2013 Higher Education Directory®

Published by
Higher Education Publications, Inc.

Edited by
Mary Pat Rodenhouse

Editor Emerita
Jeanne M. Burke

Reston, Virginia

2013

2013 Edition

Higher Education Publications, Inc.
1801 Robert Fulton Drive, Suite 340
Reston, VA 20191-4387
(888) 349-7715
(571) 313-0478
FAX (571) 313-0526
Email: info@hepinc.com
Internet address: www.hepinc.com

Carnegie classification codes with permission from The Carnegie Foundation for the Advancement of Teaching.

Internet addresses (URL's) were originally drawn from lists maintained by Washington and Lee University and the University of North Carolina-Chapel Hill and through the annual survey sent out by Higher Education Publications, Inc.

Printed in the United States of America

ISBN-10: 0-914927-69-8; ISBN-13: 978-0-914927-69-3
ISSN 0736-0797
Library of Congress Catalogue Card Number: 83-641119
Library of Congress Cataloging-in Publication Data

HEP. . . Higher Education Directory®
Reston, VA; Higher Education Publications.
V.: 28cm
Annual
Began with issue for 1983.

A directory of accredited postsecondary, degree-granting institutions in the U.S., its possessions and territories accredited by regional, national, professional and specialized agencies recognized as accrediting bodies by the U.S. Secretary of Education and the Council for Higher Education Accreditation (CHEA) which honors recognition provided by the former Council on Postsecondary Accreditation (COPA)/Commission on Recognition of Postsecondary Accreditation (CORPA)
Description based on 2013.
Cover title: 2013 Higher Education Directory®
Spine title: 2013 Higher Education Directory® Thirty-first Edition

ISSN 0736-0797 = The Higher Education Directory®.

1. Education, Higher—United States—Directories.
2. Recognized accrediting agencies and associations—United States—Directories.
3. Acronyms, explanatory notes and symbols—United States—Directories.
4. Institution changes (additions, deletions, mergers and name changes)—United States—Directories.
5. Administrative officers, titles and title codes—United States—Directories.
6. United States Department of Education offices, statewide agencies for higher education and educational associations (and consortia)—United States—Directories.
7. Religious affiliation by denomination.
8. Carnegie classification codes.
9. Statistics.
10. Universities and colleges—United States—Directories.
11. College administrators alphabetical listing, phone numbers—United States—Directories.
12. Regional, national, professional and specialized accreditation alphabetical listing—United States—Directories.
13. Institutional FICE & Unit ID Number listing—United States—Directories.
14. Institutional alphabetical listing—United States—Directories.

I. Higher Education Publications, Inc.
II. Title: Higher Education Directory®.

L901.E34 378.73-dc19 83-641119 AACR 2 MARC-S

Table of Contents

Acknowledgments

Thirty years ago on September 26, 1982, Higher Education Publications, Inc. was formed to produce a directory to succeed the Department of Education's *Education Directory: Colleges and Universities.*

When we undertook the *Higher Education Directory* project, we worked toward three main goals: To publish accurate data, to make the directory more usable, and to have the directory ready for distribution much earlier in the academic year.

We continue to meet these objectives and more, while keeping the changing landscape of reference publishing in mind. We upgraded our HED-Connect online updating system again this year based on feedback from our users. HED-Connect users can now access our accurate data from any Web-enabled device. A special thanks to everyone who helped to improve the online updating system by giving us their comments.

The response to the HED-Connect online update system was excellent again this year. Sixty percent of this year's survey updates were submitted online. You can expect more innovations and improvements to the HED-Connect update system in the coming months.

We continue to work on a tight schedule starting in mid-June to distribution in November—especially when you consider the complexity and increase in the size of the database.

We thank the thousands of people who have supplied us the necessary data contained in the directory. We had a response/update rate of 99.5%—truly outstanding! We are most appreciative of the many subscribers who have supported us in our efforts to bring you the most accurate and current information available. And, a special thanks to Ted Manning and Judith Eaton.

The accuracy and completeness of the contents of the 2013 edition was assured by a group of editors, updating and proofing specialists including Mary Pat Rodenhouse, Jodi Mondragon, Emmy Brown, Doris Jean Schreiber, Jackie Hafner and Pat Parks. Barbara Herrman handled our in-house typesetting. Mark Schreiber managed the HED-Connect update system and the database.

You may have already seen our new website, but if you have not yet visited it, I encourage you to go to www.hepinc.com. The new site features the latest news on higher education, accreditations and administrative changes along with many new helpful resources. We feel that our increased Internet presence will continue to allow us to meet the goals we established for ourselves thirty years ago and provide you with the most authoritative, timely and accurate information on the higher education community.

Frederick F. Hafner
Publisher

Reston, Virginia

Preface

Within the past several years, the traditional guidelines for recognition of accrediting agencies by the U.S. Secretary of Education have changed.

The *Higher Education Directory* (HED) makes use of accreditation at four points: (a) selection of institutions to be listed; (b) noting the institutional accreditation and accredited programs within each institution listing; (c) providing a listing of accrediting agencies with names, addresses, etc.; (d) index of accreditations.

Before 1998, the HED had relied on the recognition of accrediting agencies by the U.S. Secretary of Education to identify accrediting agencies whose actions are used in these four ways.

The Secretary (or the predecessor, the Commissioner of Education) has recognized accrediting agencies since 1952. From the beginning the recognition has been limited by statute to those agencies whose accreditation was used for Federal purposes. For the first forty years the interpretation of "Federal purposes" was expansive: the use of a list of institutions or programs to advise service members, or the possibility of future need for a list of accredited programs was sufficient to allow an agency access to the recognition process. In that period the recognition criteria were phrased in general terms of good practice. As a result the Federal list came to include almost all legitimate accrediting agencies, both agencies that accredited institutions and agencies that accredited programs.

With the passage of the 1992 amendments to the Higher Education Act the Congress introduced two significant changes of policy: (a) Federal recognition was restricted to those agencies whose accreditation was used to establish institutional eligibility for participation in federal programs; (b) the Secretary was obliged to place in the criteria for recognition a number of requirements of recognized accrediting agencies focused squarely on the administration of Federal student financial aid.

As a result a number of well-established, legitimate accrediting agencies were excluded from Federal recognition. In practice, the Secretary has dropped these from the list as their terms of recognition have expired. In each case the agency has received a letter from the Secretary emphasizing that this action does not reflect on the quality or integrity of the agency's activities, but is a result of the statutory changes in the understanding of "Federal purposes" for recognizing accrediting agencies. Since the "Federal purpose" is restricted to agencies accrediting institutions, the agencies dropped from the list are those accrediting programs exclusively. For example, among them are the agencies dealing with programs in architecture, in library and information studies, and in business (including graduate programs in business administration.)

From the start of the publication the HED relied on the federal list. This reliance and the changes in the federal recognition criteria led to the elimination from the HED listings of programs accredited by the accrediting agencies dropped from the Secretary's recognition. Thus, well known institutions were not shown as having an accredited program in architecture or business administration, while others were not shown as having accredited programs in library and information studies; yet in many cases the programs were among the premier programs in their disciplines.

The HED seeks to be both a comprehensive and an accurate guide to higher education and the HED has sought to identify reliable recognition of accrediting agencies other than that of the Secretary of Education. Beginning in 1975 the Council on Postsecondary Accreditation conducted a well-respected recognition process for accrediting agencies, and published a list of the agencies, both institutional and programmatic, that it recognized. From 1975 through the dissolution of COPA in 1993 there was substantial overlap of the COPA list and the Federal list. After 1993 the COPA recognition process was continued by the Commission on the Recognition of Postsecondary Accreditation (CORPA).

The Council on Higher Education Accreditation (CHEA), formed in 1996, now conducts recognition reviews based on its recognition policies and procedures. The recognition provisions deal with matters of good practice, and do not include the specific Federal student aid provisions now in the federal regulations. This is a two-tier process: an accreditor is first reviewed for its eligibility for CHEA recognition and, if the accreditor is deemed eligible for a recognition review, it then submits material for recognition consideration. Fifty-six (56) accreditors are recognized by CHEA as of 2011. CHEA eligibility and recognition standards are contained in the CHEA *Recognition of Accrediting Organizations: Policy and Procedures* (2010, revised), available on the CHEA web-site at www.chea.org.

In this edition, the HED has used the Secretary's list, supplemented by the most recent COPA/CORPA/CHEA list for agencies that accredit only programs within accredited institutions. Reference has been made to the Secretary's list of earlier years to identify agencies that were recognized and have been dropped because of the eligibility change noted above. No accreditation by an agency not recognized by either the Secretary or COPA/CORPA/CHEA has been included.

A footnote for clarity: some agencies, especially in the health sciences, accredit both programs within institutions and institutions whose sole program is the accredited program. Such agencies continue to meet the Secretary's eligibility requirements and many are on the Secretary's list although they are primarily program accrediting agencies. The agencies dropped from the Secretary's list are those that accredit programs only, and for the most part require a program to be within the offerings of an already-accredited institution.

Thurston E. Manning[1]

[1]Thurston Manning is a former president of North Central Association of Colleges and Schools and former president of the Council on Postsecondary Accreditation, COPA.

Foreword

The 2013 edition of the *Higher Education Directory®* contains listings of accredited, degree-granting institutions of postsecondary education in the United States and its territories.

Criteria for Listing in this Directory

To be listed in this Directory, an institution must meet the following guidelines:

(1) They are degree-granting (legally authorized to offer and are offering a program of college-level studies leading toward a degree[1]);
(2) They have submitted the information required for listing; and
(3) They meet one of the following criteria for listing:
   A. The institution is accredited at the college level by an accrediting agency that is recognized by the U.S. Secretary of Education;
   B. The institution holds pre-accredited status with an accrediting agency recognized by the U.S. Secretary of Education whose recognition includes the pre-accreditation status;
   C. The institution is accredited at the college level by an accrediting agency recognized by the Council for Higher Education Accreditation (CHEA).

"College level" means a postsecondary associate, baccalaureate, post-baccalaureate, or rabbinical education program.

Verification of Accreditations

Verification of each accreditation for all institutions was done by comparing the accreditation against the current Directory (and updated lists) for each respective regional, national, professional and specialized association or agency, along with telephone calls to numerous accrediting associations whenever there was a question of accuracy. Over 19,000 accreditations were verified through September 2012.

The reader is reminded that many institutions have programs which may not be recognized by a professional or specialized association, but are considered fine programs. The institutions may or may not have sought such recognition.

General Organization of the Directory

Our approach to the organization of the material is to make the desired information readable and easy to find. There are four indexes which are cross-referenced to the main institutional listing.

A. Prologue
   1. Accrediting agencies with addresses. Regional accrediting commissions are listed alphabetically while national, professional and specialized bodies are listed alphabetically under headings showing their specialties.
   2. Acronyms used in the Directory for accrediting bodies are listed alphabetically.
   3. Explanatory notes and symbols.
   4. U.S. postal abbreviations of states.
   5. Institution changes.
   6. Administrative officers' description and job codes.
   7. U.S. Department of Education offices.
   8. Statewide agencies of higher education.
   9. Higher education associations.
   10. Consortia of institutions of higher education.
   11. Association name index.
   12. Religious affiliation by denomination.
   13. Carnegie classification codes.
   14. Statistical data.

B. College and university listings by state with institutional characteristics and administrative officers.
   1. Institution Name. If an * appears before the institution's name, it is a part of a system. A line between institutions separates two systems.
   2. Alpha Code. The first institution listed on a page is coded (A), the second (B), etc. The Administrators' index is also coded to enable the reader to locate the desired institution quickly.
   3. Address.
   4. County.
   5. FICE Identification. This was the Federal Interagency Commission on Education number originally assigned by the Department of Education. We continue to use the term FICE. However, the Department of Education in their Office of Student Financial Assistance uses OPEID, Office of Postsecondary Education Identification. OPEID consists of the first six digits of the FICE plus two more digits indicating branch campuses. Numbers beginning with 66 are for accredited institutions for which we cannot locate a FICE or OPEID number. These are identification numbers only.
   6. Telephone Number.
   7. Unit ID Number. A unique number developed by the National Center for Education Statistics (NCES) for the Education Department's IPEDS Reports.
   8. Carnegie Classification Code. (see page **xlix**)
   9. Main FAX Number.
   10. School Calendar.
   11. URL (Universal Resource Locator).
   12. Date Established.
   13. Annual Tuition & Fees for 2012-13 school year.
   14. Fall 2011 Enrollment. Head count (not FTE) in degree programs as reported on the latest IPEDS survey.
   15. Type of Student Body.
   16. Affiliation or Control.
   17. IRS Status.
   18. Highest Degree Offered.
   19. Program. This is the general type of education offered.
   20. Accreditation (see page **viii**). **N.B. Institutional accreditation is in bold face.**
   21. Administrative and academic officers with job classification code (see page **xxvii** for descriptions).

C. Index of administrators is an alphabetical listing of all the administrators with their most direct phone number and E-mail address. The page and reference letter indicate the page on which the administrator's institution listing begins.

D. Index of regional, national, professional and specialized accreditation alphabetically by state. This index standardizes and simplifies reviewing of the 131 accrediting classifications.

E. FICE number index. Numeric listing of FICE number and school.

F. Alphabetic index of institutions.

---

[1]The *Higher Education Directory®* lists degree-granting institutions approved by regional, national, professional or specialized accrediting agencies.

Accrediting Agencies

The following regional, national, professional and specialized accrediting agencies are recognized by the U.S. Secretary of Education or the Council for Higher Education Accreditation (CHEA). The U.S. Department of Education (USDE) dates specified are the date of initial listing as a U.S. Department of Education recognized agency, the date of the U.S. Secretary's most recent grant of renewed recognition based on the last full review of the agency by the National Advisory Committee on Institutional Quality and Integrity, and the date of the agency's next scheduled review for renewal of recognition.[1] The Council for Higher Education (CHEA) date reflects initial or continued recognition by CHEA.

Regional Accrediting Bodies

Delaware, District of Columbia, Maryland, New Jersey, New York, Pennsylvania, Puerto Rico, Virgin Islands

Commission on Higher Education
Middle States Association of Colleges and Schools M
USDE: 1952/2007/2012 CHEA: 2002
3624 Market Street, Second Floor West
Philadelphia, PA 19104
(267) 284-5000 Fax (215) 662-5001
Elizabeth H. Sibolski, President
E-mail: info@msche.org
URL: www.msche.org

Connecticut, Maine, Massachusetts, New Hampshire, Rhode Island, Vermont

Commission on Institutions of Higher Education
New England Association of Schools and Colleges EH
USDE: 1952/2008/2013 CHEA: 2002
209 Burlington Road
Bedford, MA 01730-1433
(781) 271-0022 Fax (781) 271-0950
Barbara E. Brittingham, Director
E-mail: bbrittingham@neasc.org
URL: www.neasc.org

Arizona, Arkansas, Colorado, Illinois, Indiana, Iowa, Kansas, Michigan, Minnesota, Missouri, Nebraska, New Mexico, North Dakota, Ohio, Oklahoma, South Dakota, West Virginia, Wisconsin, Wyoming

Higher Learning Commission
North Central Association NH
USDE: 1952/2008/2012 CHEA: 2003
230 South LaSalle Street, Suite 7-500
Chicago, IL 60604-1413
(800) 621-7440 Fax (312) 263-7462
Sylvia Manning, President
E-mail: info@hlcommission.org
URL: www.ncahlc.org

Alaska, Idaho, Montana, Nevada, Oregon, Utah, Washington

Northwest Commission on Colleges and Universities NW
USDE: 1952/2008/2013
8060 165th Avenue, NE, Suite 100
Redmond, WA 98052
(425) 558-4224 Fax (425) 376-0596
Sandra E. Elman, President
E-mail: selman@nwccu.org
URL: www.nwccu.org

Alabama, Florida, Georgia, Kentucky, Louisiana, Mississippi, North Carolina, South Carolina, Tennessee, Texas, Virginia

Commission on Colleges
Southern Association of Colleges and Schools SC
USDE: 1952/2006/2012 CHEA: 2003
1866 Southern Lane
Decatur, GA 30033-4097
(800) 248-7701 Fax (404) 679-4528
Belle S. Wheelan, President
E-mail: bwheelan@sacscoc.org
URL: www.sacscoc.org

California, Hawaii, American Samoa, Guam, Commonwealth of the Northern Marianas, Federated States of Micronesia, Republic of the Marshall Islands, Republic of Palau

Accrediting Commission for Senior Colleges and Universities
Western Association of Schools and Colleges WC
USDE: 1952/2007/2012 CHEA: 2003
985 Atlantic Avenue, Suite 100
Alameda, CA 94501
(510) 748-9001 Fax (510) 748-9797
Ralph A. Wolff, Executive Director
E-mail: wascsr@wascsenior.org
URL: www.wascweb.org

Accrediting Commission for Community and Junior Colleges
Western Association of Schools and Colleges WJ
USDE: 1952/2008/2013 CHEA: 2003
10 Commercial Boulevard, Suite 204
Novato, CA 94949
(415) 506-0234 Fax (415) 506-0238
Barbara A. Beno, President
E-mail: accjc@accjc.org
URL: www.wascweb.org

[1]U.S. Department of Education, Nationally Recognized Accrediting Agencies, www2.ed.gov/admins/finaid/accred/accreditation.html.

National, Professional and Specialized Accrediting Bodies

Acupuncture

Accreditation Commission for Acupuncture and Oriental Medicine (ACAOM)
USDE: 1988/2011/2013
Maryland Trade Center 3
14502 Greenview Drive, Suite 300B
Laurel, MD 20708
(301) 313-0855 Fax (301) 313-0912
William W. Goding, Interim Executive Director
E-mail: william.goding@acaom.org
URL: www.acaom.org

First-professional master's degree, professional master's level certificate and diploma programs and professional post-graduate doctoral programs in acupuncture and Oriental medicine, and freestanding institutions that offer such programs **ACUP**

Allied Health

Accrediting Bureau of Health Education Schools (ABHES)
USDE: 1969/2011/2012
7777 Leesburg Pike, Suite 314N
Falls Church, VA 22043
(703) 917-9503 Fax (703) 917-4109
Carol Moneymaker, Executive Director
E-mail: cmoneymaker@abhes.org
URL: www.abhes.org

Institutions specializing in allied health education **ABHES**
Specialized programs for
- Medical laboratory technician **MLTAB**
- Medical assistant **MAAB**
- Surgical technologist **SURTEC**

Commission on Accreditation of Allied Health Education Programs (CAAHEP)
CHEA: 2011
1361 Park Street
Clearwater, FL 33756
(727) 210-2350 Fax (727) 210-2354
Kathleen Megivern, Executive Director
E-mail: mail@caahep.org
URL: www.caahep.org

The Commission on Accreditation of Allied Health Education Programs (CAAHEP) is recognized as an accrediting agency for accreditation of education for the allied health occupations. In carrying out its accreditation activities, CAAHEP cooperates with the Committees on Accreditation sponsored by various allied health and medical specialty organizations. CAAHEP is the coordinating agency for accreditation of education for the following allied health occupations:
- Anesthesiologist assistant **AA**
- Blood bank technology **BBT**
- Cardiovascular technologist **CVT**
- Cytotechnologist **CYTO**
- Diagnostic medical sonographer **DMS**
- Emergency medical technician-paramedic **EMT**
- Exercise science **EXSC**
- Kinesiotherapy **KIN**
- Medical assistant **MAC**
- Medical illustrator **MIL**
- Neurodiagnostic technologist **NDT**
- Orthotist/prosthetist **OPE**
- Perfusionist **PERF**
- Polysomnographic technologist **POLYT**
- Surgeon assistant **SURGA**
- Surgical technologist **SURGT**

Anesthesiologist Assistant

Commission on Accreditation of Allied Health Education Programs (see listing under Allied Health)
Accreditation Review Committee for the Anesthesiologist Assistant
2027 Burnside Drive
Allen, TX 75013
(469) 656-1103
Jennifer Anderson Warwick, Executive Director
E-mail: jennifer@arc-aa.org
URL: www.caahep.org/arc-aa

Post-baccalaureate programs for anesthesiologist assistant **AA**

Art

Commission on Accreditation
National Association of Schools of Art and Design (NASAD)
USDE: 1966/2008/2013
11250 Roger Bacon Drive, Suite 21
Reston, VA 20190
(703) 437-0700 Fax (703) 437-6312
Samuel Hope, Executive Director
E-mail: info@arts-accredit.org
URL: www.arts-accredit.org

Institutions and departments within institutions offering degree and non-degree granting programs in art/design and art/design-related programs **ART**

Audiology

Accreditation Commission for Audiology Education
CHEA: 2012
1718 M Street, NW #297
Washington, DC 20036-4504
(202) 986-9500 Fax (202) 986-9550
Doris Gordon, Executive Director
E-mail: info@acaeaccred.org
URL: www.acaeaccred.org

Programs leading to the Doctor of Audiology degree **ACAE**

Aviation

Aviation Accreditation Board International
CHEA: 2002
3410 Skyway Drive
Auburn, AL 36830
(334) 844-2431 Fax (334) 844-2432
Gary W. Kiteley, Executive Director
E-mail: bavenva@auburn.edu
URL: www.aabi.aero

Non-engineering programs for aviation **AAB**

Bible College Education

Commission on Accreditation
Association for Biblical Higher Education (ABHE)
USDE: 1952/2007/2012 CHEA: 2011
5850 T. G. Lee Boulevard, Suite 130
Orlando, FL 32822
(407) 207-0808 Fax (407) 207-0840
Ron Kroll, Director
E-mail: info@abhe.org
URL: www.abhe.org

Bible colleges and programs offering undergraduate and graduate programs **BI**

Blood Bank Technology

Commission on Accreditation of Allied Health Education Programs (see listing under Allied Health)
American Association of Blood Banks (AABB)
Committee on Accreditation of Specialists in Blood Bank Technology Schools
8101 Glenbrook Road
Bethesda, MD 20814-2749
(301) 907-6977 Fax (301) 907-6895
Anne Chenoweth, Manager Accreditation Programs
E-mail: aabb@aabb.org
URL: www.aabb.org

Programs for blood bank technologist **BBT**

Business

AACSB International-The Association to Advance Collegiate Schools of Business
CHEA: 2002
777 South Harbour Island Boulevard, Suite 750
Tampa, FL 33602
(813) 769-6500 Fax (813) 769-6559
Jerry Trapnell, Executive Vice President and Chief Accreditation Officer
E-mail: accreditation@aacsb.edu
URL: www.aacsb.edu

Programs for:
- Business administration education **BUS**
- Accounting **BUSA**

Accrediting Council for Independent Colleges and Schools (ACICS)
USDE: 1956/2011/2013 CHEA: 2001
750 First Street NE, Suite 980
Washington, DC 20002-4223
(202) 336-6780 Fax (202) 842-2593
Albert C. Gray, Executive Director
E-mail: agray@acics.org
URL: www.acics.org

Private, postsecondary institutions offering specialized associate, associate, baccalaureate and master's degree programs to educate students for professional, technical, or occupational careers **ACICS**

Accreditation Council for Business Schools and Programs (ACBSP)
CHEA: 2011
11520 West 119th Street
Overland Park, KS 66213
(913) 339-9356 Fax (913) 339-6226
Douglas Viehland, Executive Director
E-mail: info@acbsp.org
URL: www.acbsp.org

Business administration, management, accounting and related business fields **ACBSP**

International Assembly for Collegiate Business Education
CHEA: 2011
11374 Strang Line Rd
Lenexa, KS 66215
(913) 631-3009 Fax (913) 631-9154
Dennis N. Gash, President
E-mail: iacbe@iacbe.org
URL: www.iacbe.org

Undergraduate and graduate level business programs in institutions that grant bachelor's and/or graduate degrees **IACBE**

Cardiovascular Technology

Commission on Accreditation of Allied Health Education Programs (see listing under Allied Health)
Joint Review Committee on Education in Cardiovascular Technology (JRC-CVT)
6 Pine Knoll Drive
Beverly, MA 01915-1425
(978) 456-5594
William W. Goding, Executive Director

E-mail: office@jrccvt.org
URL: www.jrccvt.org

Programs for cardiovascular technology **CVT**

Chiropractic

The Council on Chiropractic Education (CCE)
USDE: 1974/2011/2013 CHEA: 2005
8049 North 85th Way
Scottsdale, AZ 85258-4321
(480) 443-8877 Fax (480) 483-7333
S. Ray Bennett, Director Accreditation Services
E-mail: cce@cce-usa.org
URL: www.cce-usa.org

Programs leading to and institutions offering the Doctorate of Chiropractic (D.C.) degree **CHIRO**

Christian Studies Education

Accreditation Commission
Transnational Association of Christian Colleges and Schools (TRACS)
USDE: 1991/2011/2013 CHEA: 2011
15935 Forest Road
Forest, VA 24551
(434) 525-9539 Fax (434) 525-9538
T. Paul Boatner, President
E-mail: info@tracs.org
URL: www.tracs.org

Christian liberal arts institutions which offer certificates/diplomas and associate, baccalaureate and graduate degrees **TRACS**

Clinical Laboratory Sciences

National Accrediting Agency for Clinical Laboratory Sciences (NAACLS)
CHEA: 2002
5600 North River Road, Suite 720
Rosemont, IL 60018
(773) 714-8880 Fax (773) 714-8886
Dianne M. Cearlock, Chief Executive Officer
E-mail: info@naacls.org
URL: www.naacls.org

Programs for:
- diagnostic molecular scientist **DMOLS**
- histologic technician/technologist **HT**
- medical laboratory technician **MLTAD**
- medical technologist **MT**
- pathologists' assistant **PA**

Clinical Pastoral Education

Accreditation Commission
Association for Clinical Pastoral Education, Inc. (ACPEI)
USDE: 1969/2007/2012
1549 Clairmont Road, Suite 103
Decatur, GA 30033-4635
(404) 320-1472 Fax (404) 320-0849
Teresa E. Snorton, Executive Director
E-mail: acpe@acpe.edu
URL: www.acpe.edu

Basic, advanced and supervisory clinical pastoral education programs **PAST**

Construction Education

American Council for Construction Education (ACCE)
CHEA: 2011
1717 North Loop 1604 East, Suite 320
San Antonio, TX 78232-1570
(210) 495-6161 Fax (210) 495-6168
Michael Holland, Executive Vice President
E-mail: mholland@acce-hq.org
URL: www.acce-hq.org

Associate and baccalaureate degree programs **CONST**

Continuing Education

Accrediting Commission
Accrediting Council for Continuing Education and Training (ACCET)
USDE: 1978/2008/2013
1722 N Street NW
Washington, DC 20036
(202) 955-1113 Fax (202) 955-1118
Roger J. Williams, Executive Director
E-mail: rjwilliams@accet.org
URL: www.accet.org

Institutions offering noncollegiate continuing education and institutions offering occupational associate degree programs **CNCE**

Cosmetology

National Accrediting Commission of Career Arts and Sciences (NACCAS)
USDE: 1970/2010/2015
4401 Ford Avenue, Suite 1300
Alexandria, VA 22302-1432
(703) 600-7600 Fax (703) 379-2200
Anthony Mirando, Executive Director
E-mail: naccas@naccas.org
URL: www.naccas.org

Postsecondary schools and departments of cosmetology arts and sciences and massage therapy **COSME**

Counseling and Related Educational Programs

Council for Accreditation of Counseling and Related Educational Programs (CACREP)
CHEA: 2002
1001 North Fairfax Street, Suite 510
Alexandria, VA 22314
(703) 535-5990 Fax (703) 739-6209
Carol L. Bobby, Executive Director
E-mail: cacrep@cacrep.org
URL: www.cacrep.org

Master's degree programs in addiction counseling, career counseling, marriage, couple and family counseling, mental health counseling, school counseling, student affairs and college counseling and doctorate degree programs in counselor education and supervision **CACREP**

Culinary Arts

Accrediting Commission
American Culinary Federation
CHEA: 2004
180 Center Place Way
St. Augustine, FL 32095
(904) 824-4468 Fax (904) 825-4758
Candice Childers, Director of Accreditation
E-mail: acf@acfchefs.net
URL: www.acfchefs.org

Programs in culinary arts which award certificates, diplomas or associate degrees and bachelor degree programs in culinary management **ACFEI**

Cytotechnology

Commission on Accreditation of Allied Health Education Programs (see listing under Allied Health)
Cytotechnology Programs Review Committee
American Society of Cytopathology
100 West 10th Street, Suite 605
Wilmington, DE 19801
(302) 543-6583 Fax (302) 543-6597
Debby MacIntyre, CPRC Coordinator
E-mail: dmacintyre@cytopathology.org
URL: www.cytopathology.org

Programs for the cytotechnologist **CYTO**

Dance

Commission on Accreditation
National Association of Schools of Dance (NASD)
USDE: 1983/2008/2013
11250 Roger Bacon Drive, Suite 21
Reston, VA 20190
(703) 437-0700 Fax (703) 437-6312
Samuel Hope, Executive Director
E-mail: info@arts-accredit.org
URL: www.arts-accredit.org

Institutions and departments within institutions offering degree and non-degree-granting programs in dance and dance-related disciplines **DANCE**

Dental and Dental Auxiliary Programs

Commission on Dental Accreditation
American Dental Association (ADA)
USDE: 1952/2006/2012
211 East Chicago Avenue
Chicago, IL 60611
(800) 621-8099 Fax (312) 440-2915
Anthony Ziebert, Director
E-mail: zieberta@ada.org
URL: www.ada.org

Programs leading to:
- D.D.S. or D.M.D. degree, advanced general dentistry and specialty programs **DENT**
- Dental hygiene **DH**
- Dental assisting **DA**
- Dental laboratory technology **DT**

Diagnostic Medical Sonography

Commission on Accreditation of Allied Health Education Programs (see listing under Allied Health)
Joint Review Committee on Education in Diagnostic Medical Sonography
6021 University Boulevard, Suite 500
Ellicot City, MD 21043-6090
(443) 973-3251 Fax (866) 738-3444
Cindy Weiland, Executive Director
E-mail: mail@jrcdms.org
URL: www.jrcdms.org

Programs for the diagnostic medical sonographer **DMS**

Dietetics

Accreditation Council for Education in Nutrition and Dietetics
Academy of Nutrition and Dietetics
USDE: 1974/2007/2012
120 South Riverside Plaza, Suite 2000
Chicago, IL 60606-6995
(312) 899-4872 Fax (312) 899-4817
Ulric K. Chung, Executive Director
E-mail: uchung@eatright.org
URL: www.eatright.org/cade

Coordinated programs in dietetics **DIETC**
Didactic programs **DIETD**
Post-baccalaureate internships **DIETI**
Dietetic technician programs **DIETT**

Distance Education and Training

Accrediting Commission
Distance Education and Training Council (DETC)
USDE: 1959/2007/2012 CHEA: 2001
1601 18th Street NW, Suite 2
Washington, DC 20009
(202) 234-5100 Fax (202) 332-1386
Michael P. Lambert, Executive Director
E-mail: detc@detc.org
URL: www.detc.org

Distance education institutions including associate, baccalaureate, master's, and doctoral degree-granting programs primarily through the distance learning method **DETC**

Emergency Medical Services

Commission on Accreditation for Allied Health Programs (see listing under Allied Health)
Committee on Educational Programs for the Emergency Medical Services Professions
8301 Lakeview Parkway, Suite 111-312
Rowlett, TX 75088
(214) 703-8445 Fax (214) 703-8992
George Hatch, Executive Director
E-mail: george@coaemsp.org
URL: www.coaemsp.org

Programs for the emergency medical technician-paramedic **EMT**

Engineering

ABET, Inc.
CHEA: 2003
111 Market Place, Suite 1050
Baltimore, MD 21202
(410) 347-7700 Fax (410) 625-2238
Michael Milligan, Executive Director
E-mail: accreditation@abet.org
URL: www.abet.org

Baccalaureate programs in computer science **CS**
Basic (baccalaureate) and advanced (master's) level programs in engineering **ENG**
Applied science programs at the associate, baccalaureate and master's level **ENGR**
Associate and baccalaureate degree programs in engineering technology **ENGT**

English Language

Commission on English Language Program Accreditation (CEA)
USDE: 2003/2011/2013
801 North Fairfax Drive, Suite 402A
Alexandria, VA 22314
(703) 519-2070 Fax (703) 519-2071
Teresa D. O'Donnell, Executive Director
E-mail: todonnell@cea-accredit.org
URL: www.cea-accredit.org

English language programs **CEA**

Exercise Sciences

Commission on Accreditation of Allied Health Education Programs (see listing under Allied Health)
Committee on Accreditation for the Exercise Sciences
401 West Michigan Street
Indianapolis, IN 46202
(317) 637-9200 Fax (317) 634-7817
Traci Sue Rush, Executive Director
E-mail: trush@acsm.org
URL: www.coaes.org

Programs for exercise science and related departments **EXSC**

Family and Consumer Sciences

Council for Accreditation
American Association of Family and Consumer Sciences (AAFCS)
CHEA: 2001
400 North Columbus Street, Suite 202
Alexandria, VA 22314
(703) 706-4600 Fax (703) 706-4663
Carolyn W. Jackson, Executive Director
E-mail: accreditation@aafcs.org
URL: www.aafcs.org

Baccalaureate programs in family and consumer sciences **AAFCS**

Fire and Emergency

International Fire Service Accreditation Congress Degree Assembly
CHEA: 2011
1700 West Tyler
Oklahoma State University
Stillwater, OK 74078
(405) 744-8303 Fax (405) 744-8802
Clayton Moorman, Manager
E-mail: cmoorman@ifsac.org
URL: www.ifsac.org

Undergraduate fire and emergency related programs **IFSAC**

Forestry

Society of American Foresters (SAF)
CHEA: 2001
5400 Grosvenor Lane
Bethesda, MD 20814-2198
(301) 897-8720 Fax (301) 897-3690
Carol Redelsheimer, Director of Science and Education
E-mail: redelsheimerc@safnet.org
URL: www.safnet.org

Programs leading to a bachelor's or higher first-professional degree in forestry **FOR**

Funeral Service Education

Committee on Accreditation
American Board of Funeral Service Education (ABFSE)
USDE: 1972/2010/2012 CHEA: 2012
3414 Ashland Avenue, Suite G
St. Joseph, MO 64506
(816) 233-3747 Fax (816) 233-3793
Gretchen Warner, Executive Director
E-mail: exdir@abfse.org
URL: www.abfse.org

Institutions and programs awarding diplomas, associate and bachelor's degrees in funeral service or mortuary science **FUSER**

Healthcare Management

Commission on Accreditation of Healthcare Management Education (CAHME)
USDE: 1970/2007/2013 CHEA: 2003
2111 Wilson Boulevard, Suite 700
Arlington, VA 22201
(703) 351-5010 Fax (703) 991-5989
Anthony Wisniewski, JD, President and CEO
E-mail: awisniewski@cahme.org
URL: www.cahme.org

Graduate programs in healthcare management **HSA**

Histologic Technology

See Clinical Laboratory Sciences

Home Study Education

See Distance Education and Training

Industrial Technology

The Association of Technology, Management, and Applied Engineering
CHEA: 2002
1390 Eisenhower Place
Ann Arbor, MI 48108
(734) 677-0720 Fax (734) 677-0046
Rick Coscarelli, Executive Director
E-mail: atmae@atmae.org
URL: http://atmae.org

Technology, applied technology, engineering technology and technology-related programs at the associate, baccalaureate and master's degree level **NAIT**

Interior Design

Council for Interior Design Accreditation (CIDA)
CHEA: 2002
206 Grandville Avenue, Suite 350
Grand Rapids, MI 49503
(616) 458-0400 Fax (616) 458-0460
Holly Mattson, Executive Director
E-mail: info@accredit-id.org
URL: www.accredit-id.org

First professional degree level programs (master's and baccalaureate degrees) **CIDA**

Journalism and Mass Communications

Accrediting Committee
Accrediting Council on Education in Journalism and Mass Communications (ACEJMC)
CHEA: 2002
University of Kansas School of Journalism
Stauffer-Flint Hall
1435 Jayhawk Boulevard
Lawrence, KS 66045-7575
(785) 864-3973 Fax (785) 864-5225
Susanne Shaw, Executive Director
E-mail: sshaw@ku.edu
URL: www2.ku.edu/~acejmc

Units within institutions offering professional baccalaureate and master's degree programs in journalism and mass communications **JOUR**

Kinesiotherapy

Commission on Accreditation of Allied Health Education Programs (see listing under Allied Health)
Committee on Accreditation of Education Programs for Kinesiotherapy
118 College Drive #5142
Hattiesburg, MS 39406-0002
(601) 266-5371 Fax (601) 266-4445
Jerry W. Purvis, Executive Director
E-mail: jerry.purvis@usm.edu
URL: www.akta.org

Kinesiotherapy programs **KIN**

Landscape Architecture

Landscape Architectural Accreditation Board
American Society of Landscape Architects (ASLA)
CHEA: 2003
636 Eye Street, NW
Washington, DC 20001-3736
(202) 898-2444 Fax (202) 898-1185
Ron Leighton, Executive Director
E-mail: rleighton@asla.org
URL: www.asla.org

Baccalaureate and master's programs leading to the first professional degree **LSAR**

Law

Council of the Section of Legal Education and Admissions to the Bar
American Bar Association (ABA)
USDE: 1952/2011/2013
321 North Clark Street, 21st Fl
Chicago, IL 60654
(312) 988-6738 Fax (312) 988-5681
Hulett H. Askew, Consultant on Legal Education
E-mail: legaled@americanbar.org
URL: www.americanbar.org/groups/legal_education.html

Programs in legal education; professional schools of law **LAW**

Librarianship

Committee on Accreditation
American Library Association (ALA)
CHEA: 2001
50 East Huron Street
Chicago, IL 60611-2729
(312) 280-2432 Fax (312) 280-2433
Karen O'Brien, Director of Accreditation
E-mail: accred@ala.org
URL: www.ala.org/accreditation

Master's programs leading to the first professional degree **LIB**

Marriage and Family Therapy

Commission on Accreditation for Marriage and Family Therapy Education
American Association for Marriage and Family Therapy (AAMFT)
USDE: 1978/2011/2013 CHEA: 2003
112 South Alfred Street
Alexandria, VA 22314-3061
(703) 838-9808 Fax (703) 838-9805
Tanya A. Tamarkin, Director of Education Affairs
E-mail: ttamarkin@aamft.org
URL: www.aamft.org

Clinical training programs at the master's, doctorate and post-graduate levels **MFCD**

Massage Therapy

Commission on Massage Therapy Accreditation
USDE: 2002/2010/2012
5335 Wisconsin Avenue NW, Suite 440
Washington, DC 20015
(202) 895-1518 Fax (202) 895-1519
Kate Zulaski, Executive Director
E-mail: kzulaski@comta.org
URL: www.comta.org

Institutions that award postsecondary certificates, diplomas, and associate degrees in the practice of massage therapy, bodywork, aesthetics/esthetics and skin care **COMTA**

Medical Assistant Education

(see listing under Allied Health)
Accrediting Bureau of Health Education Schools (ABHES)

Medical assistant programs **MAAB**

Commission on Accreditation of Allied Health Education Programs (see listing under Allied Health)
Medical Assisting Education Review Board
20 North Wacker Drive, Suite 1575
Chicago, IL 60606-2963
(312) 899-1500 Fax (312) 899-1259
Anna L. Johnson, Executive Director of Accreditation
E-mail: ajohnson@maerb.org
URL: www.maerb.org

One and two year medical assistant programs **MAC**

Medical Illustrator Education

Commission on Accreditation of Allied Health Education Programs (see listing under Allied Health)
Accreditation Review Committee for the Medical Illustrator
Saint Luke's Hospital Instructional Resources
32531 Meadowlark Way
Pepper Pike, OH 44124
(216) 595-9363 Fax (216) 595-9360
Kathy Jung, Chair, ARC-MI
E-mail: kijung@aol.com
URL: www.ami.org

Programs for medical illustrator **MIL**

Medical Laboratory Technician Education

(see listing under Allied Health)
Accrediting Bureau of Health Education Schools (ABHES)

Schools and programs for the medical laboratory technician **MLTAB**

(see listing under Clinical Laboratory Sciences)
National Accrediting Agency for Clinical Laboratory Sciences (NAACLS)

Programs for medical laboratory technician
(certificate) **MLTC**
(associate degree) **MLTAD**

Medical Technology

(see listing under Clinical Laboratory Sciences)
National Accrediting Agency for Clinical Laboratory Sciences (NAACLS)

Programs for medical technologist **MT**

Medicine

Liaison Committee on Medical Education (LCME) of the Council on Medical Education of the American Medical Association and the Association of American Medical Colleges
USDE: 1952/2007/2012
The LCME is administered in odd-numbered years, beginning each July 1, by:
Council on Medical Education of the American Medical Association (AMA)
515 North State Street
Chicago, IL 60610
(312) 464-4690 Fax (312) 464-5830
Barbara Barzansky, Secretary
E-mail: barbara.barzansky@ama-assn.org
URL: www.ama-assn.org

The LCME is administered in even-numbered years, beginning each July 1, by:
Association of American Medical Colleges (AAMC)
2450 N Street NW
Washington, DC 20037-1127
(202) 828-0596 Fax (202) 828-1125
Dan Hunt, LCME Secretary
E-mail: dhunt@aamc.org
URL: www.aamc.org

Programs leading to the M.D. degree **MED**

Midwifery Education

Midwifery Education Accreditation Council (MEAC)
USDE: 2001/2010/2012
1935 Pauline Boulevard, Suite 100B
Ann Arbor, MI 48103
(360) 466-2080 Fax (480) 907-2936
Sandra Bitonti Stewart, Executive Director
E-mail: sandra@meacschools.org
URL: www.meacschools.org

Accreditation of direct-entry midwifery educational institutions and programs conferring degrees and certificates **MEAC**

Montessori Teacher Education

Montessori Accreditation Council for Teacher Education (MACTE)
USDE: 1995/2010/2012
313 Second Street, SE, Suite 112
Charlottesville, VA 22902
(434) 202-7793 Fax (888) 525-8838
Rebecca Pelton, Executive Director
E-mail: rebecca@macte.org
URL: www.macte.org

Montessori teacher-education programs and institutions **MACTE**

Music

Commission on Accreditation
National Association of Schools of Music (NASM)
USDE: 1952/2008/2013
11250 Roger Bacon Drive, Suite 21
Reston, VA 20190
(703) 437-0700 Fax (703) 437-6312
Samuel Hope, Executive Director
E-mail: info@arts-accredit.org
URL: www.arts-accredit.org

Institutions and departments within institutions offering degree and non-degree-granting programs in music and music-related disciplines **MUS**

Naturopathic Medical Education

Council on Naturopathic Medical Education (CNME)
USDE: 2003/2010/2015
PO Box 178
Great Barrington, MA 01230
(413) 528-8877 Fax (413) 528-8880
Daniel Seitz, Executive Director
E-mail: council@cnme.org

URL: www.cnme.org

Graduate-level, four-year naturopathic medical education programs **NATUR**

Neurodiagnostic Technology

Commission on Accreditation of Allied Health Education Programs (see listing under Allied Health)
Committee on Accreditation for Education in Neurodiagnostic Technology
6654 South Sycamore Street
Littleton, CO 80120
(303) 738-0770 Fax (303) 738-3223
Theresa Sisneros, Executive Director
E-mail: office@coa-ndt.org
URL: http://coa-ndt.org

Programs for the electroneurodiagnostic technologist **NDT (formerly EEG)**

Nuclear Medicine Technology

Joint Review Committee on Educational Programs in Nuclear Medicine Technology
CHEA: 2002
2000 West Danforth Road, Suite 130 #203
Edmund, OK 73003
(405) 285-0546 Fax (405) 285-0579
Jan M. Winn, Executive Director
E-mail: jrcnmt@coxinet.net
URL: www.jrcnmt.org

Programs for the nuclear medicine technologist **NMT**

Nurse Anesthetists

Council on Accreditation of Nurse Anesthesia Educational Programs
USDE: 1955/2007/2013 CHEA: 2011
222 South Prospect Avenue, Suite 304
Park Ridge, IL 60068-4001
(847) 655-1160 Fax (847) 692-7137
Francis Gerbasi, Executive Director
E-mail: accreditation@coa.us.com
URL: home.coa.us.com

Nurse anesthesia educational institutions and programs at the certificate, master's and doctoral degree levels **ANEST**

Nurse-Midwifery

Accreditation Commission for Midwifery Education
USDE: 1982/2006/2012
8403 Colesville Road, Suite 1550
Silver Spring, MD 20910
(240) 485-1802 Fax (240) 485-1818
Susan E. Stone, Chair, Accreditation Commission
E-mail: susan.stone@frontierschool.edu
URL: www.midwife.org/accreditation

Pre-certification, basic certificate and master's degree nurse-midwifery educational programs **MIDWF**

Nursing

Commission on Collegiate Nursing Education (CCNE)
USDE: 2000/2007/2012
One Dupont Circle NW, Suite 530
Washington, DC 20036-1120
(202) 887-6791 Fax (202) 887-8476
Jennifer Butlin, Executive Director
E-mail: jbutlin@aacn.nche.edu
URL: www.aacn.nche.edu/accreditation

Baccalaureate and higher degree nursing education **NURSE**

Accrediting Commission
National League for Nursing (NLNAC)
USDE: 1952/2007/2012 CHEA: 2011
3343 Peachtree Road NE, Suite 850
Atlanta, GA 30326
(404) 975-5000 Fax (404) 975-5020
Sharon J. Tanner, Executive Director
E-mail: stanner@nlnac.org
URL: www.nlnac.org

Programs in:
- Practical nursing (certificate) **PNUR**
- Diploma nurse education **DNUR**
- Associate degree **ADNUR**
- Baccalaureate and higher degree nurse education **NUR**

Occupational Education

Council on Occupational Education (COE)
USDE: 1969/2011/2013
7840 Roswell Road, Bldg 300, Suite 325
Atlanta, GA 30350
(770) 396-3898 Fax (770) 396-3790
Gary Puckett, Executive Director
E-mail: info@council.org
URL: www.council.org

Occupational/vocational institutions that grant the applied associate degree in specific career and technical education **COE**

Occupational Therapy

Accreditation Council for Occupational Therapy Education
American Occupational Therapy Association
USDE: 1952/2012/2017 CHEA: 2002
4720 Montgomery Lane, PO Box 31220
Bethesda, MD 20824-1220
(301) 652-2682 Fax (301) 652-7711
Neil Harvison, Director of Accreditation
E-mail: nharvison@aota.org
URL: www.aota.org

Occupational therapy programs **OT**
Occupational therapy assistant programs **OTA**

Opticianry

Commission on Opticianry Accreditation
CHEA: 2010
PO Box 592
Canton, NY 13617
(703) 468-0566
Debra White, Director of Accreditation
E-mail: director@COAccreditation.com
URL: www.coaccreditation.com

Two-year opticianry degree programs **OPD**
One year programs for opthalmic laboratory technician **OPLT**

Optometry

Accreditation Council on Optometric Education
American Optometric Association (AOA)
USDE: 1952/2008/2013 CHEA: 2001
243 North Lindbergh Boulevard
St. Louis, MO 63141
(314) 991-4100 Fax (314) 991-4101
Joyce L. Urbeck, Administrative Director
E-mail: jlurbeck@aoa.org
URL: www.theacoe.org

Programs in:
- First professional **OPT**
- Optometric residency **OPTR**
- Optometric technology **OPTT**

Orthotic and Prosthetic Education

Commission on Accreditation of Allied Health Education Programs (see listing under Allied Health)
National Commission on Orthotic and Prosthetic Education (NCOPE)
330 John Carlyle Street, Suite 200
Alexandria, VA 22314
(703) 836-7114 Fax (703) 836-0838
Robin C. Seabrook, Executive Director
E-mail: rseabrook@ncope.org
URL: www.ncope.org

Programs for orthotic and prosthetic education **OPE**

Osteopathic Medicine

Commission on Osteopathic College Accreditation
American Osteopathic Association
USDE: 1952/2011/2016
Department of Education
142 East Ontario Street
Chicago, IL 60611-2864
(312) 202-8048 Fax (312) 202-8202
Konrad C. Miskowicz-Retz, Director
E-mail: kretz@osteopathic.org
URL: www.osteopathic.org

Programs leading to and institutions offering the D.O. (Doctor of Osteopathy/Osteopathic Medicine) degree **OSTEO**

Perfusion

Commission on Accreditation of Allied Health Education Programs (see listing under Allied Health)
Accreditation Committee - Perfusion Education
6654 South Sycamore Street
Littleton, CO 80120
(303) 738-0770 Fax (303) 738-3223
Theresa Sisneros, Executive Director
E-mail: ac-pe@msn.com
URL: www.ac-pe.org

Programs for the perfusionist **PERF**

Pharmacy

Accreditation Council for Pharmacy Education (ACPE)
USDE: 1952/2006/2012 CHEA: 2004
135 South LaSalle Street, Suite 4100
Chicago, IL 60603
(312) 664-3575 Fax (312) 664-4652
Peter H. Vlasses, Executive Director
E-mail: csinfo@acpe-accredit.org
URL: www.acpe-accredit.org

Professional degree programs in pharmacy **PHAR**

Physical Therapy

Commission on Accreditation in Physical Therapy Education
American Physical Therapy Association (APTA)
USDE: 1977/2007/2012 CHEA: 2002
Trans Potomac Plaza
1111 North Fairfax Street
Alexandria, VA 22314
(703) 706-3245 Fax (703) 684-7343

Mary Jane Harris, Director
E-mail: maryjaneharris@apta.org
URL: www.apta.org

Professional programs for the physical therapist **PTA**
Programs for the physical therapist assistant **PTAA**

Physician Assistant

Accreditation Review Commission on Education for the Physician Assistant (ARC-PA)
CHEA: 2004
12000 Findley Road, Suite 150
John's Creek, GA 30097
(770) 476-1224 Fax (770) 476-1738
John McCarty, Executive Director
E-mail: arc-pa@arc-pa.org
URL: www.arc-pa.org

Programs for the physician assistant **ARCPA**

Planning (City and Regional)

Planning Accreditation Board
CHEA: 2001
53 West Jackson Boulevard, Suite 1315
Chicago, IL 60604
(312) 662-1440 Fax (312) 662-1460
Shonagh Merits, Executive Director
E-mail: smerits@planningaccreditationboard.org
URL: www.planningaccreditationboard.org

Bachelor and master's level programs in planning **PLNG**

Podiatry

Council on Podiatric Medical Education
American Podiatric Medical Association (APMA)
USDE: 1952/2011/2013 CHEA: 2004
9312 Old Georgetown Road
Bethesda, MD 20814-1621
(301) 581-9200 Fax (301) 571-4903
Alan R. Tinkleman, Director
E-mail: artinkleman@apma.org
URL: www.cpme.org

Colleges and programs of podiatric medicine, including first professional and doctorate degree programs **POD**

Polysomnographic Technology

Commission on Accreditation of Allied Health Education Programs (see listing under Allied Health)
Committee on Accreditation for Polysomnographic Technologists Education
1711 Frank Avenue
New Bern, NC 28560
(252) 626-3238
Karen Monarchy Rowe, Executive Director
E-mail: office@coapsg.org
URL: www.coapsg.org

Programs for polysomnographic technology **POLYT**

Psychology

Commission on Accreditation
American Psychological Association (APA)
USDE: 1970/2011/2013 CHEA: 2002
750 First Street NE
Washington, DC 20002-4242
(202) 336-5979 Fax (202) 336-5978
Susan F. Zlotlow, Director Program Consultation and Accreditation
E-mail: apaaccred@apa.org
URL: www.apa.org/ed/accred.html

Doctoral programs in:
- Clinical psychology **CLPSY**
- Counseling psychology **COPSY**
- Combined professional-scientific psychology **PSPSY**
- School psychology **SCPSY**
- Pre-doctoral internship program in professional psychology **IPSY**
- Post-doctoral residency in professional psychology **PDPSY**

Public Affairs and Administration

Commission on Peer Review and Accreditation
National Association of Schools of Public Affairs and Administration (NASPAA)
CHEA: 2004
1029 Vermont Avenue, NW, Suite 1100
Washington, DC 20005
(202) 628-8965 Fax (202) 626-4978
Crystal Calarusse, Chief Accreditation Officer
E-mail: copra@naspaa.org
URL: www.naspaa.org

Master's degree programs in public affairs, public policy and administration **SPAA**

Public Health

Council on Education for Public Health (CEPH)
USDE: 1974/2007/2013
1010 Wayne Avenue, Suite 220
Silver Spring, MD 20910-5600
(202) 789-1050 Fax (202) 789-1895
Laura Rasar King, Executive Director
E-mail: lking@ceph.org
URL: www.ceph.org

Baccalaureate and graduate level programs in schools of public health and public health programs outside of schools of public health **PH**

Rabbinical and Talmudic Education

Accreditation Commission
Association of Advanced Rabbinical and Talmudic Schools (AARTS)
USDE: 1974/2007/2013 CHEA: 2011
11 Broadway, Suite 405
New York, NY 10004
(212) 363-1991 Fax (212) 533-5335
Bernard Fryshman, Executive Vice President
E-mail: BFryshma@nyit.edu

Advanced rabbinical and Talmudic schools **RABN**

Radiologic Technology

Joint Review Committee on Education in Radiologic Technology
USDE: 1957/2011/2013 CHEA: 2004
20 North Wacker Drive, Suite 2850
Chicago, IL 60606-3182
(312) 704-5300 Fax (312) 704-5304
Leslie F. Winter, Chief Executive Officer
E-mail: mail@jrcert.org
URL: www.jrcert.org

Programs for:
- Magnetic resonance **RADMAG**
- Medical dosimetry **RADDOS**
- Radiographer **RAD**
- Radiation therapist technologist **RTT**

Recreation, Park and Leisure Studies

Council on Accreditation of Parks, Recreation, Tourism and Related Professions
National Recreation and Park Association
CHEA: 2003
22377 Belmont Ridge Road
Ashburn, VA 20148-4501
(703) 858-2195 Fax (703) 858-0794
Danielle Price, Accreditation Manager
E-mail: coaprt@nrpa.org
URL: www.nrpa.org

Baccalaureate degree programs in recreation, park resources and leisure studies **NRPA**

Rehabilitation Education

Commission on Standards and Accreditation
Council on Rehabilitation Education (CORE)
CHEA: 2001
1699 Woodfield Road, Suite 300
Schaumburg, IL 60173
(847) 944-1345 Fax (847) 944-1346
Frank Lane, Executive Director
E-mail: lane@iit.edu
URL: www.core-rehab.org

Rehabilitation counselor education programs at the master's level **CORE**

Social Work

Commission on Accreditation
Council on Social Work Education (CSWE)
CHEA: 2003
1701 Duke Street, Suite 200
Alexandria, VA 22314-3457
(703) 683-8080 Fax (703) 683-8099
Stephen M. Holloway, Director, Office of Social Work Accreditation
E-mail: info@cswe.org
URL: www.cswe.org

Master's and baccalaureate degree programs **SW**

Speech-Language Pathology and Audiology

Council on Academic Accreditation
American Speech-Language-Hearing Association (ASHA)
USDE: 1967/2010/2015 CHEA: 2003
2200 Research Boulevard
Rockville, MD 20850-3289
(301) 296-5700 Fax (301) 296-8580
Patrima L. Tice, Director Credentialing
E-mail: accreditation@asha.org
URL: www.asha.org

Master's and doctoral degree programs in:
- Audiology **AUD**
- Speech-language pathology **SP**

Surgical Assisting and Technology

(see listing under Allied Health)
Accrediting Bureau of Health Education Schools (ABHES)

Surgical technologist programs **SURTEC**

Commission on Accreditation of Allied Health Education Programs (see listing under Allied Health)
Accreditation Review Council On Education in Surgical Technology and Surgical Assisting

6 West Dry Creek Circle, Suite 110
Littleton, CO 80120
(303) 694-9262 Fax (303) 741-3655
Keith Orloff, Executive Director
E-mail: info@arcstsa.org
URL: www.arcst.org

Programs for the surgical technologist **SURGT**
Programs for the surgical assistant **SURGA**

Teacher Education

National Council for Accreditation of Teacher Education (NCATE)
USDE: 1952/2006/2013 CHEA: 2002
2010 Massachusetts Avenue NW, Suite 500
Washington, DC 20036-1023
(202) 466-7496 Fax (202) 296-6620
James G. Cibulka, President
E-mail: ncate@ncate.org
URL: www.ncate.org

Baccalaureate and graduate programs for the preparation of teachers and other professional personnel for elementary and secondary schools **TED**

Accreditation Committee
Teacher Education Accreditation Council (TEAC)
USDE: 2003/2005/2013 CHEA: 2012
One Dupont Circle NW, Suite 320
Washington, DC 20036
(202) 466-7236 Fax (202) 466-7238
Mark LaCelle-Peterson, President
E-mail: teac@teac.org
URL: www.teac.org

Professional teacher education programs in institutions offering baccalaureate and graduate degrees for the preparation of K-12 teachers **TEAC**

Theatre

Commission on Accreditation
National Association of Schools of Theatre (NAST)
USDE: 1982/2008/2013
11250 Roger Bacon Drive, Suite 21
Reston, VA 20190
(703) 437-0700 Fax (703) 437-6312
Samuel Hope, Executive Director
E-mail: info@arts-accredit.org
URL: www.arts-accredit.org

Institutions and departments within institutions offering degree granting and non-degree-granting programs in theatre and theatre-related disciplines **THEA**

Theology

Commission on Accrediting
Association of Theological Schools (ATS)
USDE: 1952/2011/2013 CHEA: 2012
10 Summit Park Drive
Pittsburgh, PA 15275-1103
(412) 788-6505 Fax (412) 788-6510
Daniel O. Aleshire, Executive Director
E-mail: ats@ats.edu
URL: www.ats.edu

Freestanding schools, as well as schools or programs affiliated with larger institutions, offering graduate professional education for ministry and graduate study of theology **THEOL**

Trade and Technical Education

Accrediting Commission of Career Schools and Colleges (ACCSC)
USDE: 1967/2005/2016
2101 Wilson Boulevard, Suite 302
Arlington, VA 22201
(703) 247-4212 Fax (703) 247-4533
Michale McComis, Executive Director
E-mail: info@accsc.org
URL: www.accsc.org

Private, postsecondary degree-granting and non-degree-granting institutions that are predominantly organized to educate students for trade, occupational or technical careers **ACCSC**

Veterinary Medicine

Council on Education
American Veterinary Medical Association (AVMA)
USDE: 1952/2007/2012 CHEA: 2012
1931 North Meacham Road, Suite 100
Schaumburg, IL 60173
(800) 248-2862 Fax (847) 925-1329
David E. Granstrom, Director Education and Research
E-mail: avmainfo@avma.org
URL: www.avma.org

Colleges of veterinary medicine offering programs leading to a D.V.M./D.M.V. professional degree **VET**

Other

New York State Board of Regents
USDE: 1952/2007/2012
State Education Department
The University of the State of New York
89 Washington Avenue, Room 1106B
Albany, NY 12234
(518) 474-5844 Fax (518) 473-4909
John B. King, Jr., Commissioner of Education
E-mail: jking@mail.nysed.gov
URL: www.nysed.gov

Degree-granting institutions of higher education in New York that designate the agency as their sole or primary nationally recognized accrediting agency for purposes of establishing elibility to participate in Higher Education Act programs **NY**

Accrediting Agencies Recognized for their Pre-accreditation Categories[1]

Under the terms of the Higher Education Act and other Federal legislation providing funding assistance to postsecondary education, an institution or program is eligible to apply for participation in certain Federal programs if, in addition to meeting other statutory requirements, it is accredited by a nationally recognized accrediting agency—or if it is an institution with respect to which the U.S. Secretary of Education has determined that there is satisfactory assurance the institution or program will meet the accreditation standards of such agency or association within a reasonable time. An institution or program may establish satisfactory assurance of accreditation by acquiring pre-accreditation status with a nationally recognized accrediting agency which has been recognized by the U.S. Secretary of Education for the award of such status. According to the Criteria for Nationally Recognized Accrediting Agencies, if an accrediting agency has developed a pre-accreditation status, it must demonstrate that it applies criteria and follows procedures that are appropriately related to those used to award accreditation status. The criteria for recognition also requires an agency's standards for pre-accreditation to permit an institution or program to hold pre-accreditation no more than five years.

The following is a list of accrediting agencies recognized by the U.S. Secretary of Education for their pre-accreditation categories and the categories which are recognized.

Regional Institution Accrediting Bodies

Middle States Association of Colleges and Schools
Commission on Higher Education: *Candidate for Accreditation*

New England Association of Schools and Colleges:
Commission on Institutions of Higher Education: *Candidate for Accreditation*

Higher Learning Commission
North Central Association: *Candidate for Accreditation*

Northwest Commission on Colleges and Universities:
Candidate for Accreditation

Southern Association of Colleges and Schools
Commission on Colleges: *Candidate for Accreditation*

Western Association of Schools and Colleges
Accrediting Commission for Community and Junior Colleges: *Candidate for Accreditation*

Western Association of Schools and Colleges
Accrediting Commission for Senior Colleges and Universities: *Candidate for Accreditation*

National, Institutional and Specialized Accrediting Bodies

Academy of Nutrition and Dietetics
Accreditation Council for Education in Nutrition and Dietetics: *Pre-accreditation*

Accreditation Commission for Acupuncture and Oriental Medicine: *Candidate for Accreditation*

Accreditation Commission for Midwifery Education: *Pre-accreditation*

Accreditation Council for Pharmacy Education: *Candidate, Pre-candidate*

American Association for Marriage and Family Therapy,
Commission on Accreditation for Marriage and Family Therapy Education: *Candidate for Accreditation*

American Optometric Association
Accreditation Council on Optometric Education: *Preliminary Approval* (for professional degree programs); *Candidacy Pending* (for optometric residency programs in Veterans Administration facilities)

American Osteopathic Association
Commission on Osteopathic College Accreditation: *Provisional Accreditation*

American Physical Therapy Association
Commission on Accreditation in Physical Therapy Education: *Candidate for Accreditation*

American Podiatric Medical Association
Council on Podiatric Medical Education: *Candidate for Accreditation*

American Speech-Language-Hearing Association
Council on Academic Accreditation: *Candidate for Accreditation*

American Veterinary Medical Association
Council on Education: *Reasonable Assurance of Accreditation*

Association for Biblical Higher Education
Commission on Accreditation: *Candidate for Accreditation*

Association of Advanced Rabbinical and Talmudic Schools
Accreditation Commission: *Correspondent, Candidate for Accreditation*

Association of Theological Schools
Commission on Accrediting: *Candidate for Accredited Membership*

Council on Naturopathic Medical Education: *Pre-accreditation*

Council on Occupational Education: *Candidate for Accreditation*

Midwifery Education Accreditation Council: *Pre-accreditation*

Teacher Education Accreditation Council Accreditation Committee: *Pre-accreditation*

Transnational Association of Christian Colleges and Schools
Accreditation Commission: *Candidate for Accreditation*

[1]U.S. Department of Education, Nationally Recognized Accrediting Agencies and Associations, www2.ed.gov/admins/finaid/accred/accreditation_pg8.html.

Abbreviations, Explanatory Notes and Symbols

Abbreviations

Listed below are the abbreviations used in this Directory for the recognized regional accrediting commissions and the recognized national, professional and specialized accrediting bodies. Addresses for these associations can be found under our listing of Accrediting Agencies beginning on page viii.

The recognized regional accrediting commissions are indicated throughout this Directory by the following abbreviations:

EH New England Association of Schools and Colleges, Commission on Institutions of Higher Education

M Middle States Association of Colleges and Schools, Commission on Higher Education

NH Higher Learning Commission, North Central Association

NW Northwest Commission on Colleges and Universities

SC Southern Association of Colleges and Schools, Commission on Colleges

WC Western Association of Schools and Colleges, Accrediting Commission for Senior Colleges and Universities

WJ Western Association of Schools and Colleges, Accrediting Commission for Community and Junior Colleges

National, professional and specialized accrediting agencies and associations are listed below. Wherever possible, degree levels are shown by the following symbols: (C) diploma/certificate; (A) associate; (B) baccalaureate; (M) master's; (S) beyond master's but less than doctorate; (FP) first professional; (D) doctorate.

AA Commission on Accreditation of Allied Health Education Programs: anesthesiologist assistant (M)

AAB Aviation Accreditation Board International: aviation (A,B,M)

AAFCS American Association of Family and Consumer Sciences: family and consumer sciences (B)

ABHES Accrediting Bureau of Health Education Schools: allied health (C,A,B)

ACAE Accreditation Commission for Audiology Education: audiology (D)

ACBSP Accreditation Council for Business Schools and Programs: business administration, management, accounting and related business fields (A,B,M,D)

ACCSC Accrediting Commission of Career Schools and Colleges: occupational, trade and technical education (C,A,B,M)

ACFEI American Culinary Federation, Inc.: culinary arts and culinary management (C,A,B)

ACICS Accrediting Council for Independent Colleges and Schools: business and business-related programs (C,A,B,M)

ACUP Accreditation Commission for Acupuncture and Oriental Medicine: acupuncture (C,M,D)

ADNUR National League for Nursing: nursing (A)

ANEST Council on Accreditation of Nurse Anesthesia Educational Programs: nurse anesthesia (C,M,D)

ARCPA Accreditation Review Commission on Education for the Physician Assistant: physician assisting programs (C,A,B,M)

ART National Association of Schools of Art and Design: art and design (C,A,B,M,D)

AUD American Speech-Language-Hearing Association: audiology (D)

BBT Commission on Accreditation of Allied Health Education Programs: blood bank technology (C,M)

BI Association for Biblical Higher Education: bible college education (C,A,B,M,FP,D)

BUS AACSB-The Association to Advance Collegiate Schools of Business: business and management (B,M,D)

BUSA AACSB-The Association to Advance Collegiate Schools of Business: accounting (B,M,D)

CACREP Council for Accreditation of Counseling & Related Education programs: addiction counseling, career counseling, marriage, couple and family counseling, mental health counseling, school counseling, student affairs and college counseling (M) and counselor education and supervision (D)

CEA Commission on English Language Program Accreditation: english language (C)

CHIRO Council on Chiropractic Education: chiropractic education (FP,D)

CIDA Council for Interior Design Accreditation: interior design (B,M)

CLPSY American Psychological Association: clinical psychology (D)

CNCE Accrediting Council for Continuing Education and Training: continuing education (C,A)

COE Council on Occupational Education: occupational, trade, and technical education (C,A)

COMTA Commission on Massage Therapy Accreditation: massage therapy, bodywork, aesthetics/esthetics and skin care (C,A)

CONST American Council for Construction Education: construction education (A,B)

COPSY American Psychological Association: counseling psychology (D)

CORE Council on Rehabilitation Education: rehabilitation counseling (M)

COSME National Accrediting Commission of Career Arts and Sciences: cosmetology and massage therapy (C)

CS ABET, Inc.: computer science (B)

CVT Commission on Accreditation of Allied Health Education Programs: cardiovascular technology (C,A,B)

CYTO Commission on Accreditation of Allied Health Education Programs: cytotechnology (C,B,M)

DA American Dental Association: dental assisting (C,A)

DANCE National Association of Schools of Dance: dance (C,A,B,M,D)

DENT American Dental Association: dentistry (FP,D)

DETC Distance Education and Training Council: home study schools (A,B,M,D)

DH American Dental Association: dental hygiene (C,A,B,M)

DIETC Academy of Nutrition and Dietetics: coordinated dietetics programs (B,M)

DIETD Academy of Nutrition and Dietetics: didactic dietetics programs (B,M)

DIETI Academy of Nutrition and Dietetics: dietetic post-baccalaureate internships

DIETT Academy of Nutrition and Dietetics: dietetic technician (A)

DMOLS National Accrediting Agency for Clinical Laboratory Sciences: diagnostic molecular scientist (C,B,M)

DMS Commission on Accreditation of Allied Health Education Programs: diagnostic medical sonography (C,A,B,M)

DNUR National League for Nursing: nursing (C)

DT American Dental Association: dental laboratory technology (C,A)

EMT Commission on Accreditation of Allied Health Education Programs: emergency medical technician-paramedic (C,A,B)

ENG ABET, Inc.: engineering (B,M)

ENGR ABET, Inc.: applied science (A,B,M)

ENGT ABET, Inc.: engineering technology (A,B)

EXSC Commission on Accreditation of Allied Health Education Programs: exercise science (B,M)

FOR Society of American Foresters: forestry (B,M)

FUSER American Board of Funeral Service Education: funeral service education (C,A,B)

HSA Commission on Accreditation of Healthcare Management Education: healthcare management (M)

HT National Accrediting Agency for Clinical Laboratory Sciences: histologic technology (C,A,B)

IACBE International Assembly for Collegiate Business Education: business programs in institutions that grant bachelor/graduate degrees (A,B,M,D)

IFSAC International Fire Service Accreditation Congress Degree Assembly: fire and emergency related degree (A,B)

IPSY American Psychological Association: pre-doctoral internships in professional psychology

JOUR Accrediting Council on Education for Journalism and Mass Communications: journalism and mass communications (B,M)

KIN Commission on Accreditation of Allied Health Education Programs: kinesiotherapy (B)

LAW American Bar Association: law (FP,D)

LIB American Library Association: librarianship (M)

LSAR American Society for Landscape Architects: landscape architecture (B,M)

MAAB Accrediting Bureau of Health Education Schools: medical assisting (C,A)

MAC Commission on Accreditation of Allied Health Education Programs: medical assisting (C,A)

MACTE Montessori Accreditation Council for Teacher Education: Montessori teacher education (C)

MEAC Midwifery Education Accreditation Council: midwifery education (C,A,B,M,D)

MED Liaison Committee on Medical Education: medicine (FP,D)

MFCD American Association for Marriage and Family Therapy: marriage and family therapy (M,D)

MIDWF Accreditation Commission for Midwifery Education: nurse midwifery (C,M,D)

MIL Commission on Accreditation of Allied Health Education Programs: medical illustrator (M)

MLTAB Accrediting Bureau of Health Education Schools: medical laboratory technician (C,A)

MLTAD National Accrediting Agency for Clinical Laboratory Sciences: medical laboratory technician (A)

MT National Accrediting Agency for Clinical Laboratory Sciences: medical technology (C,B)

MUS National Association of Schools of Music: music (C,A,B,M,D)

NAIT The Association of Technology, Management, and Applied Engineering: technology, applied technology, engineering technology and technology-related programs (A,B,M)

NATUR Council on Naturopathic Medical Education: naturopathic medical education (FP,D)

NDT Commission on Accreditation of Allied Health Education Programs: neurodiagnostic technology (C,A)

NMT Joint Review Committee on Educational Programs in Nuclear Medicine Technology: nuclear medicine technology (C,A,B)

NRPA National Recreation and Park Association: recreation, park resources, and leisure studies (B)

NUR National League for Nursing: nursing (B,M,D)

NURSE Commission on Collegiate Nursing Education: nursing (B,M,D)

NY New York State Board of Regents:
Degree-granting institutions of higher education in New York that designate the agency as their sole or primary nationally recognized accrediting agency for purposes of establishing elibility to participate in Higher Education Act programs

OPD Commission on Opticianry Accreditation: opticianry (A)

OPE Commission on Accreditation of Allied Health Education Programs: orthotics and prosthetics (C,B,M)

OPLT Commission on Opticianry Accreditation: opthalmic laboratory technician (C)

OPT American Optometric Association: optometry (FP,D)

OPTR American Optometric Association: optometric residency programs

OPTT American Optometric Association: optometric technician (A)

OSTEO American Osteopathic Association, Office of Osteopathic Education: osteopathic medicine (FP,D)

OT American Occupational Therapy Association: occupational therapy (M,D)

OTA American Occupational Therapy Association: occupational therapy assistant (C,A)

PA National Accrediting Agency for Clinical Laboratory Sciences: pathologist's assistant (C,A,B,M)

PAST Association for Clinical Pastoral Education: clinical pastoral education

PDPSY American Psychological Association: post-doctorate residency in professional psychology

PERF Commission on Accreditation of Allied Health Education Programs: perfusionist (C,B,M)

PH Council on Education for Public Health: public health (B,M,D)

PHAR Accreditation Council for Pharmaceutical Education: pharmacy (FP,D)

PLNG Planning Accreditation Board: certified planning (B,M)

PNUR National League for Nursing: practical nursing (C)

POD American Podiatric Medical Association: podiatry (FP,D)

POLYT Commission on Accreditation of Allied Health Education Programs: polysomnographic technologist education (C,A)

PSPSY American Psychological Association: combined professional-scientific psychology (D)

PTA American Physical Therapy Association: physical therapy (M,D)

PTAA American Physical Therapy Association: physical therapy assistant (A)

RABN Association of Advanced Rabbinical and Talmudic Schools: rabbinical and Talmudic education (B,M,D)

RAD Joint Review Committee on Education in Radiologic Technology: radiography (C,A,B)

RADDOS Joint Review Committee on Education in Radiologic Technology: medical dosimetry (C,B,M)

RADMAG Joint Review Committee on Education in Radiologic Technology: magnetic resonance (C,B)

RTT Joint Review Committee on Education in Radiologic Technology: radiation therapist/technologist (C,A,B)

SCPSY American Psychological Association: school psychology (D)

SP American Speech-Language-Hearing Association: speech-language pathology (M,D)

SPAA National Association of Schools of Public Affairs and Administration: public affairs and administration (M)

SURGA Commission on Accreditation of Allied Health Education Programs: surgical assistant (C,A)

SURGT Commission on Accreditation of Allied Health Education Programs: surgical technology (C,A)

SURTEC Accrediting Bureau of Health Education Schools: surgical technologist (C,A)

SW Council on Social Work Education: social work (B,M)

TEAC Teacher Education Accreditation Council: teacher education (B, M,D)

TED National Council for Accreditation of Teacher Education: teacher education (B,M,S,D)

THEA National Association of Schools of Theatre: theatre (C,A,B,M,D)

THEOL Association of Theological Schools: theology (M,FP,D)

TRACS Transnational Association of Christian Colleges and Schools: christian studies education (C,A,B,M,D)

VET American Veterinary Medical Association: veterinary medicine (FP,D)

Explanatory Notes and Symbols

Associate degree: includes junior colleges, community colleges, technical institutes, and schools offering at least a two-year program of college-level studies, either leading to an associate degree wholly or principally creditable toward a baccalaureate degree.

Baccalaureate: includes those institutions offering programs of studies leading to the customary bachelor of arts or bachelor of science degrees.

First professional degree: includes those institutions that offer the academic requirements for selected professions based on programs that require at least two academic years of previous college work for entrance and a total of at least six years of college work for completion.

Master's: includes those institutions offering the customary first graduate degree, master of arts or master of science degree in the liberal arts and sciences, or the next degree in the same field after the first professional degree.

Beyond master's but less than doctorate: includes those institutions offering "postgraduate pre-doctoral degrees".

Graduate non-degree granting: includes institutions offering work beyond the bachelor's level but not conferring degrees. In some instances the degrees are conferred by cooperating institutions.

Doctorate: includes those institutions offering a Ph.D. or its equivalent in any field.

Postdoctoral research only: includes institutions operating solely for the purpose of research at the postdoctoral level.

First Talmudic degree: undergraduate degree granted by accredited Rabbinical schools. The schools in New York "using this designation do not imply that the 'First Talmudic Degree' is equivalent to any secular academic degree recognized by the Board of Regents".*

Second Talmudic degree: graduate degree granted by accredited Rabbinical schools. The schools in New York "using this designation do not imply that the 'Second Talmudic Degree' is equivalent to any secular academic degree recognized by the Board of Regents".*

---

*The University of the State of New York, The State Education Department, Albany, New York, letter August 17, 1983.

Type of Program

Occupational: refers to programs beyond high school designed to provide students with knowledge and skills necessary for immediate employment.

Two-year principally bachelor's creditable: refers to the first two years of college work.

Liberal arts and general: refers to four or five year baccalaureate or postbaccalaureate degree programs in the liberal arts and sciences.

Teacher preparatory programs: refers to programs of at least four years duration.

Professional programs: refers to separate programs of at least four years beyond high school and organized around a professionally oriented academic discipline.

Business, fine arts, music, nursing, religious, or technical emphasis: refers to programs that are organized around a specific discipline.

Symbols

* The institution is part of a system.

Used preceding any of the acronyms for the accrediting agencies the following symbols indicate that:

The accrediting agency has stated publicly that the institution or program is preliminary or provisionally accredited, accredited with some reservations, or approved on probation.

@ The institution or program has attained a pre-accredited status.

& The institution is covered under the regional accreditation of the parent institution.

U.S. Postal Abbreviation of States and Territories

Alabama .... AL
Alaska .... AK
American Samoa .... AS
Arizona .... AZ
Arkansas .... AR
California .... CA
Colorado .... CO
Connecticut .... CT
Delaware .... DE
District of Columbia .... DC
Florida .... FL
Georgia .... GA
Guam .... GU
Hawaii .... HI
Idaho .... ID
Illinois IL
Indiana .... IN
Iowa .... IA
Kansas .... KS
Kentucky .... KY
Louisiana .... LA
Maine .... ME
Maryland .... MD
Marshall Islands .... MH
Massachusetts .... MA
Michigan .... MI
Micronesia .... FM
Minnesota .... MN
Mississippi .... MS
Missouri .... MO
Montana .... MT
Nebraska .... NE
Nevada .... NV
New Hampshire .... NH
New Jersey .... NJ
New Mexico .... NM
New York .... NY
North Carolina .... NC
North Dakota .... ND
Northern Marianas .... MP
Ohio .... OH
Oklahoma .... OK
Oregon .... OR
Palau .... PW
Pennsylvania .... PA
Puerto Rico .... PR
Rhode Island .... RI
South Carolina .... SC
South Dakota .... SD
Tennessee .... TN
Texas .... TX
Utah .... UT
Vermont .... VT
Virgin Islands VI
Virginia .... VA
Washington .... WA
West Virginia .... WV
Wisconsin .... WI
Wyoming .... WY

Institution Changes

Institutions and Offices Added

California

	FICE/ID Number
Academy of Couture Art	041855
American Evangelical University	667090
Apollos University	667096
Bergin University of Canine Studies	041763
Fresno Pacific Biblical Seminary	010368
Grace Communion Seminary	667115
High Tech High Graduate School of Education	667118
LA Music Academy	038684
Rudolf Steiner College	667088
Southern States University	667108
Teachers College of San Joaquin	667087
Theatre of Arts	667098
Veritas Evangelical Seminary	667103

Colorado

	FICE/ID Number
Colorado State University-Global Campus	042087
Memorial Hospital/Memorial Health System School of Radiologic Technology	667097
Remington College-Colorado Springs	030121
Yeshiva Toras Chaim Talmudical Seminary of Denver	667113

Florida

	FICE/ID Number
Aerosim Flight Academy	041571
Azure College	667116
Health Career Institute	667104
Millennia Atlantic University	041825
Pensacola Christian College	667101

Idaho

	FICE/ID Number
College of Western Idaho	042118

Indiana

	FICE/ID Number
St. Anthony School of Echocardiography	667119

Iowa

	FICE/ID Number
Shiloh University	667095

Kansas

	FICE/ID Number
Salina Area Technical College	005499

Michigan

	FICE/ID Number
Compass College of Cinematic Arts	041633
Puritan Reformed Theological Seminary	667099
Van Andel Institute Graduate School	667085

Missouri

	FICE/ID Number
Heartland Christian College	667091

Nebraska

	FICE/ID Number
Mary Lanning Healthcare School of Radiology	004431

New Jersey

	FICE/ID Number
Yeshiva Yesodei Hatorah	667109

New York

	FICE/ID Number
Beth Medrash Meor Yitzchok	667111
Relay Graduate School of Education	667117
Yeshiva Gedolah Kesser Torah	667112
Yeshiva Zidvon Aryeh	667110

North Carolina

	FICE/ID Number
Daoist Traditions College of Chinese Medical Arts	041464
Native American Bible College	667092

Ohio

	FICE/ID Number
Valor Christian College	667093

Pennsylvania

	FICE/ID Number
YTI Career Institute-Capital Region	023044

Puerto Rico

	FICE/ID Number
Instituto de Banca y Comercio	667107

South Carolina

	FICE/ID Number
University of South Carolina School of Medicine-Greenville	667114

Texas

	FICE/ID Number
B.H. Carroll Theological Institute	667089
Grace School of Theology	667100
Lighthouse College	667106
North American College	041795
Sanford-Brown College	026150
Texas A & M University - Central Texas	667086

Virginia

	FICE/ID Number
Everest College	009267
Fortis College	023427
Global Health College	041400
iGlobal University	667105
Southside Regional Medical Center Professional Schools	012744
University of Fairfax	667094

FICE/ID Number

Institutions and Offices Dropped

Arizona

Arizona Automotive Institute 010847
(No longer degree granting)

California

Aviation & Electronic Schools of America 041253
(No longer accredited)
Cleveland Chiropractic College 021474
(Closed)
CNI College 032423
(No longer degree granting)
DeVry University - Irvine Center 666192
(Closed)
Everest College-Hayward 011121
(No longer degree granting)
International Reformed University and Seminary 041357
(No longer accredited)
Kaplan College 030445
(Closed)
Oxman College 667025
(No longer accredited)
Perelandra College 666475
(No longer accredited)

Colorado

Yorktown University 666409
(No longer accredited)

Florida

Angley College 035954
(Closed)
FastTrain of Ft. Lauderdale 041320
(Closed)
FastTrain of Jacksonville 041322
(Closed)
FastTrain of Miami 041319
(Closed)
FastTrain of Tampa 041321
(Closed)

Hawaii

Kona University 666650
(No longer accredited)

Illinois

Argosy University (Corporate Offices) 021799
(Corporate office relocated to Califorinia)
DeVry University - Lincolnshire Center 666206
(Closed)

Kansas

Kansas College of Chinese Medicine 041453
(No longer accredited)

FICE/ID Number

Louisiana

Blue Cliff College 034225
(No longer degree granting)
Camelot College 030235
(No longer degree granting)
Gretna Career College 030951
(No longer degree granting)

Massachusetts

Atlantic Union College 002119
(No longer accredited)

Minnesota

DeVry University - St. Louis Park 666559
(Closed)

New Hampshire

Chester College of New England 004733
(Closed)

New York

Long Island College Hospital School of Nursing 021187
(Closed)

Ohio

Carnegie Career College 036933
(No longer accredited)

Pennsylvania

Le Cordon Bleu Institute of Culinary Arts in Pittsburgh 030068
(Closed)

Puerto Rico

Universal Career Community College 033263
(Closed)

Texas

Court Reporting Institute of Houston 666730
(Closed)
Texas School of Business-Southwest 666729
(No longer degree granting)

Virginia

ACT College 030911
(Closed)
Heritage Institute-Manassas 023045
(Closed)
RSHT 034095
(Closed)

Washington

Northwest Aviation College 041352
(Closed)

FICE/ID Number

West Virginia

Valley College - Princeton Campus 030842
(No longer degree granting)

Wisconsin

Lakeside School of Massage Therapy 030074
(Closed)

Saint Francis Seminary 667023
(Closed)

Merged Institutions

California

Hebrew Union College-Jewish Institute of Religion (California Branch) *into* 004055
Hebrew Union College-Jewish Institute of Religion 004054

Connecticut

Board of Trustees of Community-Technical Colleges *into* 666784
Connecticut Board of Regents for Higher Education 666656

Indiana

Kaplan College *into* 022018
Kaplan College 666436

Louisiana

Northshore Technical College Florida Parishes Campus *into* 005483
Northshore Technical Community College 006756

Northshore Technical College Hammond Area Campus *into* 005481
Northshore Technical Community College 006756

Maryland

Baltimore International College *into* 023148
Stratford University 025412

Massachusetts

Longy School of Music of Bard College *into* 021430
Bard College 002671

The Art Institute of Boston at Lesley University *into* 008174
Lesley University 002160

Ohio

Hebrew Union College-Jewish Institute of Religion *into* 003047
Hebrew Union College-Jewish Institute of Religion 004054

FICE/ID Number

Hebrew Union College-Jewish Institute of Religion Central Office *into* 008798
Hebrew Union College-Jewish Institute of Religion 004054

Texas

Texas Southmost College *into* 003643
The University of Texas at Brownsville
to become
The University of Texas at Brownsville and Texas Southmost College 030646

Name Changes

Alabama

from: Andrew Jackson University 041292
to: New Charter University

from: Concordia College 010554
to: Concordia College Alabama

from: Prince Institute of Professional Studies 022960
to: Prince Institute - Southeast

from: Tri-State Institute 666683
to: Fortis Institute

Alaska

from: Career Academy 025410
to: Alaska Career College

Arizona

from: American Graduate School of Education 667017
to: Acacia University

Arkansas

from: Arkansas State University 001090
to: Arkansas State University-Jonesboro

California

from: Alliant International University-Fresno & Sacramento 011117
to: Alliant International University-San Diego

from: Alliant International University-San Diego 001158
to: Alliant International University-Fresno & Sacramento

from: Bethesda Christian University 032663
to: Bethesda University of California

from: Charles Drew University of Medicine & Science 010365
to: Charles R. Drew University of Medicine & Science

from: DeVry University - San Diego Center 666193
to: DeVry University - San Diego Campus

from: Institute of Transpersonal Psychology 022676
to: Sofia University (formerly Institute of Transpersonal Psychology)

Institution Changes

	FICE/ID Number
from: Kensington College *to:* Bristol University	033083
from: School of Urban Missions *to:* SUM Bible College and Theological Seminary	666021
from: The Art Institute of California-Hollywood *to:* The Art Institute of California, A College of Argosy University - Hollywood	031254
from: The Art Institute of California-Inland Empire *to:* The Art Institute of California, A College of Argosy University - Inland Empire	016471
from: The Art Institute of California-Los Angeles *to:* The Art Institute of California, A College of Argosy University - Los Angeles	666045
from: The Art Institute of California-Orange County *to:* The Art Institute of California, A College of Argosy University - Orange County	666182
from: The Art Institute of California-Sacramento *to:* The Art Institute of California, A College of Argosy University - Sacramento	666619
from: The Art Institute of California-San Diego *to:* The Art Institute of California, A College of Argosy University - San Diego	023276
from: The Art Institute of California-San Francisco *to:* The Art Institute of California, A College of Argosy University - San Francisco	007236
from: The Art Institute of California-Sunnyvale *to:* The Art Institute of California, A College of Argosy University - Sunnyvale	666620

Colorado

from: Adams State College *to:* Adams State University	001345
from: Metropolitan State College of Denver *to:* Metropolitan State University of Denver	001360
from: Western State College *to:* Western State Colorado University	001372

Connecticut

from: Saint Joseph College *to:* University of Saint Joseph	001409

Delaware

from: Delaware Technical and Community College Central Office *to:* Delaware Technical Community College, Office of the President	008074

District of Columbia

from: Sanz College *to:* Medtech College	666591
from: University System of the District of Columbia *to:* University of the District of Columbia	001441

Florida

	FICE/ID Number
from: DeVry University - Tampa Center *to:* DeVry University - Tampa Bay Campus	666199
from: Florida Hospital College of Health Sciences *to:* Adventist University of Health Sciences	031155
from: Florida Medical Training Institute-Coconut Creek *to:* Florida Medical Training Institute-Coral Springs	666612
from: Florida National College Hialeah Campus *to:* Florida National University Hialeah Campus	025476
from: Florida National College South Campus *to:* Florida National University South Campus	666691
from: Florida National College Training Center *to:* Florida National University Training Center	666690
from: Full Sail Real World Education *to:* Full Sail University	023621
from: Keiser Career College *to:* Southeastern College	031239
from: Keiser Career College *to:* Southeastern College	035533
from: Keiser Career College *to:* Southeastern College	666290
from: Keiser Career College *to:* Southeastern College	666758
from: Meridian Career Institute *to:* Meridian College	023268
from: South Florida Community College *to:* South Florida State College	001522

Georgia

from: Ashworth University *to:* Ashworth College	666106
from: Atlanta Metropolitan College *to:* Atlanta Metropolitan State College	012165
from: DeKalb Technical College *to:* Georgia Piedmont Technical College	005622
from: East Georgia College *to:* East Georgia State College	010997
from: Gordon College *to:* Gordon State College	001575

Hawaii

from: Traditional Chinese Medical College of Hawaii *to:* Hawaii College of Oriental Medicine	039994

Illinois

from: Methodist College of Nursing *to:* Methodist College	006228

Indiana

from: Associated Mennonite Biblical Seminary *to:* Anabaptist Mennonite Biblical Seminary	001823
from: Indiana Institute of Technology *to:* Indiana Tech	001805

FICE/ID Number

from: Indiana University System — 008002
to: Indiana University

from: Manchester College — 001820
to: Manchester University

from: Saint Meinrad Seminary and School of Theology — 007276
to: Saint Meinrad School of Theology

Louisiana

from: Acadiana Technical College Charles B Coreil Campus — 022402
to: South Louisiana Community College Charles B Coreil Campus

from: Acadiana Technical College Gulf Area Campus — 005482
to: South Louisiana Community College Gulf Area Campus

from: Acadiana Technical College Lafayette Campus — 022148
to: South Louisiana Community College Ardoin Campus

from: Acadiana Technical College T.H. Harris Campus — 005466
to: South Louisiana Community College T.H. Harris Campus

from: Acadiana Technical College Teche Area Campus — 005528
to: South Louisiana Community College Teche Area Campus

from: Central Louisiana Technical College Alexandria Campus — 005489
to: Central Louisiana Technical Community College

from: Delta School of Business & Technology — 020555
to: Delta School of Business & Technology, DBA Delta Tech

Massachusetts

from: Gibbs College of Boston, Inc. — 007481
to: Sanford-Brown College of Boston, Inc.

from: University of Massachusetts at Worcester — 009756
to: University of Massachusetts Medical School

Michigan

from: Sacred Heart Major Seminary/College and Theologate — 002313
to: Sacred Heart Major Seminary

Minnesota

from: Minnesota School of Business — 666453
to: Globe University/Minnesota School of Business

from: Northwest Technical Institute — 008267
to: Globe University Northwest Technical Institute

FICE/ID Number

Montana

from: Fort Belknap College — 025175
to: Aaniiih Nakoda College

from: Montana State University - Billings College of Technology — 010166
to: City College at Montana State University Billings

from: Montana State University - Great Falls College of Technology — 009314
to: Great Falls College Montana State University

from: Montana Tech College of Technology — 009282
to: Highlands College of Montana Tech

New Mexico

from: Institute of American Indian and Alaska Native Culture and Arts Development — 021464
to: Institute of American Indian Arts

New York

from: Adirondack Community College — 002860
to: SUNY Adirondack

from: Long Island University Riverhead Campus — 666174
to: LIU Riverhead

from: Paul Smith's College of Arts and Sciences — 002795
to: Paul Smith's College

from: State University of New York at Albany — 002835
to: University at Albany, SUNY

from: State University of New York at Buffalo — 002837
to: University at Buffalo-SUNY

from: Swedish Institute College of Health Sciences — 021700
to: Swedish Institute--College of Health Sciences

North Carolina

from: Bennett College for Women — 002911
to: Bennett College

from: Peace College — 002953
to: William Peace University (formerly Peace College)

from: Saint Augustine's College — 002968
to: Saint Augustine's University

from: St. Andrews Presbyterian College — 002967
to: St. Andrews University

Ohio

from: Academy of Court Reporting — 021521
to: Miami-Jacobs Career College

from: Belmont Technical College — 009941
to: Belmont College

from: Kent State University Ashtabula Campus — 003052
to: Kent State University at Ashtabula

from: Northeastern Ohio Universities Colleges of Medicine and Pharmacy — 024544
to: Northeast Ohio Medical University

Institution Changes

	FICE/ID Number
from: Ohio College of Podiatric Medicine *to:* Kent State University College of Podiatric Medicine	003088
from: Temple Baptist College *to:* Ohio Mid-Western College (Formerly Temple Baptist College)	037263

Oklahoma

from: Platt College *to:* Platt College-OKC Central	666341

Pennsylvania

from: Central Pennsylvania College *to:* Central Penn College	004890
from: CHI Institute *to:* Kaplan Career Institute	022898
from: Commonwealth Technical Institute *to:* Commonwealth Technical Institute at the Hiram G. Andrews Center	025366
from: Lock Haven University of Pennsylvania *to:* Lock Haven University	003323
from: Mercyhurst College *to:* Mercyhurst University	003297

Puerto Rico

from: Atlantic College *to:* Atlantic University College	025054
from: Colegio Biblico Pentecostal De Puerto Rico *to:* Universidad Teologica Del Caribe	023355
from: National College of Business and Technology *to:* National University College	022606
from: National College of Business and Technology *to:* National University College	666489
from: Ponce School of Medicine *to:* Ponce School of Medicine & Health Sciences	024824

South Carolina

from: Forrest Junior College *to:* Forrest College	004924
from: Lutheran Theological Southern Seminary *to:* Lutheran Theological Southern Seminary of Lenoir-Rhyne University	003437

Tennessee

from: Northeast State Technical Community College *to:* Northeast State Community College	005378

Texas

	FICE/ID Number
from: Cisco Junior College *to:* Cisco College	003553
from: International Business College *to:* Franklin College	009082
from: The Academy of Health Care Professions *to:* The College of Health Care Professions	031281
from: The Academy of Health Care Professions *to:* The College of Health Care Professions	034263
from: The College of Saint Thomas More *to:* The College of Saints John Fisher & Thomas More	031894
from: University of Texas Southwestern Medical Center at Dallas *to:* University of Texas Southwestern Medical Center	010019

Utah

from: Careers Unlimited *to:* The Utah College of Dental Hygiene at Careers Unlimited	034633
from: Latter-Day Saints Business College *to:* LDS Business College	003672

Vermont

from: School for International Training *to:* SIT	008860

Virginia

from: Sanford-Brown College *to:* Sanford-Brown College-Tysons Corner	009420
from: Sanz School *to:* Medtech College	025889

Washington

from: Lake Washington Technical College *to:* Lake Washington Institute of Technology	005373
from: Northwest College of Art *to:* Northwest College of Art & Design (NCAD)	026021

Wisconsin

from: Silver Lake College *to:* Silver Lake College of the Holy Family	003850

Wyoming

from: Wyoming Technical Institute *to:* WyoTech	009157

Codes and Descriptions of Administrative Officers

(01) **Chief Executive Officer (President/Chancellor)** - Directs all affairs and operations of a higher education institution.

(02) **Chief Executive Officer Within a System (President/Chancellor)** - Directs all affairs and operations of a campus or an institution which is part of a university-wide system.

(03) **Executive Vice President** - Responsible for all or most functions and operations of an institution under the direction of the Chief Executive Officer.

(04) **Administrative Assistant to the President** - Senior administrative assistant to the Chief Executive Officer.

(05) **Chief Academic Officer** - Directs the academic program of the institution. Typically includes academic planning, teaching, research, extensions and coordination of interdepartmental affairs.

(06) **Registrar** - Responsible for student registration, scheduling of classes, examinations and classroom facilities, student records and related matters.

(07) **Director of Admissions** - Responsible for the recruitment, selection and admission of students.

(08) **Head Librarian** - Directs the activities of all institutional libraries.

(09) **Director of Institutional Research** - Conducts research and studies on the institution including design of studies, data collection, analysis and reporting.

(10) **Chief Financial/Business Officer** - Directs business and financial affairs including accounting, purchasing, investments, auxiliary enterprises and related business matters.

(11) **Chief of Operations/Administration** - Responsible for administrative functions that are generally non-academic and non-financial.

(12) **Director of Branch Campus** - Official who is in charge of a branch campus.

(13) **Director, Computing and Information Management** - Coordinates computing systems and the flow of information to and from computing operations.

(14) **Director, Computer Center** - Directs the institution's major data processing facilities and services.

(15) **Director, Personnel Services** - Administers the institution's personnel policies and programs for staff or faculty and staff.

(16) **Chief, Personnel** - Responsible for establishing and directing personnel policies including government related requirements.

(17) **Chief, Health Care Professions** - Senior administrator of academic health care programs, hospitals, clinic or affiliated healthcare programs.

(18) **Chief, Facilities/Physical Plant** - Responsible for the construction, rehabilitation and maintenance of buildings and grounds.

(19) **Director, Security/Safety** - Manages campus police. Responsible for security programs, training, traffic and parking regulations.

(20) **Associate Academic Officer** - Responsible for many of the functions and operations under the direction of the Chief Academic Officer.

(21) **Associate Business Officer** - Assists and reports to the Chief Business Officer.

(22) **Director, Affirmative Action/Equal Opportunity** - Responsible for the institution's program relating to affirmative action and equal opportunity.

(23) **Director, Health Services** - Directs the operation of clinics, medical staff and other programs which provide institutional health services.

(24) **Director, Educational Media** - Responsible for audio-visual services and multimedia learning devices.

(25) **Contract Administrator** - Conducts administrative activities in connection with contracts and grants.

(26) **Chief Public Relations Officer** - Directs public relations program. May include alumni relations, publication, marketing and development.

(27) **Chief Information Officer** - Provides information about the institution to students, faculty, staff and the public.

(28) **Director of Diversity** - Responsible for the institution's programs relating to diversity.

(29) **Director, Alumni Relations** - Coordinates alumni activities between the institution and the alumni.

(30) **Chief, Development** - Organizes and directs programs connected with the fund raising activities of the institution.

(31) **Chief Community Relations Officer** - Directs the educational (usually non-credit), cultural and recreational services to the community.

(32) **Chief Student Life Officer** - Responsible for the direction of student life programs including counseling and testing, housing, placement, student union, relationships with student organizations and related functions.

(33) **Dean of Men** - Directs student life activities solely concerned with male students.

(34) **Dean of Women** - Directs student life activities solely concerned with female students.

(35) **Director, Student Affairs** - Assists Chief Student Life Officer in the non-academic student life activities.

(36) **Director, Student Placement** - Directs the operation of the student placement office to provide career counseling and job placement services to undergraduates, graduates and alumni.

(37) **Director, Student Financial Aid** - Directs the administration of all forms of student aid.

(38) **Director, Student Counseling** - Directs non-academic counseling and testing for students including referral to outside agencies.

(39) **Director, Student Housing** - Manages student housing operations.

(40) **Director, Bookstore** - Responsible for the operation of the bookstore including purchasing, advertising, sales, employment, inventory and related functions.

(41) **Athletic Director** - Manages intramural and intercollegiate programs including employment, scheduling, promotion, maintenance and related functions.

(42) **Chaplain, Director Campus Ministry** - Plans, directs the pastoral ministry and religious activities.

(43) **Director, Legal Services (General Counsel)** - Salaried staff person responsible for advising on legal rights, obligations and related matters.

(44) **Director, Annual or Planned Giving** - Operates the annual giving from all supporters of the institutions.

(45) **Chief Planning Officer** - Directs the long-range planning and the allocation of the institution's resources.

(46) **Chief, Research and Development (not fundraising)** - Initiates and directs research in using the facilities and personnel in new areas of academic and scientific exploration.

Dean or Director. Serves as the principal administrator for the institutional program indicated:

(47) **Agriculture**
(48) **Architecture**
(49) **Art and Sciences**
(50) **Business**
(51) **Continuing Education**
(52) **Dentistry**
(53) **Education**
(54) **Engineering**
(55) **Evening Division**
(56) **Extension**
(57) **Fine Arts**
(58) **Graduate Programs**
(59) **Home Economics**
(60) **Journalism/Communications**
(61) **Law**
(62) **Library Services**
(63) **Medicine**
(64) **Music**
(65) **Natural Resources**
(66) **Nursing**
(67) **Pharmacy**
(68) **Physical Education**
(69) **Public Health**
(70) **Social Work**
(71) **Special Session**
(72) **Technology**
(73) **Theology**
(74) **Veterinary Medicine**
(75) **Vocational/Occupational Education**
(76) **Allied Health Sciences**
(77) **Computer Science**
(78) **Cooperative Education**
(79) **Humanities**
(80) **Government/Public Affairs**
(81) **Mathematics/Sciences**
(82) **Political Science/International Affairs**
(83) **Social and Behavioral Sciences**
(87) **Summer School/Session**
(89) **Freshmen Studies**
(92) **Honors Program**
(93) **Minority Students**
(94) **Women's Studies**
(97) **General Studies**
(106) **Online Education/E-learning**
(107) **Professional Studies**

(84) **Director, Enrollment Management** - Plans, develops, and implements strategies to sustain enrollment. Supervises administration of all admissions and financial aid operations.

(85) **Director, Foreign Students** - Directs student life activities solely concerned with foreign students.

(86) **Director, Government Relations** - Coordinates institution's relations with local, state, and federal government.

(90) **Director, Academic Computing** - Responsible for operation and coordination of the institution's various academic computer facilities and labs.

(91) **Director, Administrative Computing** - Responsible for operation of the institution's administrative computing facility.

(96) **Director of Purchasing** - Coordinates purchasing of goods and services.

(100) **Chief of Staff** - Senior non-secretarial staff assistant to the President/Chancellor. Manages administration and operations of The Office of the President.

(101) **Secretary of the Institution/Board of Governors** - Responsible for liaison between the Board and the institution. Maintains governance and official Board records.

(102) **Director, Foundation/Corporate Relations** - Directs institution's efforts in the area of soliciting grants and gifts from foundations and corporations.

(103) **Director, Workforce Development** - Directs the institution's efforts in course development and instruction for students and the community in skills necessary to gain employment.

(104) **Director, Study Abroad** - Coordinates and advises students and faculty on academic studies conducted internationally.

(105) **Director, Web Services** - Directs the development, operations and content of the institution's web sites.

(108) **Director, Institutional Assessment** - Facilitates and directs institution-wide assessment activities for academic programs and non-academic departments.

(88) Use this code for those titles that do not fit the above positions.

(00) **President Emeritus**

United States Department of Education Offices

Arne Duncan (A)
Secretary of Education
United States Department of Education
400 Maryland Avenue, SW
Washington, DC 20202
(202) 401-3000
FAX: (202) 260-7867
URL: www.ed.gov

Martha Kanter (B)
Under Secretary of Education
United States Department of Education
400 Maryland Avenue, SW
Room 7E304
Washington, DC 20202
(202) 401-0429
FAX: (202) 205-0063
E-MAIL: carmine.perrotti@ed.gov
URL: www.ed.gov

David Bergeron (C)
Acting Assistant Secretary
Office of Postsecondary Education
United States Department of Education
1990 K Street, NW
Washington, DC 20006
(202) 502-7750
FAX: (202) 502-7677
E-MAIL: david.bergeron@ed.gov
URL: www2.ed.gov/about/offices/list/ope/index.html

Ms. Carol Griffiths (D)
Executive Director
National Advisory Committee on Institutional Quality & Integrity
Office of Postsecondary Education
United States Department of Education
1990 K Street, NW
Room 8073
Washington, DC 20006
(202) 219-7009
FAX: (202) 219-7005
E-MAIL: carol.griffiths@ed.gov
URL: www.ed.gov/about/bdscomm/list/naciqi.html

Ms. Kay Gilcher (E)
Director
Accreditation Division
Office of Postsecondary Education
U.S. Department of Education
1990 K Street, NW
Room 8027
Washington, DC 20006-8509
(202) 502-7693
URL: www.ed.gov/admins/finaid/accred/index.html

(F)
Postsecondary, Adult and Career Education Division
National Center for Education Statistics
1990 K Street, NW
Room 8107
Washington, DC 20006
(202) 219-1385
E-MAIL: contact.IES@ed.gov
URL: www.nces.ed.gov

Ms. Carol Griffiths (G)
Executive Director
National Committee on Foreign Medical Education
and Accreditation (NCFMEA)
U.S. Department of Education
1990 K Street, NW
Room 8073
Washington, DC 20006
(202) 219-7009
FAX: (202) 219-7005
E-MAIL: carol.griffiths@ed.gov
URL: www2.ed.gov/about/bdscomm/list/ncfmea.html

Statewide Agencies of Higher Education

ALABAMA

Alabama Commission on Higher Education (H)
PO Box 302000
Montgomery, AL 36130-2000
(334) 242-1998
FAX: (334) 242-0268
Dr. Gregory G. Fitch
Executive Director
E-MAIL: gregory.fitch@ache.alabama.gov
URL: www.ache.alabama.gov

State of Alabama Department of Postsecondary Education (I)
135 South Union Street
PO Box 302130
Montgomery, AL 36130
(334) 293-4524
FAX: (334) 293-4526
Susan Yvette Price
Interim Chancellor
E-MAIL: susan.price@dpe.edu
URL: www.accs.cc

ALASKA

Alaska Commission on Postsecondary Education (J)
PO Box 110505
Juneau, AK 99811-0505
(907) 465-6740
FAX: (907) 465-3293
Ms. Diane Barrans
Executive Director
E-MAIL: ACPE.execdirector@alaska.gov
URL: www.acpe.alaska.gov

ARIZONA

Arizona Board of Regents (K)
2020 North Central Avenue
Suite 230
Phoenix, AZ 85004-4593
(602) 229-2500
FAX: (602) 229-2555
Thomas K. Anderes Ph.D.
President
E-MAIL: tom.anderes@azregents.edu
URL: www.azregents.edu

Arizona Commission for Postsecondary Education (L)
2020 North Central Avenue
Suite 650
Phoenix, AZ 85004-4503
(602) 258-2435
FAX: (602) 258-2483
Dr. April L. Osborn
Executive Director
E-MAIL: acpe@azhighered.gov
URL: www.azhighered.gov

ARKANSAS

Arkansas Department of Higher Education (M)
114 East Capitol Avenue
Little Rock, AR 72201
(501) 371-2030
FAX: (501) 371-2003
Mr. Shane Broadway
Interim Director of Higher Education
E-MAIL: shane.broadway@adhe.edu
URL: www.adhe.edu

CALIFORNIA

California Community Colleges Chancellor's Office (N)
1102 Q Street
4th Floor
Sacramento, CA 95811
(916) 322-4005
FAX: (916) 322-4783
Dr. Jack Scott
Chancellor
E-MAIL: jscott@cccco.edu
URL: www.cccco.edu

COLORADO

Colorado Department of Higher Education (O)
1560 Broadway
Suite 1600
Denver, CO 80202
(303) 866-2723
FAX: (303) 866-4266
Lt.Gov. Joseph Garcia
Executive Director
E-MAIL: josephgarcia.executivedirector@dhe.state.co.us
URL: highered.colorado.gov

Colorado Community College System (P)
9101 East Lowry Boulevard
Denver, CO 80230-6011
(303) 595-1552
FAX: (303) 620-4043
Dr. Nancy J. McCallin
President
E-MAIL: president@cccs.edu
URL: www.cccs.edu

CONNECTICUT

Board of Regents for Higher Education (Q)
Connecticut State Colleges & Universities
39 Woodland Street
Hartford, CT 06105
(860) 493-0011
Dr. Robert A. Kennedy
President
E-MAIL: kennedyr@ct.edu
URL: www.ctregents.org

Office of Higher Education (R)
61 Woodland Street
Hartford, CT 06105-2326
(860) 947-1801
Jane A. Ciarleglio
Executive Director
E-MAIL: janeciarleglio@ctohe.org
URL: www.ctohe.org

DELAWARE

Delaware Higher Education Office (S)
Townsend Building
401 Federal Street
Dover, DE 19901
(302) 735-4120
FAX: (302) 739-5894
Ms. Maureen Laffey
Director
E-MAIL: dheo@doe.k12.de.us
URL: www.doe.k12.de.us/dheo

Delaware Technical Community College (T)
PO Box 897
Dover, DE 19903
(302) 739-4053
FAX: (302) 739-6225
Dr. Orlando J. George Jr.
President
E-MAIL: pres@dtcc.edu
URL: www.dtcc.edu

DISTRICT OF COLUMBIA

Office of the State Superintendent of Education Government of the District of Columbia (U)
810 First Street, NE
9th Floor
Washington, DC 20002
(202) 727-6436
FAX: (202) 727-2019
Hosanna Mahaley
State Superintendent of Education
E-MAIL: osse@dc.gov
URL: www.osse.dc.gov

District of Columbia Education Licensure Commission (V)
810 First Street, NE
2nd Floor
Washington, DC 20002
(202) 724-2095
FAX: (202) 741-0229
Ms. Robin Y. Jenkins
Executive Director
E-MAIL: robin.jenkins@dc.gov
URL: www.osse.dc.gov

FLORIDA

Board of Governors State University System of Florida (W)
325 West Gaines Street
Suite 1614
Tallahassee, FL 32399-0400
(850) 245-0466
FAX: (850) 245-9685
Frank T. Brogan
Chancellor
E-MAIL: chancellor@flbog.edu
URL: www.flbog.edu

State of Florida Department of Education Division of Florida Colleges (X)
325 West Gaines Street
1544 Turlington Building
Tallahassee, FL 32399-0400
(850) 245-9449
FAX: (850) 245-9525
Mr. Randall W. Hanna
Chancellor
E-MAIL: randy.hanna@fldoe.org
URL: www.fldoe.org/cc

GEORGIA

Board of Regents of the University System of Georgia (Y)
270 Washington Street, SW
Atlanta, GA 30334
(404) 656-2202
FAX: (404) 657-6979
Mr. Henry Huckaby
Chancellor
E-MAIL: chancellor@usg.edu
URL: www.usg.edu

University System of Georgia (Z)
270 Washington Street, SW
Atlanta, GA 30334
(404) 962-3069
FAX: (404) 962-3093
Dr. Susan Campbell Lounsbury
Asst Vice Chanc for Research & Policy Analysis
E-MAIL: susan.campbell@usg.edu
URL: www.usg.edu

HAWAII

State Post-Secondary Education Commission (a)
University of Hawaii at Manoa
2444 Dole Street
Bachman Hall, Room 209
Honolulu, HI 96822
(808) 956-8213
FAX: (808) 956-5156
Compliance Officer/Director
E-MAIL: bor@hawaii.edu

IDAHO

Idaho State Board of Education (A)
PO Box 83720
Boise, ID 83720-0037
(208) 334-2270
Fax: (208) 334-2632
Dr. Mike Rush
Executive Director
E-mail: mike.rush@osbe.idaho.gov
URL: boardofed.idaho.gov

ILLINOIS

Illinois Board of Higher Education (B)
431 East Adams
2nd Floor
Springfield, IL 62701-1404
(217) 782-2551
Fax: (217) 782-8548
Dr. George W. Reid
Executive Director
E-mail: reid@ibhe.org
URL: www.ibhe.org

Illinois Community College Board (C)
401 East Capitol Avenue
Springfield, IL 62701-1874
(217) 785-0123
Fax: (217) 785-7495
Mr. Geoffrey S. Obrzut
President/CEO
E-mail: geoffrey.obrzut@illinois.gov
URL: www.iccb.org

INDIANA

Indiana Commission for Higher Education (D)
101 West Ohio Street
Suite 550
Indianapolis, IN 46204
(317) 464-4400
Fax: (317) 464-4410
Mrs. Teresa Lubbers
Commissioner for Higher Education
E-mail: Teresal@che.in.gov
URL: www.che.in.gov

IOWA

Board of Regents, State of Iowa (E)
11260 Aurora Avenue
Urbandale, IA 50322-7905
(515) 281-3934
Fax: (515) 281-6420
Mr. Robert Donley
Executive Director
E-mail: bdonley@iastate.edu
URL: www.regents.iowa.gov

Iowa College Student Aid Commission (F)
603 East 12th Street
5th Floor
Des Moines, IA 50319
(515) 725-3410
Fax: (515) 725-3401
Ms. Karen Misjak
Executive Director
E-mail: karen.misjak@iowa.gov
URL: www.iowacollegeaid.org

Iowa Department of Education Division of Community Colleges (G)
400 East 14th Street
Grimes State Office Building
Des Moines, IA 50319-0146
(515) 281-8260
Fax: (515) 242-5988
Colleen Hunt
Interim Administrator
E-mail: colleen.hunt@iowa.gov
URL: www.educateiowa.gov

KANSAS

Kansas Board of Regents (H)
1000 SW Jackson
Suite 520
Topeka, KS 66612-1368
(785) 296-3421
Fax: (785) 296-0983
Dr. Andy Tompkins
President and CEO
E-mail: atompkins@ksbor.org
URL: www.kansasregents.org

Kansas Legislative Research Department (I)
Room 68 West, State Capitol Building
300 SW 10th Avenue
Topeka, KS 66612-1504
(785) 296-3181
Fax: (785) 296-3824
Mr. Raney L. Gilliland
Interim Director
E-mail: kslegres@klrd.ks.gov
URL: www.kslegislature.org/klrd

KENTUCKY

Kentucky Council on Postsecondary Education (J)
1024 Capital Center Drive
Suite 320
Frankfort, KY 40601-8204
(502) 573-1555
Fax: (502) 573-1535
Mr. Robert L. King
President
E-mail: mary.morse@ky.gov
URL: cpe.ky.gov

Kentucky Community & Technical College System (K)
300 North Main Street
Versailles, KY 40383
(859) 256-3132
Fax: (859) 256-3116
Dr. Michael B. McCall
President
E-mail: president@kctcs.edu
URL: www.kctcs.edu

LOUISIANA

Board of Regents (L)
PO Box 3677
Baton Rouge, LA 70821-3677
(225) 342-4253
Fax: (225) 342-9318
Dr. James E. Purcell
Commissioner of Higher Education
E-mail: jim.purcell@la.gov
URL: www.regents.state.la.us

Department of Education (M)
P.O. Box 94064
Baton Rouge, LA 70804-9064
(225) 342-3607
Fax: (225) 342-7316
Mr. John White
State Superintendent of Education
URL: www.louisianaschools.net

MAINE

Maine Department of Education Office of Higher Education (N)
23 State House Station
Augusta, ME 04333-0023
(207) 624-6600
Fax: (207) 624-6700
Mr. Stephen Bowen
Commissioner
URL: www.maine.gov/doe/

MARYLAND

Maryland Higher Education Commission (O)
6 North Liberty Street
Baltimore, MD 21201
(410) 767-3301
Fax: (410) 332-0270
Dr. Danette G. Howard
Secretary of Higher Education
E-mail: dhoward@mhec.state.md.us
URL: www.mhec.state.md.us

MASSACHUSETTS

Massachusetts Department of Higher Education (P)
1 Ashburton Place
Room 1401
McCormack Building
Boston, MA 02108
(617) 994-6901
Fax: (617) 727-6656
Richard M. Freeland Ph.D.
Commissioner
URL: www.mass.edu

MICHIGAN

Department of Licensing and Regulatory Affairs Bureau of Commercial Services, Licensing Division Private Postsecondary Schools (Q)
PO Box 30714
Lansing, MI 48909-8214
(517) 241-1017
Fax: (517) 373-3085
Mr. Michael Beamish
Manager
E-mail: beamishm@michigan.gov
URL: www.michiganps.net

Workforce Development Agency, State of Michigan Division of Education and Career Success (R)
201 North Washington Square
Victor Building, 2nd Floor
Lansing, MI 48913
(517) 373-3430
Fax: (517) 373-2759
Ms. Dianne Duthie
Director
E-mail: duthied@michigan.gov
URL: www.michigan.gov/adulteducation

MINNESOTA

Minnesota Office of Higher Education (S)
1450 Energy Park Drive
Suite 350
St. Paul, MN 55108-5227
(651) 642-0567
Fax: (651) 642-0597
Mr. Larry Pogemiller
Director
E-mail: info.ohe@state.mn.us
URL: www.ohe.state.mn.us

Minnesota State Colleges and Universities (T)
30 7th Street East
Suite 350
St. Paul, MN 55101
(651) 201-1696
Fax: (651) 297-7465
Dr. Steven J. Rosenstone
Chancellor
E-mail: steven.rosenstone@so.mnscu.edu
URL: www.mnscu.edu

MISSISSIPPI

Board of Trustees of State Institutions of Higher Learning (U)
3825 Ridgewood Road
Jackson, MS 39211
(601) 432-6623
Fax: (601) 432-6972
Dr. Hank Bounds
Commissioner of Higher Education
URL: www.mississippi.edu

Mississippi Community College Board (V)
3825 Ridgewood Drive
Jackson, MS 39211
(601) 432-6684
Fax: (601) 432-6480
Dr. Eric Clark
Executive Director
E-mail: info@mccb.edu
URL: www.mccb.edu

MISSOURI

Coordinating Board for Higher Education Department of Higher Education (W)
205 Jefferson Street, 11th Floor
PO Box 1469
Jefferson City, MO 65102-1469
(573) 751-2361
Fax: (573) 751-6635
Dr. David R. Russell
Commissioner of Higher Education
E-mail: david.russell@dhe.mo.gov
URL: www.dhe.mo.gov

MONTANA

Office of the Commissioner of Higher Education (X)
PO Box 203201
Academic, Research & Student Affairs
Helena, MT 59620-3201
(406) 444-0312
Fax: (406) 444-1469
Dr. Sylvia Moore
Deputy Commissioner
E-mail: smoore@montana.edu
URL: www.mus.edu

NEBRASKA

Coordinating Commission for Postsecondary Education (Y)
PO Box 95005
Lincoln, NE 68509-5005
(402) 471-2847
Fax: (402) 471-2886
Dr. Marshall A. Hill
Executive Director
E-mail: marshall.hill@nebraska.gov
URL: www.ccpe.state.ne.us

NEVADA

Nevada System of Higher Education (Z)
2601 Enterprise Road
Reno, NV 89512
(775) 784-4901
Fax: (775) 784-1127
Mr. Daniel J. Klaich
Chancellor
E-mail: chancellor@nevada.edu
URL: www.nevada.edu

NEW HAMPSHIRE

New Hampshire Department of Education Division of Higher Education Higher Education Commission (a)
101 Pleasant Street
Concord, NH 03301
(603) 271-0257
Fax: (603) 271-1953
Director
URL: www.education.nh.gov/highered

Community College System of New Hampshire (b)
26 College Drive
Concord, NH 03301-7407
(603) 271-2739
Fax: (603) 271-2725
Dr. Ross Gittell
Chancellor
E-mail: rgittell@ccsnh.edu
URL: www.ccsnh.edu

NEW JERSEY

Office of the Secretary of Higher Education (c)
20 West State Street, 4th Floor
PO Box 542
Trenton, NJ 08625-0542
(609) 292-4310
Fax: (609) 292-7225
E-mail: njhe@njhe.state.nj.us
URL: www.state.nj.us/highereducation

NEW MEXICO

New Mexico Higher Education Department (d)
2048 Galisteo Street
Santa Fe, NM 87505
(505) 476-8404
Fax: (505) 476-8454
Dr. Jose Garcia
Cabinet Secretary
E-mail: jose.garcia@state.nm.us
URL: www.hed.state.nm.us

NEW YORK

New York State Education Department (e)
89 Washington Avenue
Room 111
Albany, NY 12234
(518) 474-5844
Fax: (518) 473-4909
John B. King Jr.
Commissioner
E-mail: commissioner@mail.nysed.gov

Statewide Agencies of Higher Education

State University of New York (A)
Room S411A
SUNY Plaza
353 Broadway
Albany, NY 12246
(518) 320-1276 or (518) 320-1303
FAX: (518) 320-1543 or (518) 320-1570
Ms. Johanna Duncan-Poitier
Sr Vice Chanc, Community Colleges & Educ Pipeline
E-MAIL: johanna.duncan-poitier@suny.edu
URL: www.suny.edu

New York State Education Department (B)
Education Building Annex
Room 977
Albany, NY 12234
(518) 486-3633
FAX: (518) 486-2254
Mr. John D'Agati
Deputy Commissioner
E-MAIL: jdagati@mail.nysed.gov
URL: www.highered.nysed.gov

NORTH CAROLINA

The University of North Carolina (C)
910 Raleigh Road
Chapel Hill, NC 27514
(919) 962-9000
FAX: (919) 843-9695
Mr. Thomas W. Ross
President
E-MAIL: tomross@northcarolina.edu
URL: www.northcarolina.edu

North Carolina Community College System (D)
200 West Jones Street
Raleigh, NC 27603
(919) 807-6950
FAX: (919) 807-7166
Dr. Scott Ralls
President
E-MAIL: ralls@nccommunitycolleges.edu
URL: www.nccommunitycolleges.edu

NORTH DAKOTA

North Dakota University System (E)
600 East Boulevard Avenue
Department 215
State Capitol, 10th Floor
Bismarck, ND 58505-0230
(701) 328-2960
FAX: (701) 328-2961
H. A. Shirvani Ph.D.
Chancellor
URL: www.ndus.edu

OHIO

Ohio Board of Regents (F)
30 East Broad Street
36th Floor
Columbus, OH 43215
(614) 466-6000
FAX: (614) 466-5866
Mr. Jim M. Petro
Chancellor
E-MAIL: regents@regents.state.oh.us
URL: www.regents.ohio.gov

OKLAHOMA

Oklahoma State Regents for Higher Education (G)
655 Research Parkway
Suite 200
Oklahoma City, OK 73104
(405) 225-9100
FAX: (405) 225-9230
Dr. Glen D. Johnson
Chancellor
E-MAIL: gjohnson@osrhe.edu
URL: www.okhighered.org

OREGON

Oregon State Board of Higher Education (H)
PO Box 751
Portland, OR 97207-0751
(541) 346-5716
FAX: (503) 725-5709
Mr. Charles L. Triplett III
Board Secretary
E-MAIL: charles_triplett@ous.edu
URL: www.ous.edu/dept/board

Department of Community Colleges and Workforce Development (I)
255 Capitol Street, NE
Salem, OR 97310
(503) 947-2433
FAX: (503) 378-8434
Dr. Camille Preus
Commissioner
E-MAIL: camille.preus@state.or.us
URL: www.odccwd.state.or.us

PENNSYLVANIA

Pennsylvania Department of Education Liaison to Postsecondary and Higher Education Institutions (J)
333 Market Street
12th Floor
Harrisburg, PA 17126-0333
(717) 787-5041
FAX: (717) 772-3622
L. Jill Hans
Deputy Secretary, Ofc Postsecondary & Higher Educ
E-MAIL: jhans@pa.gov
URL: www.education.state.pa.us

Pennsylvania Department of Education Liaison to Postsecondary and Higher Education Institutions (K)
333 Market Street
12th Floor
Harrisburg, PA 17126-0333
(717) 783-8228
FAX: (717) 772-3622
Ms. Patricia Landis
Division Chief - Higher and Career Education
E-MAIL: plandis@state.pa.us
URL: www.education.state.pa.us

RHODE ISLAND

Rhode Island Board of Governors for Higher Education (L)
80 Washington Street
Suite 524
Providence, RI 02903
(401) 456-6000
FAX: (401) 456-6028
Mr. Ray M. DiPasquale
Commissioner of Higher Education
E-MAIL: rmdipasquale@ribghe.org
URL: www.ribghe.org

Community College of Rhode Island (M)
400 East Avenue
Warwick, RI 02886
(401) 825-2188
FAX: (401) 825-2166
Mr. Ray M. Di Pasquale
President
E-MAIL: rmdipasquale@ccri.edu
URL: www.ccri.edu

SOUTH CAROLINA

South Carolina Commission on Higher Education (N)
1122 Lady Street
Suite 300
Columbia, SC 29201
(803) 737-2275
FAX: (803) 737-2297
Ms. Julie J. Carullo
Acting Executive Director
E-MAIL: jcarullo@che.sc.gov
URL: www.che.sc.gov

South Carolina State Board for Technical and Comprehensive Education (O)
111 Executive Center Drive
Columbia, SC 29210
(803) 896-5280
FAX: (803) 896-5281
Dr. Darrel Staat
System President
E-MAIL: staatd@sctechsystem.edu
URL: www.sctechsystem.edu

SOUTH DAKOTA

South Dakota Board of Regents (P)
306 East Capitol Avenue
Suite 200
Pierre, SD 57501-2545
(605) 773-3455
FAX: (605) 773-5320
Dr. Jack R. Warner
Executive Director and Chief Executive Officer
E-MAIL: jack.warner@sdbor.edu
URL: www.sdbor.edu

South Dakota Department of Education (Q)
Office of the Secretary
800 Governors Drive
Pierre, SD 57501-2291
(605) 773-5669
FAX: (605) 773-6139
Dr. Melody Schopp
Secretary
E-MAIL: melody.schopp@state.sd.us
URL: www.doe.sd.gov

TENNESSEE

Tennessee Higher Education Commission (R)
404 James Robertson Parkway
Parkway Towers
Suite 1900
Nashville, TN 37243-0830
(615) 741-3605
FAX: (615) 741-6230
Dr. Richard G. Rhoda
Executive Director
E-MAIL: richard.rhoda@tn.gov

Tennessee Board of Regents (S)
1415 Murfreesboro Road
Suite 324
Nashville, TN 37217
(615) 366-4482
FAX: (615) 366-3903
Dr. Kay Clark
Interim Vice Chancellor for Academic Affairs
E-MAIL: kay.clark@tbr.edu
URL: www.tbr.edu

University of Tennessee Board of Trustees (T)
719 Andy Holt Tower
Knoxville, TN 37996-0170
(865) 974-3245
FAX: (865) 974-3074
Ms. Catherine S. Mizell
General Counsel and Secretary
E-MAIL: cmizell@tennessee.edu
URL: www.tennessee.edu/system/

TEXAS

Texas Higher Education Coordinating Board (U)
PO Box 12788
Austin, TX 78711
(512) 427-6101
FAX: (512) 427-6127
Dr. Raymund A. Paredes
Commissioner of Higher Education
E-MAIL: raymund.paredes@thecb.state.tx.us
URL: www.thecb.state.tx.us

Texas Higher Education Coordinating Board P-16 Initiatives (V)
PO Box 12788
Austin, TX 78711-2788
(512) 427-6545
FAX: (512) 427-6444
Dr. Judith Loredo
Assistant Commissioner
E-MAIL: judy.loredo@thecb.state.tx.us
URL: www.thecb.state.tx.us

UTAH

Utah State Board of Regents (W)
60 South 400 West
Salt Lake City, UT 84101-1284
(801) 321-7103
FAX: (801) 321-7156
Mr. David Buhler
Commissioner of Higher Education
E-MAIL: dbuhler@utahsbr.edu
URL: www.utahsbr.edu

VERMONT

Vermont Department of Education School Finance Team (X)
120 State Street
Montpelier, VT 05620-2501
(802) 828-0471
FAX: (802) 828-1631
URL: www.education.vermont.gov

VIRGINIA

State Council of Higher Education for Virginia (Y)
101 North Fourteenth Street
James Monroe Building
9th Floor
Richmond, VA 23219
(804) 225-2600
FAX: (804) 371-7911
Mr. Peter Blake
Director
E-MAIL: peterblake@schev.edu
URL: www.schev.edu

Virginia Community College System (Z)
101 North Fourteenth Street
James Monroe Building
Richmond, VA 23219
(804) 819-4903
FAX: (804) 819-4760
Dr. Glenn DuBois
Chancellor
E-MAIL: gdubois@vccs.edu
URL: www.vccs.edu

WASHINGTON

Washington Student Achievement Council (a)
917 Lakeridge Way, SW
PO Box 43430
Olympia, WA 98504-3430
(360) 753-7810
FAX: (360) 753-7808
Mr. Don Bennett
Executive Director
E-MAIL: info@wsac.wa.gov
URL: www.wsac.wa.gov

State Board for Community and Technical Colleges (b)
PO Box 42495
1300 Quince Street, SE
Olympia, WA 98504-2495
(360) 704-4355
FAX: (360) 704-4415
Mr. Marty Brown
Executive Director
URL: www.sbctc.edu

WEST VIRGINIA

West Virginia Higher Education Policy Commission (c)
1018 Kanawha Boulevard, East
Suite 700
Charleston, WV 25301-2800
(304) 558-0699
FAX: (304) 558-1011
Dr. Paul L. Hill
Chancellor
E-MAIL: paul.hill@hepc.wvnet.edu
URL: wvhepcnew.wvnet.edu

WISCONSIN

Higher Educational Aids Board (d)
PO Box 7885
Madison, WI 53707-7885
(608) 267-2206
FAX: (608) 267-2808
E-MAIL: heabmail@wisconsin.gov
URL: heab.wi.gov

Wisconsin Technical College System (e)
PO Box 7874
Madison, WI 53707-7874
(608) 266-7983
FAX: (608) 266-1285
Mr. Daniel Clancy
President
E-MAIL: dan.clancy@wtcsystem.edu
URL: www.wtcsystem.edu

WYOMING

Wyoming Community College Commission (A)
2020 Carey
8th Floor
Cheyenne, WY 82002
(307) 777-7763
FAX: (307) 777-6567
Dr. Jim Rose
Executive Director
E-MAIL: jrose@commission.wcc.edu
URL: www.communitycolleges.wy.edu

AMERICAN SAMOA

Board of Higher Education (American Samoa) American Samoa Community College (B)
PO Box 2609
Pago Pago, AS 96799
(684) 699-9155
FAX: (684) 699-6259
URL: www.amsamoa.edu

FEDERATED STATES OF MICRONESIA

Board of Regents College of Micronesia-FSM (C)
PO Box 159
Kolonia Pohnpei, FM 96941
(691) 320-2480
FAX: (691) 320-2479
E-MAIL: national@comfsm.fm
URL: www.comfsm.fm

PUERTO RICO

Puerto Rico Council on Education (D)
PO Box 19900
San Juan, PR 00910-1900
(787) 641-7100, ext. 2047
FAX: (787) 641-2573
Ms. Carmen Luz Berrios Rivera
Executive Director
E-MAIL: cberrios@ce.pr.gov
URL: www.ce.pr.gov

Higher Education Associations

AACSB International-The Association to Advance Collegiate Schools of Business (A)
777 South Harbour Island Boulevard
Suite 750
Tampa, FL 33602-5730
(813) 769-6500
Fax: (813) 769-6559
Mr. John J. Fernandes
President and Chief Executive Officer
E-mail: mediarelations@aacsb.edu
URL: www.aacsb.edu

AAUW (B)
1111 Sixteenth Street, NW
Washington, DC 20036
(800) 326-2289
Fax: (202) 872-1425
E-mail: connect@aauw.org
URL: www.aauw.org

ABET (C)
111 Market Place
Suite 1050
Baltimore, MD 21202
(410) 347-7700
Fax: (410) 625-2238
Michael K. J. Milligan Ph.D., PE
Executive Director
E-mail: info@abet.org
URL: www.abet.org

Academy of Legal Studies in Business (D)
Miami University
Department of Finance
3111 FSB
Oxford, OH 45056
(513) 529-1574
Fax: (513) 523-8180
Dr. Daniel J. Herron
Executive Secretary
E-mail: herrondj@muohio.edu
URL: www.alsb.org

Academy of Nutrition and Dietetics Accreditation Council for Education in Nutrition and Dietetics (ACEND) (E)
120 South Riverside Plaza
Suite 2000
Chicago, IL 60606-6995
(312) 899-0040, ext. 5400
Fax: (312) 899-4817
Dr. Ulric Chung
Executive Director
E-mail: uchung@eatright.org
URL: www.eatright.org/acend

Accreditation Commission for Acupuncture and Oriental Medicine (ACAOM) (F)
14502 Greenview Drive
Suite 300B
Laurel, MD 20708
(301) 313-0855
Fax: (301) 313-0912
Dr. Annette M. Donawa
Director of Accreditation Services
E-mail: annette.donawa@acaom.org
URL: www.acaom.org

Accreditation Commission for Midwifery Education (G)
8403 Colesville Road
Suite 1550
Silver Spring, MD 20910
(240) 485-1802
Fax: (240) 485-1818
Ms. Susan E. Stone
Chair ACME
E-mail: jburke@acnm.org
URL: www.midwife.org/accreditation

Accreditation Committee for Perfusion Education (H)
6663 South Sycamore Street
Littleton, CO 80120
(303) 738-0770
Fax: (303) 738-3223
Ms. Theresa Sisneros
Executive Director
E-mail: ac-pe@msn.com
URL: www.ac-pe.org

Accreditation Council for Business Schools and Programs (I)
11520 West 119th Street
Overland Park, KS 66213
(913) 339-9356
Fax: (913) 339-6226
Mr. Douglas Viehland CAE
Executive Director
E-mail: info@acbsp.org
URL: www.acbsp.org

Accreditation Council for Pharmacy Education (J)
135 S. LaSalle Street
Suite 4100
Chicago, IL 60603
(312) 664-3575
Fax: (312) 664-4652
Peter H. Vlasses, PharmD BCPS
Executive Director
E-mail: pvlasses@acpe-accredit.org
URL: www.acpe-accredit.org

Accreditation Review Commission on Education for the Physician Assistant (ARC-PA) (K)
12000 Findley Road
Suite 150
John's Creek, GA 30097
(770) 476-1224
Fax: (770) 476-1738
Mr. John McCarty
Executive Director
E-mail: arc-pa@arc-pa.org
URL: www.arc-pa.org

Accreditation Review Committee for the Anesthesiologist's Assistant (L)
2027 Burnside Drive
Allen, TX 75013
(469) 656-1103
Ms. Jennifer Anderson Warwick
Executive Director
E-mail: arcaamember@gmail.com
URL: www.caahep.org/arc-aa

Accreditation Review Committee for the Medical Illustrator (M)
32531 Meadowlark Way
Pepper Pike, OH 44124
(216) 595-9363
Fax: (216) 595-9360
E-mail: kijung@aol.com
URL: www.caahep.org/arc-mi

Accreditation Review Council on Education in Surgical Technology and Surgical Assisting (N)
6 West Dry Creek Circle
Suite 110
Littleton, CO 80120
(303) 694-9262
Fax: (303) 741-3655
Mr. Keith Orloff
Executive Director
E-mail: info@arcstsa.org
URL: www.arcst.org

Accrediting Bureau of Health Education Schools (O)
7777 Leesburg Pike
Suite 314 N
Falls Church, VA 22043
(703) 917-9503
Fax: (703) 917-4109
Ms. Carol Moneymaker
Executive Director
E-mail: info@abhes.org
URL: www.abhes.org

Accrediting Commission of Career Schools and Colleges (P)
2101 Wilson Boulevard
Suite 302
Arlington, VA 22201
(703) 247-4212
Fax: (703) 247-4533
Dr. Michale McComis
Executive Director
E-mail: info@accsc.org
URL: www.accsc.org

Accrediting Council for Continuing Education & Training (ACCET) (Q)
1722 N Street, NW
Washington, DC 20036
(202) 955-1113
Fax: (202) 955-1118
Mr. Roger J. Williams
Executive Director
E-mail: rjwilliams@accet.org
URL: www.accet.org

Accrediting Council for Independent Colleges and Schools (R)
750 First Street, NE
Suite 980
Washington, DC 20002-4223
(202) 336-6780
Fax: (202) 464-5621
Dr. Albert Gray
Executive Director & CEO
E-mail: agray@acics.org
URL: www.acics.org

Accrediting Council on Education in Journalism and Mass Communications (S)
University of Kansas, School of Journalism
1435 Jayhawk Boulevard
Stauffer-Flint Hall
Lawrence, KS 66045-7575
(785) 864-3973
Fax: (785) 864-5225
Prof. Susanne Shaw
Executive Director
E-mail: sshaw@ku.edu
URL: www.ku.edu/~acejmc

ACT, Inc. (T)
500 ACT Drive
Box 168
Iowa City, IA 52243
(319) 337-1079
Fax: (319) 337-1059
Dr. Jon S. Whitmore
CEO
URL: www.act.org

ACUTA: The Association for Information Communications Technology Professionals in Higher Education (U)
152 West Zandale Drive
Suite 200
Lexington, KY 40503-2486
(859) 278-3338
Fax: (859) 278-3268
Ms. Corinne Hoch
Executive Director
E-mail: choch@acuta.org
URL: www.acuta.org

Alabama Association of Independent Colleges and Universities (V)
5950 Carmichael Place
Suite 213
Montgomery, AL 36117
(334) 356-2220
Fax: (334) 356-2202
Gen. Paul M. Hankins
President
E-mail: hankinsp@knology.net
URL: www.aaicu.net

American Academy for Liberal Education (AALE) (W)
127 S. Peyton Street
Suite 210
Alexandria, VA 22314
(703) 717-9719
Prof. Charles Butterworth
President
E-mail: aaleinfo@aale.org
URL: www.aale.org

American Anthropological Association (X)
2200 Wilson Boulevard
Suite 600
Arlington, VA 22201
(703) 528-1902
Fax: (703) 528-3546
Mr. William E. Davis
Executive Director
E-mail: bdavis@aaanet.org
URL: www.aaanet.org

American Association for Adult and Continuing Education (AAACE) (Y)
10111 Martin Luther King, Jr. Highway
Suite 200C
Bowie, MD 20720
(301) 459-6261
Fax: (301) 459-6241
Dr. Henry Merrill
President
E-mail: aaace10@aol.com
URL: www.aaace.org

American Association for Employment in Education (Z)
947 East Johnstown Road #170
Gahanna, OH 43230
(614) 485-1111
Fax: (360) 244-7802
Mr. Doug Peden
Executive Director
E-mail: execdir@aaee.org
URL: www.aaee.org

American Association for Marriage and Family Therapy Education (a)
112 South Alfred Street
Alexandria, VA 22314-3061
(703) 253-0457
Fax: (703) 253-0508
Ms. Tatiana A. Tamarkin
Director of Educational Affairs
E-mail: ttamarkin@aamft.org
URL: www.aamft.org

American Association for Vocational Instructional Materials (b)
220 Smithonia Road
Winterville, GA 30683
(706) 742-5355
Fax: (706) 742-7005
Mr. Gary Farmer
Director
E-mail: gary@aavim.com
URL: www.aavim.com

American Association for Women in Community Colleges (AAWCC) (c)
PO Box 3098
Gaithersburg, MD 20855
(503) 399-5012
Dr. Maureen Murphy
President
E-mail: info@aawccnatl.org
URL: www.aawccnatl.org

American Association of Blood Banks Committee on Accreditation of Specialist in Blood Banking Technology Schools (d)
8101 Glenbrook Road
Bethesda, MD 20814-2749
(301) 215-6482
Fax: (301) 907-6895
Ms. Sharon D. Moffett CAE
Director Education
E-mail: professionaldevelopment@aabb.org
URL: www.aabb.org

American Association of Colleges for Teacher Education (e)
1307 New York Avenue, NW
Suite 300
Washington, DC 20005-4701
(202) 293-2450
Fax: (202) 457-8095
Dr. Sharon P. Robinson
President & Chief Executive Officer
E-mail: aacte@aacte.org
URL: www.aacte.org

American Association of Colleges of Nursing (f)
1 Dupont Circle, NW
Suite 530
Washington, DC 20036-1120
(202) 463-6930
Fax: (202) 785-8320
Dr. Geraldine Bednash
CEO and Executive Director
E-mail: pbednash@aacn.nche.edu
URL: www.aacn.nche.edu

American Association of Colleges of Osteopathic Medicine (g)
5550 Friendship Boulevard
Suite 310
Chevy Chase, MD 20815-7231
(301) 968-4142
Fax: (301) 968-4101
Stephen C. Shannon DO, MPH
President and CEO
E-mail: president@aacom.org
URL: www.aacom.org

American Association of Collegiate Registrars and Admissions Officers (AACRAO) (A)
1 Dupont Circle, NW
Suite 520
Washington, DC 20036-1135
(202) 293-9161
FAX: (202) 872-8857
Mr. Michael Reilly
Executive Director
E-MAIL: reillym@aacrao.org
URL: www.aacrao.org

American Association of Community Colleges (B)
1 Dupont Circle, NW
Suite 410
Washington, DC 20036
(202) 728-0200, ext. 235
FAX: (202) 452-1461
Dr. Walter G. Bumphus
President/CEO
E-MAIL: wbumphus@aacc.nche.edu
URL: www.aacc.nche.edu

American Association of Family and Consumer Sciences (AAFCS) (C)
400 North Columbus Street
Suite 202
Alexandria, VA 22314
(703) 706-4600
FAX: (703) 706-4663
Ms. Carolyn W. Jackson
Executive Director
E-MAIL: accreditation@aafcs.org
URL: www.aafcs.org

American Association of Medical Assistants (D)
20 North Wacker Drive
Suite 1575
Chicago, IL 60606
(312) 899-1500
FAX: (312) 899-1259
Mr. Donald A. Balasa J.D., MBA
Executive Director
E-MAIL: dbalasa@aama-ntl.org
URL: www.aama-ntl.org

American Association of Physics Teachers (E)
One Physics Ellipse
College Park, MD 20740-3845
(301) 209-3311
FAX: (301) 209-0845
Dr. Beth A. Cunningham
Executive Officer
E-MAIL: eo@aapt.org
URL: www.aapt.org

American Association of Presidents of Independent Colleges and Universities (F)
Box 7070
Provo, UT 84602-7070
(801) 422-5625
FAX: (801) 422-0617
Mr. John B. Stohlton
Executive Director
E-MAIL: john_stohlton@byu.edu
URL: www.aapicu.org

American Association of School Administrators (G)
1615 Duke Street
Alexandria, VA 22314
(703) 528-0700
FAX: (703) 841-1543
Dr. Daniel A. Domenech
Executive Director
E-MAIL: ddomenech@aasa.org
URL: www.aasa.org

American Association of State Colleges and Universities (H)
1307 New York Avenue, NW
5th Floor
Washington, DC 20005-4701
(202) 293-7070
FAX: (202) 296-5819
Dr. Muriel A. Howard
President
E-MAIL: howardm@aascu.org
URL: www.aascu.org

American Association of Teachers of Slavic and East European Languages (I)
University of Southern California
3501 Trousdale Parkway
THH 255L
Los Angeles, CA 90089-4353
(213) 740-2734
FAX: (213) 740-8550
Dr. Elizabeth Durst
Executive Director
E-MAIL: aatseel@usc.edu
URL: www.aatseel.org

American Association of University Professors (J)
1133 19th Street, NW
Suite 200
Washington, DC 20036
(202) 737-5900
FAX: (202) 737-5526
Dr. Martin D. Snyder
Senior Associate General Secretary
E-MAIL: aaup@aaup.org
URL: www.aaup.org

American Bar Association Office of the Consultant on Legal Education and Admissions to the Bar (K)
321 North Clark Street
21st Floor
Chicago, IL 60654
(312) 988-6738
FAX: (312) 988-5681
Mr. Barry A. Currier
Interim Consultant on Legal Education
E-MAIL: legaled@americanbar.org
URL: www.americanbar.org/groups/legal_education

American Board of Funeral Service Education Committee on Accreditation (L)
3414 Ashland Avenue
Suite G
St. Joseph, MO 64506
(816) 233-3747
FAX: (816) 233-3793
Dr. Gretchen Warner
Executive Director
E-MAIL: exdir@abfse.org
URL: www.abfse.org

American Catholic Philosophical Association (M)
University of St. Thomas
3800 Montrose Boulevard
Houston, TX 77006
(713) 942-3483
FAX: (713) 942-3464
Dr. R. E. Houser
National Secretary
E-MAIL: acpa@stthom.edu
URL: www.acpaweb.org

American Chemical Society Committee on Professional Training (N)
1155 Sixteenth Street, NW
Washington, DC 20036
(202) 872-4589
FAX: (202) 872-6066
Ms. Cathy A. Nelson
Assistant Director
E-MAIL: cpt@acs.org
URL: www.acs.org/cpt

American College of Microbiology Committee on Postgraduate Educational Programs (O)
1752 N Street, NW
Washington, DC 20036-2804
(202) 942-9225
FAX: (202) 942-9353
Ms. Peggy McNult
Assistant Director
E-MAIL: college@asmusa.org
URL: www.asm.org/cpep

American College of Nurse-Midwives (P)
8403 Colesville Road
Suite 1550
Silver Spring, MD 20910
(240) 485-1800
FAX: (240) 485-1818
Ms. Lorrie Kaplan
Executive Director
E-MAIL: info@acnm.org
URL: www.midwife.org

American College Personnel Association (ACPA) (Q)
1 Dupont Circle, NW
Suite 300
Washington, DC 20036-1188
(202) 835-2272
FAX: (202) 296-3286
Mr. Gregory Roberts
Executive Director
E-MAIL: info@acpa.nche.edu
URL: www.myacpa.org

American Collegiate Retailing Association (R)
Sam Walton College of Business
University of Arkansas
WJWH 538
Fayetteville, AR 72701
(479) 575-2643
Mr. Barry Berman
President
E-MAIL: mktbxb@hofstra.edu
URL: www.acraretail.org

American Conference of Academic Deans (ACAD) (S)
1818 R Street, NW
Washington, DC 20009
(202) 884-7419
FAX: (202) 265-9532
Mrs. Laura A. Rzepka
Executive Director
E-MAIL: info@acad-edu.org
URL: www.acad-edu.org

American Council for Construction Education (T)
1717 North Loop 1604 East
Suite 320
San Antonio, TX 78232-1570
(210) 495-6161
FAX: (210) 495-6168
Mr. Michael Holland
Executive Vice President
E-MAIL: acce@acce-hq.org
URL: www.acce-hq.org

American Council of Trustees and Alumni (U)
1726 M Street, NW
Suite 802
Washington, DC 20036-4525
(202) 467-6787
FAX: (202) 467-6784
Ms. Anne D. Neal
President
E-MAIL: info@goacta.org
URL: www.goacta.org

American Council on Education (V)
1 Dupont Circle, NW
Washington, DC 20036
(202) 939-9300
FAX: (202) 659-2122
Molly Corbett Broad
President
E-MAIL: acepresident@acenet.edu
URL: www.acenet.edu

American Council on Education Center for Lifelong Learning (W)
1 Dupont Circle, NW
Suite 250
Washington, DC 20036
(202) 939-9470
FAX: (202) 833-3005
Patricia Book
Assistant Vice President, Lifelong Learning
E-MAIL: credit@ace.nche.edu
URL: www.acenet.edu

American Council on Education Division of Leadership and Lifelong Learning (X)
1 Dupont Circle, NW
Suite 73-A
Washington, DC 20036
(202) 939-9389
FAX: (202)939-9302
Dr. Claire Van Ummersen
Senior Adviser
E-MAIL: cvanummersen@acenet.edu
URL: www.acenet.edu

American Counseling Association (Y)
5999 Stevenson Avenue
Alexandria, VA 22304
(800) 347-6647
FAX: (800) 473-2329
Mr. Richard Yep
Executive Director
E-MAIL: ryep@counseling.org
URL: www.counseling.org

American Culinary Federation Education Foundation Accrediting Commission (Z)
180 Center Place Way
St. Augustine, FL 32095
(904) 824-4468
FAX: (904) 825-4758
E-MAIL: cchilders@acfchefs.net
URL: www.acfchefs.org

American Educational Research Association (a)
1430 K Street, NW
Suite 1200
Washington, DC 20005
(202) 238-3200
FAX: (202) 238-3250
Dr. Felice J. Levine
Executive Director
E-MAIL: flevine@aera.net
URL: www.aera.net

American Forensic Association (b)
Box 256
River Falls, WI 54022-0256
(800) 228-5424
FAX: (715) 425-9533
Dr. James W. Pratt
Executive Secretary
E-MAIL: amforensicassoc@aol.com
URL: www.americanforensics.org

American Institute of Architecture Students (c)
1735 New York Avenue, NW
Washington, DC 20006-5209
(202) 626-7472
FAX: (202) 626-7414
Mr. Joshua Caulfield
Executive Director
E-MAIL: mailbox@aias.org
URL: www.aias.org

American Library Association Office for Accreditation (d)
50 East Huron Street
Chicago, IL 60611-2729
(312) 280-2432
FAX: (312) 280-2433
Karen O'Brien
Director, Office for Accreditation
E-MAIL: accred@ala.org
URL: www.ala.org/accreditation

American Mathematical Association of Two Year Colleges (e)
Southwest Tennessee Community College
5983 Macon Cove
Memphis, TN 38134
(901) 333-6243
FAX: (901) 333-6251
Dr. Cheryl Cleaves
Interim Executive Director
E-MAIL: amatyc@amatyc.org
URL: www.amatyc.org

American Occupational Therapy Association (f)
4720 Montgomery Lane
PO Box 31220
Bethesda, MD 20824-1220
(301) 652-6611 Ext. 2202
FAX: (301) 652-1417
Dr. Neil Harvison
Dir Accreditation & Acad Affs
E-MAIL: accred@aota.org
URL: www.aota.org

American Optometric Association Accreditation Council on Optometric Education (g)
243 North Lindbergh Boulevard
St. Louis, MO 63141
(314) 991-4100
FAX: (314) 991-4101
Ms. Joyce L. Urbeck
Administrative Director
E-MAIL: jlurbeck@aoa.org
URL: www.theacoe.org

American Osteopathic Association (h)
142 East Ontario Street
Commission on Osteopathic College Accreditation
Chicago, IL 60611-2864
(312) 202-8048
FAX: (312) 202-8202
Konrad C. Miskowicz-Retz Ph.D.
Secretary
E-MAIL: kretz@osteopathic.org
URL: www.aoacoca.org

Higher Education Associations

American Physical Therapy Association (A)
1111 North Fairfax Street
Alexandria, VA 22314
(703) 684-2782
FAX: (703) 684-7343
Mr. John D. Barnes
Chief Executive Officer
E-MAIL: dorisellmore@apta.org
URL: www.apta.org

American Political Science Association (B)
1527 New Hampshire Avenue, NW
Washington, DC 20036
(202) 483-2512
FAX: (202) 483-2657
Dr. Michael Brintnall
Executive Director
E-MAIL: apsa@apsanet.org
URL: www.apsanet.org

American Psychological Association Commission on Accreditation (C)
750 First Street, NE
Washington, DC 20002-4242
(202) 336-5979
FAX: (202) 336-5978
Dr. Susan F. Zlotlow
Dir. Program Consultation & Accred
E-MAIL: apaaccred@apa.org
URL: www.apa.org/ed/accreditation.html

American Real Estate and Urban Economics Association (D)
PO Box 3061110
Tallahassee, FL 32306-1110
(850) 644-7898
FAX: (850) 644-4077
E-MAIL: elaffitte@fsu.edu
URL: www.areuea.org

American Society for Engineering Education (E)
1818 N Street, NW
Suite 600
Washington, DC 20036
(202) 331-3545
FAX: (202) 265-8504
Mr. Norman L. Fortenberry
Executive Director
E-MAIL: n.fortenberry@asee.org
URL: www.asee.org

American Society for Microbiology (F)
1752 N Street, NW
Washington, DC 20036
(202) 942-9264
FAX: (202) 942-9329
Ms. Amy Chang
Director, Education Department
E-MAIL: education@asmusa.org
URL: www.asm.org

American Society of Cytopathology Cytotechnology Programs Review Committee (CPRC) (G)
100 West 10th Street
Suite 605
Wilmington, DE 19801
(302) 543-6583
FAX: (302) 543-6597
Ms. Deborah A. MacIntyre
Coordinator, CPRC
E-MAIL: asc@cytopathology.org
URL: www.cytopathology.org

American Society of Landscape Architects Landscape Architectural Accreditation Board (H)
636 Eye Street, NW
Washington, DC 20001-3736
(202) 898-2444
FAX: (202) 898-1185
Mr. Ron Leighton
Education/Academic Affairs Director
E-MAIL: rleighton@asla.org
URL: www.asla.org

American Speech-Language-Hearing Association Council on Academic Accreditation in Audiology and Speech-Language Pathology (I)
2200 Research Boulevard
Rockville, MD 20850
(800) 498-2071
FAX: (301) 296-8570
Dr. Arlene A. Pietranton
Chief Executive Officer
E-MAIL: accreditation@asha.org
URL: www.asha.org

American Student Government Association (J)
412 NW 16th Avenue
Gainesville, FL 32601-4203
(352) 373-6907
FAX: (352) 373-8120
Mr. W. H. Oxendine Jr.
Executive Director
E-MAIL: info@asgaonline.com
URL: www.asgaonline.com

American Veterinary Medical Association (K)
1931 North Meacham Road
Suite 100
Schaumburg, IL 60173
(800) 248-2862
FAX: (847) 925-1329
Dr. David E. Granstrom
Director Education and Research
E-MAIL: dgranstrom@avma.org
URL: www.avma.org

APPA (L)
1643 Prince Street
Alexandria, VA 22314-2818
(703) 684-1446, ext. 229
FAX: (703) 549-2772
E. Lander Medlin
Executive Vice President
E-MAIL: lander@appa.org
URL: www.appa.org

Association for Asian Studies (M)
825 Victors Way
Suite 310
Ann Arbor, MI 48108
(734) 665-2490
FAX: (734) 665-3801
Mr. Michael Paschal
Executive Director
E-MAIL: mpaschal@asian-studies.org
URL: www.asian-studies.org

Association for Biblical Higher Education Commission on Accreditation (N)
5850 T.G. Lee Boulevard
Suite 130
Orlando, FL 32822
(407) 207-0808
FAX: (407) 207-0840
Dr. Ronald C. Kroll
Director, Commission on Accreditation
E-MAIL: coa@abhe.org
URL: www.abhe.org

Association for Business Communication (O)
355 Shanks Hall (0112)
180 Turner Street NW
Blacksburg, VA 24061
(540) 231-8460
FAX: (540) 231-1452
Dr. James Dubinsky
Executive Director
E-MAIL: exec_director@businesscommunication.org
URL: www.businesscommunication.org

Association for Business Simulation and Experiential Learning (P)
c/o School of Global Business
Arcadia University
450 South Easton Road
Glenside, PA 19038
(215) 572-2849
FAX: (215) 572-4489
Dr. Annette Halpin
VP/Executive Director
E-MAIL: absel@email.com
URL: www.absel.org

The Association for Canadian Studies in the United States (ACSUS) (Q)
2030 M Street, NW
Suite 350
Washington, DC 20036
(202) 775-9007
FAX: (202) 775-0061
Mr. David Archibald
Executive Director
E-MAIL: info@acsus.org
URL: www.acsus.org

Association for Clinical Pastoral Education, Inc. (R)
1549 Clairmont Road
Suite 103
Decatur, GA 30033-4635
(404) 320-1472
FAX: (404) 320-0849
Mr. Deryck Durston
Interim Executive Director
E-MAIL: acpe@acpe.edu
URL: www.acpe.edu

Association for Consortium Leadership (S)
4900 Powhatan Avenue
Norfolk, VA 23529-0293
(757) 683-3183
FAX: (757) 683-4515
Dr. Lawrence G. Dotolo
Executive Director
E-MAIL: lgdotolo@aol.com
URL: www.national-acl.com

Association for Continuing Higher Education (T)
University of Oklahoma Outreach
OCCE Administration Building
1700 Asp Avenue
Norman, OK 73072-6400
(800) 807-2243
FAX: (405) 325-4888
Ynez Walske
Executive Secretary
E-MAIL: admin@acheinc.org
URL: www.acheinc.org

Association for Education in Journalism and Mass Communication (U)
234 Outlet Pointe Boulevard
Suite A
Columbia, SC 29210-5667
(803) 798-0271
FAX: (803) 772-3509
Ms. Jennifer H. McGill
Executive Director
E-MAIL: aejmchq@aol.com
URL: www.aejmc.org

Association for General and Liberal Studies (V)
c/o Rebecca Amato, University College
Ball State University
Muncie, IN 47306
(765) 285-8406
FAX: (765) 285-2167
Executive Director
E-MAIL: bamato@bsu.edu
URL: www.agls.org

Association for Institutional Research (W)
1435 East Piedmont Drive
Suite 211
Tallahassee, FL 32308
(850) 385-4155
FAX: (850) 385-5180
Dr. Randy L. Swing
Executive Director
E-MAIL: executivedirector@airweb.org
URL: www.airweb.org

Association for Library and Information Science Education (ALISE) (X)
65 East Wacker Place
Suite 1900
Chicago, IL 60601
(312) 795-0996
FAX: (312) 419-8950
Ms. Kathleen Combs
Executive Director
E-MAIL: contact@alise.org
URL: www.alise.org

Association for Prevention Teaching and Research (Y)
1001 Connecticut Avenue, NW
Suite 610
Washington, DC 20036
(202) 463-0550
FAX: (202) 463-0555
E-MAIL: info@aptrweb.org
URL: www.aptrweb.org

Association for the Study of Higher Education (ASHE) (Z)
UNLV
4505 South Maryland Parkway
Box 3068
Las Vegas, NV 89154-3068
(702) 895-2737
FAX: (702) 895-4269
Dr. Kimberly Nehls
Executive Director
E-MAIL: ASHE@unlv.edu
URL: www.ashe.ws

Association for Theatre in Higher Education (ATHE) (a)
PO Box 1290
Boulder, CO 80306-1290
(888) 284-3737
FAX: (303) 530-2168
Ms. Nancy Erickson
Executive Director
E-MAIL: executivedirector@athe.org
URL: www.athe.org

Association of Advanced Rabbinical and Talmudic Schools Accreditation Commission (b)
11 Broadway
Suite 405
New York, NY 10004
(212) 363-1991
FAX: (212) 533-5335
Dr. Bernard Fryshman
Executive Vice President

Association of American Colleges and Universities (c)
1818 R Street, NW
Washington, DC 20009
(202) 387-3760
FAX: (202) 265-9532
Dr. Carol G. Schneider
President
E-MAIL: info@aacu.org
URL: www.aacu.org

Association of American Law Schools (d)
1201 Connecticut Avenue, NW
Suite 800
Washington, DC 20036-2605
(202) 296-8851
FAX: (202) 296-8869
Ms. Susan Westerberg Prager
Executive Director
E-MAIL: aals@aals.org
URL: www.aals.org

Association of American Medical Colleges (e)
2450 N Street, NW
Washington, DC 20037-1127
(202) 828-0400
FAX: (202) 828-1125
Dr. Darrell G. Kirch
President/CEO
E-MAIL: aamcpresident@aamc.org
URL: www.aamc.org

Association of American Universities (f)
1200 New York Avenue, NW
Suite 550
Washington, DC 20005
(202) 408-7500
FAX: (202) 408-8184
Dr. Hunter R. Rawlings III
President
URL: www.aau.edu

Association of American University Presses (g)
28 West 36th Street
Suite 602
New York, NY 10018
(212) 989-1010
FAX: (212) 989-0275
Mr. Peter Givler
Executive Director
E-MAIL: info@aaupnet.org
URL: www.aaupnet.org

Association of Catholic Colleges and Universities (h)
1 Dupont Circle, NW
Suite 650
Washington, DC 20036
(202) 457-0650
FAX: (202) 728-0977
Michael Galligan-Stierle Ph.D.
President/CEO
E-MAIL: accu@accunet.org
URL: www.accunet.org

Association of College and University Housing Officers-International (A)
941 Chatham Lane
Suite 318
Columbus, OH 43221-2416
(614) 292-0099
Fax: (614) 292-3205
Ms. Sallie Traxler
Executive Director
E-mail: office@acuho-i.org
URL: www.acuho-i.org

Association of College and University Religious Affairs (B)
Macalester College
1600 Grand Avenue
St. Paul, MN 55105
(651) 696-6293
RevDr. Lucy Forster-Smith
President
E-mail: forstersmith@macalester.edu
URL: www.site.acuraonline.net

Association of College Unions International (C)
One City Centre
Suite 200
120 West Seventh Street
Bloomington, IN 47404-3925
(812) 245-2284
Fax: (812) 245-6710
Ms. Marsha Herman-Betzen
Executive Director
E-mail: acui@acui.org
URL: www.acui.org

Association of Collegiate Conference and Events Directors-International (D)
419 Canyon Avenue
#311
Fort Collins, CO 80521
(970) 449-4960
Fax: (970) 449-4965
Ms. Monica Nesbit Schultz
Director of Sales & Marketing
E-mail: monica@acced-i.org
URL: www.acced-i.org

Association of Collegiate Schools of Architecture (E)
1735 New York Avenue, NW
Washington, DC 20006
(202) 785-2324
Fax: (202) 628-0448
Michael Monti Ph.D.
Executive Director
E-mail: info@acsa-arch.org
URL: www.acsa-arch.org

Association of Collegiate Schools of Planning (F)
c/o Donna Dodd, Association Manager
6311 Mallard Trace Drive
Tallahassee, FL 32312
(850) 385-2054
Fax: (850) 385-2084
Dr. Charles Connerly
President
E-mail: president@acsp.org
URL: www.acsp.org

Association of Community College Trustees (G)
1233 20th Street, NW
Suite 301
Washington, DC 20036
(202) 775-4667
Fax: (202) 223-1297
Mr. J. Noah Brown
President and CEO
E-mail: nbrown@acct.org
URL: www.acct.org

Association of Departments of English (H)
26 Broadway
3rd Floor
New York, NY 10004-1789
(646) 576-5130
Fax: (646) 458-0033
Dr. David Laurence
Director
E-mail: ade@mla.org
URL: www.ade.org

Association of Departments of Foreign Languages (I)
26 Broadway
3rd Floor
New York, NY 10004-1789
(646) 576-5140
Fax: (646) 458-0033 or (646) 835-4069
Dr. Nelly Furman
Director
E-mail: adfl@mla.org
URL: www.adfl.org

The Association of Educational Publishers (J)
300 Martin Luther King Boulevard
Suite 200
Wilmington, DE 19801
(302) 295-8350
Fax: (302) 778-1110
Ms. Charlene F. Gaynor
Chief Executive Officer
E-mail: mail@aepweb.org
URL: www.aepweb.org

Association of Governing Boards of Universities and Colleges (K)
1133 20th Street, NW
Suite 300
Washington, DC 20036
(202) 296-8400
Fax: (202) 223-7053
Mr. Richard Legon
President
E-mail: rickl@agb.org
URL: www.agb.org

Association of Graduate Liberal Studies Programs (L)
c/o Duke University
Box 90095
Durham, NC 27708-0095
(919) 684-1987
Fax: (919) 681-8905
Mr. David L. Gitomer
President
E-mail: info@aglsp.org
URL: www.aglsp.org

Association of International Education Administrators (M)
Campus Box 90404
Duke University
Durham, NC 27708-0404
(919) 668-1928
Fax: (919) 684-8749
Dr. Darla K. Deardorff
Executive Director
E-mail: aiea@duke.edu
URL: www.aieaworld.org

Association of Jesuit Colleges and Universities (N)
1 Dupont Circle, NW
Suite 405
Washington, DC 20036
(202) 862-9893
Fax: (202) 862-8523
Rev. Gregory F. Lucey S.J.
President
E-mail: glucey@ajcunet.edu
URL: www.ajcunet.edu

Association of Military Colleges and Schools of the United States (O)
3604 Glenbrook Road
Fairfax, VA 22031-3211
(703) 272-8406
Fax: (703) 280-1082
Dr. Rudy Ehrenberg
Executive Director
E-mail: amcsus@cox.net
URL: www.amcsus.org

Association of Performing Arts Presenters (P)
1211 Connecticut Avenue, NW
Suite 200
Washington, DC 20036
(202) 833-2787
Fax: (202) 833-1543
E-mail: info@artspresenters.org
URL: www.apap365.org

Association of Practical Theology (Q)
Princeton Theological Seminary
Tennent Hall
108 Stockton Street
Princeton, NJ 08540
(609) 497-7739
Fax: (609) 279-9014
Mr. Gordon Mikoski
President
E-mail: gordon.mikoski@ptsem.edu
URL: www.practicaltheology.org

Association of Presbyterian Colleges and Universities (R)
100 Witherspoon Street
Louisville, KY 40202-1396
(502) 569-5509
Fax: (502) 569-8077
Mr. Gary Luhr
Executive Director
E-mail: gary.luhr@pcusa.org
URL: www.presbyteriancolleges.org

Association of Private Sector Colleges and Universities (APSCU) (S)
1101 Connecticut Avenue, NW
Suite 900
Washington, DC 20036
(202) 336-6700
Fax: (202) 336-6828
Mr. Brian Moran
Executive Vice President of Government Relations
E-mail: brian.moran@apscu.org
URL: www.apscu.org

Association of Public and Land-Grant Universities (T)
1307 New York Avenue, NW
Suite 400
Washington, DC 20005-4722
(202) 478-6040
Fax: (202) 478-6046
M. Peter McPherson
President
E-mail: pmcpherson@aplu.org
URL: www.aplu.org

Association of Research Libraries (U)
21 Dupont Circle, NW
Suite 800
Washington, DC 20036
(202) 296-2296
Fax: (202) 872-0884
Mr. Charles B. Lowry
Executive Director
E-mail: clowry@arl.org
URL: www.arl.org

Association of Schools of Allied Health Professions (V)
4400 Jenifer Street, NW
Suite 333
Washington, DC 20015
(202) 237-6481
Fax: (202) 237-6485
Dr. Thomas Elwood
Executive Director
E-mail: thomas@asahp.org
URL: www.asahp.org

Association of Specialized and Professional Accreditors (W)
3304 North Broadway Street, #214
Chicago, IL 60657
(773) 857-7900
Fax: (773) 857-7901
Mr. Joseph Vibert
Executive Director
E-mail: aspa@aspa-usa.org
URL: www.aspa-usa.org

Association of Teacher Educators (X)
PO Box 793
Manassas, VA 20113
(703) 331-0911
Fax: (703) 331-3666
Dr. David Ritchey
Executive Director
E-mail: dritchey@ate1.org
URL: www.ate1.org

Association of Teachers of Technical Writing (Y)
University of North Texas
Dept. of Linguistics & Technical Communication
1155 Union Circle #305298
Denton, TX 76203-5017
(940) 565-4458
Dr. Brenda R. Sims
Executive Secretary
E-mail: sims@unt.edu
URL: www.attw.org

The Association of Technology, Management, and Applied Engineering (ATMAE) (Z)
1390 Eisenhower Place
Ann Arbor, MI 48108
(734) 677-0720
Fax: (734) 677-0046
Mr. Rick Coscarelli
Executive Director
E-mail: rcoscarelli@atmae.org
URL: atmae.org

Association of Theological Schools in the United States and Canada The Commission on Accrediting (a)
10 Summit Park Drive
Pittsburgh, PA 15275-1103
(412) 788-6505
Fax: (412) 788-6510
Dr. Daniel O. Aleshire
Executive Director
E-mail: ats@ats.edu
URL: www.ats.edu

Association of University Programs in Health Administration (b)
2000 14th Street North
Suite 780
Arlington, VA 22201-2543
(703) 894-0940
Fax: (703) 894-0941
Ms. Lydia Middleton MBA, CAE
President & CEO
E-mail: lmiddleton@aupha.org
URL: www.aupha.org

Association of University Research Parks (c)
6262 North Swan Road
Suite 100
Tucson, AZ 85718
(520) 529-2521
Fax: (520) 529-2499
Ms. Eileen Walker
CEO
E-mail: info@aurp.net
URL: www.aurp.net

Association of University Summer Sessions (d)
PO Box 210066, Room 221
University of Arizona
Tucson, AZ 85721-0066
(520) 626-8488
Fax: (520) 621-2099
Ms. Debbie Milora
Recorder
E-mail: dmiller@u.arizona.edu

Aviation Accreditation Board International (e)
3410 Skyway Drive
Auburn, AL 36830
(334) 844-2431
Fax: (334) 844-2432
Mr. Gary W. Kiteley
President
E-mail: kitelgw@auburn.edu
URL: www.aabi.aero

Broadcast Education Association (f)
1771 N Street, NW
Washington, DC 20036-2891
(202) 429-5355
Fax: (202) 775-2981
Ms. Heather Birks
Executive Director
E-mail: hbirks@nab.org
URL: www.beaweb.org

The Carnegie Foundation for the Advancement of Teaching (g)
51 Vista Lane
Stanford, CA 94305
(650) 566-5100
Fax: (650) 326-0278
Dr. Anthony S. Bryk
President
E-mail: milligan@carnegiefoundation.org
URL: www.carnegiefoundation.org

Center for Women Policy Studies (A)
1776 Massachusetts Avenue, NW
Suite 450
Washington, DC 20036
(202) 872-1770
FAX: (202) 296-8962
Leslie R. Wolfe
President
E-MAIL: cwps@centerwomenpolicy.org
URL: www.centerwomenpolicy.org

Center on Education and Training for Employment (B)
The Ohio State University
1900 Kenny Road
Columbus, OH 43210-1016
(614) 292-9072
FAX: (614) 292-1260
Mr. Robert A. Mahlman
Director
E-MAIL: mahlman.1@osu.edu
URL: www.cete.org

College and University Professional Association for Human Resources (CUPA-HR) (C)
1811 Commons Point Drive
Knoxville, TN 37932
(865) 637-7673
FAX: (865) 637-7674
Mr. Andy Brantley
President and Chief Executive Officer
E-MAIL: memberservice@cupahr.org
URL: www.cupahr.org

College Art Association (D)
50 Broadway, Floor 21
New York, NY 10004
(212) 691-1051
FAX: (212) 627-2381
Ms. Linda Downs
Executive Director
E-MAIL: nyoffice@collegeart.org
URL: www.collegeart.org

The College Board (E)
45 Columbus Avenue
New York, NY 10023
(212) 713-8000
David Coleman
President
URL: www.collegeboard.org

College English Association (F)
James Madison University
English Department
MC 1801
Harrisonburg, VA 22807
(540) 434-2738
FAX: (540) 568-2983
Mr. Robert Hoskins
Executive Director
E-MAIL: hoskinrv@jmu.edu
URL: cea-web.org

College Media Association (G)
2301 Vanderbilt Place
VU Station B351669
Nashville, TN 37235-1669
(615) 322-6610
Mr. Christopher Carroll
Interim Executive Director
E-MAIL: chris.carroll@vanderbilt.edu
URL: www.cma.cloverpad.org

Columbia Scholastic Press Association (H)
Columbia University
Mail Code 5711
New York, NY 10027-6902
(212) 854-9400
FAX: (212) 854-9401
Mr. Edmund J. Sullivan
Executive Director
E-MAIL: cspa@columbia.edu
URL: www.columbia.edu/cu/cspa

Commission on Accreditation for Health Informatics and Information Management Education (CAHIIM) (I)
233 North Michigan Avenue
21st Floor
Chicago, IL 60601-5800
(312) 233-1100
FAX: (312) 233-1483
Dr. Claire Dixon-Lee
Executive Director CAHIIM
E-MAIL: info@cahiim.org
URL: www.cahiim.org

Commission on Accreditation of Allied Health Education Programs (J)
1361 Park Street
Clearwater, FL 33756
(727) 210-2350
FAX: (727) 210-2354
Dr. Kathleen Megivern J.D., CAE
Executive Director
E-MAIL: megivern@caahep.org
URL: www.caahep.org

Commission on Accreditation of Healthcare Management Education (CAHME) (K)
2111 Wilson Boulevard
Suite 700
Arlington, VA 22201
(703) 351-5010
FAX: (703) 991-5989
Mr. Anthony Wisniewski JD
President & CEO
E-MAIL: awisniewski@cahme.org
URL: www.cahme.org

Commission on Accreditation of Rehabilitation Facilities (CARF) (L)
6951 E. Southpoint Road
Tucson, AZ 85756
(520) 325-1044
FAX: (520) 318-1129
Dr. Brian J. Boon Ph.D.
President & CEO
E-MAIL: info@carf.org
URL: www.carf.org

Commission on Collegiate Nursing Education (CCNE) (M)
One Dupont Circle, NW
Suite 530
Washington, DC 20036-1120
(202) 887-6791
FAX: (202) 887-8476
Dr. Jennifer Butlin
Executive Director
E-MAIL: jbutlin@aacn.nche.edu
URL: www.aacn.nche.edu/accreditation

Commission on Dental Accreditation (N)
211 East Chicago Avenue
Chicago, IL 60611
(312) 440-4653
FAX: (312) 440-2915
Dr. Anthony Ziebert
Director
E-MAIL: zieberta@ada.org
URL: www.ada.org/117.aspx

Commission on English Language Program Accreditation (CEA) (O)
801 North Fairfax Street
Suite 402A
Alexandria, VA 22314
(703) 519-2070
FAX: (703) 519-2071
Ms. Teresa D. O'Donnell
Executive Director
E-MAIL: todonnell@cea-accredit.org
URL: www.cea-accredit.org

Commission on Independent Colleges and Universities (CICU) (P)
17 Elk Street
PO Box 7289
Albany, NY 12224
(518) 436-4781
FAX: (518) 436-0417
Ms. Laura L. Anglin
President
E-MAIL: mail@cicu.org
URL: www.cicu.org, www.nycolleges.org

Commission on Massage Therapy Accreditation (Q)
5335 Wisconsin Avenue, NW
Suite 440
Washington, DC 20015
(202) 895-1518
FAX: (202) 895-1519
Ms. Kate Ivane Henri Zulaski
Executive Director
E-MAIL: kzulaski@comta.org
URL: www.comta.org

Commission on Opticianry Accreditation (R)
PO Box 592
Canton, NY 13617
(703) 468-0566
Mrs. Debra White
Director of Accreditation
E-MAIL: director@coaccreditation.com
URL: www.coaccreditation.com

Committee on Accreditation for Education in Neurodiagnostic Technology (S)
22 Railroad Avenue
Suite 3
Beverly, MA 01915
(978) 338-6300
FAX: (978) 832-2638
Dr. Jackie Long-Goding RRT-NPS
Executive Director
E-MAIL: office@coa-ndt.org
URL: www.coa-ndt.org

Committee on Accreditation for Polysomnographic Technologist Education (T)
1711 Frank Avenue
New Bern, NC 28560
(252) 626-3238
Ms. Karen Monarchy Rowe
Executive Director
E-MAIL: office@coapsg.org
URL: www.coapsg.org

Committee on Accreditation for the Exercise Sciences (U)
401 West Michigan Street
Indianapolis, IN 46202
(317) 637-9200
FAX: (317) 634-7817
E-MAIL: trush@acsm.org
URL: www.coaes.org

Committee on Accreditation of Education Programs for Kinesiotherapy (V)
University of Southern Mississippi
118 College Drive, #5142
Hattiesburg, MS 39406-0002
(601) 266-5371
FAX: (601) 266-4445
Jerry W. Purvis
E-MAIL: jerry.purvis@usm.edu
URL: www.akta.org

Committee on Accreditation of Educational Programs for the Emergency Medical Services Professions (W)
8301 Lakeview Parkway
Suite 111-312
Rowlett, TX 75088
(214) 703-8445
FAX: (214) 703-8992
Dr. George Hatch
Executive Director
E-MAIL: george@coaemsp.org
URL: www.coaemsp.org

Committee on Institutional Cooperation (X)
1819 South Neil Street
Suite D
Champaign, IL 61820
(217) 333-8475
FAX: (217) 244-7127
Ms. Barbara McFadden Allen
Director
E-MAIL: cic@staff.cic.net
URL: www.cic.net

Conference on College Composition and Communication (Y)
1111 West Kenyon Road
Urbana, IL 61801-1096
(800) 369-6283
FAX: (217) 328-0977
Mr. Kent Williamson
Executive Secretary-Treasurer
E-MAIL: kwilliamson@ncte.org
URL: www.ncte.org/cccc

Council for Accreditation of Counseling and Related Educational Programs (CACREP) (Z)
1001 North Fairfax Street, Suite 510
Alexandria, VA 22314
(703) 535-5990
FAX: (703) 739-6209
Dr. Carol L. Bobby
President and CEO
E-MAIL: cacrep@cacrep.org
URL: www.cacrep.org

Council for Adult and Experiential Learning (a)
55 East Monroe
Suite 1930
Chicago, IL 60603
(312) 499-2600
FAX: (312) 499-2601
Ms. Pamela Tate
President
E-MAIL: ptate@cael.org
URL: www.cael.org

Council for Advancement and Support of Education (b)
1307 New York Avenue, NW
Suite 1000
Washington, DC 20005-4701
(202) 328-2273
FAX: (202) 387-4973
Mr. John Lippincott
President
E-MAIL: lippincott@case.org
URL: www.case.org

Council for Agricultural Science and Technology (CAST) (c)
4420 West Lincoln Way
Ames, IA 50014-3447
(515) 292-2125
FAX: (515) 292-4512
Dr. John M. Bonner
Executive Vice President
E-MAIL: cast@cast-science.org
URL: www.cast-science.org

Council for Aid to Education (d)
215 Lexington Avenue
New York, NY 10016-6023
(212) 661-5800
FAX: (212) 661-9766
Dr. Roger Benjamin
President & CEO
E-MAIL: rbenjamin@cae.org
URL: www.cae.org

Council for Christian Colleges & Universities (e)
321 8th Street, NE
Washington, DC 20002-6158
(202) 546-8713
FAX: (202) 546-8913
Dr. Edward O. Blews Jr.
President
E-MAIL: council@cccu.org
URL: www.cccu.org

Council for Economic Education (f)
122 East 42nd Street
Suite 2600
New York, NY 10168
(212) 730-7007 or (800) 338-1192
FAX: (212) 730-1793
Ms. Nan Morrison
President and CEO
E-MAIL: njmorrison@councilforeconed.org
URL: www.councilforeconed.org

Council for Higher Education Accreditation (g)
1 Dupont Circle, NW
Suite 510
Washington, DC 20036-1135
(202) 955-6126
FAX: (202) 955-6129
Dr. Judith Eaton
President
E-MAIL: chea@chea.org
URL: www.chea.org

Council for Interior Design Accreditation (formerly FIDER) (h)
206 Grandville Avenue
Suite 350
Grand Rapids, MI 49503
(616) 458-0400
FAX: (616) 458-0460
Ms. Holly Mattson
Executive Director
E-MAIL: info@accredit-id.org
URL: www.accredit-id.org

Council for Research in Music Education (i)
University of Illinois at Urbana-Champaign
1114 West Nevada
Urbana, IL 61801
(217) 333-1027
Dr. Eve Harwood
Editor
E-MAIL: crme@illinois.edu
URL: bcrme.press.illinois.edu

Council for the Advancement of Standards in Higher Education (j)
One Dupont Circle, NW
Suite 300
Washington, DC 20036-1188
(202) 862-1400
FAX: (202) 296-3286
Dr. Marybeth Drechsler Sharp
Executive Director
E-MAIL: executive_director@cas.edu
URL: www.cas.edu

Council of Colleges of Acupuncture and Oriental Medicine (CCAOM) (A)
600 Wyndhurst Avenue
Suite 112
Baltimore, MD 21210
(410) 464-6041
FAX: (410) 464-6042
Mr. David M. Sale
Executive Director
E-MAIL: executivedirector@ccaom.comcastbiz.net
URL: www.ccaom.org

Council of Colleges of Arts and Sciences (B)
PO Box 8795
c/o The College of William and Mary
Williamsburg, VA 23187-8795
(757) 221-1784
Dr. Anne-Marie McCartan
Executive Director
E-MAIL: ccas@wm.edu
URL: www.ccas.net

Council of Graduate Schools (C)
1 Dupont Circle, NW
Suite 230
Washington, DC 20036
(202) 223-3791
FAX: (202) 331-7157
Dr. Debra W. Stewart
President
E-MAIL: president@cgs.nche.edu
URL: www.cgsnet.org

Council of Independent Colleges (D)
1 Dupont Circle, NW
Suite 320
Washington, DC 20036-1142
(202) 466-7230
FAX: (202) 466-7238
Dr. Richard Ekman
President
E-MAIL: cic@cic.nche.edu
URL: www.cic.edu

The Council of Writing Program Administrators (E)
Grand Valley State University
Department of Writing
326 Lake Ontario Hall
Allendale, MI 49401
(616) 331-8147
Dr. Keith Rhodes
Secretary
E-MAIL: rhodekei@gvsu.edu
URL: www.wpacouncil.org

Council on Accreditation of Nurse Anesthesia Educational Programs (COA) (F)
222 South Prospect Avenue
Park Ridge, IL 60068-4001
(847) 655-1154
FAX: (847) 692-7137
Francis Gerbasi CRNA,Ph.D.
Executive Director
E-MAIL: fgerbasi@coa.us.com
URL: www.home.coa.us.com

Council on Chiropractic Education (G)
8049 North 85th Way
Scottsdale, AZ 85258-4321
(480) 443-8877
FAX: (480) 483-7333
Tom Benberg
President
E-MAIL: cce@cce-usa.org
URL: www.cce-usa.org

Council on Education for Public Health (H)
1010 Wayne Avenue
Suite 220
Silver Spring, MD 20910-5600
(202) 789-1050
FAX: (202) 789-1895
Ms. Laura Rasar King
Executive Director
E-MAIL: lking@ceph.org
URL: www.ceph.org

Council on Governmental Relations (I)
1200 New York Avenue, NW
Suite 750
Washington, DC 20005
(202) 289-6655
FAX: (202) 289-6698
Mr. Anthony DeCrappeo
President
E-MAIL: tdecrappeo@cogr.edu
URL: www.cogr.edu

Council on Higher Education Solutions for Adults (J)
104 Johnson Street
Marshall, TX 75670
(903) 472-2762
FAX: (903) 935-3890
Dr. Tracy Andrus
President/CEO
E-MAIL: chesa1962@gmail.com
URL: www.chesa1.com

Council on Law in Higher Education (K)
9386 Via Classico West
Wellington, FL 33411
(561) 792-4440
FAX: (561) 792-4441
Mr. Daren Bakst
President
E-MAIL: moss@clhe.org
URL: www.clhe.org

Council on Naturopathic Medical Education (L)
PO Box 178
Great Barrington, MA 01230
(413) 528-8877
FAX: (413) 528-8880
Dr. Daniel Seitz J.D., Ed.D
Executive Director
E-MAIL: danseitz@cnme.org
URL: www.cnme.org

Council on Occupational Education (M)
7840 Roswell Road
Building 300, Suite 325
Atlanta, GA 30350
(800) 917-2081
FAX: (770) 396-3790
Dr. Gary Puckett
President
E-MAIL: puckettg@council.org
URL: www.council.org

Council on Podiatric Medical Education (N)
9312 Old Georgetown Road
Bethesda, MD 20814
(301) 581-9200
FAX: (301) 571-4903
Mr. Alan R. Tinkleman
Director
E-MAIL: artinkleman@apma.org
URL: www.cpme.org

Council on Rehabilitation Education (CORE) (O)
1699 Woodfield Road
Suite 300
Schaumburg, IL 60173
(847) 944-1345
FAX: (847) 944-1346
Dr. Frank Lane
Executive Director
E-MAIL: lane@iit.edu
URL: www.core-rehab.org

Council on Social Work Education (P)
1701 Duke Street
Suite 200
Alexandria, VA 22314-3457
(703) 683-8080
FAX: (703) 683-8099
Dr. Stephen Holloway
Director Office of Social Work Accreditation
E-MAIL: sholloway@cswe.org
URL: www.cswe.org

Council on Undergraduate Research (Q)
734 15th Street, NW
Suite 550
Washington, DC 20005
(202) 783-4810
FAX: (202) 783-4811
Dr. Elizabeth L. Ambos
Executive Officer
E-MAIL: cur@cur.org
URL: www.cur.org

CSAB, Inc. (R)
817 Loyola Drive
Towson, MD 21204
(410) 339-5456
Ms. Liz Glazer
Executive Director
E-MAIL: csab@csab.org
URL: www.csab.org

Cultural Vistas (S)
10400 Little Patuxent Parkway
Suite 250
Columbia, MD 21044-3519
(410) 997-2200
FAX: (410) 992-3924
Mr. Robert Fenstermacher
President & CEO
E-MAIL: info@culturalvistas.org
URL: www.culturalvistas.org

Decision Sciences Institute (T)
75 Piedmont Road
Suite 340
Atlanta, GA 30303
(404) 413-7711
FAX: (404) 413-7714
Ms. Carol J. Latta
Executive Director
E-MAIL: clatta@gsu.edu
URL: www.decisionsciences.org

Direct Marketing Association, Inc. (U)
1120 Avenue of the Americas
New York, NY 10036-6700
(212) 768-7277
FAX: (212) 768-7353
Ms. Linda M. Wolley Esq.
CEO
E-MAIL: ceo@the-dma.org
URL: www.newdma.org

Direct Marketing Educational Foundation, Inc. (V)
1120 Avenue of the Americas
14th Floor
New York, NY 10036-6700
(212) 768-7277
FAX: (212) 790-1561
Terri L. Bartlett
President
E-MAIL: dmef@directworks.org
URL: www.directworks.org

Distance Education and Training Council (W)
1601 Eighteenth Street, NW
Suite 2
Washington, DC 20009
(202) 234-5100
FAX: (202) 332-1386
Mr. Michael P. Lambert
Executive Director
E-MAIL: info@detc.org
URL: www.detc.org

Education Commission of the States (X)
700 Broadway
Suite 810
Denver, CO 80203-3460
(303) 299-3600
FAX: (303) 296-8332
Mr. Roger Sampson
President
E-MAIL: ecs@ecs.org
URL: www.ecs.org

Education Development Center, Inc. (Y)
43 Foundry Avenue
Waltham, MA 02453
(617) 969-7100
FAX: (617) 969-5979
Mr. Luther S. Luedtke
President
E-MAIL: comment@edc.org
URL: www.edc.org

EDUCAUSE (Z)
1150 18th Street, NW
Suite 900
Washington, DC 20036-3816
(202) 872-4200
FAX: (202) 872-4318
Diana Oblinger Ph.D.
President
E-MAIL: doblinger@educause.edu
URL: www.educause.edu

FHI360 (a)
1825 Connecticut Avenue, NW
Washington, DC 20009-5721
(202) 884-8000
FAX: (202) 884-8400
Dr. Albert J. Siemens
Chief Executive Officer
E-MAIL: contact@fhi.org
URL: www.fhi360.org

Financial Management Association International (b)
University of South Florida
College of Business Administration
4202 East Fowler Avenue, BSN 3331
Tampa, FL 33620-5500
(813) 974-2084
FAX: (813) 974-3318
Mr. Jack S. Rader
Executive Director
E-MAIL: fma@coba.usf.edu
URL: www.fma.org

Friends Association for Higher Education (c)
1501 Cherry Street
Philadelphia, PA 19102
(215) 241-7116
FAX: (215) 241-7028
Ms. Kimberly Haas
FAHE Coordinator
E-MAIL: fahe@quaker.org
URL: www.earlham.edu/~fahe

The George Washington University HEATH Resource Center at the National Youth Transitions Center Graduate School of Education & Human Development (d)
2134 G Street, NW
Washington, DC 20052-0001
E-MAIL: askheath@gwu.edu
URL: www.heath.gwu.edu

The Gerontological Society of America (e)
1220 L Street, NW
Suite 901
Washington, DC 20005-4018
(202) 587-2821
FAX: (202) 587-2850
Mr. James Appleby
Executive Director
E-MAIL: geron@geron.org
URL: www.geron.org

Graduate Record Examinations Board (f)
Educational Testing Service
Mail Stop 57L
Rosedale Road
Princeton, NJ 08541
(609) 683-2014
FAX: (609) 683-2040
Dr. David G. Payne
Vice President & COO of Higher Education Division
E-MAIL: dpayne@ets.org
URL: www.ets.org

H. Wiley Hitchcock Institute for Studies in American Music (g)
Brooklyn College/CUNY
2900 Bedford Avenue
Brooklyn, NY 11210-2889
(718) 951-5655
Dr. Jeffrey Taylor
Director
E-MAIL: hisam@brooklyn.cuny.edu
URL: www.hisam.org

Higher Education Resource Services (HERS) (h)
University of Denver
1901 East Asbury Avenue
Denver, CO 80208
(303) 871-6866
FAX: (303) 871-6766
Dr. Judith White
President/Executive Director
E-MAIL: jwhite28@du.edu
URL: www.hersnet.org

Higher Learning Commission North Central Association (i)
230 South LaSalle Street
Suite 7-500
Chicago, IL 60604-1413
(312) 263-0456 / (800) 621-7440
FAX: (312) 263-7462
Ms. Sylvia Manning
President
E-MAIL: info@hlcommission.org
URL: www.ncahlc.org

Hispanic Association of Colleges and Universities (A)
8415 Datapoint Drive
Suite 400
San Antonio, TX 78229
(210) 692-3805
Fax: (210) 692-0823
Dr. Antonio R. Flores
President and CEO
E-mail: hacu@hacu.net
URL: www.hacu.net

IACLEA (International Association of Campus Law Enforcement Administrators) (B)
342 North Main Street
West Hartford, CT 06117-2507
(860) 586-7517
Fax: (860) 586-7550
Mr. Peter J. Berry CAE
Chief Staff Officer
E-mail: info@iaclea.org
URL: www.iaclea.org

The Institute for Higher Education Policy (C)
1320 19th Street, NW
Suite 400
Washington, DC 20036
(202) 861-8223
Fax: (202) 861-9307
Michelle A. Cooper Ph.D.
President
E-mail: institute@ihep.org
URL: www.ihep.org

Institute of International Education (D)
809 United Nations Plaza
New York, NY 10017-3580
(212) 883-8200
Fax: (212) 984-5496
E-mail: info@iie.org
URL: www.iie.org

Institute of International Education Council for International Exchange of Scholars (E)
1400 K Street, NW
Suite 700
Washington, DC 20005
(202) 686-4000
Fax: (202) 686-4029
Jamie Bellis
Deputy Executive Director
E-mail: scholars@iie.org
URL: www.cies.org

Intercollegiate Broadcasting System, Inc. (F)
367 Windsor Highway
New Windsor, NY 12553-7900
(845) 565-0003
Fax: (845) 565-7446
Mr. Fritz Kass
Director-Operations
E-mail: ibshq@aol.com
URL: www.collegeradio.tv

International Assembly for Collegiate Business Education (G)
11374 Strang Line Road
Lenexa, KS 66215
(913) 631-3009
Fax: (913) 631-9154
Mr. Dennis N. Gash
President
E-mail: iacbe@iacbe.org
URL: www.iacbe.org

International Association of Baptist Colleges and Universities (H)
8120 Sawyer Brown Road
Suite 108
Nashville, TN 37221-1410
(615) 673-1896
Dr. Michael Arrington
Executive Director
E-mail: marrington@baptistschools.org
URL: www.baptistschools.org

International Communication Association (I)
1500 21st Street, NW
Washington, DC 20036
(202) 955-1444
Fax: (202) 955-1448
Dr. Michael Haley
Executive Director
E-mail: mhaley@icahdq.org
URL: www.icahdq.org

International Council on Education for Teaching (J)
National-Louis University
1000 Capitol Drive
Wheeling, IL 60090
(847) 947-5622
Fax: (847) 947-5622
James O'Meara
President
E-mail: ICET_Secretariat@nl.edu
URL: www.icet4u.org

International Fire Service Accreditation Congress (K)
1700 West Tyler
Stillwater, OK 74078
(405) 744-8303
Fax: (405) 744-8802
Mr. Clayton Moorman
Manager
E-mail: cmoorman@ifsac.org
URL: www.ifsac.org

Iowa Association of Community College Trustees (L)
855 East Court Avenue
Des Moines, IA 50309
(515) 282-4692
Fax: (515) 282-3743
M. J. Dolan J.D.
Executive Director
E-mail: mjdolan@iacct.com
URL: www.iacct.com

Joint Review Committee on Education in Cardiovascular Technology (JRC-CVT) (M)
6 Pine Knoll Drive
Beverly, MA 01915-1425
(978) 456-5594
Mr. William W. Goding
Executive Director
E-mail: office@jrccvt.org
URL: www.jrccvt.org

Joint Review Committee on Education in Diagnostic Medical Sonography (N)
6021 University Boulevard
Suite 500
Ellicott City, MD 21043-6090
(443) 973-3251
Mr. Gerry Magat
Accreditation Coordinator
E-mail: mail@jrcdms.org
URL: www.jrcdms.org

Joint Review Committee on Education in Radiologic Technology (O)
20 North Wacker Drive
Suite 2850
Chicago, IL 60606-3182
(312) 704-5300
Fax: (312) 704-5304
Leslie F. Winter
Chief Executive Officer
E-mail: mail@jrcert.org
URL: www.jrcert.org

Joint Review Committee on Educational Programs in Nuclear Medicine Technology (P)
2000 West Danforth Road
Suite 130, #203
Edmond, OK 73003
(405) 285-0546
Fax: (405) 285-0579
Ms. Jan M. Winn
Executive Director
E-mail: jrcnmt@coxinet.net
URL: www.jrcnmt.org

Journalism Association of Community Colleges (Q)
PO Box 163509
Sacramento, CA 95816
(562) 860-2451, ext 2619
Fax: (562) 467-5044
Mr. Rich Cameron
Communications Director
E-mail: rich@rcameron.com
URL: www.jacconline.org

LASPAU: Academic and Professional Programs for the Americas (R)
25 Mount Auburn Street
Suite 300
Cambridge, MA 02138-6095
(617) 495-5255
Fax: (617) 495-8990
Dr. Peter DeShazo
Executive Director
E-mail: laspau-info@calists.harvard.edu
URL: www.laspau.harvard.edu

Law School Admission Council (S)
662 Penn Street
Newtown, PA 18940
(215) 968-1001
Fax: (215) 968-1119
Mr. Daniel Bernstine
President
URL: www.lsac.org

Liaison Committee on Medical Education (LCME) American Medical Association (T)
515 North State Street
Chicago, IL 60654
(312) 464-4933
Fax: (312) 464-5830
Barbara Barzansky Ph.D.,MHPE
LCME Secretary, 2011-2012
E-mail: barbara.barzansky@ama-assn.org
URL: www.lcme.org

Linguistic Society of America (U)
1325 Eighteenth Street, NW
Archibald A. Hill, Suite #211
Washington, DC 20036-6501
(202) 835-1714
Fax: (202) 835-1717
Ms. Alyson Reed
Executive Director
E-mail: lsa@lsadc.org
URL: www.lsadc.org

Literacy Research Association, Inc. (V)
7044 South 13th Street
Oak Creek, WI 53154-1429
(414) 908-4924
Fax: (414) 768-8001
Betsy Purcell
Executive Director
E-mail: b.purcell@LiteracyResearchAssociation.org
URL: www.LiteracyResearchAssociation.org

Lutheran Educational Conference of North America (W)
PMB #377
2601 South Minnesota Avenue
Suite 105
Sioux Falls, SD 57105-4750
(605) 271-9894
Fax: (605) 271-9895
Mr. William E. Hamm
President
E-mail: hamm@lutherancolleges.org
URL: www.lutherancolleges.org

Medical Assisting Education Review Board (X)
20 North Wacker Drive
Suite 1575
Chicago, IL 60606-2963
(312) 899-1500
Fax: (312) 899-1259
Ms. Anna L. Johnson
Executive Director of Accreditation
E-mail: ajohnson@maerb.org
URL: www.maerb.org

Middle States Commission on Higher Education (Y)
3624 Market Street
2nd Floor West
Philadelphia, PA 19104-2680
(267) 284-5000
Fax: (215) 662-5501
E-mail: info@msche.org
URL: www.msche.org

Midtown Detroit, Inc. (Z)
3939 Woodward Avenue
Suite 100
Detroit, MI 48201
(313) 420-6000
Fax: (313) 420-6200
Ms. Susan Mosey
President
E-mail: info@midtowndetroitinc.org
URL: www.midtowndetroitinc.org

Midwest Association of Colleges and Employers (a)
5024R Campbell Boulevard
Baltimore, MD 21236
(410) 931-8100
Fax: (410) 931-8111
Ms. Laura Kestner
President
E-mail: admin@mwace.org
URL: www.mwace.org

Midwestern Higher Education Compact (MHEC) (b)
105 Fifth Avenue South
Suite 450
Minneapolis, MN 55401
(612) 677-2777
Fax: (612) 767-3353
Mr. Larry A. Isaak
President
E-mail: mhec@mhec.org
URL: www.mhec.org

Midwifery Education Accreditation Council (MEAC) (c)
1935 Pauline Boulevard
Suite 100B
Ann Arbor, MI 48103
(360) 466-2080
Fax: (480) 907-2936
Ms. Sandra Stewart
Executive Director
E-mail: executivedirector@meacschools.org
URL: www.meacschools.org

Modern Language Association (d)
26 Broadway
3rd Floor
New York, NY 10004-1789
(646) 576-5000
Fax: (646) 458-0030
Dr. Rosemary G. Feal
Executive Director
URL: www.mla.org

Montessori Accreditation Council for Teacher Education (MACTE) (e)
313 Second Street S.E.
Suite 112
Charlottesville, VA 22902
(434) 202-7793
Fax: (888) 525-8838
Dr. Rebecca Pelton
Executive Director
E-mail: rebecca@macte.org
URL: www.macte.org

NACAS (f)
3 Boar's Head Lane
Suite B
Charlottesville, VA 22903-4610
(434) 245-8425
Fax: (434) 245-8453
Jeff Perdue
Deputy Executive Director
E-mail: info@nacas.org
URL: www.nacas.org

NASH (g)
1250 H Street, NW
Suite 700
Washington, DC 20005
(202) 248-5149
Fax: (202) 293-2605
Jane V. Wellman
Executive Director
E-mail: jane@nash-dc.org
URL: www.nashonline.org

NASPA-Student Affairs Administrators in Higher Education (h)
111 K Street, NE
10th Floor
Washington, DC 20002-4409
(202) 265-7500
Fax: (202) 898-5737
Mr. Kevin Kruger
President
E-mail: office@naspa.org
URL: www.naspa.org

National Academic Advising Association (i)
2323 Anderson Avenue
Suite 225
Manhattan, KS 66502-2912
(785) 532-5717
Fax: (785) 532-7732
Dr. Charlie L. Nutt
Executive Director
E-mail: nacada@ksu.edu
URL: www.nacada.ksu.edu

The National Academy of Education (A)
500 5th Street, NW
Suite 307
Washington, DC 20001
(202) 334-2341
Fax: (202) 334-2350
E-mail: info@naeducation.org
URL: www.naeducation.org

National Academy of Kinesiology (B)
1607 North Market Street
Champaign, IL 61820
(217) 403-7545
Fax: (217) 351-2674
Ms. Kim Scott
Business Manager
E-mail: kims@hkusa.com
URL: www.nationalacademyofkinesiology.org

National Accreditation Council for Blind and Low Vision Services (C)
7017 Pearl Road
Middleburg Heights, OH 44130
(440) 545-1601
Mr. William A. Robinson III
Executive Director
E-mail: bill@nacasb.org
URL: www.nacasb.org

National Accrediting Agency for Clinical Laboratory Sciences (D)
5600 North River Road
Suite 720
Rosemont, IL 60018
(773) 714-8880
Fax: (773) 714-8886
Dr. Dianne M. Cearlock Ph.D
CEO
E-mail: dcearlock@naacls.org
URL: www.naacls.org

National Accrediting Commission of Career Arts and Sciences (E)
4401 Ford Avenue
Suite 1300
Alexandria, VA 22302-1432
(703) 600-7600
Fax: (703) 379-2200
Tony Mirando M.S., D.C.
Executive Director
E-mail: naccas@naccas.org
URL: www.naccas.org

National Association for College Admission Counseling (F)
1050 North Highland Street
Suite 400
Arlington, VA 22201
(703) 836-2222
Fax: (703) 836-8015
Ms. Joyce E. Smith
Chief Executive Officer
E-mail: jsmith@nacacnet.org
URL: www.nacacnet.org

National Association for Equal Opportunity in Higher Education (G)
209 Third Street, SE
Washington, DC 20003
(202) 552-3300
Fax: (202) 552-3330
Lezli Baskerville Esquire
President & CEO
E-mail: presidentsoffice@nafeo.org
URL: www.nafeo.org

National Association for Ethnic Studies, Inc. (H)
Colorado State University
Department of Ethnic Studies
1790 Campus Delivery
Fort Collins, CO 80523-1790
970-491-3927
Fax: 970-491-2717
E-mail: naes@ethnicstudies.org
URL: www.ethnicstudies.org

National Association for Legal Support of Alternative Schools (I)
PO Box 2823
Santa Fe, NM 87504-2823
(505) 474-0300
Fax: (505) 474-0300
Mr. Ed Nagel
Coordinator
E-mail: nalsas@msn.com

National Association for Practical Nurse Education and Service, Inc. (J)
1940 Duke Street
Suite 200
Alexandria, VA 22314
(703) 933-1003
Fax: (703) 940-4089
Helen Larsen J.D.
Executive Director
E-mail: education@napnes.org
URL: www.napnes.org

National Association of Agricultural Educators (K)
300 Garrigus Building
University of Kentucky
Lexington, KY 40546-0215
(859) 257-2224
Fax: (859) 323-3919
Dr. Wm. Jay Jackman
Executive Director
E-mail: jjackman.naae@uky.edu
URL: www.naae.org

National Association of College and University Attorneys (L)
1 Dupont Circle, NW
Suite 620
Washington, DC 20036
(202) 833-8390
Fax: (202) 296-8379
Ms. Kathleen Curry Santora Esq.
CEO
E-mail: ksantora@nacua.org
URL: www.nacua.org

National Association of College and University Business Officers (M)
1110 Vermont Avenue, NW
Suite 800
Washington, DC 20005
(202) 861-2500
Fax: (202) 861-2583
Mr. John Walda
President
E-mail: john.walda@nacubo.org
URL: www.nacubo.org

The National Association of College & University Food Services (N)
2525 Jolly Road
Suite 280
Okemos, MI 48864
(517) 332-2494
Fax: (517) 332-8144
Dr. Joseph H. Spina Ph.D., CAE
Executive Director
E-mail: jspina@nacufs.org
URL: www.nacufs.org

National Association of College Stores (O)
500 East Lorain Street
Oberlin, OH 44074-1294
(440) 775-7777
Fax: (440) 775-4769
Mr. Brian E. Cartier CAE
Chief Executive Officer
E-mail: info@nacs.org
URL: www.nacs.org

National Association of College Wind and Percussion Instructors (P)
Division of Fine Arts
Truman State University
308 Hillcrest Drive
Kirksville, MO 63501
(660) 665-2558
Dr. Richard Weerts
Executive Secretary-Treasurer
URL: www.nacwpi.org

National Association of Colleges and Employers (Q)
62 Highland Avenue
Bethlehem, PA 18017-9085
(610) 868-1421
Fax: (610) 868-0208
Dr. Marilyn Mackes
Executive Director
E-mail: cnader@naceweb.org
URL: www.naceweb.org

National Association of Educational Procurement (R)
5523 Research Park Drive
Suite 340
Baltimore, MD 21228
(443) 543-5540
Fax: (443) 543-5550
Mrs. Doreen Murner
CEO
E-mail: dmurner@naepnet.org
URL: www.naepnet.org

National Association of Independent Colleges and Universities (S)
1025 Connecticut Avenue, NW
Suite 700
Washington, DC 20036-5405
(202) 785-8866
Fax: (202) 835-0003
Dr. David L. Warren
President
E-mail: geninfo@naicu.edu
URL: www.naicu.edu

National Association of Schools of Art and Design (T)
11250 Roger Bacon Drive
Suite 21
Reston, VA 20190
(703) 437-0700
Fax: (703) 437-6312
Samuel Hope
Executive Director
E-mail: info@arts-accredit.org
URL: www.arts-accredit.org

National Association of Schools of Dance (U)
11250 Roger Bacon Drive
Suite 21
Reston, VA 20190
(703) 437-0700
Fax: (703) 437-6312
Samuel Hope
Executive Director
E-mail: info@arts-accredit.org
URL: www.arts-accredit.org

National Association of Schools of Music (V)
11250 Roger Bacon Drive
Suite 21
Reston, VA 20190
(703) 437-0700
Fax: (703) 437-6312
Samuel Hope
Executive Director
E-mail: info@arts-accredit.org
URL: www.arts-accredit.org

National Association of Schools of Public Affairs and Administration (NASPAA) (W)
1029 Vermont Avenue, NW
Suite 1100
Washington, DC 20005
(202) 628-8965
Ms. Laurel McFarland
Executive Director
E-mail: naspaa@naspaa.org
URL: www.naspaa.org

National Association of Schools of Theatre (X)
11250 Roger Bacon Drive
Suite 21
Reston, VA 20190
(703) 437-0700
Fax: (703) 437-6312
Samuel Hope
Executive Director
E-mail: info@arts-accredit.org
URL: www.arts-accredit.org

National Association of State Directors of Teacher Education and Certification (Y)
1629 K Street NW
Suite 300
Washington, DC 20006
(202) 204-2208
Fax: (202) 204-2210
Dr. Phillip Rogers
Executive Director
E-mail: philrogers@nasdtec.com
URL: www.nasdtec.org

National Association of Student Financial Aid Administrators (Z)
1101 Connecticut Avenue, NW
Suite 1100
Washington, DC 20036-4303
(202) 785-0453
Fax: (202) 785-1487
Mr. Justin Draeger
President
E-mail: web@nasfaa.org
URL: www.nasfaa.org

National Catholic Educational Association (a)
1005 North Glebe Road
Sutie 525
Arlington, VA 22201-5792
(571) 257-0010
Fax: (703) 243-0025
Ms. Karen M. Ristau Ed.D.
President
E-mail: kristau@ncea.org
URL: www.ncea.org

National Coalition for Campus Childrens Centers (b)
950 Glenn Drive
Suite 150
Folsom, CA 95630
(877) 736-6222
Fax: (916) 932-2209
Ms. Betty McIntire
Executive Director
E-mail: info@campuschildren.org
URL: www.campuschildren.org

National Collegiate Athletic Association (c)
PO Box 6222
Indianapolis, IN 46206
(317) 917-6222
Fax: (317) 917-6364
Mr. Todd Petr
Managing Director of Research
E-mail: tpetr@ncaa.org
URL: www.ncaa.org

National Commission on Orthotic and Prosthetic Education (NCOPE) (d)
330 John Carlyle Street
Suite 200
Alexandria, VA 22314
(703) 836-7114
Fax: (703) 836-0838
Ms. Robin C. Seabrook
Executive Director
E-mail: rseabrook@ncope.org
URL: www.ncope.org

National Communication Association (e)
1765 N Street, NW
Washington, DC 20036
(202) 464-4622
Fax: (202) 464-4600
Nancy Kidd Ph.D.
Executive Director
E-mail: inbox@natcom.org
URL: www.natcom.org

National Council for Accreditation of Teacher Education (f)
2010 Massachusetts Avenue, NW
Suite 500
Washington, DC 20036
(202) 466-7496
Fax: (202) 296-6620
Dr. James G. Cibulka
President
E-mail: ncate@ncate.org
URL: www.ncate.org

National Council for Continuing Education and Training (g)
PO Box 2916
Columbus, OH 43216-2916
(888) 771-0179
Fax: (888) 853-2213
Rob Clancey
President
E-mail: nccet@nccet.org
URL: www.nccet.org

Higher Education Associations

National Council of Instructional Administrators (NCIA) Dept of Educational Administration (A)
141 Teachers College Hall
PO Box 880360
University of Nebraska - Lincoln
Lincoln, NE 68588-0360
(402) 472-3727
FAX: (402) 472-4300
Kathy Wesley
Executive Director
E-MAIL: ncia@unl.edu
URL: ncia.unl.edu

National Council of University Research Administrators (B)
1015 18th Street, NW
Suite 901
Washington, DC 20036
(202) 466-3894
FAX: (202) 223-5573
Mrs. Kathleen M. Larmett
Executive Director
E-MAIL: info@ncura.edu
URL: www.ncura.edu

National Education Association (C)
1201 Sixteenth Street, NW
Washington, DC 20036
(202) 822-7110
FAX: (202) 822-7624
Ms. Valerie Wilk
Higher Education Coordinator
E-MAIL: vwilk@nea.org
URL: www.nea.org/he

National Forensic Association (D)
Illinois State University
School of Communication
Campus Box 4480
Normal, IL 61790-4480
(309) 438-8447
FAX: (309) 438-3048
Prof. Megan Koch
National Secretary
E-MAIL: mkoch@ilstu.org
URL: www.nationalforensics.org

National League for Nursing (E)
61 Broadway
33rd Floor
New York, NY 10006
(212) 363-5555 / (800) 669-1656
FAX: (212) 812-0392
Dr. Beverly L. Malone
Chief Executive Officer
E-MAIL: oceo@nln.org
URL: www.nln.org

National League for Nursing Accrediting Commission (NLNAC) (F)
3343 Peachtree Road NE
Suite 850
Atlanta, GA 30326
(404) 975-5000
FAX: (404) 975-5020
Dr. Sharon J. Tanner
CEO
E-MAIL: sjtanner@nlnac.org
URL: www.nlnac.org

National Recreation and Park Association Council on Accreditation for Parks, Recreation, Tourism and Related Professions (COAPRT) (G)
22377 Belmont Ridge Road
Ashburn, VA 20148-4501
(703) 858-2195
FAX: (703) 858-0794
Ms. Danielle Price
Accreditation Manager
E-MAIL: coaprt@nrpa.org
URL: www.nrpa.org

National Rural Education Association (H)
Purdue University
Beering Hall of Liberal Arts & Education
100 North University Street
West Lafayette, IN 47907
(765) 494-0086
FAX: (765) 496-1228
Dr. John Hill
Executive Director
E-MAIL: jehill@purdue.edu
URL: www.nrea.net

National Safety Council College and University Initiative (I)
1121 Spring Lake Drive
Itasca, IL 60143
(630) 775-2227
FAX: (630) 775-2310
Ms. Sloane Grubb
Volunteer Manager, (College&University Oversight)
E-MAIL: sloane.grubb@nsc.org
URL: www.nsc.org

National Society for Experiential Education (J)
c/o Talley Management Group, Inc.
19 Mantua Road
Mt. Royal, NJ 08061
(856) 423-3427
FAX: (856) 423-3420
Haley Brust
Executive Director
E-MAIL: nsee@talley.com
URL: www.nsee.org

National Writing Project (K)
2105 Bancroft Way
#1042
University of California
Berkeley, CA 94720-1042
(510) 642-0963
FAX: (510) 642-4545
Dr. Sharon J. Washington
Executive Director
E-MAIL: nwp@nwp.org
URL: www.nwp.org

New England Association of Schools and Colleges, Inc. Commission on Institutions of Higher Education (L)
209 Burlington Road
Bedford, MA 01730-1433
(781) 541-5447
FAX: (781) 271-0950
Dr. Barbara Brittingham
Director of the Commission
E-MAIL: cihe@neasc.org
URL: cihe.neasc.org

New England Board of Higher Education (M)
45 Temple Place
Boston, MA 02111
(617) 357-9620, ext. 128
FAX: (617) 338-1577
Dr. Michael K. Thomas
President and CEO
E-MAIL: mthomas@nebhe.org
URL: www.nebhe.org

New Leadership Alliance for Student Learning and Accountability (N)
1825 K Street, NW
Suite 705
Washington, DC 20006
(202) 263-7478
FAX: (202) 234-7640
Dr. David C. Paris
Executive Director
E-MAIL: office@newleadershipalliance.org
URL: www.newleadershipalliance.org

North American Association of Summer Sessions (O)
1501 W. Bradley Avenue
Peoria, IL 61625
(866) 880-9607
FAX: (309) 677-3321
Ms. Janet Lange
Executive Secretary
E-MAIL: lange@bradley.edu
URL: www.naass.org

North Central Association Commission on Accreditation and School Improvement (P)
9115 Westside Parkway
Alpharetta, GA 30009
(678) 392-2285
FAX: (770) 346-9260
Mr. Mark A. Elgart
President/CEO
E-MAIL: contactus@advanc-ed.org
URL: www.advanc-ed.org

North Central Conference on Summer Sessions (Q)
Bradley University
Peoria, IL 61625
(309) 677-2374
FAX: (309) 677-3321
Mr. Jon C. Neidy
Director of Summer and Interim Sessions
E-MAIL: neidy@bradley.edu

Northwest Commission on Colleges and Universities (R)
8060 165th Avenue, NE
Suite 100
Redmond, WA 98052
(425) 558-4224
FAX: (425) 376-0596
Dr. Sandra E. Elman
President
E-MAIL: ruthb@nwccu.org
URL: www.nwccu.org

Organizational Systems Research Association (S)
Morehead State University
Department of Information Systems
150 University Boulevard, Box 2478
Morehead, KY 40351-1689
(606) 783-2718
FAX: (606) 783-5025
Dr. Donna R. Everett
Executive Director
E-MAIL: d.everett@moreheadstate.edu
URL: www.osra.org

Pennsylvania Association of Colleges and Universities (T)
950 Walnut Bottom Road
Suite 15-214
Carlisle, PA 17015
(800) 687-9010
FAX: (717) 240-0673
URL: www.pacu.org

Planning Accreditation Board (U)
53 West Jackson Boulevard
Suite 1315
Chicago, IL 60604
(312) 662-1440
Shonagh Merits
Executive Director
URL: www.planningaccreditationboard.org

Quality Education for Minorities (QEM) Network (V)
1818 N Street, NW
Suite 350
Washington, DC 20036
(202) 659-1818
FAX: (202) 659-5408
Dr. Shirley M. McBay
President
E-MAIL: qemnetwork@qem.org
URL: qemnetwork.qem.org

Society for College and University Planning (W)
1330 Eisenhower Place
Ann Arbor, MI 48108
(734) 764-2000
FAX: (734) 661-0157
Ms. Jolene Knapp, CAE
Executive Director
E-MAIL: info@scup.org
URL: www.scup.org

Society for Slovene Studies (X)
Suzzallo Library
Box 352900
University of Washington
Seattle, WA 98195
(206) 543-5588
Mr. Michael Biggins
Secretary
E-MAIL: mbiggins@uw.edu
URL: www.slovenestudies.com

Society for the Advancement of Scandinavian Study (Y)
Brigham Young University
3168 JFSB
Provo, UT 84602-6702
(801) 422-5598
Mr. Steven P. Sondrup
Managing Editor
E-MAIL: sass.subscriptions@gmail.com
URL: www.scandinavianstudy.org

Society for Values in Higher Education (Z)
Portland State University
PO Box 751-SVHE
Portland, OR 97207-0751
(503) 725-2575
FAX: (503) 725-2577
Ms. Pamela Montgomery
Director
E-MAIL: society@pdx.edu
URL: www.svhe.org

Society of American Foresters (a)
5400 Grosvenor Lane
Bethesda, MD 20814-2198
(866) 897-8720
FAX: (301) 897-3690
Mr. Michael T. Goergen Jr.
Executive Vice President & CEO
E-MAIL: goergenm@safnet.org
URL: www.safnet.org

Society of American Foresters (SAF) (b)
5400 Grosvenor Lane
Bethesda, MD 20814-2198
(301) 897-8720
FAX: (301) 897-3690
Director of Science and Education
E-MAIL: ScienceEd@safnet.org
URL: www.safnet.org

Society of Professors of Education (c)
University of West Georgia
Department of LAI
1600 Maple Street
Carrollton, GA 30118-5160
(678) 839-6132
FAX: (678) 839-6097
Dr. Robert C. Morris
Secretary-Treasurer
E-MAIL: rmorris@westga.edu

Southeastern Universities Research Association (d)
1201 New York Avenue, NW
Suite 430
Washington, DC 20005
(202) 408-7872
FAX: (202) 408-8250
Dr. Jerry Draayer
President
E-MAIL: draayer@sura.org
URL: www.sura.org

Southern Association for College Student Affairs (e)
Armstrong Atlantic State University
11935 Abercorn Street
Savannah, GA 31419
(912) 344-2510
FAX: (912) 344-3468
Dr. Joe Buck
Executive Director
E-MAIL: joe.buck@armstrong.edu
URL: www.sacsa.org

Southern Association of Colleges and Schools Commission on Colleges (f)
1866 Southern Lane
Decatur, GA 30033-4097
(404) 679-4500
FAX: (404) 679-4528
Dr. Belle S. Wheelan
President
E-MAIL: bwheelan@sacscoc.org
URL: www.sacscoc.org

Southern States Communication Association (g)
Valdosta State University
Communication Arts
1500 N. Patterson
Valdosta, GA 31698
(229) 333-5820
FAX: (229) 293-6182
Dr. Carl M. Cates
Executive Director
E-MAIL: director@ssca.net
URL: www.ssca.net

State Higher Education Executive Officers (h)
3035 Center Green Drive
Suite 100
Boulder, CO 80301-2205
(303) 541-1600
FAX: (303) 541-1639
Dr. Paul E. Lingenfelter
President
E-MAIL: sheeo@sheeo.org
URL: www.sheeo.org

Teacher Education Accreditation Council (TEAC) (i)
One Dupont Circle, NW
Suite 320
Washington, DC 20036
(202) 466-7236
FAX: (202) 466-7238
Mr. Mark LaCelle-Peterson
President
E-MAIL: teac@teac.org
URL: www.teac.org

Tennessee Independent Colleges and Universities Association (A)
1031 17th Avenue South
Nashville, TN 37212
(615) 242-6400
Fax: (615) 242-8033
Dr. Claude O. Pressnell Jr.
President
E-mail: pressnell@ticua.org
URL: www.ticua.org

Transnational Association of Christian Colleges and Schools (TRACS) (B)
15935 Forest Road
Forest, VA 24551
(434) 525-9539
Fax: (434) 525-9538
Dr. T. Paul Boatner
President
E-mail: info@tracs.org
URL: www.tracs.org

The Tuition Exchange, Inc. (C)
3 Bethesda Metro Center
Suite 700
Bethesda, MD 20814
(301) 941-1827
Fax: (301) 657-9776
Mr. Robert D. Shorb
Executive Director/CEO
E-mail: rshorb@tuitionexchange.org
URL: www.tuitionexchange.org

UNCF (D)
8260 Willow Oaks Corporate Drive
PO Box 10444
Fairfax, VA 22031-8044
(800) 331-2244
Fax: (703) 205-3575
Dr. Michael L. Lomax
President & CEO
URL: www.uncf.org

University Aviation Association (E)
3410 Skyway Drive
Auburn, AL 36830-6444
(334) 844-2434
Fax: (334) 844-2432
Ms. Carolyn Williamson
Executive Director
E-mail: uaamail@uaa.aero
URL: www.uaa.aero

University Film and Video Association (F)
University of Southern California
School of Cinematic Arts
900 West 34th Street, SCA 428
Los Angeles, CA 90089-2211
(866) 647-8382
Mr. Norman Hollyn
E-mail: ufvahome@gmail.com
URL: www.ufva.org

University Photographers' Association of America (G)
Moraine Valley Community College
9000 West College Park
Palos Hills, IL 60465
(708) 974-5495
Fax: (708) 974-0681
Mr. Glenn Carpenter
UPAA President
E-mail: carpenter@morainevalley.edu
URL: www.upaa.org

University Professional & Continuing Education Association (UPCEA) (H)
1 Dupont Circle, NW
Suite 615
Washington, DC 20036
(202) 659-3130
Fax: (202) 785-0374
Dr. Robert J. Hansen
CEO
E-mail: rhansen@upcea.edu
URL: www.upcea.edu

Urban Affairs Association (I)
University of Wisconsin-Milwaukee
PO Box 413
Milwaukee, WI 53201-0413
(414) 229-3025
E-mail: info@uaamail.org
URL: www.urbanaffairsassociation.org

Western Association of Schools and Colleges Accrediting Commission for Community and Junior Colleges (J)
10 Commercial Boulevard
Suite 204
Novato, CA 94949
(415) 506-0234
Fax: (415) 506-0238
Dr. Barbara A. Beno
President
E-mail: accjc@accjc.org
URL: www.accjc.org

Western Association of Schools and Colleges Accrediting Commission for Schools (K)
533 Airport Boulevard
Suite 200
Burlingame, CA 94010
(650) 696-1060
Fax: (650) 696-1867
Dr. David E. Brown
Executive Director
E-mail: mail@acswasc.org
URL: www.acswasc.org

Western Association of Schools and Colleges Accrediting Commission for Senior Colleges and Universities (L)
985 Atlantic Avenue
Suite 100
Alameda, CA 94501
(510) 748-9001
Fax: (510) 748-9797
Mr. Ralph A. Wolff
President
E-mail: wascsr@wascsenior.org
URL: www.wascsenior.org

Western Interstate Commission for Higher Education (M)
3035 Center Green Drive
Suite 200
Boulder, CO 80301-2204
(303) 541-0201
Fax: (303) 541-0245
Dr. David A. Longanecker
President
E-mail: dlonganecker@wiche.edu
URL: www.wiche.edu

Women in Higher Education (N)
5376 Farmco Drive
Madison, WI 53704
(608) 251-3232
Fax: (608) 284-0601
Ms. Mary Dee Wenniger
E-mail: women@wihe.com
URL: www.wihe.com

Consortia of Institutions of Higher Education

Alliance for Higher Education (A)
PO Box 836696
Richardson, TX 75083-6696
(972) 883-4920
FAX: (972) 883-4919
Maria Smith
Executive Director
E-MAIL: marias@ntxrcic.org
URL: www.ntxrcic.org

Arkansas' Independent Colleges and Universities (B)
One Riverfront Place
Suite 610
US Bank Building
North Little Rock, AR 72114
(501) 378-0843
FAX: (501) 374-1523
Mr. Rex Nelson
President
E-MAIL: rnelson@arkindcolleges.org
URL: www.arkindcolleges.org

Associated Colleges of Central Kansas (C)
210 South Main Street
McPherson, KS 67460
(620) 241-5150
FAX: (620) 241-5153
URL: www.acck.edu

Associated Colleges of the Midwest (D)
205 West Wacker Drive
Suite 220
Chicago, IL 60606
(312) 263-5000
FAX: (312) 263-5879
Dr. Christopher Welna
President
E-MAIL: acm@acm.edu
URL: www.acm.edu

Associated Colleges of the Twin Cities (ACTC) (E)
570 Asbury Street
Suite 109
St. Paul, MN 55104
(651) 556-1863
FAX: (651) 294-8959
Dr. Carole Chabries
Executive Director
E-MAIL: info@actc-mn.org
URL: www.actc-mn.org

Association of Independent California Colleges and Universities (F)
1100 Eleventh Street
Suite 10
Sacramento, CA 95814
(916) 446-7626
FAX: (916) 446-7948
Ms. Kristen Soares
President
E-MAIL: aiccu@aiccu.edu
URL: www.aiccu.edu

Association of Independent Colleges and Universities in Massachusetts (G)
11 Beacon Street
Suite 1224
Boston, MA 02108-3093
(617) 742-5147
FAX: (617) 742-3089
Mr. Richard Doherty
President
E-MAIL: richard.doherty@bc.edu
URL: www.masscolleges.org -or- www.aicum.org

Association of Independent Colleges and Universities in New Jersey (H)
797 Springfield Avenue
Summit, NJ 07901-1107
(908) 277-3738
FAX: (908) 277-0851
Mr. John B. Wilson
President and CEO
E-MAIL: jbwilson@njcolleges.org
URL: www.njcolleges.org

Association of Independent Colleges and Universities of Michigan (I)
124 West Allegan Street
Suite 650
Lansing, MI 48933-1707
(517) 372-9160
FAX: (517) 372-9165
Dr. Edward O. Blews Jr.
President

Association of Independent Colleges and Universities of Nebraska (J)
635 South 14th Street
Suite 310
Lincoln, NE 68508
(402) 434-2818
FAX: (402) 434-2825
Mr. Thomas O'Neill
President
E-MAIL: tiponeill2@aol.com

Association of Independent Colleges and Universities of Ohio (K)
41 South High Street
Suite 2424
Columbus, OH 43215
(614) 228-2196
FAX: (614) 228-8406
Mr. C. Todd Jones
President & General Counsel
E-MAIL: tjones@aicuo.edu
URL: www.aicuo.edu

Association of Independent Colleges and Universities of Pennsylvania (L)
101 North Front Street
Harrisburg, PA 17101-1405
(717) 232-8649
FAX: (717) 233-8574
Dr. Don L. Francis
President
E-MAIL: francis@aicup.org
URL: www.aicup.org

Association of Independent Colleges and Universities of Rhode Island (M)
30 Exchange Terrace
Providence, RI 02903
(401) 272-8270
FAX: (401) 272-9194
Mr. Daniel Egan
President
E-MAIL: pmulcahey@aicuri.org
URL: www.aicuri.org

Association of Independent Colleges of Art & Design (N)
236 Hope Street
Providence, RI 02906
(401) 270-5991
FAX: (401) 270-5993
Ms. Deborah Obalil
Executive Director
URL: www.aicad.org

Association of Independent Kentucky Colleges and Universities (O)
484 Chenault Road
Frankfort, KY 40601
(502) 695-5007
FAX: (502) 695-5057
Dr. Gary S. Cox
President
E-MAIL: gary.cox@aikcu.org
URL: www.aikcu.org

Association of Vermont Independent Colleges (P)
PO Box 254
Montpelier, VT 05601
(802) 828-8826
Susan Stitely
President
E-MAIL: sstitely@vermont-icolleges.org
URL: www.vermont-icolleges.org

Atlanta Regional Council for Higher Education (Q)
133 Peachtree Street NE
Suite 4925
Atlanta, GA 30303-2923
(404) 651-2668
FAX: (404) 880-9816
Mr. Michael A. Gerber
President
E-MAIL: arche@atlantahighered.org
URL: www.atlantahighered.org

Boston Theological Institute (R)
210 Herrick Road
Newton Centre, MA 02459
(617) 527-4880
FAX: (617) 527-1073
Dr. Rodney Petersen
Executive Director
E-MAIL: btioffice@bostontheological.org
URL: www.bostontheological.org

Central Pennsylvania Consortium (S)
c/o Franklin & Marshall College
PO Box 3003
Lancaster, PA 17604-3003
(717) 291-4282
FAX: (717) 358-4455
Ms. Kathryn Missildine
Executive Assistant
E-MAIL: kathy.missildine@fandm.edu
URL: www.centralpennsylvaniaconsortium.org

CHESLA (T)
10 Columbus Boulevard
Hartford, CT 06106-1978
(860) 761-8453
Ms. Jeanette W. Weldon
Executive Director
E-MAIL: jweldon@chefa.com
URL: www.chesla.org

Christian College Consortium (U)
255 Grapevine Road
Wenham, MA 01984-1813
(978) 867-4755
FAX: (978) 867-4650
Dr. Stan Gaede
President
E-MAIL: stan.gaede@gordon.edu
URL: www.ccconsortium.org

Colleges of Worcester Consortium, Inc. (V)
484 Main Street
Suite 500
Worcester, MA 01608
(508) 754-6829
FAX: (508) 797-0069
Mr. Mark Bilotta
CEO
E-MAIL: mbilotta@cowc.org
URL: www.cowc.org

Community College Leadership Consortium & Futures Assembly (W)
University of Florida, College of Education
Box 117049
229 Norman Hall
Gainesville, FL 32611-7049
(352) 273-4300
FAX: (352) 846-2697
Dr. Dale F. Campbell
Director
E-MAIL: dfc@coe.ufl.edu
URL: futures.education.ufl.edu/index.html

The Consortium for Graduate Study in Management (X)
5585 Pershing Avenue
Suite 240
St. Louis, MO 63112-1795
(314) 877-5500
FAX: (314) 877-5505
Mr. Peter J. Aranda III
Executive Director and CEO
E-MAIL: recruiting@cgsm.org
URL: www.cgsm.org

Consortium for the Advancement of Adult Higher Education (Y)
4025 South Riverpoint Parkway
Mail Stop CF-K601
Phoenix, AZ 85040
(602) 557-1153
Dr. Sue Salter Dietrich
Executive Director
E-MAIL: sue.dietrich@ipd.org
URL: www.caahe.org

Consortium of College & University Media Centers (Z)
Indiana University
601 East Kirkwood Ave
Franklin Hall 0009
Bloomington, IN 47405-1223
(812) 855-6049
FAX: (812)855-2103
Aileen Scales
Executive Director
E-MAIL: ccumc@ccumc.org
URL: www.ccumc.org

Consortium of Universities of the Washington Metropolitan Area (a)
1100 H Street, NW
Suite 500
Washington, DC 20005
(202) 331-8080
FAX: (202) 331-7925
Mr. John B. Childers
President & CEO
E-MAIL: childers@consortium.org
URL: www.consortium.org

Consortium on Financing Higher Education (b)
238 Main Street
Suite 402
Cambridge, MA 02142-1046
(617) 253-5030
FAX: (617) 258-8280
Dr. Kristine E. Dillon
President
E-MAIL: kedillon@mit.edu
URL: www.cofhe.org

Cooperating Raleigh Colleges (c)
Meredith College
3800 Hillsborough Street
Raleigh, NC 27607-5298
(919) 760-8538
FAX: (919) 760-2194
Ms. Jenny Spiker
Director
E-MAIL: crc@meredith.edu
URL: www.crcraleighcolleges.org

Council of Independent Colleges in Virginia (d)
PO Box 1005
Bedford, VA 24523
(540) 586-0606
FAX: (540) 586-2630
Mr. Robert B. Lambeth Jr.
President
E-MAIL: lambeth@cicv.org
URL: www.cicv.org

Council of North Central Two Year Colleges (e)
200 South 14th Street
Parsons, KS 67357
(620) 820-1223
FAX: (620) 421-0921
Dr. George Knox
Executive Director
E-MAIL: cnctyc@labette.edu
URL: www.labette.edu/cnctyc

Council of Presidents (f)
410 Eleventh Avenue, SE
Suite 101
Olympia, WA 98501
(360) 292-4100
FAX: (360) 292-4110
Ms. Jane Sherman
Interim Executive Director
E-MAIL: jsherman@cop.wsu.edu
URL: www.councilofpresidents.org

Federation of Independent Illinois Colleges and Universities (g)
1123 South Second Street
Springfield, IL 62704
(217) 789-1400
FAX: (217) 789-6259
Mr. David W. Tretter
President
E-MAIL: davetretter@federationedu.org
URL: www.federationedu.org

Five Colleges, Incorporated (h)
97 Spring Street
Amherst, MA 01002
(413) 542-4009
FAX: (413) 542-4029
Dr. Neal B. Abraham
Executive Director
E-MAIL: nabraham@fivecolleges.edu
URL: www.fivecolleges.edu

Georgia Independent College Association (i)
600 West Peachtree St. NW
Suite 1510
Atlanta, GA 30308
(404) 233-5433
FAX: (404) 233-6309
Dr. Susanna Baxter
President
E-MAIL: sbaxter@georgiacolleges.org
URL: www.georgiacolleges.org

Graduate Theological Foundation Oxford/Rome/Indiana Consortia (j)
Dodge House
415 Lincoln Way East
Mishawaka, IN 46544-2213
(800) 423-5983
Bethany Morgan MBA
Registrar
E-MAIL: information@gtfeducation.org
URL: www.gtfeducation.org

Great Lakes Colleges Association (A)
535 West William
Suite 301
Ann Arbor, MI 48103
(734) 661-2350
FAX: (734) 661-2349
Dr. Richard A. Detweiler
President
E-MAIL: detweiler@glca.org
URL: www.glca.org

Greater Cincinnati Consortium of Colleges and Universities (B)
Northern Kentucky University
241 Campbell Hall
Highland Heights, KY 41099
(859) 392-2424
FAX: (859) 392-2416
Ms. Janet Piccirillo
Executive Director
E-MAIL: gcccu@nku.edu
URL: www.gcccu.org

Hartford Consortium for Higher Education (C)
31 Pratt Street
4th Floor
Hartford, CT 06103
(860) 702-3801
FAX: (860) 241-1130
Dr. Martin Estey
Executive Director
E-MAIL: mestey@metrohartford.com
URL: www.hartfordconsortium.org

Higher Education Consortium for Urban Affairs, Inc. (HECUA) (D)
2233 University Avenue West
Suite 210
St. Paul, MN 55114
(651) 287-3300
FAX: (651) 659-9421
Dr. Jenny Keyser
Executive Director
E-MAIL: hecua@hecua.org
URL: www.hecua.org

Higher Education Consortium of Metropolitan St. Louis (E)
8420 Delmar Boulevard
Suite 504
St. Louis, MO 63124
(314) 991-2700
FAX: (314) 991-2874
URL: www.heccstl.com

Higher Education Data Sharing Consortium (F)
Wabash College
PO Box 352
Crawfordsville, IN 47933
(765) 361-6331
FAX: (717) 361-6475
Charles Blaich
Director
E-MAIL: blaich.cila.heds@me.com
URL: www.hedsconsortium.org

Independent Colleges and Universities of Missouri (G)
PO Box 1865
Jefferson City, MO 65102-1865
(573) 635-9160
FAX: (573) 635-6258
Dr. Ronald A. Slepitza
President
E-MAIL: bill@molobby.com
URL: www.icum.org

Independent Colleges and Universities of Texas, Inc. (H)
PO Box 13105
Austin, TX 78701-3105
(512) 472-9522
FAX: (512) 472-2371
Dr. Carol McDonald
President
E-MAIL: carol.mcdonald@icut.org
URL: www.icut.org

Independent Colleges of Indiana Inc. (I)
3135 North Meridian Street
Indianapolis, IN 46208
(317) 236-6090
FAX: (317) 236-6086
Dr. Richard Ludwick
President and CEO
E-MAIL: rludwick@icindiana.org
URL: www.icindiana.org

Independent Colleges of Washington (J)
600 Stewart Street
Suite 600
Seattle, WA 98101
(206) 623-4494
FAX: (206) 625-9621
Ms. Violet A. Boyer
President & CEO
E-MAIL: violet@icwashington.org
URL: www.icwashington.org

Inter-University Consortium for Political and Social Research (K)
The University of Michigan
Institute for Social Research
PO Box 1248
Ann Arbor, MI 48106-1248
(734) 615-8400
FAX: (734) 647-8200
Dr. George Alter
Acting Director
E-MAIL: netmail@icpsr.umich.edu
URL: www.icpsr.umich.edu

Iowa Association of Independent Colleges and Universities (L)
505 Fifth Avenue
Suite 1030
Des Moines, IA 50309
(515) 282-3175
FAX: (515) 282-8177
Mr. Gary W. Steinke
President
E-MAIL: president@iaicu.org
URL: www.iowaprivatecolleges.org

Kansas Independent College Association (M)
700 S. Kansas Avenue
Suite 622 A
Topeka, KS 66603
(785) 235-9877
FAX: (785) 235-1437
Mr. Matthew Lindsey
President
E-MAIL: matt@kscolleges.org
URL: www.kscolleges.org

Kentuckiana Metroversity (N)
200 West Broadway
Suite 800
Louisville, KY 40202
(502) 213-4562
Kathleen Mandlehr Ed.D.
Executive Director
E-MAIL: ktmand01@louisville.edu
URL: www.metroversity.org

Lehigh Valley Association of Independent Colleges (O)
130 West Greenwich Street
Bethlehem, PA 18018
(610) 625-7888
FAX: (610) 625-7891
Diane Dimitroff
Executive Director
E-MAIL: dimitroffd@lvaic.org
URL: www.lvaic.org

Louisiana Association of Independent Colleges and Universities (P)
320 Third Street
Suite 104
Baton Rouge, LA 70801
(225) 389-9885
FAX: (225) 389-0149
Ms. Mary Ann Coleman
President
E-MAIL: maryann@laicu.org
URL: www.laicu.org

Maine Independent Colleges Association (Q)
University of New England
11 Hills Beach Road
Biddeford, ME 04005
(207) 602-2306
FAX: (207) 602-5925
Dr. Danielle N. Ripich
President
E-MAIL: dripich@une.edu
URL: www.une.edu

Maryland Independent College and University Association (R)
60 West Street
Suite 201
Annapolis, MD 21401
(410) 269-0306
FAX: (410) 269-5905
Ms. Tina M. Bjarekull
President
E-MAIL: lstrayer@micua.org
URL: www.micua.org

Midwest Universities Consortium for International Activities, Inc. (S)
4700 South Hagadorn Road
Suite 150
East Lansing, MI 48823-6808
(517) 432-0661
FAX: (517) 432-4457
Dr. Philip R. Smith
President & Executive Director
E-MAIL: mucia@msu.edu
URL: www.muciainc.org

Minnesota Private College Council (T)
445 Minnesota Street
Suite 500
St. Paul, MN 55101
(651) 228-9061
FAX: (651) 228-0379
E-MAIL: colleges@mnprivatecolleges.org
URL: www.mnprivatecolleges.org

Mississippi Association of Independent Colleges and Universities (U)
PO Box 2933
Ridgeland, MS 39158-2933
(601) 957-2052
FAX: (601) 977-0233
Dr. E. Harold Fisher
Executive Director
E-MAIL: ehfisher@bellsouth.net

National Student Exchange (V)
4656 West Jefferson
Suite 140
Fort Wayne, IN 46804
(260) 436-2634
FAX: (260) 436-5676
Ms. Bette Worley
President
E-MAIL: bworley@nse2.org
URL: www.nse.org

New England Faculty Development Consortium (W)
New England Institute of Technology
1408 Division Road
East Greenwich, RI 02818
(401) 739-5000
Mr. Thomas R. Thibodeau
President
E-MAIL: tthibodeau@neit.edu
URL: www.nefdc.org

New Hampshire College & University Council (X)
3 Barrell Court
Suite 100
Concord, NH 03301-8543
(603) 225-4199
FAX: (603) 225-8108
Thomas R. Horgan
President and CEO
E-MAIL: horgan@nhcuc.org
URL: www.nhcuc.org

New Jersey Association of State Colleges and Universities (Y)
150 West State Street
Trenton, NJ 08608
(609) 989-1100
FAX: (609) 989-7017
Dr. Michael W. Klein
CEO
E-MAIL: njascu@njascu.org
URL: www.njascu.org

New Jersey Council of County Colleges (Z)
330 West State Street
Trenton, NJ 08618
(609) 392-3434
FAX: (609) 392-8158
Dr. Lawrence A. Nespoli
President
E-MAIL: info@njccc.org
URL: www.njccc.org

New Mexico Independent College Fund (a)
c/o St. John's College
Office of the President
1160 Camino Cruz Blanca
Santa Fe, NM 87505
(505) 984-6098
FAX: (505) 984-6031
E-MAIL: president@sjcsf.edu
URL: www.sjcsf.edu

New Orleans Educational Telecommunications Consortium, Inc. (b)
5000 West Esplanade Avenue
#290
Metairie, LA 70006
(504) 524-0350
E-MAIL: noetc@noetc.org
URL: www.noetc.com

North Carolina Independent Colleges and Universities (c)
530 North Blount Street
Raleigh, NC 27604
(919) 832-5817
FAX: (919) 833-0794
Dr. A. Hope Williams
President
E-MAIL: williams@ncicu.org
URL: www.ncicu.org

North Carolina Piedmont Automated Library System (NC-PALS) (d)
Bennett College
900 E. Washington Street
Greensboro, NC 27401
(336) 517-2158
FAX: (336) 370-8653
Dr. Millicent Rainey
Chair of the Executive Board
E-MAIL: mrainey@bennett.edu
URL: www.nc-pals.org

North Dakota Independent College Fund (e)
University of Mary
7500 University Drive
Bismarck, ND 58504-9652
(701) 355-8222
FAX: (701) 255-7687
Mr. Neal Kalberer
Executive Director
E-MAIL: kalberer@umary.edu

Northeast Consortium of Colleges and Universities in Massachusetts (NECCUM) (f)
North Shore Community College
1 Ferncroft Road
PO Box 3340
Danvers, MA 01923
(781) 477-2143
FAX: (781) 477-2142
Ms. Donna L. Richemond
Vice President for Student and Enrollment Services
E-MAIL: drichemo@northshore.edu
URL: www.northshore.edu

Northeast Ohio Council on Higher Education (g)
1422 Euclid Avenue
Suite 840
Cleveland, OH 44115
(216) 420-9200
FAX: (216) 420-9292
Ms. Ann Womer Benjamin
Executive Director
E-MAIL: awomerbenjamin@noche.org
URL: www.noche.org

Oak Ridge Associated Universities (h)
MC-100-22
PO Box 117
Oak Ridge, TN 37831-0117
(865) 576-3300
FAX: (865) 576-3816
Mr. Harry A. Page
President and CEO
E-MAIL: andy.page@orau.org
URL: www.orau.org

The Ohio College Association, Inc. (i)
10 West Broad Street
Suite 450
Columbus, OH 43215
(614) 464-1266
FAX: (614) 464-9281
Ms. Cindy McQuade
URL: www.ohiocollege.org

Consortia of Institutions of Higher Education

Oklahoma Independent Colleges and Universities (A)
PO Box 57148
Oklahoma City, OK 73157-7148
(405) 371-1780
Lesa Smaligo
Executive Director
E-MAIL: lesa@oicu.org
URL: www.oicu.org

Oregon Alliance of Independent Colleges & Universities (B)
16101 SW 72nd Avenue
Suite 100
Portland, OR 97224
(503) 639-4541
FAX: (503) 639-4851
Dr. Larry D. Large
President
E-MAIL: larry@oaicu.org
URL: www.oaicu.org

Pennsylvania State System of Higher Education Foundation, Inc. (C)
2986 North Second Street
Harrisburg, PA 17110
(717) 720-4056
FAX: (717) 720-7082
Ms. Jennifer S. Scipioni
President/CEO
E-MAIL: jscipioni@thepafoundation.org
URL: www.thepafoundation.org

Pittsburgh Council on Higher Education (D)
201 Wood Street
Pittsburgh, PA 15222-1912
(412) 392-4217
FAX: (412) 392-4218
Mr. Kenneth P. Service
Executive Director
E-MAIL: kservice@pointpark.edu
URL: www.pchepa.org

Quad-Cities Graduate Study Center (E)
331 W. 3rd Street
Suite 100, Room 128
Davenport, IA 52801
(563) 322-0016
Marti Clyde
Director
E-MAIL: qc@gradcenter.org
URL: www.gradcenter.org

Quad-Cities Graduate Study Center (F)
WIU - QC Campus
3561 60th Street
Moline, IL 61265
(309) 762-9481
Shirley Moore
Administrative Assistant
E-MAIL: shirley@gradcenter.org
URL: www.gradcenter.org

South Carolina Independent Colleges & Universities, Inc. (G)
PO Box 12007
Columbia, SC 29211
(803) 799-7122
FAX: (803) 254-7504
Mr. Michael G. LeFever
President & CEO
E-MAIL: mike@scicu.org
URL: www.scicu.org

South Metropolitan Higher Education Consortium (H)
One University Parkway
University Park, IL 60484
(708) 534-4984
FAX: (708) 534-8458
Ms. Genevieve Boesen
Executive Director
E-MAIL: gboesen@govst.edu
URL: www.southmetroed.org

Southern Regional Education Board (I)
592 Tenth Street, NW
Atlanta, GA 30318-5776
(404) 875-9211
FAX: (404) 872-1477
Dr. David S. Spence
President
E-MAIL: dave.spence@sreb.org
URL: www.sreb.org

Southwestern Ohio Council for Higher Education (SOCHE) (J)
3155 Research Boulevard
Suite 204
Dayton, OH 45420-4015
(937) 258-8890
FAX: (937) 258-8899
Dr. Sean Creighton
Executive Director
E-MAIL: soche@soche.org
URL: www.soche.org

Texas International Education Consortium (K)
1103 West 24th Street
Austin, TX 78705
(512) 477-9283, ext. 114
FAX: (512) 322-9079
Dr. Ronald Aqua
President & CEO
E-MAIL: ron.aqua@tiec.org
URL: www.tiec.org

Tuition Plan Consortium (L)
7425 Forsyth Boulevard
St. Louis, MO 63105
(314) 727-0900
FAX: (314) 727-0930
Ms. Nancy Farmer
President
E-MAIL: nancy@pc529.com
URL: www.tomorrowstuitiontoday.org

University City Science Center (M)
3711 Market Street
8th Floor
Philadelphia, PA 19104
(215) 966-6000
FAX: (215) 966-6002
Dr. Stephen Tang
President & CEO
E-MAIL: info@sciencecenter.org
URL: www.sciencecenter.org

The Virginia College Fund (N)
4900 Augusta Avenue
Suite 101
Richmond, VA 23230
(804) 355-3271
FAX: (804) 359-5765
Mr. James K. Dill
President
E-MAIL: jkdill@thevcf.org
URL: www.thevcf.org

Virginia Tidewater Consortium for Higher Education (O)
4900 Powhatan Avenue
Norfolk, VA 23508-1836
(757) 683-3183
FAX: (757) 683-4515
Dr. Lawrence G. Dotolo
President
E-MAIL: lgdotolo@aol.com
URL: www.vtc.odu.edu

Washington Theological Consortium (P)
487 Michigan Avenue, NE
Washington, DC 20017
(202) 832-2675
FAX: (202) 526-0818
Dr. Larry Golemon
Executive Director
E-MAIL: wtc@washtheocon.org
URL: www.washtheocon.org

West Virginia Independent Colleges & Universities, Inc. (Q)
900 Lee Street
Suite 910
Charleston, WV 25301
(304) 345-5525
FAX: (304) 345-5526
Mr. Ben Exley IV
Executive Director
E-MAIL: benexley@wvicu.org
URL: www.wvicu.org

Wisconsin Association of Independent Colleges and Universities (R)
122 West Washington Avenue
Suite 700
Madison, WI 53703-2723
(608) 256-7761
FAX: (608) 256-7065
Dr. Rolf Wegenke
President
E-MAIL: mail@waicu.org
URL: www.waicu.org

NAME INDEX

US Department of Education Offices, Statewide Agencies of Higher Education, Higher Education Associations, Consortia of Institutions of Higher Education

Institutions By Religious Affiliation

African Methodist Episcopal
- Allen University ... SC
- Edward Waters College ... FL
- Paul Quinn College ... TX
- Payne Theological Seminary ... OH
- Shorter College ... AR
- Wilberforce University ... OH

African Methodist Episcopal Zion Church
- Clinton Junior College ... SC
- Hood Theological Seminary ... NC
- Livingstone College ... NC

Alabama Baptist State Convention
- Judson College ... AL

American Baptist
- Alderson Broaddus College ... WV
- American Baptist Seminary of the West .. CA
- Bacone College ... OK
- Eastern University ... PA
- Franklin College of Indiana ... IN
- Judson University ... IL
- Linfield College ... OR
- Northern Seminary ... IL
- Ottawa University ... KS
- Ottawa University Arizona ... AZ
- Ottawa University Jeffersonville ... IN
- Ottawa University Kansas City ... KS
- Ottawa University Wisconsin ... WI
- Palmer Theological Seminary of Eastern University ... PA
- University of Sioux Falls ... SD

Assemblies Of God Church
- American Indian College of the Assemblies of God ... AZ
- Assemblies of God Theological Seminary MO
- Bethel College ... VA
- Central Bible College ... MO
- Evangel University ... MO
- Global University ... MO
- Native American Bible College ... NC
- North Central University ... MN
- Northwest University ... WA
- Southeastern University ... FL
- Southwestern Assemblies of God University ... TX
- Trinity Bible College ... ND
- Valley Forge Christian College ... PA
- Vanguard University of Southern California ... CA
- Zion Bible College ... MA

Baptist
- American Baptist College ... TN
- Arkansas Baptist College ... AR
- Arlington Baptist College ... TX
- Baptist Bible College ... MO
- Baptist Bible College and Seminary ... PA
- Baptist Missionary Association Theological Seminary ... TX
- Baptist University of the Americas ... TX
- Baylor University ... TX
- Bethel University ... MN
- Bluefield College ... VA
- Boston Baptist College ... MA
- Brewton-Parker College ... GA
- Campbell University ... NC
- Campbellsville University ... KY
- Cedarville University ... OH
- Central Baptist College ... AR
- Central Baptist Theological Seminary ... KS
- Central Baptist Theological Seminary ... VA
- Central Baptist Theological Seminary of Minneapolis ... MN
- Chowan University ... NC
- Dallas Baptist University ... TX
- Gardner-Webb University ... NC
- Georgetown College ... KY
- Hardin-Simmons University ... TX
- Howard Payne University ... TX
- Huntsville Bible College ... AL
- International Baptist College ... AZ
- Jacksonville College ... TX
- Liberty University ... VA
- Maple Springs Baptist Bible College & Seminary ... MD
- Missouri Baptist University ... MO
- Morris College ... SC
- Northland International University ... WI
- Oakland City University ... IN
- Ohio Mid-Western College (Formerly Temple Baptist College) ... OH
- Selma University ... AL
- Shaw University ... NC
- Shorter University ... GA
- Simmons College of Kentucky ... KY
- Southeastern Baptist College ... MS
- Tennessee Temple University ... TN
- The John Leland Center for Theological Studies ... VA
- Trinity Baptist College ... FL
- Truett McConnell College ... GA
- University of the Cumberlands ... KY
- Virginia Baptist College ... VA
- Virginia Intermont College ... VA
- Virginia Union University ... VA
- Washington Baptist University ... VA

Brethren Church
- Ashland University ... OH

Christian Church (Disciples Of Christ)
- Barton College ... NC
- Bethany College ... WV
- Chapman University ... CA
- Christian Theological Seminary ... IN
- Columbia College ... MO
- Culver-Stockton College ... MO
- Eureka College ... IL
- Jarvis Christian College ... TX
- Lexington Theological Seminary ... KY
- Lynchburg College ... VA
- Midway College ... KY
- Northwest Christian University ... OR
- Phillips Theological Seminary ... OK
- Texas Christian University ... TX
- Transylvania University ... KY
- William Woods University ... MO

Christian Churches And Churches of Christ
- Boise Bible College ... ID
- Central Christian College of the Bible ... MO
- Cincinnati Christian University ... OH
- Crossroads College ... MN
- Dallas Christian College ... TX
- Emmanuel Christian Seminary ... TN
- Great Lakes Christian College ... MI
- Johnson University ... TN
- Kentucky Christian University ... KY
- Lincoln Christian University ... IL
- Manhattan Christian College ... KS
- Nebraska Christian College ... NE
- Piedmont College ... GA
- Point University ... GA

Christian Methodist Episcopal
- Lane College ... TN
- Miles College ... AL
- Texas College ... TX

Christian Reformed Church
- Calvin College ... MI
- Calvin Theological Seminary ... MI
- Dordt College ... IA

Church Of Christ
- Pepperdine University ... CA

Church Of God
- Anderson University ... IN
- Lee University ... TN
- Mid-America Christian University ... OK
- Pentecostal Theological Seminary ... TN
- The University of Findlay ... OH
- Universidad Teologica Del Caribe ... PR
- Warner Pacific College ... OR
- Warner University ... FL

Church of God in Christ
- All Saints Bible College ... TN

Church of New Jerusalem
- Bryn Athyn College of the New Church ... PA

Church Of The Brethren
- Bethany Theological Seminary ... IN
- Bridgewater College ... VA
- Elizabethtown College ... PA
- Manchester University ... IN
- McPherson College ... KS

Church Of The Nazarene
- Eastern Nazarene College ... MA
- MidAmerica Nazarene University ... KS
- Mount Vernon Nazarene University ... OH
- Nazarene Bible College ... CO
- Nazarene Theological Seminary ... MO
- Northwest Nazarene University ... ID
- Olivet Nazarene University ... IL
- Point Loma Nazarene University ... CA
- Southern Nazarene University ... OK
- Trevecca Nazarene University ... TN

Churches Of Christ
- Abilene Christian University ... TX
- Amridge University ... AL
- Crowley's Ridge College ... AR
- Faulkner University ... AL
- Freed-Hardeman University ... TN
- Harding School of Theology ... TN
- Harding University Main Campus ... AR
- Heritage Christian University ... AL
- Lipscomb University ... TN
- Lubbock Christian University ... TX
- Mid-Atlantic Christian University ... NC
- Ohio Valley University ... WV
- Southwestern Christian College ... TX
- York College ... NE

Cumberland Presbyterian
- Bethel University ... TN
- Memphis Theological Seminary ... TN

Evangelical Congregational Church
- Evangelical Theological Seminary ... PA

Evangelical Covenant Church Of America
- North Park University ... IL

Evangelical Free Church Of America
- Trinity International University ... IL
- Trinity International University, Florida Regional Center ... FL

Evangelical Lutheran Church In America
- Augsburg College ... MN
- Augustana College ... IL
- Augustana College ... SD
- Bethany College ... KS
- California Lutheran University ... CA
- Capital University ... OH
- Carthage College ... WI
- Concordia College ... MN
- Finlandia University ... MI
- Gettysburg College ... PA
- Grand View University ... IA
- Gustavus Adolphus College ... MN
- Lenoir-Rhyne University ... NC
- Luther College ... IA
- Luther Seminary ... MN
- Lutheran School of Theology at Chicago IL
- Lutheran Theological Seminary at Gettysburg ... PA
- Lutheran Theological Seminary at Philadelphia ... PA
- Lutheran Theological Southern Seminary of Lenoir-Rhyne University ... SC
- Midland University ... NE
- Muhlenberg College ... PA
- Newberry College ... SC
- Pacific Lutheran Theological Seminary ... CA
- Pacific Lutheran University ... WA
- Roanoke College ... VA
- St. Olaf College ... MN
- Susquehanna University ... PA
- Texas Lutheran University ... TX
- Thiel College ... PA
- Trinity Lutheran Seminary ... OH
- Wartburg College ... IA
- Wartburg Theological Seminary ... IA
- Wittenberg University ... OH

Evangelical Lutheran Synod
- Bethany Lutheran College ... MN

Fellowship Of Grace Brethren Churches
- Grace College and Seminary ... IN

Free Methodist
- Central Christian College of Kansas ... KS
- Greenville College ... IL
- Seattle Pacific University ... WA
- Spring Arbor University ... MI

Free Will Baptist Church
- California Christian College ... CA
- Free Will Baptist Bible College ... TN
- Hillsdale Free Will Baptist College ... OK

Friends
- Earlham College and Earlham School of Religion ... IN
- George Fox University ... OR
- Guilford College ... NC
- Malone University ... OH
- William Penn University ... IA
- Wilmington College ... OH

Greek Orthodox
- Hellenic College-Holy Cross Greek Orthodox School of Theology ... MA

Interdenominational
- Carolina Graduate School of Divinity ... NC
- Denver Seminary ... CO
- Evangelical Seminary of Puerto Rico ... PR
- Faith Evangelical College & Seminary ... WA
- God's Bible School and College ... OH
- Inste Bible College ... IA
- Interdenominational Theological Center .. GA
- Messiah College ... PA
- Oak Hills Christian College ... MN
- Palm Beach Atlantic University ... FL
- Phoenix Seminary ... AZ
- Rocky Mountain College ... MT
- Shepherd University School of Theology . CA
- South Florida Bible College ... FL
- Wesley Biblical Seminary ... MS

Jewish
- Academy for Jewish Religion ... CA
- Hebrew Union College-Jewish Institute of Religion ... NY
- Rabbi Isaac Elchanan Theological Seminary ... NY
- Reconstructionist Rabbinical College ... PA

Latter-day Saints
- Brigham Young University ... UT
- Brigham Young University Hawaii ... HI
- Brigham Young University-Idaho ... ID
- LDS Business College ... UT

Lutheran
- Valparaiso University ... IN

Lutheran Church - Missouri Synod
- Concordia College ... NY
- Concordia College Alabama ... AL
- Concordia Seminary ... MO
- Concordia Theological Seminary ... IN
- Concordia University ... CA
- Concordia University ... MI
- Concordia University ... NE
- Concordia University ... OR
- Concordia University Chicago ... IL
- Concordia University Texas ... TX
- Concordia University Wisconsin ... WI
- Concordia University, St. Paul ... MN

Mennonite Brethren Church
- Fresno Pacific Biblical Seminary ... CA
- Fresno Pacific University ... CA
- Tabor College ... KS

Mennonite Church
- Anabaptist Mennonite Biblical Seminary .. IN
- Bethel College ... KS
- Bluffton University ... OH
- Eastern Mennonite University ... VA
- Goshen College ... IN
- Hesston College ... KS
- Rosedale Bible College ... OH

Missionary Church
- Bethel College ... IN

Moravian Church
- Moravian College ... PA
- Salem College ... NC

Multiple Protestant Denominations
- Huston-Tillotson University ... TX
- LeMoyne-Owen College ... TN
- Paine College ... GA

Non-denominational
- Belmont University ... TN
- Carolina Bible College ... NC
- Clearwater Christian College ... FL
- Faith Theological Seminary ... MD
- Heartland Christian College ... MO

Montreat College NC
Providence Christian College CA
University of Fort Lauderdale FL
Williamson Christian College TN

North American Baptist
Sioux Falls Seminary SD

Original Free Will Baptist Church
Mount Olive College NC

Other Protestant
Beulah Heights University GA
Grace College of Divinity NC
Mars Hill College NC
Ohio Christian University OH
Saint Louis Christian College MO
Urshan Graduate School of Theology MO

Pentecostal Church of God
Messenger College MO
Universidad Pentecostal Mizpa PR

Pentecostal Holiness Church
Emmanuel College GA
Southwestern Christian University OK

Pentecostal/Charismatic Non-Denominational
Christian Life College IL

Presbyterian Church (U.S.A.)
Agnes Scott College GA
Austin College TX
Austin Presbyterian Theological Seminary TX
Belhaven University MS
Blackburn College IL
Bloomfield College NJ
Buena Vista University IA
Carroll University WI
Columbia Theological Seminary GA
Davidson College NC
Davis & Elkins College WV
Eckerd College FL
Grove City College PA
Hampden-Sydney College VA
Hanover College IN
Hastings College NE
Jamestown College ND
King College TN
Lees-McRae College NC
Louisville Presbyterian Theological Seminary KY
Lyon College AR
Macalester College MN
Mary Baldwin College VA
Maryville College TN
McCormick Theological Seminary IL
Millikin University IL
Missouri Valley College MO
Monmouth College IL
Muskingum University OH
Pittsburgh Theological Seminary PA
Presbyterian College SC
Princeton Theological Seminary NJ
Queens University of Charlotte NC
Rhodes College TN
San Francisco Theological Seminary CA
Schreiner University TX
St. Andrews University NC
Sterling College KS
Stillman College AL
Tusculum College TN
Union Presbyterian Seminary VA
University of Dubuque IA
University of Pikeville KY
University of the Ozarks AR
Warren Wilson College NC
Waynesburg University PA
Westminster College PA
Whitworth University WA
William Peace University (formerly Peace College) NC
Wilson College PA

Presbyterian Church In America
Covenant College GA
Covenant Theological Seminary MO
Grace Mission University CA
Knox Theological Seminary FL
Presbyterian Theological Seminary in America CA

Protestant Episcopal
Church Divinity School of the Pacific CA
Episcopal Divinity School MA
General Theological Seminary NY
Nashotah House WI
Protestant Episcopal Theological Seminary in Virginia VA
Saint Augustine's University NC
Saint Paul's College VA
Seabury-Western Theological Seminary IL
Seminary of the Southwest TX
Sewanee: The University of the South TN
Trinity Episcopal School for Ministry PA
Voorhees College SC

Reformed Church In America
Central College IA
Hope College MI
New Brunswick Theological Seminary NJ
Northwestern College IA
Western Theological Seminary MI

Reformed Episcopal Church
Reformed Episcopal Seminary PA

Reformed Presbyterian Church
Evangelia University CA
Geneva College PA
Reformed Presbyterian Theological Seminary PA

Roman Catholic
Alvernia University PA
Ancilla College IN
Anna Maria College MA
Aquinas College MI
Aquinas College TN
Aquinas Institute of Theology MO
Assumption College MA
Assumption College for Sisters NJ
Athenaeum of Ohio OH
Ave Maria School of Law FL
Avila University MO
Barry University FL
Bayamon Central University PR
Belmont Abbey College NC
Benedictine College KS
Benedictine University IL
Blessed John XXIII National Seminary MA
Boston College MA
Brescia University KY
Briar Cliff University IA
Cabrini College PA
Caldwell College NJ
Calumet College of Saint Joseph IN
Canisius College NY
Cardinal Stritch University WI
Carlow University PA
Carroll College MT
Catholic Theological Union IL
Chestnut Hill College PA
Christ the King Seminary NY
Christendom College VA
Christian Brothers University TN
Clarke University IA
College of Mount St. Joseph OH
College of Our Lady of the Elms MA
College of Saint Benedict MN
College of Saint Elizabeth NJ
College of Saint Mary NE
College of St. Joseph VT
College of the Holy Cross MA
Conception Seminary College MO
Creighton University NE
DePaul University IL
DeSales University PA
Divine Word College IA
Dominican School of Philosophy and Theology CA
Dominican University IL
Donnelly College KS
Duquesne University PA
Edgewood College WI
Emmanuel College MA
Fairfield University CT
Felician College NJ
Fontbonne University MO
Franciscan University of Steubenville OH
Gannon University PA
Georgetown University DC
Georgian Court University NJ
Gonzaga University WA
Gwynedd-Mercy College PA
Holy Apostles College and Seminary CT
Holy Cross College IN
Holy Family University PA
Immaculata University PA
Immaculate Conception Seminary of Seton Hall University NJ
John Carroll University OH
Kenrick-Glennon Seminary-Kenrick School of Theology MO
King's College PA
La Roche College PA
La Salle University PA
Laboure College MA
Lewis University IL
Loras College IA
Lourdes University OH
Loyola Marymount University CA
Loyola University Chicago IL
Loyola University Maryland MD
Loyola University New Orleans LA
Madonna University MI
Marian Court College MA
Marian University IN
Marian University WI
Marquette University WI
Marygrove College MI
Marymount College CA
Marymount University VA
Marywood University PA
Mercy College of Health Sciences IA
Mercy College of Ohio OH
Mercyhurst University PA
Merrimack College MA
Misericordia University PA
Mount Angel Seminary OR
Mount Carmel College of Nursing OH
Mount Marty College SD
Mount Mary College WI
Mount Mercy University IA
Mount St. Mary's College CA
Mount St. Mary's University MD
Neumann University PA
Newman University KS
Notre Dame College OH
Notre Dame of Maryland University MD
Notre Dame Seminary, Graduate School of Theology LA
Oblate School of Theology TX
Ohio Dominican University OH
Our Lady of Holy Cross College LA
Our Lady of the Lake College LA
Our Lady of the Lake University TX
Pontifical Catholic University of Puerto Rico-Arecibo Campus PR
Pontifical Catholic University of Puerto Rico-Mayaguez Campus PR
Pontifical College Josephinum OH
Pontifical Faculty of the Immaculate Conception at the Dominican House of Studies DC
Pontifical John Paul II Institute for Studies on Marriage and Family DC
Presentation College SD
Providence College RI
Quincy University IL
Regis University CO
Rivier College NH
Rockhurst University MO
Rosemont College PA
Sacred Heart Major Seminary MI
Sacred Heart School of Theology WI
Saint Anselm College NH
Saint Bernard's School of Theology & Ministry NY
Saint Charles Borromeo Seminary PA
Saint Francis Medical Center College of Nursing IL
Saint Francis University PA
Saint Gregory the Great Seminary NE
Saint John's Seminary CA
Saint John's Seminary MA
Saint John's University MN
Saint Joseph Seminary College LA
Saint Joseph's College IN
Saint Joseph's College of Maine ME
Saint Joseph's Seminary NY
Saint Joseph's University PA
Saint Leo University FL
Saint Louis University MO
Saint Martin's University WA
Saint Mary Seminary and Graduate School of Theology OH
Saint Mary's College IN
Saint Mary's College of California CA
Saint Mary's Seminary and University MD
Saint Mary's University of Minnesota MN
Saint Mary-of-the-Woods College IN
Saint Meinrad School of Theology IN
Saint Michael's College VT
Saint Norbert College WI
Saint Patrick's Seminary & University CA
Saint Peter's College NJ
Saint Vincent College PA
Saint Vincent Seminary PA
Saint Xavier University IL
Salve Regina University RI
Seattle University WA
Seminary of the Immaculate Conception NY
Seton Hall University NJ
Seton Hall University School of Law NJ
Seton Hill University PA
Siena Heights University MI
Silver Lake College of the Holy Family WI
Spring Hill College AL
SS. Cyril and Methodius Seminary MI
St. Ambrose University IA
St. Anthony College of Nursing IL
St. Bonaventure University NY
St. Catharine College KY
St. Catherine University MN
St. Gregory's University OK
St. John Vianney College Seminary FL
St. John Vianney Theological Seminary CO
St. John's University NY
St. Mary's University TX
St. Thomas University FL
St. Vincent De Paul Regional Seminary FL
Stonehill College MA
The Catholic University of America DC
The College of Saint Scholastica MN
The College of Saints John Fisher & Thomas More TX
The Pontifical Catholic University of Puerto Rico PR
The University of Scranton PA
Thomas More College KY
Trinity Washington University DC
University of Dallas TX
University of Dayton OH
University of Detroit Mercy MI
University of Great Falls MT
University of Mary ND
University of Notre Dame IN
University of Saint Francis IN
University of Saint Joseph CT
University of Saint Mary KS
University of Saint Mary of the Lake-Mundelein Seminary IL
University of Saint Thomas MN
University of San Diego CA
University of San Francisco CA
University of St. Francis IL
University of St. Thomas TX
University of the Incarnate Word TX
University of the Sacred Heart PR
Ursuline College OH
Villanova University PA
Viterbo University WI
Walsh University OH
Wheeling Jesuit University WV
Xavier University OH
Xavier University of Louisiana LA

Russian Orthodox
Holy Trinity Orthodox Seminary NY

Seventh-day Adventist
Adventist University of Health Sciences FL
Andrews University MI
Griggs University MI
Kettering College of Medical Arts OH
La Sierra University CA
Loma Linda University CA
Oakwood University AL
Pacific Union College CA
Southern Adventist University TN
Southwestern Adventist University TX
Union College NE
Universidad Adventista de las Antillas PR
Walla Walla University WA
Washington Adventist University MD

Southern Baptist
B.H. Carroll Theological Institute TX
Blue Mountain College MS
California Baptist University CA
Carson-Newman College TN
Charleston Southern University SC
Clear Creek Baptist Bible College KY
East Texas Baptist University TX
Golden Gate Baptist Theological Seminary CA
Hannibal-La Grange University MO
Houston Baptist University TX
Louisiana College LA
Mid-Continent University KY
Midwestern Baptist Theological Seminary MO
Mississippi College MS
New Orleans Baptist Theological Seminary LA
North Greenville University SC
Oklahoma Baptist University OK
Ouachita Baptist University AR
Samford University AL
Southeastern Baptist Theological Seminary NC
Southwest Baptist University MO
Southwestern Baptist Theological Seminary TX
The Baptist College of Florida FL
The Southern Baptist Theological Seminary KY
Union University TN
University of Mary Hardin-Baylor TX
University of Mobile AL
Wayland Baptist University TX

William Carey University .... MS
Williams Baptist College .... AR
Wingate University .... NC

The Christian And Missionary Alliance

Crown College .... MN
Nyack College .... NY
Simpson University .... CA

Unification Church

Unification Theological Seminary .... NY

Unitarian Universalist

Meadville Lombard Theological School IL
Starr King School for the Ministry .... CA

United Brethren Church

Huntington University .... IN

United Church Of Christ

Bangor Theological Seminary .... ME
Catawba College .... NC
Cedar Crest College .... PA
Chicago Theological Seminary IL
Doane College .... NE
Eden Theological Seminary .... MO
Elmhurst College IL
Heidelberg University .... OH
Lakeland College .... WI
Lancaster Theological Seminary .... PA
Northland College .... WI
The Defiance College .... OH
Tougaloo College .... MS
United Theological Seminary of the Twin Cities .... MN

United Methodist

Adrian College .... MI
Albion College .... MI
Albright College .... PA
American University .... DC
Andrew College .... GA
Baker University .... KS
Baldwin Wallace University .... OH
Bennett College .... NC
Bethune Cookman University .... FL
Birmingham-Southern College .... AL
Brevard College .... NC
Centenary College of Louisiana .... LA
Central Methodist University .... MO
Claflin University .... SC
Claremont School of Theology .... CA
Clark Atlanta University .... GA
Columbia College .... SC
Cornell College .... IA
Dakota Wesleyan University .... SD
DePauw University .... IN
Dillard University .... LA
Emory & Henry College .... VA
Emory University .... GA
Ferrum College .... VA
Florida Southern College .... FL
Garrett-Evangelical Theological Seminary IL
Greensboro College .... NC
Hamline University .... MN
Hendrix College .... AR
High Point University .... NC
Hiwassee College .... TN
Huntingdon College .... AL
Iliff School of Theology .... CO
Iowa Wesleyan College .... IA
Kansas Wesleyan University .... KS
Kentucky Wesleyan College .... KY
LaGrange College .... GA
Lebanon Valley College .... PA
Lindsey Wilson College .... KY
Lon Morris College .... TX
Louisburg College .... NC
Lycoming College .... PA
MacMurray College IL
Martin Methodist College .... TN
McKendree University IL
McMurry University .... TX
Methodist Theological School in Ohio .... OH
Methodist University .... NC
Millsaps College .... MS
Morningside College .... IA
Nebraska Wesleyan University .... NE
North Carolina Wesleyan College .... NC
North Central College IL
Ohio Northern University .... OH
Ohio Wesleyan University .... OH
Oklahoma City University .... OK
Otterbein University .... OH
Pfeiffer University .... NC
Philander Smith College .... AR
Randolph College .... VA
Randolph-Macon College .... VA
Reinhardt University .... GA
Rust College .... MS
Saint Paul School of Theology .... MO
Shenandoah University .... VA
Simpson College .... IA
Southern Methodist University .... TX
Southwestern College .... KS
Southwestern University .... TX
Spartanburg Methodist College .... SC
Tennessee Wesleyan College .... TN
Texas Wesleyan University .... TX
Union College .... KY
United Theological Seminary .... OH
University of Evansville .... IN
University of Indianapolis .... IN
University of Mount Union .... OH
Virginia Wesleyan College .... VA
Wesley College .... DE
Wesley Theological Seminary .... DC
Wesleyan College .... GA
West Virginia Wesleyan College .... WV
Wiley College .... TX
Wofford College .... SC
Young Harris College .... GA

Wesleyan Church

Allegheny Wesleyan College .... OH
Houghton College .... NY
Indiana Wesleyan University .... IN
Oklahoma Wesleyan University .... OK
Somerset Christian College .... NJ
Southern Wesleyan University .... SC

Wisconsin Evangelical Lutheran Synod

Martin Luther College .... MN

Carnegie Classification Code Definitions*

This year, the Higher Education Directory lists the updated 2010 Carnegie Classifications. The 2010 Classification update retains the same structure of classifications initially adopted in 2005. Due to space limitation, the *Higher Education Directory* ® only lists the original classification framework—now called the basic classification—which was substantially revised in 2005. These new codes are listed below:

Associate's Colleges: Includes institutions where all degrees are at the associate's level, or where bachelor's degrees account for less than 10 percent of all undergraduate degrees. Excludes institutions eligible for classification as Tribal Colleges or Special Focus Institutions.

Assoc/Pub-R-S: Associate's — Public Rural-serving Small
Assoc/Pub-R-M: Associate's — Public Rural-serving Medium
Assoc/Pub-R-L: Associate's — Public Rural-serving Large
Assoc/Pub-S-SC: Associate's — Public Suburban-serving Single Campus
Assoc/Pub-S-MC: Associate's — Public Suburban-serving Multicampus
Assoc/Pub-U-SC: Associate's — Public Urban-serving Single Campus
Assoc/Pub-U-MC: Associate's — Public Urban-serving Multicampus
Assoc/Pub-Spec: Associate's — Public Special Use
Assoc/PrivNFP: Associate's — Private Not-for-profit
Assoc/PrivFP: Associate's — Private For-profit
Assoc/Pub2in4: Associate's — Public 2-year Colleges under Universities
Assoc/Pub4: Associate's — Public 4-year, Primarily Associate's
Assoc/PrivNFP4: Associate's — Private Not-for-profit 4-year, Primarily Associate's
Assoc/PrivFP4: Associate's — Private For-profit 4-year, Primarily Associate's

Doctorate-granting Universities. Includes institutions that award at least 20 doctoral degrees per year (excluding doctoral-level degrees that qualify recipients for entry into professional practice, such as the JD, MD, PharmD, DPT, etc.). Excludes Special Focus Institutions and Tribal Colleges.

RU/VH: Research Universities (very high research activity)
RU/H: Research Universities (high research activity)
DRU: Doctoral/Research Universities

Master's Colleges and Universities. Includes institutions that award at least 50 master's degrees per year. Excludes Special Focus Institutions and Tribal Colleges.

Master's/L: Master's Colleges and Universities (larger programs)
Master's/M: Master's Colleges and Universities (medium programs)
Master's/S: Master's Colleges and Universities (smaller programs)

Baccalaureate Colleges. Includes institutions where baccalaureate degrees represent at least 10 percent of all undergraduate degrees and that award fewer than 50 master's degrees or fewer than 20 doctoral degrees per year. Excludes Special Focus Institutions and Tribal Colleges.

Bac/A&S: Baccalaureate Colleges — Arts & Sciences
Bac/Diverse: Baccalaureate Colleges — Diverse Fields
Bac/Assoc: Baccalaureate/Associate's Colleges

Special Focus Institutions. Institutions awarding baccalaureate or higher-level degrees where a high concentration of degrees is in a single field or set of related fields. Excludes Tribal Colleges.

Spec/Faith: Theological seminaries, Bible colleges, and other faith-related institutions
Spec/Medical: Medical schools and medical centers
Spec/Health: Other health profession schools
Spec/Engg: Schools of engineering
Spec/Tech: Other technology-related schools
Spec/Bus: Schools of business and management
Spec/Arts: Schools of art, music, and design
Spec/Law: Schools of law
Spec/Other: Other special-focus institutions

Tribal Colleges. Colleges and universities that are members of the American Indian Higher Education Consortium, as identified in IPEDS Institutional Characteristics.

Tribal: Tribal Colleges

---

*All data provided by The Carnegie Foundation for the Advancement of Teaching. For more detailed information on the revised Carnegie Codes, please visit www.carnegiefoundation.org/classifications/

Statistics

Institutions of Higher Education by Control, Level and State

STATE	TWO YEAR		FOUR YEAR		TOTAL		SYSTEM	GRAND
	PRIVATE	PUBLIC	PRIVATE	PUBLIC	PRIVATE	PUBLIC	OFFICE	TOTAL
AL	6	27	27	16	33	43	2	78
AK	2	1	3	3	5	4	1	10
AZ	20	19	46	4	66	23	1	90
AR	3	22	13	11	16	33	2	51
CA	84	115	276	36	360	151	29	540
CO	25	14	40	15	65	29	3	97
CT	1	12	23	8	24	20	1	45
DE	1	3	4	2	5	5	1	11
DC	2	0	15	3	17	3	0	20
FL	56	6	128	35	184	41	1	226
GA	10	28	55	33	65	61	1	127
HI	2	6	10	4	12	10	2	24
ID	1	4	8	4	9	8	0	17
IL	17	47	117	12	134	59	5	198
IN	11	14	65	15	76	29	2	107
IA	2	18	45	3	47	21	3	71
KS	7	25	24	11	31	36	0	67
KY	11	16	46	8	57	24	1	82
LA	14	35	15	17	29	52	4	85
ME	3	7	14	8	17	15	2	34
MD	4	16	28	15	32	31	1	64
MA	5	16	85	14	90	30	2	122
MI	3	29	60	15	63	44	1	108
MN	6	30	57	11	63	41	3	107
MS	5	15	11	9	16	24	0	40
MO	25	21	77	13	102	34	3	139
MT	6	8	5	6	11	14	1	26
NE	8	7	19	7	27	14	2	43
NV	5	1	6	6	11	7	1	19
NH	2	7	13	5	15	12	2	29
NJ	3	19	32	21	35	40	2	77
NM	2	18	11	8	13	26	0	39
NY	40	39	200	44	240	83	5	328
NC	2	59	64	16	66	75	2	143
ND	1	4	10	7	11	11	1	23
OH	54	27	89	34	143	61	1	205
OK	8	12	20	18	28	30	0	58
OR	6	16	28	8	34	24	1	59
PA	81	16	118	46	199	62	1	262
RI	0	1	9	3	9	4	0	13
SC	5	20	28	14	33	34	0	67
SD	1	5	10	6	11	11	1	23
TN	11	13	68	10	79	23	2	104
TX	35	64	91	48	126	112	8	246
UT	3	5	19	6	22	11	1	34
VT	0	1	17	5	17	6	1	24
VA	18	24	76	17	94	41	1	136
WA	6	27	34	12	40	39	2	81
WV	11	10	13	12	24	22	2	48
WI	3	17	41	13	44	30	2	76
WY	2	7	0	1	2	8	0	10
AS	0	0	0	1	0	1	0	1
GU	0	1	1	1	1	2	0	3
MH	0	1	0	0	0	1	0	1
MP	0	0	0	1	0	1	0	1
PR	7	0	44	14	51	14	3	68
FM	0	1	0	0	0	1	0	1
PW	0	1	0	0	0	1	0	1
VI	0	0	0	1	0	1	0	1
Total	**646**	**977**	**2358**	**716**	**3004**	**1693**	**113**	**4810**

50 Largest Universities by Fall 2011 Enrollment

Institution	Enrollment
1. Ashford University	74596
2. Arizona State University	72254
3. Liberty University	65951
4. University of Central Florida	58052
5. The Ohio State University Main Campus	56867
6. Kaplan University	56606
7. Strayer University	54900
8. Air University	53887
9. University of Minnesota-Twin Cities	52557
10. University of Texas at Austin	51112
11. American Public University System	50838
12. Texas A & M University	49861
13. University of Florida	49589
14. Walden University	48982
15. Michigan State University	47954
16. University of South Florida	47362
17. Ohio University (all campuses)	46146
18. Florida International University	44686
19. Penn State University Park	44485
20. New York University	43911
21. Indiana University Bloomington	42731
22. University of Michigan-Ann Arbor	42716
23. University of Maryland University College	42713
24. University of Washington	42446
25. University of Wisconsin-Madison	42441
26. University of Cincinnati Main Campus	42421
27. Florida State University	41087
28. Grand Canyon University	40487
29. Rutgers the State University of New Jersey New Brunswick Campus	39950
30. University of Houston	39820
31. Purdue University Main Campus	39637
32. University of California-Los Angeles	39271
33. University of Arizona	39236
34. University of Southern California	38010
35. University of Maryland College Park	37200
36. California State University-Northridge	36911
37. Temple University	36855
38. Capella University	36375
39. California State University-Fullerton	36156
40. University of North Texas	35694
41. California State University-Long Beach	34870
42. University of Georgia	34816
43. North Carolina State University	34767
44. Brigham Young University	34101
45. Texas State University-San Marcos	34087
46. Western Governors University	34000
47. University of Missouri - Columbia	33805
48. The University of Alabama	33602
49. The University of Texas at Arlington	33439
50. Utah Valley University	33395

Institutions by Control and Tuition Range

Tuition	Public*	Private	Total
0 - 1,000	61	267	328
1,001 - 2,000	201	11	212
2,001 - 4,000	605	39	644
4,001 - 6,000	326	89	415
6,001 - 8,000	241	116	357
8,001 - 10,000	123	125	248
Over 10,000	136	2357	2493
Total	**1693**	**3004**	**4697**

* Figures for Public Institutions are In-State Tuitions

Universities, Colleges and Schools

by State*

*Includes the District of Columbia and, separately, U.S. Service Schools, American Samoa, Federated States of Micronesia, Guam, Marshall Islands, Northern Marianas, Palau, Puerto Rico, and Virgin Islands.

ALABAMA

Alabama Agricultural and Mechanical University (A)

4900 Meridian Street, Normal AL 35762-1357
County: Madison FICE Identification: 001002
Unit ID: 100654
Telephone: (256) 372-5230 Carnegie Class: Master's L
FAX Number: (256) 372-5244 Calendar System: Semester
URL: www.aamu.edu
Established: 1875 Annual Undergrad Tuition & Fees (In-State): $8,490
Enrollment: 5,085 Coed
Affiliation or Control: State IRS Status: 501(c)3
Highest Offering: Doctorate
Program: Liberal Arts And General; Teacher Preparatory; Professional
Accreditation: SC, AAFCS, CORE, CS, DIETD, ENG, ENGT, FOR, PLNG, SP, SW, TED

01 President .... Dr. Andrew HUGINE, JR.
03 Executive VP/COO .... Dr. Kevin A. ROLLE
05 Vice Pres Academic Affairs .... Dr. Daniel K. WIMS
10 VP of Business & Finance .... Mr. Ralph JOHNSON
26 Vice Pres Mktg/Commun/Advancement .... Ms. Wendy KOBLER
32 VP Student Affairs .... Dr. Jeffery BURGIN
41 Director of Athletics .... Mr. Bryan HICKS
46 Interim VP Inst Rsrch/Spons Pgms .... Dr. Vann NEWKIRK
22 AVP Budget & Planning .... Mr. Gregory JACKSON
21 Comptroller .... Mr. Norman JONES
15 Director Human Resources .... Ms. Cassandra TARVER-ROSS
18 Director Physical Facilities .... Mr. Walter ALEXANDER
06 Registrar .... Mr. Cedric ARRINGTON
30 Director of Development .... Mr. Archie TUCKER
84 AVP of Enrollment Management .... Ms. Venita KING
35 Director of Student Activities .... Ms. Jasmine BUXTON
37 Director of Financial Aid .... Mr. Darryl JACKSON
88 Director of Emergency Management .... Ms. Monica RAY
23 Dir Student Health & Counseling .... Dr. Jennifer PARKER-AYERS
36 Dir Career Development Services .... Ms. Carolyn LEWIS
09 Dir Institutional Research .... Dr. Thomas COAXUM
88 Director Marketing & PR .... Mr. Jerome SAINTJONES
39 Dir of Residential Housing .... Mr. Kenneth MADDOX
27 Chief Information Officer .... Mr. Greg MARROW
19 Chief of Police .... Ms. Monica RAY
08 Interim Dean Learn Resources Center .... Dr. Gary BUSH
96 Director of Purchasing .... Ms. Delores HUDSON
58 Dean Graduate School .... Dr. Vann NEWKIRK
47 Dean College Agricultural .... Dr. Lloyd WALKER
53 Dean College of Education .... Dr. Curtis MARTIN
54 Dean College of Engineering .... Dr. Trent MONTGOMERY
50 Dean College of Business .... Dr. Amin SARKAR
88 Interim Dean University College .... Dr. Juarine STEWART

Alabama Southern Community College (B)

PO Box 2000, Monroeville AL 36461-2000
County: Monroe FICE Identification: 001034
Unit ID: 101949
Telephone: (251) 575-3156 Carnegie Class: Assoc/Pub-R-S
FAX Number: (251) 575-5356 Calendar System: Semester
URL: www.ascc.edu
Established: 1965 Annual Undergrad Tuition & Fees (In-State): $4,080
Enrollment: 1,432 Coed
Affiliation or Control: State IRS Status: 501(c)3
Highest Offering: Associate Degree
Program: Occupational; 2-Year Principally Bachelor's Creditable
Accreditation: SC, ADNUR

01 President .... Dr. Reginald SYKES
05 Vice Pres Academic & Student Affs .... Dr. Lee L. TAYLOR
10 VP Finance/Administrative Services .... Mr. Roger CHANDLER
20 Dean of Instruction .... Mrs. Ann CLANTON
08 Dean of Library Services .... Ms. LaShannon HOLLINGER
06 Registrar .... Ms. Jana HORTON
37 Director of Financial Aid .... Ms. Amy ROWELL
26 Director of Public Information .... Ms. Stephanie PETTIS
18 Chief Facilities/Physical Plant .... Mr. Tom REED

Alabama State University (C)

915 S Jackson Street, Montgomery AL 36101-0271
County: Montgomery FICE Identification: 001005
Unit ID: 100724
Telephone: (334) 229-4200 Carnegie Class: Master's L
FAX Number: (334) 834-6861 Calendar System: Semester
URL: www.alasu.edu
Established: 1867 Annual Undergrad Tuition & Fees (In-State): $7,932
Enrollment: 5,429 Coed
Affiliation or Control: State IRS Status: 501(c)3
Highest Offering: Doctorate
Program: Liberal Arts And General; Teacher Preparatory
Accreditation: SC, ACBSP, CORE, MUS, OT, PTA, SW, TED, THEA

01 President .... Dr. Joseph H. SILVER, JR.
03 Chief Operating Ofcr/Exec Vice Pres .... Dr. John F. KNIGHT, JR.
05 Int Provost/Vice Pres Academic Affs .... Dr. Alfred SMITH
10 Vice President Business & Finance .. Mr. Freddie C. GALLOT, JR.
26 Vice Pres Marketing/ Communications .... Ms. Danielle KENNEDY-LAMAR
18 Int Vice Pres Buildings & Grounds .... Mr. Brian THORNTON
15 Vice Pres Human Resources .... Mrs. Carmen DOUGLAS
32 Assoc Provost/VP Student Affairs .... Dr. William P. HYTCHE
84 Assoc Provost/Dir Enrollment Mgmt .... Mrs. Cherise PETERS
20 Assoc Vice Pres Academic Affairs .... Dr. Alfred S. SMITH
35 Asst Vice Pres Student Affairs .... Mr. Ricky DRAKE
21 Asst VP Business & Finance/ Comptrol .... Mrs. Alondrea J. PRITCHETT
09 Director Institutional Research .... Dr. Kimbrely CLARK
08 Dean Libraries/Learning Resource .... Dr. Janice FRANKLIN
06 Director Records Registration .... Ms. Karen PRESTAGE
07 Director Admissions/Recruitment .... Mr. Freddie WILLIAMS, JR.
13 Director of Academic Computing/MIS .... Mr. Larry COBB
37 Director Student Financial Aid .... Mrs. Dorenda ADAMS
36 Dir Placement Svcs/Cooperative Educ .... Mrs. Mary K. WILLIAMS
26 Director University Relations .... Mr. Kenneth MULLINAX
50 Dean College Business Admin .... Dr. LaQuita BOOTH
89 Dean University College .... Dr. Evelyn HODGE
53 Int Dean College of Education .... Dr. Charlie GIBBONS
64 Dean Visual & Performing Arts .... Dr. Tommie T. STEWART
58 Dean Graduate Studies .... Dr. William PERSONS
81 Dean College of Sci Math & Tech .... Dr. Cajetan AKAJUOBI
49 Dean Col of Liberal Arts/Social Sci .... Dr. Leon C. WILSON
51 Director Cmty Svcs/Cont Education .... Mr. Olan L. WESLEY
30 Assoc Vice President of Development .... Ms. Zillah FLUKER
29 Director Alumni Relations .... Mr. Cromwell HANDY
23 Director Student Health Services .... Ms. Gwendolyn MANN
19 Exec Dir Police & Campus Security .... Mr. Henry C. DAVIS
38 Dir Counseling & Development Svcs .... Mrs. Jessyca M. DARRINGTON
39 Director Housing/Residential Life .... Mr. Hosea LEWIS
41 Director of Athletics .... Mr. Stacy DANLEY
25 Director Grants & Contracts .... Dr. Linda PHAIRE-WASHINGTON
88 Director Internal Audit .... Vacant
96 Director of Purchasing .... Ms. Ann SMITH

Amridge University (D)

1200 Taylor Road, Montgomery AL 36117-3553
County: Montgomery FICE Identification: 025034
Unit ID: 100690
Telephone: (800) 351-4040 Carnegie Class: Bac/A&S
FAX Number: (334) 387-3878 Calendar System: Semester
URL: www.amridgeuniversity.edu
Established: 1967 Annual Undergrad Tuition & Fees: $6,800
Enrollment: 780 Coed
Affiliation or Control: Churches Of Christ IRS Status: 501(c)3
Highest Offering: Doctorate
Program: Liberal Arts And General; Professional; Religious Emphasis
Accreditation: SC, @THEOL

01 President .... Dr. Michael C. TURNER
05 Academic Vice President/Dean .... Dr. Stanley PATTERSON
06 Registry Officer .... Mrs. Elaine P. TARENCE
07 Admissions .... Mrs. Ora DAVIS
08 Director of Library .... Ms. Kay S. NEWMAN
10 Chief Business Officer .... Mrs. B. P. TURNER
88 Chief Accountant .... Mrs. Anita L. CROSBY
13 Director of Computing/Information .... Mr. Clayton F. SCHMIDT
37 Financial Aid Director .... Ms. Starr FAIN
42 Director of Church Relations .... Mr. Curtis SAMPLEY
88 Director of World Missions .... Mr. Demar ELAM
29 Director of Alumni Relations .... Mr. Ed SMITH
09 Director of Institutional Research .... Dr. J. H. WHITE
14 Director of Computer Center .... Mr. Jack TEMPLE
18 Chief Facilities/Physical Plant .... Mr. Robert SHIRLEY
24 Director of Educational Media .... Mr. Thomas PATTERSON
38 Director of Student Counseling .... Dr. Wayne PERRY
26 Chief Public Relations Officer .... Mrs. Laina COSTANZA
42 Chaplain/Director Campus Ministry .... Dr. Leon F. ESTEP
44 Director Annual/Planned Giving .... Mr. Ed SMITH
73 Dean of School of Religion .... Dr. Rodney CLOUD
88 Actg Dean School of Human Services .... Dr. Kenyetta MCCURTY
90 Director Academic Computing .... Mr. Donnie E. CROSBY
15 Director Personnel Services .... Vacant

Athens State University (E)

300 N Beaty Street, Athens AL 35611-1902
County: Limestone FICE Identification: 001008
Unit ID: 100812
Telephone: (256) 233-8100 Carnegie Class: Bac/Diverse
FAX Number: (256) 216-3324 Calendar System: Semester
URL: www.athens.edu
Established: 1822 Annual Undergrad Tuition & Fees (In-State): $5,340
Enrollment: 3,389 Coed
Affiliation or Control: State IRS Status: 501(c)3
Highest Offering: Baccalaureate
Program: Liberal Arts And General; Teacher Preparatory
Accreditation: SC, ACBSP, TED

01 President .... Dr. Robert K. GLENN
05 Provost & VP for Academic Affs .... Dr. Ronald CROMWELL
20 Asst VP for Academic Affairs .... Vacant
32 Vice Pres for Enroll & Student Supp .... Mr. Jim HUTTO
10 Vice President for Financial Aff .... Mr. Mike MCCOY
21 Associate Business Officer .... Mr. Evan THORNTON
26 Vice Pres for University Advance .... Mr. Richard MOULD
08 Director of Libraries .... Dr. Robert BURKHARDT
50 Dean College of Business .... Dr. Linda SHONESY
53 Dean College of Education .... Dr. Debra BAIRD
49 Dean College of Arts & Sciences .... Dr. Ronald FRITZE
36 Dir of Career Services .... Ms. Saralyn MITCHELL
37 Dir of Student Financial Services .... Ms. Sarah MCABEE
06 Registrar .... Ms. Teresa SUIT
07 Director of Admissions & Records ..... Ms. Necedah HENDERSON
35 Director of Student Activities .... Ms. Tena BULLINGTON
29 Director of Alumni Affairs/Ann Giv .... Ms. Trish DI LULLO
30 Director of Development .... Mr. Ronnie KNOX
88 Director of Printing & Public Rels .... Mr. Guy MCCLURE
09 Director of Institutional Research .... Ms. Sylvia CORREA
18 Director of Physical Plant .... Mr. Jerry BRADFORD
15 Director of Human Resources .... Ms. Suzanne SIMS
102 Director of Gov Corp & Found Rel .... Vacant
36 Director of Student Recruitment .... Ms. Deborah SCHAUS
51 Director of Ctr for Lifelong Lrng .... Dr. Diane SAUERS
88 Director of Transfer Advising Cente .... Ms. Lisa PAYNE

Auburn University (F)

Auburn AL 36849
County: Lee FICE Identification: 001009
Unit ID: 100858
Telephone: (334) 844-4000 Carnegie Class: RU/H
FAX Number: N/A Calendar System: Semester
URL: www.auburn.edu
Established: 1856 Annual Undergrad Tuition & Fees (In-State): $9,446
Enrollment: 25,190 Coed
Affiliation or Control: State IRS Status: 501(c)3
Highest Offering: Doctorate
Program: Liberal Arts And General; Teacher Preparatory; Professional
Accreditation: SC, AAB, ART, AUD, BUS, BUSA, CACREP, CIDA, CLPSY, CONST, COPSY, CORE, CS, DIETD, ENG, FOR, #JOUR, LSAR, MFCD, MUS, NURSE, PHAR, PLNG, SP, SPAA, SW, TED, THEA, VET

01 President .... Dr. Jay GOGUE
03 Executive Vice President .... Dr. Donald L. LARGE
05 Provost/VP Acad Affairs .... Dr. Timothy R. BOOSINGER
29 Vice President Alumni Affairs .... Dr. Deborah L. SHAW
30 Vice President Development .... Ms. Jane DIFOLCO PARKER
32 Vice President Student Affaris .... Dr. Ainsley CARRY
46 Assoc Provost/VP Research .... Dr. John M. MASON
20 Associate Provost .... Dr. Emmett WINN
56 Assistant Vice President Outreach .... Dr. Royrickers COOK
58 Dean Graduate School .... Dr. George FLOWERS
84 Dean of Enrollment Services .... Dr. Charles W. ALDERMAN
11 Asst Vice Pres Auxiliary Services ..... Mr. Robert C. RITENBAUGH
15 Asst Vice Pres Human Resources .... Ms. Lynne B. HAMMOND
26 Acting Exec Dir Comm/Marketing .... Ms. Camille BARKLEY
28 Assoc Provost Multicultural Affs .... Dr. Overtoun JENDA
20 Assoc Provost Undergrad Studies .... Dr. Constance C. RELIHAN
21 Assoc Vice Pres Business & Finance .... Ms. Marcie SMITH
43 General Counsel .... Mr. Lee F. ARMSTRONG
101 Secretary to Board of Trustees .... Mr. C. Grant DAVIS
14 Exec Dir Information Technology .... Mr. Bliss BAILEY
37 Exec Dir Student Financial Services ... Mr. Michael C. REYNOLDS
11 Director Public Affairs .... Mr. Brian C. KEETER
22 Director Affirmative Action/EEO .... Ms. Kelley G. TAYLOR
86 Director Governmental Affairs .... Ms. Sherri FULFORD
09 Director Inst Research & Assessment .... Dr. James A. CLARK
41 Director of Athletics .... Mr. John O. JACOBS, JR.
06 Registrar .... Ms. Laura Ann FOREST
40 Director University Bookstore .... Ms. Catherine LEE
88 Director JCS Museum of Art .... Dr. Marilyn LAUFER
56 Dir AL Cooperative Extension Syst .... Dr. Gary D. LEMME
39 Director Housing & Residential Life .... Ms. Kim L. TRUPP
92 Director Honors College .... Dr. James R. HANSEN
10 Chief Business Officer .... Dr. Donald L. LARGE
36 Director Career Center .... Mrs. Nancy M. BERNARD
13 Associate Executive Director IT .. Dr. Nickolas A. BACKSCHEIDER
96 Asst Director Procurement Services .... Ms. Marilyn SANFORD
47 Dean of Agriculture .... Dr. William D. BATCHELOR
48 Dean Architect Design/Construction .... Dr. Vini NATHAN
49 Dean of Liberal Arts .... Dr. Anne-Katrin GRAMBERG
50 Dean of Business .... Dr. Bill HARDGRAVE
53 Dean of Education .... Dr. Betty Lou WHITFORD
54 Dean of Engineering .... Dr. Christopher B. ROBERTS
65 Dean of Forestry/Wildlife Sciences .... Dr. James P. SHEPARD
59 Dean of Human Sciences .... Dr. June M. HENTON
66 Dean of Nursing .... Dr. Gregg NEWSCHWANDER
67 Dean of Pharmacy .... Dr. R. Lee EVANS, JR.
81 Interim Dean Sciences & Mathematics .... Dr. Charles SAVRDA
74 Interim Dean Veterinary Medicine .... Dr. Calvin M. JOHNSON
08 Dean University Libraries .... Dr. Bonnie MACEWAN

Auburn University at Montgomery (G)

PO Box 244023, Montgomery AL 36124-4023
County: Montgomery FICE Identification: 008310
Unit ID: 100830
Telephone: (334) 244-3000 Carnegie Class: Master's L
FAX Number: (334) 244-3762 Calendar System: Semester
URL: www.aum.edu
Established: 1967 Annual Undergrad Tuition & Fees (In-State): $6,602
Enrollment: 5,305 Coed
Affiliation or Control: State IRS Status: 501(c)3
Highest Offering: Doctorate
Program: Teacher Preparatory; Professional
Accreditation: SC, BUS, BUSA, CACREP, CYTO, MT, NURSE, SPAA, TED

01 Chancellor .... Dr. John G. VERES, III
05 Provost .... Dr. Joe KING
30 Vice Chanc Advancement/Alumni Svcs .... Ms. Carolyn GOLDEN
10 Vice Chancellor Finance .... Ms. Wanda MEADOWS

88 Vice Chanc University Outreach .... Dr. Katherine JACKSON
20 Assoc Provost Academic/Grad Affairs .... Dr. Matthew RAGLAND
28 Asst Prov Diversity/MultiCultural ....Mr. Timothy SPRAGGINS
85 Asst Provost International Affairs ....Mr. Jacques L. FUQUA, JR.
15 Senior Human Resources Director ... Ms. Jeanine BODDIE-LAVAN
18 Sr Director of Facilities ....Mr. Dorsey SMITH
19 Sr Director of Public Safety ....Mr. Ricky ADAMS
08 Dean of Library ....Ms. Lucy L. FARROW
07 Dean of Admissions/Recruiting ....Mr. Tyler PETERSON
32 Dean of Students ....Ms. Janice LYN
84 Dean of Enrollment Management ....Mr. Tyler PETERSON
41 Athletic Director ....Mr. Steve CROTZ
37 Director of Financial Aid ....Mr. Anthony RICHEY
07 Director of Admissions ....Ms. Valerie S. CRAWFORD
39 Dir Housing & Residence Life ....Mr. Daryl MORRIS
27 Chief Information Officer ....Dr. Jeffery ANDERSON
38 Director Student Counseling ....Dr. Yulanda TYRE
88 Dir Writing Across the Curriculum ....Ms. Jennifer GOOD
19 Chief Campus Police ....Ms. Nell ROBINSON
13 Asst Chief Information Officer ....Ms. Carolyn D. RAWL
13 Asst Chief Information Officer ....Mr. Jon FISHER
21 Chief Accounting Officer ....Ms. Kim DECKER
36 Director Career Development ....Mr. Keith CULLEN
40 Director of Bookstore ....Mr. Jeffrey P. VINZANT
06 Registrar ....Vacant
25 Director of Sponsored Programs ....Ms. Fariba S. DERAVI
35 Director Student Life ....Mrs. Lakecia HARRIS
26 Communications Manager ....Mr. Frank MILES
85 Coord Intl Student Admissions ....Mr. Ron BLAESING
49 Dean of Liberal Arts ....Dr. Michael BURGER
50 Dean of Business ....Dr. Wanda Rhea INGRAM
53 Dean of Education ....Dr. Samuel FLYNT
66 Dean of Nursing ....Dr. Gregg NEWSCHWANDER
81 Dean of Sciences ....Dr. Karen STINE
51 Sr Director of Continuing Education ....Ms. Kathy GUNTER

Bevill State Community College (A)

1411 Indiana Avenue, Jasper AL 35501
County: Walker FICE Identification: 005733
Unit ID: 102429
Telephone: (205) 387-0511 Carnegie Class: Assoc/Pub-R-M
FAX Number: (205) 387-5192 Calendar System: Semester
URL: www.bscc.edu
Established: 1965 Annual Undergrad Tuition & Fees (In-State): $4,170
Enrollment: 4,069 Coed
Affiliation or Control: State IRS Status: 501(c)3
Highest Offering: Associate Degree
Program: Occupational; 2-Year Principally Bachelor's Creditable
Accreditation: SC, ADNUR, #EMT, PNUR, SURGT

01 President ....Dr. Anne MCNUTT
03 Executive Vice President ....Mr. Mark ELLARD
05 Dean of Instruction ....Dr. Charles MURRAY
32 Dean of Students ....Dr. Kim ENNIS

Birmingham-Southern College (B)

900 Arkadelphia Road, Birmingham AL 35254-0001
County: Jefferson FICE Identification: 001012
Unit ID: 100937
Telephone: (205) 226-4600 Carnegie Class: Bac/A&S
FAX Number: (205) 226-4627 Calendar System: 4/1/4
URL: www.bsc.edu
Established: 1856 Annual Undergrad Tuition & Fees: $29,600
Enrollment: 1,305 Coed
Affiliation or Control: United Methodist IRS Status: 501(c)3
Highest Offering: Baccalaureate
Program: Liberal Arts And General; Teacher Preparatory; Professional
Accreditation: SC, MUS, TED

01 President ....Gen. Charles C. KRULAK
05 Provost ....Dr. Mark SCHANTZ
10 Vice President of Finance ....Mr. Eli H. PHILLIPS
11 Vice President Administration ....Mr. Lane ESTES
30 VP Institutional Advancement ....Mr. Robert BLAKELY
27 Vice President Communications ....Mr. Bill WAGNON
13 Vice Pres Information Technology ....Mr. Anthony HAMBEY
84 Vice Pres of Enrollment Management ...Ms. Kathleen ROSSMANN
32 Vice Pres Student Development ....Dr. David EBERHARDT
07 Assoc Vice President of Admissions ....Ms. Sheri SALMON
04 Assistant to the President ....Ms. Lauren MCCURDY
20 Associate Provost ....Dr. Susan HAGEN
20 Assistant Provost ....Ms. Martha A. STEVENSON
06 Dean of Records ....Mr. Danny K. BROOKS
42 Chaplain ....Rev. Jack HINNEN
29 Director of Alumni Affairs ....Ms. Lisa HARRISON
23 Director of Health Services ....Ms. Yvette SPENCER
04 Exec Asst to the President ....Ms. Maggie MCDONALD
08 Director of the Library ....Ms. Charlotte FORD
18 Director of Facilities & Events ....Ms. Anne CURRY
37 Director of Financial Aid ....Ms. Jo Ann BENNETT
15 Director of Human Resources ....Ms. Susan E. KINNEY
26 Director of Church Relations ....Ms. Laura SISSON
38 Director Personal Counseling ....Ms. Sara HOOVER
41 Athletic Director ....Mr. Joe DEAN, JR.
19 Chief of Campus Police ....Mr. Randy YOUNGBLOOD
36 Director of Career Counseling ....Mr. Michael LEBEAU
30 Director Advancement Services ....Mr. Jeff SHERRELL
88 Dir of Interim & Contract Learning ....Dr. Katy LEONARD
28 Director of Multi-Cultural Affairs ....Ms. Erica BROWN
68 Dir Physical Fitness & Recreation ....Mr. Mike ROBINSON

88 Director of Leadership Studies ....Mr. Kent ANDERSEN
88 Director of Service Learning ....Ms. Kristin HARPER
88 Sports Information Director ....Ms. Sarah ERRECA
27 Communications Specialist ....Ms. Patricia COLE
88 Communications Specialist ....Mr. Richard RUSH
27 Assoc Dir of Comm Publications ....Ms. Tracy THOMAS
88 Assc Dir Communications-New Media ....Mr. Mike HAMILTON
88 Assoc Dir of International Programs ....Ms. Anne LEDVINA
88 Manager of Printing Services ....Mr. Jerome DAVIS
40 Manager of the Bookstore ....Mr. William ALEXANDER
96 Coordinator of Purchasing ....Ms. Cassandra BROWN
100 Chief of Staff ....Ms. Linda FLAHERTY-GOLDSMITH
27 Director of Communications ....Mrs. Hannah WOLFSON
108 Director of Inst Effective/Assess ....Dr. Noreen GAUBATZ

Bishop State Community College (C)

351 N Broad Street, Mobile AL 36603-5898
County: Mobile FICE Identification: 001030
Unit ID: 102030
Telephone: (251) 405-7000 Carnegie Class: Assoc/Pub-U-MC
FAX Number: (251) 438-3249 Calendar System: Semester
URL: www.bishop.edu
Established: 1965 Annual Undergrad Tuition & Fees (In-State): $3,312
Enrollment: 3,984 Coed
Affiliation or Control: State IRS Status: 501(c)3
Highest Offering: Associate Degree
Program: Occupational; 2-Year Principally Bachelor's Creditable
Accreditation: SC, ACBSP, ACFEI, ADNUR, EMT, FUSER, PNUR, PTAA

01 President ....Dr. James LOWE, JR.
05 Dean of Instructional Services ....Dr. Latitia MCCANE
12 Director of Southwest Campus ....Mr. Roderick MCSWAIN
12 Director of Carver Campus ....Dr. Betty LESLIE
12 Director of Central Campus ....Mrs. Madeline STOKES
05 Dean of Technical School ....Vacant
32 Dean of Students ....Dr. Terry HAZZARD
10 Dean of Business/Finance ....Mrs. Bonita ALLEN
35 Assistant to the Dean of Students ....Mrs. Wanda DANIELS
09 Coordinator Institutional Planning ....Ms. Aundrea WHEELER-DUNNER
15 Director of Human Resources ....Mrs. Marcella SIMS
18 Director of Physical Plant ....Mr. Lorenzo GRAYSON
26 Director of Public Relations ....Mr. Herb JORDAN
103 Coordinator Workforce Development ....Mr. Jim KELLEN
103 Dir Workforce Dev/Lifelong Learning ....Mr. Charles PORTER
37 Mgr Student Fin Aid/Veterans Svcs ....Dr. Samuel CHUKS

Calhoun Community College (D)

PO Box 2216, Decatur AL 35609-2216
County: Limestone FICE Identification: 001013
Unit ID: 101514
Telephone: (256) 306-2500 Carnegie Class: Assoc/Pub-R-L
FAX Number: (256) 306-2877 Calendar System: Semester
URL: www.calhoun.edu
Established: 1963 Annual Undergrad Tuition & Fees (In-State): $3,192
Enrollment: 12,033 Coed
Affiliation or Control: State IRS Status: 501(c)3
Highest Offering: Associate Degree
Program: Occupational; 2-Year Principally Bachelor's Creditable
Accreditation: SC, ACBSP, ADNUR, DA, EMT, MLTAD, PNUR, PTAA, SURGT

01 President ....Dr. Marilyn C. BECK
05 Vice Pres Instruction/Student Succ ....Ms. Alicia TAYLOR
32 Dean of Student Affairs ....Dr. Kermit CARTER
10 Dean for Business & Finance ....Mr. Jack BURROW
07 Dir Admissions & Records/Registrar ....Ms. Pauletta BURNS
08 Head Librarian ....Ms. Lucinda BEDDOW
37 Director Student Financial Aid ....Mrs. Deborah BYRD
13 Int Director Information Systems ....Mr. Nathan TYLER
102 Executive Director Foundation ....Ms. Terri BRYSON
12 Dean Research Park Campus ....Ms. Terri BRYSON
55 Director Evening Program ....Dr. Vinetta WESLEY
29 Director of Alumni Relations .. Ms. Janet KINCHERLOW-MARTIN
18 Director of Physical Plant ....Mr. Bruce CAUSEY
09 Dean Planning/Research & Grants ....Dr. Debra HENDERSHOT
103 Director of Workforce Development ....Mr. Jim SWINDELL
84 Coord Enrollment Management ....Ms. Samantha NELSON
26 Chief Public Relations Officer ....Ms. Janet KINCHERLOW-MARTIN

Central Alabama Community College (E)

1675 Cherokee Road, Alexander City AL 35010
County: Tallapoosa FICE Identification: 001007
Unit ID: 100760
Telephone: (256) 234-6346 Carnegie Class: Assoc/Pub-R-M
FAX Number: (256) 234-0384 Calendar System: Semester
URL: www.cacc.edu
Established: 1963 Annual Undergrad Tuition & Fees (In-State): $3,780
Enrollment: 2,512 Coed
Affiliation or Control: State IRS Status: 501(c)3
Highest Offering: Associate Degree
Program: Occupational; 2-Year Principally Bachelor's Creditable
Accreditation: SC, ADNUR

01 President ....Dr. Stephen B. FRANKS
05 Provost/CAO/Dean of Instruction ....Dr. Melenie BOLTON
32 Provost/Dean of Students ....Ms. Amanda HARKINS

10 Dean of Business Operations ....Mr. Lynn SPRAGGINS
35 Associate Dean of Student Services ....Ms. Glenda BLAND
09 Asc Dean Instruction/Instl Effectiv ....Ms. Sherie FLEMING
08 Librarian ....Ms. Denita OLIVER
06 Registrar ....Ms. Janice STEPHENS
26 Chief Public Relations Officer ....Mr. Brett PRITCHARD
37 Director Student Financial Aid ....Ms. Cindy ENTREKIN
38 Director Student Counseling ....Vacant
30 Advancement Officer ....Mr. Michael LOVETT

Chattahoochee Valley Community College (F)

2602 College Drive, Phenix City AL 36869-7960
County: Russell FICE Identification: 012182
Unit ID: 101028
Telephone: (334) 291-4900 Carnegie Class: Assoc/Pub-R-M
FAX Number: (334) 291-4944 Calendar System: Semester
URL: www.cv.edu
Established: 1973 Annual Undergrad Tuition & Fees (In-State): $4,480
Enrollment: 1,704 Coed
Affiliation or Control: State IRS Status: 501(c)3
Highest Offering: Associate Degree
Program: Occupational; 2-Year Principally Bachelor's Creditable
Accreditation: #SC

01 President ....Dr. Donald G. CANNON
05 Vice President/Dean of the College ....Dr. David HODGE
05 Dean of Instruction ....Vacant
32 Dean of Student Services ....Dr. Joy HAMM
103 Dean of Workforce Development ....Ms. Janet ORMOND
81 Chair of Mathematics & Science ....Mr. Earl COOK
57 Chair of Language & Fine Arts ....Ms. Susan LOCKWOOD
76 Chair of Health Sciences ....Ms. Resa LORD
88 Program Dir Public Safety Academy ....Ms. Mary SIMONTON
83 Chair of Social Sciences ....Dr. Ellen GUNTER
50 Chair Business & Information Tech ....Ms. Debra PLOTTS
08 Director Learning Resources Center ....Ms. Xueying CHEN
37 Director of Financial Aid ....Mrs. Joan WATERS
18 Director Facilities & Maintenance ....Mr. Johann WELLS
45 Dir of Institutional Effectiveness ....Dr. Joree JONES
26 Director of Marketing ....Vacant
41 Director of Athletics ....Mr. Adam THOMAS
38 Director of Counseling & Advising ....Ms. Cynthia FLOYD
27 Director of Information Systems ....Mr. Jody NOLES
88 Director of Student Development ....Mrs. Vickie WILLIAMS
51 Director of Adult Education ....Ms. Darlene THOMPSON
15 Director of Human Resources ....Ms. Debbie BOONE
30 Director of Development ....Ms. Karen KELLY
10 Chief Financial Officer ....Ms. Brenda KELLEY
55 Evening Coordinator ....Mr. Reggie GORDY
88 Dir Trng for Existing Bus & Indus ....Vacant

Columbia Southern University (G)

21982 University Lane, Orange Beach AL 36561-3845
County: Baldwin FICE Identification: 041215
Unit ID: 450933
Telephone: (251) 981-3771 Carnegie Class: Master's L
FAX Number: (251) 981-3815 Calendar System: Other
URL: www.columbiasouthern.edu
Established: 1993 Annual Undergrad Tuition & Fees: $4,800
Enrollment: 27,916 Coed
Affiliation or Control: Proprietary IRS Status: Proprietary
Highest Offering: Doctorate
Program: Occupational; 2-Year Principally Bachelor's Creditable; Liberal Arts And General; Professional; Business Emphasis
Accreditation: DETC

01 President ....Mr. Robert G. MAYES, JR.
03 Provost ....Dr. Terry DIXON
09 VP IR/Ext Compliance/Accreditation ....Dr. Karen J. SMITH
27 VP of Marketing and Outreach ....Mr. Billy HAYES
13 Chief Information Officer ....Mr. Ken STYRON
88 VP of Business Development ....Mr. Rick COOPER
07 Associate VP of Admissions ....Ms. Kathy COLE
10 Associate VP of Business Affairs ....Mr. Pat TROUP
24 Dean of Instructional Design ....Dr. Jon CRISPIN
16 Associate VP of Human Resources ....Ms. Sue BUTTS
05 Dean of Academic Services ....Mr. Elwin JONES
97 Dean of Undergraduate Programs ....Ms. Nichole GOTSCHALL
32 Dean of Students ....Mr. F. Poche WAGUESPACK
58 Dean of Graduate Programs ....Dr. Mark PANTALEO
09 Director of Institutional Research ....Dr. Katherine ODOM
06 Registrar ....Ms. Rachel FARRIS
37 Director of Financial Aid ....Mr. Aaron COLLINS
45 Director of Quality Assurance ....Ms. Tina SHIPP
08 Director of Learning Resources ....Ms. Marsha HINNEN
108 Director of Outcomes Assessment ....Dr. Michael DANIEL
26 Director of Marketing ....Mr. Beau VIGNES

Concordia College Alabama (H)

1712 Broad Street, Selma AL 36701
County: Dallas FICE Identification: 010554
Unit ID: 101073
Telephone: (334) 874-5700 Carnegie Class: Bac/Diverse
FAX Number: (334) 874-5755 Calendar System: Semester
URL: www.ccal.edu
Established: 1922 Annual Undergrad Tuition & Fees: $8,090
Enrollment: 719 Coed
Affiliation or Control: Lutheran Church - Missouri Synod
IRS Status: 501(c)3

Highest Offering: Baccalaureate
Program: 2-Year Principally Bachelor's Creditable; Liberal Arts And General; Teacher Preparatory; Business Emphasis
Accreditation: SC

01 President/Chief Executive Officer .... Dr. Tilahun M. MENDEDO
03 Executive Vice President .... Dr. Fee HABTES
05 Vice Pres Academic Affs .... Dr. Cheryl WASHINGTON
32 Acting VP of Student Services .... Mr. Bien HARBIN
30 VP of Advancement and Development .... Mr. Howard J. MOORE, JR.
10 Chief Financial Officer .... Mr. Dexter JACKSON
37 Director Financial Aid .... Mrs. Tharsteen BRIDGES
09 Effectiveness/Research and Plng .... Mrs. Ruthie J. ORSBORN
64 Director of Music .... Mr. Bobby MCKENZIE
08 Librarian .... Mr. Scott WHITING
06 Registrar .... Mrs. Chinester GRAYSON
07 Admissions Manager .... Ms. Meseret ALEMU
29 Director Alumni Affairs/Development .... Mrs. Minnie MCMILLAN
26 Public Relations .... Ms. Desiree TAYLOR
36 Dir Student Placement/Counseling .... Ms. Sadie JARETT
15 Director of Human Respources .... Ms. Xaviere J. IRBY
84 Director of Recruitment .... Mrs. Gwendolyn MOORE
27 Chief Information Officer .... Mr. Wayne GREEN
41 Director of Athletics .... Mr. Shepherd SKANES
85 Director of International Students .... Mr. Katiso ALEMU
42 Chaplain .... Rev. Lavaugn WIGGINS

*Education Corporation of America (A)

3660 Grandview Parkway Suite 300,
Birmingham AL 35243
County: Jefferson — Identification: 666006
Telephone: (205) 329-7900 — Carnegie Class: N/A
FAX Number: (205) 329-7906
URL: www.ecacolleges.com

01 President & Chief Executive Officer .... Mr. Tom A. MOORE, JR.
03 Exec VP/Chief Operations Officer .... Mr. Roger M. MILLER
05 Exec VP/Chf Compl Ofcr/Gen Counsel .... Mr. Roger L. SWARTZWELDER
26 Exec VP/Chief Marketing Officer .... Mr. Charles S. TRIERWEILER
10 Exec VP/Chief Financial Officer .... Mr. Christopher BOEHM
16 Exec VP/Human Resource & People Dev .... Mr. Michael C. WILLIAMS
13 Exec VP/Chief Info & Security Ofcr .... Mr. Ronald G. MAILLETTE
84 Exec VP Campus Development .... Mr. William R. OWENS
05 Interim Exec VP Academics .... Dr. Sara LAWHORNE
20 SVP Academic Compliance .... Ms. Judy E. LIMA
20 SVP Academic Operations & Training .... Ms. Shirley S. WILKINSON
36 SVP Career Services .... Mr. Scot STAPLETON
37 SVP Student Finance .... Ms. Kathy CHEATHAM
21 SVP Financial Ops & Controller .... Mr. Ryan BREWER
88 Regional VP & Operations Mgr .... Mr. Michael LARGENT
88 Regional VP & Operations Mgr .... Mr. Jack CLARK
88 Regional VP Operations Gen Mgr .... Ms. Pamela LONG
18 SVP Facilities & Interior Design .... Ms. Celeste PRESTENBACH

*Virginia College (B)

488 Palisades Boulevard, Birmingham AL 35209
County: Jefferson — FICE Identification: 030106
Unit ID: 420307
Telephone: (205) 802-1200 — Carnegie Class: Master's S
FAX Number: (205) 271-8225 — Calendar System: Quarter
URL: www.vc.edu
Established: 1993 — Annual Undergrad Tuition & Fees: $14,000
Enrollment: 1,900 — Coed
Affiliation or Control: Proprietary — IRS Status: Proprietary
Highest Offering: Master's
Program: Occupational; 2-Year Principally Bachelor's Creditable
Accreditation: ACICS, ACFEI, CIDA, DMS, SURGT

02 Campus President .... Mr. Chris MOORE
05 VP Academics .... Ms. Cathy PLUNKETT
07 Director of Admissions .... Mr. Bevin YESKEVICZ
06 Registrar .... Mr. Jim CUMMINGS

*Virginia College (C)

2021 Drake Avenue SW, Huntsville AL 35801
County: Madison — Identification: 666400
Unit ID: 420316
Telephone: (256) 533-7387 — Carnegie Class: Bac/Assoc
FAX Number: (256) 533-7785 — Calendar System: Quarter
URL: www.vc.edu
Established: 1993 — Annual Undergrad Tuition & Fees: $14,000
Enrollment: 731 — Coed
Affiliation or Control: Proprietary — IRS Status: Proprietary
Highest Offering: Baccalaureate
Program: 2-Year Principally Bachelor's Creditable
Accreditation: ACICS

02 Campus President .... Mr. James D. FOSTER
05 Academic Dean .... Ms. Rebecca BLALOCK
07 Director of Admissions .... Mr. Daryl W. COLEMAN
08 Librarian .... Ms. Dorothy J. BOWDEN
06 Registrar .... Ms. Bridget K. DAVIS

*Virginia College (D)

3725 Airport Boulevard, Suite 165, Mobile AL 36608
County: Mobile — Identification: 666069
Unit ID: 445090
Telephone: (251) 343-7227 — Carnegie Class: Assoc/PrivFP
FAX Number: (251) 343-7287 — Calendar System: Quarter
URL: www.vc.edu
Established: 2001 — Annual Undergrad Tuition & Fees: $18,320
Enrollment: 731 — Coed
Affiliation or Control: Proprietary — IRS Status: Proprietary
Highest Offering: Associate Degree
Program: Occupational
Accreditation: ACICS, SURGT

02 Campus President .... Mr. Eric BERRIOS
05 Academic Dean .... Mr. Dale CONLEY
06 Registrar .... Ms. Sidna K. UTSEY
07 Director of Admissions .... Ms. April MARTIN

*Virginia College (E)

6200 Atlanta Highway, Montgomery AL 36117-2802
County: Montgomery — Identification: 666408
Unit ID: 452115
Telephone: (334) 277-3390 — Carnegie Class: Not Classified
FAX Number: (334) 277-0773 — Calendar System: Quarter
URL: www.vc.edu
Established: 2008 — Annual Undergrad Tuition & Fees: $21,900
Enrollment: 878 — Coed
Affiliation or Control: Proprietary — IRS Status: Proprietary
Highest Offering: Associate Degree
Program: 2-Year Principally Bachelor's Creditable
Accreditation: ACICS, MAAB, SURGT

02 Campus President .... Madeline LITTLE
05 Academic Dean .... Kimberly ALEXANDER
07 Director of Admissions .... Lawrence BROWN
06 Registrar .... Holly BENSON

Enterprise State Community College (F)

PO Box 1300, Enterprise AL 36331-1300
County: Coffee — FICE Identification: 001015
Unit ID: 101143
Telephone: (334) 347-2623 — Carnegie Class: Assoc/Pub-R-M
FAX Number: (334) 393-6223 — Calendar System: Semester
URL: www.escc.edu
Established: 1963 — Annual Undergrad Tuition & Fees (In-State): $3,990
Enrollment: 2,731 — Coed
Affiliation or Control: State — IRS Status: 501(c)3
Highest Offering: Associate Degree
Program: Occupational; 2-Year Principally Bachelor's Creditable
Accreditation: SC

01 President .... Dr. Nancy W. CHANDLER
05 Dean of Instruction .... Dr. Matthew HUGHES
84 Associate Dean Enrollment Mgmt .... Mr. M. Gary DEAS
32 Dean of Students .... Dr. Jeffrey COATS
10 Dean Administration & Finance .... Ms. Alonzetta LANDRUM-SIMS
12 Dean Alabama Aviation Center Ozark .... Mr. Tucson ROBERTS
45 Assoc Dean Planning/Inst Effective .... Ms. Veronica CROCK
26 Dir Marketing & Media Relations .... Ms. Deidre FRITH
37 Director Student Financial Aid .... Dr. Henry L. QUISENBERRY, JR.
13 Director Information Technology .... Vacant
55 Director Evening Division .... Mr. Carl HOLBROOK
15 Director Personnel Services .... Ms. Angel LYNK

Faulkner University (G)

5345 Atlanta Highway, Montgomery AL 36109-3398
County: Montgomery — FICE Identification: 001003
Unit ID: 101189
Telephone: (334) 272-5820 — Carnegie Class: Bac/Diverse
FAX Number: (334) 386-7107 — Calendar System: Semester
URL: www.faulkner.edu
Established: 1942 — Annual Undergrad Tuition & Fees: $17,380
Enrollment: 3,574 — Coed
Affiliation or Control: Churches Of Christ — IRS Status: 501(c)3
Highest Offering: Doctorate
Program: Liberal Arts And General; Teacher Preparatory; Professional
Accreditation: SC, LAW, TED

01 President .... Dr. Billy D. HILYER
05 Vice President Academic Affairs .... Dr. Jack E. TUCCI
10 Vice President Financial Services .... Mrs. Wilma D. PHILLIPS
30 Vice President for Advancement .... Dr. Ben BRUCE
56 Vice Pres Extended Education Svcs .... Mr. Jim SPRATLIN
32 Vice President Student Services .... Vacant
84 Vice President Enrollment .... Mr. Keith MOCK
61 Dean Jones School of Law .... Mr. Charles NELSON
49 Dean College Arts & Sciences .... Dr. Dave RAMPERSAD
50 Dean College Business/Exec Educ .... Dr. Dave KHADANGA
73 Dean College of Biblical Studies .... Dr. Cecil MAY
53 Dean College of Education .... Dr. Jendia GRISSETT
88 Assoc Dean Acad/Dir of Law Library .... Mr. Tim CHINARIS
43 General Counsel/Assoc Dean Business .... Mr. Gerald JONES
88 Assoc Dean College Biblical Studies .... Dr. Scott GLEAVES
21 Associate Vice President of Finance .... Mr. Jamie HORN
88 Assoc Vice President Development .... Mr. Billy CAMP
88 Assoc Vice President Extended Svcs .... Mr. Mark HUNT
20 Assoc Vice President Acad Affairs .... Mrs. Marci JOHNS
16 Asst VP Human Resources/Diversity .... Mrs. Renee DAVIS
06 Registrar .... Mr. Don REYNOLDS
35 Dean of Students .... Mr. Faires AUSTIN
37 Director Student Financial Aid .... Mr. Buddy JACKSON
12 Director Mobile Center .... Mrs. Diane NEWELL
12 Director Birmingham Center .... Mr. Tim PARKER
12 Director Huntsville Center .... Ms. Barbara GAMBLE
41 Athletic Director .... Mr. Brent BARKER
08 Director of Libraries .... Mrs. Barbara KELLY
09 Director of Institutional Research .... Dr. Brenda TURNER
104 Director of International Studies .... Dr. Ed HICKS
26 Director of Public Relations .... Mr. Dave HOGAN
07 Director of Admissions .... Mr. Neil SCOTT
88 Director Student Success .... Mrs. Michelle OTWELL
29 Director of Alumni Relations .... Mr. Joel DILBECK
88 Director Quality Enhancement Plng .... Dr. Cindy WALKER
92 Director of Honors Program .... Dr. Robert WOODS
36 Director Career Services .... Mrs. Marie OTTINGER
38 Counselor .... Ms. Donna PUTNAM
04 Exec Assistant to the President .... Mrs. Darlene GREGORY

Fortis College (H)

3590 Pleasant Valley Road, Mobile AL 36609
County: Mobile — FICE Identification: 023410
Unit ID: 371052
Telephone: (251) 344-1203 — Carnegie Class: Assoc/PrivFP
FAX Number: (251) 344-1299 — Calendar System: Other
URL: www.fortiscollege.edu
Established: 1978 — Annual Undergrad Tuition & Fees: N/A
Enrollment: 309 — Coed
Affiliation or Control: Proprietary — IRS Status: Proprietary
Highest Offering: Associate Degree
Program: Occupational; 2-Year Principally Bachelor's Creditable; Technical Emphasis
Accreditation: ABHES, DA

Fortis Institute (I)

100 London Parkway Suite 150, Birmingham AL 35211
County: Jefferson — Identification: 666683
Unit ID: 455628
Telephone: (205) 940-7800 — Carnegie Class: Not Classified
FAX Number: (205) 942-6708 — Calendar System: Other
URL: www.fortisinstitute.edu
Established: 2008 — Annual Undergrad Tuition & Fees: N/A
Enrollment: 988 — Coed
Affiliation or Control: Proprietary — IRS Status: Proprietary
Highest Offering: Associate Degree
Program: Occupational
Accreditation: ACICS, DH

01 Campus President .... Ms. Carolyn H. PRITCHETT
05 Academic Dean .... Mr. Bob PALMATIER

† Branch campus of Fortis Institute, Erie, PA.

Gadsden State Community College (J)

1001 Geo Wallace Drive, PO Box 227,
Gadsden AL 35902-0227
County: Etowah — FICE Identification: 001017
Unit ID: 101240
Telephone: (256) 549-8200 — Carnegie Class: Assoc/Pub-R-L
FAX Number: (256) 549-8444 — Calendar System: Semester
URL: www.gadsdenstate.edu
Established: 1925 — Annual Undergrad Tuition & Fees (In-State): $3,840
Enrollment: 6,733 — Coed
Affiliation or Control: State — IRS Status: 501(c)3
Highest Offering: Associate Degree
Program: Occupational; 2-Year Principally Bachelor's Creditable
Accreditation: SC, ACBSP, ADNUR, EMT, MLTAD, PNUR, RAD

01 President .... Dr. Raymond W. STAATS
03 Vice President .... Dr. Valerie RICHARDSON
05 Dean of Instructional Services .... Dr. Jim L. JOLLY
10 Dean Financial/Administrative Svcs .... Dr. James R. PRUCNAL
72 Dean Tech Educ/Workforce Develop .... Mr. Tim GREEN
30 Assoc Dean Instnl Advance/Cmty Svc .... Ms. Pam JOHNSON
20 Assoc Dean Instructional Services .... Dr. Karen BLYTHE-SMITH
56 Assoc Dean for Distance Education .... Ms. Sara POOVEY
32 Asc Dean Stdnt Svcs/Instl Effective .... Dr. Teresa C. RHEA
26 Coordinator Public Relations .... Ms. Kay S. FOSTER
19 Director Safety & Security .... Mr. Sam LEDBETTER
21 Director of Financial Services .... Ms. Jacqueline CLARK
28 Director of Diversity & Compliance .... Ms. Michele BRADFORD
13 Director of Computer Services .... Mr. Jeff W. GREEN
16 Director Human Resources .... Ms. Kim S. COBB
41 Athletic Director .... Mr. Mike CANCILLA
38 Assoc Dean Stdnt Svcs & Counse Svcs .... Dr. Cheryl C. VICKERS
75 Director HBCU Initiatives .... Ms. Tarva VAUGHN
51 Director Adult Education .... Mr. Johnny BAKER
37 Director of Financial Aid .... Ms. Kelly D'EATH
18 Chief Facilities/Physical Plant .... Mr. Stewart DAVIS
06 Assistant to President/Registrar .... Mrs. Jennie P. DOBSON

George C. Wallace Community College - Dothan (A)

1141 Wallace Drive, Dothan AL 36303-9234
County: Dale FICE Identification: 001018
Unit ID: 101286
Telephone: (334) 983-3521 Carnegie Class: Assoc/Pub-R-M
FAX Number: (334) 983-6066 Calendar System: Semester
URL: www.wallace.edu
Established: 1947 Annual Undergrad Tuition & Fees (In-State): $3,072
Enrollment: 4,950 Coed
Affiliation or Control: State IRS Status: 501(c)3
Highest Offering: Associate Degree
Program: Occupational; 2-Year Principally Bachelor's Creditable; Business Emphasis
Accreditation: SC, ADNUR, EMT, MAC, PNUR, PTAA, RAD

01 President ..... Dr. Linda C. YOUNG
32 Dean of Student Affs/Sparks Campus . Ms. Jacqueline B. SCREWS
32 Dean of Student Dev/Wallace Campus ..... Mr. Mark SHOPE
05 Dean of Instructional Affairs ..... Mr. Tony HOLLAND
10 Dean of Business Affairs ..... Mr. Lynn BELL
07 Director Enroll Svcs/Registrar ..... Mr. Keith SAULSBERRY
08 Dir Learning Resources Ctrs System ..... Mr. A. P. HOFFMAN
37 Director of Financial Aid ..... Ms. Erma PERRY
14 AS-400 Progm/Sys Admin ..... Mr. Gordon FREE
15 Director of Human Resources ..... Ms. Brooke STRICKLAND
09 Dir Institutional Effectiveness ..... Mr. Frank BAREFIELD
40 Interim Bookstore Manager ..... Ms. Kerri SHIVER
38 Director Student Counseling ..... Ms. Jean DAGOSTIN
21 Director of Accounting & Finance ..... Ms. Kay GAMBLE
26 Dir Public Relations & Marketing ..... Ms. Barbara THOMPSON
30 Dean Institutional Svcs/Com Dev ..... Dr. Ashli BOUTWELL

George Corley Wallace State Community College - Selma (B)

PO Box 2530, 3000 Earl Goodwin Pkwy, Selma AL 36702-2530
County: Dallas FICE Identification: 005699
Unit ID: 101301
Telephone: (334) 876-9227 Carnegie Class: Assoc/Pub-R-M
FAX Number: (334) 876-9250 Calendar System: Semester
URL: www.wccs.edu
Established: 1963 Annual Undergrad Tuition & Fees (In-State): $3,048
Enrollment: 2,066 Coed
Affiliation or Control: State IRS Status: 501(c)3
Highest Offering: Associate Degree
Program: Occupational; 2-Year Principally Bachelor's Creditable
Accreditation: SC, ADNUR, PNUR

01 President ..... Dr. James M. MITCHELL
05 Vice President for Instruction ..... Dr. Robert MCCONNELL
20 Instructional Administrator ..... Mr. Raji GOURDINE
10 Director of Fiscal Affairs ..... Ms. Jacqueline SMITH
32 Dean of Students ..... Mrs. Donitha GRIFFIN
08 Librarian ..... Ms. Minnie CARSTARPHEN
66 Director Associate Degree Nursing ..... Ms. Becky CASEY
37 Director of Financial Aid/Cmty Educ ..... Mrs. Chenetta LEE
38 Counselor College Division ..... Ms. Anessa KIDD
09 Director of Institutional Research ..... Mr. Robby BENNETT
26 Coord College Rels/Instl Research ..... Mrs. Rita LETT
19 Director Security/Safety ..... Mr. Ray MOORE
41 Athletic Director ..... Mr. Marcus HANNAH
15 Personnel Specialist ..... Mrs. Helen COSBY
18 Act Chief Facilities/Physical Plant ..... Mr. Jimmie GOLDSBY
28 Director of Diversity ..... Vacant
40 Bookstore Manager ..... Ms. Chezra HALL

Heritage Christian University (C)

PO Box HCU, Florence AL 35630-0050
County: Lauderdale FICE Identification: 021997
Unit ID: 101453
Telephone: (256) 766-6610 Carnegie Class: Spec/Faith
FAX Number: N/A Calendar System: Semester
URL: www.hcu.edu
Established: 1971 Annual Undergrad Tuition & Fees: $11,792
Enrollment: 86 Coed
Affiliation or Control: Churches Of Christ IRS Status: 501(c)3
Highest Offering: Master's
Program: Religious Emphasis
Accreditation: BI

01 President ..... Mr. Dennis H. JONES
05 Vice President of Academic Affairs ..... Dr. Bill BAGENTS
10 VP Business/Finance/Operations ..... Mr. Freddie P. MOON
32 Dean of Students ..... Mr. Brad MCKINNON
58 Director of Graduate Studies ..... Dr. Jeremy BARRIER
30 Director Institutional Advancement ..... Mr. Philip GOAD
06 Registrar ..... Mrs. Charlotte ORR
08 Librarian ..... Miss Jamie S. COX
42 Director of Christian Service ..... Mr. Brad MCKINNON
84 Dir Enrollment Svcs/Stdnt Fin Aid ..... Mr. Jim COLLINS

Herzing University (D)

280 W Valley Avenue, Birmingham AL 35209-4816
County: Jefferson FICE Identification: 010193
Unit ID: 101365
Telephone: (205) 916-2800 Carnegie Class: Bac/Diverse
FAX Number: (205) 916-2807 Calendar System: Semester
URL: www.herzing.edu
Established: 1965 Annual Undergrad Tuition & Fees: $11,040
Enrollment: 330 Coed
Affiliation or Control: Proprietary IRS Status: Proprietary
Highest Offering: Baccalaureate
Program: Occupational; Technical Emphasis
Accreditation: &NH

01 President ..... Donald E. LEWIS

† Regional accreditation is carried under the parent institution in Madison, WI.

Huntingdon College (E)

1500 East Fairview Avenue, Montgomery AL 36106-2148
County: Montgomery FICE Identification: 001019
Unit ID: 101435
Telephone: (334) 833-4222 Carnegie Class: Bac/Diverse
FAX Number: (334) 833-4486 Calendar System: Semester
URL: www.huntingdon.edu
Established: 1854 Annual Undergrad Tuition & Fees: $22,500
Enrollment: 1,123 Coed
Affiliation or Control: United Methodist IRS Status: 501(c)3
Highest Offering: Baccalaureate
Program: Liberal Arts And General
Accreditation: SC, MUS

01 President ..... Rev. J. Cameron WEST
10 Treasurer & Sr VP for Plng & Admin ..... Mr. Jay A. DORMAN
30 VP for College & Alumni Relations ..... Mr. Anthony J. LEIGH
84 VP for Enrollment Management ..... Ms. Laura H. DUNCAN
05 Provost & Dean of the College ..... Dr. Sidney J. STUBBS
32 VP Student Life & Dean of Students . Dr. Frank R. PARSONS, JR.
27 Assoc VP for Comm and Marketing ..... Ms. Suellen S. OFE
35 Coordinator of Student Activities ..... Ms. Sara Beth TERRY
06 Registrar ..... Ms. Maryann M. BECK
13 Dir of Institutional Technology ..... Mr. Frank O. GRIER
36 Dir of the Center for Career & Voc ..... Ms. Francis H. TAYLOR
37 Dir Student Financial Services ..... Mr. Tommy G. DISMUKES, JR.
37 Dir of Student Financial Aid ..... Ms. Belinda G. DUETT
18 Director of Facilities and Grounds ..... Mr. T. Michael DUNN
40 Manager Follett Bookstore ..... Ms. Pam BELL
23 Director of Student Health ..... Ms. Camilla IRVIN
04 Exec Asst to President/Corp Secy ..... Ms. Sandra B. KELSER
08 Director Houghton Memorial Library ..... Mr. Eric A. KIDWELL
21 Comptroller ..... Ms. Tina S. NIXON
39 Director of Residence Life ..... Ms. Sandra Betts HALL
41 Director of Athletics ..... Mr. Hugh H. PHILLIPS
42 Chaplain and Dir of Community Svcs ..... Rev. Brian L. SMITH
19 Chief of Security ..... Mr. Michael S. WARD
104 Coordinator Travel & Event Planning ..... Ms. Tricia S. GRIER

Huntsville Bible College (F)

904 Oakwood Avenue NW, Huntsville AL 35811-1632
County: Madison FICE Identification: 038943
Unit ID: 449348
Telephone: (256) 539-0834 Carnegie Class: Assoc/PrivNFP4
FAX Number: (256) 539-0854 Calendar System: Semester
URL: www.hbc1.edu
Established: 1986 Annual Undergrad Tuition & Fees: $4,005
Enrollment: 119 Coed
Affiliation or Control: Baptist IRS Status: 501(c)3
Highest Offering: Baccalaureate
Program: Liberal Arts And General; Religious Emphasis
Accreditation: BI

01 President ..... Dr. John L. CLAY
05 Academic Dean ..... Dr. Willie T. BROWN
20 Dean of Instruction ..... Dr. Willie T. BROWN
06 Registrar ..... Ms. Belinda F. HARDIN

ITT Technical Institute (G)

6270 Park South Drive, Bessemer AL 35022-5655
County: Jefferson Identification: 666530
Unit ID: 414568
Telephone: (205) 497-5700 Carnegie Class: Spec/Tech
FAX Number: (205) 497-5799 Calendar System: Quarter
URL: www.itt-tech.edu
Established: 1994 Annual Undergrad Tuition & Fees: N/A
Enrollment: 803 Coed
Affiliation or Control: Proprietary IRS Status: Proprietary
Highest Offering: Baccalaureate
Program: Technical Emphasis
Accreditation: ACICS

† Branch campus of ITT Technical Institute, Indianapolis, IN.

ITT Technical Institute (H)

9238 Madison Boulevard, Suite 500, Madison AL 35758
County: Madison Identification: 666695
Unit ID: 451945
Telephone: (256) 542-2900 Carnegie Class: Assoc/PrivFP4
FAX Number: (256) 542-2950 Calendar System: Quarter
URL: www.itt-tech.edu
Established: N/A Annual Undergrad Tuition & Fees: N/A
Enrollment: 454 Coed
Affiliation or Control: Proprietary IRS Status: Proprietary
Highest Offering: Baccalaureate
Program: Technical Emphasis
Accreditation: ACICS

† Branch campus of ITT Technical Institute, Indianapolis, IN.

ITT Technical Institute (I)

3100 Cottage Hill Road, Bldg 3, Mobile AL 36606-2913
County: Mobile Identification: 666165
Unit ID: 450252
Telephone: (251) 472-4760 Carnegie Class: Assoc/PrivFP4
FAX Number: N/A Calendar System: Quarter
URL: www.itt-tech.edu
Established: 2006 Annual Undergrad Tuition & Fees: N/A
Enrollment: 527 Coed
Affiliation or Control: Proprietary IRS Status: Proprietary
Highest Offering: Baccalaureate
Program: Technical Emphasis
Accreditation: ACICS

† Branch campus of ITT Technical Institute, Indianapolis, IN.

J.F. Drake State Technical College (J)

3421 Meridian Street N, Huntsville AL 35811-1584
County: Madison FICE Identification: 005260
Unit ID: 101462
Telephone: (256) 539-8161 Carnegie Class: Assoc/Pub-R-S
FAX Number: (256) 539-6439 Calendar System: Semester
URL: www.drakestate.edu
Established: 1961 Annual Undergrad Tuition & Fees (In-State): $3,192
Enrollment: 1,231 Coed
Affiliation or Control: State IRS Status: 501(c)3
Highest Offering: Associate Degree
Program: Occupational; 2-Year Principally Bachelor's Creditable; Technical Emphasis
Accreditation: SC, COE

01 President ..... Dr. Helen T. MCALPINE
05 Dean of Instruction/Student Svcs ..... Dr. Patricia SIMS
10 Business Manager/Treasurer ..... Vacant
103 Director of Workforce Development ..... Mr. Ricky WILLINGHAM
45 Dir of Planning/Title III Admin ..... Dr. John REUTTER
20 Associate Dean of Instruction ..... Dr. Kemba CHAMBERS
15 Director of Human Resources ..... Vacant
14 Director Computer Services ..... Vacant
08 Director of Library Services ..... Ms. Carla CLIFT
07 Director of Admissions ..... Ms. Monica SUDEALL
37 Director Student Financial Aid ..... Ms. Jennifer O'LINGER
26 Director of Public Relations ..... Mrs. Lisa BURTON
36 College Counselor ..... Ms. Denise GAYMON
09 Dir of Institutional Effectiveness ..... Dr. Alice RAYMOND
32 Student Services Management Dir ..... Mr. Ryan SMITH
51 Director of Adult Education ..... Dr. Nicole BARNETT
18 Director of Operations ..... Mr. Bruce BULLUCK

J.F. Ingram State Technical College (K)

PO Box 220350, Deatsville AL 36022-0350
County: Elmore FICE Identification: 030025
Unit ID: 101471
Telephone: (334) 285-5177 Carnegie Class: Assoc/Pub-R-S
FAX Number: (334) 285-5328 Calendar System: Semester
URL: www.ingram.edu
Established: 1965 Annual Undergrad Tuition & Fees (In-State): $4,068
Enrollment: 1,129 Coed
Affiliation or Control: State IRS Status: 501(c)3
Highest Offering: Associate Degree
Program: Occupational; Technical Emphasis
Accreditation: COE

01 President ..... Dr. Hank DASINGER
05 Interim Dean of Instruction ..... Mr. William GRISWOLD
32 Dean of Students & Support Services ..... Mr. James WILSON
45 Dean of Strategic Planning and Eval ..... Vacant
15 Human Resources Coordinator ..... Ms. Erica PORTIS-TURNER
07 Director of Admissions & Registrar ..... Vacant
10 Interim Director of Fiscal Affairs ..... Mrs. Lisa THACKER
36 Asst Transition Specialist ..... Mrs. Mary KING

Jacksonville State University (L)

700 Pelham Road N, Jacksonville AL 36265-1602
County: Calhoun FICE Identification: 001020
Unit ID: 101480
Telephone: (256) 782-5781 Carnegie Class: Master's L
FAX Number: (256) 782-5291 Calendar System: Semester
URL: www.jsu.edu
Established: 1883 Annual Undergrad Tuition & Fees (In-State): $6,360
Enrollment: 9,490 Coed
Affiliation or Control: State IRS Status: 501(c)3
Highest Offering: Doctorate
Program: Liberal Arts And General; Teacher Preparatory; Professional
Accreditation: SC, ART, BUS, CACREP, CS, DIETD, JOUR, MUS, NAIT, NURSE, SW, TED, THEA

01 President ..... Dr. William A. MEEHAN
05 Provost/VP Academic/Student Affairs ..... Dr. Rebecca O. TURNER
10 Vice Pres Admin/Business Affairs ..... Mr. Clint CARLSON
30 Vice Pres University Advancement ..... Dr. Charles R. LEWIS

13 Vice Pres Information Technology ....Mr. Vinson HOUSTON
20 Assoc Vice Pres Academic Affairs ....Dr. Joe DELAP
84 Assoc VP Enrol Mgmt/Student Affairs ....Dr. Tim KING
08 Dean of Library Services ....Mr. John-Bauer GRAHAM
58 Dean College Graduate Studies .... Dr. William D. CARR
49 Dean College Arts & Sciences ....Dr. James E. WADE
66 Dean College Nursing/Hlth Sciences .... Dr. Sarah V. LATHAM
53 Dean College Education/Prof Studies ....Dr. John HAMMETT
50 Dean Col Commerce/Business Admin .... Dr. William FIELDING
21 University Controller .... Ms. Allyson BARKER
07 Director of Admissions .... Mr. Andy GREEN
45 Dir Institutional Support Services .... Mr. Joe WHITMORE
44 Director Institutional Development .... Mr. Earl WARREN
39 Director Residence Life ....Mr. Kevin HOULT
88 Dir International House/Programs ....Dr. John J. KETTERER
29 Director of Alumni Relations ....Ms. Kaci OGLE
15 Director of Human Resources ....Ms. Rosalynn MARTIN
37 Director Financial Aid .... Ms. Vickie ADAMS
72 Director Department of Technology ....Mr. Terry MARBUT
41 Director Athletics .... Mr. Warren KOEGEL
09 Director Inst Research & Assessment .... Dr. Alicia SIMMONS
06 Registrar ....Ms. Kelly OSTERBIND
18 Director Physical Plant ....Mr. George F. LORD
36 Director Career Placement Services ....Ms. Rebecca E. TURNER
38 Dir Counseling/Disability Sppt Svcs ....Ms. Julie NIX
35 Director Student Life ....Mr. Terry CASEY
96 Director of Purchasing ....Ms. Pamela L. FINDLEY
26 Dir of Marketing/Communications .... Mr. Tim GARNER

James H. Faulkner State Community College (A)

1900 Highway 31 S, Bay Minette AL 36507-2698
County: Baldwin FICE Identification: 001060
Unit ID: 101161
Telephone: (251) 580-2100 Carnegie Class: Assoc/Pub-S-MC
FAX Number: (251) 580-2253 Calendar System: Semester
URL: www.faulknerstate.edu
Established: 1965 Annual Undergrad Tuition & Fees (In-State): $3,312
Enrollment: 4,430 Coed
Affiliation or Control: State IRS Status: 501(c)3
Highest Offering: Associate Degree
Program: Occupational; 2-Year Principally Bachelor's Creditable
Accreditation: SC, ACFEI, ADNUR, DA, EMT, PNUR, SURGT

01 President .... Dr. Gary L. BRANCH
05 Dean of Instruction ....Ms. Emily MARTIN
32 Dean of Student Development ....Dr. Brenda J. KENNEDY
35 Dean of Student Services .... Mr. Michael NIKOLAKIS
11 Dean Administrative Services ....Mr. Jim FITZ-GERALD
103 Dean of Workforce Development .... Ms. Patty HUGHSTON
26 Director College Relations ....Vacant
06 Registrar ....Ms. Betty SHEFFIELD
08 Dir Learning Resource .... Ms. Rheena ELMORE
37 Financial Aid Officer .... Dr. Jim THEEUWES
88 Director High School Relations ....Ms. Carmelita MIKKELSEN
18 Director of Buildings & Ground ....Mr. Jim FITZ-GERALD
51 Director of Continuing Education ....Vacant
19 Chief of Police ....Mr. David CONNOR
15 Director Human Resources .... Mrs. Laura BURKS
09 Dir Institutional Effectiveness/Dev .... Ms. Linda CALDWELL
66 Director Nursing & Allied Health .... Ms. Jean GRAHAM
13 Coordinator Technology Services ....Mr. Brian STRICKLAND

Jefferson Davis Community College (B)

PO Box 958, Brewton AL 36427-0958
County: Escambia FICE Identification: 001021
Unit ID: 101499
Telephone: (251) 867-4832 Carnegie Class: Assoc/Pub-R-S
FAX Number: (251) 867-7399 Calendar System: Semester
URL: www.jdcc.edu
Established: 1965 Annual Undergrad Tuition & Fees (In-State): $3,848
Enrollment: 1,251 Coed
Affiliation or Control: State IRS Status: 501(c)3
Highest Offering: Associate Degree
Program: Occupational; 2-Year Principally Bachelor's Creditable
Accreditation: SC, ADNUR

01 President ....Dr. Daniel BAIN
05 Dean of Instruction ....Ms. Kathleen HALL
10 Dean of Business Affairs ....Mr. Bernie WALL
32 Dean of Student Affairs ....Mr. David JONES
20 Associate Dean of Instruction ....Vacant
15 Director of Human Resources ....Ms. Veronica MCKINNEY
06 Registrar .... Ms. Robin SESSIONS
13 Director of MIS ....Mr. Anthony HARDY
26 Director Mktg & Community Relations ....Vacant
08 Librarian .... Mr. Jeffrey FAUST
37 Financial Aid Director ....Ms. Vanessa M. KYLES
09 Dir Institutional Research/Testing ....Ms. Carolyn WOODS
18 Chief Facilities/Physical Plant ....Mr. Richard LYNN
88 Dir Stdnt Support Svcs/Development .... Dr. Beth BILLY

Jefferson State Community College (C)

2601 Carson Road, Birmingham AL 35215-3098
County: Jefferson FICE Identification: 001022
Unit ID: 101505
Telephone: (205) 853-1200 Carnegie Class: Assoc/Pub-U-MC
FAX Number: (205) 983-5918 Calendar System: Semester
URL: www.jeffstateonline.com
Established: 1963 Annual Undergrad Tuition & Fees (In-State): $4,200
Enrollment: 9,466 Coed
Affiliation or Control: State IRS Status: 501(c)3
Highest Offering: Associate Degree
Program: Occupational; 2-Year Principally Bachelor's Creditable
Accreditation: SC, ACBSP, ACFEI, ADNUR, CONST, EMT, FUSER, MLTAD, PNUR, PTAA, RAD

01 President ....Dr. Judy M. MERRITT
03 Vice President .... Dr. Joe E. MORRIS
05 Dean of Instruction ....Ms. Danielle COBURN
75 Dean Career & Technical Education ....Ms. Norma G. BELL
30 Dean Campus Development/Campus Svcs ....Mr. Keith A. BROWN
10 Director Financial Services .... Ms. Mary WATSON
21 Business Manager ....Vacant
32 Director of Student Services ....Dr. Linda J. HOOTON
97 Assoc Dean Transf Gen Stds Shelby ....Ms. Jeanette ROGERS
97 Assoc Dean Transf Gen Stds Jeffrsn ....Dr. Aliakbar R. YAZDI
106 Associate Dean Distance Education ....Mr. Alan B. DAVIS
51 Director College/Cmty/Corp Educ .... Ms. Kay C. POTTER
09 Info Svc/Institutional Research ....Ms. Peggy L. VANDERGRIFT
13 Director Information Technology ......Ms. Peggy L. VANDERGRIFT
37 Director Financial Aid ....Ms. Tracy R. ADAMS
84 Dean of Enrollment Services ....Dr. Phillip M. HOBBS
18 Director Maintenance ....Mr. Bill MIXON
08 Director of Learning Resources .... Ms. Barbara GOSS
36 Director Career/Job Resource
Center .... Ms. Nancy F. BEAUCHAMP
07 Director Admissions and Retention ....Ms. Lillian OWENS
15 Director Human Resources .... Ms. Ruby RUSSELL
26 Director Media Relations ....Mr. David BOBO
96 Purchasing Coordinator ....Mr. Andy TERRY
19 Director Safety & Security ....Mr. Mark BAILEY

Judson College (D)

302 Bibb Street, Marion AL 36756-2504
County: Perry FICE Identification: 001023
Unit ID: 101541
Telephone: (334) 683-5100 Carnegie Class: Bac/A&S
FAX Number: (334) 683-5147 Calendar System: Semester
URL: www.judson.edu
Established: 1838 Annual Undergrad Tuition & Fees: $14,200
Enrollment: 367 Female
Affiliation or Control: Alabama Baptist State Convention
IRS Status: 501(c)3
Highest Offering: Baccalaureate
Program: Liberal Arts And General; Teacher Preparatory
Accreditation: SC, MUS, @SW

01 President .... Dr. David E. POTTS
05 Vice Pres & Academic Dean .... Dr. Sara B. KISER
32 Vice Pres & Dean of Students ....Mrs. Sandra S. FOWLER
07 Vice President Admissions ....Mrs. Charlotte S. CLEMENTS
10 Vice President Business Affairs ....Mr. Dennis W. FRODSHAM
30 VP Institutional Advancement ....Dr. Terry SMITH MORGAN
43 VP and General Counsel .... Mr. Bill MATHEWS

Lawson State Community College (E)

3060 Wilson Road, SW, Birmingham AL 35221-1798
County: Jefferson FICE Identification: 001059
Unit ID: 101569
Telephone: (205) 925-2515 Carnegie Class: Assoc/Pub-U-MC
FAX Number: (205) 925-8526 Calendar System: Semester
URL: www.lawsonstate.edu
Established: 1949 Annual Undergrad Tuition & Fees (In-State): $4,160
Enrollment: 4,206 Coed
Affiliation or Control: State IRS Status: 501(c)3
Highest Offering: Associate Degree
Program: Occupational; 2-Year Principally Bachelor's Creditable
Accreditation: SC, ACBSP, ADNUR, DA, PNUR

01 President .... Dr. Perry W. WARD
05 Vice Pres Instructional Services ....Dr. Bruce CRAWFORD
11 Vice President of Administration .... Mrs. Sharon CREWS
35 Dean of Students .... Dr. Cynthia ANTHONY
09 Director of Institutional Research ....Dr. Randy GLAZE
20 Academic Dean ....Dr. Sherri DAVIS
75 Asc Dean Business/Information Tech .... Dr. Alice MILTON
49 Asc Dn Liberal Arts/Coll Trans Pgms ....Dr. Karl PRUITT
76 Assoc Dean of Health Occupations ....Dr. Shelia MARABLE
75 Asst Dean Career Technical Programs ....Mr. Donald SLEDGE
84 Asst Dean of Admissions/Records .... Mr. Darren ALLEN
07 Director of Admissions ....Mr. Jeff SHELLEY
08 Librarian ....Ms. Sandra HENDERSON
37 Director Student Financial Aid .... Ms. Cassandra MATTHEWS
15 Director of Personnel Services .... Mrs. Vergie SPEARS
30 Chief Development .... Dr. Myrtes GREEN
26 Chief Public Relations Officer ....Mrs. Geri ALBRIGHT
18 Chief Facilities/Physical Plant .... Mr. Chad YANCY
19 Director Safety/Security ....Mr. Walter WILLIAMS
13 Dir Computing and Information Mgmt ....Dr. Randy GLAZE
40 Director Bookstore .... Mr. Al YOUNG
31 Director Auxiliary Services ....Dr. Craig LAWRENCE
41 Athletic Director ....Mrs. Eleanor PITTS
06 Registrar ....Ms. Lori CHISEM
91 Director of Academic Computing .... Dr. Alice MILTON
24 Director Educational Media ....Ms. Sandra HENDERSON
39 Director Student Housing ....Mr. Robert SMITH
29 Coordinator Alumni Relations .... Mrs. Janice ORANGE
35 Coordinator Student Affairs ....Mrs. Sandra HOWARD
38 Coordinator Student Counseling ....Mrs. Janice WILLIAMS
84 Coordinator Enrollment Management ....Mrs. Phyllis YOUNGER

Lurleen B. Wallace Community College (F)

PO Drawer 1418, 1000 Dannelly Blvd,
Andalusia AL 36420-1224
County: Covington FICE Identification: 008988
Unit ID: 101602
Telephone: (334) 222-6591 Carnegie Class: Assoc/Pub-R-S
FAX Number: (334) 881-2300 Calendar System: Semester
URL: www.lbwcc.edu
Established: 1969 Annual Undergrad Tuition & Fees (In-State): $3,960
Enrollment: 1,779 Coed
Affiliation or Control: State IRS Status: 501(c)3
Highest Offering: Associate Degree
Program: Occupational; 2-Year Principally Bachelor's Creditable; Technical Emphasis
Accreditation: SC, ADNUR, DMS, EMT, SURGT

01 President ....Dr. Herbert H. RIEDEL
05 Dean of Instruction ....Ms. Peggy LINTON
32 Dean of Student Affairs .... Ms. Judy H. HALL
10 Chief Financial Officer ....Mrs. Linda A. HARTIN
12 Vice Pres/Greenville Campus Direct ....Dr. James D. KRUDOP
103 Assoc Dean Adult Educ/Workforce Dev ....Mr. Jimmy HUTTO
14 Assoc Dean Instr/Info Technology .... Mr. Greg APLIN
15 Director of Human Resources ....Ms. Peige JOSEY
09 Dir Inst Effectiveness & Quality .... Mr. Terry ZHU
18 Dir College Facilities/Maintenance ....Mr. Tim JONES
07 Director Admissions & Records ....Ms. Jan RILEY
41 Athletic Director .... Mr. Steve HELMS
08 Director of Learning Resources .... Ms. Mary Beth GREEN
88 Director Student Support Services ....Ms. Patricia POWELL
88 Dir Upward Bound/Andalusia Camp Dir ..Mr. Bridges ANDERSON
21 Comptroller .... Ms. Lynne PATTERSON
37 Dir Financial Aid MacArthur/Luverne ....Ms. Wanda S. BASS
37 Dir Fin Aid Andalusia/Greenville ....Ms. Donna BASS
26 Public Info Officer/Dir Mktg & Dev ....Ms. Renee LEMAIRE

Marion Military Institute (G)

1101 Washington Street, Marion AL 36756-3213
County: Perry FICE Identification: 001026
Unit ID: 101648
Telephone: (800) 664-1842 Carnegie Class: Assoc/Pub-R-S
FAX Number: (334) 683-2380 Calendar System: Semester
URL: www.marionmilitary.edu
Established: 1842 Annual Undergrad Tuition & Fees (In-State): $6,700
Enrollment: 409 Coed
Affiliation or Control: State IRS Status: 501(c)3
Highest Offering: Associate Degree
Program: 2-Year Principally Bachelor's Creditable
Accreditation: SC

01 President ....Col. David J. MOLLAHAN
03 Executive Vice President .... Dr. Susan G. STEVENSON
10 Int VP for Finance & Business Affs ... Mrs. Jennifer C. BARNETTE
05 Academic Dean ....Mr. David TIPMORE
32 VP for Student Affairs & Commandant ....Col. Thomas L. TATE
30 VP for Institutional Advancement .... Mrs. Suzanne MCKEE
84 VP for Enrollment Mgmt ....LtCol. James G. LAKE
41 Director of Athletics ....Dr. Michelle IVEY
29 Director of Alumni Affairs ....Vacant
88 ROTC Professor of Military Science ....LtCol. Sean RYAN
09 Director of Institutional Research ....Mrs. Donna LEEMON
06 Registrar ....Mrs. Wanda CALAME
38 Director of Guidance .... Ms. Brenda A. COOK
37 Director of Financial Aid .... Ms. Jacqueline WILSON
08 Library Director .... Mrs. Kelly A. GRIFFITHS
18 Supt of Buildings & Grounds ....Mr. Brian HALE
17 Director of Health Services .... Mr. Brandon TAYLOR

Miles College (H)

5500 Myron Massey Boulevard, Fairfield AL 35064-2621
County: Jefferson FICE Identification: 001028
Unit ID: 101675
Telephone: (205) 929-1000 Carnegie Class: Bac/Diverse
FAX Number: (205) 929-1453 Calendar System: Semester
URL: www.miles.edu
Established: 1898 Annual Undergrad Tuition & Fees: $11,014
Enrollment: 1,668 Coed
Affiliation or Control: Christian Methodist Episcopal IRS Status: 501(c)3
Highest Offering: Baccalaureate
Program: Liberal Arts And General; Teacher Preparatory
Accreditation: SC, SW, TED

01 President ....Dr. George T. FRENCH, JR.
05 Dean Academic Affairs ....Dr. Emmanuel CHEKWA
100 Special Asst/Chief of Staff ....Mr. Kenneth COACHMAN
10 Chief Financial Ofcr/Business Affs ....Mrs. Diana W. KNIGHTON
07 Director Admissions &
Recruitment ....Mr. Christopher ROBERTSON
06 Registrar ....Ms. Jennifer WYCOFF
08 Librarian .... Dr. Geraldine BELL
30 Director Institutional Development ....Mr. W. Frank TOPPING
32 Dean Student Affairs ....Ms. Griena KNIGHT

36 Director Career Planning/Placement ... Dr. Glenda BROWN-WADE
26 Director College Relations ... Vacant
09 Dir Institutional Effective/Rsrch ... Dr. Ba-Shen WELCH
37 Director Financial Aid ... Mr. Percy LANIER
18 Director Physical Plant ... Mr. Edward JENKINS
25 Director Sponsored Programs ... Vacant
38 Dir Counseling/Advising/Testing ... Ms. Keisha LEWIS
29 Director Alumni Affairs ... Mr. Charles CROCKROM, SR.
15 Director Personnel Services ... Mrs. Verlanda TATE
42 Chaplain ... Rev. Larry BATIE
14 Manager of Data Processing ... Ms. Jackie HUDSON

Northeast Alabama Community College (A)

PO Box 159, 138 Alabama Highway 35, Rainsville AL 35986-0159

County: DeKalb/Jackson — FICE Identification: 001031
Unit ID: 101897
Telephone: (256) 638-4418 — Carnegie Class: Assoc/Pub-R-M
FAX Number: (256) 638-3052 — Calendar System: Semester
URL: www.nacc.edu
Established: 1963 — Annual Undergrad Tuition & Fees (In-State): $4,140
Enrollment: 3,296 — Coed
Affiliation or Control: State — IRS Status: 501(c)3
Highest Offering: Associate Degree
Program: Occupational; 2-Year Principally Bachelor's Creditable; Business Emphasis
Accreditation: SC, ADNUR, EMT, PNUR

01 President ... Dr. J. David CAMPBELL
05 Dean of Instruction ... Dr. Joseph D. BURKE
56 Dean of Extended Day Program ... Ms. Marilyn REECE
32 Dean of Student Services ... Ms. Tonie M. NIBLETT
11 Dean of Admin Services/Registrar ... Mr. Larry D. GUFFEY
37 Director of Financial Aid ... Mr. Nixon WILLMON
103 Dir Workforce Devel/Skills Training ... Mr. Mike KENNAMER
26 Chief Public Relations Officer ... Mrs. Debra A. BARRENTINE
07 Dir Admissions & Student Services ... Mrs. Tonie M. NIBLETT
09 Dir Instl Planning & Assessment ... Mr. Brad FRICKS
18 Chief Facilities/Physical Plant ... Mr. Kent JONES
06 Registrar/Chief Bus Ofcr/Dir Purchg ... Mr. Larry D. GUFFEY
30 Development Director ... Ms. Heather RICE
19 Director of Security ... Mr. Norman SMITH

Northwest - Shoals Community College (B)

800 George Wallace Boulevard, Muscle Shoals AL 35661-3205

County: Colbert — FICE Identification: 005697
Unit ID: 101736
Telephone: (256) 331-5200 — Carnegie Class: Assoc/Pub-R-M
FAX Number: (256) 331-5222 — Calendar System: Semester
URL: www.nwscc.edu
Established: 1963 — Annual Undergrad Tuition & Fees (In-State): $3,220
Enrollment: 4,312 — Coed
Affiliation or Control: State — IRS Status: 501(c)3
Highest Offering: Associate Degree
Program: Occupational; 2-Year Principally Bachelor's Creditable
Accreditation: SC, ADNUR, EMT

01 President ... Dr. Humphrey LEE
05 Vice President of Instruction ... Dr. Glenda COLAGROSS
10 Chief Fiscal Officer ... Mr. Paul MERRILL
35 Assoc Dean Students/Athletic Admin ... Mr. Charles TAYLOR
09 Assc Dean Instl Effect/Dist Ed/Dev ... Mr. John MCINTOSH
20 Assoc Dean Instructional Programs ... Dr. Timmy JAMES
30 Director of Foundation/Advancement ... Vacant
37 Director of Financial Aid ... Ms. Laurel TURBYFILL
07 Dir Recruitment/Admissions/Records ... Mr. Tom CARTER
15 Dir of HR/Senior Personnel Officer ... Ms. Pam TOWNSEND
29 Director of Alumni Relations ... Vacant
36 Director of the Career Center ... Ms. Linda WAIDE
14 Director of Management Info Systems ... Mr. Alan MITCHELL
19 Chief Safety Officer ... Vacant
07 Coordinator Admissions ... Vacant
103 Assoc Dean of Workforce Develop ... Ms. Rose JONES
21 Controller ... Ms. Janet JONES
88 Director of Adult Education ... Mr. Donnie SWEENEY
88 Dir College and Career Readiness ... Mr. Ed CARTER
88 Dir of Ready to Work ... Ms. Donna PECK

Oakwood University (C)

7000 Adventist Boulevard, NW, Huntsville AL 35896-0003

County: Madison — FICE Identification: 001033
Unit ID: 101912
Telephone: (256) 726-7000 — Carnegie Class: Bac/Diverse
FAX Number: (256) 726-8335 — Calendar System: Semester
URL: www.oakwood.edu
Established: 1896 — Annual Undergrad Tuition & Fees: $14,678
Enrollment: 2,006 — Coed
Affiliation or Control: Seventh-day Adventist — IRS Status: 501(c)3
Highest Offering: Master's
Program: Occupational; Liberal Arts And General; Teacher Preparatory
Accreditation: SC, ACBSP, DIETD, DIETI, NUR, SW, TED

01 President ... Dr. Leslie POLLARD
05 Provost & Sr Vice President ... Dr. Tim MCDONALD
20 Vice President Academic Affairs ... Dr. Garland DULAN
10 Vice President Financial Affairs ... Ms. Sabrina COTTON
32 Vice President Student Services ... Vacant
30 Vice President Development ... Vacant
13 Vice Pres Information Technology ... Vacant
20 Asst Vice Pres Academic Affairs ... Dr. Roy MALCOLM
21 Asst VP Financial Affs/Controller ... Mrs. Gail CALDWELL
35 Asst Vice Pres Student Services ... Mr. Philip NIXON
16 Director Human Resources ... Mrs. Sylvia GERMANY
25 Director Sponsored Programs ... Mrs. Marcia BURNETTE
26 Director Public Relations ... Mrs. Michelle SOLOMON
07 Director Enrollment Management ... Mrs. Joyce SMITH
37 Director Financial Aid ... Ms. Joylyn TROTMAN
06 Director Records ... Mrs. Shirley SCOTT
39 Residence Life Coordinator-Men ... Mr. Tracey HOLIDAY
08 Director Library Services ... Mrs. Paulette JOHNSON
09 Director Inst Effectiveness ... Mrs. Janis NEWBORN
18 Director Physical Plant ... Mr. Colins ALEXANDER
19 Director Security ... Mr. Lewis EAKINS
29 Director Alumni Relations ... Ms. Barbara STOVALL
36 Director Career Services & Testing ... Mrs. Sonia PAUL
38 Dir Counseling & Health Services ... Dr. Janice LEWIS-THOMAS
51 Dir Adult & Continuing Education ... Dr. Rachel WILLIAMS
42 Chaplain ... Mr. T. Marshall KELLY
46 Dir Research & Faculty Dev ... Vacant
89 Director Freshmen Studies ... Mr. James HUTCHINSON
50 Chair Business & Info Systems ... Vacant
53 Chair Education ... Dr. James MBYIRUKIRA
59 Chair Family & Consumer Sciences ... Dr. Marta SOVYANHADI
60 Chair English & Foreign Languages ... Dr. Derek BOWE
64 Chair Music ... Dr. Audley CHAMBERS
65 Chair Biological Sciences ... Dr. Safawo GULLO
65 Chair Chemistry ... Dr. Kenneth LAI HING
66 Chair Nursing ... Dr. Flora FLOOD
68 Chair Health & Physical Education ... Dr. Howard SHAW
70 Chair Social Work ... Dr. George ASHLEY
73 Chair Religion & Theology ... Dr. Agniel SAMSON
81 Chair Math & Computer Science ... Mrs. Kathleen DOBBINS
82 Chair History ... Dr. Ciro SEPULVEDA
83 Chair Psychology ... Dr. Howard WEEMS
60 Chair Communication ... Dr. Rennae ELLIOTT
96 Director Purchasing ... Mrs. Belita NEWBY

Prince Institute - Southeast (D)

7735 Atlanta Highway, Montgomery AL 36117-4231

County: Montgomery — FICE Identification: 022960
Unit ID: 101958
Telephone: (334) 271-1670 — Carnegie Class: Assoc/PrivFP
FAX Number: (334) 271-1671 — Calendar System: Quarter
URL: www.princeinstitute.edu
Established: 1976 — Annual Undergrad Tuition & Fees: $12,380
Enrollment: 122 — Coed
Affiliation or Control: Proprietary — IRS Status: Proprietary
Highest Offering: Associate Degree
Program: Occupational
Accreditation: ACICS

01 Director ... Mrs. Patricia L. HILL
05 Dean of Academic Affairs ... Ms. Ann C. SCHMIDT
03 Assistant Director ... Mrs. Candace H. SHEPHERD
37 Financial Aid Administrator ... Mr. Reginald JAMES
07 Admissions Representative ... Mrs. Sherry A. HILL

Reid State Technical College (E)

PO Box 588, Evergreen AL 36401-0588

County: Conecuh — FICE Identification: 005692
Unit ID: 101994
Telephone: (251) 578-1313 — Carnegie Class: Assoc/Pub-R-S
FAX Number: (251) 578-5355 — Calendar System: Semester
URL: www.rstc.edu
Established: 1966 — Annual Undergrad Tuition & Fees (In-State): $3,360
Enrollment: 698 — Coed
Affiliation or Control: State — IRS Status: 501(c)3
Highest Offering: Associate Degree
Program: Occupational; Technical Emphasis
Accreditation: COE

01 President ... Dr. Douglas M. LITTLES
05 Dean of Students & Instruction ... Dr. Tangela PURIFOY
103 Assoc Dean Workforce Development ... Dr. Alesia K. STUART
09 Assoc Dean for Institutional Effect ... Ms. Wilma Quarker SMITH
37 Director Financial Aid ... Ms. Christy GOODWIN
07 Dir of Recruiting/Retention/Plcmt ... Ms. Coretta BOYKIN
38 Director of Counseling ... Ms. Monica ROBINSON
21 Business Manager ... Mr. David J. RHODES
06 Registrar/Enrollment Management ... Ms. Vickie NICHOLSON

Remington College, Mobile Campus (F)

828 Downtowner Loop W, Mobile AL 36609-5404

County: Mobile — FICE Identification: 026055
Unit ID: 366535
Telephone: (251) 343-8200 — Carnegie Class: Assoc/PrivFP4
FAX Number: (251) 343-0577 — Calendar System: Quarter
URL: www.remingtoncollege.edu
Established: 1986 — Annual Undergrad Tuition & Fees: $30,900
Enrollment: 525 — Coed
Affiliation or Control: Proprietary — IRS Status: Proprietary
Highest Offering: Associate Degree
Program: Occupational; 2-Year Principally Bachelor's Creditable; Technical Emphasis
Accreditation: ACCSC

01 President ... Mr. Stephen M. BACKMAN
05 Director of Education ... Ms. Cindy MCMILLAN
37 Financial Aid Director ... Ms. Linda K. CALVANESE
07 Director of Admissions ... Mr. Brent MALVEAUX
36 Dir of Career Services & Placement ... Ms. Ellen JONES
06 Registrar ... Mr. Donald SCHERMERHORN
15 Director Personnel Services ... Ms. Kristy KING
26 Chief Public Relations Officer ... Ms. Kristy KING
35 Director Student Affairs ... Ms. Bonnie LEDBETTER

Samford University (G)

800 Lakeshore Drive, Birmingham AL 35229-0001

County: Jefferson — FICE Identification: 001036
Unit ID: 102049
Telephone: (205) 726-2011 — Carnegie Class: Master's M
FAX Number: (205) 726-2171 — Calendar System: 4/1/4
URL: www.samford.edu
Established: 1841 — Annual Undergrad Tuition & Fees: $25,150
Enrollment: 4,758 — Coed
Affiliation or Control: Southern Baptist — IRS Status: 501(c)3
Highest Offering: Doctorate
Program: Liberal Arts And General; Teacher Preparatory; Professional
Accreditation: SC, ANEST, BUS, CIDA, DIETD, LAW, MUS, NURSE, PHAR, TED, THEOL

01 President ... Dr. T. Andrew WESTMORELAND
03 Provost/Exec Vice President ... Dr. J. Bradley CREED
32 Vice President for Student Affairs ... Dr. Phil KIMREY
30 Vice President of Advancement ... Mr. W. Randall PITTMAN
10 Vice President Business Affairs ... Mr. Harry B. BROCK, III
11 Vice Pres Operations/Planning ... Dr. Sarah C. LATHAM
05 Associate Provost ... Dr. Mary Sue BALDWIN
20 Assistant Provost ... Dr. Nancy BIGGIO
04 Assistant to the President ... Dr. Michael D. MORGAN
13 Chief Information Officer ... Mr. David HAKANSON
21 Controller ... Mr. Mike DARWIN
41 Athletic Director ... Mr. Martin NEWTON
88 Dir of Ethics & Leadership ... Mr. John C. KNAPP
88 Director of Advancement Services ... Mrs. Judi F. AUCOIN
29 Director of Alumni ... Mr. David GOODWIN
44 Director of Planned Giving ... Mr. Stan DAVIS
88 Dir Orientation/Parent Prgm ... Ms. Kelia FURR
21 Director of Business Services ... Mr. Mike MCCORMACK
88 Director of Capital Planning & Imp ... Mr. David T. WHITT
88 Dir Event Management & Space Utiliz ... Vacant
18 Director of Facilities Management ... Mr. Mark FULLER
37 Director of Financial Aid ... Mr. Lane M. SMITH
15 Director of Human Resources ... Mr. Fred R. ROGAN
09 Director Inst Effectiveness ... Mrs. Karen G. HAMBY
104 Director of International Studies ... Dr. David SHIPLEY
43 Director Investments and Legal Svcs ... Ms. Lisa IMBRAGULIO
08 Director of Library ... Ms. Kimmetha D. HERNDON
30 Director of Univ Advancement ... Mr. Douglas WILSON
19 Director of Pub Safety & Emer Mgmt ... Mr. Wayne PITTMAN
39 Director Residence Life & Univ Svcs ... Ms. Lauren M. TAYLOR
88 Director of Risk Mmgt & Insurance ... Mr. James A. CLEMENT
10 Budget Director ... Mr. Matt DEFORE
102 Dir of Advancement ... Ms. Sharon SMITH
07 Dean of Admissions ... Mr. Jason BLACK
42 Assistant Dean for Spritual Life ... Dr. Matthew S. KERLIN
35 Assistant Dean of Student Services ... Mr. Garry L. ATKINS
35 Assistant Dean for Campus Life ... Ms. Renie MOSS
88 Dir Business Intelligence/Strategy ... Ms. Chez SHAEFFER
26 Dir Marketing & Communications ... Mr. Philip POOLE
88 Dir of University Fellows ... Mr. Bryan M. JOHNSON
53 Dean Education/Professional Studies ... Dr. Jean A. BOX
49 Dean Howard College Arts/Sciences ... Dr. David W. CHAPMAN
67 Dean McWhorter School of Pharmacy ... Dr. Charlie SANDS
73 Dean Beeson School of Divinity ... Dr. Timothy F. GEORGE
50 Dean Brock School of Business ... Dr. J. Howard FINCH
61 Dean Cumberland School of Law ... Dr. John L. CARROLL
66 Dean Ida Moffett School of Nursing ... Dr. Nena F. SANDERS
57 Dean School of the Arts ... Dr. Joseph HOPKINS

Selma University (H)

1501 Lapsley Street, Selma AL 36701-5232

County: Dallas — FICE Identification: 001037
Unit ID: 102058
Telephone: (334) 872-2533 — Carnegie Class: Spec/Faith
FAX Number: (334) 872-7746 — Calendar System: Semester
URL: www.selmauniversity.org
Established: 1878 — Annual Undergrad Tuition & Fees: $5,750
Enrollment: 547 — Coed
Affiliation or Control: Baptist — IRS Status: 501(c)3
Highest Offering: Master's
Program: Liberal Arts And General; Religious Emphasis
Accreditation: BI

01 President ... Dr. Alvin A. CLEVELAND, SR.
05 Dean ... Dr. Kayarda LOWE

Shelton State Community College (I)

9500 Old Greensboro Road, Tuscaloosa AL 35405-8522

County: Tuscaloosa — FICE Identification: 005691
Unit ID: 102067
Telephone: (205) 391-2211 — Carnegie Class: Assoc/Pub-R-L
FAX Number: (205) 391-2426 — Calendar System: Semester
URL: www.sheltonstate.edu
Established: 1953 — Annual Undergrad Tuition & Fees (In-State): $4,416

Enrollment: 5,013 Coed
Affiliation or Control: State IRS Status: 501(c)3
Highest Offering: Associate Degree
Program: Occupational; 2-Year Principally Bachelor's Creditable
Accreditation: SC, ADNUR, PNUR

01 President Dr. Mark A. HEINRICH
05 Dean of Academic Services Dr. Peggy Shaddock PALOMBI
26 Spec Asst to Pres for External Affs Ms. Camille P. COCHRANE
10 Comptroller Mrs. Ann BRACKNELL
32 Dean of Student Services Dr. Thomas HUEBNER
13 Dean Technology/Instl Rsrch Dr. Michelle JARRELL
12 Director Fredd Campus/Title III Mr. Ronald RANGE
20 Assoc Dn Trng Existing Bus/Industry Mr. Jason MOORE
06 Asst Dean Student Svcs/Registrar Mr. Byron ABSTON
76 Assistant Dean for Health Services Ms. Gladys HILL
37 Asst Dean Financial Aid Ms. Amanda HARBISON
84 Asst Dean Stdnt Support & Retention Dr. Fran TURNER
15 Director of Personnel Services Vacant
88 Director Special Projects Ms. Channing HOWINGTON
08 Director Library Services Dr. Debbie J. GRIMES
30 Director Institutional Advancement Vacant
103 Director Workforce Development Mr. Lew DRUMMOND
25 Director Grant/Resource Development Vacant
88 Director Adult Education Mr. Phillip JOHNSON
38 Counseling Center Coordinator Ms. Holly ELLIOTT
88 Dean of Technical Services Mr. Steve FAIR
88 Dean of Auxiliary Services Dr. Thomas TAYLOR

Snead State Community College (A)

PO Box 734, Boaz AL 35957-0734
County: Marshall FICE Identification: 001038
Unit ID: 102076
Telephone: (256) 593-5120 Carnegie Class: Assoc/Pub-R-M
FAX Number: (256) 593-7180 Calendar System: Semester
URL: www.snead.edu
Established: 1898 Annual Undergrad Tuition & Fees (In-State): $4,480
Enrollment: 2,417 Coed
Affiliation or Control: State IRS Status: Exempt
Highest Offering: Associate Degree
Program: Occupational; 2-Year Principally Bachelor's Creditable
Accreditation: SC, ADNUR

01 President Dr. Robert EXLEY
10 Chief Financial Officer Mr. Mark RICHARD
05 Chief Academic Officer Dr. Jason WATTS
13 Chief IT Officer Mr. Randy MALTBIE
26 Director of PR/Marketing Ms. Shelley SMITH
38 Director of Testing Ms. Jessamine HUFFMAN
07 Interim Chief Student Svcs Officer Mr. Jason CANNON
09 Assoc Dean Acad Planning/Research Dr. Annette CEDERHOLM
81 Science Division Director Ms. Deborah RHODEN
79 Humanities Division Director Dr. Cynthia DENHAM
83 Social Science Division Director Mr. Alan BATES
81 Mathematics Division Director Mr. Blake LEETH
50 Business Division Director Mr. Vann SCOTT
75 Technology Division Director Mr. Greg RANDALL
103 Director Community Education Ms. Teresa WALKER
76 Director Health Sciences Ms. Amy LANGLEY
41 Athletic Director Mr. Mark RICHARD
08 Head Librarian Mr. John MILLER
15 Director of Human Resources Ms. Arlene BROWN
18 Director of Physical Plant Mr. Steve WILLIAMS
37 Director of Financial Aid Mr. Steve SMITH

South University (B)

5355 Vaughn Road, Montgomery AL 36116-1120
County: Montgomery FICE Identification: 004463
Unit ID: 101116
Telephone: (334) 395-8800 Carnegie Class: Bac/Assoc
FAX Number: (334) 395-8859 Calendar System: Quarter
URL: www.southuniversity.edu
Established: 1887 Annual Undergrad Tuition & Fees: $16,125
Enrollment: 754 Coed
Affiliation or Control: Proprietary IRS Status: Proprietary
Highest Offering: Master's
Program: Occupational; 2-Year Principally Bachelor's Creditable; Professional
Accreditation: &SC, MAC, NURSE, PTAA

01 President Mr. Victor K. BIEBIGHAUSER
05 Dean of Academic Affairs Mr. Donald A. EDWARDS, JR.
32 Dean of Student Affairs Ms. Patricia MCCORMICK
37 Director of Financial Aid Ms. Yvonne R. MILLER
07 Director of Admissions Ms. Anna M. PEARSON

† Regional accreditation is carried under the parent institution in Savannah, GA.

Southeastern Bible College (C)

2545 Valleydale Road, Birmingham AL 35244-2083
County: Shelby FICE Identification: 022704
Unit ID: 102261
Telephone: (205) 970-9200 Carnegie Class: Spec/Faith
FAX Number: (205) 970-9207 Calendar System: Semester
URL: www.sebc.edu
Established: 1935 Annual Undergrad Tuition & Fees: $12,080
Enrollment: 175 Coed
Affiliation or Control: Independent Non-Profit IRS Status: 501(c)3
Highest Offering: Baccalaureate
Program: Liberal Arts And General; Religious Emphasis
Accreditation: BI

01 President Dr. Don HAWKINS
05 Vice President for Educ/Provost Dr. Vicki L. WOLFE
10 Vice President for Operations Mr. Paul WILLARD
32 Dean of Students Ms. Kristie HARRICK
42 Campus Pastor Mr. Micah SIMPSON
49 Chair Dept of Arts & Sciences Dr. Dwain WALDREP
53 Chair Dept of Education Dr. Lynn GANNETT-MALICK
73 Chair Dept of Biblical Studies Dr. Jason SNYDER
04 Admin Asst to the President Mrs. Anita SCROGGINS
06 Registrar Mr. Joel WOLFE
08 Director of Library Services Mr. Paul ROBERTS
09 Coordinator of Inst Effectiveness Mrs. Michelle HOWER
18 Facilities Director Mr. David POWLESS
37 Financial Aid Director Mr. Jay POWELL
55 Director of ACHIEVE Adult Educ Mr. Steven CLECKLER

Southern Union State Community College (D)

PO Box 1000, Wadley AL 36276-1000
County: Randolph FICE Identification: 001040
Unit ID: 251260
Telephone: (256) 395-2211 Carnegie Class: Assoc/Pub-R-M
FAX Number: (256) 395-2215 Calendar System: Semester
URL: www.suscc.edu
Established: 1922 Annual Undergrad Tuition & Fees (In-State): $3,840
Enrollment: 5,088 Coed
Affiliation or Control: State IRS Status: 501(c)3
Highest Offering: Associate Degree
Program: Occupational; 2-Year Principally Bachelor's Creditable
Accreditation: SC, ADNUR, EMT, RAD, SURGT

01 President Dr. Amelia PEARSON
05 Dean of Academics Dr. Mary Jean WHITE
32 Dean of Students Ms. Tiffany SANDERS
97 Assoc Dean of Instruction Mr. Steve SPRATLIN
72 Assoc Dean of Technology Mr. Darin BALDWIN
20 Assoc Dean Student Development Mr. Gary BRANCH
13 Director Management Info Systems Ms. Cherly JORDAN
41 Athletic Director Mr. Ron RADFORD
30 Director Institutional Advancement Vacant
06 Registrar Ms. Catherine STRINGFELLOW
26 Chief Public Relations Officer Ms. Shondae BROWN
10 Chief Business Officer Mr. Ben JORDAN
35 Coordinator of Student Life Ms. Lori DANIEL

Spring Hill College (E)

4000 Dauphin Street, Mobile AL 36608-1791
County: Mobile FICE Identification: 001041
Unit ID: 102234
Telephone: (251) 380-4000 Carnegie Class: Master's S
FAX Number: (251) 460-2182 Calendar System: Semester
URL: www.shc.edu
Established: 1830 Annual Undergrad Tuition & Fees: $29,450
Enrollment: 1,460 Coed
Affiliation or Control: Roman Catholic IRS Status: 501(c)3
Highest Offering: Master's
Program: Liberal Arts And General; Teacher Preparatory
Accreditation: SC, NURSE

01 President Rev. Richard P. SALMI, SJ
05 Provost/Vice Pres Academic Affairs Dr. George E. SIMS
10 Vice President Business & Finance Ms. Rhonda SHIRAZI
32 Vice Pres Student Affs/Dn Stdnts Mr. Joe DEIGHTON
20 Assistant VP for Academic Affairs Vacant
58 Assoc Provost Grad & Cont Studies Vacant
35 Associate Dean of Students Ms. Margarita PEREZ
07 Director of Admissions Vacant
21 Controller Vacant
37 Director of Financial Aid Mrs. Ellen FOSTER
06 Registrar Mr. Stuart MOORE
88 Director Student Development Center Ms. Josetta MULLOY
29 Director of Alumni & Parents Mrs. Monde DONALDSON
91 Director Administrative Computing Mr. Mac HORTON
90 Dir Information Technology Services Mr. Glenn R. BELL
16 Director of Personnel Ms. Patricia A. DAVIS
19 Director of Public Safety/Security Mr. Todd WARREN
23 Director of Health Services Mrs. Melissa MELTON
38 Counselor Ms. Lynda OLEN
42 Director of Campus Ministry Ms. Maureen BERGAN
40 Bookstore Manager Ms. Genevieve MORRIS
41 Director Athletics & Recreation Mr. James HALL
31 Dir Foley CommunityService Center Dr. Kathleen ORANGE
26 Dir Communications/Instl Mktng Mr. John KERR
36 Coordinator of Career Services Ms. Elizabeth DEXTER-WILSON

Stillman College (F)

3601 Stillman Boulevard, POB 1430, Tuscaloosa AL 35403-1430
County: Tuscaloosa FICE Identification: 001044
Unit ID: 102270
Telephone: (205) 349-4240 Carnegie Class: Bac/A&S
FAX Number: (205) 366-8996 Calendar System: Semester
URL: www.stillman.edu
Established: 1876 Annual Undergrad Tuition & Fees: $15,088
Enrollment: 1,072 Coed
Affiliation or Control: Presbyterian Church (U.S.A.) IRS Status: 501(c)3
Highest Offering: Baccalaureate
Program: Liberal Arts And General; Teacher Preparatory
Accreditation: SC, IACBE, MUS, NURSE, TED

01 President Dr. Ernest MCNEALEY
10 Vice President Fiscal Affairs Mr. Sama MONDEH
84 Vice President Retention Dr. Charlotte CARTER
32 Vice President for Students Affairs Dr. Sharon WHITTAKER-DAVIS
31 Vice Pres External Affairs Mr. Eddie B. THOMAS
30 Associate VP for Development Mr. Gregory EUBANKS
21 Asst Vice Pres/Business Manager Mrs. Lois GWINN
09 Director of Institutional Research Ms. Cynthia D. LEATHERWOOD
26 Asst Vice President/Marketing & PR Miss Veronica CLARK
29 Asst Vice Pres Alumni Affairs Mr. Renwick JONES
53 Dean of Professional Educ/Asst VP Dr. Linda BRADFORD
49 Dean of Arts & Sciences/Asst VP Dr. Mary Jane KROTZER
06 Registrar Mrs. Barbara SMITH
08 Dean of Library Mr. Robert HEATH
37 Director of Financial Aid Mrs. Jacqueline MORRIS
38 Director of Student Development Ctr Ms. Jacqueline CURRIE
13 Director of Info Tech Mr. Dominic MURUAKO
07 Director of Admissions Mrs. Victoria BOMAN
19 Chief of Campus Police Mr. James TAGGART
41 Athletic Director Mr. Curtis CAMPBELL
15 Human Resources Director Mrs. Patricia WILSON
42 College Chaplain Dr. Mark MCCORMICK

Talladega College (G)

627 W Battle Street, Talladega AL 35160-2354
County: Talladega FICE Identification: 001046
Unit ID: 102298
Telephone: (256) 362-0206 Carnegie Class: Bac/A&S
FAX Number: (256) 761-9206 Calendar System: Semester
URL: www.talladega.edu
Established: 1867 Annual Undergrad Tuition & Fees: $17,996
Enrollment: 702 Coed
Affiliation or Control: Independent Non-Profit IRS Status: 501(c)3
Highest Offering: Baccalaureate
Program: Liberal Arts And General; Teacher Preparatory; Professional; Business Emphasis
Accreditation: SC, SW

01 President Dr. Billy C. HAWKINS
05 Provost/Vice Pres Academic Affairs Dr. Evelyn M. WHITE
10 Vice President of Finance and Admin Dr. Gerald WILLIAMS
32 Vice President Student Affairs Mrs. Jacqueline PADDIO
30 Vice Pres Institutional Advancement Vacant
18 Director Facilities Management Mr. Gary LAWSON
26 Director of Public Relations Vacant
37 Director Financial Aid Mrs. Russelle KEESE
07 Director of Admissions Mr. Charles HANKS
09 Director of Institutional Research Vacant
32 Director of Student Activities Mr. Anthony JONES
41 Athletic Director Mr. Wilberto RAMOS
08 Librarian Dr. Joseph MCDONALD
14 Information Technology Director Mr. Quintin LATIN
36 Director of Career Placement Ms. Delores TRAYLOR
40 Materials Management/Convenience St Ms. Sharonda HUTCHINSON
15 Director of Human Resources Mrs. Brenda RHODEN
19 Chief Campus Police Mr. Jefferson WALKER
50 Dean Div Administration & Business Mr. Eric HELVY
79 Dean Div Humanities/Fine Arts Vacant
81 Dean Div of Natural Sci/Math Dr. Charlie STINSON
83 Dean Div EWJ Social Sciences/Educ Dr. Lisa LONG
23 Health Services on Campus Mrs. Valarie ALFRED
25 Title III Coor/Grants Administrator Mrs. Nicola LAWLER
29 Director Alumni Relations Vacant
06 Registrar Mr. Lindsey BARNETTE
38 Director Student Counseling Ms. Delores TRAYLOR

Trenholm State Technical College (H)

PO Box 10048, Montgomery AL 36108
County: Montgomery FICE Identification: 005734
Unit ID: 102313
Telephone: (334) 420-4200 Carnegie Class: Assoc/Pub-R-S
FAX Number: (334) 420-4206 Calendar System: Semester
URL: www.trenholmstate.edu
Established: 1963 Annual Undergrad Tuition & Fees (In-State): $4,860
Enrollment: 1,721 Coed
Affiliation or Control: State IRS Status: 501(c)3
Highest Offering: Associate Degree
Program: Occupational; 2-Year Principally Bachelor's Creditable; Technical Emphasis
Accreditation: COE, ACFEI, DA, DMS, EMT, MAC, PNUR, RAD

01 President Mr. Samuel MUNNERLYN
10 Dean of Finance/Administrative Svcs Ms. Deborah GRIGGS
05 Dean of Instruction Ms. Barbara A. SPEARS
30 Dean of Development Dr. Suresh C. KAUSHIK
32 Dean of Students Ms. Beverly ROSS
103 Dean of Workforce Development Mr. Wilford HOLT
13 Assoc Dean of IT Mr. Charles HARRIS
09 Director of Institutional Research Dr. Mimi JOHNSON
18 Director Physcial Facilities Mr. Dennis MONROE
37 Director Student Financial Aid Ms. Betty EDWARDS
07 Director of Admissions/Registrar Mrs. Tennie S. MCBRYDE
27 Public Information Officer Mr. Michael EVANS
15 Director of Human Resources Ms. Pam ROLLINS
51 Dir Title III/Marketing/Cont Educ Ms. Arlinda KNIGHT
36 Coordinator Job Placement Ms. Benee EDWARDS

Troy University (A)

University Avenue, Troy AL 36082-0001

County: Pike FICE Identification: 001047
Unit ID: 102368
Telephone: (334) 670-3100 Carnegie Class: Master's L
FAX Number: (334) 670-3774 Calendar System: Semester
URL: www.troy.edu
Established: 1887 Annual Undergrad Tuition & Fees (In-State): $6,844
Enrollment: 27,270 Coed
Affiliation or Control: State IRS Status: 501(c)3
Highest Offering: Doctorate
Program: Liberal Arts And General; Teacher Preparatory; Professional
Accreditation: SC, ACBSP, ADNUR, CACREP, CORE, ENGR, MUS, NUR, SPAA, SW, TED

Code	Title	Name
01	Chancellor	Dr. Jack HAWKINS, JR.
05	Sr Vice Chanc for Academic Affairs	Dr. Earl INGRAM
32	Sr Vice Chanc Student Svcs/Admin	Dr. John R. DEW
30	Sr Vice Chanc Advance/External Affs	Dr. John SCHMIDT
10	Sr VC for Finance & Business Affs	Dr. James BOOKOUT
12	Vice Chancellor Troy Global Campus	Dr. Lance TATUM
12	Vice Chancellor Troy Dothan	Dr. Don JEFFREY
12	Vice Chancellor Troy Phenix City	Dr. David WHITE
35	Dean of Student Svcs Troy Dothan	Mr. Bob WILLIS
49	Assoc Dean Col Arts/Sci Troy Dothan	Dr. Robert SAUNDERS
50	Assoc Dean Col Bus Troy Dothan	Dr. Orrin AMES
53	Assoc Dean Col of Educ Troy Dothan	Dr. Robin BYNUM
12	Vice Chanc Troy Montgomery	Mr. Ray WHITE
49	Assoc Dean Arts/Sci Troy Montgomery	Dr. Fred BEATTY
53	Assoc Dean Col Educ Troy Montgomery	Dr. Pamela ARRINGTON
30	Assoc Vice Chanc for Development	Dr. Jean LALIBERTE
37	Assoc Vice Chanc for Financial Aid	Ms. Carol BALLARD
20	Associate Provost for Academics	Dr. Lee VARDAMAN
27	Assoc VC for Mktg/Communication	Mrs. Donna SCHUBERT
06	Registrar	Mrs. Vickie MILES
84	Dean Enrollment Services	Mr. Buddy STARLING
08	Dean Library Services	Dr. Henry STEWART
15	Senior Director Human Resources	Dr. Toni TAYLOR
13	Chief Technology Officer	Mr. Greg PRICE
26	Director University Relations	Mr. Tom DAVIS
29	Director Alumni Affairs	Ms. Faith W. WARD
36	Coordinator Career Services	Ms. Lauren COLE
18	Director Facilities/Physical Plant	Mr. Mark SALMON
60	Director of Journalism	Dr. Steven PADGETT
04	Exec Assistant to the Chancellor	Mr. Dave BARRON
38	Director Student Counseling	Ms. Teresa P. RODGERS
07	Director of Graduate Admissions	Mrs. Brenda CAMPBELL
88	Dir Not for Profit/Assoc Controller	Mrs. Lauri DORRILL
106	eTROY Dir Educational Technology	Mr. Ronnie CREEL
86	Director of Federal/State Govt Rels	Mr. Marcus PARAMORE
86	Dir of Local Governmental Relations	Mr. Alan BOOTHE
44	Director of Annual Giving	Mrs. Bronda DENISON
25	Director Sponsored Programs	Mrs. Judy FULMER
62	Dir of Library Svcs Troy Dothan	Mr. Chris SHAFFER
62	Dir of Library Svcs Troy Montgomery	Mr. Kent SNOWDEN
20	Dean Undergrad Pgms/Assoc Provost	Dr. Hal FULMER
35	Dean of Student Svcs Troy Campus	Mr. Herbert REEVES
49	Dean Arts & Sciences	Dr. James RINEHART
50	Dean Business	Dr. Judson EDWARDS
53	Interim Dean Education	Dr. Don JEFFREY
58	Dean Graduate Pgms/Assoc Provost	Dr. Dianne BARRON
76	Dean Health/Human Services	Dr. Damon ANDREW
57	Dean Communication/Fine Arts	Dr. Maryjo COCHRAN
35	Assoc Dean Student Svcs Troy Mont	Dr. James SMITH
35	Assoc Dean Student Svcs Troy Phenix	Mr. Jack MILLER
50	Assoc Dean Col Bus Troy Montgomery	Dr. Anthony RHEE

Tuskegee University (B)

Tuskegee AL 36088

County: Macon FICE Identification: 001050
Unit ID: 102377
Telephone: (334) 727-8011 Carnegie Class: Bac/Diverse
FAX Number: (334) 727-5276 Calendar System: Semester
URL: www.tuskegee.edu
Established: 1881 Annual Undergrad Tuition & Fees: $17,870
Enrollment: 3,152 Coed
Affiliation or Control: Independent Non-Profit IRS Status: 501(c)3
Highest Offering: Doctorate
Program: Liberal Arts And General; Teacher Preparatory; Professional
Accreditation: SC, BUS, DIETD, ENG, MT, NUR, #OT, SW, TED, VET

Code	Title	Name
01	President	Dr. Gilbert L. ROCHON
05	Provost	Dr. Luther S. WILLIAMS
10	Chief Financial Officer	Mr. Cecil LUCY
46	Vice Pres Sponsored Pgms/Research	Dr. Shaik JEELANI
30	Vice Pres for Development	Ms. Cheryl M. THOMAS
84	VP Student Affairs/Enrollment Mgmt	Dr. Cynthia SELLERS
101	Exec Asst to Pres/Secy to the Board	Mrs. Verna S. LITTLE
13	Chief Information Officer	Mr. Fred JUDKINS
45	Asst VP & Dir Budget & Planning	Ms. Belinda HOGUE
20	Assoc Provost & Director Intl Pgms	Dr. Eloise CARTER
49	Dean School of Education	Dr. Carlton E. MORRIS
47	Dean Agric/Enviro/Nutrition Sci	Dr. Walter A. HILL
50	Int Dean Col Business/Orgnztn/Mgmt	Dr. Tejnder SARA
54	Dean Col Engr/Architecture/Phys Sci	Dr. Legand L. BURGE
74	Dean Col Vet Med/Nurs/Allied Health	Dr. Tsegaye HABTEMARIAM
08	Director of Library Services	Mrs. Juanita ROBERTS
29	Alumni Affairs Director	Ms. Kimberly WOODARD
86	Director Federal Relations	Mrs. Willa HALL SMITH
42	Dean of the Chapel	Dr. Gregory S. GRAY
26	VP Communications/Public Rels/Mktg	Mr. Kevin J. MCLIN, SR.
51	Int Assoc Prov Cont Educ/Extension	Dr. Ntam BAHARANYI
36	Assoc Dir Career Devel/Placement	Ms. Sarah STRINGER
21	Bursar	Ms. Barbara CHISHOLM
37	Director of Financial Aid	Mr. A. D. JAMES
09	Assoc Dir Inst Analysis/Evaluation	Mr. Willie J. JACKSON
15	Director Personnel Services	Ms. Kathy WEBB
18	Project Mgr Sodexho/Physical Plant	Mr. Tony WARD
91	Director of Applications Support	Mr. James E. COOPER
06	Registrar	Mrs. Edrice LEFTWICH
38	Director Student Counseling	Dr. Joyce RHODEN
96	Director of Purchasing	Vacant

United States Sports Academy (C)

One Academy Drive, Daphne AL 36526-7055

County: Baldwin FICE Identification: 021706
Unit ID: 102395
Telephone: (251) 626-3303 Carnegie Class: Spec/Other
FAX Number: (251) 626-3874 Calendar System: Semester
URL: www.ussa.edu
Established: 1972 Annual Undergrad Tuition & Fees: $8,520
Enrollment: 571 Coed
Affiliation or Control: Independent Non-Profit IRS Status: 501(c)3
Highest Offering: Doctorate
Program: Professional
Accreditation: SC

Code	Title	Name
01	President	Dr. Thomas P. ROSANDICH
05	Vice President & CAO	Dr. Thomas J. ROSANDICH
20	Dean of Academic Affairs	Dr. Marion W. EVANS
10	Dean of Admin & Finance	Ms. Holly H. MCLELLAN
32	Director of Student Services	Dr. Timothy FOLEY
51	Assoc Dn Cont Ed/Distance Learning	Ms. Betsy R. SMITH
27	Director of Communications	Mr. Duwayne ESCOBEDO
06	Registrar	Ms. Sarah COLE
08	Director of Library/Archivist	Mr. Greg TYLER
37	Director of Financial Aid	Vacant
18	Building and Grounds	Mr. Matthew COPE

*University of Alabama System Office (D)

401 Queen City Avenue, Tuscaloosa AL 35401-1551

County: Tuscaloosa FICE Identification: 008004
Unit ID: 100733
Telephone: (205) 348-5861 Carnegie Class: N/A
FAX Number: (205) 348-9788
URL: www.uasystem.ua.edu

Code	Title	Name
01	Chancellor	Dr. Robert E. WITT
101	Sec Board & Exec Asst to Chanc	Mr. Michael A. BOWNES
05	Vice Chancellor Academic Affairs	Dr. Charles R. NASH
10	Vice Chancellor Financial Affairs	Mr. Ray HAYES
26	Vice Chancellor System Relations	Mrs. Kellee C. REINHART
43	General Counsel	Mr. R. Cooper SHATTUCK
21	General Auditor	Ms. Sabrina B. HEARN

*The University of Alabama (E)

Tuscaloosa AL 35487-0100

County: Tuscaloosa FICE Identification: 001051
Unit ID: 100751
Telephone: (205) 348-6010 Carnegie Class: RU/H
FAX Number: (205) 348-9046 Calendar System: Semester
URL: www.ua.edu
Established: 1831 Annual Undergrad Tuition & Fees (In-State): $11,475
Enrollment: 33,602 Coed
Affiliation or Control: State IRS Status: 501(c)3
Highest Offering: Doctorate
Program: Liberal Arts And General; Teacher Preparatory; Professional
Accreditation: SC, AAFCS, ART, BUS, BUSA, CACREP, CEA, CIDA, CLPSY, CORE, CS, DANCE, DIETC, DIETD, ENG, JOUR, LAW, LIB, MUS, NURSE, SP, SW, TED, THEA

Code	Title	Name
02	President	Dr. Guy BAILEY
05	Provost/Executive Vice President	Dr. Judy L. BONNER
10	Vice Pres for Financial Affairs	Dr. Lynda GILBERT
30	Interim Vice Pres for Advancement	Dr. Karen BALDWIN
46	Vice President for Research	Dr. Joe BENSON
32	Vice Pres for Student Affairs	Dr. Mark NELSON
31	Vice Pres for Community Affairs	Dr. Samory T. PRUITT
14	Vice Provost/Chief Information Ofcr	Dr. John MCGOWAN
18	Assistant VP University Facilities	Mr. Duane LAMB
18	Ast VP Univ Facilities/Construction	Mr. Tim LEOPARD
19	Asst Vice Pres Public Safety	Mr. W. Steven TUCKER
20	Vice Provost Academic Affairs	Dr. Mark NELSON
11	Asst Provost for Administration	Ms. Dorothy J. MARTIN
15	Assoc Vice Pres Human Resources	Ms. Charlotte M. HARRIS
21	Assoc Vice President for Finance	Ms. Reba J. ESSARY
21	Assoc Vice Pres Financial Affairs	Ms. Dana S. KEITH
26	Asst VP University Relations	Ms. Deborah LANE
29	Asst VP for Alumni Affs/Annual Fund	Mr. Calvin BROWN
85	Asst VP Internatl Ed/Global Affairs	Dr. Teresa WISE
06	University Registrar	Mr. W. Michael GEORGE
09	Director Inst Research/Assessment	Dr. Lorne KUFFELL
36	Exec Director of Career Center	Mr. Travis RAILSBACK
07	Dir of Undergraduate Admissions	Ms. Mary K. SPIEGEL
22	Dir & University Compliance Officer	Ms. Gwendolyn D. HOOD
11	Chief Admin Officer CCHS/RSHC	Mr. John B. MAXWELL, JR.
37	Director of Student Financial Aid	Ms. Helen ALLEN
84	Director Enrollment Management	Mrs. Terri TERRY
39	Director Dept of Housing/Res Cmty	Dr. Steven HOOD
40	Director of University Supply Store	Ms. Teresa SHREVE
41	Athletic Director	Mr. Mal M. MOORE
43	University Counsel	Mr. George B. GORDON
08	Dean of University Libraries	Dr. Louis A. PITSCHMANN
49	Dean of Arts & Sciences	Dr. Robert F. OLIN
50	Dean Col Commerce & Business Admin	Dr. J. Michael HARDIN
51	Dean College of Continuing Studies	Dr. Carolyn C. DAHL
53	Dean College of Education	Dr. James E. MCLEAN
54	Dean College of Engineering	Dr. Charles L. KARR
58	Dean Graduate School/Asst Acad VP	Dr. David A. FRANCKO
59	Dean Human Environmental Sciences	Dr. Milla BOSCHUNG
60	Dean Col of Communication/Info Sci	Dr. Loy SINGLETON
61	Dean School of Law	Mr. Kenneth C. RANDALL
62	Dir Sch of Library/Info Studies	Dr. Heidi JULIEN
38	Manager Stdnt Support Svcs-Trio Pgm	Ms. Wendy L. COGBURN
96	Asc Purchasing Mgr Genl Procurement	Ms. Pollye HARDY
96	Asc Purchas Mgr Facil Procurement	Mr. Lane COX
76	Dean Cmty Health Sciences	Dr. Rick STREIFFER
66	Dean Capstone College of Nursing	Dr. Sara E. BARGER
70	Interim Dean School of Social Work	Dr. Lucinda L. ROFF
92	Dean of Honors College	Dr. Shane SHARPE
94	Chair of Women's Studies	Dr. DoVeanna F. MINOR

*University of Alabama at Birmingham (F)

1720 2nd Avenue South, Birmingham AL 35294-0001

County: Jefferson FICE Identification: 001052
Unit ID: 100663
Telephone: (205) 934-4011 Carnegie Class: RU/VH
FAX Number: N/A Calendar System: Semester
URL: www.uab.edu
Established: 1969 Annual Undergrad Tuition & Fees (In-State): $6,798
Enrollment: 17,575 Coed
Affiliation or Control: State IRS Status: 501(c)3
Highest Offering: Doctorate
Program: Liberal Arts And General; Teacher Preparatory; Professional
Accreditation: SC, ANEST, ARCPA, ART, BUS, BUSA, CACREP, CLPSY, CORE, CS, CYTO, DENT, DIETI, ENG, HSA, IPSY, MED, MT, MUS, NMT, NURSE, OPT, OPTR, OT, PH, PTA, SPAA, SW, TED, THEA

Code	Title	Name
02	President	Dr. Carol Z. GARRISON
05	Provost	Dr. Linda C. LUCAS
10	Vice Pres Financial Affairs/Admin	Mr. Richard L. MARGISON
17	CEO UAB Health System	Dr. Will FERNIANY
30	Vice Pres Dev/Alumni/External Rels	Dr. Shirley S. KAHN
13	Int Vice Pres Info Technology	Dr. Doug RIGNEY
28	Vice Pres for Equity and Diversity	Dr. Louis DALE
46	Vice Pres for Research/Economic Dev	Dr. Richard B. MARCHASE
63	Vice Pres/Dean School of Medicine	Dr. Ray L. WATTS
11	Vice Prov Admin/Quality Improvement	Mr. Harlan M. SANDS
20	Vice Prov Student/Faculty Success	Dr. Suzanne E. AUSTIN
43	University Counsel	Mr. W. John DANIEL
49	Dean College of Arts & Sciences	Dr. Thomas DILORENZO
50	Dean School of Business	Dr. David R. KLOCK
52	Dean School of Dentistry	Dr. Michael S. REDDY
53	Dean School of Education	Dr. Deborah L. VOLTZ
54	Interim Dean School of Engineering	Dr. Melinda M. LALOR
76	Dean School of Health Professions	Dr. Harold P. JONES
66	Dean School of Nursing	Dr. Doreen C. HARPER
88	Dean School of Optometry	Dr. Rodney NOWAKOWSKI
69	Dean School of Public Health	Dr. Max MICHAEL, III
58	Dean Graduate School	Dr. Bryan D. NOE
18	Assoc Vice President Facilities	Mr. Brooks H. BAKER, III
21	Assoc VP Business/Auxillary Svcs	Mr. Christopher CLIFFORD
29	Assoc VP Alumni/Annual Giving	Ms. Rebecca WATSON
44	Asst Vice Pres Development	Mr. Alton WHITT
26	Assoc VP Public Relations & Mktg	Ms. Dale TURNBOUGH
84	Assoc Provost Enrollment Management	Dr. Brent GAGE
21	Assoc Vice Pres Financial Affairs	Ms. Patricia A. RACZYNSKI
35	Asst Vice Pres for Student Life	Mr. Andrew J. MARSCH, III
08	Director Mervyn Sterne Library	Dr. Jerry W. STEPHENS
08	Director Lister Hill Library	Mr. Scott PLUTCHAK
41	Athletic Director	Mr. Brian W. MACKIN
15	Chief Human Resources Officer	Ms. Alesia M. JONES
09	Associate Director Inst Research	Ms. Mary Beth ADAMS
19	Assistant VP & Chief of Police	Mr. Anthony B. PURCELL
07	Director Undergraduate Admissions	Mr. Kirk KLUVER
88	Exec Director Enrollment Operation	Ms. Chenise RYAN
37	Director of Financial Aid	Ms. Janet B. MAY
06	University Registrar	Ms. Tina COLLINS
39	Director Student Housing/Resid Life	Mr. Marc BOOKER
36	Exective Director Career Services	Ms. Suzanne SCOTT-TRAMMELL

*University of Alabama in Huntsville (G)

301 Sparkman Drive, Huntsville AL 35899-1911

County: Madison FICE Identification: 001055
Unit ID: 100706
Telephone: (256) 824-1000 Carnegie Class: RU/VH
FAX Number: (256) 824-6073 Calendar System: Semester
URL: www.uah.edu
Established: 1950 Annual Undergrad Tuition & Fees (In-State): $8,794
Enrollment: 7,629 Coed
Affiliation or Control: State IRS Status: 501(c)3
Highest Offering: Doctorate
Program: Liberal Arts And General; Teacher Preparatory; Professional

Accreditation: SC, ART, BUS, CS, ENG, MUS, NURSE, TED

Code	Title	Name
02	President	Dr. Robert A. ALTENKIRCH
05	Provost & Exec VP Academic Affairs	Dr. Vistasp KARBHARI
10	VP Finance & Administration	Mr. Ray PINNER
28	VP Diversity	Ms. Delois SMITH
30	Interim VP University Advancement	Mr. Ray PINNER
46	VP Research	Vacant
43	University Counsel	Mr. Robert W. RIEDER, JR.
20	Assoc Provost UG Studies/Inst Effec	Dr. Brent M. WREN
08	Interim Dean Library	Dr. David P. MOORE
58	Dean Graduate Studies	Dr. Rhonda K. GAEDE
66	Dean College of Nursing	Dr. C. Fay RAINES
81	Dean College of Science	Dr. John FIX
79	Dean College of Liberal Arts	Mr. Glenn DASHER
32	Dean of Students/Assoc VP Stdnt Aff	Dr. Regina G. HYATT
54	Dean College of Engineering	Dr. Shankar MAHALINGAM
50	Dean College Business Admin	Dr. Caron ST. JOHN
88	Assoc VP Research	Dr. Thomas M. KOSHUT
29	Assoc VP for Advancement-Alumni Rel	Mr. Joel C. LONERGAN
29	Assoc VP Advancement	Ms. April HARRIS
39	Assoc VP Auxiliary Services	Mr. John MAXON
18	Asst VP Facilities & Operations	Mr. Michael S. FINNEGAN
11	Asst VP Finance & Business Services	Mr. Robert LEONARD
21	Associate VP Budgets & Fin Planning	Mr. Chih LOO
84	Assist Provost Enrollment Services	Ms. Ingrid HAYES
102	Asst VP Corporate Relations	Mr. Joe VALLELY
88	Asst VP Human Resources	Ms. Laurel LONG
06	Registrar	Ms. Janet WALLER
13	Interim CIO	Dr. John P. MCGOWAN
09	Director Institutional Research	Ms. Deborah STOWERS
88	Interim Director CAO	Dr. Pat REARDON
88	Dir Center Space Plsm & Aeron Res	Dr. Gary ZANK
88	Interim Director Propulsion Res	Dr. Robert FREDERICK
88	Dir Ctr for Mgmt of Science & Tech	Dr. P. J. BALLENGER
88	Director Research Institute	Dr. Richard G. RHOADES
88	Director CMSA	Dr. Mikel D. PETTY
88	Director Institute for Science Educ	Dr. James A. MILLER
88	Director ITSC	Dr. Sara J. GRAVES
88	Director Lab for Structural Biology	Dr. Edward J. MEEHAN
88	Dir Small Business Develop Center	Mr. Ralph F. PERRY
88	Exec Dir Center for System Studies	Dr. Michael D. GRIFFIN
88	Director SMAP Center	Dr. Gary MADDUX
88	Acting Director Rotocraft Center	Ms. Susan O'BRIEN
104	Director Global Studies Program	Dr. David JOHNSON
88	Director Earth Systems Science Ctr	Dr. John R. CHRISTY
88	Int Dir Ctr Mgmt & Econ Research	Mr. Jeff S. THOMPSON
88	Director Humanities Center	Dr. Brian J. MARTINE
92	Director Honors Program	Dr. Harry S. DELUGACH
85	Dir Office of International Pgms	Dr. John R. POTTENGER
37	Director Financial Aid	Mr. Andrew M. WEAVER
51	Director Div Continuing Education	Dr. Karen CLANTON
41	Director Intercollegiate Athletics	Dr. William E. BROPHY, JR.
88	Exec Dir Student Success Center	Vacant
38	Dir Student Counseling Svcs	Dr. Larry CANTOR
89	Director Freshman Year Experience	Dr. Carylyn I. SANDERS
29	Director Alumni Relations	Ms. Rachel V. OSBY
30	Director Advancement	Ms. Marcie T. EPPLING
23	Director Student Health Services	Ms. Kathleen S. RHODES
86	Director Public Affairs	Mr. Ray GARNER
21	Director Internal Audit	Ms. Tharanee M. RAVINDRAN
88	Director University Center	Mr. William M. HALL
19	Director Public Safety	Mr. Michael R. SNELLGROVE
25	Director Sponsored Programs	Ms. Gloria GREENE
91	Director Administrative Computing	Mr. Malcolm RICE
07	Director Admissions	Ms. Sandra BARINOWSKI
93	Coord Undergrad Minority Mentor Pgm	Ms. Rosemary ROBINSON
23	Dir Family Staff Clinic	Ms. Louise O'KEEFE
40	Bookstore Manager	Ms. Amber YOUNG

University of Mobile (A)

5735 College Parkway, Mobile AL 36613-2842

County: Mobile FICE Identification: 001029
Unit ID: 101693

Telephone: (251) 675-5990 Carnegie Class: Bac/Diverse
FAX Number: (251) 675-6293 Calendar System: Semester
URL: www.umobile.edu
Established: 1961 Annual Undergrad Tuition & Fees: $17,110
Enrollment: 1,734 Coed
Affiliation or Control: Southern Baptist IRS Status: 501(c)3
Highest Offering: Master's
Program: 2-Year Principally Bachelor's Creditable; Liberal Arts And General; Teacher Preparatory; Professional
Accreditation: SC, ACBSP, ADNUR, MUS, NURSE

Code	Title	Name
01	President	Dr. Mark R. FOLEY
05	Vice Pres for Academic Affairs	Dr. Audrey C. EUBANKS
10	Vice President for Business Affairs	Mr. J. Steve LEE
30	VP Institutional Advancement	Mr. Brian BOYLE
84	VP Enrollment Svcs/Campus Life	Mrs. Kim LEOUSIS
44	Dir of Development for Major Gifts	Mrs. Hali GIVENS
20	Associate VP for Academic Affairs	Dr. Anne B. LOWERY
21	Associate VP for Business Affairs	Mrs. Carol CAMP
20	Assoc VP Academic Svcs/Registrar	Dr. Donald K. BERRY
84	Assoc VP for Enrollment Services	Ms. Marie BATSON
04	Assistant to the President	Dr. Fred G. LACKEY
26	Executive Director of Marketing	Ms. Lesa MOORE
41	Athletic Director	Mr. Joe NILAND
07	Director of Enrollment Services	Mrs. Charity WITTNER
08	Director of Library Services	Mr. Jeffrey D. CALAMETTI
27	Director of Media Relations	Mrs. Kathy L. DEAN
09	Director of Inst Effectiveness	Dr. Anne B. LOWERY
50	Dean School of Business	Dr. Jane FINLEY
49	Dean College of Arts & Sciences	Dr. Dwight STEEDLEY
53	Dean School of Education	Dr. Peter KINGSFORD
66	Dean School of Nursing	Dr. Jan WOOD
64	Dean School of Music	Dr. Al MILLER
88	Dean Sch of Worship Leadership	Dr. Al MILLER
88	Exec Dean Sch of Christian Ministry	Dr. Joe SAVAGE
51	Dean Center for Adult Programs	Dr. Pam BUCHANAN
73	Dean School of Christian Ministries	Dr. Doug WILSON
58	Dean of Graduate Programs	Dr. Anne B. LOWERY
39	Director of Residential Life	Mr. Kris NELSON
29	Director Alumni/Parent Relations	Mrs. Hali GIVENS
90	Director Academic Computing Lab	Mr. Mitch DAVIS
42	Director of Campus Ministries	Mr. Neal LEDBETTER
15	Director of Human Resources	Mrs. Diane BLACK
13	Director of Information Technology	Mr. Buck NORRED
18	Director of Campus Operations	Mrs. Vicki BURGIN
38	Director Student Retention	Mrs. Shirley SUTTERFIELD
88	Exec Dir Col of Christian Leadershp	Dr. Roger BRELAND

University of Montevallo (B)

Station 6001, Montevallo AL 35115-6001

County: Shelby FICE Identification: 001004
Unit ID: 101709

Telephone: (205) 665-6000 Carnegie Class: Master's M
FAX Number: (205) 665-6003 Calendar System: Semester
URL: www.montevallo.edu
Established: 1896 Annual Undergrad Tuition & Fees (In-State): $9,120
Enrollment: 3,067 Coed
Affiliation or Control: State IRS Status: 501(c)3
Highest Offering: Beyond Master's But Less Than Doctorate
Program: Liberal Arts And General; Teacher Preparatory; Professional
Accreditation: SC, AAFCS, ART, BUS, CACREP, DIETD, MUS, SP, SW, TED

Code	Title	Name
01	President	Dr. John W. STEWART, III
05	Provost and VP Academic Affairs	Dr. Suzanne OZMENT
32	Dean of Students	Dr. Tammi DAHLE
30	VP for Enrollment Management	Dr. Rick BARTH
10	VP Business Affairs	Ms. DeAnna M. SMITH
11	Sr VP for Administratiave Affairs	Dr. Michelle JOHNSTON
18	Director Physical Plant	Mr. Billy HUGHES
35	Director Student Life	Ms. Jenny BELL
06	Assoc Registrar	Ms. Amanda T. FOX
08	Director Libraries	Ms. Kathy LOWE
07	Director Admissions	Mr. Greg EMBRY
29	Dir Development/Alumni Relations	Vacant
14	Interim Chief Information Officer	Mr. John HALLIS
26	Director of University Relations	Mr. Jamie BESSETTE
37	Dir of Student Financial Services	Ms. Maria D. PARKER
38	Director Counseling Center	Dr. Tammi S. DAHLE
19	Chief of Police	Mr. Chadd ADAMS
39	Dir Housing & Residence Life	Mr. John DENSON
41	Director Athletics	Mr. James E. HERLIHY
15	Director Personnel Services	Ms. Barbara FORREST
51	Dir Reg Insvc & Continuing Ed	Ms. Rebecca L. RICHARDSON
58	Dir Graduate Admissions & Records	Ms. Rebecca HARTLEY
49	Dean College Arts & Sciences	Dr. Mary Beth ARMSTRONG
50	Dean College of Business	Dr. Stephen CRAFT
53	Dean College of Education	Dr. Anna E. MCEWAN
57	Interim Dean College of Fine Arts	Dr. Scott STEPHENS

University of North Alabama (C)

One Harrison Plaza, Florence AL 35632-0001

County: Lauderdale FICE Identification: 001016
Unit ID: 101879

Telephone: (256) 765-4100 Carnegie Class: Master's L
FAX Number: (256) 765-4329 Calendar System: Semester
URL: www.una.edu
Established: 1830 Annual Undergrad Tuition & Fees (In-State): $6,648
Enrollment: 7,128 Coed
Affiliation or Control: State IRS Status: 501(c)3
Highest Offering: Beyond Master's But Less Than Doctorate
Program: Liberal Arts And General; Teacher Preparatory; Professional
Accreditation: SC, ACBSP, ART, CACREP, CS, ENGR, MUS, NURSE, SW, TED

Code	Title	Name
01	President	Dr. William G. CALE, JR.
05	Vice Pres Acad Affairs & Provost	Dr. John THORNELL
88	Vice Provost for Intl Affairs	Dr. Chunsheng ZHANG
10	VP for Business/Financial Affairs	Dr. Steve SMITH
32	Vice President Student Affairs	Mr. David P. SHIELDS, JR.
30	Interim VP for Advancement	Dr. Judy T. JACKSON
49	Dean College of Arts & Sciences	Dr. Vagn K. HANSEN
50	Dean College of Business	Dr. Kerry P. GATLIN
53	Dean College of Education	Dr. Donna P. LEFORT
66	Dean College of Nursing	Dr. Birdie I. BAILEY
20	Assoc VP Academic Support	Dr. Thomas C. CALHOUN, JR.
31	Director University Events	Mr. Bret JENNINGS
41	Director of Athletics	Mr. Mark LINDER
21	Controller	Ms. Donna F. TIPPS
86	Director Governmental Relations	Ms. Rita F. FOSTER
44	Dir Annual Giving/Donor Research	Dr. Judy T. JACKSON
39	Director of Housing	Ms. Audrey MITCHELL
37	Director Student Financial Services	Mr. Ben J. BAKER
15	Asst Dir Human Resources/Affirm Act	Vacant
26	Director University Communications	Mr. Joshua L. WOODS
24	Dir Educational Technology Services	Ms. Debbie CHAFFIN
18	Director Facilities Admin/Planning	Mr. Michael B. GAUTNEY
19	Director of University Police	Mr. Robert G. PASTULA
51	Dir Continuing Studies and Outreach	Ms. Lavonne GATLIN
23	Director University Health Services	Dr. Kyrel L. BUCHANAN
35	Dir Judicial Affairs/Stdnt Aff Plng	Dr. Kimberly GREENWAY
40	Manager University Bookstore	Vacant
91	Director Information Tech Services	Mr. Stephen J. PUTMAN
07	Director of Admissions	Ms. Kim MAULDIN
09	Dir Inst Rsrch/Plng & Assessment	Dr. Andrew L. LUNA
29	Director Alumni Relations	Ms. Carol S. LYLES
96	Director of Procurement	Ms. Cindy H. CONLON
28	Dir Diversity/Institutional Equity	Vacant
36	Dir Career Planning & Development	Ms. Melissa T. MEDLIN
06	Registrar	Ms. Tina SHARP

University of South Alabama (D)

307 University Boulevard, N, Mobile AL 36688-0002

County: Mobile FICE Identification: 001057
Unit ID: 102094

Telephone: (251) 460-6101 Carnegie Class: RU/H
FAX Number: N/A Calendar System: Semester
URL: www.usouthal.edu
Established: 1963 Annual Undergrad Tuition & Fees (In-State): $7,950
Enrollment: 15,009 Coed
Affiliation or Control: State IRS Status: 501(c)3
Highest Offering: Doctorate
Program: Liberal Arts And General; Teacher Preparatory; Professional
Accreditation: SC, ARCPA, AUD, BUS, CS, EMT, ENG, MED, MUS, NURSE, OT, PTA, RAD, RTT, SP, SW, TED

Code	Title	Name
01	President	Mr. V. Gordon MOULTON
05	Sr Vice Pres Academic Affairs	Dr. G. David JOHNSON
30	Vice Pres Developmental/Alumni Rels	Dr. Joseph F. BUSTA
10	Vice President Financial Affairs	Mr. M. Wayne DAVIS
23	Vice President Health Sciences	Dr. Ronald FRANKS
32	VP Stdnt Affairs/Special Asst Pres	Dr. John SMITH
46	Vice President for Research	Dr. Lynne CHRONISTER
84	Assoc Vice Pres Enrollment Services	Dr. J. David STEARNS
58	Assoc VP Acad Affs/Dean Grad Sch	Dr. B. Keith HARRISON
13	Exec Director of Information Tech	Mr. Chris CANNON
46	Assoc VP IRPA & Regional Campuses	Dr. Joan EXLINE
15	Asst Vice President Human Resources	Ms. Pamela HENDERSON
17	Dean College of Medicine	Dr. Samuel J. STRADA
86	Exec Dir Government Relations	Mr. William J. FULFORD
88	Dir Student Acad Success/Retention	Dr. Nicole T. CARR
88	Director of Assessment	Ms. Cecelia MARTIN
26	Director of Public Relations	Mr. Keith AYERS
41	Director of Athletics	Dr. Joel ERDMANN
07	Director of Admissions	Ms. Norma J. TANNER
85	Director Intl Student Services	Ms. Donna PIGG
07	Director New Student Recruitment	Mr. Christopher LYNCH
09	Director of Institutional Research	Dr. Gordon E. MILLS, JR.
06	Registrar	Ms. Melissa WOLD
29	Director Alumni Relations	Ms. Karen EDWARDS
19	Director Campus Security	Mr. Zeke AULL, JR.
37	Director of Financial Aid	Ms. Emily JOHNSTON
36	Director Career Services	Ms. Bevley W. GREEN
12	Director USA Baldwin County	Ms. Cynthia WILSON
18	Director Facilities Management	Mr. Randy MOON
38	Director Student Counseling/Test	Dr. Alvah E. CLARK
88	Manager New Student Orientation	Mr. Scott R. SMITH
28	Manager Multicultural Student Affs	Dr. Carl G. CUNNINGHAM
96	Purchasing Agent	Mr. Robert M. BROWN
54	Dean College of Engineering	Dr. John STEADMAN
51	Dean Continuing Educ/Spec Pgms	Dr. Vaughn S. MILLNER
49	Dean of Arts and Sciences	Dr. Andrzej WIERZBICKI
08	Dean of University Libraries	Dr. Richard J. WOOD
50	Dean Mitchell College of Business	Dr. Carl C. MOORE
53	Dean of Education	Dr. Richard L. HAYES
66	Dean of College of Nursing	Dr. Debra C. DAVIS
76	Dean of Allied Health Professions	Dr. Richard TALBOTT
77	Dean Computer & Information Science	Dr. Alec YASINSAC

The University of West Alabama (E)

205 N Washington Street, Livingston AL 35470-2099

County: Sumter FICE Identification: 001024
Unit ID: 101587

Telephone: (205) 652-3400 Carnegie Class: Master's L
FAX Number: (205) 652-3718 Calendar System: Semester
URL: www.uwa.edu
Established: 1835 Annual Undergrad Tuition & Fees (In-State): $7,239
Enrollment: 5,258 Coed
Affiliation or Control: State IRS Status: 501(c)3
Highest Offering: Beyond Master's But Less Than Doctorate
Program: Liberal Arts And General; Teacher Preparatory; Professional
Accreditation: SC, ACBSP, ADNUR, TED

Code	Title	Name
01	President	Dr. Richard D. HOLLAND
05	Provost	Dr. David M. TAYLOR
10	Vice President Financial Affairs	Mr. T. Raiford NOLAND
30	Vice Pres Institutional Advancement	Mr. Clemit W. SPRUIELL
32	Vice President for Student Affairs	Mr. Thomas D. BUCKALEW
49	Dean of Liberal Arts	Dr. Tim EDWARDS
50	Dean of Business	Dr. Ken TUCKER
53	Dean of Teacher Education	Dr. Kathy CHANDLER
81	Dean of Natural Science/Math	Dr. Venkat SHARMA
58	Dean of Graduate Studies	Dr. Kathy CHANDLER
51	Dean Continuing Education	Dr. Tina N. JONES
106	Dean Online Programs	Dr. Martha HOCUTT
66	Chairperson of Nursing	Mrs. Marsha CANNON
08	Director of Library	Dr. Neil SNIDER
09	Dir Institutional Effectiveness	Mrs. Angel JOWERS
41	Athletic Director	Mr. Stan WILLIAMSON
35	Director of Student Life & Housing	Mr. Luther GREMMELS

06 Registrar ... Mrs. Susan SPARKMAN
37 Director Student Financial Aid ... Mr. Don RAINER
13 Director Information Systems ... Mr. Michael PRATT
18 Director of Physical Plant ... Mr. Robert L. HOLYCROSS
40 Director of Auxiliary Services ... Ms. Mamie REED
36 Director Career Services/Placement ... Ms. Tammy S. WHITE
29 Director Alumni Relations ... Mrs. Tyanne S. STONE
38 Director Student Success Center ... Dr. Vicki P. SPRUIELL
86 Director Government Relations ... Mr. Clemit W. SPRUIELL
07 Dir of Admissions/Enrollment Mgmt ... Mr. Olivier CHARLES
96 Director of Purchasing ... Mr. Lawson C. EDMONDS
89 Director Freshmen Studies ... Dr. James GENTSCH
92 Director Honors Program ... Dr. Lesa SHAUL
15 Director Personnel Services ... Mrs. Jessie W. EGBERT
30 Director of Development ... Mr. Tom TARTT
20 Associate Academic Officer ... Mrs. Angel JOWERS
26 Chief Public Relations Officer ... Ms. Betsy COMPTON
19 Director of Security/Safety ... Mr. Jeff MANUEL
103 Director Workforce Development ... Mr. Kenneth WALKER
105 Director of Web Services ... Mrs. Christi GEORGE
101 Secretary Board of Trustees ... Mrs. Earlene LINDSEY
28 Director of Diversity ... Dr. David M. TAYLOR
85 Director of Foreign Students ... Mr. John KEY

Wallace State Community College - Hanceville (A)

PO Box 2000, 801 Main Street, NW,
Hanceville AL 35077-2000
County: Cullman FICE Identification: 007871
Unit ID: 101295
Telephone: (256) 352-8000 Carnegie Class: Assoc/Pub-R-M
FAX Number: (256) 352-8228 Calendar System: Semester
URL: www.wallacestate.edu
Established: 1966 Annual Undergrad Tuition & Fees (In-State): $3,312
Enrollment: 5,535 Coed
Affiliation or Control: State IRS Status: 501(c)3
Highest Offering: Associate Degree
Program: Occupational; 2-Year Principally Bachelor's Creditable
Accreditation: **SC**, ACBSP, ACFEI, ADNUR, DA, DH, DMS, EMT, MAC, MLTAD, OTA, POLYT, PTAA, RAD

01 President ... Dr. Vicki HAWSEY
03 Executive Vice President ... Dr. Tomesa SMITH
10 Dean of Finance & Admin Svcs ... Jason MORGAN
05 College Dean ... Johnny MCMOY
20 Dean of Applied Technologies ... Jimmy HODGES
26 Dean of Institutional Outreach ... Melinda EDWARDS
72 Dean of Technical Education ... Vacant
76 Dean of Health Sciences ... Lisa GERMAN
88 Auxiliary Director ... Sid BORDEN
08 Librarian ... Lisa HULLETT
07 Director Admissions & Registrar ... Linda SPERLING
09 Director of Planning & Assessment ... Vacant
37 Director of Financial Aid ... Becky GRAVES
56 Extended Day Program Director ... Wayne MANORD
15 Director of Human Resources ... Alyce FLANAGAN
30 Director of Advancement ... Suzanne HARBIN
18 Director of Plant Operations ... Phil STUDDARD
26 Director of Communication/Marketing ... Kristen HOLMES
38 Director of Advising ... Donnie RICE
84 Director Enrollment Management ... Jennifer HILL

ALASKA

Alaska Bible College (B)

Box 289, 200 College Road, Glennallen AK 99588-0289
FICE Identification: 008843
Unit ID: 102580
Telephone: (907) 822-3201 Carnegie Class: Not Classified
FAX Number: (907) 822-5027 Calendar System: Semester
URL: www.akbible.edu
Established: 1966 Annual Undergrad Tuition & Fees: $7,030
Enrollment: 55 Coed
Affiliation or Control: Independent Non-Profit IRS Status: 501(c)3
Highest Offering: Baccalaureate
Program: Religious Emphasis
Accreditation: **BI**

01 President ... Mr. Nick RINGGER
05 Vice President Academic Affairs ... Mr. John FERCH
32 VP Student Development/Dean of Men ... Mr. Hal GIVENS
10 Vice Pres Business Administration ... Vacant
06 Registrar/Bookkeeper ... Miss Carol REIMER
08 Librarian ... Mrs. Pamela HORST
07 Director Admissions/Recruiting ... Mrs. Nikki PALMER
27 Director of Communications ... Ms. Michelle EASTTY

Alaska Career College (C)

1415 E. Tudor Road, Anchorage AK 99507-1033
County: Anchorage FICE Identification: 025410
Unit ID: 103501
Telephone: (907) 563-7575 Carnegie Class: Not Classified
FAX Number: (907) 563-8330 Calendar System: Other
URL: www.alaskacareercollege.edu
Established: N/A Annual Undergrad Tuition & Fees: $12,850
Enrollment: 400 Coed
Affiliation or Control: Proprietary IRS Status: Proprietary
Highest Offering: Associate Degree
Program: Occupational; 2-Year Principally Bachelor's Creditable; Technical Emphasis
Accreditation: **ACCSC**

01 Director ... Ms. Linda STURE

Alaska Pacific University (D)

4101 University Drive, Anchorage AK 99508-4672
County: Anchorage FICE Identification: 001061
Unit ID: 102669
Telephone: (907) 561-1266 Carnegie Class: Master's S
FAX Number: (907) 562-4276 Calendar System: Semester
URL: www.alaskapacific.edu
Established: 1957 Annual Undergrad Tuition & Fees: $27,000
Enrollment: 692 Coed
Affiliation or Control: Independent Non-Profit IRS Status: 501(c)3
Highest Offering: Master's
Program: Liberal Arts And General; Teacher Preparatory
Accreditation: **NW**, TED

01 President ... Dr. Don BANTZ
04 Assistant to the President ... Ms. Debbie ROLL
05 Academic Dean ... Ms. Tracy STEWART
10 Dean of Administration & Finance ... Ms. Deborah JOHNSTON
32 Dean of Students ... Mr. Kelly SMITH
06 Registrar ... Ms. Michelle WHEELER
07 Director of Admissions ... Mr. Barclay ROEDER
37 Director of Financial Aid ... Mr. Phong MOUA
18 Director Facilities Management ... Ms. Kathy MINCKS
13 Director Information Technology ... Mr. Michael BAKER
30 Chief Development Officer ... Ms. Stephanie HAYDN
42 Chaplain ... Rev. Doug LINDSAY
15 Director Human Resources ... Ms. Roxanna MOE
40 Assistant Campus Store Manager ... Ms. Lydia HARVEY
29 Alumni Relations Coord ... Ms. Heather HANSEN

† Granted candidacy at the Doctorate level.

Charter College (E)

2221 E Northern Lights Blvd, #120,
Anchorage AK 99508-4157
County: Anchorage FICE Identification: 025769
Unit ID: 102845
Telephone: (907) 277-1000 Carnegie Class: Bac/Assoc
FAX Number: (907) 274-3342 Calendar System: Quarter
URL: www.chartercollege.edu
Established: 1985 Annual Undergrad Tuition & Fees: $17,725
Enrollment: 1,651 Coed
Affiliation or Control: Proprietary IRS Status: Proprietary
Highest Offering: Baccalaureate
Program: Occupational; 2-Year Principally Bachelor's Creditable
Accreditation: **ACICS**

01 President ... Dr. Richard MACLEAN
05 Dean of Education ... Mr. David HERMAN
37 Director of Financial Aid ... Ms. Kristal SMITH
36 Director of Career Services ... Ms. Wendy NOVAK
08 Librarian ... Ms. Lisa DEBUSK
07 Director of Admission ... Ms. Irene LEE
11 Administrative Coordinator ... Ms. Traci RICKETTS
32 Director of Student Success ... Ms. Catherine HEBDON

Ilisagvik College (F)

PO Box 749, Barrow AK 99723-0749
County: North Slope Borough FICE Identification: 034613
Unit ID: 434584
Telephone: (907) 852-3333 Carnegie Class: Tribal
FAX Number: (907) 862-2729 Calendar System: Semester
URL: www.ilisagvik.cc
Established: 1996 Annual Undergrad Tuition & Fees: $6,270
Enrollment: 601 Coed
Affiliation or Control: Independent Non-Profit IRS Status: 501(c)3
Highest Offering: Associate Degree
Program: Occupational; 2-Year Principally Bachelor's Creditable
Accreditation: **NW**

01 President ... Ms. Pearl K. BROWER
06 Registrar ... Ms. Amm CAHOON
05 Chief Academic Officer ... Mrs. Birgit MEANY
10 Chief Business Officer ... Ms. Mary Ann GALLIPEO
15 Director Human Resources ... Ms. Martha MONNIN
18 Chief Facilities/Physical Plant ... Mr. Chris SMITH
26 Chief Public Relations Officer ... Mrs. Annie PATTERSON
32 Chief Student Life Officer ... Mr. Saga AINA
36 Director Student Placement ... Ms. Janelle EVERETT
37 Director Student Financial Aid ... Mr. Fred MILLER

*University of Alaska System (G)

910 Yukon Drive, Suite 202, Fairbanks AK 99775-5000
County: Fairbanks FICE Identification: 008005
Unit ID: 103529
Telephone: (907) 450-8000 Carnegie Class: N/A
FAX Number: (907) 450-8012
URL: www.alaska.edu

01 President ... Mr. Patrick K. GAMBLE
26 Vice President for Univ Relations ... Ms. Carla BEAM
05 Vice Pres for Academic Affairs ... Dr. Dana L. THOMAS
10 Vice Pres for Finance ... Mr. Ashok ROY
46 Associate Vice President Budget ... Ms. Michelle RIZK
09 AVP Institutional Research/Analysis ... Ms. Gwen GRUENIG
43 General Counsel ... Mr. Michael HOSTINA
15 Chief Human Resources Officer ... Mr. Donald SMITH
102 President of Foundation ... Ms. Carla BEAM
13 Chief Info Technology Officer ... Mr. Karl KOWALSKI
26 Director of Public Affairs ... Ms. Kate WATTUM

*University of Alaska Anchorage (H)

3211 Providence Drive, Anchorage AK 99508-8000
County: Anchorage FICE Identification: 011462
Unit ID: 102553
Telephone: (907) 786-1800 Carnegie Class: Master's L
FAX Number: (907) 786-4888 Calendar System: Semester
URL: www.uaa.alaska.edu
Established: 1954 Annual Undergrad Tuition & Fees (In-State): $5,632
Enrollment: 20,699 Coed
Affiliation or Control: State IRS Status: 501(c)3
Highest Offering: Master's
Program: Occupational; 2-Year Principally Bachelor's Creditable; Liberal Arts And General; Teacher Preparatory; Professional
Accreditation: **NW**, ADNUR, ART, BUS, DA, DH, @DIETD, DIETI, ENG, ENGR, JOUR, MAC, MT, MUS, NUR, PH, SW, TED

02 Chancellor ... Gen. Tom CASE
05 Interim Provost ... Dr. Elisha (Bear) BAKER
11 Vice Chancellor Administrative Svcs ... Dr. William SPINDLE
09 Sr Vice Provst Inst Effectiveness ... Ms. Renee M. CARTER-CHAPMAN
84 Assoc Vice Chanc Enrollment Mgmt ... Mr. Eric R. PEDERSEN
30 Vice Chancellor Univ Advancement ... Ms. Megan OLSON
32 Vice Chancellor Student Affairs ... Dr. Bruce SCHULTZ
26 Asst Vice Chanc University Rels ... Ms. Kristin DESMITH
91 Assoc Vice Chanc Information Tech ... Dr. Richard A. WHITNEY
09 Assoc VP of Institutional Research ... Dr. Gary RICE
18 Assoc Vice Chanc Facilities ... Mr. Christopher TURLETES
96 Assoc VC Financial Services ... Ms. Sandi CULVER
44 AVC of Development ... Ms. Beth ROSE
20 Assc VC Acad/Multicul Stdnt Success ... Ms. Vara ALLEN-JONES
35 Dean of Students ... Dr. Dewain LEE
37 Director Student Financial Aid ... Vacant
88 Director AHAINA Student Programs ... Vacant
35 Director Student Life & Leadership ... Ms. Annie ROUTE
07 Director of Admissions ... Vacant
28 Dir Campus Diversity & Compliance ... Ms. Marva WATSON
29 Director Alumni Relations ... Vacant
41 Director Athletics ... Dr. Steve COBB
06 Interim University Registrar ... Ms. Lora VOLDEN
36 Director Career Services Center ... Ms. Diane KOZAK
15 Director Human Resources ... Mr. Ron KAMAHELE
08 Dean Consortium Library ... Mr. Stephen J. ROLLINS
63 Director Biomedical Program ... Dr. Dennis VALEZENO
88 Director Native Student Services ... Mr. William TEMPLETON
50 Int Dean Col Business/Public Policy ... Dr. Rashmi PRASAD
51 Dean Community/Tech College ... Dr. Karen R. SCHMITT
83 Int Dean Col Health/Social Welfare ... Dr. William HOGAN
54 Dean School of Engineering ... Dr. Orson SMITH
49 Dean Arts & Sciences College ... Dr. John STALVEY
53 Interim Dean College of Education ... Dr. Ed MCLAIN
92 Dean Honors College ... Mr. Ronald SPATZ

† Granted candidacy at the Doctorate level.

*University of Alaska Fairbanks (I)

215 Signers' Hall, Admissions, Fairbanks AK 99775-7480
County: Fairbanks North Star Borough FICE Identification: 001063
Unit ID: 102614
Telephone: (907) 474-7500 Carnegie Class: RU/H
FAX Number: (907) 474-5379 Calendar System: Semester
URL: www.uaf.edu
Established: 1917 Annual Undergrad Tuition & Fees (In-State): $5,907
Enrollment: 9,582 Coed
Affiliation or Control: State IRS Status: 501(c)3
Highest Offering: Doctorate
Program: Occupational; 2-Year Principally Bachelor's Creditable; Liberal Arts And General; Teacher Preparatory; Professional
Accreditation: **NW**, BUS, BUSA, CLPSY, CS, DH, EMT, ENG, FOR, JOUR, MAC, MUS, SW, TED

02 Chancellor ... Mr. Brian D. ROGERS
05 Provost ... Dr. Susan M. HENRICHS
11 Vice Chancellor Administrative Svcs ... Ms. Pat PITNEY
18 Assoc Vice Chancellor Facilities ... Mr. Scott BELL
32 VC University & Student Advancement ... Dr. Mike SFRAGA
45 Vice Chancellor Research ... Dr. Mark MYERS
21 Assoc VC for Financial Services ... Mr. Raaj KURAPATI
44 Director of Development ... Ms. Emily DRYGAS
58 Dean Graduate School ... Dr. John EICHELBERGER
81 Dean Col of Natural Science/Math ... Dr. Paul LAYER
35 Assoc Vice Chanc for Student Life ... Mr. Don FOLEY
31 VC Rural/Cmty & Native Educ ... Ms. Bernice JOSEPH
12 Dean UAF Comm & Tech College ... Ms. Michele STALDER
47 Dean Sch of Natural Res/Ag Sciences ... Dr. Carol E. LEWIS
88 Dean Sch Fisheries & Ocean Sciences ... Dr. Mike CASTELLINI
50 Dean School of Management ... Dr. Mark HERRMANN
54 Dean Col of Engineering & Mines ... Dr. Doug GOERING
88 Dir Intl Arctic Research Center ... Dr. Larry HINZMAN
88 Dir Institute of Arctic Biology ... Dr. Brian M. BARNES
54 Director Inst Northern Engineering ... Dr. Daniel WHITE
15 Interim Director Human Resources ... Mr. Brad LOBLAND
19 Chief of Police ... Mr. Sean MCGEE

37 Director Financial Aid ... Ms. Deanna L. DIERINGER
26 Director of Community Advocacy ... Ms. Ann RINGSTAD
41 Director Athletics ... Dr. Gary GRAY
39 Director Residence Life ... Ms. Laura L. MCCOLLOUGH
56 Vice Provost for Extension/Outreach ... Mr. Fred SCHLUTT
40 Director of Aux/Recharge/Cntrct Ops ... Vacant
85 Director International Programs ... Ms. Donna ANGER
88 Fire Chief ... Mr. Doug SCHRAGE
88 Dir Institute of Marine Science ... Dr. Terry WHITLEDGE
49 Dean College of Liberal Arts ... Mr. Todd SHERMAN
53 Dean School of Education ... Dr. Allan MOROTTI
12 Director Bristol Bay Campus ... Dr. Deborah MCLEAN
12 Director Chukchi Campus ... Ms. Pauline HARVEY
12 Director Interior Aleutians Campus ... Ms. Teisha SIMMONS
12 Director Kuskokwim Campus ... Ms. Mary C. PETE
12 Interim Director Northwest Campus ... Mr. Robert METCALF
28 Dir Diversity & Equal Opportunity ... Ms. Mae MARSH
23 Director Health and Counseling ... Dr. B.J ALDRICH
29 Exec Director Alumni Association ... Mr. Joe HAYES
07 Interim Registrar & Dir Admissions ... Ms. Libby EDDY
88 Director Geophysical Institute ... Mr. Robert MCCOY
21 Director Business Operations ... Ms. Amanda WALL
36 Director Career Services ... Ms. Patti PICHA
38 Director Academic Advising Center ... Ms. Linda M. HAPSMITH
92 Director Honors Program ... Dr. Gary LAURSEN
94 Coordinator Women's Studies ... Dr. Sine ANAHITA
45 Dir Planning/Analysis/Inst Research ... Mr. Ian OLSON
49 Assoc Dean College of Liberal Arts ... Ms. Anita HARTMANN
26 Director Marketing/Communications ... Ms. Michelle RENFREW
08 Dean of Libraries ... Dr. Bella GERLICH
88 Director UA Museum of the North ... Dr. Carol DIEBEL
14 Dir Arctic Reg Supercomputing Ctr ... Dr. Greg NEWBY
13 Chief Info Technology Officer ... Mr. Karl KOWALSKI
20 Vice Provost & Accreditation Ofcr ... Vacant
88 Director for Disability Services ... Ms. Mary MATTHEWS
96 Dir of Procurement & Contract Svcs ... Mr. John HEBARD
88 Director Wood Center Student Union ... Mrs. Lydia ANDERSON
46 AVC Research ... Dr. John BLAKE
46 AVC Research ... Dr. Nettie LABELLE-HAMER
30 AVC for Univ & Student Advancement ... Ms. Kris RACINA
97 Interim Dean of General Studies ... Dr. Alex FITTS

*University of Alaska Southeast (A)

11120 Glacier Highway, Juneau AK 99801-8681
County: Juneau　FICE Identification: 001065
Unit ID: 102632
Telephone: (907) 796-6000　Carnegie Class: Master's S
FAX Number: N/A　Calendar System: Semester
URL: www.uas.alaska.edu
Established: 1956　Annual Undergrad Tuition & Fees (In-State): $5,249
Enrollment: 4,043　Coed
Affiliation or Control: State　IRS Status: 501(c)3
Highest Offering: Master's
Program: Occupational; Liberal Arts And General; Teacher Preparatory; Professional
Accreditation: NW, TED

02 Chancellor ... Mr. John PUGH
05 Provost & Executive Dean SCE ... Dr. Richard CAULFIELD
75 Associate Dean Sch of Career Educ ... Ms. Robin GILCRIST
46 Vice Provost for Research ... Dr. Marsha SOUSA
20 Vice Provost for Academic Affairs ... Ms. Carol HEDLIN
11 Vice Chanc & Director Admin Svcs ... Mr. James DANIELSON
12 Sitka Campus Director ... Dr. Jeffrey JOHNSTON
12 Interim Ketchikan Campus Director ... Dr. Priscilla SCHULTE
49 Dean of Arts & Sciences ... Dr. Marsha SOUSA
88 Dean of School of Management ... Mr. John BLANCHARD
88 Director UAS Ctr for Mine Training ... Mr. Mike BELL
53 Dean Education & Graduate Studies ... Dr. Deborah LO
37 Financial Aid Officer ... Ms. Corinne SOLTIS
26 Dir of Marketing/Public Relations ... Ms. Katie BAUSLER
06 Registrar ... Ms. Barbara HEGEL
11 Vice Chanc Enrollment Management ... Mr. Joseph NELSON
09 Institutional Effectiveness Manager ... Ms. Diane MEADOR
10 Director Business Services ... Mr. Tom DIENST
15 Director Personnel Services ... Mr. Kirk MCALLISTER
18 Director Facilities Services ... Mr. Keith GERKEN
08 Interim Director Library Services ... Ms. Elise TOMLINSON
13 Director Information/Technology ... Mr. Michael CIRI
30 Dir Development/Alumni Relations ... Ms. Lynne JOHNSON
29 Annual Fund Alumni Rels Manager ... Ms. Keni CAMPBELL
21 Chief Budget Officer ... Ms. Barbara HYDE
88 Director Learning Center ... Ms. Hildegard SELLNER
11 Vice Chanc Student Services ... Mr. Joseph NELSON

*Prince William Sound Community College (B)

PO Box 97, Valdez AK 99686-0097
County: Valdez-Cordova-Glennallen　Identification: 666659
Unit ID: 103361
Telephone: (907) 834-1600　Carnegie Class: Assoc/Pub-R-M
FAX Number: (907) 834-1611　Calendar System: Semester
URL: www.pwscc.edu
Established: 1978　Annual Undergrad Tuition & Fees (In-State): $3,700
Enrollment: 2,000　Coed
Affiliation or Control: State　IRS Status: 501(c)3
Highest Offering: Associate Degree
Program: Occupational; 2-Year Principally Bachelor's Creditable
Accreditation: NW

02 President ... Mr. Wes LUNDBURG
05 Dean of Instruction ... Mr. Jed PALMER
10 Business Manager ... Mr. Steve SHIELL
06 Registrar ... Ms. Shannon FOSTER
07 Director Admiss/Fin Aid/ Stdnt Svc ... Mr. Chris WASHKO
15 Director Personnel Services ... Ms. Ana HINKLE
26 Chief Public Relations Officer ... Ms. Wendy GOLDSTEIN
38 Director Student Counseling ... Vacant
88 Director of Training ... Mr. BJ WILLIAMS

ARIZONA

Acacia University (C)

7665 South Research Drive, Tempe AZ 85284-1812
County: Maricopa　Identification: 667017
Telephone: (480) 428-6034　Carnegie Class: Not Classified
FAX Number: (480) 428-6033　Calendar System: Semester
URL: www.acacia.edu
Established: 2006　Annual Undergrad Tuition & Fees: $7,300
Enrollment: 200　Coed
Affiliation or Control: Other　IRS Status: 501(c)3
Highest Offering: Master's
Program: Occupational; 2-Year Principally Bachelor's Creditable; Teacher Preparatory
Accreditation: DETC

01 President ... Mr. Michael TURICO
106 Exec VP Trainining/Online Learning ... Dr. Marilynn D. HENLEY
32 Exec VP Student Affairs ... Mr. Tim MOMAN

American Indian College of the Assemblies of God (D)

10020 N 15th Avenue, Phoenix AZ 85021-2199
County: Maricopa　FICE Identification: 021999
Unit ID: 103787
Telephone: (602) 944-3335　Carnegie Class: Bac/Diverse
FAX Number: (602) 943-8299　Calendar System: Semester
URL: www.aicag.edu
Established: 1957　Annual Undergrad Tuition & Fees: $11,550
Enrollment: 86　Coed
Affiliation or Control: Assemblies Of God Church　IRS Status: 501(c)3
Highest Offering: Baccalaureate
Program: 2-Year Principally Bachelor's Creditable; Teacher Preparatory; Religious Emphasis
Accreditation: NH

01 President ... Dr. David L. DEGARMO
05 Vice President for Academic Affairs ... Dr. Joseph J. SAGGIO
32 Vice President Student Development ... Rev. Vincent ROUBIDEAUX
10 Exec Director of Financial Services ... Rev. Paul HENNING
42 Campus Pastor ... Vacant
06 Registrar ... Ms. Jennifer ROUBIDEAUX
84 Director Enrollment Mgmt/ Admissions ... Ms. Sandra M. GONZALES
37 Student Financial Aid Director ... Ms. Nadine WALDROP
08 Library Director ... Rev. John S. ROSE
30 Director of Advancement ... Vacant
26 Chief Public Relations Officer ... Mr. Troy VANDERHULE
35 Director Student Services ... Rev. Steven CLINDANIEL
38 Director Student Counseling ... Mr. Blair SCHLEPP

Anthem College (E)

1515 East Indian School Road, Phoenix AZ 85014
County: Maricopa　FICE Identification: 022631
Unit ID: 104805
Telephone: (602) 279-9700　Carnegie Class: Assoc/PrivFP4
FAX Number: N/A　Calendar System: Other
URL: www.anthem.edu
Established: 1982　Annual Undergrad Tuition & Fees: $27,909
Enrollment: 2,663　Coed
Affiliation or Control: Proprietary　IRS Status: Proprietary
Highest Offering: Baccalaureate
Program: Occupational
Accreditation: ACICS

01 Campus President ... Dr. James HADLEY

Argosy University, Phoenix (F)

2233 W Dunlap Avenue, Phoenix AZ 85021
County: Maricopa　Identification: 666790
Unit ID: 436094
Telephone: (602) 216-2600　Carnegie Class: Spec/Health
FAX Number: (602) 216-3151　Calendar System: Semester
URL: www.argosy.edu/phoenix
Established: 1997　Annual Undergrad Tuition & Fees: $13,224
Enrollment: 868　Coed
Affiliation or Control: Proprietary　IRS Status: Proprietary
Highest Offering: Doctorate
Program: Professional
Accreditation: &WC, CLPSY

01 Campus President ... Hugh I. JENSEN
05 Vice President of Academic Affairs ... Norma J. PATTERSON
07 Senior Director of Admissions ... Lori A. SMITH
32 Director of Student Services ... Jacqueline MARTINEZ
37 Dir of Student Finance ... Alissa M. HOUSKER
06 Registrar ... Elizabeth MIRABAL
15 Human Resources ... Lonna J. MINARDI
11 Dir of Admin and Financial Svcs ... Richard BINDER

† Regional accreditation is carried under the parent institution in Orange, CA.

Arizona Christian University (formerly Southwestern College) (G)

2625 E Cactus Road, Phoenix AZ 85032-7042
County: Maricopa　FICE Identification: 007113
Unit ID: 105899
Telephone: (602) 489-5300　Carnegie Class: Bac/Diverse
FAX Number: (602) 404-2159　Calendar System: Semester
URL: www.arizonachristian.edu
Established: 1960　Annual Undergrad Tuition & Fees: $20,880
Enrollment: 600　Coed
Affiliation or Control: Independent Non-Profit　IRS Status: 501(c)3
Highest Offering: Baccalaureate
Program: Liberal Arts And General; Teacher Preparatory
Accreditation: NH

01 President ... Mr. Len MUNSIL
05 Senior Vice President and Provost ... Dr. Gary P. DAMORE
10 Senior VP & Chief Financial Officer ... Ms. Diane CATLIN
11 Vice Pres for Operations/Athletics ... Mr. Don MITCHELL
84 Vice Pres Enrollment & Marketing ... Ms. Heather KIM
100 Chief of Staff ... Mr. Brant NYHART
04 Executive Assistant to President ... Ms. Tiffani EDWARDS
30 Director of Advancement ... Mr. Daniel MILLS
20 Academic Dean ... Dr. William P. BAKER
32 Dean of Student Services ... Mr. Charles HUNTER
21 Controller ... Ms. June TAYLOR
06 Registrar & Asst Dir of Enroll Mgmt ... Mr. Lambert CRUZ
37 Director Financial Aid ... Ms. Michelle ELIZER
34 Dean of Women ... Ms. Peg FORREST
08 Director of Library Services ... Mr. Sean J. MCNULTY
39 Director of Residence Life ... Mr. Anthony SUAREZ
13 Information Technology Director ... Mr. Joel HAYS

Arizona College of Allied Health (H)

4425 W Olive Avenue, Suite 300,
Glendale AZ 85302-3851
County: Maricopa　FICE Identification: 031150
Unit ID: 421708
Telephone: (602) 222-9300　Carnegie Class: Assoc/PrivFP
FAX Number: (602) 200-8726　Calendar System: Other
URL: www.arizonacollege.edu
Established: 1991　Annual Undergrad Tuition & Fees: $14,935
Enrollment: 691　Coed
Affiliation or Control: Proprietary　IRS Status: Proprietary
Highest Offering: Associate Degree
Program: 2-Year Principally Bachelor's Creditable; Nursing Emphasis
Accreditation: ABHES

01 President ... Mr. Nick MANSOUR
11 Regional Vice Pres of Operations ... Mr. Kevin LAMOUNTAIN
37 Financial Aid Director ... Mr. Matthew CALHOUN

Arizona School of Acupuncture and Oriental Medicine (I)

4646 E Fort Lowell Road, Suite 103,
Tucson AZ 85712-1100
County: Pima　FICE Identification: 036955
Unit ID: 446039
Telephone: (520) 795-0787　Carnegie Class: Spec/Health
FAX Number: (877) 222-4606　Calendar System: Quarter
URL: www.asaom.edu
Established: 1996　Annual Graduate Tuition & Fees: $51,596
Enrollment: 45　Coed
Affiliation or Control: Proprietary　IRS Status: Proprietary
Highest Offering: Master's; No Undergraduates
Program: Professional
Accreditation: ACUP

01 CEO/Founder ... Mr. David EPLEY
11 Administrative Dean ... Vacant
37 Financial Aid Advisor ... Ms. Susan WAGNER
05 Academic/Clinic Dean ... Mr. Don LIGHTNER
20 Assistant Dean ... Ms. Melissa HOLMAN
07 Admissions Director ... Mr. Tim DUNN

Arizona State University (J)

300 E. University Drive, Tempe AZ 85281
County: Maricopa　FICE Identification: 001081
Unit ID: 104151
Telephone: (480) 965-9011　Carnegie Class: RU/VH
FAX Number: N/A　Calendar System: Semester
URL: www.asu.edu
Established: 1885　Annual Undergrad Tuition & Fees (In-State): $9,724
Enrollment: 72,254　Coed
Affiliation or Control: State　IRS Status: 501(c)3
Highest Offering: Doctorate
Program: Liberal Arts And General; Professional

Accreditation: NH, AAB, ART, AUD, BUS, BUSA, CACREP, CIDA, CLPSY, CONST, COPSY, CS, DIETD, DIETI, ENG, ENGT, HSA, IPSY, JOUR, LAW, LSAR, MUS, NRPA, NURSE, PLNG, SCPSY, SP, SPAA, SW

01 President .... Dr. Michael M. CROW
05 Exec Vice President and Provost .... Dr. Elizabeth D. CAPALDI
10 Exec Vice President/Treasurer & CFO .... Dr. Morgan R. OLSEN
03 Sr Vice Pres/Sec of the University .... Dr. Christine K. WILKINSON
102 CEO ASU Foundation .... Mr. Richard H. STANLEY
43 Sr Vice President & General Counsel .... Mr. Jose A. CARDENAS
32 Sr VP Educ Outreach & Student Svcs .... Dr. James A. RUND
41 Vice Pres of University Athletics .... Mr. Stephen PATTERSON
13 Chief Information Officer .... Mr. Gordon D. WISHON
26 Vice President for Public Affairs .... Mr. Virgil N. RENZULLI
20 Vice President Academic Personnel .... Dr. Mark S. SEARLE
106 Exec Vice Provost/Dean ASU Online .... Dr. Philip R. REGIER
16 Asst VP & Chief Human Resources Ofc .... Mr. Kevin J. SALCIDO
46 Univ Chief Research Officer .... Dr. Sethuraman PANCHANATHEN
100 VP/Chief of Staff .... Mr. Jim O'BRIEN
57 Dean Herberger Inst for Design/Arts .... Dr. Kwang-Wu KIM
50 Dean WP Carey School of Business .... Mr. Robert E. MITTELSTAEDT
54 Dean Ira A Fulton Schls of Engr .... Dr. Paul C. JOHNSON
58 Exec Vice Prov/Dean Graduate Col .... Dr. Maria T. ALLISON
92 Dean of Barrett Honors College .... Dr. Mark JACOBS
12 VP of West Campus /Dean New College .... Dr. Elizabeth LANGLAND
60 Dean Cronkite Sch Journal/Mass Comm .... Mr. Christopher CALLAHAN
61 Dean College of Law .... Mr. Douglas SYLVESTER
49 Dean of Social Sciences/LA&S .... Dr. Patrick KENNEY
66 Dean College of Nursing & Health In .... Dr. Teri BRITT PIPE
88 Dean School of Sustainability .... Dr. Sander VAN DER LEEUW
53 Dean Mary Lou Fulton Teachers Col .... Dr. Mari E. KOERNER
72 Vice Prov/Dean College Tech & Innov .... Dr. Mitzi M. MONTOYA
88 Vice Prov/Dean University College .... Dr. Frederick C. COREY
88 Dean College of Health Solutions .... Dr. Keith D. LINDER
88 Dean College of Public Programs .... Jonathan KOPPELL
88 Dean School of Life Sciences CLAS .... Dr. Robert E. PAGE

Arizona Western College (A)

2020 Avenue 8E, Yuma AZ 85365
County: Yuma FICE Identification: 001071
Unit ID: 104160
Telephone: (928) 317-6000 Carnegie Class: Assoc/Pub-R-L
FAX Number: (928) 344-7730 Calendar System: Semester
URL: www.azwestern.edu
Established: 1963 Annual Undergrad Tuition & Fees (In-District): $2,170
Enrollment: 8,418 Coed
Affiliation or Control: State/Local IRS Status: 501(c)3
Highest Offering: Associate Degree
Program: Occupational; 2-Year Principally Bachelor's Creditable
Accreditation: NH, ADNUR, RAD

01 President .... Dr. Glenn MAYLE
05 Vice Pres Academic & Student Svcs .... Dr. Eric SOULSBY
10 Vice Pres Finance/Administration .... Mrs. Carole T. COLEMAN
26 Dean Public Relations & Marketing .... Mrs. Lori STOFFT
09 Dean Instnl Effect/Rsrch/Grants .... Dr. Mary SCHAAL
20 Dean of Instruction .... Mrs. Linda ELLIOTT-NELSON
84 Dean of Enrollment Services .... Dr. Llewellyn YOUNG
103 Dean of Business & Workforce Devel .... Mrs. Lynn LABRIE
38 Dean Student Retention/Support Svcs .... Mr. Bryan DOAK
75 Dean of Career & Technical Educ .... Mr. Daniel BARAJAS
102 Executive Director AWC Foundation .... Mrs. Christina HAWKEY
21 Director of Financial Services .... Ms. Diana G. DOUCETTE
15 Director of Human Resources .... Dr. Ruth WHISLER
96 Director of Purchasing & Aux Svcs .... Mr. Denis PONDER
18 Director Facilities Mgmt & Planning .... Mr. Bill SMITH
14 Co-Dir Tech & Network Services .... Mr. Chad COLEMAN
14 Co-Dir Tech & Network Services .... Ms. Brenda WARNOCK
08 Director of Library Services .... Ms. Angie CREEL
41 Director of Athletics .... Mr. Jerry SMITH
19 Chief of Police .... Mr. John EDMUNDSON
35 Dean for Campus Life .... Ms. Mary Kay HARTON
12 Associate Dean La Paz County Svcs .... Mr. Rich TOZER
12 Assoc Dean for South Yuma County .... Mr. Everardo MARTINEZ
37 Director of Financial Aid .... Ms. Lisa SEALE
85 Coordinator of Intl Student Program .... Mr. Ken KUNTZELMAN
07 Director of Admissions/Registrar .... Ms. Amy PIGNATORE
106 Associate Dean for Distance Educ .... Mrs. Jana MOORE
88 Director of Testing Services .... Mrs. Leticia MARTINEZ
105 Webmaster II .... Mr. Damien BATES

The Art Institute of Phoenix (B)

2233 W Dunlap Avenue, Phoenix AZ 85021-2859
County: Maricopa FICE Identification: 040513
Unit ID: 428444
Telephone: (602) 331-7500 Carnegie Class: Spec/Arts
FAX Number: (602) 331-5301 Calendar System: Quarter
URL: www.artinstitutes.edu/phoenix
Established: 1995 Annual Undergrad Tuition & Fees: $28,860
Enrollment: 1,000 Coed
Affiliation or Control: Proprietary IRS Status: Proprietary
Highest Offering: Baccalaureate
Program: 2-Year Principally Bachelor's Creditable; Professional; Fine Arts Emphasis
Accreditation: ACICS, ACFEI, CIDA

01 President .... Mr. Chad WILLIAMS
05 Dean of Academic Affairs .... Dr. Meryl EPSTEIN
07 Senior Director of Admissions .... Ms. Terri SPENCER
32 Dean of Student Affairs .... Ms. Tanisha WASHINGTON
36 Director of Career Services .... Ms. Kristin FRANK
10 Director of Admin & Fin Svcs .... Ms. Lori RYAN
15 Human Resources Generalist .... Ms. Jennifer BOHNSACK
09 Dir of Institutional Effectiveness .... Ms. Jessica MARQUIS
13 Technology Support Supervisor .... Mr. Nate YOUNG
37 Director of Student Financial Svcs .... Ms. Abigail GARCIA
06 Registrar .... Ms. Bonnie BOWERS

The Art Institute of Tucson (C)

5099 East Grant Road, Suite 100, Tucson AZ 85712-2733
County: Pima FICE Identification: 037405
Unit ID: 444927
Telephone: (520) 318-2700 Carnegie Class: Spec/Arts
FAX Number: (520) 881-4794 Calendar System: Quarter
URL: www.artinstitutes.edu/tucson
Established: 1996 Annual Undergrad Tuition & Fees: $17,316
Enrollment: 491 Coed
Affiliation or Control: Proprietary IRS Status: Proprietary
Highest Offering: Baccalaureate
Program: 2-Year Principally Bachelor's Creditable; Professional
Accreditation: ACICS

01 Campus Director .... Mr. R. William VAN ZWOL
05 Dean .... Mr. Mark HINRICHS

Asian Institute of Medical Studies (D)

3131 N Country Club Road Ste 100, Tucson AZ 85716-1650
County: Pima FICE Identification: 041193
Telephone: (520) 322-6330 Carnegie Class: Not Classified
FAX Number: (520) 322-5661 Calendar System: Quarter
URL: www.asianinstitute.edu
Established: 2000 Annual Undergrad Tuition & Fees: $49,998
Enrollment: 24 Coed
Affiliation or Control: Independent Non-Profit IRS Status: 501(c)3
Highest Offering: Master's
Program: Professional
Accreditation: #ACUP

01 President .... Mr. Alex HOLLAND
07 Admissions Director .... Ms. Sonia TORRES

Brighton College (E)

7332 E Butherus Drive, Suite 102, Scottsdale AZ 85260
County: Maricopa Identification: 666710
Telephone: (800) 231-3803 Carnegie Class: Not Classified
FAX Number: (602) 212-0502 Calendar System: Other
URL: www.brightoncollege.edu
Established: 1961 Annual Undergrad Tuition & Fees: $7,800
Enrollment: 500 Coed
Affiliation or Control: Proprietary IRS Status: Proprietary
Highest Offering: Associate Degree
Program: Occupational; 2-Year Principally Bachelor's Creditable; Technical Emphasis
Accreditation: DETC

01 President .... Kathleen MIRABILE

Brookline College (F)

2445 West Dunlap Avenue, Suite 100, Phoenix AZ 85021
County: Maricopa FICE Identification: 022188
Unit ID: 104090
Telephone: (602) 242-6265 Carnegie Class: Bac/Assoc
FAX Number: (602) 973-2572 Calendar System: Other
URL: www.brooklinecollege.edu
Established: 1979 Annual Undergrad Tuition & Fees: $19,975
Enrollment: 1,585 Coed
Affiliation or Control: Proprietary IRS Status: Proprietary
Highest Offering: Baccalaureate
Program: Occupational
Accreditation: ACICS, @PTAA

01 Director .... Mr. Louis ARMENDARIZ

Brookline College (G)

1140 South Priest Drive, Tempe AZ 85281
County: Maricopa Identification: 666403
Unit ID: 404055
Telephone: (480) 545-8755 Carnegie Class: Assoc/PrivFP
FAX Number: (480) 926-1371 Calendar System: Other
URL: www.brooklinecollege.edu
Established: 1979 Annual Undergrad Tuition & Fees: $13,750
Enrollment: 575 Coed
Affiliation or Control: Proprietary IRS Status: Proprietary
Highest Offering: Associate Degree
Program: Occupational; Technical Emphasis
Accreditation: ACICS

01 Campus Director .... Mrs. Cheryl KINDRED

† Branch campus of Brookline College, Phoenix, AZ.

Brookline College (H)

5441 E 22nd Street, Suite 125, Tucson AZ 85711-5444
County: Pima Identification: 666402
Unit ID: 438179
Telephone: (520) 748-9799 Carnegie Class: Assoc/PrivFP
FAX Number: (520) 748-9355 Calendar System: Semester
URL: www.brooklinecollege.edu
Established: 1995 Annual Undergrad Tuition & Fees: $14,500
Enrollment: 849 Coed
Affiliation or Control: Proprietary IRS Status: Proprietary
Highest Offering: Baccalaureate
Program: Occupational; Liberal Arts And General
Accreditation: ACICS

01 Director .... Mr. Rodney FITZSIMMONS

† Branch campus of Brookline College, Phoenix, AZ.

Brown Mackie College-Phoenix (I)

13430 North Black Canyon Highway, Phoenix AZ 85029
County: Maricopa Identification: 666782
Unit ID: 456612
Telephone: (602) 337-3044 Carnegie Class: Assoc/PrivFP4
FAX Number: (480) 375-2450 Calendar System: Other
URL: www.brownmackie.edu
Established: N/A Annual Undergrad Tuition & Fees: $11,124
Enrollment: 459 Coed
Affiliation or Control: Proprietary IRS Status: Proprietary
Highest Offering: Baccalaureate
Program: Occupational; 2-Year Principally Bachelor's Creditable; Business Emphasis
Accreditation: ACICS, OTA, SURTEC

01 President .... Connie SHARP
07 Senior Director of Admissions .... Angie BACINO
05 Dean of Academic Affairs .... Vacant

† Branch campus of Brown Mackie College, Tuscon, AZ.

Brown Mackie College-Tucson (J)

4585 E Speedway Boulevard, Tucson AZ 85712-5300
County: Pima FICE Identification: 009451
Unit ID: 104364
Telephone: (520) 319-3300 Carnegie Class: Bac/Diverse
FAX Number: (520) 325-0108 Calendar System: Other
URL: www.brownmackie.edu
Established: 1972 Annual Undergrad Tuition & Fees: $12,204
Enrollment: 619 Coed
Affiliation or Control: Proprietary IRS Status: Proprietary
Highest Offering: Baccalaureate
Program: Occupational; 2-Year Principally Bachelor's Creditable; Business Emphasis
Accreditation: ACICS, OTA, SURTEC

01 President .... Mr. Tim BUSH
05 Dean of Academic Affairs .... Mr. Michael O'DONNELL
07 Senior Director of Admissions .... Vacant
06 Registrar .... Vacant
32 Director of Student Services .... Mr. Kris JOHNSON
36 Director of Career Services .... Mr. Frank MAISH

The Bryman School (K)

2250 W Peoria Avenue, Suite A100, Phoenix AZ 85029-4923
County: Maricopa FICE Identification: 030764
Unit ID: 384209
Telephone: (602) 274-4300 Carnegie Class: Assoc/PrivFP
FAX Number: (602) 248-9087 Calendar System: Other
URL: www.brymanschool.edu
Established: N/A Annual Undergrad Tuition & Fees: $14,112
Enrollment: 757 Coed
Affiliation or Control: Proprietary IRS Status: Proprietary
Highest Offering: Associate Degree
Program: Occupational; 2-Year Principally Bachelor's Creditable; Technical Emphasis
Accreditation: ACICS, MAAB

01 Campus President .... Mr. Erick ANDERSON
05 Dean of Education .... Ms. Sue WHITE
37 Director of Financial Aid .... Mrs. Patricia SIMON
07 Director of Admissions .... Mr. Karri PREA
36 Career Service Director .... Mr. Rick RUSCH
11 Office Manager .... Ms. Sarah ROSE

Carrington College - Mesa (L)

1001 W Southern Avenue, Suite 130, Mesa AZ 85210
County: Maricopa FICE Identification: 023352
Unit ID: 103909
Telephone: (480) 212-1600 Carnegie Class: Not Classified
FAX Number: (480) 827-0022 Calendar System: Other
URL: www.carrington.edu
Established: 1992 Annual Undergrad Tuition & Fees: $13,700
Enrollment: 853 Coed
Affiliation or Control: Proprietary IRS Status: Proprietary
Highest Offering: Associate Degree
Program: Occupational; 2-Year Principally Bachelor's Creditable

Accreditation: ACICS, DH, PTAA

01 Executive Campus Director .... Mr. Steve TEMPLE

Carrington College - Phoenix (A)

8503 N 27th Avenue, Phoenix AZ 85051-4096
County: Maricopa FICE Identification: 021006
Unit ID: 103893
Telephone: (602) 393-5900 Carnegie Class: Assoc/PrivFP
FAX Number: N/A Calendar System: Other
URL: www.carrington.edu
Established: 1976 Annual Undergrad Tuition & Fees: $14,212
Enrollment: 785 Coed
Affiliation or Control: Proprietary IRS Status: Proprietary
Highest Offering: Associate Degree
Program: Occupational; 2-Year Principally Bachelor's Creditable
Accreditation: ACICS, ADNUR

01 Executive Campus Director .... Ms. Val COLMONE
05 Dean Academic Affairs .... Ms. Susan OPALKA

Carrington College - Tucson (B)

3550 N Oracle Road, Tucson AZ 85705-3591
County: Pima FICE Identification: 030898
Unit ID: 103927
Telephone: (520) 888-5885 Carnegie Class: Not Classified
FAX Number: (520) 887-3005 Calendar System: Semester
URL: www.carrington.edu
Established: 1984 Annual Undergrad Tuition & Fees: $14,212
Enrollment: 592 Coed
Affiliation or Control: Proprietary IRS Status: Proprietary
Highest Offering: Associate Degree
Program: Occupational; 2-Year Principally Bachelor's Creditable
Accreditation: ACICS

01 Executive Campus Director .... Mr. Antonio THOMPSON

Carrington College - Westside (C)

2701 W Bethany Home Road, Phoenix AZ 85017-1705
County: Maricopa Identification: 666248
Unit ID: 250601
Telephone: (602) 433-1333 Carnegie Class: Not Classified
FAX Number: (602) 433-1414 Calendar System: Semester
URL: www.carrington.edu
Established: 1986 Annual Undergrad Tuition & Fees: $46,715
Enrollment: 600 Coed
Affiliation or Control: Proprietary IRS Status: Proprietary
Highest Offering: Associate Degree
Program: 2-Year Principally Bachelor's Creditable
Accreditation: ACICS, RAD

01 Campus Director .... Vacant

† Branch campus of Carrington College-Phoenix, Phoenix, AZ.

Central Arizona College (D)

8470 N Overfield Road, Coolidge AZ 85128-9779
County: Pinal FICE Identification: 007283
Unit ID: 104346
Telephone: (520) 494-5444 Carnegie Class: Assoc/Pub-S-MC
FAX Number: (520) 494-5008 Calendar System: Semester
URL: www.centralaz.edu
Established: 1962 Annual Undergrad Tuition & Fees (In-District): $2,160
Enrollment: 7,442 Coed
Affiliation or Control: Local IRS Status: 501(c)3
Highest Offering: Associate Degree
Program: Occupational; 2-Year Principally Bachelor's Creditable
Accreditation: NH, ADNUR, DIETT, MAC, RAD

01 Interim President .... Dr. Doris HELMICH
05 Acting VP Learning Servcies .... Dr. James MOORE
20 Acting Assoc VP Academic Affairs .... Dr. Steven GONZALES
32 Acting Assoc VP Student Affairs .... Dr. Philip TOMPKINS
76 Dean of Health Careers & Sciences .... Mr. Julian EASTER
107 Acting Asst Dean Prof & Tech Educ .... Dr. Janice PRATT
49 Dean of Arts & Social Sciences .... Ms. Terri ACKLAND
35 Acting Asst Dean Student Affairs .... Ms. Jenni GONZALES
10 Vice President Financial & Admn Svc .... Mr. Chris WODKA
13 Associate VP Technology Svcs .... Mr. Richard KING
09 Associate VP Inst Effectiveness .... Mr. Bruce MOSES
16 Vice President Human Resources .... Mr. James KIMSEY
15 Acting Associate VP HR .... Mr. T.J FERRER
09 Exec Dir Institutional Research .... Mr. William BROWN
08 Director Library Services .... Ms. Adrianna SAAVEDRA
26 Dir Public Relations & Marketing .... Mr. Thomas DICAMILLO
37 Director of Financial Aid .... Ms. Elisa JUAREZ
41 Acting Athletic Director .... Mr. Chuck SCHNOOR
39 Director of Residence/ Life .... Mr. Nev KRAGULJEVIC
19 Chief Campus Police Officer .... Mr. Luis MARTINEZ
18 Exec Director of Facilities .... Mr. Ernesto VALENZUELA
96 Director of Purchasing .... Mr. Mark SALAZ
06 Registrar .... Ms. Veronica DURAN
07 Director of Recruitment .... Mr. Luis SANCHEZ
21 Exec Dir Accounting Svc/Comptroller .... Ms. Luisa OTT
84 Dean Recruitment & Admissions .... Vacant
81 Dean of Comm/Math & Learning Supp .... Vacant

Cochise College (E)

4190 W Highway 80, Douglas AZ 85607-6190
County: Cochise FICE Identification: 001072
Unit ID: 104425
Telephone: (800) 966-7943 Carnegie Class: Assoc/Pub-R-L
FAX Number: (520) 417-4006 Calendar System: Semester
URL: www.cochise.edu
Established: 1961 Annual Undergrad Tuition & Fees (In-District): $2,100
Enrollment: 4,912 Coed
Affiliation or Control: Local IRS Status: 170(c)1
Highest Offering: Associate Degree
Program: Occupational; 2-Year Principally Bachelor's Creditable
Accreditation: NH, ADNUR

01 President .... Dr. J. D. ROTTWEILER
05 Vice Pres for Instruction/Provost .... Dr. Verlyn FICK
10 Vice Pres Administration .... Mr. Kevin S. BUTLER
13 Vice Pres Information Technology .... Mr. Carlos CARTAGENA
15 Vice Pres Human Resources .... Ms. Wendy DAVIS
49 Dean of Liberal Arts .... Mr. Chuck HOYACK
56 Dean of Extended Learning .... Ms. Sheila DEVOE HEIDMAN
32 Dean of Student Services .... Dr. James (Bo) HALL
09 Director of Institutional Research .... Dr. Jerome V. WARD
20 Director Curr/Learning/Assessment .... Dr. Judith E. DOERR
06 Director Admissions & Rec/Registrar .... Ms. Debbie QUICK
08 Director of College Libraries .... Ms. Pat HOTCHKISS
21 Director of Budgeting Services .... Ms. Sandy BRYAN
18 Dir Facilities Mgmt & Planning .... Mr. Frank DYKSTRA
29 Director Office of External Affairs .... Ms. Denise MERKEL
106 Director of Online Campus .... Mr. George SELF
37 Director of Financial Aid .... Ms. Karen BENNETT
39 Dir of Residental & Student Life .... Ms. Marisol ARENIVAS
88 Director Ctr for Economic Research .... Dr. Robert CARREIRA
51 Director Ctr for Lifelong Learning .... Ms. Sharon GILMAN
26 Dir Marketing & Creative Services .... Mr. Ed ROSKOWSKI
72 Dean of Business & Technology .... Mr. Bruce RICHARDSON
81 Dean of Math/Science & Health Sci .... Dr. Richard (Bubba) HALL
35 Asst Dean of Student Services .... Mr. Mark BOGGIE

Coconino Community College (F)

2800 S Lone Tree Road, Flagstaff AZ 86001-2701
County: Coconino FICE Identification: 031004
Unit ID: 404426
Telephone: (928) 527-1222 Carnegie Class: Assoc/Pub-R-M
FAX Number: (928) 226-4106 Calendar System: Semester
URL: www.coconino.edu
Established: 1991 Annual Undergrad Tuition & Fees (In-State): $2,700
Enrollment: 4,245 Coed
Affiliation or Control: State IRS Status: 501(c)3
Highest Offering: Associate Degree
Program: 2-Year Principally Bachelor's Creditable
Accreditation: NH

01 President .... Dr. Leah L. BORNSTEIN
05 Vice President for Academic Affairs .... Dr. Russ ROTHAMER
10 VP for Business & Administration .... Ms. Jami VAN ESS
32 Director of Student Services .... Ms. Veronica HIPOLITO
12 Executive Dean for Page Campus .... Mr. Lloyd HAMMONDS
51 Exec Dir of Cmty & Corp Learning .... Mr. John CARDANI
49 Dean of Art & Sciences .... Dr. Ingrid LEE
15 Director for Human Resources .... Ms. Theresa ALVARADO
09 Dir Institutional Research/Assess .... Dr. Stephen CHAMBERS
37 Director for Financial Aid .... Mr. Robert VOYTEK
06 Registrar/Dir Enrollment Services .... Ms. Kimmi GRULKE
88 Dean of Occupational/Profess Tech .... Dr. Monica BAKER
18 Director Facilities .... Mr. Mark EASTON
13 Chief Technical Officer .... Mr. Joe TRAINO
96 Director Purchasing/Auxiliary Svcs .... Mr. Robert SEDILLO
21 Director of Accounting & Finance .... Ms. Siri MULLANEY
30 Director Institutional Advancement .... Mr. Scott TALBOOM
04 Exec Assistant to the President .... Ms. Joan WHITE

CollegeAmerica-Flagstaff (G)

3012 East Route 66, Flagstaff AZ 86004-6323
County: Coconino FICE Identification: 031203
Unit ID: 103945
Telephone: (928) 213-6060 Carnegie Class: Assoc/PrivFP
FAX Number: (928) 526-3468 Calendar System: Other
URL: www.collegeamerica.edu
Established: 1964 Annual Undergrad Tuition & Fees: N/A
Enrollment: 265 Coed
Affiliation or Control: Proprietary IRS Status: Proprietary
Highest Offering: Baccalaureate
Program: Occupational
Accreditation: ACCSC

01 Executive Director .... Ms. Suzanne SCALES

CollegeAmerica-Phoenix (H)

9801 N Metro Parkway East, Phoenix AZ 85051
County: Maricopa Identification: 666017
Telephone: (602) 257-7522 Carnegie Class: Not Classified
FAX Number: (602) 246-3063 Calendar System: Semester
URL: www.collegeamerica.edu
Established: 2004 Annual Undergrad Tuition & Fees: N/A
Enrollment: N/A Coed
Affiliation or Control: Proprietary IRS Status: Proprietary
Highest Offering: Baccalaureate
Program: Occupational; 2-Year Principally Bachelor's Creditable
Accreditation: ACCSC

01 Assoc Director .... Mr. Marty JIUNTA

† Branch campus of CollegeAmerica-Flagstaff

DeVry University - Mesa Center (I)

1201 S Alma School Road, Suite 5450,
Mesa AZ 85210-2011
County: Maricopa Identification: 666190
Unit ID: 405137
Telephone: (480) 827-1511 Carnegie Class: Not Classified
FAX Number: (480) 827-2552 Calendar System: Semester
URL: www.devry.edu
Established: 1931 Annual Undergrad Tuition & Fees: $16,156
Enrollment: 389 Coed
Affiliation or Control: Proprietary IRS Status: Proprietary
Highest Offering: Master's
Program: Occupational; Professional; Business Emphasis
Accreditation: &NH

01 Center Dean .... Wallis STEMM

† Regional accreditation is carried under the parent institution in Downers Grove, IL.

DeVry University - Northeast Phoenix Center (J)

18500 N Allied Way, Suite 150, Phoenix AZ 85054-3102
County: Maricopa Identification: 666191
Unit ID: 437307
Telephone: (480) 657-3223 Carnegie Class: Not Classified
FAX Number: (480) 657-3222 Calendar System: Semester
URL: www.devry.edu
Established: 1931 Annual Graduate Tuition & Fees: $18,384
Enrollment: 77 Coed
Affiliation or Control: Proprietary IRS Status: Proprietary
Highest Offering: Master's; No Undergraduates
Program: Occupational; Professional; Business Emphasis
Accreditation: &NH

01 Center Dean .... Mr. Gary STARK, JR.

† Regional accreditation is carried under the parent institution in Downers Grove, IL.

DeVry University - Phoenix Campus (K)

2149 W Dunlap Avenue, Phoenix AZ 85021-2995
County: Maricopa FICE Identification: 008322
Unit ID: 104531
Telephone: (602) 870-9222 Carnegie Class: Master's M
FAX Number: (602) 870-1209 Calendar System: Semester
URL: www.devry.edu
Established: 1931 Annual Undergrad Tuition & Fees: $16,156
Enrollment: 1,596 Coed
Affiliation or Control: Proprietary IRS Status: Proprietary
Highest Offering: Master's
Program: Occupational; Professional; Business Emphasis
Accreditation: &NH, ENGT, MT

01 Metro President .... Mr. Craig JACOB
03 Group Vice President .... Mr. James DUGAN
05 Dean of Academic Affairs .... Mr. Geoffrey GATES
07 Director of Admissions .... Ms. Cathy TELLES
08 Director of Library Services .... Ms. Margot CASSIDY
06 Registrar .... Ms. Jill JAMERSON
32 Dean of Student Central .... Mr. Michael CHASE
11 Sr Director Finance & Admin .... Ms. Vicki L. MAY
15 Human Resources Business Partner .... Ms. Yamilay LEGER
31 Director of Community Outreach .... Ms. Cheryl BUNTING
36 Director of Career Services .... Ms. Deena HANDLER

† Regional accreditation is carried under the parent institution in Downers Grove, IL.

Diné College (L)

One Circle Drive, Tsaile AZ 86556-9998
County: Apache FICE Identification: 008246
Unit ID: 105297
Telephone: (928) 724-6671 Carnegie Class: Tribal
FAX Number: (928) 724-3327 Calendar System: Semester
URL: www.dinecollege.edu
Established: 1968 Annual Undergrad Tuition & Fees (In-District): $850
Enrollment: 2,021 Coed
Affiliation or Control: Local IRS Status: 501(c)3
Highest Offering: Baccalaureate
Program: Occupational; 2-Year Principally Bachelor's Creditable
Accreditation: NH

01 President .... Dr. Maggie GEORGE
05 Vice President of Academics .... Ms. Rebecca M. BENALLY
11 Vice President for Admin & Finance .... Mr. Ronald BELLOLI
32 Vice Pres of Student Success .... Ms. Glennita HASKEY
30 Director of Development .... Mr. Darryl R. BEGAY
06 Registrar .... Ms. Louise LITZIN
20 Interim Dean .... Mr. Edison CURTIS

37 Director Student Financial Aid .... Mr. Gary SEGAY
15 Dir Department of Human Resources .... Ms. Evelyn MEADOWS
18 Supt Maintenance Operations .... Mr. Delbert PAQUIN
21 Controller .... Ms. Jolene WHEELER
26 Public Relations Director .... Mr. Ed MCCOMBS
09 Director of Institutional Research .... Ms. Marie R. ETSITTY

Dunlap-Stone University (A)

19820 North 7th Street, Suite 100, Phoenix AZ 85024

County: Maricopa Identification: 666315
Telephone: (602) 648-5750 Carnegie Class: Not Classified
FAX Number: (602) 648-5755 Calendar System: Other
URL: www.dunlap-stone.edu
Established: 1995 Annual Undergrad Tuition & Fees: $8,290
Enrollment: 492 Coed
Affiliation or Control: Proprietary IRS Status: Proprietary
Highest Offering: Baccalaureate
Program: Professional; Business Emphasis
Accreditation: DETC

01 President .... Dr. Donald N. BURTON
106 Vice Pres Online Programs/Registrar .... Mrs. Caulyne BARRON

Eastern Arizona College (B)

615 N Stadium Avenue, Thatcher AZ 85552-0769

County: Graham FICE Identification: 001073
Unit ID: 104577
Telephone: (928) 428-8233 Carnegie Class: Assoc/Pub-R-L
FAX Number: (928) 428-2578 Calendar System: Semester
URL: www.eac.edu
Established: 1888 Annual Undergrad Tuition & Fees (In-District): $1,520
Enrollment: 6,997 Coed
Affiliation or Control: State/Local IRS Status: 501(c)3
Highest Offering: Associate Degree
Program: Occupational; 2-Year Principally Bachelor's Creditable
Accreditation: NH

01 President .... Mr. Mark BRYCE
03 Executive Vice President .... Mr. Brent MCEUEN
10 Chief Business Officer .... Mr. Timothy CURTIS
05 Provost .... Mrs. Jeanne BRYCE
20 Dean of Instruction .... Mr. Michael CROCKETT
20 Dean of Instruction .... Dr. Phil MCBRIDE
20 Dean of Curriculum and Instruction .... Dr. Janice LAWHORN
32 Dean of Students .... Dr. Gary SORENSEN
06 Associate Dean/Registrar .... Dr. Randall SKINNER
38 Assistant Dean of Counseling .... Ms. Sharon ALLEN
12 Director of Discovery Park Campus .... Mr. Paul ANGER
21 Director Fiscal Control/Controller .... Mr. Darwin WEECH
37 Director of Financial Aid .... Mrs. Sharon MONTOYA
14 Director of Information Resources .... Mr. Thomas THOMPSON
09 Director of Institutional Research .... Mr. Glen SNIDER
08 Director of Library Services .... Mrs. Karen JAGGERS
26 Director of Marketing & Public Rels .... Mr. Todd HAYNIE
18 Director of Physical Resources .... Mr. Dan WELKER
30 Executive Director EAC Foundation .... Mr. David UDALL
35 Director of Student Life .... Mr. Danny BATTRAW
41 Athletic Director .... Mr. James BAGNALL
15 Assoc Director Admin Support EEO Co .... Ms. Lauri AVILA
04 Exec Asst to the President and DGB .... Mrs. Laurie PENNINGTON

Embry-Riddle Aeronautical University-Prescott Campus (C)

3200 Willow Creek Road, Prescott AZ 86301-3270

County: Yavapai FICE Identification: 021047
Unit ID: 104586
Telephone: (800) 888-3728 Carnegie Class: Bac/Diverse
FAX Number: (928) 777-3740 Calendar System: Semester
URL: www.erau.edu
Established: 1978 Annual Undergrad Tuition & Fees: $29,520
Enrollment: 1,723 Coed
Affiliation or Control: Independent Non-Profit IRS Status: 501(c)3
Highest Offering: Master's
Program: Occupational; Liberal Arts And General; Professional
Accreditation: &SC, AAB, ENG

01 President .... Dr. John P. JOHNSON
05 Exec Vice President and CAO .... Mr. Frank AYERS
20 Associate VP for Academics .... Dr. Richard BLOOM
32 Dean of Students .... Mr. Larry STEPHAN
50 Director of Business & Finance .... Mr. David HALL
84 Dean of Enrollment Management .... Mr. Thomas RAJALA
15 Manager HR & Student Employment ..... Ms. Sara HEFFELFINGER
13 Director of Information Technology .... Ms. Nancy BARRETT
37 Director Financial Aid .... Mr. Daniel LUPIN
06 Director Records & Registration .... Ms. Mary LAHANN
26 Asst Director of Media Relations .... Mr. Bob ROSS
30 Senior Director of Development .... Mr. Steven BOBINSKY
09 Director of Institutional Research .... Ms. Maria FRANCO
07 Director of Admissions .... Mr. Bryan R. DOUGHERTY

† Regional accreditation is carried under the parent institution in Daytona Beach, FL.

Everest College Phoenix (D)

10400 N 25th Avenue, Suite 190, Phoenix AZ 85021-1610

County: Maricopa FICE Identification: 022950
Unit ID: 103644
Telephone: (602) 942-4141 Carnegie Class: Assoc/PrivFP4
FAX Number: (602) 943-0960 Calendar System: Other
URL: www.everest-college.com
Established: 1982 Annual Undergrad Tuition & Fees: $12,420
Enrollment: 2,254 Coed
Affiliation or Control: Proprietary IRS Status: Proprietary
Highest Offering: Baccalaureate
Program: Occupational; 2-Year Principally Bachelor's Creditable
Accreditation: NH

01 Campus President .... Mr. Todd M. MCDONALD
07 Director of Admissions .... Mr. Nick THORESON

Fortis College, Phoenix (E)

555 N 18th Street, Suite 110, Phoenix AZ 85006

County: Maricopa Identification: 666761
Unit ID: 456180
Telephone: (602) 254-3099 Carnegie Class: Assoc/PrivFP
FAX Number: (602) 254-3183 Calendar System: Semester
URL: www.fortis.edu
Established: 2008 Annual Undergrad Tuition & Fees: $13,471
Enrollment: 316 Coed
Affiliation or Control: Proprietary IRS Status: Proprietary
Highest Offering: Baccalaureate
Program: Occupational
Accreditation: ACCSC

01 Campus Director .... Glen THARP

† Branch campus of Fortis College, Centerville, OH. Tuition varies by degree program.

Frank Lloyd Wright School of Architecture (F)

Taliesin W, PO Box 4430, Scottsdale AZ 85261-4430

County: Maricopa FICE Identification: 025332
Unit ID: 104665
Telephone: (480) 860-2700 Carnegie Class: Spec/Arts
FAX Number: (480) 860-8472 Calendar System: Other
URL: www.taliesin.edu
Established: 1932 Annual Undergrad Tuition & Fees: $30,000
Enrollment: 24 Coed
Affiliation or Control: Independent Non-Profit IRS Status: 501(c)3
Highest Offering: Master's
Program: Professional
Accreditation: NH

01 Academic Dean & Dir of Curriculum .... Mr. Victor SIDY
08 Dean of Libraries .... Ms. Elizabeth AL-HAZZAM DAWASARI
07 Dir Admissions/Fin Aid/Registrar .... Ms. Pamela STEFANSSON
10 Vice President Finance .... Ms. Lisa MURPHY
30 Director of Development .... Mr. Ralph PHILLIPS
05 Director of Academic Affairs .... Ms. Madalena MAESTRI

Golf Academy of America (G)

2031 N. Arizona Ave Suite 2, Chandler AZ 85225

County: Maricopa Identification: 666023
Unit ID: 430166
Telephone: (800) 342-7342 Carnegie Class: Assoc/PrivFP
FAX Number: (480) 857-1580 Calendar System: Semester
URL: www.golfacademy.edu
Established: 1996 Annual Undergrad Tuition & Fees: $33,390
Enrollment: 204 Coed
Affiliation or Control: Proprietary IRS Status: Proprietary
Highest Offering: Associate Degree
Program: Occupational; Business Emphasis
Accreditation: ACICS

01 President .... Mr. Michael LARGENT
12 Campus Director .... Mr. Tim EBERLEIN

† Branch campus of Virginia College, Birmingham, AL.

Grand Canyon University (H)

3300 W Camelback Road, Phoenix AZ 85017-3030

County: Maricopa FICE Identification: 001074
Unit ID: 104717
Telephone: (602) 639-7500 Carnegie Class: Master's L
FAX Number: N/A Calendar System: Semester
URL: www.gcu.edu
Established: 1949 Annual Undergrad Tuition & Fees: $16,500
Enrollment: 40,487 Coed
Affiliation or Control: Proprietary IRS Status: Proprietary
Highest Offering: Doctorate
Program: Liberal Arts And General; Teacher Preparatory; Professional
Accreditation: NH, ACBSP, NURSE

01 President .... Dr. Kathy PLAYER
00 Chief Executive Officer .... Mr. Brian MUELLER
03 Executive Vice President .... Mr. Stan MEYER
11 Chief Administrative Officer .... Vacant
15 Vice President Human Resources .... Vacant
05 Chief Academic Officer .... Dr. Cheri ST. ARNAULD
26 Vice Pres of Marketing .... Ms. Christel MOSBY
50 Dean Ken Blanchard Col of Business .... Dr. Kevin BARKSDALE
53 Dean College of Education .... Dr. Kimberly LAPRADE
66 Dean College of Nursing .... Dr. Anne MCNAMARA
49 Dean of College of Arts and Science .... Dr. Mark WOODEN
58 Dean Graduate Studies .... Dr. Hank RAADA
57 Dean of Fine Arts and Production .... Mr. Claude PENSIS

Harrison Middleton University (I)

1105 East Broadway Road, Tempe AZ 85282-1505

County: Maricopa Identification: 666169
Telephone: (877) 248-6724 Carnegie Class: Not Classified
FAX Number: (800) 762-1622 Calendar System: Other
URL: www.hmu.edu
Established: 1998 Annual Undergrad Tuition & Fees: $7,900
Enrollment: 400 Coed
Affiliation or Control: Proprietary IRS Status: Proprietary
Highest Offering: Doctorate
Program: Liberal Arts And General
Accreditation: DETC

01 President .... Mr. David CURD
05 Director of Education .... Mr. Michael CURD
06 Director of Accreditation/Registrar ...... Ms. Susan CHIARAMONTE
10 Director of Finance .... Mr. Walter MILLER

International Baptist College (J)

2211 W Germann Road, Chandler AZ 85286

County: Maricopa FICE Identification: 033473
Unit ID: 436614
Telephone: (480) 245-7903 Carnegie Class: Spec/Faith
FAX Number: (480) 245-7908 Calendar System: Semester
URL: www.ibconline.edu
Established: 1980 Annual Undergrad Tuition & Fees: $10,800
Enrollment: 75 Coed
Affiliation or Control: Baptist IRS Status: 501(c)3
Highest Offering: Doctorate
Program: Occupational; 2-Year Principally Bachelor's Creditable; Teacher Preparatory; Religious Emphasis
Accreditation: TRACS

01 President .... Mr. David W. BROCK
00 Chancellor .... Dr. Jerry C. TETREAU
32 Student Life Director .... Mr. Nathan MESTLER
05 Academic Dean .... Mr. Jeffrey G. CAUPP
10 Chief Financial Officer .... Mr. Walt BAINES
08 Media Center Director .... Mr. Lee WILL
33 Dean of Men .... Mr. Nathan MESTLER
34 Dean of Women .... Ms. Marcia GAMMON
06 Registrar .... Mr. Stephen PENA
37 Financial Aid Administrator .... Mrs. Jane BUSHEY

ITT Technical Institute (K)

10220 North 25th Avenue, Suite 100, Phoenix AZ 85021

County: Maricopa Identification: 666696
Unit ID: 451972
Telephone: (602) 749-7900 Carnegie Class: Assoc/PrivFP4
FAX Number: (602) 749-7950 Calendar System: Quarter
URL: www.itt-tech.edu
Established: N/A Annual Undergrad Tuition & Fees: N/A
Enrollment: 463 Coed
Affiliation or Control: Proprietary IRS Status: Proprietary
Highest Offering: Baccalaureate
Program: Technical Emphasis
Accreditation: ACICS

† Branch campus of ITT Technical Institute, Indianapolis, IN.

ITT Technical Institute (L)

5005 S Wendler Drive, Tempe AZ 85282-6321

County: Maricopa FICE Identification: 020652
Unit ID: 105172
Telephone: (602) 437-7500 Carnegie Class: Spec/Tech
FAX Number: (602) 437-7505 Calendar System: Quarter
URL: www.itt-tech.edu
Established: 1963 Annual Undergrad Tuition & Fees: N/A
Enrollment: 721 Coed
Affiliation or Control: Proprietary IRS Status: Proprietary
Highest Offering: Baccalaureate
Program: Technical Emphasis
Accreditation: ACICS

† Branch campus of ITT Technical Institute, Indianapolis, IN.

ITT Technical Institute (M)

1455 W River Road, Tucson AZ 85704-5829

County: Pima FICE Identification: 023611
Unit ID: 105163
Telephone: (520) 408-7488 Carnegie Class: Spec/Tech
FAX Number: (520) 292-9899 Calendar System: Quarter
URL: www.itt-tech.edu
Established: 1984 Annual Undergrad Tuition & Fees: N/A
Enrollment: 518 Coed
Affiliation or Control: Proprietary IRS Status: Proprietary
Highest Offering: Baccalaureate
Program: Technical Emphasis
Accreditation: ACICS

† Branch campus of ITT Technical Institute, Indianapolis, IN.

Kaplan College (A)

13610 N Black Canyon Highway, #104,
Phoenix AZ 85029-6323

County: Maricopa FICE Identification: 020712
Unit ID: 105118
Telephone: (602) 548-1955 Carnegie Class: Assoc/PrivFP
FAX Number: (602) 548-1956 Calendar System: Semester
URL: www.kaplancollege.com
Established: 1972 Annual Undergrad Tuition & Fees: $11,900
Enrollment: 487 Coed
Affiliation or Control: Proprietary IRS Status: Proprietary
Highest Offering: Associate Degree
Program: Occupational
Accreditation: ACCSC, MAC

01 Campus President Mr. Jake ELSEN

Lamson College (B)

875 West Elliot Road, Suite 206, Tempe AZ 85284-1141

County: Maricopa FICE Identification: 025215
Unit ID: 104984
Telephone: (480) 898-7000 Carnegie Class: Assoc/PrivFP
FAX Number: (480) 967-6645 Calendar System: Other
URL: www.lamsoncollege.edu
Established: 1889 Annual Undergrad Tuition & Fees: N/A
Enrollment: 180 Coed
Affiliation or Control: Proprietary IRS Status: Proprietary
Highest Offering: Associate Degree
Program: Occupational; 2-Year Principally Bachelor's Creditable
Accreditation: ACICS

01 Campus Director Mr. Dino MEYER

Le Cordon Bleu College of Culinary Arts in Scottsdale (C)

8100 E Camelback Road, Ste 1001,
Scottsdale AZ 85251-3940

County: Maricopa FICE Identification: 026167
Unit ID: 262332
Telephone: (480) 990-3773 Carnegie Class: Spec/Other
FAX Number: (480) 990-0351 Calendar System: Other
URL: www.chefs.edu/scottsdale
Established: 1986 Annual Undergrad Tuition & Fees: $15,298
Enrollment: 1,560 Coed
Affiliation or Control: Proprietary IRS Status: Proprietary
Highest Offering: Baccalaureate
Program: Occupational
Accreditation: ACCSC, ACICS, ACFEI

01 President Mr. Lloyd KIRSCH
11 Vice President Administration Ms. Jennifer JILOT
37 Vice Pres/Director of Financial Aid Ms. Maria IARKOVA
36 Director Career Services Ms. Kathleen DOELLER
06 Registrar Ms. Polly GIBSON
07 Director of Admission Ms. Shannon FERRER

*Maricopa County Community College District Office (D)

2411 W 14th Street, Tempe AZ 85281-6941

County: Maricopa FICE Identification: 001075
Unit ID: 105136
Telephone: (480) 731-8000 Carnegie Class: N/A
FAX Number: (480) 731-8850
URL: www.maricopa.edu

01 Chancellor Dr. Rufus GLASPER
05 Executive Vice Chancellor/ Provost Dr. Maria HARPER-MARINICK
26 VC Resource Devel/Community Rels Dr. Steven HELFGOT
10 Vice Chanc Business Services Ms. Debra THOMPSON
16 Vice Chancellor Human Resources Ms. Nikki R. JACKSON
13 Vice Chanc Information Technologies Mr. George KAHKEDJIAN
21 Assoc Vice Chanc Business Services Ms. Gaye MURPHY
22 Dir Center Workforce Development Mr. Randy KIMMENS
30 Exec Director Resource Development Ms. Mary O'CONNOR
09 Assoc VC Inst Strategy/Rsrch/Effect Dr. Sherri ONDRUS
18 Assoc Vice Chanc Cap Plng/Spec Proj Mr. J. Lionel DIAZ
88 Special Assistant to the Chancellor Dr. Sue KATER

*Chandler-Gilbert Community College (E)

2626 E Pecos Road, Chandler AZ 85225-2499

County: Maricopa FICE Identification: 030722
Unit ID: 364025
Telephone: (480) 732-7000 Carnegie Class: Assoc/Pub-U-MC
FAX Number: (480) 732-7090 Calendar System: Semester
URL: www.cgc.maricopa.edu
Established: 1992 Annual Undergrad Tuition & Fees (In-District): $1,854
Enrollment: 14,030 Coed
Affiliation or Control: State/Local IRS Status: 501(c)3
Highest Offering: Associate Degree
Program: 2-Year Principally Bachelor's Creditable
Accreditation: NH, ADNUR, DIETT

02 President Dr. Linda LUJAN
05 Vice President Academic Affairs Dr. William GUERRIERO
32 Vice President Student Affairs Dr. William H. CRAWFORD, III
11 Vice Pres Administrative Services Dr. Jacalyn A. ASKIN
12 Provost Williams Campus Mr. John SCHROEDER
49 Interim Dean of Arts and Sciences Dr. Maria WISE
31 Dean of Community Affairs Dr. Cindy BARNES PHARR
32 Dean of Student Affairs Mr. Daniel HERBST
10 Assoc Dean Finance/Business Svcs Mr. Bradley KENDREX
07 Dir Admissions/Registr & Records Ms. Linda SHAW
13 Director Information Technology Mr. Victor NAVARRO
09 Dir Research/Planning/Development Ms. Mary DAY
24 Dir Instructional Tech & Media Svcs Mr. Tim KEEFE
36 Dir Career/Education Planning Svcs Mrs. Mary FREDERICK
85 Director International Education Ms. Annie JIMENEZ
32 Director College Student Services Ms. Dawn GRUICHICH
18 Director Buildings and Grounds Mr. Bruce SCHARBACH
35 Director Student Life Mr. Mike GREENE
41 Director Athletics Mr. Ed YEAGER
19 Director College Safety Mr. Robert EVERETT
37 Director Financial Aid Vacant
21 Manager College Fiscal Services Vacant
15 Manager College Employee Services Ms. Lynda ANDERSON
26 Coordinator Marketing/Public Rels Vacant
27 Coordinator of Marketing Ms. Carol CRANE
28 Coordinator of Diversity Ms. Lori GIRSHICK
28 Coordinator of Diversity Ms. Caryl TERRELL-BAMIRO
25 Project Coordinator Admin Svcs Ms. Trina LARSON

*Estrella Mountain Community College (F)

3000 N Dysart Road, Avondale AZ 85392

County: Maricopa FICE Identification: 031563
Unit ID: 384333
Telephone: (623) 935-8000 Carnegie Class: Assoc/Pub-U-MC
FAX Number: (623) 935-8008 Calendar System: Semester
URL: www.estrellamountain.edu
Established: 1990 Annual Undergrad Tuition & Fees (In-District): $2,280
Enrollment: 8,243 Coed
Affiliation or Control: State/Local IRS Status: 501(c)3
Highest Offering: Associate Degree
Program: Occupational; 2-Year Principally Bachelor's Creditable
Accreditation: NH, ADNUR

02 President Dr. Ernest LARA
05 Vice President of Academic Affairs Dr. Bryan TIPPETT
32 Vice President Student Affairs Dr. Debbie KUSHIBAB
11 Vice President Admin Services Ms. Sue TAVAKOLI
75 Vice President Occupational Educ Dr. Clay GOODMAN
20 Dean of Academic Affairs Ms. Joyce M. JACKSON
20 Dean of Academic Affairs Dr. Sylvia ORR
13 Director Information Technology Mr. Richard MARMON
35 Interim Dean of Student Services Ms. Laura DULGAR
08 Division Chair Information Resource Ms. Nikol PRICE
09 Dean Planning/Rsrch/Effectiveness Dr. Rene G. WILLEKENS
18 Director Facilities Planning/Devel Mr. Randy MAULDIN
07 Director of Enrollment Services Mr. Frank AMPARO
10 Manager College Fiscal Services Ms. Leda JOHNSON
26 Chief Public Relations Officer Mr. Ralph CAMPBELL
37 Director Student Financial Aid Ms. Rosanna SHORT
21 Manager College Budget Ms. Maggie CASTILLO

*Gateway Community College (G)

108 N 40th Street, Phoenix AZ 85034-1795

County: Maricopa FICE Identification: 008303
Unit ID: 105145
Telephone: (602) 286-8000 Carnegie Class: Assoc/Pub-U-MC
FAX Number: (602) 286-8072 Calendar System: Semester
URL: www.gatewaycc.edu/
Established: 1968 Annual Undergrad Tuition & Fees (In-District): $1,824
Enrollment: 6,801 Coed
Affiliation or Control: State/Local IRS Status: 501(c)3
Highest Offering: Associate Degree
Program: Occupational; 2-Year Principally Bachelor's Creditable
Accreditation: NH, ADNUR, DMS, NDT, NMT, POLYT, PTAA, RAD, RTT, SURGT

02 President Dr. Eugene GIOVANNINI
05 Vice President Academic Affairs Dr. Paula NORBY
32 Vice President Student Affairs Dr. Diana MUNIZ
11 Vice President Administrative Svcs Ms. Janet LANGLEY
35 Dean Student Services Dr. Dan LUFKIN
20 Associate Dean Academic Affairs Ms. Gloria STAHMER
07 Supervisor Admissions/Reg & Rec Ms. Brenda STARCK
09 Dir Research Planning & Development Ms. Cathy HERNANDEZ
88 College Budget Analyst Mr. Mark VELARDE
10 Manager College Fiscal Services Mr. Sidney DIETZ
18 Chief Facilities/Physical Plant Vacant
26 Director Marketing/Public Relations Ms. Christine LAMBRAKIS
30 Director Inst Advance & Entrep Pgm Ms. Susie PULIDO
37 Director Student Financial Aid Ms. Suzanne RINGLE
84 Coordinator Enrollment Services Ms. Kelly MCPHEE
16 Manager College Employee Services Ms. Alice CORNELIUS

*Glendale Community College (H)

6000 W Olive Avenue, Glendale AZ 85302-3006

County: Maricopa FICE Identification: 001076
Unit ID: 104708
Telephone: (623) 845-3000 Carnegie Class: Assoc/Pub-U-MC
FAX Number: (623) 845-3329 Calendar System: Semester
URL: www.gc.maricopa.edu
Established: 1965 Annual Undergrad Tuition & Fees (In-District): $1,854
Enrollment: 21,376 Coed
Affiliation or Control: State/Local IRS Status: 170(c)1
Highest Offering: Associate Degree
Program: Occupational; 2-Year Principally Bachelor's Creditable
Accreditation: NH, ADNUR

02 President Dr. Irene KOVALA
05 VP Academic & Student Affairs Dr. Ronald D. NATALE, II
11 VP Admin Services & Planning Mr. Greg ROGERS
20 Dean of Academic Affairs Dr. Fernando CAMOU
20 Dean of Academic Affairs Dr. Linda MAIER
20 Dean of Academic Affairs Mr. Eric LESHINSKIE
84 Dean Enrollment Services Ms. Mary D. BLACKWELL
35 Dean Student Life Dr. Osaro IGHODARO
12 Dean GCC North Site Mr. Charles F. JEFFERY
37 Director Financial Aid Ms. Ellen NEEL
18 Director Facilities Mr. Al GONZALES
21 Director College Business Services Mr. Herman GONZALEZ
30 Interim Dir Inst Advancement Ms. Tressa JUMPS
09 Director Research Planning & Devel Dr. Alka ARORA SINGH
15 Manager College Employee Svcs Ms. June S. FESSENDEN
44 Asst Director of Development Ms. Judy SANCHEZ
38 Dept Chair Counseling Mr. David GERKIN
08 Dept Chair Librarian Mr. Frank TORRES
19 Director College Safety Ms. Debra PALOK
04 Admin Assistant to College Pres Vacant

*Mesa Community College (I)

1833 W Southern Avenue, Mesa AZ 85202-4866

County: Maricopa FICE Identification: 001077
Unit ID: 105154
Telephone: (480) 461-7000 Carnegie Class: Assoc/Pub-U-MC
FAX Number: (480) 461-7805 Calendar System: Semester
URL: www.mesacc.edu/
Established: 1965 Annual Undergrad Tuition & Fees (In-District): $1,824
Enrollment: 25,695 Coed
Affiliation or Control: State/Local IRS Status: 501(c)3
Highest Offering: Associate Degree
Program: Occupational; 2-Year Principally Bachelor's Creditable
Accreditation: NH, ADNUR, DH, FUSER

02 President Dr. Shouan PAN
05 Vice Pres Academic Affairs Dr. James MABRY
32 Vice Pres Student Affairs Dr. Sonya PEARSON
11 Vice Pres Admin Services Mr. Jeff DARBUT
13 Vice Pres Information Technology Mr. Sasan POUREETEZADI
12 Provost Red Mountain/Downtown Ctr Ms. Jo WILSON
09 Dean of Inst Planning & Analysis Mr. Matthew ASHCRAFT
35 Dean of Student Affairs Dr. Barbara BOROS
20 Dean Instruction Dr. Rodney HOLMES
20 Dean Instruction Ms. Phebe BLITZ
20 Dean Instruction Ms. Carol ACHS
20 Dean Instruction Mr. Roger YOHE
06 Registrar Dr. Barbara BOROS
15 Associate Dean Human Resources Dr. Emily WEINACKER
18 Director Facilities Mr. Richard CLUFF
21 Dean Administrative Services Mr. John MOLL
26 Director of Institutional Advance Ms. Sonia FILAN
30 Director of Development Mr. Jared LANGKILDE
37 Dir Fin Aid/Scholarships Ms. Patricia PEPPIN
38 Dept Chair Counseling Dr. Karen HARDIN

*Paradise Valley Community College (J)

18401 N 32nd Street, Phoenix AZ 85032-1210

County: Maricopa FICE Identification: 026236
Unit ID: 364016
Telephone: (602) 787-6500 Carnegie Class: Assoc/Pub-U-MC
FAX Number: (602) 787-6625 Calendar System: Semester
URL: www.paradisevally.edu
Established: 1985 Annual Undergrad Tuition & Fees (In-District): $2,280
Enrollment: 9,874 Coed
Affiliation or Control: State/Local IRS Status: 501(c)3
Highest Offering: Associate Degree
Program: Occupational; 2-Year Principally Bachelor's Creditable
Accreditation: NH, ADNUR, DIETT

02 President Dr. Paul DALE
05 Vice President of Academic Affairs Dr. Mary Lou MOSLEY
11 VP Administrative Services Vacant
20 Dean of Academic Affairs Dr. Denise DIGIANFILIPPO
32 Vice President of Student Affairs Dr. Sandra MILLER HOLST
35 Dean of Student Affairs Dr. Shirley GREEN
13 Dean of Information Technology Mr. Paul GOLISCH
07 Supervisor of Admissions Ms. Stella NAPOLES
10 Chief Business Officer Ms. Sandy MCDILL
15 Director Personnel Services Vacant
18 Chief Facilities/Physical Plant Mr. David MATUS
37 Director Student Financial Aid Mr. Kenneth CLARKE
38 Director Student Counseling Dr. James RUBIN
06 Registrar Dr. Shirley GREEN
36 Director Student Placement Ms. Norma CHANDLER
26 Chief Public Relations Officer Vacant
09 Director of Institutional Research Mr. John SNELLING
19 Director Security/Safety Mr. Scott MEEK
41 Athletic Director Mr. Greg SILCOX

*Phoenix College (A)

1202 W Thomas Road, Phoenix AZ 85013-4234
County: Maricopa FICE Identification: 001078
Unit ID: 105428
Telephone: (602) 285-7800 Carnegie Class: Assoc/Pub-U-MC
FAX Number: (602) 285-7700 Calendar System: Semester
URL: www.pc.maricopa.edu
Established: 1920 Annual Undergrad Tuition & Fees (In-District): $2,160
Enrollment: 12,565 Coed
Affiliation or Control: State/Local IRS Status: 501(c)3
Highest Offering: Associate Degree
Program: Occupational; 2-Year Principally Bachelor's Creditable; Technical Emphasis
Accreditation: NH, ADNUR, DA, DH, HT, MAAB, MLTAD

02 President .... Dr. Anna SOLLEY
05 VP of Academic Affairs .... Ms. Casandra KAKAR
11 VP Administrative Services .... Mr. Paul DEROSE
32 Vice Pres Student Affairs .... Ms. Yira BRIMAGE
35 Dean of Student Affairs .... Ms. Chris HAINES
20 Dean of Academic Affairs .... Mr. Wilbert NELSON
103 Dean of Workforce Development .... Dr. Sharon HALFORD
14 Dean of Technology .... Mr. Mark KOAN
08 Department Chair Library .... Ms. Elizabeth SALIBA
38 Department Chair Counseling .... Ms. Nancy NAVARRETE
06 Dir Admissions/Registration/Records .... Vacant
41 Athletic Director .... Ms. Samantha EZELL
37 Director Financial Aid .... Vacant
88 Director Student Leadership .... Ms. Genesis TOOLE
84 Director Advisement Enrollment .... Vacant
09 Dir Instl Plng/Rsrch/Effectiveness .... Ms. Jan BINDER
19 Director of College Safety .... Vacant
30 Director Institutional Advancement .... Ms. Eileen ARCHIBALD
18 Director of Facilities .... Mr. Douglas MCCARTHY
10 Manager Business Services .... Ms. Angela GENNA
15 Supv College Employee Services .... Ms. Mary Helen ESCALANTE
29 Coord Alumni/Comm Relations .... Mr. Frank LUNA
04 Assistant to the President .... Ms. Renee PERRY

*Rio Salado College (B)

2323 W 14th Street, Tempe AZ 85281-6950
County: Maricopa FICE Identification: 021775
Unit ID: 105668
Telephone: (480) 517-8000 Carnegie Class: Assoc/Pub-U-MC
FAX Number: (480) 377-4719 Calendar System: Semester
URL: www.riosalado.edu
Established: 1978 Annual Undergrad Tuition & Fees (In-District): $2,310
Enrollment: 31,890 Coed
Affiliation or Control: State/Local IRS Status: 501(c)3
Highest Offering: Associate Degree
Program: Occupational; 2-Year Principally Bachelor's Creditable; Business Emphasis
Accreditation: NH, DA, DH

02 President .... Dr. Chris BUSTAMANTE
05 Vice President Teaching & Learning .... Dr. Dana OFFERMAN
10 Vice Pres Business & Employee Svcs .... Mr. Todd SIMMONS
32 Vice President Student Services .... Ms. Kishia BROCK
13 Vice President Information Services .... Mr. Edward KELTY
20 Dean of Instruction .... Mr. Rick KEMP
105 Dean of Instruction .... Ms. Dana REID
20 Dean of Instruction .... Dr. Jo JORGENSON
84 Dean Student Enrollment Services .... Vacant
26 Director Inst Advancement .... Mr. Kevin BILDER
07 Assoc Dean of Enrollment Services .... Ms. Ruby MILLER
37 Director of Financial Aid .... Mr. Ryan CHASE
09 Dir Research Planning & Development .... Vacant
18 Director of Facilities .... Mr. Ernest ADKINS
19 Director College Safety .... Ms. Margaret TURNER-SAMPLE
21 Director College Business Services .... Ms. Devi BALA
15 Manager College Employee Services .... Ms. Ginger MARTINDALE
28 Director of Diversity .... Dr. Sharon KOBERNA
08 Faculty Chair Library .... Ms. Hazel DAVIS
17 Faculty Chair Nursing .... Vacant
25 Assoc Dir Grants/Corp Development .... Ms. Barbara KHALSA
85 Director International Education .... Ms. Erma ABEYTA

*Scottsdale Community College (C)

9000 E Chaparral, Scottsdale AZ 85256-2626
County: Maricopa FICE Identification: 008304
Unit ID: 105747
Telephone: (480) 423-6000 Carnegie Class: Assoc/Pub-U-SC
FAX Number: (480) 423-6200 Calendar System: Semester
URL: www.scottsdalecc.edu
Established: 1969 Annual Undergrad Tuition & Fees (In-District): $1,950
Enrollment: 11,235 Coed
Affiliation or Control: State/Local IRS Status: 501(c)3
Highest Offering: Associate Degree
Program: Occupational; 2-Year Principally Bachelor's Creditable
Accreditation: NH, ACFEI, ADNUR

02 President .... Dr. Jan L. GEHLER
05 Vice Pres Academic/Student Affairs .... Dr. Daniel P. CORR
11 Vice Pres Administrative Services .... Mr. Carl COUCH
20 Vice Pres Occupational Educ .... Dr. Dean E. HERMANSON
32 Dean of Student Affairs .... Dr. Donna YOUNG
84 Dean of Student Enrollment .... Ms. Gia TAYLOR
07 Director of Admissions .... Ms. Fran VITALE
09 Director of Institutional Research .... Dr. Laurie COHEN
30 Director of Development .... Mr. Christopher STUDENKA
08 Director of Library Services .... Dr. Pat LOKEY
37 Director Financial Aid/Placement .... Ms. Stacie BECK
18 Director Buildings/Grounds .... Mr. Samuel J. VAN CLEAVE
19 Director of College Safety .... Mr. Les STRICKLAND
26 Dir of Marketing/Public Relations .... Vacant
51 Director Continuing Education .... Vacant
41 Athletic Director Men .... Mr. Marcus CLAPP
41 Athletic Director Women .... Vacant
88 Dir of Southwest Studies Program .... Mr. Marshall TRIMBLE
38 Director Student Advisement .... Mr. Michael CORNELIUS

*South Mountain Community College (D)

7050 S 24th Street, Phoenix AZ 85042-5806
County: Maricopa FICE Identification: 021466
Unit ID: 105792
Telephone: (602) 243-8000 Carnegie Class: Assoc/Pub-U-MC
FAX Number: (602) 243-8329 Calendar System: Semester
URL: www.southmountaincc.edu
Established: 1979 Annual Undergrad Tuition & Fees (In-District): $2,310
Enrollment: 4,738 Coed
Affiliation or Control: State/Local IRS Status: 501(c)3
Highest Offering: Associate Degree
Program: Occupational; 2-Year Principally Bachelor's Creditable
Accreditation: NH, MACTE

02 President .... Dr. Shari L. OLSON
05 Interim Vice Pres Academic Affairs .... Ms. Helen SMITH
11 Int Vice Pres Administrative Svcs .... Ms. Janet ORTEGA
32 Interim Vice Pres Student Affairs .... Dr. Lauren SHELLENBARGER
20 Assoc Dean Career Tech Educ .... Ms. Cindy ODGERS
84 Int Assoc Dean Enrollment Services .... Mr. Chris HAINES
35 Assoc Dean Student Development .... Mr. Raul MONREAL
12 Assoc Dean Extended Campuses .... Dr. Cheryl CRUTCHER
37 Director Financial Aid .... Ms. Inez MORENO-WEINERT
07 Director of Admission & Records .... Ms. Della GARCIA
09 Dean Research/Plng & Development .... Ms. Damita KALOOSTIAN
10 Director College Business Services .... Ms. Dzung TRAN
18 Director of Facilities .... Mr. Jim THARP
26 Director Marketing/Public Relations .... Mr. Robert PRICE
21 Manager Fiscal Services .... Mr. David MORRIS
15 Coordinator Human Resources .... Ms. Vanessa LOGAN
07 Coordinator Advisement/Recruitment .... Ms. Christine NEILL
36 Coordinator Job Placement .... Ms. Suzanne HIPPS

Midwestern University (E)

19555 N 59th Avenue, Glendale AZ 85308-6814
County: Maricopa Identification: 666001
Unit ID: 423643
Telephone: (623) 572-3400 Carnegie Class: Spec/Med
FAX Number: (623) 572-3410 Calendar System: Quarter
URL: www.midwestern.edu
Established: 1900 Annual Undergrad Tuition & Fees: N/A
Enrollment: 2,787 Coed
Affiliation or Control: Independent Non-Profit IRS Status: 501(c)3
Highest Offering: First Professional Degree
Program: Professional
Accreditation: &NH, ANEST, ARCPA, CLPSY, DENT, @OPT, OSTEO, OT, PERF, PHAR, POD, @PTA

01 President & CEO .... Dr. Kathleen H. GOEPPINGER
03 Exec Vice Pres/Chief Operating Ofcr . Dr. Arthur G. DOBBELAERE
10 Sr Vice Pres/Chief Financial Ofcr .... Mr. Gregory J. GAUS
05 VP/CAO Pharmacy & Health Sci Educ .... Dr. Mary LEE
05 VP/CAO Medicine & Dentistry Educ .... Dr. Dennis PAULSON
21 Vice President Finance .... Mr. Dean MALONE
26 Vice President University Relations .... Dr. Karen JOHNSON
15 VP Human Resources/Administration .... Ms. Angela MARTY
32 Dean of Student Services .... Dr. Ross KOSINSKI
76 Dean College of Health Sciences .... Dr. Jacquelyn SMITH
63 Dean Arizona Coll Osteopathic Med .... Dr. Lori KEMPER
67 Dean College of Pharmacy-Glendale .... Dr. Dennis MCCALLIAN
52 Dean College of Dental Medicine .... Dr. Russell GILPATRICK
06 Registrar .... Ms. Christy SCHENK
07 Director of Admissions .... Mr. James WALTER
18 Chief Facilities/Physical Plant .... Mr. William FRANTZ
30 Director Development .... Ms. Christine CLOUSE
37 Director Student Financial Aid .... Mr. Edmund Thomas BILLARD
09 Director of Institutional Research .... Dr. Kevin HYNES
96 Director of Purchasing .... Ms. Carol VANDIJK
13 Director Information Technology .... Mr. Erik CARROLL
19 Director Security/Safety .... Mr. Ronald ENOS

† Regional accreditation is carried under the parent institution in Downers Grove, IL.

Mohave Community College (F)

1971 E. Jagerson Avenue, Kingman AZ 86409-1238
County: Mohave FICE Identification: 011864
Unit ID: 105206
Telephone: (928) 757-0879 Carnegie Class: Assoc/Pub-S-MC
FAX Number: (928) 757-0836 Calendar System: Semester
URL: www.mohave.edu
Established: 1971 Annual Undergrad Tuition & Fees (In-District): $2,224
Enrollment: 10,706 Coed
Affiliation or Control: State/Local IRS Status: 501(c)3
Highest Offering: Associate Degree
Program: Occupational; 2-Year Principally Bachelor's Creditable; Technical Emphasis
Accreditation: NH, ADNUR, DH, EMT, PTAA, SURGT

01 President .... Dr. Michael KEARNS
03 Vice President for Administration .... Dr. H. Lynn CUNDIFF
05 Dean of Instruction .... Dr. Michael ROURKE
32 Dean of Student Services .... Ms. Jann WOODS
10 Dean of Business Services .... Mr. Dick MACDONALD
30 Assoc Vice Pres College Advancement .... Dr. Alan KLAAS
27 Chief Information Officer .... Mr. Ted MCKEVER
106 Campus Dean Distance Education .... Ms. Diana STITHEM
12 Campus Dean Bullhead City .... Mr. Shawn BRISTLE
12 Campus Dean Lake Havasu .... Dr. Nicolas SANCHEZ
12 Campus Dean Neal Kingman .... Dr. Fred GILBERT
12 Campus Dean North Mohave .... Ms. Carolyn HAMBLIN
06 Registrar .... Mr. John WILSON
21 Bursar .... Ms. Camille HOLDEN
37 Director Student Financial Aid .... Mr. Bill OSBORN
09 Dir of Institutional Research .... Mr. Bob FAUBERT
26 Chief Public Relations Officer .... Ms. Charlotte KELLER
07 Director of Recruitment/Admissions .... Mr. David SHABAZZ
35 Dir Student Services Distance Educ .... Ms. Ana MASTERSON
35 Dir Stdnt Svcs Neal Campus Kingman .... Ms. Shirley JOHNSON-CRAFT
35 Dir Student Svcs Lake Havasu Campus .... Ms. Bree KARLIN
35 Dir Stdnt Svcs Bullhead Cty Campus .... Vacant
15 Director Personnel Services .... Ms. Jenny DIXON

National Paralegal College (G)

717 East Maryland Avenue, Phoenix AZ 85014-1561
County: Maricopa FICE Identification: 041574
Unit ID: 461023
Telephone: (800) 371-6105 Carnegie Class: Not Classified
FAX Number: (866) 347-2744 Calendar System: Other
URL: nationalparalegal.edu
Established: 2003 Annual Undergrad Tuition & Fees: $5,691
Enrollment: 837 Coed
Affiliation or Control: Proprietary IRS Status: Proprietary
Highest Offering: Baccalaureate
Program: Occupational; 2-Year Principally Bachelor's Creditable; Business Emphasis
Accreditation: DETC

01 President .... Avi KATZ
05 Dean/Director .... Mark GELLER
32 Student Services Director .... David COHEN
20 Educational Director .... Stephen HAAS

Northcentral University (H)

10000 E University Drive, Prescott Valley AZ 86314-2336
County: Yavapai FICE Identification: 038133
Unit ID: 444130
Telephone: (928) 541-7777 Carnegie Class: DRU
FAX Number: (928) 541-7817 Calendar System: Other
URL: www.ncu.edu
Established: 1996 Annual Undergrad Tuition & Fees: $8,800
Enrollment: 9,662 Coed
Affiliation or Control: Proprietary IRS Status: Proprietary
Highest Offering: Doctorate
Program: Teacher Preparatory; Professional; Business Emphasis
Accreditation: NH, ACBSP, @TEAC

01 President .... Dr. Clinton D. GARDNER
05 Interim Provost .... Dr. Clinton D. GARDNER
10 Executive VP & Chief Financial Ofcr .... Mr. Christopher LYNNE
04 Director Office of the President .... Ms. Stephnie HOPPLE
50 Dean School of Business & Tech Mgmt .... Dr. Lee SMITH
53 Dean School of Education .... Dr. Cindy KNOTT
83 Dean School of Psychology .... Dr. Heather FREDERICK
97 Chair of General Education .... Ms. Melinda LYONS
21 Controller .... Ms. Shannyn STERN
11 Vice President Operations .... Mr. Eric STODDARD
06 Registrar .... Ms. Barbara HICKS
37 Dir of Learner Financial Services .... Ms. Valerie STEINBOCK
08 Director of Library Services .... Mr. Ed SALAZAR
15 Director of Human Resources .... Mr. Rodd RUSSOW
26 Director of Marketing .... Mr. Kevin LUSTIG
88 Director of Writing Program .... Vacant
45 Director of Planning & Quality Assu .... Vacant
50 Director of Strategic Business Know .... Vacant
83 Director of Marriage & Family Ther .... Dr. Branden H. HENLINE
84 Enrollment Manager .... Mr. Bob HANKS

Northern Arizona University (I)

South San Francisco Street, Flagstaff AZ 86011-0001
County: Coconino FICE Identification: 001082
Unit ID: 105330
Telephone: (928) 523-9011 Carnegie Class: RU/H
FAX Number: (928) 523-1848 Calendar System: Semester
URL: www.nau.edu
Established: 1899 Annual Undergrad Tuition & Fees (In-State): $9,271
Enrollment: 25,364 Coed
Affiliation or Control: State IRS Status: 501(c)3
Highest Offering: Doctorate
Program: Liberal Arts And General; Teacher Preparatory; Professional
Accreditation: NH, ACBSP, #ARCPA, BUS, CACREP, CONST, CS, DH, ENG, FOR, MUS, NRPA, NURSE, PTA, SP, SW, TED

01 President .... Dr. John D. HAEGER
03 Executive Vice President .... Dr. M.J MCMAHON

Code	Title	Name
05	Provost and VP for Academic Affairs	Dr. Laura HUENNEKE
30	VP University Advancement	Dr. Mason GERETY
84	Sr VP Enrollment Mgmt/Student Affs	Mr. David BOUSQUET
09	VP Planning/Budget/Inst Research	Dr. Patricia N. HAEUSER
10	VP Finance and Administration	Dr. Jennus L. BURTON
46	Vice President Research	Dr. William GRABE
56	Sr VP Extended Campuses	Mr. Fred HURST
14	Chief Information Tech Officer	Mr. Fred ESTRELLA
35	Associate VP Student Affairs	Dr. Sarah L. BICKEL
28	Associate VP of Diversity	Dr. David E. CAMACHO
84	Director Enrollment Services	Mr. James CASEBEER
12	Assoc VP/Campus Executive Officer	Mr. Larry GOULD
86	VP Govt Affairs/Business Ptnr	Ms. Christy FARLEY
20	Vice Provost Undergraduate Studies	Dr. Karen L. PUGLIESI
85	Vice Provost Center Intl Education	Mr. Harvey CHARLES
08	Dean/University Librarian	Ms. Cynthia A. CHILDREY
53	Dean College of Education	Mr. Michael SAMPSON
58	Dean of Graduate College	Dr. Ramona N. MELLOTT
54	Dean College Eng/Forestry/Nat Sci	Dr. Paul JAGODZINSKI
50	Dean W.A. Franke Col of Business	Dr. Craig VAN SLYKE
49	Dean College of Arts & Letters	Dr. Michael VINCENT
83	Int Dean Col Social/Behavioral Sci	Dr. Stephen WRIGHT
17	Exec Dean Col of Health/Human Svcs	Dr. Leslie SCHULZ
06	University Registrar	Ms. Pamela L. ANASTASSIOU
43	Office of Legal Affairs	Mr. Mark NEUMAYR
37	Director Financial Aid	Mr. Charles Andrew GRIFFIN
15	Associate VP Human Resources	Ms. Diane VERKEST
19	Director University Police	Mr. Gregory T. FOWLER
22	Director Affirmative Action	Ms. Priscilla L. MILLS
23	Director Campus Health Services	Ms. Elizabeth M. APPLEBEE
29	Director Alumni Relations	Ms. Georgette VIGIL
41	VP Intercollegiate Athletics	Ms. Lisa CAMPOS
36	Dir Gateway Student Success Center	Dr. Eileen MAHONEY
07	Interim Director of Admissions	Ms. Anika OLSEN
26	Interim Director of Public Affairs	Mr. Thomas BAUER
35	Dean of Students	Dr. Rick L. BRANDEL
38	Dir Counseling & Testing Center	Ms. Carol O'SABEN
96	Director of Purchasing	Ms. Becky E. MCGAUGH

Northland Pioneer College (A)

PO Box 610, Holbrook AZ 86025-0610

County: Navajo — FICE Identification: 011862 — Unit ID: 105349

Telephone: (928) 524-7311 — Carnegie Class: Assoc/Pub-R-L

FAX Number: (928) 524-7312 — Calendar System: Semester

URL: www.npc.edu

Established: 1973 — Annual Undergrad Tuition & Fees (In-State): $1,688

Enrollment: 3,917 — Coed

Affiliation or Control: State — IRS Status: 501(c)3

Highest Offering: Associate Degree

Program: Occupational; 2-Year Principally Bachelor's Creditable

Accreditation: NH, ADNUR

Code	Title	Name
01	President	Dr. Jeanne SWARTHOUT
05	Vice Pres Learning/Student Services	Mr. Mark H. VEST
11	Vice Pres Administrative Services	Mr. Blaine HATCH
13	Director of Information Services	Mr. Eric BISHOP
06	Registrar/Dir Enrollment Mgmt	Mr. Jake HINTON-RIVERA
04	Assistant to the President	Vacant
10	Director of Financial Services	Ms. Maderia ELLISON
21	Comptroller	Mr. John H. BREMER
15	Director of Human Resources	Vacant
37	Financial Aid Coordinator	Ms. Beaulah BOB-PENNYPACKER
88	Director of Developmental Services	Mr. Rickey JACKSON
50	Dean of Career & Technical Educ	Ms. Peggy BELKNAP
49	Dean of Arts & Sciences	Dr. Eric HENDERSON
66	Dean of Nursing	Ms. Peg ERDMAN
18	Chief Facilities/Physical Plant	Mr. David HUISH
26	Dir of Marketing/Public Relations	Ms. Ann HESS
09	Director of Institutional Effective	Dr. Leslie WASSON
88	Network and Systems Administrator	Mr. Robert GODFREY
88	Director Small Business Development	Ms. Tracy MANCUSO
08	Head Librarian	Ms. Trudy BENDER

Ottawa University Arizona (B)

10020 N 25th Avenue, Phoenix AZ 85021-1660

County: Maricopa — Identification: 666066 — Unit ID: 105367

Telephone: (602) 371-1188 — Carnegie Class: Master's M

FAX Number: (602) 371-0035 — Calendar System: Semester

URL: www.ottawa.edu

Established: 1977 — Annual Undergrad Tuition & Fees: $10,920

Enrollment: 775 — Coed

Affiliation or Control: American Baptist — IRS Status: 501(c)3

Highest Offering: Master's

Program: Liberal Arts And General; Teacher Preparatory

Accreditation: &NH

Code	Title	Name
01	President	Mr. Kevin EICHNER
05	Univ Provost/Chief Academic Officer	Dr. Terry HAINES
10	Vice Pres Administration/CFO	Mr. J. Clark RIBORDY
26	Mgr Public Relations & Publications	Ms. Paula PAINE
30	Vice Pres University Advancement	Mr. Paul BEAN
86	VP Regulatory/Governmental Affairs	Dr. Donna LEVENE
88	Vice President Enterprise Division	Dr. Brian SANDUSKY
07	Assist VP & Exec Dir Enrollment	Mr. Bill HAMMOND
06	University Registrar	Ms. Karen ADAMS
21	Director Business Operations	Mr. Tom CORLEY
37	Director Student Financial Aid	Mr. Howard FISCHER
11	Director of Administration	Ms. Peggie LANZONE
21	Director Finance/Controller	Ms. Noelle TESTA
15	Director Human Resources	Ms. Joanna WALTERS
20	Dean of Instruction	Dr. Karen MILLS
106	Vice President for Online	Mr. Brian MESSER
12	Campus Executive	Dr. Mary VANIS
88	VP and COO APOS	Mr. Shane SMEED

† Regional accreditation is carried under the parent institution in Ottawa, KS.

The Paralegal Institute (C)

7332 E Butherus Drive, Scottsdale AZ 85260

County: Maricopa — FICE Identification: 030737 — Unit ID: 105385

Telephone: (800) 354-1254 — Carnegie Class: Not Classified

FAX Number: (602) 212-0502 — Calendar System: Other

URL: www.theparalegalinstitute.edu

Established: 1974 — Annual Undergrad Tuition & Fees: $9,000

Enrollment: 360 — Coed

Affiliation or Control: Proprietary — IRS Status: Proprietary

Highest Offering: Associate Degree

Program: Occupational; 2-Year Principally Bachelor's Creditable; Business Emphasis

Accreditation: DETC

Code	Title	Name
01	President	Kathleen MIRABILE
26	Vice President Marketing	Chris CARAWAY

Penn Foster College (D)

14300 N Northsight Blvd, Suite 120, Scottsdale AZ 85260-3673

County: Maricopa — FICE Identification: 004049 — Unit ID: 211486

Telephone: (480) 947-6644 — Carnegie Class: Not Classified

FAX Number: (480) 951-6030 — Calendar System: Semester

URL: www.pennfostercollege.edu

Established: 1974 — Annual Undergrad Tuition & Fees: $2,100

Enrollment: 24,800 — Coed

Affiliation or Control: Proprietary — IRS Status: Proprietary

Highest Offering: Baccalaureate

Program: Occupational

Accreditation: DETC, MAAB

Code	Title	Name
01	President	Dr. Richard W. FERRIN
05	Chief Learning Officer	Mr. Ray MCNULTY
88	Chief Certification/Licensing Ofcr	Ms. Connie DEMPSEY

Phoenix Institute of Herbal Medicine and Acupuncture (E)

301 E Bethany Home Road, Ste A-100, Phoenix AZ 85012-1275

County: Maricopa — FICE Identification: 036175 — Unit ID: 447698

Telephone: (602) 274-1885 — Carnegie Class: Spec/Health

FAX Number: (602) 274-1895 — Calendar System: Semester

URL: www.pihma.edu

Established: 1996 — Annual Graduate Tuition & Fees: $12,473

Enrollment: 129 — Coed

Affiliation or Control: Proprietary — IRS Status: Proprietary

Highest Offering: Master's; No Undergraduates

Program: Professional

Accreditation: ACUP

Code	Title	Name
01	President	Ms. Catherine NIEMIEC
06	Admissions	Ms. Yvette MORAN

Phoenix School of Law (F)

4041 N Central Avenue, Suite 100, Phoenix AZ 85012

County: Maricopa — FICE Identification: 041314 — Unit ID: 450942

Telephone: (602) 682-6800 — Carnegie Class: Spec/Law

FAX Number: (602) 682-6999 — Calendar System: Semester

URL: www.phoenixlaw.edu

Established: N/A — Annual Graduate Tuition & Fees: $39,643

Enrollment: 368 — Coed

Affiliation or Control: Proprietary — IRS Status: Proprietary

Highest Offering: First Professional Degree; No Undergraduates

Program: Professional

Accreditation: LAW

Code	Title	Name
01	Dean	Ms. Shirley L. MAYS
05	Assoc Dean for Academic Affairs	Ms. Penny L. WILLRICH

Phoenix Seminary (G)

4222 E Thomas Road, Suite 400, Phoenix AZ 85018-7607

County: Maricopa — FICE Identification: 034784 — Unit ID: 381459

Telephone: (602) 850-8000 — Carnegie Class: Spec/Faith

FAX Number: (602) 850-8080 — Calendar System: Semester

URL: www.phoenixseminary.edu

Established: 1988 — Annual Graduate Tuition & Fees: $10,740

Enrollment: 209 — Coed

Affiliation or Control: Interdenominational — IRS Status: 501(c)3

Highest Offering: Doctorate; No Undergraduates

Program: Religious Emphasis

Accreditation: @NH, THEOL

Code	Title	Name
01	President	Dr. Darryl L. DELHOUSAYE
03	Executive Vice President/Provost	Dr. W. B. HUNTER
11	Vice President of Administration	Mr. Grant GASSON
32	Vice President Student Development	Dr. Charles MOODY
20	Dir Acad Services/Admiss/Assess	Ms. Roma ROYER
06	Registrar	Mr. Lee P. RICHARDS
84	Director of Enrollment	Mr. Eric CHANNING
08	Director of Library Services	Mr. Doug OLBERT
10	Director of Finance	Mr. Dave HESTON
37	Financial Aid Officer	Mrs. Lynn GORDON
30	Vice President of Advancement/Mktg	Ms. Patti SELLERS

Pima County Community College District (H)

4905 C East Broadway Boulevard, Tucson AZ 85709-1005

County: Pima — FICE Identification: 007266 — Unit ID: 105525

Telephone: (520) 206-4500 — Carnegie Class: Assoc/Pub-U-MC

FAX Number: (520) 206-4535 — Calendar System: Semester

URL: www.pima.edu

Established: 1966 — Annual Undergrad Tuition & Fees (In-District): $2,060

Enrollment: 33,568 — Coed

Affiliation or Control: State/Local — IRS Status: 501(c)3

Highest Offering: Associate Degree

Program: Occupational; 2-Year Principally Bachelor's Creditable

Accreditation: NH, ADNUR, DA, DH, DT, EMT, MLTAD, RAD, SURGT

Code	Title	Name
01	Chancellor	Dr. Suzanne L. MILES
05	Provost/Exec Vice Chancellor	Dr. Jerome MIGLER
10	Exec Vice Chanc for Administration	Dr. David BEA
16	Vice Chanc for Human Resources	Ms. Janet MAY
14	Vice Chanc Information Tech	Mr. Keith MCINTOSH
26	Vice Chanc Public Info & Govt Rels	Mr. C.J KARAMARGIN
12	President Downtown Campus	Dr. Luba CHLIWNIAK
12	President Northwest Campus	Dr. Alex KAJSTURA
12	President East Campus	Ms. Charlotte A. FUGETT
12	Actg President Community Campus	Dr. Lorraine MORALES
12	President West Campus	Dr. Louis ALBERT
12	President Desert Vista Campus	Dr. Johnson BIA
88	Actg Assistant Vice Chancellor	Dr. Dolores DURAN-CERDA
21	Asst Vice Chanc for Finance	Ms. Diane GROOVER
21	Asst VC for Business Services	Mr. William HOWARD
91	Asst VC Information Technology	Vacant
15	Asst VC for Employee Services	Ms. Doreen ARMSTRONG
20	Vice Provost Academic Svcs	Dr. Mary Ann MARTINEZ-SANCHEZ
32	Asst Vice Chanc for Student Dev	Ms. Leticia MENCHACA
18	Asst Vice Chancellor Facilities	Mr. Bill WARD
09	Exec Dir Planning & Inst Research	Dr. Nicola RICHMOND
37	Executive Director Financial Aid	Ms. Anna REESE
102	Executive Director Foundation	Ms. Cheryl HOUSE
41	Executive Director of Athletics	Mr. Edgar SOTO
19	Exec Director Dept of Public Safety	Ms. Stella BAY
66	Dean Nursing/Health Rel Prof	Ms. Marty MAYHEW
06	Director Admissions/Registrar	Ms. Terra BENSON
96	Director of Purchasing	Mr. Thomas HARRINGTON

Pima Medical Institute-Mesa (I)

957 S Dobson Road, Mesa AZ 85202-2903

County: Maricopa — FICE Identification: 011570 — Unit ID: 260691

Telephone: (480) 644-0267 — Carnegie Class: Assoc/PrivFP

FAX Number: (480) 649-5249 — Calendar System: Other

URL: www.pmi.edu

Established: 1972 — Annual Undergrad Tuition & Fees: N/A

Enrollment: 1,500 — Coed

Affiliation or Control: Proprietary — IRS Status: Proprietary

Highest Offering: Associate Degree

Program: Occupational

Accreditation: ABHES, OTA, PTAA, RAD

Code	Title	Name
01	Campus Director	Ms. Kristen TORRES

Pima Medical Institute-Tucson (J)

3350 E Grant Road, Suite 200, Tucson AZ 85716-2932

County: Pima — FICE Identification: 022171 — Unit ID: 105534

Telephone: (520) 326-1600 — Carnegie Class: Assoc/PrivFP

FAX Number: (520) 326-4125 — Calendar System: Other

URL: www.pmi.edu

Established: 1972 — Annual Undergrad Tuition & Fees: N/A

Enrollment: 1,263 — Coed

Affiliation or Control: Proprietary — IRS Status: Proprietary

Highest Offering: Baccalaureate

Program: Occupational

Accreditation: ABHES, OTA, PTAA, RAD

Code	Title	Name
01	Director	Mr. Dale BERG

Prescott College (K)

220 Grove Avenue, Prescott AZ 86301-2912

County: Yavapai — FICE Identification: 020653 — Unit ID: 105589

Telephone: (928) 350-2100 — Carnegie Class: Master's S

FAX Number: (928) 776-5137 — Calendar System: Semester

URL: www.prescott.edu

Established: 1966 — Annual Undergrad Tuition & Fees: $27,408

Enrollment: 1,134 Coed
Affiliation or Control: Independent Non-Profit IRS Status: 501(c)3
Highest Offering: Doctorate
Program: Liberal Arts And General; Teacher Preparatory
Accreditation: NH

01 President Dr. Kristin R. WOOLEVER
05 Exec VP of Academic Affairs/Provost Dr. Paul BURKHARDT
10 Vice President of Financial Affairs Ms. Catherine BOLAND
30 VP for Insitutional Advancement Ms. Marjory SENTE
32 VP of Student Life Vacant
84 Director Enrollment Services Ms. Jerri BROWN
06 Registrar Ms. Mary TREVOR
37 Financial Aid Director Ms. Mary Frances CAUSEY
04 Executive Assistant Ms. Cathy CHURCH
88 Dean On-Campus Delivery/Research Dr. Jack HERRING
106 Dean Distance Learning and Acad Aff Dr. Jan KEMPSTER
20 Director of Academic Operations Vacant
18 Director of Facilities Mr. Greg LAZZELL
08 Director of Library Mr. Richard LEWIS
90 Director of Instructional Tech Ms. Kistie SIMMONS
91 Director of Information Technology Mr. Jordan AMERMAN
21 Director of Financial Services Ms. Anne LABRUZZO
07 Director of ADGP Admissions Vacant
07 Director of RDP Admissions Vacant

The Refrigeration School (A)

4210 E Washington Street, Phoenix AZ 85034-1816
County: Maricopa FICE Identification: 011689
Unit ID: 105659
Telephone: (602) 275-7133 Carnegie Class: Assoc/PrivFP
FAX Number: (602) 267-4805 Calendar System: Other
URL: www.refrigerationschool.com
Established: 1965 Annual Undergrad Tuition & Fees: $29,825
Enrollment: 500 Coed
Affiliation or Control: Proprietary IRS Status: Proprietary
Highest Offering: Associate Degree
Program: Occupational
Accreditation: ACCSC

01 Campus President Ms. Heather HASKELL
37 Assistant Director of Financial Aid Ms. Angela CROSSLEY
07 Admissions Director Mr. Michael ADKINS

Sanford-Brown College (B)

9630 North 25th Avenue, Phoenix AZ 85021
County: Maricopa Identification: 666739
Unit ID: 458654
Telephone: (480) 444-1112 Carnegie Class: Not Classified
FAX Number: (480) 444-1200 Calendar System: Semester
URL: www.sanfordbrown.edu/phoenix
Established: 2009 Annual Undergrad Tuition & Fees: N/A
Enrollment: 879 Coed
Affiliation or Control: Proprietary IRS Status: Proprietary
Highest Offering: Associate Degree
Program: 2-Year Principally Bachelor's Creditable
Accreditation: ACICS, MAAB

01 Campus President Mr. George FITZPATRICK
05 Director of Education Ms. Cheryl PIETKIEWICZ

Sessions College for Professional Design (C)

398 South Mill Avenue, Suite 300, Tempe AZ 85281
County: Maricopa Identification: 667018
Telephone: (480) 212-1704 Carnegie Class: Not Classified
FAX Number: (480) 212-1705 Calendar System: Semester
URL: www.sessions.edu
Established: 1997 Annual Undergrad Tuition & Fees: $9,100
Enrollment: 30 Coed
Affiliation or Control: Proprietary IRS Status: Proprietary
Highest Offering: Associate Degree
Program: Occupational; 2-Year Principally Bachelor's Creditable
Accreditation: DETC

00 CEO Ms. Doris GRANATOWSKI
01 President Mr. Gordon DRUMMOND
03 Executive Vice President Mr. Louis J. SCHILT
05 Chief Academic Officer Ms. Tara MACKAY
10 Chief Financial Officer/Bursar Ms. Carole Anne BAILO
32 Director of Student Services Ms. Nomi ALTABEF

Sonoran Desert Institute (D)

10245 East Via Linda, Ste 110, Scottsdale AZ 85258-5316
County: Maricopa Identification: 667057
Telephone: (480) 314-2102 Carnegie Class: Not Classified
FAX Number: (480) 314-2138 Calendar System: Semester
URL: www.sdi.edu
Established: 2000 Annual Undergrad Tuition & Fees: $10,200
Enrollment: 152 Coed
Affiliation or Control: Proprietary IRS Status: Proprietary
Highest Offering: Associate Degree
Program: Occupational
Accreditation: DETC

01 President Thomas A. KUBE

Southwest College of Naturopathic Medicine & Health Sciences (E)

2140 E Broadway Road, Tempe AZ 85282-1751
County: Maricopa FICE Identification: 031070
Unit ID: 420246
Telephone: (480) 858-9100 Carnegie Class: Spec/Health
FAX Number: (480) 858-9116 Calendar System: Quarter
URL: www.scnm.edu
Established: 1993 Annual Graduate Tuition & Fees: $25,947
Enrollment: 383 Coed
Affiliation or Control: Independent Non-Profit IRS Status: 501(c)3
Highest Offering: First Professional Degree; No Undergraduates
Program: Professional
Accreditation: NH, NATUR

01 President/Chief Executive Officer Paul A. MITTMAN
17 Exec VP Academic & Clinical Affairs Christine L. GIRARD
10 Vice Pres Finance & Administration Dawn RECTOR
32 Vice President Student Affairs Melissa WINQUIST

Southwest Institute of Healing Arts (F)

1100 E Apache Boulevard, Tempe AZ 85281-5822
County: Maricopa FICE Identification: 035933
Unit ID: 442879
Telephone: (480) 994-9244 Carnegie Class: Assoc/PrivFP
FAX Number: (480) 994-3228 Calendar System: Other
URL: www.swiha.edu
Established: 1992 Annual Undergrad Tuition & Fees: $18,280
Enrollment: 1,054 Coed
Affiliation or Control: Proprietary IRS Status: Proprietary
Highest Offering: Associate Degree
Program: Occupational
Accreditation: CNCE

01 President/Owner Mrs. K. C. MILLER
05 Director of Education Mr. Michael DYE
07 Director of Admissions Mr. Matt BILACH
32 Director Student Services Ms. Maria HUNTER
106 Exec Director Online Education Mr. Brad BOUTÉ

Southwest University of Visual Arts (G)

2525 N Country Club Road, Tucson AZ 85716-2505
County: Pima FICE Identification: 024915
Unit ID: 104188
Telephone: (520) 325-0123 Carnegie Class: Spec/Arts
FAX Number: (520) 325-5535 Calendar System: Semester
URL: www.theartcenter.edu
Established: 1983 Annual Undergrad Tuition & Fees: $27,665
Enrollment: 258 Coed
Affiliation or Control: Proprietary IRS Status: Proprietary
Highest Offering: Master's
Program: Fine Arts Emphasis
Accreditation: NH, CIDA

01 President Mrs. Sharmon WOODS
07 Director of Admissions Ms. Amy WOODS
32 Director of Student Services Ms. Amy WOODS
12 Director of Albuquerque Campus Ms. Cindy WHITAKER
06 Registrar Ms. Stephanie GASSER

Thunderbird School of Global Management (H)

1 Global Place, Glendale AZ 85306-3236
County: Maricopa FICE Identification: 001070
Unit ID: 103778
Telephone: (602) 978-7011 Carnegie Class: Spec/Bus
FAX Number: (602) 978-8238 Calendar System: Trimester
URL: www.thunderbird.edu
Established: 1946 Annual Graduate Tuition & Fees: $44,080
Enrollment: 1,275 Coed
Affiliation or Control: Independent Non-Profit IRS Status: 501(c)3
Highest Offering: Master's; No Undergraduates
Program: Professional; Business Emphasis
Accreditation: NH, BUS

01 Interim President Amb. Barbara BARRETT
05 Int Chief Acad Officer/Provost Dr. Larry E. PENLEY
88 SVP Executive Education Dr. Dennis BALTZLEY
10 Chief Business Officer Mr. Timothy PROPP
30 Vice Pres & Chief Development Ofcr Vacant
84 VP of Enrollment Management Ms. Rebecca HENRIKSEN
08 Assoc VP Information Services Ms. Carol HAMMOND
07 Asst VP Admissions & Recruiting Mr. Jay BRYANT
27 VP Global Communication & Outreach Ms. Kathryn MCMANUS
36 Assoc VP for Prof Career Devel Vacant
20 Dean of Faculty Dr. Dale DAVISON
13 Director IT Operations Mr. Jim HERNDON
06 Registrar/Assoc VP Acad Operations Mr. James SCOTT
37 Director Student Financial Aid Mrs. Catherine KING-TODD
43 Vice President and General Counsel Ms. Kathryn KRECKE
20 Assoc Dir Acad/International Svcs Ms. Felicia WELCH
04 Exec Assistant to the President Ms. Mary Ellen PRUNENCA

Tohono O'odham Community College (I)

PO Box 3129, Sells AZ 85634-3129
County: Pima FICE Identification: 037844
Unit ID: 442781
Telephone: (520) 383-8401 Carnegie Class: Tribal
FAX Number: (520) 383-0029 Calendar System: Semester
URL: www.tocc.cc.az.us
Established: 1998 Annual Undergrad Tuition & Fees: $1,435
Enrollment: 295 Coed
Affiliation or Control: Tribal Control IRS Status: 501(c)3
Highest Offering: Associate Degree
Program: Occupational; 2-Year Principally Bachelor's Creditable
Accreditation: NH

01 President Mr. James VANDER HOOVEN
05 Vice President for Education Ms. Juana Clare JOSE
32 Vice Pres of Student Services Ms. Sylvia HENDRICKS
11 Vice Pres Admin Services/Finance Dr. Robert LEDMAN
46 Vice Pres Inst Research/Development Ms. Jane LATANE
75 Dept Chair Occupational Pgms Mr. George MIGUEL
07 Director of Admissions/Records Mr. Leslie LUNA
25 Sponsored Projects Mr. Samuel OROZCO
97 Dept Chair for General Education Vacant
08 Librarian Ms. Elaine CUBBINS
37 Director of Financial Aid Mr. Al RIVERA
88 Director Project NATIVE Ms. Camille MARTINEZ-YADEN
88 Director Project NATIVE Dr. Sandra LUCAS
30 Director of Fundraising Ms. Andrea AHMED
15 Human Resources Director Ms. Stacy OWSLEY

Universal Technical Institute (J)

10695 W Pierce Street, Avondale AZ 85323-7946
County: Maricopa FICE Identification: 008221
Unit ID: 106041
Telephone: (623) 245-4600 Carnegie Class: Assoc/PrivFP
FAX Number: (623) 245-4601 Calendar System: Other
URL: www.uti.edu
Established: 1965 Annual Undergrad Tuition & Fees: $30,600
Enrollment: 1,800 Coed
Affiliation or Control: Proprietary IRS Status: Proprietary
Highest Offering: Associate Degree
Program: Occupational
Accreditation: ACCSC

01 Campus President Mr. Michael ROMANO
05 Director of Education Ms. Maria WALTERS
32 Director of Student Services Mrs. Heather GONZALES
10 Director of Campus Accounting Mr. Dale KENNEDY
07 Admissions Director Mr. Adam HELLER
36 Director of Graduate Employment Ms. Cheryl RADKE
37 Director of Financial Aid Ms. Terri MEIXSEL-CORDERO
38 Counselor Ms. Ashley SZYMANSKI
18 Maintenance Director Mr. George MICKENS

University of Advancing Technology (K)

2625 W Baseline Road, Tempe AZ 85283-1056
County: Maricopa FICE Identification: 025590
Unit ID: 363934
Telephone: (602) 383-8228 Carnegie Class: Bac/Diverse
FAX Number: (602) 383-8250 Calendar System: Other
URL: www.uat.edu
Established: 1983 Annual Undergrad Tuition & Fees: $19,500
Enrollment: 1,052 Coed
Affiliation or Control: Proprietary IRS Status: Proprietary
Highest Offering: Master's
Program: Technical Emphasis
Accreditation: NH

01 President Mr. Jason PISTILLO
03 Executive Vice President Vacant
10 Treasurer/General Counsel Vacant
05 Provost Mr. Dave BOLMAN

University of Arizona (L)

1401 E University Blvd, Tucson AZ 85721-0001
County: Pima FICE Identification: 001083
Unit ID: 104179
Telephone: (520) 621-2211 Carnegie Class: RU/VH
FAX Number: (520) 621-9323 Calendar System: Semester
URL: www.arizona.edu
Established: 1885 Annual Undergrad Tuition & Fees (In-State): $10,035
Enrollment: 39,236 Coed
Affiliation or Control: State IRS Status: 501(c)3
Highest Offering: Doctorate
Program: Liberal Arts And General; Teacher Preparatory; Professional
Accreditation: NH, ART, AUD, BUS, BUSA, CEA, CLPSY, CORE, DANCE, DIETD, DIETI, ENG, IPSY, JOUR, LAW, LIB, LSAR, MED, MUS, NURSE, PERF, PH, PHAR, PLNG, SCPSY, SP, SPAA, THEA

01 President Dr. Ann WEAVER HART
05 Sr VP for Acad Affairs & Provost Dr. Jacqueline L. MOK
10 Sr VP and CFO/Business Affairs Mr. Milton M. CASTILLO
46 Sr VP for Research Dr. Leslie P. TOLBERT

17 Sr VP Health Sciences .... Dr. Lyle BOOTMAN
16 Vice Pres Human Resources ....Ms. Allison M. VAILLANCOURT
20 Vice Provost Academic Affairs .... Dr. Gail D. BURD
26 Vice President External Relations ....Mr. Jaime P. GUTIERREZ
32 Vice President Student Affairs .... Ms. Melissa VITO
43 Int VP Legal Affs/General Counsel .... Ms. Lynne O. WOOD
88 VP Reg Devel Outreach Global Init ....Mr. Michael A. PROCTOR
13 CIO/Exec Director UITS .... Ms. Michele L. NORIN
88 Vice President Health Affairs .... Dr. William M. CRIST
09 Assoc Vice Provost Inst Research .... Dr. Richard J. KROC
21 Assoc VP/Comptroller/Financial Svc ....Mr. Mark A. MCGURK
21 Sr Associate VP Business Affairs .... Mr. Robert R. SMITH
35 Assoc VP Student Affairs .... Mr. Frank FARIAS
45 Assoc VP Academic Res/Plng/Mgmt ....Mr. Edward G. FRISCH
86 Assoc VP Federal Relations .... Mr. Shay D. STAUTZ
86 Assoc VP State Relations .... Mr. Timothy S. BEE
88 Assoc Provost Faculty Affairs .... Mr. Thomas P. MILLER
88 Assoc VP External Relations-Phoenix ....Ms. Judith A. BERNAS
88 Assoc VP Finance & Admin Pres Ofc ....Ms. Karen S. FILIPPELLI
88 Asst VP Institutional Analysis .... Mr. James S. FLORIAN
88 Assoc VP Research .... Ms. Caroline M. GARCIA
88 Assoc VP Univ Research Parks .... Mr. Bruce A. WRIGHT
07 Asst VP Dean of Admissions .... Ms. Kasandra URQUIDEZ
18 Asst VP Facilities Management ....Mr. Christopher M. KOPACH
18 Asst VP Plng/Design & Construction .... Mr. Peter DOURLEIN
19 Asst VP Risk Management/Safety ....Mr. Steven C. HOLLAND
27 Asst Vice President Communications .... Mr. Johnny CRUZ
28 Asst VP Inclusive Excellence ....Mr. Raji A. RHYS WIETECHA
39 Asst VP Student Affs & Univ Housing .... Mr. James D. VAN ARSDEL
88 Asst VP Budget .... Ms. Kathryn E. WHISMAN
88 Asst VP Finance Administration .... Ms. Marilyn TAYLOR
88 Asst VP Financial Services .... Mr. Duc MA
88 Asst VP Health Sciences/Pub Affairs ..Mr. George D. HUMPHREY
88 Asst VP Marketing .... Ms. Kathleen M. JENSEN
88 Asst VP Student Affairs .... Mr. Jeffrey M. ORGERA
88 Asst VP Student Affs/Dean of Stdnts ......Mr. Keith B. HUMPHREY
88 Asst VP Tribal Relations .... Ms. Karen F. BEGAY
88 Asst Provost Off of Instruc/Assess ....Ms. Debra J. TOMANEK
88 Sr Asst VP Student Affairs .... Ms. Lynette S. COOK-FRANCIS
08 Dean of Libr/Ctr for Creative Photo ....Ms. Carla J. STOFFLE
12 Dean UA South .... Dr. James W. SHOCKEY
47 V Provost/Dean Col Agri/Life Sci .... Mr. Shane C. BURGESS
48 Dean Col Arch & Landscape Arch ....Dr. Janice A. CERVELLI
49 Exec Dean Col of Letters Arts & Sci .... Dr. Joaquin RUIZ
50 Dean Eller College of Management ....Dr. Leonard M. JESSUP
53 Dean College of Education .... Dr. Ronald W. MARX
54 Dean College of Engineering .... Dr. Jeffrey B. GOLDBERG
57 Dean College of Fine Arts .... Dr. Jory L. HANCOCK
58 Assoc VP Research/Dean Grad College .....Dr. Andrew C. COMRIE
61 Dean College of Law .... Mr. Lawrence PONOROFF
63 Dean College of Med-Phoenix Campus ....Mr. Stuart D. FLYNN
63 Dean College of Medicine .... Dr. Steven GOLDSCHMID
66 Dean College of Nursing .... Dr. Joan L. SHAVER
69 Dean Zuckerman AZ Col Public Hlth .... Dr. Iman A. HAKIM
79 Dean College of Humanities .....Dr. Mary E. WILDNER-BASSETT
81 Dean College of Optical Sciences .... Mr. Thomas L. KOCH
83 Dean Col of Social/Behav Science .... Dr. John P. JONES
92 Dean Honors College .... Dr. Patricia MACCORQUODALE
06 Registrar/Enrollment Management ....Dr. Elizabeth A. ACREE
22 Dir Office of Institutional Equity .... Ms. Mary E. TUCKER
23 Director Campus Health .... Dr. Harry MCDERMOTT
29 Exec Director Alumni Office .... Ms. Melinda W. BURKE
36 Director Career Services .... Ms. Eileen MCGARRY
37 Director Student Financial Aid .... Mr. John NAMETZ
40 Director Univ of Arizona Bookstores .... Ms. Debby L. SHIVELY
41 Director Athletics .... Mr. Greg K. BYRNE
102 President UA Foundation .... Mr. James H. MOORE

University of Phoenix (A)

4615 E Elwood Street, Phoenix AZ 85040-1958
County: Maricopa FICE Identification: 020988
Unit ID: 105516
Telephone: (480) 557-2000 Carnegie Class: Master's L
FAX Number: N/A Calendar System: Other
URL: www.phoenix.edu
Established: 1976 Annual Undergrad Tuition & Fees: N/A
Enrollment: 404,408 Coed
Affiliation or Control: Proprietary IRS Status: Proprietary
Highest Offering: Doctorate
Program: Liberal Arts And General; Teacher Preparatory; Professional
Accreditation: NH, ACBSP, CACREP, NURSE, TEAC

01 President University of Phoenix .... Dr. William PEPICELLO
00 President & COO Apollo Group .... Mr. Joseph L. D'AMICO
05 Provost/Exec VP Academic Affairs .... Dr. Alan DRIMMER
88 Sr VP & CFO Apollo Group .... Mr. Brian L. SWARTZ
100 SVP/Chief of Staff .... Ms. Nina MUNSON
45 Sr VP University Strategy .... Mr. Thomas MCCARTY
10 SVP Finance & Analysis .... Ms. Karen WHITNEY
15 SVP Human Resources .... Mr. Jose MARTIN
88 SVP Student Experience .... Ms. Ruth VELORIA
26 SVP Ext Affairs/Public Relations .... Mr. Mark BRENNER
88 Sr VP Strategic Intg & Org Effect .... Ms. Jodie PLOESSL
03 EVP Chief Std & Campus Ops Officer .... Mr. Jerrad TAUSZ
102 Exec VP Corp Rels & Educ Alliances ....Mr. Barry FEIERSTEIN
31 Exec Vice Pres External Affairs .... Ms. Terri BISHOP
13 Executive VP Strategy & Innovations .... Mr. Jay GOIN
88 EVP Integration/Design Improvement .... Mr. Vince GRELL
88 Exec VP Ops Efficiency & Effective .... Mr. Vince GRELL
37 EVP Admin Svcs StAS Fin Aid INST .... Mr. Jeff SONNENBERG
43 General Counsel .... Mr. Sean MARTIN
27 Chief Information Officer .... Mr. Mike SAJOR
88 Regional VP Central Region .... Mr. Brent FITCH
88 Regional VP Midwest Region .... Mr. John DURLING
88 Regional VP Northeast Region .... Mr. Chad BANDY
88 Regional VP Southeast Region .... Ms. Lynn MULHERIN
88 Regional VP West Region .... Ms. Jennifer CISNA
12 Campus Director Albuquerque .... Ms. Cara ATENCIO
12 Vice President/Director Atlanta GA .... Mr. Michael HEARON
12 Campus Director Augusta .... Ms. Ericka HILLIARD
12 Campus Director Austin .... Mr. Michael CULLUP
12 Campus Director Birmingham .... Mr. Chris BREEDING
12 Campus Director Boston .... Ms. Jodi ASHBROOK
12 VP Dir Canada/Europe/Middle East .... Mr. Pete MARTINEZ
12 Campus Director Central Florida .... Mr. Aaron KNOWLES
12 Campus Director Central Valley .... Ms. Ann TYE
12 Campus Director Charlotte NC .... Ms. Shannon ECKARD
12 Campus Dir Chattanooga .... Mr. Marc CROSBY
12 Campus Director Chicago IL .... Mr. Jeremiah HOOD
12 Campus Director Cincinnati Campus .... Mr. Ryan HAMPTON
12 Campus Director Cleveland .... Ms. Gina CUFFARI
12 Campus Director Columbia SC .... Ms. Stephanie JACKSON
12 Campus Director Columbus GA .... Ms. Shelby FRUTCHEY
12 Campus Director Columbus OH .... Ms. Heather LOUGHLEY
12 Campus Director Connecticut .... Ms. Nancy PLUZDRAK
12 Campus Director Dallas Campus ....Ms. Jennifer RODRIGUEZ
12 Campus Director Delaware .... Mr. Tim GILRAIN
12 Campus Director Des Moines .... Ms. Christine WILLIAMS
12 Campus Director Eastern Washington .... Mr. Paul GREEN
12 Campus Dir El Paso TX/Santa Teresa ..... Ms. Barbara JANOWSKI
12 Vice President Director Far East .... Mr. Jason SCHROTT
12 Campus Director Harrisburg PA .... Vacant
12 Campus Director Hawaii Campus .... Ms. Kristine AVERILL
12 Campus Director Houston .... Mr. Jason MORGAN
12 Campus Director Idaho Campus .... Mr. Bill BACH
12 Campus Director Indianapolis .... Ms. Jennifer KHADIVAR
12 Campus Director Jersey City Campus .... Mr. Gary WILLIAMS
12 Campus Director Kansas City .... Ms. Jeannine LAKE
12 Campus Director Knoxville .... Mr. Mark AMREIN
12 Campus Dir Lafayette & Baton Rouge .... Ms. Michelle SMITH
12 Campus Director Las Vegas .... Ms. Kathy GAMBOA
12 Assoc Campus Dir Little Rock AR .... Mr. Randy MCCORMICK
12 Campus Director Louisville Campus .... Mr. Scot MALL
12 Campus Directir Madison .... Ms. Briana HOULIHAN
12 Campus Director Maryland .... Mr. Josh CHUMLEY
12 Campus Director McAllen .... Mr. Mikal POWERS
12 Campus Director Memphis .... Ms. Raquel FORD
12 Campus Director Minneapolis .... Mr. Robert ZALABAK
12 Campus Director Nashville TN .... Mr. Mark MENDOZA
12 Campus Director Online Netherlands .... Mr. Stephen ZEMBLE
12 Campus Director New Orleans .... Ms. Tiffany DILLER
12 Campus Director North Florida .... Mr. Dan MACFERRAN
12 Campus Dir NW Arkansas (Rogers) .... Mr. Luke CAMPBELL
12 Campus Director Northern Virginia .... Mr. Erik GREENBERG
12 Campus Director Oklahoma City OK .... Mr. Troy THOMAS
12 Campus Director Omaha .... Ms. Sarah GLODEN-CARLSON
12 Campus Director Oregon .... Mr. Flint HOLLAND
12 Campus Director Philadelphia .... Mr. Joe MARZANO
12 Campus Director Phoenix Campus .... Mr. David FITZGERALD
12 Campus Director Pittsburg PA .... Mr. Troy MALOVEY
12 Campus Director Raleigh NC .... Ms. Candice MORGAN
12 Director Reno Campus .... Dr. Bob LARKIN
12 Campus Director Richmond VA .... Ms. Beth SIGLER
12 Campus Director Sacramento CA .... Mr. Scott LEWIS
12 Campus Director St Louis .... Mr. Adam WRIGHT
12 VP/Director San Antonio Campus .... Mr. Wally HEDGECOCK
12 Campus Director San Diego .... Ms. Kim LYDA-SAVICH
12 Campus Director Savannah GA .... Ms. Melissa JACKSON
12 Campus Dir Shreveport/Bossier City .... Ms. Julie MARBLE
12 Campus Director South Florida .... Ms. Leslie KRISTOF
12 Campus Director SoCal Campus .... Ms. Kendra ANGIER
12 Campus Director Southern Colorado .... Ms. Brittany NIELSON
12 Campus Director Springfield .... Ms. Heather FINLEY
12 Campus Director Tucson .... Mr. Gregg JOHNSON
12 Campus Director Tulsa .... Ms. Lori SANTIAGO
12 Campus Director Utah Campus .... Mr. Darris HOWE
12 Acting Campus Dir Washington DC .... Mr. Jason PFAFF
12 VP/Director West Florida .... Ms. Lisa NUCCI
12 Campus Director West Michigan .... Mr. Brian GLEASON
12 Campus Director Western Washington .... Mr. Bruce WILLIAMS
12 Campus Director Wyoming & Colorado .... Mr. Brent SEIFRIED
50 Exec Dir/Dean Sch Advanced Studies .... Dr. Freda HARTMAN
65 Exec Dir/Dean College Natural Sci .... Dr. Hinrich EYLERS
53 Exec Dir/Dean of Education .... Dr. Meredith CURLEY
88 Exec Dir/Dean Sch Advanced Studies ......Dr. Jeremy MORELAND
66 Exec Dir/College of Nursing .... Dr. Pam FULLER
88 Exec Dir/Dean College of IS&T .... Dr. Blair SMITH
79 Exec Dir/Dean College of Humanities .... Dr. Robert RIDEL
05 Senior VP Academic Research .... Dr. Adam HONEA
88 Exec Dir/Dean Criminal Justice/Sec .... Dr. James NESS
20 Associate Provost .... Dr. Brian LINDQUIST
10 Sr VP of Financial Services .... Mr. Jeff SONNENBERG
84 Senior Vice President Enrollment .... Ms. Trish ELLIOTT
32 Sr Vice President Student Services .... Ms. Nancy CERVASIO
106 Regional Vice President NGO Region .... Ms. Cheri SORENSEN
88 Vice President of University Svcs .... Ms. Evelyn GASKIN
83 Exec Dir/Dean College Social Sci .... Dr. Lynn HALL
100 VP Academic Administration .... Mr. Lee FINKEL
102 VP Cmty Investment & Foundation .... Ms. Pat GOTTFRIED
20 Vice President Academic Operations .... Dr. Russ PADEN
46 VP Academic Affair/Apollo Publishng .... Mr. David BICKFORD
43 VP University Legal/General Counsel .... Mr. Dan LITTERAL
11 Vice President Operations Support .... Mr. Ernie PRICE
88 VP Research & Analytics .... Ms. Jessica LILIE
88 VP Strategic Analytics .... Mr. Sameer KASARGOD
88 VP Strategy .... Mr. Rick BILODEAU
09 Assoc Vice Pres Inst Research .... Mr. Jay KLAGGE
20 Vice Provost/Senior VP .... Dr. Dawn IWAMOTO
20 Associate Provost .... Dr. Marla KELSEY
29 Exec Director Alumni Relations .... Ms. Nikki SANDOVAL
26 Chief Mktg & Prod Development .... Mr. Rob WRUBEL
07 Sr Director of Admissions .... Mr. Marc BOOKER
06 Registrar .... Ms. Audra MCQUARIE
16 Chief Human Resources Officer .... Mr. Fred NEWTON
108 Sr Director Institutional Assess .... Mr. Wayne FORAKER
28 Org Diversity Officer .... Ms. Dominique BROWN
04 Assistant to the President .... Ms. Sandy MEYER

Western International University (B)

9215 N Black Canyon Highway, Phoenix AZ 85021-2718
County: Maricopa FICE Identification: 021715
Unit ID: 106102
Telephone: (602) 943-2311 Carnegie Class: Master's M
FAX Number: (602) 371-8637 Calendar System: Other
URL: www.west.edu
Established: 1978 Annual Undergrad Tuition & Fees: $13,360
Enrollment: 3,239 Coed
Affiliation or Control: Proprietary IRS Status: Proprietary
Highest Offering: Master's
Program: Professional; Business Emphasis
Accreditation: NH

01 President .... Ms. Tracy LORENZ
05 Provost/Sr VP .... Dr. Barbara BADERMAN
06 Registrar/Sr Dir of University .... Ms. Hue HASLIM
45 VP Strategy & Development .... Ms. Allison POOLEY
13 VP InformationTechnology .... Ms. Stephanie LEACH
11 VP of Administration .... Mr. Kris MCCALL
09 Executive Director of Curriculum .... Mr. Steven OXMAN
26 VP of Marketing .... Ms. Debbie MCKEAN
10 Regional Director of Finance .... Ms. Heidi PHHIPPS
21 Sr Dir of Finance/Administration .... Ms. Beth CARLISLE
07 Director of Enrollment .... Ms. Melilssa MACHUCA
07 Director of Enrollment .... Ms. Amy KWIATKOWSKI

Yavapai College (C)

1100 E Sheldon Street, Prescott AZ 86301-3297
County: Yavapai FICE Identification: 001079
Unit ID: 106148
Telephone: (928) 445-7300 Carnegie Class: Assoc/Pub-R-L
FAX Number: (928) 776-2119 Calendar System: Semester
URL: www.yc.edu
Established: 1966 Annual Undergrad Tuition & Fees (In-District): $1,824
Enrollment: 7,837 Coed
Affiliation or Control: Local IRS Status: 501(c)3
Highest Offering: Associate Degree
Program: Occupational; 2-Year Principally Bachelor's Creditable
Accreditation: NH, ADNUR, EMT, IFSAC, RAD

01 President .... Dr. Penelope WILLS
05 Vice Pres Instruction/Student Affs .... Dr. Gregory GILLESPIE
10 Vice Pres Finance/Admin Svcs .... Dr. Clint EWELL
30 VP College Development/Foundation .... Mr. Steve WALKER
20 Dean Instruct Support & Improvement .... Ms. Stacey HILTON
12 Dean Verde Valley Campus .... Mr. James PEREY
75 Dean Career Technical Education .... Mr. John MORGAN
66 Dn Sci/Nursing/Allied Hlth/Dir Athl .... Mr. Scott FARNSWORTH
32 Dean Student Services .... Ms. Sandy GARBER
26 Director of Marketing/Public Info .... Vacant
37 Director of Financial Aid .... Ms. Terri ECKEL
09 Dir Inst Planning/Research/Assess .... Mr. Tom HUGHES
15 Director for Human Resources .... Ms. Rose HURLEY
19 Director of Campus Safety .... Mr. Joe CAPELLI
21 Dir of Business Svcs & Controller .... Mr. Frank D'ANGELO
07 Recruitment Officer .... Ms. Kornelia MARKOV
18 Director for Facilities .... Mr. David LAURENCE
13 Chief Information Officer .... Mr. Patrick BURNS
88 Paralegal Director .... Ms. Ruth HARRISON
06 Registrar .... Ms. Sheila JARRELL
29 Director Alumni Relations .... Ms. Barbara CLAY BAUGH
96 Director of Purchasing .... Ms. Phyllis LEWELLEN
88 Custom Training Coordinator .... Ms. Ginger JOHNSON
36 Coordinator Career Services .... Mr. Michael BROWN

ARKANSAS

Arkansas Baptist College (D)

1621 Martin Luther King Drive, Little Rock AR 72202-6099
County: Pulaski FICE Identification: 001087
Unit ID: 106306
Telephone: (501) 370-4000 Carnegie Class: Bac/Assoc
FAX Number: (501) 372-7992 Calendar System: Semester
URL: www.arkansasbaptist.edu
Established: 1884 Annual Undergrad Tuition & Fees: $7,800
Enrollment: 1,193 Coed
Affiliation or Control: Baptist IRS Status: 501(c)3
Highest Offering: Baccalaureate
Program: 2-Year Principally Bachelor's Creditable; Liberal Arts And General
Accreditation: NH

01 President .... Dr. Fitz HILL
04 President's Executive Assistant .... Ms. Patsy BIGGS
10 Exec VP/Chief Financial Officer .... Mr. Billy OWENS

100 Chief of Staff ... Mrs. LaCresha NEWTON
05 Interim VP of Academic Affairs ... Dr. Howard GIBSON
32 Vice President Student Affairs ... Dr. Vicki WILLIAMS
30 Director of Development ... Vacant
09 Director of Institutional Research ... Mrs. Jerelyn L. DUNCAN
103 Dir of Adult Ed & Workforce Dev ... Ms. Arma HART
07 Director of Admissions/Recruitment ... Ms. Jocelyn SPRIGGS
84 Dean of Enrollment Management ... Ms. Rosie TONEY
06 Registar ... Ms. Delores VOLIBER
37 Director of Financial Aid ... Ms. Patricia PROCTOR
08 Director of Library/Media Services ... Mrs. Joyce CAMPBELL
26 Assoc Dir Public Relations/Mktg ... Mrs. Terri CLARK
21 Business Manager ... Ms. Rita NEWBURN
34 Dean of Women ... Vacant
35 Asst Dean of Student Affairs ... Mr. Brian MILLER
33 Dean of Men ... Mr. Donald NORTHCROSS
19 Chief of Campus Safety ... Mr. Curtis JOHNSON
18 Facilities Director ... Mr. Bryan RUSHER

Arkansas Northeastern College (A)

2501 S Division Street, Blytheville AR 72315-5111
County: Mississippi FICE Identification: 012860
Unit ID: 107327
Telephone: (870) 762-1020 Carnegie Class: Assoc/Pub-R-M
FAX Number: (870) 763-3704 Calendar System: Semester
URL: www.anc.edu
Established: 1974 Annual Undergrad Tuition & Fees (In-District): $2,000
Enrollment: 1,996 Coed
Affiliation or Control: State/Local IRS Status: 501(c)3
Highest Offering: Associate Degree
Program: Occupational; 2-Year Principally Bachelor's Creditable
Accreditation: NH, ADNUR, DA, #EMT

01 Interim President ... Mrs. June WALTERS
05 Vice President of Instruction ... Ms. Mary DEMENT
10 Vice President for Finance ... Dr. James SHEMWELL
32 Vice Pres Student Svcs/Registrar ... Mrs. Laura YARBROUGH
30 Vice President for Advancement ... Mrs. Sherri BENNETT
09 Vice President MITS/Human Resources ... Mr. James W. MCCLAIN
26 Dean Development/College Relations ... Ms. Rachel GIFFORD
72 Dean Tech Programs & Training ... Mrs. Robin SINGLETON
49 Dean Arts & Sciences ... Mrs. Deborah PARKER
12 Dean Occupatl Pgms/Ext Campus Ops ... Mr. Gene BENNETT
66 Dean Nursing/Allied Hlth/PE/Rec ... Mrs. Brenda HOLIFIELD
83 Chair Communications/Humanities ... Mrs. Deanita HICKS
88 Coordinator University Center ... Mrs. Candice BLANKENSHIP
31 Coordinator Community Education ... Mrs. Sharyn STEVENSON
08 Director of College Library ... Mrs. Bronwyn MORGAN
07 Counselor Admissions & Careers ... Mr. Johnny MOORE
36 Coordinator of Placement Services ... Mr. Louis PARCHMAN
37 Director Financial Aid ... Vacant
72 Dean MITS ... Mrs. Ruby MEADOR
21 Controller ... Ms. Pacey BOWENS
15 Human Resources & ADA Coordinator ... Mrs. Carol WILF
90 Director Academic Tech Services ... Mr. James ODOM
18 Director Physical Plant and Grounds ... Mr. Ralph HILL
88 Director Talent Search/Educ Opp Ctr ... Mrs. Tonya HARRIS
88 Director Student Support Services ... Ms. Lisa MCGHEE
04 Assistant to Board/President ... Mrs. Courtney FISHER

*Arkansas State University System (B)

2222 Cottondale Lane, Suite 230, Little Rock AR 72202
County: Pulaski Identification: 666187
Telephone: (501) 660-1000 Carnegie Class: N/A
FAX Number: (501) 660-1010
URL: www.asusystem.edu

01 President ... Dr. Charles L. WELCH
04 Exec Assistant to the President ... Ms. Pam KAIL
10 Vice President for Finance ... Ms. Julie BATES
86 Vice Pres Governmental Relations ... Mr. Robert EVANS
102 System VP/President ASU Foundation ... Mr. Steve OWENS
43 Legal Counsel ... Ms. Lucinda MCDANIEL
88 Internal Auditor ... Ms. Jo LUNBECK

*Arkansas State University-Beebe (C)

PO Box 1000, Beebe AR 72012-1000
County: White FICE Identification: 001091
Unit ID: 106449
Telephone: (501) 882-3600 Carnegie Class: Assoc/Pub2in4
FAX Number: (501) 882-8970 Calendar System: Semester
URL: www.asub.edu
Established: 1927 Annual Undergrad Tuition & Fees (In-State): $2,880
Enrollment: 4,701 Coed
Affiliation or Control: State IRS Status: 501(c)3
Highest Offering: Associate Degree
Program: Occupational; 2-Year Principally Bachelor's Creditable
Accreditation: NH, EMT, MLTAD

02 Chancellor ... Dr. Eugene MCKAY
100 Executive Assistant to Chancellor ... Mr. Joe BERRY
03 Vice Chancellor ASU-Heber Springs ... Dr. James C. BOYETT
03 Vice Chancellor of ASU-Searcy ... Mr. Don HARLAN
05 Vice Chanc External/Advanced Pgms ... Mr. Barry N. FARRIS
05 Vice Chancellor Academic Affairs ... Dr. Theodore J. KALTHOFF
32 Vice Chancellor Student Services ... Dr. Deborah A. GARRETT
10 Vice Chanc Finance & Administration ... Mr. Jerry H. CARLISLE
30 Vice Chanc Inst Advancement ... Dr. Keith PINCHBACK
26 Director of Public Information ... Ms. Frances HART
06 Registrar ... Ms. Amy J. MAHAN
08 Head Librarian ... Ms. Tracy D. SMITH
15 Director of Human Resources ... Ms. Susan A. COLLIE
19 Chief of Police ... Mr. James J. MARTIN
18 Director of Physical Plant ... Mr. Jerry L. THOMPSON
37 Director Student Financial Aid ... Ms. Louise DRIVER
09 Director of Institutional Research ... Ms. Bonnie SMYTH-MCGAHA
14 Director of Computer Service ... Mr. Wade FINCHER
21 Business Manager ... Ms. Charlette MOORE
21 Controller ... Ms. Sharon A. BEEN
84 Director of Enrollment Management ... Mr. David M. MAYES
38 Dir Student Success and Retention ... Mr. Roger MOORE
36 Job Placement Coordinator ... Mr. Louis SCIVALLY
39 Director of Student Life ... Ms. Angie D. TOTTY
24 Director of Learning Center ... Ms. Rebecca E. WOLF
72 Director Advanced Tech/Allied Hlth ... Dr. Keith MCCLANAHAN
106 Director of Distance Learning ... Ms. Rhonda DURHAM
96 Dir Administrative Support Services ... Ms. Stephanie CREED
12 Dir ASU-Beebe Degree Ctr at LRAFB . Ms. Nancy A. SHEFFLETTE
07 Director of Admissions ... Ms. Robin A. HAYES
35 Coordinator of Campus Life ... Vacant
105 Website Coordinator ... Mr. Rikky L. FREE
31 Coord Marketing/Community Relations ... Mrs. Rose Mary JACKSON

*Arkansas State University-Jonesboro (D)

PO Box 600, State University AR 72467
County: Craighead FICE Identification: 001090
Unit ID: 106458
Telephone: (870) 972-2100 Carnegie Class: Master's L
FAX Number: (870) 972-3465 Calendar System: Semester
URL: www.astate.edu
Established: 1909 Annual Undergrad Tuition & Fees (In-State): $7,180
Enrollment: 13,900 Coed
Affiliation or Control: State IRS Status: 501(c)3
Highest Offering: Doctorate
Program: Liberal Arts And General; Teacher Preparatory; Professional
Accreditation: NH, ADNUR, ANEST, ART, BUS, CACREP, CEA, CORE, @DIETC, DMS, ENG, JOUR, MLTAD, MT, MUS, NUR, PTA, PTAA, RAD, RADMAG, RTT, SP, SPAA, SW, TED

02 Chancellor ... Dr. Tim HUDSON
04 Exec Assistant to the Chancellor ... Mr. Thomas MOORE
05 Exec Vice Chancellor & Provost ... Dr. Dan HOWARD
10 VC Finance & Administration ... Dr. Len FREY
32 Vice Chancellor Student Affairs ... Dr. William R. STRIPLING
30 VC University Advancement ... Mr. Cristian MURDOCK
86 Exec Dir Governmental Relations ... Mr. Robert EVANS
41 Director of Athletics ... Dr. Dean LEE
88 Assoc Vice Chanc Academic Affairs ... Dr. Lynita M. COOKSEY
21 Assoc Vice Chancellor Finance ... Mr. Russ HANNAH
11 Assoc Vice Chanc Administration ... Dr. J. W MASON
35 Assoc Vice Chanc Student Affairs ... Dr. Lonnie R. WILLIAMS
46 Int Assoc VC Research/Technology ... Dr. Andrew SUSTICH
88 Asst Vice Chanc Student Affairs ... Mr. Craig JOHNSON
13 Asst VC Information Technology/CIO ... Mr. Mark HOETING
18 Asst Vice Chancellor Facilities ... Mr. Al STOVERINK
51 Dean Continuing Educ/Cmty Outreach ... Dr. Beverly BOALS-GILBERT
88 Interim Executive Director of ABI ... Dr. Andrew SUSTICH
37 Dir of Financial Aid & Scholarship ... Mr. Terry FINNEY
09 Dir Instnl Research/Plng/Assessment ... Dr. Kathryn C. JONES
06 Registrar ... Ms. Tracy FINCH
07 Director of Admissions ... Ms. Tammy FOWLER
39 Director of Residence Life ... Mr. Patrick DIXON
38 Dean of Student Development ... Mr. Randall TATE
19 Interim Dir of University Police ... Mr. Randy MARTIN
28 Director of Disability Services ... Dr. Jenifer R. MASON
36 Interim Director of Career Services ... Dr. Lonnie WILLIAMS
38 Director Student Counseling ... Dr. Phil HESTAND
23 Director Student Health Center ... Ms. Renata VAUGHN
29 Director of Alumni Relations ... Ms. Beth SMITH
26 Director of University Relations ... Ms. Christy VALENTINE
27 Director of Media Relations ... Ms. Gina BOWMAN
88 Director Pub & Creative Services ... Mr. Mark REEVES
44 Executive Director of Development ... Dr. Jim PROCK
96 Director of Purchasing ... Ms. Carol BARNHILL
62 Int Dean of Library/Info Resources ... Mr. Jeff BAILEY
47 Int Dean Col Agriculture/Technology ... Dr. David BEASLEY
81 Interim Dean College of Sci & Math ... Dr. John PRATTE
50 Dean College of Business ... Vacant
53 Dean College of Education ... Dr. Thillainatarajan SIVAKUMARAN
58 Dean of Graduate School ... Dr. Andrew SUSTICH
60 Dean College of Communications ... Dr. Brad RAWLINS
66 Dean College of Nursing Health Prof ... Dr. Susan N. HANRAHAN
88 Dean University College ... Dr. Lynita M. COOKSEY
57 Dean Fine Arts ... Dr. Donald BOWYER
79 Dean College Humanities/Social Sci ... Dr. Lauri UMANSKY
92 Dean Honors Program ... Dr. Andrew SUSTICH
54 Dean College of Engineering ... Dr. David BEASLEY

*Arkansas State University-Mountain Home (E)

1600 S College Street, Mountain Home AR 72653-5326
County: Baxter Identification: 666311
Unit ID: 420538
Telephone: (870) 508-6100 Carnegie Class: Assoc/Pub2in4
FAX Number: (870) 508-6287 Calendar System: Semester
URL: www.asumh.edu
Established: 1995 Annual Undergrad Tuition & Fees (In-District): $3,150
Enrollment: 1,472 Coed
Affiliation or Control: State/Local IRS Status: 501(c)3
Highest Offering: Associate Degree
Program: Occupational; Business Emphasis
Accreditation: NH, EMT, FUSER

02 Chancellor ... Dr. Robin MYERS
05 Provost/VC Academic/Student Affairs ... Dr. Patricia A. BAILEY
11 Vice Chanc Administrative Affairs ... Mr. John DAVIDSON
30 Vice Chancellor Development ... Vacant
84 Assoc VC Enrollment Management ... Mrs. Rosalyn R. BLAGG
46 Assoc VC Rsrch/Sp Prog/Dist Lrng ... Mrs. Karen S. HOPPER
06 Registrar ... Mrs. Rosalyn R. BLAGG
18 Chief Facilities/Physical Plant ... Mr. Nickey L. ROBBINS
26 Chief Public Relations Officer ... Mrs. Christy C. KEIRN
35 Director Student Affairs ... Vacant
37 Director Student Financial Aid ... Mr. Clay BERRY

*Arkansas State University-Newport (F)

7648 Victory Boulevard, Newport AR 72112-8912
County: Jackson Identification: 666153
Unit ID: 440402
Telephone: (870) 512-7800 Carnegie Class: Assoc/Pub2in4
FAX Number: (870) 512-7807 Calendar System: Semester
URL: www.asun.edu
Established: 1991 Annual Undergrad Tuition & Fees (In-State): $2,850
Enrollment: 2,005 Coed
Affiliation or Control: State IRS Status: 501(c)3
Highest Offering: Associate Degree
Program: Occupational; 2-Year Principally Bachelor's Creditable
Accreditation: NH

02 Chancellor ... Dr. Larry N. WILLIAMS
04 Assistant to the Chancellor ... Ms. Laura KING
05 Vice Chancellor Academic Affairs ... Dr. Sandra MASSEY
10 Vice Chancellor Fiscal Affairs ... Mr. Adam ADAIR
32 Vice Chancellor Student Affairs ... Dr. Mary ROBERTSON
12 Vice Chancellor Jonesboro Campus ... Ms. Linda SHARP
12 Vice Chancellor Marked Tree Campus ... Mr. Jeff BOOKOUT
88 Division Chair ... Mr. Ike WHEELER
88 Division Chair ... Dr. Allen MOONEYHAN
88 Director of Business/Transportation ... Mr. Bentley WALLACE
06 Registrar/Director of Admissions ... Mr. Robert SUMMERS
13 Director of Computer Services ... Ms. Tamya STALLINGS
15 Director Human Resources ... Ms. Bettye DAVIS
18 Director of Physical Plant ... Mr. David WINSTON
21 Controller ... Ms. Melissa WATSON
25 Director of Grants Management ... Ms. Monika PHILLIPS
37 Director Student Financial Aid ... Ms. Deana TIMS
32 Director Student Services ... Ms. Ashley BUCHMAN
38 Counselor ... Ms. Amber GRADY
08 Librarian ... Ms. Jennifer BALLARD
24 Director of Learning Resource Ctr ... Ms. Christy MANN
19 Public Safety Officer ... Mr. Jeff GRIZZLE
96 Director of Procurement ... Ms. Lee WEBB
17 Director of Nursing ... Mr. Scott COWELL
108 Director of Career Pathways ... Ms. Kimberly LONG
75 Adult Education Coordinator ... Ms. Martha TAUSSIG

Arkansas Tech University (G)

1509 North Boulder Avenue, Russellville AR 72801-2222
County: Pope FICE Identification: 001089
Unit ID: 106467
Telephone: (479) 968-0389 Carnegie Class: Master's L
FAX Number: (479) 964-0522 Calendar System: Semester
URL: www.atu.edu
Established: 1909 Annual Undergrad Tuition & Fees (In-State): $5,286
Enrollment: 10,464 Coed
Affiliation or Control: State IRS Status: 501(c)3
Highest Offering: Beyond Master's But Less Than Doctorate
Program: Liberal Arts And General; Teacher Preparatory; Professional
Accreditation: NH, BUS, CS, EMT, ENG, MAC, MUS, NRPA, NUR, PTAA, TED

01 President ... Dr. Robert C. BROWN
32 VP Student Services/Univ Rels ... Ms. Susie S. NICHOLSON
05 Vice President Academic Affairs ... Dr. John WATSON
11 Sr Vice Pres Administration/Finance ... Mr. David MOSELEY
30 Vice President for Development ... Ms. Jayne W. JONES
86 Vice President Government Relations ... Mr. Phillip JACOBS
20 Assoc Vice Pres Academic Affairs ... Dr. David UNDERWOOD
88 Assistant VP for Academic Affairs ... Dr. Hanna NORTON
84 Assistant VP Enrollment Management ... Ms. Shauna H. DONNELL
06 Registrar ... Ms. Tammy RHODES
09 Director of Institutional Research ... Mr. Wyatt WATSON
08 Librarian ... Mr. William PARTON
21 Controller ... Ms. Donna RANKIN
38 Dir Learning Asst/Testing Center ... Ms. Christy RAINES
14 Director Computer Services ... Mr. Merrell E. SHOPTAW
27 Director News Bureau ... Vacant
15 Director Human Resources ... Ms. Angela REYNOLDS
37 Director Student Financial Aid ... Ms. Shirley M. GOINES
29 Director Alumni Association ... Mr. Kelly DAVIS
24 Associate Director Computer Service ... Mr. Ken WESTER
85 Director of International Students ... Mr. Yasushi ONODERA
18 Director of Physical Plant Services ... Mr. Brian LASEY
26 Chief Public Relations Officer ... Ms. Susie S. NICHOLSON
96 Director of Purchasing ... Ms. Jessica HOLLOWAY
92 Director of Honors Program ... Dr. Jan JENKINS
22 Director of Affirmative Action ... Ms. Jennifer FLEMING
35 Director Student Affairs ... Vacant

58 Dean of Graduate College ... Dr. Mary GUNTER
53 Dean of College of Education ... Dr. Sherry FIELD
49 Dean College of Arts & Humanities ... Dr. Micheal TARVER
50 Dean of College of Business ... Dr. Edward BASHAW
77 Dean of College of Applied Science ... Dr. William HOEFLER
81 Dean College of Natural & Health Sc ... Dr. Richard R. COHOON
51 Dn Col Prof Studies Cmty Outreach ... Dr. Mary Ann ROLLANS
10 Chief Business Officer ... Vacant

Black River Technical College (A)

PO Box 468, Pocahantas AR 72455-0468
County: Randolph FICE Identification: 020522
Unit ID: 106625
Telephone: (870) 248-4000 Carnegie Class: Assoc/Pub-R-M
FAX Number: (870) 248-4100 Calendar System: Semester
URL: www.blackrivertech.org
Established: 1991 Annual Undergrad Tuition & Fees (In-State): $2,790
Enrollment: 2,505 Coed
Affiliation or Control: State IRS Status: 501(c)3
Highest Offering: Associate Degree
Program: Occupational; 2-Year Principally Bachelor's Creditable
Accreditation: NH, DIETT, EMT

01 President ... Dr. Wayne HATCHER
05 Vice President General Education ... Dr. Roger JOHNSON
72 Vice President Technical Education ... Mrs. Angela CALDWELL
10 Vice President of Finance ... Mrs. Loretta WILLIAMS
32 Vice President Student Affairs ... Dr. Michael A. SULLENS
30 Vice President of Development ... Dr. Jan ZIEGLER
37 Director Student Financial Aid ... Mrs. Brandi CHESTER
06 Registrar ... Mrs. Kimberly BIGGER

Bryan College (B)

3704 West Walnut, Rogers AR 72756-1825
County: Benton Identification: 666252
Unit ID: 454458
Telephone: (479) 899-6644 Carnegie Class: Assoc/PrivFP
FAX Number: (417) 862-9554 Calendar System: Semester
URL: www.bryancolleges.edu
Established: 2007 Annual Undergrad Tuition & Fees: $28,800
Enrollment: 257 Coed
Affiliation or Control: Proprietary IRS Status: Proprietary
Highest Offering: Associate Degree
Program: Occupational; 2-Year Principally Bachelor's Creditable
Accreditation: ACICS

01 President ... Mr. Brian STEWART
03 Executive Director ... Mr. James FINLEY

† Branch campus of Bryan College, Springfield, MO.

Central Baptist College (C)

1501 College Avenue, Conway AR 72034-6470
County: Faulkner FICE Identification: 001093
Unit ID: 106713
Telephone: (501) 329-6872 Carnegie Class: Bac/Diverse
FAX Number: (501) 329-2941 Calendar System: Semester
URL: www.cbc.edu
Established: 1952 Annual Undergrad Tuition & Fees: $11,600
Enrollment: 858 Coed
Affiliation or Control: Baptist IRS Status: 501(c)3
Highest Offering: Baccalaureate
Program: Liberal Arts And General; Teacher Preparatory
Accreditation: NH

01 President ... Mr. Terry KIMBROW
05 Vice President Academic Affairs ... Dr. Gary MCALLISTER
10 Vice President Financial Affairs ... Mrs. Donna GRAY
30 VP for Advancement ... Mrs. Sancy FAULK
84 Assoc VP for Enrollment ... Mr. Ryan JOHNSON
06 Registrar ... Mrs. Phylis HOFFMANN
08 Librarian ... Mrs. Rachel WHITTINGHAM
26 Director of Public Relations ... Mrs. Deanna OTT
30 Development Officer ... Mr. Michael MAYO
37 Financial Aid Director ... Mrs. Tonya HAMMONTREE
88 Director of Special Events ... Ms. Jessica FAULKNER
91 Director of Technical Services ... Mr. Doug BIBLE
41 Athletic Director ... Mr. Lyle MIDDLETON
32 Asst Director of Student Services ... Ms. Sarah HEADLEY
15 Human Resource Analyst ... Mrs. Karen MARSHALL
29 Alumni & Communications Coord ... Miss Jessica MYRICK

College of the Ouachitas (D)

One College Circle, Malvern AR 72104-0816
County: Hot Spring FICE Identification: 009976
Unit ID: 107521
Telephone: (501) 337-5000 Carnegie Class: Assoc/Pub-R-S
FAX Number: (501) 337-9382 Calendar System: Semester
URL: www.coto.edu
Established: 1991 Annual Undergrad Tuition & Fees (In-State): $2,507
Enrollment: 1,407 Coed
Affiliation or Control: State IRS Status: 501(c)3
Highest Offering: Associate Degree
Program: Occupational; 2-Year Principally Bachelor's Creditable; Technical Emphasis
Accreditation: NH

01 President ... Dr. Stephen SCHOONMAKER
10 Vice Pres Finance & Administration ... Dr. Roger COOMER
05 Vice President of Instruction ... Dr. Martin EGGENSPERGER
09 Vice Pres for Planning & Assessment ... Ms. Carla CRUTCHFIELD
103 VP Workforce and Adult Education ... Dr. Blake ROBERTSON
32 Vice President Student Affairs ... Ms. Donna HILL
06 Registrar ... Ms. Linda JOHNSON
08 Library Director ... Ms. Mary Ann HARPER
37 Director of Financial Aid ... Ms. Teresa AVERY
13 Director of Computer Services ... Mr. David SEE
30 Dir Develop/Chief Public Rels Ofcr ... Ms. Amber CHILDERS
36 Director Career Center ... Mr. Ruben KEISLER
88 Dir TRIO Student Support Services ... Ms. Marshel JOHNSON
88 Director Career Pathways ... Mr. Billy FRANCIS

Crowley's Ridge College (E)

100 College Drive, Paragould AR 72450-9775
County: Greene FICE Identification: 001095
Unit ID: 106810
Telephone: (870) 236-6901 Carnegie Class: Assoc/PrivNFP4
FAX Number: (870) 236-7748 Calendar System: Semester
URL: www.crc.edu
Established: 1964 Annual Undergrad Tuition & Fees: $10,350
Enrollment: 221 Coed
Affiliation or Control: Churches Of Christ IRS Status: 501(c)3
Highest Offering: Baccalaureate
Program: Liberal Arts And General
Accreditation: NH

01 President ... Mr. Ken HOPPE
05 Vice President for Academic Affairs ... Mr. Phil WILKERSON
32 Vice President for Student Affairs ... Mr. Art SMITH
30 Vice President for Advancement ... Mr. Richard JOHNSON
06 Registrar ... Mr. Paul MCFADDEN
37 Director Student Financial Services ... Mr. David W. GOFF
26 Director Public Information ... Mrs. Andrea JOHNSON
07 Director Admissions/Student Life ... Mrs. Nancy JONESHILL
41 Athletic Director/Campus Minister ... Mr. Paul MCFADDEN
08 Director Learning Center ... Mr. Mark WARNICK
21 Business Office Manager ... Mrs. Sonia JOHNSON
18 Physical Plant Manager ... Mr. Larry KITCHENS
27 Director of Information Services ... Mr. Larry JOHNSON

East Arkansas Community College (F)

1700 Newcastle Road, Forrest City AR 72335-9598
County: Saint Francis FICE Identification: 012260
Unit ID: 106883
Telephone: (870) 633-4480 Carnegie Class: Assoc/Pub-R-S
FAX Number: (870) 633-7222 Calendar System: Semester
URL: www.eacc.edu
Established: 1974 Annual Undergrad Tuition & Fees (In-District): $2,430
Enrollment: 1,302 Coed
Affiliation or Control: Local IRS Status: 501(c)3
Highest Offering: Associate Degree
Program: Occupational; 2-Year Principally Bachelor's Creditable
Accreditation: NH, ADNUR, EMT

01 President ... Dr. Coy F. GRACE
05 Vice President Academic Affairs ... Mrs. Janie BAILEY
10 Vice President Business Affairs ... Mr. Vernie MEADOR
32 Vice President Student Affairs ... Mrs. Catherine T. COLEMAN
37 Director Student Financial Aid ... Mr. Alvin COLEMAN
88 Assoc VP for Applied Sciences ... Mrs. Joanne LAWSON
88 AVP for Community/Business Outreach ... Mrs. Tiffany BILLINGSLEY
97 Assoc VP for General Studies ... Dr. Cathie CLINE
08 Director Library Services ... Mrs. Paige LAWS
84 Director Enrollment Mgmt/Registrar ... Mrs. Sharon COLLIER
26 Director of Public Relations/Mktg ... Mrs. Elizabeth C. LOEB
15 Director Personnel Services ... Mrs. Yvonne RUCKER-FRANKLIN
18 Director Physical Plant ... Mr. Glenn FORD
38 Director Educational Guidance Svcs ... Mrs. Michelle WILSON
96 Director of Purchasing ... Mrs. Nancy HERBERT
04 Assistant to the President ... Mr. Christopher A. HEIGLE
51 Director of Continuing Education ... Mrs. Lindsay MIDKIFF

Ecclesia College (G)

9653 Nations Drive, Springdale AR 72762-8159
County: Benton FICE Identification: 038553
Unit ID: 446233
Telephone: (479) 248-7236 Carnegie Class: Spec/Faith
FAX Number: (479) 248-1455 Calendar System: Semester
URL: www.ecollege.edu
Established: 1975 Annual Undergrad Tuition & Fees: $16,000
Enrollment: 141 Coed
Affiliation or Control: Independent Non-Profit IRS Status: 501(c)3
Highest Offering: Baccalaureate
Program: Liberal Arts And General; Religious Emphasis
Accreditation: BI

01 President ... Mr. Oren PARIS, III
05 Vice President of Academics ... Dr. Robert HEADRICK
10 Vice Pres of Business & Finance ... Mr. Shannon WORTHEN
32 Vice Pres of Student Development ... Mr. Jesse E. WADKINS
30 Vice President of Advancement ... Mr. Mike NOVAK
26 Vice Pres of Communications ... Ms. Angie P. SNYDER
07 Director of Admissions ... Mr. Titus W. HOFER
37 Director Student Financial Aid ... Mr. Jesse E. WADKINS
41 Athletic Director ... Mr. Oren PARIS, III
06 Registrar ... Mrs. Donna BROWN
08 Head Librarian ... Mrs. Joanne CAMPBELL
88 Director Work Learning ... Mr. Nic STICE

Harding University Main Campus (H)

915 E Market, Searcy AR 72149-0001
County: White FICE Identification: 001097
Unit ID: 107044
Telephone: (501) 279-4000 Carnegie Class: Master's L
FAX Number: (501) 279-4600 Calendar System: Semester
URL: www.harding.edu
Established: 1924 Annual Undergrad Tuition & Fees: $16,226
Enrollment: 7,155 Coed
Affiliation or Control: Churches Of Christ IRS Status: 501(c)3
Highest Offering: Doctorate
Program: Occupational; Liberal Arts And General; Teacher Preparatory; Professional
Accreditation: NH, ACBSP, ARCPA, CIDA, DIETD, ENG, MUS, NUR, PHAR, @PTA, @SP, SW, TED

01 President ... Dr. David B. BURKS
03 Executive Vice President ... Dr. James W. CARR
05 Provost ... Dr. Larry LONG
30 Sr Vice President for Development ... Mr. Floyd DANIEL
10 Vice President Finance ... Mr. Mel SANSOM
44 Vice President Advancement ... Dr. Mike WILLAMS
42 Vice President of Spiritual Life ... Dr. Bruce MCLARTY
07 Assistant Vice President Admissions ... Mr. Glenn DILLARD
06 Registrar ... Mrs. Janice HURD
38 Director of Counseling ... Dr. Lew MOORE
26 Director of Public Relations ... Mr. David CROUCH
37 Director Student Financial Aid ... Mr. Jon ROBERTS
58 Director of Graduate Studies ... Mr. Pat BASHAW
08 Librarian ... Mrs. Ann DIXON
09 Director of Institutional Research ... Dr. Marty SPEARS
18 Chief Facilities/Physical Plant ... Mr. Danny DERAMUS
29 Director Alumni Relations ... Mrs. Liz HOWELL
93 Director of Minority Students ... Dr. Butch GARDNER
15 Director Personnel Services ... Mr. David ROSS
36 Director Student Placement ... Mr. Butch GARDNER
96 Director of Purchasing ... Vacant
32 Dean of Students/Vice Pres ... Dr. David COLLINS
35 Assistant Dean of Students ... Mr. Zeal NEAL
33 Assistant Dean of Students ... Mr. Stu VARNER
34 Assistant Dean of Students ... Mrs. Ranan HESTER
92 Dean of Honors College ... Dr. Warren CASEY
50 Dean School of Business ... Dr. Bryan BURKS
53 Dean School of Education ... Dr. Tony FINLEY
66 Dean School of Nursing ... Dr. Cathleen M. SHULTZ
79 Dean College of Arts & Humanities ... Dr. Warren CASEY
81 Dean College of Sciences ... Dr. Travis THOMPSON
04 Assistant to the President ... Mr. Nate COPELAND

† See Also Affiliate: Harding Graduate School of Religion, TN.

Henderson State University (I)

1100 Henderson Street, Arkadelphia AR 71999-0001
County: Clark FICE Identification: 001098
Unit ID: 107071
Telephone: (870) 230-5000 Carnegie Class: Master's M
FAX Number: (870) 230-5144 Calendar System: Semester
URL: www.hsu.edu
Established: 1890 Annual Undergrad Tuition & Fees (In-State): $7,010
Enrollment: 3,774 Coed
Affiliation or Control: State IRS Status: 501(c)3
Highest Offering: Beyond Master's But Less Than Doctorate
Program: Liberal Arts And General; Teacher Preparatory; Professional
Accreditation: NH, BUS, CACREP, DIETD, MUS, NURSE, TED

01 President ... Dr. Glendell JONES
05 Provost/VPAA ... Dr. Vernon MILES
10 Vice Pres Finance & Administration ... Mr. Bobby G. JONES
32 Int Vice President Student Services ... Mr. Chad FIELDING
04 VP External Programs ... Dr. Lewis SHEPHERD
43 General Counsel ... Ms. Elaine KNEEBONE
35 Dean of Student Services ... Mr. Chad FIELDING
36 Assoc Dean of Student Services ... Ms. Pam LIGON
13 Director Computer/Communication Svc ... Mr. David H. EPPERHART
30 Director Development ... Ms. Carrie ROBERSON
41 Director Athletics ... Mr. T. Kale GOBER
26 Director of Public Relations ... Ms. Penny A. MURPHY
49 Dean Ellis College Arts/Sciences ... Dr. Maralyn T. SOMMER
50 Dean of School of Business ... Dr. Jeff HAMM
53 Dean Teachers College Henderson ... Dr. Judy HARRISON
58 Interim Dean of Graduate School ... Dr. Kenneth TAYLOR
06 Registrar ... Mr. Tom GATTIN
08 Director Huie Library ... Mr. Robert F. YEHL
18 Director Physical Plant ... Mr. John C. CORLEY
15 Director of Human Resources ... Ms. Kathy TAYLOR
19 Director of University Police ... Mr. Jonathan CAMPBELL
38 Director of Counseling ... Ms. Deborah COLLINS
07 Director Univ Relations/Admissions ... Ms. Vikita B. HARDWRICK
37 Director of Financial Aid ... Ms. Vicki TAYLOR
92 Director of Honors College ... Dr. David T. THOMSON
88 Director of Student Research ... Dr. Martin CAMPBELL
96 Director of Purchasing ... Mr. Tim JONES
24 Dir Multi Media Learning Center ... Ms. Jennifer HOLBROOK
39 Director Residence Life ... Mr. Dan MABERY
85 Director International Students ... Dr. Drew SMITH
29 Coordinator of Alumni Services ... Ms. Sherry WRIGHT

Hendrix College (A)

1600 Washington Avenue, Conway AR 72032-3080
County: Faulkner FICE Identification: 001099
Unit ID: 107080
Telephone: (501) 329-6811 Carnegie Class: Bac/A&S
FAX Number: (501) 450-1200 Calendar System: Semester
URL: www.hendrix.edu
Established: 1876 Annual Undergrad Tuition & Fees: $46,308
Enrollment: 1,418 Coed
Affiliation or Control: United Methodist IRS Status: 501(c)3
Highest Offering: Master's
Program: Liberal Arts And General
Accreditation: NH, MUS, TED

01 President .... Dr. J. Timothy CLOYD
04 Executive Assistant to President .... Ms. Donna PLEMMONS
30 Exec Vice Pres/Dean Inst Advance .... Mr. W. Ellis ARNOLD, III
05 Provost .... Dr. Robert L. ENTZMINGER
27 Exec Vice Pres & Chief Communicat .... Mr. Frank COX
10 Executive Vice President and CFO .... Mr. Tom SIEBENMORGEN
45 Exec Vice Pres and Strategic Plng .... Ms. Karen R. FOUST
18 Assoc VP Operations & Facilities .... Mr. Loyd RYAN
32 Vice President Student Affairs .... Mr. Jim WILTGEN
35 Dean of Students .... Dr. James N. WILTGEN, JR.
26 Exec Director of Communications .... Ms. Helen S. PLOTKIN
06 Registrar .... Ms. Xinying WANG
08 Director of Libraries .... Ms. Amanda MOORE
13 Exec Vice Pres & Chief Info Office .... Mr. David J. HINSON
29 Director Alumni Relations .... Ms. Pamela OWEN
37 Director of Financial Aid .... Ms. Kristina BURFORD
40 Bookstore Manager .... Ms. Dee Dee ALLEN
79 Area Head/Humanities .... Dr. Alex VERNONE
81 Area Head/Natural Sciences .... Dr. Carl BURCH
83 Area Head/Social Sciences .... Dr. Allison SHUTT
42 Chaplain .... Rev. Wayne CLARK
07 Director of Admission .... Mr. Fred BAKER
15 Director Personnel Services .... Ms. Vicki LYNN
20 Associate Academic Officer .... Dr. David SUTHERLAND
21 Associate Business Officer .... Mr. Shawn MATHIS
36 Director Career Services .... Ms. Christy COKER
38 Director Student Counseling .... Ms. Mary Anne SIEBERT

ITT Technical Institute (B)

12200 Westhaven Drive, Little Rock AR 72211
County: Pulaski Identification: 666531
Unit ID: 413839
Telephone: (501) 565-5550 Carnegie Class: Spec/Tech
FAX Number: (501) 565-4747 Calendar System: Quarter
URL: www.itt-tech.edu
Established: 1993 Annual Undergrad Tuition & Fees: N/A
Enrollment: 466 Coed
Affiliation or Control: Proprietary IRS Status: Proprietary
Highest Offering: Baccalaureate
Program: Technical Emphasis
Accreditation: ACICS

† Branch campus of ITT Technical Institute, Indianapolis, IN.

John Brown University (C)

2000 W University Street, Siloam Springs AR 72761-2121
County: Benton FICE Identification: 001100
Unit ID: 107141
Telephone: (479) 524-9500 Carnegie Class: Bac/Diverse
FAX Number: (479) 524-9548 Calendar System: Semester
URL: www.jbu.edu
Established: 1919 Annual Undergrad Tuition & Fees: $21,774
Enrollment: 2,183 Coed
Affiliation or Control: Independent Non-Profit IRS Status: 501(c)3
Highest Offering: Master's
Program: Liberal Arts And General; Teacher Preparatory
Accreditation: NH, CONST, ENG, IACBE, TED

01 President .... Dr. Charles POLLARD
03 Executive Vice President .... Vacant
10 Vice Pres Finance & Administration .... Mrs. Kim HADLEY
84 Vice Pres Enrollment Management .... Mr. Donald W. CRANDALL
30 Vice Pres of University Advancement .... Dr. Jim KRALL
32 Vice Pres for Student Development .... Dr. Stephen T. BEERS
05 VP Academic Affairs/Dean of Faculty .... Dr. Ed ERICSON, III
88 Dean Degree Completion Program .... Mrs. Susan DEWOODY
42 Campus Pastor/Assoc Dean of Stdnts .... Mr. Rod REED
06 Registrar .... Mrs. Rebecca LAMBERT
21 Controller .... Mr. Tom PERRY
13 Chief Information Systems Ofcr .... Mr. Paul NAST
18 Director of Facilities Services .... Mr. Steve BRANKLE
44 Director of Planned Giving .... Mr. Eric GREENHAW
08 Director of Library .... Mrs. Mary HABERMAS
85 Director International Programs .... Mr. Bill STEVENSON
29 Director of Alumni/Parent Relations .... Mr. Jerry ROLLENE
37 Director of Financial Aid .... Mr. Kim ELDRIDGE
41 Athletic Director .... Ms. Robyn DAUGHERTY
38 Director of Counseling .... Dr. Tim DINGER

Lyon College (D)

PO Box 2317, Batesville AR 72503-2317
County: Independence FICE Identification: 001088
Unit ID: 106342
Telephone: (870) 307-7000 Carnegie Class: Bac/A&S
FAX Number: (870) 307-7001 Calendar System: Semester
URL: www.lyon.edu
Established: 1872 Annual Undergrad Tuition & Fees: $31,154
Enrollment: 600 Coed
Affiliation or Control: Presbyterian Church (U.S.A.) IRS Status: 501(c)3
Highest Offering: Baccalaureate
Program: Liberal Arts And General; Teacher Preparatory
Accreditation: NH, TED

01 President .... Dr. Donald V. WEATHERMAN
05 VP Academic Svcs/Dean of Faculty .... Dr. Virginia F. WRAY
10 Vice President Business & Finance .... Mr. Kenneth J. RUETER
11 Vice Pres for Administration .... Mr. David L. HERINGER
32 Vice President Student Life .... Dr. F. Bruce JOHNSTON
06 Registrar/Dir Inst Research/Comm .... Mr. Donald R. TAYLOR
08 Director Library .... Mr. Dean COVINGTON
26 Director Public Relations .... Mr. Bob R. QUALLS
29 Dir Alumni Services & Development .... Ms. Gina GARRETT
15 Director Personnel .... Mrs. Clarinda L. FOOTE
37 Director of Financial Assistance .... Mr. Tommy TUCKER
36 Director Career Development .... Ms. Vicki WEBB
13 Director Information Services .... Mr. Karl KEMP
41 Director of Athletics .... Mr. Kevin JENKINS
42 Chaplain .... Rev. Nancy MCSPADDEN
104 Director Nichols Intl Studies Pgm .... Dr. Virginia F. WRAY
53 Int Director of Teacher Education .... Ms. Kim CROSBY
07 Director of Admissions .... Mr. Josh MANNING
09 Director of Institutional Research .... Mr. Donald R. TAYLOR
38 Director Student Counseling .... Ms. Diane ELLIS

Mid-South Community College (E)

2000 W Broadway, West Memphis AR 72301-3829
County: Crittenden FICE Identification: 023482
Unit ID: 107318
Telephone: (870) 733-6722 Carnegie Class: Assoc/Pub-S-SC
FAX Number: (870) 733-6799 Calendar System: Semester
URL: www.midsouthcc.edu
Established: 1992 Annual Undergrad Tuition & Fees (In-District): $2,700
Enrollment: 2,168 Coed
Affiliation or Control: State/Local IRS Status: 501(c)3
Highest Offering: Associate Degree
Program: Occupational; 2-Year Principally Bachelor's Creditable
Accreditation: NH

01 President .... Dr. Glen F. FENTER
03 Executive Vice President .... Dr. Barbara C. BAXTER
05 Vice Pres Learning & Instruction .... Dr. Cliff JONES
10 Vice Pres Finance & Administration .... Mrs. Susan MARSHALL
32 Vice President Student Affairs .... Mr. Dwayne SCOTT
26 Director Marketing/Public Rels .... Mr. Len GRICE
37 Director of Financial Aid .... Ms. Amy CABLE
08 Director of Library Media Center .... Ms. Rene JONES
06 Registrar/Dir Institutional Rsrch .... Ms. Leslie ANDERSON
07 Director of Admissions .... Mr. Jeremy REECE
15 Director of Human Resources .... Ms. Jackie BRUBAKER
18 Director Facilities/Physical Plant .... Mr. Randy WEBB
30 Director of Advancement .... Vacant
38 Director of Student Counseling .... Vacant

National Park Community College (F)

101 College Drive,
Hot Springs National Park AR 71913-9174
County: Garland FICE Identification: 012105
Unit ID: 106980
Telephone: (501) 760-4222 Carnegie Class: Assoc/Pub-R-M
FAX Number: (501) 760-4100 Calendar System: Semester
URL: www.npcc.edu
Established: 1973 Annual Undergrad Tuition & Fees (In-District): $2,750
Enrollment: 2,540 Coed
Affiliation or Control: State/Local IRS Status: 501(c)3
Highest Offering: Associate Degree
Program: Occupational; 2-Year Principally Bachelor's Creditable; Technical Emphasis
Accreditation: NH, ADNUR, COE, EMT, MLTAD, RAD

01 President .... Dr. Sally CARDER
05 Exec Vice Pres for Instruction .... Dr. Gordon WATTS
10 Vice President for Business Affairs .... Ms. Janis SAWYER
32 Vice President Student Services .... Ms. Margaret PICKING
72 Assoc Vice Pres Technical Education .... Mr. David HUGHES
04 Assistant to the President .... Dr. Susan ALDRIDGE
20 Assoc Dean for Academic Affairs .... Dr. Brad MOODY
35 Director of Student Affairs .... Ms. Holly GARRETT-MILLER
15 Director of Human Resources .... Ms. Janet BREWER
08 Director of the Library .... Ms. Sara SEAMAN
37 Director of Financial Aid .... Ms. Lisa HOPPER
26 Chief Public Relations Officer .... Ms. Jill JOHNSON
30 Chief Development .... Ms. Lisa CAREY
38 Director Student Counseling .... Mr. Ron CHESSER

North Arkansas College (G)

1515 Pioneer Drive, Harrison AR 72601-5599
County: Boone FICE Identification: 012261
Unit ID: 107460
Telephone: (870) 743-3000 Carnegie Class: Assoc/Pub-R-M
FAX Number: (870) 391-3250 Calendar System: Semester
URL: www.northark.edu
Established: 1974 Annual Undergrad Tuition & Fees (In-District): $2,190
Enrollment: 2,307 Coed
Affiliation or Control: State/Local IRS Status: 501(c)3
Highest Offering: Associate Degree
Program: Occupational; 2-Year Principally Bachelor's Creditable; Nursing Emphasis
Accreditation: NH, ACBSP, ADNUR, EMT, MLTAD, RAD, SURGT

01 President .... Dr. Jacquelyn ELLIOTT
05 Exec Vice President of Learning .... Dr. Gwen GRESHAM
10 Vice Pres Finance & Administration .... Mr. Donald SUGG
30 Vice Pres Institutional Advancement .... Dr. Jim STOCKTON
04 Executive Assistant to President .... Mrs. Trish VILLINES
49 Dean Arts and Science .... Dr. Laura BERRY
50 Dean Business and Tech Programs .... Vacant
66 Dean of Nursing/Allied Health .... Mrs. Cindy MAYO
08 Director of Libraries .... Mr. Jim ROBB
44 Dir Institutional Effectiveness .... Mrs. Katherine VAUGHN
32 Director of Student Success .... Mrs. Nell BONDS
41 Athletic Director .... Mr. Jerry THOMASON
15 Director Human Resources .... Mrs. Kris GREENING
18 Chief Facilities/Physical Plant .... Mr. Kevin SOMERS
96 Director of Purchasing .... Mrs. Sandra JONES
37 Director Student Financial Aid .... Mrs. Jennifer HADDOCK
06 Registrar .... Mrs. Charla JENNINGS
07 Director of Admissions .... Vacant
26 Director of Public Relations .... Mrs. Micki SOMERS
90 Director Academic Computing .... Mr. Rick WILLIAMS
91 Director Administrative Computing .... Mr. Glenn COLMAN
31 Director of Community Education .... Mrs. Amy BELL

NorthWest Arkansas Community College (H)

1 College Drive, Bentonville AR 72712-5091
County: Benton FICE Identification: 030633
Unit ID: 367459
Telephone: (479) 636-9222 Carnegie Class: Assoc/Pub-R-L
FAX Number: (479) 619-4335 Calendar System: Semester
URL: www.nwacc.edu
Established: 1989 Annual Undergrad Tuition & Fees (In-District): $2,870
Enrollment: 8,528 Coed
Affiliation or Control: State/Local IRS Status: 501(c)3
Highest Offering: Associate Degree
Program: Occupational; 2-Year Principally Bachelor's Creditable
Accreditation: NH, EMT, IFSAC, PTAA

01 President .... Dr. Becky PANEITZ
05 Sr Vice Pres Learning/Provost .... Dr. Steve GATES
10 Sr VP Admin Svcs/Chief Finan Svcs .... Mr. Marty PARSONS
20 Vice Pres for Learning .... Dr. Teddy PHILLIPS
26 VP Public Relations & Development .... Mr. Wyley ELLIOTT
32 Vice Pres Learner Services .... Dr. Todd KITCHEN
21 VP Finance & Treasury Services .... Mr. Chuck RAMSEYER
103 Assoc VP Corporate Learning .... Ms. Susan PIKE
91 Assoc VP Information Technology Svc .... Ms. Paige FRANCIS
46 Assoc VP of Research & Planning .... Dr. Ricky TOMPKINS
88 AVP Global Bus & External Program .... Mr. Tim CORNELIUS
88 AVP Retail & Supplier Education .... Ms. Renee CAMPBELL
88 Interim AVP for Operations .... Mr. Jack THOMPSON
51 Dean of Adult Education .... Mr. Ben ALDAMA
32 Int Dean Learner Administrative Svc .... Mr. Dale MONTGOMERY
88 Dean of Learner Success .... Ms. Brooke HOLT
102 Executive Director of Foundation .... Ms. Meredith BRUNEN
88 Exec Director of Public Relations .... Mr. Steven HINDS
86 Exec Dir Community/Government Rels .... Mr. Jim HALL
21 Director of Accounting .... Mr. John HIXSON
21 Dir of Budget/Analytical Services .... Ms. Gulizar BAGGSON
26 Director of Marketing .... Mr. Rob HANLON
15 Director of Human Resources .... Ms. Wendi CADLE
56 Director of Distance Learning .... Dr. Kate BURKES
50 Exec Dir of Business Development .... Ms. Teresa WHITMIRE
88 Director of Building Sciences .... Mr. Rick MAYES
88 Coordinator Culinary & Hospitality .... Mr. Michael KUEFNER
88 Exec Dir for High School Rels .... Dr. Diana JOHNSON
88 Director of Learning Resources .... Vacant
25 Exec Dir Grants and Effectiveness .... Dr. Shauna STERLING
06 Director Student Records .... Ms. Taysha CARTER
07 Director of Admissions .... Ms. Michelle WALLACE
37 Director Student Financial Aid .... Ms. Michelle CORDELL
35 Director of Learner Success .... Mr. Eric VEST
28 Director of Diversity & Inclusion .... Ms. Kathryn BIRKHEAD
29 Director Alumni Relations .... Ms. Jasmine POPE
51 Business Manager & Continuing Educ .... Vacant
88 Event Coordinator .... Ms. Diane BOSS

Ouachita Baptist University (I)

410 Ouachita Street, Arkadelphia AR 71998-0001
County: Clark FICE Identification: 001102
Unit ID: 107512
Telephone: (870) 245-5000 Carnegie Class: Bac/A&S
FAX Number: (870) 245-5500 Calendar System: Semester
URL: www.obu.edu
Established: 1886 Annual Undergrad Tuition & Fees: $21,440
Enrollment: 1,594 Coed
Affiliation or Control: Southern Baptist IRS Status: 501(c)3
Highest Offering: Baccalaureate
Program: Liberal Arts And General; Teacher Preparatory
Accreditation: NH, BUS, DIETD, MUS, TED

01 President .... Dr. Rex M. HORNE, JR.
44 Vice Pres Institutional Advancement .... Dr. Keldon HENLEY
05 Vice President Academic Affairs .... Dr. Stan POOLE
11 Vice President for Admin Services .... Dr. Brett POWELL
32 Vice President for Student Services .... Dr. Wesley KLUCK

30 Vice President for Development ... Mrs. Terry G. PEEPLES
27 Vice Pres for Communications ... Mr. Trennis HENDERSON
04 Asst to President/Administration ... Mr. Philip W. HARDIN
07 Director of Admissions Counseling ... Mrs. Lori MOTL
09 Director of Institutional Research ... Mr. Phil HARDIN
15 Director of Human Resources ... Mrs. Sherri PHELPS
18 Chief Facilities/Physical Plant ... Mr. John HARDMAN
29 Director of Alumni Relations ... Mr. Jon MERRYMAN
35 Dean of Students ... Dr. Scott HAYNES
20 Assoc Vice Pres Academic Affairs ... Dr. Doug REED
26 Vice Pres for Communications ... Mr. Trennis HENDERSON
36 Director of Career Services ... Mrs. Lauren LAND
38 University Counselor ... Mr. Dan JARBOE
08 Librarian ... Dr. Ray GRANADE
06 Registrar/Director of Admissions ... Mrs. Judy JONES
37 Director Student Financial Svcs ... Mrs. Susan HURST
96 Director of Purchasing ... Ms. Kim HUNTER
92 Director Honors Program ... Dr. Barbara PEMBERTON
13 Dir Information Technology Services ... Mr. Bill PHELPS
39 Director of Housing ... Ms. Margaret FRAZIER
41 Athletic Director ... Mr. David SHARP
43 General Counsel ... Mr. Bryan MCKINNEY
21 Director of Financial Services ... Mrs. Kim HUNTER
40 Bookstore Manager ... Mrs. Yvonne CLOUD
57 Dean of School of Fine Arts ... Dr. Scott HOLSCLAW
50 Dean of the School of Business ... Mr. Bryan MCKINNEY
53 Dean Sch of Interdisciplinary Stds ... Dr. Stan POOLE
73 Dean School of Christian Studies ... Dr. Danny HAYS
53 Dean School of Education ... Dr. Merribeth BRUNING
79 Dean School of Humanities ... Dr. Jeff ROOT
81 Dean School of Natural Sciences ... Dr. Tim KNIGHT
83 Dean School of Social Sciences ... Dr. Randall WIGHT

Ozarka College (A)

PO Box 10, Melbourne AR 72556-0010

County: Izard FICE Identification: 020870
Unit ID: 107549
Telephone: (870) 368-7371 Carnegie Class: Assoc/Pub-R-S
FAX Number: (870) 368-2091 Calendar System: Semester
URL: www.ozarka.edu
Established: 1991 Annual Undergrad Tuition & Fees (In-State): $2,720
Enrollment: 1,621 Coed
Affiliation or Control: State IRS Status: 501(c)3
Highest Offering: Associate Degree
Program: Occupational; 2-Year Principally Bachelor's Creditable
Accreditation: NH

01 President ... Dr. Richard L. DAWE
05 Vice President Academic Affairs ... Dr. Dennis RITTLE
10 Vice President Finance ... Ms. Tina WHEELIS
32 Vice President of Student Services ... Mr. Ron C. HELM
45 Director Planning/IR ... Mrs. Joan R. STIRLING
13 Chief Information Officer ... Mr. Scott PINKSTON
04 Assistant to the President ... Mrs. Nancy DUST
30 Director of College Advancement ... Ms. Suellen DAVIDSON
29 Development Officer/Dir Alumni Rels . Ms. Hannah MCWILLIAMS
37 Director of Financial Aid ... Ms. Laura LAWRENCE
07 Director of Admissions ... Mrs. Amanda DOBBS
18 Chief Facilities/Physical Plant ... Mr. Ronny RUSH
06 Registrar ... Mrs. Zeda WILKERSON

Philander Smith College (B)

900 W. Daisy L. Gatson Bates Drive,
Little Rock AR 72202-3799

County: Pulaski FICE Identification: 001103
Unit ID: 107600
Telephone: (501) 375-9845 Carnegie Class: Bac/Diverse
FAX Number: (501) 370-5277 Calendar System: Semester
URL: www.philander.edu
Established: 1877 Annual Undergrad Tuition & Fees: $11,804
Enrollment: 732 Coed
Affiliation or Control: United Methodist IRS Status: 501(c)3
Highest Offering: Baccalaureate
Program: Liberal Arts And General; Teacher Preparatory; Business Emphasis
Accreditation: NH, ACBSP, SW, TED

01 President ... Dr. Johnny M. MOORE
04 Assistant to the President ... Mr. Michael HUTCHINSON
05 Vice President of Academic Affairs ... Dr. Frank R. JAMES
10 Vice President for Fiscal Affairs ... Mr. Terry WALLACE
32 Vice President of Student Affairs ... Dr. Stacey DOWNING
30 Vice Pres Inst Advancement ... Dr. Shannon FLEMING
43 General Counsel ... Mr. Eric WALKER
06 Registrar ... Ms. Bertha OWENS
42 Chaplain/Dir Ofc Religious Life ... Rev. Ronnie MILLER-YOW
20 Associate Dean of Instruction ... Dr. Jesse HARGROVE
35 Dean of Students/Residential Life ... Mr. Kevin HAMILTON
15 Director of Human Resources ... Mr. Christopher NEWTON
37 Director of Financial Aid ... Mr. David PAGE
18 Director of Physical Plant ... Mr. Henry JEMISON
26 Director Marketing/Public Relations ... Ms. Shareese KONDO
08 Director of the Library ... Ms. Theresa OJEZUA
07 Dir of Admissions/Recruitment ... Mr. Al DORSEY
29 Director of Alumni Relations ... Ms. Yvonne ALEXANDER
41 Athletic Director ... Mr. Sam WEAVER
13 Director Computer Information Sys ... Mr. Cedric KONYAOLE
09 Director of Institutional Research ... Ms. Beverly RICHARDSON
19 Chief of Security ... Mr. Jack MATLOCK
51 Director of Continuing Education ... Mr. Bruce JAMES
88 Mission Center Director ... Dr. Cynthia BURROUGHS
38 Director Student Counseling ... Vacant
40 Bookstore Manager ... Ms. Veda MAXWELL
17 Nurse ... Ms. Christal WALLER
88 Director Integrated Campus Center ... Ms. Rhonda LOVELACE
49 Division Chair Natural Sciences ... Dr. Samar SWAID
50 Division Chair of Business ... Dr. Adrian PRICE
53 Division Chair of Education ... Dr. Jesse HARGROVE
70 Director of Social Work ... Ms. Angela SANDERS
79 Int Chair Division of Humanities ... Dr. Jesse HARGROVE
83 Chair Division of Social Sciences ... Ms. Angela SANDERS

Pulaski Technical College (C)

3000 W Scenic Drive, North Little Rock AR 72118-3399

County: Pulaski FICE Identification: 020753
Unit ID: 107664
Telephone: (501) 812-2200 Carnegie Class: Assoc/Pub-U-SC
FAX Number: (501) 771-2844 Calendar System: Semester
URL: www.pulaskitech.edu
Established: 1991 Annual Undergrad Tuition & Fees (In-State): $3,000
Enrollment: 11,946 Coed
Affiliation or Control: State IRS Status: 501(c)3
Highest Offering: Associate Degree
Program: Occupational; 2-Year Principally Bachelor's Creditable; Technical Emphasis
Accreditation: NH, ACFEI, DA, OTA

01 President ... Dr. Margaret ELLIBEE
05 Executive Vice President/Provost ... Mr. Michael DELONG
20 Interim Vice President for Learning ... Ms. Mary Ann SHOPE
32 Vice President for Student Services ... Ms. Cindy HARKEY
10 Vice President for Finance ... Ms. Patricia PALMER
30 Vice President College Advancement ... Ms. Carol LANGSTON
88 Interim VP for Economic Development ... Mr. Jimmie JONES
44 Chief Development Officer ... Ms. Joyce TAYLOR
84 Dean Enrollment Svcs ... Ms. Beth TRAFFORD
07 Director of Admissions ... Mr. Clark ATKINS
38 Director of Counseling/Advising ... Ms. Lisa FISHER
08 Library Director ... Ms. Wendy DAVIS
18 Director of Physical Plant ... Mr. Stuart SMITH
09 Director of Institutional Research ... Vacant
96 Director of Purchasing ... Mr. Tim WALBERT
13 Chief Information Officer ... Mr. David HARRIS
15 Director of Human Resources ... Vacant
04 Assistant to the President ... Ms. Tena CARRIGAN
37 Director of Financial Aid ... Ms. Lavonne JUHL
26 Dir of Public Relations/Marketing ... Mr. Tim JONES
72 Dean Technical Education Division ... Mr. Mike SNEED
81 Dean Mathematics/Nat Social Scis ... Mr. Ben RAINS
50 Dean Business Division ... Ms. Christy SHERRILL
88 Dean Information Technology Div ... Mr. David DURR
57 Dean Fine Arts & Humanities ... Mr. Joey COLE
06 Registrar ... Ms. Virginia PEYTON
76 Dean Allied Health/Human Services ... Ms. Pam CICIRELLO

Remington College-Little Rock (D)

19 Remington Drive, Little Rock AR 72204-8202

County: Pulaski Identification: 666286
Unit ID: 438869
Telephone: (501) 312-0007 Carnegie Class: Assoc/PrivFP
FAX Number: (501) 225-3819 Calendar System: Quarter
URL: www.remingtoncollege.edu
Established: 1998 Annual Undergrad Tuition & Fees: $15,495
Enrollment: 362 Coed
Affiliation or Control: Proprietary IRS Status: Proprietary
Highest Offering: Associate Degree
Program: Occupational
Accreditation: ACCSC

01 President ... Dr. Rosalie LAMPONE
05 Director of Education ... Ms. Jennifer OWENS

† Branch campus of Remington College, Mobile, AL.

Rich Mountain Community College (E)

1100 College Drive, Mena AR 71953-2500

County: Polk FICE Identification: 021111
Unit ID: 107743
Telephone: (479) 394-7622 Carnegie Class: Assoc/Pub-R-S
FAX Number: (479) 394-7295 Calendar System: Semester
URL: www.rmcc.edu
Established: 1983 Annual Undergrad Tuition & Fees (In-District): $2,500
Enrollment: 1,108 Coed
Affiliation or Control: State/Local IRS Status: 501(c)3
Highest Offering: Associate Degree
Program: Occupational; 2-Year Principally Bachelor's Creditable; Liberal Arts And General
Accreditation: NH

01 President ... Mr. Phillip WILSON
05 Vice Pres Academic Affairs ... Dr. Steve ROOK
32 Vice Pres Student Affairs/Registrar ... Dr. Steve ROOK
10 VP Administration/CFO ... Mr. Morris BOYDSTUN
13 Dir of Information Technology ... Mr. J. Mark BARTON
08 Director Library Services ... Ms. Mary SHEAHAN
37 Financial Aid Director ... Ms. Mary STANDERFER
30 Director of Development ... Ms. Tammy YOUNG
18 Director of Physical Plant ... Mr. Dennis HILL
53 Director of Adult Basic Education ... Ms. Shannon ROGERS
09 Director of Institutional Research ... Ms. Tammy ODOM
15 Director of Human Resources ... Ms. Amy LUDWIG
07 Director of Admissions ... Mr. Brandon BURK
21 Controller ... Ms. Patricia HALL
26 Chief Public Relations Officer ... Ms. Tammy YOUNG
40 Bookstore Manager ... Mr. Andrew MATTHEWS
21 Fiscal Project Coordinator ... Ms. Amy LUDWIG

Shorter College (F)

604 Locus Street, North Little Rock AR 72114

County: Pulaski Identification: 667054
Telephone: (501) 374-6305 Carnegie Class: Not Classified
FAX Number: (501) 374-9333 Calendar System: Semester
URL: www.shorterjrcollege.com
Established: 1886 Annual Undergrad Tuition & Fees: N/A
Enrollment: N/A Coed
Affiliation or Control: African Methodist Episcopal IRS Status: 501(c)3
Highest Offering: Associate Degree
Program: Occupational; 2-Year Principally Bachelor's Creditable
Accreditation: @TRACS

01 President ... Dr. O. Jerome GREEN

South Arkansas Community College (G)

300 S West Avenue, PO Box 7010,
El Dorado AR 71731-7010

County: Union FICE Identification: 020746
Unit ID: 107974
Telephone: (870) 862-8131 Carnegie Class: Assoc/Pub-R-S
FAX Number: (870) 864-7190 Calendar System: Semester
URL: www.southark.edu
Established: 1992 Annual Undergrad Tuition & Fees (In-State): $3,590
Enrollment: 1,773 Coed
Affiliation or Control: State IRS Status: 501(c)3
Highest Offering: Associate Degree
Program: Occupational; 2-Year Principally Bachelor's Creditable
Accreditation: NH, EMT, OTA, PTAA, RAD, SURGT

01 President ... Dr. Barbara JONES
05 VP of Academic Learning ... Dr. Valeriano CANTU
10 Vice President for Fiscal Affairs ... Mr. Lathan HAIRSTON
32 Vice Pres of Student Services ... Dr. Curtis HILL
84 Dean of Enrollment Services ... Mr. Dean INMAN
08 Director Library Media Center ... Mrs. Francis KUYKENDALL
31 Dean of Community Education ... Ms. Jamie MCCONATHY
37 Director of Financial Aid ... Ms. Veronda TATUM
04 Admin Assistant to the President ... Ms. Susan JORDAN
26 Chief Information Officer ... Dr. Tim KIRK
27 Public Information Officer ... Mr. Heath WALDROP
15 Director Personnel Services ... Ms. Becky RIGGS
18 Director of Physical Plant ... Mr. Graham PETERSON
30 Institutional Advance/Foundation ... Ms. Cynthia REYNA
09 Director of Institutional Research ... Dr. Stephanie TULLY-DARTEZ
96 Director of Purchasing ... Ms. Ann SOUTHALL
07 Student Recruitment & Activities ... Ms. Brittany VICK
49 Dean of Liberal Arts ... Mr. Phillip BALLARD
76 Dean Health/Nursing Sciences ... Vacant
50 Dean Business/Technical Education ... Mr. Jim ROOMSBURG

Southeast Arkansas College (H)

1900 Hazel Street, Pine Bluff AR 71603-3900

County: Jefferson FICE Identification: 005707
Unit ID: 107637
Telephone: (870) 543-5900 Carnegie Class: Assoc/Pub-R-M
FAX Number: (870) 850-8636 Calendar System: Semester
URL: www.seark.edu
Established: 1991 Annual Undergrad Tuition & Fees (In-State): $2,892
Enrollment: 3,675 Coed
Affiliation or Control: State IRS Status: 501(c)3
Highest Offering: Associate Degree
Program: Occupational; 2-Year Principally Bachelor's Creditable; Technical Emphasis
Accreditation: NH, ADNUR, EMT, RAD, SURGT

01 President ... Dr. Stephen HILTERBRAN
05 Vice President Academic Affairs ... Ms. Linda E. LEWIS
32 Vice President Student Affairs ... Dr. Michael GUNTER
10 Vice President Financial Affairs ... Ms. Debbie WALLACE
76 VP Assessment/Nursing/Allied Health ... Ms. Diann W. WILLIAMS
30 VP College Affairs/Advancement ... Dr. Kaleybra M. MOREHEAD
21 Controller ... Mr. Steve BALLARD
13 Director of Technology Services ... Ms. JoAnn DUPRA
06 Assistant Registrar ... Ms. Laqueta HILL
07 Director of Admissions ... Ms. Barbara DUNN
15 Director of Personnel Services ... Ms. Dena CHILDS
18 Chief Facilities/Physical Plant ... Mr. Joel BARBAREE
28 Director of Diversity ... Dr. Kaleybra MOREHEAD
29 Dir Alumni Relations/Development ... Dr. Kaleybra MOREHEAD
37 Director Student Financial Aid ... Ms. Donna COX

Southern Arkansas University (I)

100 E University Street, Magnolia AR 71753-5000

County: Columbia FICE Identification: 001107
Unit ID: 107983
Telephone: (870) 235-4000 Carnegie Class: Master's M
FAX Number: (870) 235-5005 Calendar System: Semester
URL: www.saumag.edu

Established: 1909 Annual Undergrad Tuition & Fees (In-State): $6,018
Enrollment: 3,382 Coed
Affiliation or Control: State IRS Status: 501(c)3
Highest Offering: Master's
Program: Liberal Arts And General; Teacher Preparatory; Professional
Accreditation: NH, ADNUR, BUS, MUS, NUR, SW, TED

01 President ... Dr. David F. RANKIN
05 Vice President Academic Affairs ... Dr. Trey BERRY
11 VP Administration/General Counsel ... Mr. Roger W. GILES
32 Vice President Student Affairs ... Dr. Donna Y. ALLEN
18 Vice President of Facilities ... Mr. C. Jasper LEWIS
10 Vice President for Finance ... Mr. Paul MCLENDON
49 Dean Col Liberal/Perform Arts ... Dr. David CROUSE
50 Dean College of Business ... Dr. Lisa C. TOMS
53 Dean College of Education ... Dr. Zaidy MOHDZAIN
72 Dean College of Sci & Technology ... Dr. Scott MCKAY
58 Dean School of Graduate Studies ... Dr. Kim K. BLOSS
06 Registrar ... Dr. G. Edward NIPPER
84 Dean Enrollment Services ... Ms. Sarah E. JENNINGS
08 Director of Library ... Mr. Daniel R. PAGE
14 Director Info Technology Services ... Mr. Mike A. ARGO
38 Director Counsel/Testing Center ... Ms. Paula WASHINGTON-WOODS
35 Interim Dean of Students ... Ms. Sandra E. SMITH
29 Director of Alumni Affairs ... Ms. Ceil L. BRIDGES
30 Director of Development ... Ms. Jeanie BISMARK
37 Director of Financial Aid ... Ms. Bronwyn C. SNEED
51 Director of Continuing Education ... Ms. Sandra L. WALKER
41 Director of Athletics ... Mr. Steve BROWNING
88 Director Student Support Services ... Ms. Eunice E. WALKER
36 Director of Placement Services ... Ms. Wilma L. WILLIAMS
27 Director of Communications Center ... Mr. Aaron J. STREET
28 Director of Diversity ... Mr. Cledis D. STUART
21 Coordinator of Fringe Benefits ... Mr. D. Alan DAVIS

Southern Arkansas University Tech (A)

Post Office Box 3349, Camden AR 71711
County: Calhoun FICE Identification: 007738
Unit ID: 107992
Telephone: (870) 574-4500 Carnegie Class: Assoc/Pub2in4
FAX Number: (870) 574-4520 Calendar System: Semester
URL: www.sautech.edu
Established: 1967 Annual Undergrad Tuition & Fees (In-State): $3,630
Enrollment: 2,142 Coed
Affiliation or Control: State IRS Status: 501(c)3
Highest Offering: Associate Degree
Program: Occupational; 2-Year Principally Bachelor's Creditable
Accreditation: NH

01 Chancellor ... Dr. Corbet J. LAMKIN
10 VC for Finance & Administration ... Mrs. Gaye MANNING
05 VC for Academics ... Mr. Robert GUNNELS
32 VC for Student Services ... Dr. Reginald COOPER
13 VC for Information Technology ... Mrs. Valerie WILSON
26 Director of Communications ... Mrs. Kim COKER
09 Director of Research ... Mr. Lee SANDERS
84 Director of Enrollment Services ... Mrs. Patricia SINDLE
103 Director of Career Pathways ... Ms. LaTonya REED
31 Director of Special Programs ... Mr. Robert WHITE
75 Director of B & I Training ... Mr. Mike BASHFORD
88 Director of Career Academy ... Mr. Terry STARKEY
88 Director of AETA ... Mr. Randy HARPER
88 Director of AFTA ... Mrs. Rachel NIX
14 Director of ITS ... Mrs. Laura JOHNSON
37 Director of Financial Aid ... Mr. Jeff JEFFERSON
18 Director of Physical Plant ... Mr. Gerald MANNING
32 Director of Student Life ... Mr. David MCLEANE
06 Registrar ... Mr. Wayne BANKS
08 Director of LRC ... Ms. Allison MALONE
04 Assistant to the Chancellor ... Mrs. Paula BERGSTROM
15 Human Resources Director ... Mrs. Olivia CLACK
21 Controller ... Mr. Dale TOMMEY
45 Vice Chancellor for PAD ... Dr. Diane BETTS
39 Residential Advisor ... Mrs. LaDonna FUSILIER
96 Buyer/Bookstore Manager ... Mrs. Angela FRY
43 Legal Counsel ... Ms. Mary THOMASON
51 Director of Adult Education ... Mrs. Barbara HAMILTON

*University of Arkansas System Office (B)

2404 N University Avenue, Little Rock AR 72207-3608
County: Pulaski FICE Identification: 008008
Unit ID: 108056
Telephone: (501) 686-2500 Carnegie Class: N/A
FAX Number: (501) 686-2507
URL: www.uasys.edu

01 President ... Dr. Donald R. BOBBITT
04 Assistant to the President ... Ms. Angela HUDSON
05 Vice President Academic Affairs ... Dr. Daniel E. FERRITOR
10 Vice President for Finance ... Ms. Barbara GOSWICK
11 Vice President for Administration ... Ms. Ann KEMP
26 Vice President University Relations ... Ms. Melissa RUST
47 Vice President Agriculture ... Dr. Mark J. COCHRAN
43 General Counsel ... Mr. Fred H. HARRISON
88 Director Internal Audit ... Mr. Jacob W. FLOURNOY
21 Assoc Vice President for Finance ... Ms. Rita FLEMING

*University of Arkansas Main Campus (C)

Fayetteville AR 72701-1201
County: Washington FICE Identification: 001108
Unit ID: 106397
Telephone: (479) 575-2000 Carnegie Class: RU/VH
FAX Number: (479) 575-2361 Calendar System: Semester
URL: www.uark.edu
Established: 1871 Annual Undergrad Tuition & Fees (In-State): $7,554
Enrollment: 23,199 Coed
Affiliation or Control: State IRS Status: 501(c)3
Highest Offering: Doctorate
Program: Liberal Arts And General; Teacher Preparatory; Professional
Accreditation: NH, AAFCS, BUS, BUSA, CACREP, CEA, CIDA, CLPSY, CORE, CS, DIETD, ENG, JOUR, LAW, LSAR, MUS, NURSE, SP, SW, TED

02 Chancellor ... Dr. G. David GEARHART
04 Executive Asst to the Chancellor ... Ms. Gloria SUTHERLAND
05 Provost & Vice Chanc Academic Affs ... Dr. Sharon GABER
10 Vice Chanc Finance & Administration ... Dr. Donald O. PEDERSON
30 Vice Chanc University Advancement ... Mr. Brad E. CHOATE
86 Vice Chanc Govt & Cmty Relations ... Mr. Richard B. HUDSON
09 Vice Provost Planning/Dir Inst Res ... Dr. Kathy M. VAN LANINGHAM
46 Vice Provost Research/Econ Dev ... Dr. James M. RANKIN
35 Vice Prov Stdnt Affs/Dean Students ... Dr. Daniel PUGH
28 Vice Provost for Diversity ... Mr. Charles ROBINSON
84 Vice Prov Enrol Mgt/Dean Admissions ... Dr. Suzanne MCCRAY
26 Assoc Vice Chanc Univ Relations ... Mr. John N. DIAMOND
15 Assoc Vice Chanc Human Resources ... Ms. Debbie MCLOUD
18 Assoc Vice Chanc Facilities Mgmt ... Mr. Mike JOHNSON
21 Assoc Vice Chanc Business Affairs ... Mr. David O. MARTINSON
08 Dean of Libraries ... Ms. Carolyn H. ALLEN
49 Dean of Arts & Sciences ... Dr. Robin ROBERTS
50 Dean Sam Walton College of Business ... Dr. Dan L. WORRELL
47 Dean of Agriculture ... Dr. Michael E. VAYDA
53 Dean Education/Health Professions ... Dr. Tom SMITH
48 Dean of Architecture ... Mr. Jeff SHANNON
51 Interim Dean of Graduate School ... Dr. Todd SHIELDS
54 Dean of Engineering ... Dr. Ashok SAXENA
92 Dean Honors College ... Dr. Robert MCMATH
61 Dean of the Law School ... Ms. Stacy LEEDS
29 Assoc Vice Chanc for Alumni ... Mr. Graham G. STEWART
22 Director of Affirmative Action ... Mr. Willyerd R. COLLIER
37 Director of Financial Aid ... Ms. Kattie WING
38 Dir of Counseling/Psych Services ... Dr. Jonathan C. PERRY
25 Director Research & Sponsored Pgms ... Ms. Rosemary H. RUFF
19 Director University Police ... Mr. Steve GAHAGANS
36 Dir of Career Development Center ... Ms. Barbara BATSON
14 Director of Computing Services ... Mr. Robert E. ZIMMERMAN
06 Registrar ... Mr. Dave DAWSON
96 Director of Purchasing ... Ms. Linda FAST
58 Director Graduate & Intl Admissions ... Ms. Lynn MOSESSO

*University of Arkansas at Fort Smith (D)

PO Box 3649, Fort Smith AR 72913-3649
County: Sebastian FICE Identification: 001110
Unit ID: 108092
Telephone: (479) 788-7000 Carnegie Class: Bac/Assoc
FAX Number: (479) 788-7003 Calendar System: Semester
URL: www.uafs.edu
Established: 1928 Annual Undergrad Tuition & Fees (In-District): $5,436
Enrollment: 7,587 Coed
Affiliation or Control: State/Local IRS Status: 501(c)3
Highest Offering: Baccalaureate
Program: Occupational; Liberal Arts And General; Teacher Preparatory
Accreditation: NH, ADNUR, DH, DMS, MUS, NAIT, NUR, RAD, SURGT, TED

02 Chancellor ... Dr. Paul B. BERAN
05 Provost and Sr Vice Chancellor ... Dr. Ray WALLACE
04 Vice Chancellor Univ Relations ... Mr. Mark HORN
30 Vice Chancellor Univ Advancement ... Dr. Marta LOYD
10 Vice Chanc Finance ... Mr. Darrell MORRISON
32 Vice Chancellor Student Affairs ... Dr. Lee KREHBIEL
11 Vice Chanc for Operations ... Vacant
20 Assoc Provost Academic Affairs ... Dr. Brenda MITCHELL
31 Assoc Vice Chanc Campus/Cmty Events ... Mr. Stacey JONES
79 Dean Col Humanities/Social Sci ... Dr. Henry RINNE
76 Dean College of Health Sciences ... Dr. Carolyn MOSLEY
53 Dean College of Education ... Dr. John R. JONES
50 Dean College of Business ... Dr. Steve WILLIAMS
72 Dean Col Applied Science/Technology ... Dr. Georgia HALE
72 Dean Col Sci/Tech/Engineering/Math ... Dr. Mark ARANT
60 Dean Col of Languages/Communication ... Dr. Joe HARDIN
88 Dean Student Success ... Ms. Diana ROWDEN
84 Dean of Enrollment Management ... Ms. Penny PENDLETON
16 Dir Human Resources/EEO Officer ... Ms. Bev MCCLENDON
51 Director of Lifelong Learning ... Mr. Jeff ADAMS
12 Dir Western Arkansas Tech Ctr ... Dr. Darrel C. RINK
45 Ex Dir Institutional Effectiveness ... Mr. Darin DOUBRAVA
36 Exec Director Career Services ... Mr. Pat WIDDERS
88 Exec Dir of International Relations ... Mr. Takeo SUZUKI
88 Director of Instructional Support ... Dr. Tara MISHRA
06 Registrar ... Mr. Wayne WOMACK
08 Director of Library Services ... Mr. Robert FRIZZELL
39 Director of Student Housing ... Ms. Beth EPPINGER
37 Director Student Financial Aid ... Mr. Alan PIXLEY
38 Director of Advisement ... Ms. Julie MOSLEY
36 Director of Career Services ... Mr. Ron ORICK
29 Exec Director of Alumni Affairs ... Ms. Elizabeth UNDERWOOD
07 Director of Admissions ... Mr. Mark LLOYD
26 Director Marketing & Communications ... Mr. Jeff HARMON
41 Director of Athletics ... Mr. Dustin SMITH
27 Director of Public Information ... Ms. Sondra LAMAR
18 Director of Plant Operations ... Mr. Bill PIERCE
21 Controller ... Mr. John BOGNER
96 Associate Controller ... Ms. Debbie BREEDLOVE

*University of Arkansas at Little Rock (E)

2801 S University Avenue, Little Rock AR 72204-1099
County: Pulaski FICE Identification: 001101
Unit ID: 106245
Telephone: (501) 569-3000 Carnegie Class: DRU
FAX Number: (501) 569-8915 Calendar System: Semester
URL: www.ualr.edu
Established: 1927 Annual Undergrad Tuition & Fees (In-State): $7,041
Enrollment: 13,068 Coed
Affiliation or Control: State IRS Status: 501(c)3
Highest Offering: Doctorate
Program: Occupational; Liberal Arts And General; Teacher Preparatory; Professional
Accreditation: NH, ADNUR, ART, AUD, BUS, CONST, CORE, CS, ENG, ENGT, LAW, MUS, NUR, NURSE, RADDOS, SP, SPAA, SW, TED, THEA

02 Chancellor ... Dr. Joel E. ANDERSON
05 Provost & VC Academic Affairs ... Dr. Sandra L. ROBERSTSON
32 Vice Chanc Education/Student Svcs ... Dr. Charles W. DONALDSON
10 Vice Chanc Finance & Administration ... Dr. Robert H. ADAMS
30 Vice Chanc University Advancement ... Mr. Bill M. WALKER
58 Vice Prov Rsrch/Dn Grad School ... Dr. Patrick J. PELLICANE
13 Vice Chanc Information Services ... Ms. Jeannie WINSTON
100 Chief of Staff/Director of Budget ... Dr. Sandra L. ROBERTSON
11 Assoc Vice Chanc Facilities Mgt ... Mr. David MILLAY
21 Associate Vice Chancellor Finance ... Mr. Steven J. MCCLELLAN
44 Executive Director Development ... Mr. Bob G. DENMAN
88 Assoc Vice Chanc for Advancement ... Ms. Joni C. LEE
35 Div Chief Student Dev/Dean Students ... Vacant
84 Div Chief Enrollment Plng/Registrar ... Dr. Charles DONALDSON
06 Registrar Records & Registration ... Ms. Joyce HAIL
15 Director of Human Resource Devel ... Ms. Annette MURDOCK-TANGYE
21 Director of Financial Services ... Ms. Stacey L. HOGUE
18 Director of Physical Plant ... Mr. David L. MILLAY
80 Director Arkansas Institute of Govt ... Dr. Roby D. ROBERTSON
88 Director Ark Institute Econ Advance ... Mr. Jim L. YOUNGQUIST
27 Director of Communications ... Ms. Judy G. WILLIAMS
09 Director Institutional Research ... Ms. Rita M. STERLING
08 Director of the Library ... Ms. Wanda DOLE
19 Director of Public Safety ... Mr. Brad KING
40 Director of Bookstore ... Ms. Brenda R. THOMAS
46 Director of Research/Sponsored Pgms ... Mr. Allen D. STANLEY
37 Director Financial Aid ... Ms. Tammy HARRISON
41 Director of Athletics ... Mr. Chris PETERSON
29 Director of Alumni Relations ... Mr. Christian O'NEAL
36 Director of Student Placement ... Vacant
07 Director of Admissions ... Ms. Tammy HARRISON
38 Director Student Counseling ... Vacant
96 Director of Purchasing ... Mr. J. D. LOCHALA
20 Associate Academic Officer ... Dr. Christina S. DRALE
20 Associate Academic Officer ... Dr. Karen J. WHEELER
50 Dean of Business Administration ... Dr. Jane P. WAYLAND
53 Dean of Education ... Dr. Angela M. SEWALL
79 Dean Arts/Human/Social Science ... Dr. Deborah J. BALDWIN
54 Dean of Eng & Information Technolog ... Dr. Eric SANDGREN
81 Dean of Science & Mathematics ... Dr. Michael GEALT
61 Dean of Bowen School of Law ... Mr. John M. DIPIPPA
107 Dean of Professional Studies ... Vacant

*University of Arkansas for Medical Sciences (F)

4301 W Markham, Little Rock AR 72205-7199
County: Pulaski FICE Identification: 001109
Unit ID: 106263
Telephone: (501) 686-5000 Carnegie Class: Spec/Med
FAX Number: (501) 686-5905 Calendar System: Semester
URL: www.uams.edu
Established: 1879 Annual Undergrad Tuition & Fees (In-State): $7,446
Enrollment: 2,918 Coed
Affiliation or Control: State IRS Status: 501(c)3
Highest Offering: Doctorate
Program: Occupational; 2-Year Principally Bachelor's Creditable; Liberal Arts And General; Professional
Accreditation: NH, CYTO, DH, DIETI, DMS, EMT, HSA, IPSY, MED, MT, NMT, NURSE, PH, PHAR, RAD, SURGT

02 Chancellor ... Dr. Daniel RAHN
05 Vice Chancellor Academic Affairs ... Dr. Jeanne K. HEARD
10 Vice Chancellor Finance & CEO ... Mrs. Melony GOODHAND
26 Vice Chancellor Communications ... Ms. Pat TORVESTAD
30 Vice Chancellor Development ... Mr. Lance BURCHETT
11 Vice Chancellor Campus Operations ... Mr. Mark KENNEDAY
08 Director of Library ... Ms. Mary RYAN
27 Chief Information Officer ... Mr. David MILLER
15 Director Human Resources ... Mr. Hosea LONG
37 Director Financial Services ... Ms. Gloria KEMP

63 Dean College of Medicine ... Dr. Debra H. FISER
76 Dean Col Health Related Professions ... Dr. Douglas MURPHY
66 Dean College of Nursing ... Dr. Lorraine FRAZIER
67 Dean College of Pharmacy ... Dr. Stephanie F. GARDNER
58 Dean of the Graduate School ... Dr. Robert E. MCGEHEE, JR.

*University of Arkansas at Monticello (A)

346 University Drive, Monticello AR 71656-3596

County: Drew FICE Identification: 001085
Unit ID: 106485
Telephone: (870) 367-1020 Carnegie Class: Master's S
FAX Number: (870) 460-1321 Calendar System: Semester
URL: www.uamont.edu
Established: 1909 Annual Undergrad Tuition & Fees (In-State): $5,560
Enrollment: 3,920 Coed
Affiliation or Control: State IRS Status: 501(c)3
Highest Offering: Master's
Program: Occupational; 2-Year Principally Bachelor's Creditable; Liberal Arts And General; Teacher Preparatory
Accreditation: NH, COE, EMT, FOR, MUS, NUR, SW, TED

02 Chancellor ... Dr. Jack LASSITER
05 Interim Provost/VC for Acad Affairs ... Dr. Ranelle EUBANKS
10 Vice Chanc Finance & Administration ... Mr. Jay JONES
30 Vice Chanc Advancement/Univ Rels ... Dr. Clay BROWN
32 Vice Chanc Student Affairs ... Mr. Jay HUGHES
12 Vice Chanc UAM Col of Tech Crossett ... Ms. Linda RUSHING
12 Vice Chanc UAM Col of Tech McGehee ... Mr. Bob WARE
21 Assoc VC for Finance ... Ms. Debbie GASAWAY
06 Assc Vice Chanc Acad Affs/Registrar ... Dr. Debbie BRYANT
21 Business Manager ... Ms. Melodie COLWELL
07 Director of Admissions ... Ms. Mary WHITING
84 Director of Enrollment Mgmt ... Ms. Mary WHITING
41 Director of Athletics ... Mr. Chris RATCLIFF
35 Dean of Students/Dir Govt Relations ... Mr. Scott KUTTENKULER
13 Director Information Technology ... Mr. Bobby HOYLE
08 Director of Library ... Ms. Sandra CAMPBELL
26 Director of Media Services ... Mr. Jim L. BREWER
37 Director of Financial Aid ... Ms. Susan BREWER
09 Director of Institutional Research ... Dr. Debbie BRYANT
18 Chief Facilities/Physical Plant ... Mr. Jim HUDGINS
38 Dir Counseling/Testing Services ... Ms. Laura HUGHES
96 Director of Purchasing ... Ms. Gay PACE
29 Director of Alumni Affairs ... Vacant

*University of Arkansas at Pine Bluff (B)

1200 N University Drive, Pine Bluff AR 71601-2799

County: Jefferson FICE Identification: 001086
Unit ID: 106412
Telephone: (870) 575-8000 Carnegie Class: Bac/Diverse
FAX Number: (870) 543-8009 Calendar System: Semester
URL: www.uapb.edu
Established: 1873 Annual Undergrad Tuition & Fees (In-State): $5,624
Enrollment: 3,188 Coed
Affiliation or Control: State IRS Status: 501(c)3
Highest Offering: Doctorate
Program: Liberal Arts And General; Teacher Preparatory; Professional
Accreditation: NH, AAFCS, ART, @DIETD, MUS, NAIT, NUR, SW, TED

02 Interim Chancellor ... Dr. Calvin JOHNSON
04 Assistant to the Chancellor ... Mrs. Liz F. STRICKLAND
05 Vice Chancellor Academic Affairs ... Dr. Mary E. BENJAMIN
10 Vice Chanc Finance & Admin ... Ms. Pauline THOMAS
30 Director of Development ... Mrs. Margaret MARTIN-HALL
20 Associate Academic Officer ... Dr. Verma JONES
08 Librarian ... Mr. Edward J. FONTENETTE
91 Director of Technical Services ... Mrs. Willette TOTTEN
37 Director of Financial Aid ... Mrs. Janice KEARNEY
09 Director of Institutional Research ... Mrs. Margaret TAYLOR
15 Director Human Resources ... Ms. Gladys BENFORD
36 Director Career Services/Admissions ... Mrs. Mary JONES
26 Director Public Relations/Info ... Mrs. Tisha ARNOLD
35 Dir Student Life/Enrollment Mgmt ... Mr. Leon CRUMBLIN
38 Director Student Counseling ... Ms. Joyce VAUGHN
06 Registrar ... Mrs. Erica FULTON
19 Chief of Police ... Mr. Maxcie THOMAS
18 Chief Facilities/Physical Plant ... Mr. Robert WALL
29 Director of Alumni Affairs ... Mr. John KUYKENDALL
96 Director of Purchasing ... Mrs. A. Kay TURNER
32 Admin Coordinator Student Affairs ... Mr. Elbert BENNETT
47 Dean Agricult/Fisheries/Hum Sci ... Dr. James GARNER
49 Dean Arts & Sciences ... Dr. Yolanda PAGE
53 Interim Dean School of Education ... Dr. Fredda CARROLL
51 Interim Dean Continuing Education ... Dr. George HERTS
50 Dean School of Business/Management ... Dr. Carla MARTIN
92 Dean Honors College ... Dr. Jewell WALKER
41 Director of Athletics ... Mr. Lonza HARDY, JR.

*Cossatot Community College of the University of Arkansas (C)

183 College Drive, PO Box 960,
De Queen AR 71832-0960

County: Sevier FICE Identification: 022209
Unit ID: 106795
Telephone: (870) 584-4471 Carnegie Class: Assoc/Pub2in4
FAX Number: (870) 642-3320 Calendar System: Semester
URL: cccua.edu
Established: 1991 Annual Undergrad Tuition & Fees (In-District): $2,042
Enrollment: 1,442 Coed
Affiliation or Control: State/Local IRS Status: 501(c)3
Highest Offering: Associate Degree
Program: Occupational; 2-Year Principally Bachelor's Creditable
Accreditation: NH, ACBSP

02 Chancellor ... Mr. Steve COLE
05 Vice Chancellor of Academics ... Mrs. Maria PARKER
45 VC of Planning and Facilities ... Mr. Mike KINKADE
10 Vice Chancellor Business/Finance ... Mrs. Charlotte JOHNSON
30 Exec Director Inst Advancement ... Vacant
32 Director of Student Services ... Mr. Shaun CLARK
37 Director Student Financial Aid ... Mrs. Denise HAMMOND
26 Director of Marketing ... Ms. Alisha LEWIS
09 Director of Inst Research/Registrar ... Mrs. Brenda MORRIS
103 Dir of Public Svc/Workforce Dev ... Mrs. Tammy COLEMAN
12 Dean of Ashdown Campus ... Mr. Barrett REED
15 Director of Human Resources ... Mrs. Lilly BELL-JOHNSON
13 Information Manager ... Mr. David BLACKWELL
102 Executive Director of Foundation ... Mrs. Melanie CARLTON

*Phillips Community College of the University of Arkansas (D)

PO Box 785, Helena AR 72342-0785

County: Phillips FICE Identification: 001104
Unit ID: 107619
Telephone: (870) 338-6474 Carnegie Class: Assoc/Pub2in4
FAX Number: (870) 338-7542 Calendar System: Semester
URL: www.pccua.edu
Established: 1965 Annual Undergrad Tuition & Fees (In-District): $2,360
Enrollment: 2,199 Coed
Affiliation or Control: State/Local IRS Status: 501(c)3
Highest Offering: Associate Degree
Program: Occupational; 2-Year Principally Bachelor's Creditable
Accreditation: NH, ACBSP, ADNUR, MLTAD

02 Chancellor ... Dr. Steven MURRAY
05 Vice Chancellor for Instruction ... Dr. Deborah KING
10 Vice Chanc Finance & Administration ... Vacant
32 Vice Chanc Student Svcs/Registrar ... Mr. Lynn BOONE
30 Vice Chanc Col Advancement/Bus Dev ... Mrs. Rhonda ST. COLUMBIA
12 Vice Chancellor Stuttgart Campus ... Dr. Susan LUEBKE
12 Vice Chancellor DeWitt Campus ... Mrs. Carolyn TURNER

*University of Arkansas Community College at Batesville (E)

2005 White Drive, PO Box 3350,
Batesville AR 72503-3350

County: Independence FICE Identification: 020735
Unit ID: 106999
Telephone: (870) 612-2000 Carnegie Class: Assoc/Pub2in4
FAX Number: (870) 793-4988 Calendar System: Semester
URL: www.uaccb.edu
Established: 1975 Annual Undergrad Tuition & Fees (In-District): $2,540
Enrollment: 1,573 Coed
Affiliation or Control: State/Local IRS Status: 501(c)3
Highest Offering: Associate Degree
Program: Occupational; 2-Year Principally Bachelor's Creditable
Accreditation: NH, ADNUR, EMT

02 Chancellor ... Ms. Deborah J. FRAZIER
04 Assistant to the Chancellor ... Ms. Kim WHITTEN
05 Vice Chancellor for Academics ... Vacant
32 VC Enrollment Mgmt/Student Services ... Mr. Brian BERRY
10 Vice Chancellor Finance and Admin ... Mr. Gayle COOPER
09 VC Research/Planning/Assessment ... Dr. Anne AUSTIN
09 Dir of Institutional Research ... Mr. Blake CANNON
84 Director of Enrollment Management ... Mr. Scott POST
106 Director of Distance Learning ... Ms. Tammy JOLLEY
49 Chair Div of Arts & Humanities ... Ms. Susan BESHEARS
50 Chair Div Business/Tech/Public Svc ... Ms. Tamara GRIFFIN
76 Chair Div Nursing/Allied Health ... Ms. Rebecca KING
81 Chair Div of Math and Science ... Mr. Douglas MUSE
51 Chair Div Community and Tech Educ ... Ms. Kathleen MCNAMEE
13 Director Information Services ... Mr. Steve COLLINS
06 Dir Student Information/Registrar ... Ms. Shelly MOSER
37 Director of Financial Aid ... Ms. Kristen CROSS
30 Director of Development ... Ms. Tina PAUL
18 Director of Maintenance ... Mr. Heath WOOLDRIDGE
36 Director Student Development ... Ms. Louise HUGHES
38 Career & Counseling Services Coord ... Mr. Christopher DICKIE
08 Director Library ... Ms. Linda BENNETT
21 Controller ... Ms. Waynna DOCKINS
15 Personnel Officer ... Ms. Alexa SMITH
96 Purchasing Agent ... Ms. Peggy JACKSON
40 Bookstore Manager ... Ms. Luanne BARBER

*University of Arkansas Community College at Hope (F)

PO Box 140, 2500 S Main Street, Hope AR 71802-0140

County: Hempstead FICE Identification: 005732
Unit ID: 107725
Telephone: (870) 777-5722 Carnegie Class: Assoc/Pub2in4
FAX Number: (870) 777-5957 Calendar System: Semester
URL: www.uacch.edu
Established: 1991 Annual Undergrad Tuition & Fees (In-State): $2,348
Enrollment: 1,383 Coed
Affiliation or Control: State IRS Status: 501(c)3
Highest Offering: Associate Degree
Program: Occupational; 2-Year Principally Bachelor's Creditable; Business Emphasis
Accreditation: NH, EMT, FUSER

02 Chancellor ... Mr. Chris THOMASON
05 Vice Chancellor for Academics ... Mrs. Jennifer METHVIN
32 Vice Chancellor Student Services ... Mr. Bobby JAMES
10 Vice Chancellor for Finance ... Mr. Jerald BARBER
08 Librarian ... Ms. Marielle MCFARLAND
51 Director of Cont Educ/Ind Relations ... Ms. Jolane COOK
26 Communications Coordinator ... Mr. Brent TALLEY
24 Director of Telecommunications ... Mr. Dave PHILLIPS
15 Human Resources Officer ... Ms. Kathryn HOPKINS

*University of Arkansas Community College at Morrilton (G)

1537 University Boulevard, Morrilton AR 72110-9601

County: Conway FICE Identification: 005245
Unit ID: 107585
Telephone: (501) 354-2465 Carnegie Class: Assoc/Pub2in4
FAX Number: (501) 977-2134 Calendar System: Semester
URL: www.uaccm.edu
Established: 1961 Annual Undergrad Tuition & Fees (In-State): $3,360
Enrollment: 2,296 Coed
Affiliation or Control: State IRS Status: 501(c)3
Highest Offering: Associate Degree
Program: Occupational; 2-Year Principally Bachelor's Creditable
Accreditation: NH

02 Chancellor ... Dr. Larry D. DAVIS
05 Vice Chancellor Academic Services ... Ms. Diana ARN
10 Vice Chancellor for Finance ... Ms. Lisa GUNDERMAN
11 Vice Chancellor for Administration ... Dr. Linda M. BIRKNER
32 Vice Chancellor Student Services ... Mr. Darren JONES
09 Director of Institutional Research ... Ms. Wanda F. HENSLEY
08 Librarian ... Mr. Vincent TINERELLA
06 Registrar ... Ms. Linda HOLLAND
37 Financial Aid Director ... Mrs. Teresa Y. CASH
13 Director of Computer Services ... Mr. Richard O. GROWNS
18 Director of the Physical Plant ... Mr. C. Allen HOLLOWAY
27 Chief Information Officer ... Ms. Mary CLARK
07 Director of Admissions ... Ms. Susan DEWEY
103 Coord Workforce Develop/Cmty Educ ... Ms. Stephanie ELLIS

University of Central Arkansas (H)

201 Donaghey Avenue, Conway AR 72035-0001

County: Faulkner FICE Identification: 001092
Unit ID: 106704
Telephone: (501) 450-5000 Carnegie Class: Master's L
FAX Number: (501) 450-5003 Calendar System: Semester
URL: www.uca.edu
Established: 1907 Annual Undergrad Tuition & Fees (In-State): $7,332
Enrollment: 11,163 Coed
Affiliation or Control: State IRS Status: 501(c)3
Highest Offering: Doctorate
Program: Occupational; Liberal Arts And General; Teacher Preparatory; Professional
Accreditation: NH, ART, BUS, CIDA, CS, DIETD, DIETI, MUS, NURSE, OT, PTA, SCPSY, SP, TED, THEA

01 President ... Mr. Tom COURTWAY
05 Interim Provost/VP Academic Affairs ... Dr. Steve RUNGE
10 VP Finance/Administration ... Ms. Diane D. NEWTON
32 Vice President Student Services ... Mr. Ronnie D. WILLIAMS
84 Vice President for Enrollment Mgmt ... Dr. Robert W. PARRENT
43 Interim General Counsel ... Ms. Katie HENRY
26 VP for University & Govt Relations ... Mr. Jeffery L. PITCHFORD
30 VP for UCA Advancement ... Ms. Shelley MEHL
41 Athletics Director ... Dr. Brad TEAGUE
15 Assoc Vice Pres for Human Resources ... Dr. Graham GILLIS
85 Asst Provost/Dir Intl Engagement ... Dr. Jane Ann WILLIAMS
20 Assoc VP Academic Dev/Dir Diversity ... Vacant
46 Asst Provost/Dir Sponsored Pgms ... Dr. Timothy N. ATKINSON
20 Associate Provost ... Ms. Laura YOUNG
21 Controller ... Ms. Mary Kay DUNAWAY
58 Assoc Provost/Dean of Graduate Sch ... Dr. Elaine M. MCNIECE
51 Dean Academic Outreach/Extended Pgm ... Vacant
50 Interim Dean of Col Business Admin ... Dr. Michael CASEY
53 Dean of College of Education ... Dr. Diana G. POUNDER
76 Dean of Col Health/Applied Science ... Dr. Neil W. HATTLESTAD
49 Dean of Liberal Arts ... Dr. Maurice A. LEE
81 Interim Dean Col Natural Sci/Math ... Dr. Steve ADDISON
57 Dean Fine Arts & Communication ... Dr. Rollin R. POTTER
35 Dean of Students ... Dr. Gary A. ROBERTS
92 Dean of Honors College ... Dr. Richard I. SCOTT
07 Director Admissions ... Dr. Ron PATTERSON
08 Library Director ... Mr. Art LICHTENSTEIN
06 Registrar ... Ms. Beth D. DURFF
09 Interim Dir Institutional Research ... Ms. Amber L. HALL
13 Chief Information Officer ... Dr. Jonathan A. GLENN
37 Director Student Financial Aid ... Ms. Cheryl C. LYONS
36 Dir Career Svcs/Cooperative Educ ... Dr. Kathy RICE-CLAYBORN
19 Director University Police ... Mr. Larry K. JAMES
38 Director Counseling Center ... Dr. Maurice E. NESS
39 Asst VP for Housing & Contract Svcs ... Mr. Rick L. MCCOLLUM
29 Director of Alumni Services ... Ms. Jan A. NEWCOMER
21 Director Internal Audits ... Ms. Pamela L. MASSEY
18 Director Physical Plant ... Mr. Larry D. LAWRENCE

27 Dir Publications/Creative Services ... Mr. Richard R. HANCOCK
96 Director of Purchasing ... Ms. Cassandra MCCUIEN-SMITH
21 Director Student Accounts ... Mr. Jason A. RANKIN

University of the Ozarks (A)

415 College Avenue, Clarksville AR 72830-2880
County: Johnson FICE Identification: 001094
Unit ID: 107558
Telephone: (479) 979-1000 Carnegie Class: Bac/Diverse
FAX Number: (479) 979-1355 Calendar System: Semester
URL: www.ozarks.edu
Established: 1834 Annual Undergrad Tuition & Fees: $30,040
Enrollment: 630 Coed
Affiliation or Control: Presbyterian Church (U.S.A.) IRS Status: 501(c)3
Highest Offering: Baccalaureate
Program: Liberal Arts And General; Teacher Preparatory; Professional
Accreditation: **NH**, IACBE, TED

01 President ... Dr. Rick D. NIECE
05 Provost ... Dr. Daniel L. TADDIE
10 Chief Financial Officer ... Mr. Jeff SCACCIA
84 Director of Admission ... Mr. Brian HULL
07 Dean of Admissions & Financial Aid ... Ms. Jana D. HART
42 Chaplain ... Rev. Nancy BENSON-NICOL
35 Dean of Students ... Mr. Joe W. HOING
39 Dean of Residential & Campus Life ... Ms. Sherrie AREY
06 Registrar ... Ms. Wilma K. HARRIS
08 Librarian ... Mr. Stuart P. STELZER
27 Director of Public Information ... Mr. Larry A. ISCH
36 Director Student Placement ... Ms. Kim A. SPICER
29 Director Alumni Affairs ... Ms. Lori A. MCBEE
41 Athletic Director ... Mr. Jimmy CLARK
31 Director Campus/Community Relations ... Ms. Sheree A. NIECE
26 Chief Public Relations Officer ... Mr. Larry A. ISCH
30 Director of Development ... Ms. Reba PRIDGIN
18 Chief Facilities/Physical Plant ... Mr. Mike QUALLS
88 Director Jones Learning Center ... Ms. Julia H. FROST
90 Director Academic Computing ... Mr. Nathan SAIN
09 Director of Institutional Research ... Mr. Randolph L. PETERSON
96 Director of Purchasing ... Mr. Darrell W. WILLIAMS
89 Director of Freshmen Studies ... Mr. Stacy KEY
14 Director Computer Services ... Mr. Rick OTTO
32 Chief Student Life Officer ... Ms. Sherrie AREY
20 Associate Academic Dean ... Dr. Elissa HEIL
21 Business Manager ... Mr. Darrell W. WILLIAMS
81 Chair Division Sciences/Mathematics ... Dr. Frank KNIGHT
50 Chair Division of Business ... Dr. Robert C. HILTON
53 Chair Division of Education ... Dr. Glenda EZELL
79 Chair Division Humanities/Fine Arts ... Dr. David M. STRAIN
37 Student Financial Aid Counselor ... Ms. Melody JOHNSON

Williams Baptist College (B)

60 W Fulbright Avenue, Walnut Ridge AR 72476
County: Lawrence FICE Identification: 001106
Unit ID: 107877
Telephone: (870) 886-6741 Carnegie Class: Bac/Diverse
FAX Number: (870) 886-3924 Calendar System: Semester
URL: www.wbcoll.edu
Established: 1941 Annual Undergrad Tuition & Fees: $13,150
Enrollment: 596 Coed
Affiliation or Control: Southern Baptist IRS Status: 501(c)3
Highest Offering: Baccalaureate
Program: Liberal Arts And General
Accreditation: **NH**, TED

01 President ... Dr. Tom O. JONES
05 Acting Vice Pres Academic Affairs ... Dr. Kenneth M. STARTUP
10 Vice President for Business Affairs ... Mr. Dale LEATHERMAN
30 Vice Pres Institutional Advancement ... Dr. Eric A. TURNER
84 VP for Enrollment Mgmt/Student Svcs ... Mrs. Angela D. FLIPPO
26 Vice President of College Relations ... Dr. Brett COOPER
32 Dean of Students ... Mrs. Susan M. WATSON
44 Director of Development ... Vacant
06 Registrar ... Mrs. Tonya D. BOLTON
04 Administrative Asst to President ... Mrs. Jo C. PHILLIPS
08 Librarian ... Mrs. Pamela MERIDITH
37 Director Student Financial Aid ... Mrs. Barbara J. TURNER
38 Director Student Counseling ... Ms. Aneita COOPER
42 Director Campus Ministry ... Mr. Josh MCCARTY
18 Chief Facilities/Physical Plant ... Vacant
36 Director Student Placement ... Ms. Aneita COOPER
29 Director of Alumni Relations ... Mr. Aaron ANDREWS
13 Director Information Technology ... Mr. Blake MCGINNIS
41 Athletic Director ... Mr. Jeff RIDER

CALIFORNIA

Abraham Lincoln University (C)

3530 Wilshire Blvd, Ste 1430, Los Angeles CA 90010
County: Los Angeles Identification: 667049
Telephone: (213) 252-5100 Carnegie Class: Not Classified
FAX Number: (213) 252-5112 Calendar System: Semester
URL: www.alu.edu
Established: 1996 Annual Undergrad Tuition & Fees: $7,500
Enrollment: 138 Coed
Affiliation or Control: Proprietary IRS Status: Proprietary
Highest Offering: First Professional Degree
Program: 2-Year Principally Bachelor's Creditable; Liberal Arts And General; Professional
Accreditation: **DETC**

01 President & CEO ... Mr. Roy WINTER
11 Director of Compliance ... Ms. Jessica PARK
61 Dean School of Law ... Ms. Carole BUCKNER
32 Dean of Student Affairs ... Dr. Daryl FISHER-OGDEN
07 Director of Admissions ... Mr. Bryan PACPACO
06 Registrar ... Ms. Elizabeth GOMEZ
35 Student Services Coordinator ... Ms. Jin CHUNG
13 Technology Manager ... Mr. Myeong KIM

Academy for Jewish Religion (D)

574 Hilgard Avenue, Los Angeles CA 90024-3234
County: Los Angeles FICE Identification: 041555
Unit ID: 457271
Telephone: (310) 824-1586 Carnegie Class: Not Classified
FAX Number: (310) 824-1614 Calendar System: Trimester
URL: www.ajrca.org
Established: 2001 Annual Graduate Tuition & Fees: $22,000
Enrollment: 58 Coed
Affiliation or Control: Jewish IRS Status: 501(c)3
Highest Offering: Master's; No Undergraduates
Program: Professional; Religious Emphasis
Accreditation: **@WC**

01 President ... Rabbi Mel GOTTLIEB
05 Dean of Academic Affairs ... Dr. Tamar FRANKIEL
37 Director Student Financial Aid ... Ms. Lauren GOLDNER
06 Registrar ... Ms. Reesa ROTMAN
07 Director of Admissions ... Ms. Robin FEDERMAN
26 Chief Public Relations Officer ... Ms. Cheryl AZAIR
88 Dean of Cantorial School ... Cantor Nathan LAM
73 Dean of Rabbinical School ... Rabbi Michael MENITOFF
88 Associate Dean of Cantorial School ... Cantor Perryne ANKER

Academy of Art University (E)

79 New Montgomery Street,
San Francisco CA 94105-3410
County: San Francisco FICE Identification: 007531
Unit ID: 108232
Telephone: (415) 274-2200 Carnegie Class: Spec/Arts
FAX Number: (415) 274-8665 Calendar System: Semester
URL: www.academyart.edu
Established: 1929 Annual Undergrad Tuition & Fees: $22,950
Enrollment: 18,093 Coed
Affiliation or Control: Proprietary IRS Status: Proprietary
Highest Offering: Master's
Program: Fine Arts Emphasis
Accreditation: **WC**, ART, CIDA

01 President ... Ms. Elisa STEPHENS

Academy of Chinese Culture and Health Sciences (F)

1601 Clay Street, Oakland CA 94612-1540
County: Alameda FICE Identification: 032883
Unit ID: 108269
Telephone: (510) 763-7787 Carnegie Class: Spec/Health
FAX Number: (510) 834-8646 Calendar System: Other
URL: www.acchs.edu
Established: 1982 Annual Undergrad Tuition & Fees: $16,600
Enrollment: 111 Coed
Affiliation or Control: Independent Non-Profit IRS Status: 501(c)3
Highest Offering: Master's; No Lower Division
Program: Professional
Accreditation: **ACUP**

01 President ... Mr. John NIETERS
03 Vice President ... Mr. Phillip TOU
11 Dean of Administration ... Ms. Jane ZHANG

Academy of Couture Art (G)

5700 Wilshire Blvd, Suite 275, Los Angeles CA 90036
County: Los Angeles FICE Identification: 041855
Telephone: (310) 360-8888 Carnegie Class: Not Classified
FAX Number: (310) 857-6974 Calendar System: Quarter
URL: www.academyofcoutureart.edu
Established: 2005 Annual Undergrad Tuition & Fees: $21,638
Enrollment: N/A Coed
Affiliation or Control: Proprietary IRS Status: Proprietary
Highest Offering: Baccalaureate
Program: Occupational
Accreditation: **ACICS**

01 CEO ... Sonia ETE

Acupuncture and Integrative Medicine College-Berkeley (H)

2550 Shattuck Avenue, Berkeley CA 94704-2724
County: Alameda FICE Identification: 033274
Unit ID: 384306
Telephone: (510) 666-8248 Carnegie Class: Spec/Health
FAX Number: (510) 666-0111 Calendar System: Quarter
URL: www.aimc.edu
Established: 1990 Annual Undergrad Tuition & Fees: $15,000
Enrollment: 108 Coed
Affiliation or Control: Independent Non-Profit IRS Status: 501(c)3
Highest Offering: Master's; No Lower Division
Program: Professional
Accreditation: **ACUP**

01 President ... Mr. Yasuo TANAKA
05 Academic Dean ... Ms. Yeaji SUH
20 Clinic Dean ... Mr. Mike MORGAN
06 Registrar ... Ms. May MOK
51 Continuing Education/Events Dir ... Ms. Vim OSATHANUGRAH
07 Director of Admissions ... Mr. Jon DISKIN

Advanced College (I)

13180 Paramount Boulevard, South Gate CA 90280-7956
County: Los Angeles FICE Identification: 037863
Unit ID: 444343
Telephone: (562) 408-6969 Carnegie Class: Assoc/PrivFP
FAX Number: (562) 408-0471 Calendar System: Other
URL: www.advancedcollege.edu
Established: 1999 Annual Undergrad Tuition & Fees: $27,175
Enrollment: 193 Coed
Affiliation or Control: Proprietary IRS Status: Proprietary
Highest Offering: Associate Degree
Program: Occupational
Accreditation: **COE**

01 Chief Executive Officer ... Dr. Mehdi KARIMPOR
66 Director Vocational Nursing ... Dr. Minnie L. DOUGLAS
11 Director of Operations ... Dr. Mehdi KARIMPOUR

Advanced Training Associates (J)

1810 Gillespie Way, Suite 104, El Cajon CA 92020-1234
County: San Diego FICE Identification: 035324
Unit ID: 444361
Telephone: (619) 596-2766 Carnegie Class: Not Classified
FAX Number: (619) 596-4526 Calendar System: Other
URL: www.advancedtraining.edu
Established: 2000 Annual Undergrad Tuition & Fees: $11,650
Enrollment: 68 Coed
Affiliation or Control: Proprietary IRS Status: Proprietary
Highest Offering: Associate Degree
Program: Occupational; Technical Emphasis
Accreditation: **COE**

01 President ... Joann ZAKARIN
03 Operations Manager ... Valerie PHILLIPS

Alhambra Medical University (K)

25 S. Raymond Ave., Suite 201, Alhambra CA 91801
County: Los Angeles Identification: 667052
Telephone: (626) 289-7719 Carnegie Class: Not Classified
FAX Number: (626) 289-8641 Calendar System: Quarter
URL: www.amuedu.com
Established: 2005 Annual Graduate Tuition & Fees: $13,282
Enrollment: N/A Coed
Affiliation or Control: Proprietary IRS Status: Proprietary
Highest Offering: Master's; No Undergraduates
Program: Professional
Accreditation: **@ACUP**

01 President ... Dr. Jonathan WU
05 Academic Dean ... Jerome JIANG
23 Director of University Clinic ... Megan HAH
07 Director of Admissions ... Fanny HSU
06 Registrar ... Qing MA
08 Librarian ... Yue LU

Allan Hancock College (L)

800 S College Drive, Santa Maria CA 93454-6399
County: Santa Barbara FICE Identification: 001111
Unit ID: 108807
Telephone: (805) 922-6966 Carnegie Class: Assoc/Pub-R-L
FAX Number: (805) 928-7905 Calendar System: Semester
URL: www.hancockcollege.edu
Established: 1920 Annual Undergrad Tuition & Fees (In-District): $1,150
Enrollment: 10,211 Coed
Affiliation or Control: State/Local IRS Status: 501(c)3
Highest Offering: Associate Degree
Program: Occupational; 2-Year Principally Bachelor's Creditable
Accreditation: **WJ**

01 Interim Superintendent/President ... Dr. Elizabeth MILLER
10 Assoc Supt/VP Administrative Svcs ... Dr. Elizabeth MILLER
05 Assoc Supt/VP Academic Affairs ... Mr. Luiz P. SANCHEZ
32 VP Student Services ... Vacant
18 Vice Pres Facilities & Operations ... Mr. Felix HERNANDEZ
35 Dean Student Services ... Mr. Rob PARISI
88 Dean Counseling & Matriculation ... Dr. Charles OSIRIS
20 Dean Academic Affairs ... Ms. Roanna BENNIE
20 Dean Academic Affairs ... Ms. Nancy MEDDINGS
20 Dean Acad Afrs/Dir HSI STEM ... Dr. Paul MURPHY
20 Dean Academic Affairs ... Ms. Ardis NEILSEN
12 Dean The Extended Campus ... Mr. Rick RANTZ
41 Assoc Dean Athletics/Kinesiology ... Ms. Kim ENSING
102 Executive Director AHC Foundation ... Mr. Jeff COTTER
88 Artistic Director PCPA ... Mr. Mark BOOHER
13 Director Information Technology ... Ms. Carol VAN NAME

15 Director Human Resources ..... Ms. Cyndi MESAROS
21 Director Business Services ..... Mr. Richard CARMODY
07 Director Admissions & Records ..... Ms. Adela ESQUIVEL-SWINSON
37 Director Student Financial Aid ..... Mr. Robert PARISI
26 Dir Public Affairs & Publications ..... Mrs. Rebecca ALARCIO
40 Director Bookstore Services ..... Mr. William HOCKENSMITH
88 Director EOPS & Special Outreach ..... Mr. Will BRUCE
18 Director Plant Services ..... Mr. Rex VAN DEN BERG
09 Director Inst Research & Planning ..... Dr. Laurie PEMBERTON
19 Dir Public Safety/Chief of Police ..... Lt. Kim GRAHAM
88 Director College Achvmt Now (CAN) ..... Mr. Francisco DORAME
88 Dir Title V Learning College Grant ..... Ms. Carmela VIGNOCCHI
88 Director Cal-SOAP ..... Ms. Diana PEREZ
25 Director Institutional Grants ..... Dr. Suzanne VALERY
81 Counselor/Coordinator MESA ..... Ms. Christine REED
88 Managing Director PCPA ..... Mr. Michael BLACK

*Alliant International University President's Office (A)

One Beach Street, Suite 200,
San Francisco CA 94133-1221
County: San Francisco Identification: 666132
Unit ID: 110431
Telephone: (415) 955-2000 Carnegie Class: N/A
FAX Number: (414) 955-2062
URL: www.alliant.edu

01 President ..... Dr. Geoffrey COX
05 Provost/Vice Pres Academic Affairs ..... Dr. Russ NEWMAN
30 Exec VP Intl & Strategic Develop ..... Mr. Tarun BHATIA
11 VP Administration/General Counsel ..... Ms. Jennifer TREESE WILSON
10 Vice Pres Finance & CFO ..... Ms. Jeanine HAWK
21 Asst VP Budget/Fin Plng/Analysis ..... Mr. Rohinton BHANDARI
09 Assoc Provost Inst Research ..... Ms. Patty MULLEN
53 Dean Grad School of Education ..... Dr. Karen Schuster WEBB
88 Systemwide Dean CSPP ..... Dr. Morgan SAMMONS
32 Dean of Students ..... Dr. Craig BREWER
15 Chief Human Resources Officer ..... Ms. Kristine COMBS
88 University Ombudsperson ..... Ms. Jacyn LEWIS
96 Director of Procurement ..... Mr. Mehdi RAJABZADEH
88 Controller ..... Ms. Sheryl KOGA

*Alliant International University-Fresno & Sacramento (B)

5130 E Clinton Way, Fresno CA 93727-2014
County: Fresno FICE Identification: 001158
Unit ID: 110440
Telephone: (559) 456-2777 Carnegie Class: Not Classified
FAX Number: (559) 253-2267 Calendar System: Semester
URL: www.alliant.edu
Established: 1973 Annual Graduate Tuition & Fees: $28,350
Enrollment: 311 Coed
Affiliation or Control: Independent Non-Profit IRS Status: 501(c)3
Highest Offering: Doctorate; No Undergraduates
Program: Liberal Arts And General; Teacher Preparatory; Professional
Accreditation: **WC**, CLPSY, MFCD

02 Dir Campus/Student Services-Fresno ..... Mr. Xavier ROMANO
12 Dir Campus/Student Svcs-Sacramento ..... Ms. Penny SCHAFER
88 Dean of Forensic Studies ..... Dr. Eric HICKEY
83 Dir Clinical PsyD & PhD Program ..... Dr. Kevin J. O'CONNOR
88 Assoc Dean Forensic Studies ..... Dr. Diana CONCANNON
88 Director Organizational Psych Pgm ..... Dr. Toni KNOTT
07 Director of Admissions ..... Mr. Brian EVANS
08 Director of Library Service ..... Ms. Louise COLBERT-MAR

*Alliant International University-Irvine (C)

2855 Michelle Drive, Suite 300, Irvine CA 92606
County: Orange Identification: 666157
Unit ID: 11046804
Telephone: (949) 812-7440 Carnegie Class: Not Classified
FAX Number: (714) 508-6926 Calendar System: Semester
URL: www.alliant.edu
Established: 1991 Annual Graduate Tuition & Fees: $30,000
Enrollment: 230 Coed
Affiliation or Control: Independent Non-Profit IRS Status: 501(c)3
Highest Offering: Doctorate; No Undergraduates
Program: Teacher Preparatory; Professional
Accreditation: **WC**, MFCD

02 Director Campus/Student Services ..... Ms. Nicole CAMARAS
53 Director Educational Psych Program ..... Dr. Donald WOFFORD
88 Dir Couples/Family Therapy Program ..... Dr. Stephen W. BROWN

*Alliant International University-Los Angeles (D)

1000 S Fremont Avenue, Unit 5,
Alhambra CA 91803-1360
County: Los Angeles FICE Identification: 010013
Unit ID: 110459
Telephone: (626) 284-2777 Carnegie Class: Not Classified
FAX Number: (626) 284-0550 Calendar System: Semester
URL: www.alliant.edu
Established: 1970 Annual Graduate Tuition & Fees: $29,700
Enrollment: 729 Coed
Affiliation or Control: Independent Non-Profit IRS Status: 501(c)3
Highest Offering: Doctorate; No Undergraduates
Program: Professional
Accreditation: **WC**, CLPSY, MFCD

02 Dir of Campus & Student Services ..... Ms. Stephanie BYERS-BELL
83 Dir Clin PhD Pgm & Field Training ..... Dr. Robert GORE
88 Int Dn Indust-Organizational Psych ..... Dr. Denise LOPEZ
53 Dir Clinical Psychology PsyD Pgm ..... Dr. Beth HOUSKAMP
53 Director Educational Psy Pgm ..... Dr. Carlton PARKS
88 Int Forensic Academic Pgm Director ..... Dr. Tracy FASS
28 Director I-MERIT ..... Dr. Sheila HENDERSON
53 Teacher Education Program Director ..... Dr. Barbara STEIN-STOVER
20 Associate Dean CSPP ..... Dr. Ron DURAN
07 Admissions Recruitment Coordinator ..... Mr. Mike GIOVANINI

*Alliant International University-San Diego (E)

10455 Pomerado Road, San Diego CA 92131-1799
County: San Diego FICE Identification: 011117
Unit ID: 110468
Telephone: (858) 635-4000 Carnegie Class: DRU
FAX Number: (858) 693-8562 Calendar System: Semester
URL: www.alliant.edu
Established: 1952 Annual Undergrad Tuition & Fees: $18,600
Enrollment: 4,282 Coed
Affiliation or Control: Independent Non-Profit IRS Status: 501(c)3
Highest Offering: Doctorate
Program: Liberal Arts And General; Teacher Preparatory; Professional
Accreditation: **WC**, CLPSY, MFCD

02 President ..... Dr. Geoffrey COX
05 Provost/Vice Pres Academic Affairs ..... Dr. Russ NEWMAN
43 Vice President and Univ Counsel ..... Ms. Jennifer WILSON
32 Assoc Vice Pres for Student Life ..... Dr. Mike PITTENGER
09 Assoc Provost for Rsrch & Scholar ..... Dr. Sharon FOSTER
11 Assoc Provost for Administration ..... Dr. Tracy HELLER
26 Chief Marketing Officer ..... Mrs. Madeleine WIENER
06 University Registrar ..... Mr. Paul WELCH
37 Director of Financial Aid ..... Ms. Deborah SPINDLER
08 University Librarian ..... Mr. Scott ZIMMER

*Alliant International University-San Francisco (F)

One Beach Street, San Francisco CA 94133-1221
County: San Francisco FICE Identification: 011881
Unit ID: 110477
Telephone: (415) 955-2100 Carnegie Class: Not Classified
FAX Number: (415) 955-2179 Calendar System: Semester
URL: www.alliant.edu
Established: 1970 Annual Graduate Tuition & Fees: $21,614
Enrollment: 975 Coed
Affiliation or Control: Independent Non-Profit IRS Status: 501(c)3
Highest Offering: Doctorate; No Undergraduates
Program: Teacher Preparatory; Professional
Accreditation: **WC**, CLPSY

02 Interim Director of Campus Services ..... Mr. Joseph TALLY
07 Director of Admissions ..... Ms. Julie AQUINO
08 Director Library Services ..... Mr. Joseph TALLY
83 Associate Dean CSPP ..... Dr. Dalia DUCKER
83 Dir Clinical Psychology PhD Pgm ..... Dr. Michael LOEWY
83 Dir Clinical Psychology PsyD Pgm ..... Dr. Valata JENKINS-MONROE
83 Dir Japan Clinical Psychology Pgm ..... Dr. Reiko TRUE
83 Dir HK Clinical Psychology PsyD Pgm ..... Dr. Alex LEUNG
88 Int Dir Organizational Psych Pgms ..... Dr. Rebecca TURNER
53 Asst Dean Graduate Sch of Education ..... Dr. Trudy DAY
53 Dir Educational Psychology Program ..... Dr. Diane DIBARI
88 Director Office of Accessability ..... Dr. Nina GHISELLI

Allied American University (G)

22952 Alcalde Drive, Laguna Hills CA 92653-1337
County: Orange Identification: 666452
Telephone: (888) 384-0849 Carnegie Class: Not Classified
FAX Number: (949) 707-2978 Calendar System: Other
URL: www.allied.edu
Established: 2008 Annual Undergrad Tuition & Fees: $8,400
Enrollment: 1,714 Coed
Affiliation or Control: Proprietary IRS Status: Proprietary
Highest Offering: Baccalaureate
Program: Liberal Arts And General
Accreditation: **DETC**

01 President ..... Charli HISLOP
06 Registrar ..... Christopher BISHOP
32 Director of Student Affairs ..... Frank VAZQUEZ
07 Director of Admissions ..... Lindsay OGLESBY

AMDA College and Conservatory of the Performing Arts (H)

6305 Yucca Street, Los Angeles CA 90028
Identification: 666721
Telephone: (323) 469-3300 Carnegie Class: Not Classified
FAX Number: (323) 469-5246 Calendar System: Semester
URL: www.amda.edu
Established: 1964 Annual Undergrad Tuition & Fees: $31,308
Enrollment: 1,258 Coed
Affiliation or Control: Independent Non-Profit IRS Status: 501(c)3
Highest Offering: Baccalaureate
Program: Liberal Arts And General; Fine Arts Emphasis
Accreditation: **THEA**

01 Artistic Director/President ..... David MARTIN
05 Executive Director/Vice President ..... Jan MARTIN
07 Sr Director of Admissions ..... Karen JACKSON

American Academy of Dramatic Arts, Los Angeles Campus (I)

1336 N La Brea Avenue, Hollywood CA 90028-7504
County: Los Angeles FICE Identification: 021069
Unit ID: 108852
Telephone: (323) 464-2777 Carnegie Class: Assoc/PrivNFP
FAX Number: (323) 464-1250 Calendar System: Other
URL: www.aada.org
Established: 1974 Annual Undergrad Tuition & Fees: $30,500
Enrollment: 195 Coed
Affiliation or Control: Independent Non-Profit IRS Status: 501(c)3
Highest Offering: Associate Degree
Program: 2-Year Principally Bachelor's Creditable; Fine Arts Emphasis
Accreditation: **&M**, THEA

01 President/COO ..... Ms. Susan ZECH
12 Managing Director ..... Mr. William FARMER
07 Director of Admissions ..... Mr. Steven HONG
05 Director of Instruction ..... Ms. Theresa HAYES
37 Associate Director Financial Aid ..... Mr. Kyle ROUMILLAT
06 Registrar ..... Ms. Irma ROA
08 Head Librarian ..... Ms. Sally LAPORTE
18 Manager Facilities/Maintenance ..... Mr. Gary RICE

† Regional accreditation is carried under the parent institution in New York, NY.

American Baptist Seminary of the West (J)

2606 Dwight Way, Berkeley CA 94704-3097
County: Alameda FICE Identification: 001120
Unit ID: 108861
Telephone: (510) 841-1905 Carnegie Class: Spec/Faith
FAX Number: (510) 841-2446 Calendar System: Semester
URL: www.absw.edu
Established: 1871 Annual Undergrad Tuition & Fees: $16,200
Enrollment: 105 Coed
Affiliation or Control: American Baptist IRS Status: 501(c)3
Highest Offering: Doctorate
Program: Professional; Religious Emphasis
Accreditation: **THEOL**

01 President ..... Dr. Paul MARTIN
03 Vice President ..... Rev. Michelle M. HOLMES
05 Academic Dean ..... Dr. LeAnn SNOW FLESHER
10 Chief Financial Officer ..... Rev. Michelle M. HOLMES
06 Registrar/Dir Academic Admin ..... Ms. Nancy SVENSSON
07 Director of Admissions ..... Ms. Marie ONWUBUARIRI

American Career College-Los Angeles (K)

4021 Rosewood Avenue, Los Angeles CA 90004
County: Los Angeles FICE Identification: 022418
Unit ID: 441052
Telephone: (323) 668-7555 Carnegie Class: Assoc/PrivFP
FAX Number: (322) 953-3654 Calendar System: Other
URL: www.americancareercollege.edu
Established: 1978 Annual Undergrad Tuition & Fees: $16,590
Enrollment: 1,828 Coed
Affiliation or Control: Proprietary IRS Status: Proprietary
Highest Offering: Associate Degree
Program: Occupational
Accreditation: **ABHES**, SURGT, SURTEC

01 Director ..... Ms. Lani TOWNSEND

American Career College-Ontario (L)

3130 East Sedona Court, Ontario CA 91764
County: San Bernardino FICE Identification: 039713
Unit ID: 447768
Telephone: (909) 218-3253 Carnegie Class: Assoc/PrivFP
FAX Number: N/A Calendar System: Other
URL: www.americancareercollege.edu
Established: 2006 Annual Undergrad Tuition & Fees: $16,590
Enrollment: 1,707 Coed
Affiliation or Control: Proprietary IRS Status: Proprietary
Highest Offering: Associate Degree
Program: Occupational
Accreditation: **ABHES**, SURTEC

01 Campus President ..... Mr. Scott WARDALL

American Career College-Orange County (A)

1200 North Magnolia Avenue, Anaheim CA 92801-2607

County: Orange Identification: 667073
Unit ID: 441052
Telephone: (714) 952-9066 Carnegie Class: Assoc/PrivFP
FAX Number: (714) 952-1819 Calendar System: Other
URL: www.americancareercollege.edu
Established: 2000 Annual Undergrad Tuition & Fees: $34,110
Enrollment: 1,928 Coed
Affiliation or Control: Proprietary IRS Status: Proprietary
Highest Offering: Associate Degree
Program: Occupational
Accreditation: ABHES, SURGT, SURTEC

01 Executive Director .... Ms. Rita TOTTEN

American College of Traditional Chinese Medicine (B)

455 Arkansas Street, San Francisco CA 94107-2813

County: San Francisco FICE Identification: 030782
Unit ID: 430591
Telephone: (415) 282-7600 Carnegie Class: Spec/Health
FAX Number: (415) 282-0856 Calendar System: Quarter
URL: www.actcm.edu
Established: 1980 Annual Undergrad Tuition & Fees: $15,404
Enrollment: 267 Coed
Affiliation or Control: Independent Non-Profit IRS Status: 501(c)3
Highest Offering: Doctorate; No Lower Division
Program: Professional; Technical Emphasis
Accreditation: ACUP

01 President .... Lixin HUANG
05 Vice President for Academic Affairs .... Bingzeng ZOU
17 Dean of Clinical Education .... Steve GIVEN
20 Chief Academic & Clinic Adviser .... Stanley LEUNG
06 Registrar .... Jim HABLE
32 Director of Student Services .... Lee SWAIN
84 Dir of Recruitment/Enrollment Mgmt .... Yuwen CHIU
10 Controller .... Reno GOLEZ
20 Asst Dean of Clinical Education .... Jung KIM
20 Asst to the Dean of Master's Pgm .... Richard ALBERTA
45 Director of Institutional Planning .... Elizabeth GOLDBLATT
24 Director of Learning Resources .... Aileen HUANG
27 Director of Communications .... Alissa COHAN
37 Financial Aid Administrator .... Daryl CULLEN
14 Network Administrator .... Yan LI
08 Library Administrator .... Sara WANG
07 Admissions Counselor .... Yumiko TOMOBE
88 Academic Advisor .... Andrea NATTA
04 Admn Asst/Asst to President .... Lena LIU
30 Development Officer .... Tami GROVES
18 Facilities Manager .... Jorge MEJIA

American Conservatory Theater (C)

30 Grant Avenue, 6th floor, San Francisco CA 94108-5800

County: San Francisco FICE Identification: 020992
Unit ID: 109086
Telephone: (415) 439-2350 Carnegie Class: Spec/Arts
FAX Number: (415) 834-3210 Calendar System: Semester
URL: www.act-sf.org
Established: 1969 Annual Graduate Tuition & Fees: $20,500
Enrollment: 25 Coed
Affiliation or Control: Independent Non-Profit IRS Status: 501(c)3
Highest Offering: Master's; No Undergraduates
Program: Professional; Fine Arts Emphasis
Accreditation: WC

01 Executive Director .... Ellen RICHARD
88 Artistic Director .... Carey PERLOFF
05 Conservatory Director .... Melissa SMITH
20 Director of Academic Affairs .... Jack SHARRAR
37 Director of Financial Aid .... Jerry LOPEZ

American Evangelical University (D)

1818 S. Western Ave #409, Los Angeles CA 90006

County: Los Angeles Identification: 667090
Telephone: (323) 643-0301 Carnegie Class: Not Classified
FAX Number: (323) 643-0302 Calendar System: Semester
URL: www.aeui.org
Established: 2001 Annual Undergrad Tuition & Fees: $4,400
Enrollment: N/A Coed
Affiliation or Control: Independent Non-Profit IRS Status: 501(c)3
Highest Offering: Master's
Program: Religious Emphasis
Accreditation: @BI

01 President .... Dr. Jong KIL RYU
05 Chief Academic Officer .... Dr. Mark SUKKIL YOON
32 Chief Student Development Officer .... Rev. Jason CHOI
10 CFO .... Rev. Timothy LEE
30 Chief Development Officer .... Dr. Eui JUNG WHANG
08 Chief Librarian .... Dr. Duk YOUNG WON

American Film Institute Conservatory (E)

2021 N Western Avenue, Los Angeles CA 90027-1657

County: Los Angeles FICE Identification: 022220
Unit ID: 108870
Telephone: (323) 856-7600 Carnegie Class: Spec/Arts
FAX Number: (323) 467-4578 Calendar System: Semester
URL: www.afi.com
Established: 1969 Annual Graduate Tuition & Fees: $39,760
Enrollment: 351 Coed
Affiliation or Control: Independent Non-Profit IRS Status: 501(c)3
Highest Offering: Master's; No Undergraduates
Program: Professional; Fine Arts Emphasis
Accreditation: WC, ART

01 Director American Film Institute .... Mr. Bob GAZZALE
11 Chief Operating Officer .... Ms. Nancy HARRIS
05 Exec Vice Dean of Conservatory .... Mr. Joe PETRICCA
20 Vice Dean for Production/Post Prod .... Mr. Phil LINSON
20 Dean of Conservatory .... Mr. Robert MANDEL
32 Vice Dean Fellow Affairs .... Ms. Carolyn BROOKS
57 Artistic Director .... Mr. Frank PIERSON
57 Artistic Director .... Mr. Roger BIRNBAUM
06 Registrar .... Ms. Sheryl REINSCHMIDT
15 Manager Human Resources .... Ms. Roschoune FRANKLIN
37 Financial Aid Director .... Ms. Trina RODLER
07 Admissions Manager .... Ms. Karin T. TUCKER
30 Sr Vice President Advancement .... Mr. Tom WEST
08 Librarian .... Mr. Robert VAUGHN
13 Chief Information Officer .... Mr. Paul JACQUES

American Graduate University (F)

733 N Dodsworth Avenue, Covina CA 91724-2408

County: Los Angeles Identification: 666982
Unit ID: 109095
Telephone: (626) 966-4576 Carnegie Class: Not Classified
FAX Number: (626) 915-1709 Calendar System: Other
URL: www.agu.edu
Established: 1969 Annual Graduate Tuition & Fees: $2,475
Enrollment: 1,165 Coed
Affiliation or Control: Proprietary IRS Status: Proprietary
Highest Offering: Master's; No Undergraduates
Program: Professional; Business Emphasis
Accreditation: DETC

01 President/Dir Academic Affairs .... Mr. Paul R. MCDONALD
11 Vice President Administration .... Ms. Marie SIRNEY
32 Director of Student Services .... Ms. Sherrie ANGSTER
06 Registrar .... Ms. Debbie MCDONALD

American Jewish University (G)

15600 Mulholland Drive, Los Angeles CA 90077-1599

County: Los Angeles FICE Identification: 002741
Unit ID: 116846
Telephone: (310) 476-9777 Carnegie Class: Bac/A&S
FAX Number: (310) 471-1278 Calendar System: Semester
URL: www.ajula.edu
Established: 1947 Annual Undergrad Tuition & Fees: $27,080
Enrollment: 268 Coed
Affiliation or Control: Independent Non-Profit IRS Status: 501(c)3
Highest Offering: Master's
Program: Liberal Arts And General; Teacher Preparatory; Professional
Accreditation: WC

01 President .... Dr. Robert WEXLER
05 Provost .... Dr. Stuart SIGMAN
73 VP/Dean Ziegler Sch Rabbinic Stds .... Rabbi Bradley ARTSON
51 VP/Dean Whizin Center for Cont Educ .... Dr. Gady LEVY
10 VP Finance/Admin & Technology .... Ms. Zofia YALOVSKY
30 Sr VP Development .... Rabbi Jay STREAR
42 Rector .... Dr. Elliot DORFF
08 Director of Library Services .... Mr. Paul MILLER
06 Registrar .... Mr. Arnie WEISBERG
27 Sr Director of Comm & Recruitment .... Ms. Iris WASKOW
37 Director of Financial Aid .... Ms. Larisa ZADOYEN
53 Dean Fingerhut School of Education .... Ms. Miriam HELLER-STERN
49 Dean College of Arts & Sciences .... Dr. Stuart SIGMAN
88 Dean Nonprofit Management Program .... Ms. Nina LIEBERMAN GILADI
39 Director Residence Life .... Mr. Jacob GOWN
07 Director Undergraduate Admissions .... Mr. Matt SPOONER

American University of Armenia (H)

300 Lakeside Drive, 12th Floor, Oakland CA 94612

County: Alameda Identification: 666013
Telephone: (510) 987-9452 Carnegie Class: Not Classified
FAX Number: (510) 208-3576 Calendar System: Semester
URL: www.aua.am
Established: 1991 Annual Graduate Tuition & Fees: $6,400
Enrollment: 302 Coed
Affiliation or Control: Independent Non-Profit IRS Status: 501(c)3
Highest Offering: Master's; No Undergraduates
Program: Professional
Accreditation: WC

01 President .... Dr. Bruce M. BOGHOSIAN

American University of Health Sciences (I)

1600 E Hill St Building #1, Signal Hill CA 90755

County: Los Angeles FICE Identification: 032253
Unit ID: 433004
Telephone: (562) 988-2278 Carnegie Class: Assoc/PrivFP4
FAX Number: (562) 988-1791 Calendar System: Quarter
URL: www.auhs.edu
Established: 1994 Annual Undergrad Tuition & Fees: $32,000
Enrollment: 214 Coed
Affiliation or Control: Proprietary IRS Status: Proprietary
Highest Offering: Master's
Program: Professional
Accreditation: ACICS, NURSE

01 President .... Mr. Philip G. WOLFSON
11 Chief Operating Officer .... Pastor Gregory A. JOHNSON

Anaheim University (J)

1240 S State College Blvd, Ste 110, Anaheim CA 92806-5152

County: Orange Identification: 666651
Telephone: (714) 772-3330 Carnegie Class: Not Classified
FAX Number: (714) 772-3331 Calendar System: Other
URL: www.anaheim.edu
Established: 1996 Annual Graduate Tuition & Fees: N/A
Enrollment: N/A Coed
Affiliation or Control: Proprietary IRS Status: Proprietary
Highest Offering: Master's; No Undergraduates
Program: Professional
Accreditation: DETC

01 President .... Dr. William B. HARTLEY
05 Vice President of Academic Affairs .... Dr. David NUNAN

Antelope Valley College (K)

3041 W Avenue K, Lancaster CA 93536-5426

County: Los Angeles FICE Identification: 001113
Unit ID: 109350
Telephone: (661) 722-6300 Carnegie Class: Assoc/Pub-S-SC
FAX Number: (661) 722-6333 Calendar System: Semester
URL: www.avc.edu
Established: 1929 Annual Undergrad Tuition & Fees (In-District): $1,123
Enrollment: 14,295 Coed
Affiliation or Control: State/Local IRS Status: 501(c)3
Highest Offering: Associate Degree
Program: Occupational; 2-Year Principally Bachelor's Creditable
Accreditation: WJ, RAD

01 President/Superintendent .... Dr. Jackie L. FISHER, SR.
05 VP Academic Affairs .... Ms. Sharon LOWRY
32 VP Student Services .... Mr. Newton CHELETTE
10 Vice Pres Administrative Services .... Dr. Willard WRIGHT
15 Vice President Human Resources .... Mr. Michael TURNER
07 Dean Enrollment Svcs & Counseling .... Ms. LaDonna TRIMBLE
88 Director Disabled Students .... Dr. Louis LUCERO
26 Director Public Relations .... Mr. Steve STANDERFER
18 Dir Facilities Services .... Mr. Doug JENSEN
13 Director Information Technology .... Mr. Calvin MADLOCK
30 Dir Inst Advancement & Foundation .... Ms. Bridget RAZO
46 Director Inst Research & Planning .... Vacant
96 Buyer .... Ms. Angela MUSIAL
37 Director Financial Aid .... Ms. Sherrie PADILLA
68 Dean PE/Athlet/Visual and Perf Arts .... Mr. Newton CHELETTE
79 Dean of Inst Res/Language Arts ... Dr. Charlotte FORTE-PARNELL
83 Dean Soc & Beh Sci/Bus/Comp Stds .... Dr. Tom O'NEIL
38 Dean Counseling & Matriculation .... Vacant
76 Dean Health Sciences/Tech Ed .... Dr. Karen COWELL
35 Dean of Student Develop & Services .... Dr. Jill ZIMMERMAN
75 Dean of Technical Education .... Vacant
81 Dean of Math/Science & Engineering .... Dr. Les UHAZY

Antioch University Los Angeles (L)

400 Corporate Pointe, Culver City CA 90230

County: Los Angeles Identification: 666236
Unit ID: 245838
Telephone: (310) 578-1080 Carnegie Class: Master's L
FAX Number: (310) 822-4824 Calendar System: Quarter
URL: www.antiochla.edu
Established: 1972 Annual Undergrad Tuition & Fees: $26,260
Enrollment: 808 Coed
Affiliation or Control: Independent Non-Profit IRS Status: 501(c)3
Highest Offering: Master's
Program: Liberal Arts And General
Accreditation: &NH

01 President .... Dr. Tex BOGGS
05 Provost/VP Academic Affairs .... Dr. Luis PEDRAJA
10 Chief Financial Officer .... Mr. David HOUSER
30 Vice Pres Inst Advancement .... Ms. Amy SMITH
06 Registrar .... Ms. Emelita DACANAY
07 Director of Admissions .... Ms. Karen MAGNER
15 Director Human Resources .... Mr. Robert STAPP
18 Chief Operations Officer .... Ms. Sandy LEE
26 Dir Communications/Public Relations .... Ms. Joanna GERBER
37 Dir Student Financial Aid .... Mr. Chris FREEMAN

32 Dir Student Advocacy & Services .... Mr. Josh WILLIAMS
09 Dir Institutional Research .... Mr. Mark RIDDLE

† Regional accreditation is carried under the parent institution in Yellow Springs, OH.

Antioch University Santa Barbara (A)

602 Anacapa Street, Santa Barbara CA 93101
County: Santa Barbara Identification: 666231
Unit ID: 245847
Telephone: (805) 962-8179 Carnegie Class: Master's S
FAX Number: (805) 962-4786 Calendar System: Quarter
URL: www.antiochsb.edu
Established: 1977 Annual Undergrad Tuition & Fees: $16,812
Enrollment: 388 Coed
Affiliation or Control: Independent Non-Profit IRS Status: 501(c)3
Highest Offering: Doctorate
Program: Liberal Arts And General; Professional
Accreditation: &NH

01 President .... Dr. Nancy LEFFERT
05 Provost/VP Academic Affairs .... Dr. Barbara LIPINSKI
09 Executive Dean Institutional Rsrch .... Mr. Richard WHITNEY
30 Associate Director of Development ....Ms. Robin ELANDER
06 Registrar .... Ms. Julia DUBIEL
84 Director of Enrollment Management ....Mr. Steve WEIR
37 Assistant Director of Financial Aid ....Ms. Babette WILLENS
10 Chief Financial Officer ....Ms. Deb CARAWAY
15 Director of Human Resources ..... Ms. Nanci BRAUNSCHWEIGER
58 Chair Graduate Psychology Programs ......Dr. Elizabeth WOLFSON
53 Chair Education Program ....Dr. Marianne D'EMIDIO CASTON
88 Chair Psychology Doctoral Program .... Dr. Juliet ROHDE-BROWN
97 Chair Undergraduate Studies ....Dr. Dawn OSBORN
57 Chair Master of Fine Arts ....Vacant
50 Chair Global Business/Management ....Vacant

† Regional accreditation is carried under the parent institution in Yellow Springs, OH.

Apollos University (B)

17011 Beach Blvd, Ste 900, Huntington Beach CA 92647
County: Orange Identification: 667096
Telephone: (714) 841-6252 Carnegie Class: Not Classified
FAX Number: (866) 287-1938 Calendar System: Quarter
URL: www.apollos-university.com
Established: 2005 Annual Graduate Tuition & Fees: N/A
Enrollment: N/A Coed
Affiliation or Control: Proprietary IRS Status: Proprietary
Highest Offering: Doctorate; No Undergraduates
Program: Business Emphasis
Accreditation: DETC

01 President & CEO ....Dr. Paul EIDSON

Applied Professional Training, Inc. (C)

5751 Palmer Way, Suite D, Carlsbad CA 92010-7247
County: San Diego Identification: 666245
Telephone: (800) 431-8488 Carnegie Class: Not Classified
FAX Number: (888) 431-8588 Calendar System: Semester
URL: www.aptc.edu
Established: 1993 Annual Undergrad Tuition & Fees: $5,500
Enrollment: 1,500 Coed
Affiliation or Control: Proprietary IRS Status: Proprietary
Highest Offering: Associate Degree
Program: Occupational; 2-Year Principally Bachelor's Creditable
Accreditation: DETC

01 President/Chief Executive Officer ....Mr. Steven W. BLUME

Argosy University, Inland Empire (D)

3401 Centre Lake Drive, Suite 200, Ontario CA 91761
County: San Bernardino Identification: 666007
Unit ID: 450526
Telephone: (909) 472-0800 Carnegie Class: Bac/A&S
FAX Number: N/A Calendar System: Semester
URL: www.argosy.edu/inlandempire
Established: 2006 Annual Undergrad Tuition & Fees: $13,224
Enrollment: 733 Coed
Affiliation or Control: Proprietary IRS Status: Proprietary
Highest Offering: Doctorate
Program: Professional
Accreditation: &WC

01 Campus Director ....Vacant
05 Vice President Academic Affairs ....Dr. Marilyn AL-HASSAN
07 Senior Director of Admissions .... Wendy VASQUEZ-OSBORN
32 Assoc Director of Student Services ....Michelle CORTEZ
37 Assoc Director of Student Finance ....Tanesha WELLS
06 Registrar ....Vacant
15 Human Resources ....Vacant
11 Dir of Admin and Financial Svcs .... Mike ANDRUSKI

† Regional accreditation is carried under the parent institution in Orange, CA.

Argosy University, Los Angeles (E)

5230 Pacific Concourse Drive, Los Angeles CA 90045
County: Los Angeles Identification: 666011
Unit ID: 447272
Telephone: (310) 531-9700 Carnegie Class: Bac/A&S
FAX Number: (310) 531-9801 Calendar System: Semester
URL: www.argosy.edu/losangeles
Established: 2005 Annual Undergrad Tuition & Fees: $13,224
Enrollment: 598 Coed
Affiliation or Control: Proprietary IRS Status: Proprietary
Highest Offering: Doctorate
Program: Professional
Accreditation: &WC

01 Campus Director ....Valerie CURRY
05 Asst VP of Academic Affairs .... Dr. Carolyn MILLER
07 Senior Director of Admissions .... Daniel A. BANYAI
32 Assoc Dir of Student Services ....Jacqueline GOMEZ-JURADO
37 Assoc Dir of Student Finance .... Elisa MONTANO
11 Dir of Admin and Financial Svcs .... Mike ANDRUSKI

† Regional accreditation is carried under the parent institution in Orange, CA.

Argosy University, Orange County (F)

601 South Lewis Street, Orange CA 92868
County: Orange FICE Identification: 021799
Unit ID: 145770
Telephone: (714) 620-3700 Carnegie Class: DRU
FAX Number: (714) 620-3802 Calendar System: Semester
URL: www.argosy.edu/orangecounty
Established: 1999 Annual Undergrad Tuition & Fees: $13,224
Enrollment: 863 Coed
Affiliation or Control: Proprietary IRS Status: Proprietary
Highest Offering: Doctorate
Program: Professional
Accreditation: WC, CLPSY

01 University President ....Dr. Craig D. SWENSON
05 Vice President of Academic Affairs ....Vacant
32 GVP West .... Mr. Michael FALOTICO
32 GVP East .... Dr. William BROWN
03 Executive Vice President .... Mr. Eric EVENSON
07 VP Admissions ....Mr. Jeff CROSS
26 VP of Marketing .... Mr. Daron RODRIGUEZ
15 Vice President Human Resources .... Ms. Sheri NESHIEM
32 VP Academic Ops & Student Services .... Ms. Julie JOHNSON
106 VP for Online & Distance Learning ....Ms. Kate NOONE
10 Vice President of Finance .... Mr. Ken STEVENS
50 Dean College of Business .... Ms. Cynthia LARSON
83 Dean Psychology and Behav Sciences ....Vacant
76 Dean College of Health Sciences ....Ms. Kristin BENSON
53 Dean College of Education ....Vacant
97 Dean Undergraduate Studies .... Ms. Ruki JAYARAMAN
12 Campus President Twin Cities ....Mr. Scott TJADEN
12 Campus President Atlanta .... Dr. Ronald SWANSON
12 Campus President Dallas ....Mr. Ronald HYSON
12 Campus President Hawaii .... Dr. Warren EVANS
12 Campus President Washington D.C. .... Mr. David EREKSON
12 Campus President Seattle ....Mr. Tom DYER
12 Campus President Sarasota ....Vacant
12 Campus President Orange County ....Dr. James COX
12 Campus President Schaumburg .... Mr. James CHITWOOD
12 Campus President Tampa .... Dr. Patricia MEREDITH
12 Campus President Phoenix ....Mr. Bart LERNER
12 Campus Pres San Francisco Bay Area .... Dr. Lucille SANSING
12 Campus President Inland Empire ....Dr. James COX
12 Campus President Nashville ....Dr. Sandra WISE
12 Int Campus President San Diego ....Dr. James COX
12 Campus President Los Angeles ....Dr. James COX
12 Campus President Salt Lake City ....Vacant
12 Campus President Denver ....Dr. Marcia BANKIRER

† Main Campus and HQ moved from Chicago, IL to Orange, CA

Argosy University, San Diego (G)

1615 Murray Canyon Rd, Suite 100,
San Diego CA 92108-4423
County: San Diego Identification: 666034
Unit ID: 450544
Telephone: (619) 321-3000 Carnegie Class: Bac/Assoc
FAX Number: (619) 321-3005 Calendar System: Semester
URL: www.argosy.edu/sandiego
Established: 2005 Annual Undergrad Tuition & Fees: $13,224
Enrollment: 439 Coed
Affiliation or Control: Proprietary IRS Status: Proprietary
Highest Offering: Doctorate
Program: Professional
Accreditation: &WC

01 Campus Director ....Vacant
05 Asst VP of Academic Affairs ...... Dr. Suzanne FORBES-VIERLING
07 Senior Director of Admissions .... Detroit WHITESIDE
32 Assoc Director of Student Services .... Steve BURNS
37 Assoc Director of Student Finance .... David HALL
06 Registrar ....Vacant
15 Human Resources ....Miquon BRANCH
11 Dir of Admin and Financial Svcs .... Mike ANDRUSKI

† Regional accreditation is carried under the parent institution in Orange, CA.

Argosy University, San Francisco Bay Area (H)

1005 Atlantic Avenue, Alameda CA 94501-1148
County: Contra Costa Identification: 666081
Unit ID: 121983
Telephone: (510) 217-4700 Carnegie Class: Spec/Health
FAX Number: (510) 217-4800 Calendar System: Semester
URL: www.argosy.edu/sanfrancisco
Established: 1998 Annual Undergrad Tuition & Fees: $13,224
Enrollment: 783 Coed
Affiliation or Control: Proprietary IRS Status: Proprietary
Highest Offering: Doctorate
Program: Professional
Accreditation: &WC, #CLPSY

01 Campus President .... Dr. Lance GARRISON
05 Vice President of Academic Affairs ....Dr. Gladys ATO
07 Senior Director of Admissions .... John STOFAN
32 Director of Student Services ....Lewis BUNDY
37 Director of Student Finance ....Juan MALDONADO
06 Registrar ....Konami CHISHOLM
15 Human Resources ....Sophia WARITH
11 Dir of Admin and Financial Svcs .... Michael TOLIVER

† Regional accreditation is carried under the parent institution in Orange, CA.

Art Center College of Design (I)

1700 Lida Street, Pasadena CA 91103-1999
County: Los Angeles FICE Identification: 001116
Unit ID: 109651
Telephone: (626) 396-2200 Carnegie Class: Spec/Arts
FAX Number: N/A Calendar System: Semester
URL: www.artcenter.edu
Established: 1930 Annual Undergrad Tuition & Fees: $35,052
Enrollment: 1,650 Coed
Affiliation or Control: Independent Non-Profit IRS Status: 501(c)3
Highest Offering: Master's
Program: Professional
Accreditation: WC, ART

01 President ....Dr. Lorne M. BUCHMAN
10 Sr VP/Chief Financial Officer ....Mr. Rich HALUSCHAK
05 Provost ....Mr. Fred FEHLAU
30 Sr VP Development &External Affairs ....Ms. Arwen DUFFY
18 Senior Vice President Operations .... Mr. George FALARDEAU
07 VP Admissions/Enrollment Mgmt ....Ms. Kit BARON
32 Dean of Students .... Mr. Jeffrey HOFFMAN
88 VP Exhibitions ....Mr. Steve NOWLIN
08 VP Library Director ....Mrs. Elizabeth GALLOWAY
13 VP Information Technology .... Ms. Theresa ZIX
26 Assoc VP Marketing & Communication ....Ms. Wendy SHATTUCK
15 Executive Director Human Resources ....Ms. Nancy TORRES DUGGAN
21 Controller ....Ms. Diane WITTENBERG
37 Managing Director Financial Aid ....Ms. Brenda NIEVES
29 Director of Alumni Affairs ....Ms. Kristine BOWNE
06 Director of Enrollment & Registrar .... Mr. William GARTRELL
09 Director of Institutional Research ....Ms. Esmeralda NAVA
19 Dir Environmental Health & Safety .... Ms. Vicky MCCORMICK
102 Director Foundation Relations ....Mr. Darryl MORI
36 Director of Career Development .... Ms. Cathy KARRY
18 Director of Facilities .... Mr. Jess RIVAS
96 Director of Purchasing .... Ms. Monica MATSUO

The Art Institute of California, A College of Argosy University - Hollywood (J)

5250 Lankershim Boulevard, North Hollywood CA 91601
County: Los Angeles FICE Identification: 031254
Unit ID: 410502
Telephone: (213) 251-3636 Carnegie Class: Spec/Arts
FAX Number: (213) 385-3545 Calendar System: Quarter
URL: www.artinstitutes.edu/hollywood
Established: 1991 Annual Undergrad Tuition & Fees: $18,948
Enrollment: 1,780 Coed
Affiliation or Control: Proprietary IRS Status: Proprietary
Highest Offering: Baccalaureate
Program: Occupational
Accreditation: &WC

01 President .... Mr. AJ ANTUN
05 Assoc Dean of Academic Affairs .... Dr. Karen NOWAK
37 Director of Student Financial Svcs ....Ms. Adis CEBALLOS
32 Dean of Student Affairs .... Ms. Michelle ESTRELLADO
06 Registrar ....Ms. Lorena LOPEZ
04 Executive Assistant ....Ms. Alexa ROMEO

† Regional accreditation is carried under the parent institution, Argosy University in Orange, CA.

The Art Institute of California, A College of Argosy University - Inland Empire (K)

674 East Brier Drive, San Bernardino CA 92408-2800
County: San Bernardino FICE Identification: 016471
Unit ID: 448576

Telephone: (909) 915-2100 Carnegie Class: Spec/Arts
FAX Number: (909) 915-2130 Calendar System: Semester
URL: www.artinstitutes.edu/inlandempire
Established: 2006 Annual Undergrad Tuition & Fees: $24,864
Enrollment: 2,292 Coed
Affiliation or Control: Proprietary IRS Status: Proprietary
Highest Offering: Baccalaureate
Program: Liberal Arts And General
Accreditation: &WC

01 President ...Mr. Eman EL-HOUT

† Regional accreditation is carried under the parent institution, Argosy University in Orange, CA.

The Art Institute of California, A College of Argosy University - Los Angeles (A)

2900 31st Street, Santa Monica CA 90405-3035
County: Los Angeles Identification: 666045
Unit ID: 432533
Telephone: (310) 752-4700 Carnegie Class: Spec/Arts
FAX Number: (310) 752-4708 Calendar System: Quarter
URL: www.aila.artinstitutes.edu
Established: 1997 Annual Undergrad Tuition & Fees: $30,550
Enrollment: 2,175 Coed
Affiliation or Control: Proprietary IRS Status: Proprietary
Highest Offering: Baccalaureate
Program: Occupational; 2-Year Principally Bachelor's Creditable
Accreditation: &WC, ACFEI, CIDA

01 President ...Laura SOLOFF
05 Dean of Academic Affairs ...Shelley GLICKSTEIN
36 Director of Career Services ...Scott SAUNDERS
07 Director of Admissions ...AJ ANTUN
10 Dir Administrative/Financial Svcs ...Mohamed AMMAR
16 Director of Human Resources ...Rebecca ELLIS
06 Registrar ...Dave ANTER
08 Director Learning Resource Center ...Mary EDWARDS
26 Director of Public Relations ...Michelles ESTRELLADO
37 Director Student Financial Services ...Cynthia GALARZA
88 Culinary Arts Program Director ...Christophe BERNARD
20 Graphic Arts Program Director ...Susanne MANHEIMER
20 Media Arts/Animation Prgm Director ...Aaron LYLE
20 Video Production Program Director ...David SCHREIBER
13 Director Technology ...Glenn BELL
24 Interactive Media Design Prgm Dir ...Jan MCWILLIAM
88 Interior Design Program Director ...Joanne KRAVETZ
32 Director Student Development ...Don KOHN
35 Dean of Student Affairs ...Eric POMPEI
88 Game Art Design Program Director ...Eric ELDER

† Regional accreditation is carried under the parent institution, Argosy University in Orange, CA.

The Art Institute of California, A College of Argosy University - Orange County (B)

3601 W Sunflower Avenue, Santa Ana CA 92704-7931
County: Orange Identification: 666182
Unit ID: 441973
Telephone: (714) 830-0200 Carnegie Class: Spec/Arts
FAX Number: (714) 556-1923 Calendar System: Quarter
URL: www.artinstitutes.edu/orangecounty
Established: 2000 Annual Undergrad Tuition & Fees: $18,948
Enrollment: 2,227 Coed
Affiliation or Control: Proprietary IRS Status: Proprietary
Highest Offering: Baccalaureate
Program: Occupational; Liberal Arts And General; Fine Arts Emphasis
Accreditation: &WC, CIDA

01 President ...Mr. Gregory J. MARICK
07 Director of Admissions ...Mr. Harry RAMOS
26 Director of PR & Marketing ...Ms. Sandra BERNARDO
18 Facilities Director ...Mrs. Margaret CARROLL

† Regional accreditation is carried under the parent institution, Argosy University in Orange, CA.

The Art Institute of California, A College of Argosy University - Sacramento (C)

2850 Gateway Oaks Drive, Suite 100,
Sacramento CA 95833-4348
County: Sacramento Identification: 666619
Unit ID: 450094
Telephone: (916) 830-6320 Carnegie Class: Spec/Arts
FAX Number: (916) 830-6344 Calendar System: Quarter
URL: www.artinstitutes.edu/sacramento
Established: 2007 Annual Undergrad Tuition & Fees: $18,648
Enrollment: 1,304 Coed
Affiliation or Control: Proprietary IRS Status: Proprietary
Highest Offering: Baccalaureate
Program: Liberal Arts And General; Professional; Technical Emphasis
Accreditation: &WC

01 President ...Terry A. MARLINK

† Regional accreditation is carried under the parent institution, Argosy University in Orange, CA.

The Art Institute of California, A College of Argosy University - San Diego (D)

7650 Mission Valley Road, San Diego CA 92108-4423
County: San Diego FICE Identification: 023276
Unit ID: 117113
Telephone: (858) 598-1200 Carnegie Class: Spec/Arts
FAX Number: (619) 291-3206 Calendar System: Quarter
URL: www.the-art-institutes.info
Established: 1981 Annual Undergrad Tuition & Fees: $18,748
Enrollment: 2,101 Coed
Affiliation or Control: Proprietary IRS Status: Proprietary
Highest Offering: Baccalaureate
Program: Occupational; Liberal Arts And General
Accreditation: &WC, ACFEI, CIDA

01 President ...Elizabeth ERICKSON
05 Dean of Academic Affairs ...Rebecca BROWNING
10 Chief Financial Officer ...Beverly MILLER
32 Dean of Student Affairs ...Jennifer DONALDSON
07 Director of Admissions ...John KERNS
36 Director of Career Services ...Jean BRANAN
37 Director Student Financial Services ...Laverne ARBERRY-LAMB
06 Registrar ...Jesse ROGERS

† Regional accreditation is carried under the parent institution, Argosy University in Orange, CA.

The Art Institute of California, A College of Argosy University - San Francisco (E)

1170 Market Street, San Francisco CA 94102-4908
County: San Francisco FICE Identification: 007236
Unit ID: 117928
Telephone: (888) 493-3261 Carnegie Class: Spec/Arts
FAX Number: (415) 863-6344 Calendar System: Quarter
URL: www.aisf.artinstitutes.edu
Established: 1939 Annual Undergrad Tuition & Fees: $24,864
Enrollment: 1,582 Coed
Affiliation or Control: Proprietary IRS Status: Proprietary
Highest Offering: Master's
Program: Occupational; 2-Year Principally Bachelor's Creditable; Liberal Arts And General
Accreditation: &WC

01 President ...Mr. Byron CHUNG
05 Dean of Academic Affairs ...Dr. Joe LAVILLA
32 Dean of Student Affairs ...Ms. Michelle SKOOR
07 Director of Admissions ...Mr. Louie GARCIA
36 Director of Career Services ...Ms. Donna DESSART
37 Director of Student Financial Svcs ...Mrs. Janett CABANERO
15 HR Generalist ...Mrs. Laura DELAROZ

† Regional accreditation is carried under the parent institution, Argosy University in Orange, CA.

The Art Institute of California, A College of Argosy University - Sunnyvale (F)

1120 Kifer Road, Sunnyvale CA 94086-5303
County: Santa Clara Identification: 666620
Unit ID: 451848
Telephone: (408) 962-6400 Carnegie Class: Spec/Arts
FAX Number: (408) 962-6498 Calendar System: Other
URL: www.artinstitutes.edu/sunnyvale
Established: 2008 Annual Undergrad Tuition & Fees: N/A
Enrollment: 567 Coed
Affiliation or Control: Proprietary IRS Status: Proprietary
Highest Offering: Baccalaureate
Program: Liberal Arts And General
Accreditation: &WC

01 President ...Mr. Timothy J. HANSEN

† Regional accreditation is carried under the parent institution, Argosy University in Orange, CA.

Azusa Pacific University (G)

901 E Alosta Avenue, Azusa CA 91702-7000
County: Los Angeles FICE Identification: 001117
Unit ID: 109785
Telephone: (626) 969-3434 Carnegie Class: DRU
FAX Number: (626) 969-7180 Calendar System: Semester
URL: www.apu.edu
Established: 1899 Annual Undergrad Tuition & Fees: $37,164
Enrollment: 9,929 Coed
Affiliation or Control: Independent Non-Profit IRS Status: 501(c)3
Highest Offering: Doctorate
Program: Liberal Arts And General; Teacher Preparatory; Professional
Accreditation: WC, ART, CLPSY, IACBE, MUS, NURSE, PTA, SW, TED, THEOL

01 President ...Dr. Jon R. WALLACE
05 Provost ...Dr. Mark STANTON
26 Exec Vice Pres External Affairs ...Mr. David E. BIXBY
11 Exec Vice President Administration ...Mr. John C. REYNOLDS
32 Senior Vice Pres for Student Life ...Dr. Terry FRANSON
10 Vice President Business Affairs/CFO ...Mr. Bob L. JOHANSEN
43 VP Legal Affs/Cmty Rels/Gen Counsel ...Mr. Mark DICKERSON
84 VP for Enrollment Mangement ...Mr. David DUFAULT-HUNTER
58 Vice Provost Graduate Programs ...Dr. Diane GUIDO
20 Vice Provost Undergraduate Programs ...Dr. Kim DENU
35 AVP Student Life/Chief Judicial Ofc ...Mr. Willie HAMLETT
84 AVP Academic Enrollment/Student Svc ...Mrs. Heather PETRIDIS
26 Assoc VP University Relations ...Mr. David PECK
49 Dean College Liberal Arts/Sci ...Dr. David WEEKS
83 Int Dean School Behav/Appl Sciences ...Dr. Rose LIEGLER
50 Dean School of Business Mgmt ...Dr. Ilene BEZJIAN
53 Dean School of Education ...Dr. Anita HENCK
73 Dean Haggard School of Theology ...Dr. Scott DANIELS
64 Acting Dean School of Music ...Mr. Don NEUFELD
66 Dean School of Nursing ...Dr. Aja LESH
51 Dean Ctr Adult/Professional Studies ...Dr. Fred GARLETT
35 Assoc Dean Students/Dir Student Act ...Mrs. Shino SIMONS
15 Exec Director Human Resources ...Vacant
13 Associate Vice President/CIO ...Mr. Don DAVIS
30 Executive Director Development ...Mrs. Louise FURROW
21 Executive Director Finance ...Ms. Joyce WILLIAMS
88 Exec Director University Services ...Mr. Roger HODSDON
42 Campus Pastor ...Mr. Woody MOORWOOD
37 Dir Graduate Student Financial Svcs ...Mrs. Michelle JOHNSON
88 Registrar-Graduate ...Mrs. Norma MOCABEE
06 Registrar-Undergraduate & CAPS ...Vacant
29 Director Alumni Relations ...Mr. Craig WALLACE
09 Director Acad Info Mgmt Analysis ...Vacant
41 Director Athletics ...Mr. Gary PINE
38 Director Counseling Center ...Dr. Bill FIALA
37 Director UG/CAPS Student Finan Svcs ...Mr. Todd ROSS
18 Director Facilities Management ...Mr. Dennis ROBBINS
92 Director of Honors Program ...Dr. Vicky BOWDEN
07 Director Undergraduate Admissions ...Mr. David BURKE
36 Director Career Services ...Ms. Lynn PEARSON

Barstow Community College District (H)

2700 Barstow Road, Barstow CA 92311-6699
County: San Bernardino FICE Identification: 001119
Unit ID: 109907
Telephone: (760) 252-2411 Carnegie Class: Assoc/Pub-S-SC
FAX Number: (760) 252-1875 Calendar System: Semester
URL: www.barstow.edu
Established: 1959 Annual Undergrad Tuition & Fees (In-District): $1,104
Enrollment: 3,392 Coed
Affiliation or Control: State/Local IRS Status: 501(c)3
Highest Offering: Associate Degree
Program: Occupational; 2-Year Principally Bachelor's Creditable
Accreditation: WJ

01 President ...Dr. Thom M. ARMSTRONG
04 Exec Assistant to the President ...Mrs. Michelle HENDERSON
10 Vice President Administrative Svcs ...Mr. Virgil STANFORD
05 Vice President Academic Affairs ...Mr. Stephen B. EATON
32 Vice President Student Affairs ...Mr. James DANIELS
16 Vice President Human Resources ...Ms. Trinda BEST
09 Dean Research Dev & Planning ...Vacant
103 Dean Workforce & Economic Dev ...Mr. Ken EAVES
49 Interim Dean of Instruction ...Ms. Penny SHREVE
27 Director Public Information ...Ms. Maureen O. STOKES
18 Interim Director M&O ...Mr. Richard HERNANDEZ
21 Director Fiscal Services ...Ms. Shawna L. ROBBINS
84 Director Enrollment Services ...Ms. Heather CALDON
41 Interim Athletic Director ...Dr. Michael KARPEL
35 Director Student Dev & Outreach ...Mrs. Joann GARCIA
88 Director CTE Grants ...Ms. Sandra THOMAS
88 Director Military Programs ...Mr. Jerry PETERS
88 Interim Dir Special Pgms & Svcs ...Ms. Joann GARCIA
40 Bookstore Manager ...Mrs. Kimberly YOUNG
21 Budget Analyst ...Mrs. Debbie WYNNE

Bergin University of Canine Studies (I)

5860 Labath Avenue, Rohnert Park CA 94928
County: Sonoma FICE Identification: 041763
Unit ID: 461643
Telephone: (707) 545-3647 Carnegie Class: Not Classified
FAX Number: (707) 545-0800 Calendar System: Semester
URL: www.berginu.edu
Established: 1991 Annual Undergrad Tuition & Fees: $7,911
Enrollment: 34 Coed
Affiliation or Control: Independent Non-Profit IRS Status: 501(c)3
Highest Offering: Master's
Program: Occupational
Accreditation: ACICS

01 President ...Dr. Bonita M. BERGIN

Bethesda University of California (J)

730 N Euclid Street, Anaheim CA 92801-4115
County: Orange FICE Identification: 032663
Unit ID: 110060
Telephone: (714) 517-1945 Carnegie Class: Spec/Faith
FAX Number: (714) 683-1440 Calendar System: Semester
URL: www.buc.edu

Established: 1976 Annual Undergrad Tuition & Fees: $7,005
Enrollment: 330 Coed
Affiliation or Control: Independent Non-Profit IRS Status: 501(c)3
Highest Offering: Doctorate
Program: Religious Emphasis
Accreditation: **BI**, TRACS

01 President .... Pastor Yu Chul CHIN
05 Chief Academic Officer .... Dr. Man Tae KIM
10 Chief Business Officer .... Dr. Chan HEO
08 Head Librarian .... Ms. Ho K. WOO
07 Director of Admissions .... Ms. Jee Won HA

Biola University (A)

13800 Biola Avenue, La Mirada CA 90639-0001
County: Los Angeles FICE Identification: 001122
Unit ID: 110097
Telephone: (562) 903-6000 Carnegie Class: DRU
FAX Number: (562) 903-4748 Calendar System: 4/1/4
URL: www.biola.edu
Established: 1908 Annual Undergrad Tuition & Fees: $29,908
Enrollment: 6,251 Coed
Affiliation or Control: Independent Non-Profit IRS Status: 501(c)3
Highest Offering: Doctorate
Program: Liberal Arts And General; Teacher Preparatory; Professional
Accreditation: **WC**, ACBSP, ART, CLPSY, MUS, NURSE, THEOL

01 President .... Dr. Barry H. COREY
05 Provost/Sr Vice President .... Dr. David NYSTROM
30 Vice President Advancement .... Dr. Adam MORRIS
11 Vice President University Services .... Mr. Gregory R. BALSANO
10 Vice Pres Business/Financial Affs .... Mr. Michael PIERCE
32 Vice Pres Sudent Dev/Univ Plng/IT .... Dr. Chris GRACE
84 Vice Pres Enrollment Management .... Mr. Greg VAUGHAN
26 Vice Pres University Comm & Mktg .... Mrs. Irene NELLER
20 Vice Provost/Undergraduate Educ .... Dr. Patricia PIKE
20 Vice Provost/Fac Dev & Univ Assess .... Vacant
28 Vice Provost/Multi-Eth & Cross Cult .... Dr. Doretha O'QUINN
73 Dean Talbot School Theology .... Dr. Clinton E. ARNOLD
83 Dean Rosemead School Psychology .... Dr. Clark D. CAMPBELL
88 Dean Cook Sch Intercultural Studies .... Dr. Douglas PENNOYER
53 Dean School of Education .... Dr. June HETZEL
08 Dean of the Library .... Dr. Rodney M. VLIET
87 Director Summer Session & Interterm .... Dr. Pete MENJARES
35 Dean of Students .... Mr. Danny PASCHALL
06 Dean Academic Records/Inst Research .... Mr. Ken GILSON
15 Director Human Resources .... Mr. Ronald G. MOORADIAN
37 Director Financial Aid .... Mr. Jonathan CHOY
46 Director Financial Planning/Opers .... Ms. Sandie WEAVER
21 Director Financial Mgmt/Reporting .... Mr. David KOONTZ
13 Director Information Systems .... Mr. Gary WYTCHERLEY
29 Director Alumni Relations .... Mr. Richard BEE
19 Director Campus Safety .... Mr. John O. OJEISEKHOBA
90 Director Technology Services .... Mr. Steven R. EARLE
36 Director Career Services .... Ms. Jeanie JANG
41 Athletic Director .... Dr. David HOLMQUIST
42 Dean of Spiritual Development .... Dr. Todd PICKETT
40 Manager Bookstore .... Mr. Harry EDWARDS
24 Supervisor Media Center .... Ms. Jill WATSON
18 Director Facilities Services .... Mr. Brian PHILLIPS
38 Director Student Counseling .... Dr. Melanie TAYLOR
96 Director of Purchasing .... Mr. Jim SAMPLES
09 Dean of University Assessment .... Dr. Deborah TAYLOR

Brandman University (B)

16355 Laguna Canyon Road, Irvine CA 92618
County: Orange FICE Identification: 041618
Unit ID: 262086
Telephone: (949) 753-4774 Carnegie Class: Master's L
FAX Number: (714) 753-7875 Calendar System: Other
URL: www.brandman.edu
Established: 1958 Annual Undergrad Tuition & Fees: $15,000
Enrollment: 6,763 Coed
Affiliation or Control: Independent Non-Profit IRS Status: 501(c)3
Highest Offering: Doctorate
Program: Liberal Arts And General
Accreditation: **WC**, NURSE

01 Chancellor .... Dr. Gary BRAHM
12 Campus Director .... Ms. Jan HARTZ
05 Associate Dean of Education .... Ms. Patricia CLARK-WHITE
07 Director of Admissions .... Ms. Leticia ESPINOZA

† A member of the Chapman University System.

Bristol University (C)

2390 E. Orangewood Ave., Suite 485, Anaheim CA 92806
County: Orange FICE Identification: 033083
Unit ID: 397270
Telephone: (714) 542-8086 Carnegie Class: Not Classified
FAX Number: (714) 245-2425 Calendar System: Semester
URL: www.bristoluniversity.edu
Established: 1991 Annual Undergrad Tuition & Fees: $6,600
Enrollment: 50 Coed
Affiliation or Control: Proprietary IRS Status: Proprietary
Highest Offering: Master's
Program: Occupational; 2-Year Principally Bachelor's Creditable; Business Emphasis
Accreditation: **ACICS**

01 President .... Dr. Dwight LAYTON
03 VP Compliance .... Mr. Larry MADOSKI
05 Chief Academic Officer .... Dr. Linda MARTINEZ
37 Financial Aid Director .... Mr. Bobby PEPITO

Brooks Institute (D)

27 East Cota, Santa Barbara CA 93101
County: Santa Barbara FICE Identification: 001123
Unit ID: 110185
Telephone: (888) 304-3456 Carnegie Class: Spec/Arts
FAX Number: (805) 585-8001 Calendar System: Semester
URL: www.brooks.edu
Established: 1945 Annual Undergrad Tuition & Fees: $20,120
Enrollment: 791 Coed
Affiliation or Control: Proprietary IRS Status: Proprietary
Highest Offering: Master's
Program: Professional; Fine Arts Emphasis
Accreditation: **ACICS**

01 President .... Susan KIRKMAN
05 Dean of Education .... Vacant
10 Regional Controller .... Timothy HALSEY
07 Vice President Admissions .... Maggie BALDERAS
88 Dept Chair for Film & Communication .... Gail FISHER
108 Dir of Institutional Effectiveness .... Amanda BREY
36 Dir Career Services .... Katie HUBER
06 Registrar .... April REYES
26 Media Manager & Community Outreach .... Vacant
91 Director of Information Technology .... Greg LAWLER
08 Librarian .... Donna BURR

Brooks Institute (E)

5301 North Ventura Avenue, Ventura CA 93001-1023
County: Ventura Identification: 666250
Telephone: (805) 585-8000 Carnegie Class: Not Classified
FAX Number: (805) 585-8001 Calendar System: Semester
URL: www.brooks.edu
Established: 1945 Annual Undergrad Tuition & Fees: $20,120
Enrollment: 1,855 Coed
Affiliation or Control: Proprietary IRS Status: Proprietary
Highest Offering: Master's
Program: Occupational; Liberal Arts And General; Professional; Fine Arts Emphasis
Accreditation: **@WC**, ACICS

01 President .... Dr. Sue KIRKMAN

Bryan College (F)

2317 Gold Meadow Way, Gold River CA 95670-4443
County: Sacramento FICE Identification: 033993
Unit ID: 439826
Telephone: (916) 649-2400 Carnegie Class: Assoc/PrivFP
FAX Number: (916) 641-8649 Calendar System: Quarter
URL: www.bryancollege.edu
Established: 1996 Annual Undergrad Tuition & Fees: $17,550
Enrollment: 753 Coed
Affiliation or Control: Proprietary IRS Status: Proprietary
Highest Offering: Associate Degree
Program: Occupational; 2-Year Principally Bachelor's Creditable; Technical Emphasis
Accreditation: **ACCSC**

01 President .... Mr. Rob DILLMAN
05 Director of Education .... Ms. Christine ZMIJEWSKI
29 Dir of Student & Alumni Outreach .... Mr. Jeff HORTON
07 Director of Admissions .... Ms. Orquedia CHAVEZ
37 Director Student Financial Aid .... Mr. Ramiro ONTIVEROS
06 Registrar .... Mr. Michael KRYSHAK

Bryan College (G)

3580 Wilshire Boulevard, Suite 400,
Los Angeles CA 90010
County: Los Angeles FICE Identification: 007164
Unit ID: 110219
Telephone: (213) 484-8850 Carnegie Class: Assoc/PrivFP
FAX Number: (213) 483-3936 Calendar System: Semester
URL: www.bryancollege.edu
Established: 1940 Annual Undergrad Tuition & Fees: $12,270
Enrollment: 946 Coed
Affiliation or Control: Proprietary IRS Status: Proprietary
Highest Offering: Master's
Program: Occupational; 2-Year Principally Bachelor's Creditable
Accreditation: **ACICS**

01 President .... Mr. John KOLACINSKI

Butte College (H)

3536 Butte Campus Drive, Oroville CA 95965-8399
County: Butte FICE Identification: 008073
Unit ID: 110246
Telephone: (530) 895-2511 Carnegie Class: Assoc/Pub-R-L
FAX Number: (530) 895-2345 Calendar System: Semester
URL: www.butte.edu
Established: 1966 Annual Undergrad Tuition & Fees (In-District): $1,334
Enrollment: 14,007 Coed
Affiliation or Control: State/Local IRS Status: 501(c)3
Highest Offering: Associate Degree
Program: Occupational; 2-Year Principally Bachelor's Creditable
Accreditation: **WJ**, EMT

01 Superintendent/President .... Dr. Kimberly PERRY
05 VP Student Learning/Econ Devel .... Dr. Samia YAQUB
10 CBO/VP Administrative Services .... Mr. Andrew SULESKI
45 Vice President Planning & Info .... Mr. Les JAURON
32 Vice President Student Services .... Mr. Allen RENVILLE
20 Dean .... Mr. David DANIELSON
20 Dean .... Ms. Kam BULL
20 Dean .... Ms. Denise ADAMS
37 Director Financial Aid .... Ms. Carolyn STEPHEN
15 Director Human Resources .... Ms. Jamie CANNON
18 Dir Facilities Planning/Management .... Mr. Ken ALBRIGHT
09 Director of Institutional Research .... Dr. Baba ADAM
07 Director Admissions/Records .... Mr. Clinton SLAUGHTER
08 Director Library Services .... Dr. Luozhu CEN
12 Director Chico/Glenn Centers .... Mr. Rudy FLORES
103 Director Workforce Development .... Ms. Linda ZORN
26 Director of Marketing/Public Rels .... Ms. Lisa DELABY
41 Athletic Director .... Mr. Craig RIGSBEE
13 Director Information Services .... Mr. Doug CREMER
30 Director Institutional Advancement .... Mr. John GLIHA
21 Associate Business Officer .... Mr. Trevor STEWART
38 Coordinator of Counseling .... Ms. Susan CAREY

Cabrillo College (I)

6500 Soquel Drive, Aptos CA 95003-3194
County: Santa Cruz FICE Identification: 001124
Unit ID: 110334
Telephone: (831) 479-6100 Carnegie Class: Assoc/Pub-R-L
FAX Number: (831) 479-6425 Calendar System: Semester
URL: www.cabrillo.edu
Established: 1959 Annual Undergrad Tuition & Fees (In-District): $964
Enrollment: 15,387 Coed
Affiliation or Control: State/Local IRS Status: 501(c)3
Highest Offering: Associate Degree
Program: Occupational; 2-Year Principally Bachelor's Creditable
Accreditation: **WJ**, DH, MAC, RAD

01 President .... Dr. Brian KING
05 Vice President for Instruction .... Dr. Renee KILMER
10 Asst Supt/Vice Pres Business Svcs .... Ms. Victoria LEWIS
32 Asst Supt/Vice Pres Student Svcs .... Dr. Dennis BAILEY-FOUGNIER
13 Information Technology Director .... Dr. Dan BORGES
08 Librarian .... Mr. Georg ROMERO
27 Director Marketing & Communications .... Ms. Kristin FABOS
15 Director Personnel/Human Resources ... Ms. Loree L. MCCAWLEY
21 Director Business Services .... Mr. Graciano MENDOZA
07 Director of Enrollment Services .... Ms. Tama BOLTON
09 Dir Planning/Research/Knowledge Sys .... Vacant
18 Director Facilities Plng/Purchasing .... Mr. Joe NUGENT
40 Bookstore Manager .... Vacant

California Baptist University (J)

8432 Magnolia Avenue, Riverside CA 92504-3297
County: Riverside FICE Identification: 001125
Unit ID: 110361
Telephone: (951) 689-5771 Carnegie Class: Master's L
FAX Number: (951) 351-1808 Calendar System: Semester
URL: www.calbaptist.edu
Established: 1950 Annual Undergrad Tuition & Fees: $26,900
Enrollment: 5,413 Coed
Affiliation or Control: Southern Baptist IRS Status: 501(c)3
Highest Offering: Master's
Program: Liberal Arts And General; Teacher Preparatory; Professional
Accreditation: **WC**, ACBSP, MUS, NURSE

01 President .... Dr. Ronald L. ELLIS
04 Admin Asst to the President .... Ms. Ann CRAMER
10 Vice President for Finance & Admin .... Mr. Mark HOWE
21 Director of Financial Services .... Mr. Calvin SPARKMAN
21 Director of Accounting .... Ms. Jackie GONZALES
15 Human Resources Manager .... Ms. Julie FRESQUEZ
32 VP Enrollment & Student Services .... Mr. Kent DACUS
35 Dean of Students .... Mr. Anthony LAMMONS
39 Director of Residence Life .... Mr. Daron HUBBERT
35 Assistant Dean of Students .... Mr. Joe ADCOCK
85 Director of International Students .... Mr. Bryan DAVIS
38 Director of Enrollment Advising .... Ms. Shelly RUPARD
36 Director Career Services .... Mrs. Kushi JONES
19 Director of Public Safety .... Mr. Jim WALTERS
35 Assistant Dean of Students .... Ms. Heather HUBBERT
84 Assoc Dean Graduate Enrollment .... Ms. Gail RONVEAUX
84 Assoc Dean Enrollment Services .... Mr. Allen JOHNSON
27 Vice Pres Marketing & Communication .... Dr. Mark A. WYATT
88 Director of Conferences & Events .... Vacant
26 Director of Marketing .... Mr. Jeremy ZIMMERMAN
26 Director of Communications .... Dr. Katherine CHUTE
30 Vice Pres Institution Advancement .... Dr. Arthur CLEVELAND
44 Director of Annual Giving .... Mr. Brian BUNNELL
102 Grants Administrator .... Ms. Lauren SAVORD
29 Director Alumni & Parent Relations .... Mrs. Maria ZALESKY
106 Vice Pres for Online & Prof Studies .... Dr. David POOLE
07 Director of Enrollment Services .... Mr. Ted MEYER
13 Assoc Vice Pres of Technology .... Dr. Tran HONG
05 Provost .... Dr. Jonathan K. PARKER
46 Assoc Provost Institution Planning .... Dr. Neal MCBRIDE
20 Assoc Provost Administration .... Dr. Tracy WARD

108 Director of Assessment .... Mr. Phil MARTINEZ
24 Dir of Instructional Technology .... Mr. Keith CASTILLO
20 Dean of Academic Affairs .... Mr. Jeffrey BARNES
20 Associate Provost .... Dr. Dawn Ellen JACOBS
43 Vice Pres and General Council .... Mr. Adam BURTON
88 Vice Pres for Global Initiatives .... Dr. Larry LINAMEN
06 Registrar .... Ms. Shawnn KONING
08 Director of Library .... Mr. Steve EMERSON
18 Director Facilities/Physical Plant .... Mr. Steve SMITH
37 Director Financial Aid .... Ms. Rebecca SANCHEZ
41 Athletic Director .... Dr. Micah PARKER
105 Web Site Manager .... Mr. Waylon BAUMGARDNER
40 Director of University Bookstore .... Ms. Carol BRACEY
42 Dean Spiritual Life/Campus Minister .... Mr. John MONTGOMERY
53 Dean School of Education .... Dr. John SHOUP
54 Dean College of Engineering .... Dr. Anthony DONALDSON
64 Dean School of Music .... Dr. Judd BONNER
66 Dean School of Nursing .... Dr. Geneva OAKS
73 Dean School of Christian Ministries .... Dr. Chris MORGAN
83 Dean School of Behavioral Sciences .... Dr. H. Bruce STOKES
49 Interim Dean College of Arts & Sci .... Dr. James LU
48 Dean Architecture Art Design & Film ..... Mr. Mark A. ROBERSON
50 Dean School of Business .... Dr. Franco GANDOLFI
106 Dean for Online and Prof Studies .... Dr. Dirk DAVIS
76 Dean of College of Allied Health .... Dr. Charles SANDS

California Christian College (A)

4881 E University Avenue, Fresno CA 93703-3599

County: Fresno FICE Identification: 008844
Unit ID: 110918
Telephone: (559) 251-4215 Carnegie Class: Spec/Faith
FAX Number: (559) 251-4231 Calendar System: Semester
URL: www.calchristiancollege.edu
Established: 1955 Annual Undergrad Tuition & Fees: $7,970
Enrollment: 18 Coed
Affiliation or Control: Free Will Baptist Church IRS Status: 501(c)3
Highest Offering: Baccalaureate
Program: 2-Year Principally Bachelor's Creditable; Liberal Arts And General; Religious Emphasis
Accreditation: TRACS

01 President .... Mr. Wendell L. WALLEY
05 Academic Dean .... Dr. James H. COX
06 Registrar .... Dr. Tim POWELL
10 Chief Business Officer .... Mrs. Anna-Jean WALLEY
09 Dir Institutional Effectiveness .... Ms. Ingrid VOSS
08 Head Librarian .... Mrs. Nancy SINGH
37 Coordinator Financial Aid .... Ms. Melinda SCROGGINS
07 Admissions Representative .... Vacant
39 Director Student Housing .... Ms. Kissie TURNAGE

California Coast University (B)

925 N. Spurgeon Street, Santa Ana CA 92701-3515

County: Orange FICE Identification: 041276
Unit ID: 110936
Telephone: (714) 547-9625 Carnegie Class: Not Classified
FAX Number: (714) 547-5777 Calendar System: Other
URL: www.calcoast.edu
Established: 1973 Annual Undergrad Tuition & Fees: $9,500
Enrollment: 7,500 Coed
Affiliation or Control: Proprietary IRS Status: Proprietary
Highest Offering: Doctorate
Program: Professional; Business Emphasis
Accreditation: DETC

01 President .... Dr. Thomas M. NEAL
03 Executive Vice President .... Ms. Shelly MARQUARDT
05 Chief Academic Officer .... Dr. Cynthia TEEPLE
20 Director of Academic Affairs .... Mr. Douglas PETRIKAT

California College of the Arts (C)

1111 Eighth Street, San Francisco CA 94107-2247

County: San Francisco FICE Identification: 001127
Unit ID: 110370
Telephone: (415) 703-9500 Carnegie Class: Spec/Arts
FAX Number: (510) 655-3541 Calendar System: Semester
URL: www.cca.edu
Established: 1907 Annual Undergrad Tuition & Fees: $38,448
Enrollment: 1,966 Coed
Affiliation or Control: Independent Non-Profit IRS Status: 501(c)3
Highest Offering: Master's
Program: Professional
Accreditation: WC, ART, CIDA

01 President .... Mr. Stephen BEAL
05 Provost .... Ms. Melanie CORN
10 Sr VP Finance & Administration .... Mr. David KIRSHMAN
30 Sr Vice President of Advancement .... Ms. Susan AVILA
11 Vice President of Operations .... Ms. Jennifer STEIN
84 Vice Pres of Enrollment Management .... Ms. Sheri MCKENZIE
26 Vice President for Communications .... Ms. Chris BLISS
35 Vice President Student Affairs .... Mr. George SEDANO
15 Assoc Vice Pres Human Resources .... Ms. Sharyn SCHNEIDER
21 Assoc Vice Pres Financial Services .... Mr. Ken TANZER
20 Associate Provost .... Vacant
06 Registrar .... Mr. Jerry ALLEN
37 Director Financial Aid .... Ms. Silvia MARQUEZ
29 Director Alumni Relations .... Ms. Jessica RUSSELL
36 Director of Career Services .... Ms. Kate DEY
27 Chief Information Officer .... Ms. Mara HANCOCK
07 Director Undergrad Admissions .... Ms. Robynne ROYSTER
38 Director Student Counseling .... Dr. Tara RECH
45 Director of Campus Planning .... Mr. David MECKEL
18 Chief Facilities/Physical Plant .... Ms. Deborah FELDMANN
96 Director of Purchasing .... Ms. Jackie CRADDOCK
07 Director Graduate Admissions .... Mr. Noel DAHL

California College San Diego (D)

2820 Camino Del Rio S, Ste 300,
San Diego CA 92108-3821

County: San Diego FICE Identification: 021108
Unit ID: 110945
Telephone: (619) 680-4430 Carnegie Class: Spec/Health
FAX Number: (619) 295-5985 Calendar System: Other
URL: www.cc-sd.edu
Established: 1978 Annual Undergrad Tuition & Fees: $16,016
Enrollment: 1,455 Coed
Affiliation or Control: Proprietary IRS Status: Proprietary
Highest Offering: Master's
Program: Occupational; 2-Year Principally Bachelor's Creditable
Accreditation: ACCSC

01 Chief Operating Officer .... Mrs. Barbara THOMAS
05 Executive Director .... Dr. Ken WEBB

California Culinary Academy (E)

350 Rhode Island Street, San Francisco CA 94103

County: San Francisco FICE Identification: 022202
Unit ID: 111009
Telephone: (888) 897-3222 Carnegie Class: Assoc/PrivFP
FAX Number: (415) 771-2194 Calendar System: Other
URL: www.baychef.com
Established: 1977 Annual Undergrad Tuition & Fees: N/A
Enrollment: 749 Coed
Affiliation or Control: Proprietary IRS Status: Proprietary
Highest Offering: Associate Degree
Program: Occupational
Accreditation: ACCSC, ACICS, ACFEI

01 President .... Peter LEE
10 Vice Pres of Finance & Accounting .... Judy JIACOMETTI
07 Director of Admissions .... Donna INGENITO
37 Director of Student Finance .... Vacant
36 Director of Career Services .... Lisa WILSON

California Institute of the Arts (F)

24700 McBean Parkway, Valencia CA 91355-2397

County: Los Angeles FICE Identification: 001132
Unit ID: 111081
Telephone: (661) 255-1050 Carnegie Class: Spec/Arts
FAX Number: (661) 254-8352 Calendar System: Semester
URL: www.calarts.edu
Established: 1961 Annual Undergrad Tuition & Fees: $39,014
Enrollment: 1,441 Coed
Affiliation or Control: Independent Non-Profit IRS Status: 501(c)3
Highest Offering: Doctorate
Program: Professional; Fine Arts Emphasis
Accreditation: WC, ART, DANCE, MUS, THEA

01 President .... Dr. Steven D. LAVINE
05 Provost .... Dr. Jeannene PRZYBLYSKI
88 Vice Pres for Special Projects .... Lynn R. ROSENFELD
10 Vice Pres/Chief Financial Officer .... Donald MATTHEWSON
13 Vice President and CIO .... Michael CARTER
30 Vice Pres/Chief Advancement Officer .... Bianca ROBERTS
20 Associate Provost .... Jacqueline ELAM
21 Assoc Vice President and Controller .... Karla TALAVERA
18 Assoc Vice Pres Facilities .... Jesse SMITH
84 Assoc Provost Enrollment Management .... Audrey TANNER
20 Asst Provost for Academic Affairs .... Justine GARRETT
28 Asst Provost Equity and Diversity .... Vacant
08 Dean Div of Library & Info Resource .... Jeffrey GATTEN
88 Dean School of Critical Studies .... Amanda BEECH
88 Dean Sharon D. Lund School of Dance .... Stephan KOPLOWITZ
88 Dean School Film & Video .... Steve ANKER
88 Dean School of Theater .... Travis PRESTON
32 Dean of Students .... Yvonne GUY
57 Dean School of Art .... Thomas LAWSON
64 Dean Herb Alpert School of Music .... David ROSENBOOM
26 Executive Director Public Affairs .... Vacant
88 Director Community Arts Partnership .... Glenna AVILA
37 Interim Director of Financial Aid .... Cheryl GILLIES
29 Director Alumni Relations .... Nicole STARK LANE
15 Director of Human Resources .... Charmagne SHEARRILL
06 Registrar .... Nancy WHITTEMORE
07 Director of Admissions .... Molly RYAN

California Institute of Integral Studies (G)

1453 Mission Street, 4th Floor,
San Francisco CA 94103-2557

County: San Francisco FICE Identification: 012154
Unit ID: 110316
Telephone: (415) 575-6100 Carnegie Class: DRU
FAX Number: (415) 575-1264 Calendar System: Semester
URL: www.ciis.edu
Established: 1968 Annual Undergrad Tuition & Fees: $19,585
Enrollment: 1,423 Coed
Affiliation or Control: Independent Non-Profit IRS Status: 501(c)3
Highest Offering: Doctorate
Program: Professional
Accreditation: WC

01 President .... Mr. Joseph L. SUBBIONDO
05 Academic Vice President .... Dr. Judie WEXLER
32 Dean of Students/Director Diversity .... Ms. Shirley STRONG
29 Dean of Alumni/Dir of Travel Stds .... Dr. Richard BUGGS
20 Dean Academic Plng/Administration .... Mr. Chip B. GOLDSTEIN
10 Controller/Director Finance .... Mr. Ken ABIKO
30 Director of Development .... Ms. Dorotea REYNA
16 Director of Human Resources .... Ms. S. Michelle COLEMAN
07 Dean Admissions & Financial Aid .... Mr. Michael GRIFFIN
13 Director of Info Systems Technology .... Mr. Scott CILIBERTI
08 Library Director .... Ms. Lise DYCKMAN
06 Registrar .... Mr. Dan GURLER
26 Director of Communications .... Mr. Jim David MARTIN
37 Director of Financial Aid .... Ms. Marisol NEALON
51 Director of Public Programs .... Mr. Karim BAER
18 Director Facilities & Operations .... Mr. Jonathan MILLS
40 Bookstore Manager .... Mr. Steven SWANSON
85 International Student Advisor .... Ms. Jody O'CONNOR

California Institute of Technology (H)

1200 E California Boulevard, Pasadena CA 91125-0001

County: Los Angeles FICE Identification: 001131
Unit ID: 110404
Telephone: (626) 395-6811 Carnegie Class: RU/VH
FAX Number: (626) 795-1547 Calendar System: Trimester
URL: www.caltech.edu
Established: 1891 Annual Undergrad Tuition & Fees: $39,588
Enrollment: 2,231 Coed
Affiliation or Control: Independent Non-Profit IRS Status: 501(c)3
Highest Offering: Doctorate
Program: Liberal Arts And General; Professional
Accreditation: WC, ENG

01 President .... Dr. Jean-Lou A. CHAMEAU
04 Executive Assistant to President .... Mrs. Mary L. WEBSTER
05 Provost .... Dr. Edward M. STOLPER
88 Vice President/Director JPL .... Dr. Charles ELACHI
10 Vice President Business & Finance .... Mr. Dean W. CURRIE
30 Vice Pres Dev/Institute Relations .... Mr. Brian K. LEE
32 Vice President Student Affairs .... Dr. Anneila I. SARGENT
43 General Counsel .... Ms. Victoria D. STRATMAN
20 Vice Provost .... Dr. Melany L. HUNT
20 Vice Provost .... Dr. Morteza GHARIB
15 Assoc Vice Pres HR/Campus Svcs .... Ms. Julia M. MCCALLIN
44 Asst Vice President Development .... Vacant
31 Assoc VP Campus & Cmty Relations .Ms. Denise NELSON NASH
86 Director Govt Rels .... Mr. Hall P. DAILY
35 Senior Dir for Student Activities .... Mr. Tom N. MANNION
26 Asst VP Marketing & Communications .... Ms. Kristen BROWN
81 Chair Biology Division .... Dr. Stephen L. MAYO
81 Chair Chemistry & Chemical Engr Div .Dr. Jacqueline K. BARTON
54 Chair Engr & Applied Science Div .... Dr. Ares J. ROSAKIS
65 Chair Geology/Planet Science Div .... Dr. Kenneth FARLEY
79 Chair Humanities/Social Science Div .... Dr. Jonathan N. KATZ
81 Chair Physics/Math/Astro Division .... Dr. B. T. SOIFER
06 Registrar .... Mrs. Mary N. MORLEY
07 Director of Admissions .... Mr. Jarrid WHITNEY
08 University Librarian .... Ms. Kimberly DOUGLAS
14 Chief Information Officer .... Mr. Rich E. FAGEN
18 Assoc Vice Pres for Facilities .... Mr. James W. COWELL, JR.
18 Sr Director Facilities Management .... Mr. William R. TAYLOR
19 Manager Security Office .... Mr. Gregg HENDERSON
22 Director Employee Affirm Act/ Rels .... Ms. April WHITE CASTENADA
23 Director Health Services .... Dr. Stuart C. MILLER
25 Director Sponsored Research .... Dr. Richard P. SELIGMAN
29 Executive Director Alumni Assoc .... Ms. Alexandra C. TOBEK
37 Director Financial Aid .... Mr. Don CREWELL
36 Director Career Development .... Ms. Lauren B. STOLPER
40 Manager Bookstore .... Ms. Karyn SEIXAS
41 Director Athletics & Physical Ed .... Ms. Betsy MITCHELL
58 Dean of Graduate Studies .... Dr. Joseph E. SHEPHERD
88 Dean of Students .... Dr. D. R. KIEWIET
88 Associate Dean of Students .... Dr. Barbara C. GREEN
85 Director International Student Pgm .... Ms. Marjory GOODING
96 Dir of Purchasing & Payment Svcs .... Ms. Tina LOWENTHAL

California Intercontinental University (I)

1470 Valley Vista Drive, Suite 150,
Diamond Bar CA 91765-3954

County: Los Angeles Identification: 666670
Telephone: (909) 396-6090 Carnegie Class: Not Classified
FAX Number: (909) 804-5151 Calendar System: Other
URL: www.caluniversity.edu
Established: 2003 Annual Undergrad Tuition & Fees: $18,000
Enrollment: 215 Coed
Affiliation or Control: Proprietary IRS Status: Proprietary
Highest Offering: Doctorate
Program: Professional; Business Emphasis
Accreditation: DETC

01 Chief Executive Officer .... Mr. Senthil B. KUMAR
05 Chief Academic Ofcr/Dean Acad Affs .... Dr. Fathiah INSERTO

California International Business University (A)

520 West Ash Street 3rd Floor, San Diego CA 92101
County: San Diego Identification: 666711
Telephone: (619) 702-9400 Carnegie Class: Not Classified
FAX Number: (619) 702-9476 Calendar System: Quarter
URL: www.cibu.edu
Established: 1994 Annual Undergrad Tuition & Fees: $13,000
Enrollment: 235 Coed
Affiliation or Control: Independent Non-Profit IRS Status: 501(c)3
Highest Offering: Master's
Program: Professional; Business Emphasis
Accreditation: **ACICS**

01 President ....Dr. Phillip BABB

California Lutheran University (B)

60 W Olsen Road, Thousand Oaks CA 91360-2787
County: Ventura FICE Identification: 001133
Unit ID: 110413
Telephone: (805) 492-2411 Carnegie Class: Master's L
FAX Number: (805) 493-3513 Calendar System: Semester
URL: www.clunet.edu
Established: 1959 Annual Undergrad Tuition & Fees: $46,240
Enrollment: 4,103 Coed
Affiliation or Control: Evangelical Lutheran Church In America
IRS Status: 501(c)3
Highest Offering: Doctorate
Program: Liberal Arts And General; Teacher Preparatory; Professional
Accreditation: **WC**, TED

01 President ....Dr. Christopher KIMBALL
05 Provost/Vice Pres Academic Affairs ....Ms. Leanne NEILSON
30 Vice Pres University Advancement ....Mr. Stephen WHEATLY
10 Vice Pres Admin/Finance/Treasurer ....Ms. Karen DAVIS
32 Vice Pres Stdnt Life/Dean of Stdnts ....Mr. William ROSSER
84 VP Enrollment Mgmt & Marketing ....Dr. Matthew WARD
08 Assoc Provost for Information Svcs ....Mr. Julius BIANCHI
18 Assoc Vice Pres Facilities ....Mr. Ryan VAN OMMEREN
26 Assc Vice Pres University Relations ....Ms. Lynda FULFORD
49 Dean College Arts & Sciences ....Dr. Joan GRIFFIN
53 Dean of School of Education ....Dr. George PETERSEN
50 Dean of School of Business ....Dr. Charles MAXEY
88 Director Church Relations ....Rev. Arne BERGLAND
15 Director of Human Resources ....Ms. Susan TOLLE
06 Director Academic Svcs/Registrar ....Ms. Maria KOHNKE
42 University Pastor ....Rev. Scott MAXWELL-DOHERTY
42 University Pastor ....Rev. Melissa MAXWELL-DOHERTY
44 Director Estate & Gift ....Ms. Shannon YASMAN
41 Director Athletics ....Mr. Daniel KUNTZ
55 Director Adult Degree Program ....Dr. Lisa BUONO
36 Director of Career Services ....Ms. Cindy LEWIS
35 Director Multicultural/Intl Pgm ....Dr. Juanita HALL
21 Dir of Budget/Management Analysis ....Ms. Barbara REX
29 Director Alumni Relations ....Ms. Rachel RONNING LINDGREN
38 Director Counseling Services ....Dr. Alan GOODWIN
19 Director Security/Safety ....Mr. Frederick MILLER

California Maritime Academy (C)

200 Maritime Academy Drive, Vallejo CA 94590-0644
County: Solano FICE Identification: 001134
Unit ID: 111188
Telephone: (707) 654-1000 Carnegie Class: Bac/Diverse
FAX Number: (707) 654-1001 Calendar System: Semester
URL: www.csum.edu
Established: 1929 Annual Undergrad Tuition & Fees (In-State): $8,240
Enrollment: 889 Coed
Affiliation or Control: State IRS Status: 501(c)3
Highest Offering: Baccalaureate
Program: Occupational; Liberal Arts And General; Technical Emphasis
Accreditation: **WC**, ENG, ENGT, IACBE

01 President ....RADM. Thomas A. CROPPER, USN RET
05 Provost/VP Academic Affairs ....Dr. Gerald JAKUBOWSKI
10 Vice Pres Administration/Finance ....Mr. Kurtis D. LOHIDE
30 VP Univ Advancement/Exec Dir Found ....Ms. Beverly BYL
20 Assoc VP Academic Affairs ....Mr. Steve KRETA
20 Academic Dean ....Dr. Nael ALY
32 Dean of Students ....Dr. Debborah HEBERT
88 Master of Training Ship ....Capt. Harry BOLTON
29 Director Development/Alumni Rels ....Ms. Sylvia REGALADO
21 Budget Officer ....Mr. Steve MASTRO
06 Registrar ....Ms. Evelyn ANDREWS
08 Director of Library ....Mr. Richard ROBISON
07 Dir Admissions/Enrollment Services ....Mr. Marc MCGEE
37 Director of Financial Aid ....Ms. Nicole HILL
88 Executive Director CMA Services ....Ms. Diane RAWICZ
88 Director Ctr Excellence & Learning ....Dr. Vivienne MCCLENDON
36 Director Career Development ....Mr. James DALSKE
18 Director Facilities Planning ....Mr. Roger JAECKEL
19 Chief Security Officer ....Chief Roseann RICHARD
22 Director of Human Resources ....Ms. Kay MILLER
41 Director of Athletics ....Mr. Marv CHRISTOPHER
26 Director Public Relations ....Ms. Jennifer WHITTY
40 Bookstore Manager ....Ms. Beth AYERS
96 Purchasing Manager ....Ms. Vineeta DHILLON

California Miramar University (D)

9750 Miramar Road Suite 180, San Diego CA 92126-7501
County: San Diego Identification: 666713
Telephone: (858) 653-3000 Carnegie Class: Not Classified
FAX Number: (858) 653-6786 Calendar System: Other
URL: www.calmu.edu
Established: 2005 Annual Undergrad Tuition & Fees: $7,050
Enrollment: N/A Coed
Affiliation or Control: Proprietary IRS Status: Proprietary
Highest Offering: Doctorate
Program: Professional
Accreditation: **DETC**, ACICS

01 President ....Dr. Dominic MWENJA
07 Admissions Director ....Ms. Jeanie FOSTER

California National University for Advanced Studies (E)

8550 Balboa Boulevard, Suite 210,
Northridge CA 91325-3576
County: Los Angeles Identification: 666786
Telephone: (800) 782-2422 Carnegie Class: Not Classified
FAX Number: (818) 830-2418 Calendar System: Trimester
URL: www.cnuas.edu
Established: 1993 Annual Undergrad Tuition & Fees: $7,350
Enrollment: 703 Coed
Affiliation or Control: Proprietary IRS Status: Proprietary
Highest Offering: Master's
Program: Professional
Accreditation: **DETC**

01 President ....Dr. Carlton G. BRYANT
32 Vice Pres Student Affs/Registrar ....Ms. Stephanie M. SMITH
05 Director of Instruction ....Dr. Carol BACKER
50 Dean Business Administration ....Dr. Philip CHONG
54 Associate CNU Col of Engineering ....Dr. Robert RYAN
06 Consult to CNU VP Stdt Affs/Registr ....Dr. Philip CHONG
14 MIS Director ....Mr. Charles NG

California Northstate College of Pharmacy (F)

10811 International Drive, Rancho Cordova CA 95670
County: Sacramento Identification: 667020
Telephone: (916) 631-8108 Carnegie Class: Not Classified
FAX Number: (916) 631-8127 Calendar System: Semester
URL: www.californiacollegeofpharmacy.org
Established: 2008 Annual Graduate Tuition & Fees: $44,661
Enrollment: N/A Coed
Affiliation or Control: Independent Non-Profit IRS Status: 501(c)3
Highest Offering: Doctorate; No Undergraduates
Program: Professional
Accreditation: **WC**, @PHAR

01 President ....Dr. Alvin CHEUNG
05 Dean ....Dr. Shane DESSELLE
11 Vice President of Operations ....Mr. Norman FONG
20 Assoc Dean Academic Affs/Research ....Dr. John MARTIN
32 Asst Dean Student Affs/Admissions ....Ms. Cyndi PORTER
08 Director of Library Resources ....Mr. Scott MINOR
06 Registrar ....Ms. Lisa ERCK

California Southern University (G)

930 Roosevelt, Irvine CA 92620
County: Orange Identification: 666770
Telephone: (714) 882-7800 Carnegie Class: Not Classified
FAX Number: (714) 480-0834 Calendar System: Semester
URL: www.calsouthern.edu
Established: 1978 Annual Undergrad Tuition & Fees: $6,000
Enrollment: N/A Coed
Affiliation or Control: Independent Non-Profit IRS Status: 501(c)3
Highest Offering: Doctorate
Program: Liberal Arts And General; Professional
Accreditation: **DETC**

01 President ....Dr. Carroll RYAN

*The California State University System Office (H)

401 Golden Shore, Long Beach CA 90802-4210
County: Los Angeles FICE Identification: 001136
Unit ID: 110501
Telephone: (562) 951-4000 Carnegie Class: N/A
FAX Number: (562) 951-4986
URL: www.calstate.edu

01 Chancellor ....Dr. Charles B. REED
03 Executive Vice Chancellor & CAO ....Dr. Ephraim P. SMITH
30 Vice Chanc Univ Rels/Advancement ....Mr. Garrett ASHLEY
15 Vice Chancellor Human Resources ....Ms. Gail BROOKS
100 Chief of Staff ....Ms. Sandra B. GEORGE
10 Executive Vice Chancellor & CFO ....Dr. Benjamin F. QUILLIAN
43 General Counsel ....Ms. Christine HELWICK

*California Polytechnic State University-San Luis Obispo (I)

1 Grand Avenue, San Luis Obispo CA 93407-9000
County: San Luis Obispo FICE Identification: 001143
Unit ID: 110422
Telephone: (805) 756-1111 Carnegie Class: Master's L
FAX Number: (805) 756-5400 Calendar System: Quarter
URL: www.calpoly.edu
Established: 1901 Annual Undergrad Tuition & Fees (In-State): $9,021
Enrollment: 18,762 Coed
Affiliation or Control: State IRS Status: 501(c)3
Highest Offering: Master's
Program: Liberal Arts And General; Teacher Preparatory; Professional; Technical Emphasis
Accreditation: **WC**, ART, BUS, CONST, CS, DIETD, DIETI, ENG, FOR, LSAR, MUS, NAIT, NRPA, PLNG

02 President ....Dr. Jeffrey D. ARMSTRONG
100 Chief of Staff ....Ms. Betsy KINSLEY
05 Provost/Vice Pres Academic Affs ....Dr. Kathleen ENZ FINKEN
10 Vice Pres Administration & Finance ....Mr. Lawrence R. KELLEY
32 Interim VP Student Affairs ....Mr. Preston C. ALLEN
30 Vice Pres Univ Advance/CEO Found ....Ms. Deborah READ
88 Exec Dir CP Corp/Assoc VP Comm Svcs ....Ms. Bonnie D. MURPHY
21 Associate Vice Pres Finance ....Mr. Richard M. RAMIREZ
44 Assoc VP Univ Adv/Chief Dev Officer ....Vacant
26 Assoc VP Strategic Communications ....Mr. Chip VISCI
15 Assoc Vice Pres Academic Personnel ....Dr. Al LIDDICOAT
39 Dir Univ Housing & Assoc VP/SA ....Mr. Preston C. ALLEN
20 Vice Provost Programs & Planning ....Dr. Erling A. SMITH
46 Assoc Vice Provost Systems/Res Mgmt ....Ms. Kimi M. IKEDA
44 Assoc Vice Pres Advancement ....Ms. Cassie CARTER
07 Asst VP Admiss/Recruitment/Fin Aid ..Mr. James L. MARAVIGLIA
21 Asst Vice President Admin & Finance ....Ms. Karen WEBB
29 Asst Vice Pres Alumni Relations ....Ms. Tracee DEHAHN
06 Registrar/Dir of Academic Records ....Mr. Cem SUNATA
22 Dir Employment Eq & Fac Recruit ....Ms. Martha CODY
41 Athletic Director ....Mr. Don OBERHELMAN
18 Director Facility Services ....Mr. Mark A. HUNTER
18 Dir Facil Planning/Capital Projects ....Mr. Joel NEEL
23 Director Health/Counseling Services ....Dr. Martin E. BRAGG
38 Interim Head of Counseling Services ....Dr. Elie N. AXELROTH
32 ASI Executive Director ....Mr. Richard G. JOHNSON
32 Int Dir Student Life & Leadership ....Mr. Stephan LAMB
40 Int Director El Corral Bookstore ....Mr. Phillip DAVIS
19 University Police Department ....Chief William WATTON
35 Dean of Students ....Dr. Jean DECOSTA
51 Dean Continuing Education ....Dr. Brian TIETJE
46 Dean Research & Graduate Pgm ....Dr. Susan C. OPAVA
27 Dean of Information Services/CIO ....Dr. Michael D. MILLER
47 Dean Agriculture/Food & Env Sci ....Dr. David J. WEHNER
48 Dean Architect/Environmental Design ....Ms. Christine THEODOROPOULOS
50 Dean Orfalea College of Business ....Dr. David P. CHRISTY
54 Dean College of Engineering ....Dr. Debra LARSON
49 Dean College of Liberal Arts ....Dr. Douglas EPPERSON
81 Dean Science & Mathematics ....Dr. Philip S. BAILEY, JR.
53 Director CSM School of Education ....Dr. Bob DETWEILER
36 Dir Career Services & Testing Svcs ....Mr. Martin C. SHIBATA
09 Director Inst Planning/Analysis ....Mr. Brent S. GOODMAN
37 Director Financial Aid ....Ms. Lois M. KELLY
15 Director Human Resources ....Ms. Beth E. GALLAGHER
96 Dir Contract Procrurement Risk Mgmt ....Mr. Dru ZACHMEYER
104 Director of International Education ....Dr. Raymond ZEUSCHNER
94 Chair Women's & Gender Studies ....Dr. Thomas TRICE
92 Director University Honors Program ....Dr. Sema E. ALPTEKIN

*California State Polytechnic University-Pomona (J)

3801 W Temple Avenue, Pomona CA 91768-2557
County: Los Angeles FICE Identification: 001144
Unit ID: 110529
Telephone: (909) 869-7659 Carnegie Class: Master's L
FAX Number: (909) 869-4535 Calendar System: Quarter
URL: www.csupomona.edu
Established: 1938 Annual Undergrad Tuition & Fees (In-State): $6,624
Enrollment: 21,107 Coed
Affiliation or Control: State IRS Status: 501(c)3
Highest Offering: Master's
Program: Liberal Arts And General; Teacher Preparatory; Professional
Accreditation: **WC**, ART, BUS, CIDA, CS, DIETD, DIETI, ENG, ENGT, LSAR, PLNG, SPAA

02 President ....Dr. J. Michael ORTIZ
05 Provost/VP Academic Affairs ....Dr. Marten DENBOER
32 Vice President Student Affairs ....Dr. Douglas R. FREER
11 Vice Pres Administrative Affairs ....Dr. Edwin A. BARNES
30 Vice Pres University Advancement ....Mr. Scott C. WARRINGTON
20 Assoc Provost Academic Affairs ....Dr. Claudia L. PINTER-LUCKE
18 Assoc VP Facilities Planning & Mgmt ....Vacant
35 Assoc VP & Dean of Students ....Dr. Rebecca L. GUTIERREZ-KEETON
84 Assoc VP Enroll Management & Svcs ....Ms. Kathleen A. STREET
20 Spec Asst to the VP Faculty Affairs ....Mr. Gary HAMILTON
46 Assoc VP Research Research ....Dr. Frank W. EWERS
26 Assoc Vice Pres for Univ Relations ....Dr. Ron H. FREMONT, II
10 Assoc VP Finance/Admin Svcs ....Mr. Darwin LABORDO
35 Assoc VP Student Services ....Dr. Kevin T. COLANER

35 Assoc VP Student Affairs .... Ms. Christi R. CHISLER
13 Chief Information Officer .... Mr. John W. MCGUTHRY
28 Admin in Charge D/HR/Employee Svcs ...... Ms. Sharon L. REITER
04 Exec Assistant to the President .... Ms. Sandra L. DAVIS
47 Dean College of Agriculture .... Dr. Lester C. YOUNG
49 Int Dean Col Letters/Arts/Soc Sci .... Dr. Sharon HILLES
50 Dean Col of Business Admin .... Dr. Richard S. LAPIDUS
54 Dean College of Engineering .... Dr. Mahyar AMOUZEGAR
48 Dean Col Environmental Design .... Mr. Michael WOO
88 Dean Collins Sch of Hosp Mgmt .... Mr. Andrew H. FEINSTEIN
81 Dean College of Science .... Dr. Brian JERSKY
53 Dean College Educ/Integrat Stds .... Dr. Peggy KELLY
56 Dean Extended University .... Dr. Jerald CHESSER
44 Interim Assoc VP for Development .... Ms. Michelle L. MOYER
08 Dean University Library .... Mr. Ray WANG
41 Director of Athletics .... Mr. Brian R. SWANSON
86 Dir of Government/External Affairs .... Mr. Doug P. GLAESER
19 Chief of Police .... Mr. Michael W. GUERIN
102 Exec Dir Cal Poly Pomona Found Inc .... Mr. G. Paul STOREY
37 Director Student Financial Aid .... Ms. Diana Y. MINOR
06 Registrar/Academic Records Svcs .... Ms. Maria L. MARTINEZ
96 Director of Procurement .... Ms. Kathleen A. PRUNTY
84 Exec Dir Admissions and Outreach ..... Ms. Deborah L. BRANDON
30 Exec Director Capital Campaign .... Vacant

*California State University-Bakersfield (A)

9001 Stockdale Highway, Bakersfield CA 93311-1022
County: Kern FICE Identification: 007993
Unit ID: 110486
Telephone: (661) 654-2011 Carnegie Class: Master's L
FAX Number: (661) 654-3194 Calendar System: Quarter
URL: www.csub.edu
Established: 1965 Annual Undergrad Tuition & Fees (In-State): $7,213
Enrollment: 8,002 Coed
Affiliation or Control: State IRS Status: 501(c)3
Highest Offering: Master's
Program: Occupational; Liberal Arts And General; Teacher Preparatory; Professional; Nursing Emphasis
Accreditation: WC, BUS, NURSE, SPAA, SW, TED

02 President .... Dr. Horace MITCHELL
100 Executive Asst to the President .... Ms. Evelyn YOUNG
04 Presidential Aide .... Ms. Tina GIBLIN
05 Provost/Vice Pres Academic Affairs .... Dr. Soraya COLEY
10 Vice Pres Business/Admin Services .... Mr. Michael A. NEAL
32 Vice President Student Affairs .... Dr. Thomas WALLACE
84 Assoc VP for Enrollment Management ....Dr. Jacqueline MIMMS
12 Int Assoc VP Antelope Valley Center .... Dr. Craig KELSEY
20 Assoc VP for Academic Programs .... Dr. Carl KEMNITZ
20 Assoc VP for Faculty Affairs .... Dr. Beth RIENZI
15 AVP Human Res/Administrative Svcs .... Ms. Kellie GARCIA
88 Spec Asst to Provost Academic Aff .... Dr. Edwin SASAKI
21 Asst Vice Pres Fiscal Services .... Mr. Douglas WADE
14 Asst Vice Pres Info Technology Svcs .... Mr. Kallya SHENOY
18 Asst VP Facilities Management/Dev .... Mr. Pat JACOBS
09 Asst VP Inst Rsrch/Planning/Assess .... Dr. Laura HECHT
25 Assoc Provost for Grants & Resource .... Dr. Julio BLANCO
50 Dean Business/Public Administration .... Dr. John EMERY
53 Dean Social Sciences and Education .... Dr. Kathleen KNUTZEN
79 Dean Arts & Humanities .... Dr. Richard COLLINS
81 Dean Natural Sciences/Math/Eng .... Dr. Julio BLANCO
56 Dean Extended University Division .... Dr. Craig KELSEY
58 Dir of Academic Operation & Support .... Dr. John DIRKSE
08 Interim Dean University Library .... Dr. Curt ASHER
35 Dean Student Life .... Vacant
86 Int Exec Dir Government/Found Rels .... Dr. Soraya COLEY
06 Registrar .... Ms. Rita GUSTAFSON
88 Director Academic Advising .... Dr. Isabel SUMAYA
91 Dir Admn Computing Svcs/CMS Pgm Dir ...... Mr. Kallya SHENOY
07 Director Admissions & Records .... Mr. Min MYO
29 Director Alumni Relations .... Ms. Jennifer PATINO
41 Director Athletics .... Mr. Jeffrey KONYA
36 Dir for Cmty Engagement/Career Dev .... Ms. Jane EVARIAN
88 Director Children's Center .... Ms. Gladys GARCIA
96 Dir Contract Services/Procurement .... Mr. Michael CHAVEZ
38 Admin Supervisor Counseling Center .... Dr. Janet MILLAR
106 Director E-Learning Services .... Vacant
18 Director Facilities Operations .... Vacant
37 Director Financial Aid/Scholarships .... Dr. Ron RADNEY
92 Director CSUB Honors Program .... Dr. Michael FLACHMANN
39 Director Housing & Residential Life .... Ms. Crystal BECKS
88 Director Information Tech Support .... Vacant
26 Dir Public Affairs & Communications ....Mr. Robert MESZAROS
88 Director Safety & Risk Management .... Ms. Juli SMITH
88 Dir Svcs Students w/Disabilities .... Ms. Janice CLAUSEN
17 Director Student Health Services .... Dr. Oscar RICO
88 Director Student Recreation Center .... Mr. Mark HARRIMAN
88 Interim Director Student Union .... Mr. Mark HARRIMAN
88 Director Telecommunications .... Mr. David WATTS
88 Director Outreach Services .... Mr. Steve WATKIN
19 Director University Police .... Chief Marty WILLIAMSON
40 Bookstore Manager .... Vacant
88 Director of Food Services .... Mr. David CORRAL

*California State University-Channel Islands (B)

One University Drive, Camarillo CA 93012-8599
County: Ventura FICE Identification: 039803
Unit ID: 441937
Telephone: (805) 437-8400 Carnegie Class: Master's S
FAX Number: (805) 437-8414 Calendar System: Semester
URL: www.csuci.edu
Established: 2002 Annual Undergrad Tuition & Fees (In-District): $3,407
Enrollment: 4,179 Coed
Affiliation or Control: State/Local IRS Status: 501(c)3
Highest Offering: Master's
Program: Liberal Arts And General
Accreditation: WC, NURSE

02 President .... Dr. Richard R. RUSH
05 Provost/Vice Pres Academic Affairs .... Dr. Dawn NEUMAN
10 Vice Pres Finance/Administration .... Ms. Ysabel TRINIDAD
32 Vice President for Student Affairs .... Dr. Wm. Gregory SAWYER
13 Vice Pres Tech & Communication .... Dr. Michael BERMAN
26 Vice President for Advancement .... Vacant
100 Chief of Staff .... Dr. Therese EYERMANN
20 Associate Provost .... Dr. Renny CHRISTOPHER
88 Assistant Provost .... Dr. Dan WAKELEE
08 AVP University Library .... Ms. Amy WALLACE
56 AVP Extended University .... Dr. Gary BERG
50 AVP MVS School Business/Economics ..... Dr. William CORDEIRO
53 AVP School of Education .... Dr. Gary KINSEY
49 AVP Arts & Sciences .... Dr. Karen CAREY
30 AVP for Univ Development .... Ms. Nichole IPACH
25 AVP Research/Sponsored Programs .... Vacant
18 AVP Ops/Planning/Construction .... Mr. Dave CHAKRABORTY
21 AVP Finance & Budget .... Ms. Missy JARNAGIN
19 AVP Police & Parking .... Mr. John REID
15 AVP for Human Resources .... Ms. Anna PAVIN
88 AVP Resources & Auxiliaries .... Mr. Ed LEBIODA
88 AVP Assessment/ Co-Curricular Pgms .... Dr. George MORTEN
35 AVP Dean of Students .... Mr. Damien PENA
88 Dean of Faculty .... Vacant
84 AVP Enrollment Services .... Dr. Jane SWEETLAND
09 Director of Institutional Research .... Dr. Nelle MOFFETT
104 Dir Intl Pgms/AD Ctr Intl Affs .... Ms. Mayumi KOWTA
86 Director/Community/Govt Relations .... Ms. Celina ZACARIAS
29 Dir Development/Alumni Rels .... Ms. Tania GARCIA
88 Director Special Projects for F&A .... Ms. Caroline DOLL
06 Registrar .... Vacant
07 Director Admissions & Recruitment .... Ms. Ginger REYES
37 Dir of Financial Aid & Scholarships .... Ms. Sunshine GARCIA
39 Dir Housing & Residential Education .... Ms. Cindy DERRICO
96 Dir Procurement/Contract Services .... Ms. Valerie PATSCHECK
27 Dir of Communication/Marketing .... Ms. Nancy GILL

*California State University-Chico (C)

400 W First Street, Chico CA 95929-0001
County: Butte FICE Identification: 001146
Unit ID: 110538
Telephone: (530) 898-6116 Carnegie Class: Master's L
FAX Number: (530) 898-6824 Calendar System: Semester
URL: www.csuchico.edu
Established: 1887 Annual Undergrad Tuition & Fees (In-State): $7,438
Enrollment: 15,920 Coed
Affiliation or Control: State IRS Status: 501(c)3
Highest Offering: Master's
Program: Liberal Arts And General; Teacher Preparatory; Professional
Accreditation: WC, ART, BUS, CONST, CS, DIETD, DIETI, ENG, JOUR, MUS, NAIT, NRPA, NURSE, SP, SPAA, SW, TED, THEA

02 President .... Dr. Paul J. ZINGG
100 Chief of Staff/Dir of Govt Rels .... Ms. Karla J. ZIMMERLEE
05 Provost/Vice Pres Academic Affairs .... Dr. Belle WEI
10 Vice President Business/Finance .... Ms. Lorraine B. HOFFMAN
32 Vice President Student Affairs .... Mr. Drew CALANDRELLA
30 Vice Pres University Advancement .... Mr. Richard ELLISON
45 Vice Prov Planning/Res Allocation .... Dr. Arno RETHANS
46 Vice Provost for Reseach .... Dr. E.K. (Eun) PARK
84 Vice Provost Enrollment Management .... Ms. Meredith KELLEY
13 Vice Prov Information Resources/CIO ...... Mr. Michael SCHILLING
21 Assoc VP Financial Svcs/Univ Budget .... Ms. Stacie CORONA
15 Asst Vice Pres Faculty Affairs .... Vacant
47 Dean College of Agriculture .... Dr. Jennifer RYDER-FOX
51 Dean Continuing Education .... Ms. Debra E. BARGER
72 Dean Col Engr/Comp Sci/Const Mgmt .... Dr. Michael G. WARD
83 Dean Col Behavior & Social Sci .... Dr. Gayle E. HUTCHINSON
50 Interim Dean College of Business .... Dr. Julie INDVIK
79 Dean College Humanities/Fine Arts .... Dr. Joel ZIMBELMAN
81 Dean College Natural Sciences .... Dr. Frederika (Fraka) HARMSEN
60 Int Dean Coll Communication & Educ .... Ms. Maggie PAYNE
26 Director Public Affairs .... Mr. Joe WILLS
29 Director Alumni Relations .... Ms. Susan M. ANDERSON
09 Director Institutional Research .... Mr. William R. ALLEN
06 Registrar .... Ms. Jean H. IRVING
07 Director of Admissions .... Mr. Allan C. BEE
36 Director Student Placement .... Mr. Jamie STARMER
37 Director Financial Aid/Scholarships .... Mr. Dan REED
38 Int Dir Psyc Counslng/Wellness/Tstg .... Vacant
18 Director Facilities Management Svcs .... Mr. Luis CARABALLO
96 Director of Procurement .... Ms. Sara RUMIANO
92 Director Univ Honors Program .... Mr. John MAHONEY
35 Director Student Affairs .... Ms. Lisa ROOT
28 Coordinator of Diversity .... Mr. Tray ROBINSON

*California State University-Dominguez Hills (D)

1000 E Victoria Street, Carson CA 90747-0005
County: Los Angeles FICE Identification: 001141
Unit ID: 110547
Telephone: (310) 243-3300 Carnegie Class: Master's L
FAX Number: N/A Calendar System: Semester
URL: www.csudh.edu
Established: 1960 Annual Undergrad Tuition & Fees (In-State): $6,095
Enrollment: 10,519 Coed
Affiliation or Control: State IRS Status: 501(c)3
Highest Offering: Master's
Program: Liberal Arts And General; Teacher Preparatory; Professional
Accreditation: WC, CS, MT, MUS, NURSE, OPE, OT, SPAA, SW, TED, THEA

02 Interim President .... Dr. Willie J. HAGAN
05 Provost/Vice Pres Academic Affs .... Dr. Ramon TORRECILHA
10 Vice Pres Administration/Finance ....Ms. Mary Ann RODRIGUEZ
84 Vice Pres Enroll Mgmt/Stdnt Affairs .... Dr. Susan E. BORREGO
30 Vice President Univ Advancement .... Mr. Greg SAKS
20 Assoc VP Faculty Affairs .... Dr. Clarence "Gus" MARTIN
11 Assoc VP Administration/Finance .... Ms. Karen J. WALL
44 Assoc Vice President Development .... Ms. Andrea SALA
13 Assoc VP Information Tech .... Mr. Ronald F. BERGMANN
35 Assoc Vice President Student Life .... Dr. Daniels SONJA
21 Assoc VP Resource Management .... Dr. Janna BERSI
88 Assoc VP Student Success Services .... Dr. William FRANKLIN
15 Asst Vice Pres Human Resources/Mgmt .... Mr. Mark SEIGLE
04 Exec Assistant to the President .... Ms. Naomi GOODWIN
41 Director of Athletics .... Mr. Patrick GUILLEN
86 Dir University & Govt Relations .... Mr. David GAMBOA
26 Senior Media Relations Officer .... Ms. Brenda KNEPPER
37 Director of Financial Aid .... Ms. Delores LEE
06 Int Dir Student Records/Info Svcs .... Ms. Brandy MCLELLAND
38 Dir Student Health & Psych Services .... Dr. Janie MACHARG
09 Assoc Director Institutional Rsrch ... Mr. Pete VAN HAMERSVELD
19 Chief of Police .... Ms. Susan SLOAN
25 Director of Research/Funded Project .... Vacant
49 Acting Dean College of Liberal Arts .... Dr. Carol TUBBS
107 Actg Dean Col Professional Studies .... Dr. Anupama JOSHI
50 Dean Col of Bus Admin/Public Plcy .... Dr. H. Joseph WEN
56 Dean College of Ext & Intl Educ .... Dr. Margaret GORDON
83 Dean Col of Natural & Behav Sci .... Dr. Laura ROBLES
08 Dean of the Library .... Ms. Sandra PARHAM
18 Director of Physical Plant .... Mr. Jonathan C. SCHEFFLER
21 Accounting Director .... Ms. Cecilia PATZ
96 Director of Procurement & Contracts .... Mr. Emmit WILLIAMS
88 Director Outreach and Info Services ....Dr. Gayle BALL-PARKER

*California State University-East Bay (E)

25800 Carlos Bee Boulevard, Hayward CA 94542-3001
County: Alameda FICE Identification: 001138
Unit ID: 110574
Telephone: (510) 885-3000 Carnegie Class: Master's L
FAX Number: (510) 885-3808 Calendar System: Quarter
URL: www.csueastbay.edu
Established: 1957 Annual Undergrad Tuition & Fees (In-State): $7,047
Enrollment: 13,160 Coed
Affiliation or Control: State IRS Status: 501(c)3
Highest Offering: Doctorate
Program: Liberal Arts And General; Teacher Preparatory; Professional
Accreditation: WC, BUS, ENG, MUS, NURSE, SP, SW, TED

02 President .... Dr. Leroy M. MORISHITA
100 Chief of Staff .... Dr. Dianne RUSH WOODS
05 Provost/VP Academic Affairs .... Dr. James HOUPIS
10 Vice Pres Administration & Finance .... Mr. Brad WELLS
30 Int Vice President Univ Advancement .... Ms. Anne HARRIS
84 VP Plng/Enroll Mgmt/Student Affs .... Dr. Linda DALTON
20 Interim Assoc Provost Acad Affairs .... Ms. Linda S. DOBB
58 AVP Academic Pgms/Graduate Studies .... Dr. Susan OPP
45 Sr Dir Budget & Res for Acad Affs .... Ms. Carol REESE
21 Assoc VP Risk Mgmt/Internal Control .... Ms. Nyassa LOVE
18 Director Facilities Planning & Ops .... Mr. James ZAVAGNO
15 Director Human Resources .... Mr. Andre JOHNSON
07 Assoc VP Enrollment Dev and Mgmt .... Dr. Gregory SMITH
09 Assoc VP Planning & Inst Research ... Dr. A. Amber MACHAMER
36 Associate Vice Pres Student Affairs .... Mr. Stanley HEBERT, III
27 Assoc VP University Communications ....Mr. Jay COLOMBATTO
21 Deputy VP Finance .... Ms. Debbie BROTHWELL
46 Assoc VP Research/Sponsored Pgms .... Vacant
49 Dean Col of Ltrs/Arts/Soc Sci .... Dr. Kathleen ROUNTREE
50 Int Dean Col of Business/Economics .... Dr. Jagdish AGRAWAL
53 Dean Col of Educ/Allied Studies .... Dr. Carolyn NELSON
81 Dean College of Science .... Dr. Michael LEUNG
12 Int Exec Director Concord Campus .... Mr. Brian COOK
08 University Librarian .... Ms. Linda S. DOBB
29 Director of Alumni Relations .... Ms. Kate SHAHEED
13 Assoc VP IT Services .... Mr. Borre ULRICHSON
21 University Controller .... Mr. Darrell HAYDON
88 Exec Director of Student Retention .... Ms. Diana BALGAS
18 Director Facilities Operations .... Mr. Robert ANDREWS
23 Exec Director Student Health Svcs .... Ms. Andrea WILSON
24 Director Media & Acad Tech Svcs .... Mr. Matt COLLINS
41 Director of Athletics .... Ms. Debby DEANGELIS
19 Director University Police Dept .... Mr. James HODGES
39 Dir Housing & Residential Life .... Mr. Martin CASTILLO
38 Dir Stdnt Ctr for Acad Achieve .... Mr. John WHITMAN
51 Assoc VP Continuing/Intl Educ .... Mr. Brian COOK
38 Supervisor Counseling/Psych Svcs .... Mr. Ryan GUETERSLOH
22 Dir of Equity & Diversity .... Ms. Linda NOLAN
37 Director Student Financial Aid .... Ms. Rhonda JOHNSON
35 Dir Ofc Stdnt Dev/Judicial Affs .... Ms. Carol NOWICKI
96 Dir Procurement & Support Svcs .... Mr. Robert TODARO
36 Dir Acad Adv and Career Educ .... Mr. Lawrence BLISS

*California State University-Fresno (A)

5200 N. Barton Avenue, Fresno CA 93740-8027
County: Fresno FICE Identification: 001147
Unit ID: 110556
Telephone: (559) 278-4240 Carnegie Class: Master's L
FAX Number: (559) 278-4715 Calendar System: Semester
URL: www.csufresno.edu
Established: 1911 Annual Undergrad Tuition & Fees (In-State): $6,773
Enrollment: 21,961 Coed
Affiliation or Control: State IRS Status: 501(c)3
Highest Offering: Doctorate
Program: Liberal Arts And General; Teacher Preparatory; Professional
Accreditation: WC, BUS, CACREP, CIDA, CONST, CORE, DIETD, DIETI, ENG, MUS, NRPA, NURSE, #PH, PTA, SP, SPAA, SW, TED, THEA

02 President ... Dr. John D. WELTY
05 Provost/Vice Pres Academic Affairs ... Dr. William A. COVINO
10 VP Administration/Chief Fin Ofcr ... Ms. Cynthia TENIENTE-MATSON
30 Vice Pres University Advancement ... Dr. Peter N. SMITS
32 Vice Pres Student Affairs ... Dr. Paul M. OLIARO
15 Assoc VP Academic Personnel ... Dr. Michael CALDWELL
26 Assoc VP University Communications ... Ms. Shirley ARMBRUSTER
20 Associate Provost ... Dr. Lynnette ZELEZNY
20 Assoc VP/Dean Undergrad Students ... Dr. Dennis L. NEF
45 Assoc Vice President Research ... Dr. Thomas H. MCCLANAHAN
44 Assoc Vice Pres Univ Development ... Mr. R. Kent CLARK
21 Assoc VP for Financial Services ... Mr. Clinton MOFFITT
18 Associate Vice President Facilities ... Mr. Robert BOYD
84 Assoc Vice Pres Enrollment Services ... Mr. Bernie VINOVRSKI
51 Dean/Assoc VP Continuing/Global Ed ... Dr. Lynnette ZELEZNY
47 Dean Agricultural Science/Tech ... Dr. Charles D. BOYER
79 Dean of Arts & Humanities ... Dr. Vida SAMIIAN
50 Dean Craig School of Business ... Dr. Robert HARPER
53 Dean of Kremen School of Education ... Dr. Paul BEARE
54 Dean of Engineering ... Dr. Ramakrishna NUNNA
76 Dean of Health/Human Services ... Dr. Andrew HOFF
83 Dean of Social Sciences ... Dr. Luz GONZALEZ
81 Interim Dean of Sciences & Math ... Dr. Andrew HOFF
08 Dean of Library Services ... Mr. Peter MCDONALD
58 Dean of Graduate Studies ... Dr. Sharon BROWN-WELTY
23 Dir Univ Health/Psyc Svcs Oper ... Ms. Catherine FELIX
19 Director of Public Safety ... Mr. David HUERTA
41 Director of Athletics ... Mr. Thomas BOEH
16 Director of Human Resources ... Ms. Janice PARTEN
13 Director Technology Services ... Mr. Philip NEUFELD
09 Dir of Research Plng/Assessment ... Ms. Christina LEIMER
37 Director of Financial Aid ... Mr. Bernie OGDEN
06 Registrar ... Ms. Tina BEDDALL
27 Director of Publications ... Mr. Bruce WHITWORTH
29 Executive Director Alumni Relations ... Ms. Jacquelyn GLASENER
36 Director of Career Services ... Ms. Rita BOCCHINFUSO-COHEN
39 Director Univ Courtyard (Housing) ... Ms. Erin BOELE
96 Dir Procurement & Support Services ... Mr. Brian COTHAM
07 Director of Admissions ... Ms. Vivian FRANCO
35 Director of Student Involvement ... Ms. Sally RAMAGE
40 Bookstore Manager ... Mr. Ron DURHAM
37 Director Financial Aid ... Ms. Cecilia SCHOUWE
41 Director of Athletics ... Mr. Brian QUINN
85 Dir International Educ/Exchange ... Ms. Lay Tuan TAN
32 Assoc VP of Student Affairs ... Ms. Kandy MINK-SALAS
09 Asst VP Inst Res/Analytical Stds ... Dr. Edward SULLIVAN
96 Director of Contracts & Procurement ... Mr. Don GREEN
21 Associate VP of Financial Services ... Mr. Brian JENKINS
38 Act Exec Dir Stdnt Hlth/Counseling ... Dr. Leticia GUTIERREZ-LOPEZ
51 Dean University Extended Educ Svcs ... Dr. Harry NORMAN
79 Dean Humanities/Social Science ... Dr. Angela DELLA VOLPE
81 Actg Dean Natural Sciences & Math ... Dr. Robert KOCH
50 Dean Business & Economics ... Dr. Anil PURI
83 Dean Health & Human Development ... Dr. Shari MCMAHAN
57 Dean of the Arts ... Dr. Joseph ARNOLD
53 Dean of Education ... Dr. Claire CAVALLARO
54 Dean Engineering & Computer Science ... Dr. Raman UNNIKRISHNAN
60 Dean Communications ... Dr. William BRIGGS
35 Dean of Students ... Dr. Lea JARNAGIN
12 Dean Irvine Campus ... Dr. Susan COOPER

*California State University-Fullerton (B)

PO Box 34080, 800 N State Col Blvd, Fullerton CA 92831-3547
County: Orange FICE Identification: 001137
Unit ID: 110565
Telephone: (657) 278-2011 Carnegie Class: Master's L
FAX Number: (657) 278-2649 Calendar System: Semester
URL: www.fullerton.edu
Established: 1957 Annual Undergrad Tuition & Fees (In-State): $6,676
Enrollment: 36,156 Coed
Affiliation or Control: State IRS Status: 501(c)3
Highest Offering: Doctorate
Program: Liberal Arts And General; Teacher Preparatory; Professional
Accreditation: WC, ANEST, ART, BUS, BUSA, CACREP, CS, DANCE, ENG, JOUR, MIDWF, MUS, NURSE, PH, SP, SPAA, SW, TED, THEA

02 President ... Dr. Mildred GARCÍA
100 Chief of Staff ... Ms. Ann CAMP
05 Actg Vice President Academic Affs ... Dr. Steven MURRAY
10 Interim VP Admin & Finance/CFO ... Mr. William BARRETT
30 Interim VP University Advancement ... Ms. Theresa MENDOZA
13 VP Info Tech/Chief Info Tech Ofcr ... Mr. Amir DABIRIAN
102 AVP Operationas/CFO Foundation ... Mr. Ira UNTERMAN
44 Assoc VP University Advancement ... Mrs. Michele CESCA
58 AVP Graduate Studies/Research ... Dr. Dorota HUIZINGA
26 Assoc VP Strategic Communications ... Mr. Jeffrey COOK
20 Assoc Vice Pres Academic Affairs ... Dr. Jennifer FAUST
86 Asc VP Public Affs/Government Rels ... Mr. Owen HOLMES
84 Asst Vice Pres Enrollment Services ... Ms. Nancy DORITY
29 Exec Director Alumni Relations ... Ms. Dianna L. FISHER
06 Registrar ... Ms. Melissa WHATLEY
08 University Librarian ... Mr. Richard POLLARD
36 Director Career Development Center ... Mr. Jim CASE
45 Chief Budget Planning & Strategy ... Vacant
15 Actg Exec Director Human Resources ... Mr. Bill BARRETT
23 Acting Director Health Center ... Dr. Howard WANG
18 Director Physical Plant ... Mr. Willem VAN DER POL
19 Director University Police ... Mr. Dennis DEMAIO
28 Director Diversity/Equity Programs ... Ms. Rosamaria GOMEZ-AMARO

*California State University-Long Beach (C)

1250 Bellflower Boulevard, Long Beach CA 90840-0119
County: Los Angeles FICE Identification: 001139
Unit ID: 110583
Telephone: (562) 985-4111 Carnegie Class: Master's L
FAX Number: (562) 985-5419 Calendar System: Semester
URL: www.csulb.edu
Established: 1949 Annual Undergrad Tuition & Fees (In-State): $6,738
Enrollment: 34,870 Coed
Affiliation or Control: State IRS Status: 501(c)3
Highest Offering: Doctorate
Program: Liberal Arts And General; Teacher Preparatory; Professional
Accreditation: WC, AAFCS, ART, BUS, CEA, CS, DANCE, DIETD, DIETI, ENG, HSA, IPSY, KIN, MUS, NRPA, NURSE, PH, PTA, RTT, SP, SPAA, SW, TED, THEA

02 President ... Dr. F. K. ALEXANDER
05 Provost/Sr Vice Pres Academic Affs ... Dr. Donald PARA
11 Vice Pres Administration/Finance ... Ms. Mary E. STEPHENS
32 Vice President Student Services ... Dr. Douglas W. ROBINSON
30 Vice Pres University Rels/Devel ... Ms. Andrea TAYLOR
04 Exec Assistant to the President ... Dr. Karen NAKAI
10 Assoc VP Financial Management ... Ms. Sharon TAYLOR
20 Assoc Academic Officer/Vice Provost ... Dr. David DOWELL
35 Assoc Vice Pres Student Services ... Dr. Mary Ann TAKEMOTO
82 Assoc VP Intl Educ/Global Engagemnt ... Dr. Jeet JOSHEE
18 Assoc Vice Pres Phys Plng/Facil Mgt ... Mr. David SALAZAR
58 Assoc VP/Grad & Undergrad Programs ... Dr. Cecile LINDSAY
46 Assoc Vice Pres University Research ... Dr. T. C. YIH
16 Assoc VP Budget/Human Resource Mgmt ... Mr. Scott APEL
91 Int Assoc VP Academic Technology ... Mr. Roman KOCHAN
27 Asst Vice Pres Public Affairs ... Ms. Toni A. BERON-HUDSON
29 Asst Vice Pres Alumni Rel/Spec Proj ... Ms. Janice HATANAKA
09 Asst VP Institutional Research ... Dr. Van NOVACK
84 Asst Vice Pres Enrollment Services ... Mr. Thomas ENDERS
13 Asst VP Information Technology ... Ms. Janet FOSTER
76 Dean College Health/Human Svcs ... Dr. Kenneth MILLAR
50 Dean College of Business Admin ... Dr. Michael SOLT
53 Dean College of Education ... Dr. Marquita GRENOT-SCHEYER
54 Dean College of Engineering ... Dr. Forouzan GOLSHANI
57 Dean College of the Arts ... Dr. Raymond TORRES-SANTOS
81 Dean Col Natural Science/Math ... Dr. Laura KINGSFORD
49 Dean College of Liberal Arts ... Dr. Gerry RIPOSA
51 Dean Col Continuing & Profess Educ ... Dr. Jeet JOSHEE
08 Dean Library/Learning Resources ... Mr. Roman KOCHAN
39 Director Housing Administration ... Ms. Carol ROBERTS-CORB
15 Director Staff Personnel Services ... Vacant
41 Director Athletics ... Mr. Victor CEGLES
88 Dir Student Rels/Academic Support ... Ms. Donna GREEN
07 Director of Admissions ... Ms. Marie ALFORD
36 Director Career Plng & Placement ... Mr. Manuel PEREZ
23 Director Health Services ... Dr. Michael CARBUTO
19 Director Public Safety ... Mr. Fernando SOLORZANO
38 Director Counseling/Psych Services ... Dr. Brad COMPLIMENT
37 Director Financial Aid/Admissions ... Mr. Nicolas VALDIVIA
25 Director Found Grants/Contracts ... Ms. Sandra SHEREMAN
102 Executive Director Foundation ... Dr. Brian NOWLIN
28 Director of Equity & Diversity ... Ms. Larisa HAMADA
26 Chief Public Relations Officer ... Ms. Toni A. BERON-HUDSON
96 Director of Purchasing ... Ms. Laurinda FULLER
40 General Manager/49'er Shops ... Mr. Donald PENROD

*California State University-Los Angeles (D)

5151 State University Drive, Los Angeles CA 90032-8530
County: Los Angeles FICE Identification: 001140
Unit ID: 110592
Telephone: (323) 343-3000 Carnegie Class: Master's L
FAX Number: (323) 343-2670 Calendar System: Quarter
URL: www.calstatela.edu
Established: 1947 Annual Undergrad Tuition & Fees (In-State): $6,839
Enrollment: 21,284 Coed
Affiliation or Control: State IRS Status: 501(c)3
Highest Offering: Doctorate
Program: Liberal Arts And General; Teacher Preparatory; Professional
Accreditation: WC, ART, BUS, CACREP, CORE, CS, DIETC, DIETD, ENG, MUS, NURSE, SP, SPAA, SW, TED

02 President ... Dr. James M. ROSSER
05 Provost/Vice Pres Academic Affairs ... Dr. Ashish VAIDYA
32 Vice President Student Affairs ... Dr. Anthony R. ROSS
13 Vice Pres/Chief Technology Officer ... Mr. Peter QUAN
10 VP Administration & CFO ... Ms. Lisa M. CHAVEZ
44 Vice Pres Institutional Advancement ... Mr. Kyle C. BUTTON
20 Assoc VP Academic Affairs ... Dr. Cheryl L. NEY
11 Assoc VP Admin & Finance ... Mr. Jose GOMEZ
21 Asst VP Admin & Finance/Budget ... Ms. Mae SANTOS
35 Asst VP Student Affs/Student Svcs ... Ms. Nancy WADA-MCKEE
30 Asst VP University Development ... Ms. Collette G. ROCHA
29 Acting Exec Dir Alumni Relations ... Ms. Maria UBAGO
26 Exec Director Public Affairs ... Ms. Nancy MIRON
41 Director Intercollegiate Athletics ... Dr. Daniel BRIDGES
83 Dean Natural & Social Sciences ... Dr. James P. HENDERSON
08 University Librarian ... Ms. Alice K. KAWAKAMI
06 Univ Registrar & Dir of Enrollment ... Ms. Joan V. WOOSLEY
58 Dean Grad Studies/Research ... Dr. Lawrence M. FRITZ
88 Acting Assoc Dean Graduate Studies ... Dr. Karin A. ELLIOT BROWN
09 Director Institutional Research ... Dr. Mark PAVELCHAK
36 Director Career Placement & Plng ... Mr. Christopher LENZ
37 Director Student Financial Services ... Ms. Tamie NGUYEN
23 Director Health Center ... Dr. Monica JAZZABI
39 Director Housing Svc/Residence Life ... Mr. Stephen FLEISCHER
22 Director Equal Opportunity Pgm ... Ms. Becky HOPKINS
18 Director Facilities/Physical Plant ... Mr. Randy SHARP
19 Director Public Safety ... Mr. Joseph CURRERI
15 Asst VP Human Resources Management ... Ms. Lisa SANCHEZ
85 Director Intl Programs & Services ... Ms. Amy WANG
43 University Counsel ... Mr. Victor I. KING
07 Director of Outreach & Admissions ... Mr. Vince LOPEZ
96 Director Procurement & Contracts ... Mr. Thomas JOHNSON
09 Assoc Dir Institutional Research ... Ms. Vivien KO
28 Equity & Diversity Specialist ... Vacant
40 Manager Bookstore ... Mr. Todd MURPHY
88 Acting Dean Undergraduate Studies ... Dr. Steven JONES
49 Dean Arts & Letters ... Dr. Peter MCALLISTER
54 Dean Engr/Computer Science/Tech ... Dr. Keith MOO-YOUNG
51 Dean Extended Studies & Intl Pgms ... Dr. Jose L. GALVAN
76 Dean Health & Human Services ... Dr. Beatrice YORKER
53 Dean Charter College of Education ... Dr. Mary FALVEY
50 Dean Business & Economics ... Dr. James A. GOODRICH
92 Director Honors College ... Dr. Michelle HAWLEY

† Grants Joint Doctoral degree in cooperation with the University of California-Los Angeles.

*California State University-Monterey Bay (E)

100 Campus Center, Seaside CA 93955-8000
County: Monterey FICE Identification: 032603
Unit ID: 409698
Telephone: (831) 582-3000 Carnegie Class: Master's S
FAX Number: (831) 582-3783 Calendar System: Semester
URL: www.csumb.edu
Established: 1994 Annual Undergrad Tuition & Fees (In-State): $5,970
Enrollment: 5,173 Coed
Affiliation or Control: State IRS Status: 501(c)3
Highest Offering: Master's
Program: Liberal Arts And General
Accreditation: WC, @SW, TED

02 President ... Dr. Eduardo M. OCHOA
05 Provost ... Dr. Kathryn CRUZ-URIBE
11 Vice Pres Admin & Finance/CFO ... Mr. Kevin SAUNDERS
30 Vice Pres University Advancement ... Dr. Patti HIRAMOTO
32 Vice Pres Student Affairs ... Dr. Ronnie HIGGS
26 Dir of Govt & External Relations ... Mr. Justin WELLNER
35 Dean of Student Life ... Dr. Christine ERICKSON
10 Assoc Vice President for Finance ... Mr. John FITZGIBBON
100 Chief of Staff to President ... Ms. Anna BARTKOWSKI
06 Registrar ... Ms. Sheila HERNANDEZ
22 Director Employee Rels/EEO & ADA ... Ms. Tamberly PETROVICH
37 Director Financial Aid ... Ms. Angeles FUENTES
15 Assoc VP for Human Resources ... Ms. Mary ROBERTS
19 Chief of Police ... Chief Earl LAWSON
18 Chief Facilities/Physical Plant ... Mr. John MARKER
21 Associate Business Officer ... Mr. John FITZGIBBON
07 Dir for Admissions & Recruitment ... Mr. David LINNEVERS
29 Director Alumni Relations ... Ms. Pilar GOSE
41 Athletic Director ... Mr. Vince OTOUPAL
20 Associate Academic Officer ... Dr. Mary BOYCE
84 Assoc VP Enrollment Management ... Dr. Ronnie HIGGS
96 Director of Purchasing ... Mr. Art EVJEN

*California State University-Northridge (F)

18111 Nordhoff Street, Northridge CA 91330-0001
County: Los Angeles FICE Identification: 001153
Unit ID: 110608
Telephone: (818) 677-1200 Carnegie Class: Master's L
FAX Number: N/A Calendar System: Semester
URL: www.csun.edu
Established: 1958 Annual Undergrad Tuition & Fees (In-State): $7,002
Enrollment: 36,911 Coed
Affiliation or Control: State IRS Status: 501(c)3
Highest Offering: Doctorate
Program: Liberal Arts And General; Teacher Preparatory; Professional

Accreditation: WC, AAFCS, ART, BUS, CACREP, CIDA, CONST, CS, DIETD, DIETI, ENG, IPSY, JOUR, MUS, NURSE, PH, PTA, RAD, SP, SW, TED, THEA

02 President ... Dr. Dianne F. HARRISON
05 Provost/Vice Pres Academic Affairs ... Dr. Harry HELLENBRAND
10 Vice President Admin/Finance ... Mr. Thomas MCCARRON
32 VP Student Affairs/Dean of Students ... Dr. William WATKINS
44 Vice Pres University Advancement ... Dr. Vance T. PETERSON
13 Vice President IT/CIO ... Ms. Hilary BAKER
88 Exec Director University Corp ... Mr. Rick EVANS
20 Vice Provost Academic Affairs ... Dr. Cynthia Z. RAWITCH
100 Chief of Staff ... Dr. Barbara L. GROSS
18 Assoc VP Facilities Dev/Operations ... Mr. Colin J. DONAHUE
58 Assoc VP Grad Studies/Intl Pgms ... Vacant
30 Assoc Vice Pres Development ... Ms. Maureen F. FITZGERALD
21 Associate VP Financial Services ... Ms. Deborah WALLACE
15 Interim Assoc VP of Human Resources ... Ms. Jill A. SMITH
29 Asst Vice Pres Alumni Relations ... Mr. D. G. (Gray) MOUNGER
26 Assoc VP Marketing/Communications ... Ms. Stacy LIEBERMAN
20 Senior Dir Undergraduate Studies ... Dr. Elizabeth T. ADAMS
91 Assoc VP of Academic Resources ... Ms. Diane S. STEPHENS
07 Director of Admissions and Records ... Ms. Patty R. LORD
08 Dean University Library ... Dr. Mark STOVER
51 Dean College of Extended Learning ... Dr. Joyce A. FEUCHT-HAVIAR
79 Dean College of Humanities ... Dr. Elizabeth A. SAY
50 Dean College Business/Economics ... Dr. William P. JENNINGS
53 Dean College of Education ... Dr. Michael E. SPAGNA
57 Dean College Arts/Media/Commun ... Dr. Robert BUCKER
83 Dean Col Social/Behavioral Sci ... Dr. Stella Z. THEODOULOU
76 Dean Col Health/Human Development ... Dr. Sylvia A. ALVA
81 Dean College Science & Math ... Dr. Jerry STINNER
54 Dean College Engr/Computer Science ... Dr. S. K. RAMESH
09 Director Institutional Research ... Dr. Bettina HUBER
37 Director Financial Aid/Scholarships ... Mrs. Lili C. VIDAL
38 Director Univ Counseling Services ... Dr. Mark STEVENS
36 Director Career Center ... Ms. Ann N. MOREY
25 Dir Research/Sponsored Projects ... Mr. Scott L. PEREZ
18 Int Exec Dir Physical Plant Mgmt ... Mr. Lynn WIEGERS
19 Director of Police Services ... Ms. Anne P. GLAVIN
28 Interim Dir of Equity and Diversity ... Ms. Susan HUA
86 Dir Government/Community Relations ... Ms. Brittny MCCARTHY
23 Director Student Health Center ... Dr. Linda REID-CHASSIAKOS
39 Dir Student Housing/Conf Services ... Mr. Timothy J. TREVAN
40 Director Matador Bookstore ... Ms. Amy C. BERGER
41 Director of Athletics ... Mr. Rick MAZZUTO
85 Dir Student Devel/Intl Programs ... Mr. Thomas E. PIERNIK
92 Dir General Education Honors Pgm ... Dr. Beth A. WIGHTMAN
96 Manager Purchasing ... Ms. Deborah FLUGUM
84 Director Enrollment Management ... Dr. William WATKINS

*California State University-Sacramento (A)

6000 J Street, Sacramento CA 95819-2694
County: Sacramento FICE Identification: 001150
Unit ID: 110617
Telephone: (916) 278-6011 Carnegie Class: Master's L
FAX Number: (916) 278-6664 Calendar System: Semester
URL: www.csus.edu
Established: 1947 Annual Undergrad Tuition & Fees (In-State): $7,100
Enrollment: 28,016 Coed
Affiliation or Control: State IRS Status: 501(c)3
Highest Offering: Doctorate
Program: Liberal Arts And General; Teacher Preparatory; Professional
Accreditation: WC, ART, BUS, CACREP, CIDA, CONST, CORE, CS, DIETD, DIETI, EMT, ENG, HT, MUS, NRPA, NURSE, PTA, SP, SW

02 President ... Dr. Alexander GONZALEZ
05 Provost/Vice Pres Academic Affairs ... Dr. Charles GOSSETT
11 Vice President Administration & CFO .. Dr. Ming-Tung "Mike" LEE
26 Vice Pres University Advancement ... Mr. Vince SALES
32 Vice President Student Affairs ... Dr. Lori VARLOTTA
15 Vice President for Human Resources ... Ms. Christine D. LOVELY
25 Asst VP Research/Contract Admin ... Mr. David EARWICKER
20 Vice Provost ... Vacant
45 Assoc VP Academic Affs/Planning ... Vacant
18 Assoc Vice Pres Facilities Mgmt ... Dr. Ali IZADIAN
27 Assoc Vice President Public Affairs ... Vacant
30 Assoc Vice President Development ... Vacant
84 AVP Enrollment Mgmt/Student Support ... Mr. Edward MILLS
35 AVP Student Affairs/Campus Life ... Mr. Michael SPEROS
21 Interim Assoc VP Financial Svcs ... Ms. Justine HEARTT
13 VP & Chief Information Officer ... Dr. Larry GILBERT
43 University Counsel ... Ms. Jill PETERSON
09 Director Institutional Research ... Dr. Jing WANG
07 Director Outreach & Admissions ... Mr. Emiliano DIAZ
08 Dean University Library ... Ms. Tabzeera DOSU
29 Director Alumni Relations ... Ms. Jennifer BARBER
19 Director Public Safety ... Mr. Mark IWASA
39 Director Residential Life ... Mr. Michael SPEROS
41 Director Intercollegiate Athletics ... Dr. Terry WANLESS
36 Director Academic Adv/Career Ctrs ... Dr. Beth MERRITT MILLER
37 Director Financial Aid ... Ms. Anita KERMES
22 Director of Employment Equity ... Dr. Susan HOUGH
40 Bookstore Director ... Ms. Julia MILARDOVICH
100 Chief of Staff ... Ms. Carol ENSLEY
06 University Registrar ... Mr. Dennis GEYER
85 Director Global Education ... Dr. Jack GODWIN
23 Dir Student Health Ctr & Psych Svcs . Dr. Joy STEWART-JAMES
96 Mgr Procurement/Contract Services ... Mr. John GUION
49 Dean College of Arts & Letters ... Dr. Edward INCH
50 Dean College of Business Admin ... Dr. Sanjay VARSHNEY
53 Dean College of Education ... Dr. Vanessa SHEARED
54 Dean College of Engr/Computer Sci ... Dr. Emir J. MACARI
76 Dean College of Health/Human Svcs ... Dr. Fred BALDINI
81 Dean College of Natural Sci/Math ... Dr. Jill TRAINER
51 Dean College Continuing Education ... Mr. Guido KRICKX
83 Dean College Soc Sci/Interdisc Stds ... Dr. Charles W. GOSSETT
58 Acting Dean Graduate Studies ... Dr. Chevelle NEWSOME

*California State University-San Bernardino (B)

5500 University Parkway, San Bernardino CA 92407-2393
County: San Bernardino FICE Identification: 001142
Unit ID: 110510
Telephone: (909) 537-5000 Carnegie Class: Master's L
FAX Number: N/A Calendar System: Quarter
URL: www.csusb.edu
Established: 1960 Annual Undergrad Tuition & Fees (In-State): $7,047
Enrollment: 17,250 Coed
Affiliation or Control: State IRS Status: 501(c)3
Highest Offering: Doctorate
Program: Liberal Arts And General; Teacher Preparatory; Professional
Accreditation: WC, ART, BUS, CORE, CS, DIETD, MUS, NURSE, SPAA, SW, TED, THEA

02 President ... Dr. Tomas MORALES
05 Provost/Vice Pres Academic Affairs ... Dr. Andrew R. BODMAN
10 Vice Pres Administration/Finance ... Mr. Robert GARDNER
32 Vice President Student Affairs ... Dr. Frank L. RINCON
30 Vice Pres University Advancement ... Mr. Larry SHARP
13 Interim Vice Pres Info Tech/CIO ... Ms. Lorraine FROST
04 Spec Asst to Pres Ext Govt Rel ... Ms. Pamela LANGFORD
86 Spec Asst to Pres Federal Relations ... Dr. Clifford YOUNG
20 Assoc Provost Academic Programs ... Dr. Jenny ZORN
88 Assoc Provost Research ... Dr. Jeffrey M. THOMPSON
16 Assoc Provost Academic Personnel ... Dr. Risa DICKSON
21 Assoc VP Budget & Financial Opers ... Mr. Bob WILSON
84 Assoc VP Enrollment Mgmt ... Ms. Olivia ROSAS
35 Assoc VP Student Development ... Ms. Helga KRAY
88 Assoc VP IRT ... Ms. Lorraine FROST
88 Associate VP Development ... Ms. Cindi PRINGLE
26 Asst VP Public Affairs ... Mr. Sid ROBINSON
15 Asst VP Human Resources ... Mr. Dale T. WEST
09 Director Institutional Research ... Ms. Muriel LOPEZ-WAGNER
36 Int Placement Services Coordinator ... Ms. Carol DIXON
06 Dir Student Recs/Regis/Eval ... Ms. Grace DEMPSEY
07 Director Admissions/Recruitment ... Ms. Olivia ROSAS
38 Director Counseling Center ... Dr. Patricia SMITH
08 University Librarian ... Mr. Cesar CABALLERO
37 Director Financial Aid ... Ms. Roseanna RUIZ
45 Director Plng Design/Construction ... Mr. Hamid U. AZHAND
18 Sr Director Facilities Services ... Mr. Tony SIMPSON
41 Director Athletics ... Dr. Kevin L. HATCHER
29 Director Alumni Affairs ... Ms. Pam LANGFORD
96 Director Purchasing ... Ms. Kathy HANSEN
28 Director Diversity (faculty) ... Dr. Risa DICKSON
28 Director Diversity (staff) ... Mr. Dale T. WEST
40 Director Bookstore ... Ms. Lyly BIRD
94 Dir Gender & Sexuality Studies ... Dr. Todd JENNINGS
92 Director University Honors Program ... Dr. Allen BUTT
56 Dean of Extended Learning ... Dr. Tatiana KARMANOVA
49 Dean College of Arts & Letters ... Dr. Eri F. YASUHARA
81 Dean Col Natural Sciences ... Dr. Kirsten FLEMING
83 Dean Col Social/Behavioral Sciences ... Dr. Jamal R. NASSAR
53 Dean College of Education ... Dr. Jay FIENE
50 Dean College of Business ... Dr. Lawrence D. ROSE
58 Dean Graduate Studies ... Dr. Sandra KAMUSIKIRI
12 Dean CSUSB Palm Desert ... Dr. Fred E. JANDT
89 Dean Freshman Studies ... Dr. J. Milton CLARK

*California State University-San Marcos (C)

333 S Twin Oaks Valley Road, San Marcos CA 92096-0001
County: San Diego FICE Identification: 030113
Unit ID: 366711
Telephone: (760) 750-4000 Carnegie Class: Master's M
FAX Number: (760) 750-4030 Calendar System: Semester
URL: www.csusm.edu
Established: 1989 Annual Undergrad Tuition & Fees (In-State): $6,044
Enrollment: 10,276 Coed
Affiliation or Control: State IRS Status: 501(c)3
Highest Offering: Doctorate
Program: Liberal Arts And General; Teacher Preparatory
Accreditation: WC, NURSE, @SP, TED

02 President ... Dr. Karen S. HAYNES
04 Executive Assistant ... Ms. Joyce BRUGGEMAN
10 Vice President Finance/Admin Svcs ... Ms. Linda HAWK
05 Vice President Academic Affairs ... Dr. Emily CUTRER
32 Vice President of Student Affairs ... Dr. Eloise STIGLITZ
30 Vice Pres University Advancement ... Mr. Neal HOSS
20 Assoc Vice Pres Academic Affairs ... Dr. David BARSKY
20 Assoc VP Planning/Acad Resources ... Vacant
84 Assoc Vice Pres Enrollment Mgmt ... Vacant
15 Assoc VP Human Resource/Equal Oppty ... Ms. Joanne SHYDIAN
44 Assoc VP Development/Campaign Dir ... Mr. Bruce GENUNG
22 Assoc VP Diversity & Educ Equity ... Mr. Derrick CRAWFORD
49 Dean Col Hum Arts/Behav & Soc Sci ... Dr. Adam SHAPIRO
50 Dean Col Business Administration ... Dr. Sharon LIGHTNER
53 Dean Col Educ/Health & Human Svcs ... Dr. Don CHU
08 Dean of Library Services ... Ms. Barbara PREECE
81 Dean Col of Science & Mathematics ... Dr. Katherine KANTARDJIEFF
56 Dean of Extended Studies ... Mr. Michael SCHRODER
88 Dean Instructional/Info Technology ... Mr. Wayne VERES
37 Director Financial Aid ... Ms. Vonda GARCIA
06 Registrar ... Mr. Thomas SWANGER
07 Dir of Admissions & Recruitment ... Ms. Carol MCALLISTER
09 Chief of Staff/Dir Inst Plng & Anal ... Mr. Matthew CEPPI
18 Director Facility Services ... Mr. Gary CINNAMON
21 Associate Business Officer ... Vacant
29 Director Alumni/Parent Relations ... Ms. Lori BROCKETT
96 Director Procurment/Support Svcs ... Ms. Bella NEWBERG
38 Director Undergraduate Advising ... Mr. Andres FAVELA

† Grants Joint Doctoral degree in cooperation with the University of California-San Diego.

*California State University-Stanislaus (D)

1 University Circle, Turlock CA 95382-0299
County: Stanislaus FICE Identification: 001157
Unit ID: 110495
Telephone: (209) 667-3012 Carnegie Class: Master's L
FAX Number: (209) 667-3206 Calendar System: Semester
URL: www.csustan.edu
Established: 1957 Annual Undergrad Tuition & Fees (In-State): $7,124
Enrollment: 9,246 Coed
Affiliation or Control: State IRS Status: 501(c)3
Highest Offering: Doctorate
Program: Liberal Arts And General; Teacher Preparatory; Professional
Accreditation: WC, ART, BUS, MUS, NURSE, SPAA, SW, TED, THEA

02 Interim President ... Dr. Joseph SHELEY
05 Provost/VP Academic Affairs ... Dr. James T. STRONG
10 Vice President Business/Finance ... Mr. Russell GIAMBELLUCA
15 Int Vice Pres Faculty Affairs/HR ... Mr. Dennis W. SHIMEK
32 VP Enrollment/Student Affairs ... Dr. Suzanne M. ESPINOZA
30 Vice President Univ Advancement ... Vacant
35 AVP Student Affair/Dean of Students ... Mr. Ronald J. NOBLE
20 Associate Vice President/ALO ... Vacant
13 Assoc Vice Pres for Info Technology ... Mr. Carl E. WHITMAN
18 Int Assoc VP Facilities Services ... Ms. Melody MAFFEI
88 Assoc Vice Pres Auxiliary Services ... Mr. John W. REHO
27 Assoc Vice Pres Communications/PA ... Mr. David L. TONELLI
49 Dean College of the Arts ... Mr. Daryl J. MOORE
50 Dean College of Business Admin ... Dr. Linda I. NOWAK
53 Dean College of Education ... Dr. Kathy NORMAN
76 Dean College Human & Health Sci ... Vacant
79 Int Dean Col Humanities/Social Sci ... Dr. James A. TUEDIO
65 Dean College Natural Sciences ... Dr. Reza KAMALI
08 Interim Dean Library Services ... Ms. Annie Y. HOR
51 Dean Extended Education ... Mr. Kevin NEMETH
06 Registrar ... Ms. Lisa M. BERNARDO
15 Senior Manager HR & Compliance ... Ms. Gina B. LEGURIA
88 Int Director Retention Svcs/EOP ... Mr. Fernando BELTRAN
29 Int Dir Alumni Rel/AnnualGiving ... Ms. Shannon NICHOLS
37 Director Financial Aid ... Ms. Noelia GONZALEZ
41 Director Athletics ... Mr. Michael MATOSO
09 Director of Institutional Research ... Dr. Angel A. SANCHEZ
96 Director University Business Svcs ... Vacant
38 Director Psychological Counseling ... Dr. Daniel BERKOW
22 Campus Compliance Officer ... Vacant

*Humboldt State University (E)

1 Harpst Street, Arcata CA 95521-8222
County: Humboldt FICE Identification: 001149
Unit ID: 115755
Telephone: (707) 826-3011 Carnegie Class: Master's M
FAX Number: (707) 826-5555 Calendar System: Semester
URL: www.humboldt.edu
Established: 1913 Annual Undergrad Tuition & Fees (In-State): $7,622
Enrollment: 8,046 Coed
Affiliation or Control: State IRS Status: 501(c)3
Highest Offering: Master's
Program: Liberal Arts And General; Teacher Preparatory; Professional
Accreditation: WC, ART, ENG, FOR, MUS, NURSE, SW

02 President ... Dr. Rollin C. RICHMOND
04 Special Assistant to the President ... Ms. Denice HELWIG
05 Provost/Vice Pres Academic Affairs ... Dr. Robert A. SNYDER
20 Vice Prov Acad Pgms/Undergrad Stds ... Dr. Jena BURGES
32 VP Student Affairs & Enroll Mgmt ... Dr. Peg BLAKE
11 Vice Pres Administrative Affairs ... Mr. Burt NORDSTROM
30 Vice President of Advancement ... Mr. Frank WHITLATCH
88 Assoc Vice President Faculty Affs ... Dr. Colleen MULLERY
10 Assoc Vice Pres Business Services ... Ms. Carol TERRY
88 Assoc VP Development & Alumni Rels ... Ms. Laura JACKSON
26 Assoc VP for Mktg & Communications ... Vacant
18 Director Facilities Management ... Mr. Gary KRIETSCH
88 Director University Budget Office ... Mr. David ROWE
20 Director of Academic Resources ... Mr. Volga KOVAL
06 Registrar ... Vacant
07 Director of Admissions ... Mr. Scott HAGG
15 Associate VP for Human Resources ... Mr. David BUGBEE
08 Dean of Library ... Ms. Teresa GRENOT
29 Director Alumni Relations ... Mr. Dean HART
44 Director Planned Giving ... Ms. Kimberley PITTMAN-SCHULZ
19 Chief of University Police ... Chief Lynn SODERBERG

41 Athletic Director ... Mr. Dan COLLEN
39 Director of Housing ... Mr. John CAPACCIO
40 Asst Director Bookstore ... Ms. Roberta DUGGAN
13 Chief Information Officer ... Ms. Anna KIRCHER
36 Director Career Devel Center ... Ms. Annie BOLICK-FLOSS
28 Director Diversity & Inclusion ... Ms. Radha WEBLEY
46 Dean of Research & Sponsored Prgms ... Dr. Rhea WILLIAMSON
85 Director International Programs ... Vacant
104 Study Abroad Advisor ... Ms. Penelope SHAW
35 Dean Student Affairs ... Ms. Randi DARNALL BURKE
37 Director Student Financial Aid ... Vacant
09 Dir Institutional Research & Plng ... Dr. Jacqueline NAGATSUKA
96 Director of Contracts & Procurement ... Mr. Michael BURGHART
90 Manager Desktop IT ... Mr. Steve DARNALL
14 Director Central IT ... Mr. Josh CALLAHAN
23 Dir Health/Counseling/Psych Svcs ... Ms. Mary Grooms VANCOTT
56 Director Extended Education ... Mr. Carl F. HANSEN
79 Dean Col Arts/Humanities/Soc Sci ... Dr. Kenneth AYOOB
107 Dean College Professional Studies ... Dr. John LEE
81 Dean Col Natural Resources/Science ... Dr. Steven SMITH
21 Director Financial Services ... Ms. Lynne SANDSTROM

*San Diego State University (A)

5500 Campanile Drive, San Diego CA 92182-8000
County: San Diego FICE Identification: 001151
Unit ID: 122409
Telephone: (619) 594-5200 Carnegie Class: RU/H
FAX Number: (619) 594-8894 Calendar System: Semester
URL: www.sdsu.edu
Established: 1897 Annual Undergrad Tuition & Fees (In-State): $7,076
Enrollment: 30,000 Coed
Affiliation or Control: State IRS Status: 501(c)3
Highest Offering: Doctorate
Program: Teacher Preparatory; Professional
Accreditation: WC, ART, AUD, BUS, BUSA, CIDA, CLPSY, CORE, DIETD, ENG, HSA, JOUR, KIN, MFCD, MIDWF, NURSE, PH, @PTA, SP, SPAA, SW, TED, THEA

02 President ... Dr. Elliot HIRSHMAN
05 Provost ... Dr. Nancy A. MARLIN
10 Vice President Business Affairs ... Ms. Sally F. ROUSH
32 Vice President Student Affairs ... Dr. James R. KITCHEN
30 VP University Relations/Development ... Ms. Mary Ruth CARLETON
46 Vice President for Research ... Dr. Stephen WELTER
20 Assoc Vice Pres Academic Affairs ... Dr. Ethan A. SINGER
11 Assoc Vice President Operations ... Mr. Robert SCHULZ
88 Assoc Vice Pres Faculty Affairs ... Dr. Edith BENKOV
21 Assoc VP for Financial Operations ... Mr. Scott BURNS
15 Interim Assoc VP Administration ... Ms. Jessica RENTTO
85 Asst Vice President Intl Programs ... Dr. Alan R. SWEEDLER
27 Assoc VP Marketing & Communications ... Mr. Jack F. BERESFORD
35 Associate Vice Pres Student Affairs ... Mr. Eric RIVERA
88 Exec Dir St Affs Ldrshp/Cmpus Life ... Ms. Martha RUEL
29 Exec Director Alumni Association ... Mr. James S. HERRICK
23 Int Director Student Health Svcs ... Ms. Martha RUEL
100 Chief of Staff President's Office ... Dr. Andrea ROLLINS
23 Student Health Svcs Medical Dir ... Dr. Gregg LICHTENSTEIN
88 Asst Vice Pres Academic Affairs ... Dr. Sandra COOK
38 Director Counseling/Psych Services ... Dr. Sandy JORGENSEN-FUNK
08 Int Dean Library/Information Access ... Ms. Gale ETSCHMAIER
37 Dir Financial Aid & Scholarships ... Ms. Joanne FERCHLAND-PARELLA
45 Exec Dir Research Foundation ... Mr. Bob E. WOLFSON
51 Dean of Extended Studies ... Dr. Joe SHAPIRO
58 Assoc Dean of Graduate Affairs ... Dr. Radmilla PRISLIN
49 Dean of Undergraduate Studies ... Dr. Geoffrey W. CHASE
79 Dean of College Arts & Letters ... Dr. Paul WONG
81 Dean College of Sciences ... Dr. Stanley MALOY
54 Dean of College of Engineering ... Dr. David T. HAYHURST
50 Dean of College of Business Admin ... Dr. Michael CUNNINGHAM
76 Dean of Col Health/Human Services ... Dr. Marilyn NEWHOFF
53 Dean of College of Education ... Dr. Ric A. HOVDA
12 Dean Imperial Valley Campus ... Mr. David PEARSON
57 Dean of Profess Studies/Fine Arts ... Dr. Joyce M. GATTAS
84 Assoc Exec Dir Enrollment Services ... Ms. Rita GAJOLI
19 Director Public Safety ... Mr. John BROWNING
28 Chief Diversity Officer ... Dr. Aaron I. BRUCE
06 Registrar ... Ms. Rayanne WILLIAMS
07 Director of Admissions ... Ms. Beverly ARATA
36 Director Career Services ... Mr. James TARBOX
39 Director Housing Administration ... Vacant
40 CEO Aztec Shops ... Mrs. Donna TUSACK
41 Director Intercollegiate Athletics ... Mr. Jim STERK
85 Asc Dir Intl Stdt Ctr/Int Std Advis ... Ms. Jane KALIONZES
88 Director Environ Health & Safety ... Mr. Terry GEE
13 Sr Director Information & Tech/CIO ... Mr. Rich PICKETT
09 Dir Univ Analytic Stds/Instnl Rsrch ... Vacant
31 Dir Community Rels/Special Projects ... Mr. Tyler SHERER
96 Mgr Contract/Procurement Mgmt ... Ms. Cathy GARCIA
21 Controller ... Ms. Lorretta LEAVITT

*San Francisco State University (B)

1600 Holloway Avenue, San Francisco CA 94132-1740
County: San Francisco FICE Identification: 001154
Unit ID: 122597
Telephone: (415) 338-1111 Carnegie Class: Master's L
FAX Number: (415) 338-2514 Calendar System: Semester
URL: www.sfsu.edu
Established: 1899 Annual Undergrad Tuition & Fees (In-State): $6,888
Enrollment: 29,541 Coed
Affiliation or Control: State IRS Status: 501(c)3
Highest Offering: Doctorate
Program: Liberal Arts And General
Accreditation: WC, AAFCS, ART, BUS, CACREP, CORE, CS, DIETD, DIETI, ENG, JOUR, MT, MUS, NRPA, NURSE, PH, PTA, SP, SPAA, SW, TED, THEA

02 President ... Dr. Leslie E. WONG
05 Provost & VP Academic Affairs ... Dr. Sue V. ROSSER
44 Vice Pres University Advancement ... Mr. Robert J. NAVA
10 VP Administration and Finance ... Ms. Nancy K. HAYES
32 VP Student Affairs ... Dr. J.E.(Penny) SAFFOLD
100 Chief of Staff ... Ms. Patricia B. BARTSCHER
45 AVP Academic Planning/Development ... Dr. Linda BUCKLEY
20 Assoc VP Academic Resources ... Dr. John J. KIM
46 Assoc VP Research Sponsored Pgms ... Dr. Jaylan TURKKAN
20 Assoc VP Academic Affairs Operation ... Vacant
85 Assoc VP International Education ... Dr. Yenbo WU
18 Assoc VP Capital Plan Design Const ... Mr. Simon Y. LAM
13 AVP Division Info Tech ... Ms. Phoebe KWAN
84 Senior AVP Enrollment Management ... Dr. Jo VOLKERT
18 Sr Assoc VP Physical Plng & Develop ... Ms. Marilyn LANIER
21 Assoc VP Fiscal Affairs ... Ms. Agnes WONG-NICKERSON
16 Assoc VP HR/Safety & Risk Mgt ... Ms. Lori GENTLES
45 AVP Strategic Plng/Univ Compliance ... Mr. Gene CHELBERG
50 Dean College Business ... Ms. Linda OUBRE
53 Interim Dean College Education ... Dr. Betsy KEAN
88 Dean College Ethnic Studies ... Dr. Kenneth P. MONTEIRO
51 AVP/Dean College Extended Learning ... Vacant
69 Dean Col Health & Social Justice ... Dr. Don TAYLOR
79 Dean Col Liberal & Creative Arts ... Dr. Paul SHERWIN
81 Dean College Science & Engineering ... Dr. Sheldon AXLER
15 Dean Faculty Affairs & Prof Dev ... Dr. Sacha BUNGE
58 Dean Graduate Studies ... Dr. Ann HALLUM
88 Dean Undergraduate Studies ... Dr. Gail EVANS
43 University Counsel ... Ms. Patricia B. BARTSCHER
102 SF State President Foundation ... Mr. Robert J. NAVA
08 University Librarian ... Ms. Deborah C. MASTERS
24 Director Academic Technology ... Dr. Maggie BEERS
85 Director International Programs ... Ms. Hildy HEATH
88 Director Testing Center ... Vacant
30 Associate Vice Pres Development ... Ms. Donna BLAKEMORE
86 Director Government & Community Rel ... Ms. Lisbet SUNSHINE
27 Director University Communications ... Ms. Ellen GRIFFIN
88 Exec Dir Univ Property Management ... Mr. Mark GOODRICH
88 Director EHOS ... Mr. Aaron NEVATT
39 Dir Resident Life/Assc Dean of Stdn ... Dr. Mary Ann BEGLEY
37 Director Student Financial Aid ... Ms. Barbara HUBLER
88 Director Student Outreach Services ... Dr. Frieda LEE
07 Director Undergraduate Admissions ... Mr. John PLISKA
21 Director Univ Budget Planning ... Mr. Andrew SOM
06 Registrar ... Ms. Suzanne DMYTRENKO
41 Director Athletics ... Dr. Michael J. SIMPSON
36 Acting Director Career Center ... Vacant
38 Director Counseling & Psych Svcs ... Dr. Derethia DUVAL
88 Director Disability Pgms/Res Ctr ... Ms. Nicole BOHN
88 Dir Education Opportunity Program ... Mr. Oscar M. GARDEA
19 Chf of Police/Dir of Public Safety ... Chief Patrick WASLEY
23 Medical Dir Student Health Svcs ... Dr. Alastair SMITH
35 Dean of Students ... Mr. Joseph D. GREENWELL
96 Director Procurement Department ... Mr. Stephen C. SMITH
29 Director Alumni Relations ... Mr. Doug HUPKE
88 Budget Officer ... Mr. Franz LOZANO
88 Sr Dir Facilitites Svcs Enterp ... Mr. Chuck MEYER
88 Dir Campus Space Administration ... Ms. Zelinda ZINGARO
88 Dir LEAD ... Ms. Sarah BAUER

† Grants additional Doctoral degrees in cooperation with the UC-Berkeley and UC-San Francisco.

*San Jose State University (C)

One Washington Square, San Jose CA 95192-0001
County: Santa Clara FICE Identification: 001155
Unit ID: 122755
Telephone: (408) 924-1000 Carnegie Class: Master's L
FAX Number: (408) 924-1018 Calendar System: Semester
URL: www.sjsu.edu
Established: 1857 Annual Undergrad Tuition & Fees (In-State): $7,587
Enrollment: 30,000 Coed
Affiliation or Control: State IRS Status: 501(c)3
Highest Offering: Master's
Program: Liberal Arts And General; Teacher Preparatory; Professional; Business Emphasis
Accreditation: WC, ART, BUS, CEA, CS, DANCE, DIETD, DIETI, ENG, JOUR, LIB, MT, MUS, NAIT, NRPA, NURSE, OT, PH, PLNG, SP, SPAA, SW, TED, THEA

02 President ... Dr. Mohammed QAYOUMI
11 Vice Pres Administration & Finance ... Mr. Shawn BIBB
32 Int Vice President Student Affairs ... Mr. William NANCE
30 VP University Advancement ... Ms. Nancy BUSSANI
13 CIO ... Mr. Chip LENNO
45 Vice Provost Academic Budgets/Plng ... Vacant
14 Int Assoc VP Univ Computing/Telecom ... Mr. Don BAKER
09 Assoc VP Institutional Research ... Dr. Sutee SUJITPARAPITAYA
05 Provost/Vice Pres Acad Affairs ... Dr. Ellen JUNN
100 Chief of Staff ... Ms. Dorothy POOLE
20 Associate Vice Pres Faculty Affairs ... Dr. Joan MERDINGER
58 Assoc VP Graduate Studies/Research ... Dr. Pamela STACKS
20 Assoc VP Undergrad Studies ... Dr. Dennis JAEHNE
21 VP Admin Systems/Finance ... Ms. Josee LAROCHELLE
18 Assoc VP for Facilities/Operations ... Mr. Chris BROWN
15 Associate VP Human Resources ... Vacant
26 Assoc VP Public Affairs ... Mr. Lawrence CARR
44 Director Devel/Alumni Rels ... Mr. Brian BATES
51 Assoc VP/Dean Intl/Extended Stds ... Dr. Mark NOVAK
84 Int Assoc VP Enroll/Academic Svcs ... Ms. Sharon WILLEY
08 Dean of the University Library ... Dr. Ruth KIFER
28 Equal Opportunity Manager ... Ms. Julie PAISANT
27 Director Communications/Public Affs ... Vacant
29 Director Alumni Relations ... Ms. Janikke KLEM
06 Registrar ... Ms. Marion SOFISH
41 Director Intercollegiate Athletics ... Mr. Gene BLEYMAIER
96 Director Procurement Services ... Vacant
40 Director Spartan Bookstore ... Vacant
19 Chief of Police ... Mr. Peter DECENA
36 Director Career Center ... Ms. Cheryl ALLMEN-VINNEDGE
38 Director Counseling Services ... Ms. Ellen LIN
37 Director Fin Aid/Schlarship Ofc ... Ms. Coleetta MCELROY
39 Dir University Housing Svcs ... Mr. Victor CULATTA
23 Dir Student Health Center ... Dr. Roger ELROD
49 Dean College of Applied Sci & Art ... Dr. Charles BULLOCK
50 Dean College of Business ... Dr. David STEELE
53 Dean College of Education ... Dr. Elaine CHIN
54 Dean College of Engineering ... Dr. Belle WEI
79 Dean College of Humanities/Arts ... Dr. Lisa VOLLENDORF
81 Dean College of Science ... Dr. J. Michael PARRISH
83 Dean College Social Sciences ... Dr. Sheila BIENENFELD

*Sonoma State University (D)

1801 E Cotati Avenue, Rohnert Park CA 94928-3609
County: Sonoma FICE Identification: 001156
Unit ID: 123572
Telephone: (707) 664-2880 Carnegie Class: Master's L
FAX Number: (707) 664-2505 Calendar System: Semester
URL: www.sonoma.edu
Established: 1960 Annual Undergrad Tuition & Fees (In-State): $7,546
Enrollment: 8,668 Coed
Affiliation or Control: State IRS Status: 501(c)3
Highest Offering: Master's
Program: Liberal Arts And General; Teacher Preparatory; Professional
Accreditation: WC, ART, BUS, CACREP, MUS, NUR, TED

02 President ... Dr. Ruben ARMINANA
05 Provost & Vice Pres Academic Affs ... Dr. Andrew ROGERSON
10 Vice Pres Administration & Finance ... Mr. Laurence FURUKAWA-SCHLERETH
26 Vice President University Affairs ... Mr. Dan CONDRON
30 Interim Vice President Development ... Mr. Erik GREENY
32 Chief Student Affairs Officer ... Mr. Matthew LOPEZ-PHILLIPS
20 Assoc VP for Faculty Affairs ... Dr. Melinda BARNARD
21 Assoc VP for Admin & Finance ... Ms. Letitia COATE
35 Asst VP Stdnt Affs/Enrollment Mgmt ... Mr. Chuck RHODES
09 Director Institutional Research ... Mr. Sean JOHNSON
14 Acting CIO/Sr Dir Common Mgmt Sys ... Mr. Jason WENRICK
08 Library Dean ... Ms. Barbara BUTLER
79 Dean School of Arts & Humanities ... Dr. Thaine STEARNS
50 Dean Sch of Business/Economic ... Dr. William SILVER
53 Interim Dean School of Education ... Dr. Carlos AYALA
81 Interim Dean School Science & Tech ... Dr. Lynn STAUFFER
83 Dean School of Social Sciences ... Dr. Elaine A. LEEDER
56 Dean School of Extended Education ... Dr. Mark MERICKEL
38 Dir of Counseling/Psych Services ... Dr. Lisa WYATT
37 Director of Financial Aid ... Mrs. Susan GUTIERREZ
18 Sr Dir Facilities Services/CPDC ... Mr. Christopher DINNO
27 Assoc VP for Communications & Mktg ... Ms. Susan KASHACK
41 Director Athletics ... Mr. William J. FUSCO
19 Interim Chief Police Services ... Ms. Sally MILLER
21 Sr Director Univ Business Services ... Ms. Gloria OGG
88 Sr Director Entrepreneurial Srvcs ... Mr. Neil MARKLEY
06 Registrar ... Ms. Lisa NOTO
07 Director of Admissions ... Mr. Gustavo FLORES
29 Dir Alumni Relations/Annual Giving ... Ms. Laurie OGG
28 Mg Dir Employee Rel/Comp Svcs ... Ms. Joyce SUZUKI

California University of Management and Sciences (E)

721 North Euclid Street, Anaheim CA 92801
County: Orange FICE Identification: 041331
Telephone: (714) 533-3946 Carnegie Class: Not Classified
FAX Number: (714) 533-7778 Calendar System: Quarter
URL: www.calums.edu
Established: 1998 Annual Undergrad Tuition & Fees: $10,560
Enrollment: 370 Coed
Affiliation or Control: Independent Non-Profit IRS Status: 501(c)3
Highest Offering: Master's
Program: 2-Year Principally Bachelor's Creditable; Professional; Business Emphasis
Accreditation: ACICS

01 President ... David PARK
03 Vice President ... Jason SHIN
05 Academic Dean ... Mohammad SAFARZADEH
20 Program Director ... Woo Jin HAN
11 Registrar/Director Administration ... Jeffrey BEASCA
07 Admissions Officer ... Lisa LEE
32 Director of Student Services ... Janet LAURIN
08 Library Director ... Edwin FOLLICK
90 Academic Computing/Network Support ... James KIM
88 Chair Dept of Sports Management ... Anthony CHOI
88 Taekwondo Instructor & Dept Chair ... Andrew CHOI

California Western School of Law (F)

225 Cedar Street, San Diego CA 92101-3090
County: San Diego FICE Identification: 013103
Unit ID: 111391

Telephone: (619) 239-0391 Carnegie Class: Spec/Law
FAX Number: (619) 525-7092 Calendar System: Trimester
URL: www.cwsl.edu
Established: 1928 Annual Graduate Tuition & Fees: $43,600
Enrollment: 906 Coed
Affiliation or Control: Independent Non-Profit IRS Status: 501(c)3
Highest Offering: First Professional Degree; No Undergraduates
Program: Professional
Accreditation: LAW

01 President & Dean .... Dean Neils SCHAUMANN
05 Associate Dean Academic Affairs .... Prof. William C. ACEVES
11 Associate Dean Administration .... Prof. Laura M. PADILLA
30 Assistant Dean External Affairs .... Mr. David D. BOWERS
32 Asst Dean Students/Diversity Svcs .... Ms. Kathleen SEIBEL
36 Assistant Dean Career Services .... Ms. Courtney MIKLUSAK
88 Asst Dean Mission Development .... Mr. James M. COOPER
37 Exec Director Financial Aid .... Mr. William KAHLER
40 Exec Dir Swortwood Bookstore .... Ms. Crystal L. HENGEL
13 Exec Director Computer Services .... Ms. Mary Lou MITCHELL
18 Exec Dir Facilities Management .... Ms. Jolie L. CARTIER
88 Ex Dir Inst for Criminal Def Advoc .... Prof. Justin P. BROOKS
88 Exec Dir Inst of Health Law Studies .... Prof. Bryan A. LIANG
08 Director Law Library .... Prof. Phyllis C. MARION
10 Chief Financial Officer .... Ms. Pamela A. DUFFY
07 Director of Admissions .... Ms. Traci D. HOWARD
06 Registrar .... Ms. Diane SHRAGG
88 Director MCL/LLM Program .... Prof. Jacquelyn H. SLOTKIN
26 Chief Public Relations Officer .... Ms. Pamela HARDY
29 Director Alumni Relations .... Ms. Lori BOYLE
15 Director Personnel Services .... Ms. Rikklyn S. UEDA
28 Director of Diversity .... Ms. Marion E. CLOETE
21 Associate Business Officer .... Ms. Ruth GOULDING
35 Director Student Affairs .... Ms. Kathleen SEIBEL

Cambridge Junior College (A)

990-A Klamath Lane, Yuba City CA 95993-8978
County: Sutter FICE Identification: 038743
Unit ID: 446093
Telephone: (530) 674-9199 Carnegie Class: Assoc/PrivFP
FAX Number: (530) 671-7319 Calendar System: Other
URL: www.cambridge.edu
Established: N/A Annual Undergrad Tuition & Fees: $15,000
Enrollment: 165 Coed
Affiliation or Control: Proprietary IRS Status: Proprietary
Highest Offering: Associate Degree
Program: Occupational
Accreditation: ACICS

01 Director .... Ms. Sandy FOWLER

*Carrington College California - Administrative Office (B)

7801 Folsom Boulevard, Suite 210,
Sacramento CA 95826-2620
County: Sacramento Identification: 666086
Unit ID: 125532
Telephone: (916) 388-2800 Carnegie Class: N/A
FAX Number: (916) 381-1609
URL: www.carrington.edu/california

01 President .... Dr. Jeff AKENS

*Carrington College California - Antioch (C)

2157 Country Hills Drive, Antioch CA 94509-7435
County: Contra Costa Identification: 666041
Unit ID: 437927
Telephone: (925) 522-7777 Carnegie Class: Assoc/PrivFP
FAX Number: (925) 755-0079 Calendar System: Other
URL: www.carrington.edu
Established: 2006 Annual Undergrad Tuition & Fees: $17,236
Enrollment: 391 Coed
Affiliation or Control: Proprietary IRS Status: Proprietary
Highest Offering: Associate Degree
Program: Occupational; 2-Year Principally Bachelor's Creditable
Accreditation: &WJ, MAC

02 Executive Campus Director .... Mr. Richard CLARK

† Regional accreditation is carried under the parent institution in Sacramento, CA.

*Carrington College California - Citrus Heights (D)

7301 Greenback Lane, Suite A, Citrus Heights CA 95621
County: Sacramento Identification: 667042
Unit ID: 450702
Telephone: (916) 722-8200 Carnegie Class: Assoc/PrivFP
FAX Number: (916) 722-6883 Calendar System: Other
URL: www.carrington.edu
Established: N/A Annual Undergrad Tuition & Fees: $17,236
Enrollment: 520 Coed
Affiliation or Control: Proprietary IRS Status: Proprietary
Highest Offering: Associate Degree
Program: Occupational; 2-Year Principally Bachelor's Creditable
Accreditation: &WJ, MAC, SURGT

02 Executive Campus Director .... Mr. Jeff ORTEGA

† Regional accreditation is carried under the parent institution in Sacramento, CA.

*Carrington College California - Emeryville (E)

6001 Shellmound Street, Suite 145,
Emeryville CA 94608-1020
County: Alameda Identification: 666372
Unit ID: 445355
Telephone: (510) 420-5400 Carnegie Class: Assoc/PrivFP
FAX Number: (510) 601-0793 Calendar System: Other
URL: www.carrington.edu
Established: 2001 Annual Undergrad Tuition & Fees: $17,236
Enrollment: 205 Coed
Affiliation or Control: Proprietary IRS Status: Proprietary
Highest Offering: Associate Degree
Program: Occupational; 2-Year Principally Bachelor's Creditable
Accreditation: &WJ, MAC

02 Executive Campus Director .... Vacant

† Regional accreditation is carried under the parent institution in Sacramento, CA.

*Carrington College California - Pleasant Hill (F)

380 Civic Drive, Suite 300, Pleasant Hill CA 94523-1984
County: Contra Costa Identification: 666043
Unit ID: 438258
Telephone: (925) 609-6650 Carnegie Class: Assoc/PrivFP
FAX Number: (925) 609-6666 Calendar System: Other
URL: www.carrington.edu
Established: 1997 Annual Undergrad Tuition & Fees: $30,694
Enrollment: 399 Coed
Affiliation or Control: Proprietary IRS Status: Proprietary
Highest Offering: Associate Degree
Program: Occupational; 2-Year Principally Bachelor's Creditable
Accreditation: &WJ, MAC, PTAA

02 Executive Campus Director .... Mr. La Shawn WELLS
05 Dean of Academic Affairs .... Tracye LAUN

† Regional accreditation is carried under the parent institution in Sacramento, CA.

*Carrington College California - Sacramento (G)

8909 Folsom Boulevard, Sacramento CA 95826-9823
County: Sacramento FICE Identification: 009748
Unit ID: 125532
Telephone: (916) 361-1660 Carnegie Class: Assoc/PrivFP
FAX Number: (916) 361-6666 Calendar System: Other
URL: www.carrington.edu
Established: 1983 Annual Undergrad Tuition & Fees: $17,236
Enrollment: 1,283 Coed
Affiliation or Control: Proprietary IRS Status: Proprietary
Highest Offering: Associate Degree
Program: Occupational; 2-Year Principally Bachelor's Creditable
Accreditation: WJ, DH, MAC

02 Executive Director .... Ms. Sue SMITH
06 Registrar .... Ms. Ryanne GREEN-QUARLES
07 Director Enrollment Services .... Mr. Vance KLINKE
05 Dean of Academic Affairs .... Mr. James CRAIG

*Carrington College California - San Jose (H)

6201 San Ignacio Avenue, San Jose CA 95119-1325
County: Santa Clara Identification: 666042
Unit ID: 437936
Telephone: (408) 360-0840 Carnegie Class: Assoc/PrivFP
FAX Number: (408) 360-0848 Calendar System: Other
URL: www.carrington.edu
Established: 1999 Annual Undergrad Tuition & Fees: $30,694
Enrollment: 711 Coed
Affiliation or Control: Proprietary IRS Status: Proprietary
Highest Offering: Baccalaureate
Program: Occupational; 2-Year Principally Bachelor's Creditable
Accreditation: &WJ, DH, MAC, SURGT

02 Executive Campus Director .... Mr. Frederick HOLLAND

† Regional accreditation is carried under the parent institution in Sacramento, CA.

*Carrington College California - San Leandro (I)

15555 E 14th Street, Suite 500,
San Leandro CA 94578-9930
County: Alameda Identification: 666751
Unit ID: 246974
Telephone: (510) 276-3888 Carnegie Class: Assoc/PrivFP
FAX Number: (510) 276-3653 Calendar System: Other
URL: www.carrington.edu
Established: 1986 Annual Undergrad Tuition & Fees: $17,236
Enrollment: 611 Coed
Affiliation or Control: Proprietary IRS Status: Proprietary
Highest Offering: Associate Degree
Program: Occupational; 2-Year Principally Bachelor's Creditable
Accreditation: &WJ, MAC

02 Executive Campus Director .... Vacant
05 Dean of Academic Affairs .... Ms. Pat CHANNELL
06 Registrar .... Mr. Michael BORGES
07 Director Enrollment Services .... Ms. Kathryn COLLINS DUBA
36 Director of Career Services .... Ms. Lynne JACKSON

† Regional accreditation is carried under the parent institution in Sacramento, CA.

*Carrington College California - Stockton (J)

1313 W Robinhood Drive, Suite B,
Stockton CA 95207-5509
County: San Joaquin Identification: 666140
Unit ID: 450696
Telephone: (209) 956-1240 Carnegie Class: Assoc/PrivFP
FAX Number: (209) 956-1244 Calendar System: Semester
URL: www.carrington.edu
Established: 2005 Annual Undergrad Tuition & Fees: $30,694
Enrollment: 416 Coed
Affiliation or Control: Proprietary IRS Status: Proprietary
Highest Offering: Associate Degree
Program: Occupational; 2-Year Principally Bachelor's Creditable
Accreditation: &WJ, MAC

02 Executive Campus Director .... Mr. David KAYE
07 Director Enrollment Services .... Vacant

† Regional accreditation is carried under the parent institution in Sacramento, CA.

Casa Loma College-Van Nuys (K)

6725 Kester Avenue, Van Nuys CA 91405
County: Los Angeles FICE Identification: 006731
Unit ID: 111638
Telephone: (818) 785-2726 Carnegie Class: Assoc/PrivNFP
FAX Number: (818) 785-2191 Calendar System: Other
URL: www.casalomacollege.edu
Established: N/A Annual Undergrad Tuition & Fees: $32,006
Enrollment: 500 Coed
Affiliation or Control: Independent Non-Profit IRS Status: 501(c)3
Highest Offering: Associate Degree
Program: Occupational; Nursing Emphasis
Accreditation: ABHES, @PTAA

01 Campus Director/Controller .... Ms. Veronica PANTOJA
66 Director of Nursing .... Ms. Barbara BRIDGES
06 Registrar .... Ms. Lindsay ANTENUCCI
07 Director of Admissions .... Ms. Deanna BERNAL
26 Director Public Relations .... Mr. Paul ROOS
36 Director Career Services .... Mr. Paul BOYCHUK
37 Director Studend Financial Aid .... Ms. Rosleen AURORA

CBD College (L)

3699 Wilshire Boulevard, 4th Floor,
Los Angeles CA 90010
County: Los Angeles FICE Identification: 032503
Unit ID: 439367
Telephone: (213) 427-2200 Carnegie Class: Assoc/PrivNFP
FAX Number: (213) 427-9278 Calendar System: Other
URL: www.cbd.edu
Established: 1982 Annual Undergrad Tuition & Fees: $27,845
Enrollment: 214 Coed
Affiliation or Control: Independent Non-Profit IRS Status: 501(c)3
Highest Offering: Associate Degree
Program: Occupational
Accreditation: CNCE, SURTEC

01 President .... Mr. Alan HESHEL

Cedars-Sinai Medical Center Graduate Program in Biomedical Sciences and Translational Medicine (M)

8700 Beverly Blvd Atrium Bld 2nd Fl,
Los Angeles CA 90048
County: Los Angeles Identification: 667071
Telephone: (310) 423-6252 Carnegie Class: Not Classified
FAX Number: N/A Calendar System: Trimester
URL: www.cedars-sinai.edu
Established: N/A Annual Graduate Tuition & Fees: N/A
Enrollment: 10 Coed
Affiliation or Control: Independent Non-Profit IRS Status: 501(c)3
Highest Offering: Doctorate; No Undergraduates
Program: Professional
Accreditation: WC

01 President .... Thomas PRISELAC
05 Graduate Educ Program Coordinator .... Emma YATES

Cerritos College (A)

11110 Alondra Boulevard, Norwalk CA 90650-6298
County: Los Angeles FICE Identification: 001161
Unit ID: 111887
Telephone: (562) 860-2451 Carnegie Class: Assoc/Pub-S-SC
FAX Number: (562) 467-5005 Calendar System: Semester
URL: www.cerritos.edu
Established: 1955 Annual Undergrad Tuition & Fees (In-District): $1,156
Enrollment: 20,518 Coed
Affiliation or Control: State/Local IRS Status: 501(c)3
Highest Offering: Associate Degree
Program: Occupational; 2-Year Principally Bachelor's Creditable
Accreditation: WJ, ADNUR, DA, DH, PTAA

01 President .... Dr. Linda L. LACY
05 Vice President Academic Affairs .... Dr. JoAnna SCHILLING
10 Vice President Business Services .... Mr. David EL FATTAL
32 Vice President Student Services .... Dr. Stephen JOHNSON
16 Vice President Human Resources .... Dr. Mary Anne GULARTE
20 Dean of Academic Affairs .... Mr. Edmund (Rick) MIRANDA
07 Dean of Admissions/Records & Svcs .... Ms. Stephanie MURGUIA
38 Dean of Counseling Services .... Dr. Renee DeLong CHOMIAK
08 Dean of Library & Special Programs .... Mr. Carl BENGSTON
88 Dean Disabled Student Pgms & Svcs .... Dr. Lucinda ABORN
88 Dean of Student Support Services .... Ms. Kim WESTBY
50 Instr Dean Business/Humanities/SS .... Ms. Rachel MASON
57 Instr Dean Fine Arts/Communications .... Dr. Connie MAYFIELD
76 Instr Dean Health Occupations .... Ms. Sandra MARKS
83 Dean Academic Success .... Dr. Bryan REECE
49 Instr Dean Liberal Arts .... Mr. David FABISH
68 Instr Dean Physical Educ/Athletics .... Dr. Daniel SMITH
54 Instr Dean Science/Engineering/Math .... Dr. Carolyn CHAMBERS
73 Instruction Dean Technology .... Dr. Yannick REAL
14 Director of Information Technology .... Ms. Lee KRICHMAR
21 Director of Fiscal Services .... Mr. Noorali DELAWALLA
35 Director of Student Activities .... Ms. Holly BOGDANOVICH
36 Dir of Career/Assessment Services .... Ms. Theresa LOPEZ
18 Director Physical Plant & Const Svc .... Mr. David C. MOORE
44 Executive Director Foundation .... Mr. Steven RICHARDSON
88 Director Community Advancement .... Ms. Bellegran GOMEZ
26 Director Public & Governmental Rels .... Mr. Mark WALLACE
96 Director of Purchasing .... Mr. Mark LOGAN
15 Director Human Resources .... Dr. Adriana FLORES-CHURCH
104 Web Administrator .... Mr. Ty BOWMAN
19 Chief of Campus Police .... Mr. Richard BUKOWIECKI
28 Dir Adult Edu/Diversity Programs .... Ms. Graciela VASQUEZ
31 Director Community Education .... Dr. Patricia ROBBINS SMITH
88 Director Child Development Center .... Ms. Debra WARD
88 Operations Manager .... Mr. Arcadio AVILA
18 Facilities Manager .... Mr. Thomas RICHEY
88 Payroll Manager .... Ms. Deanna HART
21 Accounting Manager .... Mr. Shawn JONES
21 Budget Manager .... Ms. Suzie PAYNE
13 Manager Information Technology .... Mr. Patrick O'DONNELL
23 Assoc Dean Student Health Wellness .... Ms. Nancy MONTGOMERY
88 Director of CalWORKs Services .... Ms. Norma RODRIGUEZ
09 Dir of Research & Planning .... Ms. Kay NGUYEN
88 Director Adv Trans Tech Proj .... Ms. Jannet MALIG
88 PeopleSoft Database Administrator .... Ms. Maria MENDEZ
88 PeopleSoft Database Administrator .... Mr. Michael SALAZAR
88 Director of Pathway Programs .... Ms. Maggie CORDERO
22 Director Emp/Diversity/Legal Svcs .... Ms. Cynthia CONVEY
88 EOPS Assistant Director .... Ms. Yvette TAFOYA

*Chabot-Las Positas Community College District (B)

5020 Franklin Drive, Pleasanton CA 94588-3354
County: Alameda Identification: 666925
Telephone: (925) 485-5208 Carnegie Class: N/A
FAX Number: (925) 485-5256
URL: www.clpccd.org

01 Interim Chancellor .... Dr. Susan A. COTA
10 Vice Chanc Business Services .... Mr. Lorenzo LEGASPI
05 Vice Chanc Educational Svcs/Plng .... Vacant
18 Vice Chanc Facilities/Bond .... Mr. Jeffrey KINGSTON
16 Vice Chanc HR Svcs/Org Dev .... Vacant

*Chabot College (C)

25555 Hesperian Boulevard, Hayward CA 94545-2400
County: Alameda FICE Identification: 001162
Unit ID: 111920
Telephone: (510) 723-6600 Carnegie Class: Assoc/Pub-S-MC
FAX Number: (510) 782-9315 Calendar System: Semester
URL: www.chabotcollege.edu
Established: 1961 Annual Undergrad Tuition & Fees (In-District): $622
Enrollment: 15,148 Coed
Affiliation or Control: State/Local IRS Status: 501(c)3
Highest Offering: Associate Degree
Program: Occupational; 2-Year Principally Bachelor's Creditable
Accreditation: WJ, DH, MAC

02 President .... Dr. Susan S. SPERLING
05 Vice President Academic Services .... Dr. George A. RAILEY, JR.
32 Vice President Student Services .... Dr. Howard J. IRVIN
10 Int Vice President Business Svcs .... Mr. Dale WAGONER
04 Exec Asst to the College President .... Ms. Karen L. SILVA
08 Dean Instr-Learning Resource .... Vacant
38 Dean Counseling/Guidance .... Dr. Matt KRITSCHER
41 Dean Health/PE/Athletics .... Mr. Dale WAGONER
07 Director of Admissions & Records .... Mrs. Paulette LINO
37 Director of Financial Aid .... Ms. Kathryn LINZMEYER
19 Director Safety & Security .... Sgt. Keith STIVER
09 Director of Institutional Research .... Dr. Carolyn ARNOLD
15 Director Human Resources .... Dr. Wyman FONG
18 Chief Facilities/Physical Plant .... Mr. Tim NELSON
26 Chief Public Relations Officer .... Vacant
35 Director Student Life .... Ms. Danielle PRECIADO
96 Manager Purchasing/Warehouse Svcs .... Ms. Victoria LAMICA

*Las Positas College (D)

3000 Campus Hill Drive, Livermore CA 94551-7623
County: Alameda FICE Identification: 030357
Unit ID: 366401
Telephone: (925) 424-1000 Carnegie Class: Assoc/Pub-S-MC
FAX Number: (925) 443-0742 Calendar System: Semester
URL: www.laspositascollege.edu
Established: 1975 Annual Undergrad Tuition & Fees (In-District): $1,784
Enrollment: 8,500 Coed
Affiliation or Control: State/Local IRS Status: 501(c)3
Highest Offering: Associate Degree
Program: Occupational; 2-Year Principally Bachelor's Creditable
Accreditation: WJ, SURGT

02 President .... Dr. Kevin G. WALTHERS
05 Vice President Academic Svcs .... Dr. Janice NOBLE
32 Vice President Student Svcs .... Ms. Diana RODRIGUEZ
10 Vice Pres Business Services .... Vacant
04 Exec Assistant to the President .... Ms. Jennifer ADAMS
35 Dean of Student Services .... Vacant
88 Dean Arts and Communication .... Vacant
81 Dean Math/Sci/Engr/Public Safety .... Dr. Neal ELY
76 Dean Kinesiology/Health/Wellness .... Ms. Dyan MILLER
07 Dean of Admissions/Records .... Ms. Sylvia RODRIQUEZ
45 Director of Research & Planning .... Mr. Rajinder SAMRA
37 Financial Aid/Veterans Assistance .... Ms. Andi SCHREIBMAN
19 Campus Safety Supervisor .... Mr. Sean PRATHER
26 Exec Dir Public Info & Marketing .... Vacant
08 Head Librarian .... Ms. Cheryl WARREN
102 LPC Foundation Executive Director .... Dr. Ted KAYE
41 Athletic Director .... Ms. Dyan MILLER
18 Project Planner/Manager Facilities .... Mr. Jeffrey KINGSTON

Chaffey College (E)

5885 Haven Avenue, Rancho Cucamonga CA 91737-3002
County: San Bernardino FICE Identification: 001163
Unit ID: 111939
Telephone: (909) 652-6000 Carnegie Class: Assoc/Pub-S-MC
FAX Number: (909) 652-6006 Calendar System: Semester
URL: www.chaffey.edu
Established: 1883 Annual Undergrad Tuition & Fees (In-District): $1,380
Enrollment: 19,432 Coed
Affiliation or Control: State/Local IRS Status: 501(c)3
Highest Offering: Associate Degree
Program: Occupational; 2-Year Principally Bachelor's Creditable
Accreditation: WJ, ADNUR, DA, RAD

01 Superintendent/President .... Dr. Henry D. SHANNON
11 Vice Pres Administrative Services .... Ms. Lisa BAILEY
11 VP/Chief Admin Officer Chino Campus .... Vacant
05 Assoc Supt Instruction/Student Svcs .... Dr. Sherrie L. GUERRERO
10 Assoc Supt Business Svcs/Econ Devel .... Dr. Ciriaco PINEDO
09 Int Dean Inst Research/Research Dev .... Mr. Jim FILLPOT
21 Exec Director Administrative Svcs .... Ms. Melanie SIDDIQI
29 Director Alumni Relations .... Mr. Nick NAZARIAN
85 Director Transfer Center/Intl Pgms .... Ms. Jenny DANNELLEY
32 Director Student Activities .... Ms. Susan STEWART
07 Administrator Admissions/Records .... Ms. Kathy LUCERO
19 Dir Public Safety/Chief of Police .... Mr. David RAMIREZ
96 Dir Accounting/Purchasing Services .... Ms. Kim ERICKSON
06 Registrar .... Vacant
88 Director Technical Services .... Mr. Michael FINK
88 Director Childrens Center .... Ms. Birgit MONKS
23 Director Student Health Services .... Ms. Katherine PEEK
75 Dean DD/PD/Vocation .... Vacant
18 Dir Maintenance and Central Plant .... Mr. Bruce COOK
37 Director Financial Aid .... Ms. Patricia BOPKO
31 Director Auxiliary Services .... Mr. Jared CEJA
26 Director Marketing/Public Relations .... Ms. Peggy CARTWRIGHT
21 Int Exec Dir Budgeting Services .... Ms. Anita UNDERCOFFER
88 Director Museum Gallery .... Ms. Rebecca TRAWICK
18 Manager Facilities Development .... Ms. Sarah RILEY
12 Dean Chino Campus & Health Sciences .... Dr. Teresa HULL
88 Dean Visual Perf Arts/Language Arts .... Mr. Michael DINIELLI
50 Dean Business & Applied Technology .... Mr. Sid BURKS
81 Dean Mathematics & Science .... Mr. Theodore YOUNGLOVE
83 Dean Social & Behavioral Sci .... Dr. Corene SCHWARTZ
38 Dean Counseling & Matriculation .... Vacant
68 Dean Fontana Campus/Physical Educ .... Dr. Eric BISHOP
08 Dean Instructional Support .... Ms. Laura HOPE
04 Exec Assistant Supt/Pres Office .... Ms. Kathy NAPOLI

Chapman University (F)

One University Drive, Orange CA 92866-1099
County: Orange FICE Identification: 001164
Unit ID: 111948
Telephone: (714) 997-6815 Carnegie Class: Master's L
FAX Number: (714) 997-6713 Calendar System: 4/1/4
URL: www.chapman.edu
Established: 1861 Annual Undergrad Tuition & Fees: $42,084
Enrollment: 7,155 Coed
Affiliation or Control: Christian Church (Disciples Of Christ)
IRS Status: 501(c)3
Highest Offering: Doctorate
Program: Liberal Arts And General; Teacher Preparatory; Professional
Accreditation: WC, BUS, DANCE, LAW, MFCD, MUS, PTA, @SP, TEAC, THEA

01 President .... Dr. James L. DOTI
05 Chancellor .... Dr. Daniele C. STRUPPA
03 Executive Vice President & COO .... Mr. Harold W. HEWITT, JR.
30 Exec VP University Advancement .... Ms. Sheryl BOURGEOIS
32 Vice Chancellor & Dean of Students .... Dr. Jerry PRICE
84 Vice Chancellor/Dean Enrollment Mgt .... Mr. Michael PELLY
20 Vice Chancellor for Academic Admin .... Dr. Raymond SFEIR
09 Vice Chan Inst Eff & Fac Affairs .... Mr. Joseph SLOWENSKY
49 Dean Wilkinson Col Hum/Soc Sci .... Dr. Patrick QUINN
61 Dean School of Law .... Dr. Tom CAMPBELL
50 Dean School Business/Economics .... Mr. Reginald GILYARD
53 Dean College of Educational Studies .... Dr. Donald CARDINAL
88 Dean College of Film & Media Arts .... Mr. Robert BASSETT
88 Dean College of Performing Arts .... Mr. Dale MERRILL
81 Dean Col of Science & Technology .... Dr. Menas KAFATOS
88 Dean/Artistic Dir Center for Arts .... Dr. William HALL
88 Director Ctr for Global Education .... Dr. James COYLE
97 Vice Chancellor Undergrad Education .... Dr. Jeanne GUNNER
45 Vice President Campus Planning .... Mr. Kris OLSEN
16 Vice President of Human Resources .... Ms. Becky CAMPOS
43 Assoc Vice Pres of Legal Affairs .... Ms. Janine DUMONTELLE
21 Assoc Vice President & Controller .... Mr. Behzad BINESH
07 Asst VC/Chief Admissions Officer .... Mr. Michael DRUMMY
88 Assistant Chancellor .... Ms. Iris GERBASI
18 Director of Facilities .... Mr. Alan SMITH
26 Director Public Relations .... Ms. Mary PLATT
08 Dean of Library .... Ms. Charlene BALDWIN
29 Director Alumni Relations .... Ms. Dea MARCANO
13 Chief Information Officer .... Ms. Shari WATERS
09 Director of Institutional Research .... Dr. Marisol ARREDONDO
06 Registrar .... Dr. Jack FARRELL
46 Director Sponsored Research .... Ms. Yolanda UZZELL
37 Director Financial Aid .... Mr. Jack MILLIS
85 Director Intl Student Services .... Ms. Susan SAMS
19 Chief of Public Safety .... Mr. Randy BURBA
39 Assoc Dean/Director Residence Life .... Ms. Deborah MILLER
41 Athletic Director .... Mr. David CURREY
42 Dean of the Chapel .... Dr. Gail STEARNS
04 Associate to the President .... Ms. Ann CAMERON
88 Exec Assistant to the Chancellor .... Ms. Christina ZERMENO
22 Equal Opportunity Officer .... Mr. Eduardo MONGE
23 Director Student Health Services .... Ms. Jacqueline DEATS
35 Director Student LEAD .... Ms. Tami OTSUKA
36 Director Career Development .... Ms. Barbara HUBERT
38 Assoc Dean/Dir Student Psych Couns .... Ms. Jeannie WALKER
96 Director of Purchasing .... Ms. Pam AMES
04 Assistant to the President .... Ms. Dorothy FAROL

Charles R. Drew University of Medicine & Science (G)

1730 E 118th Street, Los Angeles CA 90059-3025
County: Los Angeles FICE Identification: 010365
Unit ID: 111966
Telephone: (323) 563-4800 Carnegie Class: Spec/Health
FAX Number: (323) 563-5987 Calendar System: Semester
URL: www.cdrewu.edu
Established: 1966 Annual Undergrad Tuition & Fees: $14,500
Enrollment: 410 Coed
Affiliation or Control: Independent Non-Profit IRS Status: 501(c)3
Highest Offering: Master's
Program: Occupational; 2-Year Principally Bachelor's Creditable; Liberal Arts And General; Professional
Accreditation: WC, DMS, NUR, PH, RAD

01 President & CEO .... Dr. David M. CARLISLE
100 Chief of Staff .... Ms. Edna YOHANNES
10 Chief Operating Officer .... Mr. Jim E. MAIN
45 EVP Research & Health Affairs .... Dr. Keith NORRIS
30 VP for Strategic Advancement .... Ms. Angela L. MINNIEFIELD
15 Chief Human Resources Officer .... Dr. Toni C. ELBOUSHI
11 Senior Administrator .... Mr. Nathaniel CLARK
63 Interim Dean College of Medicine .... Dr. Daphne CALMES
66 Dean School of Nursing .... Dr. Gloria J. MCNEAL
76 Dean College of Science & Health .... Dr. Gail ORUM-ALEXANDER
32 Assoc Dean of Medical Students .... Dr. Nancy HANNA
05 Assoc Provost Academic Affairs .... Dr. Ronald A. EDELSTEIN
09 Director Inst Effectiveness .... Mr. Al HEARD
27 Director Information Systems .... Mr. Matt CULLEN
08 Director Health Sciences Library .... Ms. Darlene PARKER-KELLY
37 Director Student Financial Aid .... Mr. Pierre FLOOD
84 Director of Admissions .... Dr. Rita GLORIA SAWYER
06 Registrar .... Mr. Damon A. BLUE

Charter College-Oxnard (H)

2000 Outlet Center Drive, Suite 150, Oxnard CA 93036
County: Ventura Identification: 666675
Telephone: (805) 973-1240 Carnegie Class: Not Classified
FAX Number: (775) 284-9900 Calendar System: Other
URL: www.chartercollege.edu
Established: 2009 Annual Undergrad Tuition & Fees: N/A
Enrollment: N/A Coed

Affiliation or Control: Proprietary IRS Status: Proprietary
Highest Offering: Baccalaureate
Program: Occupational; 2-Year Principally Bachelor's Creditable
Accreditation: ACICS

01 Campus President .... Ms. Cecelia BURRILL

† Branch campus of Charter College, Anchorage, AK.

Church Divinity School of the Pacific (A)

2451 Ridge Road, Berkeley CA 94709-1217
County: Alameda FICE Identification: 001165
Unit ID: 112127
Telephone: (510) 204-0700 Carnegie Class: Spec/Faith
FAX Number: (510) 644-0712 Calendar System: Semester
URL: www.cdsp.edu
Established: 1893 Annual Graduate Tuition & Fees: $16,690
Enrollment: 76 Coed
Affiliation or Control: Protestant Episcopal IRS Status: 501(c)3
Highest Offering: Doctorate; No Undergraduates
Program: Professional
Accreditation: THEOL

01 President & Dean .... Dr. W. Mark RICHARDSON
05 Dean Academic Affairs .... Dr. Ruth MEYERS
10 Chief Financial Officer .... Mr. Steve ARGYRIS
30 Vice President for Advancement .... Ms. Caitlin F. CURTIN
32 Dean of Students .... Rev. L. Ann HALLISEY
06 Registrar .... Ms. Margo WEBSTER
07 Director of Recruitment .... Ms. Dianne SMITH
27 Dir of Marketing/Communications .... Mr. Barry HOLTZCLAW
37 Director of Financial Aid .... Ms. Kathleen ANTOKHIN

Citrus College (B)

1000 W Foothill Boulevard, Glendora CA 91741-1899
County: Los Angeles FICE Identification: 001166
Unit ID: 112172
Telephone: (626) 963-0323 Carnegie Class: Assoc/Pub-S-SC
FAX Number: (626) 914-8618 Calendar System: Semester
URL: www.citruscollege.edu
Established: 1915 Annual Undergrad Tuition & Fees (In-District): $864
Enrollment: 11,000 Coed
Affiliation or Control: State/Local IRS Status: 501(c)3
Highest Offering: Associate Degree
Program: Occupational; 2-Year Principally Bachelor's Creditable; Business Emphasis
Accreditation: WJ, DA

01 Superintendent/President .... Dr. Geraldine M. PERRI
05 Vice President Academic Affairs .... Dr. Irene MALMGREN
32 Vice President Student Services .... Dr. Arvid SPOR
10 Vice Pres Finance/Admin Services .... Mrs. Carol R. HORTON
07 Dean Admissions & Records .... Vacant
51 Dean Career/Technical/Continuing Ed .... Mr. James LANCASTER
38 Dean of Counseling .... Dr. Lucinda OVER
16 Director Human Resources .... Dr. Robert SAMMIS
102 Director Development & Alumni Rels .... Ms. Christina GARCIA
35 Dean of Students .... Dr. Martha MCDONALD
18 Director Facilities & Construction .... Mr. Fred DIAMOND
09 Director of Institutional Research .... Dr. Lan HAO
06 Registrar .... Ms. Kristina SPALDING
37 Director Financial Aid .... Vacant
96 Director of Purchasing .... Mr. Robert IVERSON
21 Director of Fiscal Services .... Ms. Rosalinda BUCHWALD
26 Director of Communication .... Ms. Paula GREEN
23 Director of Health Sciences .... Dr. Maureen RENAGHAN
28 Staff Diversity Officer .... Mrs. Brenda FINK
13 Chief Information Services Officer .... Ms. Linda WELZ
19 Campus Security Supervisor .... Vacant
83 Dean Social/Behavioral Sciences/DE .... Dr. Mike HURTADO
41 Dean of Kinesiology & Athletics .... Ms. Jody WISE
79 Dean of Lang Arts & Enrollment Mgt .... Dr. Samuel LEE
65 Dean Physical/Natural Science & Lib .... Dr. Eric RABITOY
57 Dean of Fine & Performing Arts .... Mr. Robert SLACK
81 Dean Math/Business/Health Sciences .... Mr. James MCCLAIN
15 Director of Human Resources .... Dr. Robert SAMMIS
88 Dir EOPS CARE CalWORKS .... Ms. Sarah GONZALES-TAPIA
88 Project Dir RACE to STEM .... Ms. Marianne SMITH

City College of San Francisco (C)

33 Gough Street, San Francisco CA 94103-1292
County: San Francisco FICE Identification: 001167
Unit ID: 112190
Telephone: (415) 239-3000 Carnegie Class: Assoc/Pub-U-MC
FAX Number: (415) 239-3919 Calendar System: Semester
URL: www.ccsf.edu
Established: 1935 Annual Undergrad Tuition & Fees (In-District): $720
Enrollment: 35,760 Coed
Affiliation or Control: State/Local IRS Status: 501(c)3
Highest Offering: Associate Degree
Program: Occupational; 2-Year Principally Bachelor's Creditable
Accreditation: WJ, ACFEI, DA, EMT, MAC, RAD, RTT

01 Interim Chancellor .... Dr. Pamila FISHER
10 Vice Chanc Finance/Administration .... Mr. Peter A. GOLDSTEIN
05 Vice Chancellor Academic Affairs .... Dr. Alice MURILLO
32 Vice Chanc Student Development .... Ms. Lindy MCKNIGHT
46 Vice Chanc Research & Policy .... Ms. Phyllis MCGUIRE
11 Vice Chanc Campuses & Enroll Svcs .... Mr. Jorge BELL
43 Vice Chanc Legal Services .... Vacant
12 Dean Civic Center Campus .... Mr. Carl JEW
12 Dean Southeast Campus .... Mr. Jorge BELL
12 Dean Mission Campus .... Mr. Jorge BELL
12 Dean Downtown/Business School .... Dr. David DORE
26 Dean of Marketing/Public Relations .... Vacant
35 Dean Student Affairs .... Dr. Veronica HUNNICUTT
37 Dean Financial Aid & EOPS .... Mr. Roland MONTEMAYOR
07 Dean Admissions & Records .... Ms. Marylou LEYBA
20 Int Dean Instruction/Curriculum .... Mr. Tom BOEGEL
16 Dean Human Resourc/Library/Lrng Res .... Ms. Clara H. STARR
38 Dean/Dir Counseling/Student Support .... Vacant
06 Dean Matriculation .... Vacant
51 Dean Contract Educ/Voc Educ .... Vacant
85 Dean Chinatown/Intl Educ/ESL .... Ms. Joanne LOW
49 Dean Liberal Arts .... Mr. Bob DAVIS
83 Dean Behavioral/Social Sciences .... Dr. Fred CHAVARIA
81 Dean Science & Math .... Mr. David YEE
68 Dean J Adams Campus/Sch Hlth Educ .... Mr. Terry HALL
30 Dean College Development .... Dr. Kathleen SULLIVAN ALIOTO
88 Assoc Dean (Non-Credit) Admiss/Recs .... Ms. Lidia JENKINS
13 Director Information Services .... Mr. Doug RE
15 Director Employee Relations .... Mr. Steve HALE
18 Superintendent Buildings/Grounds .... Vacant
103 Dir Cal Works Education & Training . Mr. Roland MONTEMAYOR
09 Asst Dir of Institutional Research .... Mr. Steven SPURLING
27 Chief Information Technology Office .... Dr. David HOTCHKISS
96 Director of Purchasing .... Ms. Kathy HENNIG
19 Chief of Police .... Mr. Andre BARNES
88 ADA Compliance Officer .... Dr. Leilani BATTISTE
21 Assoc Vice Chanc/CFO .... Mr. John BILMONT
25 Dean Grants & Resource Dev .... Ms. Kristin CHARLES
86 Assoc Vice Chanc Governmtl Rel .... Ms. Leslie SMITH
06 Assoc Dean Registration/Records .... Ms. Monika LIU
37 Director Financial Aid .... Dr. Rose ROBERSON
88 Director Small Bus Dev Ctr .... Mr. Albert DIXON
88 Dean Faculty Support Svcs .... Dr. Minh-Hoa TA
23 Assoc Dean Student Health Svcs .... Ms. Sunny CLARK

City of Hope (D)

1500 East Duarte Road, Duarte CA 91010-3000
County: Los Angeles FICE Identification: 035924
Unit ID: 441238
Telephone: (626) 256-4673 Carnegie Class: Spec/Med
FAX Number: (626) 301-8105 Calendar System: Semester
URL: cityofhope.org
Established: 1994 Annual Graduate Tuition & Fees: N/A
Enrollment: 82 Coed
Affiliation or Control: Independent Non-Profit IRS Status: 501(c)3
Highest Offering: Doctorate; No Undergraduates
Program: Professional
Accreditation: WC

01 Dean .... John J. ROSSI
05 Director/Associate Dean Prof Educ .... Steven NORVAC

*Claremont University Consortium (E)

101 South Mills Avenue, Claremont CA 91711-5053
County: Los Angeles Identification: 666003
Telephone: (909) 621-8026 Carnegie Class: N/A
FAX Number: (909) 621-8517
URL: www.cuc.claremont.edu

01 Chief Executive Officer .... Mr. Robert WALTON
03 Executive VP/COO .... Mr. M.L. (Mel) DINKEL
10 Vice President/Treasurer .... Mr. Ken PIFER
32 Vice President of Student Affairs .... Dr. Denise HAYES
18 VP Facilities Management/Planning .... Mr. Tim MORRISON
101 Sec to Brd of Overseers/Asst to CEO .... Dr. Bonnie CLEMENS

*Claremont Graduate University (F)

150 E 10th Street, Claremont CA 91711-5909
County: Los Angeles FICE Identification: 001169
Unit ID: 112251
Telephone: (909) 621-8000 Carnegie Class: RU/H
FAX Number: (909) 621-8390 Calendar System: Semester
URL: www.cgu.edu
Established: 1925 Annual Graduate Tuition & Fees: $38,140
Enrollment: 2,177 Coed
Affiliation or Control: Independent Non-Profit IRS Status: 501(c)3
Highest Offering: Doctorate; No Undergraduates
Program: Liberal Arts And General; Teacher Preparatory; Professional
Accreditation: WC, BUS, PH

02 President .... Dr. Deborah A. FREUND
04 Exec Asst to the President .... Ms. Donna STANDLEA
05 Exec Vice President and Provost .... Dr. Jacob ADAMS
10 Senior VP for Finance and Admin .... Dr. Steven N. GARCIA
30 Vice President for Advancement .... Mr. Bedford MCINTOSH
84 Vice Prov Enroll Svc/Dean of Stdnts .... Mr. Fred SIEGEL
46 Vice Provost/Research .... Dr. Dean GERSTEIN
88 Vice Provost/Transdisciplin Studies .... Dr. Wendy MARTIN
108 Director Institutional Effectivenes .... Ms. Alana OLSCHWANG
16 Assoc VP for Human Resources .... Ms. Brenda LESWICK
47 Botany Center .... Dr. Lucinda MCDADE
50 Drucker-Ito Grad School of Mgt .... Dr. Bernie JAWORSKI
83 Behavioral & Organizational Sci .... Dr. Stewart DONALDSON
69 Community & Global Health .... Dr. Anderson JOHNSON
53 Educational Studies .... Dr. Scott THOMAS
77 Center for Information Science .... Dr. Thomas HORAN
81 Institute for Math Sciences .... Dr. Henry SCHELLHORN
82 Politics & Economics .... Dr. Stewart DONALDSON
73 Arts Humanities & Religion .... Dr. Tammi SCHNEIDER
09 Institutional Research Officer .... Ms. Jeannette GURROLA
44 Senior Director of Development .... Mr. Mike AVILA
21 Asst VP/Asst Treasurer .... Mr. Dean CALVO
29 Director Alumnae /Alumni Relations .... Ms. Monika MOORE
26 Director University Communications .... Ms. Esther WILEY
06 Registrar .... Mr. Cliff RAMIREZ
37 Director Student Financial Aid .... Ms. Susie GUILBAULT
85 International Student Coordinator .... Ms. Marsha HABIB
07 Director of Admissions .... Ms. Julia EVANS
36 Director Career Management .... Vacant
18 Director of Facilities .... Mr. DeWayne HURST
39 Housing Manager .... Mr. Chris BASS
13 Exec Dir Office Information Tech .... Mr. Travis WYNBERRY
27 Chief Information Officer .... Mr. Daris BOUTHILLIER
91 Application Services Director .... Mr. Manoj CHITRE
101 Secretary to the Board .... Ms. Louise WEBBER

*Claremont McKenna College (G)

500 E 9th Street, Claremont CA 91711-6400
County: Los Angeles FICE Identification: 001170
Unit ID: 112260
Telephone: (909) 621-8000 Carnegie Class: Bac/A&S
FAX Number: (909) 621-8790 Calendar System: Semester
URL: www.claremontmckenna.edu
Established: 1946 Annual Undergrad Tuition & Fees: $44,085
Enrollment: 1,321 Coed
Affiliation or Control: Independent Non-Profit IRS Status: 501(c)3
Highest Offering: Master's
Program: Liberal Arts And General
Accreditation: WC

02 President and CEO .... Pamela B. GANN
05 VP Academic Affairs/Dean of Faculty .... Gregory HESS
30 Vice President for Development .... Ernie ISEMINGER
10 Vice Pres Business Admin/Treasurer .... Robin J. ASPINALL
11 VP for Planning and Administration .... Matthew G. BIBBENS
32 VP Student Affs/Admiss/Fin Aid .... Jefferson HUANG
07 AVP & Dean Admission/Financial Aid .... Georgette DEVERES
21 VP and Chief Investment Officer .... James J. FLOYD
26 Assoc VP Public Affs/Communications .... Max BENAVIDEZ
13 Assoc VP/Chief Technology Officer .... Cynthia HUMES
29 Vice President for Alumni Relations .... John P. FARANDA
06 Registrar/Dir Institutional Rsrch .... Elizabeth MORGAN
36 Assoc Dean/Dir Career Services .... Diana SEDER
18 Dir Facilities and Campus Services .... Brian WORLEY
15 Director of Human Resources .... Andrea GALE
32 Dean of Students .... Mary SPELLMAN
104 Director of Off-Campus Study .... Kristen MALLORY
41 Athletic Director .... Michael SUTTON
04 Special Assistant to the President .... Cheryl M. AGUILAR

*Claremont School of Theology (H)

1325 N College Avenue, Claremont CA 91711-3199
County: Los Angeles FICE Identification: 001288
Unit ID: 124283
Telephone: (909) 447-2500 Carnegie Class: Spec/Faith
FAX Number: (909) 626-7062 Calendar System: Semester
URL: www.cst.edu
Established: 1885 Annual Graduate Tuition & Fees: $16,550
Enrollment: 225 Coed
Affiliation or Control: United Methodist IRS Status: 501(c)3
Highest Offering: Doctorate; No Undergraduates
Program: Professional
Accreditation: WC, THEOL

02 President .... Dr. Jerry D. CAMPBELL
05 Vice President Academic Affs & Dean .... Dr. Philip CLAYTON
10 VP for Administration & Finance/ CFO .... Dr. Lynn O'LEARY-ARCHER
30 Vice President of Development .... Mr. Duane DYER
21 Assoc VP for Finance & Planning .... Mr. Gamward QUAN
27 Director of Communications .... Mr. Jon HOOTEN
06 Registrar .... Ms. Jennie ALLEN
07 Director of Admission .... Ms. Jennifer MCLEAN
08 Dir of Library/Technological Svcs .... Mr. John DICKASON
42 Dir Church Rels & Ministry Resource .... Dr. Karen DALTON
37 Director of Financial Aid .... Ms. LaNae HERRERA
22 Affirmative Action Officer .... Ms. Elaine WALKER

*Keck Graduate Institute (I)

535 Watson Drive, Claremont CA 91711-4817
County: Los Angeles FICE Identification: 038533
Unit ID: 440031
Telephone: (909) 607-7855 Carnegie Class: Assoc/PrivNFP4
FAX Number: (909) 607-8086 Calendar System: Semester
URL: www.kgi.edu
Established: 1997 Annual Graduate Tuition & Fees: $38,550
Enrollment: 161 Coed
Affiliation or Control: Independent Non-Profit IRS Status: 501(c)3
Highest Offering: Doctorate; No Undergraduates
Program: Professional; Technical Emphasis
Accreditation: WC

02 President ....Dr. Sheldon M. SCHUSTER
06 Registrar ....Adam D. PAVE

*Coast Community College District Administration Offices (A)

1370 Adams Avenue, Costa Mesa CA 92626-5429
County: Orange FICE Identification: 008711
Unit ID: 112376
Telephone: (714) 438-4600 Carnegie Class: N/A
FAX Number: (714) 438-4882
URL: www.cccd.edu

01 Chancellor ....Dr. Andrew C. JONES
10 Vice Chancellor Finance & Adm Svcs ....Mr. Andrew DUNN
16 Vice Chancellor Human Resources ....Dr. Deborah D. HIRSH
05 Vice Chanc Educ Svcs & Technology ....Dr. Andreea SERBAN
26 Dir Public Affairs/Mktg & Govt Rels ....Dr. Martha PARHAM
96 Director of Purchasing ....Mr. John ERIKSEN

*Coastline Community College (B)

11460 Warner Avenue, Fountain Valley CA 92708-2597
County: Orange FICE Identification: 020635
Unit ID: 112385
Telephone: (714) 546-7600 Carnegie Class: Assoc/Pub-S-MC
FAX Number: (714) 241-6277 Calendar System: Semester
URL: www.coastline.edu
Established: 1976 Annual Undergrad Tuition & Fees (In-District): $1,136
Enrollment: 10,159 Coed
Affiliation or Control: State/Local IRS Status: 501(c)3
Highest Offering: Associate Degree
Program: Occupational; 2-Year Principally Bachelor's Creditable
Accreditation: WJ

02 President ....Dr. Loretta P. ADRIAN
05 VP of Instruction/Student Services ....Mr. Vince RODRIGUEZ
11 VP of Administrative Services ....Ms. Christine NGUYEN
84 Dean of Enrollment Services ....Ms. Lois WILKERSON
46 Admin Dean Instr Systems Devel ....Mr. Dan JONES
38 Dean of Counseling & Matriculation ....Ms. Christine LEON
106 Assoc Dean of Distance Learning ....Mr. Bob NASH
12 Actg Dean of Instruction Costa Mesa ....Dr. Ted BOEHLER
12 Actg Dean Instruction Garden Grove ....Dr. Ted BOEHLER
12 Dean Instruction Westminster ....Mr. Vinicio LOPEZ
26 Director of Mktg/PR & Govt Affairs ....Mrs. Michelle MA
06 Registrar/Director of Admissions ....Ms. Jennifer MCDONALD
37 Dir Student Financial Aid & EOPS ....Ms. Cynthia PIENKOWSKI
18 Director Maintenance & Operations ....Mr. David CANT
21 Interim Director Fiscal Services ....Mr. Richard KUDLIK
102 Executive Director Foundation ....Ms. Mariam KHOSRAVANI
40 Director Bookstore ....Mr. Michael BARE
14 Interim Director Computer Services ....Mr. Anthony MACIEL
09 Director Research/Planning/Develop ....Dr. Jorge R. SANCHEZ
88 Acting Dean of Military Programs ....Mr. Bill KERWIN
88 Manager Contract Education Programs ....Mr. Peter MAHARAJ
72 Dean of Lrng Tech Innovation & Supp ....Mr. Ted BOEHLER
24 Director of Electronic Media ....Ms. Judy GARVEY
15 Director of Personnel Services ....Vacant
88 Director of EBUS program ....Ms. Laurie MELBY
88 Director of eLearning Rsrch and Dev ....Mr. Dave THOMPSON
103 Interim Dir Workforce & Econ Dev ....Ms. Sallie SALINAS

*Golden West College (C)

15744 Golden West Street,
Huntington Beach CA 92647-2748
County: Orange FICE Identification: 001206
Unit ID: 115126
Telephone: (714) 892-7711 Carnegie Class: Assoc/Pub-S-MC
FAX Number: (714) 895-8243 Calendar System: Semester
URL: www.gwc.info
Established: 1966 Annual Undergrad Tuition & Fees (In-District): $1,126
Enrollment: 13,493 Coed
Affiliation or Control: State/Local IRS Status: Exempt
Highest Offering: Associate Degree
Program: Occupational; 2-Year Principally Bachelor's Creditable
Accreditation: WJ, ADNUR

02 President ....Mr. Wes BRYAN
05 Vice President Student Success ..Dr. Fabienne MCPHAIL NAPLES
11 Vice Pres Student & Admin Support ....Ms. Janet M. HOULIHAN
38 Dean Counseling ....Dr. David L. BAIRD
08 Assoc Dean Learning Res/Online Inst ....Mr. Jorge ASCENCIO
72 Dean Career & Tech Ed and Business ..Dr. Omid POURZANJANI
81 Dean Soc Science/Math & Sciences ....Mr. Jeff COURCHAINE
49 Dean Arts & Letters ....Dr. David D. HUDSON
23 Assoc Dean/Dir Student Health Svcs ....Mr. Robin BACHMANN
09 Assoc Dean Inst Research/Planning ..Mr. Dwayne E. THOMPSON
88 Dean Criminal Justice & Health Prof ....Mr. Ron LOWENBERG
35 Administrative Director Stdnt Svcs ....Ms. Shirley A. DONNELLY
15 Director Personnel Services ....Mrs. Crystal D. CRANE
21 Director Fiscal Services ....Mr. Paul WISNER
102 Director Foundation/Community Rels ....Ms. Margie J. BUNTEN
88 Director Emer Prep & Spec Events ....Ms. Valerie A. VENEGAS
07 Director of Admissions ....Ms. Jennifer L. ORTBERG
37 Director of Financial Aid ....Mr. Steve SKILLE
18 Chief Facilities/Physical Plant ....Mr. Joseph B. DOWLING
68 Dean Health PE & Athleics ....Mr. Albert GASPARIAN

*Orange Coast College (D)

2701 Fairview Road, POB 5005,
Costa Mesa CA 92628-5005
County: Orange FICE Identification: 001250
Unit ID: 120342
Telephone: (714) 432-0202 Carnegie Class: Assoc/Pub-S-MC
FAX Number: (714) 432-5609 Calendar System: Semester
URL: www.orangecoastcollege.edu
Established: 1947 Annual Undergrad Tuition & Fees (In-District): $1,458
Enrollment: 23,058 Coed
Affiliation or Control: State/Local IRS Status: 501(c)3
Highest Offering: Associate Degree
Program: Occupational; 2-Year Principally Bachelor's Creditable
Accreditation: WJ, ACFEI, CVT, DA, DIETT, DMS, MAC, NDT, POLYT, RAD

02 President ....Dr. Dennis HARKINS
05 Vice President Instruction ....Dr. John G. WEISPFENNING
32 Vice President Student Services ....Dr. Kristin CLARK
11 Vice Pres Administrative Services ....Dr. Richard PAGEL
84 Dean Enrollment Services ....Mr. Madjid NIROUMAND
38 Dean of Counseling ....Dr. Hue PHAM
35 Dean of Student Services ....Dr. Kathyrn MUELLER
26 Director Community Relations ....Mr. Jeffrey HOBBS
102 Director Foundation ....Mr. Douglas BENNETT
09 Director of IR/Planning and IE ....Ms. Sheri STERNER
07 Director Admiss/Records/Enroll Tech ....Mr. Efren GALVAN
15 Director Personnel Services ....Ms. Laurel FRANCIS
18 Director M & O ....Mr. Mark GOODE
37 Director Student Financial Aid ....Ms. Melissa MOSER
13 Director Infomration Technology ....Mr. Craig OBERLIN
23 Associate Dean Health Services ....Ms. Sylvia WORDEN
88 Manager Child Care Center ....Ms. Sue BIERLICH
35 Associate Dean Student Services ....Vacant
40 Director Bookstore ....Mr. William KIRCHINGER
41 Athletic Director ....Dr. Michael SUTLIFF
88 Dean of Consumer & Health Sciences ....Mr. Kevin BALLINGER
68 Dean of Kiniseology & Athletics ....Dr. Michael SUTLIFF
72 Dean of Technology ....Dr. Doug BENOIT
50 Dean of Business & Computer Science ....Dr. Doug BENOIT
83 Dean of Social & Behavioral Science ....Dr. Paul ASIM
88 Dean of Literature & Languages ....Dr. Michael MANDELKERN
81 Dean of Math & Sciences ....Dr. Robert MENDOZA
57 Dean of Visual & Performing Arts ....Mr. Joe POSHEK
62 Dean of Library and Media Services ....Mr. Joe POSHEK
103 Director Career & Cmty Education ....Ms. Raine HAMBLY
105 Director Web Services ....Mr. Glen PROFETA

Cogswell Polytechnical College (E)

1175 Bordeaux Drive, Sunnyvale CA 94089-1299
County: Santa Clara FICE Identification: 001177
Unit ID: 112394
Telephone: (408) 541-0100 Carnegie Class: Bac/Diverse
FAX Number: (408) 747-0764 Calendar System: Semester
URL: www.cogswell.edu
Established: 1887 Annual Undergrad Tuition & Fees: $24,540
Enrollment: 288 Coed
Affiliation or Control: Independent Non-Profit IRS Status: 501(c)3
Highest Offering: Baccalaureate
Program: Liberal Arts And General; Professional; Technical Emphasis
Accreditation: WC

01 Chancellor/President ....Mr. Charles (Chuck) HOUSE
05 Dean of the College ....Mr. Michael MARTIN
10 Vice President Finance ....Mr. Rejino CASTANEDA
07 Director Admissions & Recruiting ....Mr. Abraham CHACKO
06 Registrar ....Ms. Milla ZLATANOV
08 Librarian ....Ms. Vivian KOBAYASHI
04 Executive Assistant ....Ms. Debbie PAVAO

The Colburn School (F)

200 S Grand Avenue, Los Angeles CA 90012-3007
County: Los Angeles Identification: 666233
Telephone: (213) 621-2200 Carnegie Class: Not Classified
FAX Number: (213) 621-2110 Calendar System: Semester
URL: www.colburnschool.edu
Established: 2003 Annual Undergrad Tuition & Fees: N/A
Enrollment: 114 Coed
Affiliation or Control: Independent Non-Profit IRS Status: 501(c)3
Highest Offering: Baccalaureate
Program: Music Emphasis
Accreditation: MUS

01 President & CEO ....Mr. Sal KARDAN
10 Chief Financial Officer ....Mr. Seth WEINTRAUB

† Full room, board, and tuition are provided to accepted students through the school's endowment.

Coleman University (G)

8888 Balboa Avenue, San Diego CA 92123-1506
County: San Diego FICE Identification: 007296
Unit ID: 112446
Telephone: (858) 499-0202 Carnegie Class: Bac/Assoc
FAX Number: (858) 499-0233 Calendar System: Quarter
URL: www.coleman.edu
Established: 1963 Annual Undergrad Tuition & Fees: $35,200
Enrollment: 791 Coed
Affiliation or Control: Independent Non-Profit IRS Status: 501(c)3
Highest Offering: Master's
Program: Occupational; Professional; Technical Emphasis
Accreditation: ACICS

01 President ....Mr. Paul S. PANESAR
12 Vice Pres/Branch Mgr San Marcos ....Ms. Darlene S. ANKTON
05 Vice President/Dean of Academics ....Ms. Sheryl L. RIDENS
10 Chief Financial Officer ....Mr. Mohsen GHARAHBAGHIAN
06 Registrar ....Ms. Karen S. HYNES
36 Director Career Services ....Mr. John D. BULLOCK
07 Director of Admissions ....Mr. David PEARSON
09 Director of Institutional Research ....Mr. Bruce F. GILDEN
20 Associate Academic Officer ....Mr. Jason ABEL
28 Director of Diversity ....Ms. Ariana MARRON
29 Director Alumni Relations ....Ms. Ariana MARRON
38 Director Student Counseling ....Ms. Karen S. HYNES
08 Head Librarian ....Mr. Manuel A. BERNAD
105 Web Master ....Mr. Chris J. CAREY
37 Director Student Financial Aid ....Dr. Christina MILLER
26 Chief Public Relations Officer ....Ms. Bobbie A. STROHM
21 Business Manager ....Ms. Elizabeth A. GALINDO
18 Site Manager ....Mr. Keith R. WISSWELL
15 Human Resource Generalist ....Ms. Maria HAMZAVI

Coleman University (H)

1284 West San Marcos Boulevard,
San Marcos CA 92078-4073
County: San Diego Identification: 666259
Telephone: (760) 747-3990 Carnegie Class: Not Classified
FAX Number: (760) 752-9808 Calendar System: Quarter
URL: www.coleman.edu
Established: 1963 Annual Undergrad Tuition & Fees: $35,200
Enrollment: 121 Coed
Affiliation or Control: Independent Non-Profit IRS Status: 501(c)3
Highest Offering: Associate Degree
Program: Occupational; 2-Year Principally Bachelor's Creditable; Technical Emphasis
Accreditation: ACICS

01 President ....Mr. Paul PANESAR

College of the Canyons (I)

26455 Rockwell Canyon Road,
Santa Clarita CA 91355-1899
County: Los Angeles FICE Identification: 008903
Unit ID: 111461
Telephone: (661) 259-7800 Carnegie Class: Assoc/Pub-S-SC
FAX Number: (661) 259-8302 Calendar System: Semester
URL: www.canyons.edu
Established: 1967 Annual Undergrad Tuition & Fees (In-District): $1,152
Enrollment: 14,867 Coed
Affiliation or Control: State/Local IRS Status: 501(c)3
Highest Offering: Associate Degree
Program: Occupational; 2-Year Principally Bachelor's Creditable
Accreditation: WJ, ADNUR

01 Chancellor SCCCD & President COC ...Dr. Dianne G. VAN HOOK
10 Asst Supt/VP Business Services ....Ms. Sharlene COLEAL
15 Asst Supt/Vice Pres Human Resources ....Ms. Diane FIERO
46 Asst Supt/VP Inst Dev/Tech/Online ....Dr. Barry GRIBBONS
18 Asst Supt/VP Facil Plan Op/Const ....Mr. Jim SCHRAGE
32 Asst Superintendent/VP Student Svcs ....Dr. Michael WILDING
05 Int Asst Supt/Vice Pres Instruction ....Mr. Joe GERDA
20 Assoc Vice Pres Academic Affairs ....Ms. Audrey GREEN
13 Assoc VP Information Technology ....Mr. Jim TEMPLE
57 Div Dean Fine & Performing Arts ....Dr. Carmen DOMINGUEZ
76 Div Dean Allied Health & Pub Safety ....Ms. Cynthia DORROH
79 Division Dean Humanities ....Dr. Jennifer BREZINA
41 Division Dean PE/Athletic Director ....Mr. Len MOHNEY
83 Div Dean Social Sci & Business ....Dr. Patricia ROBINSON
81 Div Dean Math/Science & Engineering ....Mr. Omar TORRES
106 Dean Educ Tech/Lrng Resrc/Dist Educ ....Mr. James GLAPA-GROSSKLAG
75 Dean Career Technical Education ....Ms. Kristin HOUSER
35 Dean Student Services ....Mr. Mike JOSLIN
88 Dean Instructional Support ....Dr. Kevin KISTLER
06 Dean Enrollment Services ....Ms. Deborah RIO
88 Dean ECE and Teacher Training ....Ms. Diane STEWART
35 Dean of Students CCC ....Mr. Ryan THEULE
103 Dean Economic Development ....Mr. Peter BELLAS
66 Asst Dean Allied Health/Dir Nursing ....Dr. Diane MOREY
88 Assoc Dean Inst & Supp Svs CCC ....Ms. Denee PESCARMONA
21 Controller Fiscal Services ....Ms. Cindy GRANDGEORGE
102 COO COC Foundation/Int Dir UC ....Ms. Cathy RITZ
30 Chief Devel Officer COC Foundation ....Mr. Murray WOOD
86 Spec Asst Chan/Int Man Dir Gov Rels ....Mr. Eric HARNISH
26 Int Managing Director PR/Marketing ....Mr. Bruce BATTLE
96 Director Contracts Proc & Risk Mgmt ....Mr. Jon AASTED
88 Director Student Business Office ....Ms. Kathleen BENZ
37 Director Financial Aid ....Mr. Tom BILBRUCK
88 Director Professional Development ....Ms. Leslie CARR
19 Director Campus Safety ....Ms. Tammy CASTOR
88 Director MESA ....Ms. Susan CROWTHER
88 Director Student Development ....Ms. Allison KORSE-DEVLIN
30 Director Development ....Ms. Michele EDMONSON
106 Dir Distance & Accelerated Learning ....Mr. John MAKEVICH
09 Director of Institutional Research ....Dr. Daylene MEUSCHKE
36 Director Career Services ....Mr. Anthony MICHAELIDES
06 Dir Admissions/Records/Online Svcs ....Ms. Jasmine RUYS
88 Dir Outreach & School Relations ....Ms. Kari SOFFA
88 Exec Dir Small Business Dev Ctr ....Mr. Steven TANNEHILL

88 Dir Reentry Pgm & Veterans Affair ....Mr. Renard THOMAS
16 Interim Director Human Resources ....Ms. Christina CHUNG
25 Director Grants Development ....Ms. Theresa ZUZEVICH
23 Director Student Health & Wellness ....Ms. Colleen REEVES
88 Int Director Pub Safety Instr Pgms ....Mr. Steven MCLEAN

College of the Desert (A)

43-500 Monterey Avenue, Palm Desert CA 92260-9399
County: Riverside FICE Identification: 001182
Unit ID: 113573
Telephone: (760) 346-8041 Carnegie Class: Assoc/Pub-S-MC
FAX Number: (760) 341-8678 Calendar System: Semester
URL: www.collegeofthedesert.edu
Established: 1958 Annual Undergrad Tuition & Fees (In-District): $1,008
Enrollment: 10,412 Coed
Affiliation or Control: State/Local IRS Status: 501(c)3
Highest Offering: Associate Degree
Program: Occupational; 2-Year Principally Bachelor's Creditable
Accreditation: WJ

01 Superintendent/President ....Dr. Joel L. KINNAMON
05 Vice Pres Academic Affairs ....Mr. Farley HERZEK
11 Vice President Business Affairs ....Dr. Edwin DEAS
32 Interim Vice Pres Student Affairs ....Mr. Adrian GONZALES
15 Interim Exec Dir Human Res ....Mr. Stan DUPREE
30 Instnl Advance & Title V Director ....Ms. Pam HUNTER
84 Dean of Enrollment Services ....Dr. Annebelle NERY
38 Dean Student Support Programs ....Mr. Adrian GONZALES
102 Exec Dir of Foundation ....Mr. Jim HUMMER
09 Dean Info Tech & Inst Research ....Ms. Bina ISAAC
18 Director of Maintenance/Operations ....Mr. Steve RENEW
29 Director Alumni Relations ....Mr. Gene MARCHU
37 Director Financial Aid ....Mr. Ken LIRA
96 Director of Fiscal Services ....Mr. Wade ELLIS
06 Registrar/Director of Admissions ....Ms. Sally TIAGA

College of Marin (B)

835 College Avenue, Kentfield CA 94904-2590
County: Marin FICE Identification: 001178
Unit ID: 118347
Telephone: (415) 457-8811 Carnegie Class: Assoc/Pub-S-MC
FAX Number: (415) 456-6017 Calendar System: Semester
URL: www.marin.edu
Established: 1926 Annual Undergrad Tuition & Fees (In-District): $1,380
Enrollment: 7,075 Coed
Affiliation or Control: State/Local IRS Status: 501(c)3
Highest Offering: Associate Degree
Program: Occupational; 2-Year Principally Bachelor's Creditable
Accreditation: WJ, ADNUR, DA

01 Superintendent/President ....Dr. David W. COON
05 Int Vice President Student Learning ....Dr. Rebecca J. KENNEY
32 Int Vice President Student Services ....Ms. Angelina DUARTE
10 Vice President Operations ....Mr. Albert J. HARRISON, II
16 Exec Dean Human Res/Labor Relations ....Ms. Linda BEAM
84 Dean Enrollment Services ....Ms. Patricia GANT
49 Dean Arts & Humanities ....Dr. David SNYDER
103 Dean Wkfce Dev/Col & Cmty Prntrshps ....Ms. Nanda SCHORSKE
81 Dean Math/Sciences ....Mr. Jim ARNOLD
21 Director Fiscal Services ....Ms. Peggy ISOZAKI
09 Dir Plng/Rsch/Inst Effectiveness ....Dr. Chialin HSIEH
37 Director Financial Aid/Career Pgms ....Mr. David COOK
18 Director Maintenance & Operations ....Mr. Robert H. THOMPSON
13 Director Information Technology ....Mr. Marshall NORTHCOTT
35 Dir Student Affairs/Health Center ....Dr. Arnulfo CEDILLO
19 Chief of Police/Director of Safety ....Mr. Mitch LEMAY
68 Dir Physical Educ/Athletics ....Mr. Matt MARKOVICH
76 Interim Director Health Sciences ....Ms. Debra LEWIS
31 Dir Cmty Svc/Lifelong Lrng ....Dr. Jason LAU
26 Dir Communications/Community Rels ....Ms. Cathy SUMMA-WOLFE
08 Director of Learning Resources ....Ms. Susan ANDRIEN
88 Dir of Academic Svcs/Articulation ....Ms. Cari TORRES

College of the Redwoods Community College District (C)

7351 Tompkins Hill Road, Eureka CA 95501-9300
County: Humboldt FICE Identification: 001185
Unit ID: 121707
Telephone: (707) 476-4100 Carnegie Class: Assoc/Pub-R-L
FAX Number: (707) 476-4400 Calendar System: Semester
URL: www.redwoods.edu
Established: 1964 Annual Undergrad Tuition & Fees (In-District): $1,140
Enrollment: 17,343 Coed
Affiliation or Control: State/Local IRS Status: 501(c)3
Highest Offering: Associate Degree
Program: Occupational; 2-Year Principally Bachelor's Creditable
Accreditation: WJ, DA, NAIT

01 President ....Ms. Kathryn G. LEHNER
04 Assistant to the President ....Ms. Michelle ANDERSON
11 VP Administrative Services ....Mr. Lee LINDSEY
32 VP Student Services ....Dr. Keith SNOW-FLAMER
05 VP of Instruction ....Dr. Utpal GOSWAMI
15 Director Human Resources ....Ms. Ahn FIELDING
12 Vice President of Del Norte Campus ....Ms. Anita JANIS
12 Vice Pres of Mendocino Coast Campus ....Dr. Geisce LY
20 Dean Academic Affairs ....Dr. Rachel ANDERSON
17 Dean Health Occupations/Public Svcs ....Dr. Pat GIRCZYC
72 Int Dean Career & Technical Educ ....Mr. Jeff CUMMINGS
41 Athletic Director ....Mr. Joseph HASH
37 Director Financial Aid ....Ms. Lynn THIESEN
22 Director EOPS ....Ms. Cheryl TUCKER
88 Director Disabled Student Pgm Svcs ....Vacant
18 Director Facilities & Planning ....Mr. Tim FLANAGAN
19 Director Maintenance & Operations ....Mr. Gary PATRICK
26 Public Information Officer ....Mr. Paul DEMARK
08 Director Learning Resource Center ....Ms. Mary Grace BARRICK
09 Director of Institutional Research ....Ms. Angeline HILL
07 Manager Admissions & Records ....Ms. Kathy GOODLIVE
88 Coord Basic Law Enforcement Academy ....Mr. Ron WATERS

College of the Sequoias (D)

915 S Mooney Boulevard, Visalia CA 93277-2234
County: Tulare FICE Identification: 001186
Unit ID: 123217
Telephone: (559) 730-3700 Carnegie Class: Assoc/Pub-R-L
FAX Number: (559) 730-3894 Calendar System: Semester
URL: www.cos.edu
Established: 1925 Annual Undergrad Tuition & Fees (In-District): $1,104
Enrollment: 10,700 Coed
Affiliation or Control: State/Local IRS Status: 501(c)3
Highest Offering: Associate Degree
Program: Occupational; 2-Year Principally Bachelor's Creditable
Accreditation: WJ, PTAA

01 Superintendent/President ....Mr. Stan A. CARRIZOSA
05 Vice President Academic Services ....Dr. Jennifer LA SERNA
10 Dean Fiscal Services ....Ms. Leangela MILLER
32 Vice President Student Services ....Ms. Frances GUZMAN
37 Dean Student Svcs/Financial Aid ....Ms. Tamara RAVALIN
75 Dean Academic Svcs/Voc Educ ....Mr. Larry DUTTO
81 Dean Science/Math/Eng ....Dr. Robert URTECHO
76 Dean Allied Health/Phys Education ....Mrs. Cindy DELAIN
49 Dean Arts & Letters ....Vacant
15 Dean Human Resources/Legal Affairs ....Mr. John BRATSCH
18 Dean Facilities/Facilities Plng ....Mr. Eric MITTLESTEAD
30 Exec Dir Found/Inst Advancement ....Mr. Steve RENTON
66 Director Nursing & Allied Health ....Mrs. Karen ROBERTS
08 Dir Library/Instructional Tech ....Mrs. Kathie LEWIS
09 Director of Research ....Vacant
06 Registrar/Record Technician ....Ms. Velia RODRIGUEZ
27 Public Information Officer ....Mr. Steve RENTON
41 Athletic Director ....Mr. Lamel HARRIS
19 Chief Campus Police ....Mr. Robert MASTERSON
38 Div Chr Stdt Counsel/Hlth Std/Wk Ex ....Ms. Hunter CHURCH-GONZALES
40 Bookstore Manager ....Ms. Dorianna MENDIETTA
23 Head Nurse/Health Center ....Ms. Stephanie YOCUM
32 Student Activities Coordinator ....Mrs. Debbie DOUGLASS
103 Program Coord Workforce Development ....Ms. Louann WALDNER
36 Coord Career/Placement Center ....Ms. Bethany AZEVEDO

College of the Siskiyous (E)

800 College Avenue, Weed CA 96094-2899
County: Siskiyou FICE Identification: 001187
Unit ID: 123484
Telephone: (530) 938-5200 Carnegie Class: Assoc/Pub-R-M
FAX Number: (530) 938-5506 Calendar System: Semester
URL: www.siskiyous.edu
Established: 1957 Annual Undergrad Tuition & Fees (In-District): $1,410
Enrollment: 2,587 Coed
Affiliation or Control: State/Local IRS Status: 501(c)3
Highest Offering: Associate Degree
Program: Occupational; 2-Year Principally Bachelor's Creditable
Accreditation: WJ

01 Superintendent/President ....Mr. Randall C. LAWRENCE
04 Exec Assistant to the President ....Ms. Kathy GASSAWAY
05 Vice President Student Learning ....Dr. Robert FROST
11 Interim VP Administrative Svcs ....Mr. Scotty THOMASON
08 Assistant Dean Learning Resources ....Ms. Nancy SHEPARD
32 Director Student Life ....Mr. Doug HAUGEN
09 Director Planning Assess & Research ....Ms. Kristy ANDERSON
41 Director Athletics ....Mr. Dennis ROBERTS
20 Dean Student Learning ....Dr. Gregory SOUTH
12 Director Yreka Campus ....Ms. Sarah WHITIS
07 Director of Enrollment Services ....Ms. Meghan WITHERELL
15 Director Personnel ....Ms. Nancy MILLER
37 Supervisor Financial Aid ....Ms. Meghan WITHERELL
18 Interim Asst Dir MOT ....Mr. Phil ALVARADO
30 Director of Institutional Advancemt ....Ms. Sonia WRIGHT
28 Director of Diversity ....Ms. Nancy MILLER
96 Director of Purchasing ....Ms. Lori LUDDON

Columbia College Hollywood (F)

18618 Oxnard Street, Tarzana CA 91356-1411
County: Los Angeles FICE Identification: 021102
Unit ID: 112570
Telephone: (800) 785-0585 Carnegie Class: Spec/Arts
FAX Number: (818) 345-9053 Calendar System: Quarter
URL: www.columbiacollege.edu
Established: 1952 Annual Undergrad Tuition & Fees: $18,000
Enrollment: 348 Coed
Affiliation or Control: Independent Non-Profit IRS Status: 501(c)3
Highest Offering: Baccalaureate
Program: Liberal Arts And General; Fine Arts Emphasis
Accreditation: ART

01 President/CEO ....Mr. Richard KOBRITZ
05 Dean of the College ....Mr. Alan L. GANSBERG
10 Treasurer ....Mr. Theodore O'KARMA
22 Sr Compliance/Accreditation Manager ....Ms. Debra MONTOYA
21 Sr Director of Finance/New Ventures ....Mr. Richard CROWE
35 Dean of Student Services ....Dr. Yolanda DAWSON
13 Director of IT and Production Svcs ....Mr. Ronald REEVES
07 Director of Admissions ....Ms. Carmen MUNOZ
37 Financial Aid Manager ....Mr. Jan HASTINGS
36 Student Placement ....Ms. Kate MCARDLE

Community Christian College (G)

251 Tennessee Street, Redlands CA 92373-4438
County: San Bernardino FICE Identification: 038744
Unit ID: 446163
Telephone: (909) 335-8863 Carnegie Class: Assoc/PrivNFP
FAX Number: (909) 335-9101 Calendar System: Quarter
URL: www.cccollege.edu
Established: 1995 Annual Undergrad Tuition & Fees: $10,375
Enrollment: 152 Coed
Affiliation or Control: Independent Non-Profit IRS Status: 501(c)3
Highest Offering: Associate Degree
Program: 2-Year Principally Bachelor's Creditable
Accreditation: TRACS

01 President ....Mr. Troy VUGTEVEEN
05 Vice Pres Academic Affs/Registrar ....Dr. John HARBISON
10 Vice Pres for Finance ....Mr. Jason SCHROCK

Concord Law School of Kaplan University (H)

10866 Wilshire Blvd, Suite 1200,
Los Angeles CA 90024-4356
County: Los Angeles FICE Identification: 041259
Telephone: (310) 689-3200 Carnegie Class: Not Classified
FAX Number: (310) 470-3547 Calendar System: Other
URL: info.concordlawschool.edu
Established: 1998 Annual Graduate Tuition & Fees: $9,984
Enrollment: 1,200 Coed
Affiliation or Control: Proprietary IRS Status: Proprietary
Highest Offering: First Professional Degree; No Undergraduates
Program: Professional
Accreditation: &NH, DETC

01 Interim Dean ....Gregory BRANDES
03 Associate Dean ....Cassandra C. COLCHAGOFF
05 Dean of Faculty ....Gregory BRANDES
30 Director of External Affairs ....Donna SKIBBE
32 Dean of Students ....Dr. Martha SIEGEL
88 Associate Dean of EJD Program ....Kiyoko TATSUI
13 Associate Dean of Technology ....Vacant
13 Director of Technology Operations ....Christopher RUBIO
13 Director of Technology ....Erin FROYD
35 Director of Student Services ....Rick STEADMAN
26 Publicist ....Holly BARNHILL
89 Assoc Dean of First-Year Programs ....Steven BRACCI

† Regional accreditation is carried under the parent institution in Cedar Rapids, IA.

Concorde Career College (I)

12951 Euclid Street, Suite 101,
Garden Grove CA 92840-1451
County: Orange FICE Identification: 008071
Unit ID: 123679
Telephone: (714) 703-1900 Carnegie Class: Assoc/PrivFP
FAX Number: (714) 530-8421 Calendar System: Semester
URL: www.concorde.edu
Established: 1960 Annual Undergrad Tuition & Fees: N/A
Enrollment: 917 Coed
Affiliation or Control: Proprietary IRS Status: Proprietary
Highest Offering: Associate Degree
Program: Occupational; Nursing Emphasis
Accreditation: ACCSC, DH, @PTAA

12 Campus Director ....Christopher F. BECKER

Concorde Career College (J)

12412 Victory Boulevard, North Hollywood CA 91606-3134
County: Los Angeles FICE Identification: 007607
Unit ID: 124937
Telephone: (818) 766-8151 Carnegie Class: Assoc/PrivFP
FAX Number: (818) 766-1587 Calendar System: Quarter
URL: www.concordecareercolleges.com
Established: 1955 Annual Undergrad Tuition & Fees: $29,483
Enrollment: 806 Coed
Affiliation or Control: Proprietary IRS Status: Proprietary
Highest Offering: Associate Degree
Program: Occupational
Accreditation: ACCSC, PTAA, SURGT

01 Director ....Carmen BOWEN

Concorde Career College (A)

201 E Airport Drive, Suite A, San Bernadino CA 92408
FICE Identification: 008537
Unit ID: 124706
Telephone: (909) 884-8891 Carnegie Class: Assoc/PrivFP
FAX Number: (909) 884-1831 Calendar System: Semester
URL: www.concorde.edu
Established: 1970 Annual Undergrad Tuition & Fees: $28,906
Enrollment: 930 Coed
Affiliation or Control: Proprietary IRS Status: Proprietary
Highest Offering: Associate Degree
Program: Occupational
Accreditation: ACCSC, DH, SURGT

01 Campus President .... Fred FARIDIAN

Concorde Career College (B)

4393 Imperial Avenue, Suite 100,
San Diego CA 92113-1962
County: San Diego FICE Identification: 007930
Unit ID: 120661
Telephone: (619) 688-0800 Carnegie Class: Assoc/PrivFP
FAX Number: (619) 220-4177 Calendar System: Semester
URL: www.concorde.edu
Established: N/A Annual Undergrad Tuition & Fees: N/A
Enrollment: 705 Coed
Affiliation or Control: Proprietary IRS Status: Proprietary
Highest Offering: Associate Degree
Program: Occupational
Accreditation: ACCSC, @PTAA, SURGT

01 Campus President .... Mr. Mike COOLING

Concordia University (C)

1530 Concordia W, Irvine CA 92612-3299
County: Orange FICE Identification: 020705
Unit ID: 112075
Telephone: (949) 854-8002 Carnegie Class: Master's L
FAX Number: (949) 854-6854 Calendar System: Semester
URL: www.cui.edu
Established: 1972 Annual Undergrad Tuition & Fees: $27,300
Enrollment: 3,251 Coed
Affiliation or Control: Lutheran Church - Missouri Synod
IRS Status: 501(c)3
Highest Offering: Master's
Program: Liberal Arts And General; Teacher Preparatory
Accreditation: WC, NURSE

01 President .... Dr. Kurt J. KRUEGER
05 Provost/Exec Vice Pres .... Dr. Mary K. SCOTT
32 Exec Vice Pres Student & Enroll Svc .... Dr. Gary R. MCDANIEL
30 Exec Vice Pres Advancement .... Mr. Timothy J. JAEGER
10 Exec Vice Pres/Chief Finance Ofcr .... Mr. Kevin TILDEN
26 Exec Vice Pres External Relations .... Mr. Stephen CHRISTENSEN
20 Assoc Provost/VP Acad Affs .... Dr. Peter SENKBEIL
49 Dean College of Arts and Sciences .... Dr. Pamela KALBFLEISCH
50 Dean School Business/Profess Stds .... Dr. Timothy C. PETERS
53 Dean School of Education .... Dr. Janice NELSON
73 Dean Christ College .... Dr. Steven P. MUELLER
06 Registrar .... Prof. Kenneth R. CLAVIR
08 Director of Library Services .... Prof. Carolina BARTON
24 Director Educational Media .... Prof. John RANDALL
35 Dean of Students .... Mr. Derek VERGARA
38 Assoc Dean Student Affairs/Advising .... Mrs. Dian VIESELMEYER
43 General Counsel .... Mr. Ronald VAN BLARCOM
07 Exec Dir Admissions .... Mr. Rick HARDY
15 Director of Human Resources .... Mrs. Pamela CLAVIR
41 Athletic Director .... Prof. David BIRELINE
39 Director Residence Life .... Ms. Kimberly CHAMBERLAIN
19 Director Security/Safety .... Mr. Steven RODRIGUEZ
29 Director of Alumni Relations .... Mr. Michael BERGLER
37 Exec Dir Financial Services .... Ms. Lori MCDONALD
36 Director of Career Services .... Mrs. Victoria JAFFEE
44 Director Major Gift Planning .... Mr. Dennis COX
21 Bursar .... Mr. Edgar LOPEZ
85 Exec Director Global Programs .... Dr. Dan WAITE
13 IT Services Manager .... Mr. Chris HARRIS

*Contra Costa Community College District Office (D)

500 Court Street, Martinez CA 94553-1278
County: Contra Costa FICE Identification: 001189
Unit ID: 112817
Telephone: (925) 229-1000 Carnegie Class: N/A
FAX Number: (925) 370-2019
URL: www.4cd.edu

01 Chancellor .... Dr. Helen BENJAMIN
05 VC Education and Technology .... Mr. Mojden MEHDIZADEH
11 Vice Chanc Admin Services .... Dr. John AL-AMIN
15 VC Human Resources/Chief Negotiator .... Mr. Eugene C. HUFF

*Contra Costa College (E)

2600 Mission Bell Drive, San Pablo CA 94806-3195
County: Contra Costa FICE Identification: 001190
Unit ID: 112826
Telephone: (510) 235-7800 Carnegie Class: Assoc/Pub-S-MC
FAX Number: (510) 236-6768 Calendar System: Semester
URL: www.contracosta.edu
Established: 1948 Annual Undergrad Tuition & Fees (In-District): $1,104
Enrollment: 7,524 Coed
Affiliation or Control: State/Local IRS Status: 501(c)3
Highest Offering: Associate Degree
Program: Occupational; 2-Year Principally Bachelor's Creditable
Accreditation: WJ, DA

02 President .... Dr. Denise NOLDON
03 Interim Vice President .... Ms. Donna FLOYD
32 Interim Sr Dean of Student Services .... Ms. Vicki FERGUSON
05 Senior Dean of Instruction .... Vacant
75 Dean Economic Development .... Ms. Priscilla LEADON
07 Actg Director Admissions & Records .... Ms. Jeanette MOORE
10 Director Business Services .... Ms. Mariles MAGALONG
09 Director of Institutional Research .... Vacant
37 Director Student Financial Aid .... Ms. Viviane LAMOTHE
18 Chief Facilities/Physical Plant .... Mr. Bruce KING

*Diablo Valley College (F)

321 Golf Club Road, Pleasant Hill CA 94523-1544
County: Contra Costa FICE Identification: 001191
Unit ID: 113634
Telephone: (925) 685-1230 Carnegie Class: Assoc/Pub-S-MC
FAX Number: (925) 685-1551 Calendar System: Semester
URL: www.dvc.edu
Established: 1949 Annual Undergrad Tuition & Fees (In-District): $1,104
Enrollment: 20,910 Coed
Affiliation or Control: State/Local IRS Status: 501(c)3
Highest Offering: Associate Degree
Program: Occupational; 2-Year Principally Bachelor's Creditable
Accreditation: WJ, ACFEI, CEA, DA, DH

02 President .... Mr. Peter GARCIA
05 Vice President Instruction .... Ms. Susan E. LAMB
32 Vice President Student Services .... Vacant
10 Vice President Finance and Admin .... Mr. Chris LEIVAS
12 Exec Dean San Ramon Campus .... Dr. Kevin HORAN
20 Senior Dean of Instruction .... Vacant
84 Dean Outreach/Enroll Mgt/ Matric .... Ms. Elizabeth HAUSCARRIAGUE
12 Dean San Ramon Campus .... Ms. Kathleen COSTA
41 Dean of PE/Athl/Dance/Athletic Dir .... Ms. Christina WORSLEY
62 Director of the Library Services .... Mr. Andy KIVEL
26 Director of Media & Communications .... Ms. Chrisanne KNOX
57 Dean Applied & Fine Arts .... Mr. Michael ALMAGUER
54 Dean Physical Sci/Engr/Bio Sci .... Dr. Patricia YOUNG
50 Dean English & Social Science .... Dr. Marcia SOMER
81 Dean Math/Computer Science & Bus .... Ms. Rachel WESTLAKE
37 Dean EOPS/Fin Aid/CalWORKS/DSS .... Ms. Emily STONE
75 Dean Career Tech Ed & Econ Develop .... Ms. Kim SCHENK

*Los Medanos College (G)

2700 E Leland Road, Pittsburg CA 94565-5197
County: Contra Costa FICE Identification: 010340
Unit ID: 117894
Telephone: (925) 439-2181 Carnegie Class: Assoc/Pub-S-MC
FAX Number: (925) 427-1599 Calendar System: Semester
URL: www.losmedanos.edu
Established: 1973 Annual Undergrad Tuition & Fees (In-District): $1,124
Enrollment: 9,023 Coed
Affiliation or Control: State/Local IRS Status: 501(c)3
Highest Offering: Associate Degree
Program: Occupational; 2-Year Principally Bachelor's Creditable
Accreditation: WJ

02 President .... Mr. Bob KRATOCHVIL
03 Vice President .... Vacant
10 Director of Business Services .... Ms. Sandy SMITH
04 Int Senior Executive Assistant .... Ms. Eileen VALENZUELA
26 Dir of Marketing & Media Design .... Ms. Barbara CELLA
102 Senior Foundation Director .... Ms. Ruth GOODIN
05 Senior Dean Instruction .... Mr. Richard LIVINGSTON
32 Senior Dean of Student Svcs .... Ms. Gail NEWMAN
88 Dean Career Technical Education .... Ms. Kiran KAMATH
32 Dean Student Development .... Dr. Blas GUERRERO
49 Dean Liberal Arts and Sciences .... Vacant
07 Director of Admissions .... Ms. Robin ARMOUR
37 Director of Financial Aid .... Ms. Loretta CANTO-WILLIAMS
14 Computer & Network Svcs Supervisor .... Mr. Mike BECKER
20 Senior Academic Mgr Instruction .... Ms. Tawny BEAL
18 Buildings & Grounds Manager .... Mr. Russ HOLT

Copper Mountain College (H)

6162 Rotary Way, Box 1398, Joshua Tree CA 92252-6102
County: San Bernardino FICE Identification: 035424
Unit ID: 395362
Telephone: (760) 366-3791 Carnegie Class: Assoc/Pub-S-SC
FAX Number: (760) 366-5255 Calendar System: Semester
URL: www.cmccd.edu
Established: 1999 Annual Undergrad Tuition & Fees (In-District): $1,380
Enrollment: 2,149 Coed
Affiliation or Control: State/Local IRS Status: 501(c)3
Highest Offering: Associate Degree
Program: Occupational; 2-Year Principally Bachelor's Creditable
Accreditation: WJ

01 Superintendent/President .... Dr. Roger WAGNER
05 Vice Pres for Academic Affairs .... Dr. Wei ZHOU
32 Vice President of Student Services .... Mr. Greg BROWN
15 Manager of Human Resources .... Ms. Andrea RIESGO
18 Chief of Facilities .... Mr. Dan CAIN
12 Coordinator of Base Programs .... Mr. Gregg CHESTERMAN
102 Executive Director of Foundation .... Ms. Sandy SMITH
10 Chief Business Officer .... Ms. Meredith PLUMMER
37 Director of Financial Aid .... Mr. Brian HEINEMANN
76 Dir Hlth Science-Registered Nursing .... Ms. Christi BLAUWKAMP
91 Director of Information Systems .... Mr. Steve KEMP
26 Dir Marketing & Community Relations .... Vacant

Cuesta College (I)

PO Box 8106, San Luis Obispo CA 93403-8106
County: San Luis Obispo FICE Identification: 001192
Unit ID: 113193
Telephone: (805) 546-3100 Carnegie Class: Assoc/Pub-R-L
FAX Number: (805) 546-3904 Calendar System: Semester
URL: www.cuesta.edu
Established: 1963 Annual Undergrad Tuition & Fees (In-District): $1,400
Enrollment: 10,759 Coed
Affiliation or Control: State/Local IRS Status: 501(c)3
Highest Offering: Associate Degree
Program: Occupational; 2-Year Principally Bachelor's Creditable
Accreditation: WJ, EMT

01 Superintendent/President .... Dr. Gilbert H. STORK
05 VP/Asst Supt Academic Affairs .... Dr. A. Cathleen GREINER
10 VP/Asst Supt Administrative Svcs .... Ms. Toni SOMMER
32 VP/Asst Supt Student Services .... Dr. Linda FONTANILLA
12 Exec Dean North Co Campus/S Co Ctrs .... Ms. Sandee MCLAUGHLIN
35 Dean of Students .... Vacant
30 Exec Dir Foundation/Inst Adv .... Ms. Shannon HILL
08 Director Library/Lrng Resources/DE .... Mr. Mark STENGEL
35 Coordinator Student Life/Leadership .... Mr. Anthony GUTIERREZ
13 Director of Computer Services .... Ms. Janice M. HOUSE
37 Director of Financial Aid .... Ms. Nohemy ORNELAS
66 Director of Nursing .... Ms. Marcia SCOTT
15 Exec Dir Human Res Labor Relations .... Mr. William BENJAMIN
19 Director of Public Safety .... Mr. Joseph ARTEAGA
40 Director of Bookstore .... Ms. Trudy BELL
41 Director of Athletics .... Mr. Robert MARIUCCI
18 Dir Maintenance/Operations/Grounds .... Mr. Terry REECE
38 Director Counseling Services .... Mr. Candelario MUNOZ
103 Dir Workforce Econ Devel Cmty Pgm .... Dr. Matthew GREEN
23 Coordinator of Health Services .... Ms. Vicki SAWZAK
81 Dean Ac Aff Sci/Math/Nursing/PE .... Ms. Deborah WULFF
79 Dean Ac Aff Arts/Humanities/Soc Sci .... Dr. Pamela RALSTON
103 Dean Ac Aff Workforce Econ Dev .... Mr. John CASCAMO
76 Associate Director of Allied Health .... Ms. Lisa WEARDA
07 Director of Admissions & Records .... Vacant
09 Director of Institutional Research .... Dr. Ryan CARTNAL
21 Director Fiscal Services .... Mr. Christopher GREEN
102 Director Foundation Programs .... Ms. Karen TACKET

The Culinary Institute of America at Greystone (J)

2555 Main Street, Saint Helena CA 94574-9504
County: Napa Identification: 666260
Unit ID: 19050301
Telephone: (707) 967-1100 Carnegie Class: Not Classified
FAX Number: (707) 967-1113 Calendar System: Semester
URL: www.ciachef.edu/california/
Established: 1997 Annual Undergrad Tuition & Fees: $28,770
Enrollment: 247 Coed
Affiliation or Control: Independent Non-Profit IRS Status: 501(c)3
Highest Offering: Associate Degree
Program: Occupational; Technical Emphasis
Accreditation: &M

01 President .... Dr. Tim RYAN
05 Provost .... Mr. Mark ERICKSON
11 Managing Director .... Vacant
20 Director of Education .... Mr. Adam BUSBY

† Regional accreditation is carried under the parent institution in Hyde Park, NY.

Deep Springs College (K)

HC 72 Box 45001, Via Dyer, NV 89010-9803
County: Inyo FICE Identification: 001194
Unit ID: 113528
Telephone: (760) 872-2000 Carnegie Class: Not Classified
FAX Number: (760) 874-7077 Calendar System: Other
URL: www.deepsprings.edu
Established: 1917 Annual Undergrad Tuition & Fees: $0
Enrollment: 28 Male
Affiliation or Control: Independent Non-Profit IRS Status: 501(c)3
Highest Offering: Associate Degree
Program: 2-Year Principally Bachelor's Creditable
Accreditation: WJ

01 President .... Mr. David NEIDORF
05 Dean of College .... Mr. Kenneth CARDWELL
88 Ranch Manager .... Ms. Janice HUNTER
11 VP Operations .... Ms. Jill LAWRENCE

21 Office Manager .... Ms. Iris POPE
18 Mechanic & Plant Manager .... Mr. Padraic MACLEISH
88 Chef .... Ms. Donna BLAGDAN
88 Farm Manager .... Mr. Adam NYBORG

Dell'Arte International School of Physical Theatre (A)

P.O. Box 816, 131 H Street, Blue Lake CA 95525
County: Humboldt FICE Identification: 030256
Unit ID: 113537
Telephone: (707) 668-5663 Carnegie Class: Spec/Arts
FAX Number: (707) 668-5665 Calendar System: Other
URL: www.dellarte.com
Established: 1975 Annual Graduate Tuition & Fees: $12,000
Enrollment: 41 Coed
Affiliation or Control: Independent Non-Profit IRS Status: 501(c)3
Highest Offering: Master's; No Undergraduates
Program: Professional; Fine Arts Emphasis
Accreditation: THEA

01 Producing Artistic Director .... Mr. Michael FIELDS
10 Financial Officer .... Ms. Stephanie WETZEL
26 Marketing Director/IT Development .... Mr. Gannon ROGERS

Design Institute of San Diego (B)

8555 Commerce Avenue, San Diego CA 92121-2685
County: San Diego FICE Identification: 022980
Unit ID: 113582
Telephone: (858) 566-1200 Carnegie Class: Spec/Arts
FAX Number: (858) 566-2711 Calendar System: Semester
URL: www.disd.edu
Established: 1977 Annual Undergrad Tuition & Fees: $18,600
Enrollment: 340 Coed
Affiliation or Control: Proprietary IRS Status: Proprietary
Highest Offering: Baccalaureate
Program: Professional
Accreditation: ACICS, CIDA

01 President .... Mr. Arthur ROSENSTEIN
05 Vice President .... Ms. Gloria ROSENSTEIN
12 Campus Director .... Ms. Margot BLANK DOUCETTE
07 Director of Admissions .... Ms. Paula PARRISH
37 Director Financial Aid .... Ms. Jackie GLORIA
32 Director of Student Services .... Ms. Tena MOIOLA
08 Librarian .... Ms. Lisa SCHATTMAN
06 Registrar .... Ms. Tracy GULINO
07 Outreach & Admissions .... Ms. Liz BARRY

DeVry University - Bakersfield (C)

3000 Ming Avenue, Bakersfield CA 93304-4136
County: Kern Identification: 666486
Telephone: (661) 833-7120 Carnegie Class: Not Classified
FAX Number: N/A Calendar System: Semester
URL: www.devry.edu
Established: 1931 Annual Undergrad Tuition & Fees: $16,156
Enrollment: 400 Coed
Affiliation or Control: Proprietary IRS Status: Proprietary
Highest Offering: Baccalaureate
Program: Occupational; Professional; Business Emphasis
Accreditation: &NH

01 Center Dean .... George SHEARER

† Regional accreditation is carried under the parent institution in Downers Grove, IL.

DeVry University - Colton (D)

1090 E. Washington Street, Suite H,
Colton CA 92324-8180
County: San Bernadino Identification: 666487
Telephone: (909) 514-1808 Carnegie Class: Not Classified
FAX Number: (909) 514-1836 Calendar System: Semester
URL: www.devry.edu
Established: 1931 Annual Undergrad Tuition & Fees: $16,156
Enrollment: 441 Coed
Affiliation or Control: Proprietary IRS Status: Proprietary
Highest Offering: Master's
Program: Professional; Business Emphasis
Accreditation: &NH

01 Center Dean .... Vacant

† Regional accreditation is carried under the parent institution in Downers Grove, IL.

DeVry University - Daly City (E)

2001 Junipero Serra Blvd, Ste 161,
Daly City CA 94014-3899
County: San Mateo Identification: 666493
Telephone: (650) 991-3520 Carnegie Class: Not Classified
FAX Number: (650) 992-3840 Calendar System: Semester
URL: www.devry.edu
Established: 1931 Annual Undergrad Tuition & Fees: $16,156
Enrollment: 266 Coed
Affiliation or Control: Proprietary IRS Status: Proprietary
Highest Offering: Master's
Program: Professional; Business Emphasis
Accreditation: &NH

01 Center Dean .... William MINNICH

† Regional accreditation is carried under the parent institution in Downers Grove, IL.

DeVry University - Fremont Campus (F)

6600 Dumbarton Circle, Fremont CA 94555-3615
County: Alameda Identification: 666829
Unit ID: 432171
Telephone: (510) 574-1200 Carnegie Class: Not Classified
FAX Number: (510) 742-0868 Calendar System: Semester
URL: www.devry.com
Established: 1931 Annual Undergrad Tuition & Fees: $16,156
Enrollment: 1,740 Coed
Affiliation or Control: Proprietary IRS Status: Proprietary
Highest Offering: Master's
Program: Occupational; Professional; Business Emphasis
Accreditation: &NH, ENGT

01 Metro President .... Michael CUBBIN
07 Sr Director of Admissions .... Brian CICERO
37 Dean Student Central .... Carolyn TORRES
13 Information Technology Director .... Muhammad KHAN
06 Registrar .... Contiza COLLANTES
15 Human Resources Business Partner .... Mary BIBBS
05 Dean of International Admissions .... Chow LEE
32 Manager of Student Services .... Stefanie CORNELL
36 Director of Career Services .... Sandra DIXON
39 Manager Residence Life .... Danielle GILLINGWATER
54 Dean of Engineering Tech Programs .... Dennis MUELLER

† Regional accreditation is carried under the parent institution in Downers Grove, IL.

DeVry University - Fresno (G)

7575 North Fresno Street, Fresno CA 93720-2458
County: Fresno Identification: 666494
Telephone: (559) 439-8595 Carnegie Class: Not Classified
FAX Number: (559) 439-8598 Calendar System: Semester
URL: www.devry.edu
Established: 1931 Annual Undergrad Tuition & Fees: $16,156
Enrollment: 599 Coed
Affiliation or Control: Proprietary IRS Status: Proprietary
Highest Offering: Baccalaureate
Program: Professional; Business Emphasis
Accreditation: &NH

01 Campus President .... Joseph COPPOLA

† Regional accreditation is carried under the parent institution in Downers Grove, IL.

DeVry University - Long Beach Campus (H)

3880 Kilroy Airport Way, Long Beach CA 90806-2452
County: Los Angeles Identification: 666988
Unit ID: 420282
Telephone: (562) 427-0861 Carnegie Class: Not Classified
FAX Number: (562) 997-5368 Calendar System: Semester
URL: www.devry.edu
Established: 1931 Annual Undergrad Tuition & Fees: $16,156
Enrollment: 1,220 Coed
Affiliation or Control: Proprietary IRS Status: Proprietary
Highest Offering: Master's
Program: Occupational; Professional; Business Emphasis
Accreditation: &NH, ENGT

01 Campus President .... Ivonna EDKINS
07 Senior Director of Admissions .... Paul SALLENBACH
32 Dean Student Central .... Danielle REEVES
15 HR Business Partner .... Vacant
05 Assoc Dean Academic Affairs .... Tennille ZEILER
08 Librarian .... Heather BURKE

† Regional accreditation is carried under the parent institution in Downers Grove, IL.

DeVry University - Oakland Center (I)

505 14th St., Ste. 100, Oakland CA 94612
County: Alameda Identification: 666194
Telephone: (510) 267-1340 Carnegie Class: Not Classified
FAX Number: N/A Calendar System: Semester
URL: www.devry.edu
Established: 1931 Annual Undergrad Tuition & Fees: $16,156
Enrollment: 224 Coed
Affiliation or Control: Proprietary IRS Status: Proprietary
Highest Offering: Master's
Program: Occupational; Professional; Business Emphasis
Accreditation: &NH

01 Center Dean .... Ben ELIAS

† Regional accreditation is carried under the parent institution in Downers Grove, IL.

DeVry University - Palmdale (J)

39115 Trade Center Dr. Ste. 100,
Palmdale CA 93551-3649
County: Los Angeles Identification: 666495
Telephone: (661) 224-2920 Carnegie Class: Not Classified
FAX Number: (661) 266-4986 Calendar System: Semester
URL: www.devry.edu
Established: 1931 Annual Undergrad Tuition & Fees: $16,176
Enrollment: 494 Coed
Affiliation or Control: Proprietary IRS Status: Proprietary
Highest Offering: Master's
Program: Professional; Business Emphasis
Accreditation: &NH

01 Center Dean .... Ms. Susan ISHII

† Regional accreditation is carried under the parent institution in Downers Grove, IL.

DeVry University - Pomona Campus (K)

901 Corporate Center Drive, Pomona CA 91768-2642
County: Los Angeles FICE Identification: 023329
Unit ID: 113607
Telephone: (909) 622-8866 Carnegie Class: Master's L
FAX Number: (909) 623-5666 Calendar System: Semester
URL: www.devry.edu
Established: 1931 Annual Undergrad Tuition & Fees: $16,176
Enrollment: 2,969 Coed
Affiliation or Control: Proprietary IRS Status: Proprietary
Highest Offering: Master's
Program: Occupational; Professional; Business Emphasis
Accreditation: &NH, ENGT

01 Metro President .... Scott SAND
05 Dean Academic Affairs .... Walter BROWN
37 Director of Student Finance .... Catherine THOMAS
32 Dean Student Central .... Stacey WEINSTEIN
07 Senior Director of Admissions .... Devin DODSON
36 Assoc Director of Career Services .... Kristy AMOS
08 Director of Library Services .... Nicole BIRD
15 Human Resources Business Partner .... Makisha ALEXANDER
10 Director of Finance/Administration .... Raymond WONG
31 Director of Community Outreach .... Kenneth CHAN

† Regional accreditation is carried under the parent institution in Downers Grove, IL.

DeVry University - Sacramento (L)

2216 Kausen Drive, Ste. 1, Sacramento CA 95758-7115
County: Sacramento Identification: 666497
Telephone: (916) 478-2847 Carnegie Class: Not Classified
FAX Number: (916) 478-2849 Calendar System: Semester
URL: www.devry.edu
Established: 1931 Annual Undergrad Tuition & Fees: $16,156
Enrollment: 853 Coed
Affiliation or Control: Proprietary IRS Status: Proprietary
Highest Offering: Master's
Program: Professional; Business Emphasis
Accreditation: &NH, ENGT

01 Campus Director .... Marcela IGLESIAS

† Regional accreditation is carried under the parent institution in Downers Grove, IL.

DeVry University - San Diego Campus (M)

2655 Camino Del Rio North, Ste 201,
San Diego CA 92108-1633
County: San Diego Identification: 666193
Unit ID: 437264
Telephone: (619) 683-2446 Carnegie Class: Not Classified
FAX Number: (619) 683-2448 Calendar System: Semester
URL: www.devry.edu
Established: 2002 Annual Undergrad Tuition & Fees: $16,156
Enrollment: 914 Coed
Affiliation or Control: Proprietary IRS Status: Proprietary
Highest Offering: Master's
Program: Occupational; Professional; Business Emphasis
Accreditation: &NH

01 Campus President .... Pamela DALY

† Regional accreditation is carried under the parent institution in Downers Grove, IL.

DeVry University - San Jose (N)

2160 Lundy Avenue, Suite 250, San Jose CA 95131-1862
County: Santa Clara Identification: 666523
Telephone: (408) 571-3760 Carnegie Class: Not Classified
FAX Number: (408) 577-1246 Calendar System: Semester
URL: www.devry.edu
Established: 1931 Annual Undergrad Tuition & Fees: $16,156
Enrollment: 401 Coed
Affiliation or Control: Proprietary IRS Status: Proprietary
Highest Offering: Master's

Program: Professional; Business Emphasis
Accreditation: &NH

01 Center Dean ..... Nils SEDWICK

† Regional accreditation is carried under the parent institution in Downers Grove, IL.

DeVry University - Sherman Oaks Campus (A)

15301 Ventura Blvd, #100, Bldg D,
Sherman Oaks CA 91403-6654
County: Los Angeles — Identification: 666065
Unit ID: 439181
Telephone: (818) 713-8111 — Carnegie Class: Not Classified
FAX Number: N/A — Calendar System: Semester
URL: www.devry.edu
Established: 1931 — Annual Undergrad Tuition & Fees: $16,156
Enrollment: 1,110 — Coed
Affiliation or Control: Proprietary — IRS Status: Proprietary
Highest Offering: Master's
Program: Occupational; Professional; Business Emphasis
Accreditation: &NH, ENGT

01 Campus President ..... Brian PORTER
05 Dean of Academic Affairs ..... Sue MCDONALD
07 Senior Director of Admissions ..... Allen HERNDON
36 Director of Career Services ..... Vacant

† Regional accreditation is carried under the parent institution in Downers Grove, IL.

Dominican School of Philosophy and Theology (B)

2301 Vine Street, Berkeley CA 94708-1816
County: Alameda — FICE Identification: 001296
Unit ID: 113704
Telephone: (510) 849-2030 — Carnegie Class: Spec/Faith
FAX Number: (510) 849-1372 — Calendar System: Semester
URL: www.dspt.edu
Established: 1932 — Annual Undergrad Tuition & Fees: $15,000
Enrollment: 103 — Coed
Affiliation or Control: Roman Catholic — IRS Status: 501(c)3
Highest Offering: Master's
Program: Professional
Accreditation: WC, THEOL

01 President ..... Rev. Michael SWEENEY
05 Academic Dean ..... Rev. Christopher M. RENZ
11 Vice President Administration ..... Mr. Peter MACLEOD
30 Director Advancement/Donor Rels ..... Mr. Michael CHINNAVASO
07 Director of Admissions ..... Mr. John D. KNUTSEN
06 Registrar ..... Ms. Teresa OLSON
21 Office Manager/Dir Student Services ..... Ms. Colleen POWER
26 Director of Communications ..... Ms. Heidi MCKENNA
84 Recruitment/Development Officer ..... Ms. Justyna KRUKOWSKA

Dominican University of California (C)

50 Acacia Avenue, San Rafael CA 94901-2298
County: Marin — FICE Identification: 001196
Unit ID: 113698
Telephone: (415) 457-4440 — Carnegie Class: Master's M
FAX Number: (415) 485-3205 — Calendar System: Semester
URL: www.dominican.edu
Established: 1890 — Annual Undergrad Tuition & Fees: $38,600
Enrollment: 2,278 — Coed
Affiliation or Control: Independent Non-Profit — IRS Status: 501(c)3
Highest Offering: Master's
Program: Occupational; Liberal Arts And General; Teacher Preparatory; Professional
Accreditation: WC, NURSE, OT

01 President ..... Dr. Mary B. MARCY
05 Exec VP and Chief Academic Officer ..... Vacant
10 Vice President Business & Finance ..... Ms. Michele HINKEN
26 Vice Pres External Relations ..... Vacant
32 VP Student Life/Dean of Students ..... Dr. John F. KENNEDY
84 Vice Pres of Enrollment Management ..... Dr. John BAWOROWSKY
20 Associate VP Academic Affairs ..... Ms. Martha NELSON
27 Director of Marketing ..... Ms. Nancy BULETTE
04 Assistant to the President ..... Mrs. Sarita PURECE
100 Asst Spec Projects/Trustee Liaison ..... Dr. Francoise LEPAGE
79 Dean Sch Arts/Humanities/Social Sci ..... Dr. Nicola PITCHFORD
76 Dean of School Health/Natural Sci ..... Dr. Ching-Hua WANG
53 Dean School of Educ/Counsel Psych ..... Dr. Edward KUJAWA
50 Dean School of Business/Leadership ..... Dr. Dan MOSHAVI
88 Asc Dean Sch of Health/Natural Sci ..... Dr. Sibdas GHOSH
35 Associate Dean of Students ..... Mr. Paul RACCANELLO
18 Exec Dir Facilities/Physical Plant ..... Mr. Jacques CHARTON
08 Executive Director Library Services ..... Mr. Gary GORKA
09 Exec Dir of Institutional Research ..... Mr. Scott CLARK
37 Director of Financial Aid ..... Ms. Shanon LITTLE
07 Asst VP of Undergrad Admissions ..... Ms. Rebecca FINN KENNEY
13 Chief Technology Officer ..... Mr. Jackson RATCLIFFE
06 Registrar ..... Ms. Marianne STICKEL
29 Director of Alumni Relations ..... Ms. Tracy HOGAN
88 President Alumni Association ..... Mr. James SALTER
15 Director of Human Resources ..... Ms. Christine GODFREY
36 Director Student Placement ..... Ms. Susan FYLES
28 Director Diversity ..... Dr. Suresh APPAVOO
92 Director Honors Program ..... Dr. Diara SPAIN
38 Director Student Counseling ..... Dr. Chuck BILLINGS
26 Public Relations Officer ..... Mr. David ALBEE
85 Exec Director Intl & Global Educ ..... Dr. Jayati GHOSH
30 Director of Advancement ..... Ms. Sarah ANDREWS

Dongguk University (D)

440 Shatto Place, Los Angeles CA 90020-1704
County: Los Angeles — FICE Identification: 031095
Unit ID: 122117
Telephone: (213) 487-0110 — Carnegie Class: Spec/Health
FAX Number: (213) 487-0527 — Calendar System: Quarter
URL: www.dula.edu
Established: 1979 — Annual Undergrad Tuition & Fees: $11,600
Enrollment: 215 — Coed
Affiliation or Control: Independent Non-Profit — IRS Status: 501(c)3
Highest Offering: Master's; No Lower Division
Program: Professional
Accreditation: ACUP

01 President ..... Dr. Un Kyo SEO
05 Office of the Provost/Admissions ..... Mr. Seok Joo AUM
10 Director of Finance ..... Mr. Albert KIM
37 Financial Aid Officer ..... Ms. Julia PARK
06 Registrar ..... Mr. Hoon SEO
63 Director of Oriental Medical Center ..... Mr. Chul WON
18 Director of Facilities ..... Mr. Arturo AGUIRRE
21 Office Manager ..... Ms. Bo Yoon CHOI
85 International Student Advisor ..... Mr. Phillip YEW

El Camino College (E)

16007 Crenshaw Boulevard, Torrance CA 90506-0002
County: Los Angeles — FICE Identification: 001197
Unit ID: 113980
Telephone: (310) 660-3670 — Carnegie Class: Assoc/Pub-S-SC
FAX Number: (310) 660-7798 — Calendar System: Semester
URL: www.elcamino.edu
Established: 1947 — Annual Undergrad Tuition & Fees (In-District): $1,140
Enrollment: 24,224 — Coed
Affiliation or Control: State/Local — IRS Status: 501(c)3
Highest Offering: Associate Degree
Program: Occupational; 2-Year Principally Bachelor's Creditable
Accreditation: WJ, ADNUR, RAD

01 President ..... Dr. Thomas M. FALLO
05 Vice President Academic Affairs ..... Dr. Francisco M. ARCE
11 Vice Pres Administrative Services ..... Ms. Jo Ann HIGDON
32 Vice Pres Student/Community Advance ..... Dr. Jeanie NISHIME
15 Vice Pres of Human Resources ..... Ms. Linda BEAM
30 Dean Community Advancement ..... Mr. Jose ANAYA
45 Dean Planning/Research/Development ..... Vacant
72 Dean Industry & Technology ..... Dr. Stephanie RODRIGUEZ
81 Dean Math/Physical Sciences ..... Dr. Donald GOLDBERG
50 Dean of Business ..... Dr. Virginia RAPP
83 Dean Behavioral & Social Science ..... Dr. Gloria MIRANDA
68 Dean Health/Exer/Science/Sport ..... Mr. Rory NATIVIDAD
57 Dean Fine Arts ..... Dr. Connie FITZSIMONS
76 Dean Natural Sciences ..... Dr. Jean SHANKWEILER
79 Dean Humanities ..... Mr. Tom LEW
38 Dean Counseling Matriculation Svcs ..... Dr. Regina SMITH
84 Dean of Enrollment Services ..... Vacant
27 Director of Information Systems ..... Mr. John WAGSTAFF
31 Director of Community Relations ..... Ms. Ann GARTEN
66 Director of Nursing ..... Ms. Theresa KYLE
07 Dir Admissions/Records/Registrar ..... Mr. Bill MULROONEY
10 Chief Business Officer ..... Dr. Jo Ann HIGDON
20 Associate Academic Officer ..... Vacant
26 Chief Public Relations Officer ..... Ms. Ann M. GARTEN
102 Executive Director Foundation ..... Ms. Katie GLEASON
36 Director Student Placement ..... Dr. Regina SMITH
96 Acting Director of Purchasing ..... Mr. Rocky BONURA
40 Director of Bookstore ..... Ms. Julie BOURLIER
19 Chief of Campus Police ..... Mr. Michael TREVIS
18 Director of Facilities Plng/Svcs ..... Mr. Robert GANN
35 Director of Student Affairs ..... Mr. Harold TYLER
37 Director Student Financial Aid ..... Ms. Hortense COOPER
09 Director Institutional Research ..... Ms. Irene GRAFF
28 Director of Diversity ..... Ms. Leisa BIGGERS
21 Business Manager ..... Ms. Janice ELY
25 Resource Devel/Grants Coordinator ..... Vacant

El Camino College Compton Center (F)

1111 E Artesia Boulevard, Compton CA 90221-5393
County: Los Angeles — FICE Identification: 001188
Unit ID: 112686
Telephone: (310) 900-1600 — Carnegie Class: Assoc/Pub-S-SC
FAX Number: (310) 605-1458 — Calendar System: Semester
URL: www.compton.edu
Established: 1927 — Annual Undergrad Tuition & Fees (In-State): $1,104
Enrollment: 7,912 — Coed
Affiliation or Control: State — IRS Status: 501(c)3
Highest Offering: Associate Degree
Program: Occupational; 2-Year Principally Bachelor's Creditable
Accreditation: &WJ

01 Interim Chief Executive Officer ..... Dr. Keith CURRY
05 Vice President Academic Affairs ..... Ms. Barbara PEREZ
32 Dean Student Services ..... Dr. Ricky SHABAZZ
15 Dean Human Resources/Risk Mgmt ..... Mrs. Rachelle SASSER
20 Dean Academic Affairs ..... Dr. Susan DEVER
76 Dean Health/Human Services ..... Ms. Wanda MORRIS
88 Dir Student Development ..... Mr. Robert BUTLER
08 Librarian ..... Ms. Estina PRATT
88 Director CalWORKs & DSPS ..... Ms. Patricia BONACIC
22 Director EOP & S ..... Ms. Valarie O'GUYNN
41 Director of Athletics ..... Mr. Albert OLGUIN
09 Director Institutional Research ..... Ms. Irene GRAFF
37 Director Financial Aid ..... Dr. Mytha PASCUAL
31 Director Outreach & Relations ..... Ms. Elizabeth MARTINEZ
10 Chief Business Officer ..... Mr. Felipe LOPEZ
18 Director Facilities ..... Vacant
13 Supervisor MIS ..... Mr. Rudy RAMOS

† Regional accreditation is carried under the parent institution in Torrance, CA.

Emperor's College of Traditional Oriental Medicine (G)

1807-B Wilshire Boulevard, Santa Monica CA 90403-5678
County: Los Angeles — FICE Identification: 026090
Unit ID: 114114
Telephone: (310) 453-8300 — Carnegie Class: Spec/Health
FAX Number: (310) 829-3838 — Calendar System: Quarter
URL: www.emperors.edu
Established: 1983 — Annual Undergrad Tuition & Fees: $15,000
Enrollment: 243 — Coed
Affiliation or Control: Proprietary — IRS Status: Proprietary
Highest Offering: Doctorate
Program: Professional
Accreditation: ACUP

01 Chief Executive Officer ..... Yun KIM
05 Academic Dean ..... Jacques MORAMARCO
07 Director of Admissions ..... Lisa ROCCHETTI
37 Financial Aid Officer ..... Farida LUGEMBE
11 COO/Administrator ..... George PARK
58 Dean Doctoral Programs ..... John FANG

† Candidate at the Doctorate level.

Empire College School of Business (H)

3035 Cleveland Avenue, Santa Rosa CA 95403-2100
County: Sonoma — FICE Identification: 009032
Unit ID: 114123
Telephone: (707) 546-4000 — Carnegie Class: Assoc/PrivFP
FAX Number: (707) 546-4058 — Calendar System: Other
URL: www.empcol.edu
Established: 1961 — Annual Undergrad Tuition & Fees: $16,775
Enrollment: 536 — Coed
Affiliation or Control: Proprietary — IRS Status: Proprietary
Highest Offering: Associate Degree
Program: Occupational; Technical Emphasis
Accreditation: ACICS

01 President ..... Mr. Roy HURD
26 Vice Pres Marketing/Administration ..... Mrs. Sherie HURD
05 Director of Education ..... Mrs. Vickie SAVINO
07 Director of Admissions ..... Ms. Dahnja STRAUB
37 Director Student Financial Aid ..... Mrs. Mary O'BRIEN
11 Director of Administrative Svcs ..... Ms. Eleanor NORIEL
10 Director of Accounting ..... Mr. David YARBROUGH
36 Director Student Placement ..... Ms. Lucille INMAN
40 Bookstore Manager ..... Ms. Kass VON DER MEHDEN
06 Registrar ..... Ms. Margareta CAMPBELL
38 Student Success Advisor ..... Ms. April HURD-MATOS
38 Student Success Advisor ..... Ms. Nora SONGSTER

Epic Bible College (I)

4330 Auburn Blvd., Sacramento CA 95841
County: Sacramento — FICE Identification: 034033
Unit ID: 124487
Telephone: (916) 348-4689 — Carnegie Class: Spec/Faith
FAX Number: (916) 334-2315 — Calendar System: Trimester
URL: www.EPIC.edu
Established: 1974 — Annual Undergrad Tuition & Fees: $9,166
Enrollment: 320 — Coed
Affiliation or Control: Independent Non-Profit — IRS Status: 501(c)3
Highest Offering: Baccalaureate
Program: Liberal Arts And General; Religious Emphasis
Accreditation: TRACS

01 President ..... Dr. Ronald W. HARDEN
05 Vice President of Academics ..... Dr. Greg L. HARTLEY
09 Director of Assessment ..... Ms. Rosemarie HOWELL
08 Director Learning Resource ..... Carol SIMON
10 Chief Financial Officer ..... C. Steven CHANEY
37 Director of Financial Services ..... David PINESCHI
06 Director of Records ..... Kathy CLARKE

Eternity Bible College (J)

2136 Winifred Street, Simi Valley CA 93063
County: Ventura — Identification: 667045
Telephone: (805) 581-1233 — Carnegie Class: Not Classified

FAX Number: (805) 581-1245 Calendar System: Semester
URL: www.eternitybiblecollege.com
Established: 2004 Annual Undergrad Tuition & Fees: $5,000
Enrollment: 180 Coed
Affiliation or Control: Independent Non-Profit IRS Status: 501(c)3
Highest Offering: Baccalaureate
Program: Religious Emphasis
Accreditation: @BI

01 President Joshua WALKER
05 Academic Dean Spencer MACCUISH
07 Director of Admissions Nicole MCGLADDERY

Evangelia University (A)

2660 West Woodland Drive, Suite 200,
Anaheim CA 92801-2650
County: Orange Identification: 666640
Telephone: (714) 527-0691 Carnegie Class: Not Classified
FAX Number: (714) 527-0693 Calendar System: Other
URL: www.evangelia.edu
Established: 1999 Annual Undergrad Tuition & Fees: $3,470
Enrollment: 50 Coed
Affiliation or Control: Reformed Presbyterian Church IRS Status: 501(c)3
Highest Offering: Master's
Program: Liberal Arts And General; Religious Emphasis
Accreditation: TRACS

01 President Dr. David H. SHIN
05 Academic Dean Bo Min LEE
11 Dean Admin/Chief Operating Officer Benjamin JEONG
06 Registrar/Foreign Student Advisor Charley LEE
57 Chair Masters of Arts Program Cha Hi WON
32 Dean of Students Ki Won HAN
20 Associate Academic Dean David KIM

Everest College-Anaheim (B)

511 N. Brookhurst, Ste 300, Anaheim CA 92801
County: Orange FICE Identification: 011107
Unit ID: 371982
Telephone: (714) 953-6500 Carnegie Class: Not Classified
FAX Number: (714) 953-4163 Calendar System: Quarter
URL: www.everest.edu/campus/anaheim
Established: 1969 Annual Undergrad Tuition & Fees: $13,860
Enrollment: 664 Coed
Affiliation or Control: Proprietary IRS Status: Proprietary
Highest Offering: Associate Degree
Program: Occupational
Accreditation: ACCSC, MAC

01 President Ms. Connie ANTENORCRUC

Everest College-City of Industry (C)

12801 Crossroads Parkway S,
City of Industry CA 91746-3412
County: Los Angeles FICE Identification: 030426
Unit ID: 372037
Telephone: (562) 908-2500 Carnegie Class: Assoc/PrivFP
FAX Number: (562) 908-7656 Calendar System: Quarter
URL: www.everest-college.com
Established: 1989 Annual Undergrad Tuition & Fees: $14,176
Enrollment: 980 Coed
Affiliation or Control: Proprietary IRS Status: Proprietary
Highest Offering: Associate Degree
Program: Occupational
Accreditation: ACCSC, MAAB

01 President Ms. Sherry TOMAN

Everest College-Gardena (D)

1045 W. Redondo Beach Blvd, Ste 275,
Gardena CA 90247
County: Los Angeles FICE Identification: 011123
Unit ID: 119456
Telephone: (310) 527-7105 Carnegie Class: Not Classified
FAX Number: (310) 527-7985 Calendar System: Quarter
URL: www.everest.edu/campus/gardena
Established: N/A Annual Undergrad Tuition & Fees: $21,388
Enrollment: 569 Coed
Affiliation or Control: Proprietary IRS Status: Proprietary
Highest Offering: Associate Degree
Program: Occupational
Accreditation: ACCSC, MAC

01 Director/Admissions Mr. Victor ARIOLA

Everest College-LA Wilshire (E)

3460 Wilshire Blvd, Ste 500, Los Angeles CA 90010
County: Los Angeles FICE Identification: 007606
Unit ID: 119368
Telephone: (213) 388-9950 Carnegie Class: Assoc/PrivFP
FAX Number: (213) 388-9907 Calendar System: Quarter
URL: www.everest.edu/campus/la_wilshire
Established: 1960 Annual Undergrad Tuition & Fees: $14,994
Enrollment: 302 Coed
Affiliation or Control: Proprietary IRS Status: Proprietary
Highest Offering: Associate Degree
Program: Occupational
Accreditation: ACCSC, MAC

01 President Mr. Rob LADENDECKER

Everest College-Ontario Metro (F)

1819 South Excise Avenue, Ontario CA 91761-8525
County: San Bernadino Identification: 666621
Unit ID: 440299
Telephone: (909) 484-4311 Carnegie Class: Bac/Assoc
FAX Number: (909) 484-1162 Calendar System: Other
URL: www.everestcollege.edu
Established: 2002 Annual Undergrad Tuition & Fees: $14,238
Enrollment: 1,089 Coed
Affiliation or Control: Proprietary IRS Status: Proprietary
Highest Offering: Baccalaureate
Program: Occupational
Accreditation: ACICS

01 College President Mr. Richard MALLOW

† Branch campus of Everest College, Springfield, MO.

Everest College-Reseda (G)

18040 Sherman Way, Ste 400, Reseda CA 91335-4631
County: Los Angeles FICE Identification: 011109
Unit ID: 119359
Telephone: (818) 774-0550 Carnegie Class: Not Classified
FAX Number: (818) 774-1577 Calendar System: Quarter
URL: www.everest.edu/campus/reseda
Established: 1969 Annual Undergrad Tuition & Fees: $14,364
Enrollment: 746 Coed
Affiliation or Control: Proprietary IRS Status: Proprietary
Highest Offering: Associate Degree
Program: Occupational
Accreditation: ACCSC, SURGT

01 President Ms. Lani TOWNSEND

Everest College-San Bernardino (H)

217 Club Center Drive, Suite A, San Bernardino CA 92408
County: San Bernardino FICE Identification: 004494
Unit ID: 119508
Telephone: (909) 777-3300 Carnegie Class: Assoc/PrivFP
FAX Number: (909) 777-3550 Calendar System: Other
URL: www.everest.edu/campus/san_bernardino
Established: 1969 Annual Undergrad Tuition & Fees: N/A
Enrollment: 755 Coed
Affiliation or Control: Proprietary IRS Status: Proprietary
Highest Offering: Associate Degree
Program: Occupational
Accreditation: ACICS, MAC

01 President Ms. Jennifer WHITE

† Tuition varies by degree program.

Everest College-West LA (I)

3000 S Robertson Boulevard, Ste 300,
Los Angeles CA 90034-3158
County: Los Angeles Identification: 666749
Unit ID: 368805
Telephone: (310) 840-5777 Carnegie Class: Assoc/PrivFP
FAX Number: (310) 287-2344 Calendar System: Quarter
URL: www.everest.edu/campus/west_los_angeles
Established: 1987 Annual Undergrad Tuition & Fees: $16,937
Enrollment: 320 Coed
Affiliation or Control: Proprietary IRS Status: Proprietary
Highest Offering: Associate Degree
Program: Occupational; 2-Year Principally Bachelor's Creditable; Technical Emphasis
Accreditation: ACCSC, MAAB

01 College President Mr. Michael NIELSEN

Expression College for Digital Arts (J)

6601 Shellmound Street, Emeryville CA 94608-1021
County: Alameda FICE Identification: 039733
Unit ID: 447458
Telephone: (510) 654-2934 Carnegie Class: Spec/Arts
FAX Number: (510) 658-3414 Calendar System: Quarter
URL: www.expression.edu
Established: 1999 Annual Undergrad Tuition & Fees: $22,625
Enrollment: 808 Coed
Affiliation or Control: Proprietary IRS Status: Proprietary
Highest Offering: Baccalaureate
Program: Professional
Accreditation: ACCSC

01 Executive Director Mr. Kirk ENGEL
88 Chief Creative Officer Mr. Spencer NILSEN

Fashion Careers College (K)

1923 Morena Boulevard, San Diego CA 92110-3555
County: San Diego FICE Identification: 022343
Unit ID: 114372
Telephone: (619) 275-4700 Carnegie Class: Assoc/PrivFP
FAX Number: (619) 275-0635 Calendar System: Quarter
URL: www.fashioncareerscollege.com
Established: 1979 Annual Undergrad Tuition & Fees: $23,150
Enrollment: 90 Coed
Affiliation or Control: Proprietary IRS Status: Proprietary
Highest Offering: Associate Degree
Program: Occupational
Accreditation: ACICS

00 Founder Ms. Patricia G. O'CONNOR
01 President Ms. Judy THACKER
10 Vice President/CFO Mr. Andrew BISAHA
05 Campus Director Ms. Karen ROQUE-SHAVER
06 Registrar Mrs. Adriana GONZALEZ-MORENO
37 Financial Aid Director Ms. Alexis LYTLE
07 Admissions Advisor Ms. Rebecca HOEHLEIN
21 Director of the Business Office Mr. Peter MAMONIS, JR.
36 Career Services Representative Mr. Sean FOUST
04 Administrative Assistant Ms. Kelley PHELAN
20 Education Coordinator Mrs. Darlene RITZ

Fashion Institute of Design and Merchandising-Los Angeles (L)

919 S Grand Avenue, Los Angeles CA 90015-1421
County: Los Angeles FICE Identification: 011112
Unit ID: 114354
Telephone: (213) 624-1200 Carnegie Class: Spec/Arts
FAX Number: (213) 624-9354 Calendar System: Quarter
URL: www.fidm.edu
Established: 1969 Annual Undergrad Tuition & Fees: $25,469
Enrollment: 4,419 Coed
Affiliation or Control: Proprietary IRS Status: Proprietary
Highest Offering: Baccalaureate
Program: Occupational; 2-Year Principally Bachelor's Creditable; Business Emphasis
Accreditation: WC, WJ, ART

01 President Mrs. Tonian HOHBERG
10 Vice President Finance Ms. Annie JOHNSON
45 Vice President Planning Mrs. Vivien LOWY
05 Vice President Education Mrs. Barbara BUNDY
20 Dean of Academic Development Dr. Carol ROOKSTOOL
12 Director Orange County Campus Ms. Dorothy METCALFE
12 Director San Francisco Campus Ms. Barbara CUPPER
27 Exec Director Industry Relations Ms. Sharon RYAN
08 Director Library Ms. Kathy BAILON
06 Registrar Mr. Michael GILBERT
37 Director Financial Aid Ms. Norine FULLER
26 Director Public Relations Ms. Shirley WILSON
88 Director Adv Fashion Design Ms. Mary STEPHENS
09 Director Institutional Research Mrs. Andrea HELEKAR
38 Articulation Officer Mr. Ben WEINBERG
21 Director Student Financial Services Mr. Chris JENNINGS
96 Director of Purchasing Mrs. Darlene LATINVILLE
97 Chair General Educ/Dean Education Ms. Sheryl RABINOVICH
72 Chair Apparel Manufacturing Mgmt Ms. Roni MILLER START

Fashion Institute of Design and Merchandising-Orange County (M)

17590 Gillette Avenue, Irvine CA 92614-5610
County: Orange Identification: 666004
Unit ID: 114415
Telephone: (888) 974-3436 Carnegie Class: Assoc/PrivFP
FAX Number: N/A Calendar System: Quarter
URL: www.fidm.edu
Established: 1981 Annual Undergrad Tuition & Fees: $26,010
Enrollment: 395 Coed
Affiliation or Control: Proprietary IRS Status: Proprietary
Highest Offering: Baccalaureate
Program: Occupational; 2-Year Principally Bachelor's Creditable; Business Emphasis
Accreditation: &WJ, ART

01 Regional Campus Director Dorothy METCALFE
05 Regional Education Director Jim NEMMERT
07 Admission Director Mike MIRABELLA
36 Career Center Director Michelle PALTY
08 Branch Librarian Rebecca MARKMAN

† Regional accreditation is carried under the parent institution in Los Angeles, CA.

Fashion Institute of Design and Merchandising-San Diego (N)

350 10th Avenue, 3rd Floor, San Diego CA 92101
County: San Diego Identification: 666005
Unit ID: 248846
Telephone: (619) 235-2049 Carnegie Class: Assoc/PrivFP
FAX Number: (619) 232-4322 Calendar System: Quarter
URL: www.fidm.edu
Established: 1985 Annual Undergrad Tuition & Fees: $27,910
Enrollment: 250 Coed
Affiliation or Control: Proprietary IRS Status: Proprietary
Highest Offering: Associate Degree
Program: Occupational; 2-Year Principally Bachelor's Creditable; Business Emphasis

Accreditation: &WJ, ART

01 Campus Director .... Ms. Denise BACA
05 Education Director .... Ms. Katherine SLAUTA
07 Admissions Director .... Ms. Denise BACA

† Regional accreditation is carried under the parent institution in Los Angeles, CA.

Fashion Institute of Design and Merchandising-San Francisco (A)

55 Stockton Street, San Francisco CA 94108-5829

County: San Francisco | FICE Identification: 013041
Unit ID: 114390
Telephone: (415) 675-5200 | Carnegie Class: Assoc/PrivFP
FAX Number: (415) 296-7299 | Calendar System: Quarter
URL: www.fidm.edu
Established: 1973 | Annual Undergrad Tuition & Fees: $26,010
Enrollment: 933 | Coed
Affiliation or Control: Proprietary | IRS Status: Proprietary
Highest Offering: Associate Degree
Program: Occupational; 2-Year Principally Bachelor's Creditable; Business Emphasis
Accreditation: &WJ, ART

01 Campus Director .... Ms. Barbara CUPPER
05 Education Director .... Ms. Kim WETZEL

† Regional accreditation is carried under the parent institution in Los Angeles, CA.

Feather River College (B)

570 Golden Eagle Avenue, Quincy CA 95971-9124

County: Plumas | FICE Identification: 008597
Unit ID: 114433
Telephone: (530) 283-0202 | Carnegie Class: Assoc/Pub-R-M
FAX Number: (530) 283-3757 | Calendar System: Semester
URL: www.frc.edu
Established: 1968 | Annual Undergrad Tuition & Fees (In-District): $1,446
Enrollment: 1,453 | Coed
Affiliation or Control: State/Local | IRS Status: 501(c)3
Highest Offering: Associate Degree
Program: 2-Year Principally Bachelor's Creditable
Accreditation: WJ

01 Interim Superintendent/President .... Dr. Kevin TRUTNA
10 Chief Financial Officer .... Mr. Jim SCOUBES
05 Chief Instructional Officer .... Dr. Derek LERCH
32 Chief Student Services Officer .... Dr. Karen PIERSON
15 Director Human Resources/EEO .... Mr. David BURRIS
18 Director of Facilities/CTO .... Mr. Nick BOYD
06 Registrar/Dir of Admissions .... Ms. Leslie MIKESELL
37 Director Student Financial Aid .... Ms. Barbara CORMACK
96 Purchasing Agent .... Ms. Tamara CLINE

Fielding Graduate University (C)

2112 Santa Barbara Street,
Santa Barbara CA 93105-3538

County: Santa Barbara | FICE Identification: 020961
Unit ID: 114549
Telephone: (805) 687-1099 | Carnegie Class: DRU
FAX Number: (805) 687-4590 | Calendar System: Trimester
URL: www.fielding.edu
Established: 1974 | Annual Graduate Tuition & Fees: $23,160
Enrollment: 1,360 | Coed
Affiliation or Control: Independent Non-Profit | IRS Status: 501(c)3
Highest Offering: Doctorate; No Undergraduates
Program: Professional
Accreditation: WC, #CLPSY

01 President .... Dr. Richard S. MEYERS
101 Exec Asst to Pres/Sec Brd of Trust .... Ms. Monika KRAJEWSKA
05 Provost & Senior Vice President .... Dr. Katrina ROGERS
10 VP and Chief Financial Officer .... Ms. Lisa LEWIS
15 VP Administration & Human Resources .... Dr. Anna MCDONALD
30 VP Advancement & Development .... Mr. David EDELMAN
84 Assoc Provost Acad/Enrollment Mgmt .... Dr. Monique L. SNOWDEN
53 Dean School of Educ Ldrshp & Change .... Dr. Mario R. BORUNDA
88 Assoc Dean School Human & Org Dev .... Dr. Nancy WALLIS
83 Interim Dean School of Psychology .... Dr. Gerardo RODRIGUEZ-MENENDEZ

Five Branches University: Graduate School of Traditional Chinese Medicine (D)

3031 Tisch Way, Ste 507, San Jose CA 95128

County: Santa Clara | Identification: 667008
Telephone: (408) 260-0208 | Carnegie Class: Not Classified
FAX Number: (408) 261-3166 | Calendar System: Semester
URL: www.fivebranches.edu
Established: 2005 | Annual Undergrad Tuition & Fees: $14,000
Enrollment: 300 | Coed
Affiliation or Control: Independent Non-Profit | IRS Status: 501(c)3
Highest Offering: Doctorate; No Lower Division
Program: Professional
Accreditation: ACUP

01 President/CEO .... Ron ZAIDMAN
05 VP Academic Affairs .... Joanna ZHAO
06 Registrar .... Gina HUANG
07 Associate Director of Admissions .... Nancy BURNS
10 Chief Financial Officer .... Liana CHEN
88 Associate Director Doctoral .... Maung WAI HLA
88 Associate Director Doctoral .... E-Sing HONG
88 Director Chinese Masters of TCM .... Jasmine HUANG
88 Director Korean Masters of TCM .... Heerei PARK
88 Director of Extension Program .... Phan GOH
88 Clinic Manager .... Yee CHING
88 Director of Mind-Body Center .... Laury RAPAPPORT

Five Branches University, Graduate School of Traditional Chinese Medicine (E)

200 7th Avenue, Santa Cruz CA 95062-4669

County: Santa Cruz | FICE Identification: 031313
Unit ID: 114585
Telephone: (831) 476-9424 | Carnegie Class: Spec/Health
FAX Number: (831) 476-8928 | Calendar System: Semester
URL: www.fivebranches.edu
Established: 1984 | Annual Undergrad Tuition & Fees: $14,000
Enrollment: 287 | Coed
Affiliation or Control: Independent Non-Profit | IRS Status: 501(c)3
Highest Offering: Master's; No Lower Division
Program: Professional
Accreditation: ACUP

01 President .... Ron ZAIDMAN
05 Academic Dean .... Joanna ZHAO
07 Admissions Director .... Eleonor MENDELSON
32 Director of Student Services .... Ana LOBATO
37 Director Student Financial Aid .... Mecca MATILDA
08 Librarian .... Jim EMDY
17 Clinic Director .... Joanna ZHAO
84 Director of Enrollment Management .... Ali POLK

*Foothill-De Anza Community College District System Office (F)

12345 El Monte Road, Los Altos Hills CA 94022-4597

County: Santa Clara | FICE Identification: 009020
Unit ID: 114831
Telephone: (650) 949-6100 | Carnegie Class: N/A
FAX Number: (650) 941-1638
URL: www.fhda.edu

01 Chancellor .... Dr. Linda M. THOR
10 Vice Chancellor Business Services .... Mr. Kevin MCELROY
16 Vice Chancellor Human Resources .... Ms. Dorene NOVOTNY
13 Vice Chancellor Technology .... Mr. Joseph MOREAU
18 Exec Dir Facility Oper/Constr Mgmt .... Mr. Charles ALLEN

*De Anza College (G)

21250 Stevens Creek Boulevard,
Cupertino CA 95014-5793

County: Santa Clara | FICE Identification: 004480
Unit ID: 113333
Telephone: (408) 864-5678 | Carnegie Class: Assoc/Pub-S-MC
FAX Number: (408) 864-5698 | Calendar System: Quarter
URL: www.deanza.edu
Established: 1967 | Annual Undergrad Tuition & Fees (In-District): $1,116
Enrollment: 24,187 | Coed
Affiliation or Control: State/Local | IRS Status: 501(c)3
Highest Offering: Associate Degree
Program: Occupational; 2-Year Principally Bachelor's Creditable
Accreditation: WJ, MLTAD

02 President .... Dr. Brian MURPHY
05 Vice Pres of Instruction .... Dr. Christina ESPINOSA-PIEB
32 Vice Pres of Student Services .... Ms. Stacy A. COOK
10 Vice Pres Finance/Educ Resources .... Ms. Letha JEANPIERRE
20 Dean of Academic Services .... Ms. Christina ESPINOSA PIEB
35 Dean Student Development/EOPS .... Ms. Michele LEBLEU BURNS
38 Dean Counseling & Matriculation .... Ms. Angela CABALLERO DE CORDERO
07 Dean Admissions & Records .... Ms. Kathleen MOBERG
37 Director Student Financial Aid .... Ms. Cindy CASTILLO
15 Director Personnel Services .... Ms. Margaret MICHAELIS
18 Director Facilities/Physical Plant .... Mr. Frank NUNEZ
21 Director Budget & Personnel .... Ms. Margaret MICHAELIS
26 Director Marketing/Communications .... Ms. Marisa SPATAFORE
30 Chief Development .... Ms. Marie FOX
84 Director Enrollment Management .... Ms. Christina ESPINOSA PIEB
28 Director of Diversity .... Vacant
96 Director of Purchasing .... Ms. Carmen REDMOND
09 Institutional Research Specialist .... Ms. Mallory NEWELL

*Foothill College (H)

12345 El Monte Road, Los Altos Hills CA 94022-4599

County: Santa Clara | FICE Identification: 001199
Unit ID: 114716
Telephone: (650) 949-7777 | Carnegie Class: Assoc/Pub-S-MC
FAX Number: (650) 949-7375 | Calendar System: Quarter
URL: www.foothill.edu
Established: 1958 | Annual Undergrad Tuition & Fees (In-District): $1,116
Enrollment: 15,500 | Coed
Affiliation or Control: State/Local | IRS Status: 501(c)3
Highest Offering: Associate Degree
Program: Occupational; 2-Year Principally Bachelor's Creditable
Accreditation: WJ, DA, DH, DMS, EMT, RAD

02 President .... Dr. Judy C. MINER
45 VP Instr/Educational Resources .... Dr. Shirley TREANOR
09 VP Instr/Institutional Research .... Ms. Kimberlee MESSINA
05 VP Instr/Student Development .... Dr. Denise SWETT
103 Interim VP of Workforce Education .... Mr. John MUMMERT
32 Dean Instruction/Student Affairs .... Ms. Patricia HYLAND
31 Dean Community Services .... Vacant
56 Dean Intl & Distance Education .... Mr. George S. BEERS
32 Dean Counseling/Student Services .... Ms. Laureen BALDUCCI
12 Dean Middlefield College .... Vacant
15 Vice Chancellor Personnel Services .... Dr. Doreen NOVOTNY
102 Executive Director Foundation .... Ms. Sheryl ALEXANDER
26 Assoc VP of External Relations .... Mr. Kurt HUEG
19 Director & Chief of Police .... Mr. Ronald LEVINE
35 Dir Student Services & Activities .... Ms. Daphne SMALL
10 Chief Business Officer .... Mr. Kevin MCELROY
96 Director of Purchasing .... Ms. Carmen REDMOND
18 Manager Buildings & Grounds .... Ms. Marilyn WILLIAMS
40 Bookstore Manager .... Mr. Romeo PAULE
37 Manager Financial Aid .... Mr. Kevin HARRAL
88 Pgm Admin NASA Ames Internship .... Vacant
23 Coordinator Student Health Services .... Ms. Lorraine N. KITAJIMA
76 Int Div Dean Biology/Health Science .... Ms. Eloise ORRELL
50 Interim Div Dean Bus/Social Science .... Mr. Glenn VIOLETTE
77 Div Dean Computer/Tech/Info Systems .... Ms. Judy BAKER
57 Div Dn Fine Arts/Communications .... Mr. Mark ANDERSON
88 Division Dean Language Arts .... Mr. Paul STARER
68 Int Div Dean PE/Human Performance .... Ms. Susan GUTKIND
81 Div Dean Physical Science/Math/Engr .... Dr. Peter MURRAY

Franciscan School of Theology (I)

1712 Euclid Avenue, Berkeley CA 94709-1294

County: Alameda | FICE Identification: 011792
Unit ID: 114734
Telephone: (510) 848-5232 | Carnegie Class: Spec/Faith
FAX Number: (510) 549-9466 | Calendar System: Semester
URL: www.fst.edu
Established: 1968 | Annual Graduate Tuition & Fees: $13,620
Enrollment: 36 | Coed
Affiliation or Control: Independent Non-Profit | IRS Status: 501(c)3
Highest Offering: Master's; No Undergraduates
Program: Professional; Religious Emphasis
Accreditation: WC, THEOL

01 President .... Fr. Joseph CHINNICI, OFM
05 Dean .... Br. William SHORT, OFM
06 Registrar .... Ms. Jenna NIELSEN
07 Director of Admissions .... Mr. Vince NIMS
30 Associate Development Director .... Ms. Randi QUAID
10 Chief Financial Officer .... Ms. Carolyn RODKIN

Fremont College (J)

3440 Wilshire Blvd. 10th Floor, Los Angeles CA 90010

County: Los Angeles | FICE Identification: 030399
Unit ID: 372073
Telephone: (213) 355-7777 | Carnegie Class: Assoc/PrivFP
FAX Number: (213) 355-8088 | Calendar System: Other
URL: www.fremont.edu
Established: 1985 | Annual Undergrad Tuition & Fees: N/A
Enrollment: 350 | Coed
Affiliation or Control: Proprietary | IRS Status: Proprietary
Highest Offering: Baccalaureate
Program: Occupational; 2-Year Principally Bachelor's Creditable
Accreditation: ACCSC

01 Chairman/CEO .... Dr. Sabrina KAY
11 Director of Operations .... Mr. Tony WONG

Fresno Pacific Biblical Seminary (K)

1717 South Chestnut Avenue, Fresno CA 93727-5097

County: Fresno | FICE Identification: 010368
Unit ID: 118709
Telephone: (559) 453-2310 | Carnegie Class: Spec/Faith
FAX Number: (559) 453-2355 | Calendar System: Semester
URL: www.seminary.fresno.edu
Established: 1955 | Annual Graduate Tuition & Fees: $12,360
Enrollment: 118 | Coed
Affiliation or Control: Mennonite Brethren Church | IRS Status: 501(c)3
Highest Offering: Master's; No Undergraduates
Program: Professional; Religious Emphasis
Accreditation: WC, THEOL

01 Fresno Pacific University President .... Dr. Pete C. MENJARES
03 Vice President/Seminary Dean .... Dr. Lynn JOST
32 Seminary Dean of Students .... Dr. Valerie REMPEL
44 Director of Seminary Advancement .... Mr. Mark ISAAC
07 Director of Seminary Admissions .... Mr. Andrew JOHNSON
06 University Registrar .... Ms. Linda PRYCE-SHEEHAN
26 University Communications Director .... Ms. Diana MOCK
04 Dean's Assistant .... Ms. Sheryl BUSBY
39 University Housing Director .... Ms. Pam SCHOCK

Fresno Pacific University (A)

1717 S Chestnut Avenue, Fresno CA 93702-4798
County: Fresno FICE Identification: 001253
Unit ID: 114813
Telephone: (559) 453-2000 Carnegie Class: Master's M
FAX Number: (559) 453-2007 Calendar System: Semester
URL: www.fresno.edu
Established: 1944 Annual Undergrad Tuition & Fees: $25,336
Enrollment: 3,918 Coed
Affiliation or Control: Mennonite Brethren Church IRS Status: 501(c)3
Highest Offering: Master's
Program: Liberal Arts And General; Teacher Preparatory
Accreditation: WC, NURSE

01 President ... Dr. Pete C. MENJARES
05 Provost ... Dr. Stephen VARVIS
10 Int Vice Pres Business Affairs ... Mr. Dick HERRINTON
30 Vice President for Advancement ... Mr. Mark DEFFENBACHER
13 Vice Pres of Information Services ... Mr. Alan OURS
50 Interim Dean School of Business ... Dr. John KILROY
79 Dean Sch of Humanities/Rel/Soc Sci ... Dr. Kevin REIMER
53 Dean School of Education ... Dr. Gary GRAMENZ
78 Dean School of Natural Sciences ... Dr. Karen CIANCI
42 Dean of Spiritual Formation ... Rev. Angulus WILSON
32 Dean of Student Life ... Dr. Randy WORDEN
06 Registrar ... Ms. Linda PRYCE-SHEEHAN
08 Director of Library ... Mr. Kevin ENNS-REMPEL
36 Director of Career Resource Center ... Ms. Alicia ANDRADE
18 Facilities Manager ... Mr. Barry LOCKTON
15 Human Resources Director ... Mrs. Marylou MILLER
25 Director of Grants & Research ... Vacant
27 Publications Director ... Mr. Wayne STEFFEN
29 Alumni Director ... Mrs. Charity BROWN
37 Director of Financial Aid ... Ms. April POWELL
38 Counseling Coordinator ... Vacant
40 Bookstore Manager ... Ms. Erin NOEL
41 Athletic Director ... Mr. Dennis JANZEN
19 Director of Security ... Mr. Gary MEJIA
26 Chief Public Relations Officer ... Ms. Diana MOCK
28 Director of Diversity ... Vacant
07 Director of Admissions ... Ms. Rina CAMPBELL

Fuller Theological Seminary (B)

135 N Oakland, Pasadena CA 91182-1780
County: Los Angeles FICE Identification: 001200
Unit ID: 114840
Telephone: (626) 584-5200 Carnegie Class: Spec/Faith
FAX Number: (626) 584-5672 Calendar System: Quarter
URL: www.fuller.edu
Established: 1947 Annual Graduate Tuition & Fees: $17,388
Enrollment: 2,568 Coed
Affiliation or Control: Independent Non-Profit IRS Status: 501(c)3
Highest Offering: Doctorate; No Undergraduates
Program: Professional
Accreditation: WC, CLPSY, THEOL

01 President ... Dr. Richard J. MOUW
05 Provost & Sr Vice President ... Dr. C. Douglas MCCONNELL
10 Vice President for Finance ... Mr. John WARD
30 Vice President Seminary Advancement ... Mr. Joe B. WEBB
11 Executive VP for Administration ... Vacant
84 VP for Enrollment & Student Affairs ... Dr. Wendy WAKEMAN
73 Dean School of Theology ... Dr. Howard J. LOEWEN
88 Dean School of Psychology ... Dr. Winston E. GOODEN
88 Dean School Intercultural Studies ... Dr. Scott W. SUNQUIST
56 Assoc Provost Cont/Extended Educ ... Vacant
26 Assoc Vice Pres for Public Affairs ... Mr. Fred MESSICK
29 Assoc VP Alumni & Church Rels ... Mrs. Mary HUBBARD GIVEN
08 Assoc Provost Library Services & IT ... Vacant
73 Assoc Dean/Advanced Theol Studies ... Dr. Joel GREEN
88 Assoc Dean Doctor of Ministry Pgm ... Dr. Kurt FREDRICKSON
88 Assoc Dean School of Psychology ... Vacant
27 Asst Provost Library/IT & CIO ... Mr. Michael MURRAY
06 Registrar ... Mr. David E. KIEFER
13 Director Management Info Svcs ... Vacant
15 Director of Human Resources ... Mrs. Bernadette (BJ) BARBER
32 Director of Student Affairs ... Mr. Sam BANG
21 Director of Budget ... Dr. David R. ADAMS
39 Director of Student Housing ... Mr. David SMITH
04 Exec Asst to President & Trustees ... Ms. Wendy WALKER
18 Director of Campus Facilities ... Mr. Randall R. SMITH
31 Director of Auxiliary Services ... Mrs. Jeanne HANDOJO
24 Director of Academic Tech Center ... Vacant
43 General Counsel ... Ms. Rita K. ROWLAND
96 Director of Purchasing ... Ms. Silvia GUTIERREZ
36 Asst to Dean of Stdnts/Career Svcs ... Vacant
85 Dir Student Affs/International Svcs ... Mr. Sam BANG
37 Director Student Financial Services ... Mr. David RICHARDS
07 Assoc Director of Admissions ... Mr. Chad CAIN

Gavilan College (C)

5055 Santa Teresa Boulevard, Gilroy CA 95020-9599
County: Santa Clara FICE Identification: 001202
Unit ID: 114938
Telephone: (408) 848-4800 Carnegie Class: Assoc/Pub-S-SC
FAX Number: (408) 848-4801 Calendar System: Semester
URL: www.gavilan.edu
Established: 1919 Annual Undergrad Tuition & Fees (In-District): $918
Enrollment: 6,041 Coed
Affiliation or Control: State/Local IRS Status: 501(c)3
Highest Offering: Associate Degree
Program: Occupational; 2-Year Principally Bachelor's Creditable
Accreditation: WJ

01 Superintendent/President ... Dr. Steven M. KINSELLA
05 Exec Vice Pres Instructional Svcs ... Dr. Kathleen A. ROSE
11 Vice Pres Administrative Services ... Mr. Joseph KEELER
32 Vice President Student Services ... Mr. John PRUITT
06 Registrar ... Ms. Candice WHITNEY
08 Head Librarian ... Dr. Douglas ACHTERMAN
37 Director Student Financial Aid ... Ms. Veronica MARTINEZ
09 Director of Institutional Research ... Dr. Randy BROWN
15 Director Personnel Services ... Mr. Eric RAMONES
18 Chief Facilities/Physical Plant ... Mr. Jeff GOPP
13 Dir Computing & Information Mgmt ... Ms. Mimi ARVIZU
19 Director Security/Safety ... Ms. Ana HIPOL
26 Director Public Information ... Ms. Jan CHARGIN
23 Director Health Services ... Ms. Alice DUFRESNE-REYES
41 Athletic Director ... Mr. Ron HANNON
40 Director Bookstore ... Ms. Alexis BOLIN
49 Dean Liberal Arts/Sci/Dir Cont Educ ... Ms. Fran LOZANO
72 Dean Career Technical Education ... Ms. Sherrean CARR
07 Director of Admissions ... Ms. Candice WHITNEY

Glendale Community College (D)

1500 N Verdugo Road, Glendale CA 91208-2894
County: Los Angeles FICE Identification: 001203
Unit ID: 115001
Telephone: (818) 240-1000 Carnegie Class: Assoc/Pub-S-SC
FAX Number: (818) 549-9436 Calendar System: Semester
URL: www.glendale.edu
Established: 1927 Annual Undergrad Tuition & Fees (In-District): $1,104
Enrollment: 16,610 Coed
Affiliation or Control: State/Local IRS Status: 501(c)3
Highest Offering: Associate Degree
Program: Occupational; 2-Year Principally Bachelor's Creditable
Accreditation: WJ

01 Interim Superintendent/President ... Dr. Jim RIGGS
11 Exec Vice Pres Administrative Svcs ... Mr. Ron NAKASONE
05 Vice Pres Instructional Services ... Dr. Mary MIRCH
32 Vice President Student Services ... Dr. Ricardo PEREZ
13 Assoc VP Information & Technology ... Mr. Wayne KELLER
51 Int Admn Dn Inst Svcs Cont/Cmty Ed ... Mr. Alfred RAMIREZ
15 Administrative Dean Human Resources ... Ms. Donna VOOGT
45 Dean Research/Planning/Grants ... Dr. Edward KARPP
07 Director Admissions & Records ... Ms. Michelle MORA
20 Dean Instructional Services ... Mr. Michael RITTERBROWN
32 Dean Student Affairs ... Dr. Paul SCHLOSSMAN
35 Dean of Student Services ... Dr. Jewel A. PRICE
08 Assoc Dean Library/Lrng Resource ... Mr. James KRUSLING
37 Associate Dean Financial Aid ... Dr. Patricia HURLEY
10 Int Director Business Services ... Ms. Susan COURTEY

Golden Gate Baptist Theological Seminary (E)

201 Seminary Drive, Mill Valley CA 94941-3197
County: Marin FICE Identification: 001204
Unit ID: 115047
Telephone: (415) 380-1300 Carnegie Class: Not Classified
FAX Number: (415) 383-1302 Calendar System: Semester
URL: www.ggbts.edu
Established: 1944 Annual Graduate Tuition & Fees: $5,560
Enrollment: 1,599 Coed
Affiliation or Control: Southern Baptist IRS Status: 501(c)3
Highest Offering: Doctorate; No Undergraduates
Program: Professional; Religious Emphasis
Accreditation: WC, THEOL

00 President Emeritus ... Dr. William O. CREWS
01 President/Chairman of the Faculty ... Dr. Jeff IORG
30 Vice Pres Institutional Advancement ... Vacant
10 Vice President Business & Finance ... Mr. Gary GROAT
05 Vice President Academic Affairs ... Dr. D. Michael MARTIN
84 VP Enrollment/Student Svcs/Dn Stdts ... Dr. Adam GROZA
21 Controller ... Mr. Harrison WEAVER
06 Registrar ... Ms. Jennifer PEACH
08 Director of Library Services ... Ms. Kelly CAMPBELL
12 Director SC Campus ... Dr. Earl WAGGONER
12 Director PNW Campus ... Dr. Mark BRADLEY
12 Director Arizona Campus ... Dr. David JOHNSON
12 Director Rocky Mountain Campus ... Dr. Steve VETETO
13 Director Information Technology ... Mr. Jeff COLBERT
15 Director Personnel Services ... Vacant
18 Chief Facilities/Physical Plant ... Mr. Robert DVORAK
40 Director Bookstore ... Mr. Darren DRAEGER
07 Director Admissions ... Ms. Karen ROBINSON
44 Director of Development ... Mr. Victor VANLOO
84 Director Enrollment Management ... Ms. Karen ROBINSON
39 Resident Life Manager ... Mr. Shane TANIGAWA

Golden Gate University (F)

536 Mission Street, San Francisco CA 94105-2968
County: San Francisco FICE Identification: 001205
Unit ID: 115083
Telephone: (415) 442-7000 Carnegie Class: Master's L
FAX Number: (415) 495-2671 Calendar System: Trimester
URL: www.ggu.edu
Established: 1901 Annual Undergrad Tuition & Fees: $17,700
Enrollment: 3,605 Coed
Affiliation or Control: Independent Non-Profit IRS Status: 501(c)3
Highest Offering: Doctorate
Program: Professional; Business Emphasis
Accreditation: WC, LAW

01 President ... Dr. Daniel D. ANGEL
05 VP of Academic Affairs ... Ms. Barbara H. KARLIN
10 VP of Business Affairs & CFO ... Mr. Robert D. HITE
30 VP of University Advancement ... Ms. Elizabeth A. BRADY
13 Assoc VP Technology & Telecom ... Vacant
61 Interim Dean School of Law ... Ms. Rachel VAN CLEAVE
50 Dean Ageno School of Business ... Dr. Paul FOUTS
88 Dean School of Taxation & Acctng ... Ms. Mary CANNING
49 Dean Undergraduate Programs ... Dr. Cherron HOPPES
100 Executive Director Ofc of President ... Dr. John FYFE
12 Dean Cyber Campus ... Mr. Marvin WEINBAUM
32 Dean of Students & Student Affairs ... Ms. Janine MIXON
08 Director University Library ... Ms. Janice CARTER
08 Associate Dean Law Library ... Mr. Michael DAW
15 Director Human Resources/EEO ... Ms. Terri SHULTIS
84 Director Enrollment Services ... Mr. Louis D. RICCARDI, JR.
06 University Registrar ... Mr. Steven LIND
27 Chief Information Officer ... Mr. Scott CILIBERTI
26 Director Marketing & Communications ... Ms. Tasia S. NEEVE
88 Director PLUS Program ... Dr. Karen MCROBIE
09 Dir Planning/Resources/Analysis ... Dr. Mercy LIM
18 Director Business Svcs/Facilities ... Mr. Mike KOPERSKI
21 Controller ... Ms. Sheryl KOGA
37 Director Student Financial Aid ... Mr. Steven LIND
38 Clinical Director/Counseling Svcs ... Ms. Michael Anne CONLEY

Golf Academy of America (G)

1950 Camino Vida Roble, Suite 125, Carlsbad CA 92008
County: San Diego FICE Identification: 015609
Unit ID: 122366
Telephone: (800) 342-7342 Carnegie Class: Assoc/PrivFP
FAX Number: (760) 734-1642 Calendar System: Semester
URL: www.golfacademy.edu
Established: 1974 Annual Undergrad Tuition & Fees: $33,390
Enrollment: 295 Coed
Affiliation or Control: Proprietary IRS Status: Proprietary
Highest Offering: Associate Degree
Program: Occupational; Business Emphasis
Accreditation: ACICS

01 President ... Mr. Michael LARGENT
12 Campus Director ... Mr. Richard IORIO

† Branch campus of Virginia College, Birmingham, AL.

Grace Communion Seminary (H)

2011 E. Financial Way, PO Box 5015,
Glendova CA 91740-0730
County: Los Angeles Identification: 667115
Telephone: (626) 650-2306 Carnegie Class: Not Classified
FAX Number: (626) 650-2307 Calendar System: Semester
URL: www.gcs.edu
Established: 2004 Annual Graduate Tuition & Fees: N/A
Enrollment: 49 Coed
Affiliation or Control: Independent Non-Profit IRS Status: 501(c)3
Highest Offering: Master's; No Undergraduates
Program: Religious Emphasis
Accreditation: DETC

01 President/CEO ... Dr. Russell DUKE
05 Dean of Faculty ... Dr. Michael MORRISON
06 Registrar ... Ms. Susan EARLE

Grace Mission University (I)

1645 West Valencia Drive, Fullerton CA 92833-3860
County: Orange Identification: 666642
Telephone: (714) 525-0088 Carnegie Class: Not Classified
FAX Number: (714) 525-0089 Calendar System: Semester
URL: www.gmuedu.org
Established: 1995 Annual Undergrad Tuition & Fees: $5,420
Enrollment: 145 Coed
Affiliation or Control: Presbyterian Church In America IRS Status: 501(c)3
Highest Offering: Master's
Program: Professional; Religious Emphasis
Accreditation: @BI, TRACS

01 President ... Kwangsin KIM
03 Executive Vice President & CEO ... Dr. Kyunam CHOI
05 Academic Dean ... Dr. Hyun Wan KIM
11 Dir Administration/Financial Aid ... Mr. James KOO

Graduate Theological Union (J)

2400 Ridge Road, Berkeley CA 94709-1212
County: Alameda FICE Identification: 001207
Unit ID: 115214
Telephone: (510) 649-2400 Carnegie Class: Spec/Faith
FAX Number: (510) 649-1417 Calendar System: Semester
URL: www.gtu.edu
Established: 1962 Annual Graduate Tuition & Fees: $27,840
Enrollment: 225 Coed
Affiliation or Control: Independent Non-Profit IRS Status: 501(c)3
Highest Offering: Doctorate; No Undergraduates
Program: Professional; Religious Emphasis
Accreditation: WC, THEOL

01 President ....Dr. James A. DONAHUE
05 Dean/Vice Pres Academic Affairs ....Dr. Arthur HOLDER
10 Vice Pres Administration/Finance ....Mr. Steven G. ARGYRIS
30 Vice President for Advancement ....Mr. Eric ALEXANDER
32 VP Student Affairs/Dean Students ....Dr. Maureen A. MALONEY
07 Assistant Dean for Admissions ....Dr. Kathleen KOOK
37 Director of Financial Aid ....Ms. Kathleen ANTOKHIN
08 Library Director ....Mr. Robert BENEDETTO
06 Consortial Registrar ....Mr. John SEAL
13 Chief Information Officer ....Mr. Jeffrey DIGREORIO
26 Director of Marketing & Comm ....Mr. Jake STAFFORD
18 Building & Grounds Engineer ....Mr. Curtis OSBORNE
15 Personnel Officer ....Ms. Debi WALKER
04 Executive Assistant to President ....Ms. Teresa JOYE

*Grossmont-Cuyamaca Community College District (A)

8800 Grossmont College Drive, El Cajon CA 92020-1799
County: San Diego FICE Identification: 007006
Unit ID: 115287
Telephone: (619) 644-7010 Carnegie Class: N/A
FAX Number: (619) 644-7936
URL: www.gcccd.edu

01 Chancellor ....Dr. Cindy MILES
10 Vice Chanc Business Services ....Ms. Sue REARIC
15 Vice Chanc Human Resources ....Ms. Victoria SIMMONS

*Cuyamaca College (B)

900 Rancho San Diego Parkway, El Cajon CA 92019-4304
County: San Diego FICE Identification: 021113
Unit ID: 113218
Telephone: (619) 660-4000 Carnegie Class: Assoc/Pub-S-MC
FAX Number: (619) 660-4399 Calendar System: Quarter
URL: www.cuyamaca.edu
Established: 1978 Annual Undergrad Tuition & Fees (In-District): $1,336
Enrollment: 8,756 Coed
Affiliation or Control: State/Local IRS Status: 501(c)3
Highest Offering: Associate Degree
Program: Occupational; 2-Year Principally Bachelor's Creditable
Accreditation: WJ

02 President ....Dr. Mark J. ZACOVIC
05 Vice President Instruction ....Dr. Robin STEINBACK
32 Vice Pres Student Services ....Dr. Julianna BARNES
11 Vice Pres Administrative Services ....Dr. Arleen SATELE
20 Interim Dean of Instruction Div I ....Dr. Scott HERRIN
20 Dean of Instruction Div II ....Ms. Danene BROWN
51 Int Dean Cont Ed/Workforce Training ....Ms. Jennifer LEWIS
08 Dean Learning & TechnologyResources ....Ms. Connie ELDER
88 Acting Assistant Dean EOPS ....Ms. Nanyamka HILL
41 Assoc Dean Athletics/Athletic Dir ....Dr. Scott HERRIN
35 Assoc Dean Student Affairs ....Dr. Lauren WEINER
38 Dean Counseling & Enrollment Svc ....Ms. Susan TOPHAM
37 Director of Financial Aid ....Mr. Ray REYES
07 Supervisor Admissions & Records ....Mr. Victor DEVORE
18 Facilities/Physical Plant ....Mr. Bruce FARNHAM

*Grossmont College (C)

8800 Grossmont College Drive, El Cajon CA 92020-1799
County: San Diego FICE Identification: 001208
Unit ID: 115296
Telephone: (619) 644-7000 Carnegie Class: Assoc/Pub-S-MC
FAX Number: (619) 644-7922 Calendar System: Semester
URL: www.grossmont.edu
Established: 1961 Annual Undergrad Tuition & Fees (In-District): $1,110
Enrollment: 19,809 Coed
Affiliation or Control: State/Local IRS Status: 501(c)3
Highest Offering: Associate Degree
Program: Occupational; 2-Year Principally Bachelor's Creditable
Accreditation: WJ, ADNUR, CVT, OTA

02 President ....Dr. Sunita COOKE
05 Vice Pres of Academic Affairs ....Dr. Barbara BLANCHARD
32 Vice President of Student Services ....Mr. Jeff BAKER
38 Dean Counseling Svcs ....Vacant
72 Dean Career & Technical Workforce ....Mrs. Sheridan DEWOLF
81 Dean Math/Natural Sci/Phys Educ ....Dr. Mike REESE
60 Dean Arts/Languages/Communication ....Mr. Steve BAKER
79 Dean English/Social & Behav Sci ....Vacant
08 Dean of Learning Resources ....Ms. Kerry KILBER
35 Associate Dean Student Affairs ....Mr. Agustin ALBARRAN
09 Director of Institutional Research ....Ms. Leonor PEREZ
10 Chief Business Officer ....Mr. Tim FLOOD
15 Director Personnel Services ....Ms. Amber GREEN
18 Chief Facilities/Physical Plant ....Mr. Tim FLOOD
26 Int Chief Public Relations Officer ....Mr. Rick GRIFFIN
36 Director Student Placement ....Ms. Nancy DAVIS
37 Director Student Financial Aid ....Mr. Michael COPENHAVER
96 Director of Purchasing ....Ms. Linda BERTOLUCCI

Hands-on Medical Massage School (D)

2015 Park Avenue, Redlands CA 92373
County: San Bernardino FICE Identification: 041789
Unit ID: 461777
Telephone: (909) 793-4263 Carnegie Class: Not Classified
FAX Number: (909) 793-5763 Calendar System: Semester
URL: www.handsonmedicalmassage.com
Established: 2003 Annual Undergrad Tuition & Fees: $19,500
Enrollment: 12 Coed
Affiliation or Control: Proprietary IRS Status: Proprietary
Highest Offering: Associate Degree
Program: Occupational
Accreditation: COE

01 CEO/Director ....Ms. Carola JANIAK

Hartnell College (E)

411 Central Avenue, Salinas CA 93901-1697
County: Monterey FICE Identification: 001209
Unit ID: 115393
Telephone: (831) 755-6700 Carnegie Class: Assoc/Pub-R-L
FAX Number: (831) 755-6751 Calendar System: Semester
URL: www.hartnell.edu
Established: 1920 Annual Undergrad Tuition & Fees (In-District): $562
Enrollment: 17,864 Coed
Affiliation or Control: State/Local IRS Status: 501(c)3
Highest Offering: Associate Degree
Program: Occupational; 2-Year Principally Bachelor's Creditable
Accreditation: WJ

01 Superintendent/President ....Dr. Willard C. LEWALLEN
32 VP Student Affairs/Athletics ....Dr. Esteban SORIANO
11 Interim VP Support Operations ....Mr. Al MUNOZ
13 VP Information & Tech Systems ....Mr. Matt COOMBS
20 VP Academic Affairs ....Vacant
44 Exec Dir of Advancement ....Ms. Jackie CRUZ
68 Interim Director Athletics ....Mr. Daniel TERESA
15 Assoc VP Human Resources/EEO ....Dr. Terri PYER
21 Controller ....Ms. Maria Dolorez JAVIER
06 VP Student Affairs ....Ms. Mary DOMINGUEZ
07 Manager of Admissions ....Ms. Irene HANETA
18 Director of Facilities ....Mr. Joseph REYES
37 Manager of Financial Aid ....Ms. Jessica TOVAR

Harvey Mudd College (F)

301 Platt Boulevard, Claremont CA 91711-5990
County: Los Angeles FICE Identification: 001171
Unit ID: 115409
Telephone: (909) 621-8000 Carnegie Class: Bac/A&S
FAX Number: (909) 621-8360 Calendar System: Semester
URL: www.hmc.edu
Established: 1955 Annual Undergrad Tuition & Fees: $44,442
Enrollment: 784 Coed
Affiliation or Control: Independent Non-Profit IRS Status: 501(c)3
Highest Offering: Baccalaureate
Program: Liberal Arts And General; Professional; Technical Emphasis
Accreditation: WC, ENG

01 President ....Dr. Maria M. KLAWE
30 Vice President Advancement ....Mr. Daniel MACALUSO
10 Vice President/Treasurer ....Mr. Andrew R. DORANTES
05 Dean of the Faculty ....Dr. Jeffrey GROVES
07 Vice Pres/Dean of Admissions ....Ms. Thyra BRIGGS
32 Vice Pres/Dean of Students ....Dr. Marguerite BROWNING
13 VP/CIO ....Mr. Joseph VAUGHAN
09 Asst VP Institutional Research ....Dr. Janel H. HASTINGS
15 AVP of Human Resources ....Ms. Cynthia A. BECKWITH
18 AVP Facilities/Physical Plant ....Ms. Theresa POTTER
06 Registrar ....Mr. Mark ASHLEY
26 Director of College Relations ....Ms. Stephanie GRAHAM
28 Assoc Dean Institutional Diversity ....Ms. Sumun (Sumi) PENDAKUR
29 Director of Alumni Relations ....Ms. Jennifer GREEN
37 Director of Student Financial Aid ....Ms. Gilma LOPEZ
20 Associate Academic Officer ....Vacant
101 Exec Asst to the Pres/Secy to Board ....Ms. Karen ANGEMI

*Heald College, Central Office (G)

601 Montgomery Street, 14th Floor,
San Francisco CA 94111-2618
County: San Francisco Identification: 666712
Telephone: (415) 808-1400 Carnegie Class: N/A
FAX Number: (415) 808-1598
URL: www.heald.edu

01 President/CEO ....Ms. Eeva DESHON
05 Sr VP/Chief Academic Ofcr ....Mr. Terry RAWLS

*Heald College, Concord (H)

5130 Commercial Circle, Concord CA 94520-5617
County: Contra Costa FICE Identification: 020798
Unit ID: 115533
Telephone: (925) 288-5800 Carnegie Class: Assoc/PrivFP
FAX Number: (925) 288-5896 Calendar System: Quarter
URL: www.heald.edu
Established: 1863 Annual Undergrad Tuition & Fees: $17,300
Enrollment: 1,772 Coed
Affiliation or Control: Proprietary IRS Status: Proprietary
Highest Offering: Associate Degree
Program: Occupational
Accreditation: &WJ, DA, MAC

02 Campus President ....Ms. Shirley LLAFET
03 Campus Vice President ....Mr. Keith WOODMAN
05 Dean of Educational Programs ....Mr. Kevin KENNY
07 Director of Admissions ....Mr. Dan CHEW
36 Director of Career Services ....Ms. Kimberly BOUTTE
10 Business Office Manager ....Ms. Amalia COTA

† Regional accreditation is carried under the parent institution Heald College, Central Office in San Francisco, CA

*Heald College, Fresno (I)

255 W Bullard Avenue, Fresno CA 93704-1706
County: Fresno FICE Identification: 008093
Unit ID: 115472
Telephone: (559) 438-4222 Carnegie Class: Assoc/PrivFP
FAX Number: (559) 438-6368 Calendar System: Quarter
URL: www.heald.edu
Established: 1863 Annual Undergrad Tuition & Fees: $14,790
Enrollment: 2,109 Coed
Affiliation or Control: Proprietary IRS Status: Proprietary
Highest Offering: Associate Degree
Program: Occupational
Accreditation: &WJ, MAC

02 Campus President ....Ms. Carolyn PIERCE
07 Senior Director of Admissions ....Ms. Tina MATHIS
05 Director of Academic Affairs ....Ms. Jenny SAECHAO
36 Director of Career Services ....Vacant
10 Director of Financial Services ....Ms. Hortencia HODGE
37 Director of Financial Aid ....Mr. Kevin HOOVER
38 Director of Student Services ....Mr. Michael NEWTON
20 Assoc Director of Academic Affairs ....Vacant
50 Business Program Director ....Mr. Randey PORTER
97 General Education Program Director ....Ms. Krista HALL
61 Criminal Justice Program Director ....Mr. Mike ROBISON
88 Paralegal Program Director ....Ms. Joanne ALLEN
72 Technology Program Director ....Mr. Michael BLACKSTON
76 Healthcare Program Director ....Ms. Darlene LISTOPAD
88 Med Insurance Billing/Codng Pgm Dir ....Ms. Pamela LOCKE
67 Pharmacy Technology Program Dir ....Ms. Denise WALSH

† Regional accreditation is carried under the parent institution Heald College, Central Office in San Francisco, CA

*Heald College, Hayward (J)

25500 Industrial Boulevard, Hayward CA 94545-2349
County: Alameda FICE Identification: 025929
Unit ID: 371779
Telephone: (510) 783-2100 Carnegie Class: Assoc/PrivFP
FAX Number: (510) 783-3287 Calendar System: Quarter
URL: www.heald.edu
Established: 1967 Annual Undergrad Tuition & Fees: $17,300
Enrollment: 1,848 Coed
Affiliation or Control: Proprietary IRS Status: Proprietary
Highest Offering: Associate Degree
Program: Occupational
Accreditation: &WJ, DA, MAC

02 Campus President ....Dr. Douglas DEN HARTOG
05 Dean of Educational Programs ....Vacant
36 Director of Career Services ....Ms. Caren FLORES
07 Director of Admissions ....Mr. Jose SAES

† Regional accreditation is carried under the parent institution Heald College, Central Office in San Francisco, CA

*Heald College, Milpitas (K)

341 Great Mall Parkway, Milpitas CA 95035-8008
County: Santa Clara FICE Identification: 025932
Unit ID: 115490
Telephone: (408) 934-4900 Carnegie Class: Assoc/PrivFP
FAX Number: (408) 934-7777 Calendar System: Quarter
URL: www.heald.edu
Established: 1863 Annual Undergrad Tuition & Fees: $17,300
Enrollment: 1,719 Coed
Affiliation or Control: Proprietary IRS Status: Proprietary
Highest Offering: Associate Degree
Program: Occupational
Accreditation: &WJ, MAC

02 Campus President ....Mr. Elmo FRAZER
05 Dean of Educational Programs ....Dr. Nelly MANGRO
07 Director of Admissions ....Mr. Clarence HARDIMAN
36 Director of Career Services ....Ms. Joellen SUTTERFIELD
10 Business Office Manager ....Ms. Merrynoll BARRERA

† Regional accreditation is carried under the parent institution Heald College, Central Office in San Francisco, CA

*Heald College, Modesto (L)

5260 Pirrone Court, Salida CA 95368
County: Stanislaus Identification: 667043
Unit ID: 459930
Telephone: (209) 416-3700 Carnegie Class: Not Classified
FAX Number: (209) 416-3690 Calendar System: Quarter
URL: www.heald.edu
Established: N/A Annual Undergrad Tuition & Fees: $17,300
Enrollment: 759 Coed
Affiliation or Control: Proprietary IRS Status: Proprietary
Highest Offering: Associate Degree
Program: Occupational

Accreditation: &WJ

02 Campus President .... Mr. Ezra SALAS

† Regional accreditation is carried under the parent institution Heald College, Central Office in San Francisco, CA

*Heald College, Rancho Cordova (A)

2910 Prospect Park Drive,
Rancho Cordova CA 95670-6005

County: Sacramento FICE Identification: 007477
Unit ID: 115454
Telephone: (916) 638-1616 Carnegie Class: Assoc/PrivFP
FAX Number: (916) 638-1580 Calendar System: Quarter
URL: www.heald.edu
Established: 1863 Annual Undergrad Tuition & Fees: $14,650
Enrollment: 1,448 Coed
Affiliation or Control: Proprietary IRS Status: Proprietary
Highest Offering: Associate Degree
Program: Occupational; 2-Year Principally Bachelor's Creditable
Accreditation: &WJ, MAC

02 Campus President .... Ms. Ada GERARD
07 Director of Admissions .... Ms. Christi ARMES
05 Director of Academic Affairs .... Ms. Nancy PLUNKETT
36 Director of Career Services .... Ms. Lorraine BEAMAN
10 Director of Financial Services .... Ms. Jennifer RICARDI

† Regional accreditation is carried under the parent institution Heald College, Central Office in San Francisco, CA

*Heald College, Roseville (B)

7 Sierra Gate Plaza, Roseville CA 95678-6602

County: Sacramento FICE Identification: 025931
Unit ID: 363387
Telephone: (916) 789-8600 Carnegie Class: Assoc/PrivFP
FAX Number: (916) 896-8616 Calendar System: Quarter
URL: www.heald.edu
Established: 1863 Annual Undergrad Tuition & Fees: $14,650
Enrollment: 1,551 Coed
Affiliation or Control: Proprietary IRS Status: Proprietary
Highest Offering: Associate Degree
Program: Occupational
Accreditation: &WJ, MAC

02 Campus President .... Mr. Guy ADAMS
05 Director Academic Affairs .... Mr. John ROTH
10 Business Manager .... Ms. Kaia RHODES
36 Director Career Services .... Ms. Tina RIVERA

† Regional accreditation is carried under the parent institution Heald College, Central Office in San Francisco, CA

*Heald College, Salinas (C)

1450 N Main Street, Salinas CA 93906-5100

County: Salinas FICE Identification: 030340
Unit ID: 409874
Telephone: (831) 443-1700 Carnegie Class: Assoc/PrivFP
FAX Number: (831) 443-1050 Calendar System: Quarter
URL: www.heald.edu
Established: 1863 Annual Undergrad Tuition & Fees: $13,095
Enrollment: 1,490 Coed
Affiliation or Control: Proprietary IRS Status: Proprietary
Highest Offering: Associate Degree
Program: Occupational
Accreditation: &WJ, MAC

02 Interim Campus President .... Mr. Richard COX
07 Director of Admissions .... Mr. Christian MORENO
10 Director of Financial Services .... Ms. Lolita PARIAN
05 Director of Academic Affairs .... Mr. Jorge GARCIA
36 Director of Career Services .... Ms. Belyn WILSON

† Regional accreditation is carried under the parent institution Heald College, Central Office in San Francisco, CA

*Heald College, San Francisco (D)

875 Howard Street, Suite 100,
San Francisco CA 94105-2206

County: San Francisco FICE Identification: 007234
Unit ID: 115515
Telephone: (415) 808-3000 Carnegie Class: Assoc/PrivFP
FAX Number: (415) 808-3005 Calendar System: Quarter
URL: www.heald.edu
Established: 1863 Annual Undergrad Tuition & Fees: $17,300
Enrollment: 1,507 Coed
Affiliation or Control: Proprietary IRS Status: Proprietary
Highest Offering: Associate Degree
Program: Occupational
Accreditation: &WJ, MAC

02 Campus President .... Ms. Debbie JONES
05 Director of Academic Affairs .... Mr. Robb ERSKINE
36 Director of Career Services .... Ms. Carolyn BURNS
07 Director of Admissions .... Mr. Cary KEPLAN
10 Business Manager .... Ms. Toi KAWAII

† Regional accreditation is carried under the parent institution Heald College, Central Office in San Francisco, CA

*Heald College, Stockton (E)

1605 E March Lane, Stockton CA 95210-6632

County: San Joaquin FICE Identification: 025933
Unit ID: 371760
Telephone: (209) 473-5200 Carnegie Class: Assoc/PrivFP
FAX Number: (209) 477-2739 Calendar System: Quarter
URL: www.heald.edu
Established: 1863 Annual Undergrad Tuition & Fees: $14,650
Enrollment: 1,945 Coed
Affiliation or Control: Proprietary IRS Status: Proprietary
Highest Offering: Associate Degree
Program: Occupational
Accreditation: &WJ, DA, MAC

02 Campus President .... Mr. Sandy LAMBA
05 Director of Academic Affairs .... Mrs. Lisa DIANDA
06 Registrar .... Mr. John WHEETLEY
07 Director of Admission .... Mrs. Hola MOTOUAPUAKA
10 Director of Financial Services .... Ms. Karen BOWERS
36 Director of Career Services .... Vacant

† Regional accreditation is carried under the parent institution Heald College, Central Office in San Francisco, CA

Henley-Putnam University (F)

2804 Mission College Blvd #240, Santa Clara CA 95054

County: Santa Clara Identification: 666120
Telephone: (408) 453-9900 Carnegie Class: Not Classified
FAX Number: (408) 453-9700 Calendar System: Quarter
URL: www.henley-putnam.edu
Established: 2001 Annual Undergrad Tuition & Fees: $23,760
Enrollment: N/A Coed
Affiliation or Control: Proprietary IRS Status: Proprietary
Highest Offering: Doctorate
Program: Professional
Accreditation: DETC

01 Chief Executive Officer .... Jim P. KILLIN
05 Provost of Academics .... Dr. Amy DIMAIO
88 Provost of Co-Curricular Activites .... Amanda MORROW-JENSEN
10 Director of Finance .... Marlys YOSHIMURA
07 Director of Admissions .... Nancy REGGIO

High Tech High Graduate School of Education (G)

2861 Womble Road, San Diego CA 92106-6025

Identification: 667118
Telephone: (619) 398-4902 Carnegie Class: Not Classified
FAX Number: (619) 758-1960 Calendar System: Other
URL: gse.hightechhigh.org
Established: N/A Annual Graduate Tuition & Fees: $12,500
Enrollment: N/A Coed
Affiliation or Control: Independent Non-Profit IRS Status: 501(c)3
Highest Offering: Master's; No Undergraduates
Program: Teacher Preparatory
Accreditation: @WC

01 President .... Rob RIORDAN
05 Chief Academic Officer .... Ben DALEY
10 Chief Financial Officer .... Kay MCELRATH

Holy Names University (H)

3500 Mountain Boulevard, Oakland CA 94619-1699

County: Alameda FICE Identification: 001183
Unit ID: 115728
Telephone: (510) 436-1000 Carnegie Class: Master's M
FAX Number: (510) 436-1199 Calendar System: Semester
URL: www.hnu.edu
Established: 1868 Annual Undergrad Tuition & Fees: $31,640
Enrollment: 1,331 Coed
Affiliation or Control: Independent Non-Profit IRS Status: 501(c)3
Highest Offering: Master's
Program: Liberal Arts And General; Teacher Preparatory; Professional
Accreditation: WC, NURSE

01 President .... Dr. William J. HYNES
05 Vice President for Academic Affairs .... Dr. Lizbeth J. MARTIN
10 Vice President for Finance/Admin .... Mr. Stuart KOOP
32 Vice President for Student Affairs .... Mr. Michael S. MILLER
30 Vice President for Inst Advancement .... Mr. Richard ORTEGA
37 Dean of Student Financial Services .... Mr. Murad DIBBINI
07 Dean of Admission & Recruiting .... Mr. Brian O'ROURKE
58 Director of ABD Program .... Ms. Nancy FLINN
06 Associate Registrar .... Ms. Jeanette CALIXTO
08 Director of Library Services .... Ms. Karen SCHNEIDER
37 Dir Student Financial Assistance .... Mr. Jeff HARDIE
31 Director Campus Services .... Mr. Luis GUERRA
42 Director of Campus Ministry .... Ms. Carrie REHAK
41 Director of Athletics .... Mr. Dennis JONES
26 Director Marketing/Communications .... Ms. Lesley SIMS
29 Director of Alumni Relations .... Mr. John MCCOY
13 Director Information Technology .... Ms. Elena OLKHOVSKAYA
19 Director Campus Safety .... Ms. Dana KIRKPATRICK
15 Director Human Resources .... Ms. Patricia BARTON

Hope International University (I)

2500 E Nutwood Avenue, Fullerton CA 92831-3104

County: Orange FICE Identification: 001252
Unit ID: 120537
Telephone: (714) 879-3901 Carnegie Class: Bac/Diverse
FAX Number: (714) 681-7451 Calendar System: 4/1/4
URL: www.hiu.edu
Established: 1928 Annual Undergrad Tuition & Fees: $24,800
Enrollment: 1,365 Coed
Affiliation or Control: Independent Non-Profit IRS Status: 501(c)3
Highest Offering: Master's
Program: 2-Year Principally Bachelor's Creditable; Liberal Arts And General; Teacher Preparatory; Professional; Religious Emphasis
Accreditation: WC, BI, MFCD

01 President .... Dr. John L. DERRY
05 Vice President for Academic Affairs .... Dr. Paul ALEXANDER
10 Vice President for Business/Finance .... Mr. Frank SCOTTI
30 Vice Pres Institutional Advancement .... Mr. Michael MULRYAN
32 Vice President for Student Affairs .... Mr. Mark COMEAUX
84 Vice Pres for Enrollment Management .... Mrs. Teresea I. SMITH
08 Librarian .... Mrs. Robin HARTMAN
06 Registrar .... Mr. Ron ARCHER
07 Director Undergraduate Admissions .... Mr. Butch ELLIS
37 Director of Financial Aid .... Mrs. Shannon O'SHIELDS
41 Athletic Director .... Mr. John G. TUREK
18 Director of Campus Facilities .... Mr. Steve MULLINS
09 Assc VP for Education Effectiveness .... Dr. Tamsen MURRAY
26 Chief Public Relations Officer .... Mr. Michael MULRYAN
36 Dir Student Career Svcs & Retention .... Ms. Beth I. LEE
38 Director Student Counseling .... Dr. Laura L. STEELE
42 Chaplain/Director Campus Ministry .... Mr. Bryan A. SANDS
85 Director of International Studies .... Ms. Sasha CHANG
49 Dean College of Arts and Sciences .... Dr. Steve EDGINGTON
53 Dean College of Education .... Dr. George E. WEST
50 Dean College of Business & Mgmt .... Dr. James WOEST
88 Dean College of Ministry & Bib Stds .... Dr. Joe GRANA
83 Dean College of Psych & Counseling .... Dr. Laura L. STEELE

Horizon College of San Diego (J)

5331 Mt Alifan Drive, San Diego CA 92111

County: San Diego FICE Identification: 041405
Unit ID: 457226
Telephone: (858) 695-8587 Carnegie Class: Not Classified
FAX Number: (858) 695-9527 Calendar System: Semester
URL: www.horizoncollege.org
Established: 1993 Annual Undergrad Tuition & Fees: $18,900
Enrollment: 110 Coed
Affiliation or Control: Independent Non-Profit IRS Status: 501(c)3
Highest Offering: Baccalaureate
Program: Liberal Arts And General; Religious Emphasis
Accreditation: @BI

01 President .... Mr. F. Chapin MARSH, III
32 Dean of Students .... Mr. Wayne KINDE

Humphreys College (K)

6650 Inglewood Street, Stockton CA 95207-3896

County: San Joaquin FICE Identification: 001212
Unit ID: 115773
Telephone: (209) 478-0800 Carnegie Class: Bac/Diverse
FAX Number: (209) 478-8721 Calendar System: Quarter
URL: www.humphreys.edu
Established: 1896 Annual Undergrad Tuition & Fees: $12,863
Enrollment: 1,209 Coed
Affiliation or Control: Independent Non-Profit IRS Status: 501(c)3
Highest Offering: First Professional Degree
Program: Liberal Arts And General; Professional
Accreditation: WC

01 President .... Dr. Robert G. HUMPHREYS
05 Dn Instruction/Dir Arts & Sciences .... Dr. Robert G. HUMPHREYS, JR.
11 Dean Administration/Ofc Admin Pgm .... Ms. Wilma OKAMOTO-VAUGHN
09 Dean of Institutional Research .... Dr. Jess BONDS
61 Dean Law School .... Mr. Patrick L. PIGGOTT
20 Associate Dean of Instruction .... Ms. Cynthia BECERRA
06 Registrar .... Ms. Maria GARCIA-MILLER
07 Dir Admission/Placement/Public Rels .... Ms. Santa LOPEZ
26 Chief Public Relations Officer .... Vacant
08 Head Librarian .... Dr. Stanislav PERKNER
88 Director Paralegal Studies .... Ms. Rowena WALKER
88 Director Court Reporting Program .... Mrs. Kay REINDL
10 Chief Business Officer .... Ms. Carol KRAMLICH
37 Director Student Financial Aid .... Ms. Rita FRANCO
13 Director of Information Services .... Mr. Fabian ECHEVARRIA

ICDC College (L)

5422 West Sunset Boulevard, Los Angeles CA 90027

County: Los Angeles FICE Identification: 033953
Unit ID: 437662
Telephone: (323) 468-0404 Carnegie Class: Assoc/PrivFP
FAX Number: (323) 468-0420 Calendar System: Other
URL: www.icdccollege.edu
Established: N/A Annual Undergrad Tuition & Fees: $15,157
Enrollment: 4,350 Coed
Affiliation or Control: Proprietary IRS Status: Proprietary
Highest Offering: Associate Degree

Program: Occupational; 2-Year Principally Bachelor's Creditable
Accreditation: ACCSC

01 Campus Director .... Steve MIRANDA

Imperial Valley College (A)

380 E Aten Road, Imperial CA 92251-0158
County: Imperial FICE Identification: 001214
Unit ID: 115861
Telephone: (760) 352-8320 Carnegie Class: Assoc/Pub-R-L
FAX Number: (760) 355-2663 Calendar System: Semester
URL: www.imperial.edu
Established: 1922 Annual Undergrad Tuition & Fees (In-District): $1,326
Enrollment: 8,073 Coed
Affiliation or Control: Local IRS Status: 501(c)3
Highest Offering: Associate Degree
Program: Occupational; 2-Year Principally Bachelor's Creditable
Accreditation: WJ, EMT

01 Superintendent/President .... Dr. Victor JAIME
05 Vice President Academic Services .... Mrs. Kathy BERRY
32 Vice President Student Services .... Vacant
10 Vice President Business Services .... Mr. John LAU
15 Administrative Dean Human Services .... Mr. Travis GREGORY
13 Vice Pres Info Technology .... Mr. Todd FINNELL
103 Dean Economic & Worforce Develop .... Mr. Efrain SILVA
76 Dean of Health and Public Safety .... Mrs. Tina AGUIRRE
62 Dean Lrng Svcs/Instructional Tech .... Dr. Taylor RUHL
38 Dean of Counseling .... Mr. Ted CEASAR
35 Dean Student Develop/Campus Events .... Mr. Sergio LOPEZ
07 Director of Admissions and Records .... Ms. Gloria CARMONA
37 Director of Financial Aid .... Ms. Lisa SEALS
09 Dir Research/Planning/Grant Admin .... Vacant
59 Dir Child/Family/Consumer Sciences .... Ms. Rebecca GREEN

Infotech Career College (B)

16900 Lakewood Boulevard, Suite 209,
Bellflower CA 90706
County: Los Angeles FICE Identification: 041327
Unit ID: 450960
Telephone: (562) 804-1239 Carnegie Class: Not Classified
FAX Number: (562) 866-7739 Calendar System: Other
URL: www.infotech.edu
Established: 1998 Annual Undergrad Tuition & Fees: $14,700
Enrollment: 265 Coed
Affiliation or Control: Proprietary IRS Status: Proprietary
Highest Offering: Associate Degree
Program: Occupational
Accreditation: #COE

01 School Director .... Ms. Amita GARG

Institute of Technology (C)

564 West Herndon Avenue, Clovis CA 93612
County: Fresno FICE Identification: 030675
Unit ID: 431141
Telephone: (559) 297-4500 Carnegie Class: Assoc/PrivFP
FAX Number: (559) 297-5822 Calendar System: Semester
URL: www.it-colleges.edu
Established: N/A Annual Undergrad Tuition & Fees: N/A
Enrollment: 1,310 Coed
Affiliation or Control: Proprietary IRS Status: Proprietary
Highest Offering: Associate Degree
Program: Occupational; Technical Emphasis
Accreditation: ACCSC, ACFEI

01 President .... Joseph HAYDOCK

Interior Designers Institute (D)

1061 Camelback Road, Newport Beach CA 92660-3228
County: Orange FICE Identification: 025203
Unit ID: 116226
Telephone: (949) 675-4451 Carnegie Class: Spec/Arts
FAX Number: (949) 759-0667 Calendar System: Quarter
URL: www.idi.edu
Established: 1984 Annual Undergrad Tuition & Fees: $17,950
Enrollment: 310 Coed
Affiliation or Control: Proprietary IRS Status: Proprietary
Highest Offering: Master's
Program: Professional
Accreditation: ACCSC, CIDA

01 Executive Director .... Ms. Judy DEATON
37 Financial Aid Director .... Ms. Sharon DEATON

International Academy of Design and Technology (E)

2450 Del Paso Road, Sacramento CA 95834
Identification: 666740
Unit ID: 450447
Telephone: (916) 285-9468 Carnegie Class: Assoc/PrivFP4
FAX Number: (916) 285-6986 Calendar System: Other
URL: www.iadtsacramento.com
Established: 1977 Annual Undergrad Tuition & Fees: $12,850
Enrollment: 453 Coed
Affiliation or Control: Proprietary IRS Status: Proprietary
Highest Offering: Baccalaureate
Program: Fine Arts Emphasis
Accreditation: ACICS

01 President .... Ms. Patricia A. HOFFMAN

† Branch campus of International Academy of Design & Technology, Tampa, FL.

International Technological University (F)

355 W. San Fernando Street, San Jose CA 95113
County: Santa Clara Identification: 667070
Telephone: (888) 488-4968 Carnegie Class: Not Classified
FAX Number: (408) 331-1026 Calendar System: Semester
URL: www.itu.edu
Established: 1994 Annual Graduate Tuition & Fees: N/A
Enrollment: 1,189 Coed
Affiliation or Control: Independent Non-Profit IRS Status: 501(c)3
Highest Offering: Doctorate; No Undergraduates
Program: Professional
Accreditation: @WC

01 Acting President .... Yau-Gene CHAN
05 Academic & Exec VP/CFO .... Dr. Gerald A. CORY

International Theological Seminary (G)

3225 Tyler Avenue, El Monte CA 91731-3355
County: Los Angeles Identification: 666360
Unit ID: 396985
Telephone: (626) 448-0023 Carnegie Class: Not Classified
FAX Number: (626) 350-6343 Calendar System: Quarter
URL: www.itsla.edu
Established: 1982 Annual Undergrad Tuition & Fees: $9,770
Enrollment: 89 Coed
Affiliation or Control: Independent Non-Profit IRS Status: 501(c)3
Highest Offering: Doctorate
Program: Religious Emphasis
Accreditation: THEOL

01 President .... Dr. C. Melvin LOUCKS
05 Vice President for Academics .... Dr. Joy Jimena J. PALMER
11 Vice President for Administration .... Ms. Monica KAO
30 Vice Pres Seminary Advancement .... Dr. Edmund RHEE

ITT Technical Institute (H)

362 N Clovis Avenue, Clovis CA 93612-0300
County: Fresno Identification: 666144
Unit ID: 448451
Telephone: (559) 325-5400 Carnegie Class: Assoc/PrivFP4
FAX Number: N/A Calendar System: Quarter
URL: www.itt-tech.edu
Established: 2006 Annual Undergrad Tuition & Fees: N/A
Enrollment: 559 Coed
Affiliation or Control: Proprietary IRS Status: Proprietary
Highest Offering: Baccalaureate
Program: Technical Emphasis
Accreditation: ACICS

† Branch campus of ITT Technical Institute, Indianapolis, IN.

ITT Technical Institute (I)

1140 Galaxy Way, Suite 400, Concord CA 94520
County: Contra Costa Identification: 666697
Unit ID: 456427
Telephone: (925) 674-8200 Carnegie Class: Assoc/PrivFP4
FAX Number: N/A Calendar System: Quarter
URL: www.itt-tech.edu
Established: N/A Annual Undergrad Tuition & Fees: N/A
Enrollment: 392 Coed
Affiliation or Control: Proprietary IRS Status: Proprietary
Highest Offering: Baccalaureate
Program: Technical Emphasis
Accreditation: ACICS

† Branch campus of ITT Technical Institute, Indianapolis, IN.

ITT Technical Institute (J)

16916 S Harlan Road, Lathrop CA 95330-8737
County: San Joaquin Identification: 666533
Unit ID: 437219
Telephone: (209) 858-0077 Carnegie Class: Spec/Tech
FAX Number: (209) 858-0277 Calendar System: Quarter
URL: www.itt-tech.edu
Established: 1997 Annual Undergrad Tuition & Fees: N/A
Enrollment: 635 Coed
Affiliation or Control: Proprietary IRS Status: Proprietary
Highest Offering: Baccalaureate
Program: Technical Emphasis
Accreditation: ACICS

† Branch campus of ITT Technical Institute, Indianapolis, IN.

ITT Technical Institute (K)

4000 West Metropolitan Dr, Ste. 100, Orange CA 92868
County: Orange FICE Identification: 023219
Unit ID: 116484
Telephone: (714) 941-2400 Carnegie Class: Spec/Tech
FAX Number: (714) 535-1802 Calendar System: Quarter
URL: www.itt-tech.edu
Established: 1983 Annual Undergrad Tuition & Fees: N/A
Enrollment: 1,002 Coed
Affiliation or Control: Proprietary IRS Status: Proprietary
Highest Offering: Baccalaureate
Program: Technical Emphasis
Accreditation: ACICS

† Branch campus of ITT Technical Institute, Indianapolis, IN.

ITT Technical Institute (L)

2051 Solar Drive, Suite 150, Oxnard CA 93036-0641
County: Ventura Identification: 666534
Unit ID: 413848
Telephone: (805) 988-0143 Carnegie Class: Bac/Assoc
FAX Number: (805) 988-1813 Calendar System: Quarter
URL: www.itt-tech.edu
Established: 1993 Annual Undergrad Tuition & Fees: N/A
Enrollment: 461 Coed
Affiliation or Control: Proprietary IRS Status: Proprietary
Highest Offering: Baccalaureate
Program: Technical Emphasis
Accreditation: ACICS

† Branch campus of ITT Technical Institute, Indianapolis, IN.

ITT Technical Institute (M)

10863 Gold Center Drive,
Rancho Cordova CA 95670-6034
County: Sacramento FICE Identification: 021209
Unit ID: 108250
Telephone: (916) 851-3900 Carnegie Class: Spec/Tech
FAX Number: (916) 851-9225 Calendar System: Quarter
URL: www.itt-tech.edu
Established: 1954 Annual Undergrad Tuition & Fees: N/A
Enrollment: 660 Coed
Affiliation or Control: Proprietary IRS Status: Proprietary
Highest Offering: Baccalaureate
Program: Technical Emphasis
Accreditation: ACICS

† Branch campus of ITT Technical Institute, Indianapolis, IN.

ITT Technical Institute (N)

670 E Carnegie Drive, San Bernardino CA 92408-3519
County: San Bernardino FICE Identification: 030704
Unit ID: 381909
Telephone: (909) 806-4600 Carnegie Class: Bac/Assoc
FAX Number: (909) 806-4699 Calendar System: Quarter
URL: www.itt-tech.edu
Established: 1986 Annual Undergrad Tuition & Fees: N/A
Enrollment: 1,249 Coed
Affiliation or Control: Proprietary IRS Status: Proprietary
Highest Offering: Baccalaureate
Program: Technical Emphasis
Accreditation: ACICS

† Branch campus of ITT Technical Institute, Indianapolis, IN.

ITT Technical Institute (O)

9680 Granite Ridge Drive, San Diego CA 92123-2662
County: San Diego FICE Identification: 022916
Unit ID: 116466
Telephone: (858) 571-8500 Carnegie Class: Spec/Tech
FAX Number: (858) 571-1277 Calendar System: Quarter
URL: www.itt-tech.edu
Established: 1981 Annual Undergrad Tuition & Fees: N/A
Enrollment: 1,656 Coed
Affiliation or Control: Proprietary IRS Status: Proprietary
Highest Offering: Baccalaureate
Program: Technical Emphasis
Accreditation: ACICS

† Branch campus of ITT Technical Institute, Indianapolis, IN.

ITT Technical Institute (P)

650 W Cienega Avenue, San Dimas CA 91773-2933
County: Los Angeles FICE Identification: 022915
Unit ID: 116475
Telephone: (909) 971-2300 Carnegie Class: Spec/Tech
FAX Number: (626) 337-5271 Calendar System: Quarter
URL: www.itt-tech.edu
Established: 1982 Annual Undergrad Tuition & Fees: N/A
Enrollment: 650 Coed
Affiliation or Control: Proprietary IRS Status: Proprietary
Highest Offering: Baccalaureate
Program: Technical Emphasis

Accreditation: ACICS

† Branch campus of ITT Technical Institute, Indianapolis, IN.

ITT Technical Institute (A)

12669 Encinitas Avenue, Sylmar CA 91342-3664
County: Los Angeles FICE Identification: 023218
Unit ID: 244011
Telephone: (818) 364-5151 Carnegie Class: Bac/Assoc
FAX Number: (818) 364-5150 Calendar System: Quarter
URL: www.itt-tech.edu
Established: 1982 Annual Undergrad Tuition & Fees: N/A
Enrollment: 905 Coed
Affiliation or Control: Proprietary IRS Status: Proprietary
Highest Offering: Baccalaureate
Program: Technical Emphasis
Accreditation: ACICS

† Branch campus of ITT Technical Institute, Indianapolis, IN.

ITT Technical Institute (B)

2555 West 190th Street, Suite 125, Torrance CA 90504
County: Los Angeles FICE Identification: 030874
Unit ID: 378406
Telephone: (310) 965-5900 Carnegie Class: Spec/Tech
FAX Number: (310) 380-1557 Calendar System: Quarter
URL: www.itt-tech.edu
Established: 1986 Annual Undergrad Tuition & Fees: N/A
Enrollment: 776 Coed
Affiliation or Control: Proprietary IRS Status: Proprietary
Highest Offering: Baccalaureate
Program: Technical Emphasis
Accreditation: ACICS

† Branch campus of ITT Technical Institute, Indianapolis, IN.

John F. Kennedy University (C)

100 Ellinwood Way, Pleasant Hill CA 94523-4817
County: Contra Costa FICE Identification: 004484
Unit ID: 116712
Telephone: (925) 969-3300 Carnegie Class: Master's M
FAX Number: (925) 969-3399 Calendar System: Quarter
URL: www.jfku.edu
Established: 1964 Annual Undergrad Tuition & Fees: $19,853
Enrollment: 1,443 Coed
Affiliation or Control: Independent Non-Profit IRS Status: 501(c)3
Highest Offering: Doctorate
Program: Liberal Arts And General; Professional
Accreditation: WC, #CLPSY, IACBE

01 President .... Dr. Steven A. STARGARDTER
10 Int Chief Financial Officer .... Mr. James HYATT
05 Vice President of Academic Affairs .... Dr. Donald CAMPBELL
30 Vice President of Advancement .... Mrs. Anne Marie TAYLOR
09 Vice Pres of Institutional Research .... Vacant
26 Assoc VP Marketing/Admissions .... Ms. Cathy SANTINI
13 Director of Information Technology .... Ms. Mary HUNTER
15 Director of Human Resources .... Ms. Theresa ROGERS
61 College of Law Dean .... Mr. Dean BARBIERI
97 College of Undergraduate Studies .... Dr. Michael GRANEY-MULHOLLAND
58 College of Professional Studies .... Dr. Ruth FASSINGER
37 Director Financial Aid .... Ms. Mindy BERGERON
06 Registrar .... Mr. Micheal RAINE
08 Acting University Librarian .... Mrs. Claudia CHESTER
18 Director of Facilities .... Mr. David L. SADLER

John Paul the Great Catholic University (D)

10174 Old Grove Road, Ste 200, San Diego CA 92131
County: San Diego FICE Identification: 041937
Unit ID: 462354
Telephone: (858) 653-6740 Carnegie Class: Not Classified
FAX Number: (858) 653-3791 Calendar System: Quarter
URL: www.jpcatholic.com
Established: 2006 Annual Undergrad Tuition & Fees: N/A
Enrollment: N/A Coed
Affiliation or Control: Independent Non-Profit IRS Status: 501(c)3
Highest Offering: Master's
Program: Professional; Religious Emphasis
Accreditation: @WC

01 President .... Derry CONNOLLY
05 Provost & ALO .... Halyna KORNUTA
10 CFO .... Greg BREEN
11 Sr VP for Administration .... Lidy CONNOLLY
88 VP for Strategic Partnerships .... Joe SZALKIEWICZ
07 Vice Pres Admissions .... Martin HAROLD
32 Dean of Students .... Mark KALPAKGIAN
13 Director of IT .... Kevin MEZIERE
37 Director of Financial Aid .... Lisa WILLIAMS
06 Registrar & IR .... Liz MAMARIL
42 Chaplain .... Fr. Richard HUSTON

Kaplan College (E)

1914 Wible Road, Bakersfield CA 93304
County: Kerns Identification: 666291
Unit ID: 447102
Telephone: (661) 836-6300 Carnegie Class: Assoc/PrivFP
FAX Number: (661) 394-6056 Calendar System: Semester
URL: www.kaplancollege.edu
Established: 2005 Annual Undergrad Tuition & Fees: $14,476
Enrollment: 581 Coed
Affiliation or Control: Proprietary IRS Status: Proprietary
Highest Offering: Associate Degree
Program: Occupational
Accreditation: ACICS

01 President .... Ms. Mary WHITLOCK

† Branch campus of Kaplan College, Sacramento, CA.

Kaplan College (F)

4330 Watt Avenue, Suite 400, Sacramento CA 95821-7000
County: Sacramento FICE Identification: 023519
Unit ID: 118259
Telephone: (916) 649-8168 Carnegie Class: Assoc/PrivFP
FAX Number: (916) 649-8344 Calendar System: Quarter
URL: www.kaplancollege.edu
Established: 1982 Annual Undergrad Tuition & Fees: N/A
Enrollment: 468 Coed
Affiliation or Control: Proprietary IRS Status: Proprietary
Highest Offering: Associate Degree
Program: Occupational
Accreditation: ACICS

01 Executive Director .... Lisia MOORE
05 Director of Education .... Vacant
37 Director of Student Financial Aid .... Ryan SMITH
07 Director of Admissions .... Vacant
36 Director of Career .... Julie MUIR

Kaplan College (G)

5172 Kiernan Court, Salida CA 95368
County: Stanislaus FICE Identification: 023063
Unit ID: 366960
Telephone: (209) 543-7000 Carnegie Class: Assoc/PrivFP
FAX Number: (209) 543-1755 Calendar System: Other
URL: www.kaplancollege.edu
Established: 2005 Annual Undergrad Tuition & Fees: $13,246
Enrollment: 755 Coed
Affiliation or Control: Proprietary IRS Status: Proprietary
Highest Offering: Associate Degree
Program: Occupational
Accreditation: ACCSC, MAAB

01 Executive Director .... Mr. Bill JONES

Kaplan College (H)

9055 Balboa Avenue, San Diego CA 92123-1509
County: San Diego FICE Identification: 020917
Unit ID: 118277
Telephone: (858) 279-4500 Carnegie Class: Assoc/PrivFP
FAX Number: (858) 279-4885 Calendar System: Other
URL: www.kaplancollege.com
Established: 1976 Annual Undergrad Tuition & Fees: $32,922
Enrollment: 1,256 Coed
Affiliation or Control: Proprietary IRS Status: Proprietary
Highest Offering: Associate Degree
Program: Occupational
Accreditation: ACCSC, MAAB

01 President .... Mr. Kevin PREHN
05 Director of Education .... Mr. Michael TURNER
11 Director of Operations .... Mr. David MOVSESIAN

Kaplan College (I)

722 West March Lane, Stockton CA 95207
County: San Joaquin FICE Identification: 025654
Unit ID: 384193
Telephone: (209) 462-8777 Carnegie Class: Assoc/PrivFP
FAX Number: (209) 462-3219 Calendar System: Other
URL: stockton.kaplancollege.com
Established: 2005 Annual Undergrad Tuition & Fees: $13,155
Enrollment: 392 Coed
Affiliation or Control: Proprietary IRS Status: Proprietary
Highest Offering: Associate Degree
Program: Occupational
Accreditation: ACCSC, MAAB

01 Executive Director .... Mr. Robert BAYLES

Kaplan College (J)

2022 University Drive, Vista CA 92083-7736
County: San Diego FICE Identification: 025490
Unit ID: 118286
Telephone: (760) 630-1555 Carnegie Class: Assoc/PrivFP
FAX Number: (760) 630-1656 Calendar System: Other
URL: www.kaplancollege.com
Established: 1976 Annual Undergrad Tuition & Fees: $33,023
Enrollment: 782 Coed
Affiliation or Control: Proprietary IRS Status: Proprietary
Highest Offering: Associate Degree
Program: Occupational; Technical Emphasis
Accreditation: ACCSC, MAAB

01 Executive Director .... Ms. Laura STINSON
05 Director of Education .... Mr. Mike WITTEMAN
07 Director of Admissions .... Ms. Renee CODNER
36 Director of Career Services .... Ms. Jaye BEATTY
37 Director of Financial Aid .... Ms. Kathy SMITH
66 Director of Nursing .... Ms. Beth BUNYI

*Kern Community College District (K)

2100 Chester Avenue, Bakersfield CA 93301-4099
County: Kern FICE Identification: 006994
Unit ID: 436313
Telephone: (661) 336-5100 Carnegie Class: N/A
FAX Number: (661) 336-5134
URL: www.kccd.edu

01 Chancellor .... Ms. Sandra V. SERRANO
05 Vice Chanc Educational Services .... Vacant
11 Vice Chanc Operations Management .... Mr. Sean P. JAMES
16 Vice Chanc Human Resources .... Mr. Abe ALI
30 Assoc Vice Chanc Govt/External Rels .... Ms. Michele BRESSO
10 Chief Financial Officer .... Mr. Tom J. BURKE
13 Director Information Technology .... Mr. David W. PALINSKY
91 Asst Dir Information Technology .... Mr. Eddie D. ALVARADO
43 General Counsel .... Vacant

*Bakersfield College (L)

1801 Panorama Drive, Bakersfield CA 93305-1299
County: Kern FICE Identification: 001118
Unit ID: 109819
Telephone: (661) 395-4011 Carnegie Class: Assoc/Pub-U-MC
FAX Number: (661) 395-4241 Calendar System: Semester
URL: www.bakersfieldcollege.edu
Established: 1913 Annual Undergrad Tuition & Fees (In-District): $902
Enrollment: 17,157 Coed
Affiliation or Control: State/Local IRS Status: 501(c)3
Highest Offering: Associate Degree
Program: Occupational; 2-Year Principally Bachelor's Creditable
Accreditation: WJ, EMT, RAD

02 President .... Ms. Nan GOMEZ-HEITZEBERG
05 Exec VP Academic Affairs/Stdnt Svcs .... Ms. Nan GOMEZ-HEITZEBERG
09 Dir Institutional Research/Planning .... Dr. Ann MORGAN
20 Dean of Student Learning .... Vacant
90 Dean Learning Resources/Info Tech .... Dr. Bonnie SUDERMAN
88 Dean Learning Support Services .... Ms. Joyce COLEMAN
30 Director Foundation & Development .. Mr. Michael STEPANOVICH
11 Exec Dir Administrative Services .... Mr. Sean JAMES
12 Director Delano Center .... Mr. Rich MCCROW
37 Director Financial Aid .... Vacant
07 Director Enrollment Services .... Mrs. Suzanne A. VAUGHN
26 Director Marketing & Public Info .... Mrs. Amber CHIANG
04 Admin Assistant to the President .... Ms. Debborah SPOHN
13 Director Information Services .... Mr. Todd COSTON
20 Dean of Student Learning .... Vacant
66 Director of Nursing .... Ms. Cindy COLLIER
41 Director of Athletics .... Mr. Ryan BECKWITH
75 Dean Career & Tech Education .... Dr. Hamid EYDGAHI
20 Dean Instruction .... Dr. Daniel O'CONNOR
20 Dean of Instruction .... Dr. Emmanuel MOURTZANOS

*Cerro Coso Community College (M)

College Heights Boulevard, Ridgecrest CA 93555-7777
County: Kern FICE Identification: 010111
Unit ID: 111896
Telephone: (760) 384-6100 Carnegie Class: Assoc/Pub-U-MC
FAX Number: (760) 375-4776 Calendar System: Semester
URL: www.cerrocoso.edu
Established: 1973 Annual Undergrad Tuition & Fees (In-District): $1,106
Enrollment: 5,802 Coed
Affiliation or Control: State/Local IRS Status: 501(c)3
Highest Offering: Associate Degree
Program: Occupational; 2-Year Principally Bachelor's Creditable
Accreditation: WJ

02 President .... Ms. A. Jill BOARD
05 Vice President Academic Affairs .... Dr. Corey MARVIN
32 Vice President of Student Services .... Ms. Heather OSTASH
12 Dir Eastern Sierra College Center .... Ms. Deanna CAMPBELL
12 Dir South Kern & Kern River Valley .... Dr. Erie JOHNSON
75 Dean Career Technical Education .... Ms. Valerie KARNES
21 Director of Admin Services .... Ms. Gale LEBSOCK
38 Dir of Students & Counseling Svcs .... Ms. Paula SUOREZ
37 Dir Financial Aid & Scholarships .... Vacant
07 Dir Admiss/Records/Veteran Affs .... Vacant
10 Accounting Manager .... Ms. Lisa COUCH
15 Human Resources Manager .... Mr. Clint DOUGHERTY
88 Child Development Coordinator .... Ms. Jennifer SAN NICOLAS
26 Public Rel/Marketing & Dev Mgr .... Ms. Natalie DORRELL
13 Information Technology Manager .... Mr. Michael CAMPBELL
41 Dir Student Programs & Athletics .... Vacant
106 Director Distance Education .... Mr. Charles OSTEEN

*Porterville College (A)

100 E College Avenue, Porterville CA 93257-6058
County: Tulare FICE Identification: 001268
Unit ID: 121363
Telephone: (559) 791-2200 Carnegie Class: Assoc/Pub-U-MC
FAX Number: (559) 784-4779 Calendar System: Semester
URL: www.portervillecollege.edu
Established: 1927 Annual Undergrad Tuition & Fees (In-District): $1,178
Enrollment: 3,974 Coed
Affiliation or Control: State/Local IRS Status: 501(c)3
Highest Offering: Associate Degree
Program: Occupational; 2-Year Principally Bachelor's Creditable
Accreditation: WJ

02 President .... Dr. Rosa F. CARLSON
05 Vice President Academic Affairs .... Mr. Bill HENRY
32 Vice President Student Services .... Mr. Steven SCHULTZ
04 Administrative Asst to President .... Ms. Carol BROWN
20 Dean Academic Affairs .... Dr. Antonia ECUNG
75 Dean Career & Technical Education .... Vacant
23 Assoc Dean Health Careers .... Ms. Kim BEHRENS
18 Maintenance & Operations Manager .... Mr. John WORD
07 Director Admissions/Records .... Ms. Virginia GURROLA
10 Director Finance & Admin Services .... Ms. Arlitha WILLIAMS-HARMON
15 Human Resources Manager .... Ms. Resa HESS
37 Interim Director Financial Aid .... Ms. Erin CRUZ
09 Institutional Researcher .... Mr. Michael CARLEY
13 Director Information Technology .... Mr. Chris CRAIG
88 Director CalWorks/EOPS .... Ms. Maria ROMAN
21 Accounting Manager .... Ms. Sonia HUCKABAY
88 Program Manager Child Dev Center .... Ms. Karen BALL
08 Interim Director Library .... Ms. Lorie BARKER
35 Student Programs/Athletics .... Mr. Eric MENDOZA
27 Public Information Officer .... Vacant
105 Graphic Designer/Website Coord .... Ms. Randy MORGAN

The King's University (B)

14800 Sherman Way, Los Angeles CA 91405-2233
County: Los Angeles FICE Identification: 035163
Unit ID: 439701
Telephone: (818) 779-8040 Carnegie Class: Spec/Faith
FAX Number: (818) 779-8241 Calendar System: Quarter
URL: www.kingsuniversity.edu
Established: 1997 Annual Undergrad Tuition & Fees: $10,495
Enrollment: 549 Coed
Affiliation or Control: Independent Non-Profit IRS Status: 501(c)3
Highest Offering: Doctorate
Program: Professional; Religious Emphasis
Accreditation: BI, TRACS

01 President .... Dr. Steve E. RIGGLE
05 Exec VP & Chief Academic Officer .... Dr. Paul G. CHAPPELL
10 Chief Business Officer .... Mr. Dan J. DEHART
106 Dean/Administrator Online Education .... Prof. Donald C. BRUBAKER
09 Dir Inst Rsrch/Dean Doctoral Pgms .... Dr. Wesley M. PINKHAM
32 Chief Student Life Officer .... Dr. Michael J. GREGG
07 Director of Admissions .... Mrs. Marilyn J. CHAPPELL
06 Registrar .... Mrs. Martha S. BRANTLEY
37 Director Student Financial Aid ... Mr. Norman V. STOPPENBRINK
08 Head Librarian .... Prof. Barbara L. TARR
30 Chief Development .... Mr. Lee S. MIMMS
18 Chief Facilities Physical Plant .... Dr. Michael J. GREGG
13 Director Computing & Info Mgmt ... Mr. Edmond M. MUGWANYA
15 Director Personnel Services .... Mr. Michael B. CLEMENS
38 Director Stdnt Counseling/Chaplain .... Dr. Dale A. BUFFINGTON
36 Director Student Placement .... Dr. Jody D. SMITH
40 Director Bookstore .... Mr. Michael B. CLEMENS
21 Student Accounts Officer .... Ms. June M. HADLEY
90 Dir Acad Computing/Dir Student Affs .... Prof. Donald C. BRUBAKER
29 Director Alumni Relations .... Ms. Maureen A. BRODERSON
96 Director of Purchasing .... Mr. Michael B. CLEMENS
24 Director Educational Media .... Mr. Irwin K. LOUIE
85 Director Foreign Students .... Mrs. Marilyn J. CHAPPELL
28 Director of Diversity .... Dr. Michael J. GREGG
102 Dir Foundation/Corporate Relations .... Mr. Lee S. MIMMS
26 Chief Public Relations Officer .... Mrs. Janis A. GORAIEB

LA College International (C)

3200 Wilshire Boulevard, #400,
Los Angeles CA 90010-1308
County: Los Angeles FICE Identification: 023124
Unit ID: 116040
Telephone: (213) 381-3333 Carnegie Class: Bac/Assoc
FAX Number: (213) 383-9369 Calendar System: Other
URL: www.lac.edu
Established: 1982 Annual Undergrad Tuition & Fees: $21,963
Enrollment: 682 Coed
Affiliation or Control: Proprietary IRS Status: Proprietary
Highest Offering: Baccalaureate
Program: Occupational; 2-Year Principally Bachelor's Creditable; Technical Emphasis
Accreditation: ACICS

01 Campus Director .... Mr. Dean DUNBAR
05 Vice President of Academic Affairs .... Ms. Jodie RICE
07 Sr Dir of Marketing & Admissions .... Mr. Brian JENETTE
37 Dir of StudentFinancial Services .... Ms. Anastasia KLINE
06 Registrar .... Ms. Diane ERICKSON
36 Career Services Director .... Ms. Lori WHITE
13 IT Director .... Mr. David KOPACK

LA Music Academy (D)

370 South Fair Oaks Avenue, Pasadena CA 91105
County: Los Angeles FICE Identification: 038684
Unit ID: 446385
Telephone: (626) 568-8850 Carnegie Class: Assoc/PrivFP
FAX Number: (626) 568-8854 Calendar System: Quarter
URL: www.lamusicacademy.edu
Established: 1996 Annual Undergrad Tuition & Fees: N/A
Enrollment: 150 Coed
Affiliation or Control: Proprietary IRS Status: Proprietary
Highest Offering: Associate Degree
Program: Occupational
Accreditation: MUS

01 President .... Tom AYLESBURY
05 Dean .... Dave POZZI
11 Director of Administration .... Miranda TALBOT
07 Director of Admissions .... Scott KIEL

La Sierra University (E)

4500 Riverwalk Parkway, Riverside CA 92515-8247
County: Riverside FICE Identification: 001215
Unit ID: 117627
Telephone: (951) 785-2000 Carnegie Class: Master's M
FAX Number: (951) 785-2901 Calendar System: Quarter
URL: www.lasierra.edu
Established: 1922 Annual Undergrad Tuition & Fees: $27,231
Enrollment: 2,199 Coed
Affiliation or Control: Seventh-day Adventist IRS Status: 501(c)3
Highest Offering: Doctorate
Program: Liberal Arts And General; Teacher Preparatory; Professional; Business Emphasis
Accreditation: WC, MUS, SW, @THEOL

01 President .... Dr. Randal R. WISBEY
05 Provost .... Dr. Steve PAWLUK
10 Vice President for Finance .... Mr. David GERIGUIS
32 Vice President for Student Life .... Ms. Yamilet BAZAN
30 Vice President Development .... Mr. Norman YERGEN
84 Vice Pres Enrollment Services .... Mr. David R. LOFTHOUSE
26 VP Communication/Integrated Mktg .... Dr. Marilyn THOMSEN
21 Associate Vice President Finance .... Ms. Pamela CHRISPENS
20 Associate Provost .... Dr. Barbara FAVORITO
49 Int Dean College Arts/Sciences .... Dr. Adeny SCHMIDT
50 Dean School of Business .... Dr. John THOMAS
53 Int Dean School of Education .... Dr. Ed BOYATT
73 Dean School of Religion .... Dr. John W. WEBSTER
35 Dean of Students .... Ms. Marjorie ROBINSON
26 Exec Dir University Relations .... Mr. Larry BECKER
55 Director Adult Evening Program .... Ms. Nancy DITTEMORE
29 Director Alumni Relations .... Ms. Julie NARDUCCI
15 Director Human Resources .... Ms. Dell Jean VAN FOSSEN
08 Director Library .... Ms. Kitty SIMMONS
37 Director Student Financial Services .... Ms. Esther KINZER
42 Director Campus Ministries .... Mr. Samuel E. LEONOR, JR.
13 Director Information Technology .... Mr. Geoff INGRAM
09 Director of Institutional Research .... Mr. Guru UPPALA
18 Director Physical Plant .... Mr. Al VALDEZ
38 Director Counseling Center .... Ms. Debra WRIGHT
92 Director Honors Program .... Dr. Douglas R. CLARK
07 Director of Admissions/Registrar .... Mr. Issmael NZAMUTUNA
36 Director Career Services .... Mr. Natan VIGNA

Laguna College of Art & Design (F)

2222 Laguna Canyon Road,
Laguna Beach CA 92651-1136
County: Orange FICE Identification: 023305
Unit ID: 117168
Telephone: (949) 376-6000 Carnegie Class: Spec/Arts
FAX Number: (949) 376-6009 Calendar System: Semester
URL: www.lcad.edu
Established: 1961 Annual Undergrad Tuition & Fees: $23,730
Enrollment: 468 Coed
Affiliation or Control: Independent Non-Profit IRS Status: 501(c)3
Highest Offering: Master's
Program: Professional
Accreditation: WC, ART

01 President .... Dr. Jonathan BURKE
05 Vice President Academic Affairs .... Dr. Helene GARRISON
30 Vice Pres of Development .... Mr. Domenick IETTO
07 Dean of Admissions .... Mr. Christopher BROWN
10 Chief Financial Officer .... Mr. Jim GODEK
06 Registrar .... Ms. Laura PATRICK
08 Library Director .... Ms. Jennifer WORMSER
04 Assistant to the President .... Ms. Jennifer DANIELS
37 Dir Financial Aid/Student Services .... Mr. Christopher BROWN

Lake Tahoe Community College (G)

1 College Drive, South Lake Tahoe CA 96150-4524
County: El Dorado FICE Identification: 012907
Unit ID: 117195
Telephone: (530) 541-4660 Carnegie Class: Assoc/Pub-S-SC
FAX Number: (530) 541-7852 Calendar System: Quarter
URL: www.ltcc.edu
Established: 1975 Annual Undergrad Tuition & Fees (In-District): $1,128
Enrollment: 3,241 Coed
Affiliation or Control: State/Local IRS Status: 501(c)3
Highest Offering: Associate Degree
Program: Occupational; 2-Year Principally Bachelor's Creditable; Business Emphasis
Accreditation: WJ

01 Superintentent/President .... Dr. Kindred MURILLO
04 Admin Assistant to President .... Ms. Julie BOOTH
05 VP Academic Affs/Stdnt Svcs .... Dr. Thomas GREENE
10 Vice President Administrative Svcs .... Mr. Jeff DEFRANCO
20 Dean of Instruction .... Ms. Cynthea PRESTON
20 Interim Dean of Instruction .... Mr. Kurt GREEN
08 Director of Library .... Ms. Lisa FOLEY
13 Int Exec Dir Tech & Education Svcs .... Ms. Cheri JONES
07 Interim Director Admissions/Records .... Ms. Gayle BRADSHAW
21 Director of Administrative Services .... Mr. Marc SABELLA
15 Director of Human Resources .... Ms. Susan WALTER
18 Director of Maintenance .... Vacant
14 Director Ofc Info & Tech Services .... Mr. Bill KING
88 Director Child Development Center .... Ms. Michelle SOWER
37 Director Financial Aid .... Ms. Julie CATHIE
75 Director of Career & Tech Education .... Dr. Virginia BOYAR
09 Director of Institutional Research .... Mr. Aaron MCVEAN
26 Public Information Officer .... Ms. Christina PROCTOR
102 Foundation Director .... Ms. Melonie GUTTRY
40 Bookstore Manager .... Mr. Lor COLLIN
96 Purchasing Agent .... Mr. Bob ROSEBLADE

Lassen Community College (H)

PO Box 3000, 478-200 Highway 139,
Susanville CA 96130-3000
County: Lassen FICE Identification: 001217
Unit ID: 117274
Telephone: (530) 257-6181 Carnegie Class: Assoc/Pub-R-M
FAX Number: (530) 251-8872 Calendar System: Semester
URL: www.lassencollege.edu
Established: 1925 Annual Undergrad Tuition & Fees (In-District): $647
Enrollment: 2,503 Coed
Affiliation or Control: State/Local IRS Status: 501(c)3
Highest Offering: Associate Degree
Program: Occupational; 2-Year Principally Bachelor's Creditable
Accreditation: WJ

01 District Superintendent/President .... Dr. Marlon R. HALL
04 Assistant to President .... Ms. Julie L. JOHNSTON
05 Exec Vice Pres of Academic Services .... Ms. Susan S. MOUCK
11 Vice Pres Administrative Services .... Mr. Dave CLAUSEN
09 Dir Research/Asc Dean Instruct Svcs .... Vacant
08 Librarian .... Vacant
37 Director Financial Aid .... Mr. Matt LEVINE
35 Director Student Life .... Mr. Francis BEAUJON
41 Athletic Director .... Mr. John JONES
18 Chief Facilities/Physical Plant .... Mr. Eric RULOFSON
15 Human Resources Manager .... Ms. Vickie RAMSEY
14 Data Processing Manager .... Vacant
40 Bookstore Manager .... Ms. Dorothy NEELY

Le Cordon Bleu College of Culinary Arts in Los Angeles (I)

530 East Colorado Boulevard, Pasadena CA 91101
County: Los Angeles FICE Identification: 032103
Unit ID: 423980
Telephone: (626) 229-1300 Carnegie Class: Assoc/PrivFP
FAX Number: (626) 204-3907 Calendar System: Quarter
URL: www.chefs.edu/los-angeles
Established: 1994 Annual Undergrad Tuition & Fees: $40,140
Enrollment: 2,258 Coed
Affiliation or Control: Proprietary IRS Status: Proprietary
Highest Offering: Associate Degree
Program: Occupational
Accreditation: ACICS, ACFEI

01 President .... Mr. Tony BONDI

Life Chiropractic College West (J)

25001 Industrial Boulevard, Hayward CA 94545-2801
County: Alameda FICE Identification: 022285
Unit ID: 117520
Telephone: (510) 780-4500 Carnegie Class: Spec/Health
FAX Number: (510) 780-4525 Calendar System: Quarter
URL: www.lifewest.edu
Established: 1976 Annual Undergrad Tuition & Fees: $22,650
Enrollment: 311 Coed
Affiliation or Control: Independent Non-Profit IRS Status: 501(c)3
Highest Offering: First Professional Degree; No Lower Division
Program: Professional
Accreditation: CHIRO

01 President .... Dr. Brian KELLY
03 Executive Vice President .... Dr. Anatole BOGATSKI
05 Dean of the College .... Dr. Deborah LINDEMANN
23 Dean of the Health Center .... Dr. Kathy KINNEY
10 Acting Chief Financial Officer .... Mr. Richard PHILPOT

17 Vice President of Academic Affairs ....Dr. Scott DONALDSON
51 Dean Postgraduate & Cont Education ......Dr. Kendra HOLLOWAY
32 Dean of Students ....Mrs. Jackie BIRON
30 Director Institutional Advancement ....Mr. Drew BOSTER
88 Director of Special Projects ....Dr. George C. CASEY
46 Research Director ....Dr. Dale JOHNSON
08 Director Library ....Ms. Annette OSENGA
07 Director of Admissions & Recruiting ....Mr. Carlos ALICEA
16 Human Resources Director ....Ms. Megan SEDIQUI
40 Bookstore Director ....Mr. Robert BISHOP
37 Director Financial Aid ....Ms. Brenda R. JOHNSON
108 Director of Institutional Effective ....Dr. Kuan YANG
18 Chief Facilities/Physical Plant ....Mr. Ralph ROGERS
06 Manager Student Records ....Mrs. Robbie SHERWOOD
38 Academic Counselor ....Ms. Lori PINO

Life Pacific College (A)

1100 Covina Boulevard, San Dimas CA 91773-3298
County: Los Angeles FICE Identification: 022706
Unit ID: 117104
Telephone: (909) 599-5433 Carnegie Class: Spec/Faith
FAX Number: (909) 599-6690 Calendar System: Semester
URL: www.lifepacific.edu
Established: 1923 Annual Undergrad Tuition & Fees: $12,600
Enrollment: 598 Coed
Affiliation or Control: Other IRS Status: 501(c)3
Highest Offering: Master's
Program: Teacher Preparatory; Religious Emphasis
Accreditation: WC, BI

01 President ....Dr. Robert FLORES
04 Exec Assistant to the President ....Ms. Beth BOULTER
05 Vice President Academic Affairs ....Mr. Michael SALMEIER
32 Director Student Life ....Mr. Scott MARTZ
10 Chief Financial Officer ....Rev. Jarrod KULA
08 Librarian ....Mr. Keith DAWSON
06 Registrar ....Ms. Brittany ADAMS
18 Director of Campus Operations ....Mr. Scott MARTZ
37 Director of Financial Aid ....Mrs. Becky HUYCK
20 Assoc Acad Dean NonTrad Pgms ....Rev. Brian TOMHAVE
30 Advancement Director ....Ms. Lynnette LOZOYA
40 Bookstore Director ....Mrs. Marilyn CLARK
09 Director of Institutional Research ....Rev. Bruce PRIMROSE
13 Director Information Technology ....Mr. Lawrence LIU

Lincoln University (B)

401 15th Street, Oakland CA 94612-2801
County: Alameda FICE Identification: 006975
Unit ID: 117557
Telephone: (510) 628-8010 Carnegie Class: Master's S
FAX Number: (510) 628-8012 Calendar System: Semester
URL: www.lincolnuca.edu
Established: 1919 Annual Undergrad Tuition & Fees: $11,170
Enrollment: 379 Coed
Affiliation or Control: Independent Non-Profit IRS Status: 501(c)3
Highest Offering: Master's
Program: Liberal Arts And General; Professional; Business Emphasis
Accreditation: ACICS

01 President/Rector ....Dr. Mikhail BRODSKY
05 Dean of Faculty ....Dr. Michael GUERRA
32 Dean of Students ....Mr. William HESS
07 Director of Admissions & Records ....Ms. Peggy AU
58 Director of Graduate Programs ....Dr. Marshall J. BURAK
08 Head Librarian ....Ms. Nicole Y. MARSH
32 Director of Student Services ....Ms. Annique DALLEY
37 Chief Financial Aid Director ....Mr. James PETERSON
06 Registrar ....Ms. Maggie HUA
10 Controller ....Ms. Sherry LIANG
20 Asst Dean Academic Affairs ....Ms. Mariya ORSHANSKY

Logos Evangelical Seminary (C)

9358 Telstar Avenue, El Monte CA 91731-2816
County: Los Angeles FICE Identification: 039454
Unit ID: 397553
Telephone: (626) 571-5110 Carnegie Class: Not Classified
FAX Number: (626) 571-5119 Calendar System: Semester
URL: www.logos-seminary.edu
Established: 1989 Annual Graduate Tuition & Fees: $8,420
Enrollment: 148 Coed
Affiliation or Control: Other IRS Status: 501(c)3
Highest Offering: Doctorate; No Undergraduates
Program: Religious Emphasis
Accreditation: WC, THEOL

01 President ....Dr. Felix LIU
05 Academic Dean ....Dr. Ekron CHEN
10 Director of Business Affairs ....Mr. Sonny GAN
32 Associate Dean of Students ....Mr. Godwin NGAI
30 Director of Advancement ....Mr. James YU

Loma Linda University (D)

Loma Linda CA 92350-0001
County: San Bernardino FICE Identification: 001218
Unit ID: 117636
Telephone: (909) 558-1000 Carnegie Class: Spec/Med
FAX Number: (909) 558-0242 Calendar System: Quarter
URL: www.llu.edu
Established: 1905 Annual Undergrad Tuition & Fees: $28,422
Enrollment: 4,455 Coed
Affiliation or Control: Seventh-day Adventist IRS Status: 501(c)3
Highest Offering: Doctorate
Program: Occupational; Liberal Arts And General; Professional
Accreditation: WC, ANEST, ARCPA, CLPSY, CYTO, DENT, DH, DIETC, DMS, IPSY, MED, MFCD, MT, NURSE, OT, PH, PHAR, PTA, PTAA, RAD, RADDOS, RTT, SP, SW

01 President ....Dr. Richard H. HART
05 Provost ....Dr. Ronald L. CARTER
10 Sr Vice President Financial Affairs ....Mr. Rodney NEAL
30 Sr Vice President Advancement ....Mrs. Rachelle BUSSELL
27 Vice President Information Systems ....Dr. David P. HARRIS
84 VP Enrollment Mgmt/Student Services ....Dr. Rick E. WILLIAMS
63 Dean of Medicine ....Dr. H. Roger HADLEY
52 Dean of Dentistry ....Dr. Charles J. GOODACRE
69 Dean of Public Health ....Dr. Tricia Y. PENNIECOOK
66 Dean of Nursing ....Dr. Marilyn M. HERRMANN
76 Dean of Allied Health Professions ....Dr. Craig R. JACKSON
67 Dean School of Pharmacy ....Dr. W. William HUGHES
83 Dean School of Behavioral Health ....Dr. Beverly J. BUCKLES
73 Dean of School of Religion ....Dr. Jon PAULIEN
58 Dean Faculty of Graduate Studies .....Dr. Anthony J. ZUCCARELLI
06 Director of Records ....Ms. Erin SEHEULT
08 Director of University Libraries ....Ms. Carlene DRAKE
38 Director of Counseling ....Dr. William G. MURDOCH
43 General Legal Counsel ....Mr. Kent A. HANSEN
33 Dean of Men ....Mr. John NAFIE
34 Dean of Women ....Ms. Lynette BATES
37 Director Student Financial Aid ....Ms. Verdell SCHAEFER
09 Dir Educational Effectiveness ....Dr. Kirk CAMPBELL
15 Exec Director Human Services ....Ms. Charlene WILSON
18 Director Campus Engineering ....Mr. Randy STEVENS
96 Director of Purchasing ....Mr. Tim HICKMAN
40 Campus Bookstore Manager ....Ms. Melodi HAMILTON
42 Campus Chaplain ....Pastor Terry SWENSON

Long Beach City College (E)

4901 E Carson Street, Long Beach CA 90808-1780
County: Los Angeles FICE Identification: 001219
Unit ID: 117645
Telephone: (562) 938-4111 Carnegie Class: Assoc/Pub-U-MC
FAX Number: (562) 938-4118 Calendar System: Semester
URL: www.lbcc.edu
Established: 1927 Annual Undergrad Tuition & Fees (In-District): $1,182
Enrollment: 20,065 Coed
Affiliation or Control: State/Local IRS Status: 501(c)3
Highest Offering: Associate Degree
Program: Occupational; 2-Year Principally Bachelor's Creditable
Accreditation: WJ, ADNUR

01 Superintendent-President ....Mr. Eloy OAKLEY
05 Vice President Academic Affairs ....Dr. Gaither LOEWENSTEIN
10 Vice Pres Administrative Services ....Ms. Ann-Marie GABEL
25 Vice Pres Econ & Resourc Devel ....Ms. Lou Anne BYNUM
16 Vice President Human Resources ....Ms. Rose DELGAUDIO
32 Vice Pres Student Support Services ....Dr. Greg PETERSON
12 Assoc Vice President PCC Campus ....Dr. Byron BRELAND
15 Assoc VP Human Resources ....Ms. Cindy VYSKOCIL
13 Assoc VP Instruct & Info Tech ....Mr. Jay FIELD
07 Dean Admissions/Records ....Mr. Ross MIYASHIRO
09 Dean Academic Services ....Dr. Meena SINGHAL
38 Dean Counseling/Stdt Support Svcs ....Dr. Kaneesha TARRANT
57 Dean Creative Arts/Applied Sciences ....Mrs. Dina HUMBLE
37 Interim Dir Financial Aid Programs ....Mr. Richard YENTCH
88 Dean of Language Arts ....Dr. Jose Ramon NUNEZ
32 Dean Student Affairs ....Ms. Connie SEARS
76 Dean School Health & Science ....Mr. Paul CREASON
102 Exec Director Foundation ....Dr. Ginny BAXTER
26 Exec Dir Public Affairs & Marketing ....Mr. Mark TAYLOR
96 Director Business Support Services ....Mr. Mike COLLINS
45 Assoc Dean Inst Effectiveness ....Dr. Eva BAGG
18 Director of Facilities ....Mr. Tim WOOTTON
21 Director Fiscal Services & Payroll ....Mr. John THOMPSON
50 Dean Business and Social Science ....Dr. Laura WAN
88 Dean Student Success ....Dr. Bobbi VILLALOBOS

*Los Angeles Community College District Office (F)

770 Wilshire Boulevard, Los Angeles CA 90017
County: Los Angeles FICE Identification: 001221
Unit ID: 117681
Telephone: (213) 891-2000 Carnegie Class: N/A
FAX Number: N/A
URL: www.laccd.edu

01 Chancellor ....Dr. Daniel J. LAVISTA
43 General Counsel ....Ms. Camille A. GOULET
03 Deputy Chancellor ....Dr. Adriana D. BARRERA
05 VC Educ Support Svcs/Inst Effective ....Dr. Yasmin DELAHOUSSAYE
103 Vice Chanc Econ Workforce Devel ....Mr. Felicito CAJAYON

*East Los Angeles College (G)

1301 Avenida Cesar Chavez,
Monterey Park CA 91754-6001
County: Los Angeles FICE Identification: 022260
Unit ID: 113856
Telephone: (323) 265-8650 Carnegie Class: Assoc/Pub-U-MC
FAX Number: (323) 265-8763 Calendar System: Semester
URL: www.elac.edu
Established: 1945 Annual Undergrad Tuition & Fees (In-District): $1,380
Enrollment: 37,057 Coed
Affiliation or Control: State/Local IRS Status: 501(c)3
Highest Offering: Associate Degree
Program: Occupational; 2-Year Principally Bachelor's Creditable
Accreditation: WJ

02 Interim President ....Mr. Farley HERZEK
05 VP Academic Affairs ....Dr. Richard MOYER
103 VP Workforce & Econ Devel ....Ms. Renee D. MARTINEZ
32 VP Student Services/Special Pgms ....Mr. Oscar VALERIANO
11 VP Administrative Services ....Mr. Tom FURUKAWA
88 Assoc VP Administrative Services ....Ms. Erlinda DE OCAMPO
20 Dean Academic Affairs Sciences ....Ms. Karen DAAR
88 Dean Academic Affairs Economic Dev ....Ms. Gayle BROSSEAU
36 Dean Academic Affs/Career Tech Educ .....Ms. Laura M. RAMIREZ
49 Dean Academic Affairs Liberal Arts ....Ms. Kerrin MCMAHAN
49 Dean Academic Affairs Liberal Arts ....Ms. Vi LY
07 Dean Admissions & Records ....Mr. Jeremy P. ALLRED
12 Dean Academic Affairs Southgate Ctr ....Mr. Alfonso RIOS
30 Dean Resource & Cmty Rels ....Ms. Selina CHI
09 Dean Institutional Effectiveness ....Dr. Ryan CORNNER
51 Dean Continuing Education ....Ms. Adrienne A. MULLEN
35 Dean Student Activities ....Ms. Sonia LOPEZ
88 Dean EOP&S ....Ms. Danelle FALLERT
88 Dean CalWORKS ....Ms. Angelica TOLEDO
25 Assoc Dean Resource Development ....Dr. John RUDE
25 Assistant Dean Grants Management ....Ms. Martha ERMIAS
26 Chief Public Relations Officer ....Mr. Richard ANDERSON
22 Affirmative Action Officer ....Ms. Maria E. YEPES
37 Financial Aid Manager ....Ms. Lindy FONG
40 Director Student Store ....Ms. Joyce GARCIA
41 Athletic Director (Men/Women) ....Mr. Allen J. CONE
28 Director of Diversity ....Ms. Maria Elena YEPES
88 Child Development Director ....Mr. Michael SIMONE
38 Department Chair Counseling ....Mr. Daniel ORNELAS
21 College Fiscal Administrator ....Ms. Erlinda N. DEOCAMPO
08 Library Coordinator ....Ms. Choonhee L. RHIM
85 Foreign Student Advisement ....Ms. Nancy C. WONG
88 Director Vincent Price Art Museum ....Ms. Karen RAPP

*Los Angeles City College (H)

855 N Vermont Avenue, Los Angeles CA 90029-9990
County: Los Angeles FICE Identification: 001223
Unit ID: 117788
Telephone: (323) 953-4000 Carnegie Class: Assoc/Pub-U-MC
FAX Number: (323) 953-4013 Calendar System: Semester
URL: www.lacitycollege.edu
Established: 1929 Annual Undergrad Tuition & Fees (In-District): $1,104
Enrollment: 23,220 Coed
Affiliation or Control: Local IRS Status: 501(c)3
Highest Offering: Associate Degree
Program: Occupational; 2-Year Principally Bachelor's Creditable
Accreditation: WJ, DIETT, DT, RAD

02 Interim President ....Mrs. Renee D. MARTINEZ
05 Int Vice President Academic Affairs ....Dr. Mary CALLAHAN
11 Vice President of Administration ....Mr. Paul CARLSON
32 Vice President of Student Services ....Dr. Lawrence BRADFORD
20 Acting Dean of Academic Affairs ....Dr. Thelma DAY
20 Dean of Academic Affairs ....Ms. Allison JONES
45 Dean Planning/Instl Effectiveness ....Dr. Edward PAI
84 Dean of Enrollment Services ....Mr. William MARMOLEJO
103 Dean Workforce Development ....Ms. A. Alex DAVIS
35 Assoc Dean Student Svcs Access ....Mr. Jeremy VILLAR
37 Assoc Dean Financial Aid ....Mr. Jeremy VILLAR
35 Assoc Dean Office of Student Life ....Mr. Earic PETERS
40 Bookstore Director ....Ms. Christi O'CONNOR
85 Director International Students ....Dr. Reginald BRADY
15 Human Resources Manager ....Ms. Lenore SAUNDERS
66 Nursing Department Chair ....Ms. Betsy MANCHESTER
38 Counseling Chairperson ....Ms. Reri PUMPHREY

*Los Angeles Harbor College (I)

1111 Figueroa Place, Wilmington CA 90744-2397
County: Los Angeles FICE Identification: 001224
Unit ID: 117690
Telephone: (310) 233-4000 Carnegie Class: Assoc/Pub-U-MC
FAX Number: (310) 233-4223 Calendar System: Semester
URL: www.lahc.edu
Established: 1949 Annual Undergrad Tuition & Fees (In-District): $1,162
Enrollment: 10,205 Coed
Affiliation or Control: State/Local IRS Status: 501(c)3
Highest Offering: Associate Degree
Program: Occupational; 2-Year Principally Bachelor's Creditable
Accreditation: #WJ, ADNUR

02 President ....Mr. Marvin MARTINEZ
04 Executive Assistant to President ....Ms. Danielle JACK
05 Vice President Academic Affairs ....Mr. Luis M. ROSAS
11 Vice Pres Administrative Services ....Dr. Ann W. TOMLINSON
32 Vice President Student Services ....Mrs. Abbie L. PATTERSON
21 Assoc Vice Pres Administrative Svcs ....Mr. Nestor TAN
09 Dean of Institutional Effectiveness ....Dr. Kristi V. BLACKBURN
20 Dean of Academic Affairs ....Vacant
07 Dean Admissions/Records/Eve Ops ....Mr. David M. CHING
35 Dean Student Life ....Ms. Nina R. MALONE
20 Dean of Academic Affairs ....Mrs. Leige DOFFONEY
103 Dean of Economic/Workforce Devel ....Mrs. Sandra SANCHEZ
83 Div Chair Behavioral/Social Sci ....Mr. Bradley J. YOUNG

50 Division Chairperson Business ... Mr. Stanley C. SANDELL
60 Div Chairperson Communications ... Ms. Carmen CARRILLO
57 Div Chair Humanities/Fine Arts ... Mr. Mark D. WOOD
81 Div Chairperson Math/Phys Science ... Mr. Lauren J. MCKENZIE
76 Div Chairperson Health Sciences ... Mrs. Lynn YAMAKAWA
68 Div Chairperson Physical Education ... Mr. Nabeel M. BARAKAT
88 Div Chrp Sci & Fam/Consum Stds ... Mrs. Joyce E. PARKER
08 Division Chairperson Library ... Mr. Jonathan LEE
38 Division Chairperson Counseling ... Ms. Elizabeth COLOCHO
41 Athletic Director ... Mr. Nabeel BARAKAT
37 Director Student Financial Aid ... Mrs. Sheila U. MILLMAN
18 Facilities Manager ... Mr. William C. ENGLERT
31 Community Services Manager .. Ms. Carla R. MUSSA-MULDOON
40 College Enterprise Manager ... Mr. Mark A. ZANKICH
85 Foreign Student Advisor ... Mr. Paul GRADY

*Los Angeles Mission College (A)

13356 Eldridge Avenue, Sylmar CA 91342-3244
County: Los Angeles | FICE Identification: 012550 | Unit ID: 117867
Telephone: (818) 364-7600 | Carnegie Class: Assoc/Pub-U-MC
FAX Number: (818) 364-7826 | Calendar System: Semester
URL: www.lamission.edu
Established: 1975 | Annual Undergrad Tuition & Fees (In-District): $1,220
Enrollment: 10,045 | Coed
Affiliation or Control: State/Local | IRS Status: 501(c)3
Highest Offering: Associate Degree
Program: Occupational; 2-Year Principally Bachelor's Creditable
Accreditation: WJ

02 President ... Dr. Monte E. PEREZ
05 Vice President Academic Affairs ... Vacant
11 Vice President Administrative Svcs ... Mr. Daniel G. VILLANUEVA
32 Vice President of Student Services ... Mr. Joe RAMIREZ
20 Dean of Academic Affairs ... Dr. Nadia SWERDLOW
20 Dean of Academic Affairs ... Ms. Stephanie ATKINSON-ALSTON
35 Dean of Student Services ... Ms. Ludi VILLEGAS-VIDAL
88 Associate Dean of Academic Affairs ... Ms. Cathy BRINKMAN
88 Assistant Dean of Title V HSI ... Mrs. Susan RHI-KLEINERT
09 Act Dean Inst Rsrch/Plng/Info Tech ... Ms. Hanh TRAN
26 Chief Public Relations Officer ... Ms. Darlene MONTES
88 Director Child Development Center ... Ms. Monica MORENO
41 Athletic Director ... Mr. John KLITSNER
08 Head Librarian ... Ms. Sandy THOMSEN
38 Head Student Counseling ... Ms. Diana BONILLA
37 Student Financial Aid Manager ... Mr. Dennis J. SCHROEDER
31 Community Services Manager ... Vacant
18 Chief Facilities/Physical Plant ... Mr. Walter J. BORTMAN
88 EOP & S/Care Director ... Ms. Ludi VILLEGAS-VIDAL

*Los Angeles Pierce College (B)

6201 Winnetka Avenue, Woodland Hills CA 91371-0001
County: Los Angeles | FICE Identification: 001226 | Unit ID: 117706
Telephone: (818) 347-0551 | Carnegie Class: Assoc/Pub-U-MC
FAX Number: (818) 710-9844 | Calendar System: Semester
URL: www.piercecollege.edu
Established: 1947 | Annual Undergrad Tuition & Fees (In-District): $958
Enrollment: 20,453 | Coed
Affiliation or Control: State/Local | IRS Status: 501(c)3
Highest Offering: Associate Degree
Program: Occupational; 2-Year Principally Bachelor's Creditable
Accreditation: WJ, ADNUR

02 President ... Dr. Kathleen BURKE-KELLY
05 Vice President Academic Affairs ... Ms. Anna DAVIES
11 Vice President Administration ... Vacant
32 Vice President Student Services .Ms. Alma JOHNSON-HAWKINS
10 Assoc Vice President Admin Services ... Mr. Bruce ROSKY
10 Assoc Vice President Admin Services ... Mr. Larry KRAUS
08 Chairman Library Services ... Vacant
38 Chair Student Counseling ... Mr. Rudy DOMPE
20 Interim Dean of Academic Affairs ... Dr. Crystal KIEKEL
20 Dean of Academic Affairs ... Dr. Donna Mae VILLANUEVA
07 Dean Admissions/Records ... Mr. Marco DE LA GARZA
35 Dean Student Services ... Ms. Phyllis BRAXTON
35 Dean Student Services ... Mr. David FOLLOSCO
37 Dean Financial Aid ... Mr. Marco DE LA GARZA
09 Director Institutional Research ... Ms. Carol KOZERACKI
26 Public Information Officer ... Ms. Doreen CLAY
31 Director Community Services ... Ms. Cindy CHANG
102 Director of Foundation ... Mr. Brian CHASE
36 Director Student Placement ... Vacant
22 Compliance Officer ... Vacant
18 Director of College Facilities ... Mr. Paul NIEMAN

*Los Angeles Southwest College (C)

1600 W Imperial Highway, Los Angeles CA 90047-4899
County: Los Angeles | FICE Identification: 007047 | Unit ID: 117715
Telephone: (323) 241-5225 | Carnegie Class: Assoc/Pub-U-MC
FAX Number: (323) 241-5220 | Calendar System: Semester
URL: www.lasc.edu
Established: 1967 | Annual Undergrad Tuition & Fees (In-District): $1,102
Enrollment: 8,427 | Coed
Affiliation or Control: State/Local | IRS Status: 501(c)3
Highest Offering: Associate Degree
Program: Occupational; 2-Year Principally Bachelor's Creditable
Accreditation: #WJ

02 President ... Dr. Jack E. DANIELS, III
03 Executive Vice President ... Ms. Trudy J. WALTON
10 Vice President Admin Services ... Mr. Ferris E. TRIMBLE
46 Dean Resource Development ... Ms. Felicia DUENAS
09 Dean Institutional Effectiveness ... Dr. Daniel WALDEN
103 Dean Workforce Development ... Dr. Elmer BUGG
05 Dean Academic Affairs ... Dr. Michael A. SUTLIFF
05 Dean Academic Affairs ... Ms. Stephanie L. BRASLEY
32 Dean Student Services ... Dr. Patrick JEFFERSON
38 Chairperson Counseling ... Mr. Reggie MORRIS
08 Chairperson Library ... Ms. Shelley WERTS
07 Sr Admissions & Records Supervisor .Ms. Kimberly CARPENTER
18 Director of College Facilities ... Mr. Randy CRAIG
37 Manager Student Financial Aid ... Ms. Kathleen STIGER
88 Dean TRIO ... Dr. Oscar COBIAN

*Los Angeles Trade-Technical College (D)

400 W Washington Boulevard, Los Angeles CA 90015-4108
County: Los Angeles | FICE Identification: 001227 | Unit ID: 117724
Telephone: (213) 763-7000 | Carnegie Class: Assoc/Pub-U-MC
FAX Number: (213) 763-5393 | Calendar System: Semester
URL: www.lattc.edu
Established: 1925 | Annual Undergrad Tuition & Fees (In-District): $1,273
Enrollment: 15,483 | Coed
Affiliation or Control: State/Local | IRS Status: 501(c)3
Highest Offering: Associate Degree
Program: Occupational; 2-Year Principally Bachelor's Creditable
Accreditation: WJ, ACFEI

02 President ... Dr. Roland CHAPDELAINE
09 VP Inst Effectiveness & Innov ... Ms. Marcy DRUMMOND
11 Vice President Administration ... Dr. Mary GALLAGHER
05 VP Academic Affs & Workforce Devel ... Ms. Leticia BARAJAS
32 Vice President Student Services ... Mr. Ramon S. CASTILLO
21 Assoc Vice Pres Administrative Svcs ... Mr. William GASPER
35 Dean Student Services ... Vacant
20 Dean of Academic Affairs ... Mr. Vincent JACKSON
20 Dean Academic Affairs ... Ms. Cynthia MORLEY-MOWER
20 Dean Academic Affairs ... Mr. Joe GUERRIERI
84 Dean Enrollment Management ... Vacant
37 Manager Financial Aid/EOP&S ... Ms. Cecilia KWAN
88 Dean Inst Effective & Innovation ... Ms. Anna BADALYAN
88 Dean Matriculation/Student Success ... Ms. Dorothy SMITH
35 Dean Student Services ... Mr. Luis DORADO
18 Chief Facilities/Physical Plant ... Mr. Bill SMITH
06 Registrar ... Ms. Carolyn CLARK
10 Chief Business Officer ... Mr. Marcus ANGLIN
38 Chair Student Counseling ... Mr. Maurice BURNETT
96 Director of Purchasing ... Mr. Galen BULLOCK
102 Director Foundation/Corporate Rels ... Dr. Rhea CHUNG
26 Public Relations Manager ... Mr. David YSAIS

*Los Angeles Valley College (E)

5800 Fulton Avenue, Valley Glen CA 91401-4096
County: Los Angeles | FICE Identification: 001228 | Unit ID: 117733
Telephone: (818) 947-2600 | Carnegie Class: Assoc/Pub-U-MC
FAX Number: (818) 947-2602 | Calendar System: Semester
URL: www.lavc.edu
Established: 1949 | Annual Undergrad Tuition & Fees (In-District): $1,104
Enrollment: 18,571 | Coed
Affiliation or Control: State/Local | IRS Status: 501(c)3
Highest Offering: Associate Degree
Program: Occupational; 2-Year Principally Bachelor's Creditable
Accreditation: WJ, ADNUR

02 President ... Dr. A. Susan CARLEO
05 Vice President Academic Affairs ... Dr. Sandra L. MAYO
10 Vice Pres Administrative Services ... Mr. Tom V. JACOBSMEYER
32 Vice Pres Student Services ... Mr. Florentino MANZANO
11 Assoc Vice Pres Administrative Svcs ... Mr. Raul D. GONZALEZ
21 Financial Analyst ... Vacant
45 Chief Financial Anaylist ... Ms. Violet AMRIKHAS
20 Dean Academic Affairs ... Dr. Laurie NALEPA
20 Dean Academic Affairs ... Mr. Dennis J. REED
88 Dean Economic Development ... Dr. Deborah A. DICESARE
08 Chairperson of Library Service ... Ms. Georgianna W. SAMPLER
37 Financial Aid Manager ... Mr. Vernon D. BRIDGES
09 Dean Research & Planning ... Ms. Michelle R. FOWLES
35 Associate Dean Student Services ... Ms. Elizabeth ORTIZ
88 Associate Dean of EOPS ... Dr. Sherri RODRIGUEZ
88 Associate Dean DSPS ... Mr. David M. GREEN
35 Assoc Dean of Student Services ... Ms. Annie G. REED
102 Director Foundation/Alumni Rels ... Mr. Raul V. CASTILLO
26 Public Relations Manager ... Ms. Jennifer C. FONG
18 Director of College Facilities ... Mr. Tom LOPEZ
40 Bookstore Manager ... Vacant
13 Manager College Info Svcs ... Mr. Aaron WEATHERSBY
31 Community Services Manager ... Mr. Michael B. ATKIN
38 Director Student Counseling ... Ms. Barbara GOLDBERG
41 Athletic Director ... Vacant

*West Los Angeles College (F)

9000 Overland Avenue, Culver City CA 90230-5002
County: Los Angeles | FICE Identification: 008596 | Unit ID: 125471
Telephone: (310) 287-4200 | Carnegie Class: Assoc/Pub-U-MC
FAX Number: (310) 841-0396 | Calendar System: Semester
URL: www.wlac.edu
Established: 1969 | Annual Undergrad Tuition & Fees (In-District): $960
Enrollment: 10,703 | Coed
Affiliation or Control: State/Local | IRS Status: 501(c)3
Highest Offering: Associate Degree
Program: Occupational; 2-Year Principally Bachelor's Creditable
Accreditation: WJ, DH

02 President ... Mr. Nabil S. ABU-GHAZALEH
11 Vice President Administrative Svcs ... Mr. Kenneth B. TAKEDA
05 Vice President Academic Affairs ... Mr. Robert L. SPRAGUE
32 Vice President Student Services ... Ms. Betsy A. REGALADO
84 Dean Student Svcs Enrollment ... Mr. John M. GOLTERMANN
97 Dean General Education/Transfer ... Dr. Judith Ann FRIEDMAN
20 Dean Advance Program Development ... Mr. Mark PRACHER
75 Dean Career/Technology Education ... Ms. Ara AGUIAR
35 Dean of Student Support Services ... Dr. Shalamon DUKE
09 Dean of Research and Planning ... Ms. Rebecca TILLBERG
56 Dean Distance Learning/Inst Tech ... Mr. Eric ICHON
35 Assoc Dean Student Svcs Activities ... Ms. Celena ALCALA
11 Associate Dean Contract Ed ... Mr. Barry SLOAN
20 Associate Dean Trio ... Ms. Kathy S. WALTON
88 Academic Senate President ... Dr. Adrienne FOSTER
21 Chief Financial Administrator ... Ms. Maureen O'BRIEN
102 Actg Exec Director WLAC Foundation ... Mr. Kenneth B. TAKEDA
26 Dir Advtg/Marketing/Public Rels ... Ms. Michelle LONG-COFFEE
41 Athletic Director ... Mr. Steve AGGERS
18 Facilities Manager ... Mr. Allan HANSEN
19 Sheriff/Deputy ... Mr. Alfred A. GUERRERO
37 Financial Aid Manager ... Mr. Glenn SCHENK
40 College Enterprise Manager ... Mr. Larry PACKHAM
88 Operations Manager ... Mr. Bruce HICKS
22 Compliance Officer ... Vacant

Los Angeles County College of Nursing and Allied Health (G)

1237 N Mission Road, Los Angeles CA 90033-1083
County: Los Angeles | FICE Identification: 006165 | Unit ID: 117803
Telephone: (323) 226-4911 | Carnegie Class: Assoc/Pub-Spec
FAX Number: (323) 226-6343 | Calendar System: Semester
URL: www.ladhs.org/wps/portal/CollegeOfNursing/
Established: 1895 | Annual Undergrad Tuition & Fees (In-District): $4,925
Enrollment: 233 | Coed
Affiliation or Control: Local | IRS Status: 501(c)3
Highest Offering: Associate Degree
Program: Occupational; 2-Year Principally Bachelor's Creditable
Accreditation: WJ

01 Provost ... Ms. Nancy W. MILLER
05 Dean of Nursing Programs ... Ms. Barbara COLLIER
32 Dean Administrative/Student Svcs ... Ms. Maria C. CABALLERO
53 Dean Education/Consulting Services ... Ms. Tammy BLASS

Los Angeles Film School (H)

6353 Sunset Boulevard, Hollywood CA 90028
County: Los Angeles | FICE Identification: 040373 | Unit ID: 436429
Telephone: (323) 464-5200 | Carnegie Class: Assoc/PrivFP
FAX Number: (323) 646-0770 | Calendar System: Other
URL: www.lafilm.edu
Established: 1999 | Annual Undergrad Tuition & Fees: $43,300
Enrollment: 2,881 | Coed
Affiliation or Control: Proprietary | IRS Status: Proprietary
Highest Offering: Baccalaureate
Program: 2-Year Principally Bachelor's Creditable; Fine Arts Emphasis
Accreditation: ACCSC

01 President/CEO ... Ms. Diana DERYCZ-KESSLER

Los Angeles ORT College (I)

6435 Wilshire Blvd, Los Angeles CA 90048
County: Los Angeles | FICE Identification: 025703 | Unit ID: 368780
Telephone: (323) 966-5444 | Carnegie Class: Assoc/PrivNFP
FAX Number: (323) 966-5455 | Calendar System: Other
URL: www.laort.edu
Established: 1985 | Annual Undergrad Tuition & Fees: $11,450
Enrollment: 369 | Coed
Affiliation or Control: Independent Non-Profit | IRS Status: 501(c)3
Highest Offering: Associate Degree
Program: Occupational; Technical Emphasis
Accreditation: CNCE

*Los Rios Community College District Office (J)

1919 Spanos Court, Sacramento CA 95825-3981
County: Sacramento | FICE Identification: 001231 | Unit ID: 117900
Telephone: (916) 568-3021 | Carnegie Class: N/A
FAX Number: (916) 568-3023
URL: www.losrios.edu

01 Chancellor ... Dr. Brice W. HARRIS

04 Chancellor's Executive Assistant .... Ms. Jennifer DELUCCHI
10 Deputy Chancellor .... Mr. Jon SHARPE
05 Vice Chancellor Education/Tech .... Dr. Susan L. LORIMER
30 Vice Chanc Resource/Economic Dev .... Dr. Beverly A. SANDEEN
26 Assoc Vice Chanc Communications .... Ms. Susie S. WILLIAMS
18 Assoc Vice Chanc Facilities Mgmt .... Mr. Pablo MANZO
21 Assoc Vice Chancellor Finance .... Ms. Theresa MATISTA
15 Assoc Vice Chanc Human Resouces .... Mr. Ryan COX
13 Assoc Vice Chanc Information Tech .... Mr. Mick HOLSCLAW
32 Assoc Vice Chanc Student Services .... Dr. Victoria ROSARIO
103 Assoc Vice Chanc Workforce/Econ Dev .... Dr. Daniel THROGMORTON
43 General Counsel .... Mr. J.P SHERRY
37 Director Financial Aid .... Mr. Roy BECKHORN
96 Director General Services .... Mr. O.D BURR
09 Director Institutional Research .... Ms. Flora B. YEN

*American River College (A)

4700 College Oak Drive, Sacramento CA 95841-4286

County: Sacramento FICE Identification: 001232
Unit ID: 109208
Telephone: (916) 484-8011 Carnegie Class: Assoc/Pub-U-MC
FAX Number: (916) 484-8674 Calendar System: Semester
URL: www.arc.losrios.edu
Established: 1955 Annual Undergrad Tuition & Fees (In-District): $1,200
Enrollment: 33,210 Coed
Affiliation or Control: State/Local IRS Status: 501(c)3
Highest Offering: Associate Degree
Program: Occupational; 2-Year Principally Bachelor's Creditable
Accreditation: WJ, EMT, FUSER

02 President .... Dr. David VIAR
05 Vice President of Instruction .... Ms. Colleen H. OWINGS
32 Vice President of Student Services .... Dr. Pamela D. WALKER
10 Vice President of Admin Services .... Mr. Raymond DI GUILIO
20 Assoc Vice President of Instruction .... Dr. Lisa LAWRENSON
62 Assoc VP of Instruction/Lrng Res .... Dr. David REDFIELD
103 Assoc VP Workforce Development .... Dr. Cris MCCULLOUGH
09 Dean Planning/Rsch/Tech/Prof Dev .... Dr. Jane DE LEON
27 Public Information Officer .... Dr. Stephen PEITHMAN
30 Director of College Advancement .... Ms. Kirsten DUBRAY
37 Interim Financial Aid Supervisor .... Mr. Chad FUNK
07 Dean of Enrollment Services .... Dr. Robin NEAL
57 Dean Fine & Applied Arts .... Dr. Adam KARP
83 Interim Dean Behavioral Sci/Soc Sci .... Mr. Carlos REYES
79 Dean Humanities .... Ms. Kate JAQUES
38 Dean Counseling & Student Svcs .... Mr. Jeffrey STEPHENSON
88 Dean of English .... Ms. Tammy MONTGOMERY
81 Dean of Mathematics .... Ms. Nancy REITZ
68 Int Dean of Kinesiology/Athletics .... Mr. Greg WARZECKA
81 Dean Science/Engineering .... Dr. Rina ROY
75 Dean of Technical/Vocational Educ .... Ms. Gabriel M. MEEHAN
56 Dean Off-Campus Education .... Mr. James V. THOMPSON
38 Dean Student Support Services .... Ms. Eddie WEBB
66 Dean Health & Education .... Dr. Steven BOYD
56 Dean Natomas Education Center .... Ms. Sheryl GESSFORD
35 Dean Student Development .... Mr. Manuel PEREZ
50 Dean Business/Computer Science .... Dr. Derrick BOOTH

*Cosumnes River College (B)

8401 Center Parkway, Sacramento CA 95823-5799

County: Sacramento FICE Identification: 007536
Unit ID: 113096
Telephone: (916) 691-7344 Carnegie Class: Assoc/Pub-U-MC
FAX Number: (916) 691-7375 Calendar System: Semester
URL: www.crc.losrios.edu
Established: 1970 Annual Undergrad Tuition & Fees (In-District): $1,104
Enrollment: 15,205 Coed
Affiliation or Control: State/Local IRS Status: 501(c)3
Highest Offering: Associate Degree
Program: Occupational; 2-Year Principally Bachelor's Creditable
Accreditation: WJ, MAC

02 President .... Dr. Deborah J. TRAVIS
05 VP Instruction & Student Learning .... Mr. Whitney YAMAMURA
11 VP Admin Svcs & Student Support .... Dr. Donald WALLACE
32 VP Student Svcs/Enrollment Mgmt ...... Ms. Celia ESPOSITO-NOY
84 Dean Student Svcs/Enrollment Mgmt .... Ms. Christine THOMAS
20 Dean Instruction/Student Learning .... Dr. Judith BEACHLER
08 Dean Learning Res/College Tech ..... Mr. Stephen MCGLOUGHLIN
38 Dean Counseling & Student Services .... Dr. Michael MARION
50 Dean Business & Family Science .... Mr. Jamey NYE
79 Dean Humanities & Social Science .... Ms. Virginia REYNOLDS
41 Dean Kinesiology & Athletics .... Ms. Elizabeth BELYEA
81 Dean Science/Math/Engineering .... Dr. Robert MONTANEZ
72 Dean Careers & Technology .... Mr. Robert JOHNSON
60 Dean Comm/Visual/Performing Arts .... Mr. Torence POWELL
45 Dean of College Planning & Research .... Ms. Katherine MCLAIN
06 Registrar/Admissions & Records .... Mr. Richard ANDREWS
18 Chief Facilities/Physical Plant .... Mr. Cory WATHEN
26 Public Information Officer .... Ms. Kristie WEST

*Folsom Lake College (C)

10 College Parkway, Folsom CA 95630-6798

County: Sacramento FICE Identification: 038713
Unit ID: 444219
Telephone: (916) 608-6500 Carnegie Class: Assoc/Pub-U-MC
FAX Number: (916) 608-6584 Calendar System: Semester
URL: www.flc.losrios.edu
Established: 2004 Annual Undergrad Tuition & Fees (In-District): $1,318
Enrollment: 9,033 Coed
Affiliation or Control: State/Local IRS Status: 501(c)3
Highest Offering: Associate Degree
Program: 2-Year Principally Bachelor's Creditable
Accreditation: WJ

02 President .... Dr. Rachel ROSENTHAL
11 Vice President Administration .... Kathleen KIRKLIN
05 Vice President Instruction .... Dr. David NEWNHAM
32 Int VP Student Dev/Enroll Mgmt .... Dr. David HILL
88 Executive Director VAPAC .... David PIER
20 Dean of Instruction .... Dr. Monica PACTOL
20 Dean of Instruction & Technology .... Gary HARTLEY
20 Dean of Career & Tech Educ .... Dr. Stu VAN HORN
20 Dean of Instruction/EDC .... Dale VAN DAM
20 Dean of Instruction/VAPA .... David WILLIAMS
35 Director Student Affairs .... Aiden ELY
07 Admissions & Records Supervisor .... Christine WURZER
40 Bookstore Manager .... Rob MULLIGAN
10 Business Services Supervisor .... Joany HARMAN
18 Campus Operations Supervisor .... Colleen JOHNSON
12 Educational Center Supervisor .... Adrienne ANDREWS
37 Financial Aid Supervisor .... Carol THOMAS
26 Public Information Officer .... Scott CROW
04 Assistant to the President .... Beth SPRINKEL
09 Research Analyst .... Chris OLSON

*Sacramento City College (D)

3835 Freeport Boulevard, Sacramento CA 95822-1386

County: Sacramento FICE Identification: 001233
Unit ID: 122180
Telephone: (916) 558-2111 Carnegie Class: Assoc/Pub-U-MC
FAX Number: (916) 558-2449 Calendar System: Semester
URL: www.scc.losrios.edu
Established: 1916 Annual Undergrad Tuition & Fees (In-State): $1,396
Enrollment: 23,887 Coed
Affiliation or Control: State Related IRS Status: 501(c)3
Highest Offering: Associate Degree
Program: Occupational; 2-Year Principally Bachelor's Creditable
Accreditation: WJ, DA, DH, OTA, PTAA

02 President .... Dr. Kathryn JEFFERY
05 Vice Pres Instructional Services .... Dr. Mary TURNER
10 Vice Pres Administrative Services .... Mr. Robert J. MARTINELLI
32 Vice President Student Services ... Mr. Michael C. POINTDEXTER
20 Associate Vice Pres Instruction .... Mr. Rick IDA
20 Associate Vice Pres Instruction .... Mrs. Julia A. JOLLY
35 Associate Vice Pres Student Svcs .... Dr. Debra LUFF
13 Dean Information Technology .... Dr. Elaine ADER
07 Dean Financial Aid/Enrollment .... Ms. Christine HERNANDEZ
46 Dean Planning/Research/Development ... Dr. Marybeth BUECHNER
08 Dean Learning Resources .... Ms. Rhonda RIOS-KRAVITZ
36 Dean Counseling/Student Success .... Mr. David RASUL
40 Director College Store .... Mr. Randy CLEM
66 Director Nursing .... Ms. Dale S. COHEN
18 Director College Operations .... Mr. Gregory HAYMAN
26 Director College Advancement .... Mrs. Mary LELAND
27 Public Information Officer .... Ms. Amanda DAVIS
76 Dean Science & Allied Health .... Mr. James COLLINS
50 Dean Business .... Dr. Deborah SAKS
79 Dean Humanities/Fine Arts .... Mr. Chris IWATA
88 Dean Languages/Literature .... Mr. Albert GARCIA
72 Dean Advanced Technology .... Mrs. Donnetta WEBB
41 Dean PE/Health/Athletics .... Mr. Mitchell L. CAMPBELL
81 Dean Statistics/Math/Engineering .... Mrs. Anne LICCIARDI
83 Dean Behavioral & Social Science .... Dr. Frank MALARET
56 Dean Davis Center Center .... Mr. Don PALM
56 Interim Dean West Sacramento Ctr .... Ms. Shirley SHORT

Loyola Marymount University (E)

1 LMU Drive, Los Angeles CA 90045-2659

County: Los Angeles FICE Identification: 011649
Unit ID: 117946
Telephone: (310) 338-2700 Carnegie Class: Master's L
FAX Number: N/A Calendar System: Semester
URL: www.lmu.edu
Established: 1911 Annual Undergrad Tuition & Fees: $38,900
Enrollment: 9,352 Coed
Affiliation or Control: Roman Catholic IRS Status: 501(c)3
Highest Offering: Doctorate
Program: Liberal Arts And General; Teacher Preparatory; Professional
Accreditation: WC, ART, BUS, DANCE, ENG, LAW, MUS, TED, THEA, THEOL

01 President .... Mr. David W. BURCHAM
00 Chancellor .... Rev. Patrick J. CAHALAN, SJ
03 Exec Vice President & Provost .... Dr. Joseph HELLIGE
04 Special Assistant to the President .... Rev. Joseph LABRIE, SJ
05 Vice Provost for Academic Affairs ..... Dr. Michael J. O'SULLIVAN
10 Sr Vice Pres/Chief Financial Ofcr .... Mr. Tom O. FLEMING
26 Sr Vice Pres University Relations .... Mr. Dennis SLON
32 Sr Vice Pres for Student Affairs .... Dr. Elena M. BOVE
11 Sr Vice Pres for Administration .... Ms. Lynne B. SCARBORO
85 Vice President Intercultural Affs .... Dr. Abbie ROBINSON-ARMSTRONG
15 Vice President for Human Resources ..... Ms. Rebecca CHANDLER
86 VP for Comm/Government Relations ...... Ms. Kathleen FLANAGAN
84 Actg VP Enrollment Management .... Dr. James LANDRY
18 Vice Pres Facilities Management .... Mr. Rick GARCIA
20 Vice Pres Undergraduate Studies .... Dr. Rae Linda BROWN
21 Vice Pres for Finance/Controller .... Ms. Lori A. HUSEIN
35 Assoc VP Student Affairs .... Mr. Marshall SAUCEDA
21 AVP Auxiliary Mgmt & Business Affs .... Mr. Raymond A. DENNIS
39 Assoc Vice Pres of Student Life .... Mr. Richard ROCHELEAU
09 Assoc Vice Pres Inst Effectiveness .... Ms. Margaret KASIMATIS
35 Dean of Students .... Dr. Linda MCMURDOCK
08 Dean of University Libraries .... Ms. Kristine BRANCOLINI
06 University Registrar .... Ms. Kathy REED
61 Dean Loyola Law School/Sr VP .... Mr. Victor J. GOLD
50 Dean Business Administration .... Dr. Dennis DRAPER
57 Dean Communication/Fine Arts .... Dr. Bryant K. ALEXANDER
88 Dean School of Film & TV .... Prof. Stephen G. UJLAKI
49 Dean Liberal Arts .... Dr. Paul T. ZELEZA, SJ
54 Dean Science & Engineering .... Dr. Richard PLUMB
53 Dean School of Education .... Dr. Shane MARTIN
30 Ex Dir Dev Plnd Gvng/Princpal Gifts .... Ms. Joanie POHAS
29 Exec Dir Alumni Rels/Annual Giving .... Ms. Lisa PIUMETTI FARLAND
102 Exec Dir Corporate/Foundation Rels .... Mr. David A. TILLIPMAN
42 Director of Campus Ministry .... Rev. James D. ERPS
07 Director of Admissions .... Mr. Matthew X. FISSINGER
37 Director of Financial Aid .... Ms. Catherine GRAHAM
36 Dir Career Devel/Placement Svcs .... Mr. Jeffrey HARDT
23 Medical Director .... Daniel HYSLOP, M.D.
41 Athletic Director .... Dr. William HUSAK
19 Chief of Public Safety .... Mr. Hampton CANTRELL
44 Director of Annual Giving .... Mr. Kevin J. DELANEY
92 Director of Honors Program .... Dr. Brad STONE
94 Director of Women's Studies .... Dr. Nancy JABBRA
88 Dir Real Estate/Faculty Housing .... Ms. Kirsten ANDRESEN
38 Dir of Student Counseling .... Ms. Cassandra L. BAILEY

Marymount College (F)

30800 Palos Verdes Drive E,
Rancho Palos Verdes CA 90275-6299

County: Los Angeles FICE Identification: 010474
Unit ID: 118541
Telephone: (310) 377-5501 Carnegie Class: Assoc/PrivNFP
FAX Number: (310) 377-6223 Calendar System: Semester
URL: www.marymountpv.edu
Established: 1932 Annual Undergrad Tuition & Fees: $28,870
Enrollment: 1,045 Coed
Affiliation or Control: Roman Catholic IRS Status: 501(c)3
Highest Offering: Baccalaureate
Program: 2-Year Principally Bachelor's Creditable; Liberal Arts And General; Business Emphasis
Accreditation: WC

01 President .... Dr. Michael S. BROPHY
10 Vice President of Finance .... Mr. James REEVES
05 Dean of Academic Affairs .... Dr. Ariane SCHAUER
30 Dean Institutional Advancement .... Dr. Brenda SOLOMON
07 Dean of Admission & Enrollment Mgmt .... Dr. Barry WARD
32 Dean of Students .... Ms. Shane ARMSTRONG
20 Associate Academic Officer .... Ms. Susie MARTIN
08 Librarian .... Ms. Mary MCMILLAN
37 Director Student Financial Aid .... Ms. Tracie HUNTER
15 Director Personnel Services .... Ms. Karen THORDARSON
18 Chief Facilities/Physical Plant .... Mr. Richard SCHULT
26 Chief Public Relations Officer .... Ms. Kelly CURTIS
29 Director Alumni Relations .... Ms. Megan MCCORMICK
36 Director Student Placement .... Ms. Virginia WADE
38 Director Student Counseling .... Dr. David DRAPER
96 Director of Purchasing .... Ms. Denise FESSENBECKER
06 Registrar .... Vacant
35 Dir Student Life & Engagement .... Ms. Kelly KRUSEE
84 Director of Enrollment Management .... Ms. Paula AVERY
09 Director of Institutional Research .... Mr. Michael SEMENOFF
21 Associate Business Officer .... Ms. Kathleen RUIZ

The Master's College and Seminary (G)

21726 Placerita Canyon Road,
Santa Clarita CA 91321-1200

County: Los Angeles FICE Identification: 001220
Unit ID: 117751
Telephone: (661) 259-3540 Carnegie Class: Bac/Diverse
FAX Number: N/A Calendar System: Semester
URL: www.masters.edu
Established: 1927 Annual Undergrad Tuition & Fees: $27,300
Enrollment: 1,197 Coed
Affiliation or Control: Independent Non-Profit IRS Status: 501(c)3
Highest Offering: Doctorate
Program: Liberal Arts And General; Teacher Preparatory
Accreditation: WC, MUS

01 President .... Dr. John MACARTHUR
03 Exec Vice President and Provost .... Dr. Mark TATLOCK
05 Vice President Academic Affairs .... Dr. Alex GRANADOS
32 Dean of Student Life .... Mr. Joe KELLER
58 Vice President Graduate School .... Dr. Richard L. MAYHUE
11 Vice President of Operations .... Mr. Bob HOTTON
30 Int Vice President for Development .... Dr. Mark TATLOCK
46 Vice Pres Institutional Research .... Dr. John HUGHES
88 Director of Educational Partnership .... Vacant
10 Chief Financial Officer .... Mr. Jason HARTUNG
18 Chief of Operations .... Mr. Jason HARTUNG
06 Registrar .... Mr. Don GILMORE
08 Director Library Services .... Mr. John STONE
20 Associate Dean of Students .... Vacant
07 Director Enrollment .... Miss Hollie GORSH

41 Athletic Director ..... Mr. Steve WALDECK
37 Director Financial Aid ..... Mr. Gary EDWARDS
35 Director Campus Activities ..... Mr. Peter BARGAS
29 Director Alumni Affairs ..... Mr. Steve CRAWFORD
09 Director of Institutional Research ..... Mr. John M. WALTER
36 Director Student Placement ..... Mr. Rick WAHLER
85 International Students Advisor ..... Miss Lisa LAGEORGE

† The Master's Seminary is located at 13248 Roscoe Boulevard, Sun Valley, CA 91352.

Mendocino College (A)

1000 Hensley Creek Road, Ukiah CA 95482-7821

County: Mendocino | FICE Identification: 011672 | Unit ID: 118684
Telephone: (707) 468-3000 | Carnegie Class: Assoc/Pub-R-L
FAX Number: (707) 468-3120 | Calendar System: Semester
URL: www.mendocino.edu
Established: 1973 | Annual Undergrad Tuition & Fees (In-District): $850
Enrollment: 3,831 | Coed
Affiliation or Control: State/Local | IRS Status: 501(c)3
Highest Offering: Associate Degree
Program: Occupational; 2-Year Principally Bachelor's Creditable
Accreditation: WJ, #EMT

01 Superintendent/President ..... Dr. Roe DARNELL
05 VP of Education & Student Services ..... Vacant
11 Vice Pres Administrative Services ..... Dr. Larry PERRYMAN
08 Head Librarian ..... Mr. John KOETZNER
20 Dean of Instruction ..... Ms. Virginia GULEFF
12 Dean Lake & Willits Centers ..... Mr. Mark RAWITSCH
75 Dean Career and Technical Education ..... Ms. Susan GOFF
15 Director Human Resources ..... Ms. Karen CHATY
18 Director Maintenance and Operations ..... Mr. Steve OLIVERIA
26 Director Public Info & Marketing ..... Vacant
32 Director Student Life & Athletics ..... Mr. Mike MARI
21 Director Fiscal Services ..... Ms. Eileen CICHOCKI
14 Director Information Technology .. Ms. Karen CHRISTOPHERSON
09 Director of Institutional Research ..... Dr. Charles DUFFY
07 Director Admissions/Registrar ..... Ms. Kristie A. ANDERSON
37 Asst Dean Stdnt Financial Aid/EOPS ..... Ms. Jacquline BRADLEY

Menlo College (B)

1000 El Camino Real, Atherton CA 94027-4301

County: San Mateo | FICE Identification: 001236 | Unit ID: 118693
Telephone: (800) 556-3656 | Carnegie Class: Bac/Diverse
FAX Number: (650) 543-4496 | Calendar System: Semester
URL: www.menlo.edu
Established: 1927 | Annual Undergrad Tuition & Fees: $36,110
Enrollment: 642 | Coed
Affiliation or Control: Independent Non-Profit | IRS Status: 501(c)3
Highest Offering: Baccalaureate
Program: Liberal Arts And General; Business Emphasis
Accreditation: WC

01 President ..... Dr. James KELLY
05 Provost ..... Dr. James WOOLEVER
84 VP Enrollment Mgmt & Planning ..... Mr. David PLACEY
30 VP for Institutional Advancement ..... Vacant
10 Chief Financial Officer ..... Mr. Nilo VENTURA
20 Dean for Academic Affairs ..... Dr. Dale HOCKSTRA
107 Dean of Professional Studies Pgm ..... Dr. James WOOLEVER
18 Director Facilities & Operations ..... Mr. Robert TALBOTT
08 Dean Library Services ..... Dr. William WALTERS
41 Director of Athletics ..... Mr. Keith SPATARO
35 Associate Dean of Student Affairs ..... Ms. Sharyn MOORE
37 Director Office of Financial Aid ..... Ms. Anne HEATON-DUNLAP
36 Director of Career Services ..... Ms. Mary ROBINS
09 Assessment Coordinator ..... Ms. Ivana IZVONAR
21 Controller ..... Ms. Raagini ALI
26 Director of Commun/PR & Marketing ..... Ms. Darcy BLAKE
32 Dean of Student Affairs ..... Ms. Yasmin LAMBIE-SIMPSON
39 Director of Housing ..... Mr. Jessie GUILLIOT
07 Director Office of Admissions ..... Ms. Priscila DE SOUZA
06 Registrar ..... Ms. Mary RANDERS
29 Director of Alumni Relations ..... Vacant

Merced College (C)

3600 M Street, Merced CA 95348-2898

County: Merced | FICE Identification: 001237 | Unit ID: 118718
Telephone: (209) 384-6000 | Carnegie Class: Assoc/Pub-R-L
FAX Number: (209) 384-6043 | Calendar System: Semester
URL: www.mccd.edu
Established: 1962 | Annual Undergrad Tuition & Fees (In-District): $901
Enrollment: 9,542 | Coed
Affiliation or Control: State/Local | IRS Status: 501(c)3
Highest Offering: Associate Degree
Program: Occupational; 2-Year Principally Bachelor's Creditable; Business Emphasis
Accreditation: WJ, DMS, RAD

01 President ..... Dr. Ron TAYLOR
04 Executive Assistant to President ..... Mrs. Stacey HICKS
05 Vice President Instruction ..... Dr. Marianne TORTORICI
32 Vice Pres Student Personnel Svcs ..... Dr. Anne NEWINS
12 Dean Los Banos Campus ..... Dr. Brenda LATHAM
81 Dean Instructional Services ..... Dr. Douglas KAIN
71 Dean Instructional Services ..... Mr. Kevin KISTLER
47 Dean Instructional Services ..... Mr. Jim ANDERSEN
50 Dean Instructional Services ..... Dr. Bobby ANDERSON
83 Dean Instructional Services ..... Mr. John ALBANO
103 Dean Instructional Services ..... Mrs. Karyn DOWER
35 Dean of Student Services ..... Dr. Everett LOVELACE
26 Chief Public Relations Officer ..... Mr. Robin SHEPARD
14 Director Info Technology Services ..... Mr. Don PETERSON
18 Dir Maint/Transport/Facilities ..... Mr. Rick SOUHRADA
06 Registrar & Dir Financial Aid ..... Mrs. Sharon REINHARDT
08 Director Learning Resources Center ..... Dr. Susan WALSH

Mills College (D)

5000 MacArthur Boulevard, Oakland CA 94613-1301

County: Alameda | FICE Identification: 001238 | Unit ID: 118888
Telephone: (510) 430-2255 | Carnegie Class: Master's M
FAX Number: (510) 430-3314 | Calendar System: Semester
URL: www.mills.edu
Established: 1852 | Annual Undergrad Tuition & Fees: $38,850
Enrollment: 1,555 | Female
Affiliation or Control: Independent Non-Profit | IRS Status: 501(c)3
Highest Offering: Doctorate
Program: Liberal Arts And General; Teacher Preparatory
Accreditation: WC

01 President ..... Ms. Alecia A. DECOUDREAUX
05 Provost & Dean of the Faculty ..... Dr. Sandra C. GREER
10 Interim VP Finance & Treasurer ..... Ms. Jamie NICKEL
26 VP for Opers/Chief Public Rels Ofcr ... Ms. Renee JADUSHLEVER
30 VP for Institutional Advancement .. Ms. Cynthia BRANDT STOVER
43 Vice President & General Counsel ..... Ms. Therese M. LEONE
20 Associate Provost ..... Vacant
21 Assoc VP for Student Fin/Admin Svcs ..... Mr. David GIN
07 Dean of Undergraduate Admission ..... Ms. Giulietta AQUINO
32 Dean Student Life/Vice Provost ..... Ms. Joi LEWIS
101 Asst Secretary of Board of Trustees ..... Dr. Marianne SHELDON
38 Assoc Dean/Dir Counsel/Psych Svcs ..... Ms. Dorian NEWTON
06 Registrar ..... Mr. David GIN
18 Director of Campus Facilities ..... Ms. Linda ZITZNER
41 Director of Athletics ..... Ms. Themy ADACHI
29 Exec Director of Alumnae Relations ..... Ms. Laura GOBBI
09 Dir Acad Assess/Inst Research/Plng ..... Ms. Alice KNUDSEN

MiraCosta Community College District (E)

One Barnard Drive, Oceanside CA 92056-3899

County: San Diego | FICE Identification: 001239 | Unit ID: 118912
Telephone: (760) 757-2121 | Carnegie Class: Assoc/Pub-S-MC
FAX Number: (760) 795-6609 | Calendar System: Semester
URL: www.miracosta.edu
Established: 1934 | Annual Undergrad Tuition & Fees (In-District): $1,424
Enrollment: 14,494 | Coed
Affiliation or Control: State/Local | IRS Status: 501(c)3
Highest Offering: Associate Degree
Program: Occupational; 2-Year Principally Bachelor's Creditable
Accreditation: WJ, SURGT

01 Superintendent/President ..... Dr. Francisco RODRIGUEZ
04 Exec Assistant to Supt/President ..... Ms. Evelyn DALBY
04 Exec Assistant to Supt/President ..... Ms. Jeanne SWANSON
05 Vice President Instructional Svcs ..... Ms. Mary BENARD
32 Vice President Student Services ..... Dr. Richard J. ROBERTSON
10 Vice President Business/Admin Svcs ..... Mr. James AUSTIN
12 Dean San Elijo Campus ..... Ms. Dana SMITH
20 Dean Academic Information Svcs ..... Mr. Mario VALENTE
38 Dean Counseling/Student Develop ..... Ms. Wendy STEWART
07 Dean Admissions/Student Support ..... Mr. Gilbert HERMOSILLO
88 Associate Dean San Elijo Campus ..... Ms. Nikki SCHAPER
51 Interim Dean Community Education ..... Dr. Alketa WOJCIK
49 Dean Arts/Letters ..... Ms. Dana SMITH
81 Dean Math/Sciences ..... Mr. Carlos LOPEZ
75 Dean Career/Technical Education ..... Dr. Al TACCONE
88 Director Small Business Dev Ctr ..... Mr. Sudershan SHAUNAK
31 Director Community Services ..... Ms. Linda KUROKAWA
06 Registrar ..... Ms. Alicia TERRY
09 Director Institutional Research ..... Ms. Kimberly COUTTS
26 Interim Director Marketing/Commun ..... Ms. Cheryl BROOM
102 Director Foundation/Fund Devel ..... Ms. Linda FOGERSON
18 Director Facilities ..... Mr. Tom MACIAS
37 Interim Director Financial Aid ..... Ms. Cindy SILBERBERGER
88 Director Risk Management ..... Mr. Joseph MAZZA
88 Director Cashiering Services ..... Ms. Jo FERRIS
15 Director Human Resources ..... Ms. Sheri WRIGHT
36 Director Career Center ..... Ms. Donna DAVIS
88 Director Transfer Center ..... Ms. Lise FLOCKEN
96 Director Purchasing/Material Mgmt ..... Ms. Susan ASATO
88 Director Retention Services ..... Dr. Edward POEHLERT
21 Director Fiscal Services ..... Ms. Myeisha ARMSTRONG
19 Director Campus Police ..... Chief Robert NORCROSS
106 Director Online Education ..... Dr. James JULIUS

Monterey Institute of International Studies (F)

460 Pierce Street, Monterey CA 93940-2691

County: Monterey | FICE Identification: 001241 | Unit ID: 119058
Telephone: (831) 647-4100 | Carnegie Class: Master's L
FAX Number: (831) 647-4199 | Calendar System: Semester
URL: www.miis.edu
Established: 1955 | Annual Undergrad Tuition & Fees: $33,950
Enrollment: 780 | Coed
Affiliation or Control: Other | IRS Status: 501(c)3
Highest Offering: Master's
Program: Professional
Accreditation: &EH, BUS

01 President ..... Dr. Sunder RAMASWAMY
10 Exec Dir Finance/Business Ops/Admin ..... Mr. Jai SHANKAR
05 Provost & Chief Academic Officer ..... Dr. Amy SANDS
30 Exec Director of Inst Advancement ..... Mr. Kevin WASBAUER
45 Exec Director of Strategic Planning ..... Ms. Amy MCGILL
04 Exec Asst to the President ..... Ms. Barbara BURKE
06 Registrar ..... Mr. Seamus DORRIAN
84 Exec Director of Enrollment Mgmt ..... Ms. Jill STOFFERS
07 Admissions Officer ..... Ms. Sherre KRUFT
36 Dean of Advising & Career Services ..... Mr. Tate MILLER
37 Director Financial Aid ..... Ms. Regina GARNER
08 Librarian ..... Mr. Peter LIU
88 Program Mgr/Custom Language Svcs ..... Ms. Alicia BRENT
15 Manager Human Resources ..... Mr. Michael ULIBARRI
13 Dir Information Technology Services ..... Mr. John GRUNDER
35 Director Student Services ..... Ms. Ashley ARROCHA
29 Director Alumni Relations ..... Ms. Leah GOWRON
19 Director of Security ..... Mr. Jeremy VONDENBENKEN
24 Media Services Supervisor ..... Mr. Vince MASCAL
18 Director of Facilities Services ..... Mr. Jon GARNER
79 Dean School Trans Inter & Lang Ed ..... Dr. Renee JOURDENAIS
82 Dean School Intl Policy & Mgmt ..... Dr. Yuwei SHI
26 Exec Director of Communications ..... Mr. Jason WARBURG

† Regional accrediation is carried under parent institution Middlebury College, VT.

Monterey Peninsula College (G)

980 Fremont Street, Monterey CA 93940-4799

County: Monterey | FICE Identification: 001242 | Unit ID: 119067
Telephone: (831) 646-4000 | Carnegie Class: Assoc/Pub-R-L
FAX Number: (831) 655-2627 | Calendar System: Semester
URL: www.mpc.edu
Established: 1947 | Annual Undergrad Tuition & Fees (In-District): $1,264
Enrollment: 1,174 | Coed
Affiliation or Control: State/Local | IRS Status: 501(c)3
Highest Offering: Associate Degree
Program: Occupational; 2-Year Principally Bachelor's Creditable
Accreditation: WJ, ADNUR

01 Superintendent/President ..... Dr. Douglas GARRISON
05 Vice President Academic Affairs ..... Dr. Celine PINET
11 Vice Pres Administrative Services ..... Mr. Stephen MA
32 Vice President Student Services ..... Mr. Carsbia ANDERSON
20 Dean Instruction ..... Ms. Laura FRANKLIN
45 Dean Instructional Planning ..... Mr. Michael GILMARTIN
15 Associate Dean of Human Resources ..... Ms. Barbara LEE
35 Dean of Student Services ..... Mr. Larry WALKER
09 Director of Institutional Research ..... Dr. Rosaleen RYAN
06 Director of Admissions & Records ..... Ms. Nicole DUNNE
08 Librarian ..... Ms. Stephanie TETTER
37 Financial Aid Officer ..... Vacant
41 Athletic Director ..... Mr. Lyndon SCHUTZLER
18 Facilities Operations Supervisor ..... Mr. Pete OLSEN
26 Public Relations Officer ..... Vacant
96 Purchasing Agent ..... Ms. Mary WEBER

Mount St. Mary's College (H)

12001 Chalon Road, Los Angeles CA 90049-1599

County: Los Angeles | FICE Identification: 001243 | Unit ID: 119173
Telephone: (310) 954-4000 | Carnegie Class: Master's S
FAX Number: (310) 954-4379 | Calendar System: Semester
URL: www.msmc.la.edu
Established: 1925 | Annual Undergrad Tuition & Fees: $31,924
Enrollment: 2,936 | Female
Affiliation or Control: Roman Catholic | IRS Status: 501(c)3
Highest Offering: Doctorate
Program: Occupational; 2-Year Principally Bachelor's Creditable; Liberal Arts And General; Teacher Preparatory; Professional
Accreditation: WC, NURSE, PTA

01 President ..... Dr. Ann MCELANEY-JOHNSON
05 Provost ..... Dr. Eleanor SIEBERT
30 Vice Pres Institutional Advancement ..... Dr. Stephanie CUBBA
10 Vice Pres Administration & Finance ..... Mr. Chris MCALARY
13 VP Info Support Svcs/Enroll Mgmt ..... Mr. Larry SMITH
32 Vice President Student Affairs ..... Dr. Jane LINGUA
20 Assistant Provost ..... Vacant
09 Asst VP Inst Planning & Research ..... Dr. Heather BROWN
35 Asst VP Student Affairs ..... Ms. Bernadette ROBERT
58 Graduate Dean ..... Dr. Linda MOODY
55 Dean of Weekend College ..... Mr. Merrill RODIN
84 Director Enrollment Management ..... Mr. Dean KILGOUR
06 Registrar ..... Ms. Rocio DELEON
26 Director of Public Relations ..... Ms. Debbie REAM
15 Director of Human Resources ..... Ms. Susan LUSK
18 Director of Facilities Mgmt ..... Ms. Barbara TELL
37 Director of Student Financing ..... Ms. La Royce HOUSLEY
08 Director of MSMC Libraries ..... Ms. Claudia REED
28 Director of Diversity ..... Dr. Pam HALDEMAN

29 Director Alumni Relations ....Ms. Elizabeth ROBLES
38 Director Student Counseling ....Dr. Susan SALEM
07 Director of Admissions ....Ms. Yvonne BERUMEN
36 Director Career Services ....Ms. Marlene SIMON

Mt. San Antonio College (A)

1100 N Grand, Walnut CA 91789-1399
County: Los Angeles FICE Identification: 001245
Unit ID: 119164
Telephone: (909) 594-5611 Carnegie Class: Assoc/Pub-S-SC
FAX Number: (909) 598-2303 Calendar System: Semester
URL: www.mtsac.edu
Established: 1946 Annual Undergrad Tuition & Fees (In-District): $1,380
Enrollment: 28,388 Coed
Affiliation or Control: State/Local IRS Status: 501(c)3
Highest Offering: Associate Degree
Program: Occupational; 2-Year Principally Bachelor's Creditable
Accreditation: WJ, EMT, HT, RAD

01 President/CEO ....Dr. William T. SCROGGINS
05 Vice President Instruction ....Dr. Virginia BURLEY
11 Vice President Administrative Svcs ....Mr. Michael D. GREGORYK
32 Vice President Student Services ....Dr. Audrey YAMAGATA-NOJI
15 Vice President Human Resources ....Ms. Annette LORIA
20 Dean Instructional Services ....Ms. Terri LONG
35 Dean Student Services ....Ms. Carolyn KEYS
08 Dean Library/Learning Resources ....Ms. Megan CHEN
38 Dean Counseling ....Mr. Tom MAUCH
13 Chief Technology Officer/Info Tech ....Mr. Victor BELINSKI
84 Dean Enrollment Management ....Dr. George BRADSHAW
21 Director Fiscal Services ....Ms. Linda BALDWIN
102 Int Exec Director of Foundation ....Dr. Lisa SUGIMOTO
37 Director Financial Aid ....Ms. Susan Y. JONES
46 Director Grants ....Ms. Adrienne PRICE
26 Director Marketing & Public Affairs ....Mr. Clarence BROWN
09 Dir Research & Inst Effectiveness ....Ms. Barbara MCNEICE-STALLARD
18 Director Facilities Planning & Mgmt ....Mr. Gary NELLESEN
35 Director Student Life ....Dr. Maryann TOLANO-LEVEQUE
36 Director Career & Transfer Services ....Ms. Heidi LOCKHART
96 Purchasing Manager ....Mr. Tom MIEKLE
50 Dean Business Division ....Dr. Joumana MCGOWAN
68 Dean Physical Education ....Mr. Joe JENNUM
79 Dean Humanities & Social Science ....Mr. Jim JENKINS
72 Dean Tech/Health Science ....Dr. Sarah DAUM
65 Dean Natural Sciences ....Mr. Larry L. REDINGER
57 Dean Arts ....Dr. Susan LONG
51 Dean Continuing Education ....Ms. Donna BURNS

Mt. San Jacinto College (B)

1499 N State Street, San Jacinto CA 92583-2399
County: Riverside FICE Identification: 001246
Unit ID: 119216
Telephone: (951) 487-6752 Carnegie Class: Assoc/Pub-S-MC
FAX Number: (951) 654-9712 Calendar System: Semester
URL: www.msjc.edu
Established: 1962 Annual Undergrad Tuition & Fees (In-District): $1,052
Enrollment: 13,720 Coed
Affiliation or Control: State/Local IRS Status: 501(c)3
Highest Offering: Associate Degree
Program: Occupational; 2-Year Principally Bachelor's Creditable
Accreditation: WJ

01 Superintendent/President ....Dr. Roger W. SCHULTZ
100 Director President's Office ....Ms. Kathy S. DONNELL
05 Vice Pres Instructional Svcs ....Dr. William K. VINCENT
32 Vice President Student Services ....Dr. William K. VINCENT
35 Dean Student Services ....Ms. JoAnna QUEJADA
10 Vice President Business Svcs ....Ms. Becky ELAM
16 Vice President of Human Resources ....Ms. Irma RAMOS
18 Supervisor Maint & Operations ....Mr. Brian TWITTY
19 Chief of Police ....Vacant
20 Dean of Academic Programs ....Dr. Richard ROWLEY
21 Dean of Business Services ....Ms. Beth GOMEZ
72 Dean Instruct Acad Success/Tech ....Ms. Patricia JAMES
13 Assoc Dean of Information Tech ....Mr. Brian ORLAUSKI
41 Dean of Athletics ....Mr. Patrick SPRINGER
38 Dean Counseling/Stdnt Sppt Svcs ....Mr. Tom SPILLMAN
56 Dean of Off-Site Programs ....Mrs. Laurie MCLAUGHLIN
103 Dean Career Education - MVC ....Ms. Joyce JOHNSON
103 Dean Career Education - SJC ....Dr. Michael CONNER
27 Public Information Officer ....Ms. Karin MARRIOTT
09 Associate Dean of Research ....Mr. Charles HAWKINS
37 Supervisor Financial Aid ....Ms. Shanae WILLIAMS
07 Director Enrollment Management-SJC ....Ms. Cheri NAISH
84 Assoc Dean Enrollment Mgmt ....Ms. Susan LOOMIS
88 Assoc Dean Institutional Planning ....Ms. Rebecca TEAGUE
102 Foundation Director ....Vacant
66 Dean of Nursing and Allied Health ....Dr. Kathleen WINSTON
96 Assoc Dean Purchasing ....Ms. Teri SISCO

† The correct 2009/2010 Fall Enrollment is 15543

Mount Sierra College (C)

101 E Huntington Drive, Monrovia CA 91016-3414
County: Los Angeles FICE Identification: 031287
Unit ID: 398130
Telephone: (626) 873-2144 Carnegie Class: Bac/Diverse
FAX Number: (626) 359-5961 Calendar System: Quarter
URL: www.mtsierra.edu
Established: 1991 Annual Undergrad Tuition & Fees: $20,350
Enrollment: 624 Coed
Affiliation or Control: Proprietary IRS Status: Proprietary
Highest Offering: Baccalaureate
Program: Occupational; Professional
Accreditation: ACCSC

01 President ....Vacant
03 Vice President ....Mr. John DAVIS
11 Chief Operating Officer ....Mr. Z. Greg KAHWAJIAN
07 Director of Admissions ....Mr. Patrick AZADIAN
37 Director of Student Accounts ....Ms. Joyce BOYLAN
06 Registrar ....Ms. Jeanette ANDERSON

MTI College (D)

5221 Madison Avenue, Sacramento CA 95841-3037
County: Sacramento FICE Identification: 012912
Unit ID: 118198
Telephone: (916) 339-1500 Carnegie Class: Assoc/PrivFP
FAX Number: (916) 339-0305 Calendar System: Quarter
URL: www.mticollege.edu
Established: 1965 Annual Undergrad Tuition & Fees: $27,550
Enrollment: 813 Coed
Affiliation or Control: Proprietary IRS Status: Proprietary
Highest Offering: Associate Degree
Program: Occupational
Accreditation: WJ

01 President ....Mr. John A. ZIMMERMAN
10 Vice Pres/Chief Financial Officer ....Mr. David W. ALLEN

Musicians Institute (E)

6752 Hollywood Boulevard, Hollywood CA 90028
County: Los Angeles FICE Identification: 021618
Unit ID: 119270
Telephone: (323) 462-1384 Carnegie Class: Spec/Arts
FAX Number: (323) 462-6978 Calendar System: Quarter
URL: www.mi.edu
Established: 1977 Annual Undergrad Tuition & Fees: $23,175
Enrollment: 1,337 Coed
Affiliation or Control: Proprietary IRS Status: Proprietary
Highest Offering: Baccalaureate
Program: Music Emphasis
Accreditation: MUS

01 President ....Mr. Hisatake SHIBUYA
03 Executive Vice President ....Mr. Jose FERRO
11 Vice Pres Operations/General Mgr ....Mr. Tak SAKIMOTO
05 Director of Education ....Mr. Donny GRUENDLER
05 Director of Education ....Mr. Jon CLAYDEN

Napa Valley College (F)

2277 Napa-Vallejo Highway, Napa CA 94558-6236
County: Napa FICE Identification: 001247
Unit ID: 119331
Telephone: (707) 256-7000 Carnegie Class: Assoc/Pub-U-MC
FAX Number: (707) 253-3015 Calendar System: Semester
URL: www.napavalley.edu
Established: 1942 Annual Undergrad Tuition & Fees (In-District): $1,177
Enrollment: 6,864 Coed
Affiliation or Control: State/Local IRS Status: 501(c)3
Highest Offering: Associate Degree
Program: Occupational; 2-Year Principally Bachelor's Creditable
Accreditation: WJ, EMT

01 Interim Superintendent/President ....Dr. Ronald D. KRAFT
10 Vice President Business & Finance ....Mr. John NAHLEN
05 Vice President Instruction ....Ms. Sue NELSON
32 Vice President Student Service/NMA ....Mr. Oscar DE HARO
15 Dean Human Resources ....Ms. Laura ECKLIN
103 Dean Instruction/Econ Workforce Dev ....Ms. Faye SMYLE
45 Dean Research/Planning/Development ....Vacant
37 Dean Fin Aid/EOPS/Pre-Col TRIO Pgms ....Ms. Patricia MORGAN
13 Dean Institutional Technology ....Mr. Robert BUTLER
12 Assoc Dean Upper Valley Campus ....Ms. Judi WATKINS
07 Assoc Dean Admissions/Records ....Ms. Jessica MILLIKAN
18 Dir Camp Plng/Constr/Risk Mgmt Svcs ....Mr. Daniel J. TERAVEST
102 Foundation Exec Dir/Chf Grants Ofcr ....Ms. Melissa GIBBS
38 Division Chair Counseling ....Mr. Jose HURTADO
26 Director Community Relations ....Ms. Betty M. MALMGREN
19 Director College Police ....Mr. Kenneth L. ARNOLD
18 Director Facilities Services ....Mr. Matt CHRISTENSEN
09 Director Institutional Research ....Ms. Robyn WORNALL
29 Assoc Dir Alumni & Annual Fund Dev ....Ms. Kathy BAIRD
40 Bookstore Manager ....Vacant
96 Business Services Assistant ....Ms. Solange KADA
84 Enrollment Management ....Ms. Sue NELSON
88 Counselor/Coord Trans Center ....Ms. Gwen KELL
36 Counselor/Coordinator WA III ....Ms. Natalie BRADLEY

The National Hispanic University (G)

14271 Story Road, San Jose CA 95127-3823
County: Santa Clara FICE Identification: 025184
Unit ID: 119544
Telephone: (408) 254-6900 Carnegie Class: Bac/A&S
FAX Number: (408) 254-1369 Calendar System: 4/1/4
URL: www.nhu.edu
Established: 1981 Annual Undergrad Tuition & Fees: $9,810
Enrollment: 609 Coed
Affiliation or Control: Proprietary IRS Status: Proprietary
Highest Offering: Baccalaureate
Program: 2-Year Principally Bachelor's Creditable; Liberal Arts And General; Teacher Preparatory; Business Emphasis
Accreditation: WC

01 President ....Dr. David P. LOPEZ
05 Interim Provost ....Dr. Adriana AYALA
03 Vice President ....Mr. Jorge ESCOBAR
06 Director Admiss & Records/Registrar ....Ms. Pamela BUSTILLO
84 Director of Outreach & Recruitment ....Mr. Augustin CERVANTES
77 Director Computer Science ....Dr. Julio GARCIA
09 Director Institutional Research ....Dr. Isabel VALLEJO
37 Director Student Financial Aid ....Mr. Diondrae COLLIER
81 Coordinator Mathematics & Science ....Ms. Cynthia WAMBSGANS
88 Dir Childhood Development ....Dr. Edirle MENEZES
97 Chair Liberal Studies ....Dr. Carlos NAVARRO
53 Chair of Teacher Education ....Ms. Neva HOFEMANN
50 Chair of Business Administration ....Dr. George GUIM

National Test Pilot Institute (H)

PO Box 658, Mojave CA 93502-0658
County: Kern Identification: 667009
Telephone: (661) 824-2977 Carnegie Class: Not Classified
FAX Number: (661) 824-2943 Calendar System: Other
URL: www.ntps.edu
Established: 1981 Annual Graduate Tuition & Fees: N/A
Enrollment: N/A Coed
Affiliation or Control: Independent Non-Profit IRS Status: 501(c)3
Highest Offering: Master's; No Undergraduates
Program: Professional
Accreditation: ENG

01 President/CEO ....Al L. PETERSON
05 Director Natl Test Pilot School ....Gregory V. LEWIS
10 Director of Business Operations ....Mike HILL

National University (I)

11255 N Torrey Pines Road, La Jolla CA 92037-1011
County: San Diego FICE Identification: 011460
Unit ID: 119605
Telephone: (858) 642-8000 Carnegie Class: Master's L
FAX Number: (858) 642-8714 Calendar System: Other
URL: www.nu.edu
Established: 1971 Annual Undergrad Tuition & Fees: $17,604
Enrollment: 16,671 Coed
Affiliation or Control: Independent Non-Profit IRS Status: 501(c)3
Highest Offering: Master's
Program: 2-Year Principally Bachelor's Creditable; Liberal Arts And General; Teacher Preparatory; Professional
Accreditation: WC, ANEST, IACBE, NURSE

01 Interim University President ....Ms. Patricia E. POTTER
05 Provost ....Dr. Eileen HEVERON
11 Exec Vice Pres Admin & Business ....Mr. Richard E. CARTER
20 Associate Provost ....Ms. Debra BEAN
32 Vice President for Student Services ....Dr. Joseph ZAVALA
13 Vice President of Info Technology ....Mr. Christopher KRUG
07 Vice Chancellor of Marketing ....Ms. Ginny BENEKE
30 VP of Dev & Alumni Relations ....Mr. Robert FREELEN
09 AVP Inst Rsrch/Planning & Analysis ....Ms. Marilyn SARGENT
12 AVP Regional Oper So Cal Region ....Mr. Daren UPHAM
12 AVP Regional Oper LAX Region ....Dr. Mahvash YADEGAR
15 AVP Human Resources ....Dr. Alan HONEYCUTT
12 AVP Regional Oper Northern Region ....Ms. Marianne FINGADO
12 AVP Military and VA Programs ....Mr. Vernon TAYLOR
50 Dean School Business & Management ....Dr. Ronald UHLIG
53 Interim Dean School of Education ....Dr. Kenneth FAWSON
54 Dean School Engineer/Tech & Media ....Dr. John CICERO
49 Dean College of Letters & Sciences ....Dr. Michael MCANEAR
76 Dean Health and Human Services ....Dr. Michael LACOURSE
06 Registrar ....Ms. Veronica GARCIA
27 Director Communications ....Mr. Michael BURGOS
08 Director Library Services ....Ms. Anne-Marie SECORD
37 Director Financial Aid ....Ms. Valerie RYAN
26 Dir Information/Community Relations ....Mr. David NEVILLE
18 Director of Facilities ....Mr. Craig CROSBY
88 Director of Credentials ....Mr. Brad DAMON

New Charter University (J)

543 Howard Street, 5th Floor, San Francisco CA 94105
FICE Identification: 041292
Unit ID: 420361
Telephone: (415) 813-5970 Carnegie Class: Not Classified
FAX Number: (415) 813-5980 Calendar System: Trimester
URL: www.new.edu
Established: 1994 Annual Undergrad Tuition & Fees: $2,323
Enrollment: 510 Coed
Affiliation or Control: Proprietary IRS Status: Proprietary
Highest Offering: Master's
Program: Liberal Arts And General; Business Emphasis
Accreditation: DETC

00 CEO ....Mr. Eugene V. WADE
01 President ....Dr. Salvatore MONACO
05 Provost ....Dr. Karen BALDESCHWIELER
06 Senior Registrar ....Ms. Tamica WARD
53 Dean General Education/Liberal Arts ....Dr. Trevor BELCHER

New York Film Academy, Los Angeles (A)

3801 Barham Boulevard, Los Angeles CA 90068
County: Los Angeles FICE Identification: 041188
Telephone: (818) 733-2600 Carnegie Class: Not Classified
FAX Number: (818) 733-4074 Calendar System: Semester
URL: www.nyfa.edu
Established: 2006 Annual Undergrad Tuition & Fees: $40,000
Enrollment: 855 Coed
Affiliation or Control: Proprietary IRS Status: Proprietary
Highest Offering: Master's
Program: Fine Arts Emphasis
Accreditation: ART

05 Provost .... Mr. Michael YOUNG
20 Academic Dean .... Mr. Sonny CALDERON
11 Senior Director .... Ms. Jean SHERLOCK

NewSchool of Architecture and Design (B)

1249 F Street, San Diego CA 92101-6634
County: San Diego FICE Identification: 030439
Unit ID: 119775
Telephone: (619) 684-8800 Carnegie Class: Spec/Arts
FAX Number: (619) 684-8880 Calendar System: Quarter
URL: www.newschoolarch.edu
Established: 1980 Annual Undergrad Tuition & Fees: $23,700
Enrollment: 613 Coed
Affiliation or Control: Proprietary IRS Status: Proprietary
Highest Offering: Master's
Program: Professional
Accreditation: @WC, ACICS

01 President .... Dr. Steven ALTMAN
05 Acting Provost .... Mr. Kurt HUNKER
10 Director Finance & Administration .... Mr. Robert GIROLAMO
32 Director Student Affairs .... Vacant
48 Acting Chair Graduate Arch .... Dr. Vuslat DEMIRCAY
48 Chair Undergraduate Architecture .... Mr. Len ZEGARSKI
88 Chair Construction Management .... Dr. Linda THOMAS-MOBLEY
88 Chair Landscape Architecture .... Ms. Leslie RYAN
88 Chair Digital Media Arts .... Mr. Avery CALDWELL
97 Director General Education Programs .... Mr. Bruce MATTHES
09 Director of Institutional Research .... Ms. Nga PHAN
06 Registrar .... Ms. Maureen QUINLAN
07 Director Field Enrollment .... Mr. John KIM
07 Director Enrollment .... Ms. Dahlia NAJOR
37 Director Financial Aid .... Mr. Mike NELSON
38 Advising Manager .... Ms. Laura WILSON
21 Business Services .... Ms. Terre CORTEZ-FARAH
36 Director Career Services .... Ms. Ellyn LESTER
08 Librarian .... Ms. Karen KINNEY
20 Faculty Coordinator .... Mr. Michael STEPNER
27 Marketing Manager .... Ms. Lisa APOLINSKI
26 Public Relations Manager .... Ms. Anna CEARLEY
35 Student Success Manager .... Ms. Virginia PHILLIPS

*North Orange County Community College District (C)

1830 W Romneya Drive, Anaheim CA 92801-1819
County: Orange FICE Identification: 009742
Unit ID: 120023
Telephone: (714) 808-4500 Carnegie Class: N/A
FAX Number: (714) 808-4791
URL: www.nocccd.edu

01 Chancellor .... Dr. Ned DOFFONEY
10 Vice Chancellor Finance/Facilities .... Mr. Fred WILLIAMS
15 Vice Chancellor Human Resources .... Mr. Jeff O. HORSLEY
05 Vice Chancellor of Instruction .... Vacant
13 District Director Information Svcs .... Ms. Deborah LUDFORD
04 Exec Admin Aide to Chancellor .... Ms. Violet R. AYON
26 District Dir Public & Govt Affairs .... Ms. Kai STEARNS MOORE
22 Dist Director Equity & Diversity .... Mr. Kenneth I. ROBINSON

*Cypress College (D)

9200 Valley View, Cypress CA 90630-5897
County: Orange FICE Identification: 001193
Unit ID: 113236
Telephone: (714) 484-7000 Carnegie Class: Assoc/Pub-S-MC
FAX Number: (714) 527-8238 Calendar System: Semester
URL: www.cypresscollege.edu
Established: 1966 Annual Undergrad Tuition & Fees (In-District): $1,117
Enrollment: 15,889 Coed
Affiliation or Control: State/Local IRS Status: 501(c)3
Highest Offering: Associate Degree
Program: Occupational; 2-Year Principally Bachelor's Creditable
Accreditation: WJ, ADNUR, DA, DH, DMS, FUSER, RAD

02 President .... Dr. Robert G. SIMPSON
03 Executive Vice President .... Vacant
11 Vice Pres of Administrative Svcs .... Ms. Karen CANT
07 Dean Admissions & Records/Business .... Mr. Dave WASSENAAR
08 Dean Language Arts/Lib/Lrng Res Ctr .... Mr. Eldon YOUNG
38 Dean Counseling/Student Devel .... Mr. Paul DEDIOS
06 Registrar .... Ms. Regina FORD
102 Exec Dir Foundation/Community Devel .... Mr. Raul ALVAREZ
32 Dean Student Support Services .... Dr. Richard RAMS
88 Director Disabled Student Services .... Dr. Kimberly BARTLETT
90 Manager Systems Technology Svcs .... Mr. Michael KAVANAUGH
37 Manager Financial Aid .... Mr. Keith COBB
84 Matriculation Manager .... Ms. Kristine NELSON
09 Dir Institutional Research/ Planning .... Dr. Santanu BANDYOPADHYAY
18 Director Physical Plant/Facilities .... Mr. Albert MIRANDA
19 Director Campus Security .... Ms. Shirley SMITH
04 Executive Assistant to President .... Ms. Patricia HUMPRES
68 Dean Physical Education .... Ms. Diane HENRY
57 Dean Fine Arts .... Ms. Joyce CARRIGAN
83 Dean Social Sciences .... Ms. Nina DEMARKEY
53 Dean Science Engineering & Math .... Dr. Richard FEE

*Fullerton College (E)

321 E Chapman Avenue, Fullerton CA 92832-2095
County: Orange FICE Identification: 001201
Unit ID: 114859
Telephone: (714) 992-7000 Carnegie Class: Assoc/Pub-S-MC
FAX Number: (714) 992-9930 Calendar System: Semester
URL: www.fullcoll.edu
Established: 1913 Annual Undergrad Tuition & Fees (In-District): $1,380
Enrollment: 18,827 Coed
Affiliation or Control: State/Local IRS Status: 501(c)3
Highest Offering: Associate Degree
Program: Occupational; 2-Year Principally Bachelor's Creditable; Liberal Arts And General
Accreditation: WJ

02 President .... Dr. Rajen VURDIEN
05 Vice President Instruction .... Dr. Terry GIUGNI
32 Vice President Student Services .... Dr. Toni DUBOIS
11 Vice President Administrative Svcs .... Vacant
50 Dean Business & CIS .... Ms. Ann HOVEY
57 Dean Fine Arts .... Mr. Robert JENSEN
79 Dean Humanities .... Mr. Dan WILLOUGHBY
81 Dean Math/Computer Science .... Mr. Mark GREENHALGH
49 Interim Dean Natural Sciences .... Dr. Carol MATTSON
68 Interim Dean Physical Education .... Dr. Susan BEERS
83 Dean Social Sciences .... Mr. Daniel TESAR
72 Dean Technology & Engr .... Mr. Scott MCKENZIE
37 Director of Financial Aid .... Mr. Greg RYAN
23 Director Health Services .... Ms. Christine KIGER
18 Dir Facilities/Physical Plant .... Ms. Christine FIGHERA
40 Director of Bookstore .... Mr. Nick KARVIA
88 Dean Student Support Services .... Mr. Robert MIRANDA
35 Director Student Affairs .... Ms. Darlene JENSEN
06 Registrar .... Ms. Rena MARTINEZ
19 Director Campus Safety .... Mr. Steve SELBY
38 Dean Counseling/Student Development .... Ms. Lisa CAMPBELL
62 Dean Library Services .... Ms. Jackie BOLL
07 Dean Admissions & Records .... Mr. Albert ABUTIN
90 Academic Computing Technologies .... Mr. Co HO
09 Actg Dir of Institutional Research .... Dr. Anne HOVEY
88 Int Director Transfer Center .... Ms. Delores COMEJO
26 Public Information Officer .... Ms. Andrea HANSTEIN
04 Exec Assistant to the President .... Vacant

North-West College (F)

2121 W Garvey Avenue N, West Covina CA 91790-2051
County: Los Angeles FICE Identification: 011707
Unit ID: 120078
Telephone: (626) 960-5046 Carnegie Class: Not Classified
FAX Number: (626) 960-9190 Calendar System: Semester
URL: www.northwestcollege.com
Established: N/A Annual Undergrad Tuition & Fees: $26,622
Enrollment: 527 Coed
Affiliation or Control: Proprietary IRS Status: Proprietary
Highest Offering: Associate Degree
Program: Occupational; 2-Year Principally Bachelor's Creditable
Accreditation: ACCSC, SURGT

01 Vice President .... Mr. Mitchell FUERST

Northwestern Polytechnic University (G)

47671 Westinghouse Drive, Fremont CA 94539-7474
County: Alameda Identification: 666759
Unit ID: 120166
Telephone: (510) 592-9688 Carnegie Class: Spec/Engg
FAX Number: (510) 657-8975 Calendar System: Trimester
URL: www.npu.edu
Established: 1984 Annual Undergrad Tuition & Fees: $9,000
Enrollment: 809 Coed
Affiliation or Control: Independent Non-Profit IRS Status: 501(c)3
Highest Offering: Master's
Program: Technical Emphasis
Accreditation: ACICS

01 President .... Dr. George HSIEH
05 Dean of Academic Affairs .... Dr. Pochang HSU
07 Director of Admissions .... Ms. Monica SINHA
06 Registrar .... Ms. Lily HSIAO
10 Director of Operations .... Dr. Bill WU
46 Director of Institutional Research .... Dr. Tai HSU
15 Director Personnel Services .... Ms. Linda REN
18 Chief Facilities/Physical Plant .... Mr. Dennis YU
32 Director Student Affairs .... Ms. Wen HSIEH
36 Director Student Placement .... Mr. Michael TANG
38 Director Student Counseling .... Dr. Mariam GHAZVINI
35 Chief Student Life Officer .... Mr. Jeff LO

Notre Dame de Namur University (H)

1500 Ralston Avenue, Belmont CA 94002-1908
County: San Mateo FICE Identification: 001179
Unit ID: 120184
Telephone: (650) 508-3500 Carnegie Class: Master's M
FAX Number: (650) 508-3660 Calendar System: Semester
URL: www.ndnu.edu
Established: 1851 Annual Undergrad Tuition & Fees: $30,202
Enrollment: 1,966 Coed
Affiliation or Control: Independent Non-Profit IRS Status: 501(c)3
Highest Offering: Master's
Program: Liberal Arts And General; Teacher Preparatory; Professional
Accreditation: WC

01 President .... Dr. Judith M. GREIG
05 Provost .... Dr. Diana DEMETRULIAS
10 Vice Pres Finance & Administration .... Mr. Henry ROTH
20 Dean of Students .... Ms. Jean CONDE
84 Vice President of Enrollment .... Mr. Hernan BUCHELI
30 Vice Pres Institutional Advancement .... Mr. Michael ROMO
04 Exec Assistant to the President .... Ms. Gina DORST
49 Dean Arts & Sciences .... Dr. John LEMMON
50 Dean Business & Management .... Ms. Barbara CAULLEY
53 Dean Education & Leadership .... Dr. Joanne ROSSI
06 Registrar .... Ms. Sandra LEE
36 Director Career Development .... Ms. Carrie MCKNIGHT
37 Director Financial Aid .... Ms. Susan PACE
38 Director Student Counseling .... Dr. Dennis C. DOW
41 Athletic Director .... Mr. Josh DOODY
42 Director Spirituality .... Ms. Amy JOBIN
19 Chief Public Safety .... Vacant
23 Director Health Services .... Ms. Karen HACKETT
29 Director Events/Alumni Relations .... Vacant
26 Director Communication .... Mr. Richard ROSSI
15 Director Human Resources .... Ms. Mary HAESLOOP

Occidental College (I)

1600 Campus Road, Los Angeles CA 90041-3314
County: Los Angeles FICE Identification: 001249
Unit ID: 120254
Telephone: (323) 259-2500 Carnegie Class: Bac/A&S
FAX Number: (323) 259-2958 Calendar System: Semester
URL: www.oxy.edu
Established: 1887 Annual Undergrad Tuition & Fees: $44,571
Enrollment: 2,132 Coed
Affiliation or Control: Independent Non-Profit IRS Status: 501(c)3
Highest Offering: Master's
Program: Liberal Arts And General
Accreditation: WC

01 President .... Dr. Jonathan VEITCH
05 Dean of the College .... Dr. Jorge GONZALEZ
11 Vice President Administration .... Mr. Michael GROENER
30 Vice Pres Institutional Advancement .... Ms. Shelby RADCLIFFE
07 Vice Pres Admission & Financial Aid .... Mr. Vincent CUSEO
43 General Counsel .... Mr. Carl BOTTERUD
13 VP for Information Technology Svcs .... Dr. Pamela MCQUESTEN
10 Vice Pres for Finance & Planning .... Mr. Amos HIMMELSTEIN
10 Assoc Vice President & Controller .... Ms. Barbara VALIENTE
18 Assoc VP for Facilities Management .... Mr. Michael STEPHENS
04 Exec Assistant to the President .... Ms. Rebecca STOLZ
32 Dean of Students .... Dr. Barbara AVERY
06 Registrar .... Mr. Victor T. EGITTO
08 Librarian .... Dr. Robert KIEFT
37 Director of Financial Aid .... Ms. Maureen MCRAE
29 Director of Alumni Relations .... Ms. Dana VALK
36 Director Career Development Center .... Ms. Valerie SAVIOR
15 Director of Human Resources .... Mr. Richard LEDWIN
26 Director of Communications .... Mr. Jim TRANQUADA
09 Director Institutional Research .... Mr. Michael D. TAMADA
44 Int Dir Advance Svc Operations .... Ms. Regan REMULLA
39 Ast Dn Stdnts Resid Life/Hsng Svc .... Mr. Tim CHANG
19 Director of Campus Safety .... Ms. Hollis B. NIETO

Ohlone College (J)

43600 Mission Boulevard, Fremont CA 94539-0390
County: Alameda FICE Identification: 004481
Unit ID: 120290
Telephone: (510) 659-6000 Carnegie Class: Assoc/Pub-S-SC
FAX Number: N/A Calendar System: Semester
URL: www.ohlone.edu
Established: 1966 Annual Undergrad Tuition & Fees (In-District): $1,472
Enrollment: 9,904 Coed
Affiliation or Control: State/Local IRS Status: 501(c)3
Highest Offering: Associate Degree
Program: Occupational; 2-Year Principally Bachelor's Creditable
Accreditation: WJ, ADNUR, PTAA

01 President/Superintendent .... Dr. Gari BROWNING
10 Vice Pres Administrative Services .... Mr. Ron LITTLE, II
05 Vice President Academic Affairs .... Dr. James WRIGHT
32 Vice President Student Services .... Dr. Ron TRAVENICK

13 Assoc Vice Pres Information Tech ... Mr. Bruce GRIFFIN
20 Assoc Vice Pres Academic Affairs ... Dr. Leta STAGNARO
15 Assoc Vice Pres Human Resources ... Ms. Shairon ZINGSHEIM
08 Dean Learning Resource/Instruc Tech ... Ms. Lesley BUEHLER
39 Dean Counseling & Intl Programs ... Mr. Eddie WEST
09 Dean Institutional Research ... Mr. Michael BOWMAN
57 Dean Arts and Social Science ... Mr. Walter BIRKEDAHL
76 Dean Health Sciences & Env Studies ... Ms. Gale CARLI
83 Dean Language & Communication ... Mr. Mark LIEU
81 Dean Science/Engineering & Math ... Dr. Mike HOLTZCLAW
88 Dean Deaf Studies ... Dr. Genie GERTZ
102 Executive Director Foundation ... Ms. Susan HOUGHTON
35 Director EOPS/Student Services ... Ms. Debra TRIGG
21 Dean Business Services ... Ms. Joanne SCHULTZ
30 Director College Advancement ... Ms. Patrice BIRKEDAHL
19 Chief Safety & Security ... Mr. Steve OSAWA
18 Director Facilities/Physical Plant ... Mr. Thomas MOORE
37 Director Financial Aid ... Ms. Deborah GRIFFIN
96 Director of Purchasing ... Mr. Alex LEBEDEFF
104 Director International Programs ... Mr. Bill SHARAR
84 Director Enrollment Mgmt ... Ms. Kimberly ROBBIE

Olivet University (A)

250 Fourth Street, San Francisco CA 94103-3117

County: San Francisco — Identification: 666176
Telephone: (415) 371-0002 — Carnegie Class: Not Classified
FAX Number: (415) 371-0003 — Calendar System: Quarter
URL: www.olivetuniversity.edu
Established: 1992 — Annual Undergrad Tuition & Fees: $12,888
Enrollment: 1,079 — Coed
Affiliation or Control: Independent Non-Profit — IRS Status: 501(c)3
Highest Offering: Master's
Program: Liberal Arts And General; Professional; Religious Emphasis
Accreditation: BI

01 University President ... Dr. William WAGNER
03 Vice President ... Dr. Joseph Ray TALLMAN
05 Academic Dean ... Dr. Tracy DAVIS
32 Dean of Students ... Dr. Julia TZENG
10 Chief Financial Officer ... Mr. Barnabas JUNG
11 Chief Operating Officer ... Dr. Walker TZENG

Otis College of Art and Design (B)

9045 Lincoln Boulevard, Westchester CA 90045-3550

County: Los Angeles — FICE Identification: 001251
Unit ID: 120403
Telephone: (310) 665-6800 — Carnegie Class: Spec/Arts
FAX Number: (310) 665-6805 — Calendar System: Semester
URL: www.otis.edu
Established: 1918 — Annual Undergrad Tuition & Fees: $38,300
Enrollment: 1,209 — Coed
Affiliation or Control: Independent Non-Profit — IRS Status: 501(c)3
Highest Offering: Master's
Program: Professional
Accreditation: WC, ART

01 President ... Mr. Samuel HOI
05 Chief Academic Officer/Provost ... Dr. Kerry WALK
10 VP of Administration & Finance Svcs ... Mr. William SCHAEFFER
84 VP Enrollment Management ... Mr. Marc MEREDITH
30 VP Institutional Advancement ... Ms. Carrie STEWART
32 Dean of Students ... Dr. Laura KIRALLA
51 Dean of Continuing Education ... Ms. Amy GANTMAN
07 Dean of Admissions ... Ms. Yvette SOBKY-SHAFFER
06 Registrar ... Ms. Anna MANZANO
08 Director of Library ... Ms. Sue MABERRY
37 Director of Financial Aid ... Ms. Jessika VASQUEZ-HUERTA
88 Director of Galleries & Exhibitions ... Ms. Meg LINTON
15 Director of Human Resources ... Ms. Dana LOPEZ
36 Career Services Specialist ... Ms. Denise GIANOUSSOPOULOS
13 Director of Information Systems ... Mr. Robert WALTERS
18 Director of Facilities ... Mr. Claude NICA
26 Chief Public Relations Officer ... Ms. Margi REEVE
29 Director Alumni Relations ... Ms. Laura DAROCA
96 Director of Purchasing ... Ms. Barbara TECLE
38 Director Student Counseling ... Dr. Fred BARNES

Pacific College (C)

3160 Redhill Avenue, Costa Mesa CA 92626-3402

County: Orange — FICE Identification: 032993
Unit ID: 422695
Telephone: (800) 867-2243 — Carnegie Class: Assoc/PrivFP
FAX Number: (714) 662-1702 — Calendar System: Semester
URL: www.pacific-college.edu
Established: 1993 — Annual Undergrad Tuition & Fees: $26,900
Enrollment: 250 — Coed
Affiliation or Control: Proprietary — IRS Status: Proprietary
Highest Offering: Baccalaureate
Program: Occupational; 2-Year Principally Bachelor's Creditable; Nursing Emphasis
Accreditation: ACCSC

01 President ... Mr. William L. NELSON

Pacific College of Oriental Medicine (D)

7445 Mission Valley Road, #105, San Diego CA 92108-4408

County: San Diego — FICE Identification: 030277
Unit ID: 378576
Telephone: (619) 574-6909 — Carnegie Class: Spec/Health
FAX Number: (619) 574-6641 — Calendar System: Trimester
URL: www.pacificcollege.edu
Established: 1986 — Annual Undergrad Tuition & Fees: $11,085
Enrollment: 622 — Coed
Affiliation or Control: Proprietary — IRS Status: Proprietary
Highest Offering: Doctorate
Program: Professional
Accreditation: ACCSC, ACUP

01 President ... Mr. Jack MILLER
11 Chief Operating Officer ... Ms. Elaine GATES-MILINER
07 Vice Pres of Admissions/Marketing ... Ms. Suzanne KARSTEN
12 Campus Director NY Campus ... Mr. Malcolm YOUNGREN
12 Campus Director CH Campus ... Mr. Edward LAMADRID
05 Director of Academic Affairs ... Ms. Stacy GOMES
06 Registrar ... Mr. Troy HALL
20 Academic Dean ... Mr. Bob DAMONE
37 Financial Aid Director ... Ms. Kyle POSTON
26 Director of Adv and Marketing ... Ms. Gail VOGT
23 Director of Clinical Services ... Mr. Greg SPERBER
08 Head Librarian ... Ms. Naomi BROERING
13 Director of Information Technology ... Mr. Roland ZAKARIA
15 Office Manager ... Ms. Cindy FLOYD
40 Bookstore Manager ... Ms. Nayeli CORONA
21 Bursar/Property Manager ... Ms. Patti HINES
27 Pacific Symposium & Events Coord ... Ms. Tiffany HANSEN

Pacific Lutheran Theological Seminary (E)

2770 Marin Avenue, Berkeley CA 94708-1597

County: Alameda — FICE Identification: 001254
Unit ID: 120740
Telephone: (510) 559-5264 — Carnegie Class: Spec/Faith
FAX Number: (510) 559-2408 — Calendar System: Semester
URL: www.plts.edu
Established: 1950 — Annual Graduate Tuition & Fees: $13,568
Enrollment: 100 — Coed
Affiliation or Control: Evangelical Lutheran Church In America
IRS Status: 501(c)3
Highest Offering: Master's; No Undergraduates
Program: Professional; Religious Emphasis
Accreditation: THEOL

01 President ... Dr. Phyllis ANDERSON
05 Dean of the Faculty ... Dr. Alicia VARGAS
10 VP for Finance and Operations ... Ms. Debora OW
30 Director of Development ... Mr. Brian STEIN-WEBBER
07 Director of Admissions ... Dr. Steve CHURCHILL
08 Library Director ... Mr. Robert BENEDETTO

Pacific Oaks College (F)

55 Eureka Street, Pasadena CA 91103

County: Los Angeles — FICE Identification: 001255
Unit ID: 120768
Telephone: (877) 314-2380 — Carnegie Class: Spec/Other
FAX Number: N/A — Calendar System: Semester
URL: www.pacificoaks.edu
Established: 1945 — Annual Undergrad Tuition & Fees: $24,080
Enrollment: 736 — Coed
Affiliation or Control: Independent Non-Profit — IRS Status: 501(c)3
Highest Offering: Master's
Program: Teacher Preparatory; Professional
Accreditation: WC

01 President ... Dr. Ezat PARNIA
05 Dean of the College ... Dr. Carl KALANI BEYER
30 Vice Pres Advancement ... Mr. Kerry NEAL
07 Associate Vice Pres Admissions ... Ms. Crystal MILLER
32 Assoc Vice Pres Student Services ... Mr. Frank FRIAS
88 Exec Director Children's School ... Ms. Jane ROSENBERG
15 Director of Human Resources ... Ms. Carolyn MATHIS
10 Director of Finance ... Ms. Yug Fon CHIQUITO
53 Pgm Dir Early Childhood Education ... Dr. Wei LI-CHEN
08 Dir Instruct Sites/Library Svcs ... Ms. Diane GRAY-REED
35 Dir Ctr Stdnt Achievmt/Res/Enrich ... Ms. Pat MEDA
06 Registrar ... Ms. Jeanne GENTILLON
13 IT Director ... Ms. Terry UTTER
04 Executive Assistant to President ... Ms. Amy SEYERLE
88 Program Director Human Development ... Dr. Joseph T. SUNDEEN
37 Director of Financial Aid ... Mr. Seph RODRIGUEZ
88 Academic Dir/Instructional Sites ... Dr. Laila AAEN
88 Academic Director MFT ... Ms. Connie DESTITO

Pacific School of Religion (G)

1798 Scenic Avenue, Berkeley CA 94709-1323

County: Alameda — FICE Identification: 001256
Unit ID: 120795
Telephone: (510) 849-8200 — Carnegie Class: Spec/Faith
FAX Number: (510) 845-8948 — Calendar System: Semester
URL: www.psr.edu
Established: 1866 — Annual Graduate Tuition & Fees: $14,910
Enrollment: 229 — Coed
Affiliation or Control: Independent Non-Profit — IRS Status: 501(c)3
Highest Offering: Doctorate; No Undergraduates
Program: Professional; Religious Emphasis
Accreditation: WC, THEOL

01 President ... Dr. Riess POTTERVELD
05 Vice President & Academic Dean ... Dr. Tat-Siong Benny LIEW
10 Chief Financial Officer ... Vacant
30 VP for Institutional Advancement ... Ms. Kathi MCSHANE
20 Asst Dean Academic Pgms/Registrar ... Ms. Delphine HWANG
32 Asst Dean Students & of Cmty Life ... Mr. Donnel MILLER-MUTIA
08 Library Director GTU ... Mr. Robert BENEDETTO
07 Dir of Recruitment & Admissions ... Ms. Nicole NAFFAA
15 Personnel Director ... Ms. Deborah WALKER
04 Executive Asst to President ... Ms. Jen GALL

Pacific States University (H)

1516 S Western Avenue, Los Angeles CA 90006-4298

County: Los Angeles — FICE Identification: 031633
Unit ID: 120838
Telephone: (323) 731-2383 — Carnegie Class: Spec/Bus
FAX Number: (323) 731-7276 — Calendar System: Quarter
URL: www.psuca.edu
Established: 1928 — Annual Undergrad Tuition & Fees: $18,900
Enrollment: 192 — Coed
Affiliation or Control: Independent Non-Profit — IRS Status: 501(c)3
Highest Offering: Master's
Program: Liberal Arts And General; Professional; Business Emphasis
Accreditation: ACICS

01 President ... Dr. Jin Q. KIM
04 Special Assistant to President ... Mr. Jin Song KIM
100 Chief Secretary ... Mr. Jae Young CHUNG
82 Actg Vice Pres/Dean Intl Affairs ... Dr. Zukweon KIM
05 University Dean Emeritus ... Mr. Meyer POLLACK
88 Assoc Dean General Affairs ... Dr. Joan B. WILSON
10 Assoc Dean Strategy/Finance ... Mr. Keith K. KIM
20 Associate Dean Academic Affairs ... Dr. Min Sang KIM
32 Associate Dean Student Affairs ... Mr. Moonsik KIM
50 Director College of Business ... Dr. Kamol SOMVICHIAN
77 Dir Col Computer Sci/Info Systems ... Dr. John MA
88 Director ESL Program ... Ms. Karen CHEN
08 University Librarian ... Ms. Deborah HULL
06 Registrar/Student Financial Aid ... Ms. Namyoung CHAH

Pacific Union College (I)

One Angwin Avenue, Angwin CA 94508-9797

County: Napa — FICE Identification: 001258
Unit ID: 120865
Telephone: (707) 965-6311 — Carnegie Class: Bac/A&S
FAX Number: (707) 965-6390 — Calendar System: Quarter
URL: www.puc.edu
Established: 1882 — Annual Undergrad Tuition & Fees: $33,990
Enrollment: 1,530 — Coed
Affiliation or Control: Seventh-day Adventist — IRS Status: 501(c)3
Highest Offering: Master's
Program: 2-Year Principally Bachelor's Creditable; Liberal Arts And General; Teacher Preparatory; Professional
Accreditation: WC, ADNUR, IACBE, MUS, NUR, SW

01 President ... Dr. Heather J. KNIGHT
05 Vice Pres Admin & Academic Dean ... Dr. Nancy LECOURT
10 Vice Pres Financial Administration ... Dr. Dave LAWRENCE
32 Vice President Student Life ... Dr. Lisa BISSELL PAULSON
30 Vice President Advancement ... Mrs. Carolyn K. HAMILTON
84 Vice Pres Marketing and Enrollment ... Vacant
33 Dean of Men ... Mr. James I. BOYD, JR.
34 Dean of Women ... Miss Janice R. WOOD
08 Director Library Services ... Mr. Adu WORKU
37 Director Student Financial Services ... Ms. Laurie WHEELER
13 Director Information Technology ... Mrs. Maria VANCE
06 Director Registration & Records ... Mrs. Marlo WATERS
15 Director Human Resources ... Mr. Gayln K. BOWERS
21 Director Budgets & Fiscal Services ... Mrs. Joy L. HIRDLER
38 Director Counseling Center ... Mr. Michael JEFFERSON
18 Chief Facilities/Facil Management ... Mr. Dale WITHERS
20 Associate Academic Officer ... Mr. Edwin MOORE

Pacifica Graduate Institute (J)

249 Lambert Road, Carpinteria CA 93013-3019

County: Carpinteria — FICE Identification: 031268
Unit ID: 115746
Telephone: (805) 969-3626 — Carnegie Class: DRU
FAX Number: (805) 565-1932 — Calendar System: Quarter
URL: www.pacifica.edu
Established: 1974 — Annual Graduate Tuition & Fees: $26,484
Enrollment: 674 — Coed
Affiliation or Control: Proprietary — IRS Status: Proprietary
Highest Offering: Doctorate; No Undergraduates
Program: Professional
Accreditation: WC

00 Chancellor ... Dr. Stephen AIZENSTAT
01 President ... Dr. Carol S. PEARSON
11 Chief Administrative Officer ... Dr. Alex MIRANDA
10 Chief Financial Officer ... Mr. David HENKEL
05 Provost ... Dr. Patricia KATSKY

07 Director of Admissions ... Ms. Wendy OVEREND
37 Director of Financial Aid ... Ms. Tracie TEAGUE

Palmer College of Chiropractic, West Campus (A)

90 E Tasman Drive, San Jose CA 95134-1617
County: Santa Clara FICE Identification: 021849
Unit ID: 120944
Telephone: (408) 944-6000 Carnegie Class: Spec/Health
FAX Number: (408) 944-6111 Calendar System: Quarter
URL: www.palmer.edu
Established: 1978 Annual Graduate Tuition & Fees: $8,195
Enrollment: N/A Coed
Affiliation or Control: Independent Non-Profit IRS Status: 501(c)3
Highest Offering: First Professional Degree; No Undergraduates
Program: Professional
Accreditation: &NH, CHIRO

00 Chancellor ... Dr. Dennis M. MARCHIORI
01 President ... Dr. William C. MEEKER
05 Vice Chancellor for Academics ... Dr. Robert E. PERCUOCO
32 Vice Chancellor Student Success ... Dr. Kevin A. CUNNINGHAM
11 Vice Chancellor Support Services ... Mr. Robert E. LEE
84 Vice Chancellor for Enrollment ... Mr. J. Michael NOVAK
10 Vice Chancellor for Administration ... Mr. Thomas L. TIEMEIER
30 VC for Institutional Advancement ... Vacant
17 Vice Chancellor for Clinic Affairs ... Dr. Kurt W. WOOD
46 Vice Chancellor for Research ... Dr. Christine G. GOERTZ
26 Exec Dir for Marketing & PR ... Mr. Darren R. GARRETT
29 Executive Director for Alumni ... Dr. Mickey G. BURT
88 Exec Dir Office of Strategic Dev ... Dr. Judy M. SILVESTRONE
20 Dean of Academic Affairs ... Dr. Thomas A. SOUZA
23 Dean of Clinics ... Dr. Gregory J. SNOW
35 Dean of Student Services ... Dr. William N. DUMONTHIER
09 Sr Dir Institutional Plng/Research ... Dr. Dustin C. DERBY
21 Senior Dir for Financial Affairs ... Ms. Alexis A. VANDER HORN
13 Senior Director of IT ... Mr. Mike A. BENEDICT
15 Senior Human Resources Director ... Ms. Michelle K. WALKER
40 Senior Director of Bookstores ... Ms. Carol A. HOYT
108 Senior Director for Assessment ... Dr. Robert E. PERCUOCO
24 Sr Dir Center for Teaching/Lrng ... Vacant
09 Director of Research ... Dr. Robert COOPERSTEIN
06 Registrar ... Ms. Eliana NATHAN
07 Campus Enrollment Director ... Ms. Julie J. BEHN

† Regional accreditation is carried under the parent institution in Davenport, IA.

Palo Alto University (B)

1791 Arastradero Road, Palo Alto CA 94304
County: San Mateo FICE Identification: 021383
Unit ID: 120698
Telephone: (800) 818-6136 Carnegie Class: Spec/Health
FAX Number: (650) 433-3888 Calendar System: Quarter
URL: www.paloaltou.edu
Established: 1975 Annual Undergrad Tuition & Fees: $17,901
Enrollment: 798 Coed
Affiliation or Control: Independent Non-Profit IRS Status: 501(c)3
Highest Offering: Doctorate
Program: Professional
Accreditation: WC, CLPSY

01 President ... Dr. Allen CALVIN
05 Academic Vice President ... Dr. William FROMING
32 Vice President Student Services ... Ms. Elizabeth HILT
88 Vice President for Prof Development ... Dr. Luli EMMONS
30 Vice Pres Institutional Advancement ... Mr. John KAPLAN
08 VP Information Resource/Library Dir ... Ms. Christine KIDD
10 Vice Pres Business Affairs/CFO ... Ms. June KLEIN
17 Dir of Clinical Training-Ph.D. Pgm ... Dr. Robert RUSSELL
17 Dir of Clinical Training-Psy.D. Pgm ... Dr. Jim BRECKENRIDGE
23 Director of Clinic ... Dr. Sandy MACIAS
06 Registrar ... Ms. Nora MARQUEZ
37 Director of Financial Aid ... Ms. America BRYANT
42 Chaplain ... Rev. Byron BLAND

Palo Verde College (C)

One College Drive, Blythe CA 92225-9561
County: Riverside FICE Identification: 001259
Unit ID: 120953
Telephone: (760) 921-5500 Carnegie Class: Assoc/Pub-S-MC
FAX Number: (760) 921-5590 Calendar System: Semester
URL: www.paloverde.edu
Established: 1947 Annual Undergrad Tuition & Fees (In-District): $1,380
Enrollment: 3,315 Coed
Affiliation or Control: State/Local IRS Status: 501(c)3
Highest Offering: Associate Degree
Program: Occupational; 2-Year Principally Bachelor's Creditable
Accreditation: #WJ

01 Interim Superintendent/President ... Ms. Denise WHITTAKER
05 Vice Pres Instructional Services ... Mr. William SMITH
32 Int Vice President of Student Svcs ... Dr. Kay RAGAN
04 Admin Asst to Supt/Pres/Foundation ... Ms. Denise HUNT
66 Nursing & Allied Health Coord ... Ms. Sharron BURGESON
08 Librarian ... Ms. June TURNER
06 Registrar ... Ms. Melinda WALNOHA
88 Site Supervsr Child Dev/Teacher Ctr ... Ms. Maria KEHL
09 Institutional Research/Professor ... Mr. Brian THIEBAUX
18 Facilities & Operations Manager ... Mr. Albert BRAMBILA
13 Director of Information Technology ... Mr. Adam HOUSTON
26 Outreach & Events Coordinator ... Ms. Sarah FRID
36 Transfer & Career Ctr Dir/Counselor ... Ms. Hortensia RIVERA
45 Dir Econ Dev Center/Inst Research ... Vacant
40 Bookstore Assistant ... Ms. Denise TAYLOR
15 Human Resource Manager ... Ms. Debbie MITCHELL
21 Fiscal Services Manager ... Ms. Russi EGAN
20 Instructional Service Manager ... Ms. Lisa HOLMES

Palomar College (D)

1140 W Mission Road, San Marcos CA 92069-1487
County: San Diego FICE Identification: 001260
Unit ID: 120971
Telephone: (760) 744-1150 Carnegie Class: Assoc/Pub-S-MC
FAX Number: (760) 744-8123 Calendar System: Semester
URL: www.palomar.edu
Established: 1946 Annual Undergrad Tuition & Fees (In-District): $1,212
Enrollment: 27,452 Coed
Affiliation or Control: State/Local IRS Status: 501(c)3
Highest Offering: Associate Degree
Program: Occupational; 2-Year Principally Bachelor's Creditable
Accreditation: WJ, ADNUR, DA, EMT

01 Superintendent/President ... Mr. Robert P. DEEGAN
05 Asst Supt/Vice Pres Instruction ... Ms. Berta CUARON
32 Asst Supt/VP Student Services ... Mr. Mark VERNOY
10 Asst Supt/VP Finance/Admin Svcs ... Mr. Ron PEREZ
16 Asst Supt/VP Human Resources ... Mr. John TORTAROLO
04 Assistant to the President ... Ms. Cheryl ASHOUR
79 Int Dean Languages & Literature ... Ms. Shayla SIVERT
81 Dean Math/Natural & Health Sciences ... Mr. Dan SOURBEER
38 Dean Counseling Services ... Ms. Lynda HALTTUNEN
75 Dean Career/Tech/Extended Educ Div ... Ms. Wilma G. OWENS
50 Dean Arts/Media/Bus & Computer Sci ... Ms. Norma MIYAMOTO
83 Int Dean Social/Behavioral Sciences ... Ms. Judy CATER
13 Director Info Systems & Services ... Mr. Jose VARGAS
84 Director Enrollment Svcs/Admissions ... Vacant
09 Director Institutional Research ... Ms. Michelle BARTON
18 Int Director of Facilities ... Ms. Kelley HUDSON-MACISAAC
35 Director Student Affairs ... Ms. Sherry TITUS
37 Director Student Financial Aid ... Ms. Mary SANAGUSTIN
21 Associate Business Officer ... Vacant
26 Int Chief Public Relations Officer ... Ms. Laura GROPEN
30 Chief of Development ... Mr. Richard TALMO
51 Director Extended Education ... Vacant
19 Interim Chief of Police ... Mr. Tony CRUZ
23 Director Health Services ... Ms. Jayne CONWAY
41 Director Athletics ... Mr. Scott CATHCART
24 Supervisor Media Equipment ... Vacant

Pardee RAND Graduate School of Policy Studies (E)

1776 Main Street, Santa Monica CA 90407-2138
County: Los Angeles FICE Identification: 010441
Unit ID: 121628
Telephone: (310) 393-0411 Carnegie Class: Spec/Other
FAX Number: (310) 451-6978 Calendar System: Quarter
URL: www.prgs.edu
Established: 1970 Annual Graduate Tuition & Fees: $25,000
Enrollment: 100 Coed
Affiliation or Control: Independent Non-Profit IRS Status: 501(c)3
Highest Offering: Doctorate; No Undergraduates
Program: Professional
Accreditation: WC

01 Dean ... Dr. Susan MARQUIS
05 Associate Dean ... Ms. Rachel SWANGER
06 Registrar ... Ms. Mary PARKER

Pasadena City College (F)

1570 E Colorado Boulevard, Pasadena CA 91106-2041
County: Los Angeles FICE Identification: 001261
Unit ID: 121044
Telephone: (626) 585-7123 Carnegie Class: Assoc/Pub-S-SC
FAX Number: (626) 585-7910 Calendar System: Semester
URL: www.pasadena.edu
Established: 1924 Annual Undergrad Tuition & Fees (In-District): $1,152
Enrollment: 26,195 Coed
Affiliation or Control: State/Local IRS Status: 501(c)3
Highest Offering: Associate Degree
Program: Occupational; 2-Year Principally Bachelor's Creditable
Accreditation: WJ, DA, DH, DT, MAC, RAD

01 Superintendent/President ... Dr. Mark W. ROCHA
05 Vice President for Instruction ... Dr. Robert H. BELL
11 Int Vice Pres Admin Services ... Mr. Robert B. MILLER
32 Vice Pres Student/Learning Svcs ... Dr. Robert H. BELL
88 Vice Pres Educational Services ... Mr. Robert B. MILLER
13 Vice Pres Info Technology ... Mr. Dwayne P. CABLE
15 Int Vice Pres of Human Resources ... Mr. Robert B. MILLER
43 General Counsel ... Ms. Gail S. COOPER
30 Interim Dean External Relations ... Mrs. Elaine F. CHAPMAN
09 Int Dir Inst Planning/Research ... Ms. Crystal KOLLROSS
35 Asst Dean Student Affairs ... Dr. Scott W. THAYER
31 Director Extension ... Ms. Elaine CHAPMAN
38 Assoc Dean Counseling/Curr Liaison ... Dr. Cynthia D. OLIVO
88 Assistant Dean Special Services ... Dr. Kent YAMAUCHI
07 Assoc Dean Admissions/Records ... Ms. Dina CHASE
37 Assistant Dean Financial Aid ... Ms. Kim MILES
91 Dir Mgmt Info Svcs/Admin Comp Svcs ... Mr. Dale PITTMAN
26 Director of Public Relations ... Mr. Juan F. GUTIERREZ
18 Int Chief Facilities/Physical Plant ... Mr. Robert B. MILLER

Patten University (G)

2433 Coolidge Avenue, Oakland CA 94601-2699
County: Alameda FICE Identification: 004490
Unit ID: 121071
Telephone: (510) 261-8500 Carnegie Class: Bac/Diverse
FAX Number: (510) 534-4344 Calendar System: Semester
URL: www.patten.edu
Established: 1944 Annual Undergrad Tuition & Fees: $13,440
Enrollment: 963 Coed
Affiliation or Control: Independent Non-Profit IRS Status: 501(c)3
Highest Offering: Master's
Program: 2-Year Principally Bachelor's Creditable; Liberal Arts And General; Teacher Preparatory; Religious Emphasis
Accreditation: #WC

01 President ... Dr. Janet L. HOLMGREN
05 Int Vice Pres for Academic Affairs ... Dr. Richard GIARDINA
10 Vice Pres Finance/Administration ... Ms. Kim PENITENTI
32 Vice Pres for Student Services ... Ms. Darla CUADRA
26 Vice Pres of Communications ... Ms. Deborah DALLINGER
21 Chief Business Officer ... Mr. Andy GANES
06 Registrar ... Ms. Cindi HOGEBOOM
07 Director of Admissions ... Ms. Sharon BARTA
08 Library Director ... Mr. Joshua ADARKWA
84 Dean Enrollment Services ... Mr. Robert OLIVERA
19 Director Security/Safety ... Mr. Richard SWANSON
32 Dean of Students ... Ms. Tatiana GUADAMUZ
37 Director Student Financial Aid ... Mr. Dennis CLARK
39 Director Student Housing ... Ms. Marche SIMON
41 Athletic Director ... Mr. Robert OLIVERA
20 Associate Academic Officer ... Ms. Darlene WILLIAMS
26 Chief Public Relations Officer ... Dr. Glenn KUNKEL

Pepperdine University (H)

24255 Pacific Coast Highway, Malibu CA 90263-0001
County: Los Angeles FICE Identification: 010149
Unit ID: 121150
Telephone: (310) 506-4000 Carnegie Class: DRU
FAX Number: (310) 506-4861 Calendar System: Semester
URL: www.pepperdine.edu
Established: 1937 Annual Undergrad Tuition & Fees: $42,772
Enrollment: 7,539 Coed
Affiliation or Control: Church Of Christ IRS Status: 501(c)3
Highest Offering: Doctorate
Program: Liberal Arts And General; Teacher Preparatory; Professional
Accreditation: WC, BUS, CLPSY, DIETD, LAW, MUS

01 President ... Dr. Andrew K. BENTON
100 Chief of Staff ... Ms. Marne D. MITZE
03 Executive Vice President ... Mr. Gary A. HANSON
04 Execute Assistant ... Ms. Beverly GANDY
05 Provost ... Dr. Darryl TIPPENS
00 Chancellor Emeritus ... Dr. Charles B. RUNNELS
30 Sr VP Advancement & Public Affairs ... Mr. Keith HINKLE
10 Senior Vice President Investments ... Mr. Jeff PIPPIN
43 General Counsel ... Mr. Marc P. GOODMAN
11 Chief Administrative Officer ... Mr. Phil E. PHILLIPS
10 Chief Business Officer ... Mrs. Edna POWELL
27 Chief Information Officer ... Mr. Jonathan SEE
26 Assoc Vice Pres for Public Affairs ... Mr. Rick GIBSON
10 Chief Financial Officer ... Mr. Paul B. LASITER
21 Assoc VP Campus Ops/Business Svcs ... Mr. Alex PANG
06 Assoc VP & University Registrar ... Mr. Hung V. LE
104 Dean of International Programs ... Dr. Charles F. HALL
84 Dean of Admission/Enrollment Mgmt ... Mr. Michael E. TRUSCHKE
32 Dean of Student Affairs ... Dr. Mark DAVIS
08 Dean of Libraries ... Mr. Mark S. ROOSA
61 Dean of the School of Law ... Dr. Deanell TACHA
50 Dean of School of Business/Mgmt ... Dr. Linda LIVINGSTON
53 Dean of Graduate School Educ/Psych ... Dr. Margaret J. WEBER
49 Dean of Seaver College ... Dr. Rick R. MARRS
80 Dean School of Public Policy ... Dr. James R. WILBURN
42 University Chaplain ... Mr. David LEMLEY
46 Vice Provost for Research and Strat ... Dr. Lee KATS
108 Assistant Provost for Assessment ... Dr. Lisa BORTMAN
29 Exec Director for Alumni Affairs ... Mr. Bob CLARK
16 Assoc VP Center for Human Resources ... Mrs. Lauren COSENTINO
88 Director for Church Relations ... Dr. Jerry RUSHFORD
88 Managing Dir Center for the Arts ... Ms. Rebecca CARSON
88 Director of Special Programs ... Ms. Kanet THOMAS
39 Director Housing and Residence Life ... Ms. Kerri HEATH
85 Director Intl Student Services ... Mr. Rich DAWSON
26 Dir Public Relations and News ... Mr. Jerry DERLOSHON
23 Director of Student Health Services ... Ms. Nancy SAFINICK
36 Director Career Center ... Mr. Brad D. DUDLEY
41 Director of Athletics ... Dr. Steven POTTS
19 Director of Public Safety ... Mr. Earl CARPENTER
18 Managing Dir Fac/Physical Plant ... Mr. Robert E. BULLARD
37 Director Student Financial Aid ... Mrs. Janet LOCKHART
38 Director Student Counseling ... Ms. Connie HORTON
96 Assistant Controller ... Mr. David BRANT
09 Director of Institutional Research ... Ms. Lily PANG
88 Director of Educational Research ... Dr. Teresa KALDOR
44 Director Estate & Gift Planning ... Ms. Stephanie BUCKLEY

*Peralta Community Colleges District Office (A)

333 E Eighth Street, Oakland CA 94606-2889
County: Alameda FICE Identification: 001265
Unit ID: 121178
Telephone: (510) 466-7200 Carnegie Class: N/A
FAX Number: (510) 835-4078
URL: www.peralta.edu

01 Chancellor .... Dr. Jose M. ORTIZ
27 Assoc VC Information Technology .... Mr. Minh LAM
26 Exec Dir Public Info/Commun & Media .... Mr. Jeffrey HEYMAN

*Berkeley City College (B)

2050 Center Street, Berkeley CA 94704-1183
County: Alameda FICE Identification: 022427
Unit ID: 125170
Telephone: (510) 981-2800 Carnegie Class: Assoc/Pub-U-MC
FAX Number: (510) 841-7333 Calendar System: Semester
URL: www.berkeleycitycollege.edu
Established: 1974 Annual Undergrad Tuition & Fees (In-District): $1,288
Enrollment: 6,525 Coed
Affiliation or Control: State/Local IRS Status: 501(c)3
Highest Offering: Associate Degree
Program: 2-Year Principally Bachelor's Creditable
Accreditation: WJ

02 President .... Dr. Deborah BUDD
05 Vice President of Instruction .... Dr. Linda BERRY
32 Vice President of Student Services .... Dr. May K. CHEN
88 Division Dean II .... Dr. Harinder SINGH
35 Dean of Student Support Services .... Ms. Brenda JOHNSON
10 Business Services Manager .... Ms. Shirley SLAUGHTER
51 Dir Program Adult College Education . Dr. Nola HADLEY TORRES
88 Dir of Special Projects .... Ms. Denise JENNINGS
27 Public Information Officer .... Ms. Shirley FOGARINO

*College of Alameda (C)

555 Ralph Appezzato Memorial Pkwy,
Alameda CA 94501-2109
County: Alameda FICE Identification: 006720
Unit ID: 108667
Telephone: (510) 522-7221 Carnegie Class: Assoc/Pub-U-MC
FAX Number: (510) 337-0619 Calendar System: Semester
URL: www.peralta.edu
Established: 1968 Annual Undergrad Tuition & Fees (In-District): $1,380
Enrollment: 6,238 Coed
Affiliation or Control: State/Local IRS Status: 501(c)3
Highest Offering: Associate Degree
Program: Occupational; 2-Year Principally Bachelor's Creditable
Accreditation: WJ, DA

02 President .... Dr. Jannett N. JACKSON
05 Vice President of Instruction .... Mr. Duncan GRAHAM
32 Vice President of Student Services .... Vacant
88 Dean Special Programs .... Ms. Toni COOK
26 Chief Public Relations Officer .... Vacant
84 Dean Enrollment Services .... Mr. Alexis S. MONTEVIRGEN
10 Business & Administrative Svcs Mgr .... Ms. Mary Beth BENVENUTTI
88 Dean Acad Pathways/Student Success .... Mr. Maurice JONES

*Laney College (D)

900 Fallon Street, Oakland CA 94607-4893
County: Alameda FICE Identification: 001266
Unit ID: 117247
Telephone: (510) 834-5740 Carnegie Class: Assoc/Pub-U-MC
FAX Number: (510) 464-3528 Calendar System: Semester
URL: www.laney.edu
Established: 1953 Annual Undergrad Tuition & Fees (In-District): $1,144
Enrollment: 13,531 Coed
Affiliation or Control: State/Local IRS Status: 501(c)3
Highest Offering: Associate Degree
Program: Occupational; 2-Year Principally Bachelor's Creditable
Accreditation: WJ

02 President .... Dr. Elnora T. WEBB
05 Vice President .... Dr. Steven COHEN
10 Business/Admin Services Manager .... Ms. Connie WILLIS
49 Div Dean Liberal Arts .... Mr. Marco MENENDEZ
81 Div Dean Mathematics and Science .... Dr. Inger STARK
75 Div Dean Career & Technical Educ .... Mr. Peter CRABTREE
20 Dean Student Wellness & Development .... Dr. Tina VASCONCELLOS
31 Dean Cmty Leadership & Civic Engag .... Mr. Newin P. ORANTE
04 Executive Assistant to President .... Ms. Maisha JAMESON
37 Int Director Student Financial Aid .... Mr. Gary NICHOLES
41 Director Athletics .... Mr. John BEAM
88 Director APASS Program .... Ms. Lilia CELHAY
88 Director Gateway to College Pgm .... Mr. Anthony FLORES
88 Director TRIO Supp Services Pgm .... Dr. Amy H. LEE
88 Director Green Jobs Program .... Vacant

*Merritt College (E)

12500 Campus Drive, Oakland CA 94619-3196
County: Alameda FICE Identification: 001267
Unit ID: 118772
Telephone: (510) 531-4911 Carnegie Class: Assoc/Pub-U-MC
FAX Number: (510) 436-2405 Calendar System: Semester
URL: www.merritt.edu
Established: 1953 Annual Undergrad Tuition & Fees (In-District): $1,380
Enrollment: 5,966 Coed
Affiliation or Control: State/Local IRS Status: 501(c)3
Highest Offering: Associate Degree
Program: Occupational; 2-Year Principally Bachelor's Creditable
Accreditation: WJ, DIETT, RAD

02 Interim President .... Dr. Patricia A. STANLEY
05 Vice President of Instruction .... Ms. Anita BLACK
32 Vice President of Student Services .... Dr. Eric GRAVENBERG
96 Vice Chancellor of General Services .... Dr. Sadiq IKHARO
35 Vice Chancellor Student Services .... Dr. Jacob NG
15 Vice Chancellor for Human Resources .... Ms. Trudy LARGENT
20 Int Vice Chanc Educational Services .... Dr. Michael ORKIN
26 Exec Dir Marketing/Public Rels/Comm .... Mr. Jeffrey HEYMAN
08 Head Librarian .... Mr. Timothy HACKETT
06 Registrar .... Ms. Susana DE LA TORRE
18 Director of Facilities & Operations .... Mr. Robert BECKWITH
10 Int Business/Admin Service Mgr .... Ms. Dativa DEL ROSARIO

Phillips Graduate Institute (F)

19900 Plummer Street, Chatsworth CA 91311
County: Los Angeles FICE Identification: 022372
Unit ID: 110307
Telephone: (818) 386-5600 Carnegie Class: Spec/Health
FAX Number: (818) 386-5636 Calendar System: Semester
URL: www.pgi.edu
Established: 1971 Annual Graduate Tuition & Fees: $22,206
Enrollment: 242 Coed
Affiliation or Control: Independent Non-Profit IRS Status: 501(c)3
Highest Offering: Doctorate; No Undergraduates
Program: Professional
Accreditation: WC

01 President .... Dr. Yolanda J. GORMAN
05 Vice President Academic Affairs .... Dr. Deborah BUTTITTA
10 Vice President Finance - CFO .... Ms. Tanya PONTEP
11 Vice Pres Administrative Affairs .... Ms. Karen L. SEMIEN
07 Director of Admissions .... Dr. Melinda VALENTE
08 Director Library .... Ms. Caroline SISNEROS
37 Financial Aid Director .... Ms. Cristina LOMELI
13 IT/Operations Director .... Mr. Ed NILA
06 Registrar .... Ms. Kacey GUILFOIL
09 Dir Institutional Rsrch/Assess/Plng .... Dr. Elizabeth TREBOW
15 Director Human Resources .... Ms. Theresa WRAY
51 Coordinator Continuing Education .... Ms. Jocceline HERNANDEZ

Pima Medical Institute-Chula Vista (G)

780 Bay Boulevard, Suite 101,
Chula Vista CA 91910-5261
County: San Diego Identification: 666272
Unit ID: 434140
Telephone: (619) 425-3200 Carnegie Class: Assoc/PrivFP
FAX Number: (619) 425-3450 Calendar System: Semester
URL: www.pmi.edu
Established: 1972 Annual Undergrad Tuition & Fees: $10,830
Enrollment: 1,236 Coed
Affiliation or Control: Proprietary IRS Status: Proprietary
Highest Offering: Associate Degree
Program: Occupational
Accreditation: ABHES, RAD

01 Campus Director .... Ms. Kathy HOERSCH

† Branch campus of Pima Medical Institute, Tucson, AZ.

Pitzer College (H)

1050 N Mills Avenue, Claremont CA 91711-6110
County: Los Angeles FICE Identification: 001172
Unit ID: 121257
Telephone: (909) 621-8129 Carnegie Class: Bac/A&S
FAX Number: (909) 621-8770 Calendar System: Semester
URL: www.pitzer.edu
Established: 1963 Annual Undergrad Tuition & Fees: $43,402
Enrollment: 1,099 Coed
Affiliation or Control: Independent Non-Profit IRS Status: 501(c)3
Highest Offering: Baccalaureate
Program: Liberal Arts And General
Accreditation: WC

01 President .... Dr. Laura SKANDERA TROMBLEY
05 Vice Pres Acad Affs/Dean of Faculty .... Dr. Muriel POSTON
10 Treasurer/Vice Pres Administration .... Mr. Yuet LEE
30 Vice Pres College Advancement .... Dr. Adrian STEVENS
07 Vice Pres Admissions/Financial Aid .... Mr. Angel PEREZ
32 Vice Pres Student Affairs .... Mr. Jim MARCHANT
26 VP Marketing/Public Relations .... Mr. Mark BAILEY
44 Associate Vice Pres of Development .... Ms. Holly PREBLE
20 Associate Dean of Faculty .... Mr. Tom POON
88 Assistant Dean of Faculty .... Mrs. Barbara JUNISBAI
06 Registrar .... Ms. Eva PETERS
37 Director Financial Aid .... Vacant
07 Director Admission .... Vacant
09 Director of Institutional Research .... Mr. Jason RIVERA
15 Director Human Resources .... Ms. Marni BOBICH
18 Director Facilities .... Mr. Larry BURIK
21 Associate Treasurer .... Ms. Lori YOSHINO
36 Director Career Services .... Mr. Matt DONATO
29 Director Alumni Relations .... Ms. Brooke HENDRICKSON
38 Director Student Counseling .... Dr. Rebecca KORNBLUH

Platt College (I)

1000 S Fremont Avenue, Building A9W,
Alhambra CA 91803-8845
County: Los Angeles FICE Identification: 030627
Unit ID: 260789
Telephone: (626) 300-5444 Carnegie Class: Bac/Assoc
FAX Number: (626) 457-8295 Calendar System: Other
URL: www.plattcollege.edu
Established: 1987 Annual Undergrad Tuition & Fees: $17,991
Enrollment: 449 Coed
Affiliation or Control: Proprietary IRS Status: Proprietary
Highest Offering: Baccalaureate
Program: Occupational
Accreditation: ACCSC, DMS

01 Executive Director .... Mr. Nicholas EWELL

Platt College (J)

3700 Inland Empire Blvd, Ste 400, Ontario CA 91764-4906
County: San Bernardino Identification: 666056
Unit ID: 432384
Telephone: (909) 941-9410 Carnegie Class: Bac/Assoc
FAX Number: (909) 941-9660 Calendar System: Other
URL: www.plattcollege.edu
Established: 1997 Annual Undergrad Tuition & Fees: $17,991
Enrollment: 594 Coed
Affiliation or Control: Proprietary IRS Status: Proprietary
Highest Offering: Baccalaureate
Program: Occupational
Accreditation: ACCSC

01 Campus President .... Mr. Daryl GOLDBERG
05 Regional Dean of Academics .... Ms. Crystal NASIO
60 Visual Communication Dept Chair .... Ms. Patricia DENYS
75 Paralegal Studies Dept Chair .... Mr. Ugo NWAOHA
75 Info Tech Networking Dept Chair .... Mr. Jeffrey JACKSON
36 Career Services Director .... Ms. Megan FEYER
37 Financial Aid Director .... Mr. Daniel RAMOS
07 Admissions Director .... Mr. Steven WILLIAMS

† Branch campus of Platt College, Ahambra, CA.

Platt College (K)

6250 El Cajon Boulevard, San Diego CA 92115-3919
County: San Diego FICE Identification: 023043
Unit ID: 121275
Telephone: (619) 265-0107 Carnegie Class: Spec/Arts
FAX Number: (619) 265-8655 Calendar System: Semester
URL: www.platt.edu
Established: 1980 Annual Undergrad Tuition & Fees: $27,957
Enrollment: 360 Coed
Affiliation or Control: Proprietary IRS Status: Proprietary
Highest Offering: Baccalaureate
Program: Occupational; Professional
Accreditation: ACCSC

00 Chairman .... Mr. Robert D. LEIKER
01 President .... Mrs. Meg LEIKER
03 Vice President .... Mr. Alfred MEDRO
05 Dean of Education .... Ms. Marketa HANCOVA

Point Loma Nazarene University (L)

3900 Lomaland Drive, San Diego CA 92106-2899
County: San Diego FICE Identification: 001262
Unit ID: 121309
Telephone: (619) 849-2200 Carnegie Class: Master's L
FAX Number: (619) 849-2579 Calendar System: Semester
URL: www.pointloma.edu
Established: 1902 Annual Undergrad Tuition & Fees: $29,510
Enrollment: 3,317 Coed
Affiliation or Control: Church Of The Nazarene IRS Status: 501(c)3
Highest Offering: Beyond Master's But Less Than Doctorate
Program: Liberal Arts And General; Teacher Preparatory; Professional
Accreditation: WC, ACBSP, DIETD, EMT, MUS, NURSE, @SW

01 President .... Dr. Bob BROWER
05 Provost/Chief Academic Officer .... Dr. Kerry FULCHER
10 VP Finance/Administrative Svcs .... Mr. George LATTER
26 Vice President External Relations .... Dr. Joe WATKINS
32 Vice Pres for Student Development .... Dr. Caye SMITH
88 Vice Pres Spiritual Development .... Dr. Mary PAUL
15 Assoc VP for Human Resources .... Mrs. Joyce FALK
37 Assoc Vice President for Finance .... Mrs. Cindy CHAPPELL
35 Assc VP Stdnt Dev/Chf Diversity Ofc .... Dr. Jeffrey CARR
30 Assoc VP University Advancement .... Mr. David MCCURRY
21 Assoc VP for Budget/Accounting .... Ms. Sonia CHIN
84 Assoc VP Enrollment .... Dr. Scott SHOEMAKER
20 Vice Prov Academic Administration .... Dr. Mark PITTS
88 Vice Prov Program Dev and Accred .... Dr. Maggie BAILEY
35 Dean of Students .... Dr. Jeff BOLSTER
13 Chief Information Officer .... Vacant

09 Dir Institutional Effectiveness ..... Vacant
12 Director of Wesleyan Center ..... Dr. Mark MANN
36 Executive Dir Strengths & Vocation ..... Ms. Jeanne COCHRAN
18 Director of Physical Plant ..... Mr. Bruce KUNKEL
86 Dir Cmty Outreach/Government Rels ..... Ms. Megan EKARD COLLINS
107 Dir of External Program Development ..... Dr. Alana NICASTRO
88 Director Center Pastoral Leadship ..... Dr. Norm SHOEMAKER
42 Director of Church Relations ..... Rev. Ron FAY
88 Director of Outreach Ministries ..... Vacant
88 Director of Worship Ministries ..... Mr. George WILLIAMSON
49 Dean College of Arts & Sciences ..... Dr. Kathy MCCONNELL
83 Dean College of Social Sciences ..... Dr. Holly IRWIN
07 Director Graduate Admissions ..... Ms. Laura LEINWEBER
07 Director Undergraduate Admissions ..... Mr. Eric GROVES
08 Director of Ryan Library ..... Dr. Frank QUINN
31 Director Community Life ..... Ms. Melissa BURT-GRACIK
06 Dir Records/Institutional Research ..... Ms. Cheryl GAUGHAN
26 Director Marketing/Creative Svcs ..... Ms. Michele CORBETT
88 Assoc Dean Stdnt Success/Wellness ..... Dr. Kim BOGAN
19 Director of Public Safety ..... Mr. Mark GALBRAITH
29 Director of Alumni Relations ..... Ms. Sheryl SMEE
40 Bookstore Manager ..... Mrs. Janet RAMPENTHAL
28 Dir Multicultural/Intnl Stdnt Svcs ..... Ms. Lily DAVIS
41 Athletic Director ..... Mr. Ethan HAMILTON
88 Director of Nicholson Commons ..... Mr. Milton KARAHADIAN
94 Dir Stevenson Ctr for Women's Stds ..... Dr. Linda BEAIL
104 Director Study Abroad ..... Mr. Frank SERNA
88 Dir of Programs & Operations ..... Ms. Reyna SUND

Pomona College (A)

550 N College Avenue, #206, Claremont CA 91711-6301

County: Los Angeles FICE Identification: 001173
Unit ID: 121345
Telephone: (909) 621-8000 Carnegie Class: Bac/A&S
FAX Number: (909) 621-8403 Calendar System: Semester
URL: www.pomona.edu
Established: 1887 Annual Undergrad Tuition & Fees: $41,438
Enrollment: 1,567 Coed
Affiliation or Control: Independent Non-Profit IRS Status: 501(c)3
Highest Offering: Baccalaureate
Program: Liberal Arts And General
Accreditation: WC

01 President ..... Dr. David W. OXTOBY
05 Vice President/Dean of College ..... Dr. Cecilia CONRAD
45 Vice President Planning ..... Dr. Richard A. FASS
10 Vice President/Treasurer ..... Dr. Karen SISSON
30 VP for Institutional Advancement ..... Mr. Chris B. PONCE
32 Vice President/Dean of Students ..... Mrs. Miriam FELDBLUM
07 VP of Admissions & Financial Aid ..... Mr. Seth ALLEN
04 Special Assistant to President ..... Dr. Teresa SHAW
06 Registrar ..... Ms. Margaret ADORNO
26 Director Public Relations ..... Mr. Mark WOOD
29 Director Alumni Relations ..... Ms. Nancy J. TRESER-OSGOOD
37 Director Financial Aid ..... Ms. Mary BOOKER
36 Director Career Development ..... Ms. Mary RAYMOND
15 Director Human Resources ..... Ms. Brenda RUSHFORTH
41 Director Physical Education ..... Mr. Charles KATSIAFICAS
44 Director Annual Giving ..... Mr. Craig ARTEAGA-JOHNSON
21 Assoc Treasurer/Controller ..... Ms. Mary Lou WOODS
09 Director of Institutional Research ..... Dr. Jennifer RACHFORD
18 Chief Facilities/Physical Plant ..... Mr. Robert ROBINSON

Presbyterian Theological Seminary in America (B)

15605 Carmenita Rd., Santa Fe Springs CA 90670

County: Los Angeles FICE Identification: 041228
Telephone: (562) 926-1023 Carnegie Class: Not Classified
FAX Number: (562) 926-1025 Calendar System: Semester
URL: www.ptsa.edu
Established: 1977 Annual Undergrad Tuition & Fees: $5,760
Enrollment: 211 Coed
Affiliation or Control: Presbyterian Church In America IRS Status: 501(c)3
Highest Offering: First Professional Degree
Program: Professional; Religious Emphasis
Accreditation: BI

01 President ..... Dr. Sang Meyng LEE
05 Academic Dean ..... Vacant
11 Dean of Administration ..... Vacant
32 Dean of Students/Student Ministry ..... Rev. Choong Gi PARK
85 Dean/Director of Intl Students ..... Mr. Mankyung SUNG
08 Head Librarian ..... Mrs. Ruth CHO
06 Registrar ..... Mrs. Mi PARK
88 Administrator ..... Mrs. Michelle YOON

Professional Golfers Career College (C)

26109 Ynez Road, Temecula CA 92591-6013

County: Riverside FICE Identification: 033673
Unit ID: 437750
Telephone: (951) 719-2994 Carnegie Class: Assoc/PrivFP
FAX Number: (951) 719-1643 Calendar System: Semester
URL: www.golfcollege.edu
Established: 1990 Annual Undergrad Tuition & Fees: $28,800
Enrollment: 407 Coed
Affiliation or Control: Proprietary IRS Status: Proprietary
Highest Offering: Associate Degree
Program: Occupational; 2-Year Principally Bachelor's Creditable; Business Emphasis
Accreditation: ACICS

01 President ..... Dr. Tim SOMERVILLE

Providence Christian College (D)

1539 E. Howard Street, Pasadena CA 91104

County: Los Angeles FICE Identification: 041539
Unit ID: 455770
Telephone: (866) 323-0233 Carnegie Class: Bac/A&S
FAX Number: N/A Calendar System: Semester
URL: www.providencecc.net
Established: 2002 Annual Undergrad Tuition & Fees: $21,789
Enrollment: 71 Coed
Affiliation or Control: Non-denominational IRS Status: 501(c)3
Highest Offering: Baccalaureate
Program: Liberal Arts And General
Accreditation: @WC

01 President ..... Dr. Dominic AQUILA
05 Academic Dean ..... Dr. Russ REEVES
06 Registrar ..... Patty TSAI
11 Director of Operations ..... Dawn DIRKSEN
84 Director of Enrollment Management ..... Larissa KAMPS
30 Director of Development ..... Jack HOEKSTRA
32 Dean of Student Life ..... Justin BLEEKER

*Rancho Santiago Community College District (E)

2323 N. Broadway, Santa Ana CA 92706-1640

County: Orange FICE Identification: 006991
Unit ID: 438665
Telephone: (714) 480-7300 Carnegie Class: N/A
FAX Number: (714) 796-3915
URL: www.rsccd.edu

01 Chancellor ..... Dr. Raul RODRIGUEZ
16 Exec Vice Chanc Human Resources ..... Mr. John DIDION
10 Vice Chanc Business & Fiscal Svcs ..... Mr. Peter HARDASH
05 Asst Vice Chanc Education Svcs ..... Mr. Enrique PEREZ
04 Exec Asst to the Chancellor ..... Ms. Debra GERARD

*Santa Ana College (F)

1530 W 17th Street, Santa Ana CA 92706-3398

County: Orange FICE Identification: 001284
Unit ID: 121619
Telephone: (714) 564-6000 Carnegie Class: Assoc/Pub-S-MC
FAX Number: (714) 564-6379 Calendar System: Semester
URL: www.sac.edu
Established: 1915 Annual Undergrad Tuition & Fees (In-District): $1,388
Enrollment: 25,387 Coed
Affiliation or Control: State/Local IRS Status: 501(c)3
Highest Offering: Associate Degree
Program: Occupational; 2-Year Principally Bachelor's Creditable
Accreditation: WJ, ADNUR, OTA

02 President ..... Dr. Erlinda MARTINEZ
05 Vice President Academic Affairs ..... Dr. Linda ROSE
32 Vice President Student Services ..... Dr. Sara LUNDQUIST
51 Int Vice President Continuing Educ ..... James KENNEDY
35 Dean Student Affairs ..... Dr. Lilia TANAKEYOWMA
11 Vice Pres Administrative Svcs ..... Vacant
07 Director Admissions & Records ..... Mark LIANG
06 Registrar ..... Chris TRUONG
50 Dean Business Division ..... Dr. Allen DOOLEY
35 Assoc Dean Student Development ..... Dr. Loy NASHUA
38 Dean Counseling ..... Dr. Micki BRYANT
37 Director of Financial Aid ..... Robert MANSON
41 Dean Exercise Sci/Health/Athletics ..... Avie BRIDGES
57 Dean Fine & Performing Arts ..... Sylvia C. TURNER
30 Director College Advancement ..... Christina ROMERO
18 Interim Plant Manager ..... Ron JONES
79 Dean Humanities & Social Siences ..... Shelly JAFFRAY
81 Dean Science/Math/Health Sciences ..... Vacant
72 Dean Career Educ/Workforce Develop ..... Bart HOFFMAN
56 Associate Dean EOPS ..... Dr. Marsha GABLE
88 Associate Dean DSPS ..... Dr. Elyse CHAPLIN

*Santiago Canyon College (G)

8045 E Chapman Avenue, Orange CA 92869-4512

County: Orange FICE Identification: 036957
Unit ID: 399212
Telephone: (714) 628-4900 Carnegie Class: Assoc/Pub-S-MC
FAX Number: (714) 628-4723 Calendar System: Semester
URL: www.sccollege.edu
Established: 1997 Annual Undergrad Tuition & Fees (In-District): $1,134
Enrollment: 8,942 Coed
Affiliation or Control: State/Local IRS Status: 501(c)3
Highest Offering: Associate Degree
Program: Occupational; 2-Year Principally Bachelor's Creditable
Accreditation: WJ

02 President ..... Mr. Juan A. VAZQUEZ
04 Assistant to the President ..... Ms. Lynn MANZANO
32 Vice President Student Services ..... Dr. John HERNANDEZ
05 Vice President Academic Affairs ..... Dr. Aracely MORA
51 Vice President Continuing Educ ..... Mr. Jose VARGAS
11 Vice Pres Administrative Services ..... Mr. Steve KAWA
38 Dean Counseling ..... Ms. Ruth BABESHOFF
41 Dean Math and Sciences ..... Mr. Martin STRINGER
79 Dean Arts/Hum/Soc Sci/Library ..... Mr. John WEISPFENNING
36 Dean Business/Career Tech Education ..... Ms. Corinne DOUGHTY
20 Dean Instruction/Student Services ..... Ms. Lori FASBINDER
20 Dean Instruction/Student Services ..... Mr. Jim KENNEDY
35 Assoc Dean Student Development ..... Ms. Lorrie JORDAN
07 Assoc Dean of Admissions & Records ..... Ms. Linda MISKOVIC
37 Associate Dean Financial Aid ..... Mr. Syed RIZVI
06 Interim Registrar ..... Mr. Tuyen NGUYEN
18 Physical Plant Manager ..... Vacant

Rio Hondo College (H)

3600 Workman Mill Road, Whittier CA 90601-1699

County: Los Angeles FICE Identification: 001269
Unit ID: 121886
Telephone: (562) 692-0921 Carnegie Class: Assoc/Pub-S-SC
FAX Number: (562) 699-7386 Calendar System: Semester
URL: www.riohondo.edu
Established: 1960 Annual Undergrad Tuition & Fees (In-District): $1,104
Enrollment: 21,262 Coed
Affiliation or Control: State/Local IRS Status: 501(c)3
Highest Offering: Associate Degree
Program: Occupational; 2-Year Principally Bachelor's Creditable
Accreditation: WJ

01 Interim Superintendent/President ..... Ms. Teresa DREYFUSS
05 Int Vice President Academic Svcs ..... Mr. Kenn PIERSON
10 Vice President Finance/Business ..... Ms. Teresa DREYFUSS
32 Vice President Student Services ..... Mr. Henry GEE
86 Dir Govt & Community Relations ..... Mr. Russell CASTANEDA-CALLEROS
16 Director Human Resources ..... Ms. Yolanda EMERSON
26 Director Mktg & Communications ..... Ms. Susan HERNEY
35 Director Student Activities ..... Vacant
07 Dir Admissions & Records/Registrar ..... Ms. Judy G. PEARSON
38 Dean Counseling & Student Dev ..... Dr. Walter JONES
30 Executive Director RHC Foundation ..... Ms. Kerry FRANCO
37 Director Financial Aid & Veteran's ..... Ms. Elizabeth CORIA
18 Interim Dir Facilities Services ..... Mr. John S. RAMIREZ
96 Director of Purchasing ..... Mr. Timothy CONNELL

*Riverside Community College District (I)

450 E Alessandro Blvd., Riverside CA 92508

County: Riverside Identification: 667039
Telephone: (951) 222-8000 Carnegie Class: N/A
FAX Number: (951) 222-8036
URL: www.rccd.edu

01 Chancellor ..... Dr. Gregory W. GRAY
05 Vice Chancellor Academic Affairs ..... Dr. Ray MAGHROORI
10 Vice Chancellor Admin & Finance ..... Dr. Jim BUYSSE
28 Vice Chanc Diversity/Human Resource ..... Ms. Melissa KANE
100 Chief of Staff/Exec Asst to Chanc ..... Ms. Chris CARLSON
12 President Moreno Valley College ..... Dr. Sandra MAYO
12 President Norco College ..... Dr. Paul PARTNEL
12 President Riverside City College ..... Dr. Cynthia AZARI
09 Dean Institutional Research ..... Mr. David TORRES
66 Dean School of Nursing ..... Dr. Sandy BAKER
84 Dean Enrollment Services ..... Ms. Joy CHAMBERS

*Moreno Valley College (J)

16130 Lasselle Street, Moreno Valley CA 92551

County: Riverside FICE Identification: 041735
Unit ID: 460394
Telephone: (951) 571-6100 Carnegie Class: Not Classified
FAX Number: N/A Calendar System: Semester
URL: www.rcc.edu
Established: 2010 Annual Undergrad Tuition & Fees (In-District): $1,117
Enrollment: 9,928 Coed
Affiliation or Control: State/Local IRS Status: 501(c)3
Highest Offering: Associate Degree
Program: 2-Year Principally Bachelor's Creditable
Accreditation: WJ, DA, DH, EMT

02 President ..... Dr. Sandra MAYO
05 Int Vice President Academic Affairs ..... Dr. Cordell BRIGGS
10 Interim Vice Pres Business Services ..... Mr. David BOBBITT
32 Vice President Student Services ..... Dr. Greg SANDOVAL
20 Interim Dean of Instruction ..... Dr. Carlos TOVARES
35 Dean of Student Services ..... Ms. Eugenia VINCENT

*Norco College (K)

2001 Third Street, Norco CA 92860

County: Riverside FICE Identification: 041761
Unit ID: 460464
Telephone: (951) 372-7000 Carnegie Class: Not Classified
FAX Number: N/A Calendar System: Semester
URL: www.norcocollege.edu
Established: 2010 Annual Undergrad Tuition & Fees (In-District): $1,080
Enrollment: 9,131 Coed
Affiliation or Control: State/Local IRS Status: 501(c)3
Highest Offering: Associate Degree
Program: 2-Year Principally Bachelor's Creditable

Accreditation: WJ

02 President .... Dr. Paul PARNELL
05 Vice President Academic Affairs .... Dr. Diane DIECKMEYER
32 Vice President Student Services .... Dr. Debbie DITHOMAS
10 Int Vice Pres Business Services .... Mr. David BOBBITT
20 Dean Instruction .... Dr. Carol FARRAR
35 Dean Student Services .... Dr. Monica GREEN
88 Dean Student Success .... Dr. Greg AYCOCK
08 Dean Technology Learning Resources .... Mr. Damon NANCE
75 Assoc Dean Career & Technical Educ .... Mr. Kevin FLEMING

*Riverside City College (A)

4800 Magnolia Avenue, Riverside CA 92506

County: Riverside FICE Identification: 001270
Unit ID: 121901
Telephone: (951) 222-8000 Carnegie Class: Assoc/Pub-U-MC
FAX Number: (951) 222-8036 Calendar System: Semester
URL: www.rcc.edu
Established: 1916 Annual Undergrad Tuition & Fees (In-District): $35,000
Enrollment: 35,225 Coed
Affiliation or Control: State/Local IRS Status: 501(c)3
Highest Offering: Associate Degree
Program: Occupational; 2-Year Principally Bachelor's Creditable
Accreditation: WJ, ADNUR, ARCPA

01 Chancellor .... Dr. Gregory GRAY
02 President .... Dr. Cynthia AZARI
10 Vice President Business Services .... Mr. Normand GODIN
32 Vice President Student Services .... Dr. Edward BUSH
28 VC Diversity/Human Resources .... Ms. Melissa KANE
20 Dean of Instruction .... Mrs. Virginia MCKEE-LEONE
75 Vice Pres Career/Technical Programs .... Mr. Ron VITO
18 Assoc Vice Chancellor Facilities .... Mr. Orin WILLIAMS
21 Assoc Vice Chanc Finance .... Mr. Aaron BROWN
30 AVC Strategic Comm and Relations .... Mr. James PARSONS
20 Assoc Vice Chanc Educational Svcs .... Ms. Sylvia THOMAS
88 District Dean Open Campus .... Vacant
66 Dean School of Nursing .... Dr. Sandy BAKER
08 Exec Dean Technology/Lrng Resource .... Dr. Bernard FRADKIN
103 Exec Dean Workforce Development .... Dr. Shelagh CAMAK
70 Dean Public Safety Educ/Trng .... Dr. Cordell BRIGGS
88 Assoc Dean Early Childhood Educ .... Ms. Debbie WHITAKER
24 Prod/Artistic Dir Perform Riverside .... Vacant
25 Director Grant & Contract Services .... Mr. Richard KEELER
07 Dean Enrollment Services .... Ms. Joy CHAMBERS
35 Dean Student Services .... Mrs. Eugenia VINCENT
28 Director Diversity/HR .... Mr. Arturo ALCARAZ
41 Dean PE/Athletics .... Vacant
09 District Dir Institutional Research .... Mr. David TORRES
96 Director Purchasing .... Ms. Majd ASKAR
23 District Director Health Services .... Ms. Renee KIMBERLING
19 Chief of Police .... Mr. James MIYASHIRO
72 Dean Technology/Economic Dev .... Dr. John TILLQUIST
14 Director Software Development .... Mr. Rick HERMAN
102 Director Foundation/Alumni Affairs .... Mrs. Amy CARDULLO

Rudolf Steiner College (B)

9200 Fair Oaks Blvd, Fair Oaks CA 95628

County: Sacramento Identification: 667088
Telephone: (916) 961-8727 Carnegie Class: Not Classified
FAX Number: (916) 961-8731 Calendar System: Other
URL: www.steinercollege.edu
Established: 1976 Annual Graduate Tuition & Fees: $13,050
Enrollment: N/A Coed
Affiliation or Control: Independent Non-Profit IRS Status: 501(c)3
Highest Offering: Master's; No Undergraduates
Program: Teacher Preparatory
Accreditation: @WC

01 CEO and President .... Ms. Gayle DAVIS

Sage College (C)

12125 Day Street, Building L,
Moreno Valley CA 92557-6720

FICE Identification: 030695
Unit ID: 410520
Telephone: (951) 781-2727 Carnegie Class: Assoc/PrivFP
FAX Number: (951) 781-0570 Calendar System: Semester
URL: www.sagecollege.edu
Established: 1973 Annual Undergrad Tuition & Fees: $11,825
Enrollment: 587 Coed
Affiliation or Control: Proprietary IRS Status: Proprietary
Highest Offering: Associate Degree
Program: Occupational; 2-Year Principally Bachelor's Creditable
Accreditation: ACICS

01 Executive Director .... Ms. Lauren SOMMA
03 Assistant Director .... Ms. Sharon GOUPIL

Sage College (D)

2820 Camino Del Rio South Ste 100,
San Diego CA 92108-3821

County: San Diego Identification: 666304
Telephone: (619) 683-2727 Carnegie Class: Not Classified
FAX Number: (619) 683-2777 Calendar System: Other
URL: www.sagecollege.edu
Established: 1973 Annual Undergrad Tuition & Fees: N/A
Enrollment: N/A Coed
Affiliation or Control: Proprietary IRS Status: Proprietary
Highest Offering: Associate Degree
Program: Occupational; 2-Year Principally Bachelor's Creditable
Accreditation: ACICS

01 Administrator .... Ms. Tiffany LEWIS

Saint John's Seminary (E)

5012 Seminary Road, Camarillo CA 93012-2500

County: Ventura FICE Identification: 001299
Unit ID: 123855
Telephone: (805) 482-2755 Carnegie Class: Spec/Faith
FAX Number: (805) 482-3470 Calendar System: Semester
URL: www.stjohnsem.edu
Established: 1939 Annual Graduate Tuition & Fees: $29,200
Enrollment: 100 Male
Affiliation or Control: Roman Catholic IRS Status: 501(c)3
Highest Offering: Master's; No Undergraduates
Program: Professional; Religious Emphasis
Accreditation: WC, THEOL

01 Rector .... RevMgr. Craig A. COX
05 Academic Dean .... Rev. Joel HENSON
07 Director of Admissions .... Dr. Mark FISCHER
06 Registrar .... Ms. Esme TAKAHASHI

Saint Mary's College of California (F)

1928 Saint Mary's Road, Moraga CA 94556-2744

County: Contra Costa FICE Identification: 001302
Unit ID: 123554
Telephone: (925) 631-4000 Carnegie Class: Master's L
FAX Number: (925) 376-8497 Calendar System: 4/1/4
URL: www.stmarys-ca.edu
Established: 1863 Annual Undergrad Tuition & Fees: $38,300
Enrollment: 4,099 Coed
Affiliation or Control: Roman Catholic IRS Status: 501(c)3
Highest Offering: Doctorate
Program: Liberal Arts And General; Teacher Preparatory; Professional
Accreditation: WC, MACTE

01 President .... Bro. Ronald J. GALLAGHER
05 Provost/Vice President Acad Affairs .... Dr. Bethami DOBKIN
32 Vice Provost Student Affairs .... Dr. Jane CAMARILLO
20 Vice Provost Undergrad Academics .... Dr. Richard M. CARP
10 Vice President for Finance/CFO .... Mr. Peter MICHELL
30 Vice President Development .... Dr. Keith E. BRANT
26 Vice Pres College Communications .... Mr. Michael G. BESEDA
88 Vice President for Mission .... Dr. Carole SWAIN
84 Vice Provost Enrollment Services .... Mr. Michael BESEDA
107 Vice Prov Graduate/Professnl Stds .... Dr. Christopher SINDT
27 Asst Vice Pres of Communications .... Ms. Elizabeth SMITH
30 Asst Vice President of Development .... Ms. Lisa MOORE
43 General Counsel .... Mr. Larry NUTI
53 Dean School of Education .... Dr. Phyllis METCALF-TURNER
50 Dean School Econ & Business Admin .... Dr. Zhan LI
81 Dean School of Science .... Dr. Roy WENSLEY
49 Dean School Liberal Arts .... Dr. Steve WOOLPERT
35 Dean of Students .... Mr. Scott KIER
08 Dean Academic Resources .... Ms. Patricia KREITZ
42 Director Mission & Ministry .... Br. Michael MURPHY
07 Dean of Admissions .... Mr. Michael MCKEON
15 Director Human Resources .... Mr. Eduardo SALAZ
58 Asc Dean/Dir Graduate Business Pgms .... Dr. Shyam KAMATH
06 Registrar .... Ms. Julia ODOM
20 Assistant Dean of Students .... Mr. Jim SCIUTO
37 Director of Financial Aid .... Ms. Priscilla MUHA
88 Director of Kinesiology .... Dr. Stephen MILLER
57 Director MFA in Creative Writing .... Ms. Brenda HILLMAN
29 Director Alumni/Volunteer Engagemnt .... Mr. Chris CARTER
14 Director of Information Technology .... Mr. Dennis RICE
13 Chief Technology Officer .... Mr. Peter GRECO
19 Director of Public Safety .... Vacant
38 Director of Counseling Center .... Ms. Dai L. TO
41 Dir of Athletic & Recreation Sports .... Mr. Mark C. ORR
88 Director Saint Mary's Art Museum .... Ms. Carrie BREWSTER
71 Director of January Term Program .... Dr. Sue FALLIS
18 Exec Director of Physical Plant .... Mr. Joseph KEHOE
102 Director of Foundation & Corp Rels .... Ms. Elizabeth GALLAGHER
30 Director of Development .... Mr. Daniel G. LEWIS
36 Director of Career Devel Center .... Ms. Patty BISHOP
23 Director Health & Wellness Center .... Ms. Sue PETERS
26 Media Relations Officer .... Mr. Michael MCALPIN
86 Director Community & Govt Relations .... Mr. Tim FARLEY
94 Director Women's Resource Ctr .... Ms. Sharon SOBOTTA
88 Director of CILSA .... Mr. Marshall WELCH
88 Associate Director of CILSA .... Ms. Jennifer PIGZA
21 Director of Finance/Controller .... Ms. Jeanne DEMATTEO
88 Director Ctr International Programs . Ms. M. Susan MILLER-REID
88 Director of Food Services .... Mr. Matt CARROLL
39 Director Conferences & Housing .... Ms. Marie LUCERO
92 Director High Potential Program .... Ms. Angelica GARCIA
28 Dir of Delphine Intercultural Ctr .... Ms. Joan CUBE
09 Director of Institutional Research .... Mr. Sam AGRONOW
88 Dir New Student/Family Programs .... Ms. Jennifer HERZOG
96 Purchasing/Buyer .... Ms. Janie KLEIN

Saint Patrick's Seminary & University (G)

320 Middlefield Road, Menlo Park CA 94025-3596

County: San Mateo FICE Identification: 010074
Unit ID: 122250
Telephone: (650) 325-5621 Carnegie Class: Not Classified
FAX Number: (650) 322-0997 Calendar System: Semester
URL: www.stpatricksseminary.org
Established: 1894 Annual Undergrad Tuition & Fees: $15,382
Enrollment: 93 Male
Affiliation or Control: Roman Catholic IRS Status: 501(c)3
Highest Offering: Master's
Program: Professional; Religious Emphasis
Accreditation: WC, THEOL

01 President/Rector & Vice Chancellor .... Rev. James L. MCKEARNEY
05 Vice Rector/Academic Dean .... Rev. Gladstone H. STEVENS
10 Vice Pres of Business & Finance .... Ms. Jennifer M. MORRIS
26 Vice President for External Affairs .... Rev. James MYERS
32 Dean of Students .... Rev. Vincent BUI
08 Librarian .... Ms. Lauren JOHN
06 Registrar .... Ms. Nuria ORTIZ

The Salvation Army College for Officer Training at Crestmont (H)

30840 Hawthorne Boulevard,
Rancho Palos Verdes CA 90275-5301

County: Los Angeles FICE Identification: 036954
Unit ID: 122269
Telephone: (310) 377-0481 Carnegie Class: Not Classified
FAX Number: (310) 541-1697 Calendar System: Quarter
URL: www.crestmont.edu
Established: 1878 Annual Undergrad Tuition & Fees: $7,335
Enrollment: 106 Coed
Affiliation or Control: Other IRS Status: 501(c)3
Highest Offering: Associate Degree
Program: 2-Year Principally Bachelor's Creditable; Religious Emphasis
Accreditation: WJ

01 CEO/Principal Col for Officer Trng .... Major Tim FOLEY
03 Assistant Principal .... Major Brian SAUNDERS
05 Director of Curriculum .... Major Brian JONES
10 Director of Business Administration .... Capt. Kelly NOLAN
32 Director of Campus Services .... Major Cindy FOLEY

Samra University of Oriental Medicine (I)

3545 Wilshire Boulevard, Suite 350,
Los Angeles CA 90010

County: Los Angeles FICE Identification: 026193
Unit ID: 122287
Telephone: (213) 381-2221 Carnegie Class: Spec/Health
FAX Number: (213) 381-1701 Calendar System: Quarter
URL: www.samra.edu
Established: 1969 Annual Undergrad Tuition & Fees: $7,200
Enrollment: 177 Coed
Affiliation or Control: Independent Non-Profit IRS Status: 501(c)3
Highest Offering: Master's; No Lower Division
Program: Professional
Accreditation: ACUP

01 President .... Dr. Tae Cheong CHOO
05 Academic Dean .... Ms. Deannie JANOWITZ
88 Assoc Dean Chinese/English Section .... Ms. Deannie JANOWITZ
88 Associate Dean Korean Section .... Dr. Youngjune YOON
37 Financial Aid Administrator .... Vacant
10 Senior Fiscal Officer .... Mr. David HAN
23 Clinic Manager .... Ms. Munghwa CHUNG
08 Librarian .... Vacant

Samuel Merritt University (J)

370 Hawthorne Avenue, Oakland CA 94609-3108

County: Alameda FICE Identification: 007012
Unit ID: 122296
Telephone: (510) 869-6511 Carnegie Class: Spec/Health
FAX Number: (510) 869-6525 Calendar System: Semester
URL: www.samuelmerritt.edu
Established: 1909 Annual Undergrad Tuition & Fees: $39,456
Enrollment: 1,473 Coed
Affiliation or Control: Independent Non-Profit IRS Status: 501(c)3
Highest Offering: Doctorate
Program: Professional
Accreditation: WC, ANEST, ARCPA, NURSE, OT, POD, PTA

01 President .... Dr. Sharon C. DIAZ
05 Academic Vice President/Provost .... Dr. Scot FOSTER
10 Vice President Business Affairs/CFO .... Mr. Gregory GINGRAS
84 Vice President Enrollment Services . Mr. John GARTEN-SHUMAN
20 Assistant Academic Vice President .... Dr. Penny BAMFORD
32 Asst Vice President Student Affairs .... Mr. Craig ELLIOTT
21 Asst VP Finance & Admin/Controller .... Mr. Kenneth BOXTON
04 Assistant to the President .... Ms. Margrette PETERSON
66 Dean & Professor of Nursing .... Dr. Audrey BERMAN
63 Dean Podiatric Medicine .... Dr. John VENSON
88 Chair Dept Physical Therapy .... Dr. Terry NORDSTROM
88 Chair Dept Occupational Therapy .... Dr. Kate HAYNER
66 Chair ABSN .... Dr. Nancy HAUGEN
66 Chairperson Undergraduate Nursing .... Dr. Margaret EARLY
09 Director Institutional Research .... Ms. Nandini DASGUPTA
06 Registrar .... Ms. Anne SCHER
08 Library Director .... Mr. Marcus BANKS
37 Director Financial Aid .... Ms. Tanya GRIGGS

07 Director Admission Ms. Anne SEED
88 Dir Family Nurse Practitioner Pgm Ms. Suzanne AUGUST-SCHWARTZ
29 Director of Alumni Relations Ms. Carla ROSS
18 Director Facilities Management Ms. Lillian HARVIN
88 Director Physician Assistant Pgm Dr. Michael DEROSA
15 Exec Director Human Resources Ms. Elaine LEMAY
100 Exec Director Ofc of the President Ms. Stephanie BANGERT
30 Chief Development Officer Ms. Sue VALENCIA
12 Site Manager Sacramento Ms. Rene ENGELHART
12 Site Manager San Mateo Dr. Mileva LEWIS SAULO
13 Dir of Information Technology Svcs Mr. Blair SIMMONS
26 Assoc Dir Media Rels/Publication Ms. Elizabeth VALENTE

*San Bernardino Community College District (A)

114 S. Del Rosa Drive, San Bernardino CA 92401
County: San Bernardino Identification: 667040
Telephone: (909) 382-4091 Carnegie Class: N/A
FAX Number: (909) 382-0153
URL: www.sbccd.edu

01 Chancellor Bruce BARRON
10 Int Vice Chancellor Fiscal Services Charlie NG
15 Vice Chancellor Human Resources Vacant

*Crafton Hills College (B)

11711 Sand Canyon Road, Yucaipa CA 92399-1799
County: San Bernardino FICE Identification: 009272
Unit ID: 113111
Telephone: (909) 794-2161 Carnegie Class: Assoc/Pub-U-MC
FAX Number: (909) 794-0423 Calendar System: Semester
URL: www.craftonhills.edu
Established: 1972 Annual Undergrad Tuition & Fees (In-District): $1,380
Enrollment: 5,635 Coed
Affiliation or Control: State/Local IRS Status: 501(c)3
Highest Offering: Associate Degree
Program: Occupational; 2-Year Principally Bachelor's Creditable
Accreditation: WJ, EMT

02 Interim President Dr. Cheryl A. MARSHALL
05 Vice President of Instruction Dr. Cheryl A. MARSHALL
11 Vice President Administrative Svcs Mr. Mike STRONG
32 Exec VP Instruction/Student Svcs Ms. Rebeccah WARREN-MARLATT
88 Dean Stdnt Svcs/Stdnt Development Mr. Joe CABRALES
49 Dean of Arts & Sciences Mr. Richard HOGREFE
81 Dean Math/English/Reading/Inst Supp Mr. Raju HEGDE
36 Dean Career Educ & Human Devel Ms. June Y. YAMAMOTO
35 Dean Student Services Ms. Kirsten S. COLVEY
09 Dean Instl Effect/Research/Planning Mr. Keith WURTZ
30 Director Resource Development Ms. Cheryl BARDOWELL
40 Director Bookstore Ms. Gloriann CHAVEZ
88 Director EOPS/CARE Ms. Rejoice CHAVIRA
25 Director Grant Mgt & Development Ms. Karen CHILDERS
37 Director Financial Aid Mr. John W. MUSKAVITCH
32 Director Student Life Ms. Ericka PADDOCK
18 Director Facilities Mr. Larry COOK
13 Director Technology Services Mr. Wayne BOGH
26 Director Marketing/Public Relations Ms. Alisa SPARKIA MOORE
08 Librarian Ms. Laura WINNINGHAM

*San Bernardino Valley College (C)

701 S Mt. Vernon Avenue,
San Bernardino CA 92410-2798
County: San Bernardino FICE Identification: 001272
Unit ID: 123527
Telephone: (909) 384-4400 Carnegie Class: Assoc/Pub-U-MC
FAX Number: N/A Calendar System: Semester
URL: www.valleycollege.edu
Established: 1926 Annual Undergrad Tuition & Fees (In-District): $1,380
Enrollment: 12,380 Coed
Affiliation or Control: State/Local IRS Status: 501(c)3
Highest Offering: Associate Degree
Program: Occupational; 2-Year Principally Bachelor's Creditable
Accreditation: WJ, ADNUR

02 Interim President Dr. Larry BUCKLEY
05 Interim Vice President Instruction Dr. Haragewen KINDE
11 Vice President Administrative Svcs Mr. Jim HANSEN
32 Vice President Student Services Mr. Damon BELL
08 Dean Library/Learning Support Serv Ms. Marie MESTAS
38 Dean Counseling/Matriculation Mr. Marco COTA
07 Assoc Dean Admissions/Records Mr. Dan ANGELO
26 Director Marketing/Public Relations Mr. Craig PETINAK
88 Director Child Development Ctr Mr. Mark MERJIL
23 Director Health Services Ms. Elaine AKERS
45 Director Resource Development Mrs. Donna HOFFMAN
40 Director Bookstores Ms. Gloriann CHAVEZ
09 Director Institutional Research Dr. James SMITH
37 Director Student Financial Aid Mr. Joseph NGUYEN
68 Dean SS/Human Development & PE Dr. Cory SCHWARTZ
50 Int Dean Math/Bus/Computer Tech Mr. Roger POWELL
76 Dean Sciences Dr. Susan BANGASSER
79 Dean Arts & Humanities Dr. Kay WEISS
72 Int Dean AT/TRANS/CULA Dr. Achala CHATTERJEE
75 Dean Stdnt Success/Special Services Dr. Zelma RUSS

San Diego Christian College (D)

2100 Greenfield Drive, El Cajon CA 92019-1157
County: San Diego FICE Identification: 012031
Unit ID: 112084
Telephone: (619) 201-8700 Carnegie Class: Bac/A&S
FAX Number: (619) 201-8749 Calendar System: Semester
URL: www.sdcc.edu
Established: 1970 Annual Undergrad Tuition & Fees: $25,208
Enrollment: 410 Coed
Affiliation or Control: Independent Non-Profit IRS Status: 501(c)3
Highest Offering: Baccalaureate
Program: Liberal Arts And General; Teacher Preparatory
Accreditation: WC

01 President Dr. Paul E. AGUE
04 Exec Assistant to the President Mrs. Sarah CLARK
10 Dean for Administration and Finance Mr. Robert JENSEN
05 VP for Academic Affairs Dr. Jon DEPRIEST
32 VP for Student Services Mr. David MADDOX
07 Director of Enrollment Services Mrs. Susie M. PARKS
37 Director of Financial Aid Vacant
07 Director of Admissions Ms. Candice DELGIUDICE
42 Director of Spiritual Life Mr. Steve JENKINS
30 Director of Advancement Mr. Victor CONNER
15 Director of Human Resources Mr. Robert JENSEN
08 Director of Library Services Ms. Ruth MARTIN
29 Manager of Alumni/Donor Relations Ms. Amanda GRAHAM
09 Dean of Assessment and Planning Mrs. Lundie CARSTENSEN
41 Athletic Director Mr. Chris BANDO
23 Director of Health Services Mrs. Malia JENKINS
28 Director of Diversity Mr. Carl CALDERSON

*San Diego Community College District Administrative Offices (E)

3375 Camino Del Rio South, San Diego CA 92108-3883
County: San Diego FICE Identification: 008895
Unit ID: 122339
Telephone: (619) 388-6500 Carnegie Class: N/A
FAX Number: (619) 388-6913
URL: www.sdccd.edu

01 Chancellor Dr. Constance M. CARROLL
05 Vice Chanc Instructional Svcs Dr. Otto LEE
10 Exec Vice Chanc Business Services Dr. Bonnie Ann DOWD
15 Vice Chancellor Human Resources Mr. Will SURBROOK
18 Vice Chanc Facilities Management Mr. David UMSTOT
32 Vice Chancellor Student Services Ms. Lynn C. NEAULT
26 Director Pub Info & Govt Relations Mr. Richard DITTBENNER
43 Director Legal Services & EEO Ms. Mary ROGERS

*San Diego City College (F)

1313 Park Boulevard, San Diego CA 92101-4787
County: San Diego FICE Identification: 001273
Unit ID: 122320
Telephone: (619) 388-3400 Carnegie Class: Not Classified
FAX Number: (619) 388-3063 Calendar System: Semester
URL: www.sdcity.edu
Established: 1914 Annual Undergrad Tuition & Fees (In-District): $2,765
Enrollment: 17,593 Coed
Affiliation or Control: State/Local IRS Status: 501(c)3
Highest Offering: Associate Degree
Program: Occupational; 2-Year Principally Bachelor's Creditable
Accreditation: WJ, ADNUR

02 President Dr. Terrence BURGESS
05 Acting Vice President Instruction Dr. Randall BARNES
32 Vice President Student Services Mr. Peter WHITE
11 Vice President of Admin Services Ms. Jacquelin BELL
35 Dean of Student Affairs Ms. Denise WHISENHUNT
08 Dean Information/Learning Tech Mr. Robbi EWELL
79 Int Dean School of Arts/Humanities Ms. Trudy GERALD
50 Dean Sch Business/Info Tech Dr. Randall BARNES
88 Dean Student Develop/Matriculation Ms. Helen ELIAS
88 Dean Engr & Tech/Math/Sci/Nurs Dr. Minou SPRADLEY
56 Director Off-Campus Programs Ms. Jeanie TYLER
18 Chief Facilities/Physical Plant Mr. Derrall CHANDLER
92 Director Honors Program Dr. Kelly MAYHEW
07 Admissions & Records Supervisor Ms. Lou HUMPHRIES
22 Affirmative Action Officer Mr. Edwin HIEL
40 Bookstore Supervisor Ms. DeeDee PORTER
26 Public Information Officer Ms. Heidi BUNKOWSKE
88 PgmMgr Disabled Student Services Ms. Debra WRIGHT-HOWARD
37 Financial Aid Supervisor Mr. Gregory SANCHEZ
88 Director EOPS Vacant
83 Dean Behav & Soc Sci/Consumer Stds Ms. Lori ERRECA
68 Dean Health/Exercise Sci/Athletics Ms. Kathy MCGINNIS

*San Diego Mesa College (G)

7250 Mesa College Drive, San Diego CA 92111-4998
County: San Diego FICE Identification: 001275
Unit ID: 122375
Telephone: (619) 388-2721 Carnegie Class: Assoc/Pub-U-MC
FAX Number: (619) 388-2929 Calendar System: Semester
URL: www.sdmesa.edu
Established: 1962 Annual Undergrad Tuition & Fees (In-District): $900
Enrollment: 24,667 Coed
Affiliation or Control: State/Local IRS Status: 501(c)3
Highest Offering: Associate Degree
Program: Occupational; 2-Year Principally Bachelor's Creditable
Accreditation: WJ, DA, PTAA, RAD

02 President Dr. Pamela T. LUSTER
05 Vice President Instruction Dr. Tim MCGRATH
32 Interim VP Student Services Ms. Denise WHISENHUNT
11 Actg VP Administrative Services Mr. William CRAFT
88 Actg Dean Student Development Ms. Ashanti HANDS
79 Dean Arts & Languages Mr. Jonathan FOHRMAN
76 Dean Health Sciences/Public Svc Ms. Margie FRITCH
81 Dean School Math/Natural Sciences Dr. Saeid EIDGAHY
50 Dean Sch Business Technology Dr. Jill BAKER
62 Dean Lrng Resource/Educational Tech Mr. William P. CRAFT
68 Dean PE/Health Educ & Athletics Mr. Dave EVANS
79 Dean Humanities Mr. Andrew J. MACNEILL
83 Int Dean Social/Behav Sci/Mult Stds Dr. Charlotta ROBERTSON
35 Int Dean Student Affairs Mr. Larry MAXEY
20 Dn Instruct Svcs/Resource Dev/Rsrch Vacant
27 Public Information Officer Ms. Lina HEIL
37 Financial Aid Officer Ms. Gilda MALDONADO
07 Student Svcs Supervisor Admission Ms. Ivonne ALVAREZ
04 Exec Asst to the President Ms. Sara Beth CAIN

*San Diego Miramar College (H)

10440 Black Mountain Road, San Diego CA 92126-2999
County: San Diego FICE Identification: 011820
Unit ID: 122384
Telephone: (619) 388-7800 Carnegie Class: Assoc/Pub-U-MC
FAX Number: (619) 388-7901 Calendar System: Semester
URL: www.sdmiramar.edu
Established: 1969 Annual Undergrad Tuition & Fees (In-District): $1,104
Enrollment: 12,589 Coed
Affiliation or Control: State/Local IRS Status: 501(c)3
Highest Offering: Associate Degree
Program: 2-Year Principally Bachelor's Creditable
Accreditation: WJ

02 President Dr. Patricia HSIEH
05 Vice President Instruction Dr. Jerry BUCKLEY
32 Vice President Student Services Mr. Gerald RAMSEY
10 Vice President Admin Services Mr. Brett BELL
49 Dean of Liberal Arts Dr. Louis ASCIONE
36 Dean Career Tech/Wrkfce Initiatives Mr. Greg NEWHOUSE
50 Dean Business/Mathematics/Science Dr. Paulette HOPKINS
61 Dean of Public Safety Mr. George BEITEY
20 Physical Sciences Co-Chair Dr. Linda WOODS
26 Public Info Ofcr/Dir Alumni Rels Ms. Sandi TREVISAN
37 Financial Aid Officer Ms. Teresa VILABOY
06 Registrar Ms. Lynn NEAULT
15 Vice Chancellor Human Resources Mr. Will SURBROOK
18 Chief Facilities/Physical Plant Mr. Dane LINDSAY
88 Child Development Ms. Dawn BURGESS
35 Dean of Student Affairs Ms. Adela JACOBSON
08 Library Chair Ms. Mary HART
07 Admissions Supervisor Ms. Dana STACK
88 Chair Admin Justice/Police Acad Mr. Steve LICKISS
50 Chair Business Mr. Alan VIERSEN
72 Chair Fire Science Ms. Mary KJARTANSON
79 Chair Arts & Humanities Mr. Robert FRITSCH
81 Chair Math Mr. Harvey WILENSKY
83 Chair Social Sciences Mr. Thomas SCHILZ
88 Chair Trade/Ind/Aviation Mtn Tech Mr. David BUSER
88 Spec Proj Mgr/Advanc Transp Tech Mr. Greg NEWHOUSE
88 Chair Diesel Technology Mr. Dan WILLKIE
38 Chair Counseling Mr. David NAVARRO
76 Chair Dept of Natural Sciences Dr. Marie MCMAHON
68 Chair Exercise Science Mr. Rod PORTER
60 Chair Comm/English & World Language Ms. Sheryl GOBBLE
88 Co-Chair Automotive Mr. Joseph YOUNG

San Francisco Art Institute (I)

800 Chestnut Street, San Francisco CA 94133-2206
County: San Francisco FICE Identification: 003948
Unit ID: 122454
Telephone: (415) 771-7020 Carnegie Class: Spec/Arts
FAX Number: (415) 749-4590 Calendar System: Semester
URL: www.sfai.edu
Established: 1871 Annual Undergrad Tuition & Fees: $35,748
Enrollment: 668 Coed
Affiliation or Control: Independent Non-Profit IRS Status: 501(c)3
Highest Offering: Master's
Program: Professional; Fine Arts Emphasis
Accreditation: WC, ART

01 President Charles DESMARAIS
05 Acting VP and Dean Academic Affairs Jennifer RISSLER
88 VP Exhibitions and Public Programs Vacant
07 VP Enrollment and Student Affairs Elizabeth O'BRIEN
30 VP of Institutional Advancement Cynthia COLEBROOK
10 Chief Operating Officer Espi SANJANA
04 Exec Assistant to the President Michelle BLADE
32 Dean of Students Megann SEPT
25 Director of Academic Administration Sarah EWICK
06 Registrar Ken SCHWARTZ
88 Area Mgr School of Studio Practice Sherry KNUTSON
88 Dir Dgtl Studies & Trans-Disc Tech Paul KLEIN
20 Asst Dean for Academic Success Susan MARTIN
58 Director of Graduate Administration Zeina BARAKEH
58 Dir MA Pgm and Co-Dir Low-Resd MFA Claire DAIGLE
58 Director of MFA Programs Tony LABAT
08 Director of Library Services Jeff GUNDERSON

88 Director of City Studio ... JD BELTRAN
51 Director of Community Education ... Barbara GARBER
35 Assistant Dean of Students ... Anthony MOLINAR
38 Director of Counseling Services ... Marina CHATTERTON
26 Dir Marketing & Inst Messaging ... Janette ANDRAWES
37 Director of Financial Aid ... Larry BLAIR
13 Director of Information Technology ... Andrew SIMAS
21 Controller ... Susan WAYLAND
18 Administrative Services Director ... Heather HICKMAN
09 Inst Research & Acad Planning Assoc ... Jose DE LOS REYES
88 Director of the Writing Program ... Christina BOUFIS
88 Graduate Center Director ... Ian KIMMERLY
58 Co-Dir Low-Residency MFA Program ... Allan DE SOUZA
104 Asst Dir Student Life Global Pgm ... Shannon PLATH
88 Assoc Dir of Admissions Operations ... Jeremy SIMMONS
44 Director of Institutional Giving ... Polly SPRINGHORN
29 Manager of Alumni Relations ... Julie WEINBERG
15 Human Resources Administrator ... Joanie PACHECO
90 Academic Computing Manager ... Jeremy HOBBS

San Francisco Conservatory of Music (A)

50 Oak Street, San Francisco CA 94102-6011
County: San Francisco FICE Identification: 001278
Unit ID: 122506
Telephone: (415) 864-7326 Carnegie Class: Spec/Arts
FAX Number: (415) 503-6299 Calendar System: Semester
URL: www.sfcm.edu
Established: 1917 Annual Undergrad Tuition & Fees: $37,600
Enrollment: 380 Coed
Affiliation or Control: Independent Non-Profit IRS Status: 501(c)3
Highest Offering: Beyond Master's But Less Than Doctorate
Program: Professional; Music Emphasis
Accreditation: WC, MUS

01 President ... Colin MURDOCH
05 Dean ... Mary Ellen POOLE
32 Associate Dean of Student Life ... Jason SMITH
10 Vice Pres Finance & Administration ... Kathryn WITTENMYER
30 Vice President of Advancement ... Elizabeth TOUMA
07 Director of Admission ... Melissa COCCO-MITTEN
56 Director Preparatory/Extension ... Joan GORDON
26 Director of Communications ... Sam SMITH
30 Director of Development ... Murrey NELSON
04 Executive Assistant to President ... Jennifer SEAMAN
31 Performance Outreach Manager ... Elisabeth LOWRY
20 Assistant to the Dean ... Alice BECKETT
15 Human Resources Manager ... Michael PATTERSON
37 Director of Financial Aid ... Doris HOWARD
18 Chief Facilities Engineer ... David MITCHELL
06 Registrar ... Jonas WRIGHT
08 Head Librarian ... Kevin MCLAUGHLIN

San Francisco Theological Seminary (B)

105 Seminary Road, San Anselmo CA 94960-2997
County: Marin FICE Identification: 001279
Unit ID: 122603
Telephone: (415) 451-2800 Carnegie Class: Spec/Faith
FAX Number: (415) 451-2852 Calendar System: Semester
URL: www.sfts.edu
Established: 1871 Annual Graduate Tuition & Fees: $11,400
Enrollment: 205 Coed
Affiliation or Control: Presbyterian Church (U.S.A.) IRS Status: 501(c)3
Highest Offering: Doctorate; No Undergraduates
Program: Professional; Religious Emphasis
Accreditation: WC, THEOL

01 President ... Dr. James L. MCDONALD
05 Dean of the Seminary ... Dr. Elizabeth LIEBERT
30 VP Inst Advancement ... Ms. Cecilia TONSING
10 Vice Pres Administration/Finance ... Ms. Barbara BRENNER-BUDER
26 VP Communications ... Ms. Kay CARNEY
84 Director of Enrollment ... Ms. Elizabeth MCCORD
04 Exec Administrator to President ... Ms. Bonnie JOHNSTON
42 Chaplain & Assoc Dean Student Srvce ... Mr. Scott CLARK
36 Dir Vocational Formation Placement ... Rev. Leslie VEEN
06 Registrar ... Dr. Polly COOTE
21 Controller ... Ms. Susan BURNNETT
18 Chief of Physical Plant ... Mr. Gary MILLER
91 Director of IT ... Mr. Larry PICKARD
39 Director Student Housing ... Ms. Gail LU
15 Dir Human Resources ... Ms. Bonnie BLANK
44 Director of Annual Gifts ... Ms. Sarah CAMPBELL

San Joaquin College of Law (C)

901 Fifth Street, Clovis CA 93612-1312
County: Fresno FICE Identification: 025000
Unit ID: 122649
Telephone: (559) 323-2100 Carnegie Class: Spec/Law
FAX Number: (559) 323-5566 Calendar System: Semester
URL: www.sjcl.edu
Established: 1969 Annual Graduate Tuition & Fees: $18,113
Enrollment: 201 Coed
Affiliation or Control: Independent Non-Profit IRS Status: 501(c)3
Highest Offering: Doctorate; No Undergraduates
Program: Professional
Accreditation: WC

01 Dean ... Janice L. PEARSON
05 Dean Academic Affairs ... Sally A. PERRING
11 Director of Operations ... Joan K. LASSLEY
10 Chief Financial Officer ... Jill A. RANDLES
32 Director of Student Services ... Joyce K. MORODOMI
37 Financial Aid Administrator ... Jeannie M. LEWIS
08 Library Director ... Peter K. ROONEY
26 Public Relations Director ... Missy M. CARTIER
15 Chief of Personnel ... Beth PITCOCK
30 Chief Development ... Janice L. PEARSON
84 Director Enrollment Management ... Diane M. STEEL
61 Law Program Coordinator ... Pat A. SMITH

San Joaquin Delta College (D)

5151 Pacific Avenue, Stockton CA 95207-6370
County: San Joaquin FICE Identification: 001280
Unit ID: 122658
Telephone: (209) 954-5151 Carnegie Class: Assoc/Pub-U-MC
FAX Number: (209) 954-5644 Calendar System: Semester
URL: www.deltacollege.edu
Established: 1935 Annual Undergrad Tuition & Fees (In-District): $1,104
Enrollment: 18,968 Coed
Affiliation or Control: State/Local IRS Status: 501(c)3
Highest Offering: Associate Degree
Program: Occupational; 2-Year Principally Bachelor's Creditable
Accreditation: WJ, ACFEI, ADNUR

01 Superintendent/President ... Dr. Kathleen HART
05 Interim VP of Instruction ... Dr. Matt WETSTEIN
32 Interim Asst Supt/VP of Student Svc ... Mr. Michael KERNS
11 Vice Pres of Administrative Svcs ... Mr. Chris YATOOMA
15 Director of Human Resources ... Ms. Dianna GONZALES
13 Vice Pres Information Technology ... Vacant
09 Dean Plng Research/Regional Educ ... Vacant
103 Dean Workforce/Economic Development ... Vacant
97 Dean General Education & Transfer ... Dr. Charles JENNINGS
08 Div Dean Library/Learning Res/Lang ... Mr. Joe GONZALES
12 Associate Dean of Tracy Center ... Dr. Jessie GARZA-RODERICK
27 Dir Public Information/Marketing ... Vacant
21 Interim Director of Finance ... Mr. Jerry MCCLEAN
18 Director Facilities Management ... Mr. Michael GARR
07 Director of Admissions ... Ms. Catherine MOONEY
37 Director of Financial Aid/Vet Svcs ... Ms. Denise C. DONN
96 Director of Purchasing ... Ms. Maria BERNARDINO

San Joaquin Valley College, Inc. (E)

8400 W Mineral King Avenue, Visalia CA 93291-9283
County: Tulare FICE Identification: 021207
Unit ID: 122685
Telephone: (559) 651-2500 Carnegie Class: Assoc/PrivFP
FAX Number: (559) 651-0574 Calendar System: Quarter
URL: www.sjvc.edu/campus/Visalia/
Established: 1977 Annual Undergrad Tuition & Fees: $15,500
Enrollment: 818 Coed
Affiliation or Control: Proprietary IRS Status: Proprietary
Highest Offering: Associate Degree
Program: Occupational; 2-Year Principally Bachelor's Creditable
Accreditation: WJ, #ARCPA, DH

01 President ... Mr. Mark PERRY
00 Chief Executive Officer ... Mr. Michael PERRY
05 College Director ... Mr. Don WRIGHT
11 Vice President of Administration ... Ms. Wendy MENDES
84 Vice Pres of Enrollment Services ... Mr. Joseph HOLT
10 Chief Financial Officer ... Mr. Russ LEBO
37 Director of Student Financial Aid ... Mr. Kevin ROBINSON
96 Director of Purchasing ... Mr. Ralph ORTIZ

San Joaquin Valley College-Bakersfield (F)

201 New Stine Road, Suite 200,
Bakersfield CA 93309-2668
County: Kern FICE Identification: 023135
Unit ID: 122694
Telephone: (661) 834-0126 Carnegie Class: Assoc/PrivFP
FAX Number: (661) 834-1021 Calendar System: Quarter
URL: www.sjvc.edu/campus/Bakersfield/
Established: 1981 Annual Undergrad Tuition & Fees: $15,500
Enrollment: 613 Coed
Affiliation or Control: Proprietary IRS Status: Proprietary
Highest Offering: Associate Degree
Program: Occupational; 2-Year Principally Bachelor's Creditable
Accreditation: &WJ, SURGT

12 Campus Director ... Kelly WALTERS

† Regional accreditation is carried under the parent institution in Visalia, CA.

San Joaquin Valley College-Fresno (G)

295 E Sierra Avenue, Fresno CA 93710-3616
County: Fresno Identification: 666008
Unit ID: 262457
Telephone: (559) 448-8282 Carnegie Class: Assoc/PrivFP
FAX Number: (559) 448-8250 Calendar System: Quarter
URL: www.sjvc.edu/campus/Fresno/
Established: 1981 Annual Undergrad Tuition & Fees: $15,500
Enrollment: 653 Coed
Affiliation or Control: Proprietary IRS Status: Proprietary
Highest Offering: Associate Degree
Program: Occupational; 2-Year Principally Bachelor's Creditable
Accreditation: &WJ, SURGT

01 President ... Mr. Mark A. PERRY
12 Campus Director ... Dr. John SWIGER

† Regional accreditation is carried under the parent institution in Visalia, CA.

San Joaquin Valley College-Fresno Aviation Campus (H)

4985 E Andersen Avenue, Fresno CA 93721-1501
County: Fresno Identification: 666009
Unit ID: 422020
Telephone: (559) 453-0123 Carnegie Class: Assoc/PrivFP
FAX Number: (559) 453-0133 Calendar System: Quarter
URL: www.sjvc.edu
Established: 1991 Annual Undergrad Tuition & Fees: $12,850
Enrollment: 67 Coed
Affiliation or Control: Proprietary IRS Status: Proprietary
Highest Offering: Associate Degree
Program: Occupational; 2-Year Principally Bachelor's Creditable; Technical Emphasis
Accreditation: &WJ

01 President ... Mr. Mark PERRY
12 Campus Director ... Mr. Jack P. MACFARLANE

† Regional accreditation is carried under the parent institution in Visalia, CA.

San Joaquin Valley College-Hesperia (I)

9329 Mariposa Road, Hesperia CA 92344-8000
County: San Barnardino Identification: 667044
Unit ID: 456852
Telephone: (760) 948-1947 Carnegie Class: Assoc/PrivFP
FAX Number: (760) 948-1704 Calendar System: Quarter
URL: www.sjvc.edu/campus/Hesperia/
Established: N/A Annual Undergrad Tuition & Fees: $16,650
Enrollment: 569 Coed
Affiliation or Control: Proprietary IRS Status: Proprietary
Highest Offering: Associate Degree
Program: Occupational; 2-Year Principally Bachelor's Creditable
Accreditation: &WJ

12 Campus Director ... Ms. Melanie BLACKWELL

† Regional accreditation is carried under the parent institution in Visalia, CA.

San Joaquin Valley College-Modesto (J)

5380 Pirrone Road, Salida CA 95368-9090
County: Stanislaus Identification: 666128
Unit ID: 447351
Telephone: (209) 543-8800 Carnegie Class: Assoc/PrivFP
FAX Number: (209) 543-8320 Calendar System: Other
URL: www.sjvc.edu/campus/Modesto/
Established: 1977 Annual Undergrad Tuition & Fees: $15,500
Enrollment: 272 Coed
Affiliation or Control: Proprietary IRS Status: Proprietary
Highest Offering: Associate Degree
Program: Occupational; 2-Year Principally Bachelor's Creditable
Accreditation: &WJ

12 Director ... Mr. Sean C. HANCOCK

† Regional accreditation is carried under the parent institution in Visalia, CA.

San Joaquin Valley College-Rancho Cordova (K)

11050 Olson Drive, Suite 210,
Rancho Cordova CA 95670-5600
County: Sacramento Identification: 666133
Unit ID: 448372
Telephone: (916) 638-7582 Carnegie Class: Assoc/PrivFP
FAX Number: (916) 638-7553 Calendar System: Quarter
URL: www.sjvc.edu/campus/Rancho_Cordova/
Established: N/A Annual Undergrad Tuition & Fees: $21,560
Enrollment: 137 Coed
Affiliation or Control: Proprietary IRS Status: Proprietary
Highest Offering: Associate Degree
Program: Occupational; 2-Year Principally Bachelor's Creditable
Accreditation: &WJ

01 President ... Mr. Mark PERRY
12 Campus Director ... Mr. Jeff RUTHERFORD

† Regional accreditation is carried under the parent institution in Visalia, CA.

San Joaquin Valley College-Rancho Cucamonga (A)

10641 Church Street, Rancho Cucamonga CA 91730-6862
County: San Bernardino Identification: 666096
Unit ID: 442444
Telephone: (909) 948-7582 Carnegie Class: Assoc/PrivFP
FAX Number: (909) 948-3860 Calendar System: Quarter
URL: www.sjvc.edu/campus/Rancho_Cucamonga/
Established: N/A Annual Undergrad Tuition & Fees: $16,650
Enrollment: 709 Coed
Affiliation or Control: Proprietary IRS Status: Proprietary
Highest Offering: Associate Degree
Program: Occupational; 2-Year Principally Bachelor's Creditable
Accreditation: &WJ

01 President .... Mr. Mark PERRY
12 Campus Director .... Ms. Sherril HEIN

† Regional accreditation is carried under the parent institution in Visalia, CA.

*San Jose/Evergreen Community College District (B)

4750 San Felipe Road, San Jose CA 95135-1599
County: Santa Clara FICE Identification: 029042
Unit ID: 122737
Telephone: (408) 274-6700 Carnegie Class: N/A
FAX Number: (408) 531-8722
URL: www.sjeccd.edu

01 Chancellor .... Dr. Rita CEPEDA
11 Vice Chanc Administrative Services .... Mr. Douglas SMITH
05 Vice Chanc Educational Services .... Vacant
15 Vice Chanc Human Resources .... Ms. Kim L. GARCIA
84 Dean Enrollment Services .... Vacant
09 Int Ex Dir Rsrch & Instnl Effect .... Ms. Oleg BESPALOV
18 Dir Facilities/Const Mgmt/Operation .... Mr. Robert DIAS
07 Director Admiss/Records San Jose .... Mr. Carlo SANTOS
10 Director of Fiscal Services .... Mr. Peter FITZSIMMONS
13 Dir Information Technology Sys Svc .... Mr. Thomas ONWILER
28 Dir of Employment Svcs/Diversity .... Mr. Sam HO

*Evergreen Valley College (C)

3095 Yerba Buena Road, San Jose CA 95135-1598
County: Santa Clara FICE Identification: 012452
Unit ID: 114266
Telephone: (408) 274-7900 Carnegie Class: Assoc/Pub-U-MC
FAX Number: (408) 238-3179 Calendar System: Semester
URL: www.evc.edu
Established: 1975 Annual Undergrad Tuition & Fees (In-District): $1,152
Enrollment: 10,000 Coed
Affiliation or Control: State/Local IRS Status: 501(c)3
Highest Offering: Associate Degree
Program: 2-Year Principally Bachelor's Creditable
Accreditation: WJ, ADNUR

02 President .... Mr. Henry C. YONG
05 VP Academic Affairs .... Mr. Keith AYTCH
32 Vice Pres Student Services .... Ms. Irma ARCHULETA
10 VP Administrarive Services .... Mr. Henry GEE
50 Int Dean Business & Workforce Devel .... Ms. Sandra DEWOLFE
66 Dean Nursing & Allied Health .... Ms. Sandra DEWOLFE
62 Int Dean Library/Lrng Res .... Mr. Mark GONZALES
81 Dean Math/Science/Engineering .... Mr. Michael HIGHERS
83 Dean Soc Sci/PE/Arts/Humanities .... Mr. Mark GONZALES
84 Dean Enrollment Services .... Mr. Octavio CRUZ
38 Dean Student Counseling .... Vacant
35 Director Student Life .... Mr. Victor GARZA, JR.
37 Director Financial Aid .... Ms. Alma TANON
88 Director Student Services Pgm .... Mr. Savander PARKER
88 Director CalWorks/WIN .... Ms. Elizabeth TYRRELL
11 Supervisor Administrative Services .... Ms. Lauren MCKEE
19 District Police Chief .... Mr. Ray AGUIRRE
88 Int Dean Language Arts .... Mr. William SILVER
14 Supervisor Campus Tech Svcs .... Mr. Eugenio CANOY

*San Jose City College (D)

2100 Moorpark Avenue, San Jose CA 95128-2799
County: Santa Clara FICE Identification: 001282
Unit ID: 122746
Telephone: (408) 298-2181 Carnegie Class: Assoc/Pub-U-MC
FAX Number: (408) 298-1935 Calendar System: Semester
URL: www.sjcc.edu
Established: 1921 Annual Undergrad Tuition & Fees (In-District): $1,334
Enrollment: 10,237 Coed
Affiliation or Control: State/Local IRS Status: 501(c)3
Highest Offering: Associate Degree
Program: Occupational; 2-Year Principally Bachelor's Creditable
Accreditation: #WJ, DA

02 President .... Dr. Barbara KAVALIER
11 Vice President Administrative Svcs .... Mr. Greg NELSON
32 Vice President Student Services .... Dr. Marie-Elaine BURNS
07 Dir Admiss/Records/Financial Aid .... Mr. Takeo KUBO
88 Executive Director WIN Program .... Ms. Marilyn BRODIE
92 Director Honors Program .... Vacant
41 Athletic Director .... Ms. Deborah HUNTZE-ROONEY
04 Assistant to the President .... Ms. Isabel MACIAS
50 Dean Business & Technology .... Mr. Kishan VUJJENI
79 Dean Humanities/Social Science .... Dr. Patrick GERSTER
38 Dean Couns/Retention/Spec Pgms .... Dr. Romero JALOMO
88 Dean Language Arts .... Dr. Keiko KIMURA
81 Dean Mathematics/Sciences Division .... Dr. Leandra MARTIN

*San Mateo County Community College District Office (E)

3401 CSM Drive, San Mateo CA 94402-3651
County: San Mateo FICE Identification: 004697
Unit ID: 122782
Telephone: (650) 574-6500 Carnegie Class: N/A
FAX Number: (650) 574-6566
URL: www.smccd.edu

01 Chancellor .... Mr. Ron D. GALATOLO
03 Interim Executive Vice Chancellor .... Ms. Kathy BLACKWOOD
16 Vice Chanc Employee Rels/Human Res .... Mr. Harry JOEL
05 Vice Chanc Educational Svcs/Plng .... Dr. Jing LUAN
18 Vice Chanc Facil Plng/Maint/Oper .... Mr. Jose NUNEZ
88 Vice Chanc Auxilliary Services .... Mr. Tom BAUER
31 Director of Community/Govt Rels .... Ms. Barbara W. CHRISTENSEN
10 Interim Chief Financial Officer .... Mr. Raymond CHOW
14 Chief Technology Officer .... Mr. Frank M. VASKELIS

*Cañada College (F)

4200 Farm Hill Boulevard, Redwood City CA 94061-1099
County: San Mateo FICE Identification: 006973
Unit ID: 111434
Telephone: (650) 306-3100 Carnegie Class: Assoc/Pub-S-MC
FAX Number: (650) 306-3457 Calendar System: Semester
URL: www.canadacollege.net
Established: 1968 Annual Undergrad Tuition & Fees (In-District): $1,104
Enrollment: 6,992 Coed
Affiliation or Control: State/Local IRS Status: 501(c)3
Highest Offering: Associate Degree
Program: Occupational; 2-Year Principally Bachelor's Creditable
Accreditation: WJ, RAD

02 Interim President .... Mr. James KELLER
32 Vice President of Student Services .... Ms. Robin RICHARDS
05 Vice President of Instruction .... Ms. Linda HAYES
84 Dean Enrollment Services .... Ms. Kim LOPEZ
06 Registrar .... Ms. Ruth MILLER
10 Chief Business Officer .... Ms. Victoria NUNES
26 Director of Marketing .... Mr. Robert HOOD
45 Dir Plng/Research/Student Success .... Mr. Gregory STOUP
18 Facilities Manager .... Mr. Danny GLASS
37 Director Financial Aid .... Ms. Margie CARRINGTON
103 Dean Business/Workforce/Athletics .... Ms. Jan ROECKS
79 Dean of Humanities & Social Science .... Mr. David JOHNSON
81 Dean Science & Technology .... Dr. Janet STRINGER

*College of San Mateo (G)

1700 W Hillsdale Boulevard, San Mateo CA 94402-3795
County: San Mateo FICE Identification: 001181
Unit ID: 122791
Telephone: (650) 574-6161 Carnegie Class: Assoc/Pub-S-MC
FAX Number: (650) 574-6680 Calendar System: Semester
URL: www.collegeofsanmateo.edu
Established: 1922 Annual Undergrad Tuition & Fees (In-District): $1,380
Enrollment: 10,049 Coed
Affiliation or Control: State/Local IRS Status: 501(c)3
Highest Offering: Associate Degree
Program: Occupational; 2-Year Principally Bachelor's Creditable
Accreditation: WJ, DA

02 President .... Mr. Michael CLAIRE
05 Vice President Instruction .... Dr. Susan ESTES
32 Vice President Student Services .... Ms. Jennifer HUGHES
07 Dean Admissions & Records .... Dr. Henry VILLAREAL
38 Dean Counsel/Advis/Matriculation .... Ms. Marsha RAMEZANE
46 Dean Articulation & Research .... Dr. John J. SEWART
30 Dir College Development & Marketing .... Ms. Beverly MADDEN
18 Facilities Operations Manager .... Ms. Karen POWELL
88 Dean Language Arts Division .Dr. Sandra STEFANI COMERFORD
68 Dean Phys Educ/Athletics Division .... Mr. Andreas WOLF
81 Dean Math/Science Division .... Dr. Charlene FRONTIERA
83 Dean Creative Arts/Social Sci Div .... Dr. Kevin HENSON
50 Dean Business & Technology Division .... Ms. Kathleen ROSS

*Skyline College (H)

3300 College Drive, San Bruno CA 94066-1698
County: San Mateo FICE Identification: 007713
Unit ID: 123509
Telephone: (650) 738-4100 Carnegie Class: Assoc/Pub-S-MC
FAX Number: (650) 738-4338 Calendar System: Semester
URL: www.skylinecollege.edu
Established: 1969 Annual Undergrad Tuition & Fees (In-District): $780
Enrollment: 10,250 Coed
Affiliation or Control: State/Local IRS Status: 501(c)3
Highest Offering: Associate Degree
Program: Occupational; 2-Year Principally Bachelor's Creditable
Accreditation: WJ, ACBSP, SURGT

02 President .... Dr. Regina STANBACK STROUD
05 Vice President Instruction .... Ms. Sarah PERKINS
32 Vice President Student Services .... Dr. Joi BLAKE
84 Dean Enrollment Svcs/Financial Aid .... Dr. John MOSBY
09 Dean Plng/Rsrch/Instl Effective .... Dr. David ULATE
10 Director Business Service .... Ms. Eloisa BRIONES
83 Dean Social Science/Creative Arts .... Ms. Donna J. BESTOCK
50 Dean Business Division .... Mr. Don CARLSON
60 Dean Language Arts .... Ms. Connie BERINGER
68 Dean Physical Education .... Mr. Joseph MORELLO
81 Dean Science/Math/Technology .... Mr. Raymond HERNANDEZ
38 Dean Counsel/Advising/Matriculation .... Mr. Richard WALLACE
18 Chief Facilities/Physical Plant .... Mr. Richard INOKUCHI
103 Director SparkPoint Center .... Dr. William WATSON
37 Director Financial Aid/CalWk .... Ms. Regina MORRISON
26 Interim Communications Manager .... Ms. Cherie M. NAPIER

Sanford-Burnham Graduate School of Biomedical Sciences (I)

10901 North Torrey Pines Road, La Jolla CA 92037
County: San Diego Identification: 667069
Telephone: (858) 646-3100 Carnegie Class: Not Classified
FAX Number: (858) 646-3199 Calendar System: Quarter
URL: sanfordburnham.org
Established: 2005 Annual Graduate Tuition & Fees: N/A
Enrollment: N/A Coed
Affiliation or Control: Independent Non-Profit IRS Status: 501(c)3
Highest Offering: Master's; No Undergraduates
Program: Professional
Accreditation: @WC

01 President .... Dr. Kristiina VUORI
10 Exec VP/Chief Admin Officer/CFO .... Dr. Gary RAISL
05 Dean .... Dr. Guy SALVESEN
15 Vice Pres Human Res/Org Effect .... Ms. Beth ALTON
26 Sr Vice Pres External Relations .... Ms. Ann CAROLLO
30 Vice President Inst Advancement .... Mr. Philip GRAHAM

Santa Barbara Business College (J)

5300 California Ave, Bakersfield CA 93309-2139
County: Kern FICE Identification: 025779
Unit ID: 122834
Telephone: (661) 835-1100 Carnegie Class: Assoc/PrivFP
FAX Number: (661) 835-0242 Calendar System: Semester
URL: www.sbbcollege.edu
Established: 1982 Annual Undergrad Tuition & Fees: N/A
Enrollment: 223 Coed
Affiliation or Control: Proprietary IRS Status: Proprietary
Highest Offering: Baccalaureate
Program: Occupational; 2-Year Principally Bachelor's Creditable
Accreditation: ACICS

01 President .... Matthew JOHNSTON
07 Director of Admissions .... Holly ORTIZ
26 Marketing Coordinator .... Monica RAYMOND

Santa Barbara Business College (K)

34275 Monterey Ave, Rancho Mirage CA 92270
Identification: 666582
Telephone: (760) 341-7602 Carnegie Class: Not Classified
FAX Number: (760) 341-2607 Calendar System: Semester
URL: www.sbbcollege.com
Established: 2008 Annual Undergrad Tuition & Fees: N/A
Enrollment: 131 Coed
Affiliation or Control: Proprietary IRS Status: Proprietary
Highest Offering: Baccalaureate
Program: Occupational; 2-Year Principally Bachelor's Creditable
Accreditation: ACICS

01 President .... Matthew JOHNSON
07 Director of Admissions .... Holly ORTIZ
26 Marketing Coordinator .... Monica RAYMOND

Santa Barbara Business College (L)

506 Chapala Street, Santa Barbara CA 93101-3412
County: Santa Barbara Identification: 666099
Telephone: (805) 967-9677 Carnegie Class: Not Classified
FAX Number: (805) 967-4248 Calendar System: Semester
URL: www.sbbcollege.edu
Established: 1888 Annual Undergrad Tuition & Fees: N/A
Enrollment: 39 Coed
Affiliation or Control: Proprietary IRS Status: Proprietary
Highest Offering: Master's
Program: Occupational; 2-Year Principally Bachelor's Creditable
Accreditation: ACICS

01 President .... Matthew JOHNSTON
07 Director of Admissions .... Holly ORTIZ

† Branch campus of Santa Barbara Business College, Ventura, CA.

Santa Barbara Business College (M)

303 E Plaza Drive, Santa Maria CA 93454
County: Santa Barbara FICE Identification: 025780
Unit ID: 122852
Telephone: (805) 922-8256 Carnegie Class: Assoc/PrivFP
FAX Number: (805) 346-1857 Calendar System: Semester

URL: www.sbbcollege.edu
Established: 1980 Annual Undergrad Tuition & Fees: N/A
Enrollment: 100 Coed
Affiliation or Control: Proprietary IRS Status: Proprietary
Highest Offering: Baccalaureate
Program: Occupational; 2-Year Principally Bachelor's Creditable
Accreditation: ACICS

01 President .... Matthew JOHNSTON
07 Director of Admissions .... Holly ORTIZ
26 Marketing Coordinator .... Monica RAYMOND

Santa Barbara Business College (A)

4839 Market Street, Ventura CA 93003
County: Ventura FICE Identification: 009989
Unit ID: 433420
Telephone: (805) 339-2999 Carnegie Class: Assoc/PrivFP
FAX Number: (805) 339-2994 Calendar System: Other
URL: www.sbbcollege.edu
Established: 2003 Annual Undergrad Tuition & Fees: N/A
Enrollment: 39 Coed
Affiliation or Control: Proprietary IRS Status: Proprietary
Highest Offering: Baccalaureate
Program: Occupational; 2-Year Principally Bachelor's Creditable
Accreditation: ACICS

01 President .... Matthew JOHNSTON
07 Director of Admissions .... Holly ORTIZ
26 Marketing Coordinator .... Monica RAYMOND

Santa Barbara City College (B)

721 Cliff Drive, Santa Barbara CA 93109-2394
County: Santa Barbara FICE Identification: 001285
Unit ID: 122889
Telephone: (805) 965-0581 Carnegie Class: Assoc/Pub-R-L
FAX Number: (805) 963-7222 Calendar System: Semester
URL: www.sbcc.edu
Established: 1909 Annual Undergrad Tuition & Fees (In-District): $1,376
Enrollment: 20,372 Coed
Affiliation or Control: State/Local IRS Status: 501(c)3
Highest Offering: Associate Degree
Program: Occupational; 2-Year Principally Bachelor's Creditable
Accreditation: WJ, ACFEI, ADNUR, DMS, RAD

01 Superintendent/President .... Dr. Lori GASKIN
05 Exec Vice Pres Educational Programs ..... Dr. Jack FRIEDLANDER
51 Vice President Continuing Education .... Dr. Ofelia ARELLANO
10 Vice President Business Services .... Mr. Joseph SULLIVAN
15 Int Vice Pres Human Resources .... Ms. Patricia ENGLISH
14 Vice President Info Technology .... Dr. Paul BISHOP
72 Dean Educational Programs .... Mr. Ben PARTEE
76 Dean Educational Programs .... Dr. Betty PAZICH
81 Dean Educational Programs .... Ms. Marilynn SPAVENTA
57 Dean Educational Programs .... Dr. Alice SCHARPER
53 Dean Educational Programs .... Dr. Diane HOLLEMS
72 Dean Educational Programs .... Dr. Doug HERSH
08 Librarian .... Mr. Kenley NEUFELD
102 Exec Dir Foundation for SBCC .... Ms. Vanessa PATTERSON
09 Sr Director Institutional Research .... Mr. Robert ELSE
27 College Information Officer .... Ms. Joan GALVAN
37 Director of Student Financial Aid .... Mr. Brad HARDISON
18 Director of Facilities & Operations .... Ms. Julie HENDRICKS
07 Director of Admissions .... Ms. Allison CURTIS
85 Director International Students .... Ms. Carola SMITH
96 Manager of Purchasing .... Mr. Robert MORALES

Santa Clara University (C)

500 El Camino Real, Santa Clara CA 95053-0001
County: Santa Clara FICE Identification: 001326
Unit ID: 122931
Telephone: (408) 554-4000 Carnegie Class: Master's L
FAX Number: (408) 554-2700 Calendar System: Quarter
URL: www.scu.edu
Established: 1851 Annual Undergrad Tuition & Fees: $40,572
Enrollment: 8,800 Coed
Affiliation or Control: Independent Non-Profit IRS Status: 501(c)3
Highest Offering: Doctorate
Program: Liberal Arts And General; Teacher Preparatory; Professional
Accreditation: WC, BUS, BUSA, CS, ENG, LAW, THEOL

01 President .... Rev. Michael E. ENGH, SJ
05 Provost .... Mr. Dennis JACOBS
10 Vice President Admin & Finance .... Mr. Robert D. WARREN
43 General Counsel .... Mr. John OTTOBONI
26 Vice President University Relations .... Mr. Robert GUNSALUS
04 Exec Assistant to the President .... Ms. Molly MC DONALD
49 Dean of Arts & Sciences .... Dr. Atom YEE
50 Dean of Business .... Dr. S. Andrew STARBIRD
53 Dean Educ & Counseling Psychology .... Vacant
54 Dean of Engineering .... Dr. Godfrey MUNGAL
61 Dean of Law .... Dr. Donald J. POLDEN
73 Dean Jesuit School of Theology .... Rev. Thomas MASSARO, SJ
88 Dean Academic Support Services .... Vacant
20 Special Assistant to the President .... Dr. Don C. DODSON
20 Vice Provost Academic Affairs .... Dr. Diane E. JONTE-PACE
32 Vice Provost for Student Life .... Ms. Jeanne ROSENBERGER
84 Vice Provost for Enrollment Mgmt .... Mr. Mike SEXTON
20 Vice Provost Planning/Admin .... Dr. Charles F. EREKSON
27 Vice Provost Info Services/CIO .... Dr. Ronald L. DANIELSON
88 Assoc Provost Undergraduate Studies .... Dr. Philip R. KESTEN
88 Assoc Provost Research Initiatives .... Dr. Amy M. SHACHTER
88 Assoc Provost Faculty Development .... Dr. Eileen R. ELROD
07 Dean Admission .... Ms. Sandra L. HAYES
84 Assoc Vice Provost Enrollment Mgt .... Dr. Richard TOOMEY
27 Assoc Vice President Mktg/Comm .... Mr. Richard GIACCHETTI
21 Assoc Vice President Finance .... Mr. Harry M. FONG
15 Asst Vice President Human Resources .... Ms. Maria Elena DE GUEVARA
88 Asst Vice President University Oper .... Mr. Joe SUGG
30 Asst Vice President Development .... Ms. Nancy CALDERON
31 Asst Vice Pres Auxiliary Services .... Ms. Jane BARRANTES
35 Assoc Dean for Student Life .... Mr. Matthew DUNCAN
06 University Registrar .... Ms. Monica L. AUGUSTIN
29 Executive Dir of Alumini Relations .... Ms. Kathy KALE
41 Director Athletics and Recreation .... Dr. Daniel COONAN
08 University Librarian .... Ms. Jennifer NUTEFALL
08 Law Librarian .... Dr. Mary D. HOOD
14 Director of Information Technology .... Mr. Carl FUSSELL
24 Director Media Services .... Ms. Nancy CUTLER
36 Director Career Center .... Ms. Elspeth ROSSETTI
09 Director Institutional Research .... Ms. Barbara A. STEWART
25 Director Sponsored Projects .... Vacant
38 Director Health & Counseling Svcs .... Ms. Jill ROVARIS
85 Int Exec Dir International Programs .... Ms. Susan POPKO
21 Director Budget .... Vacant
88 Chief Investment Officer .... Mr. John E. KERRIGAN
21 Controller .... Ms. Suzanne GAUMONT
18 Director of Facilities .... Mr. Jeffrey R. CHARLES
96 Director University Support Service .... Mr. Ed MERRYMAN
19 Director Campus Safety Services .... Mr. Philip BELTRAN
40 General Manager Bookstore .... Mrs. Deborah KENDALL
42 Director of Campus Ministry .... Rev. Jack R. TREACY, SJ
22 Director of Affirmative Action .... Ms. Deborah HIRSCH
88 Director de Saisset Museum .... Ms. Rebecca M. SCHAPP
88 Exec Dir Ignatian Ctr Jesuit Educ ... Rev. Michael MCCARTHY, SJ
88 Executive Dir Ctr Sci/Tech/Society .... Mr. Thane KREINER
88 Exec Dir Markkula Ctr Applied Ethic .... Mr. Kirk O. HANSON

Santa Monica College (D)

1900 Pico Boulevard, Santa Monica CA 90405-1628
County: Los Angeles FICE Identification: 001286
Unit ID: 122977
Telephone: (310) 434-4000 Carnegie Class: Assoc/Pub-S-MC
FAX Number: (310) 434-4386 Calendar System: Semester
URL: www.smc.edu
Established: 1929 Annual Undergrad Tuition & Fees (In-District): $1,205
Enrollment: 34,072 Coed
Affiliation or Control: State/Local IRS Status: 501(c)3
Highest Offering: Associate Degree
Program: Occupational; 2-Year Principally Bachelor's Creditable
Accreditation: WJ, ADNUR

01 Superintendent/President .... Dr. Chui L. TSANG
03 Executive Vice President .... Mr. Randal R. LAWSON
10 Vice President Business/Admin .... Mr. Robert G. ISOMOTO
16 Vice President Human Resources .... Ms. Marcia WADE
05 Vice President Academic Affairs .... Mr. Jeffery SHIMIZU
45 Vice Pres Planning & Development .... Vacant
84 Vice Pres Enrollment Development .... Ms. Teresita RODRIGUEZ
32 Vice President Student Affairs .... Mr. Michael TUITASI
20 Dean Academic Affairs .... Ms. Erica LEBLANC
46 Dean Institutional Effectiveness .... Vacant
15 Dean Human Resources .... Ms. Sherri LEE-LEWIS
08 Dean Learning Resources .... Ms. Mona MARTIN
85 Dean International Education .... Ms. Kelley BRAYTON
56 Dean External Programs .... Ms. Katharine MULLER
38 Dean Counseling/Retention .... Ms. Brenda BENSON
14 Dean Information Technology .... Ms. Jocelyn CHONG
43 Campus Counsel .... Mr. Robert MYERS
106 Director Online Services & Support .... Ms. Julie YARRISH
51 Associate Dean Emeritus College .... Mr. Ron FURUYAMA
35 Dean Student Life .... Ms. Deyna HEARN
20 Dean Instructional Services .... Dr. Georgia LORENZ
17 Associate Dean of Health Sciences .... Dr. Ida DANZEY
07 Dean Enrollment Services .... Ms. Kiersten ELLIOTT
86 Sr Director Government Relations .... Mr. Don GIRARD
37 Assoc Dean Financial Aid/Scholarshp .... Mr. Steve MYROW
18 Chief Dir Facilities Management .... Ms. J.C SAUNDERS-KEURJIAN
21 Director Fiscal Services .... Mr. Chris BONVENUTO
09 Director Institutional Research .... Ms. Hannah ALFORD
104 Assoc Dean International Education .... Ms. Denise KINSELLA
41 Project Manager Athletics .... Mr. Joe CASCIO
88 Dean of Special Programs .... Vacant
102 Director of Grants .... Ms. Laurel MCQUAY-PENINGER
88 Director Performing Arts Center .... Ms. Dale FRANZEN
30 Actg Dir Institutional Advancement .... Mr. Charles POTTS
31 Director Community Relations .... Ms. Judy NEVEAU
88 Director of Classified Personnel .... Ms. Dori MACDONALD
88 Director Network Services .... Mr. Bob DAMMER
25 Director of Contracts .... Mr. Charlie YEN
96 Director of Purchasing .... Ms. Cynthia MOORE
19 Dean Camp Security Stdnt Hlth/Safe .... Dr. Albert VASQUEZ
27 Public Information Officer .... Mr. Bruce SMITH
04 Admin Asst to the President .... Ms. Lin D. CALDWELL
13 Director Management Info Systems .... Mr. Dexter L. JOHNSTON
24 Mgr Media & Reprographic Services .... Mr. Albert DESALLES
40 Bookstore Manager .... Mr. David DEVER
103 Dean Workforce Development .... Dr. Patricia RAMOS
101 Coordinator Board of Trustees .... Ms. Lisa ROSE
88 Assoc Dean Outreach & Recruitment .... Ms. Sonali PERERA-BRIDGES
88 Director Radio Station (KCRW) .... Ms. Jennifer FERRO
88 Director Facilities Programming .... Ms. Linda SULLIVAN
30 Dean Institutional Development .... Vacant
88 Assoc Dean Stdnt Success Initiative .... Mr. Roberto GONZALEZ
88 Dir Sustainability Coordination .... Ms. Genevieve BERTONE
75 Dir Career & Contract Education .... Ms. Michelle KING
88 Assoc Dir Dual Enroll/Instr Svcs .... Ms. Maral HYELER

Santa Rosa Junior College (E)

1501 Mendocino Avenue, Santa Rosa CA 95401-4395
County: Sonoma FICE Identification: 001287
Unit ID: 123013
Telephone: (707) 527-4011 Carnegie Class: Assoc/Pub-R-L
FAX Number: (707) 527-4816 Calendar System: Semester
URL: www.santarosa.edu
Established: 1918 Annual Undergrad Tuition & Fees (In-District): $1,278
Enrollment: 28,265 Coed
Affiliation or Control: State/Local IRS Status: 501(c)3
Highest Offering: Associate Degree
Program: Occupational; 2-Year Principally Bachelor's Creditable
Accreditation: WJ, DA, DH, @DIETT, EMT, RAD

01 Superintendent/President .... Dr. Frank CHONG
12 Vice President Petaluma Campus ..... Dr. Jane SALDANA-TALLEY
05 VP Acad Affs/Asst Superintendent .... Dr. Mary Kay RUDOLPH
10 Vice President Business Services .... Mr. Doug ROBERTS
32 VP Student Svcs/Asst Superindendent .... Mr. Ricardo D. NAVARRETTE
16 VP Human Resources .... Ms. Karen FURUKAWA
04 Executive Assistant to CEO/BOT .... Ms. Maria GAITAN
75 Dean Career/Tech Ed/Economic Dev .... Ms. Lorraine WILSON
11 Dean Facilities Planning/Operations .... Mr. Tony ICHSAN
88 Dean Curriculum/Education Support .... Dr. Abraham FARKAS
49 Dean Liberal Arts & Sciences .... Dr. Kris ABRAHAMSON
08 Dean Learning Res/Educ Tech .... Ms. Cherry LI-BUGG
88 Dean Counseling/Support Services .... Mr. Marty LEE
88 Dean Public Safety .... Ms. April CHAPMAN
81 Dean Sci/Tech/Engr/Math .... Ms. Karen FRINDELL TEUSCHER
17 Dean Health Sciences .... Dr. Ezbon JEN
50 Dean Business/Professional Studies .... Mr. Steve COHEN
83 Dean Arts/Comm/Behav & Soc Sci .... Dr. Tyra BENOIT
79 Dean Language Arts/Acad Foundation .... Mr. Victor CUMMINGS
41 Dean Kinesiology/Dance/Athletic Dir .... Mr. James FORKUM
88 Dean Disabled Students Pgm & Svcs .... Ms. Patie WEGMAN
72 Dean Instruction & Technical Svcs .... Mr. Robert CHUDNOFSKY
35 Dean Student Services Petaluma .... Ms. Lauralyn LARSEN
88 Dean Early Childhood Education .... Mr. Joel GORDON
88 Dean Student Success & Retention .... Ms. Ruth MCMULLEN
47 Dean Agriculture/Natural Resources .... Mr. Ganesan SRINIVASAN
19 Interim Chief of Police .... Mr. Joe PALLA
13 Director Information Technology .... Mr. Scott CONRAD
103 Director Economic/Workforce Dev .... Mr. Charles ROBBINS
21 Director of Fiscal Services .... Ms. Kate JOLLEY
37 Director Student Financial Services .... Ms. Kris SHEAR
18 Director Facilities Operations .... Mr. Paul BIELEN
23 Director Student Health Services .... Ms. Susan QUINN
09 Director Institutional Research .... Dr. KC GREANEY
35 Dir Student Affs/New Student Pgm .... Mr. Robert ETHINGTON
96 Director Purchasing & Graphics .... Mr. Tim BOSMA
40 Director Bookstore .... Ms. Lorraine FAZZOLARE
44 Director Alumni Rels & Foundation .... Ms. Kate MCCLINTOCK
66 Interim Director Nursing Program .... Ms. Anna VALDEZ
06 Dir Acad Records/Intl Admissions .... Ms. Freyja PEREIRA
07 Director Admissions/Enrollment Svcs .... Ms. Diane TRAVERSI
31 Director Community Education .... Ms. Betsy ROBERTS
15 Assistant Director Human Resources .... Ms. Sabrina MEYER
26 Interim Public Relations Manager .... Ms. Janet PARMER
90 Manager Instructional Computing .... Mr. Josh ADAMS
36 Manager Career Development Svcs .... Ms. Catherine WILSON
24 Manager Media Services .... Mr. Russ BOWDEN
24 Manager Media Services Petaluma .... Mr. Matt PEARSON

Saybrook University (F)

747 Front Street, 3rd Floor, San Francisco CA 94111-1920
County: San Francisco FICE Identification: 021206
Unit ID: 123095
Telephone: (800) 825-4480 Carnegie Class: Spec/Health
FAX Number: (415) 433-9271 Calendar System: Semester
URL: www.saybrook.edu
Established: 1971 Annual Graduate Tuition & Fees: $21,900
Enrollment: 604 Coed
Affiliation or Control: Independent Non-Profit IRS Status: 501(c)3
Highest Offering: Doctorate; No Undergraduates
Program: Professional
Accreditation: WC

01 President .... Dr. Mark SCHULMAN
05 Provost and Executive VP .... Dr. Daniel R. SEWELL
11 VP for Finance and Administration .... Mr. Michael CAIRNS
26 VP Communications/External Affairs .... Ms. Sigrid BADINELLI
06 Registrar .... Mr. Aaron HIATT
08 Director of Library Services .... Vacant
37 Director Student Financial Aid .... Ms. Shandel ROBERTS
04 Exec Assistant to the President .... Ms. Ann LUCKIESH
07 Director of Admissions .... Ms. Cathy FUSCO
16 Director of Human Resources .... Ms. Kim SRODA
13 Director IT and Network Resource .... Mr. Laurens DEHAAN
29 Director Alumni Relations .... Dr. George AIKEN
09 Director of Institutional Research .... Mr. Scott KERLIN

Scripps College (A)

1030 Columbia, Claremont CA 91711-3948
County: Los Angeles FICE Identification: 001174
Unit ID: 123165
Telephone: (909) 621-8000 Carnegie Class: Bac/A&S
FAX Number: (909) 621-8323 Calendar System: Semester
URL: www.scrippscollege.edu
Established: 1926 Annual Undergrad Tuition & Fees: $43,620
Enrollment: 950 Female
Affiliation or Control: Independent Non-Profit IRS Status: 501(c)3
Highest Offering: Baccalaureate
Program: Liberal Arts And General
Accreditation: WC

01 President ... Dr. Lori BETTISON-VARGA
05 Vice Pres/Dean of the Faculty ... Dr. Amy MARCUS-NEWHALL
30 VP for Institutional Advancement ... Mr. Michael ARCHIBALD
10 Vice President for Business Affairs ... Ms. Joanne COVILLE
32 Vice President of Student Affairs ... Ms. Rebecca LEE
07 Vice President for Enrollment ... Ms. Victoria ROMERO
26 VP for Communications & Marketing ... Ms. MaryLou J. FERRY
29 Director of Alumnae Relations ... Ms. Emily RANKIN
100 Chief of Staff/Secy to Bd of Trust ... Ms. Sally STEFFEN
04 Executive Asst to the President ... Ms. Claire BRIDGE
20 Associate Dean of Faculty ... Dr. Gretchen EDWALDS-GILBERT
15 Director of Human Resources ... Vacant
09 Director of Assessment & Research ... Ms. Junelyn PEEPLES
08 Librarian ... Ms. Judy B. HARVEY-SAHAK
06 Registrar ... Ms. Kelly HOGENCAMP
37 Director of Financial Aid ... Mr. David LEVY
36 Director of Career Planning ... Ms. Vicki P. KLOPSCH
13 Director of Information Technology ... Mr. Jeff SESSLER
18 Director of Facilities ... Mr. Niel ERRICKSON
104 Director of Off-Campus Study ... Ms. Neva BARKER

The Scripps Research Institute (B)

10550 N Torrey Pines Road, TPC19,
La Jolla CA 92037-1000
County: San Diego FICE Identification: 033213
Unit ID: 435338
Telephone: (858) 784-8469 Carnegie Class: Not Classified
FAX Number: (858) 784-2802 Calendar System: Quarter
URL: www.scripps.edu
Established: 1989 Annual Graduate Tuition & Fees: $5,000
Enrollment: 244 Coed
Affiliation or Control: Independent Non-Profit IRS Status: 501(c)3
Highest Offering: Doctorate; No Undergraduates
Program: Professional
Accreditation: WC

01 Director ... Ms. Marylyn RINALDI
05 Dean Graduate Studies ... Dr. James R. WILLIAMSON

Shasta Bible College and Graduate School (C)

2951 Goodwater Avenue, Redding CA 96002-1544
County: Shasta FICE Identification: 023593
Unit ID: 123280
Telephone: (530) 221-4275 Carnegie Class: Spec/Faith
FAX Number: (530) 221-6929 Calendar System: Semester
URL: www.shasta.edu
Established: 1972 Annual Undergrad Tuition & Fees: $10,370
Enrollment: 62 Coed
Affiliation or Control: Independent Non-Profit IRS Status: 501(c)3
Highest Offering: Master's
Program: Religious Emphasis
Accreditation: TRACS

01 President ... Dr. David R. NICHOLAS
04 Exec Assistant to the President ... Ms. Lanell E. WREN
05 Academic Dean ... Dr. Stephen G. BROWN
32 Vice President for Student Life ... Dr. Keith H. STONE
07 Dean of Admissions & Records ... Mr. George A. GUNN
18 Coordinator Grounds & Maintenance ... Mr. Gary KELLOGG
06 Registrar ... Mrs. Faith MCCARTHY
10 Asst Dir Business Affs/Controller ... Mrs. Mary MCENTIRE
37 Financial Aid Officer ... Ms. Linda ILES
56 Director External Studies ... Mrs. Faith MCCARTHY

Shasta College (D)

PO Box 496006, 11555 Old Oregon Tr,
Redding CA 96049-6006
County: Shasta FICE Identification: 001289
Unit ID: 123299
Telephone: (530) 242-7500 Carnegie Class: Assoc/Pub-R-L
FAX Number: (530) 225-4990 Calendar System: Semester
URL: www.shastacollege.edu
Established: 1950 Annual Undergrad Tuition & Fees (In-District): $1,231
Enrollment: 9,775 Coed
Affiliation or Control: State/Local IRS Status: Exempt
Highest Offering: Associate Degree
Program: Occupational; 2-Year Principally Bachelor's Creditable
Accreditation: #WJ, DH

01 Superintendent/President ... Mr. Joe WYSE
05 VP Academic Affairs ... Ms. Meridith RANDALL
11 VP Administrative Services ... Mr. Morris RODRIGUE
15 Assoc VP of Human Resources ... Ms. Laura CYPHERS BENSON
14 Assoc VP Info Services/Technology ... Mr. Doug MELINE
13 Supv Info Services Technology ... Mr. James CRANDALL
45 Director of Research & Planning ... Mr. Marc BEAM
21 Comptroller ... Ms. Nancy FUNK
32 Int Assoc VP Student Services/DOS ... Mr. Kevin O'RORKE
84 Interim Dean of Enrollment Services ... Ms. Sandra HAMILTON SLANE
57 Dean Arts/Communications/Soc Sci ... Dr. Ralph PERRIN
65 Dean Bus/Ag/Industry/Technology ... Ms. Eva JIMENEZ
66 Dean Health Sciences & Univ Prog ... Ms. Wanda SPRATT
41 Dean Safety/PE/Con Sci/Athletic Dir ... Mr. Gary HOUSER
79 Int Dean Science/Language Arts/Math ... Mr. Frank NIGRO
56 Dean Extended Education ... Mr. Thomas ORR, II
103 Dean Economic & Workforce Devel ... Ms. Eva JIMENEZ
08 Associate Dean Library Services ... Ms. Janet ALBRIGHT
37 Financial Aid Director ... Ms. Connie BARTON
88 Int Director DSPS-EOPS/CARE ... Mr. David TRAVIS
06 Chief Records Technician ... Ms. Sheree WHALEY
18 Director Physical Plant ... Mr. George ESTRADA
88 Director Food Services ... Ms. Denise AXTELL
19 Director of Campus Safety ... Vacant
88 Supervisor HazMat Compliance Pgm ... Mr. Dave FREEMAN
102 Executive Director SC Foundation ... Mr. Scott THOMPSON
40 Bookstore Manager ... Ms. Josee GENDRON

Shepherd University School of Theology (E)

1111 W. Sunset Boulevard, Los Angeles CA 90012
County: Los Angeles Identification: 667056
Telephone: (213) 481-1313 Carnegie Class: Not Classified
FAX Number: N/A Calendar System: Semester
URL: shepherduniversity.edu
Established: 1999 Annual Undergrad Tuition & Fees: $7,400
Enrollment: 50 Coed
Affiliation or Control: Interdenominational IRS Status: 501(c)3
Highest Offering: Doctorate
Program: Religious Emphasis
Accreditation: @THEOL

05 Vice Pres & Academic Dean ... Shalom Y. KIM

Sierra College (F)

5000 Rocklin Road, Rocklin CA 95677-3397
County: Placer FICE Identification: 001290
Unit ID: 123341
Telephone: (916) 624-3333 Carnegie Class: Assoc/Pub-S-MC
FAX Number: (916) 630-4530 Calendar System: Semester
URL: www.sierracollege.edu
Established: 1914 Annual Undergrad Tuition & Fees (In-District): $1,142
Enrollment: 18,915 Coed
Affiliation or Control: State/Local IRS Status: 501(c)3
Highest Offering: Associate Degree
Program: Occupational; 2-Year Principally Bachelor's Creditable
Accreditation: WJ

01 Superintendent/President ... Mr. William H. DUNCAN
05 Vice President Instruction ... Dr. Debra SUTPHEN
10 Vice Pres Finance & Administration ... Vacant
32 Vice Pres Student Services ... Ms. Mandy DAVIES
15 Vice Pres Human Resources ... Vacant
04 Exec Assistant Presidents Office ... Ms. Jeannette BISCHOFF
08 Dean Library/Learning Resource Ctr ... Mr. Brian HALEY
50 Dean Business & Technology ... Vacant
81 Dean Science & Mathematics ... Ms. Heather ROBERTS
49 Dean Liberal Arts ... Dr. Rebecca BOCCHICCHIO
68 Dean PE & Athletics ... Vacant
66 Associate Dean Nursing ... Vacant
21 Director of Finance ... Ms. Kerri HESTER
18 Dir of Facilities & Construction ... Ms. Laura DOTY
88 Director Economic Development ... Vacant
37 Financial Svcs Program Manager ... Ms. Linda WILLIAMS
31 Community Education Pgm Manager ... Ms. Adele HAMLETT
22 EEO Program Manager ... Mr. Cameron ABBOTT
26 Marketing/PR Supervisor ... Ms. Sue MICHAELS
39 Residence Life Supervisor ... Mr. Jon HAMBLEN

Silicon Valley University (G)

2160 Lundy Avenue, Suite 110, San Jose CA 95131
County: Santa Clara FICE Identification: 038103
Unit ID: 444848
Telephone: (408) 435-8989 Carnegie Class: Master's S
FAX Number: (408) 955-0887 Calendar System: Trimester
URL: www.svuca.edu
Established: 1997 Annual Undergrad Tuition & Fees: $10,000
Enrollment: 582 Coed
Affiliation or Control: Independent Non-Profit IRS Status: 501(c)3
Highest Offering: Master's
Program: Professional
Accreditation: ACICS

01 President ... Mr. Jerry SHIAO

Simpson University (H)

2211 College View Drive, Redding CA 96003-8606
County: Shasta FICE Identification: 001291
Unit ID: 123457
Telephone: (530) 224-5600 Carnegie Class: Bac/A&S
FAX Number: (530) 226-4860 Calendar System: Other
URL: www.simpsonu.edu
Established: 1921 Annual Undergrad Tuition & Fees: $22,400
Enrollment: 1,297 Coed
Affiliation or Control: The Christian And Missionary Alliance
IRS Status: 501(c)3
Highest Offering: Master's
Program: Liberal Arts And General; Teacher Preparatory
Accreditation: WC

01 President ... Dr. Larry J. MCKINNEY
03 Executive Vice President ... Mr. Bradley E. WILLIAMS
05 Provost ... Dr. Stanley A. CLARK
32 Vice President Student Development ... Dr. Richard W. BROWN
102 VP Marketing & Dev/Foundation ... Mr. Gordon B. FLINN
84 VP Enrollment Management ... Dr. Herb TOLBERT
10 Controller ... Mrs. Jill K. AULT
20 Associate Provost & UG Dean ... Dr. Robin K. DUMMER
18 Director of Facilities ... Mr. Merlin D. WEBER
04 Exec Assistant to the President ... Mrs. Regina ERICKSON
08 Dir Lib Svcs/Ast Prof Librarianship ... Mr. Larry L. HAIGHT
06 Interim Registrar ... Mrs. Dannielle STAHLY
06 Registrar ... Vacant
84 Director of Undergraduate Admission ... Mrs. Kendell M. KLUTTZ
13 Director of IT ... Mr. S. Curtis DODDS
41 Director of Athletics ... Mr. Joseph E. GRIFFIN
35 Director of Student Life ... Vacant
44 Director of Advancement Services ... Mrs. Elizabeth A. SPENCER
38 Director of Wellness Center ... Dr. Michael C. SCHILL
09 Director Institutional Rsrch/Assess ... Mrs. Brooks CLARK
39 Bookstore Manager ... Mrs. Karen COFFELT
15 Director of Human Resources ... Mrs. Kori D. OECHSLI
19 Director of Auxiliary Services ... Mr. Edward D. SCHNEIDER
39 Residence Life Supervisor ... Mr. Mark L. RIPPETOE
26 Director of Marketing ... Mr. Mark U. WOOD
29 Director of University Relations ... Mr. Matthew B. KLUTTZ
42 Director of Spiritual Formation ... Mr. Travis G. OSBORNE
13 Database Administrator ... Mr. Richard L. ARCHIBALD
23 Health Center Coordinator ... Mrs. Connie C. ECHOLS
36 Career Services Counselor ... Mrs. Pamela A. SCHALO
51 Dean of Continuing Studies ... Mrs. Patty A. TAYLOR
73 Dean AW Tozer Seminary ... Dr. Sarah C. SUMNER
54 Dean Educ/Assoc Prof Education ... Dr. Glee R. BROOKS
37 Director Student Financial Services ... Mrs. Melissa A. HUDSON
66 Dean School of Nursing ... Mrs. Georgianne DINKEL
88 Director MA in Counseling ... Dr. Addie JACKSON

Sofia University (formerly Institute of Transpersonal Psychology) (I)

1069 E Meadow Circle, Palo Alto CA 94303-4231
County: Santa Clara FICE Identification: 022676
Unit ID: 110778
Telephone: (650) 493-4430 Carnegie Class: Spec/Health
FAX Number: (650) 493-6835 Calendar System: Quarter
URL: www.sofia.edu
Established: 1975 Annual Graduate Tuition & Fees: $29,547
Enrollment: 515 Coed
Affiliation or Control: Independent Non-Profit IRS Status: 501(c)3
Highest Offering: Doctorate; No Undergraduates
Program: Professional
Accreditation: WC

01 President & CEO ... Dr. Neal KING
05 Provost/VP for Academic Affairs ... Dr. Paul ROY
10 CFO/VP for Finance/Compliance Ofcr ... Mr. Charles RANDALL

Soka University of America (J)

1 University Drive, Aliso Viejo CA 92656-8081
County: Orange FICE Identification: 038144
Unit ID: 399911
Telephone: (949) 480-4000 Carnegie Class: Bac/A&S
FAX Number: (949) 480-4001 Calendar System: Semester
URL: www.soka.edu
Established: 2001 Annual Undergrad Tuition & Fees: $27,950
Enrollment: 400 Coed
Affiliation or Control: Independent Non-Profit IRS Status: 501(c)3
Highest Offering: Master's
Program: Liberal Arts And General
Accreditation: WC

01 President/Professor of Economics ... Dr. Daniel Y. HABUKI
04 Exec Asst to the President ... Mr. Hiro SAKAI
10 Vice President Finance & Admin/CFO ... Mr. Archibald E. ASAWA
05 Provost/Vice Pres Academic Affairs ... Dr. Tomoko TAKAHASHI
20 Dean of Faculty/Prof of Economics ... Dr. Edward M. FEASEL
58 Dean of Graduate School ... Dr. Tomoko TAKAHASHI
07 Dean of Enrollment Svcs/Records ... Mr. Andrew WOOLSEY
32 Dean of Students ... Dr. Jay HEFFRON
88 Dir Envir Hlth/Sfty/Security/Event ... Mr. Cliff MOSHER
31 Director of Community Relations ... Ms. Wendy WETZEL HARDER
41 Director of Athletics & Recreation ... Mr. Mike MOORE
35 Director of Student Services ... Dr. Hyon MOON
39 Dir Stdt Activities/Resident Life ... Ms. Michelle HOBBY-MEARS
30 Director of Philanthropy ... Ms. Linda KENEDY
13 Director Info Tech/Int Dir Library ... Mr. Saeed FAKHRI RAVARI
84 Mgr Student Recruitment Programs ... Ms. Marilyn GOVE
44 Dir of International Development ... Mr. Hideki ABERA
15 Director of Human Resources ... Ms. Katherine KING
104 Dir Study Abroad & Intl Internships ... Mr. Alex H. OKUDA

06 Registrar .... Ms. Nancy YOSHIMURA
18 Chief of Operations .... Mr. Tom HARKENRIDER

Solano Community College (A)

4000 Suisun Valley Road, Fairfield CA 94534-3197

County: Solano FICE Identification: 001292
Unit ID: 123563
Telephone: (707) 864-7000 Carnegie Class: Assoc/Pub-S-SC
FAX Number: (707) 864-0361 Calendar System: Semester
URL: www.solano.edu
Established: 1945 Annual Undergrad Tuition & Fees (In-District): $1,080
Enrollment: 11,033 Coed
Affiliation or Control: State/Local IRS Status: 501(c)3
Highest Offering: Associate Degree
Program: Occupational; 2-Year Principally Bachelor's Creditable
Accreditation: WJ

01 Superintendent/President .... Dr. Jowel C. LAGUERRE
05 Exec VP Academic & Student Affairs .... Mr. Arturo REYES
10 Vice President Finance & Admin .... Mr. Yulian LIGIOSO
13 Dir Technology Systems & Support .... Vacant
07 Director of Admissions/Records .... Ms. Barbara FOUNTAIN
38 Dean Counseling/Special Services .... Mr. Erin VINES
37 Dean Financial Aid .... Ms. Robin DARCANGELO
21 Interim Director of Fiscal Services . Mr. Patrick KILLINGSWORTH
84 Director Enrollment Management .... Vacant
16 Interim Director Human Resources .... Ms. Charo ALBARRON
18 Director Facilities .... Mr. Dwight CALLOWAY
35 Dir Student Development/Mesa .... Mr. Mostafa GHOUS
06 Registrar .... Ms. Barbara FOUNTAIN
09 Director Research and Planning .... Mr. Peter CAMMISH
30 Exec Dir of Institutional Advancmnt .... Vacant
13 Int Director Technology Services .... Mr. Kimo CALILAN
49 Interim Dean School of Liberal Arts .... Dr. Jeffrey LAMB
88 Dean School Human Performance/Devel .... Ms. Lily ESPINOZA
79 Dean School of Sciences .... Vacant
76 Dn Sch Career Technical Ed/Business .... Mrs. Maire MORINEC
12 Center Dean Vallejo .... Dr. Jerry KEA
12 Center Dean Vacaville/TAFB/Nut Tree .... Dr. Shirley LEWIS
88 Director Children's Programs .... Ms. Christie SPECK
88 Director Small Bus Development Ctr .... Mr. Charles EASON
88 Director Theater Operations .... Vacant
96 Purchasing Tech/Buyer .... Ms. Laura SCOTT
36 Career & Job Placement Coordinator .... Ms. Patricia YOUNG

South Baylo University (B)

1126 N Brookhurst Street, Anaheim CA 92801-1702

County: Orange FICE Identification: 025973
Unit ID: 123633
Telephone: (714) 533-1495 Carnegie Class: Spec/Health
FAX Number: (714) 533-6040 Calendar System: Quarter
URL: www.southbaylo.edu
Established: 1977 Annual Undergrad Tuition & Fees: $12,104
Enrollment: 607 Coed
Affiliation or Control: Independent Non-Profit IRS Status: 501(c)3
Highest Offering: Doctorate
Program: Professional
Accreditation: ACUP

01 President .... Dr. Jason SHIN
05 Academic Dean .... Dr. Pia MELEN
11 Vice President Administration .... Dr. David KWON
07 Director of Admission .... Dr. Young Jin AHN
06 Registrar .... Ms. Michelle PARK
10 Director of Finance .... Ms. Michelle JANG
15 Operations/Personnel Director .... Dr. Sohila MOHIYEDDINI
36 Program Student Advisor .... Dr. Henry CHOI
08 Director of Libraries .... Dr. Edwin FOLLICK
13 Dir Computer Information System .... Mr. James KIM
88 Director of Clinics .... Dr. Sang Jo KIM
37 Financial Aid Officer .... Ms. Mimi PARK
35 Stdnt/Alumni/English LG Coordinator .... Ms. Rocio SALAS-BELTRAN
85 International Student Advisor .... Ms. Michelle PARK
88 Doctoral Clerkship Coordinator .... Dr. Sheng LI
88 Doctoral Program Director .... Dr. Wayne CHENG
88 Master Program Director .... Dr. Hanjik KIM
18 Chief Facilities/Physical Plant .... Mr. Yong Hee PARK

† Candidate at the Doctorate level.

South Coast College (C)

2011 W Chapman Avenue, Orange CA 92868-2609

County: Orange FICE Identification: 022774
Unit ID: 123642
Telephone: (714) 867-5009 Carnegie Class: Assoc/PrivFP
FAX Number: (714) 867-5026 Calendar System: Quarter
URL: www.southcoastcollege.com
Established: 1961 Annual Undergrad Tuition & Fees: $37,994
Enrollment: 392 Coed
Affiliation or Control: Proprietary IRS Status: Proprietary
Highest Offering: Associate Degree
Program: Occupational
Accreditation: ACICS

01 President .... Ms. Jean GONZALEZ
03 Vice President .... Ms. Lonnie SKELTON
11 Director of Operations .... Mr. Kevin MAGNER
37 Director of Financial Aid .... Ms. Melanie SARACCO

*South Orange County Community College District (D)

28000 Marguerite Parkway, Mission Viejo CA 92692-3697

County: Orange FICE Identification: 033433
Unit ID: 432144
Telephone: (949) 582-4500 Carnegie Class: N/A
FAX Number: (949) 364-2726
URL: www.socccd.edu

01 Chancellor .... Mr. Gary POERTNER
05 Vice Chanc Technology/Learning Svcs .. Dr. Robert S. BRAMUCCI
16 Vice Chancellor Human Resources .... Dr. David P. BUGAY
26 Dir Public Affairs/Intergovtl Rels .... Ms. Tere FLUEGEMAN
10 Vice Chancellor Business Services .... Ms. Debra FITZSIMONS

*Irvine Valley College (E)

5500 Irvine Center Drive, Irvine CA 92618-4399

County: Orange FICE Identification: 025395
Unit ID: 116439
Telephone: (949) 451-5100 Carnegie Class: Assoc/Pub-S-MC
FAX Number: (949) 451-5270 Calendar System: Semester
URL: www.ivc.edu
Established: 1979 Annual Undergrad Tuition & Fees (In-District): $1,380
Enrollment: 13,258 Coed
Affiliation or Control: State/Local IRS Status: 501(c)3
Highest Offering: Associate Degree
Program: Occupational; 2-Year Principally Bachelor's Creditable
Accreditation: WJ

02 President .... Dr. Glenn R. ROQUEMORE
05 Vice President Instruction .... Dr. Stephen C. JUSTICE
32 Vice President Student Services .... Dr. Linda FONTANILLA
20 Dean of Academic Programs .... Dr. Kathy WERLE
38 Dean Counseling Services .... Dr. Elizabeth CIPRES
49 Dean School of Liberal Arts .... Dr. Karima FELDHUS
106 Dean Online Educ/Learning Resources .... Dr. Roger OWENS
76 Dean Kinesiology/Health/Athletics .... Mr. Keith SHACKLEFORD
81 Dean Math/Sciences/Engineering .... Dr. Lianna ZHAO
57 Dean Fine Arts/Business Services .... Dr. David GATEWOOD
102 Exec Director IVC Foundation .... Mr. Richard H. MORLEY
10 Director Fiscal Services .... Mr. Davit KHACHATRYAN
07 Director Admiss/Records/Enroll Svcs .... Ms. Arleen ELSEROAD
18 Dir Facilities & Maintenance .... Mr. John EDWARDS
19 Chief of Police .... Mr. Will GLEN
37 Director Financial Aid .... Mr. Darryl COX
35 Director Student Development .... Ms. Helen LOCKE
14 Director Technology Services .... Mr. Bruce HAGAN
51 Int Director Extended Education .... Ms. Sharon LOUIE
09 Dir Research/Planning/Accreditation .... Mr. Craig HAYWARD
26 Director of Public Info & Marketing .... Ms. Diane G. OAKS
88 Child Development Center Manager .... Ms. Becky THOMAS
06 Registrar/Admissions/Records .... Mr. Ben GUZMAN

*Saddleback College (F)

28000 Marguerite Parkway, Mission Viejo CA 92692-3635

County: Orange FICE Identification: 008918
Unit ID: 122205
Telephone: (949) 582-4500 Carnegie Class: Assoc/Pub-S-MC
FAX Number: (949) 347-0438 Calendar System: Semester
URL: www.saddleback.edu
Established: 1968 Annual Undergrad Tuition & Fees (In-District): $1,184
Enrollment: 27,992 Coed
Affiliation or Control: State/Local IRS Status: 501(c)3
Highest Offering: Associate Degree
Program: Occupational; 2-Year Principally Bachelor's Creditable
Accreditation: WJ, ADNUR, EMT

02 President .... Dr. Tod A. BURNETT
05 Actg Vice President of Instruction .... Dr. Donald BUSCHE
32 Vice President of Student Services .... Dr. Juan AVALOS
07 Director Admissions & Records .... Ms. Jane ROSENKRANS
45 Director Planning/Research/Grants .... Dr. Caroline DURDELLA
06 Registrar .... Ms. Joyce SEMANIK
19 Acting Director Security/Safety .... Mr. James PYLE
26 Director Public Information .... Ms. Jennie MCCUE
102 Director College Foundation .... Mr. Donald RICKNER
35 Director Student Development .... Ms. Audra DIPADOVA
31 Director of Community Education .... Ms. Estella GARRISON
88 Director Emeritus Institute .... Mr. David ANDERSON
66 Director of Nursing .... Ms. Tammy RICE
10 VP College Administrative Services .... Ms. Carol HILTON
15 Director Human Resources .... Ms. Teddi LORCH
18 Dir Facilities/Maint/Operation .... Mr. John OZUROVICH
37 Director Financial Assistance .... Mr. Christian ALVARADO
96 Director of Purchasing .... Ms. Brandye D'LENA
85 Intl Student Program Specialist .... Ms. Monika CONNOLLY
92 Honors Program .... Ms. Alannah ROSENBERG
38 Dean Counseling Svcs/Special Pgms .... Ms. Jerilyn CHUMAN
57 Dean Fine Arts .... Mr. Bart MCHENRY
75 Dean Bus Sci/Voc Educ/Econ Devel .... Mr. Rocky CIFONE
76 Dean Hlth Sci/Human Svcs & Emeritus .... Dr. Donna RANE-SZOSTAK
81 Dean Math/Science & Engineering ... Dr. Christopher MCDONALD
79 Dean Liberal Arts/Learning Res .... Dr. Kevin O'CONNOR
106 Dean Online Education/Learning Res .... Dr. Patricia FLANIGAN
72 Dean Advance Tech Appl Science .... Mr. Don TAYLOR
68 Dean Kinesiology/Athletic Director .... Mr. Tony LIPOLD
83 Dean Social & Behavioral Sciences .... Dr. Cadence WYNTER
35 Asst Dean Couns Svcs/Spec Pgms .... Mr. Terence NELSON
84 Chair Enrollment Management .... Vacant

Southern California College of Optometry (G)

2575 Yorba Linda Boulevard, Fullerton CA 92831-1699

County: Orange FICE Identification: 001230
Unit ID: 123943
Telephone: (714) 870-7226 Carnegie Class: Spec/Health
FAX Number: (714) 879-9834 Calendar System: Quarter
URL: www.scco.edu
Established: 1904 Annual Undergrad Tuition & Fees: $29,100
Enrollment: 398 Coed
Affiliation or Control: Independent Non-Profit IRS Status: 501(c)3
Highest Offering: Doctorate
Program: Professional
Accreditation: WC, OPT, OPTR

01 President .... Dr. Kevin L. ALEXANDER
05 Vice Pres/Dean Academic Affairs .... Dr. Morris S. BERMAN
30 Vice Pres Advancement/Marketing .... Mr. Paul A. STOVER
88 Vice Pres Interprofessional Affairs .... Dr. John H. NISHIMOTO
17 Vice Pres & Dean Clinical Affairs .... Dr. Julie A. SCHORNACK
32 Vice President of Student Affairs .... Dr. Lorraine I. VOORHEES
15 Vice Pres Human Resources .... Ms. Gail S. DEUTSCH
04 Special Assistant to President .... Mr. William HEATON, JR.
10 Controller .... Mr. Bill TOLMASOFF
46 Associate Dean for Research .... Dr. Jerry PAUGH
18 Director Campus Operations .... Mr. Gregory SMITH
51 Director Continuing Education .... Ms. Susan ATKINSON
25 Director Invest & Restricted Funds .... Mr. Glenn Y. KOJIMA
15 Director Human Resources .... Mr. Dennis GABY
27 Director of Communications .... Ms. Debra J. MARKS
13 Director of Information Technology .... Mr. Gary W. GRAY
37 Director Financial Aid .... Ms. Tami A. SATO
07 Director of Admissions .... Dr. Jane Ann MUNROE
30 Dir Development/Alumni Affairs .... Ms. Frances ROZNER
08 Director of Library Services .... Ms. Donnajean MATTHEWS
23 Dir Special Clinic Programs .... Ms. Michele WHITECAVAGE
40 Manager Campus Store .... Ms. Debra WOODS

Southern California Institute of Architecture (H)

960 E 3rd Street, Los Angeles CA 90013-1822

County: Los Angeles FICE Identification: 020758
Unit ID: 123952
Telephone: (213) 613-2200 Carnegie Class: Spec/Arts
FAX Number: (213) 613-2260 Calendar System: Semester
URL: www.sciarc.edu
Established: 1972 Annual Undergrad Tuition & Fees: $35,876
Enrollment: 458 Coed
Affiliation or Control: Independent Non-Profit IRS Status: 501(c)3
Highest Offering: Master's
Program: Professional
Accreditation: WC

01 Director .... Mr. Eric O. MOSS
04 Director's Assistant .... Ms. Stephanie ATLAN
05 Director Academic Affairs .... Ms. Hsin-Ming FUNG
11 Chief Operating Officer .... Mr. Jamie BENNETT
30 Chief Development Officer .... Ms. Sarah SULLIVAN
58 Graduate Program Director .... Mr. Hernan DIAZ-ALONSO
88 Undergraduate Program Director .... Mr. John ENRIGHT
05 Academic Affairs Manager .... Mr. Paul HOLLIDAY
20 Academic Programs Assistant .... Ms. Emily REITER
10 Finance Director .... Mr. Christopher BANKS
15 Human Resources Director .... Ms. Melissa BURGESS
07 Admissions Director .... Ms. Sandy FRIGO
37 Financial Aid Director .... Ms. Helen LARA
08 Library Manager .... Mr. Kevin MCMAHON
90 Director of IT .... Mr. Vic JABRASSIAN
88 Wood & Metal Shopmaster .... Mr. Rodney ROJAS
88 Wood & Metal Shopmaster .... Mr. Katsumi MOROI
20 Academic Counselor .... Mr. Peter DUNG
06 Registrar/Chf of Staff/Intl Advisor .... Ms. Lisa RUSSO

Southern California Institute of Technology (I)

222 S Harbor Boulevard, Suite 200,
Anaheim CA 92805-3758

County: Orange FICE Identification: 031136
Unit ID: 399869
Telephone: (714) 300-0300 Carnegie Class: Bac/Diverse
FAX Number: (714) 300-0311 Calendar System: Quarter
URL: www.scitech.edu
Established: 1987 Annual Undergrad Tuition & Fees: $16,000
Enrollment: 546 Coed
Affiliation or Control: Proprietary IRS Status: Proprietary
Highest Offering: Baccalaureate
Program: Technical Emphasis
Accreditation: ACCSC

01 President .... Dr. Parviz SHAMS
03 Vice President .... Mrs. Nazila SHAMS
05 Dean of Education .... Mr. Saravana RAMAN
13 MIS .... Mr. Arian SHAMS

Southern California Seminary (J)

2075 E Madison Avenue, El Cajon CA 92019-1108

County: San Diego FICE Identification: 033323
Unit ID: 117575

Telephone: (619) 201-8999 Carnegie Class: Spec/Faith
FAX Number: (619) 201-8975 Calendar System: Trimester
URL: www.socalsem.edu
Established: 1946 Annual Undergrad Tuition & Fees: $13,692
Enrollment: 219 Coed
Affiliation or Control: Independent Non-Profit IRS Status: 501(c)3
Highest Offering: Doctorate
Program: Religious Emphasis
Accreditation: TRACS

00 Chancellor ... Dr. George W. HARE
01 President ... Dr. Gary F. COOMBS
03 Executive Vice President ... Vacant
05 Vice President for Academics ... Dr. Edward J. HERRELKO, III
32 Vice President of Student Services ... Vacant
58 Dean of Graduate Biblical Studies ... Dr. Peter OH
83 Dean of Behavioral Science ... Dr. Julie M. HAYDEN
73 Dean of Undergrad Biblical Studies ... Mr. James I. FAZIO
06 Registrar ... Mrs. Cheryl OBST
37 Director of Financial Aid ... Mrs. Yuli MARTINEZ
08 Seminary Librarian ... Miss Jennifer EWING

Southern California University of Health Sciences (A)

16200 E Amber Valley Drive, Whittier CA 90604-4051
County: Los Angeles FICE Identification: 001229
Unit ID: 117672
Telephone: (562) 947-8755 Carnegie Class: Spec/Health
FAX Number: (562) 947-5724 Calendar System: Trimester
URL: www.scuhs.edu
Established: 1911 Annual Undergrad Tuition & Fees: $28,158
Enrollment: 965 Coed
Affiliation or Control: Independent Non-Profit IRS Status: 501(c)3
Highest Offering: First Professional Degree
Program: Professional
Accreditation: WC, ACUP, CHIRO

01 President ... Dr. John SCARINGE
05 Vice President of Academic Affs ... Dr. J. Todd KNUDSEN
10 VP Admin & Finance/CFO ... Mr. Thomas K. ARENDT
84 Assoc VP Enroll Mgmt/Stdnt Affs ... Ms. Debra MITCHELL
88 Dean of Chiropractic ... Dr. Mike SACKETT
11 Director Administrative Svcs ... Ms. Theresa EGGLESTON
88 Dean Acupuncture/Oriental Medicine ... Dr. Wen-Shuo WU
21 Controller ... Mrs. Kelly GALLO
09 Dean Supportive/Inst Research ... Dr. Melea FIELDS
07 Exec Director of Enrollment Svcs ... Dr. Peter HANNA
06 Registrar ... Ms. Debra MITCHELL
13 Senior Programmer/Operations Mgr ... Mr. Mike ROCKE
32 Director of Student Affairs ... Dr. Steven JAFFE
23 Chf Clinical Ofcr/Dir Univ Hlth Ctr ... Dr. Melissa KIMURA
30 Exec Director of Inst Mktg/Advance ... Dr. Hubert CHANG
18 Chief Facilities/Physical Plant ... Vacant
37 Financial Aid Counselor ... Ms. Nida LABAO
08 Exec Dir of Seabury Learning Center ... Ms. Kathleen E. SMITH
29 Director of Alumni ... Vacant
96 Accounts Payable/Purchasing Coord ... Mrs. Catherine MCBRIDE

Southern California University School of Oriental Medicine and Acupuncture (B)

1541 Wilshire Boulevard, 3rd Floor,
Los Angeles CA 90017-2211
County: Los Angeles FICE Identification: 041720
Unit ID: 459222
Telephone: (213) 413-9500 Carnegie Class: Spec/Health
FAX Number: (213) 413-5400 Calendar System: Quarter
URL: www.scusoma.edu
Established: N/A Annual Undergrad Tuition & Fees: $12,000
Enrollment: 155 Coed
Affiliation or Control: Proprietary IRS Status: Proprietary
Highest Offering: Master's
Program: Professional
Accreditation: ACUP

01 President ... Brian H. KIM
05 Academic Dean ... Dr. Katherine H S. CHO

Southern States University (C)

123 Camino de la Reina Ste 100 East,
San Diego CA 92108
County: San Diego Identification: 667108
Telephone: (619) 298-1829 Carnegie Class: Not Classified
FAX Number: (619) 704-0175 Calendar System: Quarter
URL: www.ssu.edu
Established: 1985 Annual Undergrad Tuition & Fees: N/A
Enrollment: N/A Coed
Affiliation or Control: Proprietary IRS Status: Proprietary
Highest Offering: Master's
Program: Business Emphasis
Accreditation: ACICS

00 Chancellor ... John D. TUCKER
01 President ... Danny HSING
05 Vice Chanc Academic Affairs ... Dr. Stephanie L. DIERINGER
06 University Registrar ... Sean SELL
32 Dean of Students & Acad Advis ... William AMOKE
10 Chief Financial Officer ... Frank PARKER
08 Librarian ... Svetlana KONDRATENKO

Southwestern College (D)

900 Otay Lakes Road, Chula Vista CA 91910-7299
County: San Diego FICE Identification: 001294
Unit ID: 123800
Telephone: (619) 421-6700 Carnegie Class: Assoc/Pub-S-SC
FAX Number: (619) 482-6413 Calendar System: Semester
URL: www.swccd.edu
Established: 1961 Annual Undergrad Tuition & Fees (In-District): $1,080
Enrollment: 19,476 Coed
Affiliation or Control: State/Local IRS Status: 501(c)3
Highest Offering: Associate Degree
Program: Occupational; 2-Year Principally Bachelor's Creditable
Accreditation: WJ, ADNUR, DH, EMT, MLTAD, SURGT

01 Superintendent/President ... Dr. Melinda NISH
05 Int Vice President Academic Affairs ... Ms. Kathy TYNER
10 VP Business & Financial Affairs ... Mr. Steven CROW
32 Vice President Student Affairs ... Dr. Angelica SUAREZ
16 Vice Pres Human Resources ... Dr. Albert J. ROMAN
12 Dean Ed Ctr Otay Mesa/San Ysidr . Ms. Silvia CORNEJO-DARCY
12 Dean HEC Natl City/Crown Cove ... Ms. Christine PERRI
79 Dean Language & Literature ... Dr. Joel LEVINE
81 Int Dean Math/Science Engineering ... Mr. Richard FIELDING
35 Dean Student Services ... Ms. Mia C. MCCLELLAN
83 Dean Social Sciences & Humanities ... Dr. Mark MEADOWS
38 Dean Counseling & Matriculation ... Ms. Beatrice ZAMORA-AGUILAR
68 Dean Health/Exercise Sci/Athletics ... Mr. Terry DAVIS
60 Dean Arts & Communication ... Ms. Donna C. ARNOLD
88 Dean Instructional Support Services ... Dr. Mink STAVENGA
26 Chief Comm Cmty & Gov Rels Officer ... Ms. Lillian LEOPOLD
15 Interim Director Human Resources ... Mr. Robert A. UNGER
09 Dir Inst Rsrch Grants & Planning ... Ms. Linda HENSLEY
18 Dir Facilities Ops & Planning ... Mr. John BROWN
13 Director Computer Systems & Svcs ... Dr. Ben SEABERRY
40 Director Food Services/Bookstore ... Mr. Joe FIGHERA
88 Dir Center Ops San Ysidro ... Ms. Silvia CORNEJO-DARCY
37 Director Financial Aid ... Ms. Linda THROWER
96 Dir Contract Purchasing & Cntrl Svc ... Ms. Priya JEROME

Southwestern Law School (E)

3050 Wilshire Boulevard, Los Angeles CA 90010-1106
County: Los Angeles FICE Identification: 001295
Unit ID: 123970
Telephone: (213) 738-6700 Carnegie Class: Spec/Law
FAX Number: (213) 383-1688 Calendar System: Semester
URL: www.swlaw.edu
Established: 1911 Annual Graduate Tuition & Fees: $43,650
Enrollment: 1,121 Coed
Affiliation or Control: Independent Non-Profit IRS Status: 501(c)3
Highest Offering: Master's; No Undergraduates
Program: Professional
Accreditation: LAW

01 Interim Dean/Chief Exec Officer ... Mr. Austen L. PARRISH
03 Chief Operating Officer ... Ms. Janice A. MANIS
10 Chief Financial Officer ... Mr. Paul KALUSH
04 Corporate Secretary ... Ms. Janis K. YOKOYAMA
05 Vice Dean for Academic Affairs ... Ms. Anahid GHARAKHANIAN
46 Associate Dean of Research ... Mr. Arthur F. MCEVOY
08 Associate Dean of Library Services ... Ms. Linda A. WHISMAN
32 Assoc Dean/Dean of Stdnts & Div Aff ... Ms. Nyree GRAY
20 Associate Dean for Academic Admin ... Ms. Doreen E. HEYER
88 Sr Assoc Dean Career/Admiss/Fin Aid ... Mr. Gary J. GREENER
43 Associate Dean/General Counsel ... Mr. Patrick PYLE
30 Assoc Dean for Institutional Advanc ... Ms. Debra L. LEATHERS
27 Associate Dean for Public Affairs ... Ms. Leslie R. STEINBERG
07 Asst Dean of Admissions ... Ms. Lisa L. GEAR
06 Asst Dean Regist/Academic Records ... Ms. Carolyn HAITH
35 Asst Dean of Student Affairs ... Dr. Robert MENA
104 Asst Dean for Gen LLM/Intl Pgms ... Ms. Anne WILSON
37 Asst Dean for Financial Aid ... Mr. Wayne MAHONEY
13 Chief Information Systems Officer ... Ms. Bo SUZOW
88 Associate Dean of Special Projects ... Dr. Jane POWELL
88 Assoc Dean Interdisciplinary Prgms ... Ms. Molly SELVIN
88 Asst Dean Prop Admin/Development ... Mr. James C. CAMP
88 Dean Emeritus/Prof of Law ... Mr. Bryant G. GARTH

Stanbridge College (F)

2041 Business Center Drive, Irvine CA 92612
County: Orange FICE Identification: 038893
Unit ID: 446561
Telephone: (949) 794-9090 Carnegie Class: Assoc/PrivFP
FAX Number: (949) 794-9098 Calendar System: Other
URL: www.stanbridge.edu
Established: 1996 Annual Undergrad Tuition & Fees: $33,995
Enrollment: 740 Coed
Affiliation or Control: Proprietary IRS Status: Proprietary
Highest Offering: Baccalaureate
Program: Occupational; 2-Year Principally Bachelor's Creditable; Nursing Emphasis
Accreditation: ACCSC, OTA, @PTAA

01 Chief Executive Officer ... Yasith WEERASURIYA
10 Chief Financial Officer ... Nazi MASOUM
37 Director of Financial Aid ... Brian SILVANO
07 Director of Admissions ... Edward RIEPMA
05 VP of Instruction ... Dr. Everett PROCTER
66 Director of Nursing ... Debbie LIEU
75 Director of Occupational Therapy ... Satch PURCELL
88 Director of Physical Therapy ... Dr. Scott BENNIE
106 Director of Online Programs ... Dr. Jon INOUYE
20 Dean of Instruction ... Tim POWERS
32 Dean of Students ... John WALKER
105 VP of Internet and Media Technology ... Monir BOKTOR

Stanford University (G)

Stanford CA 94305-1684
County: Santa Clara FICE Identification: 001305
Unit ID: 243744
Telephone: (650) 723-2300 Carnegie Class: RU/VH
FAX Number: (650) 725-6847 Calendar System: Quarter
URL: www.stanford.edu
Established: 1885 Annual Undergrad Tuition & Fees: $41,250
Enrollment: 15,723 Coed
Affiliation or Control: Independent Non-Profit IRS Status: 501(c)3
Highest Offering: Doctorate
Program: Liberal Arts And General; Professional
Accreditation: WC, ARCPA, BUS, ENG, IPSY, LAW, MED, TED

01 President ... Mr. John L. HENNESSY
43 Vice President & General Counsel ... Ms. Debra L. ZUMWALT
05 Provost ... Mr. John W. ETCHEMENDY
30 Vice President for Development ... Mr. Martin SHELL
10 Vice President Business Affairs/CFO ... Mr. Randy LIVINGSTON
26 Vice President for Public Affairs ... Mr. David F. DEMAREST
15 Vice President of Human Resources ... Mr. David JONES
29 President of Alumni Associaton ... Mr. Howard E. WOLF
46 Vice Provost/Dean of Research ... Dr. Ann ARVIN
20 Vice Provost for Academic Affairs ... Dr. Stephanie KALFAYAN
88 Vice Provost Faculty Development ... Ms. Karen COOK
20 Vice Provost Undergrad Education ... Mr. Harry J. ELAM
18 Vice Provost for Land & Buildings ... Mr. Robert C. REIDY
21 Vice Provost Budget & Auxiliaries ... Mr. Timothy R. WARNER
32 Vice Provost Student Affairs ... Mr. Gregory E. BOARDMAN
04 Sr Assistant to the President ... Mr. Jeffrey H. WACHTEL
63 Dean School of Medicine ... Vacant
50 Dean Graduate School Business ... Dr. Garth SALONER
65 Dean School of Earth Sciences ... Dr. Pamela A. MATSON
53 Dean School of Education ... Dr. Claude STEELE
54 Dean School of Engineering ... Dr. James D. PLUMMER
49 Dean School Humanities & Sciences ... Mr. Richard P. SALLER
61 Dean School of Law ... Vacant
87 Dean Summer Session/Cont Stds ... Dr. Charles L. JUNKERMAN
42 Dean for Religious Life ... Rev. William L. MCLENNAN
88 Director Hoover Institution ... Dr. John RAISIAN
88 Director Stanford Lin Accelerator ... Vacant
13 Executive Director IT Services ... Mr. Bill CLEBSCH
86 Director Government Relations ... Mr. Larry N. HORTON
08 University Librarian ... Mr. Michael A. KELLER
41 Athletic Director ... Vacant
07 Director of Admission ... Vacant
88 CEO Stanford Management Company ... Mr. John POWERS
16 Director of Compensation ... Ms. Linda S. LEE
21 Director of Business Development ... Ms. Susan L. WEINSTEIN
06 Registrar ... Mr. Thomas BLACK
36 Director Career Development Center ... Mr. Lance M. CHOY
09 Director of Institutional Research ... Ms. Kathleen DETTMAN
37 Director of Student Financial Aid ... Ms. Karen S. COOPER
27 Director Stanford News Service ... Mr. Dan STOBER
19 Director Public Safety ... Ms. Laura L. WILSON
96 Chief Procurement Officer ... Mr. Stuart DAVIS
35 Director of Student Activities ... Ms. Nanci HOWE
28 Director of Diversity ... Mr. Tommy Lee WOO
38 Director Student Counseling ... Dr. Ronald ALBURCHER

Stanton University (H)

12666 Brookhurst Street, Garden Grove CA 92840
County: Orange Identification: 667053
Telephone: (714) 539-6561 Carnegie Class: Not Classified
FAX Number: (714) 539-6542 Calendar System: Quarter
URL: www.stantonuniversity.com
Established: N/A Annual Undergrad Tuition & Fees: N/A
Enrollment: N/A Coed
Affiliation or Control: Proprietary IRS Status: Proprietary
Highest Offering: Master's
Program: Professional
Accreditation: @ACUP

01 President ... Dr. Franklin R. TURNER

Starr King School for the Ministry (I)

2441 Le Conte Avenue, Berkeley CA 94709-1299
County: Alameda FICE Identification: 004080
Unit ID: 123916
Telephone: (510) 845-6232 Carnegie Class: Spec/Faith
FAX Number: (510) 845-6273 Calendar System: Semester
URL: www.sksm.edu
Established: 1904 Annual Graduate Tuition & Fees: $18,236
Enrollment: 75 Coed
Affiliation or Control: Unitarian Universalist IRS Status: 501(c)3
Highest Offering: Master's; No Undergraduates
Program: Professional

Accreditation: THEOL

01 President ... Dr. Rebecca PARKER
05 Dean of the Faculty ... Dr. Gabriella LETTNI
32 Dean of Students ... Ms. Becky LEYSER
06 Registrar ... Ms. Kat CROSWELL
07 Director of Admissions ... Ms. Crystal WESTON
30 Advancement Director ... Mr. Federico PACHECO

*State Center Community College District (A)

1525 E Weldon Avenue, Fresno CA 93704-6398
County: Fresno FICE Identification: 001306
Unit ID: 123925
Telephone: (559) 226-0720 Carnegie Class: N/A
FAX Number: (559) 229-7039
URL: www.scccd.edu

01 Chancellor ... Dr. Deborah G. BLUE
10 Vice Chancellor Finance & Admin ... Mr. Edwin ENG
16 Int Assoc Vice Chanc Human Res ... Ms. Diane CLEROU
11 Assoc Vice Chanc District Ops ... Mr. Brian SPEECE
20 Act Vice Ch Educ Svcs/Instl Effect ... Mr. Robert FOX
09 Int Vice Pres Adm Recs & Inst Res ... Ms. Doris GRIFFITH
15 Act District Dean Human Resources ... Mr. Ron CATARAHA
26 Exec Dir Public/Legislative Rels ... Dr. Teresa PATTERSON
102 Executive Director of Foundation . Ms. Gurdeep SIHOTA HE'BERT
25 Director Grants/External Funding ... Ms. Shelly CONNER
96 Director of Purchasing ... Mr. Randy VOGT
21 Director of Finance ... Mr. Wil SCHOFIELD
13 Director of Information Systems ... Mr. John BENGTSON
88 Director of Classified Personnel ... Ms. Elba GOMEZ
18 Director Maintenance/Operations ... Mr. Carl SIMMS
43 General Counsel ... Mr. Gregory TAYLOR
19 Chief of Police ... Chief Joseph CALLAHAN

*Fresno City College (B)

1101 E University Avenue, Fresno CA 93741-0002
County: Fresno FICE Identification: 001307
Unit ID: 114789
Telephone: (559) 442-4600 Carnegie Class: Assoc/Pub-U-MC
FAX Number: (559) 237-4232 Calendar System: Semester
URL: www.fresnocitycollege.edu
Established: 1910 Annual Undergrad Tuition & Fees (In-District): $1,104
Enrollment: 20,481 Coed
Affiliation or Control: State/Local IRS Status: 501(c)3
Highest Offering: Associate Degree
Program: Occupational; 2-Year Principally Bachelor's Creditable
Accreditation: WJ, DH, EMT, RAD, SURGT

02 President ... Mr. Tony CANTU
05 Vice President of Instruction ... Ms. Kelly FOWLER
32 Vice President of Student Services ... Dr. Christopher M. VILLA
10 Vice Pres Administrative Services ... Ms. Cheryl SULLIVAN
07 Vice Pres Admissions/Records ... Ms. Doris GRIFFIN
08 Dean Library/Stdnt Lrng Support Svc ... Vacant
50 Dean Business Division ... Dr. Timothy WOODS
57 Dean Fine Perform Commun Arts ... Dr. Jothany L. BLACKWOOD
79 Dean Humanities Division ... Dr. Jennifer JOHNSON
54 Dean Math/Science/Engineering Div ... Dr. Ashok V. NAIMPALLY
83 Dean Social Sciences Division ... Dr. Margaret E. MERICLE
76 Dean Health Sciences Division ... Dr. Carolyn C. DRAKE
72 Dean Applied Technology Div ... Mr. Christopher WHITESIDE
38 Dean Counseling-Guidance ... Dr. Mark SANCHEZ
88 Dean of Students/EOPS ... Dr. Lee FARLEY
103 Dean Workforce Dev & CalWorks ... Dr. Natalie C. DOCKINS
75 Director FCC Training Institute ... Mr. Charles FRANCIS
88 Director Disabled Stdnt Pgms & Svcs ... Dr. Janice EMERZIAN
09 Director Institutional Research ... Dr. Lijuan ZHAI
88 Director Police Academy ... Mr. Richard LINDSTROM
35 Director of Student Activities ... Mr. Sean HENDERSON
26 Director Marketing/Communications ... Ms. Cris M. BREMER
37 Director Financial Aid ... Ms. Kira TIPPINS
27 Public Information Officer ... Ms. Kathleen BONILLA
41 Athletic Director ... Ms. Susan YATES
38 Director Student Support Svcs & ETS ... Vacant
72 Director of Technology ... Mr. Don LOPEZ
36 Director Career Advancement ... Vacant
66 Director of Nursing ... Ms. Stephanie R. ROBINSON
88 Director CalWORKs Program ... Ms. Anne WATTS

*Reedley College (C)

995 N Reed Avenue, Reedley CA 93654-2099
County: Fresno FICE Identification: 001308
Unit ID: 117052
Telephone: (559) 638-3641 Carnegie Class: Assoc/Pub-U-MC
FAX Number: (559) 638-5040 Calendar System: Semester
URL: www.reedleycollege.edu
Established: 1926 Annual Undergrad Tuition & Fees (In-District): $898
Enrollment: 14,057 Coed
Affiliation or Control: State/Local IRS Status: 501(c)3
Highest Offering: Associate Degree
Program: Occupational; 2-Year Principally Bachelor's Creditable
Accreditation: WJ

02 Acting President ... Mr. Michael WHITE
05 Vice President of Instruction ... Vacant
11 Int Vice Pres Administrative Svcs ... Ms. Donna BERRY
32 Vice President of Student Services ... Mr. Michael WHITE
75 Dean of Instruction/Vocational Educ ... Mr. David CLARK
79 Dean of Instruction/Humanities ... Dr. John FIRZER
81 Dean Instruct/Math/Sci/Tech/PE/Hlth ... Mr. Jan DEKKER
27 Public Information Officer ... Ms. Lucy RUIZ
88 Director Disabled Stdnt Prgms/Svcs ... Dr. Janice EMERZIAN
22 Director EOPS ... Mr. Mario GONZALES
13 Director of Technology ... Mr. Gary SAKAGUCHI
37 Financial Aid Manager ... Ms. Chris CORTES
07 Admissions & Records Mgr/Registrar ... Ms. Leticia ALVAREZ

SUM Bible College and Theological Seminary (D)

735 105th Avenue, Oakland CA 94603-3603
County: Alameda Identification: 666021
Unit ID: 447953
Telephone: (510) 567-6174 Carnegie Class: Spec/Faith
FAX Number: (510) 568-1024 Calendar System: Trimester
URL: www.sum.edu
Established: 1999 Annual Undergrad Tuition & Fees: $7,905
Enrollment: 305 Coed
Affiliation or Control: Independent Non-Profit IRS Status: 501(c)3
Highest Offering: Baccalaureate
Program: Occupational; Liberal Arts And General; Professional; Religious Emphasis
Accreditation: BI

01 President/Chancellor ... Rev. George NEAU
05 Chief Academic Officer ... Dr. Elsie COOK
10 Vice President Finance ... Mrs. Judith LITTLETON
30 Chief Development/Dir of Admissions ... Mr. Roy TRUITT
42 Dean of Student Ministry ... Rev. Rondale TERRY
08 Director of the Library ... Mrs. Kristin ABRAHAM
32 Dean of Student Life ... Ms. Sharon JIMENEZ
06 Institutional Research/Registrar .. Ms. D'Lonika JENKINS-CARTER
37 Director of Financial Aid ... Mrs. Kathryn MANGAN
07 Director Recruitment ... Mr. Roy TRUITTT

† Affiliated with School of Urban Missions-New Orleans, Gretna, LA.

Taft College (E)

29 Emmons Park Drive, Taft CA 93268-1437
County: Kern FICE Identification: 001309
Unit ID: 124113
Telephone: (661) 763-7700 Carnegie Class: Assoc/Pub-S-SC
FAX Number: (661) 763-7705 Calendar System: Semester
URL: www.taftcollege.edu
Established: 1922 Annual Undergrad Tuition & Fees (In-District): $1,380
Enrollment: 5,143 Coed
Affiliation or Control: State/Local IRS Status: 501(c)3
Highest Offering: Associate Degree
Program: Occupational; 2-Year Principally Bachelor's Creditable
Accreditation: WJ, DH

01 Superintendent/President ... Dr. Dena MALONEY
05 Vice President of Instruction ... Ms. Patricia BENCH
32 Vice Pres of Student Services ... Mr. Brock MCMURRAY
04 Assistant to the President ... Ms. Shelley KLEIN
30 Director Foundation & Development ... Ms. Sheri HORN BUNK
13 Director Information Services ... Mr. Adrian AGUNDEZ
20 Associate Dean of Instruction ... Mr. Val GARCIA
38 Lead Counselor ... Ms. Darcy BOGLE
08 Director of Library & LRC ... Vacant
46 Coord Inst Research/Assessment/Plng ... Dr. Eric BERUBE
41 Director Athletics ... Ms. Kanoe BANDY
15 Director Human Resources ... Ms. Jana PETERS
21 Director of Business Services ... Mr. Jim NICHOLAS
06 Registrar/Director of Admissions ... Ms. Michelle HINES
18 Supervisor Maintenance/Operations ... Mr. Michael CAPELA
10 Chief Business Officer ... Mr. Ronald ERREA
37 Director Student Financial Aid ... Ms. Barbara AMERIO

Taft Law School (F)

3700 South Susan Street, Office 200,
Santa Ana CA 92704-6954
County: Orange Identification: 666398
Unit ID: 454689
Telephone: (714) 850-4800 Carnegie Class: Spec/Law
FAX Number: (714) 708-2082 Calendar System: Other
URL: www.taftu.edu
Established: 1976 Annual Undergrad Tuition & Fees: $7,920
Enrollment: 431 Coed
Affiliation or Control: Proprietary IRS Status: Proprietary
Highest Offering: Doctorate
Program: Professional
Accreditation: DETC

01 President ... Mr. David L. BOYD
05 Dean ... Mr. Robert K. STROUSE
86 VP of Governmental Relations ... Ms. Joan L. SLAVIN
20 Associate Dean ... Ms. Melody JOLLY

Teachers College of San Joaquin (G)

2857 Transworld Dr, Stockton CA 95206
County: San Joaquin Identification: 667087
Telephone: (209) 468-9155 Carnegie Class: Not Classified
FAX Number: (209) 468-9124 Calendar System: Semester
URL: teacherscollegesj.edu
Established: 2009 Annual Graduate Tuition & Fees: $11,550
Enrollment: N/A Coed
Affiliation or Control: State IRS Status: 501(c)3
Highest Offering: Master's; No Undergraduates
Program: Teacher Preparatory
Accreditation: WC

01 CEO ... Dr. Gary DEI ROSSI
05 Chief Academic Officer ... Dr. Catherine KEARNEY

Theatre of Arts (H)

6755 Hollywood Blvd, Ste 200, Hollywood CA 90028
County: Los Angeles Identification: 667098
Telephone: (323) 463-2500 Carnegie Class: Not Classified
FAX Number: (323) 463-2645 Calendar System: Other
URL: www.toa.edu
Established: 1927 Annual Undergrad Tuition & Fees: $19,800
Enrollment: N/A Coed
Affiliation or Control: Proprietary IRS Status: Proprietary
Highest Offering: Associate Degree
Program: Occupational
Accreditation: THEA

01 President ... James WARWICK

Thomas Aquinas College (I)

10,000 Ojai Road, Santa Paula CA 93060-9621
County: Ventura FICE Identification: 023580
Unit ID: 124292
Telephone: (805) 525-4417 Carnegie Class: Bac/A&S
FAX Number: (805) 525-9342 Calendar System: Semester
URL: www.thomasaquinas.edu
Established: 1971 Annual Undergrad Tuition & Fees: $23,600
Enrollment: 355 Coed
Affiliation or Control: Independent Non-Profit IRS Status: 501(c)3
Highest Offering: Baccalaureate
Program: Liberal Arts And General
Accreditation: WC

01 President ... Dr. Michael F. MCLEAN
04 Secretary to the President ... Mrs. Kelly BAILEY
26 Asst to Pres/Dir College Relations ... Mrs. Anne S. FORSYTH
30 Vice President for Development ... Dr. Paul J. O'REILLY
43 General Counsel ... Mr. John Q. MASTELLER
11 Vice President for Admn & Finance ... Mr. Peter L. DELUCA
05 Academic Dean ... Dr. Brian KELLY
46 Director of Development ... Mr. Robert A. BAGDAZIAN
44 Director of Gift Planning ... Mr. Thomas J. SUSANKA
07 Director of Admissions ... Mr. Jonathan P. DALY
21 Supervisor Business/Finance ... Mr. Michael COLLINS
37 Director of Financial Aid ... Mr. Gregory J. BECHER
32 Asst Dean for Student Affairs ... Mr. Steven R. CAIN
06 Registrar ... Mr. Mark KRETSCHMER
36 Director of Student Placement ... Mr. Mark R. KRETSCHMER
08 Librarian ... Mrs. Viltis A. JATULIS
42 Chaplain ... Fr. Cornelius M. BUCKLEY
27 Communications Manager ... Mr. Christopher WEINKOPF
13 Development Database Manager ... Mr. Aaron DUNKEL

Thomas Jefferson School of Law (J)

1155 Island Avenue, San Diego CA 92101
County: San Diego FICE Identification: 010854
Unit ID: 126049
Telephone: (619) 961-1247 Carnegie Class: Spec/Law
FAX Number: (619) 294-4713 Calendar System: Semester
URL: www.tjsl.edu
Established: 1969 Annual Graduate Tuition & Fees: $42,000
Enrollment: 1,254 Coed
Affiliation or Control: Independent Non-Profit IRS Status: 501(c)3
Highest Offering: Doctorate; No Undergraduates
Program: Professional
Accreditation: LAW

01 Dean and President ... Rudolph C. HASL
05 Assoc Dean Academic Affairs ... Eric MITNICK
32 Assoc Dean for Student Affairs ... M. Elizabeth (Beth) KRANSBERGER
26 Asst Dean Communications/Admin ... Lori WULFEMEYER
18 Asst Dean Facilities Services ... Lisa BRUCE
36 Director for Career Services ... Beverly BRACKER
08 Interim Library Director ... Leigh INMAN
10 Chief Financial Officer ... Nancy VU
37 Director Financial Assistance ... Marc BERMAN
06 Registrar ... Kim GRENNAN
35 Student Services Director ... Lisa FERREIRA
21 Director of Business Office ... Christine MOORE
88 Dir Clin/Judicial Educ & Acad Cnslr ... Judybeth TROPP
07 Director of Admissions ... Tim SPEARMAN
15 Director of Personnel Services ... Lisa CHIGOS

Touro College Los Angeles (K)

1317 N Crescent Heights Boulevard,
West Hollywood CA 90046-4506
County: Los Angeles FICE Identification: 041425
Unit ID: 459727
Telephone: (323) 822-9700 Carnegie Class: Not Classified
FAX Number: (310) 654-2086 Calendar System: Semester
URL: www.touro.edu/losangeles/
Established: 2005 Annual Undergrad Tuition & Fees: $15,900
Enrollment: 175 Coed

Affiliation or Control: Independent Non-Profit IRS Status: 501(c)3
Highest Offering: Master's
Program: Liberal Arts And General
Accreditation: WC

01	President	Dr. Alan KADISH
05	Founding Dean/Chief Academic Ofcr	Dr. Esther LOWY
07	Director of Admissions	Mrs. Samira MILLER
09	Dir Inst Research/Assessment	Ms. Shana ROBINSON
10	Chief Business Officer/Bursar	Mr. Kamran MANUEL
37	Dir Student Fin Aid/Registrar	Ms. Rivka WEINBERG

Touro University-California (A)

1310 Club Drive, Vallejo CA 94592
County: Solano FICE Identification: 041426
Unit ID: 459736
Telephone: (707) 638-5200 Carnegie Class: Not Classified
FAX Number: (707) 638-5255 Calendar System: Trimester
URL: www.tu.edu
Established: 1997 Annual Undergrad Tuition & Fees: $42,800
Enrollment: 1,403 Coed
Affiliation or Control: Independent Non-Profit IRS Status: 501(c)3
Highest Offering: Doctorate
Program: Teacher Preparatory; Professional
Accreditation: WC, ARCPA, OSTEO, PH, PHAR

01	President & CEO	Dr. Alan KADISH
05	Provost & COO	Dr. Marilyn HOPKINS
32	Dean of Students	Dr. Donald HAIGHT
35	Associate Dean of Students	Dr. James BINKERD
06	Registrar	Dr. Harold BORRERO
07	Director of Admissions	Dr. Donald HAIGHT
09	Director of Institutional Research	Dr. Meiling TANG
10	Chief Business Officer/CFO	Mr. Reed GOERTLER
15	Director Human Resources	Ms. Kathy LOWE
11	Associate VP of Administration	Mr. Jay RITCHIE
08	Director University Library	Ms. Tamara TRUJILLO
63	Dean College of Osteopathic Med	Dr. Michael CLEARFIELD
67	Dean College of Pharmacy	Dr. Katherine KNAPP
53	Dean Col of Education & Health Sci	Dr. Jim O'CONNOR
13	Director of Information Technology	Ms. Julia WELCH
26	Director of External Relations	Ms. Andrea GARCIA
37	Director of Student Financial Aid	Ms. Lynne MOSELEY
30	Chief Officer of Advancement	Mr. James SOTIROS
35	Director of Student Activities	Rabbi Elchonon TENENBAUM
23	Director of Student Health Center	Ms. Lorraine NALLEY

Trident University International (B)

5757 Plaza Drive, Suite 100, Cypress CA 90630
County: Orange FICE Identification: 041279
Unit ID: 450979
Telephone: (714) 816-0366 Carnegie Class: DRU
FAX Number: (714) 816-0367 Calendar System: Semester
URL: www.trident.edu
Established: 1998 Annual Undergrad Tuition & Fees: $9,440
Enrollment: 5,699 Coed
Affiliation or Control: Proprietary IRS Status: Proprietary
Highest Offering: Doctorate
Program: Liberal Arts And General; Professional; Business Emphasis
Accreditation: #WC

01	President/CEO	Dr. Lucille SANSING
10	Exec Vice President Finance/CFO	Ms. Lisa KEMP
05	Exec Vice Pres/Provost	Vacant
13	VP Computing/Info Management	Mr. Vahid SHARIAT
86	Vice Pres Compliance	Dr. Afshin AFROOKHTEH
30	Vice Pres Institutional Advancement	Dr. Steven J. GOLD
04	Executive Assistant	Ms. Patricia PARKS
15	Sr Director Human Resources	Ms. Brenda DUNBAR
88	Director Business Development	Mr. Rafael ITZHAKI
06	Registrar	Ms. Nimala SHARMA
37	Director Student Financial Aid	Ms. Taisha AZLIN WRIGHT
09	Director of Institutional Research	Dr. Pedro PIFFAUT
08	Head Librarian	Dr. Klaus MUSMANN
21	Director of Financial Operation	Mr. Scott PAK
50	Dean Business/Info Tech Management	Dr. Scott AMUNDSEN
76	Dean Educ/Health Sciences	Dr. Holly AROZCO

United Education Institute (C)

6055 Pacific Blvd, Huntington Park CA 90255
County: Los Angeles FICE Identification: 025593
Telephone: (323) 319-9500 Carnegie Class: Not Classified
FAX Number: N/A Calendar System: Other
URL: www.uei.edu
Established: 1986 Annual Undergrad Tuition & Fees: $16,650
Enrollment: 12,317 Coed
Affiliation or Control: Proprietary IRS Status: Proprietary
Highest Offering: Associate Degree
Program: Occupational
Accreditation: CNCE

01	Area President	Mr. Al NEDERHOOD

United States University (D)

830 Bay Boulevard, Chula Vista CA 91911
County: San Diego FICE Identification: 040053
Unit ID: 447050
Telephone: (619) 477-6310 Carnegie Class: Bac/A&S
FAX Number: (619) 477-7340 Calendar System: Semester
URL: www.usuniversity.edu
Established: 1997 Annual Undergrad Tuition & Fees: $6,500
Enrollment: 443 Coed
Affiliation or Control: Proprietary IRS Status: Proprietary
Highest Offering: Master's
Program: Liberal Arts And General; Teacher Preparatory; Professional; Nursing Emphasis
Accreditation: WC

01	President and CEO	Timothy P. COLE
05	Interim Provost	Dr. Shelia LEWIS
11	COO	Vacant
10	Interim CFO	Timothy FISCHER
27	CIO	Roy FINALY
20	Associate Provost	Vacant
06	Registrar	Maria Raquel CHANG
76	Director School of Health Science	Dr. Rosalinda MILLA
97	Director School of Liberal Studies	Vacant
53	Director School of Education	Roberta MASO-FLEISHMAN
66	Director School of Nursing	Pilar DE LA CRUZ-REYES

† Additional campus located in Cypress, CA.

Unitek College (E)

4670 Auto Mall Parkway, Fremont CA 94538
County: Alameda FICE Identification: 041697
Telephone: (888) 735-4355 Carnegie Class: Not Classified
FAX Number: (510) 249-9125 Calendar System: Other
URL: www.unitekcollege.edu
Established: 1992 Annual Undergrad Tuition & Fees: $23,071
Enrollment: 659 Coed
Affiliation or Control: Proprietary IRS Status: Proprietary
Highest Offering: Baccalaureate
Program: Occupational; 2-Year Principally Bachelor's Creditable; Nursing Emphasis
Accreditation: ACCSC

University of Antelope Valley (F)

44055 Sierra Hwy, Lancaster CA 93534
County: Los Angeles FICE Identification: 034275
Unit ID: 442930
Telephone: (661) 726-1911 Carnegie Class: Assoc/PrivFP
FAX Number: (661) 726-5158 Calendar System: Other
URL: www.uav.edu
Established: N/A Annual Undergrad Tuition & Fees: N/A
Enrollment: 922 Coed
Affiliation or Control: Proprietary IRS Status: Proprietary
Highest Offering: Master's
Program: Occupational; 2-Year Principally Bachelor's Creditable
Accreditation: ACICS, EMT

01	President	Mr. Marco JOHNSON
03	Vice President/CEO	Ms. Sandra JOHNSON
05	Dean of Academic Affairs	Mr. Ronald FELTS
06	Dean of Records	Mrs. Jaime MYERS
37	Financial Aid Officer	Mr. Araceli JIMENEZ
10	Director of Operations	Ms. Crystal STEPHENS

*University of California Office of the President (G)

1111 Franklin Street, Oakland CA 94607-5200
County: Alameda FICE Identification: 001311
Unit ID: 124557
Telephone: (510) 987-0700 Carnegie Class: N/A
FAX Number: (510) 987-0328
URL: www.ucop.edu

01	President	Mark G. YUDOF
05	Provost/Exec Vice Pres Acad Affairs	Aimee DORR
10	Exec Vice President/CFO	Peter J. TAYLOR
11	Exec Vice Pres Business Operations	Nathan E. BROSTROM
26	Sr Vice Pres External Relations	Daniel M. DOOLEY
47	Vice Pres Agriculture/Nat Resources	Barbara H. ALLEN-DIAZ
17	Sr Vice Pres Health Sciences & Svcs	John D. STOBO
43	General Counsel/VP Legal Affairs	Charles F. ROBINSON
32	Vice President Student Affairs	Judy K. SAKAKI
88	Exec Vice Pres Laboratory Mgmt	Glenn L. MARA
25	Sr Vice Pres Compliance/Audit	Sheryl S. VACCA
27	CIO/Vice Pres for Investments	Marie N. BERGGREN
15	Vice Pres Human Resources	Dwaine B. DUCKETT
46	Vice Pres Research/Graduate Studies	Steven V W. BECKWITH
21	VP Budget & Capital Resources	Patrick J. LENZ

*University of California-Berkeley (H)

Berkeley CA 94720-0001
County: Alameda FICE Identification: 001312
Unit ID: 110635
Telephone: (510) 642-6000 Carnegie Class: RU/VH
FAX Number: (510) 643-5499 Calendar System: Semester
URL: www.berkeley.edu
Established: 1868 Annual Undergrad Tuition & Fees (In-State): $12,874
Enrollment: 25,885 Coed
Affiliation or Control: State IRS Status: 501(c)3
Highest Offering: Doctorate
Program: Liberal Arts And General; Teacher Preparatory; Professional
Accreditation: WC, BUS, CLPSY, CS, DIETD, ENG, FOR, IPSY, JOUR, LAW, LSAR, OPT, OPTR, PH, PLNG, SCPSY, SW

02	Chancellor	Robert J. BIRGENEAU
05	Exec Vice Chancellor & Provost	George W. BRESLAUER
11	Vice Chanc Administration & Finance	John WILTON
32	Vice Chancellor Student Affairs	Harry LE GRANDE
26	Vice Chanc University Relations	Scott BIDDY
46	Vice Chancellor for Research	Graham R. FLEMING
18	Vice Chancellor Facilities Services	Edward DENTON
88	Vice Chanc Equity & Inclusion	Gibor BASRI
100	Assc Chancellor/Chief of Staff	Beata FITZPATRICK
31	Assc Chanc Govt/Cmty Campus Liaison	Linda M. WILLIAMS
25	Asst VC Research Admin & Compliance	Patrick SCHLESINGER
13	Int Assc Vice Chanc Info Technology	Lyle NEVELS
10	Assc Vice Chancellor/CFO	Erin S. GORE
84	Assc Vice Chanc Admiss & Enrollment	Anne DE LUCA
43	Chief Campus Counsel	Christopher M. PATTI
26	Assoc Vice Chanc Public Affairs	Claire HOLMES
21	Assoc VC Business & Admin Svcs	Ron T. COLEY
88	Asst Vice Chanc Finance/Controller	Delphine REGALIA
07	Asst VV & Dir Undergrad Admissions	Amy JARICH
35	Asst Vice Chanc/Dean of Students	Jonathan POULLARD
37	Asst VC & Dir Fin Aid & Scholarship	Rachelle FELDMAN
08	University Librarian	Thomas C. LEONARD
06	Registrar	Walter WONG
88	Associate Registrar	Johanna METZGAR
38	Dir Counseling & Psychological Svcs	Jeff PRINCE
36	Director Career Center	Thomas C. DEVLIN
87	Dean Sum Sess/Study Abr/Life Lrng	Richard RUSSO
41	Director of Athletics	Sandy BARBOUR
58	Dean of the Graduate Division	Andrew J. SZERI
61	Dean of Law	Christopher EDLEY, JR.
88	Dean of Optometry	Dennis M. LEVI
54	Dean School of Engineering	S. Shankar SASTRY
88	Dean of Environmental Design	Jennifer WOLCH
65	Dean of Natural Resources	J. Keith GILLESS
50	Dean of Haas School of Business	Richard K. LYONS
70	Dean of Social Welfare	Lorraine T. MIDANIK
88	Dean School of Information	AnnaLee SAXENIAN
69	Dean of Public Health	Stephen M. SHORTELL
53	Dean of Education	Judith W. LITTLE
60	Dean of Journalism	Ed WASSERMAN
88	Dean of Chemistry	Richard MATHIES
80	Dean Goldman School/Public Pol	Henry BRADY
79	Dean of Arts and Humanities	Anthony CASCARDI
88	Interim Dean of Biological Sciences	G. Steven MARTIN
81	Dean Mathematical/Physical Sciences	Mark RICHARDS
83	Dean of Social Sciences	Carla HESSE
56	Dean of University Extension	Diana WU
97	Dean of the Undergraduate Division	Tyler STOVALL

*University of California-Davis (I)

One Shields Avenue, Davis CA 95616-5270
County: Yolo FICE Identification: 001313
Unit ID: 110644
Telephone: (530) 752-1011 Carnegie Class: RU/VH
FAX Number: N/A Calendar System: Quarter
URL: www.ucdavis.edu
Established: 1905 Annual Undergrad Tuition & Fees (In-State): $13,877
Enrollment: 32,653 Coed
Affiliation or Control: State IRS Status: 501(c)3
Highest Offering: Doctorate
Program: Liberal Arts And General; Teacher Preparatory; Professional
Accreditation: WC, ARCPA, BUS, CS, DIETD, DIETI, ENG, IPSY, LAW, LSAR, MED, MT, NURSE, PDPSY, PH, VET

02	Chancellor	Dr. Linda P. KATEHI
05	Provost & Exec Vice Chancellor	Dr. Ralph J. HEXTER
03	Associate Chancellor	Mr. Karl M. ENGELBACH
46	Vice Chancellor Research	Dr. Harris A. LEWIN
88	Int Asst Executive Vice Chancellor	Mr. Karl F. MOHR
32	Int Vice Chancellor Student Affairs	Dr. Adela I. DE LA TORRE
45	VC Administrative & Resource Mgmt	Mr. John A. MEYER
76	Vice Chanc Human Health Sciences	Dr. Claire POMEROY
17	CEO UCD Medical Center	Ms. Ann M. RICE
66	Assoc VC/Dean Sch of Nursing	Dr. Heather M. YOUNG
31	Assoc Exec VC Campus Cmty Relations	Mr. Rahim REED
15	Assoc VC Human Resources	Ms. Susan M. GILBERT
10	Assoc VC Accounting/Financial Svcs	Mr. J. Michael ALLRED
30	Vice Chanc Dev/Alumni Relations	Dr. Shaun B. KEISTER
35	Assoc Vice Chanc Student Affairs	Ms. Emily GALINDO
35	Assoc Vice Chanc Student Affairs	Ms. Lora J. BOSSIO
21	Assoc Vice Chancellor Budget	Ms. Kelly M. RATLIFF
18	Assoc Vice Chancellor Safety Svcs	Ms. Jill PARKER
45	Asst Vice Chanc Campus Planning	Mr. Robert B. SEGAR
88	Asst VC Environmental Stewardship	Dr. Sid ENGLAND
86	Asst VC Govt & Community Relations	Ms. Marjorie M. DICKINSON
35	Int Assoc VC Student Affairs	Dr. Rich SHINTAKU
12	Exec Director Mondavi Center	Dr. Don F. ROTH
13	Vice Provost Info/Educ Tech	Mr. Peter M. SIEGEL
53	Vice Provost Undergraduate Studies	Dr. Pat A. TURNER
85	Vice Prov Univ Outreach/Intl Pgms	Dr. William B. LACY
20	Vice Provost Academic Affairs	Dr. Maureen L. STANTON
88	Assoc Vice Provost Internatl Pgms	Dr. Adrienne MARTIN
43	Campus Counsel	Mr. Steven A. DROWN
06	Registrar	Dr. Elias S. LOPEZ
08	University Librarian	Ms. Mackenzie SMITH
58	Dean of Graduate Studies	Dr. Jeffery C. GIBELING
47	Int Dean of Agricultural/Envir Scis	Dr. Mary DELANY
81	Dean of Biological Sciences	Dr. James E. HILDRETH
54	Dean of Engineering	Dr. Enrique J. LAVERNIA
83	Dean Social Sciences	Dr. George R. MANGUN
81	Dean Math & Physical Science	Dr. Winston T. KO

79 Dean Humanities/Arts & Culture ... Dr. Jessie A. OWENS
61 Dean School of Law ... Dr. Kevin R. JOHNSON
50 Dean Graduate School of Management ... Dr. Steven C. CURRALL
63 Dean School of Medicine ... Dr. Claire POMEROY
74 Dean Veterinary Medicine ... Dr. Michael D. LAIRMORE
53 Dean School of Education ... Dr. Harold G. LEVINE
56 Dean of University Extension ... Mr. Dennis F. PENDLETON
37 Director Financial Aid ... Ms. Kathryn A. MALONEY
88 Dir Student Research & Information ... Ms. Gillian BUTLER
09 Dir Institutional Analysis ... Mr. Robert J. LOESSBERG-ZAHL
29 AVC/Exec Director Alumni Relations ... Mr. Richard R. ENGEL
23 Director Student Health Services ... Dr. Michelle S. FAMULA
38 Director Counseling & Psych Srvcs ... Dr. Emil R. RODOLFA
36 Director Internship & Career Center ... Dr. Subhash H. RISBUD
39 Director Student Housing ... Ms. Emily GALINDO
40 Director Bookstore ... Mr. Charles P. KRATOCHVIL
41 Director Intercollegiate Athletics ... Mr. Terrance J. TUMEY
27 Int Exec Dir Strategic Commun ... Mr. Barry SHILLER
96 Director Material Management ... Ms. Janice KING
07 Director Admissions ... Mr. Walter A. ROBINSON
88 Dir Internal Audit Services ... Mr. Jeremiah MAHER
19 Chief of Police ... Chief Matt CARMICHAEL

*University of California-Hastings College of the Law (A)

200 McAllister Street, San Francisco CA 94102-4978
County: San Francisco FICE Identification: 003947
Unit ID: 110398
Telephone: (415) 565-4600 Carnegie Class: Spec/Law
FAX Number: (415) 565-4865 Calendar System: Semester
URL: www.uchastings.edu
Established: 1878 Annual Graduate Tuition & Fees: $46,806
Enrollment: 1,287 Coed
Affiliation or Control: State IRS Status: 501(c)3
Highest Offering: First Professional Degree; No Undergraduates
Program: Professional
Accreditation: WC, LAW

02 Chancellor and Dean ... Mr. Frank H. WU
05 Academic Dean ... Ms. Shauna MARSHALL
43 General Counsel ... Ms. Elise TRAYNUM
10 Chief Financial Officer ... Mr. David SEWARD
20 Associate Academic Dean ... Mr. C. Keith WINGATE
08 Director Law Library ... Ms. Jenni PARRISH
15 Executive Director Human Resources ... Ms. Marie HAIRSTON
19 Chief Public Safety ... Mr. Bill PALMINI
06 Registrar ... Ms. Gina BARNETT
07 Assistant Dean Admissions ... Mr. Greg CANADA
32 Director Student Services ... Ms. Rupa BHANDARI
27 Chief Information Officer ... Mr. Jacob HORNSBY
36 Asst Dean Career & Profess Devel ... Ms. Sari ZIMMERMAN
26 Assistant Dean Communications ... Vacant
22 Director LEOP ... Ms. Jan JEMISON
23 Student Health Manager/Admin Nurse ... Ms. Laurie BROOKNER
21 Controller ... Ms. Deborah TRAN
37 Assistant Dean Financial Aid ... Ms. Linda BISESI
40 Bookstore Manager ... Vacant
18 Property Manager ... Ms. Pansy MAR
96 Director of Purchasing ... Mr. Darryl SWEET
30 Asst Dean Institutional Advance ... Ms. Shino NOMIYA

*University of California-Irvine (B)

Campus Drive, Irvine CA 92697-0001
County: Orange FICE Identification: 001314
Unit ID: 110653
Telephone: (949) 824-5011 Carnegie Class: RU/VH
FAX Number: (949) 824-5451 Calendar System: Quarter
URL: www.uci.edu
Established: 1965 Annual Undergrad Tuition & Fees (In-State): $12,749
Enrollment: 27,889 Coed
Affiliation or Control: State IRS Status: 501(c)3
Highest Offering: Doctorate
Program: Liberal Arts And General; Teacher Preparatory; Professional
Accreditation: WC, BUS, CEA, ENG, IPSY, #LAW, MED, MT, NURSE, PLNG

02 Chancellor ... Michael V. DRAKE
05 Interim Exec Vice Chanc & Provost ... Susan V. BRYANT
10 Vice Chanc Admin/Business Services ... Wendell C. BRASE
46 Vice Chancellor for Research ... John C. HEMMINGER
32 Vice Chanc Student Affairs ... Thomas A. PARHAM
30 Vice Chanc Univ Advancement ... Gregory R. LEET
45 Vice Chanc Planning & Budget ... Meredith MICHAELS
20 Vice Provost for Academic Planning ... Michael P. CLARK
16 Vice Provost for Academic Personnel ... Herbert KILLACKEY
21 Assoc Vice Chanc Admin/Business Svc ... Paige L. MACIAS
29 Asst Vice Chanc Alumni Relations ... Jorge ANCONA
35 Assoc Vice Chancellor Stdnt Affairs ... Daniel J. DOOROS
22 Asst Executive Vice Chancellor OEOD ... Kirsten K. QUANBECK
100 Associate Chancellor ... Ramona AGRELA
20 Associate Exec Vice Chancellor ... Michael R. ARIAS
35 Asst Vice Chanc/Dean of Students ... Rameen A. TALESH
84 Asst Vice Chanc Enrollment Services ... Brent W. YUNEK
06 University Registrar ... Elizabeth C. BENNETT
43 Chief Campus Counsel ... Diane F. GEOCARIS
51 Dean Continuing Education ... Gary W. MATKIN
08 Interim University Librarian ... Lorelei A. TANJI
37 Director Financial Aid ... Christopher SHULTZ
36 Interim Director Career Center ... Linda R. DRAKE
41 Director Athletics ... Michael A. IZZI
09 Acting Dir Institutional Research ... Kimberly RAMS
58 Dean Graduate Division ... Frances M. LESLIE
20 Dean Undergraduate Education ... Sharon V. SALINGER
63 Dean School of Medicine ... Ralph V. CLAYMAN
61 Dean of Law School ... Erwin CHEMERINSKY
81 Dean Biological Sciences ... Albert F. BENNETT
81 Dean Physical Sciences ... Kenneth C. JANDA
83 Dean School of Social Sciences ... Barbara DOSHER
50 Dean Paul Merage School of Business ... Andrew J. POLICANO
79 Dean Humanities ... Vicki L. RUIZ
49 Dean Arts ... Joseph S. LEWIS
83 Dean Social Ecology ... Valerie JENNESS
54 Dean School of Engineering ... Gregory WASHINGTON
77 Dean Bren Sch of Info & Comp Sci ... Hal S. STERN
88 Chair Academic Senate ... Craig MARTENS
53 Chair School of Education ... Deborah L. VANDELL
13 CIO and Asst Vice Chancellor IT ... Dana F. ROODE
96 Director Materiel & Risk Management ... Richard COULON
26 Director Media Relations ... Cathy LAWHON
28 Director ADVANCE Program ... Douglas M. HAYNES

*University of California-Los Angeles (C)

405 Hilgard Avenue, Los Angeles CA 90095-1405
County: Los Angeles FICE Identification: 001315
Unit ID: 110662
Telephone: (310) 825-4321 Carnegie Class: RU/VH
FAX Number: N/A Calendar System: Quarter
URL: www.ucla.edu
Established: 1919 Annual Undergrad Tuition & Fees (In-State): $12,692
Enrollment: 39,271 Coed
Affiliation or Control: State IRS Status: 501(c)3
Highest Offering: Doctorate
Program: Liberal Arts And General; Professional
Accreditation: WC, BUS, CLPSY, CS, CYTO, DENT, DIETI, EMT, ENG, ENGR, HSA, IPSY, LAW, LIB, MED, #NMT, NURSE, PDPSY, PH, PLNG, RAD, SW, THEA

02 Chancellor ... Gene D. BLOCK
03 Exec Vice Chancellor/Provost ... Scott WAUGH
10 Administrative Vice Chancellor ... Jack J. POWAZEK
32 Vice Chancellor Student Affairs ... Janina MONTERO
26 Vice Chancellor External Affairs ... Rhea TURTELTAUB
45 VC Finance/Budget/Capital Pgms ... Steven A. OLSEN
17 VC Med Sciences/Dean Med School ... A. Eugene WASHINGTON
46 Vice Chancellor Research ... James S. ECONOMOU
58 VC Grad Studies/Dean Grad Div ... Claudia MITCHELL-KERNAN
16 Vice Chanc Academic Personnel ... Thomas RICE
43 Vice Chancellor Legal Affairs ... Kevin REED
82 Vice Provost International Studies ... Nicholas J. ENTRIKIN
88 Vice Provost/Dean Undergrad Educ ... Judith L. SMITH
88 Assoc VC and CEO Hospital Systems ... David T. FEINBERG
24 Assoc V Provost Instr Development ... Larry L. LOEHER
28 Vice Prov Faculty Diversity/Develop ... Rosina BECERRA
88 Asst Provost ... Margaret LEAL-SOTELO
13 Vice Provost Information Technology ... James DAVIS
88 Assoc Vice Chanc Acad Plng/Budget ... Glyn DAVIES
27 Assoc Vice Chanc Univ Communication ... Lawrence H. LOKMAN
86 Asst Vice Chanc Govt/Cmty Rels ... Keith S. PARKER
18 Assoc Vice Chanc General Services ... Jack POWAZEK
30 Assoc Vice Chancellor Development ... Tracie CHRISTENSEN
21 Assoc Vice Chancellor/Controller ... Susan K. ABELES
15 Assoc Vice Chanc Campus Human Res ... Lubbe LEVIN
35 Assoc VC Dean Student & Campus Life ... Robert J. NAPLES
29 Asst Vice Chanc/Exec Dir Alumni Rel ... Ralph AMOS
88 Executive Director Volunteer Center ... Antoinette MONGELLI
84 Assoc Vice Chanc Enrollment Mgmt ... Youlonda COPELAND-MORGAN
25 Asst VC Res Policy & Compliance ... Ann M. POLLACK
23 Asst VC Student Development/Health ... Vacant
06 Registrar ... Anita COTTER
88 Vice Prov Intel Prop/Indust Rels ... Kathryn ATCHISON
20 Assistant Provost ... Maryann J. GRAY
87 Asst Prov Academic Program Dev ... David UNRUH
09 Dir Analysis/Information Management ... Caroline S. WEST
08 University Librarian ... Gary E. STRONG
19 Chief of Police ... James HERREN
07 Dir Undergrad Admiss/Rels w/Schools ... Vu TRAN
36 Director Career Center ... Kathy L. SIMS
37 Director Financial Aid Office ... Ronald W. JOHNSON
38 Dir Student Psychological Services ... Elizabeth GONG-GUY
85 Dir Ctr for Intl Students/Scholars ... Robert B. ERICKSEN
91 Asst Vice Chanc Adm Info Systems ... Andrew WISSMILLER
41 Director Intercollegiate Athletics ... Daniel G. GUERRERO
39 Asst VC Housing & Hospitality Svcs ... Peter ANGELIS
22 Director Staff Affirmative Action ... Linda C. AVILA
96 Director of Purchasing ... William S. PROPST
88 Executive Director ASUCLA ... Robert WILLIAMS
51 Dean of Extension ... Cathy SANDEEN
53 Dean Grad Sch Educ/Info Studies ... Vacant
54 Dean Sch of Engr & Applied Sci ... Vijay K. DHIR
61 Interim Dean School of Law ... Stephen C. YEAZELL
50 Dean Anderson Grad Sch Management ... Judy D. OLIAN
52 Dean School of Dentistry ... No Hee PARK
66 Dean School of Nursing ... Courtney LYDER
88 Dean Sch of the Arts/Architecture ... Christopher WATERMAN
88 Dean School of Theater/Film/TV ... Teri SCHWARTZ
69 Dean School of Public Health ... Linda ROSENSTOCK
80 Dean School of Public Affairs ... Franklin D. GILLIAM, JR.
79 Dean of Humanities ... Timothy STOWELL
88 Dean of Life Sciences ... Victoria SORK
88 Dean of Physical Sciences ... Joseph RUDNICK
83 Dean of Social Sciences ... Alessandro DURANTI
90 Director Academic Tech Svcs ... William LABATE
40 Divisional Manager Textbooks ... Anne COLLUM

*University of California-Merced (D)

5200 North Lake Road, Merced CA 95343
County: Merced FICE Identification: 041271
Unit ID: 445188
Telephone: (209) 228-4400 Carnegie Class: Not Classified
FAX Number: (209) 228-4424 Calendar System: Semester
URL: www.ucmerced.edu
Established: 1868 Annual Undergrad Tuition & Fees (In-District): $13,070
Enrollment: 5,198 Coed
Affiliation or Control: State/Local IRS Status: 501(c)3
Highest Offering: Doctorate
Program: Liberal Arts And General; Teacher Preparatory; Professional
Accreditation: WC

02 Chancellor ... Dr. Dorothy LELAND
03 Int Exec Vice Chancellor & Provost ... Dr. Samuel TRAINA
11 Vice Chancellor Administration ... Mary E. MILLER
32 Vice Chancellor Student Affairs ... Dr. Jane F. LAWRENCE
46 Vice Chancellor Research ... Dr. Samuel TRAINA
04 Associate Chancellor ... Janet YOUNG
35 Associate Vice Chancellor Students ... Dr. Charles NIES
84 Assoc Vice Chanc Enrollment Mgmt ... J. Michael THOMPSON
23 Assoc Vice Chanc Health & Wellness ... Dr. Fuji COLLINS
06 University Registrar ... Dr. Laurie HERBRAND
07 Director of Admissions ... Encarnacion RUIZ
08 Int University Librarian ... Donald A. BARCLAY
37 Director of Financial Aid ... Diana RALLS
85 Director of International Programs ... Rebecca SWEELEY
56 Director of Extension & Summer Pgms ... Kevin M. BROWNE
19 Chief of Police ... Rita SPAUR
27 Asst Vice Chanc Univ Communications ... Patti W. WAID
41 Director of Campus Athletics & Rec ... David DUNHAM
39 Director of Student Housing ... Leslie SANTOS
58 Dean Graduate Studies ... Dr. Christopher KELLO
65 Dean Natural Sciences ... Dr. Juan MEZA
54 Dean Engineering ... Dr. E. Daniel HIRLEMAN
79 Dean School of SSHA ... Dr. Mark S. ALDENDERFER

*University of California-Riverside (E)

900 University Avenue, Riverside CA 92521
County: Riverside FICE Identification: 001316
Unit ID: 110671
Telephone: (951) 827-1012 Carnegie Class: RU/VH
FAX Number: (951) 827-3800 Calendar System: Quarter
URL: www.ucr.edu
Established: 1954 Annual Undergrad Tuition & Fees (In-State): $12,935
Enrollment: 20,956 Coed
Affiliation or Control: State IRS Status: 501(c)3
Highest Offering: Doctorate
Program: Liberal Arts And General; Teacher Preparatory; Professional
Accreditation: WC, BUS, CS, ENG, SCPSY

02 Chancellor ... Dr. Timothy P. WHITE
04 Associate Chancellor ... Ms. Cynthia R. GIORGIO
05 Exec Vice Chancellor/Provost ... Dr. Dallas RABENSTEIN
11 Vice Chanc Finance/Business Opers ... Mr. Charles J. ROWLEY
32 Vice Chancellor Student Affairs ... Mr. James W. SANDOVAL
26 Vice Chanc University Advancement ... Mr. Peter A. HAYASHIDA
46 Vice Chancellor Research ... Dr. Michael J. PAZZANI
17 VC Hlth Affs/Dean School of Med ... Dr. G. Richard OLDS
20 Vice Provost Academic Personnel ... Dr. David F. BOCIAN
58 Dean Graduate Division ... Dr. Joseph CHILDERS
50 Int Dean School of Business Admin ... Dr. Yungzeng WANG
53 Interim Dean Grad School of Educ ... Dr. Douglas MITCHELL
54 Dean Bourns College of Engineering ... Dr. Reza ABBASCHIAN
88 Dean College of Humanities Arts SS ... Dr. Steven CULLENBERG
88 Dean Col of Nat and Agr Sciences ... Dr. Marylynn YATES

*University of California-San Diego (F)

9500 Gilman Drive, La Jolla CA 92093-0014
County: San Diego FICE Identification: 001317
Unit ID: 110680
Telephone: (858) 534-2230 Carnegie Class: RU/VH
FAX Number: (858) 534-6523 Calendar System: Quarter
URL: www.ucsd.edu
Established: 1960 Annual Undergrad Tuition & Fees (In-State): $12,138
Enrollment: 28,593 Coed
Affiliation or Control: State IRS Status: 501(c)3
Highest Offering: Doctorate
Program: Liberal Arts And General; Professional
Accreditation: WC, AUD, BUS, CEA, CLPSY, @DIETI, DMS, ENG, IPSY, MED, MT, PHAR

02 Chancellor ... Dr. Pradeep K. KHOSLA
05 Executive VC Academic Affairs ... Dr. Suresh SUBRAMANI
30 VC External and Business Affairs ... Mr. Steven W. RELYEA
32 Vice Chancellor Student Affairs ... Ms. Penny E. RUE
11 Vice Chanc Resource Mgmt/Planning ... Mr. Gary C. MATTHEWS
65 Vice Chancellor Marine Sciences ... Dr. Anthony D. HAYMET
63 VC Health Science/Dean Sch Med ... Dr. David A. BRENNER
46 Vice Chancellor Research ... Dr. Sandra BROWN
18 Vice Chanc Resource Mgmt/Planning ... Mr. Gary C. MATTHEWS
100 Associate Chancellor/Chief of Staff ... Ms. Clare M. KRISTOFCO
56 Assoc VC Public Pgms/Dean Univ Ext ... Dr. Mary L. WALSHOK
43 Chief Campus Counsel ... Mr. Daniel W. PARK
21 AVC Business Fin Svcs/Controller ... Mr. Don A. LARSON
23 AVC Student Health/Wellness ... Ms. Karen J. CALFAS
26 University Communications ... Ms. Clare M. KRISTOFCO

20 Asst Vice Chanc Academic Affairs Ms. Kristina L. LARSEN
35 Assoc Vice Chanc Student Affairs Mr. Edward J. SPRIGGS
16 Asst Vice Chanc Human Resources Mr. Thomas R. LEET
88 Associate Vice Chancellor Research Dr. Miroslav KRSTIC
84 Asst Vice Chanc Admiss/Enroll Svcs Ms. Mae W. BROWN
14 Asst VC Admin Computing/Teleco Mr. Min YAO
08 University Librarian Mr. Brian E C. SCHOTTLAENDER
06 University Registrar Mr. William R. HAID
23 CEO UCSD Medical Center Mr. Paul VIVIANO
28 VC for Equity Diversity & Inclusion Vacant
29 Assistant Vice Chancellor Mr. Armin AFSAHI
96 Senior Director Purchasing Mr. Ted JOHNSON
54 Dean Jacobs Sch of Engineering Dr. Frieder SEIBLE
49 Dean Arts & Humanities Dr. Seth LERER
81 Dean Div of Biological Sciences Dr. Steve A. KAY
83 Dean of Social Sciences Dr. Jeffrey ELMAN
88 Dean Rady School of Management Mr. Robert S. SULLIVAN
81 Dean Physical Science Dr. Mark H. THIEMENS
82 Dean Sch Intl Rels/Pacific Stds Dr. Peter F. COWHEY
58 Dean Graduate Studies Dr. Kim E. BARRETT
12 Provost John Muir College Dr. Susan SMITH
12 Prov Thurgood Marshall Coll Mr. Allan HAVIS
12 Provost Earl Warren College Mr. Steven ADLER
12 Provost Revelle College Dr. Don WAYNE
12 Provost Eleanor Roosevelt College Dr. Alan C. HOUSTON
12 Provost Sixth College Dr. Daniel J. DONOGHUE
38 Director Stdt Psych/Counseling Svcs Dr. Reina JUAREZ

*University of California-San Francisco (A)

513 Parnassus Avenue, Room S-126,
San Francisco CA 94143-0402

County: San Francisco FICE Identification: 001319
Unit ID: 110699
Telephone: (415) 476-9000 Carnegie Class: Spec/Med
FAX Number: (415) 476-9634 Calendar System: Quarter
URL: www.ucsf.edu
Established: 1864 Annual Graduate Tuition & Fees: N/A
Enrollment: 2,940 Coed
Affiliation or Control: State IRS Status: 501(c)3
Highest Offering: Doctorate; No Undergraduates
Program: Professional
Accreditation: WC, DENT, DIETI, IPSY, MED, MIDWF, NURSE, PHAR, PTA

02 Chancellor Dr. Susan DESMOND-HELLMANN
03 Executive Vice Chancellor & Provost Dr. Jeffrey A. BLUESTONE
100 Assistant Chancellor Ms. Angelique LOSCAR
10 Sr Vice Chanc Finance & Admin Mr. John E. PLOTTS
05 Vice Provost Academic Affairs Dr. Sally MARSHALL
17 Dean School of Medicine/VC Med Affs Dr. Samuel HAWGOOD
20 Vice Chanc Student Academic Affairs Dr. Joseph I. CASTRO
21 Vice Chancellor Finance Mr. Eric VERMILLION
30 Int Head Univ Develop & Alumni Rels Ms. Jennifer ARNETT
26 VC Strat Communications & Univ Rels Ms. Barbara FRENCH
91 VC & Chief Info Officer - ITS Mr. Elazar HAREL
28 VC Diversity & Outreach Dr. Renee NAVARRO
32 Assoc VC Camp Life Svcs & FM Ms. Angela HAWKINS
15 Assoc VC Human Resources Mr. David ODATO
18 Asst VC Cap Pgms/Camp Architect Mr. Michael BADE
20 Vice Dean Acad Affairs/Faculty Dev Dr. Elena FUENTES-AFFLICK
06 Associate Registrar Ms. Jina SHAMIM
37 Director Student Financial Services Ms. Carrie STEERE-SALAZAR
43 Chief Campus Counsel Ms. Marcia J. CANNING
08 University Librarian/AVC Ms. Karen BUTTER
19 Chief of Police Ms. Pamela ROSKOWSKI
22 Dir Affirm Action/Equal Oppty/Diver Mr. Michael B. ADAMS
66 Dean School of Nursing Dr. David VLAHOV
52 Dean School of Dentistry Dr. John FEATHERSTONE
67 Interim Dean School of Pharmacy Dr. B. Joseph GUGLIELMO
35 Director Student Life Mr. Eric KOENIG
39 Assoc Director of Housing Services Mr. Jim JACOBS
96 Exec Dir Camp Procurmt/Bus Contract Mr. James HINE
07 Registrar Mr. Douglas CARLSON
36 Dir Career/Professional Development Mr. William LINDSTAEDT
23 Director Student Health Services Mr. Henry KAHN
40 Bookstore Manager Mr. Jim SOBCZYK

*University of California-Santa Barbara (B)

552 University Road, Santa Barbara CA 93106-0001

County: Santa Barbara FICE Identification: 001320
Unit ID: 110705
Telephone: (805) 893-8000 Carnegie Class: RU/VH
FAX Number: N/A Calendar System: Quarter
URL: www.ucsb.edu
Established: 1909 Annual Undergrad Tuition & Fees (In-State): $13,595
Enrollment: 21,685 Coed
Affiliation or Control: State IRS Status: 501(c)3
Highest Offering: Doctorate
Program: Liberal Arts And General; Teacher Preparatory
Accreditation: WC, CS, DANCE, ENG, IPSY, PSPSY

02 Chancellor Dr. Henry T. YANG
04 Exec Assistant to the Chancellor Mr. Kevin R. MCCAULEY
05 Exec Vice Chanc/Chief Academic Ofcr Dr. Glenn E. LUCAS
46 Vice Chancellor Research Dr. Michael S. WITHERELL
11 Sr Assoc Vice Chancellor Admin Svcs Mr. Marc FISHER
88 Assoc Vice Chancellor Admin Svcs Mr. Ronald CORTEZ
26 Vice Chanc Inst Advancement Vacant
32 Vice Chancellor Student Affairs Dr. Michael D. YOUNG
45 Assistant Chanc Budget & Planning Mr. Todd G. LEE
16 Assoc Vice Chanc Acad Personnel Dr. John E. TALBOTT
28 Asc VC Diversity/Equity/Acad Policy Dr. Maria HERRERA-SOBEK
20 Acting AVC Academic Programs Dr. Ronald W. TOBIN
30 Assoc Vice Chancellor Development Mr. Gary A. GREINKE
27 Assoc Vice Chanc Public Affairs Vacant
84 Asst Vice Chanc Enrollment Svcs/ Mgt Ms. Christine N. VAN GIESON
88 Exec Dir Student Acad Support Svc Ms. Mary JACOB
29 Asst Vice Chanc Alumni Affairs Mr. George THURLOW, III
88 Dean College Creative Studies Dr. Bruce H. TIFFNEY
54 Acting Dean College of Engineering Dr. Larry COLDREN
58 Dean Graduate Division Ms. Gale M. MORRISON
53 Dean Gevirtz Graduate Sch Educ Ms. Jane CONOLEY
65 Dean Bren School of Env Sci & Mgmt Dr. Steven D. GAINES
56 Dean UC Santa Barbara Extension Dr. Michael T. BROWN
35 Dean of Students Dr. Yonie HARRIS
79 Dean Humanities/Fine Arts Dr. David B. MARSHALL
81 Dean Math/Life & Physical Sciences Dr. Pierre WILTZIUS
87 Dean Summer Sessions Dr. Carol BRAUN PASTERNACK
83 Dean Social Sciences Dr. Melvin L. OLIVER
85 Director Intl Students/Scholars Ms. Mary J. JACOB
06 Acting Registrar Ms. Marsha BANKSTON
15 Interim Director Human Resources Ms. Tricia HIEMSTRA
21 Director Accounting Svcs & Controls Mr. Jim R. CORKILL
37 Acting Director Financial Aid Mr. Michael MILLER
88 Acting Dir Audit & Advisory Service Mr. Robert TARSIA
07 Director Admissions & Outreach Ms. Christine N. VAN GIESON
09 Director Institutional Research Dr. Steven C. VELASCO
23 Director Student Health Svcs Dr. Mary FERRIS
39 Exec Dir Housing Residential Svcs Mr. Wilfred E. BROWN
40 Director of UCSB Bookstore Mr. Alan KIRBY
19 Chief of Police Mr. Dustin OLSON
41 Director Intercollegiate Athletics Mr. Mark MASSARI
86 Dir Governmental Relations Ms. Kirsten DESHLER
88 Director Finance/Administration Mr. Eric J. SONQUIST
08 Co-Acting University Librarian Ms. Sherry DEDECKER
08 Co-Acting University Librarian Ms. Lucia SNOWHILL
88 Director Orientation Programs Ms. Kim R. PARENT
44 Interim Dir Capital Development Mr. Chuck HAINES
46 Acting Dir Campus Planning & Design Ms. Alissa HUMMER
44 Assoc Vice Chancellor Development Mr. Gary A. GREINKE
31 Director Arts & Lectures Ms. Celesta BILLECI
88 Director Disabled Students Pgm Mr. Gary R. WHITE
104 Campus Dir Education Abroad Program Dr. Juan E. CAMPO
88 Director Env Health & Safety Ms. Pam LOMBARDO
88 Director MultiCultural Center Ms. Zaveeni KHAN-MARCUS
38 Director Counseling Services Dr. Jeanne STANFORD
94 Director Women's Center Ms. Alka ARORA
88 Ombudsperson Ms. Priscilla MORI
88 Exec Dir Instructional Devel Mr. George H. MICHAELS
36 Director Career Services Mr. Micael S. KEMP
13 Assoc VC for IT and CIO Mr. Tom PUTNAM
43 UCSB Legal Counsel Mr. David BIRNBAUM
88 Equal Opport Sexual Harras/Title IX Mr. Ricardo ALCAINO
18 Director Design & Construction Mr. Jack WOLEVER
88 Director Univ Center/Events Center Mr. Alan KIRBY
68 Director of Recreation Mr. Jon SPAVENTA
24 Director Instructional Computing Mr. William KOSELUK
92 Honors Coord/Academic Advisor Ms. Rocio ANGELES
92 Honors Coord/Academic Advisor Mr. Scott KASSNER
96 Strategic Sourcing Specialist Mr. Chris CURLESS

*University of California-Santa Cruz (C)

1156 High Street, Santa Cruz CA 95064-1077

County: Santa Cruz FICE Identification: 001321
Unit ID: 110714
Telephone: (831) 459-0111 Carnegie Class: RU/VH
FAX Number: (831) 459-0146 Calendar System: Quarter
URL: www.ucsc.edu
Established: 1962 Annual Undergrad Tuition & Fees (In-State): $13,417
Enrollment: 17,454 Coed
Affiliation or Control: State IRS Status: 501(c)3
Highest Offering: Doctorate
Program: Liberal Arts And General; Professional
Accreditation: WC, ENG, IPSY

02 Chancellor Dr. George R. BLUMENTHAL
05 Campus Provost/Exec Vice Chancellor Dr. Alison GALLOWAY
10 Vice Chanc Business/Admin Services Christina L. VALENTINO
45 Vice Chancellor Planning/Budget Ms. Peggy DELANEY
46 Vice Chancellor Research Dr. Bruce MARGON
30 Vice Chanc of University Relations Ms. Donna M. MURPHY
13 Vice Provost Information Technology Dr. Mary DOYLE
20 V Prov/Dean Undergrad Educ Dr. Richard HUGHEY
20 Vice Provost Academic Affairs Dr. Herbert LEE
88 Sr Dir Silicon Valley Initiative Mr. Gordon RINGOLD
16 Asst VC Academic Personnel Dr. Pamela PETERSON
08 University Librarian Ms. Virginia STEEL
07 Assoc VC Enrollment Mgmt Ms. Michelle WHITTINGHAM
49 Dean of Humanities Dr. William LADUSAW
81 Dean Physical & Biological Sci Dr. Paul KOCH
49 Dean of the Arts Dr. David YAGER
83 Dean of Social Sciences Dr. Sheldon KAMIENIECKI
54 Dean of Engineering Dr. Arthur RAMIREZ
58 Vice Prov/Dean of Graduate Studies Dr. Tyrus MILLER
65 Director Institute Marine Sciences Dr. Gary B. GRIGGS
81 Director Institute Particle Physics Dr. Steven RITZ
88 Director UCO/Lick Observatory Dr. Michael BOLTE
12 Provost Stevenson College Dr. Alice YANG
12 Provost Cowell College Dr. Faye CROSBY
12 Provost Crown College Dr. F. Joel FERGUSON
12 Provost Merrill College Dr. Elizabeth ABRAMS
12 Provost Porter College Dr. Kate EDMUNDS
12 Provost Kresge College Dr. Juan POBLETE
12 Provost Oakes College Dr. Kimberly LAU
12 Provost College Eight Dr. Ronnie LIPSCHUTZ
12 Provost College Nine & Ten Dr. Helen SHAPIRO
06 Registrar Ms. Pamela HUNT-CARTER
09 Director Institutional Research Dr. Julian L. FERNALD
15 Director Staff Human Resources Ms. Charlotte MORENO
18 Int Assoc VC & Campus Arthitect Mr. John BARNES
29 Exec Director of Alumni Relations Ms. Carolyn CHRISTOPHERSON
37 Staff Director Financial Aid Ms. Ann DRAPER
22 Staff Dir EEO/Affirmative Action Mr. Ashish SAHNI
86 Director Government Relations Ms. Donna M. BLITZER
38 Interim Director Student Counseling Dr. Maryjan MURPHY
96 Director of Purchasing Mr. John BONO
35 Asst Vice Chanc Student Affairs Ms. Alma SIFUENTES

University of East-West Medicine (D)

595 Lawrence Expressway, Sunnyvale CA 94085

County: Santa Clara FICE Identification: 039953
Unit ID: 447801
Telephone: (408) 733-1878 Carnegie Class: Spec/Health
FAX Number: (408) 636-7705 Calendar System: Trimester
URL: www.uewm.edu
Established: 1997 Annual Undergrad Tuition & Fees: $33,660
Enrollment: 500 Coed
Affiliation or Control: Proprietary IRS Status: Proprietary
Highest Offering: Doctorate
Program: Professional
Accreditation: ACUP

01 President Dr. Ying Qiu WANG
11 COO Doreen SIMMONS

† Candidate at the Doctorate level.

University of LaVerne (E)

1950 Third Street, La Verne CA 91750-4443

County: Los Angeles FICE Identification: 001216
Unit ID: 117140
Telephone: (909) 593-3511 Carnegie Class: DRU
FAX Number: (909) 593-0965 Calendar System: Semester
URL: www.laverne.edu
Established: 1891 Annual Undergrad Tuition & Fees: $33,350
Enrollment: 8,370 Coed
Affiliation or Control: Independent Non-Profit IRS Status: 501(c)3
Highest Offering: Doctorate
Program: Liberal Arts And General; Teacher Preparatory; Professional
Accreditation: WC, CLPSY, #LAW, SPAA, TED

01 President Dr. Devorah A. LIEBERMAN
05 Provost Dr. Gregory DEWEY
03 Executive Vice President Mr. Philip A. HAWKEY
10 Vice Pres for Finance & Treasurer Mr. Avedis (Avo) KECHICHIAN
30 Vice President Univ Advancement Dr. Jean BJERKE
20 Vice Provost Dr. Homa SHABAHANG
49 Dean College Arts & Sciences Dr. Jonathan REED
50 Dean College Business/Public Mgmt Dr. Ibrahim (Abe) HELOU
53 Dean College of Educ/Org Leadership Dr. Mark GOOR
61 Dean College of Law Vacant
32 Dean Student Affairs Dr. Loretta RAHMANI
12 Dean Regional Campus Admin Dr. Stephen L. LESNIAK
07 Dean of Admissions Mr. Chris KRZAK
84 Assoc VP Academic Sppt/Retent Svcs Ms. Adeline CARDENAS-CLAGUE
21 Associate Vice President of Finance Ms. Lori K. GORDIEN CASE
20 Assoc VP Academic/Faculty Affairs Dr. Alfred P. CLARK
09 Assoc VP University-Wide Assessment Dr. Aghop DER-KARABETIAN
16 Assoc VP of Human Resources Ms. Jody L. BOMBA
13 Assoc VP Facil & Tech Svcs/ CIO Dr. Clive K. HOUSTON-BROWN
35 Associate Dean Student Affairs Ms. Ruby S. MONTANO-CORDOVA
88 Asst Dean Grad Acad Supp/Ret Svcs Ms. Jo Nell BAKER
27 Chief Marketing Officer Mr. Fred A. CHYR
88 Director Intl Recruitment/Admission Dr. Jeffrey NONEMAKER
18 Dir Physical Plant Operations/Svs Mr. Robert D. BEEBE
37 Int Director of Financial Aid Mr. Jason NEAL
26 Int Director of Public Relations Mrs. Alisha ROSAS
29 Director Alumni Relations Ms. Beth ELMORE
38 Director Student Counseling Dr. Richard R. ROGERS
88 Director Student Accounts Ms. Xochitl E. MARTINEZ
104 Director Intl/Study Abroad Ctr Mr. Philip HOFER
96 Director of Purchasing Mrs. Deborah S. DEACY
28 Director Multicultural Affairs Mr. Daniel L. LOERA
23 Dir Health Svcs/Svcs for Stds-Disab Ms. Cynthia K. DENNE
39 Asst Dean/Dir Housing/Res Life Ed Mr. Juan REGALADO
36 Director Career Services Mrs. Paula E. VERDUGO
88 Int Dir Center Teaching/Learning Dr. Lisa R. RODRIGUEZ
19 Int Director Campus Safety Mr. Jeffrey A. CLARK
41 Athletic Director Ms. Julie KLINE
06 Registrar Mrs. Marilyn S. DAVIES
08 University Librarian Ms. Vinaya L. TRIPURANENI
28 Chief Diversity/Inclusivity Officer Ms. Joy LEI

University of the Pacific (A)

3601 Pacific Avenue, Stockton CA 95211-0197

County: San Joaquin FICE Identification: 001329
Unit ID: 120883
Telephone: (209) 946-2011 Carnegie Class: DRU
FAX Number: (209) 946-2845 Calendar System: Semester
URL: www.pacific.edu
Established: 1851 Annual Undergrad Tuition & Fees: $38,320
Enrollment: 6,710 Coed
Affiliation or Control: Independent Non-Profit IRS Status: 501(c)3
Highest Offering: Doctorate
Program: Liberal Arts And General; Teacher Preparatory; Professional
Accreditation: WC, ART, BUS, CS, DENT, DH, ENG, IPSY, LAW, MUS, PHAR, PTA, SP, TED

01 President .... Pamela A. EIBECK
05 Provost .... Maria G. PALLAVICINI
10 Vice President Business & Finance .... Patrick D. CAVANAUGH
32 Vice President Student Life .... Elizabeth B. GRIEGO
30 Vice President Development .... Vacant
26 Vice Pres External Relations .... Ted LELAND
101 VP & Secretary to Board of Regents .... Mary Lou LACKEY
21 Associate VP Business/Finance .... Larry BREHM
84 Assoc Provost for Enrollment Svcs .... Robert ALEXANDER
26 Assoc VP Marketing/Univ Relations .... Richard ROJO
51 Asst Provost Ctr Prof & Cont Educ .... Barbara L. SHAW
08 Dean of the Library .... C. Brigid WELCH
58 Dean Research/Graduate Studies .... Jin GONG
25 Sponsored Pgms Administrator .... Carol BRODIE
29 Exec Dir of Alumni Relations .... William COEN
37 Director of Financial Aid .... Lynn FOX
07 Director of Admissions .... Rich TOLEDO
06 Registrar .... Ann GILLEN
09 Director Institutional Research .... Mike ROGERS
35 Director Student Activities .... Jason VELO
96 Director of Purchasing .... Ronda MARR
92 Director Honors Program .... George RANDELS
93 Director Multicultural Affairs .... Ines RUIZ-HUSTON
94 Director Gender Studies .... Jeffrey BECKER
38 Director of Counseling Services .... Stacie TURKS
39 Director of Housing .... Steven JACOBSON
36 Director of Career Resource Center .... Vacant
41 Director of Athletics .... Ted LELAND
42 University Chaplain .... Joel LOHR
13 Chief Information Officer .... Malik RAHMAN
15 Director of Human Resources .... Jane L. LEWIS
40 Director of Bookstore .... Nicole CASTILLO
19 Director of Public Safety .... Michael BELCHER
18 Director of Physical Plant .... Scott HEATON
28 Dir of Div/Asst to Prov for Acad .... Vacant
61 Dean McGeorge School of Law .... Jay MOOTZ
54 Dean Sch of Eng/Comp Science .... Ravi JAIN
67 Dean Sch of Pharm/Hlth Sciences .... Phillip R. OPPENHEIMER
64 Dean Conservatory of Music .... Giulio ONGARO
52 Dean School of Dentistry .... Patrick FERRILLO
53 Dean School of Education .... Lynn BECK
49 Dean College of the Pacific .... Vacant
50 Dean School Business/Public Admin .... Lewis GALE
82 Int Dean Sch International Studies .... Cynthia WAGNER WEICK

University of Philosophical Research (B)

3910 Los Feliz Boulevard, Los Angeles CA 90027

County: Los Angeles Identification: 666373
Telephone: (323) 663-2167 Carnegie Class: Not Classified
FAX Number: (323) 663-9443 Calendar System: Quarter
URL: www.uprs.edu
Established: 1998 Annual Graduate Tuition & Fees: $5,500
Enrollment: 205 Coed
Affiliation or Control: Independent Non-Profit IRS Status: 501(c)3
Highest Offering: Master's; No Undergraduates
Program: Liberal Arts And General
Accreditation: DETC

01 President/Chief Executive Officer .... Dr. Obadiah HARRIS
05 Dean of Academic Affairs .... Dr. Debashish BANERJI
06 Registrar .... Mr. John CHASE

University of Redlands (C)

PO Box 3080, Redlands CA 92373-0999

County: San Bernardino FICE Identification: 001322
Unit ID: 121691
Telephone: (909) 793-2121 Carnegie Class: Master's L
FAX Number: (909) 793-2029 Calendar System: Semester
URL: www.redlands.edu
Established: 1907 Annual Undergrad Tuition & Fees: $39,037
Enrollment: 4,404 Coed
Affiliation or Control: Independent Non-Profit IRS Status: 501(c)3
Highest Offering: Doctorate
Program: Liberal Arts And General; Teacher Preparatory; Professional
Accreditation: WC, MUS, SP

01 President .... Dr. Ralph W. KUNCL
03 Executive Vice President/COO .... Mr. Phillip L. DOOLITTLE
05 Vice President Academic Affairs .... Dr. David FITE
26 Vice President University Relations .... Mr. Neil A. MACREADY
32 Vice President/Dean Student Life .... Ms. Charlotte G. BURGESS
27 Vice Pres Mktg/Strategic Commun .... Vacant
30 Assoc Vice Pres Development .... Mr. Ray WATTS
84 Assoc Vice Pres of Enrollment Mgmt .... Ms. Nancy SVENSON
91 Assoc VP Integrated Tech Sys/CIO .... Mr. Hamid ETESAMNIA
10 Treasurer/Chief Financial Officer .... Mr. Cory NOMURA
21 Director Financial Ops & Controller .... Ms. Patricia M. CAUDLE
58 Dean School of Business .... Dr. Stuart NOBLE-GOODMAN
53 Dean School of Education .... Dr. James VALADEZ
49 Interim Dean Arts & Sciences .... Dr. Kathy OGREN
07 Vice Pres of Enrollment .... Mr. Kevin DYERLY
28 Asc Dean Campus Diversity/Inclusion .. Ms. Leela MADHAVARAU
42 Chaplain .... Rev. John T. WALSH
06 Registrar .... Vacant
104 Director Study Abroad .... Ms. Sarah N. FALKENSTIEN
37 Director of Financial Aid .... Ms. Alisha AGUILAR
90 Dir Academic Computing/Instruct .... Vacant
64 Dean School of Music .... Dr. Andrew GLENDENING
81 Director Center of Sciences & Math .... Dr. Barbara M. MURRAY
88 Director of Environmental Programs .... Dr. Lamont C. HEMPEL
08 Director of Library Services .... Ms. Gabriela SONNTAG
15 Director of Human Resources .... Ms. Roberta G. DELLHIME
22 EEO & Employee Relations Manager .... Vacant
09 Director of Institutional Research .... Ms. Wendy MCEWEN
19 Director of Public Safety .... Mr. Jeffrey TALBOTT
18 Interim Director of Physical Plant .... Mr. Roger CELLINI
29 Director of Alumni Relations .... Mr. John SERBEIN
20 Director of Acad Support Services .... Vacant
38 Director Student Counseling .... Mr. Ruben ROBLES
41 Director of Athletics .... Mr. Jeffrey MARTINEZ
96 Director of Purchasing .... Ms. Sandi TAYLOR
36 Director Student Placement .... Ms. Kathryn WOOD

University of San Diego (D)

5998 Alcala Park, San Diego CA 92110-2492

County: San Diego FICE Identification: 010395
Unit ID: 122436
Telephone: (619) 260-4600 Carnegie Class: DRU
FAX Number: (619) 260-6833 Calendar System: 4/1/4
URL: www.sandiego.edu
Established: 1949 Annual Undergrad Tuition & Fees: $39,970
Enrollment: 8,317 Coed
Affiliation or Control: Roman Catholic IRS Status: 501(c)3
Highest Offering: Doctorate
Program: Liberal Arts And General; Teacher Preparatory; Professional
Accreditation: WC, BUS, BUSA, CACREP, ENG, IPSY, LAW, MFCD, NURSE, TED

01 President .... Dr. Mary E. LYONS
04 Special Assistant to the President .... Ms. Elaine ATENCIO
05 Executive Vice President & Provost .... Dr. Julie H. SULLIVAN
10 Vice Pres Business & Admin .... Vacant
42 Vice President Mission & Ministry .... Msgr. Daniel J. DILLABOUGH
32 Vice President Student Affairs .... Ms. Carmen M. VAZQUEZ
30 Vice President Univ Relations .... Dr. Timothy L. O'MALLEY
49 Dean College of Arts & Sciences .... Dr. Mary K. BOYD
50 Dean School of Business Admin .... Dr. David F. PYKE
61 Dean School of Law .... Mr. Stephen C. FERRUOLO
53 Dean Sch Leadership/Educ Sciences .... Dr. Paula A. CORDEIRO
66 Dean School Nursing/Health Science .... Dr. Sally B. HARDIN
88 Dean School of Peace Studies .... Dr. Edward C. LUCK
51 Dean Prof & Continuing Education .... Dr. Jason LEMON
35 Asst VP & Dean of Students .... Dr. Donald R. GODWIN
20 Vice Provost .... Dr. Thomas R. HERRINTON
20 Associate Provost .... Dr. Andrew T. ALLEN
20 Assoc Provost International Affairs .... Dr. Denise DIMON
28 Assoc Provost for Incl & Diversity .... Vacant
13 Vice Provost & Chief Info Officer .... Mr. Christopher W. WESSELLS
41 Executive Director Athletics .... Mr. Ky L. SNYDER
21 Assoc Vice Pres Business Admin .... Ms. Patricia T. OLIVER PUTNAM
16 Chief Human Resources Officer .... Dr. David M. BLAKE
18 Asst VP Facilities Management .... Mr. Mark NORITA
26 Asst Vice Pres Public Affairs .... Ms. Pamela GRAY PAYTON
19 Asst Vice President Public Safety .... Mr. Larry E. BARNETT
43 General Counsel .... Ms. Kelly C. DOUGLAS
06 University Registrar .... Ms. Susan H. BUGBEE
84 Asst VP Enrollment Management .... Mr. Stephen F. PULTZ
07 Director of Admissions .... Ms. Minh-Ha HOANG
08 University Librarian .... Dr. Theresa BYRD
09 Exec Dir Inst Research & Planning .... Dr. Cel JOHNSON
54 Director Engineering Programs .... Dr. Kathleen A. KRAMER
90 Sr Director Academic Tech Services .... Ms. Shahra MESHKATY
91 Dir Enterprise Admin Sys & Services .... Ms. Indra BISHOP
102 Sr Director Foundation Relations .... Ms. Annette KETNER
86 Sr Dir Community/Govt Relations .... Mr. Thomas R. CLEARY
44 Senior Director Planned Giving .... Mr. John A. PHILLIPS
29 Director Alumni Relations .... Mr. Charles BASS
44 Director Annual Giving .... Mr. Philip GARLAND
40 Director Bookstore .... Ms. Katherine MISSELL
36 Director Career Services .... Ms. Linda M. SCALES
38 Director Counseling Center .... Dr. Stephen D. SPRINKLE
37 Director Financial Aid Services .... Ms. Judith LEWIS LOGUE
92 Director Honors Program .... Dr. Roger C. PACE
39 Director Housing .... Mr. Rick HAGAN
85 Dir International Students/Scholars .... Ms. Yvette M. FONTAINE
104 Dir International Studies Abroad .... Ms. Kira A. ESPIRITU
93 Director Multicultural Center .... Dr. Mayte PEREZ-FRANCO
27 Senior Director Media Relations .... Ms. Elizabeth HARMAN
96 Director Procurement Services .... Ms. Dawn L. ANDERSON
25 Director Sponsored Programs .... Ms. Kim EUDY
23 Director Student Health Center .... Ms. Pamela J. SIKES

University of San Francisco (E)

2130 Fulton Street, San Francisco CA 94117-1080

County: San Francisco FICE Identification: 001325
Unit ID: 122612
Telephone: (415) 422-5555 Carnegie Class: DRU
FAX Number: (415) 422-2303 Calendar System: 4/1/4
URL: www.usfca.edu
Established: 1855 Annual Undergrad Tuition & Fees: $38,884
Enrollment: 9,793 Coed
Affiliation or Control: Roman Catholic IRS Status: 501(c)3
Highest Offering: Doctorate
Program: Liberal Arts And General; Teacher Preparatory; Professional
Accreditation: WC, BUS, LAW, NURSE

01 President .... Rev. Stephen A. PRIVETT, SJ
05 Provost/Vice Pres Academic Affairs .... Dr. Jennifer E. TURPIN
00 Chancellor .... Rev. John J. LO SCHIAVO, SJ
10 Vice President Business & Finance .... Mr. Charles E. CROSS
26 Vice Pres for Communications .... Mr. David F. MACMILLAN
30 Vice President Development .... Mr. Peter J. WILCH
32 Vice Provost University Life .... Dr. Peter J. NOVAK
43 University Counsel .... Ms. Donna J. DAVIS
20 Vice Provost .... Dr. Gerardo MARIN
20 Vice Provost .... Dr. Ana KARAMAN
20 Vice Provost/Dean Academic Svcs .... Dr. Elizabeth J. JOHNSON
15 Asst Vice Pres Human Resource .... Ms. Martha A. PEUGH-WADE
21 Asst Vice Pres Financial Reporting .... Ms. Kimberly L. KVAAL
18 Asst Vice Pres Facilities Mgmt .... Mr. Michael LONDON
28 Assoc Vice Provost Diversity .... Dr. Mary J. WARDELL
42 Director University Ministry .... Ms. Julia A. DOWD
04 Exec Assistant to the President .... Ms. Jaci E. NEESAM
08 Dean of Libraries .... Mr. Tyrone H. CANNON
37 Assoc Dean Acad Svcs/Dir Fin Aid .... Ms. Susan L. MURPHY
06 Assoc Dean University Registrar .... Mr. Robert L. BROMFIELD
85 Dir International Student Services .... Ms. Lisa KOSIEWICZ
41 Executive Director of Athletics .... Mr. Scott A. SIDWELL
07 Director of Admissions .... Mr. Michael HUGHES
09 Director of Institutional Research .... Dr. Alan L. ZIAJKA
36 Director of Career Services .... Mr. James CATIGGAY
29 Director of Alumni Relations .... Ms. Cortes SAUNDERS-STORNO
13 Chief Info Officer/Info Tech Svcs .... Mr. Stephen GALLAGHER
26 Director of Media Relations .... Mr. Gary MCDONALD
38 Director Counseling Center .... Dr. Barbara J. THOMAS
19 Director of Public Safety .... Mr. Daniel LAWSON
39 Director of Residence Life .... Mr. Steve NYGAARD
24 Dir Ctr for Instruction/Technology .... Dr. John BANSAVICH
96 Director of Purchasing .... Ms. Janet L. TEYMOURTASH
35 Chief Student Life Officer .... Dr. Peter J. NOVAK
88 Asst Human Resources Director .... Ms. Diane L. NELSON
50 Dean School of Management .... Dr. Mike WEBBER
49 Dean College Arts & Sciences .... Dr. Marcelo F. CAMPERI
53 Dean School of Education .... Dr. Walter H. GMELCH
66 Dean School of Nursing .... Dr. Judith KARSHMER
61 Dean of the School of Law .... Mr. Jeffrey S. BRAND

University of Southern California (F)

University Park, Los Angeles CA 90089-0012

County: Los Angeles FICE Identification: 001328
Unit ID: 123961
Telephone: (213) 740-2311 Carnegie Class: RU/VH
FAX Number: (213) 740-8502 Calendar System: Semester
URL: www.usc.edu
Established: 1880 Annual Undergrad Tuition & Fees: $44,400
Enrollment: 38,010 Coed
Affiliation or Control: Independent Non-Profit IRS Status: 501(c)3
Highest Offering: Doctorate
Program: Occupational; Liberal Arts And General; Teacher Preparatory; Professional
Accreditation: WC, ANEST, ARCPA, BUS, BUSA, CEA, CLPSY, CS, DENT, DH, DIETI, ENG, HSA, IPSY, JOUR, LAW, LSAR, MED, MUS, OT, PDPSY, PH, PHAR, PLNG, PTA, SPAA, SW

01 President .... Dr. C. L. M. NIKIAS
05 Provost and Sr VP Academic Affairs .... Prof. Elizabeth GARRETT
11 Sr Vice Pres Administration .... Mr. Todd R. DICKEY
10 Sr Vice President & CFO .... Mr. Robert ABELES
26 Sr Vice Pres University Relations .... Mr. Thomas SAYLES
30 Sr VP University Advancement .... Mr. Albert R. CHECCIO
23 Sr Vice Pres & CEO for USC Health .... Mr. Thomas E. JACKIEWICZ
88 Chief Investment Officer .... Ms. Lisa MAZZOCCO
43 General Counsel/Secretary of Univ .... Ms. Carol MAUCH AMIR
32 Vice President Student Affairs .... Dr. Michael L. JACKSON
07 VP Admissions and Planning .... Dr. L. Katharine HARRINGTON
46 VP for Research .... Dr. Randolph W. HALL
88 VP for Real Estate Dev & Asset .... Ms. Kristina E. RASPE
88 VP for Athletic Compliance .... Mr. David M. ROBERTS
88 VP Capital Construction/Facilities .... Mr. Thomas S. LEARY, JR.
21 VP for Finance .... Ms. Margo STEURBAUT
88 VP for Health Sciences Development .... Mr. William WATSON
26 VP Public Relations & Marketing .... Ms. Brenda K. MACEO
41 Athletic Director .... Mr. Patrick C. HADEN
100 Chief of Staff/Dir of Protocol .... Mr. Dennis CORNELL
00 President Emeritus .... Dr. Steven B. SAMPLE
88 Dean Leventhal School of Accounting .... Dr. William W. HOLDER
60 Dean Annenberg School Communication .... Dr. Ernest J. WILSON, III
48 Dean School of Architecture .... Mr. Qingyun MA
50 Dean Marshall School of Business .... Mr. James G. ELLIS
88 Dean School of Cinematic Arts .... Dr. Elizabeth M. DALEY

52 Dean Ostrow School of Dentistry .... Dr. Avishai SADAN
53 Dean Rossier School of Education .... Dr. Karen S. GALLAGHER
54 Dean Viterbi School of Engineering .... Dr. Yannis C. YORTSOS
57 Dean Roski School of Fine Arts .... Dr. Rochelle STEINER
88 Dean Davis School of Gerontology .... Dr. Pinchas COHEN
61 Dean Gould School of Law .... Mr. Robert K. RASMUSSEN
63 Dean Keck School of Medicine .... Dr. Carmen A. PULIAFITO
64 Dean Thornton School of Music .... Dr. Robert A. CUTIETTA
67 Dean School of Pharmacy .... Dr. R. Pete L. VANDERVEEN
70 Dean School of Social Work .... Dr. Marilyn L. FLYNN
88 Dean School of Dramatic Arts .... Ms. Madeline PUZO
88 Dean Price School of Public Policy .... Dr. Jack H. KNOTT
49 Dean Dornsife Col Ltrs Arts & Sci .... Dr. Steve A. KAY
42 Dean Religious Life .... Mr. Varun SONI
06 Dean Academic Records & Registrar .... Dr. Douglas SHOOK
08 Dean University Libraries .... Ms. Catherine QUINLAN
07 Dean of Admission .... Mr. Timothy BRUNOLD
37 Dean of Financial Aid .... Mr. Thomas MCWHORTER
36 Assoc Sr VP Career/Protective Svcs .... Dr. Charles E. LANE
29 Assoc Sr VP and CEO Alumni Assn .... Mr. Scott M. MORY
36 Asst VP Career Services .... Dr. Mary K. CAMPBELL
51 Exec Dir Cont Ed & Summer Programs .... Ms. Eileen B. KOHAN
28 Exec Dir Office of Equity/Diversity .... Ms. Jody SHIPPER
38 Director Student Counseling Service .... Dr. Ilene ROSENSTEIN
20 Executive Vice Provost .... Dr. Michael W. QUICK
88 Vice Provost and Senior Advisor .... Dr. Martin L. LEVINE
20 Vice Prov for Graduate Programs .... Dr. Sarah PRATT
20 Vice Prov for Undergraduate Program .... Dr. Eugene N. BICKERS
27 Vice Prov for Info Tech Svcs/CIO .... Mr. Ilee RHIMES
88 Vice Prov Acad Operations & Strate .... Mr. Robert A. COOPER
88 Vice Prov for Innovation .... Ms. Krisztina HOLLY
88 Int Vice Prov Global Initiatives .... Dr. Anthony BAILEY
20 Vice Provost for Faculty Affairs .... Dr. Beth E. MEYEROWITZ

University of the West (A)

1409 Walnut Grove Avenue, Rosemead CA 91770-3709
County: Los Angeles FICE Identification: 036963
Unit ID: 449870
Telephone: (626) 571-8811 Carnegie Class: Bac/Diverse
FAX Number: (626) 571-1413 Calendar System: Semester
URL: www.uwest.edu
Established: 1991 Annual Undergrad Tuition & Fees: $13,800
Enrollment: 238 Coed
Affiliation or Control: Independent Non-Profit IRS Status: 501(c)3
Highest Offering: Doctorate
Program: Liberal Arts And General
Accreditation: WC

01 President .... Dr. Chin Shun WU
04 Special Advisor to President .... Dr. Arthur PETERSON
05 Dean of Academic Affairs .... Dr. William HOWE
32 Dean of Student Affairs .... Dr. Arthur PETERSON
10 Cheif Financial Officer .... Mr. Jeffrey LIN
08 Director of Library .... Ms. Ling Ling KUO
06 Registrar .... Ms. Laura IBARRA
07 Admissions Officer .... Ms. Grace HSIAO
39 Director of Student Life .... Mr. Thomas THING
73 Chair Dept of Religious Studies .... Dr. William HOWE
50 Chair Dept of Business Admin .... Dr. Bill CHEN

Vanguard University of Southern California (B)

55 Fair Drive, Costa Mesa CA 92626-6597
County: Orange FICE Identification: 001293
Unit ID: 123651
Telephone: (714) 556-3610 Carnegie Class: Bac/Diverse
FAX Number: (714) 957-9317 Calendar System: Semester
URL: www.vanguard.edu
Established: 1920 Annual Undergrad Tuition & Fees: $28,500
Enrollment: 2,115 Coed
Affiliation or Control: Assemblies Of God Church IRS Status: 501(c)3
Highest Offering: Master's
Program: Liberal Arts And General; Teacher Preparatory; Professional
Accreditation: WC, NURSE, THEA

01 President .... Dr. Carol A. TAYLOR
04 Exec Assistant to the President .... Ms. Shree CARTER
05 Provost/Vice President Acad Affairs .... Dr. Jeff HITTENBERGER
20 Assoc Provost/Dean Col Arts & Sci .... Dr. Michael D. WILSON
107 Director Sch Professional Studies .... Ms. Jamie BROWNLEE
73 Director for Graduate Religion .... Dr. Richard ISRAEL
53 Director for Graduate Education .... Dr. Doug GROVE
83 Director for Graduate Psychology .... Dr. Jerre WHITE
06 Registrar .... Ms. Judy HAMILTON
09 Director of Institutional Research .... Dr. Ludmilla PRASLOVA
08 Head Librarian .... Ms. Alison ENGLISH
41 Athletic Director .... Mr. Bob WILSON
10 Vice President Business/Finance .... Ms. Lettie COWIE
21 Director of Fiscal Management .... Ms. Jill ROBINSON
21 Director of Accounting Operations .... Ms. Beverly MOORE
96 Director of Purchasing .... Ms. Jennifer PAUL
19 Director of Campus Safety Services .... Mr. Paul TURGEON
27 Chief Information Officer .... Mr. Derek DENSBERGER
15 Director of Human Resources .... Mr. Joe BAFFA
18 Director of Facility Services .... Mr. Bruce CROUCH
40 Bookstore Manager .... Ms. Carol KNIGHT
101 Exec Assistant to the President .... Ms. Shree CARTER
42 University Campus Pastor .... Vacant
32 Dean of Student Life .... Mr. Tim YOUNG
39 Student Housing Coordinator .... Ms. Allison HESSE

24 Director of Learning Skills .... Ms. Barbi ROUSE
38 Director of Counseling Services .... Dr. Beth LORANCE
36 Dir of Career Planning/Placement .... Mr. Hassan ARCHER
28 Director of Diversity .... Ms. Thandiwe DINANI
84 VP for Enrollment Management .... Ms. Kim JOHNSON
07 Director of Undergrad Admissions .... Vacant
07 Director of Graduate Admissions .... Mr. Drake LEVASHEFF
37 Director of Student Financial Svcs .... Ms. Robyn FOURNIER
30 VP University Advancement .... Ms. Kelly KANNWISCHER
44 Director of Annual Fund .... Ms. Jennifer J. SMITH
29 Director of Alumni Relations .... Mr. Joel GACKLE
26 Chief Communications Officer .... Ms. Kelly KANNWISCHER
86 Director of Veteran/Government Rels .... Mr. Brent THEOBALD

*Ventura County Community College District (C)

255 W Stanley Avenue, Suite 150,
Ventura CA 93001-1348
County: Ventura FICE Identification: 006863
Unit ID: 125019
Telephone: (805) 652-5500 Carnegie Class: N/A
FAX Number: (805) 652-7700
URL: www.vcccd.edu

01 Chancellor .... Dr. Jamillah MOORE
10 Vice Chanc Business Svcs/Fin Mgmt .... Ms. Susan JOHNSON
15 Vice Chanc of Human Resources .... Ms. Patricia PARHAM

*Moorpark College (D)

7075 Campus Road, Moorpark CA 93021-1695
County: Ventura FICE Identification: 007115
Unit ID: 119137
Telephone: (805) 378-1400 Carnegie Class: Assoc/Pub-U-MC
FAX Number: (805) 378-1499 Calendar System: Semester
URL: www.moorparkcollege.edu
Established: 1967 Annual Undergrad Tuition & Fees (In-State): $1,142
Enrollment: 15,385 Coed
Affiliation or Control: State IRS Status: 501(c)3
Highest Offering: Associate Degree
Program: Occupational; 2-Year Principally Bachelor's Creditable
Accreditation: #WJ, ADNUR, RAD

02 President .... Dr. Pam EDDINGER
03 Interim Executive Vice President .... Dr. Jane HARMON
10 Vice President Business Services .... Ms. Iris INGRAM
04 Executive Assistant to President .... Ms. Louise CHRISTENER
66 Dean Student Learning .... Dr. Lori BENNETT
57 Dean Student Learning .... Ms. Patricia EWINS
50 Dean Student Learning .... Dr. Kim HOFFMANS
88 Dean of Student Learning .... Dr. Lisa MILLER
79 Dean Student Learning .... Ms. Inajane NICKLAS
49 Dean Student Learning .... Dr. Julius SOKENU
18 Director Maintainence/Operations .... Mr. John SINUTKO
88 College Business Services Manager .... Ms. Darlene MELBY
41 Athletic Director .... Mr. Howard DAVIS
06 Registrar .... Ms. Kathy COLBORN
37 Student Financial Aid Officer .... Ms. Kim KORINKE

*Oxnard College (E)

4000 S Rose Avenue, Oxnard CA 93033-6699
County: Ventura FICE Identification: 012842
Unit ID: 120421
Telephone: (805) 986-5800 Carnegie Class: Assoc/Pub-U-MC
FAX Number: (805) 986-5908 Calendar System: Semester
URL: www.oxnardcollege.edu
Established: 1975 Annual Undergrad Tuition & Fees (In-District): $1,336
Enrollment: 7,440 Coed
Affiliation or Control: State/Local IRS Status: 501(c)3
Highest Offering: Associate Degree
Program: Occupational; 2-Year Principally Bachelor's Creditable
Accreditation: #WJ, DH

02 President .... Dr. Richard DURAN
05 Exec Vice Pres of Student Learning .... Dr. Erika ENDRIJONAS
10 Vice President of Business Services .... Dr. Michael BUSH
32 Dean of Student Services .... Dr. Karen ENGELSEN
79 Dean Liberal Studies .... Ms. Marjorie PRICE
41 Director of Athletics .... Mr. Jonas CRAWFORD
88 Dean Career &Technical Education .... Ms. Carmen GUERRERO
81 Dean Math Science/Health .... Dr. Carolyn INOUYE
18 Director Maintenance/Operations .... Mr. Will DEITS
06 Registrar .... Mr. Joel DIAZ
88 Director STEM .... Dr. Cynthia HERRERA
40 Bookstore Manager .... Ms. Diane RAUSCH

*Ventura College (F)

4667 Telegraph Road, Ventura CA 93003-3899
County: Ventura FICE Identification: 001334
Unit ID: 125028
Telephone: (805) 654-6400 Carnegie Class: Assoc/Pub-U-MC
FAX Number: (805) 654-6466 Calendar System: Semester
URL: www.venturacollege.edu
Established: 1925 Annual Undergrad Tuition & Fees (In-District): $1,104
Enrollment: 13,763 Coed
Affiliation or Control: State/Local IRS Status: 501(c)3
Highest Offering: Associate Degree
Program: Occupational; 2-Year Principally Bachelor's Creditable
Accreditation: WJ, EMT

02 President .... Dr. Robin CALOTE
05 Exec Vice Pres Student Learning .... Dr. Ramiro SANCHEZ
10 Vice President Business Services .... Mr. David KEEBLER
04 Exec Assistant to the President .... Ms. Laura BROWER
75 Dean Career & Tech Education .... Dr. Kathleen SCHRADER
88 Dean Inst Effec/Eng/Learn Res Ctr .... Ms. Kathleen SCOTT
81 Dean Mathematics & Sciences .... Vacant
60 Dean Comm/Kinesiology/Athl/OS Pgm .... Mr. Tim HARRISON
83 Dean Dist Ed/Prof Dev/Soc Sci/Hum .... Ms. Gwen HUDDLESTON
32 Dean Student Services .... Ms. Victoria LUGO
106 Asst Dean Distance Education .... Vacant
35 Asst Dean Student Services .... Mr. David BRANSKY
102 Executive Director Foundation .... Mr. Norbert N. TAN
30 Director Development Foundation .... Ms. Diana DUNBAR
06 Registrar .... Ms. Susan BRICKER
18 Director Maintenance/Operations .... Mr. Jay MOORE
35 Coordinator Student Activities .... Mr. Rick TREVINO
37 Financial Aid Officer .... Ms. Alma RODRIGUEZ
09 Institutional Research .... Mr. Michael CALLAHAN
85 International Students .... Ms. Rosie STUTTS
12 Coordinator Off Campus Programs .... Dr. Art SANDFORD
25 Coordinator Resource Development .... Vacant
103 Dir Center of Excellence .... Ms. Sharon DWYER
84 Enrollment Management .... Ms. Connie BAKER
23 Director Student Health Center .... Ms. Mary JONES
19 Campus Police .... Lt. Greg BECKLEY

Veritas Evangelical Seminary (G)

39407 Murrieta Hot Springs Rd, Murrieta CA 92563
County: Riverside Identification: 667103
Telephone: (951) 698-6389 Carnegie Class: Not Classified
FAX Number: (951) 677-7017 Calendar System: Semester
URL: www.veritasseminary.com
Established: 2008 Annual Graduate Tuition & Fees: N/A
Enrollment: N/A Coed
Affiliation or Control: Independent Non-Profit IRS Status: 501(c)3
Highest Offering: Master's; No Undergraduates
Program: Religious Emphasis
Accreditation: @TRACS

00 Chancellor .... Norman L. GEISLER
01 President .... Joseph M. HOLDEN

Victor Valley College (H)

18422 Bear Valley Road, Victorville CA 92395-5850
County: San Bernardino FICE Identification: 001335
Unit ID: 125091
Telephone: (760) 245-4271 Carnegie Class: Assoc/Pub-S-SC
FAX Number: (760) 245-9744 Calendar System: Semester
URL: www.vvc.edu
Established: 1961 Annual Undergrad Tuition & Fees (In-District): $11,500
Enrollment: 12,665 Coed
Affiliation or Control: State/Local IRS Status: 501(c)3
Highest Offering: Associate Degree
Program: Occupational; 2-Year Principally Bachelor's Creditable
Accreditation: #WJ, EMT

01 Superintendent/President .... Dr. Christopher O'HEARN
05 Int Exec VP/Instruction/Stdnt Svcs .... Mr. Peter ALLAN
11 Vice President Admin Services .... Dr. G. H. JAVAHERIPOUR
15 Vice President Human Resources .... Ms. Fusako YOKOTOBI
76 Dean Health Science & Public Safety .... Dr. Patricia LUTHER
81 Dean STEM .... Dr. Lori KILDAL
79 Dean Acad Pgms Humanities/Soc Sci .... Dr. Paul WILLIAMS
75 Dean Vocational Education .... Vacant
21 Director Fiscal Services .... Ms. Karen HARDY
07 Director of Admissions .... Mrs. Greta MOON
26 Director Public Info & Marketing .... Mr. William GREULICH
41 Director Athletics/Athletic Trainer .... Mrs. Jaye TASHIMA
18 Director Maintenance/Operations .... Mr. Christopher HYLTON
37 Interim Director Financial Aid .... Mr. Arthur LOPEZ
13 Director MIS .... Mr. Sergio OKLANDER
40 Director Auxiliary Services/ASB Adv .... Mr. Robert SEWELL
35 Dean Student Services .... Dr. Tim JOHNSTON
18 Director Facilities Construction .... Mr. Steve GARCIA
19 Chief Campus Police .... Mr. Leonard KNIGHT
72 Exec Dean Technology/Info Resource .... Mr. Frank SMITH
22 Dir Disabled Student/ADA Compl Ofcr .... Vacant
88 Director Child Development Center .... Ms. Kelley JOHNSON
88 Dir Extended Optnty Pgms/Svcs/CARE .... Mr. Carl SMITH
09 Exec Dean Inst Effectiveness .... Mrs. Virginia MORAN
55 Dir Evening Opers/Inst Support Pgm .... Mr. Rolando REGINO

West Coast Ultrasound Institute (I)

291 S. La Cienega Blvd, Ste 500, Beverly Hills CA 90211
County: Los Angeles FICE Identification: 036393
Unit ID: 441229
Telephone: (310) 289-5123 Carnegie Class: Not Classified
FAX Number: (310) 289-5136 Calendar System: Quarter
URL: www.wcui.edu
Established: 1998 Annual Undergrad Tuition & Fees: $22,339
Enrollment: 777 Coed
Affiliation or Control: Proprietary IRS Status: Proprietary
Highest Offering: Associate Degree
Program: Occupational
Accreditation: ACCSC

01 Campus Director .... Mr. Josh ROSENTHAL

West Coast University (A)

12215 Victory Boulevard, North Hollywood CA 91606-3206
County: Los Angeles FICE Identification: 036983
Unit ID: 443331
Telephone: (818) 299-5500 Carnegie Class: Spec/Health
FAX Number: (818) 299-5545 Calendar System: Semester
URL: www.westcoastuniversity.edu
Established: 1909 Annual Undergrad Tuition & Fees: $32,873
Enrollment: 1,257 Coed
Affiliation or Control: Proprietary IRS Status: Proprietary
Highest Offering: Master's
Program: Professional; Nursing Emphasis
Accreditation: WC, ACICS, DH, NURSE

01 President .... Dr. Barry T. RYAN
03 Executive Director .... Mr. Ladd GRAHAM
05 Provost .... Dr. Jeb EGBERT
66 Dean of Nursing Los Angeles Campus . Dr. Rosanne SILBERLING
20 Academic Dean .... Dr. Miriam KAHAN
76 Founding Dean Occupational Therapy .... Dr. Nicolaas VAN DEN HEEVER
67 Founding Dean School of Pharmacy .... Dr. Naushad GHILZAI
52 Campus Dean Dental Hygiene .... Dr. Susan DULEY
07 Director of Admissions .... Mr. Herman WHITAKER
37 Director of Financial Aid .... Ms. Tracy CABUCO

*West Hills Community College District (B)

9900 Cody Street, Coalinga CA 93210
County: Fresno Identification: 667041
Telephone: (559) 934-2100 Carnegie Class: N/A
FAX Number: (559) 934-2810
URL: www.westhillscollege.com

01 Chancellor .... Dr. Frank P. GORNICK
10 Vice Chancellor Business Services .... Mr. Ken STOPPENBRINK
05 VC Educ Svcs/Workforce Development .... Dr. Carole GOLDSMITH
13 Director of Info Tech Services .... Ms. Michelle KOZLOWSKI
90 Assoc VC Academic & Info Systems .... Mr. Keith STEARNS
102 Exec Director WHCC Foundation .... Ms. Frances SQUIRE
15 Director of Human Resources .... Vacant
26 Director of Marketing/PIO .... Vacant
21 Director of Fiscal Services .... Ms. Tammy WEATHERMAN
25 Director of Grants .... Ms. Cathy BARABE
25 Director of Special Grant Programs .... Ms. Angela ALLISON
25 Director of Special Grant Programs .... Mr. David CASTILLO
25 Director of Special Grant Programs .... Ms. Anita WRIGHT
103 Interim Director of C6 Project .... Mr. Robert PIMENTEL
88 Director of Child Dev Centers .... Ms. Kathy WATTS
66 District Director of Health Careers .... Mr. Charles FREEMAN

*West Hills College Coalinga (C)

300 Cherry Lane, Coalinga CA 93210-1399
County: Fresno FICE Identification: 001176
Unit ID: 125462
Telephone: (559) 934-2000 Carnegie Class: Assoc/Pub-S-MC
FAX Number: N/A Calendar System: Semester
URL: www.westhillscollege.com/coalinga
Established: 1932 Annual Undergrad Tuition & Fees (In-District): $690
Enrollment: 1,672 Coed
Affiliation or Control: State/Local IRS Status: 501(c)3
Highest Offering: Associate Degree
Program: Occupational; 2-Year Principally Bachelor's Creditable; Business Emphasis
Accreditation: WJ

02 Interim President .... Dr. Tom HARRIS
05 Interim VP of Educational Services .... Ms. Stephanie DROKER
32 Vice President of Student Services .... Mr. Pedro AVILA
35 Assoc Dean of Student Services .... Mr. Mark GRITTON
20 Assoc Dean of Student Learning .... Ms. Raquel RODRIGUEZ
88 Director of CAMP Grant .... Mr. Eliseo GAMINO
47 Director of Farm of the Future .... Mr. Richard LARSON
85 Dir of International Student Svcs .... Mr. Daniel TAMAYO
88 Director of Title IV Projects .... Ms. Bertha FELIX-MATA
12 Director of North District Center .... Dr. Marcel HETU
37 Director of Financial Aid .... Dr. Joseph KOROMA

*West Hills College Lemoore (D)

555 College Avenue, Lemoore CA 93245-9248
County: Kings FICE Identification: 041113
Unit ID: 448594
Telephone: (559) 925-3000 Carnegie Class: Assoc/Pub-R-M
FAX Number: (559) 924-1243 Calendar System: Semester
URL: www.westhillscollege.com/lemoore
Established: 2002 Annual Undergrad Tuition & Fees (In-District): $690
Enrollment: 3,034 Coed
Affiliation or Control: State/Local IRS Status: 501(c)3
Highest Offering: Associate Degree
Program: Occupational; 2-Year Principally Bachelor's Creditable; Business Emphasis
Accreditation: WJ

02 President .... Mr. Don WARKENTIN
05 Vice President of Educational Svcs .... Mr. Dave BOLT
32 Vice President of Student Services .... Ms. Sylvia DORSEY-ROBINSON
35 Dean of Student Services .... Mr. Jose LOPEZ
20 Dean of Educational Svcs .... Mr. James PRESTON
88 Dean of Categorical Programs .... Mr. Joel RUBLE
37 Director of Financial Aid .... Ms. Deborah SORIA

---

*West Valley-Mission Community College District (E)

14000 Fruitvale Avenue, Saratoga CA 95070-5698
County: Santa Clara FICE Identification: 029139
Unit ID: 125222
Telephone: (408) 741-2011 Carnegie Class: N/A
FAX Number: (408) 867-8273
URL: www.wvm.edu

01 Chancellor .... Dr. Patrick SCHMITT
11 Vice Chancellor Admin Services .... Mr. Ed MADULI
15 Assoc Vice Chanc Human Resources .... Mr. Brad DAVIS
14 Director Information Systems .... Mr. Ron SMITH
18 Director of Facilities .... Mr. Javier CASTRUITA
30 Dean Advancement .... Ms. Cynthia SCHELCHER
19 Interim Director Public Safety .... Mr. Chris ROLEN
26 Director Public Affs/Community Rels .... Vacant
04 Special Assistant to the Chancellor .... Mr. Albert MOORE

*Mission College (F)

3000 Mission College Boulevard, Santa Clara CA 95054-1897
County: Santa Clara FICE Identification: 021191
Unit ID: 118930
Telephone: (408) 988-2200 Carnegie Class: Assoc/Pub-S-MC
FAX Number: (408) 496-0462 Calendar System: Semester
URL: www.missioncollege.org
Established: 1976 Annual Undergrad Tuition & Fees (In-District): $1,354
Enrollment: 9,686 Coed
Affiliation or Control: State/Local IRS Status: 501(c)3
Highest Offering: Associate Degree
Program: Occupational; 2-Year Principally Bachelor's Creditable
Accreditation: WJ

02 President .... Dr. Laurel JONES
05 Vice Pres of Instruction .... Dr. Norma AMBRIZ-GALAVIZ
32 Vice President Student Services .... Dr. Penny JOHNSON
11 Vice Pres Administrative Services .... Mr. Rick BENNETT
35 Dean of Student Support Services .... Mr. Daniel SANIDAD
103 Dean of Workforce Dev & Cmty Educ .... Mr. Danny NGUYEN
27 Dir of Public Info & Graphic Design .... Mr. Peter ANNING
20 Dean of Instruction .... Mr. Tim KARAS
24 Dean Instructional Technology .... Ms. Mina JAHAN
19 Chief of Police .... Lt. Kenneth TANAKA
18 Manager of Facilities .... Mr. Don HOUSTON
07 Assistant Director of Admissions .... Mr. Ed GREEN
37 Director of Financial Aid .... Ms. Rita GROGAN
04 Exec Assistant to the President .... Ms. Linda ANGELOTTI
81 Applied Science Division .... Ms. Janice MORGAN
88 Language Arts Division .... Mr. Myo MYINT
60 Communications Division .... Mr. Rob DEWIS
81 Mathematics and Science Division .... Ms. Thais WINSOME
83 Liberal Studies Division .... Mr. Keith JOHNSON
35 Student Services Division .... Ms. Char PERLAS

*West Valley College (G)

14000 Fruitvale Avenue, Saratoga CA 95070-5698
County: Santa Clara FICE Identification: 001338
Unit ID: 125499
Telephone: (408) 867-2200 Carnegie Class: Assoc/Pub-S-MC
FAX Number: (408) 867-5033 Calendar System: Semester
URL: www.westvalley.edu
Established: 1963 Annual Undergrad Tuition & Fees (In-District): $936
Enrollment: 11,013 Coed
Affiliation or Control: State/Local IRS Status: 501(c)3
Highest Offering: Associate Degree
Program: Occupational; 2-Year Principally Bachelor's Creditable
Accreditation: WJ

02 Interim President .... Mr. Bradley DAVIS
05 Vice President Instruction .... Ms. Kuni HAY
32 Vice President Student Services .... Dr. Victoria HINDES
11 Interim VP Administrative Services .... Mr. Patrick FENTON
20 Dean Instruction & Student Success .... Ms. Stephanie KASHIMA
30 Dean Advancement .... Ms. Cindy SCHELCHER
36 Dean Career Programs/Workforce Dev .... Mr. Frank KOBAYASHI
72 Dean Info Technology & Services .... Mr. Fred CHOW
32 Dean of Student Services .... Vacant
15 Director Human Resources .... Ms. Sarah CARAVALHO-KAHN
07 Director of Admissions .... Ms. Herlisa HAMP
18 Chief Facilities/Physical Plant .... Mr. Bill TAYLOR
26 Chief Public Relations Officer .... Mr. Bradley DAVIS
37 Director Student Financial Aid .... Ms. Maritza CANTARERO
09 Director of Institutional Research .... Ms. Inge BOND
35 Director Student Affairs .... Dr. Michelle DONOHUE-MENDOZA
29 Director Alumni Relations .... Ms. Cindy SCHELCHER
56 Coord Instruct Tech/Distance Lrng .... Ms. Lisa KAAZ

Western State University College of Law (H)

1111 N State College Boulevard, Fullerton CA 92831-3014
County: Orange FICE Identification: 010832
Unit ID: 126030
Telephone: (714) 459-1000 Carnegie Class: Spec/Law
FAX Number: (714) 526-1062 Calendar System: Semester
URL: www.wsulaw.edu
Established: 1966 Annual Graduate Tuition & Fees: $39,600
Enrollment: 500 Coed
Affiliation or Control: Proprietary IRS Status: Proprietary
Highest Offering: Doctorate; No Undergraduates
Program: Professional
Accreditation: &WC, LAW

01 Dean .... Mr. William E. ADAMS
05 Associate Dean for Academic Affairs .... Ms. Susan KELLER
07 Director of Admissions .... Ms. Gloria SWITZER
32 Assistant Dean of Students .... Mr. Charles SHEPPARD
15 Director Human Resources .... Ms. Peggy SAVALA
06 Asst Dir Student Services/Registrar .... Ms. Shari HARTMANN
37 Director Financial Assistance .... Ms. Donna ESPINOZA
36 Director of Career Services .... Ms. Ana BIDOGLIO
08 University Librarian .... Prof. Patricia O'CONNOR
18 Director Facilities .... Mr. Jon EVANS
10 Business Office Manager .... Ms. Theresa CARROLL
30 Director of Development .... Mr. James CHEYDLEUR
29 Asst Dir of Alumni Relations .... Mr. Tim MALLORY

† Regional accreditation is carried under the parent institution, Argosy University in Orange, CA.

Western University of Health Sciences (I)

309 E 2nd Street, Pomona CA 91766-1854
County: Los Angeles FICE Identification: 024827
Unit ID: 112525
Telephone: (909) 623-6116 Carnegie Class: Spec/Med
FAX Number: N/A Calendar System: Semester
URL: www.westernu.edu
Established: 1977 Annual Graduate Tuition & Fees: N/A
Enrollment: 3,293 Coed
Affiliation or Control: Independent Non-Profit IRS Status: 501(c)3
Highest Offering: Doctorate; No Undergraduates
Program: Professional
Accreditation: WC, ARCPA, DENT, NURSE, @OPT, OSTEO, PHAR, @POD, PTA, VET

01 President .... Dr. Philip PUMERANTZ
05 Provost/COO .... Dr. Gary GUGELCHUK
46 Exec Vice Provost for Academic Dev .... Dr. Elizabeth REGA
30 Senior Vice Pres of Advancement .... Dr. Thomas FOX
20 Vice Provost .... Dr. Sheree ASTON
32 Vice President of Student Affairs .... Dr. Beverly SANKS GUIDRY
25 Asst VP Spnsrd Pgms/Contract Mgt .... Mr. Matthew KATZ
06 Asst Vice Pres Univ Enroll/Registr .... Ms. Kimberly DEKRUIF
10 Chief Financial Officer/Treasurer .... Mr. Kevin SHAW
15 Executive Director Human Resources .... Ms. Linda EMILIO
18 Exec Dir Facilities/Physical Plant .... Mr. Todd CLARK
07 Director Admiss COP/CGN .... Ms. Kathy FORD
07 Director Admissions COMP/MSHS .... Ms. Susan HANSON
07 Director Admissions CO/CPM/CDM .... Ms. Marie ANDERSON
07 Director Admissions CVM/PT/PA .... Ms. Karen HUTTON-LOPEZ
23 Medical Director .... Dr. David CONNETT
08 Director of University Library .... Ms. Patricia VADER
37 Director Financial Aid .... Mr. Otto REYER
88 Dir Ctr Disability Issues/Hlth Prof .... Ms. Brenda PREMO
91 Exec Director Information Tech .... Ms. Denise WILCOX
96 Director of Procurement Services .... Mr. Michael BUTLER
26 Exec Director of Public Affairs .... Mr. Jeff KEATING
88 Dir Learning Enhancement/Acad Devel .... Mr. David HACKER
09 Director of Institutional Research .... Dr. Juan RAMIREZ
40 Bookstore Director .... Ms. Elizabeth GUERRA
52 Dean College of Dentistry .... Dr. Steven W. FRIEDRICHSEN
67 Dean College of Pharmacy .... Dr. Daniel ROBINSON
88 Founding Dean College of Optometry .... Dr. Elizabeth HOPPE
88 Founding Dean College of Podiatry .... Dr. Lawrence HARKLESS
63 Dn Col Osteopath Med/VP Clinic Affs .... Dr. Clinton ADAMS
76 Dean College Allied Health Profess .... Dr. Stephanie BOWLIN
66 Dean College of Graduate Nursing .... Dr. Karen HANFORD
58 Dean Grad Col Biomedical Sciences .... Dr. Michel BAUDRY
74 Dean College of Veterinary Medicine .... Dr. Phil NELSON
88 Chair Dept of Physical Therapy .... Dr. Denise SCHILLING
76 Chair Dept of Health Sciences .... Dr. Tina MEYER
88 Chair Physician Assistant Program .... Mr. Roy GUIZADO
63 Chair Department Family Medicine .... Dr. Alan CUNDARI

Westminster Theological Seminary in California (J)

1725 Bear Valley Parkway, Escondido CA 92027-4128
County: San Diego FICE Identification: 022768
Unit ID: 125718
Telephone: (760) 480-8474 Carnegie Class: Spec/Faith
FAX Number: (760) 480-0252 Calendar System: Semester
URL: www.wscal.edu
Established: 1979 Annual Graduate Tuition & Fees: $12,500
Enrollment: 145 Coed
Affiliation or Control: Independent Non-Profit IRS Status: 501(c)3
Highest Offering: Master's; No Undergraduates
Program: Professional
Accreditation: WC, THEOL

01 President .... Dr. W. Robert GODFREY
03 Executive Vice President .... Mr. Steven OEVERMAN

05 Academic Dean .... Dr. John FESKO
10 Business Manager .... Mr. Dan TERHORST
08 Library Director .... Mr. John G. BALES
32 Dean of Students .... Dr. Julius KIM
06 Registrar .... Ms. Heather GIDEON

Westmont College (A)

955 La Paz Road, Santa Barbara CA 93108-1089

County: Santa Barbara
FICE Identification: 001341
Unit ID: 125727
Telephone: (805) 565-6000
Carnegie Class: Bac/A&S
FAX Number: (805) 565-7006
Calendar System: Semester
URL: www.westmont.edu
Established: 1937
Annual Undergrad Tuition & Fees: $48,760
Enrollment: 1,344
Coed
Affiliation or Control: Independent Non-Profit
IRS Status: 501(c)3
Highest Offering: Baccalaureate
Program: Liberal Arts And General; Teacher Preparatory
Accreditation: WC, MUS

01 President .... Dr. Gayle D. BEEBE
05 Provost .... Dr. Mark L. SARGENT
10 Vice President Finance .... Mr. Douglas W. JONES
11 Vice President for Administration .... Mr. Christopher D. CALL
32 Vice President & Dean of Students .... Mrs. Jane H. HIGA
30 Vice President for Advancement .... Dr. Reed SHEARD
88 Vice President External Relations .... Mr. Cliff LUNDBERG
06 Registrar .... Mr. Robert KUNTZ
07 Dean of Admissions .... Mr. Silvio VAZQUEZ
08 Director Library/Information Svcs .... Mrs. Debra QUAST
09 Assoc Provost/Dir of Inst Research .... Dr. William A. WRIGHT
13 VP Information Technology & CIO .... Dr. Reed SHEARD
15 Director of Human Resources .... Ms. Beth CAUWELS
18 Director of Physical Plant .... Mr. Thomas BEVERIDGE
19 Manager Security & Public Safety .... Mr. Thomas G. BAUER
21 Controller .... Mr. Paul V. LARSON
23 Director of Student Health Services .... Dr. David HERNANDEZ
24 Coord Media Services/Asst Librarian .... Ms. Mary LOGUE
26 Director of Public Affairs .... Mrs. Nancy L. PHINNEY
29 Exec Director Alumni & Parent Rels .... Mrs. Teri BRADFORD ROUSE
35 Associate Dean of Students .... Mr. Timothy B. WILSON
88 Assoc Dean of Students for Res Life .... Mr. Stu CLEEK
36 Director of Career/Life Planning .... Mr. Dana C. ALEXANDER
88 Director of Campus Life .... Ms. Angela L. D'AMOUR
88 Director of Internships/Practica .... Mrs. Jennifer TAYLOR
37 Director of Financial Aid .... Mr. Sean SMITH
38 Director Counseling Services .... Mrs. Marcy O'HARA
39 Director of Housing .... Mr. David W. KING
40 Bookstore Manager .... Mrs. Marilyn LOPPNOW
41 Athletic Director .... Mr. David ODELL
42 Campus Pastor .... Rev. Ben PATTERSON
44 Director of Planned Giving .... Mr. Bob FREELOVE
45 Director of Campus Planning .... Mr. Randy JONES
96 Director Procurement/Auxiliary Svcs .... Mr. Troy HARRIS
28 Director of Intercultural Programs .... Mr. Jason CHA
43 College Counsel .... Ms. Toya COOPER
20 Associate Academic Officer .... Dr. Tatiana NAZARENKO

Westwood College-Anaheim (B)

1551 S Douglass Road, Anaheim CA 92806-5949

County: Orange
Identification: 666047
Unit ID: 437848
Telephone: (714) 704-2727
Carnegie Class: Bac/Diverse
FAX Number: (714) 939-2011
Calendar System: Quarter
URL: www.westwood.edu
Established: 1953
Annual Undergrad Tuition & Fees: $14,317
Enrollment: 1,049
Coed
Affiliation or Control: Proprietary
IRS Status: Proprietary
Highest Offering: Baccalaureate
Program: 2-Year Principally Bachelor's Creditable; Liberal Arts And General
Accreditation: ACICS

01 Executive Director .... Mr. Lou OSBORN

† Branch campus of Westwood College-Denver North. Denver, CO.

Westwood College-Inland Empire (C)

20 W Seventh Street, Upland CA 91786-7148

County: San Bernardino
Identification: 666104
Unit ID: 440484
Telephone: (909) 931-7550
Carnegie Class: Bac/Diverse
FAX Number: (909) 931-9195
Calendar System: Other
URL: www.westwood.edu
Established: 2001
Annual Undergrad Tuition & Fees: $15,020
Enrollment: 1,214
Coed
Affiliation or Control: Proprietary
IRS Status: Proprietary
Highest Offering: Baccalaureate
Program: Occupational; Technical Emphasis
Accreditation: ACICS

01 Campus President .... Mrs. Tina MILLER
05 Campus Academic Dean .... Dr. Luka MBEWE
07 Director of Admissions .... Ms. Alma SALAZAR
32 Director of Student Services .... Ms. Debi MALDONADO
37 Director of Financial Aid .... Ms. Erin VARGAS
06 Registrar .... Ms. Connie KUANG

† Branch campus of Westwood College-Denver North, Denver, CO.

Westwood College - Los Angeles Campus (D)

3250 Wilshire Boulevard, Suite 400, Los Angeles CA 90010-1437

County: Los Angeles
FICE Identification: 030727
Unit ID: 122843
Telephone: (213) 739-9999
Carnegie Class: Bac/Diverse
FAX Number: (213) 382-2468
Calendar System: Quarter
URL: www.westwood.edu
Established: 1997
Annual Undergrad Tuition & Fees: N/A
Enrollment: 5,257
Coed
Affiliation or Control: Proprietary
IRS Status: Proprietary
Highest Offering: Master's
Program: Occupational
Accreditation: ACICS

01 Campus President .... Mr. DeWayne JOHNSON
07 Director of Admissions .... Mr. Fred POLK

Westwood College-South Bay (E)

19700 S Vermont Avenue, #100, Torrance CA 90502-1148

County: Los Angeles
FICE Identification: 011626
Unit ID: 121381
Telephone: (310) 965-0888
Carnegie Class: Bac/Diverse
FAX Number: (310) 516-8232
Calendar System: Other
URL: www.westwood.edu
Established: 2002
Annual Undergrad Tuition & Fees: $24,900
Enrollment: 662
Coed
Affiliation or Control: Proprietary
IRS Status: Proprietary
Highest Offering: Baccalaureate
Program: Occupational; Technical Emphasis
Accreditation: ACICS

01 Campus President .... Mr. Christopher TUREN

Whittier College (F)

13406 E Philadelphia St, PO Box 634, Whittier CA 90608-4413

County: Los Angeles
FICE Identification: 001342
Unit ID: 125763
Telephone: (562) 907-4200
Carnegie Class: Bac/A&S
FAX Number: (562) 907-4242
Calendar System: 4/1/4
URL: www.whittier.edu
Established: 1887
Annual Undergrad Tuition & Fees: $49,228
Enrollment: 1,779
Coed
Affiliation or Control: Independent Non-Profit
IRS Status: 501(c)3
Highest Offering: Doctorate
Program: Liberal Arts And General; Teacher Preparatory; Professional
Accreditation: WC, LAW, SW

01 President .... Dr. Sharon D. HERZBERGER
10 Vice Pres Finance & Administration .... Mr. James DUNKELMAN
05 VP Academic Affs/Dean of Faculty .... Dr. Charlotte BORST
61 VP Legal Education/Dean Sch of Law .... Ms. Penelope BRYAN
30 Vice President College Advancement .... Ms. Elizabeth POWER ROBISON
84 Vice President Dean of Enrollment .... Mr. Fred PFURSICH
32 Dean of Students .... Dr. Jeanne ORTIZ
37 Director of Student Financial Aid .... Mr. David CARNEVALE
06 Registrar .... Mr. Wayne VAN ELLIS
08 Librarian .... Vacant
20 Dir Whtr Scholar Pgm/Assc Acad Dean .... Ms. Doreen O'CONNOR-GOMEZ
29 Director of Alumni Relations .... Vacant
27 Director of Communications .... Ms. Dana RAKOCZY
14 Director of Computing Services .... Mr. Troy GREENUP
09 Director of Institutional Research .... Mr. Fritz SMITH
39 Director for Resident Life .... Mrs. Delaphine HUDSON
41 Director of Athletics .... Mr. Rob COLEMAN
53 Dir Lib Educ Pgm/Assoc Acad Dean .... Dr. Fritz SMITH
07 Director of Admissions .... Mr. Kieron MILLER
15 Director of Human Resources .... Vacant
21 Exec Director Finance/Business Svcs .... Ms. Hoang HAU
35 Director Student Activies .... Mr. Rick CLARK
18 Director Facilities/Physical Plant .... Mr. Ken BOHAN
26 Director Public Relations .... Mrs. Dana RAKOCZY
19 Director of Campus Safety .... Mr. Timm BROWNE

William Jessup University (G)

333 Sunset Boulevard, Rocklin CA 95765-3707

County: Placer
FICE Identification: 001281
Unit ID: 122728
Telephone: (916) 577-2200
Carnegie Class: Spec/Faith
FAX Number: (916) 577-2203
Calendar System: Semester
URL: www.jessup.edu
Established: 1939
Annual Undergrad Tuition & Fees: $22,900
Enrollment: 896
Coed
Affiliation or Control: Independent Non-Profit
IRS Status: 501(c)3
Highest Offering: Baccalaureate
Program: 2-Year Principally Bachelor's Creditable; Liberal Arts And General; Teacher Preparatory; Religious Emphasis
Accreditation: WC, BI

01 President .... Dr. John JACKSON
05 Provost/Chief Academic Officer .... Dr. Dennis JAMESON
32 Vice Pres for Student Development .... Dr. Paul BLEZIEN
11 Vice Pres Finance/Administration .... Mr. Gene DEYOUNG
30 Vice President for Development .... Mr. Eric HOGUE
88 Accreditation Liason Officer .... Dr. Kay LLOVIO
107 School of Professional Studies Dir .... Mr. Sam HEINRICH
15 Director of Human Resources .... Ms. DeDe HUDAK
10 Controller .... Ms. Diane KIM
08 Library Director .... Mr. Kevin PISCHKE
88 Director of Church Relations .... Mr. Jim JESSUP
35 Dean of Students .... Mr. Ezra JOHNSON
06 Registrar .... Mrs. Tina PETERSEN
07 Director of Admission .... Mr. Vance PASCUA
37 Financial Aid Director .... Mr. Korey COMPAAN
09 Institutional Research Director .... Mrs. Karen LAMBRECHTSEN
42 Director of Campus Ministries .... Mr. Daniel GLUCK
41 Athletic Director .... Mr. Farnum SMITH
18 Facilities Director .... Mr. Brian SULLIVAN

Woodbury University (H)

7500 Glenoaks Boulevard, Burbank CA 91504-7520

County: Los Angeles
FICE Identification: 001343
Unit ID: 125897
Telephone: (818) 767-0888
Carnegie Class: Master's M
FAX Number: (818) 767-7520
Calendar System: Semester
URL: www.woodbury.edu
Established: 1884
Annual Undergrad Tuition & Fees: $31,444
Enrollment: 1,254
Coed
Affiliation or Control: Independent Non-Profit
IRS Status: 501(c)3
Highest Offering: Master's
Program: Professional; Business Emphasis
Accreditation: WC, ACBSP, ART, CIDA

01 President .... Luis CALINGO
05 Vice Pres Academic Affairs .... M. Victoria LIPTAK
10 Vice Pres Finance & Administration .... Ken JONES
84 VP Enrollment Mgmt/Univ Marketing .... Don E. ST. CLAIR
30 Vice Pres University Advancement .... Richard M. NORDIN
13 VP Information Technology/Planning .... Steve DYER
32 Vice Pres Student Development .... Phyllis A. CREMER
04 Exec Assistant to the President .... Seta JAVOR
35 Dean of Students .... Anne R. EHRLICH
50 Dean School of Business .... Andre VAN NIEKERK
48 Dean School of Architecture .... Norman MILLAR
88 Dean School of Media/Culture/Design .... Edward CLIFT
44 Sr Director of Development .... Rose NIELSEN
88 Ex Dir Inst for Exclnce Teach/Lrng .... Paul W. DECKER
06 Assistant Registrar .... Tamara L. BLOK
84 Director of Enrollment Services .... Celeastia WILLIAMS
88 Dean of Faculty .... Nedra PETERSON
15 Director of Human Resources .... Natalie AVALOS
36 Director of Career Services .... Liana JINDARYAN
18 Director of Physical Plant .... Jerry W. TRACY
38 Director of Student Counseling .... Tania ROSELLO
07 Director of Admissions .... Ruth G. LORENZANA
88 Dean Institute of Transdisciplinary .... Douglas CREMER

World Mission University (I)

500 Shatto Place, Suite 600, Los Angeles CA 90020-1789

County: Los Angeles
FICE Identification: 038683
Unit ID: 401223
Telephone: (213) 385-2322
Carnegie Class: Spec/Faith
FAX Number: (213) 385-2332
Calendar System: Semester
URL: www.wmu.edu
Established: 1989
Annual Undergrad Tuition & Fees: $5,100
Enrollment: 295
Coed
Affiliation or Control: Independent Non-Profit
IRS Status: 501(c)3
Highest Offering: First Professional Degree
Program: Religious Emphasis
Accreditation: BI, @THEOL, TRACS

01 President .... Dr. John M. SONG
05 Exec Vice Pres/Chief Acad Officer .... Dr. Sung Jin LIM
26 Vice Pres of Collegiate Relations .... Dr. John E. MCKENNA
42 Vice President of Church Relations .... Vacant
32 Dean of Student Svcs/Financial Aid .... Mr. John B. PARK
30 Director of Development .... Ms. Keum Hee LEE
10 Director of Business .... Mr. Sun Young CHOI
06 Registrar .... Mr. Solomon BAHK

The Wright Institute (J)

2728 Durant Avenue, Berkeley CA 94704-1796

County: Alameda
FICE Identification: 008846
Unit ID: 126012
Telephone: (510) 841-9230
Carnegie Class: Spec/Health
FAX Number: (510) 841-0167
Calendar System: Trimester
URL: www.wi.edu
Established: 1969
Annual Graduate Tuition & Fees: $28,900
Enrollment: 426
Coed
Affiliation or Control: Independent Non-Profit
IRS Status: 501(c)3
Highest Offering: Doctorate; No Undergraduates
Program: Professional
Accreditation: WC, CLPSY

01 President .... Mr. Peter DYBWAD
05 Dean .... Dr. Chuck ALEXANDER
10 VP of Finance & Administrative Affs .... Ms. Tricia O'REILLY
07 Dir of Admissions/Student Services .... Ms. Melissa DELANEY
08 Librarian .... Mr. Jason STRAUSS
06 Registrar .... Ms. Ginny MORGAN

WyoTech-Fremont (A)

420 Whitney Place, Fremont CA 94539-7663
County: Alameda FICE Identification: 007190
Unit ID: 123208
Telephone: (510) 490-6900 Carnegie Class: Assoc/PrivFP
FAX Number: (510) 490-8599 Calendar System: Quarter
URL: www.wyotech.com
Established: 1965 Annual Undergrad Tuition & Fees: $27,513
Enrollment: 2,015 Coed
Affiliation or Control: Proprietary IRS Status: Proprietary
Highest Offering: Associate Degree
Program: Occupational; Technical Emphasis
Accreditation: ACCSC

01 President ... Mr. Joe PAPPALY
07 Director of Admissions ... Mr. Gary WEBSTER
05 Director of Education ... Ms. Joan LYONS
36 Director of Career Services ... Vacant
37 Director of Financial Aid ... Vacant
06 Registrar ... Ms. Liz GUSTAFSON
11 Dir Compliance/Administrative Svcs ... Mrs. Lisa-Marie CUSPARD

WyoTech-Long Beach (B)

2161 Technology Place, Long Beach CA 90810-3800
County: Los Angeles FICE Identification: 012873
Unit ID: 398574
Telephone: (562) 624-9530 Carnegie Class: Assoc/PrivFP
FAX Number: (562) 437-8111 Calendar System: Quarter
URL: www.wyotech.edu
Established: 1969 Annual Undergrad Tuition & Fees: $25,133
Enrollment: 1,633 Coed
Affiliation or Control: Proprietary IRS Status: Proprietary
Highest Offering: Associate Degree
Program: Occupational; Technical Emphasis
Accreditation: ACCSC, MAAB

01 Interim President ... Mr. John L. ANDREWS

WyoTech-Sacramento (C)

980 Riverside Parkway, West Sacramento CA 95605-1507
County: Yolo Identification: 666292
Unit ID: 445452
Telephone: (916) 376-8888 Carnegie Class: Assoc/PrivFP
FAX Number: (916) 617-2069 Calendar System: Quarter
URL: www.wyotech.com
Established: 2004 Annual Undergrad Tuition & Fees: $29,250
Enrollment: 1,380 Coed
Affiliation or Control: Proprietary IRS Status: Proprietary
Highest Offering: Associate Degree
Program: Occupational; Technical Emphasis
Accreditation: ACCSC

01 Campus President ... Mr. Kurt SCHAKE

† Branch campus of Wyoming Technical Institute, Laramie, WY.

Yeshiva Ohr Elchonon Chabad/ West Coast Talmudical Seminary (D)

7215 Waring Avenue, Los Angeles CA 90046-7660
County: Los Angeles FICE Identification: 022624
Unit ID: 126076
Telephone: (323) 937-3763 Carnegie Class: Spec/Faith
FAX Number: (323) 937-9456 Calendar System: Semester
URL: www.yoec.edu
Established: 1953 Annual Undergrad Tuition & Fees: $11,900
Enrollment: 138 Male
Affiliation or Control: Independent Non-Profit IRS Status: 501(c)3
Highest Offering: Baccalaureate
Program: Professional
Accreditation: RABN

01 Chief Executive Officer ... Rabbi Ezra B. SCHOCHET
03 Executive Vice President ... Rabbi Mendel SPALTER
05 Curriculum Suprv/Education Counsel ... Rabbi Shimon RAICHIK
37 Director Student Financial Aid ... Mrs. Hendy TAUBER
06 Registrar ... Rabbi Chaim CITRON
38 Director Student Counseling ... Rabbi Mendel SCHAPIRO
08 Head Librarian ... Rabbi Ben Zion OSTER

Yo San University of Traditional Chinese Medicine (E)

13315 W Washington Boulevard, Los Angeles CA 90066
County: Los Angeles FICE Identification: 030982
Unit ID: 401250
Telephone: (310) 577-3000 Carnegie Class: Spec/Health
FAX Number: (310) 577-3033 Calendar System: Trimester
URL: www.yosan.edu
Established: 1989 Annual Undergrad Tuition & Fees: $12,670
Enrollment: 202 Coed
Affiliation or Control: Independent Non-Profit IRS Status: 501(c)3
Highest Offering: Doctorate; No Lower Division
Program: Professional
Accreditation: ACUP

01 President ... Lawrence RYAN
05 Dean of Academic & Clinical Educ ... Lawrence LAU
11 Dean of Admin & Student Affairs ... Steven CARTER
10 Chief Financial Officer ... Tracy WANG
20 Assistant Academic Dean ... Andrea MURCHISON
07 Admissions Director ... Daouia AMRIR
37 Financial Aid Coordinator ... Ed MERVINE
21 Controller ... Mariani MAY

† Candidate at the Doctorate level.

*Yosemite Community College District (F)

PO Box 4065, Modesto CA 95352-4065
County: Stanislaus FICE Identification: 009146
Unit ID: 126100
Telephone: (209) 575-6509 Carnegie Class: N/A
FAX Number: (209) 575-6565
URL: www.yosemite.edu

01 Chancellor ... Dr. Joan E. SMITH
03 Executive Vice Chancellor ... Ms. Teresa M. SCOTT
13 Asst Chancellor Information Tech ... Ms. Gina ROSE
16 Vice Chancellor Human Resources ... Ms. Diane WIRTH

*Columbia College (G)

11600 Columbia College Drive, Sonora CA 95370-8580
County: Tuolumne FICE Identification: 007707
Unit ID: 112561
Telephone: (209) 588-5100 Carnegie Class: Assoc/Pub-R-M
FAX Number: (209) 588-5104 Calendar System: Semester
URL: www.columbia.yosemite.cc.ca.us
Established: 1968 Annual Undergrad Tuition & Fees (In-District): $1,162
Enrollment: 3,764 Coed
Affiliation or Control: State/Local IRS Status: 501(c)3
Highest Offering: Associate Degree
Program: Occupational; 2-Year Principally Bachelor's Creditable
Accreditation: WJ, ACFEI

02 President ... Dr. Dennis GERVIN
05 Vice President Student Learning ... Dr. Leslie BUCKALEW
11 VP College & Administrative Svcs ... Mr. Gary WHITFIELD
20 Dean Instructional Svcs/Voc Educ ... Mr. Chris VITELLI
49 Dean of Instruction/Arts & Sciences ... Mr. Michael TOROK
24 Director of Info Tech & Media Svcs ... Mr. Brian DEMOSS
41 Athletic Director ... Mr. Michael TOROK
37 Financial Aid Manager ... Ms. Marnie SHIVELY
27 Public Information Officer ... Vacant
31 Director Community Services ... Vacant
30 Director of Development ... Ms. Beccie MICHAEL
40 Bookstore Manager ... Mr. Jeff WHALEN
18 Manager Facilities/Operations ... Ms. Judy LANCHESTER

*Modesto Junior College (H)

435 College Avenue, Modesto CA 95350-9977
County: Stanislaus FICE Identification: 001240
Unit ID: 118976
Telephone: (209) 575-6498 Carnegie Class: Assoc/Pub-R-L
FAX Number: (209) 575-6630 Calendar System: Semester
URL: www.mjc.edu
Established: 1921 Annual Undergrad Tuition & Fees (In-District): $1,004
Enrollment: 18,086 Coed
Affiliation or Control: State/Local IRS Status: 501(c)3
Highest Offering: Associate Degree
Program: Occupational; 2-Year Principally Bachelor's Creditable
Accreditation: #WJ, DA, MAC

02 President ... Ms. Jill STEARNS
05 Int Vice President for Instruction ... Dr. James FAY
32 Vice Pres for Student Services ... Ms. Brenda THAMES
11 Vice President Administrative Svcs ... Mr. Michael GUERRA
57 Div Dean Arts/Humanit & Communicat ... Mr. Mike SUNDQUIST
83 Div Dean Busi/Behav/Social Sci ... Ms. Cece HUDELSON-PUTNAM
76 Div Dean Inst/All Hlth/Fam/Con Sci ... Dr. Maurice MCKINNON
79 Div Dean Literature/Language Arts ... Mr. Patrick BETTENCOURT
54 Div Dean Science/Math/Engineering ... Mr. Brian SANDERS
47 Dean Agri/Envir Science/Tech Ed ... Mr. Mark ANGLIN
31 Dean of Community & Economic Devel ... Mr. George J. BOODROOKAS
68 Dean Phys/Rec/Health Educ/Athl Dir ... Dr. William KAISER
84 Director Matriculation/Enroll Svcs ... Vacant
09 Director of Institutional Research ... Vacant
37 Director Student Financial Aid ... Vacant
40 Manager College Bookstore ... Ms. Rhonda T. GREEN

*Yuba Community College District (I)

2088 North Beale Road, Marysville CA 95901
County: Yuba Identification: 666478
Telephone: (530) 741-6700 Carnegie Class: N/A
FAX Number: (530) 634-7704
URL: www.yccd.edu

01 Chancellor ... Dr. Douglas B. HOUSTON
05 VC Educ Planning & Services ... Dr. Kayleigh CARABUJAL
13 Director Information Technologies ... Karen TRIMBLE
86 Director Public & Governmental Rels ... Dr. Adrian LOPEZ
30 Director Institutional Development ... Dr. Phil KREBS
15 Director HR & Personnel ... Vacant
10 Chief Business Officer ... Kuldeep KAUR
18 Director Facilities Planning ... George PARKER
96 Director Purchasing ... Malinda BOGDONOFF

*Woodland Community College (J)

2300 East Gibson Road, Woodland CA 95776-5156
County: Yolo FICE Identification: 041438
Unit ID: 455512
Telephone: (530) 661-5711 Carnegie Class: Assoc/Pub-R-M
FAX Number: (530) 666-9028 Calendar System: Semester
URL: www.yccd.edu/woodland/
Established: 2008 Annual Undergrad Tuition & Fees (In-District): $1,124
Enrollment: 4,900 Coed
Affiliation or Control: State/Local IRS Status: 501(c)3
Highest Offering: Associate Degree
Program: Occupational; 2-Year Principally Bachelor's Creditable
Accreditation: WJ

02 President ... Dr. Angela R. FAIRCHILDS
03 Vice President ... Dr. Alfred B. KONUWA

*Yuba College (K)

2088 N Beale Road, Marysville CA 95901-7699
County: Yuba FICE Identification: 001344
Unit ID: 126119
Telephone: (530) 741-6700 Carnegie Class: Assoc/Pub-R-L
FAX Number: (530) 741-3541 Calendar System: Semester
URL: www.yccd.edu
Established: 1927 Annual Undergrad Tuition & Fees (In-District): $1,124
Enrollment: 8,356 Coed
Affiliation or Control: State/Local IRS Status: 501(c)3
Highest Offering: Associate Degree
Program: Occupational; 2-Year Principally Bachelor's Creditable
Accreditation: WJ, RAD

02 President ... Dr. Kay ADKINS
05 Vice Pres Academic/Student Services ... Dr. Kevin TRUTNA
07 Dir Admissions & Enrollment Svcs ... Dr. Kendyl MAGNUSON
88 Director Disabled Students/Pgm/Svcs ... Ms. Jan PONTICELLI
37 Dean Financial Aid/EOPS/TRIO ... Dr. Marisela ARCE
50 Dean Bus/Soc Sci/Cosmetology ... Dr. Ed DAVIS
88 Dir Child Dev Ctr/AmeriCorps ... Ms. Laurie SCHEUERMANN
106 Dean Distributive Ed & Media Svcs ... Ms. Martha MILLS
88 Dir Upward Bound/SSS ... Ms. Yvette SANTANA-SOTO
57 Dean Fine Arts/Language Arts ... Mr. Walter MASUDA
68 Dn Hlth/PE/Rec/Ath/Pub Safety ... Mr. Rod BEILBY
19 Director Public Safety ... Vacant
81 Dn Math/Engr/Sci/Hlth/Applied Tech ... Vacant
09 Dir Plng/Rsrch & Student Success ... Mr. Erik COOPER
38 Dn Stdnt Dev/DSPS/Vets/Stdnt Succ ... Vacant
26 Pub Info Ofcr/Dir Cmty Ed/Camp Life ... Ms. Miriam ROOT
66 Dir Nursing/Allied Health ... Ms. Sheila SCROGGINS

COLORADO

Adams State University (L)

208 Edgemont Boulevard, Alamosa CO 81101-2320
County: Alamosa FICE Identification: 001345
Unit ID: 126182
Telephone: (719) 587-7011 Carnegie Class: Master's M
FAX Number: (719) 587-7522 Calendar System: Semester
URL: www.adams.edu
Established: 1921 Annual Undergrad Tuition & Fees (In-State): $6,448
Enrollment: 3,302 Coed
Affiliation or Control: State IRS Status: 501(c)3
Highest Offering: Master's
Program: 2-Year Principally Bachelor's Creditable; Liberal Arts And General; Teacher Preparatory
Accreditation: NH, CACREP, MUS, NURSE, TEAC

01 President ... Dr. David P. SVALDI
05 Vice President for Academic Affairs ... Dr. Frank J. NOVOTNY
10 VP Finance/Governmental Relations ... Mr. Bill MANSHEIM
84 Sr VP Enrollment Mgmt/Program Devel ... Dr. Michael MUMPER
30 Vice President Inst Advancement ... Vacant
18 AVP Facil Plng/Design/Construction ... Mr. Eric VAN DE BOOGAARD
56 Asst VP Extended Campus - Academics ... Mr. Walter ROYBAL
21 Asst Vice Pres Budget & Technology ... Ms. Heather HEERSINK
20 Assoc Provost Academic Affairs ... Vacant
32 Dean Student Affairs ... Mr. Kenneth L. MARQUEZ
09 Senior Analyst Inst Research ... Mrs. Andrea BENTON-MESTAS
08 Director Library ... Mr. David GOETZMAN
37 Director Student Financial Aid ... Mr. Philip SCHROEDER
07 Director of Admissions ... Mr. Eric CARPIO
06 Registrar ... Ms. Belen MAESTAS
31 Exec Dir Community Partnerships ... Ms. Mary HOFFMAN
13 Chief Information Officer ... Mr. Kevin S. DANIEL
41 Athletic Director ... Mr. Larry MORTENSEN
27 Asst to President Communications ... Ms. Julie WAECHTER
31 Director of Auxiliary Services ... Mr. Bruce DEL TONDO
38 Director Counseling/Career Services ... Mr. Gregg ELLIOTT
15 Director Human Resources ... Ms. Tracy ROGERS
102 Executive Director ASU Foundation ... Ms. Tammy L. LOPEZ
29 Director Alumni Relations ... Ms. Lori L. LASKE

96 Director of Purchasing ... Ms. Renee VIGIL
19 Dir Adams State Univ Police Dept ... Mr. Joel SHULTS
40 Director Bookstore ... Mr. Darrell MEIS
27 Interim Director of Communications ... Mr. Mark SCHOENECKER
88 Chair English/Theatre/Communication ... Dr. David MAZEL
50 Chair Business & Economics ... Dr. Michael TOMLIN
53 Chair Education ... Dr. Edward CROWTHER
81 Chair Chemistry/Computer Sci/Math ... Dr. Matthew S. NEHRING
81 Chair Biology/Earth Science ... Dr. Brent YBARRONDO
28 Director of Diversity ... Ms. Isabel MEDINA-KEISER

Aims Community College (A)

Box 69, Greeley CO 80632-0069
County: Weld FICE Identification: 007582
Unit ID: 126207
Telephone: (970) 330-8008 Carnegie Class: Assoc/Pub-R-M
FAX Number: (970) 330-5705 Calendar System: Semester
URL: www.aims.edu
Established: 1967 Annual Undergrad Tuition & Fees (In-District): $2,621
Enrollment: 5,290 Coed
Affiliation or Control: Local IRS Status: 501(c)3
Highest Offering: Associate Degree
Program: Occupational; 2-Year Principally Bachelor's Creditable
Accreditation: NH, ADNUR, EMT, IFSAC, SURGT

01 President ... Dr. Marilynn LIDDELL
10 Chief Administrative Officer ... Mr. Mike KELLY
27 Chief Information Officer ... Vacant
05 Chief Academic Officer ... Ms. Donna SOUTHER
20 Academic Dean ... Mr. Jeff REYNOLDS
20 Academic Dean ... Dr. Dan DOHERTY
32 Dean for Student Services ... Dr. Patricia MATIJEVIC
20 Academic Dean ... Dr. Albert BUYOK
43 Chief Legal Counsel ... Ms. Sandra OWENS
30 Dir Inst Advancement/Foundation ... Ms. Julie BUDERUS
15 Interim Director Human Resources ... Mr. Damion CORDOVA
21 Budget Director ... Mr. Daniel ERBERT
21 Controller ... Vacant
18 Chief Facilities Management Officer ... Mr. Michael MILLSAPPS
37 Director Student Financial Assist ... Ms. Teri DORCHUCK
06 Registrar/Director Admissions ... Mr. Stuart THOMAS
38 Director Student Success Center ... Ms. Paula YANISH
09 Dir Inst Effectiveness & Assessment ... Ms. Lee Ann SAPPINGTON
13 Director Information Technology ... Mr. Bill WAGGONER
35 Director Student Life ... Mr. Ron FAY
12 Director Loveland Campus ... Ms. Heather LELCHOOK
12 Assoc Dean Ft Lupton Campus ... Ms. Brenda RASK
88 Director Windsor Auto/Tech Ctr ... Mr. Fred BROWN
75 Associate Dean Career & Tech Ed ... Ms. Brenda RASK
08 Assoc Dean Learning/Org Dev ... Mr. Rob UMBAUGH
66 Associate Dean Nursing ... Ms. Nina KIRK

American Sentinel University (B)

2260 South Xanadu Way, Ste 310, Aurora CO 80014
County: Arapahoe FICE Identification: 041277
Telephone: (303) 991-1575 Carnegie Class: Not Classified
FAX Number: (303) 991-1577 Calendar System: Other
URL: www.americansentinel.edu
Established: 2000 Annual Undergrad Tuition & Fees: $10,595
Enrollment: 1,980 Coed
Affiliation or Control: Proprietary IRS Status: Proprietary
Highest Offering: Doctorate
Program: Occupational; 2-Year Principally Bachelor's Creditable; Professional; Nursing Emphasis
Accreditation: DETC, NURSE

01 President ... Ms. Mary A. ADAMS
05 Provost/CEO ... Dr. John BOURNE
50 Dean Business & Technology ... Dr. Devon CANCILLA

Anthem College (C)

350 Blackhawk Street, Aurora CO 80011-8754
County: Arapahoe Identification: 666510
Unit ID: 410539
Telephone: (720) 859-7900 Carnegie Class: Assoc/PrivFP
FAX Number: (303) 344-1376 Calendar System: Other
URL: www.anthemcollege.edu
Established: 1993 Annual Undergrad Tuition & Fees: $31,995
Enrollment: 302 Coed
Affiliation or Control: Proprietary IRS Status: Proprietary
Highest Offering: Associate Degree
Program: Occupational
Accreditation: ACICS, MAAB, SURTEC

01 Campus President ... Mr. Bobby HODGE
05 Dean of Education ... Ms. Reylynda DIDONATO
07 Director of Admissions ... Mr. Dedric PHILLIPS

† Branch campus of The Bryman School, AZ.

Arapahoe Community College (D)

5900 S Santa Fe Drive, PO Box 9002,
Littleton CO 80160-9002
County: Arapahoe FICE Identification: 001346
Unit ID: 126289
Telephone: (303) 797-4222 Carnegie Class: Assoc/Pub-S-MC
FAX Number: (303) 797-5935 Calendar System: Semester
URL: www.arapahoe.edu
Established: 1965 Annual Undergrad Tuition & Fees (In-State): $4,385
Enrollment: 9,995 Coed
Affiliation or Control: State IRS Status: 501(c)3
Highest Offering: Associate Degree
Program: Occupational; 2-Year Principally Bachelor's Creditable
Accreditation: NH, ADNUR, EMT, FUSER, MLTAD, PTAA

01 President ... Dr. Diana DOYLE
11 Vice President Admin Services ... Vacant
05 Vice President Instruction ... Dr. Diane HEGEMAN
10 Chief Financial Officer ... Mr. Joseph LORENZO, JR.
103 Dean Community/Workforce Partnershp ... Mr. Matt MCKEEVER
32 Dean of Student Services ... Ms. Connie SIMPSON
38 Director of Advising and Retention ... Mr. Michael MCMANUS
07 Director Admissions & Records ... Ms. Darcy BRIGGS
37 Dir of Student Financial Services ... Ms. Dorothy SHALLCROSS
31 Exec Dir of Community/Workforce Pgm ... Ms. Kim K. LARSON-COONEY
79 Dean Liberal Arts & Prof Programs ... Vacant
76 Dean Health/Sciences & Engineering ... Ms. Linda COMEAUX
50 Dean Math/Business & Technology ... Dr. Cindy SOMERS
49 Dean Arts/Design/Social/Behav Sci ... Ms. Rebecca WOULFE
102 Executive Director Foundation ... Ms. Courtney LOEHFELM
21 Controller ... Ms. Xochil QUIJANO
19 Chief of Police ... Mr. Dennis GOODWIN
09 Director Institutional Research ... Vacant
08 Director Learning Resource Center ... Mr. Malcolm BRANTZ
26 Dir of Marketing/Public Relations ... Mr. Murry UNELL
35 Director Student Affairs ... Ms. Heather WILCOX
96 Director of Purchasing ... Ms. Amy DEMROVSKY
18 Facilities Manager ... Vacant

Argosy University, Denver (E)

7600 East Eastman Avenue, Denver CO 80231
County: Denver Identification: 666654
Unit ID: 448734
Telephone: (303) 923-4110 Carnegie Class: Bac/A&S
FAX Number: (303) 923-4112 Calendar System: Semester
URL: www.argosy.edu
Established: 2006 Annual Undergrad Tuition & Fees: $13,224
Enrollment: 485 Coed
Affiliation or Control: Proprietary IRS Status: Proprietary
Highest Offering: Doctorate
Program: Professional
Accreditation: &WC, CACREP

01 Campus President ... Dr. Richard BOOROM
07 Senior Director of Admissions ... Diane ROTONDO
32 Director of Student Services ... Irving H. PEREZ
15 Human Resources ... Nichole NORTON
37 Director of Student Finance ... Mary MURO
06 Registrar ... Timothy LANKFORD

† Regional accreditation is carried under the parent institution in Orange, CA.

The Art Institute of Colorado (F)

1200 Lincoln Street, Denver CO 80203-2172
County: Denver FICE Identification: 020789
Unit ID: 126702
Telephone: (303) 837-0825 Carnegie Class: Spec/Arts
FAX Number: (303) 860-8520 Calendar System: Quarter
URL: www.artinstitutes.edu/denver
Established: 1952 Annual Undergrad Tuition & Fees: $31,168
Enrollment: 2,206 Coed
Affiliation or Control: Proprietary IRS Status: Proprietary
Highest Offering: Baccalaureate
Program: Occupational
Accreditation: NH, ACFEI, CIDA

01 President ... Mr. David C. ZORN
05 Dean of Education ... Mr. Jon KERBAUGH
07 Senior Director of Admissions ... Ms. Sarah JOHNSON
32 Director of Student Services ... Mr. John RICHARDSON
10 Director Admin & Financial Services ... Ms. Wendy BUTLER
37 Director of Financial Aid ... Ms. Sophia LEUTH
06 Registrar ... Ms. Angel BLACK

Aspen University (G)

720 S Colorado Blvd, Suite 1150N, Denver CO 80246
County: Denver FICE Identification: 040803
Unit ID: 454829
Telephone: (800) 441-4746 Carnegie Class: Master's M
FAX Number: (303) 336-1144 Calendar System: Other
URL: www.aspen.edu
Established: 1987 Annual Undergrad Tuition & Fees: $9,000
Enrollment: 1,046 Coed
Affiliation or Control: Proprietary IRS Status: Proprietary
Highest Offering: Doctorate
Program: Business Emphasis
Accreditation: DETC, NURSE

01 President ... Dr. Gerry WILLIAMS
11 Vice Pres of Operations ... Ms. Barbara MAX
06 Registrar ... Ms. Suzanne PARTAIN

Bel-Rea Institute of Animal Technology (H)

1681 S Dayton Street, Denver CO 80247-3048
County: Arapahoe FICE Identification: 012670
Unit ID: 126359
Telephone: (800) 950-8001 Carnegie Class: Assoc/PrivFP
FAX Number: (303) 751-9969 Calendar System: Quarter
URL: www.bel-rea.com
Established: 1971 Annual Undergrad Tuition & Fees: $10,087
Enrollment: 797 Coed
Affiliation or Control: Proprietary IRS Status: Proprietary
Highest Offering: Associate Degree
Program: Occupational
Accreditation: ACCSC

01 Director ... Paulette KAUFMAN
37 Director Student Financial Aid ... Stasi BONTINELLI
32 Director Student Services ... Cynthia MEDINA

Boulder College of Massage Therapy (I)

6255 Longbow Drive, Boulder CO 80301-3295
County: Boulder FICE Identification: 030131
Unit ID: 126410
Telephone: (800) 442-5131 Carnegie Class: Assoc/PrivNFP
FAX Number: (303) 530-2204 Calendar System: Quarter
URL: www.bcmt.org
Established: 1975 Annual Undergrad Tuition & Fees: $16,299
Enrollment: 12,100 Coed
Affiliation or Control: Independent Non-Profit IRS Status: 501(c)3
Highest Offering: Associate Degree
Program: Occupational
Accreditation: ACCSC

01 President ... Mr. Dirk S. MCCUISTION
05 Director of Education ... Ms. Christa FORSYTHE
37 Financial Aid Advisor ... Ms. Kira CLARK
06 Registrar ... Ms. Wendy BERUTO

College for Financial Planning (J)

8000 E Maplewood Avenue, Suite 200,
Greenwood Village CO 80111-4727
County: Denver Identification: 666809
Unit ID: 126526
Telephone: (303) 220-1200 Carnegie Class: Not Classified
FAX Number: (303) 220-4940 Calendar System: Other
URL: www.cffp.edu
Established: 1972 Annual Undergrad Tuition & Fees: $4,295
Enrollment: 6,500 Coed
Affiliation or Control: Proprietary IRS Status: Proprietary
Highest Offering: Master's
Program: Professional
Accreditation: NH

01 President ... Mr. John SEARS
05 Vice President Academic Affairs ... Dr. Jesse ARMAN
10 Vice President Business Development ... Mr. Dirk PANTONE
07 Sr Dir Enrollment & Student Svcs ... Mr. Brett SANBORN
06 Registrar ... Ms. Viviane PRICE
38 Director Student Service Center ... Mr. Brett SANBORN

CollegeAmerica Colorado Springs (K)

3645 Citadel Drive S, Colorado Springs CO 80909-5320
County: El Paso Identification: 666293
Unit ID: 448752
Telephone: (719) 637-0600 Carnegie Class: Bac/Assoc
FAX Number: (719) 637-0806 Calendar System: Other
URL: www.collegeamerica.edu
Established: 1964 Annual Undergrad Tuition & Fees: $15,957
Enrollment: 564 Coed
Affiliation or Control: Proprietary IRS Status: Proprietary
Highest Offering: Baccalaureate
Program: Occupational
Accreditation: ACCSC

01 Executive Director ... Mrs. Rozann R. KUNSTLE

† Branch campus of CollegeAmerica Denver, Denver, CO.

CollegeAmerica Denver (L)

1385 S Colorado Blvd, 5th Floor, Denver CO 80222
County: Denver FICE Identification: 025943
Unit ID: 126872
Telephone: (303) 300-8740 Carnegie Class: Bac/Assoc
FAX Number: (303) 692-9156 Calendar System: Other
URL: www.collegeamerica.edu
Established: 1964 Annual Undergrad Tuition & Fees: $22,500
Enrollment: 614 Coed
Affiliation or Control: Proprietary IRS Status: Proprietary
Highest Offering: Baccalaureate
Program: Occupational
Accreditation: ACCSC

01 Executive Director ... Mr. Nathan LARSON

05 Academic Director ... Ms. Jeanne LIPP
37 Director of Financial Aid ... Ms. Sonia MARTINEZ
07 Director of Admissions ... Ms. Jaclyn MILLER
06 Registrar ... Ms. Gwen ESTRIDGE

CollegeAmerica Fort Collins (A)

4601 S Mason, Fort Collins CO 80525-3740
County: Larimer | Identification: 666362 | Unit ID: 448761
Telephone: (970) 225-4860 | Carnegie Class: Spec/Health
FAX Number: (970) 225-6059 | Calendar System: Other
URL: www.collegeamerica.edu
Established: 2001 | Annual Undergrad Tuition & Fees: $22,500
Enrollment: 246 | Coed
Affiliation or Control: Proprietary | IRS Status: Proprietary
Highest Offering: Baccalaureate
Program: 2-Year Principally Bachelor's Creditable; Professional; Business Emphasis
Accreditation: ACCSC

01 Campus Director ... Mr. Joel SCIMECA
07 Assistant Director of Admission ... Ms. Kristy MCNEAR
37 Financial Aid Director ... Ms. Laura MITCHELL
14 Network Administrator ... Mr. David WILD
32 Director Student Services/Placement ... Mr. Michael REY
06 Registrar ... Ms. Linda KLINE
08 Librarian ... Ms. Devon YOST
35 Student Services Coordinator ... Ms. Amanda FOX
50 Dept Chair of Business & Computers ... Mrs. Tresban RIVERA
76 Dept Chair of Healthcare ... Ms. Kai SCOTT

† Branch campus of CollegeAmerica Denver, Denver, CO.

Colorado Academy of Veterinary Technology (B)

2766 Janitell Road, Colorado Springs CO 80906
County: El Paso | FICE Identification: 041850 | Unit ID: 461953
Telephone: (719) 219-9636 | Carnegie Class: Not Classified
FAX Number: (719) 302-5577 | Calendar System: Quarter
URL: www.coloradovettech.com
Established: 2007 | Annual Undergrad Tuition & Fees: $15,595
Enrollment: 22 | Coed
Affiliation or Control: Proprietary | IRS Status: Proprietary
Highest Offering: Associate Degree
Program: Occupational
Accreditation: COE

01 Site Director/Admissions ... Dr. Steve RUBIN
05 Chief Academic Officer ... Mrs. Ramona CRANE
38 Dir Student Counseling/Fin Aid ... Mrs. Lisa BRUBAKER

Colorado Christian University (C)

8787 W Alameda Avenue, Lakewood CO 80226-7499
County: Jefferson | FICE Identification: 009401 | Unit ID: 126669
Telephone: (303) 963-3000 | Carnegie Class: Master's M
FAX Number: (303) 963-3001 | Calendar System: Semester
URL: www.ccu.edu
Established: 1914 | Annual Undergrad Tuition & Fees: $23,870
Enrollment: 3,122 | Coed
Affiliation or Control: Independent Non-Profit | IRS Status: 501(c)3
Highest Offering: Master's
Program: 2-Year Principally Bachelor's Creditable; Liberal Arts And General; Teacher Preparatory; Professional
Accreditation: NH, CACREP, MUS, NURSE

01 President ... Mr. William L. ARMSTRONG
10 Senior Vice President & CFO ... Mr. Daniel COHRS
05 VP College Adult & Graduate Studies ... Vacant
05 VP Acad Affairs College UG Studies ... Dr. Cherri S. PARKS
30 VP of Development ... Mr. Paul ELDRIDGE
32 VP for Student Development ... Mr. Jim S. MCCORMICK
20 Asst VP of Acad Affairs/Dean CAGS ... Mrs. Sarah SCHERLING
11 Asst VP for Administrative Services ... Mr. Ronald W. BENTON
35 Asst VP Stdnt Pgm/Dean of Students ... Mrs. Sharon M. FELKER
42 Asst VP of Student Life/Ministry ... Mr. Joe WALTERS
07 Asst VP Enrollment & Marketing ... Mr. Chuck KLIJEWSKI
88 Asst VP of Student Success ... Mr. Roger CHANDLER
50 Dean School of Business ... Dr. Gary EWEN
72 Dean of Business and Technology ... Dr. Mellani J. DAY
53 Dean School of Education ... Dr. Sara E. DALLMAN
53 Dean of Ed/Curriculum & Instruction ... Dr. Wendy WENDOVER
79 Dean Sch Humanities & Sciences ... Dr. William R. SAXBY
64 Dean School of Music ... Mr. Steven T. TAYLOR
73 Dean School of Theology ... Dr. Sidney S. BUZZELL
41 Athletic Director ... Mr. Darren A. RICHIE
21 Controller ... Mrs. Teresa ROBERTSON
38 Director of Counseling Services ... Dr. Joannie L. DEBRITO
44 Director of Development ... Mr. David J. NYE
18 Director of Facilities ... Mr. Mathew J. GOTHARD
37 Director of Financial Aid ... Mr. Steve M. WOODBURN
23 Director of Health Services ... Mrs. Donna HORWATH
15 Director of Human Resources ... Mr. Rick GARRIS
13 Sr Dir of Information Systems/Tech ... Mr. Bryan SHOLTEN
08 Library Director ... Mrs. Gayle C. GUNDERSON
36 Director of Life Directions Center ... Mrs. Joy STRICKLAND
06 Registrar ... Mrs. Linda K. PERCIANTE
39 Director of Residence Life ... Mr. Josh KUSCH
19 Director of Security ... Mr. Harry G. CAROTHERS
26 Dir of University Communications ... Mrs. Lisa L. ZELLER
07 Dean of Admissions ... Mr. Derry EBERT
29 Director Alumni Relations ... Mrs. Christi KIRCHNER

Colorado College (D)

14 E La Cache Poudre St., Colorado Springs CO 80903-3294
County: El Paso | FICE Identification: 001347 | Unit ID: 126678
Telephone: (719) 389-6000 | Carnegie Class: Bac/A&S
FAX Number: (719) 634-4180 | Calendar System: Other
URL: www.coloradocollege.edu
Established: 1874 | Annual Undergrad Tuition & Fees: $41,742
Enrollment: 2,043 | Coed
Affiliation or Control: Independent Non-Profit | IRS Status: 501(c)3
Highest Offering: Master's
Program: Liberal Arts And General; Teacher Preparatory
Accreditation: NH

01 President ... Dr. Jill TIEFENTHALER
05 Dean of College & Faculty ... Dr. Sandra WONG
100 Cheif of Staff ... Mr. Jermyn DAVIS
84 Vice Pres Enrollment Management ... Mr. Mark HATCH
30 Vice Pres for College Advancement ... Mr. Sean PIERI
10 Vice Pres Business/Finance & Treas ... Mr. Robert G. MOORE
41 Director of Athletics ... Mr. Ken RALPH
32 VP Student Life/Dean of Students ... Mr. Mike EDMONDS
13 VP for Information Management ... Mr. Dave ARMSTRONG
45 Asst VP for Institutional Planning ... Ms. Lyrae WILLIAMS
20 Associate Dean of the College ... Dr. Regula M. EVITT
20 Associate Dean of the Faculty ... Dr. Jeffrey NOBLETT
35 Associate Dean of Students ... Ms. Rochelle MASON
87 Dean of Summer Programs ... Mr. Eric POPKIN
07 Director of Admissions ... Mr. Roberto GARCIA
37 Director of Financial Aid ... Mr. Jim M. SWANSON
06 Registrar ... Mr. Phillip C. APODACA
26 Director of Communications ... Ms. Jane TURNIS
104 Director International Programs ... Dr. Inger BULL
15 Director Human Resources ... Ms. Barbara WILSON
18 Director of Facilities ... Mr. Chris COULTER
19 Director Campus Safety ... Mr. Pat CUNNINGHAM
08 Library Director ... Mr. Ivan GAETZ
96 Director of Purchasing ... Ms. Gina ARMS
36 Director Career Center ... Vacant
85 Dir Minority/Internatl Students ... Mr. Roger SMITH
29 Director Alumni & Parent Relations ... Mr. Jay ENGLN
88 Director Advancement Services ... Ms. Cathey BARBEE
91 Director Enterprise Info Svcs ... Mr. Vishvas PARADKAR
09 Dir Assessment/Program Review ... Ms. Amanda UDIS-KESSLER
88 Controller/Asst Treasurer ... Ms. Stacy DAVIDSON
24 Director of Media Services ... Mr. Randy BABB
39 Director Residential Life ... Mr. John LAUER
105 Director Web Communications ... Ms. Karen TO
88 Director of Budget ... Ms. Lyrae WILLIAMS
88 Director Internal Audit ... Ms. Yolanda LYONS
38 Counseling Sup/Clin Psychologist ... Mr. Bill DOVE
38 Dir Disability Services ... Ms. Jan EDWARDS
27 College News Director ... Ms. Leslie WEDDELL
90 Director Educational Tech Svcs ... Mr. Chad SCHOENWILL
88 Director of Network & Systems ... Mr. Daniel ARMSTRONG
88 Dir Collab Cmty Engagement ... Ms. Jessica COPELAND
46 College Research Professor ... Dr. Kevin RASK
42 Chaplain ... Dr. Bruce CORIELL

Colorado Heights University (E)

3001 S Federal Boulevard, Denver CO 80236-2711
County: Denver | FICE Identification: 032893 | Unit ID: 367839
Telephone: (303) 937-4225 | Carnegie Class: Spec/Bus
FAX Number: (303) 937-4224 | Calendar System: Semester
URL: www.chu.edu
Established: 1990 | Annual Undergrad Tuition & Fees: $5,166
Enrollment: 122 | Coed
Affiliation or Control: Independent Non-Profit | IRS Status: 501(c)3
Highest Offering: Master's
Program: Professional; Business Emphasis
Accreditation: ACICS

01 President ... Vacant
05 Dean of Academic Affairs ... Vacant
10 Chief Financial Officer ... Ms. Erin ONSAGER
50 Dir of MBA and BA Intl Business ... Vacant
06 Registrar ... Ms. Jennifer JOLY
08 Librarian ... Vacant
15 Director of Human Resources ... Ms. Debra POWELL
37 Director of Financial Aid ... Ms. Beba PREDIC
32 Exec Director of Student Affairs ... Ms. Lori SISNEROS
39 Director of Public Safety ... Mr. Daniil YUSUFOV
07 Exec Dir of Mktg & Admissions ... Ms. Pam SMITH
13 Director Information Technology ... Vacant
18 Director of Facilities ... Mr. Jose GALLEGOS

Colorado Mesa University (F)

1100 North Avenue, Grand Junction CO 81501-3122
County: Mesa | FICE Identification: 001358 | Unit ID: 127556
Telephone: (970) 248-1020 | Carnegie Class: Bac/A&S
FAX Number: (970) 248-1076 | Calendar System: Semester
URL: www.coloradomesa.edu
Established: 1925 | Annual Undergrad Tuition & Fees (In-State): $5,496
Enrollment: 9,005 | Coed
Affiliation or Control: State | IRS Status: 501(c)3
Highest Offering: Doctorate
Program: Occupational; Liberal Arts And General; Professional
Accreditation: NH, EMT, MUS, NURSE, RAD, TED

01 President ... Mr. Tim FOSTER
05 Vice Pres Academic/Student Affairs ... Dr. Carol FUTHEY
10 Vice President Financial/Admin Svcs ... Mr. Patrick DOYLE
31 Vice Pres Community College Affairs ... Mrs. Brigitte SUNDERMANN
96 Asst Vice Pres Auxiliary Services ... Mr. Andy RODRIGUEZ
32 Dean of Students ... Mr. John MARSHALL
13 Director Information Technology ... Mr. Jeremy BROWN
09 Director Institutional Research ... Ms. Sonia BRANDON
08 Library Director ... Ms. Elizabeth BRODAK
25 Director Sponsored Programs ... Ms. Cindy LUEB
20 Assistant Academic Officer ... Mr. Steve WERMAN
21 Controller ... Mr. Joe TAYLOR
21 Director Budget ... Ms. Whitney SUTTON
30 Director of Development ... Ms. Peggy LAMM
37 Director Financial Aid ... Mr. Curt MARTIN
18 Director of Facilities Services ... Mr. Kent MARSH
29 Director of Alumni Association ... Mr. Rick ADLEMAN
41 Athletic Director ... Mr. Butch MILLER
26 Act Director Marketing/Publications ... Ms. Dana NUNN
39 Director Housing & Residence Life ... Mr. Troy SEPPELT
06 Registrar ... Ms. Holly TEAL
07 Director of Admissions ... Mr. Jared MEIER
15 Director of Human Resources ... Ms. Barbara CASE-KING
20 Interim Director Academic Services ... Ms. Millie MOLAND
40 Bookstore Manager ... Ms. Tracy BRODRICK

Colorado Mountain College (G)

802 Grand Avenue, Glenwood Springs CO 81602-3961
County: Garfield | FICE Identification: 004506 | Unit ID: 126711
Telephone: (970) 945-8691 | Carnegie Class: Assoc/Pub-R-L
FAX Number: (970) 947-8385 | Calendar System: Semester
URL: www.coloradomtn.edu
Established: 1965 | Annual Undergrad Tuition & Fees (In-District): $1,680
Enrollment: 5,823 | Coed
Affiliation or Control: Local | IRS Status: 501(c)3
Highest Offering: Baccalaureate
Program: Occupational; 2-Year Principally Bachelor's Creditable
Accreditation: NH, ADNUR, EMT

01 President ... Dr. Stanley JENSEN
03 Senior Vice President ... Dr. Jill BOYLE
05 Sr Vice President Academic Affairs ... Dr. Brad TYNDALL
12 VP CMC/Aspen Campus ... Mr. Joseph MAESTAS
10 CFO ... Ms. Linda ENGLISH
09 VP Institutional Effectiveness ... Dr. Meeta GOEL
32 VP Student Affairs ... Mr. Brad BANKHEAD
15 Vice President of Human Resources ... Ms. Jan ASPELUND
26 Public Relations Officer ... Ms. Debbie CRAWFORD
13 Chief Information Officer ... Vacant
07 Dir Pre-Enrollment Svcs/Registrar ... Mr. Bill SOMMERS
37 Director of Financial Aid ... Ms. Rita BAYLESS
18 Director of College Facilities ... Mr. Peter WALLER
27 Director of Marketing/Publications ... Mr. Doug STEWART
96 Director of Purchasing ... Mr. Steve BOYD
20 Developmental Education Coordinator ... Vacant

Colorado Northwestern Community College (H)

500 Kennedy Drive, Rangely CO 81648-3598
County: Rio Blanco | FICE Identification: 001359 | Unit ID: 126748
Telephone: (970) 675-2261 | Carnegie Class: Assoc/Pub-R-M
FAX Number: (970) 675-5046 | Calendar System: Semester
URL: www.cncc.edu
Established: 1962 | Annual Undergrad Tuition & Fees (In-District): $3,329
Enrollment: 1,291 | Coed
Affiliation or Control: State/Local | IRS Status: 170(c)1
Highest Offering: Associate Degree
Program: Occupational; 2-Year Principally Bachelor's Creditable
Accreditation: NH, ADNUR, DH

01 President ... Mr. Russell GEORGE
12 Vice Pres Craig Campus ... Mr. Gene BILODEAU
05 Vice Pres Instruction/Student Svcs ... Mr. David SMITH
10 Vice Pres Business/Administration ... Mr. Christopher BISHOP
84 Dean of Enrollment Svcs/Registrar ... Ms. Tresa ENGLAND
08 Library Director ... Ms. Leana COX
15 Human Resource Specialist ... Ms. Kim TUCKER
26 Marketing Director ... Ms. Tresa ENGLAND
18 Facilities Director ... Mr. John BOTTELBERGHE
102 Foundation Director ... Ms. Becky NIEMI
09 Director of Institutional Research ... Ms. Mindy SHUE
38 Director Student Counseling ... Ms. Charity STOLWORTHY
96 Director of Purchasing ... Mr. Roger HANNA
56 Director of Distance Learning ... Ms. Kellie DIPPEL
37 Financial Aid Technician ... Ms. Merrie BYERS
20 Dean of Instruction in Rangely ... Ms. Judy ALLRED
20 Dean of Instruction in Craig ... Ms. Pamela GARDNER

Colorado School of Healing Arts (A)

7655 W Mississippi, Suite 100, Lakewood CO 80226-4332

County: Jefferson FICE Identification: 035844
Unit ID: 381732
Telephone: (303) 986-2320 Carnegie Class: Assoc/PrivFP
FAX Number: (303) 980-6594 Calendar System: Quarter
URL: www.csha.net
Established: 1986 Annual Undergrad Tuition & Fees: $12,600
Enrollment: 190 Coed
Affiliation or Control: Proprietary IRS Status: Proprietary
Highest Offering: Associate Degree
Program: Occupational; 2-Year Principally Bachelor's Creditable; Technical Emphasis
Accreditation: ACCSC

01 Executive Director & Owner .... Mr. Dennis SIMPSON
03 Director .... Ms. Gina SIMPSON
05 Director of Education Deg Pgm .... Mr. Mark BRAUKMAN
06 Registrar .... Ms. Ranata NOVOTNY
53 Director of Education Cert Pgm .... Ms. Chris SMITH
08 Head Librarian .... Ms. Kris WILL
11 Office Manager .... Ms. Tiffany LAYNE
40 Bookstore Manager .... Mr. Greg SENICH
36 Career Advisor/Placement .... Mr. Mark SOBOLESKE
37 Financial Aid Advisor .... Ms. Andrea NIECE
07 Admissions Representative .... Ms. Rosa TORRES

Colorado School of Mines (B)

1500 Illinois Street, Golden CO 80401-1843

County: Jefferson FICE Identification: 001348
Unit ID: 126775
Telephone: (303) 273-3000 Carnegie Class: RU/H
FAX Number: (303) 273-3278 Calendar System: Semester
URL: www.mines.edu
Established: 1874 Annual Undergrad Tuition & Fees (In-State): $15,654
Enrollment: 5,346 Coed
Affiliation or Control: State IRS Status: 501(c)3
Highest Offering: Doctorate
Program: Professional; Technical Emphasis
Accreditation: NH, ENG

01 President .... Dr. M. W. SCOGGINS
05 Provost .... Dr. Terry PARKER
10 Sr Vice Pres Finance & Admin .... Mr. Joseph TRUBACZ
88 Sr Vice Pres Strat Enterprises .... Dr. Nigel T. MIDDLETON
32 Vice Pres Student Life .... Dr. Dan FOX
30 VP for Institutional Advancement .... Mr. Brian WINKELBAUER
100 Chief of Staff .... Mr. Peter HAN
06 Registrar .... Ms. Lara MEDLEY
07 Director of Admissions .... Mr. Bruce P. GOETZ
08 Librarian .... Ms. Joanne V. LERUD-HECK
14 Director of Computer Center .... Mr. Derek J. WILSON
26 Director Integrated Marketing Comm .... Ms. Karen GILBERT
37 Director of Financial Aid .... Ms. Jill ROBERTSON
51 Director of Special Programs .... Dr. Barry MARTIN
58 Dean Graduate Studies/Research .... Dr. Thomas BOYD
18 Director of Plant Facilities .... Mr. Gary BOWERSOCK
22 Affirmative Action Officer .... Mr. Michael DOUGHERTY
39 Director of Student Housing .... Ms. Rebecca FLINTOFT
38 Director Student Development .... Mr. Ronald L. BRUMMETT
41 Athletic Director .... Mr. Thomas SPICER
04 Spec Assistant to the President .... Ms. Kristi GITKIND
09 Director of Institutional Research .... Ms. Tricia DOUTHIT
15 Director Personnel Services .... Mr. Michael DOUGHERTY
84 Director Enrollment Management .... Ms. Heather BOYD
35 Director Student Affairs .... Mr. Derek MORGAN
36 Director Student Placement .... Mr. Ronald L. BRUMMETT
19 Director Public Safety .... Mr. Keith TURNEY
94 Exec Dir Women in Sci Eng & Math .... Ms. Deb LASICH
92 Director Honors Program .... Dr. Ken OSGOOD
45 Dir Financial Planning & Budget .... Ms. Vicki NICHOL
93 Director Minority Engineering Pro .... Mr. Khahn VU
91 Director Enterprise Systems .... Mr. David LEE
29 Director Alumni Relations .... Ms. Anita PARISEAU

Colorado School of Trades (C)

1575 Hoyt Street, Lakewood CO 80215-2996

County: Jefferson FICE Identification: 011572
Unit ID: 126784
Telephone: (800) 234-4594 Carnegie Class: Assoc/PrivFP
FAX Number: (303) 233-4723 Calendar System: Other
URL: www.schooloftrades.edu
Established: 1947 Annual Undergrad Tuition & Fees: $18,900
Enrollment: 162 Coed
Affiliation or Control: Proprietary IRS Status: Proprietary
Highest Offering: Associate Degree
Program: Occupational
Accreditation: ACCSC

01 President .... Mr. Robert E. MARTIN

Colorado School of Traditional Chinese Medicine (D)

1441 York Street, Suite 202, Denver CO 80206-2127

County: Denver FICE Identification: 036863
Unit ID: 381352
Telephone: (303) 329-6355 Carnegie Class: Spec/Health
FAX Number: (303) 388-8165 Calendar System: Trimester
URL: www.cstcm.edu
Established: 1989 Annual Undergrad Tuition & Fees: $16,170
Enrollment: 144 Coed
Affiliation or Control: Proprietary IRS Status: Proprietary
Highest Offering: Master's
Program: Occupational; Professional
Accreditation: ACUP

01 Administrative Director .... Vladimir DIBRIGIDA

*Colorado State University System Office (E)

410 17th Street, Suite 2440, Denver CO 80202-4426

County: Denver FICE Identification: 033437
Telephone: (303) 534-6290 Carnegie Class: N/A
FAX Number: (303) 534-6298
URL: www.csusystem.edu

01 Chancellor .... Dr. Michaeld MARTIN
05 Chief Academic Officer .... Dr. George DENNISON
43 General Counsel .... Mr. Michael NOLSER
10 Chief Financial Officer .... Mr. Rich SCHWEIGERT
26 Director of Public Relations .... Mr. Brad BOHLANDER
86 Government Relations Coordinator .... Vacant
04 Executive Asst to President .... Ms. Melanie GEARY

*Colorado State University (F)

Fort Collins CO 80523-0015

County: Larimer FICE Identification: 001350
Unit ID: 126818
Telephone: (970) 491-1101 Carnegie Class: RU/VH
FAX Number: (970) 491-0501 Calendar System: Semester
URL: www.colostate.edu
Established: 1870 Annual Undergrad Tuition & Fees (In-State): $8,649
Enrollment: 26,735 Coed
Affiliation or Control: State IRS Status: 501(c)3
Highest Offering: Doctorate
Program: Liberal Arts And General; Teacher Preparatory; Professional
Accreditation: NH, BUS, CACREP, CEA, CIDA, CONST, COPSY, DIETC, DIETD, ENG, ENGR, FOR, IPSY, JOUR, #LSAR, MFCD, MUS, OT, PH, SW, TEAC, VET

02 President .... Dr. Anthony A. FRANK
05 Senior Executive VP/Provost .... Dr. Rick MIRANDA
46 Vice President for Research .... Dr. William H. FARLAND
10 Assoc VP for Finance and Budgets .... Ms. Lynn JOHNSON
11 VP for University Operations .... Ms. Amy PARSONS
30 VP Advancement/Strategic Initiative .... Mr. Brett B. ANDERSON
84 Vice Pres for Enrollment/Access .... Dr. Robin C. BROWN
20 Vice Prov for Undergraduate Affairs .... Dr. Alan LAMBORN
58 Dean Graduate School .... Dr. Jodie R. HANZLIK
27 VP for External Relations .... Mr. Tom MILLIGAN
90 VP for IT/Dean of Libraries .... Dr. Patrick BURNS
91 Director of Acad Comp/Network Svc .... Mr. Scott BAILY
15 Dir Human Resource Svcs .... Mr. Tony DECROSTA
36 Director Career Services .... Ms. Ann MALEN
08 Exec Assoc Dean of Libraries .... Vacant
07 Assoc VP Enroll/VP for Diversity .... Ms. Mary R. ONTIVEROS
29 Exec Director Alumni Relations .... Ms. Colleen D. MEYER
41 Athletic Director .... Mr. Jack GRAHAM
43 Deputy General Counsel .... Mr. Jason L. JOHNSON
47 Dean Agriculture Sciences .... Dr. Craig BEYROUTY
88 Dean Applied Human Sciences .... Dr. Jeff MCCUBBIN
50 Dean of Business .... Dr. Ajay MENON
54 Dean of Engineering .... Dr. Sandra L. WOODS
49 Dean of Liberal Arts .... Dr. Ann M. GILL
62 VP for IT/Dean of Libraries .... Dr. Patrick BURNS
65 Dean of Natural Resources .... Dr. Joyce BERRY
81 Dean of Natural Sciences .... Dr. Janice L. NERGER
74 Dean of Veterinary Med & Biomed Sci .... Dr. Mark STETTER
56 Director Cooperative Extension Svcs .... Dr. Lou SWANSON
06 Registrar .... Mr. Chris SENG
18 Chief Facilities/Physical Plant .... Mr. Steve R. HULTIN
22 Dir of Equal Opportunity .... Ms. Diana PRIETO
37 Director of Student Financial Aid .... Ms. Sandy CALHOUN
39 Exec Dir Housing & Dining Services .... Dr. James DOLAK
40 Director of Bookstore .... Mr. John PARRY
96 Director of Purchasing .... Mr. Frank KRAPPES
92 Director University Honors Program .... Dr. Robert KELLER
94 Dir Women & Gender Advocacy Center .... Ms. Kathy SISNEROS
09 Director of Institutional Research .... Dr. Laura JENSEN

*Colorado State University-Global Campus (G)

8000 E Maplewood Ave, Bld 5 Ste 250, Greenwood Village CO 80111-4766

County: Arapahoe FICE Identification: 042087
Telephone: (720) 279-0159 Carnegie Class: Not Classified
FAX Number: N/A Calendar System: Semester
URL: www.csuglobal.edu
Established: N/A Annual Undergrad Tuition & Fees (In-State): $10,500
Enrollment: N/A Coed
Affiliation or Control: State IRS Status: 501(c)3
Highest Offering: Master's
Program: Professional
Accreditation: NH

02 President & CEO .... Dr. Becky TAKEDA-TINKER

*Colorado State University-Pueblo (H)

2200 Bonforte Boulevard, Pueblo CO 81001-4901

County: Pueblo FICE Identification: 001365
Unit ID: 128106
Telephone: (719) 549-2100 Carnegie Class: Master's S
FAX Number: (719) 549-2650 Calendar System: Semester
URL: www.colostate-pueblo.edu
Established: 1933 Annual Undergrad Tuition & Fees (In-State): $7,327
Enrollment: 7,174 Coed
Affiliation or Control: State IRS Status: 501(c)3
Highest Offering: Master's
Program: Liberal Arts And General; Teacher Preparatory; Professional
Accreditation: NH, BUS, ENG, ENGT, MUS, NUR, SW, TEAC

02 President .... Dr. Lesley DI MARE
05 Provost/VP for Academic Affairs .... Vacant
10 VP Finance & Administration .... Vacant
84 Asst Vice Pres Enrollment Mgmt .... Mr. Joe MARSHALL
88 Asst Provost Assess/Student Lrng .... Dr. Erin FREW
32 Interim Dean Student Affairs .... Vacant
08 Dean Library .... Ms. Rhonda GONZALES
51 Dean Continuing Education .... Dr. James MALM
50 Dean Hasan School of Business .... Dr. Bruce RAYMOND
79 Dean Col of Humanities/Soc Sci .... Dr. Roy SONNEMA
54 Dean Engr/Educ/Profess Studies .... Dr. Hector CARRASCO
81 Dean Science/Math .... Dr. Richard KREMINSKI
102 Executive Director Foundation .... Mr. Todd KELLY
26 Exec Director External Affairs .... Ms. Cora ZALETEL
09 Dir Institutional Research/Analysis .... Dr. Lin CHANG
21 Controller .... Vacant
37 Director Student Financial Services .... Mr. Sean MCGIVNEY
06 Registrar .... Ms. Katie VELARDE
36 Director Career Center .... Mrs. Michelle B. GJERDE
14 Dir Info Tech Svcs/Chief Tech Ofcr .... Vacant
41 Director Athletics .... Mr. Joe FOLDA
18 Dir Facilities/Construction/Plng .... Mr. Craig CASON
15 Interim Director Human Resources .... Ms. Susan BENESCH
39 Director Residence Life & Housing .... Vacant
31 Director Auxiliary Services .... Mr. A. Ramon GARCIA
23 Student Health Services Nurse .... Ms. Carlotta FENDRICH
29 Director Alumni Relations .... Ms. Tracy SAMORA
38 Director Student Counseling .... Vacant
89 Director First Year Programs .... Dr. Derek LOPEZ
22 Director Affirmative Action .... Ms. LaNeeca WILLIAMS
85 Assoc Dir International Programs .... Ms. Annie WILLIAMS
04 Executive Asst to the President .... Ms. Trisha MACIAS

Colorado Technical University (I)

3151 South Vaughn Way, Suite 400, Aurora CO 80014

County: Arapahoe Identification: 666732
Unit ID: 430087
Telephone: (303) 632-2300 Carnegie Class: Master's M
FAX Number: (303) 694-6673 Calendar System: Quarter
URL: www.coloradotech.edu
Established: 1996 Annual Undergrad Tuition & Fees: $16,903
Enrollment: 1,200 Coed
Affiliation or Control: Proprietary IRS Status: Proprietary
Highest Offering: Doctorate
Program: Professional; Technical Emphasis
Accreditation: &NH

01 President .... Dr. Mark PIEFFER
05 Director of Education .... Dr. Bruce PETRIE
37 Director of Financial Aid .... Ms. Terry BARGAS
07 Director of Admissions .... Vacant

† Regional accreditation is carried under the parent institution in Colorado Springs, CO.

Colorado Technical University (J)

4435 N Chestnut Street, Colorado Springs CO 80907-3896

County: El Paso FICE Identification: 010148
Unit ID: 126827
Telephone: (719) 598-0200 Carnegie Class: DRU
FAX Number: (719) 598-3740 Calendar System: Quarter
URL: www.coloradotech.edu
Established: 1965 Annual Undergrad Tuition & Fees: $10,665
Enrollment: 3,020 Coed
Affiliation or Control: Proprietary IRS Status: Proprietary
Highest Offering: Doctorate
Program: Occupational; 2-Year Principally Bachelor's Creditable; Professional; Technical Emphasis
Accreditation: NH, ENG

00 Interim CEO .... Mr. Jack KOEHN
01 Campus President .... Mr. Tim GRAMLING
07 Vice President of Admissions .... Ms. Beth BRAATEN
10 Regional Director of Operations .... Mr. Jeremy WALKER
08 Dir of University Libraries .... Ms. Joanna PRIMUS
37 Dir of Student Financial Services .... Ms. Cindy RUBEK
36 Director of Career Services .... Mr. Jason RAMSEY
13 Manager of Information Systems .... Mr. Thomas LEIGH
54 Dean Engineering/Computer Science .... Dr. Bruce HARMON

Community College of Aurora (K)

16000 E Centre Tech Parkway, Aurora CO 80011-9036

County: Arapahoe FICE Identification: 022769
Unit ID: 126863
Telephone: (303) 360-4700 Carnegie Class: Assoc/Pub-S-MC

FAX Number: (303) 360-4761 Calendar System: Semester
URL: www.ccaurora.edu
Established: 1983 Annual Undergrad Tuition & Fees (In-State): $4,000
Enrollment: 7,842 Coed
Affiliation or Control: State IRS Status: 501(c)3
Highest Offering: Associate Degree
Program: Occupational; 2-Year Principally Bachelor's Creditable
Accreditation: NH, EMT

01 President ... Mr. Alton D. SCALES
05 Vice President Instruction ... Ms. Xeturah WOODLEY
11 Vice Pres Administrative Services ... Mr. Richard MAESTAS
84 VP Enrollment Mgmt/Student Services ... Dr. Elizabeth OUDENHOVEN
07 Director Admissions & Registrar ... Ms. Kristen CUSACK
21 Controller ... Ms. Mercy ABRAHAM
15 Director of Human Resources ... Ms. Cindy HESSE
08 Director Library Services ... Ms. Megan KINNEY
13 Director Information Technology ... Vacant
37 Director Financial Aid and Advising ... Mr. John YOUNG
32 Director Student Life ... Ms. Angie TIEDEMAN
27 Director College Communications ... Ms. Liz VANLANDINGHAM
09 Director of Institutional Research ... Dr. David BAILEY
18 Facilities Manager ... Mr. Jim MARSHALL
25 Coordinator of Grants & Funding ... Dr. Chris WARD

Community College of Denver (A)

Campus Box 250 P.O. Box 173363,
Denver CO 80217-3363
County: Denver FICE Identification: 009542
Unit ID: 126942
Telephone: (303) 556-2400 Carnegie Class: Assoc/Pub-U-MC
FAX Number: (303) 556-8555 Calendar System: Semester
URL: www.ccd.edu
Established: 1967 Annual Undergrad Tuition & Fees (In-State): $4,028
Enrollment: 8,900 Coed
Affiliation or Control: State IRS Status: 501(c)3
Highest Offering: Associate Degree
Program: Occupational; 2-Year Principally Bachelor's Creditable
Accreditation: NH, DH, MAC, RAD

01 Interim President ... Mr. Cliff RICHARDSON
05 Provost/Vice Pres Learning ... Dr. Bernice HARRIS
10 Vice Pres Finance & Admin/CFO ... Mr. Duane RISSE
32 Vice Pres Student Development ... Ms. Leslie MCCLELLON
102 Vice Pres Economic/Resource Devel ... Vacant
75 Dean Career/Technical Education ... Dr. Chris BUDDEN
49 Dean Language/Arts/Behavioral Sci ... Dr. Amy RELL
88 Dean Educational Advancement ... Ms. Nancy STORY
35 Dean of Students/Ed Plng/Advising ... Mr. Ryan ROSS
84 Dean of Enrollment Svcs/Registrar ... Ms. Lori KESTER
35 Director Office of Student Life ... Vacant
37 Director Financial Aid ... Mr. Thad SPAULDING
07 Director Recruit/Student Outreach ... Mr. Ari Senghor ROSNER-SALAZAR
15 Director Human Resources ... Ms. Rhonda PYLICAN
13 Executive Director IT Services ... Mr. Andy CORBETT
09 Exec Dir Inst Research & Planning ... Ms. Margaret PURYEAR

Concorde Career College (B)

111 N Havana Street, Aurora CO 80010-4314
County: Arapahoe FICE Identification: 008871
Unit ID: 126687
Telephone: (303) 861-1151 Carnegie Class: Assoc/PrivFP
FAX Number: (303) 839-5478 Calendar System: Other
URL: www.concorde.edu
Established: 1969 Annual Undergrad Tuition & Fees: $28,767
Enrollment: 795 Coed
Affiliation or Control: Proprietary IRS Status: Proprietary
Highest Offering: Associate Degree
Program: Occupational
Accreditation: ACCSC, @PTAA, RAD, SURGT

01 Campus President ... Vacant
05 Academic Dean ... Ms. Cindy COBB
37 Director of Financial Aid ... Ms. Nancy DISATE
07 Director of Admissions ... Mr. Shebon KELIN

Denver School of Nursing (C)

1401 19th Street, Denver CO 80202
County: Denver FICE Identification: 041483
Unit ID: 454856
Telephone: (303) 292-0015 Carnegie Class: Spec/Health
FAX Number: (720) 974-0290 Calendar System: Quarter
URL: www.denverschoolofnursing.edu
Established: 2003 Annual Undergrad Tuition & Fees: $51,254
Enrollment: 638 Coed
Affiliation or Control: Proprietary IRS Status: Proprietary
Highest Offering: Baccalaureate
Program: Nursing Emphasis
Accreditation: @NH, ACCSC, ADNUR, NUR

01 President ... Dr. Marcia BANKIRER
05 Director of Business Operations ... Ms. Renee MCMILLIN
32 Director of Student Services ... Mr. Michael RUSCHIVAL
66 Dean/Dir of Nursing Education Pgms ... Dr. Shelley MORISTON

Denver Seminary (D)

6399 S Santa Fe Drive, Littleton CO 80120-2912
County: Arapahoe FICE Identification: 001352
Unit ID: 126979
Telephone: (303) 761-2482 Carnegie Class: Spec/Faith
FAX Number: (303) 761-8060 Calendar System: Semester
URL: www.denverseminary.edu
Established: 1950 Annual Graduate Tuition & Fees: $14,550
Enrollment: 1,018 Coed
Affiliation or Control: Interdenominational IRS Status: 501(c)3
Highest Offering: Doctorate; No Undergraduates
Program: Professional; Religious Emphasis
Accreditation: NH, CACREP, THEOL

01 President ... Dr. Mark S. YOUNG
00 Chancellor ... Dr. Gordon MACDONALD
05 Provost/Dean ... Dr. Randolph M. MACFARLAND
10 Vice President of Finance ... Ms. Deborah KELLAR
30 Vice President of Advancement ... Dr. Jim HOWARD
32 Vice President of Student Services ... Mr. Robert JONES
20 Associate Academic Dean ... Dr. W. David BUSCHART
20 Associate Academic Dean ... Dr. Don PAYNE
06 Registrar/Dir Educ Services ... Ms. Pam BETKER
35 Dean of Student Services ... Vacant
07 Director of Admissions ... Ms. Christine MULLER
44 Director of Development ... Mr. Chris JOHNSON
40 Director of Auxiliary Services ... Mr. Kent B. QUACKENBUSH
13 Director of Information Systems ... Mr. Jason ADAMS
27 Director of Communications ... Ms. Pam BURTON
88 Dir Educational Technology ... Dr. Venita DOUGHTY
88 Dir Educational Projects ... Mrs. Lisa LINHART
18 Director of Physical Plant ... Vacant
37 Director of Financial Aid ... Mr. Joel LAOS
08 Director of Library ... Dr. Keith P. WELLS
73 Director of DMin Program ... Dr. David R. OSBORN
21 Director of Financial Services ... Mrs. Kristy EDLUND
15 Director of Human Resources ... Ms. Zandy WENNERSTROM

DeVry University - Colorado Springs Center (E)

1175 Kelly Johnson Boulevard,
Colorado Springs CO 80920-3928
County: El Paso Identification: 666511
Unit ID: 363378
Telephone: (719) 632-3000 Carnegie Class: Not Classified
FAX Number: (719) 866-6770 Calendar System: Semester
URL: www.devry.edu
Established: 2001 Annual Undergrad Tuition & Fees: $16,156
Enrollment: 452 Coed
Affiliation or Control: Proprietary IRS Status: Proprietary
Highest Offering: Master's
Program: Occupational; Professional; Business Emphasis
Accreditation: &NH

01 Center Dean ... Judy LESSER

† Regional accreditation is carried under the parent institution in Downers Grove, IL.

DeVry University - Denver South Center (F)

6312 S Fiddlers Green Circle #150E,
Greenwood Village CO 80111-4943
County: Arapahoe FICE Identification: 007648
Unit ID: 127042
Telephone: (303) 329-3000 Carnegie Class: Not Classified
FAX Number: (303) 329-4486 Calendar System: Semester
URL: www.devry.edu
Established: 2001 Annual Undergrad Tuition & Fees: $16,156
Enrollment: 283 Coed
Affiliation or Control: Proprietary IRS Status: Proprietary
Highest Offering: Master's
Program: Occupational; Professional; Business Emphasis
Accreditation: &NH

01 Center Dean ... Vacant

† Regional accreditation is carried under the parent institution in Downers Grove, IL.

DeVry University - Westminster Campus (G)

1870 W 122nd Avenue, Westminster CO 80234-2010
County: Adams Identification: 666227
Unit ID: 440590
Telephone: (303) 280-7400 Carnegie Class: Master's S
FAX Number: (303) 452-3606 Calendar System: Semester
URL: www.devry.edu
Established: 1931 Annual Undergrad Tuition & Fees: $16,156
Enrollment: 935 Coed
Affiliation or Control: Proprietary IRS Status: Proprietary
Highest Offering: Master's
Program: Occupational; Professional; Business Emphasis
Accreditation: &NH, ENGT

01 Metro President ... Mr. James CALDWELL
06 Registrar ... Ms. Lisa BARRY
10 Director of Finance and Admin ... Mr. Cliff DEFFKE
07 Director of Admissions ... Mr. Joseph OLIVER
05 Dean of Academic Affairs ... Mr. Martin GLOEGE
15 Human Resources Business Partner ... Mr. Daryl SMITH
32 Director Student Central ... Ms. Loriann WEISS
36 Director of Career Services ... Ms. Laurie DRESSEL

† Regional accreditation is carried under the parent institution in Downers Grove, IL.

Everest College (H)

14280 E Jewell Avenue, Suite 100, Aurora CO 80012
County: Arapahoe Identification: 666412
Unit ID: 366544
Telephone: (303) 745-6244 Carnegie Class: Assoc/PrivFP
FAX Number: (303) 745-6245 Calendar System: Other
URL: www.everest.edu
Established: 1895 Annual Undergrad Tuition & Fees: $17,216
Enrollment: 485 Coed
Affiliation or Control: Proprietary IRS Status: Proprietary
Highest Offering: Associate Degree
Program: Occupational
Accreditation: ACICS, MAC

01 President ... Ms. Carissa BARTON

† Branch campus of Everest College, Denver, CO.

Everest College (I)

1815 Jet Wing Drive, Colorado Springs CO 80916
County: El Paso FICE Identification: 004503
Unit ID: 126401
Telephone: (719) 638-6580 Carnegie Class: Assoc/PrivFP
FAX Number: (719) 638-6818 Calendar System: Quarter
URL: www.everest-college.com
Established: 1897 Annual Undergrad Tuition & Fees: $14,271
Enrollment: 498 Coed
Affiliation or Control: Proprietary IRS Status: Proprietary
Highest Offering: Associate Degree
Program: Occupational; 2-Year Principally Bachelor's Creditable
Accreditation: ACICS, MAC

01 President ... Mr. Robert LANTZY
05 Dean of Education ... Ms. Heidi GODBOLD
07 Director Admissions ... Mr. Dan NOEL
37 Director Student Finance ... Ms. Carrie IVERSON
36 Director Career Services ... Mr. James PROBY

Everest College (J)

9065 Grant Street, Denver CO 80229-4339
County: Adams FICE Identification: 004507
Unit ID: 127787
Telephone: (303) 457-2757 Carnegie Class: Assoc/PrivFP
FAX Number: (303) 457-4030 Calendar System: Quarter
URL: www.cci.edu
Established: 1895 Annual Undergrad Tuition & Fees: $15,660
Enrollment: 460 Coed
Affiliation or Control: Proprietary IRS Status: Proprietary
Highest Offering: Associate Degree
Program: Occupational
Accreditation: ACICS, MAC, #SURGT

01 President ... Ms. Pat SCHLOTTER
05 Academic Dean ... Mr. Raines GUINN
07 Director of Admissions ... Ms. Jennifer HEDRICK
37 Director of Student Finance ... Ms. Kim MARTINEZ
36 Director of Career Services ... Ms. Diane BOOREN
06 Registrar ... Mr. Bruce DOUGHTY

Fort Lewis College (K)

1000 Rim Drive, Durango CO 81301-3999
County: La Plata FICE Identification: 001353
Unit ID: 127185
Telephone: (970) 247-7010 Carnegie Class: Bac/A&S
FAX Number: (970) 247-7175 Calendar System: Semester
URL: www.fortlewis.edu
Established: 1911 Annual Undergrad Tuition & Fees (In-State): $6,462
Enrollment: 3,841 Coed
Affiliation or Control: State IRS Status: 170(c)1
Highest Offering: Baccalaureate
Program: Liberal Arts And General; Teacher Preparatory
Accreditation: NH, BUS, ENG, MUS, TEAC

01 President ... Dr. Dene Kay THOMAS
05 Provost/Vice Pres Academic Affairs ... Dr. Barbara MORRIS
10 Vice Pres Finance & Administration ... Mr. Steven J. SCHWARTZ
84 Assoc Vice Pres Enrollment Mgmt ... Dr. Carol SMITH
32 Vice President Student Affairs ... Dr. Glenna W. SEXTON
20 Assoc Vice Pres Academic Affairs ... Dr. Kenneth PEPION
09 Exec Dir of Institutional Research ... Mr. Richard A. MILLER
21 Director Budget ... Ms. Michele PETERSON
06 Registrar ... Ms. Kathy KENDALL
21 Controller ... Ms. Cheryl WIESCAMP
25 Director of Grants Management ... Ms. Angela ROCHAT
37 Interim Director Financial Aid ... Mr. Conrad L. CHAVEZ
07 Director of Admission ... Mr. Andrew BURNS

38 Int Dir Counseling/Student Dev Ctr .... Ms. Karen NAKAYAMA
08 Director of the Library .... Ms. Astrid OLIVER
18 Dir Physical Plant/College Engr .... Mr. Wayne KJONAAS
15 Dir Human Resources/Equal Opptnty .... Mr. Darren MATHEWS
39 Dir Stdnt Housing/Conferences Svcs .... Ms. Julie N. LOVE
41 Athletic Director .... Mr. Gary HUNTER
13 Director Computing & Telecomm .... Mr. Matt MCGLAMERY
83 Dean Sch Natural & Behavioral Sci .... Dr. Maureen BRANDON
50 Dean School of Business Admin .... Dr. Doug LYON
49 Ast Dean School Arts/Hum/Social Sci .... Ms. Bridget IRISH
28 Coord Equal Opport/Judicial Affs .... Dr. Haeryon KIM
29 Director Alumni Relations .... Mr. Ross NELSON
96 Director of Purchasing .... Mr. Wayne J. HERMES
40 Bookstore Manager .... Ms. Brooke INGLE

Front Range Community College (A)

3645 W 112th Avenue, Westminster CO 80031-2105

County: Adams FICE Identification: 007933
Unit ID: 127200

Telephone: (303) 404-5000 Carnegie Class: Assoc/Pub-S-MC
FAX Number: (303) 466-1623 Calendar System: Semester
URL: www.frontrange.edu
Established: 1968 Annual Undergrad Tuition & Fees (In-State): $2,962
Enrollment: 20,568 Coed
Affiliation or Control: State IRS Status: 501(c)3
Highest Offering: Associate Degree
Program: Occupational; 2-Year Principally Bachelor's Creditable
Accreditation: NH, ADNUR, DA, MAC, PNUR

01 President .... Mr. Andrew R. DORSEY
04 Asst to the President .... Ms. Kimberly STEFANSKI
10 Vice Pres Finance & Administration .... Ms. Jennifer SOBANET
05 Chief Academic Officer .... Dr. Sandra VELTRI
21 Controller .... Ms. Acqunetta LIKKEL
21 Director of Budget & Contracts .... Ms. Stephanie MORAN
12 Vice Pres Westminster Camp .... Ms. Therese BROWN
12 Vice Pres Larimer Campus .... Mr. Bruce WALTHERS
12 Vice Pres Boulder County Campus .... Dr. Linda CURRAN
06 Registrar .... Ms. Yolanda ESPINOZA
72 Dean of Career Technical Ed .... Vacant
106 Dean of OnLine Learning .... Ms. Tammy VERCAUTEREN
88 Dean of Transfer Education .... Ms. Lisa DONALDSON
20 Dean of Instruction Larimer .... Vacant
20 Dean of Instruction Boulder County .... Mr. Matt JAMISON
20 Dean of Instruction Westminster .... Ms. Catherine PELLISH
84 Assoc VP Enroll Mgmt & Student Svcs .... Dr. Kris BINARD
32 Dean of Student Svcs Boulder County .... Ms. Carla STEIN
32 Dean of Student Svcs Westminister .... Ms. Renee TASTAD
88 Dean/Exec Dir of Secondary Programs .... Dr. Phyllis ABT
16 Exec Director of Human Resources .... Mr. Paul MEESE
09 Director of Institutional Research .... Ms. Kim WALLACE
37 Dir of Financial Aid Campus Wide .... Ms. Carolee GOLDSMITH
08 Director of Library Services .... Vacant
18 Director of Facilities Westminster .... Mr. Patrick O'NEILL
18 Director of Facilities Larimer .... Mr. Scott MCKELVEY
35 Director Student Life Westminister .... Ms. Amy ROSDIL
35 Director Student Life Larimer .... Ms. Mary BRANTON-HOUSLEY
35 Dir Student Life Boulder County .... Ms. Amanda CLANCY
102 Director of Foundation .... Mr. Chuck CROWE
26 Dir of Marketing & Communications .... Ms. Marian MAHARAS
27 Public Information Officer .... Mr. John FEELEY
13 Director of Information Technology .... Ms. Janet WAGGONER
40 Director of Auxiliary Services .... Mr. Wes GEARY

Heritage College (B)

12 Lakeside Lane, Denver CO 80212-7413

County: Jefferson FICE Identification: 026110
Unit ID: 262509

Telephone: (303) 477-7240 Carnegie Class: Assoc/PrivFP
FAX Number: (303) 477-7276 Calendar System: Other
URL: www.heritage-education.com
Established: 1986 Annual Undergrad Tuition & Fees: $24,875
Enrollment: 622 Coed
Affiliation or Control: Proprietary IRS Status: Proprietary
Highest Offering: Associate Degree
Program: Occupational
Accreditation: ABHES

01 College Director Denver .... Jennifer SPRAGUE
03 President of Residential Schools .... Richard K. SHEPARD
05 Director of Education .... Kai STONE
07 Director of Admissions .... Elyse SCHMINKE
06 Registrar .... Julia WILLIAMS
36 Director of Career Services .... Michelle TYMOCZKO
37 Director of Financial Aid .... Anne RUSK
11 Senior Vice President .... Shannon BEELER
22 Director of Compliance .... Bill PASCHALL

Holmes Institute of Consciousness Studies (C)

573 Park Point Drive, Golden CO 80401

County: Jefferson Identification: 666255
Telephone: (720) 496-1370 Carnegie Class: Not Classified
FAX Number: (303) 526-0913 Calendar System: Quarter
URL: www.holmesinstitute.org
Established: 1972 Annual Graduate Tuition & Fees: $21,000
Enrollment: 100 Coed
Affiliation or Control: Other IRS Status: 501(c)3
Highest Offering: Master's; No Undergraduates
Program: Religious Emphasis
Accreditation: DETC

01 Dir of HICS/Dir of Education .... Rev Dr. Lynn CONNOLLY
06 Registrar .... Ms. Maureen THURSTON

Iliff School of Theology (D)

2201 S University Boulevard, Denver CO 80210-4798

County: Denver FICE Identification: 001354
Unit ID: 127273

Telephone: (303) 744-1287 Carnegie Class: Spec/Faith
FAX Number: (303) 777-3387 Calendar System: Quarter
URL: www.iliff.edu
Established: 1892 Annual Graduate Tuition & Fees: $16,920
Enrollment: 361 Coed
Affiliation or Control: United Methodist IRS Status: 501(c)3
Highest Offering: Doctorate; No Undergraduates
Program: Professional; Religious Emphasis
Accreditation: NH, THEOL

01 President .... Dr. David G H. TRICKETT
05 Vice Pres/Dean Academic Affairs .... Dr. Albert HERNANDEZ
10 Vice President for Business Affairs .... Ms. Kelly L. MCCORMICK
30 VP of Institutional Advancement .... Ms. Peggy SANDGREN
26 VP of Marketing Communications .... Ms. Greta GLOVEN
32 Dean Enrollment & Student Services .... Mr. David WORLEY
06 Registrar .... Ms. Carmen E. DOSTER
08 Director Library & Information Svcs .... Dr. Deborah CREAMER
07 Director Admission/Financial Aid .... Ms. Peggy J. BLOCKER
28 Associate Dean of Diversities .... Dr. Edward ANTONIO

Institute of Business and Medical Careers (E)

3842 South Mason Street, Fort Collins CO 80526

County: Larimer FICE Identification: 030063
Unit ID: 372329

Telephone: (970) 223-2669 Carnegie Class: Assoc/PrivFP
FAX Number: (970) 223-2796 Calendar System: Quarter
URL: www.ibmc.edu
Established: 1987 Annual Undergrad Tuition & Fees: $14,250
Enrollment: 305 Coed
Affiliation or Control: Proprietary IRS Status: Proprietary
Highest Offering: Associate Degree
Program: Occupational
Accreditation: ACICS

00 CEO .... Mr. Richard LAUB
01 President .... Mr. Steven STEELE

Institute of Taoist Education and Acupuncture (F)

325 West South Boulder Road, Ste 2, Louisville CO 80027

County: Boulder FICE Identification: 041212
Unit ID: 454838

Telephone: (720) 890-8922 Carnegie Class: Spec/Health
FAX Number: (720) 890-7719 Calendar System: Other
URL: www.itea.edu
Established: 1996 Annual Graduate Tuition & Fees: $18,500
Enrollment: 36 Coed
Affiliation or Control: Independent Non-Profit IRS Status: 501(c)3
Highest Offering: Master's; No Undergraduates
Program: Professional
Accreditation: ACUP

01 President .... Sandra LILLIE
05 Director .... Hilary SKELLON
06 Registrar .... Claudia O'NIELL
10 Financial Administrator .... Angela SMITH

IntelliTec College (G)

2315 E Pikes Peak Avenue, Colorado Springs CO 80909-6096

County: El Paso FICE Identification: 022537
Unit ID: 128179

Telephone: (719) 632-7626 Carnegie Class: Assoc/PrivFP
FAX Number: (719) 632-7451 Calendar System: Quarter
URL: www.intelliteccollege.com
Established: 1965 Annual Undergrad Tuition & Fees: $19,700
Enrollment: 580 Coed
Affiliation or Control: Proprietary IRS Status: Proprietary
Highest Offering: Associate Degree
Program: Occupational
Accreditation: ACCSC

01 COO/Executive Director .... Mr. Edwin KRAUS
06 Registrar .... Ms. Tammy ALESH

IntelliTec College (H)

772 Horizon Drive, Grand Junction CO 81506-3994

County: Mesa FICE Identification: 030669
Unit ID: 128188

Telephone: (970) 245-8101 Carnegie Class: Assoc/PrivFP
FAX Number: (970) 243-8074 Calendar System: Quarter
URL: www.intelliteccollege.edu
Established: 1984 Annual Undergrad Tuition & Fees: $21,840
Enrollment: 350 Coed
Affiliation or Control: Proprietary IRS Status: Proprietary
Highest Offering: Associate Degree
Program: Occupational
Accreditation: ACCSC

01 President .... Mr. Michael SCHRANZ
05 Director .... Mr. Mike GROVES

IntelliTec College (I)

3673 Parker Boulevard, Suite 250, Pueblo CO 81008-2211

County: Pueblo Identification: 666366
Telephone: (719) 542-3181 Carnegie Class: Not Classified
FAX Number: (719) 242-6686 Calendar System: Other
URL: www.intelliteccollege.com
Established: 2004 Annual Undergrad Tuition & Fees: $11,343
Enrollment: 225 Coed
Affiliation or Control: Proprietary IRS Status: Proprietary
Highest Offering: Associate Degree
Program: Occupational; Technical Emphasis
Accreditation: ACCSC

01 President .... Mr. Michael V. SCHRANZ
12 Director .... Mr. Andreas NILSSON

IntelliTec Medical Institute (J)

6805 Corporate Drive, Suite 100, Colorado Springs CO 80919

County: El Paso FICE Identification: 008635
Unit ID: 127839

Telephone: (719) 596-7400 Carnegie Class: Assoc/PrivFP
FAX Number: (719) 596-2464 Calendar System: Other
URL: www.intellitecmedical.edu
Established: 1966 Annual Undergrad Tuition & Fees: $21,849
Enrollment: 478 Coed
Affiliation or Control: Proprietary IRS Status: Proprietary
Highest Offering: Associate Degree
Program: Occupational
Accreditation: ABHES, DA

01 Campus Director .... Mr. Todd MATTHEWS

ITT Technical Institute (K)

500 E 84th Avenue, Suite B12, Thornton CO 80229-5338

County: Arapahoe FICE Identification: 023217
Unit ID: 244154

Telephone: (303) 288-4488 Carnegie Class: Spec/Tech
FAX Number: (303) 288-8166 Calendar System: Quarter
URL: www.itt-tech.edu
Established: 1984 Annual Undergrad Tuition & Fees: N/A
Enrollment: 568 Coed
Affiliation or Control: Proprietary IRS Status: Proprietary
Highest Offering: Baccalaureate
Program: Technical Emphasis
Accreditation: ACICS

† Branch campus of ITT Technical Institute, Indianapolis, IN.

Johnson & Wales University - Denver Campus (L)

7150 Montview Boulevard, Denver CO 80220-1866

County: Denver Identification: 666411
Unit ID: 439288

Telephone: (303) 256-9300 Carnegie Class: Bac/Assoc
FAX Number: (303) 256-9333 Calendar System: Quarter
URL: www.jwu.edu/denver
Established: 2000 Annual Undergrad Tuition & Fees: $26,112
Enrollment: 1,672 Coed
Affiliation or Control: Independent Non-Profit IRS Status: 501(c)3
Highest Offering: Baccalaureate
Program: Occupational; 2-Year Principally Bachelor's Creditable
Accreditation: &EH, DIETD

01 President .... Ms. Robin KRAKOWSKY
05 VP and Dean of Academic Affairs .... Dr. Richard WISCOTT
32 Dean of Students .... Mr. Jeff EDERER
20 Associate Dean of Academic Affairs .... Mr. Antonio BARREIRO
30 Asst Dir Devel/Scholarship/Advance .... Ms. Kara JOHNSTON
11 Director of Operations .... Mr. JD SAWYER
07 Director of Admissions .... Ms. Kim MEDINA
06 Dir of Student Acad & Financial Svc .... Ms. Kimberly BUXTON-HAMEL
35 Director Student Affairs .... Ms. Denise KUPETZ
36 Dir Experiential Educ/Career Svcs .... Ms. Laura DEAN
26 Dir Public Relations/Cmty Affairs .... Ms. Lindsay TRACY
15 Human Resources Representative .... Ms. Rodena BARR
41 Athletic Director .... Mr. Jeff CULVER
88 Dean of Culinary Education .... Mr. Jorge DE LA TORRE
88 Dean of Experiential Education .... Dr. Gregory F. LORENZE

† Regional accreditation is carried under the parent institution in Providence, RI.

Jones International University (M)

9697 E Mineral Avenue, Centennial CO 80112-3408

County: Arapahoe FICE Identification: 035343
Unit ID: 444723

Telephone: (800) 811-5663 Carnegie Class: Master's L
FAX Number: (303) 799-0966 Calendar System: Other

URL: www.jiu.edu
Established: 1993 Annual Undergrad Tuition & Fees: $12,720
Enrollment: 4,508 Coed
Affiliation or Control: Proprietary IRS Status: Proprietary
Highest Offering: Doctorate
Program: Teacher Preparatory; Professional; Business Emphasis
Accreditation: NH

01 President ... Mr. Richard COX, JR.
05 Chief Academic Officer ... Dr. Marijane AXTELL PAULSEN
10 Chief Financial Officer ... Ms. Christine SPATH
50 Dean School of Business ... Dr. Danette LANCE
53 Dean School of Education ... Dr. Joanne MAYPOLE

Kaplan College (A)

500 E 84th Avenue, Suite W200,
Thornton CO 80229-5316
County: Adams FICE Identification: 021676
Unit ID: 381796
Telephone: (303) 295-0550 Carnegie Class: Assoc/PrivFP
FAX Number: (303) 295-0102 Calendar System: Quarter
URL: www.kaplancollege.com
Established: 1977 Annual Undergrad Tuition & Fees: $14,706
Enrollment: 184 Coed
Affiliation or Control: Proprietary IRS Status: Proprietary
Highest Offering: Associate Degree
Program: Occupational
Accreditation: ACCSC

01 Executive Director ... Ms. Shannon ERICKSON

Lamar Community College (B)

2401 S Main, Lamar CO 81052-3999
County: Prowers FICE Identification: 001355
Unit ID: 127389
Telephone: (719) 336-2248 Carnegie Class: Assoc/Pub-R-S
FAX Number: (719) 336-2448 Calendar System: Semester
URL: www.lamarcc.edu
Established: 1937 Annual Undergrad Tuition & Fees (In-State): $4,511
Enrollment: 935 Coed
Affiliation or Control: State IRS Status: 501(c)3
Highest Offering: Associate Degree
Program: Occupational; 2-Year Principally Bachelor's Creditable
Accreditation: NH, ADNUR

01 President ... Mr. John MARRIN
05 VP Academic Services/Student Svcs ... Mrs. Cheryl SANCHEZ
11 VP Admin Svcs/Institutional Rsrch ... Mr. Chad DE BONO
20 Dean of Academic Services ... Mr. Curtis TURNER
26 Director of Communication ... Mrs. Anne-Marie CRAMPTON
06 Registrar ... Mrs. Amber THOMPSON
08 Library Tech ... Ms. Ellen LOVELL
18 Director of Facilities ... Mr. Sean LIRLEY
15 Director Personnel Services ... Ms. Gwen GRUENLOH
39 Director Student Housing ... Mr. Chad DEBONO
38 Director Student Counseling ... Ms. Deanna SIEMSEN
96 Director of Purchasing ... Mrs. Ava BAIR
40 Director Bookstore ... Mrs. Sheila DIETERLE
41 Athletic Director ... Mr. Craig BROOKS
37 Director Financial Aid ... Mrs. Teale HEMPHILL
07 Director of Admissions ... Mrs. Jenna DAVIS
09 Coordinator Institutional Research ... Mrs. Kim WALLACE

Lincoln College of Technology (C)

11194 East 45th Avenue, Denver CO 80239
County: Denver FICE Identification: 007547
Unit ID: 126951
Telephone: (303) 722-5724 Carnegie Class: Assoc/PrivFP
FAX Number: (303) 778-8264 Calendar System: Other
URL: www.lincolnedu.com
Established: 1963 Annual Undergrad Tuition & Fees: N/A
Enrollment: 1,195 Coed
Affiliation or Control: Proprietary IRS Status: Proprietary
Highest Offering: Associate Degree
Program: Occupational
Accreditation: ACCSC

01 Executive Director ... Mr. Al SHORT
07 Director Admissions ... Ms. Jennifer HASH
05 Director of Education ... Mr. Ted HRDLICKA

McKinley College (D)

2001 Lowe Street, Fort Collins CO 80525-3474
County: Larimer Identification: 666237
Telephone: (970) 207-4550 Carnegie Class: Not Classified
FAX Number: (877) 599-5863 Calendar System: Other
URL: www.mckinleycollege.edu
Established: 2004 Annual Undergrad Tuition & Fees: $3,100
Enrollment: N/A Coed
Affiliation or Control: Proprietary IRS Status: Proprietary
Highest Offering: Associate Degree
Program: Occupational; 2-Year Principally Bachelor's Creditable
Accreditation: DETC

01 President ... Ann ROHR

Memorial Hospital/Memorial Health System School of Radiologic Technology (E)

1400 East Boulder Street, Colorado Springs CO 80909
County: El Paso Identification: 667097
Telephone: (719) 365-8291 Carnegie Class: Not Classified
FAX Number: N/A Calendar System: Semester
URL: www.memorialhealthsystem.com
Established: 1969 Annual Undergrad Tuition & Fees: $5,000
Enrollment: 36 Coed
Affiliation or Control: Independent Non-Profit IRS Status: 501(c)3
Highest Offering: Associate Degree
Program: Occupational
Accreditation: RAD

01 Director ... Elaine R. IVAN

Metropolitan State University of Denver (F)

PO Box 173362, Denver CO 80217-3362
County: Denver FICE Identification: 001360
Unit ID: 127565
Telephone: (303) 556-3022 Carnegie Class: Bac/Diverse
FAX Number: (303) 556-3912 Calendar System: Semester
URL: www.msudenver.edu
Established: 1963 Annual Undergrad Tuition & Fees (In-State): $5,337
Enrollment: 23,538 Coed
Affiliation or Control: State IRS Status: 501(c)3
Highest Offering: Master's
Program: Liberal Arts And General; Teacher Preparatory; Professional
Accreditation: NH, ART, CS, DIETD, ENGT, EXSC, IPSY, MT, MUS, NRPA, NUR, SW, TED, THEA

01 President ... Dr. Stephen M. JORDAN
04 Exec Asst to President ... Ms. Mary Lou LAWRENCE
05 Vice President Academic Affairs ... Dr. Vicki GOLICH
10 Vice Pres Administration Finance ... Ms. Natalie LUTES
30 Vice Pres Advancement/External Rela ... Dr. Erin TRAPP
20 Deputy Provost Academic Affairs ... Dr. Luis TORRES
43 Gen Counsel/Sec to Board ... Ms. Loretta P. MARTINEZ
102 Assoc VP External Relations/Advanc ... Mr. Gregory J. GEISSLER
88 Assoc VP Academic Centers/ Programs ... Dr. Maurice F. HAMINGTON
27 Assoc VP/CIO ... Dr. James LYALL
20 Assoc VP for Academic Affairs ... Dr. Sheila THOMPSON
15 Assoc VP & Director Human Resources ... Ms. Judith L. ZEWE
84 Assoc VP for Enrollment Services ... Mrs. Judi DIAZ-BONACQUISTI
21 Assoc VP Admin & Finance ... Mr. George M. MIDDLEMIST
13 Assoc VP & CTO ... Ms. Joan ZERKOVICH
26 Assoc to Pres/Marketing & Comm ... Ms. Catherine LUCAS
29 Director of Alumni Relations ... Mr. Mark JASTORFF
50 Dean School Business ... Dr. Ann B. MURPHY
107 Dean School Professional Studies ... Dr. Sandra HAYNES
49 Dean School Letters/Arts/Science ... Dr. Joan L. FOSTER
35 Dean Student Life ... Ms. Emilia PAUL
22 Exec Director EEO/Asst to President ... Dr. Percy A. MOREHOUSE, JR.
09 Dir Sponsored Research/Programs ... Ms. Gwendolyn MAMI
56 Director of Extended Education ... Ms. Carol SVENDSEN
06 Registrar ... Ms. Paula MARTINEZ
37 Director Financial Aid ... Ms. Cindy HEJL
38 Director Counseling Center ... Dr. Gail BRUCE-SANFORD
41 Athletic Director ... Ms. Joan MCDERMOTT
35 Director Student Activities ... Ms. Angela LEVALLEY
36 Director Career Services ... Ms. Bridgette COBLE
28 Assoc to Pres Inst Diversity ... Dr. Myron ANDERSON

Morgan Community College (G)

920 Barlow Road, Fort Morgan CO 80701-4399
County: Morgan FICE Identification: 009981
Unit ID: 127617
Telephone: (970) 542-3100 Carnegie Class: Assoc/Pub-R-M
FAX Number: (970) 542-3115 Calendar System: Semester
URL: www.morgancc.edu
Established: 1967 Annual Undergrad Tuition & Fees (In-State): $2,962
Enrollment: 1,885 Coed
Affiliation or Control: State IRS Status: Exempt
Highest Offering: Associate Degree
Program: Occupational; 2-Year Principally Bachelor's Creditable
Accreditation: NH, ADNUR, PTAA

01 President ... Dr. Kerry HART
10 Vice Pres Finance/Admin Services ... Ms. Susan CLOUGH
05 Vice President of Instruction ... Ms. Betty MCKIE
84 Vice President of Student Success ... Mr. Kent BAUER
04 Assistant to the President ... Ms. Jane FRIES
12 Center Director ... Ms. Mary ANDERSEN
12 Center Director ... Ms. Nancy BARDEN
12 Center Director ... Ms. Kellie OVERTURF
12 Center Director ... Ms. Valerie RHOADES
09 Dir of Institutional Effectiveness ... Mr. Derek GRUBB
26 Dir of Communications & Marketing ... Ms. Katie BARRON
30 Dir Community Relations/Development ... Mr. David WILLARD
37 Director of Financial Aid ... Ms. Sally NESTOR
07 Director of Admissions ... Ms. Kim MAXWELL
15 Director of Personnel Services ... Vacant
08 Director of Learning Resources ... Ms. April AMACK
96 Director of Purchasing ... Ms. Julie BEYDLER
40 Director of Bookstore ... Ms. Anita ERTLE
18 Coordinator of M & O ... Mr. Seth NOBLE
36 Voc Guidance/Placement Counselor ... Mr. Dan MARLER
14 Director Information Technology ... Mr. Michael SHRIVER
66 Div Chr Hlth Occup/Dir Nursing Educ ... Ms. Kathy FRISBIE
49 Division Chair Arts & Sciences ... Mr. Todd SCHNEIDER
50 Division Chair Business ... Ms. Jaylene EVANS

Naropa University (H)

2130 Arapahoe Avenue, Boulder CO 80302-6697
County: Boulder FICE Identification: 021175
Unit ID: 127653
Telephone: (303) 444-0202 Carnegie Class: Master's L
FAX Number: (303) 444-0410 Calendar System: Semester
URL: www.naropa.edu
Established: 1974 Annual Undergrad Tuition & Fees: $27,670
Enrollment: 1,090 Coed
Affiliation or Control: Independent Non-Profit IRS Status: 501(c)3
Highest Offering: Master's
Program: Liberal Arts And General
Accreditation: NH

01 Interim President ... Mr. John WHITEHOUSE COBB
04 Assistant to the President ... Ms. Cathy CHEN-ORTEGA
10 Vice President Business & Finance ... Vacant
05 Int Provost/Vice Pres Academic Affs ... Dr. Carol A. BLACKSHIRE-BELAY
11 Chief Administrative Officer ... Mr. Todd KILBURN
30 Vice Pres Development/Ext Relations ... Ms. Jill GRAMMER
84 VP Student Affairs/Enrollment Mgmt ... Ms. Cheryl BARBOUR
13 Assistant Vice President for IT ... Mr. Harvey NICHOLS
07 Dean of Admissions ... Ms. Janet ERICKSON
97 Associate Dean Undergrad Educ ... Mr. Mark A. MILLER
35 Dean of Students ... Mr. Robert CILLO
39 Director of Student Housing ... Ms. Lisa CONSTANTINO
06 Registrar ... Ms. Jamie PETA
08 Librarian ... Mr. Mark KILLE
18 Director of Facilities ... Mr. Don RASMUSSEN
37 Dir Student Financial Services ... Ms. Nancy MORRELL
15 Director of Human Resources ... Ms. Angie GOSSETT
106 Director of Online Curriculum Devel ... Mr. Jirka HLADIS
29 Alumni Relations Officer ... Ms. Melissa HOLLAND
14 Assistant Director Technical ... Mr. Mike PAXTON
28 Chief Diversity Officer ... Ms. Suzanne BENALLY
19 Safety & Security Manager ... Mr. Steve JEWELL

National Theatre Conservatory (I)

1101 13th Street, Denver CO 80204-2157
County: Denver FICE Identification: 025179
Unit ID: 260196
Telephone: (303) 446-4855 Carnegie Class: Not Classified
FAX Number: (303) 623-0693 Calendar System: Semester
URL: www.denvercenter.org
Established: 1983 Annual Graduate Tuition & Fees: N/A
Enrollment: 28 Coed
Affiliation or Control: Independent Non-Profit IRS Status: 501(c)3
Highest Offering: Master's; No Undergraduates
Program: Professional
Accreditation: NH

01 President/COO ... Mr. Randy WEEKS
05 Director of Education ... Mr. Daniel RENNER
06 Registrar ... Ms. Jeannette MATUSIAK
10 Chief Financial Officer ... Ms. Vicky MILES

Nazarene Bible College (J)

1111 Academy Park Loop,
Colorado Springs CO 80910-3704
County: El Paso FICE Identification: 013007
Unit ID: 127714
Telephone: (719) 884-5000 Carnegie Class: Spec/Faith
FAX Number: (719) 884-5199 Calendar System: Trimester
URL: www.nbc.edu
Established: 1964 Annual Undergrad Tuition & Fees: $10,800
Enrollment: 860 Coed
Affiliation or Control: Church Of The Nazarene IRS Status: 501(c)3
Highest Offering: Baccalaureate
Program: Professional; Religious Emphasis
Accreditation: NH, BI

01 President ... Dr. Harold B. GRAVES
05 Vice President for Academic Affairs ... Dr. Gary W. STREIT
32 Vice Pres for Student Development ... Prof. Laurel L. MATSON
10 Vice President for Finance ... Mr. J. Mike ARRAMBIDE
106 Dean of Online Education ... Dr. Alan D. LYKE
84 Vice President Marketing/Recruiting ... Prof. Laurel L. MATSON
08 Library Director ... Prof. Ann M. ATTIG
37 Financial Aid Officer ... Mr. Malcolm E. BRITTON
09 Director of Institutional Research ... Vacant
06 Registrar ... Dr. Jay W. OTT

Northeastern Junior College (K)

100 College Drive, Sterling CO 80751-2399
County: Logan FICE Identification: 001361
Unit ID: 127732
Telephone: (970) 521-6600 Carnegie Class: Assoc/Pub-R-M
FAX Number: (970) 521-6636 Calendar System: Semester

URL: www.njc.edu
Established: 1941 Annual Undergrad Tuition & Fees (In-State): $3,278
Enrollment: 2,154 Coed
Affiliation or Control: State IRS Status: 501(c)3
Highest Offering: Associate Degree
Program: Occupational; 2-Year Principally Bachelor's Creditable
Accreditation: NH, ADNUR, PNUR

01 President .... Mr. Jay LEE
05 Vice President Academic Services .... Mr. Stanton GARTIN
10 Vice Pres Finance & Administration .... Ms. Brenda LAUER
32 Dean of Student Success .... Mr. Steve SMITH
84 Dean New Student Enroll/Admissions .... Mr. Andrew LONG
29 Alumni Director .... Mr. Jack ANNAN
102 Executive Director NJC Foundation .... Vacant
06 Director Records/Admission Process .... Ms. Angela ANDERSON
37 Director of Financial Aid .... Ms. Alice WEINGARDT
35 Dir Resident Life & Student Activit .... Mr. David MCNABB
18 Physical Plant Director .... Mr. David CRAWFORD
15 Human Resources Director .... Ms. Tammy KALLSEN
41 Athletic Director .... Ms. Marci HENRY
96 Director of Purchasing/AR .... Ms. Annie SHALLA
09 Dir of Inst Research/Plng/Devel .... Mr. Derek HERBERT
26 Director of Marketing .... Ms. Barbara BAKER
21 Assistant Controller .... Vacant
13 Director Information Technology .... Ms. Cherie BRUNGARDT
40 Bookstore Director .... Vacant

Otero Junior College (A)

1802 Colorado Avenue, La Junta CO 81050-3346
County: Otero FICE Identification: 001362
Unit ID: 127778
Telephone: (719) 384-6831 Carnegie Class: Assoc/Pub-R-S
FAX Number: (719) 384-6933 Calendar System: Semester
URL: www.ojc.edu
Established: 1941 Annual Undergrad Tuition & Fees (In-State): $3,987
Enrollment: 1,200 Coed
Affiliation or Control: State IRS Status: 501(c)3
Highest Offering: Associate Degree
Program: Occupational; 2-Year Principally Bachelor's Creditable
Accreditation: NH, ADNUR

01 President .... Mr. James T. RIZZUTO
11 Vice Pres Administrative Services .... Mr. Pat MALOTT
05 Vice Pres Instructional Services .... Dr. James HERRELL
32 Vice President Student Services .... Mr. Jeff PAOLUCCI
20 Assoc VP Instructional Services .... Mr. David COCKRELL
08 Director Learning Resources .... Ms. Sue KEEFER
38 Director Advising/Guidance/Recruit .... Mr. Brad SMITH
41 Athletic Director .... Mr. Gary ADDINGTON
15 Director of Human Resources .... Mrs. Marlene F. BOETTCHER
18 Director of Physical Plant .... Mr. John CANADAY
40 Bookstore Manager .... Mrs. Debra NICHOLSON
37 Director of Financial Aid .... Ms. Angela BENFATTI
88 Director of Auxilliary Services .... Ms. Leah REED
26 Director Marketing/Public Relations .... Mrs. Almabeth KAESS
14 Director of Computer Services .... Mr. Mark ALLEN

Pikes Peak Community College (B)

5675 S Academy Boulevard,
Colorado Springs CO 80906-5498
County: El Paso FICE Identification: 008896
Unit ID: 127820
Telephone: (719) 502-2000 Carnegie Class: Assoc/Pub-U-MC
FAX Number: (719) 502-2201 Calendar System: Semester
URL: www.ppcc.edu
Established: 1968 Annual Undergrad Tuition & Fees (In-State): $6,584
Enrollment: 14,651 Coed
Affiliation or Control: State IRS Status: 501(c)3
Highest Offering: Associate Degree
Program: Occupational; 2-Year Principally Bachelor's Creditable
Accreditation: NH, ACFEI, ADNUR, DA, EMT

01 President .... Dr. Lance BOLTON
04 Exec Assistant to the President .... Ms. Kimberly BARNETT
05 Vice Pres Instructional Services .... Ms. Cindy BUCKLEY
88 Vice President Student Success .... Mr. Felix M. LOPEZ
10 Vice Pres Administrative Services .... Mr. Mike YOUNG
32 Vice Pres Enrollment Services .... Dr. Randy WEBER
20 Asst to VP Instructional Services .... Ms. Julie HAZEL
84 Director Enrollment Services .... Mr. Jeff HORNER
37 Director of Financial Aid .... Ms. Sherri MCCULLOUGH
08 Director of Libraries .... Ms. Carole OLDS
16 Exec Dir of Human Resource Services .... Mr. Carlton BROOKS
26 Exec Dir Marketing/Communications .... Ms. Allison SWICKARD
21 Director of Business Svcs .... Ms. Eileen HOGUE
06 Registrar .... Ms. Twila HUMPHREY
102 Exec Dir Found/Res/Cmty Development .... Mr. Jon STEPLETON
18 Dir Facilities/Maintenance/Opers .... Mr. Bob LUND
13 Director Information Technology .... Mr. Cyrille PARENT
19 Director Public Safety .... Mr. Ken HILTE
88 Director Student Support Services .... Mr. Edmond QUESADA
88 Dir Military & Veteran Programs .... Ms. Cheri ARFSTEN
76 Dean Health and Science .... Vacant
81 Dean Mathematics & English .... Ms. Carol JONAS-MORRISON
50 Dean Business//Public Service/SS .... Ms. Bree LANGEMO
60 Dean Comm/Humanities/Tech Studies .... Ms. Taffy MULLIKEN
36 Dir of Career Planning & Advising .... Mr. Lincoln WULF
35 Dean of Students .... Ms. Jennifer SENGENBERGER
96 Director of Purchasing .... Ms. Rockie HURRELL

38 Director Student Counseling .... Ms. Yolanda HARRIS
88 Dean of High School Programs .... Ms. Chelsy HARRIS
09 Director of Institutional Research .... Dr. Tim GRIFFIN

Pima Medical Institute-Denver (C)

7475 Dakin Street, Westminster CO 80221
County: Denver Identification: 666171
Unit ID: 404912
Telephone: (303) 426-1800 Carnegie Class: Assoc/PrivFP
FAX Number: (303) 430-4048 Calendar System: Other
URL: www.pmi.edu
Established: 1988 Annual Undergrad Tuition & Fees: $10,550
Enrollment: 1,235 Coed
Affiliation or Control: Proprietary IRS Status: Proprietary
Highest Offering: Associate Degree
Program: Occupational
Accreditation: ABHES, OTA, PTAA, RAD

01 Campus Director .... Ms. Sue ANDERSON

† Branch campus of Pima Medical Institute, Tucson, AZ.

Platt College (D)

3100 S Parker Road, Suite 200, Aurora CO 80014-3141
County: Arapahoe FICE Identification: 030149
Unit ID: 260813
Telephone: (303) 369-5151 Carnegie Class: Bac/Diverse
FAX Number: (303) 745-1433 Calendar System: Quarter
URL: www.plattcolorado.edu
Established: 1986 Annual Undergrad Tuition & Fees: $19,320
Enrollment: 202 Coed
Affiliation or Control: Proprietary IRS Status: Proprietary
Highest Offering: Baccalaureate
Program: Nursing Emphasis
Accreditation: ACCSC, NUR

01 President/CEO .... Mr. Jerald B. SIRBU
05 Vice President of Academic Affairs .... Dr. Julie BASLER
10 Director of Financial Services .... Mr. Robert CRAVER
37 Director of Financial Aid/Registrar .... Ms. Margie ROSE
08 Head Librarian .... Ms. Laura CULLERTON
66 Dean College of Nursing .... Mr. Glenn RAUP
66 Dean of Nursing Program .... Ms. Hollie CALDWELL

Prince Institute-Rocky Mountains (E)

9051 Harlan Street, Suite 20, Westminster CO 80030-2901
County: Jefferson FICE Identification: 021887
Unit ID: 126924
Telephone: (303) 427-5292 Carnegie Class: Assoc/PrivFP
FAX Number: (303) 427-5383 Calendar System: Quarter
URL: www.princeinstitute.edu
Established: 1976 Annual Undergrad Tuition & Fees: $11,800
Enrollment: 143 Coed
Affiliation or Control: Proprietary IRS Status: Proprietary
Highest Offering: Associate Degree
Program: Occupational; Technical Emphasis
Accreditation: ACICS

01 Campus Director .... Vacant

Pueblo Community College (F)

900 W Orman Avenue, Pueblo CO 81004-1499
County: Pueblo FICE Identification: 021163
Unit ID: 127884
Telephone: (719) 549-3200 Carnegie Class: Assoc/Pub-R-L
FAX Number: (719) 544-1179 Calendar System: Semester
URL: www.pueblocc.edu
Established: 1933 Annual Undergrad Tuition & Fees (In-State): $3,175
Enrollment: 8,055 Coed
Affiliation or Control: State IRS Status: 501(c)3
Highest Offering: Associate Degree
Program: Occupational; 2-Year Principally Bachelor's Creditable
Accreditation: NH, ACFEI, ADNUR, DA, DH, EMT, OTA, PNUR, POLYT, PTAA

01 President .... Ms. Patricia ERJAVEC
10 Vice Pres Administration & Finance .... Ms. Colleen ARMSTRONG
05 Vice Pres of Learning .... Ms. Laura SOLANO
32 Vice President of Student Services .... Ms. Lucinda MIHELICH
12 Dean Fremont Campus .... Mr. Sterling JENKINS
12 Dean of SCCC East Campus .... Dr. Lynn URBAN
12 Dean of SCCC West Campus .... Ms. Shannon SOUTH
76 Dean Health & Public Safety .... Ms. Mary CHAVEZ
49 Exec Dean/Dean of Arts & Science .... Dr. Lana CARTER
50 Dean of Business & Technology .... Dr. Jennifer SHERMAN
102 Exec Dir Foundation/Alumni Rels .... Ms. Diane PORTER
07 Director Admissions & Records .... Ms. Maija KURTZ
21 Controller .... Ms. Gayle PETTINARI
37 Director Financial Aid .... Mr. Ron SWARTWOOD
15 Director Human Resources .... Mr. Ken NUFER
14 Director of Computer Services .... Mr. Bryan CRAWFORD
18 Director Facility Svcs/Capital Plng .... Mr. Clifford KITCHEN
35 Director Student Activities/Col Ctr .... Mr. Joel ZARR
38 Director Learning Center .... Mr. Ross BARNHART
08 Director Library Services .... Ms. Jeanne W. GARDNER
27 Dir Communications/Community Rels .... Ms. Erin HERGERT
36 Director of Career & Counseling .... Mr. Dennis JOHNSON
84 Director of Recruitment .... Ms. Carriann MARTINEZ

06 Registrar .... Ms. Maija KURTZ
09 Dir Plng/Accreditation/Effective .... Dr. Patricia DIAWARA
96 Purchasing Agent .... Ms. Leanne CORSENTINO
26 Chief Public Relations Officer .... Mr. Gary FRANCHI
31 Dean of Community Educ & Training .... Ms. Juanita FUENTES
103 Exec Dir Economic & Workforce Devel .... Mr. Vukich JOHN
88 Director of Academic Advising .... Mr. Gage MICHAEL

Red Rocks Community College (G)

13300 W Sixth Avenue, Lakewood CO 80228-1255
County: Jefferson FICE Identification: 009543
Unit ID: 127909
Telephone: (303) 914-6600 Carnegie Class: Assoc/Pub-S-MC
FAX Number: (303) 914-6666 Calendar System: Semester
URL: www.rrcc.edu
Established: 1969 Annual Undergrad Tuition & Fees (In-State): $2,951
Enrollment: 9,541 Coed
Affiliation or Control: State IRS Status: 501(c)3
Highest Offering: Associate Degree
Program: Occupational; 2-Year Principally Bachelor's Creditable
Accreditation: NH, ARCPA, MAC, RAD

01 President .... Dr. Michele HANEY
04 Assistant to the President .... Ms. Kathy SCHISSLER
11 Vice Pres Administrative Services .... Ms. Peggy MORGAN
05 Vice President Instruction .... Ms. Colleen JORGENSEN
32 Vice Pres Stdnt Svc/Enrollment Mgt .... Vacant
20 Dean Support Learning Svcs .... Ms. Marilyn SMITH
20 Dean .... Mr. Rick REEVES
13 Dean Technology CTE .... Mr. Bill MCGREEVY
88 Dean of Instruct/Exec Dir RMEC-OSHA .... Ms. Joan SMITH
85 Director International Education .... Ms. Linda YAZDANI
07 Dir Student Recruitment/Advising .... Ms. Linda CROOK
21 Controller .... Ms. Kathy KAOUDIS
37 Director Financial Aid .... Ms. Linda CROOK
06 Registrar Enrollment Services .... Dr. Dean RATHE
36 Director Advising .... Ms. Nancy CARLSON
18 Director Facilities .... Mr. Mark BANA
16 Director Human Resources .... Mr. Bill DIAL
102 Exec Director RRCC Foundation .... Mr. Ron SLINGER
27 Director Marketing/Communications .... Ms. Kim REIN
35 Director Student Activities .... Ms. Carolyn MATTERN
88 Dir Childhood Ed & Support Svcs .... Ms. Kathleen DEVRIES
09 Director Institutional Research .... Mr. Andrew STEVENS
96 Coordinator Purchasing .... Ms. Renee ARCHULETA

Redstone College (H)

10851 W 120th Avenue, Broomfield CO 80021-3401
County: Broomfield FICE Identification: 007297
Unit ID: 126605
Telephone: (303) 466-1714 Carnegie Class: Assoc/PrivFP
FAX Number: (303) 469-3797 Calendar System: Other
URL: www.redstone.edu
Established: 1965 Annual Undergrad Tuition & Fees: $26,000
Enrollment: 831 Coed
Affiliation or Control: Proprietary IRS Status: Proprietary
Highest Offering: Associate Degree
Program: Occupational
Accreditation: ACICS

01 Campus President .... Mr. Frank DE MONBRUN
05 Campus Academic Dean .... Mr. Tim GUERRERO
07 Senior Director of Admissions .... Ms. Cate CLARK
11 Director of Campus Operations .... Ms. Alicia HARBIN
06 Senior Registrar .... Ms. Vicki MIDDEKER

Regis University (I)

3333 Regis Boulevard, Denver CO 80221-1099
County: Denver FICE Identification: 001363
Unit ID: 127918
Telephone: (303) 458-4100 Carnegie Class: Master's L
FAX Number: (303) 458-4921 Calendar System: Semester
URL: www.regis.edu
Established: 1877 Annual Undergrad Tuition & Fees: $31,800
Enrollment: 11,253 Coed
Affiliation or Control: Roman Catholic IRS Status: 501(c)3
Highest Offering: Doctorate
Program: Liberal Arts And General; Teacher Preparatory; Professional
Accreditation: NH, CACREP, CS, NURSE, @PHAR, PTA, TEAC

01 President .... Rev. John FITZGIBBONS
43 Legal Counsel .... Mr. Stanley ERECKSON
05 Provost .... Dr. Patricia A. LADEWIG
30 Vice President University Relations .... Ms. Julie A. CROCKETT
11 Vice President Administration .... Ms. Karen B. WEBBER
32 Vice President Mission .... Dr. Thomas E. REYNOLDS
10 Vice President/CFO .... Mr. Chuck DAHLMAN
88 VP New Ventures/Strategic Alliances .... Dr. William J. HUSSON
26 Chief Marketing Officer/Assoc VP .... Dr. Soon Beng YEAP
84 Assoc VP Enrollment Services .... Mr. Bill HATHAWAY-CLARK
88 Assoc VP University Services .... Ms. Susan LAYTON
15 Assoc VP Human Resources .... Mr. Tony L. CROW
18 Assoc VP Physical Plant .... Mr. Michael J. REDMOND
20 Asst VP Academic Affairs .... Mr. Steve JACOBS
28 Asst VP for Diversity .... Ms. Sandra L. MITCHELL
26 Asst VP University Relations .... Ms. Marycate LUMPP
29 Exec Asst VP Alumni Engagement Pgms .... Ms. Sarah BEHUNEK
27 Interim Chief Information Officer .... Mr. Erich DELCAMP

107 Dean Professional Studies .... Dr. Roxanne GONZALES
76 Dean Health Professions .... Dr. Janet HOUSER
49 Dean of Regis College .... Dr. Paul D. EWALD
08 Dean of Libraries .... Dr. Ivan K. GAETZ
35 Dean of Students .... Ms. Diane M. MCSHEEHY
07 Director of Admissions .... Mr. Victor L. DAVOLT
07 Director of Admissions .... Ms. Kathy RANK
88 Dir/RHCHP Admissions and Student Op .... Ms. Kim FRISCH
37 Director Financial Aid .... Ms. Elinor MILLER
06 Director Registration .... Ms. Cathy GORRELL
06 Director Academic Records .... Ms. Terry GAURMER
38 Director Personal Counseling .... Dr. Chaney GIVENS
19 Director of Campus Safety .... Mr. William T. WILLIAMS
09 Director of Institutional Research .... Ms. Paula HARMER
25 Director Academic Grants .... Mr. Donald BRIDGER
42 Director of University Ministry . Ms. Kristi GONSALVES-MCCABE
36 Director of Career Services .... Mr. Richard DELLIVENERI
41 Director Athletics .... Ms. Ann MARTIN

Remington College-Colorado Springs (A)

6050 Erin Park Drive, Suite 250,
Colorado Springs CO 80918

County: El Paso — FICE Identification: 030121
Unit ID: 381741
Telephone: (719) 532-1234 — Carnegie Class: Bac/Assoc
FAX Number: (719) 264-1234 — Calendar System: Quarter
URL: www.remingtoncollege.edu
Established: N/A — Annual Undergrad Tuition & Fees: $14,695
Enrollment: 149 — Coed
Affiliation or Control: Independent Non-Profit — IRS Status: 501(c)3
Highest Offering: Associate Degree
Program: Occupational
Accreditation: ACICS

Rocky Mountain College of Art & Design (B)

1600 Pierce Street, Lakewood CO 80214-1433

County: Denver — FICE Identification: 007649
Unit ID: 127945
Telephone: (303) 753-6046 — Carnegie Class: Spec/Arts
FAX Number: (303) 759-4970 — Calendar System: Semester
URL: www.rmcad.edu
Established: 1963 — Annual Undergrad Tuition & Fees: $27,648
Enrollment: 635 — Coed
Affiliation or Control: Proprietary — IRS Status: Proprietary
Highest Offering: Master's
Program: Fine Arts Emphasis
Accreditation: NH, ART, CIDA

01 President .... Dr. Maria PUZZIFERRO
45 Chief Financial Officer .... Mr. Mark FULLER
07 VP Admissions .... Mr. Dave HOBLICK
13 VP of Information Technology .... Mr. Chris MINCHEFF
37 Financial Aid Director .... Ms. Tammy DYBDAHL
05 Dean of Academic Affairs .... Dr. Kiki GILDERHUS
06 Registrar .... Mr. Chuck KING
09 Dir Institutional Effectiveness .... Dr. Stephanie FUENTES
15 Human Resources Director .... Ms. Carrie BRANCHEAU
10 Controller .... Ms. Becky SKOUGSTAD
08 Head Librarian .... Mr. Hugh THURLOW
35 Director Student Activities .... Ms. Krista REEVE

Rocky Vista University (C)

8401 South Chambers Road, Parker CO 80134

County: Douglas — Identification: 667002
Telephone: (303) 373-2008 — Carnegie Class: Not Classified
FAX Number: N/A — Calendar System: Other
URL: www.rockyvistauniversity.org
Established: 1983 — Annual Graduate Tuition & Fees: $44,686
Enrollment: 321 — Coed
Affiliation or Control: Independent Non-Profit — IRS Status: 501(c)3
Highest Offering: Doctorate; No Undergraduates
Program: Professional
Accreditation: @NH, @OSTEO

01 Acting President .... Dr. Bruce DUBIN
05 Acting Dean/Vice Dean .... Dr. Thomas MOHR
43 Vice Pres & General Counsel .... Mr. J. Andrew USERA
20 Sr Assoc Dean of Academic Affairs .... Dr. Stephen PUTTHOFF
10 Chief Operating Officer/CFO .... Mr. Peter FREYTAG

St. John Vianney Theological Seminary (D)

1300 S Steele Street, Denver CO 80210-2526

County: Denver — Identification: 666127
Telephone: (303) 282-3427 — Carnegie Class: Not Classified
FAX Number: (303) 282-3453 — Calendar System: Semester
URL: www.sjvdenver.org
Established: 1999 — Annual Graduate Tuition & Fees: $27,205
Enrollment: 130 — Male
Affiliation or Control: Roman Catholic — IRS Status: 501(c)3
Highest Offering: Master's; No Undergraduates
Program: Professional; Religious Emphasis
Accreditation: THEOL

01 Rector .... Msgr. Michael GLENN
03 Vice Rector .... Rev. Jorge RODRIGUEZ
05 Academic Dean .... Rev. Andreas HOECK
06 Registrar .... Dr. Richard NEYENS

Southwest Acupuncture College (E)

6620 Gunpark Drive, Boulder CO 80301-3339

County: Boulder — Identification: 666618
Unit ID: 436261
Telephone: (303) 581-9955 — Carnegie Class: Spec/Health
FAX Number: (303) 581-9933 — Calendar System: Semester
URL: www.acupuncturecollege.edu
Established: 1997 — Annual Graduate Tuition & Fees: N/A
Enrollment: 140 — Coed
Affiliation or Control: Proprietary — IRS Status: Proprietary
Highest Offering: Master's; No Undergraduates
Program: Professional
Accreditation: ACUP

01 Campus Director .... Valerie HOBBS

† Branch campus of Southwest Acupuncture College, Santa Fe, NM.

Trinidad State Junior College (F)

600 Prospect, Trinidad CO 81082-2396

County: Las Animas — FICE Identification: 001368
Unit ID: 128258
Telephone: (719) 846-5621 — Carnegie Class: Assoc/Pub-R-M
FAX Number: (719) 846-5667 — Calendar System: Semester
URL: www.trinidadstate.edu
Established: 1925 — Annual Undergrad Tuition & Fees (In-State): $3,988
Enrollment: 1,864 — Coed
Affiliation or Control: State — IRS Status: 501(c)3
Highest Offering: Associate Degree
Program: Occupational; 2-Year Principally Bachelor's Creditable
Accreditation: NH, ENGR

01 Interim President .... Dr. Charles BOHLEN
05 Vice President of Academic Affairs .... Dr. Paula DAVIS
11 Vice President Administrative Svcs .... Mr. Michael JOLLY
12 Assoc Vice President/Alamosa Campus .... Vacant
32 VP Stdnt Affairs & Sponsored Pgm .... Ms. Kerry GABRIELSON
49 Dean Arts & Sciences .... Ms. Debbie ULIBARRI
35 Associate Dean Student Services VC .... Mr. Robert MARTINEZ
20 Dean of Instruction/Alamosa Campus .... Mr. Rolando RAEL
30 Director of Devel/College Relations .... Ms. Toni DEANGELIS
15 Human Resources Director .... Ms. Lorrie VELASQUEZ
37 Director Financial Aid .... Ms. Wilma ATENCIO
06 Registrar/Institutional Research .... Ms. Annette LUJAN
07 Admission/Recruitment Specialist .... Vacant
18 Director Facilities/Physical Plant .... Mr. Louis MANTELLI
10 Controller .... Ms. Juanita PENA
32 Dir Stdnt Spprt Svcs/Advisory Coord .... Vacant
14 Distance Lrng/Audio Visual Coord .... Mr. Doug BAK
08 Library Resource Manager .... Mr. Wayne RIVERA
35 Coordinator of Student Life .... Vacant

*University of Colorado System Office (G)

1800 Grant Street, Suite 800, Denver CO 80203

County: Denver — FICE Identification: 007996
Unit ID: 128300
Telephone: (303) 860-5600 — Carnegie Class: N/A
FAX Number: (303) 860-5610
URL: www.cu.edu

01 President .... Mr. Bruce D. BENSON
05 Assoc VP & Academic Affairs Officer .... Dr. Kathleen BOLLARD
100 Senior VP & Chief of Staff .... Mr. Leonard DINEGAR
10 VP & Chief Financial Officer .... Mr. Todd SALIMAN
43 VP University Counsel/Secy Board .... Mr. Pat O'ROURKE
16 Sr AVP/Chief Human Resource Ofcr .... Ms. Jill POLLOCK
86 VP Government Relations .... Ms. Tanya KELLY-BOWRY
26 Assoc VP University Relations .... Mr. Ken MCCONNELLOGUE
21 Asst VP & University Controller .... Mr. Robert KUEHLER
13 Asst VP & Chief Information Ofcr .... Mr. Robert WEIR
31 Dir Business & Community Relations .... Ms. Elizabeth COLLINS

*University of Colorado Boulder (H)

Boulder CO 80309-0001

County: Boulder — FICE Identification: 001370
Unit ID: 126614
Telephone: (303) 492-1411 — Carnegie Class: RU/VH
FAX Number: N/A — Calendar System: Semester
URL: www.colorado.edu
Established: 1876 — Annual Undergrad Tuition & Fees (In-State): $9,482
Enrollment: 29,884 — Coed
Affiliation or Control: State — IRS Status: 501(c)3
Highest Offering: Doctorate
Program: Liberal Arts And General; Teacher Preparatory; Professional
Accreditation: NH, AUD, BUS, CEA, CLPSY, CS, ENG, IPSY, #JOUR, LAW, MUS, SP, TED

02 Chancellor .... Dr. Phillip P. DISTEFANO
05 Provost & Exec Vice Chancellor .... Dr. Russell MOORE
10 Sr Vice Chanc Budget & Finance .... Ms. Kelly L. FOX
46 Vice Chancellor for Research .... Dr. Stein STURE
11 Int Vice Chanc Administration .... Mr. Jeffrey LIPTON
32 Vice Chanc Student Affairs .... Ms. Deborah J. COFFIN
28 Vice Chanc for Diversity/Equity .... Dr. Robert BOSWELL
26 Vice Chanc for Strategic Relations .... Ms. Frances DRAPER
21 Assc VC Budget & Finance/Controller .... Mr. Steven L. MCNALLY
13 Assoc VC & Chief Information Offcr .... Dr. Lawrence M. LEVINE
100 Senior Advisor to the Chancellor .... Ms. Mary Jo WHITE
30 Vice President for Development .... Ms. Carolyn WHITEHEAD
29 Exec Director for Alumni Relations .... Ms. Deborah W. FOWLKES
58 Dean of the Graduate School .... Dr. John A. STEVENSON
61 Dean of Law .... Dr. Philip J. WEISER
49 Dean of Arts & Science .... Dr. Steven R. LEIGH
54 Dean of Engineering .... Dr. Robert H. DAVIS
50 Dean of Business .... Dr. David L. IKENBERRY
53 Dean of Education .... Dr. Loretta SHEPARD
64 Dean of Music .... Dr. Daniel P. SHER
60 Dir Journalism/Mass Communication ... Dr. Christopher BRAIDER
51 Dean Continuing Ed & Prof Studies .... Ms. Anne K. HEINZ
62 Dean of Libraries .... Mr. James F. WILLIAMS
35 Dean of Students .... Ms. Christina GONZALES
37 Director of Financial Aid .... Ms. Gwen E. POMPER
07 Director of Admissions .... Mr. Kevin L. MACLENNAN
06 Registrar .... Ms. Barbara J. TODD
09 Director of Institutional Research .... Dr. Lou MCCLELLAND
25 Director of Contracts Grants .... Mr. Randall W. DRAPER
15 Asst Vice Chanc of Human Resources .... Ms. Candice BOWEN
41 Athletic Director .... Mr. Michael R. BOHN
19 Director of Public Safety .... Mr. Joe E. ROY, II
23 Director of Student Health Center .... Dr. Donald MISCH
36 Director of Career Services .... Dr. Lisa E. SEVERY
88 Director of Museum .... Dr. Patrick KOCIOLEK

*University of Colorado Colorado Springs (I)

1420 Austin Bluffs Parkway, Colorado Springs CO 80918

County: El Paso — FICE Identification: 004509
Unit ID: 126580
Telephone: (719) 255-8227 — Carnegie Class: Master's L
FAX Number: (719) 255-3362 — Calendar System: Semester
URL: www.uccs.edu
Established: 1965 — Annual Undergrad Tuition & Fees (In-State): $8,238
Enrollment: 9,339 — Coed
Affiliation or Control: State — IRS Status: 501(c)3
Highest Offering: Doctorate
Program: Teacher Preparatory; Professional
Accreditation: NH, BUS, CACREP, CLPSY, CS, DIETD, ENG, NURSE, TED

02 Chancellor .... Dr. Pam SHOCKLEY-ZALABAK
05 Provost .... Vacant
10 Vice Chanc Administration & Finance .... Dr. Brian BURNETT
11 Assoc Vice Chanc Admin & Finance .... Susan SZPYRKA
32 Vice Chanc Student Success .... Dr. Homer A. WESLEY, III
30 Vice Chanc Univ Advancement .... Martin WOOD
20 Sr Vice Chanc Academic Affairs .... Dr. David MOON
43 Legal Counsel .... Jenny WILLITS
25 Director of Sponsored Programs .... Gwen GENNARO
08 Dean of Library .... Teri SWITZER
07 Director of Admissions & Records .... Vacant
09 Director of Institutional Research .... Dr. Robyn MARSCHKE
15 Human Resources .... Cynthia CORWIN
19 Director of Public Safety .... Jim SPICE
29 Director Alumni & Community Rels .... Jennifer HANE
37 Director Finan Aid/Stdnt Employment .... Jevita ROGERS
40 Manager of Bookstore .... Jason VOTRUBA
18 Chief Facilities/Physical Plant .... Gary REYNOLDS
26 Director Media Relations .... Tom HUTTON
38 Director Student Counseling .... Dr. Z. Benek ALTAYLI
41 Director of Athletics .... Stephen W. KIRKHAM
13 Director of Information Technology .... Jerry WILSON
21 Director Resource Management .... Gayanne SCOTT
49 Dean of Letters/Arts/Science .... Dr. Peter BRAZA
50 Dean of Business .... Dr. Venkateshwar REDDY
53 Dean of Education .... Dr. Mary SNYDER
54 Dean of Engineering/Applied Science .... Dr. Ramaswami DANDAPANI
80 Assoc Dean of Public Affairs .... Dr. Terry SCHWARTZ
66 Dean Nursing/Health Sciences .... Dr. Nancy SMITH
58 Dean of Graduate School .... Dr. Kelli KLEBE
28 Director of Diversity .... Dr. Kee WARNER
39 Director Campus Housing .... Ralph GIESE
88 Director of Sustainability .... Linda KOGAN

*University of Colorado Denver|Anschutz Medical Campus (J)

1250 14th Street, Denver CO 80217

County: Denver — FICE Identification: 004508
Unit ID: 126562
Telephone: (303) 556-2400 — Carnegie Class: RU/H
FAX Number: N/A — Calendar System: Semester
URL: www.ucdenver.edu
Established: 1912 — Annual Undergrad Tuition & Fees (In-State): $7,394
Enrollment: 18,114 — Coed
Affiliation or Control: State — IRS Status: 501(c)3
Highest Offering: Doctorate
Program: Liberal Arts And General; Teacher Preparatory; Professional
Accreditation: NH, ARCPA, BUS, BUSA, CACREP, CS, DENT, DMS, ENG, HSA, IPSY, LSAR, MED, MIDWF, MUS, NURSE, PH, PHAR, PLNG, PTA, SPAA, TED

02 Interim Chancellor .... Dr. Don ELLIMAN

03 VP Health Affairs/Exec VC AMC .... Ms. Lilly MARKS
10 Vice Chancellor Admin/Finance .... Mr. Jeffrey PARKER
46 Vice Chancellor for Research .... Dr. Richard TRAYSTMAN
17 VC Health Affairs/Dean of Medicine .... Dr. Richard D. KRUGMAN
26 VC of Mkting & Community Engagement .... Ms. Leanna CLARK
05 Provost & VC Academic/Student Affs .... Dr. Roderick NAIRN
52 Dean School of Dental Medicine .... Dr. Denise KASSEBAUM
66 Dean College of Nursing .... Dr. Patricia MORITZ
67 Dean School of Pharmacy .... Dr. Ralph ALTIERE
69 Dean CO School of Public Health .... Dr. David GOFF
58 Dean Graduate School .... Dr. Barry SHUR
64 Dean College of Arts and Media .... Dr. David DYNAK
80 Dean School of Pubilc Affairs .... Dr. Paul TESKE
49 Dean College of Liberal Arts & Sci .... Dr. Dan J. HOWARD
48 Dean College of Arch/Planning .... Mr. Mark GELERNTER
50 Dean Business School .... Ms. Sueann AMBRON
53 Dean School of Education .... Dr. Rebecca KANTOR
54 Dean College of Engineering .... Dr. Marc INGBER
46 Assoc VC for Research .... Dr. Mary COUSSONS-READ
20 Assoc VC Academic Affairs .... Dr. Laura GOODWIN
32 Assoc VC Student Affairs .... Dr. Raul CARDENAS
21 Assoc VC Budget/Finance .... Ms. Lisa DOUGLAS
18 Assoc VC Facilities Management .... Mr. David C. TURNQUIST
15 Asst VC Human Resources .... Mr. Kevin JACOBS
13 Asst VC Information Technology Svcs .... Mr. Russell POOLE
88 Asst VC Academic Tech/Extd Learning .... Mr. Robert TOLSMA
84 Asst VC Enrollment Management .... Ms. Barbara EDWARDS
88 Asst VC Student Success .... Ms. Peggy LORE
09 Asst VC Institutional Research .... Dr. Christine STROUP-BENHAM
35 Asst VC Univ Life/Dean of Students .... Dr. Samantha ORTIZ
06 Registrar .... Ms. Ingrid ESCHHOLZ
28 Director Diversity/Inclusion .... Mr. Dominic MARTINEZ
08 Director Auraria Library .... Dr. Mary SOMERVILLE
08 Director Health Sciences Library .... Mr. Jerry PERRY
26 Director PR/Media Relations .... Ms. Jacque MONTGOMERY
37 Director Financial Aid Svcs .... Mr. James BROSCHEIT
19 Chief of Police .... Mr. Doug ABRAHAM
29 Director Alumni Relations .... Ms. Joy FRENCH
43 Assistant University Counsel .... Mr. Christopher PUCKETT

University of Denver (A)

2199 S. University Blvd., Denver CO 80208-0001

County: Denver FICE Identification: 001371
Unit ID: 127060
Telephone: (303) 871-2000 Carnegie Class: RU/H
FAX Number: (303) 871-3301 Calendar System: Quarter
URL: www.du.edu
Established: 1864 Annual Undergrad Tuition & Fees: $39,177
Enrollment: 11,797 Coed
Affiliation or Control: Independent Non-Profit IRS Status: 501(c)3
Highest Offering: Doctorate
Program: Liberal Arts And General; Teacher Preparatory; Professional
Accreditation: **NH**, ART, BUS, BUSA, CEA, CLPSY, COPSY, ENG, IPSY, LAW, LIB, MUS, SW

01 Chancellor .... Dr. Robert D. COOMBE
05 Provost .... Dr. Gregg O. KVISTAD
43 University Counsel .... Mr. Paul H. CHAN
10 Vice Chanc Business/Financial Affs .... Mr. Craig WOODY
41 Vice Chanc Athletics and Recreation .... Ms. Peg BRADLEY-DOPPES
30 Vice Chanc University Advancement .... Mr. Scott R. LUMPKIN
26 Vice Chancellor Communications .... Mr. Kevin CARROLL
13 VC Technology/Chief Tech Officer .... Mr. Tim BROOKS
84 Vice Chancellor for Enrollment .... Mr. Thomas WILLOUGHBY
37 Director of Financial Aid .... Mr. Chris GEORGE
04 Assistant to the Chancellor .... Ms. Claire BROWNELL
20 Associate Provost Academic Program .... Dr. Jennifer KARAS
32 Assoc Provost Student Life .... Dr. Patti HELTON
28 Assoc Provost Multicult Excellence .... Mr. Frank TUITT
58 Vice Provost Graduate Studies .... Dr. Barbara WILCOTS
08 Dean Libraries .... Ms. Nancy T. ALLEN
34 Dean The Women's College .... Dr. Lynn GANGONE
45 Associate Provost Planning/Budget .... Ms. Julia MCGAHEY
102 Assc Vice Chanc Annual Giving/Found .... Ms. Kristine CECIL
44 Assoc Vice Chanc Major Gifts .... Mr. Mike MCCALL
06 Registrar .... Mr. Dennis M. BECKER
21 Controller/Assistant Treasurer .... Ms. Margaret HENRY
36 Director Career Center .... Ms. Mary M. HAWKINS
22 EO/ADA Compliance Director .... Ms. Kathryne GROVE
18 Director Facilities Management .... Mr. Jeff BEMELEN
09 Director Institutional Research .... Dr. Ali WALTON
15 Director Human Resources .... Ms. Amy KING
19 Director Campus Safety .... Mr. Donald ENLOE
96 Director University Business Svcs .... Mr. Joe BENSON
91 Director Admin Information Systems .... Ms. Susan LUTZ
23 Dir of Univ Health Services .... Mr. Chris WERA
79 Dean Arts/Humanities/Social Science .... Dr. Anne MCCALL
81 Dean Natural Science/Math .... Dr. Andrei KUTATELADZE
50 Dean College of Business .... Dr. Christine RIORDAN
61 Dean College of Law .... Mr. Martin J. KATZ
82 Dean Graduate Sch Intl Studies .... Mr. Christopher R. HILL
70 Dean Graduate Sch Social Work .... Dr. James WILLIAMS
55 Interim Dean University College .... Mr. Michael MCGUIRE
53 Dean College of Education .... Dr. Greg M. ANDERSON
64 Director Lamont School of Music .... Ms. Nancy COCHRAN
88 Dir Special Community Programs .... Dr. Cathy GRIEVE
57 Director School of Art/Art History .... Dr. Gwen CHANZIT
07 Director of Enrollment Services .... Ms. Anne GROSS
35 Exec Dir of Campus Life .... Mr. Carl JOHNSON

University of Northern Colorado (B)

501 20th Street, Greeley CO 80639-6900

County: Weld FICE Identification: 001349
Unit ID: 127741
Telephone: (970) 351-1890 Carnegie Class: DRU
FAX Number: (970) 351-1880 Calendar System: Semester
URL: www.unco.edu
Established: 1889 Annual Undergrad Tuition & Fees (In-State): $6,576
Enrollment: 12,360 Coed
Affiliation or Control: State IRS Status: 501(c)3
Highest Offering: Doctorate
Program: Liberal Arts And General; Teacher Preparatory; Professional
Accreditation: **NH**, ART, AUD, BUS, BUSA, CACREP, COPSY, CORE, DIETD, DIETI, MUS, NURSE, PH, #SCPSY, SP, TED

01 President .... Ms. Kay NORTON
05 Provost/Vice Pres Academic Affairs .... Ms. Robbyn WACKER
11 Vice President Administration .... Ms. Michelle QUINN
43 Vice President & University Counsel .... Mr. Dan SATRIANA
26 VP Univ Advancement/Univ Relations .... Mr. Chuck LEONHARDT
30 Vice Pres Development/Alumni Rels .... Ms. Victoria GORRELL
58 Actg Dean Grad School .... Ms. Linda BLACK
20 Ast VP Undergrad Stds/Dean Univ Col .... Dr. Thomas SMITH
10 Asst Vice President Budgets/Analysi .... Ms. Susan SIMMERS
13 Asst VP Information Technology .... Ms. Jeanette VANGALDER
84 Asst Vice Pres for Enrollment Mgmt .... Mr. Tobias GUZMAN
49 Dean Humanities & Social Sciences .... Dr. David CALDWELL
50 Dean Business Administration .... Dr. Donald GUDMUNDSON
53 Dean Education/Behavorial Sciences .... Dr. Eugene SHEEHAN
76 Dean Natural & Health Sciences .... Dr. Denise BATTLES
57 Dean Performing Visual Arts .... Dr. Andrew SVEDLOW
08 Dean University Libraries .... Ms. Helen REED
35 Dean of Students .... Dr. Katrina RODRIGUEZ
102 Exec Director University Foundation .... Ms. Polly KURTZ
06 Registrar .... Mr. Charlie COUCH
07 Director of Admissions .... Mr. Randall LANGSTON
25 Dir Sponsored Pgms/Academic Res .... Ms. Michele SCHWIETZ
37 Dir Student Financial Resources .... Mr. Marty SOMERO
36 Director of Career Services .... Ms. Renee WELCH
15 Director of Human Resources .... Mr. Marshall PARKS
29 Asst VP Alumni/Donor Relations .... Mr. Matt MANFRA
18 Director Facilities Management .... Mr. Kirk LEICHLITER
41 Director Intercollegiate Athletics .... Mr. Jay HINRICHS
39 Director of Residence Life .... Ms. Jenna FINLEY
38 Director Student Counseling .... Ms. Kim WILCOX
19 Chief of University Police .... Mr. Dennis PUMPHREY
44 Director of Annual Giving .... Vacant
27 Dir Communications/Media Relations .... Mr. Nate HAAS
96 Director of Purchasing .... Ms. Cristal SWAIN

University of the Rockies (C)

555 E Pikes Peak Ave, Suite 108,
Colorado Springs CO 80903-3612

County: El Paso FICE Identification: 035453
Unit ID: 441308
Telephone: (719) 442-0505 Carnegie Class: Spec/Health
FAX Number: (719) 389-0359 Calendar System: Other
URL: www.rockies.edu
Established: 1998 Annual Graduate Tuition & Fees: $14,249
Enrollment: 1,810 Coed
Affiliation or Control: Proprietary IRS Status: Proprietary
Highest Offering: Doctorate; No Undergraduates
Program: Professional
Accreditation: **NH**

01 President .... Dr. Charlita SHELTON
03 Vice President/Campus Director .... Dr. Robert EDELBROCK
05 Provost .... Dr. Tina PARSCAL
20 Vice President of Academic Services .... Vacant
20 Vice Pres of Academic Affs Online .... Ms. Linda HIEMER
32 Director of Student Affairs .... Ms. Janet BRUGGER
58 Dean School of Prof Psychology .... Dr. David STEPHENS
106 Dean Sch Organizational Leadership .... Vacant
26 Campus PR/Marketing Specialist .... Ms. Melissa BLEVINS
37 Director of Financial Aid .... Ms. Jami FLEMING
15 Director of Human Resources .... Ms. Barbara HENRY-QUINN
06 Associate Campus Registrar .... Ms. Katina JORDAN
07 Campus Enrollment Services Manager .... Ms. Carolyn HARRIS
28 Director of Diversity .... Dr. Amy KAHN

U.S. Career Institute (D)

2001 Lowe Street, Fort Collins CO 80525

County: Larimer Identification: 666776
Telephone: (970) 207-4500 Carnegie Class: Not Classified
FAX Number: (970) 223-1678 Calendar System: Other
URL: www.uscareerinstitute.edu
Established: 1981 Annual Undergrad Tuition & Fees: N/A
Enrollment: N/A Coed
Affiliation or Control: Proprietary IRS Status: Proprietary
Highest Offering: Associate Degree
Program: Occupational; Business Emphasis
Accreditation: **DETC**

01 President .... Ann ROHR
03 Chief Executive Officer .... Cole P. THOMPSON
11 Vice President Student Affairs .... Joyce LINDQUIST
10 Vice President Finance .... Jason STANSBERRY
13 Vice President Information Tech .... Scott LYNCH
05 Director of Education .... Janet PERRY

Western State Colorado University (E)

600 North Adams, Gunnison CO 81231-0001

County: Gunnison FICE Identification: 001372
Unit ID: 128391
Telephone: (970) 943-0120 Carnegie Class: Bac/A&S
FAX Number: (970) 943-7069 Calendar System: Semester
URL: www.western.edu
Established: 1911 Annual Undergrad Tuition & Fees (In-State): $6,449
Enrollment: 2,242 Coed
Affiliation or Control: State IRS Status: 501(c)3
Highest Offering: Master's
Program: Liberal Arts And General; Teacher Preparatory; Professional
Accreditation: **NH**, MUS, @TEAC

01 President .... Dr. Jay W. HELMAN
05 Provost/Vice Pres Academic Affairs .... Dr. Patricia MANZANARES-GONZALES
10 Vice Pres Finance & Administration .... Mr. W. Bradley BACA
32 Vice President of Student Affairs .... Mr. Gary PIERSON
30 Vice Pres Institutional Advancement .... Mr. Thomas F. BURGGRAF, JR.
20 Assoc Vice Pres Academic Affairs .... Dr. Kevin NELSON
21 Assoc Vice Pres Finance & Admin .... Ms. Julie FEIER
07 Director of Admissions .... Vacant
35 Assoc Vice Pres Student Affairs .... Ms. Shelley JANSEN
06 Registrar .... Ms. Debra CLARK
37 Director Student Financial Aid .... Mr. Jerry MARTINEZ
104 Dir Intl Student Pgms/Study Abroad .... Mr. John MAHONEY
41 Athletic Director .... Dr. R. Greg WAGGONER
15 Director of Human Resources .... Ms. Kim GAILEY
40 Director Retail Operations .... Ms. Teri HAUS
91 Director Administrative Computing .... Mr. Chad ROBINSON
08 Director Library Services .... Ms. Nancy GAUSS
51 Director Extended Studies .... Ms. Layne Meredith NELSON
39 Director Residence Life .... Ms. Carrie BUCHANAN
36 Director Career Svcs/Internships .... Ms. Svea WHITING
26 Director of Public Relations .... Vacant
29 Director of Alumni Relations .... Ms. Tonya VANHEE
44 Director Annual & Special Gifts .... Ms. Deb HOSKINS
09 Director Institutional Research .... Mr. Doug DRIVER
18 Chief Facilities/Physical Plant .... Mr. Paul MORGAN
35 Director of Student Affairs .... Vacant
84 Director of Enrollment Management .... Vacant
28 Director of Multicultural Center .... Ms. Sally ROMERO
96 Director of Purchasing .... Ms. Patty LOVE

*Westwood College (F)

7604 Technology Way Suite 400, Denver CO 80237

County: Denver Identification: 667029
Telephone: (303) 846-1700 Carnegie Class: N/A
FAX Number: N/A
URL: www.westwood.edu

01 Chief Executive Officer .... Mr. Dean GOUIN

*Westwood College-Denver North (G)

7350 N Broadway, Denver CO 80221-3653

County: Adams FICE Identification: 007548
Unit ID: 127024
Telephone: (303) 650-5050 Carnegie Class: Bac/Diverse
FAX Number: (303) 426-4647 Calendar System: Other
URL: www.westwood.edu
Established: 1953 Annual Undergrad Tuition & Fees: $14,923
Enrollment: 550 Coed
Affiliation or Control: Proprietary IRS Status: Proprietary
Highest Offering: Baccalaureate
Program: Occupational; Technical Emphasis
Accreditation: **ACICS**

02 Campus President .... Ms. Natalie WILLIAMS

*Westwood College-Denver South (H)

3150 S Sheridan Boulevard, Denver CO 80227-5507

County: Denver Identification: 666512
Unit ID: 381787
Telephone: (303) 934-1122 Carnegie Class: Bac/Diverse
FAX Number: (303) 934-2583 Calendar System: Quarter
URL: www.westwood.edu
Established: 1953 Annual Undergrad Tuition & Fees: $25,840
Enrollment: 369 Coed
Affiliation or Control: Proprietary IRS Status: Proprietary
Highest Offering: Baccalaureate
Program: Occupational
Accreditation: **ACICS**

02 Executive Director .... Daniel C. SNYDER
04 Executive Assistant .... Donna REICHERT
05 Campus Academic Dean .... Bob STUDINGER
07 Director of Admissions .... Daniel VOPAT
06 Registrar .... Kristin HUSBY
08 Librarian .... Jessica KING
10 Director of Finance .... Abigail BARNES
36 Director of Career Services .... Lansford HOLNESS
32 Assistant Director Student Support .... Jennifer LEV

† Branch campus of Westwood College-Denver North, Denver, CO. The significant tuition increase from last year to this is due to the correction of an error in the 2012 edition.

William Howard Taft University (A)

600 South Cherry Street, Suite 525, Denver CO 80246
County: Denver FICE Identification: 041004
Telephone: (303) 867-1155 Carnegie Class: Not Classified
FAX Number: (303) 867-1156 Calendar System: Trimester
URL: www.taft.edu
Established: 1976 Annual Undergrad Tuition & Fees: N/A
Enrollment: N/A Coed
Affiliation or Control: Proprietary IRS Status: Proprietary
Highest Offering: Doctorate
Program: 2-Year Principally Bachelor's Creditable; Liberal Arts And General; Professional
Accreditation: DETC

01 President .... Mr. Jerome ALLEY
03 Chief Operating Officer .... Mr. Robert K. STROUSE
11 Director of Administration .... Ms. Christine A. BALDWIN

† Tuition varies by degree program.

Yeshiva Toras Chaim Talmudical Seminary of Denver (B)

1555 Stuart Street, Denver CO 80204
County: Denver Identification: 667113
Unit ID: 128425
Telephone: (303) 629-8200 Carnegie Class: Spec/Faith
FAX Number: (303) 623-5949 Calendar System: Semester
Established: 1967 Annual Undergrad Tuition & Fees: $17,550
Enrollment: 82 Male
Affiliation or Control: Independent Non-Profit IRS Status: 501(c)3
Highest Offering: Second Talmudic Degree
Program: Religious Emphasis
Accreditation: RABN

01 President/CEO .... Rabbi Ahron WASSERMAN
00 Board Chair .... H. Michael MILLER
03 Vice President .... Rabbi Aaron KAGAN
30 Dir of Development & Admissions .... Shlomo FISHEROWITZ
33 Dean of Men .... Rabbi Israel KAGAN
40 Events Manager/Bookstore Director .... Sara Gittie NUSSBUAM
10 Business Manager .... Tannis HALEY

CONNECTICUT

Albertus Magnus College (C)

700 Prospect Street, New Haven CT 06511-1189
County: New Haven FICE Identification: 001374
Unit ID: 128498
Telephone: (203) 773-8550 Carnegie Class: Master's L
FAX Number: (203) 773-9539 Calendar System: Semester
URL: www.albertus.edu
Established: 1925 Annual Undergrad Tuition & Fees: $39,877
Enrollment: 2,010 Coed
Affiliation or Control: Independent Non-Profit IRS Status: 501(c)3
Highest Offering: Master's
Program: Liberal Arts And General
Accreditation: EH, IACBE

01 President .... Dr. Julia M. MCNAMARA
05 Interim Vice Pres Academic Affairs .... Dr. Sean O'CONNELL
10 Vice President Finance/Treasurer .... Mrs. Jeanne E. MANN
13 VP Information Technology Services .... Mr. Steven GSTALDER
29 VP Development/Alumni Relations .... Ms. Carolyn A. BEHAN KRAUS
32 Dean for Student Services .... Ms. Maureen V. MORRISON
07 Dean for Admission/Financial Aid .... Mr. Richard J. LOLATTE
35 Assistant Dean for Student Life .... Ms. Jennifer DUROCHER
06 Registrar .... Ms. Claudia SCHIAVONE
08 Director Library/Information Svcs .... Ms. Anne LEENEY-PANAGROSSI
55 Dean for School of New Dimensions .... Dr. Irene RIOS
09 Dir Assessment/Institutional Rsrch .... Dr. Phyllis DELEO
37 Director Financial Aid .... Mr. Andrew FOSTER
90 Director Academic Computing .... Mr. Robert HUBBARD
41 Director of Athletics .... Mr. Michael S. SPINNER
58 Director MALS Program .... Ms. Julia COASH
89 Director of Freshmen Advising .... Vacant
92 Director of Honors Program .... Dr. Christine ATKINS
96 Dir Purchas/Pub Sfty/Spec Projects .... Mr. James A. SCHAFRICK
15 Director Human Resources .... Mrs. Diane L. NUNN
26 Dir Communications/Community Rels .... Ms. Rosanne ZUDEKOFF
36 Director Career Services .... Ms. Suzanne YURKO WALL
42 Director of Campus Ministry .... Sr. Helen KIERAN, OP
18 Supervisor of Facilities Services .... Mr. Edward J. THOMASI, SR.

Beth Benjamin Academy of Connecticut (D)

132 Prospect Street, Stamford CT 06901-1202
County: Fairfield FICE Identification: 029120
Unit ID: 414975
Telephone: (203) 325-4351 Carnegie Class: Not Classified
FAX Number: (203) 323-6073 Calendar System: Trimester
Established: 1976 Annual Undergrad Tuition & Fees: $5,945
Enrollment: 60 Male
Affiliation or Control: Independent Non-Profit IRS Status: 501(c)3
Highest Offering: First Talmudic Degree
Program: Teacher Preparatory; Professional
Accreditation: RABN

01 Rosh Hayeshiva .... Rabbi S. SCHUSTAL
04 Associate Rosh Hayeshiva .... Rabbi M. HERSHKOWITZ
05 Dean .... Rabbi Michael BENDER

Charter Oak State College (E)

55 Paul Manafort Drive, New Britain CT 06053-2142
County: Hartford FICE Identification: 032343
Unit ID: 128780
Telephone: (860) 515-3800 Carnegie Class: Bac/A&S
FAX Number: (860) 606-9615 Calendar System: Other
URL: www.charteroak.edu
Established: 1973 Annual Undergrad Tuition & Fees (In-State): $6,222
Enrollment: 2,263 Coed
Affiliation or Control: State IRS Status: 501(c)3
Highest Offering: Baccalaureate
Program: Liberal Arts And General
Accreditation: EH

01 President .... Mr. Edward KLONOSKI
05 Provost .... Dr. Shirley M. ADAMS
20 Dean Undergraduate Programs .... Dr. Dana WILKIE
10 Chief Financial/Administrative Ofcr .... Mr. Clifford S. WILLIAMS
13 Chief Information Officer .... Mr. George F. CLAFFEY, JR.
09 Dir Institutional Effectiveness .... Vacant
06 Registrar .... Ms. Jennifer WASHINGTON
37 Dir Financial Aid/Veterans Benefits .... Ms. Deborah FLINN
20 Director Academic Services .... Ms. Linda LARKIN
07 Director Admissions .... Ms. Lori GAGNE PENDLETON
45 Coordinator Special Assessments .... Dr. Maryanne LEGROW
106 Director Distance Learning .... Ms. Susan H. ISRAEL
26 Director Marketing/Public Relations .... Ms. Carolyn HEBERT

*Connecticut Board of Regents for Higher Education (F)

39 Woodland Street, Hartford CT 06105-2337
County: Hartford Identification: 666656
Unit ID: 129011
Telephone: (860) 493-0000 Carnegie Class: N/A
FAX Number: (860) 493-0009
URL: www.ctregents.org

01 President .... Dr. Robert A. KENNEDY
03 Executive Vice President .... Mr. Michael P. MEOTTI
88 Vice President for CSU .... Dr. Elsa NUNEZ
88 Vice President for CCC .... Dr. David LEVINSON
15 VP for Human Resources .... Mr. Steve WEINBERGER
100 Chief of Staff/Director PR & Mktg .... Ms. Colleen FLANAGAN
10 Chief Financial Officer .... Mr. William BOWES
13 Chief Information Officer .... Dr. Wendy CHANG
21 Exec Dir Finance & Administration .... Vacant
101 Assoc Board Affairs/Secy to BOT .... Ms. Erin FITZGERALD
04 Administrative Assistant .... Ms. Judith S. NOSAL

*Central Connecticut State University (G)

1615 Stanley Street, New Britain CT 06050-4010
County: Hartford FICE Identification: 001378
Unit ID: 128771
Telephone: (860) 832-3200 Carnegie Class: Master's L
FAX Number: (860) 832-2522 Calendar System: Semester
URL: www.ccsu.edu
Established: 1849 Annual Undergrad Tuition & Fees (In-State): $8,321
Enrollment: 12,521 Coed
Affiliation or Control: State IRS Status: 501(c)3
Highest Offering: Doctorate
Program: Liberal Arts And General; Teacher Preparatory; Professional
Accreditation: EH, ANEST, CACREP, CONST, CORE, CS, ENG, ENGT, EXSC, MFCD, MUS, NAIT, NURSE, SW, TED

02 President .... Dr. John W. MILLER
04 Assistant to the President .... Ms. Courtney MCDAVID
05 Provost/Vice Pres Academic Affs .... Dr. Carl R. LOVITT
30 Vice Pres Institutional Advancement .... Mr. Chris GALLIGAN
32 Vice President Student Affairs .... Dr. Laura TORDENTI
35 Asst Vice Pres/Dean of Students .... Vacant
20 Associate VP Academic Affairs .... Dr. Joseph P. PAIGE
44 Assoc VP Institutional Advancement .... Mr. Nicholas PETTINICO, JR.
58 Associate VP Graduate Studies .... Dr. Paulette LEMMA
26 Assoc VP Marketing/ Communications .... Dr. Mark W. MCLAUGHLIN
88 Special Assistant to the President .... Ms. Carolyn MAGNAN
11 Chief Administrative Officer .... Dr. Richard R. BACHOO
10 Chief Financial Officer .... Mrs. Charlene CASAMENTO
15 Chief Human Resources Officer .... Mr. Lou PISANO
13 Chief Information Officer .... Mr. James ESTRADA
28 Interim Chief Diversity Officer .... Ms. Rosa RODRIGUEZ
49 Dean School Arts & Sciences .... Dr. Susan PEASE
50 Dean School of Business .... Dr. Siamack SHOJAI
53 Dean School Educ & Prof Studies .... Dr. Mitch SAKOFS
54 Dean School Engineering/Technology .... Dr. Zdzislaw KREMENS
82 Dir Center International Education .... Dr. Nancy B. WAGNER
51 Dir Continuing Educ/Cmty Engagement .... Vacant
07 Director Admissions & Recruitment .... Mr. Lawrence HALL
41 Director Athletics .... Mr. Paul SCHLICKMANN
39 Director Residence Life .... Ms. Jean ALICANDRO
19 Director Public Safety .... Mr. Jason B. POWELL
37 Director Student Financial Aid .... Mr. Richard BISHOP
44 Director Institutional Advancement .... Ms. Cynthia B. CAYER
27 Media Relations Officer .... Ms. Janice PALMER
08 Interim Director Library Services .... Mr. Carl ANTONUCCI
36 Dir Ctr Advising/Career Exploration .... Mr. Kenneth POPPE
23 Director Health Services .... Dr. Christopher R. DIAMOND
24 Director Academic Technology .... Mr. Scott M. ERARDI
06 Registrar .... Mr. Patrick TUCKER
38 Director Counseling & Wellness .... Mr. Timothy CORBITT
18 Asst Chief Admin Ofcr/Dir Facil Mgt .... Mr. Salvatore CINTORINO
21 Director of Business Services .... Ms. Lori JAMES
96 Purchasing Manager .... Mr. Thomas BRODEUR
09 Director of Institutional Research .... Ms. Yvonne KIRBY

*Eastern Connecticut State University (H)

83 Windham Street, Willimantic CT 06226-2295
County: Windham FICE Identification: 001425
Unit ID: 129215
Telephone: (860) 465-5000 Carnegie Class: Master's S
FAX Number: (860) 465-4485 Calendar System: Semester
URL: www.easternct.edu
Established: 1889 Annual Undergrad Tuition & Fees (In-State): $8,555
Enrollment: 5,586 Coed
Affiliation or Control: State IRS Status: 501(c)3
Highest Offering: Master's
Program: 2-Year Principally Bachelor's Creditable; Liberal Arts And General; Teacher Preparatory; Professional
Accreditation: EH, SW, TED

02 President .... Dr. Elsa M. NUNEZ
03 Executive Vice President .... Dr. Michael E. PERNAL
05 Vice President for Academic Affairs .... Dr. Rhona C. FREE
10 Int VP Finance/Administration .... Mr. James R. HOWARTH
32 Vice Pres Student Affairs .... Mr. Ken BEDINI
30 Vice Pres Institutional Advance .... Mr. Kenneth J. DELISA
21 Assoc Vice Pres Finance & Admin .... Mr. James HOWARTH
09 Asst Dir of Institutional Research .... Dr. Brian R. LASHLEY
41 Acting Director of Athletics .... Mr. Michael STENKO
08 Director of Library Services .... Ms. Patricia S. BANACH
37 Actg Director of Financial Aid .... Mr. Patrick KELLY
07 Interim Director of Admissions .... Mr. Christopher DORSEY
36 Director of Career Services .... Mr. Clifford MARRETT
29 Director of Alumni Affairs .... Mr. Michael STENKO
06 Interim Registrar .... Ms. Jennifer HUOPPI
19 Director of Public Safety .... Mr. Jeffrey A. GAREWSKI
39 Acting Director Housing/Res Life .... Ms. Angela BAZIN
40 Director of Bookstore .... Mr. Ben BLAKE
42 Director of Campus Ministry .... Rev. Laurence LAPOINTE
18 Dir of Facilities Mgmt/Planning .... Ms. Nancy TINKER
26 Director University Relations .... Mr. Edward H. OSBORN
49 Dean of Arts & Sciences .... Dr. Carmen R. CID
51 Assoc Dean Continuing Education .... Dr. Carol J. WILLIAMS
58 Int Dean Educ/Prof Studies/Grad Pgm .... Dr. Jaime GOMEZ
96 Assoc Dir Fiscal Affs/Acquisition .... Mr. David ROBERTS
38 Director of Counseling & Psych Svcs .... Dr. Mercy ARAIS

*Southern Connecticut State University (I)

501 Crescent Street, New Haven CT 06515-0901
County: New Haven FICE Identification: 001406
Unit ID: 130493
Telephone: (203) 392-5200 Carnegie Class: Master's L
FAX Number: (203) 392-7149 Calendar System: Semester
URL: www.southernct.edu
Established: 1893 Annual Undergrad Tuition & Fees (In-State): $8,541
Enrollment: 11,533 Coed
Affiliation or Control: State IRS Status: 501(c)3
Highest Offering: Doctorate
Program: Liberal Arts And General; Teacher Preparatory; Professional
Accreditation: EH, CACREP, CS, EXSC, #LIB, MFCD, NURSE, PH, SP, SW, TED

02 President .... Dr. Mary A. PAPAZIAN
04 Admin Assistant to the President .... Ms. Beth Ann H. JOHNSON
05 Int Provost/Vice Pres Acad Affairs .... Dr. Marianne KENNEDY
03 Executive Vice President .... Mr. James E. BLAKE
32 Int Vice Pres Student/Univ Affairs .... Dr. Peter F. TROIANO
30 Int Vice President Inst Advancement .... Mr. Gregg CRERAR
16 Assoc VP for Human Resources .... Ms. Jaye BAILEY
20 Assoc VP Academic Student Services .... Ms. Kimberly M. CRONE
43 Employment and Labor .... Ms. Diane MAZZA
18 Assoc VP Capitol Budgeting/Fac Ops .... Mr. Robert G. SHEELEY
13 Interim Chief Info Tech Officer .... Dr. Kenneth SPELKE
49 Dean School Arts & Sciences .... Dr. Donna Jean A. FREDEEN
50 Dean School of Business .... Dr. Ellen DURNIN
53 Interim Dean School Education .... Dr. Deborah NEWTON
58 Dean School Graduate Studies .... Dr. Holly CRAWFORD
70 Dean School Health/Human Svcs .... Dr. Gregory PAVEZA
44 Assoc to VP Dir Major/Planned Gifts .... Vacant
41 Director Intercollegiate Athletics .... Ms. Patricia NICOL
26 Director of Public Affairs .... Mr. Patrick DILGER
29 Director Alumni Affairs .... Ms. Michelle JOHNSTON
07 Dir Admissions/Enrollment Mgmt .... Vacant
06 Registrar .... Vacant
08 Director of Library Services .... Dr. Christina BAUM
09 Director of Institutional Research .... Vacant
91 Director Computer Svcs/Admin .... Mr. John O. YOUNG
90 Director Computer Svcs/Academic .... Vacant

15 Director of Human Resources Vacant
19 Director of Public Safety Mr. Joseph M. DOOLEY
25 Director of Sponsored Research Ms. Patricia M. ZIBLUK
37 Director of Financial Aid Ms. Gloria LEE
36 Director of Career Services Vacant
23 Director of Health Services Dr. Diane S. MORGENTHALER
35 Director of Student Affairs Dr. Peter F. TROIANO
46 Director Ofc of Mgmt/Info/Research Mr. Richard RICCARDI
28 Exec Asst to Pres Divers/Equity Pgm Dr. Marcia SMITH-GLASPER
38 Director of Counseling Services Dr. Julie LIEFELD
96 Purchasing Manager Ms. Jane MAILHIOT
21 University Controller Ms. Lise M. BRULE
92 Director of Honors Program Dr. Terese GEMME
94 Director of Women's Studies Dr. Yi-Chun Tricia LIN

*Western Connecticut State University (A)

181 White Street, Danbury CT 06810-6885
County: Fairfield FICE Identification: 001380
Unit ID: 130776
Telephone: (203) 837-8200 Carnegie Class: Master's M
FAX Number: (203) 837-8276 Calendar System: Semester
URL: www.wcsu.edu
Established: 1903 Annual Undergrad Tuition & Fees (In-State): $8,440
Enrollment: 6,407 Coed
Affiliation or Control: State IRS Status: 501(c)3
Highest Offering: Doctorate
Program: Liberal Arts And General; Teacher Preparatory; Professional
Accreditation: EH, CACREP, MUS, NURSE, SW, TED

02 President Dr. James W. SCHMOTTER
05 Provost/Vice Pres Academic Affairs Dr. Jane MCBRIDE GATES
10 Vice Pres Finance & Administration Mr. Paul REIS
30 Int Assoc VP Inst Advancement Mr. Paul M. STEINMETZ
32 Vice Pres Student Affs/Ext Affs Dr. Walter B. BERNSTEIN
88 Dean of Visual/Performing Arts Dr. Daniel GOBLE
35 Dean of Student Affairs Dr. Walter CRAMER
49 Dean of Arts & Sciences Dr. Mary STEWART ALEXANDER
50 Dean of Ancell Business Dr. Allen MORTON
107 Dean of Professional Studies Dr. Jess HOUSE
16 Assoc Vice Pres Human Resources Mr. Charles P. SPIRIDON
14 Chief Information Officer Ms. Lorraine CAPOBIANCO
21 Director Fiscal Affairs/Controller Mr. Sean LOUGHRAN
44 Director of Development Ms. Jane VON TRAPP
22 Ex Asst to Pres/Chief Diversity Ofc Ms. Carolyn LANIER
06 Registrar Ms. Lourdes CRUZ
84 Int Enrollment Mgmt Officer Mr. William HAWKINS
08 Director of Library Services Dr. Edward O'HARA
09 Director of Inst Research/Assess Dr. Jerry WILCOX
25 Director of Grant/Programs Ms. Gabrielle E. JAZWIECKI
38 Director of Counseling Svcs Vacant
37 Dir Financial Aid/Veterans Affairs Ms. Nancy BARTON
36 Director of Career Devel Center Ms. Maureen C. GERNERT
26 Director University Relations Mr. Paul STEINMETZ
39 Dir of Housing & Residence Life Mr. Ron MASON
35 Director Student Life Dr. Paul M. SIMON
41 Director of Athletics Mr. Edward FARRINGTON
29 Director of Alumni Affairs Ms. Tammy MCINERNEY
07 Director of Admissions Vacant
15 Director of Employee Relations Mr. Frederic CRATTY
45 Dir of Facilities Plng & Engr Mr. Peter VISENTIN
11 Director of Administrative Services Mr. Mark R. CASE
88 Dir Environmental & Facilities Svcs Mr. Luigi MARCONE
88 Dir Facil Utilization & Promotion Mr. John MURPHY
21 Director of Fin Planning & Budgets Ms. Mary Ann DEASE
19 Director of University Police Mr. Neil MCLAUGHLIN

*Asnuntuck Community College (B)

170 Elm Street, Enfield CT 06082-3800
County: Hartford FICE Identification: 011150
Unit ID: 128577
Telephone: (860) 253-3000 Carnegie Class: Assoc/Pub-S-SC
FAX Number: (860) 253-3007 Calendar System: Semester
URL: www.asnuntuck.edu
Established: 1972 Annual Undergrad Tuition & Fees (In-State): $3,490
Enrollment: 1,687 Coed
Affiliation or Control: State IRS Status: 501(c)3
Highest Offering: Associate Degree
Program: Occupational; 2-Year Principally Bachelor's Creditable
Accreditation: EH

02 President Dr. Martha MCLEOD
05 Dean of Academic Affairs Ms. Barbara MCCARTHY
10 Acting Dean of Administration Mr. James LOMBELLA
32 Dean Student Services Ms. Kathleen KELLEY
15 Director of Human Resources Mr. Joe BLEICHER
51 Act Director Continuing Education Mr. Thomas GOODROW
07 Director Admissions Mr. Tim ST. JAMES
06 Registrar Ms. Gail LABBADIA
37 Director Financial Aid Ms. Donna JONES-SEARLE
09 Director Institutional Research Ms. Qing L. MACK
30 Director Institutional Advancement Vacant
18 Chief Facilities/Physical Plant Mr. Joseph MULLER
96 Fiscal Administrative Officer Mr. Duncan D. MORRIS

*Capital Community College (C)

950 Main Street, Hartford CT 06103-1207
County: Hartford FICE Identification: 007635
Unit ID: 129367
Telephone: (860) 906-5000 Carnegie Class: Assoc/Pub-U-SC
FAX Number: (860) 520-7906 Calendar System: Semester
URL: www.ccc.commnet.edu
Established: 1967 Annual Undergrad Tuition & Fees (In-State): $3,570
Enrollment: 4,512 Coed
Affiliation or Control: State IRS Status: 501(c)3
Highest Offering: Associate Degree
Program: Occupational; 2-Year Principally Bachelor's Creditable
Accreditation: EH, ADNUR, EMT, MAC, PTAA, RAD

02 President Dr. Wilfredo NIEVES
05 Academic Dean Dr. Mary Ann AFFLECK
32 Dean of Student Services Ms. Doris B. ARRINGTON
11 Dean of Administration Mr. Lester PRIMUS
51 Dean Continuing Educ/Community Svcs Ms. Linda GUZZO
09 Director of Institutional Research Ms. Jenny WANG
10 Director Finance/Administration Mr. Ted HALE
06 Registrar Ms. Waynette ARNUM
08 Director of Library Services Ms. Jessica VANDERHOFF
88 Disabilities Coordinator Ms. Glaisma PEREZ-SILVA
07 Director of Admissions Ms. Marsha BALL-DAVIS
37 Director of Financial Aid Ms. Margaret MALASPINA
14 Director of Computer Services Mr. Roger FERRARO
66 Dir Cont Educ Nurse/Allied Health Ms. Ruth KREMS
36 Dir of Career Planning/Development Ms. Linda DOMENITZ
26 Director of Information/Marketing Ms. Jane BRONFMAN
15 Director of Human Resources Mr. Henry BURGOS
20 Associate Academic Officer Mr. C. Raymond HUGHES
30 Director Institutional Advancement Mr. John MCNAMARA

*Gateway Community College (D)

60 Sargent Drive, New Haven CT 06511-5970
County: New Haven FICE Identification: 008037
Unit ID: 130396
Telephone: (203) 285-2000 Carnegie Class: Assoc/Pub-U-MC
FAX Number: (203) 285-2018 Calendar System: Semester
URL: www.gwcc.commnet.edu
Established: 1968 Annual Undergrad Tuition & Fees (In-State): $3,598
Enrollment: 7,261 Coed
Affiliation or Control: State IRS Status: 501(c)3
Highest Offering: Associate Degree
Program: Occupational; 2-Year Principally Bachelor's Creditable
Accreditation: EH, ADNUR, DIETT, NMT, RAD, RTT

02 President Dr. Dorsey L. KENDRICK
11 Dean of Administrative Services Mr. Louis S. D'ANTONIO
46 Dean of Research & Development Ms. Mary Ellen CODY
05 Dean of Learning Dr. Mark KOSINSKI
31 Dean Community Services Ms. Victoria BOZZUTO
15 Director Personnel/Contract Admin Ms. Lucille BROWN
04 Executive Assistant to President Ms. Carol G. MCHUGH
09 Director Institutional Research Dr. Vincent P. TONG
27 Director Public Info & Marketing Ms. Evelyn GARD
10 Director Finance & Admin Svcs Ms. Jill RAIOLA
30 Director Institutional Advancement Vacant
08 Director Learning Resources Center Ms. Clara OGBAA
07 Director of Admissions Ms. Kim SHEA
36 Director Career Development Center Mr. Michael BUCCILLI
06 Registrar Vacant
37 Director Financial Aid Mr. Raymond ZEEK
38 Director Student Counseling Vacant
35 Director of College Life Ms. Roberta PRIOR
24 Director Educational Technologies Ms. Wendy SAMBERG
25 Grants Facilitator Vacant
13 Director Computer Services Mr. Lawrence SALAY
24 Director Early Learning Center Ms. Marjorie WEINER
51 Coord Center for Education Svcs Mr. Luis F. MELENDEZ
50 Chair Business Department Mr. Richard REES
79 Chair Humanities Department Mr. Chester H. SCHNEPF
83 Chair Social Sciences Department Mr. Victor MEDINA
88 Coord Early Childhood Education Ms. Susan E. LOGSTON
88 Coord Drug/Alcohol Rehab Counseling Ms. Cheryl SHANNON
16 Coordinator Human Services Programs Mr. Jonah COHEN
67 Coordinator Pharmacy Tech Program Ms. Louise A. PETROKA
81 Chair Math/Natural Sci Department Mr. Rocky TREMBLAY
50 Director Business & Industry Svcs Mr. John VINCZE
88 Director Dietetic Technician Pgm Ms. Elaine LICKTIEG
76 Director Allied Health Ms. Marcia DORAN
20 Associate Dean of Learning Vacant
88 Director Credit Free Programming Vacant
54 Dir Engineering/Applied Technology Mr. Paul SILBERQUIT
18 Chief Facilities/Physical Plant Mr. Lucian SIMONE

*Housatonic Community College (E)

900 Lafayette Boulevard, Bridgeport CT 06604-4704
County: Fairfield FICE Identification: 004513
Unit ID: 129543
Telephone: (203) 332-5000 Carnegie Class: Assoc/Pub-R-M
FAX Number: (203) 332-5123 Calendar System: Semester
URL: www.hcc.commnet.edu
Established: 1966 Annual Undergrad Tuition & Fees (In-State): $3,598
Enrollment: 5,975 Coed
Affiliation or Control: State IRS Status: 501(c)3
Highest Offering: Associate Degree
Program: Occupational; 2-Year Principally Bachelor's Creditable
Accreditation: EH, OTA, PTAA

02 President Ms. Anita GLINIECKI
05 Academic Dean Ms. Elizabeth ROOP
11 Dean of Administration Mr. Ralph TYLER
31 Dean of Outreach Vacant
32 Dean of Students Dr. Avis D. HENDRICKSON
20 Associate Dean Academics Mr. Alan BARKLEY
06 Registrar Mr. Jim CONNOLLY
07 Director of Admissions Ms. Deloris Y. CURTIS
08 Librarian Ms. Shelly STROHM
37 Director of Financial Aid Ms. Barbara SUROWIEC
26 Public Relations Associate Mr. Anson SMITH
19 Director of Security Mr. Christopher GOUGH
09 Director of Institutional Research Ms. Jan SCHAEFFLER
14 Director of Computer Services Mr. Anthony VITOLA
16 Director Personnel/Labor Relations Ms. Theresa EISENBACH
30 Director University Advancement Mr. Chris CAROLLO
35 Director of Student Life Ms. Linda BAYUSIK
10 Director of Finance/Admin Svcs Ms. Teresa ORAVETZ
18 Coordinator of Facilities Mr. Richard HENNESSEY

*Manchester Community College (F)

PO Box 1046, Great Path, Manchester CT 06045-1046
County: Hartford FICE Identification: 001392
Unit ID: 129695
Telephone: (860) 512-3000 Carnegie Class: Assoc/Pub-S-SC
FAX Number: (860) 512-3631 Calendar System: Semester
URL: www.mcc.manchestercc.edu
Established: 1963 Annual Undergrad Tuition & Fees (In-State): $3,598
Enrollment: 7,499 Coed
Affiliation or Control: State IRS Status: 501(c)3
Highest Offering: Associate Degree
Program: Occupational; 2-Year Principally Bachelor's Creditable
Accreditation: EH, ACFEI, OTA, PTAA, SURGT

02 President Dr. Gena GLICKMAN
05 Dean of Academic Affairs Dr. Joanne RUSSELL
32 Dean of Student Affairs Dr. G. Duncan HARRIS
11 Dean of Administrative Affairs Mr. James MCDOWELL
30 Dean of Advancement Ms. Leia BELL
51 Dean of Continuing Education Ms. Melanie HABER
20 Associate Dean of Academic Affairs Dr. Pamela MITCHELL-CRUMP
10 Director Finance & Admin Services Ms. Regina FERRANTE
07 Director of Admissions Mr. Peter HARRIS
06 Registrar Ms. Natalie DURANT
08 Director of Library Services Vacant
13 Director of Information Technology Mr. Barry GRANT
09 Director Plng/Research & Assessment Mr. David NIELSEN
15 Director of Human Resources Ms. Deborah WILSON
18 Dir Facilities Management/ Planning Ms. Darlene MANCINI-BROWN
26 Dir Marketing and Public Relations Ms. Charlene TAPPAN
37 Director of Financial Aid Ms. Ivette RIVERA-DREYER
72 Director Business/Engineering/Tech Ms. Catherine SEAVER
83 Director Social Science/Hospitality Dr. Christopher PAULIN
81 Dir Math/Science/Health Careers Ms. Marcia JEHNINGS
79 Director of Liberal Arts Mr. Michael STEFANOWICZ
35 Director of Student Life Ms. Cynthia WASHBURNE
19 Director of Public Safety Ms. Susan GIBBENS
44 Coordinator Annual Giving Ms. Sara VINCENT
38 Dir Counseling and Career Svcs Mr. Carl OCHNIO
84 Director of Enrollment Management Mr. Peter HARRIS
102 Associate Dean of Advancement Ms. Endia DECORDOVA
04 Executive Assistant to President Ms. Patricia LINDO
103 Director of Business & Industry Ms. Janet ALAMPI
90 Director of Academic Support Ctr Mr. Brian CLEARY
85 Dir Multicultural/Intl Affairs Mr. Joseph MESQUITA

*Middlesex Community College (G)

100 Training Hill Road, Middletown CT 06457-4889
County: Middlesex FICE Identification: 008038
Unit ID: 129756
Telephone: (860) 343-5800 Carnegie Class: Assoc/Pub-S-SC
FAX Number: (860) 344-7488 Calendar System: Semester
URL: www.mxcc.commnet.edu
Established: 1966 Annual Undergrad Tuition & Fees (In-State): $3,598
Enrollment: 2,876 Coed
Affiliation or Control: State IRS Status: 501(c)3
Highest Offering: Associate Degree
Program: Occupational; 2-Year Principally Bachelor's Creditable
Accreditation: EH, OPD, RAD

02 President Dr. Anna WASESCHA
05 Dean of Academics Dr. Steven MINKLER
10 Dean Finance & Administration Mr. David SYKES
32 Dean of Students Dr. Adrienne MASLIN
51 Dean Continuing Education Mr. Reid SMALLEY
06 Registrar Ms. Susan SALOWITZ
08 Director Library Services Ms. Lan LIU
37 Director Financial Aid Ms. Irene MARTIN
30 Director Institutional Advancement Mr. Greg KLINE
07 Interim Director of Admissions Dr. Darryl REOME
09 Director of Institutional Research Dr. Paul CARMICHAEL
13 Director Information Technology Ms. Annie SCOTT
35 Coordinator Student Activities Ms. Judy MAZGULSKI
88 Director Child Care Services Ms. Hilary PHELPS
18 Chief Facilities/Physical Plant Mr. Steven CHESTER
103 Director of Business & Industry Vacant
15 Director Personnel Services Vacant
26 Chief Public Relations Officer Ms. Marlene OLSON
50 Chair Business Ms. Patricia RAYMOND
83 Chair Social & Behavioral Ms. Judith FELTON
81 Chair Mathematics Ms. Pamela FROST
49 Chair Arts & Humanities Dr. Donna BONTATIBUS
81 Chair Science & Health Dr. Marci SWEDE

*Naugatuck Valley Community College (A)

750 Chase Parkway, Waterbury CT 06708-3089

County: New Haven FICE Identification: 006982
Unit ID: 129729
Telephone: (203) 575-8044 Carnegie Class: Assoc/Pub-R-L
FAX Number: (203) 575-8096 Calendar System: Semester
URL: www.nvcc.commnet.edu
Established: 1964 Annual Undergrad Tuition & Fees (In-State): $3,618
Enrollment: 7,361 Coed
Affiliation or Control: State IRS Status: 501(c)3
Highest Offering: Associate Degree
Program: Occupational; 2-Year Principally Bachelor's Creditable
Accreditation: EH, ADNUR, ENGT, PTAA, RAD

Code	Title	Name
02	President	Dr. Daisy Cocco DE FILIPPIS
11	Dean of Administration	Mr. James TROUP
05	Dean Learning/Student Development	Dr. Sandra PALMER
31	Dean Community/Economic Development	Vacant
35	Dean of Student Services	Ms. Lillian ORTIZ
30	Actg Assoc Dean of Resource Devel	Mr. Waldemar KOSTRZEWA
13	Assoc Dean Information Technology	Mr. Conal LARKIN
20	Actg Assoc Dean of Academic Affairs	Ms. Estela LOPEZ
06	Registrar	Ms. Joan ARBUSTO
37	Director of Financial Aid	Ms. Catherine HARDY
07	Director of Admissions	Ms. Linda STANGO
22	Affirmative Action Officer	Mr. Ron CLYMER
08	Director of Learning Resource Ctr	Dr. Samuel BROWN
10	Director of Finance/Admin Services	Ms. Lisa PALEN
32	Director of Student Activities	Ms. Karen BLAKE
18	Chief Facilities/Physical Plant	Mr. Robert DIVJAK
09	Director of Institutional Research	Ms. Lauren FRIEDMAN
38	Director Student Development Svcs	Mr. Bernd MATTHEIS
15	Director of Human Resources	Mr. Arthur DUBOIS
44	Director Institutional Advancement	Ms. Sydney VOGHEL-OCHS
26	Public Relations Associate	Ms. Allison O'LEARY

*Northwestern Connecticut Community-Technical College (B)

Park Place E, Winsted CT 06098-1798

County: Litchfield FICE Identification: 001398
Unit ID: 130040
Telephone: (860) 738-6300 Carnegie Class: Assoc/Pub-S-SC
FAX Number: (860) 738-6488 Calendar System: Semester
URL: www.nwctc.commnet.edu
Established: 1965 Annual Undergrad Tuition & Fees (In-State): $3,598
Enrollment: 1,701 Coed
Affiliation or Control: State IRS Status: 501(c)3
Highest Offering: Associate Degree
Program: Occupational; 2-Year Principally Bachelor's Creditable
Accreditation: EH, MAC, PTAA

Code	Title	Name
02	President	Dr. Barbara DOUGLASS
11	Dean of Administration	Dr. Steven R. FRAZIER
05	Dean of Academic & Student Affairs	Dr. Patricia A. BOUFFARD
07	Director of Admissions	Ms. Joanne NARDI
08	Director of Library Services	Mr. James PATTERSON
06	Registrar	Ms. Debra REYNOLDS
15	Director of Human Resources	Ms. Fran PISTILLI
37	Financial Aid Officer	Mr. Louis BRISTOL
14	Director of Computer Services	Mr. Joseph DANAJOVITS
88	Dir CEDHH	Mr. Gary GRECO
38	Dir of Student Development	Ms. Ruth GONZALEZ
09	Director of Institutional Research	Ms. Caitlin BOGER-HAWKINS
26	Director Marketing/Public Relations	Mr. Grantley ADAMS
10	Director Financial/Admin Services	Ms. Kimberly DRAGAN

*Norwalk Community College (C)

188 Richards Avenue, Norwalk CT 06854-1655

County: Fairfield FICE Identification: 001399
Unit ID: 130004
Telephone: (203) 857-7000 Carnegie Class: Assoc/Pub-R-L
FAX Number: (203) 857-7287 Calendar System: Semester
URL: www.ncc.commnet.edu
Established: 1961 Annual Undergrad Tuition & Fees (In-State): $3,598
Enrollment: 6,700 Coed
Affiliation or Control: State IRS Status: 501(c)3
Highest Offering: Associate Degree
Program: Occupational; 2-Year Principally Bachelor's Creditable
Accreditation: EH, ADNUR, MAC, PTAA

Code	Title	Name
02	President	Dr. David L. LEVINSON
05	Provost & Dean of Academic Affairs	Dr. Pamela EDINGTON
11	Dean of Administration	Dr. Rose R. ELLIS
32	Dean of Students	Dr. Robert BAER
09	Dean of Institutional Effectiveness	Dr. Vanessa MOREST
30	Executive Director of Development	Ms. Jane KIEFER
51	Director of Continuing Education	Mr. David CHASE
08	Director of Library Services	Ms. Linda LERMAN
37	Financial Aid Officer	Ms. Norma L. MCNERNEY
66	Int Director of Nursing Education	Ms. Coral PRESTI
06	Registrar	Ms. Danita BROWN
15	Director Human Resources	Ms. Virginia C. DELLAMURA
26	Director of Public Relations	Ms. Madeline K. BARILLO
36	Director Career Development	Mr. Patrick O. BOLAND
38	Director Student Counseling	Ms. Catherine MILLER
35	Acting Director Student Activities	Ms. Adrienne CONLEY
10	Director Finance/Administration	Ms. Carrie MCGEE-YUROF
18	Chief Facilities/Physical Plant	Mr. Anthony (Tony) CENTOPANTI

*Quinebaug Valley Community College (D)

742 Upper Maple Street, Danielson CT 06239-1440

County: Windham FICE Identification: 010530
Unit ID: 130217
Telephone: (860) 412-7200 Carnegie Class: Assoc/Pub-R-M
FAX Number: (860) 412-7222 Calendar System: Semester
URL: www.qvcc.commnet.edu
Established: 1971 Annual Undergrad Tuition & Fees (In-State): $3,598
Enrollment: 2,101 Coed
Affiliation or Control: State IRS Status: 501(c)3
Highest Offering: Associate Degree
Program: Occupational; 2-Year Principally Bachelor's Creditable
Accreditation: EH, MAC

Code	Title	Name
02	President	Dr. Ross TOMLIN
32	Dean of Student Services	Mr. David BATY
11	Dean of Administrative Services	Mr. Paul MARTLAND
08	Director of Library Services	Ms. Sharon MOORE
37	Director of Student Financial Aid	Mr. Alfred WILLIAMS
84	Director Enrollment & Research	Vacant
51	Director Ctr for Cmty/Profess Lrng	Ms. Jill O'HAGAN
14	Director Computer/Telecomm Svcs	Mr. Kevin ANDERSON
07	Director of Admissions	Vacant
09	Director of Institutional Research	Dr. Donna SOHAN
10	Chief Business Officer	Ms. Michelle WEISS
15	Dir Personnel Svcs/Aff Action Ofcr	Mr. Dennis SIDOTI
18	Chief Facilities/Physical Plant	Mr. David STIFEL
26	Chief Public Relations Officer	Ms. Susan BREAULT
30	Director of College Development	Ms. Monique WOLANIN
05	Chief Academic Office	Dr. Amy DESONIA
06	Registrar	Mr. Antonio VELOSO

*Three Rivers Community College (E)

574 New London Turnpike, Norwich CT 06360

County: New London FICE Identification: 009765
Unit ID: 129808
Telephone: (860) 886-0177 Carnegie Class: Assoc/Pub-R-M
FAX Number: (860) 886-0691 Calendar System: Semester
URL: www.trcc.commnet.edu
Established: 1963 Annual Undergrad Tuition & Fees (In-State): $3,598
Enrollment: 5,154 Coed
Affiliation or Control: State IRS Status: 501(c)3
Highest Offering: Associate Degree
Program: Occupational; 2-Year Principally Bachelor's Creditable
Accreditation: EH, ACBSP, ADNUR, ENGT

Code	Title	Name
02	President	Dr. Grace S. JONES
05	Academic Dean	Ms. Ann Z. BRANCHINI
11	Dean of Administration	Mr. Michael LOPEZ
32	Dean of Student Services	Dr. Karin EDWARDS
06	Registrar	Ms. Christine LANGUTH
38	Director of Counseling	Mrs. Jacqueline PHILLIPS
08	Director Learning Resources	Ms. Mildred HODGE
15	Director Human Resources	Ms. Louise J. SUMMA
37	Director Student Financial Aid	Ms. Hong Yu KOVIC
18	Director of Facilities	Mr. Arnie DE LA ROSSA
30	Int Dir Institutional Advancement	Ms. Robie CIRZYB
09	Director of Institutional Research	Dr. George REZENDES
26	Public Relations Associate	Ms. Tracy ROSIENE

*Tunxis Community College (F)

271 Scott Swamp Road, Farmington CT 06032-3187

County: Hartford FICE Identification: 009764
Unit ID: 130606
Telephone: (860) 255-3500 Carnegie Class: Assoc/Pub-S-SC
FAX Number: N/A Calendar System: Semester
URL: www.tunxis.commnet.edu
Established: 1969 Annual Undergrad Tuition & Fees (In-State): $3,598
Enrollment: 4,376 Coed
Affiliation or Control: State IRS Status: 501(c)3
Highest Offering: Associate Degree
Program: Occupational; 2-Year Principally Bachelor's Creditable
Accreditation: EH, ACBSP, DA, DH, PTAA

Code	Title	Name
02	President	Dr. Cathryn L. ADDY
05	Dean of Academic Affairs	Dr. Michael ROOKE
32	Dean of Student Services	Dr. Kirk PETERS
11	Dean of Administration	Mr. Charles CLEARY
45	Dean of Institutional Effectiveness	Dr. David C. ENGLAND
10	Dir Finance/Administrative Services	Ms. Nancy ESCHENBRENNER
30	Dir of Institutional Advancement	Vacant
15	Director Human Resources	Ms. Pamela KOWAR
08	Director Library Services	Dr. Lisa LAVOIE
13	Director Information Technology	Mr. Robert WAHL
07	Director of Admissions	Mr. Peter MCCLUSKEY
35	Director Academic Support Center	Ms. Kathleen SCHWAGER
09	Director of Institutional Research	Vacant
37	Director Financial Aid Services	Mr. David WELSH
26	Dir of Marketing/Public Relations	Vacant
18	Director of Facilities	Mr. John LODOVICO
90	Coord Academic Info Technology	Mr. Steven MEAD
91	Coord Admin Information Technology	Mrs. Mary Ann DIORIO

Connecticut College (G)

270 Mohegan Avenue, New London CT 06320-4125

County: New London FICE Identification: 001379
Unit ID: 128902
Telephone: (860) 447-1911 Carnegie Class: Bac/A&S
FAX Number: (860) 439-2700 Calendar System: Semester
URL: www.conncoll.edu
Established: 1911 Annual Undergrad Tuition & Fees: $44,890
Enrollment: 1,903 Coed
Affiliation or Control: Independent Non-Profit IRS Status: 501(c)3
Highest Offering: Master's
Program: Liberal Arts And General; Teacher Preparatory
Accreditation: EH

Code	Title	Name
01	President	Mr. Leo I. HIGDON, JR.
05	Dean of the Faculty	Dr. Roger L. BROOKS
10	Vice President for Finance	Mr. Paul L. MARONI
30	Vice President College Advancement	Mr. Gregory T. WALDRON
08	Vice Pres of Info Svcs/Librarian	Dr. W. Lee HISLE
11	Vice President for Administration	Mr. Ulyssess B. HAMMOND
26	Vice President College Relations	Ms. Patricia M. CAREY
07	VP of Admission & Financial Aid	Ms. Martha C. MERRILL
15	Asst VP HR/Professional Development	Ms. Cheryl L. MILLER
20	Dean of the College	Vacant
35	Dean of Student Life	Dr. Jocelyn BRIDDELL
28	Dean of Multicultural Affairs	Dr. Elizabeth GARCIA
20	Dean of Studies	Dr. Theresa P. AMMIRATI
20	Associate Dean of Faculty	Prof. Abigail A. VAN SLYCK
06	Registrar	Ms. Elisabeth S. LABRIOLA
09	Director of Institutional Research	Dr. John D. NUGENT
21	Controller	Ms. Amanda B. MAYFIELD
36	Director of Placement	Vacant
37	Director of Financial Aid	Ms. Elaine F. SOLINGA
41	Director of Athletics	Mr. Francis SHIELDS
29	Director of Alumni Relations	Ms. Bridget MCSHANE
38	Director Student Counseling	Dr. Janet D. SPOLTORE
84	Director Enrollment Management	Vacant
18	Chief Facilities/Physical Plant	Mr. James NORTON
96	Director of Purchasing	Mr. Scott A. SLABODEN
88	Secretary of the College	Ms. Bonnie WELLS

Fairfield University (H)

1073 N Benson Road, Fairfield CT 06824-5195

County: Fairfield FICE Identification: 001385
Unit ID: 129242
Telephone: (203) 254-4000 Carnegie Class: Master's L
FAX Number: (203) 254-4101 Calendar System: Semester
URL: www.fairfield.edu
Established: 1942 Annual Undergrad Tuition & Fees: $41,090
Enrollment: 4,991 Coed
Affiliation or Control: Roman Catholic IRS Status: 501(c)3
Highest Offering: Doctorate
Program: Liberal Arts And General; Teacher Preparatory; Professional
Accreditation: EH, ANEST, BUS, CACREP, ENG, MFCD, NURSE, TED

Code	Title	Name
01	President	Rev. Jeffrey P. VON ARX, SJ
04	Special Asst to the President	Rev. Charles H. ALLEN, SJ
05	Sr Vice President Academic Affairs	Rev. Paul J. FITZGERALD, SJ
11	VP Administration & Chief of Staff	Dr. Mark C. REED
10	Vice President Finance/Treasurer	Ms. Julie L. DOLAN
30	Vice President Univ Advancement	Ms. Stephanie FROST
26	Vice Pres Mktg & Communications	Ms. Rama SUDHAKAR
32	Vice President of Student Affairs	Dr. Thomas C. PELLEGRINO
20	Assoc Vice Pres Academic Affairs	Dr. Mary Frances MALONE
20	Assoc Vice Pres Academic Affairs	Dr. Elizabeth BOQUET
18	Assoc Vice Pres Facilities Mgmt	Mr. David W. FRASSINELLI
38	Asst Vice Pres/Dir Counseling Svcs	Dr. Susan N. BIRGE
88	Asst VP Admin/Stdnt Affs	Mr. James D. FITZPATRICK
44	Asst Vice President of Advancement	Ms. Julianna DAVIS
09	Int Dir Institutional Research/Plng	Ms. Amy BOCZER
84	Dean of Enrollment	Ms. Karen A. PELLEGRINO
07	Director of Graduate Admission	Ms. Marianne L. GUMPPER
06	University Registrar	Mr. Robert C. RUSSO
14	Dir Computing/Network Services	Mr. Michael GRAHAM-CORNELL
37	Director of Financial Aid	Vacant
36	Director of Career Planning	Ms. Cathleen M. BORGMAN
29	Director of Alumni Relations	Ms. Janet A. CANEPA
42	Director of Campus Ministry	Rev. George COLLINS, SJ
19	Director of Public Safety	Mr. Todd A. PELAZZA
41	Director of Athletics	Mr. Eugene P. DORIS
49	Dean College Arts & Science	Dr. Robbin D. CRABTREE
50	Dean Charles F Dolan Sch of Bus	Dr. Donald E. GIBSON
54	Dean School of Engineering	Dr. Jack BEAL
66	Dean School of Nursing	Dr. Lynn BABINGTON
53	Dean Grad Sch of Educ/Allied Prof	Dr. Susan D. FRANZOSA
35	Dean of Students	Ms. Karen A. DONOGHUE
88	Sr Assoc Dean Stdnts/Dir Univ Act	Mr. Matthew A. DINNAN
35	Assoc Dean Stdnts/Dir Stdnt Devel	Dr. Joseph DEFEO
28	Assoc Dn Stdnts/Dir Stdnt Div Pgm	Mr. William H. JOHNSON
85	Dir of International Programs	Mr. Christopher JOHNSON
92	Director of Honors Program	Dr. John E. THIEL
08	Univ Librarian/Dir of Library Svcs	Ms. Joan T. OVERFIELD
23	Director of Student Health Center	Ms. Judith KAECHELE
15	Director Human Resources	Mr. Mark J. GUGLIELMONI
96	Director of Purchasing	Mr. Nicholas J. PAPILLO

Goodwin College (I)

One Riverside Drive, East Hartford CT 06118-2777

County: Hartford FICE Identification: 022449
Unit ID: 129154
Telephone: (860) 528-4111 Carnegie Class: Assoc/PrivNFP
FAX Number: (860) 291-9550 Calendar System: Semester
URL: www.goodwin.edu
Established: 1999 Annual Undergrad Tuition & Fees: $18,800

Enrollment: 3,100 Coed
Affiliation or Control: Independent Non-Profit IRS Status: 501(c)3
Highest Offering: Baccalaureate
Program: 2-Year Principally Bachelor's Creditable
Accreditation: EH, ADNUR, HT, MAAB, MAC, OTA

01 President .... Mr. Mark E. SCHEINBERG
03 Executive Vice President/Provost .... Ms. Ann B. CLARK
10 Vice President for Finance/CFO .... Mr. Jerry D. EMLET
05 Vice President for Academic Affairs ... Ms. Judith D. ZIMMERMAN
45 Vice Pres for Inst Effectiveness .... Ms. Janet L. JEFFORD
30 Vice Pres Col Rels & Advancement .... Mr. Todd J. ANDREWS
18 Vice Pres for Phys Facilities & IT .... Mr. Bryant L. HARRELL
84 Vice President for Enrollment .... Mr. Daniel NOONAN
30 Vice President for Advancement .... Ms. Brooke PENDERS
20 Asst Vice Pres Academic Affairs .... Ms. Danielle S. WILKEN
88 Dean of Magnet Schools .... Mr. Alan KRAMER
35 Dean of Students .... Dr. Sandy WIRTH
07 Director of Admissions .... Mr. Nicholas LENTINO
36 Director of Career Services .... Mr. David ZOPPOLI
26 Director of Communications .... Mr. Lee SAWYER
44 Assoc Dir of Developmnt/Annual Fund .... Ms. Leia BELL
21 Director of Finance & Business Svcs .... Ms. Sharon N. DADDONA
37 Director of Financial Aid .... Mr. William MANGINI
09 Dir Inst Research/Educ Assessment .... Dr. Alan J. STURTZ
08 Director of Library Services .... Ms. Marilyn L. NOWLAN
106 Director of Online Learning .... Dr. Mark FAZIOLI
06 Assistant Dean/Registrar .... Ms. Denise SCHWABE
32 Assistant Dean for Student Life ...... Ms. Joy CASTELLO-BUTLER
13 Director of Information Technology .... Mr. Dan REGO
29 Alumni Relations Coordinator .... Ms. Vanessa PERGOLIZZI
04 Executive Assistant to President .... Ms. Ann ZAJCHOWSKI
20 Dean of the Faculty .... Dr. Henriette M. PRANGER
66 Dept Chair/Director Nursing .... Ms. Janice COSTELLO
83 Dept Chair Social Sci & Education .... Dr. Clifford THERMER

Hartford Seminary (A)

77 Sherman Street, Hartford CT 06105-2260
County: Hartford FICE Identification: 001387
Unit ID: 129491
Telephone: (860) 509-9500 Carnegie Class: Spec/Faith
FAX Number: (860) 509-9509 Calendar System: Semester
URL: www.hartsem.edu
Established: 1834 Annual Graduate Tuition & Fees: $11,340
Enrollment: 155 Coed
Affiliation or Control: Independent Non-Profit IRS Status: 501(c)3
Highest Offering: Doctorate; No Undergraduates
Program: Professional; Religious Emphasis
Accreditation: EH, THEOL

01 President .... Dr. Heidi HADSELL
05 Academic Dean .... Dr. Uriah KIM
11 Director of Admin and Facilities ...... Ms. Roseann LEZAK JANOW
30 Chief Development Officer .... Rev. Jonathan LEE
07 Admissions Manager .... Ms. Tina DEMO
88 Director Religion Research Inst .... Dr. David A. ROOZEN
88 Director Doctor of Ministry Program .... Dr. Scott THUMMA
88 Director of Islamic Center .... Dr. Ingrid MATTSON
08 Library Director .... Dr. Steven BLACKBURN
44 Dir of Annual Fund & Database Admin .... Ms. Janine HEWITT
10 Comptroller .... Ms. Lilyne HOLLINGWORTH
84 Dir Enrollment Management/Registrar .... Ms. Karen ROLLINS
04 Exec Assistant to the President .... Ms. Mary ZEMAN
27 Director of Communications .... Mr. David BARRETT

Holy Apostles College and Seminary (B)

33 Prospect Hill Road, Cromwell CT 06416-2005
County: Middlesex FICE Identification: 001389
Unit ID: 129534
Telephone: (860) 632-3010 Carnegie Class: Spec/Faith
FAX Number: (860) 632-3030 Calendar System: Semester
URL: www.holyapostles.edu
Established: 1956 Annual Undergrad Tuition & Fees: $10,200
Enrollment: 360 Coed
Affiliation or Control: Roman Catholic IRS Status: 501(c)3
Highest Offering: Beyond Master's But Less Than Doctorate
Program: Liberal Arts And General; Professional
Accreditation: EH

01 President & Rector .... V.Rev. Douglas L. MOSEY
03 Vice Rector .... Rev. Richard FINEO
03 Vice President .... Rev. Gregoire J. FLUET
05 Academic Dean .... Dr. Gerrard NADAL
07 Director of Admissions .... Rev. Bradley W. PIERCE
10 Finance Officer .... Mr. William RUSSELL
08 Director of Library Services .... Ms. Clare ADAMO
06 Registrar .... Dr. Cynthia TOOLIN

Lincoln College of New England (C)

2279 Mount Vernon Road, Southington CT 06489-1057
County: Hartford FICE Identification: 009407
Unit ID: 128683
Telephone: (860) 628-4751 Carnegie Class: Bac/Assoc
FAX Number: (860) 628-6444 Calendar System: Semester
URL: www.lincolncollegene.edu
Established: 1966 Annual Undergrad Tuition & Fees: $18,780
Enrollment: 1,230 Coed
Affiliation or Control: Proprietary IRS Status: Proprietary
Highest Offering: Baccalaureate
Program: Occupational; 2-Year Principally Bachelor's Creditable
Accreditation: EH, DA, DH, DIETT, FUSER, MAC, NMT, OTA

01 President .... Mrs. Kathryn REGJO
04 Executive Assistant to President .... Mrs. Rita W. SCHOOLNIK
05 Vice Pres Academic Affairs .... Dr. Gil LINNE
11 Vice Pres Operations & Stdnt Affs .... Mr. Spencer MCNIVEN
10 Chief Financial Officer .... Mr. Kevin MILLER
07 Director of Admissions On Ground .... Mr. John ALONSO
07 Vice Pres Admissions .... Mr. Richard EINSTEIN
10 Director of Administrative Services .... Mrs. Denise LEWICKI
32 Associate Dean of Student Life .... Mr. Dwayne CAMERON
35 Assoc Dean of Student Services .... Mrs. Cynthia A. CLARK
35 Dir Student Services On-Line .... Mr. Daryl VALLERIE
20 Dean of Academic Affairs/Assessment ..... Mr. Steven GOLDSMITH
20 Dean of Academic Affairs On-Line .... Mrs. Denise ALBERLE-CANNATA
20 Dean of Academic Affairs-Hartford .... Mr. Ken ZANE
06 Registrar .... Mr. Christopher DISTISO
06 Dir of Academic Records/Registratio .... Mr. Fletcher BROWN
08 Director of Library Services .... Mrs. Valeri E. WALLACE
37 Regional Director of Financial Aid .... Mrs. Gina D. SWENTON
09 Dir Institutional Research .... Dr. Kristy HUNTLEY
19 Director Campus Safety & Security .... Mr. David C. ALLING
36 Director of Career Services .... Mr. Christopher FRYER
36 VP of Career Services .... Mr. Bob MCNAMARA
18 Supt of Buildings & Grounds .... Mr. Leonard ROY
13 IT Administrator-Southington .... Mr. Edward D. CONNELLY
13 IT Administrator - Hartford .... Mr. David HEINTZ
13 IT Administrator On-Line .... Mr. Steve MEANS
07 Director of Admissions Online .... Ms. Gretchen LAMMLE
10 Dir/Administrative Services Online .... Mr. James WILSON
37 Dir of FA & Student Affairs Online .... Ms. Cortni NESBIT

Lyme Academy College of Fine Arts (D)

84 Lyme Street, Old Lyme CT 06371-2333
County: New London FICE Identification: 030794
Unit ID: 129686
Telephone: (860) 434-5232 Carnegie Class: Spec/Arts
FAX Number: (860) 434-8725 Calendar System: Semester
URL: www.lymeacademy.edu
Established: 1976 Annual Undergrad Tuition & Fees: $41,696
Enrollment: 89 Coed
Affiliation or Control: Independent Non-Profit IRS Status: 501(c)3
Highest Offering: Baccalaureate
Program: Fine Arts Emphasis
Accreditation: EH, ART

01 President .... Ms. Debra PETKE
30 Vice President External Affairs .... Ms. Joanne DONAGHUE
10 Controller .... Ms. Wendy MASSE
05 Actg Dean/Vice Pres Academic Affs .... Ms. Sally SEAMAN
07 Director Admissions/Cont Educ .... Ms. Sarah CHURCHILL
06 Registrar & Financial Aid .... Mr. James FALCONER
51 Int Director Continuing Education .... Ms. Renee BEYAR

Mitchell College (E)

437 Pequot Avenue, New London CT 06320-4498
County: New London FICE Identification: 001393
Unit ID: 129774
Telephone: (860) 701-5000 Carnegie Class: Bac/Diverse
FAX Number: (860) 701-5090 Calendar System: Semester
URL: www.mitchell.edu
Established: 1938 Annual Undergrad Tuition & Fees: $28,494
Enrollment: 952 Coed
Affiliation or Control: Independent Non-Profit IRS Status: 501(c)3
Highest Offering: Baccalaureate
Program: Liberal Arts And General; Teacher Preparatory; Business Emphasis
Accreditation: EH

01 President .... Dr. Mary Ellen JUKOSKI
03 Senior Vice President .... Mr. Kevin MAYNE
05 VP Acad Affs/Dean of the College .... Dr. Laurence CONNER
10 Vice Pres Administration & Finance .... Ms. Dyann J. BAKER
32 Vice Pres Student Affs/Dean Stdnts .... Mr. Jason EBBELING
84 Assoc VP Enrollment Mgmt .... Ms. Susan BIBEAU
41 Director Of Athletics .... Ms. Maureen WHITE
06 Registrar .... Mr. Kevin P. KELLY
88 Director of Thames Academy .... Ms. Tammy VUKSINIC
08 Director of Library Services .... Ms. Suzanne M. BARTELS
15 Director of Human Resources .... Ms. Susan L. DEVLIN
09 Dir Institutional Rsrch & Assesment ..... Ms. Melanie R. SULLIVAN
37 Director of Financial Aid .... Ms. Jacklyn C. STOLTZ
38 Director FYC and Ctr for Teaching .... Dr. David J. BRAILEY
35 Director of Student Activities .... Ms. Cheri HENAULT
27 Director of Communications .... Ms. Renee K. FOURNIER
29 Director of Alumni Relations .... Ms. Carol BROWN
102 Director of Parent Programs .... Ms. Kimberly S. HODGES
36 Director of Career Center .... Dr. Catherine ERIK-SOUSSI
88 Director of Learning Resource Ctr .... Dr. Peter LOVE
31 Title III Activity Director & PM .... Ms. Kathleen E. NEAL
96 Purchasing Manager .... Ms. Jill RAKOFF
26 Dir Public Relations & Marketing .... Ms. Renee K. FOURNIER
39 Assoc Director of Residence Life .... Ms. Jamia DANZY
18 Director of Facilities .... Vacant
88 Bursar .... Ms. Leah BRENNAN
13 Chief Technology Officer .... Mr. Chuck KEELER
07 Assoc Director of Admissions .... Mr. Sean CORCORAN
21 Accounting Manager .... Ms. Wendy HODGE

Paier College of Art (F)

20 Gorham Avenue, Hamden CT 06514-3902
County: New Haven FICE Identification: 007459
Unit ID: 130110
Telephone: (203) 287-3031 Carnegie Class: Spec/Arts
FAX Number: (203) 287-3021 Calendar System: Semester
URL: www.paiercollegeofart.edu
Established: 1946 Annual Undergrad Tuition & Fees: $12,960
Enrollment: 220 Coed
Affiliation or Control: Proprietary IRS Status: Proprietary
Highest Offering: Baccalaureate
Program: Liberal Arts And General
Accreditation: ACCSC

01 President .... Mr. Jonathan E. PAIER
03 Vice President .... Mr. Daniel L. PAIER
05 Dean of the College .... Mr. Francis COOLEY
10 Director Finance .... Mrs. Maureen E. PAIER
57 Director Design/Graphics .... Mr. Peter MISERENDINO
102 Director Foundation/Arts .... Mr. Robert E. ZAPPALORTI
08 Librarian .... Ms. Beth HARRIS
37 Director Student Financial Aid .... Mr. John DE ROSE
32 Director of Student Services .... Mrs. Maureen DEROSE
20 Assistant to the Dean .... Ms. Angela DEROSE
88 Director Interior Design .... Mr. Pierre STRAUCH
88 Director Photography .... Mr. Peter BENSON
07 Admissions Secretary .... Ms. Lynn PASCALE

Post University (G)

800 Country Club Road, Waterbury CT 06723-2540
County: New Haven FICE Identification: 001401
Unit ID: 130183
Telephone: (203) 596-4500 Carnegie Class: Bac/Diverse
FAX Number: (203) 756-5810 Calendar System: Semester
URL: www.post.edu
Established: 1890 Annual Undergrad Tuition & Fees: $2727450
Enrollment: 812 Coed
Affiliation or Control: Proprietary IRS Status: Proprietary
Highest Offering: Master's
Program: Occupational; 2-Year Principally Bachelor's Creditable; Liberal Arts And General; Professional
Accreditation: EH

01 President & CEO .... Dr. Thomas SAMPH
05 Provost .... Dr. Donald MROZ
10 CFO/Vice President Finance & Admin .... Mr. Scott T. ALLEN
07 Director of Admissions .... Mr. Jay E. MURRAY
06 Registrar .... Mr. Keith GAUVIN
41 Director of Athletics .... Mr. Anthony FALLACARO
15 Human Resources Director .... Ms. Madelaine KELSEY
08 Library Director .... Ms. Tracy RALSTON
27 Chief Information Officer .... Mr. Michael STATMORE
26 Director of Communications .... Ms. Kelly STATMORE
36 Director Career Services .... Dr. Mary RIGALI
35 Dean of Students .... Ms. Erica KLUGE
40 Campus Store Manager .... Mrs. Frances R. KAMINSKY
19 Director of Campus Safety .... Mr. Robert TANSLEY
38 Director Student Counseling .... Ms. Lisa ANTEL
84 Vice President OEI Enrollment Mgmt ... Ms. Veronica MONTALVO
37 Director Financial Aid .... Ms. Regina FAULDS
37 Director Office of Student Finance .... Ms. Michelle GAMBACINI
106 President Online Education Institut .... Mr. Frank MULGREW
26 Chief Marketing Officer .... Mr. Marcelo S. PARRAVICINI
88 Director of Military Programs .... Mr. Edmund LIZOTTE
50 Dean of School of Business .... Dr. Donald MROZ
53 Dean of School of Education .... Dr. Jane BAILEY
49 Dean of Post College .... Dr. James NARDOZZI
80 Dean John P Burke Sch Pub Service .... Dr. Richard STROMPF
04 Executive Asst to the President .... Ms. Melissah KOCHERA

Quinnipiac University (H)

275 Mount Carmel Avenue, Hamden CT 06518-1908
County: New Haven FICE Identification: 001402
Unit ID: 130226
Telephone: (203) 582-8200 Carnegie Class: Master's L
FAX Number: (203) 582-4703 Calendar System: Semester
URL: www.quinnipiac.edu
Established: 1929 Annual Undergrad Tuition & Fees: $38,000
Enrollment: 8,352 Coed
Affiliation or Control: Independent Non-Profit IRS Status: 501(c)3
Highest Offering: First Professional Degree
Program: Liberal Arts And General; Professional
Accreditation: EH, ARCPA, BUS, CS, LAW, NUR, OT, PA, PERF, PTA, RAD, TED

01 President .... Dr. John L. LAHEY
03 Vice President/Exec Assoc to Pres .... Ms. Jean L. HUSTED
05 Sr Vice Pres Academic/Student Affs .... Dr. Mark A. THOMPSON
10 Sr Vice Pres Financial Affairs .... Dr. Patrick J. HEALY
11 Sr Vice Pres Administration .... Dr. Richard C. FERGUSON
30 Vice President Devel/Alumni Affairs ..... Mr. Donald J. WEINBACH
07 Vice Pres/Dean of Admissions .... Ms. Joan I. MOHR
32 Vice President & Dean of Students .... Dr. Manuel C. CARREIRO
26 Vice President for Public Affairs .... Ms. Lynn M. BUSHNELL
18 Vice Pres Facilities/Capital Plng .... Mr. Salvatore FILARDI
15 Vice President for Human Resources .... Mr. Ronald MASON
20 Int Assoc Vice Pres Academic Affs .... Dr. Annalisa ZINN
29 Assoc VP Alumni Affairs/ParentRels .... Ms. Dianna PATEGAS
27 Assoc VP for Information Services .... Ms. Janice WACHTARZ

88 Assoc VP for Human Resources ... Ms. Anna SPRAGG
88 Assoc VP for Faculty Relations ... Ms. Sarah STEELE
28 AVP Acad Affs/Chief Diversity Ofcr ... Dr. Diana M. ARIZA
35 Assoc Dean of Student Affairs ... Ms. Carol T. BOUCHER
38 Asst Dean Career Svcs Sch Comm ... Vacant
38 Asst Dean Career Svcs Sch Hlth Sci ... Ms. Cynthia L. CHRISTIE
19 Chief of Security ... Mr. David BARGER
08 Director of Arnold Bernhard Library ... Vacant
35 Dir Stdnt Ctr/Stdnt Leadership Dev ... Mr. Daniel W. BROWN
41 Director of Athletics & Recreation ... Mr. Jack J. MCDONALD
40 Campus Store Manager ... Mr. Andrew A. TRANQUILLI
104 Director for Global Education ... Ms. Andrea HOGAN
21 Controller ... Mr. Daniel R. JOHNSON
96 Assoc Dir of Administrative Svcs ... Ms. Maria BIMONTE-YERGANIAN
30 Director of Development ... Mr. Nicholas George WORMLEY
06 Registrar ... Ms. Dorothy M. LAURIA
37 Sr Director of Financial Aid ... Mr. Dominic YOIA
84 Director Enrollment Management ... Ms. Joan I. MOHR
09 Director of Institutional Research ... Mr. Edward GILLEN
72 Director of Academic Technology ... Ms. Lauren ERARDI
50 Dean School of Business ... Dr. Matthew L. O'CONNOR
49 Dean College of Arts & Sciences ... Dr. Hans BERGMANN
76 Dean School of Health Sciences ... Dr. Edward R. O'CONNOR
61 Dean School of Law ... Mr. Brad SAXTON
60 Dean School of Communications ... Mr. Lee KAMLET
53 Int Dean School of Education ... Dr. Gary ALGER
63 Dean of the School of Medicine ... Dr. Bruce KOEPPEN
94 Dean/Director of Women's Studies ... Ms. Michele HOFFNUNG
36 Asst Dean Career Devel Sch Bus ... Ms. Jill Anne FERRALL
88 Asst Dean Career Svcs Col Arts/Sci ... Vacant
61 Associate Dean School of Law ... Mr. David S. KING

Rensselaer at Hartford (A)

275 Windsor Street, Hartford CT 06120-2991
County: Hartford | FICE Identification: 002804 | Unit ID: 129428
Telephone: (860) 548-2400 | Carnegie Class: Master's L
FAX Number: (860) 548-7887 | Calendar System: Semester
URL: www.ewp.rpi.edu/hartford
Established: 1955 | Annual Graduate Tuition & Fees: $33,840
Enrollment: 381 | Coed
Affiliation or Control: Independent Non-Profit | IRS Status: 501(c)3
Highest Offering: Master's; No Undergraduates
Program: Professional
Accreditation: &M

01 Acting Dean ... Dr. David L. RAINEY
06 Registrar ... Ms. Doris M. MATSIKAS
32 Student Services Administrator ... Ms. Natalie SUTERA
08 Library Director ... Ms. Mary DIXEY
13 Director Technical & Info Services ... Mr. Brian CLEMENT
18 Director Operations & Facilities ... Mr. Paul J. MURPHY
37 Financial Aid Officer ... Mr. John GONYEA
05 Asst Dean for Academic Programs ... Dr. Houman YOUNESSI
84 Director Enrollment & Marketing ... Mrs. Kristin GALLIGAN

† Regional accreditation is carried under the parent institution, Rensselaer Polytechnic Institute, NY.

Sacred Heart University (B)

5151 Park Avenue, Fairfield CT 06825-1000
County: Fairfield | FICE Identification: 001403 | Unit ID: 130253
Telephone: (203) 371-7999 | Carnegie Class: Master's L
FAX Number: (203) 365-7652 | Calendar System: Semester
URL: www.sacredheart.edu
Established: 1963 | Annual Undergrad Tuition & Fees: $34,030
Enrollment: 6,407 | Coed
Affiliation or Control: Independent Non-Profit | IRS Status: 501(c)3
Highest Offering: Doctorate
Program: Liberal Arts And General; Teacher Preparatory; Professional; Business Emphasis
Accreditation: EH, BUS, NURSE, OT, PTA, SW, TED

01 President ... Dr. John J. PETILLO
11 Sr VP for Finance & Administration ... Mr. Michael J. KINNEY
05 Provost/Vice Pres Academic Affairs ... Dr. Laura NIESEN DE ABRUNA
32 Sr VP Student Affairs & Athletics ... Mr. James M. BARQUINERO
15 Vice President for Human Resources ... Mr. Robert M. HARDY
26 VP Marketing & Communication ... Mr. Michael L. IANNAZZI
88 VP for Mission & Catholic Identity ... Dr. Michael J. HIGGINS
10 Vice President for Finance ... Mr. Philip J. MCCABE
13 VP for Information Tech & Security ... Mr. Michael D. TRIMBLE
45 VP for Strategic Planning & Admin ... Dr. David L. COPPOLA
30 Vice Pres University Advancement ... Ms. Megan ROCK
20 Vice Provost for Special Acad Pgms ... Ms. Mary Lou DEROSA
07 Interim VP Enrollment Management ... Mr. Jim BARQUINERO
43 University General Counsel ... Mr. Michael D. LAROBINA
49 Dean College of Arts & Sciences ... Dr. Seamus CAREY
50 Dean College of Business ... Dr. John CHALYKOFF
76 Dean College of Health Professions ... Dr. Patricia W. WALKER
53 Dean College of Education ... Dr. James C. CARL
35 Dean of Students ... Mr. Larry J. WIELK
21 Controller ... Mr. Peter J. WARD
06 Registrar ... Mrs. Dona J. PERRONE
88 Bursar ... Ms. Alice M. AVERY
08 University Librarian ... Dr. Peter G. FERRIBY
16 Exec Dir for Human Resources ... Mrs. Julia E. NOFRI
37 Exec Dir Univ Financial Asst ... Ms. Julie SAVINO
27 Exec Director of Public Relations ... Mrs. Funda F. ALP
105 Director Web Content Management ... Mrs. Nancy D. BOUDREAU
44 Director of Annual Giving ... Ms. Judite VAMVAKIDES
41 Exec Director of Athletics ... Mr. Donald COOK
88 Exec Dir Student Affairs Research ... Ms. Deanna FIORENTINO
09 Director of Institutional Research ... Vacant
19 Director of Public Safety ... Mr. Jack FERNANDEZ
25 Director of Foundations and Grants ... Dr. Virginia M. HARRIS
36 Exec Director of Career Developmt ... Mrs. Patricia A. KLAUSER
88 Exec Dir Budgets Student Affairs ... Mrs. JudyAnn RICCIO
38 Director Counseling Center ... Dr. Mary Jo MASON
92 Director Honors Program ... Dr. Jason J. MOLITIERNO
39 Director of Residential Life ... Mr. Joel R. QUINTONG
42 Director Campus Ministry & Chaplain ... Fr. Jerry RYLE
88 Dir GE Foundations Scholar Pgm ... Ms. Virginia L. STEPHENS
88 General Manager WSHU ... Mr. George J. LOMBARDI
96 Purchasing Manager ... Mrs. Donna STERN
29 Director of Alumni Relations ... Ms. Emily GILLETTE

St. Vincent's College (C)

2800 Main Street, Bridgeport CT 06606-4292
County: Fairfield | FICE Identification: 006191 | Unit ID: 130448
Telephone: (203) 576-5235 | Carnegie Class: Assoc/PrivNFP
FAX Number: (203) 576-5893 | Calendar System: Semester
URL: www.stvincentscollege.edu
Established: 1991 | Annual Undergrad Tuition & Fees: $18,600
Enrollment: 731 | Coed
Affiliation or Control: Independent Non-Profit | IRS Status: 501(c)3
Highest Offering: Baccalaureate
Program: Occupational; 2-Year Principally Bachelor's Creditable; Nursing Emphasis
Accreditation: EH, ADNUR, MAC, RAD

01 President ... Dr. Martha K. SHOULDIS
10 Chief Financial Officer ... Mr. Christopher GIVEN
05 Vice President/Dean ... Dr. Joanne R. WOLFERTZ
20 Dean of Academic Services ... Dr. Susan CAPASSO
11 Director of Administrative Services ... Mrs. Janice N. FAYE
16 Human Resources Officer ... Dr. Joanne R. WOLFERTZ
37 Director of Financial Aid ... Mrs. Mary L. RICH
06 Registrar ... Mr. Joseph MACIONUS
07 Director of Admissions & Marketing ... Mr. Joseph MARRONE
51 Director Education ... Ms. Tatiana RAMPINO
08 Librarian ... Ms. Vicky JACOBSON
66 Chair of Nursing-ADN ... Mrs. Margo M. MCCARTHY
66 Chair of Nursing-BSN ... Dr. Sharon MAKOWSKI
88 Chair of Radiography ... Ms. Terry HINE
97 Chair of General Education ... Dr. Susan CAPASSO
88 Chair of Medical Assisting ... Ms. Holly MULRENAN
21 Associate Business Officer ... Mrs. Alfreda MOZDZER

Sanford-Brown College-Farmington (D)

270 Farminton Avenue, Suite 245, Farmington CT 06032-1909
County: Hartford | FICE Identification: 012877 | Unit ID: 129613
Telephone: (860) 882-1690 | Carnegie Class: Assoc/PrivFP
FAX Number: (860) 882-1691 | Calendar System: Quarter
URL: www.sanfordbrown.edu
Established: N/A | Annual Undergrad Tuition & Fees: $11,453
Enrollment: 318 | Coed
Affiliation or Control: Proprietary | IRS Status: Proprietary
Highest Offering: Associate Degree
Program: Occupational
Accreditation: ACICS, MAAB

01 President ... Mr. Kurtis M. PETERSON

Trinity College (E)

300 Summit Street, Hartford CT 06106-3100
County: Hartford | FICE Identification: 001414 | Unit ID: 130590
Telephone: (860) 297-2000 | Carnegie Class: Bac/A&S
FAX Number: (860) 297-2257 | Calendar System: Semester
URL: www.trincoll.edu
Established: 1823 | Annual Undergrad Tuition & Fees: $45,730
Enrollment: 2,178 | Coed
Affiliation or Control: Independent Non-Profit | IRS Status: 501(c)3
Highest Offering: Master's
Program: Liberal Arts And General
Accreditation: EH, ENG

01 President ... Dr. James F. JONES, JR.
05 Dean of the Faculty ... Dr. Rena FRADEN
10 Vice Pres Finance & Ops/Treasurer ... Mr. Paul MUTONE
30 Vice Pres College Advancement ... Mr. Ronald A. JOYCE
32 Dean of Students ... Mr. Frederick ALFORD
101 Secretary of the College ... Mrs. MaryJo KEATING
07 Dean Admissions/Financial Aid ... Mr. Larry DOW
20 Associate Academic Dean ... Dr. Sheila FISHER
20 Associate Academic Dean ... Dr. Melanie STEIN
27 Director of Media Relations ... Ms. Michele J. JACKLIN
31 Director of Community Relations ... Mr. Jason ROJAS
37 Director of Financial Aid ... Ms. Kelly O'BRIEN
06 Registrar ... Ms. Patricia MCGREGOR
18 Dir of Facilities Mgmt/Plng & Svcs ... Mr. Gary BRICHER
15 Director of Human Resources ... Ms. Beth IACAMPO
21 Director of Business Operations ... Mr. Alan R. SAUER
21 Budget Director ... Ms. Marcia PHELAN JOHNSON
19 Director of Campus Safety ... Mr. James PERROTTI
44 Director of Development ... Ms. Gretchen ORSCHIEDT
44 Director of Institutional Support ... Ms. Amy F. BROUGH
36 Director of Career Services ... Mr. Peter BENNETT
21 Comptroller ... Mr. Guy DRAPEAU
13 Director of Computer/Commun Systems ... Ms. Suzanne ABER
41 Director of Athletics ... Mr. Michael D. RENWICK
09 Director of Institutional Research ... Dr. James J. HUGHES
32 Director of Campus Life ... Ms. Amy DEBAUN
42 College Chaplain ... Rev. Allison READ
28 Dean of Multicultural Affairs ... Ms. Karla SPURLOCK-EVANS
38 Director Student Counseling ... Dr. Randolph LEE
96 Director of Purchasing ... Mr. Michael S. ELLIOTT
88 Dean of Urban and Global Studies ... Dr. Xiangming CHEN
29 Director of Alumni Relations ... Ms. Katherine DECONTI
08 Head Librarian ... Dr. Richard S. ROSS
26 Director of Communications ... Ms. Jenny HOLLAND

University of Bridgeport (F)

126 Park Avenue, Bridgeport CT 06604-5620
County: Fairfield | FICE Identification: 001416 | Unit ID: 128744
Telephone: (203) 576-4000 | Carnegie Class: Master's L
FAX Number: (203) 576-4653 | Calendar System: Semester
URL: www.bridgeport.edu
Established: 1927 | Annual Undergrad Tuition & Fees: $28,140
Enrollment: 4,805 | Coed
Affiliation or Control: Independent Non-Profit | IRS Status: 501(c)3
Highest Offering: Doctorate
Program: Occupational; Liberal Arts And General; Teacher Preparatory; Professional
Accreditation: EH, ACBSP, ACUP, #ARCPA, ART, CHIRO, DH, ENG, NATUR

01 President ... Mr. Neil Albert SALONEN
04 Executive Assistant to President ... Ms. Joan E. FLORCZAK
05 Provost & VP for Academic Affairs ... Dr. Hans VAN DER GIESSEN
10 VP Administration & Finance ... Dr. Susan D. WILLIAMS
88 Vice Pres International Programs ... Dr. Thomas J. WARD
30 Vice Pres for University Relations ... Ms. Mary Jane FOSTER
18 VP of Facilities ... Mr. George ESTRADA
09 Exec Asst Pres Plng/Inst Research ... Ms. Barbara A. GABIANELLI
07 Dean of Admissions ... Ms. Karissa L. PECKHAM
32 Dean of Students ... Vacant
08 University Librarian ... Ms. Deborah L. DULEPSKI
15 Dir Human Resources/Affirm Act Ofcr ... Dr. Melitha R. PRZYGODA
21 Controller ... Mr. Thomas A. DEBRIZZI, JR.
27 Systems Architect & Interim CIO ... Mr. Matanya ELCHANANI
37 Director of Financial Aid ... Ms. Ciara M. NEGRON
13 Director Information Technology ... Mr. Arthur DYE
90 Director of Academic Computing ... Mr. Abdelshakour A. ABUZNEID
19 Exec Director of Campus Security ... Ms. April J. VOURNELIS
38 Director of Counseling Services ... Ms. Glory A. BLANCEAGLE
06 University Registrar ... Mr. Christian HANSEN
85 Director of Intl Student Affairs ... Ms. Yumin WANG
39 Dir Residential Life/Stdnt Conduct ... Mr. Robert VASS
96 Director of Purchasing ... Ms. Jacqueline A. REEVES
35 Dir Campus Activit & Cmty Service ... Vacant
12 Director of Waterbury Center ... Ms. Karen K. RINGWOOD
12 Director of Stamford Center ... Ms. Maureen L. MALONEY
29 Director Alumni Relations ... Ms. Susan BUTLER
26 Dir Public Info & Media Affairs ... Ms. Leslie H. GEARY
43 University Counsel ... Mr. Michael D. BROMLEY
41 Athletic Director ... Mr. James M. MORAN
51 Dean Continuing/Profess Studies ... Mr. Michael J. GIAMPAOLI
23 Director of Health Center ... Ms. Melissa H. LOPEZ
88 Director of Acupuncture Institute ... Dr. Jennifer BRETT
40 Manager of the Bookstore ... Mr. Gary M. REEVES
42 Director of Interfaith Center ... Vacant
36 Director of Career Services ... Vacant
54 VP Grad Stds/Research & Dean Engr ... Dr. Tarek M. SOBH
49 Dean Arts & Sciences ... Dr. Stephen E. HEALEY
53 Dean School of Education ... Dr. Allen P. COOK
88 Dean College of Chiropractic ... Dr. Frank A. ZOLLI
88 Dean College Naturopathic Medicine ... Dr. Elizabeth W. PIMENTEL
50 Dean School of Business ... Dr. Robert F. GILMORE
17 Vice Provost Div of Health Science ... Dr. David M. BRADY
97 Director Div of General Studies ... Dr. Edward V. GEIST
89 Director First Year Studies ... Ms. Roxie L. RAY
52 Dir Fones Sch of Dental Hygiene ... Dr. Margaret H. ZAYAN
56 Director for Distance Learning ... Mr. Kris BICKELL
24 Media Services Coordinator ... Ms. Lynn DORSEY
57 Dir Shintaro Akatsu Sch of Design ... Mr. Richard W. YELLE
88 Dir Physician Assistant Institute ... Dr. Daniel CERVONKA

University of Connecticut (G)

Storrs CT 06269-0001
County: Tolland | FICE Identification: 001417 | Unit ID: 129020
Telephone: (860) 486-2000 | Carnegie Class: RU/VH
FAX Number: N/A | Calendar System: Semester
URL: www.uconn.edu
Established: 1881 | Annual Undergrad Tuition & Fees (In-State): $11,242
Enrollment: 30,525 | Coed
Affiliation or Control: State | IRS Status: 501(c)3
Highest Offering: Doctorate
Program: Liberal Arts And General; Teacher Preparatory; Professional

Accreditation: EH, ART, AUD, BUS, BUSA, CACREP, CEA, CLPSY, CS, DIETC, DIETD, DIETI, DMOLS, ENG, JOUR, LAW, LSAR, MFCD, MUS, NURSE, PHAR, PTA, SCPSY, SP, SPAA, SW, TED

01 President .... Susan HERBST
100 Chief of Staff .... Rachel RUBIN
05 Interim Prov/Ex VP Academic Affairs .... Mun CHOI
17 Executive VP for Health Affairs .... Frank TORTI
10 Exec VP for Administration and CFO .... Richard D. GRAY
32 Vice President for Student Affairs .... John SADDLEMIRE
46 Senior Vice Provost/VP for Research .... Suman SINGHA
88 Vice Pres for Economic Development .... Mary HOLZ-CLAUSE
101 Executive Secretary to the Board .... Rachel RUBIN
26 Int Assoc Vice Pres/Communications .... David MARTEL
41 Director of Athletics .... Warde J. MANUEL
43 Asst Attorney General .... Ralph URBAN
43 General Counsel .... Richard ORR
13 Vice Provost & IT Leader .... Nancy BULL
28 Vice Provost for Diversity .... Jeffrey OGBAR
21 Assoc VP for Budget & Finance .... Lysa TEAL
18 AVP Arch/Engr & Bldg Services .... Kenneth EGEBERG
19 Dir Public Safety/Chief of Police .... Barbara O'CONNOR
28 Int Assoc VP for Diversity & Equity .... Elizabeth CONKLIN
35 Asst Vice Pres for Student Affairs .... Cynthia F. JONES
45 Asst V Prov for Inst Effectiveness .... Suresh NAIR
102 Pres Univ Connecticut Foundation .... John MARTIN
20 Int Vice Provost for Acad Admin .... Sally REIS
20 Chief Ops Officer/Academic Admin .... Amy DONAHUE
84 VP Enrollment Planning & Mgmt .... Wayne LOCUST
08 V Provost for University Libraries .... Brinley FRANKLIN
12 Director Stamford Campus .... Sharon WHITE
12 Director Avery Point Campus .... Michael ALFULTIS
12 Director Waterbury Campus .... William J. PIZZUTO
12 Director Hartford Campus .... Michael MENARD
12 Director Torrington Campus .... Barry FELDMAN
92 Assoc Vice Prov/Director Honors Pgm .... Lynne GOODSTEIN
25 Interim Exec Dir Sponsrd Pgms .... Antje HARNISH
86 Director Government Relations .... Gail GARBER
86 Dir Govt Relations/Health Affairs .... Joann LOMBARDO
06 Interim Registrar .... Lauren DIGRAZIA
27 Manager Media Communications .... Michael KIRK
09 Director Institutional Research .... Pamela J. ROELFS
07 Director Undergrad Admissions .... Nathan FUERST
37 Director Student Financial Aid .... Mona LUCAS
29 Director Alumni Relations .... Lisa LEWIS
23 Director Student Health Services .... Michael KURLAND
15 Director of Human Resources .... Aliza WILDER
96 Dir Procurement/Logistical Svcs .... Matthew LARSON
47 Dean Col of Agric/Natural Resources .... Gregory WEIDEMANN
50 Dean School of Business .... John ELLIOT
53 Dean Neag School of Education .... Thomas DEFRANCO
54 Interim Dean of Engineering .... Kazem KAZEROUNIAN
51 Int Dir Center Continuing Studies .... Peter DIPLOCK
57 Dean of Fine Arts .... Brid GRANT
58 Int Vice Prov Grad Ed/Dean Grad Sch .... Kent HOLSINGER
82 Exec Director Office Intl Affairs .... Elizabeth MAHAN
61 Dean School of Law .... Jeremy PAUL
49 Dean College of Lib Arts/Sciences .... Jeremy TEITELBAUM
66 Interim Dean School of Nursing .... Regina CUSSON
67 Dean School of Pharmacy .... Robert L. MCCARTHY
70 Dean School of Social Work .... Salome RAHEIM
52 Dean of Dental Medicine .... Roderick L. MACNEIL
63 Dean School of Medicine .... Frank TORTI
38 Int Dir Stdnt Couns/Mental Hlth Svc .... Elizabeth CRACCO
39 Exec Director Residential Life .... Steve KREMER

University of Connecticut Health Center (A)

263 Farmington Avenue, Farmington CT 06030-1827
County: Hartford FICE Identification: 009867
Unit ID: 243762
Telephone: (860) 679-2000 Carnegie Class: Not Classified
FAX Number: (860) 679-1255 Calendar System: Other
URL: www.uchc.edu
Established: 1961 Annual Undergrad Tuition & Fees (In-State): $34,040
Enrollment: 975 Coed
Affiliation or Control: State IRS Status: 501(c)3
Highest Offering: First Professional Degree
Program: Professional
Accreditation: &EH, DENT, MED, PH

01 President .... Dr. Susan HERBST
10 Assoc VP/Chief Financial Ofcr .... Mr. John BIANCAMANO
45 Assoc Vice President of Budget .... Ms. M. Lisa DANVILLE
30 Assoc VP Development .... Ms. Dina PLAPLER
16 Assoc Vice Pres Human Resources .... Vacant
46 Assoc VP Research Admin (Emeritus) .... Mr. Leonard P. PAPLAUSKAS
21 Assistant Vice President Finance .... Mr. Jeffrey P. GEOGHEGAN
08 Associate Director Library .... Ms. Evelyn B. MORGEN
52 Dean School of Dental Medicine .... Dr. Monty R. MACNEIL
63 Dean School of Medicine .... Dr. Frank M. TORTI
53 Assoc Dean Education/Patient Care .... Dr. Steven LEPOWSKY
35 Assoc Dean Medical Student Affairs .... Dr. David HENDERSON
93 Asc Dn/Dir Dept Hlth Career Op Pgms .... Dr. Marja M. HURLEY
17 Hospital Director .... Dr. Mike SUMMERER

† Regional accreditation is carried under the parent institution in Storrs, CT.

University of Hartford (B)

200 Bloomfield Avenue, West Hartford CT 06117-1599
County: Hartford FICE Identification: 001422
Unit ID: 129525
Telephone: (860) 768-4100 Carnegie Class: Master's L
FAX Number: (860) 768-4070 Calendar System: Semester
URL: www.hartford.edu
Established: 1877 Annual Undergrad Tuition & Fees: $32,172
Enrollment: 7,025 Coed
Affiliation or Control: Independent Non-Profit IRS Status: 501(c)3
Highest Offering: Doctorate
Program: Liberal Arts And General; Teacher Preparatory; Professional
Accreditation: EH, ART, BUS, CLPSY, DANCE, ENG, ENGT, MT, MUS, NURSE, OPE, PTA, RAD, TED, THEA

01 President .... Dr. Walter HARRISON
05 Provost .... Ms. Sharon VASQUEZ
10 Vice Pres Finance & Administration .... Mr. Arosha JAYAWICKREMA
30 Vice Pres Institutional Advancement .... Ms. Christine M. PINA
32 Vice Pres Student Affs/Dean Stdnts .... Dr. J. Lee PETERS
26 Vice Pres of Univ Relations .... Mr. John J. CARSON
21 Asst Vice Pres Finance/Controller .... Ms. Kimberly KENNISON
35 Asst Vice Pres Student Development .... Ms. DeLois LINDSEY
04 Senior Advisor to the President .... Ms. Susan FITZGERALD
35 Assoc Vice Pres for Student Life .... Mr. Irwin NUSSBAUM
21 Assoc Vice Pres/Treasurer .... Mr. Thomas J. PERRA
43 Vice Pres/Gen Counsel & Secretary .... Mr. Thomas DORER
20 Assoc Provost/Dean UG Studies .... Dr. Guy C. COLARULLI
20 Asst Provost/Dean of Faculty Devel .... Dr. Frederick SWEITZER
07 Dean of Admission .... Mr. Richard A. ZEISER
04 Exec Assistant to the President .... Ms. Ilena ROSENSTEIN
15 Exec Dir Human Resources & Devel .... Ms. Lisa BELANGER
08 Director University Libraries .... Ms. Randi L. ASHTON-PRITTING
37 Director Student Financial Aid .... Ms. Jennifer FUHRMANN
06 Director Registration & Records .... Ms. Doreen LAY
38 Dir Counsel & Personal Development .... Dr. David ALBERT
36 Director Career Center .... Mr. John KNIERING
14 Chief Info Ofcr/Ex Dir Info Tech .... Mr. George BROPHY
19 Director Public Safety .... Mr. John SCHMALTZ
23 Director Health Services .... Ms. Mary NORRIS
24 Director Media Technology Services .... Mr. Sebastian SORRENTINO
25 Dir Inst Prtnrshp/Sponsored Rsrch .... Dr. Peter LISI
29 Senior Director Alumni Relations .... Ms. Kandyce AUST
18 Assoc Vice Pres for Facilities/Mgmt .... Mr. Norman YOUNG
88 Asst Provost for Financial Planning .... Dr. James A. MELLO
41 Director Athletics .... Ms. Patricia MEISER
104 Director International Studies .... Ms. Sarah REUTER
09 Director Institutional Research .... Ms. Sarah NOELL
94 Director of Women's Center .... Ms. Patricia MCKENNA-GRANT
88 Director of Judicial Process .... Ms. Helena SAJKO
96 Director of Purchasing .... Mr. Dennis M. GACIOCH
92 Director of University Honors .... Dr. Donald JONES
88 Dean University Programs .... Mr. R. J. MCGIVNEY
57 Dean Hartford Art School .... Dr. Nancy M. STUART
72 Dean College Engineer/Tech/Arch .... Dr. Louis MANZIONE
58 Interim Dean Graduate Studies .... Dr. Frederick SWEITZER
49 Dean College Arts & Science .... Dr. Joseph VOELKER
50 Dean Barney School of Business .... Dr. James W. FAIRFIELD-SONN
12 Dean Hillyer College .... Dr. David H. GOLDENBERG
53 Dean College of Education .... Dr. Ralph MUELLER
88 Dean Hartt School .... Dr. Aaron FLAGG

University of New Haven (C)

300 Boston Post Road, West Haven CT 06516-1999
County: New Haven FICE Identification: 001397
Unit ID: 129941
Telephone: (203) 932-7000 Carnegie Class: Master's L
FAX Number: (203) 931-6060 Calendar System: Other
URL: www.newhaven.edu
Established: 1920 Annual Undergrad Tuition & Fees: $32,125
Enrollment: 6,385 Coed
Affiliation or Control: Independent Non-Profit IRS Status: 501(c)3
Highest Offering: Doctorate
Program: Liberal Arts And General; Professional
Accreditation: EH, CS, DH, DIETD, ENG

01 President .... Dr. Steven H. KAPLAN
05 Provost/Vice Pres Academic Affs .... Dr. David P. DAUWALDER
10 Vice Pres Finance/Treasurer of Univ .... Mr. George S. SYNODI
30 Vice President Univ Advancement .... Mr. Richard J. TUCHMAN
32 Vice President for Student Affairs .... Dr. Margaret JABLONSKI
100 Chief of Staff & Univ Secretary .... Ms. Gayle S. TAGLIATELA
84 Vice Pres Enrollment Management .... Mr. James MCCOY
18 Assoc Vice President for Facilities .... Mr. Louis ANNINO
15 Vice President Human Resources .... Ms. Caroline KOZIATEK
20 Asc Prov Grad Stds/Rsrch/Fac Devel .... Dr. Ira H. KLEINFELD
21 Assoc Vice Pres for Finance .... Mr. Patrick TORRE
13 Assoc VP Institutional Technology .... Mr. Vincent P. MANGIACAPRA
35 Assc VP Stdnt Affs/Dean of Students .. Ms. Rebecca D. JOHNSON
88 Assoc VP Enrollment Management .... Mr. Kevin J. PHILLIPS
41 Assc Vice Pres Athletics/Recreation .... Ms. Deborah CHIN
37 Assoc Vice Pres Financial Aid .... Ms. Karen FLYNN
88 Asst Provost Undergrad Stds/Assess .... Dr. Gordon SIMERSON
08 University Librarian .... Ms. Hanko H. DOBI
44 Director of Development .... Ms. Roslyn REABACK
06 Registrar for Undergraduate Records .... Ms. Nancy BAKER
06 Registrar for Graduate Records .... Ms. Virginia KLUMP
30 Director Advancement Services .... Mr. Carl PITRUZZELLO
07 Director of Graduate Admissions .... Ms. Eloise GORMLEY
28 Director of Intercultural Relations .... Ms. Wanda TYLER
29 Director of Alumni Events .... Ms. Jennifer PJATAK
38 Director of Counseling .... Dr. Deborah EVERHART
09 Director Institutional Research .... Dr. Elizabeth JOHNSTON-O'CONNOR
19 Chief of University Police .... Chief Henry A. STARKEL
85 Director of Intl Student Services .... Ms. Andrea HOGAN
35 Director Student Activities .... Mr. Gregory OVEREND
96 Director of Procurement Services .... Mr. David ROBERTS
85 Director International Admissions .... Mr. Joseph SPELLMAN
88 Dir Student Accounts/Risk Manager .... Mr. Marc MANIATIS
26 Director of Recruiting & Marketing .... Mr. Wayne LEON
88 Dean of University College .... Mr. Arthur GOON
49 Dean College Arts & Sciences .... Dr. Lourdes ALVAREZ
50 Exec Dean College Business .... Dr. Lawrence FLANAGAN
54 Dean Tagliatela Col Engineering .... Dr. Ronald HARICHANDRAN
88 Dn HCL Col Crimnl Just/Forensic Sci .... Dr. Mario GABOURY
106 AVP & Dean Col Lifelong & eLearning .... Dr. Marsha K. HAM

University of Saint Joseph (D)

1678 Asylum Avenue, West Hartford CT 06117-2791
County: Hartford FICE Identification: 001409
Unit ID: 130314
Telephone: (860) 232-4571 Carnegie Class: Master's L
FAX Number: (860) 233-5695 Calendar System: Semester
URL: www.usj.edu
Established: 1932 Annual Undergrad Tuition & Fees: $31,826
Enrollment: 2,439 Female
Affiliation or Control: Roman Catholic IRS Status: 501(c)3
Highest Offering: Doctorate
Program: Liberal Arts And General; Teacher Preparatory; Professional
Accreditation: EH, DIETD, DIETI, MFCD, NURSE, @PHAR, SW

01 President .... Dr. Pamela T. REID
05 Provost .... Dr. Michelle KALIS
10 Vice President Finance & Admin .... Mr. Shawn M. HARRINGTON
30 VP Institutional Advancement .... Mr. Douglas NELSON
84 VP Enrollment Management .... Mr. Gary SHERMAN
32 VP Student Affairs .... Dr. Cheryl A. BARNARD
21 Assoc VP of Finance/Controller .... Mr. William HAWKINS
15 Director of Human Resources .... Ms. Deborah SPENCER
58 Dean Sch of Grad & Prof Studies .... Dr. Daniel NUSSBAUM
67 Dean School of Pharmacy .... Dr. Joseph OFOSU
53 Dean School of Education .... Dr. Kathleen BUTLER
76 Dean School of Health/Nat Sci .... Dr. Sandra AFFENITO
79 Dean School of Humanities/Soc Sci .... Dr. Wayne STEELY
08 Librarian .... Ms. Linda O. GEFFNER
06 Interim Registrar .... Mr. Herb RILEY
26 Dir of Marketing & Communications .... Ms. Cynthia MARIANI
18 Director of Facilities .... Mr. Kevin COCHRAN
29 Dir of Alumni Rels/Annual Giving .... Mr. Stephen KUMNICK
07 Director of Admissions .... Ms. Eileen HOCKING
37 Director of Financial Aid .... Ms. Elizabeth BAKER
36 Director of Career Services .... Mr. Stephen SEWARD
92 Director of Honors Program .... Dr. Elizabeth VOZZOLA
35 Director Student Activities .... Ms. Tracy LAKE
09 Director of Institutional Research .... Mr. Michael BRODERICK
101 Exec Asst to Pres/Secy to Board .... Ms. Ruth FOXMAN
04 Exec Asst to Pres/Dir Spec Event .... Ms. Kelley STREETER

Wesleyan University (E)

Middletown CT 06459-0001
County: Middlesex FICE Identification: 001424
Unit ID: 130697
Telephone: (860) 685-2000 Carnegie Class: Bac/A&S
FAX Number: (860) 685-2001 Calendar System: Semester
URL: www.wesleyan.edu
Established: 1831 Annual Undergrad Tuition & Fees: $45,358
Enrollment: 3,202 Coed
Affiliation or Control: Independent Non-Profit IRS Status: 501(c)3
Highest Offering: Doctorate
Program: Liberal Arts And General
Accreditation: EH

01 President .... Dr. Michael S. ROTH
05 Vice Pres Academic Affairs/Provost .... Dr. Robert ROSENTHAL
10 Vice President/Treasurer .... Dr. John MEERTS
26 Vice President University Relations .... Ms. Barbara-Jan WILSON
28 Vice President for Diversity .... Dr. Sonia B. MAÑJON
32 Vice Pres of Student Affairs .... Mr. Michael J. WHALEY
07 Dean of Admissions & Financial Aid .... Ms. Nancy H. MEISLAHN
35 Asst Vice Pres/Dean of Students .... Mr. Richard CULLITON
09 Director of Institutional Research .... Mr. Michael E. WHITCOMB
37 Director Financial Aid .... Vacant
29 Asst VP Alumni/Parent Relations .... Ms. Gemma F. EBSTEIN
27 Asst Vice Pres University Relations .... Ms. Ann GOODWIN
20 Associate Provost .... Dr. Karen L. ANDERSON
18 Asst Vice President for Facilities .... Ms. Joyce TOPSHE
58 Director of Graduate Liberal Stds .... Ms. Sheryl CULOTTA
06 Registrar .... Ms. Anna VAN DER BURG
08 Librarian .... Ms. Patricia TULLY
36 Director Career Development .... Mr. Michael A. SCIOLA
15 Director Human Resources .... Ms. Julia HICKS
19 Director Public Safety .... Mr. David A. MEYER
31 Dir Community Svcs/Volunteerism .... Ms. Catherine CRIMMINS LECHOWICZ
41 Director of Athletics .... Mr. John S. BIDDISCOMBE
45 Director of Strategic Initiatives .... Dr. Charles G. SALAS

Yale University (A)

New Haven CT 06520
County: New Haven FICE Identification: 001426
Unit ID: 130794
Telephone: (203) 432-4771 Carnegie Class: RU/VH
FAX Number: N/A Calendar System: Semester
URL: www.yale.edu
Established: 1701 Annual Undergrad Tuition & Fees: $42,300
Enrollment: 11,875 Coed
Affiliation or Control: Independent Non-Profit IRS Status: 501(c)3
Highest Offering: Doctorate
Program: Liberal Arts And General; Professional
Accreditation: EH, ARCPA, BUS, CLPSY, ENG, FOR, IPSY, LAW, MED, MIDWF, MUS, NURSE, PH, THEOL

01 President .... Richard C. LEVIN
05 Provost .... Peter SALOVEY
86 Vice Pres & Dir New Haven/State Aff .... Bruce D. ALEXANDER
101 Vice President & Secretary .... Linda K. LORIMER
10 Vice Pres Finance & Business Ops .... Shauna KING
30 Vice President Development .... Vacant
43 Vice President & General Counsel .... Dorothy K. ROBINSON
16 Vice Pres/Chief HR Officer .... Michael A. PEEL
32 Secretary/Vice Pres Student Life .... Kimberly M. GOFF-CREWS
20 Deputy Provost Science & Tech .... Steven M. GIRVIN
20 Deputy Provost of the Arts .... Barbara SHAILOR
20 Deputy Provost Arts and Humanities .... Emily P. BAKEMEIR
20 Deputy Prov Health Affairs .... Stephanie SPANGLER
20 Deputy Provost Academic Resources .... J. Lloyd SUTTLE
11 Assoc VP of Administration .... Janet E. LINDNER
18 Assoc VP Facilities .... John H. BOLLIER
21 Assoc VP Finance & Univ Controller .... Stephen C. MURPHY
27 Chief Comm Ofcr/Dir Ofc Public Affs .... Elizabeth STAUDERMAN
96 Assoc VP & Chief Procurement Ofcr .... John A. MAYES
102 Assoc VP/Dir Corp & Found Rels .... Patricia E. PEDERSEN
08 University Librarian .... Susan GIBBONS
09 Acting Dir Institutional Research .... Rebecca J. FRIEDKIN
13 Assoc VP & Univ CIO .... Leonard PETERS
19 Chief University Police .... Ronnell A. HIGGINS
06 University Registrar .... Gabriel G. OLSZEWSKI
07 Dean Undergraduate Admissions .... Jeffrey BRENZEL
20 Dean Undergraduate Education .... Joseph W. GORDON
35 Dean Student Affairs .... Mr. W. Marichal GENTRY
29 Exec Director Assoc of Yale Alumni .... Mark R. DOLLHOPF
37 Director University Financial Aid .... Caesar T. STORLAZZI
27 Assoc CIO .... Charles POWELL
22 Dir Ofc Equal Opportunities .... Valarie J. STANLEY
23 Director University Health Services .... Dr. Paul GENECIN
90 Sr Dir Academic Technology .... Peggy A. MCCREADY
25 Exec Dir Univ Grant & Contract Admn .... Michael GLASGOW
36 Director Career Services .... Allyson L. MOORE
44 Univ Director Planned Giving .... Eileen B. DONAHUE
39 Dir Grad & Prof Student Housing .... George E. LONGYEAR, JR.
41 Director Athletics .... Thomas A. BECKETT
42 University Chaplain .... Sharon KUGLER
85 Director Intl Students & Scholars .... Ann KUHLMAN
48 Dean of the School of Architecture .... Robert A M. STERN
49 Dean of Yale College .... Mary MILLER
50 Dean School of Management .... Edward A. SNYDER
54 Dean Faculty of Engineering .... Ms. T. Kyle VANDERLICK
57 Dean of the School of Art .... Robert STORR
58 Dean of Grad Sch Arts & Science .... Thomas D. POLLARD
57 Dean of the School of Drama .... James A. BUNDY
61 Dean of the Law School .... Robert C. POST
64 Dean of the School of Music .... Robert L. BLOCKER
65 Dean Sch of Forestry & Environ Stds .... Sir Peter CRANE
73 Dean of the Divinity School .... Gregory E. STERLING
88 Director Inst of Sacred Music .... Martin D. JEAN
63 Dean of School of Medicine .... Dr. Robert J. ALPERN
66 Dean of the School of Nursing .... Margaret GREY
69 Dean of Public Health .... Paul C. CLEARY
28 Chief Diversity Officer .... Deborah STANLEY-MCAULAY
104 Dean Intl & Professional Experience .... Jane EDWARDS

DELAWARE

Delaware College of Art and Design (B)

600 N Market Street, Wilmington DE 19801-3007
County: New Castle FICE Identification: 041398
Unit ID: 432524
Telephone: (302) 622-8000 Carnegie Class: Assoc/PrivNFP
FAX Number: (302) 622-8870 Calendar System: Semester
URL: www.dcad.edu
Established: 1997 Annual Undergrad Tuition & Fees: $20,624
Enrollment: 245 Coed
Affiliation or Control: Independent Non-Profit IRS Status: 501(c)3
Highest Offering: Associate Degree
Program: 2-Year Principally Bachelor's Creditable; Fine Arts Emphasis
Accreditation: M, ART

01 President .... Mr. Stuart BARON

Delaware State University (C)

1200 N DuPont Highway, Dover DE 19901-2275
County: Kent FICE Identification: 001428
Unit ID: 130934
Telephone: (302) 857-6060 Carnegie Class: Master's M
FAX Number: (302) 857-6069 Calendar System: Semester
URL: www.desu.edu
Established: 1891 Annual Undergrad Tuition & Fees (In-State): $7,056
Enrollment: 4,154 Coed
Affiliation or Control: State IRS Status: 501(c)3
Highest Offering: Doctorate
Program: Liberal Arts And General; Teacher Preparatory; Professional
Accreditation: M, BUS, #DIETD, NUR, SW, TED

01 President .... Dr. Harry L. WILLIAMS
04 Assistant to the President .... Ms. Natasha A. ADAMS
05 Int Provost & V Chair Academic Affs .... Dr. Alton THOMPSON
10 Vice Pres Finance & Administration .... Mr. Amir MOHAMMADI
30 Vice Pres Institutional Advancement .... Mrs. Carolyn CURRY
32 Vice Pres Student Affairs .... Mr. Kemal ATKINS
13 Assoc VP Information Technology .... Mr. Arthur LEIBLE
43 General Counsel .... Mr. Thomas PRESTON
46 Vice President for Research .... Dr. Noureddine MELIKECHI
18 Director of Facilities .... Mr. Randy JONES
06 Registrar .... Mr. Terrell HOLMES
07 Director of Admissions .... Ms. Erin HILL
62 Dean of Library Services .... Ms. Rebecca BATSON
37 Director of Financial Aid .... Ms. Lynn IOCANO
09 Director of Institutional Research .... Dr. Phyllis Y. EDAMATSU
29 Director of Alumni Relations .... Ms. Lorene K. ROBINSON
36 Director Career Planning/Placement .... Mrs. Robin ROBERTS
38 Director of Student Counseling .... Mr. Ralph ROBINSON
27 News Director .... Mr. Carlos HOLMES
41 Director of Athletics .... Ms. Candy YOUNG SANDERS
15 Director of Human Resources .... Ms. Irene HAWKINS

*Delaware Technical Community College, Office of the President (D)

Box 897, Dover DE 19903-0897
County: Kent FICE Identification: 008074
Unit ID: 130882
Telephone: (302) 739-3737 Carnegie Class: N/A
FAX Number: (302) 739-6225
URL: www.dtcc.edu

01 President .... Dr. Orlando J. GEORGE, JR.
05 Vice President for Academic Affairs .... Ms. Stephanie S. SMITH
10 Vice President for Finance .... Mr. Gerard M. MCNESBY
15 Vice Pres Inst Effect/College Rels .... Dr. Judith A. SCIPLE
43 Vice Pres Legal Affs & Human Res .... Mr. Brian D. SHIREY
102 Assoc VP Institutional Advancement .... Dr. Barbara S. RIDGELY
20 Asst Vice Pres Educational Support .... Dr. Kimberly L. JOYCE
21 Asst Vice President for Finance .... Ms. Carol C. RHODES
15 Asst Vice Pres Human Resources .... Ms. Patricia A. DEPLASCO
26 Acting Asst VP for Marketing & PR .... Ms. Lisa C. HASTINGS-SHEPPARD
20 Asst VP Curriculum & Instruction .... Dr. June S. TURANSKY
09 Director of Institutional Research .... Ms. Tracy L. BAKOWSKI
13 Chief Technology Officer .... Mr. Robert H. MESSNER
106 Director of E-Learning .... Dr. Richard C. KRALEVICH
104 International Education Director .... Ms. Taryn E. GASSNER

*Delaware Technical Community College, Owens Campus (E)

Box 610, Georgetown DE 19947-0610
County: Sussex FICE Identification: 007053
Unit ID: 130891
Telephone: (302) 856-5400 Carnegie Class: Assoc/Pub-R-M
FAX Number: (302) 858-5455 Calendar System: Semester
URL: www.dtcc.edu/owens
Established: 1967 Annual Undergrad Tuition & Fees (In-State): $3,242
Enrollment: 4,741 Coed
Affiliation or Control: State IRS Status: 501(c)3
Highest Offering: Associate Degree
Program: Occupational; 2-Year Principally Bachelor's Creditable
Accreditation: M, ACBSP, ADNUR, DMS, ENGT, MLTAD, OTA, PTAA, RAD

02 Vice President & Campus Director .... Dr. Ileana M. SMITH
05 Dean of Instruction .... Bobbi J. BARENDS
32 Dean of Student Services .... Dr. Ann L. DELNEGRO
20 Assistant Dean of Instruction .... Ms. Christy A. MORIARTY
04 Assistant to the Campus Director .... Ms. Elizabeth A. RODIER
31 Director Corporate/Community Pgms .... Mr. Christopher M. MOODY
15 Human Resources Director .... Ms. Maribeth B. DOCKETY
11 Director of Administrative Services .... Mr. Linford P. FAUCETT
06 Registrar & Director of Admissions .... Mr. Willie G. THOMAS
08 Head Librarian .... Dr. Shirin JAMASB
26 Chief Public Relations Officer .... Ms. Christine GILLAN
37 Director of Student Financial Aid .... Ms. Veronica E. ONEY
84 Director of Enrollment Management .... Vacant
18 Asst Dir of Administrative Services .... Mr. George E. BOOTH
10 Business Manager .... Mr. Robert W. HEARN, JR.
29 Alumni Coordinator .... Ms. Alison BUCKLEY

*Delaware Technical Community College, Stanton-Wilmington Campus (F)

400 Stanton-Christiana Road, Newark DE 19713-2197
County: New Castle FICE Identification: 021449
Unit ID: 130916
Telephone: (302) 454-3900 Carnegie Class: Assoc/Pub-U-MC
FAX Number: (302) 368-6620 Calendar System: Semester
URL: www.dtcc.edu/stanton
Established: 1968 Annual Undergrad Tuition & Fees (In-State): $3,242
Enrollment: 6,978 Coed
Affiliation or Control: State IRS Status: 501(c)3
Highest Offering: Associate Degree
Program: Occupational; 2-Year Principally Bachelor's Creditable
Accreditation: M, ACBSP, ACFEI, ADNUR, DH, DMS, ENGT, HT, MAC, NMT, OTA, PTAA, RAD

02 Vice President & Campus Director .... Mr. Mark T. BRAINARD
03 Assistant Campus Director .... Dr. Frances H. LEACH
05 Dean Instruction Stanton/Wilmington .... Dr. Kathy A. JANVIER
32 Dean Stdnt Svcs Stanton/Wilmington .... Dr. Regan HICKS-GOLDSTEIN
35 Asst Dean Student Services Stanton .... Mrs. Cornelia JOHNSON
35 Asst Dean Student Svcs Wilmington .... Mrs. Margaret Rose HENRY
20 Asst Dean of Instruction Stanton .... Mr. Robert J. BRADLEY
20 Asst Dean of Instruction Wilmington .... Dr. Kathern R. FRIEL
04 Assistant to the Campus Director .... Dr. Jacquita L. WRIGHT-HENDERSON
91 Systems Admin Director DIET .... Mr. Kenneth J. WEAVERLING
31 Dir of Corporate/Community Pgms .... Dr. Susan E. ZAWISLAK
15 Director of Human Resources .... Dr. Jacqueline D. JENKINS
11 Director Administrative Services .... Mr. John A. FOGELGREN
37 Financial Aid Officer .... Dr. Debra J. TROXLER
06 Registrar Stanton/Wilmington .... Mrs. Collette M. HAYES
08 Head Librarian Stanton .... Mrs. Regina A. WELLS
08 Head Librarian Wilmington .... Mrs. Donna M. ABED
10 Business Manager .... Mr. Daniel R. EHMANN
21 Assistant Business Manager .... Dr. Mary M Y. CHEN
88 Asst Director Admin Services .... Mr. Eddie CUNNINGHAM

*Delaware Technical Community College, Terry Campus (G)

100 Campus Drive, Dover DE 19904-1383
County: Kent FICE Identification: 011727
Unit ID: 130907
Telephone: (302) 857-1000 Carnegie Class: Assoc/Pub-R-M
FAX Number: (302) 857-1296 Calendar System: Semester
URL: www.dtcc.edu/terry
Established: 1972 Annual Undergrad Tuition & Fees (In-State): $3,242
Enrollment: 3,336 Coed
Affiliation or Control: State IRS Status: 501(c)3
Highest Offering: Associate Degree
Program: Occupational; 2-Year Principally Bachelor's Creditable
Accreditation: M, ACBSP, ACFEI, ADNUR, EMT, PNUR

02 Vice President & Campus Director .... Dr. June S. TURANSKY
05 Dean Instruction .... Mr. John M. BUCKLEY
32 Dean Student Services .... Ms. Jennifer P. MOSLEY
04 Assistant to the Campus Director .... Dr. Martha J. HOFSTETTER
31 Director Corporate & Community Pgms .... Vacant
15 Director of Human Resources .... Ms. Charlotte T. LISTER
11 Director of Administrative Services .... Mr. William J. AYERS
37 Director Student Financial Aid .... Ms. Jennifer J. GRUNDEN
08 Head Librarian .... Dr. Margaret R. PROUSE
10 Business Manager .... Mr. James A. GREENWELL
06 Registrar/Admissions Coordinator .... Ms. Nauleen A. PERRY

Goldey-Beacom College (H)

4701 Limestone Road, Wilmington DE 19808-0551
County: New Castle FICE Identification: 001429
Unit ID: 130989
Telephone: (302) 998-8814 Carnegie Class: Spec/Bus
FAX Number: (302) 998-8631 Calendar System: Semester
URL: www.gbc.edu
Established: 1886 Annual Undergrad Tuition & Fees: $21,120
Enrollment: 1,156 Coed
Affiliation or Control: Independent Non-Profit IRS Status: 501(c)3
Highest Offering: Master's
Program: Liberal Arts And General; Professional; Business Emphasis
Accreditation: M, ACBSP, IACBE

01 President .... Dr. Mohammad ILYAS
26 Vice President External Affairs .... Dr. Gary L. WIRT
10 Vice Pres Finance/Administration .... Mrs. Kristine M. SANTOMAURO
05 Dean of Academic Affairs .... Mrs. Alison Boord WHITE
32 Dean of Students .... Mrs. Bernadette H. WIMBERLEY
07 Director of Admissions .... Mr. Larry EBY
84 Dean Enrollment Mgmt/Registrar .... Mrs. Jane H. LYSLE
91 Dean of Information Technology/ACC .... Mrs. Emily S. JACKSON
21 Controller .... Mrs. Susan M. MANNERING
40 Director of Auxiliary Services .... Mrs. Valerie J. HASTINGS-CANDELORO
39 Director of Housing/Residence Life .... Mr. Kevin MARTIN
36 Career Service Specialist .... Ms. Elizabeth KIRKER
36 Career Service Specialist .... Ms. Kimberly PLUSCH
18 Director of Facilities .... Mr. Meezie FOSTER
41 Athletic Director .... Mr. Charles A. HAMMOND

University of Delaware (I)

104 Hullihen Hall, Newark DE 19716
County: New Castle FICE Identification: 001431
Unit ID: 130943
Telephone: (302) 831-2000 Carnegie Class: RU/VH
FAX Number: N/A Calendar System: 4/1/4
URL: www.udel.edu
Established: 1743 Annual Undergrad Tuition & Fees (In-State): $11,682
Enrollment: 21,489 Coed
Affiliation or Control: State Related IRS Status: 501(c)3
Highest Offering: Doctorate
Program: Liberal Arts And General; Teacher Preparatory; Professional

Accreditation: M, BUS, BUSA, CEA, CLPSY, DIETD, DIETI, ENG, ENGT, IPSY, MT, MUS, NURSE, PTA, SPAA, TED

01 President ... Dr. Patrick T. HARKER
05 Interim Provost ... Dr. Nancy BRICKHOUSE
03 Exec Vice President/Univ Treasurer ... Mr. Scott R. DOUGLASS
11 Vice President for Finance & Admin ... Ms. Jennifer DAVIS
30 VP Development & Alumni Relations ... Ms. Monica M. TAYLOR
26 Vice Pres Communications/Marketing ... Vacant
13 Vice Pres Information Technologies ... Mr. Carl JACOBSON
43 Vice Pres and General Counsel ... Mr. Lawrence WHITE
100 VP/Chief of Staff ... Ms. Patricia WILSON
18 VP Facilities & Auxillary Services ... Mr. David SINGLETON
46 Senior Vice Provost for Research ... Dr. Mark A. BARTEAU
58 Vice Provost Graduate and Prof Educ ... Dr. Charles RIORDAN
20 Interim Deputy Provost ... Dr. Ann ARDIS
51 Asst Provost Prof Cont Studies ... Dr. James K. BROOMALL
88 Assoc Provost Academic Affairs ... Dr. Margaret ANDERSEN
84 Assoc Provost Admin/Enrollment Svcs ... Ms. Margaret B. BOTTORFF
32 Vice Pres for Student Life ... Dr. Michael A. GILBERT
09 Director Institutional Research ... Dr. Heather A. KELLY
29 Director Alumni Relations ... Ms. Cynthia B. CAMPANELLA
08 Vice Provost/Director Libraries ... Ms. Susan BRYNTESON
37 Director Student Financial Services ... Ms. Melissa STONE
36 Director Career Services Center ... Mr. Matthew BRINK
19 Exec Director Public Safety ... Mr. Albert J. HOMIAK, JR.
47 Dean Agriculture/Natural Resources ... Dr. Mark RIEGER
49 Dean Arts & Sciences ... Dr. George H. WATSON
50 Dean Business & Economics ... Dr. Bruce W. WEBER
54 Interim Dean College of Engineering ... Dr. Babatunde A. OGUNNAIKE
65 Dean of Earth/Ocean/Environment ... Dr. Nancy M. TARGETT
76 Dean of Health Sciences ... Dr. Kathleen S. MATT
53 Dean Education/Human Development ... Dr. Lynn OKAGAKI
92 Director University Honors Program ... Dr. Michael A. ARNOLD
107 Assoc Prov Grad/Professional Edu ... Dr. John E. SAWYER
07 Director Admissions ... Dr. José AVILES
15 Director Human Resources ... Mr. Jerry CUTLER
96 Director of Procurement Services ... Ms. Debra C. REESE
06 University Registrar ... Mr. Jeffrey L. PALMER
21 Director Budget ... Mr. Michael S. JACKSON
28 Director Equity and Inclusion ... Ms. Rebecca R. FOGERTY
35 Dean of Students/AVP Student Life ... Ms. Dawn M. THOMPSON
38 Director Ctr for Couns/Student Dev ... Dr. Charles L. BEALE
39 Director Housing Assignment Service ... Ms. Linda CAREY
41 Director Athletics & Recreation ... Mr. Bernard MUIR

Wesley College (A)

120 N State Street, Dover DE 19901-3876

County: Kent
FICE Identification: 001433
Unit ID: 131098
Telephone: (302) 736-2300
Carnegie Class: Bac/Diverse
FAX Number: (302) 736-2301
Calendar System: Semester
URL: www.wesley.edu
Established: 1873
Annual Undergrad Tuition & Fees: $22,392
Enrollment: 1,892
Coed
Affiliation or Control: United Methodist
IRS Status: 501(c)3
Highest Offering: Master's
Program: Liberal Arts And General; Teacher Preparatory; Professional
Accreditation: M, NUR

01 President ... Dr. William N. JOHNSTON
05 Vice President for Academic Affairs ... Dr. Patricia DWYER
10 VP Finance/Dir Human Resource ... Mr. Eric NELSON
30 Vice Pres Institutional Advancement ... Mr. Chris WOOD
20 Assoc VP for Academic Affairs ... Dr. Colleen DI RADDO
32 Dean of Students ... Ms. Mary-Alice OZECHOSKI
51 Exec Dir Wesley College New Castle ... Dr. Zoann PARKER
84 Dean of Enrollment Management ... Dr. Howard BALLENTINE
42 Dir Spiritual Life and Comm Involv ... Rev. Steve LAMOTTE
21 Dir Acctg and Business Systems ... Mr. Scott SLACUM
43 General Counsel ... Mr. David WILKS
06 Registrar ... Ms. Rayann FRYATT
88 Head of School Campus/Community Sch ... Ms. Patricia HERMANCE
12 Part-time Admin Coord DAFB ... Ms. Tracey LUNDBLAD
08 Director of the Parker Library ... Mr. Roger GETZ
20 Director of Academic Support Svcs ... Ms. Charlene STEPHENS
36 Asst Dir Academic Support Services ... Ms. Christine MCDERMOTT
26 Director of Marketing ... Ms. Jessica COOK
09 Director of Institutional Research ... Vacant
46 Dir Data Analy & Inst Assessment ... Vacant
07 Director of Undergrad Admissions ... Vacant
41 Exec Dir of Sports & Recreation ... Mr. Mike DRASS
18 Director of the Physical Plant ... Mr. Rick RICHARDSON
40 Director of the Bookstore ... Mr. Kris MCGLOTHIN
19 Director of Safety/Security ... Mr. Walter BEAUPRE
23 Director Student Health Services ... Ms. Jill MASER
44 Dir of the Annual Wesley Fund ... Ms. Cathy NOSEL
88 Dir of The Wesley Fund ... Ms. Cathy ANDERSON
39 Director of Residence Life ... Mr. Kevin HANSBURY
35 Director of Student Activities ... Ms. Sarah SMITH
37 Dir of Student Financial Planning ... Mr. Michael HALL
38 Director of Counseling ... Ms. Ann ROGGE
85 Director of Global Initiatives ... Mr. Kevin CULLEN
29 Director Alumni Affairs ... Ms. Amanda DOWNES
88 Dir Campus Community High School ... Ms. Heidi GREENE
41 Assoc Dir of Sports & Rec ... Vacant
04 Assistant to the President ... Ms. Ellen COLEMAN
88 Supervisor Finance Office ... Ms. Zoe BELL

Widener University School of Law (B)

PO Box 7474, Wilmington DE 19803-0474

County: New Castle
FICE Identification: 012962
Unit ID: 211945
Telephone: (302) 477-2100
Carnegie Class: Not Classified
FAX Number: (302) 477-2282
Calendar System: Semester
URL: www.law.widener.edu
Established: 1971
Annual Undergrad Tuition & Fees: $38,160
Enrollment: 1,598
Coed
Affiliation or Control: Independent Non-Profit
IRS Status: 501(c)3
Highest Offering: First Professional Degree
Program: Professional
Accreditation: LAW

01 President ... Dr. James T. HARRIS, III
05 Interim Sr Vice President & Provost ... Dr. Stephn C. WILHITE
20 Dean ... Ms. Linda L. AMMONS
11 Sr Vice Pres Administration/Finance ... Mr. Joseph J. BAKER
30 Vice Pres University Advancement ... Ms. Linda S. DURANT
12 Vice Dean Delaware Campus ... Mr. Patrick KELLY
12 Vice Dean Harrisburg Campus ... Ms. Robyn L. MEADOWS
32 Dean of Students Harrisburg Campus ... Mr. Keith E. SEALING
35 Assoc Dean Student Academic Svcs ... Ms. Susan GOLDBERG
07 Assistant Dean Admission ... Ms. Barbara L. AYARS
29 Asst Director Alumni Relations ... Ms. Nancy RAVERT WARD
06 Assistant Dean Registrar ... Ms. Tamara L. GRAHAM
37 Director of Financial Aid ... Ms. Eleanor A. KELLY
61 Assistant Dean Legal Education Inst ... Ms. Eileen A. GRENA
36 Asst Dean Career Development ... Ms. Lea Nora RUFFIN
21 Assistant Dean Business & Admin ... Mr. Verne R. SMITH
13 Chief Information Officer ... Mr. Peter D. SHOUDY
18 Director of Operations ... Mr. Carl G. PIERCE
08 Director Legal Information Center ... Mr. Michael J. SLINGER
09 Dir IR & Effectiveness ... Dr. Stephen W. THORPE
26 Chief Public Relations Officer ... Ms. Mary E. ALLEN
35 Assistant Dean for Student Affairs ... Mr. Edmund LUCE

† Branch campus of Widener University in Pennsylvania. This listing reflects the administrators for the school of law for the Harrisburg (PA) and Delaware campuses.

Wilmington University (C)

320 N Dupont Highway, New Castle DE 19720-6491

County: New Castle
FICE Identification: 007948
Unit ID: 131113
Telephone: (302) 356-4636
Carnegie Class: DRU
FAX Number: (302) 328-5902
Calendar System: Trimester
URL: www.wilmu.edu
Established: 1967
Annual Undergrad Tuition & Fees: $9,710
Enrollment: 10,848
Coed
Affiliation or Control: Independent Non-Profit
IRS Status: 501(c)3
Highest Offering: Doctorate
Program: Liberal Arts And General; Professional
Accreditation: M, CACREP, IACBE, NURSE, TED

01 President ... Dr. Jack P. VARSALONA
32 University Vice Pres Student Affs ... Dr. LaVerne T. HARMON
11 University Vice Pres Admin Affs ... Ms. Carole D. PITCHER
10 Vice President/CFO Financial Affs ... Ms. Heather A. O'CONNELL
88 Vice Pres Academic Support Services ... Ms. Erin DIMARCO
88 Vice President External Affairs ... Dr. Peter A. BAILEY
05 Vice President Academic Affairs ... Dr. James D. WILSON, JR.
88 Asst Vice Pres/Dean of Locations ... Dr. Richard D. GOCHNAUER
21 Asst Vice President/Controller ... Mr. David R. LEWIS
15 Asst Vice Pres/Chief Human Res Ofcr ... Mr. P. Donald HAGERMANN
26 Asst Vice Pres Public Relations ... Mr. Christopher G. PITCHER
30 Asst Vice Pres Inst Advancement ... Dr. Thomas B. CUPPLES
100 Asst Vice Pres/President's Office ... Dr. Angela C. SUCHANIC
88 Asst VP Administrative Affairs ... Ms. Eileen G. DONNELLY
35 Asst VP Student Affairs ... Ms. Tina M. SCOTT
20 Asst VP Academic Affairs ... Dr. Sheila M. SHARBAUGH
19 Asst VP/University Safety/Athletic ... Dr. Jack L. CUNNINGHAM
08 Director Library ... Mr. James M. MCCLOSKEY
105 Director of Web Communications ... Mr. Kevin G. BARRY
13 Dir Information Technology ... Mr. Bryan E. STEINBERG
41 Director Athletics ... Ms. Linda M. ANDRZJEWSKI
07 Director of Admissions ... Ms. Laura M. MORRIS
18 Chief Facilities/Physical Plant ... Mr. William P. QUINN
29 Director Alumni Relations ... Ms. Patricia L. JENNINGS
36 Director Student Placement ... Dr. Regina C. ALLEN-SHARPE
96 Director of Purchasing ... Mr. Mark S. PARIS
26 Director University Relations ... Ms. Jacque R. VARSALONA
37 Director Student Financial Services ... Ms. Trudy E. HITE
88 Executive Director Academic Support ... Mrs. Peg P. MITCHELL
27 Director University Information ... Mrs. Meghan R. SCHMEUSSER
78 Director Cooperative Learning ... Mr. David C. CAFFO
16 Director Human Resources ... Mrs. Nicole ROMANO
50 Dean College of Business ... Dr. Donald W. DURANDETTA
53 Dean College of Education ... Dr. John C. GRAY
76 Dean College of Health Professions ... Ms. Denise Z. WESTBROOK
83 Dean College Social/Behavioral Sci ... Dr. Christian A. TROWBRIDGE
49 Dean College of Arts and Sciences ... Dr. Doreen B. TURNBO
72 Dean College of Technology ... Dr. Edward L. GUTHRIE

DISTRICT OF COLUMBIA

American University (D)

4400 Massachusetts Avenue, NW, Washington DC 20016

FICE Identification: 001434
Unit ID: 131159
Telephone: (202) 885-1000
Carnegie Class: DRU
FAX Number: N/A
Calendar System: Semester
URL: www.american.edu
Established: 1893
Annual Undergrad Tuition & Fees: $39,499
Enrollment: 12,980
Coed
Affiliation or Control: United Methodist
IRS Status: 501(c)3
Highest Offering: Doctorate
Program: Liberal Arts And General; Teacher Preparatory; Professional
Accreditation: M, BUS, CLPSY, IPSY, JOUR, LAW, MUS, SPAA, TED

01 President ... Dr. Cornelius M. KERWIN
05 Provost ... Dr. Scott A. BASS
30 Vice President Development ... Dr. Thomas MINAR
10 Vice President Finance & Treasurer ... Mr. Donald MYERS
32 Vice President Campus Life ... Dr. Gail S. HANSON
43 Vice President General Counsel ... Ms. Mary E. KENNARD
11 Vice Provost for Academic Admin ... Ms. Violeta ETTLE
18 Asst VP Facilities Dev/Real Estate ... Mr. Jorge J. ABUD
21 Asst VP Finance & Asst Treasurer ... Mr. Douglas KUDRAVETZ
35 Asst Vice Pres and Dean of Students ... Dr. Robert HRADSKY
35 Asst Vice President Campus Life ... Dr. Fanta AW
29 Asst Vice Pres of Alumni Relations ... Ms. Raina LENNEY
84 Vice Provost Undergrad Enrollment ... Dr. Sharon ALSTON
13 Asst Vice Pres and CIO ... Mr. David L. SWARTZ
100 Chief of Staff President's Office ... Mr. David E. TAYLOR
20 Sr Vice Provost & Dean Acad Affairs ... Dr. Phyllis PERES
58 Vice Provost Grad Studies & Rsrch ... Dr. Jonathan G. TUBMAN
20 Vice Provost Undergrad Studies ... Dr. Virginia (Lyn) STALLINGS
49 Dean College Arts & Sciences ... Dr. Peter STARR
60 Dean Sch of Communication ... Dr. Jeffrey RUTENBECK
50 Dean Kogod School of Business ... Dr. Michael J. GINZBERG
61 Dean Washington College of Law ... Dr. Claudio GROSSMAN
82 Dean School of Intl Service ... Dr. James GOLDGEIER
80 Dean School of Public Affairs ... Dr. Barbara ROMZEK
15 Exec Director Human Resources ... Ms. Beth MUHA
36 Exec Director Career Center ... Mr. Gihan FERNANDO
09 Dir Institutional Rsrch/ Assessment ... Ms. Karen L. FROSLID JONES
26 Vice Pres University Communications ... Dr. Teresa (Terry) FLANNERY
06 University Registrar ... Dr. Alice POEHLS
08 Interim University Librarian ... Ms. Nancy DAVENPORT
21 Controller ... Mr. John R. SMIELL
88 Dir Student Finance and Collections ... Mr. Mark WELCH
21 Asst Vice Pres Budget & Finance ... Ms. Nana AN
88 Asst VP Risk Mgmt/Safety Svcs ... Ms. Patricia L. KELSHIAN
88 Assoc Director Student Billing ... Ms. Minh N. PHUNG
88 Assoc Dir Student Account Operation ... Mr. Darrell COOK
42 University Chaplain ... Dr. Joseph T. ELDRIDGE
30 Asst Vice President Development ... Ms. Abbey FAGIN
19 Exec Dir Univ Safety Programs ... Mr. Daniel NICHOLS
37 Director Financial Aid ... Mr. Brian LEE SANG
38 Director of Counseling Center ... Dr. Wanda COLLINS
25 Director Contracting & Procurement ... Mr. Brian BLAIR
07 Director of Admissions ... Mr. Gregory GRAUMAN
85 Director Intl Student/Scholar Svcs ... Dr. Fanta AW
92 Interim Dir Univ Honors Program ... Dr. Michael L. MANSON
41 Director Athletics & Recreation ... Mr. Keith GILL
28 Director of Multicultural Affairs ... Ms. Tiffany SPEAKS
96 Asst Director of Purchasing ... Ms. Hallie PORTER
104 Director AU Abroad ... Ms. Sara E. DUMONT

The Catholic University of America (E)

620 Michigan Avenue, NE, Washington DC 20064-0002

FICE Identification: 001437
Unit ID: 131283
Telephone: (202) 319-5000
Carnegie Class: RU/H
FAX Number: (202) 319-4441
Calendar System: Semester
URL: www.cua.edu
Established: 1887
Annual Undergrad Tuition & Fees: $36,570
Enrollment: 6,894
Coed
Affiliation or Control: Roman Catholic
IRS Status: 501(c)3
Highest Offering: Doctorate
Program: Liberal Arts And General; Teacher Preparatory; Professional
Accreditation: M, CLPSY, ENG, IPSY, LAW, LIB, MUS, NURSE, SW, TED, THEOL

01 President ... Mr. John H. GARVEY
100 VP University Rels/Chief of Staff ... Mr. Frank G. PERSICO
05 Provost ... Dr. James F. BRENNAN
10 Vice Pres Finance & Treasurer ... Ms. Cathy R. WOOD
30 Vice Pres Institutional Advancement ... Mr. H. Ken DEDOMINICIS
32 Vice President Student Life ... Mrs. Susan D. PERVI
21 Vice President Business Services ... Vacant
84 Vice Pres Enrollment Management ... Mr. Michael HENDRICKS
35 Assoc VP Student Life/Dean Students ... Mr. Jonathan C. SAWYER
26 Assoc Vice Pres for Public Affairs ... Mr. Victor B. NAKAS
43 University Counsel ... Mr. Lawrence J. MORRIS
15 Assoc VP/Chief Human Resources ... Ms. Christine SPORTES
18 Assoc VP Facilities Operations ... Mr. Jerry CONRAD
41 Assoc VP & Director Athletics ... Dr. Michael S. ALLEN
88 Assoc VP for Campus Services ... Mr. Timothy CARNEY
44 Asst Vice Pres Development ... Vacant
25 Assoc Prov Sponsored Research ... Mr. Ralph ALBANO

58 Dean Graduate Studies ... Dr. James GREENE
48 Dean of Architecture ... Mr. Randall OTT
49 Dean of Arts & Sciences ... Dr. Lawrence R. POOS
54 Dean of Engineering ... Dr. Charles C. NGUYEN
61 Dean of Law ... Ms. Veryl V. MILES
64 Dean of Music ... Dr. Grayson WAGSTAFF
70 Dean Natl Catholic Sch Social Svcs ... Dr. James R. ZABORA
66 Dean of Nursing ... Dr. Patricia MCMULLEN
73 Act Dean Theology/Religious Studies ... Rev. Mark MOROZOWICH
55 Dean Metropolitan Sch Profess Stds ... Dr. Sara M. THOMPSON
62 Acting Dean Library/Information Sci ... Dr. Ingrid HSIEH-YEE
79 Dean of Philosophy ... Dr. John C. MCCARTHY
88 Dean of Canon Law ... Rev. Robert J. KASLYN, SJ
07 Dean of Admissions ... Ms. Christine MICA
13 Chief Information Officer ... Mr. Ziaeddin MAFAHER
08 Director of Libraries ... Mr. Stephen CONNAGHAN
06 Registrar ... Ms. Adriana FARELLA
36 Director of Career Services ... Mr. Anthony CHIAPPETTA
29 Exec Director Alumni Relations ... Ms. Kyra A. LYONS
19 Director of Public Safety ... Ms. Thomasine JOHNSON
38 Director of Counseling Center ... Dr. T. Monroe RAYBURN
23 Medical Director of Health Center ... Dr. Loretta STAUDT
37 Director of Financial Aid ... Vacant
39 Director of Housing Services ... Ms. Heidi E. ZEICH
44 Director Annual Giving ... Vacant
42 Dir Univ Campus Ministry ... Rev. Jude DEANGELO, OFM CONV
09 Dir Inst Research/Assessment ... Mr. Brian A. JOHNSTON
92 Director Univ Honors Program ... Dr. Peter SHOEMAKER
96 Director of Procurement Services ... Mr. Norman BROWN
22 Equal Opportunity Officer ... Ms. Lisa WOOD
88 Compliance and Ethics Officer ... Mr. Vincent A. LACOVARA
40 Manager Bookstore ... Ms. Tammy ROGERS

Corcoran College of Art and Design (A)

500 17th Street, NW, Washington DC 20006-4804

FICE Identification: 011950
Unit ID: 131308

Telephone: (202) 639-1801 Carnegie Class: Spec/Arts
FAX Number: (202) 639-1802 Calendar System: Semester
URL: www.corcoran.edu
Established: 1890 Annual Undergrad Tuition & Fees: $30,930
Enrollment: 696 Coed
Affiliation or Control: Independent Non-Profit IRS Status: 501(c)3
Highest Offering: Master's
Program: Liberal Arts And General
Accreditation: M, ART

01 Director & CEO of Gallery & College ... Mr. Fred BOLLERER
05 Provost & Chief Academic Officer ... Ms. Catherine ARMOUR
10 Vice President of Finance ... Mr. Stephen GOLDSMITH
26 Vice President of Communications ... Ms. Kristin GUITER
20 Assoc Provost/Dean Undergrad Stds ... Mr. Andy GRUNDBERG
32 Dean of Students ... Mr. John DICKSON
84 Dean of Enrollment ... Ms. Christine LEICHLITER
15 Sr Director of Human Resources ... Ms. Karen WITT
11 Senior Director of Operations ... Mr. Steve BROWN
06 Registrar ... Ms. Curren MCLANE
08 Library Director ... Mr. Mario ASCENCIO
37 Director of Financial Aid ... Ms. Diane MORRIS
51 Director of Continuing Education ... Ms. Doris OSTRANDER

Gallaudet University (B)

800 Florida Avenue, NE, Washington DC 20002-3695

FICE Identification: 001443
Unit ID: 131450

Telephone: (202) 651-5000 Carnegie Class: Master's S
FAX Number: (202) 651-5508 Calendar System: Semester
URL: www.gallaudet.edu
Established: 1864 Annual Undergrad Tuition & Fees: $13,898
Enrollment: 1,488 Coed
Affiliation or Control: Independent Non-Profit IRS Status: 501(c)3
Highest Offering: Doctorate
Program: Liberal Arts And General; Teacher Preparatory; Professional
Accreditation: M, ACBSP, AUD, CACREP, CLPSY, SP, SW, TED

01 President ... Dr. T. Alan HURWITZ
05 Provost ... Dr. Stephen F. WEINER
10 Vice Pres Admin & Finance/Treasurer ... Mr. Paul KELLY
30 Vice Pres Dev & Alumni Relations ... Dr. Lynne MURRAY
100 Chief of Staff ... Mr. Don BEIL
101 Spec Asst to Pres/Board Liaison ... Vacant
84 Interim Chief Enrollmt Mgmt Officer ... Ms. Charity REEDY-HINES
28 Assoc Provost Diversity/Inclusion ... Dr. Angela MCCASKILL
27 Chief Information Officer ... Dr. Cynthia KING
88 Dean Laurent Clerc Nat Deaf Ed Ctr ... Mr. Edward H. BOSSO
49 Dean Arts/Sciences/Technologies ... Dr. Isaac AGBOOLA
58 Dean Graduate Sch & Prof Pgms ... Dr. Carol ERTING
32 Dean Student Affairs ... Mr. Dwight BENEDICT
88 Actg Dean Prof Services & Outreach ... Vacant
88 Exec Dir Academic Quality ... Dr. Patricia HULSEBOSCH
21 Executive Director Finance ... Ms. Jean CIBUZAR
45 Director University Budget ... Ms. Debra LIPKEY
96 Exec Dir Business Support Services ... Mr. Gary ALLER
18 Executive Director Facilities ... Dr. Meloyde BATTEN-MICKENS
11 Interim Asst Vice Pres Admin ... Mr. Fred WEINER
102 Dir Corp and Foundations Relations ... Vacant
26 Exec Dir Comm & Public Relations ... Ms. Catherine MURPHY
09 Dir Research & Info Services ... Ms. Sarah DUCRAY
29 Director Alumni Relations ... Mr. Samuel SONNENSTRAHL
16 Director Human Resources Svcs ... Ms. Elaine VANCE
90 Exec Dir Technology Services ... Mr. Earl PARKS
88 Dir Technology Servcies Enterprise ... Mr. Harvey GROSSINGER
14 Info Security Officer/Network Dir ... Vacant
88 Director Library Public Services ... Ms. Sarah HAMRICK
88 University Ombuds ... Ms. Suzanne ROSEN SINGLETON
88 Dir Library Deaf Collection/Archive ... Mr. Ulf HEDBERG
22 Director Equal Opportunity Programs ... Ms. Sharrell MCCASKILL

George Washington University (C)

2121 I Street, NW, Washington DC 20052-0002

FICE Identification: 001444
Unit ID: 131469

Telephone: (202) 994-1000 Carnegie Class: RU/VH
FAX Number: (202) 994-0458 Calendar System: Semester
URL: www.gwu.edu
Established: 1821 Annual Undergrad Tuition & Fees: $45,780
Enrollment: 25,260 Coed
Affiliation or Control: Independent Non-Profit IRS Status: 501(c)3
Highest Offering: Doctorate
Program: 2-Year Principally Bachelor's Creditable; Liberal Arts And General; Teacher Preparatory; Professional
Accreditation: M, ARCPA, BUS, BUSA, CACREP, CIDA, CLPSY, CORE, CS, DMS, ENG, HSA, LAW, MED, MT, MUS, NURSE, PH, PTA, SP, SPAA, TED

01 President ... Dr. Steven KNAPP
100 Chief of Staff President's Office ... Ms. Barbara A. PORTER
05 Provost & Exec VP Academic Affairs ... Dr. Steven LERMAN
30 Vice Pres for Dev/Alumni Relations ... Mr. Michael J. MORSBERGER
10 Exec Vice President & Treasurer ... Mr. Louis H. KATZ
43 Senior Vice Pres & General Counsel ... Ms. Beth NOLAN
32 Sr VP Student/Acad Support Svcs ... Dr. Robert A. CHERNAK
26 Vice President External Relations ... Ms. Lorraine A. VOLES
20 Sr Vice Provost Academic Affairs ... Dr. Forrest MALTZMAN
28 Vice Provost Diversity & Inclusion ... Dr. Terri Harris REED
20 Vice Provost Teaching and Learning ... Dr. Stephen C. EHRMAN
15 Chief Human Resources Officer ... Ms. Sabrina ELLIS
13 Chief Information Officer ... Mr. David STEINOUR
20 Vice Provost, Faculty Affairs ... Dr. Diane C. MARTIN
20 Sr Assoc VP for Academic Operations ... Dr. Craig W. LINEBAUGH
21 Senior Associate VP for Finance ... Mr. David D. LAWLOR
11 Senior Assoc VP of Operations ... Ms. Alicia M. O'NEIL
35 Senior Assoc VP & Dean of Students ... Dr. Peter A. KONWERSKI
89 Assoc VP & Dean of Freshmen . Ms. Helen CANNADAY SAULNY
90 Assoc VP for Acad Technologies ... Ms. P. B. GARRETT
88 Assoc VP of IR/Acad Plng/Assessment ... Dr. Cheryl BEIL
46 Vice President for Research ... Dr. Leo M. CHALUPA
21 Chief Budget Officer ... Ms. Vanessa R. ROSE
21 University Comptroller ... Ms. Debra L. DICKENSON
09 Director Inst Research & Planning ... Mr. Joachim W. KNOP
86 Assistant Vice President DC Affairs ... Mr. Bernard DEMCZUK
87 Associate VP for International Pgms ... Dr. Donna SCARBORO
08 University Librarian ... Mr. Jack A. SIGGINS
26 Asst VP for Communications ... Ms. Sarah GEGENHEIMER BALDASSARO
27 Exec Director of Media Relations ... Ms. Candace E. SMITH
29 Associate VP Alumni Relations ... Ms. Adrienne A. RULNICK
06 Registrar ... Ms. Elizabeth A. AMUNDSON
07 Assoc VP & Dean Undergrad Admiss ... Dr. Kathryn M. NAPPER
38 Director Counseling Center ... Dr. John R. DAGES
37 Assoc VP & Director Financial Aid ... Mr. Daniel E. SMALL
36 Exec Director Career Center ... Ms. Marva GUMBS
18 Associate VP Facilities ... Vacant
85 Director International Services ... Mr. Joseph G. LEONARD
19 Sr Assoc VP Safety & Security ... Mr. Darrell L. DARNELL
22 Exec Dir Equal Employ Opportunity ... Ms. Lydia M. MARTINEZ
23 Director Student Health Services ... Dr. Isabel GOLDENBERG
40 Director GW Bookstore ... Mr. Robert C. BLAKE
107 Dean Col of Professional Studies ... Dr. Ali ESKANDARIAN
49 Dean Columbian Col Arts/Sciences ... Dr. Marguerite BARRATT
63 Interim Dean Medicine & Health Sci ... Dr. Jeffrey S. AKMAN
69 Dean School of Public Health ... Dr. Lynn R. GOLDMAN
61 Dean Law School ... Dr. Paul S. BERMAN
54 Dean Engineer/Applied Science ... Dr. David DOLLING
53 Dean Education/Human Development ... Dr. Michael J. FEUER
50 Dean School of Business ... Dr. Doug GUTHRIE
82 Dean Elliott School Intl Affairs ... Dr. Michael E. BROWN
66 Dean School of Nursing ... Dr. Jean JOHNSON
12 Dean GW Virginia Sci/Tech Campus ... Dr. Ali ESKANDARIAN
41 Director Athletics/Recreation ... Mr. Patrick NERO
84 Asst VP Grad Student Enroll Mgmt ... Dr. Kristin WILLIAMS
92 Director University Honors Program ... Dr. Maria H. FRAWLEY
93 Director Multicultural Student Svc ... Mr. Michael R. TAPSCOTT

Georgetown University (D)

37th & O Streets, NW, Washington DC 20057-1947

FICE Identification: 001445
Unit ID: 131496

Telephone: (202) 687-0100 Carnegie Class: RU/VH
FAX Number: N/A Calendar System: Semester
URL: www.georgetown.edu
Established: 1789 Annual Undergrad Tuition & Fees: $42,870
Enrollment: 17,130 Coed
Affiliation or Control: Roman Catholic IRS Status: 501(c)3
Highest Offering: Doctorate
Program: Liberal Arts And General; Professional
Accreditation: M, ANEST, BUS, CEA, HSA, LAW, MED, MIDWF, NURSE

01 President ... Dr. John (Jack) J. DEGIOIA
03 Sr Vice Pres/Chief Admin Officer ... Dr. Spiros DIMOLITSAS
101 Secretary of the University ... Mr. Edward M. QUINN
100 Chief of Staff ... Mr. Joseph FERRARA
05 Provost ... Dr. Robert M. GROVES
17 Exec Vice Pres Health Sciences ... Dr. Howard J. FEDEROFF
61 Exec Vice Pres/Dean of Law School ... Dr. William M. TREANOR
26 Vice Pres for Advancement ... Mr. R. Bartley MOORE
42 Vice Pres for Mission and Ministry ... Rev. Philip L. BOROUGHS, SJ
11 Sr Vice Pres and COO ... Mr. Christopher L. AUGOSTINI
10 Vice Pres Administrative Services ... Mr. David RUBENSTEIN
13 Vice Pres/CIO ... Ms. Lisa DAVIS
15 VP/Chief Human Resources Ofcr ... Ms. Mary Anne MAHIN
27 VP Public Affairs & Strategic Dev ... Mr. Erik SMULSON
18 VP Univ Facilities/Student Housing ... Ms. Karen S. FRANK
32 Vice President for Student Affairs ... Dr. Todd OLSON
28 VP for Inst Diversity & Equity ... Ms. Rosemary KILKENNY
19 Vice President University Safety ... Mr. Rocco DELMONACO, JR.
29 Associate VP Alumni Relations ... Mr. William G. REYNOLDS
88 Assoc VP for Auxiliary Services ... Ms. Margie BRYANT
30 Assoc VP University Development ... Mr. Matthew T. LAMBERT
90 Assoc VP Univ Information Svcs ... Dr. Ardoth HASSLER
43 Interim VP & General Counsel ... Ms. Lisa KRIM
06 Registrar ... Mr. John Q. PIERCE, IV
07 Dean Undergraduate Admissions ... Mr. Charles A. DEACON
08 University Librarian ... Ms. Artemis G. KIRK
09 Exec Director Inst Research ... Dr. Michael D. MCGUIRE
37 Dean Student Financial Svcs ... Ms. Patricia A. MCWADE
25 Associate Dean for Research Admin ... Ms. Mary E. SCHMIEDEL
49 Dean Georgetown College ... Dr. Chester GILLIS
82 Dean School Foreign Service ... Dr. Carol LANCASTER
50 Dean School of Business ... Dr. David A. THOMAS
63 Dean Medical School ... Dr. Stephen R. MITCHELL
66 Dean Sch of Nursing/Health Stds ... Dr. Martin Y. IGUCHI
51 Interim Dean Cont Studies ... Dr. Walter RANKIN
58 Interim Dean of Graduate School ... Dr. Gerald MARA
86 Asst to President Federal Relations ... Mr. Scott S. FLEMING
31 Asst Vice Pres for External Rels ... Ms. Linda GREENAN
85 Exec Dir International Programs ... Ms. Kathryn S. BELLOWS
36 Exec Director Career Center ... Dr. J. Michael SCHAUB
22 Int Dir Diversity Equity & Aff Act ... Mr. Michael W. SMITH
24 Exec Dir Classroom Educ/Tech Svcs ... Mr. Mark J. COHEN
38 Director Student Health ... Dr. Philip W. MEILMAN
41 Director Athletics ... Mr. Lee REED
20 Associate Provost ... Ms. Marcia B. MINTZ
20 Associate Provost Academics ... Ms. Marjory S. BLUMENTHAL
96 Director Financial Operations ... Ms. Geneva THORNE

Howard University (E)

2400 Sixth Street, NW, Washington DC 20059-0001

FICE Identification: 001448
Unit ID: 131520

Telephone: (202) 806-6100 Carnegie Class: RU/H
FAX Number: (202) 806-5934 Calendar System: Semester
URL: www.howard.edu
Established: 1867 Annual Undergrad Tuition & Fees: $22,883
Enrollment: 10,583 Coed
Affiliation or Control: Independent Non-Profit IRS Status: 501(c)3
Highest Offering: Doctorate
Program: Occupational; Liberal Arts And General; Teacher Preparatory; Professional
Accreditation: M, ARCPA, ART, BUS, BUSA, CLPSY, #COPSY, CS, DENT, DH, DIETC, ENG, IPSY, JOUR, LAW, MED, MT, MUS, NURSE, OT, PHAR, PTA, RTT, SP, SW, TED, THEA, THEOL

01 President ... Dr. Sidney RIBEAU
05 Provost/Chief Academic Officer ... Dr. Wayne H. FREDERICK
10 Senior Vice President & CFO ... Mr. Robert TAROLA
45 Sr VP Strategic Planning ... Dr. Hassan MINOR, JR.
101 Senior Vice Pres/Secretary of Univ ... Ms. Artis G. HAMPSHIRE-COWAN
43 General Counsel ... Mr. Kurt L. SCHMOKE
30 Vice President Development ... Ms. Nesta BERNARD
100 Chief of Staff ... Mr. Andrew RIVERS
17 CEO University Hospital ... Mr. Larry WARREN
20 Associate Provost ... Dr. Joseph P. REIDY
46 AVP for Research Health Sciences ... Dr. Kristy F. WOODS
32 Vice President Student Affairs ... Dr. Barbara GRIFFIN
13 Interim Chief Information Officer ... Mr. Tilmon SMITH
21 Deputy Chief Financial Officer ... Ms. Bridget SARIKAS
58 Interim Dean Graduate School ... Dr. Charles BETSEY
49 Interim Dean College Arts/Sciences ... Dr. Segun GBADEGESIN
50 Dean School of Business ... Dr. Barron H. HARVEY
61 Interim Dean School of Law ... Ms. Okianer CHRISTIAN DARK
63 Dean College of Medicine ... Dr. Mark S. JOHNSON
52 Dean College of Dentistry ... Dr. Leo E. ROUSE
54 Dean Col Engr/Arch/Computr Sciences ... Dr. James W. MITCHELL
53 Dean School of Education ... Dr. Leslie T. FENWICK
60 Interim Dean School Communications ... Dr. Chuka ONWUMECHILI
88 Dean Col Nursing/Allied Hlth Sci ... Dr. Mary HILL
70 Dean School of Social Work ... Dr. Cudore L. SNELL
73 Dean School of Divinity ... Dr. Alton B. POLLARD, III
67 Dean School of Pharmacy ... Dr. Anthony WUTOH
48 Director School of Architecture ... Prof. Bradford C. GRANT
76 Assoc Dean/Div Allied Health Sci ... Dr. Allan JOHNSON
57 Assoc Dean/Division of Fine Arts ... Dr. Tritobia H. BENJAMIN
84 Director of Enrollment Management ... Vacant
07 Director of Admissions ... Ms. Linda SANDERS-HAWKINS
37 Director Financial Aid ... Mr. Derek KINDLE
42 Dean Andrew Rankin Chapel ... Dr. Bernard L. RICHARDSON
35 Dean Student Life & Activities ... Ms. Tonya L. GUILLORY

39 Dean of Residence Life ... Mr. Marc D. LEE
36 Director Career Services Office ... Dr. Joan M. BROWNE
23 Director Student Health Center ... Dr. Evelyn TREAKLE-MOORE
09 Dir University Research & Plng ... Vacant
08 Director University Libraries ... Mr. Howard DODSON, JR.
88 Director Health Sciences Library ... Ms. Cynthia L. HENDERSON
88 Director Law Library ... Ms. Rhea BALLARD-THROWER
24 Dir Teaching Learning & Assmnt Ctr ... Dr. Theresa M. REDD
92 Director of Honors Program ... Dr. Daniel A. WILLIAMS, III
94 Director of Women's Studies ... Vacant
30 Sr Dir for Advancement Services ... Mr. Brent E. SWINTON
29 Acting Director Alumni Relations ... Mr. Spencer CHENIER
44 Director of Annual Giving ... Ms. Christie ASKEW
26 Acting Dir Comm & Marketing ... Dr. Kerry-Ann HAMILTON
15 Chief Human Resources Officer ... Mr. Jimmy JONES
16 Director of Employment ... Ms. Kym WILSON
22 Dir Equal Employment Opportunity ... Mr. Antwan LOFTON
40 Director University Bookstore ... Mr. Antwan D. CLINTON
19 Chief of Campus Police ... Mr. Leroy K. JAMES
41 Athletics Director ... Mr. Louis PERKINS, JR.
31 Director HU Community Association ... Ms. Maybelle T. BENNETT
18 Exec Dir Physical Facilities ... Mr. Chris CALHOUN

The Institute of World Politics (A)

1521 16th Street, NW, Washington DC 20036-1464

FICE Identification: 041144
Unit ID: 455804
Telephone: (202) 462-2101 | Carnegie Class: Spec/Other
FAX Number: (202) 464-0335 | Calendar System: Semester
URL: www.iwp.edu
Established: 1990 | Annual Graduate Tuition & Fees: $26,950
Enrollment: 143 | Coed
Affiliation or Control: Independent Non-Profit | IRS Status: 501(c)3
Highest Offering: Master's; No Undergraduates
Program: Professional
Accreditation: M

01 President ... Dr. John LENCZOWSKI
03 Executive Vice President ... Mr. Douglas MILLS
30 Vice Pres Institutional Advancement ... Ms. Tricia LLOYD
05 VP Academic Aff/Chief Academic Ofcr ... Dr. Charles Roger SMITH
32 Vice Pres Student Affs/Admissions ... Mr. Jason C. JOHNSRUD
10 Director Financial Operations ... Mrs. Elaine PINDER
06 Registrar & Institutional Research ... Mrs. Hasanna BENSON-TYUS
30 Director of Development ... Ms. Whitney ATHAYDE
84 Director Student Recruitment ... Mr. Colin PARKS
08 Director Libraries/Info Svcs ... Mr. Jim STAMBAUGH
21 Controller ... Mr. Kevin KORYCANSKY
04 Asst to President/Development Ofcr ... Ms. Kathy CARROLL
27 Communications Officer ... Mr. Charles VAN SOMEREN
37 Director of Financial Aid ... Ms. La Nae HERRARA

Medtech College (B)

529 14th Street, NW, Washington DC 20045

Identification: 666591
Telephone: (202) 872-4700 | Carnegie Class: Not Classified
FAX Number: (202) 872-9009 | Calendar System: Semester
URL: www.medtech.edu
Established: 1939 | Annual Undergrad Tuition & Fees: $14,781
Enrollment: 13 | Coed
Affiliation or Control: Proprietary | IRS Status: Proprietary
Highest Offering: Associate Degree
Program: Occupational; 2-Year Principally Bachelor's Creditable
Accreditation: COE

01 Campus Director ... Dr. Aamir QURESHI
05 Director of Education ... Ms. Rene DAVIS

† National accreditation is carried under parent institution in Falls Church, VA.

Pontifical Faculty of the Immaculate Conception at the Dominican House of Studies (C)

487 Michigan Avenue, NE, Washington DC 20017-1585

FICE Identification: 012803
Unit ID: 131405
Telephone: (202) 495-3820 | Carnegie Class: Spec/Faith
FAX Number: (202) 495-3873 | Calendar System: Semester
URL: www.dhs.edu
Established: 1902 | Annual Graduate Tuition & Fees: $15,370
Enrollment: 104 | Coed
Affiliation or Control: Roman Catholic | IRS Status: 501(c)3
Highest Offering: Master's; No Undergraduates
Program: Professional; Religious Emphasis
Accreditation: M, THEOL

01 President ... Fr. Steven BOGUSLAWSKI, OP
05 Vice President/Academic Dean ... Fr. Gabriel O'DONNELL, OP
30 Vice President for Advancement ... Vacant
20 Secretary of Studies ... Fr. Brian CHRZASTEK, OP
08 Librarian ... Fr. John Martin RUIZ, OP
18 Director of Facilities ... Br. Gerard THAYER, OP
42 Chaplain to Commuter Students ... Fr. Andrew HOFER, OP
06 Registrar ... Dr. Tobias NATHE
10 Treasurer/Director of Financial Aid ... Ms. Shauna ROYE
29 Director Alumni and Friends ... Ms. Margaret PERRY
14 IT Director ... Mr. Carlos MOLINA

88 Writing Tutor ... Fr. Raymond VANDEGRIFT, OP
36 Director of Career Placement ... Dr. Jem SULLIVAN
04 Admin Assistant to President ... Mrs. Honya WEEKS
88 Faculty Secretary ... Mrs. Joan BUTLER

Pontifical John Paul II Institute for Studies on Marriage and Family (D)

620 Michigan Ave, NE, McGivney Hall, Washington DC 20064

FICE Identification: 041427
Unit ID: 455813
Telephone: (202) 526-3799 | Carnegie Class: Spec/Other
FAX Number: (202) 269-6090 | Calendar System: Other
URL: www.johnpaulii.edu
Established: 1988 | Annual Graduate Tuition & Fees: $15,800
Enrollment: 83 | Coed
Affiliation or Control: Roman Catholic | IRS Status: 501(c)3
Highest Offering: Doctorate; No Undergraduates
Program: Professional; Religious Emphasis
Accreditation: M

01 President ... Rev. Livio MELINA
03 Vice President ... Carl A. ANDERSON
05 Provost ... Fr. Antonio LOPEZ
06 Registrar ... Joseph C. ATKINSON
07 Director of Admissions ... Sara L. TRUDEAU
20 Dean ... Rev. Antonio LOPEZ
20 Associate Dean for Academic Affairs ... David S. CRAWFORD
11 Assoc Dean Progams & Administration ... Nick J. BAGILEO

† Affiliated with The Catholic University of America, DC.

Potomac College (E)

4000 Chesapeake Street, NW, Washington DC 20016-1860

FICE Identification: 032183
Unit ID: 384412
Telephone: (202) 686-0876 | Carnegie Class: Spec/Bus
FAX Number: (202) 686-0818 | Calendar System: Semester
URL: www.potomac.edu
Established: 1991 | Annual Undergrad Tuition & Fees: $11,680
Enrollment: 267 | Coed
Affiliation or Control: Proprietary | IRS Status: Proprietary
Highest Offering: Baccalaureate
Program: Business Emphasis
Accreditation: M

01 CEO ... Dr. Laura PALMER NOONE
108 Director Inst Assessment & Effectiv ... Walter PERSON
08 Director of Learning Resource Ctr ... Edward ROBINSON

Radians College (F)

1025 Vermont Avenue, Suite 200, Washington DC 20005

Identification: 667005
Telephone: (202) 291-9020 | Carnegie Class: Not Classified
FAX Number: (202) 291-8013 | Calendar System: Trimester
URL: www.radianscollege.edu
Established: 2005 | Annual Undergrad Tuition & Fees: N/A
Enrollment: N/A | Coed
Affiliation or Control: Proprietary | IRS Status: Proprietary
Highest Offering: Associate Degree
Program: Occupational; 2-Year Principally Bachelor's Creditable; Nursing Emphasis
Accreditation: ACICS

01 President ... Mr. Seelan ABRAHAM
05 VP Academic Administration ... Ms. India MEDLEY

Strayer University (G)

1133 15th Street, NW, Washington DC 20005-2710

FICE Identification: 001459
Unit ID: 131803
Telephone: (202) 408-2400 | Carnegie Class: Master's L
FAX Number: (202) 419-1423 | Calendar System: Quarter
URL: www.strayer.edu
Established: 1892 | Annual Undergrad Tuition & Fees: $19,985
Enrollment: 54,900 | Coed
Affiliation or Control: Proprietary | IRS Status: Proprietary
Highest Offering: Master's
Program: Occupational; Liberal Arts And General; Professional
Accreditation: M, @TEAC

01 Interim President ... Dr. Michael PLATTER
05 Int Provost/Chief Academic Ofcr ... Dr. Randi REICH COSENTINO
20 Sr Vice Provost of Academic Admin ... Dr. Deborah SNYDER
10 Senior VP/Chief Financial Officer ... Mr. Mark C. BROWN
32 Senior Vice Provost Student Affairs ... Ms. Mariana VALDEZ-FAULI
37 Vice Pres Student Financial Svcs ... Mr. Richard M. ANTHONY
13 VP/Chief Technology Officer ... Mr. Kevin P. O'REAGAN
106 Online Academic Dean Global Region ... Mr. Matthew MIKO
35 Dean of Students ... Ms. Jacqueline PALMER
08 University Librarian ... Mr. David A. MOULTON
20 Dir of Acad Program Administration ... Ms. Cyndi L. WASTLER
06 University Registrar ... Mr. Robert BERWICK
20 Chamblee Campus Dean ... Dr. Charles M. SMITH
12 Chamblee Campus Director ... Mr. Paul LAWSON
20 Chesterfield Campus Dean ... Ms. Carol WILLIAMS
12 Chesterfield Campus Director ... Ms. Cheryl VAUGHAN
20 Christiana Campus Dean ... Dr. Antony JACOB
12 Christiana Campus Director ... Ms. Hannah RICHARDSON
20 Charleston Campus Dean ... Mr. Rufus ROBINSON
12 Charleston Campus Director ... Ms. Keona TIMMONS
20 Cobb County Campus Dean ... Ms. LaRoyce MORGAN
12 Cobb County Campus Director ... Mr. Bruce REESE
20 Columbia Campus Dean ... Dr. Pender GBENEDIO
12 Columbia Campus Director ... Ms. Florence SPENCER
20 Delaware County Campus Dean ... Dr. Joseph GRECO
12 Delaware County Campus Director ... Ms. Lauren ZUCKER
20 Fredericksburg Campus Dean ... Mr. James BLACKER
12 Fredericksburg Campus Director ... Ms. Amy RIDPATH
20 Greensboro Campus Dean ... Dr. Johnny ELUKA
12 Greensboro Campus Director ... Ms. Nashanta WHITAKER
20 Henrico Campus Dean ... Mr. Bob NOLLEY
12 Henrico Campus Director ... Ms. Carla GREEN
20 Lower Bucks Campus Dean ... Mr. Gary WHITE
12 Lower Bucks Campus Director ... Mr. Lamar FARR
20 Greenville Campus Dean ... Mr. Peter MCDANIEL
12 Greenville Campus Director ... Ms. Kelly HUMPHRIES
20 King of Prussia Campus Dean ... Dr. Eugene GARONE
12 King of Prussia Campus Director ... Ms. Monique STERLING
20 Loudoun Campus Dean ... Ms. Myra ROBINSON
12 Loudoun Campus Director ... Mr. Tyrone TINDELL
20 Manassas Campus Dean ... Ms. Melba WILLIAMS
12 Manassas Campus Director ... Ms. Shirin SAGHAFI
20 North Raleigh Campus Dean ... Dr. Pang-Jen CRAIG KUNG
12 North Raleigh Campus Director ... Ms. Kenya DUKES
20 Morrow Campus Dean ... Dr. Virgil MENSAH-DARTEY
12 Morrow Campus Director ... Ms. Toni STURDIVANT
20 Nashville Campus Dean ... Dr. Udoh UDOM
12 Nashville Campus Director ... Ms. Denise SILVA
20 Newport News Campus Dean ... Dr. Gianpaolo CAPPUZZO
12 Newport News Campus Director ... Ms. D'Andre H. WILSON
20 North Charlotte Campus Dean ... Dr. Kazem KAN-SHAGHAGHI
12 North Charlotte Campus Director ... Ms. Dianna ANDERSON
20 Owings Mills Campus Dean ... Mr. Barry THOMAS
12 Owings Mills Campus Director ... Dr. Doreen LUCAS
20 Roswell Campus Dean ... Dr. Keva YARBROUGH
12 Roswell Campus Director ... Ms. Diana BONSIGNORE
20 Shelby Oaks Campus Dean ... Dr. Ron DAVIS
12 Shelby Oaks Campus Director ... Mr. Torrence EDDIE
20 Penn Center West Campus Dean ... Dr. George MARUSCHOCK
12 Penn Center West Campus Director ... Ms. Carly BROWN
20 Prince Georges Campus Dean ... Mr. Willie STRAIT
12 Prince Georges Campus Director ... Ms. Chinneta COLLINS
20 Research Triangle Park Campus Dean ... Mr. Donald WEST
12 Research Triangle Park Campus Dir ... Ms. Cherry CLARK
20 Rockville Campus Dean ... Dr. Jerald L. FEINSTEIN
12 Rockville Campus Director ... Mr. Huot HE
20 South Charlotte Campus Dean ... Dr. Johnnie D. WOODARD
12 South Charlotte Campus Director ... Mr. Mark LOMAS
20 Virginia Beach Campus Dean ... Dr. Hermann BAYER
12 Virginia Beach Campus Director ... Mr. Tom LOTITO
12 Takoma Park Campus Director ... Mr. Melvin MENNS
20 Takoma Park Campus Dean ... Mr. Doug EARHART
20 Tampa East Campus Dean ... Dr. Yamil GUEVARA
12 Tampa East Campus Director ... Mr. Jeffrey KEITH
20 Tampa Westshore Campus Dean ... Dr. Mohammad SUMADI
12 Tampa Westshore Campus Director ... Ms. Jennifer PORTER
20 Woodbridge Campus Dean ... Dr. Michael I. OTAIGBE
12 Woodbridge Campus Director ... Ms. Niaomi CARTER
12 Thousand Oakes Campus Director ... Ms. Lottie MINOR
20 Thousand Oaks Campus Dean ... Dr. Jeannie OLIVER
20 Washington Campus Dean ... Dr. Chandra QUAYE
12 Washington Campus Director ... Mr. Haroon MOKEL
20 White Marsh Campus Dean ... Ms. A. Kobina ARMOO
12 White Marsh Campus Director ... Ms. Yanka CAMPBELL
20 Arlington Campus Dean ... Ms. E. Maggie SIZER
12 Arlington Campus Director ... Ms. Corey ROSSO
20 Alexandria Campus Dean ... Dr. Abed H. ALMALA
12 Alexandria Campus Director ... Ms. Amy PROPER
20 Center City Campus Dean ... Mr. Izzeldin BAKHIT
12 Center City Campus Director ... Mr. Isaac WALTERS
20 Anne Arundel Campus Dean ... Dr. Twila LINDSAY
12 Anne Arundel Campus Director ... Mr. Valtroud HARVEY
20 Birmingham Campus Dean ... Dr. Vidal ADADEVOH
12 Birmingham Campus Director ... Ms. Stephanie GOWER
20 Chesapeake Campus Dean ... Dr. Muleka KIKWEBATI
12 Chesapeake Campus Director ... Ms. Jeanne POINDEXTER

Trinity Washington University (H)

125 Michigan Avenue, NE, Washington DC 20017-1090

FICE Identification: 001460
Unit ID: 131876
Telephone: (202) 884-9000 | Carnegie Class: Master's L
FAX Number: (202) 884-9229 | Calendar System: Semester
URL: www.trinitydc.edu
Established: 1897 | Annual Undergrad Tuition & Fees: $20,975
Enrollment: 2,556 | Female
Affiliation or Control: Roman Catholic | IRS Status: 501(c)3
Highest Offering: Master's
Program: Liberal Arts And General; Teacher Preparatory; Professional
Accreditation: M, NURSE, TED

01 President ... Ms. Patricia A. MCGUIRE
04 Assistant to the President ... Ms. Cassandra BOSTON
05 Vice President Academic Affairs ... Ms. Virginia BROADDUS
84 Vice Pres Enrollment Services ... Ms. Cathy GEIER
30 Vice Pres Institutional Advancement ... Ms. Ann PAULEY

07 Vice President of CAS Admissions .... Ms. Kelly GOSNELL
49 Dean College of Arts & Science .... Dr. Elizabeth CHILD
53 Dean School of Education .... Vacant
107 Dean School of Professional Studies .... Dr. Telaekah BROOKS
66 Dean Sch Nursing/Health Professions .... Dr. Mary ROMANELLO
84 Executive Director Enrollment Devel .... Vacant
44 Director of Development .... Ms. Judy TART
32 Dean of Student Services .... Ms. Michelle BOWIE
15 Director of Human Resources .... Ms. Carole KING
41 Athletic Director .... Ms. Tracy RENKEN
18 Exec Director Facilities Services .... Mr. Tim KNIGHT
29 Director Alumnae Affairs .... Ms. Margy REAGAN

University of the District of Columbia (A)

4200 Connecticut Avenue, NW,
Washington DC 20008-1174

FICE Identification: 001441
Unit ID: 131399
Telephone: (202) 274-5000 Carnegie Class: Master's S
FAX Number: (202) 274-5304 Calendar System: Semester
URL: www.udc.edu
Established: 1976 Annual Undergrad Tuition & Fees (In-District): $7,244
Enrollment: 5,286 Coed
Affiliation or Control: Local IRS Status: 501(c)3
Highest Offering: Doctorate
Program: Occupational; 2-Year Principally Bachelor's Creditable; Liberal Arts And General; Teacher Preparatory; Professional
Accreditation: M, ACBSP, ADNUR, CACREP, CS, DIETD, ENG, FUSER, LAW, NUR, SP, SW, TED

01 President .... Dr. Allen SESSOMS
05 Provost/Vice Pres Academic Affairs .... Dr. Ken BAIN
32 Vice President for Student Affairs .... Dr. Valerie EPPS
16 Vice President Human Resources .... Ms. Myrtho BLANCHARD
18 VP Facilities & Real Estate .... Ms. Barbara JUMPER
07 Assoc VP Admission/Recruit .... Mr. Dwight SHANCHEZ
09 Assoc Provost Inst Rsrch & Acc .... Vacant
12 CEO UDC Community College .... Dr. Calvin WOODLAND
20 Executive Asst to the Provost .... Mr. Herman PRESCOTT
10 Chief Financial Officer .... Mr. Ibrahim H. KOROMA
49 Acting Dean Arts & Sciences .... Dr. April MASSEY
50 Dean Sch Business & Public Mgmt .... Dr. Richard BEBEE
61 Dean School of Law .... Ms. Katherine S. BRODERICK
54 Dean Engineering/Applied Scis .... Dr. Devdas SHETTY
56 Dean Agriculture Urban Stablity .... Dr. Sabine O'HARA
06 University Registrar .... Ms. LaVerne M. HILL-FLANAGAN
21 Director of Finance .... Mr. Steven GRAUBART
37 Director Student Financial Aid .... Mr. James CONTRERAS
26 Dir Marketing & Communications .... Vacant
08 Dean Learning Resources .... Mr. Albert J. CASCIERO
88 Director Institute Gerontology .... Ms. Jessyna MCDONALD
88 Director Ctr for Res & Urban Policy .... Vacant
86 Director of Government Affairs .... Ms. Aimee OCCHETTI
25 Director Grants Administration .... Ms. Cassandra PARKER
15 Director Human Resources .... Vacant
41 Athletic Director .... Ms. Patricia A. THOMAS
43 Deputy University Counsel .... Ms. Andrea BAGWELL
88 General Manager UDC Cable TV .... Mr. Edward JONES, JR.
18 Chief Facilities/Physical Plant .... Mr. Armando PRIETO
29 Exec Director of Alumni Affairs .... Vacant
30 Exec Director of Development .... Ms. Felicia BRANT
09 Director of Institutional Research .... Vacant
38 Director Student Counseling .... Dr. Jane D. OFFEL
96 Director of Procurement .... Ms. Mary A. HARRIS
27 Media Liaison and Univ Spokesperson .... Mr. Alan ETTER
88 Dean Student Achievement .... Ms. Hermina P. PETERS
103 Acting Dean Workforce Dept .... Ms. Kim R. FORD
19 Dir Public Safety/Chief of Police .... Mr. Larry E. VOLTZ
92 Director TRIO Program .... Ms. Saundra M. CARTER
36 Director Career Services .... Ms. Katie NAILLER
86 Director State & Local Affairs .... Mr. Thomas E. REDMOND
85 Director International Affairs .... Mr. Paul N. TENNASSEE
11 Director Financial Operations .... Mr. William C. NELSON
88 Director STEM .... Ms. Barbara J. HOLMES
29 Director Alumni Affairs .... Mr. Joseph LIBERTELLI
89 Dir 1st Yr Experience Programs .... Mr. Esteban OLIVERAS
102 Diretor Sponsored Programs .... Ms. Jovita WELLS
13 Dir Information Technology .... Vacant
88 Dir Small Business Develop Ctr .... Ms. Candice MILES

Washington Theological Union (B)

6896 Laurel Street, NW, Washington DC 20012-2016

FICE Identification: 010065
Unit ID: 164243
Telephone: (202) 726-8800 Carnegie Class: Spec/Faith
FAX Number: (202) 726-1716 Calendar System: Semester
URL: www.wtu.edu
Established: 1969 Annual Graduate Tuition & Fees: $17,160
Enrollment: 123 Coed
Affiliation or Control: Independent Non-Profit IRS Status: 501(c)3
Highest Offering: Doctorate; No Undergraduates
Program: Professional; Religious Emphasis
Accreditation: M, THEOL

01 President .... Vacant
05 Academic Dean .... Sr. Anne E. MCLAUGHLIN
10 Chief Financial Officer .... Mr. Wayne WISSMAN
06 Registrar/Dir Student Financial Aid .... Deacon Bartholomew J. MERELLA
08 Librarian .... Mr. Steven BROWN
32 Dean of Students .... Vacant
07 Dir of Enrollment/Admiss Services .... Vacant
30 Director of Development .... Ms. Joan KNETEMANN
13 Director of Technology .... Ms. Neha PAUL

Wesley Theological Seminary (C)

4500 Massachusetts Avenue, NW,
Washington DC 20016-5690

FICE Identification: 001464
Unit ID: 131973
Telephone: (202) 885-8600 Carnegie Class: Spec/Faith
FAX Number: (202) 885-8605 Calendar System: Semester
URL: www.wesleyseminary.edu
Established: 1882 Annual Graduate Tuition & Fees: $16,532
Enrollment: 645 Coed
Affiliation or Control: United Methodist IRS Status: 501(c)3
Highest Offering: Doctorate; No Undergraduates
Program: Professional; Religious Emphasis
Accreditation: M, THEOL

01 President .... Dr. David MCALLISTER-WILSON
10 Vice Pres Finance/Administration .... Ms. June STOWE
30 Vice President for Development .... Rev. Terry BRADFIELD
04 Special Assistant to the President .... Ms. Jane S. DELAND
05 Dean .... Dr. Amy G. ODEN
32 Assoc Dean Acad Admin/Cmty Life ...... Rev. Shelby M. HAGGRAY
07 Director of Admissions .... Rev. William D. ALDRIDGE
06 Registrar .... Ms. Eleanor GEASE
08 Director of Library .... Dr. William FAUPEL
15 Director Human Resources .... Ms. Yasmin LEWIS-WHITE
18 Chief Facilities/Physical Plant .... Mr. Randall ADAMS
37 Director Student Financial Aid .... Ms. Mary VIBERT
29 Director Alumni Relations .... Ms. Mauri BISHOP
26 Director of Marketing .... Ms. Laurie ENCENEAT

FLORIDA

Academy for Five Element Acupuncture (D)

305 SE Second Avenue, Gainesville FL 32601-6811
County: Alachua FICE Identification: 035243
Unit ID: 451079
Telephone: (352) 335-2332 Carnegie Class: Spec/Health
FAX Number: (352) 337-2535 Calendar System: Trimester
URL: www.acupuncturist.edu
Established: 1998 Annual Graduate Tuition & Fees: $41,200
Enrollment: 80 Coed
Affiliation or Control: Independent Non-Profit IRS Status: 501(c)3
Highest Offering: Master's; No Undergraduates
Program: Professional
Accreditation: ACUP

01 President .... Ms. Misti OXFORD-PICKERAL
11 Vice President Administration .... Ms. Joanne EPSTEIN
05 Academic Dean .... Mr. Chuck GRAHAM
37 Financial Aid Administrator .... Mr. Glenn MORRIS
06 Registrar .... Ms. Angela XISTRIS

Academy for Practical Nursing and Health Occupations (E)

5154 Okeechobee Blvd #201, West Palm Beach FL 33417
County: Palm Beach FICE Identification: 033463
Unit ID: 412173
Telephone: (561) 683-1400 Carnegie Class: Not Classified
FAX Number: (561) 683-6773 Calendar System: Other
URL: www.apnho.com
Established: 1978 Annual Undergrad Tuition & Fees: $18,571
Enrollment: 407 Coed
Affiliation or Control: Independent Non-Profit IRS Status: 501(c)3
Highest Offering: Associate Degree
Program: Occupational; 2-Year Principally Bachelor's Creditable; Nursing Emphasis
Accreditation: COE

01 President .... Lois M. GACKENHEIMER

Acupuncture & Massage College (F)

10506 N Kendall Drive, Miami FL 33176-1509
County: Miami-Dade FICE Identification: 034145
Unit ID: 439969
Telephone: (305) 595-9500 Carnegie Class: Spec/Health
FAX Number: (305) 595-2622 Calendar System: Semester
URL: www.amcollege.edu
Established: 1983 Annual Undergrad Tuition & Fees: $45,000
Enrollment: 216 Coed
Affiliation or Control: Proprietary IRS Status: Proprietary
Highest Offering: Master's
Program: Professional; Technical Emphasis
Accreditation: ACCSC, ACUP

00 Chief Executive Officer .... Ms. Nancy E. BROWNE
01 President .... Dr. Richard M. BROWNE
05 Academic Dean .... Dr. Lana MONCHEK
17 Clinic Director .... Dr. Wel LU
37 Financial Aid Director .... Ms. Judith GALVIS
07 Admissions Director .... Mr. Joe CALARESO
06 Registrar/Student Services .... Ms. Maria GARCIA

Adventist University of Health Sciences (G)

671 Winyah Drive, Orlando FL 32803-1204
County: Orange FICE Identification: 031155
Unit ID: 133872
Telephone: (407) 303-9798 Carnegie Class: Spec/Health
FAX Number: (407) 303-9408 Calendar System: Trimester
URL: www.fhchs.edu
Established: 1992 Annual Undergrad Tuition & Fees: $10,780
Enrollment: 2,668 Coed
Affiliation or Control: Seventh-day Adventist IRS Status: 501(c)3
Highest Offering: Master's
Program: Occupational; 2-Year Principally Bachelor's Creditable; Professional
Accreditation: SC, ADNUR, ANEST, DMS, MT, NMT, NUR, OTA, RAD

01 President .... Dr. David E. GREENLAW
05 Sr VP for Academic Administration .... Dr. Donald E. WILLIAMS
10 Sr VP for Finance/CFO .... Mr. Robert A. CURREN
11 VP for Operations .... Mr. Ruben O. MARTINEZ
32 VP for Student Services .... Mr. Stephen H. ROCHE
26 VP Marketing & Public Relations .... Mr. Lewis HENDERSHOT
106 VP for Educational Tech/Distance Ed .... Dr. Dan LIM
20 Associate VP for Academic Admin .... Dr. Len ARCHER
09 Dir of Accreditation & Inst Effect .... Dr. Roy LUKMAN
37 Director of Financial Aid .... Mrs. Starr S. BENDER
06 Registrar .... Dr. Janet CALDERON
45 Dir of Grant Management .... Ms. Stefanie JOHNSON
88 Director Ctr for Acad Achievement .... Ms. Yvette C. SALIBA
08 Library Director .... Ms. Deanna L. FLORES
42 Campus Chaplain .... Mr. Reynold ACOSTA
07 Director of Enrollment Services .... Mrs. Katie R. SHAW
21 Chief Accountant .... Mr. Grayson GOODMAN
39 Director of Residence Hall .... Mr. David A. BRYANT
30 Development Officer .... Mrs. Carol BRADFIELD
16 Director of Human Resources .... Mr. Fred W. STEPHENS
13 Director of Information Technology .... Mr. Travis WOOLEY
04 Executive Asst to the President .... Mrs. Dawn H. CREFT

Aerosim Flight Academy (H)

2700 Flight Line Ave, Sanford FL 32773
County: Seminole FICE Identification: 041571
Unit ID: 429012
Telephone: (407) 330-7020 Carnegie Class: Not Classified
FAX Number: (407) 323-3817 Calendar System: Other
URL: www.aerosim.com/academy
Established: 1989 Annual Undergrad Tuition & Fees: $70,024
Enrollment: 62 Coed
Affiliation or Control: Proprietary IRS Status: Proprietary
Highest Offering: Associate Degree
Program: Occupational
Accreditation: ACCSC

01 Vice President/Campus Director .... Ed CARRASCO
05 Dir Academic Affairs/Dean .... Mike CAMPBELL
07 Manager of Admissions .... Thomas MENDENHALL

American InterContinental University (I)

2250 N Commerce Parkway, Weston FL 33326-3233
County: Broward Identification: 666336
Unit ID: 438601
Telephone: (954) 446-6100 Carnegie Class: Bac/Diverse
FAX Number: (954) 446-6301 Calendar System: Quarter
URL: www.aiuniv.edu
Established: 1998 Annual Undergrad Tuition & Fees: $19,366
Enrollment: 722 Coed
Affiliation or Control: Proprietary IRS Status: Proprietary
Highest Offering: Master's
Program: Professional; Business Emphasis
Accreditation: &NH, ACBSP

01 President .... Dr. Hisham SHABAN
10 Controller .... Mr. Don BLACKMAN
32 Interim Director of Student Affairs .... Mrs. Alice OLIVER
05 Interim VP of Academic Affairs .... Dr. John CAMPBELL
06 Coordinator Registrar Office & Rec .... Ms. Dawn LEAMING
09 Int Dir Institutional Effectiveness .... Dr. Fabian CONE
08 Head Librarian .... Ms. Sharon ARGOV
37 Director Financial Aid .... Mr. Travis BROWN
22 Director Regulatory Operations .... Vacant
16 Director of Human Resource .... Ms. Sharmane BUCHANAN
36 Director of Career Service .... Mrs. Elizabeth BALACHANDRAN
13 Director Information Technology .... Mr. Juan RODRIGUEZ
04 Admin Assistant to the President .... Ms. Lisabelle TORRES

† Regional accreditation is carried under the parent institution in Hoffman Estates, IL.

Argosy University, Sarasota (A)

5250 17th Street, Sarasota FL 34235-8246

County: Sarasota　FICE Identification: 025906
Unit ID: 137148
Telephone: (941) 379-0404　Carnegie Class: DRU
FAX Number: (941) 379-9464　Calendar System: Semester
URL: www.argosy.edu/sarasota
Established: 1976　Annual Undergrad Tuition & Fees: $13,224
Enrollment: 1,443　Coed
Affiliation or Control: Proprietary　IRS Status: Proprietary
Highest Offering: Doctorate
Program: Professional
Accreditation: &WC, CACREP

01 Campus President .... Dr. Sandra WISE
05 Vice President of Academic Affairs .... Vacant
07 Senior Director of Admissions .... Rachel MALONE
32 Director of Student Services .... Holly WHITNEY
37 Director of Student Finance .... Debra KERRIS
06 Registrar .... Diane GIFFORD
15 Human Resources .... Quinn CLEMONS
11 Dir of Admin and Financial Svcs .... John PARKER

† Regional accreditation is carried under the parent institution in Orange, CA.

Argosy University, Tampa (B)

1403 N. Howard Avenue, Tampa FL 33607

County: Hillsborough　Identification: 666082
Unit ID: 428268
Telephone: (813) 393-5290　Carnegie Class: Master's S
FAX Number: (813) 874-1989　Calendar System: Semester
URL: www.argosy.edu/tampa
Established: 1997　Annual Undergrad Tuition & Fees: $13,224
Enrollment: 631　Coed
Affiliation or Control: Proprietary　IRS Status: Proprietary
Highest Offering: Doctorate
Program: Professional
Accreditation: &WC, CLPSY

01 Campus President .... Vacant
05 Vice President of Academic Affairs .... Vacant
07 Senior Director of Admissions .... Vacant
32 Director of Student Services .... Iris CRAWFORD
37 Director of Student Finance .... Cristina PEGUERO
06 Registrar .... Vacant
15 Human Resources .... Jillian CONRAD
11 Dir of Admin and Financial Svcs .... John PARKER

† Regional accreditation is carried under the parent institution in Orange, CA.

The Art Institute of Fort Lauderdale (C)

1799 SE 17th Street, Fort Lauderdale FL 33316-3000

County: Broward　FICE Identification: 010195
Unit ID: 132338
Telephone: (954) 463-3000　Carnegie Class: Spec/Arts
FAX Number: (954) 523-7676　Calendar System: Quarter
URL: www.aifl.edu
Established: 1968　Annual Undergrad Tuition & Fees: $17,654
Enrollment: 2,552　Coed
Affiliation or Control: Proprietary　IRS Status: Proprietary
Highest Offering: Baccalaureate
Program: Occupational; Liberal Arts And General
Accreditation: ACICS, ACFEI, CIDA

01 President .... Claude W. TOLAND
10 Vice Pres Admin/Financial Services .... Maria V. BARRON
32 Dean of Student Services .... Kathy F. DEANER
05 Dean of Academic Affairs .... Peter C. WEST
20 Associate Dean of Academic Affairs .... David WALCZAK
06 Registrar .... Laura N. TENGERES
07 Senior Director of Admissions .... Judith JOCHEMS
37 Director Student Financial Services .... Joyce CUMMINGS
36 Director of Career Services .... Wendy WAGNER-LIND
15 Human Resources Generalist .... Samantha GORDON

ATI Career Training Center (D)

2890 NW 62nd Street, Fort Lauderdale FL 33309-1737

County: Broward　FICE Identification: 022159
Unit ID: 137892
Telephone: (954) 973-4760　Carnegie Class: Assoc/PrivFP
FAX Number: (954) 973-6422　Calendar System: Quarter
URL: www.aticareertraining.edu
Established: 1979　Annual Undergrad Tuition & Fees: $17,272
Enrollment: 600　Coed
Affiliation or Control: Proprietary　IRS Status: Proprietary
Highest Offering: Associate Degree
Program: Occupational
Accreditation: #ACCSC

00 CEO & Vice Chairman .... Mr. Arthur BENJAMIN
01 President & COO .... Mr. Carli STRENGTH
05 Executive Director .... Mr. Errol STEPHENSON

ATI Career Training Center (E)

7265 NW 25th Street, Miami FL 33122-1707

County: Miami-Dade　FICE Identification: 030355
Unit ID: 136738
Telephone: (305) 573-1600　Carnegie Class: Not Classified
FAX Number: (305) 599-9721　Calendar System: Other
URL: www.aticareertraining.edu
Established: 1945　Annual Undergrad Tuition & Fees: N/A
Enrollment: 878　Coed
Affiliation or Control: Proprietary　IRS Status: Proprietary
Highest Offering: Associate Degree
Program: Occupational; Technical Emphasis
Accreditation: ACCSC

01 Director .... Ms. Marcela MUNERA
05 Director of Education .... Mrs. Karen TERRY
36 Director of Career Services .... Mr. Scott DUDEK

ATI Career Training Center (F)

3501 Northwest 9th Avenue, Oakland Park FL 33309-5900

County: Broward　FICE Identification: 022932
Unit ID: 136747
Telephone: (954) 563-5899　Carnegie Class: Not Classified
FAX Number: (954) 568-0874　Calendar System: Other
URL: www.aticareertraining.edu
Established: 1988　Annual Undergrad Tuition & Fees: $25,885
Enrollment: 820　Coed
Affiliation or Control: Proprietary　IRS Status: Proprietary
Highest Offering: Associate Degree
Program: Occupational
Accreditation: #ACCSC

01 Executive Director .... Mr. Dwight BERRY
04 Assistant to Executive Director .... Ms. Lukita ALTERMA

Atlantic Institute of Oriental Medicine (G)

100 E Broward Boulevard, Suite 100,
Fort Lauderdale FL 33301-3510

County: Broward　FICE Identification: 034296
Unit ID: 439446
Telephone: (954) 763-9840　Carnegie Class: Spec/Health
FAX Number: (954) 763-9844　Calendar System: Trimester
URL: www.atom.edu
Established: 1994　Annual Graduate Tuition & Fees: $15,000
Enrollment: 135　Coed
Affiliation or Control: Independent Non-Profit　IRS Status: 501(c)3
Highest Offering: Master's; No Undergraduates
Program: Professional
Accreditation: ACUP

01 President .... Johanna C. YEN
05 Academic Dean .... Yan CHENG

Ave Maria School of Law (H)

1025 Commons Circle, Naples FL 34119

County: Collier　FICE Identification: 036914
Unit ID: 442295
Telephone: (239) 687-5300　Carnegie Class: Spec/Law
FAX Number: (239) 353-3173　Calendar System: Semester
URL: www.avemarialaw.edu
Established: 2000　Annual Graduate Tuition & Fees: $36,490
Enrollment: 489　Coed
Affiliation or Control: Roman Catholic　IRS Status: 501(c)3
Highest Offering: First Professional Degree; No Undergraduates
Program: Professional
Accreditation: LAW

01 President and Dean .... Mr. Eugene R. MILHIZER
04 Executive Assistant to the Dean .... Ms. Pamela KRAMER
05 Assoc Dean Academic Affairs .... Mr. Patrick QUIRK
32 Assoc Dean for Student Affairs .... Ms. Kaye A. CASTRO
08 Assoc Dean Library/Information Svcs .... Ms. Roberta STUDWELL
42 Chaplain .... Fr. Michael ORSI
06 Registrar .... Ms. Angela KOJIRO
37 Director of Financial Aid .... Mr. Kevin MCGOWAN
30 Director of Develop & External Affs .... Mr. John KNOWLES
07 Assistant Dean of Admissions .... Ms. Monique MCCARTHY
36 Director of Career Services .... Ms. Victoria RYAN
24 Audio-Visual Coordinator .... Mr. Tony PETRO
11 Director Finance & Administration .... Ms. Virginia TRAVER
13 Technology Solutions Manager .... Mr. John DEPRISCO
91 Database Applications Manager .... Mr. Ken THIONGO
40 Bookstore Manager .... Ms. Kathryn LOVE

Ave Maria University (I)

5050 Ave Maria Boulevard, Ave Maria FL 34142-9505

County: Collier　FICE Identification: 039413
Unit ID: 446048
Telephone: (239) 280-2500　Carnegie Class: Bac/A&S
FAX Number: (239) 352-2392　Calendar System: Semester
URL: www.avemaria.edu
Established: 2003　Annual Undergrad Tuition & Fees: $30,000
Enrollment: 850　Coed
Affiliation or Control: Independent Non-Profit　IRS Status: 501(c)3
Highest Offering: Doctorate
Program: Liberal Arts And General; Religious Emphasis
Accreditation: SC

00 Chancellor .... Mr. Thomas S. MONAGHAN
01 President/CEO .... Mr. James TOWEY
05 Acting VP Academic Affairs .... Dr. Micahael DAUPHINAIS
13 VP Technology Systems & Engineering .... Mr. Eddie DEJTHAI
26 ViP for Institutional Advancement .... Dr. Lou TRAINA
32 Vice President for Student Affairs .... Dr. Dan A. DENTINO
10 Chief Financial Officer .... Mr. Eugene MUNIN
84 Vice Pres Enrollment and Marketing .... Dr. Dennis GRACE
08 Director of Library Services .... Ms. Jennifer NODES
15 Human Resources & Privacy Ofcr .... Ms. Rebecca ZMUDA
18 Director Physical Plant & Security .... Mr. Thomas R. MINICK
21 Controller .... Mr. Anthony BEATA
44 Director Planned Giving .... Mr. Jeffrey MCMANUS
88 Director of Mission/Outreach .... Vacant
35 Director of Student Life .... Ms. Julie COSDEN
42 Director of Campus Ministry .... Fr. Robert MCTEIGUE
07 Director of Admissions .... Mr. Jason FABAZ
37 Managing Financial Aid Director .... Mrs. Anne HART
39 Director Resident Life .... Mr. Lucas CONDIT
29 Phoneathon Manager .... Mr. Gary HUBER
38 Mental Health Counselor .... Ms. Sharon O'REILLY
41 Athletic Director .... Mr. Kevin JOYCE

Aviator College of Aeronautical Science & Technology (J)

3800 St. Lucie Blvd, Fort Pierce FL 34946

County: Saint Lucie　FICE Identification: 039863
Unit ID: 447847
Telephone: (772) 466-4822　Carnegie Class: Not Classified
FAX Number: (772) 462-4886　Calendar System: Semester
URL: www.aviator.edu
Established: 1984　Annual Undergrad Tuition & Fees: $67,373
Enrollment: 47　Coed
Affiliation or Control: Proprietary　IRS Status: Proprietary
Highest Offering: Associate Degree
Program: Occupational; 2-Year Principally Bachelor's Creditable; Technical Emphasis
Accreditation: ACCSC

01 President .... Mr. Michael E. COHEN
10 Vice Pres & Chief Financial Officer .... Ms. T.J METE
05 Director of Education .... Mr. Pierre LAVIAL
06 Registrar .... Ms. Roxanne PALMER

Azure College (K)

871 NW 167th Street, Miami Gardens FL 33169

County: Miami-Dade　Identification: 667116
Telephone: (305) 751-0001　Carnegie Class: Not Classified
FAX Number: (305) 751-9991　Calendar System: Quarter
URL: www.azurecollege.edu
Established: 2004　Annual Undergrad Tuition & Fees: N/A
Enrollment: N/A　Coed
Affiliation or Control: Proprietary　IRS Status: Proprietary
Highest Offering: Associate Degree
Program: Occupational
Accreditation: ABHES

01 CEO .... Mr. Jhonson NAPOLEON

The Baptist College of Florida (L)

5400 College Drive, Graceville FL 32440-3306

County: Jackson　FICE Identification: 021596
Unit ID: 132408
Telephone: (850) 263-3261　Carnegie Class: Spec/Faith
FAX Number: (850) 263-7506　Calendar System: Semester
URL: www.baptistcollege.edu
Established: 1943　Annual Undergrad Tuition & Fees: $9,400
Enrollment: 606　Coed
Affiliation or Control: Southern Baptist　IRS Status: 501(c)3
Highest Offering: Master's
Program: 2-Year Principally Bachelor's Creditable; Teacher Preparatory; Religious Emphasis
Accreditation: SC, MUS

01 President .... Dr. Thomas A. KINCHEN
03 Senior Vice President/CFO .... Dr. R. C. HAMMACK
30 Vice President for Development .... Mr. Charles R. PARKER
05 Dean of Faculty .... Dr. G. Robin JUMPER
06 Registrar .... Ms. Stephanie W. ORR
26 Director of Marketing .... Mrs. Sandra K. RICHARDS
09 Director of Institutional Research .... Vacant
37 Director of Financial Aid & VA .... Mrs. Stephanie E. POWELL
32 Dean of Students .... Dr. Roger C. RICHARDS
07 Director of Admissions .... Mrs. Sandra K. RICHARDS
18 Maintenance Director .... Mr. Huie G. WILSON
21 Associate Business Officer .... Ms. Polly K. FLOYD
30 Director of Development .... Vacant

Barry University (M)

11300 NE Second Avenue, Miami Shores FL 33161-6695

County: Dade　FICE Identification: 001466
Unit ID: 132471
Telephone: (305) 899-3000　Carnegie Class: DRU
FAX Number: (305) 899-3054　Calendar System: Semester
URL: www.barry.edu
Established: 1940　Annual Undergrad Tuition & Fees: $28,160

Enrollment: 8,905 Coed
Affiliation or Control: Roman Catholic IRS Status: 501(c)3
Highest Offering: Doctorate
Program: Liberal Arts And General; Teacher Preparatory; Professional
Accreditation: **SC**, ANEST, ARCPA, BUS, CACREP, HT, LAW, MACTE, NURSE, OT, PERF, POD, SW, THEOL

01 President ... Sr. Linda BEVILACQUA
00 President Emerita ... Sr. Jeanne O'LAUGHLIN
05 Provost ... Dr. Linda PETERSON
10 Vice President Business & Finance ... Mr. Bruce EDWARDS
11 VP Bus Development & Operations ... Dr. Michael GRIFFIN
32 Vice President Student Affairs ... Dr. Scott F. SMITH
30 VP Inst Adv & External Affairs ... Mrs. Sara B. HERALD
09 VP Mission & Inst Effectiveness ... Dr. Christopher STARRATT
43 General Counsel ... Mr. David DUDGEON
49 Dean College of Arts/Sciences ... Dr. Karen A. CALLAGHAN
76 Int Dean College of Health Sciences ... Dr. John MCFADDEN
51 Int Dean School of Adult/Cont Ed ... Dr. Andrea ALLEN
50 Dean School of Business ... Dr. Tomislav MANDAKOVIC
53 Dean School of Education ... Dr. Terry PIPER
88 Dean Human Perf/Leisure Sci ... Dr. Darlene KLUKA
61 Dean School of Law ... Dr. Leticia M. DIAZ
63 Dean School of Podiatric Medicine ... Dr. Jeffrey JENSEN
70 Dean School of Social Work ... Dr. Phyllis SCOTT
90 Chief Technology Officer ... Ms. Yvette BROWN
84 Assoc Vice Pres Enrollment Mgmt ... Ms. Angela SCOTT
35 Assoc VP Student Affs/Dean Students ... Dr. Maria L. ALVAREZ
35 Assoc Vice Pres Student Affairs ... Dr. Eileen MCDONOUGH
18 Assoc VP Business Svcs & Fac Mgmt ... Ms. Monica SOTO
30 Assoc Vice Pres Inst Advancement ... Mr. Tom SEVERINO
21 Assoc VP Finance & Chief Acc Office ... Ms. Nicole DIEZ
26 Asst VP Communication/Marketing ... Mr. Michael S. LADERMAN
15 Associate VP Human Resources ... Ms. Jennifer N. BOYD-PUGH
29 Asst VP Alumni Relations ... Mrs. Elizabeth REED
91 Assoc VP Admin Information Systems ... Ms. Traci SIMPSON
42 Director Campus Ministry ... Dr. Anthony BONTA
105 Assistant VP Web Marketing ... Mr. Michel SILY
19 Executive Director of Public Safety ... Mr. George E. WILHELM
08 Dir Library Svcs/Libr Dir ... Mr. Thomas MESSNER
44 Director for Major Gifts ... Ms. Victoria CHAMPION
44 Director Annual Fund ... Mr. Paul MUITE
06 University Registrar ... Ms. Cynthia A. CHRUSZCZYK
36 Director Career Services ... Mr. John MORIARTY
39 Director Housing and Residence Life ... Mr. Matthew R. CAMERON
92 Director Honors Program ... Dr. Pawena SIRIMANGKALA
96 Director of Purchasing ... Ms. Sandra MADISON
37 Director Financial Aid ... Mr. Howard D. HUMESTON
38 Director Student Counseling Center ... Dr. James SCOTT
40 Manager Bookstore ... Ms. Claudia HADJEZ

Bay Medical Center (A)

615 N Bonita Avenue, Panama City FL 32401-3600
County: Bay FICE Identification: 011127
Unit ID: 439464
Telephone: (800) 422-2418 Carnegie Class: Not Classified
FAX Number: (850) 747-6115 Calendar System: Semester
URL: www.baymedical.org/Career-Center.aspx
Established: 1969 Annual Graduate Tuition & Fees: $21,825
Enrollment: 52 Coed
Affiliation or Control: Independent Non-Profit IRS Status: 501(c)3
Highest Offering: Master's; No Undergraduates
Program: Occupational; Professional
Accreditation: **ANEST**

01 President/CEO ... Mr. Steve JOHNSON
10 Chief Financial Officer ... Mr. Chris BROOKS
05 Chief Nursing Officer ... Ms. Marsha WHITE

Beacon College (B)

105 E Main Street, Leesburg FL 34748-5162
County: Lake FICE Identification: 033733
Unit ID: 384254
Telephone: (352) 787-7660 Carnegie Class: Bac/A&S
FAX Number: (352) 787-0721 Calendar System: Semester
URL: www.beaconcollege.edu
Established: 1989 Annual Undergrad Tuition & Fees: $29,510
Enrollment: 154 Coed
Affiliation or Control: Independent Non-Profit IRS Status: 501(c)3
Highest Offering: Baccalaureate
Program: Liberal Arts And General
Accreditation: **SC**

01 Interim President ... Dr. John HUTCHINSON
05 Vice President of Academic Affairs ... Dr. Shelly CHANDLER
32 Vice President of Student Services ... Dr. Robert BRIDGEMAN
30 VP of Institutional Advancement ... Dr. Walter ZIELINSKI
10 VP of Finance & Administration ... Mr. Calvin SANSON
06 Registrar ... Mr. David BROWN
18 Director of Facilities ... Mr. Chris HALL
35 Director of Student Life ... Mr. Rob ROGERS
37 Director of Financial Aid ... Ms. Shawna WELLS-BOOTH
08 Coordinator of Library Resources ... Vacant
13 Director Information Technology ... Mr. Scott HUGHES
04 Exec Assistant to the President ... Ms. Tamara SYNDER

Bethune Cookman University (C)

640 Dr. Mary McLeod Bethune Blvd,
Daytona Beach FL 32114-3099
County: Volusia FICE Identification: 001467
Unit ID: 132602
Telephone: (386) 481-2000 Carnegie Class: Bac/Diverse
FAX Number: (386) 481-2010 Calendar System: Semester
URL: www.cookman.edu
Established: 1904 Annual Undergrad Tuition & Fees: $14,410
Enrollment: 3,578 Coed
Affiliation or Control: United Methodist IRS Status: 501(c)3
Highest Offering: Master's
Program: Liberal Arts And General; Teacher Preparatory; Nursing Emphasis
Accreditation: **SC**, NUR, TED

01 Interim President ... Dr. Edison O. JACKSON
10 VP Admin Services/Fiscal Affairs ... Dr. Ronald DOWDY
05 Provost ... Dr. Hiram POWELL
30 Vice Pres Institutional Advancement ... Vacant
32 VP Enrollment Mgmt/Student Dev ... Dr. Dwaun J. WARMACK
09 Vice Pres Inst Research/Plng & Eff ... Dr. Willis WALTER
21 Assoc Vice Pres Finance/Budget ... Mrs. Melissa PETERS
39 Director Resident Life ... Mr. Fulton POSTON
29 Director Alumni Affairs ... Ms. Sharon BOSTICK-ISSAC
44 Planned/Major Gifts Officer ... Vacant
26 Assoc Dir/Communications/Mktg ... Mrs. Meredith RODRIGUEZ
20 Assoc Vice President Acad Affs ... Vacant
36 Dir Career and Program Services ... Ms. Davita BONNER
08 Director Library/LRC ... Dr. Tasha LUCAS-YOUMANS
06 Registrar ... Mrs. Annie REDD
07 Director Admissions ... Mr. Reynolda BROWN
37 Director Financial Aid ... Mr. Joseph L. COLEMAN
23 Director Health Services ... Ms. Colleen O'BRIEN
41 Athletics Director ... Mr. Lynn THOMPSON
42 Chaplain/Dir of Religious Life ... Rev. Walter MONROE
19 Director of Security ... Capt. Melvin WILLIAMS
15 VP HR/Reg/Legal Aff/Counsel to Pres ... Ms. Pamela BROWNE
18 Chief Facilities/Physical Plant ... Mr. Ervin ROSS, JR.
92 Director of Honors Program ... Dr. Masood POORANDI
27 VP Info Tech/Chief Info Officer ... Mr. Franklin PATTERSON
66 Dean School of Nursing ... Dr. Willie M. SESSION
50 Dean School of Business ... Dr. Aubrey E. LONG
53 Dean School of Education ... Dr. Carol B. JOHNSON
79 Dean Sch of Arts & Humanities ... Dr. James BROOKS
81 Dean Sch Science/Engineering/Math ... Dr. Herbert THOMPSON
83 Dean School of Social Sciences ... Dr. Ian PAYTON
58 Dean of Graduate Studies ... Dr. Darryl FRAZIER

Brevard Community College (D)

1519 Clearlake Road, Cocoa FL 32922-6597
County: Brevard FICE Identification: 001470
Unit ID: 132693
Telephone: (321) 632-1111 Carnegie Class: Assoc/Pub-R-L
FAX Number: (321) 633-4565 Calendar System: Semester
URL: www.brevardcc.edu
Established: 1960 Annual Undergrad Tuition & Fees (In-District): $2,820
Enrollment: 17,891 Coed
Affiliation or Control: Local IRS Status: 501(c)3
Highest Offering: Associate Degree
Program: Occupational; 2-Year Principally Bachelor's Creditable
Accreditation: **SC**, DA, DH, EMT, MLTAD, RAD, SURGT

01 President ... Dr. James H. RICHEY
10 VP Financial & Technology Services ... Mr. Richard LAIRD
84 VP Enrollment Mgmt/Student Success ... Dr. John F. DIETRICH
45 Vice Pres for Planning/Assessment ... Dr. Linda L. MIEDEMA
04 Exec Advisor to the President ... Dr. Joe L. SMITH
18 AVP Facilities ... Dr. Richard PARADISE
10 Chief Financial Officer ... Mr. Mark CHERRY
15 AVP/Exec Dir Human Resources ... Ms. Darla FERGUSON
31 AVP Communications ... Mr. John GLISCH
12 Provost Palm Bay Campus ... Dr. Ethel NEWMAN
12 Provost Melbourne Campus ... Ms. Sandy HANDFIELD
12 Provost Cocoa Campus ... Dr. Beverly J. SLAUGHTER
12 Provost Titusville Campus ... Dr. Philip SIMPSON
12 Provost eBrevard ... Dr. Kathy COBB
103 Exec Dir/Workforce Trng & Devel ... Ms. Mildred COYNE
37 Director Student Financial Aid ... Ms. Indira DZADOVSKY
07 Dir Collegewide Admiss & Advsmnt ... Ms. Linda EICHAS
102 Executive Director Foundation ... Ms. Michele MURRELL
04 Executive Asst to the President ... Ms. Gina CLINE
06 Registrar ... Ms. Stephanie BURNETTE

Broward College (E)

111 E Las Olas Boulevard,
Fort Lauderdale FL 33301-2298
County: Broward FICE Identification: 001500
Unit ID: 132709
Telephone: (954) 201-6500 Carnegie Class: Assoc/Pub-U-MC
FAX Number: (954) 201-7576 Calendar System: Trimester
URL: www.broward.edu
Established: 1959 Annual Undergrad Tuition & Fees (In-State): $3,057
Enrollment: 4,176 Coed
Affiliation or Control: State IRS Status: 501(c)3
Highest Offering: Baccalaureate
Program: Occupational; 2-Year Principally Bachelor's Creditable; Teacher Preparatory
Accreditation: **SC**, ADNUR, DA, DH, DMS, EMT, MAC, MUS, NUR, PTAA

01 President ... Mr. J. David ARMSTRONG
32 Vice Pres Student Affs/Enroll Mgmt ... Mrs. Angelia MILLENDER
05 Sr Vice Pres Acad Affairs/Provost ... Dr. Linda HOWDYSHELL
10 Sr Vice Pres Finance/Administration ... Mr. Thomas OLLIFF
26 VP Public Affairs and Marketing ... Ms. Aileen IZQUIERDO
11 Vice President of Operations ... Mr. Alex DENIS
102 VP Advanc/Exec Dir BC Foundation ... Ms. Nancy BOTERO
15 Assoc Vice President HR & Equity ... Ms. Denese EDSALL
13 Vice President Info Technology ... Ms. Patti BARNEY
86 VP Govt Policy/Regulatory Affairs ... Mr. Gregory A. HAILE
12 President Central Campus ... Dr. Mercedes A. QUIROGA
12 President North Campus ... Dr. Barbara J. BRYAN
12 President South Campus ... Dr. S. (Sean) MADISON
88 Assoc Vice President Economic Dev ... Mr. Norm SEAVERS
09 Assoc VP Inst Research/Plng/ Effect ... Dr. Rigoberto RINCONES-GÓMEZ
21 Comptroller ... Mr. Jayson IROFF
37 Director of Student Financial Svcs ... Mr. Robert ROBBINS
06 Registrar ... Mr. Willie ALEXANDER
08 Dean of Libraries/Learning Res ... Ms. Jacqueline HENNING
88 Director Enterprise Business Intel ... Ms. Wendy CLINK
84 Director Enrollment Management ... Vacant
29 Director Alumni Relations ... Ms. Danielle SYLVESTER

Brown Mackie College-Miami (F)

One Herald Plaza, Miami FL 33132-1418
County: Miami-Dade Identification: 666110
Unit ID: 447290
Telephone: (305) 341-6600 Carnegie Class: Assoc/PrivFP4
FAX Number: (305) 373-8814 Calendar System: Other
URL: www.brownmackie.edu
Established: 2004 Annual Undergrad Tuition & Fees: $13,896
Enrollment: 934 Coed
Affiliation or Control: Proprietary IRS Status: Proprietary
Highest Offering: Baccalaureate
Program: Occupational; 2-Year Principally Bachelor's Creditable; Business Emphasis
Accreditation: **ACICS**

01 President ... Ms. Julia M. DENNISTON
05 Dean of Academic Affairs ... Mr. Thomas CHAMBERLAIN
07 Senior Director of Admissions ... Mr. Greg KING
06 Registrar ... Ms. Lourdes PAONESSA

† Branch campus of Brown Mackie College, Cincinnati, OH.

Cambridge Institute of Allied Health & Technology (G)

5150 Linton Boulevard, Suite 340, Delray Beach FL 33484
County: Palm Beach FICE Identification: 040834
Unit ID: 454865
Telephone: (561) 381-4990 Carnegie Class: Assoc/PrivFP
FAX Number: (561) 381-4992 Calendar System: Other
URL: www.cambridgehealth.edu
Established: N/A Annual Undergrad Tuition & Fees: $15,665
Enrollment: 183 Coed
Affiliation or Control: Proprietary IRS Status: Proprietary
Highest Offering: Associate Degree
Program: Occupational
Accreditation: **ABHES**, DMS, NMT, #RAD, RTT

01 President ... Mr. Terry LAPIER

Carlos Albizu University Miami Campus (H)

2173 NW 99th Avenue, Miami FL 33172-2209
County: Miami-Dade Identification: 666814
Unit ID: 132842
Telephone: (305) 593-1223 Carnegie Class: Master's M
FAX Number: (305) 592-7930 Calendar System: Semester
URL: www.albizu.edu
Established: 1980 Annual Undergrad Tuition & Fees: $12,048
Enrollment: 1,047 Coed
Affiliation or Control: Independent Non-Profit IRS Status: 501(c)3
Highest Offering: Doctorate
Program: Professional
Accreditation: **&M**, CLPSY

01 President ... Dr. Ileana RODRIGUEZ-GARCIA
05 Chanc/Chf Acad Ofcr/Coord Cont Educ ... Dr. Carmen ROCA
32 Director Student Service/Counseling ... Mr. Peter RUBIO
83 Director of Undergrad Psychology ... Dr. Francisco MARTINEZ-MESA
53 Dir Education/Undergrad Programs ... Mr. Rafael MARTINEZ
88 Director of Clinical Training ... Dr. Gerald SPECTER
88 Director of Psychological Services ... Vacant
58 Director of Masters Programs ... Ms. Diana BARROSO
30 Director of Development ... Vacant
10 Director of Finance ... Ms. Eunice PIERRE-LOUIS
11 Director of Administration ... Mr. Magdiel BELETTE
37 Financial Aid Officer ... Dr. Ramona MORALES
06 Registrar ... Mrs. Fina CAMPA
08 Library Director ... Ms. Mary BISHOP
13 Director of ITS ... Ms. Gabriel NUNEZ
15 Director of Human Resources ... Vacant
09 Director of Institutional Research ... Mrs. Mirta MIRANDA
50 Int Director Business Program ... Mr. Orlando RIVERO
18 Administration Facilities Manager ... Mr. Magdiel BELETTE
20 Associate Academic Officer ... Vacant
29 Alumni Relations Officer ... Mr. Marco BOWER
36 Director Career & Retention ... Dr. Claudia DOLINSKY
84 Director Enrollment Management ... Mr. Rafeal VASQUEZ
96 Director of Purchasing ... Ms. Elsa VEGA

07 Asst Director of Admissions ... Ms. Carmen VAZQUEZ

† Regional accreditation is carried under the parent institution in San Juan, PR.

Central Florida Institute (A)

6000 Cinderland Pkwy, Orlando FL 32810

County: Orange
Identification: 667022
Unit ID: 439525
Telephone: (407) 253-5354
Carnegie Class: Assoc/PrivFP
FAX Number: (407) 294-3453
Calendar System: Other
URL: www.cfi.edu
Established: 1997
Annual Undergrad Tuition & Fees: N/A
Enrollment: N/A
Coed
Affiliation or Control: Proprietary
IRS Status: Proprietary
Highest Offering: Associate Degree
Program: Occupational
Accreditation: **ABHES**, DMS

01 School Director ... Mr. Carlos ROMAY

Central Florida Institute (B)

30522 US Highway 19 N, Ste 300,
Palm Harbor FL 34684-4436

County: Pinellas
FICE Identification: 034254
Unit ID: 439525
Telephone: (727) 784-0003
Carnegie Class: Assoc/PrivFP
FAX Number: (727) 781-9421
Calendar System: Other
URL: www.cfinstitute.com
Established: 1998
Annual Undergrad Tuition & Fees: N/A
Enrollment: 322
Coed
Affiliation or Control: Proprietary
IRS Status: Proprietary
Highest Offering: Associate Degree
Program: Occupational; Technical Emphasis
Accreditation: **ABHES**, CVT, DMS, POLYT, SURGT, SURTEC

01 School Director ... Mrs. Rose Lynn GREENE
05 Director of Education ... Mr. Michael SHELBY
06 Registrar ... Mr. Steve COLEMAN
07 Director of Admissions ... Mr. Nelson ZAYAS
76 Director of Health Education ... Ms. Sondra CRANFORD
37 Director of Financial Aid ... Mr. David ROCK
32 Dir Career/Student Support Svcs ... Ms. Lolita JOHNS
88 Compliance Specialist ... Ms. Caitlin DEVERS-JONES

† Tuition is variable based on program.

Centura Institute (C)

6359 Edgewater Drive, Orlando FL 32810

County: Orange
FICE Identification: 039394
Unit ID: 446446
Telephone: (407) 275-9696
Carnegie Class: Assoc/PrivFP
FAX Number: (407) 275-4499
Calendar System: Semester
URL: www.centura.edu
Established: 2002
Annual Undergrad Tuition & Fees: N/A
Enrollment: 97
Coed
Affiliation or Control: Proprietary
IRS Status: Proprietary
Highest Offering: Associate Degree
Program: Occupational
Accreditation: **ACCSC**

01 Director ... Mrs. Danielle BROWN

Chipola College (D)

3094 Indian Circle, Marianna FL 32446-3065

County: Jackson
FICE Identification: 001472
Unit ID: 133021
Telephone: (850) 526-2761
Carnegie Class: Assoc/Pub4
FAX Number: (850) 718-2388
Calendar System: Semester
URL: www.chipola.edu
Established: 1947
Annual Undergrad Tuition & Fees (In-District): $3,060
Enrollment: 2,338
Coed
Affiliation or Control: State/Local
IRS Status: 501(c)3
Highest Offering: Baccalaureate
Program: Occupational; 2-Year Principally Bachelor's Creditable
Accreditation: **SC**

01 President ... Dr. Gene PROUGH
05 Sr VP Instructional/Student Svcs ... Dr. Sarah CLEMMONS
10 Vice President of Finance ... Mr. Steve YOUNG
05 VP Baccalaureate/Workforce Dev ... Dr. Jason HURST
13 Associate VP Information Systems ... Mr. Dennis F. EVERETT
16 Assoc VP of Human Resources ... Mrs. Karan P. DAVIS
32 Vice Pres of Student Affairs ... Dr. Jayne ROBERTS
45 Assoc Dean Institutional Dev/Plng ... Mrs. Gail C. HARTZOG
18 Physical Plant Manager ... Mr. Harry FLEENER
26 Director Public Relations ... Mr. Bryan C. CRAVEN
37 Director of Financial Aid ... Ms. Sybil CLOUD
41 Director of Athletics ... Dr. Steven GIVENS
40 Bookstore Manager ... Ms. Greer STANTON

City College (E)

177 Montgomery Road, Altamonte Springs FL 32714

County: Seminole
FICE Identification: 030799
Unit ID: 417327
Telephone: (407) 831-9816
Carnegie Class: Assoc/PrivNFP
FAX Number: (407) 831-1147
Calendar System: Quarter
URL: www.citycollegeorlando.edu
Established: 1997
Annual Undergrad Tuition & Fees: $14,000
Enrollment: 320
Coed
Affiliation or Control: Independent Non-Profit
IRS Status: 501(c)3
Highest Offering: Associate Degree
Program: Occupational
Accreditation: **ACICS**

01 President ... Mrs. Esther FIKE
05 Executive Director ... Mr. Cliff PHILLIPS

City College (F)

2000 W Commercial Boulevard,
Fort Lauderdale FL 33309-1916

County: Broward
FICE Identification: 025154
Unit ID: 244233
Telephone: (954) 492-5353
Carnegie Class: Bac/Assoc
FAX Number: (954) 491-1965
Calendar System: Quarter
URL: www.citycollege.edu
Established: 1983
Annual Undergrad Tuition & Fees: $19,200
Enrollment: 1,652
Coed
Affiliation or Control: Independent Non-Profit
IRS Status: 501(c)3
Highest Offering: Baccalaureate
Program: Occupational; Business Emphasis
Accreditation: **ACICS**, EMT

01 President ... Esther FIKE
03 Executive Director ... Ilia MARTIN
36 Director of Career Development ... Traci ACKERMAN
05 Director of Education ... Anie BONILLA
07 Director of Admissions ... Lesa-Gaye FRANCIS
10 Director of Financial Affairs ... Ginger RUBACK
13 Director of Technologies ... Jeffrey A. CLAYTON
08 Director of Library ... Vicki BRINER
06 Registrar ... James CIRONE
15 Human Resources Generalist ... Patricia BURKHART
37 Director Student Financial Aid ... Kathy JOHNSON

City College (G)

7001 NW Fourth Boulevard, Gainesville FL 32607

County: Alachua
Identification: 666413
Unit ID: 406547
Telephone: (352) 335-4000
Carnegie Class: Bac/Assoc
FAX Number: (352) 335-4303
Calendar System: Quarter
URL: www.citycollege.edu
Established: 1986
Annual Undergrad Tuition & Fees: $13,200
Enrollment: 480
Coed
Affiliation or Control: Independent Non-Profit
IRS Status: 501(c)3
Highest Offering: Baccalaureate
Program: Occupational; 2-Year Principally Bachelor's Creditable
Accreditation: **ACICS**, EMT

01 Executive Director ... Mr. Steve SCHWAB

† Branch campus of City College, Fort Lauderdale, FL.

City College (H)

9300 S Dadeland Blvd, Suite PH, Miami FL 33156

County: Miami-Dade
Identification: 666414
Unit ID: 434539
Telephone: (305) 666-9242
Carnegie Class: Bac/Assoc
FAX Number: (305) 666-9243
Calendar System: Quarter
URL: www.citycollege.edu
Established: 1997
Annual Undergrad Tuition & Fees: $14,532
Enrollment: 318
Coed
Affiliation or Control: Independent Non-Profit
IRS Status: 501(c)3
Highest Offering: Baccalaureate
Program: Occupational; 2-Year Principally Bachelor's Creditable
Accreditation: **ACICS**, EMT

01 Executive Director ... Ms. Marciela HOWARD
05 Director of Education ... Dr. Mathew ABRAHAM
06 Registrar ... Ms. Donysha GIVENS
07 Director of Admissions ... Ms. Alison POLANCO

† Branch campus of City College, Fort Lauderdale, FL.

Clearwater Christian College (I)

3400 Gulf-to-Bay Boulevard, Clearwater FL 33759-4595

County: Pinellas
FICE Identification: 001473
Unit ID: 133085
Telephone: (727) 726-1153
Carnegie Class: Bac/A&S
FAX Number: (727) 723-8566
Calendar System: Semester
URL: www.clearwater.edu
Established: 1966
Annual Undergrad Tuition & Fees: $16,550
Enrollment: 519
Coed
Affiliation or Control: Non-denominational
IRS Status: 501(c)3
Highest Offering: Master's
Program: Liberal Arts And General; Teacher Preparatory
Accreditation: **SC**

01 President ... Dr. John H. KLEM
05 Vice President for Academic Affairs ... Dr. Mary C. DRAPER
10 Vice Pres for Financial Affairs ... Mr. Randy T. LIVINGSTON
30 Vice Pres Institutional Advancement ... Mr. Terry D. WILD
32 Vice President for Student Life ... Mr. Ryan DUPEE
06 Registrar ... Mr. Thomas CANNON
26 Dean of Institutional Advancement ... Mr. Benjamin PUCKETT
35 Dean of Students ... Mr. Todd BARTON
09 Director Institutional Research ... Dr. Mary DRAPER
37 Director of Financial Aid ... Mr. Ryan MCNAMARA
38 Director of Guidance & Career Svcs ... Mrs. Lisa DOLLENMAYER
41 Athletic Director ... Vacant
29 Alumni Director ... Mr. Benjamin PUCKETT
08 Director of the Library ... Mrs. Elizabether WERNER
50 Chair of Business Studies Division ... Dr. Ian DUNCAN
49 Chair of Humanities Division ... Dr. Dan HURST
73 Chair of Biblical Studies Division ... Dr. Philip BURGGRAFF
53 Chair of Education Division ... Dr. Philip LARSEN
81 Chair of Science Division ... Dr. Jonathan HENRY
57 Chair of Fine Arts Division ... Dr. Craig RALSTON
07 Director of Admissions ... Mr. Anthony WILSON
15 Director of Human Resources ... Mrs. Vicki LIVINGSTON
21 Accounting Manager ... Miss Bethany KAPPLAN
18 Director of Campus Plant ... Mr. Roy SQUIRES
13 Director of Information Technology ... Mr. Kevin GAULT
19 Chief of Campus Security ... Mr. Terry BAUMANN
88 Director of Custodial Services ... Mrs. Kelly MACLEOD
88 Director of Food Service ... Mr. Dennis BURGGRAFF
96 Director of Auxiliary Services ... Mr. Joe VALENTIN

College of Business and Technology (J)

8991 SW 107th Avenue, Suite 200, Miami FL 33176-1412

County: Miami-Dade
FICE Identification: 030716
Unit ID: 417318
Telephone: (305) 273-4499
Carnegie Class: Assoc/PrivFP
FAX Number: (305) 270-0779
Calendar System: Semester
URL: www.cbt.edu
Established: 1988
Annual Undergrad Tuition & Fees: $11,800
Enrollment: 314
Coed
Affiliation or Control: Proprietary
IRS Status: Proprietary
Highest Offering: Associate Degree
Program: Occupational; 2-Year Principally Bachelor's Creditable; Technical Emphasis
Accreditation: **ACICS**

01 President ... Mr. Fernando N. LLERENA
03 Executive Director ... Mr. Luis E. LLERENA
05 Regional Director of Education ... Mrs. Gladys P. LLERENA
37 Financial Aid Director ... Mrs. Yazmin PALMA
36 Career Services Director ... Ms. Vanessa RODRIGUEZ
06 Registrar ... Ms. Maria GONZALEZ
07 Director of Admissions ... Mr. Roger ALONSO
50 Program Director ... Ms. Carolyn SMITH
10 Finance Director ... Ms. Maricel SPEZZACATENA
26 Corporate Dir of Public Affairs ... Ms. Monica LLERENA
84 Managing Director of Strategy ... Vacant
85 International Relations Director ... Vacant
12 Campus Director ... Mr. Kennedy FERNANDEZ
12 Campus Director ... Mr. Hector DUENAS
12 Campus Director ... Vacant

College of Central Florida (K)

3001 S.W. College Road, Ocala FL 34474

County: Marion
FICE Identification: 001471
Unit ID: 132851
Telephone: (352) 237-2111
Carnegie Class: Assoc/Pub-R-L
FAX Number: (352) 291-4450
Calendar System: Semester
URL: www.cf.edu
Established: 1957
Annual Undergrad Tuition & Fees (In-District): $3,104
Enrollment: 8,965
Coed
Affiliation or Control: Local
IRS Status: 501(c)3
Highest Offering: Baccalaureate
Program: Occupational; 2-Year Principally Bachelor's Creditable; Liberal Arts And General; Teacher Preparatory; Professional
Accreditation: **SC**, ADNUR, DA, EMT, PNUR, PTAA, SURGT

01 President ... Dr. James D. HENNINGSEN
03 Senior Vice President ... Vacant
10 Interim Vice President Adm & Fin ... Mr. Steve ASH
05 Vice President Academic Affairs ... Dr. Mark PAUGH
30 Vice Pres Institutional Advancement ... Mrs. Joan STEARNS
32 Vice President Student Affairs ... Dr. Timothy WISE
12 Provost/VP Citrus County Campus ... Dr. Vernon LAWTER, JR.
12 Provost Levy Center/Exec Dir Plng ... Mrs. Marilyn LADNER
31 Exec Dir College/Cmty Relations ... Dr. Jillian RAMSAMMY
75 Assoc VP for Careers & Tech Educ ... Dr. Cheryl FANTE
49 Dean Liberal Arts & Sciences ... Dr. June JONES
08 Interim Dean Learning Resources ... Ms. Susan BRADSHAW
53 Dean Teacher Education ... Ms. Debbie BOWE
15 Human Resources Director ... Ms. Gilda CROCKER
37 Director Financial Aid ... Ms. Judy MENADIER
84 Dean Enrollment Management ... Ms. Lyn POWELL
26 Director Marketing/Public Rels ... Dr. Joe WALLACE
09 Director Inst Effectiveness ... Dr. Lawrence J. KUSZYNSKI
13 Chief Information Officer ... Ms. Kathy ANDERSON
06 Registrar ... Ms. Devona SEWELL
18 Director Facilities ... Mr. Tommy MORELOCK
19 Manager Public Safety ... Mr. Don UGLIANO
96 Director of Purchasing ... Mr. Stewart TRAUTMAN
29 Annual Fund/Alumni Devel Coord ... Ms. Pamela CALERO
07 Director of Admissions/Records ... Mrs. Teri LITTLE-BERRY

Concorde Career Institute (A)

7960 Arlington Expressway, Ste 120,
Jacksonville FL 32211-7429

County: Duval FICE Identification: 020896
Unit ID: 133845
Telephone: (904) 725-0525 Carnegie Class: Assoc/PrivFP
FAX Number: (904) 721-9944 Calendar System: Semester
URL: www.concorde.edu
Established: 1988 Annual Undergrad Tuition & Fees: $24,500
Enrollment: 491 Coed
Affiliation or Control: Proprietary IRS Status: Proprietary
Highest Offering: Associate Degree
Program: Occupational
Accreditation: ACCSC, @PTAA, SURGT

01 Campus Director .... Melissa RYAN

Concorde Career Institute (B)

10933 Marks Way, Miramar FL 33025

County: Broward FICE Identification: 022751
Unit ID: 133854
Telephone: (954) 731-8880 Carnegie Class: Not Classified
FAX Number: (954) 484-2961 Calendar System: Other
URL: www.concorde.edu
Established: N/A Annual Undergrad Tuition & Fees: N/A
Enrollment: 511 Coed
Affiliation or Control: Proprietary IRS Status: Proprietary
Highest Offering: Associate Degree
Program: Occupational; 2-Year Principally Bachelor's Creditable
Accreditation: ACCSC, SURGT

01 Campus President .... Dan GRIMM

Concorde Career Institute (C)

4202 West Spruce, Tampa FL 33607-4127

County: Hillsborough FICE Identification: 021727
Unit ID: 133863
Telephone: (813) 874-0094 Carnegie Class: Not Classified
FAX Number: (813) 872-6884 Calendar System: Other
URL: www.concorde.edu
Established: N/A Annual Undergrad Tuition & Fees: N/A
Enrollment: 501 Coed
Affiliation or Control: Proprietary IRS Status: Proprietary
Highest Offering: Associate Degree
Program: Occupational
Accreditation: ACCSC, SURGT

01 Campus President .... Donna HALLAM

Dade Medical College (D)

3401 NW 7th Street, Miami FL 33125-4013

County: Miami-Dade FICE Identification: 038323
Unit ID: 444574
Telephone: (305) 644-1171 Carnegie Class: Assoc/PrivFP
FAX Number: (305) 644-1129 Calendar System: Other
URL: www.dademedical.edu
Established: 1999 Annual Undergrad Tuition & Fees: N/A
Enrollment: 1,800 Coed
Affiliation or Control: Proprietary IRS Status: Proprietary
Highest Offering: Baccalaureate
Program: 2-Year Principally Bachelor's Creditable; Nursing Emphasis
Accreditation: ABHES, RAD

01 Chief Executive Officer .... Mr. Ernesto PEREZ
10 Chief Financial Officer .... Mr. Chris GRESSETT
11 Exec Vice President of Operations .... Mr. Roger LOPEZ

Daytona College (E)

425 South Nova Road, Ormond Beach FL 32174-8449

County: Volusia FICE Identification: 039396
Unit ID: 447014
Telephone: (386) 267-0565 Carnegie Class: Assoc/PrivFP
FAX Number: (386) 267-0567 Calendar System: Semester
URL: www.daytonacollege.edu
Established: 1996 Annual Undergrad Tuition & Fees: $9,800
Enrollment: 280 Coed
Affiliation or Control: Proprietary IRS Status: Proprietary
Highest Offering: Associate Degree
Program: Occupational
Accreditation: ACCSC

01 President .... Mr. Roger BRADLEY
05 Director .... Mr. Justin BERKOWITZ

Daytona State College (F)

PO Box 2811, Daytona Beach FL 32120-2811

County: Volusia FICE Identification: 001475
Unit ID: 133386
Telephone: (386) 506-3000 Carnegie Class: Assoc/Pub4
FAX Number: (386) 506-4440 Calendar System: Semester
URL: www.DaytonaState.edu
Established: 1958 Annual Undergrad Tuition & Fees (In-District): $3,074
Enrollment: 16,951 Coed
Affiliation or Control: Local IRS Status: 501(c)3
Highest Offering: Baccalaureate
Program: Occupational; 2-Year Principally Bachelor's Creditable
Accreditation: SC, ADNUR, DA, DH, EMT, MAC, OTA, PTAA, SURGT

01 President .... Dr. Carol EATON
03 Executive Vice President .... Mr. Brian T. BABB
05 VP Academic Affairs .... Dr. Michael VITALE
18 AVP Administrative Services .... Mr. Peter X. MCCARTHY
13 VP Information Services .... Mr. Roberto LOMBARDO
86 VP Governmental Relations .... Ms. Sharon CROW
84 VP Student Development & IE .... Dr. Thomas LOBASSO
50 AVP College of Business Admin .... Dr. Eileen HAMBY
15 Assoc VP Human Resources .... Ms. Robin BARR
103 AVP College of Workforce & CE .... Mrs. Mary BRUNO
84 AVP Enrollment Development .... Mr. Buckley JAMES
46 AVP Institutional Effectiveness .... Dr. Nancy MORGAN
08 Head Librarian .... Ms. Mercedes CLEMENT
108 Director Assessment .... Ms. Janet SLEDGE
17 Assoc VP Col Health Human Pub Svc .... Dr. James GREENE
72 Assoc VP College of Technology .... Dr. Ron EAGLIN
08 Assoc VP/Div Library & Acad Support ... Dr. Michelle MCCRANEY
53 Assoc VP College of Education .... Ms. Kristy PRESSWOOD
106 Exec Director Col of Online Studies .... Dr. Rob SAUM
88 Director Center for Women & Men .... Ms. Judy CAMPBELL
49 AVP College Arts/Music/Science .... Ms. Susan PATE
20 AVP Academic Affairs .... Dr. Rhodella BROWN
35 Dean Student Development .... Mr. Keith KENNEDY
88 Director Facilities Planning .... Mr. Steven ECKMAN
09 Dean Institutional Research .... Ms. Susan ANTILLON
37 Dean Financial Aid .... Mr. Kevin MCCRARY
88 Dean School of Health & Wellness .... Mr. Will DUNNE
19 Director Campus Safety .... Mr. Bill TILLARD
12 Provost DeLand & Deltona Campuses .... Mr. Bill WETHERELL
12 Provost Flagler/Palm Coast Campus .... Mr. Kent RYAN
88 VP Internal Auditor .... Ms. Isalene MONTGOMERY
43 College Counsel .... Mr. Brian BABB
51 Director Ctr for Business/Industry .... Mr. Frank MERCER
32 Asst Dean Student Activities .... Mr. Bruce COOK
96 Assoc VP Purch & Business Svcs .... Ms. Janet PARISH
38 Director Academic Advising .... Ms. LeeAnn DAVIS
07 Director Admissions/Recruitment .... Ms. Karen SANDERS
22 Director of Equity Inclusion .... Mr. Lonnie THOMPSON
21 Assoc VP Accounting .... Ms. Cass FOWLER
06 Director Student Accounts .... Ms. Amy IVERSON
26 Director of Marketing .... Ms. Laurie WHITE

DeVry University - Fort Lauderdale (G)

600 Corporate Drive, Suite 200,
Ft. Lauderdale FL 33334-3603

County: Broward Identification: 666525
Telephone: (954) 938-3083 Carnegie Class: Not Classified
FAX Number: (954) 938-7446 Calendar System: Semester
URL: www.devry.edu
Established: 1931 Annual Undergrad Tuition & Fees: $16,156
Enrollment: 303 Coed
Affiliation or Control: Proprietary IRS Status: Proprietary
Highest Offering: Master's
Program: Professional; Business Emphasis
Accreditation: &NH

01 Center Dean .... Antoinette CUPPARI

† Regional accreditation is carried under the parent institution in Downers Grove, IL.

DeVry University - Jacksonville (H)

5200 Belfort Road, Suite 175, Jacksonville FL 32256-6040

County: Duval Identification: 666527
Telephone: (904) 367-4942 Carnegie Class: Not Classified
FAX Number: (904) 731-4121 Calendar System: Semester
URL: www.devry.edu
Established: 1931 Annual Undergrad Tuition & Fees: $16,156
Enrollment: 266 Coed
Affiliation or Control: Proprietary IRS Status: Proprietary
Highest Offering: Master's
Program: Professional; Business Emphasis
Accreditation: &NH

01 Campus Director .... Abel OKAGBARE

† Regional accreditation is carried under the parent institution in Downers Grove, IL.

DeVry University - Miami Center (I)

8700 W Flagler St., Suite 100, Miami FL 33174-2535

County: Dade Identification: 666197
Unit ID: 438762
Telephone: (305) 229-4833 Carnegie Class: Not Classified
FAX Number: (305) 221-8887 Calendar System: Semester
URL: www.devry.edu
Established: 1931 Annual Undergrad Tuition & Fees: $16,156
Enrollment: 227 Coed
Affiliation or Control: Proprietary IRS Status: Proprietary
Highest Offering: Master's
Program: Occupational; Professional; Business Emphasis
Accreditation: &NH

01 Center Dean .... David COLE

† Regional accreditation is carried under the parent institution in Downers Grove, IL.

DeVry University - Miramar Campus (J)

2300 SW 145th Avenue, Miramar FL 33027-4150

County: Broward Identification: 666196
Unit ID: 439163
Telephone: (954) 499-9775 Carnegie Class: Master's L
FAX Number: N/A Calendar System: Semester
URL: www.devry.edu
Established: 1931 Annual Undergrad Tuition & Fees: $16,156
Enrollment: 1,234 Coed
Affiliation or Control: Proprietary IRS Status: Proprietary
Highest Offering: Master's
Program: Occupational; Professional; Business Emphasis
Accreditation: &NH, ENGT

01 Metro President .... Mr. Joshua PADRON
37 Manager Student Finance .... Ms. Maria MAURO
05 Associate Provost Curriculum .... Mr. Jesus FERNANDEZ
15 HR Business Partner .... Ms. Maria VALDESPINO
07 Senior Director of Admissions .... Mr. Oronde BAYLOR
06 Assistant Registrar .... Ms. Frances TOUS
72 Dean of Technology Programs .... Mr. Raef YASSIN
50 Dean of Business & CIS .... Mr. Willie WILBORN
08 Director of Library Services .... Dr. Mary HOWREY
36 Director of Career Services .... Mr. Antonio COBAS
31 Director of Community Outreach .... Ms. Keisha SMITH

† Regional accreditation is carried under the parent institution in Downers Grove, IL.

DeVry University - Orlando Campus (K)

4000 Millenia Boulevard, Orlando FL 32839-2426

County: Orange Identification: 666112
Unit ID: 439163
Telephone: (407) 345-2800 Carnegie Class: Master's L
FAX Number: (407) 345-2829 Calendar System: Semester
URL: www.devry.com
Established: 1931 Annual Undergrad Tuition & Fees: $16,156
Enrollment: 1,970 Coed
Affiliation or Control: Proprietary IRS Status: Proprietary
Highest Offering: Master's
Program: Occupational; Professional; Business Emphasis
Accreditation: &NH, ENGT

01 Metro President .... Mr. Steven BROOKS
08 Director of Library Services .... Ms. Candace KELLER-RABER
10 Sr Dir of Finance/Administration .... Mr. Wes CAMPBELL
32 Manager Student Services .... Mr. Jameer ABASS
07 Sr Director of Admissions .... Ms. Elizabeth MEYER
05 Dean of Academic Affairs .... Dr. Eddie WACHTER
97 Dean General Education .... Ms. Dusty MADDOX
37 Manager Student Finance .... Mr. Dale THOMAS
15 HR Business Partner .... Ms. Anita SPINELLI
36 Director of Career Services .... Ms. Kathleen EMERY
06 Registrar .... Ms. Sheila DIAL

† Regional accreditation is carried under the parent institution in Downers Grove, IL.

DeVry University - Orlando North Center (L)

1800 Pembrook Drive, Suite 160, Orlando FL 32810-6372

County: Orange Identification: 666198
Unit ID: 437334
Telephone: (407) 659-0900 Carnegie Class: Not Classified
FAX Number: (407) 659-0901 Calendar System: Semester
URL: www.devry.edu
Established: 1931 Annual Undergrad Tuition & Fees: $16,176
Enrollment: 273 Coed
Affiliation or Control: Proprietary IRS Status: Proprietary
Highest Offering: Master's
Program: Occupational; Professional; Business Emphasis
Accreditation: &NH

01 Center Dean .... Elisabeth SAUTNER

† Regional accreditation is carried under the parent institution in Downers Grove, IL.

DeVry University - Tampa Bay Campus (M)

5540 W Executive Dr., Ste. 100, Tampa FL 33609-1002

County: Hillsborough Identification: 666199
Unit ID: 434885
Telephone: (813) 287-6700 Carnegie Class: Not Classified
FAX Number: (813) 288-8980 Calendar System: Semester
URL: www.devry.edu
Established: 1931 Annual Undergrad Tuition & Fees: $16,156
Enrollment: 356 Coed
Affiliation or Control: Proprietary IRS Status: Proprietary
Highest Offering: Master's
Program: Occupational; Professional; Business Emphasis
Accreditation: &NH

01 Campus Dean .... Lynn KOHLER

† Regional accreditation is carried under the parent institution in Downers Grove, IL.

DeVry University - Tampa East (A)

6700 Lakeview Center Drive, Ste 150,
Tampa FL 33619-1121

County: Hillsborough | Identification: 666528
Telephone: (813) 664-4260 | Carnegie Class: Not Classified
FAX Number: (813) 740-2790 | Calendar System: Semester
URL: www.devry.edu
Established: 1931 | Annual Undergrad Tuition & Fees: $16,156
Enrollment: 358 | Coed
Affiliation or Control: Proprietary | IRS Status: Proprietary
Highest Offering: Master's
Program: Professional; Business Emphasis
Accreditation: &NH

01 Center Dean .... Nicole BETHUNE-WALKER

† Regional accreditation is carried under the parent institution in Downers Grove, IL.

Digital Media Arts College (B)

5400 Broken Sound Blvd, Suite 100,
Boca Raton FL 33487

County: Palm Beach | FICE Identification: 041274
Unit ID: 451060
Telephone: (561) 391-1148 | Carnegie Class: Bac/Diverse
FAX Number: (561) 998-3430 | Calendar System: Semester
URL: www.dmac.edu
Established: 2002 | Annual Undergrad Tuition & Fees: $24,000
Enrollment: 400 | Coed
Affiliation or Control: Proprietary | IRS Status: Proprietary
Highest Offering: Master's
Program: Professional; Fine Arts Emphasis
Accreditation: ACICS

01 President .... Mr. Alfred MCCLOY
03 Exec Vice President/Dir of Finance .... Mr. David MURVIN

Dragon Rises College of Oriental Medicine (C)

1000 NE 16th Ave., Building F, Gainesville FL 32601-4557

County: Alachua | FICE Identification: 038883
Unit ID: 449481
Telephone: (352) 371-2833 | Carnegie Class: Spec/Health
FAX Number: (352) 244-0003 | Calendar System: Semester
URL: www.dragonrises.edu
Established: 2001 | Annual Undergrad Tuition & Fees: $15,495
Enrollment: 60 | Coed
Affiliation or Control: Proprietary | IRS Status: Proprietary
Highest Offering: Master's
Program: Professional
Accreditation: ACUP

01 Director .... Mr. Bruce PAGEL
05 Academic Dean .... Mr. Kenney EBERSOLE
23 Clinic Director .... Mr. Jamin NICHOLS
32 Dean of Student Services .... Ms. Ruth HAYES-MORRISON
37 Financial Aid Administrator .... Ms. Kate ELLISON

East West College of Natural Medicine (D)

3808 N Tamiami Trail, Sarasota FL 34234-5362

County: Sarasota | FICE Identification: 034297
Unit ID: 439394
Telephone: (941) 355-9080 | Carnegie Class: Spec/Health
FAX Number: (941) 355-3243 | Calendar System: Trimester
URL: www.ewcollege.org
Established: 1994 | Annual Undergrad Tuition & Fees: $47,000
Enrollment: 105 | Coed
Affiliation or Control: Proprietary | IRS Status: Proprietary
Highest Offering: Master's
Program: Professional
Accreditation: ACUP

01 President/CEO .... Dr. Joseph T. ROGALSKI
05 Academic Dean .... Mr. Jonathan D. WALD

Eckerd College (E)

4200 54th Avenue S, Saint Petersburg FL 33711-4700

County: Pinellas | FICE Identification: 001487
Unit ID: 133492
Telephone: (727) 867-1166 | Carnegie Class: Bac/A&S
FAX Number: (727) 864-1877 | Calendar System: 4/1/4
URL: www.eckerd.edu
Established: 1958 | Annual Undergrad Tuition & Fees: $35,926
Enrollment: 2,346 | Coed
Affiliation or Control: Presbyterian Church (U.S.A.) | IRS Status: 501(c)3
Highest Offering: Baccalaureate
Program: Liberal Arts And General
Accreditation: SC

01 President .... Dr. Donald R. EASTMAN, III
05 Exec Vice Pres/Provost/Dean Faculty .... Dr. Suzan HARRISON
10 CFO .... Mr. Christopher P. BRENNAN
03 Vice President .... Dr. Lisa A. METS
30 Vice President Advancement .... Mr. Matthew S. BISSET
51 Vice Pres/Dean of Special Programs .... Mr. Kelly KIRSCHNER
32 Vice Pres/Dean for Student Life .... Dr. James J. ANNARELLI
07 Dean of Admissions & Financial Aid .... Mr. John SULLIVAN
20 Assistant to the Pres Academic Affs .... Dr. Kathryn J. WATSON
26 Exec Dir Marketing/Communication .... Ms. Valerie GLIEM
21 Associate Chief Financial Officer .... Ms. Luz ARCILA
20 Assoc Dean Institutional Effective .... Dr. David A. EUBANKS
30 Assoc VP Advancement .... Mr. Tom SCHNEIDER
88 Academic Director of PEL .... Dr. Margret SKAFTADOTTIR
105 Dir Web/Marketing/Communication .... Mr. Casey PAQUET
27 Director Media Relations .... Ms. Alizza PUNZALAN HALL
88 Director of ASPEC .... Mr. Ken WOLFE
88 Director of CALA .... Dr. Norman SMITH
88 Director of International Education .... Ms. Diane L. FERRIS
85 Dir International Student Programs .... Mr. Olivier DEBURE
13 Dir of Information Tech .... Dr. John A. DUFF
09 Director Institutional Research .... Vacant
06 Registrar .... Ms. Linda SWINDALL
06 Student Enrollment Manager PEL .... Ms. Lin JORGENSEN
08 Director of Library .... Ms. Jamie W. GILL
38 Director Counseling Center .... Dr. Scott C. STRADER
29 Director Alumni Engagement .... Mr. Chris CONNORS
19 Director Campus Safety .... Mr. Adam COLBY
36 Educ Career Plng/Applied Learning .... Ms. Jessica NEANDER
37 Director Financial Aid .... Dr. Pat E. WATKINS
41 Athletic Director .... Dr. Robert FORTOSIS
07 Director of Admission .... Ms. Maria FURTADO
42 Chaplain .... Rev. Doug MCMAHON
88 Director of Sponsored Research .... Vacant
21 Controller .... Ms. Robin SMALLEY
35 Assistant Dean of Student Affairs .... Ms. Lorisa LORENZO
88 Asst Dean Students for Campus Act .... Mr. Fred SABOTA
28 Assoc Dn Stdnt Affs/Dir Mltcltl-Div .... Ms. Lena L. WILFALK
87 Dir Conferences and Summer School .... Ms. Cheryl GOLD

Edison State College (F)

8099 College Parkway, SW, Fort Myers FL 33919-5566

County: Lee | FICE Identification: 001477
Unit ID: 133508
Telephone: (239) 489-9300 | Carnegie Class: Assoc/Pub4
FAX Number: (239) 489-9103 | Calendar System: Semester
URL: www.edison.edu
Established: 1961 | Annual Undergrad Tuition & Fees (In-State): $3,469
Enrollment: 17,310 | Coed
Affiliation or Control: State | IRS Status: 501(c)3
Highest Offering: Baccalaureate
Program: Occupational; 2-Year Principally Bachelor's Creditable; Liberal Arts And General; Teacher Preparatory; Professional
Accreditation: #SC, ADNUR, CVT, DH, EMT, NUR, RAD

01 District President .... Dr. Jeffery ALLBRITTEN
10 VP Financial Services .... Ms. Gina DOEBLE
30 Vice President of Development .... Vacant
88 Vice President Inst Research .... Vacant
05 Int Vice President Academic Affairs .... Dr. Erin HARREL
12 Pres Charlotte County Campus .... Dr. Patricia LAND
12 Pres Collier County Campus .... Dr. Robert R. JONES
06 Registrar .... Mrs. Billee SILVA
15 Dir Human Resources/Asst Gen Couns .... Mr. Ron DENTE
96 Director of Purchasing .... Mrs. Lisa TUDOR
49 Dn Arts & Sciences/Assoc Acad Ofcr .... Vacant
09 Dean Inst Research .... Mr. Kevin COUGHLIN
107 Dean Professional/Tech Studies .... Mrs. Mary MYERS
66 Dean School of Nursing .... Vacant
32 Dean Student Services .... Dr. Amy TEPROVICH
20 Assoc Dn Arts & Sci/Assoc Acad Ofcr .... Dr. Rodney DENNISON
88 Dean College and Career Readiness .... Dr. Eileen DELUCA
29 Coordinator Alumni Relations .... Ms. Rio DE ARMOND
18 Director Facilities Plant/Mgmt .... Mr. Steve NICE
26 Director of Marketing .... Ms. Catherine BERGERSON
88 Director Student Support Services .... Ms. Paula DAILY
35 Director of Student Life .... Ms. Amy TEPROVICH
38 Director of Student Counseling .... Vacant
13 Director Technology Services .... Mr. Mark TRASK
08 Campus Dir Lrng Resources Collier .... Mr. Antony VALENTI
08 Campus Dir Lrng Resources Charlotte .... Ms. Mary Ann WALTON
08 Dir Learning Resources Lee .... Mr. William SHULUK

Edward Waters College (G)

1658 Kings Road, Jacksonville FL 32209-6199

County: Duval | FICE Identification: 001478
Unit ID: 133526
Telephone: (904) 470-8000 | Carnegie Class: Bac/Diverse
FAX Number: (904) 470-8039 | Calendar System: Semester
URL: www.ewc.edu
Established: 1866 | Annual Undergrad Tuition & Fees: $11,158
Enrollment: 751 | Coed
Affiliation or Control: African Methodist Episcopal | IRS Status: 501(c)3
Highest Offering: Baccalaureate
Program: Liberal Arts And General
Accreditation: SC, IACBE

01 President .... Mr. Nathaniel GLOVER
03 Executive Vice President/VPIA .... Dr. Eurmon HERVEY
25 Dir of Title III/Sponsored Programs .... Mrs. Lois M. WASHBURN
88 Executive Business Auditor .... Mr. George DANDELAKE
10 Vice Pres Business & Finance .... Mr. Randolph MITCHELL
32 Vice President Student Affairs .... Dr. James EWERS
84 Asst VP Enrollment Management .... Dr. Kimberly DAVIS
05 Interim VP of Academic Affairs .... Dr. Marvin GRANT
101 Secy of the College/Clerk BOT .... Mrs. Linda FOSTER
06 Registrar .... Ms. Loretta LATIMER
08 Director Library Services .... Ms. Carmella MARTIN
15 Director Human Resources .... Mr. Arthur BENDOLPH
37 Director Financial Aid .... Ms. Janice NOWAK
88 Dir of Teacher Education .... Dr. Marie SNOW
20 Assistant VP Academic Affairs .... Dr. Reuben PERECHI
50 Chair Business Administration .... Dr. Francis IKEOKWU
43 General Counsel .... Mr. Michael FREED
09 Interim Dir OIPRE .... Ms. Bernice PARKER-BELL
88 Director Upward Bound .... Dr. Delacy SANFORD
36 Director Career Planning .... Vacant
30 Assistant VP Inst Advancement .... Ms. Wanda J. WILLIS
96 Director of Auxiliary Services .... Vacant
07 Director of Admissions .... Vacant
26 Coord Comm & Marketing .... Mr. Blake HACHT
88 Interim Director of TRIO .... Mr. Selah BISHOP
31 Director Community Resource Center .... Mrs. Marie HEATH
88 Exec Director of CTL .... Dr. Mammie JEFFRIES
89 Director of First-Year Experience .... Dr. Mel C. NORWOOD, II
88 Director of FAME .... Mrs. Gladys CLAY
41 Director of Athletics .... Mr. Johnny REMBERT
13 Assistant CIO .... Mr. David SIMFUKWE

Embry-Riddle Aeronautical University (H)

600 S Clyde Morris Boulevard,
Daytona Beach FL 32114-3900

County: Volusia | FICE Identification: 001479
Unit ID: 133553
Telephone: (386) 226-6000 | Carnegie Class: Master's M
FAX Number: (386) 226-6459 | Calendar System: Semester
URL: www.erau.edu
Established: 1926 | Annual Undergrad Tuition & Fees: $29,520
Enrollment: 5,205 | Coed
Affiliation or Control: Independent Non-Profit | IRS Status: 501(c)3
Highest Offering: Doctorate
Program: Occupational; Liberal Arts And General; Professional
Accreditation: SC, AAB, ACBSP, ENG

01 President .... Dr. John P. JOHNSON
05 Exec Vice President and CAO .... Mr. Richard HEIST
10 Vice Pres/Chief Financial Officer .... Mr. Eric B. WEEKES
15 Vice President Human Resources .... Ms. Irene MCREYNOLDS
32 Dean of Students .... Ms. Sonja TAYLOR
84 Assoc VP Enrollment Management .... Mr. Eduardo PRIETO
26 Assistant Director Communications .... Ms. Mary VAN BUREN
37 Director Financial Aid .... Ms. Barbara DRYDEN
09 Director Institutional Research .... Ms. Maria FRANCO
36 Executive Director Career Services .... Ms. Lisa KOLLAR
07 Director UG Admissions .... Mr. Robert J. ADAMS
13 Chief Information Officer .... Ms. Cindy BIXLER
29 Assistant VP Alumni Relations .... Ms. Michele BERG
06 Director Records & Registration .... Mrs. Valerie KRUSE
88 Director Univ Veterans Affairs .... Ms. Faith DESLAURIERS
41 Director of Athletics .... Mr. Steven G. RIDDER
28 Director of Diversity Initiatives .... Mr. Richard M. STICKNEY
35 Assoc Director Student Activities .... Ms. Lauren E. MORAN
38 Director Student Academic Support .... Mr. Richard NICOLS

Embry-Riddle Aeronautical University-Worldwide (I)

600 S Clyde Morris Boulevard,
Daytona Beach FL 32114-3900

County: Volusia | Identification: 666089
Unit ID: 426314
Telephone: (800) 522-6787 | Carnegie Class: Spec/Tech
FAX Number: (386) 226-6984 | Calendar System: Other
URL: www.erau.edu
Established: 1970 | Annual Undergrad Tuition & Fees: $11,700
Enrollment: 16,244 | Coed
Affiliation or Control: Independent Non-Profit | IRS Status: 501(c)3
Highest Offering: Master's
Program: Occupational; Liberal Arts And General; Professional
Accreditation: &SC

01 President .... Dr. John P. JOHNSON
05 Exec Vice President & CAO Worldwide .... Dr. John WATRET
20 Assoc VP Academic Affairs .... Dr. Barry FARBROTHER
84 Assoc VP Enrollment Management .... Mr. Eduardo PRIETO
45 Assoc VP Institutional Effectivenes .... Ms. Joan MILLER
10 Assoc VP & Chief Business Officer .... Mr. Robert JOST
26 Executive Director of Marketing .... Mr. Mark DIFABIO
09 Director of Institutional Research .... Ms. Maria FRANCO
29 Assistant VP for Alumni Relations .... Ms. Michele BERG
07 Director of Admissions .... Ms. Linda DAMMER

† Regional accreditation is carried under the parent institution in Daytona Beach, FL.

Everest Institute (J)

530 West 49th Street, Hialeah FL 33012-3605

County: Dade | Identification: 666271
Unit ID: 136011
Telephone: (305) 558-9500 | Carnegie Class: Assoc/PrivFP

FAX Number: (305) 558-4419 Calendar System: Other
URL: www.everest.edu/hialeah
Established: 1977 Annual Undergrad Tuition & Fees: $15,552
Enrollment: 592 Coed
Affiliation or Control: Proprietary IRS Status: Proprietary
Highest Offering: Associate Degree
Program: Occupational
Accreditation: ACICS, SURGT

01 President .... Ms. Fran HEASTON

† Branch campus of Everest Institute, Miami, FL.

Everest Institute (A)

9020 SW 137th Avenue, Miami FL 33186-1410
County: Miami-Dade FICE Identification: 030032
Unit ID: 409670
Telephone: (305) 386-9900 Carnegie Class: Assoc/PrivFP
FAX Number: (305) 388-1740 Calendar System: Other
URL: www.everest.edu
Established: 1977 Annual Undergrad Tuition & Fees: $15,732
Enrollment: 676 Coed
Affiliation or Control: Proprietary IRS Status: Proprietary
Highest Offering: Associate Degree
Program: 2-Year Principally Bachelor's Creditable
Accreditation: ACICS, MAAB, SURGT

01 President .... Darrell RHOTEN
04 Assistant to the President .... Carolina MARTE
05 Academic Dean .... Claudette THOMPSON

Everest Institute (B)

111 NW 183rd Street, Suite 200, Miami FL 33169-4538
County: Miami-Dade FICE Identification: 021218
Unit ID: 135957
Telephone: (305) 949-9500 Carnegie Class: Assoc/PrivFP
FAX Number: (305) 949-7303 Calendar System: Other
URL: www.everest.edu
Established: 1977 Annual Undergrad Tuition & Fees: $15,732
Enrollment: 659 Coed
Affiliation or Control: Proprietary IRS Status: Proprietary
Highest Offering: Associate Degree
Program: Occupational; 2-Year Principally Bachelor's Creditable; Technical Emphasis
Accreditation: ACICS

01 Campus President .... Peter BASTIONY
05 Academic Dean .... Mike GIACCHINO
20 Associate Dean .... Rose-Marie MURRAY
07 Director of Admissions .... Kevin WILKINSON
37 Director of Finance .... Angela MACKEY
36 Director of Career Services .... Natalia MEJIA
06 Registrar .... Tonia SMITH
10 Business Office Manager .... Mauricio ROSAS

Everest University-Brandon Campus (C)

3924 Coconut Palm Drive, Tampa FL 33619-1354
County: Hillsborough Identification: 666416
Unit ID: 260293
Telephone: (813) 621-0041 Carnegie Class: Master's M
FAX Number: (813) 623-5769 Calendar System: Quarter
URL: www.everest.edu
Established: 1890 Annual Undergrad Tuition & Fees: $16,452
Enrollment: 10,635 Coed
Affiliation or Control: Proprietary IRS Status: Proprietary
Highest Offering: Master's
Program: Occupational; 2-Year Principally Bachelor's Creditable; Business Emphasis
Accreditation: ACICS, MAC, RAD

01 President .... Mr. Todd PEARSON
03 Vice President .... Mr. Rod KIRKWOOD
05 Associate Academic Dean .... Mr. Thomas MOORE-PIZON
04 Assistant to the President .... Ms. Amanda LONG
06 Dean of Registration .... Ms. Lori VANG
07 Director of Admissions .... Ms. Shandretta POINTER
08 Head Librarian .... Ms. Madeline LOCK
10 Director Student Accounts .... Ms. Courtenay LOPEZ
36 Director Student Placement .... Ms. Millie REED
37 Director Student Financial Aid .... Mr. Michael WERNON
32 Director Student Services .... Ms. Dolly BROWN

† Branch campus of Everest University, Tampa, FL.

Everest University-Jacksonville Campus (D)

8226 Phillips Highway, Jacksonville FL 32256-1240
County: Duval Identification: 666994
Unit ID: 438902
Telephone: (904) 731-4949 Carnegie Class: Assoc/PrivFP4
FAX Number: (904) 731-0599 Calendar System: Quarter
URL: www.everest.edu
Established: 2000 Annual Undergrad Tuition & Fees: $14,976
Enrollment: 787 Coed
Affiliation or Control: Proprietary IRS Status: Proprietary
Highest Offering: Master's
Program: Liberal Arts And General; Professional
Accreditation: ACICS, MAAB

01 Acting President .... Ms. Donna WILHELM
04 Assistant to the President .... Ms. Loraine PARR
05 Acad Dean Lanier/Modular Programs .... Dr. James ARTLEY
20 Associate Academic Dean .... Dr. Tameiko ALLEN GRANT
07 Director of Admissions .... Mr. Robin MANNING
36 Director of Career Service .... Ms. Marta ROTH
37 Director Student Financial Aid .... Ms. Cathy KIMBALL
10 Director Student Accounts .... Ms. Donna WILHELM

† Branch campus of Everest University, Largo, FL.

Everest University-Lakeland Campus (E)

995 E Memorial Boulevard, Suite 110, Lakeland FL 33801-1919
County: Polk Identification: 666415
Unit ID: 367909
Telephone: (863) 686-1444 Carnegie Class: Bac/Assoc
FAX Number: (863) 688-9881 Calendar System: Quarter
URL: www.everest.edu
Established: 1890 Annual Undergrad Tuition & Fees: $16,272
Enrollment: 450 Coed
Affiliation or Control: Proprietary IRS Status: Proprietary
Highest Offering: Baccalaureate
Program: Occupational; Business Emphasis
Accreditation: ACICS, MAC

01 President .... Mr. Rod KIRKWOOD
05 Academic Dean .... Mr. Charlie ZARUBA
07 Admissions Director .... Mr. Allen GOFF
36 Career Services Director .... Ms. Carly THOMPSON
37 Student Finance Director .... Ms. Linda WAGNER
10 Business Director .... Ms. Ariel MILLIGAN
08 Librarian .... Ms. Betty MARTINEZ

† Branch campus of Everest University, Largo, FL.

Everest University-Largo (F)

1199 East Bay Drive, Largo FL 33770-2556
County: Pinellas FICE Identification: 025998
Unit ID: 137810
Telephone: (727) 725-2688 Carnegie Class: Bac/Assoc
FAX Number: (727) 373-4412 Calendar System: Quarter
URL: www.everest.edu
Established: 1890 Annual Undergrad Tuition & Fees: $20,420
Enrollment: 442 Coed
Affiliation or Control: Proprietary IRS Status: Proprietary
Highest Offering: Master's
Program: Occupational; 2-Year Principally Bachelor's Creditable; Business Emphasis
Accreditation: ACICS

01 President .... Mr. Sami FANEK
05 Chief Academic Officer .... Mr. Oluyemi AWOLOLA
07 Director of Admissions .... Ms. Jill MALONE
07 Director of High School Admissions .... Ms. Theresa AMICO
37 Director of Student Finance .... Mr. Will SCOTT
36 Director of Career Services .... Ms. Lindsey DEMITH
10 Business Manager .... Mr. Will SCOTT
08 Librarian .... Ms. Candice PASCUAL
32 Director of Student Services .... Vacant
20 Assoc Dean of Academics .... Ms. Heidi DINDIAL-THOMPSON

Everest University-Melbourne Campus (G)

2401 N Harbor City Boulevard, Melbourne FL 32935-6609
County: Brevard Identification: 666417
Unit ID: 420006
Telephone: (321) 253-2929 Carnegie Class: Bac/Assoc
FAX Number: (321) 255-2017 Calendar System: Quarter
URL: www.everest.edu
Established: 1996 Annual Undergrad Tuition & Fees: $14,616
Enrollment: 679 Coed
Affiliation or Control: Proprietary IRS Status: Proprietary
Highest Offering: Master's
Program: Occupational; Business Emphasis
Accreditation: ACICS, MAC

01 President .... Mr. Mark W. JUDGE
05 Academic Dean .... Ms. Jennie LESSER
07 Admissions Director .... Mr. Timothy ALEXANDER
37 Director of Student Finance .... Mr. Bryan CAPPS
36 Career Plan Placement Director .... Mrs. Catherine MALLOZZI
10 Director of Student Accounts .... Mr. Bryan CAPPS

† Branch campus of Everest University-North Orlando Campus, Orlando, FL.

Everest University-North Orlando Campus (H)

5421 Diplomat Circle, Orlando FL 32810-5674
County: Orange FICE Identification: 001499
Unit ID: 136288
Telephone: (407) 628-5870 Carnegie Class: Bac/Assoc
FAX Number: (407) 628-1344 Calendar System: Quarter
URL: www.everest.edu
Established: 1918 Annual Undergrad Tuition & Fees: $14,616
Enrollment: 1,047 Coed
Affiliation or Control: Proprietary IRS Status: Proprietary
Highest Offering: Master's
Program: Business Emphasis
Accreditation: ACICS, MAC

01 President .... Charlie HARDIMAN
03 Vice President .... Vacant
12 President of Branch Campus .... Louise A. STEINKEOWAY
12 President of Melbourne Branch .... Mark JUDGE
05 Academic Dean .... William FORD
07 Director of Admissions .... Kenny ANDERSON
08 Librarian .... Tamara DUJARDIAN
37 Financial Aid Supervisor .... Linda KAISRLIK
06 Registrar .... Katonia WARREN
36 Director Student Placement .... Danielle THORNTON
10 Chief Business Officer .... Jessica KINESKEY
35 Director Student Service .... Liane PARDO

Everest University-Orange Park (I)

805 Wells Road, Orange Park FL 32073-2301
County: Clay Identification: 666590
Unit ID: 445434
Telephone: (904) 264-9122 Carnegie Class: Bac/Assoc
FAX Number: (904) 264-9952 Calendar System: Quarter
URL: www.everest.edu
Established: 2003 Annual Undergrad Tuition & Fees: $14,976
Enrollment: 817 Coed
Affiliation or Control: Proprietary IRS Status: Proprietary
Highest Offering: Baccalaureate
Program: Business Emphasis
Accreditation: ACICS, MAAB

01 President .... Mr. Scot HAYNES
05 Academic Dean .... Ms. Tameiko GRANT
37 Director Financial Aid .... Ms. Kristine HIBBARD
32 Director Student Services .... Vacant

† Branch campus of Everest University, Tampa, FL.

Everest University-Pompano Beach Campus (J)

225 N Federal Highway, Pompano Beach FL 33062
County: Broward FICE Identification: 008146
Unit ID: 134149
Telephone: (954) 783-7339 Carnegie Class: Master's S
FAX Number: (954) 943-2547 Calendar System: Quarter
URL: www.everest.edu
Established: 1940 Annual Undergrad Tuition & Fees: $14,976
Enrollment: 1,713 Coed
Affiliation or Control: Proprietary IRS Status: Proprietary
Highest Offering: Master's
Program: 2-Year Principally Bachelor's Creditable; Professional; Business Emphasis
Accreditation: ACICS, MAAB

01 President .... Mr. Stephen GUIDRY
05 Academic Dean .... Mr. Esmail ZARIAROW
07 Director Admissions .... Mr. Martin LEVERT
07 Director Admissions .... Ms. Amanda MCLURE
37 Director Student Finance .... Mr. Todd FOX
06 Registrar .... Ms. Dana NGUYEN
20 Associate Academic Dean .... Ms. Indira ST. ONER
36 Director Career Planning/Placement .... Ms. Andrea MITCHELL
08 Librarian .... Ms. Keri ENTERLINE
10 Director Student Accounts .... Mr. Trevor BLOW
04 Admin Assistant to the President .... Ms. Fumiko NYE

Everest University-South Orlando Campus (K)

9200 Southpark Center Loop, Orlando FL 32819-8606
County: Orange Identification: 666418
Unit ID: 390701
Telephone: (407) 851-2525 Carnegie Class: Bac/Assoc
FAX Number: (407) 345-8671 Calendar System: Quarter
URL: www.everest.edu
Established: 1953 Annual Undergrad Tuition & Fees: $20,000
Enrollment: 1,100 Coed
Affiliation or Control: Proprietary IRS Status: Proprietary
Highest Offering: Master's
Program: 2-Year Principally Bachelor's Creditable; Professional; Business Emphasis
Accreditation: ACICS, MAC

01 President .... Mr. Jay WILMOTH
10 Vice President of Finance .... Vacant
05 Dean of Academics .... Dr. M. Brad MILLER
07 Director of Admissions .... Mr. Shawn WENNER
37 Director of Student Finance .... Ms. Sherri WILLIAMS
88 Director of Student Accounts .... Mr. Jerry THOMPSON
36 Director of Career Services .... Ms. Veena GARIB
32 Director of Student Services .... Mr. Tony GAFFNEY

† Branch campus of Everest University-North Orlando Campus, Orlando, FL.

Everest University-Tampa Campus (A)

3319 W Hillsborough Avenue, Tampa FL 33614-5801
County: Hillsborough FICE Identification: 001534
Unit ID: 137801
Telephone: (813) 879-6000 Carnegie Class: Bac/Assoc
FAX Number: (813) 871-2483 Calendar System: Quarter
URL: www.everest.edu
Established: 1890 Annual Undergrad Tuition & Fees: $23,396
Enrollment: 687 Coed
Affiliation or Control: Proprietary IRS Status: Proprietary
Highest Offering: Master's
Program: Occupational; 2-Year Principally Bachelor's Creditable; Professional; Business Emphasis
Accreditation: ACICS, MAC

01 President ... Mr. Thomas M. BARLOW
04 Assistant to the President ... Ms. Maida AVELLANET
05 Academic Dean ... Ms. Theo EGGLESTON
07 Director of Admissions ... Vacant
37 Director of Financial Aid ... Mr. Brian JONES
32 Director of Student Services ... Ms. Yolanda WILLIAMS
10 Director of Student Accounts ... Ms. Janet GENAO
36 Director of Career Services ... Ms. Regina HODGSON
20 Associate Academic Dean ... Ms. Dena SEIDEN
06 Lead Registrar ... Ms. Kim LARKIN
08 University Librarian ... Ms. Judith COLE

Everglades University (B)

5002 T-Rex Avenue, Suite 100,
Boca Raton FL 33431-4493
County: Palm Beach FICE Identification: 031085
Unit ID: 385619
Telephone: (888) 772-6077 Carnegie Class: Bac/Diverse
FAX Number: (561) 912-1191 Calendar System: Semester
URL: www.evergladesuniversity.edu
Established: 1990 Annual Undergrad Tuition & Fees: $22,200
Enrollment: 1,111 Coed
Affiliation or Control: Independent Non-Profit IRS Status: 501(c)3
Highest Offering: Master's
Program: Professional
Accreditation: SC

01 President/CEO ... Ms. Kristi L. MOLLIS
05 Vice President of Academic Affairs ... Dr. Jayne MOSCHELLA
37 Regional Director of Financial Aid ... Mrs. Seeta SINGH MOONILALL
84 Regional Dir Enrollment Management ... Mrs. Marci TULLY
88 Director of Fundraising ... Vacant
09 Director Inst Effectiveness ... Mr. Chee PIONG
08 Director of Library Services ... Ms. Amanda SARRA
12 Vice President Boca Raton Campus ... Ms. Carla SANOIR
12 Vice President Online Division ... Ms. Suzanne CROWLEY
12 Vice President Sarasota Campus ... Ms. Caroline KING
12 Vice President of Orlando Campus ... Ms. Sherry PARKER
20 Dean of Academics Online ... Vacant
20 Dean of Academics Sarasota ... Dr. Christine GRAHAM
20 Dean of Academics Orlando ... Dr. Melissa DEGESO
20 Assistant Dean Boca Raton ... Mr. Jared BEZET
07 Director of Admissions Boca ... Vacant
07 Director of Admissions Online Boca ... Ms. Susan ARONBERG
07 Director of Admissions Orlando ... Mr. Richard FOSA
07 Director of Admission Sarasota ... Vacant
04 Assistant to the President ... Ms. Christina OAKLEY
37 Online Financial Aid Director Boca ... Vacant
37 Asst Financial Aid Director Online ... Ms. Fatima FLORES
37 Financial Aid Director Sarasota ... Mrs. Courtney ROBERTSON
37 Financial Aid Director Orlando ... Mr. Anthony CHAMBERS
37 Asst Financial Aid Director Boca ... Ms. Anne RODNE
06 Registrar-Online Division ... Mr. Adrian KACZOR
06 Registrar Online Division ... Ms. Tanecia NATTO
06 Registrar Boca ... Ms. Katie ROBERSON
06 Registrar Orlando ... Mr. Clifton HURD
06 Registrar Sarasota ... Ms. Donna BARANOWSKI
50 Business Department ... Mr. David SMITH
50 Dept Chair of Construction Mgmt ... Mr. William FLUELLEN
88 Department Chair of Aviation ... Mr. Michael VAN DUSEN
76 Department Chair Allied Health ... Vacant
97 Department Chair General Education ... Vacant
88 Librarian Boca Raton ... Mr. Zachary ENGLISH
88 Librarian Sarasota ... Ms. Anisa THOMAS
08 Librarian Orlando ... Ms. Sara GONZALEZ
21 Business Manager ... Vacant
32 Dir of Student Services Online ... Vacant
32 Dir of Student Services Boca Raton ... Ms. Casi HASKINS
32 Dir of Student Services Sarasota ... Vacant
32 Dir of Student Services Orlando ... Ms. Kayli LEWIS
88 Bursar Manager Online Division ... Mr. Tyree WHITEHEAD
88 Bursar Online Division ... Ms. Samantha ISAAC
40 Bursar/Bookstore Manager Boca ... Vacant
40 Bookstore Manager Online Division ... Ms. Pamela PETERSON
40 Bursar/Bookstore Manager Sarasota ... Ms. Anita WENDZEL
40 Bursar/Bookstore Manager Orlando ... Ms. Mabel RASMUSSEN
88 Online Trainer ... Mr. Ronnie ABUKHALAF

Flagler College (C)

74 King Street, Saint Augustine FL 32084-4342
County: Saint Johns FICE Identification: 007893
Unit ID: 133711
Telephone: (904) 829-6481 Carnegie Class: Bac/Diverse
FAX Number: (904) 824-6017 Calendar System: Semester
URL: www.flagler.edu
Established: 1968 Annual Undergrad Tuition & Fees: $15,340
Enrollment: 2,591 Coed
Affiliation or Control: Independent Non-Profit IRS Status: 501(c)3
Highest Offering: Baccalaureate
Program: Liberal Arts And General; Teacher Preparatory; Business Emphasis
Accreditation: SC, @TEAC

01 President ... Dr. William T. ABARE, JR.
00 Chancellor ... Dr. William L. PROCTOR
10 Vice President Business Services ... Mr. Kenneth S. RUSSOM
30 Vice President Inst Advancement ... Mr. Mark WHITTAKER
05 Dean Academic Affairs ... Dr. Alan WOOLFOLK
26 Exec Director College Relations ... Ms. Donna DELORENZO
21 Executive Director of Finance ... Ms. Pamela F. LEYDON
09 Director Inst Research & Planning ... Dr. Randi HAGEN
27 Director of News and Information ... Mr. Brian L. THOMPSON
84 Vice President for Enrollment Mgmt ... Mr. Marc G. WILLIAR
32 Dean of Student Services ... Mr. Daniel P. STEWART
20 Associate Dean of Academic Affairs ... Mr. Yvan J. KELLY
35 Assistant Dean of Student Services ... Dr. Dirk HIBLER
38 Associate Dean of Counseling ... Dr. Glenn GOLDBERG
06 Registrar ... Mrs. Miriam C. ROBERSON
37 Director of Financial Aid ... Mr. Christopher D. HAFFNER
36 Director of Career Services ... Ms. Tara STEVENSON
08 Director of Library Services ... Mr. Michael A. GALLEN
41 Director Intercollegiate Athletics ... Mr. Jud DAMON
19 Director of Safety & Security ... Mr. Kerry DAVIS
40 Bookstore Manager ... Mr. Bob SMITH
24 Director Educational Media Services ... Mr. Steven I. SKIPP
13 Director Technology Services ... Mr. Joseph S. PROVENZA
39 Director of Residence Life ... Ms. Rachel T. GREEN
35 Director of Student Activities ... Ms. Carley JAMES
12 Dean Flagler College - Tallahassee ... Dr. Donald K. PARKS
88 Dir of Disability Services ... Ms. Eva Lynn FRANCISCO
18 Superintendent of Plant & Grounds ... Mr. Victor CHENEY
04 Assistant to the President ... Ms. Mary Jane DILLON
21 Director of Business Services ... Mr. Larry D. WEEKS
29 Director Alumni Relations ... Ms. Margo BROWN
44 Director Annual Fund ... Mr. Jeffrey DAVITT
15 Human Resource Analysis ... Ms. Tricia KRISTOFF
31 Director of College Relations ... Ms. Laura STEVENSON
88 Senior Woman Admin Athletic Dept ... Ms. Jennifer RINNERT

Florida Career College (D)

410 Park Place Boulevard, Clearwater FL 33759-3924
County: Pinellas FICE Identification: 025862
Unit ID: 364885
Telephone: (727) 724-1037 Carnegie Class: Assoc/PrivFP
FAX Number: (727) 723-7630 Calendar System: Other
URL: www.careercollege.edu
Established: 2006 Annual Undergrad Tuition & Fees: $16,744
Enrollment: 175 Coed
Affiliation or Control: Proprietary IRS Status: Proprietary
Highest Offering: Associate Degree
Program: Occupational
Accreditation: ACICS, COE

01 Chief Executive Officer ... Mr. Julio SOCORRO
03 Executive Director ... Mr. Steeve DEMERVE

Florida Career College (E)

3750 West 18th Avenue, Hialeah FL 33012-7028
County: Miami-Dade Identification: 666624
Telephone: (305) 825-3231 Carnegie Class: Not Classified
FAX Number: (305) 825-3436 Calendar System: Other
URL: www.careercollege.edu
Established: 2006 Annual Undergrad Tuition & Fees: N/A
Enrollment: N/A Coed
Affiliation or Control: Proprietary IRS Status: Proprietary
Highest Offering: Baccalaureate
Program: Occupational; 2-Year Principally Bachelor's Creditable
Accreditation: ACICS

01 Executive Director ... Ms. Muriel GUTIERREZ

Florida Career College (F)

3383 North State Road 7,
Lauderdale Lakes FL 33319-5617
County: Broward Identification: 666622
Telephone: (954) 535-8700 Carnegie Class: Not Classified
FAX Number: (954) 733-7558 Calendar System: Other
URL: www.careercollege.edu
Established: 1982 Annual Undergrad Tuition & Fees: N/A
Enrollment: N/A Coed
Affiliation or Control: Proprietary IRS Status: Proprietary
Highest Offering: Baccalaureate
Program: Occupational; 2-Year Principally Bachelor's Creditable
Accreditation: ACICS

01 Executive Director ... Ms. Marion DAMOUR

Florida Career College (G)

1321 SW 107th Avenue, Suite 201B,
Miami FL 33174-2521
County: Miami-Dade FICE Identification: 023058
Unit ID: 133997
Telephone: (305) 553-6065 Carnegie Class: Assoc/PrivFP4
FAX Number: (305) 225-0128 Calendar System: Quarter
URL: www.careercollege.edu
Established: 1982 Annual Undergrad Tuition & Fees: $17,100
Enrollment: 3,651 Coed
Affiliation or Control: Proprietary IRS Status: Proprietary
Highest Offering: Baccalaureate
Program: Occupational; 2-Year Principally Bachelor's Creditable; Technical Emphasis
Accreditation: ACICS

01 President/CEO ... Mr. David KNOBEL
03 Executive Director ... Ms. Erica MATTHEW
88 Associate Executive Director ... Mr. Eduardo SAMA
88 Associate Executive Director ... Ms. Muriel GUTIERREZ
88 Area Executive Director ... Mr. Gilbert DELGADO
88 Area Executive Director ... Mr. Michael SCHWAM
05 Director of Education ... Mr. Anthony RICHIEZ
37 Financial Aid Director ... Ms. Vanessa ALFARO
06 Registrar ... Ms. Jessica RIVERA
07 Director of Admission ... Ms. Heidi CRUZ

Florida Career College (H)

7891 Pines Boulevard, Pembroke Pines FL 33024-6916
County: Broward Identification: 666025
Telephone: (954) 965-7272 Carnegie Class: Not Classified
FAX Number: (954) 983-2707 Calendar System: Quarter
URL: www.careercollege.edu
Established: 1982 Annual Undergrad Tuition & Fees: $15,250
Enrollment: 895 Coed
Affiliation or Control: Proprietary IRS Status: Proprietary
Highest Offering: Baccalaureate
Program: Occupational; 2-Year Principally Bachelor's Creditable
Accreditation: ACICS

01 Executive Director ... Dr. Gilbert DELGADO
05 Director of Education ... Mr. Max ANER
26 Vice Pres Communication ... Mr. Peter LUNDBERG

Florida Christian College (I)

1011 Bill Beck Boulevard, Kissimmee FL 34744-5301
County: Osceola FICE Identification: 021567
Unit ID: 132879
Telephone: (407) 847-8966 Carnegie Class: Spec/Faith
FAX Number: (321) 206-2007 Calendar System: Semester
URL: www.fcc.edu
Established: 1976 Annual Undergrad Tuition & Fees: $15,380
Enrollment: 380 Coed
Affiliation or Control: Independent Non-Profit IRS Status: 501(c)3
Highest Offering: Baccalaureate
Program: 2-Year Principally Bachelor's Creditable; Teacher Preparatory; Professional; Religious Emphasis
Accreditation: #SC, #BI, MUS

01 President ... Mr. William BEHRMAN
03 Exec Vice President ... Dr. Terry ALLCORN
10 Vice President of Finance ... Mrs. Renee COOK
05 Vice President Academics ... Dr. Brian SMITH
43 General Counsel ... Dr. David PETERS
06 Registrar ... Mrs. Diane ADAMS
08 Librarian ... Mrs. Linda STARK
88 Director of Student Services ... Dr. Joe HARVEY
07 Director of Traditional Admissions ... Mrs. Kellie SPENCER
07 Director of LEAD Admissions ... Mrs. Tina TARRANCE
18 Executive Director of Operations ... Mr. Paul PEPPARD
35 Executive Director of Student Life ... Mrs. Sandra PEPPARD
37 Director of Financial Aid ... Mr. Bryce FOULKE
21 Executive Director of Finance ... Mrs. Ann BECKMAN
21 Director of Financial Reporting ... Mr. Jim JACOBS
15 Director of Human Resources ... Mrs. Eileen ADAMS
13 Director of Information Technology ... Mr. Glenn FEASTER
09 Director of Institutional Research ... Mr. Bruce DUSTERHOFT
106 Asst Director of Online Initiatives ... Mr. James BYRD
88 Director of Special Events ... Mrs. Glinda CAMERON
41 Athletic Director ... Mr. Bryce BOW
39 Residence Director ... Mr. Robert MEHLENBACHER
30 Director of Development ... Vacant
29 Alumni Director ... Mr. Alan TISON
26 Director of Communications ... Ms. Crystal HUTCHESON
04 Exec Assistant to the President ... Mrs. Nancy BRADDS
04 Assistant to the President ... Mr. Mark DURBIN

Florida Coastal School of Law (J)

8787 Baypine, Jacksonville FL 32256-8528
County: Duval FICE Identification: 033743
Unit ID: 434715
Telephone: (904) 680-7700 Carnegie Class: Spec/Law
FAX Number: (904) 680-7777 Calendar System: Semester
URL: www.fcsl.edu
Established: 1995 Annual Graduate Tuition & Fees: $39,465
Enrollment: 1,830 Coed
Affiliation or Control: Proprietary IRS Status: Proprietary
Highest Offering: First Professional Degree; No Undergraduates
Program: Professional
Accreditation: LAW

01 Dean & Professor of Law ... Mr. C. Peter GOPLERUD
05 Vice Dean ... Mrs. Cynthia STROUD
10 Vice Pres Finance & Administration ... Mr. Bruce WILSON
30 Dir of Institutional Advancement ... Mrs. Margaret DEES

20 Associate Dean Academic Affairs .... Mrs. Cynthia IRVIN
32 Assistant Dean of Students .... Mr. Thomas TAGGART
08 Professor/Director of Law Library .... Mrs. Alma (Nickie) SINGLETON
04 Assistant to the Dean .... Ms. Denise SACCO
36 Director of Career Services .... Mrs. Ellen SEFTON
06 Registrar .... Ms. Bridgette WAINES
37 Director Financial Aid .... Mr. Roger COLLINS
14 Director Information Technology .... Mr. Mark SABATTINI
26 Asst Dir Marketing/Communications .... Mr. Brooks TERRY
15 Director of Human Resources .... Mrs. Stacie SMITH
18 Facilities Manager .... Mr. Jay LEHMANN
20 Assistant Dean of Academic Affairs .... Ms. Danielle NOE

Florida College (A)

119 N Glen Arven Avenue,
Temple Terrace FL 33617-5578
County: Hillsborough FICE Identification: 001482
Unit ID: 133809
Telephone: (813) 988-5131 Carnegie Class: Bac/Assoc
FAX Number: (813) 899-6772 Calendar System: Semester
URL: www.floridacollege.edu
Established: 1944 Annual Undergrad Tuition & Fees: $14,000
Enrollment: 502 Coed
Affiliation or Control: Independent Non-Profit IRS Status: 501(c)3
Highest Offering: Baccalaureate
Program: Liberal Arts And General; Religious Emphasis
Accreditation: **SC**, MUS

01 President .... Dr. Harry E. PAYNE, JR.
05 Vice Pres of Acad & Student Affairs .... Dr. Douglas H. NORTHCUTT
20 Dean of Academics .... Dr. Daniel W. PETTY
32 Dean of Student Services .... Dr. Brian CRISPELL
10 Chief Business Officer .... Mr. Ronnie STACKPOLE
37 Director Student Financial Aid .... Mrs. Lisa MCCLISTER
84 Director of Enrollment Management .... Mr. Paul CASEBOLT
09 Director of Institutional Research .... Dr. M. Thaxter DICKEY
06 Registrar .... Ms. Beth A. GRANT
44 Director of Planned Giving .... Mr. Douglas R. NERLAND
08 Director of Library .... Mrs. Wanda DICKEY
90 Director of Academic Computing .... Mr. M. Ray HINDS
91 Director of Information Technology ...... Mr. William J. MCKINNEY
30 Director Institutional Development .... Mr. Douglas R. NERLAND
26 Director of Alumni/Public Relations .... Mr. Ralph R. WALKER, JR.
27 Director of Marketing .... Mr. Jared BARR
40 Manager of Bookstore .... Mr. Jeff NUNLEY

Florida College of Integrative Medicine (B)

7100 Lake Ellenor Drive, Orlando FL 32809-5721
County: Orange FICE Identification: 032383
Unit ID: 434441
Telephone: (407) 888-8689 Carnegie Class: Spec/Health
FAX Number: (407) 888-8211 Calendar System: Semester
URL: www.fcim.edu
Established: 1990 Annual Undergrad Tuition & Fees: $15,125
Enrollment: 135 Coed
Affiliation or Control: Proprietary IRS Status: Proprietary
Highest Offering: Master's; No Lower Division
Program: Professional
Accreditation: **ACUP**

01 President .... Mr. Larry LAN
03 Vice President .... Ms. Jenjen HAN
11 Chief Administrative Officer .... Mr. Robert P. LYNCH
05 Academic Dean .... Dr. Lin CHAI

Florida College of Natural Health (C)

616 67th Street Circle East, Bradenton FL 34208-6087
County: Sarasota Identification: 666830
Unit ID: 438294
Telephone: (941) 744-1244 Carnegie Class: Assoc/PrivFP
FAX Number: (941) 744-1242 Calendar System: Other
URL: www.fcnh.com
Established: 1998 Annual Undergrad Tuition & Fees: N/A
Enrollment: 205 Coed
Affiliation or Control: Proprietary IRS Status: Proprietary
Highest Offering: Associate Degree
Program: Occupational
Accreditation: **ACCSC**, COMTA

01 Director .... Mrs. Ronnie FULTON

† Branch campus of Florida College of Natural Health, Pompano Beach, FL.

Florida College of Natural Health (D)

2600 Lake Lucien Drive, Suite 240,
Maitland FL 32751-7253
County: Seminole Identification: 666513
Unit ID: 438285
Telephone: (407) 261-0319 Carnegie Class: Assoc/PrivFP
FAX Number: (407) 261-0342 Calendar System: Other
URL: www.fcnh.com
Established: 1995 Annual Undergrad Tuition & Fees: $12,072
Enrollment: 646 Coed
Affiliation or Control: Proprietary IRS Status: Proprietary
Highest Offering: Associate Degree
Program: Occupational
Accreditation: **ACCSC**, COMTA

01 Director .... Ms. Stephanie DUCKSWORTH

† Branch campus of Florida College of Natural Health, Pompano Beach, FL.

Florida College of Natural Health (E)

7925 NW 12th Street, #201, Miami FL 33126-1821
County: Miami-Dade Identification: 666514
Unit ID: 420103
Telephone: (305) 597-9599 Carnegie Class: Assoc/PrivFP
FAX Number: (305) 597-9110 Calendar System: Other
URL: www.fcnh.com
Established: 1993 Annual Undergrad Tuition & Fees: N/A
Enrollment: 228 Coed
Affiliation or Control: Proprietary IRS Status: Proprietary
Highest Offering: Associate Degree
Program: Occupational
Accreditation: **ACCSC**, COMTA

01 Campus Director .... Ms. Debra STARR-COHEN

† Branch campus of Florida College of Natural Health, Pompano Beach, FL.

Florida College of Natural Health (F)

2001 W Sample Road, #100,
Pompano Beach FL 33064-1342
County: Broward FICE Identification: 030086
Unit ID: 387925
Telephone: (954) 975-6400 Carnegie Class: Assoc/PrivFP
FAX Number: (954) 975-9633 Calendar System: Other
URL: www.fcnh.com
Established: 1986 Annual Undergrad Tuition & Fees: $12,072
Enrollment: 380 Coed
Affiliation or Control: Proprietary IRS Status: Proprietary
Highest Offering: Associate Degree
Program: Occupational
Accreditation: **ACCSC**, COMTA

01 President .... Mr. Stephen LAZARUS
10 Controller .... Ms. Barbara KRANE
03 Vice President of Compliance .... Ms. Melissa WADE
05 Vice President of Education .... Ms. Dawnette CABALUNA

Florida Gateway College (G)

149 SE College Place, Lake City FL 32025-2007
County: Columbia FICE Identification: 001501
Unit ID: 135160
Telephone: (386) 752-1822 Carnegie Class: Assoc/Pub-R-M
FAX Number: (386) 755-1521 Calendar System: Semester
URL: www.fgc.edu
Established: 1947 Annual Undergrad Tuition & Fees (In-State): $3,070
Enrollment: 3,228 Coed
Affiliation or Control: State IRS Status: 501(c)3
Highest Offering: Baccalaureate
Program: Occupational; 2-Year Principally Bachelor's Creditable; Liberal Arts And General; Teacher Preparatory; Nursing Emphasis
Accreditation: **SC**, ADNUR, EMT, #PTAA

01 President .... Dr. Charles W. HALL
10 Vice President Business Services .... Ms. Marilyn HAMM
04 Assistant to the President .... Ms. Karyn CONGRESSI
05 Vice President for Academic Pgms .... Dr. Brian DOPSON
75 Vice President Occupational Pgms .... Ms. Tracy HICKMAN
32 Vice President for Student Services .... Dr. Linda CROLEY
14 Exec Dir Info Technology/CIO .... Mr. Mike DAVIS
47 Exec Dir of Industrial & Agricult .... Mr. John PIERSOL
08 Exec Dir Library & Community Svcs .... Mr. Jim MORRIS
53 Exec Dir Teacher Prep Academy .... Ms. Pamela CARSWELL
102 Executive Director Foundation .... Mr. Mike LEE
26 Exec Dir Media & Community Info .... Mr. Mike MCKEE
37 Director Financial Aid .... Mrs. Debberin TUNSIL
84 Director Enrollment Management .... Ms. Sandra JOHNSTON
15 Director Human Resources .... Ms. Sharon BEST
06 Registrar .... Ms. Gayle HUNTER
21 Director Business Services .... Mr. Van SMITHEY
66 Director Nursing Programs .... Ms. Mattie JONES
25 Director of Grants .... Dr. Laurel SEMMES
09 Director of Research/Institutional .... Ms. Patty ANDERSON
18 Chief Facilities/Physical Plant .... Mr. George SCOTT
96 Director of Purchasing .... Mr. Bill BROWN
36 Director Advising/Student Dev .... Dr. Margaret MCLAUGHLIN
88 Director for Water Resources .... Mr. Tim ATKINSON
88 Director for Criminal Justice .... Mr. John JEWETT
88 Director Title III/Develop Educ .... Ms. Carrie RODESILER

Florida Institute of Technology (H)

150 W University Boulevard, Melbourne FL 32901-6975
County: Brevard FICE Identification: 001469
Unit ID: 133881
Telephone: (321) 674-8000 Carnegie Class: DRU
FAX Number: (321) 984-8461 Calendar System: Semester
URL: www.fit.edu
Established: 1958 Annual Undergrad Tuition & Fees: $36,020
Enrollment: 8,980 Coed
Affiliation or Control: Independent Non-Profit IRS Status: 501(c)3
Highest Offering: Doctorate
Program: Liberal Arts And General; Teacher Preparatory; Professional; Technical Emphasis
Accreditation: **SC**, AAB, CLPSY, CS, ENG

01 President .... Dr. Anthony J. CATANESE
04 Exec Asst to Pres & Ombudsman .... Mrs. Suzee S. LOUCHE
05 Executive Vice Pres & COO .... Dr. T. Dwayne MCCAY
10 Sr Vice Pres Financial Affairs/CFO .... Dr. Robert E. NIEBUHR
88 Sr Vice Pres External Relations .... Capt. Winston SCOTT
30 Sr Vice Pres/Chief Development Ofcr .... Ms. Susan ST. ONGE
20 Deputy COO .... Dr. Donn MILLER-KERMANI
88 Dean College of Aeronautics .... Dr. Kenneth STACKPOOLE
50 Dean College of Business .... Dr. S. Ann BECKER
54 Dean College of Engineering .... Dr. Frederic HAM
83 Dean Col of Psychology/Liberal Arts .... Dr. Mary Beth KENKEL
81 Dean College of Science .... Dr. Hamid RASSOUL
08 Dean of Libraries .... Dr. Celine LANG
18 Vice Pres Facilities Ops/Architect .... Mr. Gregory TSARK
13 Vice Pres IT/CIO .... Mr. Eric KLEDZIK
27 Vice Pres Marketing & Communication .... Mr. Wesley SUMNER
46 Vice President Research .... Mr. Frank KINNEY
32 Vice President Student Affairs .... Dr. Randall L. ALFORD
11 Vice Pres Support Services .... Dr. Joni OGLESBY
21 Assoc Vice Pres/Fin Plng & Control .... Ms. Claire WURMFELD
84 Assoc Vice Pres Enrollment Mgmt .... Mr. Gary HAMME
108 Assoc Vice Pres Inst Compliance .... Dr. Monica BALOGA
35 Assoc VP Student Affs/Dean of Stdnt .... Mr. Rodney BOWERS
106 Asst Vice Pres/Dir Online Learning .... Mr. Brian EHRLICH
29 Asst VP Alum Rel/Exec Dir Alum Assn .... Mr. Bino CAMPANINI
06 Registrar .... Ms. Charlotte YOUNG
88 Director Academic Support Services .... Mr. Rodd NEWCOMBE
41 Director Athletics .... Mr. William K. JURGENS
19 Director Campus Security .... Mr. Kevin GRAHAM
36 Director Career Services .... Ms. Dona E. GAYNOR
38 Dir Counseling/Psychological Svcs .... Dr. Robyn TAPLEY
88 Director Creative Services .... Ms. Judi E. TINTERA
88 Dir Environ & Regulatory Compliance .... Mr. Greg PEEBLES
18 Director Facilities Operations .... Mr. John M. MILBOURNE
37 Director Financial Aid .... Mr. Jay LALLY
07 Director Grad Adm Online Learning .... Ms. Carolyn P. FARRIOR
58 Director Graduate Programs .... Ms. Rosemary LAYNE
85 Director Intl Students/Scholar Svcs .... Ms. Judith BROOKE
09 Director Institutional Research .... Ms. Leslie L. SAVOIE
07 Director Undergraduate Admission .... Mr. Michael PERRY
88 Director University Museums .... Ms. Carla FUNK
07 Assoc Director Graduate Admissions .... Ms. Cheryl-Ann BROWN

Florida Keys Community College (I)

5901 College Road, Key West FL 33040-4397
County: Monroe FICE Identification: 001485
Unit ID: 133960
Telephone: (305) 296-9081 Carnegie Class: Assoc/Pub-R-S
FAX Number: (305) 292-5155 Calendar System: Trimester
URL: www.fkcc.edu
Established: 1963 Annual Undergrad Tuition & Fees (In-District): $3,776
Enrollment: 1,374 Coed
Affiliation or Control: State/Local IRS Status: 501(c)3
Highest Offering: Associate Degree
Program: Occupational; 2-Year Principally Bachelor's Creditable; Fine Arts Emphasis
Accreditation: **SC**

01 President .... Dr. Jonathan GUEUERRA
05 Provost .... Mrs. Brittany SYNDER
10 Vice Pres Financial & Admin Svcs .... Mrs. Jean MAUK
32 Director Student Services .... Ms. Michelle CHERRY
51 Dir Lifelong Learning and Cont Educ .... Mrs. Cathy TORRES
04 Director Pres Office .... Mrs. Debbie LEONARD
26 Director College and Public Rels .. Mrs. Amber ERNST-LEONARD
06 Registrar .... Mrs. Cheryl MALSHEIMER
08 Director Learning Resources .... Mrs. Juana CAREAGA
37 Dir Student Fin Aid/Enrollment Svcs .... Ms. Susan URBAN
35 Dean Student Affairs .... Mrs. Erika MACWILLIAMS
18 Dir Purchasing and Plant Opers .... Mr. Douglas PRYOR
13 Director of IT .... Mr. Bryan GILCHRIST
15 Director Human Resources .... Mr. Charles MCGINNIS
25 Director Sponsored Programs .... Ms. Joanne PRESTON
102 Dir Of FKCC Foundation .... Mrs. Patti CAREY
21 Controller .... Ms. LeeAnne HOLLAND
88 Centers Director .... Mr. Christopher FLETCHER
09 Dir Institutional Effectiveness .... Ms. Julie BAILEY
84 Director Enrollment Management .... Ms. Gavin MCKIERNAN
76 Int Dean of Allied Health & Nursing .... Ms. Mary TURNER
88 Dean of Marine Sciences and Tech .... Dr. Patrick RICE
49 Interim Dean Arts & Sciences .... Mr. Michael MCPHERSON

Florida Medical Training Institute-Coral Springs (J)

7451 Wiles Road, Suite 105, Coral Springs FL 33067
County: Broward Identification: 666612
Telephone: (954) 752-1414 Carnegie Class: Not Classified
FAX Number: (954) 752-2721 Calendar System: Other
URL: www.fmti.edu
Established: 1999 Annual Undergrad Tuition & Fees: N/A
Enrollment: N/A Coed
Affiliation or Control: Proprietary IRS Status: Proprietary
Highest Offering: Associate Degree
Program: Occupational

Accreditation: ABHES

01 Campus Director ..... Mr. William DRAGONETTI

Florida Memorial University (A)

15800 NW 42nd Avenue, Miami Gardens FL 33054-6199
County: Miami-Dade FICE Identification: 001486
Unit ID: 133979
Telephone: (305) 626-3600 Carnegie Class: Master's S
FAX Number: (305) 626-3769 Calendar System: Semester
URL: www.fmuniv.edu
Established: 1879 Annual Undergrad Tuition & Fees: $14,445
Enrollment: 1,776 Coed
Affiliation or Control: Independent Non-Profit IRS Status: 501(c)3
Highest Offering: Master's
Program: Liberal Arts And General; Teacher Preparatory
Accreditation: SC, ACBSP, CS, MUS, SW

01 President ..... Dr. Henry LEWIS, III
05 Provost and VP Academic Affairs ..... Dr. Makola ABDULLAH
20 Associate Provost ..... Dr. Denise CALLWOOD-BRATHWAITE
04 Assistant to President ..... Ms. Rachel TURNER
49 Dean of Arts and Sciences ..... Dr. William HOPPER
88 Associate VP for Auxiliary Services ..... Mr. Archie BOUIE
100 Chief of Staff ..... Dr. Mary O'BANNER
10 Vice Pres Business/Fiscal Affairs ..... Mr. Tony VALENTINE
11 Vice President for Administration ..... Dr. Harold CLARKE, JR.
32 Vice Pres for Student Affairs ..... Ms. Danneal JONES
30 Vice Pres Institutional Advancement ..... Dr. Adriene WRIGHT
45 Assoc VP Intitutional Effectiveness ..... Dr. Sandra THOMPSON
88 Director of Aviation ..... Dr. Arnold TOLBERT
50 Dean Business Administration ..... Dr. Abbass ENTESSARI
53 Dean Division Education ..... Dr. Mildred BERRY
81 Chair Natural Science ..... Dr. Rose Mary STIFFIN
83 Chair Social Sciences ..... Dr. Priye TORULAGHA
88 Chair Visual and Performing Arts ..... Dr. Dawn BATSON-BOREL
77 Chair Comp Science/Math & Tech ..... Dr. Ben WONGSAROJ
79 Chair Division Humanities ..... Dr. William JONG-EBOT
89 Director Freshman Studies Dept ..... Dr. Jeffrey SWAIN
08 Director University Library ..... Mrs. Gloria OSWALD
84 Director of Enrollment Mgmt ..... Mr. Roscoe WARREN
06 Registrar ..... Mrs. Lelia A. EFFORD
09 Director of Institutional Research ..... Dr. Carlos CANAS
42 Director of Church Relations ..... Mrs. Patricia CARTER
15 Director Human Resources Management ..... Mrs. Valerie A. WILLIAMS
88 Dir Property and Risk Management ..... Mr. Alphonso BURNSIDE
41 Director of Athletics ..... Mr. Robert SMITH
36 Director Career Development ..... Ms. Athena JACKSON
37 Interim Director Financial Aid ..... Mr. Kozman STROMAN
39 Director Residential Life ..... Mrs. Jacklan ALEXANDER
07 Director of Admissions ..... Mrs. Peggy Murray MARTIN
19 Chief of Security ..... Chief Terrance WILSON
18 Dir Facility Mgmt/Plant Operations ..... Mr. David JACCARINO
42 Campus Minister ..... Rev. Wendell PARIS
29 Director Alumni Affairs ..... Mrs. Sheila POWELL-COHEN
38 Lead Counselor ..... Mr. Michael MOSS
35 Director Student Affairs ..... Mr. C. Vernon MARTIN, JR.
85 Actg International Student Advisor ..... Mr. Trevor LEWIS
13 Actg Chief Information Officer ..... Mr. Orlando HUERTAS
55 Dir of Evening and Weekend Program ..... Mrs. Gladys GONZALEZ
88 Director of Assessment ..... Dr. Richard YAKLICH

Florida National University Hialeah Campus (B)

4425 W. Jose Regueiro (20th Avenue),
Hialeah FL 33012-4108
County: Dade FICE Identification: 025476
Unit ID: 408844
Telephone: (305) 821-3333 Carnegie Class: Assoc/PrivFP4
FAX Number: (305) 362-0595 Calendar System: Semester
URL: www.fnc.edu
Established: 1982 Annual Undergrad Tuition & Fees: $13,170
Enrollment: 1,704 Coed
Affiliation or Control: Proprietary IRS Status: Proprietary
Highest Offering: Master's
Program: 2-Year Principally Bachelor's Creditable
Accreditation: SC

01 President/CEO ..... Mrs. Maria REGUEIRO
09 VP of Assessment & Research/FA Dir ..... Mr. Omar SANCHEZ
11 Vice President of Operations ..... Mr. Frank ANDREU
05 Vice President of Academic Affairs ..... Mrs. Caridad SANCHEZ
10 Controller ..... Mrs. Lourdes NIEVES
88 Accreditation Liaison ..... Mrs. Barbara RODRIGUEZ
07 Director of Admissions ..... Mr. Joseph FORTON
06 College Registrar ..... Mr. Jose L. VALDES
08 Library Director ..... Mr. Patrick BYRNES
32 Director of Student Services ..... Mrs. Makeda MEEKS
105 Distance Learning Director ..... Mrs. Sandra LOMENA
12 Campus Dean ..... Mr. Jorge ALFONSO
88 Academic Advisor ..... Mr. Bernardo NAVARRO
88 Academic Advisor ..... Mrs. Jelenny HERNANDEZ
36 Job Placement Officer ..... Mr. Candido AVEILLE
50 Business & Economics Division Head ..... Dr. James BULLEN
76 Allied Health Division Head ..... Dr. Loreto ALMONTE
66 RN Program Director ..... Mrs. Oneida SEGURA
66 PN Nursing Division Director ..... Mrs. Maida BURGOS
79 Humanities and Fine Arts Division ..... Mrs. Barbara RODRIGUEZ
88 ESL Division Head ..... Mr. Oscar PEREZ
15 Human Resources Generalist ..... Mr. Tony SOLANA
88 Military Recruiter ..... Mrs. Vilma ROSARIO

Florida National University South Campus (C)

11865 SW 26th Street Unit H-3, Miami FL 33175
Identification: 666691
Unit ID: 40884401
Telephone: (305) 226-9999 Carnegie Class: Not Classified
FAX Number: (305) 226-4439 Calendar System: Semester
URL: www.fnc.edu
Established: 2002 Annual Undergrad Tuition & Fees: $13,170
Enrollment: 891 Coed
Affiliation or Control: Proprietary IRS Status: Proprietary
Highest Offering: Baccalaureate
Program: 2-Year Principally Bachelor's Creditable
Accreditation: &SC

01 President/CEO ..... Mrs. Maria C. REGUEIRO
09 VP of Assessment & Research/FA ..... Mr. Omar SANCHEZ
11 Vice President of Operations ..... Mr. Frank ANDREU
05 Vice President of Academic Affairs ..... Mrs. Caridad SANCHEZ
10 Controller ..... Mrs. Lourdes NIEVES
88 Accreditation Liaison ..... Mrs. Barbara RODRIGUEZ
07 Director of Admissions ..... Mr. Joseph FORTON
06 College Registrar ..... Mr. Jose L. VALDES
08 Library Director ..... Mr. Patrick BYRNES
32 Director of Student Services ..... Mrs. Makeda MEEKS
12 Campus Dean ..... Mr. Guillermo ARAYA
36 Job Placement Officer ..... Mrs. Heydee CUERVO
88 Academic Advisor ..... Mrs. Melissa LOPEZ
50 Business & Economics Division Head ..... Dr. James BULLEN
76 Allied Health Division Head ..... Dr. Loreto ALMONTE
66 PN Nursing Division Director ..... Mrs. Maida BURGOS
66 RN Program Director ..... Mrs. Oneida SEGURA
79 Humanities and Fine Arts Division ..... Mrs. Barbara RODRIGUEZ
15 Human Resources Generalist ..... Mr. Tony SOLANA
88 ESL Division Head ..... Mr. Oscar PEREZ

† Regional accreditation is carried under the parent institution Florida National College, Hialeah, FL.

Florida National University Training Center (D)

4206 West 12th Avenue, Hialeah FL 33012
Identification: 666690
Unit ID: 40884402
Telephone: (305) 231-3326 Carnegie Class: Not Classified
FAX Number: (305) 819-9616 Calendar System: Semester
URL: www.fnc.edu
Established: 2004 Annual Undergrad Tuition & Fees: $13,170
Enrollment: 161 Coed
Affiliation or Control: Proprietary IRS Status: Proprietary
Highest Offering: Baccalaureate
Program: 2-Year Principally Bachelor's Creditable
Accreditation: &SC

01 President/CEO ..... Mrs. Maria C. REGUEIRO
09 VP of Assessment & Research/FA ..... Mr. Omar SANCHEZ
11 Vice President of Operations ..... Mr. Frank ANDREU
05 Vice President of Academic Affairs ..... Mrs. Caridad SANCHEZ
10 Controller ..... Mrs. Lourdes NIEVES
88 Accreditation Liaison ..... Mrs. Barbara RODRIGUEZ
07 Director of Admissions ..... Mr. Joseph FORTON
06 College Registrar ..... Mr. Jose L. VALDES
08 Library Director ..... Mr. Patrick BYRNES
32 Director of Student Services ..... Mrs. Makeda MEEKS
12 Interim Campus Dean ..... Mr. Jose L. VALDEZ
36 Job Placement Officer ..... Mrs. Genobeba DELGADO
88 Academic Advisor ..... Mr. Bernardo GARCIA
76 Allied Health Division Head ..... Dr. Loreto ALMONTE
88 ESL Division Head ..... Mr. Ocar PEREZ

† Regional accreditation is carried under the parent institution Florida National College, Hialeah, FL.

Florida Southern College (E)

111 Lake Hollingsworth Drive, Lakeland FL 33801-5698
County: Polk FICE Identification: 001488
Unit ID: 134079
Telephone: (863) 680-4111 Carnegie Class: Bac/Diverse
FAX Number: (863) 680-4112 Calendar System: Semester
URL: www.flsouthern.edu
Established: 1885 Annual Undergrad Tuition & Fees: $27,200
Enrollment: 2,442 Coed
Affiliation or Control: United Methodist IRS Status: 501(c)3
Highest Offering: Master's
Program: Liberal Arts And General
Accreditation: SC, NURSE

01 President ..... Dr. Anne B. KERR
05 Provost ..... Dr. Kyle FEDLER
10 Vice President Finance & Admin ..... Mr. Terry DENNIS
26 Vice President External Relations ..... Dr. Robert H. TATE
32 Dean of Student Development ..... Mr. Bill C. LANGSTON, II
84 Vice Pres/Dean Enrollment Mgmt ..... Mr. John GRUNDIG
30 Vice President Advancement ..... Dr. Matthew R. THOMPSON
26 Vice President of Marketing & Comm ..... Mr. David A. WEAGLE
08 Director of the Library ..... Mr. Randall M. MACDONALD
07 Director of Admissions ..... Ms. Erin ERVIN
06 Registrar ..... Ms. Sally L. THISSEN
09 Dir Inst Research/Effectiveness ..... Dr. Kenneth M. REAVES
36 Director of Career Development ..... Ms. Xuchitl COSO
37 Director of Student Financial Aid ..... Mr. William L. HEALY
29 Coordinator of Alumni Services ..... Ms. Meredith PROKUSKI
41 Athletic Director ..... Mr. Peter E. MEYER
42 Chaplain Director Campus Ministry ..... Rev. Timothy S. WRIGHT
19 Director Security/Safety ..... Mr. William CAREW
15 Director of Human Resources ..... Ms. Katherine PAWLAK
20 Assoc Provost Experiential Educ ..... Dr. Mary L. CROWE
31 Director of Community Living ..... Ms. Elizabeth CHING-BUSH
38 Director Student Counseling ..... Dr. Carol BALLARD

Florida State College at Jacksonville (F)

501 W State Street, Jacksonville FL 32202-4097
County: Duval FICE Identification: 001484
Unit ID: 133702
Telephone: (904) 646-2300 Carnegie Class: Assoc/Pub4
FAX Number: N/A Calendar System: Semester
URL: www.fscj.edu
Established: 1963 Annual Undergrad Tuition & Fees (In-District): $3,086
Enrollment: 39,376 Coed
Affiliation or Control: Local IRS Status: Exempt
Highest Offering: Baccalaureate
Program: Occupational; 2-Year Principally Bachelor's Creditable
Accreditation: SC, ACBSP, ACFEI, ADNUR, DA, DH, DIETT, EMT, FUSER, HT, MLTAD, NUR, OTA, PTAA, SURGT

01 College President ..... Dr. Steven R. WALLACE
05 Exec Vice President Instruction ..... Dr. Donald W. GREEN, JR.
12 Campus President Downtown ..... Dr. Christal M. ALBRECHT
12 Campus President Urban Resource Ctr ..... Ms. Jana KOOI
12 Campus President-Kent ..... Dr. Margarita A. CABRAL-MALY
12 Campus President-North ..... Dr. Barbara A. DARBY
12 Campus President-South ..... Dr. Denis G. WRIGHT
13 Vice President of Technology ..... Dr. Robert J. RENNIE
11 Vice Pres of Administrative Svcs ..... Mr. Steven P. BOWERS
15 Vice President of Human Resources ..... Dr. Christine C. ARAB
30 VP Student Devel/Cmty Education ..... Dr. Tracy A. PIERCE
43 Gen Counsel/VP Strategic Intiative ..... Ms. Jeanne M. MILLER
20 Assoc VP of Educational Tech ..... Mr. Dennis M. REIMAN
103 Assoc VP Workforce Devel/Adult Ed ..... Mr. James D. SIMPSON, III
18 Assoc VP Facilities Mgmt and Const ..... Mr. Charles M. STRATMANN
10 Assoc Vice Pres of Financial Svcs ..... Ms. Peggy L. BOORD
96 Assoc VP of Purchasing/Bus Svcs ..... Mr. Laurence I. SNELL
15 Employee Svcs Dir/Col Equity Ofcr ..... Ms. Elaine TISDALE
31 Exec Director of Cultural Programs ..... Dr. Milton A. RUSSOS
88 Exec Dir Military Educ Institute ..... Adm. James E. STEVENSON
102 Exec Director of the Foundation ..... Mr. Robert L. STAMP
88 Dir Svcs for Stdnts w/Disabilities ..... Ms. Denise J. GIARRUSSO
41 Dir Athletics and Physical Educ ..... Mr. George E. SANDERS
84 Dist Dir Enroll Svcs/Coll Registrar ..... Mr. Peter J. BIEGEL
37 Director Student Financial Aid ..... Ms. Michele BOWLES
45 Director of Resource Development ..... Dr. Phyllis R. RENNIGER
88 Director Aviation Ctr of Excellence ..... Mr. Gene V. MILOWICKI
06 Registrar ..... Ms. Lori G. COLLINS
07 Director of Admissions ..... Ms. Roz DEXTER-HARRIS
09 Director of Institutional Research ..... Mr. Greg MICHALSKI

Florida Technical College (G)

1199 S Woodland Boulevard, Deland FL 32720-7415
County: Volusia Identification: 666419
Unit ID: 432393
Telephone: (386) 734-3303 Carnegie Class: Not Classified
FAX Number: (386) 734-5150 Calendar System: Quarter
URL: www.ftccollege.edu
Established: 1997 Annual Undergrad Tuition & Fees: $26,500
Enrollment: 346 Coed
Affiliation or Control: Proprietary IRS Status: Proprietary
Highest Offering: Baccalaureate
Program: 2-Year Principally Bachelor's Creditable
Accreditation: ACICS

01 Executive Director ..... Mr. Alex RODRIGUEZ
06 Registrar ..... Ms. Sabiana MONTANEZ
07 Director of Admissions ..... Mr. Christopher MERCADO

Florida Technical College (H)

4715 South Florida Avenue, Suite 4,
Lakeland FL 33813-2101
County: Polk FICE Identification: 025981
Unit ID: 432409
Telephone: (866) 967-8822 Carnegie Class: Not Classified
FAX Number: (866) 619-7600 Calendar System: Quarter
URL: www.ftccollege.edu
Established: 1990 Annual Undergrad Tuition & Fees: $16,339
Enrollment: 300 Coed
Affiliation or Control: Proprietary IRS Status: Proprietary
Highest Offering: Baccalaureate
Program: Occupational
Accreditation: ACICS

01 Executive Director ..... Lisa Marie VELARDI

Florida Technical College (A)

12900 Challenger Parkway, Orlando FL 32826
County: Orange FICE Identification: 022187
Unit ID: 134112
Telephone: (407) 447-7300 Carnegie Class: Assoc/PrivFP
FAX Number: (407) 447-7301 Calendar System: Quarter
URL: www.ftccollege.edu
Established: 1982 Annual Undergrad Tuition & Fees: $22,450
Enrollment: 3,500 Coed
Affiliation or Control: Proprietary IRS Status: Proprietary
Highest Offering: Baccalaureate
Program: Occupational; 2-Year Principally Bachelor's Creditable; Liberal Arts And General; Technical Emphasis
Accreditation: ACICS

00 President/CEO .... Mr. David RUGGIERI
01 Executive Director .... Mr. Gabriel GARCES
05 Director of Education .... Dr. David PENN
07 Director of Admissions .... Ms. Audrey HARDEN
37 Director of Financial Aid .... Ms. Deborah DIAZ

Fortis College (B)

7757 West Flagler Street, Ste 230, Miami FL 33144
County: Miami-Dade FICE Identification: 030542
Telephone: (305) 717-7000 Carnegie Class: Not Classified
FAX Number: (786) 388-5464 Calendar System: Quarter
URL: www.fortis.edu
Established: 1978 Annual Undergrad Tuition & Fees: $12,100
Enrollment: 705 Coed
Affiliation or Control: Proprietary IRS Status: Proprietary
Highest Offering: Associate Degree
Program: Occupational
Accreditation: COE

01 President .... Mr. Sylvio FREEMAN

Fortis College (C)

560 Wells Road, Orange Park FL 32073-2999
County: Clay FICE Identification: 034343
Unit ID: 439792
Telephone: (904) 269-7086 Carnegie Class: Assoc/PrivFP
FAX Number: (904) 269-6664 Calendar System: Semester
URL: www.fortis.edu
Established: 1985 Annual Undergrad Tuition & Fees: $14,975
Enrollment: 521 Coed
Affiliation or Control: Proprietary IRS Status: Proprietary
Highest Offering: Associate Degree
Program: Occupational; 2-Year Principally Bachelor's Creditable
Accreditation: ACICS, SURGT

01 Campus President .... Mr. Wyman DICKEY

Fortis College (D)

3910 US Highway 301N, Suite 200,
Tampa FL 33619-1283
County: Hillsborough FICE Identification: 023057
Unit ID: 136075
Telephone: (813) 620-1446 Carnegie Class: Assoc/PrivFP
FAX Number: (813) 620-1641 Calendar System: Quarter
URL: www.fortis.edu
Established: 1978 Annual Undergrad Tuition & Fees: $19,300
Enrollment: 525 Coed
Affiliation or Control: Proprietary IRS Status: Proprietary
Highest Offering: Associate Degree
Program: 2-Year Principally Bachelor's Creditable; Nursing Emphasis
Accreditation: ACICS

01 Director .... Mr. Mark GUTMANN
05 Director of Education .... Ms. Tonja HELTON
66 Director of Nursing .... Dr. Joanna HILL

Fortis College (E)

1573 W Fairbanks Avenue, Suite 100,
Winter Park FL 32789-4679
County: Orange FICE Identification: 022455
Unit ID: 132806
Telephone: (407) 843-3984 Carnegie Class: Assoc/PrivFP
FAX Number: (407) 843-9828 Calendar System: Quarter
URL: www.fortiscollege.edu
Established: 1985 Annual Undergrad Tuition & Fees: $18,350
Enrollment: 482 Coed
Affiliation or Control: Proprietary IRS Status: Proprietary
Highest Offering: Associate Degree
Program: Occupational
Accreditation: ACCSC, MAC

01 School Director .... Mr. Ray NUNZIATIA
06 Registrar/Business Manager .... Ms. Lisa BEARD
36 Career Services Director .... Ms. Andro MEDA-POLLACK
37 Financial Aid Director .... Ms. Keisha WHITAKER
07 Admissions Director .... Mr. Antivan HARRINGTON

Full Sail University (F)

3300 University Boulevard, Winter Park FL 32792
County: Orange FICE Identification: 023621
Unit ID: 134237
Telephone: (407) 679-0100 Carnegie Class: Master's L
FAX Number: (407) 679-9685 Calendar System: Other
URL: www.fullsail.edu
Established: 1979 Annual Undergrad Tuition & Fees: $36,905
Enrollment: 20,160 Coed
Affiliation or Control: Proprietary IRS Status: Proprietary
Highest Offering: Master's
Program: Occupational; 2-Year Principally Bachelor's Creditable
Accreditation: ACCSC

01 President .... Mr. Garry JONES
07 Vice President of Admissions .... Mr. Matt PENGRA

Golf Academy of America (G)

510 South Hunt Club Blvd., Apopka FL 32703
County: Seminole Identification: 666186
Unit ID: 430157
Telephone: (800) 342-7342 Carnegie Class: Assoc/PrivFP
FAX Number: (407) 699-6653 Calendar System: Semester
URL: www.golfacademy.edu
Established: 1986 Annual Undergrad Tuition & Fees: $33,390
Enrollment: 228 Coed
Affiliation or Control: Proprietary IRS Status: Proprietary
Highest Offering: Associate Degree
Program: Occupational; Business Emphasis
Accreditation: ACICS

01 President .... Mr. Michael LARGENT
12 Campus Director .... Mr. Bradley G. TURNER

† Branch campus of Virginia College, Birmingham, AL.

Gulf Coast State College (H)

5230 W Highway 98, Panama City FL 32401-1058
County: Bay FICE Identification: 001490
Unit ID: 134343
Telephone: (850) 769-1551 Carnegie Class: Assoc/Pub-R-L
FAX Number: (850) 913-3319 Calendar System: Semester
URL: www.gulfcoast.edu
Established: 1957 Annual Undergrad Tuition & Fees (In-State): $2,370
Enrollment: 6,436 Coed
Affiliation or Control: State Related IRS Status: 501(c)3
Highest Offering: Baccalaureate
Program: Occupational; 2-Year Principally Bachelor's Creditable; Teacher Preparatory
Accreditation: SC, ACFEI, ADNUR, DA, DH, EMT, PTAA, RAD, SURGA, SURGT

01 President .... Dr. Jim KERLEY
11 Vice Pres Administration & Finance .... Mr. John D. MERCER
05 VP Academic Affairs & Learn Support .... Dr. George BISHOP
75 Chief Economic Dev Officer .... Dr. Jeffry J. STEVENSON
32 VP Student Affairs .... Dr. Melissa LAVENDER
20 Assoc VP Academic Affairs .... Dr. Cheryl L. FLAX-HYMAN
27 Chief Information Officer .... Mr. Herman G. DANIELS
08 Director of Library .... Ms. Lori DRISCOLL
07 Director of Enrollment Services .... Ms. Sharon O. TODD
15 Exec Director of Human Resources .... Ms. Roberta MACKEY
18 Superintendent Grounds & Bldg Svcs .... Mr. Dennis STORCK
28 Assoc Dir Retention/Stdnt Diversity .... Dr. Carrie B. BAKER
26 Exec Director Media & Community Rel .... Mr. Christopher P. THOMES
96 Coordinator of Purchasing .... Ms. Tonia E. LAWSON
37 Director of Financial Aid .... Mr. Christopher J. WESTLAKE
09 Coordinator Institutional Research .... Ms. Dee NIELSEN
30 Chief Development Officer .... Vacant

Health Career Institute (I)

1764 N. Congress Avenue, West Palm Beach FL 33409
County: Palm Beach Identification: 667104
Telephone: (561) 586-0121 Carnegie Class: Not Classified
FAX Number: (561) 471-4010 Calendar System: Semester
URL: www.hci.edu
Established: N/A Annual Undergrad Tuition & Fees: N/A
Enrollment: N/A Coed
Affiliation or Control: Independent Non-Profit IRS Status: 501(c)3
Highest Offering: Associate Degree
Program: Occupational
Accreditation: ACCSC

01 President .... Tina PALERMO
03 Vice President .... Marty PALERMO
10 Financial Director .... Cathy WALDRON

Heritage Institute-Fort Myers (J)

6630 Orion Drive, Suite 200, Fort Meyers FL 33912-7130
County: Lee FICE Identification: 025971
Unit ID: 135124
Telephone: (239) 936-5822 Carnegie Class: Assoc/PrivFP
FAX Number: (239) 225-9117 Calendar System: Other
URL: www.heritage-education.com
Established: 2001 Annual Undergrad Tuition & Fees: $24,950
Enrollment: 804 Coed
Affiliation or Control: Proprietary IRS Status: Proprietary
Highest Offering: Associate Degree
Program: Occupational
Accreditation: ABHES

01 Director .... Ms. Eva HUTSON

Heritage Institute-Jacksonville (K)

4130 Salisbury Road, Suite 1100, Jacksonville FL 32216
County: Duval FICE Identification: 030358
Unit ID: 372772
Telephone: (904) 332-0910 Carnegie Class: Assoc/PrivFP
FAX Number: (904) 332-0920 Calendar System: Other
URL: www.heritage-education.com/campus_jacksonville.htm
Established: 2001 Annual Undergrad Tuition & Fees: N/A
Enrollment: 389 Coed
Affiliation or Control: Proprietary IRS Status: Proprietary
Highest Offering: Associate Degree
Program: Occupational
Accreditation: ABHES

01 Director .... Ms. Michelle GRANT

Herzing University (L)

1865 SR 436, Winter Park FL 32792
County: Orange Identification: 666422
Unit ID: 386472
Telephone: (407) 478-0500 Carnegie Class: Bac/Assoc
FAX Number: (407) 478-0501 Calendar System: Trimester
URL: www.herzing.edu
Established: 1965 Annual Undergrad Tuition & Fees: $17,200
Enrollment: 399 Coed
Affiliation or Control: Proprietary IRS Status: Proprietary
Highest Offering: Master's
Program: 2-Year Principally Bachelor's Creditable; Nursing Emphasis
Accreditation: &NH, PTAA, SURTEC

01 President .... Mrs. Heather ANTONACCI
37 Director Financial Aid .... Ms. Krista KUHR
07 Director of Admissions .... Ms. Lauren RUSTON
05 Academic Dean .... Ms. Pat EDWARDS
06 Registrar .... Ms. Lori GUISEPPI
29 Director Alumni Relations .... Ms. Sharon ROSEN

† Regional accreditation is carried under the parent institution in Madison, WI.

Hillsborough Community College (M)

PO Box 31127, 39 Columbia Drive, Tampa FL 33631-3127
County: Hillsborough FICE Identification: 007870
Unit ID: 134495
Telephone: (813) 253-7000 Carnegie Class: Assoc/Pub-U-MC
FAX Number: (813) 253-7183 Calendar System: Semester
URL: www.hccfl.edu
Established: 1968 Annual Undergrad Tuition & Fees (In-State): $2,481
Enrollment: 28,329 Coed
Affiliation or Control: State IRS Status: 501(c)3
Highest Offering: Associate Degree
Program: Occupational; 2-Year Principally Bachelor's Creditable
Accreditation: SC, ACFEI, ADNUR, DA, DH, @DIETT, DMS, EMT, MUS, NMT, OPD, RAD, RTT

01 President .... Dr. Ken ATWATER
10 Vice President Administration/CFO .... Ms. Barbara LARSON
03 Senior Vice President .... Mr. Robert WOLF
05 Vice President for Academic Affairs .... Mr. Craig JOHNSON
14 Int Vice Pres Info Technology .... Mr. Stephen GORHAM
32 VP Student Services/Enrollment Mgt .... Dr. Ken RAY
12 Campus President Dale Mabry .... Dr. Robert P. CHUNN
12 Campus President Ybor City Campus .... Dr. Shawn ROBINSON
12 Campus President Plant City Campus .... Dr. Martyn CLAY
12 Campus President Brandon Campus .... Dr. Carlos SOTO
12 Campus President South Shore Campus .... Dr. Allen WITT
22 Asst to Pres Equity/Special Pgms .... Dr. Joan HOLMES
26 Exec Dir Marketing/Public Relations .... Ms. Ashley CARL
09 Spc Asst to Pres Strat Plng & Analy .... Dr. Paul NAGY
102 Director HCC Foundation .... Dr. Adrienne GARCIA
43 College Attorney .... Ms. Martha K. KOEHLER
15 Director Human Resources .... Ms. Sue FLAIG
21 Controller .... Ms. Bonnie J. CARR
75 Director Technical Programs .... Dr. Ginger CLARK
20 Director Assoc in Arts Programs .... Dr. Karen GRIFFIN
90 Director of Academic Technology .... Mr. Richard SENKER
75 Dean Public Services Programs .... Mr. Jack EVANS
88 Dean Environmental Programs .... Vacant
88 Dean Assoc in Science Programs .... Dr. Ellen CANGI
88 Dean Assoc in Arts/Hum/Comm Pgms .... Dr. Mary BENDICKSON
81 Dean Assoc in Math/Science .... Mr. Robert WYNEGAR
76 Dean Health/Wellness & Sports Tech .... Dr. Amy ANDERSON
37 Financial Aid Director .... Ms. Tierra SMITH
06 Registrar .... Ms. Katherine DURKEE
18 Director Facilities/Physical Plant .... Mr. David CABECEIRAS
96 Director of Purchasing .... Ms. Vonda MELCHIOR
31 Dir of Community & Govt Relations .... Ms. Sarah (Sally) EVERETT

Hobe Sound Bible College (N)

PO Box 1065, Hobe Sound FL 33475-1065
County: Martin FICE Identification: 021889
Unit ID: 134510
Telephone: (772) 546-5534 Carnegie Class: Spec/Faith

FAX Number: (772) 545-1422 Calendar System: Semester
URL: www.hsbc.edu
Established: 1960 Annual Undergrad Tuition & Fees: $5,280
Enrollment: 100 Coed
Affiliation or Control: Independent Non-Profit IRS Status: 501(c)3
Highest Offering: Baccalaureate
Program: Liberal Arts And General; Religious Emphasis
Accreditation: BI

01 President ... Mr. P. Daniel STETLER
05 Academic Dean ... Dr. Clifford W. CHURCHILL
10 Director of Finances ... Mr. Kendall STRAIGHT
11 Director of Administration ... Mr. Wesley HOLDEN
32 Dean of Students ... Mr. John S. JONES
33 Dean of Men ... Mr. Jonathan STRATTON
08 Librarian ... Mr. Phil JONES
26 Public Relations Director ... Mr. Paul STETLER
06 Registrar ... Mrs. Faye PARSONS
07 Director of Admissions ... Ms. Joanna WETHERALD
30 Director of Development ... Mr. Patrick DAVIS
51 Dean of External Studies ... Mr. Dalbert N. WALKER

Hodges University (A)

2655 Northbrooke Drive, Naples FL 34119-7932
County: Collier FICE Identification: 030375
Unit ID: 367884
Telephone: (239) 513-1122 Carnegie Class: Master's S
FAX Number: (239) 598-6253 Calendar System: Trimester
URL: www.hodges.edu
Established: 1990 Annual Undergrad Tuition & Fees: $14,700
Enrollment: 2,900 Coed
Affiliation or Control: Independent Non-Profit IRS Status: 501(c)3
Highest Offering: Master's
Program: Liberal Arts And General
Accreditation: SC, IACBE, MAC, @PTAA

01 President ... Dr. Terry MCMAHAN
05 Exec Vice Pres Academic Affairs ... Dr. Jeanette BROCK
10 Exec Vice Pres of Finance ... Mr. John WHITE
11 Exec Vice Pres Administration ... Dr. Joseph PEPE
06 Vice Pres of Student Records Mgt ... Ms. Carol MORRISON
84 Vice President of Enrollment Mgt ... Ms. Rita LAMPUS
35 Vice Pres of Student Development ... Mr. Ron BOWMAN
37 VP of Student Financial Assistance ... Mr. Joseph GILCHRIST
30 Vice Pres University Advancement ... Mr. Phil MEMOLI
38 Director Student Counseling ... Mr. Micki ERICKSON
26 Chief Public Relations Officer ... Mr. Joe TURNER
09 Dir Institutional Effective/Rsrch ... Dr. Diane BALL

Indian River State College (B)

3209 Virginia Avenue, Fort Pierce FL 34981-5596
County: Saint Lucie FICE Identification: 001493
Unit ID: 134608
Telephone: (772) 462-4772 Carnegie Class: Assoc/Pub4
FAX Number: (772) 462-4796 Calendar System: Semester
URL: www.irsc.edu
Established: 1960 Annual Undergrad Tuition & Fees (In-District): $2,804
Enrollment: 17,528 Coed
Affiliation or Control: Local IRS Status: 501(c)3
Highest Offering: Baccalaureate
Program: Occupational; 2-Year Principally Bachelor's Creditable; Liberal Arts And General; Teacher Preparatory
Accreditation: SC, ADNUR, DA, DH, DT, EMT, MAC, MLTAD, NUR, PTAA, RAD, SURGT

01 President ... Dr. Edwin R. MASSEY
32 Vice President Student Affairs ... Mr. Frank WATKINS
05 Vice President Academic Affairs ... Dr. Anthony IACONO
10 Vice Pres Administration/Finance ... Mr. Barry A. KEIM
88 Vice Pres Applied Science & Tech ... Dr. Alan L. ROBERTS
45 Associate VP Institutional Effectiv ... Dr. Christina HART
04 Exec Assistant to the President ... Mr. Andrew TREADWELL
12 Vice Pres/Provost-Fort Pierce ... Dr. Mary G. LOCKE
12 Provost Pt St Lucie/St Lucie W ... Dr. Harvey E. ARNOLD
12 Provost Okeechobee ... Mr. Russ BROWN
12 Provost Stuart ... Ms. Patricia ALAN
12 Provost Vero Beach ... Dr. David SULLIVAN
12 Dean Northwest Center ... Mr. Andre HAWKINS
18 Dean Auxiliary Services/Facility ... Mr. Allen BOTTORFF
72 Dean Institutional Tech ... Mr. Paul R. O'BRIEN
80 Dean of Public Services ... Mr. Evan BERRY
72 Dean Advanced Technology ... Mr. Jose L. FARINOS
93 Associate Dean Minority Affairs ... Ms. Adriene JEFFERSON
51 Associate Dean Developmental Ed ... Ms. Libby LIVINGS-EASSA
20 Asst Dean Educational Services ... Mr. Steven W. PAYNE
50 Assistant Dean Business Technology ... Mr. Cedric GIBSON
15 Associate Dean Human Resources ... Vacant
14 Associate Dean Data Processing ... Ms. Patricia D. PFEIFFER
21 Assistant Dean Finance ... Mr. Joe MAZUR
08 Associate Dean Learning Resources ... Ms. Patricia C. PROFETA
49 Associate Dean of Arts & Sciences ... Mr. Casey LUNCEFORD
11 Assoc Dean Administrative Services ... Ms. Jan PAGANO
75 Associate Dean Industrial Education ... Ms. Donna RIVETT
76 Associate Dean of Health Science ... Ms. Jane P. CEBELAK
09 Associate Dean Research/Reports ... Mr. Gerald L. MOCK
66 Administrative Director of Nursing ... Ms. Ann HUBBARD
102 Executive Director Foundation ... Ms. Ann DECKER
30 Director Institutional Advancement ... Ms. Michelle ABALDO
41 Director Athletics ... Mr. Scott KIMMELMAN
36 Director Student Success Services ... Ms. Flossie JACKSON
84 Director Enrollment Management ... Ms. Eileen STORCK
37 Director Student Financial Aid ... Ms. Mary LEWIS
06 Registrar/Dir Student Affs/Admiss ... Ms. Karen CHAPDELAINE
96 Purchasing Agent ... Mr. Don WINDHAM
38 Director Student Counseling ... Ms. Dale HAYES
51 Admin Dir Baccalaureate Programs ... Mr. Ian NEUHARD
35 Director Student Affairs ... Ms. Sharon LOWE

International Academy of Design and Technology (C)

5104 Eisenhower Boulevard, Tampa FL 33634-6313
County: Hillsborough FICE Identification: 030314
Unit ID: 134680
Telephone: (813) 881-0007 Carnegie Class: Spec/Arts
FAX Number: (813) 884-9327 Calendar System: Quarter
URL: www.academy.edu
Established: 1984 Annual Undergrad Tuition & Fees: $19,080
Enrollment: 971 Coed
Affiliation or Control: Proprietary IRS Status: Proprietary
Highest Offering: Baccalaureate
Program: Fine Arts Emphasis
Accreditation: ACICS, CIDA

01 President ... Dr. Karen O'DONNELL
10 Vice President of Finance ... Tim COPPOLA
05 Dean/Chief Academic Officer ... Phil BULONE
07 Director of Admissions ... Dewey MCGUIRK
32 Director of Student Services ... Amanda WILLIAMS
36 Director of Career Services ... Carl STORCK
08 Learning Resource Center Coord ... Elaine NERI
37 Director Student Financial Aid ... Jameson STEVENS
35 Manager of Student Services ... Kimberly FORTENBERRY

International Academy of Design and Technology-Online (D)

5104 Eisenhower Boulevard, Tampa FL 33634-6313
County: Hillsborough Identification: 666631
Unit ID: 456296
Telephone: (813) 881-0007 Carnegie Class: Assoc/PrivFP4
FAX Number: (813) 357-2505 Calendar System: Quarter
URL: www.iadt.edu
Established: 1977 Annual Undergrad Tuition & Fees: $14,400
Enrollment: 1,896 Coed
Affiliation or Control: Proprietary IRS Status: Proprietary
Highest Offering: Baccalaureate
Program: Professional; Fine Arts Emphasis
Accreditation: ACICS

01 President ... Mr. Mark PAGE
05 Director of Education ... Ms. Dawn CARLSON
06 Registrar ... Ms. Nicole BELLFIELD
07 VP of Admissions ... Mr. Michael WASHINGTON

† Branch campus of International Academy of Design and Technology, FL.

ITT Technical Institute (E)

3401 S University Drive, Fort Lauderdale FL 33328-2021
County: Broward Identification: 666536
Unit ID: 409069
Telephone: (954) 476-9300 Carnegie Class: Spec/Tech
FAX Number: (954) 476-6889 Calendar System: Quarter
URL: www.itt-tech.edu
Established: 1991 Annual Undergrad Tuition & Fees: N/A
Enrollment: 683 Coed
Affiliation or Control: Proprietary IRS Status: Proprietary
Highest Offering: Baccalaureate
Program: Technical Emphasis
Accreditation: ACICS

† Branch campus of ITT Technical Institute, Indianapolis, IN.

ITT Technical Institute (F)

13500 Powers Court, Suite 100, Fort Myers FL 33912
County: Lee Identification: 666669
Unit ID: 456436
Telephone: (239) 603-8700 Carnegie Class: Assoc/PrivFP4
FAX Number: N/A Calendar System: Quarter
URL: www.itt-tech.edu
Established: N/A Annual Undergrad Tuition & Fees: N/A
Enrollment: 299 Coed
Affiliation or Control: Proprietary IRS Status: Proprietary
Highest Offering: Baccalaureate
Program: Technical Emphasis
Accreditation: ACICS

† Branch campus of ITT Technical Institute, Indianapolis, IN.

ITT Technical Institute (G)

7011 A.C. Skinner Parkway, Ste. 140, Jacksonville FL 32256-6954
County: Duval Identification: 666537
Unit ID: 407063
Telephone: (904) 573-9100 Carnegie Class: Spec/Tech
FAX Number: (904) 573-0512 Calendar System: Quarter
URL: www.itt-tech.edu
Established: 1990 Annual Undergrad Tuition & Fees: N/A
Enrollment: 749 Coed
Affiliation or Control: Proprietary IRS Status: Proprietary
Highest Offering: Baccalaureate
Program: Technical Emphasis
Accreditation: ACICS

† Branch campus of ITT Technical Institute, Indianapolis, IN.

ITT Technical Institute (H)

1400 International Parkway South, Lake Mary FL 32746-1607
County: Seminole FICE Identification: 030876
Unit ID: 372578
Telephone: (407) 660-2900 Carnegie Class: Spec/Tech
FAX Number: (407) 660-2566 Calendar System: Quarter
URL: www.itt-tech.edu
Established: 1989 Annual Undergrad Tuition & Fees: N/A
Enrollment: 555 Coed
Affiliation or Control: Proprietary IRS Status: Proprietary
Highest Offering: Baccalaureate
Program: Technical Emphasis
Accreditation: ACICS

† Branch campus of ITT Technical Institute, Indianapolis, IN.

ITT Technical Institute (I)

7955 NW 12th Street, Suite 119, Miami FL 33126-1823
County: Miami-Dade Identification: 666026
Unit ID: 430263
Telephone: (305) 477-3080 Carnegie Class: Spec/Tech
FAX Number: (305) 477-7561 Calendar System: Quarter
URL: www.itt-tech.edu
Established: 1996 Annual Undergrad Tuition & Fees: N/A
Enrollment: 680 Coed
Affiliation or Control: Proprietary IRS Status: Proprietary
Highest Offering: Baccalaureate
Program: Technical Emphasis
Accreditation: ACICS

† Branch campus of ITT Technical Institute, Indianapolis, IN.

ITT Technical Institute (J)

877 Executive Ctr. Dr. W, Ste. 100, St. Petersburg FL 33702
County: Pinellas Identification: 666163
Unit ID: 450207
Telephone: (727) 209-4700 Carnegie Class: Assoc/PrivFP4
FAX Number: N/A Calendar System: Quarter
URL: www.itt-tech.edu
Established: 2006 Annual Undergrad Tuition & Fees: N/A
Enrollment: 258 Coed
Affiliation or Control: Proprietary IRS Status: Proprietary
Highest Offering: Baccalaureate
Program: Technical Emphasis
Accreditation: ACICS

† Branch campus of ITT Technical Institute, Indianapolis, IN.

ITT Technical Institute (K)

4809 Memorial Highway, Tampa FL 33634-7350
County: Hillsborough FICE Identification: 022865
Unit ID: 134909
Telephone: (813) 885-2244 Carnegie Class: Spec/Tech
FAX Number: (813) 888-8451 Calendar System: Quarter
URL: www.itt-tech.edu
Established: 1981 Annual Undergrad Tuition & Fees: N/A
Enrollment: 803 Coed
Affiliation or Control: Proprietary IRS Status: Proprietary
Highest Offering: Baccalaureate
Program: Technical Emphasis
Accreditation: ACICS

† Branch campus of ITT Technical Institute, Indianapolis, IN.

Jacksonville University (L)

2800 University Boulevard N, Jacksonville FL 32211-3394
County: Duval FICE Identification: 001495
Unit ID: 134945
Telephone: (904) 256-8000 Carnegie Class: Master's M
FAX Number: N/A Calendar System: Semester
URL: www.ju.edu
Established: 1934 Annual Undergrad Tuition & Fees: $29,100
Enrollment: 3,715 Coed
Affiliation or Control: Independent Non-Profit IRS Status: 501(c)3
Highest Offering: Doctorate
Program: Liberal Arts And General; Teacher Preparatory; Professional; Business Emphasis
Accreditation: SC, AAB, BUS, DANCE, DENT, MUS, NURSE

01 President ... Dr. Kerry D. ROMESBURG
05 Senior VP for Academic Affairs ... Dr. Lois S. BECKER
10 VP for Finance & Administration ... Mr. George C. SCADUTO
84 Vice Pres Enrollment Management ... Mr. Terry E. WHITTUM
32 Vice President for Student Life ... Dr. John A. BALOG

30 Vice Pres University Advancement .... Mr. Michael HOWLAND
26 VP Univ Rel & External Affairs .... Dr. Derek J. HALL
13 VP Info Tech & Chief Info Officer .... Mr. Tom HALL
04 Exec Assistant to the President .... Ms. Dolores STARR
41 Interim Athletic Director .... Mr. Joel LAMP
06 Registrar .... Ms. Carolyn BARRETT
09 Director of Institutional Research .... Vacant
07 Director of Admissions .... Vacant
08 Director of the Library .... Mr. David JONES
35 Dean of Students .... Dr. Bryan F. COKER
36 Director of Career Development .... Ms. Devan COUGHLIN
37 Dir Student Financial Assistance .... Ms. Breanne SIMKIN
29 Asst VP for Institutional Advance .... Vacant
21 Controller .... Ms. Liza MULLINS
11 Exec Dir Budgets/Business Opers .... Ms. Ellen M. PAIGE
96 Director of Purchasing .... Mr. Michael J. BOBBIN
40 Director of the Bookstore .... Ms. Kimberly BANKS
42 Campus Minister .... Mr. Mark SMITH
15 Director of Human Resources .... Mr. James V. WILLIAMS
57 Dean College of Fine Arts .... Mr. William E. HILL
49 Dean Col of Arts & Sciences .... Dr. Douglas HAZZARD
50 Dean College of Business .... Dr. Don CAPENER
51 Assoc Dean of Continuing Studies .... Vacant
53 Interim Dean School of Education .... Dr. Douglas HAZZARD
64 Chairman Division of Music .... Dr. Thomas HARRISON
66 Dean School of Nursing .... Dr. Judith ERICKSON
79 Chair Div of Humanitites .... Dr. Scott KIMBROUGH
81 Chair Division of Science & Math ...... Dr. Lee Ann J. CLEMENTS
38 Director Student Counseling .... Ms. Kristin R. ALBERTS
83 Chair Division of Social Science .... Dr. Sherry JACKSON
88 Chair Division of Naval Science .... Capt. Herbert HADLEY
88 Chair Div of Theatre Arts & Dance .... Mr. Brian PALMER
57 Chair Division Art/Art History .... Ms. Dana L. CHAPMAN
18 Chief Facilities/Physical Plant .... Mr. Joe COLEMAN

Johnson & Wales University (A)

1701 NE 127th Street, North Miami FL 33181-2518

County: Miami-Dade | Identification: 666423
Unit ID: 414823
Telephone: (305) 892-7000 | Carnegie Class: Bac/Assoc
FAX Number: (305) 892-7030 | Calendar System: Quarter
URL: www.jwu.edu
Established: 1992 | Annual Undergrad Tuition & Fees: $26,112
Enrollment: 2,153 | Coed
Affiliation or Control: Independent Non-Profit | IRS Status: 501(c)3
Highest Offering: Baccalaureate
Program: Occupational; 2-Year Principally Bachelor's Creditable
Accreditation: &EH

01 President North Miami Campus .... Mrs. Loreen M. CHANT
03 Vice Pres/Dean of Academic Affairs .... Mr. Larry RICE
05 Dean of Culinary Education .... Mr. Bruce M. OZGA
100 Executive Administrator .... Mr. Jordan FICKESS
32 Director of Student Acad Services .... Ms. Maheen CARROLL
07 Director of Admissions .... Mr. Jeffrey GREENIP
11 Director of Administration .... Mr. Barry VOGEL
18 Director of Facilities Management .... Mr. Paul ZAHN
26 Dir of Comm & Media Relations .... Mrs. Tonya EVANS
30 Director of Development & Alumni .... Mr. Peter ROOD
35 Dean of Students .... Ms. Ismare MONREAL
37 Director of Student Financial Svcs .... Mr. Chris MAGNAN
88 Director of the Center for Academic .... Ms. Martha SACKS
13 Director of Campus IT Services .... Mr. Michael GRAZIOTTI
19 Interim Dir Campus Safety & Sec .... Mr. Kelvin DARROUGH
23 Director of Student Health Services .... Ms. Roberta ADAMONIS
36 Director Exp Education & Career Svc .... Ms. Darlene CANTOR
39 Director of Residential Life .... Mr. Dan OFSTEIN
41 Director of Athletics & Campus Rec .... Mr. David GRAHAM
96 Director of Purchasing .... Mr. Shawn RAY
29 Manager of Alumni Relations .... Ms. Karen MCGIBBON
44 Development Relations Officer .... Ms. Yudit ARTEAGA
15 Campus Human Resources Manager .... Ms. Dolly DURAN
40 Bookstore Manager .... Mr. Darryl LERNER
08 Director of Library Services .... Ms. Nicole COVONE
85 International Student Advisor .... Ms. Nicole GRAHAM
92 Honors Program Coordinator .... Ms. Carol KORIS

† Regional accreditation is carried under the parent institution in Providence, RI.

Jones College (B)

5353 Arlington Expressway, Jacksonville FL 32211-5588

County: Duval | FICE Identification: 001497
Unit ID: 135063
Telephone: (904) 743-1122 | Carnegie Class: Bac/Diverse
FAX Number: (904) 743-4446 | Calendar System: Trimester
URL: www.jones.edu
Established: 1918 | Annual Undergrad Tuition & Fees: $7,410
Enrollment: 699 | Coed
Affiliation or Control: Independent Non-Profit | IRS Status: 501(c)3
Highest Offering: Baccalaureate
Program: Business Emphasis
Accreditation: ACICS

00 Corporate President & CEO .... Dorothy D. JONES
01 President of the College .... Frank M. MCCAFFERTY
05 Dean of the College .... Dee THORNTON
10 Business Officer .... Kathy DANE
37 Director of Financial Assistance .... Becky DAVIS
07 Diretor of Admissions .... Linda VAUGHN
36 Director of Career Development .... Mona WEBB
13 Director IT .... Holly KELLEY
08 Librarian .... Kevin DOBYNS

Jose Maria Vargas University (C)

8300 S Palm Drive, Pembroke Pines FL 33025

FICE Identification: 041620
Telephone: (954) 322-4460 | Carnegie Class: Not Classified
FAX Number: (954) 322-4131 | Calendar System: Semester
URL: www.jmvu.edu
Established: N/A | Annual Undergrad Tuition & Fees: $8,240
Enrollment: 167 | Coed
Affiliation or Control: Proprietary | IRS Status: Proprietary
Highest Offering: Master's
Program: Occupational; 2-Year Principally Bachelor's Creditable; Teacher Preparatory; Professional
Accreditation: ACICS, @TEAC

01 President .... Dr. Alicia F. PARRA DE ORTIZ
05 Vice President of Academic Affairs .... Clara GONZALEZ
10 Vice President of Finance .... Lelis Antonio ORTIZ ALVAREZ
08 Library Director .... Yrenes FORNES
18 Facilities/Purchasing Director .... Erika Jose ORTIZ PARRA
21 Director of Budgeting .... Edith PAREDES
06 Registrar .... Lelis ORTIZ PARRA
32 Director of Student Development .... Erika ORTIZ
58 Coord of Research/Grad Studies .... Lori N. KIJANCA
53 Coordinator of Education .... Claudia PARRA
88 Coordinator of Graphic Design .... Henry BALLATE
50 Coordinator of Business Programs .... Minelba MARTINEZ

Kaplan College (D)

10131 Pines Boulevard, Pembroke Pines FL 33026

Identification: 666752
Unit ID: 458238
Telephone: (954) 885-3500 | Carnegie Class: Not Classified
FAX Number: (954) 431-0823 | Calendar System: Semester
URL: www.kaplancollege.com
Established: N/A | Annual Undergrad Tuition & Fees: N/A
Enrollment: 67 | Coordinate
Affiliation or Control: Proprietary | IRS Status: Proprietary
Highest Offering: Associate Degree
Program: 2-Year Principally Bachelor's Creditable
Accreditation: ACICS

01 Executive Director .... Mr. Steve NELSON

† Branch campus of Kaplan Career Institute, Harrisburg, PA.

Keiser University (E)

1500 NW 49th Street, Fort Lauderdale FL 33309-3700

County: Broward | FICE Identification: 021519
Unit ID: 135081
Telephone: (954) 776-4456 | Carnegie Class: Bac/Assoc
FAX Number: (954) 771-4894 | Calendar System: Semester
URL: www.keiseruniversity.edu
Established: 1977 | Annual Undergrad Tuition & Fees: $15,064
Enrollment: 18,765 | Coed
Affiliation or Control: Proprietary | IRS Status: Proprietary
Highest Offering: Doctorate
Program: Occupational
Accreditation: SC, ACFEI, ADNUR, ARCPA, DMS, MAAB, MLTAD, NURSE, OTA, PTAA, RAD

00 Chancellor .... Dr. Arthur KEISER
01 Campus President .... Mr. John SITES
26 Reg Dir Media & Public Relations .... Ms. Kimberly DALE

Keiser University (F)

10330 S Federal Highway,
Port Saint Lucie FL 34952-5605

County: Saint Lucie | Identification: 666289
Unit ID: 437990
Telephone: (772) 398-9990 | Carnegie Class: Not Classified
FAX Number: (772) 335-9619 | Calendar System: Semester
URL: www.keiseruniversity.edu
Established: 1977 | Annual Undergrad Tuition & Fees: $8,250
Enrollment: 488 | Coed
Affiliation or Control: Proprietary | IRS Status: Proprietary
Highest Offering: Associate Degree
Program: Occupational
Accreditation: &SC, SURGT

01 Campus President .... Dr. Thomas CREOLA

† Regional accreditation is carried under the parent institution Keiser University, Fort Lauderdale, FL.

Keiser University (G)

2085 Vista Parkway, West Palm Beach FL 33411-2719

County: Palm Beach | Identification: 667032
Unit ID: 428170
Telephone: (561) 471-6000 | Carnegie Class: Assoc/PrivFP
FAX Number: (561) 471-7849 | Calendar System: Quarter
URL: www.keiseruniversity.edu
Established: N/A | Annual Undergrad Tuition & Fees: $14,176
Enrollment: 1,790 | Coed
Affiliation or Control: Proprietary | IRS Status: Proprietary
Highest Offering: Doctorate
Program: Occupational
Accreditation: &SC, ADNUR, OTA

01 Campus President .... Ms. Kimberly LEA
03 Executive Vice Chancellor/COO .... Mr. Peter CROCITTO

† Regional accreditation is carried under the parent institution Keiser University, Fort Lauderdale, FL.

Key College (H)

225 E Dania Beach Blvd, Suite 130,
Dania Beach FL 33004-3042

County: Broward | FICE Identification: 023251
Unit ID: 134422
Telephone: (954) 923-4440 | Carnegie Class: Assoc/PrivFP
FAX Number: (954) 923-9226 | Calendar System: Quarter
URL: www.keycollege.edu
Established: 1982 | Annual Undergrad Tuition & Fees: $10,815
Enrollment: 82 | Coed
Affiliation or Control: Proprietary | IRS Status: Proprietary
Highest Offering: Associate Degree
Program: 2-Year Principally Bachelor's Creditable; Business Emphasis
Accreditation: ACICS

01 President .... Mr. Ronald DOOLEY
05 Director of Academic Affairs .... Ms. Marella KING
07 Director of Admissions .... Vacant
37 Director of Financial Aid .... Mrs. Rachael GONZALES
06 Registrar .... Mr. Rashad BENNETT

Knox Theological Seminary (I)

5554 N Federal Highway, Fort Lauderdale FL 33308-3209

County: Broward | FICE Identification: 039923
Telephone: (954) 771-0376 | Carnegie Class: Not Classified
FAX Number: (954) 351-3343 | Calendar System: Semester
URL: www.knoxseminary.edu
Established: 1989 | Annual Undergrad Tuition & Fees: $7,080
Enrollment: 112 | Coed
Affiliation or Control: Presbyterian Church In America | IRS Status: 501(c)3
Highest Offering: Doctorate
Program: Religious Emphasis
Accreditation: THEOL

01 President & CEO .... Dr. Luder WHITLOCK
05 Dean of Faculty .... Dr. Warren GAGE
32 Dir Student Svcs/Dean of Students ...... Mr. Jonathan LINEBAUGH

Lake-Sumter Community College (J)

9501 US Highway 441, Leesburg FL 34788-8751

County: Lake | FICE Identification: 001502
Unit ID: 135188
Telephone: (352) 787-3747 | Carnegie Class: Assoc/Pub-S-MC
FAX Number: (352) 365-3548 | Calendar System: Semester
URL: www.lscc.edu
Established: 1962 | Annual Undergrad Tuition & Fees (In-District): $3,142
Enrollment: 4,759 | Coed
Affiliation or Control: State/Local | IRS Status: 501(c)3
Highest Offering: Baccalaureate
Program: Occupational; 2-Year Principally Bachelor's Creditable
Accreditation: SC, ADNUR

01 President .... Dr. Charles R. MOJOCK
10 VP Business Affairs .... Mr. Richard M. SCOTT
05 VP Academic-Student Affairs .... Dr. Barbara C. HOWARD
21 Controller .... Mr. John FROMAN
75 Dean Career & Technical Programs .... Dr. Mary Jo RAGER
53 Dean General Ed & Transfer Programs .... Mr. Gary SLIGH
15 Exec Director Human Resources .... Mr. Tim KANE
13 Chief Information Officer .... Mr. Douglas GUILER
09 Exec Dir Planning & IE .... Dr. Kristy LISLE
32 Assistant VP Student Affairs .... Dr. Michelle BALON
30 Exec Dir Inst Advance & Foundation .... Ms. Rosanne BRANDEBURG
18 Director College Facilities .... Mr. Donald BALL
08 Director Libraries .... Ms. Denise K. ENGLISH
35 Director Student Development .... Ms. Claire BRADY
21 Director Budget & Accounting .... Ms. Sue FAGAN
66 Director Nursing .... Dr. Margaret WACKER
08 Director Learning Center .... Ms. Marion J. KANE
26 Director College Relations .... Vacant
37 Director Financial Aid .... Ms. Audrey WILLIAMS
84 Director Enrollment Management .... Ms. Debra MARVEL
41 Athletic Director .... Mr. Michael K. MATULIA
88 Director Youth Outreach Programs .... Mr. Reinaldo CORTES
106 Director Distance Learning .... Mr. Mike NATHANSON

Le Cordon Bleu College of Culinary Arts in Miami (K)

3221 Enterprise Way, Miramar FL 33025-3929

County: Broward | Identification: 666369
Unit ID: 446835
Telephone: (954) 438-8882 | Carnegie Class: Assoc/PrivFP
FAX Number: (954) 438-9519 | Calendar System: Other
URL: www.chefs.edu/miami
Established: 2002 | Annual Undergrad Tuition & Fees: $14,170
Enrollment: 1,553 | Coed
Affiliation or Control: Proprietary | IRS Status: Proprietary

Highest Offering: Associate Degree
Program: Occupational
Accreditation: ACCSC, ACFEI, ACICS

01 President .... Mr. Bob KANE

† Branch campus of Le Cordon Bleu Institute of Culinary Arts, Pittsburgh, PA.

Le Cordon Bleu College of Culinary Arts in Orlando (A)

8511 Commodity Circle, Orlando FL 32819-9002
County: Orange Identification: 666064
Unit ID: 442231
Telephone: (407) 888-4000 Carnegie Class: Assoc/PrivFP
FAX Number: (407) 888-4019 Calendar System: Quarter
URL: www.chefs.edu/orlando
Established: 2002 Annual Undergrad Tuition & Fees: $17,500
Enrollment: 1,000 Coed
Affiliation or Control: Proprietary IRS Status: Proprietary
Highest Offering: Associate Degree
Program: 2-Year Principally Bachelor's Creditable; Professional; Technical Emphasis
Accreditation: ACICS, ACFEI

01 President .... Joe HARDIMAN
07 Vice President of Admissions .... Ken FIIGUEROA
22 Director of Regulatory Operations .... Sean MURPHY
05 Director of Education .... Chef William MATHER
06 Registrar .... Laura HARRELSON

† Branch campus of International Academy of Design & Technology, Tampa, FL.

Lincoln College of Technology (B)

2410 Metrocentre Boulevard,
West Palm Beach FL 33407-3155
County: Palm Beach FICE Identification: 022808
Unit ID: 136066
Telephone: (561) 842-8324 Carnegie Class: Assoc/PrivFP4
FAX Number: (561) 842-9503 Calendar System: Other
URL: www.lincolncollegeoftechnology.com
Established: 1982 Annual Undergrad Tuition & Fees: $18,564
Enrollment: 1,599 Coed
Affiliation or Control: Proprietary IRS Status: Proprietary
Highest Offering: Baccalaureate
Program: Occupational; Technical Emphasis
Accreditation: ACICS, ACFEI

01 President .... Ms. Helen CARVER

Lincoln Tech Fern Park Orlando Campus (C)

7275 Estapona Circle, Fern Park FL 32730-2351
County: Seminole FICE Identification: 033903
Unit ID: 439437
Telephone: (407) 673-7406 Carnegie Class: Assoc/PrivFP
FAX Number: (407) 339-0295 Calendar System: Quarter
URL: www.lincolntech.com
Established: 1991 Annual Undergrad Tuition & Fees: N/A
Enrollment: 425 Coed
Affiliation or Control: Proprietary IRS Status: Proprietary
Highest Offering: Associate Degree
Program: Occupational; 2-Year Principally Bachelor's Creditable; Nursing Emphasis
Accreditation: ABHES, DA, SURTEC

01 Executive Director .... Mr. Carl BUTTS
05 Director of Education .... Mr. Jim WILBOUR

Lynn University (D)

3601 N Military Trail, Boca Raton FL 33431-5598
County: Palm Beach FICE Identification: 001505
Unit ID: 132657
Telephone: (561) 237-7000 Carnegie Class: DRU
FAX Number: (561) 237-7100 Calendar System: Semester
URL: www.lynn.edu
Established: 1962 Annual Undergrad Tuition & Fees: $32,600
Enrollment: 2,102 Coed
Affiliation or Control: Independent Non-Profit IRS Status: 501(c)3
Highest Offering: Doctorate
Program: Liberal Arts And General; Business Emphasis
Accreditation: SC, IACBE, MUS

01 President .... Dr. Kevin M. ROSS
100 Chief of Staff .... Dr. Jason L. WALTON
00 President Emeritus .... Dr. Donald E. ROSS
11 Sr Vice Pres Administration .... Mr. Gregory J. MALFITANO
05 Vice President Academic Affairs .... Dr. Gregg COX
84 Vice Pres Enrollment Management .... Dr. Gareth FOWLES
10 Vice President Business & Finance .... Ms. Laurie LEVINE
32 Vice President for Student Life .... Dr. Phil RIORDAN
26 Vice Pres Marketing & Communication .Ms. Michele M. MORRIS
30 Vice Pres Development/Alumni Affs .... Ms. Judith L. NELSON
13 Chief Information Officer .... Mr. Chris G. BONIFORTI
88 Dean of Administration .... Mr. Thomas J. HEFFERNAN
35 Dean of Students .... Mr. Paul S. TURNER
20 Academic Dean .... Dr. Gregg C. COX
43 General Counsel .... Ms. Margaret E. RUDDY
88 Exec Dir Stdnt Administrative Svcs .... Ms. Evelyn C. NELSON
08 Library Director .... Vacant
39 Director Housing & Residence Life .... Ms. Joy DOLIBER
36 Director Career Development .... Vacant
41 Director of Athletics .... Dr. Kristen L. MORAZ
18 Director Auxiliary Services .... Mr. Matthew P. CHALOUX
23 Director Health Center .... Ms. Rita ALBERT
27 Director of Marketing .... Mrs. Carol A. HERZ
31 Director of Public Relations .... Mr. Joshua GLANZER
44 Director of Regional Development .... Mr. Jay J. BRANDT
29 Director Alumni Affairs .... Mr. Matthew R. ROOS
42 Chaplain .... Fr. Martin C. DEVEREAUX
07 Dir Undergraduate Admissions .... Mr. Stefano PAPALEO
37 Dir Student Financial Assistance .... Mrs. Chan J. PARK
38 Director of the Counseling Center .... Ms. Nicole R. OVEDIA
96 Director of Purchasing .... Mr. Alfredo H. BONIFORTI
06 Registrar .... Ms. Angela K. ROGERS
21 Director of Accounting .... Mr. Michael C. BOLDUC
07 Dir Graduate & UG Evening Admiss .... Mr. Steven PRUITT
51 Director Distance Learning .... Dr. Mary L. TEBES
09 Director of Institutional Research .... Mrs. Lara MARTIN
15 Director of Employee Services .... Mrs. Carole E. DODGE
40 Bookstore Manager .... Ms. Rita D. LOUREIRO
50 Dean College Business & Management ..... Mr. Thomas KRUCZEK
49 Dean College of Liberal Educ ...... Dr. Katrina CARTER-TELLISON
88 Dean School of Aeronautics .... Dr. Jeffrey C. JOHNSON
53 Dean Ross College of Education .... Dr. Craig MERTLER
60 Dean College Intl Communications .... Dr. David L. JAFFE
88 Dean College Hospitality Mgmt .... Vacant
64 Dean Conservatory of Music .... Dr. Jon H. ROBERTSON
88 Dean Inst Achievement Learning .... Dr. Marsha A. GLINES

MedVance Institute of Fort Lauderdale (E)

4850 W Oakland Park Blvd, Suite 200,
Lauderdale Lakes FL 33313-7261
County: Broward Identification: 666269
Unit ID: 443438
Telephone: (954) 587-7100 Carnegie Class: Assoc/PrivFP
FAX Number: (954) 587-7704 Calendar System: Other
URL: www.medvance.edu
Established: 2003 Annual Undergrad Tuition & Fees: $13,600
Enrollment: 425 Coed
Affiliation or Control: Proprietary IRS Status: Proprietary
Highest Offering: Associate Degree
Program: Occupational
Accreditation: ABHES, MLTAD, RAD, SURGT, SURTEC

01 Director .... Mr. Michael BEAUREGARD

† Branch campus of MedVance Institute, Baton Rouge, LA.

Meridian College (F)

7020 Professioinal Pkwy E, Sarasota FL 34240
County: Sarasota FICE Identification: 023268
Unit ID: 244279
Telephone: (941) 377-4880 Carnegie Class: Not Classified
FAX Number: (941) 378-2842 Calendar System: Other
URL: www.meridian.edu
Established: 1982 Annual Undergrad Tuition & Fees: $15,600
Enrollment: 89 Coed
Affiliation or Control: Proprietary IRS Status: Proprietary
Highest Offering: Associate Degree
Program: Occupational
Accreditation: ACCSC

01 President .... Mr. Wayne A. SLATER

Miami Ad School (G)

955 Alton Road, Miami Beach FL 33139-5203
County: Miami-Dade FICE Identification: 031256
Unit ID: 428000
Telephone: (305) 538-3193 Carnegie Class: Assoc/PrivFP
FAX Number: (305) 538-3724 Calendar System: Quarter
URL: www.miamiadschool.com
Established: 1993 Annual Undergrad Tuition & Fees: $17,400
Enrollment: 181 Coed
Affiliation or Control: Proprietary IRS Status: Proprietary
Highest Offering: Associate Degree
Program: Occupational
Accreditation: COE

01 President .... Ms. Pipa SEICHRIST

Miami Dade College (H)

300 NE Second Avenue, Miami FL 33132-2296
County: Miami-Dade County FICE Identification: 001506
Unit ID: 135717
Telephone: (305) 237-8888 Carnegie Class: Assoc/Pub4
FAX Number: (305) 237-7913 Calendar System: Semester
URL: www.mdc.edu/main/
Established: 1960 Annual Undergrad Tuition & Fees (In-State): $3,366
Enrollment: 59,570 Coed
Affiliation or Control: State IRS Status: 501(c)3
Highest Offering: Baccalaureate
Program: Occupational; 2-Year Principally Bachelor's Creditable; Liberal Arts And General; Teacher Preparatory
Accreditation: SC, ADNUR, ARCPA, ART, DANCE, DH, DMS, EMT, FUSER, HT, MLTAD, MUS, NUR, OPD, PTAA, RAD, THEA

01 College President .... Dr. Eduardo J. PADRON
05 College Provost .... Dr. Rolando MONTOYA
10 Sr Vice Provost Business Affairs .... Mr. E. H. LEVERING
13 Interim Vice Provost Info Tech .... Ms. Ruth Ann BALLA
18 Interim Vice Provost Facilities .... Mr. Patrick REBULL
15 Vice Provost Human Resources .... Ms. Iliana CASTILLO-FRICK
09 Assoc Provost Inst Effectiveness .... Dr. Joanne BASHFORD
20 Vice Provost for Education .... Dr. Pamela MENKE
12 Campus President Hialeah .... Vacant
12 Campus President Kendall .... Dr. Lourdes OROZA
12 Campus President Medical .... Dr. Armando FERRER
12 Campus President North .... Dr. Jose VICENTE
12 Interim Campus President Wolfson .... Ms. Madeline PUMARIEGA
12 Campus President Homestead .... Dr. Jeanne JACOBS
12 Campus President InterAmerican .... Dr. Gina CORTES-SUAREZ
21 Assoc Vice Prov Business Affs .... Mr. Gregory KNOTT
32 Director Student Services .... Dr. Rene GARCIA
102 Exec Director MDC Foundation .... Mr. L. J RODRIGUEZ
37 Collegewide Financial Aid Director .... Ms. Mercedes AMAYA
93 Director Employee Relations/EOP/ADA .... Dr. Joy C. RUFF
07 Collegewide Director Admissions .... Ms. Dulce BELTRAN
26 Chief Public Rels Officer/Dir Comm .... Mr. Juan MENDIETA
29 Director Annual Giving/Alumni Rels .... Ms. Nairobi ABRAMS
35 Chief Student Life Officer .... Ms. Teresa REIGOSA
36 Dir Testing Admin/Pgm Evaluation .... Mr. Silvio RODRIGUEZ
28 Director of Diversity .... Dr. Joy C. RUFF
38 Director Student Advisement .... Ms. Paola DOCUMET
84 Director Enrollment Management .... Dr. Rene GARCIA
96 Director of Purchasing .... Mr. Roman MARTINEZ
41 Director Athletics & Student Life .... Mr. Anthony FIORENZA
06 Collegewide Registrar .... Ms. Dulce BELTRAN
09 Director of Institutional Research .... Dr. David M. KAISER
43 Legal Counsel .... Ms. Carmen DOMINGUEZ
86 Director Governmental Affairs .... Ms. Victoria HERNANDEZ
100 Chief of Staff .... Mr. George ANDREWS
103 Dean Workforce Education & Develop .... Vacant
104 Int Program Manager Study Abroad .... Ms. Eva FERNANDEZ
105 College Webmaster .... Mr. Andrew SEAGA
08 Head Librarian/Dir Learning Resourc .... Ms. Isabel HERNANDEZ
85 Director Foreign Students .... Ms. Tere COLLADA

Miami International University of Art & Design (I)

1501 Biscayne Boulevard, Suite 100,
Miami FL 33132-1418
County: Miami-Dade FICE Identification: 008878
Unit ID: 134811
Telephone: (305) 428-5700 Carnegie Class: Spec/Arts
FAX Number: (305) 374-7946 Calendar System: Quarter
URL: www.aimiu.aii.edu
Established: 1965 Annual Undergrad Tuition & Fees: $17,704
Enrollment: 4,068 Coed
Affiliation or Control: Proprietary IRS Status: Proprietary
Highest Offering: Master's
Program: Fine Arts Emphasis
Accreditation: SC, CIDA

01 President .... Ms. Erika FLEMING
05 Chief Academic Officer .... Mr. Paul COX
10 Dir Admin & Financial Services .... Mr. Joseph GIANNATTASIO
32 Dean of Student Affairs .... Mr. John OSBORNE
07 Director of Admissions .... Mr. Kevin RYAN
08 Librarian .... Mr. Daniel CROMER

Millennia Atlantic University (J)

3801 NW 97th Avenue, Doral FL 33178
County: Miami-Dade FICE Identification: 041825
Unit ID: 461883
Telephone: (786) 331-1000 Carnegie Class: Not Classified
FAX Number: (305) 591-9507 Calendar System: Semester
URL: www.maufl.edu
Established: N/A Annual Undergrad Tuition & Fees: $7,400
Enrollment: 70 Coed
Affiliation or Control: Proprietary IRS Status: Proprietary
Highest Offering: Master's
Program: Business Emphasis
Accreditation: ACICS

01 President .... Dr. Aristides MAZA-DUERTO

North Florida Community College (K)

325 NW Turner Davis Drive, Madison FL 32340-1610
County: Madison FICE Identification: 001508
Unit ID: 136145
Telephone: (850) 973-2288 Carnegie Class: Assoc/Pub-R-S
FAX Number: (850) 973-1696 Calendar System: Semester
URL: www.nfcc.edu
Established: 1958 Annual Undergrad Tuition & Fees (In-State): $2,994
Enrollment: 1,610 Coed
Affiliation or Control: State IRS Status: 501(c)3
Highest Offering: Associate Degree
Program: Occupational; 2-Year Principally Bachelor's Creditable
Accreditation: SC

01 President Mr. John GROSSKOPF
05 Dean of Academic Affairs/CAO Dr. Sharon ERLE
11 Dean Administrative Svcs & CBO Ms. Amelia MULKEY
07 Dean of Enrollment/Student Services Ms. Mary Anne WHEELER
09 Manager of Networking Systems Mr. John SIRMON
15 Director of Personnel Services Mr. Bill HUNTER
08 Head Librarian Ms. Kay HOGAN
88 SSS and Disability Coordinator Ms. Nancy LILLIS
88 Director of Public Safety Academy Mr. Rick DAVIS
06 Registrar Ms. Lori PLEASANT
18 Chief Facilities/Physical Plant Mr. Dale HACKLE
21 Controller Ms. Edna EALY
26 Public Information Officer Ms. Kim SCARBORO
29 Dir Foundation Alumni Relations Mrs. Gina RUTHERFORD
37 Director Student Financial Aid Ms. Peggy HARRIS
28 Director of Diversity Ms. Denise BELL
32 Director Student Services Ms. Kim HALFHILL
96 Director of Purchasing Ms. Sarah NEWSOME

Northwest Florida State College (A)

100 College Boulevard, Niceville FL 32578-1295
County: Okaloosa FICE Identification: 001510
Unit ID: 136233
Telephone: (850) 678-5111 Carnegie Class: Assoc/Pub4
FAX Number: (850) 729-5215 Calendar System: Semester
URL: www.nwfsc.edu
Established: 1963 Annual Undergrad Tuition & Fees (In-District): $3,070
Enrollment: 10,051 Coed
Affiliation or Control: Local IRS Status: 501(c)3
Highest Offering: Baccalaureate
Program: Occupational; 2-Year Principally Bachelor's Creditable; Liberal Arts And General; Teacher Preparatory; Professional
Accreditation: SC, DA, NURSE

01 President Dr. Ty HANDY
05 Vice Pres for Instruction Dr. Sasha JARRELL
11 Vice Pres Administrative Services Dr. Gary YANCEY
27 Chief Information Officer Mr. Greg ELLER
09 Director of Institutional Research Dr. Diane W. HODGINS
10 Assoc Vice Pres Business Services Ms. Donna K. UTLEY
25 Contract Administrator Dr. Anne SOUTHARD
15 Director Human Resources/Diversity Ms. Nancy MURPHY
07 Director of Admissions Ms. Martha LITTLE
29 Assoc Director for Resource/Alumni Ms. Carla REINLIE
41 Interim Athletic Director Mr. Ramsey ROSS
37 Director Financial Aid/Veteran Affs Ms. Patricia BENNETT
18 Facilities Director Mr. Sam JONES
44 Dir Resource Dev/College Foundation Mrs. Cristie KEDROSKI
36 Director Student Counseling Ms. Dianne AVILLION
08 Director Learning Resources Center Ms. Janice HENDERSON
26 Director Marketing/Public Relations Ms. Sylvia BRYAN
96 Coordinator of Purchasing Ms. Dedria LUNDERMAN
06 Dean of Students Ms. Christine C. BISHOP
04 Adm Assistant to President Ms. Carolyn LAUX

Nova Southeastern University (B)

3301 College Avenue, Fort Lauderdale FL 33314-7796
County: Broward FICE Identification: 001509
Unit ID: 136215
Telephone: (954) 262-7300 Carnegie Class: RU/H
FAX Number: (954) 262-3800 Calendar System: Other
URL: www.nova.edu
Established: 1964 Annual Undergrad Tuition & Fees: $23,850
Enrollment: 28,457 Coed
Affiliation or Control: Independent Non-Profit IRS Status: 501(c)3
Highest Offering: Doctorate
Program: Liberal Arts And General; Teacher Preparatory; Professional
Accreditation: SC, AA, ACAE, ARCPA, AUD, CLPSY, DENT, DMS, IACBE, IPSY, LAW, MFCD, NURSE, OPT, OPTR, OSTEO, OT, PH, PHAR, PTA, SP

01 President Dr. George L. HANBURY, II
05 Exec VP & Provost for Acad Affs Dr. Frank DE PIANO
11 Exec Vice Pres/COO Vacant
10 Executive Director Finance Ms. Alyson SYLVA
00 Chancellor Nova Southeastern Univ Mr. Ray FERRERO, JR.
17 Chancellor Health Professions (HPD) Dr. Fred LIPPMAN
20 Vice Chancellor/Provost (HPD) Dr. Irving ROSENBAUM
09 VP Institutional Effectiveness Dr. Ronald CHENAIL
86 Vice Pres Community/Govt Affairs Dr. Larry A. CALDERON
08 Vice Pres Info Svcs/Univ Librarian Ms. Lydia M. ACOSTA
43 Vice President Legal Affairs Mr. Joel BERMAN
46 Vice Pres Research Tech Transfer Dr. Gary S. MARGULES
30 Vice President Inst Advancement Vacant
18 Executive Director Facilities Mgmt Mr. Peter J. WITSCHEN
13 Vice Pres Info Tech/Chief Info Ofcr Mr. Tom WEST
15 Vice President Human Resources Mr. Robert J. PIETRYKOWSKI
37 Asc VP Stdnt Enrollment/Stdnt Svcs Dr. Stephanie BROWN
21 Assoc Vice Pres Business Services Mr. Marc CROCQUET
20 Exec Dean/Program Professor Dr. Kimberly DURHAM
26 Exec Director University Relations Mr. David DAWSON
19 Director Public Safety Mr. James EWING
09 Exec Dir of Institutional Research Vacant
45 Exec Dir Accreditation Planning Dr. Dian MOORHOUSE
24 Exec Dir Ed Tech/Digital Media Prod Vacant
25 Exec Director Grants & Contracts Ms. Barbara STERRY
86 Director Licensure/State Relations Dr. Greg F. STIBER
84 Director Enrollment Management Ms. Maria P. DILLARD
12 Headmaster University School Dr. Jerry CHERMAK
27 Director University Publications Mr. Ron RYAN
29 Director Alumni Relations Ms. Sara DUCUENNOIS
36 Director of Career Development Ms. Shari SAPERSTEIN
06 University Registrar Ms. Elaine G. POFF
41 Director of Athletics Mr. Michael MOMINEY
39 Dir Residential Life & Housing Ms. Aarika CAMP
96 Director of Purchasing Mr. Mike COROMINAS
23 Asst Dir of Campus Recreation Mr. Tom VIRTUCCI
26 Director of Public Affairs Ms. Julie SPECHLER
63 Dean College Osteopathic Medicine Dr. Anthony SILVAGNI
67 Dean College Pharmacy Dr. Andres MALAVE
88 Dean College Optometry Dr. David LOSHIN
76 Dean College Allied Health Dr. Richard E. DAVIS
77 Dean Grad Sch Computer/Info Sci Dr. Eric ACKERMAN
61 Dean Shepard Broad Law Center Mr. Athornia STEELE
65 Dean Oceanographic Center Dr. Richard DODGE
50 Int Dn W Huizenga Grad Sch Bus/Entr Dr. J. Preston JONES
49 Dean Farquhar Col Arts & Sciences Dr. Donald ROSENBLUM
88 Dean Center Psychological Stds Ms. Karen GROSBY
83 Dean Grad Sch Humanities/Social Sci Dr. Honggang YANG
53 Dean Sch Education & Human Services Dr. H. Wells SINGLETON
88 Dean Mailman Segal Institute Dr. Roni LEIDERMAN
63 Dean College of Medical Sciences Dr. Harold LAUBAUCH
52 Dean College of Dental Medicine Dr. Robert A. UCHIN
35 Dean of Student Affairs Dr. Brad WILLIAMS

Palm Beach Atlantic University (C)

901 S. Flagler Drive, West Palm Beach FL 33401
County: Palm Beach FICE Identification: 008849
Unit ID: 136330
Telephone: (561) 803-2000 Carnegie Class: Master's M
FAX Number: (561) 803-2186 Calendar System: Semester
URL: www.pba.edu
Established: 1968 Annual Undergrad Tuition & Fees: $24,800
Enrollment: 3,663 Coed
Affiliation or Control: Interdenominational IRS Status: 501(c)3
Highest Offering: Doctorate
Program: Occupational; Liberal Arts And General; Teacher Preparatory; Professional
Accreditation: SC, IACBE, MUS, NURSE, PHAR

01 President Mr. William B. FLEMING
05 Provost Dr. Joseph A. KLOBA
11 Sr VP for Finance Admin & Plng Mr. John KAUTZ, III
04 Executive Asst to President Mr. Tim WORLEY
30 Vice President Development Mrs. Viki PUGH
32 Vice President Student Development Vacant
09 Asst Vice Pres Rsrch/Effectiveness Mrs. Carolanne BROWN
27 Assoc VP Campus Information Svcs Mr. Phillip MAJOR
26 Assoc VP Univ Relations & Marketing Mrs. Rebecca PEELING
51 Dean MacArthur School of Leadership Dr. James A. LAUB
49 Dean School of Arts & Sciences Dr. J. Barton STARR
50 Interim Dean School of Business Dr. Leslie TURNER
53 Dean School of Education Dr. Gene SALE
57 Dean School of Music/Fine Arts Dr. Lloyd MIMS
66 Dean School of Nursing Dr. Joanne MASELLA
67 Dean Gregory School of Pharmacy Dr. Mary FERRILL
60 Dean School Communication/Media Dr. J. Duane MEEKS
73 Dean School of Ministry Dr. Randy RICHARDS
06 Registrar Ms. Audrey SCHOFIELD
08 Dean of the Library Mr. Steven BAKER
20 Dean of Faculty Vacant
15 Assoc VP of Human Resources Ms. Mona L. HICKS
18 Director of Physical Plant Mr. Michael STEGER
21 Controller Mrs. Renae MURRAY
29 AVP Alumni Relations/Annual Fund Ms. Delesa MORRIS
31 Coordinator Community Services Mrs. Cindy LAMERSON
38 Director of Student Success Center Mrs. Andrea DYBEN
37 Director of Financial Aid Mr. Todd MARTIN
35 Dean of Students Mr. Kevin ABEL
40 Director of Campus Store Mrs. Abbie ROSEMEYER
41 Director of Athletics Mrs. Carolyn STONE
42 Director of Campus Ministries Mr. Mark KAPRIVE
19 Director of Safety & Security Mr. Terry WHEELER
92 Director of Supper Honors Program Dr. Tom ST. ANTOINE
07 Dean of Admissions Mr. Joe SHARP

Palm Beach State College (D)

4200 Congress Avenue, Lake Worth FL 33461-4796
County: Palm Beach FICE Identification: 001512
Unit ID: 136358
Telephone: (561) 967-7222 Carnegie Class: Assoc/Pub-S-MC
FAX Number: (561) 868-3504 Calendar System: Semester
URL: www.palmbeachstate.edu
Established: 1933 Annual Undergrad Tuition & Fees (In-District): $2,947
Enrollment: 29,354 Coed
Affiliation or Control: Local IRS Status: 501(c)3
Highest Offering: Baccalaureate
Program: Occupational; 2-Year Principally Bachelor's Creditable
Accreditation: SC, ADNUR, DA, DH, DMS, EMT, MAC, RAD, SURGT

01 President Dr. Dennis P. GALLON
05 Vice President for Academic Affairs Dr. Sharon A. SASS
10 Vice President Admin/Business Svcs Mr. Richard A. BECKER
32 Vice President for Student Services Dr. Peter BARBATIS
102 CEO Foundation Ms. Suellen MANN
12 Provost Glades Center Vacant
12 Provost South Campus Dr. Bernadette MENDONEZ RUSSELL
12 Provost Eissey Campus Dr. Jean WIHBEY
12 Provost Central Campus Dr. Maria M. VALLEJO
35 Dean Student Services/Central Ms. Penny J. MCISAAC
35 Dean Student Services/Boca Raton Ms. Nicole P. BANKS
35 Dean Student Services/Eissey Mr. Scott MACLACHLAN
35 Dean Educational Services/Glades Dr. Barry L. MOORE
84 Dean Enrollment Management Vacant
103 Dean Workforce Ms. Patricia V. RICHIE
37 Director Financial Aid Ms. Susan KADIR
41 Dir Student Activities/Athletics Mr. David HOLSTEIN
09 Dir Institutional Effectiveness Dr. Jennifer D. CAMPBELL
86 Director Government Relations Ms. Erin S. MCCOLSKEY
18 Director Facilities Mr. John T. WASUKANIS
15 Director Human Resources Dr. Ellen GRACE
26 Dir College Relations & Marketing Dr. Grace H. TRUMAN
21 Controller Mr. James E. DUFFIE
06 Registrar/Director Admissions Mr. Edward MUELLER
96 Director of Purchasing Ms. Jodi HART
27 Chief Information Officer Mr. Anthony PARZIALE
13 Director Information Technology Mr. Chuck H. ZETTLER
29 Director Alumni Relations Ms. Suellen MANN
25 Manager Grant Development Ms. Maureen CAPP
88 Project Reports Coordinator Ms. Karen M. LIPPE

Palmer College of Chiropractic, Florida Campus (E)

4777 City Center Parkway, Port Orange FL 32129-4153
County: Volusia Identification: 666330
Telephone: (386) 763-2709 Carnegie Class: Not Classified
FAX Number: (386) 763-2635 Calendar System: Quarter
URL: www.palmer.edu
Established: 2002 Annual Undergrad Tuition & Fees: $8,195
Enrollment: N/A Coed
Affiliation or Control: Independent Non-Profit IRS Status: 501(c)3
Highest Offering: First Professional Degree
Program: Professional
Accreditation: &NH, CHIRO

00 Chancellor Dr. Dennis M. MARCHIORI
01 President Dr. Peter A. MARTIN
05 Vice Chancellor for Academics Dr. Robert E. PERCUOCO
32 Vice Chancellor Student Success Dr. Kevin A. CUNNINGHAM
11 Vice Chancellor Support Services Mr. Robert E. LEE
84 Vice Chancellor for Enrollment Mr. J. Michael NOVAK
10 Vice Chancellor for Administration Mr. Thomas L. TIEMEIER
17 Vice Chancellor for Clinic Affairs Dr. Kurt W. WOOD
46 Vice Chancellor for Research Dr. Christine G. GOERTZ
26 Exec Dir for Marketing & PR Mr. Darren R. GARRETT
29 Executive Director for Alumni Dr. Mickey G. BURT
88 Exec Dir Office of Strategic Dev Dr. Judy M. SILVESTRONE
20 Dean of Academic Affairs Dr. Donald F. GRAN
21 Senior Dir for Financial Affairs Ms. Alexis A. VANDERHORN
13 Senior Director IT Mr. Mike A. BENEDICT
09 Sr Dir Institutional Plng/Research Dr. Dustin C. DERBY
40 Senior Director of Bookstores Ms. Carol A. HOYT
15 Sr Director of Human Resources Ms. Michelle K. WALKER
24 Sr Dir/Center for Teaching/Lrng Dr. Dana J. LAWRENCE
108 Senior Director for Assessment Vacant
07 Campus Enrollment Director Ms. Jessica BLUMENFELD
46 Director of Research Dr. Liang ZHANG
37 Manager of Financial Planning Ms. Carmen AFGHANI
35 Director of Student Services Ms. Melissa L. LINGO
23 Dean of Clinics Dr. Albert J. LUCE
06 Registrar Mr. Jason BREWER
08 Librarian Mr. Daniel W. WRIGHT

† Regional accreditation is carried under the parent institution in Davenport, IA.

Pasco-Hernando Community College (F)

10230 Ridge Road, New Port Richey FL 34654-5199
County: Pasco FICE Identification: 010652
Unit ID: 136400
Telephone: (727) 847-2727 Carnegie Class: Assoc/Pub-S-MC
FAX Number: (727) 816-1815 Calendar System: Semester
URL: www.phcc.edu
Established: 1972 Annual Undergrad Tuition & Fees (In-District): $3,035
Enrollment: 11,390 Coed
Affiliation or Control: State/Local IRS Status: 501(c)3
Highest Offering: Associate Degree
Program: Occupational; 2-Year Principally Bachelor's Creditable
Accreditation: SC, ADNUR, DH, EMT

01 President Dr. Katherine M. JOHNSON
05 VP Instruction/Prov West Campus Dr. Burt H. HARRES, JR.
32 VP Stdnt Devel/Enrollment Mgmt Dr. Timothy L. BEARD
10 Vice Pres Administration & Finance Mr. Kenneth R. BURDZINSKI
12 Provost of the East Campus Dr. Randall H. STOVALL
12 Provost of the North Campus Dr. Stanley M. GIANNET
12 Assoc Provost Spring Hill Campus Ms. Bonnie M. CLARK
103 Dean of Workforce Development Mr. Edwin G. GOOLSBY
24 Dean of Institutional Technology Mr. Paul G. WRIGHT
20 Asst Dean Instructional Services Ms. Jeanne F. GASQUE
17 Dean Health Occupations Ms. Jayme S. ROTHBERG
49 Dean Arts and Sciences Dr. John L. WHITLOCK
35 Assoc Dean Student Act/Engagement Mr. Robert E. BADE
21 Dean Admin/Finance/Comptroller Mr. Brian S. HORN
84 Dean Student Enroll/Retention Ms. Donna R. BURDZINSKI
09 Assoc Dean Institutional Effective Dr. Gerardine COCHRAN
13 Director of Management Info Svcs Ms. Janice L. SCOTT
30 Dea Inst Advancement/Exec Dir Found Ms. Arla S. ALTMAN

66 Associate Dean of Nursing .... Ms. Billie J. GABBARD
07 Dir Admissions & Student Records .... Vacant
37 Asst Dean Financial Aid/Vet Svcs ..... Ms. Rebecca S. SHANAFELT
43 Gen Counsel/Exec Dir Govt Relations .... Mr. Stephen C. SCHROEDER
08 Director of Libraries .... Mr. Raymond J. CALVERT
41 Athletics Director/Instructor .... Mr. James E. JOHNSON
26 Exec Dir Marketing/Public Relation .... Ms. Lucy T. MILLER
18 Director of Facilities .... Mr. Keith V. BRAUN
15 Exec Director of Human Resources .... Ms. Vivian M. FRIEND
40 Auxiliary Services Manager .... Mr. John D. COLLINS
28 Coord of Disabilities Services .... Mr. Ron THIESSEN
22 Dist Coord Multicul Std Affs/Eq Svc .... Mr. Imani D. ASUKILE
96 Purchasing Agent .... Ms. Debra B. WHITTAKER

Pensacola Christian College (A)

250 Brent Lane, Pensacola FL 32503

County: Escambia — Identification: 667101
Telephone: (850) 478-8496 — Carnegie Class: Not Classified
FAX Number: (850) 479-6577 — Calendar System: Semester
URL: www.pcci.edu
Established: 1974 — Annual Undergrad Tuition & Fees: $5,420
Enrollment: N/A — Coed
Affiliation or Control: Independent Non-Profit — IRS Status: 501(c)3
Highest Offering: Doctorate
Program: Religious Emphasis
Accreditation: @TRACS

01 President .... Dr. Troy SHOEMAKER
05 Acting Academic Vice President .... Dr. Raylene COCHRAN

Pensacola State College (B)

1000 College Boulevard, Pensacola FL 32504-8998

County: Escambia — FICE Identification: 001513
Unit ID: 136473
Telephone: (850) 484-1000 — Carnegie Class: Assoc/Pub-R-L
FAX Number: (850) 484-1826 — Calendar System: Semester
URL: www.pensacolastate.edu
Established: 1948 — Annual Undergrad Tuition & Fees (In-District): $2,902
Enrollment: 11,531 — Coed
Affiliation or Control: Local — IRS Status: 501(c)3
Highest Offering: Baccalaureate
Program: 2-Year Principally Bachelor's Creditable
Accreditation: SC, ACFEI, ADNUR, DH, EMT, MAC, PTAA, RAD, SURGT

01 President .... Dr. Ed MEADOWS
05 Vice Pres for Academic Affairs .... Dr. Erin SPICER
32 Vice President Student Affairs .... Mr. Tom GILLIAM
10 Vice President for Business .... Mrs. Gean Ann EMOND
103 VP Workforce Educ/Academic Support .... Mr. Dan BUSSE
12 Dean Milton Campus .... Ms. Anthea AMOS
12 Dean Warrington Campus .... Ms. Frances DUNCAN
28 Assoc Vice Pres Inst Diversity .... Dr. Gael FRAZER
30 Exec Dir Col Devel/Alumni Affairs .... Ms. Patrice WHITTEN
13 Int Director MIS/Telecom Systems .... Mr. Bert MERRITT
86 Exec Director of Govt Relations .... Mr. Larry BRACKEN
26 Director Marketing & College Info .... Ms. Sheila NICHOLS
06 Registrar .... Ms. Martha CAUGHEY
09 Dean Instnl Effectiveness & Grants .... Dr. Debbie DOUMA
18 Director Physical Plant .... Mr. Walt WINTER
14 Director Computer Svcs/Telecommun .... Mr. William MELOY
15 Director Human Resources/EA/EO .... Ms. Tammy HENDERSON
37 Dir Fin Aid/Veteran Affairs/Scholar .... Ms. Karen KESSLER
36 Director Student Job Services .... Mr. Gil BIXEL
19 Public Safety Director .... Mr. Hank SHIRAH
43 General Counsel .... Mr. Thomas J. GILLIAM
35 Director Student Life .... Mr. Peter WILKIN
08 Int District Dept Head Libraries .... Ms. Winifred BRADLEY
96 Director of Purchasing .... Ms. Cassie BOATWRIGHT
21 Associate Business Officer .... Ms. Jackie PADILLA
29 Director Alumni Relations .... Vacant
07 Director of Admissions .... Ms. Martha CAUGHEY
38 Director Student Counseling .... Ms. Kathy DUTREMBLE
41 Director Athletics .... Mr. Bill HAMILTON
84 Director Enrollment Management .... Ms. Kathy DUTREMBLE
12 Director South Santa Rosa Center .... Ms. Michele HORTON
12 Director Century Center .... Ms. Paula JERNIGAN
31 Coordinator Community Education .... Ms. Frances YEO

Polk State College (C)

999 Avenue H, NE, Winter Haven FL 33881-4299

County: Polk — FICE Identification: 001514
Unit ID: 136516
Telephone: (863) 297-1000 — Carnegie Class: Assoc/Pub-R-L
FAX Number: (863) 297-1065 — Calendar System: Trimester
URL: www.polk.edu
Established: 1964 — Annual Undergrad Tuition & Fees (In-District): $3,114
Enrollment: 11,529 — Coed
Affiliation or Control: Local — IRS Status: 501(c)3
Highest Offering: Baccalaureate
Program: Occupational; 2-Year Principally Bachelor's Creditable; Technical Emphasis
Accreditation: SC, ADNUR, CVT, DMS, EMT, OTA, PTAA, RAD

01 President .... Dr. Eileen HOLDEN
05 Vice Pres Academic/Student Svcs .... Dr. Ken ROSS
30 Vice Pres Development .... Ms. Tracy PORTER
10 Vice President Administration/CFO .... Mr. Peter A. ELLIOTT
26 Assoc VP Communications/Public Affs .... Mr. David STEELE
32 Dean Student Services-Lakeland .... Mr. Reggie WEBB
32 Dean Student Services-Winter Haven .... Dr. Saul REYES
20 District Dn Academic/Student Svcs .... Dr. Patricia JONES
12 Provost Lakeland Campus .... Mr. Stephen E. HULL
12 Provost Winter Haven Campus .... Dr. Sharon MILLER
66 Director of Nursing .... Dr. Annette HUTCHERSON
06 Registrar .... Ms. Kathy BUCKLEW
21 Comptroller .... Ms. Teresa VOROUS
18 District Director Facilities .... Mr. George URBANO
37 Director Financial Aid .... Ms. Marcia CONLIFFE
22 Director of Equity & Diversity .... Ms. Val BAKER
41 Athletic Diredtor .... Mr. Bing TYUS
09 Dir Inst Research/Effective/Plng .... Mr. Peter USINGER
15 Director Personnel Services .... Ms. Jill HALL
84 Director Enrollment Management .... Mr. Reginald WEBB
96 Director of Purchasing .... Ms. Wendy GELTCH

Polytechnic University Puerto Rico (D)

8180 NW 36th Street, Suite 401, Miami FL 33166-6674

County: Miami-Dade — Identification: 666238
Unit ID: 456481
Telephone: (305) 418-4220 — Carnegie Class: Spec/Bus
FAX Number: (305) 418-4325 — Calendar System: Trimester
URL: www.pupr.edu
Established: 2001 — Annual Undergrad Tuition & Fees: $12,900
Enrollment: 136 — Coed
Affiliation or Control: Independent Non-Profit — IRS Status: 501(c)3
Highest Offering: Master's
Program: Professional; Technical Emphasis
Accreditation: &M

01 President .... Mr. Ernesto VAZQUEZ-BARQUET
03 VP & Campus Director .... Mr. Jose ORLANDO RIVERA
05 Vice Pres Academic Affairs .... Dr. Miguel RIESTRA
20 Academic Director .... Mr. Ernesto CASTRO
11 Vice Pres Administration/Finance .... Mr. Ernesto R. VASQUEZ-MARTINEZ
07 Director of Admissions .... Ms. Teresa CARDONA
37 Dir of Financial Aid/HR Coordinator .... Mr. Sergio VILLOLDO
06 Registrar .... Ms. Diana DEL NODAL
04 Administrative Assistant .... Ms. Haydee OPERO

† Regional accreditation is carried under the parent institution, Universidad Politecnica de Puerto Rico, San Juan, PR.

Professional Golfers Career College (E)

16349 Phil Ritson Way, Winter Garden FL 34787

County: Orange — Identification: 666300
Telephone: (407) 905-2200 — Carnegie Class: Not Classified
FAX Number: (407) 905-2241 — Calendar System: Semester
URL: www.golfcollege.edu
Established: 2005 — Annual Undergrad Tuition & Fees: $13,000
Enrollment: 185 — Coed
Affiliation or Control: Proprietary — IRS Status: Proprietary
Highest Offering: Associate Degree
Program: Occupational
Accreditation: ACICS

01 President .... Mr. Tim SOMMERVILLE
10 Chief Financial Officer .... Ms. Sandi SOMMERVILLE

Professional Training Center (F)

13926 SW 47th Street, Miami FL 33175-4404

County: Miami-Dade — FICE Identification: 033484
Unit ID: 436702
Telephone: (305) 220-4120 — Carnegie Class: Assoc/PrivFP
FAX Number: (305) 220-2889 — Calendar System: Other
URL: www.ptcmatt.com
Established: 1994 — Annual Undergrad Tuition & Fees: $38,595
Enrollment: 544 — Coed
Affiliation or Control: Proprietary — IRS Status: Proprietary
Highest Offering: Baccalaureate
Program: Occupational; 2-Year Principally Bachelor's Creditable
Accreditation: ACICS, RAD

01 Chief Executive Officer .... Mr. Antonio MATTIA
11 Vice President Operations .... Mr. Marc MATTIA
06 Academic Registrar .... Mr. John KRAMER
07 Director of Admissions .... Vacant
15 Human Resources Director .... Ms. Jeannie HIDALGO
37 Student Finance Director .... Ms. Angie GUTIERREZ
32 Student Services Director .... Vacant
36 Placement Director .... Vacant
08 Librarian .... Ms. Ophelia WIETZ
51 Continuing Education Dept Director .... Ms. Michelle PENA
97 Dir of Assoc & General Education .... Vacant
67 Pharmacy Director .... Mrs. Alicia TUMA
76 Diagnostic Med Sonography Pgm Dir .. Dr. Victor M. FERNANDEZ
88 Imaging Director .... Vacant

Rasmussen College - Fort Myers (G)

9160 Forum Corporate Parkway, Fort Myers FL 33905

County: Lee — Identification: 667062
Unit ID: 13830902
Telephone: (239) 477-2100 — Carnegie Class: Not Classified
FAX Number: (239) 477-2101 — Calendar System: Quarter
URL: www.rasmussen.edu
Established: 1900 — Annual Undergrad Tuition & Fees: $16,340
Enrollment: 676 — Coed
Affiliation or Control: Proprietary — IRS Status: Proprietary
Highest Offering: Baccalaureate
Program: Occupational; 2-Year Principally Bachelor's Creditable
Accreditation: &NH, MAAB

01 Campus Director .... Eric WHITEHOUSE

† Regional accreditation is carried under the parent institution in Lake Elmo, MN.

Rasmussen College - New Port Richey (H)

7660 Little Road, New Port Richey FL 34654

Identification: 666425
Unit ID: 138336
Telephone: (727) 942-0069 — Carnegie Class: Bac/Assoc
FAX Number: (727) 938-5709 — Calendar System: Quarter
URL: www.rasmussen.edu
Established: 1968 — Annual Undergrad Tuition & Fees: $16,340
Enrollment: 946 — Coed
Affiliation or Control: Proprietary — IRS Status: Proprietary
Highest Offering: Baccalaureate
Program: Occupational; 2-Year Principally Bachelor's Creditable
Accreditation: &NH, MAAB

01 Campus Director .... Mrs. Claire WALKER

† Regional accreditation is carried under parent institution in Lake Elmo, MN.

Rasmussen College - Ocala (I)

4755 SW 46th Court, Ocala FL 34474

County: Marion — FICE Identification: 008501
Unit ID: 138309
Telephone: (352) 629-1941 — Carnegie Class: Bac/Assoc
FAX Number: (352) 629-0926 — Calendar System: Quarter
URL: www.rasmussen.edu
Established: 1968 — Annual Undergrad Tuition & Fees: $16,340
Enrollment: 1,318 — Coed
Affiliation or Control: Proprietary — IRS Status: Proprietary
Highest Offering: Baccalaureate
Program: Occupational; 2-Year Principally Bachelor's Creditable
Accreditation: &NH, MAAB

01 Campus Director .... Mr. Pete BEASLEY

† Regional accreditation carried under the parent institution in Lake Elmo, MN.

Rasmussen College - Tampa/Brandon (J)

4042 Park Oaks Boulevard, Tampa FL 33610

County: Hillsborough — Identification: 667067
Unit ID: 13830903
Telephone: (813) 246-7600 — Carnegie Class: Not Classified
FAX Number: (813) 621-4835 — Calendar System: Quarter
URL: www.rasmussen.edu
Established: 1900 — Annual Undergrad Tuition & Fees: $16,340
Enrollment: 18 — Coed
Affiliation or Control: Proprietary — IRS Status: Proprietary
Highest Offering: Baccalaureate
Program: Occupational; 2-Year Principally Bachelor's Creditable
Accreditation: &NH

01 Campus Director .... Margaret COOK

† Regional accreditation is carried under the parent institution in Lake Elmo, MN.

Reformed Theological Seminary (K)

1231 Reformation Drive, Oviedo FL 32765-7197

County: Seminole — Identification: 666628
Unit ID: 372763
Telephone: (407) 366-9493 — Carnegie Class: Not Classified
FAX Number: (407) 366-9425 — Calendar System: Semester
URL: www.rts.edu
Established: 1989 — Annual Graduate Tuition & Fees: $14,665
Enrollment: 502 — Coed
Affiliation or Control: Independent Non-Profit — IRS Status: 501(c)3
Highest Offering: Doctorate; No Undergraduates
Program: Professional; Religious Emphasis
Accreditation: &SC, &THEOL

00 Chancellor & CEO .... Dr. Michael A. MILTON
01 President .... Dr. Donald W. SWEETING
11 Vice President of Administration .... Mr. Robert E. EMEOTT
30 Chief Development Officer .... Rev. Lynwood C. PEREZ
05 Academic Dean .... Dr. Scott R. SWAIN
32 Dean of Students .... Dr. Robert H. ORNER
07 Director of Admissions .... Dr. Kevin COLLINS
06 Registrar .... Mr. Lanny CONLEY
58 Director of Doctor of Ministry .... Dr. Steven L. CHILDERS
08 Library Director .... Mr. John R. MUETHER
40 Bookstore Manager .... Mr. Greg THOMPSON
18 Superv Facilities/Physical Plant .... Mr. Gary MILLER

04 Assistant to the President .... Ms. Cristi MANSFIELD

† Regional accreditation is carried under the parent institution in Jackson, MS.

Remington College-Tampa Campus (A)

6302 E Martin Luther King Dr, #400, Tampa FL 33619
County: Hillsborough FICE Identification: 007586
Unit ID: 135939
Telephone: (813) 935-5700 Carnegie Class: Bac/Assoc
FAX Number: (813) 935-7415 Calendar System: Quarter
URL: www.remingtoncollege.edu
Established: 1948 Annual Undergrad Tuition & Fees: $15,478
Enrollment: 177 Coed
Affiliation or Control: Proprietary IRS Status: Proprietary
Highest Offering: Baccalaureate
Program: Occupational; Technical Emphasis
Accreditation: ACCSC, NURSE

01 President .... Dr. Ken HEINEMANN
06 Registrar .... Ms. Mary BALTES
36 Director Student Placement .... Ms. Deborah HOFFMAN
37 Director Student Financial Aid .... Ms. Brittany REMLIN

Ringling College of Art and Design (B)

2700 N Tamiami Trail, Sarasota FL 34234-5895
County: Sarasota FICE Identification: 012574
Unit ID: 136774
Telephone: (941) 351-5100 Carnegie Class: Spec/Arts
FAX Number: (941) 359-7517 Calendar System: Semester
URL: www.ringling.edu
Established: 1931 Annual Undergrad Tuition & Fees: $34,840
Enrollment: 1,376 Coed
Affiliation or Control: Independent Non-Profit IRS Status: 501(c)3
Highest Offering: Baccalaureate
Program: Professional; Fine Arts Emphasis
Accreditation: SC, ART, CIDA

01 President .... Dr. Larry R. THOMPSON
04 Spec Asst to Pres Media & Cmty Rels ... Ms. Christine M. LANGE
05 Vice President for Academic Affairs .... Ms. Melody WEILER
30 Vice Pres Advancement .... Mr. Michael MOORE
10 Vice President for Finance & Admin .... Ms. Tracy A. WAGNER
15 VP Human/Organizational Development .... Ms. Christine C. DEGEORGE
32 Vice Pres Student Life/Dean Stdnts .... Dr. Tammy WALSH
20 Assoc Vice Pres Faculty Affairs .... Mr. David JACKSON
21 Asst VP for Fin & Admn/Controller .... Ms. Monica K. WAID
18 Asst VP/Dir Facilities Operations .... Mr. Jeffrey A. POLESHEK
29 Asst VP Alumni Relations/Advance .... Ms. Terri J. ARNELL
07 Dean of Admissions .... Mr. James H. DEAN
51 Director of Continuing Studies .... Ms. Diane ZORN
06 Dir Advising/Records & Registration ... Ms. Donna M. ANDERSON
44 Director of Development .... Ms. Christine P. JOHNSON
90 Director Institutional Technology .... Dr. Mahmoud PEGAH
36 Director Career Services .... Mr. Charles KOVACS
26 Dir of Marketing & Communications .... Mr. James H. DEAN
37 Director of Financial Aid .... Mr. Kurt WOLF
19 Director of Public Safety .... Mr. Richard E. TUBBS
08 Director of Library Services .... Ms. Kathleen L. LIST
09 Dir of Student Outcomes Assessment .... Dr. Alison L. WATKINS

The Robert E. Webber Institute for Worship Studies (C)

151 Kingsley Avenue, Orange Park FL 32073-5640
County: Clay Identification: 666616
Telephone: (904) 264-2172 Carnegie Class: Not Classified
FAX Number: (904) 278-2878 Calendar System: Semester
URL: www.iws.edu
Established: 1998 Annual Graduate Tuition & Fees: $4,816
Enrollment: 130 Coed
Affiliation or Control: Independent Non-Profit IRS Status: 501(c)3
Highest Offering: Doctorate; No Undergraduates
Program: Professional; Religious Emphasis
Accreditation: BI

01 Chief Executive Officer .... Dr. James R. HART
05 Chief Academic Officer .... Dr. Andrew E. HILL
10 Chief Financial Officer .... Ms. Tracie M. HARLEY
06 Registrar .... Vacant
84 Director of Enrollment Management .... Mr. Mark J. MURRAY
08 Library Director .... Ms. Carol B. SITTEMA
29 Director Alumni Relations .... Dr. Kent L. WALTERS
42 Dean of the Chapel .... Dr. Darrell A. HARRIS
106 Dir of Distance Learning Technology .... Dr. Sam L. HOROWITZ
88 Administrative Support Coordinator .... Ms. Dianna L. ANDREWS
32 Dir Student Services/Adm Asst Advan .... Ms. Sandy E. DINKINS
45 Dir Strategic Plng/Accreditation .... Dr. Steve E. HUNTLEY
13 Director of Information Technology . Dr. James Kenneth RUSHING

Rollins College (D)

1000 Holt Avenue, Winter Park FL 32789-4499
County: Orange FICE Identification: 001515
Unit ID: 136950
Telephone: (407) 646-2000 Carnegie Class: Master's L
FAX Number: (407) 646-2600 Calendar System: Semester
URL: www.rollins.edu
Established: 1885 Annual Undergrad Tuition & Fees: $39,900
Enrollment: 3,272 Coed
Affiliation or Control: Independent Non-Profit IRS Status: 501(c)3
Highest Offering: Master's
Program: Liberal Arts And General; Teacher Preparatory; Professional
Accreditation: SC, BUS, CACREP, MUS

01 President .... Dr. Lewis DUNCAN
05 Vice President Acad Affairs/Provost .... Dr. Carol BRESNAHAN
32 Interim VP for Student Affairs .... Mr. Steven NEILSON
10 Vice President Business/Finance .... Mr. Jeffrey EISENBARTH
30 VP for Institutional Advancement .... Dr. Ronald KORVAS
27 Chief Information Officer .... Dr. Pat SCHOKNECHT
49 Dean of College of Arts & Sciences .... Dr. Robert SMITHER
107 Interim Dean Col of Prof Studies .... Dr. Debra WELLMAN
51 Dean of Hamilton Holt School .... Dr. David RICHARD
35 Dean of Student Affairs .... Dr. Karen HATER
84 Dean of Enrollment Management .... Mr. David ERDMANN
50 Dean of Graduate Business School .... Dr. Craig MCALLASTER
42 Dean of the Chapel .... Dr. Patrick POWERS
08 Director of Olin Library .... Dr. Jonathan MILLER
41 Athletic Director .... Ms. Pennie PARKER
21 Assoc VP Finance/Asst Treasurer .... Mr. William SHORT
30 Assoc Vice Pres Development .... Ms. Lisa THOMSON
26 Assoc VP Marketing & Communications .... Mr. Thomas HOPE
15 Asst VP Human Res/Risk Management .... Ms. Maria MARTINEZ
20 Assistant Provost .... Dr. Toni STROLLO HOLBROOK
88 Exec Director Student Services .... Ms. Meghan HARTE
37 Director of Financial Aid .... Mr. Steve BOOKER
09 Director of Institutional Research .... Mr. Udeth LUGO
104 Director of International Programs .... Ms. Giselda BEAUDIN
07 Director of Admission .... Ms. Holly POHLIG
39 Director of Residential Life .... Mr. Leon HAYNER
36 Director of Career Services .... Mr. Ray ROGERS
38 Director of Personal Counseling .... Dr. Joanne VOGEL
35 Dir Student Involvement Leadership .... Mr. Brent TURNER
18 Director of Facilities Management .... Mr. Scott BITIKOFER
96 Director of Business Services .... Ms. Kathy WELCH
19 Campus Security Director .... Mr. Ken MILLER
29 Interim Director Alumni Relations .... Ms. Leslie CARNEY
44 Director of Annual Giving .... Ms. Leslie CARNEY
44 Director of Planned Giving .... Ms. Amanda HOPKINS
102 Director of Foundation Relations .... Mr. Joseph MONTI
40 Manager of Bookstore .... Ms. Mary VITELLI
04 Exec Assistant to the President .... Dr. Lorrie KYLE

St. John Vianney College Seminary (E)

2900 SW 87th Avenue, Miami FL 33165-3244
County: Miami-Dade FICE Identification: 008075
Unit ID: 137272
Telephone: (305) 223-4561 Carnegie Class: Spec/Faith
FAX Number: (305) 223-0650 Calendar System: Semester
URL: www.sjvcs.edu
Established: 1959 Annual Undergrad Tuition & Fees: $17,000
Enrollment: 77 Male
Affiliation or Control: Roman Catholic IRS Status: 501(c)3
Highest Offering: Baccalaureate
Program: Liberal Arts And General
Accreditation: SC

01 Rector & President .... Rev. Roberto GAZA
05 Academic Dean .... Dr. Ramon SANTOS
06 Registrar .... Mrs. Bonnie DE ANGULO
08 Librarian .... Mrs. Maria RODRIGUEZ
32 Dean of Students .... Rev. Lucian PIERRE
38 Director of Counseling .... Vacant
09 Institutional Research Director .... Dr. Jose ORTA
42 Spiritual Director .... Rev. Juan Carlos RIOS

St. Johns River State College (F)

5001 St. Johns Avenue, Palatka FL 32177-3897
County: Putnam FICE Identification: 001523
Unit ID: 137281
Telephone: (386) 312-4200 Carnegie Class: Assoc/Pub-R-L
FAX Number: (386) 312-4229 Calendar System: Semester
URL: www.sjrstate.edu
Established: 1958 Annual Undergrad Tuition & Fees (In-District): $3,120
Enrollment: 7,448 Coed
Affiliation or Control: State/Local IRS Status: 501(c)3
Highest Offering: Baccalaureate
Program: Occupational; 2-Year Principally Bachelor's Creditable; Teacher Preparatory
Accreditation: SC

01 President .... Mr. Joe PICKENS
03 Exec Vice President/General Counsel .... Dr. Melissa C. MILLER
32 Vice President Student Affairs .... Dr. Gilbert L. EVANS, JR.
05 Vice President Academic Affairs .... Dr. Melanie A. BROWN
10 Vice President Finance & Admin/CFO .... Mr. Albert P. LITTLE
30 Vice Pres Develop/External Affairs .... Mrs. Caroline D. TINGLE
108 VP for Research & Inst Effective .... Dr. Rosalind M. HUMERICK
103 Vice Pres Workforce Development .... Dr. Anna M. LEBESCH
13 Chief Information Officer .... Mr. Paul M. HAWKINS
12 Provost St Augustine Campus .... Dr. Gregory K. MCLEOD
12 Provost Orange Park/Dir Govt Rels .... Mr. James C. ROY
49 Dean of Arts & Sciences .... Dr. Laura L. BOILINI
57 Dean of Florida School of the Arts .... Mr. Alain R. HENTSCHEL
08 Dean of Library Services .... Mrs. Carmen M. CUMMINGS
66 Dean Nursing .... Dr. Mary A. LANEY
88 Dean of Adult & Secondary Education ...... Dr. Edward K. JORDAN
53 Associate Dean of Teacher Education .... Dr. Myrna L. ALLEN
88 Exec Director TH Center for the Art .... Mr. James A. WALSH
88 Director of Dual Enrollment .... Mrs. Melissa PERRY
103 Director of Workforce Services .... Mrs. Melissa E. O'CONNELL
51 Dir of Cont/Community Education .... Mrs. Meghan DEPUTY
26 Director of Public Relations .... Mrs. Susan B. KESSLER
88 Director Criminal Justice .... Mr. Gary A. KILLAM
38 Dir of Counsel/Acad Advising .... Ms. Sara J. MYERS
88 Director of Testing & Acad Success ...... Mrs. Jane T. CRAWFORD
07 Director of Admissions and Records .... Mrs. Susanne B. LINEBERGER

Saint Leo University (G)

33701 State Road 52 W, Saint Leo FL 33574-6665
County: Pasco FICE Identification: 001526
Unit ID: 137032
Telephone: (352) 588-8200 Carnegie Class: Master's L
FAX Number: (352) 588-8654 Calendar System: Semester
URL: www.saintleo.edu
Established: 1889 Annual Undergrad Tuition & Fees: $18,870
Enrollment: 15,564 Coed
Affiliation or Control: Roman Catholic IRS Status: 501(c)3
Highest Offering: Beyond Master's But Less Than Doctorate
Program: Liberal Arts And General; Teacher Preparatory; Professional
Accreditation: SC, IACBE, SW

01 President .... Dr. Arthur F. KIRK, JR.
05 VP Academic Affairs .... Dr. Maribeth DURST
51 VP Continuing Ed/Student Services .... Dr. Edward DADEZ
84 VP Enrollment & Online Programs .... Ms. Kathryn MCFARLAND
10 VP Business Affairs .... Mr. Frank MEZZANINI
30 VP University Advancement .... Mr. David OSTRANDER
04 Assistant to the President .... Vacant
20 Associate VP Academic Affairs .... Dr. Jeffrey ANDERSON
108 Director of Assessment .... Dr. Robert LUCIO
51 Associate VP Continuing Education .... Dr. Beth CARTER
43 Associate VP/General Counsel .... Ms. Deborah BROWN
84 Associate VP Enrollment .... Ms. Dana DAVIES
90 Associate VP/CIO .... Mr. Les LLOYD
42 Asst to the Pres for Univ Ministry .... Fr. Stephan BROWN
32 Associate VP Student Services .... Mr. Kenneth POSNER
38 Director Counseling Services .... Mr. Lawson JOLLY
49 Dean School of Arts & Sciences .... Dr. Mary SPOTO
75 Dean School of Educ/Social Svcs .... Dr. Carol WALKER
50 Dean School of Business .... Dr. Michael NASTANSKI
58 Dir Graduate Studies in Business .... Dr. Lorrie MCGOVERN
58 Dir Grad Studies in Crim Justice .... Dr. Robert DIEMER
58 Dir Grad Studies in Education .... Dr. Sharyn DISABATO
58 Dir Grad Studies in Social Work .... Dr. Cindy LEE
58 Dir Graduate Studies in Theology .... Fr. Anthony KISSEL
06 Registrar .... Mrs. Karen HATFIELD
08 Director Library Services .... Mr. Brent SHORT
07 Assoc VP of UG Admission/Advising .... Mr. Jeff WALSH
88 Asst VP Instructional Technology .... Dr. Susan COLARIC
88 Dir Academic Student Support Svcs .... Dr. Joanne MACEACHRAN
11 Director Academic Administration .... Mr. Joseph TADEO
41 Director Athletics .... Mr. Fran REIDY
26 Director University Communications .... Ms. Maureen MOORE
18 Director Physical Plant .... Mr. Jose CABAN
19 Exec Dir Campus Security & Safety .... Mr. Robert SULLIVAN
23 Director Health Center .... Ms. Teresa DADEZ
88 Asst Director Disability Services .... Ms. Christine GEORGALLIS
35 Asst VP for Student Services .... Ms. Ana DI DONATO
29 Director Alumni Relations .... Mr. Eddie KENNY
88 Director Parent Relations .... Mr. Stephen KUBASEK
44 Exec Director Development .... Ms. Dawn PARISI
85 Assoc Director International Svcs .... Ms. Paige RAMSEY-HAMACHER
15 Human Resources Manager .... Ms. Theresa KLUENDER
36 Director of Career Planning .... Mr. Robert LIDDELL
21 Assoc VP Business Affairs .... Ms. Christine GIBSON
12 Asst VP Continuing Ed Virginia .... Ms. Susan PAULSON
12 Asst VP Continuing Ed Central Reg .... Mr. Jack NUSSEN
12 Asst VP Continuing Ed Florida .... Mr. Stephen HESS
103 Director Professional Development .... Ms. Anne KIBBE
88 Director Dining Services .... Mr. Rich VOGEL

St. Petersburg College (H)

PO Box 13489, Saint Petersburg FL 33733-3489
County: Pinellas FICE Identification: 001528
Unit ID: 137078
Telephone: (727) 341-4772 Carnegie Class: Bac/Assoc
FAX Number: (727) 341-3318 Calendar System: Semester
URL: www.spcollege.edu
Established: 1927 Annual Undergrad Tuition & Fees (In-District): $3,171
Enrollment: 33,128 Coed
Affiliation or Control: Local IRS Status: 501(c)3
Highest Offering: Baccalaureate
Program: Occupational; 2-Year Principally Bachelor's Creditable; Teacher Preparatory; Professional
Accreditation: SC, ADNUR, DH, EMT, FUSER, IFSAC, MLTAD, NURSE, OPE, PTAA, RAD

01 President .... Dr. William D. LAW
05 Sr Vice Pres Academic/Student Affs .... Dr. Anne M. COOPER
88 VP Bacc Pgms & University Ptnrshps .... Vacant
32 VP Academic/Student Affairs .... Dr. Tonjua L. WILLIAMS
11 VP Admin/Bus Svcs & Info Technology .. Dr. Douglas S. DUNCAN
46 VP Economic Dev & Innov Projects .... Dennis L. JONES

18 VP Facilities Plng/Inst Svcs .... Vacant
15 Vice Pres Human Resources .... Patty JONES
30 VP Inst Advance/Exec Dir Foundation .... Frances NEU
45 Assoc VP Business Svcs .... Jamelle CONNER
84 Assoc VP Enrollment Mgmt .... Dr. Pat RINARD
37 Assoc VP Financial Asst Svcs .... Michael J. BENNETT
104 Assoc VP Univ Partnership Center .... Catherine C. KENNEDY
41 Director Athletics .... Mark STRICKLAND
26 Dir Marketing/Public Information .... Michael O'KEEFFE
103 Director Workforce Services .... Dr. Jason KRUPP
43 Acting General Counsel .... Suzanne GARDNER
12 Campus Exec Officer Allstate Center .... J. C. BROCK
12 Provost Clearwater Campus .... Dr. Stanley VITTETOE
12 Provost/Health Education Center .... Dr. Phil NICOTERA
12 Provost St Petersburg Campus .... Dr. Karen K. WHITE
12 Provost Seminole Campus .... Dr. James OLLIVER
12 Provost Tarpon Springs Campus .... Dr. Conferlete CARNEY
12 Campus Exec Officer Downtown Center .... Dr. Kevin GORDON
22 Dir Equal Access/Equal Opportunity .... Pam SMITH
96 Dir Procurement & Asset Mgmt .... Paul SPINELLI
38 Dir Student Success .... Joe DVORACSEK
88 Dean College of Public Safety Admin .... Brian FRANK
88 Dean Col of Policy/Legal Studies .... Susan S. DEMERS
83 Dean Social & Behavioral Sciences .... Dr. Joseph SMILEY
88 Principal St Pete Collegiate High .... Starla METZ
88 President Faculty Senate .... Dr. Richard MERCADANTE

St. Thomas University (A)

16401 NW 37th Avenue, Miami Gardens FL 33054-6498
County: Miami-Dade FICE Identification: 001468
Unit ID: 137476
Telephone: (305) 625-6000 Carnegie Class: Master's L
FAX Number: (305) 628-6510 Calendar System: Semester
URL: www.stu.edu
Established: 1961 Annual Undergrad Tuition & Fees: $25,110
Enrollment: 2,472 Coed
Affiliation or Control: Roman Catholic IRS Status: 501(c)3
Highest Offering: Doctorate
Program: Liberal Arts And General; Teacher Preparatory; Professional
Accreditation: SC, LAW

01 President .... Msgr. Franklyn M. CASALE
05 Provost & Chief Academic Officer .... Dr. Gregory S. CHAN
10 Vice Pres Finance/Administration .... Mr. Terrence O'CONNER
61 Dean of Law School .... Mr. Douglas RAY
30 Vice Pres University Advancement .... Dr. Beverly BACHRACH
45 Vice Pres for Planning & Enrollment .... Dr. Beatriz G. ROBINSON
20 Assoc Provost Academic Support Svcs .... Dr. Susan B. ANGULO
84 Dean Enrollment Management .... Mr. Andre LIGHTBOURN
26 Director Marketing/Communications .... Ms. Marivi PRADO
06 Assoc Prov Records/Acad Computing .... Ms. Maria ABDEL
37 Assoc Director Financial Aid .... Ms. Yaidany RIVERO
08 University Librarian .... Mr. Larry TREADWELL
21 Controller .... Ms. Maribel SMITH
18 Director Facilities/Physical Plant .... Mr. Juan ZAMORA
09 Director Institutional Research .... Dr. Jerry A. WEINBERG
36 Director Career Services .... Mr. Timothy DEPALMA
41 Athletic Director .... Ms. Laura COURTLEY-TODD
32 Dean of Students .... Mr. Isaac CARTER
15 Assoc Director Human Resources .... Ms. Lenore PRADO
25 Assoc Dir Grant Writing/Publication .... Ms. Susan L. SMITH
38 Assoc Director Health & Wellness .... Vacant
73 Dean School of Theology .... Dr. Maria PASCUZZI
12 Dean Biscayne College .... Dr. Scott ZERMAN
27 Chief Information Officer .... Mr. Rudy IBARRA
29 Director Alumni Relations .... Vacant
44 Director Annual Giving .... Ms. Cheryl LAWKO
11 Director for Administration .... Ms. Sylvia RODRIGUEZ

St. Vincent De Paul Regional Seminary (B)

10701 S Military Trail, Boynton Beach FL 33436-4899
County: Palm Beach FICE Identification: 008223
Unit ID: 136701
Telephone: (561) 732-4424 Carnegie Class: Spec/Faith
FAX Number: (561) 737-2205 Calendar System: Semester
URL: www.svdp.edu
Established: 1963 Annual Graduate Tuition & Fees: $32,000
Enrollment: 86 Coed
Affiliation or Control: Roman Catholic IRS Status: 501(c)3
Highest Offering: Master's; No Undergraduates
Program: Religious Emphasis
Accreditation: SC, THEOL

01 Rector/President .... Rev. David L. TOUPS
03 Vice Rector .... Rev. Jose ALFARO
05 Academic Dean/Registrar .... Deacon Dennis DEMES
10 Treasurer .... Mr. Keith PARKER
08 Director of the Library .... Mr. Arthur QUINN

Sanford-Brown Institute (C)

1201 W Cypress Creek Road, Ste 101,
Fort Lauderdale FL 33309
County: Broward Identification: 667031
Unit ID: 385008
Telephone: (954) 308-7400 Carnegie Class: Assoc/PrivFP
FAX Number: (954) 375-6900 Calendar System: Other
URL: www.sanfordbrown.edu/Fort-Lauderdale
Established: 1989 Annual Undergrad Tuition & Fees: $14,500
Enrollment: 871 Coed
Affiliation or Control: Proprietary IRS Status: Proprietary
Highest Offering: Associate Degree
Program: Occupational; Technical Emphasis
Accreditation: ACICS, CVT, DA, DH, DMS, MAAB, SURTEC

01 Campus President .... Mr. Mark CONROY

† Branch campus of Sanford-Brown College, Atlanta, GA.

Sanford-Brown Institute (D)

10255 Fortune Parkway, Suite #501,
Jacksonville FL 32256-0757
County: Duval FICE Identification: 026164
Unit ID: 404505
Telephone: (904) 363-6221 Carnegie Class: Assoc/PrivFP
FAX Number: (904) 363-6824 Calendar System: Other
URL: www.sanfordbrown.edu/Jacksonville
Established: 1977 Annual Undergrad Tuition & Fees: $12,647
Enrollment: 776 Coed
Affiliation or Control: Proprietary IRS Status: Proprietary
Highest Offering: Associate Degree
Program: Occupational
Accreditation: ACICS, DA, DH, MAAB, SURTEC

01 President .... Mr. Doug GOODWIN

Sanford-Brown Institute (E)

5701 E Hillsborough Ave, Suite 1417,
Tampa FL 33610-5428
County: Hillsborough Identification: 666027
Unit ID: 379029
Telephone: (813) 393-4250 Carnegie Class: Assoc/PrivFP
FAX Number: (813) 626-0392 Calendar System: Other
URL: www.sanfordbrown.edu/Tampa
Established: 1984 Annual Undergrad Tuition & Fees: $14,100
Enrollment: 1,063 Coed
Affiliation or Control: Proprietary IRS Status: Proprietary
Highest Offering: Associate Degree
Program: Occupational
Accreditation: ACICS, MAAB

01 President .... Mr. Ben SEDRINE

† Branch campus of Sanford-Brown Institute, Jacksonville, FL.

Santa Fe College (F)

3000 NW 83rd Street, Gainesville FL 32606-6200
County: Alachua FICE Identification: 001519
Unit ID: 137096
Telephone: (352) 395-5000 Carnegie Class: Assoc/Pub-R-L
FAX Number: (352) 395-5581 Calendar System: Semester
URL: www.sfcollege.edu
Established: 1965 Annual Undergrad Tuition & Fees (In-District): $3,071
Enrollment: 17,596 Coed
Affiliation or Control: Local IRS Status: 501(c)3
Highest Offering: Baccalaureate
Program: Occupational; 2-Year Principally Bachelor's Creditable
Accreditation: SC, ADNUR, CONST, CVT, DA, DH, DMS, EMT, NMT, PNUR, RAD, SURGT

01 President .... Dr. Jackson N. SASSER
05 Provost/Vice Pres Academic Affairs .... Dr. Edward BONAHUE
10 Chief Financial Ofcr/VP Admin Affs .... Ms. Ginger GIBSON
32 Int Vice President Student Affairs .... Dr. Naima BROWN
30 Vice President Development .... Mr. Chuck CLEMONS
108 VP Assessment/Research/Technology .... Dr. Lisa ARMOUR
04 Assistant to the President .... Ms. Cathy KEEN
20 Associate VP Academic Affairs .... Dr. Curtis JEFFERSON
13 Assoc VP Information Tech Services .... Mr. Timothy C. NESLER
18 Assoc VP Facilities Services .... Mr. William REESE
35 Assoc VP Student Affs/Financial Aid .... Mr. Steven H. FISHER
88 Assoc Vice Pres Educational Centers .... Ms. Bennye J. ALLIGOOD
25 Asst VP/Development/Grants/Projects .... Ms. Joan M. SUCHORSKI
20 Asst Vice Pres Academic Affairs .... Dr. Dave YONUTAS
35 Asst Vice Pres Student Affairs .... Mr. John COWART
43 Legal Counsel .... Ms. Patti P. LOCASCIO
06 College Registrar .... Ms. Lynn SULLIVAN
88 Dir High Sch Dual Enrollment Pgm .... Ms. Linda LANZA-KADUCE
88 Interim Director Advisement Center .... Ms. Sharon LOSCHIAVO
41 Athletic Director .... Mr. Jim KEITES
08 Director Library Service .... Ms. Myra STERRETT
19 Director Institute of Public Safety .... Capt. Daryl JOHNSTON
35 Director Student Life .... Mr. Dan RODKIN
96 Director of Purchasing .... Mr. David SHLAFER
28 Director of Diversity .... Ms. Elizabeth O'REGGIO
37 Director Student Financial Aid .... Ms. Maureen MCFARLANE
15 Director Human Resources .... Ms. Lela FRYE

Schiller International University (G)

8560 Ulmerton Road, Largo FL 33771
County: Pinellas FICE Identification: 023141
Unit ID: 404338
Telephone: (727) 736-5082 Carnegie Class: Spec/Bus
FAX Number: (727) 734-0359 Calendar System: Semester
URL: www.schiller.edu
Established: 1964 Annual Undergrad Tuition & Fees: $18,360
Enrollment: 163 Coed
Affiliation or Control: Proprietary IRS Status: Proprietary
Highest Offering: Master's
Program: Occupational; Liberal Arts And General; Business Emphasis
Accreditation: ACICS

01 President .... Dr. Michele Z. GEIGLE
05 Provost .... Vacant
07 Director of Admissions .... Mr. Phillip CLARK

Seminole State College of Florida (H)

100 Weldon Boulevard, Sanford FL 32773-6199
County: Seminole FICE Identification: 001520
Unit ID: 137209
Telephone: (407) 708-4722 Carnegie Class: Assoc/Pub-S-SC
FAX Number: (407) 708-2139 Calendar System: Semester
URL: www.seminolestate.edu
Established: 1965 Annual Undergrad Tuition & Fees (In-District): $3,131
Enrollment: 18,886 Coed
Affiliation or Control: Local IRS Status: 501(c)3
Highest Offering: Baccalaureate
Program: Occupational; 2-Year Principally Bachelor's Creditable
Accreditation: SC, ADNUR, EMT, PTAA

01 President .... Dr. E. Ann MCGEE
10 Executive VP/CFO .... Dr. Joseph SARNOVSKY
05 VP Academic Affairs/CAO .... Dr. Laura ROSS
32 VP Student Affairs/CSAO .... Dr. Marcia ROMAN
13 VP Information Resources/CIO .... Mr. Dick T. HAMANN
102 Executive Director Foundation .... Mr. John GYLLIN
21 AVP Finance & Budget .... Ms. Lynn POWERS
26 AVP College Relations .... Mr. Michael GARLICH
12 Provost Altamonte Springs .... Ms. Lynn COLON
12 Provost Oviedo Campus .... Mr. Robert LEDFORD
28 Director Diversity and Inclusion .... Dr. Yolanda WILLIAMS
08 Dean Learning Resources .... Ms. Patricia D. DESALVO
36 AVP Career Programs .... Ms. Angela M. KERSENBROCK
35 AVP Student Development .... Ms. Patry ENGLISH
54 Dean Engineering and Design .... Mr. Michael STALEY
51 Dean Academic Foundations .... Dr. Terri DANIELS
86 Director Government Relations .... Mr. Donald PAYTON
91 Director Networks .... Mr. Julio VALENTIN
38 Director Counseling and Advising .... Ms. Deborah LYNCH
20 Director Curriculum .... Ms. Christine BROEKER
15 AVP Human Resources .... Ms. Mae KLINE
06 Int Dir Enrollment Svcs/Registrar .... Mr. Nate JONES
37 Director Student Financial Aid .... Ms. Carmen AFGHANI
09 AVP Institutional Effectiveness .... Dr. Mark MORGAN
41 Director Intercollegiate Athletics .... Mr. John SCARPINO
07 AVP Student Recruitment .... Mrs. Pamela MENNECHEY
36 Director Career Development .... Mrs. Christy KING
14 AVP Information Technology .... Ms. Pilar ACOSTA

South Florida Bible College (I)

1100 South Federal Highway, Deerfield Beach FL 33441
County: Broward FICE Identification: 032643
Unit ID: 366003
Telephone: (954) 545-4500 Carnegie Class: Spec/Faith
FAX Number: (954) 480-9755 Calendar System: Semester
URL: www.sfbc.edu
Established: 1985 Annual Undergrad Tuition & Fees: $5,365
Enrollment: 68 Coed
Affiliation or Control: Interdenominational IRS Status: 501(c)3
Highest Offering: Doctorate
Program: Professional; Religious Emphasis
Accreditation: @BI

01 President .... Dr. Joseph GUADAGNINO
03 Provost .... Mary A. DRABIK
10 Chief Financial Officer .... Beatrice GUADAGNINO
06 Registrar .... Tom DAVIS
08 Librarian .... Paula STEVENSON
05 Dean of Faculty .... Dr. Thomas DRABIK
32 Dean of Students .... Dr. John STEVENSON

South Florida State College (J)

600 W College Drive, Avon Park FL 33825-9399
County: Highlands FICE Identification: 001522
Unit ID: 137315
Telephone: (863) 453-6661 Carnegie Class: Assoc/Pub-R-M
FAX Number: (863) 453-0165 Calendar System: Trimester
URL: www.southflorida.edu
Established: 1965 Annual Undergrad Tuition & Fees (In-District): $3,136
Enrollment: 2,742 Coed
Affiliation or Control: Local IRS Status: 501(c)3
Highest Offering: Baccalaureate
Program: Occupational; 2-Year Principally Bachelor's Creditable
Accreditation: SC, DA, DH, RAD

01 President .... Dr. Norman L. STEPHENS, JR.
05 Vice Pres Educational/Stdnt Svcs .... Dr. Leana REVELL
11 Vice Pres Administrative Services .... Mr. Glenn W. LITTLE
51 Dean Adult & Continuing Education .... Dr. Michael MCLEOD
75 Dean Applied Science & Tech .... Mr. J. Kevin BROWN
49 Dean Arts & Sciences .... Dr. Kimberly BATTY-HERBERT
88 Dean Cultural Programming .... Mr. Douglas M. ANDREWS
45 Dean Resource Development .... Mr. Donald L. APPELQUIST
32 Dean Student Services .... Mrs. Annie ALEXANDER-HARVEY
84 Assoc Dean Enrollment Svcs/Univ Rel .... Mrs. Laura M. WHITE
12 Director DeSoto Campus .... Mrs. Suzanne DEMERS
12 Director Hardee Campus .... Ms. Teresa CRAWFORD
12 Director Lake Placid Center .... Mr. Randall K. PAEPLOW

21 Controller ... Mrs. Anita A. KOVACS
26 Director Community Relations ... Ms. Deborah BELL
72 Director Educational Tech Center ... Mrs. Melanie M. JACKSON
15 Director Human Res/EA-EO & ADA Ofcr ... Mrs. Susie HALE
18 Dir Phys Plant/Opers/Maintenance ... Mr. Roberto FLORES
06 Registrar ... Dr. Deborah M. FUSCHETTI
41 Athletic Director ... Mr. Richard J. HITT
36 Director Career Development Center ... Mrs. Colleen RAFATTI
37 Director Financial Aid ... Ms. Susie JOHNSON
13 Dir Information Tech/Inst Research ... Dr. Chris VAN DER KAAY
38 Director Student Counseling ... Ms. Felicia DOZIER
08 Library Services ... Ms. Lena PHELPS-ELLERKER
40 Manager College Bookstore ... Mr. Gene HALEY
96 Coordinator Purchasing ... Mr. Richard PEAVY
10 Chief Business Officer ... Mrs. Anita A. KOVACS

South University (A)

9801 Belevedere Road, Royal Palm Beach FL 33411
County: Palm Beach Identification: 666117
Unit ID: 133465
Telephone: (561) 273-6500 Carnegie Class: Bac/Diverse
FAX Number: (561) 273-6420 Calendar System: Quarter
URL: www.southuniversity.edu
Established: 1899 Annual Undergrad Tuition & Fees: $15,910
Enrollment: 991 Coed
Affiliation or Control: Proprietary IRS Status: Proprietary
Highest Offering: Master's
Program: Occupational; 2-Year Principally Bachelor's Creditable; Liberal Arts And General
Accreditation: &SC, NURSE, PTAA

01 President ... Mr. David MCGUIRE
05 Dean of Academic Affairs ... Vacant
32 Dean of Student Affairs ... Ms. Maria SANTOS
07 Director of Admissions ... Mr. Gary MALISOS
37 Director of Financial Aid ... Ms. Kacey ATKINSON
10 Director of Finance ... Ms. Luz ARROYO
13 Director Computing/Info Management ... Ms. Sharon JACKSON
21 Business Officer ... Ms. Melodi RAMTALLIE
06 Registrar ... Ms. Michelle BELKIN
08 Head Librarian ... Mr. David BOSCA
36 Career Services Coordinator ... Ms. Jessica RENARD

† Regional accreditation is carried under the parent institution in Savannah, GA.

Southeastern College (B)

6812 Forest Hills Blvd, Suite D-1, Greenacres FL 33413
County: Palm Beach FICE Identification: 031239
Telephone: (561) 433-2330 Carnegie Class: Not Classified
FAX Number: (561) 433-9025 Calendar System: Other
URL: www.sec.edu
Established: 1988 Annual Undergrad Tuition & Fees: $15,064
Enrollment: 1,490 Coed
Affiliation or Control: Proprietary IRS Status: Proprietary
Highest Offering: Associate Degree
Program: Occupational
Accreditation: ACCSC, MAAB, SURGT

01 Vice President ... Ms. Christine HOOVER

Southeastern College (C)

6700 South Point Pkwy, Ste 400, Jacksonville FL 32216
County: Duval FICE Identification: 035533
Unit ID: 443270
Telephone: (904) 448-9499 Carnegie Class: Assoc/PrivFP
FAX Number: (904) 448-9270 Calendar System: Other
URL: www.sec.edu
Established: 1988 Annual Undergrad Tuition & Fees: $15,064
Enrollment: 187 Coed
Affiliation or Control: Proprietary IRS Status: Proprietary
Highest Offering: Associate Degree
Program: Occupational
Accreditation: ACCSC

01 Campus Vice President ... Mr. Shawn HUMPHREY

Southeastern College (D)

17395 NW 59th Avenue, Miami Lakes FL 33015-5111
County: Miami-Dade Identification: 666290
Unit ID: 42817001
Telephone: (305) 820-5003 Carnegie Class: Not Classified
FAX Number: (305) 820-5455 Calendar System: Quarter
URL: www.sec.edu
Established: 2002 Annual Undergrad Tuition & Fees: $29,968
Enrollment: 350 Coed
Affiliation or Control: Proprietary IRS Status: Proprietary
Highest Offering: Associate Degree
Program: Occupational
Accreditation: ACCSC, MAAB, SURGT

01 Vice President ... Enrique CARO
05 Dean Academics ... Craig MUNNS

† Branch campus of Southeastern College, Greenacres, FL.

Southeastern College (E)

11208 Blue Heron Boulevard, Suite A, St. Petersburg FL 33716
County: Pinellas Identification: 666758
Unit ID: 42817002
Telephone: (727) 576-6500 Carnegie Class: Not Classified
FAX Number: (727) 576-6589 Calendar System: Semester
URL: www.sec.edu
Established: 1988 Annual Undergrad Tuition & Fees: $7,492
Enrollment: 300 Coed
Affiliation or Control: Proprietary IRS Status: Proprietary
Highest Offering: Associate Degree
Program: Occupational; 2-Year Principally Bachelor's Creditable; Nursing Emphasis
Accreditation: ACCSC, MAAB, SURGT

03 Vice President ... Mr. Jeff SLAGLE

† Branch campus of Southeastern College, Greenacres, FL.

Southeastern University (F)

1000 Longfellow Boulevard, Lakeland FL 33801-6099
County: Polk FICE Identification: 001521
Unit ID: 137564
Telephone: (863) 667-5000 Carnegie Class: Bac/Diverse
FAX Number: (863) 667-5200 Calendar System: Semester
URL: www.seu.edu
Established: 1935 Annual Undergrad Tuition & Fees: $18,596
Enrollment: 2,546 Coed
Affiliation or Control: Assemblies Of God Church IRS Status: 501(c)3
Highest Offering: Master's
Program: Liberal Arts And General; Teacher Preparatory; Religious Emphasis
Accreditation: SC, IACBE, SW

01 President ... Dr. Kent INGLE
03 Executive Vice President ... Mr. Del CHITTIM
05 Provost ... Dr. William C. HACKET, JR.
10 Vice Pres Finance/Administration ... Dr. Dan MORTENSEN
30 VP for University Advancement ... Mr. Brian C. CARROLL
35 VP for Student Development ... Mr. James (Chris) OWEN
84 VP for Enrollment Management ... Mr. Roy ROWLAND, IV
09 Assoc Provost/Dean Inst Research ... Dr. Andrew H. PERMENTER
08 Dean of Library Services ... Mrs. Grace VEACH
06 Dir Student Records/Registrar ... Mrs. Linda M. KELSO
37 Director Student Financial Services ... Mrs. Carol B. BRADLEY
07 Director of Admission ... Ms. Betania TORRES
15 Director Human Resources ... Mr. Jeff M. HERMAN
29 Director Alumni Relations ... Ms. Jebapriya ARUL
18 Chief Facilities/Physical Plant ... Mr. Norman M. ALDERMAN
88 Director of Academic Success ... Mrs. Pamela CROSBY
36 Director of Career Services ... Mrs. Jacquelyn SMALL
21 Controller ... Mr. Frederick S. GORE
26 Public Relations Officer ... Mr. Edward MANER
38 Director Student Counseling ... Dr. James (Emory) WELCH
88 Dir of Institutional Effectiveness ... Mr. Andrew MILLER

Southern Career College (G)

9550 Regency Square Blvd,Suite 1100, Jacksonville FL 32225
County: Duval FICE Identification: 025982
Unit ID: 134121
Telephone: (904) 724-2229 Carnegie Class: Assoc/PrivFP
FAX Number: (904) 520-7295 Calendar System: Quarter
URL: www.southerncareercollege.edu
Established: 1960 Annual Undergrad Tuition & Fees: $23,000
Enrollment: 185 Coed
Affiliation or Control: Proprietary IRS Status: Proprietary
Highest Offering: Associate Degree
Program: Occupational
Accreditation: ACICS

01 Campus Director ... Mr. Jardiel VASQUEZ

Southern Technical College (H)

1485 Florida Mall Avenue, Orlando FL 32809-7733
County: Orange FICE Identification: 039035
Unit ID: 446552
Telephone: (407) 438-6000 Carnegie Class: Assoc/PrivFP
FAX Number: (407) 438-6005 Calendar System: Semester
URL: www.southerntech.edu
Established: 1956 Annual Undergrad Tuition & Fees: $30,975
Enrollment: 1,398 Coed
Affiliation or Control: Proprietary IRS Status: Proprietary
Highest Offering: Associate Degree
Program: Occupational
Accreditation: ACICS

01 Dean ... Mr. Dwayne ORE

Southwest Florida College (I)

1685 Medical Lane, Fort Myers FL 33907-1158
County: Lee FICE Identification: 022788
Unit ID: 366553
Telephone: (239) 939-4766 Carnegie Class: Bac/Assoc
FAX Number: (239) 790-2118 Calendar System: Quarter
URL: www.swfc.edu
Established: 1974 Annual Undergrad Tuition & Fees: $33,600
Enrollment: 1,685 Coed
Affiliation or Control: Proprietary IRS Status: Proprietary
Highest Offering: Baccalaureate
Program: Occupational; 2-Year Principally Bachelor's Creditable; Teacher Preparatory; Professional; Business Emphasis
Accreditation: ACICS, MAAB, SURTEC

01 President ... Dr. Stephen CALABRO
05 VP of Academic Affairs ... Dr. Melanie YERK

State College of Florida, Manatee-Sarasota (J)

PO Box 1849, Bradenton FL 34206-7046
County: Manatee FICE Identification: 001504
Unit ID: 135391
Telephone: (941) 752-5000 Carnegie Class: Assoc/Pub-U-MC
FAX Number: (941) 758-6830 Calendar System: Semester
URL: www.scf.edu
Established: 1957 Annual Undergrad Tuition & Fees (In-District): $3,074
Enrollment: 11,141 Coed
Affiliation or Control: Local IRS Status: 501(c)3
Highest Offering: Baccalaureate
Program: Occupational; 2-Year Principally Bachelor's Creditable
Accreditation: SC, ADNUR, DH, NUR, OTA, PTAA, RAD

01 President ... Dr. Lars A. HAFNER
04 Exec Assistant to President ... Vacant
10 Vice President Business/Admin Svcs ... Dr. Carol F. PROBSTFELD
05 VP Academic Quality & Success ... Dr. W. Jack CROCKER
20 Assoc VP Acad Quality & Success ... Mr. Gary RUSSELL
32 VP Educational & Student Services ... Dr. Donald R. BOWMAN
12 Provost Bradenton/VP Baccalaureate ... Dr. Michael J. MEARS
12 Provost Lakewood Ranch/Dean BSN ... Dr. Bonnie HESSELBERG
12 Provost Venice Campus ... Ms. Darlene WEDLER-JOHNSON
102 Exec Dir SCF Foundation Inc ... Ms. Peg LOWERY
15 Executive Director Human Resources ... Ms. Margaret Z. BECK
21 Assoc VP Finance ... Ms. Karen A. KESTER
38 Assoc VP Student Development ... Ms. Lynn DREES
06 Assoc VP Student Services ... Ms. MariLynn J. LEWY
31 Assoc VP Corporate & Community Dev ... Ms. Daisy VULOVICH
25 Assoc VP Eval & Compl & Inst Effect ... Mr. Bradley W. DAVIS
45 Assoc VP Facilities & Planning ... Ms. Traci STEEN
51 Director Inst of Continuing/Cmty Ed ... Ms. Cynthia HUNTER
19 Director Business Svc/Public Safety ... Mr. Timothy LANGENBACK
22 Equity Officer ... Ms. Gloria TRACY
72 Director Career & Technical Ed ... Dr. Idelia P. PHILLIPS
08 Director Library Services ... Ms. Tracy ELLIOTT
09 Director Institutional Research ... Ms. Su-hua MEN
14 Chief Information Officer ... Mr. Feng HOU
26 Director Public Affairs & Marketing ... Ms. Katherine WALKER
37 Director Financial Aid ... Mr. Jack TONEY
40 Manager Bookstore ... Mrs. Betty J. GIBSON
36 Director Career Resource Centers ... Ms. Denise D. GATCH
41 Director Athletics ... Mr. Matt ENNIS
103 Director Inst Workforce Development ... Mr. David AUXIER
88 Director Academic Resource Centers ... Ms. Jacquelyn MCNEIL
43 General Counsel ... Mr. Steve PROUTY
88 Head of SCF Collegiate School ... Ms. Kelly MONOD

*State University System of Florida, Board of Governors (K)

325 W Gaines Street, Suite 1614, Tallahassee FL 32399-0400
County: Leon FICE Identification: 008068
Unit ID: 137449
Telephone: (850) 245-0466 Carnegie Class: N/A
FAX Number: (850) 245-9685
URL: www.flbog.edu

01 Chancellor ... Mr. Frank T. BROGAN
05 Vice Chanc Academic/Student Affairs ... Dr. Jan IGNASH
10 Vice Chanc Budget & Finance ... Mr. Tim JONES
43 General Counsel ... Ms. Vikki SHIRLEY
22 Inspector General & Compliance ... Mr. Derry HARPER
101 Interim Corporate Secretary ... Ms. Monoka VENTERS
100 Chief of Staff ... Mr. Randy A. GOIN, JR.

*Florida Agricultural and Mechanical University (L)

1601 S. Martin Luther King Jr., Bl, Tallahassee FL 32307
County: Leon FICE Identification: 001480
Unit ID: 133650
Telephone: (850) 599-3000 Carnegie Class: DRU
FAX Number: (850) 599-3952 Calendar System: Semester
URL: www.famu.edu
Established: 1887 Annual Undergrad Tuition & Fees (In-State): $5,887
Enrollment: 13,207 Coed
Affiliation or Control: State IRS Status: 501(c)3
Highest Offering: Doctorate
Program: Occupational; Liberal Arts And General; Teacher Preparatory; Professional
Accreditation: SC, CS, ENG, ENGT, JOUR, LAW, LSAR, NUR, #OT, PH, PHAR, PTA, SW, TED

02 President ... Dr. James H. AMMONS
05 Provost/Vice Pres Academic Affs ... Dr. Larry ROBINSON

10 Vice Pres Admin & Financial Svcs .... Dr. Teresa HARDEE
32 Vice Pres Student Affairs .... Dr. William HUDSON, JR.
30 VP University Relations .... Dr. Thomas HAYNES
25 Interim VP for Sponsored Research .... Dr. Kinfe K. REDDA
88 VP Audit and Compliance .... Mr. Richard GIVENS
13 Interim CIO Enterprise Technology .... Mr. Michael JAMES
35 Assoc Vice Pres Student Affairs .... Mr. Henry KIRBY
44 Asst VP University Development .... Vacant
20 Associate VP for Academic Affairs .... Vacant
21 Asst Vice Pres Planning & Budgeting .... Vacant
06 University Registrar .... Dr. Agatha ONWUNLI
43 VP for Legal Affs & General Counsel .... Atty. Avery MCKNIGHT
07 Director of Admissions .... Ms. Barbara COX
08 Director of University Libraries .... Dr. Lauren SAPP
37 Director of Financial Aid .... Ms. Lisa STEWART
36 Director of The Career Center .... Dr. Delores DEAN
09 Director of Institutional Research .... Dr. Kwadwo OWUSU-ADUEMIRI
28 Director of EEO .... Ms. Carrie GAVIN
26 Chief Public Relations Officer .... Mrs. Sharon SAUNDERS
21 University Controller .... Dr. William FEATHERSTONE
15 Assistant VP for Human Resources .... Ms. Nellie WOODRUFF
29 Director of Alumni Affairs .... Mrs. Carmen CUMMINGS
51 Director of Continuing Education .... Mrs. Phyllis WATSON
49 Dean of Arts & Sciences .... Dr. Ralph TURNER
50 Dean of Business and Industry .... Dr. Shawnta FRIDAY-STROUD
66 Interim Dean of Nursing .... Dr. Ruena NORMAN
67 Dean of Pharmacy .... Dr. Michael THOMPSON
53 Dean of Education .... Dr. Genniver BELL
54 Interim Dean Engr Sci/Tech/Agricult .... Dr. Samuel DONALD
48 Dean of Architecture .... Mr. Rodner B. WRIGHT
97 Dean of General Studies .... Dr. Dorothy HENDERSON
60 Dean of Journalism .... Dr. James M. HAWKINS
58 Interim Dean of Graduate Studies .... Dr. Verian THOMAS
76 Dean of Allied Health Sciences .... Dr. Cynthia HUGHES HARRIS
54 Interim Dean FAMU/FSU Engineering .... Dr. John COLLIER
61 Dean College of Law .... Mr. Leroy PERNELL
19 Interim Director of Security .... Mr. John EARST
23 Director of Student Health Services .... Ms. Tanya TATUM
41 Director of Athletics .... Mr. Derek HORNE
18 Assoc VP Facilities/Plng/Phys Plnt .... Mr. Joseph BAKKER
38 Director Counseling Services .... Dr. Yolanda BOGAN
96 Director of Purchasing .... Ms. Stephany FALL
101 COS/BOT Liaison/Interim Title III D .... Mrs. Rosalind FUSE-HALL
04 Assistant to the President .... Mrs. Patricia WOODARD
88 Int Director Environmental Sciences .... Dr. Michael ABAZINGE
86 Director of Governmental Relations .... Mr. Tola THOMPSON

*Florida Atlantic University (A)

PO Box 3091, 777 Glades Road,
Boca Raton FL 33431-0991

County: Palm Beach — FICE Identification: 001481
Unit ID: 133669

Telephone: (561) 297-3000 — Carnegie Class: RU/H
FAX Number: (561) 297-3942 — Calendar System: Semester
URL: www.fau.edu
Established: 1961 — Annual Undergrad Tuition & Fees (In-State): $4,761
Enrollment: 29,313 — Coed
Affiliation or Control: State — IRS Status: 501(c)3
Highest Offering: Doctorate
Program: Liberal Arts And General; Teacher Preparatory; Professional
Accreditation: SC, BUS, CACREP, CORE, CS, ENG, #MED, MUS, NURSE, PLNG, SP, SPAA, SW, TED

02 President .... Dr. Mary Jane SAUNDERS
45 Vice President Strategic Planning .... Dr. Gitanjali KAUL
05 Univ Prov/Chief Academic Officer .... Dr. Brenda CLAIBORNE
10 VP Finance/Chief Fiscal Officer .... Mr. Dennis CRUDELE
32 Vice President Student Affairs .... Dr. Charles L. BROWN
46 Vice President Research .... Dr. Barry ROSSON
102 VP Cmty Engagement/Exec Dir FAU Fdn .... Dr. Jennifer O'FLANNERY ANDERSON
88 Assoc Vice Pres Univ Architect Ofc .... Mr. Tom DONAUDY
46 Associate Vice President Research .... Dr. Jeffrey ANDERSON
20 Assoc Provost Acad Budget/Planning .... Dr. Norman KAUFMAN
13 Assoc Provost Info Resource Mgmt .... Mr. Jason BALL
29 Vice President Alumni Relations .... Mr. Bradford W. CREWS
27 Dir of Marketing and Creative Svcs .... Mr. William PLATE
21 Assoc Bus Ofcr/Assoc VP For Admin .... Ms. Dorothy RUSSELL
35 Assoc Dean Student Affairs .... Mr. Terry MENA
43 General Counsel .... Mr. David KIAN
27 University Ombudsman .... Ms. Patricia SINGER
22 Director EEO Programs .... Ms. Paula BEHUL
84 Assoc VP Enrollment Management .... Dr. Robert SELTZER
63 Dean C E Schmidt Col of Medicine .... Dr. David J. BJORKMAN
20 Assoc Provost Personnel & Programs .... Dr. Diane ALPERIN
80 Dean of Design and Social Inquiry .... Dr. Rosalyn Y. CARTER
49 Interim Dean of Arts & Letters .... Dr. Heather COLTMAN
50 Interim Dean of Business .... Dr. Somnath BHATTACHARYA
53 Dean of Education .... Dr. Valerie BRISTOR
54 Int Dean of Engineering/Comp Sci .... Dr. Mohammad ILYAS
66 Dean of Nursing .... Dr. Marlaine SMITH
81 Dean of Science .... Dr. Gary PERRY
92 Dean of Honors College .... Dr. Jeff BULLER
58 Dean Graduate College .... Dr. Barry T. ROSSON
20 Dean Undergraduate Studies .... Dr. Edward E. PRATT
53 Asst Dean/PK-12 Sch/Educational Pgm .... Mr. Joel HERBST
07 Director Undergraduate Admissions .... Ms. Barbara PLETCHER
90 Director Enterprise Computing Svcs .... Mr. Mehran BASIRATMAND
91 Dir Univ Administrative Systems .... Ms. Kay RECKTENWALD
25 Dir Sponsored Programs .... Ms. JoAnn MORETTI
09 Director Inst Effective/Analysis .... Vacant
24 Dir University Learning Resources .... Mrs. Molly MUNRO
06 Interim Registrar .... Mr. Jeffrey HENDRICKS
08 Dean University Library .... Dr. William MILLER
15 Director Human Resources .... Mr. James ACTON
41 Athletics Director .... Mr. Patrick CHUN
39 Director Student Housing .... Ms. Jill ECKARDT
36 Dir Career Devel Ctr/Student Place .... Ms. Sandra JAKUBOW
21 Director Business Services .... Ms. Stacy VOLNICK
85 Director Intl Students/Scholar Svcs .... Dr. Mihaela METIANU
37 Director Student Financial Aid .... Ms. Tracy BOULUKOS
23 Director Student Health Services .... Ms. Cathie L. WALLACE
19 Dir Safety & Security/Chief Police .... Chief Charles LOWE
86 Director Government Relations .... Mr. David MANN
45 Director Facilities Planning .... Mr. Robert RICHMAN
18 Director Physical Plant .... Mr. John SINGER
42 Director Campus Ministries .... Ms. Elise ANGIOLLIO
38 Dir Counseling & Psychological Svcs .... Dr. Kirk M. DOUGHER
96 Director of Purchasing .... Mr. Ed SCHIFF
28 Assoc Dir Multicultural Affairs .... Dr. Ingrid JONES
88 Director Student Union .... Dr. Larry FAERMAN
88 Dir Office Students w/Disabilities .... Ms. Nicole ROKOS
88 Assoc Director Student Orientation .... Ms. Heather BISHARA
88 Assoc Dir Student Dev/Activities .... Ms. Michele PERKINS
21 University Controller .... Mrs. Stacey SEMMEL
57 Director School of the Arts .... Vacant
60 Dir Sch of Comm/Multimedia Studies .... Dr. Noemi MARIN
88 Director School of Accounting .... Dr. Somnath BHATTACHARYA
88 Dir Complex Systems/Brain Sciences .... Dr. Janet BLANKS
70 Director School of Social Work .... Dr. Michele HAWKINS
80 Dir School of Public Administration .... Dr. Khi THAI
48 Director School of Architecture .... Dr. Deirdre HARDY
88 Dir Center for Env/Urban Solutions .... Dr. James MURLEY
104 Director of International Programs .... Dr. Catherine MESCHIEVITZ
88 Assoc Provost Lifelong Learning .... Dr. Herbert SHAPIRO
94 Director Women's Studies .... Dr. Josephine A. BEOKU-BETTS
65 Dir Pine Jog Environ Education Ctr .... Mr. Ray COLEMAN
53 Dir K Slattery Educ Research Ctr .... Ms. Lydia BARTRAM
54 Dir SeaTech Inst for Ocean Engr .... Dr. Manhar DHANAK
54 Dir Intermodal Trans Safety/Sec Ctr .... Dr. Pete SCARLATOS
88 Dir Harbor Brnch Oceanographic Inst .... Dr. Margaret LEINEN

*Florida Gulf Coast University (B)

10501 FGCU Boulevard S, Fort Myers FL 33965-6565

County: Lee — FICE Identification: 032553
Unit ID: 433660

Telephone: (239) 590-1000 — Carnegie Class: Master's L
FAX Number: (239) 590-1166 — Calendar System: Semester
URL: www.fgcu.edu
Established: 1991 — Annual Undergrad Tuition & Fees (In-State): $6,068
Enrollment: 12,655 — Coed
Affiliation or Control: State — IRS Status: 501(c)3
Highest Offering: Doctorate
Program: Liberal Arts And General; Teacher Preparatory; Professional
Accreditation: SC, ANEST, BUS, CACREP, ENG, MT, NURSE, OT, PTA, SPAA, SW

02 President .... Dr. Wilson G. BRADSHAW
05 Provost & VP Academic Affairs .... Dr. Ronald B. TOLL
10 Vice Pres Admin Services/Finance .... Mr. Steve L. MAGIERA
30 VP Univ Advance/Exec Dir Foundation .... Dr. Rosemary M. THOMAS
32 Vice President Student Affairs .... Dr. J. Michael ROLLO
20 Assoc VP Academic/Curriculum Sppt .... Dr. Cathy DUFF
45 Asc Prov/Asc VP Plng & Inst Perfrmc .... Dr. Paul SNYDER
58 Assoc VP Research/Dean Grad Studies .... Dr. T. C YIH
26 Asst VP Community Rels/Marketing .... Mr. Ken SCHEXNAYDER
04 Asst to Pres/University Ombudsman .... Ms. Helen MAMARCHEV
88 Asst Vice Pres Business Services .... Mr. Joseph MCDONALD
13 Asst VP Business Technology Svcs .... Ms. Mary BANKS
15 Asst Vice Pres Human Resources .... Dr. David KAKKURI
21 Controller/Asst VP Admin Services .... Ms. Linda BACHELER
35 Dean Student Affairs .... Dr. Michele YOVANOVICH
49 Dean College Arts & Sciences .... Dr. Donna P. HENRY
20 Dean of Undergraduate Studies .... Dr. Jim WOHLPART
50 Dean Lutgert College of Business .... Dr. Hudson ROGERS
53 Dean College of Education .... Dr. Marcia GREENE
76 Dean College Health Professions .... Dr. Mitchell CORDOVA
54 Dean Whitaker Col of Engineering .... Dr. Richard A. BEHR
62 Dean Library Services .... Dr. Kathleen MILLER
45 Assoc Dean Plng/Inst Performance .... Dr. George ALEXANDER
38 Asst Dean Counselng/Stdnt Hlth Svcs .... Dr. Jon L. BRUNNER
43 Asst Dean Judicial Affairs .... Ms. Cindy LYONS
07 Director of Admissions .... Mr. Marc LAVIOLETTE
96 Director of Procurement Services .... Ms. Maryan EGAN
19 Director Campus Police & Safety .... Chief Steven C. MOORE
100 Chief of Staff/Univ Spokesperson .... Ms. Susan EVANS
18 Director Facilities Planning .... Mr. Barrett GENSON
37 Director Student Financial Aid .... Mr. Jorge LOPEZ-ROSADO
06 University Registrar .... Ms. Susan BYARS
23 Director Student Health Services .... Ms. Eileen DONDERO
41 Director Intercollegiate Athletics .... Mr. Kenneth KAVANAGH
28 Director Equity & Diversity .... Mr. Jimmy MYERS
85 Director International Services .... Ms. Elaine HOZDIK
106 Dir Web/E-learning/Publication Svcs .... Mr. David JAEGER
72 Director Academic & Event Tech .... Ms. Pat O'CONNOR-BENSON
36 Director Career Development Svcs .... Mr. Reid LENNERTZ
31 Dir Center for Civic Engagement .... Ms. Jessica RHEA
29 Director Alumni Relations .... Ms. Lindsey TOUCHETTE
43 General Counsel .... Ms. Vee LEONARD
92 Director Honors Program .... Dr. Sean KELLY
09 Director Inst Research/Analysis .... Dr. Robert VINES
21 Director University Budgets .... Mr. David VAZQUEZ
39 Director University Housing .... Dr. Brian FISHER
86 Director Government Relations .... Ms. Jennifer GOEN
51 Exec Dir Cont Educ/Off-Campus Pgms .... Dr. Paul THORNTON
88 General Manager/WGCU .... Mr. Rick JOHNSON
40 Manager The University Store .... Ms. Laura JENSEN

*Florida International University (C)

University Park, 11200 SW 8 Street, Miami FL 33199-0001

County: Miami-Dade — FICE Identification: 009635
Unit ID: 133951

Telephone: (305) 348-2000 — Carnegie Class: RU/H
FAX Number: N/A — Calendar System: Semester
URL: www.fiu.edu
Established: 1965 — Annual Undergrad Tuition & Fees (In-State): $6,416
Enrollment: 44,686 — Coed
Affiliation or Control: State — IRS Status: 501(c)3
Highest Offering: Doctorate
Program: Liberal Arts And General; Teacher Preparatory; Professional
Accreditation: SC, ANEST, ART, BUS, BUSA, CACREP, CIDA, CONST, CS, DIETC, DIETD, ENG, IPSY, JOUR, LAW, LSAR, #MED, MUS, NURSE, OT, #PH, PTA, SP, SPAA, SW, TED, THEA

02 President .... Dr. Mark ROSENBERG
100 Chief of Staff .... Mr. Javier MARQUES
05 Exec VP Academic Affs/Provost .... Dr. Douglas WARTZOK
88 Int VP for Engagement .... Dr. Irma BECERRA-FERNANDEZ
20 Vice Provost Academic Affairs .... Dr. Elizabeth BEJAR
10 CFO & Sr VP for Administration .... Dr. Kenneth JESSELL
30 Vice President for Advancement .... Mr. Howard LIPMAN
32 Int VP Student Affairs .... Dr. Larry LUNSFORD
09 Assoc VP Planning & Inst Research .... Mr. Jeffery GONZALEZ
46 VP for Research .... Dr. Andres GIL
13 Vice President/CIO .... Mr. Robert GRILLO
12 Vice Prov Biscayne Bay Campus .... Mr. Stephen MOLL
84 Assoc VP Enrollment Management .... Vacant
35 Assoc VP Stdnt Affs Biscayne Bay .... Ms. Cathy AKENS
45 Assoc VP Strategic Development .... Ms. Liane MARTINEZ
15 Assoc Vice Pres Human Resources .... Dr. Jaffus HARDRICK
18 Assoc VP Facilities Operations .... Mr. John CAL
07 Director/Undergraduate Admissions .... Mr. Barry TAYLOR
20 Assoc VP Academic Administration .... Ms. Tonja MOORE
49 Dean College Arts & Sciences .... Dr. Kenneth FURTON
50 Exec Dean College Business Admin .... Dr. David KLOCK
54 Dean Col Engineering/Computing .... Dr. Amir MIRMIRAN
53 Dean College of Education .... Dr. Delia GARCIA
88 Dean Sch Hospitality Management .... Dr. Mike HAMPTON
60 Dean School Journ/Mass Communic .... Dr. Raul REIS
66 Dean Col Nursing/Health Science .... Dr. Ora STRICKLAND
69 Int Dean College of Public Health .... Dr. Michele CICCAZZO
61 Dean College of Law .... Mr. R. Alexander ACOSTA
63 Dean College of Medicine .... Dr. John ROCK
88 Dean Undergraduate Education .... Dr. Douglas ROBERTSON
58 Dean University Graduate School .... Dr. Lakshmi REDDI
92 Dean Honors College .... Dr. Lesley NORTHUP
48 Dean Col Architecture & the Arts .... Mr. Brian SCHRINER
77 Int Dir Sch Computing/Info Sciences .... Dr. Sundararaj IYENGAR
64 Director School of Music .... Mr. Orlando GARCIA
38 Director Counseling/Psych Svcs .... Dr. Cheryl NOWELL
22 Director Equal Opportunity Program .... Ms. Shirlyon J. MCWHORTER
88 Director School Accounting .... Dr. Ruth MCEWEN
88 Director Multicultural Pgms & Svcs .... Mr. Robert M. COATIE
62 Int Dean of Libraries .... Dr. Thomas BRESLIN
25 Assoc VP Sponsored Research .... Dr. Joseph BARABINO
41 Athletics Director .... Mr. Pete GARCIA
86 Asst VP for Government Affairs .... Ms. Michelle PALACIO
06 Int University Registrar .... Ms. Andrea JAY
86 VP for Government Relations .... Mr. Steve SAULS
88 Dir Community Rel/Special Events .... Ms. Dania RIVERO
37 Director Student Financial Aid .... Mr. Francisco VALINES
36 Int Director Career Services .... Ms. Ivette DUARTE
23 Director Univ Health Services .... Dr. Oscar LOYNAZ
39 Executive Director Student Housing .... Mr. James R. WASSENAAR, JR.
85 Director Intl Student/Scholar Svcs .... Ms. Ana M. SIPPIN
88 Director Disability Student Svcs .... Ms. Amanda NIGUIDULA
88 Director Internal Audit .... Mr. Allen VANN
24 Director Media & Technology Support .... Ms. Debra SHERIDAN
21 Associate VP and Univ Controller .... Ms. Cecilia HAMILTON
14 Assistant VP Univ Technology Svcs .... Mr. Robert GRILLO
88 Int Dir Environmentl Health/Safety .... Mr. William YOUNGBLUT
19 Chief of Police .... Chief Alexander CASAS
29 Assoc Vice Pres Alumni Affairs .... Mr. Bill DRAUGHON
27 Director Media Relations .... Ms. Maydel SANTANA-BRAVO
43 General Counsel .... Ms. Kristina RAATTAMA

*Florida State University (D)

Tallahassee FL 32306-9936

County: Leon — FICE Identification: 001489
Unit ID: 134097

Telephone: (850) 644-2525 — Carnegie Class: RU/VH
FAX Number: (850) 644-9936 — Calendar System: Semester
URL: www.fsu.edu
Established: 1851 — Annual Undergrad Tuition & Fees (In-State): $6,403
Enrollment: 41,087 — Coed
Affiliation or Control: State — IRS Status: 501(c)3
Highest Offering: Doctorate
Program: Liberal Arts And General; Teacher Preparatory; Professional
Accreditation: SC, AAFCS, ART, BUS, BUSA, CACREP, CIDA, CLPSY, CORE, CS, DANCE, DIETD, DIETI, ENG, IPSY, LAW, LIB, MED, MFCD, MUS, NURSE, PLNG, PSPSY, SP, SPAA, SW, TED, THEA

02 President ... Dr. Eric J. BARRON
05 Prov/Ex Vice Pres Academic Affs ... Dr. Garnett S. STOKES
10 Sr Vice Pres Finance & Admin ... Mr. John R. CARNAGHI
32 Vice President Student Affairs ... Dr. Mary B. COBURN
46 Vice President Research ... Dr. Kirby KEMPER
26 Vice President University Relations ... Ms. Elizabeth MARYANSKI
45 VP Planning and Programs ... Dr. Robert E. BRADLEY
30 VP University Advancement ... Mr. Thomas W. JENNINGS
102 Exec VP FSU Foundation ... Mr. Andy A. JHANJI
100 Chief of Staff to President ... Ms. Dawn RANDLE
88 Assoc Vice President for Research ... Dr. Ross ELLINGTON
18 Associate VP for Facilities ... Mr. Dennis A. BAILEY
21 Assoc VP Budget/Planning/Fin Svcs ... Mr. Rafael G. ALVAREZ
20 Associate VP for Academic Affairs ... Ms. Anne BLANKENSHIP
16 Asst Vice Pres for Human Resources ... Ms. Joyce A. INGRAM
11 Asst VP for Administrative Services ... Dr. Perry CROWELL
88 Dir Academic Pgm Professional Svcs ... Mr. Bill LINDNER
20 Interim Dean Faculties/Dep Provost ... Dr. Jennifer N. BUCHANAN
49 Interim Dean Arts & Sciences ... Dr. Sam HUCKABA
50 Dean Business ... Dr. Caryn BECK-DUDLEY
53 Dean Education ... Dr. Marcy P. DRISCOLL
59 Dean Human Sciences ... Dr. Billie COLLIER
88 Dean Communication & Information ... Dr. Larry DENNIS
66 Interim Dean Nursing ... Dr. Dianne SPEAKE
88 Dean Criminology ... Dr. Thomas BLOMBERG
61 Dean Law ... Mr. Donald WEIDNER
83 Dean Social Sciences ... Dr. David W. RASMUSSEN
70 Dean Social Work ... Dr. Nicholas MAZZA
88 Dean Motion Picture Arts ... Mr. Frank PATTERSON
64 Dean Music ... Dr. Don GIBSON
57 Dean Visual Arts/Theatre/Dance ... Dr. Sally E. MCRORIE
88 Director of Theatre ... Mr. Charles C. JACKSON
54 Dean Engineering ... Dr. Yaw YEBOAH
63 Dean Medicine ... Dr. John FOGARTY
58 Dean Graduate Studies ... Dr. Nancy MARCUS
88 Dean Undergraduate Studies ... Dr. Karen L. LAUGHLIN
35 Dean of Students ... Dr. Jeanine WARD-ROOF
12 Dean Panama City Branch Campus ... Dr. George DEPUY
07 Asst VP Admissions and Records ... Mr. John BARNHILL
06 University Registrar ... Ms. Kimberly BARBER
07 Director Admissions ... Ms. Janice FINNEY
92 Director University Honors Program ... Dr. James MATHES
37 Director Student Financial Aid ... Mr. Darryl MARSHALL
08 Director Libraries ... Ms. Julia ZIMMERMAN
27 Chief Information Officer ... Mr. Michael BARRETT
90 Dir University Computing Services ... Mr. Randy MCCAUSLAND
43 Interim University Attorney ... Ms. Carolyn EGAN
88 Asst VP of University Relations ... Dr. Jeanette DEDIEMAR
104 Director International Programs ... Dr. James E. PITTS
88 Chief Budget Officer ... Mr. Michael P. LAKE
09 Director Institutional Research ... Dr. Richard BURNETTE
86 Director Governmental Relations ... Ms. Kathleen M. DALY
41 Director Intercollegiate Athletics ... Mr. Randy SPETMAN
38 Director Student Counseling ... Dr. Nikki PRITCHETT
19 Director Public Safety ... Mr. David L. PERRY
23 Director Student Health Services ... Dr. Lesley SACHER
36 Director Career Center ... Ms. Myrna HOOVER
29 Director Alumni Affairs ... Mr. Scott ATWELL
88 Inspector General ... Mr. David COURY
28 Dir Office of Diversity/Equal Oppty ... Ms. Renisha L. GIBBS
96 Director of Purchasing ... Ms. Martha DOOLITTLE
39 Director Student Housing ... Ms. Adrienne FRAME
88 Director Technology Service/Support ... Mr. Harvey BUCHANAN
106 Director Distance Learning ... Ms. Susann RUDASILL
88 Director Sponsored Research ... Mr. Gregory THOMPSON
88 Director IT Security ... Mr. Joseph LAZOR

*New College of Florida (A)

5800 Bay Shore Road, Sarasota FL 34243-2109

County: Sarasota | FICE Identification: 001507 | Unit ID: 262129
Telephone: (941) 487-4100 | Carnegie Class: Bac/A&S
FAX Number: (941) 487-4101 | Calendar System: 4/1/4
URL: www.ncf.edu
Established: 1960 | Annual Undergrad Tuition & Fees (In-State): $6,783
Enrollment: 845 | Coed
Affiliation or Control: State | IRS Status: 501(c)3
Highest Offering: Baccalaureate
Program: Liberal Arts And General
Accreditation: SC

02 President ... Dr. Donal E. O'SHEA
05 Provost ... Dr. Stephen MILES
10 Vice Pres Finance & Administration ... Mr. John U. MARTIN
79 Chair of Humanities ... Dr. Aron EDIDIN
81 Chair of Natural Sciences ... Dr. Paul SCUDDER
83 Chair of Social Sciences ... Dr. David HARVEY
08 Dean Cook Library ... Dr. Brian DOHERTY
84 Dean of Enrollment & Info Tech ... Ms. Kathleen KILLION
32 Dean of Students ... Dr. Wendy BASHANT
07 Associate Dean of Admissions ... Ms. Sonia WU
20 Associate Academic Officer ... Dr. Raymonda BURGMAN
21 Associate Business Officer ... Mr. William LAWHON
13 Director of Information Support ... Mr. Jeff SMITH
29 Director Alumnae/i Association ... Ms. Jessica ROGERS
06 Registrar ... Ms. Lynn FOWLER
26 Director Public Affairs ... Mr. Jake HARTVIGSEN
38 Director Counseling ... Dr. Anne E. FISHER
39 Director Residence Life ... Mr. Tracy MURRY
09 Director of Institutional Research ... Ms. Hui-Men WEN
15 Director Personnel Services ... Mr. Mark LEVENSON
18 Chief Facilities/Physical Plant ... Mr. Robert MASON
28 Director of Diversity ... Vacant
96 Director of Purchasing ... Mr. Mark LILLQUIST
37 Director Student Financial Aid ... Ms. Tara KARAS
43 Director Legal Svcs/General Counsel ... Mr. David SMOLKER
25 Contract Administrator ... Ms. Jeanne WARE
72 Director of Technology Support ... Mr. Jeff SMITH
04 Assistant to the President ... Ms. Suzanne L. JANNEY
30 Chief Development ... Mr. Clint MONTS DE OCA
35 Director Student Affairs ... Mr. Tracy MURRY

*University of Central Florida (B)

PO Box 160000, Orlando FL 32816-0001

County: Orange | FICE Identification: 003954 | Unit ID: 132903
Telephone: (407) 823-2000 | Carnegie Class: RU/VH
FAX Number: N/A | Calendar System: Semester
URL: www.ucf.edu
Established: 1963 | Annual Undergrad Tuition & Fees (In-State): $5,584
Enrollment: 58,052 | Coed
Affiliation or Control: State | IRS Status: 501(c)3
Highest Offering: Doctorate
Program: Occupational; Liberal Arts And General; Teacher Preparatory; Professional
Accreditation: SC, BUS, BUSA, CACREP, CEA, CLPSY, CS, ENG, HSA, IPSY, #MED, MT, MUS, NURSE, PTA, SP, SPAA, SW, TED

02 President ... Dr. John C. HITT
05 Provost/Executive Vice President ... Dr. Tony G. WALDROP
100 Vice President and Chief of Staff ... Dr. John SCHELL
10 Vice Pres Administration & Finance ... Mr. William F. MERCK, II
26 Vice President University Relations ... Dr. Daniel HOLSENBECK
43 Vice President/General Counsel ... Mr. W. Scott COLE
46 VP Research and Commercialization ... Dr. M. J. SOILEAU
26 VP Strategy/Mktg/Comm/Admissions .. VAdm. Alfred HARMS, JR.
32 VP Student Dev/Enrollment Svcs ... Dr. Maribeth EHASZ
30 Vice Pres Development/Alumni Rels ... Mr. Robert HOLMES, JR.
31 Vice President for Community Rels ... Ms. Helen DONEGAN
63 VP Medical Affairs/Dean Med College ... Dr. Deborah GERMAN
49 Dean College of Arts & Humanities ... Dr. Jose B. FERNANDEZ
50 Dean College of Business Admin ... Dr. Paul JARLEY
53 Dean College of Education ... Dr. Sandra L. ROBINSON
54 Int Dean College of Engr/Comp Sci ... Dr. Michael GEORGIOPOULOS
76 Dean College of Hlth/Pub Affs ... Dr. Michael FRUMKIN
88 Dean Rosen College Hospitality Mgt ... Dr. Abraham PIZAM
66 Dean College of Nursing ... Dr. Jean LEUNER
88 Dean College of Optics & Photonics ... Dr. Bahaa SALEH
81 Dean College of Sciences ... Dr. Michael D. JOHNSON
92 Dean Burnett Honors College ... Dr. Alvin WANG
20 Vice Provost Academic Affairs ... Dr. Diane CHASE
13 Vice Provost Info Tech/Resources ... Dr. Joel L. HARTMAN
20 Vice Provost Academic Admin ... Dr. Edward NEIGHBOR
12 Int Vice Provost Regional Campuses ... Dr. Joyce DORNER
58 Int Vice Provost/Dean Graduate ... Dr. Charles R. HINKLE
88 Interim Vice Provost/Dean Undergrad ... Dr. Elliot VITTES
18 Assoc VP Facilities and Safety ... Ms. Lee KERNEK
29 Assoc Vice Pres Alumni Relations ... Mr. Tom MESSINA
86 Assoc VP for University Relations ... Mr. Fred KITTINGER
88 Assoc VP Rsrch & Commercialization ... Mr. Tom O'NEAL
07 Assoc VP Undergrad Admissions ... Dr. Gordon CHAVIS
21 Assoc Vice Pres Admin/Finance ... Ms. Judith MONROE
27 Assoc VP Dir News & Information ... Mr. Grant HESTON
88 Int Assoc Vice Provost Fac Relation ... Dr. Lyman BRODIE
09 Asst VP Institutional Research ... Dr. M. Paige BORDEN
37 Exec Dir Student Financial Asst ... Ms. Mary MCKINNEY
06 University Registrar ... Mr. Brian BOYD
08 Director Libraries ... Mr. Barry BAKER
15 Asst VP Human Resources ... Mr. Mark A. ROBERTS
19 Director Public Safety/Police ... Mr. Richard BEARY
93 Director Multicul Acad Suppt Svcs ... Mr. Wayne JACKSON
14 Dir Comp Svcs/Telecommunications ... Mr. Robert YANCKELLO
38 Director Counseling Center ... Dr. Stacey PEARSON
41 Vice Pres & Director of Athletics ... Mr. Todd STANSBURY
22 Director EEO Affirmative Action ... Ms. Janet BALANOFF
23 Director Health Center ... Dr. Michael G. DEICHEN
39 Director Housing and Residence Life ... Mrs. Christi HARTZLER
28 Director of Diversity Initiatives ... Dr. Valarie G. KING
96 Director of Purchasing ... Mr. Gregory ROBINSON
36 Director Career Services ... Ms. Lynn HANSEN

*University of Florida (C)

235 Tigert Hall, Gainesville FL 32611-9500

County: Alachua | FICE Identification: 001535 | Unit ID: 134130
Telephone: (352) 392-3261 | Carnegie Class: RU/VH
FAX Number: N/A | Calendar System: Semester
URL: www.ufl.edu
Established: 1853 | Annual Undergrad Tuition & Fees (In-State): $6,143
Enrollment: 49,589 | Coed
Affiliation or Control: State | IRS Status: 501(c)3
Highest Offering: Doctorate
Program: Liberal Arts And General; Teacher Preparatory; Professional
Accreditation: SC, ARCPA, ART, AUD, BUS, BUSA, CACREP, CEA, CIDA, CLPSY, CONST, COPSY, DANCE, DENT, DIETD, DIETI, ENG, ENGR, FOR, HSA, IPSY, JOUR, LAW, LSAR, MED, MIDWF, MUS, NURSE, OT, PH, PHAR, PLNG, PTA, SCPSY, SP, TED, THEA, VET

02 President ... Dr. James B. MACHEN
05 Provost & Senior Vice President ... Dr. Joseph GLOVER
47 Sr Vice Pres Agric/Natural Res ... Dr. Jack M. PAYNE
17 Sr Vice Pres Health Affairs ... Dr. David S. GUZICK
11 Sr Vice Pres/Chief Operating Ofcr ... Dr. Winfred M. PHILLIPS
30 Vice President Dev/Alumni Affairs ... Mr. Thomas J. MITCHELL
10 Vice President Business Affairs ... Mr. Curtis REYNOLDS
32 Vice President Student Affairs ... Mr. David KRATZER
26 Vice President Univ Relations ... Ms. Jane A. ADAMS
15 Vice Pres Human Resources ... Ms. Paula V. FUSSELL
46 Vice President Research ... Dr. David P. NORTON
43 Vice President/General Counsel ... Ms. Jamie L. KEITH
13 Vice President & CIO ... Mr. Elias G. ELDAYRIE
86 Assoc VP Government Relations ... Ms. Marion S. HOFFMAN
26 Asc Vice Pres/Public Rel/Marketing ... Mr. William A. FLETCHER
21 Finance/Admin Assoc Vice President ... Mr. Fred CANTRELL
21 Finance/Admin Assoc Vice President ... Mr. Robert MILLER
18 AVP of Facilities/Plng/Construction ... Ms. Carol WALKER
20 Associate Provost ... Dr. Kathleen A. LONG
20 Associate Provost ... Dr. Angel KWOLEK-FOLLAND
92 Assoc Provost Undergrad Affairs ... Dr. Bernard A. MAIR
09 Asst Provost/Dir Inst Research/Plng ... Dr. Marie ZEGLEN
84 Vice Pres Enroll Mgmt/Assoc Provost ... Dr. Zina EVANS
35 Int Dean Stdnts/Asst VP Stdnt Affs ... Dr. Jen D. SHAW
08 Dean University Libraries ... Ms. Judith RUSSELL
50 Dean of Business Administration ... Dr. John KRAFT
49 Dean of Liberal Arts & Science ... Dr. Paul J. D'ANIERI
68 Dean Health/Human Performance ... Dr. Steve M. DORMAN
61 Dean of Law ... Mr. Robert H. JERRY
66 Dean of Nursing ... Dr. Kathleen A. LONG
67 Dean of Pharmacy ... Dr. William H. RIFFEE
54 Dean of Engineering ... Dr. Cammy ABERNATHY
47 Dean Agricultural/Life Sciences ... Dr. Teresa C. BALSER
60 Dean of Journalism/Communications ... Dr. John W. WRIGHT
76 Dean Pub Health/Health Professions ... Dr. Michael PERRI
53 Dean of Education ... Dr. Glenn GOOD
47 Int Dean IFAS Extension ... Dr. Millie FERRER
74 Dean of Veterinary Medicine ... Dr. Glen F. HOFFSIS
57 Dean of Fine Arts ... Ms. Lucinda LAVELLI
48 Dean Design Construction Planning ... Dr. Christopher SILVER
63 Dean of Medicine ... Dr. Michael L. GOOD
46 Int Dean of IFAS Research ... Dr. John HAYES
52 Dean of Dentistry ... Dr. Teresa A. DOLAN
65 Sr Asc Dn/Dir Sch Natural Res/Envir ... Dr. James C. CATO
58 Dean Graduate School ... Dr. Henry T. FRIERSON
06 University Registrar ... Mr. Stephen J. PRITZ
23 Director of Student Health ... Dr. Phillip L. BARKLEY
38 Director of Counseling Center ... Dr. Sherry BENTON
37 Int Director Student Financial Aid ... Mr. Richard D. WILDER
36 Director of Placement Services ... Dr. Wayne E. WALLACE
14 Director of Computer Center ... Mr. Timothy J. FITZPATRICK
19 Director of University Police ... Ms. Linda J. STUMP
27 Assoc Director News & Public Affs ... Mr. Frank AHERN
27 Assoc Director News & Public Affs ... Mr. Stephen F. ORLANDO
24 Director of Academic Technology ... Dr. Fedro S. ZAZUETA
65 Director of Forestry ... Dr. Timothy L. WHITE
39 Director of Housing ... Mr. Norbert W. DUNKEL
41 Athletic Director ... Mr. Jeremy N. FOLEY
29 Int Exec Director Alumni Affairs ... Ms. Katie MARQUIS
15 Director Human Resources ... Ms. Jodi D. GENTRY
28 Director of Diversity ... Ms. Tamara COHEN
96 Director of Purchasing ... Ms. Lisa DEAL

*University of North Florida (D)

1 UNF Drive, Jacksonville FL 32224-7699

County: Duval | FICE Identification: 009841 | Unit ID: 136172
Telephone: (904) 620-1000 | Carnegie Class: Master's L
FAX Number: (904) 620-2414 | Calendar System: Semester
URL: www.unf.edu
Established: 1965 | Annual Undergrad Tuition & Fees (In-State): $6,309
Enrollment: 16,368 | Coed
Affiliation or Control: State | IRS Status: 501(c)3
Highest Offering: Doctorate
Program: Liberal Arts And General; Teacher Preparatory; Professional
Accreditation: SC, ANEST, BUS, BUSA, CACREP, CONST, CS, DIETD, DIETI, ENG, HSA, MUS, NURSE, PH, PTA, SPAA, TED

02 President ... Mr. John A. DELANEY
05 Provost ... Dr. Mark E. WORKMAN
20 Associate Provost ... Dr. Bobby E. WALDRUP
20 Associate Provost ... Dr. Newton N. JACKSON
100 VP/Chief of Staff ... Dr. Thomas S. SERWATKA
86 VP Governmental Affairs ... Ms. Janet D. OWEN
43 VP/General Counsel ... Ms. Karen J. STONE
15 VP Human Resources ... Ms. Rachelle GOTTLIEB
10 VP Administration/Finance ... Ms. Shari A. SHUMAN
30 VP Institutional Advancement ... Dr. Pierre N. ALLAIRE
32 VP Student & International Affairs ... Dr. Mauricio GONZALEZ
84 Assoc VP for Enrollment Services ... Ms. Deborah M. KAYE
88 Assoc VP/Compliance Officer ... Dr. Joann N. CAMPBELL
21 Assoc VP Admin & Finance ... Mr. Scott BENNETT
13 Assoc VP Chief Info Officer ... Mr. Lance TAYLOR
44 Assoc VP Major Gifts ... Ms. Elizabeth M. HEAD
35 Assoc VP Student Affairs ... Mr. Everett J. MALCOLM, III
45 Asst VP Research ... Dr. Imeh D. EBONG
88 Asst VP Development ... Ms. Ann S. MCCULLEN
26 Asst VP Public Relations ... Ms. Sharon ASHTON
88 Asst VP Student Affairs ... Dr. Lucy S. CROFT
89 Dean of Undergraduate Studies ... Dr. Jeffrey W. COKER
58 Dean of the Graduate School ... Dr. James L. ROBERSON
08 Dean of the Library ... Dr. Shirley HALLBLADE
49 Dean College of Arts & Sciences ... Dr. Barbara HETRICK
50 Dean Coggin College of Business ... Dr. Ajay SAMANT
53 Dean College of Education ... Dr. Larry DANIEL

76 Dean Brooks College of Health .... Dr. Pam CHALLY
77 Dean Computing Engineering & Constr .... Dr. Mark A. TUMEO
51 Dean Continuing Education .... Mr. Robert WOOD
04 Executive Director Pres Office .... Mr. Donald A. SHEA
16 Dir Human Resources .... Ms. Teresa L. SANDROCK
88 Dir Internal Auditing .... Mr. Robert L. BERRY
22 Dir Equal Oppty Programs .... Ms. Cheryl N. GONZALEZ
88 Dir Professional Dev Training .... Ms. Idania R. GROPPER
21 Chief Budget Officer .... Mr. Ricky B. ARJUNE
21 Controller .... Ms. Valerie O. STEVENSON
88 Dir Environment Health/Safety .... Mr. Daniel D. ENDICOTT
88 Dir ADA Compliance .... Ms. Rocelia T. GONZALEZ
88 Treasurer .... Mr. Michael S. NEGLIA
18 Dir Univ Facilities Planning .... Mr. Zak OVADIA
88 Dir University Center .... Mr. George ANDROUIN
29 Dir Alumni Services .... Ms. Faith M. HALL
19 Dir Safety Security .... Mr. John E. DEAN
36 Dir Career Development Services .... Mr. Rick ROBERTS
85 Dir Intercultural Ctr for Peace .... Dr. Oupa SEANE
88 Dir Child Development Research Ctr .... Ms. Pam BELL
23 Chief Medical Officer .... Dr. Fred BECK
38 Dir Univ Counseling Center .... Dr. Theresa M. DINUZZO
88 Dir Women's Center .... Ms. Sheila D. SPIVEY
85 Dir The International Center .... Dr. Timothy ROBINSON
39 Dir Housing Residence Life .... Mr. Paul RIEL
41 Athletic Director .... Mr. Lee L. MOON
88 Dir Office of Faculty .... Dr. Francis D. RICHARD
88 Exec Dir of Assessment .... Dr. Judith E. MILLER
92 Dir Honors Program .... Dr. Mary O. BORG
37 Dir Student Financial Aid .... Ms. Anissa AGNE
06 Registrar .... Mrs. Megan R. KUEHNER
44 Associate Director Annual Giving .... Ms. Lynn M. BROWN
88 Associate Vice Pres for Major Gifts .... Ms. Elizabeth HEAD
07 Dir Admissions .... Mr. John YANCEY
25 Dir Contracts and Grants Acct .... Ms. Cheresa Y. HAMILTON
09 Dir Institutional Research .... Dr. Richard S. POWELL
88 Exec Dir FL Inst of Education .... Dr. Cheryl A. FOUNTAIN
104 Dir Study Abroad .... Ms. Anne S. FUGARD
88 Dir Small Business Dev Ctr .... Ms. Janice W. DONALDSON
88 Dir Disability Resource Center .... Dr. Kristine W. WEBB
96 Dir Purchasing .... Ms. Kathy RITTER
103 Dir Continuing Education .... Mr. Timothy W. GILES

*University of South Florida (A)

4202 E Fowler Avenue, Tampa FL 33620-6100
County: Hillsborough FICE Identification: 001537
Unit ID: 137351
Telephone: (813) 974-2011 Carnegie Class: RU/VH
FAX Number: (813) 974-5530 Calendar System: Semester
URL: www.usf.edu
Established: 1956 Annual Undergrad Tuition & Fees (In-State): $6,334
Enrollment: 47,362 Coed
Affiliation or Control: State IRS Status: 501(c)3
Highest Offering: Doctorate
Program: Liberal Arts And General; Teacher Preparatory; Professional
Accreditation: SC, ANEST, ART, AUD, BUS, BUSA, CACREP, CEA, CLPSY, CORE, CS, ENG, ENGR, IPSY, JOUR, LIB, MED, MUS, NURSE, PH, @PHAR, PTA, SCPSY, SP, SPAA, SW, TED, THEA

02 President .... Dr. Judy L. GENSHAFT
100 Chief of Staff/President's Office .... Dr. Cynthia S. VISOT
05 Prov/Exec Vice Pres Academic Affs .... Dr. Ralph WILCOX
82 USF Wrld-Sr VP Global Affs/Intl Res .... Dr. Karen HOLBROOK
46 Vice Pres Research & Innovation .... Dr. Paul SANBERG
17 Sr Vice Pres USF Health .... Dr. Stephen K. KLASKO
20 Sr Vice Prov Faculty & Development .... Dr. Dwayne SMITH
10 Vice Pres Business & Finance .... Mr. Nick TRIVUNOVICH
11 Vice Pres Administrative Services .... Ms. Sandy LOVINS
30 Sr Vice Pres University Advancement .... Mr. Joel MOMBERG
32 Vice President Student Affairs .... Vacant
13 Vice Pres Information Technology .... Mr. Michael PEARCE
26 VP Univ Communication/Marketing .... Vacant
35 Assoc Vice Pres Student Affairs .... Dr. Denita SISCOE
29 Assoc Vice Pres Alumni Affairs .... Mr. Bill MCCAUSLAND
44 Assoc Vice Pres Development .... Mr. Rod GRABOWSKI
14 Assoc Vice Pres Info Technologies .... Mr. George W. ELLIS
22 Assoc VP for Diversity/Equal Oppty .... Dr. Ted WILLIAMS
84 Assoc VP Enrollment Planning & Mgmt .... Dr. Paul J. DOSAL
86 Asst Vice Pres Government Rels .... Mr. Mark WALSH
35 Asst Vice Pres Student Affairs .... Dr. Kevin M. BANKS
35 Asst Vice Pres Student Affairs .... Mr. Guy CONWAY
40 Asst VP Auxillary Services .... Mr. Jeffrey A. MACK
43 General Counsel .... Mr. Steven D. PREVAUX
39 Dean Housing/Residential Educ .... Ms. Ana HERNANDEZ
83 Dean Behavioral/Community Sci .... Dr. Julianne SEROVICH
50 Dean Business Administration .... Dr. Moez LIMAYEM
53 Dean Education .... Vacant
54 Dean Engineering .... Dr. John M. WIENCEK
57 Dean College of the Arts .... Dr. James S. MOY
49 Dean Arts & Sciences .... Dr. Eric EISENBERG
66 Dean Nursing .... Dr. Dianne MORRISON-BEEDY
69 Dean Public Health .... Dr. Donna PETERSEN
58 Dean Graduate School .... Dr. Karen D. LILLER
89 Dean of Undergraduate Studies .... Dr. W. Robert SULLINS
51 Dean University College .... Dr. Judy ASHCROFT
48 Dir Sch of Architecture/Cmty Design .... Mr. Robert MACLEOD
12 Regional Chanc Sarasota-Manatee .... Dr. Arthur M. GUILFORD
12 Regional Chanc USF St Petersburg .... Dr. Margaret SULLIVAN
21 Comptroller .... Ms. Linda PETERSON
27 Director of News .... Ms. Lara WADE
06 University Registrar .... Ms. Angela W. DEBOSE
07 Director Admissions .... Mr. David HENRY
18 Director Physical Plant .... Mr. Adrian CUARTA
21 University Budget Officer .... Ms. Bertha P. ALEXANDER
37 Director Financial Aid .... Ms. Billy Jo HAMILTON
38 Interim Director Counseling Ctr .... Dr. Dale A. HICKS
36 Director of the Career Center .... Dr. Drema K. HOWARD
19 Director University Police .... Mr. Thomas F. LONGO
08 USF Libraries Dean .... Dr. William GARRISON
41 Director of Athletics .... Mr. Doug WOOLARD
28 Director of Diversity & Inclusion .... Ms. Patsy FELICIANO
96 Director Purchasing & Property Svcs .... Mr. Michael ABERNETHY

*University of South Florida Manatee-Sarasota (B)

8350 Tamiami Trail, Sarasota FL 34243-2049
County: Manatee Identification: 667058
Unit ID: 451671
Telephone: (941) 359-4200 Carnegie Class: Master's M
FAX Number: N/A Calendar System: Semester
URL: www.usfsm.edu
Established: 1956 Annual Undergrad Tuition & Fees (In-State): $4,547
Enrollment: 435 Coed
Affiliation or Control: State IRS Status: 501(c)3
Highest Offering: Master's; No Lower Division
Program: Liberal Arts And General; Teacher Preparatory; Professional
Accreditation: SC

02 Regional Chancellor .... Dr. Arthur M. GUILFORD
10 Vice Chancellor Business & Finance .... Mr. Ben ELLINOR
05 Vice Chancellor Academic Affairs .... Dr. Bonnie JONES
32 Dean of Students .... Ms. Mary Beth WALLACE
30 Vice Chancellor Advancement .... Mr. Dennis L. STOVER
49 Dean College of Arts & Sciences .... Dr. Jane ROSE
50 Dean College of Business .... Dr. Robert ANDERSON
53 Dean College of Education .... Dr. Terry OSBORN
88 Dean Sch Hotel & Restaurant Mgmt .... Dr. Cihan COBANOGLU

*University of South Florida St. Petersburg (C)

140 7th Avenue S, Saint Petersburg FL 33701-5016
County: Pinellas FICE Identification: 009016
Unit ID: 448840
Telephone: (727) 873-4873 Carnegie Class: Master's M
FAX Number: (727) 553-4131 Calendar System: Semester
URL: www.stpete.usf.edu
Established: 1966 Annual Undergrad Tuition & Fees (In-District): $5,200
Enrollment: 4,310 Coed
Affiliation or Control: State/Local IRS Status: 501(c)3
Highest Offering: Master's
Program: Liberal Arts And General; Teacher Preparatory; Professional
Accreditation: SC, BUS, BUSA, JOUR, TED

02 Int Regional Chancellor .... Dr. William T. HOGARTH
04 Special Asst to Regional Chancellor .... Ms. Pam NGO
05 Reg Vice Chanc Academic Affairs .... Dr. Norine NOONAN
11 Reg Vice Chanc Admin/Financial Svcs .... Dr. Ashok DHINGRA
26 Reg Vice Chanc External Affairs .... Dr. Helen LEVINE
32 Reg Assoc Vice Chanc Student Affs .... Dr. Julie WONG
49 Dean College of Arts & Sciences .... Dr. Frank BIAFORA
50 Dean College of Business .... Dr. Maling EBRAHIMPOUR
53 Dean College of Education .... Dr. William HELLER
08 Dean of the Library .... Ms. Carol HIXSON
09 Dir Inst Res/Effectiveness .... Dr. J. E. GONZALEZ
19 Chief of Police .... Ms. Renee CHENEVERT
13 Director of Campus Computing .... Mr. Jeff REISBERG
16 Associate Director Human Resources .... Ms. Sandra CONWAY
37 Director of Financial Aid .... Ms. Erin DUNN
06 Director Records and Registration .... Ms. Linda CROSSMAN
07 Director Admissions & Marketing .... Ms. Holly KICKLITER
30 Executive Director of Development .... Ms. Kim HALL
18 Dir Facil Plng/Construction Svcs .... Mr. John DICKSON
96 Purchasing Manager .... Mr. Bill BENJAMIN

*University of West Florida (D)

11000 University Parkway, Pensacola FL 32514-5750
County: Escambia FICE Identification: 003955
Unit ID: 138354
Telephone: (850) 474-2000 Carnegie Class: DRU
FAX Number: (850) 474-3131 Calendar System: Semester
URL: uwf.edu
Established: 1963 Annual Undergrad Tuition & Fees (In-State): $5,425
Enrollment: 11,982 Coed
Affiliation or Control: State IRS Status: 501(c)3
Highest Offering: Doctorate
Program: Liberal Arts And General; Teacher Preparatory; Professional
Accreditation: SC, BUS, ENG, MT, MUS, NURSE, PH, SW, TED

02 President .... Dr. Judy A. BENSE
05 Provost .... Dr. Chula G. KING
32 Vice President Student Affairs .... Dr. Kevin BAILEY
11 VP for Administrative Services .... Mr. Matthew ALTIER
20 Vice Provost .... Dr. George B. ELLENBERG
27 Sr Assoc VP University Affairs/CIO .... Mr. Mike F. DIECKMANN
30 Vice Pres for Development .... Dr. Kyle MARRERO
84 Assoc Vice Pres Enrollment Mgt .... Mrs. Susan J. MCKINNON
18 Assoc VP Facilities Dev/Operations .... Dr. James R. BARNETT
35 Associate Vice Pres Student Affairs .... Dr. James R. HURD
58 AVP Res & Dean of Grad Students .... Dr. Richard S. PODEMSKI
21 Asc VP Internal Audit/Mgmt Consultg .... Ms. J. Betsy BOWERS
15 Associate Vice Pres Human Resources .... Mrs. Sherell D. HENDRICKSON
96 Assoc VP Public Safety & Mgmt Svcs .... Mr. David J. O'BRIEN
28 Assoc VP Diversity/Intl Educ/Pgms .... Dr. Angela E. MCCORVEY
88 Executive Director .... Mr. J. Patrick CRAWFORD
43 Associate General Counsel .... Ms. Patricia D. LOTT
35 Assistant VP/Dean of Students .... Dr. Tammy L. MCGUCKIN
50 Dean of Business .... Dr. F. Edward RANELLI
49 Dean of Arts & Sciences .... Dr. Jane S. HALONEN
107 Dean of Professional Studies .... Dr. Pamela NORTHRUP
100 Chief of Staff .... Dr. Kimberly S. BROWN
08 Dean University Libraries .... Mr. Robert DUGAN
35 Associate Dean of Students .... Dr. LuSharon WILEY
10 Chief Budget Officer .... Dr. Susan E. STEPHENSON
21 Asst VP Financial Services .... Ms. Colleen M. ASMUS
06 Registrar .... Mrs. Ann H. DZIADON
13 Chief Technology Officer .... Mrs. Melanie J. HAVEARD
07 Director of Admissions .... Mr. Stephen MCKELLIPS
92 Director of Honors Program .... Dr. Gregory W. LANIER
37 Director of Financial Aid .... Ms. Cathy R. BROWN
19 Director of University Police .... Mr. John S. WARREN
39 Director of Housing/Residence Life .... Dr. Ruth L. DAVISON
38 Director Health & Counseling .... Dr. Rebecca E. KENNEDY
88 Director Facilities Planning .... Mr. Kenneth C. KLINDT
29 Director of Alumni Relations .... Ms. Katherine C. EHEREDGE
41 Athletic Director .... Mr. David L. SCOTT
26 Director Mktg & Creative Services .... Ms. Sabrina MCLAUGHLIN
09 Director Institutional Research .... Vacant
44 Director of Development .... Ms. Martha Lee BLODGETT
21 Director University Budgets .... Ms. Valerie Z. MONEYHAM
21 Director Business/Auxiliary Svcs .... Ms. Ellen P. TILL
57 Dir Sch Fine/Performing/Comm Arts .... Dr. Brendan B. KELLY

Stenotype Institute of Jacksonville (E)

3563 Phillips Hwy, Bldg E Suite 501, Jacksonville FL 32207
County: Duval FICE Identification: 008417
Unit ID: 137537
Telephone: (904) 398-4141 Carnegie Class: Assoc/PrivFP
FAX Number: (904) 398-7878 Calendar System: Trimester
URL: www.stenotype.edu
Established: N/A Annual Undergrad Tuition & Fees: $16,100
Enrollment: 203 Coed
Affiliation or Control: Proprietary IRS Status: Proprietary
Highest Offering: Associate Degree
Program: Occupational
Accreditation: ACICS

01 Executive Director .... Carl MCGOWAN
05 Director of Education .... Carol CLARK
07 Director of Admissions .... Tanveer AHMED

Stetson University (F)

421 N Woodland Boulevard, DeLand FL 32723-0001
County: Volusia FICE Identification: 001531
Unit ID: 137546
Telephone: (386) 822-7000 Carnegie Class: Master's L
FAX Number: (386) 822-8832 Calendar System: 4/1/4
URL: www.stetson.edu
Established: 1883 Annual Undergrad Tuition & Fees: $36,644
Enrollment: 3,877 Coed
Affiliation or Control: Independent Non-Profit IRS Status: 501(c)3
Highest Offering: Doctorate
Program: Liberal Arts And General; Teacher Preparatory; Professional
Accreditation: SC, BUS, BUSA, CACREP, LAW, MUS, TED

01 President .... Dr. Wendy B. LIBBY
05 Provost & Vice Pres Acad Affairs .... Dr. Beth PAUL
10 VP for Business Affairs & CFO .... Mr. F. Robert HUTH
88 Spec Advsr to Pres for Philanthropy .... Ms. Linda P. DAVIS
30 Vice Pres for University Relations .... Ms. Carol JULIAN
84 VP Enrollment Management .... Mr. Joel BAUMAN
26 VP for University Marketing .... Mr. Gregory CARROLL
32 Vice President for Student Affairs .... Mr. Christopher KANDUS-FISHER
61 Dean College of Law .... Mr. Christopher PIETRUSZKIEWICZ
49 Dean of College of Arts & Sciences .... Dr. Karen RYAN
50 Dean of School of Business Admin .... Dr. Thomas SCHWARZ
64 Dean of School of Music .... Dr. Jean O. WEST
20 Assoc Provost for Faculty Devlpmnt .... Dr. Karen KAIVOLA
20 Assoc VP for Boundless Learning .... Dr. Emily RICHARDSON
20 Asst Provost for Student Success .... Dr. Lua HANCOCK
06 Registrar .... Vacant
08 Dean of duPont-Ball Library .... Ms. Susan RYAN
27 Assoc VP Technology & CIO .... Mr. R. William PENNEY
15 Assoc VP for Human Resources .... Ms. Shelia DANIELS
18 Assoc Vice Pres Facilities Mgmt .... Mr. Al ALLEN
21 Assoc Vice Pres for Finance .... Mr. Jeffrey MARGHEIM
88 Asst Vice Pres for Univ Relations .... Ms. Rina TOVAR
07 Dean of Admissions .... Mr. Robert STEWART
32 Asst Dean of Students .... Ms. Rosalie CARPENTER
39 Exec Dir of Housing & Res Life .... Mr. Ben FALTER
09 Dir Institutional Research & Plng .... Dr. Ray BARCLAY
42 University Chaplain .... Rev. Michael R. FRONK
44 Director of Annual Giving .... Mr. Mark ERNEST
44 Director of Planned Giving .... Ms. Katheryn P. PEARCE
29 Director Alumni Relations .... Ms. Colleen M. COOPER
51 Director Continuing Education .... Mr. William R. O'CONNOR
36 Director Univ Career Services .... Ms. Robin KAZMAREK
104 Director of International Learning .... Mr. Eric CANNY

38 Director Counseling Center .... Ms. Cheryl HAMMOCK
41 Director of Athletics ....Mr. Jeffrey P. ALTIER
15 Director Human Resources ....Ms. Betty WHITEMAN
23 Director Health Services .... Ms. Suzanne E. VILLALOBOS
96 Director of Purchasing ....Ms. Valinda WIMER
19 Chief Pubic Safety ....Mr. Robert MATUSICK

Tallahassee Community College (A)

444 Appleyard Drive, Tallahassee FL 32304-2895
County: Leon FICE Identification: 001533
Unit ID: 137759
Telephone: (850) 201-6200 Carnegie Class: Assoc/Pub-R-L
FAX Number: (850) 201-8682 Calendar System: Semester
URL: www.tcc.fl.edu
Established: 1966 Annual Undergrad Tuition & Fees (In-District): $2,569
Enrollment: 15,275 Coed
Affiliation or Control: Local IRS Status: 501(c)3
Highest Offering: Associate Degree
Program: Occupational; 2-Year Principally Bachelor's Creditable
Accreditation: SC, DA, DH, EMT

01 President .... Dr. Jim MURDAUGH
10 Vice Pres Administrative Svcs/CFO .... Dr. Teresa SMITH
13 Int VP Information Technology .... Dr. Teresa SMITH
05 Vice President for Academic Affairs .... Dr. Barbara SLOAN
32 Vice President for Student Affs .... Ms. Sharon JEFFERSON
103 Int VP Workforce Development .... Mr. Robin JOHNSTON
88 Assoc VP Inst Effectiveness .... Dr. Lei WANG
11 Asst VP Administrative Services .... Mr. Jerry SCHILLING
100 Chief of Staff .... Mr. Scott BALOG
12 Asst VP Florida Public Safety Inst .... Vacant
57 Dean Communications & Humanities .... Dr. Marge BANOCY-PAYNE
83 Dean History & Social Sciences ....Dr. Monte FINKELSTEIN
81 Dean Science & Math ....Dr. Frank BROWN
72 Dean Technology & Professional Pgms .... Ms. Kate STEWART
20 Dean Academic Support ....Dr. Sally SEARCH
08 Director of Library Services ....Ms. Deborah P. ROBINSON
76 Dean Health Care Professions ....Ms. Alice NIED
37 Director of Financial Aid .... Mr. William SPIERS
84 Dean Enrollment Management .... Vacant
15 Director of Human Resources ....Ms. Renae TOLSON
102 Director of TCC Foundation .... Mr. Robin JOHNSTON
41 Director of Athletics ....Mr. Rob CHANEY
35 Director of Campus Life ....Mr. Douglas K. WADDELL
27 Director of Communications ....Ms. Alice MAXWELL
88 Exec Dir Florida Public Safety Inst .... Mr. E. E. EUNICE
18 Dir Facilities/Construction/Plng .... Mr. David WILDES
21 Controller .... Ms. Patricia MANNING
45 Director of Educational Research ....Dr. Barbara J. GILL
09 Director of Institutional Research ....Ms. Margaret WINGATE
72 Dir Ctr for Instruct Tech/Dist Educ .... Vacant
106 Dir Center for Distance Learning ....Dr. Marilyn DICKEY
88 Dir Ctr for Teach/Learn/Ldrshp .... Dr. Karinda BARRETT
13 Director IT & Support Services ....Mr. Chip SINGLETARY
18 Construction Coordinator .... Mr. Bill HUNTER
88 Dir Budget and General Services .... Vacant
85 International Students Coordinator .... Ms. Betty JENSEN
14 Dir Management Information Systems .... Mr. John BURCH
25 Contracts and Grants Manager .... Ms. Vanessa LAWRENCE
88 Director Grants & Special Projects .... Mr. Charles WOOD
51 Director of Adult & Continuing Educ ....Ms. Carol EASLEY
29 Coord & Development Alumni Relation .... Vacant
96 Purchasing Manager .... Mr. Bobby HINSON
19 Chief of Police .... Mr. David HENDRY

Talmudic College of Florida (B)

4000 Alton Road, Miami Beach FL 33140
County: Dade FICE Identification: 025089
Unit ID: 137777
Telephone: (305) 534-7050 Carnegie Class: Spec/Faith
FAX Number: (305) 534-8444 Calendar System: Semester
URL: www.talmudicu.edu
Established: 1974 Annual Undergrad Tuition & Fees: $12,250
Enrollment: 52 Male
Affiliation or Control: Independent Non-Profit IRS Status: 501(c)3
Highest Offering: Doctorate
Program: Teacher Preparatory; Professional; Religious Emphasis
Accreditation: RABN

01 President ....Rabbi Yitzchak ZWEIG
05 Dean/Vice President ....Rabbi Yochanan ZWEIG
06 Registrar .... Rabbi Ira HILL
37 Director Student Financial Aid ....Ms. Stacy BROWN
20 Director Educational Programs .... Rabbi Yeshaya GREENBERG
07 Director of Admissions .... Rabbi Yaakov BURSTYN

Teacher Education University (C)

1079 West Morse Boulevard, Suite B,
Winter Park FL 32789-3751
County: Orange Identification: 666342
Telephone: (800) 523-1578 Carnegie Class: Not Classified
FAX Number: (407) 740-8177 Calendar System: Semester
URL: www.TEU.edu
Established: 2005 Annual Undergrad Tuition & Fees: $5,280
Enrollment: N/A Coed
Affiliation or Control: Proprietary IRS Status: Proprietary
Highest Offering: Master's
Program: Teacher Preparatory
Accreditation: DETC

01 Chief Education/Academic Officer ....Dr. Kristi BORDELON
11 Chief Designated Admin/Dir Fin Svcs .... Ms. Amanda BOWERS
05 Director Academics/Curriculum ....Ms. Charlotte LUGERING
07 Admissions Coordinator .... Ms. Anne MARION
06 Registrar ....Ms. Jennifer MORRISON

Trinity Baptist College (D)

800 Hammond Boulevard, Jacksonville FL 32221-1398
County: Duval FICE Identification: 031019
Unit ID: 137953
Telephone: (904) 596-2400 Carnegie Class: Spec/Faith
FAX Number: (904) 596-2532 Calendar System: Semester
URL: www.tbc.edu
Established: 1974 Annual Undergrad Tuition & Fees: $14,560
Enrollment: 260 Coed
Affiliation or Control: Baptist IRS Status: 501(c)3
Highest Offering: Master's
Program: 2-Year Principally Bachelor's Creditable; Teacher Preparatory; Religious Emphasis
Accreditation: TRACS

00 Chancellor ....Dr. Thomas C. MESSER
01 President/CEO .... Mr. Mac HEAVENER
03 Senior Vice President ....Dr. Matthew BEEMER
32 Dean of Students ....Mr. Jeremiah STANLEY
84 Director of Enrollment Management ....Mr. Brandon WILLIS
37 Director of Financial Aid .... Mr. Mark ELKINS

Trinity College of Florida (E)

2430 Welbilt Boulevard, Trinity FL 34655-4401
County: Pasco FICE Identification: 030282
Unit ID: 137962
Telephone: (727) 376-6911 Carnegie Class: Spec/Faith
FAX Number: (727) 376-0781 Calendar System: Semester
URL: www.trinitycollege.edu
Established: 1932 Annual Undergrad Tuition & Fees: $12,608
Enrollment: 192 Coed
Affiliation or Control: Independent Non-Profit IRS Status: 501(c)3
Highest Offering: Baccalaureate
Program: Religious Emphasis
Accreditation: BI

01 President ....Dr. Mark T. O'FARRELL
32 Vice President Student Affairs .... Rev. Al DEPOUTOT
05 Vice President Academic Affairs .... Dr. David BENEDICT
30 Vice President for Advancement .... Dr. Charlie MARTIN
10 Vice Pres for Business & Finance ...Mr. Richard C. HENRICKSEN
07 Vice Pres for Enrollment/Adult Ed .... Vacant
06 Registrar ....Mr. Zachary T. RANES
26 Asst VP Marketing/Communications ......Mr. Kevin D. O'FARRELL

Trinity International University, Florida Regional Center (F)

8190 W State Road 84, Davie FL 33324-4611
County: Broward FICE Identification: 012314
Unit ID: 135610
Telephone: (954) 382-6400 Carnegie Class: Bac/Diverse
FAX Number: (954) 382-6470 Calendar System: Semester
URL: www.tiu.edu/florida
Established: 1949 Annual Undergrad Tuition & Fees: $10,200
Enrollment: 392 Coed
Affiliation or Control: Evangelical Free Church Of America
IRS Status: 501(c)3
Highest Offering: Master's
Program: Liberal Arts And General; Teacher Preparatory
Accreditation: &NH

01 President .... Dr. G. Craig WILLIFORD
05 Exec Vice President/Provost ....Dr. Jeanette L. HSIEH
11 Exec Director & Assoc Dean .... Mr. Scott MCCLELLAND
20 Director of Academic Operations .... Ms. Deborah WILES
32 Director Student Services ....Mrs. Sarudzayi WILSON
16 Chief Operations Ofcr/Human Res ....Mrs. Ileana GIL
06 Director of Records .... Mr. Steve DAVIS
37 Financial Aid Director .... Ms. Karen GUAL

† Regional accreditation is carried under the parent institution in Deerfield, IL.

Ultimate Medical Academy-Clearwater (G)

1255 Cleveland Street, Clearwater FL 33756
County: Pinellas FICE Identification: 035493
Unit ID: 441371
Telephone: (727) 298-8685 Carnegie Class: Not Classified
FAX Number: (727) 446-2489 Calendar System: Semester
URL: www.ultimatemedical.edu
Established: N/A Annual Undergrad Tuition & Fees: $13,150
Enrollment: 108 Coed
Affiliation or Control: Proprietary IRS Status: Proprietary
Highest Offering: Associate Degree
Program: Occupational
Accreditation: ABHES

01 Campus Director ....Ms. Lori LEGROW

University of Fort Lauderdale (H)

4093 NW 16th Street, Lauderhille FL 33313-5809
County: Broward FICE Identification: 041563
Unit ID: 457402
Telephone: (954) 486-7728 Carnegie Class: Not Classified
FAX Number: (954) 486-7667 Calendar System: Other
URL: www.uftl.edu
Established: N/A Annual Undergrad Tuition & Fees: N/A
Enrollment: 69 Coed
Affiliation or Control: Non-denominational IRS Status: 501(c)3
Highest Offering: Doctorate
Program: Professional; Religious Emphasis
Accreditation: TRACS

01 Chancellor and CEO ....Dr. Henry B. FERNANDEZ
05 Chief Academic Officer .... Dr. Winnifred MCPHERSON
10 Chief Financial Officer .... Mr. Brian HANKERSON
09 VP Inst Effective/Compliance ....Ms. Laura TUCKER
32 VP for Academic & Student Services ..Ms. Chloris UNDERWOOD
06 Registrar .... Mr. Stephen ALLISON
07 Director of Admissions ....Mr. Kelvin BAKER

University of Miami (I)

Coral Gables FL 33124
County: Miami-Dade FICE Identification: 001536
Unit ID: 135726
Telephone: (305) 284-2211 Carnegie Class: RU/VH
FAX Number: N/A Calendar System: Semester
URL: www.miami.edu
Established: 1925 Annual Undergrad Tuition & Fees: $39,654
Enrollment: 16,068 Coed
Affiliation or Control: Independent Non-Profit IRS Status: 501(c)3
Highest Offering: Doctorate
Program: Liberal Arts And General; Teacher Preparatory; Professional
Accreditation: SC, ANEST, BUS, BUSA, CEA, CLPSY, COPSY, DENT, ENG, HSA, IPSY, LAW, MED, MIDWF, MUS, NURSE, PH, PTA, @TEAC

01 President ....Dr. Donna E. SHALALA
05 Exec Vice President & Provost ....Dr. Thomas J. LEBLANC
10 Sr Vice Pres for Business & Finance ....Mr. Joseph T. NATOLI
63 Sr VP & Dean School of Medicine .... Dr. Pascal J. GOLDSCHMIDT
30 Sr VP Univ Advancement/Ext Affairs .... Mr. Sergio M. GONZALEZ
21 Vice President Finance & Treasurer ....Mr. John R. SHIPLEY
43 Vice Pres Gen Counsel/Sec of Univ ....Ms. Aileen M. UGALDE
32 Vice President Student Affairs .... Dr. Patricia A. WHITELY
17 Vice Pres Medical Administration .... Mr. Jonathan (Jack) LORD
15 Vice President Human Resources ....Ms. Nerissa E. MORRIS
13 Vice Pres Information Tech/CIO ....Mr. Steve CAWLEY
21 Vice President Budget & Planning .... Mr. Mark DIAZ
18 Vice Pres Real Estate & Facilities ....Mr. Larry D. MARBERT
27 Vice Pres University Communications .... Ms. Jacqueline R. MENENDEZ
86 Vice Pres Government Affairs .... Mr. Rodolfo J. FERNANDEZ
100 President's Chief of Staff ....Dr. Rebecca M. FOX
20 Sr Vice Prov/Dean Undergrad Educ .... Dr. William S. GREEN
46 Vice Provost for Research .... Dr. John L. BIXBY
20 Vice Provost Faculty Affairs ....Dr. David J. BIRNBACH
20 Vice Prov Acad Affs/Dean Grad Sch .... Mr. M. Brian BLAKE
41 Director of Athletics .... Mr. Shawn EICHORST
29 Associate VP Alumni Relations ....Ms. Donna A. ARBIDE
21 Assoc Vice President/Controller .... Ms. Theresa L. ASHMAN
06 Assoc Vice President & Registrar .... Dr. Scott INGOLD
21 Asst Vice Pres Business & Finance ...... Ms. Sarah N. ARTECONA
84 Asst VP of Enrollment Management ....Mr. James M. BAUER
26 Exec Director Media Relations ....Mrs. Elizabeth AMORE
86 Director of Government Affairs .... Ms. Shira KASTAN
09 Asst VP Planning & Inst Research .... Dr. Mary M. SAPP
19 Chief of Police ....Major David A. RIVERO
49 Dean College of Arts & Sciences .... Dr. Leonidas G. BACHAS
48 Dean School of Architecture ..Ms. Elizabeth M. PLATER-ZYBERK
50 Dean Business Administration .... Dr. Eugene ANDERSON
60 Dean School Communication .... Dr. Gregory J. SHEPHERD
53 Dean of Education/Human Development .... Dr. Isaac PRILLELTENSKY
54 Dean College of Engineering ....Dr. James M. TIEN
61 Dean of Law ....Ms. Patricia WHITE
64 Dean Frost School of Music ....Dr. Shelton G. BERG
65 Dean Marine & Atmospheric Science .... Dr. Roni AVISSAR
66 Dean of Nursing & Health Studies .... Dr. Nilda P. PERAGALLO
58 Dean of the Graduate School ....Dr. Teresa A. SCANDURA
08 Dean of Libraries ....Mr. William D. WALKER
35 Dean of Students ....Dr. Ricardo D. HALL
12 Director Center Hemisphere Policy ....Dr. Susan K. PURCELL
38 Director Student Counseling .... Vacant
36 Director Career Services .... Mr. Christian GARCIA
85 Director Intl Student & Scholar Svc ....Ms. Teresa S. DE LA GUARDIA
39 Director Student Housing ....Mr. James G. SMART
96 Chief Purchasing Officer .... Ms. Susan R. MONTES
28 Exec Dir Equality Administration ....Ms. Wilhemena BLACK

University of St. Augustine for Health Sciences (J)

1 University Boulevard, Saint Augustine FL 32086-5799
County: Saint Johns FICE Identification: 031713
Unit ID: 367954
Telephone: (904) 826-0084 Carnegie Class: Spec/Health
FAX Number: (904) 826-0085 Calendar System: Trimester
URL: www.usa.edu

Established: 1979 Annual Undergrad Tuition & Fees: $32,085
Enrollment: 1,478 Coed
Affiliation or Control: Proprietary IRS Status: Proprietary
Highest Offering: Doctorate
Program: Professional
Accreditation: DETC, OT, PTA

01 President .... Dr. Wanda NITSCH
03 Vice President .... Dr. Cindy MATHENA
88 Dir Inst of Occupational Therapy .... Dr. Karen HOWELL
88 Program Dir Physical Therapy - SA .... Dr. Jeffrey ROT
88 Program Dir Physical Therapy - SD .... Dr. Ellen LOWE
88 Program Dir Occupational Therapy SD .... Dr. Judith OLSON
88 Dir Trans Doctor Physical Therapy .... Dr. Jodi LIPHART
06 Registrar .... Ms. Diane RONDINELLI
07 Director of Admissions .... Mr. Steve JONES
51 Director of Continuing Education .... Ms. Lori HANKINS

University of Tampa (A)

401 W Kennedy Boulevard, Tampa FL 33606-1490
County: Hillsborough FICE Identification: 001538
Unit ID: 137847
Telephone: (813) 253-3333 Carnegie Class: Master's L
FAX Number: (813) 258-7207 Calendar System: Other
URL: www.ut.edu
Established: 1931 Annual Undergrad Tuition & Fees: $24,682
Enrollment: 6,738 Coed
Affiliation or Control: Independent Non-Profit IRS Status: 501(c)3
Highest Offering: Master's
Program: Liberal Arts And General; Teacher Preparatory; Professional
Accreditation: SC, BUS, MUS, NUR

01 President .... Dr. Ronald L. VAUGHN
05 Provost/Vice Pres Academic Affairs .... Dr. Janet M. MCNEW
10 Vice Pres Administration/Finance .... Mr. Richard W. OGOREK
84 Vice President Enrollment .... Mr. Dennis L. NOSTRAND
30 Vice Pres Development/Univ Rels .... Mr. Daniel T. GURA
45 Vice Pres Operations & Planning .... Dr. Linda W. DEVINE
13 Vice President Info Technology .... Ms. Donna R. ALEXANDER
21 Assistant Vice Pres Admin/Finance .... Mr. T. Kevin LAFFERTY
32 Dean of Students .... Ms. Stephanie R. KREBS
20 Assoc Provost & Dean of Acad Svcs .... Dr. Katharine H. COLE
06 Registrar .... Ms. Michelle PELAEZ
08 Director of the Library .... Ms. Marlyn PETHE-COOK
29 Director of Alumni Relations .... Mr. James HARDWICK
44 Director of Annual Giving .... Mrs. Taylor A. PINKE
37 Director of Financial Aid .... Ms. Jacqueline LATORELLA
27 Director of Public Information .... Mr. Eric D. CARDENAS
36 Director of Career Services .... Mr. Mark W. COLVENBACH
18 Director of Facilities Management .... Mr. David RAMSEY
91 Director Information Systems .... Mr. Jon ALBRECHT
15 Exec Director of Human Resources .... Ms. Donna B. POPOVICH
07 Sr Associate Director of Admissions .... Mr. Brent W. BENNER
41 Athletic Director .... Mr. Larry J. MARFISE
40 Manager Campus Store .... Vacant
39 Director of Residence Life .... Ms. Krystal R. SCHOFIELD
22 Affirmative Action Officer .... Ms. Donna B. POPOVICH
19 Director Safety & Security .... Mr. Kevin A. HOWELL
23 Dir Health Center/Stdnt Counseling .... Ms. Sharon P. SCHAEFER
44 Director of Planned Giving .... Mr. William F. ROTH
38 Director Student Counseling .... Ms. Sharon P. SCHAEFER
96 Director of Procurement .... Ms. Cyn D. EZELL
09 Dir Institutional Effectiveness .... Dr. Jeanne M. ROBERTS
92 Director of Honors Program .... Dr. Gary S. LUTER
50 Dean College of Business .... Dr. F. Frank GHANNADIAN
83 Dean Social Science/Math Education .... Dr. Joseph D. SCLAFANI
81 Dean College Natural/Health Sci .... Dr. James A. GORE
57 Dean College of Arts/Letters .... Dr. Haig MARDIROSIAN
51 Assoc Dean Graduate/Continuing Stds .... Dr. Donald D. MORRILL

Valencia College (B)

PO Box 3028, Orlando FL 32802-3028
County: Orange FICE Identification: 006750
Unit ID: 138187
Telephone: (407) 299-5000 Carnegie Class: Assoc/Pub-U-MC
FAX Number: (407) 426-8970 Calendar System: Semester
URL: www.valenciacollege.edu
Established: 1967 Annual Undergrad Tuition & Fees (In-State): $2,972
Enrollment: 42,631 Coed
Affiliation or Control: State IRS Status: 501(c)3
Highest Offering: Baccalaureate
Program: Occupational; 2-Year Principally Bachelor's Creditable
Accreditation: SC, ADNUR, CEA, CVT, DH, DMS, EMT, RAD

01 President .... Dr. Sanford C. SHUGART
05 Exec VP/Chief Learning Officer .... Vacant
32 Vice President Student Affairs .... Dr. Joyce C. ROMANO
10 Vice President Operations & Finance .... Mr. Keith W. HOUCK
30 Vice Pres Institutional Advancement .... Vacant
43 Vice Pres Policy & General Counsel .... Dr. William J. MULLOWNEY
16 Vice Pres Human Resources/Diversity .... Dr. Stanley H. STONE
26 Vice Pres Marketing/Strategic Comm .... Ms. Lucy BOUDET
12 Campus President East Campus .... Dr. Ruth L. PRATHER
12 Campus President Osceola Campus .... Dr. Kathleen A. PLINSKE
12 Campus President West Campus .... Dr. Falecia D. WILLIAMS
27 Chief Information Officer .... Mr. William A. WHITE
102 Pres & CEO Valencia Foundation .... Ms. Geraldine M P. GALLAGHER
18 Asst VP Facilities Services .... Ms. Helene LOISELLE
103 Asst VP Career & Workforce Ed .... Dr. Nasser HEDAYAT
21 Asst VP Financial Svcs .... Ms. Jacqueline D. LASCH
35 Asst VP Student Affairs .... Dr. Sonya F. JOSEPH
37 Asst VP Fin Aid/College Trans .... Vacant
07 Asst VP Admissions & Records .... Dr. Renee K. SIMPSON
31 Asst VP College/Community Rels .... Vacant
28 Asst VP Diversity & Inclusion .... Dr. Martha W. WILLIAMS
20 Asst VP Academic Affairs .... Vacant
19 Asst VP Safety/Security Risk Mgmt .... Mr. Thomas LOPEZ
35 Dean of Students East .... Ms. Linda B. VANCE
35 Dean of Students West .... Mr. Tyron S. JOHNSON
35 Dean of Students Osceola .... Ms. Jillian M. SZENTMIKLOSI
35 Dean of Students Winter Park .... Dr. Cheryl ROBINSON
40 Director College Bookstore .... Mr. Todd A. HUNT
92 Director Honors Program .... Dr. Valerie C. BURKS
96 Director Procurement/Aux Svcs .... Mr. W. Edward AMES
105 Director Web and Portal Services .... Mr. Jeff DANSER
09 Managing Director Research .... Vacant
04 Senior Executive Assistant .... Ms. Barbara HALSTEAD

Virginia College (C)

19 W Garden Street, Pensacola FL 32502-5678
County: Escambia FICE Identification: 031005
Unit ID: 389727
Telephone: (850) 436-8838 Carnegie Class: Assoc/PrivFP
FAX Number: (850) 436-2663 Calendar System: Quarter
URL: www.vc.edu
Established: 2001 Annual Undergrad Tuition & Fees: $17,423
Enrollment: 577 Coed
Affiliation or Control: Proprietary IRS Status: Proprietary
Highest Offering: Associate Degree
Program: Occupational
Accreditation: ACICS, SURGT

01 Campus President .... Dr. Kimberly COOLIDGE
05 Academic Dean .... Mr. Don COCKROFT
07 Director of Admissions .... Ms. Melanie PARLIER
06 Registrar .... Ms. Darlene CARSON

† Branch campus of Virginia College, Birmingham, AL.

Warner University (D)

13895 Highway 27, Lake Wales FL 33859-2549
County: Polk FICE Identification: 008848
Unit ID: 138275
Telephone: (863) 638-1426 Carnegie Class: Master's S
FAX Number: (863) 638-1472 Calendar System: Semester
URL: www.warner.edu
Established: 1968 Annual Undergrad Tuition & Fees: $24,026
Enrollment: 1,016 Coed
Affiliation or Control: Church Of God IRS Status: 501(c)3
Highest Offering: Master's
Program: Liberal Arts And General; Teacher Preparatory
Accreditation: SC, @SW

01 President .... Dr. Gregory V. HALL
05 Exec Vice Pres/Chief Academic Ofcr .... Dr. James G. MOYER
10 Vice Pres for Finance & Business .... Mr. Greg A. RODDEN
30 Vice President for Advancement .... Mrs. Doris B. GUKICH
84 VP for Enrollment Mgmt & Marketing .... Mrs. Dawn M. RAFOOL
50 Dean of School of Business .... Dr. Cathy LEWIS-BRIM
49 Dean of Ministry/Arts & Sciences .... Dr. Steven DARR
53 Dean of School of Education .... Dr. Bill RIGEL
32 Dean of Student Life .... Rev. Dawn MEADOWS
43 General Counsel .... Dr. Norman WHITE
06 Registrar .... Mrs. Sara F. KANE
07 Director of Admissions .... Mr. Bob MOBLEY
37 Director Student Financial Aid .... Mrs. Lorrie STEEDLEY
21 Controller .... Mr. Dean MEADOWS
08 Librarian .... Mrs. Sherill HARRIGER
29 Director Alumni Relations .... Miss Kareen PICKETT
106 Dean of School of Online Education .... Dr. Jeff HAYES
42 Campus Pastor .... Rev. Bob BECKLER
83 Chair Social & Natural Science .... Mrs. Erica SIRRINE
68 Chair Physical Educ/Rec/Health .... Mr. Trevor HALL
09 Director of Institutional Research .... Mrs. Lisa B. MURPHY
18 Chief Facilities/Physical Plant .... Mr. Bill BROWN
97 Director of General Studies .... Mrs. Kelly MILLS
79 Chair Ministry & Humanities .... Dr. Michael SANDERS
88 Chair of Traditional BA .... Dr. Melodi GUILBAULT
40 Director Bookstore .... Ms. Monica HAMILTON
13 Director of Institutional Tech .... Mr. Mark THOMAS
19 Director Campus Security .... Mr. Brian ROWLES

Webber International University (E)

1201 Scenic Highway N/P.O. Box 96,
Babson Park FL 33827-0096
County: Polk FICE Identification: 001540
Unit ID: 138293
Telephone: (863) 638-1431 Carnegie Class: Bac/Diverse
FAX Number: (863) 638-2823 Calendar System: Semester
URL: www.webber.edu
Established: 1927 Annual Undergrad Tuition & Fees: $22,411
Enrollment: 728 Coed
Affiliation or Control: Independent Non-Profit IRS Status: 501(c)3
Highest Offering: Master's
Program: Business Emphasis
Accreditation: SC, IACBE

01 President .... Dr. H. Keith WADE
05 Academic Dean .... Dr. Charles SHIEH
10 Vice President Finance .... Ms. Christina JORDON
30 VP Institutional Advancement .... Dr. Steve WARNER
32 Dean of Student Life .... Ms. Johanna DEVERTEUIL
06 Registrar/Dir of Financial Aid .... Mrs. Kathy A. WILSON
36 Director Career Services .... Vacant
08 Head Librarian .... Ms. Sue DUNNING
26 Dir Public Relations/Athletic Dir .... Mr. Bill HEATH
13 Director Information Technology .... Mr. Bob M. WEIS
55 Director for Adult Education .... Vacant
18 Director of Campus Svcs/Maintenance .... Mr. Matt YENTES
40 Director of Bookstore .... Mr. Jay CULVER
07 Director of Admissions .... Mr. Jeff BENNETT
09 Director of Institutional Effectiv .... Dr. Bill LOFTUS
50 Chair of Business Education .... Dr. Jeanette EBERLE
53 Chair of General Education Division .... Dr. Charles WUNKER

Wolford College (F)

1336 Creekside Boulevard, Suite 2,
Naples FL 34108-1931
County: Collier FICE Identification: 039393
Unit ID: 451130
Telephone: (239) 513-1135 Carnegie Class: Spec/Health
FAX Number: (239) 513-1368 Calendar System: Semester
URL: www.wolford.edu
Established: 2004 Annual Graduate Tuition & Fees: N/A
Enrollment: 234 Coed
Affiliation or Control: Independent Non-Profit IRS Status: 501(c)3
Highest Offering: Master's; No Undergraduates
Program: Professional
Accreditation: ANEST

01 President .... Dr. Norman R. WOLFORD
05 Dean .... Dr. John NOLAN
37 Director of Financial Aid Services .... Mr. Gilbert CHANG
84 Dir Enrollment & Student Services .... Ms. Lori ELLISON
09 Dir Institutional Effectiveness .... Ms. Victoria COPPARD

Yeshiva Gedolah Rabbinical College (G)

1140 Alton Road, Miami Beach FL 33139-4708
County: Dade FICE Identification: 032563
Unit ID: 363712
Telephone: (305) 653-8770 Carnegie Class: Spec/Faith
FAX Number: (305) 653-6790 Calendar System: Semester
Established: 1973 Annual Undergrad Tuition & Fees: $8,000
Enrollment: 32 Male
Affiliation or Control: Independent Non-Profit IRS Status: 501(c)3
Highest Offering: Master's
Program: Teacher Preparatory; Professional
Accreditation: @RABN

01 Executive Vice President .... Rabbi Benzion KORF
05 Dean .... Rabbi Abraham KORF
06 Registrar .... Ayelet BORTUNK

GEORGIA

Abraham Baldwin Agricultural College (H)

ABAC 1 - 2802 Moore Highway, Tifton GA 31793-2601
County: Tift FICE Identification: 001541
Unit ID: 138558
Telephone: (229) 391-5001 Carnegie Class: Assoc/Pub4
FAX Number: (229) 391-5051 Calendar System: Semester
URL: www.abac.edu
Established: 1908 Annual Undergrad Tuition & Fees (In-State): $3,848
Enrollment: 3,248 Coed
Affiliation or Control: State IRS Status: 501(c)3
Highest Offering: Baccalaureate
Program: Occupational; 2-Year Principally Bachelor's Creditable
Accreditation: SC, ADNUR

01 President .... Dr. David BRIDGES
05 VP for Academic Affairs .... Dr. Niles REDDICK
10 VP for Planning & Operations .... Mr. John CLEMENS
30 VP External Affairs/Chief of Staff .... Mr. Paul WILLIS
08 Director of Library Services .... Ms. Marie DAVIS
32 Dean of Students .... Ms. Bernice HUGHES
13 Chief Data Officer & Registrar .... Ms. Tarrah MIRUS
38 Director of Student Development .... Dr. Maggie MARTIN
37 Director of Student Financial Svcs .... Ms. Shawn THOMAS
44 Director of Capital Planning .... Mr. Melvin MERRILL
15 Director of Human Resources .... Mr. Richard SPANCAKE
26 Director of Public Relations .... Ms. Ashley MOCK
108 Director of Assessment .... Ms. Amy HOWELL
84 Director Enrollment Management .... Ms. Donna WEBB
96 Director of Procurement .... Ms. Teri MATHIS
19 Chief of Police .... Mr. Bryan A. GOLDEN

† Part of the University System of Georgia.

Agnes Scott College (I)

141 E College Avenue, Decatur GA 30030-3797
County: DeKalb FICE Identification: 001542
Unit ID: 138600

Telephone: (404) 471-6000 Carnegie Class: Bac/A&S
FAX Number: (404) 471-6067 Calendar System: Semester
URL: www.agnesscott.edu
Established: 1889 Annual Undergrad Tuition & Fees: $32,195
Enrollment: 871 Female
Affiliation or Control: Presbyterian Church (U.S.A.) IRS Status: 501(c)3
Highest Offering: Baccalaureate
Program: Liberal Arts And General
Accreditation: SC

01 President .... Dr. Elizabeth KISS
05 VP Acad Affs/Dean of the College .... Dr. Carolyn J. STEFANCO
32 VP Student Life/Dean of Students .... Ms. Donna A. LEE
10 Vice President Business/Finance .... Mr. John P. HEGMAN
30 Vice Pres College Advancement .... Mr. Robert PARKER
84 Vice Pres Enrollment & Admission .... Ms. Laura MARTIN
13 Assoc VP Technology .... Ms. LaNeta COUNTS
20 Associate Dean of the College .... Dr. James K. DIEDRICK
35 Associate Dean of Students .... Ms. Suzanne ONORATO
42 Chaplain .... Rev. Kate COLUSSY-ESTES
04 Director Office of the President .... Ms. Lea Ann HUDSON
27 Senior Director of Communications .... Mr. J. D. FITE
44 Senior Director of Development .... Ms. Elizabeth K. WILSON
06 Registrar .... Ms. Angela DEWBERRY
35 Associate Dean of Students .... Dr. Kijua SANDERS-MCMURTRY
08 Director of Library Services .... Ms. Elizabeth BAGLEY
29 Director of Alumnae Relations .... Ms. Kimberly VICKERS
36 Director Career Planning .... Ms. Catherine NEINER
18 Director of Facilities .... Mr. Tim BLANKENSHIP
15 Director of Human Resources .... Ms. Karen GILBERT
41 Director of Athletics .... Ms. Joeleen AKIN
28 Director of Multicultural Affairs .... Vacant
37 Director of Student Financial Aid .... Mr. Patrick BONONES
38 Director Personal Counseling .... Dr. Holly BYRD
09 Director of Institutional Research .... Ms. Katherine MCGUIRE
07 Director of Admissions .... Ms. Alexa GAETA
23 Director of Student Health .... Ms. Carole HOLCOMB

Albany State University (A)

504 College Drive, Albany GA 31705-2796
County: Dougherty FICE Identification: 001544
Unit ID: 138716
Telephone: (229) 430-4600 Carnegie Class: Master's M
FAX Number: (229) 430-4830 Calendar System: Semester
URL: www.asurams.edu
Established: 1903 Annual Undergrad Tuition & Fees (In-State): $5,912
Enrollment: 4,663 Coed
Affiliation or Control: State IRS Status: 501(c)3
Highest Offering: Beyond Master's But Less Than Doctorate
Program: Liberal Arts And General; Teacher Preparatory; Professional
Accreditation: SC, ACBSP, NUR, SPAA, SW, TED

01 President .... Dr. Everette J. FREEMAN
43 Chief of Staff & University Counsel . Ms. Sharon "Nyota" TUCKER
05 Vice President Academic Affairs .... Dr. Abiodun OJEMANKINDE
32 Vice Pres Student Affairs .... Dr. Edgar L. BERRY
10 Vice President Fiscal Affairs .... Mr. Larry WAKEFIELD
30 Vice Pres Institutional Advance .... Mr. Clifford PORTER
13 Vice Pres Information Tech/CIO .... Mr. Erwin CARROW
20 Asst Vice Pres Academic Affairs .... Dr. Linda GRIMSLEY
46 Assoc VP Research Sponsored Prog .... Dr. Mary WOHFORD
09 Asst VP Research & Effectiveness .... Dr. Ruth SALTER
06 Dean Academic Svcs and Registrar .... Mrs. Arna T. ALBRITTEN
84 Int Dean/Assoc VP Enrollment Svcs .... Mr. Mike MILLER
08 Director Library Services .... Dr. LaVerne MCLAUGHLIN
88 Director Title III .... Mrs. Connie LEGGETT
27 Director University Communications .... Ms. Vickie OLDHAN
38 Director Counseling/Disability Svcs .... Dr. Stephanie HARRIS-JOLLY
88 Director Budgets and Contracts .... Mrs. Marion RYANT
37 Director Financial Aid .... Mr. Thomas HARRIS, JR.
23 Director Student Health Services .... Dr. Vickie PHILLIPS
15 Director Human Resources Mgmt .... Mr. Steve GRANT
19 Chief of Police .... Mr. John FIELDS
41 Interim Director of Athletics .... Dr. Richard WILLIAMS
07 Director Enrollment Services .... Mr. James BURRELL
18 Director Facilities Management .... Mr. James OLIVER
35 Director Student Life/Judicial Affs .... Ms. Gwinetta L. TRICE
38 Director Career Services .... Ms. Glorya E. WILLIAMS
29 Director Alumni Affairs .... Ms. Wendy WILSON
96 Director Business Services .... Ms. Lori W. BURNETT
88 Controller .... Ms. Dorothy MARTIN
25 Director Grants and Contracts .... Mr. Andrew FLOYD
39 Director Housing Residence Life .... Mrs. Bonisha PORTER

† Part of the University System of Georgia.

Albany Technical College (B)

1704 S Slappey Boulevard, Albany GA 31701-3587
County: Dougherty FICE Identification: 005601
Unit ID: 138682
Telephone: (229) 430-3500 Carnegie Class: Assoc/Pub-R-M
FAX Number: (229) 430-3594 Calendar System: Semester
URL: www.albanytech.edu
Established: 1961 Annual Undergrad Tuition & Fees (In-State): $3,024
Enrollment: 4,727 Coed
Affiliation or Control: State IRS Status: 501(c)3
Highest Offering: Associate Degree
Program: Occupational; 2-Year Principally Bachelor's Creditable; Technical Emphasis
Accreditation: SC, DA, MAC, RAD, SURGT

01 President .... Dr. Anthony O. PARKER
05 Vice President for Academic Affairs .... Ms. Shirley ARMSTRONG
32 VP Student Affairs/Enrollment Mgmt .... Ms. Lisa DEJESUS
46 Vice President Economic Development .... Mr. Matt TRICE
11 Vice Pres Administrative Services .... Mrs. Kathy SKATES
45 Vice Pres of Inst Effectiveness .... Ms. Vicki TUCKER
88 Associate Vice Pres of Adult Educ .... Mrs. Linda COSTON
04 Special Assistant to the President .... Mr. Joe NAJJAR
07 Dean of Admissions .... Vacant
06 Registrar .... Ms. Suzann CULPEPPER
37 Director of Financial Aid .... Ms. Helen CATT
36 Dir of Job Placement/Career Svcs .... Ms. Judy JIMMERSON
21 Director of Accounting Services .... Mrs. Karen THOMAS
20 Dean of Academic Affairs .... Dr. Dorothy GARNER
20 Dean of Academic Affairs .... Ms. Corine HUGHLEY
20 Dean of Academic Affairs .... Mr. Emmett GRISWOLD
55 Dean of Evening Administration .... Dr. Ed COOPER
88 Director of Business & Industry Svc .... Mr. Gary FRAGE
51 Dir Manufacturing Tech Ctr/Contg Ed .... Ms. Valerie WILLIAMS
09 Director of Institutional Research .... Mr. Joe NAJJAR
26 Director of Public Rels/Information .... Ms. Wendy HOWELL
14 Director of Computer/Info Systems .... Mr. Bobby WIDNER
88 Director of Special Programs .... Vacant
18 Campus Operations Manager .... Mr. Lavon ACKLEY
56 Dir Spec Proj/Tech in Curriculum .... Ms. Elizabeth DEMING
35 Director Student Activities .... Dr. Mary RICHARDSON

Altamaha Technical College (C)

1777 W Cherry Street, Jesup GA 31545-0612
County: Wayne FICE Identification: 030321
Unit ID: 366447
Telephone: (912) 427-5800 Carnegie Class: Assoc/Pub-R-S
FAX Number: (912) 427-5823 Calendar System: Semester
URL: www.altamahatech.edu
Established: 1989 Annual Undergrad Tuition & Fees (In-State): $2,550
Enrollment: 1,410 Coed
Affiliation or Control: State IRS Status: 501(c)3
Highest Offering: Associate Degree
Program: Occupational; 2-Year Principally Bachelor's Creditable
Accreditation: SC, COE

01 President .... Ms. Lorette M. HOOVER
05 Vice President for Academic Affairs .... Dr. June MCCLAIN
11 Vice Pres Administrative Services .... Ms. Monica S. O'QUINN
32 Vice President for Student Affairs .... Ms. Karla C. EUBANKS
09 Dir of Institutional Effectiveness .... Mr. Lonnie V. ROBERTS
06 Registrar .... Mr. Chris MISSEL
07 Director of Admissions .... Mr. Chris JEANCAKE
15 Director Personnel Services .... Ms. Katrina HOWARD
18 Chief Facilities/Physical Plant .... Dr. June MCCLAIN
20 Dean of Academic Affairs .... Dr. Ron SHAFER
20 Dean of Academic Affairs .... Mr. Walt PINDER
20 Dean of Academic Affairs .... Ms. Patsy WILKERSON
21 Director of Accounting .... Ms. Melissa LAMB
30 Dir of Institutional Advancement .... Ms. Melinda LAAGER
36 Career Placement & Dev Coord .... Ms. Markisha BUTLER
37 Financial Aid Coordinator .... Mrs. Tina MANNING
28 Special Services Coordinator .... Ms. Tracy BRUMMETT
96 Purchasing Technician .... Ms. Kathy KOVACH
08 Director of Library Services .... Ms. Jessica EVERINGHAM
14 Director of Information Tech .... Mr. Richard COTHERN
40 Bookstore Manager .... Ms. Bertie SHIPES
18 Maintenance Manager .... Mr. Randy SMITH
38 Counseling & Special Svcs Director ... Ms. Cathy MONTGOMERY
29 Director Alumni Relations .... Vacant
20 Dean of Academic Support .... Ms. Sandra WILLIAMS

American InterContinental University (D)

6600 Pchtree-Dunwdy Rd, 500 Embassy,
Atlanta GA 30328
County: Fulton Identification: 666723
Unit ID: 438586
Telephone: (404) 965-6500 Carnegie Class: Master's M
FAX Number: (404) 965-6501 Calendar System: Quarter
URL: atlanta.aiuniv.edu
Established: 1977 Annual Undergrad Tuition & Fees: $16,691
Enrollment: 1,727 Coed
Affiliation or Control: Proprietary IRS Status: Proprietary
Highest Offering: Master's
Program: Liberal Arts And General
Accreditation: &NH, ACBSP, CIDA

01 President .... Mr. Peter CORREA
10 Vice President of Finance .... Mr. Richard HAWKSHEAD
32 Vice President Student Affairs .... Ms. Janis HENRY
09 Dir Inst Rsrch/Assess & Effective .... Mrs. Patricia HAWKINS
22 Director of Compliance .... Ms. Helen GALLAGHER

† Regional accreditation is carried under the parent institution in Hoffman Estates, IL.

Andrew College (E)

501 College Street, Cuthbert GA 39840-5550
County: Randolph FICE Identification: 001545
Unit ID: 138761
Telephone: (229) 732-2171 Carnegie Class: Assoc/PrivNFP
FAX Number: (229) 732-2176 Calendar System: Semester
URL: www.andrewcollege.edu
Established: 1854 Annual Undergrad Tuition & Fees: $20,688
Enrollment: 321 Coed
Affiliation or Control: United Methodist IRS Status: 501(c)3
Highest Offering: Associate Degree
Program: 2-Year Principally Bachelor's Creditable; Fine Arts Emphasis
Accreditation: SC

01 President .... Dr. David C. SEYLE
04 Executive Asst to the President .... Mrs. Pennie R. SCROGGINS
10 Chief Financial Officer .... Mr. Bryan HELMS
07 Director Admissions & Financial Aid .... Mr. Blake COTY
21 Controller .... Mrs. Julie CADLE
30 Director of Development .... Mr. Andy BRUBAKER
32 Director of Student Life .... Dr. Sherri TAYLOR
41 Athletic Director .... Dr. Edith SMITH
42 Chaplain .... Vacant
08 Librarian .... Mrs. Karan PITTMAN
37 Coordinator Student Financial Aid .... Mrs. Amy THOMPSON
40 Director of Bookstore .... Mrs. Karan PITTMAN
88 Student Support Services Director .... Ms. Santee ARCHER
05 Dean of Academic Affairs .... Mr. Jason GOODNER
06 Registrar .... Ms. Rachel BUSH
13 Director Computer Services .... Mr. Paul MOORE
18 Director of Maintenance .... Mr. David HARPER
19 Chief of Police .... Vacant
39 Director of Resident Housing .... Ms. Desi FRAZIER
105 Web Services .... Mr. Brice HERRIN
88 Director of AndrewServes .... Mrs. Rebecca WHITE
88 FOCUS Director .... Mrs. Bennie MATTOX
88 Director of Student Success Center .... Mr. Stephen ADAMS

Argosy University, Atlanta (F)

980 Hammond Drive, Suite 100, Atlanta GA 30328-6162
County: Fulton Identification: 666735
Unit ID: 367936
Telephone: (770) 671-1200 Carnegie Class: DRU
FAX Number: (770) 407-1110 Calendar System: Semester
URL: www.argosy.edu/atlanta
Established: 1990 Annual Undergrad Tuition & Fees: $13,224
Enrollment: 2,591 Coed
Affiliation or Control: Proprietary IRS Status: Proprietary
Highest Offering: Doctorate
Program: Professional
Accreditation: &WC, CACREP, CLPSY

01 Campus President .... Dr. Ronald SWANSON
05 Vice President Academic Affairs .... Dr. Murray BRADFIELD
07 Senior Director of Admissions .... Johanna COLLINS
32 Director Student Services .... Kim P. OUSLEY
37 Director of Student Finance .... Monica M. CONOVER
06 Registrar .... Tanya CRUMP
15 Human Resources .... Thomas TUCKER
11 Dir of Admin & Financial Services .... Brian GARDNER

† Regional accreditation is carried under the parent institution in Orange, CA.

Armstrong Atlantic State University (G)

11935 Abercorn Street, Savannah GA 31419-1997
County: Chatham FICE Identification: 001546
Unit ID: 138789
Telephone: (912) 344-2503 Carnegie Class: Master's L
FAX Number: N/A Calendar System: Semester
URL: www.armstrong.edu
Established: 1935 Annual Undergrad Tuition & Fees (In-State): $4,942
Enrollment: 7,493 Coed
Affiliation or Control: State IRS Status: 501(c)3
Highest Offering: Doctorate
Program: Occupational; Liberal Arts And General; Teacher Preparatory; Professional
Accreditation: SC, CS, HSA, MT, MUS, NMT, NURSE, PH, PTA, RAD, RTT, SP, TED

01 President .... Dr. Linda M. BLEICKEN
05 Provost & VP for Academic Affairs .... Dr. Carey ADAMS
10 Vice President Business & Finance .... Mr. David CARSON
32 Vice President Student Affairs .... Dr. Keith BETTS
30 Vice President for Advancement .... Mr. William KELSO
100 Chief of Staff .... Dr. Amy HEASTON
43 University Counsel .... Mr. Lee DAVIS
27 Chief Information Officer .... Mr. Robert P. HOWARD
84 Assoc VP Enrollment Mgmt .... Dr. Patrice B. MITCHELL
21 Associate VP Business & Finance .... Mr. Marc MASCOLO
20 Int Assistant VP Academic Affairs .... Dr. John KRAFT
53 Dean College of Education .... Dr. Patricia WACHHOLZ
76 Dean Health Professions .... Dr. David WARD
49 Dean College of Liberal Arts .... Dr. Laura BARRETT
72 Dean Science and Technology .... Dr. Robert GREGERSON
08 University Librarian .... Mr. Doug FRAZIER
06 Registrar .... Ms. Judy GINTER
19 Chief Campus Police .... Mr. Wayne WILLCOX
41 Athletic Director .... Ms. Lisa SWEANY
07 Director of Admissions .... Ms. Stephanie WHALEY
88 Director Faculty Development .... Dr. Teresa WINTERHALTER
37 Director Financial Aid .... Ms. Lee Ann KIRKLAND
89 Director First Year Experience .... Mr. Herbert BRUCE
92 Director Honors Program .... Dr. Jonathan ROBERTS
09 Director Institutional Research .... Ms. Abby WILLCOX
104 Director of International Education .... Dr. James ANDERSON
12 Director Liberty Center .... Mr. Peter HOFFMAN

106 Director Online & Blended Learning ... Dr. Kristen BETTS
15 Director of Human Resources ... Ms. Rebecca CARROLL
18 Director Plant Operations ... Mr. David FAIRCLOTH
38 Director Counseling Services ... Mr. John MITCHELL
39 Director Housing & Residence Life ... Ms. Amy GARBACZ-SYNDER
28 Director Multicultural Affairs ... Ms. Nashia WHITTENBURG
35 Director Student Activities ... Vacant
29 Director Alumni Affairs ... Vacant
44 Director Major & Planned Giving ... Ms. Julie GERBSCH
26 Director Marketing & Communications ... Ms. Brenda FORBIS

† Part of the University System of Georgia.

The Art Institute of Atlanta (A)

6600 Peachtree Dunwoody Road, Atlanta GA 30328-1635
County: Fulton FICE Identification: 009270
Unit ID: 138813
Telephone: (770) 394-8300 Carnegie Class: Spec/Arts
FAX Number: (770) 394-0008 Calendar System: Quarter
URL: www.artinstitutes.edu/atlanta/
Established: 1949 Annual Undergrad Tuition & Fees: $23,535
Enrollment: 3,662 Coed
Affiliation or Control: Proprietary IRS Status: Proprietary
Highest Offering: Baccalaureate
Program: Fine Arts Emphasis
Accreditation: SC, ACFEI, CIDA

01 President ... Mrs. Jo Ann KOCH
10 Dir of Admin and Financial Svcs ... Mr. Chris SCHWARZER
15 Director of Human Resources ... Ms. Joselyn CASSIDY
07 Senior Director of Admissions ... Ms. Joy MCCLURE
05 Dean of Academic Affairs ... Dr. Dan GARLAND
32 Dean of Student Affairs ... Ms. April SHAVKIN
37 Director of Student Financial Svcs ... Vacant
09 Dir of Inst Effectiveness/Research ... Dr. Michael T. HOEFER
08 Director of Library ... Ms. Gayle MEIER
13 Director of Technology ... Ms. TJ BONDS
06 Registrar ... Ms. Diana HILL
20 Associate Dean of Academic Affairs ... Vacant
36 Director of Career Services ... Mrs. Sharon BOLLING-CLAY
26 Director of Communications ... Ms. Kim RESNIK
40 Retail and Administrative Services ... Mr. Lewis HAWKINS
18 Director of Facilities ... Mr. Brandon GHOLSTON
38 Student Support Svcs Coordinator ... Ms. Elizabeth BUSH
39 Director of Residence Life/Housing ... Mr. Stephan MOORE
04 Exec Assistant to the President ... Ms. Rebecca CROWFOOT

Ashworth College (B)

6625 The Corners Parkway, Norcross GA 30092-3406
County: Gwinnett Identification: 666106
Telephone: (770) 729-8400 Carnegie Class: Not Classified
FAX Number: (770) 729-9296 Calendar System: Semester
URL: www.ashworthcollege.edu
Established: 2000 Annual Undergrad Tuition & Fees: $4,153
Enrollment: 12,000 Coed
Affiliation or Control: Proprietary IRS Status: Proprietary
Highest Offering: Master's
Program: Occupational; 2-Year Principally Bachelor's Creditable; Professional
Accreditation: DETC

01 President ... Mr. Robert KLAPPER
05 Chief Academic Officer ... Dr. Leslie GARGIULO

Athens Technical College (C)

800 US Highway 29 N, Athens GA 30601-1500
County: Clarke FICE Identification: 005600
Unit ID: 246813
Telephone: (706) 355-5000 Carnegie Class: Assoc/Pub-R-M
FAX Number: (706) 369-5753 Calendar System: Semester
URL: www.athenstech.edu
Established: 1958 Annual Undergrad Tuition & Fees (In-State): $3,765
Enrollment: 5,111 Coed
Affiliation or Control: State IRS Status: 501(c)3
Highest Offering: Associate Degree
Program: Occupational; 2-Year Principally Bachelor's Creditable; Technical Emphasis
Accreditation: SC, ACBSP, ADNUR, DA, DH, DMS, PTAA, RAD, SURGT

01 President ... Dr. Flora W. TYDINGS
05 Vice President Academic Affairs ... Dr. Joyce SANSING
32 Vice President Student Affairs ... Ms. Andrea DANIEL
11 Vice Pres Administrative Services ... Ms. Kathryn S. THOMAS
45 Vice Pres Economic Devel Services ... Mr. Jerry BARROW
12 Vice President of Off Campus Sites ... Dr. Larry D. SIEFFERMAN
09 Vice President Inst Effectiveness ... Dr. Daniel J. SMITH
13 Vice Pres Information Technology ... Mr. Dennis ASHWORTH
72 Dean Technical Education ... Ms. Susan LARSON
76 Dean Life Sciences ... Dr. Scott MARTIN
06 Registrar ... Ms. Caroline ANGELO
07 Director Admissions ... Mr. Lenzy REID
08 Director Library Services ... Ms. Carol STANLEY
08 Librarian Elbert County Campus ... Ms. Marci MANGLITZ
36 Director Student Support/Career Dev ... Ms. Celeste TAYLOR
37 Director Financial Aid ... Ms. Wanda HICKS
88 Director Adult Education Programs ... Ms. Temple BENNETT
12 Director Walton County Campus ... Mr. James E. HOGG
12 Director Greene County Campus ... Mr. Sibley BRYAN

50 Dean Business/Personal Services Div ... Ms. Diane CAMPBELL
35 Student Activities Director ... Dr. Yancey GULLEY
15 Director Human Resources ... Dr. Leslie CRICKENBERGER
18 Facilities Director ... Mr. Jim WALTER
30 Director Institutional Advancement ... Ms. Liz DALTON
21 Director of Accounting ... Ms. April ROBERTSON
97 Dean of General Education ... Dr. Carol MYERS
108 Director of Research and Assessment ... Ms. Stephanie G. BENSON

Atlanta Metropolitan State College (D)

1630 Metropolitan Parkway, SW, Atlanta GA 30310-4498
County: Fulton FICE Identification: 012165
Unit ID: 138901
Telephone: (404) 756-4000 Carnegie Class: Assoc/Pub-U-SC
FAX Number: (404) 756-4460 Calendar System: Semester
URL: www.atlm.edu
Established: 1974 Annual Undergrad Tuition & Fees (In-State): $3,462
Enrollment: 2,737 Coed
Affiliation or Control: State IRS Status: 501(c)3
Highest Offering: Baccalaureate
Program: Occupational; 2-Year Principally Bachelor's Creditable
Accreditation: SC, ACBSP

01 President ... Dr. Gary A. MCGAHA, SR.
05 Vice Pres Academic Affairs ... Dr. Jerome DRAIN
10 Vice President Fiscal Affairs ... Mr. Freddie L. JOHNSON
32 Vice President Student Affairs ... Mrs. Cynthia EVERS
30 Vice Pres Institutional Advancement ... Mr. Larion WILLIAMS
20 Assoc Vice Pres Academic Affairs ... Vacant
21 Assoc VP Fiscal Affs/ Comptroller ... Mrs. Michelle ALSTON-BROWN
50 Dean Div Business/Computer Sci ... Ms. Cheryl BARNES
79 Dean Div Humanities/Fine Arts ... Dr. Frank JOHNSON
81 Dean Div of Sci/Math/Health Profess ... Dr. Bonita FLOURNOY
83 Dean Div of Social Science ... Dr. Grady CULPEPPER
06 Dir Enrollment Services/Registrar ... Mrs. Candace PERRY
15 Director of Human Resources ... Ms. Regina Ray SIMMONS
08 Director of the Library ... Mr. Robert QUARLES
35 Director of Student Activities ... Ms. Iris SHANKLIN
37 Director of Financial Aid ... Mrs. Alicia SCOTT
38 Director Counseling/Disability Svcs ... Ms. Tammy YOUNG
14 Data Processing Manager ... Mr. Walter CUMMINGS
13 Chief Information Officer ... Mr. Antonio W. TRAVIS
09 Director Inst Effectiveness ... Dr. Mark CUNNINGHAM
19 Director of Campus Safety ... Mr. Antonio LONG
35 Dir of Student Outreach & Access ... Mr. Stephen WOODALL
18 Dir Plant Operations/Facilities ... Mr. E. Keith WILLIAMS
40 Bookstore Manager ... Ms. Barbara SMITH

† Part of the University System of Georgia.

Atlanta Technical College (E)

1560 Metropolitan Parkway, SW, Atlanta GA 30310-4446
County: Fulton FICE Identification: 008543
Unit ID: 138840
Telephone: (404) 225-4000 Carnegie Class: Assoc/Pub-U-SC
FAX Number: (404) 225-4639 Calendar System: Semester
URL: www.atlantatech.edu
Established: 1967 Annual Undergrad Tuition & Fees (In-State): $2,052
Enrollment: 4,491 Coed
Affiliation or Control: State IRS Status: 501(c)3
Highest Offering: Associate Degree
Program: Occupational; 2-Year Principally Bachelor's Creditable; Technical Emphasis
Accreditation: SC, COE, DA, DT, MAC, @PTAA

01 President ... Dr. Alvetta P. THOMAS
05 Vice President Academic Affairs ... Dr. Gladys CAMP
11 Vice Pres Administrative Services ... Mrs. Teresa BROWN
32 Vice President Student Affairs ... Dr. Rushton JOHNSON
30 Vice President Economic Development ... Mr. Harold CRAIG
04 Assistant to the President ... Mrs. Joni WILLIAMS
45 Executive Vice President ... Dr. Rodney ELLIS
26 Director Communications & Marketing ... Mrs. Terreta RODGERS
37 Director of Financial Aid ... Mrs. Deborah CLARK
07 Director of Admissions ... Mr. Vory BILLUPS
88 Dean Industrial and Transportation ... Dr. Constance RUSSELL
51 Director of Continuing Education ... Dr. Deborah JOHNSON-BLAKE
36 Director Career Placement ... Mr. Michael BURNSIDE
50 Dean Business and Public Services ... Ms. Arriana DANIEL
88 Dean Health and Public Safety ... Dr. Queenston THORPE
06 Registrar ... Mrs. Niya EADY
15 Director Human Resources ... Ms. Marilyn SMITH-ROBINSON
18 Director of Facilities ... Mr. Isaac VINING
09 Director of Curriculum and Planning ... Dr. Murray J. WILLIAMS

Atlanta's John Marshall Law School (F)

1422 West Peachtree Street NW, Atlanta GA 30309
County: Fulton FICE Identification: 031733
Unit ID: 138929
Telephone: (404) 872-3593 Carnegie Class: Spec/Law
FAX Number: (404) 873-3802 Calendar System: Semester
URL: www.johnmarshall.edu
Established: 1933 Annual Graduate Tuition & Fees: $37,335
Enrollment: 736 Coed
Affiliation or Control: Proprietary IRS Status: Proprietary
Highest Offering: First Professional Degree; No Undergraduates
Program: Professional
Accreditation: LAW

01 Dean ... Mr. Richardson R. LYNN
05 Assoc Dean Academics ... Mr. Kevin CIEPLY
32 Assoc Dean of Students ... Ms. Sheryl E. HARRISON
10 Chief Financial Officer ... Mr. Allen BREZEL
11 Asst Dean for Administration ... Ms. Michelle HARRIS

Augusta State University (G)

2500 Walton Way, Augusta GA 30904-2200
County: Richmond FICE Identification: 001552
Unit ID: 138983
Telephone: (706) 737-1400 Carnegie Class: Master's L
FAX Number: (706) 737-1773 Calendar System: Semester
URL: www.aug.edu
Established: 1925 Annual Undergrad Tuition & Fees (In-State): $5,622
Enrollment: 6,741 Coed
Affiliation or Control: State IRS Status: 501(c)3
Highest Offering: Beyond Master's But Less Than Doctorate
Program: Occupational; 2-Year Principally Bachelor's Creditable; Liberal Arts And General; Teacher Preparatory
Accreditation: SC, ART, BUS, CACREP, MUS, NUR, SPAA, SW, TED

01 Interim President ... Dr. Shirley KENNY
05 Vice President Academic Affs ... Dr. Carol J. RYCHLY
10 Vice President Business Operations ... Ms. Therese ROSIER
32 Vice President Student Services ... Dr. Joyce JONES
30 Vice Pres Development/Alumni Rels ... Ms. Helen HENDEE
20 Assoc VP for Academic Affairs ... Dr. Peter BASCIANO
20 Assoc VP for Academic Affairs ... Dr. Raymond A. WHITING
45 Asst VP for Campus Development ... Mr. Jeffrey W. FOLEY
49 Dean College Arts/Humanities ... Dr. Charles W. CLARK
50 Dean College of Business ... Dr. Marc D. MILLER
53 Dean College of Education ... Dr. Lucinda CHANCE
21 Dir Fin Servs/Controller Acct Servs ... Ms. Corrina WARNER
51 Director Continuing Education ... Ms. Carolyn K. INGRAHAM
09 Director Institutional Research ... Ms. Mary FILPUS-LUYCKX
08 Librarian ... Ms. Camilla REID
07 Director Admissions/Registrar ... Ms. Katherine SWEENEY
29 Dir Alumni Relations/Annual Giving ... Ms. Rhonda OELLERICH BANKS
36 Director Career Center ... Ms. Julie GOLEY
37 Director Financial Aid ... Ms. Cynthia PARKS
15 Director Human Resources ... Mr. Walt ALEXANDERSON
38 Director Counseling Center ... Dr. Robert MAYS
35 Director Student Activities ... Mr. Eddie J. HOWARD
26 Dir Public Relations/Publications ... Ms. Kathy D. SCHOFE
41 Director Athletics ... Mr. Clint BRYANT
19 Director Public Safety ... Mr. Jasper COOKE
40 Director Business Services ... Mr. Karl MUNCHY
18 Director Plant Operations ... Mr. Dave W. FREEMAN
13 Director Information Technology ... Mr. Chip MATSON
88 Director Academic Advisement ... Ms. Kathryn T. THOMPSON
25 Director Grants Administration ... Ms. Kimberly F. GRAY
28 Director of Student Development ... Ms. Karen A. MOBLEY-BELK
21 Budget Director ... Ms. Aisha LAVIN
88 Director Testing & Disability Svcs ... Ms. Angie KITCHENS

† Part of the University System of Georgia.

Augusta Technical College (H)

3200 Augusta Tech Drive, Augusta GA 30906-3399
County: Richmond FICE Identification: 005599
Unit ID: 138956
Telephone: (706) 771-4000 Carnegie Class: Assoc/Pub-R-M
FAX Number: (706) 771-4016 Calendar System: Semester
URL: www.augustatech.edu
Established: 1961 Annual Undergrad Tuition & Fees (In-District): $3,768
Enrollment: 4,393 Coed
Affiliation or Control: State/Local IRS Status: 501(c)3
Highest Offering: Associate Degree
Program: Occupational
Accreditation: SC, CVT, DA, ENGT, MAC, OTA, PNUR, SURGT

01 President ... Mr. Terry D. ELAM
05 Vice President Academic Affairs ... Mr. C. Rick HALL
11 Vice Pres Administrative Services ... Ms. Sheila HILL
32 Vice Pres Student Affairs ... Dr. Melissa M. FRANK-ALSTON
88 Vice President Economic Development ... Dr. Lisa PALMER
12 VP Ops Thomson/McDuffie Campus ... Mr. Ted DUZENSKI
12 Dean/Director Waynesboro Campus ... Ms. Johnica MITCHELL
35 Dean Student Services ... Vacant
37 Director Financial Aid ... Ms. Beverly SMYRE HINES
07 Director Admissions ... Ms. Donna WENDT
30 Director Institutional Advancement ... Ms. Beverly PELTIER
06 Registrar ... Ms. Sabrina WHITE
45 Dir Inst Planning/Effectiveness ... Dr. Annabelle LEWIS
21 Director Accounting ... Ms. Sherrick L. JOHNSON
26 Dir Marketing/Public Relations ... Ms. Bonita JENKINS
15 Payroll/Benefits Manager ... Ms. Lori USRY
84 Enrollment Manager Thomson Campus ... Ms. Julie LANGHAM
36 Career Services Assistant ... Ms. Kerry CHARLES
88 High School Coordinator ... Ms. Deborah HEREDIA
76 Dean Allied Health Science ... Dr. Gwen TAYLOR
72 Dean Industrial Technology ... Mr. James PRICE
50 Dean Business/Personal Svcs ... Ms. Elizabeth A. JULIAN
97 Dean Gen Ed & Learning Support ... Mr. John RICHARDSON
54 Dean Information & Engineering Tech ... Ms. JoAnne ROBINSON

Bainbridge College (A)

2500 E Shotwell Street, PO Box 990,
Bainbridge GA 39818-0990

County: Decatur
FICE Identification: 011074
Unit ID: 139010
Telephone: (229) 248-2500
Carnegie Class: Assoc/Pub-R-M
FAX Number: (229) 248-2547
Calendar System: Semester
URL: www.bainbridge.edu
Established: 1970
Annual Undergrad Tuition & Fees (In-State): $2,914
Enrollment: 3,735
Coed
Affiliation or Control: State
IRS Status: 501(c)3
Highest Offering: Associate Degree
Program: Occupational; 2-Year Principally Bachelor's Creditable
Accreditation: SC, ADNUR

01 President .... Dr. Richard CARVAJAL
05 Vice Pres Academic Affairs .... Dr. Tonya STRICKLAND
10 Vice Pres of Business & Operations .... Mr. Shawn MCGEE
32 Dean of Student Services .... Ms. Connie SNYDER
49 Chair Arts & Sciences Division .... Dr. Michael KIRKLAND
75 Chair Technical Studies Division .... Dr. Adria BELK
88 Chair Dept of Learning Support .... Mr. Wesley WHITEHEAD
08 Director Library .... Ms. Susan RALPH
51 Director of Continuing Education .... Ms. Ann WELLS
26 Chief Public Relations Officer .... Ms. Meredyth EARNEST
37 Director of Financial Aid .... Vacant
21 Controller .... Ms. Kay LIVINGSTON
18 Director of Plant Operations .... Mr. Leonard DEAN
91 Director of Technology Services .... Mr. Scott DUNN
35 Director Student Affairs .... Mr. Sam MAYHEW
30 Director of Development .... Ms. Dale FULLER
07 Director of Admissions .... Mr. Spencer STEWART
09 Research Analyst .... Vacant
38 Counselor .... Ms. Arlene COOK

† Part of the University System of Georgia.

Bauder College (B)

384 Northyards Blvd, Ste 190 & 400,
Atlanta GA 30313-2439

County: Fulton
FICE Identification: 011574
Unit ID: 139074
Telephone: (404) 237-7573
Carnegie Class: Bac/Assoc
FAX Number: (404) 237-1642
Calendar System: Quarter
URL: atlanta.bauder.edu
Established: 1964
Annual Undergrad Tuition & Fees: $44,251
Enrollment: 795
Coed
Affiliation or Control: Proprietary
IRS Status: Proprietary
Highest Offering: Baccalaureate
Program: Occupational; 2-Year Principally Bachelor's Creditable
Accreditation: SC

01 President/CEO .... Dr. Charles A. TAYLOR
05 Vice President for Academic Affairs .... Dr. Katrina MALLORY
11 Vice President of Operations .... Antonio WALLACE
10 Director of Finance .... Tanya JACKSON
07 Director of Admissions .... Terri HOLTE
37 Manager Financial Aid .... Cathy DUNHAM
36 Exec Director of Career Services .... Andrea ROTH
20 Dean for Academic Affairs .... Christopher HUMPHREY
66 Director of Nursing .... Maxinee BLACK-ARIAS
06 Head Registrar .... Hannah LEONARD-HINDS
09 Director of Institutional Research .... Dr. Godfrey F. NOE
08 Head Librarian .... Mary Kaye HOOKER
04 Executive Assistant .... Shannon GILMER
21 Director of Student Accounts .... LaTanya HARTSFIELD
32 Director Student Services .... Carolyn JENKINS

Berry College (C)

2277 Martha Berry Highway, NW,
Mount Berry GA 30149-0001

County: Floyd
FICE Identification: 001554
Unit ID: 139144
Telephone: (706) 232-5374
Carnegie Class: Bac/A&S
FAX Number: (706) 236-2238
Calendar System: Semester
URL: www.berry.edu
Established: 1902
Annual Undergrad Tuition & Fees: $27,650
Enrollment: 2,093
Coed
Affiliation or Control: Independent Non-Profit
IRS Status: 501(c)3
Highest Offering: Beyond Master's But Less Than Doctorate
Program: Liberal Arts And General; Teacher Preparatory; Professional
Accreditation: SC, BUS, MUS, TED

01 President .... Dr. Stephen R. BRIGGS
05 Vice President & Provost .... Dr. Katherine M. WHATLEY
10 Vice President Finance .... Mr. Brian I. ERB
32 VP Student Affairs and Enrollment .... Ms. Debbie HEIDA
30 Vice Pres Institutional Advancement .... Ms. Bettyann O'NEILL
84 VP of Enrollment Management .... Dr. Gary WATERS
100 Chief of Staff .... Mr. Whit WHITAKER
42 Chaplain .... Rev. Jonathan HUGGINS
35 Assoc Vice Pres Student Affairs .... Ms. Julie A. BUMPUS
26 Asst VP Public Rels and Marketing .... Ms. Jeanne MATHEWS
20 Associate Provost .... Dr. Andrew BRESSETTE
50 Dean Campbell School of Business .... Dr. John GROUT
53 Dean Charter School of Education .... Dr. Jackie MCDOWELL
79 Dean School Humanities/Arts/Soc Sci .... Dr. Thomas D. KENNEDY
81 Dean School of Math/Natural Science .... Dr. Bruce CONN
78 Dean Stdnt Work/Experiential Lrng .... Mr. Rufus MASSEY
07 Director of Admissions .... Mr. Brett E. KENNEDY
08 Director of the Library .... Ms. Sherre Lee HARRINGTON
29 Director of Alumni Affairs .... Ms. Christina WATTERS
27 Chief Information Officer .... Ms. Penny EVANS-PLANTS
38 Director of Counseling Center .... Dr. J. Marshall JENKINS
37 Director of Financial Aid .... Ms. Marcia MCCONNELL
36 Director of Career Center .... Mrs. Sue TARPLEY
09 Dir Institutional Rsrch & Registrar .... Dr. Bryce DURBIN
88 Dir Faculty Rsrch & Sponsored Pgm .... Mrs. Donna DAVIN
18 Director Physical Plant .... Mr. Mark HOPKINS
89 Director First Year Experience .... Mrs. Katherine POWELL
92 Director Honors Program .... Dr. Brian CARROLL
94 Director Women's Studies .... Dr. Susan LOGSDON-CONRADSEN
96 Director Purchasing .... Mr. Brad BARRRIS
85 Director International Programs .... Ms. Sarah EGERER
15 Director Human Resources .... Mr. Harold NALLY
43 Director of Legal Services .... Mr. Danny PRICE
78 Dir Stdnt Work/Experiential Lrng .... Mr. Michael BURNES
88 Director of Employee Development .... Mr. Wes MORAN

Beulah Heights University (D)

892 Berne Street, SE, PO Box 18145,
Atlanta GA 30316-1873

County: Fulton
FICE Identification: 030763
Unit ID: 139153
Telephone: (404) 627-2681
Carnegie Class: Spec/Faith
FAX Number: (404) 627-0702
Calendar System: Semester
URL: www.beulah.org
Established: 1918
Annual Undergrad Tuition & Fees: $5,760
Enrollment: 750
Coed
Affiliation or Control: Other Protestant
IRS Status: 501(c)3
Highest Offering: Doctorate
Program: Religious Emphasis
Accreditation: BI, TRACS

01 President .... Dr. Benson M. KARANJA
05 Vice Pres/Dean Academic Affairs .... Dr. James B. KEILLER
88 VP for Academic Program Development .... Dr. Angelita HOWARD
09 Director for Assessment/Planning .... Ms. Hiuko ADAMS
32 VP Student Life/Enrollment Mgmt .... Pastor Shawn ADAMS
37 Director of Financial Aid .... Ms. Pat A. BANKS
08 Director of Library Services .... Mr. Pradeep K. DAS
06 Registrar .... Mrs. Jacquelyn B. ARMSTRONG
15 Human Resources Coordinator .... Miss Marquetta PRICE
07 Director of Admissions .... Mr. John DREHER
18 Facilities Director .... Mr. Harvey BRUMELOW
97 Chair Dept of General Studies .... Dr. Angelita HOWARD
73 Chair Dept of Religious Studies .... Mr. Walter TURNER
88 Chair Dept of Leadership Studies .... Ms. Betty G. PALMER
42 Dean of Chapel .... Bishop Johnathan E. ALVARADO
10 Vice President for Finance .... Mr. Randy BREWER
20 Associate Academic Officer .... Dr. Mark HARDGROVE
21 Associate Business Officer .... Mr. Randy BREWER
26 Chief Public Relations/Dev Officer .... Mr. Peter KARANJA
29 Dir of Marketing/Enrollment/Almuni .... Miss Debbie CHAND

Brenau University (E)

500 Washington Street, SE, Gainesville GA 30501-3668

County: Hall
FICE Identification: 001556
Unit ID: 139199
Telephone: (770) 534-6299
Carnegie Class: Master's L
FAX Number: (770) 534-6114
Calendar System: Semester
URL: www.brenau.edu
Established: 1878
Annual Undergrad Tuition & Fees: $22,218
Enrollment: 2,789
Coed
Affiliation or Control: Independent Non-Profit
IRS Status: 501(c)3
Highest Offering: Doctorate
Program: Liberal Arts And General; Teacher Preparatory; Professional
Accreditation: SC, ACBSP, CIDA, DANCE, NURSE, OT, TED

01 President .... Dr. Ed L. SCHRADER
03 Exec VP/Chief Financial Ofcr .... Dr. Wayne W. DEMPSEY
05 Provost & VP For Academic Affairs .... Dr. Nancy F. KRIPPEL
100 Chief of Staff .... Ms. Jody Y. WALL
10 Vice President Financial Services .... Ms. Sandra D. THORNTON
32 Sr VP Enrollment Mgt/Student Svcs .... Mr. Scott A. BRIELL
30 Vice Pres External Relations .... Mr. J. Matthew THOMAS
13 Chief Information Tech Officer .... Mr. Chip L. ANDREWS
09 Director of Research & Planning .... Dr. Robert E. CUTTINO
37 Assoc VP of EM & Dir Financial Aid .... Ms. Pam J. BARRETT
07 Dean Graduate Admissions .... Ms. Christina C. WHITE
21 Controller .... Ms. Holly REYNOLDS
15 Director of Human Resources .... Ms. Kelley L. MADDOX
18 Director Facilities & Logistics .... Mr. Mike HOLLIMON
26 VP Communications/Publications .... Mr. David MORRISON
35 Dean of Student Success & Retention .... Ms. Valerie SIMMONS-WALSTON
36 Director of Career Services .... Mr. George BAGEL
24 Director of Learning Center .... Dr. Vince J. YAMILKOSKI
41 Athletic Director .... Mr. Mike LOCHSTAMPFOR
23 Chaplain .... Dr. Don HARRISON
53 Dean College of Education .... Dr. Sandra LESLIE
76 Dean College of Health & Sciences .... Dr. Gale H. STARICH
66 Chair Department of Nursing .... Dr. Keeta P. WILBORN
50 Dean College Business/Mass Commun .... Dr. Bill LIGHTFOOT
79 Dean College of Fine Arts & Human .... Dr. Andrea C. BIRCH
81 Chair Math & Science Department .... Dr. Latricia SCRIVEN
08 Dean of Library Svcs & SACS Liaison .... Ms. Marlene GIGUERE
88 Executive Director for Recruitment .... Mr. Nathan R. GOSS
06 Registrar & Dir of Student Records .... Ms. Barbara WILSON
29 Director Alumni Relations .... Ms. Jennifer DELL
19 Director Campus Safety & Security .... Ms. Paula DAMPIER

Brewton-Parker College (F)

201 David-Eliza Fountain Circle,
Mount Vernon GA 30445-0197

County: Montgomery
FICE Identification: 001557
Unit ID: 139205
Telephone: (912) 583-2241
Carnegie Class: Bac/Diverse
FAX Number: (912) 583-4498
Calendar System: Semester
URL: www.bpc.edu
Established: 1904
Annual Undergrad Tuition & Fees: $11,800
Enrollment: 629
Coed
Affiliation or Control: Baptist
IRS Status: 501(c)3
Highest Offering: Baccalaureate
Program: 2-Year Principally Bachelor's Creditable; Liberal Arts And General; Teacher Preparatory; Business Emphasis
Accreditation: #SC, TED

01 President .... Dr. Mike SIMONEAUX
11 Chief Operating Officer .... Mr. Randy F. MINTON
05 Vice President Academic Affairs .... Dr. Tim SEARCY
30 Interim VP Col Advancement .... Ms. Jessica L. JAMES
84 Vice Pres of Enrollment Services .... Mr. Jim BEALL
10 Chief Financial Officer .... Mrs. Natasha MASON
09 Dir of Assessment & Inst Research .... Dr. Carol S. O'DELL
32 Dean of Students .... Mrs. Sherrie HELMS
06 Registrar .... Mrs. Sara CROWE
07 Dir of Admiss & Intl Student Svcs .... Ms. Sandra CLAY
08 Librarian .... Mrs. Ann HUGHES
26 Interim Director of Marketing .... Ms. Kelley M. ARNOLD
27 Director of News & Public Relations .... Ms. Kelley M. ARNOLD
35 Director of Student Activities .... Vacant
37 Director of Financial Aid .... Mr. Rick WOOLVERTON
42 Director of Campus Ministry .... Ms. Lauren PARNELL
18 Director of Plant Operations .... Mr. Ben HAMILTON
38 Dir Counseling & Career Services .... Mrs. Tonia SPAULDING
39 Director of Housing .... Mr. Greg COURSEY
15 Director Human Resources .... Mrs. Shirley ELLIS
40 Bookstore Manager .... Mrs. Lynn ADDISON
13 Chief Information Officer .... Mr. David KIGHT
91 Computer Program/Analyst .... Vacant
29 Director Alumni Relations .... Ms. Jessica L. JAMES
25 Director Grants/Projects .... Ms. Jessica L. JAMES
41 Athletic Director .... Ms. Sheila SIMMONS
20 Academic Assistant to the Provost .... Mrs. Sadia AJOHDA
43 General Counsel .... Mr. John MANNING
50 Chair Business Division .... Mr. Randy F. MINTON
53 Chair Education Division .... Dr. Susan E. WHITE
49 Chair Arts & Sciences Division .... Dr. Ruth Ellen PORTER
73 Chair Christian Studies .... Dr. Jerry RAY

Brown College of Court Reporting (G)

1900 Emery St. NW, Atlanta GA 30318

County: Fulton
FICE Identification: 020609
Unit ID: 139214
Telephone: (404) 876-1227
Carnegie Class: Assoc/PrivFP
FAX Number: (404) 876-4415
Calendar System: Quarter
URL: www.bccr.edu
Established: 1972
Annual Undergrad Tuition & Fees: $15,960
Enrollment: 240
Coed
Affiliation or Control: Proprietary
IRS Status: Proprietary
Highest Offering: Associate Degree
Program: Occupational; 2-Year Principally Bachelor's Creditable
Accreditation: COE

01 Executive Director .... Sue C. SCHMITH
07 Director of Admissions .... Marita CAREY
05 Director of Education .... Shirley SOTONA

Brown Mackie College-Atlanta (H)

4370 Peachtree Road NE, Atlanta GA 30319

County: Gwinnett
FICE Identification: 026214
Unit ID: 410283
Telephone: (404) 799-4500
Carnegie Class: Assoc/PrivFP
FAX Number: (404) 799-4522
Calendar System: Other
URL: www.brownmackie.edu
Established: 1987
Annual Undergrad Tuition & Fees: $11,124
Enrollment: 845
Coed
Affiliation or Control: Proprietary
IRS Status: Proprietary
Highest Offering: Baccalaureate
Program: Occupational; 2-Year Principally Bachelor's Creditable; Business Emphasis
Accreditation: ACICS, OTA, SURTEC

01 President .... Mr. Reggie MORTON
05 Dean of Academic Affairs .... Ms. Dominica AUSTIN
07 Senior Director of Admissions .... Mr. Carmichael JAMES
06 Registrar .... Ms. Pat HILDERBRANT

Carver College (I)

3870 Cascade Road SW, Atlanta GA 30331-2184

County: Fulton
FICE Identification: 036353
Unit ID: 139287
Telephone: (404) 527-4520
Carnegie Class: Not Classified
FAX Number: (404) 527-4526
Calendar System: Semester
URL: www.carver.edu

Established: 1943 Annual Undergrad Tuition & Fees: $7,920
Enrollment: 117 Coed
Affiliation or Control: Independent Non-Profit IRS Status: 501(c)3
Highest Offering: Baccalaureate
Program: Religious Emphasis
Accreditation: BI

01 President and CEO ... Mr. Robert W. CRUMMIE
05 Vice Pres Academic Affs/Acad Dean ... Dr. Sujaya JAMES
10 Vice President of Business Affairs ... Mr. Terry ALEXANDER
30 Vice President of Advancement ... Mrs. Carla M. CRUMMIE
32 Dean of Students ... Mr. Damon D. BYRD
07 Director of Admissions ... Mr. Richard A. FEILDS
06 Registrar ... Mrs. Olive JACKS
09 Dir Institutional Effectiveness ... Ms. Traonah PATTERSON
29 Director Alumni Affairs ... Mr. Troy MAMON
42 Stdnt Director of Chapel Services ... Mr. Robert ROSS
73 Director of Bible/Theology Division ... Dr. Sujaya JAMES
97 Director of General Studies ... Dr. Benjamin JACKS
107 Director of Professional Studies ... Dr. John JENKINS
08 Director of Library Services ... Mrs. Tosha BUSSEY
18 Chief of Facilities/Physical Plant ... Mr. Bill WORST
40 Director of Bookstore ... Mr. Dimanche DIDEROT

Central Georgia Technical College (A)

3300 Macon Tech Drive, Macon GA 31206-3699
County: Bibb FICE Identification: 005763
Unit ID: 140304
Telephone: (478) 757-3400 Carnegie Class: Assoc/Pub-R-L
FAX Number: (478) 757-3454 Calendar System: Quarter
URL: www.centralgatech.edu
Established: 1966 Annual Undergrad Tuition & Fees (In-State): $3,515
Enrollment: 6,038 Coed
Affiliation or Control: State IRS Status: 501(c)3
Highest Offering: Associate Degree
Program: Occupational; Technical Emphasis
Accreditation: SC, DH, MLTAD, SURGT

01 Interim President ... Dr. Ivan ALLEN
05 Vice President Academic Affairs ... Mr. Hank GRIFFETH
10 Vice President Administrative Svcs ... Ms. Elaine TRUELOVE
32 Vice President Student Affairs ... Dr. Eddy DIXON
31 Vice President Econ Dev ... Ms. Rebecca LEE
11 Vice Pres Facilities/Ancillary Svcs ... Ms. Dana DAVIS
13 Vice Pres Technology ... Mr. Gardner LONG, II
20 Assoc Vice Pres Academic Affairs ... Ms. Joan THOMPSON
35 Dean of Student Affairs ... Vacant
88 Dean Curriculum & Staff Dev ... Dr. Hazel STRUBY
06 Registrar ... Mr. Brandon ELAM
07 Director of Admissions ... Dr. Jasper FOUST
21 Director of Accounting Services ... Mr. Chris JOHNSON
26 Exec Dir Advancement & Public Rels ... Mrs. Tonya MCCLURE
36 Director Career Services ... Mr. Tony TURNER
08 Director Library & Media Services ... Mr. Neil MCARTHUR
37 Director of Financial Aid ... Ms. Jackie WHITE
15 Director Human Resources ... Ms. Linda HAMPTON
105 Web Developer/Data Analyst ... Ms. Margo S. KENIREY
18 Facilities Director ... Mr. Robert DOMINY
13 Director of Information Technology ... Mr. Ben HALL
51 Director of Continuing Education ... Mr. Clay TEAGUE

Chattahoochee Technical College (B)

980 South Cobb Drive, Marietta GA 30060
County: Barton FICE Identification: 030290
Unit ID: 366456
Telephone: (770) 528-4545 Carnegie Class: Not Classified
FAX Number: (770) 975-4126 Calendar System: Quarter
URL: www.chattahoocheetech.edu
Established: 1981 Annual Undergrad Tuition & Fees (In-State): $2,250
Enrollment: 11,564 Coed
Affiliation or Control: State IRS Status: 501(c)3
Highest Offering: Associate Degree
Program: Occupational
Accreditation: SC, ACFEI, MAC, PTAA, RAD

01 President ... Dr. Ron NEWCOMB
04 Administrative Asst to President ... Ms. Tammy COLLUM
05 Vice President Academic Affairs ... Dr. Trina BOTELER
10 Vice President for Finance ... Ms. Catrice HUFSTETLER
32 VP Student Affairs/Enrollment Mgmt ... Dr. Scott RULE
31 Vice Pres Community/Econ Develop ... Mr. Glenn RASCO
18 Vice President for Facilities ... Mr. David SIMMONS
26 Exec Dir External Affs/Brd Liaison ... Ms. Jennifer NELSON
30 Exec Dir Advancement/Resource Devel ... Ms. Chris KNIFE
06 Registrar ... Ms. Shannon POLLOCK

Clark Atlanta University (C)

223 James P. Brawley Drive, SW, Atlanta GA 30314-4391
County: Fulton FICE Identification: 001559
Unit ID: 138947
Telephone: (404) 880-8000 Carnegie Class: DRU
FAX Number: N/A Calendar System: Semester
URL: www.cau.edu
Established: 1988 Annual Undergrad Tuition & Fees: $19,830
Enrollment: 3,843 Coed
Affiliation or Control: United Methodist IRS Status: 501(c)3
Highest Offering: Doctorate
Program: Liberal Arts And General; Teacher Preparatory; Professional
Accreditation: SC, BUS, CACREP, SPAA, SW, TED

01 President ... Dr. Carlton E. BROWN
05 Provost/VP for Academic Affairs ... Vacant
30 VP for Inst Advancement/Univ Rels ... Vacant
10 VP for Finance/Business Svcs ... Ms. Lucille MAUGE
84 VP for Enroll Svcs/Student Affairs ... Dr. Carl JONES
88 VP for Research & Sponsored Pgms ... Dr. Marcus W. SHUTE
20 Assoc VP for Academic Affairs ... Dr. Jeffrey J. PHILLIPS
13 Assoc VP/Chief Info Ofcr ... Mr. Reginald BRINSON
21 Assoc VP/Controller ... Mr. Edward PATRICK
35 Assoc VP Student Affairs/Dean ... Ms. Ernita HEMMITT
09 Director Planning/Assessment/Rsrch ... Mr. Narendra H. PATEL
43 General Counsel ... Mr. Lance DUNNINGS
06 Registrar ... Ms. Angela FREEMAN
26 Director Strategic Communications ... Ms. Donna BROCK
29 Director Alumni Relations ... Ms. Gay-linn GATEWOOD-JASHO
15 Director Human Resources ... Ms. Valerie VINSON
07 Asst Director of Admissions ... Ms. Danette D. ADAMS
38 Director University Counseling Ctr ... Dr. Marilyn LINEBERGER
36 Director Career Planning/Placement ... Ms. Ernita HEMMITT
37 Director Student Financial Aid ... Mr. Nigel EDWARDS
96 Director of Purchasing ... Ms. Donna BYRD
41 Director of Athletics ... Dr. Tamica JONES
42 University Chaplain ... Dr. Valerie EVERETT
49 Dean Arts & Sciences ... Dr. Shirley WILLIAMS-KIRKSEY
50 Dean Business Admin ... Dr. Lydia FLOYD
53 Dean Education ... Dr. Sean WARNER
70 Dean Social Work ... Dr. Vimala PILLARI
58 Dean Graduate Studies ... Dr. Bettye CLARK
19 Chief of Public Safety ... Chief Thomas TRAWICK
23 Director Health Services ... Ms. Janet SINGLETON
25 Manager Grants & Contracts Accting ... Mr. G. Keith WILLIAMS
39 Director of Residence Life ... Mr. Ernest MOORE
88 Director Instructional Media ... Mr. Frank EDWARDS
101 Coordinator for Board Relations ... Ms. Natalie BAKER
104 Dir International Educ/Study Abroad ... Dr. Paul M. BROWN
22 University Compliance Officer ... Mr. Robert CLARK
100 Chief of Staff/Spec Asst to Pres ... Ms. Cynthia BUSKEY
44 Exec Dir for Fund Dev & Annual Giv ... Ms. Nicole BLOUNT
18 Director of Facilities ... Mr. Victor PANCHUK

Clayton State University (D)

2000 Clayton State Boulevard, Morrow GA 30260-0285
County: Clayton FICE Identification: 008976
Unit ID: 139311
Telephone: (678) 466-4000 Carnegie Class: Bac/Diverse
FAX Number: (770) 961-3700 Calendar System: Semester
URL: www.clayton.edu
Established: 1969 Annual Undergrad Tuition & Fees (In-State): $5,012
Enrollment: 6,860 Coed
Affiliation or Control: State IRS Status: 501(c)3
Highest Offering: Master's
Program: Occupational; Liberal Arts And General; Teacher Preparatory
Accreditation: SC, BUS, DH, MUS, NURSE, TED

01 President ... Dr. Thomas HYNES
05 Provost/Vice Pres Academic Affairs ... Dr. Michael CRAFTON
10 VP for Operations/Planning/Budget ... Ms. Corlis CUMMINGS
32 Vice President for Student Affairs ... Dr. Brian HAYNES
26 Vice President External Affairs ... Ms. Kate TROELSTRA
13 Vice Pres Information Tech & Svcs ... Dr. John S. BRYAN
20 Assoc Vice President Academic Affs ... Dr. Robert A. VAUGHAN, JR.
35 Assoc Vice Pres Student Affairs ... Dr. Elaine MANGLITZ
84 Assoc VP Enroll Mgmt/Acad Success ... Dr. Mark DADDONA
41 Executive Director of Athletics ... Mr. Carl MCALOOSE
88 Executive Director of Spivey Hall ... Mr. Samuel DIXON
15 Exec Dir Human Resources & Services ... Mr. John BROOKS
49 Dean of Arts & Sciences ... Dr. Nasser MOMAYEZI
36 Dean of Retention & Stdnt Placement ... Vacant
50 Dean of Business ... Dr. Alphonso OGBUEHI
76 Dean of Health Sciences ... Dr. Lisa EICHELBERGER
81 Dean Information/Mathematical Sci ... Dr. Lila ROBERTS
08 Dean of Library Services ... Dr. Gordon BAKER
46 Dean Assessmnt/Instructnl Developmt ... Dr. Jill LANE
51 Director of Continuing Education ... Ms. Janet WINKLER
06 University Registrar ... Ms. Rebecca GMEINER
07 Director of Admissions ... Ms. Betty MOMAYEZI
31 Director of Auxiliary Services ... Ms. Carolina AMERO
26 Director of University Relations ... Mr. John SHIFFERT
18 Director of Plant Operations ... Mr. Harun BISWAS
19 Director of Public Safety ... Mr. Bobby HAMIL
30 Dir of Development/Alumni Relations ... Ms. Reda ROWELL
09 Director of Institutional Research ... Dr. Narem REDDY
24 Director Media Services ... Mr. Paul BAILEY
38 Director of Counseling Services ... Dr. Christine SMITH
37 Director Student Financial Aid ... Ms. Pat BARTON
96 Director of Purchasing ... Ms. Marcia JONES
29 Director Alumni Relations ... Mr. Gid ROWELL

† Part of the University System of Georgia.

College of Coastal Georgia (E)

One College Drive, Brunswick GA 31520-3632
County: Glynn FICE Identification: 001558
Unit ID: 139250
Telephone: (912) 279-5700 Carnegie Class: Assoc/Pub-R-M
FAX Number: (912) 262-3072 Calendar System: Semester
URL: www.ccga.edu
Established: 1961 Annual Undergrad Tuition & Fees (In-State): $4,496
Enrollment: 3,474 Coed
Affiliation or Control: State IRS Status: 501(c)3
Highest Offering: Baccalaureate
Program: Occupational; 2-Year Principally Bachelor's Creditable; Liberal Arts And General; Teacher Preparatory; Professional
Accreditation: SC, ACFEI, ADNUR, MLTAD, NUR, RAD

01 President ... Dr. Valerie HEPBURN
05 Vice President Academic Affairs ... Dr. Phil MASON
10 Vice President Business Affairs ... Mr. Jeffrey H. PRESTON
32 Vice President Student Affairs ... Ms. Heidi LEMING
20 Associate VP Academic Affairs ... Ms. Kay HAMPTON
20 Asst VP Academic Services ... Dr. Ann CROWTHER
84 Asst VP Enrollment Management ... Mr. Clayton DANIELS
29 Asst VP Alumni & Annual Giving ... Ms. Elizabeth WEATHERLY
21 Asst VP Business Affairs ... Mr. C. Tom SAUNDERS
88 Asst VP Construction and Design ... Mr. Greg CARVER
37 Director Student Financial Aid ... Ms. Terral HARRIS
06 Registrar ... Ms. Lisa LESSEIG
08 Dean of Library Services ... Ms. Debra HOLMES
09 Director Institutional Effectivenes ... Dr. Jim Hughes LYNCH
12 Director Camden Center ... Ms. Holly CHRISTENSEN
15 Interim Director Human Resources ... Ms. Phyllis BROADWELL
18 Chief Facilities/Physical Plant ... Mr. Gary STRICKLAND
50 Dean Sch of Business & Public Affs ... Dr. William MOUNTS
49 Dean Sch Art/Humanities & Soc Sci ... Dr. M. Karen HAMBRIGHT
81 Dean School of Math and Natural Sci ... Dr. Keith E. BELCHER
53 Dean School of Education & Teacher ... Dr. Michael HAZELKORN
66 Dean School of Nursing & Health Sci ... Dr. Patricia KRAFT
19 Chief of Police ... Mr. Brian SIPE
39 Director of Residence Life ... Dr. Michael BUTCHER
41 Director of Athletics ... Dr. William "Bee" CARLTON
27 Chief Information Officer ... Mr. Tim MOODY
13 Director of Technology Services ... Ms. Geri CULBREATH
26 Director of Marketing & Public Rels ... Mr. John CORNELL
88 Coordinator Faculty & Admin Svcs ... Ms. Sandra J. BUNN
96 Purchasing Officer ... Ms. Karen O. MARTIN

† Part of the University System of Georgia.

Columbia Theological Seminary (F)

P.O. Box 520, 701 Columbia Drive,
Decatur GA 30031-0520
County: DeKalb FICE Identification: 001560
Unit ID: 139348
Telephone: (404) 378-8821 Carnegie Class: Spec/Faith
FAX Number: (404) 377-9696 Calendar System: 4/1/4
URL: www.ctsnet.edu
Established: 1828 Annual Graduate Tuition & Fees: N/A
Enrollment: 387 Coed
Affiliation or Control: Presbyterian Church (U.S.A.) IRS Status: 501(c)3
Highest Offering: Doctorate; No Undergraduates
Program: Professional; Religious Emphasis
Accreditation: SC, THEOL

01 President ... Dr. Stephen A. HAYNER
05 Exec VP Acad Affs/Dean of Faculty ... Dr. Deborah F. MULLEN
10 Vice Pres Business and Finance ... Mr. Martin SADLER
32 Vice President Student Services ... Rev. John WHITE
30 Vice Pres Institutional Advancement ... Mr. Doug TAYLOR
20 Assoc Dean Academic Administration ... Dr. Ann Clay ADAMS
08 Director of Library ... Vacant
107 Assoc Dean Advanced Prof Studies ... Dr. Kevin PARK
06 Registrar ... Mr. Mike MEDFORD
07 Director of Admissions & Recruiting ... Rev. Monica WEDLOCK
26 Director of Communications ... Mr. Michael THOMPSON

Columbus State University (G)

4225 University Avenue, Columbus GA 31907-5645
County: Muscogee FICE Identification: 001561
Unit ID: 139366
Telephone: (706) 507-8800 Carnegie Class: Master's L
FAX Number: (706) 568-2123 Calendar System: Semester
URL: www.columbusstate.edu
Established: 1958 Annual Undergrad Tuition & Fees (In-State): $6,592
Enrollment: 8,307 Coed
Affiliation or Control: State IRS Status: 501(c)3
Highest Offering: Doctorate
Program: 2-Year Principally Bachelor's Creditable; Liberal Arts And General; Teacher Preparatory; Professional
Accreditation: SC, ART, BUS, CACREP, MUS, NURSE, TED, THEA

01 President ... Dr. Timothy S. MESCON
05 Provost/VP Academic Affairs ... Dr. Tom HACKETT
10 Vice President Business & Finance ... Mr. Tom HELTON
32 VP Student Affairs & Enrollment Mgt ... Dr. Gina SHEEKS
30 VP University Advancement ... Dr. Alan MEDDERS
14 Chief Information Officer ... Mr. Abraham GEORGE
20 Assoc Provost Undergraduate Educ ... Dr. Tina BUTCHER
20 Assoc Provost Graduate Educ ... Dr. Greg DOMIN
30 Assoc VP for Development ... Mr. Spence SEALY
21 Asst Vice Pres Business & Finance ... Mrs. Lougene BROWN
35 Assistant VP Student Affairs ... Dr. Darryl B. HOLLOMAN
84 Asst VP for Enrollment Mgmt ... Mr. John MCELVEEN
26 Asst VP for University Relations ... Mr. John LESTER
50 Dean College of Business & Comp Sci ... Dr. Linda HADLEY
81 Dean College of Letters & Sciences ... Dr. David LANOUE
53 Dean College of Education ... Dr. Barbara BUCKNER
57 Dean College of the Arts ... Dr. Richard L. BAXTER
08 Dean of Libraries ... Mr. Mark FLYNN
35 Dean of Students ... Mr. Aaron J. REESE
35 Sr Dir Student Life & Development ... Dr. Kimberly MULLEN
44 Dir Annual Giving/Alumni Relations ... Ms. Meri ROBINSON
29 Director Alumni Relations ... Mrs. Jennifer JOYNER
15 Human Resources Director ... Ms. Laurie S. JONES
09 Director Institutional Research ... Dr. Sri SITHARAMAN

41 Athletic Director ... Mr. Jay SPARKS
19 Chief Campus Police ... Mr. Rus DREW
51 Director Continuing Education ... Ms. Susan WIRT
39 Director Residence Life ... Mr. Jonathan LUCIA
37 Director Financial Aid ... Ms. Janis BOWLES
38 Director Counseling Center ... Dr. Dan ROSE
85 Director Center International Educ ... Dr. Neal R. MCCRILLIS
07 Director of Admissions ... Ms. Susan LOVELL
06 Registrar ... Mr. John H. BROWN
92 Director Honors Program ... Dr. Cindy HENNING
23 Director Student Health Services ... Ms. Rebecca TEW

† Part of the University System of Georgia.

Columbus Technical College (A)

928 Manchester Expressway, Columbus GA 31904-6572

County: Muscogee | FICE Identification: 005624
Unit ID: 139357
Telephone: (706) 649-1800 | Carnegie Class: Assoc/Pub-R-M
FAX Number: (706) 649-1885 | Calendar System: Semester
URL: www.columbustech.edu
Established: 1961 | Annual Undergrad Tuition & Fees (In-State): $3,150
Enrollment: 3,906 | Coed
Affiliation or Control: State | IRS Status: 501(c)3
Highest Offering: Associate Degree
Program: Occupational; 2-Year Principally Bachelor's Creditable; Technical Emphasis
Accreditation: SC, ADNUR, DA, DH, MAC, PNUR, RAD, SURGT

01 President ... Mr. J. Robert JONES
11 Vice President Administrative Svcs ... Ms. Betty JACKSON
05 Vice President Academic Affairs ... Dr. Linn STOREY
32 Vice President Student Affairs ... Ms. Tara ASKEW
18 Vice President Operations ... Mr. Tommy WILSON
46 VP Institutional Effectiveness ... Dr. Michael LAMB
88 Vice President Economic Development ... Mr. James LOYD
06 Assoc VP of Stdnt Affairs/Registrar ... Dr. Sarah BEECHAM
15 Director of Human Resources ... Ms. Patricia HOOD
26 Director of Communications ... Ms. Cheryl MYERS
37 Associate VP of Financial Aid ... Ms. Debbie HENSHAW
38 Director Student Counseling ... Ms. Olive VIDAL-KENDALL
30 Director Institutional Advancement ... Ms. Gloria DODDS

Covenant College (B)

14049 Scenic Highway, Lookout Mountain TN 30750-4164

County: Dade | FICE Identification: 003484
Unit ID: 139393
Telephone: (706) 820-1560 | Carnegie Class: Bac/Diverse
FAX Number: (706) 820-2165 | Calendar System: Semester
URL: www.covenant.edu
Established: 1955 | Annual Undergrad Tuition & Fees: $28,270
Enrollment: 1,094 | Coed
Affiliation or Control: Presbyterian Church In America | IRS Status: 501(c)3
Highest Offering: Master's
Program: Liberal Arts And General; Teacher Preparatory
Accreditation: SC

01 President ... Dr. J. Derek HALVORSON
05 Vice Pres Academic Affairs & CFO ... Dr. Jeffrey B. HALL
30 Vice President Advancement ... Mr. Troy DUBLE
32 Vice Pres Student Development ... Mr. Brad VOYLES
08 Librarian ... Mr. Tad MINDEMAN
06 Dean of Records ... Mr. Rodney E. MILLER
42 Chaplain ... Mr. Aaron MESSNER
58 Director of Master of Education Pgm ... Dr. Jim DREXLER
21 Controller ... Mr. Robert E. HARBERT
18 Director of Physical Plant ... Mr. David NORTHCUTT
37 Director of Student Financial Plng ... Mrs. Brenda RAPIER
15 Director of Human Resources ... Mr. Pat SEMTNER
41 Athletic Director ... Ms. Tami SMIALEK
13 Chief Information Officer ... Ms. Marjorie CROCKER
29 Director of Alumni Relations ... Mr. Marshall K. ROWE
24 Director of AV Services ... Mr. Matt WRIGHT
23 Director of Health Services ... Mrs. Barbara M. MICHAL
07 Dir Admissions & Church Relations ... Mr. Matthew BRYANT
09 Director of Institutional Research ... Dr. Karen NELSON
26 Chief Public Relations Officer ... Ms. Jen ALLEN
20 Director of Academic Support ... Mrs. Janet HULSEY
36 Dir of Center for Calling & Career ... Mr. Anthony TUCKER

Dalton State College (C)

650 College Drive, Dalton GA 30720-3797

County: Whitfield | FICE Identification: 003956
Unit ID: 139463
Telephone: (706) 272-4436 | Carnegie Class: Bac/Assoc
FAX Number: (706) 272-4588 | Calendar System: Semester
URL: www.daltonstate.edu
Established: 1963 | Annual Undergrad Tuition & Fees (In-State): $3,622
Enrollment: 5,750 | Coed
Affiliation or Control: State | IRS Status: 501(c)3
Highest Offering: Baccalaureate
Program: Occupational; 2-Year Principally Bachelor's Creditable; Liberal Arts And General; Teacher Preparatory; Professional
Accreditation: SC, ADNUR, BUS, MAC, MLTAD, RAD, SW, TED

01 President ... Dr. John O. SCHWENN
05 Vice President for Academic Affairs ... Dr. Sandra STONE
10 Vice President Fiscal Affairs ... Mr. Scott BAILEY
84 Vice Pres Enrollment & Student Svcs ... Dr. Jodi S. JOHNSON
20 Asst Vice President Academic Affs ... Dr. Andy MEYER
37 Director of Financial Aid/Vet Svcs ... Ms. Carol JONES
08 Librarian ... Ms. Lydia KNIGHT
09 Director Inst Research & Planning ... Dr. Henry M. CODJOE
21 Asst Director of Business Office ... Mr. Nick HENRY
07 Asst VP for Enrollment Services ... Dr. Angela HARRIS
18 Chief Facilities/Physical Plant ... Mr. Jack REYNOLDS
26 Director Marketing & Communication ... Ms. Pam PARTAIN
102 Director Foundation ... Mr. David ELROD
32 Director Student Life ... Ms. Jami HALL
38 Director Student Counseling ... Ms. Linda WHEELER
15 Director Human Resources ... Ms. Faith MILLER
96 Interim Director of Purchasing ... Ms. Penny CORDELL
13 Director Computing & Info Services ... Mr. Terry BAILEY
19 Director Public Safety ... Mr. Billy GEE
29 Director Alumni Relations ... Mr. Josh WILSON
39 Director Student Housing ... Mr. Jonathan JOHNSON
50 Interim Dean School of Business ... Dr. Larry JOHNSON
53 Dean School of Education ... Dr. Calvin MEYER
49 Dean School of Liberal Arts ... Ms. Mary NIELSEN
81 Dean School of Science/Tech/Math ... Mr. Randall GRIFFUS
66 Dean School of Health Professions ... Ms. Cordia STARLING
70 Dean of Social Work ... Mr. Spencer ZEIGER
56 Dean External Programs ... Mr. Charles JOHNSON

† Part of the University System of Georgia.

Darton College (D)

2400 Gillionville Road, Albany GA 31707-3098

County: Dougherty | FICE Identification: 001543
Unit ID: 138691
Telephone: (229) 317-6000 | Carnegie Class: Assoc/Pub-R-M
FAX Number: (229) 317-6604 | Calendar System: Semester
URL: www.darton.edu
Established: 1963 | Annual Undergrad Tuition & Fees (In-State): $3,164
Enrollment: 6,097 | Coed
Affiliation or Control: State | IRS Status: 501(c)3
Highest Offering: Baccalaureate
Program: Occupational; 2-Year Principally Bachelor's Creditable
Accreditation: SC, ADNUR, CVT, DH, HT, MLTAD, OTA, PTAA

01 President ... Dr. Peter J. SIRENO
10 Vice Pres Business/Financial Svcs ... Mr. Ronnie A. HENRY
05 VP Academic Affairs ... Dr. F. Gary BARNETTE
32 VP Student Affs/Dean of Students ... Dr. F. Gary BARNETTE
21 Asst VP Business/Financial Svcs ... Mr. Stan BROWN
51 Interim Dir Cont Ed/Economic Dev ... Mr. Michael WHITE
08 Director Learning Resources Ctr ... Mrs. Mary WASHINGTON
07 Director Admissions ... Ms. Susan BOWEN
13 Director Office of Information Tech ... Mr. Tracy COSPER
18 Director Physical Plant ... Mr. D. Steve HARRIS
26 Director College Relations ... Mr. Tracy GOODE
41 Athletic Director ... Mr. Michael KIEFER
06 Registrar ... Mrs. Frances CARR
37 Director Student Financial Aid ... Ms. Haley HOOKS
15 Director Personnel Services ... Mr. Ronnie HENRY
85 International Student Coordinator ... Ms. Diana GARNER
29 Director Alumni Relations ... Vacant
36 Director Student Placement ... Mr. Jason SWORDS
38 Director Student Counseling ... Ms. Carol Ann HAM
96 Director of Purchasing ... Mrs. Joy CAUSEY
89 Director Freshmen Studies ... Ms. Kristi STIMPSON
92 Director Honors Program ... Ms. Shani CLARK
93 Director Minority Students ... Ms. Simonee PATTON
09 Director of Institutional Research ... Dr. Richard BALSLEY

† Part of the University System of Georgia.

DeVry University - Alpharetta Campus (E)

2555 Northwinds Parkway, Alpharetta GA 30009-2232

County: DeKalb | Identification: 666989
Unit ID: 432162
Telephone: (770) 619-3600 | Carnegie Class: Not Classified
FAX Number: (770) 664-8824 | Calendar System: Semester
URL: www.devry.edu
Established: 1997 | Annual Undergrad Tuition & Fees: $16,156
Enrollment: 762 | Coed
Affiliation or Control: Proprietary | IRS Status: Proprietary
Highest Offering: Master's
Program: Occupational; Professional; Business Emphasis
Accreditation: &NH, ENGT

01 Campus Dean ... Tonya GIBSON
07 Director of Admissions ... Lance STRIBLING
08 Librarian ... Vacant

† Regional accreditation is carried under the parent institution in Downers Grove, IL.

DeVry University - Atlanta Buckhead Center (F)

3575 Piedmont Road NE, Atlanta GA 30305-1543

County: Fulton | Identification: 666200
Unit ID: 437291
Telephone: (404) 760-1400 | Carnegie Class: Not Classified
FAX Number: N/A | Calendar System: Semester
URL: www.keller.edu
Established: 1998 | Annual Graduate Tuition & Fees: $18,384
Enrollment: 162 | Coed
Affiliation or Control: Proprietary | IRS Status: Proprietary
Highest Offering: Master's; No Undergraduates
Program: Occupational; Professional; Business Emphasis
Accreditation: &NH

01 Center Dean ... Stephanie O'NEAL

† Regional accreditation is carried under the parent institution in Downers Grove, IL.

DeVry University - Atlanta Cobb/ Galleria Center (G)

100 Galleria Parkway, SE, Suite 100, Atlanta GA 30339-3122

County: DeKalb | Identification: 666257
Telephone: (770) 916-3704 | Carnegie Class: Not Classified
FAX Number: N/A | Calendar System: Semester
URL: www.devry.edu
Established: 1931 | Annual Undergrad Tuition & Fees: $16,156
Enrollment: 538 | Coed
Affiliation or Control: Proprietary | IRS Status: Proprietary
Highest Offering: Master's
Program: Occupational; Professional; Business Emphasis
Accreditation: &NH

01 Center Dean ... Mr. Angelo BROWN

† Regional accreditation is carried under the parent institution in Downers Grove, IL.

DeVry University - Atlanta/ Perimeter Center (H)

2 Ravinia Drive, Suite 250, Atlanta GA 30346-2104

County: Fulton | Identification: 666201
Unit ID: 437282
Telephone: (770) 391-6200 | Carnegie Class: Not Classified
FAX Number: N/A | Calendar System: Semester
URL: www.keller.edu
Established: 1993 | Annual Undergrad Tuition & Fees: $16,156
Enrollment: 223 | Coed
Affiliation or Control: Proprietary | IRS Status: Proprietary
Highest Offering: Master's
Program: Occupational; Professional; Business Emphasis
Accreditation: &NH

01 Center Dean ... Elizabeth COOK

† Regional accreditation is carried under the parent institution in Downers Grove, IL.

DeVry University - Decatur Campus (I)

One West Court Square, Ste. 100, Decatur GA 30030-2556

County: DeKalb | FICE Identification: 009224
Unit ID: 139533
Telephone: (404) 270-2700 | Carnegie Class: Master's L
FAX Number: (404) 292-8117 | Calendar System: Semester
URL: www.devry.edu
Established: 1931 | Annual Undergrad Tuition & Fees: $16,156
Enrollment: 3,156 | Coed
Affiliation or Control: Proprietary | IRS Status: Proprietary
Highest Offering: Master's
Program: Occupational; Professional; Business Emphasis
Accreditation: &NH, ENGT

01 Metro President ... Mr. Chris CHAVEZ
05 Dean of Academic Affairs ... Mr. John DUNBAR
08 Director Library Services ... Ms. Tiia KUNNAPAS
32 Student Services Manager ... Ms. Penny SAWYER
50 Dean of Business & Technology ... Mr. Charles THOMPSON
37 Director Student Finance ... Ms. Loucha SIMON-FRANCOIS
36 Director of Career Services ... Mr. Brian SHADIX
06 Registrar ... Ms. Heather HOFFMAN
07 Director of Admissions ... Mr. Jimmy COPLES
31 Director of Community Outreach ... Mrs. Jeanne JOHNSON-WHATLEY
49 Dean of Arts & Sciences ... Mr. Dale BURGESS
15 HR Business Partner ... Mr. Felix ALEJANDRO

† Regional accreditation is carried under the parent institution in Downers Grove, IL.

DeVry University - Gwinnett Center (J)

3505 Koger Boulevard, Suite 170, Duluth GA 30096-7671

County: Gwinnett | Identification: 666202
Unit ID: 440554
Telephone: (770) 381-4400 | Carnegie Class: Not Classified
FAX Number: (770) 381-4411 | Calendar System: Semester
URL: www.devry.edu
Established: 2001 | Annual Undergrad Tuition & Fees: $16,156
Enrollment: 571 | Coed
Affiliation or Control: Proprietary | IRS Status: Proprietary
Highest Offering: Master's
Program: Occupational; Professional; Business Emphasis
Accreditation: &NH

01 Center Dean ..... Gregory PACE

† Regional accreditation is carried under the parent institution in Downers Grove, IL.

DeVry University - Henry County (A)

675 Southcrest Parkway, Suite 100,
Stockbridge GA 30281-7973

County: Henry | Identification: 666532
Telephone: (678) 284-4700 | Carnegie Class: Not Classified
FAX Number: (770) 474-5011 | Calendar System: Semester
URL: www.devry.edu
Established: 1931 | Annual Undergrad Tuition & Fees: $16,156
Enrollment: 590 | Coed
Affiliation or Control: Proprietary | IRS Status: Proprietary
Highest Offering: Master's
Program: Professional; Business Emphasis
Accreditation: &NH

01 Center Dean ..... Mr. Pete JOINES

† Regional accreditation is carried under the parent institution in Downers Grove, IL.

East Georgia State College (B)

131 College Circle, Swainsboro GA 30401-3643

County: Emanuel | FICE Identification: 010997
Unit ID: 139621
Telephone: (478) 289-2000 | Carnegie Class: Assoc/Pub-R-S
FAX Number: (478) 289-2038 | Calendar System: Semester
URL: www.ega.edu
Established: 1973 | Annual Undergrad Tuition & Fees (In-State): $3,368
Enrollment: 3,436 | Coed
Affiliation or Control: State | IRS Status: 501(c)3
Highest Offering: Baccalaureate
Program: Occupational; 2-Year Principally Bachelor's Creditable
Accreditation: SC

01 Interim President ..... Dr. Bob BOEHMER
05 Vice President for Academic Affairs ..... Dr. Timothy D. GOODMAN
10 Vice President for Business Affairs ..... Mr. Cliff GAY
32 Vice Pres for Student Affairs ..... Mr. Donald AVERY
13 Vice Pres Information Technology ..... Mr. Mike ROUNTREE
100 Chief of Staff/Legal Counsel ..... Mrs. Mary C. SMITH
04 Executive Assistant to President ..... Mrs. Susan GRAY
08 Librarian ..... Vacant
06 Registrar ..... Mrs. Janet STRACHER
27 Director of Public Information ..... Mr. Gerald D. HOOKS
09 Director of Institutional Research ..... Mr. David GRIBBIN
37 Director of Financial Aid ..... Mrs. Karen S. JONES
15 Director of Human Resources ..... Mrs. Tracy WOODS
30 Director of External Affairs ..... Ms. Elizabeth GILMER
18 Director of Facilities ..... Mrs. Michelle GOFF
26 Director of Marketing ..... Ms. Norma WOODS
12 Director of EGSC-Statesboro ..... Ms. Caroline MCMILLAN
19 Director of Security ..... Mr. Drew DURDEN
35 Director of Student Life ..... Ms. Vicki SHERROD
07 Director of Admissions ..... Vacant
21 Comptroller ..... Ms. Natasha W. MASON
38 Dir Counseling/Disability Services ..... Ms. Anna Marie REICH
39 Director of Housing ..... Ms. Missie CRAWFORD
41 Director of Athletics ..... Mr. Neil BAILEY
12 Dir Judie A Fulford Cmty Lrng Ctr ..... Mrs. Jean D. SCHWABE
18 Director of Plant Operations ..... Mr. David STEPTOE
88 Director of Accounting Services ..... Ms. Becky FOSKEY

† Part of the University System of Georgia.

Emmanuel College (C)

181 Spring Street, Franklin Springs GA 30639

County: Franklin | FICE Identification: 001563
Unit ID: 139630
Telephone: (706) 245-7226 | Carnegie Class: Bac/Diverse
FAX Number: (706) 245-4424 | Calendar System: Semester
URL: www.ec.edu
Established: 1919 | Annual Undergrad Tuition & Fees: $14,575
Enrollment: 788 | Coed
Affiliation or Control: Pentecostal Holiness Church | IRS Status: 501(c)3
Highest Offering: Baccalaureate
Program: Liberal Arts And General; Teacher Preparatory; Professional; Business Emphasis
Accreditation: SC

01 President ..... Dr. Michael S. STEWART
32 Vice President for Student Life ..... Mr. Jason CROY
05 Vice President for Academic Affairs ..... Dr. John R. HENZEL, JR.
10 Vice President for Finance ..... Dr. Kevin CRAWFORD
30 Vice President for Development ..... Mr. Brian JAMES
84 Vice Pres Enrollment Mgmt/Marketing ..... Ms. Wendy VINSON
08 Director of Library Services ..... Ms. Austina JORDAN
06 Registrar ..... Mrs. Debra F. GRIZZLE
37 Director of Financial Aid ..... Mr. Vince WELCH
13 Director of Information Technology ..... Mr. Glenn TONEY
11 Director of Campus Operations ..... Mr. Ron MCCULLAR
41 Director of Athletics ..... Mr. Mike BONA
42 Director of Spiritual Life ..... Mr. Chris MAXWELL
15 Director of Human Resources ..... Mrs. Joann HARPER
26 Chief Public Relations Officer ..... Mrs. Paula DIXON
38 Director of Student Counseling ..... Mr. Sean WILLIAMSON
96 Director of Accounting Services ..... Mrs. Anita RAY
18 Physical Plant Director ..... Mr. Wayne CRIDER
09 Diredtor of Institutional Research ..... Dr. Brian PEEK
29 Director Alumni Relations ..... Mr. Harrell W. QUEEN

Emory University (D)

201 Dowman Drive, Atlanta GA 30322-0001

County: DeKalb | FICE Identification: 001564
Unit ID: 139658
Telephone: (404) 727-6123 | Carnegie Class: RU/VH
FAX Number: (404) 727-5997 | Calendar System: Semester
URL: www.emory.edu
Established: 1836 | Annual Undergrad Tuition & Fees: $42,980
Enrollment: 13,893 | Coed
Affiliation or Control: United Methodist | IRS Status: 501(c)3
Highest Offering: Doctorate
Program: Occupational; 2-Year Principally Bachelor's Creditable; Liberal Arts And General; Teacher Preparatory; Professional
Accreditation: SC, AA, ARCPA, BUS, CLPSY, DENT, DIETI, IPSY, LAW, MED, MIDWF, NURSE, PH, PTA, RAD, TED, THEOL

01 President ..... Dr. James W. WAGNER
05 Provost/Exec VP Acad Affs ..... Dr. Earl LEWIS
03 Exec Vice Pres for Finance/Admin ..... Mr. Michael J. MANDL
17 Exec Vice Pres Health Affairs ..... Dr. S. Wright CAUGHMAN
101 VP/Secretary of the University ..... Dr. Rosemary MAGEE
04 VP/Deputy to the President ..... Dr. Gary S. HAUK
43 Sr Vice Pres & General Counsel ..... Mr. Stephen D. SENCER
30 Sr Vice Pres Devel/Alumni Rels ..... Ms. Susan CRUSE
32 Sr Vice President/Dean Campus Life ..... Dr. Ajay NAIR
46 Vice President for Research Admin ..... Dr. David L. WYNES
29 Vice President Alumni Relations ..... Ms. Allison DYKES
10 Vice President for Finance ..... Ms. Edith C. MURPHREE
58 Vice Provost/Dean Graduate Sch ..... Dr. Lisa A. TEDESCO
15 Vice President Human Resources ..... Mr. Peter BARNES
26 Vice Pres Communications/Marketing ..... Mr. Ron SAUDER
22 Vice President Equal Opportunity ..... Vacant
86 Vice President Governmental Affairs ..... Mr. John T. ENGELEN
18 Vice President Campus Services ..... Mr. Matthew EARLY
25 Assoc Vice Pres for Research Admin ..... Ms. Kerry PELUSO
10 Assoc Vice President & Controller ..... Ms. Belva WHITE
35 Special Asst to Sr VP Campus Life ..... Dr. Carolyn LIVINGSTON
28 Sr Vice Provost Community/Diversity ..... Mr. Ozzie HARRIS
20 Sr Vice Prov for Academic Affairs ..... Dr. Claire E. STERK
44 Sr Assoc Vice Pres Annual Giving ..... Mr. Raymond REYNOLDS, JR.
20 Sr Vice Prov for Undergrad Acad Aff ..... Dr. Lynn ZIMMERMAN
88 Assoc Vice Prov Oper Student Svcs ..... Ms. Heather MUGG
08 Interim Vice Provost/Dir Libraries ..... Dr. Richard A. MENDOLA
14 CIO/Vice Provost Information Tech ..... Dr. Richard A. MENDOLA
07 AVP Undergrad Enroll/Dean of Admiss ..... Dr. John LATTING
49 Dean of Emory College ..... Dr. Robin FORMAN
12 Dean & CEO Oxford College ..... Dr. Stephen H. BOWEN
63 Dean of Medicine ..... Dr. Thomas J. LAWLEY
66 Dean of Nursing ..... Dr. Linda MCCAULEY
73 Dean of Theology ..... Dr. Jan LOVE
61 Dean of Law ..... Mr. David PARTLETT
50 Dean of the Business School ..... Dr. Lawrence M. BENVENISTE
69 Dean of Public Health ..... Dr. James W. CURRAN
85 Dir Intl Student Scholar Program ..... Ms. Lelia CRAWFORD
80 Pres & CEO of the Carter Center ..... Dr. John HARDMAN
42 Dean of the Chapel & Religious Life ..... Rev. Susan HENRY-CROWE
06 University Registrar ..... Mr. Tom MILLEN
27 Executive Director Marketing ..... Ms. Jan GLEASON
37 Director Financial Aid ..... Mr. Dean BENTLEY
36 Director Placement Service ..... Mr. Paul FOWLER
19 Chief of Police ..... Mr. Craig T. WATSON
23 Pres & CEO Emory Healthcare ..... Mr. John T. FOX
41 Director Athletics/Recreation ..... Mr. Timothy DOWNES
88 Director Yerkes Research Ctrs ..... Dr. Stuart M. ZOLA
49 Director Institute Liberal Arts ..... Dr. Kevin CORRIGAN
88 Director M C Carlos Museum ..... Ms. Bonnie SPEED
40 University Bookstore Liaison ..... Mr. Bruce COVEY
39 Exec Dir Res Life & Housing ..... Dr. Andrea TRINKLEIN
38 Director Univ Counseling Center ..... Dr. Mark MCLEOD
09 Director Institutional Research ..... Dr. Daniel TEODORESCU
96 Director Contract Admin/Compliance ..... Mr. Rex HARDAWAY

Everest Institute (E)

2460 Wesley Chapel Road, Suite 100,
Decatur GA 30035-3420

County: DeKalb | Identification: 666285
Unit ID: 438638
Telephone: (404) 327-8787 | Carnegie Class: Assoc/PrivFP
FAX Number: (404) 327-8980 | Calendar System: Quarter
URL: www.everest.edu
Established: N/A | Annual Undergrad Tuition & Fees: $16,568
Enrollment: 717 | Coed
Affiliation or Control: Proprietary | IRS Status: Proprietary
Highest Offering: Associate Degree
Program: Occupational
Accreditation: ACCSC, SURGT

01 President ..... Mr. Chris KEY

† Branch campus of Everest Institute, Cross Lanes, WV.

Fort Valley State University (F)

1005 State University Drive, Fort Valley GA 31030-4313

County: Peach | FICE Identification: 001566
Unit ID: 139719
Telephone: (478) 825-6211 | Carnegie Class: Bac/Diverse
FAX Number: (478) 825-6394 | Calendar System: Semester
URL: www.fvsu.edu
Established: 1895 | Annual Undergrad Tuition & Fees (In-State): $5,278
Enrollment: 3,755 | Coed
Affiliation or Control: State | IRS Status: 501(c)3
Highest Offering: Beyond Master's But Less Than Doctorate
Program: Occupational; Liberal Arts And General; Teacher Preparatory
Accreditation: SC, AAFCS, CACREP, #CORE, DIETD, ENGT, TED

01 President ..... Dr. Larry E. RIVERS
03 Inerim Exeutive Vice President ..... Dr. Canter BROWN, JR.
32 Vice Pres Student Affairs ..... Mr. Willie WILLIAMS
10 Int Vice Pres Business & Finance ..... Mr. Henry SPINKS
31 Vice President External Affairs ..... Dr. Melody CARTER
05 Int Vice Pres for Academic Affairs ..... Dr. Julius SCIPIO
09 VP Inst Research/Plng & Effec ..... Dr. B. Donta TRUSS
88 Assoc VP for Land Grant Affair ..... Dr. Mark LATTIMORE
04 Spec Asst to the Pres/Legal Counsel ..... Dr. Canter BROWN
49 Int Dean of Arts/Sciences ..... Dr. Keith MURPHY
21 Comptroller ..... Mr. Kevin HOWARD
06 Registrar ..... Mrs. Sharee LAWRENCE
13 Director for Information Technology ..... Mr. Gary MILLER
08 Dir University Libraries ..... Dr. Annie PAYTON
07 Director Admissions ..... Mr. Johnny C. NIMES
37 Int Director Financial Aid ..... Ms. Lakisia SANDERS
88 Director Title III ..... Dr. Melody CARTER
29 Director Alumni Affairs ..... Ms. Clara BRASWELL
15 Director of Human Resources ..... Ms. Erika GRAVETT
19 Director Campus Safety ..... Mr. Ken MORGAN
47 Int Dean Agriculture ..... Dr. Gavindarajan KANNON
23 Director Health Services ..... Vacant
18 Director Plant & Maintenance ..... Dr. Dwayne CREW
36 Director Counsel/Career Development ..... Ms. Simmons ROMELDA
26 Director Marketing/Communications ..... Vacant
41 Director of Athletics ..... Vacant
88 Int Exec Dir Academic Success Ctr ..... Dr. Jerry HAYWOOD
58 Dean Grad Studies/Extended Educ ..... Dr. Anna HOLLOWAY
53 Dean College of Education ..... Dr. Edward HILL

† Part of the University System of Georgia.

Gainesville State College (G)

3820 Mundy Mill Rd, Oakwood GA 30566-3414

County: Hall | FICE Identification: 001567
Unit ID: 139773
Telephone: (678) 717-3639 | Carnegie Class: Assoc/Pub4
FAX Number: (678) 717-3859 | Calendar System: Semester
URL: www.gsc.edu
Established: 1964 | Annual Undergrad Tuition & Fees (In-State): $3,031
Enrollment: 8,571 | Coed
Affiliation or Control: State | IRS Status: 501(c)3
Highest Offering: Baccalaureate
Program: Occupational; 2-Year Principally Bachelor's Creditable
Accreditation: SC, ACBSP, TED

01 Interim President ..... Dr. Randy PIERCE
05 Vice President Academic Affairs ..... Dr. Al PANU
10 Int Vice President Business/Finance ..... Ms. Wanda ALDRIDGE
32 Vice Pres Student Activities ..... Dr. Tom G. WALTER
30 Vice President Advancement ..... Ms. Mary TRANSUE
12 Vice Pres/CEO Oconee Campus ..... Dr. Margaret VENABLE
35 Assoc Vice Pres Student Development ..... Dr. Alicia CAUDILL
20 Assoc Vice Pres Academic Affairs ..... Dr. Chaudron GILLE
84 Assoc VP Enrollment Management ..... Mr. Mack PALMOUR
88 Int Asst VP Academic Enrichment ..... Dr. Kristen RONEY
06 Registrar ..... Ms. Janice HARTSOE
07 Director of Admissions ..... Mr. Mack PALMOUR
13 Director Information Technology ..... Mr. Brandon A. HAAG
51 Director Cont Educ/Public Service ..... Ms. Wendy THELLMAN
09 Director Institutional Research ..... Ms. Betsy CANTRELL
35 Director Student Activities ..... Dr. Cara RAY
37 Director Financial Aid ..... Ms. Susan A. SMITH
28 Director Diversity Initiatives ..... Dr. Robert ROBINSON
22 Affirmative Action/EEO Officer ..... Dr. Joan H. MARLER
29 Director Alumni Affairs ..... Ms. Jennifer HENDRICKSON
26 Director Public Rels/Marketing ..... Ms. Sloan W. JONES
08 Director ACTT & Library ..... Dr. Deborah PROSSER
15 Personnel Services Director ..... Ms. Amy COLLINS
18 Director Plant Operations ..... Mr. Bill MOODY
19 Director Public Safety ..... Mr. Clifford POOLE
96 Director of Purchasing ..... Ms. Bonnie JONES
38 Director Student Counseling ..... Dr. Joy EVANS
40 Bookstore Manager ..... Ms. Jackie MAULDIN
25 Grant Administrator ..... Ms. Debbra PILGRIM
89 Director First Year Experience ..... Mr. Abdul ROUX
88 Director of Academic Advising ..... Ms. Terri CARROLL
50 Dean Sch Bus Educ/Health/Wellness ..... Dr. Maryellen COSGROVE
83 Dean School of Social Sciences ..... Dr. Lee CHEEK, JR.
79 Int Dean Sch Humanities & Fine Arts ..... Dr. Eric SKIPPER
81 Interim Dean STEM ..... Dr. Danny LAU
36 Director Student Placement ..... Vacant

† Part of the University System of Georgia.

Georgia Christian University (A)

6789 Peachtree Industrial Boulevard, Atlanta GA 30360
County: DeKalb | FICE Identification: 041565
Unit ID: 461236
Telephone: (770) 279-0507 | Carnegie Class: Not Classified
FAX Number: (770) 279-0308 | Calendar System: Other
URL: www.gcuniv.edu
Established: 1986 | Annual Undergrad Tuition & Fees: $21,500
Enrollment: 320 | Coed
Affiliation or Control: Independent Non-Profit | IRS Status: 501(c)3
Highest Offering: Doctorate
Program: Professional; Religious Emphasis
Accreditation: @TRACS

01 President ... Dr. Paul C. KIM
07 Director of Admissions ... Ms. Eungjo LEE
05 Chief Academic Officer ... Dr. Hee Sook SONG
45 Director Of Planning ... Dr. SamYoung KIM
10 Chief Financial Officer ... Ms. Eunice KIM
12 Director of Branch Campus ... Ms. Sun Hee CHOI
25 Assc Director Strategic Advancement ... Mr. Peter CHOE
18 Chief Facilities/Physical Plant ... Rev. Min Soo KIM
19 Director Security/Safety ... Mr. Samuel KIM
21 Director of Business Affairs ... Mr. James D. CHONG
29 Director Alumni Relations ... Rev. Min Soo KIM
26 Chief Public Relations Officer ... Dr. Hyun Sung CHO
96 Director Purchasing ... Mr. Daniel KIM
06 Registrar ... Dr. Seung-Ju BAICK
37 Director Student Financial Aid ... Dr. Hee Sook SONG
50 Dean Business ... Dr. Auther H KIM
53 Dean Education ... Dr. Young Jun KIM
88 Dean Divinity School ... Dr. Ho Woo LEE
64 Dean Music ... Dr. Soo Jin KIM
88 Dn Mission Stds/World Christianity ... Dr. Young Hwan KIM
73 Dean Theology ... Dr. Jong Sik CHANG
88 International Student Advisor ... Vacant
30 Dir of Institutional Advancement ... Dr. Yong Soo JO
42 Associate Chaplain ... Rev. Chang Sun PYO

Georgia College & State University (B)

231 West Hancock Street, Milledgeville GA 31061-0490
County: Baldwin | FICE Identification: 001602
Unit ID: 139861
Telephone: (478) 445-5004 | Carnegie Class: Master's L
FAX Number: (478) 445-1191 | Calendar System: Semester
URL: www.gcsu.edu
Established: 1889 | Annual Undergrad Tuition & Fees (In-State): $8,618
Enrollment: 6,636 | Coed
Affiliation or Control: State | IRS Status: 501(c)3
Highest Offering: Doctorate
Program: Liberal Arts And General; Teacher Preparatory; Professional
Accreditation: SC, BUS, MUS, NUR, SPAA, TED

01 President ... Dr. Steve DORMAN
04 Exec Assistant to the President ... Ms. Monica STARLEY
05 Interim Provost/VP Academic Affairs ... Dr. Matthew LIAO-TROTH
11 VP Administration & Operations ... Dr. Paul A. JONES
32 VP Student Affairs/Dean of Students ... Dr. Bruce HARSHBARGER
30 VP External Rel/University Advance ... Ms. Amy AMASON
20 Assoc Provost for Academic Affs ... Dr. Tom ORMOND
51 Assoc VP Extended University ... Dr. Mark PELTON
35 Associate Vice Pres Student Affairs ... Dr. Paul K. JAHR
26 Assoc VP Strategic Communications ... Vacant
84 Asst VP Enrollment Management ... Ms. Suzanne PITTMAN
31 Asst VP for Auxiliary Services ... Mr. Kyle CULLARS
21 Asst VP Institutional Budget/Plng ... Ms. Susan ALLEN
49 Dean College of Arts & Sciences ... Mr. Ken PROCTER
50 Interim Dean College of Business ... Dr. Dale YOUNG
53 Dean College of Education ... Dr. Jane HINSON
76 Dean College of Health Sciences ... Dr. Sandra GANGSTEAD
39 Exec Director University Housing ... Mr. Larry CHRISTENSON
88 Univ Architect/Dir Facilities Plng ... Mr. Michael RICKENBAKER
18 Director of Plant Operations ... Mr. John GADSON
19 Director of Public Safety ... Mr. Scott BECKNER
09 Director of Institutional Research ... Dr. Ed HALE
12 Director Macon Graduate Center ... Dr. Kendra RUSSELL
12 Director Robins Center ... Dr. Howard WOODARD
13 Chief Information Officer ... Mr. Robert ORR
08 Director of University Libraries ... Dr. Joe MOCNIK
36 Director Career Center ... Ms. Mary ROBERTS
40 Director of University Bookstores ... Ms. Lynda GRABLE
16 Director Human Resources ... Mr. Rod KELLY
22 Int Director Instl Equity/Diversity ... Dr. Veronica WOMACK
91 Director Data Management Resources ... Ms. Michelle HIGHTOWER
07 Director of Admissions ... Mr. Kevin CHAMBERS
06 Registrar ... Ms. Kay ANDERSON
41 Director of Athetics ... Mr. Wendell STATON
29 Director Alumni & Parent Relations ... Mr. Matt MIZE
43 General Counsel ... Mr. Marc CARDINALLI
38 Director of Counseling Services ... Dr. Anne REYNOLDS
37 Director Financial Aid ... Ms. Cathy CRAWLEY
88 Dir Materials Mgmt/Central Services ... Mr. Mark MEEKS
88 Director of Audit/Advisory Services ... Ms. Julia HANN
35 Director of Campus Life ... Mr. Tom MILES

Georgia Gwinnett College (C)

1000 University Center Lane, Lawrenceville GA 30043
County: Gwinnett | FICE Identification: 041429
Unit ID: 447689
Telephone: (678) 407-5000 | Carnegie Class: Bac/Diverse
FAX Number: N/A | Calendar System: Semester
URL: www.ggc.usg.edu
Established: 2005 | Annual Undergrad Tuition & Fees (In-District): $5,290
Enrollment: 7,742 | Coed
Affiliation or Control: State/Local | IRS Status: 501(c)3
Highest Offering: Baccalaureate
Program: Liberal Arts And General
Accreditation: SC

01 President ... Dr. Daniel J. KAUFMAN
05 Vice Pres Academic/Student Affairs ... Dr. Stanley PRECZEWSKI
18 Vice Pres Facilities/Operations ... Mr. Eddie BEAUCHAMP
88 Vice Pres Educational Technology ... Dr. Mark IKEN
44 Vice President for Resources ... Ms. Laura MAXWELL
30 Vice President Advancement ... Ms. Renee BYRD-LEWIS
41 Athletic Director ... Dr. Darin WILSON

Georgia Health Sciences University (D)

1120 Fifteenth Street, Augusta GA 30912-0004
County: Richmond | FICE Identification: 001579
Unit ID: 140401
Telephone: (706) 721-0211 | Carnegie Class: Spec/Med
FAX Number: N/A | Calendar System: Semester
URL: www.georgiahealth.edu
Established: 1828 | Annual Undergrad Tuition & Fees (In-State): $8,908
Enrollment: 2,442 | Coed
Affiliation or Control: State | IRS Status: 501(c)3
Highest Offering: Doctorate
Program: Occupational; Professional
Accreditation: SC, ANEST, ARCPA, DENT, DH, DMS, IPSY, MED, MIL, MT, NMT, NURSE, OT, PH, PTA, RTT

01 President ... Dr. Ricardo AZZIZ
05 Exec VP for Acad Affairs/Provost ... Dr. Gretchen CAUGHMAN
10 Sr VP Finance & Admin/CFO ... Vacant
46 Senior Vice President for Research ... Dr. Mark W. HAMRICK
30 Sr VP Advance/Cmty Relations/CDO ... Ms. Susan L. BARCUS
17 Exec Vice Pres Clinical Affairs ... Mr. David S. HEFNER
27 Chief Information Officer ... Mr. Charles ENICKS
32 Vice Pres for Student Svcs & Dev ... Dr. Kevin B. FRAZIER
26 Interim VP Comm & Marketing ... Dr. Roman M. CIBIRKA
20 VP Instruction & Enrollment Mgmt ... Dr. Roman M. CIBIRKA
21 Interim Chief Audit Officer ... Mr. Michael W. FOXMAN
43 General Counsel ... Mr. Andrew NEWTON
63 Dean of Medical College ... Dr. Peter F. BUCKLEY
52 Dean College of Dental Med ... Dr. Connie L. DRISKO
58 Interim Dean College of Grad Stds ... Dr. Edward INSCHO
66 Dean College of Nursing ... Dr. Lucy N. MARION
76 Dean Col of Allied Health Sciences ... Dr. E. Andrew BALAS
88 Dept Chair Biostatistics ... Dr. Varghese T. GEORGE
88 VP Institutional Effectiveness ... Mrs. Beth P. BRIGDON
46 Sr Assoc VP Research Administration ... Ms. Betty J. ALDRIDGE
21 Assoc VP for Finance/Controller ... Mr. Jim JONES
18 VP Facilities Service ... Mr. Philip HOWARD
51 Director Continuing Education ... Ms. Caro CASSELS
22 Dir Affirm Action/Equal Employ Opty ... Mr. Glenn POWELL
08 Interim Director of Libraries ... Dr. David KING
88 Director, Supply Chain Mgmt ... Mr. Clay TROVER
15 Interim Enterprise VP Human Res ... Ms. Susan A. NORTON
19 Director Public Safety Division ... Mr. William E. MCBRIDE, JR.
06 Registrar ... Ms. Heather METRESS
28 Director Student Diversity Intl ... Ms. Beverly TARVER
35 Director Student & Auxiliary Svcs ... Mr. Dale HARTENBURG
39 Director of Residence Life ... Mr. Thomas J. FITTS, JR.
29 Sr Director Alumni Affairs ... Mr. Scott HENSON
88 Director Human Research Protection ... Ms. Ivy TILLMAN
102 Director of Development ... Ms. Eileen BRANDON
27 Director of University Comm ... Mr. Jack EVANS
04 Exec Admin Assist to the President ... Ms. Laura SHERROUSE
07 Interim Director of Admissions ... Mr. John ENGEL
09 Director of Institutional Research ... Mrs. Holly GOODSON
28 VP for Diversity & Inclusion ... Dr. Kent GUION
88 Managing Director, GCHC ... Mr. Robert BRADFORD
88 VP Finance, GHSMA ... Ms. Patricia BROWNLOW
88 Director Economic Development ... Ms. Annie H. BURRISS
88 VP Financial Svcs, GHSMC ... Mr. Greg DAMRON
88 VP Finance, GHSMA ... Ms. Patricia BROWNLOW
88 Exec Dir, GA War Veterans Nur Home ... Mr. Charles ESPOSITO
88 Assoc VP Tech Trans & Economic Dev ... Dr. Chris MCKINNEY
86 VP Gov Rel/Chief Advocacy Officer ... Mr. Michael SHAFFER
88 VP Partnerships & Strategic Affil ... Mr. Shawn VINCENT
88 Chief Integrity Officer ... Mr. James RUSH, JR.

† Part of the University System of Georgia.

Georgia Highlands College (E)

3175 Cedartown Highway SE, Rome GA 30161-3897
County: Floyd | FICE Identification: 009507
Unit ID: 139700
Telephone: (706) 802-5000 | Carnegie Class: Assoc/Pub-R-M
FAX Number: (706) 295-6610 | Calendar System: Semester
URL: www.highlands.edu
Established: 1970 | Annual Undergrad Tuition & Fees (In-State): $2,532
Enrollment: 5,530 | Coed
Affiliation or Control: State | IRS Status: 501(c)3
Highest Offering: Baccalaureate
Program: Occupational; 2-Year Principally Bachelor's Creditable
Accreditation: SC, ADNUR, DH

01 Interim President ... Dr. Renva WATTERSON
03 Interim Vice President ... Dr. Laura MUSSELWHITE
10 Vice Pres Finance/Administration ... Mr. Rob WHITAKER
15 Director Human Resources ... Ms. Ginni SILER
38 Student Support Services Coord ... Ms. Sheryl MCKINNEY
37 Director Financial Aid ... Ms. Megan SIMPSON
06 Registrar ... Ms. Sandie DAVIS
09 Director of Institutional Research ... Dr. Laura MUSSELWHITE
21 Director of Accounting ... Mr. Jamie PETTY
29 Director Alumni Relations ... Ms. Alison LAMPKIN
32 Student Life Coordinator ... Mr. John SPRANZA
08 Librarian ... Mr. Elijah SCOTT
19 Director Security ... Mr. John UPTON
26 Chief Public Relations Officer ... Ms. Dana DAVIS
40 Manager Bookstore ... Ms. Annette MITCHELL
30 Development Officer ... Mr. John SOUTHWOOD
18 Chief Facilities/Physical Plant ... Mr. Phillip KIMSEY
96 Director of Purchasing ... Ms. Cynthia PARKER
12 Campus Dean Marietta Campus ... Dr. Kirk NOOKS
12 Campus Dean Paulding Campus ... Dr. Cathy LEDBETTER
12 Cmapus Dean Douglasville Campus ... Mr. Ken REAVES
12 Campus Dean Floyd Campus ... Mr. Todd JONES
12 Campus Dean Cartersville Campus ... Ms. Carolyn HAMRICK
83 Dean Social Sciences ... Dr. Robert PAGE
76 Dean Health Sciences ... Ms. Rebecca MADDOX
88 Dean Acadamic Success ... Dr. Diane LANGSTON
68 Dean Science/PE ... Ms. Donna DAUGHERTY
81 Dean Mathematics ... Dr. Carla MOLDAVAN
79 Dean Humanities ... Dr. Jonathan HERSHEY
14 Dir Info Tech/Inst Computer Ctr ... Mr. Jeff PATTY
41 Director of Athletics ... Mr. Phillip GAFFNEY
28 Director of Diversity ... Dr. Kirk NOOKS

† Part of the University System of Georgia.

Georgia Institute of Technology (F)

225 North Avenue, NW, Atlanta GA 30332-0002
County: Fulton | FICE Identification: 001569
Unit ID: 139755
Telephone: (404) 894-2000 | Carnegie Class: RU/VH
FAX Number: (404) 894-1277 | Calendar System: Semester
URL: www.gatech.edu
Established: 1885 | Annual Undergrad Tuition & Fees (In-State): $10,098
Enrollment: 20,941 | Coed
Affiliation or Control: State | IRS Status: 501(c)3
Highest Offering: Doctorate
Program: Professional
Accreditation: SC, ART, BUS, CONST, CS, ENG, IPSY, OPE, PLNG

01 President ... Dr. G. P. (Bud) PETERSON
05 Provost/Exec VP Academic Affairs ... Dr. Rafael BRAS
10 Executive Vice Pres Admin/Finance ... Mr. Steven SWANT
46 Executive Vice President Research ... Dr. Stephen CROSS
100 Assistant Vice Pres/Chief of Staff ... Ms. Lynn DURHAM
30 Vice President Development ... Mr. Barrett H. CARSON
26 Vice Pres Communications/Marketing ... Mr. Michael L. WARDEN
32 Vice President Student Affairs ... Dr. William SCHAFER
88 VP/ Director Ga Tech Res Inst ... Dr. Robert MCGRATH
46 Vice President Research ... Ms. Jilda GARTON
86 Exec Dir Government/Cmty Relations ... Mr. Dene SHEHEANE
88 Vice Prov Entrprse Innovation Inst ... Mr. Stephen FLEMING
29 President Georgia Tech Alumni Assoc ... Mr. Joseph IRWIN
20 Vice Prov Grad Ed & Faculty Affairs ... Dr. Susan COZZENS
84 Vice Prov Enrollment Services ... Dr. Paul KOHN
88 Vice Prov Undergraduate Education ... Dr. Colin POTTS
43 Vice Pres Legal Affairs/Risk Mgt ... Mr. Patrick MCKENNA
21 Senior Vice Pres Admin & Finance ... Dr. Amir RAHNAMAY-AZAR
16 Assoc VP Human Resources ... Mr. M. Scott MORRIS
18 Vice President Facilities ... Mr. Charles G. RHODE
31 Vice President Campus Services ... Mr. Paul STROUTS
13 Vice President Information Tech/CIO ... Mr. James O'CONNOR
41 Director of Athletics ... Mr. Dan RADAKOVICH
22 Senior Director Diversity Mgmt ... Ms. Pearl ALEXANDER
12 Dean Ivan Allen College ... Dr. Jacqueline J. ROYSTER
35 Dean of Students/Asst Vice Pres ... Mr. John STEIN
48 Dean College of Architecture ... Mr. Alan BALFOUR
77 Dean College of Computing ... Dr. Zvi GALIL
54 Dean College of Engineering ... Dr. Gary S. MAY
08 Vice Prov Lrng Excel/Dean Libraries ... Ms. Catherine MURRAY-RUST
82 Dean College of Management ... Dr. Steven C. SALBU
81 Dean College of Sciences ... Dr. Paul HOUSTON
06 Registrar ... Ms. Reta PIKOWSKY
40 Director Bookstore ... Mr. Gerald J. MALONEY
19 Director of Security & Police ... Ms. Teresa CROCKER
107 Dean Professional Education ... Dr. Nelson BAKER
78 Exec Dir Prof Practice Div ... Dr. Patrick ANTHONY
37 Director Student Financial Aid ... Ms. Marie MONS
23 Sr Director Student Health Svcs ... Dr. Gregory MOORE
39 Executive Director Housing ... Mr. Michael BLACK
09 Exec Dir Inst Research & Planning ... Ms. Sandra J. BRAMBLETT
85 Vice Provost Intl Initiatives ... Dr. Steven MCLAUGHLIN
104 Exec Dir International Education ... Ms. Amy HENRY
93 Dir Minority Education Development ... Mr. Gordon MOORE
36 Director Career Services ... Mr. Ralph MOBLEY
38 Director Counseling Center ... Dr. Ruperto PEREZ
53 AVP Learning Excel/Director CETL ... Dr. Donna C. LLEWELLYN
88 Senior Director Auxiliary Svcs ... Mr. Richard STEELE
07 Director Undergraduate Admission ... Mr. Richard CLARK
96 Director of Procurement Services ... Mr. Frans BARENDS
88 Exec Dir Inst Budget Plng & Admin ... Mr. James KIRK
88 Director Capital Planning/Spce Mgt ... Mr. Howard WERTHEIMER
88 Exec Director Organizational Devel ... Mr. Chet WARZYNSKI
88 Bursar ... Ms. Carol PAYNE

88	Associate Vice President Fin Svcs	Mr. James FORTNER

† Part of the University System of Georgia.

Georgia Military College (A)

201 E Greene Street, Milledgeville GA 31061-3398

County: Baldwin
FICE Identification: 001571
Unit ID: 139904
Telephone: (478) 445-2700
Carnegie Class: Assoc/Pub-Spec
FAX Number: (478) 445-2688
Calendar System: Quarter
URL: www.gmc.cc.ga.us
Established: 1879
Annual Undergrad Tuition & Fees: $4,959
Enrollment: 1,555
Coed
Affiliation or Control: Independent Non-Profit
IRS Status: 501(c)3
Highest Offering: Associate Degree
Program: 2-Year Principally Bachelor's Creditable
Accreditation: SC

01	President	MajGen. Peter J. BOYLAN
03	Executive Vice President	Col. Fred VAN HORN
05	Vice Pres Academic Affs/Dn Faculty	Dr. Phillip M. HOLMES
10	Vice President Business Affairs	Mr. Charles E. MADDEN
84	Vice Pres for Enrollment/Retention	Ms. Donna FINDLEY
32	Vice Pres Student Svcs/Commandant	Col. Patrick BEER
30	Vice Pres Institutional Advancement	Mrs. Elizabeth SHEPPARD
13	Vice Pres Information Technology	Ms. Jody YEARWOOD
21	Assoc Vice Pres Business Affairs	Ms. Susan MEEKS
09	Director Institutional Research	Ms. Wendy KALLINA
41	Athletic Director	Mr. Bert WILLIAMS
18	Director Facilities/Engineer	Mr. Jeff GRAY
06	Registrar	Mrs. Robin KNIGHT
08	Librarian	Mr. Glen PHILLIPS
19	Chief of Security/Safety	Mr. James HODNETT

Georgia Northwestern Technical College (B)

One Maurice Culberson Drive, Rome GA 30161

County: Floyd
FICE Identification: 005257
Unit ID: 141273
Telephone: (706) 295-6963
Carnegie Class: Not Classified
FAX Number: (706) 295-6944
Calendar System: Semester
URL: www.gntc.edu
Established: 1966
Annual Undergrad Tuition & Fees (In-State): $2,048
Enrollment: 6,187
Coed
Affiliation or Control: State
IRS Status: 501(c)3
Highest Offering: Associate Degree
Program: Occupational; 2-Year Principally Bachelor's Creditable
Accreditation: SC, ADNUR, COE, DA, DMS, EMT, MAC, OTA, RAD, RTT, SURGT

01	President	Dr. Craig MCDANIEL
05	Provost	Mr. Jeff KING
30	Vice Pres Econ Development	Mr. Pete MCDONALD
20	Vice President Academic Affairs	Dr. Mindy MCCANNON
09	Vice Pres Inst Effectiveness	Ms. Heidi POPHAM
51	Vice President Adult Education	Ms. Susan HACKNEY
11	Vice Pres Administrative Services	Ms. Kelly BARNES
32	Assoc Vice Pres Student Services	Dr. Steve BRADSHAW
06	Registrar	Ms. Selena MAGNUSSON
08	Director of Library Services	Ms. Linda FLOYD
35	Director of Student Affairs	Mr. David MCBURNETT
37	Director of Financial Aid	Ms. Sarah TWIGGS
18	Director Facilities Management	Mr. Johnny TROTTER
26	Dir Marketing/Public Relations	Ms. Amber JORDAN
15	Director of Human Resources	Ms. Peggy CORDELL

Georgia Perimeter College (C)

3251 Panthersville Road, Decatur GA 30034-3897

County: DeKalb
FICE Identification: 001562
Unit ID: 244437
Telephone: (678) 891-2300
Carnegie Class: Assoc/Pub-S-MC
FAX Number: N/A
Calendar System: Semester
URL: www.gpc.edu
Established: 1963
Annual Undergrad Tuition & Fees (In-State): $3,502
Enrollment: 26,404
Coed
Affiliation or Control: State
IRS Status: 501(c)3
Highest Offering: Baccalaureate
Program: Occupational; 2-Year Principally Bachelor's Creditable
Accreditation: SC, ADNUR, DH

01	Interim President	Mr. Robert E. WATTS
05	Int Vice President Academic Affairs	Mr. Philip SMITH
10	Exec Vice Pres Financial/Admin Affs	Mr. Ronald STARK
30	Vice Pres Institutional Advancement	Mr. Jeffrey TARNOWSKI
32	Vice Pres Student Affairs	Dr. Vincent JUNE
88	Dir of Organizational Development	Mr. Wallace WIEHE
35	Asst Vice Pres for Student Affairs	Ms. Coletta HASSELL
84	Assistant VP Enrollment Management	Ms. Lisa FOWLER
88	Dir Center for Teaching & Learning	Dr. Pamela MOOLENAR-WIRSY
13	Assoc VP/Chief Information Officer	Mr. Reid J. CHRISTENBERRRY
12	Academic Dean Alpharetta Campus	Dr. Susan CODY
106	Int Academic Dean Online Campus	Dr. Ingrid THOMPSON-SELLERS
12	Int Academic Dean Clarkston Campus	Dr. Stuart NOEL
12	Academic Dean Dunwoody Campus	Dr. Margaret EHRLICH
12	Academic Dean Newton Campus	Dr. Ronald KEY
15	Dir HR Employment/Acad Svcs	Mr. Thomas GEORGE
26	Director Public Relations	Ms. Barbara OBRENTZ
88	Dir Human Res Conflict Management	Ms. Karen TRUESDALE
45	Int Dir Institutional Research/Plng	Ms. Patti GREGG
41	Director Athletics	Mr. Alfred BARNEY
21	Asst Vice Pres Finance	Ms. Diane HICKEY
29	Director Alumni Relations	Mr. Collins FOSTER
37	Dir Student Financial Services	Ms. Robin WINSTON
25	Director Grants/Sponsored Programs	Ms. Ethel BROWN
28	Director of Disability Services	Ms. Bonnie MARTIN
88	Dir Hum Res Cmp/Aff Act/Opn Rec Ofr	Ms. Amanda REDDICK
96	Director of Logistical Services	Mr. Brian Keith CHAPMAN
07	Assoc Dir Admissions & Records	Mr. Doug RUCH

† Part of the University System of Georgia.

Georgia Piedmont Technical College (D)

495 N Indian Creek Drive, Clarkston GA 30021-2397

County: DeKalb
FICE Identification: 005622
Unit ID: 244446
Telephone: (404) 297-9522
Carnegie Class: Assoc/Pub-S-MC
FAX Number: (404) 297-4234
Calendar System: Semester
URL: www.gptc.edu
Established: 1961
Annual Undergrad Tuition & Fees (In-State): $4,044
Enrollment: 4,308
Coed
Affiliation or Control: State
IRS Status: 501(c)3
Highest Offering: Associate Degree
Program: Occupational; 2-Year Principally Bachelor's Creditable; Technical Emphasis
Accreditation: SC, ENGT, MAC, MLTAD

01	Acting President	Mr. Larry TEEMS
11	Vice Pres of Business & Financial	Ms. Heather PENCE
03	Executive Vice President	Vacant
05	Vice President Academic Affairs	Dr. Tanya GORMAN
46	Vice Pres of Economic Development	Mr. Richard SMITH
30	Vice President Inst Advancement	Ms. Cynthia EDWARDS
20	Dean Academic Operations	Mr. Julian P. WADE
20	Dean Academic Delivery	Mr. Marcus HICKS
20	Dean Academic Accountability & Outc	Dr. Daisy DAVIS
20	Dean Academic Support	Dr. Debra GORDON
32	Acting VP Student Affairs	Ms. Amanda TAYLOR-RODRIGUEZ
15	Director of Human Resources	Ms. Gale BELTON
26	Public Relations & Info Director	Mr. Cory THOMPSON
06	Registrar	Ms. Karen SILLS
07	Director of Admissions	Mr. Terry RICHARDSON
108	Dir Inst Assess/Eval/Effectiveness	Dr. Sue CHANDLER
50	Director Business & Comm Services	Ms. Loretta HICKS
37	Director of Financial Aid	Ms. Jerri HUEWITT
18	Director of Facilities & Auxil Svcs	Vacant
88	Director of Adult Literacy	Dr. Martha COURSEY
29	Director Alumni Relations	Vacant
36	Director Assessment & Career Svcs	Mr. Keith SAGERS

Georgia Southern University (E)

PO Box 8033, Statesboro GA 30460-8033

County: Bulloch
FICE Identification: 001572
Unit ID: 139931
Telephone: (912) 478-4636
Carnegie Class: DRU
FAX Number: N/A
Calendar System: Semester
URL: www.georgiasouthern.edu
Established: 1906
Annual Undergrad Tuition & Fees (In-State): $6,724
Enrollment: 20,253
Coed
Affiliation or Control: State
IRS Status: 501(c)3
Highest Offering: Doctorate
Program: Liberal Arts And General; Teacher Preparatory; Professional
Accreditation: SC, ART, BUS, BUSA, CACREP, CIDA, CONST, CS, DIETD, ENGT, MUS, NRPA, NURSE, PH, SPAA, TED, THEA

01	President	Dr. Brooks A. KEEL
05	Provost/Vice Pres Academic Affairs	Dr. Jean BARTELS
10	Vice Pres Business & Finance	Dr. Ron CORE
32	VP Student Affairs & Enroll Mgmt	Dr. Teresa THOMPSON
30	VP Univ Advance/GSU Foundation Pres	Ms. Salinda ARTHUR
27	VP Information Technology/CIO	Mr. Steve BURRELL
86	VP Governmtl Rels/Cmty Engagement	Mr. Russell KEEN
46	Vice Pres for Research	Dr. Charles PATTERSON
09	Assoc VP Strategic Rsrch & Analysis	Dr. Jayne PERKINS BROWN
20	Vice Provost Academic Affairs	Dr. Michael SMITH
35	Assoc VP & Dean of Students	Ms. Patrice BUCKNER
43	Assoc Vice Pres for Legal Affairs	Ms. Maura COPELAND
04	Exec Associate to the President	Ms. Marilyn BRUCE
07	Director of Admissions	Ms. Sarah SMITH
58	Dean College of Graduate Studies	Dr. Charles PATTERSON
50	Dean College Business Admin	Dr. Bill WELLS
53	Dean College Education	Dr. Thomas KOBALLA
76	Dean College Health/Human Sci	Vacant
49	Dean Col Liberal Arts/Social Sci	Dr. Curtis RICKER
81	Dean College Science & Tech	Dr. Martha ABELL
54	Int Dean AEP Col Engrng/Info Tech	Dr. Mohammad DAVOUD
51	Assoc Provost Continuing Education	Dr. Anthony BRETTI
69	Dean College of Public Health	Dr. R. Gregory EVANS
62	Dean University Library	Dr. Bede MITCHELL
88	Dir NCAA Compliance/Stdnt-Athl Svcs	Mr. Keith ROUGHTON
88	Director Audit & Advisory Services	Ms. Jana BRILEY
43	Associate University Attorney	Mr. Geoffrey CARSON
26	Director Marketing & Communications	Mr. Christian FLATHMAN
88	Director Academic Success Center	Ms. Janet L. O'BRIEN
37	Director Financial Aid	Ms. Connie MURPHEY
06	Registrar	Ms. Velma BURDEN
88	Director Auxiliary Services	Mr. Edward D. MILLS
21	Controller	Ms. Kim THOMPSON BROWN
15	Director Human Resources	Mr. Paul MICHAUD
41	Athletic Director	Mr. Sam BAKER
18	Director Physical Plant	Vacant
19	Director Public Safety	Mr. Michael RUSSELL
36	Director Career Services	Vacant
38	Director Counseling Services	Dr. Jodi K. CALDWELL
88	Director Educ Opportunity Programs	Ms. Joyya SMITH
23	Administrator Health Services	Mr. Paul FERGUSON
39	Director University Housing	Mr. Christopher MACDONALD
28	Dir Multicultural Student Center	Vacant
88	Director Leadership/Outreach Pgms	Dr. Todd DEAL
88	Director Advancement IT	Ms. Janice WEST
29	Sr Dir Alumni Rels/Annual Giving	Mr. Wendell TOMPKINS, JR.
88	Director Botanical Garden	Ms. Carolyn ALTMAN
13	Director Computing & Info Mgmt	Mr. David EWING
90	Director Info Tech for Acad Affairs	Ms. Pamela DEAL
31	Director Museum	Dr. Brent THARP
40	Director Stores & Shops	Mr. Richie AKINS
88	Director Wildlife Educ/Raptor Ctr	Mr. Steven M. HEIN
96	Director of Materials Management	Mr. George HORN
28	Director of Diversity Services	Mr. Gary P. GAWEL

† Part of the University System of Georgia.

Georgia Southwestern State University (F)

800 GA Southwestern State Univ Dr, Americus GA 31709-4693

County: Sumter
FICE Identification: 001573
Unit ID: 139764
Telephone: (800) 338-0082
Carnegie Class: Master's S
FAX Number: N/A
Calendar System: Semester
URL: www.gsw.edu
Established: 1906
Annual Undergrad Tuition & Fees (In-State): $12,006
Enrollment: 3,046
Coed
Affiliation or Control: State
IRS Status: 501(c)3
Highest Offering: Beyond Master's But Less Than Doctorate
Program: Occupational; Liberal Arts And General; Teacher Preparatory; Professional
Accreditation: SC, BUS, NUR, TED

01	President	Dr. Kendall A. BLANCHARD
05	Vice President Academic Affairs	Dr. Brian U. ADLER
10	Vice Pres Business & Finance	Mr. W. Cody KING
32	Vice President for Student Affairs	Dr. Samuel T. MILLER
26	Vice Pres for University Relations	Vacant
84	Vice Pres Enroll Mgmt/Dir Admiss	Dr. Gaye HAYES
09	Director Institutional Research	Dr. Lisa A. COOPER
08	Interim Dean Library Services	Ms. Ru STORY-HUFFMAN
91	Dir Information/Instructional Tech	Mr. Royce HACKETT
30	Director of Development	Mr. Stephen E. SNYDER
06	Registrar	Ms. Krista SMITH
36	Director Career Services Center	Ms. Etrat FATHI
37	Director Student Financial Aid	Ms. Angela V. BRYANT
85	Director Foreign Students	Mr. John FOX
27	Director Public Relations	Mr. Stephen E. SNYDER
32	Dean of Students	Dr. Gaye HAYES
53	Dean of Education	Dr. Lettie WATFORD
50	Dean of Business	Dr. Elizabeth WILSON
66	Dean of Nursing	Dr. Sandra D. DANIEL
49	Dean of Arts & Sciences	Dr. J. Kelly MCCOY
77	Dean Computing & Mathematics	Dr. Boris PELTSVERGER
15	Director of Human Resources	Ms. Janet SIDERS
41	Athletic Director	Ms. Jaclyn DONOVAN
51	Director of Continuing Education	Ms. Karen HOLLOWAY
18	Director of Physical Plant	Mr. George L. SMITH
38	Director Student Counseling	Ms. Alma G. KEITA
96	Director of Purchasing	Ms. Nancy ROOKS
29	Coord Alumni Relations/Annual Fund	Ms. Kimberly COMER

† Part of the University System of Georgia.

Georgia State University (G)

PO Box 3999, Atlanta GA 30302-3999

County: Fulton
FICE Identification: 001574
Unit ID: 139940
Telephone: (404) 413-2000
Carnegie Class: RU/VH
FAX Number: (404) 413-1380
Calendar System: Semester
URL: www.gsu.edu
Established: 1913
Annual Undergrad Tuition & Fees (In-State): $9,664
Enrollment: 32,022
Coed
Affiliation or Control: State
IRS Status: 501(c)3
Highest Offering: Doctorate
Program: Liberal Arts And General; Teacher Preparatory; Professional
Accreditation: SC, ART, BUS, BUSA, CACREP, CEA, CLPSY, COPSY, CORE, DIETC, DIETD, EXSC, HSA, IPSY, LAW, MUS, NURSE, PH, PTA, SCPSY, SP, SPAA, SW, TED

01	President	Dr. Mark P. BECKER
05	Sr VP Academic Affairs & Provost	Dr. Risa I. PALM
10	Sr VP Finance & Administration	Dr. Jerry J. RACKLIFFE
46	Vice President Research & Econ Dev	Dr. James A. WEYHENMEYER
32	Vice President Student Affairs	Dr. Douglass F. COVEY
30	Vice President Development	Mr. Walter T. MASSEY
26	VP Communications & Marketing	Vacant
43	University Attorney	Dr. Kerry L. HEYWARD

49 Dean Arts & Sciences .... Dr. William J. LONG
50 Dean Business .... Dr. H. Fenwick HUSS
53 Interim Dean Education .... Dr. Paul A. ALBERTO
76 Dean Nursing/Health Professions .... Dr. Margaret C. WILMOTH
69 Dean Public Health .... Dr. Michael P. ERIKSEN
61 Dean Law .... Dr. Steven J. KAMINSHINE
80 Dean Policy Studies .... Dr. Mary Beth WALKER
92 Dean Honors College .... Dr. Larry S. BERMAN
08 Dean University Library .... Dr. Nancy H. SEAMANS
20 Assoc Provost Academic Programs .... Dr. Timothy M. RENICK
88 Assoc Provost Strategic Initiatives .... Dr. Robert D. MORRIS
09 Assoc Provost Inst Effectiveness .... Dr. Peter LYONS
13 Assoc Provost Info Sys & Technology .... Mr. J. L. ALBERT
82 Assc Prov International Initiatives .... Dr. Jun LIU
20 Assoc Provost Faculty Affairs .... Dr. Lynda BROWN WRIGHT
45 Assoc VP Research Integrity .... Dr. Brenda J. CHAPMAN
45 Assoc Vice President Research .... Dr. Monica H. SWAHN
18 Assoc VP Facilities .... Mr. Ramesh VAKAMUDI
21 Assoc Vice President Finance .... Ms. Elizabeth R. JONES
30 Assoc VP Central Development .... Mr. John D. CLARK
30 Assoc VP Advancement Resources .... Ms. Charlotte P. PARKS
30 Assoc VP Constituent Programs Dev .... Mr. David J. FRABONI
102 Assoc VP GSU Foundation .... Mr. Dale J. PALMER
35 Assoc VP Stdnt Affs/Dean Students .... Dr. Rebecca Y. STOUT
07 Asst VP Undergraduate Admissions .... Mr. Scott M. BURKE
84 Asst VP Student Retention .... Dr. Allison CALHOUN-BROWN
88 Asst VP Student Affairs Admin .... Mr. Jeff W. WALKER
29 Asst VP Alumni Relations .... Ms. Christina C. MILLION
40 Asst VP Auxiliary Enterprises .... Mr. Wayne E. REED
21 Asst VP Finance & Comptroller .... Mr. Bruce R. SPRATT
15 Asst VP Human Resources .... Ms. Linda J. NELSON
22 Asst VP Opp Dev/Diversity Educ .... Ms. Linda J. NELSON
19 Asst VP/Chief University Police .... Ms. Connie B. SAMPSON
25 Asst VP Research/Awards Admin .... Vacant
06 Registrar .... Ms. Shari PIOTROWSKI
85 Dir Intl Students/Scholars Svcs .... Ms. Heather L. HOUSLEY
39 Director University Housing .... Ms. Marilyn A. DE LAROCHE
38 Director Psychological & Health Svc .... Dr. Jill LEE-BARBER
28 Director Diversity Programs .... Mr. John R. DAY
14 Director Business Support Services .... Mr. William F. PARASKA
13 Director Professional Services .... Mr. Julian O. ALLEN
88 Director Application Engineering .... Mr. John M. BANDY, JR.
13 Director Technology Engineering .... Mr. Keith E. CAMPBELL
88 Director Production Services .... Mr. William GRUSZKA
13 Director Technical Support Services .... Ms. June M. MOSS
36 Director University Career Svcs .... Mr. Kevin E. GAW
37 Director Financial Aid .... Mr. Louis B. SCOTT
96 Director of Business Services .... Mr. Larry J. MCCALOP
88 Dir Univ Auditing & Advisory Svcs .... Mr. Sterling ROTH
88 Director Design/Construction Svcs .... Ms. Kimberly P. BAUER
88 Director Emergency Management .... Mr. D. Michael RADERSTORF
26 Director Govt & Community Affairs .... Ms. Julia M. KERLIN
41 Athletic Director .... Ms. Cheryl L. LEVICK
88 Special Advisor to President .... Mr. Thomas C. LEWIS
88 Spec Asst Univ Ceremonies/Events .... Ms. DeAnna J. HINES
04 Assistant to the President .... Ms. Ethel M. BROWN
88 Assistant to the Provost .... Dr. Edgar C. TORBERT

† Part of the University System of Georgia.

Gordon State College (A)

419 College Dr., Barnesville GA 30204-1746
County: Lamar FICE Identification: 001575
Unit ID: 139968
Telephone: (678) 359-5021 Carnegie Class: Assoc/Pub4
FAX Number: (678) 359-5080 Calendar System: Semester
URL: www.gdn.edu
Established: 1972 Annual Undergrad Tuition & Fees (In-State): $3,642
Enrollment: 4,664 Coed
Affiliation or Control: State IRS Status: 501(c)3
Highest Offering: Baccalaureate
Program: Occupational; 2-Year Principally Bachelor's Creditable; Teacher Preparatory
Accreditation: SC, ADNUR, NUR

01 President .... Dr. Max BURNS
05 VP Academic Affairs .... Dr. Ed R. WHEELER
20 Associate VP Academic Affairs .... Dr. Richard BASKIN
10 VP Business Affairs .... Mr. Lee FRUITTICHER
32 VP Student Affairs .... Dr. Dennis R. CHAMBERLAIN
30 VP Institutional Advancement .... Mrs. Rhonda TOON
08 Head Librarian .... Ms. Nancy D. ANDERSON
37 Director of Financial Aid .... Mr. Larry G. MITCHAM
06 Registrar .... Ms. Janet BARRAS
15 Director of Human Resources .... Ms. Tonya L. JOHNSON
18 Director of Facilities .... Mr. Richard VEREEN
38 Director of Counseling Services .... Mrs. Laura BOWEN
07 Director of Admissions .... Mr. Bennett FERGUSON
27 Chief Public Information Officer .... Mrs. Tamara BOATWRIGHT
09 Director of Institutional Research .... Vacant
19 Director of Public Safety .... Chief Jeff MASON
40 Bookstore Manager .... Mrs. Connie H. WADE
41 Athletic Director .... Mr. Todd DAVIS
39 Director of Resident Life .... Ms. Tonya R. COLEMAN
35 Director of Student Activities .... Mrs. Sharon LLOYD
13 Director of Computer Services .... Mr. Jeff HAYES
20 Director of Student Success Center .... Mr. Peter J. HIGGINS
21 Director of Business Services .... Ms. Sharon ELLIS
88 Comptroller .... Mr. Clint CHASTAIN
29 Director of Alumni Relations .... Mrs. Natalie RISCHBIETER

† Part of the University System of Georgia.

Gupton Jones College of Funeral Service (B)

5141 Snapfinger Woods Drive, Decatur GA 30035-4022
County: DeKalb FICE Identification: 010771
Unit ID: 139995
Telephone: (770) 593-2257 Carnegie Class: Assoc/PrivNFP
FAX Number: (770) 593-1891 Calendar System: Quarter
URL: www.gupton-jones.edu
Established: 1920 Annual Undergrad Tuition & Fees: $9,000
Enrollment: 130 Coed
Affiliation or Control: Independent Non-Profit IRS Status: 501(c)3
Highest Offering: Associate Degree
Program: Occupational; 2-Year Principally Bachelor's Creditable; Technical Emphasis
Accreditation: FUSER

01 President .... Ms. Patty S. HUTCHESON
05 Dean .... Mr. James HINZ
06 Registrar .... Ms. Felicia SMITH

Gwinnett College (C)

4230 Highway 29, Suite 11, Lilburn GA 30047-3447
County: Gwinnett FICE Identification: 025830
Unit ID: 140003
Telephone: (770) 381-7200 Carnegie Class: Assoc/PrivFP
FAX Number: (770) 381-0454 Calendar System: Other
URL: www.gwinnettcollege.com
Established: 1976 Annual Undergrad Tuition & Fees: $9,550
Enrollment: 318 Coed
Affiliation or Control: Proprietary IRS Status: Proprietary
Highest Offering: Associate Degree
Program: Occupational; 2-Year Principally Bachelor's Creditable
Accreditation: ACICS

01 President .... Mr. Michael DAVIS

Gwinnett Technical College (D)

5150 Sugarloaf Parkway, Lawrenceville GA 30043-5702
County: Gwinnett FICE Identification: 022884
Unit ID: 140012
Telephone: (770) 962-7580 Carnegie Class: Assoc/Pub-S-SC
FAX Number: (770) 962-7985 Calendar System: Semester
URL: www.gwinnetttech.edu
Established: 1984 Annual Undergrad Tuition & Fees (In-State): $2,524
Enrollment: 6,648 Coed
Affiliation or Control: State IRS Status: 501(c)3
Highest Offering: Associate Degree
Program: Occupational; 2-Year Principally Bachelor's Creditable; Technical Emphasis
Accreditation: SC, ACFEI, ADNUR, DA, EMT, MAC, RAD, SURGT

01 President .... Mrs. Sharon J. BARTELS
05 Vice President of Academic Affairs .... Dr. Victoria SEALS
26 Vice Pres Recruitment/Marketing .... Mr. Dave MCCULLOCH
32 Vice President of Student Affairs .... Vacant
11 Vice President Administration .... Mr. David WELDEN
30 Vice Pres Institutional Advancement .... Mrs. Mary Beth BYERLY
88 Director of Economic Development .... Ms. Ann SECHRIST
16 Director Human Resources .... Ms. Becky BURTON
09 Exec Dir Inst Effectiveness .... Mrs. Julie POST
21 Director of Accounting .... Mrs. Valerie STRICKLAND
06 Registrar .... Ms. Arlene CLARKE
46 Dir Assessment/Advisement/Ed Plng .... Mrs. Brenda PYLE
36 Director of Career Services .... Ms. Ave MILLER
37 Director of Financial Aid .... Ms. Kristen GAST
53 Director of Adult Education .... Ms. Stephanie ROOKS
07 Director of Admissions .... Dr. Florence HALLORAN
18 Dir Facilities/Campus Architect .... Vacant
19 Chief of Campus Police & Security .... Mr. Joseph MARKHAM
08 Manager of Library Services .... Ms. Elissa CHECOV
04 Assistant to the President .... Mrs. Stephanie SMITH

Herzing University (E)

3393 Peachtree Road NE, Suite 1003,
Atlanta GA 30326-1332
County: Fulton FICE Identification: 020897
Unit ID: 140340
Telephone: (404) 816-4533 Carnegie Class: Bac/Diverse
FAX Number: (404) 816-5576 Calendar System: Semester
URL: www.herzing.edu/atlanta/
Established: 1949 Annual Undergrad Tuition & Fees: $16,320
Enrollment: 448 Coed
Affiliation or Control: Proprietary IRS Status: Proprietary
Highest Offering: Baccalaureate
Program: Occupational; 2-Year Principally Bachelor's Creditable; Liberal Arts And General; Technical Emphasis
Accreditation: &NH

01 President .... Mr. Frank R. WEBSTER
05 Academic Dean .... Mrs. Marsha JOHNSON
36 Director of Career Services .... Mr. William SLATON
08 College Librarian .... Mr. Eric H. MURRAY
07 Director of Admissions .... Ms. Anissa ELDER
06 Registrar .... Ms. Fiona JIMILL
37 Director of Student Financial Aid .... Mrs. Stephanie GUNBY

† Regional accreditation is carried under the parent institution in Madison, WI.

Interactive College of Technology (F)

5303 New Peachtree Road, Chamblee GA 30341-2818
County: DeKalb FICE Identification: 022843
Unit ID: 138655
Telephone: (770) 216-2960 Carnegie Class: Assoc/PrivFP
FAX Number: (770) 216-2988 Calendar System: Semester
URL: www.ict-ils.edu
Established: 1986 Annual Undergrad Tuition & Fees: $8,260
Enrollment: 266 Coed
Affiliation or Control: Proprietary IRS Status: Proprietary
Highest Offering: Associate Degree
Program: Occupational
Accreditation: COE

01 President .... Mr. Elmer R. SMITH
05 Dean of the College .... Mr. Thomas BLAIR
12 Campus Director Pasadena Texas .... Mr. Gregory WEAVER
12 Campus Dir SW Houston Texas .... Ms. Cynthia BRYSON
12 Campus Dir North Houston Texas .... Mr. John BYRNES
12 Campus Director - Newport KY .... Ms. Bobbi PALMER
12 Campus Directory - Morrow GA .... Ms. Shea MINNICK

Interdenominational Theological Center (G)

700 Martin L. King, Jr. Drive, SW, Atlanta GA 30314-4143
County: Fulton FICE Identification: 001568
Unit ID: 140146
Telephone: (404) 527-7700 Carnegie Class: Spec/Faith
FAX Number: (404) 527-0901 Calendar System: Semester
URL: www.itc.edu
Established: 1958 Annual Graduate Tuition & Fees: $11,780
Enrollment: 415 Coed
Affiliation or Control: Interdenominational IRS Status: 501(c)3
Highest Offering: Doctorate; No Undergraduates
Program: Professional; Religious Emphasis
Accreditation: SC, THEOL

01 President .... Dr. Ronald E. PETERS
05 Interim VP for Acad Svcs/Provost .... Dr. Temba L. MAFICO
10 Vice Pres Admin Services .... Dr. Kevin STEWART
30 VP for Institutional Advancement .... Ms. Christal M. CHERRY
06 Registrar .... Ms. Bobbie HALL
37 Financial Aid Director .... Ms. Tina GARNIGAN
15 Human Resource Consultant .... Ms. Kathryn J. WEBB
42 Chaplain/Counselor .... Dr. Willie GOODMAN
32 Int Director of Student Services .... Ms. Patrice EVANS

ITT Technical Institute (H)

485 Oak Place, Suite 800, Atlanta GA 30349
County: Fulton Identification: 666595
Unit ID: 450243
Telephone: (404) 765-4600 Carnegie Class: Assoc/PrivFP4
FAX Number: (770) 904-4650 Calendar System: Quarter
URL: www.itt-tech.edu
Established: N/A Annual Undergrad Tuition & Fees: N/A
Enrollment: 699 Coed
Affiliation or Control: Proprietary IRS Status: Proprietary
Highest Offering: Baccalaureate
Program: Technical Emphasis
Accreditation: ACICS

† Branch campus of ITT Technical Institute, Indianapolis, IN.

ITT Technical Institute (I)

10700 Abbotts Bridge Road, Duluth GA 30097-8460
County: Gwinnett Identification: 666325
Unit ID: 443526
Telephone: (678) 957-8510 Carnegie Class: Spec/Tech
FAX Number: (678) 417-2070 Calendar System: Quarter
URL: www.itt-tech.edu
Established: 2003 Annual Undergrad Tuition & Fees: N/A
Enrollment: 636 Coed
Affiliation or Control: Proprietary IRS Status: Proprietary
Highest Offering: Baccalaureate
Program: Technical Emphasis
Accreditation: ACICS

† Branch campus of ITT Technical Institute, Indianapolis, IN.

ITT Technical Institute (J)

2065 ITT Tech Way N.W., Kennesaw GA 30144
County: Cobb Identification: 666378
Unit ID: 446905
Telephone: (770) 426-2300 Carnegie Class: Assoc/PrivFP4
FAX Number: N/A Calendar System: Quarter
URL: www.itt-tech.edu
Established: N/A Annual Undergrad Tuition & Fees: N/A
Enrollment: 501 Coed
Affiliation or Control: Proprietary IRS Status: Proprietary
Highest Offering: Baccalaureate
Program: Technical Emphasis

Accreditation: ACICS

† Branch campus of ITT Technical Institute, Indianapolis, IN.

Kennesaw State University (A)

1000 Chastain Road #0101, Kennesaw GA 30144-5591
County: Cobb　FICE Identification: 001577
Unit ID: 140164
Telephone: (770) 423-6000　Carnegie Class: Master's L
FAX Number: (770) 423-6543　Calendar System: Semester
URL: www.kennesaw.edu
Established: 1963　Annual Undergrad Tuition & Fees (In-State): $6,486
Enrollment: 24,175　Coed
Affiliation or Control: State　IRS Status: 501(c)3
Highest Offering: Doctorate
Program: Liberal Arts And General; Teacher Preparatory; Professional
Accreditation: SC, ART, BUS, BUSA, CS, MACTE, MUS, NURSE, SPAA, SW, TED, THEA

01 President .... Dr. Daniel S. PAPP
05 Provost/Vice Pres Academic Affs .... Dr. W. Ken HARMON
30 VP University Advancement & Devel .... Mr. Michael HARDERS
32 Vice Pres Student Success .... Dr. Jerome RATCHFORD
11 Vice President for Operations .... Dr. Randy C. HINDS
58 VP Research/Dean Graduate College .... Dr. Charles J. AMLANER
26 Vice President External Affairs .... Ms. Arlethia PERRY-JOHNSON
20 Senior Vice Provost Academic Affs .... Dr. Teresa M. JOYCE
43 Univ Gen Coun/Sp Asst Pres Leg Affs .... Dr. Flora B. DEVINE
04 Faculty Exec Assistant to President .... Dr. Maureen MCCARTHY
20 Assoc Vice Pres for Curriculum .... Dr. Valerie D. WHITTLESEY
21 Assoc Vice Pres for Operations .... Ms. Maria BRITT
20 Assoc VP Acad Affairs/Dean Univ Col .... Dr. Ralph J. RASCATI
15 Asst Vice Pres Human Resources Svcs .... Mr. Rodney BOSSERT
84 Asst Vice Pres Enrollment Services .... Mr. Kim WEST
08 Asst Vice Pres for Library Services .... Mr. J. David EVANS
18 Asst Vice Pres Facilities Services .... Mr. John A. ANDERSON
26 Asst VP Strategic Comm/Marketing .... Mr. David ARNOLD
04 Exec Assistant to President .... Ms. Lynda K. JOHNSON
79 Dean Humanities/Social Science .... Dr. Robert DORFF
81 Dean Mathematics/Science .... Dr. Mark R. ANDERSON
53 Dean Bagwell College of Education .... Dr. Arlinda EATON
50 Dean Coles College of Business .... Dr. Kathy S. SCHWAIG
76 Dean WellStar Col Health/Human Svcs .... Dr. Richard L. SOWELL
49 Dean College of the Arts .... Mr. Joseph D. MEEKS
35 Dean of Student Success .... Dr. Michael L. SANSEVIRO
51 Dean Continuing/Professional Educ .... Ms. Barbara S. CALHOUN
07 Asc Dn Enrol Svs/Ex Dir Univ Admiss .... Ms. Susan N. BLAKE
38 Asst Dean/Dir Student Success Svs .... Dr. Robert J. MATTOX
28 Chief Diversity Officer .... Dr. Erik MALEWSKI
06 Interim Registrar .... Ms. Ana EDWARDS
13 Assoc Chief Info Ofcr/Chf Tech Ofcr .... Dr. John L. ISENHOUR
91 Dir Enterprise Systems & Services .... Mr. T. Wayne DENNISON
37 Director Student Financial Aid .... Mr. Rondall H. DAY
07 Dir Student Recruitment/Admissions .... Dr. Angela J. EVANS
40 Int Assoc Dir Auxiliary Svcs/Pgms .... Ms. Laura MCMILLAN
36 Director of Career Services Center .... Ms. Karen B. ANDREWS
41 Director of Athletics .... Mr. Vaughn A. WILLIAMS
29 Director Alumni Affairs .... Ms. Lisa A. DUKE
44 Director Annual Giving .... Vacant
46 Ex Dir Entrpr Info Mgt/Chf Data Ofr .... Mr. Erik R. BOWE
19 Director Public Safety .... Mr. Theodore J. COCHRAN
35 Director Student Life .... Ms. Katherine E. ALDAY
88 Dir Enterprise Academic Reporting .... Ms. Donna R. HUTCHESON
10 Chief Business Officer .... Dr. Randy C. HINDS
96 Director of Purchasing .... Vacant

† Part of the University System of Georgia.

LaGrange College (B)

601 Broad Street, La Grange GA 30240-2999
County: Troup　FICE Identification: 001578
Unit ID: 140234
Telephone: (706) 880-8000　Carnegie Class: Bac/Diverse
FAX Number: (706) 880-8358　Calendar System: 4/1/4
URL: www.lagrange.edu
Established: 1831　Annual Undergrad Tuition & Fees: $24,303
Enrollment: 957　Coed
Affiliation or Control: United Methodist　IRS Status: 501(c)3
Highest Offering: Master's
Program: Liberal Arts And General; Teacher Preparatory
Accreditation: SC, ACBSP, NUR

01 President .... Dr. Dan MCALEXANDER
05 Provost and Chief Academic Officer .... Dr. David GARRISON
11 Exec Vice President Administration .... Vacant
30 Vice President Advancement .... Mr. William JONES
84 Vice Pres Enrollment Management .... Vacant
10 Vice Pres Finance & Operations .... Mr. Martin E. PIRRMAN
42 VP Spiritual Life & Church Relation .... Dr. Quincy D. BROWN
32 Dean of Student Engagement .... Dr. Mark SHOOK
14 Director Infomation Technology .... Mr. James BLACKWOOD
06 Registrar .... Mr. Jimmy G. HERRING
08 Director Library .... Mr. Loren L. PINKERMAN
26 Director Communications/Marketing .... Mr. Dean A. HARTMAN
88 Director LaGrange Fund .... Vacant
37 Director Student Financial Aid .... Ms. Sylvia A. SMITH
41 Athletic Director .... Mrs. Jennifer D. CLAYBROOK
36 Director Student Placement .... Mrs. Diana GOLDWIRE
55 Director Evening College .... Mrs. Linda H. MCMULLEN
38 Director Student Counseling .... Mrs. Pamela TREMBLAY
44 Director Major Gifts .... Ms. Rebecca ROTH
40 Director Bookstore .... Vacant
09 Director Inst Research .... Dr. Doug FLOR
12 Director LaGrange College Albany .... Ms. Beth BROWN
35 Director Student Activities .... Vacant
18 Manager Facilities/Physical Plant .... Mr. Michael CONIGLIO
31 Events Coordinator .... Ms. Tammy ROGERS
04 Executive Assistant to President .... Mrs. Carla RHODES
29 Director Alumni & Cmty Relations .... Mrs. Martha PIRKLE
13 Director Admin Computing .... Vacant
15 Director Human Resources .... Mrs. Dawn COKER
84 Dean of Enrollment Management .... Mr. Joseph C. MILLER
44 Director of Planned Giving .... Mr. Wendell CLARK
88 Director of SOURCE Center .... Mr. Todd PRATER

Lanier Technical College (C)

2990 Landrum Education Drive, Oakwood GA 30566-3405
County: Hall　FICE Identification: 005254
Unit ID: 140243
Telephone: (770) 531-6300　Carnegie Class: Assoc/Pub-R-M
FAX Number: (770) 531-6328　Calendar System: Semester
URL: www.laniertech.edu
Established: 1964　Annual Undergrad Tuition & Fees (In-State): $3,789
Enrollment: 3,570　Coed
Affiliation or Control: State　IRS Status: 501(c)3
Highest Offering: Associate Degree
Program: Occupational; 2-Year Principally Bachelor's Creditable; Technical Emphasis
Accreditation: SC, COE, DA, DH, EMT, MAC, MLTAD, RAD, SURGT

01 President .... Mr. Russell VANDIVER
103 Vice President Economic Development .... Vacant
05 Vice President Academic Affairs .... Dr. Linda M. BARROW
12 Vice President Operations Forsyth .... Dr. Joanne P. TOLLESON
32 Vice President Student Affairs .... Ms. Lisa WILSON
10 Vice Pres Administrative Services .... Ms. Laura ELDER
13 Vice President Technology .... Mr. Robbie VICKERS
04 Executive Assistant to President .... Ms. Becky SMITH
09 Dir of Institutional Effectiveness .... Mr. Brad GADBERRY
30 Director of Development .... Ms. Carol SPIRES
26 Director Public Relations Officer .... Mr. Dave PARRISH
20 Dean Academic Affairs .... Ms. Dianne BOWERS
20 Dean Academic Affairs .... Ms. Donna BRINSON
12 Director Satellite Campus .... Ms. Lisa MALOOF
12 Director Satellite Campus .... Mr. Tim MCDONALD
12 Director Satellite Campus .... Dr. Howard LEDFORD
07 Director of Admissions .... Mr. Mike MARLOWE
06 Registrar .... Ms. Sandi J. BAKER
37 Director Student Financial Aid .... Ms. Patsy GRIFFIN
84 Director Enrollment Management .... Ms. Deanna ORZA
36 Student Placement Specialist .... Ms. Melissa LAWRENCE
28 Coord Special Svcs/Minority Affairs .... Ms. Mallory SAFLEY
21 Director Administrative Services .... Ms. Janet BOHANON
15 Director of Human Resources .... Ms. Jill CANTRELL
18 Director of Facilities .... Mr. Carl PITTS

Le Cordon Bleu College of Culinary Arts in Atlanta (D)

1927 Lakeside Parkway, Tucker GA 30084-5865
County: DeKalb　Identification: 666298
Unit ID: 443623
Telephone: (770) 938-4711　Carnegie Class: Assoc/PrivFP
FAX Number: (770) 938-4571　Calendar System: Quarter
URL: www.chefs.edu/atlanta
Established: 2003　Annual Undergrad Tuition & Fees: $19,521
Enrollment: 1,249　Coed
Affiliation or Control: Proprietary　IRS Status: Proprietary
Highest Offering: Associate Degree
Program: Occupational; 2-Year Principally Bachelor's Creditable; Technical Emphasis
Accreditation: ACICS, ACFEI

01 President .... Mr. Glenn MACK
36 Director of Career Services .... Ms. Cybil TALLEY
07 Director of Admissions .... Mr. Cristian LIUBA
88 Executive Chef .... Mr. Creighton SCHROEDER
10 Business Operations Manager .... Mr. Christopher WEINERT
96 Director of Purchasing .... Mr. Brad JOHNSON
06 Associate Registrar .... Ms. Renee WILSON

† Branch campus of Le Cordon Bleu College of Culinary Arts, Portland, OR.

Life University (E)

1269 Barclay Circle, Marietta GA 30060-2996
County: Cobb　FICE Identification: 020748
Unit ID: 140252
Telephone: (770) 426-2600　Carnegie Class: Bac/A&S
FAX Number: (770) 429-4819　Calendar System: Quarter
URL: www.life.edu
Established: 1974　Annual Undergrad Tuition & Fees: $9,395
Enrollment: 2,609　Coed
Affiliation or Control: Independent Non-Profit　IRS Status: 501(c)3
Highest Offering: Doctorate
Program: 2-Year Principally Bachelor's Creditable; Liberal Arts And General; Professional
Accreditation: SC, CHIRO, DIETD, DIETI

01 President .... Dr. Guy F. RIEKEMAN
03 Executive Vice President/Provost .... Dr. Brian MCAULAY
10 Exec Vice President for Finance .... Mr. William JARR
30 Vice Pres of University Advancement .... Mr. Greg HARRIS
32 Vice President for Student Services .... Dr. Marc SCHNEIDER
11 Vice President for Admin Services .... Dr. Tim GROSS
84 Executive Dir of Enrollment & Mktg .... Dr. Cynthia BOYD
41 Director of Athletics .... Mr. John BARRETT
15 Director of Human Resources .... Ms. Stella PETERSON
27 Chief Information Officer .... Mr. John ALTIKULAC
13 Director Information Technology .... Mr. Thorton MUIR
104 Director of Global Initiatives .... Dr. John DOWNES
76 Dean College of Chiropractic .... Dr. Leslie KING
49 Dean College Undergraduate Studies .... Dr. Michael SMITH
23 Dean of Clinics .... Dr. Ralph DAVIS
06 Registrar .... Ms. Tiffany SMITH
08 Director of Learning Resources .... Ms. Susan STEWART
46 Director of Research .... Dr. Stephanie SULLIVAN
29 Alumni Relations Manager .... Ms. Leila TATUM
108 Director of Inst Effectiveness .... Dr. Vince ERARIO
09 Director of Institutional Research .... Mr. Tiannan ZHOU
18 Director Facilities/Physical Plant .... Mr. Richard SHAW
38 Director Student Success .... Dr. Lisa RUBIN
37 Director Student Financial Aid .... Ms. Melissa WATERS
35 Dir of Student Development .... Ms. Jennifer VALTOS
36 Director of Career Planning .... Ms. Susan DUDT
88 Dir of Student Administrative Svcs .... Ms. Kay FREELAND
26 Director of Communications .... Mr. Craig DEKSHENIEKS
28 Director of Diversity .... Dr. Jerry HARDEE
21 Budget Director .... Ms. Amy MCILVANE
44 Manager of Constituent Relations .... Mr. Tom MCCLESKEY

Lincoln College of Technology (F)

2359 Windy Hill Road, Marietta GA 30067
County: Cobb　Identification: 666282
Unit ID: 434159
Telephone: (770) 226-0056　Carnegie Class: Assoc/PrivFP
FAX Number: (770) 226-0084　Calendar System: Semester
URL: www.lincolnedu.com
Established: 2001　Annual Undergrad Tuition & Fees: $19,204
Enrollment: 393　Coed
Affiliation or Control: Proprietary　IRS Status: Proprietary
Highest Offering: Associate Degree
Program: Occupational; 2-Year Principally Bachelor's Creditable
Accreditation: ACICS

01 Executive Director .... Mr. Brian CAPOZZI

Luther Rice University (G)

3038 Evans Mill Road, Lithonia GA 30038-2454
County: DeKalb　FICE Identification: 031009
Unit ID: 135364
Telephone: (770) 484-1204　Carnegie Class: Spec/Faith
FAX Number: (770) 484-1155　Calendar System: Semester
URL: www.lru.edu
Established: 1962　Annual Undergrad Tuition & Fees: $7,140
Enrollment: 1,317　Coed
Affiliation or Control: Independent Non-Profit　IRS Status: 501(c)3
Highest Offering: Doctorate
Program: Liberal Arts And General; Professional
Accreditation: TRACS

01 President .... Dr. James L. FLANAGAN
10 Vice President Financial Affairs .... Mr. Louis B. HARDCASTLE
32 Vice President for Student Affairs .... Dr. Dennis D. DIERINGER
05 Vice President for Academic Affairs .... Dr. Brad K. ARNETT
30 Vice Pres Institutional Advancement .... Mr. Russ L. SORROW
09 VP for Institutional Effectiveness .... Dr. Ralph J. MCCANN
08 Director of Library Services .... Mr. Hal HALLER
37 Director Student Financial Aid .... Mr. Gary W. COOK
88 Asst to the Pres for Asian Affairs .... Dr. Kyung C. LIM
85 Asst to the Pres Global Strategy .... Dr. Ronald B. LONG

Macon State College (H)

100 College Station Drive, Macon GA 31206-5145
County: Bibb　FICE Identification: 007728
Unit ID: 140322
Telephone: (478) 471-2700　Carnegie Class: Bac/Diverse
FAX Number: (478) 471-2846　Calendar System: Semester
URL: www.maconstate.edu
Established: 1968　Annual Undergrad Tuition & Fees (In-State): $3,714
Enrollment: 5,702　Coed
Affiliation or Control: State　IRS Status: 501(c)3
Highest Offering: Baccalaureate
Program: Liberal Arts And General
Accreditation: SC, ADNUR, CS, NUR, TED

01 Interim President .... Dr. John BLACK
05 Vice President Academic Affairs .... Dr. Martha L. VENN
10 Vice President Fiscal Affairs .... Ms. Nancy STROUD
26 Vice President External Affairs .... Mr. Albert J. ABRAMS
32 Vice Pres Student Affs/Enroll Mgmt .. Dr. Jeffrey V. STEWART, III
20 Asst VP for Student Success .... Dr. Pamela BEDWELL
84 Dean of Admissions/Enroll Mgmt .... Dr. Sherri ROWLAND
21 Asst Vice Pres Fiscal Affairs .... Vacant
30 Assoc Vice Pres Development/Alumni .... Ms. Sue CHIPMAN
09 Assoc VP Institutional Research .... Vacant
07 Director of Admissions .... Mr. Bruce APPLEWHITE
51 Director Continuing Education .... Mr. Albert J. ABRAMS

12 Dean of Warner Robins Campuses ... Mr. David CARPENTER
13 Chief Information Officer ... Mr. Roger DIXON
06 Registrar ... Mr. Tom WAUGH
08 Director Library Services ... Ms. Pat BORCK
37 Director Financial Aid ... Ms. Pat SIMMONS
15 Dir Human Resources/EEO Officer ... Ms. Holly MORRISON
18 Director of Plant Operations ... Mr. David SIMS
44 Associate Director Development ... Ms. Beth BYERS
36 Director Counseling ... Ms. Ann LOYD
35 Asst Dean of Students ... Mr. Michael STEWART
88 Director Student Support Services ... Ms. Yolanda PETTY
27 Director Communications ... Mr. William H. WEAVER
21 Dir Business Services/Comptroller ... Mr. Brian STANLEY
96 Purchasing Manager ... Ms. Barbara BURNS
50 Dean of Business ... Dr. Varkey K. TITUS
66 Dean School of Nursing/Health ... Dr. Rebecca J. CORVEY
49 Dean Arts & Sciences ... Dr. Ron WILLIAMS
50 Dean Education ... Dr. Ann LEVETT
72 Dean Information Technology ... Dr. Alex KOOHANG
36 Director Career Services ... Ms. Barbara WARREN
90 Director Academic Resource Center ... Mr. Paul JOHNSON
91 Director Administrative Systems ... Ms. Beverly BERGMAN
88 Director Wellness Program ... Mr. James HAGLER
39 Director of Residence Life ... Dr. Chris SUMMERLIN
19 Director of Public Safety ... Mr. Shawn DOUGLAS
40 Director Auxillary Services ... Mr. Kevin REID

† Part of the University System of Georgia.

Mercer University (A)

1400 Coleman Avenue, Macon GA 31207-0003
County: Bibb — FICE Identification: 001580
Unit ID: 140447
Telephone: (478) 301-2700 — Carnegie Class: Master's L
FAX Number: (478) 301-2108 — Calendar System: Semester
URL: www.mercer.edu
Established: 1833 — Annual Undergrad Tuition & Fees: $32,166
Enrollment: 8,336 — Coed
Affiliation or Control: Independent Non-Profit — IRS Status: 501(c)3
Highest Offering: Doctorate
Program: Liberal Arts And General; Teacher Preparatory; Professional
Accreditation: SC, ANEST, ARCPA, BUS, CACREP, CS, ENG, LAW, MED, MFCD, MUS, NURSE, PH, PHAR, @PTA, TED, THEOL

01 President and CEO ... Mr. William D. UNDERWOOD
00 Chancellor ... Dr. R. Kirby GODSEY
100 Senior VP and Chief of Staff ... Mr. Larry D. BRUMLEY
05 Provost ... Dr. D. Scott DAVIS
10 Executive VP for Admin & Finance ... Dr. James S. NETHERTON
12 Sr VP Atlanta Campus ... Dr. Richard V. SWINDLE
30 Sr VP for University Advancement ... Mr. John A. PATTERSON
84 Sr Vice Pres Enrollment Mgmt ... Dr. Penny L. ELKINS
43 Vice President and General Counsel ... Mr. William G. SOLOMON
13 Chief Technology Officer ... Mr. Michael R. BELOTE
17 Sr VP Health Sciences/Dean Phar/HS ... Dr. Hewitt MATTHEWS
32 Vice President & Dean of Students ... Dr. Doug R. PEARSON
46 Sr V Prov Research/Dean Grad Stds ... Dr. Wayne C. GLASGOW
21 Treasurer & Assoc VP Finance ... Ms. Julia T. DAVIS
18 Assoc Vice President for Facilities ... Mr. Russell VULLO
15 Associate Vice Pres Personnel Admin . Ms. Rhonda W. LIDSTONE
26 Sr Asst VP for Marketing Commun ... Mr. Richard L. CAMERON
37 Assoc VP Student Financial Planning ... Ms. Carol K. WILLIAMS
49 Dean College of Liberal Arts ... Dr. Lake LAMBERT
61 Dean School of Law ... Mr. Gary J. SIMSON
63 Dean School of Medicine ... Dr. William F. BINA, III
54 Dean School of Engineering ... Dr. Wade H. SHAW
50 Dean Sch Business/Econ ... Dr. D. Scott DAVIS
73 Dean School of Theology ... Dr. R. Alan CULPEPPER
53 Dean College of Education ... Dr. Carl R. MARTRAY
66 Dean College of Nursing ... Dr. Linda A. STREIT
51 Dean College Cont/Prof Stds ... Dr. Priscilla R. DANHEISER
64 Interim Dean School of Music ... Dr. C. David KEITH
08 Dean of University Libraries ... Ms. Elizabeth D. HAMMOND
06 Registrar ... Ms. Lucy P. WILSON
50 Assoc Dn Sch Business/Econ-Atlanta ... Dr. Gina L. MILLER
41 Athletic Director ... Mr. Jim COLE
19 Chief Police Department ... Mr. Gary COLLINS
09 Director of Institutional Research ... Ms. Sarah E. MAY
96 Director of Purchasing ... Mr. Charles MIZE
07 Asst VP & Director of Admissions ... Mr. C. Ray TATUM

Middle Georgia College (B)

1100 Second Street, SE, Cochran GA 31014-1599
County: Bleckley — FICE Identification: 001581
Unit ID: 140483
Telephone: (478) 934-6221 — Carnegie Class: Assoc/Pub4
FAX Number: (478) 934-3199 — Calendar System: Semester
URL: www.mgc.edu
Established: 1884 — Annual Undergrad Tuition & Fees (In-State): $3,066
Enrollment: 3,424 — Coed
Affiliation or Control: State — IRS Status: 501(c)3
Highest Offering: Baccalaureate
Program: Occupational; 2-Year Principally Bachelor's Creditable
Accreditation: SC, ADNUR, OTA

01 President ... Dr. Michael STOY
05 Vice President for Academic Affairs ... Dr. Mary Lou FRANK
10 Vice President for Fiscal Affairs ... Ms. Lynn E. HOBBS
32 Vice Pres Student & Public Affairs ... Mrs. Jennifer BRANNON
08 Director of Library Resources ... Mr. Paul ROBARDS
38 Director of Testing ... Mrs. Predita HOWARD
15 Director of Personnel ... Ms. Lisa CHASTAIN
37 Director of Financial Aid ... Mr. Josh FOSKEY
40 Director of Bookstore ... Mr. Josh FOSKEY
07 Director of Admissions/Registrar ... Mr. Jed EDGE
26 Chief Public Relations Officer ... Ms. Tricia PURSER
12 Director of Dublin Center ... Dr. Stephen SVONAVEC
12 Dir Eastman Campus/Chief Plng Ofcr ... Vacant
12 Dir of Georgia Aviation Campus ... Mrs. Jennifer BRANNON

† Part of the University System of Georgia.

Middle Georgia Technical College (C)

80 Cohen Walker Drive, Warner Robins GA 31088-2729
County: Houston — FICE Identification: 025086
Unit ID: 140085
Telephone: (478) 988-6800 — Carnegie Class: Assoc/Pub-R-M
FAX Number: (478) 988-6813 — Calendar System: Quarter
URL: www.middlegatech.edu
Established: 1973 — Annual Undergrad Tuition & Fees (In-State): $2,700
Enrollment: 3,703 — Coed
Affiliation or Control: State — IRS Status: 501(c)3
Highest Offering: Associate Degree
Program: Occupational; 2-Year Principally Bachelor's Creditable; Technical Emphasis
Accreditation: SC, DA, DH, RAD, SURGT

01 Acting President ... Dr. Jeff SCRUGGS
05 Vice President for Academic Affairs ... Dr. Amy L. HOLLOWAY
32 Vice President for Student Affairs ... Mr. Craig JACKSON
09 VP Economic Develop/Inst Support ... Mr. Jeffrey SCRUGGS
11 VP for Administrative Services ... Mrs. Michelle SINIARD
88 Vice President for Adult Education ... Ms. Brenda L. BROWN
07 Director of Admissions ... Mr. Dann WEBB
37 Director of Financial Aid ... Ms. Shirley GLOVER
06 Registrar ... Ms. Sonja JENKINS
08 Director of Library Services ... Dr. Dumont C. BUNN
15 Director of Human Resources ... Ms. Carol F. JONES
30 Int Director of Advancement ... Ms. Janet H. KELLY
26 Marketing & PR Director ... Mrs. Janet H. KELLY
18 Maintenance Superintendent ... Mr. Joe PETERSDORFF

Morehouse College (D)

830 Westview Drive SW, Atlanta GA 30314-3773
County: Fulton — FICE Identification: 001582
Unit ID: 140553
Telephone: (404) 681-2800 — Carnegie Class: Bac/A&S
FAX Number: (404) 681-2650 — Calendar System: Semester
URL: www.morehouse.edu
Established: 1867 — Annual Undergrad Tuition & Fees: $23,792
Enrollment: 2,438 — Male
Affiliation or Control: Independent Non-Profit — IRS Status: 501(c)3
Highest Offering: Baccalaureate
Program: Liberal Arts And General; Teacher Preparatory
Accreditation: SC, BUS, MUS

01 President ... Dr. Robert M. FRANKLIN
05 Int Provost/Sr Vice Pres Acad Affs ... Dr. Ann W. WATTS
11 Vice President Campus Operations ... Mr. Andre E. BERTRAND
30 Vice Pres Institutional Advancement ... Mr. Phillip D. HOWARD
100 Chief of Staff ... Ms. Fran PHILLIPS-CALHOUN
32 VP Student Svcs and Enrollment Mgmt ... Dr. William BYNUM
10 Int Vice Pres Business Affairs/CFO ... Ms. Sheila JACOBS
20 Assoc Vice Pres Special Acad Pgms ... Dr. Anne W. WATTS
15 Assoc Vice Pres Human Resource ... Ms. Pamela WESTON
44 Exec Asst to Pres-Capital Campaign ... Ms. Kathleen JOHNSON
42 Dean Martin Luther King Jr Chapel ... Dr. Lawrence E. CARTER
06 Int Assoc Dean Records/Registration ... Ms. Kasi ROBINSON
07 Dean Admissions & Recruitment ... Mr. Kevin L. WILLIAMS
37 Director of Financial Aid ... Mr. James STOTTS
29 Dir Alumni Rels/Annual Giving Pgm ... Mr. Henry GOODGAME
26 Director Public Relations ... Ms. Toni O'NEAL MOSLEY
36 Director of Placement ... Mr. Doug COOPER
41 Athletic Director ... Mr. Andre PATTILLO
39 Director Student Housing ... Mr. Maurice WASHINGTON
19 Chief of Campus Police ... Chief Vernon WORTHY
18 Int Superintendent Physical Plant ... Mr. Curtis DAVIS
85 Director Andrew Young Ctr Intl Pgms ... Mr. Julius COLES
86 Director Government Relations ... Ms. Denise MOORE
09 Director of Institutional Research ... Dr. Michael FLEMING
35 Director Student Services ... Mr. Kevin BOOKER
38 Director of Student Counseling ... Dr. Gary WRIGHT
96 Purchasing Manager ... Mr. Kevin BRANCH
27 Publications Manager ... Ms. Vickie HAMPTON
50 Dean Div of Business & Economics ... Dr. John E. WILLIAMS
81 Dean Div of Science & Mathematics ... Dr. John K. HAYNES
79 Dean Div of Humanities & Soc Sci ... Dr. Tobe JOHNSON

Morehouse School of Medicine (E)

720 Westview Drive, SW, Atlanta GA 30310-1495
County: Fulton — FICE Identification: 024821
Unit ID: 140562
Telephone: (404) 752-1500 — Carnegie Class: Spec/Med
FAX Number: (404) 752-1027 — Calendar System: Semester
URL: www.msm.edu
Established: 1975 — Annual Graduate Tuition & Fees: $41,500
Enrollment: 331 — Coed
Affiliation or Control: Independent Non-Profit — IRS Status: 501(c)3
Highest Offering: Doctorate; No Undergraduates
Program: Professional
Accreditation: SC, MED, PH

01 President ... Dr. John E. MAUPIN, JR.
05 Dean and Executive Vice President ... Dr. Valerie MONTGOMERY RICE
88 Sr Adv/Asst Dean Health Quality ... Vacant
86 Sr Adv for Strategic Mgmt/Gov Rels ... Dr. Virgina FLOYD
43 General Counsel ... Mr. Harold JORDAN
30 VP Institutional Advancement ... Mrs. Sally DAVIS
46 VP & Sr Assoc Dean for Research Af ... Dr. Sandra HARRIS-HOOKER
20 Sr Assoc Dean for Educ/Faculty Affs ... Dr. Martha ELKS
11 Assoc Dean Admin/Asst VP Finance ... Ms. Sandra E. WATSON
38 Director of Counseling ... Dr. Shawn GARRISON
37 Director of Financial Aid ... Ms. Cynthia H. HANDY
08 Interim Director of Library ... Mr. Joe SWANSON, JR.
09 Chief of Planning & Inst Research ... Ms. Andrea D. FOX
26 Exec Director of Marketing & Comm ... Ms. Rosalyn BARNES
25 Interim Dir of Grants & Contracts ... Ms. Terryl OBASANYA
29 Director of Alum Rel & Giving ... Ms. Carrie M. DUMAS
84 Director of Admissions ... Mr. Brandon HUNTER
96 Director of Purchasing ... Mr. Linwood HILTON
15 Associate VP of Human Resources ... Ms. Denise BRITT
102 Assoc VP for Inst Adv Found/Corp ... Mrs. Mary K. MURPHY
102 Assoc VP of Inst Adv Major Gifts ... Ms. Kelly BROWN MORRIS
22 Chief Compliance Officer ... Mr. Jonathan WILLIAMS
100 Chief of Staff ... Ms. Santhia CURTIS
06 Registrar ... Mrs. Adrienne L. WYATT
88 Assoc Dean for Clinical Affairs ... Dr. Derrick BEECH, JR.
27 Interim Chief Information Officer ... Ms. Annmarie EADES
19 Director of Public Safety ... Mr. Joseph CHEVALIER, JR.
105 Director of Web Services ... Ms. Chrystal NEELY
44 Dir of Alum Affairs & Annual Fund ... Mr. Robert STEPHENS

Moultrie Technical College (F)

800 Veterans Parkway North, Moultrie GA 31788-1919
County: Colquitt — FICE Identification: 005255
Unit ID: 140599
Telephone: (912) 891-7000 — Carnegie Class: Assoc/Pub-R-M
FAX Number: (912) 891-7010 — Calendar System: Semester
URL: www.moultrietech.edu
Established: 1964 — Annual Undergrad Tuition & Fees (In-State): $3,747
Enrollment: 2,610 — Coed
Affiliation or Control: State — IRS Status: 501(c)3
Highest Offering: Associate Degree
Program: Occupational; Technical Emphasis
Accreditation: @SC, COE, MAC, RAD, SURGT

01 President ... Dr. Tina K. ANDERSON
05 Vice President for Academic Affairs ... Jim GLASS
11 VP of Administrative Services ... Ken STRICKLAND
32 Vice President of Student Services ... Leigh WALLACE
21 Vice President Operations ... David EVANS
09 VP Institutional Effectiveness ... Tavarez HOLSTON
51 Asst Vice President of Adult Educ ... Jerry SMITH
12 Dean of Instruction Moultrie Campus ... Tina STRICKLAND
12 Dean of Instruction Tifton Campus ... Becky RICHARDSON
06 Registrar ... Wendi TOSTENSON
32 Director Student Affairs ... Lisa GRIFFIN
15 Director Human Resources ... Michael HEARD
18 Chief Facilities/Physical Plant ... Steve PEACOCK
26 Director of Marketing ... Jana WIGGINS
37 Director Student Financial Aid ... Judi LOVVORN
36 Career Services Specialist ... Bridgett ADAMS

North Georgia College & State University (G)

82 College Circle, Dahlonega GA 30597-1001
County: Lumpkin — FICE Identification: 001585
Unit ID: 140669
Telephone: (706) 864-1400 — Carnegie Class: Master's L
FAX Number: (706) 864-1478 — Calendar System: Semester
URL: www.northgeorgia.edu
Established: 1873 — Annual Undergrad Tuition & Fees (In-State): $6,570
Enrollment: 6,067 — Coed
Affiliation or Control: State — IRS Status: 501(c)3
Highest Offering: Doctorate
Program: 2-Year Principally Bachelor's Creditable; Liberal Arts And General; Teacher Preparatory; Professional
Accreditation: SC, ADNUR, BUS, CACREP, NUR, PTA, TED

01 President ... Dr. Bonita JACOBS
11 Vice Pres of Exec Affairs ... Mr. Billy WELLS
05 Vice Pres for Acad Affairs ... Dr. Patricia DONAT
10 Vice President Business and Finance ... Mr. Frank J. MCCONNELL
30 Vice Pres Institutional Advancement ... Dr. Andrew LEAVITT
32 Vice Pres Student Affairs ... Col. Tom PALMER
41 Athletic Director ... Ms. Lindsay REEVES
13 Chief Information Officer ... Dr. Bryson PAYNE
20 Assoc Vice Pres for Acad Affairs ... Dr. Richard OATES
20 Interim Assoc VP for Acad Affairs ... Dr. Terry MCLEOD
20 Interim Assoc VP for Acad Affairs ... Dr. Kathy SISK
07 Director of Undergrad Admissions ... Ms. Jennifer CHADWICK
07 Director Cadet Admissions ... Mr. Keith ANTONIA
92 Honors Program Director ... Dr. Stephen SMITH
06 Registrar ... Ms. Jill BRADY
25 Director of Grants & Contracts ... Ms. Kelley ROBERTS
37 Director of Student Financial Aid ... Ms. Jill RAYNER
58 Exec Director Regional Engagement ... Dr. Donna GESSELL
88 Exec Director Inst Effectiveness ... Dr. Denise YOUNG

09 Director Institutional Research ... Ms. Linda ROWLAND
08 Director of Library Services ... Ms. Shawn TONNER
51 Dir of Public Services/Cont Educ ... Ms. Jane O'GORMAN
49 Dean of Arts & Letters ... Dr. Christopher JESPERSEN
50 Dean M C School of Business ... Dr. Donna MAYO
53 Dean of School of Education ... Dr. Bob MICHAEL
65 Dean Sch of Science & Health Prof ... Dr. Michael BODRI
18 Assoc Vice Pres for Facilities ... Mr. Jeffrey DAVIS
104 Director Center Global Engagement ... Dr. Dlynn ARMSTRONG-WILLIAMS
40 Manager of Bookstore ... Ms. Laurie DAVIS
15 Director Human Resources ... Ms. Beth ARBUTHNOT
96 Director of Materials Mangement ... Mr. Alan SIBERT
16 Associate VP for Administration ... Dr. Brenda FINDLEY
18 Director of Plant Operations ... Mr. Todd BERMANN
19 Director/Chief of Public Safety ... Mr. Michael F. STAPLETON
29 Director of Alumni Relations ... Mr. Phil COLLINS
30 Director of Development ... Mr. Jeffrey S. BOGAN
26 Director of University Relations ... Ms. Kate MAINE
35 Interim Dean of Students ... Ms. Alyson PAUL
20 Commandant of Cadets ... Col. Tom PALMER
36 Director of Career Services ... Ms. Dora DITCHFIELD
38 Director Student Counseling/Dev ... Dr. Simon CORDERY
39 Interim of Residence Life ... Ms. Treva SMITH
23 Director of Student Health Services ... Ms. Karen TOMLINSON
88 Exec Director of Univ Centers ... Dr. Sherman DAY

† Part of the University System of Georgia.

North Georgia Technical College (A)

PO Box 65, Clarkesville GA 30523-0065
County: Habersham FICE Identification: 005619
Unit ID: 140678
Telephone: (706) 754-7700 Carnegie Class: Assoc/Pub-R-M
FAX Number: (706) 754-7777 Calendar System: Semester
URL: www.northgatech.edu
Established: 1943 Annual Undergrad Tuition & Fees (In-State): $3,863
Enrollment: 2,533 Coed
Affiliation or Control: State IRS Status: 501(c)3
Highest Offering: Associate Degree
Program: Occupational; 2-Year Principally Bachelor's Creditable; Technical Emphasis
Accreditation: SC, ACFEI, MAC, MLTAD

01 President ... Dr. Gail THAXTON
05 Vice President of Academic Affairs ... Rex BISHOP
35 Vice President for Student Affairs ... Dr. Michael KING
06 Registrar ... Caroline FRICK
07 Director of Admissions ... Amanda MITCHELL
10 Chief Business Officer ... Dr. Mark IVESTER
15 Director Personnel Services ... Marcia PEYTON
18 Chief Facilities/Physical Plant ... Michael BOYD
26 Chief Public Relations Officer ... Sandra MAUGHON
29 Director Alumni Relations ... Cynthia BROWN
32 Chief Student Life Officer ... Sherry SEAL
36 Director Job Placement ... Daniel GREGG
37 Director Student Financial Aid ... Kim KELLEY
38 Director Student Counseling ... Vacant
84 Director Enrollment Management ... Amanda MITCHELL
96 Director of Purchasing ... Darline CHURCH
09 Director of Institutional Research ... Vacant
46 Dir Institutional Effectiveness ... Janet HENDERSON
20 Dean of Academics ... Kathie IVESTER
20 Dean of Academics ... Dan PRESSLEY
20 Dean of Academics ... Mindy GLANDER

Oconee Fall Line Technical College-North Campus (B)

1189 Deepstep Road, Sandersville GA 31082-9337
County: Washington FICE Identification: 031555
Unit ID: 420431
Telephone: (478) 553-2050 Carnegie Class: Assoc/Pub-R-S
FAX Number: (478) 553-2118 Calendar System: Semester
URL: www.oftc.edu
Established: 1996 Annual Undergrad Tuition & Fees (In-State): $2,070
Enrollment: 1,870 Coed
Affiliation or Control: State IRS Status: 501(c)3
Highest Offering: Associate Degree
Program: Occupational
Accreditation: COE

01 President ... Dr. Lloyd HORADAN
05 Vice Pres Academic/Student Affs ... Ms. Erica HARDEN
11 Vice Pres Administrative Services ... Ms. Rosemary SELBY
30 Vice Pres Economic Development ... Ms. Leigh EVANS
49 Dean Arts & Sciences/Business Svcs ... Ms. Michele STRICKLAND
32 Dean Student Affairs ... Ms. Johnnie EDGE
06 Registrar ... Ms. Geri CLEMENTS
07 Director of Admissions ... Mr. Raydor CONEWAY
15 Director Human Resources ... Ms. Sharon VEAL
21 Director of Administrative Services ... Ms. Penny KITCHENS
18 Director Facilities/Physical Plant ... Mr. Jim HARRISON
26 Exec Director Marketing ... Ms. Jennifer AHRENS
37 Financial Aid Director ... Ms. Betty YOUNG
28 Dir of Spec Populations/Stdnt Life ... Ms. Dessie HALL

Oconee Fall Line Technical College-South Campus (C)

560 Pinehill Road, Dublin GA 31021-1599
County: Laurens FICE Identification: 022795
Unit ID: 140076
Telephone: (478) 275-6589 Carnegie Class: Assoc/Pub-R-M
FAX Number: (478) 275-6642 Calendar System: Semester
URL: www.oftc.edu
Established: 1984 Annual Undergrad Tuition & Fees (In-State): $1,662
Enrollment: 1,869 Coed
Affiliation or Control: State IRS Status: 501(c)3
Highest Offering: Associate Degree
Program: Occupational; Technical Emphasis
Accreditation: COE, MAC, RAD

01 President ... Dr. Lloyd HORADAN
05 Provost South Campus ... Mrs. Beth CRUMPTON
09 Vice Pres Inst Effectiveness ... Dr. Katie DAVIS
32 Dean Student Affairs ... Mr. Jay MULLIS
06 Assistant Registrar ... Ms. Kimberly NOLES
18 Director Facilities ... Mr. Ragan GREEN
12 Dean Little Ocmulgee Instr Center ... Vacant
30 Exec Dir Institutional Advancement ... Mrs. Jenny SHUMAN
19 Director Safety & Security ... Mr. Rick SWANSON
36 Director of Career Development ... Mrs. Cecile MILLER
76 Dean Allied Health/Prof Svcs ... Ms. Tammy BAYTO
37 Asst Director Financial Aid ... Ms. Teresa CRAFTON
08 Director Library Services ... Ms. Wendi MORRIS

Ogeechee Technical College (D)

One Joseph E. Kennedy Boulevard, Statesboro GA 30458-8049
County: Bulloch FICE Identification: 030300
Unit ID: 366465
Telephone: (912) 681-5500 Carnegie Class: Assoc/Pub-R-M
FAX Number: (912) 486-7704 Calendar System: Semester
URL: www.ogeecheetech.edu
Established: 1987 Annual Undergrad Tuition & Fees (In-State): $2,660
Enrollment: 2,181 Coed
Affiliation or Control: State IRS Status: 501(c)3
Highest Offering: Associate Degree
Program: Occupational; 2-Year Principally Bachelor's Creditable
Accreditation: COE, DA, DMS, FUSER, MAC, OPD, RAD, SURGT

01 President ... Dr. Dawn H. CARTEE
04 Exec Assistant to the President ... Ms. Karen MOBLEY
05 Vice President for Academic Affairs ... Dr. Charlene LAMAR
31 Vice President Economic Development ... Ms. Lori DURDEN
108 VP Institutional Effectiveness ... Ms. Dianne STEWART
32 Vice President Student Affairs ... Mr. Ryan FOLEY
10 Vice President for Administration ... Ms. Eyvonne HART
13 VP Technology & Institutional Supp ... Mr. Jeff DAVIS
30 VP College Advancement ... Ms. Beth MATHEWS
26 VP Community & College Relations ... Mr. Barry TURNER
09 Director Inst Research & Planning ... Ms. Brandy TAYLOR
20 Dean for Academic Affairs ... Mr. John GROOVER
20 Dean for Academic Affairs ... Ms. Julie M. STRICKLAND
20 Dean for Academic Affairs ... Mr. Bill BARTON
88 Dean for Adult Education ... Mr. Michael K. BURRELL
08 Dean for Library Services ... Dr. Lynn FUTCH
51 Dir Continuing Ed & Ind Training ... Ms. Kathleen KOSMOSKI
84 Director for Admissions ... Ms. Laura SAUNDERS
06 Registrar ... Ms. Michelle STUBBS
37 Director for Financial Aid ... Ms. Letrell THOMAS
07 Director for Recruitment/Retention ... Ms. LeAnne ROBINSON
21 Director for Accounting ... Ms. Patsy POWELL
15 Director for Human Resources ... Mr. Steve MILLER
40 Director for Auxiliary Services ... Mr. J.J ALTMAN
18 Director for Plant Operations ... Mr. Buddy SAPP
19 Director Campus Safety & Security ... Mr. Jeff SMITH

Oglethorpe University (E)

4484 Peachtree Road, NE, Atlanta GA 30319-2797
County: DeKalb FICE Identification: 001586
Unit ID: 140696
Telephone: (404) 261-1441 Carnegie Class: Bac/A&S
FAX Number: (404) 364-8500 Calendar System: Semester
URL: www.oglethorpe.edu
Established: 1835 Annual Undergrad Tuition & Fees: $29,900
Enrollment: 1,149 Coed
Affiliation or Control: Independent Non-Profit IRS Status: 501(c)3
Highest Offering: Master's
Program: Liberal Arts And General; Teacher Preparatory; Business Emphasis
Accreditation: SC

01 President ... Dr. Lawrence M. SCHALL
05 Provost ... Dr. Denise VON HERRMANN
10 Vice Pres for Business & Finance ... Mr. Michael D. HORAN
30 Vice Pres Devel & Alumni Relations ... Mr. Kevin A. SMYRL
84 Vice Pres for Enrollment Management ... Ms. Lucy LEUSCH
32 VP Stdnt Affairs/Dean of Students ... Ms. Michelle HALL
04 Exec Assistant to the President ... Ms. Terri WILLIAMS
08 Librarian ... Ms. Anne SALTER
06 Registrar ... Vacant
09 Director of Institutional Research ... Ms. Janet H. MADDOX
26 Exec Dir Marketing/Public Relations ... Mr. Todd BENNETT
41 Interim Athletic Director ... Vacant
37 Director of Financial Aid ... Ms. Meg MCGINNISS
39 Director of Residence Life ... Mr. Danny GLASSMAN
21 Director of Finance/Controller ... Ms. Amy RENTENBACH
91 Director Administrative Computing ... Vacant
27 Chief Information Officer ... Mr. Cole MADDOX
29 Director of Alumni Relations ... Ms. Barbara HENRY
36 Director of Career Counseling ... Ms. Caroline WEIMAR
44 Director of Development Operations ... Mr. John CARR
15 Director Human Resources ... Vacant
55 Director Evening Degree Program ... Ms. Lisa LITTLEFIELD
31 Dir Center for Civic Engagement ... Ms. Tamara NASH
18 Director Facilities/Physical Plant ... Mr. Walter HALL
40 Bookstore Manager ... Mr. Paul RINGHOFF

Okefenokee Technical College (F)

1701 Carswell Avenue, Waycross GA 31503-4016
County: Ware FICE Identification: 005511
Unit ID: 248776
Telephone: (912) 287-6584 Carnegie Class: Assoc/Pub-R-M
FAX Number: (912) 287-4865 Calendar System: Semester
URL: www.okefenokeetech.edu
Established: 1965 Annual Undergrad Tuition & Fees (In-State): $3,795
Enrollment: 1,333 Coed
Affiliation or Control: State IRS Status: 501(c)3
Highest Offering: Associate Degree
Program: Occupational; Technical Emphasis
Accreditation: SC, MAC, MLTAD, RAD, SURGT

01 Interim President ... Dr. Glenn DEIBERT
05 Vice Pres for Academic Affairs ... Ms. Danita CANNON
11 VP of Administrative Services ... Ms. Pamela FARR
46 Vice Pres for Economic Development ... Mr. Andy BRANNEN
32 Vice President for Student Affairs ... Ms. Danita CANNON
06 Registrar ... Ms. Tara EICHFIELD
26 Public Relations/Information Dir ... Ms. Cindy TANNER
18 Facilities Director ... Mr. Chad BOYETT
36 Career Services Director ... Mr. Charlie GIBSON
37 Director Student Financial Aid ... Mr. Josh DASHER
09 Institutional Effectiveness Dir ... Ms. Teresa ALLEN
07 Director of Admissions ... Mr. Neal MURPHY
15 Human Resources Coordinator ... Ms. Cynthia LINDER
30 Coord of Resource Development ... Ms. Cindy TANNER

Paine College (G)

1235 15th Street, Augusta GA 30901-3182
County: Richmond FICE Identification: 001587
Unit ID: 140720
Telephone: (706) 821-8200 Carnegie Class: Bac/Diverse
FAX Number: (706) 821-8373 Calendar System: Semester
URL: www.paine.edu
Established: 1882 Annual Undergrad Tuition & Fees: $12,506
Enrollment: 891 Coed
Affiliation or Control: Multiple Protestant Denominations
IRS Status: 501(c)3
Highest Offering: Baccalaureate
Program: Liberal Arts And General; Teacher Preparatory; Professional
Accreditation: SC, ACBSP, TED

01 President ... Dr. George C. BRADLEY
05 Provost and VP of Academic Affairs ... Dr. Marcus D. TILLERY
10 VP of Admin & Fiscal Affairs ... Vacant
30 VP of Inst Advancement ... Mr. Brandon BROWN
32 VP and Dean of Student Affairs ... Dr. Elias ETINGE
88 Executive Asst to the President ... Dr. Cheryl EVANS JONES
45 Dir Plng/Eval & Title III Coord ... Dr. Cheryl EVANS JONES
88 Special Asst to the President ... Dr. Walter C. HOWARD
42 Campus Pastor ... Dr. Luther FELDER
41 Athletics Director ... Mr. Timothy DUNCAN
20 Assoc VP of Acad Affairs ... Dr. Tina MARSHALL-BRADLEY
20 Asst VP for Academic Affairs ... Dr. Edem TETTEH
46 Asst to the Provost for Research ... Dr. Kenneth LEWIS
44 Asst VP of Inst Advancement ... Ms. Helene CARTER
49 Dean School Arts and Sciences ... Dr. Emily A. WILLIAMS
107 Dean School Professional Studies ... Vacant
19 Chief of Campus Safety ... Mr. James L. REID
23 College Nurse ... Ms. Harriett S. JONES
21 Controller ... Ms. Peta-Gaye SHAW
07 Director Admissions ... Mr. Joseph TINSLEY
88 Director Athletics Compliance ... Ms. Taura HATNEY
36 Director Career Services ... Mrs. April EWING
38 Director Counseling Center ... Ms. Tiffaney WILLIAMS
18 Dir Facilities Mgmt/Environ Svcs ... Mr. Michael SUMMERS
37 Director Financial Aid ... Ms. Gerri BOGAN
14 Dir Information Technology Svcs ... Mr. Michael HICKS
09 Director Inst Research ... Mrs. Alice M. SIMPKINS
08 Dir Library/Learning Res Ctr ... Mrs. Lyn DENNISON
39 Director Residence Life ... Ms. Shartrisse JUDSON
25 Director Sponsored Programs ... Mr. Geno CLARK
35 Director Student Activities ... Mr. Torrez WILSON
88 Dir Transportation/Maintenance ... Mr. Charlie WOODLEY
15 Human Resources Manager ... Mrs. Jannette HENRY-DAVENPORT
40 Manager of The Lion's Shop ... Ms. Antoinette DAWKINS
06 Registrar/Dir Enrollmt Mgt Services ... Mrs. Castine RHOADES WILLIAMS
51 Coord Continuing Studies Program ... Ms. Nazareth WARD
29 Director Alumni Relations ... Mrs. Mildred KENDRICK
26 Dir Communications & Marketing ... Ms. Natasha CARTER
96 Junior Buyer ... Mr. Curtis WHITE
105 Website Designer ... Mr. Kevin O. WILSON

Piedmont College (A)

PO Box 10, Demorest GA 30535-0010
County: Habersham FICE Identification: 001588
Unit ID: 140818
Telephone: (706) 778-3000 Carnegie Class: Master's L
FAX Number: (706) 776-0701 Calendar System: Semester
URL: www.piedmont.edu
Established: 1897 Annual Undergrad Tuition & Fees: $19,930
Enrollment: 2,834 Coed
Affiliation or Control: Christian Churches And Churches of Christ
IRS Status: 501(c)3
Highest Offering: Doctorate
Program: Liberal Arts And General; Teacher Preparatory
Accreditation: SC, ACBSP, NUR

01 President .... Dr. James F. MELLICHAMP
05 Vice Pres Academic Affairs .... Dr. James MELLICHAMP
03 Exec VP for Institutional Resources .... Dr. John MISNER
11 Asst VP for Administrative Services .... Mr. Parks MILLER
10 Asst VP Finance/Human Resources .... Ms. Margie MEANS
12 Vice President Athens Campus .... Dr. Mel PALMER
30 Assoc VP Institutional Advancement .... Mr. William S. LOYD
35 Asst VP Student Svcs/Dn Admissions . Ms. Cynthia L. PETERSON
88 Special Assistant to the President .... Ms. Jane KIDD
44 Assoc Dir Institutional Advancement .... Mr. Justin SCALI
04 Assistant to the President .... Ms. Ann SUTTON
04 Assistant to the President .... Ms. Kristen GRAY
32 Dean Student Affairs .... Mr. Andrew B. DAVIS
42 Chaplain/Church Relations .... Rev Dr. Ashley CLEERE
07 Director Graduate Admissions .... Ms. Penny LOGGINS
06 Registrar .... Ms. Linda WOFFORD
08 College Librarian .... Mr. Robert GLASS, JR.
37 Director of Financial Aid .... Mr. David MCMILLION
07 Director Undergraduate Admissions .... Ms. Brenda BOONSTRA
13 Director Information Technology .... Dr. Shahryar HEYDARI
15 Human Resources Specialist .... Ms. Debbie ZIMMERMAN
26 Director of Public Relations .... Mr. David E. PRICE
41 Dir of Intercollegiate Athletics .... Mr. John L. DZIK
21 Compliance & Treasurery Officer .... Ms. Leesa P. ANDERSON
36 Director Counseling/Career Services .... Dr. Kel Lee CUTRELL
19 Director Security/Campus Police .... Mr. Richard D. MARTIN
66 Dean School of Nursing/Health Sci .... Dr. Linda SCOTT
50 Dean School of Business Admin .... Dr. John MISNER
49 Dean School of Arts & Sciences .... Dr. Steven NIMMO
53 Dean School of Education .... Dr. Donald GNECCO

Point University (B)

507 W 10th St, West Point GA 31833
County: Troup FICE Identification: 001547
Unit ID: 138868
Telephone: (706) 385-1000 Carnegie Class: Bac/Diverse
FAX Number: N/A Calendar System: Semester
URL: www.point.edu
Established: 1937 Annual Undergrad Tuition & Fees: $17,400
Enrollment: 1,245 Coed
Affiliation or Control: Christian Churches And Churches of Christ
IRS Status: 501(c)3
Highest Offering: Baccalaureate
Program: 2-Year Principally Bachelor's Creditable; Liberal Arts And General; Teacher Preparatory; Religious Emphasis
Accreditation: SC, TED

01 President .... Mr. Dean C. COLLINS
05 Chief Academic Officer .... Dr. W. Darryl HARRISON
20 Vice Pres for Academic Affairs .... Dr. Kimberly C. MACENCZAK
09 Vice Pres for Inst Effectiveness .... Dr. Dennis E. GLENN
84 Vice Pres for Enrollment Management .... Ms. Stacy BARTLETT
11 Vice Pres for Admin and COO .... Mr. Lance FRANCIS
42 Vice Pres for Spiritual Formation .... Mr. Samuel (Wye) W. HUXFORD
30 Vice President for Advancement .... Ms. Emma W. MORRIS
13 Vice Pres for Info Technology .... Mr. Jose' DIEUDONNE'
41 Athletic Director .... Mr. Kevin PORTER
10 Chief Financial Officer .... Ms. Donna W. LANKFORD
21 Controller .... Ms. Merinda THROWER
08 Library Director .... Mr. Michael L. BAIN
07 Director of Admission .... Ms. Tiffany WOOD
06 Registrar .... Ms. Tonya CANNON
37 Director of Financial Aid .... Ms. Anna ENGLISH
32 Director of Student Life .... Mr. Chris BEIRNE
18 Dir of Facilities and Maintenance .... Mr. Jim ALDRIDGE
88 Chancellor .... Dr. R. Edwin GROOVER
29 Director of Alumni Relations .... Ms. Pam ROSS
19 Director of Security .... Mr. Fred BERKELEY

† Formerly Atlanta Christian College

Reinhardt University (C)

7300 Reinhardt Circle, Waleska GA 30183-2981
County: Cherokee FICE Identification: 001589
Unit ID: 140872
Telephone: (770) 720-5600 Carnegie Class: Bac/Diverse
FAX Number: (770) 720-5602 Calendar System: Semester
URL: www.reinhardt.edu
Established: 1883 Annual Undergrad Tuition & Fees: $18,120
Enrollment: 1,154 Coed
Affiliation or Control: United Methodist IRS Status: 501(c)3
Highest Offering: Master's
Program: Liberal Arts And General
Accreditation: SC, MUS

01 President .... Dr. J. Thomas ISHERWOOD
04 Executive Assistant to President .... Mrs. Bonnie H. DEBORD
05 VP & Dean for Academic Affairs .... Dr. Robert L. DRISCOLL
10 Vice Pres Finance & Administration .... Mr. Robert G. MCKINNON
30 VP for Advancement .... Mrs. JoEllen B. WILSON
32 VP Student Affairs/Dean of Students .... Dr. Roger R. LEE
20 Assoc VP for Academic Affairs .... Mrs. Margaret J. O'CONNOR
58 Assoc Vice Pres Graduate Studies .... Dr. Margaret M. MORLIER
101 Asst Secretary Board of Trustees .... Mrs. Bonnie H. DEBORD
18 Exec Director of Physical Plant .... Mr. John W. YOUNG
26 Exec Dir Marketing/Communications .... Mrs. Marsha S. WHITE
13 Exec Dir & CIO for Information Tech .... Mrs. Virginia R. TOMLINSON
88 Exec Director of Funk Heritage Ctr .... Dr. Joseph H. KITCHENS
07 Director of Admissions .... Mrs. Julie C. FLEMING
06 Registrar .... Ms. Janet M. RODNING
09 Dir Instnl Research/Effectiveness .... Mrs. Cheryl A. NORRIS
08 Director of Library .... Mr. Joel C. LANGFORD
19 Director of Public Safety .... Ms. Sherry N. CORNETT
29 Dir Alumni Rel & Alumni Giving .... Vacant
42 University Chaplain .... Rev. Leigh S. MARTIN
21 Controller .... Mr. Peter J. BROMSTAD
37 Director Student Financial Aid .... Mrs. Angie D. HARLOW
41 Director of Athletics .... Mr. William C. POPP
16 Director Human Resources .... Mrs. Sandy B. MILTON
39 Director Residence Life .... Ms. Shalyn J. HERNANDEZ
23 Campus Nurse .... Mrs. Allison STARTUP
35 Asst Dean of Students/Dir Stdnt Act .... Dr. Walter P. MAY
38 Director of Counseling Svcs .... Mr. Derek L. STRUCHTEMEYER
88 Dir Center for Student Success .... Dr. Catherine B. EMANUEL
36 Director of Career Services .... Mrs. Peggy C. FEEHERY
40 Bookstore Manager .... Ms. Janet TASKER
105 Web Communication Manager .... Mr. John C. PETTIBONE
106 Coordinator Online Education .... Dr. Thomas M. REED
49 Dean School of Arts & Humanities .... Dr. Arthur W. GLOWKA
81 Dean School of Maths & Sciences .... Dr. Bill J. DEANGELIS
50 Int Dean McCamish School Business .... Dr. Donald D. WILSON, JR.
53 Dean Price School of Education .... Dr. James L. CURRY, JR.
64 Int Dean School of Music .... Dr. Dennis K. MCINTIRE

Richmont Graduate University (D)

2055 Mt. Paran Road, NW, Atlanta GA 30327-2921
County: Fulton FICE Identification: 033554
Unit ID: 441104
Telephone: (404) 233-3949 Carnegie Class: Spec/Health
FAX Number: (404) 239-9460 Calendar System: Semester
URL: www.richmont.edu
Established: 1973 Annual Graduate Tuition & Fees: $13,200
Enrollment: 258 Coed
Affiliation or Control: Independent Non-Profit IRS Status: 501(c)3
Highest Offering: Master's; No Undergraduates
Program: Professional
Accreditation: SC

01 President .... Dr. C. Jeffrey TERRELL
03 Vice Pres/Chair of Integration .... Dr. Gary W. MOON
30 Vice President for Advancement .... Mr. Bob RODGERS, JR.
04 Assistant to the President .... Ms. Jennifer COOPER
05 Academic Dean .... Dr. Philip A. COYLE
10 Chief Financial Officer .... Mr. William J. MUELLER

Sanford-Brown College (E)

1140 Hammond Drive NE, Suite A 1150, Atlanta GA 30328
County: Fulton FICE Identification: 021160
Unit ID: 420495
Telephone: (770) 576-4498 Carnegie Class: Assoc/PrivFP
FAX Number: (773) 601-3881 Calendar System: Other
URL: www.sanfordbrown.edu/Atlanta
Established: N/A Annual Undergrad Tuition & Fees: $15,358
Enrollment: 1,473 Coed
Affiliation or Control: Proprietary IRS Status: Proprietary
Highest Offering: Associate Degree
Program: Occupational
Accreditation: ACICS, CVT, DH, DMS

01 Campus President .... Mr. Steven IROFF

Savannah College of Art and Design (F)

342 Bull Street, PO Box 3146, Savannah GA 31402-6263
County: Chatham FICE Identification: 021415
Unit ID: 140951
Telephone: (912) 525-5000 Carnegie Class: Spec/Arts
FAX Number: (912) 525-6263 Calendar System: Quarter
URL: www.scad.edu
Established: 1978 Annual Undergrad Tuition & Fees: $31,905
Enrollment: 11,063 Coed
Affiliation or Control: Independent Non-Profit IRS Status: 501(c)3
Highest Offering: Master's
Program: Fine Arts Emphasis
Accreditation: SC, CIDA

01 President .... Mrs. Paula WALLACE
03 COO - SCAD Group Inc. .... Mr. Brian F. MURPHY
84 VP for Enrollment Management .... Mr. Scott LINZEY
46 Sr Vice Pres College Resources .... Mr. Glenn E. WALLACE, JR.
05 Chief Academic Officer .... Mr. Tom FISCHER
10 Chief Financial Officer .... Mr. Joseph MANORY
20 VP for Academic Services .... Dr. Gokhan OZAYSIN
12 Vice President for SCAD Atlanta .... Mr. Pharris D. (PJ) JOHNSON
12 Vice President for SCAD Hong Kong .... Mr. John Paul ROWAN
13 VP for Educational Technology .... Mr. Andrew FULP
32 Vice President for Student Success .... Dr. Philip ALLETTO
15 Vice President for Human Resources .... Ms. Lesley HANAK
13 Asst VP for IM&T .... Vacant
106 Assistant VP for eLearning .... Mr. Darrell NAYLOR-JOHNSON
35 Dean of Students .... Mr. David PUGH
26 Director of Media Relations .... Ms. Sunny NELSON
29 Assoc VP Alumni & Career Success .... Ms. Alison H. DAVIS
08 Dean of Library/Academic Services .... Vacant
18 Exec Dir for Physical Resources .... Mr. John HOUSLEY
37 Director of Financial Aid .... Ms. Brenda CLARK
06 Registrar .... Vacant
96 Director Procurement/Payment Svcs .... Ms. Mary GRANT
07 Executive Director of Admission .... Ms. Sara MALBROUGH
30 Exec Dir of Inst Advancement .... Vacant
19 Director of College Security .... Mr. Jeff SMITH
41 Athletics Director .... Mr. Steve LARSON
38 Dir Counseling/Student Support Svc .. Dr. Tamara KNAPP-GROSZ
20 Dean of Undergraduate Studies .... Ms. Beth GASKIN
58 Director of Graduate Studies .... Ms. Sarah MCCARN
88 Dean of School of Building Arts .... Mr. Christian SOTTILE
88 Dean of School Communication Arts .... Mr. John LOWE
88 Dean of School of Design .... Mr. Victor ERMOLI
88 Dn Sch Film/Dig Media/PerformingArt .... Mr. Peter WEISHAR
57 Dean of School of Fine Arts .... Mr. Steve BLISS
49 Dean of School of Liberal Arts .... Mr. Robert EISINGER
88 Dean School of Fashion .... Mr. Michael FINK
88 Dean School of Foundation Studies .... Ms. Maureen GARVIN

Savannah State University (G)

3219 College Street, Savannah GA 31404-5308
County: Chatham FICE Identification: 001590
Unit ID: 140960
Telephone: (912) 358-4778 Carnegie Class: Bac/A&S
FAX Number: (912) 356-2256 Calendar System: Semester
URL: www.savannahstate.edu
Established: 1890 Annual Undergrad Tuition & Fees (In-State): $6,192
Enrollment: 4,552 Coed
Affiliation or Control: State IRS Status: 501(c)3
Highest Offering: Master's
Program: Liberal Arts And General
Accreditation: SC, BUS, ENGT, JOUR, SPAA, SW

01 University President .... Dr. Cheryl DOZIER
05 Vice Pres Academic Affairs .... Dr. Mostafa SARHAN
10 Vice Pres Business & Finance .... Mr. Edward B. JOLLEY, JR.
32 Vice President Student Affairs .... Dr. Irvin CLARK
30 Vice President Advancement .... Mr. Phillip D. ADAMS
20 Asst Vice Pres Academic Affairs .... Dr. Larry STOKES
84 Dir Enrollment Services/Registrar .... Mr. Timothy CRANFORD
07 Asst Director of Admissions .... Ms. Carol DOLAN
15 Director Human Resources .... Dr. Sandra M. BEST
08 Librarian .... Mrs. MaryJo FAYOYIN
26 Director Marketing/Communications .... Ms. Loretta HEYWARD
27 Chief Information Officer .... Mr. Jeff DELANEY
18 Director Facilities/Physical Plant .... Mr. Ervin OGDEN
09 Dir Inst Resrch/Planning/Assessment .... Dr. Michael G. CROW
29 Director Alumni Relations .... Ms. Barbara S. MYERS
37 Director Financial Aid .... Mrs. Adrienne BROWN
19 Chief of Police .... Mr. Creighton ROBERTS
35 Director of Student Development .... Ms. Jacqueline AWE
50 Asst Dean College Business Admin .... Dr. Reginald LESEANE
83 Interim Dean Col Lib Arts/Soc Sci .... Dr. Michael SCHROEDER
72 Int Dean Col Science & Technology .... Dr. Jonathan LAMBRIGHT

† Part of the University System of Georgia.

Savannah Technical College (H)

5717 White Bluff Road, Savannah GA 31405-5521
County: Chatham FICE Identification: 005618
Unit ID: 140942
Telephone: (912) 443-5700 Carnegie Class: Assoc/Pub-R-M
FAX Number: (912) 443-5705 Calendar System: Quarter
URL: www.savannahtech.edu
Established: 1967 Annual Undergrad Tuition & Fees (In-State): $2,522
Enrollment: 4,669 Coed
Affiliation or Control: State IRS Status: 501(c)3
Highest Offering: Associate Degree
Program: Occupational; 2-Year Principally Bachelor's Creditable; Technical Emphasis
Accreditation: SC, ACFEI, DA, DH, ENGT, MAC, PNUR, SURGT

01 President .... Dr. Kathy S. LOVE
03 Vice President Operations .... Mr. Jim WHEELESS
11 Vice Pres Administrative Services .... Ms. Sue Z. TURNER
32 Vice President Student Affairs .... Mr. Jim NORDONE
45 Vice Pres Econ Dev & Acad Affairs .... Dr. Ken BOYD
84 Exec Director Enroll Mgmt/Marketing .... Ms. Gail EUBANKS
07 Director of Admissions .... Ms. Gwendolyn MOORE
06 Registrar .... Ms. Regina THOMAS-WILLIAMS
18 Director Facilities .... Mr. Ken COOK
37 Exec Dir of Student Financial Svcs .... Ms. Teresa POTTS
38 Director Student Support Services .... Ms. Laurie HERRINGTON
15 Director Human Resources .... Ms. Melissa BANKS

12 Campus Dean Liberty Campus ... Ms. Terrie O. SELLERS
12 Campus Dean Effingham Campus ... Mr. Robert SOLOMON
96 Purchasing Manager ... Mr. Kevin CHIEVES
88 Dean Public Services ... Dr. Gayle TREMBLE
76 Dean Allied Health ... Mr. Larry ROBERSON
75 Dean Industrial Technology ... Mr. Tal LOOS
50 Dean Business Technology ... Ms. Carol PAULK
97 Dean General Studies ... Dr. Al CUNNINGHAM

Shorter University (A)

315 Shorter Avenue, Rome GA 30165-4298
County: Floyd FICE Identification: 001591
Unit ID: 140988
Telephone: (706) 291-2121 Carnegie Class: Bac/A&S
FAX Number: (706) 236-1515 Calendar System: Semester
URL: www.shorter.edu
Established: 1873 Annual Undergrad Tuition & Fees: $18,770
Enrollment: 3,818 Coed
Affiliation or Control: Baptist IRS Status: 501(c)3
Highest Offering: Master's
Program: Liberal Arts And General; Teacher Preparatory; Professional
Accreditation: SC, MUS, NURSE

01 President ... Dr. Donald V. DOWLESS
05 Executive Vice President & Provost ... Dr. Donald L. MARTIN
11 VP for Administrative Affairs ... Vacant
10 Vice President for Finance & CFO ... Mrs. Stephanie R. OWENS
84 Vice Pres Enrollment Management ... Vacant
30 Vice President for Advancement ... Mr. Bert EPTING
32 VP Student Affairs/Dean of Students ... Mr. Corey HUMPHRIES
26 Vice President for Public Relations ... Mrs. Dawn C. TOLBERT
06 Registrar ... Mrs. Brandi BERGER
29 Director of Alumni Relations ... Mrs. Sheri RANSOME
35 Director of Student Activities ... Ms. Emily W. MESSER
08 Director of Libraries ... Mr. DeWayne WILLIAMS
09 Director of Inst Planning/Research ... Ms. Julie ENSEL
37 Director of Financial Aid ... Ms. Tara JONES
15 Director Human Resources ... Mr. Wayne PHIPPS
90 Director of Academic Computing ... Mr. Anthony J. NICHOLS
56 Director Special Programs ... Vacant
13 Director of Information Technology ... Mr. Ryan HAYLOCK
18 Director of Facilities Management ... Mr. Dickerson E. TAYLOR
38 Director of Student Support Svcs ... Dr. Emily DERRICK
23 Director of Health Services ... Mrs. Mary SHOTWELL SMITH
41 Athletic Director ... Mr. Bill PETERSON
40 Bookstore Manager ... Ms. Jasmine RAGLAND
57 Dean School of the Arts ... Dr. Alan B. WINGARD
50 Dean College of Business ... Dr. Robert H. DARVILLE
49 Dean School of Liberal Arts ... Dr. Sabrena PARTON
53 Dean School of Education ... Dr. Norma HARPER
56 Dean Coll Adult/Professional Pgms ... Dr. Jacqueline AVANT
66 Dean School of Nursing ... Vacant
106 Dean of Online Programs ... Mr. Sean BUTCHER
81 Assoc Dean Sciences & Mathematics ... Ms. Lisa M. KEITH
79 Assoc Dean Humanities/Social Sci ... Dr. Benjamin MCFRY
73 Chair Dept of Christian Studies ... Dr. Earle KELLETT
53 Chair Department of Education ... Dr. Gary ROSS
77 Chair Dept of Math/Computer Science ... Dr. Diana SWANAGAN
60 Chair Dept of Communication Arts ... Dr. Dana HALL
83 Chr Dpt Hist/Poli Sci/Psych/Soclgy ... Dr. Barsha PICKELL
42 Campus Minister ... Rev. David E. ROLAND
44 Director of Annual Giving ... Mr. Neely RAPER
07 Director of Admissions ... Mr. Patrick MCELHANEY
39 Dir Residence Life/Student Conduct ... Mr. Joshua ARNOLD
104 Director of International Programs ... Vacant

South Georgia College (B)

100 W College Park Drive, Douglas GA 31533-5098
County: Coffee FICE Identification: 001592
Unit ID: 140997
Telephone: (912) 260-4394 Carnegie Class: Assoc/Pub-R-S
FAX Number: (912) 260-4454 Calendar System: Semester
URL: www.sgc.edu
Established: 1906 Annual Undergrad Tuition & Fees (In-State): $3,562
Enrollment: 2,269 Coed
Affiliation or Control: State IRS Status: 501(c)3
Highest Offering: Baccalaureate
Program: 2-Year Principally Bachelor's Creditable; Liberal Arts And General
Accreditation: SC, ADNUR

01 President ... Dr. Virginia M. CARSON
05 Vice Pres Academic Affairs ... Dr. Carl MCDONALD
32 Vice President for Student Success ... Mr. Wes S. BROWN
10 Vice President for Fiscal Affairs ... Mr. Mark LATHAM
30 Vice President for External Affairs ... Ms. Walda KIGHT
11 Vice President for Operations ... Mr. Keith NEWELL
08 Librarian ... Ms. Jacqueline VICKERS
06 Registrar ... Dr. Randy BRASWELL
37 Director Financial Aid ... Ms. Becky RUMKER
15 Director Human Resources ... Mr. Keith NEWELL
18 Chief Facilities/Phys Plant ... Mr. Keith NEWELL
07 Director of Admissions ... Dr. Randy BRASWELL
12 Dir of Entry Programs and Planning ... Ms. Valerie WEBSTER
72 Director of Technology ... Ms. Lena HELMBRECHT
40 Director of Bookstore ... Ms. Daphne FRENCH
21 Director of Business Services ... Ms. Peggy DOBBS
41 Interim Athletic Director ... Mr. Wes BROWN
09 Dir of Institutional Effectiveness ... Ms. Danielle BUEHRER
39 Director of Residence Life ... Mr. Andy JOHNSON
35 Director of Student Life ... Ms. Sue MILLER
19 Director of Security ... Ms. Sonja MCCULLOCH

† Part of the University System of Georgia.

South Georgia Technical College (C)

900 South Georgia Tech Parkway,
Americus GA 31709-8167
County: Sumter FICE Identification: 005617
Unit ID: 141006
Telephone: (229) 931-2394 Carnegie Class: Assoc/Pub-R-M
FAX Number: (229) 931-2924 Calendar System: Semester
URL: www.southgatech.edu
Established: 1948 Annual Undergrad Tuition & Fees (In-State): $3,240
Enrollment: 2,278 Coed
Affiliation or Control: State IRS Status: 501(c)3
Highest Offering: Associate Degree
Program: Occupational; Technical Emphasis
Accreditation: SC, COE

01 President ... Sparky REEVES
11 Vice Pres Administrative Services ... Janice DAVIS
10 Vice Pres Business & Industry Svcs ... Wally SUMMERS
05 Vice President for Academic Affairs ... John WATFORD
09 Vice Pres of Institutional Support ... Karen J. WERLING
04 Special Assistant to the President ... Don SMITH
20 Dean of Instruction ... David KUIPERS
20 Dean of Instruction ... Raymond HOLT
26 Dir of Resource Devel & Marketing ... Su Ann BIRD
13 Technology Director ... Wray SKIPPER
37 Director of Financial Aid ... Michael WRIGHT
15 Director Personnel Services ... Sandy LARSON
36 Director of Career Services ... Cynthia CARTER
32 Director of Campus Life ... Brandan HARRELL
21 Director of Accounting ... Lea COE
88 Director of Administrative Services ... Mark BROOKS
55 Director of Instruction-Evening ... Lemond HALL
06 Registrar ... Julie PARTAIN
08 Librarian ... Jerry STOVALL
07 Director of Admissions ... Whitney CRISP
28 Director of Diversity ... Sandy LARSON
29 Director Alumni Relations ... SuAnn BIRD
35 Director Student Affairs ... Don SMITH
38 Director Student Counseling ... Cynthia CARTER
84 Director Enrollment Management ... Whitney CRISP
18 Chief Facilities/Physical Plant ... Jeff WISEMAN
30 Chief Development ... Wally SUMMERS
96 Purchasing Agent ... Gail CLARY

South University (D)

709 Mall Boulevard, Savannah GA 31406-4881
County: Chatham FICE Identification: 013039
Unit ID: 139579
Telephone: (912) 201-8000 Carnegie Class: Master's L
FAX Number: (912) 201-8070 Calendar System: Quarter
URL: www.southuniversity.edu
Established: 1899 Annual Undergrad Tuition & Fees: $15,910
Enrollment: 1,443 Coed
Affiliation or Control: Proprietary IRS Status: Proprietary
Highest Offering: Doctorate
Program: 2-Year Principally Bachelor's Creditable; Liberal Arts And General; Professional; Business Emphasis
Accreditation: SC, AA, ARCPA, MAC, NURSE, PHAR, PTAA

00 Chancellor ... Mr. John T. SOUTH, III
01 Campus President Savannah ... Mr. Todd CELLINI
12 President West Palm Beach ... Mr. David MCGUIRE
12 President Montgomery ... Mr. Victor K. BIEBIGHAUSER
12 President Columbia ... Mr. Brad KAUFFMAN
05 Vice Chanc Academic Affairs ... Dr. Steven K. YOHO
15 Assoc Chanc of Human Resources ... Ms. Trisha EARLS
13 Assoc Chanc Information Technology ... Mr. James FREYBURGER
10 Assoc Chancellor of Finance ... Ms. Katrina WIGREN
26 Assoc Chancellor Marketing ... Mr. Bruce CHONG
07 Assoc Chancellor Admissions ... Mr. Matthew MILLS
06 Registrar ... Mr. Bryan LOGIE
20 Dean of Academic Affairs ... Ms. Becky HAYES
17 Dean College of Health Professions ... Dr. A. William PAULSEN
37 Director of Student Financial Aid ... Ms. Tressa BRUSH
67 Dean School of Pharmacy ... Dr. James E. WYNN
32 Asst Dean Student Affairs/Pharmacy ... Ms. Gabriella FISCHER
08 Head Librarian ... Ms. Valerie E. YAUGHN
27 Asst Chancellor Communications ... Ms. Heather R. ASKEW
36 Director of Career Services ... Mr. Don HOLLAND
19 Director of Security ... Mr. Bill LYGHT

Southeastern Technical College (E)

3001 E First Street, Vidalia GA 30474-8817
County: Toombs FICE Identification: 030665
Unit ID: 368911
Telephone: (912) 538-3100 Carnegie Class: Assoc/Pub-R-S
FAX Number: (912) 538-3156 Calendar System: Semester
URL: www.southeasterntech.edu
Established: 1989 Annual Undergrad Tuition & Fees (In-State): $3,072
Enrollment: 1,826 Coed
Affiliation or Control: State IRS Status: 501(c)3
Highest Offering: Associate Degree
Program: Occupational; Technical Emphasis
Accreditation: SC, DH, EMT, MAC, MLTAD, RAD, SURGT

01 President ... Dr. Cathryn MITCHELL
03 Provost ... Mr. Larry CALHOUN
05 Vice Pres Academic Affairs ... Ms. Teresa COLEMAN
11 Vice Pres Administrative Services ... Ms. Denise POWELL
10 Vice President Fiscal Affairs ... Vacant
32 Vice President Student Affairs ... Dr. Barry DOTSON
84 Director Enrollment Services ... Mr. Brad HART
06 Registrar ... Ms. Karen VEREEN
37 Director Financial Aid ... Mr. Mitchell FAGLER
36 Director Job Placement ... Mr. Lance HELMS
103 Special Populations Coordinator ... Ms. Helen THOMAS
88 Fatherhood Initiative Coordinator ... Vacant
40 Bookstore Manager ... Ms. Brooke SALTER

Southern Crescent Technical College (F)

501 Varsity Road, Griffin GA 30223-2042
County: Spalding FICE Identification: 005621
Unit ID: 139986
Telephone: (770) 228-7348 Carnegie Class: Assoc/Pub-S-MC
FAX Number: (770) 229-3227 Calendar System: Semester
URL: www.sctech.edu
Established: 1963 Annual Undergrad Tuition & Fees (In-State): $3,117
Enrollment: 5,156 Coed
Affiliation or Control: State IRS Status: 501(c)3
Highest Offering: Associate Degree
Program: Occupational; 2-Year Principally Bachelor's Creditable; Technical Emphasis
Accreditation: SC, DA, MAC, SURGT

01 President ... Dr. Randall PETERS
03 Provost ... Mr. Steve DANIEL
05 Vice Pres for Academic Affairs ... Dr. Dawn HODGES
32 Vice Pres for Student Affairs ... Ms. Xenia JOHNS
103 Vice Pres for Economic Development ... Mr. Mark ANDREWS
10 Vice Pres Administrative Services ... Ms. Miriam CASLIN
18 Vice Pres Facilities/Operations ... Mr. Jim BROWN
30 Vice President Advancement ... Ms. Barbara Jo COOK
09 Dir Institutional Effectiveness ... Mr. Brent MAYES
08 Director of Library Services ... Ms. Kate WILLIAMS
06 Registrar ... Ms. Kathlyn BURDEN
26 Dir Marketing & Public Relations ... Ms. Anna TAYLOR
37 Director of Financial Aid ... Ms. Kimberly MORRIS
49 Dean Business Tech Arts & Sciences/ ... Ms. Rebecca JOHNSON
76 Dean Allied Health ... Dr. John POPE
75 Dean Personal Svcs/Public Safety ... Ms. Karen WILLIAMS
75 Dean Industrial Technical Studies ... Mr. Steve CROMER
106 Dean Computer Info Services ... Ms. Tempie KITCHENS

Southern Polytechnic State University (G)

1100 South Marietta Parkway, Marietta GA 30060-2896
County: Cobb FICE Identification: 001570
Unit ID: 141097
Telephone: (678) 915-7778 Carnegie Class: Master's M
FAX Number: (678) 915-7483 Calendar System: Semester
URL: www.spsu.edu/
Established: 1948 Annual Undergrad Tuition & Fees (In-State): $6,678
Enrollment: 5,784 Coed
Affiliation or Control: State IRS Status: 501(c)3
Highest Offering: Master's
Program: 2-Year Principally Bachelor's Creditable; Liberal Arts And General; Teacher Preparatory; Professional; Technical Emphasis
Accreditation: SC, ACBSP, CONST, CS, ENG, ENGR, ENGT

01 President ... Dr. Lisa A. ROSSBACHER
05 Vice President for Academic Affairs ... Dr. Zvi SZAFRAN
32 Vice Pres Student/Enrollment Svcs ... Dr. Ron R. KOGER
30 VP for University Advancement ... Dr. Ron D. DEMPSEY
10 Vice President for Business/Finance ... Dr. Bill PRIGGE
13 Chief Information Officer ... Dr. Sam CONN
04 Exec Assistant to President ... Ms. Mary T. PHILLIPS
29 Exec Dir Strategic Mktg/Sustainblty ... Mr. James W. COOPER
22 Affirmative Action Officer ... Ms. Mary E. MCGEE
20 Assoc VP for Academic Affairs ... Mr. Dave CAUDILL
54 Dean of Engineering ... Dr. Thomas CURRIN
48 Dean of Architecture & Const Mgmt ... Dr. Wilson C. BARNES
49 Dean of Arts & Sciences ... Dr. Thomas NELSON
77 Dean of Computing/Software Eng ... Dr. Han REICHGELT
72 Dean of Engr Technology/Mgmt ... Dr. Jeffrey RAY
56 Dean of Extended University ... Dr. Ruston HUNT
93 Dir of Adv/Tutoring/Tst/Intl Center ... Dr. Jeff ORR
58 Director of Graduate Studies ... Ms. Nikki PALAMIOTIS
104 Director of International Programs ... Dr. Richard BENNETT
08 Director of Library ... Dr. Joyce W. MILLS
78 Dir Center for Teaching Excellence ... Ms. Dawn RAMSEY
92 Director of Honors Program ... Dr. Nancy L. REICHERT
35 Dean of Students ... Mr. Barry D. BIRCKHEAD
36 Director of Career/Counseling Svcs ... Ms. Phyllis N. WEATHERLY
88 Director of Recreation and Wellness ... Mr. Karl D. STABER
07 Dir Admissions/Student Recruitment ... Mr. Gary W. BUSH
09 Director of Institutional Research ... Mr. Dave CLINE
37 Dir of Scholarships/Financial Aid ... Mr. Gary MANN
06 Registrar ... Mr. Stephen A. HAMRICK
44 Director of Development ... Ms. Kit TRENSCH
26 Director of Public Relations ... Ms. Sylvia CARSON
21 Controller ... Mr. Arthur VAUGHN
21 Director of Budget and Grants ... Ms. Robin WADE
15 Director of Human Resources ... Dr. I. Charles AZEBEOKHAI

19 Chief of University Police ....Chief John BAUER
18 Dir of Facilities Management ....Mr. Steve KITCHEN
96 Director Procurement ....Mr. Robert P. FORBES
31 Director Auxillary Enterprises ....Ms. Kasey HELTON
90 Director Desktop Support ....Mr. Dave PARHAM
13 Dir of IT Enterprise Applications ....Mr. Ken HILL
91 Director IT Operations ....Mr. Ronald J. SKOPITZ
14 Dir IT Systems/Networks/Security ....Mr. Jim HERBERT
41 Director of Athletics ....Mr. Matthew GRIFFIN
88 Internal Auditor ....Mr. William KETCHUM

† Part of the University System of Georgia. Most of the tutition increase is due to a change in the definition of "full-time student" from 24 credit hour annually to 30.

Southwest Georgia Technical College (A)

15689 US Highway 19 N, Thomasville GA 31792-2622
County: Thomas FICE Identification: 005615
Unit ID: 141158
Telephone: (229) 225-4096 Carnegie Class: Assoc/Pub-R-S
FAX Number: (229) 225-4330 Calendar System: Semester
URL: www.southwestgatech.edu
Established: 1947 Annual Undergrad Tuition & Fees (In-State): $3,747
Enrollment: 1,769 Coed
Affiliation or Control: State IRS Status: 501(c)3
Highest Offering: Associate Degree
Program: Occupational
Accreditation: SC, ADNUR, MAC, MLTAD, SURGT

01 President ....Dr. Craig R. WENTWORTH
11 Vice Pres Administrative Services ....Mr. Paul ROBERTS
05 Vice Pres Academic Affairs ....Dr. Annie MCELROY
32 Vice President Student Affairs ....Ms. Joyce HALSTEAD
30 Vice President Economic Development ....Mr. Gary PITTS
09 VP Institutional Effectiveness ....Dr. Debbie GOODMAN
76 Dean Allied Health/Gen Education ....Ms. Carla BARROW
50 Dean Bus/Computer/Prof Svcs/T&I ....Mr. Dennis LEE
37 Director Financial Aid ....Ms. Amy SCOGGINS
26 Dir Marketing/Inst Devel/Pub Rels ....Ms. Amy MAISON
88 Executive Director Adult Education ....Mr. Dale ALDRIDGE
07 Director Admissions ....Ms. Wanda HANCOCK
06 Registrar ....Ms. Deborah GRAY
08 Director Library & Media Services ....Ms. Gail ROBERTS
36 Dir Career Placement & Development ....Dr. Jeanine LONG

Spelman College (B)

350 Spelman Lane, SW, Atlanta GA 30314-4399
County: Fulton FICE Identification: 001594
Unit ID: 141060
Telephone: (404) 681-3643 Carnegie Class: Bac/A&S
FAX Number: N/A Calendar System: Semester
URL: www.spelman.edu
Established: 1881 Annual Undergrad Tuition & Fees: $23,794
Enrollment: 2,170 Female
Affiliation or Control: Independent Non-Profit IRS Status: 501(c)3
Highest Offering: Baccalaureate
Program: Liberal Arts And General; Teacher Preparatory
Accreditation: SC, MUS, TED

01 President ....Dr. Beverly Daniel TATUM
05 Provost & VP of Academic Affairs ....Dr. Johnnella E. BUTLER
20 Vice Provost ....Dr. Myra BURNETT
10 VP Business/Financial Affairs/ Treas ....Mr. Robert D. FLANIGAN, JR.
32 Vice President for Student Affairs ....Dr. Darnita KILLIAN
30 Vice Pres for College Relations ....Ms. Eloise ALEXIS
84 Vice Pres Enrollment Management ....Ms. Arlene CASH
30 Vice President for Development ....Ms. Kassandra JOLLEY
21 Assoc VP Business/Financial Affairs ....Mr. John CUNNINGHAM
88 Dir Investments & Financial Plng ....Ms. Rhonda HONEGAN
21 Controller ....Ms. April AUSTIN
100 Secretary of College ....Ms. Tamaria DAVIS
26 Exec Dir of Communications ....Ms. Tomika DEPRIEST
04 Assistant to President ....Ms. Yvonne SKILLINGS
13 VP & CIO Media & Information Tech ....Ms. Delores BARTON
105 Dir Bonner Comm Svcs/Student Dev ....Vacant
20 Dean of Undergraduate Studies ....Dr. Desiree PEDESCLEAUX
42 Director Sisters Center for WISDOM ....Rev. Lisa D. RHODES
06 Registrar ....Dr. Frederick FRESH
07 Director of Admissions ....Ms. Erica JOHNSON
27 Director Publications ....Ms. Jo Moore STEWART
29 Director of Alumnae Affairs ....Ms. Sharon OWENS
37 Director of Student Financial Svcs ....Ms. Lenora JACKSON
36 Director Career Planning/Devel ....Mr. Harold BELL
78 Director of Cooperative Education ....Mr. Keith WEBB
15 Director Human Resources ....Ms. Bernadette COHEN
38 Director Counseling Services ....Dr. Ave MARSHALL
09 Dir Inst Rsrch/Assessment/Planning ....Ms. Jill TRIPLETT
88 Director Women's Resource Center ....Dr. Beverly GUY-SHEFTALL
18 Director Facilities/Mgmt & Svcs ....Mr. Arthur E. FRAZIER, III
19 Director of Public Safety ....Mr. Steve BOWSER
24 Dir Educational Technology Svcs ....Ms. Jenell SARGENT
46 Associate Provost of Research ....Dr. Carmen SIDBURY
44 Director of Annual Giving ....Ms. DeShanna BROWN
102 Dir of Corp & Foundation Relations ....Ms. Shelese LANE
88 Director of Special Events ....Ms. Heather HAWES
39 Director Housing & Residential Life ....Ms. Alison CUMMINGS
86 Director Title III/Government Rels ....Ms. Helga GREENFIELD
88 Coordinator Intl/Commuter Students ....Ms. Letitia DENARD
08 Director of Woodruff Library ....Ms. Loretta PARHAM
23 Director Health Services ....Ms. Brenda DALTON
25 Director Sponsored Programs ....Mr. T.N. Nokware ADESEGUN
102 Assoc VP for College Relations ....Ms. Helga GREENFIELD
35 Dean Students ....Ms. Kimberly FERGUSON
40 Director Bookstore ....Ms. Tiffani HODGE
41 Dir Phys Ed & Athletics/Sr Instr ....Ms. Germaine MCAULEY
96 Dir Adminstrative Support Svcs ....Ms. Jacqueline JAMES

Thomas University (C)

1501 Millpond Road, Thomasville GA 31792-7499
County: Thomas FICE Identification: 001555
Unit ID: 141167
Telephone: (229) 226-1621 Carnegie Class: Bac/Diverse
FAX Number: (229) 226-1653 Calendar System: Semester
URL: www.thomasu.edu
Established: 1950 Annual Undergrad Tuition & Fees: $14,520
Enrollment: 1,109 Coed
Affiliation or Control: Independent Non-Profit IRS Status: 501(c)3
Highest Offering: Master's
Program: Liberal Arts And General; Professional
Accreditation: SC, CORE, MT, NUR, SW

01 President ....Dr. Gary BONVILLIAN
05 Vice Pres of Academic Affairs ....Dr. Ann LANDIS
30 Vice Pres for Instnl Advancement ....Mr. Richard MUNROE
08 Univ Librarian/Dir Info Services ....Ms. Amber BROCK
06 Registrar ....Mrs. Lacey HARRISON
84 Exec Dir Enroll Mgmt/Student Svcs ....Dr. Vivian GALLMAN-DERIENZO
07 Director of Admissions ....Ms. Kerri KNIGHT
38 Director of Student Support Svcs ....Ms. Faye R. JOHNSON
37 Director of Financial Aid ....Ms. Melinda REESE
41 Director of Athletics ....Mr. Michael D. LEE
10 Controller ....Ms. Sue STONE
18 Director of Physical Plant ....Mr. Randy WILCOX
32 Director of Student Life ....Mr. John RAINEY
44 Director of Annual Fund ....Ms. Melinda FRIDDELL
26 Director of Communications ....Mrs. Cindy MONTGOMERY
04 Assistant to the President ....Ms. Linda M. HERNDON

Toccoa Falls College (D)

107 North Chapel Drive, Toccoa Falls GA 30598-0068
County: Stephens FICE Identification: 001596
Unit ID: 141185
Telephone: (706) 886-6831 Carnegie Class: Bac/Diverse
FAX Number: (706) 282-6005 Calendar System: Semester
URL: www.tfc.edu
Established: 1907 Annual Undergrad Tuition & Fees: $17,710
Enrollment: 721 Coed
Affiliation or Control: Independent Non-Profit IRS Status: 501(c)3
Highest Offering: Baccalaureate
Program: Liberal Arts And General; Teacher Preparatory
Accreditation: SC, BI, MUS

01 President ....Dr. Robert M. MYERS
04 Sr Exec Administrative Assistant ....Mrs. Paula S. ELKINS
32 VP Student Development ....Mr. Lee P. YOWELL
30 VP for Advancement ....Mr. James HANSEN
10 Vice President for Finance ....Mr. R. Gregg SCHULTE
05 VP for Academic Affairs ....Dr. W. Brian SHELTON
84 Dean of Enrollment Management ....Mr. Daniel GRIFFIN
42 Director Spiritual Form ....Dr. Stephen WOODWORTH
09 Director Institutional Research ....Dr. David W. MCCARTHY
08 Director Info Svcs/IT Dept/Library ....Miss Patricia J. FISHER
39 Director Residence/Community Life ....Mrs. Debbie MOORE
29 Director Alumni Assoc/Col Relations ....Miss Sharon SANDERSON
38 Dir Stdnt Health/Career Servs ....Mr. Johnathan C. KERR
37 Director Student Financial Aid ....Mr. Truitt FRANKLIN
07 Director of Admissions ....Ms. Joanna E. BRUCE
06 Registrar ....Mr. Kelly G. VICKERS
41 Athletic Director ....Vacant
18 Chief Facilities/Physical Plant ....Mr. Gerald WILLIAMSON
26 Chief Public Relations Officer ....Ms. Angela R. RAMAGE
15 Director Human Resources ....Ms. Mary K. RITCHEY

Truett McConnell College (E)

100 Alumni Drive, Cleveland GA 30528-1264
County: White FICE Identification: 001597
Unit ID: 141237
Telephone: (706) 865-2134 Carnegie Class: Bac/Assoc
FAX Number: (706) 219-3339 Calendar System: Semester
URL: www.truett.edu
Established: 1946 Annual Undergrad Tuition & Fees: $15,650
Enrollment: 922 Coed
Affiliation or Control: Baptist IRS Status: 501(c)3
Highest Offering: Baccalaureate
Program: Liberal Arts And General; Religious Emphasis
Accreditation: SC, MUS

01 President ....Dr. Emir CANER
05 Vice Pres Academic Services ....Dr. Brad REYNOLDS
11 Vice Pres Administrative Svcs ....Mr. David ARMSTRONG
30 Vice Pres Institutional Advancement ....Dr. Daniel P. MOOSBRUGGER
32 Vice President of Student Services ....Mr. Chris EPPLING
04 Executive Assistant to President ....Mrs. Jeanavon BURROW
41 Athletic Director ....Mr. Chris EPPLING
06 Registrar/Dir Inst Research ....Mrs. Melissa FORTNER
37 Director of Financial Aid ....Mrs. Becky MOORE
08 Librarian ....Ms. Janice E. WILSON
29 Director of Alumni Relations ....Mr. Steve PATTON
07 Director of Admissions ....Mr. Nathan RAYNOR
42 Director of Collegiate Ministries ....Mr. Keith WADE
40 Bookstore Manager ....Mr. Eddie O'BRIEN

University of Atlanta (F)

6685 Peachtree Industrial Boulevard, Atlanta GA 30360-2116
County: DeKalb Identification: 666399
Telephone: (877) 503-4588 Carnegie Class: Not Classified
FAX Number: (678) 669-2439 Calendar System: Semester
URL: www.uofa.edu
Established: 2006 Annual Undergrad Tuition & Fees: $4,075
Enrollment: 610 Coed
Affiliation or Control: Proprietary IRS Status: Proprietary
Highest Offering: Doctorate
Program: Liberal Arts And General; Professional; Business Emphasis
Accreditation: DETC

01 President ....Mr. Nick MITHANI
03 Chief Executive Officer ....Mr. Alex MITHANI
05 Dean of Faculty ....Dr. James L. WILLIAMS
32 VP Student Affairs ....Ms. Nechelle ROBINSON
84 VP Enrollment Management ....Mr. Bill KAY

† Currently in teach out phase. Accreditation expires June 30, 2013.

University of Georgia (G)

Athens GA 30602-0001
County: Clarke FICE Identification: 001598
Unit ID: 139959
Telephone: (706) 542-3000 Carnegie Class: RU/VH
FAX Number: N/A Calendar System: Semester
URL: www.uga.edu
Established: 1785 Annual Undergrad Tuition & Fees (In-State): $9,842
Enrollment: 34,816 Coed
Affiliation or Control: State IRS Status: 501(c)3
Highest Offering: Doctorate
Program: Liberal Arts And General; Teacher Preparatory; Professional
Accreditation: SC, AAFCS, ART, BUS, BUSA, CACREP, CIDA, CLPSY, COPSY, DANCE, DIETD, DIETI, ENG, FOR, JOUR, LAW, LSAR, MFCD, MUS, NRPA, PH, PHAR, SCPSY, SP, SPAA, SW, TED, THEA, VET

01 President ....Dr. Michael F. ADAMS
100 Chief of Staff ....Dr. Margaret A. AMSTUTZ
04 Assistant to the President ....Mr. Charles G. TONEY
04 Assistant to the President ....Mr. Matthew M. WINSTON, JR.
04 Assistant to the President ....Ms. Mary E. MCDONALD
05 Sr VP Academic Affs/Provost ....Mr. Jere W. MOREHEAD
10 Sr Vice Pres Finance/Administration ....Mr. Timothy P. BURGESS
26 Sr Vice Pres for External Affairs ....Mr. Thomas S. LANDRUM
20 Vice President for Instruction ....Dr. Laura D. JOLLY
46 Vice President for Research ....Dr. David C. LEE
88 Vice Pres Public Svc/Outreach ....Dr. Jennifer L. FRUM
32 Vice President Student Affairs ....Dr. Rodney D. BENNETT
86 Vice President for Govt Relations ....Mr. J. Griffin DOYLE
26 Vice President Public Affairs ....Dr. Thomas H. JACKSON, JR.
104 Assoc Prov for International Educ ....Dr. Kavita K. PANDIT
28 Assoc Prov/Chief Diversity Officer ....Dr. Michelle G. COOK
45 Int Assoc Provost Academic Planning ....Dr. Jerome S. LEGGE
88 Assoc Provost/Economic Development ....Dr. Margaret W. DAHL
13 CIO & Associate Provost ....Dr. Timothy M. CHESTER
08 University Librarian/Assoc Provost ....Dr. William G. POTTER
07 Assoc VP Admissions/Enroll Mgmt ....Ms. Nancy G. MCDUFF
21 Sr Assoc VP Finance/Administration ....Mr. Ryan A. NESBIT
18 Assoc Vice President Physical Plant ....Mr. Ralph F. JOHNSON
15 Associate VP Human Resources ....Mr. Tom E. GAUSVIK
43 Executive Director of Legal Affairs ....Mr. Stephen M. SHEWMAKER
49 Dean of Arts & Sciences ....Dr. Alan T. DORSEY
47 Dean of Agricultural & Environ Sci ....Dr. J. Scott ANGLE
61 Dean of Law ....Ms. Rebecca H. WHITE
67 Dean of Pharmacy ....Dr. Svein OIE
65 Dean Forestry & Natural Resources ....Dr. Michael L. CLUTTER
53 Dean of Education ....Dr. Arthur M. HORNE
58 Dean of the Graduate School ....Dr. Maureen GRASSO
50 Dean of Business ....Dr. Robert T. SUMICHRAST
60 Dean Journalism & Mass Comm ....Dr. E. Culpepper CLARK
59 Dean of Family/Consumer Science ....Dr. Linda K. FOX
74 Dean of Veterinary Medicine ....Dr. Sheila W. ALLEN
70 Dean of Social Work ....Dr. Maurice C. DANIELS
48 Dean of Environment & Design ....Mr. Daniel J. NADENICEK
80 Dean of Public/International Affs ....Dr. Thomas P. LAUTH
69 Dean of Public Health ....Dr. Phillip L. WILLIAMS
88 Dean School of Ecology ....Dr. John L. GITTLEMAN
92 Director of Honors Program ....Dr. David S. WILLIAMS
88 Dean GHSU/UGA Medical ....Dr. Barbara L. SCHUSTER
41 Athletic Director ....Mr. William G. MCGARITY
22 Int Director of Equal Opportunity ....Ms. Eryn J. DAWKINS
06 Registrar ....Dr. Jan M. HATHCOTE
19 Chief of Police ....Chief James E. WILLIAMSON
37 Director of Student Financial Aid ....Ms. Bonnie C. JOERSCHKE
36 Director of Career Services Center ....Mr. Scott T. WILLIAMS
39 Executive Director of Housing ....Dr. Gerard J. KOWALSKI
23 Exec Director of Health Services ....Dr. Jean E. CHIN
35 Dean of Students ....Dr. William M. MCDONALD
38 Dir Counseling/Psychological Svcs ....Dr. Gayle M. ROBBINS
51 Dir of Georgia Ctr Continuing Educ ....Dr. William R. CROWE

29 Exec Director of Alumni Relations .... Ms. Deborah H. DIETZLER
30 Assoc Vice Pres Development .... Mr. Robert S. HAWKINS
09 Int Dir of Institutional Research .... Ms. Tracie W. SAPP
88 Director of Academic Enhancement .... Dr. Earl GINTER
94 Director Inst of Women's Studies . Dr. Juanita JOHNSON-BAILEY
96 Director of Purchasing .... Ms. Annette EVANS

† Part of the University System of Georgia.

University of West Georgia (A)

1601 Maple Street, Carrollton GA 30118-0001
County: Carroll FICE Identification: 001601
Unit ID: 141334
Telephone: (678) 839-5000 Carnegie Class: Master's L
FAX Number: (678) 839-4766 Calendar System: Semester
URL: www.westga.edu
Established: 1906 Annual Undergrad Tuition & Fees (In-State): $6,710
Enrollment: 11,646 Coed
Affiliation or Control: State IRS Status: 501(c)3
Highest Offering: Doctorate
Program: Occupational; Liberal Arts And General; Teacher Preparatory; Professional
Accreditation: SC, ART, BUS, BUSA, CACREP, CS, MUS, NURSE, SP, SPAA, TED, THEA

01 President .... Dr. Beheruz N. SETHNA
05 Provost & VP for Academic Affairs .... Dr. Michael HORVATH
10 Vice President Business & Finance .... Mr. Jim SUTHERLAND
32 Vice President for Student Affairs .... Dr. Scott LINGRELL
26 Vice President of Univ Advancement .... Mr. Bill ESTES
30 Director of Development .... Ms. Diane HOMESLEY
20 Deputy Provost .... Dr. Jon ANDERSON
84 Assoc VP for Enrollment Mgt .... Vacant
20 Associate VP for Academic Affairs .... Dr. Myrna GANTNER
21 University Controller .... Mr. Richard SEARS
83 Dean of Social Sciences .... Dr. N. Jane MCCANDLESS
50 Dean of Business .... Dr. Faye S. MCINTYRE
53 Dean of Education .... Dr. Dianne HOFF
79 Dean College of Arts and Humanities .... Dr. Randy HENDRICKS
81 Dean Science and Mathematics .... Dr. Bruce LANDMAN
92 Dean & Director of Honors College .... Dr. Michael D. HESTER
06 Registrar .... Ms. Donna HALEY
07 Director of Admissions .... Mr. Justin BARLOW
08 Director of Libraries .... Ms. Lorene FLANDERS
37 Director of Financial Aid .... Ms. Kimberly L. JORDAN
36 Director of Career Services .... Ms. Wanda R. MCGUKIN
27 Chief Information Officer .... Mrs. Kathy KRAL
51 Director of Continuing Education .... Mr. James L. AGAN
15 Dir of Human Res/Affirm Action Ofcr .... Ms. Stephanie ROOKS
18 Director Facilities/Administration .... Mr. Robert S. WATKINS
19 Director of University Police .... Mr. Thomas J. MACKEL
23 Director of Health Services .... Dr. Leslie COTTRELL
35 Director of the Campus Center .... Mr. Matthew MILLER
39 Director of Residence Life .... Mr. Stephen WHITLOCK
41 Director of Athletics .... Mr. Daryl DICKEY
38 Dir of Counseling & Career Dev .... Dr. Lisa ADAMS
88 Dir Business Svcs/Auxiliary Enterpr .... Mr. Mark REEVES
09 Director Inst Research/Planning .... Dr. Ebenezer KOLAJO
29 Director of Alumni Relations .... Mr. H. Franklin PRITCHETT
89 Director of EXEL Center .... Mrs. Cheryl A. RICE
26 Asst Vice President of UA .... Ms. Jami BOWER
40 Asst Bookstore Manager .... Ms. Beth ADAMS
25 Assoc VP Research & Spons Projects .... Dr. Arlene HORNE
55 Dean of USG eCore .... Dr. Melanie N. CLAY
12 Director-Newnan Campus .... Ms. Cathy WRIGHT
44 Director of Planned Giving .... Mr. Ernie HENDERSON
28 Director of Diversity .... Vacant
24 Assistant Dir for Classroom Support .... Mr. Brian MCCRARY
43 University Legal Counsel .... Ms. Jane SIMPSON
104 Dir of International Svcs & Pgms .... Dr. William SCHANIEL
102 Assoc Exec Dir of WG Foundation .... Mr. Bart GILLESPIE
66 Dean School of Nursing .... Dr. Kathyrn GRAMS

† Part of the University System of Georgia.

*University System of Georgia Office (B)

270 Washington Street, SW, Atlanta GA 30334-9007
County: Fulton FICE Identification: 008290
Telephone: (404) 656-2202 Carnegie Class: N/A
FAX Number: (404) 657-6979
URL: www.usg.edu

01 Chancellor .... Mr. Hank M. HUCKABY
04 Executive Assistant to Chancellor .... Ms. Sabrina THOMPSON
11 Exec Vice Chanc Administration .... Mr. Steve WRIGLEY
05 Exec Vice Chanc/Chief Academic Ofcr .... Dr. Houston DAVIS
10 Vice Chancellor Fiscal Affairs .... Mr. John BROWN
21 Chief Audit Officer .... Mr. John M. FUCHKO, III
26 Sr Vice Chanc External Affairs .... Mr. Thomas E. DANIEL
18 Vice Chancellor Facilities .... Ms. Linda DANIELS
13 Vice Chanc/Chief Info Officer .... Dr. Curt CARVER
27 Assoc Vice Chanc Media/Publications .... Mr. John MILLSAPS

Valdosta State University (C)

1500 N Patterson Street, Valdosta GA 31698-0010
County: Lowndes FICE Identification: 001599
Unit ID: 141264
Telephone: (229) 333-5800 Carnegie Class: Master's L
FAX Number: (229) 333-7400 Calendar System: Semester
URL: www.valdosta.edu
Established: 1906 Annual Undergrad Tuition & Fees (In-State): $5,792
Enrollment: 13,089 Coed
Affiliation or Control: State IRS Status: 501(c)3
Highest Offering: Doctorate
Program: 2-Year Principally Bachelor's Creditable; Liberal Arts And General; Teacher Preparatory
Accreditation: SC, ART, BUS, CACREP, #LIB, MFCD, MUS, NURSE, SP, SPAA, SW, TED, THEA

01 President .... Dr. William MCKINNEY
05 Acting VP Academic Affairs .... Dr. Karla HULL
10 Vice President for Finance & Admin .... Ms. Sue E. FUCIARELLI
30 Vice President for Advancement .... Mr. John D. CRAWFORD
32 Vice Pres for Student Affairs .... Mr. Russell F. MAST
84 Assoc VP for Enrollment Management .... Mr. Andy T. CLARK
58 Asst VP for Rsrch & Dean of Grad .... Dr. Alfred FUCIARELLI
45 Asst to President Strategic Rsrch .... Vacant
49 Dean College of Arts & Sciences .... Dr. Connie L. RICHARDS
50 Dean College of Business Admin .... Dr. Wayne L. PLUMLY
57 Dean College of the Arts .... Dr. John C. GASTON
53 Acting Dean College of Education .... Dr. Brian GERBER
66 Dean College of Nursing .... Dr. Anita G. HUFFT
06 Registrar .... Mr. Stanley JONES
13 Chief Information Officer .... Mr. Joseph A. NEWTON
39 Director Housing & Residence Life .... Dr. Thomas W. HARDY
07 Director Admissions/Enrollment Mgmt .... Mr. Walter H. PEACOCK
08 University Librarian .... Dr. Alan BERNSTEIN
37 Director of Financial Aid .... Mr. Douglas R. TANNER
31 Director of Public Services .... Mr. Bill MUNTZ
88 Dir of Publication & Design Service .... Mr. Jeff GRANT
36 Dir Career Services/Cooperative Ed .... Ms. Winifred V. COLLINS
15 Director of Human Resources .... Dr. Denise BOGART
88 Director Division Aerospace Studies .... LtCol. Marsha ALEEM
22 Director of Social Equity .... Dr. Maggie J. VIVERETTE
43 University Attorney .... Ms. Laverne L. GASKINS
18 Dir Phys Plant & Facilities Plng .... Mr. Ray SABLE
26 Dir Marketing & Cmty Relations .... Ms. Mary B. GOODING
38 Director of Counseling Center .... Dr. John GROTGEN

† Part of the University System of Georgia.

Waycross College (D)

2001 S Georgia Parkway, Waycross GA 31503-0110
County: Ware FICE Identification: 020550
Unit ID: 141307
Telephone: (912) 449-7500 Carnegie Class: Assoc/Pub-R-S
FAX Number: (912) 449-7614 Calendar System: Semester
URL: www.waycross.edu
Established: 1976 Annual Undergrad Tuition & Fees (In-State): $3,174
Enrollment: 964 Coed
Affiliation or Control: State IRS Status: 501(c)3
Highest Offering: Associate Degree
Program: Occupational; 2-Year Principally Bachelor's Creditable
Accreditation: SC

01 Interim President .... Dr. Mary Ellen WILSON
05 Int Vice Pres/Dean Academic Affairs .... Ms. Sara E. SELBY
10 Vice President Business Affairs .... Ms. Melissa LEE
84 Vice Pres Enrollment/Student Svcs .... Ms. Sara E. SELBY
20 Assoc Dean for Academic Affairs .... Ms. Sara E. SELBY
08 Director of Library Services .... Ms. Sharon L. KELLY
32 Director for Student Life .... Ms. Sharon K. KOMANECKY
31 Director Development/Community Svcs ..... Mr. Taylor HEREFORD
18 Director Physical Plant .... Mr. Harbin FARR
09 Director of Institutional Research .... Vacant
15 Director Personnel Services .... Vacant
30 Chief Devel/Public & Alumni Rels .... Mr. Taylor HEREFORD
13 Director of Computer Services .... Mr. Corry JOHNSON
37 Director Student Financial Aid .... Ms. Debbie M. HOWARD
06 Registrar/Director of Admissions .... Mr. Rob WINGFIELD
26 Chief Public Relations Officer .... Mr. Taylor HEREFORD
28 Director of Diversity .... Ms. Sara SELBY
29 Director Alumni Relations .... Mr. Taylor HEREFORD
38 Director Student Counseling .... Ms. Sharon KOMANECKY
96 Director of Purchasing .... Ms. Rhonda BLOUNT
35 Asst Director Student Support .... Ms. Angela HOLLAND-WASDIN
40 Bookstore Manager .... Ms. Rhonda ANDERSON

† Part of the University System of Georgia.

Wesleyan College (E)

4760 Forsyth Road, Macon GA 31210-4462
County: Bibb FICE Identification: 001600
Unit ID: 141325
Telephone: (478) 477-1110 Carnegie Class: Bac/A&S
FAX Number: (478) 757-4030 Calendar System: Semester
URL: www.wesleyancollege.edu
Established: 1836 Annual Undergrad Tuition & Fees: $19,000
Enrollment: 683 Female
Affiliation or Control: United Methodist IRS Status: 501(c)3
Highest Offering: Master's
Program: Liberal Arts And General; Teacher Preparatory
Accreditation: SC, MUS

01 President .... Ms. Ruth A. KNOX
05 Dean of the College .... Dr. Vivia L. FOWLER
30 VP Institutional Advancement .... Ms. Susan T. WELSH
10 Vice Pres Finance/Treasurer .... Mr. Richard P. MAIER
32 Vice Pres for Student Affairs .... Ms. Patricia M. GIBBS
84 Vice Pres for Enrollment Services .... Mr. C. Stephen FARR
06 Assistant Dean/Registrar .... Ms. Patricia R. HARDEMAN
04 Assistant to the President .... Ms. Denise W. HOLLOWAY
04 Assistant to the President .... Mrs. Sally A. HEMINGWAY
08 Library Director .... Ms. Sybil MCNEIL
13 Director of Information Services .... Mr. Kevin L. ULSHAFER
29 Director of Alumnae Affairs .... Ms. Cathy C. SNOW
26 Director of Communications .... Ms. Mary Ann HOWARD
44 Director of Annual Fund .... Ms. Andrea G. WILLIFORD
37 Director of Financial Aid .... Ms. Danielle LODGE
39 Director of Residence Life .... Ms. Stefanie SWANGER
18 Director of Physical Plant .... Ms. Kelly BLEDSOE
41 Athletic Director .... Ms. Patty GIBBS
42 Chaplain .... Rev. Bill HURDLE
19 Director Security/Safety .... Mr. Clinton BRANTLEY
15 Director Human Resources .... Ms. Meagon DAVIS
07 Director of Admissions .... Ms. Danielle LODGE
09 Director of Institutional Research .... Ms. Angie WRIGHT
32 Chief Student Life Officer .... Ms. Stefanie SWANGER
36 Director Career Development .... Ms. Monica MOODY
38 Director Student Counseling .... Ms. Jamie THAMES
96 Director of Purchasing .... Ms. Lindsay TIMMS
20 Associate Academic Officer .... Ms. Patricia R. HARDEMAN
21 Associate Business Officer .... Ms. Dawn P. NASH
40 Bookstore Manager .... Ms. Lindsay TIMMS

West Georgia Technical College (F)

176 Murphy Campus Boulevard, Waco GA 30182-2407
County: Haralson FICE Identification: 010487
Unit ID: 139278
Telephone: (770) 537-6000 Carnegie Class: Assoc/Pub-S-SC
FAX Number: (770) 537-7976 Calendar System: Semester
URL: www.westgatech.edu
Established: 1968 Annual Undergrad Tuition & Fees (In-State): $3,288
Enrollment: 7,331 Coed
Affiliation or Control: State IRS Status: 501(c)3
Highest Offering: Associate Degree
Program: Occupational; 2-Year Principally Bachelor's Creditable; Technical Emphasis
Accreditation: SC, ACBSP, ADNUR, DH, MAC, MLTAD, RAD, SURGT

01 President .... Dr. Skip SULLIVAN
05 Vice President Academic Affairs .... Mr. Patrick K. HANNON
32 Vice President Student Affairs .... Mr. Eddie GORE
30 Vice Pres Institutional Advancement .... Mrs. Dawn COOK
09 VP Institutional Effectiveness .... Dr. Kristen DOUGLAS
20 Asst Vice Pres For Curriculum .... Dr. Sindi MCGOWAN
08 Director Library Services .... Mrs. Mary MCCLUNG
06 Registrar .... Mrs. Laura JAKUBIAK
13 Exec Dir Information Technology .... Mr. Brian HENDERSON
07 Director of Admissions .... Mrs. Mary ADERHOLD
18 Director Facilities .... Mr. Michael JILES

Westwood College-Atlanta Midtown (G)

1100 Spring Street, Suite 102, Atlanta GA 30309-2824
County: Fulton Identification: 666421
Unit ID: 445072
Telephone: (404) 745-9862 Carnegie Class: Bac/Assoc
FAX Number: (404) 892-7253 Calendar System: Semester
URL: www.westwood.edu
Established: 2004 Annual Undergrad Tuition & Fees: $14,923
Enrollment: 581 Coed
Affiliation or Control: Proprietary IRS Status: Proprietary
Highest Offering: Baccalaureate
Program: Occupational
Accreditation: ACICS

01 President of Campus .... Bryan GULEBIAN

† Branch campus of Westwood College-DuPage, Woodbridge, IL.

Westwood College-Atlanta Northlake (H)

2309 Parklake Drive NE, Atlanta GA 30345-2906
County: Dekalb Identification: 666597
Unit ID: 445276
Telephone: (866) 821-6145 Carnegie Class: Bac/Assoc
FAX Number: (770) 934-9539 Calendar System: Quarter
URL: www.westwood.edu
Established: N/A Annual Undergrad Tuition & Fees: $14,923
Enrollment: 491 Coed
Affiliation or Control: Proprietary IRS Status: Proprietary
Highest Offering: Baccalaureate
Program: Occupational; Liberal Arts And General
Accreditation: ACICS, MAC

01 Campus President .... Ms. Tira H. CLAY

† Branch campus of Westwood College-O'Hare Airport, Chicago, IL.

Wiregrass Georgia Technical College (I)

4089 Val Tech Road, Valdosta GA 31602
County: Lowndes FICE Identification: 005256
Unit ID: 141255
Telephone: (229) 333-2100 Carnegie Class: Assoc/Pub-R-M
FAX Number: (229) 333-2129 Calendar System: Semester
URL: www.wiregrass.edu
Established: 1963 Annual Undergrad Tuition & Fees (In-State): $2,552
Enrollment: 4,382 Coed

Affiliation or Control: State IRS Status: 501(c)3
Highest Offering: Associate Degree
Program: Occupational; 2-Year Principally Bachelor's Creditable; Technical Emphasis
Accreditation: SC, DA, DH, MLTAD, SURGT

01 President .... Dr. Ray PERREN
03 Provost .... Ms. Lisa TOMBERLIN
50 VP for Academic Affairs .... Dr. Ron O'MEARA
11 VP for Administrative Services .... Ms. Keren WYNN
32 VP for Student Affairs .... Ms. Connie SUMNER
09 VP for Institutional Effectiveness .... Dr. Helen PENNY
88 VP for Adult Education .... Mr. Alvin PAYTON
46 VP for Economic Development .... Ms. Lidell GREENWAY
26 Executive Dir for Public Relations .... Ms. Angela HOBBY

Young Harris College (A)

PO Box 694, Young Harris GA 30582-0098
County: Towns FICE Identification: 001604
Unit ID: 141361
Telephone: (706) 379-3111 Carnegie Class: Assoc/PrivNFP
FAX Number: (706) 379-4319 Calendar System: Semester
URL: www.yhc.edu
Established: 1886 Annual Undergrad Tuition & Fees: $23,004
Enrollment: 886 Coed
Affiliation or Control: United Methodist IRS Status: 501(c)3
Highest Offering: Baccalaureate
Program: Liberal Arts And General
Accreditation: SC, MUS

01 President .... Dr. Cathy COX
05 Vice Pres for Academic Affairs .... Dr. Gary MYERS
11 Senior VP for Finance & Admin .... Mr. David LEOPARD
10 Vice President for Finance .... Mr. Wade M. BENSON
32 Vice President for Student Affairs .... Ms. Susan ROGERS
84 Vice Pres for Enrollment Management .... Mr. Clinton G. HOBBS
30 Vice President of Advancement .... Mr. Jay STROMAN
45 VP for Planning and Assessment .... Ms. Rosemary R. ROYSTON
14 Vice President of Campus Technology .... Mr. Ken FANEUFF
29 Director of Alumni Relations .... Ms. Dana ENSLEY
20 Associate Academic Officer .... Dr. Keith DEFOOR
08 Librarian .... Ms. Dawn LAMADE
38 Counselor .... Ms. Lynne GRADY
06 Registrar .... Ms. Tammy GIBSON
37 Director Student Financial Aid .... Ms. Linda ADAMS
07 Director of Admissions .... Vacant
15 Director Personnel Services .... Mr. Vince ROBELOTTO
26 Chief Public Relations Officer .... Ms. Denise COOK
18 Chief Facilities/Physical Plant .... Mr. Jim RAWSKI
19 Director of Safety & Compliance .... Vacant
41 Athletic Director .... Mr. Randy DUNN
42 Campus Minister .... Rev. Tim MOORE

HAWAII

Argosy University, Hawaii (B)

400 ABS Tower, 1001 Bishop Street, Honolulu HI 96813
County: Honolulu Identification: 666787
Unit ID: 366748
Telephone: (808) 536-5555 Carnegie Class: Master's S
FAX Number: (808) 536-5505 Calendar System: Semester
URL: www.argosy.edu/hawaii
Established: 1994 Annual Undergrad Tuition & Fees: $13,224
Enrollment: 533 Coed
Affiliation or Control: Proprietary IRS Status: Proprietary
Highest Offering: Doctorate
Program: Professional
Accreditation: &WC, CLPSY

01 Campus President .... Dr. Warren EVANS
05 Vice President of Acad Affairs .... Dr. Zachary OLIVER
07 Senior Director of Admissions .... Paul BILLINGTON
32 Director of Student Services .... Cherie ANDRADE
15 Human Resources .... Maria FERNANDEZ
11 Dir of Admin and Financial Svcs .... Vacant

† Regional accreditation is carried under the parent institution in Orange, CA.

Babel University Professional School of Translation (C)

1833 Kalakaua Avenue, #208, Honolulu HI 96815
County: Honolulu Identification: 666350
Telephone: (808) 946-3773 Carnegie Class: Not Classified
FAX Number: (808) 946-3993 Calendar System: Other
URL: www.babel.edu
Established: 2000 Annual Graduate Tuition & Fees: $19,450
Enrollment: 69 Coed
Affiliation or Control: Proprietary IRS Status: Proprietary
Highest Offering: Master's; No Undergraduates
Program: Professional
Accreditation: DETC

01 Chancellor .... Dr. Miyoko YUASA
05 Head of Deans .... Mr. Yoshiharu ISHIDA

Brigham Young University Hawaii (D)

55-220 Kulanui Street, Laie Oahu HI 96762-1294
County: Honolulu FICE Identification: 001606
Unit ID: 230047
Telephone: (808) 675-3211 Carnegie Class: Bac/Diverse
FAX Number: (808) 675-3329 Calendar System: Semester
URL: www.byuh.edu
Established: 1955 Annual Undergrad Tuition & Fees: $4,630
Enrollment: 2,716 Coed
Affiliation or Control: Latter-day Saints IRS Status: 501(c)3
Highest Offering: Baccalaureate
Program: Liberal Arts And General; Teacher Preparatory; Professional
Accreditation: WC, SW

01 President .... Dr. Steven C. WHEELWRIGHT
05 Vice President for Academics .... Dr. Max L. CHECKETTS
11 VP for Administrative Services .... Mr. Michael B. BLISS
32 VP for Student Development & Svcs .... Dr. Debbie HIPPOLITE WRIGHT
18 VP Construction Facilities & Maint .... Mr. David A. LEWIS
04 Administrative Asst to the Pres .... Ms. Lisa FEHOKO
108 Assoc Academic VP for Assessment .... Dr. William G. NEAL
20 Assoc Academic VP for Instruction .... Dr. D. Chad COMPTON
20 Assoc Academic VP for Curriculum .... Dr. Jennifer LANE
81 Dean College of Math and Sciences .... Dr. W. Jeffrey BURROUGHS
88 Dean College of Bus/Computing/Govt .... Dr. Glade TEW
88 Dean College of Human Development .... Dr. John BAILEY
88 Dean College of Lang/Culture & Arts .... Dr. Phillip MCARTHUR
13 University Technology Officer .... Mr. Kevin SCHLAG
07 Director Enrollment Services .... Mr. Arapata MEHA
41 Director of Athletics .... Mr. Ken WAGNER
08 Director University Library .... Michael ALDRICH
51 Director of Educational Outreach .... Mrs. Edna OWAN
88 Director Budget Services .... Mr. Steven TUELLER
96 Director of Purchasing & Travel .... Mr. Robert OWAN
19 Director Safety/Security & Risk Mgt .... Mr. Roy YAMAMOTO
15 Director of Human Resources .... Mrs. Tessie FAUSTINO
18 Director Facilities Management .... Mr. Judd WHETTEN
10 Director Financial Services .... Mr. Eric MARLER
40 Director Bookstore .... Mr. Kenway L. KUA
23 Director Health Center .... Dr. P. Douglas NIELSON
88 Dir Compliance & Internal Audit .... Mr. Adam R. JACOBSMEYER
36 Director Career Services .... Mrs. Jodi CHOWEN
39 Director Housing & Residential Life .... Mr. John A. ELKINGTON
38 Director of Counseling Services .... Dr. Paul BUCKINGHAM
35 Director Student Leadership & Honor .... Mr. David LUCERO
88 Director Food Services .... Mr. David KEALA
26 Director Communications .... Mr. Michael JOHANSON
88 Director Testing and Assessment .... Dr. Paul H. FREEBAIRN

† Affiliated with Brigham Young University, Provo, UT.

Chaminade University of Honolulu (E)

3140 Waialae Avenue, Honolulu HI 96816-1578
County: Honolulu FICE Identification: 001605
Unit ID: 141486
Telephone: (808) 735-4711 Carnegie Class: Master's L
FAX Number: (808) 735-4870 Calendar System: Semester
URL: www.chaminade.edu
Established: 1955 Annual Undergrad Tuition & Fees: $19,200
Enrollment: 2,822 Coed
Affiliation or Control: Independent Non-Profit IRS Status: 501(c)3
Highest Offering: Master's
Program: Liberal Arts And General; Teacher Preparatory; Professional
Accreditation: WC, MACTE

01 President .... Bro. Bernard PLOEGER, SM
04 Exec Assistant to the President .... Bro. Frank DAMM, SM
05 Provost .... Dr. Larry OSBORNE
30 VP for Institutional Advancement .... Ms. Diane PETERS-NGUYEN
10 Vice President Finance/Facilities .... Ms. Aulani KAANOI
13 Dean of Info Services & Library .... Dr. Larry OSBORNE
84 Dean of Enrollment Management .... Ms. Joy BOUEY
32 Dean of Students .... Ms. Grissel BENITZ-HODGE
35 Associate Dean of Students .... Ms. Allison JEROME
88 Assoc Dean of Enrollment Mgmt .... Ms. Amy TAKIGUCHI
88 Dir Academic Advising/Retention .... Mr. Curtis WASHBURN
90 Director Network/Desktop Services .... Mr. Eddie PANG
55 Dir Adult Evening & Online Programs .... Mr. Skip LEE
91 Director of Management Info Svcs .... Mr. Jorge HERNANDEZ
29 Director of Alumni Relations .... Ms. Be-Jay KODAMA
41 Director of Athletics .... Mr. William VILLA
42 Director of Campus Ministry .... Mr. Danny O'REGAN
36 Dir Career Develop/Job Placement .... Ms. Kimberley GRAVES
18 Director of Facilities Operations .... Mr. Michael HAISEN
11 Director of Administrative Services .... Ms. Elaine OISHI
21 Director of Finance .... Vacant
07 Director of Admissions .... Ms. Joy BOUEY
08 Director of Library .... Ms. Sharon LEPAGE
15 Director Personnel Services .... Mrs. Lucy STREETER
19 Supervisor of Security .... Mr. Melvin DECOSTA
38 Director of Student Counseling .... Dr. June YASUHARA
06 Registrar .... Mr. John MORRIS
37 Director Student Financial Aid .... Ms. Amy TAKIGUCHI
09 Institutional Research Specialist .... Mr. Hieu NGUYEN

Hawaii College of Oriental Medicine (F)

93 Banyan Drive, Suite 504, Hilo HI 96720
County: Hawaii FICE Identification: 039994
Unit ID: 449579
Telephone: (808) 981-2790 Carnegie Class: Spec/Health
FAX Number: (808) 933-1369 Calendar System: Trimester
URL: www.hicom.edu
Established: 1986 Annual Graduate Tuition & Fees: $14,628
Enrollment: 8 Coed
Affiliation or Control: Independent Non-Profit IRS Status: 501(c)3
Highest Offering: Master's; No Undergraduates
Program: Professional
Accreditation: ACUP

01 President .... Dr. Jacqueline HAHN
05 Academic Dean .... Ms. Megan J. YARBERRY
11 Director of Operations .... Mr. Greg BAKER

Hawaii Pacific University (G)

1164 Bishop Street, Suite 800, Honolulu HI 96813-2882
County: Honolulu FICE Identification: 007279
Unit ID: 141644
Telephone: (808) 544-0200 Carnegie Class: Master's L
FAX Number: (808) 544-1136 Calendar System: Semester
URL: www.hpu.edu
Established: 1965 Annual Undergrad Tuition & Fees: $18,500
Enrollment: 8,071 Coed
Affiliation or Control: Independent Non-Profit IRS Status: 501(c)3
Highest Offering: Master's
Program: Liberal Arts And General; Teacher Preparatory; Professional
Accreditation: WC, NUR, NURSE, SW

01 President .... Dr. Geoff BANNISTER
00 President Emeritus .... Mr. Chatt G. WRIGHT
05 Vice President of Academic Affairs .... Dr. Andrew BRITTAIN
20 Assistant VP Academic Affairs .... Mr. Joe SCHMIEDL
56 Assoc VP Off-Campus/Military Pgm .... Mr. Robert CYBORON
88 Director Instructional Innovation .... Dr. Stephanie SCHULL
35 Exec Dir Student Academic Services .... Ms. Deborah NAKASHIMA
84 Vice Pres Enrollment Management .... Mr. Scott STENSRUD
10 VP/Chief Financial Officer .... Mr. William KLINE
09 Vice Pres Institutional Research .... Dr. Leslie H. CORREA
15 Assistant VP Human Resources .... Ms. Cecilia SHANER
30 Vice Pres Alumni & Univ Relations .... Ms. Mary Ellen MCGILLAN
21 Associate VP/Controller .... Ms. Kathleen CLARK
50 Dean Business Administration .... Dr. Deborah CROWNE
66 Acting Dean Nursing/Health Sciences .... Dr. Dale ALLISON
81 Dean Natural/Computational Sciences .... Dr. Andrew BRITTAIN
60 Dean Humanities & Social Sciences .... Dr. Steven COMBS
89 Dean of Students .... Ms. Marites MCKEY
13 Chief Application Officer .... Mr. Robert SLIKE
106 Assistant Dean Distance Ed Policy .... Dr. Asoke DATTA
85 Dir Intl Admis/Recruit/Student Srvs .... Ms. Lilian HALLSTROM
97 Assistant Dean General Education .... Dr. Malia SMITH
07 Director of Admissions .... Ms. Sara SATO
09 Academic Information Analyst .... Mr. John IGE
104 Director Intl Exchange/Study Abroad .... Dr. Jon DAVIDANN
36 Director Career Svcs Ctr/Co-op Educ .... Mr. Joseph BARRIENTOS
06 Registrar .... Vacant
37 Director Financial Aid .... Mr. Adam HATCH
41 Athletic Director .... Mr. Darren VORDERBRUEGGE
51 Assoc Dir Adult Learning Program .... Ms. Jill MERL
105 Director Web Services .... Mr. Abe TOMA
08 University Librarian .... Ms. Kathleen CHEE
42 University Chaplain .... Rev. Dale BURKE
14 Director Computing Services .... Ms. Lisa CARPENTER
88 Dir Admin Support Operations .... Ms. Jamie KEMP
19 Assoc Director Security and Safety .... Mr. Wayne FERNANDEZ
18 Manager Facilities/Physical Plant .... Mr. Steve HENDRICKS
40 Bookstore Manager .... Ms. Shellee HEEN
29 Alumni/Parent Relations Coordinator .... Ms. Kris SMITH
38 Director Counseling/Behavioral Hlth .... Dr. Kevin BOWMAN
96 Procurement Director .... Mr. Kevin WETTER

Hawaii Tokai International College (H)

2241 Kapiolani Boulevard, Honolulu HI 96826-4310
County: Honolulu FICE Identification: 037603
Telephone: (808) 983-4100 Carnegie Class: Not Classified
FAX Number: (808) 983-4107 Calendar System: Quarter
URL: www.hawaiitokai.edu
Established: 1992 Annual Undergrad Tuition & Fees: $11,430
Enrollment: 121 Coed
Affiliation or Control: Independent Non-Profit IRS Status: 501(c)3
Highest Offering: Associate Degree
Program: 2-Year Principally Bachelor's Creditable; Liberal Arts And General
Accreditation: WJ

01 Chancellor .... Dr. Naoto YOSHIKAWA
05 Vice Chancellor .... Dr. Douglas FUQUA
11 Exec Director of Administration .... Mr. Yuzo OIDA
20 Dean of Instruction .... Dr. Deanna MADDEN
46 Director Program Development .... Ms. Wanda SAKO
08 Librarian .... Ms. Suzanne HARTER
32 Director Student Services .... Ms. Jaelee HEUPEL
15 Human Resources Officer .... Ms. Janice DAWSON
21 Finance Department .... Mr. Mark GREENE
29 Alum Rel Coord/Std Sup Specialist .... Mr. Andrew FUJIMOTO

Heald College, Honolulu (A)

1500 Kapiolani Boulevard, Honolulu HI 96814-3797
County: Honolulu FICE Identification: 004546
Unit ID: 141468
Telephone: (808) 955-1500 Carnegie Class: Assoc/PrivFP
FAX Number: (808) 955-6964 Calendar System: Quarter
URL: www.heald.edu
Established: 1863 Annual Undergrad Tuition & Fees: $17,200
Enrollment: 1,844 Coed
Affiliation or Control: Proprietary IRS Status: Proprietary
Highest Offering: Associate Degree
Program: Occupational
Accreditation: &WJ, DA, MAC

01 Regional VP/Campus Operation .... Mrs. Evelyn A. SCHEMMEL
03 Campus Vice President .... Mr. Michael C. VAN LEAR
10 Director of Financial Services .... Mr. Arthur VALENZUELA
05 Director of Academic Affairs .... Mrs. Merrill W. CUTTING

† Regional accreditation is carried under the parent institution Heald College, Central Office in San Francisco, CA.

Institute of Clinical Acupuncture and Oriental Medicine (B)

100 N Beretania Street, Suite 203 B,
Honolulu HI 96817-4709
County: Honolulu FICE Identification: 037353
Unit ID: 444699
Telephone: (808) 521-2288 Carnegie Class: Spec/Health
FAX Number: (808) 521-2271 Calendar System: Semester
URL: www.orientalmedicine.edu
Established: 1996 Annual Graduate Tuition & Fees: $12,810
Enrollment: 46 Coed
Affiliation or Control: Proprietary IRS Status: Proprietary
Highest Offering: Master's; No Undergraduates
Program: Professional
Accreditation: ACUP

01 President .... Dr. Wai Hoa LOW
05 Chancellor Academic Affairs .... Dr. Edmund BERNAUER
63 Clinic Director .... Dr. Catherine Yu-Ling LOW

New Hope Christian College-Hawaii (C)

290 Sand Island Access Road, Honolulu HI 96819
County: Honolulu Identification: 667010
Unit ID: 457484
Telephone: (808) 853-1040 Carnegie Class: Not Classified
FAX Number: (808) 853-1042 Calendar System: Semester
URL: hawaii.newhope.edu/
Established: 1998 Annual Undergrad Tuition & Fees: $7,592
Enrollment: 124 Coed
Affiliation or Control: Independent Non-Profit IRS Status: 501(c)3
Highest Offering: Baccalaureate
Program: Religious Emphasis
Accreditation: @BI

00 Chancellor .... Dr. Wayne CORDEIRO
01 President .... Guy HIGASHI
05 Dean & Executive Officer .... Dr. Randall FURUSHIMA
03 Executive Director .... Gary LOU
06 Registrar .... Martha STINTON
84 Director of Enrollment Management .... Lori HIGASHI
32 Director of Student Life .... Mia BURKE
10 Director of Business Administration .... James W. KAHLER

Remington College-Honolulu Campus (D)

1111 Bishop Street, Suite 400, Honolulu HI 96813-2811
County: Honolulu Identification: 666028
Unit ID: 372958
Telephone: (808) 942-1000 Carnegie Class: Bac/Assoc
FAX Number: (808) 533-3064 Calendar System: Quarter
URL: www.remingtoncollege.edu
Established: 1999 Annual Undergrad Tuition & Fees: $16,140
Enrollment: 646 Coed
Affiliation or Control: Proprietary IRS Status: Proprietary
Highest Offering: Baccalaureate
Program: 2-Year Principally Bachelor's Creditable; Liberal Arts And General; Business Emphasis
Accreditation: ACCSC

01 President .... Mr. Louis LAMAIR
05 Director of Education .... Mr. Charles STRATTON
37 Director of Financial Services .... Ms. Debbie USO
07 Director of Admissions .... Mr. Jonathan HUGHES
36 Director of Career Services .... Mrs. Leah HARVELL
06 Registrar .... Ms. Lyann LEE
08 Director of Information Resources .... Mr. Glen ARAKAKI
04 Executive Assistant .... Ms. Alison ROMERO
76 Dept Chr Clinical Med Assisting .... Dr. Salvacion CHONG
77 Dept Chr Computer Networking Tech .... Mr. John SCOTT
83 Department Chair Criminal Justice .... Mr. Hector WEST
88 Dept Chair International Business .... Mr. Mark LANGENBACHER

† Branch campus of Remington College, Mobile, AL.

*University of Hawaii System Office (E)

2444 Dole Street, Honolulu HI 96822
County: Honolulu FICE Identification: 007885
Unit ID: 141963
Telephone: (808) 956-8207 Carnegie Class: N/A
FAX Number: (808) 956-5286
URL: www.hawaii.edu

01 President .... Dr. M. R. C GREENWOOD
05 Exec VP for Academic Affs/Provost .... Dr. Linda K. JOHNSRUD
46 Vice President for Research .... Dr. James R. GAINES
43 VP Legal Affs/Univ Gen Counsel .... Ms. Darolyn LENDIO
10 VP Budget and Finance/CFO .... Mr. Howard TODO
88 Vice President Community Colleges .... Dr. John MORTON
32 VP Student Affs and Univ/Comm Rels .... Mr. Rockne FREITAS
27 Vice President Info Tech/CIO .... Dr. David K. LASSNER
35 Assoc Vice Pres Student Affairs .... Vacant
26 Assoc VP External Affs & Univ Rels .... Ms. Lynne T. WATERS
18 Assoc VP Capital Improvements .... Mr. Brian MINAAI
102 President UH Foundation .... Ms. Donna VUCHINICH
21 Director of Budget .... Vacant
16 System Director Human Resources .... Ms. Brenna HASHIMOTO
13 Director Management Info Systems .... Ms. Susan K. INOUYE
45 Director Off Research Services .... Ms. Yaa-Yin FONG
21 Director Financial Management .... Mr. Paul Y. KOBAYASHI, JR.
09 Dir Admin Operations/EVAAP .... Ms. Sandra FURUTO
22 Director EEO/AA .... Ms. Mie WATANABE
88 Director Creative Services .... Ms. Cheryl S. ERNST
31 Dir Public Relations/Special Events .... Vacant

*University of Hawaii at Hilo (F)

200 W Kawili Street, Hilo HI 96720-4091
County: Hawaii FICE Identification: 001611
Unit ID: 141565
Telephone: (808) 974-7444 Carnegie Class: Bac/A&S
FAX Number: (808) 974-7622 Calendar System: Semester
URL: www.uhh.hawaii.edu
Established: 1947 Annual Undergrad Tuition & Fees (In-State): $5,880
Enrollment: 4,139 Coed
Affiliation or Control: State IRS Status: 501(c)3
Highest Offering: Doctorate
Program: Liberal Arts And General; Teacher Preparatory; Professional
Accreditation: WC, BUS, CEA, NUR, PHAR, @TEAC

02 Chancellor .... Dr. Donald O. STRANEY
05 Vice Chancellor Academic Affair .... Dr. Kenith SIMMONS
10 Vice Chanc Administrative Affs .... Dr. Marcia SAKAI
46 Int Vice Chancellor for Research .... Dr. Daniel E. BROWN
32 Vice Chancellor Student Affairs .... Dr. Luoluo HONG
20 Asst VC for Academic Affairs .... Vacant
21 Budget Director .... Ms. Lois M. FUJIYOSHI
88 Director University Disability Svcs .... Ms. Susan SHIRACHI
15 Director Human Resources .... Mr. Kerwin S. IWAMOTO
18 Director Facilities Planner .... Mr. Lo-Li CHIH
26 Director University Relations .... Mr. Gerald L. DE MELLO
08 University Librarian .... Dr. Linda Marie GOLIAN-LUI
24 Director Media Relations .... Ms. Alyson Y. KAKUGAWA-LEONG
07 Director Admissions .... Mr. James CROMWELL
38 Acting Director Counseling .... Ms. Barbara B. HEINTZ
39 Director Housing .... Mr. Miles K. NAGATA
35 Director Campus Center .... Ms. Ellen I. KUSANO
37 Director Financial Aid .... Mr. Jeff SCOFIELD
06 University Registrar .... Ms. Cathy ZENZ
49 Dean College of Arts & Sciences .... Dr. Randy HIROKAWA
50 Dean College of Business & Econ .... Dr. Marcia SAKAI
67 Dean College of Pharmacy .... Dr. John PEZZUTO
47 Dean Col Agri/Forestry/Nat Res Mgmt .... Dr. William W. STEINER
51 Int Dean Cont Educ/Community Svcs .... Dr. April K. SCAZZOLA
41 Director of Athletics .... Mr. Dexter IRVIN
40 Bookstore Manager .... Ms. Margot MASSA
85 Dir International Student Services .... Dr. Ruth E. ROBISON
36 Director Career Services .... Dr. Norman S. STAHL
22 Director EEO/AA .... Ms. Kelly OAKS
09 Institutional Research Analyst .... Mr. Brendan HENNESSEY
29 Director Marketing & Alumni .... Ms. Yu Yok PEARRING
30 Senior Director of Development .... Ms. Margaret SHIBA
94 Facilitator Women's Studies .... Ms. Amy GREGG
23 Acting Director Medical Services .... Ms. Lisa LYON
92 Honors Director .... Vacant
88 Dir College of Hawaiian Language .... Dr. Kalena SILVA

*University of Hawaii at Manoa (G)

2500 Campus Road, Honolulu HI 96822-2217
County: Honolulu FICE Identification: 001610
Unit ID: 141574
Telephone: (808) 956-8111 Carnegie Class: RU/VH
FAX Number: N/A Calendar System: Semester
URL: www.manoa.hawaii.edu
Established: 1907 Annual Undergrad Tuition & Fees (In-State): $9,404
Enrollment: 20,429 Coed
Affiliation or Control: State IRS Status: 501(c)3
Highest Offering: Doctorate
Program: Liberal Arts And General; Teacher Preparatory; Professional
Accreditation: WC, BUS, CEA, CLPSY, CORE, DH, DIETD, ENG, IPSY, LAW, LIB, MED, MT, MUS, NURSE, PH, PLNG, SP, SW, TED

02 Chancellor .... Dr. Thomas M. APPLE
11 Vice Chanc Admin/Finance/Operations .... Ms. Kathleen D. CUTSHAW
05 Vice Chanc Academic Affs .... Dr. Reed W. DASENBROCK
45 Vice Chanc Research/Grad Education .... Dr. Gary K. OSTRANDER
32 Vice Chancellor for Students .... Dr. Francisco J. HERNANDEZ
06 University Registrar .... Mr. Stuart LAU
07 Director of Admissions .... Dr. Alan I. YANG
08 Interim University Librarian .... Dr. Gregg GEARY
37 Director Financial Aid Services .... Ms. Jodie M. KUBA
38 Director Counsel/Student Devel Ctr .... Dr. Allyson M. TANOUYE
18 Asst Vice Chanc for Campus Svcs .... Mr. David T. HAFNER, JR.
23 Director University Health Center .... Dr. Andrew W. NICHOLS
39 Director Student Housing .... Mr. Michael W. KAPTIK
40 Director Campus Svcs (Bookstore) .... Ms. Deborah T. HEUBLER
41 Athletic Director .... Mr. James J. DONOVAN
56 Interim Dean Outreach College .... Dr. William G. CHISMAR
50 Dean Shidler College of Business .... Dr. V. Vance ROLEY
58 Dean Graduate Division .... Dr. Patricia A. COOPER
88 Int Dean Sch of Travel Industry Mgt .... Dr. Juanita C. LIU
53 Dean College of Education .... Dr. Donald B. YOUNG
54 Dean College of Engineering .... Dr. Peter E. CROUCH
47 Int Dean Col Trop Agric & Human Res .... Dr. Sylvia YUEN
63 Dean John A Burns Sch of Med .... Dr. Jerris R. HEDGES
66 Dean Sch Nursing & Dental Hygiene .... Dr. Mary G. BOLAND
70 Dean M P Thompson Sch of Soc Work .... Dr. Noreen K. MOKUAU
61 Dean Wm S Richardson Sch of Law .... Mr. Aviam SOIFER
48 Dean School of Architecture .... Mr. Clark E. LLEWELLYN
49 Int Dean College Arts & Humanities .... Mr. Thomas R. BINGHAM
65 Dean College Natural Sciences .... Dr. William L. DITTO
83 Dean College Social Sciences .... Dr. Denise E. KONAN
79 Dean College Lang Ling & Lit .... Dr. Robert BLEY-VROMAN
88 Dean Sch Ocean & Earth Sci & Tech .... Dr. Brian TAYLOR
88 Int Dean Pac and Asian Stds .... Dr. Edward SHULTZ
88 Dn Hawaiinuiakea Sch Hawn Knowledge .... Dr. Maenette BENHAM
86 Int Director of Cmty/Govt Affairs .... Ms. Diane CHANG
28 Dir Stdnt Equity/Exclnce/Diversity .... Dr. Amefil AGBAYANI
36 Dir Manoa Career Center .... Ms. Myrtle CHING-RAPPA
15 Director Human Resources .... Ms. Tammy KUNIYOSHI
88 Director Cancer Center .... Dr. Michele CARBONE
88 Director Institute for Astronomy .... Dr. Guenther HASINGER
88 Director Waikiki Aquarium .... Dr. Andrew ROSSITER
88 Int Assc Dr Pac Biosci Research Ctr .... Dr. Marilyn DUNLAP

*University of Hawaii - West Oahu (H)

96-129 Ala Ike, Pearl City HI 96782-3699
County: Honolulu FICE Identification: 021078
Unit ID: 141981
Telephone: (808) 454-4700 Carnegie Class: Bac/Diverse
FAX Number: (808) 453-6076 Calendar System: Semester
URL: www.uhwo.hawaii.edu
Established: 1976 Annual Undergrad Tuition & Fees (In-State): $5,592
Enrollment: 1,718 Coed
Affiliation or Control: State IRS Status: 501(c)3
Highest Offering: Baccalaureate
Program: Liberal Arts And General; Teacher Preparatory
Accreditation: WC

02 Chancellor .... Dr. Gene I. AWAKUNI
05 Int Vice Chanc Academic Affairs .... Dr. Neva Jacquelyn KILPATRICK
32 Int Vice Chanc for Student Affairs .... Vacant
11 Vice Chanc Administrative Services .... Ms. Donna KIYOSAKI
84 Director for Enrollment Management .... Ms. Susan S. NISHIDA
09 Director of Institutional Research .... Dr. Elaine LEE
26 Dir Public Relations & Marketing .... Ms. Kalowena KOMEIJI
08 Head Librarian .... Ms. Sarah S. GILMAN
06 Registrar .... Ms. Robyn OSHIRO
37 Financial Aid Officer .... Mr. Lester ISHIMOTO
15 Human Resources Specialist .... Ms. Nancy K. NAKASONE
18 Facilities/Auxiliary Services Mgr .... Mr. James (Kimo) YAMAGUCHI
10 Fiscal Officer .... Ms. Lori FOO

*University of Hawaii Community Colleges (I)

2444 Dole Street, Honolulu HI 96822-2411
County: Honolulu FICE Identification: 006751
Unit ID: 420592
Telephone: (808) 956-7038 Carnegie Class: N/A
FAX Number: (808) 956-9219
URL: www.hawaii.edu

01 Vice Pres for Community Colleges .... Dr. John F. MORTON
05 Assoc Vice Pres Academic Affairs .... Dr. Peter QUIGLEY
11 Assoc Vice Pres Admin/Cmty Col Oper .... Mr. Michael T. UNEBASAMI
04 Executive Assistant to the VP .... Ms. Deborah NAKAGAWA

*Kapiolani Community College (J)

4303 Diamond Head Road, Honolulu HI 96816-4496
County: Honolulu FICE Identification: 001613
Unit ID: 141796
Telephone: (808) 734-9000 Carnegie Class: Assoc/Pub2in4
FAX Number: (808) 734-9162 Calendar System: Semester
URL: www.kcc.hawaii.edu
Established: 1957 Annual Undergrad Tuition & Fees (In-State): $2,484
Enrollment: 9,023 Coed
Affiliation or Control: State IRS Status: 501(c)3
Highest Offering: Associate Degree
Program: Occupational; 2-Year Principally Bachelor's Creditable
Accreditation: WJ, ACFEI, ADNUR, MAC, MLTAD, OTA, PTAA, RAD, SURGT

02 Chancellor .... Dr. Leon RICHARDS
05 Vice Chancellor for Acad Affs .... Dr. Louise PAGOTTO
10 Vice Chancellor for Admin Services .... Mr. Milton HIGA
32 Vice Chanellor for Student Services .... Ms. Mona LEE
49 Dean Arts and Sciences .... Dr. Charles SASAKI
50 Dean Hospitality/Business/Legal .... Dr. Frank HAAS
66 Dean Health Programs .... Dr. Patricia O'HAGAN
51 Dean Community & Continuing Educ .... Ms. Carol HOSHIKO
04 Special Asst to the Chancellor .... Dr. Salvatore LANZILOTTI
88 Dir Culinary Inst of the Pacific .... Mr. Conrad NONAKA
09 Dir Institutional Effectiveness .... Dr. Robert FRANCO
08 Librarian .... Ms. Susan MURATA
06 Registrar .... Ms. Jerilyn LORENZO
37 Financial Aid Officer .... Ms. Jennifer BRADLEY
18 Auxiliary Services Officer .... Mr. Gordon MAN
29 Alumni Relations Coordinator .... Ms. Louise YAMAMOTO
30 Development Officer .... Ms. Linh HOANG
15 Director Personnel Office .... Ms. Eileen TORIGOE
21 Fiscal Officer .... Ms. Carol MASUTANI
35 Student Activities Coordinator .... Mr. Keith KASHIWADA

*University of Hawaii Hawaii Community College (A)

200 W Kawili Street, Hilo HI 96720-4091
County: Hawaii FICE Identification: 005258
Unit ID: 383190
Telephone: (808) 934-2500 Carnegie Class: Assoc/Pub2in4
FAX Number: (808) 934-2501 Calendar System: Semester
URL: www.hawaii.hawaii.edu
Established: 1941 Annual Undergrad Tuition & Fees (In-State): $2,558
Enrollment: 3,933 Coed
Affiliation or Control: State IRS Status: 501(c)3
Highest Offering: Associate Degree
Program: Occupational; 2-Year Principally Bachelor's Creditable
Accreditation: WJ, ACFEI, ADNUR, CEA

02 Chancellor .... Ms. Noreen YAMANE
05 Int Vice Chanc Academic Affairs .... Ms. Joni ONISHI
11 Vice Chanc Administrative Affairs .... Mr. James YOSHIDA
32 Vice Chanc Student Affairs .... Mr. Jason CIFRA
51 Int Dir Continuing Educ/Training .... Ms. Deborah SHIGEHARA
37 Student Financial Aid Officer .... Vacant
12 Int Dir UH Center at West Hawaii .... Ms. Beth SANDERS
06 Registrar .... Mr. David LOEDING
15 Personnel Services Officer .... Ms. Mari CHANG
07 Admissions Specialist .... Ms. Dorinna MANUEL-CORTEZ
21 Budget Specialist .... Ms. Jodi MINE

*University of Hawaii Honolulu Community College (B)

874 Dillingham Boulevard, Honolulu HI 96817-4598
County: Honolulu FICE Identification: 001612
Unit ID: 141680
Telephone: (808) 845-9211 Carnegie Class: Assoc/Pub2in4
FAX Number: (808) 845-9173 Calendar System: Semester
URL: www2.honolulu.hawaii.edu
Established: 1920 Annual Undergrad Tuition & Fees (In-State): $2,454
Enrollment: 4,600 Coed
Affiliation or Control: State IRS Status: 501(c)3
Highest Offering: Associate Degree
Program: Occupational; 2-Year Principally Bachelor's Creditable; Technical Emphasis
Accreditation: WJ

02 Chancellor .... Ms. Erika LACRO
05 Int Vice Chancellor of Acad Affairs .... Mr. Russell UYENO
11 Int Vice Chancellor of Admin Svcs .... Mr. Brian FURUTO
32 Dean of Student Services .... Vacant
88 Int Dir PCATT .... Ms. Rosemary SUMAJIT
88 Interim Dean Transport & Trades .... Mr. Michael BARROS
27 Dean Communications & Services .... Vacant
24 Director Educational Media .... Dr. Jon BLUMHARDT
21 Fiscal Officer .... Mr. Derek INAFUKU
08 Librarian in Charge .... Ms. Irene MESINA
37 Financial Aid Officer .... Ms. Jannine OYAMA
15 Director Personnel Services .... Ms. Sharene MORIWAKI
18 Chief Facilities/Physical Plant .... Mr. Brian FURUTO
35 Director Student Affairs .... Ms. Emily Ann KUKULIES
04 Executive Asst to the Chancellor .... Ms. Billie LUEDER
06 Registrar .... Ms. Farah DOIGUCHI
09 Director Management Info & Research .... Ms. Lynn INOSHITA
36 Dir Student Placement/Counselor .... Ms. Silvan CHUNG
20 Interim Dean University College .... Ms. Marcia ROBERTS-DEUTSCH

*University of Hawaii Kauai Community College (C)

3-1901 Kaumualii Highway, Lihue HI 96766-9500
County: Kauai FICE Identification: 001614
Unit ID: 141802
Telephone: (808) 245-8311 Carnegie Class: Assoc/Pub2in4
FAX Number: (808) 245-8220 Calendar System: Semester
URL: kauai.hawaii.edu/
Established: 1964 Annual Undergrad Tuition & Fees (In-State): $3,090
Enrollment: 1,433 Coed
Affiliation or Control: State IRS Status: 501(c)3
Highest Offering: Associate Degree
Program: Occupational; 2-Year Principally Bachelor's Creditable
Accreditation: WJ, ACFEI, ADNUR

02 Chancellor .... Dr. Helen COX
05 Vice Chanc Academic Affairs .... Dr. James DIRE
32 Vice Chanc Student Affairs .... Mr. Earl K. NISHIGUCHI
20 Actg Asst Dn Acad Supp/Univ Ctr Dir .... Ms. Ramona KINCAID
11 Director of Administrative Services .... Mr. Gary NITTA
51 Director Continuing Educ/Training .... Mr. Bruce GETZEN
08 Librarian .... Mr. Robert KAJIWARA
06 Registrar .... Mr. Leighton ORIDE
18 Chief Facilities/Physical Plant .... Mr. Calvin SHIRAI
21 Associate Business Officer .... Ms. Phyllis VIDINHA
37 Financial Aid Officer .... Ms. Rebecca THOMPSON
22 AA/EEO Coordinator .... Ms. Jo Rae BAPTISTE
35 Counselor .... Mr. John CONSTANTINO
09 Institutional Researcher .... Mr. Jonathan KALK

*University of Hawaii Leeward Community College (D)

96-045 Ala Ike, Pearl City HI 96782-3393
County: Honolulu FICE Identification: 004549
Unit ID: 141811
Telephone: (808) 455-0011 Carnegie Class: Assoc/Pub2in4
FAX Number: (808) 455-0471 Calendar System: Semester
URL: www.leeward.hawaii.edu
Established: 1968 Annual Undergrad Tuition & Fees (In-State): $3,030
Enrollment: 7,895 Coed
Affiliation or Control: State IRS Status: 501(c)3
Highest Offering: Associate Degree
Program: Occupational; 2-Year Principally Bachelor's Creditable
Accreditation: WJ, ACFEI

02 Chancellor .... Mr. Manuel J. CABRAL
05 Vice Chancellor/CAO .... Mr. Michael PECSOK
11 Vice Chancellor Admin Services .... Mr. Mark LANE
32 Dean Student Services .... Mr. Christopher MANASERI
72 Asst Dean Career & Tech Education .... Mr. Ron UMEHIRA
49 Asst Dean Arts & Sciences .... Mr. James GOODMAN
08 Librarian .... Mr. Christopher MATZ
06 Registrar .... Mr. Warren MAU
37 Financial Aid Officer .... Ms. Aileen LUM-AKANA
12 Coord Waianae Education Center .... Ms. Laurie LAWRENCE
91 Computer Center Manager .... Ms. Penny UYEHARA
15 Human Resources/EEO/AA Officer .... Mr. Michael WONG
19 Security Supervisor .... Mr. Talbort HOOK
24 Media Coordinator .... Ms. Leanne CHUN
35 Student Activities Coordinator .... Ms. Lexer CHOU
36 Placement Officer .... Vacant
18 Chief Facilities/Physical Plant .... Ms. Sandy MAEDA

*University of Hawaii Maui College (E)

310 Kaahumanu Avenue, Kahului HI 96732-1644
County: Maui FICE Identification: 001615
Unit ID: 141839
Telephone: (808) 984-3500 Carnegie Class: Assoc/Pub4
FAX Number: (808) 984-3546 Calendar System: Semester
URL: maui.hawaii.edu
Established: 1931 Annual Undergrad Tuition & Fees (In-State): $1,229
Enrollment: 4,529 Coed
Affiliation or Control: State IRS Status: 501(c)3
Highest Offering: Baccalaureate
Program: Occupational; 2-Year Principally Bachelor's Creditable; Nursing Emphasis
Accreditation: WC, ACFEI, ADNUR, DA, DH

02 Chancellor .... Dr. Clyde SAKAMOTO
05 Vice Chanc Academic Affairs .... Dr. Jonathon MCKEE
32 Vice Chancellor of Student Affairs .... Mr. Alvin TAGOMORI
11 Vice Chanc of Administrative Affs .... Mr. David TAMANAHA
13 Interim Vice Chanc Information Tech .... Dr. Debasis BHATTACHARYA
20 Int Assistant Dean of Instruction .... Mr. David GROOMS
51 Director Continuing Educ/Training .... Ms. Lori TERAOAWACHI
08 Librarian .... Ms. Lisa SEPA
06 Registrar .... Mr. Stephen KAMEDA
12 Director University Center Maui .... Ms. Tamone Karen HANADA
07 Director of Admissions .... Mr. Stephen KAMEDA
09 Director of Institutional Research .... Dr. Jean PEZZOLI
15 Director Personnel Services .... Ms. Debbi BROWN
18 Chief Facilities/Physical Plant .... Mr. Robert BURTON
21 Associate Fiscal Officer .... Ms. Cindy YAMAMOTO
30 Chief Development .... Mr. Ray TSUCHIYAMA
36 Director Student Placement .... Mr. Stephen KAMEDA
37 Director Student Financial Aid .... Ms. Cathy BIO
38 Director Student Counseling .... Mr. Shane PAYBA

*University of Hawaii Windward Community College (F)

45-720 Keaahala Road, Kaneohe HI 96744-3598
County: Honolulu FICE Identification: 011220
Unit ID: 141990
Telephone: (808) 235-7400 Carnegie Class: Assoc/Pub2in4
FAX Number: (808) 247-5362 Calendar System: Semester
URL: www.wcc.hawaii.edu
Established: 1972 Annual Undergrad Tuition & Fees (In-State): $3,090
Enrollment: 2,625 Coed
Affiliation or Control: State IRS Status: 501(c)3
Highest Offering: Associate Degree
Program: Occupational; 2-Year Principally Bachelor's Creditable
Accreditation: WJ

02 Chancellor .... Mr. Doug DYKSTRA
05 Vice Chancellor Academic Affairs .... Dr. Richard FULTON
32 Vice Chancellor Student Services .... Ms. Ardis ESHENBERG
11 Vice Chanc Administrative Services .... Mr. Clifford TOGO
75 Int Dir Vocational/Cmty Education .... Ms. Kristin KOREY-SMITH
08 Head Librarian .... Ms. Nancy HEU
06 Registrar .... Ms. Geri IMAI
09 Director of Institutional Research .... Mr. Jeffrey HUNT
37 Director Student Financial Aid .... Mr. Steven CHIGAWA
15 Personnel Officer .... Ms. Karen CHO
26 Marketing/Public Relations Dir .... Ms. Bonnie BEATSON

World Medicine Institute (G)

931 University Avenue, Suite 104, Honolulu HI 96826-3266
County: Honolulu FICE Identification: 030725
Unit ID: 141936
Telephone: (808) 947-4788 Carnegie Class: Spec/Health
FAX Number: (808) 373-4341 Calendar System: Semester
URL: www.worldmedicineinstitute.com
Established: 1970 Annual Graduate Tuition & Fees: $10,640
Enrollment: 57 Coed
Affiliation or Control: Independent Non-Profit IRS Status: 501(c)3
Highest Offering: Master's; No Undergraduates
Program: Professional
Accreditation: ACUP

01 President .... Dr. Lillian CHANG
05 Academic Dean .... Dr. Gayle TODOKI

IDAHO

Boise Bible College (H)

8695 W Marigold Street, Boise ID 83714-1220
County: Ada FICE Identification: 022345
Unit ID: 142090
Telephone: (208) 376-7731 Carnegie Class: Spec/Faith
FAX Number: (208) 376-7743 Calendar System: Semester
URL: www.boisebible.edu
Established: 1945 Annual Undergrad Tuition & Fees: $10,100
Enrollment: 207 Coed
Affiliation or Control: Christian Churches And Churches of Christ
IRS Status: 501(c)3
Highest Offering: Baccalaureate
Program: Religious Emphasis
Accreditation: BI

01 President .... Mr. Terry E. STINE
05 Academic Dean .... Mr. Charles FABER
32 Dean of Students .... Mr. Travis JACOB
10 Chief Business Officer .... Mr. Jim VAUGHAN
30 Director of Development .... Mr. David DAVOLT
84 Director of Enrollment Services .... Mr. Ross KNUDSEN
07 Director of Admissions .... Mr. Russell GROVE
08 Head Librarian .... Mrs. Glennis THOMAS
37 Financial Aid Director .... Mrs. Joyce ANDERSON
18 Supt of Building & Grounds .... Mr. Scott OR
04 Assistant to the President .... Mrs. Ricki CARR
40 Director of Bookstore .... Mrs. Debby GRAF
29 Alumni Relations Coordinator .... Dr. James BYERLY

Boise State University (I)

1910 University Drive, Boise ID 83725-1000
County: Ada FICE Identification: 001616
Unit ID: 142115
Telephone: (208) 426-1000 Carnegie Class: Master's L
FAX Number: (208) 426-3765 Calendar System: Semester
URL: www.boisestate.edu
Established: 1932 Annual Undergrad Tuition & Fees (In-State): $5,884
Enrollment: 19,664 Coed
Affiliation or Control: State IRS Status: 501(c)3
Highest Offering: Doctorate
Program: Liberal Arts And General; Teacher Preparatory; Professional; Business Emphasis
Accreditation: NW, ACFEI, ART, BUS, BUSA, CACREP, CONST, CS, DMS, ENG, MUS, NUR, RAD, SPAA, SW, TED, THEA

01 President .... Dr. Robert W. KUSTRA
05 Provost/Vice Pres Academic Affairs .... Dr. Martin SCHIMPF
10 Vice President Finan/Administration .... Ms. Stacy PEARSON
32 Vice President Student Affairs .... Dr. Lisa HARRIS
30 Int Vice Pres Univ Advancement .... Ms. Rosemary REINHARDT
43 Vice President/University Counsel .... Mr. Kevin SATTERLEE
20 Associate VP for Academic Planning .... Dr. James MUNGER
21 Associate Vice Pres for Finance .... Ms. Jo Ellen DI NUCCI
46 AVP Strategic Research Initiatives .... Vacant
13 Assoc VP Information Technologies .... Mr. Max DAVIS-JOHNSON
08 Dean of University Libraries .... Dr. Marilyn MOODY
84 Exec Director Enrollment Services .... Ms. Mara AFFRE
29 Executive Director Alumni Affairs .... Mr. Mark ARSTEIN
17 Medical Services Director .... Dr. Vincent SERIO
06 Registrar .... Ms. Kristine COLLINS
18 Exec Director Campus Security .... Mr. Jon UDA
40 Director Bookstore .... Mr. Mike REED
24 Director Academic Technologies .... Mr. Dale PIKE

09 Dir Inst Analysis Assessment .... Mr. Steven P. SCHMIDT
07 Director of Admissions ....Ms. Jenny CERDA
35 Director Student Affairs ....Ms. Lynn HUMPHREY
26 Dir of Communications & Marketing ....Mr. Frank ZANG
41 Director Athletics ....Mr. Mark COYLE
22 Director Affirmative Action/EEO ....Ms. Marla HENKEN
15 Exec Director Human Resources ....Mr. Pablo COBLENTZ
38 Director Counseling Center ....Dr. Dan TIMBERLAKE
37 Director Student Financial Aid ....Mr. David TOLMAN
96 Director of Purchasing ....Ms. Terri SPINAZZA
51 Dean Extended Studies ....Mr. Mark WHEELER
49 Dean of Arts & Sciences ....Dr. Tony ROARK
83 Dean of Social Science/Public Affs ....Dr. Melissa LAVITT
50 Dean of Business & Economics ....Dr. Pat SHANNON
53 Dean of Education ....Dr. Diane BOOTHE
58 Dean of the Graduate College ....Dr. Jack PELTON
76 Dean of Health Sciences ....Dr. Tim DUNNAGAN
54 Interim Dean College of Engineering ....Dr. Amy MOLL

Brigham Young University-Idaho (A)

Rexburg ID 83460-1650

County: Madison — FICE Identification: 001625
Unit ID: 142522
Telephone: (208) 496-1411 — Carnegie Class: Bac/Diverse
FAX Number: (208) 496-1103 — Calendar System: Semester
URL: www.byui.edu
Established: 1888 — Annual Undergrad Tuition & Fees: $3,570
Enrollment: 15,102 — Coed
Affiliation or Control: Latter-day Saints — IRS Status: 501(c)3
Highest Offering: Baccalaureate
Program: Occupational; Liberal Arts And General
Accreditation: NW, ADNUR, CIDA, EMT, ENG, ENGT, MAC, MUS, NUR, SW

01 President ....Dr. Kim B. CLARK
05 Academic Vice President ....Dr. Fenton L. BROADHEAD
46 University Resources Vice President ... Mr. Charles N. ANDERSEN
35 Student Svcs & Activities Vice Pres ....Mr. Kevin T. MIYASAKI
30 Advancement Vice President ....Dr. Henry J. EYRING
20 Assoc Academic VP Instruction ....Mr. Kelly T. BURGENER
20 Assoc Academic Vice Pres Curriculum ....Dr. Edwin A. SEXTON
45 Assoc Acad VP Education/Acad Devel ....Dr. Rob EATON
20 Assoc Acad VP Support Services ....Dr. Richard K. PAGE
20 Assoc Acad VP Student Connections ....Dr. Guy M. HOLLINGSWORTH
32 Dean of Students ....Mr. Kip B. HARRIS
32 Student Well Being Mng Director ....Mr. Wynn N. HILL
51 Continuing Education Director ....Mr. Chad P. PRICE
13 Chief Technology Officer ....Mr. M. Spalding JUGGANAIKLOO
09 Inst Research & Assessment Director ....Dr. Scott J. BERGSTROM
06 Student Records & Registration ....Mr. Kyle R. MARTIN
37 Student Fin Aid/Scholarship Dir ....Mr. Aaron D. SANNS
08 University Librarian ....Dr. Ralph M. KERN
72 Academic Technology Svcs Director ....Mr. Kent L. BARRUS
21 Univ Operations Managing Director ....Mr. Wayne N. CLARK
15 Human Resources Director ....Mr. Kevin L. PRICE
23 Student Health Services Director ....Mr. Shaun ORR
38 Student Counseling Center Director ....Mr. Reed J. STODDARD
19 University Security & Safety ....Mr. Garth M. GUNDERSON
07 Admissions Director ....Mr. Tyler R. WILLIAMS
29 Alumni Director ....Mr. Steven J. DAVIS
35 Student Activities Mng Director ....Mr. Derek R. FAY
26 University Rels & Services Mng Dir ....Mr. Bruce R. HOBBS
30 Philanthropies Director ....Mr. Christopher W. MOORE
44 Annual Giving Director ....Mr. D. Alton HANSEN
39 Housing & Student Living Director ....Dr. Troy J. DOUGHERTY
43 Legal Counsel ....Mr. Michael R. ORME
21 Financial Services Mng Director ....Mr. Russel K. BENEDICT
88 Academic Discovery Center Director ....Mrs. Amy R. LABAUGH
96 Purchasing & Travel Director ....Mr. Darin N. LEE
84 Enrollment Svcs Managing Director ....Mr. Rob J. GARRETT
27 University Communications Director ....Mr. Merv R. BROWN
40 University Store Manager ....Mr. Doug R. MASON
104 International Services Manager ....Mr. Mike R. OSWALD
04 Asst to Pres Strategy & Planning ....Mrs. Betty A. OLDHAM

Brown Mackie College-Boise (B)

9050 West Overland Road, Ste. 101, Boise ID 83709

County: Ada — Identification: 666780
Unit ID: 455600
Telephone: (208) 321-8800 — Carnegie Class: Assoc/PrivFP4
FAX Number: (208) 375-3249 — Calendar System: Other
URL: www.brownmackie.edu
Established: 2008 — Annual Undergrad Tuition & Fees: $11,520
Enrollment: 464 — Coed
Affiliation or Control: Proprietary — IRS Status: Proprietary
Highest Offering: Baccalaureate
Program: Occupational; 2-Year Principally Bachelor's Creditable; Business Emphasis
Accreditation: ACICS, OTA, SURGT, SURTEC

01 President ....Steve KALINA
07 Senior Director of Admissions ....Vacant
05 Dean of Academic Affairs ....Rob ROBICHAUD

† Branch campus of Brown Mackie College, South Bend, IN.

Carrington College - Boise (C)

1122 N Liberty Street, Boise ID 83704-8742

County: Ada — FICE Identification: 022180
Unit ID: 142054
Telephone: (208) 377-8080 — Carnegie Class: Assoc/PrivFP
FAX Number: (208) 322-7658 — Calendar System: Semester
URL: www.carrington.edu
Established: 1980 — Annual Undergrad Tuition & Fees: $28,473
Enrollment: 557 — Coed
Affiliation or Control: Proprietary — IRS Status: Proprietary
Highest Offering: Associate Degree
Program: Occupational; 2-Year Principally Bachelor's Creditable
Accreditation: ACICS, DA, DH, MAAB, PNUR, PTAA

01 Executive Director ....Ms. Danielle HORRAS
05 Dean of Academic Affairs ....Mr. Bradley JAHN
36 Director Career Services ....Ms. Valerie DICKERSON

The College of Idaho (D)

2112 Cleveland Boulevard, Caldwell ID 83605-9990

County: Canyon — FICE Identification: 001617
Unit ID: 142294
Telephone: (208) 459-5011 — Carnegie Class: Bac/A&S
FAX Number: (208) 454-2077 — Calendar System: Other
URL: www.collegeofidaho.edu
Established: 1891 — Annual Undergrad Tuition & Fees: $22,695
Enrollment: 1,040 — Coed
Affiliation or Control: Independent Non-Profit — IRS Status: 501(c)3
Highest Offering: Master's
Program: Liberal Arts And General; Teacher Preparatory
Accreditation: NW

01 President ....Dr. Marvin HENBERG
05 Vice President Academic Affairs ....Dr. John OTTENHOFF
10 Vice Pres Finance/Administration ....Ms. Petra CARVER
32 Vice President Student Affairs ....Mr. Paul BENNION
26 Vice Pres College Relations ....Mr. Michael VANDERVELDEN
06 Registrar ....Ms. Ann KUCK
84 Dean Enrollment Management ....Mr. Brian BAVA
41 Director of Athletics ....Mr. Marty HOLLY
26 Dir of Marketing & Communications ....Mr. Dustin WUNDERLICH
29 Dir of Alumni & Parent Relations ....Ms. Sally SKINNER
44 Director of Boone Fund ....Ms. Tara WENSEL
20 Associate Dean ....Dr. Kathy SEIBOLD
08 Librarian ....Ms. Christine SCHUTZ
18 Director Maintenance & Operations ....Mr. Kyle ABRAHAMSON
21 Controller ....Ms. Deanna ROSS
37 Director of Financial Services ....Mrs. Juanitta PEARSON
15 Human Resources Director ....Ms. Bev ROBINSON
36 Director Student Placement ....Ms. Dora GALLEGOS
85 Director of International Education ....Dr. Ellen BATT
92 Director of Honors Program ....Dr. Sue SCHAPER
89 Director of Freshman Studies ....Dr. Lynn WEBSTER
39 Director of Residential Life ....Ms. Jen NELSON
93 Director of Minority Affairs ....Mr. Arnold HERNANDEZ
42 Campus Minister ....Dr. Phil ROGERS
19 Director of Campus Safety ....Mr. Allan LAIRD
96 Director of Purchasing ....Ms. Peta CARVER
90 Director of Network Services ....Mr. Zane HOWE
09 Director Institutional Research ....Dr. Kristina MAZURAK
30 Director Development ....Mr. Jack CAFFERTY
40 Bookstore Manager ....Ms. Susan HUNSBERGER
38 Counselor ....Ms. Marilyn SIMMONDS

College of Southern Idaho (E)

PO Box 1238, 315 Falls Avenue,
Twin Falls ID 83303-1238

County: Twin Falls — FICE Identification: 001619
Unit ID: 142559
Telephone: (208) 733-9554 — Carnegie Class: Assoc/Pub-R-L
FAX Number: (208) 736-3015 — Calendar System: Semester
URL: www.csi.edu
Established: 1964 — Annual Undergrad Tuition & Fees (In-District): $2,640
Enrollment: 7,849 — Coed
Affiliation or Control: Local — IRS Status: 501(c)3
Highest Offering: Associate Degree
Program: Occupational; 2-Year Principally Bachelor's Creditable
Accreditation: NW, ADNUR, DH, EMT, MAC, RAD, SURGA, SURGT

01 President ....Dr. Gerald L. BECK
05 Exec VP/Chief Academic Officer ....Dr. D. Jeff FOX
11 Vice President of Administration ....Mr. J. Mike MASON
32 VP of Student Svc/Plng & Grant Dev ....Dr. Edit SZANTO
102 Executive Director Foundation ....Ms. Debra J. WILSON
20 Instructional Dean ....Dr. John S. MILLER
20 Instructional Dean ....Dr. Cindy R. BOND
20 Instructional Dean ....Mr. Terry L. PATTERSON
76 Dean Health Sci/Human Svcs/Biology ....Dr. Mark A. SUGDEN
21 Dean of Finance ....Mr. Jeff M. HARMON
09 Dean of Information Technology ....Dr. Ken B. CAMPBELL
35 Dean of Students ....Mr. Graydon A. STANLEY
88 Dean of Student Services ....Mr. J. Scott SCHOLES
06 Director of Admissions & Records ....Ms. Gail SCHULL
38 Director of Advising ....Mr. Cesar PEREZ GARCIA
37 Director of Student Financial Aid ....Ms. Jennifer J. ZIMMERS
15 Director Human Resources ....Mr. Monty J. ARROSSA
18 Director Physical Plant ....Mr. Randy G. DILL
08 Director Library ....Ms. Teri L. FATTIG
26 Public Information Director ....Mr. Doug L. MAUGHAN
14 Director Data Services ....Mr. Jay N. SNEDDON
19 Director Security & Safety ....Mr. Jim ELLINGTON
41 Athletic Director ....Mr. Joel C. BATE
27 Sports Information Director ....Ms. Karen D. BAUMERT
85 Director of Foreign Students ....Ms. Samra CULUM
92 Coordinator Honors Program ....Ms. Kimberly PRESTWICH
04 Admin Assistant to the President ....Ms. Kathy S. DEAHL

College of Western Idaho (F)

5500 East Opportunity Dr, Nampa ID 83687

County: Canyon — FICE Identification: 042118
Unit ID: 455114
Telephone: (208) 562-3000 — Carnegie Class: Assoc/Pub-R-M
FAX Number: (888) 562-3216 — Calendar System: Semester
URL: cwidaho.cc
Established: 2007 — Annual Undergrad Tuition & Fees (In-District): $3,264
Enrollment: 8,077 — Coed
Affiliation or Control: Local — IRS Status: 501(c)3
Highest Offering: Associate Degree
Program: Occupational; 2-Year Principally Bachelor's Creditable
Accreditation: @NW

01 President ....Dr. Bert GLANDON
10 VP Finance & Administration ....Ms. Cheryl WRIGHT
05 VP of Instruction ....Mr. Rick AMAN

Eastern Idaho Technical College (G)

1600 S 25th E, Idaho Falls ID 83404-5788

County: Bonneville — FICE Identification: 011133
Unit ID: 142179
Telephone: (208) 524-3000 — Carnegie Class: Assoc/Pub-R-S
FAX Number: (208) 524-3007 — Calendar System: Semester
URL: www.eitc.edu
Established: 1969 — Annual Undergrad Tuition & Fees (In-State): $3,515
Enrollment: 830 — Coed
Affiliation or Control: State — IRS Status: 501(c)3
Highest Offering: Associate Degree
Program: Occupational; 2-Year Principally Bachelor's Creditable; Technical Emphasis
Accreditation: NW, MAC, SURGT

01 President ....Mr. Steve K. ALBISTON
10 Vice President of Finance and Admin ....Mr. James STRATTON
05 VP of Instruction & Student Affairs ....Dr. Sharee ANDERSON
06 Registrar ....Mrs. Suzanne FELT
10 Controller ....Mr. Don E. BOURNE
103 Mgr Workforce Trng/Cmty Education . Mr. Kenneth W. ERICKSON
08 Librarian ....Mrs. Suzy RICKS
37 Financial Aid Director ....Mrs. Shayna SHARP
04 Administrative Assistant ....Mrs. Jacque LARSEN
26 Director of College Relations ....Mr. Todd WIGHTMAN
102 Foundation Director ....Mrs. Michelle P. ZIEL
07 Director of Admissions/Placement ....Mrs. Annalea AVERY
40 Bookstore Operator ....Mr. Devon H. GLOVER
50 Business/Office/Technology Div Mgr ....Mr. Christian J. GODFREY
97 General Education Division Manager ....Mrs. Peggy L. NELSON
76 Health Care Technology Div Manager ....Dr. Shirley BAME
88 Trades/Industry Division Manager ....Mr. Kent E. BERGGREN
88 Adult Basic Education Div Manager ....Mrs. Melody CLEGG
09 Director of Institutional Research ....Mr. Douglas D. DEPRIEST
15 Director Human Resources ....Mrs. Isela GUTIERREZ
18 Chief Facilities/Physical Plant ....Mr. William C. BRYANT
29 Director Alumni Relations ....Mrs. Melissa M. BEAN

Idaho State University (H)

921 S 8th, Pocatello ID 83209-0009

County: Bannock — FICE Identification: 001620
Unit ID: 142276
Telephone: (208) 282-0211 — Carnegie Class: RU/H
FAX Number: (208) 282-4000 — Calendar System: Semester
URL: www.isu.edu
Established: 1901 — Annual Undergrad Tuition & Fees (In-State): $6,070
Enrollment: 14,873 — Coed
Affiliation or Control: State — IRS Status: 501(c)3
Highest Offering: Doctorate
Program: Occupational; Liberal Arts And General; Teacher Preparatory; Professional
Accreditation: NW, ACFEI, ADNUR, ARCPA, AUD, BUS, BUSA, CACREP, CLPSY, CS, DENT, DH, DIETD, DIETI, EMT, ENG, ENGT, MAC, MT, MUS, NAIT, NURSE, OT, PH, PHAR, PTA, PTAA, SP, SW, TED, THEA

01 President ....Dr. Arthur C. VAILAS
05 Int ProvostVP for Acad Affairs ....Dr. Barbara ADAMCIK
10 Vice President for Finance & Admin ...... Mr. James A. FLETCHER
30 Vice Pres University Advancement ....Dr. Kent M. TINGEY
32 Vice Pres of Student Affairs ....Dr. Patricia TERRELL
46 Exec Dir of Research & Tech Trans ......Dr. Richard T. JACOBSEN
43 University Legal Counsel ....Mr. Bradley H. HALL
41 Athletic Director ....Mr. Jeff TINGEY
20 AVP/Exec Dean Div Health Sciences ....Dr. Linda HATZENBUEHLER
20 AVP for Academic Affairs ....Dr. Laura WOODWORTH-NEY
20 AVP for Academic Affairs ....Ms. Kay CHRISTENSEN
30 Interim AVP for Development ....Mr. Scott TURNER
18 AVP for Facilities Services ....Mr. Joseph HAN
58 Interim Dean of Graduate School .... Dr. Cynthia PEMBERTON
54 Dean College of Science & Engr ....Dr. George IMEL
67 Dean College of Pharmacy ....Dr. Paul S. CADY
50 Interim Dean College of Business ....Dr. Thomas OTTAWAY
49 Dean College of Arts & Letters ....Dr. Kandi TURLEY-AMES
53 Dean College of Education ....Dr. Deborah L. HEDEEN
75 Dean College of Technology ....Dr. Scott RASMUSSEN
12 Dean of Academic Pgm ISU-Meridian ....Dr. Bessie KATSILOMETES
12 Dean of Academic Pgm ISU-Id Falls .... Dr. Lyle W. CASTLE
08 University Librarian & Dean .... Ms. Sandra SHOPSHIRE

06 Registrar & Dir of Undergrad Admiss ... Ms. Laura MCKENZIE
14 Chief Information Officer ... Mr. Randy GAINES
29 Director Alumni Relations ... Ms. K.C FELT
09 Director Institutional Research ... Mr. Vince MILLER
37 Director Student Financial Aid ... Mr. Kent D. LARSON
15 Director Human Resources ... Mr. David J. MILLER
25 Director Sponsored Programs ... Ms. Dianne K. HORROCKS
23 Director Student Health Center ... Dr. Ronald SOLBRIG
22 Dir EEO/Affirm Action & Diversity ... Ms. Joyce HAMMOND-PERRY
19 Director Public Safety ... Mr. Stephen A. CHATTERTON
26 Director Marketing & Communication ... Mr. Mark LEVINE
86 Director Government Relations ... Mr. Kent KUNZ
88 Director Events Management ... Mr. George CASPER
35 Director of Student Life ... Dr. Jane COE-SMITH
38 Director of Counseling & Testing ... Dr. Don PAULSON
85 Director of International Programs ... Ms. Maria FLETCHER

ITT Technical Institute (A)

12302 W Explorer Drive, Boise ID 83713-1529
County: Ada FICE Identification: 004553
Unit ID: 142337
Telephone: (208) 322-8844 Carnegie Class: Spec/Tech
FAX Number: (208) 322-0173 Calendar System: Quarter
URL: www.itt-tech.edu
Established: 1969 Annual Undergrad Tuition & Fees: N/A
Enrollment: 468 Coed
Affiliation or Control: Proprietary IRS Status: Proprietary
Highest Offering: Baccalaureate
Program: Technical Emphasis
Accreditation: ACICS

† Branch campus of ITT Technical Institute, Indianapolis, IN.

Lewis-Clark State College (B)

500 8th Avenue, Lewiston ID 83501-2698
County: Nez Perce FICE Identification: 001621
Unit ID: 142328
Telephone: (208) 792-5272 Carnegie Class: Bac/Diverse
FAX Number: (208) 792-2831 Calendar System: Semester
URL: www.lcsc.edu
Established: 1893 Annual Undergrad Tuition & Fees (In-State): $5,562
Enrollment: 4,693 Coed
Affiliation or Control: State IRS Status: 501(c)3
Highest Offering: Baccalaureate
Program: Occupational; 2-Year Principally Bachelor's Creditable; Liberal Arts And General; Teacher Preparatory; Professional; Nursing Emphasis
Accreditation: NW, IACBE, MAC, NURSE, SW, TED

01 President ... Dr. J. Anthony FERNANDEZ
05 Provost/Vice Pres Academic Affairs ... Dr. Carmen SIMONE
10 VP Finance and Administration ... Mr. Chet HERBST
75 Dean Professional/Technical Pgms ... Dr. Robert LOHRMEYER
51 Dean Community Programs ... Ms. Kathy MARTIN
20 Dean Academic Programs ... Vacant
35 Dean Student Services ... Dr. Andrew HANSON
08 Director of Library Services ... Ms. Susan NIEWENHOUS
103 Director of Workforce Training ... Dr. Linda STRICKLIN
07 Director of Admissions/Registrar ... Ms. Nikol LUTHER
09 Dir Planning/Research/Assessment ... Mr. Howard ERDMAN
13 Chief Technology Officer ... Mr. Allen SCHMOOCK
41 Athletic Director ... Mr. Gary PICONE
15 Director of Human Resources ... Ms. Vikki SWIFT
27 Director of College Communications ... Mr. Bert SAHLBERG
29 Director of Alumni Relations ... Ms. Renee OLSEN
37 Director of Student Financial Aid ... Ms. Laura HUGHES
30 Director of College Advancement ... Ms. Mary HASENOEHRL
18 Director of Physical Plant ... Mr. Matt GRAVES
36 Director Career & Advising Services ... Ms. Debra LYBYER
96 Director of Purchasing ... Ms. Sheila KOM

New Saint Andrews College (C)

PO Box 9025, Moscow ID 83843-1525
County: Latah Identification: 666166
Unit ID: 440396
Telephone: (208) 882-1566 Carnegie Class: Bac/A&S
FAX Number: (208) 882-4293 Calendar System: Other
URL: www.nsa.edu
Established: 1994 Annual Undergrad Tuition & Fees: $10,750
Enrollment: 161 Coed
Affiliation or Control: Independent Non-Profit IRS Status: 170(c)1
Highest Offering: Master's
Program: Liberal Arts And General; Religious Emphasis
Accreditation: TRACS

01 President ... Dr. Roy A. ATWOOD
03 Executive Vice President ... Mr. Bob HIERONYMUS
05 Vice President ... Mr. Ed IVERSON
58 Dean of Graduate Studies ... Dr. Jonathan MCINTOSH
10 Dir Financial & Facility Services ... Mr. Eric BURNETT
08 Head Librarian ... Mr. Ed IVERSON
06 Registrar ... Mrs. Beverlee ATWOOD
20 Dean of Undergraduate Studies ... Mr. Ben MERKLE
07 Director Admissions ... Mrs. Brenda SCHLECT
40 Bookstore Manager ... Mr. Eric BURNETT
09 Dir Institutional Effectiveness ... Mr. Ed IVERSON
84 Director Student Recruitment ... Mr. John SAWYER

North Idaho College (D)

1000 W Garden Avenue, Coeur d'Alene ID 83814-2199
County: Kootenai FICE Identification: 001623
Unit ID: 142443
Telephone: (208) 769-3300 Carnegie Class: Assoc/Pub-R-M
FAX Number: (208) 765-2761 Calendar System: Semester
URL: www.nic.edu
Established: 1933 Annual Undergrad Tuition & Fees (In-District): $2,846
Enrollment: 6,751 Coed
Affiliation or Control: Local IRS Status: 501(c)3
Highest Offering: Associate Degree
Program: Occupational; 2-Year Principally Bachelor's Creditable
Accreditation: NW, ADNUR, RAD

01 President ... Dr. Joe H. DUNLAP
05 Vice President for Instruction ... Vacant
10 Vice President for Resource Mgmt ... Mr. Ronald DORN
32 Vice President for Student Services ... Vacant
26 VP for Community Relations & Mktg ... Mr. Mark BROWNING
103 Dean of Prof/Tech/Workforce Educ ... Mr. Mike MIRES
97 Dean of General Studies ... Mr. Robert MURRAY
17 Dean of Nursing & Health Care Pgms ... Dr. Lita BURNS
06 Registrar ... Ms. Tami HAFT
09 Director of Inst Effectiveness ... Ms. Ann LEWIS
08 Librarian ... Vacant
13 Director of Information Technology ... Mr. Stephen A. RUPPEL
37 Director of Financial Aid ... Mr. Joseph BEKKEN
07 Director of Admissions ... Ms. Tami HAFT
15 Director of Human Resources ... Vacant
18 Director of Facilities ... Mr. Mike HALPERN
26 Director of Comm & Marketing ... Ms. Stacy HUDSON
30 Development Director ... Ms. Rayelle ANDERSON
35 Director Student Activities ... Mr. Dean BENNETT
36 Dir of Academic & Support Services ... Ms. Sally HINDERS
21 Controller ... Ms. Sarah GARCIA
72 Technology Coordinator ... Mr. Andy FINNEY
29 Alumni Relations Coordinator ... Ms. Katie ELWELL

Northwest Nazarene University (E)

623 S. University Blvd., Nampa ID 83686-5897
County: Canyon FICE Identification: 001624
Unit ID: 142461
Telephone: (208) 467-8011 Carnegie Class: Master's L
FAX Number: (208) 467-8099 Calendar System: Semester
URL: www.nnu.edu
Established: 1913 Annual Undergrad Tuition & Fees: $25,240
Enrollment: 2,064 Coed
Affiliation or Control: Church Of The Nazarene IRS Status: 501(c)3
Highest Offering: Master's
Program: Liberal Arts And General; Teacher Preparatory; Professional
Accreditation: NW, ACBSP, CACREP, MUS, NURSE, SW, TED

01 President ... Dr. David C. ALEXANDER
05 Vice Pres Academic Affairs/Dean ... Dr. Burton J. WEBB
30 Vice Pres University Advancement ... Dr. Joel K. PEARSALL
10 Vice Pres Financial Affairs ... Mr. David S. TARRANT
84 Vice Pres Enrollment & Marketing ... Mrs. Stacey L. BERGGREN
32 Vice President Student Development ... Dr. Carey W. COOK
88 Vice Pres Spiritual & Ldrshp Dev ... Dr. Fred C. FULLERTON
06 Registrar ... Mrs. Nancy A. AYERS
08 Director of the Library ... Dr. Sharon I. BULL
29 Director of Alumni Relations ... Mr. Darl L. BRUNER
51 Dir Center for Professional Devel ... Vacant
42 Dean of the Chapel ... Rev. M. Gene SCHANDORFF
42 Director of Campus Ministry ... Ms. Julene M. TEGERSTRAND
40 Bookstore Manager ... Ms. Gail D. WALKER
39 Director of Residential Life ... Mrs. Karen L. PEARSON
38 Director of Wellness Center ... Mrs. Terri BLACKBURN
07 Director of Admissions ... Mr. Mike B. MARSTON
21 Controller ... Mrs. Shirley J. HAIDLE
26 Director of Marketing & Media ... Mrs. Hollie M. LINDNER
35 Director of Campus Life ... Mr. Tim R. MILBURN
36 Director of Career Center ... Ms. Amanda F. MARBLE
13 Exec Director of Info Technology ... Dr. Eric J. KELLERER
24 Director of Tech & Media Resources ... Mr. Frank E. ESTELL
37 Director of Financial Aid ... Mr. David KLAFFKE
93 Director of Multicultural Affairs ... Rev. Jamie COLEMAN
16 Director of Human Resources ... Ms. Sherry L. HARTMAN
41 Athletic Director ... Mr. Rich F. SANDERS
91 Dir of Administrative Computing ... Mr. Brian C. STILLMAN
90 Network Systems Administrator ... Mr. Tim A. GROSS
18 Chief Facilities/Physical Plant ... Mr. C. Richard VAN SCHYNDEL

† Granted candidacy at the Doctorate level.

Stevens-Henager College-Boise (F)

1444 S. Entertainment Avenue, Boise ID 83709
County: Ada Identification: 666329
Telephone: (208) 383-4540 Carnegie Class: Not Classified
FAX Number: (208) 345-6999 Calendar System: Other
URL: www.stevenshenager.edu
Established: 2004 Annual Undergrad Tuition & Fees: $15,790
Enrollment: 481 Coed
Affiliation or Control: Proprietary IRS Status: Proprietary
Highest Offering: Baccalaureate
Program: Occupational; Professional
Accreditation: ACCSC

01 Campus Director ... Dr. Shane REEDER

University of Idaho (G)

Campus Drive, PO Box 443151, Moscow ID 83844-3151
County: Latah FICE Identification: 001626
Unit ID: 142285
Telephone: (208) 885-6111 Carnegie Class: RU/H
FAX Number: (208) 885-5540 Calendar System: Semester
URL: www.uidaho.edu
Established: 1889 Annual Undergrad Tuition & Fees (In-State): $6,212
Enrollment: 12,312 Coed
Affiliation or Control: State IRS Status: 501(c)3
Highest Offering: Doctorate
Program: Liberal Arts And General; Teacher Preparatory; Professional
Accreditation: NW, ART, BUS, BUSA, CIDA, CORE, CS, DIETC, ENG, FOR, IPSY, LAW, LSAR, MUS, NRPA, TED

01 President ... Dr. M. Duane NELLIS
05 Provost & Executive Vice President ... Dr. Douglas D. BAKER
10 Vice Pres Finance & Administration ... Mr. Ron SMITH
30 Vice Pres University Advancement ... Mr. Christopher D. MURRAY
46 Vice President Research ... Dr. John MCIVER
12 Assoc Vice Pres for Northern Idaho ... Dr. Charles BUCK
12 Assoc VP and CEO Boise Center ... Dr. Trudy J. ANDERSON
12 Assoc Vice Pres Idaho Falls Center ... Dr. Robert W. SMITH
27 Assoc Vice Pres Mktg/Strat Comm ... Vacant
18 Assistant Vice President Facilities ... Mr. Brian D. JOHNSON
21 Asst VP Aux Svcs/Ad Ops/Cap Plng ... Mr. Tyrone W. BROOKS
84 Asst Vice Pres Enrollmnt Managemnt ... Mr. Steve NEIHEISEL
28 Asst to Pres Diversity/Equity/Cmty ... Vacant
19 Manager Parking & Trans Services ... Mr. Carl ROOT
20 Vice Provost Academic Affairs ... Dr. Jeanne M. CHRISTIANSEN
35 Vice Provost Student Affairs ... Dr. Bruce M. PITMAN
08 Dean Library Services ... Ms. Lynn N. BAIRD
15 Int Associate VP Human Resources ... Mr. Matt DORSCHEL
32 Dean of Students ... Dr. Bruce M. PITMAN
22 Dir Human Rights/Access/Inclusion ... Ms. Carmen A. SUAREZ
06 Registrar ... Ms. Nancy A. KROGH
07 Director of Admissions ... Mr. Michael LOEHRING
09 Director Inst Research & Assessment ... Dr. Archie A. GEORGE
24 Director Information Tech Services ... Mr. Daniel EWART
29 Director Alumni Relations ... Mr. Steven C. JOHNSON
36 Dir Career & Professional Planning ... Ms. Suzanne K L. BILLINGTON
37 Director Student Financial Aid ... Dr. Daniel D. DAVENPORT
38 Director Counseling & Testing Ctr ... Dr. Joan PULAKOS
39 Director University Residences ... Mr. Ray GASSER
41 Athletic Director ... Dr. Robert SPEAR
42 Director Campus Christian Center ... Ms. Sharon A. KEHOE
43 General University Counsel ... Mr. Kent E. NELSON
44 Director Annual Giving ... Ms. Mandy HANOUSEK
87 Director Summer & Dual Enrol Prog ... Ms. Nancy KROGH
92 Director Honors Program ... Dr. Alton CAMPBELL
93 Int Director Multicultural Affairs ... Mr. Eddy A. RUIZ
94 Director Women's Center ... Ms. Heather GASSER
40 Director Bookstore ... Mr. John Anthony BALES
96 Manager Purchasing ... Mr. Christopher P. JOHNSON
47 Dean College of Agri/Life Sciences ... Dr. John E. HAMMEL
48 Dean College of Art & Architecture ... Mr. Mark E. HOVERSTEN
49 Dean Col of Letters/Arts Soc Sci ... Dr. Katherine G. AIKEN
50 Dean College of Business & Econ ... Dr. Mario S. REYES
53 Dean College of Education ... Dr. Corinne MANTLE-BROMLEY
54 Dean College of Engineering ... Dr. Larry STAUFFER
58 Dean Graduate Studies ... Dr. Jie CHEN
61 Dean College of Law ... Mr. Donald L. BURNETT, JR.
65 Dean College of Natural Resources ... Dr. Kurt PREGITZER
81 Interim Dean College of Science ... Dr. Paul JOYCE

ILLINOIS

Adler School of Professional Psychology (H)

17 North Dearborn, Chicago IL 60602
County: Cook FICE Identification: 020681
Unit ID: 142832
Telephone: (312) 662-4000 Carnegie Class: Spec/Health
FAX Number: (312) 662-4099 Calendar System: Semester
URL: www.adler.edu
Established: 1952 Annual Graduate Tuition & Fees: $33,000
Enrollment: 1,186 Coed
Affiliation or Control: Independent Non-Profit IRS Status: 501(c)3
Highest Offering: Doctorate; No Undergraduates
Program: Professional
Accreditation: NH, CLPSY, CORE, IPSY

01 President ... Dr. Raymond E. CROSSMAN
101 Board Secy/Dir Ofc of the Pres ... Ms. Mitzi NORTON
11 Vice President Administration ... Mrs. Jo Beth CUP
07 Associate Vice President Admissions ... Mr. Craig HINES
07 Director of Admissions ... Ms. Michelle BRICE
26 Assoce Vice President Marketing ... Mr. Mark BRANSON
06 Registrar ... Ms. Sheba JONES
32 Assoc Vice President Student Affair ... Mr. Greg MACVARISH
35 Asst Director Student Affairs ... Vacant
37 Director Student Financial Aid ... Ms. Terri ESCH
05 Vice President Academic Affairs ... Vacant
31 VP Community Engagement & Training ... Dr. Wendy PASZKIEWICZ
31 Director Community Engagement ... Mr. Cecil THOMAS
88 Director MA Counseling Training ... Dr. Paul FITZGERALD
88 Director of Doctoral Training ... Dr. Eunice KIM

24 Director Learning & Educ Technology ... Mr. Zoaib MIRZA
10 Vice President Finance & IT ... Mr. Jeffrey GREEN
18 Director of Facilities ... Ms. Hope POPA
21 Controller ... Ms. Eve HERDEA
13 Associate VP Technology ... Mr. Paul COLLINS
16 Assoc VP Human Resources ... Ms. Elinor HITE
23 Director Adler Community Health Svc ... Dr. Dan BARNES
08 Director Library ... Ms. Kerry COCHRANE
09 Director of Institutional Research ... Mr. Don HUFFMAN
12 Dean Vancouver Campus ... Dr. Larry AXELROD
30 Vice President of Development ... Mr. Anthony CHIMERA
44 Director of Annual Giving ... Vacant
102 Director Corp & Foundation Rels ... Ms. Kate LUX
36 Director Career Services ... Vacant
28 VP Institutes on Social Change ... Dr. Lynn TODMAN
28 Director IPSSJ ... Dr. Elena QUINTANA
29 Director Alumni Relations ... Ms. Nadia WHITESIDE

American Academy of Art (A)

332 S Michigan Avenue, Chicago IL 60604-4302
County: Cook　FICE Identification: 001628
Unit ID: 142887
Telephone: (312) 461-0600　Carnegie Class: Spec/Arts
FAX Number: (312) 294-9570　Calendar System: Semester
URL: www.aaart.edu
Established: 1923　Annual Undergrad Tuition & Fees: $27,400
Enrollment: 461　Coed
Affiliation or Control: Proprietary　IRS Status: Proprietary
Highest Offering: Baccalaureate
Program: Professional; Fine Arts Emphasis
Accreditation: NH, ACCSC

01 Director ... Mr. Richard H. OTTO
05 Academic Dean ... Mr. Duncan WEBB
06 Registrar ... Ms. Marcia R. THOMAS
36 Career Services Coordinator ... Ms. Lindsay SANDBOTHE
37 Financial Aid Director ... Ms. Ione FITZGERALD
08 Faculty Librarian ... Ms. Lindsay HARMON
88 Cultural Coordinator ... Ms. Lou Ann BURKHARDT
07 Director of Admissions ... Mr. Stuart ROSENBLOOM

American InterContinental University (B)

5550 Prairie Stone Parkway Ste 400,
Hoffman Estates IL 60192-3713
County: Cook　FICE Identification: 021136
Unit ID: 445027
Telephone: (877) 701-3800　Carnegie Class: Master's L
FAX Number: N/A　Calendar System: Quarter
URL: www.aiuonline.edu
Established: 1970　Annual Undergrad Tuition & Fees: N/A
Enrollment: 16,538　Coed
Affiliation or Control: Proprietary　IRS Status: Proprietary
Highest Offering: Master's
Program: 2-Year Principally Bachelor's Creditable; Professional
Accreditation: NH, ACBSP, @TEAC

01 Chief Executive Officer/President ... Mr. George MILLER
05 Provost/Chief Academic Officer ... Dr. Gregory WASHINGTON

Argosy University, Chicago (C)

225 North Michigan Ave., Suite 1300, Chicago IL 60601
County: Cook　Identification: 666736
Unit ID: 145770
Telephone: (312) 777-7600　Carnegie Class: DRU
FAX Number: (312) 777-7748　Calendar System: Semester
URL: www.argosy.edu/chicago
Established: 1976　Annual Undergrad Tuition & Fees: $13,224
Enrollment: 1,453　Coed
Affiliation or Control: Proprietary　IRS Status: Proprietary
Highest Offering: Doctorate
Program: Professional
Accreditation: &WC, CACREP, CLPSY

02 Campus President ... Dr. C. Ronald KIMBERLING
05 Vice President of Academic Affairs ... Dr. David VANWINKLE
07 Senior Director of Admissions ... Vacant
32 Director of Student Services ... Eric ZIEHLKE
37 Dir of Student Financial Services ... Lyudmila BERKOFF
06 Registrar ... Tyler SHIPPEN
15 Human Resources ... Stan WACLAW
11 Dir of Admin & Financial Services ... Irene AYERS

† Regional accreditation is carried under the parent institution in Orange, CA.

Argosy University, Schaumburg (D)

999 N. Plaza Drive, Suite 111, Schaumburg IL 60173-5403
County: Cook　Identification: 666789
Unit ID: 420866
Telephone: (847) 969-4900　Carnegie Class: Spec/Health
FAX Number: (847) 969-4999　Calendar System: Semester
URL: www.argosy.edu/schaumburg
Established: 1994　Annual Undergrad Tuition & Fees: $13,224
Enrollment: 684　Coed
Affiliation or Control: Proprietary　IRS Status: Proprietary
Highest Offering: Doctorate
Program: Professional
Accreditation: &WC, CACREP, CLPSY, SURGT

02 Campus President ... Dr. Charles R. KIMBERLING
05 Vice President of Academic Affairs ... Dr. David B. VANWINKLE
07 Senior Director of Admissions ... Catherine CURRAN
32 Director of Student Services ... Dr. Evelyn HUMPHRIES
37 Assoc Director of Student Finance ... Vacant
06 Registrar ... Dr. Evelyn HUMPHRIES
15 Human Resources ... Stan WACLAW
11 Dir of Admin and Financial Services ... Irene AYERS

† Regional accreditation is carried under the parent institution in Orange, CA.

Augustana College (E)

639-38th Street, Rock Island IL 61201-2296
County: Rock Island　FICE Identification: 001633
Unit ID: 143084
Telephone: (309) 794-7000　Carnegie Class: Bac/A&S
FAX Number: (309) 794-7422　Calendar System: Trimester
URL: www.augustana.edu
Established: 1860　Annual Undergrad Tuition & Fees: $34,614
Enrollment: 2,500　Coed
Affiliation or Control: Evangelical Lutheran Church In America
IRS Status: 501(c)3
Highest Offering: Baccalaureate
Program: Liberal Arts And General; Teacher Preparatory
Accreditation: NH, MUS, TED

01 President ... Mr. Steven C. BAHLS
05 Dean of College ... Dr. Pareena G. LAWRENCE
10 Vice Pres Business & Finance ... Mr. David ENGLISH
30 Vice President Advancement ... Ms. Lynn E. JACKSON
32 Vice Pres/Dean of Student Services ... Dr. Evelyn S. CAMPBELL
84 VP Enrollment/Communication/Plng ... Mr. W. Kent BARNDS
20 Associate Dean of the College ... Dr. Margaret E. FARRAR
25 Director Assessments/Grants Officer ... Vacant
42 Chaplain ... Rev. Richard W. PRIGGIE
06 College Registrar ... Ms. Liesl A. FOWLER
14 Director of ITS ... Mr. Chris VAUGHAN
08 Director of the Library ... Ms. Carla B. TRACY
26 Director of Public Relations ... Ms. Keri RURSCH
36 Director of Career Development ... Ms. Johnna ADAM
29 Director Alumni/Parent Relations ... Ms. Kelly NOACK
37 Director of Student Financial Aid ... Ms. Susan STANDLEY
38 Director Student Counseling ... Mr. Michael W. TENDALL
09 Director of Institutional Research ... Mr. Mark SALISBURY
41 Director of Athletics ... Mr. Mike ZAPOLSKI
15 Director Human Resources ... Mrs. Laura C. FORD
18 Director Facilities Services ... Mr. Dennis M. HITTLE
07 Director of Admissions/Recruitment ... Ms. Meghan M. COOLEY
28 Director of Diversity ... Mr. Greg AGUILAR

Aurora University (F)

347 S Gladstone Avenue, Aurora IL 60506-4892
County: Kane　FICE Identification: 001634
Unit ID: 143118
Telephone: (630) 892-6431　Carnegie Class: Master's L
FAX Number: (630) 844-5463　Calendar System: Semester
URL: www.aurora.edu
Established: 1893　Annual Undergrad Tuition & Fees: $19,900
Enrollment: 4,378　Coed
Affiliation or Control: Independent Non-Profit　IRS Status: 501(c)3
Highest Offering: Doctorate
Program: Liberal Arts And General; Teacher Preparatory; Professional
Accreditation: NH, NURSE, SW, TED

01 President ... Dr. Rebecca L. SHERRICK
05 Provost ... Dr. Andrew P. MANION
30 Exec Vice Pres Univ Advancement ... Mr. Theodore C. PARGE
10 Vice President for Finance ... Mrs. Beth W. REISSENWEBER
11 Vice President for Administration ... Mr. Thomas HAMMOND
84 Vice President Enrollment ... Dr. Donna DE SPAIN
32 Vice President for Student Life ... Dr. Lora DE LACEY
26 Vice President Public Relations ... Mr. Steven MCFARLAND
31 Vice President Community Relations ... Ms. Sarah R. RUSSE
30 VP for Development/Alumni Relations ... Ms. Teri TOMASZKIEWICZ
35 Asst Vice Pres for Student Life ... Ms. Amy LAMPHERE
37 Dean of Student Financial Services ... Mrs. Heather L. MCKANE
13 Chief Information Officer ... Ms. Celeste E. BRANDING
91 Dir of Administrative Computing ... Mr. Robt S. LOWE
20 Assistant Provost ... Ms. Ellen J. GOLDBERG
21 Controller ... Mr. Joseph ONZICK
06 Registrar ... Ms. Lisa WISNIOWICZ
08 Director of the Library ... Mr. John W. LAW
15 Director of Human Resources ... Vacant
19 Director of Campus Safety ... Mr. Gary BOLT
88 Dir Rsrch on Retention/Tchng Effect ... Ms. Brynn LANDWEHR
44 Director Special Gifts ... Mr. Roger K. PAROLINI
41 Athletic Director ... Mr. Mark C. WALSH
28 Director of Diversity Affairs ... Vacant
38 Director of Counseling Center ... Vacant
107 Int Dean College Professional Stds ... Dr. Jodi KOSLOW-MARTIN
66 Director of School of Nursing ... Dr. Carmella MORAN
70 Director of School of Social Work ... Dr. Fred R. MCKENZIE
49 Int Dean College of Arts/Sciences ... Dr. Saib OTHMAN
88 Dean of Faculty Development ... Dr. Alicia C. COSKY
50 Director Dunham School of Business ... Dr. Charles EDWARDS
53 Dean College of Education ... Dr. Donald C. WOLD
68 Dir of School of Health/Phys Educ ... Dr. Jennifer BUCKLEY

Benedictine University (G)

5700 College Road, Lisle IL 60532-0900
County: DuPage　FICE Identification: 001767
Unit ID: 145619
Telephone: (630) 829-6000　Carnegie Class: DRU
FAX Number: (630) 960-1126　Calendar System: Semester
URL: www.ben.edu
Established: 1887　Annual Undergrad Tuition & Fees: $25,350
Enrollment: 6,857　Coed
Affiliation or Control: Roman Catholic　IRS Status: 501(c)3
Highest Offering: Doctorate
Program: Liberal Arts And General; Teacher Preparatory; Professional
Accreditation: NH, DIETD, DIETI, NURSE

01 President ... Dr. William J. CARROLL
03 Executive Vice President ... Mr. Charles GREGORY
05 Provost/Vice Pres Academic Affs ... Dr. Donald TAYLOR
10 VP Business & Finance ... Mr. Allan GOZUM
88 Exec Dir of Stewardship Development ... Ms. Pat ARIANO
30 Managing Dir of Univ Advancement ... Ms. Meagan DANIEL
32 Associate Vice Pres Student Life ... Mr. Marco MASINI
09 Assoc Prov/Dir Inst Effectiveness ... Dr. David SONNENBERGER
42 Director University Ministry ... Mr. Mark KUROWSKI
84 VP for Enrollment Services ... Ms. Kari GIBBONS
06 Acting Registrar ... Ms. Betty MORRISON
08 Director Library Services ... Mr. Jack FRITTS
37 Sr Associate Dean Financial Aid ... Ms. Diane BATTISTELLA
36 Director Career Development ... Ms. Julie COSIMO
23 Director Health Services ... Ms. Barbara ALLANACH
26 Exec Dir Marketing/Communications ... Ms. Mercy ROBB
50 Dean College of Business ... Dr. Sandra GILL
81 Dean College of Science ... Dr. Bart NG
49 Dean College of Liberal Arts ... Dr. Maria DE LA CAMARA
51 Dean Col of Adult Profess Studies ... Dr. Michael CARROLL
53 Dean Col Education/Health Services ... Dr. Alan GORR
19 Chief of Police ... Mr. Michael SALATINO
18 Director Campus Services ... Mr. Jay L. STUART
39 Director of Residence Life ... Ms. Zeina ABUSOUD
29 Director of Alumni Relations ... Vacant
31 Director Community Development ... Ms. Denise WEST
15 Director of Personnel Resources ... Ms. Betsy RHINESMITH
35 Student Activ & Commuter Svcs Coord ... Ms. Katie BUELL
27 Chief Information Officer ... Mr. Charles WILLIAMS

Black Hawk College (H)

6600 34th Avenue, Moline IL 61265-5899
County: Rock Island　FICE Identification: 001638
Unit ID: 143279
Telephone: (309) 796-5000　Carnegie Class: Assoc/Pub-R-L
FAX Number: (309) 792-5976　Calendar System: Semester
URL: www.bhc.edu
Established: 1946　Annual Undergrad Tuition & Fees (In-District): $3,225
Enrollment: 6,403　Coed
Affiliation or Control: Local　IRS Status: 501(c)3
Highest Offering: Associate Degree
Program: Occupational; 2-Year Principally Bachelor's Creditable
Accreditation: NH, ADNUR, PTAA

01 President ... Dr. Thomas B. BAYNUM
05 Interim VP of Instruction ... Dr. Bettie TRUITT
10 Chief Financial Officer ... Ms. Leslie ANDERSON
11 VP Administration ... Mr. Mike PHILLIPS
32 VP Student Services ... Dr. Richard VALLANDINGHAM
12 Vice President for East Campus ... Ms. Chanda DOWELL
15 Director of Human Resources ... Ms. Karen BOYD
13 Chief Information Officer ... Mr. Sam SCOMA
09 Director Plng & Inst Effectiveness ... Ms. Kathy MALCOLM
20 Dean Instruction/Academic Support ... Vacant
20 Dean of Business and Technology ... Dr. Michael RIVERA
32 Asst Dean of Student Support Svcs ... Dr. Kim ARMSTRONG
51 Dean Adult/Continuing Educ ... Ms. Glenda NICKE
44 Exec Dir BHC Foundation QC Campus ... Ms. Shelly CAIN
88 Director Small Business Devel Ctr ... Mr. Joel YOUNGS
26 Director Marketing/Public Relations ... Mr. John MEINEKE
37 Director of Financial Aid ... Ms. Joanna DYE
36 Director Career Services Center ... Dr. Bruce STOREY
40 Bookstore Manager Quad Cities ... Ms. Nyla WOOLARD
41 Division Director Athletics/Coach ... Mr. Gary HUBER
08 Librarian ... Ms. Charlet KEY
19 Chief of Police ... Vacant
22 EEO/Affirmative Action Officer ... Ms. Jo JOHNSON
24 Dir Teaching Lrng Ctr/Online Lrng ... Vacant
81 Dept Chair Math/Comp Science ... Mr. Peter NODZENSKI
31 Professional and Continuing Educ ... Ms. Brenda BROWN
51 Director Adult Education ... Ms. Diane FALL
35 Asst Dean of Student Support Svc/EC ... Mr. B. J MCCULLUM
06 Registrar ... Ms. Sandi GIESON
96 Purchasing Manager ... Mr. Mike MELEG
51 Department Chair Adult Education ... Ms. Constance KAPPAS
72 Dept Chair Bus & Office Tech ... Ms. Diana MCCABE
57 Dept Chair Comm & Fine Arts ... Ms. Michelle JOHNSON
79 Dept Chair Human/Languages/Journal ... Mr. Bill DESMOND
54 Dept Chair Natural Science/Engrng ... Mr. Brian GLASER
83 Dept Chair Social/Behav/Educ Stds ... Dr. Bruce LEBLANC
47 Department Chair Applied Science ... Mr. William GOOD
49 Dept Chair Liberal Arts/Sciences ... Mr. Kirk WATSON
66 Dept Chair Assoc Degree/Prac Nurs ... Ms. Karen BABER
76 Dept Chair Allied Health/HPE ... Ms. Betsey MORTHLAND
88 Dept Chair Counseling ... Ms. Wendy BOCK
62 Dept Chair Lrg Resource Center ... Ms. Charlet KEY

Blackburn College (A)

700 College Avenue, Carlinville IL 62626-1498
County: Macoupin FICE Identification: 001639
Unit ID: 143288
Telephone: (217) 854-3231 Carnegie Class: Bac/Diverse
FAX Number: (217) 854-5700 Calendar System: Semester
URL: www.blackburn.edu
Established: 1837 Annual Undergrad Tuition & Fees: $14,862
Enrollment: 554 Coed
Affiliation or Control: Presbyterian Church (U.S.A.) IRS Status: 501(c)3
Highest Offering: Baccalaureate
Program: Liberal Arts And General; Teacher Preparatory
Accreditation: NH

01 President .... Dr. Miriam R. PRIDE
05 Provost .... Dr. Jeffery P. APER
10 Vice Pres Administration & Finance .... Ms. Heather BIGARD
30 VP for Institutional Advancement .... Mr. Glen KRUPICA
04 Exec Asst to Pres/Asst Sec Bd Trust .... Ms. Ann M. ALLEN
32 Dean of Students .... Ms. Heidi HEINZ
07 Director of Admissions .... Ms. Alisha KAPP
88 Director of Transfer Admissions .... Mr. John MALIN
29 Sr Develop Ofcr/Alumni/Staff Rels .... Mr. Nate RUSH
37 Director of Financial Aid .... Ms. Jane KELSEY
08 Head Librarian .... Ms. Carol SCHAEFER
38 College Counselor .... Mr. Robert M. WEIS
06 College Registrar .... Ms. Dianna RUYLE
15 Director Personnel Services .... Ms. Ann ALLEN
36 Director Student Placement .... Ms. Suzanne KRUPICA
18 Director Physical Plant .... Mr. Samuel HARDING
41 Int Director of Athletic Programs .... Ms. Heidi HEINZ
42 Chaplain .... Vacant
26 Director of Public Relations .... Mr. Peter OSWALD
09 Director Institutional Research .... Dr. Kristi NELMS
21 Controller .... Ms. Dawn KIPER
44 Director of Annual Giving .... Ms. Jodi ROWE

Blessing-Rieman College of Nursing (B)

Broadway at 11th, PO Box 7005, Quincy IL 62305-7005
County: Adams FICE Identification: 006214
Unit ID: 143297
Telephone: (217) 228-5520 Carnegie Class: Spec/Health
FAX Number: (217) 223-4661 Calendar System: Semester
URL: www.brcn.edu
Established: 1891 Annual Undergrad Tuition & Fees: $17,840
Enrollment: 385 Coed
Affiliation or Control: Independent Non-Profit IRS Status: 501(c)3
Highest Offering: Master's
Program: Professional; Nursing Emphasis
Accreditation: NH, NURSE

01 President College of Nursing .... Dr. Pamela S. BROWN

Bradley University (C)

1501 W Bradley Avenue, Peoria IL 61625-0001
County: Peoria FICE Identification: 001641
Unit ID: 143358
Telephone: (309) 676-7611 Carnegie Class: Master's L
FAX Number: N/A Calendar System: Semester
URL: www.bradley.edu
Established: 1897 Annual Undergrad Tuition & Fees: $28,264
Enrollment: 5,640 Coed
Affiliation or Control: Independent Non-Profit IRS Status: 501(c)3
Highest Offering: Doctorate
Program: Liberal Arts And General; Teacher Preparatory; Professional
Accreditation: NH, ART, BUS, BUSA, CACREP, CONST, DIETD, @DIETI, ENG, ENGT, MUS, NUR, PTA, SW, TED, THEA

01 President .... Ms. Joanne K. GLASSER
05 Provost/Vice Pres Academic Affairs .... Dr. David GLASSMAN
20 Assistant Provost Academic Affairs .... Mrs. Linda J. PIZZUTI
10 Vice President Business Affairs .... Mr. Gary M. ANNA
30 Vice President Advancement .... Mr. Pat VICKERMAN
32 Vice Pres Student Affairs .... Dr. Alan G. GALSKY
27 Assoc VP University Communications .... Mr. Shelley EPSTEIN
26 Assoc VP University Marketing .... Ms. Susan ANDREWS
58 Dean Graduate School .... Dr. Jeffrey BAKKEN
50 Dean Foster Col Business Admin .... Dr. Darrell J. RADSON
57 Dean Slane Col Communic/Fine Arts ... Dr. Jeffrey H. HUBERMAN
53 Dean Education & Health Sciences .... Dr. Joan L. SATTLER
54 Dean Engineering & Technology .... Dr. Lex A. AKERS
49 Int Dean Liberal Arts & Sciences .... Dr. Stacey ROBERTSON
84 Ex Dir Enrollment Mgmt Office Oper .. Ms. Angela M. ROBERSON
13 Assoc Provost Info Resources & Tech .... Mr. J. Chuck RUCH
08 Exec Director of the Library .... Ms. Barbara GALIK
38 Ex Dir Ctr For Stdnt Dev/Hlth Svcs .... Dr. Joyce SHOTICK
39 Ex Dir Ctr Residential Lvgn/Ldrshp .... Mr. Nathan THOMAS
88 Exec Dir Student Involvement .... Mr. Mike KEUP
36 Exec Director Smith Career Center .... Ms. Jane C. LINNENBURGER
14 Exec Dir Computing Services .... Ms. Sandra BURY
24 Ex Dir Instruct Tech/Media Svcs .... Mr. Nial L. JOHNSON
29 Exec Director of Alumni Relations .... Ms. Lori FAN
51 Executive Director Continuing Educ .... Ms. Janet LANGE
06 Registrar .... Mrs. Katherine M. BEATY
37 Exec Dir Enroll Mgmt/Dir Fin Asst .... Mr. David L. PARDIECK
07 Exec Director Admissions .... Mr. Rodney SAN JOSE
19 Chief of Campus Police .... Mr. Brian JOSCHKO
15 Director of Human Resources .... Ms. Nena PEPLOW
18 Director Facilities Management .... Vacant
23 Medical Director .... Dr. Jessica HIGGS
27 Senior Director Public Relations .... Ms. M. Kathleen CONVER
41 Director Athletics .... Dr. Michael CROSS
78 Interim Dir Experiential Education .... Mrs. Dawn KOELTZOW
87 Assoc Dir Summer/Interim Sessions .... Mr. Jon NEIDY
25 Int Dir Off/Teaching Excel/Fac Dev .... Mrs. Kim WILLIS
22 Director Affirmative Action/EEO .... Ms. Nena PEPLOW
28 Dir Multicultural Student Services .... Ms. Frances JONES
92 Director of Honors Program .... Dr. Robert FULLER
94 Director of Women's Studies .... Dr. Stacey M. ROBERTSON
09 Dir of Institutional Improvement .... Ms. Jennifer GRUENING
40 Manager Bookstore .... Mr. Paul KROENKE
88 Dir of PreProfessional Health Adv .... Dr. Melinda MARIS
88 Dir Pre Law Center .... Mrs. Nicole MEYER

Carl Sandburg College (D)

2400 Tom L. Wilson Boulevard, Galesburg IL 61401-9576
County: Knox FICE Identification: 007265
Unit ID: 143613
Telephone: (309) 344-2518 Carnegie Class: Assoc/Pub-R-M
FAX Number: (309) 344-1395 Calendar System: Semester
URL: www.sandburg.edu
Established: 1966 Annual Undergrad Tuition & Fees: $4,054
Enrollment: 4,392 Coed
Affiliation or Control: Independent Non-Profit IRS Status: 501(c)3
Highest Offering: Associate Degree
Program: Occupational; 2-Year Principally Bachelor's Creditable
Accreditation: NH, ADNUR, DH, FUSER, PNUR

01 President .... Dr. Lori L. SUNDBERG
32 VP of Student Services/AD .... Mr. Steve NORTON
05 VP of Academic Services .... Ms. Julie GIBB
11 VP Administrative Services & CIO .... Mr. Samuel SUDHAKAR
08 Dean of Library .... Mr. Michael WALTERS
76 Dean of Career Technical and Health .... Ms. Lauri WHITE
12 Dean of Extension Services .... Ms. Debra MILLER
56 Director of Extension Services .... Ms. Linda THOMAS
96 Director of Business Services .... Mr. Larry BYRNE
37 Director Financial Aid .... Ms. Lisa HANSON
26 Director Marketing/Public Relations .... Ms. Robin DEMOTT
10 Chief Financial Officer/Treasurer .... Ms. Lisa BLAKE
102 Dir Foundation & Bus & Comm Ed .... Ms. Gena ALCORN
88 Director TRIO Upward Bound .... Mr. Tony BENTLEY
88 Dean of Student Success .... Ms. Misty LYON
07 Director of Recuitment .... Ms. Dylana CARLSON
66 Associate Dean of Nursing .... Ms. Rosemary O'DANIEL
06 Director of Admissions & Records .... Mr. Rick EDDY
46 Dean HR/Organizational Development ... Dr. Constance THURMAN
19 Director of Public Safety .... Mr. Andrew TOLLE

Catholic Theological Union (E)

5401 S Cornell Avenue, Chicago IL 60615-5698
County: Cook FICE Identification: 009232
Unit ID: 143659
Telephone: (773) 371-5400 Carnegie Class: Spec/Faith
FAX Number: (773) 324-8490 Calendar System: Semester
URL: www.ctu.edu
Established: 1967 Annual Graduate Tuition & Fees: $19,170
Enrollment: 480 Coed
Affiliation or Control: Roman Catholic IRS Status: 501(c)3
Highest Offering: Doctorate; No Undergraduates
Program: Professional; Religious Emphasis
Accreditation: THEOL

01 President .... Rev. Donald P. SENIOR, CP
05 Vice President/Academic Dean .... Sr. Barbara REID, OP
10 Vice Pres Administration & Finance .... Mr. Michael W. CONNORS
30 Director of Development .... Ms. Anne M. TIRPAK
26 Dir of Marketing & Communications .... Ms. Nancy NICKEL
08 Director of the Library .... Ms. Melody L. MCMAHON
06 Registrar .... Mrs. Maria De Jesus LEMUS
07 Director of Admissions .... Ms. Angela PAVIGLIANITI
21 Comptroller .... Mrs. Joyce E. O'CONNOR
51 Director of Continuing Education .... Ms. Keiren O'KELLY
04 Assistant to the President .... Sr. Pam PAULOSKI, SP
32 Events & Student Services Manager ... Ms. Christine HENDERSON
37 Director Student Financial Aid .... Ms. Kathy VAN DUSER

Chicago School of Professional Psychology (F)

325 N Wells Street, Chicago IL 60654-8158
County: Cook FICE Identification: 021553
Unit ID: 143978
Telephone: (312) 329-6600 Carnegie Class: Spec/Health
FAX Number: (312) 644-3333 Calendar System: Semester
URL: www.thechicagoschool.edu
Established: 1979 Annual Graduate Tuition & Fees: $32,868
Enrollment: 4,188 Coed
Affiliation or Control: Independent Non-Profit IRS Status: 501(c)3
Highest Offering: Doctorate; No Undergraduates
Program: Professional
Accreditation: NH, CLPSY

01 President .... Dr. Michele NEALON-WOODS
12 Interim Campus President Chicago .... Dr. Patricia BREEN
12 Campus President Washington DC .... Dr. Orlando TAYLOR
10 Vice Pres of Finance/Administration .... Ms. Carole ROBERTSON
11 Senior Vice President of Operations .... Vacant
102 President TCS Foundation .... Vacant
13 Vice Pres of Information Technology .... Vacant
26 Vice Pres of Marketing & Comm .... Ms. Dina SCHENK
05 Vice Pres for Academic Affairs .... Dr. Jay FINKELMAN
32 Assoc VP Engagement/Student Affairs .... Vacant
20 Assoc Dean Academic Affairs Chicago .... Dr. Breeda MCGRATH
106 Dean of Online-Blended Programs .... Dr. Patricia BREEN
32 Director of Student Services ...... Ms. Jennifer STRIPE-PORTILLO
07 Director of Admissions Chicago .... Ms. Andrea SCHMOYER
15 Director Human Resources Chicago .... Ms. Kim ORTIZ
37 Assistant Director of Financial Aid .... Ms. Tamatha CONAWAY
36 Director of Career Services .... Ms. Aisha GHORI
08 Campus Librarian .... Vacant
09 Dir Institutional/Market Research .... Dr. George HAY
26 Dir Communications/Public Relations .... Ms. Elinor GILBERT
36 Dir Office of Placement/Training .... Ms. Heather SHEETS
88 Assoc Director of Clincal Services .... Ms. Marilisa MOREA
88 Director of Community Partnerships .... Ms. Jill GLENN
07 Director of Admissions California .... Mr. Robert PETTAY
88 Dir Center for Academic Excellence .... Dr. Katia MITOVA
28 Dir Multicultural/Diversity Studies .... Vacant
27 Dir of Institutional Publications .... Ms. Judy BEAUPRE
06 Registrar Chicago .... Ms. Aubri ADKINS
88 Dept Chair Clincal Psych PsyD .... Dr. Thomas BARRETT
88 Dept Chair Business Psych PsyD .... Dr. Keith CARROLL
88 Dept Chair School Psych Master's .... Dr. James WALSH
88 Dept Ch Forensic Psych PsyD/Masters .... Dr. Michele HOY-WATKINS
88 Dept Chr Clinical-ABA PsyD/Masters .... Dr. Diana WALKER
88 Dept Chair Clincal-Counsel Master's .... Dr. Virginia QUINONEZ
35 Director of Student Affairs .... Ms. Shea WOLFE

Chicago State University (G)

9501 S King Drive, Chicago IL 60628-1598
County: Cook FICE Identification: 001694
Unit ID: 144005
Telephone: (773) 995-2000 Carnegie Class: Master's L
FAX Number: (773) 995-2563 Calendar System: Semester
URL: www.csu.edu
Established: 1867 Annual Undergrad Tuition & Fees (In-State): $10,964
Enrollment: 6,882 Coed
Affiliation or Control: State IRS Status: 501(c)3
Highest Offering: Doctorate
Program: Liberal Arts And General; Teacher Preparatory; Professional
Accreditation: NH, ACBSP, CACREP, MUS, NRPA, NUR, OT, PHAR, SW, TED

01 President .... Dr. Wayne D. WATSON
100 Chief of Staff .... Dr. Napoleon W. MOSES
05 Provost/Sr VP for Academic Affairs ..... Dr. Sandra WESTBROOKS
43 VP Gen Counsel for Labor/Legal Affs .... Mr. Patrick CAGE
21 VP of Administration and Finance .... Mr. Glenn MEEKS
10 Acting Director Budget & Risk Mgmt . Mrs. Arrileen PATAWARAN
13 Chief Information Officer .... Mrs. Ce S. COLE DILLON
84 Vice Pres of Enrollment Management ... Mrs. Angela HENDERSON
09 Director Inst Research/Evaluations .... Dr. Resche HINES
49 Interim Dean Arts & Sciences .... Dr. David R. KANIS
53 Dean Education .... Dr. Sylvia GIST
67 Dean College of Pharmacy .... Dr. Miriam MOBLEY-SMITH
76 Dean College of Health Sciences .... Dr. Joseph A. BALOGUN
50 Dean College of Business .... Mr. Derrick K. COLLINS
08 Acting Dean of Library/Instruct Svc .... Dr. Richard DARGA
51 Interim Dean Cont Educ Nontrad Pgms .... Ms. Nelly MAYNARD
06 Registrar .... Mrs. Victoria SMITH-MURPHY
21 Bursar .... Ms. Miesha V. DALEY
84 Assoc Vice President Enroll Mgmt .... Ms. Cheri SIDNEY
37 Director of Financial Aid .... Mrs. Brenda HOOKER
07 Director of Admissions .... Mr. Matthew HARRISON
29 Director Alumni Affairs .... Vacant
26 Director of Marketing & Communicati .... Mrs. Sabrina LAND
15 Director Human Resources .... Dr. Renee D. MITCHELL
36 Director of Career Development .... Dr. Renee D. MITCHELL
88 Dir Latino Resource Center .... Mr. Fernando DIAZ
96 Director of Purchasing .... Ms. Janielle GRAHAM
18 Int Dir Facilities/Physical Plant .... Mr. Alan O'NEAL
20 Associate VP Academic Officer .... Dr. Debrah JEFFERSON
35 Dir of Student Act & Leadership Dev .... Vacant
38 Director Counseling Center .... Dr. Michael C. EDWARDS
27 Dir of Public Relations & Communica ..... Ms. Deborah DOUGLAS

Chicago Theological Seminary (H)

1407 East 60th Street, Chicago IL 60637-1284
County: Cook FICE Identification: 001661
Unit ID: 144014
Telephone: (773) 896-2400 Carnegie Class: Spec/Faith
FAX Number: (773) 643-1284 Calendar System: Semester
URL: www.ctschicago.edu
Established: 1855 Annual Graduate Tuition & Fees: $13,680
Enrollment: 228 Coed
Affiliation or Control: United Church Of Christ IRS Status: 501(c)3
Highest Offering: Doctorate; No Undergraduates
Program: Professional; Religious Emphasis
Accreditation: NH, THEOL

01 President .... Dr. Alice HUNT
05 Academic Dean .... Dr. Ken STONE
10 Vice President for Finance & Admin .... Mr. Stephen MANNING
30 Vice President for Advancement .... Ms. Megan DAVIS OCHI

06 Registrar ... Ms. Elena JIMENEZ
08 Head Librarian ... Rev. Neil W. GERDES
84 Director of Enrollment ... Mr. Kim KING

Christian Life College (A)

400 E Gregory Street, Mount Prospect IL 60056-2522
County: Cook FICE Identification: 031993
Unit ID: 260947
Telephone: (847) 259-1840 Carnegie Class: Spec/Faith
FAX Number: (847) 259-3888 Calendar System: Semester
URL: www.christianlifecollege.edu
Established: 1950 Annual Undergrad Tuition & Fees: $10,590
Enrollment: 40 Coed
Affiliation or Control: Pentecostal/Charismatic Non-Denominational
IRS Status: 501(c)3
Highest Offering: Baccalaureate
Program: Religious Emphasis
Accreditation: TRACS

01 President ... Mr. Harry R. SCHMIDT
05 Academic Dean ... Mr. Wayne R. WACHSMUTH
08 Director of Library Services ... Mr. Christopher C. ULLMAN
10 Director of Finance ... Mr. Roger K. STEVENS
32 Dean of Students ... Vacant
06 Registrar ... Vacant

*City Colleges of Chicago (B)

226 W Jackson Boulevard, Chicago IL 60606-6998
County: Cook FICE Identification: 001647
Unit ID: 144500
Telephone: (312) 553-2500 Carnegie Class: N/A
FAX Number: (312) 553-2699
URL: www.ccc.edu

01 Chancellor ... Ms. Cheryl HYMAN
05 Provost ... Mr. Kojo QUARTEY
10 Interim Vice Chancellor Finance ... Mr. JR DEMPSEY
13 Vice Chanc/Chief Information Ofcr ... Ms. Arshele STEVENS
09 Vice Chanc Strategy & Instnl Intel ... Dr. Alvin BISARYA
11 Vice Chanc Administrative Services ... Ms. Diane MINOR
04 Executive Board Administrator ... Ms. Regina HAWKINS
43 General Counsel ... Mr. James REILLY
27 Vice Chanc Institutional Advan ... Mr. Laurent PERNOT

*City Colleges of Chicago Harold Washington College (C)

30 E Lake Street, Chicago IL 60601-2449
County: Cook FICE Identification: 001652
Unit ID: 144209
Telephone: (312) 553-5600 Carnegie Class: Assoc/Pub-U-MC
FAX Number: (312) 553-5964 Calendar System: Semester
URL: www.ccc.edu
Established: 1962 Annual Undergrad Tuition & Fees (In-District): $3,010
Enrollment: 8,915 Coed
Affiliation or Control: State/Local IRS Status: 501(c)3
Highest Offering: Associate Degree
Program: Occupational; 2-Year Principally Bachelor's Creditable
Accreditation: NH, ACBSP

02 President ... Mr. Donald J. LAACKMAN
05 Int Vice Pres Academic/Student Affs ... Mr. John H. METOYER
11 Vice President Operations ... Mr. Kent LUSK
37 Director of Financial Aid ... Vacant
18 Chief Facilities/Physical Plant ... Mr. Richard WREN
21 Director Bus Admin & Aux Services ... Vacant
08 Librarian ... Mr. John KIERALDO
15 Human Resources Admin ... Mr. Brandon PENDLETON
20 Dean of Instruction ... Mr. Armen SARRAFIAN
32 Dean of Student Services ... Mr. Wendell BLAIR
04 Assistant to the President ... Mr. Gabriel RAZO
88 Int Dean Public Agency/Special Pgms ... Mr. John HADER
20 Associate Dean of Instruction ... Mr. George BICKFORD
13 Director Information Technology ... Ms. Ewa BEJNAROWICZ
35 Assoc Dean of Student Services ... Mr. Robert BROWN
46 Director Research/Planning ... Mr. William EDWARDS

*City Colleges of Chicago Harry S Truman College (D)

1145 W Wilson Avenue, Chicago IL 60640-5691
County: Cook FICE Identification: 001648
Unit ID: 144184
Telephone: (773) 907-4700 Carnegie Class: Assoc/Pub-U-MC
FAX Number: (773) 907-4464 Calendar System: Semester
URL: www.trumancollege.edu
Established: 1956 Annual Undergrad Tuition & Fees (In-District): $3,070
Enrollment: 6,275 Coed
Affiliation or Control: State/Local IRS Status: 501(c)3
Highest Offering: Associate Degree
Program: Occupational; 2-Year Principally Bachelor's Creditable
Accreditation: NH, ADNUR

02 President ... Dr. Reagan F. ROMALI
05 Vice Pres Student/Academic Affs ... Dr. Pervez RAHMAN
06 Registrar ... Ms. My Linh TRAN
32 Dean of Student Services ... Ms. Brenda WEDDINGTON
35 Associate Dean of Student Services ... Ms. Indra PELAEZ
35 Director of Student Activities ... Mr. Jason WIEDENHOEFT
56 Dean of Adult Education ... Mr. Armando MATA
51 Dean of Continuing Education ... Ms. Nancy KRAMER
20 Interim Dean of Instruction ... Ms. Loretta BAILES
20 Associate Dean of Instruction ... Ms. DeShaunta STEWART
20 Associate Dean of Instruction ... Ms. Regina JENNINGS-HOLDEN
10 Exec Dir Business/Operational Svcs ... Mr. Thomas DUNHAM
19 Director of Security ... Mr. Ira HUNTER
37 Director of Financial Aid ... Mr. Robert EVANS
15 Human Resource Administrator ... Mr. Michael ROBERTS
27 Director of Public Relations ... Ms. Nikole MUZZY
18 Chief Engineer ... Mr. Brian MCCUE
72 Asst Dean Information Technology ... Mr. Mike KRITIKOS
24 Director Lakeview Learning Center ... Ms. Ellen SELLERGREN
09 Asst Dir of Research & Evaluation ... Ms. Ericka KILBURN
88 Director of Auxiliary Services ... Ms. Nina CAO
20 Director of Developmental Education ... Ms. Maggie AYALA RICE

*City Colleges of Chicago Kennedy-King College (E)

6301 South Halsted Street, Chicago IL 60621-3798
County: Cook FICE Identification: 001654
Unit ID: 144157
Telephone: (773) 602-5000 Carnegie Class: Assoc/Pub-U-MC
FAX Number: N/A Calendar System: Semester
URL: www.kennedyking.ccc.edu
Established: 1934 Annual Undergrad Tuition & Fees (In-District): $3,070
Enrollment: 7,013 Coed
Affiliation or Control: State/Local IRS Status: 501(c)3
Highest Offering: Associate Degree
Program: Occupational; 2-Year Principally Bachelor's Creditable
Accreditation: NH, DH

02 President ... Dr. Joyce C. ESTER
05 Vice President for Academic Affairs ... Ms. Katonja WEBB
32 Dean Student Services ... Ms. De Reese REID-HART
12 Dean-Dawson Tech Institute ... Mr. Selmon ASSIGNON
36 Dean Career Programs ... Ms. Kimberly CHAVIS
51 Dean Adult/Continuing Education ... Mr. John MCCLURE
35 Assistant Dean Student Services ... Vacant
37 Director Financial Aid ... Ms. Tabitha O'NEIL
20 Director Academic Support Services ... Mr. Brandon NICHOLS
10 Director Business/Operation Svcs ... Mr. Christopher STINSON
06 Registrar ... Vacant
09 Director of Institutional Research ... Ms. Tasha JARRETT
18 Chief Facilities/Physical Plant ... Mr. Jerome DABNEY
26 Marketing Director ... Vacant
15 Director Human Resources ... Mr. Rene ALVARADO
04 Assistant to the President ... Ms. Ukeyco RHYNS

*City Colleges of Chicago Malcolm X College (F)

1900 W Van Buren Street, Chicago IL 60612-3197
County: Cook FICE Identification: 001650
Unit ID: 144166
Telephone: (312) 850-7000 Carnegie Class: Assoc/Pub-U-MC
FAX Number: (312) 850-7039 Calendar System: Semester
URL: www.ccc.edu/malcolmx
Established: 1911 Annual Undergrad Tuition & Fees (In-District): $3,719
Enrollment: 5,083 Coed
Affiliation or Control: State/Local IRS Status: 501(c)3
Highest Offering: Associate Degree
Program: Occupational; 2-Year Principally Bachelor's Creditable
Accreditation: NH, #ARCPA, FUSER, RAD, SURGT

02 President ... Dr. Anthony E. MUNROE
05 Vice Pres Academic Affairs ... Dr. Darrylinn TODD
32 Dean Student Services/Enroll Mgmt ... Ms. Kimberly HOLLINGSWORTH
10 Exec Director Business Operations ... Ms. Kim TYLER
04 Executive Assistant to President ... Ms. Alanna POORE
15 Human Resources Administrator ... Mr. Stanley BEAMON
20 Dean Instruction ... Dr. Lynette STOKES-WILSON
09 Assoc Dir Inst Research & Planning ... Mr. Byron A. JAVIER
13 Asst Dean Information Technology ... Mr. Charles MCCLEANON
06 Registrar ... Mr. Alex UNDERWOOD
35 Assoc Dean Student Services ... Dr. Tasha WILLIAMS
07 Director Admissions/Financial Aid ... Mr. Marco SEPULVEDA
88 Director Child Care Center ... Ms. Aisha RUTHER
19 Director Security/Public Safety ... Mr. Lorenzo CLEMONS
18 Chief Facilities/Physical Plant ... Mr. Eduardo JONES
18 Chief Facilites/Physical Plant ... Mr. John MORLEY
08 Librarian ... Ms. CM WINTERS-PALACIO
21 Business Manager ... Ms. Latasha JOHNSON
40 Director Bookstore ... Ms. Kristen ROMAN
26 Coordinator Marketing ... Ms. Twania BREWSTER
75 Dean Career Programs ... Dr. Micah YOUNG
56 Dean Adult Education Pgms ... Ms. Sharon BRYANT
88 Assoc Dean Student Development ... Ms. Lisa WILLIS

*City Colleges of Chicago Olive-Harvey College (G)

10001 S Woodlawn Avenue, Chicago IL 60628-1645
County: Cook FICE Identification: 009767
Unit ID: 144175
Telephone: (773) 291-6100 Carnegie Class: Assoc/Pub-U-MC
FAX Number: (773) 291-6304 Calendar System: Semester
URL: www.ccc.edu/colleges/olive-harvey/pages/default.aspx
Established: 1970 Annual Undergrad Tuition & Fees (In-District): $3,130
Enrollment: 4,617 Coed
Affiliation or Control: State/Local IRS Status: 501(c)3
Highest Offering: Associate Degree
Program: Occupational; 2-Year Principally Bachelor's Creditable
Accreditation: NH

02 President ... Dr. Craig FOLLINS
04 Assistant to President ... Ms. Hakeemah SHAMSUDDIN
05 VP Academic & Student Affairs ... Dr. David MARSHALL
32 Dean Student Services ... Mr. Gregory ROBINSON
51 Dean Adult & Continuing Education ... Ms. Kathy TAYLOR
09 Asst Dean of Research/Planning ... Vacant
13 Asst Dean Information Technology ... Mr. Savio PINTO
20 Dean of Instruction ... Vacant
36 Dean of Career Programs ... Vacant
35 Assoc Dean of Student Services ... Dr. Ria PINKSTON-MCKEE
35 Assoc Dean of Student Services ... Ms. Michelle ADAMS
36 Assoc Dean of College to Career ... Ms. Joanne IVORY
10 Exec Dir Business/Admin/Aux Svc ... Dr. Nikita JOHNSON
12 Director of South Chicago Lrng Ctr ... Ms. Irma SALDANA
37 Director Financial Aid ... Mr. Stacey ROBBINS
06 Registrar ... Vacant
19 Director Security ... Mr. Reginald JOHNSON
88 Director Child Development Center ... Ms. Tiffany CARTER
41 Director of Athletics ... Mr. Norman FUTRELL
15 Human Resource Administrator ... Ms. Sharon PRAYOR
21 Business Manager ... Ms. Angela ARRINGTON-JONES
26 Director Public Relations ... Vacant

*City Colleges of Chicago Richard J. Daley College (H)

7500 S Pulaski Road, Chicago IL 60652-1299
County: Cook FICE Identification: 001649
Unit ID: 144193
Telephone: (773) 838-7500 Carnegie Class: Assoc/Pub-U-MC
FAX Number: (773) 838-7524 Calendar System: Semester
URL: daley.ccc.edu
Established: 1960 Annual Undergrad Tuition & Fees (In-District): $3,070
Enrollment: 4,547 Coed
Affiliation or Control: State/Local IRS Status: 501(c)3
Highest Offering: Associate Degree
Program: Occupational; 2-Year Principally Bachelor's Creditable
Accreditation: NH, ADNUR

02 President ... Dr. Jose M. AYBAR
03 Vice President ... Dr. Keith MCCOY
05 Dean of Instruction ... Vacant
36 Dean Career & Economic Programs ... Ms. Benita HUNTER
88 Dean Adult Education ... Mr. Victor CASTILLO
32 Dean of Student Services ... Vacant
51 Dean Continuing Education ... Mrs. Jean JOHNSON
10 Exec Director Business Operations ... Ms. Emma L. ORTIZ
37 Director Financial Aid ... Mr. James LOAGUE
18 Chief Engineer/Physical Plant ... Mr. Tim SMITH
19 Director Security ... Mr. Robert HOGAN
21 Asst Director Business/Oper Svcs ... Ms. Crystal WASHINGTON
35 Assoc Dean Student Services ... Dr. Yesenia AVALOS
06 Registrar ... Mr. Milton WRIGHT
09 Director of Institutional Research ... Ms. Mary MCLEAN
15 Administrator Human Resources ... Ms. Elinore MOORE

*City Colleges of Chicago Wilbur Wright College (I)

4300 N Narragansett Avenue, Chicago IL 60634-1591
County: Cook FICE Identification: 001655
Unit ID: 144218
Telephone: (773) 777-7900 Carnegie Class: Assoc/Pub-U-MC
FAX Number: (773) 481-8185 Calendar System: Semester
URL: www.ccc.edu/wright
Established: 1934 Annual Undergrad Tuition & Fees (In-District): $3,070
Enrollment: 12,673 Coed
Affiliation or Control: State/Local IRS Status: 501(c)3
Highest Offering: Associate Degree
Program: Occupational; 2-Year Principally Bachelor's Creditable
Accreditation: NH, ACBSP, OTA, RAD

02 President ... Mr. Jim PALOS
05 Vice President Academic Affairs ... Ms. Cynthia CORDES
32 Dean Student Services ... Ms. Romell MURDEN-WALDU
20 Dean of Instruction ... Mr. Kevin LI
35 Assoc Dean Student Svcs ... Ms. Maria LLOPIZ
07 Assistant Dean Admissions ... Vacant
20 Associate Dean of Instruction ... Mr. Jeffrey JANULIS
10 Director Business ... Mrs. Nancy BECKMAN
08 Librarian ... Ms. Linda NEIL
37 Director Financial Aid ... Ms. Ronda ROCQUEMORE
09 Dir Institutional Research/Plng ... Mr. Brian TRZEBIATOWSKI
14 Director Computer Support ... Ms. Lula WALLACE
18 Director of Facilities ... Ms. Jackie LONQUIST
15 Director Personnel Services ... Ms. Kimberly WILLIAMSON
38 Director Student Counseling ... Ms. Maria LLOPIZ
19 Director of Security ... Mr. Jack MURPHY
06 Registrar ... Vacant
41 Athletic Director ... Mr. John MCDONNELL
51 Dean of Continuing Education ... Dr. Alba PEZZAROSSI
76 Dean Allied Health ... Ms. Julie WHITE
53 Dean Adult Education ... Ms. Daisy MITCHELL
12 Dean Humboldt Park Center ... Ms. Madeline ROMAN-VARGAS
12 Assoc Dean Humboldt Park Center ... Mr. Marc SMIERCIAK

College of DuPage (A)

425 Fawell Boulevard, Glen Ellyn IL 60137-6599
County: DuPage Identification: 006656
Unit ID: 144865
Telephone: (630) 942-2800 Carnegie Class: Assoc/Pub-S-SC
FAX Number: (630) 858-9399 Calendar System: Semester
URL: www.cod.edu
Established: 1966 Annual Undergrad Tuition & Fees (In-District): $4,080
Enrollment: 26,209 Coed
Affiliation or Control: State/Local IRS Status: 501(c)3
Highest Offering: Associate Degree
Program: Occupational; 2-Year Principally Bachelor's Creditable
Accreditation: NH, ACFEI, ADNUR, ART, DH, DMS, MAC, NMT, PNUR, PTAA, RAD, SURGT

01 President ... Dr. Robert L. BREUDER
03 Executive Vice President ... Dr. Joseph COLLINS
05 Vice President Academic Affairs ... Dr. Jean V. KARTJE
11 Senior Vice Pres Administration ... Mr. Thomas J. GLASER
13 Vice Pres Information Technology ... Mr. Chuck CURRIER
45 VP Planning & Inst Effectiveness ... Mr. James BENTE
15 Vice President Human Resources ... Ms. Linda SANDS-VANKERK
30 VP Develop/Exec Dir COD Foundation ... Ms. Catherine BROD
24 Asst VP Info Sys/Multimedia Svcs ... Ms. Donna BERLINER
20 Assoc VP Academic Affairs ... Dr. Glenda GALLISATH
27 Assoc VP Marketing & External Rels ... Mr. Joseph MOORE
84 Assoc VP Enrollment Management ... Mr. Earl DOWLING
49 Dean Liberal Arts ... Dr. Daniel LLOYD
50 Dean Business & Technology ... Dr. Donna H. STEWART
75 Dean Health & Sciences ... Mr. Thomas CAMERON
51 Dean Cont Ed/Extended Learning ... Dr. Joseph CASSIDY
08 Dean Library ... Dr. Lisa A. STOCK
32 Dean Student Affairs ... Ms. Susan M. MARTIN
21 Asst VP Financial Affs/Controller ... Ms. Lynn SAPYTA
18 Dir Facilities Planning and Dev ... Mr. John WANDOLOWSKI
06 Dean Admiss/Registration/Records ... Ms. Jane L. SMITH
09 Director Research ... Dr. Harlan M. SCHWEER
30 Asst VP Resource Development ... Dr. Laura MANNION
88 Internal Auditor ... Mr. James E. MARTNER
57 Director Performing Arts ... Mr. Stephen CUMMINS
41 Director Athletics ... Mr. Paul ZAKOWSKI
25 Director of Grants ... Ms. Barbara ABROMITIS
86 Director Legislative Relations ... Ms. Mary Ann MILLUSH
19 Director & Chief COD Police Dept ... Mr. Mark FAZZINI
18 Director Facilities Operations ... Mr. Jim MA
79 Associate Dean Humanities ... Ms. Laura ORTIZ
60 Associate Dean Communications ... Ms. Beverly REED
26 Dir Marketing & Creative Svcs ... Ms. Laurie JORGENSEN
88 Dir Academic Partnerships ... Ms. Mary KLINEFELTER
57 Assoc Dean Fine & Applied Arts ... Ms. Cathryn WILKINSON
66 Director Nursing Programs ... Ms. Vickie GUKENBERGER
16 Director Labor & Emp Relations ... Ms. Mia IGYARTO
77 Assoc Dean Computer & App Tech ... Mr. John KRONENBURGER
83 Assoc Dean Social & Behav Sciences . Ms. Marianne HUNNICUTT
81 Assoc Dean Math & Physical Sciences ... Mr. Thomas SCHRADER
88 Assoc Dean Health & Bio Sciences ... Ms. Karen SOLT
88 Associate Dean Learning Resources ... Ms. Ellen SUTTON

College of Lake County (B)

19351 W Washington Street, Grayslake IL 60030-1198
County: Lake FICE Identification: 007694
Unit ID: 146472
Telephone: (847) 543-2000 Carnegie Class: Assoc/Pub-S-MC
FAX Number: (847) 223-1017 Calendar System: Semester
URL: www.clcillinois.edu
Established: 1967 Annual Undergrad Tuition & Fees (In-District): $3,136
Enrollment: 17,389 Coed
Affiliation or Control: Local IRS Status: 501(c)3
Highest Offering: Associate Degree
Program: Occupational; 2-Year Principally Bachelor's Creditable
Accreditation: NH, ADNUR, DH, MAC, RAD, SURGT

01 President ... Dr. Girard W. WEBER
05 Vice President Educ Affairs ... Dr. Richard J. HANEY
11 Vice Pres Administrative Affs ... Mr. David AGAZZI
32 Vice Pres Student Development ... Ms. Darl E. DRUMMOND
88 Asst Vice Pres of Student Devel ... Ms. Karen HLAVIN
35 Asst Dir Student Develop Operation ... Ms. Erin FOWLES
26 Exec Dir Public Relations & Mktg ... Ms. Evelyn R. SCHIELE
12 Dean Southlake Campus ... Ms. Vicky CVITKOVIC
12 Dean Lakeshore Campus ... Dr. Alphonso BALDWIN
08 Dean Libraries/Instruction Svcs ... Ms. Cornelia E. BAKKER
88 Dir Workplace Lrng/Perform/Prof Dev ... Ms. Sonia CROSIER
10 Dean Business Services/Finance ... Mr. Ted P. POULOS
21 Controller/Controller's Office ... Mr. Wright WILLIAMS
50 Dean of Business/Workforce Bus Div ... Ms. Lourdene HUHRA
76 Dean Biological/Health Sciences ... Dr. Denise ANASTASIO
83 Dean Social Sciences ... Dr. Jeffrey A. STOMPER
79 Dean Comm Arts/Humanities/Fine Arts ... Mr. Roland G. MILLER
81 Dean Engr/Math/Physical Science ... Mr. Gary MORGAN
51 Dean Adult Basic Education/GED/ESL ... Ms. Mary S. CHARUHAS
38 Dean Counsel/Advising/Transfer Ctr ... Vacant
55 Assoc Dean Adult Education ... Vacant
54 Asc Dean Engr/Math/Physical Science ... Mr. Jose VELARDE
31 Assoc Dean Community Education ... Ms. Michele VAUGHN
103 Exec Dir Workforce/Prof Dev Inst ... Ms. Roneida MARTIN
41 Dir Athletics/Physical Activities ... Mr. Chad GOOD
86 Dir Resource Dev/Legislative Affrs ... Mr. Nick C. KALLIERIS
13 Chief Info Ofcr/Info Tech Svcs ... Mr. Kamlesh SANGHVI
14 Director User Services/User Spport ... Mr. Edward BOCKMAN
88 Dir Application Svcs/Applic Develop ... Mr. Jay MEYER
35 Executive Director of Student Life ... Vacant
102 Executive Director CLC Foundation ... Mr. William DEVORE
16 Exec Director Human Resources ... Ms. Susan YASECKO
88 Director Student Services Lakeshore ... Mr. David WEATHERSPOON
18 Director Facilities ... Mr. Ted JOHNSON
88 Dir Children's Learning Center ... Ms. Sandra GROENINGER
88 Dir Ofc Students w/ Disabilities ... Mr. Thomas CROWE
19 Chief of Police/CLC Police Dept ... Mr. Thomas GUENTHER
36 Exec Dir Career/Placement Services ... Ms. Sylvia M. JOHNSON
88 Dir Educational Talent Srch Grants ... Ms. Sharon SANDERS-FUNNYE
88 Dir Illinois Small Business Dev Ctr ... Ms. Jan L. BAUER
20 Asst Vice Pres Educational Affairs ... Ms. Alyssa O'BRIEN
88 Asst Dir Educational Affairs Oper .. Ms. Arlene SANTOS-GEORGE
20 Director Academic Support Services ... Ms. Adriane W. HUTCHINSON
66 Director Nursing Education ... Dr. Deborah JEZUIT
51 Dir Center for Personal Enrichment ... Vacant
88 Exec Dir James Lumber Ctr Perf Arts ... Ms. Gwethalyn BRONNER
88 Director Procurement Tech Asst Ctr ... Mr. Marc N. VIOLANTE
88 Director Judicial Services ... Ms. Margaret C. MILLER
29 Dir Alumni Relations/Special Events ... Ms. Julie SHROKA
23 Director Health Services ... Ms. Michelle M. GRACE
37 Director Financial Aid ... Vacant
88 Dir Active Lrng Technologies ... Mr. Scott RIAL
88 Director Continuing Prof Devel ... Ms. Carol EWING
88 Director of Business Services ... Ms. Melanie SCHERER
84 Asst Director Enrollment Services ... Ms. Debra MICHELINI
15 Assistant Director Human Resources ... Ms. Kathleen SCATLIFFE-WALLACE
88 Director Green Jobs Initiative ... Mr. Stephen BELL
51 Assoc Dean/Adult Education ... Mr. Matthew HUSEBY
35 Director Student Support Services ... Ms. Zandra GENOUS
88 Director Technical Services ... Mr. James SENFT
38 Director of Advising ... Ms. Trisha ANDREWS
88 Project Dir IGEN Career Pathways ... Dr. Theresa BERRYMAN
09 Exec Dir/Inst Effect/Plan/Research ... Mr. Sean HOGAN

The College of Office Technology (C)

1520 W Division Street, Chicago IL 60642-3312
County: Cook FICE Identification: 023378
Unit ID: 143075
Telephone: (773) 278-0042 Carnegie Class: Assoc/PrivFP
FAX Number: (773) 278-0143 Calendar System: Semester
URL: www.cotedu.com
Established: 1982 Annual Undergrad Tuition & Fees: $12,273
Enrollment: 295 Coed
Affiliation or Control: Proprietary IRS Status: Proprietary
Highest Offering: Associate Degree
Program: Occupational
Accreditation: ACICS

01 President ... Ms. Karla GALVA

Columbia College Chicago (D)

600 S Michigan Avenue, Chicago IL 60605-1996
County: Cook FICE Identification: 001665
Unit ID: 144281
Telephone: (312) 369-1000 Carnegie Class: Master's M
FAX Number: (312) 369-8069 Calendar System: Semester
URL: www.colum.edu
Established: 1890 Annual Undergrad Tuition & Fees: $21,200
Enrollment: 11,625 Coed
Affiliation or Control: Independent Non-Profit IRS Status: 501(c)3
Highest Offering: Master's
Program: Liberal Arts And General
Accreditation: NH, CIDA

01 President ... Dr. Warrick L. CARTER
03 Senior Vice President ... Dr. Warren CHAPMAN
10 VP Bus Affairs/Chief Financial Ofcr ... Mr. Ken GOTSCH
43 Vice President/General Counsel ... Ms. Annice KELLY
30 Vice Pres Institutional Advancement ... Dr. Eric WINSTON
88 Vice President Campus Environment ... Ms. Alicia M. BERG
45 Vice Pres Planning & Compliance ... Ms. Anne FOLEY
20 VP Academic Affairs/Interim Provost ... Dr. Louise LOVE
35 Vice President Student Affairs ... Mr. Mark KELLY
21 Associate VP of Business Affairs ... Mr. Timothy BAUHS
100 Assoc Vice Pres/Chief of Staff ... Mr. Paul CHIARAVALLE
84 Assoc Vice Pres for Enrollment Mgmt ... Ms. Debra MCGRATH
18 Assoc VP Facilities/Operations ... Mr. John KAVOURIS
32 Assoc Vice Pres/Dean of Students ... Ms. Sharon WILSON-TAYLOR
26 Assoc VP PR/Marketing/Advertising ... Ms. Diane DOYNE
13 Assoc VP & CIO Info Technology .. Ms. Bernadette B. MCMAHON
21 Assoc Vice President & Controller ... Mr. Kevin DOHERTY
19 Assoc Vice Pres Safety & Security ... Mr. Robert KOVERMAN
07 Executive Director of Admissions ... Mr. Murphy MONROE
44 Assoc VP Institutional Advancement ... Mr. Michael ANDERSON
37 Exec Dir of Student Financial Svcs ... Ms. Jennifer WATERS
35 Asst Dean of Student Development ... Mr. William FRIEDMAN
88 Director of Degree Evaluation ... Ms. Susan SINDLINGER
26 Senior Director of Public Relations ... Mr. Steve KAUFFMAN
15 Director Human Resources ... Ms. Patricia OLALDE
29 National Director Alumni Relations ... Mr. Charles BONILLA
96 Director of Purchasing ... Mr. Thomas RUSSELL
28 Exec Director Multicultural Affs ... Ms. Sheila CARTER
85 Dir International Student Affairs ... Ms. Gigi POSEJPAL
06 Director of Records/Registrar ... Mr. Marvin COHEN
36 Director of Portfolio Center ... Mr. Tim LONG
39 Director of Residence Life ... Ms. Mary OAKES
09 AVP Planning/Dir Inst Research ... Mr. Royal DAWSON
88 Director of Latino Cultural Affairs ... Mr. Daniel ARANDA
88 Dir of New Stdnt Pgms & Orientation ... Ms. Emily EASTON
57 Dean School of Fine/Performing Arts ... Dr. Eliza NICHOLS
88 Dean School of Media Arts ... Dr. Robin BARGAR
49 Dean School Liberal Arts/Sciences ... Dr. Deborah HOLDSTEIN

Concordia University Chicago (E)

7400 Augusta Street, River Forest IL 60305-1499
County: Cook FICE Identification: 001666
Unit ID: 144351
Telephone: (708) 771-8300 Carnegie Class: Master's L
FAX Number: (708) 209-3176 Calendar System: Semester
URL: www.cuchicago.edu
Established: 1864 Annual Undergrad Tuition & Fees: $25,942
Enrollment: 5,135 Coed
Affiliation or Control: Lutheran Church - Missouri Synod
IRS Status: 501(c)3
Highest Offering: Doctorate
Program: Liberal Arts And General; Teacher Preparatory; Professional
Accreditation: NH, CACREP, MUS, TED

01 President ... Dr. John F. JOHNSON
05 Sr Vice President for Academics ... Dr. Manfred B. BOOS
30 Sr Vice Pres Development/Alumni ... Ms. Cindy SIMPSON
45 Sr VP for Planning & Research ... Mr. Alan E. MEYER
10 Vice President for Finance ... Mr. Tom HALLETT
11 Vice President for Administration ... Dr. Dennis E. WITTE
84 Vice Pres Enrollment & Marketing ... Ms. Evelyn P. BURDICK
32 Vice President Student Services ... Mr. Jeff HYNES
44 Asst Vice President of Major Gifts ... Mr. Tom J. FOOTE
84 Asst Vice President for Enrollment ... Ms. Gwen E. KANELOS
49 Dean College Arts & Sciences ... Dr. Pamela KALBFLEISCH
53 Dean College Education ... Dr. Kevin BRANDON
50 Dean College of Business ... Dr. George VUKOTICH
58 Dean Col Graduate Innovative Pgms ... Dr. Thomas JANDRIS
88 Associate Director of CURES ... Ms. Elizabeth M. BECKER
37 Director Student Financial Planning ... Ms. Aida ASENCIO-PINTO
06 Registrar ... Ms. Connie PETTINGER
08 Director of Library Services ... Ms. Yana V. SERDYUK
88 Director of Degree Completion ... Dr. Carol J. REISECK
36 Director Career Plng/Placement Svcs ... Mr. Gerald PINOTTI
27 Director Marketing Communications ... Vacant
15 Director of Human Resources ... Ms. Elizabeth WOTEN
18 Director of Physical Plant ... Ms. Linda HOLOWICKI
11 Dean of Administration ... Mr. Glen D. STEINER
29 Director of Alumni Relations ... Ms. Paige CRAIG
38 Director Schmieding Counseling Ctr ... Dr. Carol A. JABS
31 Director of Auxiliary Services ... Mr. Pete D. BECKER
41 Director of Athletics ... Mr. Peter D. GNAN
21 Director of Business Services ... Ms. Anne FARMER
88 Director of Budget Services ... Ms. Tina NEPOMUCENO
39 Director Campus Housing ... Mr. Scott HENDRICKS
42 Campus Pastor ... Rev. Jeffrey LEININGER
24 Dir of Media Production Services ... Mr. James A. KOSINSKY
19 Director of Public Safety ... Ms. Amberleigh BIRKHOLZ
88 Director of Academic Advising ... Ms. Rosemarie GARCIA-HILLS
26 Chief Public Relations Officer ... Vacant
96 Director of Purchasing ... Ms. Kathryn KLEMENT
91 Manager of Admin Information System ... Ms. Linda C. BERRY
85 International Student Advisor ... Vacant

Coyne College (F)

330 North Green Street, Chicago IL 60607-1300
County: Cook FICE Identification: 007549
Unit ID: 144485
Telephone: (773) 577-8100 Carnegie Class: Assoc/PrivFP
FAX Number: (312) 226-3818 Calendar System: Semester
URL: www.coynecollege.edu
Established: 1899 Annual Undergrad Tuition & Fees: N/A
Enrollment: 694 Coed
Affiliation or Control: Proprietary IRS Status: Proprietary
Highest Offering: Associate Degree
Program: Occupational; 2-Year Principally Bachelor's Creditable
Accreditation: ACCSC, MAAB

01 President ... Mr. Russell FREEMAN

Danville Area Community College (G)

2000 E Main Street, Danville IL 61832-5199
County: Vermilion FICE Identification: 001669
Unit ID: 144564
Telephone: (217) 443-3222 Carnegie Class: Assoc/Pub-R-L
FAX Number: (217) 443-8560 Calendar System: Semester
URL: www.dacc.edu
Established: 1946 Annual Undergrad Tuition & Fees (In-District): $3,300
Enrollment: 5,974 Coed
Affiliation or Control: State/Local IRS Status: 501(c)3
Highest Offering: Associate Degree
Program: Occupational; 2-Year Principally Bachelor's Creditable
Accreditation: NH, RAD

01 President ... Dr. Alice M. JACOBS
04 Admin Asst to the Pres/Board Sec ... Ms. Kerri L. THURMAN
05 VP Instruction & Student Svcs ... Mr. David L. KIETZMANN

15 Director Human Resources/AA Ofcr ..... Ms. Jill A. CRANMORE
10 Chief Financial Officer ..... Ms. Tammy CLARK-BETANCOURT
11 Director Administrative Services ... Mr. R. Michael CUNNINGHAM
07 Director Admissions & Registrar ..... Ms. Stacy L. EHMEN
45 Director Grants and Planning ..... Ms. Laura M. WILLIAMS
44 Foundation Executive Director ..... Ms. Tracy D. WAHLFELDT
26 Director Marketing/Col Relations ..... Ms. Lara L. CONKLIN
09 Dir Institutional Effectiveness ..... Ms. Nancy A. BOESDORFER
88 Executive Director of JTP ..... Mr. Brian C. HENSGEN
21 Controller ..... Ms. Debra L. KNIGHT
37 Director of Financial Aid ..... Ms. Janet M. INGARGIOLA
51 Dir Corporate/Community Education ..... Ms. Sara L. VANDEWALKER
91 Director of Admin Data Systems ..... Mr. Kim H. COLWELL
90 Director Computer & Network Svcs ... Mr. Jefferson D. WILLIAMS
88 Director of Adult Education ..... Mr. Thomas G. SZOTT
50 Dean Business & Technology ..... Mr. Bruce M. RAPE
49 Dean Liberal Arts and Library Servi .... Dr. Penny J. MCCONNELL
81 Dean Math & Sciences ..... Ms. Kathy R. STURGEON
41 Athletic Director ..... Mr. Tim M. BUNTON
88 Director Small Business Development ..... Mr. Michael J. O'BRIEN
35 Director Student Support Services ..... Ms. Vicky L. WELGE
36 Coordinator Career Services ..... Ms. Carla M. BOYD
24 Director Instructional Media ..... Mr. Jonathon L. SPORS
40 Coordinator Bookstore ..... Ms. Cindy A. PARR-BARRETT
88 Coordinator Retention ..... Ms. Cindy J. PECK
88 Coordinator Recruitment ..... Ms. Dawn S. NASSER

DePaul University (A)

1E Jackson Boulevard, Chicago IL 60604-2287
County: Cook FICE Identification: 001671
Unit ID: 144740
Telephone: (312) 362-8000 Carnegie Class: DRU
FAX Number: (312) 362-5322 Calendar System: Quarter
URL: www.depaul.edu
Established: 1898 Annual Undergrad Tuition & Fees: $30,618
Enrollment: 25,398 Coed
Affiliation or Control: Roman Catholic IRS Status: 501(c)3
Highest Offering: Doctorate
Program: Liberal Arts And General; Teacher Preparatory; Professional
Accreditation: NH, ANEST, BUS, BUSA, CLPSY, LAW, MUS, NURSE, SPAA, SW

01 President ..... Rev. Dennis H. HOLTSCHNEIDER
00 Chancellor ..... Rev. John T. RICHARDSON, CM
05 Interim Provost ..... Dr. Patricia P. O'DONOGHUE
03 Executive Vice President ..... Mr. Robert KOZOMAN
11 Vice President Admin/Sec of Univ ..... Rev. Edward R. UDOVIC
32 Vice President Student Affairs ..... Ms. Cynthia SUMMERS
84 Sr Vice Pres Enrollment Management ..... Dr. David H. KALSBEEK
10 Vice President for Finance ..... Ms. Bonnie FRANKEL
15 Vice President Human Resources ..... Mr. William W. SEITHEL
18 Vice President Facilities Operation ..... Mr. Robert J. JANIS
43 Vice President & General Counsel ..... Dr. Jose D. PADILLA
08 VP Teaching/Learning Resources ..... Rev. Edward R. UDOVIC
29 Asst VP Alumni Engagement/Outreac ..... Tracy KRAHL
28 Vice Pres for Inst Diversity ..... Ms. Elizabeth F. ORTIZ
27 VP Public Relations & Communication ..... Ms. Cynthia LAWSON
30 Senior Vice Pres for Development ..... Ms. Mary FINGER
20 Assoc VP Academic Affairs ..... Ms. Caryn CHADEN
20 Assoc VP Academic Affairs Online ..... Mr. GianMario BESANA
45 Sr Exec Strategic Planning ..... Dr. Jay BRAATZ
21 Sr Assoc VP Fiscal Admin ..... Ms. Alyssa KUPKA
35 AVP Student Advocacy Affairs ..... Ms. Cynthia SUMMERS
46 Assoc VP Faculty Development ..... Dr. Rafaela WEFFER
35 Assoc Vice Pres Student Development ..... Dr. Peggy BURKE
22 Assoc VP for Div Ed & Leadership ..... Mr. Rico TYLER
20 Assoc Vice Pres Academic Affairs ..... Ms. Kelly JOHNSON
09 Asst VP Inst Rsrch & Mkt Analytic ..... Dr. Liz SANDERS
36 Assoc Vice President Career Svcs ..... Ms. Carol MONTGOMERY
42 Assoc VP University Ministry ..... Mr. Mark LABOE
21 Assoc VP Operations ..... Mr. Mark TITZER
88 Asst Vice Pres Univ Marketing Comm ..... Ms. Gwyn FRIEND
26 AVP Research ..... Ms. Joanne ROMAGNI
88 Senior Executive University Mission ..... Rev. Edward R. UDOVIC, CM
88 Treasurer ..... Mr. Jeffrey BETHKE
88 Controller ..... Mr. Mark HAWKINS
90 Director Academic Technology Devel ..... Dr. Sharon GUAN
27 Director of Information Services ..... Mr. Robert MCCORMICK
37 Director Financial Aid ..... Ms. Paula LUFF
25 Director Sponsored Programs Rsrch ..... Dr. Douglas PETCHER
26 Director Media Relations ..... Mr. John HOLDEN
41 Athletic Director ..... Ms. Jean PONSETTO
19 Director Public Safety ..... Mr. Robert WACHOWSKI
38 Director Student Counseling ..... Dr. Jeffery LANFEAR
51 Dean School for New Learning ..... Ms. Marisa ALICEA
50 Dean Driehaus Business College ..... Dr. Ray WHITTINGTON
64 Dean School of Music ..... Dr. Donald E. CASEY
61 Dean College of Law ..... Judge Warren WOLFSON
49 Dean Liberal Arts & Sciences ..... Dr. Charles S. SUCHAR
57 Dean Theatre School ..... Mr. John CULBERT
53 Dean School of Education ..... Dr. Paul ZIONTS
88 Dean Computing & Digital Media ..... Dr. David MILLER
06 Registrar ..... Ms. Patricia HUERTA
07 Director of Admissions ..... Ms. Carlene KLAAS
89 Dean College of Communication ..... Dr. Jacqueline TAYLOR

*DeVry University - Home Office (B)

3005 Highland Parkway, Downers Grove IL 60515-5799
County: DuPage FICE Identification: 001672
Unit ID: 144777
Telephone: (800) 733-3879 Carnegie Class: N/A
FAX Number: (630) 571-0317
URL: www.devry.edu

00 President & Chief Executive Officer ..... Mr. Daniel HAMBURGER
01 Exec VP/President of DeVry Univ ..... Mr. David J. PAULDINE
86 Sr VP Govt & Reg Affairs/CCO . Ms. Sharon THOMAS-PARROTT
26 Chief Marketing Officer ..... Mr. John BIRMINGHAM
32 VP of Student & Career Services ..... Ms. Madeleine SLUTSKY
10 CFO/Treasurer ..... Mr. Timothy WIGGINS
27 VP/Chief Information Officer ..... Mr. Eric DIRST
43 VP/General Counsel/Corp Secretary ..... Mr. Gregory DAVIS
84 VP Enrollment Management ..... Ms. Erika ORRIS
88 VP Enrollment Management - Online ..... Mr. Ted KULAWIAK
05 Provost/VP Academic Affairs ..... Ms. Donna LORAINE
16 VP Human Resources ..... Ms. Donna JENNINGS
88 VP Regulatory Affairs ..... Mr. Thomas BABEL
88 Pres K-12/Prof & Intl Education ..... Mr. Steven RIEHS
12 Chief Operating Officer ..... Ms. Jill ALBRINCK
07 Group VP Admissions - California ..... Mr. Mark BUCK
07 Group VP Admissions - Mountain ..... Mr. Russell GILL
07 VP of Admissions - Northeast ..... Mr. Aaron MCCARDELL
07 Group VP Admissions - Southeast ..... Mr. Matt DEARSMAN
07 Group VP Admissions - North Central ..... Ms. Virginia MECHNIG
07 Group VP Admissions - South Central ..... Mr. David WOOD
12 Group VP - North Central ..... Ms. Terri JOHNSON
12 Group VP - South Central ..... Mr. Mark CAMERON
12 Group VP - California ..... Ms. Shelly DUBOIS
12 Group VP - Mountain ..... Mr. Jim DUGAN
12 Group VP - Northeast ..... Mr. Darryl FIELD
12 Group VP - Southeast ..... Mr. Julio TORRES

*DeVry University - Addison Campus (C)

1221 N Swift Road, Addison IL 60101-6106
County: DuPage FICE Identification: 022966
Unit ID: 144768
Telephone: (630) 953-1300 Carnegie Class: Not Classified
FAX Number: (630) 953-1236 Calendar System: Semester
URL: www.devry.edu
Established: 1931 Annual Undergrad Tuition & Fees: $16,156
Enrollment: 1,523 Coed
Affiliation or Control: Proprietary IRS Status: Proprietary
Highest Offering: Baccalaureate
Program: Occupational; Professional; Business Emphasis
Accreditation: &NH, ENGT

02 Metro President ..... Dr. Susan L. FRIEDBERG
07 Senior Director of Admissions ..... Ms. Michelle ALFORD
05 Dean of Academic Affairs ..... Ms. Janet ABRI
37 Director of Student Finance ..... Ms. Sejal AMIN
32 Manager Student Services ..... Mr. Michael KULCZYCKI
06 Registrar ..... Mr. Brad BURCH
15 HR Business Partner ..... Mr. Douglas OFFUTT
77 Program Dean ..... Ms. Lyn WUNSCHL
36 Director of Career Services ..... Ms. Kathleen MCCUEN

† Regional accreditation is carried under the parent institution in Downers Grove, IL.

*DeVry University - Chicago Campus (D)

3300 N Campbell Avenue, Chicago IL 60618-5994
County: Cook FICE Identification: 010727
Unit ID: 144759
Telephone: (773) 929-8500 Carnegie Class: Master's L
FAX Number: (773) 348-1780 Calendar System: Semester
URL: www.devry.edu
Established: 1931 Annual Undergrad Tuition & Fees: $16,156
Enrollment: 2,119 Coed
Affiliation or Control: Proprietary IRS Status: Proprietary
Highest Offering: Master's
Program: Occupational; Professional; Business Emphasis
Accreditation: &NH, ENGT

02 Campus President ..... Ms. Candace GOODWIN
06 Registrar ..... Ms. Jacqueline LLOYD
07 Senior Director of Admissions ..... Mr. Lennor JOHNSON
05 Dean Academic Affairs ..... Ms. Deborah ZELECHOWSKI
36 Director of Career Services ..... Vacant
37 Director of Student Finance ..... Ms. Milena DOBRINA
08 Director Library Services ..... Mr. Jason ROSSI
15 HR Business Partner ..... Vacant
26 Director of Community Outreach ..... Ms. Karen KUSHINO
32 Manager Student Services ..... Mr. Tim CALI

† Regional accreditation is carried under the parent institution in Downers Grove, IL.

*DeVry University - Chicago Loop Center (E)

225 W Washington Street, Ste 100,
Chicago IL 60606-2418
County: Cook Identification: 666203
Unit ID: 439206
Telephone: (312) 372-4900 Carnegie Class: Not Classified
FAX Number: (312) 372-4870 Calendar System: Semester
URL: www.devry.edu
Established: 1973 Annual Undergrad Tuition & Fees: $16,156
Enrollment: 1,590 Coed
Affiliation or Control: Proprietary IRS Status: Proprietary
Highest Offering: Master's
Program: Occupational; Professional; Business Emphasis
Accreditation: &NH

02 Campus President ..... Mr. Piotr LECHOWSKI
07 Director of Admissions ..... Ms. Ana THARAKAN

† Regional accreditation is carried under the parent institution in Downers Grove, IL.

*DeVry University - Chicago O'Hare Center (F)

8550 W Bryn Mawr Ave, Suite 450,
Chicago IL 60631-3224
County: Cook Identification: 666204
Unit ID: 437352
Telephone: (773) 695-1000 Carnegie Class: Not Classified
FAX Number: (773) 695-9118 Calendar System: Semester
URL: www.devry.edu
Established: 1999 Annual Undergrad Tuition & Fees: $16,156
Enrollment: 289 Coed
Affiliation or Control: Proprietary IRS Status: Proprietary
Highest Offering: Master's
Program: Occupational; Professional; Business Emphasis
Accreditation: &NH

02 Center Dean ..... Oolka DIXIT

† Regional accreditation is carried under the parent institution in Downers Grove, IL.

*DeVry University - Downers Grove (G)

3005 Highland Parkway, Downers Grove IL 60515-5799
County: DuPage Identification: 666791
Telephone: (630) 515-3000 Carnegie Class: Not Classified
FAX Number: N/A Calendar System: Semester
URL: www.devry.edu
Established: 1931 Annual Undergrad Tuition & Fees: $16,156
Enrollment: 6,843 Coed
Affiliation or Control: Proprietary IRS Status: Proprietary
Highest Offering: Master's
Program: Professional; Business Emphasis
Accreditation: &NH

02 Center Dean ..... Rowena KLEIN-ROBARTS

† Regional accreditation is carried under the parent institution in Downers Grove, IL.

*DeVry University - Elgin Center (H)

2250 Point Boulevard, Suite 250, Elgin IL 60123-7873
County: Kane Identification: 666205
Unit ID: 439215
Telephone: (847) 649-3980 Carnegie Class: Not Classified
FAX Number: (847) 622-1246 Calendar System: Semester
URL: www.devry.edu
Established: 1993 Annual Undergrad Tuition & Fees: $16,156
Enrollment: 283 Coed
Affiliation or Control: Proprietary IRS Status: Proprietary
Highest Offering: Master's
Program: Occupational; Professional; Business Emphasis
Accreditation: &NH

02 Center Dean ..... Mr. Timothy M. FLORER

† Regional accreditation is carried under the parent institution in Downers Grove, IL.

*DeVry University - Gurnee (I)

1075 Tri-State Parkway, Suite 800, Gurnee IL 60031-9126
County: Lake Identification: 666535
Telephone: (847) 855-2649 Carnegie Class: Not Classified
FAX Number: (847) 855-5932 Calendar System: Semester
URL: www.devry.edu
Established: 1931 Annual Undergrad Tuition & Fees: $16,156
Enrollment: 500 Coed
Affiliation or Control: Proprietary IRS Status: Proprietary
Highest Offering: Master's
Program: Professional; Business Emphasis
Accreditation: &NH

02 Center Dean ..... Lewis ZANON

† Regional accreditation is carried under the parent institution in Downers Grove, IL.

*DeVry University - Naperville Center (J)

2056 Westings Avenue, Suite 40,
Naperville IL 60563-2361
County: DuPage Identification: 666207
Telephone: (630) 428-9086 Carnegie Class: Not Classified
FAX Number: (630) 428-4721 Calendar System: Semester
URL: www.devry.edu
Established: 1931 Annual Undergrad Tuition & Fees: $16,156
Enrollment: 512 Coed
Affiliation or Control: Proprietary IRS Status: Proprietary
Highest Offering: Master's
Program: Occupational; Professional; Business Emphasis

Accreditation: &NH

02 Center Dean ... Mary WAHLBECK

† Regional accreditation is carried under the parent institution in Downers Grove, IL.

*DeVry University - Schaumburg Center (A)

1051 Perimeter Drive, 9th Floor,
Schaumburg IL 60173-5009

County: Cook | Identification: 666208
Unit ID: 439251
Telephone: (847) 330-0040 | Carnegie Class: Not Classified
FAX Number: (847) 330-0046 | Calendar System: Semester
URL: www.keller.edu
Established: 1931 | Annual Graduate Tuition & Fees: $18,384
Enrollment: 288 | Coed
Affiliation or Control: Proprietary | IRS Status: Proprietary
Highest Offering: Master's; No Undergraduates
Program: Occupational; Professional; Business Emphasis
Accreditation: &NH

02 Center Dean ... Megan BAKER

† Regional accreditation is carried under the parent institution in Downers Grove, IL.

*DeVry University - Tinley Park Campus (B)

18624 W Creek Drive, Tinley Park IL 60477-6243

County: Cook | Identification: 666113
Unit ID: 439242
Telephone: (708) 342-3300 | Carnegie Class: Not Classified
FAX Number: (708) 342-3712 | Calendar System: Semester
URL: www.devry.edu
Established: 1931 | Annual Undergrad Tuition & Fees: $16,156
Enrollment: 1,356 | Coed
Affiliation or Control: Proprietary | IRS Status: Proprietary
Highest Offering: Master's
Program: Occupational; Professional; Business Emphasis
Accreditation: &NH

02 Campus President ... Mr. Jamal SCOTT
10 Director of Facilities ... Mr. James MADORMA
07 Senior Director of Admissions ... Ms. Angela HOWARD
06 Registrar ... Ms. Canny WITTORP
15 HR Business Partner ... Vacant
05 Associate Dean ... Ms. Anne PERRY
37 Director of Student Finance ... Ms. Margaret CARMODY
08 Director of Library Services ... Mr. Paul BURDEN

† Regional accreditation is carried under the parent institution in Downers Grove, IL.

Dominican University (C)

7900 W Division Street, River Forest IL 60305-1099

County: Cook | FICE Identification: 001750
Unit ID: 148496
Telephone: (708) 366-2490 | Carnegie Class: Master's L
FAX Number: (708) 524-5990 | Calendar System: Semester
URL: www.dom.edu
Established: 1901 | Annual Undergrad Tuition & Fees: $27,730
Enrollment: 3,612 | Coed
Affiliation or Control: Roman Catholic | IRS Status: 501(c)3
Highest Offering: Doctorate
Program: Liberal Arts And General; Teacher Preparatory; Professional
Accreditation: NH, ACBSP, DIETC, DIETD, LIB, SW

01 President ... Dr. Donna M. CARROLL
05 Provost ... Dr. Cheryl JOHNSON-ODIM
20 Associate Provost ... Dr. David H. KRAUSE
11 Sr VP for Finance & Administration ... Ms. Amy MCCORMACK
42 Vice Pres for Mission & Ministry ... Sr. Diane KENNEDY, OP
30 Vice Pres University Advancement ... Mrs. Grace J. CICHOMSKA
84 Sr VP Enrollment Management ... Mr. Ray KENNELLY
07 AVP Enroll Mgt/Dir Undergrad Admiss ... Mr. Glenn HAMILTON
32 Dean of Students ... Ms. Trudi GOGGIN
50 Dean School of Business ... Dr. Arvid JOHNSON
62 Dean Grad School Library Science ... Dr. Susan ROMAN
53 Dean School of Education ... Dr. Colleen REARDON
70 Dean Graduate School Social Work ... Mr. Charles STOPPS
49 Dean College of Arts & Science ... Dr. Jeffrey CARLSON
88 Assistant Provost ... Mr. Matthew J. HLINAK
08 University Librarian ... Ms. Felice E. MACIEJEWSKI
26 Chief Marketing/Communications Ofcr ... Mr. Jeffrey KRAFT
27 Chief Information Officer ... Mrs. Jill ALBIN-HILL
06 Registrar ... Mr. Michael Patrick MILLER
36 Director Career Development ... Ms. Keli WOJCIECHOWSKI
29 Dir Alumnae/i Relations ... Ms. Alysha COMSTOCK
88 Promoter of Mission Integration ... Sr. Mary Ann MEUNINGHOFF, OP
09 Dir Institutional Rsch & Assessment ... Ms. Elizabeth SILK
15 Director Human Resources ... Ms. Roberta MCMAHON
18 Director/Physical Plant ... Mr. Daniel BULOW
07 Director Transfer/Adult Admission ... Mr. Michael MORSOVILLO
37 Director Financial Aid ... Ms. Marie VON EBERS
23 Director Wellness Center ... Ms. Elizabeth RITZMAN
41 Director Athletics ... Mr. Erick BAUMANN
104 Director International Studies ... Dr. Sue PONREMY

East-West University (D)

816 S Michigan Avenue, Chicago IL 60605-2185

County: Cook | FICE Identification: 021686
Unit ID: 144883
Telephone: (312) 939-0111 | Carnegie Class: Bac/A&S
FAX Number: (312) 939-0083 | Calendar System: Quarter
URL: www.eastwest.edu
Established: 1980 | Annual Undergrad Tuition & Fees: $17,595
Enrollment: 862 | Coed
Affiliation or Control: Independent Non-Profit | IRS Status: 501(c)3
Highest Offering: Baccalaureate
Program: Liberal Arts And General
Accreditation: NH

01 Chancellor ... Dr. M. Wasiullah KHAN
05 Provost ... Dr. Madhu JAIN
20 Associate Provost ... Dr. Ekkehard T. WILKE
88 Assistant Provost for Acad Quality ... Dr. Lawrence J. GORMAN
07 Associate Dean of Admissions ... Mrs. Mettha M. ROSS
30 Assoc Dean Development/Univ Rels ... Mr. Zafar A. MALIK
32 Director of Counseling/Student Affs ... Ms. Melissa A. STEC
37 Director of Financial Aid ... Ms. Arica OSTREICHER
06 Registrar ... Mr. Matt S. MCCAW
04 Assistant to the Chancellor ... Ms. Carolyn J. FOWLKES
19 Director of Security ... Mr. Tasleem RAJA
26 Chief Public Relations Officer ... Mr. John THOMAS
18 Chief Facilities/Physical Plant ... Mr. Tasleem RAJA
10 Chief Business Officer ... Dr. Madhu JAIN
44 Chief Development Officer ... Ms. Judith BACON
38 Academic Counselor ... Ms. Meco HARRIS
85 International Student Advisor ... Mr. Rashed JAHANGIR

Eastern Illinois University (E)

600 Lincoln Avenue, Charleston IL 61920-3099

County: Coles | FICE Identification: 001674
Unit ID: 144892
Telephone: (217) 581-5000 | Carnegie Class: Master's L
FAX Number: (217) 581-2722 | Calendar System: Semester
URL: www.eiu.edu
Established: 1895 | Annual Undergrad Tuition & Fees (In-State): $10,930
Enrollment: 11,178 | Coed
Affiliation or Control: State | IRS Status: 501(c)3
Highest Offering: Beyond Master's But Less Than Doctorate
Program: Liberal Arts And General; Teacher Preparatory; Professional
Accreditation: NH, AAFCS, ART, BUS, BUSA, CACREP, DIETD, DIETI, JOUR, MUS, NAIT, NRPA, NURSE, SP, TED, THEA

01 President ... Dr. William L. PERRY
05 Provost/Vice Pres Academic Affairs ... Dr. Blair M. LORD
10 Vice President Business Affairs ... Dr. William V. WEBER
32 Vice President Student Affairs ... Dr. Daniel P. NADLER
30 Vice Pres University Advancement ... Mr. Robert K. MARTIN
20 Associate VP Academic Affairs ... Mr. Jeffrey F. CROSS
35 Associate Vice Pres Student Affairs ... Vacant
13 Asst VP for Information Tech Svcs ... Ms. Kathy S. REED
08 Dean of Library Services ... Dr. Allen K. LANHAM
84 Dean Enrollment Management ... Vacant
92 Dean Honors College ... Dr. John STIMAC
15 Director Human Resources ... Dr. Richard K. ENYARD
43 General Counsel ... Mr. Robert L. MILLER
22 Director Civil Rights ... Ms. Cynthia D. NICHOLS
45 Dir Planning/Budgeting/Research ... Mr. Michael S. MAURER
07 Director of Admissions ... Ms. Brenda L. MAJOR
37 Director of Financial Aid ... Mr. Jerry A. DONNA
06 Registrar ... Ms. Gayle S. HARVEY
29 Director Alumni Svc/Community Rels ... Mr. Steven W. RICH
09 Director of Institutional Research ... Vacant
18 Int Dir Facilities/Planning Mgmt ... Mr. Dave CROCKETT
96 Int Dir Procur/Disburs/Contract Svc ... Ms. Kay E. MCELWEE
38 Director of Counseling Center ... Ms. Sandra K. COX
25 Director of Research & Grants ... Dr. Robert W. CHESNUT
41 Director of Athletics ... Ms. Barbara A. BURKE
93 Director of Minority Affairs ... Ms. Mona DAVENPORT
39 Director of Housing/Dining Service ... Mr. Mark A. HUDSON
51 Dean Continuing Education ... Dr. William C. HINE
58 Dean Graduate School ... Dr. Robert M. AUGUSTINE
81 Dean College Sciences ... Dr. W. Harold ORNES
50 Dean Lumpkin Col Bus/Appl Sci ... Dr. Mahyar IZADI
79 Dean College Arts/Humanities ... Dr. Bonnie IRWIN
53 Dean College Education ... Dr. Diane H. JACKMAN

Elgin Community College (F)

1700 Spartan Drive, Elgin IL 60123-7193

County: Kane | FICE Identification: 001675
Unit ID: 144944
Telephone: (847) 697-1000 | Carnegie Class: Assoc/Pub-S-MC
FAX Number: (847) 214-7995 | Calendar System: Semester
URL: www.elgin.edu
Established: 1949 | Annual Undergrad Tuition & Fees (In-District): $3,150
Enrollment: 11,811 | Coed
Affiliation or Control: Local | IRS Status: 501(c)3
Highest Offering: Associate Degree
Program: Occupational; 2-Year Principally Bachelor's Creditable
Accreditation: NH, ADNUR, COMTA, DA, HT, MLTAD, PTAA, RAD, SURGT

01 President ... Dr. David SAM
10 Vice Pres Business/Finance ... Ms. Sharon KONNY
05 VP Teaching/Learning/Stdnt Dev ... Ms. Rose DIGERLANDO
20 Asst VP Teach/Lrng/Stdnt Dev ... Ms. Marcy THOMPSON
20 Dean Academic Dev/Learning Resource ... Dr. Mi HU
50 Dean Business ... Vacant
88 Dean Sustain/Safety & Career Tech ... Dr. Jeff BOYD
83 Dean Comm/Behavioral Sciences ... Dr. Ruixuan MAO
57 Dean Liberal/Visual/Performing Arts ... Ms. Mary HATCH
81 Dean Math/Science & Engineer ... Dr. James MCGEE
32 Dean of Student Services ... Dr. Carol COWLES
88 Dean Adult Basic Education ... Ms. Peggy HEINRICH
76 Dean Health Professions ... Ms. Wendy MILLER
38 Assoc Dean Counsel/Career Svcs ... Mr. John COFFIN
84 Assoc Dean Enrollment Management ... Dr. Mary PERKINS
106 Assoc Dean Inst Improve/Dist Lrng ... Mr. Timothy MOORE
08 Associate Dean Library ... Mr. Brian BEECHER
88 Asc Dean TRIO/Reten/Stdnt Outreach ... Dr. L. Bruce AUSTIN
18 Managing Director Facilities ... Mr. Cal BYRD
16 Chief Human Resources Officer ... Ms. Janelle CROWLEY
13 Chief Information Officer ... Mr. Ned COONEN
26 Chief Marketing/Comm Officer ... Ms. Paula AMENTA
30 Exec Dir Inst Advance/ECC Found ... Ms. Katherine SAWYER
20 Int Managing Dir Inst Comp/Curr ... Ms. Sharon WILSON
45 Executive Dir Planning/Inst Effect ... Dr. Philip GARBER
09 Director Institutional Research ... Mr. David RUDDEN
37 Director Financial Aid/Scholarships ... Ms. Amy PERRIN
19 Chief of Police ... Mr. Emad EASSA
21 Controller ... Ms. Heather SCHOLL
06 Assoc Dean Registration/Records ... Dr. Jennifer MCCLURE
90 Director Academic Computing ... Ms. Karin STACY
22 Paralegal/EEO/AA and FOIA Officer ... Ms. Marilyn PRENTICE
07 Director of Admissions/Recruitment ... Mr. Trevell EDDINS
41 Director Athletics & Wellness ... Mr. Kent PAYNE
40 Exec Dir Aux Enterprises & Cont Ed ... Mr. Frank HERNANDEZ
96 Director Business Services ... Ms. Melissa TAIT
36 Director Career Services ... Ms. Peggy GUNDRUM
26 Senior Director of Marketing ... Mr. Jeffrey ARENA
35 Director Orientation/Student Life ... Ms. Amybeth MAURER
88 Dir Small Business Devel Center ... Mr. Kriss KNOWLES
14 Director Technology Services ... Mr. Jeffery METZGER
86 Dir Cmty Engagemnt/Legislative Affs ... Mr. Michael MULCRONE
101 Secretary to Board of Trustees ... Ms. Eleanor MACKINNEY
04 Sr Exec Asst to the President ... Ms. Kathleen J. STOVER

Ellis University (G)

111 N Canal Street, Suite 380, Chicago IL 60606-7202

County: Cook | FICE Identification: 041433
Unit ID: 452133
Telephone: (877) 355-4762 | Carnegie Class: Bac/A&S
FAX Number: (312) 589-7499 | Calendar System: Semester
URL: www.ellis.edu
Established: 2008 | Annual Undergrad Tuition & Fees: $13,410
Enrollment: 375 | Coed
Affiliation or Control: Independent Non-Profit | IRS Status: 501(c)3
Highest Offering: Master's
Program: Professional; Business Emphasis
Accreditation: DETC

01 President ... Dr. Virginia A. CARLIN
10 Interim CFO ... Randy WILLY
11 VP of Operations ... Raymond RODRIGUEZ
20 Chief Academic Officer ... Dr. Andrew CARPENTER
06 Registrar ... Yahana TEGEGNE
07 Director of Academic Advising ... LePra GEORGE

Elmhurst College (H)

190 Prospect, Elmhurst IL 60126-3296

County: DuPage | FICE Identification: 001676
Unit ID: 144962
Telephone: (630) 279-4100 | Carnegie Class: Master's M
FAX Number: (630) 617-3282 | Calendar System: 4/1/4
URL: www.elmhurst.edu
Established: 1871 | Annual Undergrad Tuition & Fees: $31,450
Enrollment: 3,455 | Coed
Affiliation or Control: United Church Of Christ | IRS Status: 501(c)3
Highest Offering: Master's
Program: Liberal Arts And General; Teacher Preparatory; Professional
Accreditation: NH, NURSE

01 President ... Dr. S. Alan RAY
10 Sr VP of Finance & Administration ... Mr. James CUNNINGHAM
05 Vice Pres Acad Affs/Dean of Faculty ... Dr. Alzada TIPTON
27 VP and Chief Information Officer ... Dr. James KULICH
26 VP for Communications & Public Affs ... Mr. James W. WINTERS
29 VP for Development/Alumni Relations ... Mr. Joseph R. EMMICK
32 Dean of Students ... Dr. Eileen G. SULLIVAN
07 Dean of Admission ... Mr. Gary F. ROLD
107 Dean School for Professional Stds ... Dr. Timothy RICORDATI
20 Associate Dean of Faculty ... Dr. Heather HALL
20 Associate Dean of Faculty ... Dr. Theodore LERUD
88 Exec Dir Center for Pro Excellence ... Dr. Lawrence B. CARROLL
18 Exec Director Facilities Management ... Mr. Bruce J. MATHER
42 Chaplain ... Rev. H. Scott MATHENEY
06 Registrar ... Mr. S. Dean ELLENS
08 Director of the Library ... Ms. Susan S. STEFFEN
36 Director of Career Education ... Ms. Peggy KILLIAN
21 Controller ... Mr. Richard A. SCHEPLER
38 Director of Counseling Services ... Dr. Amy SWARR
28 Director of Intercultural Education ... Dr. Kathleen RUST
14 Director of Computer Services ... Mr. James M. FRANCIS
88 Director Development Services ... Ms. LaTonya FOSTER
29 Director of Alumni Relations ... Vacant

88	Managing Dir of Public Affairs	Ms. Desiree CHEN
16	Director of Human Resources	Mr. John NEWTON
19	Exec Director of Campus Security	Mr. Jeff KEDROWSKI
37	Director of Financial Aid	Ms. Ruth PUSICH
07	Director of Admission	Ms. Stephanie LEVENSON
07	Director Adult/Graduate Admission	Ms. Elizabeth D. KUEBLER
39	Director of Residence Life	Ms. Christine J. SMITH
41	Director Intercollegiate Athletics	Mr. Paul KROHN

Erikson Institute (A)

451 N. Lasalle Street, Chicago IL 60654

County: Cook FICE Identification: 035103
Unit ID: 409254
Telephone: (312) 755-2250 Carnegie Class: Spec/Other
FAX Number: (312) 755-0928 Calendar System: Semester
URL: www.erikson.edu
Established: 1966 Annual Graduate Tuition & Fees: $14,680
Enrollment: 278 Coed
Affiliation or Control: Independent Non-Profit IRS Status: 501(c)3
Highest Offering: Master's; No Undergraduates
Program: Professional
Accreditation: NH

01	President	Samuel J. MEISELS
05	Sr VP Academic Affs/Dean of Faculty	Aisha RAY
10	Vice President Finance/Operations	Susan WALLACE
45	Vice President Planning/Enrollment	Jeanne LOCKRIDGE
30	Vice Pres Institutional Advancement	Randy L. HOLGATE
84	Dean of Enrollment Management	Michel FRENDIAN
13	Chief Information Officer	Jonathan FRANK
27	Chief Marketing/Communications Ofcr	Anne DIVITA KOPACZ
88	Dir of Professional Development	Deborah MANTIA
44	Asst Dir Development Data Systems	Deborah HARP

Eureka College (B)

300 E College Avenue, Eureka IL 61530-1500

County: Woodford FICE Identification: 001678
Unit ID: 144971
Telephone: (309) 467-3721 Carnegie Class: Bac/Diverse
FAX Number: (309) 467-6386 Calendar System: Semester
URL: www.eureka.edu
Established: 1855 Annual Undergrad Tuition & Fees: $18,650
Enrollment: 755 Coed
Affiliation or Control: Christian Church (Disciples Of Christ)
IRS Status: 501(c)3
Highest Offering: Baccalaureate
Program: Liberal Arts And General; Teacher Preparatory
Accreditation: NH

01	President	Dr. J. David ARNOLD
04	Administrative Asst to President	Ms. Jyl KRAUSE
05	Provost & Dean of the College	Dr. Philip Acree CAVALIER
10	VP Fin/Fac/Chief Financial Officer	Mr. Marc PASTERIS
32	Dean of Student Services	Mr. Ken A. BAXTER
30	Vice Pres Dev & Alumni Relations	Mr. Michael MURTAGH
26	Director of College Relations	Vacant
06	Registrar	Mr. Scott WIGNALL
08	Library Director	Mr. Tony GLASS
18	Director of Physical Plant	Mr. Rob MCCHESNEY
42	Chaplain	Rev. Bruce M. FOWLKES
14	Director of Computer Services	Dr. Kanaka VIJITHA-KUMARA
37	Director of Financial Aid	Mrs. Ellen M. RIGSBY
41	Athletic Director	Mr. Paul BRYANT
29	Director Alumni Relations	Mrs. Shellie SCHWANKE

Fox College (C)

6640 South Cicero Avenue, Bedford Park IL 60638

County: Cook FICE Identification: 025228
Unit ID: 145239
Telephone: (708) 444-4500 Carnegie Class: Assoc/PrivFP
FAX Number: (708) 802-6585 Calendar System: Semester
URL: www.foxcollege.edu
Established: 1932 Annual Undergrad Tuition & Fees: $15,080
Enrollment: 500 Coed
Affiliation or Control: Proprietary IRS Status: Proprietary
Highest Offering: Associate Degree
Program: Occupational; 2-Year Principally Bachelor's Creditable; Business Emphasis
Accreditation: NH, MAAB, PTAA

01	President	Mr. Carey CRANSTON
11	Operations Administrator	Ms. Nicole BROWN

Garrett-Evangelical Theological Seminary (D)

2121 Sheridan Road, Evanston IL 60201-3298

County: Cook FICE Identification: 001682
Unit ID: 145275
Telephone: (847) 866-3900 Carnegie Class: Spec/Faith
FAX Number: (847) 866-3957 Calendar System: Semester
URL: www.garrett.edu
Established: 1853 Annual Graduate Tuition & Fees: $17,835
Enrollment: 382 Coed
Affiliation or Control: United Methodist IRS Status: 501(c)3
Highest Offering: Doctorate; No Undergraduates
Program: Professional; Religious Emphasis
Accreditation: NH, THEOL

01	President	Dr. Philip A. AMERSON
11	VP for Admin/External Programming	Dr. James A. NOSEWORTHY
05	Acad Dean/Vice Pres Acad Affairs	Dr. Lallene J. RECTOR
30	Vice President for Development	Dr. David L. HEETLAND
10	Vice President Business Affairs/CFO	Mr. Arnold HENNING
32	Dean of Students	Rev. Cynthia A. WILSON
84	Assistant VP for Enrollment Mgmt	Rev. Becky J. EBERHART
04	Assistant to the President	Vacant
21	Controller	Ms. Jessica JOHNSTON
06	Registrar/Dir of Academic Studies	Rev. Vince MCGLOTHIN-ELLER
08	Acting Director of United Library	Dr. Jaeyeon L. CHUNG
13	Director of Information Technology	Mr. James D. CASH
18	Director of Buildings & Grounds	Mr. John CARTER
39	Director of Housing & Food Service	Ms. Barbara B. ADAMS
29	Dir Annual Gvg/Alum Rel/Hospitality	Ms. Kay A. BURLINGHAM
88	Director of Stewardship	Ms. Elizabeth P. CAMPBELL
37	Director of Financial Aid	Ms. Margaret C. HALLEN
26	Manager of Communications & Events	Mr. Shane NICHOLS

Governors State University (E)

1 University Parkway, University Park IL 60484-0975

County: Will FICE Identification: 009145
Unit ID: 145336
Telephone: (708) 534-5000 Carnegie Class: Master's L
FAX Number: (708) 534-4107 Calendar System: Semester
URL: www.govst.edu
Established: 1969 Annual Undergrad Tuition & Fees (In-State): $9,116
Enrollment: 5,541 Coed
Affiliation or Control: State IRS Status: 501(c)3
Highest Offering: Doctorate
Program: Liberal Arts And General; Teacher Preparatory; Professional
Accreditation: NH, ACBSP, CACREP, HSA, NUR, OT, PTA, SP, SPAA, SW, TED

01	President	Dr. Elaine P. MAIMON
03	Executive VP & Chief of Staff/Treas	Dr. Gebeyehu EJIGU
05	Provost/VP Academic Affairs	Dr. Terry C. ALLISON
10	Vice Pres Admininstration & Finance	Ms. Karen KISSEL
11	Interim Vice Pres Admin & Planning	Dr. Gebeyehu EJIGU
30	VP Advancement/CEO Foundation	Ms. Joan T. VAUGHAN
26	VP Enrollment Mgmt & Marketing	Ms. Courtney KOHN SANDERS
43	Legal Counsel	Ms. Alexis KENNEDY
22	Affirmative Action/EO	Mr. Tony A. TYMKOW
45	Director Budget Planning/Inst Rsrch	Dr. Jeffrey SLOVAK
09	Assoc Dir of Institutional Research	Vacant
29	Interim Director of Alumni Assoc	Ms. Cheri GAREY
26	Asst VP of Marketing/Communication	Ms. Rhonda BROWN
50	Dean Col Business/Public Admin	Dr. Ellen FOSTER CURTIS
49	Dean College Arts Sciences	Dr. Reinhold HILL
76	Dean Col Health Professions	Dr. Elizabeth CADA
53	Dean College Education	Dr. Deborah BORDELON
32	Dean Student Affairs & Services	Dr. Sherilyn POOLE
84	Exec Director Enrollment Services	Vacant
08	Dean Library Svc/Academic Computing	Vacant
56	Dean Extend Lrng/Community Svcs	Vacant
06	Registrar	Ms. Michelle SMITH-WILLIAMS
37	Director Financial Aid	Ms. Freda WHISETON-COMER
35	Acting Executive Dir Student Life	Ms. Vanessa NEWBY
20	Associate Provost/AVP Academic Affs	Dr. Angela LATHAM
21	Director Business Operations	Ms. Karen KISSEL
13	Exec Director Information Tech Svcs	Mr. Peter J. MIZERA
15	Director Human Resources	Ms. Gail BRADSHAW
18	Director Physical Plant	Mr. David STONE
19	Int Director Dept Public Safety	Mr. James MCGEE
38	Dir Stdnt Develop/Counseling Center	Ms. Kelly MCCARTHY
36	Director of Career Services	Ms. Darcie R. CAMPOS
96	Dir of Procurement/Auxillary Svcs	Ms. Tracy SULLIVAN

Greenville College (F)

315 E College, Greenville IL 62246

County: Bond FICE Identification: 001684
Unit ID: 145372
Telephone: (618) 664-2800 Carnegie Class: Bac/Diverse
FAX Number: (618) 664-6841 Calendar System: 4/1/4
URL: www.greenville.edu
Established: 1892 Annual Undergrad Tuition & Fees: $22,920
Enrollment: 1,501 Coed
Affiliation or Control: Free Methodist IRS Status: 501(c)3
Highest Offering: Master's
Program: Liberal Arts And General; Teacher Preparatory; Professional
Accreditation: NH, @TEAC

01	Acting President	Dr. Randy BERGEN
04	Assistant to the President	Ms. Tamie HEICHELBECK
05	Interim VPAA	Dr. Brad SHAW
30	Vice Pres for Advancement	Mr. Walter FENTON
10	Vice President for Finance	Mrs. Dana FUNDERBURK
32	Vice Pres for Student Development	Dr. Norman D. HALL
84	Vice Pres for Enrollment	Mr. Michael RITTER
45	Assoc VP Planning/Dn Prof Stds	Dr. Dave HOLDEN
08	Director of Library	Ms. Jane L. HOPKINS
06	Registrar	Mrs. Michelle SUSSENBACH
29	Director Alumni Relations	Ms. Pam TAYLOR
37	Director of Financial Aid	Mrs. Marilae LATHAM
30	Director of Advancement	Vacant
42	Dean Chapel & Dir Spiritual Form	Mrs. Lori GAFFNER
18	Director of Facilities	Mr. Chris KESTER
26	Director of Marketing	Mr. Nathan BREWER
09	Dean of College Planning/Assessment	Vacant
49	Interim Dean School Arts & Sciences	Dr. Brian HARTLEY
53	Interim Dean School of Education	Dr. Brian REINHARD
41	Athletic Director	Dr. Doug FAULKNER
13	Assoc VP Innovation & Technology	Dr. Vickie COOK

Harper College (G)

1200 W Algonquin Road, Palatine IL 60067-7398

County: Cook FICE Identification: 003961
Unit ID: 149842
Telephone: (847) 925-6000 Carnegie Class: Assoc/Pub-S-SC
FAX Number: (847) 925-6034 Calendar System: Semester
URL: www.harpercollege.edu
Established: 1965 Annual Undergrad Tuition & Fees (In-District): $3,054
Enrollment: 17,337 Coed
Affiliation or Control: State/Local IRS Status: 501(c)3
Highest Offering: Associate Degree
Program: Occupational; 2-Year Principally Bachelor's Creditable
Accreditation: NH, ACBSP, ADNUR, CEA, DH, DIETT, DMS, MAC, MUS, RAD

01	President	Dr. Kenneth L. ENDER
100	Chief of Staff	Ms. Sheila QUIRK-BAILEY
101	Senior Executive to the President	Mrs. Maria COONS
10	Exec VP Finance & Admin Services	Dr. Ron ALLY
05	Provost	Dr. Judith MARWICK
30	Interim Exec Dir Advancement/Fdn	Ms. Lisa DIETLIN
26	Chief Communications Officer	Mr. Phil BURDICK
20	Associate Provost/Interdis St Succ	Ms. Joan KINDLE
16	Chief Human Resources Officer	Mr. Roger SPAYER
27	Chief Information Officer	Mr. Patrick BAUER
21	Controller	Mr. Bret BONNSTETTER
18	Exec Director of Facilities Mgmt	Mr. Thomas CRYLEN
88	Asst Provost & Dean Career Pgm	Ms. Sally GRIFFITH
08	Dean Resources for Learning	Ms. Njambi KAMOCHE
32	Dean Stdnt Affs/Welln & Campus Act	Ms. Ashley KNIGHT
84	Dean Enrollment Services	Ms. Maria MOTEN
51	Dean Cont Education & Bus Outreach	Dr. Mark MROZINSKI
35	Dean Student Development	Ms. Sheryl OTTO
50	Dean Business & Social Science	Ms. Michele' ROBINSON
81	Interim Dean Mathematics & Sciences	Ms. Julie ELLEFSON-KUEHN
88	Asst Dean Acad Enrch/ Engmt/Dir AED	Ms. Darice TROUT
49	Dean Liberal Arts	Mr. Brian KNETL
88	Assoc Dean Ctr Adjunct Fac Engag	Ms. Barbara SMALL
93	Assoc Dean Ctr Multicultural Lrng	Ms. Laura LABAUVE-MAHER
23	Asst Dean CAFE & Dir Allied Health	Ms. Shannon LENGERICH
76	Assistant Dean/Allied Health Dir	Vacant
72	Assistant Dean CAFE	Mr. John SMITH
88	Dir New Student Programs/Retention	Ms. Vicki ATKINSON
13	Director IT Enterprise Systems	Mr. Mike BABB
26	Director Marketing Services	Mr. Mike BARZACCHINI
36	Director Career Ctr & Women's Pgm	Ms. Kathleen CANFIELD
88	Director Client Services	Ms. Sue CONTARINO
09	Director Institutional Research	Mr. Doug EASTERLING
106	Director Ctr for Innov Instruction	Mr. Matthew ENSENBERGER
88	Dir Disability Svcs/ADA Compliance	Mr. Scott FRIEDMAN
88	Director Physical Plant	Mr. Darryl KNIGHT
37	Dir Student Financial Assistance	Ms. Laura MCGEE
66	Director Nursing	Ms. Marjorie KOZLOWSKI
14	Interim Director Technical Services	Mr. James BATSON
35	Director Student Activities	Vacant
07	Dir Student Recruitment & Outreach	Mr. Robert PARZY
88	Campus Architect	Mr. Stephen PETERSEN
38	Dir Academic Advising & Counseling	Mr. Eric ROSENTHAL
44	Asc Exec Dir Found/Dir Major Gifts	Ms. Katherine SAWYER
88	Dir Inst Effect/Outcomes Assess	Ms. Darlene SCHLENBECKER
41	Director of Athletics & Fitness	Mr. Doug SPIWAK
103	Director Adult Learning	Ms. Nancy WAJLER

Harrington College of Design (H)

200 W Madison, 2nd Floor, Chicago IL 60606-3433

County: Cook FICE Identification: 020552
Unit ID: 145460
Telephone: (312) 939-4975 Carnegie Class: Spec/Arts
FAX Number: (312) 939-8005 Calendar System: Semester
URL: www.harrington.edu
Established: 1931 Annual Undergrad Tuition & Fees: $19,300
Enrollment: 620 Coed
Affiliation or Control: Proprietary IRS Status: Proprietary
Highest Offering: Master's
Program: Professional; Fine Arts Emphasis
Accreditation: NH, CIDA

01	President	Mr. Bob NACHTSHEIM
05	Director of Academic Affairs	Ms. Gretchen FRICKX
07	Director of Admissions	Ms. Jessie MCEWEN
10	Regional Controller	Mr. Matthew FIRCK
13	Manager of IT & Facilities	Mr. Bryan STYER
36	Director Career Services	Ms. Camille HARRIS
08	Head Librarian	Ms. Leigh GATES
37	Manager of Financial Aid	Mr. Victor AGAPAY
06	Registrar	Mr. Sam DELAROSA
35	Director Student Services	Mr. Sam DELAROSA
09	Director of Institutional Research	Ms. Renee DAROSKY

Heartland Community College (I)

1500 W Raab Road, Normal IL 61761-9446

County: McLean FICE Identification: 030838
Unit ID: 384342
Telephone: (309) 268-8000 Carnegie Class: Assoc/Pub-R-L
FAX Number: (309) 268-7999 Calendar System: Semester

URL: www.heartland.edu
Established: 1990 Annual Undergrad Tuition & Fees (In-District): $3,264
Enrollment: 5,610 Coed
Affiliation or Control: State/Local IRS Status: 501(c)3
Highest Offering: Associate Degree
Program: Occupational; 2-Year Principally Bachelor's Creditable
Accreditation: NH, ADNUR, RAD

01 President ... Dr. Allen GOBEN
05 Vice Pres Learning/Student Success ... Dr. Rick PEARCE
10 Vice President Business Services ... Mr. Robert D. WIDMER
30 Vice Pres Institutional Advancement ... Dr. Helen KATZ
51 Vice President Continuing Education ... Ms. Mary Beth TRAKINAT
88 Dean Student Success ... Dr. Amy MUNSON
84 Dean Enrollment Services ... Mr. Padriac SHINVILLE
18 Executive Director of Facilities ... Mr. James HUBBARD
11 Director of Administrative Services ... Ms. Valerie CRAWFORD
13 Chief Information Officer ... Mr. Doug MINTER
21 Controller ... Ms. Sue GILPIN
37 Director of Financial Aid ... Mr. Kim DONAT
15 Exec Director Human Resources ... Mrs. Barb LEATHERS
86 Exec Dir Governmental Relations ... Ms. Janet HILL GETZ
09 Exec Director Inst Effectiveness ... Mr. David COOK
41 Director of Athletics ... Mr. Nate METZGER
29 Director Alumni Relations/Outreach ... Ms. Colleen REYNOLDS
36 Director Testing Services ... Ms. Kimberly KELLEY
38 Director of Advisement & Records ... Ms. Cecilia OLIVARES
26 Director of Marketing ... Ms. Amy HUMPHREYS

Hebrew Theological College (A)

7135 N Carpenter Road, Skokie IL 60077-3263
County: Cook FICE Identification: 001685
Unit ID: 145497
Telephone: (847) 982-2500 Carnegie Class: Spec/Faith
FAX Number: (847) 674-6381 Calendar System: Semester
URL: www.htc.edu
Established: 1922 Annual Undergrad Tuition & Fees: $19,150
Enrollment: 493 Coordinate
Affiliation or Control: Independent Non-Profit IRS Status: 501(c)3
Highest Offering: Master's
Program: Liberal Arts And General; Teacher Preparatory; Professional; Religious Emphasis
Accreditation: NH

01 Chancellor ... Rabbi Jerold ISENBERG
05 Rosh Hayeshiva-Chief Academic ... Rabbi Avraham FRIEDMAN
11 Vice President for Administration ... Rabbi Sender KUTNER
20 Dean Blitstein Institute ... Dr. Esther SHKOP
20 Dean AHS & LAS Men's Division ... Rabbi Michael MYERS
33 Mashgiach Ruchani-Dean ... Rabbi Zvi ZIMMERMAN
34 Menahel Ruchani-Dean ... Rabbi Binyamin OLSTEIN
34 Assistant Dean Blitstein Institute ... Ms. Rita LIPSHITZ
06 Registrar ... Rabbi Shmuel SCHUMAN
07 Director of Admissions ... Rabbi Joshua ZISOOK
30 Director of Development ... Rabbi Gershon SEIF
44 Development Coordinator ... Rabbi Yaakov FRIEDMAN
08 Librarian ... Rabbi Elie GINSPARG
88 Israel Program Liaison - Blitstein ... Mrs. Chaya FISH
88 Israel Program Liaison - Beis Midra ... Rabbi Joshua KANTER

† Separate campuses for male and female students.

Highland Community College (B)

2998 W Pearl City Road, Freeport IL 61032-9341
County: Stephenson FICE Identification: 001681
Unit ID: 145521
Telephone: (815) 235-6121 Carnegie Class: Assoc/Pub-R-M
FAX Number: (815) 235-6130 Calendar System: Semester
URL: www.highland.edu
Established: 1961 Annual Undergrad Tuition & Fees (In-District): $3,420
Enrollment: 1,959 Coed
Affiliation or Control: State/Local IRS Status: 501(c)3
Highest Offering: Associate Degree
Program: Occupational; 2-Year Principally Bachelor's Creditable
Accreditation: NH, MAC

01 President ... Dr. Joe M. KANOSKY
05 Vice Pres Academic Services ... Mr. Tim HOOD
11 Vice Pres Administrative Services ... Ms. Jill M. JANSSEN
15 Associate VP Human Resources ... Ms. Rose A. FERGUSON
32 Assoc VP Student Services ... Mrs. Elizabeth L. GERBER
50 Dean Business & Technology ... Mr. Scott R. ANDERSON
79 Dean Humanities/Soc Science ... Dr. Thompson A. BRANDT
66 Assoc Dean Nursing & Allied Health ... Ms. Donna KAUKE
81 Assoc Dean Natural Science & Math ... Mr. George GOLDSWORTHY
51 Director Adult Education ... Mr. Mark JANSEN
41 Director Athletics ... Mr. Peter E. NORMAN
84 Director Enrollment/Records ... Mr. Jeremy BRADT
37 Director Financial Aid ... Ms. Kathy BANGASSER
90 Director ITS ... Mr. Nathan HENSAL
09 Director Institutional Research ... Dr. Michelle THRUMAN
88 Director Learning Services ... Ms. Carolyn PETSCHE
08 Director Library Services ... Mrs. Judy MOORE
31 Director Marketing & Cmty Relations ... Mr. Pete WILLGING
88 Director Partners for Employment ... Ms. Kathy K. DAY
18 Director Physical Plant/Maint ... Mr. Kurt SIMPSON
88 Director Retired & Senior Vol Pgm ... Mr. Michael J. SHORE
88 Director Title IV Student Support ... Ms. Virginia A. WARE
21 Manager Accounting ... Ms. Mary J. LLOYD
40 Manager Bookstore ... Ms. Madonna KEENEY
101 Exec Asst to President/Board Sec ... Ms. Terri A. GRIMES
96 Purchasing & Insurance Specialist ... Ms. Teresa WILLIAMS
102 Executive Director Foundation ... Mr. James M. BERBERET

Illinois Central College (C)

1 College Drive, East Peoria IL 61635-0001
County: Tazewell FICE Identification: 006753
Unit ID: 145682
Telephone: (309) 694-5422 Carnegie Class: Assoc/Pub-R-L
FAX Number: (309) 694-5450 Calendar System: Semester
URL: www.icc.edu
Established: 1966 Annual Undergrad Tuition & Fees (In-District): $3,195
Enrollment: 12,286 Coed
Affiliation or Control: State/Local IRS Status: 501(c)3
Highest Offering: Associate Degree
Program: Occupational; 2-Year Principally Bachelor's Creditable
Accreditation: NH, ADNUR, DH, MAC, MLTAD, MUS, OTA, PTAA, RAD, SURGT

01 President ... Dr. John S. ERWIN
05 Provost ... Dr. William TAMMONE
10 Exec VP Administration/Finance ... Mr. Bruce BUDDE
26 Assoc Vice President of Marketing ... Dr. Cheryl FLIEGE
20 Vice Pres of Academic Affairs ... Dr. Margaret A. SWANSON
30 Exec Dir/Chief Development Officer ... Ms. Robin BALLARD
15 Exec Director of Human Resources ... Mr. Patrick PARSONS
14 Director Technology Services ... Dr. Susan WHEELER
38 Director Advisement/Assess/Counsel ... Ms. Pam WILFINGER
37 Director Student Financial Services ... Ms. Beth MCCLAIN
07 Director Enrollment Services ... Ms. Angela DREESSEN
28 Executive Director of Diversity ... Dr. Rita ALI
18 Dir of Facilities Planning & Design ... Mr. Troy HATTERMANN
51 Dean Corporate/Community Education ... Ms. Ellen GEORGE
88 Dean Inst Innovations & Learning ... Ms. Janice KINSINGER
83 Dean Social Sciences ... Dr. Jill WRIGHT
81 Dean Math/Science/Engineering ... Mr. Tom PILAT
50 Dean Business/Info Services ... Dr. Gina MCCONOUGHEY
32 Dean of Student Services ... Mr. Guy GOODMAN
57 Dean Arts & Communications ... Mr. Christopher GRAY
47 Dean Agriculture/Industrial Tech ... Mr. Michael SLOAN
31 Dean Cmty Outreach/ICC S Coord ... Ms. Kay SUTTON
60 Dean English ... Dr. Jill WRIGHT

Illinois College (D)

1101 W College Avenue, Jacksonville IL 62650-2299
County: Morgan FICE Identification: 001688
Unit ID: 145691
Telephone: (217) 245-3000 Carnegie Class: Bac/A&S
FAX Number: (217) 245-3034 Calendar System: Semester
URL: www.ic.edu
Established: 1829 Annual Undergrad Tuition & Fees: $26,500
Enrollment: 956 Coed
Affiliation or Control: Independent Non-Profit IRS Status: 501(c)3
Highest Offering: Baccalaureate
Program: Liberal Arts And General; Teacher Preparatory
Accreditation: NH

01 President ... Dr. Axel D. STEUER
05 Vice President Academic Affairs ... Dr. Elizabeth H. TOBIN
10 Vice President Business Affairs ... Mr. Frank G. WILLIAMS
30 Vice President Advancement ... Mr. Philip R. HOOD
84 Vice President for Enrollment ... Ms. Stephanie CHIPMAN
32 VP Student Affairs/Dean of Students ... Dr. Malinda L. CARLSON
18 Asst Vice Pres Campus Facilities ... Mr. Allen R. MAYS, JR.
20 Associate Dean of the College ... Mr. Nicholas P. CAPO
07 Associate Director Admissions ... Mr. Richard L. BYSTRY
29 Director Alumni Relations ... Ms. Kristin E. JAMISON
26 Director of Marketing & Communicati ... Ms. Mary Ellen ROY
08 Librarian ... Mr. Jan FIGA
37 Director Student Financial Aid ... Ms. Katherine A. TAYLOR
36 Director of Career Center ... Ms. Susan K. DRAKE
06 Registrar ... Ms. Helen KUHN
21 Controller ... Ms. Melissa J. DYSSON
35 Director Student Activities ... Ms. Karen K. HOMOLKA
42 Chaplain ... Rev. Katrina E. JENKINS
88 Assoc Dir of Admissions/Recruitment ... Ms. Kristen REED
09 Advisor to Pres for Inst Research ... Dr. Robert A. SWEATMAN
15 Director Personnel Services ... Ms. Teresa C. SMITH
38 Director Student Counseling ... Mr. William TENNILL
28 Director of Diversity ... Mr. Justin MALLETT

Illinois College of Optometry (E)

3241 S Michigan Avenue, Chicago IL 60616-3878
County: Cook FICE Identification: 001689
Unit ID: 145628
Telephone: (312) 225-1700 Carnegie Class: Spec/Health
FAX Number: (312) 225-1724 Calendar System: Quarter
URL: www.ico.edu
Established: 1872 Annual Graduate Tuition & Fees: $31,660
Enrollment: 646 Coed
Affiliation or Control: Independent Non-Profit IRS Status: 501(c)3
Highest Offering: First Professional Degree; No Undergraduates
Program: Professional
Accreditation: NH, OPT, OPTR

01 President ... Dr. Arol R. AUGSBURGER
05 Vice Pres for Academic Affairs/Dean ... Dr. Stephanie MESSNER
11 Vice President Administration ... Ms. Laura L. ROUNCE
17 Vice Pres for Patient Care Services ... Dr. Leonard V. MESSNER
10 VP for Finance & Business/CFO ... Mr. John BUDZYNSKI
30 VP Student/Alumni/College Devel ... Dr. Mark COLIP
22 VP Compliance/Cmty Based Services ... Dr. Valarie CONRAD
20 Associate Dean Academic Affairs ... Dr. Barclay BAKKUM
06 Asst Dean Academic Admin/Registrar ... Mrs. Lavern YOUNG
07 Director of Admissions ... Ms. Teisha JOHNSON
35 Sr Director Student Development ... Ms. Beth KARMIS
37 Director Student Financial Aid ... Ms. Melissa BARTOLD
29 Director Alumni Relations ... Ms. Connie M. SCAVUZZO
18 Chief Facilities/Physical Plant ... Mr. Opie NIMON
36 Director Student Placement ... Ms. Tracy FAULKNER

*Illinois Eastern Community Colleges System Office (F)

233 E Chestnut Street, Olney IL 62450-2298
County: Richland FICE Identification: 009135
Unit ID: 443368
Telephone: (618) 393-2982 Carnegie Class: N/A
FAX Number: (618) 392-4816
URL: www.iecc.edu

01 Chief Executive Officer ... Mr. Terry BRUCE
05 Dean Acad/Student Support Svc/CAO ... Mrs. Chris CANTWELL
10 Chief Finance Officer/Treasurer ... Mr. Roger BROWNING
103 Dean Workforce Education ... Mr. Michael THOMAS
30 Assoc Dean Grants/Inst Development ... Mrs. LeAnn HARTLEROAD
20 Pgm Director College Support Svcs ... Ms. Rita S. ADAMS
88 Program Director SBDC ... Mr. Byron BRUMFIEL
85 Pgm Dir Intl Std/Dir Dist Std Rctmt ... Mrs. Pamela SWANSON-MADDEN
15 Director of Human Resources ... Mrs. Tara BUERSTER
88 Asst Director Upward Bound ... Ms. Tiffany COWGER
88 Asst Director Upward Bound East ... Mr. Brandon WEGER
88 Director Student Advantage Network ... Mrs. Cora WEGER
88 Director Talent Search ... Vacant

*Illinois Eastern Community Colleges Frontier Community College (G)

Frontier Drive, Fairfield IL 62837-9801
County: Wayne FICE Identification: 020744
Unit ID: 403469
Telephone: (618) 842-3711 Carnegie Class: Assoc/Pub-R-L
FAX Number: (618) 842-4425 Calendar System: Semester
URL: www.iecc.edu/fcc
Established: 1976 Annual Undergrad Tuition & Fees (In-District): $2,858
Enrollment: 2,194 Coed
Affiliation or Control: State/Local IRS Status: 501(c)3
Highest Offering: Associate Degree
Program: Occupational; 2-Year Principally Bachelor's Creditable
Accreditation: &NH, ADNUR

02 President ... Dr. Tim TAYLOR
05 Dean of Instruction ... Mr. Bob BOYLES
32 Asst Dean of Student Services ... Mrs. Jan WILES
51 Assoc Dean Adult & Cont Education ... Mrs. Jervaise MCDANIEL
10 Director of Business ... Ms. Mary ATKINS
08 Director of Learning Resource Ctr ... Ms. Merna YOUNGBLOOD
88 Pgm Dir Emerg Prep/Indu Qual Mgmt ... Ms. Carrie DAGG
18 Supervisor of Building & Grounds ... Mr. Galen DUNN
37 Coordinator of Financial Aid ... Mr. Adam BOWLES
26 Coord of Public Info & Marketing ... Ms. Karen BRYANT
88 Coord Literary Development Program ... Ms. Janet HERMAN
06 Coordinator of Registration/Records ... Ms. Amy LOSS

*Illinois Eastern Community Colleges Lincoln Trail College (H)

11220 State Highway 1, Robinson IL 62454-5707
County: Crawford FICE Identification: 009786
Unit ID: 403478
Telephone: (618) 544-8657 Carnegie Class: Assoc/Pub-R-M
FAX Number: (618) 544-7423 Calendar System: Semester
URL: www.iecc.edu/ltc
Established: 1969 Annual Undergrad Tuition & Fees (In-District): $2,858
Enrollment: 1,066 Coed
Affiliation or Control: State/Local IRS Status: 501(c)3
Highest Offering: Associate Degree
Program: Occupational; 2-Year Principally Bachelor's Creditable
Accreditation: &NH, ADNUR

02 President ... Mr. Mitch HANNAHS
05 Dean of the College ... Ms. Kathy HARRIS
37 Director of Financial Aid ... Ms. Jennifer BARTHELEMY
07 Director of Admissions ... Ms. Becky L. MIKEWORTH
08 Director of Learning Resource Ctr ... Ms. Vicky BONELLI
10 Director of Business ... Ms. Jamie HENRY
36 Career Advisor ... Ms. Gayle ZARING
41 Interim Sports Center Manager/Coach ... Mr. Kevin BOWERS
18 Groundskeeper ... Mr. Dan LEGGITT
26 Coord Public Information/Marketing ... Ms. Danelle HEVRON

*Illinois Eastern Community Colleges Olney Central College (I)

305 North West Street, Olney IL 62450-1099
County: Richland FICE Identification: 001742
Unit ID: 145707

Telephone: (618) 395-7777 Carnegie Class: Assoc/Pub-R-M
FAX Number: (618) 392-3293 Calendar System: Semester
URL: www.iecc.edu/occ
Established: 1962 Annual Undergrad Tuition & Fees (In-District): $2,858
Enrollment: 1,524 Coed
Affiliation or Control: State/Local IRS Status: 501(c)3
Highest Offering: Associate Degree
Program: Occupational; 2-Year Principally Bachelor's Creditable
Accreditation: &NH, ADNUR, RAD

02 President .... Mr. Rodney RANES
05 Dean of Instruction .... Mr. Jeff CUTCHIN
32 Assistant Dean Student Services .... Mrs. Chris WEBBER
76 Assoc Dean Nursing Allied Health .... Ms. Tamara FRALICKER
08 Director Learning Resource Center .... Mrs. Charlotte BRUCE
88 Director Cosmetology .... Ms. Linda MILLER
10 Director Business .... Mr. Doug SHIPMAN
41 Athletic Director/Coach .... Mr. Dennis CONLEY
37 Financial Aid Coordinator .... Mrs. Vicki STUCKEY
18 Operations/Maintenance Team Leader .... Mr. Larry GANGLOFF

*Illinois Eastern Community Colleges Wabash Valley College (A)

2200 College Drive, Mount Carmel IL 62863-2657
County: Wabash FICE Identification: 001779
Unit ID: 403487
Telephone: (618) 262-8641 Carnegie Class: Assoc/Pub-R-L
FAX Number: (618) 262-5347 Calendar System: Semester
URL: www.iecc.edu/wvc
Established: 1960 Annual Undergrad Tuition & Fees (In-District): $2,858
Enrollment: 5,456 Coed
Affiliation or Control: State/Local IRS Status: 501(c)3
Highest Offering: Associate Degree
Program: Occupational; 2-Year Principally Bachelor's Creditable
Accreditation: &NH, ADNUR

02 President .... Mr. Matt FOWLER
05 Interim Dean of Instruction .... Mr. Wayne MORRIS
32 Assistant Dean Student Services .... Mrs. Diana SPEAR
20 Director of Academic Advising .... Mr. Tim ZIMMER
08 Director of LRC .... Ms. Sandy CRAIG
60 Director of Broadcasting .... Mr. Kyle PEACH
41 Athletic Director .... Mr. Daniel SPARKS
26 Director of Public Info & Marketing .... Vacant
10 Director of Business .... Ms. Reilly BAUMGART
37 Financial Aid Coordinator .... Ms. Mary JOHNSON
18 Groundskeeper .... Mr. Ron MARTIN

The Illinois Institute of Art (B)

350 N Orleans, Suite 136, Chicago IL 60654-1514
County: Cook FICE Identification: 012584
Unit ID: 148177
Telephone: (312) 280-3500 Carnegie Class: Spec/Arts
FAX Number: (312) 777-8780 Calendar System: Quarter
URL: www.artinstitutes.edu/chicago
Established: 1916 Annual Undergrad Tuition & Fees: $21,996
Enrollment: 2,858 Coed
Affiliation or Control: Proprietary IRS Status: Proprietary
Highest Offering: Baccalaureate
Program: Professional; Technical Emphasis
Accreditation: NH, ACFEI, CIDA

01 President/Chicago .... John B. JENKINS
04 Exec Assistant to the President .... Allison SANTOS
05 Vice President of Academic Affairs .... Vesna GRBOVIC
07 VP/Senior Director of Admissions .... Janis K. ANTON
20 Associate Dean of Academic Affairs .... Karen JANKO
20 Associate Dean of Academic Affairs .... Marlene ATKINS
06 Registrar .... Donohue MICHAEL
108 Director of Assessment .... Dr. James BORLAND
08 Librarian .... Sean MCCARTHY
88 Director of Transitional Studies .... Karine BRAVAIS-SLYMAN
88 Dir Media/Game Arts/Animation .... Jason HOPKINS
88 Director Digital Film/Vis Effects .... Scott PERRY
97 Director General Education .... Deann GROSSI
88 Dir Culinary Arts & Hospitality .... Richard VALENTE
88 Dir Fashion Merch/Mktg Mgmt .... Dan ROBISON
88 Dir Fashion Design/Prod/Accessories .... Victoria SINON
88 Director Interior/Product Design .... Melissa MCATEE
88 Dir Visual Comm/Graphic Dsgn/Adv .... Perrin STAMATIS
88 Dir Foundations/Illustration/Design .... Jodie LAWRENCE
10 Dir Administration/Financial Svcs .... Robert SMETAK
21 Director of Accounting .... Diosa COLLADO
37 Director Student Financial Aid .... Paula PRICE
32 Dean of Student Affairs .... Catherine BROKENSHIRE
35 Asst Dean of Student Affairs .... Valarie RAND
38 Student Support Coordinator .... Sara SPIEGEL
40 Supply Store Manager .... Ricardo OLAVE
36 Director of Career Services .... Patricia GILLER
15 Human Resources Generalist .... Rae DEROSE
13 Director of Technology .... Terence HAHN

Illinois Institute of Technology (C)

3300 S Federal Street, Chicago IL 60616-3793
County: Cook FICE Identification: 001691
Unit ID: 145725
Telephone: (312) 567-3000 Carnegie Class: RU/H
FAX Number: (312) 567-3004 Calendar System: Semester
URL: www.iit.edu
Established: 1890 Annual Undergrad Tuition & Fees: $36,504
Enrollment: 7,787 Coed
Affiliation or Control: Independent Non-Profit IRS Status: 501(c)3
Highest Offering: Doctorate
Program: Liberal Arts And General; Teacher Preparatory; Professional; Technical Emphasis
Accreditation: NH, BUS, CLPSY, CORE, CS, ENG, LAW, LSAR

01 President .... Dr. John L. ANDERSON
05 Provost .... Dr. Alan W. CRAMB
10 VP Finance & Administration .... Dr. Patricia LAUGHLIN
21 AVP & Controller .... Mr. Brian LAFFEY
21 AVP Finance .... Mr. David ULASZEK
18 VP Facilities & Public Safety .... Mr. Bruce WATTS
30 Vice Pres Institutional Advancement .... Ms. Elizabeth HUGHES
88 Vice Pres International Affairs .... Dr. Darsh T. WASAN
86 Vice President External Affairs .... Mr. David E. BAKER
43 Vice President General Counsel .... Mr. Anthony D'AMATO
31 VP Community Affairs & Outreach .... Mr. Leroy E. KENNEDY
27 Vice Pres Marketing/Communications .... Ms. Jeanne HARTIG
88 Sr VP & Dir IIT Research Inst .... Dr. David MCCORMICK
88 VP & Dir Inst Food Safety & Health .... Dr. Robert BRACKETT
13 Chief Information Officer .... Mr. Ophir TRIGALO
04 Director President's Office .... Ms. Sandra LAPORTE
18 AVP Facilities/Real Estate & Const .... Mr. Terence FRIGO
11 Assoc Vice Pres Auxillary Services .... Ms. Jean M. BINGHAM
28 Vice Provost Student Diversity .... Mr. Gerald DOYLE
16 Associate VP Human Resources .... Ms. Antoinette MURRIL
20 Vice Provost Undergrad Education .... Dr. Michael GOSZ
26 Assoc Dir Media Relations .... Mr. Evan VENIE
32 Dean of Students .... Ms. Katherine MURPHY-STETZ
61 Dean Chicago-Kent College of Law .... Mr. Harold J. KRENT
49 Dean College of Science & Letters .... Dr. Russell BETTS
54 Dean Armour Col of Engineering .... Dr. Natacha DEPAOLA
50 Dean Stuart School of Business .... Dr. Harvey KAHALAS
48 Dean College of Architecture .... Mr. Wiel ARETS
83 Dean College of Psychology .... Dr. M. Ellen MITCHELL
88 Dean Institute of Design .... Mr. Patrick F. WHITNEY
58 Dean Graduate Col & VP Research .... Dr. Ali CINAR
72 Dean School of Applied Technology .... Dr. C. Robert CARLSON
06 Registrar .... Mr. Peter ZACHOCKI
36 VP Strategic Initiatives .... Mr. Dennis ROBERSON
25 Director Sponsored Research .... Ms. Domenica G. PAPPAS
09 Director Institutional Information .... Dr. Carol-Ann EMMONS
44 Director Annual Giving .... Mr. Jason SMITH
29 Director Alumni & Donor Relations .... Mr. James ACTON
37 Assoc Director Financial Aid .... Ms. Abigail MCGRATH
41 Athletic Director .... Mr. Enzley MITCHELL, IV
19 Director Public Safety .... Mr. Raymond MARTINEZ
08 Dean of Libraries .... Ms. Sharon BOSTICK
22 Dir Equal Opp/Affirmative Action .... Ms. Candida MIRANDA
96 Director of Purchasing .... Mr. Frank FIORITO
28 Director Student Ctr for Diversity .... Ms. Lisa MONTGOMERY
35 Director Student Life .... Ms. Erin GRAY
88 Dir Environmental Health & Safety .... Ms. Cynthia CHAFFEE

Illinois State University (D)

School and North Streets, Normal IL 61790-0001
County: McLean FICE Identification: 001692
Unit ID: 145813
Telephone: (309) 438-2111 Carnegie Class: DRU
FAX Number: (309) 438-2768 Calendar System: Semester
URL: www.ilstu.edu
Established: 1857 Annual Undergrad Tuition & Fees (In-State): $12,726
Enrollment: 21,310 Coed
Affiliation or Control: State IRS Status: 501(c)3
Highest Offering: Doctorate
Program: Liberal Arts And General; Teacher Preparatory; Professional
Accreditation: NH, AAFCS, ART, AUD, BUS, BUSA, CIDA, CONST, CS, DIETD, DIETI, IPSY, MT, MUS, NAIT, NRPA, NURSE, SCPSY, SP, SW, TED, THEA

01 President .... Dr. C. Alvin BOWMAN, JR.
05 Vice Pres Academic Affs & Provost .... Dr. Sheri N. EVERTS
10 Vice President Finance & Planning .... Dr. Daniel LAYZELL
32 Vice President Student Affairs .... Mr. Larry DIETZ
26 Vice President Univ Advancement .... Ms. Erin MINNE
20 Associate Provost .... Dr. Jan MURPHY
35 Assoc Vice Pres Student Affairs .... Dr. Brent PATERSON
21 Assoc VP Finance & Planning .... Ms. Debra K. SMITLEY
91 Assoc Vice President Technology .... Dr. Mark WALBERT
58 Assoc VP Grad Std/Res/Intern Educ .... Dr. Darrell KRUGER
84 Assoc VP Enrollment Management .... Dr. Jonathan M. ROSENTHAL
15 Assoc VP Human Resources .... Dr. Khris CLEVENGER
86 Asst to Pres/Government Relations .... Mr. Philip ADAMS
08 Dean University Libraries .... Ms. Sohair WASTAWY
06 University Registrar .... Mr. Jess D. RAY
07 Director Admissions .... Ms. Doris GROVES
20 Director University College .... Ms. Amelia NOEL-ELKINS
30 Exec Director of Development .... Ms. Joy D. HUTCHCRAFT
21 Asst VP Financial Admin/Comptroller .... Mr. Greg L. ALT
37 Director Financial Aid .... Ms. Jana ALBRECHT
29 Director Alumni Services .... Dr. Stephanie Ann EPP
36 Director Career Center .... Dr. Stephen CANTINE
18 Asst Director Facilities Planning .... Ms. Christine TSUI
19 Chief University Police .... Mr. Aaron WOODRUFF
28 Dir Off of Eq Oppty/Ethics & Access .... Mr. Shane MCCREERY
23 Director Student Health Services .... Ms. Laura KNOBLAUCH
39 Director University Housing .... Ms. Maureen BLAIR
41 Director Intercollegiate Athletics .... Mr. Gary FRIEDMAN
85 Director International Studies .... Dr. Momar NDIAYE
92 Director Honors Program .... Dr. Kim PEREIRA
94 Director Women's Studies .... Dr. Alison BAILEY
96 Director of Purchasing .... Ms. Judy JOHNSON
49 Dean College Arts & Sciences .... Dr. Gregory SIMPSON
50 Dean College Business .... Dr. Scott JOHNSON
53 Dean College Education .... Dr. Deborah J. CURTIS
72 Dean College Applied Science/Tech .... Dr. Jeffrey A. WOOD
57 Dean College Fine Arts .... Dr. James MAJOR
66 Dean Mennonite College of Nursing .... Dr. Janet KREJCI
04 Assistant to the President .... Mr. Jay GROVES

Illinois Valley Community College (E)

815 N Orlando Smith Road, Oglesby IL 61348-9692
County: La Salle FICE Identification: 001705
Unit ID: 145831
Telephone: (815) 224-2720 Carnegie Class: Assoc/Pub-R-L
FAX Number: (815) 224-3033 Calendar System: Semester
URL: www.ivcc.edu
Established: 1966 Annual Undergrad Tuition & Fees (In-District): $2,763
Enrollment: 4,355 Coed
Affiliation or Control: Local IRS Status: 501(c)3
Highest Offering: Associate Degree
Program: Occupational; 2-Year Principally Bachelor's Creditable
Accreditation: NH, ADNUR, DA

01 President .... Dr. Jerry M. CORCORAN
05 Int VP Learning/Student Development .... Dr. Lori E. SCROGGS
10 Vice Pres Business Svcs/Finance .... Ms. Cheryl E. ROELFSEMA
20 Assoc Vice Pres Academic Affairs .... Ms. Sue L. ISERMANN
32 Assoc Vice Pres Student Services .... Ms. Tracy L. MORRIS
24 Director of Learning Technologies .... Ms. Emily B. VESCOGNI
31 Director Cmty Relations & Marketing .... Mr. Francis R. BROLLEY
13 Dir of Information Technology Svcs .... Mr. Harold B. BARNES
51 Dir Cont Educ/Business Services .... Ms. Jamie L. GAHM
15 Director Human Resources .... Ms. Glenna S. JONES
37 Director of Financial Aid .... Ms. Patricia A. WILLIAMSON
07 Director of Admissions/Records .... Mr. Mark J. GRZYBOWSKI
08 Head Librarian .... Ms. Frances A. WHALEY
30 Director of Development .... Mr. Francis R. BROLLEY
96 Director of Purchasing .... Ms. Michelle L. CARBONI
18 Director of Facilities .... Mr. Gary K. JOHNSON
09 Director of Institutional Research .... Mr. Robert C. MATTSON
81 Dean Natural Science/Business .... Mr. Ron W. GROLEAU
66 Dean Health Professions/ Nursing .... Ms. Bonnie L. BENNETT-CAMPBELL
75 Dean Career/Technical Programs .... Ms. Elaine NOVAK
79 Int Dn Humanities/Fine Arts/Soc Sci .... Dr. Jeffrey M. ANDERSON
88 Dean English/Mathematics/Education .... Ms. Marianne DZIK

Illinois Wesleyan University (F)

PO Box 2900, 1312 Park Street, Bloomington IL 61702-2900
County: McLean FICE Identification: 001696
Unit ID: 145646
Telephone: (309) 556-1000 Carnegie Class: Bac/A&S
FAX Number: (309) 556-3411 Calendar System: Other
URL: www.iwu.edu
Established: 1850 Annual Undergrad Tuition & Fees: $36,572
Enrollment: 2,090 Coed
Affiliation or Control: Independent Non-Profit IRS Status: 501(c)3
Highest Offering: Baccalaureate
Program: Liberal Arts And General; Teacher Preparatory; Professional
Accreditation: NH, MUS, NURSE

01 President .... Dr. Richard F. WILSON
05 Provost & Dean of Faculty .... Dr. Jonathan D. GREEN
10 Vice President Business & Finance .... Mr. Daniel P. KLOTZBACH
30 Vice President for Advancement .... Mr. Martin W. SMITH
26 Vice President for Communications .... Mr. Matt KURZ
32 VP Student Affairs/Dean Students .... Dr. Karla CARNEY-HALL
07 Dean of Admissions .... Mr. Tony BANKSTON
84 Dean of Enrollment Management .... Mr. Robert MURRAY
09 AVP Instl Research/Plng/Evaluation .... Dr. Michael THOMPSON
86 Dir Government/Community Relations .... Mr. Carl F. TEICHMAN
04 Exec Assistant to the President .... Ms. Susan E. BASSI
20 Assoc Provost Acad Plng/Standards .... Dr. Frank A. BOYD
20 Associate Dean of Curriculum .... Dr. Zahia DRICI
16 Assoc VP for Human Resources .... Ms. Catherine SPITZ
13 Asst Provost/Chief Technology Ofcr .... Mr. Trey SHORT
44 Associate Vice Pres for Advancement .... Mr. Benjamin J. RHODES
88 Associate Vice Pres for Advancement .... Mr. Steve D. SEIBRING
35 Asc Dean Stdnts/Co-Curricular/Pgmng .... Ms. Darcy L. GREDER
38 Asst Dean/Dir Student Counseling .... Dr. Annorrah MOORMAN
35 Asst Dean of Students .... Mr. Matthew DAMSCHRODER
08 University Librarian .... Dr. Karen SCHMIDT
06 Registrar .... Dr. Leslie BETZ
42 University Chaplain .... Rev. Elyse NELSON WINGER
21 Controller .... Mr. John BRYANT
37 Director of Financial Aid .... Mr. Scott SEIBRING
64 Director of School of Music .... Dr. Mario J. PELUSI
57 Director of School of Art .... Prof. Miles C. BAIR
57 Director of School of Theatre Arts .... Dr. Curtis C. TROUT
66 Director of School of Nursing .... Dr. Victoria FOLSE
41 Director of Athletics .... Prof. Dennis BRIDGES
29 Director of Alumni Relations .... Ms. Ann HARDING
102 Dir Grants/Foundation Relations .... Mr. Carlo ROBUSTELLI
44 Dir of Wesleyan Annual Fund .... Mr. Jeffrey MAVROS
36 Director of Career Center .... Mr. Warren KISTNER
18 Director of Physical Plant .... Mr. Millard C. JORGENSON
88 Director of Sports Information .... Mr. Stewart I. SALOWITZ
93 Director Multicultural Student Affs .... Mr. George E. JACKSON, III
35 Director of Student Activities .... Mr. Colin STEWART
94 Director of Women's Studies Program .... Dr. Carole MYSCOFSKI

104 Director of International Office ....Ms. Stacey SHIMIZU
40 Bookstore Manager ....Mr. Thaddeus SUTTER

Institute for Clinical Social Work (A)

401 South State Street, Suite 822, Chicago IL 60605
County: Cook FICE Identification: 025737
Unit ID: 145886
Telephone: (312) 935-4232 Carnegie Class: Spec/Health
FAX Number: (312) 935-4255 Calendar System: Semester
URL: www.icsw.edu
Established: 1981 Annual Graduate Tuition & Fees: $22,896
Enrollment: 96 Coed
Affiliation or Control: Independent Non-Profit IRS Status: 501(c)3
Highest Offering: Doctorate; No Undergraduates
Program: Professional
Accreditation: NH

01 President ....Dr. Marty LAUB
05 Dean ....Dr. Alan LEVY
58 Director of Doctoral Studies ....Dr. R. Dennis SHELBY
88 Director of Master's Studies ....Dr. Denise DUVAL TSIOLES
20 Associate Dean ....Dr. Scott HARMS ROSE
11 Director of Operations ....Maureen A. HEWITT
37 Admin Fin Aid/Instl Operations ....Pierre SMITH
08 Librarian ....Scot AUSBORN
32 Coordinator Student/Faculty Svcs ....Elizabeth OLER

International Academy of Design and Technology (B)

1 N State Street, Suite 500, Chicago IL 60602-9736
County: Cook FICE Identification: 021603
Unit ID: 146010
Telephone: (312) 980-9200 Carnegie Class: Spec/Arts
FAX Number: (312) 541-3929 Calendar System: Other
URL: www.iadtchicago.edu
Established: 1977 Annual Undergrad Tuition & Fees: $14,400
Enrollment: 814 Coed
Affiliation or Control: Proprietary IRS Status: Proprietary
Highest Offering: Baccalaureate
Program: Occupational
Accreditation: ACICS, CIDA

01 President ....Mr. Robert NACHTSHEIM
05 Campus Director of Education ....Ms. Kathleen EMBRY
88 Regulatory Operations Consultant ....Dr. Darlene ULMER
07 Campus Director of Admissions ....Mr. A.J JABER
06 Associate Registrar ....Ms. Paris BALKCOM
08 Regional Director Library Services ....Ms. Kayte KORWITTS
36 Director of Career Services ....Ms. Cheryl PERILLO
37 Student Finance Manager ....Mr. Alia KOLOVIC

International Academy of Design and Technology-Schaumburg (C)

935-E National Parkway, Schaumburg IL 60173-5160
County: Cook Identification: 666141
Telephone: (847) 969-2800 Carnegie Class: Not Classified
FAX Number: (847) 969-2819 Calendar System: Quarter
URL: www.iadtschaumburg.com
Established: 2004 Annual Undergrad Tuition & Fees: $19,200
Enrollment: 93 Coed
Affiliation or Control: Proprietary IRS Status: Proprietary
Highest Offering: Baccalaureate
Program: Fine Arts Emphasis
Accreditation: ACICS

01 Campus Director ....Mr. Tom TIMMONS

† Branch campus of International Academy of Design and Technology, Chicago, IL.

ITT Technical Institute (D)

1401 Feehanville Drive, Mount Prospect IL 60056-6005
County: Cook Identification: 666538
Unit ID: 260974
Telephone: (847) 375-8800 Carnegie Class: Spec/Tech
FAX Number: (847) 375-9022 Calendar System: Quarter
URL: www.itt-tech.edu
Established: 1986 Annual Undergrad Tuition & Fees: N/A
Enrollment: 429 Coed
Affiliation or Control: Proprietary IRS Status: Proprietary
Highest Offering: Baccalaureate
Program: Technical Emphasis
Accreditation: ACICS

† Branch campus of ITT Technical Institute, Indianapolis, IN.

ITT Technical Institute (E)

800 Jorie Blvd., Suite 100, Oak Brook IL 60523
County: DuPage Identification: 666118
Unit ID: 434557
Telephone: (630) 472-7000 Carnegie Class: Spec/Tech
FAX Number: (630) 455-6476 Calendar System: Quarter
URL: www.itt-tech.edu
Established: 1997 Annual Undergrad Tuition & Fees: N/A
Enrollment: 451 Coed
Affiliation or Control: Proprietary IRS Status: Proprietary
Highest Offering: Baccalaureate
Program: Technical Emphasis
Accreditation: ACICS

† Branch campus of ITT Technical Institute, Indianapolis, IN.

ITT Technical Institute (F)

11551 184th Place, Orland Park IL 60467-4900
County: Cook Identification: 666539
Unit ID: 414586
Telephone: (708) 326-3200 Carnegie Class: Spec/Tech
FAX Number: N/A Calendar System: Quarter
URL: www.itt-tech.edu
Established: 1993 Annual Undergrad Tuition & Fees: N/A
Enrollment: 549 Coed
Affiliation or Control: Proprietary IRS Status: Proprietary
Highest Offering: Baccalaureate
Program: Technical Emphasis
Accreditation: ACICS

† Branch campus of ITT Technical Institute, Indianapolis, IN.

John A. Logan College (G)

700 Logan College Road, Carterville IL 62918-2500
County: Williamson FICE Identification: 008076
Unit ID: 146205
Telephone: (618) 985-3741 Carnegie Class: Assoc/Pub-R-L
FAX Number: (618) 985-2248 Calendar System: Semester
URL: www.jalc.edu
Established: 1967 Annual Undergrad Tuition & Fees (In-District): $2,800
Enrollment: 6,257 Coed
Affiliation or Control: State/Local IRS Status: 501(c)3
Highest Offering: Associate Degree
Program: Occupational; 2-Year Principally Bachelor's Creditable
Accreditation: NH, CONST, DA, DH, DMS, MLTAD, OTA

01 President ....Dr. Michael DREITH
05 Vice President Instruction Services ....Dr. Deborah PAYNE
10 VP Business Svcs/College Facilities ....Mr. Brad MCCORMICK
11 Vice President Administration ....Dr. Tim DAUGHERTY
06 Dean Student Services ....Mr. Terry CRAIN
21 Dean Financial Operations ....Ms. Stacy BUCKINGHAM
20 Dean Instruction ....Mr. Keith KRAPF
103 Dean Workforce Dev/Comm Educ ....Mr. Phil MINNIS
88 Assoc Dean Baccalaureate Transfer ....Mr. Mark HENSON
76 Assoc Dean Health/Public Svcs ....Dr. Valerie BARKO
51 Assoc Dean Continuing Education ....Mr. Barry HANCOCK
88 Assoc Dean Adult Basic/Secondary Ed ....Ms. Kay FLEMING
13 Assoc Dean Information Technology ....Mr. Robin H. PAULS
07 Associate Dean Admissions ....Vacant
37 Director of Student Financial Asst ....Ms. Sherry SUMMARY
08 Assoc Dean for Library Services ....Ms. Judy VINEYARD
30 Director of Development ....Vacant
26 Dir Community Relations/Marketing ....Mr. Steve O'KEEFE
35 Director of Student Activities ....Ms. Adrienne BARKLEY-GIFFIN
36 Director of Placement ....Ms. Lisa HUDGENS
102 Executive Director of Foundation ....Ms. Staci BYNUM
66 Director of Nursing ....Ms. Marilyn FALASTER
88 Director of Career Dev/Acad Support ....Ms. Christy MCBRIDE
15 Director of Human Resources/AAO ....Mr. Clay BREWER
18 Dir Building/Grounds/Campus Safety ....Mr. Dwight HOFFARD
09 Director Institutional Research ....Mr. Eric PULLEY
29 Dir of Scholarships/Alumni Svcs ....Ms. Stacy HOLLOWAY

John Marshall Law School (H)

315 S Plymouth Court, Chicago IL 60604-3968
County: Cook FICE Identification: 001698
Unit ID: 146241
Telephone: (312) 427-2737 Carnegie Class: Spec/Law
FAX Number: (312) 427-8307 Calendar System: Semester
URL: www.jmls.edu
Established: 1899 Annual Graduate Tuition & Fees: $41,224
Enrollment: 1,648 Coed
Affiliation or Control: Independent Non-Profit IRS Status: 501(c)3
Highest Offering: First Professional Degree; No Undergraduates
Program: Professional
Accreditation: NH, LAW

01 Dean ....Mr. John E. CORKERY
05 Assoc Dean Academic Affairs ....Dean Ralph RUEBNER
07 Assoc Dean Admissions/Stdnt Affairs ....Mr. William B. POWERS
10 Chief Financial Officer ....Ms. Cynthia SAH
13 Chief Technology Officer ....Mr. Jim VELCO
45 Dean Outreach and Planning ....Mr. Rory Dean SMITH
36 Asst Dean for Career Services ....Ms. Laurel A. HAJEK
20 Asst Dean for Academic Services ....Ms. Jodie NEEDHAM
15 Asst Dean Human Resources ....Mr. Martin D'AMBROSE
06 Registrar ....Ms. Anna JOHNSON
29 Director Alumni Relations/Aux Svcs ....Ms. Sherri BERENDT
37 Director Student Financial Aid ....Ms. Yara SANTANA

John Wood Community College (I)

1301 S 48th Street, Quincy IL 62305-8736
County: Adams FICE Identification: 012813
Unit ID: 146278
Telephone: (217) 224-6500 Carnegie Class: Assoc/Pub-R-M
FAX Number: (217) 224-4208 Calendar System: Semester
URL: www.jwcc.edu
Established: 1974 Annual Undergrad Tuition & Fees (In-District): $3,990
Enrollment: 2,390 Coed
Affiliation or Control: State/Local IRS Status: 501(c)3
Highest Offering: Associate Degree
Program: Occupational; 2-Year Principally Bachelor's Creditable
Accreditation: NH, SURGT

01 President ....Dr. John LETTS
05 Vice President for Instruction ....Dr. Ron DAVIS
10 Vice Pres for Finance/Business Svcs ....Ms. Mary ARP
32 Vice President for Student Services ....Mr. Michael ELBE
09 Dir Institutional Effectiveness ....Mr. Josh WELKER
88 Dean Transfer Education ....Dr. David SHINN
75 Dean Career/Technical/Workforce Ed ....Ms. Pam FOUST
84 Dean Enrollment Svcs/Dir Finan Aid ....Ms. Melanie LECHTENBERG
88 Associate Dean Transfer Education ....Mr. Kent HAWLEY
103 Assoc Dn Career Technical Workfc Ed ....Mr. Terry JENKINS
07 Director Admissions ....Mr. Lee WIBBELL
06 Registrar/Dir Career/Advising Svcs ....Mr. Cody BAGGETT
21 Director Fiscal Services ....Vacant
35 Director Support Services ....Dr. Sandra THOMAS
13 Director Information Services ....Mr. Joshua BRUECK
76 Director Health Sciences ....Ms. Betty MCDONNELL
08 Dir Library Svcs/Acad Spprt Center ....Ms. Barbara LIEBER
26 Director Public Relations/Marketing ....Ms. Tracy ORNE
41 Int Dir of Student Life/Athletics ....Mr. Brad HOYT
30 Director Advancement ....Ms. Barbara HOLTHAUS
36 Dir Career Services ....Mr. Cody BAGGETT
15 Director Human Resources ....Ms. Stacey O'BRIEN
18 Director Physical Plant ....Mr. Lou BARTA
19 Chief of Campus Police ....Mr. Bill LATOUR
40 Manager of Auxiliary Services ....Ms. Denise WILLIAMS
47 Dept Chair Ag Sciences ....Mr. Gary SHUPE
77 Dept Chair Ofc Technology/Comp Sci ....Ms. Carol SHARPE
50 Interim Dept Chair Business ....Ms. Cathy STEPHENS
57 Dept Chair Fine Arts ....Mr. Gary DECLUE
81 Department Chair Mathematics ....Mr. David RIGSBEE
65 Dept Chair Natural Sciences ....Dr. Ivan PAUL
79 Dept Chair Language/Literature/Hum ....Ms. Valerie VLAHAKIS
88 Dept Chair Developmental Education ....Ms. Joyce MILLER-BOREN
83 Dept Chair Social/Behavior Science ....Mr. Randall EGDORF

Joliet Junior College (J)

1215 Houbolt Road, Joliet IL 60431-8938
County: Will FICE Identification: 001699
Unit ID: 146296
Telephone: (815) 729-9020 Carnegie Class: Assoc/Pub-S-SC
FAX Number: (815) 729-4256 Calendar System: Semester
URL: www.jjc.edu
Established: 1901 Annual Undergrad Tuition & Fees (In-District): $3,210
Enrollment: 15,322 Coed
Affiliation or Control: State/Local IRS Status: 501(c)3
Highest Offering: Associate Degree
Program: Occupational; 2-Year Principally Bachelor's Creditable
Accreditation: NH, ACBSP, ACFEI, ADNUR, MUS

01 President ....Dr. Debra S. DANIELS
05 Vice President Academic Affairs ....Dr. Valerie ROBERSON
11 Interim VP Administrative Services ....Dr. Judy MITCHELL
13 Int Dir Information Technology ....Mr. Jim SERR
32 VP Student Development ....Dr. Yolanda ISAACS
31 Dean Community/Economic Development ....Mr. Daniel KREIDLER
07 Director Admissions & Recruitment ....Ms. Jennifer KLOBERDANZ
88 Dir Adult & Family Services ....Ms. Emilie MCCALLISTER
37 Director Financial Aid ....Mr. David SEWARD
15 Director Human Resources ....Ms. Joyce COLEMAN
06 Registrar ....Mr. Keith TILLMAN
18 Director Facility Services ....Mr. Patrick VAN DUYNE
21 Director Business/Auxiliary Svcs ....Dr. Judy MITCHELL
26 Dir Commun/External Relations ....Ms. Kelly ROHDER
36 Director Career Services ....Ms. Bridgett LARKIN-BEENE
41 Director Athletics ....Mr. Wayne KING
21 Director Financial Svcs/Controller ....Mr. Jeffrey HEAP
19 Dir Campus Safety & Police Chief ....Mr. Peter COMANDA
30 Dir Inst Adv Exec Dir JJC Found ....Ms. Kristin MULVEY
08 Director Library ....Mr. Thomas URBANSKI
40 Manager Bookstore ....Mr. Michael M. MAIER
88 Coord GSD ....Ms. Angie KAYSEN-LUZBETAK
74 Coord Veterinary Medicine Tech ....Dr. Scott KELLER
38 Counselor/Dept Chair ....Ms. Mildred HOLMES

Judson University (K)

1151 N State Street, Elgin IL 60123-1498
County: Kane FICE Identification: 001700
Unit ID: 146339
Telephone: (847) 628-2500 Carnegie Class: Bac/Diverse
FAX Number: (847) 628-1027 Calendar System: Semester
URL: www.judsonu.edu
Established: 1913 Annual Undergrad Tuition & Fees: $27,000
Enrollment: 1,124 Coed
Affiliation or Control: American Baptist IRS Status: 501(c)3
Highest Offering: Master's
Program: Liberal Arts And General; Teacher Preparatory; Professional
Accreditation: NH

01 Interim President ....Dr. William CROTHERS
04 Exec Assistant to the President ....Mrs. Tena ROBOTHAM
05 Provost/Vice Pres Academic Affairs ....Dr. Dale SIMMONS
10 Interim VP Business Affairs ....Mr. John POTTER
30 Vice President External Relations ....Mr. Tory GUM

32 VP/Dean of Student Development ... Mrs. LeAnn PAULEY-HEARD
84 Exec Dir of Enrollment Services ... Ms. Nancy BINGER
49 Dean Liberal Arts and Sciences ... Dr. Lanette POTEETE-YOUNG
48 Dean Art/Design and Architecture ... Dr. Curtis SARTOR
53 Dean Education ... Dr. Kathy MILLER
50 Dean Leadership and Business ... Dr. Thomas BERLINER
09 Assoc Provost Inst Research ... Ms. Jaynn TOBIAS-JOHNSON
06 University Registrar ... Ms. Virginia GUTH
08 Library Director ... Mr. Larry WILD
13 Director of Information Technology ... Mr. Brent RICHARDSON
88 Director of University Advancement ... Dr. Angelo BRAVOS
88 Dir of Advancement Operations ... Ms. Jean BEDNAR
29 Director of Alumni Relations ... Mrs. Bonnie BIENERT
37 Director of Financial Aid ... Dr. Roberto SANTIZO
07 Assoc Director of Admissions ... Mr. Ryan TROUT
27 Director of Comm & Marketing ... Ms. Mary DULABAUM
35 Assoc Dean of Students & Res Life ... Mr. Laine MCLAUGHLIN
36 Director of Career Services ... Mrs. Doris HAUGEN
38 Director of Counseling Center ... Dr. Donald FERRELL
19 Director of Campus Safety ... Mr. Nick SALZMANN
41 Athletic Director ... Mr. Tony TOMPKINS
88 Director of Faith/Learning & Life ... Mrs. Victoria KUEKER
88 Director of Student Success ... Miss Jaimee BARTHA
39 Director of Housing ... Mrs. Karen ALDRIDGE
85 Director of Intercultural Relations ... Mrs. Lisa JAROT
34 Dean of Women ... Ms. Casey SUNDSEDT
23 Campus Nurse ... Ms. Susan WEBER
88 Dir of Acad Asst & ADA Compliance ... Dr. Rolanda BURRIS
106 Director of Online Education ... Mrs. Martha JOHNSON
92 Honors Director ... Dr. Craig KAPLOWITZ
15 Director of Human Resources ... Mr. Tom RUEGER
101 Asst Sec to Board of Trustees ... Mrs. Tena ROBOTHAM

Kankakee Community College (A)

100 College Drive, Kankakee IL 60901-6505
County: Kankakee FICE Identification: 007690
Unit ID: 146348
Telephone: (815) 802-8100 Carnegie Class: Assoc/Pub-R-L
FAX Number: (815) 802-8101 Calendar System: Semester
URL: www.kcc.edu
Established: 1966 Annual Undergrad Tuition & Fees (In-District): $3,390
Enrollment: 4,178 Coed
Affiliation or Control: State/Local IRS Status: 501(c)3
Highest Offering: Associate Degree
Program: Occupational; 2-Year Principally Bachelor's Creditable
Accreditation: NH, MLTAD, PTAA

01 President ... Dr. John AVENDANO
04 Executive Secretary to President ... Ms. Rose MITCHELL
05 VP of Instructional & Stdnt Success ... Mr. Dennis SORENSEN
10 VP of Administration & Finance ... Ms. Vicki GARDNER
06 Registrar ... Ms. Michelle DRISCOLL
32 Dean of Student Development ... Ms. Julia WASKOSKY
35 Assoc Dean Student Devlp/Registrar ... Ms. Michelle DRISCOLL
09 Dir Institutional Research ... Dr. Vicki MAGEE
31 Asst Dean Adult & Community Educ ... Ms. Margaret COOPER
103 Director of Workforce Development ... Ms. Dana WASHINGTON
37 Director Financial Aid ... Mr. John PERRY
35 Coord Student Life ... Ms. Lindsey FRITZ
88 Director Fitness Center ... Mr. Dennis CLARK
41 Director Athletics ... Mr. Ted PETERSEN
15 Director Human Resources ... Mr. David CAGLE
21 Director Financial Affairs ... Ms. Beth NUNLEY
50 Assoc Dean Business & Technology ... Mr. Paul CARLSON
51 Asst Dean Cont Educ & Career Svcs ... Ms. Mary POSING
18 Dir Campus Facilities & Security ... Mr. Rich SODERQUIST
88 Coordinator Small Business Devel ... Mr. Ken CRITE
81 Assoc Dean Math/Science Division ... Ms. Virginia MAKEPEACE
76 Assoc Dean Health Careers Div ... Ms. Kim MAU
88 Director Student Advisement ... Ms. Meredith PURCELL
76 Director Respiratory Therapist Pgm ... Ms. Nancy OZEE
76 Director Medical Lab Technology ... Ms. Glenda FORNERIS
83 Assoc Dean Humanities/Social Sci ... Mr. Mark LANTING
76 Director Radiology Technology Pgm ... Ms. Darla JEPSON
13 Director Information Tech Svcs ... Mr. Michael O'CONNOR
102 Exec Director of KCC Foundation ... Ms. Kelly MYERS
07 Coord Admissions & Recruitment ... Mrs. Oshunda CARPENTER-WILLIAMS
88 Director Institutional Tech/Fac Dev ... Mr. Craig KEIGHER
62 Director Learning Resource Center ... Ms. Karen BECKER
26 Director Marketing ... Ms. Kari SARGEANT
88 Dean of Sustainability ... Dr. Bert JACOBSON

Kaskaskia College (B)

27210 College Road, Centralia IL 62801-7878
County: Clinton FICE Identification: 001701
Unit ID: 146366
Telephone: (618) 545-3000 Carnegie Class: Assoc/Pub-R-L
FAX Number: (618) 532-1990 Calendar System: Semester
URL: www.kaskaskia.edu
Established: 1940 Annual Undergrad Tuition & Fees (In-District): $3,120
Enrollment: 5,286 Coed
Affiliation or Control: State/Local IRS Status: 501(c)3
Highest Offering: Associate Degree
Program: Occupational; 2-Year Principally Bachelor's Creditable
Accreditation: NH, ADNUR, DA, MLTAD, OTA, PTAA, RAD

01 President ... Dr. James C. UNDERWOOD
11 Vice Pres Administrative Services ... Mrs. Nancy KINSEY
05 Vice Pres Instructional Services ... Dr. Gregory LABYAK
32 Vice President of Student Services ... Mr. Sedgwick HARRIS
75 Dean Career & Technical Education ... Vacant
49 Dean of Arts & Sciences ... Ms. Kellie HENEGAR
66 Dean of Nursing ... Mrs. Susan BATCHELOR
09 Int Dir Inst Effectiveness ... Mr. Jeffrey EBEL
08 Director of LRC ... Vacant
15 Dir Human Resources/Legal Counsel ... Ms. Rhonda BOEHNE
18 Director Facilities/Physical Plant ... Mr. Phillip ELLRICH
96 Director Purchasing/Auxiliary Svcs ... Mr. Craig ROPER
06 Manager of Records & Registration ... Ms. Jan RIPPERDA
37 Director of Financial Aid ... Ms. Lisa COLLIER
88 Director of Radiologic Technology ... Mrs. Mimi POLCZYNSKI
88 Dir Physical Therapist Asst Pgm ... Ms. Jane HERRMANN
91 Director of Information Technology ... Ms. Gina SCHUETZ
27 Director of Public Information ... Ms. Cathy KARRICK
26 Director of Marketing ... Mr. Travis HENSON
40 Bookstore Manager ... Ms. Cheryl JOHNSON
88 Director Adult Education ... Ms. Lisa ATKINS
88 Project Director Business Svc Ctr ... Mr. Steve GRONER
50 Business Services Field Rep ... Mr. Art BORUM
41 Athletic Director ... Vacant
10 Controller ... Ms. Mary DANT
88 Coordinator of Student Recruitment ... Ms. Amy TROUTT
38 Director of Reten & Stdnt Develop ... Ms. Christin DALAVARIS
84 Dean of Enrollment Management ... Ms. Denise DERRICK
07 Dir Admissions/Records & Dual Cred ... Mrs. Cheryl BOEHNE
88 Director of Title III Program ... Mr. Robert BLINN
88 Dir Centralia Correctional Ctr Pgm ... Mr. George EVANS
30 Coord Inst Advancement Programs ... Mrs. Suzanne CHRIST

Kendall College (C)

900 N North Branch Street, Chicago IL 60642
County: Cook FICE Identification: 001703
Unit ID: 146393
Telephone: (312) 752-2000 Carnegie Class: Bac/Diverse
FAX Number: (312) 752-2021 Calendar System: Quarter
URL: www.kendall.edu
Established: 1934 Annual Undergrad Tuition & Fees: $22,910
Enrollment: 2,225 Coed
Affiliation or Control: Proprietary IRS Status: Proprietary
Highest Offering: Baccalaureate
Program: Occupational; 2-Year Principally Bachelor's Creditable; Liberal Arts And General; Teacher Preparatory; Professional; Business Emphasis
Accreditation: NH, ACFEI

01 President ... Ms. Emily WILLIAMS KNIGHT
05 Provost ... Dr. Gwen HILLESHEIM
32 Dean of Student Affairs ... Ms. Kimberly SKARR
26 Director of Marketing ... Ms. Genevieve BURKE
04 Assistant to the President ... Mrs. Helena VASILOPOULOS
10 Director of Finance ... Mr. Roald HENDERSON
06 Registrar ... Ms. Amanda MOLLER
15 Director of Human Resources ... Ms. Stephanie TOMINO
29 Director of Alumni Affairs ... Vacant
38 Director of Advising ... Ms. Amy HERRICK
08 Director Library Services ... Mrs. Iva M. FREEMAN
84 Director of Enrollment Management ... Mr. Tom MARIGLIANO
13 Director of Information Technology ... Mr. Brian SON
37 Director of Financial Aid ... Mr. Chris MILLER
39 Director of Residence Life ... Ms. Jena HENSON
106 Academic Director ... Ms. Cheryl BONCUORE
97 Director of General Education ... Mr. Ryan BARTELMAY
18 Chief Facilities/Physical Plant ... Mr. Philip LITTLE
35 Director Student Life ... Vacant
09 Director of Institutional Research ... Mrs. Stacy VLAHAKIS
96 Procurement Manager ... Ms. Lara ENGERT

Kishwaukee College (D)

21193 Malta Road, Malta IL 60150-9600
County: De Kalb FICE Identification: 007684
Unit ID: 146418
Telephone: (815) 825-2086 Carnegie Class: Assoc/Pub-S-SC
FAX Number: (815) 825-2072 Calendar System: Semester
URL: www.kishwaukeecollege.edu
Established: 1967 Annual Undergrad Tuition & Fees (In-District): $3,100
Enrollment: 5,099 Coed
Affiliation or Control: State/Local IRS Status: 501(c)3
Highest Offering: Associate Degree
Program: Occupational; 2-Year Principally Bachelor's Creditable
Accreditation: NH, COMTA, RAD

01 President ... Dr. Thomas L. CHOICE
05 Vice President Instruction ... Mrs. Evelina CICHY
10 Vice Pres of Finance/Administration ... Mr. Robert GALICK
32 Vice President Student Services ... Mrs. Nancy PARTCH
09 Assoc VP Institutional Effectivenes ... Mr. Kevin J. FUSS
83 Dean Arts/Communic/Social Science ... Vacant
72 Dean Career Technologies ... Mrs. Sara POHL
76 Dean Health & Education ... Ms. Bette CHILTON
35 Dean of Student Services ... Ms. Nancy PARTCH
81 Dean Math/Science/Business ... Mr. Steven SQUIER
51 Dean Adult Educ/Transition Pgms ... Ms. Joanne KANTNER
21 Dean of Business Affairs ... Ms. Beth YOUNG
88 Exec Dir Bus Dev & Cont Ed ... Ms. Karen SCHMITT
102 Exec Dir Kish Col Foundation Devel ... Mr. Marshall HAYES
07 Dir Admissions/Registration/Records ... Ms. Jill BIER
27 Dir of Marketing & Public Relations ... Ms. Kayte HAMEL
37 Director Student Financial Aid ... Mrs. Pam WAGENER
14 Director Information Technology ... Mr. Scott ARMSTRONG
40 Director Bookstore ... Mrs. Lynne DURIN
08 Director Library Services ... Ms. Anne-Marie EGGLESTON
15 Director Human Resources ... Mrs. Kate NOREIKO
41 Athletic Director ... Ms. Karen WILEY
18 Chief Facilities/Physical Plant ... Mr. Gary STROTHMAN

Knowledge Systems Institute (E)

3420 Main Street, Skokie IL 60076-2453
County: Cook FICE Identification: 026227
Unit ID: 260956
Telephone: (847) 679-3135 Carnegie Class: Spec/Tech
FAX Number: (847) 679-3166 Calendar System: Semester
URL: www.ksi.edu
Established: 1978 Annual Graduate Tuition & Fees: $7,690
Enrollment: 119 Coed
Affiliation or Control: Independent Non-Profit IRS Status: 501(c)3
Highest Offering: Master's; No Undergraduates
Program: Professional; Technical Emphasis
Accreditation: NH

01 Chancellor ... Dr. Shi-Kuo CHANG
03 Executive Director ... Ms. Judy PAN
05 Academic Dean ... Dr. Cheng-Yuan HSIEH
07 Chr Computer Sci/Admiss Committee ... Dr. Cheng-Yuan HSIEH
11 Administrative Manager ... Mr. Noorjhan ALI

Knox College (F)

2 E South Street, Galesburg IL 61401-4999
County: Knox FICE Identification: 001704
Unit ID: 146427
Telephone: (309) 341-7000 Carnegie Class: Bac/A&S
FAX Number: (309) 341-7090 Calendar System: Trimester
URL: www.knox.edu
Established: 1837 Annual Undergrad Tuition & Fees: $36,492
Enrollment: 1,405 Coed
Affiliation or Control: Independent Non-Profit IRS Status: 501(c)3
Highest Offering: Baccalaureate
Program: Liberal Arts And General; Teacher Preparatory
Accreditation: NH, @TEAC

01 President ... Dr. Teresa L. AMOTT
05 VP Acad Affairs/Dean of College ... Dr. Lawrence B. BREITBORDE
10 Vice Pres for Finance & Admin Svcs ... Mr. Thomas B. AXTELL
30 Vice President for Advancement ... Ms. Beverly HOLMES
07 Vice Pres Enrollment/Dean of Admn ... Mr. Paul R. STEENIS
27 Assoc VP/Communications ... Ms. Megan SCOTT
06 Registrar ... Mr. Kevin J. HASTINGS
32 Dean of Students ... Ms. Debbie SOUTHERN
20 Associate Dean of College ... Dr. Lori HASLEM
37 Director Financial Aid ... Ms. Ann BRILL
08 Librarian ... Mr. Jeffrey A. DOUGLAS
36 Interim Dir Ctr Career Pre-Prof Dev ... Ms. Terrie SALINE
14 Dir/CIO Information Technology Svcs ... Mr. Steven HALL
15 Director Human Resources ... Ms. Gina ZINDT
18 Director Facilities Services ... Mr. Scott MAUST
21 Controller ... Ms. Bobby Jo MAURER
86 Dir Government & Community Relation ... Ms. Karrie HEARTLEIN
29 Dir Alumni & Constituent Programs ... Ms. Carol J. BROWN
38 Director of Counseling Services ... Dr. Daniel L. LARSON
41 Director of Athletics ... Mr. Chad EISELE
19 Director Campus Safety ... Mr. John SCHLAF
09 Dir Institutional Research/Assess ... Mr. Charles L. CLARK
102 Dir Corporate/Foundation Relations ... Ms. Joanne PETERSON

Lake Forest College (G)

555 N Sheridan Road, Lake Forest IL 60045-2338
County: Lake FICE Identification: 001706
Unit ID: 146481
Telephone: (847) 234-3100 Carnegie Class: Bac/A&S
FAX Number: (847) 735-6291 Calendar System: Semester
URL: www.lakeforest.edu
Established: 1857 Annual Undergrad Tuition & Fees: $38,300
Enrollment: 1,493 Coed
Affiliation or Control: Independent Non-Profit IRS Status: 501(c)3
Highest Offering: Master's
Program: Liberal Arts And General
Accreditation: NH

01 President ... Mr. Stephen D. SCHUTT
05 Provost/Dean of Faculty ... Dr. Michael ORR
10 Vice Pres of Business/Treasurer ... Mrs. Leslie T. CHAPMAN
30 VP of Development & Alumni Pgms ... Mr. Richard BARTOLOZZI
07 Vice Pres Admissions/Career Svcs ... Mr. William G. MOTZER, JR.
45 VP Budget/Planning/Controller ... Ms. Lori H. SUNDBERG
04 Executive Assistant to President ... Ms. Elizabeth A. PALM
32 Dean of Students ... Mr. Rob FLOT
35 Director of Residence Life ... Ms. Carolyn GOLZ
28 Director Intercult Relelations ... Ms. Erin HOFFMAN
20 Asc Dean Facul/Dir Ctr Chicago Pgms ... Dr. Rand SMITH
20 Assoc Dean Facul/Dir Lrng/Tchng Ctr ... Dr. Richard MALLETTE
31 Director of Community Education ... Mr. Dan LEMAHIEU
37 Director of Financial Aid ... Mr. Gerard J. CEBRZYNSKI
41 Athletic Director ... Ms. Jacqueline SLAATS
08 Librarian & Director Info Svcs/Tech ... Mr. James R. CUBIT
06 Registrar ... Ms. Ruthane I. BOPP
38 Director of Counseling Services ... Dr. Jennifer JEZIORSKI
29 Assoc Vice Pres for Alumni Relation ... Mr. Timothy STATE
09 Director of Institutional Research ... Ms. Lori H. SUNDBERG
15 Director of Human Resources ... Vacant

36 Director of Career Services ....Ms. Lisa HINKLEY
18 Director of Facilities Management ....Mr. David J. SIEBERT
26 Assoc VP for Comm//Mktg ....Ms. Elizabeth LIBBY
19 Director of Public Safety ....Mr. Richard L. COHEN

Lake Forest Graduate School of Management (A)

1905 W Field Court, Lake Forest IL 60045-4824
County: Lake FICE Identification: 023192
Unit ID: 146490
Telephone: (847) 234-5005 Carnegie Class: Spec/Bus
FAX Number: (847) 295-3656 Calendar System: Quarter
URL: www.lakeforestmba.edu
Established: 1946 Annual Graduate Tuition & Fees: $3,106
Enrollment: 710 Coed
Affiliation or Control: Independent Non-Profit IRS Status: 501(c)3
Highest Offering: Master's; No Undergraduates
Program: Professional; Business Emphasis
Accreditation: NH

01 President ....Mr. John N. POPOLI
05 Exec VP Educ Pgms & Solutions ......Mr. Christopher MULTHAUF
10 VP Finance & CFO ....Mr. Malcolm C. DOUGLAS
26 VP Marketing & Corporate Sales ....Mr. Peter DRUMMOND
46 VP R&D and Innovation ....Ms. Kathleen M. LECK
16 VP Human Resources & Fundraising ....Ms. Stasia ZWISLER
27 VP Information Technology & CIO ....Mr. Gregory KOZAK
20 Dean Degree Programs & Faculty Rel ....Ms. Ellen MCMAHON
20 Dean Corporate Learning Services ....Mr. Neil HOLMAN
06 Registrar ....Ms. Christine L. PERLSTROM
29 Manager Alumni Relations & Events ....Ms. Jessica GARDNER
37 Associate Director of Financial Aid ....Ms. Rebecca KIM
07 Director of Admissions ....Ms. Carolyn BRUNE

Lake Land College (B)

5001 Lake Land Boulevard, Mattoon IL 61938-9366
County: Coles FICE Identification: 007644
Unit ID: 146506
Telephone: (217) 234-5253 Carnegie Class: Assoc/Pub-R-L
FAX Number: (217) 234-5400 Calendar System: Semester
URL: www.lakeland.cc.il.us
Established: 1966 Annual Undergrad Tuition & Fees (In-District): $3,024
Enrollment: 8,867 Coed
Affiliation or Control: State/Local IRS Status: 501(c)3
Highest Offering: Associate Degree
Program: Occupational; 2-Year Principally Bachelor's Creditable
Accreditation: NH, ADNUR, DH, PNUR, PTAA

01 President ....Mr. Scott LENSINK
04 Admin Assistant to President ....Ms. Lana FULLER
10 Vice President Business Services ....Mr. Ray RIECK
05 VP Academic Services ....Dr. Jim HULL
32 Vice President Student Services ....Dr. Tina STOVALL
30 Vice President Development ....Ms. Pam CRISMAN
103 Assoc Vice Pres Workforce Devel ....Ms. Linda VON BEHREN
20 Assoc Vice Pres Educational Svcs ....Dr. Deb HUTTI
88 Exec Dean Correctional Pgms ....Mr. Tom KERKHOFF
07 Dean of Admissions Services ....Mr. Jon VAN DYKE
50 Dean Center for Business & Industry ....Mr. Robert WESTCOTT
88 Assoc Dean Corrections-Taylorville ....Mr. John ALLEN
88 Assoc Dean Corrections-Graham ....Mr. Dennis MIHLBACHLER
88 Assoc Dean Corrections-Dwight ....Mr. Alan MORTENSEN
88 Assoc Dean Corrections-Dixon ....Mr. Brandon YOUNG
88 Assoc Dean Corrections-Western ....Mr. Tom THEISS
88 Assoc Dean Correction-IL River ....Mr. Tom ZABORAC
88 Assoc Dean Corrections-Jacksonville ....Mr. Steve BAHNEY
88 Assoc Dean Corrections-Lawrence ....Mr. Tim WATSON
88 Assoc Dean Corrections-Robinson ....Mr. Glen DONALDSON
88 Assc Dean Corrections-SW & Vandalia ....Mr. Steve DRAKE
88 Site Director Corrections-Hill ....Ms. Christine LEHR
88 Site Director Corr-Vienna & Shawnee ......Mr. Blake MCCONNELL
21 Comptroller ....Ms. Madge SHOOT
08 Director of the LRC ....Mr. Scott DRONE-SILVERS
26 Dir Communications/Creative Svcs ....Mrs. Kelly ALLEE
14 Director of Information Systems/Svc ....Mr. Lee SPANIOL
37 Director of Financial Aid ....Ms. Paula CARPENTER
19 Director Facilities Planning ....Mr. Michael KASDORF
15 Director of Human Resources ....Ms. Dawn SCHLECHTE
88 Director Learning Technologies ....Mr. Steve GARREN
25 Director Grant Development ....Ms. Emily RAMAGE
40 Director Auxiliary Services ....Ms. Chris KRAMER
29 Director Foundation & Alumni Svcs ....Mr. Dave COX
36 Director of Career Services ....Ms. Tina MOORE
38 Director of Student Counseling ....Ms. Emily HARTKE
18 Director of Physical Plant ....Mr. Durb ASKEW
41 Director of Athletics ....Mr. Dennis THRONEBURG
09 Director of Institutional Research ....Dr. Lynn BREER

Lakeview College of Nursing (C)

903 N Logan Avenue, Danville IL 61832-3788
County: Vermilion FICE Identification: 010501
Unit ID: 146533
Telephone: (217) 709-0920 Carnegie Class: Spec/Health
FAX Number: (217) 709-0954 Calendar System: Semester
URL: www.lakeviewcol.edu
Established: 1987 Annual Undergrad Tuition & Fees: $13,500
Enrollment: 289 Coed
Affiliation or Control: Independent Non-Profit IRS Status: 501(c)3
Highest Offering: Baccalaureate
Program: Professional; Nursing Emphasis
Accreditation: NH, NURSE

01 Interim Dean of Nursing ....Ms. Irene STEWARD
11 Associate CEO ....Ms. Sheila MINGEE
06 Registrar/Dir Enrollment ....Ms. Connie YOUNG
08 Library Dir/IT Coordinator ....Ms. Miranda SHAKE

Le Cordon Bleu College of Culinary Arts in Chicago (D)

361 W Chestnut Street, Chicago IL 60610
County: Cook FICE Identification: 023522
Unit ID: 144467
Telephone: (312) 944-0882 Carnegie Class: Assoc/PrivFP
FAX Number: (312) 944-8557 Calendar System: Semester
URL: www.chefs.edu/chicago
Established: 1983 Annual Undergrad Tuition & Fees: $19,530
Enrollment: 1,389 Coed
Affiliation or Control: Proprietary IRS Status: Proprietary
Highest Offering: Associate Degree
Program: Occupational
Accreditation: NH, ACFEI

01 President ....Mr. Kirk T. BACHMANN
05 VP Academic Affs/Dean Student Svcs ....Mr. Marshall J. SHAFKOWITZ

Lewis and Clark Community College (E)

5800 Godfrey Road, Godfrey IL 62035-2466
County: Madison FICE Identification: 010020
Unit ID: 146603
Telephone: (618) 466-7000 Carnegie Class: Assoc/Pub-S-SC
FAX Number: (618) 466-2798 Calendar System: Semester
URL: www.lc.edu
Established: 1970 Annual Undergrad Tuition & Fees (In-District): $3,420
Enrollment: 8,451 Coed
Affiliation or Control: State/Local IRS Status: 501(c)3
Highest Offering: Associate Degree
Program: Occupational; 2-Year Principally Bachelor's Creditable
Accreditation: NH, ADNUR, DA, DH, OTA

01 President ....Dr. Dale T. CHAPMAN
05 Vice President Academic Affairs ....Dr. Linda CHAPMAN
84 Vice President Enrollment Services ....Mr. Kent SCHEFFEL
32 Vice President Student Services ....Dr. Sean HILL
11 Vice President Administration ....Mr. Gary AYRES
10 Assoc Vice Pres Finance ....Mrs. Mary SCHULTE
10 Assoc Vice President Accounting ....Mrs. Nancy KAISER
76 Dean Science/Math/Technology ....Dr. Sue CZERWINSKI-ALJETS
72 Dean Business & Liberal Arts ....Mrs. Jill LANE
88 Director Corp & Comm Learning ....Mrs. Kathy WILLIS
27 Assoc Vice Pres Telecommunications ....Mrs. Julie MCPIKE
18 Assoc Vice Pres Cap Proj/Campus ..Mr. Christopher BACHMANN
102 Vice Pres Media & Found Rel ....Mrs. Lori ARTIS
20 Dir Academic Operations & Planning ....Mr. Jeff COLES
09 Director Institutional Research ....Mr. Dennis KRIEB
51 Director Adult Education Program ....Mrs. Valorie HARRIS
88 Director Enrollment Center/Advising ....Mrs. Delfina DORNES
37 Dir Financial Aid/Stdnt Employment ....Mrs. Angela WEAVER
38 Dir Student Dev & Counseling ....Mrs. Kathy HABERER
35 Director Student Support Services ....Ms. Dolores PATRICK
15 Director Human Resources ....Mr. Bob BECHERER
06 Registrar ....Ms. Heidi SCOTT

Lewis University (F)

One University Parkway, Romeoville IL 60446-2200
County: Will FICE Identification: 001707
Unit ID: 146612
Telephone: (815) 838-0500 Carnegie Class: Master's L
FAX Number: (815) 838-9456 Calendar System: Semester
URL: www.lewisu.edu
Established: 1932 Annual Undergrad Tuition & Fees: $24,770
Enrollment: 6,394 Coed
Affiliation or Control: Roman Catholic IRS Status: 501(c)3
Highest Offering: Doctorate
Program: Occupational; Liberal Arts And General; Teacher Preparatory; Professional
Accreditation: NH, ACBSP, NURSE, @SW, TED

01 President ....Bro. James GAFFNEY, FSC
03 Executive Vice President ....Mr. Wayne J. DRAUDT
05 Provost ....Dr. Stephany S. SCHLACHTER
32 Vice President Student Services ....Mr. Joseph T. FALESE
10 Vice Pres for Business & Facilities ....Mr. Robert C. DE ROSE
84 Vice President Enrollment Mgmt ....Vacant
30 Vice Pres University Advancement ....Mr. Leonard BERTOLINI
07 Director of Admission ....Mr. Ryan COCKERILL
35 Dean of Student Services ....Ms. Kathryn SLATTERY
28 Assoc Vice Pres Mission ....Mr. Kurt SCHACKMUTH
49 Dean College Arts & Sciences ....Dr. Bonnie BONDAVALLI
50 Dean College Business ....Dr. Rami KHASAWNEH
66 Dean Col Nursing/Health Professions ....Dr. Peggy RICE
15 Assoc Vice Pres Human Resources ....Ms. Graciela DUFOUR
09 Dir Instl Data Analysis/Assessment ....Mrs. Vicky TUCKER
08 Director of Library ....Vacant
06 Registrar ....Mr. Robert KEMPIAK
37 Director of Financial Aid ....Ms. Janeen DECHARINTE
26 Director Marketing/Communications . Ms. Ramona LAMONTAGNE
41 Director of Athletics ....Vacant
23 Dir of Health & Counseling Services .... Ms. Michele MANASSAH
19 Director of Campus Security ....Mr. James MONTANARI
42 Director of University Ministry ....Mr. Steve ZLATIC
31 Dir of Meetings/Events/Conferences ....Mr. Robert ARNOLD
13 Chief Info Technology Officer ....Mr. John DALBY
85 Director International Student Svcs ....Mr. Michael FEKETE
14 Director Instl Data Administration ....Ms. Tammy KUSE
29 Exec Dir Alumni/Development Svcs ....Ms. Julie PENNER
96 Director of Purchasing ....Mr. Jim KOENIG
36 Director of Career Services ....Ms. Kristi KELLY

Lexington College (G)

310 S Peoria, Suite 512, Chicago IL 60607-3534
County: Cook FICE Identification: 025276
Unit ID: 146621
Telephone: (312) 226-6294 Carnegie Class: Spec/Bus
FAX Number: (312) 226-6405 Calendar System: Semester
URL: www.lexingtoncollege.edu
Established: 1977 Annual Undergrad Tuition & Fees: $24,075
Enrollment: 64 Female
Affiliation or Control: Independent Non-Profit IRS Status: 501(c)3
Highest Offering: Baccalaureate
Program: Professional
Accreditation: NH

01 President ....Ms. Mary HUNT
05 Academic Dean ....Mrs. Jolene BIRMINGHAM
10 Manager of Business Office ....Ms. Estela GODINA
26 Mgr Communications & Marketing ....Ms. Megan GOGGIN
37 Director of Financial Aid ....Ms. Maria LEBRON
06 Registrar ....Vacant
21 Associate Business Officer ....Ms. Diane MCDERMOTT
30 Director of Development ....Ms. Katherine CASKEY
35 Director Student Affairs ....Vacant

Lincoln Christian University (H)

100 Campus View Drive, Lincoln IL 62656-2167
County: Logan FICE Identification: 001708
Unit ID: 146667
Telephone: (217) 732-3168 Carnegie Class: Spec/Faith
FAX Number: (217) 732-5718 Calendar System: Semester
URL: www.lincolnchristian.edu
Established: 1944 Annual Undergrad Tuition & Fees: $15,060
Enrollment: 1,088 Coed
Affiliation or Control: Christian Churches And Churches of Christ
IRS Status: 501(c)3
Highest Offering: Doctorate
Program: Liberal Arts And General; Religious Emphasis
Accreditation: NH, BI, THEOL

01 President ....Dr. Keith H. RAY
05 Provost ....Dr. Clay HAM
10 Vice President of Finance ....Miss Andrea SHORT
32 Vice Pres of Student Development ....Mr. Brian MILLS
30 VP of University Advancement ....Mr. Gordon D. VENTURELLA
84 VP of Enrollment Management ....Mrs. Krista BROOKS
29 Assoc VP of Alumni Services ....Mr. Lynn LAUGHLIN
06 Registrar ....Mr. Shawn SMITH
08 Librarian ....Ms. Nancy OLSON
37 Director of Financial Aid ....Ms. Nancy SIDDENS
101 Admin Asst to Pres/Secy Bd of Gov ....Mrs. Linda SEGGELKE
13 Director of Campus Technology ....Mr. Mark HOUPT

Lincoln College (I)

300 Keokuk Street, Lincoln IL 62656-1699
County: Logan FICE Identification: 001709
Unit ID: 146676
Telephone: (217) 732-3155 Carnegie Class: Bac/Assoc
FAX Number: (217) 732-8859 Calendar System: Semester
URL: www.lincolncollege.edu
Established: 1865 Annual Undergrad Tuition & Fees: $17,500
Enrollment: 1,248 Coed
Affiliation or Control: Independent Non-Profit IRS Status: 501(c)3
Highest Offering: Baccalaureate
Program: 2-Year Principally Bachelor's Creditable
Accreditation: NH, IACBE

01 President ....Mr. John D. BLACKBURN
05 Vice Pres Academic Affairs ....Dr. A. Gigi FANSLER
30 Vice President for Advancement ....Ms. Debbie ACKERMAN
10 Vice Pres Finance & Administration ....Mr. Greg A. EIMER
84 VP for Enroll Mgmt & Student Svcs ...... Mr. Anthony CARDENAS
37 Director of Financial Aid ....Mr. Chris STECKMANN
06 Registrar ....Mrs. Debra J. HARMON
29 Coordinator Alumni Relations ....Ms. Kerri TAYLOR
38 Director of Counseling ....Ms. Michelle BAUER
08 Head Librarian ....Mr. Mike STARASTA
18 Director of Building & Grounds ....Ms. Ronda PIATT
23 Director of Health Services ....Ms. Diane STEPHENSON
21 Controller ....Mrs. Katherine PAPESCH
15 Director of Human Resources ....Mrs. Kathy STEFFENS
40 Bookstore Manager ....Mrs. Donna HUTCHISON
39 Director of Housing ....Mrs. Bridgett THOMAS
13 Director of Information Technology ....Mr. Tim FOSTER
27 Director of Communications ....Vacant
35 Director of Student Development ....Vacant
07 Director of Admissions ....Mrs. Gretchen BREE
09 Director of Institutional Research ....Mr. David SMALLEY

Lincoln College of Technology (A)

8317 West North Avenue, Melrose Park IL 60160-1605

FICE Identification: 010316
Unit ID: 146700
Telephone: (708) 344-4700 Carnegie Class: Assoc/PrivFP
FAX Number: (708) 345-4380 Calendar System: Semester
URL: www.lincolnedu.com
Established: 1950 Annual Undergrad Tuition & Fees: $29,830
Enrollment: 1,249 Coed
Affiliation or Control: Proprietary IRS Status: Proprietary
Highest Offering: Associate Degree
Program: Occupational
Accreditation: ACCSC

01 President ... Mr. David SCHUCHMAN

Lincoln Land Community College (B)

5250 Shepherd Road, PO Box 19256,
Springfield IL 62794-9256

County: Sangamon FICE Identification: 007170
Unit ID: 146685
Telephone: (217) 786-2200 Carnegie Class: Assoc/Pub-R-L
FAX Number: (217) 786-2468 Calendar System: Semester
URL: www.llcc.edu
Established: 1967 Annual Undergrad Tuition & Fees (In-District): $3,210
Enrollment: 7,337 Coed
Affiliation or Control: Local IRS Status: 501(c)3
Highest Offering: Associate Degree
Program: Occupational; 2-Year Principally Bachelor's Creditable
Accreditation: NH, ADNUR, OTA, RAD

01 President ... Dr. Charlotte J. WARREN
11 Vice President Administrative Svcs ... Mr. Richard W. VERTREES
05 Vice President Academic Svcs ... Dr. Eileen G. TEPATTI
32 Vice President Student Services ... Ms. Lesley J. FREDERICK
103 Vice President Workforce Systems ... Dr. Judy JOZAITIS
13 Chief Information Officer ... Mr. Esteban CRUZ
04 Asst to Pres Planning & Inst Impr ... Ms. Iva G. BERGERON
15 Assoc Vice Pres Human Resources ... Ms. Junell A. RANSDELL
84 Assoc VP Enrollment Svcs/Registrar ... Ms. Tyra TAYLOR
45 Asc VP Budget/Finan Plng/Analysis ... Ms. Mary A. MCGEE
10 Asst VP Business & Fiscal Opers ... Vacant
37 Asst Vice President Financial Aid ... Mr. Lee BURSI
86 Asst VP Corp/Gov Trng & Econ Devel ... Ms. Paula J. LUEBBERT
18 Asst VP Construction ... Mr. Hugh GARVEY
12 Exec Director Educ Service Area ... Mr. Scott R. STALLMAN
12 Exec Director Educ Service Area ... Ms. Jan M. TERRY
102 Exec Director LLCC Foundation ... Ms. Karen A. SANDERS
26 Exec Dir Public Relations/Marketing ... Ms. Lynn WHALEN
24 Exec Director Learning Lab ... Mrs. Julie CLEVENGER
88 Director Small Business Devel Ctr ... Mr. Kevin LUST
07 Director Admissions & Records ... Mr. Ronald J. GREGOIRE
22 Dir Employ Bnft Svc/Eq Opty Cmpl Of ... Ms. Nicole M. RALPH
09 Director Institutional Research ... Ms. Susan SIMPSON
30 Director Development ... Ms. Janet SEMANIK
36 Director Placement/Testing ... Ms. Tricia A. KUJAWA
32 Director Student Life ... Ms. Marci ROCKEY
19 Police Chief ... Mr. Bradley D. GENTRY
21 Controller ... Ms. Karie L. LONGHTA
50 Dean Business & Technologies ... Mr. David A. GREEN
83 Dean Social Sciences ... Dr. Victor K. BRODERICK
72 Dean District Learning Resources ... Ms. Wendy L. HOWERTER
57 Dean Arts & Humanities ... Mr. David E. LAUBERSHEIMER
81 Dean Mathematics and Sciences ... Mr. William D. BADE
76 Dean Health Professions ... Dr. Cynthia L. MASKEY
08 Assoc Dean Library ... Mrs. Tamara SCHNELL
56 Asc Dean Instruct Tech/Distance Ed ... Mrs. Becky PARTON

Loyola University Chicago (C)

1032 W. Sheridan Road, Chicago IL 60660

County: Cook FICE Identification: 001710
Unit ID: 146719
Telephone: (773) 274-3000 Carnegie Class: RU/H
FAX Number: (312) 915-7003 Calendar System: Semester
URL: www.luc.edu
Established: 1870 Annual Undergrad Tuition & Fees: $34,938
Enrollment: 16,040 Coed
Affiliation or Control: Roman Catholic IRS Status: 501(c)3
Highest Offering: Doctorate
Program: Liberal Arts And General; Teacher Preparatory; Professional; Business Emphasis
Accreditation: NH, BUS, BUSA, CLPSY, COPSY, DENT, DIETI, EMT, LAW, MED, MT, NURSE, SW, TED, THEA

01 President/CEO ... Rev. Michael J. GARANZINI, SJ
17 Sr VP & Provost Health Sciences ... Dr. Richard GAMELLI
05 Provost ... Dr. John P. PELISSERO
04 Asst to the President for Mission ... Dr. John J. HARDT
88 Special Assistant to the President ... Rev. John COSTELLO, SJ
16 Vice President Government Affairs ... Mr. Philip P. HALE
88 Asst VP/Asst to Chairman ... Ms. Donna B. CURIN
30 Sr Vice President Advancement ... Mr. Jonathan R. HEINTZELMAN
10 Sr Vice President Finance & CFO ... Mr. William G. LAIRD
45 Sr VP Cap Planning & Campus Mgmt ... Mr. Wayne MAGDZIARZ
15 Sr VP Admin Svcs & Chief HR Officer ... Mr. Thomas M. KELLY
32 Vice President Student Development ... Dr. Robert KELLY
43 Sr Vice President & General Counsel ... Ms. Ellen KANE-MUNRO
88 Chief Operating Officer/Health Sci ... Mr. Steve BERGFELD
27 Vice President Information Services ... Ms. Susan M. MALISCH
12 Vice President & Director Rome Ctr ... Mr. Emilio IODICE
26 VP Marketing & Communications ... Ms. Kelly SHANNON
04 Special Assistant to the President ... Ms. Lorraine G. SNYDER
20 Vice Provost Academic Affairs ... Dr. Nancy TUCHMAN
49 Dean of Arts & Sciences ... Dr. Reinhard ANDRESS
41 Asst VP & Director Athletics ... Dr. M.Grace CALHOUN
63 Dean School of Medicine ... Dr. Linda BRUBAKER
26 Assoc VP Community Affairs/Outreach ... Ms. Jennifer R. CLARK
88 Vice Provost Health Sciences Rsrch ... Dr. Richard KENNEDY
85 Assoc Provost Global Affairs ... Dr. Patrick M. BOYLE
84 Assoc Provost Enrollment Management ... Mr. Paul G. ROBERTS
15 Dean Faculty Rome Center ... Dr. Susana CAVALLO
90 Director Academic Tech Services ... Mr. Bruce A. MONTES
18 Associate VP of Capital Projects ... Ms. Kana WIBBENMEYER
20 Assoc Provost Academic Services ... Rev. Justin DAFFRON, SJ
21 Assoc VP for Budget & Finance ... Dr. Thomas F. HICKEY
46 Assoc Provost Research Services ... Dr. Samuel A. ATTOH
88 Deputy General Counsel/Asst Sec ... Ms. Pamela G. COSTAS
28 Assoc Dean Student Diversity ... Mr. Javier CERVANTES
21 Assoc VP Finance & Contoller ... Ms. Andrea SABITSANA
21 Assoc VP Sponsored Pgm Accounting ... Ms. Donna QUIRK
35 Associate VP Campus Services ... Mr. Timothy MCGURIMAN
88 Asst VP Bioethics & HSD Mission ... Dr. Mark G. KUCZEWSKI
11 Assistant Provost Administration ... Dr. Marian A. CLAFFEY
88 Assoc VP Administration/Finance/SSM ... Ms. Cindy D. GONYA
88 Assoc VP Informatics/Academic Systm ... Mr. Ronald N. PRICE
35 Assoc VP & Dean of Students ... Ms. Jane F. NEUFELD
50 Dean School of Business Admin ... Dr. Kathleen A. GETZ
60 Dean School of Communication ... Dr. Donald B. HEIDER
53 Dean School of Education ... Dr. David P. PRASSE
58 Dean of Graduate School ... Dr. Samuel A. ATTOH
61 Dean School of Law ... Dr. David N. YELLEN
66 Dean School of Nursing ... Dr. Vicki A. KEOUGH
70 Dean School of Social Work ... Dr. Darrell P. WHEELER
51 Acting Dean Continuing & Prof Educ ... Dr. Janet DEATHERAGE
08 Dean University Libraries ... Mr. Robert A. SEAL
06 Director of Registration & Records ... Ms. Clare M. KORINEK
23 Director Student Wellness Center ... Ms. Diane C. ASARO
07 Director Undergraduate Admissions ... Ms. Lori A. GREENE
36 Director Career Development Center ... Dr. Darby SCISM
39 Director Residence Life ... Dr. Romando A. NASH
15 Director of Human Resources ... Ms. Joan C. STASIAK
09 Director Institutional Research ... Dr. Richard S. HURST
19 Director Campus Safety ... Mr. Robert FINE
29 Director Alumni Relations ... Ms. Nicole MEEHAN
96 Manager of Purchasing ... Mr. Sam J. PERRY
88 Director Special Events ... Mr. Richard WILLIAMS
07 Dir Graduate & Professional Admiss ... Ms. Ann E. BEZBATCHENKO
21 Dir Academic Business Operations ... Ms. Joanna PAPPAS
88 Dir Budgeting & Financial Planning ... Mr. Joseph M. FILIPIAK
46 Dir Enrollment Systems Research ... Mr. Timothy HEUER
35 Assistant VP Student Development ... Mr. Jack MCLEAN
28 Dir Student Diversity & Multicultur ... Ms. Sadika SULAIMAN-HARA
44 Director Annual Giving ... Ms. Shena KEITH
88 Dir Advancement Info Services ... Ms. Stacy HUGHES
21 Treasurer ... Mr. Eric JONES
37 Director of Scholarships ... Mr. Edward MOORE
90 Dir of System Implementation & Cons ... Mr. Kevin J. SMITH
88 Director of Communications & Media ... Ms. Maeve M. KILEY
102 Dir of Corporate & Foundation Rels ... Ms. Angela LIEGEL
42 Dir Sacremental Life & MDS Chapel ... Rev. Patrick DORSEY

Lutheran School of Theology at Chicago (D)

1100 E 55th Street, Chicago IL 60615-9985

County: Cook FICE Identification: 001712
Unit ID: 146728
Telephone: (773) 256-0700 Carnegie Class: Spec/Faith
FAX Number: (773) 256-0782 Calendar System: Semester
URL: www.lstc.edu
Established: 1860 Annual Graduate Tuition & Fees: $13,554
Enrollment: 284 Coed
Affiliation or Control: Evangelical Lutheran Church In America
IRS Status: 501(c)3
Highest Offering: Doctorate; No Undergraduates
Program: Professional; Religious Emphasis
Accreditation: NH, THEOL

01 President ... Dr. James NIEMAN
04 Assistant to the President ... Ms. Patti DEBIAS
108 Exec for Administration/Assess/Plng ... Ms. Laura WILHELM
05 Dean/Vice Pres for Academic Affairs ... Dr. Michael SHELLEY
88 Director of the MDiv Programs ... Dr. Kathleen BILLMAN
88 Director of the MA Programs ... Dr. Kurt HENDEL
58 Director of Advanced Studies ... Dr. Esther MENN
88 Pastor to the Community ... Rev. Joan BECK
11 Vice President for Operations ... Mr. Bob BERRIDGE
30 Vice President for Advancement ... Mr. Mark H. VAN SCHARREL
10 Chief Financial Officer ... Mr. Jon KLAUSA
07 Director of Admissions ... Dr. Scott CHALMERS
37 Dir Financial Aid/Admissions ... Ms. Dorothy DOMINIAK
06 Registrar ... Ms. Patricia A. BARTLEY
26 Director of Communications/Mktg ... Ms. Janet BODEN
08 Director of Library ... Dr. Christine WENDEROTH
13 Dir of Information Technology Svcs ... Mr. Kenesa DEBELA

MacCormac College (E)

29 E Madison Street 2nd Floor, Chicago IL 60602-4405

County: Cook FICE Identification: 001716
Unit ID: 146816
Telephone: (312) 922-1884 Carnegie Class: Assoc/PrivNFP
FAX Number: (312) 922-4286 Calendar System: Semester
URL: www.maccormac.edu
Established: 1904 Annual Undergrad Tuition & Fees: $12,960
Enrollment: 176 Coed
Affiliation or Control: Independent Non-Profit IRS Status: 501(c)3
Highest Offering: Associate Degree
Program: 2-Year Principally Bachelor's Creditable
Accreditation: NH

01 President ... Dr. Marnelle ALEXIS
05 Academic Dean ... Dr. Pam STEINKE
10 Director of Finance/Human Resources ... Mr. Matt GAWENDA
06 Registrar ... Ms. Mariza SILVA
37 Director of Financial Aid ... Mr. Robert GOMEZ
32 Assoc Dir Admission/Student Svcs ... Mr. Marcus TROUTMAN
07 Admissions Coord/Placement Director ... Ms. Ashlee FARNEY

MacMurray College (F)

447 E College Avenue, Jacksonville IL 62650-2590

County: Morgan FICE Identification: 001717
Unit ID: 146825
Telephone: (217) 479-7041 Carnegie Class: Bac/Diverse
FAX Number: (217) 245-0405 Calendar System: 4/1/4
URL: www.mac.edu
Established: 1846 Annual Undergrad Tuition & Fees: $20,900
Enrollment: 548 Coed
Affiliation or Control: United Methodist IRS Status: 501(c)3
Highest Offering: Baccalaureate
Program: Liberal Arts And General; Teacher Preparatory; Professional
Accreditation: NH, NURSE, SW

01 President ... Dr. Colleen HESTER
03 CFO & Vice President of Finance ... Ms. Jackie LOOSER
05 VP Academic Affairs & Student Life ... Mr. John BAILEY
32 Dean of Student Affairs ... Mr. Martin SABOLO
30 Exec Dir Institutional Advancement ... Ms. Bridget PHILLIPS
84 Chief Admissions Officer ... Ms. Alicia ZEONE
10 Controller ... Mr. Andrew SIDOCK
13 Director of IT/System Administrator ... Mr. Bob LOOSER
06 Registrar ... Dr. Glen CLATTERBUCK
08 Librarian ... Ms. Susan EILERING
37 Director of Financial Aid ... Ms. Laci ENGELBRECHT
36 Coordinator Career Services ... Ms. Cori WAGNER
29 Director Alumni Relations ... Ms. Christina WELLS
09 Director of Institutional Research ... Vacant
18 Director of Facilities ... Mr. Larry TROWBRIDGE
26 Director of Public Relations ... Mr. Ted ROTH

McCormick Theological Seminary (G)

5460 S University Avenue, Chicago IL 60615-5108

County: Cook FICE Identification: 001721
Unit ID: 146977
Telephone: (773) 947-6300 Carnegie Class: Spec/Faith
FAX Number: (773) 288-2612 Calendar System: Semester
URL: www.mccormick.edu
Established: 1829 Annual Graduate Tuition & Fees: $17,200
Enrollment: 241 Coed
Affiliation or Control: Presbyterian Church (U.S.A.) IRS Status: 501(c)3
Highest Offering: Doctorate; No Undergraduates
Program: Professional
Accreditation: NH, THEOL

01 President ... Rev. Frank M. YAMADA
10 Vice Pres Administration/Finance ... Mr. David CRAWFORD
05 Vice Pres Acad Affs/Dean Faculty ... Dr. Luis R. RIVERA
32 Vice President for Student Affairs ... Rev Dr. Christine VOGEL
30 Sr Dir Seminary Rels & Development ... Mr. Sam EVANS
06 Registrar ... Mr. Jim COURTNEY
29 Int Dir of Alumni/ae & Church Rels ... Ms. Emily MCGINLEY
08 Director of JKM Library ... Dr. Christine WENDEROTH
15 Director Human Resources ... Ms. Karen PURNELL
37 Dir Student Financial Planning ... Ms. Tabitha CLARK

McHenry County College (H)

8900 US Highway 14, Crystal Lake IL 60012-2796

County: McHenry FICE Identification: 007691
Unit ID: 147004
Telephone: (815) 455-3700 Carnegie Class: Assoc/Pub-S-SC
FAX Number: (815) 455-3999 Calendar System: Semester
URL: www.mchenry.edu
Established: 1967 Annual Undergrad Tuition & Fees (In-District): $3,500
Enrollment: 7,104 Coed
Affiliation or Control: State/Local IRS Status: 501(c)3
Highest Offering: Associate Degree
Program: Occupational; 2-Year Principally Bachelor's Creditable
Accreditation: NH

01 President ... Dr. Vicky SMITH
05 VP Academic & Student Affairs ... Dr. Anthony MIKSA
11 VP Administrative Services ... Mr. Larry WEST
30 Vice Pres Institutional Advancement ... Ms. Laura J. BROWN
10 CFO/Treasurer ... Vacant

21 Controller ... Mr. Kevin IHETU
13 Chief Information Officer ... Dr. Allen P. BUTLER
15 AVP of Human Resources ... Ms. Angelina CASTILLO
32 AVP Academic & Student Affairs ... Ms. Juletta PATRICK
35 Dean of Students ... Vacant
18 Director of Physical Facilities ... Mr. Gregory EVANS
09 Director Institutional Research ... Mr. Joseph BAUMANN
19 Director Campus Public Safety ... Mr. Michael CLESCERI
26 Dir Marketing & Public Relations ... Mrs. Christina HAGGERTY
84 Director Enrollment Services ... Ms. Marianne DEVENNY
88 Dean of Student Success ... Dr. Flecia THOMAS
101 Asst to the President/Board Liaison ... Mrs. Pat KRIEGERMEIER
72 Director Communication Technologies ... Mr. Dale NALEWAY
14 Director Application Solutions ... Ms. Marilyn SCHICK
88 Director End User Services ... Mr. Geary SMITH
88 Director of Network Services ... Mr. Rob RASMUSSEN
88 Exec Dir of Shah Center Programs ... Ms. Catherine JONES
103 Dean of Adult Education ... Mr. Richard CLUTE
41 Director Athletics-Intramural & Rec ... Mr. Wally REYNOLDS
40 Director Bookstore ... Ms. Cathie SCHERMAN
44 Director Institutional Advancement ... Ms. Patricia STEJSKAL
15 Director Employment Svcs/Diversity ... Ms. Sandra HESS MOLL
102 Executive Director MCC Foundation ... Mr. Bill BRENNAN
88 Director of Children's Learning Ctr ... Vacant
79 Exec Dean Humanities & Soc Sciences .. Dr. Thomas TAKAYAMA
81 Exec Dean Math/Sciences Health Pro ... Ms. Amy MAXEINER
66 Director Nursing ... Ms. Joan FLANAGAN
51 Exec Dean Cont & Professional Ed ... Ms. Kay MOORMANN
75 Exec Dean Career & Technical Educ ... Mr. James FALCO
96 Director of Business Services ... Ms. Jennifer JONES
88 Director Food Services ... Ms. Sandra JOHNSTON
29 Director Alumni Relations ... Mr. Bill BRENNAN
37 Director of Financial Aid ... Mr. Dane KLEE
88 Director of High School Plus ... Mr. Tony CAPALBO
106 Director of Online Learning ... Dr. Raymond LAWSON
08 Dean of Library ... Ms. Kathy HARGER
51 Dir of Continuing Education ... Ms. Dori SMITH
25 Director or Resource Development ... Dr. Marcella RECA ZIPP
23 Director of Health and Wellness ... Ms. Lena KALEMBA

McKendree University (A)

701 College Road, Lebanon IL 62254-9990
County: Saint Clair FICE Identification: 001722
Unit ID: 147013
Telephone: (618) 537-4481 Carnegie Class: Master's L
FAX Number: (618) 537-6259 Calendar System: Semester
URL: www.mckendree.edu
Established: 1828 Annual Undergrad Tuition & Fees: $24,340
Enrollment: 3,250 Coed
Affiliation or Control: United Methodist IRS Status: 501(c)3
Highest Offering: Doctorate
Program: Liberal Arts And General; Teacher Preparatory; Professional
Accreditation: NH, IACBE, NURSE, TED

01 President ... Dr. James M. DENNIS
03 Senior Vice President ... Ms. Victoria A. DOWLING
04 Assistant to the President ... Ms. Patti J. DANIELS
05 Provost/Dean of the University ... Dr. Christine M. BAHR
10 Vice Pres Finance/Administration ... Mrs. Sally A. MAYHEW
07 Vice Pres Admission & Financial Aid ... Mr. Chris HALL
32 Vice President Student Affairs ... Dr. Joni BASTIAN
09 Vice Pres Research Plng & Tech ... Dr. Mary E. BORNHEIMER
30 Asst VP Dev/Alumni/Parent Relations ... Ms. Kimberly A. MAYDEN
20 Associate Dean of the University ... Dr. Tami EGGLESTON
12 Assoc Dean McKendree-at-Scott ... Mr. Thomas A. PAWLOW
56 External Programs ... Dr. Joseph J. CIPFL
13 Director Technology Information ... Mr. George KRISS
06 Registrar/Asst Dean ... Ms. Debra LARSON
08 Librarian ... Ms. Rebecca SCHREINER
21 Comptroller/Budget Manager ... Mr. Paul ZINK
26 Exec Dir Marketing/Communications ... Mrs. Krysti H. CONNELLY
29 Director Alumni Relations ... Mrs. Whitney FRAIER
44 Director of Annual Giving ... Mr. Vincent PIAZZA
37 Director Financial Aid ... Mr. James MYERS
36 Director Career Services ... Ms. Jennifer K. PICKERELL
18 Director of Operations ... Mr. Edward M. WILLETT
15 Director Human Resources ... Ms. Shirley A. RENTZ
27 Director Media Relations ... Ms. Lisa K. BRANDON
39 Director of Residence Life ... Mr. Mitch NASSER
35 Director of Campus Activities ... Mr. Craig L. ROBERTSON
41 Athletic Director ... Mr. Chuck BRUEGGEMANN
42 Chaplain/Director Church Relations ... Rev Dr. B. Timothy HARRISON
40 Bookstore Director ... Ms. Rebecca B. MATHEWS
30 Director of Advancement Services ... Mr. Scott L. BILLHARTZ
19 Director Safety & Security ... Mr. Ranodore M. FOGGS
44 Director of Major Gifts ... Ms. Tricia POETTKER
88 Director of Student Accounts ... Mrs. Marsha GILES
28 Director of Diversity ... Mr. Brent W. REEVES

Meadville Lombard Theological School (B)

610 South Michigan Avenue, Chicago IL 60605
County: Cook FICE Identification: 001723
Unit ID: 147031
Telephone: (773) 256-3000 Carnegie Class: Spec/Faith
FAX Number: (312) 327-7002 Calendar System: Semester
URL: www.meadville.edu
Established: 1844 Annual Graduate Tuition & Fees: $17,460
Enrollment: 115 Coed
Affiliation or Control: Unitarian Universalist IRS Status: 501(c)3
Highest Offering: Doctorate; No Undergraduates
Program: Professional; Religious Emphasis
Accreditation: THEOL

01 President ... Dr. Lee BARKER
05 Provost ... Dr. Sharon WELCH
10 Vice Pres Finance & Administration ... Ms. Deborah BIEBER
30 Vice President of Development ... Vacant
08 Dean of Library ... Rev. Neil W. GERDES
32 Senior Director Student Services ... Ms. Tina PORTER

Methodist College (C)

415 St. Mark Court, Peoria IL 61603
County: Peoria FICE Identification: 006228
Unit ID: 147129
Telephone: (309) 672-5530 Carnegie Class: Spec/Health
FAX Number: (309) 671-8303 Calendar System: Semester
URL: www.methodistcol.edu
Established: 2000 Annual Undergrad Tuition & Fees: $15,725
Enrollment: 523 Coed
Affiliation or Control: Independent Non-Profit IRS Status: 501(c)3
Highest Offering: Baccalaureate
Program: Nursing Emphasis
Accreditation: NH, NUR, NURSE

01 President ... Dr. Kimberly JOHNSTON
05 Dean of Academic Affairs ... Dr. Linda PENDERGAST
84 Dean Enrollment Management ... Mr. David PETERSON
20 Director of Educational Tech ... Mr. Matthew HERTZOG
30 Director Business Svcs & Marketing ... Ms. Kirstin MARSHALL
15 Director Human Resources ... Ms. Linda MOORE
45 Director Inst Effectiveness ... Vacant
13 Director Information Management ... Mr. Bud SANDY

Midstate College (D)

411 W Northmoor Road, Peoria IL 61614-3558
County: Peoria FICE Identification: 004568
Unit ID: 147165
Telephone: (309) 692-4092 Carnegie Class: Bac/Assoc
FAX Number: (309) 692-3893 Calendar System: Quarter
URL: www.midstate.edu
Established: 1888 Annual Undergrad Tuition & Fees: $15,225
Enrollment: 632 Coed
Affiliation or Control: Proprietary IRS Status: Proprietary
Highest Offering: Baccalaureate
Program: Occupational; 2-Year Principally Bachelor's Creditable; Business Emphasis
Accreditation: NH, MAC

01 President ... Meredith N. BUNCH
03 Chief Executive Officer ... Meredith N. BUNCH
05 Chief Academic Dean ... Margaret J. STARR
09 Director of Assessment ... Sheryl KRISTENSEN
10 Controller ... Angie HATTEN
37 Director of Financial Assistance ... Irene BIMROSE
26 Director of Marketing & Enrollment ... Ashley SPAIN
32 Director of Student Affairs ... Rhonda P. URBAN
36 Director of Career Services ... Jennie GREENAN
08 Director of Library Resources ... Zachary M. BROWN

Midwest College of Oriental Medicine (E)

4334 N Hazel, Suite 102, Chicago IL 60613-1429
County: Cook Identification: 666090
Unit ID: 439020
Telephone: (773) 975-1295 Carnegie Class: Spec/Health
FAX Number: (773) 975-6511 Calendar System: Quarter
URL: www.acupuncture.edu
Established: 1979 Annual Undergrad Tuition & Fees: $11,759
Enrollment: 169 Coed
Affiliation or Control: Proprietary IRS Status: Proprietary
Highest Offering: Master's
Program: Professional
Accreditation: ACUP

01 President ... Dr. William DUNBAR
05 Academic Dean/Research Director ... Dr. Hui-Yan CAI
11 Administrative Director ... Dr. Robert CHELNICK
88 Special Projects Director ... Dr. Kristine L. LA POINT
37 Financial Aid Director ... Ms. Jennifer RHYNER
07 Admissions Coord/Transfer Credit ... Ms. Kelly A. WESTERLUND
06 Records Officer/Registrar ... Ms. Amy L. BENISH
08 Librarian ... Ms. Michelle C. KOPTEROS
32 Dean of Students ... Ms. Olga GAJDOSIK
09 Research Director ... Mr. Jin Hua XIE
63 Dean of Biomedicine Science ... Dr. Donald L. MARTIN
85 Dean of Foreign Students ... Dr. Duckin SUH
17 Internship Director ... Dr. Alan D. URETZ
45 Clinic Tracking/Inst Evaluation ... Ms. Deirdre M. DUNBAR
86 Compliance Officer ... Mr. Harry S. HEIFETZ
91 Information Systems ... Mr. Iosif G. LIFSHITS
26 Marketing/Student Affairs ... Mr. Chris A. KRAJNIAK

Midwestern University (F)

555 31st Street, Downers Grove IL 60515-1200
County: DuPage FICE Identification: 001657
Unit ID: 143853
Telephone: (630) 969-4400 Carnegie Class: Spec/Med
FAX Number: N/A Calendar System: Quarter
URL: www.midwestern.edu
Established: 1900 Annual Undergrad Tuition & Fees: N/A
Enrollment: 2,339 Coed
Affiliation or Control: Independent Non-Profit IRS Status: 501(c)3
Highest Offering: Doctorate
Program: Professional
Accreditation: NH, ARCPA, DENT, OSTEO, OT, PHAR, PTA

01 President/CEO ... Dr. Kathleen H. GOEPPINGER
03 Exec VP/Chief Operating Officer ... Dr. Arthur G. DOBBELAERE
10 Sr VP/Chief Financial Officer ... Mr. Gregory J. GAUS
21 Vice President Business Services ... Mr. Dean P. MALONE
26 Vice President University Relations ... Dr. Karen D. JOHNSON
05 VP/CAO Dental & Medical Education ... Dr. Dennis J. PAULSON
05 VP/CAO Pharmacy & Health Sci Educ ... Dr. Mary W L. LEE
11 VP Human Resources & Administration ... Ms. Angela L. MARTY
63 Dean Chicago Col of Osteo Medicine ... Dr. Karen J. NICHOLS
67 Dean Chicago College of Pharmacy ... Dr. Nancy F. FJORTOFT
76 Interim Dean Col Health Sciences ... Dr. Fred D. ROMANO
52 Dean College of Dental Medicine IL ... Dr. M. A. J. Lex MACNEIL
32 Dean for Student Services ... Dr. Teresa A. DOMBROWSKI
88 Director Finance ... Dr. Kimberly A. BROWN
08 University Librarian ... Ms. Natalie K. REED
06 Registrar ... Ms. Sue C. HARDWIDGE
46 Director Research & Sponsored Pgms ... Dr. James M. WOODS
07 Director of Admissions ... Mr. Michael J. LAKEN
30 Dir Development/Alumni Relations ... Ms. Karen L. WYSOCKI
09 Director of Institutional Research ... Dr. Kevin P. HYNES
14 Director Information Technology Svc ... Mr. Erik P. CARROLL
15 Director Human Resources ... Ms. Amy B. GIBSON
24 Director Media Resources ... Ms. Kathleen A M. DOOLEY
18 Director Campus Facilities ... Mr. Kevin M. MCCORMICK
37 Director Student Financial Services ... Mr. Nathan ERNST

† Tuition rates vary by program

Millikin University (G)

1184 W Main Street, Decatur IL 62522-2084
County: Macon FICE Identification: 001724
Unit ID: 147244
Telephone: (217) 424-6211 Carnegie Class: Bac/Diverse
FAX Number: (217) 424-3993 Calendar System: Semester
URL: www.millikin.edu
Established: 1901 Annual Undergrad Tuition & Fees: $27,852
Enrollment: 2,314 Coed
Affiliation or Control: Presbyterian Church (U.S.A.) IRS Status: 501(c)3
Highest Offering: Master's
Program: Liberal Arts And General; Teacher Preparatory; Professional; Nursing Emphasis
Accreditation: NH, ACBSP, ANEST, MUS, NURSE, TED

01 President ... Dr. Harold G. JEFFCOAT
05 Vice President Academic Affairs ... Mr. Barry N. PEARSON
10 Vice Pres Finance/Business Affs ... Mr. Richard RIEDER
30 Vice Pres University Development ... Mrs. Peggy S. LUY
84 Vice President of Enrollment ... Mr. Rich L. DUNSWORTH
32 Dean of Students ... Mrs. Raphaella PRANGE
100 Chief of Staff/Board Secretary ... Ms. Marilyn S. DAVIS
49 Dean of Arts & Sciences ... Dr. Randy M. BROOKS
57 Interim Dean of Fine Arts ... Ms. Laura LEDFORD
107 Int Dean Col of Professional Stds ... Dr. Deborah L. SLAYTON
50 Dean of Tabor School of Business ... Dr. James G. DAHL
06 Registrar ... Mr. Walter G. WESSEL
29 Director of Alumni Relations ... Dr. Janice G. DEVORE
44 Director of Major Gifts/Grant Devel ... Mrs. Anne-Marie P. BERK
36 Director of Career Center ... Ms. Pamela M. FOLGER
13 Director of Technology ... Mrs. Patricia A. PETTIT
08 Director of the Library ... Ms. Cindy FULLER
44 Director of Development ... Mr. Dave E. BRANDON
41 Director of Athletics ... Dr. Craig WHITE
53 Director of School of Education ... Dr. Nancy I. GAYLEN
88 Director Kirkland Fine Arts Ctr ... Mrs. Janiece L. SADDORIS-TRAUGHBER
28 Dir Ctr for Multicultural Stdnt Aff ... Ms. Latrina L. DENSON
104 Director Center for Intl Education ... Mrs. Carmen ARAVENA
15 Director Human Resources ... Ms. Diane L. LANE
21 Director of Fiscal Operations ... Mrs. Ruby F. BRASE
21 Controller ... Mrs. Vicki A. WRIGLEY
38 Director of Counseling Services ... Mr. Kevin C. GRAHAM
92 Director of Honors Program ... Dr. Cheryl L. CHAMBLIN
35 Director Student Programs ... Ms. Elizabeth J. EVANS
37 Director of Financial Aid ... Ms. Cheryl L. HOWERTON
51 Director of Extended Programs ... Vacant
58 Director of MBA Program ... Dr. Anthony F. LIBERATORE
64 Director School of Music ... Dr. Stephen B. WIDENHOFER
87 Director of Summer School ... Dr. James G. DAHL
09 Coord of Institutional Research ... Mrs. Laura A. BIRCH
19 Director of Safety and Security ... Mr. Chris BALLARD
105 Webmaster ... Mr. Curtis D. SHIRLEY
66 Director School of Nursing ... Dr. Deborah L. SLAYTON
07 Director of Admission ... Mr. Joe HAVIS
39 Director of Residence Life ... Mrs. Molly BERRY

Monmouth College (H)

700 E Broadway, Monmouth IL 61462-1963
County: Warren FICE Identification: 001725
Unit ID: 147341
Telephone: (309) 457-2311 Carnegie Class: Bac/A&S
FAX Number: (309) 457-2141 Calendar System: Semester
URL: www.monmouthcollege.edu
Established: 1853 Annual Undergrad Tuition & Fees: $37,750
Enrollment: 1,321 Coed
Affiliation or Control: Presbyterian Church (U.S.A.) IRS Status: 501(c)3

Highest Offering: Baccalaureate
Program: Liberal Arts And General; Teacher Preparatory
Accreditation: NH

01 President .... Dr. Mauri A. DITZLER
05 Dean of Faculty .... Dr. David M. TIMMERMAN
10 Vice President Finance & Business .. Mr. Donald L. GLADFELTER
30 Vice Pres Devel/College Relations .... Ms. Molly A. BALL
32 Vice Pres Student Life/Dn Students ..... Ms. Jacquelyn S. CONDON
84 Vice President Enrollment Mgmt .... Mr. Omar G. CORREA
06 Registrar .... Ms. Christine D. JOHNSTON
08 Director Hewes Library .... Mr. Richard SAYRE
37 Director of Financial Aid .... Ms. Jayne A. SCHRECK
29 Director of Alumni Programs .... Ms. Lucy THOMPSON
26 Director College Communications .... Mr. Jeffrey D. RANKIN
44 Director of Annual Giving .... Ms. Hannah MAHER
15 Director of Personnel Services .... Mr. Mike MCNALL
18 Director Facilities Management .... Mr. Earl WILFONG
20 Associate Dean of the Faculty .... Dr. Frank GERSICH
21 Controller .... Mrs. Debbie CLARK

Moody Bible Institute (A)

820 N Lasalle Boulevard, Chicago IL 60610-3263
County: Cook　FICE Identification: 001727
Unit ID: 147369
Telephone: (312) 329-4000　Carnegie Class: Spec/Faith
FAX Number: (312) 329-4109　Calendar System: Semester
URL: www.moody.edu
Established: 1886　Annual Undergrad Tuition & Fees: $9,950
Enrollment: 3,501　Coed
Affiliation or Control: Independent Non-Profit　IRS Status: 501(c)3
Highest Offering: First Professional Degree
Program: Liberal Arts And General; Professional; Religious Emphasis
Accreditation: NH, BI, MUS, THEOL

01 President .... Dr. J. Paul NYQUIST
05 Provost & Dean of Education .... Dr. Junias V. VENUGOPAL
11 Exec VP & Chief Operating Officer .... Mr. Steven A. MOGCK
43 Vice President & General Counsel .... Mrs. Elizabeth A. BROWN
20 VP/Dean of Undergraduate School .... Dr. Larry J. DAVIDHIZAR
58 VP/Dean of Graduate School .... Dr. John A. JELINEK
16 Vice President Human Resources .... Mr. Lloyd R. DODSON
88 Vice President Broadcasting .... Mr. Collin LAMBERT
30 Vice President Stewardship .... Mr. James ELLIOTT
13 Vice President Information Systems .... Mr. Frank W. LEBER
26 Vice Pres Corporate Communications .... Mrs. Christine GORZ
45 Vice Pres/Dean of Educ Services .... Vacant
84 Vice President of Student Services .... Dr. Tom A. SHAW
18 Division Manager Facilities .... Mr. Konrad FINCK
56 Dir Customer Rels/Distance Lrng Ctr .... Mr. John KNIGHT
32 Dean of Students .... Dr. Timothy E. ARENS
07 Dean of Admissions .... Mr. Charles E. DRESSER
38 Associate Dean Counseling Services .... Mr. Steve BRASEL
35 Associate Dean for Student Programs .... Mr. Joseph M. GONZALES, JR.
36 Assoc Dean of Career Development .... Mr. Patrick FRIEDLINE
39 Associate Dean Residence Life .... Mr. Bruce R. NORQUIST
37 Director of Financial Aid .... Mrs. Berdia MARSHALL
06 Registrar/Director of Acad Records .... Mr. George MOSHER
08 Department Manager Library .... Mr. James PRESTON
29 Exec Director Alumni Association .... Mrs. Nancy HASTINGS
41 Athletic Director .... Mr. Daniel DUNN
10 Chief Fin Ofcr/Treasurer/Asst Secy .... Mr. Ken HEULITT
21 Controller .... Miss Linda WAHR
23 Admin of Health Service .... Miss Ann MEYER
96 Manager of Procurement Services .... Mr. Paul BRACKLEY
09 Institutional Researcher .... Mr. Gregory GAERTNER

† Tuition is paid through donor contributions. Fees are $1,950.00 per year.

Moraine Valley Community College (B)

9000 W College Parkway, Palos Hills IL 60465-0937
County: Cook　FICE Identification: 007692
Unit ID: 147378
Telephone: (708) 974-4300　Carnegie Class: Assoc/Pub-S-SC
FAX Number: (708) 974-1184　Calendar System: Semester
URL: www.morainevalley.edu
Established: 1967　Annual Undergrad Tuition & Fees (In-District): $3,630
Enrollment: 18,169　Coed
Affiliation or Control: State/Local　IRS Status: 501(c)3
Highest Offering: Associate Degree
Program: Occupational; 2-Year Principally Bachelor's Creditable
Accreditation: NH, COMTA, MAC, POLYT, RAD

01 President .... Dr. Sylvia JENKINS
05 Vice President Academic Affairs .... Vacant
32 Vice President Student Devel .... Dr. Normah SALLEH-BARONE
11 Exec Vice Pres Administrative Svcs .... Mr. Andrew M. DUREN
10 Chief Financial Officer .... Mr. Robert STERKOWITZ
13 Chief Information Officer .... Mr. Jack LEIFEL
50 Dean Science/Business/Comp Tech .... Dr. Pamela HANEY
49 Dean Liberal Arts .... Mr. Walter FRONCZEK
38 Dean Counseling & Advising .... Ms. Joann WRIGHT
84 Dean Enrollment Services .... Mr. Severo BALASON
51 Dean Corporate/Cmty & Cont Educ .... Mr. Albert LEWIS
36 Dean Career Programs .... Ms. Margaret MACHON
35 Dean Student Services .... Vacant
88 Dean Learn Enrich & Col Readiness .... Mr. Michael MORSCHES
56 Asst Dean/Dir Academic Outreach .... Ms. Maureen FARRELL
32 Asst Dean Code of Conduct & St Life .... Mr. Kent MARSHALL
37 Director Financial Aid .... Ms. Laurie ANEMA
09 Dir Institutional Research/Planning .... Ms. Elizabeth REIS
19 Chief of Police .... Mr. Patrick O'CONNOR
15 Director Human Resources .... Ms. Lynn HARRINGTON
07 Director of Admissions/Recruitment .... Ms. Claudia ROSELLI
26 Director College & Cmty Relations .... Mr. Mark HORSTMEYER
18 Director Campus Operations .... Mr. Rick BRENNAN
40 Director Auxiliary Svcs .... Mr. Kashif SHAH
41 Director Athletics .... Mr. William FINN
85 Asst Dean Intl Student Admissions .... Ms. Diane VIVERITO
27 Director Mktg & Creative Services .... Ms. Delores J. BROOKS
44 Dir Res Devel/Extended Programs .... Dr. Sharon KATTERMAN
21 Controller .... Ms. Theresa O'CARROLL
42 Campus Minister .... Mr. Bill DROEL
88 Director Center Disability Services .... Ms. Debbie SIEVERS
96 Director of Purchasing .... Ms. Jane BENTLEY

Morrison Institute of Technology (C)

701 Portland Avenue, Morrison IL 61270-2959
County: Whiteside　FICE Identification: 008880
Unit ID: 147396
Telephone: (815) 772-7218　Carnegie Class: Assoc/PrivNFP
FAX Number: (815) 772-7584　Calendar System: Semester
URL: www.morrisontech.edu
Established: 1973　Annual Undergrad Tuition & Fees: $15,100
Enrollment: 92　Coed
Affiliation or Control: Independent Non-Profit　IRS Status: 501(c)3
Highest Offering: Associate Degree
Program: 2-Year Principally Bachelor's Creditable; Technical Emphasis
Accreditation: COE, ENGT

01 Chief Executive Officer .... Mr. Christopher D. SCOTT
05 Vice President of Academic Affairs .... Mr. Greg J. TULLY

Morton College (D)

3801 S Central Avenue, Cicero IL 60804-4398
County: Cook　FICE Identification: 001728
Unit ID: 147411
Telephone: (708) 656-8000　Carnegie Class: Assoc/Pub-S-SC
FAX Number: (708) 656-3297　Calendar System: Semester
URL: www.morton.edu
Established: 1924　Annual Undergrad Tuition & Fees (In-District): $3,188
Enrollment: 5,321　Coed
Affiliation or Control: State/Local　IRS Status: 501(c)3
Highest Offering: Associate Degree
Program: Occupational; 2-Year Principally Bachelor's Creditable
Accreditation: NH, PTAA

01 Interim President .... Dr. R. Gene GARDNER
05 VP Academic/Student Development .... Mr. Muhammad SIDDIQI
32 Director of Student Development .... Vacant
51 Dean Adult Educ/Cmty Prgms/Outreach .... Mr. James YOUNG
08 Director of Library .... Ms. Jennifer BUTLER
15 Director of Human Resources .... Mr. Kenneth STOCK
31 Director Community & Business Svcs .... Ms. Susan FELICE
09 Director Institutional Research .... Ms. Magda BANDA
18 Director of Facilities & Operations .... Mr. John S. POTEMPA
37 Director of Financial Aid .... Ms. Yolanda FREEMON

National-Louis University (E)

122 S Michigan Avenue, Chicago IL 60603
County: Cook　FICE Identification: 001733
Unit ID: 147536
Telephone: (888) 658-8632　Carnegie Class: DRU
FAX Number: N/A　Calendar System: Quarter
URL: www.nl.edu
Established: 1886　Annual Undergrad Tuition & Fees: $18,540
Enrollment: 5,679　Coed
Affiliation or Control: Independent Non-Profit　IRS Status: 501(c)3
Highest Offering: Doctorate
Program: Teacher Preparatory; Professional
Accreditation: NH, IACBE, TED

01 President .... Dr. Nivine MEGAHED
05 Provost .... Dr. Christine J. QUINN
30 Vice Pres Institutional Advancement .... Mr. John BERGHOLZ
15 Vice President Human Resources .... Mr. Tom BERGMANN
10 Vice Pres Finance & Administration .... Mr. Marty MICKEY
84 Vice Pres Enrollment Mgmt .... Ms. Bobbi BIRINGER
14 Vice President Operational Services .... Vacant
26 Vice Pres Marketing/Communications .... Dr. Joselyn ZIVIN
09 Vice Provost Institutional Effect .... Dr. Marsha WATSON
20 Vice Prov Acad Pgm & Fac Dev .... Dr. Kathleen SHERIDAN
88 Asst Vice Prov Advising/Retention .... Mr. Stephen NEER
50 Int Dean College of Mgmt/Business .... Dr. Walter ROETTGER
53 Dean Natl College of Education .... Dr. Alison HILSABECK
49 Int Dean College of Arts & Science .... Vacant
08 Dean University Library .... Ms. Kathleen WALSH
32 Exec Dir Stdnt Affs/Ombudsperson .... Mr. Brisbane ROUZAN
12 Exec Director Milwaukee/Beloit .... Mr. Robert VANCE
12 Exec Director Florida Regional .... Dr. George VALCOURT
43 Exec Director of Legal Services .... Mrs. McCeil J. JOHNSON
28 Director of Employment/Diversity .... Ms. Erin HAULOTTE
37 Director of Student Finance .... Mr. Steve DIBENEDETTO
07 Director of Admissions/Registrar .... Mr. Ken KASPRZAK
36 Director of Career Services .... Vacant
29 President Alumni Advisory Board .... Vacant
51 Director Outreach Academic Pgm .... Ms. Karen HAWORTH
35 Director of Student Life .... Ms. Maria MEINTANIS
23 Student Health Services Coordinator .... Vacant

National University of Health Sciences (F)

200 E Roosevelt Road, Lombard IL 60148-4583
County: DuPage　FICE Identification: 001732
Unit ID: 147590
Telephone: (630) 629-2000　Carnegie Class: Spec/Health
FAX Number: (630) 889-6600　Calendar System: Trimester
URL: www.nuhs.edu
Established: 1906　Annual Undergrad Tuition & Fees: $8,884
Enrollment: 869　Coed
Affiliation or Control: Independent Non-Profit　IRS Status: 501(c)3
Highest Offering: First Professional Degree
Program: Liberal Arts And General; Professional; Technical Emphasis
Accreditation: NH, ACUP, CHIRO, COMTA, @NATUR

01 President .... Dr. James F. WINTERSTEIN
05 Vice President Academic Services .... Dr. Vincent F. DE BONO
10 Vice President Business Services .... Mr. Ron MENSCHING
11 Vice Pres Administrative Services .... Ms. Tracy MCHUGH
76 Dean College Allied Health Sciences .... Dr. Randy L. SWENSON
51 Dean Col Postprofessional Educ .... Dr. Jonathan SOLTYS
23 Dean of Clinics .... Dr. David PARISH
107 Dean Col Professional Studies FL .... Dr. Joseph STIEFEL
107 Dean Col Professional Studies IL .... Dr. Nicholas TRONGALE
46 Dean of Research .... Dr. Gregory D. CRAMER
32 Dean of Students .... Dr. Daniel R. DRISCOLL
108 Dean Academic Assessment .... Dr. Chad MAOLA
88 Dean Accreditation .... Mr. Keith WEROSH
08 Chair Learning Resource Center .... Ms. Joyce E. WHITEHEAD
06 University Registrar .... Ms. Izabela DUBAK
07 Dir Communication/Enrollment Svcs .... Ms. Victoria SWEENEY
21 Director of Financial Services .... Ms. Sue UNGER
37 Director of Financial Aid .... Mr. Robert DAME
18 Director Maintenance & Facilities .... Mr. Tom ROHNER
15 Director of Human Resources .... Mr. Andrew WOZNIAK
26 Chief Public Relations Officer .... Ms. Christine LUCENTA
30 Director Alumni & Development .... Ms. Shawna MCDONOUGH
13 Dir Management Information Services .... Mr. Kurt FALER
39 Coordinator of Housing .... Ms. Pam THOMAS
40 Bookstore Manager .... Ms. Mary BASSETT

North Central College (G)

30 N Brainard Street, Naperville IL 60540-4607
County: DuPage　FICE Identification: 001734
Unit ID: 147660
Telephone: (630) 637-5100　Carnegie Class: Master's M
FAX Number: (630) 637-5121　Calendar System: Trimester
URL: www.northcentralcollege.edu
Established: 1861　Annual Undergrad Tuition & Fees: $30,891
Enrollment: 2,989　Coed
Affiliation or Control: United Methodist　IRS Status: 501(c)3
Highest Offering: Master's
Program: Liberal Arts And General
Accreditation: NH

01 President .... Dr. Harold R. WILDE
04 Exec Secy/Assistant to President .... Ms. Margaret A. WIORA
05 Vice President Academic Affairs .... Dr. R. Devadoss PANDIAN
10 Vice President Business Affairs .... Mr. Paul H. LOSCHEIDER
30 Vice Pres Institutional Advancement .... Mr. Rick E. SPENCER
84 VP Enrollment Management/Stdnt Svcs .... Ms. Laurie M. HAMEN
16 Asst Vice Pres Human Resources .... Ms. Michelle M. SKINDER
26 Asst Vice President Mktg/Communic .... Mr. James GODO
21 Asst VP for Business Operations .... Mr. Michael J. HUDSON
20 Associate Academic Dean .... Dr. Marti S. BOGART
07 Dean of Admissions .... Mr. Marty R. SAUER
32 Dean of Students .... Ms. Kimberly SLUIS
58 Dean of Graduate Pgms/Continuing Ed .... Dr. Peter S. BARGER
06 Registrar .... Mr. Jonathan M. PICKERING
08 Director of the Library .... Mr. John J. SMALL
36 Director of Career Development .... Mr. Jeffrey D. DENARD
37 Director of Financial Aid .... Mr. Marty ROSSMAN
23 Director of the Wellness Center .... Ms. Sally CARPENTER
31 Director of Cmty Educ/Conf/Camps .... Mr. Michael E. SQUIRE
41 Athletic Director .... Mr. James MILLER
21 AVP Finance/Controller .... Vacant
39 Director of Residence Life .... Mr. Kevin E. MCCARTHY
42 Campus Chaplain .... Rev. Lynn L. PRIES
90 Director of Technology Services .... Dr. Kathy A. WILDERS
44 Director of Planned Giving .... Mr. Bruce NORTELL
09 Director of Institutional Research .... Mr. Jonathan M. PICKERING
29 Director Alumni Relations .... Mr. Adrian M. ALDRICH
28 Director of Multicultural Affairs .... Ms. Dorothy J. PLEAS

North Park University (H)

3225 W Foster Avenue, Chicago IL 60625-4895
County: Cook　FICE Identification: 001735
Unit ID: 147679
Telephone: (773) 244-6200　Carnegie Class: Master's L
FAX Number: (773) 244-4953　Calendar System: Semester
URL: www.northpark.edu
Established: 1891　Annual Undergrad Tuition & Fees: $22,090
Enrollment: 3,223　Coed
Affiliation or Control: Evangelical Covenant Church Of America
IRS Status: 501(c)3
Highest Offering: Doctorate

Program: Liberal Arts And General; Teacher Preparatory; Professional
Accreditation: NH, IACBE, MUS, NURSE, THEOL

01	President	Dr. David L. PARKYN
10	Executive Vice President/CFO	Mr. Carl E. BALSAM
05	Provost	Dr. Joseph JONES
84	Vice Pres for Enrollment/Marketing	Mr. Nathan MOUTTET
30	Vice President for Development	Ms. Mary M. SURRIDGE
73	Seminary Dean	Dr. Davide W. KERSTEN
49	Dean of Arts & Sciences	Dr. Charles I. PETERSON
51	Dean School of Adult Learning	Dr. Bryan WATKINS
50	Dean School of Business & NFP Mgmt	Dr. Wesley LINDAHL
53	Dean School of Education	Dr. Rebecca NELSON
64	Dean School of Music	Dr. Craig JOHNSON
66	Dean School of Nursing	Dr. Linda DUNCAN
09	Director of Institutional Research	Dr. Robert STANLEY
28	Dean of Diversity & Intercult Pgm	Dr. Terry LINDSAY
32	Dean of Student Development	Ms. Andrea NEVELS
08	Director of Library	Ms. Sally A. ANDERSON
07	Director of Admissions	Mr. Mark OLSON
38	Director Counseling/Health Services	Ms. Juanita BARRETT
37	Director Financial Aid Services	Dr. Lucy G. SHAKER
14	Director of Computer Center	Mr. Steven P. CLARK
15	Director of Human Resources	Ms. Ingrid K. TENGLIN
18	Director of Environmental Services	Mr. Carl H. WISTROM
19	Director of Security	Mr. Daniel GOORIS
21	Director of Finance	Mr. Lester H. CARLSTROM
26	University Marketing & Communic	Mr. Nathan MOUTTET
41	Athletic Director	Mr. Jack F. SURRIDGE
42	Director University Ministries	Mr. Anthony ZAMBLE
36	Director of Career Planning	Ms. Colette HANDS
06	Registrar	Mr. Aaron D. SCHOOF
29	Alumni Relations Manager	Ms. Melissa VELEZ LUCE

Northeastern Illinois University (A)

5500 N Saint Louis Avenue, Chicago IL 60625-4699
County: Cook — FICE Identification: 001693
Unit ID: 147776
Telephone: (773) 583-4050 — Carnegie Class: Master's L
FAX Number: (773) 442-4900 — Calendar System: Semester
URL: www.neiu.edu
Established: 1867 — Annual Undergrad Tuition & Fees (In-State): $8,089
Enrollment: 11,580 — Coed
Affiliation or Control: State — IRS Status: 501(c)3
Highest Offering: Master's
Program: Liberal Arts And General; Teacher Preparatory; Professional; Fine Arts Emphasis
Accreditation: NH, ART, CACREP, CORE, MUS, SW, TED

01	President	Dr. Sharon K. HAHS
05	Acting Provost	Dr. Victoria A. ROMAN-LAGUNAS
10	Vice Pres Finance & Administration	Mr. Mark WILCOCKSON
32	Vice President for Student Affairs	Dr. Frank E. ROSS
30	Vice President Instnl Advancement	Ms. Melba RODRIGUEZ
28	AVP Diversity & Intercultural Affs	Vacant
35	Associate VP for Student Affairs	Dr. Daniel LOPEZ, JR.
36	Dir Academic & Career Advising	Vacant
07	Associate VP Enrollment Services	Dr. Janice HARRING-HENDON
21	Executive Director of Univ Budgets	Dr. Helen C. ANG
08	Dean of Libraries & Learning Rscs	Vacant
09	Director Institutional Research	Mr. Blase E. MASINI
15	Human Resources Director	Ms. Marta E. MASO
25	Acting Director Sponsored Programs	Mr. Jonathan P. TEUBER
26	Asst VP Marketing & Public Rels	Ms. Erika M. KREHBIEL
37	Director Financial Aid	Ms. Maureen T. AMOS
50	Dean College Business/Management	Dr. Amy B. HIETAPELTO
58	Interim Dean of Graduate College	Dr. Marcelo O. SZTAINBERG
53	Dean College of Education	Dr. Maureen D. GILLETTE
49	Dean College of Arts & Sciences	Dr. Wamucii E. NJOGU
13	Exec Dir Univ Technology Services	Mr. Kim TRACY
18	Asst Vice Pres Facilities Mgmt	Ms. Nancy MEDINA
19	Director University Police Dept	Mr. James C. LYON, JR.
21	Director Financial Affs/Controller	Ms. Peggy HO
22	Dir Univ Outreach/Equal Employment	Dr. Roberto A. SANABRIA
86	Director of Government Relations	Ms. Suleyma PEREZ
06	Registrar	Mr. Daniel R. WEBER
29	Director of Alumni Relations	Ms. Damaris TAPIA
38	Director Counseling Office	Vacant
96	Director of Purchasing/Auxil Svcs	Mr. Robert FILIPP

Northern Illinois University (B)

De Kalb IL 60115-2825
County: De Kalb — FICE Identification: 001737
Unit ID: 147703
Telephone: (815) 753-1000 — Carnegie Class: RU/H
FAX Number: (815) 753-0198 — Calendar System: Semester
URL: www.niu.edu
Established: 1895 — Annual Undergrad Tuition & Fees (In-State): $11,474
Enrollment: 22,990 — Coed
Affiliation or Control: State — IRS Status: 501(c)3
Highest Offering: Doctorate
Program: Liberal Arts And General; Teacher Preparatory; Professional
Accreditation: NH, ART, AUD, BUS, BUSA, CACREP, CLPSY, CORE, DIETD, DIETI, ENG, ENGT, IPSY, LAW, MFCD, MT, MUS, NAIT, NURSE, PH, PTA, SCPSY, SP, SPAA, TED, THEA

01	President	John G. PETERS
05	Executive Vice Pres & Provost	Raymond W. ALDEN, III
20	Vice Provost Academic Planning/Dev	Carolinda DOUGLASS
10	Exec Vice Pres/Chief of Operations	Eddie R. WILLIAMS
30	Vice Pres Univ Advance/Development	Michael P. MALONE
45	Vice Prov Resource Planning	Susan MINI
11	VP Admin/University Outreach	Anne C. KAPLAN
32	Acting VP Student Affs/Enroll Mgmt	Kelly WESENER MICHAEL
46	Vice Pres for Research/Grad Studies	Lisa C. FREEMAN
26	Vice Pres External Affairs	Kathryn A. BUETTNER
43	VP/General Counsel/Legal Svcs	Jerry D. BLAKEMORE
102	President NIU Foundation/Devel	Mallory M. SIMPSON
13	Assoc Vice Pres Info Tech Services	Walter L. CZERNIAK
18	Assoc Vice Pres Finance Facility Op	Robert C. ALBANESE
15	Assoc VP Admin/Human Resources	Steven D. CUNNINGHAM
35	Assoc VP for Student Affairs	John Raymond JONES
51	Assoc Vice President NIU Outreach	John L. LEWIS
23	Director Health Services	Christine GRADY
07	Assoc VP Student Affs/Enroll Mgmt	Katherine MCCARTHY
28	Asst Vice Pres Diversity/Equity	James BRUNSEN
20	Vice Provost	Anne BIRBERICK
50	Dean of Business	Denise SCHOENBACHLER
53	Dean of Education	La Vonne NEAL
54	Dean of Engineering/Engr Tech	Promod VOHRA
61	Dean of Law	Jennifer ROSATO
49	Dean Liberal Arts & Sciences	Christopher MCCORD
76	Dean Health & Human Sciences	Derryl BLOCK
57	Dean Visual & Performing Arts	Richard HOLLY
58	Dean Grad Sch/AVP Grad Studies	Bradley BOND
85	Assoc Prov International Programs	Deborah L. PIERCE
84	Asst Vice Prov Enrollment Services	Vacant
31	Exec Dir Community Relations	Rena COTSONES
12	Director Lorado Taft Field Campus	Diana DENNIS
12	Director Outreach Centers	Brian VOLLMERT
12	Director NIU Naperville	Brian BECKER
06	Director Registration & Records	Jerry MONTAG
09	Director of Institutional Research	J. Daniel HOUSE
24	Director of Media Services	Jay ORBIK
25	Director of Sponsored Projects	David STONE
36	Exec Director of Career Services	Cindy HENDERSON
37	Director of Student Financial Aid	Kathleen D. BRUNSON
38	Director of Counseling/Student Dev	Micky M. SHARMA
40	Director of University Bookstore	Mitch KIELB
19	Police Chief/Public Safety	Donald GRADY
41	Athletic Director	Jeff COMPHER
91	Director Enterprise Info Systems	Kimberly S. HENSLEY
39	Executive Director Housing & Dining	Kelly WESENER
88	Director Access-Ability Resources	Melanie THOMPSON
29	Director Alumni Relations	Patricia ANDERSON
96	Director of Purchasing	Al MUELLER

Northern Seminary (C)

660 E Butterfield Road, Lombard IL 60148-5698
County: DuPage — FICE Identification: 001736
Unit ID: 147697
Telephone: (630) 620-2180 — Carnegie Class: Spec/Faith
FAX Number: (630) 620-2190 — Calendar System: Quarter
URL: www.seminary.edu
Established: 1913 — Annual Graduate Tuition & Fees: $12,927
Enrollment: 150 — Coed
Affiliation or Control: American Baptist — IRS Status: 501(c)3
Highest Offering: Doctorate; No Undergraduates
Program: Professional; Religious Emphasis
Accreditation: NH, THEOL

01	President/Chief Academic Officer	Dr. Alistair BROWN
05	Dean of Academic Programs	Dr. Karen WALKER-FREEBURG
20	Dean of Academic Administration	Mr. Blake WALTER
30	Exec Dir Advancement/Enroll Mgmt	Mr. Greg HENSON
06	Registrar	Ms. Marilyn R. MAST HEWITT
88	Director Doctoral Studies	Dr. Karen WALKER-FREEBURG
32	Director Student Services	Ms. Marilyn MAST HEWITT
15	Director Human Resources	Vacant
13	Director of Information Technology	Mr. Dwight HAWLEY

Northwestern College (D)

9501 Technology Blvd; Suite 425, Rosemont IL 60018
County: Cook — FICE Identification: 012362
Unit ID: 147749
Telephone: (847) 233-7700 — Carnegie Class: Assoc/PrivFP
FAX Number: (847) 233-7705 — Calendar System: Quarter
URL: www.northwesterncollege.edu
Established: 1902 — Annual Undergrad Tuition & Fees: $16,520
Enrollment: 1,625 — Coed
Affiliation or Control: Proprietary — IRS Status: Proprietary
Highest Offering: Associate Degree
Program: Occupational; 2-Year Principally Bachelor's Creditable
Accreditation: NH, ACBSP, MAC, RAD

01	President	Mr. Lawrence SCHUMACHER
03	Executive VP of Operations	Mrs. Gail SCHUMACHER
11	Vice President of Campus Operations	Mrs. Cynthia REYNOLDS
10	Controller	Ms. Leslie RODRIGUEZ
05	VP of Academic Affairs	Mrs. Diane MAREK
13	VP of Technology	Mr. David HOMAN
32	VP of Student Affairs	Mrs. Barbara ANDERSON-SAPATA
08	Director of Library Services	Ms. Sarah DULAY
12	Director of Bridgeview Campus	Mr. Tony SAPATA
12	Director of Naperville Campus	Ms. Mary REYNOLDS
12	Director of Chicago Campus	Mrs. Laura SORIA
16	Chief Human Resources Officer	Ms. Cheri CANFIELD
37	Director of Financial Assistance	Mrs. Ethel ARROYO
38	Director of Counseling	Ms. Alexandra DELLUTRI
106	Distance Education Director	Ms. Jenifer VIENCEK
07	Director of Admissions	Mr. Shahed KASEM
07	Director of Admissions	Ms. Tina FURNACE
07	Director of Admissions	Ms. Cindy SHEFFIELD
11	Dir of Administration Bridgeview	Mrs. Margie BENNECKE
11	Director of Administration Chicago	Mrs. Nubia CASTILLO
66	Director of Nursing	Ms. Lisa EVOY
06	Registrar	Ms. Sharon FORBES
36	Career Development Coordinator	Ms. Amy BUOSCIO
76	Program Director - AH	Mrs. Joyce MCNAMARA
97	Program Director - GE	Mr. David COOPER
50	Program Director - SC	Mr. Willie MORRIS
61	Program Director - LS	Mr. Joseph PECKO

Northwestern University (E)

633 Clark Street, Evanston IL 60208-3854
County: Cook — FICE Identification: 001739
Unit ID: 147767
Telephone: (847) 491-3741 — Carnegie Class: RU/VH
FAX Number: (847) 491-7364 — Calendar System: Quarter
URL: www.northwestern.edu
Established: 1851 — Annual Undergrad Tuition & Fees: $43,380
Enrollment: 20,284 — Coed
Affiliation or Control: Independent Non-Profit — IRS Status: 501(c)3
Highest Offering: Doctorate
Program: Liberal Arts And General; Teacher Preparatory; Professional
Accreditation: NH, #ARCPA, AUD, BUS, CLPSY, ENG, HSA, IPSY, JOUR, LAW, MED, MFCD, MUS, OPE, PH, PTA, SP

01	President	Dr. Morton O. SCHAPIRO
05	Provost	Dr. Daniel I. LINZER
10	Sr Vice Pres Business/Finance	Mr. Eugene S. SUNSHINE
32	Vice President Student Affairs	Dr. Patricia TELLES-IRVIN
26	Vice President University Relations	Mr. Alan K. CUBBAGE
45	Vice Pres Administration & Planning	Ms. Marilyn MCCOY
13	Vice Pres Information Technology	Mr. Sean B. REYNOLDS
30	Vice Pres for Alumni Rel & Devel	Mr. Robert MCQUINN
46	Vice President Research	Mr. Joseph T. WALSH
88	Vice Pres/Chief Investment Officer	Mr. William H. MCLEAN
43	Vice President/General Counsel	Mr. Thomas G. CLINE
84	Associate Provost Univ Enrollment	Mr. Michael E. MILLS
53	Associate Provost Undergrad Educ	Dr. Ronald R. BRAEUTIGAM
20	Associate Provost Faculty Affairs	Dr. James B. YOUNG
20	Assoc Provost Academic Initiatives	Mr. Jake JULIA
21	Assoc Prov Budget/Facil/Analysis	Ms. Jean E. SHEDD
86	Spec Asst to Pres for Govt Rels	Mr. Bruce LAYTON
04	Assistant to the President	Mr. Eugene Y. LOWE, JR.
100	Director Office of the President	Ms. Judith V. REMINGTON
41	Athletic Director	Mr. James J. PHILLIPS
72	Dean Sch Engr/Applied Science	Dr. Julio M. OTTINO
50	Dean Graduate School of Management	Dr. Sally E. BLOUNT
60	Dean School of Journalism	Dr. Bradley J. HAMM
64	Dean School of Music	Dr. Toni-Marie MONTGOMERY
63	Dean School of Medicine	Dr. Eric G. NEILSON
51	Dean/Assoc Prov Conting Educ	Dr. Thomas F. GIBBONS
58	Dean Graduate School	Mr. Dwight A. MCBRIDE
60	Dean School of Communication	Dr. Barbara J. O'KEEFE
53	Dean School of Education	Dr. Penelope L. PETERSON
49	Dean College Arts & Science	Dr. Sarah C. MANGELSDORF
61	Dean School of Law	Dr. Daniel B. RODRIGUEZ
08	University Librarian	Ms. Sarah M. PRITCHARD
36	Director of Univ Career Services	Dr. Lonnie J. DUNLAP
35	Dean of Students	Mr. Burgwell HOWARD
29	Asc VP Alum Rel/Ex Dir NW Alum Assn	Ms. Catherine L. STEMBRIDGE
88	Assoc Vice President for Research	Mr. Lewis SMITH
88	Assoc Vice President for Research	Ms. Linda HICKE
88	Assoc VP for Rsrch Innov & New Vent	Ms. Alicia LOFFLER
88	Assoc Vice President for Research	Ms. Ann ADAMS
21	Assoc Vice Pres Budget Planning	Mr. James M. HURLEY
18	Assoc Vice Pres Facilities Mgmt	Mr. Ronald NAYLER
16	Assoc Vice Pres for Human Resources	Ms. Pamela BEEMER
21	Assoc Vice Pres Finance/Controller	Ms. Ingrid S. STAFFORD
07	Dean of Undergraduate Admissions	Mr. Christopher WATSON
88	Ex Dir Technology Transfer Pgm	Ms. Indrani MUKHARJI
23	Medical Director of Health Services	Dr. John ALEXANDER
39	Director of Residential Life	Ms. Mary GOLDENBERG
38	Director of Counseling/Psych Svcs	Dr. John H. DUNKLE
42	University Chaplain	Dr. Timothy S. STEVENS
09	Director Analytical Studies	Vacant
88	Director University Housing	Ms. Theresa M. DELIN
88	Dir Program Review/Spec Project	Mr. Jeremy HUNSUCKER
71	Planning/Special Projects Director	Ms. Evelyn CALIENDO
88	Director Univ Center/Student Svcs	Mr. Richard R. THOMAS
88	Director University Services	Mr. Brian S. PETERS
06	Registrar	Ms. Michele A. NEARY
37	Director Financial Aid	Ms. Carolyn V. LINDLEY
15	Dir HR Consulting Svcs/Staffing	Mr. Paul CORONA
19	Chief of University Police	Mr. Bruce LEWIS
21	Director Auditing	Ms. Betty L. MCPHILIMY
22	Dir Equal Emply Oppprty/Affirm Act	Ms. Pamela PIRTLE
96	Director University Svcs Purchasing	Mr. Jim KONRAD

Oakton Community College (F)

1600 E Golf Road, Des Plaines IL 60016-1256
County: Cook — FICE Identification: 009896
Unit ID: 147800
Telephone: (847) 635-1600 — Carnegie Class: Assoc/Pub-S-MC
FAX Number: (847) 635-1992 — Calendar System: Semester
URL: www.oakton.edu
Established: 1969 — Annual Undergrad Tuition & Fees (In-District): $2,812
Enrollment: 5,956 — Coed

Affiliation or Control: Local IRS Status: 501(c)3
Highest Offering: Associate Degree
Program: Occupational; 2-Year Principally Bachelor's Creditable; Business Emphasis
Accreditation: NH, ADNUR, MLTAD, PTAA

01 President ... Dr. Margaret B. LEE
05 Vice President Academic Affairs ... Dr. Thomas HAMEL
20 Assistant VP Academic Affairs ... Dr. Nancy PRENDERGAST
32 Vice President Student Affairs ... Dr. Joianne SMITH
10 Vice President Business & Finance ... Mr. Carl F. COSTANZA
51 AVP Cont Ed & Trng/Wrkforce Dev ... Dr. Merrill IRVING
13 Vice Pres Information Technology ... Ms. Bonnie LUCAS
76 Dean Science & Health Careers ... Dr. Adam HAYASHI
81 Dean Math & Technology ... Dr. Robert SOMPOLSKI
60 Dean Language/Humanities & the Arts ... Ms. Linda KORBEL
83 Dean Social Science/Business ... Mr. Bradley WOOTEN
26 Exec Director College Advancement ... Dr. Carlee DRUMMER
09 Director Research ... Dr. Trudy H. BERS
08 Director Library & Media Svcs ... Mr. Gary NEWHOUSE
35 Interim Dean of Students ... Mr. Cary SCHAWEL
84 Dir of Student Recruitment/Outreach ... Ms. Michele BROWN
06 Director of Registrar Services ... Mr. Bruce OATES
35 Director of Student Life ... Ms. Ann Marie BARRY
88 Director of Student Success ... Mr. Sebastian CONTRERAS, JR.
41 Director of Athletics ... Mr. Bruce OATES
13 Director Systems & Network Svcs ... Mr. John WADE
50 Dir Business Institute/Prof Educ ... Ms. Lynn SEINFELD
21 Director of Accounting Services ... Mr. Raul GARCIA
21 Director of Business Services ... Ms. Doreen SCHWARTZ
15 Associate VP Human Resources ... Mr. D. Arnie OUDENHOVEN
18 Director of Facilities ... Ms. Leah SWANQUIST
14 Dir of Educ Computing/End User Svcs ... Ms. Renee KOZIMOR
07 Director of Enrollment Services ... Ms. Cheryl WARMANN
25 Dir of Grants & Alternative Funding ... Ms. Roxann MARSHBURN
31 Dir of Community & Adult Education ... Ms. Robyn BAILEY
28 Ethics Officer ... Mr. D. Arnie OUDENHOVEN

Olivet Nazarene University (A)

One University Avenue, Bourbonnais IL 60914-2345
County: Kankakee FICE Identification: 001741
Unit ID: 147828
Telephone: (815) 939-5011 Carnegie Class: Master's L
FAX Number: (815) 935-4998 Calendar System: Semester
URL: www.olivet.edu
Established: 1907 Annual Undergrad Tuition & Fees: $27,590
Enrollment: 4,177 Coed
Affiliation or Control: Church Of The Nazarene IRS Status: 501(c)3
Highest Offering: Doctorate
Program: Liberal Arts And General; Teacher Preparatory; Professional
Accreditation: NH, DIETD, ENG, MUS, NURSE, SW, TED

01 President ... Dr. John C. BOWLING
05 Vice President Academic Affairs ... Dr. Gregg CHENOWETH
10 Vice President for Finance ... Dr. Douglas E. PERRY
32 Vice President Student Development ... Dr. Walter W. WEBB
26 Vice Pres Institutional Advancement ... Dr. Brian ALLEN
58 Vice Pres for Grad & Adult Studies ... Mr. Ryan SPITTAL
49 Dean College of Arts & Sciences ... Dr. Janna MCLEAN
73 Dn Sch Theology/Christian Ministry ... Dr. Carl LETH
53 Dean School of Education ... Dr. Jim UPCHURCH
107 Dean School of Professional Studies ... Dr. Dennis CROCKER
29 Dir Alumni & University Relations ... Mr. Gary GRIFFIN
07 Director of Admissions ... Mrs. Susan WOLFF
06 Registrar ... Dr. Jim D. KNIGHT
08 Director of the Library ... Mrs. Kathy R. BOYENS
37 Director of Financial Aid ... Mr. Greg BRUNER
14 Director of Computer Center ... Mr. Dennis SEYMOUR
41 Athletic Director ... Mr. Gary NEWSOME
42 Chaplain ... Rev. Mark HOLCOMB
30 Exec Director of Development ... Mr. Dan J. FERRIS
35 Director Student Activities ... Mrs. Kathy STEINACKER
15 Director of Human Resources ... Mr. David PICKERING
18 Chief Facilities/Physical Plant ... Mr. Matt WHITIS
40 Bookstore Manager ... Mrs. Rachel PIAZZA
36 Career Specialist ... Mrs. Mary ANDERSON
85 International Student Advisor ... Mr. Tony GRIMM
27 Coord of Strategic Comm & Web ... Mrs. Heather DAY

Pacific College of Oriental Medicine (B)

65 East Wacker Place 21st Floor, Chicago IL 60601
County: Cook Identification: 666615
Unit ID: 442842
Telephone: (888) 729-4811 Carnegie Class: Spec/Health
FAX Number: (773) 477-4109 Calendar System: Other
URL: www.pacificcollege.edu
Established: 1999 Annual Undergrad Tuition & Fees: $15,895
Enrollment: 284 Coed
Affiliation or Control: Proprietary IRS Status: Proprietary
Highest Offering: Master's
Program: Professional
Accreditation: ACCSC, ACUP

01 Director/Chief Operating Officer ... Dr. Edward LAMADRID

† Branch campus of Pacific College of Oriental Medicine, San Diego CA.

Parkland College (C)

2400 W Bradley Avenue, Champaign IL 61821-1899
County: Champaign FICE Identification: 007118
Unit ID: 147916
Telephone: (217) 351-2200 Carnegie Class: Assoc/Pub-R-L
FAX Number: (217) 351-2581 Calendar System: Semester
URL: www.parkland.edu
Established: 1966 Annual Undergrad Tuition & Fees (In-District): $3,360
Enrollment: 9,368 Coed
Affiliation or Control: State/Local IRS Status: 501(c)3
Highest Offering: Associate Degree
Program: Occupational; 2-Year Principally Bachelor's Creditable
Accreditation: NH, ADNUR, DH, @DIETT, OTA, RAD, SURGT

01 President ... Dr. Thomas R. RAMAGE
04 Asst to President/Board of Trustees ... Ms. Nancy R. WILLAMON
05 Vice President Academic Services ... Dr. Kristine M. YOUNG
32 Vice President Student Services ... Dr. Linda H. MOORE
11 Vice Pres Administrative Svcs/CFO ... Mr. Christopher M. RANDLES
30 Vice Pres Institutional Advancement ... Dr. Seamus REILLY
35 Dean of Students ... Ms. Marietta TURNER
75 Dean of Career & Transfer Prgms ... Mr. Randy FLETCHER
50 Dept Chair Bus & Agri Industries ... Mr. Bruce HENRIKSON
77 Department Chair Comp Science & IT ... Ms. Maria MOBASSERI
54 Dept Chair Engineering Science/Tech ... Ms. Catherine STALTER
79 Dept Chair Humanities ... Mr. Tom BARNARD
57 Dept Chair Fine & Applied Arts ... Ms. Nancy SUTTON
76 Dept Chair Health Professions ... Ms. Roberta SCHOLZE
81 Department Chair Mathematics ... Mr. Geoffrey GRIFFITHS
65 Dept Chair Natural Sciences ... Ms. Kathy BRUCE
83 Dept Chair Social Sci & Human Svcs ... Mr. Paul SARANTAKOS
88 Dir Center for Academic Success ... Ms. Becky OSBORNE
09 Director Accountability & Research ... Mr. Kevin KNOTT
88 Director of Adult Basic Education ... Ms. Tawanna NICKENS
26 Dir Marketing & Public Relations ... Ms. Patty LEHN
103 Exec Director Workforce Development ... Mr. Minor JACKSON
102 Exec Director Parkland Foundation ... Mr. Carl R. MEYER
08 Director Library ... Ms. Anna Maria S. WATKIN
31 Director Community Education ... Ms. Jan SIMON
25 Director Grants and Contracts ... Mr. Ray SPENCER
07 Director Admissions/Enrollment Mgmt ... Mr. Reo WILHOUR
35 Director Student Life ... Dr. Thomas M. CAULFIELD
41 Director Athletics ... Mr. Rod M. LOVETT
36 Director Career Center ... Ms. Sandra L. SPENCER
38 Dir Counseling & Advising Center ... Mr. John SHEAHAN
37 Director Financial Aid ... Mr. Tim WENDT
19 Director Public Safety ... Mr. Von YOUNG
18 Director Physical Plant ... Mr. James BUSTARD
15 Director Human Resources ... Ms. Kathleen CHARLESTON
21 Controller ... Mr. Dave DONSBACH
40 Manager of Bookstore ... Ms. Diane M. KIEST
44 Dir Planned and Major Gifts ... Mr. Michael HAGAN
88 Dir Assessment Center ... Dr. Mügé DIZÉN

Prairie State College (D)

202 S Halsted Street, Chicago Heights IL 60411-8226
County: Cook FICE Identification: 001640
Unit ID: 148007
Telephone: (708) 709-3500 Carnegie Class: Assoc/Pub-S-SC
FAX Number: (708) 755-2587 Calendar System: Semester
URL: www.prairiestate.edu
Established: 1957 Annual Undergrad Tuition & Fees (In-District): $3,480
Enrollment: 5,697 Coed
Affiliation or Control: State/Local IRS Status: 501(c)3
Highest Offering: Associate Degree
Program: Occupational; 2-Year Principally Bachelor's Creditable
Accreditation: NH, ADNUR, DH, SURGT

01 President ... Dr. Eric C. RADTKE
10 Vice Pres Finance & Administration ... Dr. Alan D. ROBERTSON
05 Vice Pres Academic Affs/Dean Facul ... Dr. Adenuga ATEWOLOGUN
31 Vice President Community/Econ Devel ... Dr. Terri L. WINFREE
32 VP Student Affairs/Dean of Students ... Mr. Gregory A. THOMAS
49 Dean Liberal Arts ... Dr. Susan R. SOLBERG
50 Dean Business/Mathematics & Science ... Dr. Debra L. PRENDERGAST
17 Dean Health & Industrial Technology ... Dr. Marie C. HANSEL
15 Exec Dir Human Resources/Empl Rels ... Vacant
88 Director of Labor Relations ... Mr. Leo R. ALEXANDER
14 Exec Dir Info Technology Resources ... Ms. Diane CONATSER
56 Dean Adult Education ... Ms. Kim M. KUNCE
21 Controller/Dir of Business Svcs ... Mr. James M. EATON
08 Assoc Dean/Library & Instruct Svcs ... Dr. Anthony MOLARO
51 Dean Corporate/Cont Professional Ed ... Mr. Edward JODELKA
35 Dean Student Dev & Campus Life ... Dr. Shawn L. GOVAN
20 Associate Dean Faculty Affairs ... Ms. Patricia ZUCCARELLO
18 Director Facilities and Operations ... Mr. Timothy J. KOZIEK
26 Exec Dir Communications & Marketing ... Ms. Jennifer E. STONER
102 Executive Director Foundation ... Ms. Cathy K. KLOSS
91 Assoc Dir Admin Computer Services ... Mr. Roy E. MAURER
07 Exec Dir Enrollment/Fin Aid Svcs ... Ms. Jaime M. MILLER
19 Dir Camp/Pub Safety/Chief of Police ... Vacant
88 Director Children's Learning Center ... Ms. Kellie E. CLARK
88 Director Advising/Disability Svcs ... Ms. Diane J. JANOWIAK
37 Director Financial Aid/Vet Affairs ... Ms. Alice GARCIA
09 Director Institutional Research ... Vacant
88 Director Institutional Support Svcs ... Ms. Paulette A. MAURER
41 Director Physical Ed/Athletics ... Mr. Edward J. SCHAFFER

88 Director Test Svcs/Intent Advising ... Ms. Lee A. HELBERT
04 Exec Assistant to the President ... Ms. Patricia G. TROST

Principia College (E)

1 Maybeck Place, Elsah IL 62028-9799
County: Jersey FICE Identification: 001744
Unit ID: 148016
Telephone: (618) 374-2131 Carnegie Class: Bac/A&S
FAX Number: (618) 374-5500 Calendar System: Semester
URL: www.principiacollege.edu
Established: 1898 Annual Undergrad Tuition & Fees: $25,960
Enrollment: 500 Coed
Affiliation or Control: Independent Non-Profit IRS Status: 501(c)3
Highest Offering: Baccalaureate
Program: Liberal Arts And General; Teacher Preparatory
Accreditation: NH

01 President and Chief Executive ... Dr. Jonathan PALMER
05 Dean of Academics ... Dr. Scott SCHNEBERGER
88 Chief Investment Officer ... Mr. Howard E. BERNER, JR.
10 Chief Financial Officer ... Mr. Doug GIBBS
20 Associate Dean of Academics ... Dr. Joe RITTER
27 Director of Marketing ... Ms. Gretchen NEWBY
06 Registrar ... Ms. Alice DERVIN
07 Dean of Enrollment Mgt/Admissions ... Mr. Brian MCCAULEY
08 Director of Libraries ... Mrs. Lisa ROBERTS
13 Chief Technology Officer ... Mr. Richard BOOTH
104 Director of Principia Abroads ... Ms. Linda A. BOHAKER
30 Chief Advancement Officer ... Mr. Glenn WILLIAMS
41 Director of Athletics ... Mr. Lee ELLIS
15 Human Resources Manager ... Ms. SharonAnn SMITH
18 Director of Facilities ... Mr. Ed GOEWERT
11 Director of Administration ... Mrs. Karen D. GRIMMER
21 Controller ... Mrs. Sara THORNDIKE
29 Director of Alumni Relations ... Mrs. Donna GIBBS
32 Dean of Students ... Ms. Dorsie GLEN
37 Director of College Financial Aid ... Mrs. Tami GAVALETZ
96 Purchasing Manager ... Vacant
38 Director Academic Career Advising ... Mrs. Midge BROWNING
09 Director of IEP ... Vacant

Quincy University (F)

1800 College Avenue, Quincy IL 62301-2699
County: Adams FICE Identification: 001745
Unit ID: 148131
Telephone: (217) 222-8020 Carnegie Class: Master's S
FAX Number: (217) 228-5257 Calendar System: Semester
URL: www.quincy.edu
Established: 1860 Annual Undergrad Tuition & Fees: $25,180
Enrollment: 1,735 Coed
Affiliation or Control: Roman Catholic IRS Status: 501(c)3
Highest Offering: Master's
Program: Liberal Arts And General; Teacher Preparatory
Accreditation: NH

01 President ... Dr. Robert GERVASI
05 Vice Pres for Academic Affairs ... Dr. Teresa REED
42 Vice Pres for Mission & Ministry ... Fr. John DOCTOR, OFM
10 Vice President for Business/Finance ... Mr. Tim WEIS
13 Chief Information Officer ... Dr. Daniel MICHAELS
84 Vice Pres for Enrollment Management ... Mrs. Syndi PECK
32 Vice Pres for Student Affairs ... Dr. Tiffany QUINZE
101 Corporate Secretary ... Dr. Teresa REED
21 Assoc VP for Finance/Controller ... Mrs. Jean M. GREEN
30 Assoc Vice President Advancement ... Mrs. Julie BELL
50 Dean School of Business ... Dr. John GLASGOW
53 Dean School of Education ... Dr. Ann BEHRENS
79 Chair Division of Humanities ... Dr. Terrence RIDDELL
81 Chair Division Science & Technology ... Dr. Lee ENGER
83 Chair Div Behavioral/Social Sci ... Dr. Wendy BELLER
57 Chr Div Communication & Fine Arts ... Dr. Barbara SCHLEPPENBACH
20 Dean Academic Support Services ... Dr. Teresa WILLIAMS
08 Dean of Library/Info Resources ... Ms. Patricia TOMCZAK
92 Director of Honors Program ... Dr. Daniel STRUDWICK
06 Registrar ... Mrs. Barbara WELLMAN
09 Institution Research Specialist ... Mrs. Roberta PAUL
42 Director of Campus Ministry ... Fr. Ferd CHERI
37 Director of Financial Aid ... Ms. Lisa FLACK
27 Director of Communications ... Mr. Jim ROBESKY
29 Director of Alumni Services ... Mr. Bill O'DONNELL
36 Director Career Planning/Placement ... Ms. Kristen LIESEN
41 Director of Athletics ... Mr. Marty BELL
18 Director of Facilities Management ... Mr. Rob GOEBEL
39 Director of Residence Life ... Mr. Jeff SPAIN
28 Dir Multicultural/Leadership Pgms ... Ms. Natasha RAMSEY
19 Director of Security ... Mr. Sam LATHROP
15 Director of Human Resources ... Ms. Dana KEPPNER
38 Director of the Counseling Center ... Mrs. Molly DUNN-STEINKE
96 Director of Purchasing ... Mrs. Jennifer TRUITT
25 Grant Writer ... Ms. Julie BOLL
40 Manager of the Bookstore ... Mr. Ben MEANS
44 Coordinator of Development ... Mr. Matthew BERGMAN

Rasmussen College - Aurora (G)

2363 Sequoia Drive, Suite 131, Aurora IL 60506
Identification: 667060
Unit ID: 44867301
Telephone: (630) 888-3500 Carnegie Class: Not Classified
FAX Number: (630) 888-3501 Calendar System: Quarter
URL: www.rasmussen.edu

Established: 1900 Annual Undergrad Tuition & Fees: $16,340
Enrollment: 553 Coed
Affiliation or Control: Proprietary IRS Status: Proprietary
Highest Offering: Baccalaureate
Program: Occupational; 2-Year Principally Bachelor's Creditable
Accreditation: &NH, MAAB

01 Campus Director .... Susan CHENEY

† Regional accreditation is carried under the parent institution in Lake Elmo, MN.

Rasmussen College - Mokena/ Tinley Park (A)

8650 W. Spring Lake Drive, Mokena IL 60448
County: Will Identification: 667064
Unit ID: 44867303
Telephone: (815) 534-3300 Carnegie Class: Not Classified
FAX Number: (815) 534-3301 Calendar System: Quarter
URL: www.rasmussen.edu
Established: 1900 Annual Undergrad Tuition & Fees: $16,340
Enrollment: 42 Coed
Affiliation or Control: Proprietary IRS Status: Proprietary
Highest Offering: Baccalaureate
Program: Occupational; 2-Year Principally Bachelor's Creditable
Accreditation: &NH, MAAB

01 Campus Director .... Staci HEGARTY

† Regional accreditation is carried under the parent institution in Lake Elmo, MN.

Rasmussen College - Rockford (B)

6000 E. State Street, 4th Floor, Rockford IL 61108
Identification: 667065
Unit ID: 448673
Telephone: (815) 316-4800 Carnegie Class: Assoc/PrivFP
FAX Number: (815) 315-4801 Calendar System: Quarter
URL: www.rasmussen.edu
Established: 1900 Annual Undergrad Tuition & Fees: $16,340
Enrollment: 1,201 Coed
Affiliation or Control: Proprietary IRS Status: Proprietary
Highest Offering: Baccalaureate
Program: Occupational; 2-Year Principally Bachelor's Creditable
Accreditation: &NH, MAAB

01 Campus Director .... Craig STEEGE

† Regional accreditation is carried under the parent institution in Lake Elmo, MN.

Rasmussen College - Romeoville/ Joliet (C)

1400 West Normantown Road, Romeoville IL 60446
County: Will Identification: 667066
Unit ID: 44867302
Telephone: (815) 306-2600 Carnegie Class: Not Classified
FAX Number: (815) 306-2601 Calendar System: Quarter
URL: www.rasmussen.edu
Established: 1900 Annual Undergrad Tuition & Fees: $16,340
Enrollment: 382 Coed
Affiliation or Control: Proprietary IRS Status: Proprietary
Highest Offering: Baccalaureate
Program: Occupational; 2-Year Principally Bachelor's Creditable
Accreditation: &NH, MAAB

01 Campus Director .... Amy KING

† Regional accreditation is carried under the parent institution in Lake Elmo, MN.

Rend Lake College (D)

468 N Ken Gray Parkway, Ina IL 62846-9801
County: Jefferson FICE Identification: 007119
Unit ID: 148256
Telephone: (618) 437-5321 Carnegie Class: Assoc/Pub-R-L
FAX Number: (618) 437-5677 Calendar System: Semester
URL: www.rlc.edu
Established: 1967 Annual Undergrad Tuition & Fees (In-District): $3,072
Enrollment: 4,943 Coed
Affiliation or Control: State/Local IRS Status: 501(c)3
Highest Offering: Associate Degree
Program: Occupational; 2-Year Principally Bachelor's Creditable
Accreditation: NH, MLTAD, OTA, RAD

01 President .... Mr. Terry WILKERSON
05 VP of Academic Instruction .... Ms. Chris KUBERSKI
10 VP of Finance & Administration .... Mr. Robert CARLOCK
20 VP of Career Technical Instruction .... Ms. Lisa PAYNE
09 VP of Institutional Effectiveness .... Ms. Andrea WITTHOFT
38 Vice Pres of Student Services .... Ms. Lisa PRICE
26 Director Marketing & Information .... Mr. Chad COPPLE
37 Director Student Financial Aid .... Ms. Cheri RUSHING
41 Athletic Director .... Vacant
18 Director Physical Plant .... Mr. C. Randall SHIVELY
102 CEO of RLC Foundation .... Ms. Shawna HALL
06 Director of Student Records .... Ms. Vickie SCHULTE
09 Director of Institutional Research .... Ms. Christina HUTCHESON

Resurrection University (E)

3 Erie Court, Oak Park IL 60302-2519
County: Cook FICE Identification: 006250
Unit ID: 149763
Telephone: (708) 763-6530 Carnegie Class: Spec/Health
FAX Number: (708) 763-1531 Calendar System: Semester
URL: www.resu.edu
Established: 1982 Annual Undergrad Tuition & Fees: $23,278
Enrollment: 417 Coed
Affiliation or Control: Independent Non-Profit IRS Status: 501(c)3
Highest Offering: Master's
Program: Liberal Arts And General; Nursing Emphasis
Accreditation: NH, NURSE

01 President .... Dr. Beth A. BROOKS
66 Dean of Nursing .... Dr. Sandie SOLDWISCH
07 Director of Admissions/Marketing .... Mr. Scott DUNNELL
10 Chief Financial Officer .... Dr. Therese A. SCANLAN
32 Director of Student Services .... Ms. Carmelita GEE
29 Director of Alumni Relations .... Mr. Scott DUNNELL
04 Administrative Asst to President .... Ms. Barbara BAILEY
90 Program Analyst .... Mr. Zbigniew KUSNIERZ
37 Student Financial Aid .... Ms. Shirley HOWELL
06 Registrar .... Mr. Michael SHERMAN

Richland Community College (F)

One College Park, Decatur IL 62521-8513
County: Macon FICE Identification: 010879
Unit ID: 148292
Telephone: (217) 875-7200 Carnegie Class: Assoc/Pub-R-M
FAX Number: (217) 875-6961 Calendar System: Semester
URL: www.richland.edu
Established: 1971 Annual Undergrad Tuition & Fees (In-District): $2,892
Enrollment: 3,632 Coed
Affiliation or Control: State/Local IRS Status: 501(c)3
Highest Offering: Associate Degree
Program: Occupational; 2-Year Principally Bachelor's Creditable
Accreditation: NH, ADNUR, SURGT

01 President .... Dr. Gayie M. SAUNDERS
10 Vice President of Finance & Admin .... Mr. Greg E. FLORIAN
05 Vice Pres Student/Academic Affairs .... Dr. Tod TREAT
103 VP Econ Dev/Innov Wkfce Solutions .... Dr. Douglas BRAUER
106 Director Online Learning .... Mrs. Kona JONES
30 Exec Director Foundation & Develop .... Mr. Richard MCGOWAN
29 Dir Scholarships/Alumni Development ... Mrs. Tricia CORDULACK
51 Dean Continuing Education .... Mrs. Darbe BRINKOETTER
27 Exec Director of Public Information .... Ms. Lisa GREGORY
07 Dean Enrollment Services .... Mr. Marcus BROWN
06 Director Advising & Registration .... Ms. Stephanie ZIMMERMAN
32 Director Student Engagement .... Mrs. Heather KIND-KEPPEL
38 Director Counseling and Advising .... Mrs. Deborah MCGEE
53 Dean Teaching/Learning Support Svcs .... Mrs. Sheryl BLAHNIK
81 Dean of Math & Sciences .... Dr. John CORDULACK
72 Dean of Business & Technology .... Vacant
37 Dir Financial Aid/Veteran Affairs .... Ms. Carmin E. ROSS
36 Director Career Services .... Mr. Michael DIGGS
16 Director Human Resources .... Mr. Richard GSCHWEND
57 Dean of Communications/Fine Arts .... Dr. Lily SIU
76 Dean of Health Professions .... Ms. Ellen COLBECK
18 Dir Tech Services & Operations .... Mr. David HOLTFRETER
19 Dir Campus Safety .... Mr. Greg FIRKUS

Robert Morris University (G)

401 South State Street, Chicago IL 60605-1225
County: Cook FICE Identification: 001746
Unit ID: 148335
Telephone: (312) 935-6800 Carnegie Class: Master's M
FAX Number: (312) 935-6660 Calendar System: Other
URL: www.robertmorris.edu
Established: 1913 Annual Undergrad Tuition & Fees: $22,200
Enrollment: 3,630 Coed
Affiliation or Control: Independent Non-Profit IRS Status: 501(c)3
Highest Offering: Master's
Program: Occupational; 2-Year Principally Bachelor's Creditable; Liberal Arts And General; Professional; Business Emphasis
Accreditation: NH, ADNUR, IACBE, MAC, SURGT

01 President .... Michael P. VIOLLT
05 Provost .... Mablene KRUEGER
45 Sr VP for Resource Administration .... Deborah BRODZINSKI
84 Sr VP for Enrollment Management .... Nicole FARINELLA
88 Sr VP for Adult & Grad Enrollment .... Catherine LOCKWOOD
20 VP of Academic Administration .... Kathleen SUHAJDA
88 VP of Brand and Image .... Christine FISHER
10 VP of Business Affairs .... Ronald M. ARNOLD
41 VP of Extra Curricular Activities .... Megan SMITH
09 VP of External Affairs .... Marie A. GIACOMELLI
37 VP of Financial Services .... Leigh BRINSON
15 VP of Human Resources .... Nicole SKALUBA
14 VP of Information Systems .... Lisa CONTRERAS
26 VP of Marketing/Communications .... Connie ESPARZA
32 VP of Student Affairs .... Angela JORDAN
97 Dean of College of Liberal Arts .... Paula DIAZ
76 Dean of Nursing & Health Studies .... Janet DAVIS
49 Dean of Institute of Art & Design .... Janice KAUSHAL
72 Dean of Inst of Technology & Media .... Basim KHARTABIL
58 Dean of Morris Grad School of Mgmt .... Kayed AKKAWI
88 Dean of Program Development .... Lora TIMMONS
50 Dean of Business Administration .... Larry NIEMAN
88 Exec Dir/Dean Inst of Culinary Arts .... Nancy ROTUNNO
88 Dean of Day Div Enrollment .... Michelle CASINI
07 Dean of Admissions .... Ana MENDEZ
88 Dean of Morris Grad School of Mgmt .... Fernando VILLEDA
88 Dean of Admissions Athletic Enroll .... Justin MERRIS
88 Dean of Admissions Out of State .... Betsy MALM
88 Dean of Transfer Enrollment .... Dennis MUMAW
88 Dean of Experiential Technology .... Jill MCGINTY
88 Sr Dir of Academic Administration .... Kathleen VIOLLT
88 Sr Director of Academic Programming .... Carolyn SUKKAR
88 Dir of Admissions Info Systems .... Damaris RIVERA
88 Director of High School Relations .... Danielle NAFFZIGER
36 Dean of Career Development .... Stefanie CALDWELL
96 Dir of Purchasing and Facilities .... Amy KECK
88 Director of Data Administration .... Deana MIRANDA
88 Director of Communications .... Sue POLZ
88 Director of Food Service Operations .... Nick JARMUZ
88 Dir of Human Capital Management .... Gregory TALL
88 Director of Internal Relations .... Joe TAKASH
13 Director of Networking Services .... Gloria PLAZA
26 Director of Public Relations .... Nancy DONOHOE
88 Director of Student Center .... Daniel MARTIN
06 Director of Student Information .... Stella MACH
39 Dir of Student Life and Housing .... Janely RIVERA
35 Dir Student Services/Special Progms .... Monique JONES
88 Dir of Student Support Services .... Pinkey STEWART
88 Dir of System Integration/Integrity .... Arlene REGNERUS
88 Director of Title VII Grant .... Lauren MILLER
88 Dir of Upward Bound and ETS .... Carolyn BASLEY
90 Director of User Services .... Dipak PATEL
88 Associate Registrar .... Nancy SMITH-IRONS
21 Controller .... Melanie CARLIN
08 Institutional Library Director .... Sue DUTLER
18 Institutional Dir of Operations .... Nino RANDAZZO
40 Dir of Bookstore Operations .... Julie MELLER

Rock Valley College (H)

3301 N Mulford Road, Rockford IL 61114-5699
County: Winnebago FICE Identification: 001747
Unit ID: 148380
Telephone: (815) 921-7821 Carnegie Class: Assoc/Pub-R-L
FAX Number: N/A Calendar System: Semester
URL: www.rockvalleycollege.edu
Established: 1964 Annual Undergrad Tuition & Fees (In-District): $2,804
Enrollment: 8,849 Coed
Affiliation or Control: Local IRS Status: 501(c)3
Highest Offering: Associate Degree
Program: Occupational; 2-Year Principally Bachelor's Creditable
Accreditation: NH, DH, SURGT

01 President .... Dr. Jack J. BECHERER
05 Provost/CAO .... Dr. Diane L. NYHAMMER
102 Executive Director Foundation .... Ms. Pamela OWENS
10 Vice Pres Administrative Services .... Mr. Sam OVERTON, JR.
32 Assoc VP Student Development .... Ms. Amy DIAZ
51 Assoc VP Outreach & Planning .... Mr. Michael MASTROIANNI
20 Assoc VP Academic Affairs .... Vacant
13 Managing Dir Information Technology .... Ms. Diann JABUSCH
15 Managing Dir Human Resource Svc .... Ms. Jessica JONES
96 Director Business Services .... Ms. Jacki MINNIHAN
84 Dir Enroll Mgmt & Judicial Affairs .... Ms. Lynn PERKINS
18 Director Facilities Planning & POM .... Mr. Thomas VIEL
26 Director Public Relations .... Ms. Nancy CHAMBERLAIN
88 Director Theatre & Arts Park .... Mr. Michael WEBB
19 Director Public Safety .... Mr. Joe DROUGHT
21 Director Financial Services .... Vacant
37 Director Financial Aid .... Ms. Cyndi STONESIFER
09 Executive Director Inst Research .... Ms. Lisa MEHLIG
06 Registrar .... Ms. Michelle ROTHMEYER
35 Manager Student Life .... Ms. Quiana PRESTON
36 Coordinator Career Svcs/Placement .... Mr. Art DELGADO
07 Manager of Recruitment & Admissions . Ms. Jennifer THOMPSON

Rockford Career College (I)

1130 S. Alpine Road, Rockford IL 61108
County: Winnebago FICE Identification: 008545
Unit ID: 148399
Telephone: (815) 965-8616 Carnegie Class: Assoc/PrivFP
FAX Number: (815) 965-0360 Calendar System: Quarter
URL: www.rockfordcareercollege.edu
Established: 1862 Annual Undergrad Tuition & Fees: $9,200
Enrollment: 706 Coed
Affiliation or Control: Proprietary IRS Status: Proprietary
Highest Offering: Associate Degree
Program: Occupational; 2-Year Principally Bachelor's Creditable
Accreditation: ACICS, MAC

01 President/CEO .... Mr. Steven GIBSON
10 Vice President/Dir of Finance .... Mr. Guary BERNADELLE
05 Dean of Academics .... Ms. Amy SEMENCHUCK
32 Dean of Students .... Ms. Karen GILBERT
22 Dir of Institutional Compliance .... Mr. Jack MARTIN
84 Director of Enrollment .... Mr. David JULIUS
15 Director of Human Resources .... Mr. Jim LAIBLE
36 Director Student Placement .... Ms. Monica WILLIAMS
37 Director of Financial Aid .... Ms. Lisa RUCH
26 Director of College Relations .... Mr. Jeff SWANBERG

Rockford College (A)

5050 E State Street, Rockford IL 61108-2393
County: Winnebago　FICE Identification: 001748
Unit ID: 148405
Telephone: (815) 226-4000　Carnegie Class: Master's L
FAX Number: (815) 226-4119　Calendar System: Semester
URL: www.rockford.edu
Established: 1847　Annual Undergrad Tuition & Fees: $26,210
Enrollment: 1,318　Coed
Affiliation or Control: Independent Non-Profit　IRS Status: 501(c)3
Highest Offering: Master's
Program: Liberal Arts And General; Teacher Preparatory; Professional
Accreditation: NH, IACBE, NUR

01	President	Dr. Robert L. HEAD
05	VP & Dean of the College	Dr. Steven SICONOLFI
30	VP for Institutional Advancement	Mr. Bernard SUNDSTEDT
88	Senior Development Officer	Mr. John MCNAMARA
10	VP for Business/Operations/CFO	Ms. Christina ANDERSON
21	Business Office Accounting Manager	Mr. Justin KRUEGER
84	VP Enrollment Management	Mr. Barrett BELL
07	Assoc VP Undergraduate Admission	Ms. Jennifer NORDSTROM
37	Assistant VP for SAS	Mr. Todd FISCHER-FREE
11	Associate Vice President Operations	Mr. Matthew PHILLIPS
13	Director of Information Technology	Ms. Bonnie JOHNSON
32	Dean of Students	Mr. Bradley KNOTTS
58	Director of MBA	Mr. Jeffrey FAHRENWALD
58	Director of MAT	Dr. Michelle MCREYNOLDS
06	Registrar	Ms. Anna J. JATTKOWSKI-HUDSON
04	Exec Assistant to the President	Ms. Susan OSHINSKI
04	Assistant to the President	Ms. Teddy PHILLIPS
41	Athletic Director	Mrs. Kristyn KING
15	Director of Human Resources	Ms. Kim ADAMS
36	Director Career Services	Ms. Kelly COOPER
26	Director of Communications	Ms. Rita ELLIOTT
09	Coordinator of IR	Dr. Chih-Ming (Ryan) CHUNG
12	Director of Kobe-Regents Center	Ms. Michelle GRIGGS
38	Director Counseling	Mrs. Sallyann ROBERTS
23	Director Health Services	Mrs. Cecelia M. BRISTOL
18	Director Physical Plant	Mr. Jerry BERG
19	Security Officer	Mr. Roy RONCAL
08	Head Librarian	Ms. Kelly JAMES

Roosevelt University (B)

430 S Michigan Avenue, Chicago IL 60605-1394
County: Cook　FICE Identification: 001749
Unit ID: 148487
Telephone: (312) 341-3500　Carnegie Class: Master's L
FAX Number: (312) 341-3655　Calendar System: Semester
URL: www.roosevelt.edu
Established: 1945　Annual Undergrad Tuition & Fees: $25,950
Enrollment: 6,620　Coed
Affiliation or Control: Independent Non-Profit　IRS Status: 501(c)3
Highest Offering: Doctorate
Program: Liberal Arts And General; Teacher Preparatory; Professional
Accreditation: NH, ACBSP, CACREP, CLPSY, MUS, @PHAR, TED

01	President	Dr. Charles R. MIDDLETON
03	Provost & Exec Vice President	Dr. James GANDRE
45	Vice Provost for Planning & Budgets	Mr. Michael FORD
05	Vice Provost Faculty/Acad Admin	Dr. Samuel ROSENBERG
10	Sr VP of Finance/Admin and CFO	Ms. Miroslava MEJIA KRUG
86	VP Govt Relations/Univ Outreach	Ms. Lesley SLAVITT
84	VP Enrollment Mgmt & Student Svcs	Dr. Sallye MCKEE
15	Vice President Human Resources	Ms. Gretchen VAN NATTA
100	Chief of Staff & Asst Secy to BOT	Mr. Brigham J. TIMPSON
12	Schaumburg Campus Provost	Dr. Douglas KNERR
30	VP Inst Advancement and CAO	Mr. Patrick WOODS
30	Assoc VP Operations & Campaign Dir	Ms. Kim GIBSON-HARMAN
29	Director of Alumni Relations	Ms. Janice PARKIN
44	Asst Vice President Planned Giving	Ms. Denise A. BRANSFORD
07	Senior Director of Admissions	Ms. Asia MITCHELL
35	Assoc VP Communication & Retention	Mr. Eric TAMMES
09	Assoc Provost Inst Research	Mr. Joseph P. REGAN
21	Associate VP Finance	Ms. Tangella MADDOX
32	Senior Assoc VP Student Services	Ms. Tanya L. WOLTMANN
18	Assoc VP Campus Planning & Op	Mr. Steven A. HOSELTON
96	Assoc Vice President for Admin Svcs	Ms. Laurie CASHMAN
85	Asst Dir of International Programs	Ms. Dawm HOUGLAND
13	Chief Information Officer	Mr. Neeraj KUMAR
58	Int Assoc Prov Research & Grad Stds	Dr. Kimberly N. RUFFIN
49	Dean College Arts & Sciences	Dr. Lynn Y. WEINER
50	Dean College Business Admin	Dr. Terri L. FRIEL
64	Dean College of Performing Arts	Mr. Henry FOGEL
107	Int Dean Col of Professional Stds	Dr. Gregory A. BUCKLEY
53	Dean College of Education	Dr. Holly STADLER
67	Dean College of Pharmacy	Dr. George MACKINNON
39	Asst VP of Residence Life	Ms. Bridget COLLIER
26	Asst VP Public Relations	Mr. Thomas R. KAROW
88	Exec Dir of Auditorium Theatre/RU	Mr. Brett BATTERSON
08	University Librarian	Mr. Richard UTTICH
06	University Registrar	Ms. Sheila COFFIN
37	Sr Assoc VP Admission & Fin Aid	Dr. Walter J H. O'NEILL
38	Director Counseling Center	Dr. Susan STOCK
36	Director of Career Development	Ms. Tina GADDY

Rosalind Franklin University of Medicine & Science (C)

3333 Green Bay Road, North Chicago IL 60064-3095
County: Lake　FICE Identification: 001659
Unit ID: 145558
Telephone: (847) 578-3000　Carnegie Class: Spec/Med
FAX Number: (847) 578-3401　Calendar System: Quarter
URL: www.rosalindfranklin.edu
Established: 1912　Annual Undergrad Tuition & Fees: N/A
Enrollment: 2,027　Coed
Affiliation or Control: Independent Non-Profit　IRS Status: 501(c)3
Highest Offering: Doctorate; No Lower Division
Program: Professional; Technical Emphasis
Accreditation: NH, ANEST, ARCPA, CLPSY, MED, PA, @PHAR, POD, PTA

01	President/Chief Executive Officer	Dr. Michael WELCH
03	Exec Vice Pres/Chief Operating Ofcr	Ms. Margot SURRIDGE
17	VP Medical Affs/Dean Medical School	Dr. Russell ROBERTSON
05	VP Acad Affs/ Dean Col Hlth Prof	Dr. Wendy RHEAULT
46	VP Research	Dr. Ronald S. KAPLAN
67	Dean Col of Pharmacy	Dr. Gloria MEREDITH
58	Dean Sch Grad PostDoc Stds	Dr. Joseph X. DIMARIO
63	Dean Scholl Col Podiatric Med	Dr. Nancy L. PARSLEY
10	Chief Financial Officer	Ms. Roberta LANE
88	VP Faculty Affairs	Dr. Timothy R. HANSEN
30	VP Institutional Advancement	Ms. Tina M. ERICKSON
100	Director Office of the President	Ms. Donna AGNEW
88	Chief Compliance Officer	Mr. Bret MOBERG
45	Assoc VP Financial Plng/Analysis	Mr. Eugene DAUN
88	Assoc VP Learning Resources	Dr. Melanie SHURAN
09	Assoc VP Institutional Research	Ms. Maryann DECAIRE
11	Assoc VP Operations	Mr. Daniel ESTA
84	Assoc VP Stdnt Aff/Enrollment Mgmt	Ms. Rebecca DURKIN
27	Chief Information Officer	Mr. Richard LOESCH
29	Exec Dir Alumni/Community Affairs	Ms. Martha KELLY BATES
15	Exec Dir of Human Resources	Ms. Sherry BAGNO
26	Exec Dir Marketing/Communications	Ms. Lee CONCHA
19	Director Campus Security	Mr. Gordon BLANCHARD
18	Dir Facilities Management	Mr. Robert D. JACKSON
25	Dir Sponsored Research	Ms. Dora ESPINOZA
06	Registrar	Mr. Timothy CARROLL
37	Dir Student Financial Services	Ms. Maryann DECAIRE
88	Dir Academic/Retention Svcs	Mr. Steven WEIAND
07	Dir Admissions/Recruitment	Mr. La'Mont VAUGHN
32	Director Student Life	Ms. Shelly BLOHOWIAK

Rush University (D)

600 S Paulina, Chicago IL 60612-3832
County: Cook　FICE Identification: 009800
Unit ID: 148511
Telephone: (312) 942-7100　Carnegie Class: Spec/Med
FAX Number: (312) 942-2219　Calendar System: Quarter
URL: www.rushu.rush.edu
Established: 1971　Annual Undergrad Tuition & Fees: $31,440
Enrollment: 2,118　Coed
Affiliation or Control: Independent Non-Profit　IRS Status: 501(c)3
Highest Offering: Doctorate
Program: Professional
Accreditation: NH, ANEST, #ARCPA, AUD, BBT, DIETI, DMS, HSA, IPSY, MED, MT, NURSE, OT, PERF, SP

01	President	Dr. Larry J. GOODMAN
03	Executive Vice President/COO	Mr. Peter W. BUTLER
17	Sr Vice Pres Medical Affs/Provost	Dr. Thomas A. DEUTSCH
26	Sr Vice Pres Corp/External Affairs	Mr. Avery S. MILLER
10	Senior Vice President Finance	Mr. John MORDACH
30	Senior Vice President Philanthropy	Ms. Diane M. MCKEEVER
13	Sr Vice Pres/Chief Information Ofcr	Mr. Lac VAN TRAN
43	Sr Vice President Legal Affairs	Ms. Anne MURPHY
15	Sr Vice President Human Resource	Ms. Mary E. SCHOPP
46	Vice President Research	Dr. James L. MULSHINE
25	Vice Pres Chief Compliance Office	Dr. Cynthia E. BOYD
22	Assoc VP Equal Oppty Academic Affs	Ms. Beverly B. HUCKMAN
18	Vice Pres Campus Transformation	Mr. Mick ZDEBLICK
20	Vice Provost	Dr. Lois A. HALSTEAD
32	Assoc Prov Student Svcs/Registrar	Dr. Gayle WARD
76	Dean College of Health Sciences	Dr. David SHELLEDY
58	Acting Dean Graduate College	Dr. James L. MULSHINE
66	Dean College of Nursing	Dr. Melanie DREHER
63	Dean Rush Medical College	Dr. Thomas A. DEUTSCH
20	Assoc Dean Med/Student Pgm	Dr. Keith BOYD
27	Asst Vice President Marketing	Ms. Lori ALLEN
08	Director Library	Ms. Christine D. FRANK
35	Director Student Affairs	Ms. Jill GABBERT
37	Director Student Financial Aid	Mr. David J. NELSON
09	Director of Institutional Research	Dr. James L. MULSHINE
38	Director Student Counsel Center	Dr. Hilarie TEREBESSY
29	Director Alumni Relations	Mr. James LOWENBERG
85	Director International Services	Ms. Helen LAVELLE
96	Director of Purchasing	Mr. Michael MULROE
90	Asst Dir McCormick Educ Tech Ctr	Mr. William FLEMING
21	Manager of Financial Affairs	Ms. Diane HEALY

St. Anthony College of Nursing (E)

5658 E State Street, Rockford IL 61108-2468
County: Winnebago　FICE Identification: 009987
Unit ID: 149028
Telephone: (815) 395-5091　Carnegie Class: Spec/Health
FAX Number: (815) 395-2275　Calendar System: Semester
URL: www.sacn.edu
Established: 1915　Annual Undergrad Tuition & Fees: $20,134
Enrollment: 210　Coed
Affiliation or Control: Roman Catholic　IRS Status: 501(c)3
Highest Offering: Master's
Program: Professional; Nursing Emphasis
Accreditation: NH, NURSE

01	President	Dr. Terese A. BURCH
05	Dean for Undergraduate Affairs	Dr. Elizabeth M. CARSON
58	Dean for Graduate Affairs & Rsrch	Dr. Shannon K. LIZER
32	Assoc Dean for Support Services	Ms. Nancy A. SANDERS
08	College LRC/Med Library Director	Ms. Heather KLEPITSCH

St. Augustine College (F)

1333-45 W Argyle Street, Chicago IL 60640-3501
County: Cook　FICE Identification: 021854
Unit ID: 148876
Telephone: (773) 878-8756　Carnegie Class: Assoc/PrivNFP4
FAX Number: (773) 878-0937　Calendar System: Semester
URL: www.staugustine.edu
Established: 1980　Annual Undergrad Tuition & Fees: $8,760
Enrollment: 1,675　Coed
Affiliation or Control: Independent Non-Profit　IRS Status: 501(c)3
Highest Offering: Baccalaureate
Program: 2-Year Principally Bachelor's Creditable; Liberal Arts And General
Accreditation: NH, SW

01	President	Mr. Andrew C. SUND
05	Dean of Academic & Student Affairs	Dr. Bruno BONDAVALLI
20	Dean of Instruction	Mr. Lee MALTBY
10	VP for Finance	Ms. Saundra FLEMING
30	VP for Institutional Advancement	Mr. Alfredo CALIXTO
103	VP for Workforce Development	Mr. Norman RUANO
09	VP Technology/Research & Systems	Mr. Paul HECK
37	Director of Financial Aid	Ms. Maria ZAMBONINO
15	Director Human Resources	Mr. Teofilo CALERO
18	Director of Physical Facilities	Mr. Pablo RODRIGUEZ
07	Director of Recruitment	Ms. Gloria QUIROZ
12	Director Satellites	Ms. Carmen RIVERA
24	Dir of Learning Resources Center	Ms. Elizabeth GRUBY

Saint Francis Medical Center College of Nursing (G)

511 NE Greenleaf Street, Peoria IL 61603-3783
County: Peoria　FICE Identification: 006240
Unit ID: 148575
Telephone: (309) 655-2201　Carnegie Class: Spec/Health
FAX Number: (309) 624-8973　Calendar System: Semester
URL: www.sfmccon.edu
Established: 1985　Annual Undergrad Tuition & Fees: $16,366
Enrollment: 556　Coed
Affiliation or Control: Roman Catholic　IRS Status: 501(c)3
Highest Offering: Doctorate
Program: Professional; Nursing Emphasis
Accreditation: NH, NUR

01	President of the College	Dr. Patricia A. STOCKERT
05	Dean Undergraduate Program	Dr. Sue C. BROWN
58	Dean Graduate Program	Dr. Janice F. BOUNDY
32	Asst Dean of Support Services	Mr. Kevin N. STEPHENS
07	Director of Admissions/Registrar	Ms. Janice E. FARQUHARSON
08	Librarian	Ms. Leslie E. MENZ
38	College Counselor	Mrs. Jennifer CARLOCK
37	Coord Student Fin/Financial Assist	Mrs. Nancy S. PERRYMAN
21	Coord Student Finance/Accts Rec	Ms. Laura L. SIMMONS
04	Administrative Assistant	Ms. Luann MORELOCK

St. John's College (H)

729 E. Carpenter St., Springfield IL 62702-5317
County: Sangamon　FICE Identification: 030980
Unit ID: 148593
Telephone: (217) 525-5628　Carnegie Class: Spec/Health
FAX Number: (217) 757-6870　Calendar System: Semester
URL: www.stjohnscollegespringfield.edu
Established: 1991　Annual Undergrad Tuition & Fees: $15,792
Enrollment: 111　Coed
Affiliation or Control: Independent Non-Profit　IRS Status: 501(c)3
Highest Offering: Baccalaureate
Program: Professional; Nursing Emphasis
Accreditation: NH, NDT, NUR

01	Chancellor	Dr. Brenda R. JEFFERS
05	Academic Lead	Ms. Casey SCHUMACHER
07	Admissions Officer/Registrar	Ms. Linda S. QUIGLEY
32	Student Development Officer	Ms. Beth M. BEASLEY
30	Development Officer	Ms. Kristine MYSZKA
51	Director of Continuing Education	Dr. Judy SHACKELFORD
37	Financial Aid Officer	Ms. Mary BROWN

Saint Xavier University (I)

3700 W 103rd Street, Chicago IL 60655-3105
County: Cook　FICE Identification: 001768
Unit ID: 148627
Telephone: (773) 298-3000　Carnegie Class: Master's L
FAX Number: (773) 779-9061　Calendar System: Semester
URL: www.sxu.edu
Established: 1846　Annual Undergrad Tuition & Fees: $28,110
Enrollment: 4,709　Coed

Affiliation or Control: Roman Catholic IRS Status: 501(c)3
Highest Offering: Master's
Program: Liberal Arts And General; Professional
Accreditation: NH, ACBSP, MUS, NURSE, SP, TED

01 President .... Ms. Christine M. WISEMAN
05 Provost .... Dr. Angela DURANTE
10 Vice President Business & Finance .... Mr. Raymond P. CATANIA
30 Executive Director Development .... Dr. Steven J. MURPHY
26 Vice President University Relations .... Mr. Robert C. TENCZAR, JR.
32 Vice President Student Affairs .... Mr. John P. PELRINE, JR.
45 Vice Pres Administration/Planning .... Sr. Susan M. SANDERS, RSM
09 Executive Director Inst Research .... Dr. Kathleen CARLSON
13 Asst VP Instr Res & Tech .... Vacant
37 Director Financial Aid .... Ms. Susan SWISHER
35 Asst Vice Pres Student Affairs .... Ms. Carrie SCHADE
18 Asst Vice Pres Facilities Mgmt .... Mr. Peter SKACH
18 Director Auxilliary Services .... Vacant
21 Controller .... Ms. Tina FRODYMA
07 Asst VP Student Recruitment .... Vacant
20 Associate Provost .... Dr. Richard VENNERI
20 Associate Provost .... Vacant
20 Asst Provost/Director Retention .... Ms. Maureen WOGAN
26 Executive Director Media Relation .... Ms. Karla THOMAS
51 Dean School Cont Prof Studies .... Dr. Leslie PETTY
49 Dean College Arts/Sciences .... Dr. Kathleen ALAIMO
53 Dean School of Education .... Dr. S. Beverly GULLEY
50 Interim Dean School of Management .... Dr. John EBER
66 Dean School of Nursing .... Dr. Gloria JACOBSON
35 Dean of Students .... Ms. Eileen DOHERTY
24 Director Media Services .... Mr. Lee VAN SICKLE
08 Director Library .... Mr. Mark A. VARGAS
06 Director Records/Registration Svcs .... Ms. Barbara SUTTON
19 Dir Public Safety/Chief of Police .... Mr. Jack TOUHY
29 Director Alumni/Parent Relations .... Ms. Jamie MANAHAN
41 Director Athletics .... Mr. Robert HALLBERG
42 Director Campus Ministry .... Ms. Esther SANBORN
85 Director Center for Intl Education .... Ms. Colleen O'HARA
40 Director Bookstore Operations .... Ms. Donna GASIOR
96 Purchasing Coordinator .... Ms. Donna PAVLIK
36 Director of Career Services .... Ms. Jean RIORDAN

Sanford-Brown College (A)

1101 Eastport Plaza Drive, Collinsville IL 62234
Identification: 666753
Unit ID: 391582
Telephone: (618) 344-5600 Carnegie Class: Assoc/PrivFP
FAX Number: (314) 421-5256 Calendar System: Semester
URL: www.sanfordbrown.edu/Collinsville
Established: N/A Annual Undergrad Tuition & Fees: $11,891
Enrollment: 889 Coed
Affiliation or Control: Proprietary IRS Status: Proprietary
Highest Offering: Associate Degree
Program: Occupational
Accreditation: ACICS, MAAB

01 Campus Director .... Mr. Douglas GOODWIN

Sauk Valley Community College (B)

173 Illinois Route 2, Dixon IL 61021-9188
County: Lee FICE Identification: 001752
Unit ID: 148672
Telephone: (815) 288-5511 Carnegie Class: Assoc/Pub-R-M
FAX Number: (815) 288-1880 Calendar System: Semester
URL: www.svcc.edu
Established: 1965 Annual Undergrad Tuition & Fees (In-State): $3,243
Enrollment: 1,601 Coed
Affiliation or Control: State IRS Status: 501(c)3
Highest Offering: Associate Degree
Program: Occupational; 2-Year Principally Bachelor's Creditable
Accreditation: NH, RAD

01 President .... Dr. George J. MIHEL
05 Academic Vice President .... Mr. Alan D. PFEIFER
32 Dean of Student Services .... Mr. Luis S. MORENO
10 Dean of Business Services .... Ms. Paula MEYER
20 Dean of Instructional Services .... Mr. Jon MANDRELL
09 Dean Institutional Research/Plng .... Mr. Steve NUNEZ
76 Dean Health & Sciences .... Ms. Janet D. LYNCH
18 Director Buildings & Grounds .... Mr. John DITTO
15 Director of Human Resources .... Ms. Kathryn SNOW
06 Registrar .... Ms. Pam MEDEMA
102 Director of Foundation and Grants .... Ms. Amy VIERING
13 Dean of Information Services .... Ms. Chris SHELLEY
41 Director of Athletics .... Mr. Russ DAMHOFF
26 Coordinator College Relations .... Ms. Rachel MARCO
37 Coord Student Financial Assistance .... Ms. Debra STIEFEL
91 Director of Instructional Technolog .... Dr. Molly BAKER

School of the Art Institute of Chicago (C)

37 S Wabash, Chicago IL 60603-3103
County: Cook FICE Identification: 001753
Unit ID: 143048
Telephone: (312) 899-5100 Carnegie Class: Spec/Arts
FAX Number: (312) 263-0141 Calendar System: Semester
URL: www.saic.edu
Established: 1866 Annual Undergrad Tuition & Fees: $37,560
Enrollment: 3,221 Coed
Affiliation or Control: Independent Non-Profit IRS Status: 501(c)3
Highest Offering: Master's
Program: Teacher Preparatory; Fine Arts Emphasis
Accreditation: NH, ART

01 President .... Mr. Walter MASSEY
00 Chancellor .... Mr. Tony JONES
05 Provost .... Ms. Elissa TENNY
11 Senior VP Planning & COO .... Mr. Edward J. MCNULTY
84 Vice Pres Enrollment Management .... Ms. Rose MILKOWSKI
30 VP for Institutional Advancement .... Ms. Cheryl JESSOGNE
10 Vice President of Finance .... Mr. Brian ESKER
15 Vice President for Human Resources .... Mr. Michael NICOLAI
32 Vice Pres/Dean of Student Affairs .... Dr. Felice DUBLON
20 Vice Provost .... Mr. Paul COFFEY
18 Assoc VP Facilities/Operations .... Mr. Thomas BUECHELE
20 Dean of Faculty .... Ms. Lisa WAINWRIGHT
35 Dean of Student Life .... Ms. Deborah MARTIN
21 Exec Dir Academic Accounting .... Ms. Sherry MISGEN
26 Exec Dir Enroll Mktg & Operations .... Ms. Maryann SCHAEFER
27 Exec Director Mktg & Graphics .... Ms. Ann WIENS
29 Assoc Director Alumni Relations .... Ms. Emily CHAPMAN
38 Exec Director Student Counseling .... Dr. Joseph BEHEN
84 Exec Director Enrollment Services .... Ms. Jane BRUMITT
06 Director Registration & Records .... Mr. Brad ERZ
08 Director of School Library .... Ms. Claire EIKE
36 Asst Dean/Dir Career Development .... Ms. Katharine SCHUTTA
07 Director of Undergrad Admissions .... Mr. Scott RAMON
07 Director of Graduate Admissions .... Mr. Andre VAN DE PUTTE
105 Exec Director Web E-Communication .... Ms. Rae ULRICH
37 Director of Student Financial Svcs .... Mr. Patrick JAMES
28 Director of Multicultural Affairs .... Mr. James BRITT
23 Director of Health Services .... Vacant
09 Enrollment Analyst .... Mr. Bruce FELKNOR
49 Dean Undergraduate Studies .... Ms. Tiffany HOLMES
58 Chair of Graduate Division .... Ms. Barbara DEGENEVIEVE

Seabury-Western Theological Seminary (D)

8765 W. Higgins Road, Chicago IL 60631
County: Cook FICE Identification: 001754
Unit ID: 148724
Telephone: (773) 380-6780 Carnegie Class: Spec/Faith
FAX Number: (847) 328-9624 Calendar System: Semester
URL: www.seabury.edu
Established: 1858 Annual Graduate Tuition & Fees: N/A
Enrollment: 38 Coed
Affiliation or Control: Protestant Episcopal IRS Status: 501(c)3
Highest Offering: Doctorate; No Undergraduates
Program: Professional; Religious Emphasis
Accreditation: THEOL

01 President .... Rev. Roger A. FERLO
05 Academic Dean .... Rev. Ellen WONDRA
10 Interim Director of Finance .... Mr. Robert DOAK
04 Exec Assistant to the Dean .... Br. Ronald A. FOX, BSG
51 Dir of Continuing Education .... Ms. Ruth FREY
08 Director United Library .... Ms. Beth SHEPPARD
06 Registrar & Admissions .... Ms. Peggy PEARSON
30 Director of Development .... Mr. Joe FLINT
42 Dir of Congregational Development .... Ms. Susan HARLOW
15 Mgr Accting/Human Res/Spec Events .... Ms. Lynn BOWERS
44 Annual Campaign Coordinator .... Ms. Susan QUIGLEY

Shawnee Community College (E)

8364 Shawnee College Road, Ullin IL 62992-2206
County: Pulaski FICE Identification: 007693
Unit ID: 148821
Telephone: (618) 634-3200 Carnegie Class: Assoc/Pub-R-L
FAX Number: (618) 634-3300 Calendar System: Semester
URL: www.shawneecc.edu
Established: 1967 Annual Undergrad Tuition & Fees (In-District): $2,760
Enrollment: 3,913 Coed
Affiliation or Control: Local IRS Status: 501(c)3
Highest Offering: Associate Degree
Program: Occupational; 2-Year Principally Bachelor's Creditable
Accreditation: NH, MLTAD, OTA

01 President .... Dr. Larry E. PETERSON
05 Vice Pres Instructional Services .... Dr. Tim H. BELLAMEY
32 Int Vice President Student Svcs .... Ms. Carolyn KINDLE
04 Asst to President/Human Res Ofcr .... Ms. Beth DARDEN
20 Dean Instructional Services .... Ms. Jean Ellen BOYD
51 Dean Adult Educ/Alternative Instruc .... Mr. James DARDEN
10 Chief Financial Officer .... Ms. Tiffiney RYAN
38 Student Support Services Director .... Mr. Jeff MCGOY
35 Dean of Student Services .... Ms. Dee BLAKELY
37 Dir Fin Aid/Coord Vet & Mil Personl .... Dr. Tammy CAPPS
41 Athletic Director .... Mr. Mike FITZGERALD
13 Director MIS .... Mr. Chris CLARK
12 Director Metro Center .... Dr. Sally WEST
66 Director of Nursing .... Ms. Denise GRIFFITH
08 Head Librarian .... Ms. Tracey JOHNSON
06 Registrar .... Ms. Danielle BOYD
102 Dir Resource Development/Foundation .... Mr. Greg LEGAN
21 Director of Business Services .... Ms. Brandy WOODS
18 Facilities Director .... Mr. Don KOCH
40 Bookstore Manager .... Ms. Erica POAT
88 Special Needs Counselor .... Ms. Annie HUBBARD
88 Coord Ctr for Cmty/Economic Devel .... Ms. Candy EASTWOOD
26 Public Relations Coordinator .... Ms. Sharon FELKER
36 Career Services Coordinator .... Ms. Leslie WELDON
50 Div Chair Business/Occup/Tech Dp .... Mr. Jerry AINSWORTH
81 Division Chair Math/Science .... Ms. Rhonda DILLOW
79 Div Chr Social Stds/Humanities/Comm .... Ms. Sharon WALKER
76 Div Chair Allied Health .... Ms. Tracy LOHSTROH

Shimer College (F)

3424 S State Street, Second Floor, Chicago IL 60616-3893
County: Cook FICE Identification: 001756
Unit ID: 148849
Telephone: (312) 235-3500 Carnegie Class: Bac/A&S
FAX Number: (312) 235-3502 Calendar System: Semester
URL: www.shimer.edu
Established: 1853 Annual Undergrad Tuition & Fees: $24,600
Enrollment: 127 Coed
Affiliation or Control: Independent Non-Profit IRS Status: 501(c)3
Highest Offering: Baccalaureate
Program: Liberal Arts And General
Accreditation: NH

01 President .... Dr. Susan HENKING
10 Chief Financial Officer/Dir Ops .... Ms. Sandra COLLINS
05 Dean of the College .... Dr. Barbara STONE
32 Dean of Students .... Mr. B. David GALT
30 Director of Development .... Ms. Mary Pat BARBARI
37 Director of Financial Aid .... Ms. Janet HENTHORN
07 Director of Admissions .... Ms. Elaine VINCENT
08 Library Director .... Ms. Colleen MCCARROLL
06 Registrar .... Mr. James ULRICH

SOLEX College (G)

350 E. Dundee Road, Suite 200, Wheeling IL 60090
County: Cook FICE Identification: 045816
Unit ID: 459356
Telephone: (847) 229-9595 Carnegie Class: Not Classified
FAX Number: (847) 229-1919 Calendar System: Other
Established: 2004 Annual Undergrad Tuition & Fees: $17,200
Enrollment: 30 Coed
Affiliation or Control: Proprietary IRS Status: Proprietary
Highest Offering: Associate Degree
Program: Occupational; 2-Year Principally Bachelor's Creditable; Technical Emphasis
Accreditation: ACICS, COMTA

01 Executive Director .... Mr. Leon E. LINTON

South Suburban College of Cook County (H)

15800 S State Street, South Holland IL 60473-1270
County: Cook FICE Identification: 001769
Unit ID: 149365
Telephone: (708) 596-2000 Carnegie Class: Assoc/Pub-S-SC
FAX Number: (708) 210-5710 Calendar System: Semester
URL: www.ssc.edu
Established: 1927 Annual Undergrad Tuition & Fees (In-District): $3,773
Enrollment: 7,524 Coed
Affiliation or Control: State/Local IRS Status: 501(c)3
Highest Offering: Associate Degree
Program: Occupational; 2-Year Principally Bachelor's Creditable
Accreditation: NH, ADNUR, MAC, MUS, OTA, PNUR

01 President .... Mr. Don MANNING
05 Vice President Academic Services .... Dr. Diane OSTOJIC
11 Vice Pres Administrative Services .... Mr. Don MANNING
32 Vice President Student Development .... Ms. Songie ADEBIYI
84 VP Enrollment/Community Education .... Mrs. Jane Ellen STOCKER
35 Dean Student Development .... Mr. Greg LAWRENCE
83 Dean Legal Studies/Soc & Behav Sci .... Mr. Ronald KAWANNA, JR.
50 Dean Business & Technology .... Mr. James COATES
76 Dean Health Professions & Sciences .... Mr. Jeff WADDY
57 Dean Fine Arts/Soc & Behav Sci/Bus .... Mr. Tom GOVAN, JR.
66 Dean Nursing/Fine Arts/English/Hum .... Ms. Marjorie ROACHE
51 Director Continuing Education .... Ms. Shirley DREWENSKI
10 Controller/Treasurer .... Mr. Tim POLLERT
26 Director Public Rels/Pub & Found .... Mr. Patrick RUSH
14 Director Information Technology .... Mr. John MCCORMACK
35 Assoc Dean Student Services .... Mrs. Patrice BURTON
88 Dir New Student Ctr & Retenion Svcs .... Mrs. Jazaer FARRAR
84 Director Enrollment Services .... Mrs. Robin RIHACEK
37 Director of Financial Aid .... Mr. John SEMPLE
18 Director Physical Plant .... Mr. Martin LAREAU
24 Dir Communication Svcs/Media Design .... Mrs. Lisa MILLER
41 Athletic Director .... Mr. Steve RUZICH
09 Director of Institutional Research .... Mr. Kevin RIORDAN
15 Director Human Resources .... Ms. Kimberly PIGATTI

Southeastern Illinois College (I)

3575 College Road, Harrisburg IL 62946-4925
County: Saline FICE Identification: 001757
Unit ID: 148937
Telephone: (618) 252-5400 Carnegie Class: Assoc/Pub-R-L
FAX Number: (618) 252-3156 Calendar System: Semester
URL: www.sic.edu
Established: 1960 Annual Undergrad Tuition & Fees (In-District): $5,500
Enrollment: 2,138 Coed

Affiliation or Control: State/Local　IRS Status: 501(c)3
Highest Offering: Associate Degree
Program: Occupational; 2-Year Principally Bachelor's Creditable
Accreditation: NH, MLTAD, OTA

01 President ..... Dr. Jonah RICE
05 Vice President Instruction ..... Dr. Dana KEATING
10 VP Administration/Business Affairs ..... Mr. Tim WALKER
32 Dean of Enrollment Mgt & Stdnt Dev ..... Mr. Chad FLANNERY
20 Dean of Career & Technical Educ ..... Mrs. Karen WEISS
103 Assoc Dean of Workforce & Cmty Ed ..... Mrs. Lori COX
08 Head Librarian ..... Mr. Gary JONES
84 Director Enrollment Services ..... Ms. Sarah ADAMS
26 Marketing Coordinator ..... Ms. Angela WILSON
37 Financial Aid Director ..... Ms. Emily HENSON
13 Chief Information Officer ..... Mr. Greg MCCULLOCH
76 Director Allied Health & Nursing ..... Ms. Gina SIRACH
15 Human Resources Administrator ..... Mrs. Barbara POTTER
06 Registrar ..... Ms. Sarah ADAMS
18 Director of Environmental Services ..... Mr. Ed FITZGERALD

*Southern Illinois University (A)

Stone Center - 1400 Douglas Drive, Carbondale IL 6290
County: Jackson　FICE Identification: 008237
Unit ID: 149240
Telephone: (618) 536-3331　Carnegie Class: N/A
FAX Number: (618) 536-3404
URL: www.southernillinois.edu

01 President ..... Dr. Glenn POSHARD
05 Vice President Academic Affairs ..... Dr. Paul SARVELA
10 Sr VP Financial/Admin Affs/Bd Treas ..... Dr. Duane STUCKY
88 Director Risk Management ..... Ms. Chris GLIDEWELL
86 Exec Dir of Governmental Public Aff ..... Vacant
21 Exec Dir of Internal Audits ..... Ms. Kim LABONTE
43 General Couns & Legal Svcs ..... Mr. Jeffrey C. MCCLELLAN
04 Assistant to the President ..... Ms. Paula S. KEITH

*Southern Illinois University Carbondale (B)

425 Clocktower Drive, Carbondale IL 62901-4701
County: Jackson　FICE Identification: 001758
Unit ID: 149222
Telephone: (618) 453-2121　Carnegie Class: RU/H
FAX Number: (618) 453-3250　Calendar System: Semester
URL: siuc.edu/
Established: 1869　Annual Undergrad Tuition & Fees (In-State): $11,528
Enrollment: 19,817　Coed
Affiliation or Control: State　IRS Status: 501(c)3
Highest Offering: Doctorate
Program: Occupational; 2-Year Principally Bachelor's Creditable; Liberal Arts And General; Teacher Preparatory; Professional
Accreditation: NH, AAB, ARCPA, ART, BUS, BUSA, CACREP, CEA, CIDA, CLPSY, COPSY, CORE, CS, DH, DIETD, DIETI, DMS, ENG, ENGT, FOR, FUSER, IFSAC, IPSY, JOUR, LAW, MED, MLTAD, MUS, NAIT, PH, PTAA, RADDOS, RTT, SP, SPAA, SW, TED, THEA

02 Chancellor ..... Dr. Rita CHENG
05 Provost & Vice Chancellor ..... Dr. John NICKLOW
32 Assoc VC Stdnt Life & Intercul Rels ..... Dr. Peter GITAU
30 Vice Chanc Inst Advancement ..... Vacant
10 VC for Administration and Finance ..... Mr. Kevin BAME
46 Assoc VC Rsrch & Dir Rsrch Dev/Adv ..... Dr. John KOROPCHAK
28 Assoc Chancellor Diversity ..... Dr. Linda MCCABE-SMITH
102 Asst Director SIU Foundation ..... Ms. Elizabeth BANYCKY
13 Asst Provost & Chief Info Officer ..... Mr. Ronald D. CRAIN
84 Asst Provost Enrollment Mgmt ..... Vacant
20 Assoc Provost for Academic Admin ..... Ms. Susan LOGUE
20 Assoc Provost for Academic Programs ..... Dr. James S. ALLEN
04 Assistant to the Chancellor ..... Mr. Martin J. BAGGOTT
49 Dean Liberal Arts ..... Dr. Kimberly LEONARD
50 Dean College of Business ..... Dr. James D. CRADIT
53 Interim Dean Educ & Human Services ..... Dr. John J. BENSHOFF
54 Dean Engineering ..... Dr. Gary KOLB
58 Dean Graduate School ..... Dr. John A. KOROPCHAK
61 Dean School of Law ..... Dr. Cynthia FOUNTAINE
81 Interim Dean College of Science ..... Dr. Laurie ACHENBACH
63 Dean School of Medicine ..... Dr. John K. DORSEY
47 Dean Agricultural Sciences ..... Dr. Mickey A. LATOUR
72 Dean Col Applied Sciences & Arts ..... Dr. JuAn WANT
57 Interim Dean Mass Comm/Media Arts ..... Dr. Dafna P. LEMISH
08 Dean Library Affairs ..... Dr. Anne C. MOORE
07 Director Undergrad Admissions ..... Ms. Katharine J. SUSKI
37 Director Student Financial Aid ..... Ms. Terry HARFST
29 Associate VC Alumni Services ..... Ms. Michelle SUAREZ
21 Director Budget ..... Ms. Carol A. HENRY
09 Int Director Institutional Research ..... Dr. George VINEYARD
88 University Ombudsman ..... Mr. Donald BIXLER
13 Exec Dir Finance ..... Ms. Judith MARSHALL
27 Director University Communications ..... Dr. Mike RUIZ
15 Director Human Resources ..... Ms. Jennifer WATSON
39 Interim Director University Housing ..... Ms. Lisa M. MARKS
36 Director Univ Career Services ..... Ms. Keri YOUNG
85 Director Intl Pgms & Svcs ..... Ms. Carla E. COPPI
18 Director Plant/Service Operations ..... Mr. Philip S. GATTON
19 Director of Public Safety ..... Mr. Todd D. SIGLER
23 Director Student Health Services ..... Dr. Ted W. GRACE
41 Director Intercollegiate Athletics ..... Mr. Mario L. MOCCIA
51 Interim Director Continuing Educ ..... Ms. Lorrie LEFLER
06 Director Registrar's Office ..... Ms. Tiffany SPENCER
38 Director Student Counseling Center ..... Dr. Rosemary E. SIMMONS
96 Int Director Procurement Services ..... Ms. Debbie ABELL
35 Assoc Dean of Students ..... Dr. Katherine L. SERMERSHEIM

*Southern Illinois University Edwardsville (C)

Edwardsville IL 62026-0001
County: Madison　FICE Identification: 001759
Unit ID: 149231
Telephone: (618) 650-2000　Carnegie Class: Master's L
FAX Number: (618) 650-2270　Calendar System: Semester
URL: www.siue.edu
Established: 1957　Annual Undergrad Tuition & Fees (In-State): $9,251
Enrollment: 14,235　Coed
Affiliation or Control: State　IRS Status: 501(c)3
Highest Offering: Doctorate
Program: Liberal Arts And General; Teacher Preparatory; Professional
Accreditation: NH, THEA, ANEST, BUS, BUSA, CONST, CS, DENT, ENG, JOUR, MLTAD, MUS, NURSE, PHAR, SP, SPAA, SW, TED

02 Chancellor ..... Dr. Julie FURST-BOWE
05 Interim Prov & VC for Academic Affs ..... Dr. Ann M. BOYLE
11 Vice Chancellor for Administration ..... Mr. Kenneth R. NEHER
26 VC Univ Rel & CEO SIUE Foundation ..... Mr. Patrick HUNDLEY
32 Vice Chanc for Student Affairs ..... Dr. Narbeth R. EMMANUEL
100 Executive Asst to the Chancellor ..... Ms. Kimberly H. DURR
22 Asst Chanc for Institutional Compli ..... Mr. Paul PITTS
20 Assoc Prov for Acad Plng & Pgm Dev ..... Dr. Susan L. THOMAS
20 Assoc Prov Rsch/Dean Grad Sch ..... Dr. Jerry B. WEINBERG
35 Assoc VC Stdnt Affs/Dean of Stdnts ..... Dr. James W. KLENKE
35 Assoc VC for Student Affairs ..... Ms. Lora MILES
13 Assoc VC for IT & CIO ..... Ms. Jennifer VANDEVER
28 Assoc Prov Inst Diversity/Inclusion ..... Dr. Venessa BROWN
88 Asst Prov for Acad Innov & Eff ..... Dr. P. Denise COBB
41 Asst VC Athletic Dev/Dir Athletics ..... Dr. Bradley L. HEWITT
84 Asst VC for Enrollment Mgmt ..... Mr. Scott BELOBRAJDIC
45 Asst VC for Planning & Budgeting ..... Mr. Richard WALKER
49 Dean College of Arts & Sciences ..... Dr. Aldemaro ROMERO
50 Dean School of Business ..... Dr. Gary A. GIAMARTINO
52 Interim Dean Sch of Dental Medicine ..... Dr. Bruce E. ROTTER
53 Dean School of Education ..... Dr. Bette BERGERON
54 Dean School of Engineering ..... Dr. Hasan SEVIM
66 Dean School of Nursing ..... Dr. Marcia C. MAURER
67 Dean School of Pharmacy ..... Dr. Gireesh V. GUPCHUP
62 Dean Library & Information Services ..... Dr. Regina MCBRIDE
21 Budget Director ..... Mr. William F. WINTER, JR.
27 Asst VC Univ Rel/Exec Dir Univ M&C ..... Ms. Elizabeth M. KESERAUSKIS
51 Exec Director Educational Outreach ..... Vacant
12 Exec Dir of East St Louis Center ..... Dr. Venessa BROWN
88 Director Academic Advising ..... Ms. Cheryle L. TUCKER-LOEWE
07 Director Admissions ..... Mr. Todd C. BURRELL
29 Director Alumni Affairs ..... Mr. Stephen E. JANKOWSKI
36 Director Career Dev Center ..... Ms. Susan SEIBERT
38 Director Counseling Services ..... Dr. Andrew B. KING
18 Director Facilities Management ..... Mr. Paul FULIGNI
23 Director Health Services ..... Ms. Riane B. GREENWALT
15 Director Human Resources ..... Ms. Sherrie SENKFOR
09 Dir Institutional Rsrch & Studies ..... Mr. Phillip M. BROWN
85 Director Ctr for International Pgms ..... Dr. Ronald P. SCHAEFER
96 Director of Purchasing ..... Ms. Nancy J. UFERT FAIRLESS
37 Director Student Financial Aid ..... Ms. Sharon L. BERRY
102 Dir Univ Advancement/Foundation Ops ..... Mr. Kevin MARTIN
39 Director University Housing ..... Mr. Michael J. SCHULTZ
19 Director University Police ..... Ms. Regina M. HAYS
06 Registrar ..... Ms. Laura A. STROM

Southwestern Illinois College (D)

2500 Carlyle Avenue, Belleville IL 62221-5899
County: Saint Clair　FICE Identification: 001636
Unit ID: 143215
Telephone: (618) 235-2700　Carnegie Class: Assoc/Pub-S-MC
FAX Number: (618) 277-0631　Calendar System: Semester
URL: www.swic.edu
Established: 1946　Annual Undergrad Tuition & Fees (In-District): $2,912
Enrollment: 7,896　Coed
Affiliation or Control: State/Local　IRS Status: 501(c)3
Highest Offering: Associate Degree
Program: Occupational; 2-Year Principally Bachelor's Creditable
Accreditation: NH, ACFEI, ADNUR, MAC, MLTAD, PTAA, RAD

01 President - District ..... Dr. Georgia COSTELLO
10 Controller ..... Ms. Deborah MASSENA
11 VP Administrative Svcs/Treasurer ..... Mr. Bernie J. YSURSA
05 Vice Pres Instruction ..... Mr. Clay L. BAITMAN
31 Vice Pres Community Svcs ..... Dr. Mark P. EICHENLAUB
26 Vice Pres Mktg/Institutional Adv ..... Mr. Mike R. FLEMING
09 Vice Pres Planning/Evaluation/Dev ..... Mr. H. O. BROWNBACK
15 Director Human Resources ..... Ms. Sherry FAVRE
32 Vice Pres Student Development ..... Ms. Staci G. CLAYBORNE
20 Assoc Dean Instructional Services ..... Ms. Patricia POU
12 Executive Director SWGCC ..... Mr. Charles L. WHITEHEAD
12 Executive Director Red Bud Campus ..... Mr. Mike REED
30 Interim Exec Director Foundation ..... Mr. Gary E. GRAY
08 Dean Learning Resources ..... Mrs. Laurie A. BINGEL
37 Director of Financial Aid/Placement ..... Mr. Robert TEBBE
13 Chief Information Officer ..... Dr. James RIHA
18 Director of Physical Plant ..... Mr. Ron R. HENDERSON
19 Director of Public Safety ..... Mr. Mark A. GREEN
96 Director of Purchasing ..... Mr. Mike R. THOMAS
76 Dean Hlth Sci and Homeland Security ..... Ms. Julie A. MUERTZ
50 Dean of Business Division ..... Ms. Janet S. FONTENOT
72 Dean of Technical Education ..... Mr. Brad SPARKS
81 Dean of Math & Science ..... Ms. Amanda M. STARKEY
49 Dean of Liberal Arts ..... Dr. Paul W. WREFORD
51 Director Adult Education/Cont Educ ..... Dr. Suzanne C. DAILEY
07 Dean of Enrollment Services ..... Ms. Michelle L. BIRK
28 Director of Diversity ..... Ms. Donna MOODY
88 Director Green Jobs/Green Economy ..... Ms. Karen STALLMAN
88 Dean of Success Programs ..... Ms. Deborah ALFORD
88 Treasurer IL Green Economy Network ..... Mr. Robert J. HILGENBRINK

Spertus College (E)

610 S Michigan Avenue, Chicago IL 60605-1994
County: Cook　FICE Identification: 001663
Unit ID: 148982
Telephone: (312) 322-1700　Carnegie Class: Spec/Other
FAX Number: (312) 922-6406　Calendar System: Quarter
URL: www.spertus.edu
Established: 1924　Annual Graduate Tuition & Fees: $18,750
Enrollment: 320　Coed
Affiliation or Control: Independent Non-Profit　IRS Status: 501(c)3
Highest Offering: Doctorate; No Undergraduates
Program: Liberal Arts And General; Teacher Preparatory; Professional
Accreditation: NH

01 President ..... Dr. Hal M. LEWIS
05 Dean ..... Dr. Dean BELL
51 Director for Public Programing ..... Ms. Beth SCHENKER
10 Director Finance & Administration ..... Mr. Robert TENUTA
88 Director Nonprofit Admin Program ..... Dr. Karen BAIRD
37 Student Records/Financial Aid Mgr ..... Ms. Lisa DEL SESTO

Spoon River College (F)

23235 N County Road 22, Canton IL 61520-9801
County: Fulton　FICE Identification: 001643
Unit ID: 148991
Telephone: (309) 647-4645　Carnegie Class: Assoc/Pub-R-M
FAX Number: (309) 649-6235　Calendar System: Semester
URL: www.src.edu
Established: 1959　Annual Undergrad Tuition & Fees (In-District): $3,390
Enrollment: 2,375　Coed
Affiliation or Control: Local　IRS Status: 501(c)3
Highest Offering: Associate Degree
Program: Occupational; 2-Year Principally Bachelor's Creditable
Accreditation: NH

01 President ..... Mr. Curt OLDFIELD
05 Vice President Inst/Student Svcs ..... Dr. Randall GREENWELL
11 Vice President Admin Services ..... Mr. Brett STOLLER
31 Vice President Community Outreach ..... Ms. Carol DAVIS
04 Executive Asst to the President ..... Ms. Julie HAMPTON
36 Dean Career & Technical Education ..... Mr. Michael DENUM
32 Interim Dean Student Services ..... Ms. Missy WILKINSON
66 Dean Nursing ..... Ms. Cheryl A. HOFFMAN
88 Dean Transfer Education ..... Ms. Renee HIGGINS
18 Director Facilities ..... Mr. Bob A. HAILE
53 Dir Secondary Education Programs ..... Mr. Chad MURPHY
08 Director Library Services ..... Ms. Kathleen A. MENANTEAUX
13 Chief Information Officer ..... Mr. Raj SIDDARAJU
41 Director Athletics/Student Life ..... Mr. Ron CLARK
21 Director Business Services ..... Ms. Sarah GRAY
37 Director Financial Aid ..... Ms. Salinda Jo BRANSON
40 Dir Purchasing & Auxiliary Services ..... Mr. Brad T. O'BRIEN
15 Director Human Resources ..... Ms. Michelle L. BUGOS
14 Director Technology Services ..... Mr. Dean CLARY
84 Director Enrollment Services ..... Ms. Missy A. WILKINSON
13 Director Information Services ..... Ms. Patty SCHMIDT
09 Coord Institutional Reporting ..... Ms. Rani MAKKENA
26 Coordinator Marketing ..... Ms. Anna R. BUEHRER
27 Coordinator College Information ..... Ms. Sally SHIELDS

Taylor Business Institute (G)

318 W Adams Street, Suite 500, Chicago IL 60606
County: Cook　FICE Identification: 011810
Unit ID: 149310
Telephone: (312) 658-5100　Carnegie Class: Assoc/PrivFP
FAX Number: (312) 658-0867　Calendar System: Quarter
URL: www.tbiil.edu
Established: 1962　Annual Undergrad Tuition & Fees: $13,500
Enrollment: 322　Coed
Affiliation or Control: Proprietary　IRS Status: Proprietary
Highest Offering: Associate Degree
Program: Occupational
Accreditation: ACICS

01 President ..... Mrs. Janice C. PARKER

Telshe Yeshiva-Chicago (H)

3535 W Foster Avenue, Chicago IL 60625-5598
County: Cook　FICE Identification: 020732
Unit ID: 149329
Telephone: (773) 463-7738　Carnegie Class: Spec/Faith
FAX Number: (773) 463-2849　Calendar System: Semester
Established: 1960　Annual Undergrad Tuition & Fees: $12,000
Enrollment: 91　Male
Affiliation or Control: Independent Non-Profit　IRS Status: 501(c)3
Highest Offering: Second Talmudic Degree

Program: Professional
Accreditation: RABN

01 President ... Rabbi Avrohom C. LEVIN
03 Executive Vice President ... Rabbi Yitzchok LEVIN
05 Vice President ... Rabbi Chaim D. KELLER
05 Vice President ... Rabbi Moshe SCHMELCZER
11 Administrative Director/Secretary ... Rabbi Shmuel ADLER

Toyota Technological Institute at Chicago (A)

6045 South Kenwood Avenue, Chicago IL 60637
County: Cook Identification: 666367
Unit ID: 445054
Telephone: (773) 834-2500 Carnegie Class: Assoc/PrivNFP4
FAX Number: (773) 834-9881 Calendar System: Quarter
URL: www.ttic.edu
Established: 2003 Annual Graduate Tuition & Fees: $30,000
Enrollment: 22 Coed
Affiliation or Control: Independent Non-Profit IRS Status: 501(c)3
Highest Offering: Doctorate; No Undergraduates
Program: Professional; Technical Emphasis
Accreditation: NH

01 Interim President ... Dr. Stuart A. RICE
05 Chief Academic Officer ... Dr. David MCALLESTER
10 Treasurer/Secretary of the Board ... Mr. Masashi HISAMOTO
11 Chief Administrator ... Mr. Gary HAMBURG
58 Director of Graduate Studies ... Dr. Nathan SREBRO
21 Controller ... Ms. Anna RUFFULO
15 Human Resources Coordinator ... Ms. Liv LEADER

Tribeca Flashpoint Media Arts Academy (B)

28 North Clark Street, Suite 500, Chicago IL 60602
County: Cook Identification: 667083
Telephone: (312) 332-0707 Carnegie Class: Not Classified
FAX Number: (312) 506-0708 Calendar System: Semester
URL: www.tfa.edu
Established: 2007 Annual Undergrad Tuition & Fees: $25,500
Enrollment: 550 Coed
Affiliation or Control: Proprietary IRS Status: Proprietary
Highest Offering: Associate Degree
Program: Occupational; 2-Year Principally Bachelor's Creditable
Accreditation: ACICS

01 President ... Howard A. TULLMAN
05 Exec VP/Dean Academic Affairs ... Paula M. FROEHLE
10 Exec VP/Chief Financial Officer ... Mario CHRISTOPHER
11 Sr VP/Associate Academic Dean ... John MURRAY
15 Sr VP/Human Resources/Career Svcs ... Jill GEIMER
07 Sr VP/Director Admissions ... Heather SWANSON
11 Sr VP Operations ... Ernesto PARAS
26 VP Marketing/Business Development ... Edward GLASSMAN
32 VP/Assoc Dean of Students ... Benjamin J. SPANNER
06 Registrar ... Brad BERGERON
21 Controller ... Laura PETRY

Trinity Christian College (C)

6601 W College Drive, Palos Heights IL 60463-0929
County: Cook FICE Identification: 001771
Unit ID: 149505
Telephone: (708) 597-3000 Carnegie Class: Bac/Diverse
FAX Number: (708) 385-5665 Calendar System: 4/1/4
URL: www.trnty.edu
Established: 1959 Annual Undergrad Tuition & Fees: $23,098
Enrollment: 1,470 Coed
Affiliation or Control: Independent Non-Profit IRS Status: 501(c)3
Highest Offering: Baccalaureate
Program: Liberal Arts And General; Teacher Preparatory; Professional
Accreditation: NH, ACBSP, NURSE, SW

01 President ... Dr. Steven TIMMERMANS
05 Provost ... Dr. Elizabeth RUDENGA
10 Vice Pres for Business & Finance ... Mr. James E. BELSTRA
07 Dean of Admissions ... Mr. Pete HAMSTRA
32 Vice President Student Development ... Mrs. Ginny CARPENTER
30 Vice Pres for Development ... Mr. Larryl HUMME
11 Vice Pres for Campus Development ... Dr. George VANDER VELDE
08 Director of Library Services ... Ms. Marcille FREDERICK
06 Registrar ... Mr. Chris HUANG
07 Director of Admissions ... Mr. Jeremy KLYN
36 Director Career Planning/Placement ... Mrs. Jackie MEDENBLIK
55 Director of Adult Studies Programs ... Dr. Lori SCREMENTI
29 Director of Alumni Relations ... Mr. Travis BANDSTRA
27 Dir of Marketing and Communications ... Ms. Kim FABIAN
88 Asst Dir Marketing/Graphic Designer ... Mr. Peter CLEVERING
44 Campaign Gifts Manager ... Vacant
14 Director of Computer Services ... Mr. Joe VELDERMAN
41 Director of Athletics ... Mr. Bill SCHEPEL
31 Director of Community Partnerships ... Ms. Anna ROSAS
42 Chaplain ... Dr. Willis VAN GRONINGEN
85 Director of Off-Campus Programs ... Dr. Burton J. ROZEMA
37 Director Financial Aid ... Ms. Denise COLEMAN
18 Director of Building/Grounds ... Mr. Tim TIMMONS
44 Director of Planned Giving ... Mr. Ken BOSS
21 Controller ... Mr. Mike TROCHUCK
28 Dir of Diversity/Acad Dean/Ed Prof ... Mr. Don WOO
92 Director of Honors Program ... Dr. Craig MATTSON
35 Director Student Affairs/Counseling ... Mrs. Ginny CARPENTER
84 Director Enrollment Management ... Mr. Pete HAMSTRA
09 Asst Registar for Inst Research ... Ms. Kimberly WILLIAMS
15 Human Resources Manager ... Mr. Larry BOER
20 Acad Dean/Mathematics Prof ... Dr. Sharon ROBBERT
20 Acad Dean/Social Work Prof ... Dr. Mackenzi HUYSER

Trinity College of Nursing & Health Sciences (D)

2122 25th Avenue, Rock Island IL 61201-5317
County: Rock Island FICE Identification: 006225
Unit ID: 146755
Telephone: (309) 779-7700 Carnegie Class: Spec/Health
FAX Number: (309) 779-7748 Calendar System: Semester
URL: www.trinitycollegeqc.edu
Established: 1994 Annual Undergrad Tuition & Fees: $12,394
Enrollment: 222 Coed
Affiliation or Control: Independent Non-Profit IRS Status: 501(c)3
Highest Offering: Baccalaureate
Program: Professional; Nursing Emphasis
Accreditation: NH, ADNUR, NURSE, RAD

01 Chancellor ... Dr. Susan C. WAJERT
05 Dean of Nursing & Health Sciences ... Ms. Tracy L. POELVOORDE

Trinity International University (E)

2065 Half Day Road, Deerfield IL 60015-1284
County: Lake FICE Identification: 001772
Unit ID: 149514
Telephone: (847) 945-8800 Carnegie Class: DRU
FAX Number: (847) 317-8090 Calendar System: Semester
URL: www.tiu.edu
Established: 1897 Annual Undergrad Tuition & Fees: $24,610
Enrollment: 2,823 Coed
Affiliation or Control: Evangelical Free Church Of America
IRS Status: 501(c)3
Highest Offering: Doctorate
Program: Liberal Arts And General; Teacher Preparatory; Professional
Accreditation: NH, THEOL

01 President ... Dr. Craig WILLIFORD
04 Director of the President's Office ... Ms. Mindy WILKERSON
03 Exec Vice President & Provost ... Dr. Jeanette HSIEH
05 Sr VP Education/Dean Divinity Sch ... Dr. Tite TIENOU
20 Sr Vice President Academic Affairs ... Dr. Jeanette HSIEH
84 Sr VP for Enrollment Management ... Mr. Roger L. KIEFFER
32 Sr VP Stdnt Affs/Dn Stdnts/Athl Dir ... Dr. William O. WASHINGTON
13 Sr VP Information Technology/Plng ... Mr. Steven GEGGIE
30 Sr Vice Pres University Advancement ... Dr. David HOAG
10 Sr VP of Business & Finance/CFO ... Mr. Mike PICHA
44 Vice President of Development ... Mr. Carl JOHNSON
26 Director Marketing ... Ms. Rachel YANTIS
21 University Controller ... Mr. Paul EISENMENGER
73 Assoc Academic Dean Divinity School ... Dr. James R. MOORE
88 Interim Dean of Nontraditional Educ ... Mr. Jay SIMALA
35 Assoc Dean of Undergraduate Stdnts ... Ms. Karen WROBBEL
90 Director of Acad/Desktop Computing ... Mr. Chris MILLER
91 Director Administrative Computing ... Ms. Katie KEMP
23 Director of Health Services ... Ms. Barbara VIETMEIER
58 Assoc Dean of Graduate School ... Dr. Joyce A. SHELTON
61 Dean of Law School ... Mr. Myron R. STEEVES
35 Dean of Students TEDS & TGS ... Mr. Felix THEONUGRAHA
42 Chaplain ... Rev. Scott SAMUELSON
07 Director Undergraduate Admissions ... Mr. Aaron MAHL
07 Director TEDS & TGS Admissions ... Mr. Jared CHRISTIENSEN
19 Director of Security Services ... Mr. Bob TOPOREK
96 Director of Facilities ... Mr. Ryan HUST
15 Director of Human Resources ... Mr. Kevin MOON
06 Assoc University Registrar ... Mr. David SKINNER
37 Director of Financial Aid ... Ms. Patricia COLES
36 Director of Career Services ... Ms. Jan VICTOR
36 Director of Placement ... Dr. Eugene SWANSTROM
08 University Librarian ... Dr. Robert H. KRAPOHL
29 Director of Alumni ... Mr. Ryan L. FINNELLY
27 Director of Publications ... Mr. Chris DONOTO
38 Director of Counseling Center ... Ms. Cathy CONWAY
28 Director of Ethnic Diversity ... Mr. Orlando FELICIANO
92 Director of Honors Program ... Vacant
35 Director of Student Activities ... Ms. Heather CORDERO
85 International Student Coordinator ... Ms. Kate REED
39 Housing Coordinator ... Mrs. Amy HORTON

Triton College (F)

2000 Fifth Avenue, River Grove IL 60171-1995
County: Cook FICE Identification: 001773
Unit ID: 149532
Telephone: (708) 456-0300 Carnegie Class: Assoc/Pub-S-SC
FAX Number: (708) 583-3112 Calendar System: Semester
URL: www.triton.edu
Established: 1964 Annual Undergrad Tuition & Fees (In-District): $3,302
Enrollment: 15,632 Coed
Affiliation or Control: Local IRS Status: 501(c)3
Highest Offering: Associate Degree
Program: Occupational; 2-Year Principally Bachelor's Creditable; Business Emphasis
Accreditation: NH, ADNUR, CACREP, DMS, NMT, RAD, SURGT

01 President ... Dr. Patricia GRANADOS
10 Vice President Business Services ... Mr. Sean SULLIVAN
05 VP Student and Academic Affairs ... Dr. Douglas OLSON
101 Secretary for Brd of Trustees ... Ms. Susan PAGE
13 Assoc Vice Pres Information Systems ... Mr. Michael GARRITY
21 Assoc VP Business Operations ... Mr. Kevin KENNEDY
18 Assoc VP Facilities ... Mr. John LAMBRECHT
20 Assoc Vice Pres Academic Affairs ... Ms. Cheryl ANTONICH
35 Dean of Student Services ... Mr. Corey WILLIAMS
84 Dean of Enrollment Services ... Mr. Sujith ZACHARIAH
21 Director Finance ... Mr. James REYNOLDS
45 Director Planning & Accreditation ... Ms. Margaret STABILE
25 Director of Grants Development ... Dr. Sherry BURLINGAME
88 Director Teaching & Learning ... Dr. Mary Ann TOBIN
26 Executive Director Marketing ... Mr. Sam TOLIA
07 Director Admissions Services ... Ms. Izabela ZURAWSKA
37 Assoc Dean of Financial Aid ... Ms. Patricia ZINGA
19 Chief of Police ... Mr. Jeffrey SARGENT
102 Director Triton Foundation ... Vacant
31 Dir Spec Initiatives/Community Rels ... Ms. Lindsey WESTLEY
09 Dir Institutional Effectiveness ... Ms. Faon GRANDINETTI
14 Sr Data and System Admin ... Mr. Robert HAUSKNECHT
91 Director Programming Services ... Vacant
102 Asst Director Corporate Outreach ... Ms. Susan SMEDINGHOFF
90 Manager Online Technology ... Vacant
86 Outreach/Communications Assistant ... Ms. Brenda JONES WATKINS
72 Instructional Technologist ... Ms. Marie-Ange ZICHER
49 Dean Arts & Sciences ... Vacant
51 Dean of Continuing Education ... Mr. Paul JENSEN
76 Dean Health Careers & Pub Svc Pro ... Dr. Sue COLLINS
55 Dean of Adult Education ... Dr. Virginia CABASA-HESS
09 Dean of Academic Success ... Dr. Deborah BANESS KING
49 Asst Dean of Arts & Sciences ... Mr. Ric SEGOVIA
51 Asst Dean Continuing Education ... Ms. Colleen MAZZUCA-PESCE
29 Director Alumni Relations ... Ms. Lisa SCALESSI
50 Dean Business & Technology ... Vacant
100 Coord for Brd of Trustees/Exec Asst ... Ms. Mayra RIVERA
32 AVP of Student Affairs ... Dr. Quincy MARTIN
45 AVP of Strategic Planning ... Ms. Mary Rita MOORE
13 VP of Technology & Innovation ... Mr. Humberto ESPINO

University of Chicago (G)

5801 S Ellis Avenue, Chicago IL 60637-1496
County: Cook FICE Identification: 001774
Unit ID: 144050
Telephone: (773) 702-1234 Carnegie Class: RU/VH
FAX Number: N/A Calendar System: Quarter
URL: www.uchicago.edu
Established: 1891 Annual Undergrad Tuition & Fees: $43,581
Enrollment: 15,262 Coed
Affiliation or Control: Independent Non-Profit IRS Status: 501(c)3
Highest Offering: Doctorate
Program: Liberal Arts And General; Teacher Preparatory; Professional
Accreditation: NH, BUS, IPSY, LAW, MED, SW, THEOL

01 President ... Mr. Robert J. ZIMMER
05 Provost ... Mr. Thomas F. ROSENBAUM
03 Executive Vice President ... Mr. David A. GREENE
10 VP of Administration/CFO ... Mr. Nim CHINNIAH
86 Vice President for Civic Engagement ... Mr. Derek DOUGLAS
101 VP/Sec of the University ... Mr. David FITHIAN
46 VP for Research/Argonne Natl Lab ... Mr. Donald LEVY
17 EVP for Medical Affairs/Dean of BSD ... Dr. Kenneth POLONSKY
30 VP for Alumni Rel & Development ... Mr. Ken MANOTTI
43 Vice President & General Counsel ... Ms. Beth A. HARRIS
88 Vice Pres/Chief Investment Officer ... Mr. Mark A. SCHMID
84 VP/Dean Col Enroll/Financial Aid ... Mr. James NONDORF
42 Dean Rockefeller Memorial Chapel ... Ms. Elizabeth DAVENPORT
32 VP/Campus Life Student Services ... Ms. Karen W. COLEMAN
26 Vice Pres for Communications ... Ms. Julie PETERSON
88 Assoc VP University Architect ... Mr. Steve WIESENTHAL
16 Assoc VP Human Resources Mgmt ... Ms. Gwynne DILDAY
09 Assoc VP Rsrch/Dir Rsrch Admin ... Ms. Carol ZUICHES
21 Asst VP Risk Management & Audit ... Mr. Glenn KLINKSIEK
31 Assoc VP for Community Affairs ... Ms. Susan CAMPBELL
35 Ast VP Stdnt Life/Assoc Dean Col ... Ms. Eleanor DAUGHERTY
49 Dean of the College ... Mr. John W. BOYER
83 Dean of Social Sciences Division ... Mr. Mario SMALL
79 Dean of Humanities Division ... Ms. Martha T. ROTH
61 Dean of the Law School ... Mr. Michael H. SCHILL
88 Dean Harris Sch Public Policy ... Mr. Colm O'MUIRCHEARTAIGH
81 Dean Physical Sciences Division ... Mr. Robert A. FEFFERMAN
88 Dean of the Divinity School ... Ms. Margaret MITCHELL
50 Dean of Booth School of Business ... Mr. Sunil KUMAR
70 Dean Social Svcs Admin ... Mr. Neil GUTERMAN
04 Associate Provost ... Ms. Ingrid GOULD
88 Deputy Provost for Research ... Dr. Roy E. WEISS
20 Deputy Provost for Grad Education ... Ms. Deborah L. NELSON
28 Deputy Provost for Minority Affairs ... Mr. William MCDADE
22 Assoc Provost/Affirm Action Ofcr ... Ms. Aneesah ALI
45 Assoc Provost for Planning ... Ms. Blair ARCHAMBEAU
20 Associate Provost ... Mr. Stephen H. GABEL
20 Associate Provost ... Ms. Mary J. HARVEY
21 AVP for Finance ... Mr. John R. KROLL
06 Interim Registrar ... Mr. Andrew HANNAH
37 Director College Aid ... Ms. Alicia REYES
36 Co-Dir Career Adv & Planning Svcs ... Vacant
36 Director Career Adv & Planning Svcs ... Ms. Meredith DAW
08 Director University Library ... Ms. Judith NADLER
38 Dir Stdnt Counseling/Resource Svc ... Dr. Thomas A M. KRAMER
96 Exec Dir Payroll/Procurement ... Mr. Mark FEHLBERG

*University of Illinois University Administration (A)

506 S Wright Street, Urbana IL 61801-3689
County: Champaign FICE Identification: 008001
Unit ID: 149587
Telephone: (217) 333-6400 Carnegie Class: N/A
FAX Number: (217) 333-5733
URL: www.uillinois.edu

01 President ... Dr. Robert A. EASTER
02 Vice President/Chancellor (Chicago) ... Dr. Paula ALLEN-MEARES
02 Vice President/Chancellor (Sprfld) ... Dr. Susan KOCH
02 Vice President/Chancellor (Urbana) ... Dr. Phyllis WISE
10 CFO/VP and Comptroller ... Mr. Walter KNORR
05 Vice Pres for Academic Affairs ... Dr. Christophe PIERRE
17 Vice Pres for Health Affairs ... Dr. Joe GARCIA
09 Vice Pres for Research ... Dr. Lawrence SCHOOK
43 University Counsel ... Mr. Thomas R. BEARROWS
86 Exec Director for Govt Relations ... Ms. Katherine LAING
26 Exec Dir for University Relations ... Mr. Thomas P. HARDY
13 Executive CIO ... Dr. Michael HITES
16 Executive Director HR ... Ms. Maureen PARKS
101 Secretary Board of Trustees/Univ ... Dr. Susan M. KIES

*University of Illinois at Chicago (B)

601 S Morgan, M/C 102, Chicago IL 60607-7128
County: Cook FICE Identification: 001776
Unit ID: 145600
Telephone: (312) 996-7000 Carnegie Class: RU/VH
FAX Number: (312) 413-3393 Calendar System: Semester
URL: www.uic.edu
Established: 1896 Annual Undergrad Tuition & Fees (In-State): $13,938
Enrollment: 27,580 Coed
Affiliation or Control: State IRS Status: 501(c)3
Highest Offering: Doctorate
Program: Liberal Arts And General; Teacher Preparatory; Professional
Accreditation: NH, ART, BUS, BUSA, CEA, CLPSY, CS, DENT, DIETC, DIETD, ENG, ENGR, IPSY, MED, MIDWF, MIL, NURSE, OT, PH, PHAR, PLNG, PTA, SPAA, SW

02 Chancellor ... Dr. Paula ALLEN-MEARES
05 Vice Chancellor Acad Affs/Provost ... Dr. Lon KAUFMAN
32 Vice Chancellor Student Affairs ... Dr. Barbara HENLEY
11 Vice Chanc for Administrative Svcs ... Mr. Mark DONOVAN
46 Vice Chancellor for Research ... Dr. Mitra DUTTA
26 Vice Chanc for External Affairs ... Vacant
17 CEO Healthcare System ... Mr. John DENARDO
29 Vice President Alumni Association ... Ms. Arlene NORSYM
30 Vice Chancellor for Development ... Ms. Penelope C. HUNT
84 Int Vice Prov Acad/Enrollment Svcs ... Ms. Amy LEVANT
35 Assoc Vice Chanc/Dean Stdnt Affairs ... Dr. Linda DEANNA
27 Assoc Chancellor Public Affairs ... Mr. Mark ROSATI
23 Vice Pres for Health Affairs ... Dr. Skip GARCIA
10 Exec Asst VP Business/Finance ... Dr. Heather J. HABERAECKER
48 Dean College Arch & the Arts ... Ms. Judith RUSSI KIRSHNER
50 Dean College Business Admin ... Dr. Michael B. MIKHAIL
52 Dean College Dentistry ... Dr. Bruce GRAHAM
53 Dean College Education ... Dr. Victoria CHOU
54 Dean College Engineering ... Dr. Peter C. NELSON
76 Dean Col Applied Health Sciences ... Dr. Bo FERNHALL
58 Dean Graduate College ... Dr. Karen COLLEY
92 Dean of the Honors College ... Dr. Bette L. BOTTOMS
49 Dean Liberal Arts & Sciences ... Dr. Astrida ORLE TANTILLO
63 Dean College Medicine ... Dr. Dimitri AZAR
66 Dean College Nursing ... Dr. Terri E. WEAVER
67 Dean College Pharmacy ... Dr. Jerry BAUMAN
70 Dean College Social Work ... Dr. Creasie HAIRSTON
69 Dean School of Public Health ... Dr. Paul BRANDT-RAUF
26 Dean Urban Planning/Public Affs ... Dr. Michael A. PAGANO
43 University Counsel ... Mr. Thomas R. BEARROWS
08 University Librarian ... Ms. Mary CASE
88 Asst Univ Librarian Health Sciences ... Ms. Kathryn H. CARPENTER
07 Exec Director Admissions ... Mr. Kevin M. BROWNE
41 Director Athletics ... Mr. James W. SCHMIDT
38 Director Student Counseling ... Dr. Joseph HERMES
37 Director Student Financial Aid ... Mr. Timothy OPGENORTH
09 Director of Institutional Research ... Ms. Mary LELIK
15 Director Faculty Affairs HR ... Ms. Angela L. YUDT
22 Director Access & Equity ... Ms. Caryn A. BILLS-WINDT
36 Director Career Services ... Mr. Jaime VELASQUEZ
14 Director Acad Computer/ Communs ... Ms. Cynthia E. HERRERA LINDSTROM
56 Exec Director External Education ... Ms. Mary P. NIEMIEC
51 Exec Dir School Cont Studies ... Ms. Cordelia MALONEY
06 Registrar ... Mr. Robert DIXON
96 Interim Director of Purchasing ... Mr. Kevin FAIR
18 Director Operations & Maintenance ... Mr. Clarence E. BRIDGES

*University of Illinois at Springfield (C)

One University Plaza, Springfield IL 62703-5407
County: Sangamon FICE Identification: 009333
Unit ID: 148654
Telephone: (217) 206-6600 Carnegie Class: Master's L
FAX Number: (217) 206-6511 Calendar System: Semester
URL: www.uis.edu
Established: 1969 Annual Undergrad Tuition & Fees (In-State): $8,952
Enrollment: 5,137 Coed
Affiliation or Control: State IRS Status: 501(c)3
Highest Offering: Doctorate
Program: Liberal Arts And General; Teacher Preparatory; Professional
Accreditation: NH, BUS, CACREP, MT, SPAA, SW

02 Chancellor ... Dr. Susan KOCH
27 Assoc Chancellor/Constituent Rels ... Mr. Edward WOJCICKI
05 Vice Chancellor Acad Affs ... Ms. Lynn PARDIE
32 Vice Chanc Student Affairs ... Dr. Timothy L. BARNETT
20 Vice Chanc Undergrad Education ... Ms. Karen MORANSKI
29 Vice President Alumni Relations ... Mr. Charles SCHRAGE
30 Interim Assoc Chancellor for Devel ... Ms. Sarah JENNINGS
18 Asc Chanc Admin/Exec Dir Facil Svcs ... Mr. David BARROWS
22 Asc Chanc Access/Equal Opportunity ... Ms. Deanie BROWN
49 Dean College Liberal Arts/Science ... Dr. James ERMATINGER
50 Dean College Business/Management ... Dr. Ronald D. MCNEIL
80 Dean College Public Affs/Admin ... Dr. Pinky S. WASSENBERG
53 Interim Dean College Edu/Human Svcs ... Dr. James ERMATINGER
15 Acting Director of Human Resources ... Mr. Robert LAEL
84 Director of Enrollment Management ... Vacant
43 Legal Counsel ... Dr. Mark HENSS
08 University Librarian ... Ms. Jane B. TREADWELL
26 Director Public Information ... Mr. Derek SCHNAPP
20 Associate Provost ... Mr. Aaron G. SHURES
19 Chief Campus Police Department ... Mr. Donald MITCHELL
06 Registrar ... Mr. Brian CLEVENGER
35 Director of Student Life ... Ms. Cynthia THOMPSON
41 Director of Athletics ... Ms. Kim PATE
90 Director Campus Technology Service ... Vacant
09 Director Institutional Research ... Ms. Laura DORMAN
96 Director of Purchasing ... Mr. Michael BLOECHLE
37 Director Financial Assistance ... Dr. Gerard JOSEPH
38 Director Counseling Center ... Dr. Judith SHIPP
85 Director International Programs ... Dr. Jonathan GOLDBERGBELLE
24 Assoc Prov Educational Technology ... Mr. Farokh ESLAHI
39 Director Campus Housing ... Mr. John RINGLE

*University of Illinois at Urbana-Champaign (D)

601 E John Street, Champaign IL 61820-5711
County: Champaign FICE Identification: 001775
Unit ID: 145637
Telephone: (217) 333-1000 Carnegie Class: RU/VH
FAX Number: (217) 333-9758 Calendar System: Semester
URL: www.illinois.edu
Established: 1867 Annual Undergrad Tuition & Fees (In-State): $14,960
Enrollment: 31,932 Coed
Affiliation or Control: State IRS Status: 501(c)3
Highest Offering: Doctorate
Program: Occupational; Liberal Arts And General; Teacher Preparatory; Professional
Accreditation: NH, ART, AUD, BUS, BUSA, CLPSY, COPSY, CORE, CS, DANCE, DIETD, DIETI, ENG, FOR, IPSY, JOUR, LAW, LIB, LSAR, MUS, NRPA, PLNG, SP, SW, THEA, VET

02 Vice President & Chancellor ... Dr. Phyllis M. WISE
05 Vice Chancellor Acad Affs & Provost ... Dr. Ilesanmi ADESIDA
46 Vice Chancellor Research ... Dr. Peter E. SCHIFFER
32 Vice Chancellor Student Affairs ... Dr. C. Renee ROMANO
30 Int Vice Chanc for Inst Advancement ... Mr. Edward EWALD
31 Associate Chanc Public Engagement ... Dr. Pradeep KHANNA
20 Vice Provost Academic Affairs ... Dr. Barbara WILSON
88 Associate Chancellor ... Mr. Michael DELORENZO
88 Associate Chancellor ... Dr. Menah PRATT-CLARKE
26 Associate Chanc Public Affairs ... Ms. Robin KALER
04 Associate Chancellor ... Dr. Reginald ALSTON
29 Int Assoc Chanc Alumni Relations ... Ms. Vanessa FAURIE
15 Associate Provost Human Resources ... Ms. Elyne COLE
07 Asst Prov Enrollment Management ... Ms. Stacey KOSTELL
82 Int Assoc Provost Intl Pgms/Studies ... Dr. Wolfgang SCHLOER
21 Vice Provost Budgetary Planning ... Mr. Mike ANDRECHAK
09 Asst Provost Management Info ... Dr. Amy EDWARDS
49 Dean Liberal Arts & Sciences ... Dr. Ruth WATKINS
61 Dean Law ... Dr. Bruce SMITH
74 Dean Veterinary Medicine ... Dr. Herbert E. WHITELEY
54 Interim Dean Engineering ... Dr. Michael B. BRAGG
47 Dean Agric/Consumer/Environ Sci ... Dr. Robert HAUSER
50 Dean Business ... Dr. Larry DEBROCK
57 Dean Fine & Applied Arts ... Dr. Robert GRAVES
70 Dean School of Social Work ... Dr. Wynne S. KORR
68 Dean Col Applied Health Sciences ... Dr. Tanya M. GALLAGHER
60 Interim Dean College of Media ... Dr. Janet SLATER
58 Dean Graduate College ... Dr. Debasish DUTTA
62 Int Dean Grad Sch Library/Info Sci ... Dr. Allen H. RENEAR
53 Dean Education ... Dr. Mary KALANTZIS
63 Int Reg Dean Col Med/Urbana-Champ ... Dr. Uretz S. OLIPHANT
88 Int Dean Labor & Employment Rels ... Dr. Joseph J. MARTOCCHIO
08 University Librarian & Dean ... Dr. Paula KAUFMAN
88 Dir Acad Aff Institute of Aviation ... Mr. Tom EMANUEL
13 Interim Chief Information Officer ... Mr. Paul HIXSON
35 Dean of Students ... Dr. Kenneth BALLOM
56 Int Assoc Dean Extension & Outreach ... Dr. Robert HOEFT
41 Director Athletics ... Mr. Michael J. THOMAS
10 Asst Vice Pres Bus/Fin Affairs ... Ms. Maxine L. SANDRETTO
43 Campus Legal Counsel ... Mr. Scott RICE
88 Deputy CIO Information Technology ... Mr. Joseph G. GULICK
22 Dir Equal Opportunity & Access ... Dr. Menah PRATT-CLARKE
19 Director Public Safety ... Mr. Jeffrey T. CHRISTENSEN
18 Exec Director Facilities Services ... Dr. John G. DEMPSEY
23 Director McKinley Health Center ... Dr. Robert D. PALINKAS
36 Director Career Services Center ... Dr. Gail ROONEY
37 Director Student Financial Aid ... Mr. Daniel R. MANN
38 Director Counseling Center ... Dr. Carla MCCOWAN
39 Director Housing Division ... Mr. John E. COLLINS
51 Int Dir Cont Educ/Public Service ... Dr. Faye LESHT
06 Int Registrar ... Mr. Rodney E. HOEWING

University of St. Francis (E)

500 N Wilcox Street, Joliet IL 60435-6188
County: Will FICE Identification: 001664
Unit ID: 148584
Telephone: (815) 740-3400 Carnegie Class: Master's L
FAX Number: (815) 740-4285 Calendar System: Semester
URL: www.stfrancis.edu
Established: 1920 Annual Undergrad Tuition & Fees: $26,824
Enrollment: 3,321 Coed
Affiliation or Control: Roman Catholic IRS Status: 501(c)3
Highest Offering: Doctorate
Program: Liberal Arts And General; Teacher Preparatory; Professional
Accreditation: NH, ACBSP, NRPA, NURSE, SW, TED

01 President ... Dr. Michael J. VINCIGUERRA
05 Provost/VP Academic Affairs ... Dr. Frank H. PASCOE
10 VP Finance & Administration ... Ms. Elizabeth A. LAKEN
84 VP Admissions/Enrollment Svcs ... Mr. Charles M. BEUTEL
88 VP Mission Int & Ministry ... Sr. Mary Elizabeth IMLER
27 CIO ... Dr. Gerard H. KICKUL
30 Chief Advancement Officer ... Ms. Regina M. BLOCK
04 Executive Assistant to President ... Ms. Barbara S. INGOLD
26 Exec Dir Univ Rels/Pres Liaison ... Ms. Nancy A. POHLMAN
18 Exec Dir Operations & Facil Mgmt ... Mr. Mike DECMAN
30 Exec Dir Development ... Ms. Jacquelyn A. BERSANO
21 Controller ... Mr. Mark MCCABE
49 Dean Col Arts & Sciences ... Dr. Robert KASE
50 Dean Col Business/Health Admin ... Dr. Christopher CLOTT
53 Dean Col Education ... Dr. John S. GAMBRO
66 Dean Col Nursing ... Dr. Carol J. WILSON
32 Dean of Students ... Mr. Damon N. SLOAN
29 Dir Alumni Relations ... Ms. Aubrey L. DURISH
41 Dir Athletics ... Mr. Dave LAKETA
38 Dir Counseling Services ... Mr. Carlos AQUINO
28 Dir Diversity ... Dr. Billie P. TERRELL
37 Dir Financial Aid ... Ms. Mary V. SHAW
07 Dir Undergrad Admissions ... Vacant
07 Dir Grad/Degree Completion Admiss ... Ms. Sandra L. SLOKA
07 Asst Dir Undergraduate Admissions ... Mr. Eric A. RUIZ
15 Dir Human Resources ... Mr. John D. BYRNES
09 Dir Institutional Effectiveness ... Ms. Janine M. HICKS
08 Dir Library Services ... Mr. Terrance L. COTTRELL
14 Dir Network Support Services ... Mr. Mark T. SNODGRASS
39 Dir Residence Life ... Ms. Christina M. AICHELE
19 Dir Security ... Mr. Thomas S. URASKI
35 Dir Student Development ... Ms. Dominique A. ANNIS
42 Dir University Ministry ... Ms. Julie M. KRAKORA
06 Registrar ... Ms. Laura A. KOGA
23 Coordinator of Health Services ... Ms. Phyllis M. PETERSON
36 Dir Career Services ... Vacant
24 Head of Tech Svcs ... Ms. Gail GAWLIK
105 Web Communications Manager ... Mr. Michael PLANETA

University of Saint Mary of the Lake-Mundelein Seminary (F)

1000 E Maple Avenue, Mundelein IL 60060-1174
County: Lake FICE Identification: 001765
Unit ID: 148885
Telephone: (847) 566-6401 Carnegie Class: Spec/Faith
FAX Number: (847) 566-7330 Calendar System: Quarter
URL: www.usml.edu
Established: 1844 Annual Graduate Tuition & Fees: $22,185
Enrollment: 165 Male
Affiliation or Control: Roman Catholic IRS Status: 501(c)3
Highest Offering: Doctorate; No Undergraduates
Program: Professional; Religious Emphasis
Accreditation: THEOL

00 Chancellor ... Card. Francis GEORGE
01 Rector/President ... Rev. Robert E. BARRON
03 Vice Rector for Seminary Admin ... Rev. James PRESTA
05 Vice Rector for Academic Affairs ... Rev. Thomas A. BAIMA
73 Vice President/Ecclesiastical Dean ... Rev. John G. LODGE
32 Vice President/Dean of Formation ... Rev. Ronald HICKS
20 Vice President & Provost ... Rev. Thomas FRANZMAN
10 Vice President for Finance ... Mr. John F. LEHOCKY
30 Vice President Inst Advancement ... Mr. Mark TERESI
18 Vice President for Facilities ... Mr. Stanley C. RYS
20 Assistant Academic Dean ... Mr. Christopher MCATEE
73 Director Pre-Theology Program ... Rev. August J. BELAUSKAS
08 Library Director ... Mrs. Lorraine OLLEY
06 Registrar ... Mrs. Mary Ann ULZ
88 Director of Pastoral Internships ... Rev. Martin BARNUM
88 Director of Liturgy ... Rev. John S. SZMYD
88 Director of Prayer Formation ... Rev. Kevin FEENEY
39 Director of Seminary Residence Hall ... Rev. Kevin FEENEY
14 Director Computer Services ... Mr. Eric ALBERT
28 Director of Diversity ... Rev. Martin BARNUM

VanderCook College of Music (G)

3140 S Federal Street, Chicago IL 60616-3731
County: Cook FICE Identification: 001778
Unit ID: 149639
Telephone: (312) 225-6288 Carnegie Class: Spec/Arts
FAX Number: (312) 225-5211 Calendar System: Semester
URL: www.vandercook.edu
Established: 1909 Annual Undergrad Tuition & Fees: $24,116
Enrollment: 368 Coed
Affiliation or Control: Independent Non-Profit IRS Status: 501(c)3
Highest Offering: Master's

Program: Teacher Preparatory; Professional; Music Emphasis
Accreditation: NH, MUS

01 President .... Dr. Charles T. MENGHINI
06 Registrar .... Mrs. Carolyn BERGHOFF
08 Head Librarian .... Mr. Robert DELAND
05 Dean of Undergraduate Studies .... Ms. Stacey LARSON
58 Dean of Graduate Studies .... Ms. Ruth RHODES
07 Director of Admissions .... Ms. Amy LENTING
10 Controller .... Ms. Diane KELLY
37 Director of Financial Aid .... Ms. Sirena COVINGTON
13 Director Information Technologies .... Mr. Rick MALIK
04 President's Assistant .... Ms. Cindy TOVAR
51 Director of Continuing Education .... Mr. Rick PALESE

Vatterott College-Quincy (A)

3609 North Marx Drive, Quincy IL 62305
County: Adams FICE Identification: 020693
Unit ID: 148140
Telephone: (217) 224-0600 Carnegie Class: Assoc/PrivFP
FAX Number: (217) 223-6771 Calendar System: Other
URL: www.vatterott-college.edu
Established: 1995 Annual Undergrad Tuition & Fees: $11,135
Enrollment: 291 Coed
Affiliation or Control: Proprietary IRS Status: Proprietary
Highest Offering: Associate Degree
Program: Occupational; 2-Year Principally Bachelor's Creditable
Accreditation: ACCSC

01 CEO & President .... Ms. Pam BELL
10 Chief Financial Officer .... Mr. Dennis BEAVERS
05 Vice President Academic Affairs .... Mr. Brandon SHEDRON
30 VP Regulatory Affs/Strategic Devel .... Mr. Aaron LACEY
43 General Counsel/Chief Administrator .... Mr. Scott CASANOVER
12 Campus Director .... Mr. Tom LOCKETT

Waubonsee Community College (B)

Route 47 at Waubonsee Drive,
Sugar Grove IL 60554-9799
County: Kane FICE Identification: 006931
Unit ID: 149727
Telephone: (630) 466-7900 Carnegie Class: Assoc/Pub-S-SC
FAX Number: (630) 466-7550 Calendar System: Semester
URL: www.waubonsee.edu
Established: 1966 Annual Undergrad Tuition & Fees (In-District): $2,448
Enrollment: 10,717 Coed
Affiliation or Control: Local IRS Status: 501(c)3
Highest Offering: Associate Degree
Program: Occupational; 2-Year Principally Bachelor's Creditable
Accreditation: NH, MAC, SURGT

01 President .... Dr. Christine J. SOBEK
05 Exec VP Educ Affs/Chief Lrng Ofcr .... Dr. Deborah F. LOVINGOOD
10 Exec VP Finance & Operations .... Mr. David QUILLEN
09 VP Quality/Strategic Development .... Dr. Karen STEWART
56 Asst VP Pgm Devel/Distance Learning .... Ms. Jane REGNIER
20 Asst Vice President of Instruction .... Ms. Jill WOLD
32 Vice Pres of Student Development .... Ms. Melinda L. JAMES
16 Exec Director Human Resources .... Ms. Michele NEEDHAM
13 Chief Information Officer .... Mr. Terence FELTON
76 Dean Health & Life Science .... Dr. Jess TOUSSAINT
83 Dean Social Sciences & Education .... Dr. William MARZANO
79 Dean Humanities/Fine Arts/Languages .... Ms. Cynthia FISHER
88 Dean Learning Enhancement/Coll Read .... Ms. Medea RAMBISH
106 Dean Dist Learn/Instuc Tech .... Ms. Renee TONIONI
60 Dean Communications/Library Svc .... Ms. Mary Edith BUTLER
18 Director Campus Operations .... Mr. Dale WILLERTH
30 Director Fund Development .... Ms. Katharine RICHARDS
35 Dean Counseling/Student Support .... Ms. Kelli SINCLAIR
56 Dean Adult Education .... Ms. Jeri L. DIXON
72 Dean Tech/Math/Physical Science .... Dr. Paul HUMMEL
50 Dean Business/Information Systems .... Ms. Suzette MURRAY
103 Dean Workforce Development .... Ms. Lesa NORRIS
84 Dean Enrollment Mgmt .... Ms. Faith LASHURE
26 Exec Dir Marketing/Communications .... Mr. Jeff NOBLITT
21 Asst Vice President of Finance .... Ms. Darla S. CARDINE
04 Senior Executive to President .... Ms. Kimberly CAPONI
37 Director Student Fin Aid Services .... Dr. Charles BOUDREAU
28 Dir Governmental/Multicultural Affa .... Ms. Lourdes BLACKSMITH
31 Dean Community Education .... Mr. Douglas L. GRIER
09 Dir Institutional Effectiveness .... Dr. Stacey RANDALL
88 Asst VP Workforce Sol/Comm Learning .... Mr. Gary KECSKÉS
19 Dir Emergency/Preparednes/Safety .... Mr. John WU
88 Dir Accounting/Business Services .... Mr. Bruce HARTMANN

Western Illinois University (C)

1 University Circle, Macomb IL 61455-1390
County: McDonough FICE Identification: 001780
Unit ID: 149772
Telephone: (309) 295-1414 Carnegie Class: Master's L
FAX Number: (309) 298-2400 Calendar System: Semester
URL: www.wiu.edu
Established: 1899 Annual Undergrad Tuition & Fees (In-State): $10,443
Enrollment: 12,554 Coed
Affiliation or Control: State IRS Status: 501(c)3
Highest Offering: Doctorate
Program: Liberal Arts And General; Teacher Preparatory
Accreditation: NH, ART, BUS, BUSA, CACREP, CEA, DIETD, MUS, NAIT, NRPA, NURSE, SP, SW, TED, THEA

01 President .... Dr. Jack THOMAS
05 Provost/Vice Pres Academic Affairs .... Dr. Kenneth HAWKINSON
20 Assoc Provost/Assoc VP Acad Affs .... Dr. Kathleen NEUMANN
20 Asst VP for Academic Affairs .... Dr. Ronald WILLIAMS
20 Int Assoc Provost/Undergrad & Grad .... Dr. Nancy P. PARSON
11 VP Administrative Services .... Ms. Julie DEWEES
32 Vice President Student Services .... Dr. Gary M. BILLER
26 Vice Pres Advancement/Public Svcs .... Mr. Bradley BAINTER
29 Director Alumni Programs .... Ms. Amy SPELMAN
35 Assoc VP Student Support Svcs .... Mr. W. Earl BRACEY
39 Assoc Vice Pres Student Services .... Mr. John BIERNBAUM
45 VP for QC & Planning .... Dr. Joseph RIVES
86 Asst to Pres Government Relations .... Vacant
49 Dean College Arts/ Sciences .... Dr. Susan MARTINELLI-FERNANDEZ
50 Dean College Business/Technology .... Dr. Thomas L. EREKSON
53 Dean College Ed & Human Svcs .... Dr. Sterling SADDLER
57 Dean Fine Arts & Comm .... Dr. William T. CLOW
08 Dean University Libraries .... Dr. Phyllis SELF
92 Dir Illinois Centennial Honors Col .... Dr. Richard J. HARDY
64 Director School of Music .... Dr. Bart SHANKLIN
06 Registrar .... Dr. Angela LYNN
21 Director Business Services .... Ms. Dana BIERNBAUM
13 Dir Admin Information Mgmt Systems .... Ms. Brenda PARKS
90 Director of University Technology .... Mr. Daniel A. ROMANO
27 Director University Relations .... Ms. Darcie R. SHINBERGER
09 Director Inst Research & Planning .... Ms. Rhonda K. KLINE
22 Director Equal Opportunity & Access .... Ms. Andrea HENDERSON
37 Director Financial Aid .... Mr. Robert ANDERSEN
36 Director Placement .... Mr. Martin J. KRAL
15 Director Human Resources .... Ms. Pamela L. BOWMAN
18 Interim Director Physical Plant .... Mr. Scott A. COKER
19 Interim Director Public Safety .... Mr. Thomas N. CLARK
23 Director Health Center .... Ms. Mary M. HARRIS
31 Dir Distance Learning and Outreach .... Dr. Richard CARTER
40 Director University Bookstore .... Mr. Jude KIAH
41 Director Athletics .... Dr. Tim VAN ALSTINE
102 Director WIU Foundation .... Mr. Bradley BAINTER
30 Director of Development .... Vacant
07 Director Admissions .... Dr. Andrew BORST
38 Director Student Counseling .... Dr. James E. DITULIO
96 Director of Purchasing .... Ms. Dana BIERNBAUM
85 Dir Center International Studies .... Dr. Richard CARTER

Westwood College-Chicago Loop (D)

1 North State Street, Suite 1000, Chicago IL 60602
County: Cook Identification: 666424
Unit ID: 443687
Telephone: (312) 739-0850 Carnegie Class: Bac/Diverse
FAX Number: (312) 739-1004 Calendar System: Other
URL: www.westwood.edu
Established: 2003 Annual Undergrad Tuition & Fees: $29,735
Enrollment: 700 Coed
Affiliation or Control: Proprietary IRS Status: Proprietary
Highest Offering: Baccalaureate
Program: Occupational; Business Emphasis
Accreditation: ACICS

01 Campus President .... Debbie PLEMONS
05 Academic Dean .... Dillon RASMUSSEN
07 Admissions Director .... Jeff HILL

† Branch campus of Westwood College-Los Angeles, Los Angeles, CA.

Westwood College-DuPage (E)

7155 Janes Avenue, Woodridge IL 60517-2321
County: DuPage FICE Identification: 030792
Unit ID: 406194
Telephone: (866) 721-7646 Carnegie Class: Bac/Diverse
FAX Number: (630) 963-1420 Calendar System: Quarter
URL: www.westwood.edu
Established: N/A Annual Undergrad Tuition & Fees: $24,508
Enrollment: 320 Coed
Affiliation or Control: Proprietary IRS Status: Proprietary
Highest Offering: Baccalaureate
Program: Occupational; Liberal Arts And General
Accreditation: ACICS

01 Campus President .... Kelly T. MOORE
05 Campus Academic Dean .... Jennifer SHARP
11 Director of Campus Operations .... Diana GARCIA
07 Director of Admissions .... Doug LOCHBAUM
36 Assistant Director of Career Svcs .... Elliott REASONER
37 Director of Student Finance .... Pertrina BRIGGS

Westwood College-O'Hare Airport (F)

8501 W Higgins Road, Suite 100, Chicago IL 60631-2814
County: Cook FICE Identification: 023139
Unit ID: 178226
Telephone: (773) 380-6800 Carnegie Class: Bac/Diverse
FAX Number: (773) 380-6820 Calendar System: Other
URL: www.westwood.edu
Established: 2000 Annual Undergrad Tuition & Fees: $14,923
Enrollment: 655 Coed
Affiliation or Control: Proprietary IRS Status: Proprietary
Highest Offering: Baccalaureate
Program: Occupational; 2-Year Principally Bachelor's Creditable; Professional; Technical Emphasis
Accreditation: ACICS

01 President .... Mr. David BOSTICK
05 Academic Dean .... Dr. Ellen CROWE
32 Assistant Director of Student Svcs .... Vacant
10 Director of Campus Operations .... Ms. Zena WILLIAMS
07 Director of Admissions .... Mr. Lou BELLSOM
36 Director of Career Services .... Ms. Hope GREEN
37 Director of Student Finance .... Ms. Tracy WALKER

Westwood College-River Oaks (G)

80 River Oaks Center, Suite 111,
Calumet City IL 60409-5555
County: Cook Identification: 666440
Unit ID: 440147
Telephone: (708) 832-1988 Carnegie Class: Bac/Diverse
FAX Number: (708) 862-6525 Calendar System: Other
URL: www.westwood.edu
Established: 2000 Annual Undergrad Tuition & Fees: $14,923
Enrollment: 523 Coed
Affiliation or Control: Proprietary IRS Status: Proprietary
Highest Offering: Baccalaureate
Program: Occupational
Accreditation: ACICS

01 Executive Director .... Bruce MCKENZIE

† Branch campus of Westwood College-Los Angeles, Los Angeles, CA.

Wheaton College (H)

501 College Avenue, Wheaton IL 60187-5593
County: DuPage FICE Identification: 001781
Unit ID: 149781
Telephone: (630) 752-5000 Carnegie Class: Bac/A&S
FAX Number: (630) 752-5555 Calendar System: Semester
URL: www.wheaton.edu
Established: 1860 Annual Undergrad Tuition & Fees: $30,120
Enrollment: 3,069 Coed
Affiliation or Control: Independent Non-Profit IRS Status: 501(c)3
Highest Offering: Doctorate
Program: Liberal Arts And General; Teacher Preparatory; Professional
Accreditation: NH, CLPSY, MUS, TED

01 President .... Dr. Philip G. RYKEN
05 Provost .... Dr. Stanton L. JONES
03 Vice President for Finance .... Mr. Dale A. KEMP
32 Vice President Student Development .... Mr. Paul O. CHELSEN
30 Vice Pres Advancement/Alumni Rels .... Dr. R. Mark DILLON
04 Exec Asst to the President .... Miss Marilee A. MELVIN
58 Acting Dean of the Graduate School .... Dr. Nicholas PERRIN
79 Dean Humanities/Theol Studies .... Dr. Jill P. BAUMGAERTNER
49 Dean of the Conservatory of Music .... Dr. Michael WILDER
83 Dean Natural & Social Sciences .... Dr. Dorothy F. CHAPPELL
104 Dean Global & Exper Learning .... Dr. Laura M. MONTGOMERY
09 Dean Information and Technology .... Dr. Gary N. LARSON
35 Dean of Student Care and Services .... Dr. Melanie HUMPHREYS
06 Registrar .... Mrs. Peggy KING
08 College Librarian .... Mrs. Lisa T. RICHMOND
20 Director Billy Graham Center .... Dr. Lon J. ALLISON
21 Business Manager .... Mr. Stephen W. MEAD
21 Senior Dir of Financial Operations .... Mr. Patrick T. BROOKE
29 Director of Alumni Relations .... Ms. Cindra STACKHOUSE TAETZCH
24 Director of Media Resources .... Mr. J. R. SMITH
36 Director of Career Services .... Mrs. Ita FISCHER
16 Director of Human Resources .... Mrs. Karen TUCKER
13 Director of Computing Services .... Mr. Lowell W. BALLARD
07 Director Undergraduate Admissions .... Ms. Shawn B. LEFTWICH
07 Director Graduate Admissions .... Ms. Julie A. HUEBNER
37 Director of Student Financial Aid .... Ms. Karen BELLING
39 Associate Dean of Residence Life .... Mr. Justin HETH
38 Director of Counseling .... Dr. Doug B. DEMERCHANT
42 Chaplain .... Dr. Stephen B. KELLOUGH
23 Director of Student Health Services .... Ms. Britt BLACK
26 Director of Media Relations .... Ms. LaTonya TAYLOR
40 Interim Manager of Bookstore .... Mr. Wyatt WATERMAN
18 Director of Physical Plant .... Mr. James M. JOHNSON
19 Chief of Public Safety .... Mr. Robert F. NORRIS
105 Director Web Communications .... Miss Elisa M. LEBERIS
88 Editor & Director of Special Proj .... Mrs. Georgia DOUGLASS
93 Director Multicultural Development .... Mr. Rodney K. SISCO
96 Director of Purchasing .... Mr. Gregory S. DOTY
88 Director Risk Management .... Mr. Daniel CLARK

Worsham College of Mortuary Science (I)

495 Northgate Parkway, Wheeling IL 60090-2646
County: Cook FICE Identification: 001783
Unit ID: 369455
Telephone: (847) 808-8444 Carnegie Class: Assoc/PrivFP
FAX Number: (847) 808-8493 Calendar System: Quarter
URL: www.worshamcollege.com
Established: 1911 Annual Undergrad Tuition & Fees: $20,700
Enrollment: 100 Coed
Affiliation or Control: Proprietary IRS Status: Proprietary
Highest Offering: Associate Degree
Program: Occupational
Accreditation: FUSER

01 Director .... Ms. Stephanie J. KANN

Zarem/Golde ORT Technical Institute (A)

5440 W. Fargo Avenue, Skokie IL 60077
County: Cook FICE Identification: 041184
Unit ID: 393180
Telephone: (847) 324-5588 Carnegie Class: Assoc/PrivNFP
FAX Number: (847) 324-5580 Calendar System: Other
URL: www.chicagotrainingschool.com
Established: 1991 Annual Undergrad Tuition & Fees: $5,550
Enrollment: 500 Coed
Affiliation or Control: Independent Non-Profit IRS Status: 501(c)3
Highest Offering: Associate Degree
Program: Occupational; 2-Year Principally Bachelor's Creditable; Nursing Emphasis
Accreditation: CNCE

01 Director .... Marina CHUDNOVSKY

INDIANA

American College of Education (B)

101 West Ohio St., Suite 1200, Indianapolis IN 46204
County: Marion Identification: 666242
Unit ID: 449889
Telephone: (800) 280-0307 Carnegie Class: Spec/Other
FAX Number: N/A Calendar System: Semester
URL: www.ace.edu
Established: 2005 Annual Graduate Tuition & Fees: $6,950
Enrollment: 3,410 Coed
Affiliation or Control: Proprietary IRS Status: Proprietary
Highest Offering: Master's; No Undergraduates
Program: Teacher Preparatory
Accreditation: NH, @TEAC

01 President .... Ms. Sandra DORAN
05 Associate Provost .... Dr. Shawntel D. LANDRY
10 Vice President Regulatory Affairs .... Ms. Sharyl THOMPSON
26 Sr VP Marketing and Enrollment .... Ms. Rhonda HARPER

Anabaptist Mennonite Biblical Seminary (C)

3003 Benham Avenue, Elkhart IN 46517-1999
County: Elkhart FICE Identification: 001823
Unit ID: 151865
Telephone: (574) 295-3726 Carnegie Class: Spec/Faith
FAX Number: (574) 295-0092 Calendar System: 4/1/4
URL: www.ambs.edu
Established: 1946 Annual Graduate Tuition & Fees: $13,740
Enrollment: 115 Coed
Affiliation or Control: Mennonite Church IRS Status: 501(c)3
Highest Offering: Master's; No Undergraduates
Program: Professional
Accreditation: NH, THEOL

01 President .... Dr. Sara W. SHENK
05 Academic Dean .... Dr. Rebecca SLOUGH
11 Administrative Vice President .... Mr. Ron RINGENBERG
30 Director of Development .... Ms. Missy K. SCHROCK
10 Chief Financial Officer .... Mr. Jeff MILLER
06 Registrar .... Mr. Scott JANZEN
08 Librarian .... Ms. Eileen SANER
84 Director of Enrollment Services .... Mr. Bob ROSA
73 Director of Inst Mennonite Studies .... Dr. Mary H. SCHERTZ

Ancilla College (D)

PO Box 1, Donaldson IN 46513-0001
County: Marshall FICE Identification: 001784
Unit ID: 150048
Telephone: (574) 936-8898 Carnegie Class: Assoc/PrivNFP
FAX Number: (574) 935-1773 Calendar System: Semester
URL: www.ancilla.edu
Established: 1937 Annual Undergrad Tuition & Fees: $13,650
Enrollment: 518 Coed
Affiliation or Control: Roman Catholic IRS Status: 501(c)3
Highest Offering: Associate Degree
Program: 2-Year Principally Bachelor's Creditable
Accreditation: NH

01 President .... Dr. Ron MAY
04 Assistant to the President .... Ms. Diana CALDWELL
05 Dean of Academic & Student Services .... Dr. Joanna BLOUNT
10 Exec Director Finance & Admin .... Mr. Mike BROWN
30 Exec Dir of Institutional Advance .... Mr. Todd ZELTWANGER
07 Interim Exec Dir of Admissions .... Mr. Eric WIGNALL
42 Coord Mission Integration .... Sr. Carleen WRASMAN, PHJC
21 Director of Business Affairs .... Mr. Raymond GIRRES
37 Director of Financial Aid .... Mrs. Katherine MILLS
41 Athletic Director .... Mr. Robert REESE
36 Director of Advising Center .... Mr. James CAWTHON
30 Assoc Dir Inst Advancement/Alumni .... Mr. Thomas SIBAL
13 Director of Information Technology .... Mr. John LINBACK
09 Interim Dir Inst Rsrch/Assessment .... Vacant
18 Chief Facilities/Physical Plant .... Mr. Tom NOWAK
32 Director Student Development .... Mr. Gene REESE
06 Interim Registrar .... Ms. Diane ENDRES
40 Bookstore Manager .... Ms. Nena HASKINS
08 Librarian .... Ms. Cassaundra BASH
17 Director Nursing & Health Science .... Ms. Ann FITZGERALD

Anderson University (E)

1100 E Fifth Street, Anderson IN 46012-3495
County: Madison FICE Identification: 001785
Unit ID: 150066
Telephone: (765) 649-9071 Carnegie Class: Master's L
FAX Number: (765) 641-3851 Calendar System: Semester
URL: www.anderson.edu
Established: 1917 Annual Undergrad Tuition & Fees: $25,440
Enrollment: 2,611 Coed
Affiliation or Control: Church Of God IRS Status: 501(c)3
Highest Offering: Doctorate
Program: Liberal Arts And General; Teacher Preparatory; Professional
Accreditation: NH, ACBSP, MUS, NURSE, SW, TED, THEOL

01 President .... Dr. James L. EDWARDS
05 Provost .... Dr. Marie S. MORRIS
10 Vice President Finance/Treasurer .... Mrs. Dana S. STUART
30 Vice President for Advancement .... Mr. Robert L. COFFMAN
32 VP Student Affairs .... Dr. Brent A. BAKER
73 Dean School of Theology .... Dr. David L. SEBASTIAN
79 Dean College of the Arts .... Dr. Jeffrey E. WRIGHT
81 Dean College of Science/Humanities .... Dr. D. Blake JANUTOLO
50 Dean Falls School of Business .... Dr. Terry C. TRUITT
42 Campus Pastor .... Rev. J. Todd FAULKNER
06 University Registrar .... Mr. Arthur J. LEAK
26 Exec Director for Advancement .... Mr. Tom S. BRUCE
08 Director of Libraries .... Dr. Janet L. BREWER
07 Director of Admissions .... Mr. Joe M. DAVIS
21 Assistant Treasurer/Controller .... Mrs. Vanessa J. TIJERINA
36 Dir Career Development .... Mrs. Laurie L. JUDGE
14 Director of Info Technology Svcs .... Mr. Michael A. TUCKER
37 Student Financial Services .... Mr. Kenneth F. NIEMAN
27 Dir Univ Communications/Cmty Rels .... Mr. Chris J. WILLIAMS
18 Exec Dir Facilities & Property Mgmt .... Mr. Joseph M. ROYER
16 Director of Human Resources .... Mrs. Denise A T. KRIEBEL
19 Director Police & Security Services .... Mr. Walter L. SMITH
24 Director of Ctr for Educ Technology .... Mr. Shelby D. CANTLEY
51 Dean School of Adult Learning .... Dr. Aleza D. BEVERLY
40 Bookstore Manager .... Mr. Antonio S. DELAROSA
41 Athletic Director .... Ms. Marcie J. TAYLOR
38 Director Counseling Services .... Ms. Christal R. HELVERING
29 Director of Alumni Relations .... Mr. Benjamin A. DAVIS

The Art Institute of Indianapolis (F)

3500 Depauw Boulevard Suite 1010, Indianapolis IN 46268
County: Marion Identification: 666247
Unit ID: 448345
Telephone: (317) 613-4800 Carnegie Class: Spec/Arts
FAX Number: (317) 613-4808 Calendar System: Quarter
URL: www.aii.edu/indianapolis
Established: 2006 Annual Undergrad Tuition & Fees: $17,616
Enrollment: 942 Coed
Affiliation or Control: Proprietary IRS Status: Proprietary
Highest Offering: Baccalaureate
Program: Liberal Arts And General
Accreditation: ACICS

01 President .... Mr. Michael MORPHEW
05 Dean of Academic Affairs .... Mr. Gary ZELLO

† Branch campus of The Art Institute of Phoenix, AZ.

Ball State University (G)

2000 W University Avenue, Muncie IN 47306-1099
County: Delaware FICE Identification: 001786
Unit ID: 150136
Telephone: (765) 289-1241 Carnegie Class: RU/H
FAX Number: (765) 285-1461 Calendar System: Semester
URL: www.bsu.edu
Established: 1918 Annual Undergrad Tuition & Fees (In-State): $8,980
Enrollment: 22,147 Coed
Affiliation or Control: State IRS Status: 501(c)3
Highest Offering: Doctorate
Program: Occupational; Liberal Arts And General; Teacher Preparatory; Professional
Accreditation: NH, DANCE, AAFCS, ART, AUD, BUS, BUSA, CACREP, CEA, CIDA, COPSY, CORE, DIETD, DIETI, ENGT, IPSY, JOUR, LSAR, MUS, NURSE, PLNG, RAD, SCPSY, SP, SW, TED, THEA

01 President .... Dr. Jo Ann M. GORA
05 Provost/Vice Pres Academic Affs .... Dr. Terry KING
84 VP Marketing/Comm/Enroll Mgmt .... Mr. Tom TAYLOR
10 VP Business Affairs & Treasurer .... Dr. Randy B. HOWARD
30 Vice Pres University Advancement .... Mr. Hudson AKIN
13 VP for Information Technology .... Mr. Philip C. REPP
32 VP Student Affairs/Dean of Students .... Dr. Kay BALES
41 Dir Intercollegiate Athletics .... Mr. Bill SCHOLL
21 Assoc VP Business/Aux Svcs .... Ms. Leisa JULIAN
86 Assoc VP Governmental Relations .... Ms. Gretchen GUTMAN
21 Assoc VP Finance/Asst Treasurer .... Mr. Bernard HANNON
85 Dean Rinker Ctr for Intl Programs .... Dr. Kenneth M. HOLLAND
20 Assoc Provost/Dean Univ College .... Dr. Marilyn M. BUCK
18 Assoc VP Facilities Planning/Mgmt .... Mr. Kevin S. KENYON
07 Director Admissions & Orientation . Mr. Christopher T. MUNCHEL
32 Asc VP Student Affairs/Dir Housing .... Dr. Alan L. HARGRAVE
29 Exec Director Alumni Programs .... Vacant
26 Assoc VP Marketing & Communications .. Mr. Tony PROUDFOOT
38 Director Counseling/Health Services .... Dr. June P. PAYNE
14 Asst VP IT for Strategic/Fiscal Mgt .... Mr. Donald (Jr.) KING
88 Dir Unified Techonology Support .... Mr. Dan LUTZ
36 Director Career Center .... Vacant
37 Director Scholarships/Financial Aid .... Dr. John MCPHERSON
22 Exec Director University Compliance .... Ms. Sali K. FALLING
06 Reg/Dir Registration/Acad Pgms .... Mrs. Nancy L. CRONK
09 Int Dir Inst Effectiveness .... Mrs. Andrea INGLE
30 Exec Director Univ Development .... Dr. Charles R. JAGGERS
96 Director of Purchasing Services .... Mrs. Rhodene UPCHURCH
24 Director of Teleplex .... Mr. William B. CAHOE
88 Asst to Vice Pres/Ombudsperson .... Mrs. Katie SLABAUGH
25 Director Contracts & Grants .... Ms. Kathy A. LUCAS
19 Director Public Safety .... Mr. Gene BURTON
15 Director of Human Resources Svcs .... Ms. Judith A. BURKE
28 Asst Provost Diversity .... Dr. Charles R. PAYNE
08 Dean University Libraries .... Dr. Arthur W. HAFNER
57 Dean College of Fine Arts .... Dr. Robert A. KVAM
50 Dean Miller College of Business .... Dr. Rajib N. SANYAL
48 Dean College Architecture/Planning .... Dr. Guillermo P. VASQUEZ DE VELASCO
53 Dean of Teachers College .... Dr. John E. JACOBSON
58 Asc Provost/Research/Dean Grad Sch .... Dr. Robert J. MORRIS
49 Dean Col of Science/Humanities .... Dr. Michael A. MAGGIOTTO
60 Dean Col of Comm/Info/Media .... Mr. Roger LAVERY
72 Dean Col Applied Science/Technology .... Dr. Mitchell H. WHALEY
92 Dean of Honors College .... Dr. James S. RUEBEL
103 Assoc VP Econ Dev/Community Engage . Dr. John A. FALLON, III

Bethany Theological Seminary (H)

615 National Road W, Richmond IN 47374-4019
County: Wayne FICE Identification: 001637
Unit ID: 143233
Telephone: (800) 287-8822 Carnegie Class: Spec/Faith
FAX Number: (765) 983-1840 Calendar System: Semester
URL: www.bethanyseminary.edu
Established: 1905 Annual Graduate Tuition & Fees: $11,961
Enrollment: 71 Coed
Affiliation or Control: Church Of The Brethren IRS Status: 501(c)3
Highest Offering: Master's; No Undergraduates
Program: Professional
Accreditation: NH, THEOL

01 President .... Dr. Ruthann K. JOHANSEN
05 Academic Dean .... Dr. Steven J. SCHWEITZER
10 Exec Dir of Student/Business Svcs .... Ms. Brenda J. REISH
30 Exec Dir Institutional Advancement .... Mr. Lowell FLORY
20 Director of Academic Services .... Ms. April VANLONDEN
26 Director of Communications .... Ms. Jennifer L. WILLIAMS
32 Director of Student Development .... Ms. Amy S. GALL RITCHIE
12 Director Brethren Academy .... Ms. Julie M. HOSTETTER
88 Director Inst Ministry with Youth .... Mr. Russell HAITCH
07 Director of Admissions .... Ms. Tracy PRIMOZICH

Bethel College (I)

1001 Bethel Circle, Mishawaka IN 46545-5509
County: Saint Joseph FICE Identification: 001787
Unit ID: 150145
Telephone: (574) 259-8511 Carnegie Class: Bac/Diverse
FAX Number: (574) 257-3326 Calendar System: Semester
URL: www.bethelcollege.edu
Established: 1947 Annual Undergrad Tuition & Fees: $23,930
Enrollment: 2,074 Coed
Affiliation or Control: Missionary Church IRS Status: 501(c)3
Highest Offering: Master's
Program: 2-Year Principally Bachelor's Creditable; Liberal Arts And General; Teacher Preparatory; Professional; Nursing Emphasis
Accreditation: NH, ADNUR, IACBE, MUS, NUR, TED

01 President .... Dr. Steven CRAMER
03 Senior Vice President .... Dr. Dennis ENGBRECHT
05 VP for Academic Services .... Dr. Barbara BELLEFEUILLLE
30 VP for Development .... Mr. Terry ZEITLOW
10 VP & Chief Financial Officer .... Mr. Clair KNAPP
26 VP for College Relations .... Dr. Robert LAURENT
32 VP for Student Development .... Dr. Shawn HOLTGREN
36 VP for Life Calling/Stdnt Enrichmnt .... Dr. Kathy GRIBBIN
84 Asst VP for Enrollment/Marketng .... Mr. Randy BEACHY
13 Chief Technology Officer .... Vacant
66 Dean Division of Nursing .... Dr. Debra GILLUM
81 Dean Division of Sciences .... Dr. Robert MYERS
88 Director of Non-Traditional Studies .... Mr. Dale GADD
79 Dean Arts & Humanities .... Dr. Thomas VISKER
58 Dean Professional & Graduate Pgm .... Dr. Bradley SMITH
35 Dean of Students .... Mrs. Julie BEAM
06 Registrar .... Mrs. Jeanne FOX
36 Director Student Enrichment .... Vacant
37 Director Financial Aid .... Mr. Guy FISHER
26 Director Marketing & Communication .... Ms. Jaimee THIRION
41 Director Athletics .... Ms. Jody MARTINEZ
08 Director Library Services .... Dr. Clyde ROOT
88 Director Teacher Certification .... Mrs. Joyce LAURENT
18 Director Physical Plant .... Mr. Steve YAW
09 Director Institutional Research .... Dr. Ray WHITEMAN
19 Director Campus Safety .... Vacant
85 Director International Students .... Mrs. Lori GONZALEZ

91 Director Administrative Computing .... Mr. Harold RODGERS
23 Director Wellness Center .... Mrs. Carol BEMIS
29 Director Alumni Services .... Mrs. Lois PANNABECKER
28 Director Intercultural Development .... Mr. Alex GONZALEZ
07 Director Admissions .... Vacant
15 Director Human Resources .... Mrs. Lisa MALKEWICZ

Brown Mackie College-Fort Wayne (A)

3000 E Coliseum Boulevard, Ste 100,
Fort Wayne IN 46805-1565
County: Allen Identification: 666435
Unit ID: 408039
Telephone: (260) 484-4400 Carnegie Class: Assoc/PrivFP4
FAX Number: (260) 484-2678 Calendar System: Other
URL: www.brownmackie.edu
Established: 1882 Annual Undergrad Tuition & Fees: $11,124
Enrollment: 1,003 Coed
Affiliation or Control: Proprietary IRS Status: Proprietary
Highest Offering: Baccalaureate
Program: 2-Year Principally Bachelor's Creditable; Business Emphasis
Accreditation: ACICS, MAC, OTA, PTAA, SURGT, SURTEC

01 President .... Mr. Jim BISHOP
05 Dean of Academic Affairs .... Mr. Jeff GULLEY
32 Director of Student Services .... Ms. Kathy JUTT
07 Senior Director of Admissions .... Mr. Bob ALLEN
36 Director of Career Services .... Mr. Anthony DAVIS

† Branch campus of Brown Mackie-South Bend, South Bend, IN.

Brown Mackie College-Indianapolis (B)

1200 N. Meridian Street, Suite 100, Indianapolis IN 46204
County: Marion Identification: 666394
Unit ID: 451699
Telephone: (317) 554-8300 Carnegie Class: Assoc/PrivFP4
FAX Number: (317) 632-4557 Calendar System: Quarter
URL: www.brownmackie.edu
Established: 2007 Annual Undergrad Tuition & Fees: $11,772
Enrollment: 1,080 Coed
Affiliation or Control: Proprietary IRS Status: Proprietary
Highest Offering: Baccalaureate
Program: 2-Year Principally Bachelor's Creditable; Business Emphasis
Accreditation: ACICS, OTA

01 President .... Ms. Sherry JONES
05 Dean of Academic Affairs .... Ms. Christina CROSS
07 Senior Director of Admissions .... Vacant
06 Registrar .... Vacant
10 Student Account Advisor .... Ms. Marisa MALONE
37 Director of Financial Aid .... Vacant
08 Librarian .... Ms. Dawn LIPP

† Branch campus of Brown Mackie College-Findlay, Findlay, OH.

Brown Mackie College-Merrillville (C)

1000 E 80th Place, Suite 205M, Merrillville IN 46410-5602
County: Lake FICE Identification: 021032
Unit ID: 151616
Telephone: (219) 769-3321 Carnegie Class: Assoc/PrivFP4
FAX Number: (219) 738-1076 Calendar System: Other
URL: www.brownmackie.edu
Established: 1890 Annual Undergrad Tuition & Fees: $11,124
Enrollment: 542 Coed
Affiliation or Control: Proprietary IRS Status: Proprietary
Highest Offering: Baccalaureate
Program: Occupational; 2-Year Principally Bachelor's Creditable; Business Emphasis
Accreditation: ACICS, MAAB, OTA, SURGT

01 President .... Ms. Shalisa POWELL
05 Dean of Academic Affairs .... Mr. James KAPITAN
07 Senior Director of Admissions .... Vacant
36 Director of Career Services .... Ms. Julie LYNCH
06 Registrar .... Ms. Tiffany BRACK

† Branch campus of Brown Mackie College-Cincinnati, Cincinnati, OH.

Brown Mackie College-Michigan City (D)

325 E US Highway 20, Michigan City IN 46360-7362
County: La Porte Identification: 666426
Unit ID: 151625
Telephone: (219) 877-3100 Carnegie Class: Assoc/PrivFP4
FAX Number: (219) 877-3110 Calendar System: Other
URL: www.cbcaec.com
Established: N/A Annual Undergrad Tuition & Fees: $11,124
Enrollment: 321 Coed
Affiliation or Control: Proprietary IRS Status: Proprietary
Highest Offering: Beyond Master's But Less Than Doctorate
Program: Occupational; 2-Year Principally Bachelor's Creditable; Business Emphasis
Accreditation: ACICS, MAAB, SURGT

01 President .... Ms. Sheryl ELSTON
05 Dean of Academic Affairs .... Ms. Diane DIDONNA
07 Senior Director of Admissions .... Ms. Nancy SPENNY
06 Registrar .... Ms. Karry WIER
36 Director of Career Services .... Ms. Paula SCOTT

† Branch campus of Brown Mackie College-Cincinnati, Cincinnati, OH.

Brown Mackie College-South Bend (E)

3454 Douglas Road, South Bend IN 46635
County: Saint Joseph FICE Identification: 004583
Unit ID: 151944
Telephone: (574) 237-0774 Carnegie Class: Assoc/PrivFP4
FAX Number: (574) 237-3585 Calendar System: Other
URL: www.brownmackie.edu
Established: 1882 Annual Undergrad Tuition & Fees: $11,124
Enrollment: 605 Coed
Affiliation or Control: Proprietary IRS Status: Proprietary
Highest Offering: Baccalaureate
Program: 2-Year Principally Bachelor's Creditable; Business Emphasis
Accreditation: ACICS, MAC, OTA, PTAA

01 President .... Vacant
05 Dean of Academic Affairs .... Mr. Steve RICHARDS
07 Senior Director of Admissions .... Vacant
06 Registrar .... Ms. Heather RYAN
36 Director of Career Services .... Ms. Sheryl DECKER

Butler University (F)

4600 Sunset Avenue, Indianapolis IN 46208-3443
County: Marion FICE Identification: 001788
Unit ID: 150163
Telephone: (317) 940-8000 Carnegie Class: Master's M
FAX Number: (317) 940-9930 Calendar System: Semester
URL: www.butler.edu
Established: 1855 Annual Undergrad Tuition & Fees: $32,280
Enrollment: 4,667 Coed
Affiliation or Control: Independent Non-Profit IRS Status: 501(c)3
Highest Offering: Doctorate
Program: Liberal Arts And General; Teacher Preparatory; Professional
Accreditation: NH, ARCPA, BUS, CACREP, DANCE, IPSY, MUS, PHAR, TED, THEA

01 President .... Mr. James M. DANKO
05 Interim Provost .... Dr. Kathryn MORRIS
10 Vice President for Finance .... Mr. Bruce E. ARICK
30 VP University Advancement .... Mr. D. Mark HELMUS
84 Vice Pres Enrollment Management .... Mr. Thomas D. WEEDE
32 Vice President of Student Affairs .... Dr. Levester JOHNSON
20 Assoc Provost Student Acad Affs ..... Dr. Mary M. RAMSBOTTOM
20 Assoc Prov Faculty Affs .... Dr. Laura L. BEHLING
57 Dean Jordan College Fine Arts .... Dr. Ronald CALTABIANO
50 Dean Business Administration .... Dr. Chuck R. WILLIAMS
49 Dean Liberal Arts & Science .... Dr. Jay R. HOWARD
53 Dean Education .... Dr. Ena M. SHELLEY
67 Dean Pharmacy & Health Sciences .... Dr. Mary H. ANDRITZ
60 Dean College of Communication .... Dr. Gary EDGERTON
35 Dean Student Services .... Dr. Sally E. CLICK
35 Dean Student Life .... Dr. Irene E. STEVENS
38 Asst Dean & Director Counseling Ctr .... Dr. Keith B. MAGNUS
08 Dean of Libraries .... Mr. Lewis R. MILLER
29 Exec Dir Alumni/Development Pgms .... Ms. M. Rachel STEPHEN BURT
15 Exec Dir HR/Chief Diversity Officer .... Mr. Jonathan A. SMALL
88 Exec Director Clowes Memorial Hall .... Ms. Elise J. KUSHIGIAN
37 Director Financial Aid .... Ms. Melissa J. SMURDON
21 Executive Budget Director .... Mr. Robert J. MARCUS
26 Exec Director University Relations .... Ms. Marcia A. DOWELL
07 Dean of Admission .... Mr. Scott D. HAM
31 Director Conference/Special Events .... Ms. Beth A. ALEXANDER
39 Director Residence Life .... Ms. Karla K. CUNNINGHAM
09 Director Institutional Research .... Dr. Nandini RAMASWAMY
85 Director International Programs ..... Dr. C. Montgomery BROADED
06 Registrar .... Ms. Sondrea S. OZOLINS
36 Director Career Services .... Mr. Gary R. BEAULIEU
41 Director of Athletics .... Mr. Barry S. COLLIER
27 Chief Information Officer .... Mr. Scott A. KINCAID
19 Chief of Staff/Exec Dir Pub Safety .... Mr. Ben D. HUNTER
21 Controller .... Ms. Susan M. WESTERMEYER
26 Dir Print Marketing/Communications .... Ms. Sally M. CUTLER
28 Director of Diversity Programs .... Ms. Valerie J. DAVIDSON
40 Manager Bookstore .... Ms. Janine L. FRAINIER
96 Manager of Purchasing .... Ms. Shelly S. RABIDEAU
101 Executive Assistant to the Board .... Dr. Carol WROBLEWSKI

Calumet College of Saint Joseph (G)

2400 New York Avenue, Whiting IN 46394-2195
County: Lake FICE Identification: 001834
Unit ID: 150172
Telephone: (219) 473-7770 Carnegie Class: Master's S
FAX Number: (219) 473-4259 Calendar System: Semester
URL: www.ccsj.edu
Established: 1951 Annual Undergrad Tuition & Fees: $14,680
Enrollment: 1,172 Coed
Affiliation or Control: Roman Catholic IRS Status: 501(c)3
Highest Offering: Master's
Program: Liberal Arts And General; Teacher Preparatory; Professional; Business Emphasis
Accreditation: NH

01 President .... Dr. Daniel LOWERY
05 Vice President Academic Affairs .... Dr. Joi PATTERSON
30 Vice President for Development .... Vacant
32 Vice President of Student Life .... Ms. Melisha HENDERSON
10 VP Business & Finance .... Ms. Lynn MISKUS
35 Dean of Students .... Ms. Melisha HENDERSON
06 Registrar .... Ms. Diana FRANCIS
08 Librarian .... Ms. Marcia KEITH
09 Institutional Researcher .... Mr. Darren HENDERSON
26 Director of Marketing & Pub Rel .... Ms. Linda GAJEWSKI
41 Athletic Director .... Mr. Peter HARING
42 Director of Campus Ministry .... Br. Jerry SCHWIETERMAN
15 Director of Human Resources .... Ms. Jacqueline NALLS
18 VP of Facilities & Technology .... Mr. Gene KESSLER
84 Dir of Enrollment Management .... Ms. Mary SEVERA
37 Dir of Business Office & Fin Aid Op .... Ms. Gina PIRTLE
36 Director of Career Services .... Mr. Mike KENNY
13 Director of Computer Services .... Mr. Kevin KRIEPS
105 Assoc Dir of Advertising/Webmaster ...... Mr. Darren JASIENIECKI
29 Alumni Relations .... Ms. Angela HUGHES
40 Bookstore Manager .... Ms. Erren TAPIA
88 Asst to President for Development .... Mr. Michael SPICCIA

Christian Theological Seminary (H)

1000 W. 42nd Street, Indianapolis IN 46208-3301
County: Marion FICE Identification: 001789
Unit ID: 150215
Telephone: (317) 924-1331 Carnegie Class: Spec/Faith
FAX Number: (317) 923-1961 Calendar System: Semester
URL: www.cts.edu
Established: 1925 Annual Graduate Tuition & Fees: $13,620
Enrollment: 236 Coed
Affiliation or Control: Christian Church (Disciples Of Christ)
IRS Status: 501(c)3
Highest Offering: Doctorate; No Undergraduates
Program: Professional; Religious Emphasis
Accreditation: NH, MFCD, THEOL

01 President .... Dr. Matthew M. BOULTON
05 Int Vice Pres & Co-Academic Dean .... Dr. Edwin D. APONTE
30 Vice President Development .... Ms. Melissa HICKMAN
32 Dean of Students .... Rev. Mary HARRIS
10 Chief Operating Officer .... Ms. Julie SHEWMAKER
16 Executive Admin/HR Director .... Ms. Kathleen BELL
44 Director Annual Fund .... Ms. Karen HORSMAN
21 Director of Business Affairs .... Mrs. Shari CULLUMBER
42 Chaplain .... Dr. Tercio B. JUNKER
08 Director of Library .... Ms. Lorna SHOEMAKER
06 Registrar .... Mr. Matt SCHLIMGEN
75 Director of Field Education .... Dr. William KINCAID
18 Director of Physical Plant .... Mr. Richard DAVIS
37 Director of Student Financial Aid .... Mr. Ed DETAMORE
40 Director of Bookstore .... Mrs. Sarah EVANS
27 Communications Associate .... Mr. Chris VARNAU

College of Court Reporting, Inc. (I)

111 W 10th, Suite 111, Hobart IN 46342-5969
County: Lake FICE Identification: 026158
Unit ID: 150251
Telephone: (866) 294-3974 Carnegie Class: Assoc/PrivFP
FAX Number: (219) 942-1631 Calendar System: Semester
URL: www.ccr.edu
Established: 1984 Annual Undergrad Tuition & Fees: $13,500
Enrollment: 261 Coed
Affiliation or Control: Proprietary IRS Status: Proprietary
Highest Offering: Associate Degree
Program: Occupational
Accreditation: ACICS

01 President .... Mr. Jeff T. MOODY
03 Executive Director .... Mr. Jay VETTICKAL
05 Director of Education .... Ms. Kay MOODY
07 Director of Admissions .... Ms. Nicky M. RODRIQUEZ
37 Director of Financial Aid .... Ms. Lisa MORTON
32 Director of Student Services .... Ms. Kathleen LAZART

Concordia Theological Seminary (J)

6600 N Clinton Street, Fort Wayne IN 46825-4996
County: Allen FICE Identification: 020876
Unit ID: 150288
Telephone: (260) 452-2100 Carnegie Class: Spec/Faith
FAX Number: (260) 452-2121 Calendar System: Quarter
URL: www.ctsfw.edu
Established: 1846 Annual Graduate Tuition & Fees: $25,041
Enrollment: 321 Male
Affiliation or Control: Lutheran Church - Missouri Synod
IRS Status: 501(c)3
Highest Offering: Doctorate; No Undergraduates
Program: Professional
Accreditation: NH, THEOL

01 President .... Dr. Lawrence R. RAST
05 Academic Dean .... Dr. Charles A. GIESCHEN
36 Dean Pastoral Education/Placement .... Dr. Carl C. FICKENSCHER, II
32 Dean of Students .... Rev. Thomas P. ZIMMERMAN
10 Vice President Business Affairs .... Rev. Albert B. WINGFIELD
06 Registrar .... Mrs. Barbara A. WEGMAN
07 Director of Admissions .... Rev. John M. DREYER
08 Head Librarian .... Prof. Robert V. ROETHEMEYER

Crossroads Bible College (A)

601 N Shortridge Road, Indianapolis IN 46219-4912
County: Marion FICE Identification: 034567
Unit ID: 439613
Telephone: (317) 789-8255 Carnegie Class: Spec/Faith
FAX Number: (317) 789-8253 Calendar System: Semester
URL: www.crossroads.edu
Established: 1980 Annual Undergrad Tuition & Fees: $9,980
Enrollment: 203 Coed
Affiliation or Control: Independent Non-Profit IRS Status: 501(c)3
Highest Offering: Baccalaureate
Program: Religious Emphasis
Accreditation: BI

01 President ..... Dr. A. Charles WARE
03 Executive Vice President ..... Dr. John A. CRABTREE, JR.
05 Vice President Academic Affairs ..... Dr. Mark ECKEL
32 Vice President Student Affairs ..... Mr. Marcus SCHRADER
06 Registrar ..... Dr. Linda CHAVIS

DePauw University (B)

313 S Locust Street, Greencastle IN 46135-1772
County: Putnam FICE Identification: 001792
Unit ID: 150400
Telephone: (765) 658-4800 Carnegie Class: Bac/A&S
FAX Number: (765) 658-4177 Calendar System: 4/1/4
URL: www.depauw.edu
Established: 1837 Annual Undergrad Tuition & Fees: $38,750
Enrollment: 2,352 Coed
Affiliation or Control: United Methodist IRS Status: 501(c)3
Highest Offering: Baccalaureate
Program: Liberal Arts And General
Accreditation: NH, MUS, TED

01 President ..... Dr. Brian W. CASEY
100 Senior Advisor to the President ..... Mr. Christopher J. WELLS
45 VP for Comm & Strat Initiatives ..... Mr. Christopher J. WELLS
05 Vice President for Academic Affairs ..... Dr. David T. HARVEY
20 Dean of the Faculty ..... Dr. Terri BONEBRIGHT
20 Dean of Academic Life ..... Dr. Pedar W. FOSS
10 Vice Pres Finance/Administration ..... Mr. Bradley A. KELSHEIMER
21 Assoc Vice Pres for Finance ..... Mr. Kevin S. KESSINGER
30 VP for Advancement ..... Dr. Marcia S. LATTA
07 Vice Pres Admissions/Financial Aid ..... Mr. Daniel L. MEYER
32 VP Student Life/Dean of Students ..... Dr. Cynthia BABINGTON
04 Executive Assistant to President ..... Ms. Elizabeth DEMMINGS
06 Registrar ..... Dr. Kenneth J. KIRKPATRICK
27 Chief Information Officer ..... Ms. Carol L. SMITH
88 Executive Director of Development ..... Mr. Jason G. PETROVICH
64 Dean of the School of Music ..... Dr. Mark MCCOY
37 Director of Financial Aid ..... Mr. Craig A. SLAUGHTER
29 Exec Director of Alumni Relations ..... Ms. Jennifer C. SOSTER
41 Director of Athletics ..... Ms. Stevie BAKER-WATSON
36 Director of Career Services ..... Mr. Steven LANGERUD
23 Director of Student Health Services ..... Dr. Scott RIPPLE
88 Director of International Education ..... Ms. Kathleen S. KNAUL
08 Director of Libraries ..... Mr. Rick E. PROVINE
16 Director of Human Resources ..... Ms. Patricia BACON
18 Director of Facilities ..... Mr. Richard N. VANCE
19 Director of Public Safety ..... Ms. Angela D. NALLY
09 Director of Institutional Research ..... Dr. William M. TOBIN
42 University Chaplain ..... Dr. Paul T. WILSON
38 Director of Counseling Services ..... Dr. Bud EDWARDS
96 Director of Purchasing ..... Mr. Richard SHUCK
21 Exec Director of Finance/Controller ..... Mr. Keith ARCHER
26 Exec Director of Media Relations ..... Mr. Ken OWEN
44 Director of Annual Giving ..... Ms. Lindsay STEGMAN

DeVry University - Indianapolis (C)

9100 Keystone Crossing, Suite 350,
Indianapolis IN 46240-2158
County: Marion Identification: 666556
Unit ID: 432214
Telephone: (317) 581-8854 Carnegie Class: Spec/Bus
FAX Number: (317) 581-8955 Calendar System: Semester
URL: www.devry.edu
Established: 1931 Annual Undergrad Tuition & Fees: $16,156
Enrollment: 420 Coed
Affiliation or Control: Proprietary IRS Status: Proprietary
Highest Offering: Master's
Program: Professional; Business Emphasis
Accreditation: &NH

01 Campus Director ..... Bill COIT

† Regional accreditation is carried under the parent institution in Downers Grove, IL.

DeVry University - Merrillville Center (D)

1000 E 80th Place, Suite 222 Mall,
Merrillville IN 46410-5673
County: Lake Identification: 666209
Unit ID: 432214
Telephone: (219) 736-7440 Carnegie Class: Spec/Bus
FAX Number: (219) 736-7874 Calendar System: Semester
URL: www.devry.edu
Established: 1997 Annual Undergrad Tuition & Fees: $16,156
Enrollment: 368 Coed
Affiliation or Control: Proprietary IRS Status: Proprietary
Highest Offering: Master's
Program: Occupational; Professional; Business Emphasis
Accreditation: &NH

01 Center Dean ..... Mr. Ivan BAUBLITZ

† Regional accreditation is carried under the parent institution in Downers Grove, IL.

Earlham College and Earlham School of Religion (E)

801 National Road W, Richmond IN 47374-4095
County: Wayne FICE Identification: 001793
Unit ID: 150455
Telephone: (765) 983-1200 Carnegie Class: Bac/A&S
FAX Number: (765) 983-1304 Calendar System: Semester
URL: www.earlham.edu
Established: 1847 Annual Undergrad Tuition & Fees: $47,930
Enrollment: 1,057 Coed
Affiliation or Control: Friends IRS Status: 501(c)3
Highest Offering: Master's
Program: Liberal Arts And General; Teacher Preparatory; Professional; Religious Emphasis
Accreditation: NH, THEOL

01 President ..... John David DAWSON
05 Vice President Academic Affairs ..... Greg MAHLER
10 Vice President Business Affairs ..... Sena LANDEY
30 Vice President Advancement ..... Jim MCKEY
88 Vice President School of Religion ..... Jay MARSHALL
31 Vice President for Community Rels ..... Avis STEWART
44 Assoc VP for Institutional Advance ..... Kim TANNER
32 Dean of Student Development ..... Cheryl PRESLEY
07 Dean of Admissions/Financial Aid ..... Jonathan STROUD
04 Assistant to President ..... JoBeth BUCKLEY
41 Athletic Director ..... Mike BERGUM
21 Assistant VP for Business ..... Dana NORTH
21 Controller ..... Cathy HABSCHMIDT
88 Director Academic Support Services ..... Donna KEESLING
29 Director of Alumni Relations ..... Gail CLARK
42 Director of Religious Life ..... Kelly BURK
36 Director of Career Services ..... Eric LARSEN
14 Director of Computing Services ..... Thomas STEFFES
37 Director of Financial Aid ..... Robert ARNOLD
23 Director of Health Services ..... Mary Ann STIENBARGER
16 Director of Human Resources ..... Emily STEWART
09 Director of Institutional Research ..... Nelson BINGHAM
85 Director of International Programs ..... Patty O'MALEY-LAMSON
18 Director of Physical Plant ..... Ian SMITH
26 Director of Public Affairs ..... Vacant
27 Director of Public Information ..... Mark BLACKMON
19 Director of Security ..... Tom KEARNS
08 Librarian ..... Neal BAKER
40 Bookstore Manager ..... Dee Dee CUMMINGS
06 Registrar ..... Bonita WASHINGTON-LACEY
73 Admissions School of Religion ..... Matt HISRICH
06 Registrar School of Religion ..... April VANLONDEN
35 Director Student Affairs ..... Rich DORNBERGER
20 Associate Academic Officer ..... Lyn MILLER
88 Provost ..... Nelson BINGHAM
15 Director Personnel Services ..... Vacant
28 Director of Diversity ..... Trayce PETERSON
84 Director Enrollment Management ..... Nancy SINEX
96 Director of Purchasing ..... Alice LAFUZE

Franklin College of Indiana (F)

101 Branigin Boulevard, Franklin IN 46131-2623
County: Johnson FICE Identification: 001798
Unit ID: 150604
Telephone: (317) 738-8000 Carnegie Class: Bac/Diverse
FAX Number: (317) 736-6030 Calendar System: 4/1/4
URL: www.franklincollege.edu
Established: 1834 Annual Undergrad Tuition & Fees: $26,710
Enrollment: 1,051 Coed
Affiliation or Control: American Baptist IRS Status: 501(c)3
Highest Offering: Baccalaureate
Program: Liberal Arts And General; Teacher Preparatory
Accreditation: NH, TED

01 President ..... Dr. James G. MOSELEY
04 Assistant to the President ..... Ms. Janet D. SCHANTZ
10 Vice President Finance ..... Mr. Bryan SPETTER
45 Vice Pres Planning/Plant/Technology ..... Mrs. Lisa FEARS
05 Vice Pres Academic Affs/Dean of Col ..... Dr. David G. BRAILOW
84 Vice Pres Enrollment and Marketing ..... Mr. Alan P. HILL
20 Assoc VP Acad Affs/Instl Effective ..... Dr. Timothy L. GARNER
32 Dean of Students ..... Mr. Ellis F. HALL
20 Ast Dean Engaged Lrng/Dir Prof Dev .. Mrs. Brooke A. WORLAND
06 Interim Registrar ..... Mrs. Jennifer N. WHITSON
18 Dir Facilities/Energy Management ..... Mr. Thomas PATZ
39 Director of Residence Life ..... Ms. LaTika WEBSTER
38 Director of Counseling ..... Dr. John R. SHAFER
30 Int Managing Dir Inst Advancement ..... Mr. Thomas W. ARMOR
35 Dir Stdnt Activities/Organizations ..... Ms. Keri ELLINGTON
29 Director of Alumni Relations ..... Mrs. Margee STAMPER
46 Dir of Devel Research & Records ..... Ms. Betsy SCHMIDT
44 Dir Advancement/Leadership Giving ..... Mr. Thomas W. ARMOR
37 Director of Financial Aid ..... Mrs. Elizabeth SAPPENFIELD
42 Campus Minister ..... Rev. David WEATHERSPOON
41 Athletic Director ..... Mr. Kerry N. PRATHER
13 Dir of Information Tech Services ..... Ms. Lisa E. MAHAN
36 Dir Career Svcs/Asst Dean Students ..... Mr. Kirk J. BIXLER
88 Director of Leadership Development ..... Mrs. Bonnie L. PRIBUSH
85 Director of Intercultural Studies ..... Ms. Simone PILON
88 Director of Dining Services-Sodexo ..... Mr. Les PETROFF
44 Dir Development/Donor Relations ..... Mrs. Kristy BROWN
07 Director of Admissions ..... Vacant
26 Director of Public Relations ..... Ms. Deidra BAUMGARDNER
08 Director of the Library ..... Mr. Ronald L. SCHUETZ
19 Director of Campus Security ..... Mr. Steve LEONARD
105 Webmaster ..... Vacant
44 Advancement Associate ..... Mr. Daniel J. FRISCHE
15 Manager of Employee Resources ..... Mrs. Maureen PINNICK
22 Proj Mgr Organization Devel/Safety ..... Mr. Thomas PATZ
40 Bookstore Manager (Follett) ..... Ms. Paige PRIDMORE
21 Business Office Manager ..... Mr. Brad JONES
23 Coordinator of Health Services ..... Ms. Theresa NIGH
28 Coord Multicultural/Diversity Svcs ..... Ms. Terri L. ROBERTS
50 Head Business/Computing/Math Div ..... Mr. James C. WILLIAMS
53 Head Education Division ..... Mrs. Katherine M. REMSBURG
79 Head Humanities Division ..... Dr. Sara COLBURN-ALSOP
60 Head Journalism Division ..... Mr. Joel CRAMER
65 Head Natural Sciences Division ..... Dr. Steven K. BROWDER
83 Head Social Sciences Division ..... Dr. Denise M. BAIRD
57 Head Fine Arts Division ..... Mr. Robin ROBERTS

Goshen College (G)

1700 S Main Street, Goshen IN 46526-4794
County: Elkhart FICE Identification: 001799
Unit ID: 150668
Telephone: (574) 535-7000 Carnegie Class: Bac/A&S
FAX Number: (574) 535-7060 Calendar System: Semester
URL: www.goshen.edu
Established: 1894 Annual Undergrad Tuition & Fees: $26,900
Enrollment: 841 Coed
Affiliation or Control: Mennonite Church IRS Status: 501(c)3
Highest Offering: Master's
Program: Liberal Arts And General; Teacher Preparatory; Professional
Accreditation: NH, NURSE, SW, TED

01 President ..... Dr. James E. BRENNEMAN
05 VP Academic Affairs/Academic Dean ..... Dr. Anita K. STALTER
10 Vice President for Finance ..... Mr. James L. HISTAND
30 Vice Pres Institutional Advancement ..... Mr. James K. CASKEY
84 VP for Enroll Management/Marketing ... Mr. James R. TOWNSEND
28 Director of Multicultural Affairs ..... Vacant
32 VP Student Life/Dean of Students ..... Mr. Bill BORN
20 Associate Academic Dean ..... Dr. Ross PETERSON-VEATCH
66 Director of Undergraduate Nursing ..... Ms. Vicki S. KIRKTON
58 Director of Graduate Nursing ..... Dr. Brenda S. SROF
70 Director of Social Work ..... Dr. Jeanne M. LIECHTY
53 Director of Elementary Teacher Educ ..... Dr. Kathryn MEYER REIMER
08 Librarian ..... Ms. Lisa G. GUEDEA CARRENO
82 Director of International Education ..... Dr. Tom J. MEYERS
88 Director of Secondary Education ..... Dr. Kevin GARY
14 Director of Information Tech Svcs ..... Mr. Michael SHERER
09 Director of Institutional Research ..... Dr. Scott BARGE
06 Registrar ..... Mr. Stan W. MILLER
37 Director Student Financial Aid ..... Ms. Judy S. MOORE
26 Director of Public Relations ..... Mr. Richard AGUIRRE
29 Director of Alumni/Parent Relations ..... Ms. Kelli B. KING
42 Campus Minister ..... Mr. Robert E. YODER
36 Director of Career Services ..... Ms. Anita R. YODER
18 Director of Facilities ..... Mr. Clay E. SHETLER
15 Director of Human Resources ..... Mr. Norm BAKHIT
88 Exe Director of Adult/Online Pgms ..... Mr. Randy GUNDEN
35 Director of Student Activities ..... Ms. DaVonne HARRIS
38 Director Student Counseling ..... Mrs. Char HOCHSTETLER
04 Admin Assistant to the President ..... Ms. Betty SCHRAG
07 Director of Admissions ..... Dr. Dan KOOP LIECHTY

Grace College and Seminary (H)

200 Seminary Drive, Winona Lake IN 46590-1294
County: Kosciusko FICE Identification: 001800
Unit ID: 150677
Telephone: (574) 372-5100 Carnegie Class: Bac/Diverse
FAX Number: (574) 372-5139 Calendar System: Semester
URL: www.grace.edu
Established: 1948 Annual Undergrad Tuition & Fees: $23,290
Enrollment: 1,616 Coed
Affiliation or Control: Fellowship Of Grace Brethren Churches
IRS Status: 501(c)3
Highest Offering: Doctorate
Program: Liberal Arts And General; Teacher Preparatory; Religious Emphasis
Accreditation: NH, CACREP, IACBE, TED, THEOL

01 President ..... Dr. Ronald E. MANAHAN
04 Exec Assistant to the President ..... Mrs. Nancy L. WEIMER
05 Provost ..... Dr. William J. KATIP
32 VP Student Affairs & Academic Svcs ..... Dr. James E. SWANSON
10 Chief Financial Officer ..... Mr. G. Stephen POPENFOOSE
30 Chief Advancement Officer ..... Mr. John R. BOAL
11 Chief Operations Officer ..... Mr. Thomas A. DUNN
73 Dean of the Seminary ..... Dr. Jeffery A. GILL
13 Dir Information Technology ..... Mr. Donald W. FLUKE
07 Dean of Admissions ..... Mrs. Cindy N. SISSON

42 Dean of Chapel & Global Ministries .... Mr. J. Carlos TELLEZ
23 Director Student Health & Wellness .... Dr. Joe A. GRAHAM
106 Dir Online Learning .... Mr. Timothy J. ZIEBARTH
06 Registrar .... Mr. Steven T. CARLSON
08 Librarian .... Mrs. Tonya L. FAWCETT
37 Director Student Financial Aid .... Mrs. Charlette R. SAUDERS
15 Director of Human Resource .... Mrs. Audrey L. RUSSELL
27 Dir of Marketing & Communication .... Mr. David GROUT
18 Director Physical Plant .... Mr. Randy KLEINHANS
29 Director Alumni Relations .... Mrs. Tammy DENLINGER
41 Athletic Director .... Mr. Bailey WEATHERS
36 Director of Career Services .... Mrs. Denise TERRY
09 Director of Institutional Research .... Vacant
108 Director Institutional Assessment .... Vacant
51 Dean of Adult & Community Educ .... Dr. Stephen A. GRILL

Hanover College (A)

PO Box 108, Hanover IN 47243-0108

County: Jefferson FICE Identification: 001801
Unit ID: 150756
Telephone: (812) 866-7000 Carnegie Class: Bac/A&S
FAX Number: (812) 866-2164 Calendar System: Other
URL: www.hanover.edu
Established: 1827 Annual Undergrad Tuition & Fees: $30,268
Enrollment: 1,063 Coed
Affiliation or Control: Presbyterian Church (U.S.A.) IRS Status: 501(c)3
Highest Offering: Baccalaureate
Program: Liberal Arts And General; Teacher Preparatory
Accreditation: NH, TED

01 President .... Dr. Sue DEWINE
04 Executive Asst to the President .... Mrs. Treva SHELTON
05 Vice Pres/Dean of the Faculty .... Dr. Steve JOBE
30 Vice President College Advancement .... Mr. Dennis HUNT
10 Vice President Business Affairs .... Mr. J. Michael BRUCE
32 Vice President Student Life .... Dr. David YEAGER
84 Vice Pres Enrollment Management .... Mr. Jon RIESTER
37 Director of Financial Aid .... Mr. Richard NASH
88 Exec Director-Rivers Institute .... Dr. Larry DEBUHR
88 Exec Director-Center for Bus Prep .... Mr. Jerry JOHNSON
36 Director of Placement .... Mrs. Margaret KRANTZ
06 Registrar .... Dr. Ken PRINCE
08 Director of College Libraries .... Mr. Ken GIBSON
18 Chief Facilities/Physical Plant .... Mr. Scott KLEIN
26 Dir Communications & Marketing .... Mrs. Rhonda BURCH
29 Director of Alumni Relations .... Mrs. Ann INMAN
07 Dean of Admission .... Mr. Chris GAGE
38 Director of Student Counseling .... Mrs. Katie DINE YOUNG
15 Director of Human Resources .... Ms. Shelley PREOCANIN
35 Coord Student Org/Leadership Trng .... Mrs. Kathryn LOWE-SCHNEIDER

Harrison College - Anderson Campus (B)

140 E 53rd Street, Anderson IN 46013-1717

County: Madison Identification: 666030
Unit ID: 151157
Telephone: (765) 644-7514 Carnegie Class: Assoc/PrivFP
FAX Number: (765) 644-5724 Calendar System: Quarter
URL: www.harrison.edu
Established: 1902 Annual Undergrad Tuition & Fees: N/A
Enrollment: 299 Coed
Affiliation or Control: Proprietary IRS Status: Proprietary
Highest Offering: Baccalaureate
Program: Occupational; 2-Year Principally Bachelor's Creditable
Accreditation: &@NH, ACICS, MAC

01 President .... Mr. Jason T. KONESCO
12 Campus President .... Ms. Charlene STACY

† Regional accreditation is carried under the parent institution in Indianapolis (Downtown Campus), IN.

Harrison College - Columbus Indiana Campus (C)

2222 Poshard Drive, Columbus IN 47203-1843

County: Bartholomew Identification: 666428
Unit ID: 151193
Telephone: (812) 379-9000 Carnegie Class: Assoc/PrivFP
FAX Number: (812) 375-0414 Calendar System: Quarter
URL: www.harrison.edu
Established: 1902 Annual Undergrad Tuition & Fees: N/A
Enrollment: 244 Coed
Affiliation or Control: Proprietary IRS Status: Proprietary
Highest Offering: Baccalaureate
Program: Occupational; 2-Year Principally Bachelor's Creditable
Accreditation: &@NH, ACICS, MAC

01 President .... Mr. Jason T. KONESCO
12 Campus President .... Ms. Angela SHAFER

† Regional accreditation is carried under the parent institution in Indianapolis (Downtown Campus), IN.

Harrison College - Elkhart Campus (D)

56075 Parkway Avenue, Elkhart IN 46516-9325

County: Elkhart Identification: 666143
Unit ID: 450386
Telephone: (574) 522-0397 Carnegie Class: Assoc/PrivFP
FAX Number: (574) 523-0829 Calendar System: Quarter
URL: www.ibcschools.edu
Established: 1902 Annual Undergrad Tuition & Fees: N/A
Enrollment: 303 Coed
Affiliation or Control: Proprietary IRS Status: Proprietary
Highest Offering: Baccalaureate
Program: Occupational; 2-Year Principally Bachelor's Creditable
Accreditation: &@NH, ACICS, MAC

01 President .... Mr. Jason T. KONESCO
12 Campus President .... Mr. Justin ELLIOTT

† Regional accreditation is carried under the parent institution in Indianapolis (Downtown Campus), IN.

Harrison College - Evansville Campus (E)

4601 Theater Drive, Evansville IN 47715-3901

County: Vanderburgh Identification: 666429
Unit ID: 423670
Telephone: (812) 476-6000 Carnegie Class: Bac/Assoc
FAX Number: (812) 471-8576 Calendar System: Quarter
URL: www.harrison.edu
Established: 1902 Annual Undergrad Tuition & Fees: N/A
Enrollment: 266 Coed
Affiliation or Control: Proprietary IRS Status: Proprietary
Highest Offering: Baccalaureate
Program: Occupational; 2-Year Principally Bachelor's Creditable
Accreditation: &@NH, ACICS, MAC

01 President .... Mr. Jason T. KONESCO
12 Campus President .... Mr. Scott KURTZ

† Regional accreditation is carried under the parent institution in Indianapolis (Downtown Campus), IN.

Harrison College - Fort Wayne Campus (F)

6413 N Clinton Street, Fort Wayne IN 46825-4911

County: Allen Identification: 666029
Unit ID: 438966
Telephone: (260) 471-7667 Carnegie Class: Assoc/PrivFP4
FAX Number: (260) 471-6918 Calendar System: Quarter
URL: www.harrison.edu
Established: 1902 Annual Undergrad Tuition & Fees: N/A
Enrollment: 499 Coed
Affiliation or Control: Proprietary IRS Status: Proprietary
Highest Offering: Baccalaureate
Program: Occupational; 2-Year Principally Bachelor's Creditable
Accreditation: &@NH, ACICS, MAC, SURGT

01 President .... Mr. Jason T. KONESCO
12 Campus President .... Ms. Charlene STACY

† Regional accreditation is carried under the parent institution in Indianapolis (Downtown Campus), IN.

Harrison College - Indianapolis Downtown Campus (G)

550 E Washington Street, Indianapolis IN 46204-2611

County: Marion FICE Identification: 021584
Unit ID: 151166
Telephone: (317) 264-5656 Carnegie Class: Bac/Assoc
FAX Number: (317) 264-5650 Calendar System: Quarter
URL: www.harrison.edu
Established: 1902 Annual Undergrad Tuition & Fees: N/A
Enrollment: 535 Coed
Affiliation or Control: Proprietary IRS Status: Proprietary
Highest Offering: Baccalaureate
Program: Occupational; 2-Year Principally Bachelor's Creditable
Accreditation: @NH, ACICS, ACFEI, MAC

01 President .... Mr. Jason T. KONESCO
12 Regional President .... Mr. Steve D. HARDIN

Harrison College - Indianapolis East Campus (H)

8150 Brookville Road, Indianapolis IN 46239-8903

County: Marion Identification: 666430
Unit ID: 414850
Telephone: (317) 375-8000 Carnegie Class: Assoc/PrivFP
FAX Number: (317) 351-1871 Calendar System: Quarter
URL: www.harrison.edu
Established: 1902 Annual Undergrad Tuition & Fees: N/A
Enrollment: 519 Coed
Affiliation or Control: Proprietary IRS Status: Proprietary
Highest Offering: Baccalaureate
Program: 2-Year Principally Bachelor's Creditable; Nursing Emphasis
Accreditation: &@NH, ACICS, ADNUR, MAC, MLTAD, SURGT

01 President .... Mr. Jason T. KONESCO
12 Campus President .... Mr. Gary A. MCGEE

† Regional accreditation is carried under the parent institution in Indianapolis (Downtown Campus), IN.

Harrison College - Indianapolis Northwest Campus (I)

6300 Technology Center Drive, Indianapolis IN 46278-6022

County: Hamilton Identification: 666388
Unit ID: 447397
Telephone: (317) 873-6500 Carnegie Class: Assoc/PrivFP
FAX Number: (317) 733-6266 Calendar System: Quarter
URL: www.harrison.edu
Established: 1902 Annual Undergrad Tuition & Fees: N/A
Enrollment: 289 Coed
Affiliation or Control: Proprietary IRS Status: Proprietary
Highest Offering: Baccalaureate
Program: Occupational; 2-Year Principally Bachelor's Creditable
Accreditation: &@NH, ACICS

01 President .... Mr. Jason T. KONESCO
12 Campus President .... Mr. Marvin BAILEY

† Regional accreditation is carried under the parent institution in Indianapolis (Downtown Campus), IN.

Harrison College - Lafayette Campus (J)

4705 Meijer Court, Lafayette IN 47905-4859

County: Tippecanoe Identification: 666431
Unit ID: 151245
Telephone: (765) 447-9550 Carnegie Class: Assoc/PrivFP
FAX Number: (765) 447-0868 Calendar System: Quarter
URL: www.harrison.edu
Established: 1902 Annual Undergrad Tuition & Fees: N/A
Enrollment: 278 Coed
Affiliation or Control: Proprietary IRS Status: Proprietary
Highest Offering: Baccalaureate
Program: Occupational; 2-Year Principally Bachelor's Creditable
Accreditation: &@NH, ACICS, MAC

01 President .... Mr. Jason T. KONESCO
12 Campus President .... Mr. Al PARKER

† Regional accreditation is carried under the parent institution in Indianapolis (Downtown Campus), IN.

Harrison College - Muncie Campus (K)

411 West Riggin Road, Muncie IN 47303-6413

County: Delaware FICE Identification: 030097
Unit ID: 151209
Telephone: (765) 288-8681 Carnegie Class: Assoc/PrivFP4
FAX Number: (765) 288-8797 Calendar System: Quarter
URL: www.harrison.edu
Established: 1902 Annual Undergrad Tuition & Fees: N/A
Enrollment: 206 Coed
Affiliation or Control: Proprietary IRS Status: Proprietary
Highest Offering: Baccalaureate
Program: Occupational; 2-Year Principally Bachelor's Creditable
Accreditation: @NH, ACICS, MAC

01 President .... Mr. Jason T. KONESCO
12 Campus President .... Ms. Charlene SAMPLE-PURTLEBAUGH

Harrison College - Terre Haute Campus (L)

1378 S State Road 46, Terre Haute IN 47803-9787

County: Vigo Identification: 666433
Unit ID: 151236
Telephone: (812) 877-2100 Carnegie Class: Assoc/PrivFP4
FAX Number: (812) 877-4440 Calendar System: Quarter
URL: www.harrison.edu
Established: 1902 Annual Undergrad Tuition & Fees: N/A
Enrollment: 322 Coed
Affiliation or Control: Proprietary IRS Status: Proprietary
Highest Offering: Baccalaureate
Program: Occupational; 2-Year Principally Bachelor's Creditable
Accreditation: &@NH, ACICS, MAC

01 President .... Mr. Jason T. KONESCO
12 Campus President .... Ms. Pat J. MOZLEY

† Regional accreditation is carried under the parent institution in Indianapolis (Downtown Campus), IN.

Holy Cross College (M)

PO Box 308, Notre Dame IN 46556-0308

County: Saint Joseph FICE Identification: 007263
Unit ID: 150774
Telephone: (574) 239-8400 Carnegie Class: Bac/A&S
FAX Number: (574) 239-8323 Calendar System: Semester
URL: www.hcc-nd.edu
Established: 1966 Annual Undergrad Tuition & Fees: $23,900
Enrollment: 453 Coed
Affiliation or Control: Roman Catholic IRS Status: 501(c)3
Highest Offering: Baccalaureate
Program: Liberal Arts And General
Accreditation: NH

01 President Bro. John R. PAIGE, CSC
03 Senior Vice President Dr. Tina S. HOLLAND
11 VP for Operations Mr. Dan HAVERTY
30 VP for Mission Advancement Mr. Robert L. KLOSKA
04 Executive Assistant Ms. Jodie L. SWEET
20 Dean of Faculty Mr. Justin WATSON
32 Dean of Students Mr. Daniel J. COCHRAN
06 Registrar Mr. Richard J. SULLIVAN
84 Director of Enrollment Management Mr. Brian STUDEBAKER
37 Director of Financial Aid Mr. Robert BENJAMIN
38 Director of Student Counseling Svcs .Bro. Chris J. DREYER, CSC
13 Director of Campus Technology ... Bro. Charles D. DREVON, CSC
18 Director of Building & Grounds Mr. Randy MCKINLEY
39 Director of Residence Life Dr. Christopher TORRIJAS
08 Director of Library Services Mrs. Mary Ellen HEGEDUS
36 Director of Discernment & Prep Mr. Charles BALL
42 Director of Campus Ministry Mr. Andrew POLANIECKI
41 Athletic Director Mr. Robert SCHERMERHORN

Huntington University (A)

2303 College Avenue, Huntington IN 46750-9986
County: Huntington FICE Identification: 001803
Unit ID: 150941
Telephone: (260) 356-6000 Carnegie Class: Bac/Diverse
FAX Number: (260) 359-4086 Calendar System: 4/1/4
URL: www.huntington.edu
Established: 1897 Annual Undergrad Tuition & Fees: $23,780
Enrollment: 1,262 Coed
Affiliation or Control: United Brethren Church IRS Status: 501(c)3
Highest Offering: Master's
Program: Liberal Arts And General; Teacher Preparatory; Professional
Accreditation: NH, NURSE, SW, TED

01 President Dr. G. Blair DOWDEN
05 Int Sr Vice Pres Academic Affairs Dr. Delbert D. DOUGHTY
10 Interim VP for Business/Finance Mrs. Julie A. HENDRYX
84 Sr VP Enrollment Mgmt & Marketing .. Mr. Jeffrey C. BERGGREN
45 Sr VP Strategy & Grad/Adult Program ... Dr. Ann C. MCPHERREN
30 Vice President for Advancement Mr. Vincent D. HAUPERT
32 Vice President for Student Life Dr. Ron L. COFFEY
45 VP for Strategy & Innovation Mr. Troy D. IRICK
26 Vice Pres for University Relations Mr. John W. PAFF
04 Admin Assistant to President Mrs. Barbara A. THOMPSON
42 Campus Pastor Rev. Arthur L. WILSON
58 Dean of Graduate & Adult Programs Dr. Stephen D. HOLTROP
36 Assoc Dean Student Life/Career Dev Ms. Martha J. SMITH
35 Assoc Dean of Student Development Mr. Jesse M. BROWN
44 Senior Director of Gift Planning Mr. Richard W. MCCONNELL
21 Controller & Budget Director Mr. Scott A. BERRY
37 Director of Financial Aid Mrs. Sharon R. WOODS
06 Registrar Mrs. Sarah J. HARVEY
08 Director of Library Services Ms. Anita GRAY
13 Director of Technology Services Mr. Gary L. CAMPBELL
38 Director of Learning Assistance Mrs. Kristal L. CHAFIN
41 Athletic Director Ms. Lori L. CULLER
18 Director of Physical Plant Mr. Jerry A. GRESSLEY
15 Dir Human Resources/Auxiliary Svcs Mrs. Julie A. HENDRYX
29 Director of Alumni Mrs. Margaret A. ROUSH
19 Director of Campus Police Mr. Barry A. COCHRAN
88 Dir of Horizon Leadership Program Mr. Jesse M. BROWN
26 Assoc Director of Media Relations Ms. Ashley SMITH
40 Bookstore Manager Mrs. Lisa M. SNYDER

Indiana State University (B)

200 N 7th Street, Terre Haute IN 47809-1902
County: Vigo FICE Identification: 001807
Unit ID: 151324
Telephone: (812) 237-6311 Carnegie Class: DRU
FAX Number: (812) 237-2291 Calendar System: Semester
URL: web.indstate.edu
Established: 1865 Annual Undergrad Tuition & Fees (In-State): $7,898
Enrollment: 11,528 Coed
Affiliation or Control: State IRS Status: 501(c)3
Highest Offering: Doctorate
Program: Liberal Arts And General; Teacher Preparatory; Professional
Accreditation: NH, AAFCS, #ARCPA, ART, BUS, CACREP, CIDA, CLPSY, CONST, COPSY, DIETC, ENGT, MUS, NAIT, NRPA, NUR, SCPSY, SP, SW, TED

01 President Dr. Daniel J. BRADLEY
100 Chief of Staff Ms. Teresa D. EXLINE
86 Exec Dir of Government Relations Mr. Greg J. GOODE
88 Chief Strategic Officer Dr. Karl BURGHER
05 Provost/Vice Pres Academic Affs Dr. C. Jack MAYNARD
10 VP Business Affs & Fin/Treas Ms. Diann E. MCKEE
84 VP Enrollment Mgmt/Mktg/Comm Mr. John BEACON
32 VP Student Affairs/Dean of Students Ms. Carmen TILLERY
43 General Council/Univ Secretary Ms. Melony A. SACOPULOS
20 Interim Assoc VP Academic Affairs Dr. Joshua POWERS
13 Assoc VP Chief Info Officer Dr. Lisa SPENCE
18 Assoc VP Univ Facilities Management Mr. Kevin L. RUNION
26 Asst VP Communications/Marketing Ms. Tara SINGER
07 Assoc VP Enroll/Mgmt/Adm/HS Rel Mr. Richard J. TOOMEY
29 Director of Alumni Affairs Mr. Charles P. DEMAIO
15 Assoc VP Human Resources Mr. Wil DOWNS
14 Exec Dir Information Technology Mr. Yancy PHILLIPS
21 Business Officer Ms. Diann E. MCKEE
06 Registrar Ms. April HAY
22 Director of Affirm Action Vacant
28 University Diversity Officer Ms. Elonda ERVIN
41 Director of Athletics Mr. Ronald PRETTYMAN

36 Career Services Executive Director Mrs. Tracy J. POWERS
88 Assoc Vice Pres Comm Engagement Dr. Nancy B. ROGERS
25 Director Sponsored Programs Ms. Dawn UNDERWOOD
09 Director of Institutional Research Ms. Patty MCCLINTOCK
19 Director of Public Safety Mr. William C. MERCIER
96 Dir Purchasing/Central Receiving Mr. Kevin BARR
39 Director of Residential Life Mr. Rex KENDALL
38 Director of Student Counseling Dr. Kenneth CHEW
37 Interim Dir Student Financial Aid Ms. Crystal BAKER
49 Dean of Arts & Sciences Dr. John MURRAY
50 Dean of Business Dr. Brien N. SMITH
53 Dean of Education Dr. Bradley BALCH
68 Dean Nursing/Health & Human Svcs Dr. Richard (Biff) WILLIAMS
72 Dean of Technology Dr. Bradford (Brad) SIMS
58 Dean of Grad/Professional Studies Dr. Jay GATRELL
08 Dean of Library Services Ms. Alberta COMER
56 Dean of Extended Learning Dr. Ken BRAUCHLE

Indiana Tech (C)

1600 E Washington Boulevard, Fort Wayne IN 46803-1297
County: Allen FICE Identification: 001805
Unit ID: 151290
Telephone: (260) 422-5561 Carnegie Class: Spec/Bus
FAX Number: (260) 420-1453 Calendar System: Semester
URL: www.indianatech.edu
Established: 1930 Annual Undergrad Tuition & Fees: $24,370
Enrollment: 4,547 Coed
Affiliation or Control: Independent Non-Profit IRS Status: 501(c)3
Highest Offering: Doctorate
Program: Professional; Business Emphasis
Accreditation: NH, ENG

01 President Dr. Arthur E. SNYDER
05 Vice President for Academic Affairs Dr. Douglas G. PERRY
03 Exec VP Finance & Administration Ms. Judy K. ROY
107 VP College of Professional Studies Mr. Steve A. HERENDEEN
84 VP Enrollment Mgmt/Student Life Ms. Allison G. CARNAHAN
30 Vice President of Inst Advancement Mr. Mark H. RICHTER
50 Dean of Business Dr. Jeffrey A. ZIMMERMAN
06 Registrar Mr. Travis A. BLUME
97 Dean of General Studies Dr. Doty A. LATUSZEK
54 Dean of Engineering/Computer Sci Mr. David A. ASCHLIMAN
61 Dean Law School Mr. Peter C. ALEXANDER
37 Director of Financial Aid Mr. Scott W. THUM
18 Director of Facilities Management Mr. R. Mike TOWNSLEY
13 Director of Information Technology Mr. Jeff S. LEICHTY
15 Human Resources Director Mr. Christopher B. BLACK
21 Controller Ms. Shelly R. MUSOLF
77 Assoc Dean of Computer Sciences Mr. Gary A. MESSICK
58 Director Global Leadership Program Dr. Kenneth E. RAUCH
20 Assoc Dean of CPS Dr. Andrew I. NWANNE
53 Director of Teacher Education Dr. Brad L. YODER
07 Assoc VP Enrollment Management Ms. Monica L. CHAMBERLAIN
26 Marketing Director Ms. Janet L. SCHUTTE
36 Dir of Career Planning & Devel Ctr Ms. Cynthia P. VERDUCE
11 Director of Operations-CPS Ms. Sharon LOKUTA
12 Operations Manager-Indianapolis Ms. Phyllis E. HOGAN
08 Director McMillen Library Ms. Constance E. SCOTT
88 Director of Criminal Sciences Dr. Steven F. HUNDERSMARCK
106 Director of Online Learning Dr. Y. Ben LEE
89 Director of Freshman College & SSS Ms. Mary C. SCUDDER
39 Assoc VP Student Services Mr. Chris M. DICKSON
29 Dir Annual Fund & Alumni Relations .. Mr. Michael E. PETERSON
04 Executive Asst to the President Ms. Jennifer A. ROSS
42 Faith Services Coordinator Mr. Gregory P. BYMAN
41 Athletic Director Mr. Martin C. NEUHOFF
32 Director Student Life Ms. Andrea G. CHECK
35 Student Life Coordinator Vacant
84 Enrollment Manager-Fort Wayne Mr. Yiani DEMITSAS
84 Enrollment Manager-Indy Mr. Shayne D. ABRAHAMS
88 Associate VP Advancement Ms. Mary V. SLAFKOSKY
88 Associate VP Advancement Mr. Larry J. PIERKARSKI
88 CPS Development Manager Ms. A. Nicole SCOTT
88 Title III Director Ms. Danielle L. WITZIGREUTER

*Indiana University (D)

Bryan Hall, Bloomington IN 47405-7000
County: Monroe FICE Identification: 008002
Telephone: (812) 855-4613 Carnegie Class: N/A
FAX Number: N/A
URL: www.indiana.edu

01 President Dr. Michael A. MCROBBIE
05 Exec Vice President/Provost IUB Lauren ROBEL
45 Exec Vice Pres/Chancellor IUPUI Dr. Charles BANTZ
45 Exec VP Univ Regional Affs/Plng/Pol Mr. John APPLEGATE
46 Vice Pres for Research Dr. Jorge JOSE
28 VP Diversity/Equity/Multicultural Dr. Edwin MARSHALL
18 Vice Pres Facilities Dr. Thomas MORRISON
10 Vice Pres/Chief Financial Officer Dr. Neil THEOBALD
26 VP Public Affairs & Govt Relations Mr. Michael SAMPLE
100 Chief of Staff Dr. Karen H. ADAMS
13 Vice President Info Tech/CIO Dr. Brad C. WHEELER
43 Vice Pres and University Counsel Ms. Jacqueline A. SIMMONS
104 Vice Pres for International Affairs Dr. David ZARET
88 Vice President for Engagement Mr. William B. STEPHAN
41 VP & Dir of Intercoll Athletics Mr. Fred GLASS
63 VP Univ Clinical Affs/Dean Sch Med Dr. Craig BRATER
21 University Treasurer Ms. Mary Frances MCCOURT

22 Director of Affirmative Action Ms. Julie KNOST
29 Exec Dir IU Alumni Association Mr. J. Thomas FORBES
15 Director of Human Resources Mr. Dan RIVES
27 Director of Media Relations Mr. Mark LAND
102 President IU Foundation Dr. Gene TEMPEL

*Indiana University Bloomington (E)

107 S. Indiana Ave., Bloomington IN 47405-7000
County: Monroe FICE Identification: 001809
Unit ID: 151351
Telephone: (812) 855-4848 Carnegie Class: RU/VH
FAX Number: (812) 855-5678 Calendar System: Semester
URL: www.iub.edu
Established: 1820 Annual Undergrad Tuition & Fees (In-State): $10,034
Enrollment: 42,731 Coed
Affiliation or Control: State IRS Status: 501(c)3
Highest Offering: Doctorate
Program: Liberal Arts And General; Teacher Preparatory; Professional
Accreditation: NH, ART, AUD, BUS, BUSA, CACREP, CIDA, CLPSY, COPSY, DIETD, IPSY, JOUR, LAW, LIB, MUS, NRPA, OPD, OPT, OPTR, OPTT, PH, SCPSY, SP, SPAA, TED, THEA

02 President Dr. Michael MCROBBIE
05 Exec Vice Pres & Provost Ms. Lauren ROBEL
03 Exec Vice Pres & Chanc IUPUI Dr. Charles BANTZ
09 Exec VP Univ Reg Affs/Plng/Policy Mr. John S. APPLEGATE
88 Senior Advisor to Provost & Exec VP ... Dr. Maynard THOMPSON
10 Sr Vice President & CFO Dr. Neil THEOBALD
63 VP Univ Clin Affrs/Dean Sch of Med Dr. D. Craig BRATER
18 Vice Pres Capital Plng/Facilities Dr. Tom MORRISON
28 VP Diversity/Equity & Multicul Affs Dr. Edwin MARSHALL
46 Vice President for Research Dr. Jorge JOSE
26 VP for Public Affs & Govt Relations Mr. Mike SAMPLE
88 Vice President for Engagement Mr. William B. STEPHAN
20 Vice Provost for Undergraduate Educ Dr. Sonya STEPHENS
20 Vice Prov Faculty & Academic Affs Dr. Thomas GIERYN
88 Assoc VP Rsrch/Vice Provost Rsrch Dr. P. Sarita SONI
84 Vice Provost Enrollment Mgmt Dr. David JOHNSON
30 Sr Vice Pres Development/IU Fdn Ms. Marti HEIL
15 Associate Vice Pres Human Resources Mr. Dan RIVES
09 Assoc VP Univ Inst Rsrch/Reporting Dr. Vic BORDEN
91 Assoc VP Enterprise Infrastructure Mr. Dennis CROMWELL
21 Sr Assoc V Povst Budget & Admin/IUB Mr. James DONGES
13 Vice Pres Info Technology & CIO Dr. Brad WHEELER
58 Dean University Graduate School Dr. James WIMBUSH
102 Pres & CEO IU Foundation Dr. Eugene R. TEMPEL
20 Assoc Vice Prov Faculty & Acad Affs Dr. Sara PRYOR
20 Assoc Vice Prov Faculty & Acad Affs Dr. Anne MASSEY
85 Assoc VP for International Svcs Mr. Christopher VIERS
49 Dean College Arts & Sciences Dr. Larry SINGELL
08 Ruth Lilly Dean Univ Libraries Dr. Brenda JOHNSON
32 Dean of Students Dr. Pete GOLDSMITH
50 Dean Kelley School of Business Dr. Daniel SMITH
53 Dean School of Education Dr. Gerardo GONZALEZ
68 Int Dean Sch Health/Phys Ed/Recrtn Dr. Mo TORABI
88 Dean School of Optometry Dr. Joseph BONANNO
61 Interim Dean School of Law Ms. Hannah BUXBAUM
64 Dean Jacobs School of Music Mr. Gwyn RICHARDS
60 Int Dean School of Journalism Dr. Michael EVANS
88 Dean School of Informatics Dr. Bobby SCHNABEL
80 Dean SPEA Dr. John D. GRAHAM
62 Dean Sch of Library/Info Science Dr. Debora SHAW
82 Vice Pres International Affairs Dr. David ZARET
92 Dean Hutton Honors College Dr. Matthew AUER
94 Dean Women's Affairs Dr. Yvette ALEX-ASSENSOH
35 Assoc Dean for Student Affairs Ms. Carol MCCORD
29 Exec Dir IU Alumni Association Mr. J.T FORBES
39 Exec Dir Residential Pgm & Svcs Mr. Pat CONNOR
36 Exec Dir Career Dev Center Mr. Patrick DONAHUE
16 Bloomington Dir Employee Rels Svcs Ms. Suzanne RYAN
06 Assoc Vice Provost/Registrar Mr. Mark MCCONAHAY
23 Exec Dir & CFO IU Health Center Dr. Hugh JESSOP
43 VP & General Counsel Ms. Jacqueline SIMMONS
88 Director IU Press Dr. Janet RABINOWITCH
22 Director Affirmative Action Ms. Julie KNOST
40 Manager of IU Bookstore Mr. Joe BENDER
19 Chief of Police Mr. Keith CASH
88 Exec Dir Indiana Memorial Union Mr. Bruce JACOBS
88 Director Radio/TV Services Mr. Perry METZ
88 Operations Mgr Campus Bus Service Mr. Perry MAULL
88 Director IU Auditorium Mr. Doug BOOHER
18 Asst VP Facilities Operations Mr. Hank HEWETSON
38 Director Counseling & Psych Svs Dr. Nancy STOCKTON
41 VP & Dir Intercollegiate Athletics Mr. Fred GLASS
96 Asst VP for Procurement Ms. Jill SCHUNK
25 Exec Dir Grant & Contract Services Mr. Jim BECKER
90 Asocc Dean Rsrch Tech/ED PTI/Prof Dr. Craig STEWART
07 Director of Admissions Ms. Mary Ellen ANDERSON

*Indiana University East (F)

2325 Chester Boulevard, Richmond IN 47374-1289
County: Wayne FICE Identification: 001811
Unit ID: 151388
Telephone: (765) 973-8200 Carnegie Class: Bac/Diverse
FAX Number: (765) 973-8237 Calendar System: Semester
URL: www.iue.edu
Established: 1946 Annual Undergrad Tuition & Fees (In-State): $7,964
Enrollment: 3,725 Coed
Affiliation or Control: State IRS Status: 501(c)3
Highest Offering: Master's
Program: Liberal Arts And General; Teacher Preparatory

Accreditation: NH, ACBSP, NUR, TED

Code	Title	Name
02	Interim Chancellor	Dr. Lawrence D. RICHARDS
05	Interim Vice Chanc Academic Affairs	Dr. Mary BLAKEFIELD
26	Vice Chanc External Affs/Marketing	Mr. Rob ZINKAN
10	Vice Chancellor Admin & Finance	Mr. Dan DOOLEY
32	Interim Dean of Students	Ms. Carrie HELLER
13	Director Information Technology	Mr. Todd DUKE
30	Director of Gift Development	Ms. Stephanie HAYS-MUSSOINI
06	Registrar	Mr. Dennis HICKS
08	Director Library/Media Services	Dr. Frances YATES
15	Director Human Resources	Ms. Dianne S. CHANDLER
36	Director Career Services	Vacant
07	Director of Admissions	Ms. Molly VANDERPOOL
37	Dir Fin Aid & Scholarships	Ms. Sarah SOPER
20	Director University College	Ms. Carrie HELLER
40	Manager of Barnes & Noble Bookstore	Ms. Kristy FRASHER
35	Director of Campus Life	Ms. Rebeckah SNODDY
21	Interim Bursar	Ms. Shelley DODSON
22	Interim Director Affirmative Action	Ms. Dianne CHANDLER
70	Director Social Work/Human Services	Mr. Ed FITZGERALD
27	Director Communications & Marketing	Mr. John DALTON
97	Director General Studies	Dr. Ross ALEXANDER
29	Director Alumni Relations	Ms. Terry WIESEHAN
28	Director of Multicultural Affairs	Vacant
50	Dean Business/Technology	Dr. David FRANTZ
79	Dean Humanities & Social Sciences	Dr. Katherine FRANK
81	Interim Dean Natural Math & Science	Dr. Neil SABINE
66	Dean of Nursing	Ms. Karen CLARK
53	Dean Education	Dr. Marilyn WATKINS

*Indiana University Kokomo (A)

2300 S Washington, Box 9003, Kokomo IN 46904-9003

County: Howard FICE Identification: 001814

Unit ID: 151333

Telephone: (765) 453-2000 Carnegie Class: Bac/Diverse

FAX Number: (765) 455-9444 Calendar System: Semester

URL: www.iuk.edu

Established: 1945 Annual Undergrad Tuition & Fees (In-State): $6,332

Enrollment: 3,318 Coed

Affiliation or Control: State IRS Status: 501(c)3

Highest Offering: Master's

Program: Occupational; Liberal Arts And General; Teacher Preparatory; Professional

Accreditation: NH, BUS, NURSE, RAD, TED

Code	Title	Name
02	Chancellor	Dr. Michael HARRIS
05	Exec Vice Chanc Academic Affairs	Dr. Sue SCIAME-GIESECKE
10	Vice Chanc Admin/Finance	Mr. Roy TAMIR
32	Vice Chancellor Student Affairs	Dr. Jack A. THARP
30	Vice Chancellor for Advancement	Ms. Penny LEE
20	Asst Vice Chanc Academic Affairs	Dr. Kathy PARKISON
72	Director Division Purdue Tech	Ms. Christy BOZIC
08	Dean of the Library	Ms. Rhonda ARMSTRONG
37	Associate Director Financial Aid	Ms. Karen GALLATIN
84	Director of Enrollment Management	Ms. Tyana LANGE
15	Director Human Resources	Vacant
06	Registrar	Ms. Stacey THOMAS
38	Asst Vice Chanc Student Success	Ms. Gerry G. STROMAN
36	Manager Career Services	Ms. Tracy SPRINGER
29	Director Alumni Relations	Ms. Catherine VALCKE
27	Director Communications & Marketing	Ms. Marie RADEL
35	Dean of Students	Ms. Sarah SARBER
18	Chief Facilities/Physical Plant	Vacant
50	Dean School of Business	Dr. Frank WADSWORTH
49	Interim Dean School Arts & Science	Dr. Erv BOSCHMANN
66	Dean School of Nursing	Dr. Linda WALLACE
53	Dean Division of Education	Dr. Paul PAESE
81	Chair Natural/Info/Math Sciences	Dr. Christian CHAURET
79	Chair Humanities	Dr. Scott JONES

*Indiana University Northwest (B)

3400 Broadway, Gary IN 46408-1197

County: Lake FICE Identification: 001815

Unit ID: 151360

Telephone: (219) 980-6500 Carnegie Class: Master's M

FAX Number: (219) 980-6670 Calendar System: Semester

URL: www.iun.edu

Established: 1921 Annual Undergrad Tuition & Fees (In-State): $6,627

Enrollment: 6,035 Coed

Affiliation or Control: State IRS Status: 501(c)3

Highest Offering: Master's

Program: Occupational; Liberal Arts And General; Teacher Preparatory; Professional

Accreditation: NH, BUS, DA, DH, NUR, NURSE, RAD, RTT, SPAA, TED

Code	Title	Name
02	Chancellor	Dr. William J. LOWE
04	Exec Asst to the Chancellor	Mrs. Kathy MALONE
05	Exec Vice Chanc Academic Affairs	Dr. David J. MALIK
11	Vice Chancellor Administration	Dr. Joseph PELLICCIOTTI
32	Vice Chancellor Student Services	Dr. Georj LEWIS
10	Campus Chief Financial Officer	Mrs. Marianne MILICH
26	Interim Director External Rels	Ms. Kris FALZONE
27	Chief Information Officer	Ms. Beth VAN GORDON
20	Assoc Vice Chanc Academic Affs	Dr. Cynthia O'DELL
09	Asst VC Inst Effectiveness & Rsrch	Mr. John NOVAK
49	Dean College of Arts & Sciences	Dr. Mark HOYERT
88	Dean Col of Health & Human Svcs	Dr. Patrick BANKSTON
50	Dean School of Business & Economics	Dr. Anna ROMINGER
53	Dean School of Education	Dr. Stanley WIGLE
51	Division Chair Continuing Studies	Mr. Thomas SWIRSKI
80	Director Public & Environ Affs	Dr. Barbara PEAT
70	Director Social Work	Dr. Darlene LYNCH
06	Interim Registrar	Mr. Jeff JOHNSTON
51	Int Dir Extended/Continuing Study	Dr. Atilla TUNCAY
07	Director Admissions	Ms. Linda B. TEMPLETON
37	Director Financial Aid	Mr. Harold BURTLEY
36	Director Career & Placement	Ms. Sharese DUDLEY
35	Coordinator Student Life	Mr. Scott FULK
19	Director Security	Ms. Patricia NOWAK
29	Director Alumni Relations	Ms. Paulette LAFATA-JOHNSON
66	Director Division of Nursing	Dr. Linda DELUNAS
24	Director Instructional Media Svcs	Mr. Paul SHARPE
08	Director Library	Mr. Timothy SUTHERLAND
18	Director Physical Plant	Mr. Otto JEFIMENKO
21	Manager Student Accounts	Ms. Sandra MENDOZA
25	Director Research/Sponsored Pgms	Ms. T.J STOOPS
15	Director Human Resources	Ms. Carolyn HARTLEY
28	Int Dir of Diversity Programming	Mr. James WALLACE, JR.
38	Director of Student Counseling Ctr	Ms. Barbara A. BULLOCK
22	Director Affirmative Action	Ms. Ida GILLIS

*Indiana University-Purdue University Fort Wayne (C)

2101 E Coliseum Boulevard, Fort Wayne IN 46805-1499

County: Allen FICE Identification: 001828

Unit ID: 151102

Telephone: (260) 481-6100 Carnegie Class: Master's L

FAX Number: (260) 481-6880 Calendar System: Semester

URL: www.ipfw.edu

Established: 1964 Annual Undergrad Tuition & Fees (In-State): $6,876

Enrollment: 14,326 Coed

Affiliation or Control: State IRS Status: 501(c)3

Highest Offering: Master's

Program: Liberal Arts And General; Teacher Preparatory; Professional

Accreditation: NH, ADNUR, BUS, CS, DA, DH, DT, ENG, ENGT, MUS, NUR, RAD, SPAA, TED, THEA

Code	Title	Name
02	Chancellor	Dr. Vicky L. CARWEIN
05	Int Vice Chanc Academic Affairs	Dr. Steven T. SARRATORE
10	Vice Chancellor Financial Affairs	Mr. Walter J. BRANSON
32	Vice Chancellor Student Affairs	Dr. George S. MCCLELLAN
45	Assoc Vice Chancellor Inst Research	Dr. Robert WILKINSON
04	Admin Assistant to the Chancellor	Ms. Kay FOLKS
30	Executive Director Development	Ms. Linda L. RUFFOLO
26	Exec Dir Univ Relations/Commun	Ms. Irene A. WALTERS
14	Director Information Tech Services	Mr. Robert M. KOSTRUBANIC
18	Director Physical Plant	Mr. Jay H. HARRIS
29	Director Alumni Relations	Ms. Kimberly M. WAGNER
08	Library Dean	Ms. Cheryl B. TRUESDELL
15	Director Human Resources	Ms. Rose M. COSTELLO
41	Director of Athletics	Mr. Tommy BELL
21	Comptroller	Mr. Daniel L. GEBHART
06	Registrar	Mr. Patrick A. MCLAUGHLIN
96	Director Purchasing	Ms. Cynthia M. ELICK
19	Chief University Police	Mr. Jeffrey W. DAVIS
22	Director Institutional Equity	Ms. Christine M. MARCUCCILLI
85	Director International Program	Mr. Brian MYLREA
37	Director Financial Aid	Ms. Judith CRAMER
07	Director of Admissions	Ms. Carol B. ISAACS
38	Assoc Vice Chanc Student Success	Dr. Bruce BUSBY
84	Director Enrollment Management	Mr. Mark A. FRANKE
49	Dean Arts & Sciences	Dr. Carl N. DRUMMOND
76	Dean Health Sciences	Dr. Ann OBERGFELL
51	Exec Director Continuing Stds	Ms. Deborah M. CONKLIN
72	Dean Engr Tech/Computer Science	Mr. S.C. Max YEN
53	Interim Dean Educ & Public Policy	Dr. James BURG
50	Dean Business	Dr. Otto H. CHANG
57	Interim Dean Visual/Performing Arts	Dr. John O'CONNELL
46	Assoc Vice Chanc Rsrch Ext Support	Dr. J. ALBAYYARI
20	Associate Academic Officer	Dr. Steve T. SARRATORE
35	Dean of Students	Dr. Eric M. NORMAN
28	Assoc Vice Chancellor Diversity	Mr. Kenneth C. CHRISTMON

*Indiana University-Purdue University Indianapolis (D)

355 N Lansing Street, Indianapolis IN 46202-2896

County: Marion FICE Identification: 001813

Unit ID: 151111

Telephone: (317) 274-5555 Carnegie Class: RU/H

FAX Number: N/A Calendar System: Semester

URL: www.iupui.edu

Established: 1969 Annual Undergrad Tuition & Fees (In-State): $7,081

Enrollment: 30,530 Coed

Affiliation or Control: State IRS Status: 501(c)3

Highest Offering: Doctorate

Program: Occupational; Liberal Arts And General; Teacher Preparatory; Professional

Accreditation: NH, ADNUR, ART, CIDA, CLPSY, CS, CYTO, DA, DENT, DH, DIETI, EMT, ENG, ENGT, HSA, HT, IPSY, LAW, MED, MT, MUS, NDT, NMT, NUR, NURSE, OT, PA, PH, PTA, RAD, RADDOS, RTT, SPAA, SW

Code	Title	Name
02	Chancellor	Dr. Charles R. BANTZ
100	Chief of Staff	Mr. Andrew R. KLEIN
28	Asst Chanc Diversity/Equity/Incl	Mr. Kenneth B. DURGANS
04	Assistant to Chancellor for Comm	Ms. Sylvia M. PAYNE
05	Exec Vice Chanc/Chief Academic Ofcr	Dr. Nasser H. PAYDAR
10	Vice Chanc Administration & Finance	Ms. Dawn M. RHODES
26	Vice Chancellor External Affairs	Ms. Amy C. WARNER
32	Vice Chancellor Student Life	Dr. Zebulun R. DAVENPORT
46	Vice Chancellor Research	Dr. Kody VARAHRAMYAN
13	Dean Information Technologies	Dr. Anastasia MORRONE
08	Dean University Library	Mr. David W. LEWIS
84	Director Enrollment Services	Dr. Rebecca E. PORTER
06	Registrar	Ms. Mary Beth MYERS
21	Bursar	Mr. Dan YOUNGBLOOD
22	Director Equal Opportunity	Ms. Kim D. KIRKLAND
38	Director Student Counseling	Dr. Julie LASH
39	Director Campus Housing	Mr. Aaron HART
40	Bookstore Manager	Ms. Michele G. CARTER
36	Career Services Council	Mr. Joshua D. KILLEY
41	Athletic Director	Mr. Michael R. MOORE
29	Director Alumni Relations	Mr. Stefan S. DAVIS
27	Director News & Media	Ms. Margie SMITH-SIMMONS
09	Director Institutional Research	Dr. Gary PIKE
07	Dir of Undergraduate Admissions	Mr. Chris J. FOLEY
37	Director Student Financial Aid	Ms. Kathy PURVIS
15	Asst Vice Chanc Human Resources	Ms. Carlene M. THOMPSON
23	Medical Director Student Health Svc	Dr. Stephen F. WINTERMEYER
18	Director Campus Facility Services	Ms. Emily C. WREN
19	Chief Campus Police	Mr. Paul E. NORRIS
92	Dean Honors College	Dr. E. Jane LUZAR
96	Director Purchasing	Mr. Robert HALTER
45	Senior Advisor/Academic Planning	Dr. Trudy W. BANTA
12	Dean Columbus Campus	Dr. Marwan A. WAFA
76	Dean School Health/Rehab Sci	Dr. Austin O. AGHO
57	Dean Herron School of Art	Ms. Valerie EICKMEIER
51	Dean Sch of Continuing Studies	Dr. Daniel J. CALLISON
52	Dean School of Dentistry	Dr. John N. WILLIAMS
54	Dean School of Engr/Technology	Dr. David J. RUSSOMANNO
88	Exec Assoc Dean of Informatics	Dr. Anthony FAIOLA
61	Dean Sch of Law Indianapolis	Mr. Gary R. ROBERTS
49	Dean School of Liberal Arts	Dr. William A. BLOMQUIST
63	Dean School of Medicine	Dr. D. Craig BRATER
66	Dean School of Nursing	Dr. Marion E. BROOME
68	Dean School of Physical Education	Dr. James M. GLADDEN
81	Dean School of Science	Dr. Simon RHODES
70	Dean School of Social Work	Dr. Michael PATCHNER
53	Exec Assoc Dean School of Education	Dr. Patricia M. ROGAN
60	Int Ex Assoc Dean Sch of Journalism	Dr. Dan DREW
62	Exec Assoc Dean Library/Info Sci	Dr. Tomas A. LIPINSKI
80	Exec Assoc Dean Public/Environ Affs	Dr. Terry BAUMER
85	Assoc Vice Chanc International Affs	Dr. Gil LATZ
50	Assoc Dean School of Business	Dr. Philip L. COCHRAN
58	Associate Dean Graduate School	Dr. Sherry F. QUEENER
89	Dean University College	Dr. Kathy JOHNSON

*Indiana University South Bend (E)

1700 Mishawaka Avenue, South Bend IN 46634-7111

County: Saint Joseph FICE Identification: 001816

Unit ID: 151342

Telephone: (574) 520-4872 Carnegie Class: Master's M

FAX Number: (574) 520-4834 Calendar System: Semester

URL: www.iusb.edu

Established: 1940 Annual Undergrad Tuition & Fees (In-State): $6,728

Enrollment: 8,385 Coed

Affiliation or Control: State IRS Status: 501(c)3

Highest Offering: Master's

Program: Occupational; Liberal Arts And General; Teacher Preparatory; Professional

Accreditation: NH, BUS, CACREP, DH, MACTE, NURSE, RAD, SPAA, TED

Code	Title	Name
02	Chancellor	Dr. Una Mae RECK
05	Exec Vice Chanc Academic Affairs	Dr. Alfred J. GUILLAUME, JR.
10	Vice Chancellor Finance & Admin	Mr. Bill J. O'DONNELL
26	Vice Chanc Public Affs/Univ Advance	Dr. Ilene SHEFFER
32	Vice Chanc Student Affs/Enroll Mgmt	Dr. Jeff JONES
13	Regional Chief Information Officer	Ms. Elizabeth VAN GORDON
20	Assoc Vice Chanc Academic Affs	Dr. John L. MCINTOSH
88	Assoc VC Student Acad Support Svcs	Ms. Karen L. WHITE
84	Asst Vice Chanc for Enrollment Svcs	Ms. Cathy M. BUCKMAN
06	Registrar	Mr. Jeff JOHNSTON
36	Director Career Services Office	Mr. Jeffery L. JACKSON
35	Dir Student Activit Ctr/Athletics	Mr. Gary DEMSKI
18	Director Facilities Management	Mr. Michael PRATER
19	Director of Safety & Security	Mr. Martin L. GERSEY
15	Director of Human Resources	Ms. Sara ERMETI
24	Dir of Instructional Media Svcs	Mr. Jim YOCOM
29	Dir Alumni Affs/Campus Ceremonies	Ms. Jeanie METZGER
27	Director Communications/Marketing	Mr. Kenneth W. BAIERL
52	Director of Dental Auxiliary Educ	Ms. Kristyn QUIMBY
51	Director of Extended Learning	Mr. Tim RYAN
97	Director of General Studies	Dr. David A. VOLLRATH
85	Director of International Programs	Dr. Scott SERNAU
38	Director Student Counseling Ctr	Mr. James HURST
07	Director of Admissions	Vacant
09	Director of Institutional Research	Mr. Biniam TESFAMARIAM
28	Director of Diversity	Ms. Charlotte D. PFEIFFER
30	Director of Development	Ms. Dina HARRIS
39	Director of Student Housing	Mr. Paul KRIKAU
21	Director of Accounting	Vacant
37	Associate Director of Financial Aid	Ms. Cyndi LANG
49	Dean of Liberal Arts & Science	Dr. Elizabeth E. DUNN
50	Dean of Business & Economics	Dr. Robert DUCOFFE
53	Interim Dean of Education	Dr. Karen CLARK
57	Dean of the Arts	Dr. Marvin CURTIS
66	Int Dean of Nursing/Health Profess	Dr. Doug MCMILLAN
08	Dean of Library Services	Ms. Vicki BLOOM

*Indiana University Southeast (A)

4201 Grant Line Road, New Albany IN 47150-6405
County: Floyd FICE Identification: 001817
Unit ID: 151379
Telephone: (812) 941-2000 Carnegie Class: Master's L
FAX Number: (812) 941-2475 Calendar System: Semester
URL: www.ius.edu
Established: 1941 Annual Undergrad Tuition & Fees (In-State): $6,575
Enrollment: 7,256 Coed
Affiliation or Control: State IRS Status: 501(c)3
Highest Offering: Master's
Program: Occupational; Liberal Arts And General; Teacher Preparatory; Professional; Business Emphasis
Accreditation: NH, BUS, NURSE, TED

02 Chancellor .... Dr. Sandra R. PATTERSON-RANDLES
05 Vice Chancellor Academic Affairs .... Dr. Gilbert W. ATNIP
10 Vice Chanc Administration/Finance .... Mr. Dana C. WAVLE
32 Int Vice Chancellor Student Affairs .... Ms. Anne M. SKUCE
29 Int Vice Chanc Alumni/Cmty Rels .... Mr. Jerry A. WAYNE
20 Assoc Vice Chanc Academic Affairs .Dr. Annette M. WYANDOTTE
13 Chief Information Officer .... Mr. Thomas SAWYER
07 Acting Director Admissions .... Mr. Christopher M. CREWS
04 Admin Assistant to the Chancellor .... Ms. Debra A. EBERLE
35 Dean for Student Life .... Mr. Seuth CHALEUNPHONH
06 Registrar .... Mr. Patrick FAWCETT
37 Director Student Financial Aid .... Ms. Brittany HUBBARD
08 Director Library Services .... Mr. C. Martin ROSEN
14 Director IT Systems & Operations .... Mr. Kirk K. KLAPHAAK
36 Director Career Development Center .... Mr. James E. LEWIS, III
18 Director Physical Plant .... Mr. James WOLFE, JR.
14 Dir IT Communications & Support .... Mr. Nicholas T. RAY
21 Director Accounting Services .... Mr. Michael J. KERSTIENS
41 Director Athletics .... Mr. Joseph M. GLOVER
72 Purdue Pgms Site Administrator .... Dr. Andy SCHAFFER
15 Director Human Resources .... Ms. Ann B. LEE
09 Director Institutional Research .... Dr. Tanlee T. WASSON
19 Chief Safety & Security .... Mr. Charles EDELEN
38 Dir Advis Center-Exploratory Stdnts .... Ms. Rebecca B. TURNER
22 Staff Equity & Diversity .... Ms. Darlene P. YOUNG
30 Director of Development .... Vacant
26 Dir of University Communication .... Ms. Jennifer J. WOLF
39 Director Residence Life & Housing .... Ms. Amanda G. STONECIPHER
51 Manager Continuing Studies .... Ms. Saundra E. GORDON
79 Dean School Arts & Letters .... Dr. Samantha EARLEY
81 Int Dean School Natural Sciences .... Dr. Bahman NASSIM
83 Dean School Social Sciences .... Dr. Joseph L. WERT
50 Dean School Business .... Dr. A. Jay WHITE
53 Dean School Education .... Dr. Gloria J. MURRAY
66 Dean School Nursing .... Dr. Marian A. MCKAY
46 Dean for Research .... Dr. Walter F. RYAN

Indiana Wesleyan University (B)

4201 S Washington Street, Marion IN 46953-4999
County: Grant FICE Identification: 001822
Unit ID: 151801
Telephone: (765) 674-6901 Carnegie Class: Master's L
FAX Number: (765) 677-2499 Calendar System: 4/1/4
URL: www.indwes.edu
Established: 1920 Annual Undergrad Tuition & Fees: $30,576
Enrollment: 15,872 Coed
Affiliation or Control: Wesleyan Church IRS Status: 501(c)3
Highest Offering: Doctorate
Program: Liberal Arts And General; Teacher Preparatory; Professional; Business Emphasis
Accreditation: NH, CACREP, MUS, NURSE, SW, TED

01 President .... Dr. Henry L. SMITH
03 Executive Vice President .... Dr. Keith NEWMAN
05 Provost .... Dr. David W. WRIGHT
10 Vice President Finance/CFO .... Dr. Duane KILTY
49 VP & Dean College of Arts & Science .... Dr. Darlene BRESSLER
51 VP & Dean Adult & Prof Studies .... Dr. Bridget AITCHISON
88 Vice President Wesley Seminary .... Dr. Wayne SCHMIDT
58 Dean Graduate School .... Dr. Jim FULLER
88 Dean of the Seminary .... Dr. Ken SCHENCK
66 Exec Director School of Nursing .... Dr. Barbara IHRKE
32 Vice Pres Student Development .... Dr. Michael MOFFITT
84 Vice Pres Enrollment Management .... Mrs. Kris DOUGLAS
13 VP Info Tech/CIO/Facil Svcs/Cmp Pln .... Mr. John JONES
09 Asst Provost Inst Research & Accred .... Dr. Don SPROWL
88 Assistant Provost for Scholarship .... Dr. Jerry PATTENGALE
20 Assistant Provost for Acad Svcs .... Mrs. Karen ROORBACH
37 Associate VP Financial Aid .... Mr. Thomas RATLIFF
08 Director Library Resources .... Mrs. Shelia CARLBLOM
08 Director Off-campus Library Svcs .... Mrs. Jule KIND
29 Director of Alumni .... Mr. Rick CARDER
07 Director Admissions .... Mr. Daniel SOLMS
15 Director Personnel Services .... Mrs. Diane MCDANIEL
06 University Registrar .... Mrs. Kim NICHOLSON
21 Controller .... Mrs. Tiffany LEWIS
36 Director Center for Life Calling .... Dr. Bill MILLARD
41 Athletic Director .... Mr. Mark DEMICHAEL
42 Dean of the Chapel .... Dr. Jim LO
44 Director Planned Giving .... Mr. Brian LEWIS
28 Director Intercultural Student Svcs .... Mr. Don LAWRENCE
92 Exec Director of Honors College .... Mr. David RIGGS
100 Chief of Staff .... Dr. Larry LINDSAY

International Business College (C)

5699 Coventry Lane, Fort Wayne IN 46804-9990
County: Allen FICE Identification: 004579
Unit ID: 151458
Telephone: (260) 459-4500 Carnegie Class: Bac/Assoc
FAX Number: (260) 436-1896 Calendar System: Semester
URL: www.ibcfortwayne.edu
Established: 1889 Annual Undergrad Tuition & Fees: $13,500
Enrollment: 559 Coed
Affiliation or Control: Proprietary IRS Status: Proprietary
Highest Offering: Baccalaureate
Program: Occupational; 2-Year Principally Bachelor's Creditable
Accreditation: ACICS, MAC

01 President .... Mr. Steve KINZER
05 Director of Education .... Ms. Debra PETERSEN
07 Director of Admissions .... Ms. Gena HOPKINS
32 Student Services Director .... Ms. Roxanna SHULL
51 Director Continuing Education .... Mr. Amee AUGENSPEIN
36 Director of Placement .... Vacant
06 Registrar .... Ms. Cara CLAPPER

International Business College (D)

7205 Shadeland Station, Indianapolis IN 46256-3997
County: Marion Identification: 666929
Unit ID: 151467
Telephone: (317) 813-2300 Carnegie Class: Assoc/PrivFP
FAX Number: (317) 841-6419 Calendar System: Other
URL: www.intlbusinesscollege.com
Established: 1984 Annual Undergrad Tuition & Fees: $13,950
Enrollment: 310 Coed
Affiliation or Control: Proprietary IRS Status: Proprietary
Highest Offering: Associate Degree
Program: Occupational
Accreditation: ACICS, DA, MAC

01 President .... Ms. Kathy CHIUDIONI
05 Director of Education .... Ms. Judith THAMES

ITT Technical Institute (E)

2810 Dupont Commerce Court,
Fort Wayne IN 46825-2393
County: Allen FICE Identification: 008329
Unit ID: 151500
Telephone: (260) 497-6200 Carnegie Class: Spec/Tech
FAX Number: (260) 497-6299 Calendar System: Quarter
URL: www.itt-tech.edu
Established: 1967 Annual Undergrad Tuition & Fees: N/A
Enrollment: 628 Coed
Affiliation or Control: Proprietary IRS Status: Proprietary
Highest Offering: Baccalaureate
Program: Technical Emphasis
Accreditation: ACICS

† Branch campus of ITT Technical Institute, Indianapolis, IN.

ITT Technical Institute (F)

9511 Angola Court, Indianapolis IN 46268-1119
County: Marion FICE Identification: 007329
Unit ID: 151519
Telephone: (317) 875-8640 Carnegie Class: Master's S
FAX Number: (317) 875-8641 Calendar System: Quarter
URL: www.itt-tech.edu
Established: 1956 Annual Undergrad Tuition & Fees: N/A
Enrollment: 7,164 Coed
Affiliation or Control: Proprietary IRS Status: Proprietary
Highest Offering: Master's
Program: Technical Emphasis
Accreditation: ACICS

ITT Technical Institute (G)

10999 Stahl Road, Newburgh IN 47630-7429
County: Warrick FICE Identification: 007327
Unit ID: 251251
Telephone: (812) 858-1600 Carnegie Class: Spec/Tech
FAX Number: (812) 858-0646 Calendar System: Quarter
URL: www.itt-tech.edu
Established: 1959 Annual Undergrad Tuition & Fees: N/A
Enrollment: 528 Coed
Affiliation or Control: Proprietary IRS Status: Proprietary
Highest Offering: Baccalaureate
Program: Technical Emphasis
Accreditation: ACICS

† Branch campus of ITT Technical Institute, Indianapolis, IN.

ITT Technical Institute (H)

17390 Dugdale Drive, Suite 100, South Bend IN 46635
County: St. Joseph Identification: 666700
Unit ID: 450270
Telephone: (574) 247-8300 Carnegie Class: Assoc/PrivFP4
FAX Number: (574) 247-8350 Calendar System: Quarter
URL: www.itt-tech.edu
Established: N/A Annual Undergrad Tuition & Fees: N/A
Enrollment: 480 Coed
Affiliation or Control: Proprietary IRS Status: Proprietary
Highest Offering: Baccalaureate
Program: Technical Emphasis
Accreditation: ACICS

† Branch campus of ITT Technical Institute, Indianapolis, IN.

*Ivy Tech Community College of Indiana-Central Office (I)

50 W Fall Creek Parkway N Drive,
Indianapolis IN 46208-5752
County: Marion FICE Identification: 008546
Unit ID: 363563
Telephone: (317) 921-4882 Carnegie Class: N/A
FAX Number: (317) 921-4753
URL: www.ivytech.edu

01 President .... Mr. Thomas J. SNYDER
05 Sr VP Academic Affairs/Provost .... Dr. Mary E. OSTRYE
10 Vice President Finance/Treasurer .... Mr. Chris RUHL
30 Vice President Development .... Dr. Joyce ROGERS
88 Sr VP Pgm Analysis/Instl Efficiency .... Mr. Jeff TERP
32 Vice Pres Stdnt Affairs/Enrol Mgmt .... Dr. Benjamin YOUNG
103 Vice Pres Workforce & Econ Dev .... Dr. Rebecca NICKOLI
27 Vice Pres Marketing/Communications .... Mr. Jeff FANTER
12 President Corporate College .... Mr. Matt BELL
20 Assoc Vice Pres Academic Affairs .... Dr. Russell D. BAKER
18 AVP Facilities Inst Planning .... Mr. Richard B. TULLY
53 Exec Dir Academic Policy/Assessment .... Dr. Cherry K. SMITH
88 Chief Finan Student Resources Offcr .... Mr. Ben BURTON
15 Executive Director Human Resources .... Mrs. Julie LORTON-ROWLAND
09 Exec Dir Institutional Research .... Mrs. Jill KRAMER
21 Assistant Treasurer .... Mr. Mark A. HUSK
13 Chief Technology Officer .... Mrs. Anne BRINSON

*Ivy Tech Community College of Indiana-Bloomington (J)

200 N Daniels Way, Bloomington IN 47404-9772
County: Monroe FICE Identification: 035213
Unit ID: 440244
Telephone: (812) 332-1559 Carnegie Class: Assoc/Pub-R-M
FAX Number: (812) 330-6106 Calendar System: Semester
URL: www.ivytech.edu/bloomington
Established: 1963 Annual Undergrad Tuition & Fees (In-State): $3,000
Enrollment: 6,500 Coed
Affiliation or Control: State IRS Status: 501(c)3
Highest Offering: Associate Degree
Program: Occupational; 2-Year Principally Bachelor's Creditable
Accreditation: &NH, ACBSP, ACFEI, ADNUR, EMT, NAIT, PNUR, RTT

02 Chancellor .... Mr. John R. WHIKEHART
05 Vice Chancellor Academic Affairs .... Dr. Brad THURMOND
32 Vice Chancellor Student Affairs .... Ms. Jennie VAUGHAN
18 Director of Facilities .... Mr. Doug MATTICK
103 Interim Exec Dir Workfce/Econ Devel .... Ms. Katrina JONES
10 Executive Director Finance .... Mr. Doug GILES
30 Interim Exec Dir of Development .... Mr. Sam DEWEESE
13 Exec Dir of Campus Computing Svcs .... Mr. Ben ACKERMAN
26 Exec Director of Marketing .... Ms. Amanda BILLINGS
06 Registrar .... Ms. Rachel SKEENS
08 Library Director .... Ms. Susan CATT
28 Director of Outreach .... Ms. Debra VANCE
35 Director of Student Development .... Mr. Sam DEWEESE
21 Director Business Office .... Ms. Sherry DEIRTH
51 Director Continuing Education .... Ms. Susie GRAHAM
84 Director of Enrollment Services .... Ms. Vonda CLAY
37 Director Student Financial Aid .... Ms. Patt MCCAFFERTY
36 Assistant Director Career Services .... Ms. Katie ANDERSON
29 Asst Dir Alumni Relations .... Ms. Emilee MABREY
09 Institutional Research Analyst .... Ms. Lindsey PANICCIA

*Ivy Tech Community College-Central Indiana (K)

50 W Fall Creek Parkway North Drive,
Indianapolis IN 46208-5752
County: Marion FICE Identification: 009917
Unit ID: 150987
Telephone: (317) 921-4882 Carnegie Class: Assoc/Pub-U-SC
FAX Number: (317) 921-4753 Calendar System: Semester
URL: www.ivytech.edu/indianapolis/
Established: 1966 Annual Undergrad Tuition & Fees (In-State): $3,455
Enrollment: 22,353 Coed
Affiliation or Control: State IRS Status: 501(c)3
Highest Offering: Associate Degree
Program: Occupational; 2-Year Principally Bachelor's Creditable
Accreditation: &NH, FUSER, ACBSP, ACFEI, ADNUR, MAC, NAIT, PNUR, RAD, SURGT

02 Interim Chancellor .... Dr. Kathleen F. LEE
05 Interim VC of Academic Affairs .... Dr. Frank MOMAN
32 Vice Chancellor of Student Affairs .... Dr. Darrell CAIN
10 Executive Director of Finance .... Mr. Michael DAVIDSON
15 Exec Director of Human Resources .... Ms. La Veda HOWELL
11 Exec Dir of Administrative Services .... Mr. James N. BARNEY
103 Exec Dir Workforce & Economic Devel .... Ms. Stephanie TAYLOR

30 Exec Dir Institutional Advancement ....Mr. Randy ROGERS
35 Asst Vice Chanc Student Affairs ....Mr. Jerry H. HARRELL
37 Director of Financial Aid ....Ms. Lori J. HANDY
06 Registrar ....Ms. Melanie HOUGH
07 Director of Admissions ....Dr. Tracy FUNK
09 Director of Institutional Research ....Mr. Jeff CORNETT
36 Director of Career Services ....Dr. Rebecca PATTEN-LEMONS
96 Director of Purchasing ....Mr. Jerry L. KOENIG
20 Asst Vice Chanc Academic Affairs ....Mr. Gary PELLICO
26 Director Marketing/Communications ....Ms. Shannon WILSON
46 Director of Resource Development ....Mr. Paul ST. ANGELO

*Ivy Tech Community College of Indiana-Columbus (A)

4475 Central Avenue, Columbus IN 47203-1868
County: Bartholomew FICE Identification: 010038
Unit ID: 150996
Telephone: (812) 372-9925 Carnegie Class: Assoc/Pub-R-M
FAX Number: (812) 372-0311 Calendar System: Semester
URL: www.ivytech.edu/columbus
Established: 1967 Annual Undergrad Tuition & Fees (In-State): $3,454
Enrollment: 6,346 Coed
Affiliation or Control: State IRS Status: 501(c)3
Highest Offering: Associate Degree
Program: Occupational; 2-Year Principally Bachelor's Creditable
Accreditation: &NH, ART, ACBSP, ADNUR, DA, EMT, MAC, NAIT, PNUR, SURGT

02 Chancellor ....Dr. John A. HOGAN
04 Assistant to the Chancellor ....Ms. Therese A. COPELAND
05 Vice Chancellor Academic Affairs ....Dr. Steven B. COMBS
32 Vice Chancellor for Student Affairs ....Mr. Roger B. BINGHAM
10 Executive Director of Finance ....Ms. Stephanie S. AMOS
15 Exec Director of Human Resources ....Mr. John L. HATTER
88 Exec Director Corporate College ....Ms. Teresa J. BEGLEY
26 Exec Dir Marketing/Communications ......Mr. Randall K. PROFFITT
30 Exec Dir of Resource Development ....Ms. Brenda J. VOGEL
20 Asst Vice Chanc Academic Affairs ....Ms. Catherine A. WOODWARD
18 Executive Director of Facilities ....Mr. Floyd D. DONNELL
07 Director of Admissions ....Ms. Alisa DECK
37 Director of Financial Aid ....Mr. Paul R. JOHNSTON
14 Exec Director Computer Tech Svcs ....Mr. Dana L. STICKANS
06 Registrar ....Ms. Corrie A. MCGUCKIN
35 Dir Student Support & Development ....Mr. Neil S. BAGADIONG
36 Director Career/Employment Svcs ....Ms. Rebecca A. ALLEN
38 Int Dir Student Support/Development ....Ms. Janet M. SHARP

*Ivy Tech Community College of Indiana-East Central (B)

4301 Cowan Road, Muncie IN 47302-9448
County: Delaware FICE Identification: 009924
Unit ID: 151005
Telephone: (765) 289-2291 Carnegie Class: Assoc/Pub-R-L
FAX Number: (765) 289-2292 Calendar System: Semester
URL: www.ivytech.edu/eastcentral/
Established: 1968 Annual Undergrad Tuition & Fees (In-State): $2,786
Enrollment: 8,895 Coed
Affiliation or Control: State IRS Status: 501(c)3
Highest Offering: Associate Degree
Program: Occupational; 2-Year Principally Bachelor's Creditable
Accreditation: &NH, ACBSP, ACFEI, ADNUR, DA, DH, MAC, NAIT, PNUR, PTAA, RAD, SURGT

02 Chancellor ....Ms. Gail CHESTERFIELD
12 Vice Chancellor/Dean-Anderson ....Dr. Jim WILLEY
12 Vice Chancellor/Dean-Marion ....Dr. John LIGHTLE
05 Vice Chancellor Academic Affairs ....Dr. Ron SLOAN
32 Vice Chancellor Student Affairs ....Dr. Mary LEWELLEN
97 Dean General Education Division ....Mr. Neil ANTHONY
23 Dean Health Division ....Vacant
66 Dean School of Nursing ....Ms. Paula BOLEY
50 Dean Business Division ....Dr. Janet EVELYNDORSEY
72 Dean Technology Division ....Dr. Joyce WILKERSON
88 Dean Public Svcs/Academic Skills ....Mr. Jeff SCOTT
88 Exec Director Corporate College ....Mr. Roy WINKLER
15 Exec Director of Human Resources ....Mr. Tim KELSEY
26 Exec Dir Mktg & Communications ....Ms. Betty WINGROVE
30 Exec Dir of Resource Development ....Ms. Tracey DANNER-ODENWELDER
21 Regional Dir Financial Affairs ....Mr. Mike EVANS
10 Director of Business Services ....Ms. Kristin KEISLING
35 Associate Dean of Student Affairs ....Vacant
06 Registrar ....Ms. Mia BARNES
07 Director of Admissions ....Dr. Mary LEWELLEN
18 Director of Facilities ....Mr. Harry MUELLER
37 Regional Director Financial Aid ....Ms. Tammy TOMFOHRDE
84 Director Enrollment Management ....Mr. Corey SHARP
11 Administrative Services Manager ....Ms. Sheila JOHNSON
36 Coordinator Student Placement ....Vacant
09 Director of Institutional Research ....Mr. Ryan JOHNSON

*Ivy Tech Community College of Indiana-Kokomo (C)

1815 E Morgan Street, Box 1373, Kokomo IN 46903-1373
County: Howard FICE Identification: 010041
Unit ID: 151014
Telephone: (765) 459-0561 Carnegie Class: Assoc/Pub-R-M
FAX Number: (765) 454-5121 Calendar System: Semester
URL: www.ivytech.edu/kokomo
Established: 1968 Annual Undergrad Tuition & Fees (In-State): $3,454
Enrollment: 5,335 Coed
Affiliation or Control: State IRS Status: 501(c)3
Highest Offering: Associate Degree
Program: Occupational; 2-Year Principally Bachelor's Creditable; Technical Emphasis
Accreditation: &NH, ACBSP, ADNUR, DA, EMT, MAC, NAIT, PNUR, SURGT

02 Chancellor ....Mr. Steve DAILY
05 Vice Chancellor of Academic Affairs ....Dr. Pamela LEWIS
32 Vice Chancellor Student Affairs ....Mrs. Michelle SIMMONS
12 Vice Chancellor of Logansport ....Mr. Kevin BOSTIC
20 Int Asst Vice Chanc Academic Affs ....Ms. Kim KING
12 Exec Dir Instructional Site Wabash ....Mrs. Pamella GUTHRIE
31 Exec Dir Corporate/Community Svcs ....Mrs. Janice BAILEY
10 Executive Director Finance ....Mr. Greg AARON
14 Exec Dir Instructional Technology ....Mr. Montaven HUGHES
26 Exec Dir Marketing/Communications ....Mrs. Marcia WORLAND
16 Exec Director Human Resources ....Mrs. Celestine JOHNSON
37 Director Financial Aid ....Ms. Anjanetta POLK
45 Director Resource Development ....Mrs. Kelly KARICKHOFF
25 Director Grants/Projects ....Ms. Miriam THOMAS
06 Registrar ....Mr. David SCHEBLO
08 Library Director ....Ms. Julie DIESMAN
18 Director Facilities ....Mr. Michael KARICKHOFF
07 Director of Admissions ....Mr. Mike FEDERSPILL
29 Director Alumni Relations ....Ms. Michelle MARTIN
38 Director Student Counseling ....Ms. Susan MAXSON
36 Asst Director Career Services ....Ms. Jennifer NICHOLS
21 Business Office Manager ....Mrs. Cecilia (Jody) DAILY
40 Bookstore Manager ....Vacant
88 Apprenticeship Coordinator ....Mrs. M. Nadine NEWSOM

*Ivy Tech Community College of Indiana-Lafayette (D)

3101 S Creasy Lane, Box 6299, Lafayette IN 47903-6299
County: Tippecanoe FICE Identification: 010039
Unit ID: 151023
Telephone: (765) 269-5000 Carnegie Class: Assoc/Pub-R-L
FAX Number: (765) 772-9107 Calendar System: Semester
URL: www.ivytech.edu/lafayette
Established: 1968 Annual Undergrad Tuition & Fees (In-State): $3,334
Enrollment: 7,628 Coed
Affiliation or Control: State IRS Status: 501(c)3
Highest Offering: Associate Degree
Program: Occupational; 2-Year Principally Bachelor's Creditable
Accreditation: &NH, ACBSP, ADNUR, DA, MAC, NAIT, PNUR, SURGT

02 Chancellor ....Dr. David A. BATHE
05 Vice Chancellor of Academic Affairs ......Dr. Todd E. ROSWARSKI
32 Vice Chancellor of Student Affairs ....Dr. John LAWS
10 Exec Director of Administration ....Ms. Jane HARPER
15 Exec Director of Human Resources ....Ms. Carmen A. HURST
30 Exec Director Resource Development ....Ms. Pat COREY
103 Exec Dir of Work Force & Econ Devel ....Mr. Craig LAMB
26 Exec Dir Marketing & Communications ....Mr. Tom MCCOOL
20 Asst Vice Chanc Academic Affairs ....Dr. Victoria WACEK
09 Asst Vice Chanc Instnl Research ....Mr. William JONES
72 Dean School of Technology ....Ms. Susan ELY
50 Dean School of Business ....Dr. Sheryl SHIPLEY
80 Dean Sch of Public & Social Svcs ....Mr. Bill COGHILL
76 Dean School of Health Sciences ....Ms. Jolene MILLER
49 Dean School of Lib Arts & Science ....Mr. David BERRY
54 Dean Sch of Applied Sci/Engr Tech ....Mr. J. Geoff KNOWLES
12 Site Dir Montgomery Cnty Inst Ctr ....Mr. J. Geoff KNOWLES
12 Site Dir White Cnty Inst Ctr ....Ms. Judy DOPPELFELD
37 Director of Financial Aid ....Ms. Beverly COOPER
06 Registrar ....Dr. Susan STOKER
28 Exec Dir Diversity/Engagement ....Mr. Andrew ANTONIO
18 Exec Director of Facilities ....Mr. Kenneth J. LARSON
35 Dir Student Life/Dev/Leadership ....Mr. Eric VANDEVOORDE
14 Exec Dir Computer/Technology Svcs ....Ms. Nikki LEBO
07 Director of Admissions ....Mr. Ivan HERNANDEZ
08 Library Director ....Ms. Cindy MITCHELL
36 Dir of Career Services ....Ms. Dottie LARSON
38 Dir of Academic Affairs & Support ....Ms. Nancy PEARSON
96 Dir Business Office/Cash Management .....Ms. Sandra PATCHETT
12 Site Manager Renaissance Inst Ctr ....Mr. Andrew MUFFETT
04 Assistant to the Chancellor ....Ms. Jessica VARKONYI

*Ivy Tech Community College of Indiana-North Central (E)

220 Dean Johnson Boulevard, South Bend IN 46601-3415
County: Saint Joseph FICE Identification: 008423
Unit ID: 150978
Telephone: (574) 289-7001 Carnegie Class: Assoc/Pub-R-L
FAX Number: (574) 236-7165 Calendar System: Semester
URL: www.ivytech.edu/southbend
Established: 1967 Annual Undergrad Tuition & Fees (In-State): $3,355
Enrollment: 9,000 Coed
Affiliation or Control: State IRS Status: 501(c)3
Highest Offering: Associate Degree
Program: Occupational; 2-Year Principally Bachelor's Creditable
Accreditation: &NH, ART, ACBSP, ACFEI, ADNUR, DA, DH, EMT, MAC, MLTAD, NAIT, PNUR

02 Chancellor ....Dr. Thomas G. COLEY
03 Vice Chancellor/Dean ....Mr. Randy R. MAXSON
03 Vice Chancellor/Dean ....Ms. Teresa SHAFFER
05 Vice Chancellor of Academic Affairs ....Dr. Chuck PHILIP
10 Exec Director of Finance ....Ms. Karen E. VARGO
32 Vice Chanellor of Student Affairs ....Dr. Keith BRANHAM
16 Exec Director Human Resources ....Mr. Michael POPIELSKI
06 Registrar ....Mr. Ed J. GRAMS
07 Director of Admissions ....Ms. Janice AUSTIN
18 Executive Director Facilities ....Mr. James JASIEWICZ
26 Exec Dir Marketing/Communications ....Ms. Tracie L. DAVIS
30 Executive Director Development ....Mr. Thomas KILIAN
37 Director of Student Financial Aid ....Mr. Jeff A. FISHER
14 Exec Dir Computer & Technology ....Mr. Mckechney VALERIS
88 Exec Dir Corporate College ....Ms. Jean PERRIN

*Ivy Tech Community College of Indiana-Northeast (F)

3800 N Anthony Boulevard, Fort Wayne IN 46805-1489
County: Allen FICE Identification: 009926
Unit ID: 151032
Telephone: (260) 482-9171 Carnegie Class: Assoc/Pub-U-SC
FAX Number: (260) 480-4177 Calendar System: Semester
URL: www.ivytech.edu/fortwayne/
Established: 1968 Annual Undergrad Tuition & Fees (In-State): $3,258
Enrollment: 11,547 Coed
Affiliation or Control: State IRS Status: 501(c)3
Highest Offering: Associate Degree
Program: Occupational; 2-Year Principally Bachelor's Creditable
Accreditation: &NH, ACBSP, ACFEI, ADNUR, EMT, MAC, NAIT, PNUR

02 Chancellor ....Dr. Jerrilee K. MOSIER
05 Vice Chancellor Academic Affairs ....Dr. Cathy MAXWELL
32 Vice Chancellor of Student Affairs ....Mr. John C. LEWTON
10 Executive Director of Finance ....Ms. Valerie EAKINS
13 Exec Dir Computer/Tech Svcs ....Mr. Clifford M. CLARKE
26 Exec Dir Marketing & Communications ....Mr. Andrew WELCH
15 Exec Director of Human Resources ....Ms. Donna J. MARR
103 Exec Dir Workforce and Economic Dev ....Mr. James O. ASCHLIMAN
30 Exec Dir of Resource Development ....Mr. John MILENTIS
06 Registrar ....Ms. Amy J. JOHNSTON
37 Director of Financial Aid ....Mr. Norm NEWMAN
36 Director of Career Services ....Ms. Sheila BIGGS
18 Director of Facilities ....Mr. Everett L. LAWSON
08 Library Director ....Ms. Sharon S. HULTQUIST
07 Director of Admissions ....Ms. Robyn BOSS
51 Continuing Education Manager ....Ms. Amanda JONES

*Ivy Tech Community College of Indiana-Northwest (G)

1440 E 35th Avenue, Gary IN 46409-1499
County: Lake FICE Identification: 010040
Unit ID: 151087
Telephone: (219) 981-1111 Carnegie Class: Assoc/Pub-U-MC
FAX Number: (219) 981-4415 Calendar System: Semester
URL: www.ivytech.edu/northwest
Established: 1968 Annual Undergrad Tuition & Fees (In-State): $3,455
Enrollment: 10,404 Coed
Affiliation or Control: State IRS Status: 501(c)3
Highest Offering: Associate Degree
Program: Occupational; 2-Year Principally Bachelor's Creditable
Accreditation: &NH, ACBSP, ACFEI, ADNUR, FUSER, MAC, NAIT, PNUR, PTAA, SURGT

02 Chancellor ....Mr. J. Guadalupe VALTIERRA
04 Admin Assistant to the Chancellor ....Mrs. Jonetta C. ANTHONY
05 Vice Chanc of Academic Affairs ....Mrs. Margaret SEMMER
32 Vice Chanc of Student Affairs ....Mr. R. Keith HOWARD
12 Vice Chancellor Valparaiso Campus ....Mr. Aco SIKOSKI
12 Vice Chancellor East Chicago Campus ...Mr. R. Louie GONZALEZ
12 Vice Chanc Michigan City Campus ....Mr. Rick SORIA
15 Exec Dir Regional Human Resources ....Ms. Sandra KOUSEN
103 Exec Dir Workforce/Economic Devel ....Mr. Forrest THON
10 Executive Director of Finance ....Mrs. Dawn THOSTESEN
18 Executive Director of Facilities ....Mr. Terry PHILLIPS
26 Exec Dir Marketing/Communications ....Ms. Karen L. WILLIAMS
30 Exec Director Resource Development ....Ms. Cindy J. HALL
13 Exec Dir Computer Technology Svcs ....Mr. David GIDCUMB
18 Asst Director of Facilities ....Mr. Joseph PLESEK
37 Director of Financial Aid ....Mrs. Barbara JERZYK
06 Registrar ....Ms. Eva LUDWICKUZ
32 Dir of Student Life/Dev Leadership ....Ms. Uzoma OLUKA
36 Director of Career Services ....Ms. Chandra GARY
08 Director of Library Services ....Mrs. Barbara WEAVER
07 Director of Admissions ....Mr. Derek DABROWIAK
28 Director of Diversity Affairs ....Vacant
25 Manager of Grant/Project ....Ms. Eugenia SACOPULOS

*Ivy Tech Community College of Indiana-Richmond (H)

2357 Chester Boulevard, Richmond IN 47374-1298
County: Wayne FICE Identification: 010037
Unit ID: 151078
Telephone: (765) 966-2656 Carnegie Class: Assoc/Pub-R-M
FAX Number: (765) 962-8741 Calendar System: Semester
URL: www.ivytech.edu/richmond
Established: 1968 Annual Undergrad Tuition & Fees (In-State): $3,454
Enrollment: 3,968 Coed
Affiliation or Control: State IRS Status: 501(c)3
Highest Offering: Associate Degree
Program: Occupational; 2-Year Principally Bachelor's Creditable

Accreditation: &NH, ACBSP, ADNUR, MAC, NAIT, PNUR

Code	Title	Name
02	Interim Chancellor	Dr. Steven TINCHER
05	Vice Chancellor Academic Affairs	Dr. Steven TINCHER
32	Vice Chanc Student Affs/Human Res	Ms. Sabrina PENNINGTON
10	Exec Director Finance & Facilities	Ms. Valerie RAY
103	Exec Dir Corporate College	Ms. Kim THURLOW
30	Exec Dir Resource Development	Ms. Diana J. PAPPIN
31	Exec Dir External Affairs	Dr. Nancy L. GREEN
29	Alumni Relations	Ms. Diana J. PAPPIN
26	Marketing Director	Mr. Bruce MORGAN
07	Director of Admissions	Ms. Christine SEGER
20	Dir Student Success/Retention	Ms. Mary Louise EDWARDS
36	Dir Career/Employment Services	Mr. Paul LUTTMAN
06	Registrar	Ms. Jeannie HAMBLIN-FOX
37	Director Financial Aid	Ms. Ann FRANZEN-ROHA
15	Director Human Resources	Ms. Lindy COVALT
35	Director of Student Life	Ms. Tiffany ERK
28	Director of Multicultural Affairs	Vacant
24	Mgr Instructional Technology	Mr. Curtis BLAKELY
22	Equal Opportunity Official	Vacant
50	School Dean Bus/Tech/App Sci & Engr	Ms. Peg J. TERRELL
76	School Dean Hlth Sci Ed/Public Svcs	Ms. Jillene ANDERSON
49	School Dean Liberal Arts/Sciences	Mr. William GRAESSER
66	School Dean Nursing	Ms. Glenda CLINE

*Ivy Tech Community College of Indiana-Southeast (A)

590 Ivy Tech Drive, Madison IN 47250-1883
County: Jefferson FICE Identification: 009923
Unit ID: 151096
Telephone: (812) 265-2580 Carnegie Class: Assoc/Pub-R-M
FAX Number: (812) 265-4028 Calendar System: Semester
URL: www.ivytech.edu/southeast
Established: 1971 Annual Undergrad Tuition & Fees (In-State): $3,354
Enrollment: 2,753 Coed
Affiliation or Control: State IRS Status: 501(c)3
Highest Offering: Associate Degree
Program: Occupational; 2-Year Principally Bachelor's Creditable
Accreditation: &NH, ACBSP, ADNUR, MAC, PNUR

Code	Title	Name
02	Chancellor	Mr. Jim HELMS
05	Executive Dean	Mr. Donald L. HEIDERMAN, JR.
12	Assoc VC Acad Affs Lawrenceburg	Mr. Mark GRAVER
20	Vice Chancellor of Academic Affairs	Dr. Joe MOORE
32	Vice Chancellor Student Affairs	Mrs. Margaret STEWART
10	Exec Director of Business Affairs	Mr. Jeff HOLLKAMP
15	Exec Director Resource Development	Ms. Paula HEIDERMAN
103	Ex Dir Workforce/Economic Devel	Mr. Randy JOHANN
23	ASN/PSN Program Chair	Mrs. Georgia SIMMONS
06	Registrar	Mr. Kevin L. BRADLEY
26	Exec Dir Marketing/Communication	Mr. Hank BENTZ
37	Director of Financial Aid	Mr. Richard HILL
36	Asst Dir Finan Aid/Career Svcs	Ms. Anne CUSKER
07	Asst Dir Admiss/Career Counseling	Mrs. Cindy HUTCHERSON

*Ivy Tech Community College of Indiana-Southern Indiana (B)

8204 Highway 311, Sellersburg IN 47172-1897
County: Clark FICE Identification: 010109
Unit ID: 151041
Telephone: (812) 246-3301 Carnegie Class: Assoc/Pub-S-SC
FAX Number: (812) 246-9905 Calendar System: Semester
URL: www.ivytech.edu/sellersburg/
Established: 1968 Annual Undergrad Tuition & Fees (In-State): $3,234
Enrollment: 5,361 Coed
Affiliation or Control: State IRS Status: 501(c)3
Highest Offering: Associate Degree
Program: Occupational; 2-Year Principally Bachelor's Creditable
Accreditation: &NH, ACBSP, ADNUR, MAC, MLTAD, NAIT, PNUR, @PTAA

Code	Title	Name
02	Chancellor	Dr. Rita H. SHOURDS
84	Vice Chancellor of Enroll Svcs	Mr. Terry L. NOLOT
05	Vice Chancellor of Academic Affairs	Ms. Catherine E. SHERRARD
07	Asst Vice Chanc of Enroll Svcs	Mr. Benjamin G. HARRIS
30	Executive Director of Development	Mr. Andrew B. TAKAMI
15	Executive Dir of Human Resources	Ms. Lisa K. GENTNER
10	Executive Director of Finance	Ms. Janet K. STALEY
37	Director Financial Aid	Mr. Gary L. COTTRILL
21	Business Office Manager	Ms. Mary E. LEAVITT
18	Director of Facilities	Mr. Robert C. POFF
32	Asst Director of Campus Engagement	Mr. Thomas W. EVANS
103	Executive Director of Corp College	Mr. Nolan (Bill) W. WHITE
06	Registrar	Mr. John (Chris) C. GOODMAN

*Ivy Tech Community College of Indiana-Southwest (C)

3501 First Avenue, Evansville IN 47710-1881
County: Vanderburgh FICE Identification: 009925
Unit ID: 151050
Telephone: (812) 426-2865 Carnegie Class: Assoc/Pub-R-L
FAX Number: (812) 429-1483 Calendar System: Semester
URL: www.ivytech.edu/evansville/
Established: 1968 Annual Undergrad Tuition & Fees (In-State): $3,334
Enrollment: 6,272 Coed
Affiliation or Control: State IRS Status: 501(c)3
Highest Offering: Associate Degree
Program: Occupational; 2-Year Principally Bachelor's Creditable
Accreditation: &NH, ACBSP, ADNUR, ART, EMT, MAC, NAIT, PNUR, SURGT

Code	Title	Name
02	Chancellor	Dr. Daniel L. SCHENK
05	Vice Chancellor of Academic Affairs	Vacant
32	Vice Chancellor of Student Affairs	Ms. Deborah ANDERSON
72	Dean Schs of Tech/Applied Sci/Eng	Dr. Marvin D. BAUSMAN
50	Division Chair Business	Dr. Mary Jo DENTINO
97	Div Chair General Ed/Support Svcs	Dr. Michael E. PETTY
103	Exec Dir Workforce & Economic Devel	Mr. Terry W. HUBER
15	Exec Director of Human Resources	Ms. Mary MURPHY
11	Exec Director of Administration	Mrs. Alisha AMAN
30	Exec Director Resource Development	Mr. Rob HENSON
26	Director Marketing/Communications	Ms. Rachel NADEAU
06	Registrar	Ms. Jennifer BRIGGS
07	Director of Admissions	Mrs. Denise JOHNSON-KINCAID
37	Financial Aid Manager	Ms. Kristi EIDSON
36	Career & Employment Svcs Manager	Ms. Margie SCHENK

*Ivy Tech Community College of Indiana-Wabash Valley (D)

8000 S. Education Drive, Terre Haute IN 47802-4833
County: Vigo FICE Identification: 008547
Unit ID: 151069
Telephone: (812) 299-1121 Carnegie Class: Assoc/Pub-R-L
FAX Number: (812) 299-5723 Calendar System: Semester
URL: ivytech7.cc.in.us
Established: 1966 Annual Undergrad Tuition & Fees (In-State): $2,787
Enrollment: 6,221 Coed
Affiliation or Control: State IRS Status: 501(c)3
Highest Offering: Associate Degree
Program: 2-Year Principally Bachelor's Creditable; Business Emphasis
Accreditation: &NH, ACBSP, ADNUR, EMT, MAC, MLTAD, NAIT, PNUR, RAD, SURGT

Code	Title	Name
02	Chancellor	Dr. Ann M. VALENTINE
05	Dean of Academic Affairs	Ms. Deanna KING
32	Dean of Student Affairs	Ms. Leah ALLMAN
11	Exec Director for Administration	Mr. John R. ADKINS
103	Exec Dir Workforce & Economic Dev	Ms. Lea Anne CROOKS
30	Executive Director of Resource Dev	Ms. Becky MILLER
10	Executive Director of Finance	Mr. Charles RUBEY
06	Registrar	Mr. Wilson TURNER
37	Director of Financial Aid	Ms. Julie WONDERLIN
07	Director of Admissions	Mr. Michael FISHER
36	Director of Career Services	Vacant
88	Asst Director of Admissions	Ms. Brandy CANDLER
18	Director of Facilities	Mr. Larry A. SWANK

Kaplan College (E)

7833 Indianapolis Boulevard, Hammond IN 46324-3347
County: Lake Identification: 666436
Unit ID: 152415
Telephone: (219) 844-0100 Carnegie Class: Assoc/PrivFP
FAX Number: (219) 844-0105 Calendar System: Quarter
URL: www.getinfo.kaplancollege.com
Established: 1969 Annual Undergrad Tuition & Fees: $14,697
Enrollment: 499 Coed
Affiliation or Control: Proprietary IRS Status: Proprietary
Highest Offering: Associate Degree
Program: Occupational
Accreditation: ACICS

Code	Title	Name
01	Campus President	Mr. Johnny CRAIG

† Branch campus of Kaplan College, Merrillville, IN.

Kaplan College (F)

7302 Woodland Drive, Indianapolis IN 46278-1736
County: Marion FICE Identification: 009777
Unit ID: 152220
Telephone: (317) 299-6001 Carnegie Class: Assoc/PrivFP
FAX Number: (317) 298-6342 Calendar System: Semester
URL: www.getinfo.kaplancollege.com
Established: 1967 Annual Undergrad Tuition & Fees: $14,943
Enrollment: 431 Coed
Affiliation or Control: Proprietary IRS Status: Proprietary
Highest Offering: Associate Degree
Program: Occupational
Accreditation: ACCSC, DA, MAC

Code	Title	Name
01	Acting President	Mr. Jason HORTON

Lincoln College of Technology (G)

7225 Winton Drive, Building 128, Indianapolis IN 46268-4198
County: Marion FICE Identification: 007938
Unit ID: 151661
Telephone: (317) 632-5553 Carnegie Class: Assoc/PrivFP
FAX Number: (317) 687-0475 Calendar System: Semester
URL: www.lincolntech.com
Established: 1962 Annual Undergrad Tuition & Fees: $29,440
Enrollment: 1,043 Coed
Affiliation or Control: Proprietary IRS Status: Proprietary
Highest Offering: Associate Degree
Program: Occupational
Accreditation: ACCSC

Code	Title	Name
01	President	Todd CLARK
05	Vice President of Education	Dale SHEPPERSON
11	Director Administrative Services	LaTrina JOHNSON
36	Director Student Placement	Jennifer FINESILVER

Manchester University (H)

604 E College Avenue, North Manchester IN 46962-1225
County: Wabash FICE Identification: 001820
Unit ID: 151777
Telephone: (260) 982-5000 Carnegie Class: Bac/Diverse
FAX Number: (260) 982-5043 Calendar System: 4/1/4
URL: www.manchester.edu
Established: 1889 Annual Undergrad Tuition & Fees: $26,746
Enrollment: 1,320 Coed
Affiliation or Control: Church Of The Brethren IRS Status: 501(c)3
Highest Offering: Doctorate
Program: Liberal Arts And General; Teacher Preparatory; Professional
Accreditation: NH, @PHAR, SW, TED

Code	Title	Name
01	President	Dr. Jo YOUNG SWITZER
03	Executive Vice President	Dr. David F. MCFADDEN
05	Vice President Academic Affairs	Dr. Glenn R. SHARFMAN
10	Vice Pres Financial Affairs/Treas	Mr. Jack A. GOCHENAUR
32	Vice President Student Development	Dr. Beth E. SWEITZER-RILEY
30	Vice President College Advancement	Mr. Michael EASTMAN
07	Director of Admissions	Mr. Adam HOHMAN
20	Associate Academic Dean	Dr. Mark W. HUNTINGTON
29	Exec Director of Alumni Assocation	Mr. Gary E. MONTEL
30	Executive Director of Development	Ms. Melanie B. HARMON
15	Director Human Resources	Mr. Dale E. CARPENTER
08	Director of the Library	Mr. Robin J. GRATZ
06	Registrar	Ms. Lila D. HAMMER
24	Director of Audio-Visual Services	Mr. Stanley G. PITTMAN
38	Director of Counseling	Ms. Danette NORMAN TILL
36	Director of Career Services	Ms. Elizabeth J. BUSHNELL
39	Director of Residence Life	Mr. Allen J. MACHIELSON
42	Campus Pastor	Mr. Walt WILTSCHEK
41	Director of Athletics	Mr. Rick ESPESET
13	Director of Mgmt Info Services	Mr. Michael CASE
19	Director of Security	Mr. Leslie L. GAHL
44	Director of the Manchester Fund	Ms. Janeen W. KOOI
37	Director of Student Financial Aid	Ms. Sherri L. SHOCKEY
88	Director of Multicultural Affairs	Mr. Michael G. DIXON
26	Director of Public Relations	Ms. Jeri S. KORNEGAY
18	Director of Physical Plant	Mr. Christopher W. GARBER
23	Director of Health Services	Ms. Heather R. BANKS
21	Senior Accountant	Mr. Michael J. LECKRONE
35	Director Student Affairs	Ms. Shanon L. FAWBUSH
96	Director of Purchasing	Mr. Quentin J. MOUDY
40	Bookstore Manager	Ms. Heather K. GOCHENAUR

Marian University (I)

3200 Cold Spring Road, Indianapolis IN 46222-1997
County: Marion FICE Identification: 001821
Unit ID: 151786
Telephone: (317) 955-6000 Carnegie Class: Bac/Diverse
FAX Number: (317) 955-6448 Calendar System: Semester
URL: www.marian.edu
Established: 1851 Annual Undergrad Tuition & Fees: $27,300
Enrollment: 2,550 Coed
Affiliation or Control: Roman Catholic IRS Status: 501(c)3
Highest Offering: Doctorate
Program: Liberal Arts And General; Teacher Preparatory; Professional
Accreditation: NH, IACBE, NURSE, @OSTEO, TED

Code	Title	Name
01	President	Mr. Daniel J. ELSENER
05	Executive VP and Provost	Dr. Thomas ENNEKING
10	VP for Finance & Business Opers	Mr. Greg GINDER
26	VP for Marketing Communications	Mr. Robert GOLOBISH
30	VP for Institutional Advancement	Mr. John FINKE
32	VP Student Affairs/Dean of Students	Ms. Ruth RODGERS
84	AVP Enrollment Management	Dr. Jack P. POWELL
37	Dean Financial Aid/Enroll Mgmt	Mr. Chad BIR
20	Dean for Academic Affairs	Mr. William HARTING
18	Director of Facilities	Mr. Neil LANGFERMAN
41	Director of Athletics	Mr. Steve DOWNING
29	Director of Alumni Affairs	Mrs. Barbara STUCKWISCH
06	Registrar	Mr. John A. HILL
08	Director of Graduate Library Svcs	Ms. Nancy KIRKPATRICK
35	Director of Student Act/Orientation	Ms. Jill MATTINGLY
19	Director of Safety & Police Svcs	Mr. Scott RALPH
13	Chief Information Office	Mr. Peter E. WILLIAMS
27	Dir of Marketing Communications	Mrs. Julie ADAMS
36	Dir of Internships & Career Svcs	Dr. Leanne MALLOY
42	Director of Campus Ministry	Vacant
38	Director Academic Support Services	Mrs. Marjorie BATIC
07	AVP for Enrollment Management	Dr. Jack POWELL
55	Exec Director Adult Programs	Ms. Amy BENNETT
38	Director of Counseling Services	Ms. Leanne MALLOY
88	Director of Advancement Information	Mrs. Vida KOTARSKI
23	Director of Health & Wellness Svcs	Ms. Jan CARNAGHI
09	Director of Institutional Research	Mr. William HARTING
15	Director of Human Resources	Ms. Anita HERBERTZ
21	Director of Business Services	Ms. Alice SHELTON
40	Bookstore Manager	Ms. Allison BONEZ

Martin University (A)

2171 Avondale Place, PO 18567,
Indianapolis IN 46218-3878

County: Marion FICE Identification: 021408
Unit ID: 151810
Telephone: (317) 543-3235 Carnegie Class: Bac/A&S
FAX Number: (317) 543-3257 Calendar System: Semester
URL: www.martin.edu
Established: 1977 Annual Undergrad Tuition & Fees: $14,180
Enrollment: 911 Coed
Affiliation or Control: Independent Non-Profit IRS Status: 501(c)3
Highest Offering: Master's
Program: Liberal Arts And General
Accreditation: **NH**

01 President .... Dr. George E. MILLER, III
05 Vice President Academic Affairs .... Dr. Amenti SUJAI
09 Director of Institutional Research .... Dr. Brian STEUERWALD
15 Vice President Human Resources .... Ms. Ruby BOWMAN
32 Vice President Student Services .... Dr. Stanley SINGLETON
10 Fiscal Officer .... Mr. Michael MOOS
37 Director Financial Aid .... Ms. Corrine FURTICK
30 VP of Sponsored Programs .... Dr. David VANDERSTEL
18 Manager of Facilities .... Mr. William WOODSON
31 Director of Community Relations .... Mr. Ricky ELMORE
13 VP for Technology Systems .... Dr. Laura-Lee DAVIDSON
06 Registrar .... Vacant
21 Bursar .... Mrs. Virginia GOODWIN
40 Manager Bookstore .... Ms. Tanya DOUGLAS
96 Purchasing Manager .... Ms. Pam HOOD

MedTech College (B)

7230 Engle Road, Suite 200, Fort Wayne IN 46804

County: Allen Identification: 666677
Unit ID: 456366
Telephone: (317) 845-0300 Carnegie Class: Assoc/PrivFP
FAX Number: (317) 863-4895 Calendar System: Quarter
URL: www.medtechcollege.edu
Established: 2008 Annual Undergrad Tuition & Fees: $14,781
Enrollment: 539 Coed
Affiliation or Control: Proprietary IRS Status: Proprietary
Highest Offering: Associate Degree
Program: Occupational; 2-Year Principally Bachelor's Creditable
Accreditation: **ACICS**, MAC, MLTAD

01 Executive Director .... Mr. Luke KNOKE

† Branch campus of MedTech College, Indianapolis, IN.

MedTech College (C)

1500 American Way, Greenwood IN 46143

County: Johnson Identification: 666678
Unit ID: 456357
Telephone: (317) 534-0322 Carnegie Class: Assoc/PrivFP
FAX Number: (317) 863-4895 Calendar System: Quarter
URL: www.medtechcollege.edu
Established: 2007 Annual Undergrad Tuition & Fees: N/A
Enrollment: 736 Coed
Affiliation or Control: Proprietary IRS Status: Proprietary
Highest Offering: Associate Degree
Program: Occupational; 2-Year Principally Bachelor's Creditable
Accreditation: **ACICS**, MAC, MLTAD

01 Executive Director .... Mr. Mike HARDING

† Branch campus of MedTech College, Indianapolis, IN.

MedTech College (D)

6612 East 75th Street Suite 300, Indianapolis IN 46250

County: Marion FICE Identification: 007362
Unit ID: 448415
Telephone: (317) 845-0100 Carnegie Class: Assoc/PrivFP
FAX Number: (317) 845-1800 Calendar System: Quarter
URL: www.medtechcollege.edu
Established: 2004 Annual Undergrad Tuition & Fees: $14,781
Enrollment: 1,013 Coed
Affiliation or Control: Proprietary IRS Status: Proprietary
Highest Offering: Associate Degree
Program: Occupational
Accreditation: **ACICS**, #MAC, MLTAD, PNUR

01 Executive Director .... Mr. Steve ALLEN

Mid-America College of Funeral Service (E)

3111 Hamburg Pike, Jeffersonville IN 47130-9630

County: Clark FICE Identification: 010618
Unit ID: 151962
Telephone: (812) 288-8878 Carnegie Class: Spec/Other
FAX Number: (812) 288-5942 Calendar System: Quarter
URL: www.mid-america.edu
Established: 1905 Annual Undergrad Tuition & Fees: $12,000
Enrollment: 86 Coed
Affiliation or Control: Independent Non-Profit IRS Status: 501(c)3
Highest Offering: Associate Degree
Program: Occupational
Accreditation: **FUSER**

01 President .... Mr. John R. BRABOY
32 Dean of Students .... Mr. Richard D. NELSON
06 Registrar/Director of Admissions .... Ms. Amanda J. CHRISTENSEN
29 Director Alumni Relations .... Vacant
37 Director Student Financial Aid .... Mr. Richard D. NELSON

Mid-America Reformed Seminary (F)

229 Seminary Drive, Dyer IN 46311-1069

County: Lake FICE Identification: 039893
Unit ID: 373030
Telephone: (219) 864-2400 Carnegie Class: Not Classified
FAX Number: (219) 864-2410 Calendar System: Semester
URL: www.midamerica.edu
Established: 1981 Annual Undergrad Tuition & Fees: $8,250
Enrollment: 40 Coed
Affiliation or Control: Independent Non-Profit IRS Status: 501(c)3
Highest Offering: Master's
Program: Religious Emphasis
Accreditation: **THEOL**, TRACS

01 President .... Dr. Cornelius VENEMA
32 Dean of Students .... Rev. Alan STRANGE
06 Registrar .... Rev. Alan STRANGE
30 Director of Development .... Mr. Keith LEMAHIEU
96 Office Manager/Director Purchasing .... Ms. Florence KOOIMAN
36 Director of Apprenticeship Program .... Rev. Mark VANDERHART

National College (G)

6060 Castleway West Drive, Indianapolis IN 46250

County: Marion Identification: 666680
Telephone: (317) 578-7353 Carnegie Class: Not Classified
FAX Number: (317) 578-7721 Calendar System: Quarter
URL: www.ncbt.edu
Established: 1886 Annual Undergrad Tuition & Fees: N/A
Enrollment: N/A Coed
Affiliation or Control: Proprietary IRS Status: Proprietary
Highest Offering: Baccalaureate
Program: Occupational
Accreditation: **ACICS**, MAC, SURGT

01 Campus Director .... Vacant
04 Admin Asst to Campus Director .... Ms. Patricia JANVIER

Oakland City University (H)

138 N Lucretia Street, Oakland City IN 47660-1099

County: Gibson FICE Identification: 001824
Unit ID: 152099
Telephone: (812) 749-4781 Carnegie Class: Master's M
FAX Number: (812) 749-1233 Calendar System: Semester
URL: www.oak.edu
Established: 1885 Annual Undergrad Tuition & Fees: $18,000
Enrollment: 2,650 Coed
Affiliation or Control: Baptist IRS Status: 501(c)3
Highest Offering: Doctorate
Program: Occupational; 2-Year Principally Bachelor's Creditable; Liberal Arts And General; Teacher Preparatory; Professional
Accreditation: **NH**, IACBE, TED, THEOL

01 President .... Dr. Ray G. BARBER
11 Vice Pres Administration & Finance .... Dr. Robert E. YEAGER
05 Provost .... Dr. Michael J. ATKINSON
44 Vice Pres Planning & Research .... Dr. Bernard MARLEY
30 Director of Development .... Mr. Brian BAKER
32 Director Student Affairs/Housing .... Dr. James PRATT
12 Director Bedford College Center .... Dr. L. Kay COLLINS
42 Campus Chaplain .... Rev. Mark GRIMES
06 Registrar .... Ms. Betty BURNS
07 Director of Admissions .... Ms. Kim HELDT
37 Director Student Financial Aid .... Mrs. Caren RICHESON
09 Director of Institutional Research .... Dr. Morris PELZEL
15 Director Personnel Services .... Mrs. Kris PRATT
91 Director Information Technology .... Mr. Clint WOOLSEY
88 Director Institutional Assessment .... Mrs. Amy SATTERLY
08 Learning Resources Center .... Mrs. Denise PINNICK
29 Dir Alumni Rels/Chief Pub Rels Ofcr .... Ms. Susan SULLIVAN
36 Director Placement .... Dr. James PRATT
36 Dir Career & College Directions .... Mrs. Charity JULIAN
35 Director Student Support Services .... Mrs. Cinda K. PHILLIPS
88 Director Upward Bound Program .... Ms. Mary HEALY
10 Business Mgr/Chief Financial Ofcr .... Mrs. Elizabeth BARBER
88 Dean Sch Adult Degree/Prof Stds .... Dr. Micheal PELT
73 Dean Graduate School of Theology .... Dr. Douglas LOW
18 Chief Facilities/Physical Plant .... Mr. Wayne ROWLAND
53 Dean School of Education .... Dr. Mary Jo BEAUCHAMP
50 Dean School of Business .... Mr. Norman REYNOLDS
21 Assistant Chief Financial Officer .... Mrs. Elizabeth CARLISLE
49 Dean School of Arts & Sciences .... Dr. Claudine CUTCHIN
22 Compliance Officer .... Ms. Patricia ENDICOTT

Ottawa University Jeffersonville (I)

287 Quarter Master Court, Jeffersonville IN 47130-3669

County: Clark Identification: 666088
Unit ID: 442897
Telephone: (785) 242-5200 Carnegie Class: Spec/Bus
FAX Number: (812) 280-7269 Calendar System: Semester
URL: www.ottawa.edu
Established: 2002 Annual Undergrad Tuition & Fees: $10,920
Enrollment: 154 Coed
Affiliation or Control: American Baptist IRS Status: 501(c)3
Highest Offering: Master's
Program: Liberal Arts And General
Accreditation: **&NH**

01 President .... Mr. Kevin EICHNER
03 Interim Campus Executive .... Ms. Peg GERNAND
05 Univ Provost/Chief Academic Officer .... Dr. Terry HAINES
10 Vice Pres Administration/CFO .... Mr. J. Clark RIBORDY
26 Mgr Public Relations & Publications .... Ms. Paula PAINE
30 Vice Pres University Advancement .... Mr. Paul BEAN
86 VP Regulatory/Governmental Affairs .... Dr. Donna LEVENE
88 Vice President Enterprise Division .... Dr. Brian SANDUSKY
11 Administrative Manager .... Ms. Patrice FESS
07 Senior Enrollment Advisor .... Ms. Peg GERNAND
21 Director Finance/Controller .... Ms. Noelle TESTA
21 Director Business Operations .... Mr. Tom CORLEY
15 Director Human Resources .... Ms. Joanna WALTERS
06 University Registrar .... Ms. Karen ADAMS
37 Director Financial Aid .... Mr. Howard FISCHER
106 Vice President for Online .... Mr. Brian MESSER
88 VP and COO for APOS .... Mr. Shane SMEED

† Regional accreditation is carried under the parent institution in Ottawa, KS.

Purdue University Main Campus (J)

610 Purdue Mall, West Lafayette IN 47907-2040

County: Tippecanoe FICE Identification: 001825
Unit ID: 243780
Telephone: (765) 494-4600 Carnegie Class: RU/VH
FAX Number: N/A Calendar System: Semester
URL: www.purdue.edu
Established: 1869 Annual Undergrad Tuition & Fees (In-State): $9,900
Enrollment: 39,637 Coed
Affiliation or Control: State IRS Status: 501(c)3
Highest Offering: Doctorate
Program: Liberal Arts And General; Teacher Preparatory; Professional
Accreditation: **NH**, AAB, ART, AUD, BUS, CACREP, CIDA, CLPSY, CONST, COPSY, CS, DIETC, DIETD, ENG, ENGR, ENGT, FOR, IPSY, LSAR, MFCD, NAIT, NURSE, PHAR, SP, TED, THEA, VET

01 Interim President .... Dr. Timothy SANDS
10 Exec Vice President & Treasurer .... Mr. Alphonso V. DIAZ
05 Acting Exec VP Acad Affairs/Provost .... Dr. Victor LECHTENBERG
30 Vice Pres for Development .... Ms. Lisa D. CALVERT
16 Vice President Ethics & Compliance .... Prof. Alysa C. ROLLOCK
10 Sr VP Business Svcs/Asst Treas .... Mr. James S. ALMOND
13 Vice Pres Information Technology .... Dr. William G. MCCARTNEY
15 Vice President Human Resources .... Mr. Luis E. LEWIN
18 Vice President Physical Facilities .... Mr. Robert E. MCMAINS
39 Assoc Vice Pres Housing/Food Serv .... Ms. Beth M. MCCUSKEY
26 Vice Pres Marketing & Media .... Ms. Teri THOMPSON
32 Vice President of Student Affairs .... Dr. Melissa E. EXUM
20 Vice Provost Undergrad Acad Affairs .... Dr. A. Dale WHITAKER
46 Vice President for Research .... Dr. Richard O. BUCKIUS
88 Assoc VP for Engagement .... Dr. Suresh GARIMELLA
86 Assoc VP Governmental Relations .... Mr. Timothy J. SANDERS
20 Vice Provost Faculty Affairs .... Dr. Beverly D. SYPHER
20 Assistant Provost .... Dr. Nancy A. BULGER
20 Assistant Provost/Financial Affairs .... Ms. Connie L. LAPINSKAS
47 Dean College of Agriculture .... Dr. Jay T. AKRIDGE
59 Dean College Health & Human Science .... Dr. Christine M. LADISCH
53 Dean College of Education .... Dr. Maryann SANTOS DE BARONA
54 Dean College of Engineering .... Dr. Leah H. JAMIESON
49 Dean College of Liberal Arts .... Dr. Irwin H. WEISER
50 Dean School of Management .... Dr. P. Christopher EARLEY
67 Dean College of Pharmacy .... Dr. Craig K. SVENSSON
81 Dean College of Science .... Dr. Jeffrey T. ROBERTS
72 Dean College of Technology .... Dr. Gary R. BERTOLINE
74 Dean College of Veterinary Medicine .... Dr. Willie M. REED
58 Dean of Graduate School .... Dr. Mark J. SMITH
104 Dean International Programs .... Dr. Michael A. BRZEZINSKI
08 Dean of Libraries .... Dr. James L. MULLINS
29 Exec Dir & CEO Alumni Association .... Mr. Kirk R. CERNY
45 Exec Dir Strateg Planning & Assess .... Prof. Rabindra N. MUKERJEA
41 Director Intercollegiate Athletics .... Mr. Morgan J. BURKE
09 Director of Institutional Research .... Dr. Jacque L. FROST
36 Director Center Career Opportunity .... Mr. Timothy B. LUZADER
31 Assistant VP External Relations .... Mr. Chris W. SIGURDSON
85 Dir Intl Students & Scholars .... Dr. Joe D. POTTS
25 Director Sponsored Program Svcs .... Mr. Michael R. LUDWIG
94 Director Women's Studies .... Dr. Tracey J. BOISSEAU
07 Dean Admiss/Asst VP Enroll Mgmt .... Dr. Pamela T. HORNE
35 Dean of Students .... Ms. Danita M. BROWN
04 Executive Assistant to President .... Ms. Sharon K. WHITLOCK
37 Director Financial Aid .... Mr. Ted E. MALONE
06 Registrar .... Mr. Robert A. KUBAT
28 Vice Provost Diversity & Inclusion .... Dr. G. Christine TAYLOR
38 Associate Dean Student Counseling .... Mr. Robert L. MATE
96 Director of Procurement Services .... Mr. Phillip D. O'KEEFFE
21 Comptroller .... Ms. Mary Catherine GAISBAUER
84 Asst VP/Dir Enroll Mgmt/Analys/Rep .... Mr. Brent M. DRAKE

Purdue University Calumet (K)

2200 169th Street, Hammond IN 46323-2094

County: Lake FICE Identification: 001827
Unit ID: 152248
Telephone: (219) 989-2204 Carnegie Class: Master's L
FAX Number: (219) 989-2581 Calendar System: Semester

URL: www.purduecal.edu
Established: 1946 Annual Undergrad Tuition & Fees (In-State): $6,991
Enrollment: 9,786 Coed
Affiliation or Control: State IRS Status: 501(c)3
Highest Offering: Master's
Program: Liberal Arts And General; Teacher Preparatory; Professional
Accreditation: NH, CACREP, ENG, ENGT, IACBE, MFCD, NUR, TED

01 Chancellor .... Thomas L. KEON
04 Exec Asst to Chancellor Engagement .... Regina D. BIDDINGS-MURO
05 Vice Chancellor Academic Affairs .... Ralph V. ROGERS
10 Vice Chanc Administrative Services .... James K. JOHNSTON
30 Interim Vice Chanc for Advancement .... Regina D. BIDDINGS-MURO
13 Vice Chanc for Information Services .... Frank CERVONE
32 Interim Vice Chanc Student Services .... Sarah E. HOWARD
46 Interim Assoc VC Rsrch & Grad Stds .... Chenn ZHOU
26 Assoc Vice Chancellor for Marketing .... Mark LACIEN
09 Asst VC Academic Quality & Outreach .... M. Beth PELLICCIOTTI
11 Asst Vice Chancellor for Admin Svcs .... Michael KULL
27 Asst Vice Chanc Advance/Univ Rels .... Wes K. LUKOSHUS
88 Asst Vice Chanc for ED OPP Programs .... Roy HAMILTON
20 Asst Vice Chanc Enrollment Svcs .... Vacant
21 Asst VC Business Svcs/Comptroller .... Randal FREEBOURN
15 Asst Vice Chanc Human Resources .... Mary Beth RINCON
84 Asst VC Enrollment Management .... Carol CORTILET-ALBRECHT
49 Dean Sch Liberal Arts/Social Sc .... Ronald CORTHELL
54 Dean School Engr/Math/Sci .... William R. LAW
72 Dean School of Technology .... Niaz LATIF
50 Dean School of Management .... Jane MUTCHLER
66 Dean School of Nursing .... Gerard S. PEGGY
53 Dean School of Educ/Teacher Educ .... Alice ANDERSON
06 Registrar .... Anne Agosto SEVERA
21 Asst Comptroller/Budget/Fiscal Plng .... Donna ADELSPERGER
07 Interim Director of Admissions .... Dachea HILL
37 Int Dir Financial Aid & Stdnt Acct .... Sheryl SPIVEY
41 Director of Athletics .... Richard J. COSTELLO
38 Director Counseling Center .... Kenneth JACKSON
08 Dir Research/Learning & Res Svcs .... Tammy GUERRERO
29 Dir Alumni Relations/Annual Giving .... Diana VIRIJEVICH
22 Director Office of Equity Diversity .... Linda KNOX
19 Chief University Police .... Anthony MARTIN
85 Exec Dir of International Programs .... Judith PENNYWELL
96 Dir of Procurement/General Services .... Phillip BROWN
39 Director of Housng Residental Educ .... Scott IVERSON
92 Director of the Honors Program .... Rowan JOHN

Purdue University North Central Campus (A)

1401 S US 421, Westville IN 46391-9542
County: La Porte FICE Identification: 001826
Unit ID: 152266
Telephone: (219) 785-5200 Carnegie Class: Bac/Diverse
FAX Number: (219) 785-5355 Calendar System: Semester
URL: www.pnc.edu
Established: 1943 Annual Undergrad Tuition & Fees (In-State): $7,066
Enrollment: 5,279 Coed
Affiliation or Control: State IRS Status: 501(c)3
Highest Offering: Master's
Program: Liberal Arts And General; Teacher Preparatory; Professional
Accreditation: NH, ACBSP, ADNUR, ENGT, NUR, TED

01 Chancellor .... Dr. James B. DWORKIN
04 Executive Asst to the Chancellor .... Mrs. Debra A. NIELSEN
30 Interim Director of Advancement .... Mrs. Melissa C. WESTPHAL-BENEFIEL
05 Vice Chanc Academic Affairs .... Dr. Karen L. SCHMID
20 Assoc Vice Chanc Acad Affairs .... Dr. Kumara JAYASURIYA
10 Vice Chanc for Admin .... Mr. Stephen R. TURNER
84 VC for Enroll Mgmt & Student Svcs .... Mr. Paul M. MCGUINNESS
32 Asst VC & Dean of Students .... Mr. John T. COGGINS
14 Asc VC Information Technology/CIO .... Mr. Daniel A. BURNS
10 Asc Vice Chanc Business Svcs/ Budget .... Mr. Phillip E. JANKOWSKI
15 Assoc Vice Chanc Human Resources .... Mrs. Susan T. MILLER
50 Interim Dean College of Business .... Dr. Cynthia ROBERTS
72 Dean College of Engr & Tech .... Dr. Thomas F. BRADY
49 Dean College of Liberal Arts .... Dr. S. Rex MORROW
88 Dean College of Science .... Dr. Keith E. SCHWINGENDORF
66 Chair Nursing Department .... Dr. Mario ORTIZ
83 Chair Social Sciences Department .... Dr. Michael LYNN
81 Chair Biology/Chem Department .... Dr. C. Kenneth HOLFORD
81 Chair Math/Physics/Statistics Dept .... Dr. Purna DAS
53 Acting Chair Education Department .... Dr. Kam C. CHAN
88 Int Chair English/Foreign Lang Dept .... Dr. Jerry HOLT
60 Chair Communication Dept .... Dr. V. Scott SMITHSON
54 Chair Engr Tech Dept .... Vacant
88 Chair Comp Info & Tech Dept .... Mr. Mark SMITH
88 Chair Business & Leadership Dept .... Dr. Carolyn ROPER
22 Asst Dir EEO & Training .... Ms. Laura ODOM
21 Bursar .... Mrs. Beverly J. PULLER
21 Accounting Manager .... Mr. Brock MARTIN
96 Dir Auxiliary Svcs & Resource Plng .... Mrs. Elizabeth DEPEW
08 Librarian .... Mr. Kent R. JOHNSON
07 Asst Dean Enroll & Student Outreach .... Mrs. Janice WHISLER
06 Assistant Registrar .... Mrs. Jennifer WOLSZCZAK
36 Director of Career Development .... Mrs. Natalie CONNORS
37 Director Financial Aid & Compliance .... Mrs. Shelly BARNES
38 Director Student Counseling .... Ms. Diana MAROVICH
19 Director of Public Safety .... Mr. Robert GAEKLE
27 Director Media & Comm Services .... Mrs. Carol CONNELLY
41 Director Student Athletics .... Mr. John WEBER
35 Director Student Activities .... Mrs. Keri MARRS DE BARRON
18 Director Facilities Management .... Mr. L. James SALLEE
09 Data Specialist .... Mrs. Madonna TRITLE
26 Asst VC of Mktg & Campus Relations .... Mrs. Judy N. JACOBI
88 Coord Special Events & Marketing .... Ms. Liz BERNEL
29 Director Alumni Relations .... Mrs. Amy NAVARDAUSKAS
58 Dir Graduate & Extended Learning .... Dr. Kumara JAYASURIYA
50 Director MBA Program .... Mrs. Janet KNIGHT
88 Director of Food Service .... Mr. Keith PEFFERS
40 Bookstore Manager .... Ms. Susan PEARSON
88 Coord Service Learning .... Ms. Laura WEAVER
88 Dir School Partnerships .... Mrs. Susan WILSON
88 Interim Dir Academic Advising .... Ms. Kathleen JOHNSON
06 Asst Vice Chanc Enroll Mgmt .... Ms. Sandra CZEKAJ
88 Asst Dean of Enroll Access .... Ms. Mary A. BISHEL
88 Director Student Success Center .... Ms. Jane BROOKS

Rose-Hulman Institute of Technology (B)

5500 Wabash Avenue, Terre Haute IN 47803-3920
County: Vigo FICE Identification: 001830
Unit ID: 152318
Telephone: (812) 877-1511 Carnegie Class: Spec/Engg
FAX Number: (812) 877-9925 Calendar System: Quarter
URL: www.rose-hulman.edu
Established: 1874 Annual Undergrad Tuition & Fees: $38,313
Enrollment: 1,980 Coed
Affiliation or Control: Independent Non-Profit IRS Status: 501(c)3
Highest Offering: Master's
Program: Professional; Technical Emphasis
Accreditation: NH, CS, ENG

01 Interim President .... Mr. Robert A. COONS
05 Vice Pres Academic Affairs .... Dr. Phillip J. CORNWELL
30 Vice President Inst Advancement .... Mr. Rickey N. MCCURRY
32 Vice President Student Affairs .... Mr. Peter A. GUSTAFSON
26 VP Communications/Marketing .... Ms. Mary G. BARR
10 Interim Vice Pres Business/Finance .... Mr. Matthew D. DAVIS
84 Vice President Enrollment Mgmt .... Mr. James A. GOECKER
03 Vice Pres for Rose-Hulman Ventures .... Dr. Elizabeth M. HAGERMAN
20 Interim Dean of Faculty .... Dr. Richard E. STAMPER
20 Associate Dean of Faculty .... Dr. Azad SIAHMAKOUN
20 Asso Dean Online Learning/Instr Tec .... Dr. Kay C. DEE
104 Associate Dean Global Programs .... Dr. Luchen LI
13 Vice Pres Instruct/Admin/Info Tech .... Dr. Louis H. TURCOTTE
21 Controller .... Mr. Matthew D. DAVIS
18 Sr Director Facilities Operations .... Mr. Michael A. TAYLOR
36 Dir Career Services/Employer Rels .... Mr. Kevin L. HEWERDINE
07 Director of Admissions .... Ms. Lisa M. NORTON
29 Executive Director Alumni Affairs .... Mr. Jim BERTOLI
45 Exec Dir Inst Rsrch/Plng/Assessment .... Dr. Julia M. WILLIAMS
15 Director of Human Resources .... Ms. Kimberly D. MILLER
37 Director of Financial Aid .... Ms. Melinda L. MIDDLETON
41 Director of Athletics .... Mr. Jeffrey L. JENKINS
28 Director Center for Diversity .... Dr. Luanne TILSTRA
44 Senior Director of Planned Giving .... Mr. Robert F. CONRAD
44 Director of Planned Giving .... Mr. Chris AIMONE
44 Assistant Director Annual Giving .... Ms. Jennifer KENZOR
06 Registrar .... Mr. Timothy J. PRICKEL
08 Library Director .... Ms. Bernadette EWEN
19 Director of Public Safety .... Mr. John S. WOLFE
40 Bookstore Manager .... Ms. Sheryl E. FULK
85 Dir Intl Stdnt Svcs/Disability Svcs .... Ms. Karen A. DEGRANGE
04 Exec Assistant to the President .... Ms. Kerry SCHAFFER
25 Dir Fin Svcs/Sponsored Programs .... Ms. Linda L. PRICE
96 Director Administrative Services .... Mr. Dan WELLS
09 Director of Institutional Research .... Mr. Timothy CHOW
102 Director Corporate & Foundation Rel .... Mr. Richard D. BOYCE
39 Director of Residence Life .... Mr. Erik Z. HAYES
35 Dean of Student Affairs .... Mr. Thomas D. MILLER
35 Dean of Student Services .... Ms. Donna J. GUSTAFSON
101 Dir Donor Relations/Exec Asst Board .... Ms. Tammy SHAFFER
105 Web Content Director .... Ms. Marianne MESSINA
108 Director of Assessment .... Ms. Shannon M. SEXTON

St. Anthony School of Echocardiography (C)

1201 S. Main Street, Crown Point IN 46307
County: Lake Identification: 667119
Telephone: (219) 757-6132 Carnegie Class: Not Classified
FAX Number: (219) 681-6725 Calendar System: Semester
URL: www.franciscanalliance.org/hospitals/crownpoint
Established: 2004 Annual Undergrad Tuition & Fees: $12,500
Enrollment: 13 Coed
Affiliation or Control: Independent Non-Profit IRS Status: 501(c)3
Highest Offering: Associate Degree
Program: Occupational
Accreditation: DMS

01 Co-Program Director .... Tracy BULT
01 Co-Program Director .... Karin KOLISZ

Saint Joseph's College (D)

PO Box 870, US Highway 231, Rensselaer IN 47978-0870
County: Jasper FICE Identification: 001833
Unit ID: 152363
Telephone: (219) 866-6000 Carnegie Class: Bac/Diverse
FAX Number: (219) 866-6100 Calendar System: Semester
URL: www.saintjoe.edu
Established: 1889 Annual Undergrad Tuition & Fees: $27,350
Enrollment: 965 Coed
Affiliation or Control: Roman Catholic IRS Status: 501(c)3
Highest Offering: Master's
Program: Liberal Arts And General; Teacher Preparatory; Professional
Accreditation: NH, IACBE, TED

01 President .... Dr. F. Dennis RIEGELNEGG
04 Admin Asst to the President .... Mrs. Sheila K. HANEWICH
05 Vice President for Academic Affairs .... Dr. Daniel J. BLANKENSHIP
10 Vice President Business Affairs .... Mr. Hoa NGUYEN
30 Vice Pres Inst Advancement/Mrktng .... Dr. Maureen V. EGAN
84 Asst VP of Enrollment Management .... Mr. John WADELL
32 Dean of Students .... Dr. Leslie FRERE
06 Registrar .... Mrs. Maureen HEALEY
08 Librarian .... Mrs. Catherine A. SALYERS
14 Director of Computer Center .... Mr. David ADAMS
38 Director of Counseling Services .... Ms. Laura WAGNER
18 Chief Facilities/Physical Plant .... Mr. Randal FLINN
15 Director Human Resources .... Ms. Nancy STUDER
26 Director of Integrated Marketing .... Ms. Christine BABICK-SAQUI
29 Director Alumni Relations .... Mrs. Kendra ILLINGWORTH
37 Director Student Financial Services .... Mrs. Debra SIZEMORE
28 Director of Diversity .... Mr. Ernest WATSON
36 Director Career Development .... Dr. David BOOP
09 Director of Institutional Research .... Mrs. Elizabeth GRAF
41 Athletic Director .... Mr. William MASSOELS
40 Director Bookstore .... Mr. Vinse HERSHBERGER
42 Chaplain/Director Campus Ministry .... Vacant

Saint Mary-of-the-Woods College (E)

St Mary of the Woods IN 47876-0067
County: Vigo FICE Identification: 001835
Unit ID: 152381
Telephone: (812) 535-5151 Carnegie Class: Bac/Diverse
FAX Number: (812) 535-5231 Calendar System: Semester
URL: www.smwc.edu
Established: 1840 Annual Undergrad Tuition & Fees: $27,620
Enrollment: 1,441 Coed
Affiliation or Control: Roman Catholic IRS Status: 501(c)3
Highest Offering: Master's
Program: Liberal Arts And General
Accreditation: NH, MUS, TED

01 President .... Dr. Dottie KING
30 Vice President for Advancement .... Ms. Karen DYER
10 Vice Pres Finance & Administration .... Mr. Gordon AFDAHL
05 Vice President for Academic Affairs .... Dr. Janet CLARK
32 Vice President for Student Life .... Ms. Vicki KOSOWSKY
84 Vice Pres Enrollment Management .... Ms. Beth TERREL
06 Registrar .... Ms. Susan MEIER
08 Director of the Library .... Ms. Judy TRIBBLE
29 Dir Alumnae Affairs/Annual Giving .... Ms. Chanel REEDER
26 Executive Dir of College Relations .... Ms. Dee REED
106 Director Woods Online Program .... Ms. Gwen HAGEMEYER
13 Exec Dir Information Technology .... Vacant
21 Controller .... Ms. Missie SCHWAB
36 Director of Career Development .... Ms. Susan GRESHAM
15 Director Human Resources .... Ms. Diana WARREN
18 Chief Facilities/Physical Plant .... Mr. Bill ZINK
35 Director Campus Life .... Mr. Jeffrey MALLOY
37 Director Financial Aid .... Ms. Darla HOPPER
44 Dir Major and Planned Gifts .... Ms. April SIMMA
64 Dir Grad Pgm Music Therapy .... Ms. Tracy RICHARDSON
88 Dir Grad Pgm Art Therapy .... Ms. Kathy GOTSHALL
88 Dir Grad Pgm Leadership Development .... Ms. Susan DECKER

Saint Mary's College (F)

Notre Dame IN 46556
County: Saint Joseph FICE Identification: 001836
Unit ID: 152390
Telephone: (574) 284-4000 Carnegie Class: Bac/A&S
FAX Number: (574) 284-4716 Calendar System: Semester
URL: www.saintmarys.edu
Established: 1844 Annual Undergrad Tuition & Fees: $33,280
Enrollment: 1,510 Female
Affiliation or Control: Roman Catholic IRS Status: 501(c)3
Highest Offering: Baccalaureate
Program: Liberal Arts And General; Teacher Preparatory; Professional
Accreditation: NH, ART, MUS, NUR, SW, TED

01 President .... Dr. Carol Ann MOONEY
04 Executive Asst to the President .... Ms. Susan C. DAMPEER
05 Sr Vice President & Dean of Faculty .... Dr. Patricia A. FLEMING
26 Vice President College Relations .... Ms. Shari M. RODRIGUEZ
32 Vice President for Student Affairs .... Ms. Karen A. JOHNSON
10 Vice Pres Finance & Administration .... Mr. Richard SPELLER
84 Vice Pres for Enrollment Management .... Ms. Mona BOWE
88 Vice President for Mission .... Sr. Veronique WIEDOWER, CSC
89 Associate Dean for Advising .... Ms. Susan VANEK
06 Registrar .... Mr. Todd NORRIS
07 Director of Admission .... Ms. Kristin MCANDREW
08 Director of Library .... Ms. Janet S. FORE
09 Director of Institutional Research .... Ms. Jessica ICKES
29 Director of Alumnae Relations .... Ms. Kara O'LEARY
37 Director of Financial Aid .... Ms. Kathleen M. BROWN
27 Director of Publicity & Cmty Rels .... Ms. Gwen O'BRIEN
38 Director of Women's Health .... Ms. Elizabeth FOURMAN
13 Chief Information Officer .... Mr. Michael BOEHM

15 Director of Human Resources ... Vacant
19 Director of Safety & Security ... Mr. David GARIEPY
40 Manager Bookstore ... Mr. Michael G. HICKS
41 Director of Athletics ... Ms. Julie SCHROEDER-BIEK
42 Director of Campus Ministry ... Ms. Judith FEAN
18 Director of Facilities ... Mr. William HAMBLING
35 Dir Stdt Involvement/Multicult Pgm ... Ms. Stephanie STEWARD-BRIDGES
96 Director of Purchasing ... Mr. Daniel P. DEETER

Saint Meinrad School of Theology (A)

200 Hill Drive, Saint Meinrad IN 47577-1030

County: Spencer — FICE Identification: 007276
Unit ID: 152451
Telephone: (812) 357-6611 — Carnegie Class: Spec/Faith
FAX Number: (812) 357-6964 — Calendar System: Semester
URL: www.saintmeinrad.edu
Established: 1861 — Annual Graduate Tuition & Fees: $21,158
Enrollment: 254 — Coed
Affiliation or Control: Roman Catholic — IRS Status: 501(c)3
Highest Offering: Master's; No Undergraduates
Program: Professional; Religious Emphasis
Accreditation: NH, THEOL

01 President & Rector ... Rev. Denis ROBINSON, OSB
03 Vice Rector ... Rev. Tobias COLGAN, OSB
05 Academic Dean ... Dr. Robert ALVIS
84 Director of Enrollment ... Rev. Brendan MOSS, OSB
42 Director of Spiritual Formation ... Rev. Joseph MORIARTY
20 Director of Lay Degree Programs ... Mr. Kyle KRAMER
30 Vice President of Development ... Mr. Michael ZIEMIANSKI
10 Business Manager & Treasurer ... Rev. Adrian BURKE, OSB
08 Library Director ... Dr. Daniel KOLB
06 Registrar ... Mrs. Donna M. BALBACH
88 Dir Inst for Priests & Presbyterate ... Rev. Ronald KNOTT
21 Director of Budget ... Mrs. Pam DOWLAND
37 Director of Student Financial Aid ... Mrs. Ruth KRESS
26 Director of Communications ... Mrs. Mary Jeanne SCHUMACHER
29 Director of Alumni Relations ... Mr. Tim HERRMANN
38 Director of Student Counseling Ctr ... Sr. Diane PHARO, SCN
88 Dir of Info & Instructional Tech ... Vacant
09 Director of Institutional Research ... Rev. Bede CISCO, OSB
23 Director of Health Services ... Mrs. Ann ROHLEDER

Taylor University (B)

West 236 Reade Avenue, Upland IN 46989-1001

County: Grant — FICE Identification: 001838
Unit ID: 152530
Telephone: (765) 998-2751 — Carnegie Class: Bac/Diverse
FAX Number: (765) 998-4910 — Calendar System: 4/1/4
URL: www.taylor.edu
Established: 1846 — Annual Undergrad Tuition & Fees: $28,088
Enrollment: 2,424 — Coed
Affiliation or Control: Independent Non-Profit — IRS Status: 501(c)3
Highest Offering: Master's
Program: Liberal Arts And General; Teacher Preparatory; Fine Arts Emphasis
Accreditation: NH, ENG, MUS, SW, TED

01 President ... Dr. Eugene B. HABECKER
05 Provost ... Dr. Jeff MOSHIER
11 VP Business Administration ... Mr. Ronald SUTHERLAND
30 VP University Advancement ... Dr. Ben SELLS
32 VP Student Dev/Dean of Students ... Dr. Skip TRUDEAU
84 VP Enroll Mgmt & Marketing ... Mr. Stephen MORTLAND
10 VP Finance & CFO ... Mr. Stephen OLSON
49 Dean Sch Liberal Arts ... Dr. Thomas JONES
58 Dean Sch Professional/Grad Studies ... Dr. Connie LIGHTFOOT
50 Dean Sch of Business ... Dr. Larry BELCHER
81 Dean Sch Natural & Applied Sciences ... Dr. William TOLL
104 Dean International Programs ... Dr. Chris BENNETT
13 Chief Information Officer ... Mr. Rob LINEHAN
106 Dean of Online Learning ... Dr. Jeff GROELING
41 Director of Athletics ... Dr. Angie FINCANNON
20 Dean Faculty Development/Dir CTLE ... Dr. Faye CHECHOWICH
26 Assoc VP Univ Relations & Marketing ... Ms. Joyce WOOD
44 Assoc VP for Campaigns ... Mr. David RITCHIE
44 Assoc VP for Major & Planned Gifts ... Mr. Mike FALDER
29 Assoc VP Alumni & Parent Relations ... Mr. Brent RUDIN
36 Assoc Dean Students/Dir Career Dev ... Mr. Drew MOSER
37 Assoc Dean Enroll Mgmt/Dir Fin Aid ... Mr. Timothy NACE
08 Assoc Dn Stdnt Support/Un Librarian ... Mr. Daniel BOWELL
15 Director of HR Operations ... Ms. Toni NEWLIN
06 Registrar ... Ms. Janet SHAFFER
42 Campus Pastor/Assoc Dean Students ... Rev. Randall GRUENDYKE
39 Residence Life Pgm/Asc Dn Stdnt ... Mr. Steve MORLEY
18 Director of Physical Plant ... Mr. Greg ELEY
07 Director Admissions ... Ms. Amy BARNETT
38 Director of Counseling Center ... Mr. Robert NEIDECK
21 Controller ... Mr. David LLOYD
19 Chief of Police/Taylor Police ... Mr. Jeff WALLACE
09 Director IR/Assoc Registrar ... Dr. Edwin WELCH
108 Director Assessment/Quality Improv ... Mr. Brent MAHER
24 Director of Academic Technology ... Mr. Gary FRIESEN
88 University Bursar ... Ms. Cathy MOORMAN
40 Bookstore Manager ... Mr. Matthew VOSS

TCM International Institute (C)

6337 Hollister Drive, Indianapolis IN 46224

Identification: 666333
Telephone: (317) 299-0333 — Carnegie Class: Not Classified
FAX Number: (317) 290-8607 — Calendar System: Semester
URL: www.tcmi.org
Established: 1991 — Annual Graduate Tuition & Fees: N/A
Enrollment: N/A — Coed
Affiliation or Control: Independent Non-Profit — IRS Status: 501(c)3
Highest Offering: Master's; No Undergraduates
Program: Religious Emphasis
Accreditation: NH

01 President ... Dr. Tony TWIST

Trine University (D)

1 University Avenue, Angola IN 46703-1764

County: Steuben — FICE Identification: 001839
Unit ID: 152567
Telephone: (260) 665-4100 — Carnegie Class: Bac/Diverse
FAX Number: (260) 665-4292 — Calendar System: Semester
URL: www.trine.edu
Established: 1884 — Annual Undergrad Tuition & Fees: $27,660
Enrollment: 2,200 — Coed
Affiliation or Control: Independent Non-Profit — IRS Status: 501(c)3
Highest Offering: Master's
Program: Teacher Preparatory; Professional; Business Emphasis
Accreditation: NH, ACBSP, ENG, TED

01 President ... Dr. Earl D. BROOKS, II
03 Senior Vice President ... Mr. Mike BOCK
05 Vice President for Academic Affairs ... Dr. John SHANNON
10 Vice President Finance ... Ms. Jody GREER
30 Vice Pres for Alumni & Development ... Mr. Kent D. STUCKY
84 VP Enrollment Mgmt/Dean Admissions ... Mr. Scott GOPLIN
32 Vice President for Student Services ... Mr. Randy WHITE
51 Asst Vice Pres for Adult Learning ... Dr. Jean DELLER
107 Dean of Professional Studies ... Mr. David WOOD
15 Human Resources ... Mr. Robert MORELAND
41 Athletic Director ... Mr. Matt LAND
06 Registrar ... Ms. Debra F. HELMSING
27 Dir Integrated & Brand Marketing ... Ms. Jill BOGGS
04 Assistant to the President ... Ms. Gretchen MILLER
37 Director Student Financial Planning ... Ms. Kim BENNETT
13 Chief Information Officer-IT ... Ms. Michelle DUNN
08 Director of the Library ... Ms. Kristina BREWER
36 Int Director of Placement/Coop Educ ... Ms. Linda BATEMAN
09 Director Inst Planning/Research ... Ms. Christina ZAMBRUN

University of Evansville (E)

1800 Lincoln Avenue, Evansville IN 47722-1586

County: Vanderburgh — FICE Identification: 001795
Unit ID: 150534
Telephone: (812) 488-2000 — Carnegie Class: Master's S
FAX Number: (812) 488-2320 — Calendar System: Semester
URL: www.evansville.edu
Established: 1854 — Annual Undergrad Tuition & Fees: $30,556
Enrollment: 2,554 — Coed
Affiliation or Control: United Methodist — IRS Status: 501(c)3
Highest Offering: Doctorate
Program: Liberal Arts And General; Teacher Preparatory; Professional
Accreditation: NH, BUS, CS, ENG, MUS, NUR, PTA, PTAA, TED

01 President ... Dr. Thomas A. KAZEE
05 Sr Vice President Academic Affairs ... Dr. John MOSBO
30 Vice Pres Development ... Mr. John C. BARNER
10 Vice President Fiscal Affairs/Admin ... Mr. Jeffery M. WOLF
32 VP Student Affairs/Dean of Students ... Ms. Dana CLAYTON
84 Vice President Enrollment Services ... Vacant
26 VP Marketing and Communication ... Vacant
25 Assoc VP Academic Affs/Grants Dir ... Dr. Jennifer L. GRABAN
35 Asst VP Student Affs/Dir Res Life ... Mr. Michael A. TESSIER
21 Asst VP for Fiscal Affairs ... Ms. Donna O. TEAGUE
13 Asst VP & Chief Technology Office ... Mr. Donald HUDSON
49 Interim Dean of Arts & Sciences ... Dr. Ray LUTGRING
50 Dean of Business Administration ... Dr. Stephen STANDIFIRD
53 Dean of Education/Health Science ... Dr. Lynn R. PENLAND
54 Dean Engineering/Computer Science ... Dr. Phillip M. GERHART
41 Director of Athletics ... Mr. John STANLEY
26 Director of University Relations ... Ms. Lucy HIMSTEDT
06 University Registrar ... Ms. Celia TEOH
06 Asst VP Institutional Effectiveness ... Ms. Amy BRANDEBURY
08 University Librarian ... Mr. William F. LOUDEN
42 University Chaplain ... Rev. Tammy GIESELMAN
11 Director of Administrative Services ... Mr. Mark J. LOGEL
29 Director of Alumni/Parent Relations ... Ms. Sylvia Y. DEVAULT
44 Dir Gift Planning/Capital Support ... Ms. Abigail MILEY
36 Director of Career Svcs/Placement ... Mr. C. Gene WELLS
38 Director of Counseling/Health Educ ... Ms. Sylvia T. BUCK
37 Director of Financial Aid ... Ms. JoAnn E. LAUGEL
15 Director of Human Resources ... Mr. Keith GEHLHAUSEN
18 Director of Physical Plant ... Mr. Larry S. HORN
19 Director of Safety & Security ... Mr. Harold P. MATTHEWS
104 Director of Study Abroad/Harlaxton ... Mr. Earl D. KIRK
40 Director of Bookstore ... Mr. Douglas GUSTWILLER
28 Director of Diversity ... Ms. Latoya SMITH
44 Asst Director of Gift Giving ... Ms. Cathy RENNER
27 Coordinator of News Services ... Ms. Kristen LUND
07 Dean of Admissions ... Mr. Donald VOS

University of Indianapolis (F)

1400 E Hanna Avenue, Indianapolis IN 46227-3697

County: Marion — FICE Identification: 001804
Unit ID: 151263
Telephone: (317) 788-3368 — Carnegie Class: Master's L
FAX Number: (317) 788-3300 — Calendar System: Other
URL: www.uindy.edu
Established: 1902 — Annual Undergrad Tuition & Fees: $23,590
Enrollment: 5,345 — Coed
Affiliation or Control: United Methodist — IRS Status: 501(c)3
Highest Offering: Doctorate
Program: Occupational; Liberal Arts And General; Teacher Preparatory; Professional
Accreditation: NH, ACBSP, ADNUR, ART, CLPSY, EXSC, MIDWF, MUS, NURSE, OT, PTA, PTAA, SW, TED

01 President ... Dr. Robert L. MANUEL
05 Exec VP Academic Affairs/Provost ... Dr. Deborah Ware BALOGH
46 VP Research/Plng/Strategic Ptnrship ... Dr. Mary C. MOORE
10 Vice President Business & Finance . Mr. Michael L. BRAUGHTON
32 Vice President for Student Affairs ... Mr. Mark T. WEIGAND
30 Vice President for Inst Advancement ... Mr. James E. SMITH
84 Vice President for Enrollment ... Mr. Mark T. WEIGAND
35 Assoc VP for Student Affairs ... Ms. Kory M. VITANGELI
13 Associate VP Information Systems ... Mr. Steven R. HERRIFORD
49 Int Dean College of Arts/Sciences ... Dr. Jennifer A. DRAKE
50 Dean School of Business ... Dr. Sheela N. YADAV
53 Dean School of Education ... Dr. Kathryn A. MORAN
66 Dean School of Nursing ... Dr. Anne C. THOMAS
76 Dean College of Health Sciences ... Dr. Stephanie KELLY
88 Dean School of Adult Learning ... Vacant
06 Registrar ... Dr. Mary Beth BAGG
27 Exec Dir Communications & Marketing ... Ms. Mary WADE ATTEBERRY
07 Director of Admissions ... Mr. Ronald W. WILKS
08 Librarian ... Dr. Chris LAMAR
15 Director Human Resources ... Mr. Stant CLARK
26 Director Marketing ... Mr. Joe P. SOLARI
36 Dir Career Svcs/Employer Relations ... Mr. Paul W. GABONAY
37 Director Student Financial Aid ... Mrs. Linda B. HANDY
58 Director Graduate Business Pgms ... Dr. Matthew W. WILL
18 Director Physical Plant ... Mr. Kenneth M. PIEPENBRINK
19 Director Safety & Police Services ... Mr. Michael REDDICK
29 Director Alumni Relations ... Ms. Natalie A. CUMMINGS
31 Director Univ Cmty Bridge Program ... Dr. Mary E. BUSCH
41 Director Athletics ... Dr. Sue J. WILLEY
42 Co-Chaplain ... Rev. L. Lang BROWNLEE
42 Co-Chaplain ... Rev. Jeremiah GIBBS
44 Director Planned & Major Gifts ... Mr. Andy M. KOCHER
85 Director International Programs ... Ms. Marilyn O. CHASE
24 Director Media/Client Services ... Mr. Robert A. JONES
38 Director Counseling Center ... Ms. Kelly MILLER
72 Director Ctr for Instructional Tech ... Mrs. Elizabeth A. KIGGINS
09 Director Enrollment Research ... Ms. Mary E. GRANT
40 Bookstore Manager ... Ms. Lesley NORIEGA

University of Notre Dame (G)

400 Main Building, Notre Dame IN 46556

County: Saint Joseph — FICE Identification: 001840
Unit ID: 152080
Telephone: (574) 631-5000 — Carnegie Class: RU/VH
FAX Number: (574) 631-6700 — Calendar System: Semester
URL: www.nd.edu
Established: 1842 — Annual Undergrad Tuition & Fees: $42,971
Enrollment: 12,004 — Coed
Affiliation or Control: Roman Catholic — IRS Status: 501(c)3
Highest Offering: Doctorate
Program: Liberal Arts And General; Professional; Business Emphasis
Accreditation: NH, ART, BUS, BUSA, COPSY, CS, ENG, IPSY, LAW, THEOL

01 President ... Rev. John I. JENKINS, CSC
05 Provost ... Dr. Thomas G. BURISH
03 Executive Vice President ... Dr. John F. AFFLECK-GRAVES
20 Vice Pres/Sr Associate Provost ... Dr. Christine M. MAZIAR
20 Vice Pres/Associate Provost ... Dr. Daniel J. MYERS
20 Vice Pres/Associate Provost ... Dr. Donald B. POPE-DAVIS
82 VP/Provost Internationalization ... Dr. Nicholas ENTRIKIN
32 Vice President for Student Affairs ... Ms. Erin HOFFMANN HARDING
10 Vice President for Finance ... Mr. John A. SEJDINAJ
46 Vice President for Research ... Dr. Robert J. BERNHARD
43 Vice President & General Counsel ... Ms. Marianne CORR
88 Vice Pres/Chief Investment Ofcr ... Mr. Scott C. MALPASS
41 Vice Pres & Director of Athletics ... Mr. John "Jack" B. SWARBRICK
15 Vice Pres Human Resources ... Mr. Robert K. MCQUADE
26 Vice President University Relations ... Mr. Louis M. NANNI
13 VP & Chief Information Officer ... Mr. Ronald D. KRAEMER
88 VP Mission Engagmnt/Church Affairs . Rev. William M. LIES, CSC
100 Chief of Staff ... Ms. Ann M. FIRTH
28 Chief Diversity Officer ... Dr. Frances L. SHAVERS
84 Assoc VP Undergraduate Enrollment ... Mr. Donald BISHOP
18 Assoc VP Facilities & Design ... Mr. Douglas K. MARSH
06 Interim Registrar ... Mr. Charles T. HURLEY
96 Director Procurement ... Mr. Vaibhav AGARWAL
50 Interim Dean of College of Business ... Dr. Roger D. HUANG
61 Dean of Law School ... Prof. Nell J. NEWTON
54 Dean College of Engineering ... Dr. Peter K. KILPATRICK
58 Dean of the Graduate School ... Dr. Greg E. STERLING
49 Dean of Arts & Letters ... Dr. John T. MCGREEVY
81 Dean of Science ... Dr. Gregory P. CRAWFORD
48 Dean of Architecture ... Dr. Michael N. LYKOUDIS
88 Dean First Year of Studies ... Dr. Hugh R. PAGE
29 Exec Director Alumni Assoc ... Ms. Dolly DUFFY
08 Dir of University Libraries ... Ms. Diane PARR WALKER
27 Chief Communications Executive ... Mr. Matthew V. STORIN
42 Director of Campus Ministry ... Rev. James B. KING, CSC

37 Assoc Dir of Student Financial Aid ... Ms. Mary B. NUCCIARONE
36 Director of Career Center ... Mr. Lee J. SVETE
38 Director of Counseling Center ... Dr. Susan STEIBE-PASALICH
45 Interim Assoc VP Strategic Planning ... Mr. David C. BAILEY
19 Director of Security/Police ... Mr. Phillip A. JOHNSON

University of Saint Francis (A)

2701 Spring Street, Fort Wayne IN 46808-3994
County: Allen FICE Identification: 001832
Unit ID: 152336
Telephone: (260) 399-7700 Carnegie Class: Master's S
FAX Number: N/A Calendar System: Semester
URL: www.sf.edu
Established: 1890 Annual Undergrad Tuition & Fees: $24,440
Enrollment: 2,343 Coed
Affiliation or Control: Roman Catholic IRS Status: 501(c)3
Highest Offering: Master's
Program: Occupational; 2-Year Principally Bachelor's Creditable; Liberal Arts And General; Teacher Preparatory; Professional
Accreditation: NH, ACBSP, ADNUR, ARCPA, ART, NURSE, PTAA, RAD, SURGT, SW, TED

01 President ... Sr. M. Elise KRISS, OSF
20 Vice President Academic Affairs ... Dr. J. Andrew PRALL
03 Executive Vice President ... Dr. Stacy J. ADKINSON
11 Associate Vice President ... Mrs. Teresa SORDELET
10 Vice President Finance & Operations ... Mr. Richard BIENZ
30 Vice President University Relations ... Mr. Donald SCHENKEL
32 Dean of Students ... Ms. Sharon K. MEJEUR
26 Assoc Vice President Marketing ... Mrs. Trois HART
35 Associate Dean of Students ... Mrs. Beth GROMAN
49 Dean School of Arts & Sciences ... Dr. Matthew SMITH
50 Dean Keith Busse School of Business ... Ms. Helen MURRAY
57 Dean School of Creative Arts ... Mr. Rick E. CARTWRIGHT
17 Dean School of Health Sciences ... Dr. Nancy N. GILLESPIE
107 Dean School of Professional Studies ... Dr. Jane M. SWISS
06 Registrar ... Mr. Francis P. CONNOR
84 Assoc VP Enrollment Management ... Mr. Jean Paul SPAGNOLO
29 Director Alumni Relations ... Mrs. Jessica L. SWINFORD
41 Director Athletics ... Mr. Michael MCCAFFREY
88 Director Campaigns & Major Gifts ... Mr. William SLAYTON
42 Director Campus Ministry ... Mr. Joshua STAGNI
19 Director Campus Safety & Security ... Mr. Richard ROBBINS
36 Director Career Services ... Mr. William BRUNE
88 Dir Center for Service Engagement ... Ms. Katrina BOEDEKER
88 Director Co-Curricular Activities ... Ms. Melissa REESMAN
102 Dir Corp/Found Relations and Grants ... Mrs. Lynn MCKENNA-FRAZIER
12 Interim Dean Crown Point Site ... Sr. M. Elaine BROTHERS
88 Director Development ... Ms. Kristen R. RIEBENACK
13 Dir Distance/Instruc/Educ Tech ... Mr. Robert SOULLIERE
07 Executive Dir Enrollment Services ... Mrs. Jamie MCGRATH
21 Dir Financial Planning/Accounting ... Mrs. Cathy CRAWFORD
88 Director Financial Reporting ... Mr. Craig TEETSEL
35 Associate Dean Student Services ... Ms. Jenny FAWBUSH
58 Director Graduate School ... Dr. Douglas BARCALOW
88 Director Health Sciences Sim Lab ... Dr. Dawn MABRY
88 Dir Hlth Sci Strategic Initiatives ... Dr. Lorene ARNOLD
92 Director Honors Program ... Dr. Mathew FISHER
39 Director Housing & Residence Life ... Mr. Andrew MCKEE
15 Director Human Resources ... Mrs. Norma BOENKER
108 Dir Inst Effectiveness/Accredit ... Dr. Marcia K. SAUTER
09 Director Institutional Research ... Dr. Stephanie J. OETTING
08 Director Library Services ... Mrs. Karla ALEXANDER
88 Asst to Pres for Mission Integra ... Sr. Mary Evelyn GOVERT, OSF
91 Dir Network & Information Mgmt ... Mr. Mark ROBBINS
88 Director Operations ... Mr. Thomas BUCK
44 Director Planned Giving ... Sr. M. Marilyn OLIVER, OSF
88 Director Retention ... Mrs. Michelle KUHLHORST
88 Director Sports Information ... Mr. Bill SCOTT
88 Dir Student Academic Services ... Mrs. Tricia BUGAJSKI
88 Dir Tech Security & Compliance ... Mr. Randy TROY
88 Director TRiO ... Mr. Tellis YOUNG
14 Dir Tech User Support Services ... Mr. A. Drew REPP
88 Mgr AVI Food Service ... Mr. Brian SMITH
40 Mgr Barnes & Noble Campus Shoppe ... Mrs. Robin HUFFMAN

University of Southern Indiana (B)

8600 University Boulevard, Evansville IN 47712-3596
County: Vanderburgh FICE Identification: 001808
Unit ID: 151306
Telephone: (812) 464-8600 Carnegie Class: Master's L
FAX Number: (812) 464-1960 Calendar System: Semester
URL: www.usi.edu
Established: 1965 Annual Undergrad Tuition & Fees (In-State): $6,145
Enrollment: 10,820 Coed
Affiliation or Control: State IRS Status: 501(c)3
Highest Offering: Doctorate
Program: Liberal Arts And General; Teacher Preparatory; Professional
Accreditation: NH, ART, BUS, BUSA, DA, DH, @DIETD, DMS, ENG, JOUR, NURSE, OT, OTA, RAD, SW, TED

01 President ... Dr. Linda L M. BENNETT
100 Assistant to the President ... Ms. Janel S. ALLEN
05 Provost ... Dr. Ronald S. ROCHON
10 Vice President Business Affairs ... Mr. Mark ROZEWSKI
86 Vice Pres Govt and Univ Relations ... Ms. Cynthia S. BRINKER
26 Asst VP Marketing/Communications ... Mr. Todd A. WILSON
56 Assoc Provost Outreach Engagement ... Dr. Mark C. BERNHARD
20 Interim Asst Provost Acad Affairs ... Dr. Shelly B. BLUNT
32 Assoc Provost for Student Affairs ... Dr. Marcia K. KIESSLING
21 Asst Vice Pres Business Affairs ... Ms. Mary A. HUPFER
09 Exec Director Plng/Research/Assess . Dr. Katherine A. DRAUGHON
58 Interim Director Graduate Studies ... Dr. Wes T. DURHAM
06 Registrar ... Ms. Sandy K. FRANK
07 Director of Admission ... Mr. Eric H. OTTO
08 Interim Director of Library Svcs ... Ms. Martha I. NIEMEIER
30 Director of Development/USI Fndtn ... Mr. David A. BOWER
92 Director Honors Program ... Dr. Antonia D. BAMBINA
38 Director of Counseling ... Dr. B. Thomas LONGWELL
36 Director of Career Counseling ... Mr. Timothy K. BUECHER
29 Director of Alumni Affairs ... Mrs. Janet L. JOHNSON
37 Director of Student Financial Asst ... Ms. Mary J. HARPER
15 Director of Human Resources ... Ms. Donna J. EVINGER
36 Director Career Services/Placement ... Mr. Philip L. PARKER
35 Dean of Students ... Dr. Angela E. BATISTA
85 Director of Intl Student Services ... Mrs. Heidi GREGORI-GAHAN
28 Director Multicultural Center ... Ms. Pamela F. HOPSON
14 Exec Dir of Information Technology ... Mr. Richard TOENISKOETTER
90 Academic Services Coordinator ... Mr. Juzar AHMED
18 Director of Facilities Operations ... Mr. Stephen P. HELFRICH
96 Director Procurement/Distribution ... Mr. David A. GOLDENBERG
27 Director of News & Information Svcs ... Ms. Kathy W. FUNKE
19 Director of Security ... Mr. Stephen WOODALL
39 Director of Residence Life ... Ms. Laurie M. BERRY
40 Bookstore Manager ... Mr. Michael J. GOELZHAUSER
41 Athletic Director ... Mr. Jon Mark HALL
50 Dean College of Business ... Dr. Mohammed KHAYUM
49 Dean College of Liberal Arts ... Mr. Michael K. AAKHUS
66 Dean College Nursing/Health Profess ... Dr. Ann H. WHITE
81 Dean College of Science/Engineering ... Dr. Scott A. GORDON
21 Asst Vice Pres Finance Admin Treas ... Mr. Steven J. BRIDGES
51 Director Continuing Education ... Ms. Linda L. CLEEK
106 Asst Provost for Distance Learning ... Ms. Megan W. LINOS

Valparaiso University (C)

Valparaiso IN 46383-9978
County: Porter FICE Identification: 001842
Unit ID: 152600
Telephone: (219) 464-5000 Carnegie Class: Master's L
FAX Number: (219) 464-5381 Calendar System: Semester
URL: valpo.edu
Established: 1859 Annual Undergrad Tuition & Fees: $32,250
Enrollment: 3,967 Coed
Affiliation or Control: Lutheran IRS Status: 501(c)3
Highest Offering: Doctorate
Program: Liberal Arts And General; Teacher Preparatory; Professional
Accreditation: NH, BUS, CACREP, CEA, ENG, LAW, MUS, NURSE, SW, TED

01 President ... Mr. Mark A. HECKLER
05 Provost/Exec Vice Pres Acad Affs ... Dr. Mark R. SCHWEHN
20 Senior Associate Provost ... Dr. Renu JUNEJA
32 Vice President for Student Affairs ... Dr. Bonnie L. HUNTER
11 VP for Administration & Finance ... Mr. Charley E. GILLISPIE
84 Vice Pres for Enrollment Management ... Mr. Michael JOSEPH
26 VP Integrated Mktg/Communications ... Mr. Scott D. OCHANDER
58 Asc Provost/Dean Grad Sch/Cont Ed ... Dr. David L. ROWLAND
30 Vice Pres Institutional Advancement ... Ms. Lisa HOLLANDER
43 Vice President University Counsel ... Mr. Darron C. FARHA
92 Dean of Christ College ... Dr. Mel PIEHL
49 Dean College Arts & Sciences ... Dr. Jon T. KILPINEN
61 Dean School of Law ... Mr. Jay CONISON
54 Dean College of Engineering ... Dr. Eric JOHNSON
50 Dean College of Business Admin ... Dr. James BRODZINSKI
66 Dean College of Nursing ... Dr. Janet M. BROWN
08 Dean Library Services ... Dr. Bradford L. EDEN
35 Dean of Students ... Dr. Timothy S. JENKINS
37 Director of Financial Aid ... Mr. David FEVIG
42 Exec Dir of Campus Ministries ... Rev. Brian T. JOHNSON
06 Registrar ... Ms. Shelly KOOI
19 Chief University Police ... Ms. Rebecca A. WALKOWIAK
39 Asst Dean Students/Residential Life ... Mr. Ryan BLEVINS
104 Director of Study Abroad Programs ... Ms. Julie A. MADDOX
85 Dir International Students/Scholars ... Mr. Holly SINGH
29 Director Alumni Relations ... Vacant
15 Dir Human Resource Services ... Ms. Nora WIERGACZ
88 Exec Dir for Capital Planning ... Mr. Fred W. PLANT
36 Director Career Center ... Mr. Tom CATH
38 Director of Counseling Services ... Dr. Stewart E. COOPER
41 Director Athletics ... Mr. Mark LABARBERA
20 Assistant Provost ... Dr. Rick GILLMAN
21 Controller ... Ms. Dianne M. WOODS
28 Director of Multicultural Programs ... Ms. Jane M. BELLO-BRUNSON
96 Director of Procurement ... Ms. Nancy K. MURRAY
09 Exec Dir Instnl Effectiveness ... Mr. Greg STINSON
42 University Pastor ... Rev. Charlene COX
42 University Pastor ... Rev. James WETZSTEIN

Vincennes University (D)

1002 N First Street, Vincennes IN 47591-1504
County: Knox FICE Identification: 001843
Unit ID: 152637
Telephone: (812) 888-8888 Carnegie Class: Assoc/Pub4
FAX Number: (812) 888-5868 Calendar System: Semester
URL: www.vinu.edu
Established: 1801 Annual Undergrad Tuition & Fees (In-State): $4,883
Enrollment: 10,059 Coed
Affiliation or Control: State IRS Status: 501(c)3
Highest Offering: Baccalaureate
Program: Occupational; 2-Year Principally Bachelor's Creditable; Liberal Arts And General
Accreditation: NH, ACBSP, ADNUR, ART, EMT, FUSER, NUR, PNUR, PTAA, SURGT, THEA

01 President ... Dr. Richard E. HELTON
05 Provost/Vice Pres Institutional Svc ... Mr. Charles R. JOHNSON, JR.
10 Vice Pres Financial Svcs/Govt Rels ... Mr. Phillip S. RATH
103 VP Workforce Dev/Comm Services ... Mr. David C. TUCKER
12 Assistant VP/Dean Jasper Campus ... Dr. Alan D. JOHNSON
21 Associate Vice President/Controller ... Ms. Linda L. WALDROUP
32 Asst Provost Student Affairs ... Ms. Lynn WHITE
20 Asst Provost Curriculum & Inst ... Dr. Carolyn K. JONES
35 Dean of Students ... Mr. John T. LIVERS
26 Sr Director External Relations ... Ms. Kristi R. DEETZ
07 Director of Admissions ... Mr. Christian BLOME
08 Director of Learning Resources/Tech ... Mr. David PETER
09 Int Dir of Inst Research/Planning ... Ms. Kimela A. MEEKS
13 Director of Mgmt Information Center ... Mr. Carmin A. SCHNARR
27 Director Public Information ... Mr. Duane H. CHATTIN
88 Director of University Events ... Ms. Brenda L. THOMPSON
36 Dir Ctr for Career & Empl Relations ... Mr. Richard A. COLEMAN
37 Director of Student Financial Aid ... Mr. Stanley J. WERNE
88 Director Disability Services ... Vacant
38 Director of Student Counseling ... Dr. Lisa J. BISHOP
39 Director of Housing Facilities ... Ms. Patricia A. JOST
40 Manager of Bookstore ... Mr. Ronald L. KOTTER
102 President of VU Foundation ... Mr. Bumper R. HOSTETLER
41 Athletic Director ... Mr. Harry L. MEEKS
88 Director of Project Excel/Proj Link ... Ms. Heather MOFFAT
29 Director of Alumni Programs ... Ms. Jennifer D. GILMORE
85 Dir Multicultural/Intl Student Affs ... Ms. Schvalla RIVERA
18 Director of Physical Plant ... Mr. James W. MINDERMAN
19 Director of Campus Police ... Mr. James M. JONES
88 Bursar ... Ms. Lori J. HOSTETLER
23 Coordinator Student Health Office ... Ms. Margaret J. MILLIGAN
24 Director of Media Services ... Mr. Jay D. WOLF
06 Registrar/Veterans Affairs ... Ms. Rebecca K. LITTLE
39 Director Residential Life ... Ms. Dawn M. BREWER
88 Director Marketing Services ... Ms. Andrea G. TSCHERTER
96 Director of Procurement ... Mr. Daniel R. MARTENS
38 Director Academic Advising ... Mr. Thomas E. KONKLE
88 Director Architectural Services ... Mr. Andrew YOUNG
16 Director Human Resources/AAO ... Ms. Lorethea H. POTTS-RUSK
76 Dean Health Sci/Human Perf ... Ms. Jana L. VIECK
50 Int Dean Business/Public Svc Div ... Ms. Mary L. HOLLARS
72 Dean Technology Division ... Mr. Arthur H. HAASE
81 Int Dean Science/Math Division ... Mr. Jay A. BARDOLE
83 Dean Social Sci/Performing Arts ... Mr. Eric W. MARGERUM
51 Dean Extended Studies ... Mr. Donald E. KAUFMAN
79 Dean Humanities Division ... Dr. Charles W. REINHART
88 Dir Avia Tech Ctr Indianapolis ... Mr. Michael D. GEHRICH
88 Dir Marketing Communications ... Ms. Krystal F. SPENCER
88 Dir Institutional Effectiveness ... Mr. Michael GRESS

Wabash College (E)

301 W Wabash, PO Box 352,
Crawfordsville IN 47933-0352
County: Montgomery FICE Identification: 001844
Unit ID: 152673
Telephone: (765) 361-6100 Carnegie Class: Bac/A&S
FAX Number: (765) 361-6461 Calendar System: Semester
URL: www.wabash.edu
Established: 1832 Annual Undergrad Tuition & Fees: $33,950
Enrollment: 909 Male
Affiliation or Control: Independent Non-Profit IRS Status: 501(c)3
Highest Offering: Baccalaureate
Program: Liberal Arts And General
Accreditation: NH, TED

01 President ... Dr. Patrick E. WHITE
05 Dean of the College ... Dr. Gary A. PHILLIPS
10 Chief Financial Officer & Treasurer ... Mr. Larry GRIFFITH
32 Dean of Students ... Mr. Michael P. RATERS
30 Dean for Advancement ... Mr. Jonathan S. STERN
35 Associate Dean of Students ... Mr. George W. OPRISKO
06 Registrar and Assoc Dean ... Dr. Julie A. OLSEN
07 Dean of Admissions & Financial Aid ... Mr. Steven J. KLEIN
37 Director of Financial Aid ... Mr. R. Clinton GASAWAY
08 Head Librarian & Dir Lilly Library ... Mr. John E. LAMBORN
13 Director of IT Services ... Mr. Bradley K. WEAVER
36 Director of Career Development ... Mr. R. Scott CRAWFORD
29 Dir of Alumni & Parent Relations ... Mr. Thomas G. RUNGE
26 Senior Director of Communications a ... Mr. James L. AMIDON
40 Director of Purchasing & Bookstore ... Mr. Thomas E. KEEDY
41 Dir of Athletics & Campus Wellness ... Mr. Joseph R. HAKLIN
44 Director of Development ... Ms. Alison KOTHE
15 Director of Human Resources ... Ms. Catherine A. METZ
18 Director of Campus Services ... Mr. David MORGAN
96 Director of Purchasing & Bookstore ... Mr. Thomas E. KEEDY
21 Controller ... Ms. Cathy VANARSDALL
38 Director of Counseling Services ... Mr. Kevin C. SWAIM
28 Dir of Malcolm X Inst & Assoc Dean ... Dr. Michael J. BROWN
88 Dir of Ctr of Inquiry in the LA ... Dr. Charles F. BLAICH
88 Dir Wabash Ctr Teaching/Learning ... Dr. Nadine S. PENCE
19 Director of Safety and Security ... Mr. Richard G. WOODS

IOWA

AIB College of Business (F)

2500 Fleur Drive, Des Moines IA 50321-1799
County: Polk FICE Identification: 003963
Unit ID: 152822

Telephone: (515) 244-4221 Carnegie Class: Spec/Bus
FAX Number: (515) 244-6773 Calendar System: Quarter
URL: www.aib.edu
Established: 1921 Annual Undergrad Tuition & Fees: $14,040
Enrollment: 862 Coed
Affiliation or Control: Independent Non-Profit IRS Status: 501(c)3
Highest Offering: Baccalaureate
Program: Business Emphasis
Accreditation: NH

01 President Ms. Nancy WILLIAMS
05 Vice President for Academic Affairs Dr. M. Susan CIGELMAN
32 VP for Student Life Mr. Terry WILSON
20 Chief Academic Officer Ms. Christy ROLAND
10 VP & Chief Financial Officer Mr. Paul WINGET
15 Director of Human Resources Ms. Joan HITZEL
88 Faculty Assembly President Ms. Kelly SWINTON
04 Executive Assistant to President Ms. Ronette SMITH
50 Department Chair Accounting Mr. Larry MURPHY
50 Dept Chair Business Administration Ms. Ann WRIGHT
97 Dept Chair Comm & General Studies Vacant
61 Dept Chair Court Reporting Ms. Kay SMITH
18 Chief Facilities Officer Mr. Chris SCHMIDT
36 Director of Career Services Ms. Jane DEHAVEN
21 Controller Ms. Janet CRUM
37 Director of Financial Aid Services Ms. Laurie SANDERS
88 Director of Facilities Management Mr. Mike LARSON
88 Director of Academic Advising Ms. Jessica HANSEN
06 Registrar Mr. Randy TERRONEZ
88 Director of Activities Ms. Jennifer BEAL
38 Director of Student Counseling Ms. Sheila KEENE
08 Library Director Ms. Leslie BINTNER
31 Director of Community Engagement Ms. Julie SPICER
29 Alumni Director Ms. Reonna SNYDER
88 Senior Programmer/Analyst III Mr. Mark ROLAND
105 Graphic/Web Designer Ms. Rachel SORENSEN
13 Senior Director of Information Tech Ms. Denise CODY
41 Athletics Director Mr. Keith COLEMAN
90 Assistant Dean for Academic Res Ms. Danielle EDWARDS
26 Director of Public Relations Ms. Jane MEISNER
07 Director of Admissions Mr. Steve OLSEN
84 Senior Director of Enroll & Mark Mr. Terry PETERS
30 Senior Dir of Advancement Ms. Dawn ROBERTS
88 Dir of Inst Acct/Compliance Ms. Courtney SAMENTO
35 Director of Student Life Ms. Danielle SCHMIDT
40 Director of Retail Services Ms. Kristin SIEREN

Allen College (A)

1825 Logan Avenue, Waterloo IA 50703-1999
County: Black Hawk FICE Identification: 030691
Unit ID: 152798
Telephone: (319) 226-2000 Carnegie Class: Spec/Health
FAX Number: (319) 226-2020 Calendar System: Semester
URL: www.allencollege.edu
Established: 1989 Annual Undergrad Tuition & Fees: $19,303
Enrollment: 500 Coed
Affiliation or Control: Independent Non-Profit IRS Status: 501(c)3
Highest Offering: Doctorate
Program: Professional; Nursing Emphasis
Accreditation: NH, MT, NMT, NUR, NURSE, RAD

01 Chancellor Dr. Jerry DURHAM
05 Vice Chancellor of Academic Affairs Dr. Nancy KRAMER
10 Dir Business/Administrative Svcs Ms. Denise HANSON
66 Dean School of Nursing Dr. Kendra WILLIAMS-PEREZ
76 Dean School of Health Sciences Dr. Peggy FORTSCH
06 Dir of Student Services/Registrar Ms. Joanna RAMSDEN-MEIER
37 Financial Aid Coordinator Ms. Kathie WALTERS
24 Media Specialist Ms. Robin NICHOLSON
07 Admissions Counselor Ms. Michelle KOEHN
08 Coordinator Library/Media Services Dr. Ruth YAN

Antioch School of Church Planting and Leadership Development (B)

2400 Oakwood Road, Ames IA 50014
County: Story Identification: 667026
Telephone: (515) 292-9694 Carnegie Class: Not Classified
FAX Number: (515) 292-1933 Calendar System: Other
URL: www.antiochschool.edu
Established: 2006 Annual Undergrad Tuition & Fees: $1,800
Enrollment: N/A Coed
Affiliation or Control: Independent Non-Profit IRS Status: 501(c)3
Highest Offering: Doctorate
Program: Religious Emphasis
Accreditation: DETC

01 President Jeff REED
05 Academic Dean Stephen KEMP

Ashford University (C)

400 N Bluff Boulevard, Clinton IA 52732-3997
County: Clinton FICE Identification: 001881
Unit ID: 154022
Telephone: (563) 242-4023 Carnegie Class: Master's L
FAX Number: (563) 242-2003 Calendar System: Semester
URL: www.ashford.edu
Established: 1918 Annual Undergrad Tuition & Fees: $16,520
Enrollment: 74,596 Coed
Affiliation or Control: Proprietary IRS Status: Proprietary
Highest Offering: Master's
Program: Liberal Arts And General; Teacher Preparatory; Business Emphasis
Accreditation: NH, IACBE

01 University President Dr. Elizabeth TICE
05 Provost Dr. Rebecca WARDLOW
20 Vice President Academic Affairs Dr. James JEREMIAH
26 Director of Communications Mr. Larry LIBBERTON
07 Director of Admissions Mr. Jason WOODS
37 Director Financial Aid Ms. Lisa KRAMER
08 Library Director Ms. Flora LOWE
50 Dean Col Business/Professional Stds Dr. Charlie MINNICK
49 Dean College Arts & Sciences Dr. William LOWE
53 Dean College Education Dr. Joen ROTTLER
56 Center For External Studies Ms. Cynthia COMBS
39 Director of Residence Life Ms. Lettie CONNOLLY
41 Director of Athletics Ms. Meg SCHEBLER
06 University Registrar Mr. Kirk MORRISON
88 Director Prior Learning Assessment Dr. Karen CONZETT
19 Director of Security Mr. Kristopher SCHMIDT
09 Director of Institutional Research Mr. Kurt FOLKENDT

*Board of Regents, State of Iowa (D)

11260 Aurora Avenue, Urbandale IA 50322-7405
County: Polk FICE Identification: 033443
Telephone: (515) 281-3934 Carnegie Class: N/A
FAX Number: (515) 281-6420
URL: www.regents.iowa.gov

01 Executive Director Mr. Bob DONLEY
05 Chief Academic Officer Dr. Diana GONZALEZ
10 Chief Business Officer Mrs. Patrice M. SAYRE
43 General Counsel Mr. Thomas A. EVANS

*Iowa State University (E)

Ames IA 50011-0002
County: Story FICE Identification: 001869
Unit ID: 153603
Telephone: (515) 294-4111 Carnegie Class: RU/VH
FAX Number: (515) 294-2592 Calendar System: Semester
URL: www.iastate.edu
Established: 1858 Annual Undergrad Tuition & Fees (In-State): $7,726
Enrollment: 29,887 Coed
Affiliation or Control: State IRS Status: 501(c)3
Highest Offering: Doctorate
Program: Liberal Arts And General; Teacher Preparatory; Professional
Accreditation: NH, BUS, BUSA, CIDA, COPSY, CS, DIETD, DIETI, ENG, FOR, IPSY, JOUR, LSAR, #MFCD, MUS, NAIT, PLNG, SPAA, VET

02 President Dr. Steven LEATH
100 Assoc VP/Chief of Staff Mr. Miles LACKEY
05 Sr Vice President and Provost Dr. Jonathan A. WICKERT
10 Sr Vice Pres for Business & Finance Mr. Warren R. MADDEN
32 Sr Vice Pres for Student Affairs Dr. Thomas L. HILL
46 Vice President Research/Econ Dev Dr. Sharron S. QUISENBERRY
56 Vice Pres Extension/Outreach Dr. Cathann A. KRESS
24 Vice Provost Info Technology & CIO Dr. James A. DAVIS
20 Associate Provost Academic Programs Dr. David K. HOLGER
28 Assoc Prov Acad Pers/Chief Div Off Dr. Dawn BRATSCH-PRINCE
21 Associate Vice President/Univ Sec Ms. Pam ELLIOTT CAIN
18 Assoc Vice Pres Facilities Mr. David J. MILLER
15 Assoc Vice Pres Human Resources Mr. David P. TRAINOR
38 Asst VP for Counseling Service Dr. Terry W. MASON
04 Sr Policy Adv to the President Dr. Tahira K. HIRA
102 Int President of ISU Foundation Dr. Labh HIRA
29 President of Alumni Association Mr. Jeffrey W. JOHNSON
37 Director of Financial Aid Ms. Roberta L. JOHNSON
06 Registrar Ms. Laura DOERING
07 Int Director of Admissions Mr. Phil CAFFREY
22 In Director of Equal Opp/Diversity Ms. Jessica STOLEE
08 Dean of Library Services Ms. Olivia M. MADISON
09 Director of Institutional Research Dr. Gebre H. TESFAGIORGIS
19 Director of Public Safety Mr. Jerry D. STEWART
26 Director of University Relations Mr. John F. MCCARROLL
35 Dean of Students Dr. Pamela ANTHONY
23 Director of Student Health Ms. Michelle HENDRICKS
39 Director of Residence Dr. Peter D. ENGLIN
91 Associate CIO/Admin Info Systems Mr. Maury M. HOPE
25 Director of Sponsored Program Admin Ms. Rochelle ATHEY
41 Director of Athletics Mr. Jamie B. POLLARD
88 Director Ames Laboratory Dr. Alex H. KING
43 University Counsel Mr. Paul N. TANAKA
96 Director of Purchasing Ms. Nancy S. BROOKS
40 Director University Bookstore Ms. Rita M. PHILLIPS
58 Dean Graduate College Dr. David K. HOLGER
47 Dean College of Agriculture Dr. Wendy WINTERSTEEN
50 Int Dean College of Business Dr. Michael R. CRUM
48 Dean College of Design Mr. Luis C. RICO-GUTIERREZ
53 Dean College of Human Sciences Dr. Pamela WHITE
54 Int Dean College of Engineering Dr. Mufit AKINC
49 Dean Col of Lib Arts & Sciences Dr. Beate SCHMITTMANN
74 Dean College of Veterinary Medicine Dr. Lisa NOLAN

*University of Iowa (F)

Iowa City IA 52242-0001
County: Johnson FICE Identification: 001892
Unit ID: 153658
Telephone: (319) 335-3500 Carnegie Class: RU/VH
FAX Number: (319) 335-0807 Calendar System: Semester
URL: www.uiowa.edu
Established: 1847 Annual Undergrad Tuition & Fees (In-State): $8,057
Enrollment: 30,893 Coed
Affiliation or Control: State IRS Status: 501(c)3
Highest Offering: Doctorate
Program: Liberal Arts And General; Teacher Preparatory; Professional
Accreditation: NH, ANEST, ARCPA, AUD, BUS, BUSA, CACREP, CEA, CLPSY, COPSY, CORE, DANCE, DENT, DIETI, DMS, EMT, ENG, ENGR, HSA, IPSY, #JOUR, LAW, LIB, MED, MUS, NMT, NURSE, PERF, PH, PHAR, PLNG, PTA, RAD, RTT, SCPSY, SP, SW, THEA

02 President Dr. Sally MASON
05 Exec Vice President & Provost Dr. Patrick B. BUTLER
46 Vice President Research Dr. Jordan L. COHEN
10 VP Finance/Operations/Univ Treas Mr. Douglas K. TRUE
32 VP Student Life Dr. Thomas R. ROCKLIN
17 Vice President for Medical Affairs Dr. Jean E. ROBILLARD
102 Vice Pres University Foundation Mr. David R. DIERKS
26 VP Strategic Communication Mr. Tysen KENDIG
20 Associate Provost Faculty Dr. Tom W. RICE
51 Assoc Provost Continuing Education Dr. Chet S. RZONCA
28 Chief Diversity Officer/AP Dr. Georgina DODGE
88 Assoc Provost/Dean Univ College Dr. Beth INGRAM
45 Assoc Vice President Research Dr. Richard D. HICHWA
11 Assoc VP/Dir of Admin and Planning Mr. Donald J. SZESZYCKI
16 Assoc VP Finan/Univ Svcs/Dir HR Ms. Susan C. BUCKLEY
18 Assoc VP/Dir Facilities Management Mr. Donald J. GUCKERT
13 Assoc Vice President & CIO Mr. Steven R. FLEAGLE
23 Assoc VP/CEO Univ Hosp & Clinics Mr. Kenneth KATES
25 Executive Dir Sponsored Pgms Ms. Jennifer LASSNER
19 Asst VP/Director Public Safety Mr. Charles D. GREEN
85 Dean International Programs Dr. Downing THOMAS
43 VP Legal Affairs & Gen Coun Ms. Carroll REASONER
08 University Librarian Ms. Nancy L. BAKER
29 Exec Director Alumni Association Mr. Vincent C. NELSON
30 President University Foundation Ms. Lynette L. MARSHALL
07 Director Admissions Mr. Michael BARRON
37 Director Student Financial Aid Mr. Mark S. WARNER
06 Registrar Mr. Lawrence J. LOCKWOOD
36 Director Career Center Mr. David A. BAUMGARTNER
38 Director Univ Counseling Services Dr. Sam V. COCHRAN, III
39 Director Residence Services Mr. Von STANGE
41 Director Athletics Administration Mr. Gary BARTA
49 Dean Col of Liberal Arts & Sciences Dr. Chaden DJALALI
50 Dean College of Business Admin Dr. Sarah GARDIAL
52 Dean College of Dentistry Dr. David C. JOHNSEN
53 Dean College of Education Dr. Margaret CROCCO
54 Dean College of Engineering Dr. Alec SCRANTON
58 Dean Graduate College Dr. John C. KELLER
61 Dean College of Law Dr. Gail B. AGRAWAL
66 Dean College of Nursing Dr. Rita A. FRANTZ
67 Dean College of Pharmacy Dr. Donald E. LETENDRE
69 Dean College of Public Health Dr. Susan CURRY
63 Interim Dean College of Medicine Dr. Donna HAMMOND
04 Special Assistant to President Dr. Thomas K. DEAN
22 Dir Equal Opportunity/Diversity Ms. Jennifer A. MODESTOU
86 Director State Relations Mr. Keith SAUNDERS
40 Director University Bookstore Mr. George E. HERBERT
96 Director Purchasing Ms. Deborah J. ZUMBACH
92 Director Honors Program Dr. Art L. SPISAK
87 Director Summer Session Dr. Chet RZONCA
24 Manager Audiovisual Center Mr. Daniel G. LIND
35 Dean of Students Dr. David L. GRADY

*University of Northern Iowa (G)

1227 W 27th Street, Cedar Falls IA 50614-0001
County: Black Hawk FICE Identification: 001890
Unit ID: 154095
Telephone: (319) 273-2311 Carnegie Class: Master's L
FAX Number: (319) 273-2885 Calendar System: Semester
URL: www.uni.edu
Established: 1876 Annual Undergrad Tuition & Fees (In-State): $7,635
Enrollment: 13,168 Coed
Affiliation or Control: State IRS Status: 501(c)3
Highest Offering: Doctorate
Program: Liberal Arts And General; Teacher Preparatory
Accreditation: NH, BUS, CACREP, CEA, ENGT, MUS, NAIT, NRPA, SP, SW

02 President Dr. Benjamin J. ALLEN
05 Executive Vice President & Provost Dr. Gloria J. GIBSON
32 Vice Pres for Student Affairs Dr. Terrence HOGAN
10 VP Administration/Financial Svcs Mr. Michael A. HAGER
18 Assoc VP for Facilities Management Mr. Morris E. MIKKELSEN
04 Spec Asst to Pres for Board/Gov Rel Dr. Patricia L. GEADELMANN
26 Exec Director University Relations Mr. James O'CONNOR
39 Int Executive Director of Residence Ms. Carol PETERSEN
20 Assoc Provost for Academic Affairs Dr. Michael J. LICARI
13 Chief Information Officer Dr. Shashidhar KAPARTHI
62 Interim Dean of Library Services Ms. Katherine MARTIN
06 Registrar Mr. Philip L. PATTON
37 Director of Financial Aid Ms. Joyce MORROW
15 Int Dir Human Resource Services Ms. Michelle C. BYERS
36 Director of Career Services Mr. Robert J. FREDERICK
83 Int Dean Col Social/Behav Science Dr. Brenda BASS
53 Dean College of Education Dr. Dwight C. WATSON
49 Dean Col Humanities/Arts & Science Dr. Joel HAACK
51 Dean Cont Educ/Special Programs Dr. Kent M. JOHNSON
50 Dean College Business Admin Dr. Farzad MOUSSAVI
35 Dean of Students Dr. Leslie K. WILLIAMS
07 Director of Admissions Ms. Christie KANGAS
10 Controller/Secretary/Treasurer Mr. Gary B. SHONTZ
38 Counseling Center Director Dr. David C. TOWLE

22 Asst to Pres Compliance/Equity Mgmt .. Ms. Leah K. GUTKNECHT
41 Athletic Director ... Mr. Troy A. DANNEN
21 Director of Business Operations ... Ms. Kelly A. FLEGE

Briar Cliff University (A)

3303 Rebecca Street, Sioux City IA 51104-2100
County: Woodbury FICE Identification: 001846
Unit ID: 152992
Telephone: (712) 279-5321 Carnegie Class: Bac/Diverse
FAX Number: (712) 279-5410 Calendar System: 4/1/4
URL: www.briarcliff.edu
Established: 1929 Annual Undergrad Tuition & Fees: $25,642
Enrollment: 1,185 Coed
Affiliation or Control: Roman Catholic IRS Status: 501(c)3
Highest Offering: Master's
Program: Liberal Arts And General; Teacher Preparatory; Professional
Accreditation: NH, NURSE, SW

01 President ... Mrs. Beverly A. WHARTON
05 Vice President Academic Affairs ... Dr. William MANGAN
10 Vice President Finance & Treasurer ... Mrs. Beth GRIGSBY
30 Vice Pres Institutional Advancement ... Mr. Craig MCGARRY
84 Vice Pres Enrollment Management ... Mrs. Sharisue WILCOXON
32 Vice President Student Development ... Mr. Steve JANOWIAK
06 Registrar ... Mrs. Deidre ENGEL
08 Librarian/Dir Information Services ... Ms. Debora ROBERTSON
14 Director Computer Center ... Ms. Leah WARD
29 Director Alumni Relations ... Ms. Suzy HOEVET
36 Director Career Development ... Ms. Nancy MCGUIRE
37 Director Financial Aid ... Mr. Robert PIECHOTA
40 Director Bookstore ... Ms. Nancy WATSON
41 Athletic Director ... Mr. Steve GAST
42 Director Campus Ministry ... Sr. Janet MAY
18 Director Physical Plant ... Mr. Eric HOLMQUIST
26 Director Marketing & Communications ... Ms. Paula DAMON
44 Director Gift Planning ... Mr. Mike JORGENSEN
07 Director of Admissions ... Mr. Brian EBEN
15 Director Human Resources ... Mrs. JoAnn PETERSON
39 Director Residence Life ... Mr. Dave ARENS
38 Director Student Counseling ... Ms. Laurel MEINE
09 Director of Institutional Research ... Ms. Deidre ENGEL

Brown Mackie College-Quad Cities (B)

2119 East Kimberly Road, Bettendorf IA 52722
County: Scott Identification: 666792
Unit ID: 373085
Telephone: (563) 344-1500 Carnegie Class: Assoc/PrivFP
FAX Number: (563) 344-1501 Calendar System: Other
URL: www.brownmackie.edu
Established: N/A Annual Undergrad Tuition & Fees: $11,124
Enrollment: 311 Coed
Affiliation or Control: Proprietary IRS Status: Proprietary
Highest Offering: Baccalaureate
Program: Occupational; 2-Year Principally Bachelor's Creditable; Business Emphasis
Accreditation: ACICS

01 President ... Taylor BRACEY
07 Senior Director of Admissions ... Vacant
05 Dean of Academic Affairs ... Greg SMITH

Buena Vista University (C)

610 W Fourth Street, Storm Lake IA 50588-1798
County: Buena Vista FICE Identification: 001847
Unit ID: 153001
Telephone: (712) 749-2351 Carnegie Class: Bac/Diverse
FAX Number: (712) 749-2037 Calendar System: 4/1/4
URL: www.bvu.edu
Established: 1891 Annual Undergrad Tuition & Fees: $28,314
Enrollment: 1,002 Coed
Affiliation or Control: Presbyterian Church (U.S.A.) IRS Status: 501(c)3
Highest Offering: Master's
Program: Liberal Arts And General; Teacher Preparatory
Accreditation: NH, SW, @TEAC

01 President ... Dr. Frederick V. MOORE
04 Assistant to the President ... Ms. Donna L. SCHONEBOOM
05 VP Academic Affairs/Dean of Faculty ... Dr. David R. EVANS
10 Vice President Business Services ... Ms. Elizabeth MERTEN
84 Vice Pres for Enrollment Management ... Mr. Michael FRANTZ
32 VP Student Affairs/Dean Students ... Dr. Meg MCKEON
30 Vice Pres for Inst Advancement ... Mr. Kenneth L. CONVERSE
81 Dean School of Science ... Mr. Ben DONATH
50 Dean HWS School of Business ... Dr. Ashok SUBRAMANIAN
53 Dean School of Education ... Dr. Paul THEOBALD
60 Dean School Communication & Arts . Dr. Michael D. WHITLATCH
83 Dean School Social Sci/Phil/ Relig ... Dr. Dixee BARTHOLOMEW-FEIS
20 Associate Dean of Faculty ... Dr. Peter K. STEINFELD
20 AVP Acad Affs/Dn Graduate/Prof Stds ... Dr. Susan KALSOW
06 Registrar ... Ms. Nila HOUSKA
07 Director of Admissions ... Ms. Bridget KURKOWSKI
15 Human Resources Manager ... Ms. Beth MCNALLY
08 University Librarian ... Mr. James R. KENNEDY
27 Dir University Marketing & Comm ... Ms. Jennifer FELTON
29 Director of Alumni Rels/Annual Fund ... Ms. Amy J. JONES
13 Managing Director Univ Info Svcs ... Vacant
18 Director of Physical Plant ... Mr. Keith E. SCHMIDT

36 Director of Career Services ... Ms. Carol J. LYTLE
37 Director of Financial Assistance ... Ms. Leanne VALENTINE
28 Director of Intercultural Programs ... Mr. Yorgun MARCEL
41 Athletic Director ... Ms. Christyn ABARAY
42 Chaplain ... Rev. Ken MEISSNER
19 Director of Campus Security ... Mr. Mark KIRKHOLM
38 Director of Counseling Services ... Ms. Mandy BOOTHBY
09 Institutional Researcher ... Mr. James E. HEWETT
96 Purchasing Administrator ... Ms. Tanya LANDGRAF

Central College (D)

812 University, Pella IA 50219-1999
County: Marion FICE Identification: 001850
Unit ID: 153108
Telephone: (641) 628-9000 Carnegie Class: Bac/A&S
FAX Number: (641) 628-5316 Calendar System: Semester
URL: www.central.edu
Established: 1853 Annual Undergrad Tuition & Fees: $29,490
Enrollment: 1,604 Coed
Affiliation or Control: Reformed Church In America IRS Status: 501(c)3
Highest Offering: Baccalaureate
Program: Liberal Arts And General; Teacher Preparatory; Professional
Accreditation: NH, MUS

01 President ... Dr. Mark L. PUTNAM
05 VP Academic Affairs/Dean of Faculty ... Dr. Mary M. STREY
30 Vice President Advancement ... Mr. David B. SUTPHEN
84 Vice Pres Enrollment Management ... Mrs. Carol WILLIAMSON
32 Vice Pres Student Development ... Dr. Peggy FITCH
10 Vice Pres for Finance & Admin ... Ms. Margaret TUNGSETH
20 Director of Academic Resources ... Mr. Eric JONES
35 Dean of Students ... Mr. Charles STREY
07 Director of Admission ... Mr. Chevy FREIBURGER
38 Director of Counseling ... Ms. Michelle KELLAR
39 Director of Residence Life ... Ms. Melissa SHARKEY
08 Director of Library ... Mrs. Natalie N. HUTCHINSON
88 Associate Dean for Global Education ... Ms. Lyn R. ISAACSON
36 Director of Career Center ... Mrs. Patricia JOACHIM KITZMAN
29 Director of Alumni Relations ... Ms. Ann VAN HEMERT
37 Director Financial Aid ... Mr. Wayne DILLE
104 Manager On-Campus Rels/Study Abroad ... Mr. Brian ZYLSTRA
13 Chief Information Officer ... Vacant
90 Director of Academic Computing ... Ms. Debra BRUXVOORT
42 Chaplain ... Rev. Joe BRUMMEL
44 Director Planned Giving ... Mr. Don MORRISON
15 Director of Human Resources ... Ms. Gena GARBER
41 Interim Athletics Director ... Mr. Eric VAN KLEY
18 Dir Facilities Planning/Management ... Mr. Mike LUBBERDEN
28 Director of Intercultural Life ... Mr. Brandyn WOODARD

Clarke University (E)

1550 Clarke Drive, Dubuque IA 52001-3198
County: Dubuque FICE Identification: 001852
Unit ID: 153126
Telephone: (563) 588-6300 Carnegie Class: Bac/Diverse
FAX Number: (563) 588-6789 Calendar System: Semester
URL: www.clarke.edu
Established: 1843 Annual Undergrad Tuition & Fees: $26,950
Enrollment: 1,232 Coed
Affiliation or Control: Roman Catholic IRS Status: 501(c)3
Highest Offering: Doctorate
Program: Liberal Arts And General; Teacher Preparatory; Professional
Accreditation: NH, MUS, NURSE, PTA, @SW

01 President ... Dr. Joanne M. BURROWS, SC
04 Exec Admin Assistant to President ... Ms. Linda J. LAUFENBERG
05 Provost/Vice Pres Academic Affs ... Dr. Joan LINGEN, BVM
30 Vice Pres Institutional Advancement ... Mr. Bill BIEBUYCK
32 Vice President Student Life ... Ms. Kate ZANGER
10 Vice President Business & Finance ... Ms. Deanna MCCORMICK
84 Vice President Enrollment Mgmt ... Dr. Beth TRIPLETT
51 Director Adult & Continuing Educ ... Mr. Scott SCHNEIDER
06 Registrar ... Ms. Kristi BAGSTAD
08 Director of Library ... Ms. Susanne LEIBOLD
20 Academic Dean of Undergraduate Stds ... Dr. Graciela CANEIRO-LIVINGSTON
20 Academic Dean of Graduate Studies ... Vacant
37 Director of Financial Aid ... Ms. Amy NORTON
26 Exec Director of Marketing & Comm ... Vacant
14 Director of Computer Center ... Ms. Karen GERHARD
18 Director of Facilities ... Mr. Brian SCHULTES
38 Dir of Counseling/Career Services ... Ms. Lorie MURPHY-FREEBOLIN
15 Director of Human Resources ... Ms. Megan LUCAS
41 Director of Athletics ... Mr. Curt LONG
42 Director of Campus Ministry ... Ms. Amy GOLM, BVM
40 Director of the Bookstore ... Mr. James SPAULDING
23 Director of Health Services ... Ms. Julie BURGMEIER
90 Director of Academic Support Center ... Mr. Brian GOMOLL
07 Director of Admissions ... Ms. Emily KRUSE
44 Director of Development ... Ms. Wendy SCARDINO
09 Director of Institutional Research ... Mr. Glen LANTZ
29 Manager of Alumni Relations Events ... Ms. Katie BAHL
85 International Students Advisor ... Ms. Evelyn NADEAU

Coe College (F)

1220 1st Avenue, NE, Cedar Rapids IA 52402-5092
County: Linn FICE Identification: 001854
Unit ID: 153144
Telephone: (319) 399-8000 Carnegie Class: Bac/A&S
FAX Number: (319) 399-8830 Calendar System: Semester
URL: www.coe.edu
Established: 1851 Annual Undergrad Tuition & Fees: $34,220
Enrollment: 1,378 Coed
Affiliation or Control: Independent Non-Profit IRS Status: 501(c)3
Highest Offering: Master's
Program: Liberal Arts And General; Teacher Preparatory; Professional
Accreditation: NH, MUS, NURSE

01 President ... Dr. James R. PHIFER
05 Vice Pres Acad Affs/Dean of Faculty ... Dr. Marie BAEHR
11 Vice President Admin/Enrollment ... Mr. Michael L. WHITE
32 Vice President Student Affairs ... Mr. Lou W. STARK
30 Vice President Advancement ... Mr. Richard E. MEISTERLING
21 Controller ... Mr. Richard E. RHEINSCHMIDT
07 Dean of Admission ... Ms. Julie STAKER
06 Registrar ... Dr. Evelyn J. MOORE
08 Director Library Services ... Ms. Jill JACK
29 Director Alumni Programs ... Ms. Jean A. JOHNSON
09 Director of Institutional Research ... Dr. Wendy L. DUNN
26 Dir of Marketing/Public Relations ... Mr. Rod PRITCHARD
37 Director of Financial Aid ... Ms. Barbara HOFFMAN
20 Associate Dean ... Dr. Terry MCNABB
35 Dean of Students ... Mr. Erik ALBINSON
85 International Student Advisor ... Ms. Deanna L. JOBE
42 Chaplain ... Rev. Kristin E. HUTSON
23 Director of Health Services ... Ms. Melinda S. BROKAW
41 Director of Athletics ... Mr. John M. CHANDLER
18 Director of Physical Plant ... Ms. Lisa CIHA
36 Career Services Coordinator ... Ms. Michelle MCILLECE
36 Dir of Internships/Career Services ... Ms. Diana R. PATTEN

Cornell College (G)

600 First Street SW, Mount Vernon IA 52314-1098
County: Linn FICE Identification: 001856
Unit ID: 153162
Telephone: (319) 895-4000 Carnegie Class: Bac/A&S
FAX Number: (319) 895-4492 Calendar System: Other
URL: www.cornellcollege.edu
Established: 1853 Annual Undergrad Tuition & Fees: $42,605
Enrollment: 1,197 Coed
Affiliation or Control: United Methodist IRS Status: 501(c)3
Highest Offering: Baccalaureate
Program: Liberal Arts And General; Teacher Preparatory
Accreditation: NH

01 President ... Mr. Jonathan BRAND
05 VP Acad Affairs/Dean of College ... Dr. R. Joseph DIEKER
10 Vice President Business Affairs ... Ms. Karen MERCER
84 Interim VP for Enrollment ... Ms. Sharon GRICE
32 Vice President Student Affairs ... Mr. John W. HARP
44 Interim VP Alumni Advancement ... Ms. Ruth MILLER
04 Special Asst to the President ... Dr. James W. BROWN
35 Dean of Students ... Dr. Heidi LEVINE
20 Associate Dean of the College ... Dr. Gayle LUCK
09 Director of Institutional Research ... Dr. Becki S. ELKINS
37 Director of Student Financial Asst ... Ms. Cindi P. REINTS
06 Registrar ... Ms. Jonna HIGGINS-FREESE
08 College Librarian ... Mr. Paul WAELCHLI
29 Director of Alumni Programs ... Ms. Lisa C. WHITE
30 Director College Advancement Svc ... Ms. Jennifer BOETTGER
27 Director of College Communications ... Ms. Dee A. REXROAT
96 Director of Purchasing/Admin Svcs ... Ms. Lisa M. LARSON
42 Chaplain ... Ms. Catherine M. QUEHL-ENGEL
22 Affirmative Action Officer ... Ms. Vickie L. FARMER
41 Athletics Director ... Mr. John T. COCHRANE
18 Director of Facilities ... Mr. Joel C. MILLER
36 Director Career Engagement Center ... Mr. R.J HOLMES
38 Director Student Counseling ... Dr. Brenda C. LOVSTUEN
15 Director of Human Resources ... Ms. Vickie L. FARMER
07 Senior Director of Admissions ... Ms. Sharon GRICE
28 Director of Intercultural Life ... Mr. Kenneth W. MORRIS
13 Director of Information Technology ... Mr. Mike J. CERVENY
40 Manager Bookstore ... Mr. Tyler WEDIG

Des Moines Area Community College (H)

2006 S Ankeny Boulevard, Ankeny IA 50023-3993
County: Polk FICE Identification: 007120
Unit ID: 153214
Telephone: (515) 964-6200 Carnegie Class: Assoc/Pub-R-L
FAX Number: N/A Calendar System: Semester
URL: www.dmacc.edu
Established: 1966 Annual Undergrad Tuition & Fees (In-District): $3,990
Enrollment: 25,425 Coed
Affiliation or Control: State/Local IRS Status: 501(c)3
Highest Offering: Associate Degree
Program: Occupational; 2-Year Principally Bachelor's Creditable
Accreditation: NH, FUSER, ACBSP, ACFEI, ADNUR, DA, DH, MAC, MLTAD, SURGT

01 President/CEO ... Dr. Rob DENSON
05 Exec Vice Pres Academic Affairs ... Dr. Kim LINDUSKA
10 Vice President Business Svcs ... Mr. Doug WILLIAMS
103 Vice Pres Cmty/Workforce Partnershp ... Dr. Mary CHAPMAN
13 Vice Pres Information Solutions ... Mr. Greg MARTIN
12 Provost Urban Campus ... Dr. Laura DOUGLAS
12 Provost Boone Campus ... Mr. Tom LEE
12 Provost Carroll Campus ... Mr. Steve SCHULZ
12 Provost Newton Campus ... Ms. Mary ENTZ
12 Provost West Campus ... Dr. Tony PAUSTIAN

32 Exec Dean Student Services .... Dr. Laurie WOLF
15 Executive Director Human Resources .... Dr. Sandy TRYON
102 Executive Director Foundation .... Ms. Tara CONNOLLY
09 Exec Director Inst Effectiveness .... Dr. Joe DEHART
51 Exec Dir Continuing Education .... Ms. Jane HERRMANN
50 Exec Dir Business Resources .... Ms. Kim DIDIER
84 Exec Dir Enrollment Management .... Mr. Michael LENTSCH
37 Director Financial Aid .... Ms. DeLores HAWKINS
26 Director of Marketing .... Mr. Todd JONES
25 Director Grants/Contracts .... Ms. Deb KOUA
06 Registrar .... Ms. Rachel ERKKILA
18 Chief Facilities/Physical Plant .... Mr. Mark BAETHKE
38 Director Student Development .... Ms. Wendy ROBINSON
96 Director of Purchasing .... Mr. Tim HAGER
27 Media Liaison .... Mr. Dan IVIS
70 Dean Sciences & Humanities .... Mr. Jim STICK
72 Dean Industrial & Technology .... Mr. Scott OCKEN
76 Dean Health Service & Science .... Ms. Sally SCHROEDER
50 Dean Business/Mgmt/Information Tech .... Mr. Drew GOCKEN
55 Dean Evening & Weekend College .... Mr. Jeff KELLY

Des Moines University (A)

3200 Grand Avenue, Des Moines IA 50312-4198
County: Polk FICE Identification: 001855
Unit ID: 154156
Telephone: (515) 271-1400 Carnegie Class: Spec/Med
FAX Number: (515) 271-1532 Calendar System: Other
URL: www.dmu.edu
Established: 1898 Annual Graduate Tuition & Fees: N/A
Enrollment: 1,862 Coed
Affiliation or Control: Independent Non-Profit IRS Status: 501(c)3
Highest Offering: First Professional Degree; No Undergraduates
Program: Professional
Accreditation: NH, ARCPA, OSTEO, PH, POD, PTA

01 President/CEO .... Dr. Angela L. WALKER FRANKLIN
05 Provost .... Dr. Karen P. MCLEAN
32 Vice President Student Services .... Ms. Mary Ann ZUG
30 Vice Pres for Advancement .... Ms. Susan HUPPERT
46 Vice President for Research .... Dr. Jeffrey GRAY
06 Registrar .... Ms. Kathy L. SCAGLIONE
08 Director of Library .... Mr. Larry MARQUARDT
15 Director of Human Resources .... Ms. Becky LADE
27 Chief Information Officer .... Ms. Carolyn WEAVER
37 Director of Financial Aid .... Ms. Mary PAYNE
18 Director of Facilities Management .... Mr. David MCNERNEY
19 Director University Services .... Mr. John BRUECKEN
88 Chief Compliance Officer .... Ms. Erika LINDEN
21 Chief Financial Officer .... Mr. Mark J. PEIFFER
69 Director Public Health Program .... Dr. Mary Mincer HANSEN
76 Director Healthcare Administration .... Dr. Carla STEBBINS
26 Director Marketing & Communication .... Ms. Kendall DILLON
38 Director Educational Support Svcs .... Ms. Lynn MARTIN
84 Director Enrollment Management .... Ms. Jamie REHMANN
76 Dean College Health Sciences .... Dr. Jodi CAHALAN
63 Dean Col Podiatric Medicine/Surg .... Dr. Robert YOHO
63 Dean Col Osteopathic Medicine/Surg .... Dr. Kendall REED
25 Director Sponsored Programs .... Ms. Kay COURTADE

† Tuition varies by program.

Divine Word College (B)

102 Jacoby Drive, SW, PO Box 380,
Epworth IA 52045-0380
County: Dubuque FICE Identification: 001858
Unit ID: 153241
Telephone: (563) 876-3353 Carnegie Class: Spec/Faith
FAX Number: (563) 876-3407 Calendar System: Semester
URL: www.dwci.edu
Established: 1918 Annual Undergrad Tuition & Fees: $12,000
Enrollment: 126 Male
Affiliation or Control: Roman Catholic IRS Status: 501(c)3
Highest Offering: Baccalaureate
Program: Religious Emphasis
Accreditation: NH

01 President .... Fr. Timothy A. LENCHAK
05 Academic Dean/Vice President .... Dr. Mathew KANJIRATHINKAL
10 Vice Pres for Finances/Fin Aid Dir .... Mr. Mark PASKER
07 Director Admissions/VP Recruitment .... Mr. Len UHAL
30 Development Director .... Mr. Terrance SYKORA
32 Dean of Students .... Rev. Khien LUU
08 Librarian .... Mr. Daniel BOICE
06 Registrar .... Mrs. Deborah HIRSCH
38 Counselor .... Mrs. Nan PECK
26 Public Relations Director .... Ms. Sandy WILGENBUSCH

Dordt College (C)

498 4th Avenue, NE, Sioux Center IA 51250-1697
County: Sioux FICE Identification: 001859
Unit ID: 153250
Telephone: (712) 722-6000 Carnegie Class: Bac/Diverse
FAX Number: (712) 722-1185 Calendar System: Semester
URL: www.dordt.edu
Established: 1955 Annual Undergrad Tuition & Fees: $25,100
Enrollment: 1,402 Coed
Affiliation or Control: Christian Reformed Church IRS Status: 501(c)3
Highest Offering: Master's
Program: 2-Year Principally Bachelor's Creditable; Liberal Arts And General; Teacher Preparatory
Accreditation: NH, ENG, NURSE, SW

01 President .... Dr. Erik HOEKSTRA
04 Assistant to the President .... Dr. Curtis J. TAYLOR
10 Vice President Business .... Mr. Arlan NEDERHOFF
30 Vice President College Advancement .... Mr. John BAAS
20 Assoc Provost/VP Student Services .... Dr. Bethany SCHUTTINGA
84 Exec Director Enrollment .... Mr. Dale ZEVENBERGEN
07 Executive Director Admissions .... Mr. Quentin VAN ESSEN
37 Director Financial Aid .... Mr. Michael EPEMA
06 Associate Provost/Registrar .... Mr. James BOS
88 Dean for Research and Scholarship .... Dr. John H. KOK
20 Assoc Provost/Dean for Cur & Instr .... Dr. Leah ZUIDEMA
58 Director Graduate Education .... Dr. Timothy VAN SOELEN
36 Director of Career Services .... Mr. Chris DEJONG
26 Marketing and Public Relations .. Ms. Sonya JONGSMA KNAUSS
18 Director Physical Plant .... Mr. Stan OORDT
39 Director Resident Life .... Mr. Robert TAYLOR
42 Campus Pastor .... Rev. Aaron BAART
41 Director of Athletics .... Mr. Glenn BOUMA
40 Director Bookstore/Purchasing .... Ms. Lora DEVRIES
44 Director of Planned Giving .... Mr. Dave VANDER WERF
29 Director Alumni/Church Relations .... Mr. Wes FOPMA
15 Director Human Resources .... Mrs. Sue DROOG
96 Director of Purchasing .... Mr. Fred HAAN
91 Director of Computer Services .... Mr. Brian VAN DONSELAAR
44 Development Programs Coordinator .... Ms. Barbara J. MELLEMA
08 Director of Library Services .... Ms. Sheryl S. TAYLOR
23 Director of Health Sciences .... Ms. Pamela L. HULSTEIN
88 Director Academic Skills Center .... Ms. Pamala S. DE JONG

Drake University (D)

2507 University Avenue, Des Moines IA 50311-4505
County: Polk FICE Identification: 001860
Unit ID: 153269
Telephone: (515) 271-2011 Carnegie Class: Master's L
FAX Number: (515) 271-3016 Calendar System: Semester
URL: www.drake.edu
Established: 1881 Annual Undergrad Tuition & Fees: $29,410
Enrollment: 5,384 Coed
Affiliation or Control: Independent Non-Profit IRS Status: 501(c)3
Highest Offering: Doctorate
Program: Liberal Arts And General; Teacher Preparatory; Professional
Accreditation: NH, ART, BUS, BUSA, CORE, JOUR, LAW, MUS, PHAR

01 President .... Dr. David E. MAXWELL
05 Provost .... Dr. Deneese JONES
10 Vice President Business & Finance .... Ms. Deborah NEWSOM
30 Vice Pres Alumni and Development .... Mr. John SMITH
07 Vice Pres Admissions/Financial Aid .... Mr. Tom DELAHUNT
20 Associate Provost of Curriculum .... Mr. Art SANDERS
09 Associate Provost .... Dr. Raylene ROSPOND
32 Interim Vice Prov Student Affairs .... Ms. Melissa STURM-SMITH
35 Dean of Students .... Dr. Sentwali BAKARI
15 Human Resources Director .... Ms. Venessa MACRO
27 Chief Tech Information Officer .... Dr. Ann KOVALCHICK
04 Executive Asst to Pres/Secy of Univ .... Ms. Linda S. RYAN
18 Director Facility Services .... Ms. Jolene SCHMIDT
06 Director of Student Records .... Mr. Kevin P. MOENKHAUS
08 Dean Cowles Library .... Mr. Rodney N. HENSHAW
85 Vice Provost of Intl Programs .... Dr. Christa OLSON
91 Director Campus Information Svcs .... Ms. Angela EMBREE
19 Chief Campus Security Services .... Mr. Hans M. HANSON
26 Exec Dir Marketing & Communications .... Ms. Debra LUKEHART
29 Alumni/Parent Programs .... Mr. Blake CAMPBELL
49 Dean Arts & Sciences .... Dr. Joseph LENZ
53 Dean School Education .... Dr. Janet M. MCMAHILL
61 Dean Law School .... Mr. Allan VESTAL
50 Dean Business/Public Administration .... Mr. Charles EDWARDS, JR.
67 Dean Pharmacy/Health Science .... Dr. Raylene ROSPOND
60 Dean Journ/Mass Communications .. Mr. Charles EDWARDS, JR.
44 Director of Planned Giving .... Ms. Sarah PRITCHARD
88 Assistant Dean of Students .... Vacant
41 Director Intercollegiate Athletics .... Ms. Sandy Hatfield CLUBB
37 Director Financial Aid .... Ms. Susan K. LADD
38 Director University Counseling Ctr .... Dr. Mark KLOBERDANZ
92 Assistant Director Honors Program .... Ms. Charlene SKIDMORE
94 Director Women's Studies .... Dr. Nancy REINCKE
31 Dir Community Outreach/Development .... Mr. Dolph PULLIAM
39 Director Office of Residence Life .... Ms. Lorissa LIEURANCE

*Eastern Iowa Community College District (E)

306 W River Drive, Davenport IA 52801-1221
County: Scott FICE Identification: 004075
Unit ID: 153311
Telephone: (563) 336-3300 Carnegie Class: N/A
FAX Number: (563) 336-3350
URL: www.eicc.edu

01 Chancellor .... Dr. Donald S. DOUCETTE
05 Vice Chancellor for Instruction .... Dr. Jeff ARMSTRONG
30 Exec Dir Resource Development .... Dr. Ellen KABAT LENSCH
103 Vice Chanc Workforce Dev/Cont Educ .... Dr. Nancy KOTHENBEUTEL
31 Exec Dir Community & Econ Devel .... Mr. Mark KAPFER
26 Associate Director for Marketing .... Ms. Karen FARLEY
11 Exec Dir Administrative Services .... Ms. Lana J. DETTBARN
09 Dir Institutional Effectiveness .... Ms. Laurie R. HANSON
27 Associate Director Communications .... Mr. Alan CAMPBELL

*Clinton Community College (F)

1000 Lincoln Boulevard, Clinton IA 52732-6299
County: Clinton FICE Identification: 001853
Unit ID: 153135
Telephone: (563) 244-7001 Carnegie Class: Not Classified
FAX Number: (563) 244-7107 Calendar System: Semester
URL: www.eicc.edu
Established: 1966 Annual Undergrad Tuition & Fees (In-District): $131
Enrollment: 1,972 Coed
Affiliation or Control: State/Local IRS Status: 501(c)3
Highest Offering: Associate Degree
Program: Occupational; 2-Year Principally Bachelor's Creditable
Accreditation: &NH

02 President .... Dr. Karen VICKERS
05 Dean of the College .... Mr. Ron SERPLISS
32 Dean of Student Development .... Ms. Lisa MILLER
102 Asst to Pres/Exec Dir Sharar Found .... Ms. Ann EISENMAN
04 Assistant to President/Admin .... Ms. Deborah RICHTER

*Muscatine Community College (G)

152 Colorado Street, Muscatine IA 52761-5396
County: Muscatine FICE Identification: 001882
Unit ID: 154040
Telephone: (563) 288-6001 Carnegie Class: Not Classified
FAX Number: (563) 288-6074 Calendar System: Semester
URL: www.eicc.edu
Established: 1929 Annual Undergrad Tuition & Fees (In-District): $131
Enrollment: 2,007 Coed
Affiliation or Control: State/Local IRS Status: 501(c)3
Highest Offering: Associate Degree
Program: Occupational; 2-Year Principally Bachelor's Creditable
Accreditation: &NH

02 President .... Mr. Bob ALLBEE
04 Assistant to the President .... Ms. Lisa WIEGEL
05 Dean of the College .... Dr. Gail SPIES
32 Dean of Student Development .... Ms. Shelly CRAM-RAHLF
31 Director Business/Industry Center .... Mr. Marvin SMITH
06 Registrar .... Ms. Robin MITCHELL
08 Library Specialist .... Ms. Nancy LUIKART

*Scott Community College (H)

500 Belmont Road, Bettendorf IA 52722-6804
County: Scott FICE Identification: 001885
Unit ID: 154314
Telephone: (563) 441-4001 Carnegie Class: Not Classified
FAX Number: (563) 441-4154 Calendar System: Semester
URL: www.eicc.edu
Established: 1966 Annual Undergrad Tuition & Fees (In-District): $131
Enrollment: 5,860 Coed
Affiliation or Control: State/Local IRS Status: 501(c)3
Highest Offering: Associate Degree
Program: Occupational; 2-Year Principally Bachelor's Creditable
Accreditation: &NH, DA, NDT, RAD

02 President .... Dr. Teresa A. PAPER
05 Dean of the College .... Vacant
32 Dean of Student Development/Affs .... Ms. Lisa BROWN
36 Dean Career Assistance Center .... Ms. Peg GARRISON
72 Dean Applied Technologies .... Ms. Janet COOGAN
49 Dean Arts & Sciences .... Dr. R. Andrew BURT
08 Librarian .... Ms. Michelle BAILEY
11 Asst to President Administration .... Mr. Matt SCHMIT
06 Registrar .... Mr. Arnold THODE
18 Chief Facilities/Physical Plant .... Mr. Ken MIROCHA
37 Director Student Financial Aid .... Ms. Jeannine INGELSON
36 Job Placement Specialist .... Mr. Wayne COLE

Emmaus Bible College (I)

2570 Asbury Road, Dubuque IA 52001-3096
County: Dubuque FICE Identification: 023289
Unit ID: 153302
Telephone: (563) 588-8000 Carnegie Class: Spec/Faith
FAX Number: (563) 588-1216 Calendar System: Semester
URL: www.emmaus.edu
Established: 1941 Annual Undergrad Tuition & Fees: $14,500
Enrollment: 249 Coed
Affiliation or Control: Independent Non-Profit IRS Status: 501(c)3
Highest Offering: Baccalaureate
Program: Liberal Arts And General; Teacher Preparatory; Professional
Accreditation: NH, BI

01 President .... Mr. Kenneth A. DAUGHTERS
11 VP for Administration & Finance .... Mr. Mark A. PRESSON
05 Vice President for Academic Affairs .... Mrs. Lisa L. BEATTY
32 VP for Student Development .... Mr. Jon W. GLOCK
88 Dean for Biblical Studies .... Dr. David J. MACLEOD
06 Registrar .... Mrs. Kathryn L. VAN DINE
08 Librarian .... Mr. John H. RUSH
37 Financial Aid Officer .... Mr. Steve C. SEEMAN
10 Controller .... Mr. Steve M. JENSEN
07 Enrollment Services Manager .... Mr. Israel CHAVEZ

Faith Baptist Bible College and Seminary (A)

1900 NW 4th Street, Ankeny IA 50023-2152
County: Polk FICE Identification: 007121
Unit ID: 153320
Telephone: (515) 964-0601 Carnegie Class: Spec/Faith
FAX Number: (515) 964-1638 Calendar System: Semester
URL: www.faith.edu
Established: 1921 Annual Undergrad Tuition & Fees: $15,020
Enrollment: 344 Coed
Affiliation or Control: Independent Non-Profit IRS Status: 501(c)3
Highest Offering: First Professional Degree
Program: Liberal Arts And General; Teacher Preparatory; Religious Emphasis
Accreditation: NH, BI

01 President .... Dr. James D. MAXWELL, III
05 VP for Academic Services .... Dr. Jeffery G. NEWMAN
73 Dean of Seminary .... Dr. Ernest SCHMIDT
10 VP for Business/CFO .... Mr. Daniel H. BJOKNE
30 VP for Advancement/Church Rels .... Mr. Eugene M. MATLOCK
34 Dean of Women .... Mrs. Sharon S. GUTWEIN
32 Dean of Students .... Mr. Shon R. LUNDBERG
33 Dean of Men .... Mr. Lance A. AUGSBURGER
27 Director of Communications .... Mr. Don K. ANDERSON
06 Registrar .... Mr. David L. STOUT
37 Director Student Financial Aid .... Mr. Breck H. APPELL
08 Head Librarian .... Dr. John HARTOG, II

Graceland University (B)

1 University Place, Lamoni IA 50140-1699
County: Decatur FICE Identification: 001866
Unit ID: 153366
Telephone: (641) 784-5000 Carnegie Class: Master's L
FAX Number: (641) 784-5480 Calendar System: 4/1/4
URL: www.graceland.edu
Established: 1895 Annual Undergrad Tuition & Fees: $22,680
Enrollment: 2,318 Coed
Affiliation or Control: Other IRS Status: 501(c)3
Highest Offering: Doctorate
Program: Liberal Arts And General; Teacher Preparatory
Accreditation: NH, TED

01 President .... Dr. John SELLARS
05 Vice Pres Acad Affs/Dean of Faculty .... Dr. Parris R. WATTS
09 VP Institutional Effectiveness .... Dr. Kathleen M. CLAUSON
10 Vice Pres Business & Admin Svcs .... Ms. Janice TIFFANY
32 Dean of Students .... Mrs. Marian KILLPACK
84 Vice Pres Enrollment/Dean Admission .... Mr. Kirk BJORLAND
30 Vice Pres Institutional Advancement .... Mr. Kelly EVERETT
51 Director for Graduate/Continuing Ed .... Mr. Paul BINNICKER
39 Director of Residence Life .... Ms. Deb SKINNER
06 Registrar .... Mrs. M. Joyce LIGHTHILL
08 Librarian .... Mr. Francis ACLAND
29 Director of Alumni Relations .... Mr. Paul DAVIS
36 Director Career/Acad/CAP Couns Ctr .... Mrs. Michele MAGUIRE-BECK
23 Director Health Service .... Mrs. Benna EASTER
18 Director Facility Services .... Mr. Kurt REMMENGA
15 Director Human Resources .... Mrs. Ondrea DORY
26 Chief Public Relations Officer .... Mr. Randy MELINE
04 Executive Asst to President .... Ms. Jodi L. SEYMOUR
41 Athletic Director .... Mr. Jeff FALKNER
44 Director of Annual Fund/Stewardship .. Mrs. Peggy STURDEVANT
85 Director International Programs .... Ms. Diana JONES
86 Director Government Relations .... Dr. Tom MORAIN
50 Dean School of Business .... Dr. Steven ANDERS
53 Dean School of Education .... Dr. Tammy EVERETT
49 Dean Col Liberal Arts/Sciences .... Dr. Gary HEISSERER
66 Dean School of Nursing .... Dr. Claudia HORTON
07 Director of Admissions .... Mr. Kevin BROWN

Grand View University (C)

1200 Grandview Avenue, Des Moines IA 50316-1599
County: Polk FICE Identification: 001867
Unit ID: 153375
Telephone: (515) 263-2800 Carnegie Class: Bac/Diverse
FAX Number: (515) 263-6095 Calendar System: Semester
URL: www.grandview.edu
Established: 1896 Annual Undergrad Tuition & Fees: $21,826
Enrollment: 2,229 Coed
Affiliation or Control: Evangelical Lutheran Church In America
IRS Status: 501(c)3
Highest Offering: Master's
Program: Liberal Arts And General; Professional
Accreditation: NH, NURSE

01 President .... Mr. Kent L. HENNING
04 Executive Asst to the President .... Mr. Lucas J. CASEY
05 Provost/Vice Pres Academic Affairs ... Dr. Mary Elizabeth STIVERS
10 Vice Pres Administration & Finance .... Mr. Adam J. VOIGTS
30 Vice President Advancement .... Mr. William H. BURMA
84 Vice Pres Enrollment Management .... Ms. Debbie M. BARGER
26 Vice Pres Marketing/Communications .... Ms. Carol M. BAMFORD
32 Vice President Student Affairs .... Dr. Jay B. PRESCOTT
37 Director Financial Aid .... Ms. Michele A. DUNNE
20 Special Assistant to the Provost .... Ms. Pamela M. MILLOY
51 Acting Dean Graduate/Adult Programs .... Dr. Patricia A. RINKE
35 Associate VP for Student Affairs .... Mr. Jason K. BAUER
06 Registrar .... Ms. Debbie K. GANNON
42 Senior Campus Pastor .... Rev. Russell L. LACKEY
09 Director Inst Planning/Research .... Ms. Debbie M. BARGER
36 Director Career Center .... Ms. Susan M. STEARNS
91 Vice President Information Svcs/CIO .... Mr. Tim T. WHEELDON
08 Director of the Library .... Ms. Pamela D. REES
40 Director Bookstore & Campus Svcs .... Mr. Michael D. SHUPP
07 Director of Admissions .... Ms. Diane S. JOHNSON
18 Director Buildings & Grounds .... Ms. Kim I. BUTLER
38 Director Leadership & Counseling .... Mr. Kent A. SCHORNACK
28 Dir Multicultural & Cmty Outreach .... Mr. Alex H. PIEDRAS
41 Athletic Director .... Mr. Troy A. PLUMMER
15 Human Resources Manager .... Ms. Erica L. KLUVER

Grinnell College (D)

1121 Park Street, Grinnell IA 50112-1690
County: Poweshiek FICE Identification: 001868
Unit ID: 153384
Telephone: (641) 269-4000 Carnegie Class: Bac/A&S
FAX Number: (641) 269-3408 Calendar System: Semester
URL: www.grinnell.edu
Established: 1846 Annual Undergrad Tuition & Fees: $41,004
Enrollment: 1,662 Coed
Affiliation or Control: Independent Non-Profit IRS Status: 501(c)3
Highest Offering: Baccalaureate
Program: Liberal Arts And General; Teacher Preparatory
Accreditation: NH

01 President .... Raynard S. KINGTON
100 Special Assistant to the President .... Angela VOOS
05 Vice Pres Acad Affs/Dean of College .... Paula V. SMITH
26 Vice President College/Alumni Rels .... Beth HALLORAN
88 Chief Investment Officer .... David S. CLAY
32 Vice Pres Student Services .... W. Houston DOUGHARTY
88 Vice President of College Services .... John KALKBRENNER
10 Vice President for Finance/Treas .... Karen VOSS
20 Associate Dean of College .... Mark SCHNEIDER
20 Associate Dean of College .... Heather LOBBAN-VIRAVONG
07 VP Enroll/Dean Adm & Fin Aid .... Joseph P. BAGNOLI
30 Director of Development Operations .... Jacquelyn AANES
37 Director of Student Financial Aid .... Arnold A. WOODS, JR.
15 Director of Human Resources .... Kristin LOVIG
06 Registrar .... Cheryl CHASE
08 Librarian .... Richard FYFFE
29 Director of Alumni Relations .... Jayn CHANEY
14 Dir of Information Technology Svcs .... Vacant
09 Interim Assoc VP Analy/Inst Rsch .... James E. SWARTZ
85 Director Intl Student Services .... Karen K. EDWARDS
40 Manager/Bookstore .... Cassandra J. WHERRY
41 Athletic Director .... Greg WALLACE
23 Director of Health Service .... Deb SHILL
38 Assoc Dean/Dir Academic Advising .... Joyce STERN
18 Director Facilities Management .... Mark E. GODAR
19 Director of Safety & Security .... Stephen A. BRISCOE
42 Chaplain/Dean of Rel Life .... Deanna SHORB
102 Director Corp/Founda/Govt Rels .... Karen WIESE
39 Asst Dean/Director Residence Life .... Andrea CONNER
35 Dean of Students .... Travis GREENE
27 Director of Communication .... Jim REISCHE
31 Coord Community Service Center .... Deanna SHORB

Hamilton Technical College (E)

1011 E 53rd Street, Davenport IA 52807-2616
County: Scott FICE Identification: 012064
Unit ID: 153427
Telephone: (563) 386-3570 Carnegie Class: Spec/Tech
FAX Number: (563) 386-6756 Calendar System: Semester
URL: www.hamiltontechcollege.com
Established: 1969 Annual Undergrad Tuition & Fees: $11,025
Enrollment: 250 Coed
Affiliation or Control: Proprietary IRS Status: Proprietary
Highest Offering: Baccalaureate
Program: Occupational; Technical Emphasis
Accreditation: ACCSC

01 President .... Mrs. Maryanne HAMILTON

Hawkeye Community College (F)

Box 8015, Waterloo IA 50704-8015
County: Black Hawk FICE Identification: 004595
Unit ID: 153445
Telephone: (319) 296-2320 Carnegie Class: Assoc/Pub-R-L
FAX Number: (319) 296-2874 Calendar System: Semester
URL: www.hawkeyecollege.edu
Established: 1966 Annual Undergrad Tuition & Fees (In-District): $4,290
Enrollment: 6,238 Coed
Affiliation or Control: State/Local IRS Status: 501(c)3
Highest Offering: Associate Degree
Program: Occupational; 2-Year Principally Bachelor's Creditable
Accreditation: NH, DA, DH, MLTAD, @PTAA

01 President .... Dr. Linda A. ALLEN
05 Vice Pres Academic Affairs .... Dr. Samuel DOSUMU
10 Vice Pres Administration & Finance .... Mr. Dan GILLEN
30 Vice Pres Institutional Advancement .... Ms. Kathy A. FLYNN
102 Executive Director Foundation .... Ms. Peg A. BROWN
15 Exec Dir Human Resource Services .... Mr. John D. CLOPTON
81 Dean Math/Natural & Social Sciences .... Dr. Cynthia BOTTRELL
79 Dean Comm/Humanities/Educ/Fine Arts .... Ms. Laurel KLINKENBERG
75 Dean Applied Science/Eng Technology .... Mr. A. Ray BEETS
76 Dean Health Sciences .... Ms. Sarah TURNER
50 Dean Business & Public Services .... Mr. Bryan RENFRO
32 Dean of Students .... Ms. Nancy HENDERSON
07 Director Admissions & Recruitment .... Mr. Dave BALL
21 Director Business Services .... Ms. Denise BOUSKA
13 Director Communication/Info Systems .... Mr. Dan BONINE
62 Director Library Services .... Ms. Candace HAVELY
51 Director of Continuing Education .... Mr. Alan G. CLAUSEN
18 Director Plant & Facilities .... Ms. Lindsey NISSEN
06 Dir Student Records & Registration .... Ms. Patricia A. EAST
24 Director Teaching/Learning Services .... Ms. D.J CORSON
09 Director Institutional Research .... Ms. Connie BUHR
26 Director Public Relations/Mktg .... Ms. Mary Pat MOORE
28 Assoc Dir of Multicultural Affairs .... Mr. Quentin HART
35 Student Life Coordinator .... Ms. Stephanie CHERRY
44 Development Officer .... Ms. Karen GEBEL
101 Board Secretary .... Ms. Denise A. DUNN

Indian Hills Community College (G)

525 Grandview, Ottumwa IA 52501-1398
County: Wapello FICE Identification: 008403
Unit ID: 153472
Telephone: (641) 683-5111 Carnegie Class: Assoc/Pub-R-M
FAX Number: (641) 683-5184 Calendar System: Quarter
URL: www.ihcc.cc.ia.us
Established: 1966 Annual Undergrad Tuition & Fees (In-District): $4,320
Enrollment: 5,035 Coed
Affiliation or Control: State/Local IRS Status: 501(c)3
Highest Offering: Associate Degree
Program: Occupational; 2-Year Principally Bachelor's Creditable
Accreditation: NH, ACFEI, EMT, MLTAD, OTA, PTAA, RAD

01 President .... Dr. Jim LINDENMAYER
10 Chief Financial Officer .... Ms. Sue PIXLEY
05 Vice President Academic Affairs .... Dr. Marlene SPROUSE
04 Asst to Pres/College & Industry Rel .... Mr. Mick LAWSON
86 Asst to Pres/Govt Affs & Comm Rels .... Ms. Martha WICK
49 Executive Dean Arts & Sciences .... Ms. Darlas SHOCKLEY
103 Exec Dean Reg Workforce/Econ Dev .... Mr. Tom RUBEL
32 Dean Student Services .... Mr. Kelly CONRAD
76 Dean Health Occupations .... Ms. Jill BUDDE
72 Assoc Dean Advanced Technologies .... Mr. Tom RUBEL
12 Dean Centerville Campus .... Mr. Joe STARCEVICH
15 Director Human Resources .... Ms. Bonnie CAMPBELL
20 Dean Academic Services .... Dr. Lyvier LEFFLER
18 Director Maintenance .... Mr. Rick FOSDYCK
06 Registrar .... Ms. Gail LOCKRIDGE
41 Athletic Director .... Mr. Mike HAGEN
26 Director for Media/Public Rels .... Mr. Kevin PINK
37 Director Student Financial Aid .... Mr. Christopher BOWSER
88 Chair Aviation Programs .... Ms. Jane BERG

Inste Bible College (H)

2302 SW 3rd Street, Ankeny IA 50023-2453
County: Polk Identification: 666461
Telephone: (515) 289-9200 Carnegie Class: Not Classified
FAX Number: (515) 289-9201 Calendar System: Semester
URL: www.inste.edu
Established: 1982 Annual Undergrad Tuition & Fees: $2,024
Enrollment: 28 Coed
Affiliation or Control: Interdenominational IRS Status: 501(c)3
Highest Offering: Baccalaureate
Program: Liberal Arts And General; Religious Emphasis
Accreditation: DETC

01 President .... Dr. Nicholas VENDITTI
05 Vice President & Academic Dean .... Dr. Leona VENDITTI
20 Assistant Dean .... Rev. Victor COLÓN

Iowa Central Community College (I)

One Triton Circle, Fort Dodge IA 50501-5798
County: Webster FICE Identification: 001865
Unit ID: 153524
Telephone: (515) 576-7201 Carnegie Class: Assoc/Pub-R-M
FAX Number: (515) 576-7207 Calendar System: Semester
URL: www.iowacentral.edu
Established: 1966 Annual Undergrad Tuition & Fees (In-District): $4,320
Enrollment: 6,298 Coed
Affiliation or Control: Local IRS Status: 501(c)3
Highest Offering: Associate Degree
Program: Occupational; 2-Year Principally Bachelor's Creditable
Accreditation: NH, DH, MAC, MLTAD, RAD

01 President .... Dr. Daniel P. KINNEY
04 Assistant to the President .... Mrs. Karen L. LOMBARD
05 Vice President of Instruction .... Mr. David E. GROSLAND
32 Vice Pres Enroll Mgmt/Student Devel .... Mr. Thomas J. BENEKE
86 VP External Affairs/Govt Rels .... Mr. James B. KERSTEN
30 VP Development/Alumni Rels .... Mrs. Laurie M. HENDRICKS
10 Vice President of Business Affairs .... Mrs. Angela A. MARTIN
72 Dean Business & Ind Technology .... Mr. Neale J. ADAMS
66 Dean Health Sciences .... Ms. Trina J. STATON
49 Dean Liberal Arts & Sciences .... Mrs. Jennifer M. CONDON
106 Dean Distance Learning .... Mr. Timothy J. MARTIN
21 Director Business Office .... Mr. Luke J. GROVE

16 Director Human Resources ... Ms. Kimberly N. WHITMORE
15 Coordinator Human Resources ... Ms. Sandi J. PIEPER
06 Registrar ... Ms. Courtney A. KOPP
84 Director Enrollment Management ... Ms. Sara A. CONDON
37 Director Financial Aid ... Mrs. Darci M. BANGERT
09 Director Institutional Effectivenes ... Vacant
41 Director Intercollegiate Athletics ... Mr. Rick A. SANDQUIST
39 Director Housing ... Mr. Jeremy D. CONLEY
35 Coord Student Life & Activities ... Mr. Anthony E. ACKLIN
62 Director Library ... Mr. Dan C. SCHIEFELBEIN
18 Director Physical Facilities ... Mr. Troy A. BRANDT
12 Director Storm Lake Center ... Mr. Dan J. ANDERSON
12 Director Webster City Center ... Mrs. Kelly J. WIRTZ
27 Director Public Information ... Mr. Paul A. DECOURSEY
13 Director Institutional Technology ... Mr. Jeff A. NELSEN
13 Director Institutional Technology ... Mr. Troy D. CRAMPTON
14 Computer System Analyst ... Mr. Warren K. BAUER
40 Bookstore Manager ... Mrs. Samantha E. MCCLAIN

Iowa Lakes Community College (A)

19 S Seventh Street, Estherville IA 51334-2234

County: Emmet FICE Identification: 001864
Unit ID: 153533
Telephone: (712) 362-2604 Carnegie Class: Assoc/Pub-R-M
FAX Number: (712) 362-8363 Calendar System: Semester
URL: www.iowalakes.edu
Established: 1967 Annual Undergrad Tuition & Fees (In-District): $5,228
Enrollment: 3,102 Coed
Affiliation or Control: State/Local IRS Status: 501(c)3
Highest Offering: Associate Degree
Program: Occupational; 2-Year Principally Bachelor's Creditable
Accreditation: NH, MAC, SURGT

01 President ... Ms. Valerie K. NEWHOUSE
03 Vice President of Administration ... Mr. Robert W. L'HEUREUX
12 Exec Dean Emmetsburg Campus ... Mr. Thomas S. BROTHERTON
27 Exec Director of Marketing ... Ms. Jane S. CAMPBELL
05 Exec Dean Instruction/Development ... Mr. Mark A. GRUWELL
18 Exec Dir of Facilities Management ... Ms. Delaine S. HINEY
51 Exec Dir Econ Development/Cont Educ ... Mr. Clark L. MARSHALL
30 Exec Director Inst Advancement ... Ms. Jolene R. ROGERS
12 Exec Dean Estherville Campus ... Mr. Scott M. STOKES
32 Executive Dean of Students ... Ms. Julie R. WILLIAMS

*Iowa Valley Community College District (B)

3702 S Center Street, Marshalltown IA 50158-4760

County: Marshall FICE Identification: 033436
Telephone: (641) 752-4643 Carnegie Class: N/A
FAX Number: (641) 754-1336
URL: www.ivccd.com

01 Chancellor ... Mr. Christopher DUREE
51 Vice Chanc Continuing Educ/Training ... Ms. Jacque GOODMAN
11 Vice Chanc Administrative Services ... Ms. Colleen SPRINGER
10 Chief Financial Officer ... Ms. Kathleen PINK
12 Provost of ECC ... Dr. Nancy MUECKE
12 Provost of MCC ... Dr. Robin SHAFFER LILIENTHAL
12 Dean of Iowa Valley Grinnell ... Ms. Mary Anne NICKLE
26 Director of Marketing ... Ms. Robin ANCTIL
09 Institutional Researcher ... Dr. Lisa BREJA
04 Admin Assistant to the Chancellor ... Ms. Barbara JENNINGS
13 Dir Computing and Info Management ... Mr. Jim WILSON

*Ellsworth Community College (C)

1100 College Avenue, Iowa Falls IA 50126-1199

County: Hardin FICE Identification: 001862
Unit ID: 153296
Telephone: (641) 648-4611 Carnegie Class: Assoc/Pub-R-S
FAX Number: (641) 648-3128 Calendar System: Semester
URL: www.iavalley.edu
Established: 1890 Annual Undergrad Tuition & Fees (In-District): $3,456
Enrollment: 1,046 Coed
Affiliation or Control: State/Local IRS Status: 501(c)3
Highest Offering: Associate Degree
Program: Occupational; 2-Year Principally Bachelor's Creditable
Accreditation: &NH, MAC

02 Provost ... Dr. Nancy MUECKE
05 Dean of Instruction ... Dr. Kelly FAGA
08 Director of Libraries ... Ms. Sandra GREUFE
32 Dean of Student Serv/Athletic Dir ... Mr. Paul EBERHARDT
39 Director Student Housing ... Mr. O. J. PAYNE
37 Director Financial Aid ... Ms. Tara MILLER
44 Dir Annual Plan Giving/Dir Alum Rel ... Ms. Kaitlyn BARTLING
32 Associate Dean Student Services ... Ms. Annie KALOUS
84 Director Enrollment Mgmt/Registrar ... Ms. Barb KLEIN

*Marshalltown Community College (D)

3700 S Center Street, Marshalltown IA 50158-4760

County: Marshall FICE Identification: 001875
Unit ID: 153922
Telephone: (641) 752-7106 Carnegie Class: Assoc/Pub-R-S
FAX Number: (641) 752-8149 Calendar System: Semester
URL: www.iavalley.edu
Established: 1927 Annual Undergrad Tuition & Fees (In-District): $4,080
Enrollment: 2,026 Coed
Affiliation or Control: State/Local IRS Status: 501(c)3
Highest Offering: Associate Degree
Program: Occupational; 2-Year Principally Bachelor's Creditable
Accreditation: &NH, DA

02 Chancellor ... Dr. Christopher A. DUREE
11 Vice Chanc Administrative Services ... Ms. Colleen SPRINGER
10 Chief Financial Officer ... Ms. Kathy PINK
51 Vice Chancellor of Cont Educ/Trng ... Ms. Jacque GOODMAN
03 Povost ... Dr. Robin SHAFFER LILIENTHAL
05 Dean of Students & Academic Affairs ... Dr. Chris A. RUSSELL
20 Dir of Retention & Learning Svcs ... Mr. Nate CHUA
06 Registrar ... Ms. Molly M. OSMUN
76 Assoc Dean of Health Occupations ... Vacant
102 Executive Director of Foundation ... Ms. Carol GEIL
84 Assoc Dean of Enrollment Services ... Ms. Angie REDMOND
37 Director Student Financial Aid ... Mr. Matt DANIELS
26 Director of Marketing ... Ms. Robin ANCTIL
41 Athletic Director ... Mr. Daniel HUNTLEY
35 Coordinator of Student Engagement ... Ms. Abigale ALSENE
38 Senior Student Success Specialist ... Mr. Dan KEY
39 Dir Residence Life & Housing ... Mr. Phil HERNANDEZ
08 Library Supervisor ... Vacant
40 Bookstore Supervisor ... Ms. Meghan TOMLINSON

Iowa Wesleyan College (E)

601 N Main, Mount Pleasant IA 52641-1398

County: Henry FICE Identification: 001871
Unit ID: 153621
Telephone: (319) 385-8021 Carnegie Class: Bac/Diverse
FAX Number: (319) 385-6296 Calendar System: Semester
URL: www.iwc.edu
Established: 1842 Annual Undergrad Tuition & Fees: $24,300
Enrollment: 741 Coed
Affiliation or Control: United Methodist IRS Status: 501(c)3
Highest Offering: Baccalaureate
Program: Liberal Arts And General; Teacher Preparatory; Professional
Accreditation: NH, NUR

01 President ... Dr. Jay K. SIMMONS
100 Special Assistant to the President ... Ms. Carol NEMITZ
10 Senior VP/Chief Financial Officer ... Ms. Phyllis WHITNEY
05 VP Academic Affairs and Dean ... Dr. Jeffrey FAGER
30 Vice Pres Institutional Relations ... Mr. Jerry THOMAS
32 Vice Pres and Dean for Student Life ... Dr. Linda R. BUCHANAN
51 Associate VP for Extended Learning ... Mr. David C. FILE
27 Assoc VP/Chief Information Officer ... Dr. Kit NIP
07 Assoc VP & Dean for Admissions ... Mr. Mark PETTY
06 Registrar ... Ms. Patty BROKKEN
37 Director of Financial Aid ... Ms. Renae ARMENTROUT
08 Library Director ... Ms. Paula KINNEY
15 Director of Human Resources ... Ms. Kathy MOOTHART
30 Development Officer ... Ms. Dawn DUNNEGAN
44 Director of Annual Fund ... Ms. Erica MARTIN
26 Director of Marketing/Communication ... Ms. Martha POTTS-BELL
26 Publications Manager ... Ms. Sheri MICHAELS
29 Director of Alumni/Parent Relations ... Ms. Anita HAMPTON
42 Director of Church Relations ... Vacant
41 Athletic Director ... Mr. Mike HAMPTON
18 Director of Physical Plant ... Mr. Bob VITALE
35 Director of Student Activities ... Ms. Kat NIEMANN
36 Director of Career Development ... Ms. Heidi SEEGERS
40 Bookstore Director ... Ms. Teeni VITALE
04 Senior Exec Asst to the President ... Ms. Rebecca ROWE

Iowa Western Community College (F)

2700 College Road, Council Bluffs IA 51503-0567

County: Pottawattamie FICE Identification: 004598
Unit ID: 153630
Telephone: (712) 325-3200 Carnegie Class: Assoc/Pub-S-MC
FAX Number: (712) 325-3424 Calendar System: Semester
URL: www.iwcc.edu
Established: 1966 Annual Undergrad Tuition & Fees (In-District): $3,336
Enrollment: 7,200 Coed
Affiliation or Control: State/Local IRS Status: 501(c)3
Highest Offering: Associate Degree
Program: Occupational; 2-Year Principally Bachelor's Creditable
Accreditation: NH, ACFEI, DA, DH, MAC, SURGT

01 President ... Dr. Dan KINNEY
04 Assistant to the President ... Ms. Kathryn A. SCHUSTER
10 Vice Pres of Finance & Operations ... Mr. Thomas JOHNSON
05 Vice President for Academic Affairs ... Dr. Dorothy DURAN
32 Vice President for Student Services ... Ms. Tori CHRISTIE
26 Vice Pres of Marketing/Public Rels ... Mr. Donald KOHLER
09 Dean of Institutional Research ... Ms. Karna LOEWENSTEIN
84 Dean Enrollment Services ... Ms. Chris LAFERLA
35 Dean Student Support Services ... Ms. Sarah HOLLOWELL
12 Director of Clarinda Campus ... Mr. Chad WELLHAUSEN
06 Registrar ... Ms. Jill CLARK
15 Director of Personnel Services ... Vacant
29 Director of Alumni Relations ... Ms. Rachel LENHARDT
37 Director of Student Financial Aid ... Mr. Blaine DUISTERMARS
21 Director Accounting ... Mr. Eddie HOLTZ
14 Director Computer Center ... Mr. James A. MAHLBERG
76 Area Nursing Coordinator ... Ms. Rita BERTHELSEN
88 Exec Dir Economic Development ... Mr. Mark STANLEY
41 Athletic Director ... Ms. Brenda HAMPTON
08 Librarian ... Vacant
39 Director of Housing ... Ms. Kim HENRY
18 Chief Facilities/Physical Plant ... Mr. Greg CLAUSEN
07 Director of Admissions/Advising ... Ms. Keri ZIMMER
96 Director of Purchasing ... Mrs. Diane OSBAHR
36 Dir Student Placement/Counseling ... Vacant
40 Director Food Svcs/Bookstore Mgr ... Ms. Eddie HOLTZ

ITT Technical Institute (G)

1860 NW 118th Street, Suite 110, Clive IA 50325-8278

County: Polk Identification: 666596
Unit ID: 451954
Telephone: (515) 327-5500 Carnegie Class: Assoc/PrivFP4
FAX Number: (515) 327-5550 Calendar System: Quarter
URL: www.itt-tech.edu
Established: N/A Annual Undergrad Tuition & Fees: N/A
Enrollment: 257 Coed
Affiliation or Control: Proprietary IRS Status: Proprietary
Highest Offering: Baccalaureate
Program: Technical Emphasis
Accreditation: ACICS

† Branch campus of ITT Technical Institute, Indianapolis, IN.

Kaplan University (H)

3165 Edgewood Parkway SW, Cedar Rapids IA 52404-2998

County: Linn FICE Identification: 004220
Unit ID: 153418
Telephone: (319) 363-0481 Carnegie Class: Bac/Assoc
FAX Number: (319) 363-3812 Calendar System: Quarter
URL: www.cedarrapids.kaplanuniversity.edu
Established: 1900 Annual Undergrad Tuition & Fees: $15,372
Enrollment: 916 Coed
Affiliation or Control: Proprietary IRS Status: Proprietary
Highest Offering: Master's
Program: Occupational; 2-Year Principally Bachelor's Creditable
Accreditation: &NH, MAC

01 Cedar Rapids Campus President ... Mrs. Susan M. SPIVEY
05 Academic Dean ... Dr. Steve BONNETT
12 Mason City Campus Exec Director ... Ms. Destiny HASTINGS
12 Des Moines Campus President ... Mr. Jeremy WELLS
12 Cedar Falls Campus President ... Ms. Gwen BRAMLET-HECKER

† Regional accreditation is carried under the parent institution in Davenport, IA.

Kaplan University (I)

1801 East Kimberly Road, Suite 1, Davenport IA 52807-2095

County: Scott FICE Identification: 004586
Unit ID: 260901
Telephone: (563) 355-3500 Carnegie Class: Master's L
FAX Number: (563) 355-1320 Calendar System: Quarter
URL: www.kucampus.edu
Established: 1937 Annual Undergrad Tuition & Fees: $13,008
Enrollment: 56,606 Coed
Affiliation or Control: Proprietary IRS Status: Proprietary
Highest Offering: Doctorate
Program: Occupational
Accreditation: NH, MAC, NURSE

01 Campus President ... Dr. Mark GARLAND
04 Assistant to the Campus President ... Ms. Sara SKELTON
32 Director of Student Services ... Ms. Connie BONNE
37 Director of Financial Aid ... Ms. Sharon BARBER
07 Director of Admissions ... Mr. Jason WILEVSKI
36 Employment Search Coordinator ... Ms. Lisa ZERBONIA
08 Librarian ... Ms. Carole SWIFT
06 Registrar ... Ms. Janet GEHRLS

Kaplan University (J)

Plaza West 2570 4th Street, SW, Mason City IA 50401-3102

County: Cerro Gordo Identification: 666438
Unit ID: 153409
Telephone: (641) 423-2530 Carnegie Class: Bac/Assoc
FAX Number: (641) 423-7512 Calendar System: Quarter
URL: www.KU-MasonCity.com
Established: 1900 Annual Undergrad Tuition & Fees: $15,327
Enrollment: 300 Coed
Affiliation or Control: Proprietary IRS Status: Proprietary
Highest Offering: Baccalaureate
Program: Occupational; 2-Year Principally Bachelor's Creditable; Professional; Business Emphasis
Accreditation: &NH, MAC

01 Executive Director ... Ms. Destiny HASTINGS
05 Academic Dean ... Mrs. Sherri BOEDEKER
07 Director of Admissions ... Mrs. Sara TURNBULL
37 Director of Financial Aid ... Mrs. Shari GARRISON
06 Registrar ... Mrs. Eden PATTI
36 Director of Career Services ... Mrs. Karen RIES
08 Director of Library Servics ... Mrs. Kim MASHECK

† Regional accreditation is carried under the parent institution in Davenport, IA.

Kaplan University (A)

4655 121st Street, Urbandale IA 50323-2311
County: Polk Identification: 666437
Unit ID: 367024
Telephone: (515) 727-2100 Carnegie Class: Bac/Assoc
FAX Number: (515) 727-2115 Calendar System: Quarter
URL: www.kucampus.edu
Established: 1985 Annual Undergrad Tuition & Fees: $15,372
Enrollment: 905 Coed
Affiliation or Control: Proprietary IRS Status: Proprietary
Highest Offering: Baccalaureate
Program: Occupational
Accreditation: &NH, MAC

01 President ... Mr. Jeremy WELLS
05 Academic Dean ... Ms. Kacy WEBSTER
07 Director of Admissions ... Mr. Mark BANDY

† Regional accreditation is carried under the parent institution in Davenport, IA.

Kirkwood Community College (B)

PO Box 2068, Cedar Rapids IA 52406-2068
County: Linn FICE Identification: 004076
Unit ID: 153737
Telephone: (319) 398-5411 Carnegie Class: Assoc/Pub-R-L
FAX Number: (319) 398-1037 Calendar System: Semester
URL: www.kirkwood.edu
Established: 1966 Annual Undergrad Tuition & Fees (In-District): $3,990
Enrollment: 17,610 Coed
Affiliation or Control: Local IRS Status: 501(c)3
Highest Offering: Associate Degree
Program: Occupational; 2-Year Principally Bachelor's Creditable
Accreditation: NH, ACBSP, ACFEI, DA, DH, DT, EMT, MAC, NDT, OTA, PTAA, SURGT

01 President ... Dr. Mick STARCEVICH
51 VP Cont Education/Training Svcs ... Dr. Kim JOHNSON
10 Vice President/Chief Fin/Oper Ofcr ... Mr. Jim CHOATE
30 Vice President Resource Development ... Ms. Kathy HALL
05 Vice President Instruction ... Dr. Bill LAMB
32 Vice President Student Services ... Dr. Kristie FISHER
20 Assoc Vice President Instruction ... Mr. John HENIK
12 Dean Iowa City Campus ... Dr. Dale SIMON
35 Dean of Students ... Mr. Jon BUSE
15 Director Human Resources ... Mr. Mike ROBERTS
13 Associate VP IT ... Mr. Jon NEFF
09 Associate VP Institutional Research ... Mr. Al ROWE
86 Associate VP Governmental Rels ... Mr. Steven J. OVEL
106 Dean Distance Lrng & Secondary Pgm ... Mr. Todd PRUSHA
84 Director Enrollment Management ... Ms. Peg JULIUS
08 Director Library ... Mr. Aaron WINGS
07 Director Admissions ... Mr. Douglas F. BANNON
18 Associate VP Facilities ... Mr. Tom KALDENBERG
25 Director Grants & Fed Programs ... Ms. Chris O'BRIEN
41 Athletic Director ... Mr. Doug WAGEMESTER
06 Registrar ... Ms. Dena RAUCH
29 Scholarship & Alumni Director ... Ms. Jody DONALDSON
37 Director Student Financial Aid ... Ms. Peg JULIUS
47 Dean Agriculture ... Mr. Scott ERMER
72 Dean Industrial Technology ... Mr. Jeff MITCHELL
88 Dean English ... Ms. Allison YORK
79 Dean Arts & Humanities ... Dr. Jennifer BRADLEY
76 Dean Health Sciences ... Ms. Nancy GLAB
83 Dean Social Sciences/Career Option ... Dr. Milford MUSKETT
81 Dean Math/Science ... Dr. Lori WOESTE
66 Dean Nursing ... Dr. Jimmy REYES
76 Dean Health Occupations ... Dr. Mike MCLAUGHLIN
50 Dean Business & Information Tech ... Mr. Chuck HINZ
88 Dean Learning Services ... Mr. Chuck HINZ

Loras College (C)

1450 Alta Vista, Dubuque IA 52004-0178
County: Dubuque FICE Identification: 001873
Unit ID: 153825
Telephone: (563) 588-7100 Carnegie Class: Bac/Diverse
FAX Number: (563) 588-7964 Calendar System: Semester
URL: www.loras.edu
Established: 1839 Annual Undergrad Tuition & Fees: $28,148
Enrollment: 1,488 Coed
Affiliation or Control: Roman Catholic IRS Status: 501(c)3
Highest Offering: Master's
Program: Liberal Arts And General; Teacher Preparatory
Accreditation: NH, @SW

01 President ... Mr. James E. COLLINS
05 Provost & Academic Dean ... Dr. Cheryl R. JACOBSEN
10 Vice President Finance/Admin Svcs ... Dr. David W. EISINGER
84 Vice Pres Enrollment Management ... Vacant
30 Vice President Inst Advancement ... Vacant
32 Vice President Student Development ... Mr. Arthur W. SUNLEAF
04 Executive Assistant to President ... Vacant
20 Assoc Vice Pres Academic Affairs ... Dr. Mary E. CARROLL
30 Assoc VP Institutional Advancement ... Mr. Michael H. DOYLE
42 Dean of Campus Spiritual Life ... Vacant
91 Sr Dir Technology Support Services ... Mr. Tom D. KRUSE
29 Exec Dir Alumni & Communications ... Ms. Bobbi L. EARLES
15 Dir Human/Organization Development ... Ms. Gloria A. BENTLEY
09 Director of Institutional Research ... Dr. Shaun E. COWMAN
38 Director Center for Counseling ... Dr. Michael J. BOYD
07 Director of Admissions ... Ms. Sharon K. LYONS
08 Director of Academic Resource Ctr ... Ms. Joyce A. MELDREM
19 Director of Safety/Security ... Vacant
44 Director of Major & Planned Giving ... Mr. Eric J. SOLBERG
41 Director of Athletics ... Mr. Robert E. QUINN
18 Director of Physical Plant ... Mr. John R. MCDERMOTT
40 Director of Bookstore ... Ms. Renee A. MENNE
23 Director of Health Center ... Mrs. Tammy S. MARTI
85 Director of Intercultural Office ... Mr. Anthony K. DAVIS
42 Director of Campus Ministry ... Ms. Colleen M. KUHL
06 Registrar ... Mr. JT BROWN
39 Dir of Residence Life/Campus Safety ... Ms. Molly A. BURROWS-SCHUMACHER
35 Director of Student Life ... Ms. Kimberly A. WALSH
37 Director of Financial Planning ... Ms. Julie A. DUNN
25 Grant Writing Director ... Ms. Valorie A. WOERDEHOFF
26 Dir Communication/Media Relations ... Ms. Susan P. HAFKEMEYER
96 Controller for Business Office ... Ms. Sandy M. RECKER
36 Academic Internship Coordinator ... Ms. Faye A. FINNEGAN

Luther College (D)

700 College Drive, Decorah IA 52101-1045
County: Winneshiek FICE Identification: 001874
Unit ID: 153834
Telephone: (563) 387-2000 Carnegie Class: Bac/A&S
FAX Number: (563) 387-2158 Calendar System: 4/1/4
URL: www.luther.edu
Established: 1861 Annual Undergrad Tuition & Fees: $36,100
Enrollment: 2,471 Coed
Affiliation or Control: Evangelical Lutheran Church In America
IRS Status: 501(c)3
Highest Offering: Baccalaureate
Program: Liberal Arts And General; Teacher Preparatory; Professional
Accreditation: NH, MUS, NURSE, SW, TED

01 President ... Dr. Richard L. TORGERSON
05 Vice Pres Acad Affs/Dean of College ... Dr. Kevin KRAUS
20 Assistant Dean ... Ms. Arleen ORVIS
30 Vice President for Development ... Mr. Keith J. CHRISTENSEN
10 Vice President for Finance & Admin ... Ms. Diane L. TACKE
32 Vice Pres/Dean for Student Life ... Mr. Corey LANDSTROM
84 Vice Pres Enrollment Management ... Mr. Scot SCHAEFFER
13 Exec Dir Library & Info Tech Svcs ... Mr. Paul R. MATTSON
91 Director Information Systems ... Ms. Marcia A. GULLICKSON
21 Controller ... Ms. Peggy LENSING
18 Exec Director Campus Services ... Mr. Richard J. TENNESON
44 Senior Development Officer ... Mr. Thomas K. MURRAY
06 Registrar ... Mr. Douglas KOSCHMEDER
20 Associate Dean ... Dr. Jeffrey WILKERSON
15 Director Human Resources ... Ms. Lora STEIL
41 Director Intercollegiate Athletics ... Dr. Joe H. THOMPSON
29 Director of Alumni Relations ... Ms. Sherry B. ALCOCK
26 Exec Dir Communications/Marketing ... Mr. Rob K. LARSON
26 Director of Public Information ... Mr. Jerrold JOHNSON
04 Assistant to the President ... Ms. Karen B. MARTIN-SCHRAMM
35 Associate Dean Student Life ... Ms. Jane HILDEBRAND
36 Director Career Center ... Ms. Keley SMITH-KELLER
38 Director Counseling Service ... Dr. Pamela C. TORRESDAL
37 Director Student Financial Planning ... Ms. Janice K. CORDELL
42 Dir Campus Ministry & Cong Rels ... Rev. Michael R. BLAIR
40 Director Book Shop/Union Services ... Ms. Deanna CASTERTON
27 Director of Publications ... Ms. Ellen E. MODERSOHN
39 Assistant Dean & Dir Res Life ... Ms. Kristine FRANZEN
85 Exec Dir Ctr Glo Learning & Int Adm ... Mr. Jon LUND
44 Director of Planned Giving ... Mr. James ANDERSON
23 Director Health Services ... Ms. JoEllen ANDERSON
19 Director Security/Safety ... Mr. Robert HARRI
88 Director Campus Programing ... Ms. Tanya M. GERTZ
28 Exec Director of Diversity ... Dr. Sheila RADFORD-HILL
09 Director Assessment/Inst Research ... Dr. Jon A. CHRISTY
07 Director of Recruiting Services ... Mr. Kirk NEUBAUER
35 Coordinator Student Activities ... Ms. Trish NEUBAUER
88 Asst Dean & Health Res Adv ... Ms. Janet HUNTER

Maharishi University of Management (E)

1000 N 4th Street, Fairfield IA 52557-0001
County: Jefferson FICE Identification: 011113
Unit ID: 153861
Telephone: (641) 472-7000 Carnegie Class: Master's L
FAX Number: (641) 472-1179 Calendar System: Other
URL: www.mum.edu
Established: 1971 Annual Undergrad Tuition & Fees: $24,430
Enrollment: 1,134 Coed
Affiliation or Control: Independent Non-Profit IRS Status: 501(c)3
Highest Offering: Doctorate
Program: Liberal Arts And General; Teacher Preparatory
Accreditation: NH, IACBE

01 President ... Dr. Bevan H. MORRIS
03 Executive Vice President ... Dr. Craig PEARSON
05 Dean of Faculty ... Dr. Cathy GORINI
10 Treasurer ... Mr. Michael SPIVAK
88 International Vice President ... Dr. Michael DILLBECK
88 International Vice President ... Dr. Susan DILLBECK
11 Chief Administrative Officer ... Dr. David STREID
07 Dean of Admissions ... Mr. Bradford MYLETT
32 Dean of Student Life ... Ms. Ellen AKST JONES
33 Associate Dean of Men ... Mr. Jan SICKLER
34 Associate Dean of Women ... Ms. Elaine POMFREY
06 Registrar ... Mr. Tom ROWE
45 Director of Expansion ... Dr. David TODT
26 Media Director ... Mr. Ken CHAWKIN
51 Dir Distance Educ/Intl Programs ... Mr. Dennis HEATON
27 Director of Press ... Mr. Harry BRIGHT
39 Director of Housing ... Mr. Britt ZEIGER
37 Director of Student Financial Aid ... Mr. Bill CHRISTENSEN
14 Director of Information Services ... Mr. Tom HIRSCH
09 Director of Assessment ... Mr. Raoul CALDERON
15 Director of Personnel ... Mr. John KENNEDY
29 Director Alumni Relations ... Ms. Jennine FELLMER
30 Co-Director of Development ... Mr. Nick ROSANIA
30 Co-Director of Development ... Ms. Sandra ROSANIA
36 Director Student Placement ... Dr. Rachel GOODMAN
18 Chief Facilities/Physical Plant ... Mr. De Armond BRIGGS
49 Dean College of Arts & Sciences ... Dr. Scott HERRIOTT
77 Dn College of Computer Sci & Math ... Mr. Gregory GUTHRIE
58 Dean of Graduate School ... Dr. Frederick TRAVIS

Mercy College of Health Sciences (F)

928 Sixth Avenue, Des Moines IA 50309-1239
County: Polk FICE Identification: 006273
Unit ID: 153977
Telephone: (515) 643-3180 Carnegie Class: Spec/Health
FAX Number: (515) 643-6698 Calendar System: Semester
URL: www.mchs.edu
Established: 1995 Annual Undergrad Tuition & Fees: $14,460
Enrollment: 833 Coed
Affiliation or Control: Roman Catholic IRS Status: 501(c)3
Highest Offering: Baccalaureate
Program: Liberal Arts And General; Professional; Nursing Emphasis
Accreditation: NH, ADNUR, DMS, EMT, MAC, MT, NMT, NURSE, POLYT, PTAA, RAD, SURGT

01 President ... Dr. Barbara Q. DECKER
05 VP of Academic Affairs and Provost ... Dr. Steven D. LANGDON
26 VP of External Affairs ... Mr. Brian P. TINGLEFF
10 VP of Business & Regulatory Affairs ... Dr. Thomas LEAHY
66 Dean of Nursing ... Dr. Shirley BEAVER
49 Dean of Liberal Arts & Sciences ... Dr. Jeannine MATZ
76 Dean of Allied Health ... Ms. Theresa SMITH
09 Dean Inst Rsrch/Assess/Dist Educ ... Dr. Joan M. MCCLEISH
08 Dir of Library and Media Services ... Ms. Eileen HANSEN
06 Registrar ... Ms. Carolyn BUCKLIN
15 Human Resources Business Partner ... Ms. Anne DENNIS
37 Director of Financial Aid ... Ms. Lisa CROAT
38 Manager of Student Success ... Dr. Kristine OWENS
13 Director of Information Technology ... Mr. Jeff BOUZEK
18 Facilities Manager ... Mr. David STEENHOEK
07 Admissions Manager ... Ms. Kara DONOVAN
26 Marketing Manager ... Mr. Jim TAGYE
32 Director of Student Services ... Dr. Karen ANDERSON

Morningside College (G)

1501 Morningside Avenue, Sioux City IA 51106-1751
County: Woodbury FICE Identification: 001879
Unit ID: 154004
Telephone: (712) 274-5000 Carnegie Class: Bac/Diverse
FAX Number: (712) 274-5101 Calendar System: Semester
URL: www.morningside.edu
Established: 1894 Annual Undergrad Tuition & Fees: $25,000
Enrollment: 2,047 Coed
Affiliation or Control: United Methodist IRS Status: 501(c)3
Highest Offering: Master's
Program: Liberal Arts And General; Teacher Preparatory; Professional
Accreditation: NH, MUS, NURSE

01 President ... Mr. John C. REYNDERS
05 Vice President/Dean of College ... Dr. William C. DEEDS
10 Vice President Business & Finance ... Mr. Ronald A. JORGENSEN
32 Vice Pres Student Life & Enrollment ... Mrs. Terri A. CURRY
30 Vice Pres Institutional Advancement ... Mr. Thomas M. RICE
35 Dean for Advising/Assoc Dean Stdnts ... Dr. Mary LEIDA
20 Associate Dean for Acad Affairs ... Dr. Susan BURNS
09 Asc Dean Assessment/Inst Research ... Dr. John PINTO
06 Registrar ... Ms. Mary PESHEK
37 Director Student Financial Planning ... Ms. Karen GAGNON
14 Dir Info Tech/Dean Learning Center ... Mr. Andrew HEISER
26 Director Public Relations ... Mr. Rick WOLLMAN
29 Director of Alumni Relations ... Mr. Gene AMBROSON
58 Director of Graduate Studies ... Dr. Glenna J. TEVIS
18 Director of Physical Plant ... Mr. Kirk JOHNSON
19 Director of Security ... Mr. Jim CORNELIA
23 Director of Student Health ... Ms. Carol GARVEY
24 Media Center Supervisor ... Ms. Janet L. JACOBSON
36 Director of Career Services ... Ms. Stacie HAYS
40 Director of Bookstore ... Mr. Duane BENSON
41 Interim Athletic Director ... Mrs. Robbie ROHLENA
42 Campus Ministry ... Rev. Kathy MARTIN
44 Director of Gift Planning ... Mr. Fred S. ERBES
15 Director Human Resources ... Ms. Cindy WELP
38 Director Student Counseling ... Ms. Brenda CRAWFORD
21 Controller ... Mr. Paul TREFT

Mount Mercy University (H)

1330 Elmhurst Drive, NE, Cedar Rapids IA 52402-4797
County: Linn FICE Identification: 001880
Unit ID: 154013
Telephone: (319) 363-8213 Carnegie Class: Bac/Diverse

FAX Number: (319) 363-5270 Calendar System: 4/1/4
URL: www.mtmercy.edu
Established: 1928 Annual Undergrad Tuition & Fees: $25,400
Enrollment: 1,824 Coed
Affiliation or Control: Roman Catholic IRS Status: 501(c)3
Highest Offering: Master's
Program: Liberal Arts And General; Teacher Preparatory; Professional
Accreditation: NH, NURSE, SW

01 President .... Dr. Christopher R L. BLAKE
05 Acting Provost/VP Academic Affairs .... Dr. Melody GRAHAM
10 Vice President Finance .... Ms. Barbara D. PARKS POOLEY
84 Vice Pres Enrollment Management .... Mr. Robert CALLAHAN
30 Vice Pres Develop & Alumni Rels .... Mr. Duff RIDGEWAY
11 Vice President for Administration .... Ms. Vicky SMITH
20 Vice Provost Academic Affairs .... Dr. Janet R. HANDLER
07 Dean of Admissions .... Mr. Scott BAUMLER
06 Registrar .... Mr. Jason CLAPP
08 Director of Library Services .... Mrs. Marilyn J. MURPHY
36 Director of Career Services .... Ms. Cheryl TABARELLA-REED
29 Asst VP Develop & Alumni Relations .... Ms. Lonna DREWELOW
37 Director of Financial Aid .... Ms. Bethany RINDERKNECHT
26 Asst VP Communications/Marketing .... Mr. Fritz MCDONALD
41 Director of Athletics .... Mr. Scot H. REISINGER
42 Director Campus Ministry .... Mr. William MULCAHEY
32 Interim Dean of Students .... Ms. Jenifer A. HANSON
44 Director of Major & Planned Gifts .... Vacant
88 Director of Faculty Development .... Dr. Edy PARSONS
38 Director of Counseling Services .... Ms. Colleen PRENDERGAST
13 Director of Technology Operations .... Ms. Connie SNITKER
19 Director of Public Safety .... Mr. Raymond J. KESSENICH
24 Academic Technology Librarian .... Ms. Vicky MALOY
35 Director of Student Activities .... Ms. Sarah L. BOTKIN
15 Director Human Resources .... Vacant
18 Director Facilities/Physical Plant .... Mr. Dave D. DENNIS
92 Director Honors Program .... Dr. Joy E. OCHS
40 Bookstore Manager .... Ms. Janie A. MILLS
04 Exec Assistant to President .... Mrs. Dianne M. AUSTAD
09 Exec Dir of Institutional Research .... Ms. Lori HEYING

North Iowa Area Community College (A)

500 College Drive, Mason City IA 50401-7299
County: Cerro Gordo FICE Identification: 001877
Unit ID: 154059
Telephone: (641) 423-1264 Carnegie Class: Assoc/Pub-R-M
FAX Number: (641) 423-1711 Calendar System: Semester
URL: www.niacc.edu
Established: 1917 Annual Undergrad Tuition & Fees (In-District): $4,505
Enrollment: 3,557 Coed
Affiliation or Control: State/Local IRS Status: 501(c)3
Highest Offering: Associate Degree
Program: Occupational; 2-Year Principally Bachelor's Creditable
Accreditation: NH, ADNUR, MAC, PTAA

01 President .... Dr. Debra A. DERR
05 Vice Pres Academic/Student Affairs .... Dr. Lyn A. BRODERSEN
10 Vice Pres Administrative Services .... Mrs. Kathy M. GROVE
32 Dean of Student Development .... Dr. Terri L. EWERS
30 VP of Inst Advancement & JPEC .... Mr. Jamie T. ZANIOS
09 VP Inst Effectiveness & Organiz Dev .... Dr. Shelly M. SCHMIT
06 Registrar .... Mrs. Michelle L. PETZNICK
07 Director of Admissions .... Mrs. Rachel L. MCGUIRE
49 Chair Arts & Science Division .... Dr. William W. BACKLIN
47 Chair Ag & Industrial Division .... Mr. Joshua J. BYRNES
50 Chair Business Division .... Mrs. Laura L. MERFELD
66 Chair Health Division .... Mrs. Donna J. ORTON
51 Dean of Cont Ed & Economic Dev .... Mr. Terry W. SCHUMAKER
37 Director of Financial Aid .... Mrs. Mary E. BLOOMINGDALE
20 Director Learning Support Division .... Mrs. Jessica J. PUTNAM
14 Director of Technology Services .... Mr. Mark D. GREENWOOD
103 Regional Dir of Iowa Works .... Ms. Angela A. KONIG
40 Bookstore Manager .... Mrs. Rhonda K. NESHEIM-KAUFFMAN
41 Director of Athletics .... Mr. Dan J. MASON
18 Director of Facilities Management .... Mr. Tony A. PAPPAS
21 Accountant/Business Office Manager .... Ms. Mindy R. EASTMAN
24 Instructional Technology Coord .... Mr. Bruce G. MCKEE
39 Director Student Housing .... Mr. Travis J. HERGERT
08 Librarian .... Ms. Karen F. DOLE
88 Director of Food Service .... Mr. Ken P. WEBBER
31 Dir Marketing/Cmty Rels/Govt Affs .... Mrs. Michele R. APPELGATE
88 Dir Incubation & Acceleration Svcs .... Mr. Mark C. OLCHEFSKE
88 Director of School Partnerships .... Mrs. Jean M. OSTRANDER
88 Director of Operations .... Mrs. Constance J. GLANDON
88 Director of Programming & Sales .... Mrs. Jody L. EAST

Northeast Iowa Community College (B)

Box 400, Calmar IA 52132-0400
County: Winneshiek FICE Identification: 004587
Unit ID: 154110
Telephone: (563) 562-3263 Carnegie Class: Assoc/Pub-R-M
FAX Number: (563) 562-3719 Calendar System: Semester
URL: www.nicc.edu
Established: 1966 Annual Undergrad Tuition & Fees (In-District): $5,216
Enrollment: 5,051 Coed
Affiliation or Control: Local IRS Status: 501(c)3
Highest Offering: Associate Degree
Program: Occupational; 2-Year Principally Bachelor's Creditable
Accreditation: NH, DA, RAD

01 President .... Dr. Liang C. WEE
10 Vice Pres Finance & Administration .... Mr. John D. NOEL
05 Chief Acad Ofcr/VP Academic Affairs .... Vacant
46 Vice Pres Bus & Community Solutions .... Dr. Wendy A. MIHM-HEROLD
12 Peosta Provost .... Dr. Amy H. ESTERHUIZEN
12 Calmar Provost .... Ms. Rhonda K. SEIBERT
32 Vice Pres Student Services .... Dr. Linda M. PETERSON
51 Exec Dir Town Clock/Dubuque Centers .... Ms. Wendy S. KNIGHT
102 Exec Director of NICC Foundation .... Ms. Julie A. WURTZEL
21 Executive Director of Finance .... Mr. Thomas M. RIDOUT
26 Exec Dir of External Relations .... Ms. Tracy L. KRUSE
15 Exec Director of Human Resources .... Dr. Julie G. HUISKAMP
106 Director Distance Learning .... Dr. Christopher M. OSTWINKLE
13 Director Computer Information Sys .... Mr. Leonard B. FIELDS
09 Director of Institutional Research .... Ms. Dolores M. MILLER
88 Director Economic Devel/Peosta .... Mr. Gregory A. WILLGING
37 Director of Financial Aid .... Vacant
06 Registrar .... Ms. Karla R. WINTER
06 Registrar .... Ms. Sheila R. BECKER
36 Career Services Manager .... Mr. Chris E. ENTRINGER
07 Director of Admissions .... Ms. Kristi L. STRIEF

Northwest Iowa Community College (C)

603 W Park Street, Sheldon IA 51201-1046
County: Sioux FICE Identification: 004600
Unit ID: 154129
Telephone: (712) 324-5061 Carnegie Class: Assoc/Pub-R-S
FAX Number: (712) 324-4136 Calendar System: Semester
URL: www.nwicc.edu
Established: 1966 Annual Undergrad Tuition & Fees (In-District): $3,984
Enrollment: 1,545 Coed
Affiliation or Control: State/Local IRS Status: 501(c)3
Highest Offering: Associate Degree
Program: Occupational; 2-Year Principally Bachelor's Creditable; Technical Emphasis
Accreditation: NH

01 President .... Dr. Alethea F. STUBBE
05 VP Student & Academic Services .... Dr. John HARTOG
30 VP Inst Adv & External Affairs .... Dr. Jan E. SNYDER
10 VP Operations & Finance .... Mr. Mark BROWN
49 Dean Arts & Sci/Business/Health .... Dr. Rhonda R. PENNINGS
72 Dean Applied Technology .... Vacant
53 Dean Extended Learning Services .... Ms. Gretchen G. BARTELSON
21 Director of Business Services .... Mr. Dan REEVES
37 Financial Aid Director .... Ms. Karna HOFMEYER
84 Director Enrollment Management .... Ms. Lisa L. STORY
08 Director of Library Services .... Ms. Molly D. GALM
13 Director of Technology & Info Svcs .... Mr. Mike OLDENKAMP
88 Director of TRIO .... Ms. Laurie L. EDWARDS
51 Exec Dir of Econ Dev & Cont Ed Trng .... Mr. Frank DE MILIA
06 Registrar .... Ms. Beth SIBENALLER-WOODALL
15 Director of Human Resources .... Ms. Sandy BRUNS
88 Director of Alt HS/Learning Center .... Ms. Susan SCHMIDT
26 Director Community Relations .... Ms. Kristin E. KOLLBAUM
18 Director Physical Facilities .... Mr. Doug RODGER

Northwestern College (D)

101 Seventh Street, SW, Orange City IA 51041-1996
County: Sioux FICE Identification: 001883
Unit ID: 154101
Telephone: (712) 707-7000 Carnegie Class: Bac/Diverse
FAX Number: (712) 707-7247 Calendar System: Semester
URL: www.nwciowa.edu
Established: 1882 Annual Undergrad Tuition & Fees: $25,590
Enrollment: 1,211 Coed
Affiliation or Control: Reformed Church In America IRS Status: 501(c)3
Highest Offering: Baccalaureate
Program: Liberal Arts And General; Teacher Preparatory; Professional
Accreditation: NH, IACBE, NURSE, SW, TED

01 President .... Mr. Gregory E. CHRISTY
05 Provost .... Dr. Jasper LESAGE
20 Dean of Faculty .... Dr. Adrienne M. FORGETTE
32 Dean of Students .... Dr. John J. BROGAN
10 Vice President Financial Affairs .... Mr. Doug D. BEUKELMAN
30 Vice President Advancement .... Mr. Jay WIELENGA
84 Dean of Enrollment Management .... Mr. Kenton PAULS
88 Assoc Dean of Spiritual Formation .... Ms. Barb DEWALD
104 Associate Dean for Global Education .... Dr. Douglas W. CARLSON
42 Chaplain .... Rev. Harlan VAN OORT
41 Director of Athletics .... Mr. Barry M. BRANDT
08 Director of the Library .... Mr. Tim SCHLAK
06 Registrar .... Ms. Sandy VAN KLEY
37 Director of Financial Aid .... Mr. Eric ANDERSON
14 Director of Computing Services .... Mr. Harlan R. JORGENSEN
26 Director of Public Relations .... Mr. Duane L. BEESON
36 Director of Career Development .... Mr. William C. MINNICK
38 Dir Student Counseling Services .... Dr. Sally EDMAN
18 Director of Maintenance/Operations .... Mr. Scott K. SIMMELINK
29 Director Alumni Relations .... Mr. Mark R. BLOEMENDAAL
15 Director of Human Resources .... Mrs. Deb SANDBULTE
09 Director of Institutional Research .... Vacant

Palmer College of Chiropractic (E)

1000 Brady Street, Davenport IA 52803-5287
County: Scott FICE Identification: 012300
Unit ID: 154174
Telephone: (563) 884-5000 Carnegie Class: Spec/Health
FAX Number: (563) 884-5409 Calendar System: Trimester
URL: www.palmer.edu
Established: 1897 Annual Undergrad Tuition & Fees: $8,195
Enrollment: 2,198 Coed
Affiliation or Control: Independent Non-Profit IRS Status: 501(c)3
Highest Offering: First Professional Degree
Program: Professional
Accreditation: NH, CHIRO

00 Chancellor .... Dr. Dennis M. MARCHIORI
01 Campus Provost .... Dr. Daniel J. WEINERT
05 Vice Chancellor for Academics .... Dr. Robert E. PERCUOCO
32 Vice Chancellor Student Success .... Dr. Kevin A. CUNNINGHAM
11 Vice Chancellor Support Services .... Mr. Robert E. LEE
84 Vice Chancellor for Enrollment .... Mr. J. Michael NOVAK
10 Vice Chancellor for Administration .... Mr. Thomas L. TIEMEIER
17 Vice Chancellor for Clinic Affairs .... Dr. Kurt W. WOOD
46 Vice Chancellor for Research .... Dr. Christine GOERTZ
26 Exec Dir for Marketing & PR .... Mr. Darren R. GARRETT
29 Executive Director for Alumni .... Dr. Mickey G. BURT
88 Exec Dir Office of Strategic Dev .... Dr. Judy M. SILVESTRONE
20 Dean of Academic Programs .... Vacant
88 Director of Undergrad Studies .... Ms. Cathy EBERHART
06 Senior Director/Registrar .... Ms. Mindy S. LEAHY
09 Sr Dir Institutional Plng/Research .... Dr. Dustin C. DERBY
21 Senior Dir for Financial Affairs .... Ms. Alexis A. VANDER HORN
13 Senior Director of IT .... Mr. Mike A. BENEDICT
15 Senior Director of Human Resources .... Ms. Michelle K. WALKER
18 Senior Director of Facilities .... Mr. Stanley E. CARLSON
07 Senior Director of Admissions .... Ms. Karen S. EDEN
37 Senior Dir of Financial Planning .... Ms. Jennifer L. RANDAZZO
108 Senior Director for Assessment .... Vacant
24 Sr Dir/Center for Teaching/Lrng .... Dr. Dana J. LAWRENCE
51 Senior Dir of Continuing Education .... Vacant
38 Senior Dir of Counseling Services .... Dr. Lori L. NEWMAN
08 Senior Director of Library .... Mr. Dennis R. PETERSON
40 Senior Director of Bookstores .... Ms. Carol A. HOYT
88 Sr Dir Quality Assurance/Sys Organ .... Ms. Earlye A. JULIEN
35 Dir of Student Academic Affairs .... Dr. Kevin W. PAUSTIAN
96 Purchasing Manager .... Ms. Cheryl L. KOFRON

St. Ambrose University (F)

518 W Locust Street, Davenport IA 52803-2898
County: Scott FICE Identification: 001889
Unit ID: 154235
Telephone: (563) 333-6000 Carnegie Class: Master's L
FAX Number: (563) 333-6243 Calendar System: Semester
URL: www.sau.edu
Established: 1882 Annual Undergrad Tuition & Fees: $25,730
Enrollment: 3,281 Coed
Affiliation or Control: Roman Catholic IRS Status: 501(c)3
Highest Offering: Doctorate
Program: Liberal Arts And General; Fine Arts Emphasis
Accreditation: NH, ACBSP, ENG, NURSE, OT, PTA, @SP, SW, TEAC

01 President .... Sr. Joan LESCINSKI, CSJ
05 Vice President for Academic Affairs .... Dr. Paul KOCH
10 Vice President Finance .... Mr. Michael C. POSTER
42 Chaplain .... Rev. Charles A. ADAM
30 Interim Director Advancement Area .... Ms. Sally E. CRINO
84 Vice Pres Enrollment Management .... Mr. John D. COOPER
88 Assoc Vice Pres for Advancement .... Mr. Edward J. FINN
46 Assoc Vice Pres Assess/Research .... Dr. Tracy SCHUSTER-MATLOCK
21 Assistant Vice President Finance .... Ms. Carol A. GLINES
26 Asst Vice Pres Communications/Mktg .... Ms. Linda R. HIRSCH
32 Asst VP Student Svcs/Dean of Stdnts .... Mr. Timothy PHILLIPS
15 Director Human Resources .... Ms. Audrey D. HEIN
07 Director Admissions .... Ms. Meg F. HALLIGAN
14 Exec Dir of Information Resources .... Ms. Mary B. HEINZMAN
29 Director Alumni Rels & Spec Project .... Ms. Anne A. GANNAWAY
37 Director Financial Aid .... Ms. Julie A. HAACK
38 Director Counseling .... Mr. Stephen TENDALL
18 Director Physical Plant .... Mr. Jim M. HANNON
06 Registrar .... Mr. Dan L. ZEIMET
23 Director of Health Services .... Ms. Nancy A. HINES
19 Director of Security .... Mr. Robert CHRISTOPHER
39 Director of Resident Life .... Mr. Matt B. HANSEN
08 Director Library .... Ms. Mary B. HEINZMAN
36 Director Career Development .... Ms. Angela P. ELLIOTT
41 Athletic Director .... Mr. Raymond J. SHOVLAIN
94 Director of Women's Studies .... Dr. Beatrice F. JACOBSON
40 Manager of Bookstore .... Ms. Linda K. MACUMBER
85 Asst VP International Education .... Dr. Ryan D. DYE
88 Chair Masters Pastoral Studies .... Rev. Bud GRANT
88 Chair Masters Criminal Justice .... Mr. Waylyn C. MCCULLOH
49 Dean College Arts & Sciences .... Dr. Aron R. AJI
50 Dean College Business .... Dr. David J. O'CONNELL
71 Dean Education and Health Sciences .... Dr. Sandra L. CASSADY
88 Dean for Academic Adult Programming .... Dr. Regina M. MATHESON
54 Dir Ambrose Industrial Engineering .... Dr. Michael E. OPAR
57 Director Fine Arts .... Mr. Lance A. SADLEK
88 Director Occupational Therapy .... Ms. Phyllis J. WENTHE
88 Director Masters of Accounting .... Mr. Lew D. MARX
58 Director Academic Svcs MBA Pgm .... Ms. Allison S. AMBROSE
58 Director Graduate Student Recruit .... Ms. Elizabeth B. LOVELESS
28 Director of Diversity .... Dr. Paul C. KOCH

St. Luke's College (A)

2720 Stone Park Boulevard, Sioux City IA 51104-0010
County: Woodbury FICE Identification: 007291
Unit ID: 154262
Telephone: (712) 279-3149 Carnegie Class: Assoc/PrivNFP
FAX Number: (712) 233-8017 Calendar System: Semester
URL: www.stlukescollege.edu
Established: 1995 Annual Undergrad Tuition & Fees: $17,170
Enrollment: 214 Coed
Affiliation or Control: Independent Non-Profit IRS Status: 501(c)3
Highest Offering: Associate Degree
Program: Occupational; 2-Year Principally Bachelor's Creditable; Nursing Emphasis
Accreditation: NH, ADNUR, MT, RAD

01 Chancellor .... Mr. Michael D. STILES
05 Exec Dean/Chief Academic Officer .... Dr. Richard S. AYI
32 Dept Chair Student Services .... Ms. Danelle D. JOHANNSEN

Shiloh University (B)

100 Shiloh Drive, Kalona IA 52247
County: Washington Identification: 667095
Telephone: (319) 656-2447 Carnegie Class: Not Classified
FAX Number: N/A Calendar System: Trimester
URL: www.shilohuniversity.org
Established: 2006 Annual Undergrad Tuition & Fees: $4,385
Enrollment: N/A Coed
Affiliation or Control: Independent Non-Profit IRS Status: 501(c)3
Highest Offering: Master's
Program: Religious Emphasis
Accreditation: DETC

01 President .... Mr. Christopher REEVES

Simpson College (C)

701 North C Street, Indianola IA 50125-1297
County: Warren FICE Identification: 001887
Unit ID: 154350
Telephone: (515) 961-6251 Carnegie Class: Bac/A&S
FAX Number: (515) 961-1498 Calendar System: Other
URL: www.simpson.edu
Established: 1860 Annual Undergrad Tuition & Fees: $28,974
Enrollment: 1,817 Coed
Affiliation or Control: United Methodist IRS Status: 501(c)3
Highest Offering: Master's
Program: Liberal Arts And General; Teacher Preparatory; Business Emphasis
Accreditation: NH, MUS

01 President .... Dr. John W. BYRD
05 Vice Pres/Dean Academic Affairs .... Dr. Steven J. GRIFFITH
10 Vice President Business/Finance .... Mr. Kenneth I. BIRKENHOLTZ
30 Vice President College Advancement .... Mr. Robert J. LANE
32 Vice President Student Development .... Mr. James D. THORIUS
84 Vice President Enrollment .... Ms. Deborah J. TIERNEY
91 VP Info Svcs/Chief Info Officer .... Ms. Kelley L. BRADDER
37 Asst VP Enrollment/Financial Aid .... Ms. Tracie PAVON
06 Registrar & Associate Dean .... Ms. Jody RAGAN
26 Executive Director College Rels .... Vacant
08 Director of Library .... Ms. Cynthia M. DYER
27 Director of Information Services .... Mr. Allan APPENZELLER
44 Director of Annual Giving .... Ms. Sherry FULLER
15 Director of Human Resources .... Ms. Mary E. BARTLEY
36 Director of Career Services .... Ms. Jennifer DEL PINO
07 Director of Admissions .... Ms. Alison SWANSON
41 Athletic Director .... Mr. John F. SIRIANNI
96 Director of Procurement .... Ms. Marilyn J. LEEK
35 Assistant Dean of Students .... Mr. Richard O. RAMOS
42 Chaplain .... Mr. Fritz WEHRENBERG
39 Director of Residence Life .... Mr. Luke BEHAUNEK
18 Director Campus Services .... Mr. John HARRIS
21 Controller .... Ms. Heather TRAVIS
19 Coordinator of Campus Security .... Mr. Chris FRERICHS
51 Associate Dean Adult Learning .... Dr. Rosemary J. LINK
28 International Educ Coordinator .... Mr. Jay WILKINSON

Southeastern Community College (D)

1500 W Agency Road, PO Box 180,
West Burlington IA 52655-0180
County: Des Moines FICE Identification: 001848
Unit ID: 154378
Telephone: (319) 752-2731 Carnegie Class: Assoc/Pub-R-M
FAX Number: (319) 752-4957 Calendar System: Semester
URL: www.scciowa.edu
Established: 1966 Annual Undergrad Tuition & Fees (In-District): $4,260
Enrollment: 3,341 Coed
Affiliation or Control: State/Local IRS Status: 501(c)3
Highest Offering: Associate Degree
Program: Occupational; 2-Year Principally Bachelor's Creditable
Accreditation: NH, EMT, MAC

01 President .... Dr. Beverly SIMONE
05 Vice Pres of Teaching & Learning .... Mr. Phil THOMAS
32 Vice President of Student Services .... Ms. Joan WILLIAMS
11 Vice Pres Admin Services/Human Res .... Mr. Bill MECK
30 Exec Director for Inst Advancement .... Ms. Rebecca RUMP
37 Financial Aid Officer .... Mr. Ean FREELS
84 Enrollment Coordinator .... Ms. Dana CHRISMAN
06 Registrar .... Mr. Tim GRAY
15 Director Human Resources .... Ms. Michelle FOSTER
49 Dean Humanities/Social Sciences .... Dr. Tim AHERN
12 Dean Keokuk Campus/Trans Studies .... Dr. Teresa GARCIA
75 Dean Vocational-Technical Education .... Ms. Laura MENKE

Southwestern Community College (E)

1501 W Townline Street, Creston IA 50801-1098
County: Union FICE Identification: 001857
Unit ID: 154396
Telephone: (641) 782-7081 Carnegie Class: Assoc/Pub-R-S
FAX Number: (641) 782-3312 Calendar System: Semester
URL: www.swcciowa.edu
Established: 1966 Annual Undergrad Tuition & Fees (In-State): $4,440
Enrollment: 1,730 Coed
Affiliation or Control: State IRS Status: 501(c)3
Highest Offering: Associate Degree
Program: Occupational; 2-Year Principally Bachelor's Creditable
Accreditation: NH

01 Superintendent/President .... Dr. Barbara J. CRITTENDEN
03 Vice President Economic Development .... Mr. Thomas L. LESAN
10 Chief Financial Officer .... Mrs. Teresa KREJCI
05 Vice President Instruction .... Mr. Bill TAYLOR
32 Dean of Student Services .... Dr. Matt THOMPSON
30 Director Institutional Advancement .... Dr. Matt THOMPSON
20 Assoc Vice Pres of Instruction .... Dr. Jane BRADLEY
106 Director of Distance Education .... Mr. Doug GREENE
15 Director of Human Resources .... Mrs. Jolene GRIFFITH
26 Director Marketing .... Mrs. Terri HIGGINS
08 Head Librarian .... Mrs. Ann COULTER
13 Director of Information Technology .... Mr. Scott HELM
37 Director Financial Aid .... Mrs. Tracy DAVIS

University of Dubuque (F)

2000 University Avenue, Dubuque IA 52001-5099
County: Dubuque FICE Identification: 001891
Unit ID: 153278
Telephone: (563) 589-3000 Carnegie Class: Master's S
FAX Number: (563) 589-3682 Calendar System: 4/1/4
URL: www.dbq.edu
Established: 1852 Annual Undergrad Tuition & Fees: $24,530
Enrollment: 2,013 Coed
Affiliation or Control: Presbyterian Church (U.S.A.) IRS Status: 501(c)3
Highest Offering: Doctorate
Program: Liberal Arts And General; Teacher Preparatory; Professional
Accreditation: NH, AAB, NURSE, THEOL

01 President .... Dr. Jeffrey F. BULLOCK
04 Exec Assistant to the President .... Mrs. Deborah L. BUOL
05 Vice President/Dean of the College .... Dr. Mark WARD
10 Vice President Finance & Treasurer .... Mr. James D. STEINER
84 Co-Vice Pres Enrollment/Univ Rels .... Mr. Peter L. SMITH
84 Co-Vice Pres Enrollment/Univ Rels .... Ms. Susan M. SMITH
20 Vice Pres/Dean of Seminary .... Dr. Bradley J. LONGFIELD
30 Vice President for Philanthropy .... Mr. David DENDY
32 Dean of Student Life .... Dr. Michael H. MIYAMOTO
13 Network Administrator .... Ms. Sherry CUSICK
07 Dean of Admission .... Mr. Jesse L. JAMES
06 Registrar .... Ms. Elizabeth OLESON
08 Director of Libraries .... Ms. Mary Anne KNEFEL
16 Director of Human Resources .... Ms. Julie MACTAGGART
37 Dean of Student Financial Planning .... Mr. Timothy KREMER
09 Dir Institutional Research .... Ms. Keri SAMSON
36 Director of Career Services .... Dr. Amy BAUS
29 Director Alumni Relations .... Mr. David MOORE
40 Director Bookstore .... Ms. Margo KETELS
41 Athletic Director .... Mr. Dan RUNKLE
18 Director of Facilities .... Mr. Craig KLOFT
04 Special Assistant to the President .... Dr. John R. STEWART

Upper Iowa University (G)

605 Washington, Box 1857, Fayette IA 52142-1857
County: Fayette FICE Identification: 001893
Unit ID: 154493
Telephone: (563) 425-5200 Carnegie Class: Master's M
FAX Number: (563) 425-5271 Calendar System: Semester
URL: www.uiu.edu
Established: 1857 Annual Undergrad Tuition & Fees: $24,400
Enrollment: 6,822 Coed
Affiliation or Control: Independent Non-Profit IRS Status: 501(c)3
Highest Offering: Master's
Program: Liberal Arts And General; Teacher Preparatory; Business Emphasis
Accreditation: NH, NURSE

01 President .... Dr. Alan G. WALKER
05 Chief Academic Officer .... Dr. David CHOWN
10 Exec Vice President & CFO .... Mr. Donald AUNGST
20 Sr VP for Academic Extension .... Dr. William DUFFY
82 Sr VP International Programs .... Vacant
84 SVP Strategic Pos/Chief Enroll Ofcr .... Mr. Melik KHOURY
07 VP of Admissions .... Ms. Jobyna JOHNSTON
30 VP for Development .... Mr. Wendell SNODGRASS
09 Assoc VP Inst Effect & Assessment .... Ms. Janet SHEPHERD
32 Dean of Student Development .... Ms. Louise SCOTT
36 Assoc Dean Stdnts/Dir Res Life .... Ms. Jean MERKLE
12 Director South Central Region .... Ms. Shawn WILSON
12 Director Mid-West Region .... Mr. Walter BEMBRY
12 Director North Central Region .... Mr. Marshall WHITLOCK
12 Director Mid-Central Region .... Ms. Kathy FRANKEN
06 Registrar .... Mrs. Holly STREETER
08 Director Library Services .... Mrs. Becky WADIAN
41 Athletic Director .... Mr. David MILLER
04 President's Assistant .... Dr. Adriel HILTON
56 Dir Ctr for Distance Educ .... Ms. Barb SCHULTZ
105 Director Internet Development .... Mr. Joel KUNZE
21 Associate Business Ofcr/Controller .... Ms. Laura MATT
36 Director of Career Development .... Mr. Darren NOBLE
35 Dir Student Leadership & Activities .... Mr. Daryl GROVE
26 Exec Dir of Comm & Marketing .... Ms. Monica HEATON
86 Director External Affairs .... Mr. Andrew WENTHE
13 Director Information Technology .... Mr. Terry SMID
15 Director Payroll & Benefits .... Ms. Tammy CAROLAN
88 Director Sports Info Services .... Mr. Howard THOMPSON
18 Chief Facilities/Physical Plant .... Mr. Bryan JOLLEY
40 Bookstore Manager .... Mr. Brett DEVORE

Vatterott College-Des Moines (H)

7000 Fleur Drive, Des Moines IA 50321-2414
County: Polk FICE Identification: 026092
Unit ID: 373058
Telephone: (515) 309-9000 Carnegie Class: Assoc/PrivFP
FAX Number: (515) 309-0366 Calendar System: Other
URL: www.vatterott-college.edu
Established: 1997 Annual Undergrad Tuition & Fees: $11,785
Enrollment: 391 Coed
Affiliation or Control: Proprietary IRS Status: Proprietary
Highest Offering: Associate Degree
Program: Occupational
Accreditation: ACCSC, DA, MAAB

01 CEO & President .... Ms. Pam BELL
10 Chief Financial Officer .... Mr. Dennis BEAVERS
05 Chief Academic Officer .... Dr. John TUCKER
11 Chief Administrative Officer .... Mr. Erio COMICI
12 Campus Director .... Ms. Sarah BOUMA

Waldorf College (I)

106 S 6th Street, Forest City IA 50436-1713
County: Winnebago FICE Identification: 001895
Unit ID: 154518
Telephone: (641) 585-2450 Carnegie Class: Bac/Diverse
FAX Number: (641) 585-8194 Calendar System: Semester
URL: www.waldorf.edu
Established: 1903 Annual Undergrad Tuition & Fees: $19,820
Enrollment: 582 Coed
Affiliation or Control: Proprietary IRS Status: Proprietary
Highest Offering: Baccalaureate
Program: Liberal Arts And General
Accreditation: NH

01 President .... Dr. Robert ALSOP
05 Dean of Col/Vice Pres Acad Affs .... Dr. Scott SEARCY
30 Vice President Advancement .... Vacant
10 Vice President Business Affairs .... Mr. Mason HARMS
04 Assistant to the President .... Ms. Cindy CARTER
32 Dean of Students .... Mr. Jason RAMAKER
92 Dean of Honors Program .... Dr. Suzanne FALCK-YI
20 Associate Academic Dean .... Vacant
07 Director Admissions .... Mr. Scott PITCHER
08 Library Director .... Ms. Amy HILL
29 Director of Alumni Affairs .... Ms. Rita GILBERTSON
06 Registrar .... Ms. Becky STUMME
37 Director of Financial Aid .... Mr. Duane POLSDOFER
18 Director of Facilities Services .... Mr. Allan EGGEBRAATEN
27 Director of Media .... Vacant
26 Communications Director .... Ms. Barbara BARROWS
44 Director of Annual Fund .... Ms. Nancy OLSON
38 Counselor .... Mr. James AMELSBERG
41 Athletic Director .... Mr. Michael SCARANO
39 Director of Residential Life .... Vacant
36 Director Student Placement .... Ms. Mary REISETTER
40 Bookstore Manager .... Ms. Karla SCHAEFER
15 Director Human Resources .... Ms. Dawn RAMAKER

Wartburg College (J)

PO Box 1003, 100 Wartburg Boulevard,
Waverly IA 50677-0903
County: Bremer FICE Identification: 001896
Unit ID: 154527
Telephone: (319) 352-8200 Carnegie Class: Bac/A&S
FAX Number: (319) 352-8514 Calendar System: Other
URL: www.wartburg.edu
Established: 1852 Annual Undergrad Tuition & Fees: $32,740
Enrollment: 1,805 Coed
Affiliation or Control: Evangelical Lutheran Church In America
IRS Status: 501(c)3
Highest Offering: Baccalaureate
Program: Liberal Arts And General; Teacher Preparatory
Accreditation: NH, MUS, SW, TED

01 President .... Dr. Darrel D. COLSON
05 VP Acad Affs/Dean Faculty .... Dr. Mark L. BIERMANN

32 VP Student Life/Dean Students .... Dr. Deborah L. LOERS
10 Vice President for Administration .... Mr. Gary S. GRACE
30 Vice Pres Institutional Advancement .... Mr. Scott C. LEISINGER
84 Vice Pres Enrollment Management .... Dr. Edith J. WALDSTEIN
07 Asst VP Admiss/Alumni/Parent Pgms .... Mr. Jay T. COLEMAN
06 Registrar .... Ms. Sheree S. COVERT
26 Assoc VP for Mktg and Comm .... Mr. Graham GARNER
91 Dir of Info Technology Svcs/CIO .... Mr. Gary L. WIPPERMAN
08 College Librarian .... Ms. Christine L. SCHAFER
29 Dir of Alumni/Parent Rel & Ann Giv .... Mr. Jeff BECK
37 Director of Financial Aid .... Ms. Jen L. SASSMAN
41 Director of Athletics .... Mr. Eric R. WILLIS
42 Dean of the Chapel .... Rev. Ramona S. BOUZARD
18 Director of Physical Plant .... Mr. John A. WUERTZ
39 Asst Dean/Dir of Residential Life .... Mr. Wesley H. BROOKS
36 Assoc Dir of Pathways/Career Svcs .... Mr. Derek N. SOLHEIM
38 Director of Counseling Svcs .... Mrs. Stephanie R. NEWSOM
40 Bookstore Manager .... Ms. Heather PATRICK
85 Director of International Programs .... Ms. Jenna RINEHART
35 Director of Campus Programming .... Ms. Ashley LANG
88 Campus Pastor .... Rev. Brian A. BECKSTROM
23 Dir of Health & Wellness Promotion ..... Ms. Dawn R. WIEGMANN
21 Chief Business Officer & Treasurer .... Mr. Richard W. SEGGERMAN
15 Director of Human Resources .... Ms. Jane J. JUCHEMS
30 Director of Development .... Mr. Donald J. MEYER
09 Dir of Inst Research/Prof of Psych .... Dr. Fred D. RIBICH
92 Director Honors Program .... Dr. Mariah H. BIRGEN
04 Assistant to the President .... Ms. Janeen K. STEWART
20 Asst Dean for Academic Affairs .... Ms. Stephanie S. TEKIPPE

Wartburg Theological Seminary (A)

333 Wartburg Place, PO Box 5004, Dubuque IA 52004-5004

County: Dubuque FICE Identification: 001897
Unit ID: 154536
Telephone: (563) 589-0200 Carnegie Class: Spec/Faith
FAX Number: (563) 589-0333 Calendar System: 4/1/4
URL: www.wartburgseminary.edu
Established: 1854 Annual Graduate Tuition & Fees: $14,700
Enrollment: 153 Coed
Affiliation or Control: Evangelical Lutheran Church In America
IRS Status: 501(c)3
Highest Offering: Master's; No Undergraduates
Program: Professional
Accreditation: NH, THEOL

01 President .... Dr. Stanley N. OLSON
05 Academic Dean of the Seminary .... Dr. Craig L. NESSAN
10 Vice Pres for Finance & Operations ... Mr. Andy B. WILLENBORG
30 Vice President for Mission Support .... Rev. Len HOFFMANN
15 Assistant to President & Dir of HR .... Ms. Eileen LEMAY
88 Dean for Vocation .... Rev. Amy L. CURRENT
08 Library Director .... Ms. Susan J S. EBERTZ
06 Registrar/Admin Assistant to Dean .... Dr. Kevin L. ANDERSON
13 Director of Information Technology .... Ms. Lori L. BRUFLODT

Western Iowa Tech Community College (B)

PO Box 5199, 4647 Stone Avenue, Sioux City IA 51102-5199

County: Woodbury FICE Identification: 007316
Unit ID: 154572
Telephone: (712) 274-6400 Carnegie Class: Assoc/Pub-R-L
FAX Number: (712) 274-6412 Calendar System: Semester
URL: www.witcc.edu
Established: 1966 Annual Undergrad Tuition & Fees (In-District): $4,305
Enrollment: 6,789 Coed
Affiliation or Control: State/Local IRS Status: 501(c)3
Highest Offering: Associate Degree
Program: Occupational; 2-Year Principally Bachelor's Creditable
Accreditation: NH, DA, EMT, MAC, PNUR, PTAA, SURGT

01 President .... Dr. Terry MURRELL
03 Executive Vice President .... Dr. Juline ALBERT
10 VP Finance/Administrative Svcs/CFO .... Mr. Troy JASMAN
31 Dean of Corporate College .... Mr. Martin REIMER
15 Exec Director of Human Resources .... Ms. Brenda BRADLEY
13 Dean of Information Technology .... Mr. Mike LOGAN
30 Exec Director College Development ...... Ms. Carolyn ELLWANGER
32 Dean of Students .... Dr. Tricia SUTHERLAND
05 Dean of Instruction/Chief Acad Ofcr .... Vacant
31 Dean External Rels/Dir Job Trng Prt .... Dr. Julene STOIK
84 Dean of Enrollment Services .... Ms. Janet GILL
88 Director of Economic Development .... Ms. Angela LAWSON
08 Library Services Manager .... Ms. Sharon DYKSHOORN
88 KWIT/KOJI-FM General Manager .... Ms. Gretchen GONDEK
88 Director Small Business Devel Ctr .... Mr. Dan WUBBENA
18 Director Phys Plant/College Safety .... Mr. Kyle HUESER
09 Dir Instl Rsrch/Resource Dev Coord .... Mr. Larry OBERMEYER
07 Director of Recruitment .... Ms. Lora VANDER ZWAAG
26 Director Marketing/Publications .... Ms. Emma HEWITT
37 Director of Financial Aid .... Mr. Don DUZIK

William Penn University (C)

201 Trueblood Avenue, Oskaloosa IA 52577-1799

County: Mahaska FICE Identification: 001900
Unit ID: 154590
Telephone: (641) 673-1001 Carnegie Class: Bac/Diverse
FAX Number: (641) 673-1396 Calendar System: Semester
URL: www.wmpenn.edu
Established: 1873 Annual Undergrad Tuition & Fees: $21,720
Enrollment: 2,104 Coed
Affiliation or Control: Friends IRS Status: 501(c)3
Highest Offering: Master's
Program: Liberal Arts And General; Teacher Preparatory
Accreditation: NH

01 President .... Dr. Ann FIELDS
30 Vice President for Advancement .... Ms. Sherry TAYLOR
05 Vice President for Academic Affairs .... Dr. Noel STAHLE
32 Executive Vice President .... Mr. John OTTOSSON
10 VP Financial Operations .... Ms. Bonnie JOHNSON
41 VP Athletics .... Mr. Greg HAFNER
44 Assoc VP for Development .... Ms. Marsha RIORDAN
108 Assoc VP Assessment/Devel/Planning .. Dr. Mary Pat WOHLFORD
07 Director of Admissions .... Ms. Kira STRONG
06 Registrar .... Dr. Michael EDWARDS
37 Director of Financial Aid .... Ms. Cyndi PEIFFER
36 Career Services Coordinator .... Ms. Debbie STEVENS
08 Head Librarian .... Ms. Julie HANSEN
26 Dir Public Relations/Marketing .... Ms. Amber LAKE
29 Director of Alumni Relations .... Ms. Jodi GREINER
31 Director of Community Relations .... Ms. Jill DURSKY
15 Human Resource Manager .... Ms. Louise BLAINE
35 Director of Student Activities .... Mr. Levi TARBELL
38 Student Counselor .... Mr. Frank SIMS
09 Director of Institutional Research .... Vacant
42 Campus Minister .... Mr. Spencer THURY
40 Bookstore Manager .... Ms. Heidi PARKER
18 Director of Buildings & Grounds .... Mr. Milt CAMPBELL
83 Chair Div of Social/Behavioral Sci .... Dr. Michael COLLINS
72 Chair Div of Applied Technology .... Dr. Jim DROST
53 Chair Division of Education .... Dr. Pamela MARTIN
50 Chair Div of Business Admin .... Dr. Lonny L. WILSON
79 Chair Division of Humanities .... Dr. Jared PEARCE
76 Chair Div of Health & Life Sciences .... Dr. James A. NORTH

KANSAS

Allen County Community College (D)

1801 N Cottonwood, Iola KS 66749-1698

County: Allen FICE Identification: 001901
Unit ID: 154642
Telephone: (620) 365-5116 Carnegie Class: Assoc/Pub-R-M
FAX Number: (620) 365-7406 Calendar System: Semester
URL: www.allencc.edu
Established: 1923 Annual Undergrad Tuition & Fees (In-District): $2,176
Enrollment: 2,878 Coed
Affiliation or Control: State/Local IRS Status: 501(c)3
Highest Offering: Associate Degree
Program: Occupational; 2-Year Principally Bachelor's Creditable
Accreditation: NH

01 President .... Mr. John A. MASTERSON
05 Vice Pres for Academic Affairs .... Mr. Jon MARSHALL
10 Vice Pres for Finance & Operations .... Mr. Steve TROXEL
32 Vice Pres Student Affairs .... Ms. Cynthia JACOBSON
12 Dean for the Iola Campus .... Mrs. Tosca HARRIS
12 Dean for the Burlingame Campus .... Mr. Bob REAVIS
106 Dean for Online Learning .... Mrs. Regena BAILEY-AYE
08 Director of Library .... Mr. Steven ANDERSON
13 Director of MIS .... Mr. Doug DUNLAP
38 Director of Guidance Services .... Dr. Valis MCLEAN
37 Director of Financial Aid .... Mrs. Vicki CURRY
30 Director of Development .... Mrs. Cynthia ADAMS
18 Director of Physical Plant Opers .... Mr. Don BAUER
07 Director of Admissions .... Ms. Rebecca BILDERBACK
41 Director of Athletics .... Ms. Jessica PETERS
40 Director of Bookstore .... Mrs. Donna CASON
17 Allied Health Director .... Mrs. April HENRY
85 Foreign Student Advisor .... Mr. John STEEL
90 Director Academic Computing .... Ms. Anna CATTERSON
09 Director Inst Research/Assessment .... Vacant
06 Registrar .... Mrs. Bobbie HAVILAND
26 Public Relations Coordinator .... Mrs. Nancy FORD

The Art Institutes International - Kansas City (E)

8208 Melrose Drive, Lenexa KS 66214

County: Johnson Identification: 666765
Unit ID: 452018
Telephone: (913) 217-4600 Carnegie Class: Spec/Arts
FAX Number: (913) 217-2690 Calendar System: Semester
URL: www.artinstitutes.edu
Established: 2008 Annual Undergrad Tuition & Fees: $17,668
Enrollment: 560 Coed
Affiliation or Control: Proprietary IRS Status: Proprietary
Highest Offering: Baccalaureate
Program: Occupational
Accreditation: ACICS

01 President .... Ms. Cyndie SHADOW

† Branch campus of The Art Institute of Phoeniz, AZ.

Baker University (F)

618 Eighth Street, Baldwin City KS 66006-0065

County: Douglas FICE Identification: 001903
Unit ID: 154688
Telephone: (785) 594-6451 Carnegie Class: Master's L
FAX Number: (785) 594-2522 Calendar System: 4/1/4
URL: www.bakeru.edu
Established: 1858 Annual Undergrad Tuition & Fees: $24,470
Enrollment: 3,536 Coed
Affiliation or Control: United Methodist IRS Status: 501(c)3
Highest Offering: Doctorate
Program: Liberal Arts And General; Teacher Preparatory; Professional
Accreditation: NH, ACBSP, MUS, NURSE, TED

01 President .... Dr. Patricia N. LONG
11 COO & Exec VP for Admin Services .... Dr. Susan LINDAHL
05 Exec VP Acad Affs/Dn Col Arts/Scis .... Dr. Brian POSLER
58 VP/Dean Sch Prof/Grad Studies .... Dr. Peggy HARRIS
30 VP for University Advancement .... Ms. Lyn LAKIN
84 VP for Enrollment Mgmt/Student Dev .... Dr. Mark BANDRE
13 VP of Technology & SPGS Operation .... Mr. Simon MAXWELL
66 VP/Dean of School of Nursing .... Dr. Kathleen HARR
44 VP for Endowment/Planned Giving .... Mr. Jerry WEAKLEY
26 Director of Marketing & Comm .... Mr. Neil KULBISKI
06 University Registrar .... Ms. Ruth MILLER
42 Minister to the University .... Dr. Ira L. DESPAIN
32 Dean of Students .... Dr. Cassy BAILEY
30 Sr Dir of University Advancement .... Mr. Patrick MIKESIC
09 Dir of Inst Research/Math Prof .... Dr. Jean JOHNSON
88 Asst Dean Stdnt Engage & Success .... Dr. Judith SMRHA
97 Interim Asst Dean Liberal Studies .... Dr. Erin JOYCE
35 Associate Dean of Students .... Dr. Teresa CLOUNCH
45 Special Asst to Pres Planning/Accr .... Dr. Rob FLAHERTY
08 Director of Library Services .... Ms. Kay BRADT
07 Director of Enrollment Management .... Mr. Kevin KROPF
37 Director of Financial Aid .... Mrs. Jeanne MOTT
36 Director of Career Services .... Ms. Susan WADE
41 Director Of Athletics .... Ms. Theresa YETMAR
23 Dir of Student Health Services .... Ms. Ruth SARNA
18 Director of Physical Plant .... Mr. Jeremy PORTLOCK
21 University Controller .... Ms. Melissa VAN LEIDEN
29 Dir of Alumni & Corporate Relations .... Mr. Doug BARTH
38 Director Counseling Center .... Dr. Tim HODGES
28 Dir Multicultural Affs & Retention .... Mr. Silas DULAN
26 Public Relations Director .... Mr. Steve ROTTINGHAUS
15 Dir of Human Resources & Staff Dev .... Ms. Connie DEEL
88 Consultant to Pres Health Svc Exp .... Dr. Kathryn BALLOU

Barclay College (G)

607 N Kingman, Haviland KS 67059-0288

County: Kiowa FICE Identification: 001917
Unit ID: 155070
Telephone: (620) 862-5252 Carnegie Class: Spec/Faith
FAX Number: (620) 862-5242 Calendar System: Semester
URL: www.barclaycollege.edu
Established: 1917 Annual Undergrad Tuition & Fees: $13,990
Enrollment: 244 Coed
Affiliation or Control: Independent Non-Profit IRS Status: 501(c)3
Highest Offering: Baccalaureate
Program: Liberal Arts And General; Religious Emphasis
Accreditation: BI

01 President .... Dr. Royce FRAZIER
05 VP Academics .... Dr. Jim LS SHANA
10 VP Business Services .... Mr. Lee ANDERS
32 VP Student Services .... Mr. Kevin LEE
30 VP Institutional Advancement .... Dr. Herb FRAZIER
06 VP Registration and Records .... Dr. Glenn W. LEPPERT
37 Director Student Financial Aid .... Mr. Ryan HAASE
07 Admissions Counselor .... Mr. Justin KENDALL
08 Librarian .... Mr. Pat HALL
29 Alumni Relations .... Dr. Herb FRAZIER

Barton County Community College (H)

245 NE 30th Road, Great Bend KS 67530-9107

County: Barton FICE Identification: 004608
Unit ID: 154697
Telephone: (620) 792-2701 Carnegie Class: Assoc/Pub-R-L
FAX Number: (620) 792-5624 Calendar System: Semester
URL: www.bartonccc.edu
Established: 1965 Annual Undergrad Tuition & Fees (In-District): $2,963
Enrollment: 4,909 Coed
Affiliation or Control: State/Local IRS Status: 501(c)3
Highest Offering: Associate Degree
Program: Occupational; 2-Year Principally Bachelor's Creditable
Accreditation: NH, ADNUR, EMT, MLTAD

01 President .... Dr. Carl R. HEILMAN
05 VP of Instruction & Student Svcs .... Dr. Penny QUINN
11 Dean of Administration .... Mr. Mark E. DEAN
27 Dean of Information Services .... Mr. Charles PERKINS
32 Dean of Student Services .... Mrs. Angela M. MADDY
20 Dean of Academics .... Dr. Richard L. ABEL
88 Dean Ft Riley Lrng Svcs/Mil Ops .... Mr. Gene KINGSLIEN
103 Dean Workforce Training & Cmty Educ .... Mrs. Elaine R. SIMMONS
37 Asst Dean Stndt Svcs/Dir Fin Aid .... Mrs. Myrna L. PERKINS
30 Exec Dir Institutional Advancement .... Mrs. Darnell HOLOPIREK
66 Exec Dir of Nursing & Healthcare Ed .... Dr. Kathy KOTTAS
50 Exec Dir of Business/Tech/Cmty Educ .... Ms. Jane HOWARD
103 Exec Dir of Workforce Trn & Cmty Ed .... Mrs. Julie KRAMP
26 Dir of Public Relations & Marketing .... Mr. Brandon STEINERT
04 Assistant to President .... Mrs. Amye SCHNEIDER
41 Director of Athletics .... Mr. Trevor ROLFS

08 Director of Learning Resources ..... Mrs. ReGina REYNOLDS-CASPER
15 Director of Human Resources ..... Mrs. Julie A. KNOBLICH
07 Director of Admissions ..... Ms. Tana COOPER
19 Coordinator of Facility Management ..... Mr. Jim D. IRELAND
25 Director of Grants ..... Ms. Cathie R. OSHIRO
06 Registrar ..... Mrs. Lori D. CROWTHER
40 Bookstore Manager ..... Mrs. Connie M. KERNS
09 Coord of Instruct & Instnl Research ..... Mrs. Caicey L. CRUTCHER
39 Coordinator of Student Housing ..... Mr. Dan MCFADDEN

Benedictine College (A)

1020 N 2nd Street, Atchison KS 66002-1499
County: Atchison　FICE Identification: 010256
Unit ID: 154712
Telephone: (913) 367-5340　Carnegie Class: Bac/Diverse
FAX Number: (913) 367-6566　Calendar System: Semester
URL: www.benedictine.edu
Established: 1858　Annual Undergrad Tuition & Fees: $22,550
Enrollment: 2,070　Coed
Affiliation or Control: Roman Catholic　IRS Status: 501(c)3
Highest Offering: Master's
Program: Liberal Arts And General; Teacher Preparatory; Business Emphasis
Accreditation: NH, MUS, NURSE, TED

01 President ..... Mr. Stephen D. MINNIS
05 Dean of the College ..... Dr. Kimberly C. SHANKMAN
10 Chief Financial Officer ..... Mr. Ronald J. OLINGER
30 Vice President Advancement ..... Ms. Kelly J. VOWELS
84 Dean of Enrollment Management ..... Mr. Pete HELGESEN
32 Vice President of Student Life ..... Dr. Linda HENRY
35 Dean of Students ..... Dr. Joseph WURTZ
42 Director for Mission and Ministry ..... Fr. Brendan ROLLING, OSB
41 Athletic Director ..... Mr. Charles GARTENMAYER
26 Vice President for College Rels ..... Mr. Tom HOOPES
20 Assoc Dean & Registrar ..... Sr. Linda HERNDON, OSB
09 Assistant Dean of the College ..... Vacant
58 Exec Dir of Grad Business Programs ..... Mr. Dave GEENENS
58 Director of MASL/Asst Prof Educ ..... Dr. Cheryl REDING
37 Director of Student Financial Aid ..... Mr. Tony TANKING
27 Dir of Marketing & Communications ..... Mr. Steve JOHNSON
38 Director of Counseling Center ..... Mr. Kerry A. MARVIN
23 Director of Student Health Services ..... Ms. Janet ADRIAN
18 Director of Operations ..... Mr. Matt FASSERO
14 Dir of Tech & Information Sys ..... Mr. Randy ROWLAND
88 Director of International Program ..... Mr. Daniele MUSSO
08 Librarian ..... Mr. Steven GROMATZKY
39 Director of Residence Life ..... Mr. Sean MULCAHY
21 Bursar ..... Ms. Becky MILLER
35 Student Activities Director ..... Mr. Matt LITT
36 Director of Career Services ..... Ms. Becky GILMORE
29 Director of Planned Giving & Alumni ..... Mr. Tim ANDREWS

Bethany College (B)

335 E Swensson Street, Lindsborg KS 67456-1895
County: McPherson　FICE Identification: 001904
Unit ID: 154721
Telephone: (785) 227-3311　Carnegie Class: Bac/Diverse
FAX Number: (785) 227-2004　Calendar System: 4/1/4
URL: www.bethanylb.edu
Established: 1881　Annual Undergrad Tuition & Fees: $22,624
Enrollment: 589　Coed
Affiliation or Control: Evangelical Lutheran Church In America
IRS Status: 501(c)3
Highest Offering: Baccalaureate
Program: Liberal Arts And General; Teacher Preparatory; Professional
Accreditation: NH, MUS, TED

01 President ..... Dr. Edward F. LEONARD, III
05 Provost and Dean of the College ..... Dr. Kenneth M. MACUR
30 Vice President of Advancement ..... Mr. Jim RUBLE
10 VP for Finance and Operations ..... Mr. Bob SCHMOLL
21 Accountant ..... Mr. John COYKENDALL
32 Dean for Student Life ..... Vacant
84 VP for Recruitment & Marketing ..... Ms. Tricia HAWK
88 Assoc Vice Pres for Development ..... Mr. Warren OLSON
44 Exec Dir of Alumni & Advancement ..... Mr. Galen B. BUNNING
06 Registrar ..... Ms. Jill MEGREDY
08 Director of Library ..... Mrs. Denise K. CARSON
41 Athletic Director ..... Mr. Jon M. DANIELS
37 Director Financial Aid ..... Ms. Amber MANETH
18 Director Campus Facilities ..... Mr. Randy JIRAK
13 Director of Computer Services ..... Mr. Brian RICHTER
26 Director of Communications ..... Ms. Stephanie MCDOWELL
29 Director Alumni Development ..... Ms. Molly B. JOHNSON
36 Director Career Services ..... Ms. Jessica L. SCHIERLING
39 Residential Education Director ..... Ms. Trace TAYLOR
42 Campus Pastor ..... Rev. Naomi M. STRAND
35 Director Campus Activities ..... Ms. Roxie L. SJOGREN
88 Program Dir Athletic Training ..... Dr. David SLACK
53 Program Director Teacher Education ..... Mr. Gail KONZEM
64 Music Department Chair ..... Dr. Jeffrey WALL
15 Director of Human Resources ..... Mrs. Jo Ann M. MATTISON
09 Director of Assessment and Research ..... Ms. Joanne GUNSOLLEY
40 Bookstore Manager ..... Mrs. Brenda C. SMITH
92 Honors Program Coordinator ..... Dr. Kristin VAN TASSEL
38 Student Counselor ..... Ms. Valoree BARRETT
85 Coord Student Life & Intl Program ..... Ms. Charlotte ANDERSON

Bethel College (C)

300 E 27th Street, North Newton KS 67117-0531
County: Harvey　FICE Identification: 001905
Unit ID: 154749
Telephone: (316) 283-2500　Carnegie Class: Bac/Diverse
FAX Number: (316) 284-5286　Calendar System: 4/1/4
URL: www.bethelks.edu
Established: 1887　Annual Undergrad Tuition & Fees: $22,600
Enrollment: 523　Coed
Affiliation or Control: Mennonite Church　IRS Status: 501(c)3
Highest Offering: Baccalaureate
Program: Liberal Arts And General; Teacher Preparatory; Professional
Accreditation: NH, NURSE, SW, TED

01 President ..... Dr. Perry D. WHITE
04 Assistant to the President ..... Ms. Rosa BARRERA
05 Vice President Academic Affairs ..... Dr. Brad BORN
32 Vice President Student Life ..... Mr. Aaron L. AUSTIN
41 Athletic Director ..... Mr. Kent ALLSHOUSE
30 Vice President Advancement ..... Ms. Sondra KOONTZ
10 Vice Presiden for Business Affairs ..... Mr. Allen WEDEL
26 VP for Marketing and Communications ..... Ms. Lori LIVENGOOD
06 Registrar ..... Ms. Marcia K. MILLER
44 Director of Development ..... Mr. Fred GOERING
07 Vice President for Admissions ..... Mr. Todd H. MOORE
37 Director of Financial Aid ..... Mr. Tony GRABER
29 Director of Alumni Relations ..... Mr. David LINSCHEID
08 Head Librarian ..... Ms. Gail STUCKY
42 Director of Church Relations ..... Mr. Dale SCHRAG
18 Chief Facilities/Physical Plant ..... Mr. Les GOERZEN

Brown Mackie College-Kansas City (D)

9705 Lenexa Drive, Lenexa KS 66215-1345
County: Johnson　Identification: 666091
Unit ID: 154767
Telephone: (913) 768-1900　Carnegie Class: Assoc/PrivFP
FAX Number: (913) 495-9555　Calendar System: Other
URL: www.brownmackie.edu
Established: 1984　Annual Undergrad Tuition & Fees: $11,124
Enrollment: 464　Coed
Affiliation or Control: Proprietary　IRS Status: Proprietary
Highest Offering: Associate Degree
Program: Occupational; 2-Year Principally Bachelor's Creditable; Business Emphasis
Accreditation: &NH, OTA

01 President ..... Vacant
05 Dean of Academic Affairs ..... Ms. Connie BEENE
07 Senior Director of Admissions ..... Vacant
06 Registrar ..... Ms. Mary Lou WHITTON
36 Director of Career Services ..... Ms. Mickie HOLLIDAY

† Regional accreditation is carried under the parent institution in Salina, KS.

Brown Mackie College-Salina (E)

2106 S 9th Street, Salina KS 67401-7307
County: Saline　FICE Identification: 006755
Unit ID: 154776
Telephone: (785) 825-5422　Carnegie Class: Assoc/PrivFP
FAX Number: (785) 827-7623　Calendar System: Other
URL: www.brownmackie.edu
Established: 1892　Annual Undergrad Tuition & Fees: $11,124
Enrollment: 402　Coed
Affiliation or Control: Proprietary　IRS Status: Proprietary
Highest Offering: Associate Degree
Program: Occupational; 2-Year Principally Bachelor's Creditable; Business Emphasis
Accreditation: NH, OTA

01 President ..... Ms. Judy HOLMES
05 Dean of Academic Affairs ..... Mr. Dennis RITTLE
07 Senior Director of Admissions ..... Ms. Diann HEATH
06 Registrar ..... Ms. Lisa GRAVES
36 Director of Career Services ..... Ms. Garnett ZAMBONI

Bryan College (F)

1527 SW Fairlawn Road, Topeka KS 66604
County: Shawnee　FICE Identification: 030662
Unit ID: 154794
Telephone: (785) 272-0889　Carnegie Class: Assoc/PrivFP
FAX Number: (785) 272-4538　Calendar System: Other
URL: www.bryancolleges.edu
Established: N/A　Annual Undergrad Tuition & Fees: N/A
Enrollment: 200　Coed
Affiliation or Control: Proprietary　IRS Status: Proprietary
Highest Offering: Associate Degree
Program: Occupational
Accreditation: ACICS

01 Executive Director ..... Mr. Wayne MAJOR

Butler Community College (G)

901 S. Haverhill Road, El Dorado KS 67042-3225
County: Butler　FICE Identification: 001906
Unit ID: 154800
Telephone: (316) 321-2222　Carnegie Class: Assoc/Pub-S-MC
FAX Number: (316) 322-3109　Calendar System: Semester
URL: www.butlercc.edu
Established: 1927　Annual Undergrad Tuition & Fees (In-District): $2,136
Enrollment: 10,061　Coed
Affiliation or Control: Local　IRS Status: 501(c)3
Highest Offering: Associate Degree
Program: Occupational; 2-Year Principally Bachelor's Creditable; Liberal Arts And General
Accreditation: NH, ACBSP, ADNUR, ENGT

01 President ..... Dr. Jacqueline VIETTI
05 Vice President of Academics ..... Dr. Karla FISHER
10 Vice President of Finance ..... Mr. Kent WILLIAMS
32 Vice President of Student Services ..... Mr. Bill RINKENBAUGH
08 Reference Librarian ..... Ms. Judy BASTIN
06 Registrar ..... Ms. Rhonda MORRISON
09 Director of Institutional Research ..... Dr. Gene GEORGE
15 Director Personnel Services ..... Ms. Vicki LONG
21 Associate Business Officer ..... Ms. Edith WAUGH
26 Director Public Information/Rels ..... Mr. Ryan ENTZ
29 Director Alumni Relations ..... Ms. Keri MYERS
30 Chief Development ..... Ms. Stacy COFER
35 Director Student Affairs/Counseling ..... Ms. Karen GELVIN
36 Director Student Placement ..... Ms. Loretta PATTERSON
37 Director Student Financial Aid ..... Ms. Susie EDWARDS
84 Director Enrollment Management ..... Ms. Jessica OHMAN
18 Director Facilities ..... Mr. Roger NEIFERT
28 Director of Diversity ..... Vacant
96 Director of Purchasing ..... Ms. Regina KIEFFER
07 Director of Admissions ..... Ms. Kirsten ALLEN
38 Director Student Counseling ..... Ms. Jessica OHMAN

Central Baptist Theological Seminary (H)

6601 Monticello Road, Shawnee KS 66226-3513
County: Johnson　FICE Identification: 001907
Unit ID: 154837
Telephone: (913) 667-5700　Carnegie Class: Spec/Faith
FAX Number: (913) 371-8110　Calendar System: Semester
URL: www.cbts.edu
Established: 1901　Annual Graduate Tuition & Fees: $6,780
Enrollment: 189　Coed
Affiliation or Control: Baptist　IRS Status: 501(c)3
Highest Offering: Doctorate; No Undergraduates
Program: Professional; Religious Emphasis
Accreditation: NH, THEOL

01 President ..... Dr. Molly T. MARSHALL
05 Dean of the Seminary ..... Dr. Robert E. JOHNSON
03 Executive Vice President ..... Mr. George TOWNSEND
30 VP for Institutional Advancement ..... Dr. John GRAVLEY
06 Assistant to the Dean/Registrar ..... Mr. Stephen GUINN
26 Director of Seminary Relations ..... Ms. Robin SANDBOTHE
07 Director of Recruitment ..... Mrs. Debra SERMONS

Central Christian College of Kansas (I)

1200 S Main, PO Box 1403, McPherson KS 67460-5799
County: McPherson　FICE Identification: 001908
Unit ID: 154855
Telephone: (620) 241-0723　Carnegie Class: Bac/Diverse
FAX Number: (620) 241-6032　Calendar System: 4/1/4
URL: www.centralchristian.edu
Established: 1884　Annual Undergrad Tuition & Fees: $19,500
Enrollment: 650　Coed
Affiliation or Control: Free Methodist　IRS Status: 501(c)3
Highest Offering: Baccalaureate
Program: Liberal Arts And General
Accreditation: NH

01 President ..... Mr. Hal HOXIE
05 Vice President of Academics ..... Dr. Leonard FAVARA, JR.
10 Vice President of Finance ..... Dr. David FERRELL
30 Vice President of Advancement ..... Vacant
32 Chief Student Affairs Officer ..... Rev. Chris SMITH
53 Dean of Professional Education ..... Dr. Dean KROEKER
21 Director of Finance ..... Mr. Dale BURGE
06 Registrar ..... Mrs. Bev KELLEY
41 Athletic Director ..... Mr. Chad KERR
07 Director of Admissions ..... Mr. Rick WYATT
09 Director of Institutional Research ..... Mr. Marc SELLER
37 Director of Financial Aid ..... Mr. Mike REIMER

Cleveland Chiropractic College - Kansas City (J)

10850 Lowell Avenue, Overland Park KS 66210
County: Johnson　FICE Identification: 020907
Unit ID: 177038
Telephone: (913) 234-0600　Carnegie Class: Spec/Health
FAX Number: (913) 234-0904　Calendar System: Trimester
URL: www.cleveland.edu
Established: 1922　Annual Undergrad Tuition & Fees: $8,484
Enrollment: 569　Coed
Affiliation or Control: Independent Non-Profit　IRS Status: 501(c)3
Highest Offering: First Professional Degree
Program: Professional
Accreditation: NH, CHIRO

01 President Dr. Carl S. CLEVELAND, III
10 Chief Operating Officer Mr. Jeff KARP
05 Provost Dr. Ashley CLEVELAND
26 VP of Campus and Alumni Relations Dr. Clark BECKLEY
20 Dean of Pre-Clinical Education Dr. Paul BARLETT
21 Controller Ms. Marla COPE
27 Director of Communications Mr. Alan MORGAN
06 Director of Academic Records Mr. David FOOSE
37 Director of Financial Aid Ms. Caprice CALAMAIO
16 Director of Human Resources Mr. Dale MARRANT
09 Director of Institutional Reporting Dr. Christena NICHOLSON
09 Director of Research Dr. Mark T. PFEFER
35 Director of Student Services Ms. Jalonna BOWIE
07 Director of Admissions Ms. Melissa DENTON
20 Dean of Clinical Education Dr. Julia BARTLETT
08 Library Director Ms. Marcia M. THOMAS
13 Systems Administrator Mr. Calvin DANIELS
04 Assistant to the President Ms. Marjorie BRADSHAW
18 Director of Facilities Mgmt Mr. Frank HANEY

Cloud County Community College (A)

2221 Campus Drive, Concordia KS 66901-1002
County: Cloud FICE Identification: 001909
Unit ID: 154907
Telephone: (785) 243-1435 Carnegie Class: Assoc/Pub-R-M
FAX Number: (785) 243-1459 Calendar System: Semester
URL: www.cloud.edu
Established: 1965 Annual Undergrad Tuition & Fees (In-District): $2,910
Enrollment: 3,048 Coed
Affiliation or Control: State/Local IRS Status: 501(c)3
Highest Offering: Associate Degree
Program: Occupational; 2-Year Principally Bachelor's Creditable
Accreditation: NH, ADNUR

01 President Dr. Danette TOONE
05 Vice President for Academic Affairs Dr. Kimberly KRULL
84 VP Enrollment Mgmt/Student Services Mr. Joel FIGGS
11 Vice Pres for Administrative Svcs Mr. Robert MAXSON
30 Director Institutional Advancement Vacant
07 Director of Admissions Ms. Kimberly REYNOLDS
08 Director of Library Services Ms. Jennifer SCHROEDER
41 Athletic Director Mr. Matthew BECHARD
06 Registrar Mrs. Linda PETERSEN
18 Chief Facilities/Physical Plant Mr. Rex E. SICARD
26 Chief Public Relations Officer Ms. Jenny ACREE
102 Ex Dir Cloud County Cmty Col Found Mr. James LUKACEVICH
37 Director Student Financial Aid Ms. Suzi KNOETTGEN
38 Director Advising & Retention Ms. Ashley DOUGLAS
15 Coordinator of Human Resources Ms. Christine WILSON

Coffeyville Community College (B)

400 W 11th Street, Coffeyville KS 67337-5064
County: Montgomery FICE Identification: 001910
Unit ID: 154925
Telephone: (620) 251-7700 Carnegie Class: Assoc/Pub-R-S
FAX Number: (620) 252-7098 Calendar System: Semester
URL: www.coffeyville.edu
Established: 1923 Annual Undergrad Tuition & Fees (In-District): $2,080
Enrollment: 1,932 Coed
Affiliation or Control: State/Local IRS Status: 501(c)3
Highest Offering: Associate Degree
Program: Occupational; 2-Year Principally Bachelor's Creditable
Accreditation: NH, EMT, MAC

01 President Ms. Linda MOLEY
05 Vice President for Learning Mrs. Alysia JOHNSTON
32 Vice President for Student Services Mrs. Jill KOSLOSKY
10 Vice Pres for Operations & Finance Mr. Jeff MORRIS
88 VP for Innovation/Bus Initiatives Mr. Marlon THORNBURG
102 Exec Director-CCC Foundation Mr. Dickie ROLLS
26 Marketing Director/Grant Writer Mrs. Lisa KUEHN
06 Registrar Mrs. Deborah OESTMANN
08 Director Learning Resource Center Mr. Marty EVENSVOLD
37 Director of Financial Aid Mrs. Pam FEERER
18 Director of Buildings/Ground Ms. Vivian FROST
85 Director of International Students Mrs. Marla LARIMORE
51 Director of Continuing Education Vacant
106 Director of Distance Learning Mr. Brad WEBER
12 Director Columbus Technical Campus Mrs. Cindy HARROLD
35 Director of Student Life Mr. Andy MUNDAY
40 Bookstore Manager Mrs. Karen STRIMPLE
72 Dean of Technology Vacant
15 Director of Personnel Mrs. Cindy SUTHERLAND
41 Athletics Director Mr. Jeff LEIKER
36 Student Counselor/Academic Advisor Mrs. Delia NORTHRUP

Colby Community College (C)

1255 S Range, Colby KS 67701-4099
County: Thomas FICE Identification: 001911
Unit ID: 154934
Telephone: (785) 462-3984 Carnegie Class: Assoc/Pub-R-M
FAX Number: (785) 460-4699 Calendar System: Semester
URL: www.colbycc.edu
Established: 1964 Annual Undergrad Tuition & Fees (In-District): $3,040
Enrollment: 1,461 Coed
Affiliation or Control: State/Local IRS Status: 501(c)3
Highest Offering: Associate Degree
Program: Occupational; 2-Year Principally Bachelor's Creditable
Accreditation: NH, ADNUR, PTAA

01 President Dr. Stephen M. VACIK
05 Dean of Academic Affairs Mrs. Joyce WASHBURN
32 VP of Student Affairs Dr. Keegan NICHOLS
10 Vice President of Fiscal Affairs Mr. Alan WAITES
06 Registrar Ms. Brette PFEIFER
08 Librarian Mrs. Tara SCHROER
26 Director of Public Information Mrs. Deborah SCHWANKE
09 Director Institutional Research Vacant
07 Director of Admissions Mrs. Nikol NOLAN
18 Dean of External Affairs Mr. Barry KAAZ
37 Director of Student Financial Aid Mrs. Paula HALVORSON
29 Director Alumni Relations Mr. Nick WELLS
41 Athletic Director Mr. Ryan STURDY
14 Director of Computer Center Mr. Jess RANDEL

Cowley County Community College (D)

125 S Second, PO Box 1147,
Arkansas City KS 67005-1147
County: Cowley FICE Identification: 001902
Unit ID: 154952
Telephone: (620) 442-0430 Carnegie Class: Assoc/Pub-R-M
FAX Number: (620) 441-5350 Calendar System: Semester
URL: www.cowley.edu
Established: 1922 Annual Undergrad Tuition & Fees (In-District): $2,280
Enrollment: 4,304 Coed
Affiliation or Control: Local IRS Status: 501(c)3
Highest Offering: Associate Degree
Program: Occupational; 2-Year Principally Bachelor's Creditable
Accreditation: NH, EMT

01 President Dr. Patrick J. MCATEE
10 Exec Vice Pres of Business Services Mr. Tony CROUCH
05 Vice President of Academic Affairs Mr. Slade GRIFFITHS
32 Vice President of Student Affairs Mrs. Sue SAIA
41 Athletic Director Mr. Dick SPEAS
13 Vice Pres of Research & Technology Mr. Charles MCKOWN
30 Vice Pres Institutional Development Mr. Ben SCHEARS
06 Registrar Mr. Mark BRITTON
26 Dir Inst Comm/Public Relations Mr. Rama PEROO

Dodge City Community College (E)

2501 N 14th Avenue, Dodge City KS 67801-2399
County: Ford FICE Identification: 001913
Unit ID: 154998
Telephone: (620) 225-1321 Carnegie Class: Assoc/Pub-R-M
FAX Number: (620) 227-9366 Calendar System: Semester
URL: www.dc3.edu
Established: 1935 Annual Undergrad Tuition & Fees (In-District): $1,680
Enrollment: 1,924 Coed
Affiliation or Control: State/Local IRS Status: 501(c)3
Highest Offering: Associate Degree
Program: Occupational; 2-Year Principally Bachelor's Creditable
Accreditation: NH, ADNUR, PNUR

01 President Dr. Don A. WOODBURN
05 Exec VP College Affairs/Learning Mr. Michael AHERN
10 Vice Pres of Operations & Finance Ms. Vada HERMON
103 VP Innovation/Workforce Development Mr. Danny GILLUM
31 VP Community & Industry Relations Mr. Anthony LYONS
32 Dean of Student Services Mrs. Beverly TEMAAT
72 Dean Technology/Distance Education Mr. Thad RUSSELL
84 Dean of Enrollment Management Mrs. Kelly RUSSELL
51 Dir Bus/Technology/Continuing Educ Vacant
24 Director Adult Learning Center Mr. Ryan AUSMUS
26 Director Public Information Office Mr. Rick DRUSE
07 Dir Admissions Placement & Testing Mrs. Tammy TABOR
102 Exec Director of DCCC Foundation Mr. Roger PROFFITT
08 Director Learning Resource Center Mrs. Shelly HUELSMAN
66 Director Nursing Allied Health Vacant
15 Director of Human Resources Ms. Sheila BERGKAMP
41 Athletic Director Mr. Casey MALEK
06 Registrar Ms. Stephanie LANNING
37 Director of Financial Aid Mr. Russ MCBEE
21 Director of Business Services Ms. Debbie BISCH
40 Director Bookstore Mrs. Debby MALEK
13 Director Information Technology Mrs. Judith MAXFIELD
39 Director of Residence Life Mr. Lewis MIZE
18 Director of Facilities & Operations Mr. Greg PATEE
04 Exec Assistant to the President Mrs. Carla PATEE

Donnelly College (F)

608 N 18th Street, Kansas City KS 66102-4298
County: Wyandotte FICE Identification: 001914
Unit ID: 155007
Telephone: (913) 621-8700 Carnegie Class: Bac/Assoc
FAX Number: (913) 621-8719 Calendar System: Semester
URL: www.donnelly.edu
Established: 1949 Annual Undergrad Tuition & Fees: $7,074
Enrollment: 650 Coed
Affiliation or Control: Roman Catholic IRS Status: 501(c)3
Highest Offering: Baccalaureate
Program: Occupational; 2-Year Principally Bachelor's Creditable; Liberal Arts And General
Accreditation: NH

01 President Dr. Steven M. LANASA
03 Vice President Mrs. Frances SANDERS
32 Vice President of Student Affairs Ms. Donette ALONZO
85 Dean of International Students Ms. Deirdre WOODS
88 Assoc VP of Student Success Mrs. Amy NEUFELD
06 Registrar Mrs. Amber BLOOMFIELD-MARTINEZ
26 Marketing Coordinator Ms. Lynn HIRE
30 Director of Development Mrs. Emily BUCKLEY
36 Career Center Coord/Library Dir Mrs. Jane BALLAGH DE TOVAR
37 Director of Financial Aid Mrs. Belinda OGAN
10 Dir Business Affairs/Personnel Svcs Mrs. Susan SERRANO
18 Director of Facilities Mr. Terry STARR
09 Dir Institutional Rsrch/Plng/Assess Mrs. Frances SANDERS
14 Director of Computer Services Mr. Wen Li SHU
07 Director of Admissions Mr. Edward MARQUEZ
29 Alumni Relations Mr. Roger BERG

Emporia State University (G)

1200 Commercial Street, Emporia KS 66801-5087
County: Lyon FICE Identification: 001927
Unit ID: 155025
Telephone: (620) 341-1200 Carnegie Class: Master's L
FAX Number: (620) 341-5553 Calendar System: Semester
URL: www.emporia.edu
Established: 1863 Annual Undergrad Tuition & Fees (In-State): $5,272
Enrollment: 5,976 Coed
Affiliation or Control: State IRS Status: 501(c)3
Highest Offering: Doctorate
Program: Liberal Arts And General; Teacher Preparatory
Accreditation: NH, ART, BUS, CACREP, CORE, LIB, MUS, NUR, TED

01 President Dr. Michael SHONROCK
05 Provost/VP for Academic Affairs Dr. Teresa A. MEHRING
11 Vice President Admin & Fiscal Affs Mr. Raymond A. HAUKE
32 VP Strategic Partnershps/Stdnt Life Dr. James E. WILLIAMS
14 Assoc Vice Pres Tech/Computing Svcs Mr. Michael ERICKSON
85 Asst Vice Pres for Internatl Educ Mr. Gonzalo BRUCE
35 Asst Vice Pres Student Affairs Ms. Lynn M. HOBSON
10 Assoc Vice Pres Fiscal Affairs Ms. Diana E. KUHLMANN
102 President ESU Foundation Ms. DenaSue POTESTIO
29 Director of Alumni/Govt Rels Mr. K. Tyler CURTIS
88 Director Natl Teachers Hall of Fame Vacant
22 Affirmative Action Officer Ms. Judy ANDERSON
53 Dean/The Teachers College Dr. Kenneth WEAVER
49 Dean College of Liberal Arts/Sci Dr. Marie MILLER
50 Interim Dean School of Business Dr. John RICH
62 Dean School of Library/Info Mgmt Dr. Gwendolyn ALEXANDER
58 Dean Graduate Studies Dr. Kathy ERMLER
88 Exec Dir Jones Inst Educ Excel Dr. Roger CASWELL
06 Registrar Ms. M. Elaine HENRIE
08 Dean University Libraries/Archives Mr. John SHERIDAN
88 Director Assessment/Measurements Dr. Anthony L. AMBROSIO
106 Director Distance Education Dr. Kathy ERMLER
37 Director Student Financial Aid Ms. M. Elaine HENRIE
07 Director Admissions Ms. Laura M. EDDY
36 Director Career Services Ms. June COLEMAN
38 Director Student Life & Counseling Dr. Jaqueline L. SCHMIDT
26 Director Marketing & Media Relation Mr. William NOBLITT
91 Director Computing & Telecom Svcs Vacant
41 Director Athletics Mr. Kent L. WEISER
18 Director Facilities/Physical Plant Mr. Mark S. RUNGE
15 Director Human Resources Ms. Judy ANDERSON
23 Director Health Services Dr. Jaqueline L. SCHMIDT
39 Dir Residential Life/Orientation Mr. Wade REDEKER
40 Manager Bookstore Mr. Michael MCRELL
19 Director Police & Safety Capt. Chris HOOVER
43 General Counsel Vacant
21 Controller Ms. Mary MINGENBACK
09 Director Institutional Research Dr. JoLanna KORD
92 Director Honors Program Dr. William H. CLAMURRO
28 Director Multicultural Affairs Mr. Jason BROOKS

Flint Hills Technical College (H)

3301 W 18th Avenue, Emporia KS 66801-5957
County: Lyon FICE Identification: 005264
Unit ID: 155052
Telephone: (620) 343-4600 Carnegie Class: Assoc/Pub-R-S
FAX Number: (620) 343-4610 Calendar System: Semester
URL: www.fhtc.edu
Established: 1965 Annual Undergrad Tuition & Fees (In-District): $3,936
Enrollment: 706 Coed
Affiliation or Control: State/Local IRS Status: 501(c)3
Highest Offering: Associate Degree
Program: Occupational; Technical Emphasis
Accreditation: NH, DA, DH, EMT

01 President Dr. Dean HOLLENBECK
05 Vice Pres Instructional Services Mr. Steve LOEWEN
32 Vice Pres Student Services Ms. Lisa KIRMER
10 Vice Pres Business Services Mrs. Nancy THOMPSON
06 Registrar Ms. Brenda CARMICHAEL
15 Director Personnel Services Mrs. Sheri KNIGHT
37 Director Student Financial Aid Ms. Sandra SCHROEDER
84 Director Enrollment Management Ms. Brenda CARMICHAEL

Fort Hays State University (I)

600 Park Street, Hays KS 67601-4099
County: Ellis FICE Identification: 001915
Unit ID: 155061
Telephone: (785) 628-4000 Carnegie Class: Master's L
FAX Number: (785) 628-4096 Calendar System: Semester
URL: www.fhsu.edu

Established: 1902 Annual Undergrad Tuition & Fees (In-State): $4,233
Enrollment: 14,707 Coed
Affiliation or Control: State IRS Status: 501(c)3
Highest Offering: Beyond Master's But Less Than Doctorate
Program: Liberal Arts And General; Teacher Preparatory; Professional
Accreditation: NH, MUS, NURSE, RAD, SP, SW, TED

01 President ... Dr. Edward H. HAMMOND
05 Provost ... Dr. Lawrence V. GOULD
10 Vice Pres Administration & Finance ... Mr. Mike BARNETT
32 Vice President Student Affairs ... Dr. Tisa MASON
35 Asst Vice Pres Student Affairs ... Ms. Shana MEYER
09 Asst Provost Quality Improvement ... Dr. Chris CRAWFORD
58 Dean Graduate Studies and Research ... Dr. Tim CROWLEY
04 Exec Assistant to the President ... Mr. Todd POWELL
04 Assistant to President ... Ms. Lisa M. KARLIN
06 Registrar ... Dr. Joseph G. LINN
07 Admissions Director ... Ms. Tricia CLINE
29 Exec Director Alumni & Govt Rels ... Ms. Debra K. PRIDEAUX
45 Director Budget & Planning ... Mr. Larry R. GETTY
36 Director Career Services ... Mr. Daniel B. RICE
37 Director Student Financial Aid ... Mr. Craig E. KARLIN
26 Director University Relations ... Mr. Kent L. STEWARD
14 Director Computing/Telecom Center ... Dr. David E. SCHMIDT
08 Director Library ... Mr. John A. ROSS
15 Director Personnel Services ... Ms. Shannon LINDSEY
51 Dean Virtual College ... Mr. Dennis KING
53 Interim Dean College Education ... Dr. Robert F. SCOTT
49 Dean College Liberal Arts/Sciences ... Dr. Paul W. FABER
50 Dean College Business ... Dr. Mark BANNISTER
76 Dean Coll Health/Life Science ... Dr. Jeff BRIGGS
18 Co-Dir Chief Facil/Physical Plant ... Mr. Jim SCHREIBER
18 Co-Dir Chief Facil/Physical Plant ... Mr. Ken JACOBS
38 Dir Acad Advis/Career Exploration ... Dr. Patricia L. GRIFFIN
28 Diversity Coordinator ... Vacant

Fort Scott Community College (A)

2108 S Horton, Fort Scott KS 66701-3140
County: Bourbon FICE Identification: 001916
Unit ID: 155098
Telephone: (620) 223-2700 Carnegie Class: Assoc/Pub-R-M
FAX Number: (620) 223-4927 Calendar System: Semester
URL: www.fortscott.edu
Established: 1919 Annual Undergrad Tuition & Fees (In-District): $2,580
Enrollment: 2,051 Coed
Affiliation or Control: State/Local IRS Status: 501(c)3
Highest Offering: Associate Degree
Program: Occupational; 2-Year Principally Bachelor's Creditable
Accreditation: NH, ADNUR

01 President ... Dr. Clayton TATRO
05 Dean of Instruction ... Dr. Donna ESTILL
32 Dean of Student Services ... Steve ARMSTRONG
10 Dean of Finance and Operations ... Karla FARMER
07 Director Admissions ... Mert BARROWS
08 Library Director ... Wendy WILMOTH
06 Registrar ... Morgan BECK
26 Director Public Relations ... Kathleen HINRICHS
66 Director Nursing ... Bill RHOADS
41 Athletic Director ... JD ETTORE
13 Information Technology Director ... Morgan BECK
12 Associate Dean Pittsburg Campus ... Judy COLLINS
12 Associate Dean Paola ... Buddy Jo TANCK
38 Director of Advising ... Steve KRAMER
15 Director Personnel Services ... Juley MCDANIEL
18 Campus Services Director ... Joel RAMSEY
30 Director of Development ... Gary PALMER
37 Director Student Financial Aid ... Lillie GRUBB
28 Director of Diversity ... Jill WARFORD
35 Director of Student Life ... Marci MYERS
21 Director Business Operations ... Mindy RUSSELL

Friends University (B)

2100 W University Avenue, Wichita KS 67213-3397
County: Sedgwick FICE Identification: 001918
Unit ID: 155089
Telephone: (316) 295-5000 Carnegie Class: Master's L
FAX Number: (316) 295-5060 Calendar System: Semester
URL: www.friends.edu
Established: 1898 Annual Undergrad Tuition & Fees: $22,320
Enrollment: 2,905 Coed
Affiliation or Control: Independent Non-Profit IRS Status: 501(c)3
Highest Offering: Master's
Program: 2-Year Principally Bachelor's Creditable; Liberal Arts And General; Teacher Preparatory; Professional
Accreditation: NH, MFCD, MUS, TED

01 President ... Dr. TJ ARANT
04 Executive Secretary ... Ms. Nancy GRAF
10 Vice Pres Administration & Finance ... Mr. Randall C. DOERKSEN
32 Vice President of Student Life ... Dr. Carole OBERMEYER
30 Vice President University Relations ... Vacant
20 Assoc VP of Academic Affairs ... Dr. Darcy ZABEL
15 Assoc VP Admn Finance/Dir of HR ... Ms. Kelley WILLIAMS
06 Assoc VP Registrar/Enrollment Svcs ... Ms. Heidi HOSKINSON
49 Dean College of Bus/Art/Sci & Educ ... Dr. Steve PETERS
51 Dean Adult and Professional Studies ... Dr. Jo LOBERTINI
58 Dean Graduate School ... Vacant
50 Chair Business & IT ... Dr. Arlen HONTS
57 Chair Fine Arts ... Dr. Stephen EAVES
81 Chair Natural Science/Math ... Dr. Nora STRASSER
73 Chair Religion/Humanities ... Dr. Stan HARSTINE
53 Chair Teacher Education ... Dr. Jan WILSON
83 Chair Social/Behavioral Science ... Mr. Bill ALLAN
46 Dir Inst Research & Assessment ... Dr. Stephanie J. HARGRAVE
08 Director Library ... Mr. Max BURSON
18 Chief Facilities/Physical Plant ... Mr. Paul WINCHESTER
96 Director of Purchasing/Aux Services ... Mr. Ryan ARCHER
88 Exec Dir Adult Student Recruitment ... Vacant
07 Dir Traditional Undergrad Admiss ... Ms. Erin HANEBERG
41 Director Athletics ... Mr. Joe ZIMMERMAN
37 Director Financial Aid ... Mr. Brandon PIERCE
42 Chaplain ... Mr. Patrick SEHL, JR.
35 Director of Campus Life ... Mr. Gary RAPP
39 Director Residence Life ... Ms. Kelley MARTIN
26 Director Communications ... Ms. Gisele MCMINIMY
29 Exec Dir Alumni/Annual Fund ... Ms. Lisa TILMA

Garden City Community College (C)

801 Campus Drive, Garden City KS 67846-6398
County: Finney FICE Identification: 001919
Unit ID: 155104
Telephone: (620) 276-7611 Carnegie Class: Assoc/Pub-R-M
FAX Number: (620) 276-9573 Calendar System: Semester
URL: www.gcccks.edu
Established: 1919 Annual Undergrad Tuition & Fees (In-District): $2,310
Enrollment: 1,887 Coed
Affiliation or Control: Local IRS Status: 501(c)3
Highest Offering: Associate Degree
Program: Occupational; 2-Year Principally Bachelor's Creditable
Accreditation: NH, ADNUR, EMT

01 President ... Dr. Herbert SWENDER
03 Vice President ... Ms. Dee WIGNER
05 Dean Academics ... Mr. Kevin BRUNGARDT
32 Dean Student Services ... Mr. Ryan RUDA
08 Library Director ... Mr. Trent SMITH
06 Registrar ... Ms. Nancy UNRUH
07 Director of Admissions ... Ms. Nikki GEIER
15 Director of Human Resources ... Ms. Cricket TURLEY
18 Physical Plant Director ... Mr. Larry JOHNSTON
26 Dir Information Svcs/Publication ... Mr. Steve QUAKENBUSH
37 Director Student Financial Aid ... Ms. Kathy BLAU
39 Director Residential Life ... Ms. Kate COVINGTON
38 Director Student Counseling ... Mr. Colin LAMB
75 Dean Technical Education ... Ms. Lenora COOK

Haskell Indian Nations University (D)

155 Indian Avenue, #5030, Lawrence KS 66046-4800
County: Douglas FICE Identification: 010438
Unit ID: 155140
Telephone: (785) 749-8404 Carnegie Class: Tribal
FAX Number: (785) 749-8406 Calendar System: Semester
URL: www.haskell.edu
Established: 1884 Annual Undergrad Tuition & Fees: $430
Enrollment: 826 Coed
Affiliation or Control: Federal IRS Status: Exempt
Highest Offering: Baccalaureate
Program: 2-Year Principally Bachelor's Creditable; Liberal Arts And General; Teacher Preparatory
Accreditation: NH

01 President ... Mr. Chris REDMAN
05 Vice President for Academics ... Dr. Venida CHENAULT
11 Vice President University Services ... Mr. Clyde PEACOCK
10 Chief Finance Officer ... Mr. Michael LEWIS
27 Chief Information Officer ... Mr. Josh ARCE
08 Librarian/Dir Academic Support Ctr ... Dr. Marilyn RUSSELL
39 Dir Resident Housing/Mgr Stdnt Life ... Mr. Jim TUCKER
37 Financial Aid Officer ... Ms. Reta BREWER
06 Registrar ... Mr. Manny KING
07 Director of Admissions ... Ms. Dorothy D. STITES
09 Dir Instl Research/Sponsored Pgms ... Ms. Freda GIPP
36 Actg Career Development Specialist ... Mr. Burgess TAPEDO
38 Director Student Counseling ... Ms. Brenda SCHILDT
15 Human Resources Liason ... Ms. Mona GONZALES
96 Acquisitions ... Ms. Janice BEGAY
26 Executive Asst/Public Relations ... Mr. Stephen PRUE
18 Director Facilities Management ... Mr. Lee PAHCODDY, JR.

Hesston College (E)

Box 3000, Hesston KS 67062-2093
County: Harvey FICE Identification: 001920
Unit ID: 155177
Telephone: (620) 327-4221 Carnegie Class: Assoc/PrivNFP
FAX Number: (620) 327-8300 Calendar System: Semester
URL: www.hesston.edu
Established: 1909 Annual Undergrad Tuition & Fees: $22,282
Enrollment: 468 Coed
Affiliation or Control: Mennonite Church IRS Status: 501(c)3
Highest Offering: Associate Degree
Program: Occupational; 2-Year Principally Bachelor's Creditable
Accreditation: NH, ADNUR

01 President ... Dr. Howard KEIM
05 Vice President of Academics ... Dr. Sandra ZERGER
30 Vice President of Advancement ... Mrs. Yvonne SIEBER
07 Vice President of Admissions ... Mrs. Rachel S. MILLER
10 Vice Pres of Finance & Auxil Svcs ... Mr. Don WEAVER
32 Vice President of Student Life ... Mr. Lamar ROTH
29 Director of Alumni & Church Rels ... Mr. Dallas STUTZMAN
06 Registrar ... Mr. Brent YODER
21 Business Manager ... Mr. Karl BRUBAKER

Highland Community College (F)

606 W Main, Highland KS 66035-0068
County: Doniphan FICE Identification: 001921
Unit ID: 155186
Telephone: (785) 442-6000 Carnegie Class: Assoc/Pub-R-M
FAX Number: (785) 442-6100 Calendar System: Semester
URL: www.highlandcc.edu
Established: 1858 Annual Undergrad Tuition & Fees (In-District): $2,790
Enrollment: 3,534 Coed
Affiliation or Control: Local IRS Status: 501(c)3
Highest Offering: Associate Degree
Program: Occupational; 2-Year Principally Bachelor's Creditable
Accreditation: NH

01 President ... Mr. David REIST
05 Vice President for Academic Affairs ... Dr. Cia VERSCHELDEN
32 Vice President for Student Services ... Dr. Cheryl RASMUSSEN
10 Vice Pres for Finance/Operations ... Ms. Cynthia HAGGARD
88 Director of Technical Education ... Ms. Terri BALL
102 Exec Asst to Pres/Exec Dir HCC Foun ... Dr. Craig E. MOSHER
06 Registrar ... Ms. Alice HAMILTON
37 Financial Aid Director ... Ms. Christi WAGGONER
13 Director of Information Systems ... Mr. John NICHOLAS
09 Director of Institutional Research ... Dr. Harold ARNETT
38 Director Student Counseling ... Ms. Kristin WOODRUFF
41 Athletic Director ... Mr. Greg DELZEIT
08 Library Director ... Ms. Penny DONALDSON
18 Supervisor of Buildings & Grounds ... Mr. Rick CROSSLAND
26 Chief Public Relations Officer ... Dr. Craig MOSHER
29 Director Alumni Relations ... Dr. Craig MOSHER
35 Director of Student Life ... Mr. Bradley DIXON
15 Human Resource Manager ... Ms. Eileen C. GRONNIGER
40 Bookstore Coordinator ... Ms. Sarah ALBERS

Highland Community College-Technical Center (G)

1501 W Riley Street, Atchison KS 66002-1537
County: Atchison FICE Identification: 005266
Unit ID: 155609
Telephone: (913) 367-6204 Carnegie Class: Not Classified
FAX Number: (913) 367-3107 Calendar System: Quarter
URL: www.highlandcc.edu
Established: 1967 Annual Undergrad Tuition & Fees: $3,720
Enrollment: 340 Coed
Affiliation or Control: Proprietary IRS Status: Proprietary
Highest Offering: Associate Degree
Program: Occupational
Accreditation: &NH, COE

05 Dean of Curriculum & Instruction ... Mrs. Terri BALL

† Regional accreditation is carried under the parent institution in Highland, KS.

Hutchinson Community College and Area Vocational School (H)

1300 N Plum Street, Hutchinson KS 67501-5894
County: Reno FICE Identification: 001923
Unit ID: 155195
Telephone: (620) 665-3500 Carnegie Class: Assoc/Pub-R-L
FAX Number: (620) 665-3310 Calendar System: Semester
URL: www.hutchcc.edu
Established: 1928 Annual Undergrad Tuition & Fees (In-District): $2,144
Enrollment: 5,509 Coed
Affiliation or Control: State/Local IRS Status: 501(c)3
Highest Offering: Associate Degree
Program: Occupational; 2-Year Principally Bachelor's Creditable
Accreditation: NH, ACBSP, ADNUR, EMT, PNUR, PTAA, RAD, SURGT

01 President ... Dr. Edward E. BERGER
05 Vice President of Academic Affairs ... Dr. Cindy HOSS
10 Vice President Finance/Operations ... Mr. Carter FILE
103 VP Workforce Development/Outreach ... Mr. Steve PORTER
32 Vice President of Students ... Mr. Randy E. MYERS
26 Director of Marketing & Info ... Mrs. M. L. HINKLE
13 Director of Data Processing ... Mr. Loren L. MORRIS
06 Registrar ... Mrs. Christina LONG
41 Athletic Director ... Mr. Randy STANGE
15 Director of Personnel ... Mr. Brooks E. MANTOOTH
37 Financial Aid Officer ... Mr. Ron MENEFEE
07 Director of Admissions ... Mr. Corbin STROBEL
18 Director of Plant Facilities ... Mr. Don ROSE
39 Director of Residence Life ... Ms. Dana HINSHAW
29 Director Alumni Relations ... Mrs. Cindy KEAST
08 Coordinator of Library Services ... Mr. Robert KELLY
09 Coord of Institutional Research ... Mr. Mike TONN

Independence Community College (I)

Brookside Drive and College Avenue,
Independence KS 67301-0708
County: Montgomery FICE Identification: 001924
Unit ID: 155201

Telephone: (620) 331-4100 Carnegie Class: Assoc/Pub-R-S
FAX Number: (620) 331-5344 Calendar System: Semester
URL: www.indycc.edu
Established: 1925 Annual Undergrad Tuition & Fees (In-District): $2,130
Enrollment: 793 Coed
Affiliation or Control: State/Local IRS Status: 501(c)3
Highest Offering: Associate Degree
Program: Occupational; 2-Year Principally Bachelor's Creditable
Accreditation: NH

01 President ... Dr. Daniel W. BARWICK
10 VP Financial and Employee Services ... Mr. Jan FISCHER
05 VP Academic Affairs ... Dr. Sara HARRIS
32 Interim VP Student Affairs/Athletic ... Ms. Tammie GELDENHUYS
11 VP Information/Operations ... Mr. Greg EYTCHESON
26 VP Marketing/Resource Dev ... Ms. Misty GITHENS
102 Foundation Director ... Ms. Lori SHAW
06 Registrar ... Ms. Sonja CONLEY
08 Director Library/Lrng Resource Ctr ... Ms. Lily MORGAN
18 Director Maintenance/Custodial ... Mr. Mario LOPEZ
12 Director William Inge Center ... Mr. Peter ELLENSTEIN
07 Recruiting/Admissions Specialist ... Ms. Brittany THORNTON
37 Financial Aid Coordinator ... Ms. Wendy ISLE
13 MIS Coordinator ... Mr. Darrin MCFARLAND
09 Dir of Institutional Research ... Ms. Debbie PHELPS
04 Executive Asst to President ... Ms. Beverly HARRIS
40 Bookstore Manager ... Ms. Teresa VESTAL
25 Grants/New Program Development ... Vacant
88 Upward Bound Program Director ... Ms. Nicole PERCIVAL
72 Dean Tech Educ/Outreach ... Mr. Travis GITHENS

ITT Technical Institute (A)

8111 E. 32nd St. N, Suite 103, Wichita KS 67226
County: Sedgwick Identification: 666168
Unit ID: 450234
Telephone: (316) 609-4100 Carnegie Class: Assoc/PrivFP4
FAX Number: N/A Calendar System: Quarter
URL: www.itt-tech.edu
Established: 2006 Annual Undergrad Tuition & Fees: N/A
Enrollment: 407 Coed
Affiliation or Control: Proprietary IRS Status: Proprietary
Highest Offering: Baccalaureate
Program: Technical Emphasis
Accreditation: ACICS

† Branch campus of ITT Technical Institute, Indianapolis, IN.

Johnson County Community College (B)

12345 College Boulevard, Overland Park KS 66210-1299
County: Johnson FICE Identification: 008244
Unit ID: 155210
Telephone: (913) 469-8500 Carnegie Class: Assoc/Pub-S-SC
FAX Number: (913) 469-2559 Calendar System: Semester
URL: www.jccc.edu
Established: 1969 Annual Undergrad Tuition & Fees (In-District): $1,260
Enrollment: 21,033 Coed
Affiliation or Control: State/Local IRS Status: 501(c)3
Highest Offering: Associate Degree
Program: Occupational; 2-Year Principally Bachelor's Creditable
Accreditation: NH, ACBSP, ACFEI, ADNUR, DH, EMT, IFSAC, POLYT

01 President ... Dr. Terry A. CALAWAY
10 Exec Vice Pres Administrative Svcs ... Dr. Joseph M. SOPCICH
11 Exec Vice Pres Educational Planning ... Dr. Dana GROVE
05 Exec Vice Pres Academic Affairs ... Dr. Marilyn RHINEHART
15 Executive Vice Pres HR & Comm/Econ ... Dr. Judy KORB
32 Vice Pres Student Success/Engagemnt ... Dr. Dennis DAY
27 Vice President Information Services ... Ms. Denise MOORE
04 Exec Asst to the President & Board ... Ms. Terri SCHLICHT
26 AVP Marketing Communications ... Ms. Julie HAAS
21 AVP Financial Services ... Mr. Bob PRATER
18 Executive Director Campus Services ... Mr. Rex HAYS
72 Dean Technology ... Mr. Bill BROWN
88 Exec Director Academic Initiative ... Dr. Jason KOVAC
13 Director Admin Computing Services ... Ms. Sandra WARNER
49 Dean Curriculum/Academic Quality ... Ms. Ruth RANDALL
96 Executive Director Procurement ... Mr. Mitch BORCHERS
35 Dean Student Services ... Mr. Paul KYLE
76 Dean Hlth Care Professions/Wellness ... Dr. Clarissa CRAIG
37 Director Student Financial Aid ... Vacant
36 Director Testing and Assessment ... Ms. Mary Ann DICKERSON
06 Registrar ... Ms. Leslie QUINN
08 Director Library Services ... Mr. Mark DAGANAAR
68 Dir Physical Education/Athletics ... Mr. Carl HEINRICH
07 Director of Admissions ... Mr. Peter BELK
84 Asst Dean Enrollment Management ... Ms. MargE SHELLEY
92 Program Facilitator Honors ... Dr. Pat DECKER
35 Asst Dean Student Activ/Ldrshp Dev ... Ms. Pam VASSAR

Kansas City Kansas Community College (C)

7250 State Avenue, Kansas City KS 66112-3003
County: Wyandotte FICE Identification: 001925
Unit ID: 155292
Telephone: (913) 334-1100 Carnegie Class: Assoc/Pub-U-SC
FAX Number: (913) 288-7609 Calendar System: Semester
URL: www.kckcc.edu
Established: 1923 Annual Undergrad Tuition & Fees (In-District): $2,130
Enrollment: 7,555 Coed
Affiliation or Control: State/Local IRS Status: 501(c)3
Highest Offering: Associate Degree
Program: Occupational; 2-Year Principally Bachelor's Creditable
Accreditation: NH, ACBSP, ADNUR, EMT, FUSER, PTAA

01 President ... Dr. Doris F. GIVENS
11 VP Student & Administrative Svcs ... Mr. Brian BODE
05 Provost ... Dr. Tamara AGHA-JAFFAR
50 Dean Business & Continuing Educ ... Dr. Marvin HUNT
81 Dean Engineering/Math/Science ... Dr. Edward KREMER
84 Dean Enrollment Mgmt/Registrar ... Dr. Denise MCDOWELL
16 Dean Human Resources/Affirm Action ... Ms. Leota MARKS
79 Dean Humanities & Fine Arts ... Dr. Cherilee WALKER
13 Dean Information Services ... Mr. Baz ABOUELENEIN
45 Dean Institutional Services ... Dr. Sangki MIN
66 Dean Nursing Educ/Allied Health ... Dr. Shirley A. WENDEL
83 Dean Social & Behavioral Sciences ... Dr. Charles WILSON
32 Dean Student Services ... Vacant
75 Dean Technical Education Center ... Mr. Cliff SMITH
88 Exec Director Leavenworth Center ... Ms. Karalin ALSDURF
88 Director of Academic Resource Ctr ... Ms. Jaclyn ANDERSON
41 Director of Athletics ... Mr. Dan PRATT
40 Director of Bookstore Operations ... Mr. John BURRIGHT
18 Director of Buildings/Grounds ... Mr. Jeff SIXTA
19 Director of Campus Police ... Mr. Greg SCHNEIDER
36 Director of Career Planning/Plcmnt ... Ms. Linda L. WYATT
26 Director of College Advancement ... Mr. Jerry TONEY
14 Director of Computing ... Mr. James BENNETT
31 Director of Cont Educ & Cmty Svcs ... Ms. Rosemary L. LISCHKA
38 Director of Counseling ... Dr. Alda PRESTON
09 Director Ctr for Rsrch & Cmty Devel ... Ms. Kaaren FIFE
37 Director of Financial Aid ... Ms. Mary I. DORR
21 Director of Financial Records ... Ms. Marie BRANSTETTER
92 Director of Honors/Phi Theta Kappa ... Ms. Stacy TUCKER
28 Director of Intercultural Center ... Ms. Barbara CLARK-EVANS
08 Director of Library ... Ms. Cheryl POSTLEWAIT
24 Director Media Services Technology ... Mr. Michael J. KIMBROUGH
106 Director of Online Services ... Ms. Susan STUART
96 Director of Purchasing & Risk Mgr ... Mr. David ROOT
35 Director of Student Activities ... Ms. Linda SUTTON
07 Director of Admissions ... Ms. Sherri A. NEFF
06 Assistant Registrar ... Ms. Theresa HOLLIDAY
88 Director Community Outreach Counsel ... Ms. Andrea J. CHASTAIN
15 Director Human Resources ... Ms. Cheryl C. COLEMAN
88 Director Forensic Laboratory ... Mr. Alan H. COLEN
88 Director Wellness Center ... Mr. Rob M. CRANE
103 Director Emerging Workforce ... Ms. Jeanne CRANE-SMITH
88 Director Regional Prevention Center ... Ms. Carla D. GREEN
66 Director Nursing ... Ms. Anita M. KRONDAK
66 Director Practical Nursing ... Ms. Susan K. WHITE
88 Assistant Director Student Develop ... Ms. Tamara D. MILLER
88 Director EMT-MICT Program ... Ms. Donna OLAFSON
88 Director Technical Programs ... Mr. Richard PIPER
88 Director Technical Programs Perkins ... Ms. Donna S. SHAWN
88 Assistant Director Academic Resourc ... Ms. Amanda WILLIAMS
88 Director Performing Arts Center ... Mr. Bill YEAZEL

Kansas State University (D)

Manhattan KS 66506
County: Riley FICE Identification: 001928
Unit ID: 155399
Telephone: (785) 532-6250 Carnegie Class: RU/H
FAX Number: (785) 532-2120 Calendar System: Semester
URL: www.k-state.edu
Established: 1863 Annual Undergrad Tuition & Fees (In-State): $8,047
Enrollment: 23,863 Coed
Affiliation or Control: State IRS Status: 501(c)3
Highest Offering: Doctorate
Program: Liberal Arts And General; Teacher Preparatory; Professional
Accreditation: NH, ART, BUS, BUSA, CACREP, CEA, CIDA, CONST, CS, DIETC, DIETD, ENG, IPSY, JOUR, LSAR, MFCD, MUS, NRPA, PLNG, SP, SPAA, SW, TED, THEA, VET

01 President ... Dr. Kirk H. SCHULZ
05 Provost and Senior Vice President ... Dr. April C. MASON
10 Vice Pres Administration & Finance ... Mr. Bruce SHUBERT
46 Vice President Research ... Dr. Ronald W. TREWYN
32 VP Student Life/Dean of Students ... Dr. Pat J. BOSCO
26 VP for Communications & Marketing ... Mr. Jeffery B. MORRIS
31 Dir of Community Rels/Asst to Pres ... Dr. Jackie L. HARTMAN
20 Senior Vice Provost ... Dr. Ruth DYER
86 Asst to Pres/Dir for Govt Relations ... Dr. Susan K. PETERSON
04 Admin Asst to the President ... Ms. Dana M. HASTINGS
13 Vice Provost Info Tech Svcs ... Mr. Kenneth STAFFORD
108 Assoc Prov Institutional Effectiv ... Dr. Brian A. NIEHOFF
88 Director Military Affairs ... Mr. Arthur S. DE GROAT
08 Dean of Libraries ... Dr. Lori A. GOETSCH
47 Dean of Agriculture ... Dr. John FLOROS
48 Dean Architecture/Planning/Design ... Mr. Timothy DE NOBLE
49 Dean of Arts & Sciences ... Dr. Peter K. DORHOUT
50 Dean of Business Administration ... Dr. Ali R. MALEKZADEH
51 Dean of Continuing Education ... Dr. Sue C. MAES
53 Dean of Education ... Dr. Michael C. HOLEN
54 Dean of Engineering ... Dr. John R. ENGLISH
58 Dean of Graduate School ... Dr. Carol SHANKLIN
59 Dean of Human Ecology ... Dr. Virginia M. MOXLEY
72 Dean of Technology & Aviation ... Dr. Verna M. FITZSIMMONS
74 Dean of Veterinary Medicine ... Dr. Ralph C. RICHARDSON
30 President/CEO of Foundation ... Dr. Fred A. CHOLICK
29 Alumni Association President ... Ms. Amy Button RENZ
41 Athletic Director ... Mr. John CURRIE
56 Dir Research and Extension ... Dr. John FLOROS
21 Director of Budget ... Ms. Cindy A. BONTRAGER
37 Asst VP Student Financial Assist ... Mr. Lawrence E. MOEDER
36 Director Career & Employment Svcs ... Ms. Kerri D. KELLER
06 Registrar ... Dr. Monty E. NIELSEN
07 Asst VP/Director of Admissions ... Mr. Lawrence E. MOEDER
15 Asst VP for Human Resources ... Mr. Gary E. LEITNAKER
28 Assoc Prov for Diversity ... Dr. Myra E. GORDON

Kansas State University-Salina, College of Technology and Aviation (E)

2310 Centennial Road, Salina KS 67401-8196
County: Saline FICE Identification: 004611
Unit ID: 155405
Telephone: (785) 826-2601 Carnegie Class: Not Classified
FAX Number: (785) 826-2998 Calendar System: Semester
URL: www.salina.k-state.edu
Established: 1965 Annual Undergrad Tuition & Fees (In-State): $6,100
Enrollment: 835 Coed
Affiliation or Control: State IRS Status: 501(c)3
Highest Offering: Master's
Program: Occupational; 2-Year Principally Bachelor's Creditable; Liberal Arts And General
Accreditation: &NH, AAB, ENGT

01 CEO and Dean ... Dr. Verna M. FITZSIMMONS
05 Associate Dean of Academics ... Mr. David DELKER
32 Assoc Dean of Student Life ... Ms. Dixie SCHIERLMAN
10 Director of Fiscal Affairs ... Ms. Alyson ROME
37 Financial Aid Officer ... Ms. Cindy NEWELL
08 Librarian & Asst Dean of Academics ... Ms. Alysia STARKEY
06 Registrar ... Ms. Jackie LINN
18 Chief Facilities/Physical Plant ... Mr. Bill BOCHTE
26 Chief Public Rels/Dir Alumni Rels ... Ms. Natalie BLAIR
36 Director Student Placement ... Vacant
38 Director Student Counseling ... Mr. Joel MATTHEWS
96 Director of Purchasing ... Ms. Alyson ROME

† Regional accreditation is carried under the parent institution in Manhattan, KS.

Kansas Wesleyan University (F)

100 E Claflin Avenue, Salina KS 67401-6196
County: Saline FICE Identification: 001929
Unit ID: 155414
Telephone: (785) 827-5541 Carnegie Class: Bac/Diverse
FAX Number: (785) 827-0927 Calendar System: Semester
URL: www.kwu.edu
Established: 1886 Annual Undergrad Tuition & Fees: $22,600
Enrollment: 851 Coed
Affiliation or Control: United Methodist IRS Status: 501(c)3
Highest Offering: Master's
Program: Liberal Arts And General; Teacher Preparatory; Professional
Accreditation: NH, NUR, TED

01 President and CEO ... Dr. Fletcher M. LAMKIN
04 Executive Assistant to President ... Ms. Jan M. SHIRK
10 Vice Pres Finance/Administration ... Mr. Wayne R. SCHNEIDER
21 Controller/Business Officer ... Ms. Cheri L. JOHNSON
32 Vice Pres Student Services ... Mr. William P. TANNER
37 Director Enrollment/Financial Svcs ... Ms. Glenna R. ALEXANDER
06 Registrar ... Ms. Glenna R. ALEXANDER
07 Director of Admissions ... Mr. Steven M. BERRY
05 Exec Vice President/Provost ... Dr. Wayne LOWEN
30 Exec Dir Institutional Advancement ... Mr. Jeffrey D. CHAPMAN
29 Director of Alumni Relations ... Ms. Jennifer L. REIN
26 Dir PR/Marketing/Communications ... Ms. Mary J. GORDON
44 Director of Development ... Ms. Sophie A. LAMB
35 Exec Director Student Development ... Ms. Bridget WEISER
36 Director of Career Services ... Ms. Carla M. LARKIN
108 Director of Assessment ... Prof. Raymond A. TUCKER
08 Director of Library Svcs ... Mr. James CORBLY
13 Director of Information Systems ... Mr. Jay C. KROB
18 Director of Plant Operations ... Mr. Darrell D. VICTORY
40 Manager Yotee's Bookstore ... Mr. Steve CARRIER
42 Chaplain Univ United Meth Church ... Rev. Mike ROSE
41 Athletic Director ... Mr. David W. DALLAS
58 Director of MBA Program ... Prof. Monte SHADWICK
66 Director of Nursing Educaiton ... Dr. Linda M. ADAMS-WENDLING
88 Director of Teacher Education ... Dr. Martha ROBERTSON
79 Division Chair Humanities ... Dr. Philip S. MECKLEY
64 Dept of Music Chair ... Prof. Kensuke HAKODA
49 Div Chair Applied Art & Sciences ... Prof. Bryan MINNICH
83 Division Chair Social Sciences ... Prof. John K. BURCHILL
50 Dept of Business & Acct Chair ... Dr. Paul H. HEDLUND
88 Dept Behav Sci & Human Svcs Chair ... Dr. Steven J. HOEKSTRA
57 Division Chair Fine Arts ... Prof. Barbara J. MARSHALL
81 Dept Mathematics & Physics Chair ... Dr. Susan K. MCDONALD
77 Dept Computer Studies Chair ... Dr. Rasalee M. STEIMEL

Labette Community College (G)

200 S 14th, Parsons KS 67357-4299
County: Labette FICE Identification: 001930
Unit ID: 155450
Telephone: (620) 421-6700 Carnegie Class: Assoc/Pub-R-M
FAX Number: (620) 421-0921 Calendar System: Semester
URL: www.labette.edu
Established: 1923 Annual Undergrad Tuition & Fees (In-District): $2,730

Enrollment: 2,035 Coed
Affiliation or Control: Local IRS Status: 501(c)3
Highest Offering: Associate Degree
Program: Occupational; 2-Year Principally Bachelor's Creditable
Accreditation: NH, ADNUR, @PTAA, RAD

01 President .... Dr. George C. KNOX
04 Executive Assistant to President .... Ms. Megan A. FUGATE
05 Vice President Academic Affairs .... Mr. Joe BURKE
10 Vice President Finance & Operations .. Ms. Leanna J. NEWBERRY
32 Vice President Student Affairs .... Ms. Tammy FUENTEZ
20 Dean of Instruction .... Mr. Mark WATKINS
13 Director of Information Technology .... Mrs. Jody BURZINSKI
30 Dir Resource Devel/Alumni Rels .... Mrs. Lindi D. FORBES
08 Director of Library Services .... Mr. Scott M. ZOLLARS
18 Director of Physical Plant .... Mr. Kevin DOHERTY
66 Director of Nursing .... Mrs. Delyna BOHNENBLUST
41 Athletic Director .... Mr. Aaron J. KEAL
31 Director of Community Services .... Vacant
26 Director of Public Relations .... Mrs. Bethany KENDRICK
06 Registrar/Dir Student Financial Aid .... Ms. Kathy JOHNSTON
07 Director of Admissions .... Ms. Kathy JOHNSTON
15 Director of Human Relations .... Ms. Janice S. GEORGE
37 Director Student Financial Aid .... Ms. Kathy JOHNSTON
35 Student Life Coordinator .... Ms. Tarah COCKRELL
40 Bookstore Specialist .... Mrs. Lois D. HEMBREE

Manhattan Area Technical College (A)

3136 Dickens Avenue, Manhattan KS 66503-2499
County: Riley FICE Identification: 005500
Unit ID: 155487
Telephone: (785) 587-2800 Carnegie Class: Assoc/Pub-R-S
FAX Number: (785) 587-2804 Calendar System: Semester
URL: www.matc.net
Established: 1965 Annual Undergrad Tuition & Fees (In-District): $4,215
Enrollment: 715 Coed
Affiliation or Control: State/Local IRS Status: 501(c)3
Highest Offering: Associate Degree
Program: Occupational; 2-Year Principally Bachelor's Creditable; Technical Emphasis
Accreditation: NH, ADNUR, DH

01 President/CEO .... Dr. Robert J. EDLESTON
05 Vice Pres of Instructional Services .... Ms. Marilyn MAHAN
32 Vice President of Student Services .... Mr. Joel LUNDSTROM
10 Vice President of Business Services .... Ms. Jane BLOODGOOD
30 Assoc VP Institutional Advancement .... Dr. Richard FOGG
15 Director Human Resources .... Ms. Trysta WILLIAMS
07 Director of Admissions .... Ms. Nicole BOLLIG
37 Director Financial Aid .... Ms. Sarah SAUERESSIG

Manhattan Christian College (B)

1415 Anderson, Manhattan KS 66502-4081
County: Riley FICE Identification: 001931
Unit ID: 155496
Telephone: (785) 539-3571 Carnegie Class: Spec/Faith
FAX Number: (785) 539-0832 Calendar System: Semester
URL: www.mccks.edu
Established: 1927 Annual Undergrad Tuition & Fees: $12,768
Enrollment: 384 Coed
Affiliation or Control: Christian Churches And Churches of Christ
IRS Status: 501(c)3
Highest Offering: Baccalaureate
Program: Liberal Arts And General; Professional; Religious Emphasis
Accreditation: NH, BI

01 President .... Mr. J. Kevin INGRAM
05 Vice President Academic Affairs .... Mr. Randall L. INGMIRE
10 Vice President Business Affairs .... Ms. Lori J. STANFIELD
30 Vice Pres Institutional Advancement .... Mr. Vern HENRICKS
32 Vice President Student Life .... Dr. Rick L. WRIGHT
06 Registrar .... Mrs. Lauren HESKETT
26 Asst to Institutional Advancement .... Mrs. Jolene K. RUPE
37 Director of Financial Aid .... Mrs. Margaret K. CARLISLE
08 Library Director .... Mrs. Mary Ann BUHLER
41 Athletic Director .... Mr. Shawn M. CONDRA
29 Alumni Relations Director .... Mrs. Genae DENVER
04 Admin Asst to President .... Ms. Juanita (Nita) M. PRICKETT

McPherson College (C)

1600 E Euclid, PO Box 1402, McPherson KS 67460-1402
County: McPherson FICE Identification: 001933
Unit ID: 155511
Telephone: (620) 242-0400 Carnegie Class: Bac/Diverse
FAX Number: (620) 241-8443 Calendar System: 4/1/4
URL: www.mcpherson.edu
Established: 1887 Annual Undergrad Tuition & Fees: $21,801
Enrollment: 585 Coed
Affiliation or Control: Church Of The Brethren IRS Status: 501(c)3
Highest Offering: Baccalaureate
Program: Liberal Arts And General; Teacher Preparatory
Accreditation: NH, TED

01 President .... Mr. Michael P. SCHNEIDER
05 Provost .... Dr. Kent EATON
30 Vice President for Advancement .... Ms. Amanda GUTIERREZ
10 Vice President for Finance .... Mr. Rick TUXHORN
26 Vice President for Marketing .... Ms. Christi HOPKINS
07 Vice President for Admissions .... Mr. David BARRETT
32 Dean of Students .... Dr. Sharonda MACLIN
41 Athletic Director .... Mr. Doug QUINT
06 Assoc Dean of Academic Records .... Mrs. Karlene M. TYLER
88 Special Projects Coordinator .... Ms. Abbey ARCHER-RIERSON
37 Director of Financial Aid .... Ms. Brenda KREHBIEL
08 Director of Library Services .... Ms. Mary HESTER
36 Director of Career Services .... Mrs. Chris WIENS
26 Director Marketing & Communications .... Ms. Nancy YOUNG
40 Director of Bookstore .... Mrs. Linda BARRETT
42 Director of Campus Ministry .... Dr. Steve CRAIN
13 Director of Computer Services .... Mr. David GITCHELL

MidAmerica Nazarene University (D)

2030 E College Way, Olathe KS 66062-1899
County: Johnson FICE Identification: 007032
Unit ID: 155520
Telephone: (913) 782-3750 Carnegie Class: Master's M
FAX Number: (913) 971-3290 Calendar System: Semester
URL: www.mnu.edu
Established: 1966 Annual Undergrad Tuition & Fees: $20,500
Enrollment: 1,811 Coed
Affiliation or Control: Church Of The Nazarene IRS Status: 501(c)3
Highest Offering: Master's
Program: 2-Year Principally Bachelor's Creditable; Liberal Arts And General; Teacher Preparatory; Professional
Accreditation: NH, CACREP, MUS, NURSE, TED

01 President .... Dr. David J. SPITTAL
05 Vice President Academic Affairs .... Dr. Stephen W. RAGAN
10 Vice President Finance .... Mr. Kevin P. GILMORE
30 Vice Pres University Advancement .... Mr. Jon D. NORTH
32 Vice President Community Formation .... Dr. Randy BECKUM
42 University Chaplain .... Dr. Randy BECKUM
20 Associate Academic Vice President .... Dr. Mark C. FORD
27 Chief Technology Officer .... Dr. Martin CROSSLAND
88 Dean School Christian Min/Formation .... Vacant
66 Dean Sch Nursing/Health Sci .... Dr. Susan LARSON
50 Dean School of Business .... Mrs. Jamie MYRTLE
53 Dean Sch Behav Sci/Counseling .... Dr. Earl BLAND
49 Dean College Arts & Sciences .... Dr. Cindy PETERSON
06 Registrar .... Mr. James R. GARRISON
08 Director of the Library .... Mr. Bruce FLANDERS
26 Assoc VP University Advancement .... Mr. Tim KEETON
07 Interim Director of Admissions .... Ms. Lisa DOWNS
39 Director of Residential Life .... Mrs. Kristi KEETON
29 Director of Alumni .... Mr. Kevin S. GARBER
37 Director of Student Financial Svcs .... Mr. Perry DIEHM
41 Athletic Director .... Mr. Kevin L. STEELE
15 Director of Human Resources .... Ms. Nancy S. MERIMEE
27 Marketing Strategist .... Mrs. Kimberly CAMPBELL
18 Director of Facility Services .... Mr. Denis JOHNSON
40 Bookstore Manager .... Mr. Nikos KELLEPOURIS
19 Director of Campus Safety .... Mr. Emil F. SCHELLACK

Neosho County Community College (E)

800 W 14th Street, Chanute KS 66720-2699
County: Neosho FICE Identification: 001936
Unit ID: 155566
Telephone: (620) 431-2820 Carnegie Class: Assoc/Pub-R-M
FAX Number: (620) 431-0082 Calendar System: Semester
URL: www.neosho.edu
Established: 1935 Annual Undergrad Tuition & Fees (In-District): $2,310
Enrollment: 2,556 Coed
Affiliation or Control: Local IRS Status: 501(c)3
Highest Offering: Associate Degree
Program: Occupational; 2-Year Principally Bachelor's Creditable
Accreditation: NH, ACBSP, ADNUR

01 President .... Dr. Brian L. INBODY
05 Vice President Student Learning .... Mr. James GENANDT
11 Vice President for Operations .... Mr. Benjamin J. SMITH
10 Chief Financial Officer .... Ms. Sondra K. SOLANDER
32 Dean Student Development .... Mr. Jason KEGLER
51 Dean of Outreach and Workforce Dev .... Ms. Brenda L. KRUMM
12 Dean Ottawa Campus .... Mr. Dale E. ERNST
15 Director Personnel Services .... Ms. Terri DALE
106 Associate Dean for Online Campus .... Ms. Marie GARDNER
13 Associate Dean for Operations/CIO ... Mr. Kerry D. RANABARGAR
30 Director of Development/Alumni Rels .... Ms. Claudia CHRISTIANSEN
08 Director Library Services .... Ms. Susan D. WEISENBERGER
37 Director Student Financial Aid .... Ms. Kara B. HALE
66 Director of Nursing .... Ms. Pamela COVAULT
13 Director of Technology Services .... Mr. Jon SEIBERT
46 Director of Assessment/Research .... Ms. Sarah ROBB
41 Athletic Director .... Ms. Amber BURDGE
07 Director of Admissions .... Vacant
85 Dir/International Student Services .... Ms. Sarah CADWALLADER
06 Registrar .... Ms. Nikki PETERS
09 Coordinator/Institutional Research .... Ms. LuAnn HAUSER
40 Chanute Bookstore Coordinator .... Ms. Mary Jo SECHLER
40 Ottawa Bookstore Coordinator .... Ms. Diane HOWELL
26 Chief Public Relations Officer .... Ms. Nancy ISAAC
38 Director Student Counseling .... Vacant
39 Residence/Student Life Coordinator .... Vacant
04 Admin Asst to the President .... Ms. Denise GILMORE

Newman University (F)

3100 McCormick, Wichita KS 67213-2097
County: Sedgwick FICE Identification: 001939
Unit ID: 155335
Telephone: (316) 942-4291 Carnegie Class: Master's L
FAX Number: (316) 942-4483 Calendar System: Semester
URL: www.newmanu.edu
Established: 1933 Annual Undergrad Tuition & Fees: $22,238
Enrollment: 3,021 Coed
Affiliation or Control: Roman Catholic IRS Status: 501(c)3
Highest Offering: Master's
Program: Occupational; 2-Year Principally Bachelor's Creditable; Liberal Arts And General; Teacher Preparatory; Professional
Accreditation: NH, ANEST, NURSE, OTA, RAD, SW, TED

01 President .... Dr. Noreen CARROCCI
04 Exec Assistant to the President .... Ms. Tracy MCGAREY
05 Provost & Vice Pres Acad Affairs .... Dr. Michael AUSTIN
30 Vice Pres University Advancement .... Mr. Troy HORINE
10 Vice Pres Finance/Administration .... Mr. Mark DRESSELHAUS
15 Vice President Human Resources .... Ms. Rhonda CANTRELL
20 Assoc VP Acad Svcs/Student Dev .... Ms. Rosemary NIEDENS
42 Director of Campus Ministry .... Fr. Michael LINNEBUR
29 Director of Alumni Relations .... Ms. Sarah CUNDIFF
26 Director of Communications .... Ms. Kelly SNEDDEN
09 Director of Institutional Research .... Sr. JoAnn MARK, ASC
08 Library Director .... Mr. Joseph FORTE
06 Registrar .... Ms. Shirley RUEB
37 Director of Financial Aid .... Ms. Charly SMITH
41 Director of Athletics .... Mr. Victor TRILLI
40 Director of Bookstore .... Mr. Larry WILLIAMS
13 Director of Information Technology .... Mr. Icer VAUGHAN
19 Director of Safety & Security .... Mr. Richard OLIVERSON
21 Controller .... Mr. Don WIESNER
07 Dean of Admissions .... Mr. John CLAYTON
32 Dean of Students .... Ms. Laura NICHOLAS HUPACH
58 Dean College of Grad/Cont Studies .... Dr. Audrey CURTIS HANE
49 Dean College of Undergrad Studies .... Dr. David SHUBERT

North Central Kansas Technical College (G)

PO Box 507, Beloit KS 67420-0507
County: Mitchell FICE Identification: 005265
Unit ID: 155593
Telephone: (785) 738-2276 Carnegie Class: Assoc/Pub-R-S
FAX Number: (785) 738-2903 Calendar System: Semester
URL: www.ncktc.edu
Established: 1964 Annual Undergrad Tuition & Fees (In-District): $4,398
Enrollment: 811 Coed
Affiliation or Control: State/Local IRS Status: 501(c)3
Highest Offering: Associate Degree
Program: Occupational; 2-Year Principally Bachelor's Creditable; Technical Emphasis
Accreditation: NH, ADNUR

01 President .... Mr. Eric BURKS
05 Dean of Instruction .... Mr. Corey ISBELL
11 Dean of Administrative Services .... Mrs. Brandi ZIMMER
66 Director of Nursing .... Mrs. Sandy GOTTSCHALK
06 Registrar .... Ms. Judy HEIDRICK
07 Director of Admissions .... Mr. David HUGHES
09 Coordinator Institutional Research .... Mrs. Jennifer BROWN
32 Dean of Student Services .... Mr. David HUGHES
37 Director Student Financial Aid .... Mr. Gary ODLE

Northwest Kansas Technical College (H)

1209 Harrison Street, PO Box 668,
Goodland KS 67735-3441
County: Sherman FICE Identification: 005267
Unit ID: 155618
Telephone: (785) 890-3641 Carnegie Class: Assoc/Pub-R-S
FAX Number: (785) 899-5711 Calendar System: Semester
URL: www.nwktc.edu
Established: 1964 Annual Undergrad Tuition & Fees (In-District): $8,931
Enrollment: 473 Coed
Affiliation or Control: State/Local IRS Status: 501(c)3
Highest Offering: Associate Degree
Program: Occupational; Technical Emphasis
Accreditation: NH, MAC

01 President .... Dr. Ed MILLS
05 Vice Pres Instruct & Student Svcs .... Ms. Brenda L. CHATFIELD
35 Asst Vice Pres of Student Affairs .... Ms. Reina BRANUM

Ottawa University (I)

1001 S Cedar Street, Ottawa KS 66067-3399
County: Franklin FICE Identification: 001937
Unit ID: 155627
Telephone: (785) 242-5200 Carnegie Class: Bac/Diverse
FAX Number: (785) 229-1020 Calendar System: Semester
URL: www.ottawa.edu
Established: 1865 Annual Undergrad Tuition & Fees: $23,000
Enrollment: 971 Coed
Affiliation or Control: American Baptist IRS Status: 501(c)3
Highest Offering: Master's
Program: Liberal Arts And General; Teacher Preparatory

Accreditation: NH, TED

01 President Mr. Kevin C. EICHNER
05 Univ Provost/Chief Academic Officer Dr. Terry HAINES
20 Vice Pres & Provost of the College Dr. Dennis J. TYNER
10 Vice Pres Administration/CFO Mr. J. Clark RIBORDY
26 Mgr Public Relations & Publications Ms. Paula PAINE
30 Vice Pres University Advancement Mr. Paul BEAN
86 VP Regulatory/Governmental Affairs Dr. Donna LEVENE
09 Assoc VP Governmental/Reg Affairs Ms. Jan STONE
88 Vice President Enterprise Division Dr. Brian SANDUSKY
106 Vice President for Online Mr. Brian MESSER
12 Campus Executive Arizona Dr. Mary VANIS
12 Interim Campus Executive Indiana Ms. Peg GERNAND
12 Campus Executive Wisconsin Dr. Wade MAULAND
32 Dean Student Affairs Mr. Tom TALDO
84 Mgr New Student Enrollment Service Mr. Steed BELL
06 University Registrar Ms. Karen ADAMS
21 Director Finance/Controller Ms. Noelle TESTA
21 Director Business Operations Mr. Thomas CORLEY
15 Director Human Resources Mrs. Joanna L. WALTERS
37 Director Financial Aid Mr. Howard FISCHER
13 Director Information Technology Dr. Jack MAXWELL
29 Director Alumni Programs Ms. Nori HALE
08 Director Library Services Ms. Gloria CREED-DIKEOGU
41 Director Athletics Ms. Arabie CONNER
36 Dir Career Svcs/Student Employment Mrs. Susan WEBB
18 Chief Facilities/Physical Plant Mr. Herb ORR
04 Executive Assistant to President Ms. Gaynia MENNINGER
11 Chief Operations Officer Mr. Keith JOHNSON
20 Dean of Instruction Dr. Karen OHNESORGE
53 Interim Dean School of Education Dr. Amy HOGAN
88 VP and COO APOS Mr. Shane SMEED
84 Enrollment Director Online Ms. Sarah TIPPING

† The Online division is included in this institution's Enrollment count.

Ottawa University Kansas City (A)

4370 W. 109th Street, Suite 200,
Overland Park KS 66211-1302

County: Johnson — Identification: 666083
Unit ID: 155636
Telephone: (913) 266-8600 — Carnegie Class: Bac/Diverse
FAX Number: (913) 451-0806 — Calendar System: Semester
URL: www.ottawa.edu
Established: 1974 — Annual Undergrad Tuition & Fees: $10,920
Enrollment: 352 — Coed
Affiliation or Control: American Baptist — IRS Status: 501(c)3
Highest Offering: Master's
Program: Liberal Arts And General; Teacher Preparatory
Accreditation: &NH

01 President Mr. Kevin EICHNER
05 Univ Provost/Chief Academic Officer Dr. Terry HAINES
20 Dean of Instruction Ms. Kristen MOORE
10 Vice Pres Administration/CFO Mr. J. Clark RIBORDY
26 Mgr Public Relations & Publications Ms. Paula PAINE
30 Vice Pres University Advancement Mr. Paul BEAN
86 VP Regulatory/Governmental Affairs Dr. Donna LEVENE
88 Vice President Enterprise Division Dr. Brian SANDUSKY
21 Director Finance/Controller Ms. Noelle TESTA
21 Director Business Operations Mr. Tom CORLEY
15 Director Human Resources Ms. Joanna WALTERS
06 University Registrar Ms. Karen ADAMS
07 Director of Enrollment Ms. Sarah TIPPING
21 Business Administrator Mr. Chad TALDO
106 Vice President for Online Mr. Brian MESSER
88 VP and COO APOS Mr. Shane SMEED

† Regional accreditation is carried under the parent institution in Ottawa, KS.

Pinnacle Career Institute (B)

1601 W. 23rd Street, Ste 200, Lawrence KS 66046

County: Douglas — FICE Identification: 026130
Unit ID: 367097
Telephone: (785) 841-9640 — Carnegie Class: Assoc/PrivFP
FAX Number: (785) 841-4854 — Calendar System: Quarter
URL: www.pcitraining.edu
Established: 1953 — Annual Undergrad Tuition & Fees: $13,470
Enrollment: 102 — Coed
Affiliation or Control: Proprietary — IRS Status: Proprietary
Highest Offering: Associate Degree
Program: Occupational
Accreditation: ACICS

01 Executive Director Mr. Brian LAHARGOUE

Pittsburg State University (C)

1701 S Broadway, Pittsburg KS 66762-7500

County: Crawford — FICE Identification: 001926
Unit ID: 155681
Telephone: (620) 231-7000 — Carnegie Class: Master's L
FAX Number: (620) 235-4080 — Calendar System: Semester
URL: www.pittstate.edu
Established: 1903 — Annual Undergrad Tuition & Fees (In-State): $5,494
Enrollment: 7,275 — Coed
Affiliation or Control: State — IRS Status: 501(c)3
Highest Offering: Beyond Master's But Less Than Doctorate
Program: Liberal Arts And General; Teacher Preparatory; Professional
Accreditation: NH, BUS, CACREP, ENGT, MUS, NRPA, NURSE, SW, TED

01 President Dr. Steven A. SCOTT
05 Provost & VP for Academic Affairs Dr. Lynette OLSON
11 VP Administration & Campus Life Mr. John D. PATTERSON
30 Vice Pres University Advancement Dr. J. Bradford HODSON
06 Registrar Ms. Debbie GREVE
32 Assoc VP Campus Life/Auxil Svcs Dr. Steve ERWIN
88 Assoc VP for Communication & Mktg Mr. Chris KELLY
84 Assoc Vice Pres Enrollment Mgmt Dr. William IVY
51 Dean Graduate & Continuing Studies Dr. Pawan KAHOL
49 Dean of Arts & Sciences Dr. Karl KUNKEL
50 Dean of Business Dr. Paul GRIMES
53 Dean of Education Dr. Howard W. SMITH
72 Dean of Technology Dr. Bruce D. DALLMAN
08 Dean of Library Services Dr. David BUNNELL
108 Director Assessment Dr. Patricia LINDLEY
26 Director of Media Relations Mr. Ron WOMBLE
29 Dir Alumni Rels/Constituent Svcs Ms. Johnna M. SCHREMMER
27 Chief Information Officer Ms. Angela NERIA
15 Director Human Resource Svcs/Budget Dr. Michele D. SEXTON
85 Director of International Affairs Mr. Charles A. OLCESE
04 Dir of Community & Govt Relations Mr. Shawn NACCARATO
18 Director of Trades & Landscape Svcs Mr. Tom AMERSHEK
18 Director Gen & Custodial Services Ms. Wanda ENDICOTT
19 Director of University Police Mr. Mike MCCRACKEN
22 Dir Equal Opportunity/Affirm Action Ms. Cindy JOHNSON
37 Director of Financial Aid Ms. Tammy HIGGINS
41 Dir of Intercollegiate Athletics Mr. James JOHNSON
07 Director of Admissions Ms. Melinda A. ROELFS
36 Director Career Services Ms. Mindy E. CLONINGER
09 Director of Institutional Research Dr. Peggy SNYDER
38 Dir University Counseling Services Dr. Steven MAYHEW
30 Director of University Development Ms. Kathleen FLANNERY
96 Director of Purchasing Mr. Jim HUGHES
28 Director of Diversity Ms. Deatrea ROSE
10 Controller Ms. Barbara J. WINTER

Pratt Community College (D)

348 NE SR 61, Pratt KS 67124-8432

County: Pratt — FICE Identification: 001938
Unit ID: 155715
Telephone: (620) 672-5641 — Carnegie Class: Assoc/Pub-R-S
FAX Number: (620) 672-5288 — Calendar System: Semester
URL: www.prattcc.edu
Established: 1938 — Annual Undergrad Tuition & Fees (In-District): $3,003
Enrollment: 1,667 — Coed
Affiliation or Control: State/Local — IRS Status: 501(c)3
Highest Offering: Associate Degree
Program: Occupational; 2-Year Principally Bachelor's Creditable
Accreditation: NH, ACBSP, ADNUR

01 President Dr. William A. WOJCIECHOWSKI
05 Vice President Instruction Mr. James STRATFORD
10 Vice President Finance/Operations Mr. Kent ADAMS
84 Vice Pres Student Enroll Management Ms. Lisa MILLER
66 Dean of Nursing Ms. Gail WITHERS
41 Director of Athletics Mr. Kurt MCAFEE
20 Dean of Academic Instruction Vacant
75 Dean of Technical Instruction Dr. Joe VARRIENTOS
07 Director of Admissions Mr. Lynn PEREZ
06 Registrar Ms. Sally PROSSER
13 Director of Information Technology Mr. Jerry SANKO
37 Director of Financial Aid Ms. Ann RUDER
30 Director Development Ms. Jody JORNS
08 Dir Linda Hunt Memorial Library Ms. Pam DIETZ
16 Director of Personnel Ms. Rita PINKALL
38 Director Student Success Center Ms. Amy JACKSON
21 Controller Mr. Jay MIES
18 Director of Buildings & Grounds Mr. Dan PETZ
39 Director of Residence Life Vacant
26 Chief Public Relations Officer Vacant

Salina Area Technical College (E)

2562 Centennial Road, Salina KS 67401

County: Saline — FICE Identification: 005499
Telephone: (785) 309-3100 — Carnegie Class: Not Classified
FAX Number: (785) 309-3101 — Calendar System: Semester
URL: www.salinatech.edu
Established: 1965 — Annual Undergrad Tuition & Fees (In-District): $3,829
Enrollment: 402 — Coed
Affiliation or Control: State/Local — IRS Status: 501(c)3
Highest Offering: Associate Degree
Program: Occupational
Accreditation: @NH, DA

01 President Mr. Greg R. GOODE

Seward County Community College/Area Technical School (F)

1801 N Kansas Avenue, Liberal KS 67901-2054

County: Seward — FICE Identification: 008228
Unit ID: 155858
Telephone: (620) 624-1951 — Carnegie Class: Assoc/Pub-R-S
FAX Number: (620) 417-1169 — Calendar System: Semester
URL: www.sccc.edu
Established: 1967 — Annual Undergrad Tuition & Fees (In-District): $2,160
Enrollment: 1,906 — Coed
Affiliation or Control: State/Local — IRS Status: 501(c)3
Highest Offering: Associate Degree
Program: Occupational; 2-Year Principally Bachelor's Creditable
Accreditation: NH, ACBSP, ADNUR, MLTAD, SURGT

01 President Dr. Duane M. DUNN
05 Dean of Academic Affairs Ms. Cynthia K. RAPP
10 Dean of Finance & Operations Mr. Dennis M. SANDER
32 Dean of Student Services Ms. Celeste DONOVAN
88 Dean of Career and Technical Ed Vacant
06 Registrar Ms. Donetta DREITZ
13 Director of Information Technology Mr. Mark W. MERRIHEW
37 Financial Aid Director Mrs. Donna M. FISHER
26 Dir of Public and Alumni Relations Mrs. Andrea G. YOXALL
50 Director of Business & Industry Mrs. Norma Jean DODGE
24 Director of Multi-media Mr. Doug BROWNE
08 Director of Library Mr. Matthew PANNKUK
41 Athletic Director Mr. Galen W. MCSPADDEN
18 Dir of Buildings Grounds & Security Mr. Roger SCHEIB
40 Director of Bookstore Ms. Jerri L. LYDDON
30 Director of Development/Alumni Rels Ms. Tammy DOLL
39 Student Housing Manager Ms. Jacy L. SAUTTER
09 Institutional Research/Data Analyst Ms. Teresa WEHMEIER
21 Fiscal Officer/Admin Assistant Mr. Mike BAILEY
19 Security Supervisor Mr. Kelly J. CAMPBELL
15 Director of Human Resources Ms. Deborah WEILERT
07 Admissions Coordinator Ms. Nereida LUJAN
38 Counselor Ms. Star L. TRISCORNIA
35 Director Student Activities Mr. Wade LYON
04 Adm Asst to Pres & Brd of Trustees Mrs. Pamela M. PERKINS
66 Dir of Nursing and Allied Health Mrs. Veda KING
75 Director of Area Technical School Dr. Bud SMITHSON
26 Director of Marketing Mr. J.R DONEY

Southwestern College (G)

100 College Street, Winfield KS 67156-2499

County: Cowley — FICE Identification: 001940
Unit ID: 155900
Telephone: (620) 229-6000 — Carnegie Class: Master's M
FAX Number: (620) 229-6224 — Calendar System: Semester
URL: www.sckans.edu
Established: 1885 — Annual Undergrad Tuition & Fees: $22,756
Enrollment: 1,687 — Coed
Affiliation or Control: United Methodist — IRS Status: 501(c)3
Highest Offering: Doctorate
Program: Liberal Arts And General; Teacher Preparatory; Professional
Accreditation: NH, MUS, NURSE, TED

01 President Dr. William R. MERRIMAN, JR.
05 Vice President Academic Affairs Dr. James A. SHEPPARD
10 Vice President Finance Ms. Sheila R. KRUG
32 Vice President Student Life Dr. Dawn E. PLEAS-BAILEY
107 Vice President Professional Studies Ms. Pamela MONACO
45 VP Planning/New Programs Dr. Stephen K. WILKE
30 Vice Pres Institutional Advancement Mr. Mike K. FARRELL
26 Vice President Communications Ms. Sara S. WEINERT
13 Vice Pres Information Technology Mr. Ben LIM
35 Dean of Student Life Mr. Dan FALK
29 Director Alumni Programs Ms. Susan G. LOWE
44 Director Development Ms. Jessica FALK
44 Director Major Gifts Mr. Ronnie D. JENKINS
20 Director Academic Affairs Ms. Lolita REPP
08 Library Director Ms. Veronica MCASEY
07 Director Admission Ms. Marla SEXSON
37 Director Financial Aid Ms. Brenda D. HICKS
06 Registrar Ms. Stacy TOWNSLEY
35 Director Campus Life Ms. Lai-L CLEMONS
09 Director of Institutional Research Ms. Margaret A. ROBINSON
41 Director Athletics Mr. David DENLY
42 Campus Minister Ms. Ashlee E. ALLEY
87 Director Human Resources Ms. Lonnie BOYD
96 Director of Purchasing Mr. David H. DOLSEN
36 Director Advising/Student Success Ms. Tami P. PULLINS
04 Administrative Asst to President Ms. Skye BROWNING

Sterling College (H)

125 W Cooper Street, Sterling KS 67579-1533

County: Rice — FICE Identification: 001945
Unit ID: 155937
Telephone: (620) 278-2173 — Carnegie Class: Bac/Diverse
FAX Number: (620) 278-4411 — Calendar System: 4/1/4
URL: www.sterling.edu
Established: 1887 — Annual Undergrad Tuition & Fees: $20,950
Enrollment: 674 — Coed
Affiliation or Control: Presbyterian Church (U.S.A.) — IRS Status: 501(c)3
Highest Offering: Baccalaureate
Program: Liberal Arts And General; Teacher Preparatory
Accreditation: NH, TED

01 Acting President Mr. Scott RICH
05 Vice President Academic Affairs Dr. Greg KERR
30 Vice President for Inst Advancement Dr. Marvin DEWEY
10 Vice President Financial Services Mr. Scott RICH
32 VP Student Life & Student Affairs Mrs. Tina WOHLER
84 Vice Pres Enrollment & Marketing Vacant
06 Registrar Ms. Janet CAYWOOD
08 Head Librarian Mrs. Valorie STARR
37 Director of Financial Aid Vacant
29 Director of Alumni/Parent Services Ms. Amy THOMPSON
41 Athletic Director Mr. Gary KEMPF
20 Director Academic Support Mrs. Carol LUDWICK
44 Director of Annual Giving Vacant
18 Chief Facilities/Physical Plant Mr. Clay THOMAS

36 Director Student Placement ... Ms. Lisa PARSON
38 Director Student Counseling ... Ms. Teri ANDERSON
21 Associate Business Officer ... Ms. Michelle HALL
26 Chief Public Relations Officer ... Ms. Karin SWIHART

Tabor College (A)

400 S Jefferson Street, Hillsboro KS 67063-1753
County: Marion FICE Identification: 001946
Unit ID: 155973
Telephone: (620) 947-3121 Carnegie Class: Bac/Diverse
FAX Number: (620) 947-2607 Calendar System: 4/1/4
URL: www.tabor.edu
Established: 1908 Annual Undergrad Tuition & Fees: $21,740
Enrollment: 734 Coed
Affiliation or Control: Mennonite Brethren Church IRS Status: 501(c)3
Highest Offering: Master's
Program: Liberal Arts And General; Teacher Preparatory
Accreditation: NH, MUS, NURSE, TED

01 President ... Dr. Jules GLANZER
05 Vice President Academic Affairs ... Dr. Frank JOHNSON
10 Sr Vice President Business/Finance ... Mr. Kirby FADENRECHT
30 Vice President Advancement ... Mr. Ronald BRAUN
41 Vice President of Athletics ... Mr. Rusty ALLEN
32 Vice President of Student Life ... Dr. Jim PAULUS
06 Registrar ... Ms. Deanne DUERKSEN
08 Director of Library Services ... Ms. Robin OTTOSON
84 Director Enrollment Management ... Mr. Rusty ALLEN
37 Dir of Student Financial Services ... Mr. Scott FRANZ
29 Director Alumni & Parent Relations ... Ms. Marlene FAST
27 Director of Communications ... Mrs. Beth RIFFEL
18 Director Facilities/Physical Plant ... Mr. Doug GRABER
35 Director Student Success ... Mr. Kevin HADDUCK
09 Institutional Research ... Mrs. Deborah PENN
13 Director of Information Services ... Mr. Chris GLANZER
27 Chief Information Officer ... Mrs. Joy MARK
15 Human Resources Coordinator ... Mrs. Ruth FUNK

University of Kansas Main Campus (B)

1450 Jayhawk Boulevard, Room 230,
Lawrence KS 66045-7535
County: Douglas FICE Identification: 001948
Unit ID: 155317
Telephone: (785) 864-2700 Carnegie Class: RU/VH
FAX Number: N/A Calendar System: Semester
URL: www.ku.edu
Established: 1866 Annual Undergrad Tuition & Fees (In-State): $8,888
Enrollment: 28,718 Coed
Affiliation or Control: State IRS Status: 501(c)3
Highest Offering: Doctorate
Program: Liberal Arts And General; Teacher Preparatory; Professional
Accreditation: NH, ART, AUD, BUS, BUSA, CEA, CLPSY, COPSY, CS, ENG, HSA, IPSY, JOUR, LAW, MUS, PH, PHAR, PLNG, SCPSY, SP, SPAA, SW, TED

01 Chancellor ... Dr. Bernadette GRAY-LITTLE
05 Exec Vice Chancellor/Provost ... Dr. Jeffrey S. VITTER
12 Vice Chancellor/Dean Edwards Campus ... Dr. Robert M. CLARK
26 Vice Chancellor for Public Affairs ... Dr. Timothy CABONI
04 Executive Assistant to Chancellor ... Ms. Mary G. BURG
43 General Counsel ... Mr. James P. POTTORFF, JR.
20 Sr Vice Provost Academic Affairs ... Dr. Sara ROSEN
20 Vice Provost ... Dr. Mary Lee HUMMERT
20 Vice Provost ... Ms. Diane H. GODDARD
32 Vice Provost for Student Affairs ... Dr. Tammara DURHAM
46 Vice Provost Research/Grad Studies ... Dr. Steven F. WARREN
28 Vice Provost Diversity & Equity ... Dr. Fred RODRIGUEZ
13 Chief Information Officer ... Mr. Bob LIM
45 Asst Vice Provost Research ... Ms. Joanne K. ALTIERI
58 Assoc VP/Dean Research & Grad Stds ... Dr. Thomas W. HEILKE
104 Assoc VP International Programs ... Ms. Susan GRONBECK-TEDESCO
96 Assoc Vice Provost of Purchasing ... Mr. Barry K. SWANSON
84 AVP Recruitment/Enrollment ... Dr. Matt MELVIN
30 President Endowment Association ... Mr. Dale SEUFERLING
29 President Alumni Association ... Mr. Kevin J. CORBETT
07 Director Admissions ... Ms. Lisa P. KRESS
10 Chief Business/Financial Plng Ofcr ... Ms. Theresa K. GORDZICA
21 Comptroller ... Ms. Katrina M. YOAKUM
21 Director Budget Office ... Mr. Richard L. MCKINNEY
06 University Registrar ... Ms. Cindy DERRITT
09 Univ Director Inst Research Plng ... Ms. Deborah J. TEETER
15 Director Human Resources ... Ms. Ola FAUCHER
85 Director International Student Svcs ... Dr. Charles A. BANKART
38 Director Counseling/Psych Services ... Dr. Michael LYNCH MAESTAS
18 Director Design & Construction Mgmt ... Mr. James E. MODIG
37 Director Student Financial Aid ... Ms. Brenda MAIGAARD
36 Director Career/Employment Svcs ... Mr. David GASTON
41 Director Intercollegiate Athletics ... Dr. Sheahon ZENGER
18 Interim Director Facilities Service ... Mr. Vince AVILA
22 Director Equal Oppty/Recruitment ... Vacant
88 Int Director Multicultural Affairs ... Mr. Rueben PEREZ
23 Director Student Health Services ... Ms. Carol SEAGER
24 Director Media Services ... Dr. Susan M. ZVACEK
39 Director Housing ... Dr. Diana ROBERTSON
86 Director State Relations ... Ms. Kathy DAMRON
92 Director Honors Program ... Dr. Kathleen A. MCCLUSKEY-FAWCETT
86 Director Federal Relations ... Mr. Jack CLINE

40 Director Bookstores ... Ms. Estella MCCOLLUM
51 Exec Dir Continuing Education ... Mr. Frederick W. PAWLICKI
25 Manager Contract Negotiations ... Ms. Lucille MARINO
91 Project Coord Information Systems ... Mr. David M. GARDNER
49 Dean Liberal Arts/Science ... Dr. Danny J. ANDERSON
61 Dean of Law ... Mr. Stephen W. MAZZA
54 Interim Dean of Engineering ... Dr. Stanley T. ROLFE
48 Dean Architecture/Design/Planning ... Mr. John C. GAUNT
50 Dean of Business ... Dr. Neeli BENDAPUDI
67 Dean of Pharmacy ... Dr. Kenneth L. AUDUS
60 Dean of Journalism ... Dr. Ann M. BRILL
53 Dean of Education ... Dr. Rick GINSBERG
64 Dean of Music ... Dr. Robert L. WALZEL, JR.
70 Dean of Social Welfare ... Dr. Mary Ellen KONDRAT
08 Dean of Library ... Ms. Lorraine J. HARICOMBE
57 Assoc Dean School of the Arts ... Ms. Elizabeth KOWALCHUK

† Medical Center and Main campus enrollments should be combined for the total institution enrollment.

University of Kansas Medical Center (C)

3901 Rainbow Boulevard, Kansas City KS 66160-0001
County: Wyandotte FICE Identification: 024579
Unit ID: 155326
Telephone: (913) 588-5000 Carnegie Class: Not Classified
FAX Number: (913) 588-1412 Calendar System: Semester
URL: www.kumc.edu
Established: 1905 Annual Undergrad Tuition & Fees (In-State): $8,272
Enrollment: 2,491 Coed
Affiliation or Control: State IRS Status: 501(c)3
Highest Offering: Doctorate
Program: Professional
Accreditation: &NH, ANEST, CYTO, DIETI, DMOLS, DMS, MED, MIDWF, MT, NMT, NURSE, OT, PTA

01 Actg Exec Vice Chanc/Actg Dean SOM ... Dr. Steve STITES
17 President & CEO Univ of Kansas Hosp ... Mr. Bob PAGE
05 Sr Vice Chan Acad Affs/Dean SON SAH ... Dr. Karen L. MILLER
11 Vice Chancellor for Administration ... Ms. Steffani WEBB
46 Vice Chan for Research/Pres KUMC RI ... Dr. Paul TERRANOVA
20 Vice Chanc Acad Affs/Dean Grad Stds ... Dr. Allen B. RAWITCH
32 Vice Chancellor of Student Services ... Mr. Vince LOFFREDO
25 Assc Vice Chanc Res Adm/Exec Dir RI ... Dr. Gregory S. KOPF
20 Assoc Vice Chanc Educ Resources ... Dr. Heidi CHUMLEY
10 Assoc Vice Chancellor Finance ... Mr. Mike KEEBLE
13 Assoc VC Info Res/Chief Info Ofcr ... Mr. James (Jim) L. BINGHAM
19 Assoc Vice Chanc/Chief of Police ... Mr. Richard (Rick) L. JOHNSON
15 Assoc Vice Chanc Administration ... Mr. Adrian FITZMAURICE
06 Assc Vice Chanc Stdnt Svc/Registrar ... Dr. Chris MEIERS
88 Asst Vice Chan Enterprise Analytics ... Dr. Russ WAITMAN
88 Sr Assoc Dean for Clinical Affairs ... Dr. Doug GIROD
63 Dean SOM Wichita Campus ... Dr. H. David WILSON
43 Associate General Counsel ... Mr. Steve L. RUDDICK
66 Dir Acad Affairs Admin SON ... Mr. Edward WILSON
88 Senior Associate Dean Finance ... Ms. Kimberly A. MEYER
100 Chief of Staff ... Vacant
76 Assoc Dean Administration SAH ... Ms. Lou LOESCHER-JUNGE
21 Controller ... Mr. Robert W. WESELOH
26 Director of Communications ... Ms. CJ JANOVY
08 Director Dykes Library ... Ms. Karen COLE
37 Director of Student Financial Aid ... Ms. Sara HONECK
58 Director Graduate Studies ... Ms. Marcia A. JONES
09 Director Data Mgmt and Analysis ... Ms. Kathy SCHLEETER
35 Director of Student Life ... Mr. Ryan K. GOVE
29 Director Alumni Affairs ... Ms. Kim HUYETT
105 Director Internet Development ... Mr. Jameson WATKINS
18 Director Facilities Management ... Vacant
96 Director of Purchasing ... Mr. Stephen SCANLON
28 Director of Training and Diversity ... Mr. Charles ROMERO
38 Director of Student Counseling ... Dr. Larry LONG
85 Director International Programs ... Vacant

† Medical Center and Main campus enrollments should be combined for the total institution enrollment. Regional accreditation is carried under the parent institution in Lawrence, KS.

University of Saint Mary (D)

4100 S 4th Street Trafficway, Leavenworth KS 66048-5082
County: Leavenworth FICE Identification: 001943
Unit ID: 155812
Telephone: (913) 682-5151 Carnegie Class: Master's M
FAX Number: (913) 758-6140 Calendar System: Semester
URL: www.stmary.edu
Established: 1923 Annual Undergrad Tuition & Fees: $21,500
Enrollment: 1,044 Coed
Affiliation or Control: Roman Catholic IRS Status: 501(c)3
Highest Offering: Doctorate
Program: Liberal Arts And General; Teacher Preparatory; Professional
Accreditation: NH, IACBE, NURSE, @PTA, TED

01 President ... Dr. Diane STEELE
05 Academic Vice President ... Dr. Bryan LEBEAU
10 Vice President for Finance ... Mr. Dale CULVER
30 Director of Development ... Mr. Andrew DAME
26 VP for Marketing & Communication ... Ms. Laura DAVIS
32 Vice Presient for Student Life ... Dr. Wendi SANTEE
07 Director of Enrollment ... Mr. Ken WUERZEBERGER
06 Registrar ... Ms. Mary Pat DUTTON
08 Director of the Library ... Ms. Penny LONERGAN

09 Data Analyst ... Ms. Veronica DONOVAN
29 Alumni and Events Coordinator ... Ms. Sharon CLAY
37 Director of Financial Aid ... Ms. Annissa EPPERSON
42 Campus Minister ... Sr. Julie MARSH
44 Development Officer Planned Giving ... Ms. Karolyn DREILING
41 Athletic Director ... Mr. Rob MILLER
15 Director Human Resources ... Ms. Teresa LEE
39 Director of Residence Life ... Ms. Kristian JACKSON
21 Controller ... Ms. Sherry WELLS
38 Counselor ... Ms. Deborah SHADDY
18 Plant Manager ... Mr. Mark GIESEMAN
40 Bookstore Manager ... Ms. Terri MULLIS
12 Site Coordinator Johnson County ... Ms. Patricia HOWARD
14 Coordinator of Computer Operations ... Mr. Kevin GANTT
04 Executive Administrative Assistant ... Ms. Linda QUINLEY

Vatterott College - Wichita (E)

8853 East 37th Street North, Wichita KS 67226-2018
County: Sedgwick Identification: 666583
Unit ID: 440891
Telephone: (316) 634-0066 Carnegie Class: Assoc/PrivFP
FAX Number: (316) 634-0002 Calendar System: Quarter
URL: www.vatterott.edu
Established: N/A Annual Undergrad Tuition & Fees: $11,629
Enrollment: 275 Coed
Affiliation or Control: Proprietary IRS Status: Proprietary
Highest Offering: Associate Degree
Program: Occupational; 2-Year Principally Bachelor's Creditable; Technical Emphasis
Accreditation: ACCSC

01 Campus Director ... Mr. Michael HARRIS

† Branch campus of Vatterott College-North Park, Berkeley, MO.

Washburn University (F)

1700 SW College Avenue, Topeka KS 66621-0001
County: Shawnee FICE Identification: 001949
Unit ID: 156082
Telephone: (785) 670-1010 Carnegie Class: Master's M
FAX Number: (785) 670-1089 Calendar System: Semester
URL: www.washburn.edu
Established: 1865 Annual Undergrad Tuition & Fees (In-District): $5,486
Enrollment: 7,303 Coed
Affiliation or Control: Local IRS Status: 501(c)3
Highest Offering: Doctorate
Program: Liberal Arts And General; Teacher Preparatory; Professional
Accreditation: NH, ART, BUS, DMS, LAW, MUS, NURSE, OTA, PTAA, RAD, SW, TED

01 President ... Dr. Jerry B. FARLEY
05 Vice President Acad Affairs ... Dr. Randall G. PEMBROOK
10 Vice Pres Admin & Treasurer ... Mr. Rick L. ANDERSON
32 Vice President for Student Life ... Dr. Denise OTTINGER
04 Special Assistant to the President ... Dr. Cynthia A. HORNBERGER
84 Director Enrollment Management ... Mr. Richard W. LIEDTKE
43 University Legal Counsel ... Ms. Lisa R. JONES
20 Assoc Vice Pres Acad Affairs ... Dr. Nancy A. TATE
30 President WU Foundation ... Dr. Juliann MAZACHEK
06 Registrar ... Dr. Carla RASCH
08 Dean of Libraries ... Dr. Alan BEARMAN
35 Dean of Students ... Mr. Meredith KIDD
37 Director Student Financial Aid ... Ms. Gail PALMER
07 Director of Admissions ... Ms. Susan SMITH
15 Director of Human Resources ... Ms. Deborah D. MOORE
90 Director Info Systems & Services ... Mr. Floyd DAVENPORT
09 Director Institutional Research ... Ms. Melodie E. CHRISTAL
49 Dean College Arts & Sciences ... Dr. Gordon MCQUERE
88 Interim Dean School Applied Studies ... Dr. Nancy A. TATE
61 Dean School of Law ... Mr. Thomas J. ROMIG
50 Dean School of Business ... Dr. David SOLLARS
66 Dean School of Nursing ... Dr. Monica S. SCHEIBMEIR
41 Athletic Director ... Mr. Loren FERRE
35 Director Student Services ... Ms. Jeanne D. KESSLER
22 Director Equal Opportunity ... Ms. Carol L. VOGEL
18 Director Facilities Services ... Mr. Bill GLATTS
23 Interim Director Health Services ... Dr. Shirley DINKEL
29 Alumni Director ... Ms. Susie HOFFMANN
96 Director of Purchasing ... Mr. Mel RAGAR
92 Dean Honors Program ... Dr. Michael J. MCGUIRE
88 Assistant Dean of Student Success ... Dr. John DAHLSTRAND
39 Director Student Housing ... Ms. Mindy P. RENDON
40 Director Bookstore ... Ms. Kay FARLEY
35 Director Student Activities ... Ms. Jessica NEUMANN
38 Director Student Counseling ... Ms. Marilynn KOELLIKER

Wichita Area Technical College (G)

4004 N Webb Road, Wichita KS 67226-8101
County: Sedgwick FICE Identification: 005498
Unit ID: 156107
Telephone: (316) 677-9400 Carnegie Class: Assoc/Pub-U-MC
FAX Number: (316) 677-9510 Calendar System: Semester
URL: www.watc.edu
Established: 1965 Annual Undergrad Tuition & Fees (In-District): $2,700
Enrollment: 2,136 Coed
Affiliation or Control: State/Local IRS Status: 501(c)3
Highest Offering: Associate Degree
Program: 2-Year Principally Bachelor's Creditable; Technical Emphasis
Accreditation: NH, DA, MAC, PNUR, SURGT

01 President Dr. Anthony G. KINKEL
05 Vice Pres Academic Affairs Ms. Sheree UTASH
10 Vice Pres Administration & CFO Mr. Doug BRANTNER
32 Vice Pres Stdnt Svcs/Workforce Dev Mr. Jim FLY
13 Exec Dir Tech/Instl Effect/Found Mr. Randy ROEBUCK
15 Exec Director Human Resources Ms. Judy MOUNT
07 Exec Dir Recruiting & Marketing Mr. Joe ONTJES

Wichita State University (A)

1845 N Fairmount, Wichita KS 67260-0001
County: Sedgwick FICE Identification: 001950
Unit ID: 156125
Telephone: (316) 978-3456 Carnegie Class: RU/H
FAX Number: (316) 978-3770 Calendar System: Semester
URL: www.wichita.edu
Established: 1895 Annual Undergrad Tuition & Fees (In-State): $6,407
Enrollment: 14,972 Coed
Affiliation or Control: State IRS Status: 501(c)3
Highest Offering: Doctorate
Program: Liberal Arts And General; Teacher Preparatory; Professional
Accreditation: NH, ARCPA, ART, AUD, BUS, BUSA, CLPSY, DANCE, DENT, DH, ENG, IPSY, MT, MUS, NURSE, PTA, SP, SPAA, SW, TED

01 President Dr. John W. BARDO
05 Provost/VP Academic Affs/Research Dr. Keith H. PICKUS
11 Vice Pres Administration & Finance Ms. Mary L. HERRIN
32 Vice Pres Campus Life/Un Relations Dr. Wade A. ROBINSON
43 Vice Pres/General Counsel/Dir EEO Mr. Ted D. AYRES
26 Assoc VP University Relations Mr. Barth A. HAGUE
09 Asst VP/Dir Institutional Research Dr. Donna J. HAWLEY
20 Senior Assoc Provost Dr. Richard D. MUMA
27 Assoc Provost/Chief Info Officer Dr. Ravi PENDSE
20 Associate Provost Dr. Linnea GLENMAYE
46 Asc Provost Research/Dir Rsch Admin Dr. J. David MCDONALD
49 Dean Liberal Arts & Sciences Dr. Ronald R. MATSON
50 Dean Barton School of Business Dr. Douglas A. HENSLER
53 Dean Education Dr. Sharon IORIO
54 Dean Engineering Dr. Zulma TORO-RAMOS
57 Dean Fine Arts Dr. Rodney E. MILLER
76 Dean Health Professions Dr. Peter A. COHEN
58 Dean Graduate School Dr. J. David MCDONALD
08 Dean Libraries Dr. Don GILSTRAP
84 Dean of Enrollment Services Ms. Christine SCHNEIKART-LUEBBE
86 Exec Director Government Relations Mr. Andrew SCHLAPP
24 Exec Dir Media Resources Center Mr. Michael A. WOOD
29 Exec Director Alumni Association Ms. Deborah KENNEDY
41 Athletic Director Dr. Eric L. SEXTON
88 Director Creative Services Mr. Craig LINDEMAN
15 Director Human Resources Ms. Frankie M. BROWN
21 Director Budgets Mr. Paul F. WERNER
06 Registrar Ms. Gina D. CRABTREE
07 Director of Admissions Mr. Bobby GANDU
37 Director Financial Aid Ms. Deborah BYERS
36 Director Placement/Career Services Ms. Jill M. PLETCHER
38 Director Counseling & Testing Dr. Maureen DASEY-MORALES
18 Director Physical Plant Mr. Woodrow DEPONTIER
45 Director Facilities Planning Mr. John D. GIST
19 Campus Police Chief Mr. Paul W. DOTSON
23 Director Student Health Services Ms. Camille CHILDERS
39 Director Student Housing Ms. Trish INSLEE
28 Int Director Multicultural Affairs Dr. Wade ROBINSON
40 Manager Bookstore Mr. Kevin J. KONDA
21 Controller Mr. Steven D. LAFEVER
42 Campus Minister Rev. Christopher ESHELMAN
96 Director of Purchasing Mr. Steven WHITE
102 Foundation CEO & President Dr. Elizabeth KING

Wright Career College (B)

10700 Metcalf Avenue, Overland Park KS 66210
FICE Identification: 025909
Unit ID: 406200
Telephone: (913) 385-7700 Carnegie Class: Assoc/PrivNFP
FAX Number: (913) 647-8073 Calendar System: Other
URL: www.wrightcc.edu
Established: 1997 Annual Undergrad Tuition & Fees: N/A
Enrollment: 2,000 Coed
Affiliation or Control: Independent Non-Profit IRS Status: 501(c)3
Highest Offering: Baccalaureate
Program: Occupational
Accreditation: ACICS

01 Campus Director Mr. Mike SHEW

KENTUCKY

Alice Lloyd College (C)

Purpose Road, Pippa Passes KY 41844-9703
County: Knott FICE Identification: 001951
Unit ID: 156189
Telephone: (606) 368-2101 Carnegie Class: Bac/Diverse
FAX Number: (606) 368-6212 Calendar System: Semester
URL: www.alc.edu
Established: 1923 Annual Undergrad Tuition & Fees: $10,100
Enrollment: 593 Coed
Affiliation or Control: Independent Non-Profit IRS Status: 501(c)3
Highest Offering: Baccalaureate
Program: Liberal Arts And General; Teacher Preparatory
Accreditation: SC

01 President Dr. Joe A. STEPP
03 Executive Vice President Dr. Jim STEPP
05 Vice President Academic Affairs Dr. Claude CRUM
10 Vice President of Business Affairs Mr. David JOHNSON
32 Dean of Students & Community Life Mr. Scott CORNETT
07 Director of Admissions Ms. Angela PHIPPS
06 Registrar Mrs. Thelmarie THORNSBERRY
08 Director of Library Mr. Andrew BUSROE
37 Director of Financial Aid Mrs. Jacqueline STEWART
88 Director of Student Work Program Mr. Kerry RATLIFF
53 Director of Teacher Education Dr. Sherry LONG
18 Director of Physical Plant Mr. Ryan GIBSON
39 Director of Student Housing Mr. John MILLS
29 Director of Alumni Relations Mrs. Teresa GRENDER
35 Director of Student Activities Ms. Christine STUMBO
26 Dir of Marketing & Communications Ms. Tiffany OWENS
09 Director of Institutional Research Mr. Gary GIBSON
30 Director of Development Mrs. Margo SPARKMAN

† Cost of tuition is guaranteed for students from 108 county territories.

Asbury Theological Seminary (D)

204 N Lexington Avenue, Wilmore KY 40390-1199
County: Jessamine FICE Identification: 001953
Unit ID: 156222
Telephone: (859) 858-3581 Carnegie Class: Spec/Faith
FAX Number: N/A Calendar System: 4/1/4
URL: www.asburyseminary.edu
Established: 1923 Annual Graduate Tuition & Fees: $530
Enrollment: 1,529 Coed
Affiliation or Control: Independent Non-Profit IRS Status: 501(c)3
Highest Offering: Doctorate; No Undergraduates
Program: Professional
Accreditation: SC, THEOL

01 President Dr. Timothy C. TENNENT
05 Dean/Academic Affairs Dr. Leslie A. ANDREWS
10 Vice President Finance Mr. Bryan BLANKENSHIP
30 Vice President Seminary Advancement Mr. Jay MANSUR
31 Vice Pres Community Formation Dr. Marilyn ELLIOTT
84 Vice Pres Enrollment Management Mr. Kevin BISH
13 Chief Technology Officer Mr. Patrick GARDELLA
06 Registrar Mrs. Sheryl VOIGTS
07 Director of Admissions Mrs. Carolyn CLAYTON
37 Director of Student Financial Aid Mrs. Jenny BURKHART
18 Chief Facilities/Physical Plant Mr. Lanny SPEARS
26 Chief Public Relations Officer Vacant
09 Director of Institutional Research Dr. Deborah COLWILL
15 Director Personnel Services Mrs. Barbara ANTROBUS
29 Director Alumni Relations Ms. Tammy CESSNA
73 Dean School of Theology & Formation Dr. James THOBABEN
12 Dean Beeson Center Dr. Tom TUMBLIN
12 Dean E.S.J. School Dr. Gregg OKESSON

Asbury University (E)

1 Macklem Drive, Wilmore KY 40390-1198
County: Jessamine FICE Identification: 001952
Unit ID: 156213
Telephone: (859) 858-3511 Carnegie Class: Bac/Diverse
FAX Number: (859) 858-3921 Calendar System: Semester
URL: www.asbury.edu
Established: 1890 Annual Undergrad Tuition & Fees: $25,140
Enrollment: 1,638 Coed
Affiliation or Control: Independent Non-Profit IRS Status: 501(c)3
Highest Offering: Master's
Program: Liberal Arts And General; Teacher Preparatory
Accreditation: SC, MUS, SW, TED

01 President Dr. Sandra C. GRAY
05 Provost Dr. Jon S. KULAGA
10 Vice Pres Business Affairs & Treas Dr. Charlie D. FISKEAUX
84 Vice Pres of Enrollment Management Dr. Mark J. TROYER
32 Vice Pres Student Dev/Dean Students Dr. Douglas A. WILCOXSON
30 Vice President for Inst Advancement Dr. R. Gregory SWANSON
11 Asst Vice President Operations Mr. Glenn R. HAMILTON
20 Academic Dean Dr. Bonnie BANKER
49 Dir of College of Arts & Sciences Dr. Stephen K. CLEMENTS
53 Director of School of Education Dr. Sherry POWERS
60 Dir of School of Communication Arts Dr. James R. OWENS
58 Dir of School of Grad & Prof Stud Dr. Verna J. LOWE
51 Dir of Adult Professional Studies Mr. T. Joshua FEE
12 Director of Orlando Campus Rev. J. Craig WAGNER
106 Director of Online Education Mrs. Sara PORTER
44 Senior Advancement Director Rev. Stuart A. SMITH
37 Director of Financial Aid Mr. Ronald M. ANDERSON
42 Assoc Dean for Campus Ministries Rev. Gregory K. HASELOFF
39 Assoc Dean for Residence Life Mr. Joe W. BRUNER
22 Asc Dean Stdnt Success/Intercult Mrs. Deborah L. VETTER
06 Registrar Mr. William A. HALL, JR.
29 Dir of Alumni Relations/Parents Pgm Miss Carolyn L. RIDLEY
09 Institutional Research & Planning Dr. Gay L. HOLCOMB
08 Director of Library Services Mr. Morgan A. TRACY
13 Director of Information Services Mr. Paul J. DUPREE
07 Director of Admissions Mrs. Lisa D. HARPER
26 Dir of Marketing & Commununications Mr. Bradley JOHNSON
18 Director of Physical Plant Mr. Eric C. MCMILLION
23 Supervisor of Clinic Miss Carol J. AMEY
36 Dir Center for Career & Calling Mr. Jason CLAYTON
38 Director of Counseling Center Mrs. Melissa COZART
19 Dir of Security & Environ Safety Mr. Jerry MARCHAL
40 Manager of Bookstore Mr. C. David TRAMMELL
21 Associate Business Officer Mr. Gary E. HOWARD
04 Admin Asst to the President Mrs. Dana MOUTZ
85 Coordinator of Intercultural Pgms Mrs. Esther JADHAV
41 Athletics Director Mr. Mark PERDUE

ATA College (F)

10180 Linn Station Rd, Ste A-200, Louisville KY 40223
County: Jefferson FICE Identification: 040383
Unit ID: 447935
Telephone: (502) 371-8330 Carnegie Class: Assoc/PrivFP
FAX Number: (502) 371-8598 Calendar System: Quarter
URL: www.ata.edu
Established: 1994 Annual Undergrad Tuition & Fees: N/A
Enrollment: 504 Coed
Affiliation or Control: Proprietary IRS Status: Proprietary
Highest Offering: Associate Degree
Program: Occupational
Accreditation: ABHES

01 President Mr. Donald A. JONES

Beckfield College (G)

16 Spiral Drive, Florence KY 41042-4866
County: Boone FICE Identification: 024911
Unit ID: 247065
Telephone: (859) 371-9393 Carnegie Class: Assoc/PrivFP4
FAX Number: (859) 371-5096 Calendar System: Quarter
URL: www.beckfield.edu
Established: 1984 Annual Undergrad Tuition & Fees: $15,120
Enrollment: 977 Coed
Affiliation or Control: Proprietary IRS Status: Proprietary
Highest Offering: Baccalaureate
Program: Professional; Business Emphasis
Accreditation: ACICS

00 Chief Executive Officer Ms. Diane G. WOLFER
01 President Florence Campus Mr. Richard F. COSTA, JR.
05 Vice President of Academic Affairs Ms. Cindy GRIGGS
12 Campus Director of Florence Mr. Keith GRANT
32 Director of Student Services Ms. Sarah CRABTREE
37 Director of Financial Aid Ms. Patricia A. NETTLETON
13 Director of Information Technology Mr. James BRUN
07 Director Admissions Ms. Kathy BENDER
36 Director Career Services Ms. Danielle FULLER
22 Director of Compliance Mr. Peter NETTLETON
06 Registrar Ms. Leah BOERGER
08 Librarian Ms. Emily STEELE
12 Interim Campus Dean-Florence Dr. Jerry LINGER, JR.
50 Dean of Business/Technology Ms. Amy M. HEDGES
66 Dean Division of Nursing Mr. Timothy D. CURL
76 Dean of Allied Health Ms. Ruth GABBARD
97 Dean of General Education Ms. Brittaney HARP
88 Dean of Criminal Justice Dr. Jack BROWN
04 Assistant to the President Ms. Cheryl A. KUNKEL

Bellarmine University (H)

2001 Newburg Road, Louisville KY 40205-0671
County: Jefferson FICE Identification: 001954
Unit ID: 156286
Telephone: (502) 272-8000 Carnegie Class: Master's L
FAX Number: (502) 272-8033 Calendar System: Semester
URL: www.bellarmine.edu
Established: 1950 Annual Undergrad Tuition & Fees: $33,270
Enrollment: 3,432 Coed
Affiliation or Control: Independent Non-Profit IRS Status: 501(c)3
Highest Offering: Doctorate
Program: Liberal Arts And General; Teacher Preparatory; Professional
Accreditation: SC, BUS, MT, NURSE, PTA, TED

01 President Dr. Joseph J. MCGOWAN
05 Provost Dr. Doris A. TEGART
10 Vice President Admin & Finance Mr. Robert L. ZIMLICH
32 Vice President Acad & Student Life Dr. Fred W. RHODES
30 Vice President Development & Alumni Mr. Glenn F. KOSSE
26 Vice President Comm/Public Affairs Mr. Hunt C. HELM
84 Vice President Enrollment Mgmt Mr. Sean J. RYAN
100 Exec Assistant to the President Ms. Marisa ZOELLER
20 Vice President Academic Affairs Dr. Carole PFEFFER
20 Asst VP Academic Affairs Dr. Graham ELLIS
20 Asst VP for Acadeic Affairs Dr. Cindy G. GNADINGER
66 Dn Lansing Sch of Nursing/Hlth Sci Dr. Susan H. DAVIS
50 Dean Rubel School of Business Dr. Daniel L. BAUER
107 Dean of Professional Studies Dr. Mike MATTEI
53 Dean Annsley Frazier Thornton Ed Dr. Robert B. COOPER
47 Dean Regional Environmental Studies Dr. Robert KINGSOLVER
49 Dean Bellarmine College Dr. William E. FENTON
15 Chief Human Resources Officer Ms. Lynn M. BYNUM
21 Asst VP for Admin and Finance Ms. Denise BROWN-CORNELIUS
28 Asst VP & Dir Multicultural Pgms Dr. Hannah CLAYBORNE
85 Director of International Programs Ms. Gabriele BOSLEY
35 Dean of Students Dr. Helen G. RYAN
89 Dean Academic Advising Dr. Catherine SUTTON
92 Director Honors Program Dr. Hank J. ROTHGERBER
41 Athletic Director Mr. Scott P. WIEGANDT

18	Chief Facilities/Physical Plant	Mr. Jeffrey DEAN
07	Dean of Admission	Mr. Timothy A. STURGEON
08	Director of the Library	Mr. John K. STEMMER
19	Director Safety & Security	Mr. Joseph FRYE
07	Dean of Graduate School Admission	Dr. Sara YOUNT-PETTINGILL
06	Registrar	Ms. Ann E. OLSEN
96	Purchasing Manager	Mr. Patrick COONS
42	Director Campus Ministry	Dr. Melanie P. SULLIVAN
39	Director Residence Life	Ms. Leslie M. MAXIE-ASHFORD
13	Director Information Technology	Mr. Eric SATTERLY
37	Director Student Financial Aid	Ms. Heather BOUTELL
09	Director of Institutional Research	Mr. David M. MAHAN
36	Asst Dean Career Services	Mr. Todd D. REALE
29	Executive Director Alumni Relations	Mr. Peter W. KREMER
26	Director of News/Media/Social Netwk	Mr. Jason A. CISSELL
38	Director Student Counseling	Dr. Gary PETIPRIN
92	Director of Brown Scholars Program	Dr. Matisa WILBON

Berea College (A)

101 Chestnut Street, Berea KY 40404-0003

County: Madison FICE Identification: 001955
Unit ID: 156295
Telephone: (859) 985-3000 Carnegie Class: Bac/A&S
FAX Number: (859) 985-3917 Calendar System: Semester
URL: www.berea.edu
Established: 1855 Annual Undergrad Tuition & Fees: $980
Enrollment: 1,661 Coed
Affiliation or Control: Independent Non-Profit IRS Status: 501(c)3
Highest Offering: Baccalaureate
Program: Liberal Arts And General; Teacher Preparatory; Professional
Accreditation: SC, NURSE, TED

01	President	Dr. Lyle D. ROELOFS
10	Vice President Finance	Mr. Jeff S. AMBURGEY
30	Vice President Alumni College Rels	Ms. Michelle JANSSEN
32	Vice President Labor & Student Life	Ms. Gail WOLFORD
11	VP Operations & Sustainability	Mr. Steve KARCHER
100	Assistant to Pres/Chief of Staff	Ms. Tammy CLEMONS
35	Asst Vice Pres for Student Life	Mr. Gus GERASSIMIDES
05	Academic VP/Dean of the Faculty	Dr. Chad BERRY
37	Dir of Student Financial Aid Svcs	Ms. Nancy MELTON
38	Dir Counseling/Psychological Svcs	Ms. Sue REIMONDO
44	Director of Gift Planning	Ms. Amy SHEHEE
20	Dean of Curriculum/Student Learning	Dr. Scott STEELE
13	Chief Information Officer	Dr. John LYMPANY
07	Director of Admissions Operations	Mr. Luke HODSON
29	Director of Alumni Relations	Vacant
15	Director of People Services	Ms. Carolyn CASTLE
18	Director of Facilities Management	Mr. Jon METCALF
88	Director of Appalachian Center	Mr. Chris GREEN
09	Director of Inst Rsrch/Assessment	Ms. Judith WECKMAN
23	Director of College Health Service	Dr. Miriam DAVID
26	Assoc VP for Integrated Marketing	Mr. James C. MAGUIRE
08	Director of Library Services	Ms. Anne CHASE
41	Dir Athletics/Seabury Ctr Complex	Mr. Mark CARTMILL
42	Director Campus Christian Center	Rev. Gail BOWMAN
43	General Counsel	Mr. Judge WILSON
19	Director of Public Safety	Mr. V. Lavoyed HUDGINS
28	Director Black Cultural Center	Vacant
85	Director International Center	Dr. Richard CAHILL
40	College Bookstore Director	Ms. Marty WAYLAND
96	Purchasing Manager	Ms. Aurelia BRANDENBURG
24	Media Services Coordinator	Mr. Rob LEWIS
06	Director of Academic Services	Mr. Curtis SANDBERG
88	Center for Transformative Learning	Ms. Leslie ORTQUIST-AHRENS
88	Woodson Center for Interracial Educ	Dr. Alicestyne TURLEY
88	Director of CELTS	Ms. Ashley COCHRANE

Brescia University (B)

717 Frederica Street, Owensboro KY 42301-3023

County: Daviess FICE Identification: 001958
Unit ID: 156356
Telephone: (270) 685-3131 Carnegie Class: Bac/Diverse
FAX Number: (270) 686-6422 Calendar System: Semester
URL: www.brescia.edu
Established: 1950 Annual Undergrad Tuition & Fees: $18,500
Enrollment: 755 Coed
Affiliation or Control: Roman Catholic IRS Status: 501(c)3
Highest Offering: Master's
Program: Liberal Arts And General; Teacher Preparatory
Accreditation: SC, SW

01	President	Rev. Larry HOSTETTER
05	Vice President & Academic Dean	Dr. Cheryl CLEMONS
10	Vice President Business & Finance	Mr. Dale CECIL
84	Vice President of Enrollment	Mr. Christopher HOUK
30	Vice Pres Institutional Advancement	Mr. Todd BROCK
32	Vice Pres/Dean Student Development	Dr. James FITZPATRICK
39	Asst Dean Students Residence Life	Mr. Jeffrey A. RUDNIK
35	Asst Dean Stdnts Act/Leadership Dev	Mr. Lucas O. LANGDON
06	Registrar	Sr. Helena FISCHER, OSU
71	Director of Weekend College	Mr. Greg ALVEY
38	Director of Counseling Center	Ms. Eva G. ATKINSON
08	Director of Library Services	Sr. Judith N. RINEY, OSU
88	Director Student Support Services	Dr. Dolores KIESLER
15	Director of Human Resources	Ms. Tammy S. KELLER
13	Director of Information Technology	Mr. Jack T. WILSON
18	Director of Physical Plant	Mr. Larry J. YOUNGER
37	Director of Financial Aid	Ms. Marcie TILLETT
41	Director of Athletics	Mr. Larry COX
26	Director of Public Relations	Ms. Tina KASEY
29	Director of Alumni	Mr. Jason COX
44	Director of Annual Giving	Ms. Amy FRENCH
09	Director of Institutional Research	Ms. Tracy NAYLOR
58	Director of Graduate Program-MBA	Dr. Sandra O. OBILADE
58	Director of Graduate Program-MSCI	Dr. Patricia A. AKOJIE
42	Director of Campus Ministry	Sr. Pam MUELLER, OSU
07	Director of Admissions	Ms. Christy ROHNER
21	Asst Director Business & Finance	Ms. Nancy W. REYNOLDS
36	Coordinator of Career Services	Ms. Helen BENNETT
20	Associate Academic Officer	Mr. Keith HUDSON
40	Bookstore Manager	Ms. Beverly MCCANDLESS

Brown Mackie College-Hopkinsville (C)

4001 Fort Campbell Boulevard, Hopkinsville KY 42240-4948

County: Christian Identification: 666516
Unit ID: 421513
Telephone: (270) 886-1302 Carnegie Class: Assoc/PrivFP
FAX Number: (270) 886-3544 Calendar System: Other
URL: www.brownmackie.com
Established: 1995 Annual Undergrad Tuition & Fees: $11,124
Enrollment: 256 Coed
Affiliation or Control: Proprietary IRS Status: Proprietary
Highest Offering: Associate Degree
Program: 2-Year Principally Bachelor's Creditable; Business Emphasis
Accreditation: ACICS, OTA

01	President	Ms. Elaine CUE
06	Associate Registrar	Ms. Belinda DOZIER
36	Director of Career Services	Vacant
07	Senior Director of Admissions	Ms. Delanda BYARS

† Branch campus of Brown Mackie College-Findlay, Findlay, OH.

Brown Mackie College-Louisville (D)

3605 Fern Valley Road, Louisville KY 40219-1916

County: Jefferson FICE Identification: 021082
Unit ID: 157599
Telephone: (502) 810-6000 Carnegie Class: Assoc/PrivFP
FAX Number: (502) 357-9956 Calendar System: Other
URL: www.brownmackie.edu
Established: 1972 Annual Undergrad Tuition & Fees: $11,124
Enrollment: 1,665 Coed
Affiliation or Control: Proprietary IRS Status: Proprietary
Highest Offering: Baccalaureate
Program: Occupational; 2-Year Principally Bachelor's Creditable; Business Emphasis
Accreditation: ACICS, OTA, SURGT, SURTEC

01	President	Mr. Mike FONTAINE
05	Dean of Academic Affairs	Ms. Natalie HARRIS
07	Senior Director of Admissions	Mr. George NOSKO
06	Registrar	Ms. Shannon MITCHELL
36	Director of Career Services	Ms. Chasity TRZOP

† Branch campus of Brown Mackie College-Findlay, Findlay, OH.

Brown Mackie College-Northern Kentucky (E)

309 Buttermilk Pike, Fort Mitchell KY 41017-2191

County: Kenton Identification: 666446
Unit ID: 157696
Telephone: (859) 341-5627 Carnegie Class: Assoc/PrivFP
FAX Number: (859) 341-6483 Calendar System: Other
URL: www.brownmackie.edu
Established: 1981 Annual Undergrad Tuition & Fees: $11,124
Enrollment: 632 Coed
Affiliation or Control: Proprietary IRS Status: Proprietary
Highest Offering: Associate Degree
Program: Occupational; 2-Year Principally Bachelor's Creditable; Business Emphasis
Accreditation: ACICS, OTA

01	President	Ms. Christine KNOUFF
05	Dean of Academic Affairs	Ms. Marcia NEUDIGATE
07	Senior Director of Admissions	Ms. Amy WOLF
32	Director of Student Services	Ms. Jean SCHULTZ
36	Director of Career Services	Ms. Michelle DRENNEN

† Branch campus of Brown Mackie College, Cincinnati, OH.

Campbellsville University (F)

1 Universty Drive, Campbellsville KY 42718-2799

County: Taylor FICE Identification: 001959
Unit ID: 156365
Telephone: (270) 789-5000 Carnegie Class: Master's M
FAX Number: (270) 789-5050 Calendar System: Semester
URL: www.campbellsville.edu
Established: 1906 Annual Undergrad Tuition & Fees: $21,100
Enrollment: 3,607 Coed
Affiliation or Control: Baptist IRS Status: 501(c)3
Highest Offering: Master's
Program: Liberal Arts And General; Teacher Preparatory; Professional
Accreditation: SC, IACBE, MUS, SW, TED

01	President	Dr. Michael CARTER
10	Vice Pres Finance & Administration	Mr. Otto TENNANT
05	Vice President Academic Affairs	Dr. Frank CHEATHAM
30	Vice President for Development	Mr. Benji KELLY
26	VP for Church & External Rels	Mr. John E. CHOWNING
07	VP for Admissions/Student Svcs	Mr. Dave WALTERS
32	Dean of Student Services	Mrs. Jodi ALLEN
20	Associate Academic Officer	Vacant
21	Comptroller	Mr. Tim JUDD
09	Director of Institutional Research	Mr. Paul DAMERON
38	Director of Student Counseling	Vacant
28	Director of Diversity	Mr. John E. CHOWNING
92	Director of Honors Program	Dr. Craig L. ROGERS
41	Director of Athletics	Mr. Rusty HOLLINGSWORTH
40	Director of Bookstore	Mrs. Donna WRIGHT
42	Director of Campus Ministries	Mr. Edwin C. PAVY
13	Director of Computing/Communication	Mr. Hermano QUEIROZ
37	Director of Financial Aid	Ms. Chris TOLSON
29	Director of Alumni Relations	Mrs. Paula SMITH
08	Director of Library Services	Mr. John BURCH
15	Director of Personnel Services	Mr. Terry VANMETER
18	Director of Maintenance	Mr. Steve MORRIS
27	Director of News Information	Mrs. Joan C. MCKINNEY
06	Director of Student Records	Mrs. Rita A. CREASON
04	Secretary to the President	Mrs. Kellie VAUGHN
96	Dir of Purchasing/Special Projects	Mr. Marion HALL
88	Director of Custodial Services	Mr. Bob STOTTS

Centre College (G)

600 W Walnut Street, Danville KY 40422-1394

County: Boyle FICE Identification: 001961
Unit ID: 156408
Telephone: (859) 238-5200 Carnegie Class: Bac/A&S
FAX Number: (859) 238-6977 Calendar System: Other
URL: www.centre.edu
Established: 1819 Annual Undergrad Tuition & Fees: $43,800
Enrollment: 1,309 Coed
Affiliation or Control: Independent Non-Profit IRS Status: 501(c)3
Highest Offering: Baccalaureate
Program: Liberal Arts And General; Teacher Preparatory
Accreditation: SC

01	President	Dr. John A. ROUSH
05	Vice President & Dean of College	Dr. Stephanie L. FABRITIUS
10	Vice Pres for Finance & Treasurer	Mr. Robert L. KEASLER
26	Vice President College Relations	Dr. Richard W. TROLLINGER
32	Vice Pres/Dean of Student Life	Mr. Wm. Randy HAYS
30	Assoc VP Development/Alumni Affairs	Mr. Shawn LYONS
43	Assoc VP for Legal Affs/Gift Plng	Mr. James P. LEAHEY
53	Asst VP & Assoc Prof of Education	Mr. James H. ATKINS
07	Dean Admiss/Student Financial Plng	Mr. Robert M. NESMITH
20	Associate Dean of the College	Dr. Beth GLAZIER-MCDONALD
45	Asst to the President for Planning	Dr. Clarence R. WYATT
85	Director of International Programs	Dr. Milton M. REIGELMAN
08	Director of Library Services	Mr. Stanley R. CAMPBELL
04	Exec Assistant to the President	Ms. Yvonne Y. MORLEY
37	Director of Student Financial Plng	Mrs. Elaine E. LARSON
06	Registrar	Mr. Timothy P. CULHAN
15	Director Human Resources/Admin Svcs	Mrs. Kay L. DRAKE
27	Director of Communications	Dr. Michael P. STRYSICK
36	Director of Career Services	Ms. Deborah A. JONES
35	Director Student Life & Housing	Ms. Ann S. YOUNG
41	Int Dir of Athletics & Recreation	Ms. Gina M. NICOLETTI
19	Co-Director of Public Safety	Mr. Kevin S. MILBY
19	Co-Director of Public Safety	Mr. Gary D. BUGG
57	Mgr Director Norton Center for Arts	Mr. Steven A. HOFFMAN
09	Director of Institutional Research	Dr. J. Steven WINRICH
13	Director of Info Technology Service	Mr. Arthur L. MOORE
24	Director Ctr for Teaching/Learning	Dr. Sarah E. LASHLEY
18	Director of Facilities Management	Mr. D. Wayne KING
21	Controller	Mr. Steven A. JAMISON
42	College Chaplain	Dr. Richard D. AXTELL
38	Assoc Dean & Dir Residence Life	Ms. Sarah S. HALL
96	Dir Purchasing/Campus Interiors	Ms. Ann T. SMITH
29	Director of Alumni Affairs	Ms. Megan H. MILBY

Clear Creek Baptist Bible College (H)

300 Clear Creek Road, Pineville KY 40977-9754

County: Bell FICE Identification: 025356
Unit ID: 156417
Telephone: (606) 337-3196 Carnegie Class: Spec/Faith
FAX Number: (606) 337-2372 Calendar System: Semester
URL: www.ccbbc.edu
Established: 1926 Annual Undergrad Tuition & Fees: $5,882
Enrollment: 172 Coed
Affiliation or Control: Southern Baptist IRS Status: 501(c)3
Highest Offering: Baccalaureate
Program: Religious Emphasis
Accreditation: SC, BI

01	President	Dr. Donnie S. FOX
05	Academic Dean	Dr. Malcolm HESTER
32	Dean of Students	Rev. David WADE
11	Dean of Administrative Affairs	Mr. Jeremy ANDERSON
30	Dean of Institutional Advancement	Dr. Jay SULFRIDGE
08	Librarian	Mrs. Marge CUMMINGS
42	Christian Service Director	Rev. Richard BARTELS
18	Dir of Maintenance and Facilities	Mr. Ronnie WASHAM
37	Director Financial Aid	Mr. Sam RISNER

06 Registrar ...... Mrs. Brenda HESTER
07 Admissions ...... Rev. Billy HOWELL
26 Director of College Relations ...... Rev. Richard L. WITHERITE
14 Director of Computer Operations ...... Mr. Shane KAHKOLA
56 Director of Distance Education ...... Dr. Jay BARNETT

Daymar College-Bellevue (A)

119 Fairfield Avenue, Bellevue KY 41073
County: Campbell Identification: 666390
Unit ID: 447476
Telephone: (859) 291-0800 Carnegie Class: Assoc/PrivFP
FAX Number: (859) 491-7500 Calendar System: Quarter
URL: www.daymarcollege.edu
Established: 2005 Annual Undergrad Tuition & Fees: $16,610
Enrollment: 444 Coed
Affiliation or Control: Proprietary IRS Status: Proprietary
Highest Offering: Baccalaureate
Program: Technical Emphasis
Accreditation: ACICS

01 President ...... Mark A. GABIS
12 Campus President ...... Tina BARNES
05 Director of Education ...... James HUTCHINS
07 Director of Admissions ...... Cathy BARID
32 Director of Student Services ...... Raaven FLANIGAN

† Branch campus of Daymar College, Owensboro, KY.

Daymar College-Bowling Green (B)

2421 Fitzgerald Industrial Drive,
Bowling Green KY 42101-4071
County: Warren Identification: 666439
Unit ID: 363439
Telephone: (270) 843-6750 Carnegie Class: Assoc/PrivFP
FAX Number: (270) 843-6976 Calendar System: Quarter
URL: www.daymarcollege.edu
Established: 1954 Annual Undergrad Tuition & Fees: $16,610
Enrollment: 375 Coed
Affiliation or Control: Proprietary IRS Status: Proprietary
Highest Offering: Baccalaureate
Program: Technical Emphasis
Accreditation: ACICS

01 President ...... Mark GABIS
12 Campus President ...... Melva P. HALE
05 Director of Education ...... Duane DOYLE
07 Director of Admissions ...... Traci HENDERSON
37 Director of Financial Services ...... Janice CUTLIFF
32 Director of Student Services ...... Braden WILSON
36 Director or Career Services ...... Sarah ROSCOE

† Branch campus of Daymar Institute, Nashville, TN.

Daymar College-Louisville (C)

4112 Fern Valley Road, Louisville KY 40219-1973
County: Jefferson Identification: 666391
Unit ID: 406219
Telephone: (502) 495-1040 Carnegie Class: Assoc/PrivFP
FAX Number: (502) 495-1518 Calendar System: Quarter
URL: www.daymarcollege.edu
Established: 2001 Annual Undergrad Tuition & Fees: $16,610
Enrollment: 492 Coed
Affiliation or Control: Proprietary IRS Status: Proprietary
Highest Offering: Baccalaureate
Program: Technical Emphasis
Accreditation: ACICS

01 President ...... Mark GABIS
12 Campus President ...... Mark MANN
07 Senior Director of Admissions ...... Terry QUEENO
32 Director of Student Services ...... Jennifer BALL
08 Librarian ...... Jason ZARNDT

† Branch campus of Daymar College, Owensboro, KY.

Daymar College-Louisville East (D)

3309 Collins Lane, Louisville KY 40245
County: Jefferson Identification: 667081
Unit ID: 460473
Telephone: (502) 400-4075 Carnegie Class: Not Classified
FAX Number: N/A Calendar System: Quarter
URL: www.daymarcollege.edu
Established: N/A Annual Undergrad Tuition & Fees: $15,600
Enrollment: 131 Coed
Affiliation or Control: Proprietary IRS Status: Proprietary
Highest Offering: Baccalaureate
Program: Technical Emphasis
Accreditation: ACICS

01 President ...... Mark A. GABIS
12 Campus Director ...... Vacant

† Branch campus of Daymar College, Owensboro, KY.

Daymar College-Madisonville (E)

1105 National Mine Drive, Madisonville KY 42431
County: Hopkins Identification: 667079
Unit ID: 449302
Telephone: (270) 643-0312 Carnegie Class: Assoc/PrivFP
FAX Number: N/A Calendar System: Quarter
URL: www.daymarcollege.edu
Established: N/A Annual Undergrad Tuition & Fees: $15,600
Enrollment: 53 Coed
Affiliation or Control: Proprietary IRS Status: Proprietary
Highest Offering: Baccalaureate
Program: Technical Emphasis
Accreditation: ACICS

01 President ...... Mark A. GABIS
12 Campus Director ...... Pat VINCENT

† Branch campus of Daymar College, Owensboro, KY.

Daymar College-Owensboro (F)

3361 Buckland Square, PO Box 22150,
Owensboro KY 42304-2150
County: Daviess FICE Identification: 009313
Unit ID: 157465
Telephone: (270) 926-4040 Carnegie Class: Assoc/PrivFP
FAX Number: (270) 685-4090 Calendar System: Quarter
URL: www.daymarcollege.edu
Established: 1963 Annual Undergrad Tuition & Fees: $16,610
Enrollment: 324 Coed
Affiliation or Control: Proprietary IRS Status: Proprietary
Highest Offering: Baccalaureate
Program: Technical Emphasis
Accreditation: ACICS

01 President ...... Mark A. GABIS
12 Campus President ...... Pamela MOON
05 Director of Education ...... Hany NASRALLAH
07 Director of Admissions ...... Latasha SHEMWELL
06 Registrar ...... Debi SWEEDEN
08 Librarian ...... Martha LUDWICZAK
36 Dir of Career Svc & Cmty Relations ...... Vacant

Daymar College-Paducah (G)

509 S 30th Street, Paducah KY 42002-4181
County: McCracken FICE Identification: 008425
Unit ID: 156903
Telephone: (270) 444-9676 Carnegie Class: Assoc/PrivFP
FAX Number: (270) 441-7202 Calendar System: Quarter
URL: www.daymarcollege.edu
Established: 1964 Annual Undergrad Tuition & Fees: $16,610
Enrollment: 220 Coed
Affiliation or Control: Proprietary IRS Status: Proprietary
Highest Offering: Baccalaureate
Program: Technical Emphasis
Accreditation: ACICS

01 President ...... Mr. Mark A. GABIS
12 Campus President ...... Mr. Brian CARROLL
07 Director of Admissions ...... Ms. Connie HOLLEY
37 Director of Financial Services ...... Ms. Jo Ann PRICE
32 Director of Student Services ...... Ms. Peggy TIPPIN
05 Director of Education ...... Mr. Greg WEBB
36 Dir of Career Svc & Cmty Relations ...... Ms. Buffy BLANTON

Daymar College-Scottsville (H)

1138 Old Gallatin Road, Scottsville KY 42164
County: Allen Identification: 667080
Unit ID: 455646
Telephone: (270) 237-3577 Carnegie Class: Assoc/PrivFP
FAX Number: N/A Calendar System: Quarter
URL: www.daymarcollege.edu
Established: N/A Annual Undergrad Tuition & Fees: $15,600
Enrollment: 98 Coed
Affiliation or Control: Proprietary IRS Status: Proprietary
Highest Offering: Baccalaureate
Program: Technical Emphasis
Accreditation: ACICS

01 President ...... Mark A. GABIS
12 Campus Director ...... David YOUNG

† Branch campus of Daymar College, Owensboro, KY.

DeVry University - Louisville (I)

10172 Linn Station Road, Suite 300,
Louisville KY 40223-3887
County: Jefferson Identification: 666588
Unit ID: 454209
Telephone: (502) 326-2860 Carnegie Class: Assoc/PrivFP4
FAX Number: (502) 329-5894 Calendar System: Semester
URL: www.devry.edu
Established: 1931 Annual Undergrad Tuition & Fees: $16,156
Enrollment: 141 Coed
Affiliation or Control: Proprietary IRS Status: Proprietary
Highest Offering: Baccalaureate
Program: Professional; Business Emphasis
Accreditation: &NH

01 Campus Director ...... Ebony SPENCER-MULDROW

† Regional accreditation is carried under the parent institution in Downers Grove, IL.

Eastern Kentucky University (J)

521 Lancaster Avenue, Richmond KY 40475-3102
County: Madison FICE Identification: 001963
Unit ID: 156620
Telephone: (859) 622-1000 Carnegie Class: Master's L
FAX Number: (859) 622-1020 Calendar System: Semester
URL: www.eku.edu
Established: 1906 Annual Undergrad Tuition & Fees (In-State): $7,320
Enrollment: 16,062 Coed
Affiliation or Control: State IRS Status: 501(c)3
Highest Offering: Doctorate
Program: Occupational; Liberal Arts And General; Teacher Preparatory; Professional
Accreditation: SC, AAFCS, ADNUR, BUS, CACREP, CONST, CS, DIETD, DIETI, EMT, IFSAC, MLTAD, MT, MUS, NAIT, NRPA, NURSE, OT, PH, SP, SPAA, SW, TED

01 President ...... Dr. Doug WHITLOCK
05 Provost/Vice Pres Academic Affairs ...... Dr. Janna VICE
32 Int Assoc Provost/VP Student Affs ...... Dr. Claire GOOD
10 Vice Pres Financial Affs/Treasurer ...... Mr. Barry POYNTER
30 Vice Pres Univ Advancement ...... Mr. Joseph FOSTER
21 Associate Vice President Finance ...... Mrs. Linda HERZOG
84 Assoc VP/Dean of Enrollment Mgmt ...... Ms. Linda FOSSEN
45 Assoc VP University Programs ...... Dr. Sara ZEIGLER
26 Assoc VP Public Relations/Marketing ...... Mr. Marc WHITT
35 Assoc Vice Pres Student Affairs ...... Dr. Mike REAGLE
76 Dean Health Sciences ...... Dr. Deborah WHITEHOUSE
49 Dean Arts & Sciences ...... Dr. John WADE
50 Dean Business & Technology ...... Dr. Robert ROGOW
53 Dean Education ...... Dr. William PHILLIPS
88 Dean Justice & Safety ...... Dr. Allen AULT
51 Dean Continuing Education/Outreach ...... Dr. Charles HICKOX
86 Exec Dir Government Relations ...... Mr. Jim CLARK
43 University Counsel ...... Mrs. Judy SPAIN
19 Int Chief of Police ...... Mr. Brian MULLINS
08 Director Libraries ...... Ms. Betina GARDNER
06 Registrar ...... Ms. Tina DAVIS
88 Director Advising ...... Mr. Benton SHIREY
07 Director Admissions ...... Mr. Brett MORRIS
36 Director Career Services ...... Mrs. Laura MELIUS
25 Director Sponsored Programs ...... Mr. Gus BENSON
92 Director Honors Program ...... Dr. Linda FROST
09 Director Institutional Research ...... Ms. Bethany MILLER
85 Director International Education ...... Dr. William HOLMES
38 Director Counseling Center ...... Dr. Jen C. WALKER
39 Director Housing ...... Mrs. Kenna MIDDLETON
88 Director Judicial Affairs/Disabled ...... Mrs. Betsy BOHANNON
37 Director Student Financial Assist ...... Mrs. Shelley S. PARK
23 Director Student Health Services ...... Dr. Pradeep BOSE
40 Director Bookstore ...... Ms. Lisa CROWE
15 Director Human Resources ...... Mr. Gary BARKSDALE
90 Director Info Tech/Delivery Svcs ...... Ms. Mona ISAACS
29 Director Alumni Relations ...... Ms. Jackie COLLIER
88 Dir Student Involvement/Leadership ...... Ms. April BARNES
24 Director Media Resources ...... Ms. Jo BROSIUS
18 Director Facilities Services ...... Mr. Rich MIDDLETON
28 Director of Diversity ...... Ms. Sandra MOORE
96 Director of Purchasing ...... Ms. Lora SNIDER
42 Chaplain ...... Dr. Patrick C. NNOROMELE
04 Admin Asst to the President ...... Ms. Lisa KELLEY
04 Admin Asst to the President ...... Mrs. Dreidre ADAMS

Frontier Nursing University (K)

PO Box 528, Hyden KY 41749-0528
County: Leslie FICE Identification: 030070
Unit ID: 156727
Telephone: (606) 672-2312 Carnegie Class: Spec/Health
FAX Number: (606) 672-3776 Calendar System: Quarter
URL: www.frontier.edu
Established: 1939 Annual Graduate Tuition & Fees: $15,660
Enrollment: 1,346 Coed
Affiliation or Control: Independent Non-Profit IRS Status: 501(c)3
Highest Offering: Doctorate; No Undergraduates
Program: Professional; Nursing Emphasis
Accreditation: SC, MIDWF, NUR

01 President & Dean ...... Dr. Susan STONE
11 Chief Operations Officer ...... Ms. Shelley ALDRIDGE
10 Vice President of Finance ...... Mr. Michael STEINMETZ
05 Associate Dean of Academic Affairs ...... Dr. Joyce KNESTRICK
88 Assoc Dean Midwifery/Women's Health ...... Dr. Suzan ULRICH
66 Assoc Dean of Family Nursing ...... Dr. Julie MARFELL
88 Associate Dean of Research ...... Dr. Janet ENGSTROM
88 DNP Program Director ...... Dr. Barbara ANDERSON
88 Bridge Option Director ...... Dr. Trish VOSS
29 Director of Development and Alumni ...... Ms. Denise BARRETT
07 Director of Recruitment & Retention ...... Ms. Stephanie BOYD
06 Registrar ...... Ms. Sherri DAVIS
37 Director of Financial Aid ...... Ms. Rainie BOGGS
08 Director of Library Services ...... Ms. Billie Anne GEBB
13 Information Technology Manager ...... Mr. Paul STACKHOUSE

Galen College of Nursing (L)

1031 Zorn Avenue, Suite 400, Louisville KY 40207-1064
County: Jefferson FICE Identification: 030837
Unit ID: 156471
Telephone: (502) 410-6200 Carnegie Class: Assoc/PrivFP
FAX Number: (502) 581-0425 Calendar System: Quarter
URL: www.galencollege.edu
Established: 1989 Annual Undergrad Tuition & Fees: $16,365

Enrollment: 1,274 Coed
Affiliation or Control: Proprietary IRS Status: Proprietary
Highest Offering: Associate Degree
Program: 2-Year Principally Bachelor's Creditable; Nursing Emphasis
Accreditation: @SC, COE

01 President .... Mr. Mark A. VOGT
10 Executive VP and CFO .... Mr. Joseph R. PETERS
05 VP of Academic Affairs .... Ms. Tracy A. ORTELLI
84 VP of Enrollment Management .... Mr. Thomas DWYER
09 VP of Institutional Research .... Mr. David RAY
11 VP of Academic Operations .... Ms. Audria DENKER
106 VP of Online .... Dr. Steve HYNDMAN
37 Financial Aid Director .... Ms. Joni M. PENLAND
07 Director of Admissions .... Ms. Brenda SKAGGS
20 Asst VP of Academic Affairs .... Vacant
66 Dean of the Cincinnati Campus .... Ms. Carol BUSCHUR
66 Dean of the Main Campus-Louisville .... Dr. Joan L. FREY
66 Dean of the Tampa Bay Campus .... Vacant
66 Dean of the San Antonio Campus .... Dr. Vivian C. LILLY
26 Dir of Communications & Marketing .... Ms. Stephanie FRENCH
43 Director of Regulatory Affairs .... Ms. Kathleen GOOKIN
13 Director of Information Technology .... Mr. Duane HELLUMS
15 Director of Human Resources .... Ms. Lisa TWOHEY

Georgetown College (A)

400 E College Street, Georgetown KY 40324-1696
County: Scott FICE Identification: 001964
Unit ID: 156745
Telephone: (502) 863-8000 Carnegie Class: Bac/A&S
FAX Number: (502) 868-8891 Calendar System: Semester
URL: www.georgetowncollege.edu
Established: 1787 Annual Undergrad Tuition & Fees: $30,770
Enrollment: 1,818 Coed
Affiliation or Control: Baptist IRS Status: 501(c)3
Highest Offering: Master's
Program: Liberal Arts And General
Accreditation: SC, TED

01 President .... Dr. William H. CROUCH, JR.
05 Provost/Dean of the College .... Dr. Rosemary ALLEN
10 Vice President/CFO/Treasurer .... Mr. James MOAK
43 General Counsel & Spec Asst to Pres .... Mr. James H. NEWBERRY, JR.
30 Assoc VP/Chief Development Officer .... Mr. Roy LOWDENBACK
32 VP Student Life/Dean of Students .... Dr. Todd GAMBILL
84 Vice President for Enrollment .... Ms. Michelle LYNCH
13 Assoc VP for Info Tech Services .... Mr. Grover HIBBERD
26 Assoc VP Inst Adv/Dir Comm & Mktg .... Mr. Jim ALLISON
21 Controller .... Mr. David WILHITE
88 Bursar .... Ms. Marianne RIDDLE
06 Registrar .... Ms. Winnie BRATCHER
15 Director of Human Resources .... Ms. Tracie SHAPIRO
28 VP of Diversity and Inclusion .... Mr. Brian EVANS
53 Dean of Education .... Dr. Yolanda CARTER
07 Director of Admissions .... Vacant
37 Dir of Student Financial Planning .... Ms. Tiffany HORNBERGER
09 Institutional Research Associate .... Ms. Jane BENARD
08 Director of Library Services .... Ms. Susan MARTIN
29 Director of Alumni Relations .... Ms. Laura OWSLEY
41 Athletic Director .... Mr. Brian EVANS
42 Director of Religious Life .... Mr. H.K KINGKADE
36 Dir Graves Ctr for Calling & Career .... Mr. Ray CLERE
19 Director Campus Safety .... Mr. Dan BROWN
38 Director of Counseling/Health Svcs .... Dr. Lloyd CLARK
18 Dir Facilities and Grounds .... Mr. Randall FRANCIS

ITT Technical Institute (B)

2473 Fortune Drive, Suite 180, Lexington KY 40509-4253
County: Fayette Identification: 666158
Unit ID: 448488
Telephone: (859) 246-3300 Carnegie Class: Assoc/PrivFP4
FAX Number: N/A Calendar System: Quarter
URL: www.itt-tech.edu
Established: 2006 Annual Undergrad Tuition & Fees: N/A
Enrollment: 379 Coed
Affiliation or Control: Proprietary IRS Status: Proprietary
Highest Offering: Baccalaureate
Program: Technical Emphasis
Accreditation: ACICS

† Branch campus of ITT Technical Institute, Indianapolis, IN.

ITT Technical Institute (C)

9500 Ormsby Station Road, Suite 100,
Louisville KY 40223
County: Jefferson Identification: 666540
Unit ID: 413857
Telephone: (502) 327-7424 Carnegie Class: Spec/Tech
FAX Number: (502) 327-7624 Calendar System: Quarter
URL: www.itt-tech.edu
Established: 1993 Annual Undergrad Tuition & Fees: N/A
Enrollment: 856 Coed
Affiliation or Control: Proprietary IRS Status: Proprietary
Highest Offering: Baccalaureate
Program: Technical Emphasis
Accreditation: ACICS

† Branch campus of ITT Technical Institute, Indianapolis, IN.

Kentucky Christian University (D)

100 Academic Parkway, Grayson KY 41143-2205
County: Carter FICE Identification: 001965
Unit ID: 157100
Telephone: (606) 474-3000 Carnegie Class: Bac/Diverse
FAX Number: (606) 474-3155 Calendar System: Semester
URL: www.kcu.edu
Established: 1919 Annual Undergrad Tuition & Fees: $16,778
Enrollment: 606 Coed
Affiliation or Control: Christian Churches And Churches of Christ
IRS Status: 501(c)3
Highest Offering: Master's
Program: Liberal Arts And General; Fine Arts Emphasis
Accreditation: SC, NURSE, SW

01 President/CEO .... Dr. Jeff K. METCALF
05 VP of Academic Affairs .... Vacant
10 VP of Business & Finance .... Mr. William S. BONDURANT
84 VP of Enrollment Services .... Vacant
30 VP of University Advancement .... Mr. Larry D. MONROE
88 Director of Church Relations .... Mr. Jeff W. GREENE
06 Registrar .... Mrs. Andrea L. STAMPER
13 Director of Campus Technology .... Mr. Greg C. RICHARDSON
08 Librarian .... Mrs. Naulayne R. ENDERS
09 Assessment & SaBRE Director .... Mr. Kenneth L. BECK
32 Dean of Student Services .... Mr. Ron W. ARNETT
42 Campus Minister .... Mr. Larry W. MARSHALL
37 Director Financial Aid .... Mrs. Jennie M. BENDER
15 Human Resources Officer .... Mr. Terry L. YANKEY
38 Student Counseling Coordinator .... Mr. Jerry R. MORRIS
41 Athletic Director .... Mr. Bruce W. DIXON
39 Director of Residence Services .... Mr. Kris A. LANGSTAFF
18 Director of Maintenance .... Mr. Troy E. ROUSH
29 Alumni Relations Officer .... Mr. Jeff W. GREENE
58 Dean of the Graduate School .... Dr. David A. FIENSY
07 Director of Enrollment Services .... Mrs. Sheree D. GREER
26 Public Realations Officer .... Mr. David A. BENNETT
40 Bookstore Director .... Mrs. Sandra L. BROOKS

*Kentucky Community and Technical College System (E)

300 N Main Street, Versailles KY 40383-1245
County: Woodford FICE Identification: 006724
Unit ID: 157854
Telephone: (859) 256-3100 Carnegie Class: N/A
FAX Number: (859) 256-3119
URL: www.kctcs.edu

01 President .... Dr. Michael B. MCCALL
00 Chancellor .... Dr. Jay BOX
10 Vice President Finance .... Mr. Ken WALKER
13 Vice Pres Technology Solutions .... Mr. Paul CZARAPATA
30 Vice Pres Devel & Public Relations .... Mr. Timothy R. BURCHAM, CFRE
04 Sr Exec Assistant to the President .... Ms. Beth HILLIARD

*Ashland Community and Technical College (F)

1400 College Drive, Ashland KY 41101-3617
County: Boyd FICE Identification: 001990
Unit ID: 156231
Telephone: (606) 326-2000 Carnegie Class: Assoc/Pub-R-M
FAX Number: (606) 326-2187 Calendar System: Semester
URL: www.ashland.kctcs.edu
Established: 1938 Annual Undergrad Tuition & Fees (In-State): $3,240
Enrollment: 4,932 Coed
Affiliation or Control: State IRS Status: 501(c)3
Highest Offering: Associate Degree
Program: Occupational; 2-Year Principally Bachelor's Creditable
Accreditation: SC, ADNUR, IFSAC, SURGT

02 President & CEO .... Dr. Kay ADKINS
05 Dean of Academic Affairs .... Dr. Janie KITCHEN
32 Dean of Student Affairs .... Ms. Willie G. MCCULLOUGH
10 Dean of Business Affairs .... Ms. Karen J. BLEVINS
103 Dean Cmty Workforce/Economic Devel .... Dr. Larry FERGUSON
30 Dean of Advancement .... Ms. Louise SHYTLE
09 Dean of Inst Plng/Research/Effect .... Mr. Steve FLOUHOUSE
26 Dean Mktg and Community Relations .... Mr. John K. MCGLONE
11 Dean of Administrative Services .... Mr. W.S. (Stu) TAYLOR, III
08 Director of Library Services .... Mr. Matthew ONION
07 Assoc Dean Admissions/Registrar .... Mr. Chandra KUMAR
13 Assoc Dean Information Technology .... Mr. Farnoosh RAFIEE
28 Director of Cultural Diversity .... Mr. Alvin D. BAKER
15 Director of Human Resources .... Ms. Kellie L. ALLEN
25 Director of Grants & Contracts .... Ms. Sarah DIAMOND BURROWAY
37 Director of Financial Aid .... Ms. Robin LEWIS
18 Chief Facilities/Physical Plant .... Mr. Emmett BLEVINS
36 Coordinator of Career Services .... Ms. Nancy L. MENSHOUSE
79 Division Chair Humanities .... Mr. Kevin COOTS
76 Division Chair Health Sciences .... Ms. Jennifer CARROLL
81 Div Chair Math & Natural Sciences .... Dr. Keith BRAMMELL

*Big Sandy Community and Technical College (G)

1 Bert T. Combs Drive, Prestonburg KY 41653-9502
County: Floyd FICE Identification: 001996
Unit ID: 157553
Telephone: (606) 886-3863 Carnegie Class: Assoc/Pub-R-M
FAX Number: (606) 886-2677 Calendar System: Semester
URL: www.bigsandy.kctcs.edu
Established: 1964 Annual Undergrad Tuition & Fees (In-State): $3,240
Enrollment: 5,370 Coed
Affiliation or Control: State IRS Status: 501(c)3
Highest Offering: Associate Degree
Program: Occupational; 2-Year Principally Bachelor's Creditable
Accreditation: SC, DH

02 President/CEO .... Dr. George EDWARDS
03 Vice Pres Institutional Services .... Mr. Bobby MCCOOL
05 Provost .... Dr. Nancy JOHNSON
10 Vice President of Business Affairs .... Mr. John HERALD
32 Mgr Transformation Communications .... Ms. Melinda JUSTICE
35 Assoc Dean of Student Affairs .... Mr. Jimmy WRIGHT
08 Director of Library Services .... Ms. Melissa FORSYTH
15 Director of Human Resources .... Mr. Jackie CECIL
06 Registrar .... Ms. Della PACK
37 Director of Financial Aid .... Ms. Denise TRUSTY
09 Int Dir Institutional Effectiveness .... Ms. Denese ATKINSON
13 Director of Information Technology .... Mr. John DOVE
40 Bookstore Manager .... Ms. Pam WILEY
26 Public Relations .... Mr. Randall ROBERTS
07 Director of Admissions .... Vacant
28 Director of Cultural Diversity .... Ms. Tina TERRY
103 Int Director Workforce Development .... Ms. Kelli HALL

*Bluegrass Community and Technical College (H)

470 Cooper Drive, Lexington KY 40506-0001
County: Fayette FICE Identification: 009707
Unit ID: 156392
Telephone: (859) 246-6200 Carnegie Class: Assoc/Pub-R-L
FAX Number: (859) 246-4664 Calendar System: Semester
URL: www.bluegrass.kctcs.edu
Established: 1965 Annual Undergrad Tuition & Fees (In-State): $3,360
Enrollment: 14,200 Coed
Affiliation or Control: State IRS Status: 501(c)3
Highest Offering: Associate Degree
Program: Occupational; 2-Year Principally Bachelor's Creditable
Accreditation: SC, ADNUR, DA, DH, DT, IFSAC, MAC, NMT, POLYT, RAD, SURGT

02 President & CEO .... Dr. Augusta A. JULIAN
103 VP Workforce/Institutional Devel .... Mr. Mark MANUEL
13 Vice Pres of Information Technology .... Mr. Ren BATES
05 VP of Academics .... Dr. David M. HELLMICH
32 VP Student Dev/Enrollment Svcs .. Dr. Palisa WILLIAMS RUSHIN
10 VP Finance & Administration .... Ms. Lisa G. BELL
28 VP Multiculturalism & Inclusion .... Ms. Charlene WALKER
56 VP Regional Campuses/ Outreach .... Mr. Francis (Tri) A. ROBERTS, III
20 Dean of Academic Affairs .... Dr. Sandra CAREY
20 Dean of Academic Affairs .... Ms. Bonnie NICHOLSON
06 Registrar .... Ms. Becky HARP-STEPHENS
37 Financial Aid Director .... Ms. Runan PENDERGRAST
07 Admissions Director .... Ms. Shelbie HUGLE
15 Director Human Resource/Payroll .... Ms. Deborrah L. CATLETT
26 Chief Communications Officer .... Ms. Vernal L. KENNEDY
38 Advising/Assessment Int Director .... Ms. Pamela BATES
30 Chief Development Officer .... Ms. Linda EPLING
79 Assistant Dean Humanities .... Ms. Diana MARTIN
88 Assistant Dean Natural Sciences .... Ms. Tammy LILES
66 Assistant Dean Nursing .... Ms. Karen MAYO
76 Assistant Dean Allied Health .... Mr. Marty A. BAXTER
81 Asst Dean Mathematics .... Ms. Ruth SIMMS
77 Asst Dean Computer Sci/Info Systems .... Ms. Debbie HOLT
72 Asst Dean Trades/Technologies/Equn .... Mr. William FRANKLIN
88 Asst Dean Mfg Industrial Technology .... Mr. Paul TURNER
50 Asst Dean Business/Education .... Ms. Jenny JONES
83 Asst Dean Comm/Hist/Lang/Social Sci .... Ms. Vicki WILSON
08 Asst Dean Learning Resources Center .... Mr. Charles JAMES
88 Asst Dean Adult Educ/Opportunity .... Dr. Rebecca SIMMS
106 Assistant Dean Distance Learning .... Mr. Ben WORTH
18 Director of Maintenance/Operations .... Mr. Michael BALL
96 Director of Purchasing .... Ms. Tammy HORN

*Bowling Green Technical College (I)

1845 Loop Drive, Bowling Green KY 42101-9202
County: Warren FICE Identification: 005271
Unit ID: 156338
Telephone: (270) 901-1000 Carnegie Class: Assoc/Pub-R-M
FAX Number: (270) 901-1145 Calendar System: Semester
URL: www.bowlinggreen.kctcs.edu
Established: 1939 Annual Undergrad Tuition & Fees (In-State): $3,360
Enrollment: 5,718 Coed
Affiliation or Control: State IRS Status: 501(c)3
Highest Offering: Associate Degree
Program: Occupational; 2-Year Principally Bachelor's Creditable; Technical Emphasis
Accreditation: SC, ACFEI, DMS, IFSAC, POLYT, RAD, SURGT

02 President & CEO .... Dr. Nathan L. HODGES
03 Provost .... Dr. Phillip NEAL
05 Vice President Academic Affairs .... Ms. Iris DOTSON
32 Vice President Student Affairs .... Dr. Gerald NAPOLES
06 Registrar .... Ms. Brooke JUSTICE
10 Vice President Business Affairs .... Mr. Chris CUMENS
15 Director of Human Resources .... Ms. Sherri L. FORESTER
26 Director of Public Relations .... Mr. Mark D. BROOKS
30 Director of Advancement .... Ms. Donna P. MARTIN
37 Director of Financial Aid .... Mr. Rickie W. WILSON
09 Director Institutuion Effectiveness .... Mr. Mark GARRETT
103 Dean of Workforce Solutions .... Mr. Lewis BURKE, JR.

*Elizabethtown Community and Technical College (A)

600 College Street Road, Elizabethtown KY 42701

County: Hardin FICE Identification: 001991
Unit ID: 156648
Telephone: (270) 769-2371 Carnegie Class: Assoc/Pub-R-M
FAX Number: (270) 769-0736 Calendar System: Semester
URL: www.elizabethtown.kctcs.edu
Established: 1963 Annual Undergrad Tuition & Fees (In-State): $140
Enrollment: 5,759 Coed
Affiliation or Control: State IRS Status: 501(c)3
Highest Offering: Associate Degree
Program: Occupational; 2-Year Principally Bachelor's Creditable
Accreditation: SC, ADNUR, IFSAC, RAD

02 President .... Dr. Thelma WHITE
05 Provost (Interim) .... Dr. Diane OWSLEY
32 Chief Student Affairs Officer .... Dr. Dale BUCKLES
11 Chief Operations .... Mr. Keith JOHNSON
12 Campus Education Center Director .... Mr. Darrin POWELL
103 Dean of Workforce Development .... Dr. Thomas DAVENPORT
10 Dean of Business Affairs .... Mr. Jonathan THOMPSON
08 Library Director .... Ms. Ann THOMPSON
15 Director of Human Resources .... Ms. Kris WOOD
06 Registrar .... Mr. Bryan SMITH
13 Director of Information Technology .... Mr. Chris LEE
37 Director of Financial Aid .... Mr. Michael BARLOW
30 Chief Development .... Mr. Ronald HARRELL
26 Director of Public Relations .... Ms. Mary Jo KING
24 Learning Center Coordinator .... Ms. Pam HARPER
36 Counselor .... Ms. Sharon SPRATT
38 Counselor .... Mr. Charles SPATARO
40 Bookstore Manager .... Ms. Pamela BENTLEY
46 Assoc Dean of Inst Effectiveness .... Dr. Jack DILBECK
18 Maintenance/Operations Supervisor .... Mr. Charles COBB
57 Chair Div of Arts/Humanities .... Ms. Jacqueline HAWKINS
81 Chair Div of Biological Science .... Ms. Penelope LOGSDON
81 Chair Div of Physical Science .... Mr. Paul STURGEON
75 Chair Div Occupational Technology .... Mr. Mike HAZZARD
83 Chair Div Social & Behavioral Sci .... Ms. Theresia STEWART
28 Director of Diversity .... Ms. Felicia TOLIVER

*Gateway Community and Technical College (B)

500 Technology Way, Florence KY 41042

County: Boone FICE Identification: 005273
Unit ID: 157438
Telephone: (859) 441-4500 Carnegie Class: Assoc/Pub-S-MC
FAX Number: (859) 292-6415 Calendar System: Semester
URL: www.gateway.kctcs.edu
Established: 1961 Annual Undergrad Tuition & Fees (In-State): $4,200
Enrollment: 4,857 Coed
Affiliation or Control: State IRS Status: 501(c)3
Highest Offering: Associate Degree
Program: Occupational; 2-Year Principally Bachelor's Creditable
Accreditation: SC, IFSAC

02 President/CEO .... Dr. Ed HUGHES
04 Executive Assistant to President .... Ms. Sharon POORE
05 Provost/Vice Pres Academic Affairs .... Dr. Laura URBAN
30 VP Resource Devel/External Affairs .... Ms. Laura KROEGER
32 Vice Pres Student Development .... Ms. Ingrid WASHINGTON
10 VP Administration & Business Affs .... Mr. Mike BAKER
09 VP Knowledge Mgmt/Strategic Initiat .... Dr. Patricia GOODMAN
103 VP Business Solutions & Innovations .... Dr. Angie TAYLOR
20 Assoc Provost Academic Affairs .... Dr. Teri VONHANDORF
20 Assoc Provost Academic Affairs .... Ms. Marinell BROWN
20 Assoc Provost Academic Affairs .... Dr. Ross SANTELL
06 Registrar .... Mr. Robin WRIGHT
15 Director of Human Resources .... Ms. Phyllis YEAGER
18 Director Maintenance & Operations .... Mr. George HALL
26 Dir Marketing & Public Relations .... Ms. Margaret THOMSON
37 Director of Financial Aid .... Mr. Justin CRISTELLO
88 Director Early College Initiatives .... Ms. Shelby KRENTZ
84 Dean of Enrollment Services .... Mr. Andre WASHINGTON
08 Director Library/Information Svcs .... Ms. Charlene MCGRATH
25 Director of Grants .... Dr. Amber BECKER
36 Coordinator of Career Services .... Ms. Amy MONSON
35 Student Affairs Specialist .... Ms. Janet SAMPLES

*Hazard Community and Technical College (C)

One Community College Drive, Hazard KY 41701-2402

County: Perry FICE Identification: 006962
Unit ID: 156790
Telephone: (606) 436-5721 Carnegie Class: Assoc/Pub-R-M
FAX Number: (606) 439-2988 Calendar System: Semester
URL: www.hazard.kctcs.edu
Established: 1968 Annual Undergrad Tuition & Fees (In-State): $4,050
Enrollment: 4,726 Coed
Affiliation or Control: State IRS Status: 501(c)3
Highest Offering: Associate Degree
Program: Occupational; 2-Year Principally Bachelor's Creditable
Accreditation: SC, DMS, IFSAC, PTAA, RAD, SURGT

02 President/CEO .... Dr. Stephen GREINER
05 Vice Pres of Learning Services .... Dr. Kathy SMOOT
32 Vice President of Student Services .... Mr. Doug FRALEY
10 Vice President of Business Services .... Ms. Connie WATTS
04 Exec Admin Asst to President .... Ms. Delcie COMBS
86 Sr Dir of Advance & Govt Relations .... Mr. Ron DALEY
13 Chief Information Officer .... Ms. Donna ROARK
15 Senior Director of Human Resources .... Ms. Vickie COMBS
21 Dean of Business Services .... Ms. Jackie HALL
08 Director Library Services .... Mrs. Cathy BRANSON
20 Academic Dean Lees College Campus .... Ms. Leila SMITH
20 Academic Dean Technical Campus .... Ms. Jeniffer LINDON
20 Academic Dean Hazard Campus .... Ms. Anna NAPIER
09 Coordinator of Inst Research .... Mrs. Anna L. PUFFER
18 Dean of Operations .... Mr. Fred LANDRUM
26 Director of Public Relations .... Mrs. Evelyn WOOD
37 Director of Financial Aid .... Mr. Charles ANDERSON, JR.
35 Dean of Student Life/Engagement .... Mr. Cluster HOWARD
40 Bookstore Manager .... Mrs. Patricia CAUDILL
06 Registrar .... Ms. Libby PETERS
07 Director of Admissions .... Mr. Scott GROSS
88 Dean of Institutional Effectiveness .... Ms. Germaine SHAFFER
28 Director Cultural Diversity .... Mr. Elbert HAGANS
88 Director Radiology Program .... Mr. Homer TERRY
81 Div Chair Sciences & Mathematics .... Mr. Dell SASSER
88 Div Chair Occupational Technology .... Ms. Carolyn BUSH
76 Div Chair Allied Health Technology .... Ms. Gwen COLLINS
79 Div Chair Heritage/Humanities .... Mr. Thomas NEACE

*Henderson Community College (D)

2660 S Green Street, Henderson KY 42420-4699

County: Henderson FICE Identification: 001993
Unit ID: 156851
Telephone: (270) 827-1867 Carnegie Class: Assoc/Pub-R-M
FAX Number: (270) 831-9600 Calendar System: Semester
URL: www.henderson.kctcs.edu
Established: 1960 Annual Undergrad Tuition & Fees (In-State): $3,360
Enrollment: 2,142 Coed
Affiliation or Control: State IRS Status: 501(c)3
Highest Offering: Associate Degree
Program: Occupational; 2-Year Principally Bachelor's Creditable
Accreditation: SC, ADNUR, DH, MAC, MLTAD

02 President/CEO .... Dr. Kris WILLIAMS
05 Dean of Academic Affairs .... Dr. David F. BRAUER
32 Dean Student Affairs .... Ms. Patricia MITCHELL
10 Chief Business Affairs Officer .... Mr. Jerry H. GENTRY
08 Library Director .... Mr. Mike W. KNECHT
13 Chief Information Technology Ofcr .... Ms. Kimberley S. CONLEY
15 Director of Human Resources .... Ms. Doris J. LAKE
57 Director of Fine Arts Center .... Ms. Rachael BAAR
06 Registrar .... Ms. Brenda L. KNIGHT
31 Dean Workforce Solutions .... Ms. Pamala P. WILSON
28 Director of Cultural Diversity .... Mr. William DIXON
30 Chief Institutional Advance Ofcr .... Ms. Susanne WILSON
09 Asst Dean/Dir Plng & Rsrch .... Mr. Mike THURMAN
18 Maintenance/Oper Supervisor .... Mr. David CAMPBELL
35 Student Activities Coordinator .... Mr. Larry TUTT
36 Career Services Coordinator .... Ms. Angela WATSON
37 Director Financial Aid .... Mr. Andrew ZELLERS
103 Workforce Development Liaison .... Ms. Victoria REED
88 Dir Advising and Assessment .... Mr. Cary CONLEY
88 Professional Development Coord .... Ms. Cathy HUNT
57 Division Chair Arts/Humanities .... Mr. Mike A. KNECHT
81 Div Chair Physical Sciences .... Ms. Rebecca WELLS
83 Div Chair Social/Behavior Sciences .... Mr. Eugene PATSALIDES
76 Div Chair Biological Sciences .... Dr. Mary Gail WILDER

*Hopkinsville Community College (E)

720 North Drive, PO Box 2100,
Hopkinsville KY 42241-2100

County: Christian FICE Identification: 001994
Unit ID: 156860
Telephone: (270) 707-3700 Carnegie Class: Assoc/Pub-R-M
FAX Number: (270) 886-0237 Calendar System: Semester
URL: www.hopkinsville.kctcs.edu
Established: 1965 Annual Undergrad Tuition & Fees (In-State): $3,360
Enrollment: 4,464 Coed
Affiliation or Control: State IRS Status: 501(c)3
Highest Offering: Associate Degree
Program: Occupational; 2-Year Principally Bachelor's Creditable
Accreditation: SC, ADNUR

02 President/CEO .... Dr. James E. SELBE
04 Executive Administrative Assistant .... Ms. Cheryle DYMEK
05 Dean of Academic Affairs .... Ms. Alissa YOUNG
06 Registrar .... Ms. Melissa STEVENSON
08 Library Services Director .... Ms. Cynthia A. ATKINS
09 Institutional Effectiveness Dean .... Dr. Lance R. ANGELL
10 Chief Business Affairs Officer .... Ms. Beverly A. ATWOOD
12 Campus/Educ Center Director FTC .... Ms. Allisha LEE
13 Technology Solutions Director .... Mr. Terry DUNCAN
16 Human Resources Director .... Ms. Yvonne GLASMAN
18 Maintence/Operations Director .... Mr. Dan HAMBY
19 Safety Specialist .... Vacant
21 Business Affairs Associate Dean .... Ms. Ann T. HOLLAND
26 Marketing & Communication Director .... Ms. Rena YOUNG
28 Cultural Diversity Director .... Ms. Tracey Y. WILLIAMS
30 Chief Institutional Advancement Ofc .... Ms. Yvette EASTHAM
32 Chief Student Affairs Officer .... Dr. Jason D. WARREN
36 Career & Transfer Director .... Ms. Kanya ALLEN
37 Financial Aid Director .... Ms. Janet GUNTHER
38 Advising Center Director .... Ms. Deloria SCOTT
40 Bookstore Director .... Ms. Diane CUNNINGHAM
51 Continuing Education Associate Dean .... Ms. Carol KIRVES
57 Arts and Sciences Division Chair .... Dr. Ken CASEY
72 Professional & Technical Studies .... Dr. Randy WILSON
76 Allied Health Div Chair .... Ms. Peggy I. BOZARTH
81 Mathmatics & Sciences Div Chair .... Mr. Ted H. WILSON
103 Chief Cmty/Workforce/Econ Dev Ofcr .... Mr. Jerry GILLIAM

*Jefferson Community and Technical College (F)

109 E Broadway, Louisville KY 40202-2000

County: Jefferson FICE Identification: 006961
Unit ID: 156921
Telephone: (502) 213-5333 Carnegie Class: Assoc/Pub-U-MC
FAX Number: N/A Calendar System: Semester
URL: www.jefferson.kctcs.edu
Established: 1967 Annual Undergrad Tuition & Fees (In-State): $4,090
Enrollment: 15,085 Coed
Affiliation or Control: State IRS Status: 501(c)3
Highest Offering: Associate Degree
Program: Occupational; 2-Year Principally Bachelor's Creditable
Accreditation: SC, ACFEI, ADNUR, DMS, IFSAC, MAC, NMT, OTA, PTAA, RAD, SURGT

02 President .... Dr. Anthony NEWBERRY
05 Provost/Chief Academic Affairs Ofcr .... Dr. Diane CALHOUN-FRENCH
10 Chief Business Officer .... Ms. Norma NORTHERN
20 Dean Academic Affs Tech Programs .... Mr. Robert SILLIMAN
20 Dean Academic Affs Downtown .... Dr. Randy DAVIS
20 Dean Academic Affairs Southwest .... Dr. Katy VARNER
32 Dean of Student Affairs Southwest .... Dr. Denise GRAY-LACKEY
32 Dean Student Affairs Downtown .... Dr. Laura SMITH
21 Associate Dean of Business Affairs .... Vacant
08 Library Services Director .... Ms. Sheree WILLIAMS
08 Library Svcs Director Southwest .... Vacant
13 Director Information Technology .... Mr. Thomas ROGERS
09 Director of Institutional Research .... Dr. Mary C. JONES
06 Registrar .... Ms. Amanda TINDALL
28 Director of Cultural Diversity .... Ms. Janet MULLER
26 Dir of Marketing/Public Relations .... Ms. Lisa BROSKY
15 Director of Human Resources .... Mr. Kent ROBINSON
18 Facilities Director .... Mr. Craig TURPIN
37 Director of Financial Aid .... Vacant
30 Dir Inst Advance/Development Coord .... Ms. Jo Carole DICKSON
88 Director CE/CS/Business/ Industry .... Ms. Mary Ann HYLAND-MURR
07 Director of Admissions .... Ms. Melanie VAUGHAN-COOKE
38 Director of Student Counseling .... Dr. Telly SELLARS
96 Director of Purchasing .... Ms. Pamela DUMM
12 Director of Carrolton Campus .... Ms. Susan CARLISLE
12 Director of Shelby Campus .... Dr. John WIELAND
12 Int Dir Bullitt County Campus .... Ms. Donna MILLER
44 Manager of Advancement .... Ms. Karla HALL
31 Coord Cont Education/Cmty Services .... Ms. Donna HILL
24 Learning Center Coord Downtown .... Ms. Reneau WAGGONER
79 Chairperson Humanities Southwest .... Dr. Donna ELKINS
50 Chairperson Business Downtown .... Dr. Pamela BESSER
65 Div Chair Natural Sci Downtown .... Ms. Caroline MARTINSON
66 Dean Nursing/Allied Health .... Dr. Carolyn O'DANIEL
76 Chair Allied Health Jefferson Tech .... Ms. Eva OLTMAN
83 Div Chair Behav/Soc Sci Downtown .... Mr. Ron WALFORD
83 Chair Behav/Soc Sci Southwest .... Ms. Cathy WRIGHT
50 Chairperson Business Southwest .... Mr. Pete RODSKI
79 Chairperson Humanities Downtown .... Ms. Marlisa AUSTIN
81 Chrpsn Natural Science Southwest .... Mr. Gerry JOHNSON
72 Chair Technology/Related Sci-SW .... Mr. Bruce JOST
72 Chair Technology & Industry .... Mr. Andrew KORNOWSKI

*Madisonville Community College (G)

2000 College Drive, Madisonville KY 42431-9199

County: Hopkins FICE Identification: 009010
Unit ID: 157304
Telephone: (270) 824-8573 Carnegie Class: Assoc/Pub-R-M
FAX Number: (270) 824-1864 Calendar System: Semester
URL: www.madisonville.kctcs.edu
Established: 1968 Annual Undergrad Tuition & Fees (In-State): $4,200
Enrollment: 4,582 Coed
Affiliation or Control: State IRS Status: 501(c)3
Highest Offering: Associate Degree
Program: Occupational; 2-Year Principally Bachelor's Creditable
Accreditation: SC, ADNUR, IFSAC, MLTAD, OTA, PTAA, RAD, SURGA, SURGT

02 President .... Dr. Judith L. RHOADS
05 Chief Academic Affairs Officer .... Dr. Deborah M. COX
10 Chief Business Affairs Officer .... Mr. Ray GILLASPIE
32 Dean of Student Affairs .... Mr. Jonathan V. PARRENT
72 Division Chair Applied Technology .... Ms. Darlena GALLEGOS

66 Div Chr Nursing/Related Tech ... Ms. Patricia SIMMONS
79 Div Chr Humanities/Related Tech ... Dr. Scott VANDER PLOEG
83 Div Chr Social Science/Related Tech ... Mr. Chester M. CUNNINGHAM
81 Div Chr Mathematics and Sciences ... Dr. John LOWBRIDGE
76 Div Chr Allied Health/Related Tech ... Ms. Karol A. CONRAD
08 Director of Library Services ... Ms. Cherry L. BERGES
06 Registrar ... Ms. Tiffanie WITT
15 Director of Human Resources ... Ms. May F. WRIGHT
36 Counselor ... Ms. Sherry D. HEWELL
30 Director of Advancement ... Mr. John E. PETERS
37 Director of Financial Aid ... Ms. Martha PHELPS
26 Public Relations Officer ... Ms. Joyce RIGGS
56 Extended Campus Director ... Dr. George G. HUMPHREYS
40 Bookstore Manager ... Ms. Sonya L. BURNS
25 Dir Grants/Planning & Effectiveness ... Mr. David A. SCHUERMER
84 Coord of Enrollment Management ... Ms. Aimee J. WILKERSON
28 Director of Cultural Diversity ... Mr. James H. BOWLES
20 Associate Academic Officer ... Ms. Lisa A. HOWERTON
21 Manager Business Operations ... Mr. Michael L. JOHNSON
103 Director Workforce Solutions ... Mr. Mike DAVENPORT

*Maysville Community and Technical College (A)

1755 US 68, Maysville KY 41056-8910
County: Mason   FICE Identification: 006960
Unit ID: 157331
Telephone: (606) 759-7141   Carnegie Class: Assoc/Pub-R-M
FAX Number: (606) 759-7174   Calendar System: Semester
URL: www.maysville.kctcs.edu
Established: 1966   Annual Undergrad Tuition & Fees (In-State): $4,050
Enrollment: 4,634   Coed
Affiliation or Control: State   IRS Status: 501(c)3
Highest Offering: Associate Degree
Program: Occupational; 2-Year Principally Bachelor's Creditable
Accreditation: SC, IFSAC, MAC

02 President ... Dr. Ed STORY
05 Chief Academic Officer ... Dr. Juston PATE
10 Chief Finance & Facilities Officer ... Mr. George A. JONES
32 Assoc Dean Student Development ... Ms. Patricia MASSIE
09 Assoc Dean Institutional Rsch/Plng ... Ms. Pam STAFFORD
21 Associate Dean of Finance ... Mr. Steve WINFREY
08 Director Library Services ... Ms. Sonja EADS
13 Director Information Technology ... Mr. Henry JEFFERSON
30 Dir Resource Development/Foundation ... Ms. Cara CLARKE
103 Chief Officer Workforce Solutions ... Ms. Barbara CAMPBELL
37 Director Student Financial Aid ... Ms. Leslie STORIE
26 Public Relations Director ... Ms. Tina CURTIS
28 Director of Diversity ... Mr. Noel WILLIAMS
15 Director of Human Resources ... Ms. Sandi L. ESTILL
40 Bookstore Manager ... Ms. Kaye HIGH
24 Coordinator of Assessment/Testing ... Ms. Frances PETERSON
20 Coordinator of Academic Programs ... Mr. Stanley CLICK
50 Div Chr Bus/Inform Technologies ... Ms. Darla HUNT
49 Div Chair Liberal Arts/Education ... Mr. John KLEE
81 Div Chair Math/Science/Agriculture ... Dr. Angela FULTZ
66 Division Chair of Health Sciences ... Ms. Deborah NOLDER
72 Division Chair Industrial Tech ... Mr. Stanley W. CLICK

*Owensboro Community and Technical College (B)

4800 New Hartford Road, Owensboro KY 42303-1899
County: Daviess   FICE Identification: 030345
Unit ID: 247940
Telephone: (270) 686-4400   Carnegie Class: Assoc/Pub-R-M
FAX Number: (270) 686-4594   Calendar System: Semester
URL: www.octc.kctcs.edu
Established: 1986   Annual Undergrad Tuition & Fees (In-State): $4,050
Enrollment: 7,091   Coed
Affiliation or Control: State   IRS Status: 501(c)3
Highest Offering: Associate Degree
Program: Occupational; 2-Year Principally Bachelor's Creditable
Accreditation: SC, IFSAC, RAD, SURGT

02 President ... Dr. James S. KLAUBER
04 Assistant to the President ... Ms. Kittridge DANT
05 VP of Academic Affairs ... Dr. Scott WILLIAMS
32 Vice Pres of Student Affairs ... Mr. Kevin BEARDMORE
30 VP Institutional Advancement ... Mr. Larry S. MILLER
10 VP of Business Affairs ... Ms. Sarah PRICE
13 Vice Pres Information Technology ... Mr. James HARTZ
103 VP Workforce Solutions ... Ms. Cynthia FIORELLA
35 Assoc Dean of Student Affairs ... Ms. Sandy CARDEN
08 Library Services Director ... Ms. Donna ABELL
06 Registrar ... Ms. Sandy CARDEN
15 Director of Human Resources ... Ms. Victoria HOHIEMER
09 Director of Institutional Research ... Mr. Kevin BEARDMORE
29 Dir Advancement/Alumni Relations ... Ms. Linda TAYLOR
37 Financial Aid Director ... Ms. Bernice AYER
26 Director of Public Relations ... Ms. Bernadette TOY-HALE
28 Director of Diversity ... Ms. Lorna HOLLOWELL
38 Director Student Counseling ... Ms. Barbara TIPMORE
84 Director Enrollment Management ... Mr. Kevin BEARDMORE
96 Director of Purchasing ... Ms. Sarah PRICE
24 Dir of Teaching & Learning Center ... Ms. Judy COOMES
40 Bookstore Manager ... Ms. Sonya SOUTHARD
88 TV Production Manager ... Mr. John BRYENTON
07 Senior Admissions Advisor ... Ms. Linda CALHOUN

55 Evening & Weekend Coordinator ... Mr. Barry STEPHENS
36 Career Resource/Placemnt Ctr Coord ... Ms. Katie BALLARD
79 Associate Dean Humanities ... Dr. Julia LEDFORD
83 Assoc Dean Soc Sci/Bus/Public Svc ... Dr. Marc MALTBY
81 Assoc Dean Math/Sci/Allied Health ... Dr. Veena SALLAN
75 Assoc Dean Advanced Technologies ... Mr. Autry DEAN
66 Associate Dean Nursing ... Ms. Melissa ALSTOTT
88 Assc Dean Personal Svc/Skill Trades ... Mr. Mike ROGERS

*Somerset Community College (C)

808 Monticello Street, Somerset KY 42501-2973
County: Pulaski   FICE Identification: 001997
Unit ID: 157711
Telephone: (877) 629-9722   Carnegie Class: Assoc/Pub-R-L
FAX Number: N/A   Calendar System: Semester
URL: somerset.kctcs.edu
Established: 1965   Annual Undergrad Tuition & Fees (In-State): $3,240
Enrollment: 9,928   Coed
Affiliation or Control: State   IRS Status: 501(c)3
Highest Offering: Associate Degree
Program: Occupational; 2-Year Principally Bachelor's Creditable
Accreditation: SC, ADNUR, IFSAC, MLTAD, PTAA, RAD, SURGT

02 President/CEO ... Dr. Jo MARSHALL
05 Provost ... Dr. Tony L. HONEYCUTT
49 Dean of Arts and Sciences ... Ms. Sharon F. WHITEHEAD
09 Dean of Institutional Effectiveness ... Ms. Amy L. BEAUDOIN
32 Dean of Student Affairs ... Ms. Tracy L. CASADA
106 Assoc Dean for Distance Education ... Ms. Linda D. BOURNE
10 Chief Business Affairs Officer ... Mr. Timothy ZIMMERMAN
11 Chief Operations Officer ... Mr. Larry ABBOTT
30 Chief Institutional Advance Ofcr ... Ms. Ann O. ZWICK
103 Chief Cmty Wkfc & Economic Dev Ofc ... Mr. David A. WILES
76 Assoc Dean for Health Sciences ... Ms. Nancy L. POWELL
79 Assoc Dean Humanities/Fine Arts/SS ... Mr. Jon BURLEW
83 Assoc Dean Math/Natural Science ... Mr. Clint R. HAYES
88 Assoc Dean Const/Manuf/Trans ... Mr. Daniel C. BURNETT
50 Assoc Dean Bus/IT/Crim Just/Ed/Cons ... Ms. Lois A. MCWHORTER
88 Dean Academic Support Services ... Mr. Bruce GOVER
46 Dir of Prof and Org Development ... Ms. Karen M. WRIGHT
20 Assoc Dean for Learning ... Ms. Shelley J. BURGETT
37 Commons Director of Financial Aid ... Ms. Shawn R. ANDERSON
06 Registrar ... Ms. Paula J. GUFFEY
15 Director of Human Resources ... Ms. Jill N. MEECE
26 Director of Public Relations ... Ms. Cindy D. CLOUSE
26 Director of Public Relations ... Mr. David J. CAZALET, JR.
28 Director of Cultural Diversity ... Ms. Elaine WILSON
12 McCreary Center Director ... Ms. Gayle P. BORDERS
88 Dean of Applied Technology ... Mr. Roger L. ANGERINE
12 Clinton Center Director ... Ms. Dorothy E. PHILLIPS
12 Director of Casey Center ... Ms. Judy SAPP
12 Director of Russell Center ... Ms. Winfrey BATES
13 Director of Information Technology ... Mr. Gary CUNNINGHAM

*Southeast Kentucky Community and Technical College (D)

700 College Road, Cumberland KY 40823-1099
County: Harlan   FICE Identification: 001998
Unit ID: 157739
Telephone: (606) 589-2145   Carnegie Class: Assoc/Pub-R-M
FAX Number: (606) 589-4941   Calendar System: Semester
URL: www.southeast.kctcs.net
Established: 1960   Annual Undergrad Tuition & Fees (In-State): $3,360
Enrollment: 5,216   Coed
Affiliation or Control: State   IRS Status: 501(c)3
Highest Offering: Associate Degree
Program: Occupational; 2-Year Principally Bachelor's Creditable
Accreditation: SC, ADNUR, MLTAD, PNUR, PTAA, RAD, SURGT

02 President ... Dr. W. Bruce AYERS
05 Chief Academic Officer ... Dr. Wheeler CONOVER
10 Chief Business Affairs Officer ... Ms. Susan CROUSHORN
12 Branch Campus Director ... Ms. Deborah YOUNG
12 Campus/Education Center Director ... Mr. Stephen STURGILL
06 Dean Student Affairs/Registrar ... Ms. Karin GIBSON
21 Dean Administration Services ... Mr. Tom POPE
11 Chief Operations Officer ... Mr. Larry WARF
103 Chief Community Workforce ... Mr. Vic ADAMS
20 Chief Learning Officer ... Mrs. Pam WHITEHEAD
26 Director of Public Relations ... Mr. Chris JONES
16 Human Resources Director ... Ms. Billie FRANKS
08 Head Librarian ... Mr. Warren GRAY
13 Director of Information Technology ... Mr. Merrill GALLOWAY
09 Director of Institutional Research ... Dr. Rick MASON
28 Director of Diversity ... Ms. Carolyn SUNDY
30 Director of Advancement ... Ms. Susan CALDWELL
35 Dean Student Affairs ... Ms. Rebecca PARROTT-ROBBINS
96 Dean of Finance ... Ms. Angela SIMPSON
07 Director of Admissions ... Ms. Veria BALDWIN
40 Bookstore Manager ... Ms. Tammy DEAL
15 Human Resource Specialist ... Ms. Jeannie HAYES
37 Coordinator Financial Aid ... Ms. Charlotte LOCKABY
76 Div Chr Allied Hlth/Coord Clin Lab ... Ms. Kathy GUYN
83 Div Chair Soc Sci/Business/Rel Tech ... Mr. Kevin LAMBERT
79 Div Chair Humanities/Comm/Fine Arts ... Ms. Terry MACUILA
88 Div Chair Industrial Technology ... Mr. Ronnie DANIELS
65 Div Chair Natural Sciences ... Ms. Pat SCOPA

*West Kentucky Community and Technical College (E)

4810 Alben Barkley Drive, Paducah KY 42002-7380
County: McCracken   FICE Identification: 001979
Unit ID: 157483
Telephone: (270) 554-9200   Carnegie Class: Assoc/Pub-R-L
FAX Number: (270) 554-6217   Calendar System: Semester
URL: www.westkentucky.kctcs.edu
Established: 1909   Annual Undergrad Tuition & Fees (In-State): $4,200
Enrollment: 7,352   Coed
Affiliation or Control: State   IRS Status: 501(c)3
Highest Offering: Associate Degree
Program: Occupational; 2-Year Principally Bachelor's Creditable
Accreditation: SC, ACFEI, ADNUR, DA, DMS, IFSAC, POLYT, PTAA, RAD, SURGT

02 President ... Dr. Barbara VEAZEY
30 Interim VP Economic Development ... Mr. David MORRISON
05 VP of Academic Affairs ... Dr. Tena PAYNE
32 Interim VP of Student Affairs ... Dr. Belinda DALTON-RUSSELL
10 VP of Administrative Services ... Mr. John CARRICO
88 VP Learning Initiatives ... Ms. Sherry ANDERSON
45 VP Institutional Development ... Dr. Steve FREEMAN
10 VP Business Affairs ... Ms. Susan GRAVES
08 Library Services Director ... Mr. Ken BRADSHAW
37 Financial Aid Director ... Vacant
26 Public Relations Director ... Ms. Janett BLYTHE
13 Director Information Technology ... Ms. Ruby RODGERS
15 Director Human Resources ... Ms. Bridget CANTER
30 Dir Institutional Advancement ... Ms. Kay TRAVIS
40 Bookstore Manager ... Mr. Todd MITCHELL
06 Registrar/Director of Admissions ... Ms. Maria ROSA
35 Student Activities Coordinator ... Mr. Rick TIPPIN
79 Dean Humanities/Fine Arts/Soc Sci ... Ms. Sharla KRUPANSKY
66 Dean Nursing Division ... Ms. Shari GHOLSON
50 Dean Business/Comp Related Tech Div ... Ms. Tammy POTTER
76 Dean Allied Health Division ... Ms. Peggy BLOCK
75 Dean Applied Tech Division ... Ms. Stephanie MILLIKEN
81 Dean Science & Math Division ... Dr. Karen HLINKA
97 Dean Transition Education Div ... Ms. Maria FLYNN
09 Associate VP of IE ... Dr. Renea AKIN
07 Director of Admissions ... Ms. Maria ROSA
28 Director of Diversity ... Ms. Jipaum ASKEW-ROBINSON
36 Director Student Placement ... Ms. Paula ARMON

Kentucky Mountain Bible College (F)

Box 10, Vancleve KY 41385-0010
County: Breathitt   FICE Identification: 030021
Unit ID: 157030
Telephone: (606) 693-5000   Carnegie Class: Spec/Faith
FAX Number: (606) 693-4884   Calendar System: Semester
URL: www.kmbc.edu
Established: 1931   Annual Undergrad Tuition & Fees: $6,690
Enrollment: 75   Coed
Affiliation or Control: Independent Non-Profit   IRS Status: 501(c)3
Highest Offering: Baccalaureate
Program: 2-Year Principally Bachelor's Creditable; Liberal Arts And General; Religious Emphasis
Accreditation: BI

01 President ... Dr. Philip E. SPEAS
05 Exec Vice Pres/VP Academic Affs ... Rev. Thomas H. LORIMER
30 Vice President Development ... Dr. John E. NEIHOF, JR.
10 Chief Business Manager ... Ms. Joy PAUL
32 Dean of Student Affairs ... Mr. Jim NELSON
13 Director IT ... Mr. Stephen A. LORIMER
08 Head Librarian ... Ms. Patricia A. BOWEN
06 Registrar ... Mr. Richard ENGLEHARDT
07 Chief Admissions Counselor ... Mr. David W. LORIMER
37 Director Student Financial Aid ... Ms. Rosita MARSHALL
26 Dir PR/Foreign Stdnts/Dean of Men ... Mr. James H. NELSON
34 Dean of Women ... Ms. Wanda SPEAS

Kentucky State University (G)

400 E Main Street, Frankfort KY 40601-2355
County: Franklin   FICE Identification: 001968
Unit ID: 157058
Telephone: (502) 597-6000   Carnegie Class: Bac/A&S
FAX Number: (502) 597-6490   Calendar System: Semester
URL: www.kysu.edu
Established: 1886   Annual Undergrad Tuition & Fees (In-State): $8,235
Enrollment: 2,600   Coed
Affiliation or Control: State   IRS Status: 501(c)3
Highest Offering: Master's
Program: Liberal Arts And General; Teacher Preparatory; Business Emphasis
Accreditation: SC, ACBSP, ADNUR, MUS, NUR, SPAA, SW, TED

01 President ... Dr. Mary E. SIAS
05 Int Provost/Vice Pres Academic Affs ... Dr. Joel THIERSTEIN
10 Chief Financial Officer ... Ms. Alice JOHNSON
32 VP Student Success/Enrollment Mgmt ... Dr. Lorenzo ESTERS
30 Exec VP External Relation & Dev ... Mr. Hinfred MCDUFFIE
07 Director of Admissions ... Mr. Juan ALEXANDER
23 Director Student Health Services ... Ms. Floarine WILSON
31 Int Director Educational Outreach ... Ms. Irma JOHNSON
06 Director Records/Registrar ... Mr. John MARTIN
08 Director Libraries ... Ms. Sheila STUCKEY

100 Chief of Staff/Exec Asst to Pres .... Mr. Stephen MASON
36 Dir Couns/Career Plng/Placement .... Mr. Ronald BANKS
14 Director Information Technology ....Mr. Edward FIELDS
15 Director Human Resources ....Mr. Gary MEISELES
29 Director Alumni Affairs ....Mr. Garland HIGGINS
39 Director Residence Life ....Ms. Renee' WATSON
37 Director Student Financial Aid ....Ms. Victoria OWENS
25 Int Director Land Grant Programs ....Vacant
26 Director Public Relations ....Ms. Felicia LEWIS
43 General Counsel ....Ms. Lori A. DAVIS
21 Internal Auditor ....Vacant
18 Director Physical Plant ....Mr. Jack MCNEAR
41 Director Athletics ....Dr. Denisha HENDRICKS
19 Chief University Police ....Ms. Stephanie BASTIN
45 Budget Director ....Vacant
84 Director Enrollment Management ....Vacant
96 Director of Purchasing ....Ms. Tonya MONTGOMERY
49 Dean College of Arts & Science ....Dr. Sam OLEKA
107 Dean College of Prof Studies ....Dr. Gashaw LAKE
09 Coord Instl Research/Effectivenes ....Dr. Robin GEIGER

Kentucky Wesleyan College (A)

3000 Frederica Street, Owensboro KY 42301

County: Daviess — FICE Identification: 001969
Unit ID: 157076
Telephone: (270) 926-3111 — Carnegie Class: Bac/Diverse
FAX Number: (270) 926-3112 — Calendar System: Semester
URL: www.kwc.edu
Established: 1858 — Annual Undergrad Tuition & Fees: $19,640
Enrollment: 741 — Coed
Affiliation or Control: United Methodist — IRS Status: 501(c)3
Highest Offering: Baccalaureate
Program: Liberal Arts And General; Teacher Preparatory
Accreditation: **SC**, IACBE

01 President ....Dr. Craig TURNER
05 VP Acad Affairs/Dean of the College ....Dr. Paula DEHN
03 Executive Vice President ....Vacant
10 Vice Pres for Finance/Treasurer .... Ms. Cindra K. STIFF
30 VP for Development/Alumni Relations ....Vacant
32 VP of Student Affairs .... Mr. Scott E. KRAMER
07 Director of Admissions .... Mr. Rashad SMITH
06 Registrar ....Ms. Jennifer VAUGHN
09 Director of Institutional Research ....Mr. Mark C. HEDGES
15 Director of Personnel Services ....Mrs. Linda B. KELLER
37 Director of Student Financial Aid .... Ms. Samantha HAYES
89 Director of the PLUS Center .... Ms. Marisue S. COY
08 Director of Library Learning Center . Mrs. Patricia G. MCFARLING
41 Athletic Director ....Vacant
21 Controller ....Ms. Courtney LEMASTER
29 Director of Alumni Relations ....Vacant
26 Director of Public Relations .... Ms. Kathy RUTHERMAN
42 Campus Minister ....Mr. Kent LEWIS

Lexington Theological Seminary (B)

631 S Limestone, Lexington KY 40508-3288

County: Fayette — FICE Identification: 001971
Unit ID: 157207
Telephone: (859) 252-0361 — Carnegie Class: Spec/Faith
FAX Number: (859) 281-6042 — Calendar System: Semester
URL: www.lextheo.edu
Established: 1865 — Annual Graduate Tuition & Fees: $10,840
Enrollment: 66 — Coed
Affiliation or Control: Christian Church (Disciples Of Christ)
IRS Status: 501(c)3
Highest Offering: Doctorate; No Undergraduates
Program: Professional; Religious Emphasis
Accreditation: **THEOL**

01 President .... Dr. Charisse L. GILLETT
05 Dean ....Dr. Richard WEIS
30 Vice President for Advancement .... Mr. Mark BLANKENSHIP
10 Chief Financial Officer ....Mrs. Laura DAVIS
06 Registrar .... Ms. Windy KIDD
08 Librarian ....Ms. Dolores YILIBUW
36 Director Student Placement .... Rev. Jan EHRMANTRAUT
13 Director Information Services ....Mr. Ben WYATT
07 Director Admission .... Rev. Erin CASH

Lincoln College of Technology (C)

8095 Connector Drive, Florence KY 41042-1466

County: Boone — Identification: 666447
Unit ID: 245032
Telephone: (859) 282-9999 — Carnegie Class: Assoc/PrivFP
FAX Number: (859) 282-7940 — Calendar System: Quarter
URL: www.lincolnedu.com
Established: 1978 — Annual Undergrad Tuition & Fees: $17,168
Enrollment: 590 — Coed
Affiliation or Control: Proprietary — IRS Status: Proprietary
Highest Offering: Associate Degree
Program: Occupational; 2-Year Principally Bachelor's Creditable
Accreditation: **ACICS**, MAAB

01 Director .... Mr. Peter MARTINELLO
05 Academic Dean .... Ms. Laura CARNAGHI
07 Director of Admissions .... Mr. Cliff MESSINA
37 Director of Financial Aid .... Ms. Victoria HUBBARD

† Branch campus of Lincoln College of Technology, Dayton, OH.

Lindsey Wilson College (D)

210 Lindsey Wilson Street, Columbia KY 42728-1298

County: Adair — FICE Identification: 001972
Unit ID: 157216
Telephone: (270) 384-2126 — Carnegie Class: Master's M
FAX Number: (270) 384-8200 — Calendar System: Semester
URL: www.lindsey.edu
Established: 1903 — Annual Undergrad Tuition & Fees: $21,230
Enrollment: 2,600 — Coed
Affiliation or Control: United Methodist — IRS Status: 501(c)3
Highest Offering: Master's
Program: 2-Year Principally Bachelor's Creditable; Liberal Arts And General; Teacher Preparatory
Accreditation: **SC**, CACREP, IACBE

01 President ....Dr. William T. LUCKEY, JR.
03 Chancellor ....Dr. John B. BEGLEY
05 Vice President Academic Affairs .... Dr. Bettie C. STARR
10 Vice President Administration .... Dr. Roger D. DRAKE
30 Vice President Advancement ....Mr. Kevin A. THOMPSON
04 Executive Assistant ....Mrs. Nancy SINCLAIR
32 Vice President Student Services ....Dr. Dean ADAMS
37 VP Educ Outreach/Stdnt Finan Svcs ....Mrs. Denise G. FUDGE
35 Dean of Students .... Mr. Christopher SCHMIDT
20 Associate Academic Dean ....Ms. Leslie KORB
88 Dean of Chapel ....Dr. Terry W. SWAN
07 Dean of Admissions ....Mrs. Traci M. POOLER
07 Director of Admissions ....Mrs. Charity F. FERGUSON
55 Director of Evening College ....Ms. Regina HAUGEN
41 Athletic Director .... Mr. Willis POOLER, III
06 Registrar ....Mrs. Sue B. COOMER
15 Director of Human Resources ....Mrs. Karen F. WRIGHT
31 Dir of Civic Engagement & Std Ldrsp ....Mrs. Amy C. THOMPSON-WELLS
36 Director Career Services ....Mrs. Ashley MILLER
08 Librarian ....Mr. C. Phil HANNA
18 Director of Physical Plant ....Mr. Michael L. NEWTON
21 Director of Auxiliary Services ....Mr. Jeff WILLIS
40 Bookstore Manager ....Mrs. Amy M. COOPER
35 Director of Student Activities ....Mrs. Jayne S. HOPKINS
85 Dir of International Stdnt Programs .... Mrs. Suzy MCALPINE
14 Director Information Services ....Mrs. Harriet B. GOLD
13 Director of Information Systems ....Mr. Anthony MOORE
26 Public Relations Officer ....Mr. Duane BONIFER
29 Assistant to Pres Alumni Affairs ....Mr. Randy BURNS
19 Director Safety/Security ....Mr. Michael STATEN
42 Chaplain ....Rev. Troy A. ELMORE
09 Dir Plng/Instl Effective/Research ....Vacant
37 Director Student Financial Services .... Ms. Marilyn RADFORD
38 Director Student Counseling ....Dr. Jeff CRANE
66 Director of Nursing ....Mrs. Marian SMITH

Louisville Bible College (E)

8013 Damascus Road, Louisville KY 40228

County: Jefferson — FICE Identification: 041418
Unit ID: 157234
Telephone: (502) 231-5221 — Carnegie Class: Spec/Faith
FAX Number: (502) 231-5222 — Calendar System: Semester
URL: www.myLBC.us
Established: 1948 — Annual Undergrad Tuition & Fees: $4,800
Enrollment: 118 — Coed
Affiliation or Control: Independent Non-Profit — IRS Status: 501(c)3
Highest Offering: Master's
Program: Religious Emphasis
Accreditation: **@BI**

01 President .... Dr. Tracy W. MARX
05 VP for Academic Affairs ....Ronald J. DOWNS
30 VP for Operations & Advancement ....Danny L. DYE

Louisville Presbyterian Theological Seminary (F)

1044 Alta Vista Road, Louisville KY 40205-1798

County: Jefferson — FICE Identification: 001974
Unit ID: 157298
Telephone: (502) 895-3411 — Carnegie Class: Spec/Faith
FAX Number: (502) 895-1096 — Calendar System: 4/1/4
URL: www.lpts.edu
Established: 1853 — Annual Graduate Tuition & Fees: $10,546
Enrollment: 229 — Coed
Affiliation or Control: Presbyterian Church (U.S.A.) — IRS Status: 501(c)3
Highest Offering: Doctorate; No Undergraduates
Program: Professional; Religious Emphasis
Accreditation: **SC**, MFCD, THEOL

01 President .... Dr. Michael JINKINS
30 Interim VP for Inst Advancement .... Mr. Dennis RIGGS
10 Vice President & CFO ....Mr. Patrick A. CECIL
05 Dean of the Seminary .... Dr. Susan GARRETT
32 Dean of Students .... Rev. Kilen GRAY
06 Registrar .... Rev. David E. GRAY
44 Director of Seminary Fund ....Ms. Judy JOHNSTON
29 Director Alum & Church Relations ....Rev. Leah J. BRADLEY
27 Interim Director of Communications ....Ms. Melissa RUE
08 Acting Director of Library Services .... Ms. Angela MORRIS
21 Controller ....Ms. Marti F. MARSH
51 Director of DMin & Continuing Ed ....Dr. David HESTER
07 Director of Recruitment & Admiss ....Rev. Cheri HARPER

13 Acting Director of IT Services .... Mr. Jack SHARER
18 Director of Facilities ....Mr. Tim WILLIAMS

Mid-Continent University (G)

99 Powell Road E, Mayfield KY 42066-9007

County: Graves — FICE Identification: 025762
Unit ID: 157359
Telephone: (270) 247-8521 — Carnegie Class: Bac/Diverse
FAX Number: (270) 247-3115 — Calendar System: Semester
URL: www.midcontinent.edu
Established: 1949 — Annual Undergrad Tuition & Fees: $13,350
Enrollment: 2,472 — Coed
Affiliation or Control: Southern Baptist — IRS Status: 501(c)3
Highest Offering: Master's
Program: Liberal Arts And General; Business Emphasis
Accreditation: **SC**

01 President ....Dr. Robert J. IMHOFF
04 Assistant to the President ....Mrs. Mitzi TURNER
03 Executive Vice President ....Dr. Charles W. FORD
05 Vice President Academic Affairs ....Dr. Tom WALDEN
10 VP Finance & Administration ....Col. Andrew B. STRATTON
32 Dean Students/International Affairs .... Ms. Koby MILLER
55 VP Adult Pgms/Dir Advantage Pgm ....Dr. Jacquelyn IMHOFF
09 VP Inst Effectiveness/Planning ....Dr. Cynthia TWEEDELL
20 Assoc VP Academic Affairs .... Dr. Debra HUDSON
08 Dean of the Markham Library ....Mr. Ben GRAVES
30 Director of External Relations ....Mr. David SMITH
06 University Registrar .... Mrs. Yvonne YATES
21 Director of Budget & Planning ....Col. Andrew B. STRATTON
07 Director Admissions/Advantage Pgm .... Mr. Chris AUSTIN
07 Director of Graduate Admissions .... Mrs. Wendy PUCKETT
07 Assoc Dean for Trad Undergraduate .... Mr. Karl HATTON
37 Director of Financial Aid .... Mr. Kent YOUNGBLOOD
41 Athletic Director .... Mr. Larry LAMPKINS
18 Director of Facilities ....Mr. Tim BLALOCK
14 Director of Information Services ....Mr. David ROSS
15 Director of Human Resources ....Mr. Homer BURTON
19 Director of Campus Security ....Mr. Tye JACKSON
21 Business Office Manager .... Mrs. Deborah NALL
49 Dean Baptist Col of Arts & Science .....Dr. Jamie SUMMERVILLE
73 Dean Baptist College of Bible ....Dr. Stephen WILLIAMS
58 Dean of Graduate Studies .... Dr. David WILLIAMS

Midway College (H)

512 E Stephens Street, Midway KY 40347-1120

County: Woodford — FICE Identification: 001975
Unit ID: 157377
Telephone: (859) 846-4421 — Carnegie Class: Bac/Diverse
FAX Number: (859) 846-5349 — Calendar System: Semester
URL: www.midway.edu
Established: 1847 — Annual Undergrad Tuition & Fees: $20,700
Enrollment: 1,755 — Female
Affiliation or Control: Christian Church (Disciples Of Christ)
IRS Status: 501(c)3
Highest Offering: Doctorate
Program: 2-Year Principally Bachelor's Creditable; Liberal Arts And General; Teacher Preparatory; Professional
Accreditation: **SC**, ADNUR, NUR

01 Interim President ....Dr. Robert L. VOGEL
05 Vice President of Academic Affairs ....Dr. Marlene M. HELM
04 Admin Assist to the President ....Ms. Sheila K. HOLSCLAW
10 Vice Pres of Business Affairs ....Mr. Lyen C. CREWS, II
30 Vice President of Advancement ....Mr. Roy W. MUNDY, II
84 Vice Pres of Enrl Mgmt/Dean of Adm ....Dr. Johnie E. DEAN
26 Vice Pres of Marketing & Comm ....Mrs. Ellen D. GREGORY
36 Dean of School for Career Dev ....Dr. William (Bill) BROWN
106 Dean of Online College .... Mrs. Judith W. MARCUM
32 Dean of Student Life ....Vacant
07 Associate Dean of Admissions .... Mrs. Rachel LINARES
58 Director of Graduate Admissions ....Mrs. Rebecca SERRANO
20 Associate Academic Dean .... Mrs. Lesia HOLDER
06 Registrar ....Mrs. Linda P. ELDRIDGE
08 Director of Library Services ....Ms. Catherine L. REILENDER
41 Athletic Director .... Mrs. Wendy HOFFMAN
07 Director of Admissions Women's Col ....Mrs. Stacy M. SHARP
13 Director of Information Systems ....Mrs. C. Joan MCDANIEL
15 Director of Human Resources ....Mrs. Anne COCKLEY
21 Director of Student Accounts .... Mr. Robert L. NORTON
29 Director of Development/Alumni Affs ....Ms. Christy c. SMITH
37 Director of Financial Aid ....Ms. Katie A. CONRAD
18 Director of Physical Plant ....Mr. Stephen D. GOODWIN
39 Dir Residence Life/Stdnt Activities .... Ms. Leigh OAKLEY

Morehead State University (I)

150 University Boulevard, Morehead KY 40351-1689

County: Rowan — FICE Identification: 001976
Unit ID: 157386
Telephone: (606) 783-2221 — Carnegie Class: Master's L
FAX Number: N/A — Calendar System: Semester
URL: www.moreheadstate.edu
Established: 1887 — Annual Undergrad Tuition & Fees (In-State): $7,284
Enrollment: 10,971 — Coed
Affiliation or Control: State — IRS Status: 501(c)3
Highest Offering: Doctorate
Program: Occupational; Liberal Arts And General; Teacher Preparatory; Professional

Accreditation: SC, ADNUR, BUS, DMS, MUS, NAIT, NURSE, RAD, SW, TED, THEA

01 President ... Dr. Wayne D. ANDREWS
05 Provost ... Dr. Karla HUGHES
10 Vice Pres Admin Fiscal Services ... Mr. Michael R. WALTERS
32 Vice President Student Life ... Ms. Madonna WEATHERS
30 Vice Pres for Univ Advancement ... Mr. James A. SHAW
45 Chief of Staff/VP Plng Budgets/Tech ... Vacant
20 Assoc VP Academic Affairs/Programs ... Dr. Dayna S. SEELIG
04 Assistant to the President ... Ms. Carol JOHNSON
06 Registrar ... Ms. Roslyn PERRY
46 Director Undergrad Research Pgm ... Dr. Bruce MATTINGLY
51 Asst VP Adult Ed & College Access ... Dr. Dan CONNELL
84 Asst Vice Pres Enrollment Services ... Mr. Jeffrey LILES
26 Asst VP Marketing & Communication ... Ms. Jami HORNBUCKLE
18 Asst VP Facilities Management ... Mr. Gene CAUDILL
40 Asst Vice Pres Auxiliary Services ... Mr. William REDWINE
08 Interim Dean of Library Services ... Dr. David GREGORY
07 Director of Admissions ... Ms. Holly POLLOCK
09 Dir Inst Research & Analysis ... Ms. Erin D. WRIGHT
13 Dir of Enter Sys Arch & Security ... Mr. Drew HENDERSON
15 Director of Human Resources ... Mr. Phillip GNIOT
19 Director of Public Safety ... Mr. Matt SPARKS
21 Director Accounting/Budget Control ... Mrs. Kelli OWEN
21 Director of Budgets ... Ms. Teresa LINDGREN
28 Dir Multicultural Student Services ... Vacant
29 Director Alumni Relations ... Ms. Tami JONES
32 Dean of Students ... Mr. Kevin KOETT
37 Director Financial Aid ... Ms. Donna KING
36 Director Acad Advising/Career Svcs ... Ms. Julia HAWKINS
39 Director of Housing ... Ms. Dallas SAMMONS
41 Director of Athletics ... Mr. Brian A. HUTCHINSON
43 General Counsel ... Dr. Jane FITZPATRICK
44 Director of Development ... Ms. Melinda C. HIGHLEY
27 Media Relations Director ... Mr. Jason BLANTON
85 Director International Education ... Dr. Philip KRUMMRICH
96 Director Support Services ... Ms. Ladonna PURCELL
38 Director of Counseling & Health Svc ... Dr. Brenda WILBURN
50 Dean of Business ... Dr. Robert ALBERT
53 Dean Education ... Dr. Cathy GUNN
72 Dean Science & Technology ... Dr. Roger MCNEIL
79 Dean of Humanities ... Dr. Scott MCBRIDE
27 Asst VP Technology ... Mr. Steve RICHMOND
20 Asst VP Academic Affairs ... Ms. Jill RATLIFF

Murray State University (A)

218 Wells Hall, Murray KY 42071-3318
County: Calloway FICE Identification: 001977
Unit ID: 157401
Telephone: (270) 809-3011 Carnegie Class: Master's L
FAX Number: (270) 809-3413 Calendar System: Semester
URL: www.murraystate.edu
Established: 1922 Annual Undergrad Tuition & Fees (In-State): $6,840
Enrollment: 10,623 Coed
Affiliation or Control: State IRS Status: 501(c)3
Highest Offering: Doctorate
Program: 2-Year Principally Bachelor's Creditable; Liberal Arts And General; Teacher Preparatory; Professional
Accreditation: SC, ANEST, ART, BUS, DIETD, DIETI, ENG, ENGR, ENGT, JOUR, MUS, NURSE, SP, SW, TED, THEA

01 President ... Dr. Randy J. DUNN
100 Chief of Staff ... Dr. Joshua E. JACOBS
101 Sr Exec Coord for Pres/Coord Bd Rel ... Ms. Jill HUNT
05 Provost/VP Academic Affairs ... Dr. Bonnie S. HIGGINSON
10 VP Finance & Admin Svcs ... Mr. Tom W. DENTON
32 VP Student Affairs ... Dr. Don E. ROBERTSON
30 VP Institutional Advancement ... Mr. James F. CARTER
58 Assoc Provost/Grad Educ & Research ... Dr. Jay MORGAN
20 Assoc Prov/Undergrad Education ... Dr. Renae D. DUNCAN
88 Assoc VP Institutional Advancement ... Dr. Bob L. JACKSON
35 Assoc VP Student Affairs ... Mr. Michael E. YOUNG
26 Asst VP Communications ... Ms. Catherine M. SIVILLS
43 General Counsel ... Mr. John P. RALL
50 Dean Bauernfeind Col of Business ... Dr. Timothy S. TODD
53 Dean College of Education ... Dr. David WHALEY
76 Dean Col of Health Sci & Human Svcs ... Dr. Susan M. MULLER
79 Dean Col of Humanities & Fine Arts ... Dr. O. Ted BROWN
81 Dean Col Science/Engineering/Tech ... Dr. Stephen H. COBB
47 Dean Hutson School of Agriculture ... Dr. Tony L. BRANNON
66 Dean School of Nursing ... Dr. Marcia B. HOBBS
08 Dean University Libraries ... Mr. Adam L. MURRAY
51 Dn Cont Educ/Academic Outreach ... Dr. Brian W. VAN HORN
24 Asst Dn/Dir Dist Learn/Noncrdt Pgm ... Mr. Daniel A. LAVIT
97 Coordinator University Studies ... Dr. Peter F. MURPHY
92 Director Honors Program ... Dr. Warren EDMINSTER
85 Director Institute for Intl Studies ... Dr. Luis CANALES
104 Assoc Director Education Abroad ... Ms. Melanie C. MCCALLON
84 Exec Director Enrollment Mgmt ... Mr. Fred K. DIETZ
07 Dir Undgrad Admissions Svcs ... Ms. Lesa C. HARRIS
06 Registrar ... Ms. Tracy ROBERTS
37 Dir Student Fin Aid/Scholarships ... Ms. Lori A. MITCHUM
39 Director Housing ... Dr. J. David WILSON
38 Dir University Counseling Services ... Dr. Angie TRZEPACZ
28 Dir African-American Student Svcs ... Mr. Sidney G. CARTHELL
36 Director Career Services ... Dr. Ross B. MELOAN
23 Director Health Services ... Ms. Roberta M. GARFIELD
16 Director Human Resources ... Mr. Thomas E. HOFFACKER
21 Sr Director Accounting & Fin Svcs ... Ms. Jacklyn K. DUDLEY
21 Dir Fiscal Plng/Analysis/Budget Ofc ... Mr. Carl F. PRESTFELDT
102 Executive Director MSU Foundation ... Dr. Tim I. MILLER
96 Int Director Procurement Services ... Ms. Jan R. FUQUA
22 Int Dir Office of Equal Opportunity ... Ms. Cami DUFFY
88 Exec Director Regional Outreach ... Ms. Gina S. WINCHESTER
13 Chief Information Officer ... Ms. Linda G. MILLER
91 Manager Administrative Computing ... Mr. Brantly D. TRAVIS
90 Dir Ctr for Teaching/Learn/Tech ... Mr. Howard T. RICE
09 Coordinator Institutional Research ... Ms. Fugen MUSCIO
41 Athletic Director ... Mr. C. Allen WARD
18 VP Finance & Admin Svcs ... Mr. Tom W. DENTON
19 Dir Public Safety/Emergency Mgmt ... Mr. David V. DEVOSS
40 Director University Store ... Ms. R. Karol HARDISON
25 Director Sponsored Programs ... Mr. John A. ROARK
29 Assoc Director Alumni Affairs ... Ms. Sabrina K. MATHIS
105 Web Manager ... Mr. R. Tony A. POWELL
108 Director Institutional Assessment ... Dr. Kelley C. WEZNER

National College (B)

115 E Lexington Avenue, Danville KY 40422-1517
County: Boyle Identification: 666441
Unit ID: 433572
Telephone: (859) 236-6991 Carnegie Class: Not Classified
FAX Number: (859) 236-1063 Calendar System: Quarter
URL: www.ncbt.edu
Established: 1886 Annual Undergrad Tuition & Fees: $11,500
Enrollment: 450 Coed
Affiliation or Control: Proprietary IRS Status: Proprietary
Highest Offering: Associate Degree
Program: Occupational; 2-Year Principally Bachelor's Creditable
Accreditation: ACICS, MAC

01 Director ... Mr. Lee BOWLING
05 Vice President ... Ms. Charlotte BRINNEMAN

† Branch campus of National College, Lexington, KY.

National College (C)

7627 Ewing Boulevard, Florence KY 41042-1812
County: Boone Identification: 666442
Telephone: (859) 525-6510 Carnegie Class: Not Classified
FAX Number: (859) 525-8961 Calendar System: Quarter
URL: www.ncbt.edu
Established: 1970 Annual Undergrad Tuition & Fees: $11,101
Enrollment: 298 Coed
Affiliation or Control: Proprietary IRS Status: Proprietary
Highest Offering: Associate Degree
Program: Occupational; 2-Year Principally Bachelor's Creditable
Accreditation: ACICS, MAC, SURGT

01 Director ... Ms. Carole REED-MAHONEY
04 Assistant to the Director ... Mrs. Linda MERRELL
05 Vice President ... Ms. Charlotte BRINNEMAN

† Branch campus of National College, Lexington, KY.

National College (D)

2376 Sir Barton Way, Lexington KY 40509-2256
County: Fayette FICE Identification: 010489
Unit ID: 157021
Telephone: (859) 253-0621 Carnegie Class: Assoc/PrivFP4
FAX Number: (859) 254-7664 Calendar System: Quarter
URL: www.ncbt.edu
Established: 1941 Annual Undergrad Tuition & Fees: $11,101
Enrollment: 1,856 Coed
Affiliation or Control: Proprietary IRS Status: Proprietary
Highest Offering: Baccalaureate
Program: Occupational; 2-Year Principally Bachelor's Creditable
Accreditation: ACICS, MAC, SURGT

01 President ... Mr. Frank LONGAKER
05 Campus Director ... Ms. Kim THOMASSON
03 Vice President ... Ms. Charlotte BRINNEMAN
32 Director of Student Services ... Mr. Raymond BROOK
07 Regional Director of Admissions ... Ms. Donna STOUTENBOROUGH

National College (E)

4205 Dixie Highway, Louisville KY 40216-4147
County: Jefferson Identification: 666443
Unit ID: 433590
Telephone: (502) 447-7634 Carnegie Class: Not Classified
FAX Number: (502) 447-7665 Calendar System: Quarter
URL: www.national-college.edu
Established: 1886 Annual Undergrad Tuition & Fees: $15,216
Enrollment: 462 Coed
Affiliation or Control: Proprietary IRS Status: Proprietary
Highest Offering: Baccalaureate
Program: Occupational; 2-Year Principally Bachelor's Creditable
Accreditation: ACICS, MAC, SURGT

01 Director ... Mr. Vincent TINEBRA
05 Assistant Director ... Ms. Vicki STRUNK

† Branch campus of National College, Lexington, KY.

National College (F)

50 National College Boulevard, Pikeville KY 41501-3176
County: Pike Identification: 666444
Telephone: (606) 478-7200 Carnegie Class: Not Classified
FAX Number: (606) 437-4952 Calendar System: Quarter
URL: www.ncbt.edu
Established: 1970 Annual Undergrad Tuition & Fees: $7,500
Enrollment: 285 Coed
Affiliation or Control: Proprietary IRS Status: Proprietary
Highest Offering: Associate Degree
Program: Occupational; 2-Year Principally Bachelor's Creditable
Accreditation: ACICS, MAC

01 Director ... Ms. Tammy RILEY

† Branch campus of National College, Lexington, KY.

National College (G)

125 S Killarney Lane, Richmond KY 40475-2309
County: Madison Identification: 666445
Unit ID: 433615
Telephone: (859) 623-8956 Carnegie Class: Not Classified
FAX Number: (859) 624-5544 Calendar System: Quarter
URL: www.ncbt.edu
Established: 1974 Annual Undergrad Tuition & Fees: $9,450
Enrollment: 417 Coed
Affiliation or Control: Proprietary IRS Status: Proprietary
Highest Offering: Associate Degree
Program: Occupational; 2-Year Principally Bachelor's Creditable
Accreditation: ACICS, MAC

01 President ... Mr. Frank LONGAKER
03 Vice President ... Ms. Charlotte BRINNEMAN
05 Director ... Mrs. Keeley GADD

† Branch campus of National College, Lexington, KY.

Northern Kentucky University (H)

Nunn Drive, Highland Heights KY 41099-0000
County: Campbell FICE Identification: 009275
Unit ID: 157447
Telephone: (859) 572-5100 Carnegie Class: Master's L
FAX Number: (859) 572-5566 Calendar System: Semester
URL: www.nku.edu
Established: 1968 Annual Undergrad Tuition & Fees (In-State): $7,872
Enrollment: 15,738 Coed
Affiliation or Control: State IRS Status: 501(c)3
Highest Offering: Doctorate
Program: 2-Year Principally Bachelor's Creditable; Liberal Arts And General; Teacher Preparatory; Professional
Accreditation: SC, BUS, CONST, ENGT, LAW, MUS, NUR, RAD, SPAA, SW, TED

01 President ... Mr. Geoffrey S. MEARNS
04 Exec Asst to President ... Ms. Kathryn J. HERSCHEDE
05 Vice Pres Academic Affairs/Provost ... Dr. Gail W. WELLS
10 Vice Pres Admin & Finance ... Mr. Kenneth H. RAMEY
32 Interim Vice Pres Student Affairs ... Dr. Lisa RHINE
30 Vice Pres University Advancement ... Mr. Gerard A. ST. AMAND
45 Vice Pres Planning/Policy/Budget ... Dr. Sue HODGES MOORE
43 VP Legal Affairs & General Counsel ... Ms. Sara L. SIDEBOTTOM
86 Vice Pres Govt/Community Relations ... Mr. Joseph E. WIND
44 Asst VP University Development ... Mr. Donald A. GORBANDT
26 Asst VP Marketing & Communications ... Mr. Rick MEYERS
88 Assoc Provost for Reg Stewardship ... Dr. Jan HILLARD
20 Vice Provost University Programs ... Mr. J. Patrick MOYNAHAN
49 Dean College of Arts & Sciences ... Dr. Samuel ZACHARY
50 Dean College of Business ... Dr. Rick KOLBE
88 Dean College of Informatics ... Dr. Kevin KIRBY
53 Dean College of Ed & Human Services ... Dr. Mark WASICSKO
61 Dean Chase College of Law ... Mr. Dennis HONABACH
66 Dean College of Health Professions ... Dr. Denise ROBINSON
11 Director of Administration ... Ms. Linda REYNOLDS
18 Asst VP Facilities Management ... Mr. Larry BLAKE
18 Director Operations & Maintenance ... Mr. Ray MIRIZZI
21 Dir Fin & Operational Auditing ... Mr. Larry MEYER
21 Dir Business/Auxiliary Services ... Mr. Andy MEEKS
88 Dir Architecture & Construction ... Mr. Steve NIENABER
45 Director Campus Space and Planning ... Ms. Mary Paula SCHUH
15 Senior Director Human Resources ... Ms. Lori SOUTHWOOD
21 Comptroller ... Mr. Russell A. KERDOLFF
19 Director Public Safety ... Mr. Jason WILLIS
13 Director IT ... Ms. Kimberly HEIMBROCK
96 Director Procurement Services ... Mr. Jeffrey STRUNK
20 Assoc Provost Academic Affs/Admin ... Ms. Beth SWEENEY
13 Assoc Provost & CIO ... Mr. Timothy FERGUSON
08 Assoc Provost Library Services ... Mr. Arne J. ALMQUIST
92 Interim Director Honors Program ... Ms. Belle ZEMBRODT
84 Assoc VP Enrollment Management ... Mr. Paul ORSCHELN
07 Director Undergraduate Admissions ... Ms. Melissa GORBANDT
06 Registrar ... Ms. Marla HERRON
37 Dir Student Financial Assistance ... Ms. Leah STEWART
78 Exec Dir Ctr for Civic Engagement ... Mr. Mark NEIKIRK
51 Director Community Connections ... Ms. Melinda SPONG
25 Director Research/Grants/Contracts ... Mr. William THOMPSON
89 Director First Year Programs ... Dr. Mei Mei BURR
88 Sr Director Office of the Budget ... Mr. Kenneth KLINE
45 Exec Director Planning/Performance ... Ms. Vickie NATALE
09 Exec Dir Institutional Research ... Ms. Katherine A. BONTRAGER
88 Director Campus Recreation ... Mr. Matthew HACKETT
38 Dir Health/Counseling/Prevention ... Ms. Barbara SWEEN
35 Director Student Life ... Ms. Betty MULKEY
38 Int Dir Testing/Disability Services ... Mr. Ben ANDERSON
39 Interim Director University Housing ... Mr. Arnie SLAUGHTER
36 Director Career Development ... Mr. Bill FROUDE
85 Director Intl Student & Scholars ... Ms. Elizabeth LEIBACH

41 Director Athletic Administration .... Dr. Scott EATON
102 Executive Director Foundation ....Ms. Karen ZERHUSEN KRUER
29 Director Alumni Programs .... Ms. Deidra FAJACK

St. Catharine College (A)

2735 Bardstown Road, Saint Catharine KY 40061-9499
County: Washington FICE Identification: 001983
Unit ID: 157632
Telephone: (859) 336-5082 Carnegie Class: Bac/Assoc
FAX Number: (859) 336-5031 Calendar System: Semester
URL: www.sccky.edu
Established: 1931 Annual Undergrad Tuition & Fees: $17,976
Enrollment: 1,146 Coed
Affiliation or Control: Roman Catholic IRS Status: 501(c)3
Highest Offering: Master's
Program: Occupational; 2-Year Principally Bachelor's Creditable
Accreditation: SC, ADNUR, DMS, RAD, RTT, SURGT

01 President .... Mr. William D. HUSTON
03 Executive Vice President .... Mr. Roger L. MARCUM
05 Vice President for Academic Affairs .... Dr. Don GILES
10 Vice President Finance .... Mr. Gary ROBINSON
30 Vice President for Advancement .... Vacant
84 VP Enrollment Mgt/Dean of Students .... Ms. Vicki GUTHRIE
06 Registrar .... Ms. Anita FOSTER
07 Director of Admissions .... Mr. Paul PRESTA
08 Head Librarian .... Ms. Ilona BURDETTE
37 Financial Aid Officer .... Ms. Melinda LYNCH
27 Director of Communications .... Mr. Jim EARLS
38 Director of Counseling .... Vacant
15 Director of Personnel Services .... Mrs. Carlotta BRUSSELL
18 Chief Facilities/Physical Plant .... Mr. Dwight COTTON
21 Associate Business Officer .... Mr. Jim SNYDER
26 Chief Public Relations Officer .... Mr. Jimmie EARLS
35 Director of Student Affairs .... Mr. Ticha CHIKUNI
09 Director of Institutional Research .... Ms. Nora HATTON
29 Director of Alumni Relations .... Ms. Angela HOFFMAN

Simmons College of Kentucky (B)

1018 South 7th Street, Louisville KY 40203-3322
County: Jefferson FICE Identification: 041780
Unit ID: 461759
Telephone: (502) 776-1443 Carnegie Class: Not Classified
FAX Number: (502) 776-2227 Calendar System: Semester
URL: www.simmonscollegeky.edu
Established: 1879 Annual Undergrad Tuition & Fees: $7,650
Enrollment: N/A Coed
Affiliation or Control: Baptist IRS Status: 501(c)3
Highest Offering: Baccalaureate
Program: Religious Emphasis
Accreditation: @BI

01 President .... Mr. Kevin W. COSBY
05 Vice Pres Academic Affairs .... Dr. Brian J. WELLS
32 Vice Pres Student Affs/Dir Admiss .... Ms. Kathleen BROWN

The Southern Baptist Theological Seminary (C)

2825 Lexington Road, Louisville KY 40280-2899
County: Jefferson FICE Identification: 001982
Unit ID: 157748
Telephone: (502) 897-4011 Carnegie Class: Spec/Faith
FAX Number: (502) 899-1770 Calendar System: Other
URL: www.sbts.edu
Established: 1859 Annual Undergrad Tuition & Fees: $7,152
Enrollment: 3,364 Coed
Affiliation or Control: Southern Baptist IRS Status: 501(c)3
Highest Offering: Doctorate
Program: Professional; Religious Emphasis
Accreditation: SC, MUS, THEOL

01 President .... Dr. R. Albert MOHLER, JR.
100 Chief of Staff to the President .... Mr. Matthew HALL
05 Sr VP Academic Administration .... Dr. Russell D. MOORE
11 Sr VP Institutional Administration .... Mr. Dan DUMAS
10 Vice Pres of Business Operations .... Mr. Craig PARKER
11 Vice President of Operations .... Mr. Andrew VINCENT
26 Vice President Communications .... Mr. Steve WATTERS
13 Assoc VP Information Technology .... Mr. Jason HEATH
30 VP Institutional Advancement .... Dr. Jason ALLEN
32 Vice President Student Services .... Dr. Randy STINSON
106 Assoc VP Online Education .... Dr. Timothy Paul JONES
07 Assoc VP Enrollment Management ..... Dr. Phillip BETHANCOURT
09 Director of Institutional Assessmnt .... Mr. Joseph C. HARROD
15 Director Human Resources .... Mr. Jim STITZINGER
18 Chief Facilities/Physical Plant .... Mr. Bob SNIP
41 Director of Health & Recreation .... Mr. Matt EMADI
07 Director of Admissions .... Mr. John POWELL
08 Librarian .... Mr. Bruce L. KEISLING
29 Director Strategic Initiatives .... Mr. Benjamin DOCKERY
37 Manager of Financial Aid .... Mrs. Erin JOINER
73 Dean of School of Theology .... Dr. Russell D. MOORE
53 Dean School of Church Ministries .... Dr. Randy STINSON
88 Dean Missions Evang Ch Growth .... Mr. Zane PRATT
88 Dean Boyce College .... Dr. Dan DEWITT
04 Admin Assistant to the President .... Miss Rachel HULTZ

Spalding University (D)

845 S Third Street, Louisville KY 40203-2213
County: Jefferson FICE Identification: 001960
Unit ID: 157757
Telephone: (502) 585-9911 Carnegie Class: DRU
FAX Number: (502) 585-7158 Calendar System: Other
URL: www.spalding.edu
Established: 1814 Annual Undergrad Tuition & Fees: $20,550
Enrollment: 2,432 Coed
Affiliation or Control: Independent Non-Profit IRS Status: 501(c)3
Highest Offering: Doctorate
Program: Liberal Arts And General; Teacher Preparatory; Professional
Accreditation: SC, CLPSY, IACBE, NURSE, OT, SW, TED

01 President .... Ms. Tori MURDEN MCCLURE
05 Provost .... Dr. Randy STRICKLAND
30 Dir of Advancement & Philanthropy .... Ms. Bobbie RAFFERTY
32 Dean of Students .... Dr. Richard HUDSON
10 Chief Financial Officer .... Mr. Mark HOHMANN
43 General Counsel .... Ms. Emily NORRIS
84 Dean of Enrollment Management .... Mr. Chris HART
53 Dean of College of Education .... Dr. Beverly C. KEEPERS
83 Dean College Social Science/Hum .... Dr. John JAMES
88 Chair Adult Accelerated Programs .... Dr. Linda BEATTIE
76 Dean College Health & Nat Science .... Ms. Joanne BERRYMAN
26 Ex Dir Marketing/Public Relations .... Mr. Rick BARNEY
20 Sr Dir Academic Resource Center .... Ms. Judith LUTHER
06 Registrar .... Ms. Jennifer KRUMHANSL
27 Chief Information Officer .... Mr. Ezra KRUMHANSL
08 Director Library .... Ms. Jackie YOUNG
37 Director Student Financial Aid .... Ms. Gina KUZUOKA
15 Human Resources Director .... Mrs. Melissa LOWE
09 Dir of Institutional Effectiveness .... Ms. Kay VETTER
26 Director of Executive Communication .... Ms. Beth NEWBERRY
88 Dir Student Achievement/Retention .... Ms. Judith LUTHER
41 Director of Athletics .... Mr. Roger BURKMAN
88 Admin Dir/Mstr Fin Arts in Writing .... Ms. Karen MANN
21 Business Manager .... Ms. Jamie PAGE
18 JLL Facilities Manager .... Mr. Kevin WEBER
40 Bookstore Manager .... Vacant
88 Director Applied Behavior Analysis .... Vacant
88 Director Masters of Business Commu . Dr. Denise CUMBERLAND

Spencerian College (E)

1575 Winchester Road, Lexington KY 40505-4520
County: Fayette Identification: 666448
Unit ID: 433563
Telephone: (859) 223-9608 Carnegie Class: Assoc/PrivFP
FAX Number: (859) 224-7744 Calendar System: Quarter
URL: www.spencerian.edu
Established: 1997 Annual Undergrad Tuition & Fees: $20,800
Enrollment: 447 Coed
Affiliation or Control: Proprietary IRS Status: Proprietary
Highest Offering: Associate Degree
Program: Occupational; 2-Year Principally Bachelor's Creditable
Accreditation: ACICS, MAC, MLTAB, RAD

01 Executive Director .... Mr. Buddy HOSKINSON
05 Academic Dean .... Mr. Chris DOUGLAS
20 Compliance Officer .... Mr. Brian HIGHLEY
07 Director of Admissions .... Mrs. Christine WILDES
37 Director of Financial Planning .... Mrs. Patricia RAY
36 Director of Career Services .... Mr. Jesse MOYERS
06 Registrar .... Mr. Eric COMBS

† Branch campus of Spencerian College, Louisville, KY.

Spencerian College (F)

4627 Dixie Highway, Louisville KY 40216-2605
County: Jefferson FICE Identification: 004618
Unit ID: 157766
Telephone: (502) 447-1000 Carnegie Class: Assoc/PrivFP
FAX Number: (502) 447-4574 Calendar System: Quarter
URL: www.spencerian.edu
Established: 1892 Annual Undergrad Tuition & Fees: $16,320
Enrollment: 1,012 Coed
Affiliation or Control: Proprietary IRS Status: Proprietary
Highest Offering: Associate Degree
Program: Occupational
Accreditation: ACICS, CVT, MAC, MLTAB, RAD, SURGT

01 Executive Director .... Ms. Jan M. GORDON
05 Academic Dean .... Ms. Linda BLAIR
37 Director of Financial Planning .... Ms. Jill SCHULER
07 Director of Admissions .... Ms. Kathleen BELANGER
36 Director of Career Services .... Ms. Heather FUQUA
35 Associate Dean of Student Services .... Ms. Alice PHILLIPS

Sullivan College of Technology and Design (G)

3901 Atkinson Square Drive, Louisville KY 40218-4549
County: Jefferson FICE Identification: 012088
Unit ID: 157270
Telephone: (502) 456-6509 Carnegie Class: Spec/Arts
FAX Number: (502) 456-2341 Calendar System: Quarter
URL: www.sctd.edu
Established: 1961 Annual Undergrad Tuition & Fees: $17,340
Enrollment: 589 Coed
Affiliation or Control: Proprietary IRS Status: Proprietary
Highest Offering: Baccalaureate
Program: Occupational
Accreditation: ACICS

00 Chancellor .... Dr. A. R. SULLIVAN
01 President .... Mr. Glenn D. SULLIVAN
11 Senior Vice President .... Mr. Thomas F. DAVISSON
03 Executive Vice President .... Mr. Bill NOEL
05 Dean of Academic Affairs .... Dr. Sheree KOPPEL
10 Vice President Finance .... Mr. Shelton BRIDGES
84 Vice Pres Enrollment Management .... Mr. James CRICK
12 Executive Director .... Mr. David WINKLER
06 Registrar .... Ms. Cathy DRUIN
07 Director of Admissions .... Mr. Aamer CHAUHDRI
37 Dir of Student Financial Planning .... Mr. Andre DOWNING
08 Head Librarian .... Ms. Jill SHERMAN
36 Placement Director .... Mr. Sam MANNINO
55 Evening Division Dean .... Ms. Beverly LIVERS
96 Director of Purchasing .... Ms. Ann VEST
14 Chief Technology Officer .... Mr. Mike GROSSE
29 Director Alumni Relations .... Ms. Hazel MATTHEWS

Sullivan University (H)

3101 Bardstown Road, Louisville KY 40205-3000
County: Jefferson FICE Identification: 004619
Unit ID: 157793
Telephone: (502) 456-6504 Carnegie Class: Master's M
FAX Number: (502) 456-0040 Calendar System: Quarter
URL: www.sullivan.edu
Established: 1962 Annual Undergrad Tuition & Fees: $17,520
Enrollment: 5,974 Coed
Affiliation or Control: Proprietary IRS Status: Proprietary
Highest Offering: Doctorate
Program: Occupational; Professional
Accreditation: SC, ACFEI, IACBE, MAC, PHAR

00 Chancellor .... Dr. A. R. SULLIVAN
01 President .... Mr. Glenn D. SULLIVAN
03 Vice President/Chief Executive Ofcr .... Dr. Eric HARTER
03 Executive Vice President .... Mr. Bill NOEL
05 Chief Academic Officer .... Dr. Jay MARR
88 Senior Vice President .... Mr. Thomas F. DAVISSON
10 Vice President Finance .... Mr. Shelton BRIDGES
84 Vice Pres Enrollment Management .... Mr. James CRICK
32 Vice President of Student Services .... Mr. Chris ERNST
36 Vice President of Career Services .... Mr. Trace CHESSER
58 Associate Dean Graduate School .... Dr. Ken MILLER
35 Student Life Coordinator .... Ms. Kim RICHARDSON
88 Dir Natl Ctr Hospitality Studies .... Mr. Keith LERME
06 Registrar .... Ms. Kim MITCHELL
08 Librarian .... Mr. Charles BROWN
13 Chief Technology Officer .... Mr. Mike GROSSE
37 Director Student Financial Planning .... Vacant
55 Director Evening Division .... Mr. James TAYLOR
40 Director Bookstore .... Ms. Brenda HOOKS
07 Director of Admissions .... Ms. Terri THOMAS
12 Director Lexington Branch .... Mr. David KEENE
39 Director of Student Housing .... Ms. Audra SMAIL
20 Associate Dean of Students .... Ms. Aubree ALVAREZ
96 Director of Purchasing .... Ms. Ann VEST
56 Director of Extension Campus .... Ms. Barbara DEAN
88 Director of Enrollment Services .... Mr. Jim KLEIN
29 Director Alumni Relations .... Ms. Hazel MATTHEWS
09 Director Institutional Research .... Dr. Forrest HOULETTE
18 Manager Campus Facilities .... Mr. Mike FOWLER
67 Dean College of Pharmacy .... Dr. Hieu TRAN
50 Dean College of Business Admin .... Mr. Ken MORAN
72 Dean College of Technology .... Dr. Emmanuel UDOH

Thomas More College (I)

333 Thomas More Parkway,
Crestview Hills KY 41017-3495
County: Kenton FICE Identification: 002001
Unit ID: 157809
Telephone: (859) 341-5800 Carnegie Class: Master's S
FAX Number: (859) 344-3345 Calendar System: Semester
URL: www.thomasmore.edu
Established: 1921 Annual Undergrad Tuition & Fees: $26,595
Enrollment: 1,832 Coed
Affiliation or Control: Roman Catholic IRS Status: 501(c)3
Highest Offering: Master's
Program: Liberal Arts And General; Teacher Preparatory; Professional
Accreditation: SC, NUR

01 President .... Sr. Margaret A. STALLMEYER
04 Assistant to the President .... Ms. Charlene BARLOW
10 Vice President of Finance .... Mr. Peter W. AAMODT
05 Vice President for Academic Affairs .... Dr. Bradley A. BIELSKI
30 Vice Pres for Inst Advancement .... Ms. Cathy SILVERS
32 Vice Pres of Student Services .... Mr. Matthew H. WEBSTER
35 Dean of Students .... Ms. Ebony GRIGGS-GRIFFIN
09 Dir of Inst Planning/Effectiveness .... Ms. Genie M. WAMBAUGH
06 Registrar .... Ms. Kelly GOYETTE
08 Director of Library .... Mr. James M. MCKELLOGG
37 Director of Financial Aid .... Ms. Mary GIVHAN
13 Director of IT .... Mr. William K. SWISHER
26 Dir Communications/Media Relations .... Ms. Stacy ROGERS
38 Director of Counseling .... Ms. Veronica A. LUBBE
42 Chaplain .... Rev. Gerald E. TWADDELL
84 Director of Enrollment for TAP .... Dr. Bradley A. BIELSKI

41 Athletic Director .... Mr. Terry D. CONNOR
19 Director of Campus Safety .... Mr. Robert MARSHALL
15 Director of Human Resources .... Ms. Laura CUSTER
18 Director of Facilities .... Mr. Jeffrey KORDENBROCK
29 Director of Alumni .... Ms. Monica GINNEY
36 Dir of Career Planning/Coop Educ .... Ms. Kelly LANE
73 Director of Campus Ministry .... Sr. Patricia DOROBEK
21 Controller .... Ms. Debbie A. RAPIER
51 Director of Lifelong Learning .... Mr. Nathan HARTMAN
92 Director of Honors Program .... Dr. Catherine SHERRON
44 Dir Annual Giving/Special Events .... Ms. Beth MALEY
07 Associate Director of Admissions .... Mr. Billy SARGE
35 Coordinator of Student Activities .... Mr. Calvin ROBINSON
39 Coordinator of Residence Life .... Mr. Brian SHEELEY

Transylvania University (A)

300 N Broadway, Lexington KY 40508-1797
County: Fayette FICE Identification: 001987
Unit ID: 157818
Telephone: (859) 233-8300 Carnegie Class: Bac/A&S
FAX Number: (859) 233-8797 Calendar System: Other
URL: www.transy.edu
Established: 1780 Annual Undergrad Tuition & Fees: $29,865
Enrollment: 1,029 Coed
Affiliation or Control: Christian Church (Disciples Of Christ)
IRS Status: 501(c)3
Highest Offering: Baccalaureate
Program: Liberal Arts And General; Teacher Preparatory
Accreditation: SC, TED

01 President .... Dr. R. Owen WILLIAMS
20 Interim Dean of the College .... Dr. Kathleen JAGGER
10 Vice President Finance & Business .... Mr. Marc MATHEWS
30 Vice Pres Advancement .... Mr. Kirk PURDOM
32 Dean of Students .... Dr. Barbara LOMONACO
06 Registrar .... Ms. Michelle RAWLINGS
09 Director of Institutional Research .... Mr. Rhyan M. CONYERS
07 Vice President for Enrollment .... Mr. Bradley L. GOAN
08 Librarian .... Ms. Susan M. BROWN
37 Director of Financial Aid .... Mr. David J. CECIL
26 Director of Public Relations .... Ms. Sarah EMMONS
36 Director of Placement Services .... Ms. Susan S. RAYER
13 Director of Information Technology .... Mr. Jason WHITAKER
104 Dir Study Abroad & Special Programs .... Ms. Kathryn C. SIMON
15 Director Personnel Services .... Mr. Jeff MUDRAK
18 Chief Facilities/Physical Plant .... Mr. Darrell L. BANKS
96 Director of Purchasing .... Ms. Shawn T. SINGLETON
29 Director Alumni Relations .... Ms. Natasa PAJIC
28 Director of Campus Diversity .... Mr. Eduardo NINO-MORENO

Union College (B)

310 College Street, Barbourville KY 40906-1499
County: Knox FICE Identification: 001988
Unit ID: 157863
Telephone: (606) 546-4151 Carnegie Class: Master's L
FAX Number: (606) 546-1217 Calendar System: Other
URL: www.unionky.edu
Established: 1879 Annual Undergrad Tuition & Fees: $20,890
Enrollment: 1,380 Coed
Affiliation or Control: United Methodist IRS Status: 501(c)3
Highest Offering: Master's
Program: Liberal Arts And General; Teacher Preparatory
Accreditation: SC, SW

01 President .... Dr. Marcia HAWKINS
01 VP for Academic Affairs .... Dr. Thomas J. MCFARLAND
30 Vice President for Advancement .... Ms. Denise WAINSCOTT
84 Dean of Enrollment Management .... Dr. Jerry JACKSON
32 Dean of Students .... Vacant
53 Head of Educational Studies Dept .... Dr. Jason REEVES
35 Associate Dean Student Life .... Ms. Barbara TEAGUE
96 Dir Purchasing/Act Pyable/Staff Act .... Ms. Jennifer JONES
06 Registrar .... Ms. Kathy WEBB
18 Director of Physical Plant (NMRC) .... Mr. James JAMERSON
41 Athletic Director .... Vacant
29 Director of Alumni Relations .... Mr. Tommy RUTH
09 Director of Institutional Research .... Mr. Greg MYERS
10 Chief Business Officer .... Mr. Steve HOSKINS
26 Int Director of Public Relations .... Ms. Melissa REID
88 Director of Sports Information .... Mr. Jay STANCIL
88 Director of Special Programs .... Dr. Sarah HENDRIX
08 Head Librarian .... Ms. Tara L. COOPER
42 College Minister .... Rev. David MILLER
31 Director of Common Partners .... Ms. Gabrielle MELLENDORF
37 Assistant Director of Financial Aid .... Ms. Jessica COOK
38 Director of Counseling .... Mrs. Jodi CARROLL
15 Benefits Coordinator .... Ms. Lynn SMITH
19 Safety Team Leader .... Mr. Michael GRAY
50 Chair Department of Business .... Dr. Carolyn PAYNE
88 Chair Dept Wellness/Human Perf/Rec .... Dr. Larry INKSTER
79 Chair Dept Engr/Comm/Language .... Dr. James GARRETT
57 Chr Dpt Hist/Relig Std/Fn/Perf Arts .... Dr. Russell SISSON
81 Chair Dept of Natural Sciences .... Dr. Dan COVINGTON
83 Chair Dept Social/Behav Science .... Dr. Robert ARMOUR
04 Executive Assistant for President .... Mrs. Margaret SENTERS
72 Director of Technology .... Mr. Brad JONES
88 Events Coordinator .... Ms. Bobbie DOOLIN

University of the Cumberlands (C)

6191 College Station Drive, Williamsburg KY 40769-4490
County: Whitley FICE Identification: 001962
Unit ID: 156541
Telephone: (606) 549-2200 Carnegie Class: Master's M
FAX Number: (606) 549-2820 Calendar System: Semester
URL: www.ucumberlands.edu
Established: 1888 Annual Undergrad Tuition & Fees: $19,000
Enrollment: 3,747 Coed
Affiliation or Control: Baptist IRS Status: 501(c)3
Highest Offering: Doctorate
Program: Liberal Arts And General; Teacher Preparatory
Accreditation: SC, ARCPA

01 President .... Dr. James H. TAYLOR
30 Vice Pres Institutional Advancement .... Mrs. Sue WAKE
05 Vice President Academic Affairs .... Dr. Larry L. COCKRUM
32 Vice President Student Services .... Dr. Michael COLEGROVE
10 Vice President Business Services .... Mr. Steve MORRIS
21 Vice President Finance .... Ms. Jana K. BAILEY
11 Vice President Operations .... Mr. Kyle GILBERT
37 Vice Pres Student Financial Plng .... Mr. Steve ALLEN
41 Vice Pres Athletics/Athletic Dir .... Mr. Randy VERNON
07 Director of Admissions .... Mrs. Erica HARRIS
06 Registrar .... Mr. Charles DUPIER
20 Associate Dean .... Dr. Thomas E. FISH
09 Institutional Research .... Mr. Charles DUPIER
26 Dir Multimedia/Athletic Services .... Ms. Jennifer FLOYD
35 Dean Student Life .... Ms. Linda CARTER
15 Director of Human Resources .... Ms. Pearl BAKER
90 Director of Information Technology .... Mr. Donnie GRIMES
42 Dir International Pgm/Church Rels .... Dr. Rick FLEENOR
36 Director of Career Services .... Ms. Debbie HARP
08 Head Librarian .... Ms. Jan WREN
58 Director Graduate Program .... Dr. Fred SAGESTER
18 Director of Physical Plant .... Mr. David ROOT
21 Bursar .... Ms. Jo DUPIER
29 Director Alumni Relations .... Mr. Dave BERGMAN

University of Kentucky (D)

Lexington KY 40506-0003
County: Fayette FICE Identification: 001989
Unit ID: 157085
Telephone: (859) 257-9000 Carnegie Class: RU/VH
FAX Number: (859) 257-4000 Calendar System: Semester
URL: www.uky.edu
Established: 1865 Annual Undergrad Tuition & Fees (In-State): $9,676
Enrollment: 27,226 Coed
Affiliation or Control: State IRS Status: 501(c)3
Highest Offering: Doctorate
Program: Liberal Arts And General; Teacher Preparatory; Professional
Accreditation: SC, AAFCS, ARCPA, ART, BUS, BUSA, CIDA, CLPSY, COPSY, CORE, CS, DENT, DIETC, DIETD, DIETI, ENG, FOR, HSA, JOUR, LAW, LIB, LSAR, MED, MFCD, MT, MUS, NURSE, PH, PHAR, PTA, #SCPSY, SP, SPAA, SW, TED, THEA

01 President .... Dr. Eli CAPILOUTO
46 Vice President Research .... Dr. James W. TRACY
05 Interim Provost .... Dr. Timothy S. TRACY
100 President's Chief of Staff .... Mr. Bill SWINFORD
10 Exec VP Finance/Administration .... Mr. Frank A. BUTLER
17 Executive VP for Health Affairs .... Dr. Michael KARPF
13 Chief Information Technology Office .... Mr. Vincent J. KELLEN
46 VP Institutional Effectiveness .... Dr. Heidi M. ANDERSON
32 Vice Pres Student Affairs .... Dr. Robert C. MOCK, JR.
28 Vice Pres Institutional Diversity .... Dr. Judy J. JACKSON
30 Vice President for Development .... Dr. D. M. RICHEY
17 Vice Pres Health Care Operations .... Dr. Richard LOFGREN
10 VP Health Care Opers/CFO .... Mr. Sergio MELGAR
45 VP Fin Operations and Treasurer .... Ms. Angela MARTIN
18 Vice President Facilities Mgmt .... Mr. Bob WISEMAN
88 VP Commercialization/Econ Devel .... Dr. Leonard E. HELLER
88 Assoc VP Research Infrastructure .... Vacant
22 Assoc VP Institutional Equity .... Mr. Terry D. ALLEN
26 Associate VP External Affairs .... Mr. Thomas W. HARRIS
35 Assoc VP Stdnt Affs/Dean of Stdnts .... Dr. Victor A. HAZARD
15 Assoc VP Human Resource Services .... Ms. Kimberly R. WILSON
88 Asst Vice Pres Public Safety .... Mr. Anthany BEATTY
31 Assoc Vice Pres Auxiliary Services .... Mr. Ben CRUTCHER
25 Assoc VP Res Admin & Fiscal Affs .... Mr. Jack SUPPLEE, JR.
88 Assoc VP Res Spon Proj Acct .... Ms. Debbie DAVIS
44 Assoc VP University Engagement .... Dr. Philip GREASLEY
20 Assoc Provost Intl Affairs .... Dr. Susan CARVALHO
20 Assoc Prov Clncl Translational Sci .... Dr. Philip A. KERN
17 Assoc VP Clinical Network Devel .... Mr. Joe CLAYPOOL
58 Assoc Prov Acad Adm/Dean Grad Sch .... Dr. Jeannine BLACKWELL
88 Assoc Provost Educ Partnerships .... Dr. John YOPP
20 Assoc Provost Undergrad Educ .... Dr. Micheal D. MULLEN
20 Associate Provost Faculty Affairs .... Dr. Lynda BROWN-WRIGHT
84 Assoc Provost Enroll Mgmt/Registrar .... Mr. Don WITT
08 Dean of Libraries .... Dr. Terry P. BIRDWHISTELL
27 Director University Press .... Dr. Stephen WRINN
43 General Counsel .... Ms. Barbara JONES
41 Director Athletics .... Mr. Mitch BARNHART
37 Director Student Financial Aid .... Ms. Lynda GEORGE
09 Director of Institutional Research .... Dr. Roger P. SUGARMAN
18 Chief Facilities/Physical Plant .... Vacant
36 Director Career Center .... Ms. Francene GILMER
38 Director Counseling & Testing .... Dr. Mary C. BOLIN-REECE
29 Director Alumni Relations .... Mr. Stan R. KEY
26 Exec Director Public Relations .... Mr. Jay BLANTON
90 Director Technical Academic Support .... Vacant
21 Controller .... Ms. Rhonda BECK
47 Dean of Agriculture .... Dr. M. Scott SMITH
19 Chief of Police .... Mr. Joseph W. MONROE
48 Dean College of Design .... Dr. Michael A. SPEAKS
88 Director Student Center .... Mr. John H. HERBST
49 Dean of Arts & Sciences .... Dr. Mark KORNBLUH
50 Dean of Business & Economics .... Dr. David BLACKWELL
53 Dean of Education .... Dr. Mary J. O'HAIR
54 Dean of Engineering .... Dr. Thomas W. LESTER
57 Dean of Fine Arts .... Dr. Michael TICK
60 Dean of Communication/Info Studies .... Dr. Dan O'HAIR
61 Dean of Law .... Mr. David BRENNEN
70 Dean of Social Work .... Dr. James P. ADAMS, JR.
76 Interim Dean of Health Sciences .... Dr. Sharon STEWART
52 Dean of Dentistry .... Dr. Sharon P. TURNER
63 Dean of Medicine/VP Clinical Affs .... Dr. Fredrick C. DE BEER
66 Dean of Nursing .... Dr. Jane M. KIRSCHLING
67 Dean of Pharmacy .... Dr. Tim TRACY
69 Dean Public Health .... Dr. Stephen W. WYATT
96 Director of Purchasing .... Mr. William L. HARRIS
23 Director Univ Student Health Svcs .... Dr. Gregory R. MOORE

University of Louisville (E)

2301 S Third Street, Louisville KY 40292-0001
County: Jefferson FICE Identification: 001999
Unit ID: 157289
Telephone: (502) 852-5555 Carnegie Class: RU/VH
FAX Number: (502) 852-7013 Calendar System: Semester
URL: www.louisville.edu
Established: 1798 Annual Undergrad Tuition & Fees (In-State): $9,466
Enrollment: 22,249 Coed
Affiliation or Control: State IRS Status: 501(c)3
Highest Offering: Doctorate
Program: Liberal Arts And General; Teacher Preparatory; Professional
Accreditation: SC, AUD, BUS, BUSA, CIDA, CLPSY, COPSY, CS, DENT, DH, ENG, EXSC, IPSY, LAW, MED, MFCD, MUS, NURSE, PH, PLNG, SP, SPAA, SW, TED, THEA

01 President .... Dr. James R. RAMSEY
05 Exec Vice Pres/University Prov .... Dr. Shirley C. WILLIHNGANZ
17 Exec Vice Pres for Health Affairs .... Dr. David DUNN
46 Executive VP for Research .... Dr. Bill PIERCE
32 Vice President Student Affairs .... Dr. Tom JACKSON, JR.
11 Vice President for Business Affairs .... Mr. Larry L. OWSLEY
30 Vice Pres Univ Advancement .... Mr. Keith INMAN
13 Vice Pres Information Tech .... Dr. Priscilla HANCOCK
86 VP for Community Engagement .... Mr. Daniel HALL
10 Vice President for Finance .... Mr. Michael J. CURTIN
16 Vice Pres Human Resources .... Mr. Sam CONNALLY
41 Vice President for Athletics .... Mr. Tom JURICH
44 Sr Assoc VP Advancement .... Ms. Rebecca SIMPSON
18 Assoc VP Facilities/Physical Plant .... Mr. Larry DETHERAGE
29 Asst Vice Pres for Alumni Relations .... Mr. Jimmy FORD
100 Chief of Staff for the President .... Ms. Kathleen M. SMITH
43 University Counsel .... Ms. Angela D. KOSHEWA
20 Vice Prov Undergraduate Affairs .... Dr. Dale B. BILLINGSLEY
58 Int Dean Graduate School .... Dr. Beth A. BOEHM
28 Vice Prov for Diversity/Intl Affs .... Dr. Mordean TAYLOR-ARCHER
88 Assoc Prov Acad Acct/IR & Effect .... Mr. Robert S. GOLDSTEIN
106 Assoc Univ Provost Distance Ed/Delp .... Dr. Gale RHODES
88 Asst Prov for Accreditation .... Ms. Connie C. SHUMAKE
21 Controller .... Mr. Larry W. ZINK
07 Executive Director Admissions .... Ms. Jenny L. SAWYER
06 Interim University Registrar .... Mr. Scott A. BURKS
37 Exec Director Financial Aid .... Ms. Patricia O. ARAUZ
26 Director of Comm/Marketing .... Ms. Cindy HESS
25 Director Contract Admin/Risk Mgmt .... Mr. David MARTIN
15 Dir of Staff Dev/Employee Rel .... Ms. Mary E. MILES
19 Director Public Safety .... Mr. Wayne HALL
09 Director Inst Research and Planning .... Ms. Becky PATTERSON
45 Director Inst Effectiveness .... Ms. Cheryl B. GILCHRIST
39 Director Student Housing .... Ms. Shannon D. STATEN
105 Director of Digital Media .... Mr. Jeffery A. RUSHTON
27 Director Media Relations .... Mr. Mark HEBERT
88 Assoc Vice Pres for Audit Services .... Mr. David F. BARKER
14 Director IT Enterprise Security .... Ms. Brenda B. GOMBOSKY
92 Director of Honors Program .... Dr. John F. RICHARDSON
96 Director Purchasing .... Mr. David MARTIN
88 Dir Planning/Design & Construction .... Mr. Kenneth DIETZ
36 Director Career Services .... Ms. Leslye A. ERICKSON
38 Director Counseling Services .... Dr. Kathy J. PENDLETON
08 Dean of University Libraries .... Mr. Robert FOX
49 Dean College Arts & Sciences .... Dr. James B. HUDSON
50 Dean College of Business .... Dr. R. Charles MOYER
52 Dean School of Dentistry .... Dr. John J. SAUK
53 Int Dean Col of Educ/Human Develop .... Dr. Blake HASELTON
70 Dean Kent School Social Work .... Dr. Terry L. SINGER
64 Dean School of Music .... Dr. Christopher DOANE
61 Interim Dean Brandeis School of Law .... Ms. Susan DUNCAN
66 Dean School of Nursing .... Dr. Marcia J. HERN
54 Dean Speed School of Engineering .... Dr. Neville PINTO
63 Interim Dean School of Medicine .... Dr. Toni GANZEL
69 Dean Public Health/Information Sci .... Dr. Richard D. CLOVER
35 Dean of Students/Assoc VP Stdnt Aff .... Dr. Michael MARDIS

University of Pikeville (F)

147 Sycamore Street, Pikeville KY 41501-1194
County: Pike FICE Identification: 001980
Unit ID: 157535
Telephone: (606) 218-5250 Carnegie Class: Bac/A&S
FAX Number: (606) 218-5269 Calendar System: Semester

URL: www.upike.edu
Established: 1889 Annual Undergrad Tuition & Fees: $17,050
Enrollment: 1,838 Coed
Affiliation or Control: Presbyterian Church (U.S.A.) IRS Status: 501(c)3
Highest Offering: Doctorate
Program: Liberal Arts And General; Teacher Preparatory
Accreditation: SC, OSTEO, @SW

01 President .... Mr. Paul E. PATTON
03 Vice Pres/Special Asst to President .... Mr. James HURLEY
05 VPAA/Dean College Arts/Sciences .... Mr. Thomas R. HESS
10 Vice Pres Finance/Business Affairs .... Mr. Douglas J. LANGE
30 Vice President for Development .... Dr. Eric BECHER
26 Asst Vice President Public Affairs .... Mrs. Lucy HOLMAN
63 VP Health Affairs/Dean KYCOM .... Dr. Boyd R. BUSER
32 VP Student Svcs/Dean of Students .... Mr. Ron DAMRON
07 Director Admissions/Stdnt Fin Svcs .... Mr. Gary JUSTICE
08 Director of Library Services .... Ms. Karen S. CHAFIN-EVANS
06 Asst VP Academic Affairs/Registrar .... Mrs. Gia POTTER
09 Director of Institutional Research .... Dr. Meg SIDLE
14 Senior Info Services Administrator .... Mr. Randy SCARBERRY
18 Director of Facilities .... Mr. John HOLMAN
37 Asst Dean Student Financial Svcs .... Mrs. Judy BRADLEY
15 Director of Human Resources .... Mrs. Lisa LANGE

Western Kentucky University (A)

1906 College Heights Blvd, Bowling Green KY 42101-3576
County: Warren FICE Identification: 002002
Unit ID: 157951
Telephone: (270) 745-0111 Carnegie Class: Master's L
FAX Number: (270) 745-5387 Calendar System: Semester
URL: www.wku.edu
Established: 1906 Annual Undergrad Tuition & Fees (In-State): $8,472
Enrollment: 21,036 Coed
Affiliation or Control: State IRS Status: 501(c)3
Highest Offering: Doctorate
Program: 2-Year Principally Bachelor's Creditable; Liberal Arts And General; Teacher Preparatory; Professional
Accreditation: SC, THEA, ADNUR, ART, BUS, BUSA, CACREP, DH, DIETD, @DIETI, ENG, JOUR, MUS, NAIT, NRPA, NURSE, PH, SP, SPAA, SW, TED

01 President .... Dr. Gary A. RANSDELL
05 Provost/Vice Pres Academic Affairs .... Dr. Gordon EMSLIE
46 VP for Research .... Dr. Gordon BAYLIS
26 Vice President for Public Affairs .... Ms. Robbin M. TAYLOR
30 Vice Pres Development & Alumni Rels .... Ms. Kathryn COSTELLO
13 Vice Pres Information Technology .... Dr. Bob OWEN
32 Vice President Student Affairs .... Mr. Howard E. BAILEY
10 Vice President Finance & Admin .... Ms. K. Ann MEAD
100 Chief of Staff/General Counsel .... Ms. Deborah T. WILKINS
20 Vice Provost Academic Affairs .... Dr. Richard C. MILLER
11 Vice Pres Campus Svcs & Facilities .... Mr. John N. OSBORNE
84 Interim Assoc VP for Enrollment Mgt .... Dr. Brian MEREDITH
55 Assoc VP Ext Learning & Outreach .... Dr. Beth LAVES
79 Dean Arts & Letters .... Dr. David D. LEE
50 Dean Business .... Dr. Jeffrey KATZ
53 Dean Education/Behavioral Sci .... Dr. Sam EVANS
81 Dean Science/Engineering .... Dr. Cheryl L. STEVENS
58 Interim Dean Grad Studies & Researc .... Dr. Kinchel DOERNER
97 Dean University College .... Dr. Dennis K. GEORGE
62 Interim Dean Libraries .... Ms. Connie FOSTER
88 Assoc VP Enrichment & Effectiveness .... Dr. Doug MCELROY
88 Assoc VP Planning & Program Develop .... Dr. Sylvia GAIKO
21 Chief Financial Officer .... Mr. Jim CUMMINGS
21 Budget Director .... Ms. Kimberly REED
07 Director Admissions .... Mr. Scott S. GORDON
88 Assoc VP Academic Budgets & Admin .... Mr. Mike DALE
88 Assoc VP Research and Development .... Mr. Douglas ROHRER
06 Registrar .... Ms. Freida K. EGGLETON
91 Director Admin Systems/Applications .... Mr. Gordon L. JOHNSON
15 Director Human Resources .... Mr. Tony L. GLISSON
18 Director Facilities Management .... Mr. Charles E. JONES
12 Director and Assoc Dean Glasgow .... Dr. Sally RAY
12 Dir Elizabethtown & Assoc Dean .... Dr. Ronald STEPHENS
12 Dir Camp Owens & Assoc Dean .... Dr. Gene E. TICE
90 Director Academic Technology .... Mr. John BOWERS
88 Dir Acad Advising & Retention Ctr .... Mr. Kevin P. THOMAS
39 Director Housing & Residence Life .... Mr. Brian KUSTER
19 Chief of Police .... Mr. Robert DEANE
29 Asst VP WKU Alumni Association .... Mr. Donald SMITH
102 Director Corporate/Foundation Rels .... Mr. Richard A. DUBOSE
44 Assistant VP Major Gifts .... Mr. John P. BLAIR
36 Director Career Services Center .... Dr. Lynne HOLLAND
37 Dir Student Financial Assistance .... Ms. Cindy BURNETTE
38 Director Counseling & Testing Ctr .... Dr. Brian VAN BRUNT
40 Director Bookstore .... Ms. Shawna C. TURNER
09 Director Institutional Research .... Dr. Tuesdi HELBIG
22 Equal Oppty/ADA/Compliance Director .... Ms. Huda N. MELKY
24 Director Educ Telecommunications .... Mr. Jack A. HANES
41 Interim Athletics Director .... Mr. Todd M. STEWART
85 Director Intl Student & Sch Service .... Mr. Tarek EL SHAYEB
85 Exec Dir International Programs .... Dr. Richard C. SUTTON
92 Executive Director Honors College .... Dr. Craig COBANE
96 Director Purchasing/Accts Payable .... Mr. Ken BAUSHKE
28 Director Diversity Programs .... Vacant
94 Director Women's Studies .... Dr. Jane OLMSTED
101 Senior Administrative Assistant .... Ms. Julia J. MCDONALD
104 Director Study Abroad/Global Lrng .... Vacant
23 Assoc Director Health Services .... Mr. Jeffrey T. ROSE
76 Dean Health & Human Services .... Dr. John A. BONAGURO
27 Director of Media Relations .... Mr. Bob SKIPPER
86 Dir Govt/Community Relations .... Ms. Jennifer B. SMITH
04 Executive Admininstrative Assistant .... Ms. Shelia E. HOUCHINS

LOUISIANA

Baton Rouge College (B)

1900 North Lobdell Boulevard,
Baton Rouge LA 70806-2246
County: East Baton Rouge FICE Identification: 026171
Unit ID: 373447
Telephone: (225) 292-5464 Carnegie Class: Assoc/PrivFP
FAX Number: (225) 308-4582 Calendar System: Semester
URL: www.brc.edu
Established: 1981 Annual Undergrad Tuition & Fees: $18,590
Enrollment: 43 Coed
Affiliation or Control: Proprietary IRS Status: Proprietary
Highest Offering: Associate Degree
Program: Occupational
Accreditation: CNCE

00 Chancellor .... Mrs. Valencia V. LANDRY
01 President .... Dr. Mohammad AJMAL
10 Chief Financial/Business Operations .... Mr. Jay DYKES, JR.
07 Admissions/Recruiting .... Mr. Billy FAIRLEY
06 Registrar/Bursar .... Mrs. Mary MCQUEARY
88 Education Consultant/Facilitator .... Dr. Daisy SLAN
36 Dir of Career Placement/Compliance .... Ms. Jordin L. DYKES

Baton Rouge School of Computers (C)

9352 Interline Avenue, Baton Rouge LA 70809-1909
County: East Baton Rouge FICE Identification: 021975
Unit ID: 158343
Telephone: (225) 923-2524 Carnegie Class: Assoc/PrivFP
FAX Number: (225) 923-2979 Calendar System: Other
URL: www.brsc.edu
Established: 1979 Annual Undergrad Tuition & Fees: $16,504
Enrollment: 70 Coed
Affiliation or Control: Proprietary IRS Status: Proprietary
Highest Offering: Associate Degree
Program: Occupational
Accreditation: ACCSC

01 President/Director .... Mrs. Betty D. TRUXILLO
05 Chief Academic Officer .... Ms. Pauline ROBERTS
37 Financial Aid Assistant .... Vacant
06 Registrar .... Ms. Cheryl DIFFEY

Blue Cliff College (D)

120 James Comeaux Road, Lafayette LA 70508
County: Lafayette FICE Identification: 034226
Unit ID: 439491
Telephone: (337) 269-0620 Carnegie Class: Assoc/PrivFP
FAX Number: (337) 269-0688 Calendar System: Quarter
URL: www.bluecliffcollege.com
Established: 1987 Annual Undergrad Tuition & Fees: $14,644
Enrollment: 14,344 Coed
Affiliation or Control: Proprietary IRS Status: Proprietary
Highest Offering: Associate Degree
Program: Occupational; Technical Emphasis
Accreditation: ACCSC

01 Director .... Ms. Teresa RICE
32 Sr Student Services Coordinator .... Mrs. Leah HYDE
07 Director of Admissions .... Mr. Dalton DURAL

Blue Cliff College (E)

3200 Cleary Avenue, Metairie LA 70002-5714
County: Jefferson FICE Identification: 032943
Unit ID: 434821
Telephone: (504) 456-3141 Carnegie Class: Assoc/PrivFP
FAX Number: (504) 456-7849 Calendar System: Quarter
URL: www.bluecliffcollege.com
Established: 1987 Annual Undergrad Tuition & Fees: N/A
Enrollment: 555 Coed
Affiliation or Control: Proprietary IRS Status: Proprietary
Highest Offering: Associate Degree
Program: Occupational
Accreditation: ACCSC

01 President/CEO .... Mr. Reggie MOORE
05 Campus Director .... Mr. Doug ROBERTSON

Cameron College (F)

2740 Canal Street, New Orleans LA 70119-5500
County: Orleans FICE Identification: 022340
Unit ID: 158440
Telephone: (504) 821-5881 Carnegie Class: Assoc/PrivFP
FAX Number: (504) 822-3467 Calendar System: Other
URL: www.cameroncollege.com
Established: 1981 Annual Undergrad Tuition & Fees: $10,730
Enrollment: 212 Coed
Affiliation or Control: Proprietary IRS Status: Proprietary
Highest Offering: Associate Degree
Program: Occupational
Accreditation: COE

01 President .... Ms. Eleanor W. CAMERON

Career Technical College (G)

2319 Louisville Avenue, Monroe LA 71201-6126
County: Ouachita FICE Identification: 026068
Unit ID: 367112
Telephone: (318) 323-2889 Carnegie Class: Assoc/PrivFP
FAX Number: (318) 324-9883 Calendar System: Quarter
URL: www.careertc.edu
Established: 1988 Annual Undergrad Tuition & Fees: $14,160
Enrollment: 750 Coed
Affiliation or Control: Proprietary IRS Status: Proprietary
Highest Offering: Associate Degree
Program: Occupational; 2-Year Principally Bachelor's Creditable; Technical Emphasis
Accreditation: COE, ACICS, MAC, RAD, SURGT

01 College Director .... Ms. Cheryl P. LOKEY

Centenary College of Louisiana (H)

PO Box 41188, Shreveport LA 71134-1188
County: Caddo FICE Identification: 002003
Unit ID: 158477
Telephone: (318) 869-5011 Carnegie Class: Bac/A&S
FAX Number: (318) 869-5010 Calendar System: Semester
URL: www.centenary.edu
Established: 1825 Annual Undergrad Tuition & Fees: $29,500
Enrollment: 891 Coed
Affiliation or Control: United Methodist IRS Status: 501(c)3
Highest Offering: Master's
Program: Liberal Arts And General; Teacher Preparatory; Professional
Accreditation: SC, MUS, @TEAC, TED

01 President .... Dr. B. David ROWE
04 Exec Assistant to the President .... Mrs. Connie WHITTINGTON
05 Dean of the College & Provost .... Dr. Michael R. HEMPHILL
50 Dean of the School of Business .... Dr. Christopher L. MARTIN
64 Dean of the School of Music .... Dr. Gale ODOM
30 Vice President for Inst Advancement .... Mr. Scott RAWLES
84 Vice President of Enrollment Svcs .... Mr. Monty L. CURTIS
10 Vice President for Finance/Admin .... Mr. Michael PEARSON
32 VP Student Development .... Vacant
13 Director of Information Technology .... Mr. Scott MERRITT
21 Controller .... Mrs. Marie DAVIS
41 Director of Athletics & Wellness .... Mrs. Ronda SEAGRAVES
32 Dean of Students .... Dr. Mark MILLER
38 Director of Counseling .... Ms. Tina FELDT
37 Director of Financial Aid .... Mrs. Lynette VISKOZKI
06 Registrar/Director of Re-Enrollment .... Ms. Nicole DEESE
08 Librarian .... Ms. Christy WRENN
26 Director Marketing & Communications .... Ms. Margo SHIDELER
29 Director of Alumni Relations .... Ms. Saige WILHITE
38 Director of Career Services .... Mr. Dennis TAYLOR
18 Director of Facilities .... Mr. Chris SAMPITE
46 Director Sponsored Research .... Ms. Patty J. ROBERTS
88 Director of Church Relations .... Rev. Betsy EAVES
44 Sr Director of Annual Giving .... Mr. Fred LANDRY
07 Director of Admissions .... Mrs. Gail ROBERSON
15 Human Resources Director .... Ms. Tracy MARANTO-PHILLIPS
19 Director of Public Safety .... Mr. Eddie WALKER

Delta College of Arts & Technology (I)

7380 Exchange Place, Baton Rouge LA 70806-3851
County: East Baton Rouge FICE Identification: 025383
Unit ID: 366270
Telephone: (225) 928-7770 Carnegie Class: Assoc/PrivFP
FAX Number: (225) 927-9096 Calendar System: Other
URL: www.deltacollege.com
Established: 1983 Annual Undergrad Tuition & Fees: $22,100
Enrollment: 568 Coed
Affiliation or Control: Proprietary IRS Status: Proprietary
Highest Offering: Associate Degree
Program: Occupational; 2-Year Principally Bachelor's Creditable; Nursing Emphasis
Accreditation: ACCSC

01 President .... Mr. Billy L. CLARK

Delta School of Business & Technology, DBA Delta Tech (J)

517 Broad Street, Lake Charles LA 70601-4334
County: Calcasieu FICE Identification: 020555
Unit ID: 158723
Telephone: (337) 439-5765 Carnegie Class: Assoc/PrivFP
FAX Number: (337) 436-5151 Calendar System: Quarter
URL: www.deltatech.edu
Established: 1970 Annual Undergrad Tuition & Fees: $9,590
Enrollment: 300 Coed
Affiliation or Control: Proprietary IRS Status: Proprietary
Highest Offering: Associate Degree
Program: Occupational
Accreditation: ACICS

01 Chief Executive Officer .... Mr. Jeff EDWARDS
10 Chief Fiscal Officer/Corp Secretary .... Mrs. Nina LEBLANC

Dillard University (A)

2601 Gentilly Boulevard, New Orleans LA 70122-3097
County: Orleans FICE Identification: 002004
Unit ID: 158802
Telephone: (504) 283-8822 Carnegie Class: Bac/A&S
FAX Number: N/A Calendar System: Semester
URL: www.dillard.edu
Established: 1869 Annual Undergrad Tuition & Fees: $15,520
Enrollment: 1,249 Coed
Affiliation or Control: United Methodist IRS Status: 501(c)3
Highest Offering: Baccalaureate
Program: Liberal Arts And General; Teacher Preparatory; Professional
Accreditation: **SC**, NUR

01 President ... Dr. Walter M. KIMBROUGH
03 Executive Vice President ... Dr. Walter L. STRONG
05 Provost/Sr VP for Academic Affairs ... Dr. Phyllis W. DAWKINS
32 Vice President for Student Success ... Dr. Toya BARNES-TEAMER
43 VP for Legal Affairs ... Ms. Debra NEVEU
10 Interim VP for Business & Finance ... Ms. Wanda BROOKS
20 Associate Provost ... Vacant
07 Asst VP of Admissions ... Dr. Alecia CYPRIAN
18 Assoc Vice Pres Facilities Mgmt ... Mr. Keith MCKENDALL
36 Director of Career/Prof Services ... Dr. Dawn WILLIAMS
06 Director of Records & Registration ... Ms. Pamela ENGLAND
37 Int Dir Financial Aid/Scholarships ... Ms. Shannon NEAL
102 Assoc VP Research & Spons Programs ... Mr. Theodore CALLIER
30 Int Assistant VP for Development ... Dr. Troy BALDWIN
100 Assistant to the President ... Vacant
09 Director of Institutional Research ... Dr. Willie KIRKLAND
27 Asst Vice Pres Community Devel ... Mr. Nick L. HARRIS
19 Chief of Police ... Mr. Andre' MENZIES
16 Director of Human Resources ... Ms. Lori KNIGHT
26 Sr Dir of Marketing Communications ... Ms. Mona DUFFEL-JONES
97 Dean of College of General Studies ... Dr. Dorothy SMITH
08 Interim Dean of Library/Learning ... Ms. Cynthia CHARLES
49 Dean of College of Arts & Sciences ... Dr. Robert COLLINS
96 Purchasing Officer ... Ms. Anlatear KIRKLIN

Herzing University (B)

2500 Williams Boulevard, Kenner LA 70062
County: Jefferson Identification: 666450
Unit ID: 433536
Telephone: (504) 733-0074 Carnegie Class: Bac/Assoc
FAX Number: (504) 733-0020 Calendar System: Semester
URL: www.herzing.edu
Established: 1996 Annual Undergrad Tuition & Fees: $14,200
Enrollment: 393 Coed
Affiliation or Control: Proprietary IRS Status: Proprietary
Highest Offering: Baccalaureate
Program: Occupational; 2-Year Principally Bachelor's Creditable; Technical Emphasis
Accreditation: **&NH**, MAAB, SURTEC

01 President ... Mr. Mark ASPIAZU
05 Academic Dean ... Ms. Stephanie BURNS
07 Director of Admissions ... Ms. Chrissy KALIVITIS
37 Director of Financial Services ... Ms. Ava B. GOMEZ
36 Director of Career Services ... Ms. Myeshia S. AMBROSE

† Regional accreditation is carried under the parent institution in Madison, WI.

ITI Technical College (C)

13944 Airline Highway, Baton Rouge LA 70817-5998
County: East Baton Rouge FICE Identification: 021662
Unit ID: 159197
Telephone: (225) 752-4230 Carnegie Class: Assoc/PrivFP
FAX Number: (225) 756-0903 Calendar System: Quarter
URL: www.iticollege.edu
Established: 1973 Annual Undergrad Tuition & Fees: $26,650
Enrollment: 537 Coed
Affiliation or Control: Proprietary IRS Status: Proprietary
Highest Offering: Associate Degree
Program: Occupational; Technical Emphasis
Accreditation: **ACCSC**

01 President ... Mr. Earl Joe MARTIN, III
03 Vice President ... Mr. Mark WORTHY
05 Dean of Education ... Mr. Louis BABIN

ITT Technical Institute (D)

14111 Airline Hwy, Suite 101,
Baton Rouge LA 70817-6241
County: East Baton Rouge Parish Identification: 666164
Unit ID: 450216
Telephone: (225) 754-5800 Carnegie Class: Assoc/PrivFP4
FAX Number: N/A Calendar System: Quarter
URL: www.itt-tech.edu
Established: 2006 Annual Undergrad Tuition & Fees: N/A
Enrollment: 626 Coed
Affiliation or Control: Proprietary IRS Status: Proprietary
Highest Offering: Baccalaureate
Program: Technical Emphasis
Accreditation: **ACICS**

† Branch campus of ITT Technical Institute, Indianapolis, IN.

ITT Technical Institute (E)

140 James Drive East, Saint Rose LA 70087-4005
County: St. Charles Identification: 666031
Unit ID: 437042
Telephone: (504) 463-0338 Carnegie Class: Spec/Tech
FAX Number: (504) 463-0979 Calendar System: Quarter
URL: www.itt-tech.edu
Established: 1968 Annual Undergrad Tuition & Fees: N/A
Enrollment: 623 Coed
Affiliation or Control: Proprietary IRS Status: Proprietary
Highest Offering: Baccalaureate
Program: Technical Emphasis
Accreditation: **ACICS**

† Branch campus of ITT Technical Institute, Indianapolis, IN.

Louisiana College (F)

1140 College Drive, Pineville LA 71359-0001
County: Rapides FICE Identification: 002007
Unit ID: 159568
Telephone: (318) 487-7011 Carnegie Class: Bac/Diverse
FAX Number: (318) 487-7191 Calendar System: Semester
URL: www.lacollege.edu
Established: 1906 Annual Undergrad Tuition & Fees: $13,780
Enrollment: 1,557 Coed
Affiliation or Control: Southern Baptist IRS Status: 501(c)3
Highest Offering: Master's
Program: Liberal Arts And General; Teacher Preparatory
Accreditation: **SC**, ACBSP, NURSE, PTAA, SW, TED

01 President ... Dr. Joe AGUILLARD
05 Vice Pres Academic Affairs ... Vacant
10 Vice President for Business Affairs ... Mr. Randall HARGIS
30 Vice President for Inst Advancement ... Mr. Tim JOHNSON
32 Dean of Students ... Mr. Eric JOHNSON
20 Assistant Dean of the College ... Dr. Wade WARREN
06 Registrar ... Dr. Brad DUFFY
84 Director Enrollment Mgmt/Admissions ... Mr. Byron MCGEE
37 Director of Financial Aid ... Mr. Eric GOSSETT
08 Director of the Library ... Mr. Terry MARTIN
26 Director of Marketing ... Mr. John WILLIE
14 Director Computer Services ... Mr. Shane DAVIS
18 Director of Physical Plant ... Mr. Randall HARGIS
21 Director of Business Office ... Ms. Beverly INGRAM
39 Director of Housing ... Mr. Welson CESAR
41 Athletic Director ... Mr. Darrell PAYNE
42 Baptist Student Union Director ... Mr. Brandon ROBIN
44 Director Constituent Relations ... Mr. Danny MCVAY
35 Director Student Activities ... Ms. K. B THOMAS
36 Director Career Development ... Mrs. Leneil MERCER
09 Director of Institutional Research ... Mr. Bruce DEATON
38 Director Student Counseling ... Ms. Leneil MERCER
07 Director of Admissions ... Mr. Byron MCGEE
15 Director Personnel Services ... Ms. Shannon TASSIN
40 Bookstore Manager ... Mrs. Linda BILLINGSLEY
29 Coord Alumni Affairs/Fdn Rels ... Ms. Luana CUNNINGHAM
19 Coordinator of Safety & Security ... Mr. Dwayne ROGERS
23 Coordinator of Health Services ... Ms. Carla MARTIN
04 Assistant to the President ... Ms. Susan NIXON

*Louisiana Community & Technical College System (G)

265 S Foster Drive, Baton Rouge LA 70806-4104
County: East Baton Rouge Identification: 666188
Telephone: (225) 922-2800 Carnegie Class: N/A
FAX Number: (225) 922-2392
URL: www.lctcs.edu

01 President ... Dr. Joe MAY
03 Executive Vice President ... Dr. Neil MATKIN
10 Sr Vice Pres Finance & Admin ... Ms. Jan JACKSON
103 Sr VP Workforce/Career/Tech Educ ... Dr. G. Jeremiah RYAN
09 Asst VP of Institutional Research ... Dr. Albertha LAWSON
26 Director of Public Relations ... Ms. Kizzy PAYTON
30 Exec Director System Advancement ... Ms. Leah GOSS
04 Exec Assistant to the President ... Ms. Angel TETRICK
106 Executive Director of LCTCSOnline ... Dr. Robert JOHNSON

*Baton Rouge Community College (H)

201 Community College Drive,
Baton Rouge LA 70806-4156
County: East Baton Rouge FICE Identification: 037303
Unit ID: 437103
Telephone: (225) 216-8000 Carnegie Class: Assoc/Pub-U-SC
FAX Number: (225) 216-8100 Calendar System: Semester
URL: www.mybrcc.edu
Established: 1998 Annual Undergrad Tuition & Fees (In-District): $2,832
Enrollment: 8,275 Coed
Affiliation or Control: State/Local IRS Status: 501(c)3
Highest Offering: Associate Degree
Program: Occupational; 2-Year Principally Bachelor's Creditable
Accreditation: **SC**, ACBSP, ADNUR, NAIT

02 Chancellor ... Dr. Andrea L. MILLER
32 Int Vice Chancellor Student Affairs ... Dr. Girard MELANCON
30 Vice Chanc Economic Development ... Ms. Phyllis MOUTON
05 Int Vice Chancellor Acad Affairs ... Ms. Monique CROSS
10 Vice Chanc Administration & Finance ... Ms. Pam DIEZ
45 Exec Dir Strategic Planning/Analys ... Ms. Ann ZANDERS
84 Int Exec Director Enrollment Svcs ... Dr. Teresa JONES
09 Director of Inst Effectiveness ... Dr. Shana CORVERS
15 Interim Director of HR/Payroll ... Mr. William DALTON
18 Chief of Facilities/Physical Plant ... Vacant
10 Chief Financial Officer ... Ms. Helen HARRIS
26 Exec Dir Pub Rels/Performing Arts ... Mr. Steve MITCHELL
29 Director of External Resources ... Ms. Georgia SCOBEE
35 Dir Student Programs & Resources ... Ms. Stacia HARDY
36 Director Career and Job Placement ... Ms. Lisa HIBNER
37 Director Student Financial Aid ... Mr. Johnny MANELA
38 Exec Dir for Advising & Counseling ... Ms. Vinetta FRIE
41 Athletic Director ... Mr. Neil HAYHURST
88 Director of Disability Services ... Ms. Wendy DEVALL
88 Dir of Academic Learning Center ... Ms. Jeanne STACY
25 Project Director Title III ... Ms. Tanasha BROWN
88 Upward Bound Program Director ... Ms. Darica SIMON
96 Director of Purchasing ... Mr. Michael CONSTANTIN

*Bossier Parish Community College (I)

6220 E Texas Street, Bossier City LA 71111-6922
County: Bossier FICE Identification: 020554
Unit ID: 158431
Telephone: (318) 678-6000 Carnegie Class: Assoc/Pub-R-M
FAX Number: (318) 678-6389 Calendar System: Semester
URL: www.bpcc.edu
Established: 1966 Annual Undergrad Tuition & Fees (In-District): $2,730
Enrollment: 7,077 Coed
Affiliation or Control: State/Local IRS Status: 501(c)3
Highest Offering: Associate Degree
Program: Occupational; 2-Year Principally Bachelor's Creditable
Accreditation: **SC**, ACFEI, ADNUR, EMT, MAC, NAIT, OTA, PTAA, SURGT

02 Chancellor ... Mr. James B. HENDERSON
05 VC for Academic Affairs ... Dr. Stan WILKINS
11 VC Business Affs/Economic Devel ... Mr. Tom WILLIAMS
32 VC of Student Affairs ... Ms. Karen RECCHIA
10 Chief Financial Officer ... Ms. Michelle BREWER
20 Assoc VC Planning/Instruction ... Ms. Lesa TAYLOR-DUPREE
60 Dean of Comm & Performing Arts ... Mr. Ray Scott CRAWFORD
103 Dean of Workforce Develop/Cont Educ ... Ms. Lisa WARGO
08 Dean of Learning Resources ... Ms. Brenda BRANTLEY
88 Dean for Innovative Learning ... Ms. Donna WOMACK
21 Comptroller ... Ms. Carol BATES
38 Student Counselor ... Mr. Morris ROBINSON
37 Director Student Financial Aid ... Ms. Vickie TEMPLE
06 Registrar ... Ms. Patty H. STEWART
26 Director of Public Relations ... Ms. Tracy MCGILL
16 Director of Human Resources ... Mrs. Teri BASHARA
35 Director of Student Life ... Ms. Marjoree HARPER
13 Chief Information Officer ... Mr. Gary HOLLATZ
22 Diversity/Multicultural Affairs ... Ms. Cindy DARBY
72 Director of Educational Technology ... Ms. Kathleen GAY
18 Dir Physical Plant & Maintenance ... Mr. Joe ST. ANDRE
29 Director Alumni Relations ... Ms. Stephanie ROGERS
09 Dir Inst Research/Assessment/Grants ... Ms. Lisa WHEELER
96 Director of Purchasing ... Ms. Gayle DOUCET

*Capital Area Technical College Baton Rouge Campus (J)

3250 N Acadian Thruway E, Baton Rouge LA 70805-6699
County: East Baton Rouge FICE Identification: 005488
Unit ID: 158352
Telephone: (225) 359-9201 Carnegie Class: Assoc/Pub-U-MC
FAX Number: (225) 359-9306 Calendar System: Semester
URL: www.catc.edu
Established: 1944 Annual Undergrad Tuition & Fees (In-District): $1,900
Enrollment: 2,316 Coed
Affiliation or Control: State/Local IRS Status: 501(c)3
Highest Offering: Associate Degree
Program: Occupational; Technical Emphasis
Accreditation: **COE**, ACFEI, NAIT

02 Regional Director ... Dr. Kay MCDANIEL
07 Senior Admissions Officer ... Ms. Buffy BRINKLEY
05 Chief Academic Officer ... Ms. Phyllis BECKMAN
10 Chief Business Officer ... Mr. Mike HUBBS
26 Chief Development/Public Rels Ofcr ... Mrs. Tammy BROWN
103 Chief Workforce Development Officer ... Mr. LaMoyne WILLIAMS
06 Records Officer ... Ms. Buffy BRINKLEY
37 Financial Aid Officer ... Ms. Latreva WALKER
38 Director Student Counseling ... Ms. Buffy BRINKLEY
09 Director of Institutional Research ... Mrs. Rebecca LOVELL
96 Director of Purchasing ... Ms. Darlene HELM
15 Human Resources Manager ... Ms. Donna PEREZ
18 Facilities & Property Manager ... Mr. Mark VIGNES

*Capital Area Technical College Folkes Campus (K)

3337 Highway 10 E, Jackson LA 70748-6240
County: East Feliciana FICE Identification: 025099
Unit ID: 158945
Telephone: (225) 634-2636 Carnegie Class: Not Classified
FAX Number: (225) 634-4225 Calendar System: Semester
URL: www.catc.edu/folkes
Established: 1977 Annual Undergrad Tuition & Fees (In-District): $1,542
Enrollment: 475 Coed
Affiliation or Control: State/Local IRS Status: 501(c)3

Highest Offering: Associate Degree
Program: Occupational; Technical Emphasis
Accreditation: COE

02 Campus Administrator ....Mr. Johnny ARCENEAUX
18 Chf Facilities/Dir Security/Safety ....Mr. David MOFFAT
06 Registrar ....Mrs. Loretta PROFIT

† Branch campus of Capital Area Technical College Baton Rouge Campus.

*Capital Area Technical College Jumonville Campus (A)

PO Box 725, New Roads LA 70760-0725
County: Pointe Coupee FICE Identification: 005478
Unit ID: 160214
Telephone: (225) 638-8613 Carnegie Class: Not Classified
FAX Number: (225) 618-0157 Calendar System: Semester
URL: www.ltc.edu
Established: 1952 Annual Undergrad Tuition & Fees (In-District): $1,108
Enrollment: 259 Coed
Affiliation or Control: State/Local IRS Status: 501(c)3
Highest Offering: Associate Degree
Program: Occupational; Technical Emphasis
Accreditation: COE

02 Campus Dean ....Ms. Amy DAVIS

† Branch campus of Capital Area Technical College Baton Rouge Campus.

*Central Louisiana Technical College Avoyelles Campus (B)

508 Choupique Street, Cottonport LA 71327-3743
County: Avoyelles FICE Identification: 008317
Unit ID: 158237
Telephone: (318) 876-2401 Carnegie Class: Not Classified
FAX Number: (318) 876-2634 Calendar System: Semester
URL: www.ltc.edu
Established: 1938 Annual Undergrad Tuition & Fees (In-District): $1,542
Enrollment: 378 Coed
Affiliation or Control: State/Local IRS Status: 501(c)3
Highest Offering: Associate Degree
Program: Occupational; Technical Emphasis
Accreditation: COE

02 Campus Dean ....Mr. Jude PITRE

*Central Louisiana Technical College Huey P. Long Campus (C)

5960 Highway 167 N, Winnfield LA 71483-5075
County: Winn FICE Identification: 005480
Unit ID: 159090
Telephone: (318) 628-4342 Carnegie Class: Not Classified
FAX Number: (318) 628-7768 Calendar System: Semester
URL: www.ltc.edu
Established: 1938 Annual Undergrad Tuition & Fees (In-District): $1,542
Enrollment: 310 Coed
Affiliation or Control: State/Local IRS Status: 501(c)3
Highest Offering: Associate Degree
Program: Occupational; Technical Emphasis
Accreditation: COE

02 Campus Dean ....Mr. Danny KEYES

*Central Louisiana Technical College Oakdale Campus (D)

117 Highway 1152, Oakdale LA 71463-3536
County: Allen FICE Identification: 030026
Unit ID: 160047
Telephone: (318) 335-3944 Carnegie Class: Assoc/Pub-R-S
FAX Number: (318) 335-3347 Calendar System: Quarter
URL: www.ltc.edu
Established: N/A Annual Undergrad Tuition & Fees (In-District): $1,542
Enrollment: 456 Coed
Affiliation or Control: State/Local IRS Status: 501(c)3
Highest Offering: Associate Degree
Program: Occupational; Technical Emphasis
Accreditation: COE

02 Campus Coordinator ....Ms. Donnis POE

*Central Louisiana Technical Community College (E)

PO Box 5698, Alexandria LA 71307-5698
County: Rapides FICE Identification: 005489
Unit ID: 158088
Telephone: (318) 487-5443 Carnegie Class: Assoc/Pub-R-S
FAX Number: (318) 487-5970 Calendar System: Trimester
URL: www.region6.ltc.edu
Established: 1965 Annual Undergrad Tuition & Fees (In-State): $1,474
Enrollment: 2,190 Coed
Affiliation or Control: State IRS Status: 501(c)3
Highest Offering: Associate Degree
Program: Occupational; Technical Emphasis
Accreditation: COE

02 Interim Chancellor ....Mr. Michael ELAM
05 Int Asst Campus Dean/Chf Acad Ofcr ....Ms. Carol HEBERT

*Delgado Community College (F)

615 City Park Avenue, New Orleans LA 70119-4399
County: Orleans FICE Identification: 004625
Unit ID: 158662
Telephone: (504) 671-5000 Carnegie Class: Assoc/Pub-U-MC
FAX Number: (504) 361-6699 Calendar System: Semester
URL: www.dcc.edu
Established: 1921 Annual Undergrad Tuition & Fees (In-District): $3,330
Enrollment: 20,436 Coed
Affiliation or Control: State/Local IRS Status: 501(c)3
Highest Offering: Associate Degree
Program: Occupational; 2-Year Principally Bachelor's Creditable
Accreditation: SC, ACBSP, ACFEI, ADNUR, DIETT, DMS, EMT, ENGT, FUSER, MLTAD, NAIT, NMT, OTA, PTAA, RAD, RTT, SURGT

02 Chancellor ....Dr. Monty SULLIVAN
10 Vice Chanc Business/Admin Affairs ....Mr. Aristide C. EAGAN, III
05 Vice Chanc Acad Affs/Col Provost ....Ms. Deborah R. LEA
103 Asst Vice Chanc Workforce Dev/Educ ....Dr. Leroy KENDRICK
66 Exec Dean School of Nursing Campus ....Dr. Cheryl MYERS
76 Dean of Allied Health ....Mr. Ray GISCLAIR
50 Dean Business & Technology ....Mr. Warren PUNEKY
60 Dean of Communication Division ....Mr. Lester ADELSBERG
81 Dean Science & Math ....Mr. Thomas GRUBER
79 Dean of Arts and Humanities ....Ms. Patrice MOORE
106 Dean of Dist Learn and Instr Tech ....Ms. Melissa LACOUR
12 Dean Northshore ....Ms. Ashley CHITWOOD
12 Exec Dean West Bank Campus ....Ms. Larissa L. STEIB
26 Exec Director of Public Relations ....Ms. Carol GNIADY
09 Exec Dir Inst Research/Alumni Rels ....Ms. Nita HUTTER
88 Exec Dir of Curriculum & Pgm Devel ....Mr. Timothy STAMM
32 Asst VC of Student Affairs ....Ms. Arnel COSEY
15 Asst Vice Chanc for Human Resources ....Ms. Carmen WALTERS
14 Asst VC of Information Technology ....Mr. Thomas LOVINCE
21 Asst VC of Budget & Finance ....Mr. Steve CAZAUBON
18 Asst VC of Dir Facilities/Planning ....Mr. Adolfo GIRAU
21 Asst VC/Comptroller ....Mr. Ronald RODRIGUEZ
88 Senior Compliance Officer ....Mr. Steve ZERINGUE
04 Executive Asst to the Chancellor ....Ms. Traci SMOTHERS
72 Asst Dean Business & Technology ....Mr. Rene CINTRON
55 Asst Dean Evening and Weekend Div ....Ms. Mercedes MUNSTER
08 Librarian ....Ms. Denise REPMAN
37 Director Financial Aid ....Ms. Germaine EDWARDS
41 Athletic Director ....Mr. Tommy SMITH
06 College Registrar ....Ms. Maria CISNEROS
07 Director Admissions/Enrollment Svcs ....Ms. Gwen BOUTTE
25 Director of Grants Development ....Dr. Claudia SAUCIER
35 Director of Student Life ....Mrs. Michelle GRECO
88 Director Ofc of Advising & Testing ....Ms. Tania CARRADINE
96 Director of Purchasing ....Ms. Susan VARBLE
19 Director of Campus Police ....Mr. Ronald DOUCETTE
88 Director of Auxiliary Services ....Mr. Timothy GALLIANO

*L.E. Fletcher Technical Community College (G)

PO Box 5033, Houma LA 70361-5033
County: Terrebonne FICE Identification: 005761
Unit ID: 160481
Telephone: (985) 857-3655 Carnegie Class: Assoc/Pub-U-MC
FAX Number: (985) 857-3689 Calendar System: Semester
URL: www.fletcher.edu
Established: 1948 Annual Undergrad Tuition & Fees (In-State): $2,831
Enrollment: 2,486 Coed
Affiliation or Control: State IRS Status: Exempt
Highest Offering: Associate Degree
Program: Occupational; 2-Year Principally Bachelor's Creditable
Accreditation: SC, COE, NAIT, PNUR

02 Chancellor ....Mr. F. Travis LAVIGNE, JR.
05 Vice Chancellor Instruction ....Mr. William H. TULAK
06 Registrar ....Ms. Lisa HIDALGO
09 Director of Institutional Research ....Mr. Stanton MCNEELY
10 Vice Chancellor Finance & Admin ....Mr. Bryan E. GLATTER
30 Director Institutional Development ....Ms. Marianne MCCRORY
32 Dean of Student Affairs ....Vacant
75 Dean of Technical Education ....Ms. Fathia WILLIAMS
66 Dean of Nursing and Allied Health ....Ms. Sonia CLARKE
07 Director of Admissions ....Ms. Anglea HEBERT
15 HR Manager ....Mrs. Dale SHAW
37 Director of Financial Aid ....Mrs. Shawn TRAVIS
04 Assistant to the Chancellor ....Ms. Brenda FAUCHEUX
08 Head Librarian ....Mrs. Suzanne MARTIN
26 Director of Public Relations ....Mrs. Elmy SAVOIE
49 Dean Art and Sciences ....Mrs. Donna ESTRADA
103 Director of Workforce Education ....Mrs. Catherine BARBER
75 Director of LAMPI ....Mr. Breck CHAISSON

*Louisiana Delta Community College (H)

7500 Millhaven Road, Monroe LA 71203
County: Ouachita Parish FICE Identification: 041301
Unit ID: 440624
Telephone: (318) 345-9000 Carnegie Class: Assoc/Pub-R-S
FAX Number: N/A Calendar System: Semester
URL: www.ladelta.edu
Established: 2001 Annual Undergrad Tuition & Fees (In-District): $2,931
Enrollment: 2,953 Coed
Affiliation or Control: State/Local IRS Status: 501(c)3
Highest Offering: Associate Degree
Program: Occupational; 2-Year Principally Bachelor's Creditable
Accreditation: SC, ADNUR

02 Interim Chancellor ....Dr. Jerry RYAN
05 Interim V Chancellor of Academic ....Mrs. Margie MIXON
10 Interim V C of Finance & Administra ....Mrs. Melissa DUCOTE
20 Registrar ....Mr. Joe MANSOUR
32 Interim V C of Student Affairs ....Ms. Alvina THOMAS
30 Dir of Institutional Advancement ....Mr. Keith ADAMS
13 Chief Information Officer ....Mr. Bradley MASTERS

*Northeast Louisiana Technical College Bastrop Campus (I)

PO Box 1120 Kammell Street, Bastrop LA 71221-1120
County: Morehouse Identification: 667030
Telephone: (318) 283-0836 Carnegie Class: Not Classified
FAX Number: (318) 283-0871 Calendar System: Semester
URL: www.region8.ltc.edu
Established: N/A Annual Undergrad Tuition & Fees (In-District): $2,931
Enrollment: 321 Coed
Affiliation or Control: State/Local IRS Status: 501(c)3
Highest Offering: Associate Degree
Program: Occupational; Technical Emphasis
Accreditation: COE

02 Regional Director/Campus Director ....Norene R. SMITH
05 Interim Asst Campus Dean ....Loe DUNN

*Northeast Louisiana Technical College Delta-Ouachita Campus (J)

609 Vocational Parkway, West Monroe LA 71292-0128
County: Quachita FICE Identification: 005471
Unit ID: 158769
Telephone: (318) 397-6100 Carnegie Class: Assoc/Pub-R-S
FAX Number: (318) 397-6106 Calendar System: Semester
URL: www.myneltc.edu
Established: 1981 Annual Undergrad Tuition & Fees (In-District): $2,931
Enrollment: 1,531 Coed
Affiliation or Control: State/Local IRS Status: 501(c)3
Highest Offering: Associate Degree
Program: Occupational; Technical Emphasis
Accreditation: COE, NAIT

02 Regional Director ....Vacant
05 Asst Dean/Chf Acad/Stdnt Affs Ofcr ....Ms. Margie F. MIXON
07 Director of Admissions ....Ms. Kathy GARDNER
15 Chief Human Resources Officer ....Ms. Dana ILIFF
10 Chief Financial Officer ....Mrs. Margie BROWN
18 Asst Dean/Chief Facilities Officer ....Mr. Greg GROVES
21 Associate Business Officer ....Mr. Patrick TURNER
37 Director Student Financial Aid ....Mr. Adiran TURNER

*Northeast Louisiana Technical College Farmerville Campus (K)

605 W Boundary Street, Farmerville LA 71241-2067
County: Union FICE Identification: 005476
Unit ID: 159984
Telephone: (318) 368-3179 Carnegie Class: Not Classified
FAX Number: (318) 368-9180 Calendar System: Semester
URL: www.ltc.edu
Established: 1952 Annual Undergrad Tuition & Fees (In-District): $2,931
Enrollment: 95 Coed
Affiliation or Control: State/Local IRS Status: 501(c)3
Highest Offering: Associate Degree
Program: Occupational; Technical Emphasis
Accreditation: COE

02 Vice Chancellor ....Mrs. Norene R. SMITH
05 Dean ....Mr. Doug POSTEL
32 Asst Dean Student Affairs ....Ms. Lum FARR

*Northeast Louisiana Technical College Northeast Campus (L)

1710 Warren Street, Winnsboro LA 71295-2940
County: Franklin FICE Identification: 005475
Unit ID: 160001
Telephone: (318) 435-2163 Carnegie Class: Assoc/Pub-R-S
FAX Number: (318) 435-2166 Calendar System: Semester
URL: www.ltc.edu
Established: 1952 Annual Undergrad Tuition & Fees (In-District): $2,931
Enrollment: 377 Coed
Affiliation or Control: State/Local IRS Status: 501(c)3
Highest Offering: Associate Degree
Program: Occupational; Technical Emphasis
Accreditation: COE

02 Campus Dean ....Mrs. Debbie M. PRICE

*Northeast Louisiana Technicial College Ruston Campus (M)

1010 James Street, PO Box 1070, Ruston LA 71273-1070
FICE Identification: 023404
Unit ID: 160366

Telephone: (318) 251-4145 Carnegie Class: Assoc/Pub-R-S
FAX Number: (318) 251-4159 Calendar System: Semester
URL: www.region8.ltc.edu
Established: 1977 Annual Undergrad Tuition & Fees (In-District): $2,931
Enrollment: 270 Coed
Affiliation or Control: State/Local IRS Status: 501(c)3
Highest Offering: Associate Degree
Program: Occupational; Technical Emphasis
Accreditation: COE

02 Campus Dean .... Mr. Doug POSTEL

*Northshore Technical Community College (A)

1710 Sullivan Drive, Bogalusa LA 70427-5866
County: Washington FICE Identification: 006756
Unit ID: 160667
Telephone: (985) 732-6640 Carnegie Class: Assoc/Pub-U-MC
FAX Number: (985) 732-6603 Calendar System: Trimester
URL: www.northshorecollege.edu
Established: 1930 Annual Undergrad Tuition & Fees (In-District): $1,946
Enrollment: 3,349 Coed
Affiliation or Control: State/Local IRS Status: 501(c)3
Highest Offering: Associate Degree
Program: Occupational; 2-Year Principally Bachelor's Creditable; Technical Emphasis
Accreditation: COE

02 Dean .... Mr. William S. WAINWRIGHT
05 Associate Dean .... Mr. William POTTER
20 Assistant Dean .... Ms. Gayle LADNER
32 Student Services Officer .... Ms. Debra SHERMAN
09 Dir of Institutional Research & Eff .... Ms. Shelia SINGLETARY
10 Vice Chancellor Finance & Admin .... Mr. Marc CHAUVIN
15 Human Resources Director .... Ms. Joanna DILLMAN
18 Chief Facilities/Physical Plant .... Mr. Gerald BLAPPERT
103 Chief Workforce Development .... Ms. Stephanie BADEAUX
37 Director of Financial Aid .... Mr. Mack JACKSON, III
96 Director of Purchasing .... Ms. Ann LUMPKIN

*Northwest Louisiana Technical College Natchitoches Campus (B)

6587 Highway 1 Bypass (3110),
Natchitoches LA 71458-0657
County: Natchitoches FICE Identification: 021602
Unit ID: 159823
Telephone: (318) 357-3162 Carnegie Class: Assoc/Pub-R-S
FAX Number: (318) 352-2248 Calendar System: Semester
URL: www.ltc.edu
Established: 1938 Annual Undergrad Tuition & Fees (In-District): $1,542
Enrollment: 9,191 Coed
Affiliation or Control: State/Local IRS Status: 501(c)3
Highest Offering: Associate Degree
Program: Occupational; Technical Emphasis
Accreditation: COE

02 Campus Dean .... Laurie MORROW
32 Asst Dean Student Affairs .... Moses BAINES

† Branch campus of Northwest Louisiana Technical College Northwest Campus, Minden, LA.

*Northwest Louisiana Technical College Northwest Campus (C)

PO Box 835, Minden LA 71058-0835
County: Webster FICE Identification: 009975
Unit ID: 160010
Telephone: (318) 371-3035 Carnegie Class: Assoc/Pub-R-S
FAX Number: (318) 371-3055 Calendar System: Trimester
URL: www.ltc.edu
Established: 1952 Annual Undergrad Tuition & Fees (In-District): $542
Enrollment: 2,870 Coed
Affiliation or Control: State/Local IRS Status: 501(c)3
Highest Offering: Associate Degree
Program: Occupational; 2-Year Principally Bachelor's Creditable; Technical Emphasis
Accreditation: COE

02 Campus Dean .... Mr. Charles T. STRONG
05 Assistant Dean .... Mr. David RHODES
32 Director of Student Services .... Mr. David RHODES
15 Director Personnel Services .... Ms. Lisa SNIDER
05 Assistant Dean .... Ms. Diane CLARK
37 Director Student Financial Aid .... Ms. Annette CHANLER

*Northwest Louisiana Technical College Shreveport Campus (D)

Box 78527, 2010 N Market Street,
Shreveport LA 71137-8527
County: Caddo FICE Identification: 005469
Unit ID: 160427
Telephone: (318) 676-7811 Carnegie Class: Assoc/Pub-R-S
FAX Number: (318) 676-7805 Calendar System: Semester
URL: www.nwltc.edu
Established: 1936 Annual Undergrad Tuition & Fees (In-District): $1,542
Enrollment: 1,500 Coed
Affiliation or Control: State/Local IRS Status: 501(c)3
Highest Offering: Associate Degree
Program: Occupational; 2-Year Principally Bachelor's Creditable; Technical Emphasis
Accreditation: COE

02 Regional Director .... Mr. Charles STRONG
05 Campus Dean .... Ms. Angie RYMER
32 Director of Student Affairs .... Ms. Cindy MAGGIO
20 Assistant Campus Dean .... Vacant
37 Student Financial Aid Officer .... Mr. Chris MOREE
84 Enrollment Data Base Management .... Ms. Cindy FLORES
37 Student Financial Aid Officer .... Ms. Nakesha HALL
15 Admin Svcs Ofcr II/District Hum Res .... Ms. Amber SAUNDERS
10 Regional CFO .... Ms. Patti LANN
96 Procurement Specialist .... Ms. Kim HENRY

† Branch campus of Northwest Louisiana Technical College Northwest Campus, Minden, LA.

*Nunez Community College (E)

3710 Paris Road, Chalmette LA 70043-1297
County: Saint Bernard FICE Identification: 021661
Unit ID: 158884
Telephone: (504) 278-6200 Carnegie Class: Assoc/Pub-S-SC
FAX Number: (504) 278-6480 Calendar System: Semester
URL: www.nunez.edu
Established: 1992 Annual Undergrad Tuition & Fees (In-District): $2,875
Enrollment: 2,416 Coed
Affiliation or Control: State/Local IRS Status: 501(c)3
Highest Offering: Associate Degree
Program: Occupational; 2-Year Principally Bachelor's Creditable
Accreditation: SC, NAIT

02 Chancellor .... Dr. Thomas R. WARNER
05 Vice Chanc for Acad & Student Affs .... Mrs. Annette ACCOMANDO
30 Ex Dir Inst Advanc/Ex Asst to Chanc .... Ms. Teresa L. SMITH
10 Chief Financial Officer .... Mr. Louis LEHR
32 Dean for Student Affairs .... Ms. Becky MAILLET
72 Dean of Business/Technology .... Vacant
45 Dir Planning/Inst Effectiveness .... Mr. Leonard UNBEHAGEN
08 Director of Library Services .... Mr. Richard DEFOE
15 Dir Human Res/Exec Asst to Chanc .... Dr. Carol MCLEOD
38 Student Counselor .... Mr. Tommie POWELL, III
06 Registrar .... Ms. Meg GREENFIELD
37 Director Financial Aid .... Ms. Glenda DESPENZA
103 Director Workforce Development .... Mr. Ernest T. FRAZIER, JR.
25 Director of Sponsored Programs .... Ms. Carly GERVAIS
29 Director Alumni Relations .... Vacant
18 Coordinator of Facilities .... Ms. Dawn HART-THORE
41 Coord Student Activities/Athletics .... Vacant
13 Computer Services Coordinator .... Mr. Jason HOSCH

*River Parishes Community College (F)

PO Box 310, Sorrento LA 70778-0310
County: Ascension FICE Identification: 037894
Unit ID: 436304
Telephone: (225) 675-8270 Carnegie Class: Assoc/Pub-S-SC
FAX Number: (225) 675-5478 Calendar System: Semester
URL: www.rpcc.edu
Established: 1999 Annual Undergrad Tuition & Fees (In-District): $2,803
Enrollment: 2,717 Coed
Affiliation or Control: State/Local IRS Status: 501(c)3
Highest Offering: Associate Degree
Program: 2-Year Principally Bachelor's Creditable
Accreditation: SC, NAIT

02 Chancellor .... Dr. Joe Ben WELCH
03 Executive Vice Chancellor .... Dr. William MARTIN
10 VC Business/Finance/Administration .... Clen BURTON
84 Dean of Students/Enrollment Mgmt .... Allison D. VICKNAIR
05 Dean of Academic Studies .... Dr. Crystal LEE
21 Director of Accounting & Payroll .... Lisa JACKSON
30 VC for Inst Advace & Effectiveness .... Dr. Lisa WATSON
06 Registrar .... Cara LANDRY
37 Director Financial Aid .... Terry MARTIN
38 Director Student Counseling .... Jennifer KLEINPETER
08 Director of Library Services .... Wendy JOHNSON
15 Human Resource Manager .... Donna WHITTINGTON
07 Admissions Counselor .... Dianna GILBERT
09 Director of Institutional Research .... Ashley GRAY

*South Central Louisiana Technical College Lafourche Campus (G)

1425 Tiger Drive, Thibodaux LA 70301-4336
County: LaFourche FICE Identification: 030091
Unit ID: 160719
Telephone: (985) 447-0924 Carnegie Class: Assoc/Pub-S-MC
FAX Number: (985) 447-0927 Calendar System: Semester
URL: www.ltc.edu
Established: 1976 Annual Undergrad Tuition & Fees (In-District): $1,200
Enrollment: 495 Coed
Affiliation or Control: State/Local IRS Status: 501(c)3
Highest Offering: Associate Degree
Program: Occupational; Technical Emphasis
Accreditation: COE, SURGT

02 Actg Campus Administrator .... Ms. Donna PITRE
07 Actg Director Admissions & Records .... Ms. Donna PITRE
10 Campus Accountant .... Ms. Robin GEASON
11 Administrative Coordinator .... Ms. Patricia L. BAKER
12 Campus Coordinator Galliano Campus .... Ms. Donna PITRE

† Branch campus of South Central Louisiana Technical College Young Memorial Campus.

*South Central Louisiana Technical College River Parishes Campus (H)

PO Drawer AQ, 181 Regala Park Road,
Reserve LA 70084-0542
County: Saint John the Baptist FICE Identification: 023334
Unit ID: 160311
Telephone: (985) 536-4418 Carnegie Class: Assoc/Pub-S-MC
FAX Number: (985) 536-7697 Calendar System: Quarter
URL: www.ltc.edu
Established: 1973 Annual Undergrad Tuition & Fees (In-District): $1,542
Enrollment: 1,427 Coed
Affiliation or Control: State/Local IRS Status: 501(c)3
Highest Offering: Associate Degree
Program: Occupational; Technical Emphasis
Accreditation: COE, NAIT

02 Campus Administrator .... Ms. Cynthia POSKEY
32 Director Student Affairs .... Ms. Annette THORNTON

† Branch campus of South Central Louisiana Technical Colege Young Memorial Campus.

*South Central Louisiana Technical College Young Memorial Campus (I)

900 Youngs Road, Morgan City LA 70380-2931
County: Saint Mary FICE Identification: 005526
Unit ID: 160913
Telephone: (985) 380-2436 Carnegie Class: Assoc/Pub-S-MC
FAX Number: (985) 380-2440 Calendar System: Semester
URL: www.ltc.edu
Established: 1965 Annual Undergrad Tuition & Fees (In-District): $1,542
Enrollment: 3,491 Coed
Affiliation or Control: State/Local IRS Status: 501(c)3
Highest Offering: Associate Degree
Program: Occupational; Technical Emphasis
Accreditation: COE

02 Campus Administrator .... Mr. Karl J. YOUNG, JR.
05 Chief Academic Officer .... Ms. Melanie HENRY
07 Dir of Admissions/Student Affairs .... Ms. Tanya J. ANDERSON
09 Director of Institutional Research .... Ms. Katherine FALGOUT
10 Chief Business Officer .... Mr. Darryl DAIGLE
15 Director Human Resources .... Ms. Pam MILLER

*South Louisiana Community College (J)

320 Devalcourt Street, Lafayette LA 70506-4124
County: Lafayette FICE Identification: 039563
Unit ID: 434061
Telephone: (337) 521-8896 Carnegie Class: Assoc/Pub-R-M
FAX Number: (337) 262-2100 Calendar System: Semester
URL: www.southlouisiana.edu
Established: 1998 Annual Undergrad Tuition & Fees (In-District): $2,712
Enrollment: 3,898 Coed
Affiliation or Control: State/Local IRS Status: 501(c)3
Highest Offering: Associate Degree
Program: Occupational; 2-Year Principally Bachelor's Creditable
Accreditation: SC, EMT, NAIT

02 Chancellor .... Dr. Natalie HARDER
04 Assistant to the Chancellor .... Ms. Ziuta BLAES
05 Vice Chanc Academic Affairs .... Dr. Michael GLISSON
10 Vice Chanc Finance & Administration .... Mr. Rudy GONZALES
32 Vice Chanc of Student Services .... Ms. Rochelle MOORE
20 Assoc Dean Instruction .... Ms. Karol HOWERTON
32 Dean of Students .... Ms. Meltida WILSON
09 Director of Institutional Research .... Dr. Charles MILLER
06 Registrar/Dir of Admissions .... Ms. Susie BUTLER
37 Director of Financial Aid .... Ms. Shonda ROSINSKI
08 Director of Library Services .... Ms. Katherine ROLFES
21 Business Manager .... Ms. Janet LAGRANGE
96 Financial Manager .... Ms. Gloria SMITH
18 Facilities Manager .... Mr. Ed LOPEZ
15 Human Resources Manager .... Ms. Alicia HULIN

*South Louisiana Community College Ardoin Campus (K)

1101 Bertrand Drive, Lafayette LA 70506-4115
County: Lafayette FICE Identification: 022148
Unit ID: 159443
Telephone: (337) 262-5962 Carnegie Class: Assoc/Pub-R-S
FAX Number: (337) 262-5122 Calendar System: Semester
URL: www.acadiana.edu
Established: 1978 Annual Undergrad Tuition & Fees (In-State): $1,542
Enrollment: 1,398 Coed
Affiliation or Control: State IRS Status: 501(c)3
Highest Offering: Associate Degree
Program: Occupational; Technical Emphasis

Accreditation: COE, ACFEI, MLTAD, NAIT, SURGT

02 Assistant Dean .... Dr. Desiree HUGGINS
06 Registrar .... Ms. Toni AUCOIN
37 Director of Financial Aid .... Mr. Joseph GORDON

*South Louisiana Community College Charles B Coreil Campus (A)

1124 Vocational Dr Ward 1, Ville Platte LA 70586-0296
County: Evangeline FICE Identification: 022402
Unit ID: 160816
Telephone: (337) 363-2197 Carnegie Class: Not Classified
FAX Number: (337) 363-7984 Calendar System: Semester
URL: www.ltc.edu
Established: 1976 Annual Undergrad Tuition & Fees (In-District): $1,474
Enrollment: 230 Coed
Affiliation or Control: State/Local IRS Status: 501(c)3
Highest Offering: Associate Degree
Program: Occupational; Technical Emphasis
Accreditation: COE

02 Campus Dean .... Mr. Sam HARB

*South Louisiana Community College Gulf Area Campus (B)

1301 Clover Street, Abbeville LA 70510-3811
County: Vermilion FICE Identification: 005482
Unit ID: 159018
Telephone: (337) 893-4984 Carnegie Class: Assoc/Pub-R-S
FAX Number: (337) 893-4991 Calendar System: Other
URL: www.ltc.edu
Established: 1952 Annual Undergrad Tuition & Fees (In-District): $1,542
Enrollment: 422 Coed
Affiliation or Control: State/Local IRS Status: 501(c)3
Highest Offering: Associate Degree
Program: Occupational; Technical Emphasis
Accreditation: COE

02 Assistant Campus Dean .... Ms. Karol HOWERTON
32 Dir Student Services/Financial Aid .... Ms. Tobi EDWARDS

*South Louisiana Community College T.H. Harris Campus (C)

332 East South Street, Opelousas LA 70570-6114
County: Saint Landry FICE Identification: 005466
Unit ID: 160676
Telephone: (337) 948-0239 Carnegie Class: Assoc/Pub-R-S
FAX Number: (337) 948-0243 Calendar System: Semester
URL: www.ltc.edu
Established: 1938 Annual Undergrad Tuition & Fees (In-District): $1,542
Enrollment: 666 Coed
Affiliation or Control: State/Local IRS Status: 501(c)3
Highest Offering: Associate Degree
Program: Occupational; 2-Year Principally Bachelor's Creditable; Technical Emphasis
Accreditation: COE

02 Assistant Campus Dean .... Mr. Harold SCHEXSNAYDER
37 Financial Aid Officer .... Mrs. Kelly CARUSO
32 Student Affairs Officer .... Mrs. Twana BENOIT

*South Louisiana Community College Teche Area Campus (D)

PO Box 11057, 609 Ember Drive, New Iberia LA 70562-1057
County: Iberia FICE Identification: 005528
Unit ID: 160694
Telephone: (337) 373-0011 Carnegie Class: Assoc/Pub-R-S
FAX Number: (337) 373-0039 Calendar System: Semester
URL: www.techeareacampus.net
Established: 1951 Annual Undergrad Tuition & Fees (In-District): $1,542
Enrollment: 750 Coed
Affiliation or Control: State/Local IRS Status: 501(c)3
Highest Offering: Associate Degree
Program: Occupational; Technical Emphasis
Accreditation: COE

02 Assistant Campus Dean .... Dr. Camille L. JARRELL
06 Registrar .... Ms. Tammy B. FAULK

*Sowela Technical Community College (E)

PO Box 16950, Lake Charles LA 70616-6950
County: Calcasieu FICE Identification: 005467
Unit ID: 160579
Telephone: (337) 491-2698 Carnegie Class: Assoc/Pub-R-S
FAX Number: (337) 491-2135 Calendar System: Semester
URL: www.sowela.edu
Established: 1938 Annual Undergrad Tuition & Fees (In-District): $3,594
Enrollment: 3,054 Coed
Affiliation or Control: State/Local IRS Status: 501(c)3
Highest Offering: Associate Degree
Program: 2-Year Principally Bachelor's Creditable; Technical Emphasis
Accreditation: @SC, COE, NAIT

02 Chancellor .... Dr. Neil ASPINWALL
04 Assistant to the Chancellor .... Ms. Amy THIBODEAUX
05 Vice Chanc Acad Affs/Stdnt Success .... Dr. Rick BATEMAN, JR.
10 Vice Chancellor Finance .... Ms. Jeanine NEWMAN
46 Vice Chancellor Economic Devel .... Vacant
27 Chief Info Resources & Tech Officer .... Dr. Charles NWANKWO
06 Exec Dean Enrollment Mgmt/Registrar .... Vacant
21 Controller .... Mr. Francis PORCHE, JR.
37 Director of Financial Aid .... Ms. Anna DAIGLE
08 Director of Library Services .... Ms. Mary Frances SHERWOOD
15 Director of Human Resources .... Dr. Brett RICHARD
103 Director of Workforce Development .... Mr. William E. MAYO
35 Director of Student Support Service .... Ms. Christine COLLINS
18 Director Facilities Planning & Mgmt .... Mr. Davidson DARBONE
09 Exec Director Planning & Analysis ... Dr. Fitzpatrick U. ANYANWU

Louisiana Culinary Institute (F)

10550 Airline Highway, Baton Rouge LA 70816-4109
County: East Baton Rouge FICE Identification: 041123
Unit ID: 449612
Telephone: (225) 769-8820 Carnegie Class: Assoc/PrivFP
FAX Number: (225) 769-8792 Calendar System: Semester
URL: www.louisianaculinary.com
Established: 2002 Annual Undergrad Tuition & Fees: $28,075
Enrollment: 159 Coed
Affiliation or Control: Proprietary IRS Status: Proprietary
Highest Offering: Associate Degree
Program: Occupational
Accreditation: COE

01 Chief Executive Officer .... Keith RUSH

*Louisiana State University System Office (G)

3810 W Lakeshore Drive, Baton Rouge LA 70808-4600
County: East Baton Rouge FICE Identification: 002009
Unit ID: 159638
Telephone: (225) 578-2111 Carnegie Class: N/A
FAX Number: (225) 578-5524
URL: www.lsusystem.lsu.edu

01 Interim President .... Dr. William L. JENKINS
05 VP Academic Affairs .... Dr. Carolyn H. HARGRAVE
20 VP Stdnt/Acad Spprt/Chief of Staff .... Dr. Michael GARGANO
26 VP Communications/External Affairs .... Dr. Charles F. ZEWE
17 VP Health Affairs/Medical Education .... Dr. Fred P. CERISE
30 Asst VP Advancement Coordination .... Mr. Joseph CORSO
88 Asst Vice Pres for System Relations . Dr. Robert H. RASMUSSEN
10 CFO/Asst Vice Pres & Comptroller .... Mrs. Wendy SIMONEAUX
18 System Director Facility Planning .... Mr. Danny MAHAFFEY
43 General Counsel to President .... Mr. P. Raymond LAMONICA
15 System Dir Human Resource/Risk Mgt ... Ms. Sharyon LIPSCOMB
21 System Director Internal Audit .... Mr. Chad BRACKIN

*Louisiana State University and Agricultural and Mechanical College (H)

Baton Rouge LA 70803-0100
County: East Baton Rouge FICE Identification: 002010
Unit ID: 159391
Telephone: (225) 578-3202 Carnegie Class: RU/VH
FAX Number: (225) 578-6400 Calendar System: Semester
URL: www.lsu.edu
Established: 1860 Annual Undergrad Tuition & Fees (In-State): $6,954
Enrollment: 29,718 Coed
Affiliation or Control: State IRS Status: 501(c)3
Highest Offering: Doctorate
Program: Liberal Arts And General; Teacher Preparatory; Professional
Accreditation: SC, AAFCS, ART, BUS, CACREP, CIDA, CLPSY, CONST, CS, DIETD, EMT, ENG, FOR, IPSY, JOUR, LIB, LSAR, MUS, SCPSY, SP, SPAA, SW, TED, THEA, VET

02 Interim Chancellor .... Mr. William L. JENKINS
05 Exec Vice Chanc/Provost Acad Affs .... Dr. Stuart R. BELL
26 Assoc Vice Chanc Comm & Univ Rel .... Mr. Herb VINCENT
10 Vice Chanc Fin & Admin/Controller .... Mr. Eric N. MONDAY
46 Vice Chanc Research & Econ Dev .... Dr. Thomas R. KLEI
45 Vice Chanc Strategic Initiatives .... Dr. Isiah M. WARNER
32 Vice Chanc Student Life/Enroll Svcs .... Dr. Kurt J. KEPPLER
102 President/CEO LSU Foundation .... MajGen. Lee G. GRIFFIN
28 Vice Prov Campus Equity/Diversity .... Dr. Katrice A. ALBERT
20 Vice Prov Academic Affairs .... Dr. Jane CASSIDY
20 Vice Provost Academics & Planning .... Dr. Gilmore REEVE
15 Assoc VC Human Resources Mgmt .... Mr. A. G. MONACO
84 Int Assoc VC Enrollment Management .... Dr. David KURPIUS
30 Exec Director Inst Advancement .... Ms. Bunnie CANNON
43 Legislative Affairs Director .... Dr. Jason DRODDY
27 Asst Vice Chanc Comm/Univ Relations .... Mrs. Holly CULLEN
85 Assoc VC International Programs .... Dr. Lakshman VELUPILLAI
37 Assoc Dir Student Aid/Scholarships .... Ms. Amy MARIX
08 Dean LSU Libraries .... Dr. Jennifer S. CARGILL
79 Dean College of Humanities .... Dr. Gaines FOSTER
58 Dean of Graduate School .... Dr. David CONSTANT
54 Dean College of Engineering .... Dr. Richard KOUBEK
47 Dean College of Agriculture .... Dr. Kenneth L. KOONCE
50 Dean Ourso College of Business .... Dr. Eli JONES
70 Dean School of Social Work .... Dr. Christian MOLIDOR
64 Dean College Music & Dramatic Arts .... Dr. Laurence KAPTAIN
81 Dean College of Science .... Dr. Kevin R. CARMAN
62 Dean Sch of Library & Info Science .... Dr. Beth M. PASKOFF
53 Interim Dean College of Education .... Dr. Laura F. LINDSAY
49 Int Dean College of Art & Design .... Mr. Kenneth CARPENTER
74 Dean Veterinary Medicine .... Dr. Peter F. HAYNES
60 Int Dean Manship Sch of Mass Comm .... Dr. Jerry CEPPOS
92 Dean Honors College .... Dr. Nancy L. CLARK
65 Dean Sch of Coast & Environ .... Dr. Christopher D'ELIA
88 Assoc Dean University College .... Mr. Paul IVEY
38 Assc Dean Advising & Counseling Ctr .... Mr. R. Paul IVEY
35 Assistant Dean Student Services .... Ms. Angela GUILLORY
88 Sr Ex Dir SN Ctr Security Rsch Trng .... Mr. Jim FERNANDEZ
88 Exec Director Center Energy Stds .... Dr. Allan G. PULSIPHER
51 Exec Director Continuing Education .... Mr. Doug WEIMER
29 President Alumni Association .... Dr. Charlie W. ROBERTS
59 Director School Human Ecology .... Dr. Roy J. MARTIN
88 Exec Director Museum of Art .... Mr. Thomas A. LIVESAY
18 Exec Director Facility Services .... Mr. Tony LOMBARDO
13 Int Chief Info Ofcr/Info Tech Svcs .... Mr. Brian NICHOLS
75 Dir Sch Human Res Ed/Workforce Dev .. Dr. Michael F. BURNETT
80 Director Public Admin Institute .... Dr. James A. RICHARDSON
88 Director LSU Press .... Ms. MaryKatherine CALLAWAY
41 Athletic Director .... Mr. Joe ALLEVA
06 Registrar .... Mr. Robert K. DOOLOS
36 Director Career Services .... Dr. Mary D. FEDUCCIA
09 Director of Institutional Research .... Ms. Sandy J. WALKER
93 Director Multicultural Affairs .... Ms. Chaunda ALLEN
94 Director Women's/Gender Studies .... Dr. Michelle MASSE
65 Director Museum of Natural Science ... Dr. Frederick H. SHELDON
88 Director Rural Life Museum .... Mr. David J W. FLOYD
96 Exec Dir of Purch & Property Mgmt .... Ms. Marie FRANK
07 Assoc Director of Admissions .... Ms. Lupe LAMADRID

*Louisiana State University at Alexandria (I)

8100 Highway 71 S, Alexandria LA 71302-9121
County: Rapides FICE Identification: 002011
Unit ID: 159382
Telephone: (318) 445-3672 Carnegie Class: Bac/A&S
FAX Number: (318) 473-6418 Calendar System: Semester
URL: www.lsua.edu
Established: 1959 Annual Undergrad Tuition & Fees (In-State): $4,617
Enrollment: 2,613 Coed
Affiliation or Control: State IRS Status: 501(c)3
Highest Offering: Baccalaureate
Program: Liberal Arts And General; Teacher Preparatory
Accreditation: SC, ADNUR, MLTAD, NUR, RAD, TED

02 Chancellor .... Dr. David P. MANUEL
05 Vice Chanc Academic & Student Affs .... Dr. Barbara S. HATFIELD
10 Vice Chanc Finance/Admin Services .... Mr. David WESSE
30 Director Institutional Advancement ..... Ms. Melinda F. ANDERSON
20 Asst VC Academic/Student Affairs .... Dr. Eamon HALPIN
21 Asst VC Finance/Admin Services .... Ms. Belinda AARON
50 Dept Chair Business Administration .... Dr. Robert BUSH
49 Dept Chair Arts/English/Humanities .... Dr. Arthur RANKIN
83 Dept Chair Behavioral & Social Sci .... Dr. Jerry SANSON
81 Dept Chair Math & Physical Sciences .... Dr. Nathan PONDER
53 Deparment Chair Education .... Dr. Judy RUNDELL
76 Department Chair Allied Health .... Dr. Haywood JOINER
66 Department Chair Nursing .... Dr. Elizabeth BATTALORA
49 Dept Chair Biological Sciences .... Dr. Carol CORBAT
18 Exec Director of Facility Services .... Mr. Robert KARAM
84 Exec Director Enrollment Management .... Ms. Teresa SEYMOUR
08 Director Library .... Dr. Bonnie HINES
37 Director of Financial Aid .... Mr. Paul MONTELEONE
15 Director Human Resource Management .... Ms. Lynette BURLEW
14 Dir Information/Educ Technology .... Mr. Deron THAXTON
51 Director Continuing Education .... Mr. Robert S. SAVAGE
32 Director Student Services .... Dr. Eamon HALPIN
09 Dir Inst Research/Effectiveness .... Mr. Reed BLALOCK
96 Dir Procurement Svcs/Property Mgmt .... Mr. Larry WILLIAMS
27 Chief Information Officer .... Mr. Deron THAXTON
41 Director Athletics .... Mr. Charles ZEILMAN, JR.
07 Director of Admissions & Recruiting .... Ms. Shelly KIEFFER
06 Registrar .... Ms. Teresa SEYMOUR

*Louisiana State University at Eunice (J)

2048 Johnson Highway, Eunice LA 70535-6726
County: Acadia FICE Identification: 002012
Unit ID: 159407
Telephone: (337) 457-7311 Carnegie Class: Assoc/Pub2in4
FAX Number: (337) 546-6620 Calendar System: Semester
URL: www.lsue.edu
Established: 1964 Annual Undergrad Tuition & Fees (In-State): $2,500
Enrollment: 3,010 Coed
Affiliation or Control: State IRS Status: 501(c)3
Highest Offering: Associate Degree
Program: Occupational; 2-Year Principally Bachelor's Creditable
Accreditation: SC, ADNUR, DMS, RAD

02 Chancellor .... Dr. William J. NUNEZ, III
05 Vice Chancellor Academic Affairs .... Dr. Stephen GUEMPEL
32 Vice Chancellor Student Affairs .... Ms. Judy DANIELS
10 Vice Chancellor Business Affairs .... Ms. Arlene C. TUCKER
26 Director of Public Relations .... Mr. Van REED

08 Director of the Library ... Mr. Gerald PATOUT
06 Registrar/Director Admissions ... Mr. Jason SAMPLER
37 Director of Financial Aid ... Ms. Jacqueline LA CHAPELLE
30 Director Institutional Development ... Ms. Madelaine LANDRY
51 Director of Continuing Education ... Mr. David PULLING
18 Director Physical Plant ... Mr. Michael BROUSSARD
25 Director Grants ... Ms. Jane SPRADLING
15 Director Personnel Services ... Vacant
81 Head Division of Sciences ... Dr. Renee ROBICHAUX
50 Head Div Bus/Nursing/Allied Health ... Ms. Dotty MCDONALD
49 Head Division of Liberal Arts ... Dr. Luciane BERG

*Louisiana State University Health Sciences Center-New Orleans (A)

433 Bolivar Street, New Orleans LA 70112-2223
County: Orleans — FICE Identification: 002014
Unit ID: 159373
Telephone: (504) 568-4808 — Carnegie Class: Spec/Med
FAX Number: N/A — Calendar System: Semester
URL: www.lsuhsc.edu
Established: 1931 — Annual Undergrad Tuition & Fees (In-State): $5,393
Enrollment: 2,777 — Coed
Affiliation or Control: State — IRS Status: 501(c)3
Highest Offering: Doctorate
Program: Occupational; 2-Year Principally Bachelor's Creditable; Liberal Arts And General; Professional
Accreditation: SC, ANEST, AUD, CORE, CVT, DENT, DH, DT, IPSY, MED, MT, NURSE, OT, PTA, SP

00 Chancellor Emeritus ... Dr. John ROCK
02 Chancellor ... Dr. Larry H. HOLLIER
05 Vice Chanc Acad Aff/Dean Grad Stds ... Dr. Joseph M. MOERSCHBAECHER
10 Vice Chancellor Admin & Finance ... Mr. Ronald E. SMITH
17 Vice Chanc Clinic/Cmty/Security Aff ... Mr. Ronald E. GARDNER
63 Dean Medicine NO ... Dr. Steve NELSON
52 Dean School of Dentistry ... Dr. Henry GREMILLION
66 Dean of Nursing ... Dr. Demetrius PORCHE
69 Dean of Public Health ... Dr. Elizabeth FONTHAM
76 Dean Allied Health Professions ... Dr. Jim R. CAIRO
04 Assistant to the Chancellor ... Mrs. Patricia MAGEE
86 Director of Government Programs ... Ms. Rose D. CHATELAIN
14 Director Computer Services ... Ms. Petina OWENS
13 Director Information Services ... Ms. Leslie L. CAPO
08 Int Director Library Administration ... Ms. Debra H. SIBLEY
15 Director Human Resource Mgmt ... Mr. Duane LEBBE
06 Registrar ... Mr. William Bryant FAUST
37 Assoc Dir Student Financial Aid ... Ms. Kimberly BRUNO
09 Director of Institutional Research ... Dr. Ken KRATZ
31 Director of Community Relations ... Ms. Diane E. BAJOIE
18 Chief Facilities/Physical Plant ... Mr. John BALL
96 Director of Purchasing ... Mr. Brent HEROLD
26 Director of External Relations ... Mr. Christopher VIDRINE

*Louisiana State University Health Sciences Center at Shreveport (B)

1501 Kings Highway, Shreveport LA 71103
County: Caddo — FICE Identification: 008067
Unit ID: 435000
Telephone: (318) 675-5000 — Carnegie Class: Spec/Med
FAX Number: N/A — Calendar System: Semester
URL: www.lsuhscshreveport.edu
Established: N/A — Annual Undergrad Tuition & Fees (In-District): $7,723
Enrollment: 867 — Coed
Affiliation or Control: State/Local — IRS Status: 501(c)3
Highest Offering: Doctorate
Program: Professional
Accreditation: SC, DENT, MED, MT, OT, PTA, SP

02 Chancellor ... Dr. Robert A. BARISH
11 Vice Chancellor Administration ... Mr. John T. DAILEY
06 Registrar ... Ms. Kim CARMEN
10 Chief Financial Officer ... Ms. Sheila FAOUR
63 Dean School of Medicine ... Dr. Andrew L. CHESSON, JR.
76 Dean Sch Allied Health Professions ... Dr. Joseph MCCULLOCH
58 Dean School of Graduate Studies ... Dr. Sandra C. ROERIG

† Tuition varies by degree program.

*Louisiana State University Paul M. Hebert Law Center (C)

1 East Campus Drive, Baton Rouge LA 70803
County: East Baton Rouge — Identification: 667028
Telephone: (225) 578-8491 — Carnegie Class: Not Classified
FAX Number: (225) 578-8202 — Calendar System: Semester
URL: www.law.lsu.edu
Established: 1906 — Annual Graduate Tuition & Fees: $18,617
Enrollment: 737 — Coed
Affiliation or Control: State — IRS Status: 501(c)3
Highest Offering: Doctorate; No Undergraduates
Program: Professional
Accreditation: SC, LAW

02 Chancellor ... Jack M. WEISS
10 Vice Chanc Business/Financial Affs ... Gregory SMITH
05 Vice Chancellor for Academic Affair ... Cheney C. JOSEPH, JR.
20 Vice Chancellor Faculty Develop ... Raymond T. DIAMOND

*Louisiana State University in Shreveport (D)

One University Place, Shreveport LA 71115-2399
County: Caddo — FICE Identification: 002013
Unit ID: 159416
Telephone: (318) 797-5000 — Carnegie Class: Master's M
FAX Number: (318) 797-5180 — Calendar System: Semester
URL: www.lsus.edu
Established: 1967 — Annual Undergrad Tuition & Fees (In-State): $4,943
Enrollment: 4,562 — Coed
Affiliation or Control: State — IRS Status: 501(c)3
Highest Offering: Beyond Master's But Less Than Doctorate
Program: Liberal Arts And General; Teacher Preparatory; Professional
Accreditation: SC, ARCPA, BUS, CS, TED

02 Interim Chancellor ... Dr. Paul D. SISSON
05 Provost/Vice Chanc Academic Affairs ... Dr. Paul D. SISSON
10 Vice Chancellor Business Affairs ... Mr. Michael T. FERRELL
32 Interim Vice Chanc Student Affairs . Dr. Randy R. BUTTERBAUGH
30 Interim Vice Chancellor Development ... Dr. Johnette M. MAGNER
29 Director Alumni Affairs ... Ms. Dianne B. HOWELL
09 Director Planning/Inst Research ... Vacant
15 Director of Human Resource Mgmt ... Mr. Bill WOLFE
08 Dean Noel Memorial Library ... Dr. Alan D. GABEHART
37 Director of Student Financial Aid ... Mrs. Betty M. MCCRARY
07 Interim Registrar ... Ms. Darlenna M. ATKINS
36 Director of Career Services ... Ms. Gina STARNES
38 Director Student Counseling ... Mrs. Paula B. ATKINS
14 Director of Computing Services ... Mr. Shelby C. KEITH
18 Director of Facility Services ... Mr. Donald R. BLOXOM
40 Director of Bookstore ... Ms. Brenda P. BARTLEBAUGH
96 Director of Purchasing ... Mrs. Cynthia P. ARMSTRONG
26 Director of Media/Public Relations ... Mrs. Jennifer C. STEADMAN
04 Assistant to the Chancellor ... Mrs. Viki P. FENTRESS
19 Director of University Police ... Ms. Rebecca CHILES
41 Athletic Director ... Mr. Doug ROBINSON
44 Director Annual/Planning Giving ... Vacant
49 Dean of Arts and Sciences ... Dr. Larry ANDERSON
58 Dean of Graduate Programs ... Vacant
51 Director of Continuing Education ... Mrs. Tisha L. SAMHAN
53 Dean of Business/Educ/Human Devel ... Dr. David B. GUSTAVSON

*University of New Orleans (E)

2000 Lakeshore Drive, New Orleans LA 70148-2000
County: Orleans — FICE Identification: 002015
Unit ID: 159939
Telephone: (504) 280-6000 — Carnegie Class: RU/H
FAX Number: (504) 280-5522 — Calendar System: Semester
URL: www.uno.edu/
Established: 1958 — Annual Undergrad Tuition & Fees (In-State): $5,733
Enrollment: 10,903 — Coed
Affiliation or Control: State — IRS Status: 501(c)3
Highest Offering: Doctorate
Program: Liberal Arts And General; Teacher Preparatory
Accreditation: SC, ART, BUS, BUSA, CACREP, CS, ENG, MUS, PLNG, TED, THEA

02 President ... Dr. Peter J. FOS
05 Interim Provost ... Dr. Lou V. PARADISE
46 VP Research ... Dr. Scott L. WHITTENBURG
10 VP Fin Svcs/Bus Affs/Comptroller ... Ms. Linda K. ROBISON
27 VP for External Affairs ... Ms. Rachel A. KINCAID
13 Chief Information Officer ... Mr. Jim E. BURGARD
43 University/General Counsel ... Ms. Patricia A. ADAMS
50 Dean of Business Administration ... Dr. John WILLIAMS
53 Int Dean of Education & Human Dev ... Dr. April BEDFORD
54 Dean of Engineering ... Vacant
49 Dean of Liberal Arts ... Dr. Susan E. KRANTZ
08 Dean of Library ... Dr. Sharon B. MADER
81 Dean of Sciences ... Dr. Steve JOHNSON
06 University Registrar ... Mr. Matt MOORE
29 Director Alumni Affairs ... Ms. Pamela MEYER
26 Director of Public Relations ... Mr. Adam NORRIS
07 Director of Admissions ... Mr. Dave MEREDITH
19 Asst Vice Chanc for Public Safety ... Mr. Thomas HARRINGTON
19 Chief of UNO Police Operations ... Mr. H. David ALLY
85 Director International Students ... Ms. Christiana J. THOMAS
23 Director Student Health Services ... Ms. Denise G. PEREZ
96 Director of Purchasing ... Ms. Deborah K. BRIDGES
41 Director Intercollegiate Athletics ... Mr. Derek MOREL
32 Associate Dean of Student Affairs ... Dr. Pamela V. RAULT
39 Director Student Housing ... Mr. Mike BRAUNINGER

Loyola University New Orleans (F)

6363 Saint Charles Avenue, New Orleans LA 70118-6195
County: Orleans — FICE Identification: 002016
Unit ID: 159656
Telephone: (504) 865-2011 — Carnegie Class: Master's L
FAX Number: (504) 865-3851 — Calendar System: Semester
URL: www.loyno.edu
Established: 1912 — Annual Undergrad Tuition & Fees: $33,846
Enrollment: 5,178 — Coed
Affiliation or Control: Roman Catholic — IRS Status: 501(c)3
Highest Offering: Doctorate
Program: Liberal Arts And General; Teacher Preparatory; Professional
Accreditation: SC, BUS, CACREP, LAW, MUS, NUR, NURSE

01 President ... Rev. Kevin W. WILDES, SJ
101 Exec Asst to Pres for Board Rels ... Ms. Kristine D. LELONG
05 Provost/Vice Pres Academic Affs ... Dr. Marc MANGANARO
10 Vice President for Business/Finance ... Mr. John J. CALAMIA
30 Vice Pres Institutional Advance ... Mr. William BISHOP
32 VP Student Affairs/Assoc Provost ... Dr. Marcia L. PETTY
88 Vice Pres for Mission & Ministry ... Rev. Ted DZIAK, SJ
84 Vice Pres for Enrollment Management ... Mr. Salvatore LIBERTO
13 Vice Prov Information Tech/CIO ... Mr. Bret JACOBS
21 Assoc Vice Pres Financial Affairs ... Mr. Leon MATHES
44 Assoc Vice Pres Development ... Mr. Chris WISEMAN
27 Asst VP Marketing/Communications ... Mr. Terrell F. FISHER
11 Asst Vice Pres Administration ... Mr. Paul C. FLEMING
35 Asst Vice Pres of Student Affairs ... Mr. Robert A. REED
20 Sr Vice Provost of Academic Affairs ... Dr. Lydia VOIGT
45 Asst Provost Inst Effective/Assess ... Vacant
42 Dean University Ministry ... Mr. Kurt BINDEWALD
09 Co-Director Institutional Research ... Ms. Cynthia D. CAIRE
26 Dir Public Affairs/External Rels ... Ms. Meredith HARTLEY
43 General Counsel ... Ms. Gita BOLT
29 Director Alumni Relations ... Ms. Monique G. GARDNER
06 Dir Stdnt Records/Registration Svcs ... Ms. Kathy R. GROS
07 Director Admissions/Recruitment Ops ... Mr. Keith E. GRAMLING
15 Director of Human Resources ... Mr. Ross D. MATTHEWS
40 Director Bookstore ... Ms. Ivon FASCIO
41 Director Athletics & Wellness ... Dr. Michael GIORLANDO
36 Director Career Services ... Ms. Roberta KASKEL
23 Admin Director Student Health Svcs ... Dr. Alicia BOURQUE
19 Director University Police ... Mr. Patrick X. BAILEY
37 Director Scholarships/Financial Aid ... Ms. Catherine SIMONEAUX
08 Director of the Law Library ... Mr. P. Michael WHIPPLE
85 Director Ctr for International Ed ... Ms. Debra DANNA
86 Dir Government Relations ... Mr. Tommy SCREEN
38 Director Student Counseling ... Dr. Alicia BOURQUE
96 Director of Purchasing ... Mr. Bret PENNISON
28 Dir Intercultural Understanding ... Ms. Lisa MARTIN
06 Dir Admin Services-Student Records ... Mr. Michael RACHAL
39 Director of Residential Life ... Mr. Craig BEEBE
08 Dean of Libraries ... Dr. Michael OLSON
49 Int Dean Humanities/Natural Science ... Dr. Maria CALZADA
61 Dean of Law ... Ms. Maria LOPEZ
64 Dean of Music and Fine Arts ... Dr. Anthony DECUIR
50 Dean of Business ... Dr. William LOCANDER
83 Dean of Social Sciences ... Dr. Luis MIRON

MedVance Institute-Baton Rouge (G)

9255 Interline Avenue, Baton Rouge LA 70809
County: East Baton Rouge — FICE Identification: 034803
Unit ID: 439738
Telephone: (225) 248-1015 — Carnegie Class: Assoc/PrivFP
FAX Number: (225) 248-9517 — Calendar System: Other
URL: www.medvance.edu/colleges/baton-rouge-la
Established: 1991 — Annual Undergrad Tuition & Fees: $13,500
Enrollment: 751 — Coed
Affiliation or Control: Proprietary — IRS Status: Proprietary
Highest Offering: Associate Degree
Program: Occupational
Accreditation: ABHES, MLTAD, RAD, SURTEC

01 Campus Director ... Mr. William PAUL

New Orleans Baptist Theological Seminary (H)

3939 Gentilly Boulevard, New Orleans LA 70126-4858
County: Orleans — FICE Identification: 002019
Unit ID: 159948
Telephone: (504) 282-4455 — Carnegie Class: Spec/Faith
FAX Number: (504) 283-3631 — Calendar System: Semester
URL: www.nobts.edu
Established: 1917 — Annual Undergrad Tuition & Fees: $5,486
Enrollment: 2,930 — Coed
Affiliation or Control: Southern Baptist — IRS Status: 501(c)3
Highest Offering: Doctorate
Program: Professional; Religious Emphasis
Accreditation: SC, MUS, THEOL

01 President ... Dr. Charles S. KELLEY, JR.
05 Provost ... Dr. Steve W. LEMKE
09 Dir Institutional Effectiveness ... Dr. C. Scott DRUMM
10 Vice President for Business Affairs ... Mr. Clay L. CORVIN
30 Vice President for Development ... Mr. Randy DRIGGERS
58 Dean Graduate Studies ... Dr. Jerry N. BARLOW
12 Dean Leavell College ... Dr. L. Thomas STRONG, III
32 Dean of Students ... Mr. J. Craig GARRETT
07 Dean of Admissions & Registrar ... Dr. Paul E. GREGOIRE, JR.
08 Dean of Libraries ... Dr. Jeff D. GRIFFIN
18 Associate VP of Facilities ... Dr. Jim O. PARKER
13 Assoc VP Information Technology ... Dr. Laurie S. WATTS
73 Assoc Dean Prof Doctoral Pgms ... Dr. Reggie R. OGEA
106 Associate Dean of Online Learning ... Dr. W. Craig PRICE
20 Associate Dean of Graduate Studies ... Dr. Michael H. EDENS
58 Assoc Dean Research Doctoral Pgms ... Dr. Charles A. RAY, JR.
35 Assoc Dean of Students ... Dr. Judi JACKSON
88 Director of Leavell Center ... Dr. Preston L. NIX
15 Director of Human Resources ... Ms. Pattie SHOENER
26 Chief Public Relations Officer ... Mr. Gary D. MYERS
29 Director of Alumni Relations ... Dr. Dennis L. PHELPS
36 Director of Student Enlistment ... Mr. J. Craig GARRETT
37 Director of Student Financial Aid ... Mr. Owen NEASE
38 Director of Testing & Counseling ... Dr. Jeffery W. NAVE

Notre Dame Seminary, Graduate School of Theology (A)

2901 S Carrollton Avenue, New Orleans LA 70118-4391
County: Orleans FICE Identification: 002022
Unit ID: 160029
Telephone: (504) 866-7426 Carnegie Class: Spec/Faith
FAX Number: (504) 866-3119 Calendar System: Semester
URL: www.nds.edu
Established: 1923 Annual Graduate Tuition & Fees: $19,140
Enrollment: 142 Coed
Affiliation or Control: Roman Catholic IRS Status: 501(c)3
Highest Offering: Master's; No Undergraduates
Program: Professional; Religious Emphasis
Accreditation: SC, THEOL

01 President/Rector .... V.Rev. James A. WEHNER, STD
05 Academic Dean .... Rev. Minh PHAN
10 Business Manager .... Ms. Michelle W. KLEIN
08 Director of Library .... Mr. Thomas B. BENDER
06 Registrar .... Ms. Cynthia A. GARRITY
09 Director IE/Planning/Faculty Devel .... Dr. Rebecca S. MALONEY

Our Lady of Holy Cross College (B)

4123 Woodland Drive, New Orleans LA 70131-7399
County: Orleans FICE Identification: 002023
Unit ID: 160065
Telephone: (504) 394-7744 Carnegie Class: Master's S
FAX Number: (504) 391-2421 Calendar System: Semester
URL: www.olhcc.edu
Established: 1916 Annual Undergrad Tuition & Fees: $9,000
Enrollment: 900 Coed
Affiliation or Control: Roman Catholic IRS Status: 501(c)3
Highest Offering: Master's
Program: Liberal Arts And General; Teacher Preparatory; Professional; Nursing Emphasis
Accreditation: SC, CACREP, IACBE, NUR, RAD, TED

01 President .... Dr. Ronald J. AMBROSETTI
05 Provost/Vice Pres Academic Affairs .... Dr. Patricia PRECHTER
10 Vice Pres for Finance & Operations .... Mrs. Arlean WEHLE
30 Vice Pres for Philanthropy .... Mr. David CATHERMAN
20 Director of CTL .... Dr. Victoria DAHMES
07 Interim Dean of Admissions .... Ms. Meredith REED
37 Int Coordinator of Financial Aid .... Mrs. Anna VAUGHAN
08 Director of Library Services .... Sr. Helen FONTENOT
49 Dean Liberal Arts and Science .... Dr. Michael LABRANCHE
06 Registrar .... Mr. Robert MITCHELL
09 Director Inst Research & Planning .... Vacant
42 Director of Campus Ministry .... Fr. John LYDON
15 Human Resources Manager .... Ms. Cathy WAGUESPACK
44 Director of Annual Fund .... Mr. David CATHERMAN
13 Director of Technology Services .... Mr. Wayne CLEMENT

Our Lady of the Lake College (C)

7434 Perkins Road, Baton Rouge LA 70808-4380
County: East Baton Rouge FICE Identification: 031062
Unit ID: 160074
Telephone: (225) 768-1700 Carnegie Class: Spec/Health
FAX Number: (225) 768-0811 Calendar System: Semester
URL: www.ololcollege.edu
Established: 1923 Annual Undergrad Tuition & Fees: $11,640
Enrollment: 1,748 Coed
Affiliation or Control: Roman Catholic IRS Status: 501(c)3
Highest Offering: Master's
Program: Occupational; 2-Year Principally Bachelor's Creditable; Liberal Arts And General; Professional
Accreditation: SC, ADNUR, ANEST, #ARCPA, MT, NUR, PTAA, RAD, SURGT

01 President .... Dr. Sandra S. HARPER
05 Exec VP for Academics and Students .... Dr. David ENGLAND
10 VP for Finance and Administration .... Mr. Hoa NGUYEN
51 Vice President Career Training .... Ms. Marie N. KELLEY
66 Dean School of Nursing .... Dr. Jennifer BECK
49 Dean School of A&S and Health Prof .... Dr. Katherine KRIEG
32 Dean Student Services .... Dr. Phyllis SIMPSON
08 Dean of Library .... Vacant
30 Director of Institutional Advance .... Ms. Denise DOKEY
37 Director Financial Aid .... Ms. Tiffany MAGEE
06 Registrar .... Mr. Ryan GARRITY
84 Director Enrollment Management .... Ms. Rebecca CANNON
88 Director Physician Asst Studies .... Mr. John ALLGOOD
58 Director Nurse Anesthetist Program .... Ms. Phyllis PEDERSEN
76 Director Radiologic Technology .... Ms. Dianne PHILLIPS
76 Director Clinical Lab Sciences .... Dr. Debbie FOX
76 Director Physical Therapist Asst .... Ms. Leah GEHEBER
76 Director Surgical Technology .... Ms. Alice COMISH
88 Dir Health Service Administration .... Ms. Elizabeth BERZAS
76 Director Respiratory Therapy .... Ms. Sue DAVIS
88 Director Engaged Learning/Writing .... Dr. Glenn BLALOCK
106 Director Distributed Education .... Mr. Eric SENECA
91 Manager Student Info System .... Mr. Janssen BURRIS

Remington College-Baton Rouge Campus (D)

10551 Coursey Boulevard, Baton Rouge LA 70816-4040
County: East Baton Rouge Identification: 666449
Unit ID: 440271
Telephone: (225) 236-3200 Carnegie Class: Assoc/PrivFP
FAX Number: (225) 922-9569 Calendar System: Quarter
URL: www.remingtoncollege.edu
Established: 1998 Annual Undergrad Tuition & Fees: $15,995
Enrollment: 409 Coed
Affiliation or Control: Proprietary IRS Status: Proprietary
Highest Offering: Associate Degree
Program: Occupational; 2-Year Principally Bachelor's Creditable
Accreditation: ACCSC

01 President .... Mr. Michael SMITH

† Branch campus of Remington College, Cleveland, OH.

Remington College-Lafayette Campus (E)

303 Rue Louis XIV, Lafayette LA 70508-5700
County: Lafayette FICE Identification: 005203
Unit ID: 160524
Telephone: (337) 981-4010 Carnegie Class: Assoc/PrivFP
FAX Number: (337) 983-7130 Calendar System: Quarter
URL: www.remingtoncollege.edu
Established: 1940 Annual Undergrad Tuition & Fees: $14,745
Enrollment: 420 Coed
Affiliation or Control: Proprietary IRS Status: Proprietary
Highest Offering: Associate Degree
Program: Occupational
Accreditation: ACCSC

01 President .... Ms. JoAnn BOUDREAUX
07 Director of Admissions .... Ms. Heather DAIDLE

† Branch campus of Remington College, Cleveland, OH.

Remington College-Shreveport (F)

2106 Bert Kouns Industrial Loop, Shreveport LA 71118
County: Caddo Identification: 666302
Unit ID: 451866
Telephone: (318) 671-4001 Carnegie Class: Assoc/PrivFP
FAX Number: (318) 671-4065 Calendar System: Semester
URL: www.remingtoncollege.edu
Established: 2007 Annual Undergrad Tuition & Fees: $15,995
Enrollment: 445 Coed
Affiliation or Control: Proprietary IRS Status: Proprietary
Highest Offering: Associate Degree
Program: Occupational
Accreditation: ACCSC

01 President .... Mr. Jerry DRISKILL

† Branch campus of Remington College, Cleveland, OH.

Saint Joseph Seminary College (G)

75376 River Road, Saint Benedict LA 70457-9999
County: Saint Tammany FICE Identification: 002027
Unit ID: 160409
Telephone: (985) 867-2225 Carnegie Class: Spec/Faith
FAX Number: (985) 867-2270 Calendar System: Semester
URL: www.sjasc.edu
Established: 1891 Annual Undergrad Tuition & Fees: $28,200
Enrollment: 83 Male
Affiliation or Control: Roman Catholic IRS Status: 501(c)3
Highest Offering: Baccalaureate
Program: Liberal Arts And General; Religious Emphasis
Accreditation: SC

01 President - Rector .... V.Rev. Gregory M. BOQUET, OSB
05 Academic Dean .... Dr. Jude LUPINETTI
03 Vice-Rector .... Rev. Matthew CLARK, OSB
08 Librarian .... Ms. Bonnie WOOD
56 Director Extension Programs .... Vacant
10 Business Officer .... Mrs. Judith GAUBERT
37 Director Financial Aid .... Mr. George BINDER
29 Director of Alumni Affairs .... Rev. Matthew CLARK, OSB
30 Director of Development .... Mrs. Vanessa CROUERE
27 Director of Communications .... Bro. Simon STUBBS, OSB
32 Dean of Students .... Rev. Killian TOLG, OSB

*Southern University and Agricultural & Mechanical College System Office (H)

JS Clark Admin Building, 4th Floor,
Baton Rouge LA 70813-0001
County: East Baton Rouge FICE Identification: 009637
Unit ID: 160533
Telephone: (225) 771-4680 Carnegie Class: N/A
FAX Number: (225) 771-5522
URL: www.sus.edu

01 President .... Dr. Ronald F. MASON, JR.
100 Chief of Staff .... Ms. Evola C. BATES
43 General Counsel to the System/Board .... Ms. Tracie J. WOODS
10 Vice Pres Finance/Business Affairs .... Mr. Kevin APPLETON
13 Vice Pres Information Technology .... Mr. Tony MOORE
05 System Officer for Academic Affairs . Mr. Walter T. TILLMAN, JR.
30 VP Sys Advance/Exec Dir Foundation .... Dr. Ernie T. HUGHES
43 Exec Counsel/Legislative Liaison .... Mr. Byron C. WILLIAMS
29 Director of Alumni Affairs .... Ms. Robyn MERRICK
26 Director of Publications .... Mr. Henry TILLMAN
18 Director of Facilities Planning .... Mr. Endas VINCENT
21 System Director of Internal Audit .... Ms. Linda H. CATALON

*Southern University and A&M College (I)

Baton Rouge LA 70813-0001
County: East Baton Rouge FICE Identification: 002025
Unit ID: 160621
Telephone: (225) 771-4500 Carnegie Class: Master's L
FAX Number: (225) 771-2018 Calendar System: Semester
URL: www.subr.edu
Established: 1880 Annual Undergrad Tuition & Fees (In-State): $5,812
Enrollment: 6,903 Coed
Affiliation or Control: State IRS Status: 501(c)3
Highest Offering: Doctorate
Program: Liberal Arts And General; Teacher Preparatory
Accreditation: SC, AAFCS, ART, BUS, CACREP, CORE, CS, DIETD, DIETI, ENG, ENGT, #JOUR, LAW, MUS, NURSE, #SP, SPAA, SW, TED

02 Chancellor .... Dr. James LLORENS
05 Int Exec Vice Chancellor & Provost .... Dr. Janet RAMI
32 Int Asst Vice Chanc Student Affairs .... Dr. Brandon DUMAS
10 Vice Chanc of Finance & Admin ...Mr. Flandus MCCLINTON, JR.
46 VC Research/Strategic Initiative .... Dr. Michael STUBBLEFIELD
20 Int Assoc Vice Chan Academic Affs .... Dr. Ella KELLEY
26 Asst to Chanc for Media Relations .... Mr. Edward PRATT
45 Dir Planning Assess/Instnl Research .... Vacant
29 Director of Alumni Affairs .... Ms. Robyn MERRICK
15 Director Human Resources .... Mr. Lester POURCIAU
21 Chief Budget Officer .... Ms. Pamela JONES
06 Registrar .... Mr. Arthur GILLIS
07 Director Admissions/Recruitment .... Ms. Michelle L. HILL
35 Dean of Students .... Mr. Kelwin WILLIAMS
39 Director Residential Housing .... Mr. Shandon NEAL
37 Director of Financial Aid .... Ms. Ursula SHORTY
13 Chief Information Officer .... Mr. Carlos THOMAS
51 Dir Intl Educ/Dir Svc Learning/CE .... Dr. Barbara CARPENTER
41 Athletic Director .... Mr. William BROUSSARD
18 Director Facilities Planning .... Mr. Endas VINCENT
88 Director School of Accountancy .... Ms. Mary A. DARBY
96 Director of Purchasing .... Mrs. Linda B. ANTOINE
38 Director Student Counseling .... Dr. ValaRay IRVIN
62 Dean of Libraries .... Mrs. Emma BRADFORD-PERRY
88 Dean University College .... Dr. Dana CARPENTER
92 Dean of Honors College .... Dr. Ella KELLEY
58 Dean of the Graduate School .... Dr. Mwalimu J. SHUJAA
54 Dean College of Engineering .... Dr. Habib P. MOHAMADIAN
50 Dean College of Business .... Dr. Donald R. ANDREWS
53 Dean College of Education .... Dr. Verjanis PEOPLES
47 Int Dean Col Agri/Family/Consum Sci .... Dr. Doze BUTLER
49 Dean College Arts/Humanities .... Dr. Joyce O'ROURKE
80 Dean School of Public Policy .... Dr. William ARP
48 Dean School Architecture .... Mr. Lonnie WILKINSON
66 Int Dean of School of Nursing .... Dr. Cheryl TAYLOR
81 Dean of College of Science .... Dr. Robert H. MILLER

*Southern University at New Orleans (J)

6400 Press Drive, New Orleans LA 70126-1009
County: Orleans FICE Identification: 002026
Unit ID: 160630
Telephone: (504) 286-5000 Carnegie Class: Master's M
FAX Number: (504) 286-5131 Calendar System: Semester
URL: www.suno.edu
Established: 1956 Annual Undergrad Tuition & Fees (In-State): $4,008
Enrollment: 3,245 Coed
Affiliation or Control: State IRS Status: 501(c)3
Highest Offering: Master's
Program: Liberal Arts And General; Teacher Preparatory; Business Emphasis
Accreditation: SC, SW, TED

02 Chancellor .... Dr. Victor UKPOLO
04 Exec Assoc to the Chancellor .... Mr. Harold E. CLARK
05 VC for Academic Affairs & SACS .... Dr. David S. ADEGBOYE
10 VC for Admin & Finance .... Mr. Woodie WHITE
09 Dir IR & Strategic Initiatives .... Dr. Michael RALPH
09 Director Quality Enhancement Plan .Ms. Ada KWANBUNBUMPEN
108 Learning Outcomes/Assessment Coord .... Vacant
84 VC Student Affs & Enroll Services .... Dr. Donna GRANT
29 Vice Chan Cmty Outreach/Univ Advanc .... Mrs. Gloria B. MOULTRIE
21 Director of Facilities Management .... Mr. Shaun M. LEWIS
25 Dir Grants & Sponsored Programs .... Dr. William R. BELISLE
06 Registrar .... Ms. Gilda DAVIS
21 Comptroller .... Ms. Shawn M. GULLEY
08 Director of Library .... Mrs. Shatiqua A. MOSBY-WILSON
36 Dir Career Counseling & Vet Liaison .... Mr. Joseph MARION
14 Director of Information Technology ..Mr. Edmond M. CUMMINGS
15 Director of Human Resources .... Vacant
19 Police Captain Campus Police .... Mr. Ira THOMAS, SR.
20 Assoc VC Academic Affairs Faculty .... Mr. Wesley T. BISHOP
41 Director of Athletics .... Mr. Elston H. KING
07 Int Dir Financial Aid .... Ms. Leatrice D. LATIMORE
26 Director of Public Relations .... Mr. David GRUBB
96 Director of Purchasing .... Ms. Marilyn G. MANUEL
106 Director of E-Learning .... Ms. Shelia WOOD

70 Dean School of Social Work ... Dr. Beverly C. FAVRE
50 Dean College of Business/Pub Admin ... Dr. Igwe E. UDEH
88 Director of Museum Studies ... Dr. Sara HOLLIS
58 Dean of Graduate Studies ... Vacant
49 Dean College of Arts & Sciences ... Dr. Henry E. MOKOSSO
53 Int Dean College Educ & Human Dev ... Dr. Louise KALTENBAUGH
88 Dir Services for Students w/Disab ... Ms. Yolanda L. MIMS
35 Int Dir of Student Activities & Org ... Ms. Shawanda M. HOWARD
38 Dir of Student Development Center ... Mrs. Josephine OKORONKWO
39 Director of Residential Life ... Dr. Adrell L. PINKNEY
88 Director of Title III Programs ... Dr. Brenda W. JACKSON
88 Dir Student Support Services Pgm ... Ms. Linda D. FREDERICK
88 Dir Ctr for African & American Stds ... Dr. Romanus EJIAGA

*Southern University at Shreveport-Louisiana (A)

3050 Martin Luther King Drive, Shreveport LA 71107-4795
County: Caddo — FICE Identification: 007686
Unit ID: 160649
Telephone: (318) 670-6000 — Carnegie Class: Assoc/Pub2in4
FAX Number: (318) 670-6374 — Calendar System: Semester
URL: www.susla.edu
Established: 1964 — Annual Undergrad Tuition & Fees (In-State): $3,195
Enrollment: 2,831 — Coed
Affiliation or Control: State — IRS Status: 501(c)3
Highest Offering: Associate Degree
Program: Occupational; 2-Year Principally Bachelor's Creditable
Accreditation: **SC**, ADNUR, DH, MLTAD, NAIT, RAD, SURGT

02 Chancellor ... Dr. Ray L. BELTON
26 Spec Asst to Chanc/Dir Univ Rels ... Vacant
04 Admin Assistant to the Chancellor ... Mrs. Carolyn S. WEBB
05 Vice Chanc Academic Affairs ... Dr. Orella BRAZILE
10 Vice Chanc for Fiscal Affairs ... Mr. Benjamin W. PUGH
21 Comptroller ... Mrs. Brandy JACOBSEN
21 Bursar ... Ms. LaSonia MORRIS
103 VC Cmty Outreach/Workforce Develop ... Mrs. Janice SNEED
32 Vice Chanc Student Affs/Athletics ... Dr. Sharon F. GREEN
84 Assoc Vice Chanc Enrollment Mgmt ... Vacant
06 Registrar ... Ms. Mahailier L. BROOM
08 Librarian ... Mrs. Jane O'RILEY
35 Asst Vice Chanc for Student Affairs ... Vacant
20 Asst Vice Chanc for Academic Affs ... Dr. Regina ROBINSON
51 Director of Continuing Education ... Mrs. Beverly PARKER
07 Director of Admission & Recruitment ... Mrs. Rhalanda JACKSON
37 Interim Director of Financial Aid ... Ms. Taishieka DAVIS
27 Director Ofc of Univ Comm/Marketing ... Mr. William STROTHER
83 Div Chair Behavioral Sciences/Educ ... Mrs. Roslyn J. HOLT
50 Division Chair Business Studies ... Vacant
79 Division Chair for Humanities ... Mrs. June PHILLIPS
72 Div Chair Science & Technology ... Dr. Barry C. HESTER
76 Div Chair for Respiratory Therapy ... Mrs. JoAnn BROWN
46 Dir Inst Rsrch/Grants & Spnsrd Pgms ... Vacant
13 Director of Information Technology ... Dr. Gabriel FAGBEYIRO
88 Director Student Support Services ... Ms. Karen COCO
75 Director Aerospace Technology ... Mr. David FOGLEMAN
38 Director Counseling Center ... Ms. Rubie J. SCERE
15 Int Director Human Resources ... Ms. Murner JENKINS
96 Director of Purchasing ... Ms. Sophia JACKSON-LEE
18 Dir Physical Plant Facilities ... Mr. Joseph LACOUR
88 Director of Testing Center ... Ms. Kaye WASHINGTON
21 University Budget Officer ... Ms. Regina WINN
72 Director Radiologic Technology ... Ms. Sheila SWIFT
88 Ex Dir TRIO Cmty Outrch/Talent Srch ... Mrs. Carrie ROBINSON
88 Director Dental Hygiene ... Mrs. Kheysia H. WASHINGTON
09 Director Inst Plng/Assessment/Rsrch ... Mr. Martin FORTNER
66 Dean of School of Nursing ... Dr. Sandra TUCKER
88 Director Biomedical Research Devel ... Dr. Joseph ORBAN
83 Dean Behav Sci/Educ/Bus Standards ... Vacant

Southwest University (B)

2200 Veterans Memorial Boulevard,
Kenner LA 70062-4005
County: Jefferson — Identification: 666310
Telephone: (504) 468-2900 — Carnegie Class: Not Classified
FAX Number: (504) 468-3213 — Calendar System: Semester
URL: www.southwest.edu
Established: 1982 — Annual Undergrad Tuition & Fees: $9,000
Enrollment: 415 — Coed
Affiliation or Control: Proprietary — IRS Status: Proprietary
Highest Offering: Master's
Program: 2-Year Principally Bachelor's Creditable; Liberal Arts And General; Professional; Business Emphasis
Accreditation: **DETC**

01 President ... Dr. Grayce LEE
11 Administrative Officer ... Mr. Neil FESER
07 Admissions ... Mrs. Lydia OCMAND

Tulane University (C)

6823 St. Charles Avenue, New Orleans LA 70118-5698
County: Orleans — FICE Identification: 002029
Unit ID: 160755
Telephone: (504) 865-5000 — Carnegie Class: RU/VH
FAX Number: (504) 865-5202 — Calendar System: Semester
URL: www.tulane.edu
Established: 1834 — Annual Undergrad Tuition & Fees: $45,240
Enrollment: 13,359 — Coed
Affiliation or Control: Independent Non-Profit — IRS Status: 501(c)3
Highest Offering: Doctorate
Program: Liberal Arts And General; Teacher Preparatory; Professional
Accreditation: **SC**, BUS, DIETI, ENG, ENGR, HSA, IPSY, LAW, MED, PH, SCPSY, SW, TEAC

01 President ... Dr. Scott S. COWEN
05 Sr Vice Pres Acad Affairs/Provost ... Prof. Michael BERNSTEIN
26 COO/Sr VP External Affairs ... Ms. Yvette M. JONES
10 Sr Vice Pres for Operations & CFO ... Mr. Anthony P. LORINO
63 Sr Vice Pres/Dn School of Medicine ... Dr. Benjamin P. SACHS
17 VP/Vice Dean Health Sciences ... Ms. Mary BROWN
43 General Counsel ... Ms. Victoria D. JOHNSON
13 VP Information Technology/CTO ... Mr. Charles P. MCMAHON
20 Senior Associate Provost ... Ms. Ana LOPEZ
32 VP Student Affairs ... Mr. Michael HOGG
20 Associate Provost ... Dr. Brian MITCHELL
58 Assoc Prov Graduate Studies ... Dr. Brian S. MITCHELL
100 Chief of Staff & Vice President ... Ms. Anne BANOS
22 VP Inst Equity/Asst to Pres Dvrsity ... Ms. Deborah E. LOVE
32 Vice Pres Student Affs/Dn Students ... Dr. Cynthia CHERREY
84 Vice Pres Enrollment Mgmt/Registrar ... Mr. Earl RETIF
18 VP Operations & Facilities Services ... Dr. Earl F. BIHLMEYER
26 Vice Pres University Communications ... Ms. Deborah L. GRANT
46 Assoc Sr Vice President Research ... Ms. Laura LEVY
30 Vice President Development ... Ms. Luann D. DOZIER
86 Assoc VP Government Relations ... Ms. Sharon P. COURTNEY
35 Assoc VP Auxiliary Svcs/Student Ctr ... Mr. Robert C. HAILEY
18 Assoc Vice President Facilities ... Mr. Sylvester C. JOHNSON
44 Assoc Vice President Development ... Mr. Jeffrey A. BUSH
37 Assoc Vice President Financial Aid ... Mr. Michael GOODMAN
90 Director End User Support Svcs ... Mr. Adam KROB
21 Director Budget ... Mr. Gene MEYERS
22 Exec Dir Empl Rels/Inst Equity ... Ms. Stephanie ALLWEISS
29 Exec Director Alumni Affairs ... Ms. Charlotte TRAVIESO
21 Controller ... Mr. Frank (Doug) HARRELL
19 Director of Public Safety ... Mr. Kenneth DUPAQUIER
08 Dean Library & Academic Information ... Dr. Lance QUERY
38 Exec Dir Educ Resources/Couns ... Dr. Jillandra C. ROVARIS
36 Exec Director Career Svcs Ctr ... Dr. Amjad ANOUBI
12 Dir Tulane Natl Primate Res Ctr ... Mr. Andrew LACKNER
24 Executive Director Publications ... Ms. Carol J. SCHLUETER
39 Assoc VP Housing Services/Residence ... Mr. W. Ross BRYAN
96 Director Central Procurement Svcs ... Mr. William VAN CLEAVE
91 Asst VP Software Application Svcs ... Ms. Mary T. WALSH
41 Director Athletics ... Mr. Richard P. DICKSON
51 Dean Sch Cont Stds/Summer Sch ... Dr. Rick MARKSBURY
49 Dean School of Liberal Arts ... Dr. Carol HABER
49 Dean Newcomb-Tulane College ... Dr. James MACLAREN
61 Dean School of Law ... Mr. David D. MEYER
69 Dean Sch Public Health/Trop Med ... Dr. Pierre BUEKENS
54 Dean School Science & Engineering ... Dr. Nicholas J. ALTIERO
48 Dean School of Architecture ... Mr. Kenneth SCHWARTZ
50 Dean AB Freeman School of Business ... Dr. Ira SOLOMON
70 Dean School of Social Work ... Dr. Ronald MARKS
09 Director of Institutional Research ... Dr. Dave D. DAVIS
88 Exec Dir of CELT ... Dr. Michael CUNNINGHAM

*University of Louisiana System Office (D)

1201 N Third Street, Suite 7-300,
Baton Rouge LA 70802-5243
County: East Baton Rouge — FICE Identification: 033444
Unit ID: 247083
Telephone: (225) 342-6950 — Carnegie Class: N/A
FAX Number: (225) 342-6473
URL: www.ulsystem.net

01 President ... Dr. Randy MOFFETT
05 Provost & VP Acad & Student Affs ... Vacant
10 VP Business & Finance ... Mr. Robbie ROBINSON
09 VP Research & Performance Assess ... Dr. Beatrice BALDWIN
11 VP Administration and General Couns ... Ms. Dianne IRVINE
21 Asst VP for Budget & Finance ... Dr. Edwin LITOLFF

*Grambling State University (E)

Grambling LA 71245-3091
County: Lincoln — FICE Identification: 002006
Unit ID: 159009
Telephone: (318) 247-3811 — Carnegie Class: Master's M
FAX Number: (318) 274-6172 — Calendar System: Semester
URL: www.gram.edu
Established: 1901 — Annual Undergrad Tuition & Fees (In-State): $5,607
Enrollment: 5,207 — Coed
Affiliation or Control: State — IRS Status: 501(c)3
Highest Offering: Doctorate
Program: 2-Year Principally Bachelor's Creditable; Liberal Arts And General; Teacher Preparatory; Professional
Accreditation: **SC**, BUS, CS, ENGT, JOUR, MUS, NRPA, NUR, SPAA, SW, TED, THEA

02 President ... Dr. Frank G. POGUE
05 Provost/Vice Pres Academic Affairs ... Dr. Connie WALTON
10 Vice President for Finance and Admn ... Mr. Leon SANDERS
32 Vice President Student Affairs ... Dr. Stacey DUHON
30 Vice President Inst Advancement ... Dr. Kenoye EKE
86 Exec Assoc VP of CIAP ... Mr. Mahmoud LAMADANIE
18 Director of Facilties Management ... Mr. Lavoyd R. DUDLEY
14 Assoc VP of Information Technology ... Mr. Winfred JONES
45 Assoc VP of Planning & Research ... Ms. Nettie DANIELS
19 University Police Chief ... Mr. Freddie PETERSON
15 AVP of Human Resources ... Mrs. Monica BRADLEY
53 Dean College of Education ... Vacant
50 Dean College of Business ... Dr. Carl WRIGHT
58 Dean Division Grad Studies/Research ... Dr. Janet A. GUYDEN
88 Interim Dean Col of Prof Studies ... Dr. Rama TUNUGUNTLA
49 Interim Dean College of Arts & Sci ... Dr. Evelyn WYNN
92 Assistant Dean Honors College ... Dr. Ellen SMILEY
41 Director of Athletics ... Dr. Percy CALDWELL
22 EEO Officer & Wage & Salary Officer ... Mrs. Monica BRADLEY
07 Director of Admissions ... Mrs. Annie MOSS
06 University Registrar ... Mrs. Patricia J. HUTCHERSON
37 Dir Student Financial Aid ... Mr. Albert TEZENO
91 Dir of Administrative Computing ... Mrs. Peggy HANLEY
04 Executive Asst to the President ... Dr. Ellen SMILEY
29 Director Alumni Relations ... Ms. Debra JOHNSON
23 Director of Health Services ... Mrs. Patrice OUTLEY
38 Director Counseling Center ... Dr. Coleen SPEED
39 Dir of Residential Life and Housing ... Mr. James PAYNE
42 Director of Campus Ministry ... Rev. Consuella BREAUX
96 Director of Purchasing ... Ms. Connie HAMPTON
40 Manager University Bookstore ... Ms. Rosalyn LEWIS
106 Director of Distance Learning ... Mr. Eldrie HAMILTON
20 Special Assistant to Provost and VP ... Ms. Joann BROWN
36 Director of Career Services ... Mr. Johnny PATTERSON
44 Dir Annual Fund Coord ... Vacant

*Louisiana Tech University (F)

PO Box 3168, Ruston LA 71272-0001
County: Lincoln — FICE Identification: 002008
Unit ID: 159647
Telephone: (318) 257-0211 — Carnegie Class: RU/H
FAX Number: (318) 257-2928 — Calendar System: Quarter
URL: www.latech.edu
Established: 1894 — Annual Undergrad Tuition & Fees (In-State): $6,850
Enrollment: 11,581 — Coed
Affiliation or Control: State — IRS Status: 501(c)3
Highest Offering: Doctorate
Program: Liberal Arts And General; Teacher Preparatory; Professional
Accreditation: **SC**, AAB, AAFCS, ADNUR, ART, AUD, BUS, BUSA, CIDA, COPSY, CS, DIETD, DIETI, ENG, ENGT, FOR, MUS, SP, TED

02 President ... Dr. Daniel D. RENEAU
05 VP Academic Affs/Dean Grad School ... Dr. Terry M. MCCONATHY
32 Vice President for Student Affairs ... Dr. Jim M. KING
11 Vice Pres Finance/Administration ... Mr. Joe R. THOMAS
30 Vice President for Univ Advancement ... Ms. Corre A. STEGALL
10 Comptroller ... Mrs. Lisa COLE
50 Dean of Business ... Dr. James LUMPKIN
49 Dean of Liberal Arts ... Dr. Don KACZVINSKY
53 Dean of Education ... Dr. David GULLATT
54 Dean of Engineering & Science ... Dr. Stan A. NAPPER
65 Dean of Applied & Natural Sciences ... Dr. James D. LIBERATOS
84 Dean of Enrollment Management ... Mrs. Pamela R. FORD
07 Interim Director of Admissions ... Mrs. Joan B. EDINGER
21 Business Officer ... Mr. Jerry S. DREWETT
14 Director of Computer Center ... Mr. Roy S. WATERS
37 Director Student Financial Aid ... Mr. Roger VICK
09 Director Institutional Research ... Mrs. Lori C. THEIS
06 Registrar ... Mr. Robert D. VENTO
08 Director of Libraries ... Mr. Michael DICARLO
15 Director of Personnel ... Mrs. Sheila TRAMMEL
26 Chief University Communications ... Mr. David GUERIN
29 Director of Alumni Relations ... Mr. Ryan RICHARD
36 Dir Career Ctr/Student Counseling ... Mr. Ron CATHEY
89 Director of Freshmen Studies ... Vacant
92 Director of Honors Program ... Dr. Rick SIMMONS
93 Director of Multicultural Affairs ... Vacant
96 Director of Purchasing ... Ms. Karen MURPHY
18 Int Chief Facilities/Physical Plant ... Mr. Doug WILLIS
35 Director Student Affairs ... Dr. Jim KING

*McNeese State University (G)

4205 Ryan Street, Lake Charles LA 70609-4510
County: Calcasieu — FICE Identification: 002017
Unit ID: 159717
Telephone: (337) 475-5000 — Carnegie Class: Master's L
FAX Number: (337) 475-5012 — Calendar System: Semester
URL: www.mcneese.edu
Established: 1939 — Annual Undergrad Tuition & Fees (In-State): $14,605
Enrollment: 8,791 — Coed
Affiliation or Control: State — IRS Status: 501(c)3
Highest Offering: Beyond Master's But Less Than Doctorate
Program: Liberal Arts And General; Teacher Preparatory; Professional
Accreditation: **SC**, AAFCS, ADNUR, ART, BUS, CS, DIETD, DIETI, ENG, ENGT, MT, MUS, NURSE, RAD, TED

02 President ... Dr. Philip C. WILLIAMS
05 Provost/VP Academic & Student Affs ... Dr. Jeanne M. DABOVAL
10 Vice President for Business Affairs ... Mr. Eddie P. MECHE
30 Vice Pres University Advancement ... Mr. Richard H. REID
81 Dean College of Science ... Dr. George F. MEAD, JR.
58 Int Dean Dore Sch Graduate Studies ... Dr. George F. MEAD, JR.
50 Interim Dean College Business ... Dr. Banamber MISHRA
53 Dean of College of Education ... Dr. Wayne R. FETTER
49 Dean College Liberal Arts ... Dr. Ray MILES
54 Dean Col of Engr & Engr Technology ... Dr. Nikos KIRITSIS
66 Dean of College of Nursing ... Dr. Peggy L. WOLFE
84 Dean Enrollment Management ... Ms. Stephanie B. TARVER
32 AVP Enrollment Mgt/Student Affairs ... Mr. Toby W. OSBURN

18 Director Facilities & Plant Opers ... Mr. Richard R. RHODEN
13 Director of Univ Computing Services ... Mr. Stanley HIPPLER
31 Dir Community Service and Outreach ... Mrs. Betty H. ANDERSON
15 Director of Human Resources ... Ms. Charlene R. ABBOTT
09 Director Institutional Research ... Ms. Kathleen S. DOUGAY
37 Director Student Financial Aid ... Ms. Taina J. SAVOIT
08 Director of Library ... Ms. Debbie L. JOHNSON-HOUSTON
19 Dir University Police/Info Center ... Ms. Cinnamon A. SALVADOR
29 Director Alumni Affairs ... Ms. Joyce D. PATTERSON
38 Director Scholarships/Testing ... Ms. Ralynn F. CASTETE
35 Assistant Dean Student Services ... Vacant
07 Dir of Admissions and Recruiting ... Ms. Kara SMITH
36 Director Career Services ... Ms. Kathy E. BOND
41 Athletic Director ... Mr. Thomas H. MCCLELLAND, II
45 Dir Inst Effectiveness/Acad Support ... Dr. Tom DVORSKE
96 Director Purchasing/Property Cntrl ... Ms. Pamela L. WATKINS
92 Director of Honors College ... Dr. Scott E. GOINS
14 Chief Information Technology ... Mr. Chad THIBODEAUX
46 Director of Research Services/LERC ... Ms. Janet R. WOOLMAN
85 International Student Advisor ... Ms. Christine M. KAY
26 Director Public Relations ... Ms. Candace V. TOWNSEND
23 RN Supervisor-Student Health ... Ms. Sharon E. GUILLORY
40 Bookstore Manager ... Ms. Sharamie T. MOORE
06 Coordinator Alternative Learning ... Mr. Matthew D. WELCH
90 Coord of Col of Science Computing ... Dr. William G. ALBRECHT
106 Director of Electronic Learning ... Ms. Helen B. WARE
28 Chief Diversity Officer ... Dr. Michael T. SNOWDEN

*Nicholls State University (A)

University Station, Thibodaux LA 70310-0001
County: Lafourche FICE Identification: 002005
Unit ID: 159966
Telephone: (985) 446-8111 Carnegie Class: Master's M
FAX Number: (985) 448-4920 Calendar System: Semester
URL: www.nicholls.edu
Established: 1948 Annual Undergrad Tuition & Fees (In-State): $5,737
Enrollment: 6,774 Coed
Affiliation or Control: State IRS Status: 501(c)3
Highest Offering: Beyond Master's But Less Than Doctorate
Program: 2-Year Principally Bachelor's Creditable; Liberal Arts And General; Teacher Preparatory
Accreditation: SC, AAFCS, ART, BUS, BUSA, DIETD, ENGR, ENGT, JOUR, MUS, NAIT, NURSE, TED

02 President ... Dr. Stephen T. HULBERT
05 VP for Academic Affairs ... Dr. Allayne BARRILLEAUX
03 Executive Vice President ... Mr. Lawrence W. HOWELL
32 Vice Pres Student Affs/Enroll Svcs ... Dr. Eugene A. DIAL
30 Vice President for Inst Advancement ... Dr. David E. BOUDREAUX
21 Asst Vice Pres for Facilities ... Mr. Michael G. DAVIS
21 Asst Vice Pres for Finance/CFO ... Mr. Michael P. NAQUIN
45 Exec Dir of Planning/Effectiveness ... Mrs. Renee G. HICKS
49 Dean of Arts & Sciences ... Dr. John DOUCET
66 Dean of Nursing and Allied Health ... Dr. Velma S. WESTBROOK
50 Dean Business Administration ... Dr. Shawn MAULDIN
53 Dean of Education ... Dr. Leslie JONES
88 Dean of University College ... Dr. Albert DAVIS
32 Dean of Student Life ... Vacant
09 Dir Assess/Institutional Research ... Mrs. Leslie B. DISHMAN
08 Director of Library ... Dr. Robert BREMET
19 Director of University Police ... Mr. Craig M. JACCUZZO
36 Director of Student Placement ... Ms. Kristie R. TAUZIN
37 Director of Student Financial Aid ... Ms. Casie TRICHE
14 Director of Computing Center ... Mr. Charles R. ORDOYNE
15 Director of Human Resources ... Mr. John FORD
18 Dir Facility Plng/Special Projects ... Mr. Michael G. DAVIS
26 Director of University Relations ... Mrs. Renee PIPER
51 Assoc Dir of Continuing Education ... Ms. Simone HARRIS
41 Athletic Director ... Mr. Robert BERNARDI
29 Director of Alumni Affairs ... Miss Deborah A. RAZIANO
06 Director Records & Registration ... Mr. Kelly J. RODRIGUE
07 Director of Admissions ... Mrs. Becky L. DUROCHER
23 Director University Health Services ... Dr. Diane GARVEY
38 Director of Student Services ... Dr. Michele E. CARUSO
39 Director Residence Life ... Mr. Hayward GUENARD
90 Director Academic Computing ... Mr. Thomas BONVILLAIN
84 Director of Enrollment Services ... Mrs. Courtney CASSARD
96 Director of Purchasing ... Mr. Terry G. DUPRE
88 Director Research & Sponsored Pgms ... Mrs. Debra BENOIT
58 Director of Graduate Programs ... Ms. Betty KLEEN
88 Director of Printing & Design ... Mr. Bruno RUGGIERO
88 Director of Auxiliary Services ... Mrs. Brenda HASKINS
88 Coordinator of Veterans Services ... Mr. Gilberto BURBANTE

*Northwestern State University (B)

140 Central Avenue, Natchitoches LA 71497-0002
County: Natchitoches FICE Identification: 002021
Unit ID: 160038
Telephone: (318) 357-6361 Carnegie Class: Master's L
FAX Number: (318) 357-4223 Calendar System: Semester
URL: www.nsula.edu
Established: 1884 Annual Undergrad Tuition & Fees (In-State): $8,137
Enrollment: 9,191 Coed
Affiliation or Control: State IRS Status: 501(c)3
Highest Offering: Doctorate
Program: Liberal Arts And General; Teacher Preparatory; Professional
Accreditation: SC, AAFCS, ADNUR, ART, BUS, ENGT, MUS, NURSE, RAD, SW, TED, THEA

02 President ... Dr. Randall J. WEBB
04 Exec Assistant to the President ... Mr. Robert CREW
05 Provost/VP Academic & Student Affs ... Dr. Lisa ABNEY
11 Vice Pres for University Affairs ... Dr. Marcus JONES
26 Vice President for External Affairs ... Mr. Jerry D. PIERCE
46 Vice Pres for Tech/Research/Eco Dev ... Dr. Darlene WILLIAMS
10 Vice President Business Affairs ... Mr. Carl JONES
20 Vice Provost ... Dr. Steve HORTON
32 Asst Provost & Dean of Students ... Dr. Chris MAGGIO
53 Dean Col of Education & Human Dev ... Dr. Vickie GENTRY
49 Dean Col of Arts/Letters/Grad Stds ... Dr. Steve HORTON
66 Dean Col of Nursing & Allied Health ... Dr. Norann PLANCHOCK
72 Dean Col of Science/Tech/Business ... Dr. Austin TEMPLE
88 Director Scholars College ... Dr. Davina MCCLAIN
12 Director Leesville Campus ... Dr. Randy HALEY
09 Director Institutional Research ... Mr. Curtis PENROD
06 Registrar ... Mrs. Lillie F. BELL
08 Director of Libraries ... Ms. Abbie LANDRY
29 Director Alumni Affairs & Devel ... Mr. Drake OWENS
37 Director Student Financial Aid ... Mrs. Chrystal WOODARD
27 Director News Bureau ... Mr. David WEST
36 Director Counseling & Career Svcs ... Mrs. Rebecca BOONE
41 Athletic Director ... Mr. Greg BURKE
23 Director of Health Services ... Mrs. Stephanie CAMPBELL
07 Director of University Recruiting ... Mrs. Jana LUCKY
15 Director Human Resources ... Mr. Cecil KNOTTS
18 Physical Plant Director ... Mr. Chuck BOURG
96 Director of Purchasing ... Mr. Stan WRIGHT
21 Associate Business Officer ... Ms. Rita GRAVES

*Southeastern Louisiana University (C)

548 Western Avenue, Hammond LA 70402-0001
County: Tangipahoa FICE Identification: 002024
Unit ID: 160612
Telephone: (985) 549-2000 Carnegie Class: Master's L
FAX Number: (985) 549-2061 Calendar System: Semester
URL: www.selu.edu
Established: 1925 Annual Undergrad Tuition & Fees (In-State): $4,510
Enrollment: 15,414 Coed
Affiliation or Control: State IRS Status: 501(c)3
Highest Offering: Doctorate
Program: Liberal Arts And General; Teacher Preparatory; Professional
Accreditation: SC, AAFCS, ART, BUS, BUSA, CACREP, CS, ENGR, MUS, NAIT, NURSE, SP, SW, TED

02 President ... Dr. John L. CRAIN
05 Provost/VP Academic Affairs ... Dr. Tammy BOURG
10 Interim VP Administration/Finance ... Mr. Sam DOMIANO
30 Vice Pres University Advancement ... Ms. Wendy JOHNS-LAUDERDALE
32 Vice President Student Affairs ... Dr. Marvin L. YATES
20 Asst VP Academic Affairs ... Dr. Josie WALKER
13 Chief Information Officer ... Dr. Mike M. ASOODEH
04 Exec Assistant to the President ... Ms. Erin K. COWSER
21 Controller ... Ms. Nettie L. BURCHFIELD
06 Director Records & Registration ... Ms. Paulette M. POCHE
08 Director of Library ... Mr. Eric W. JOHNSON
36 Director Career Development Svcs ... Mr. Ken W. RIDGEDELL
31 Interim Director Auxiliary Services ... Ms. Connie DAVIS
29 Director of Alumni Services ... Ms. Kathy L. PITTMAN
39 Dir Student Housing & Resident Svcs ... Dr. Kay MAURIN
15 Director Human Resources ... Mr. Kevin BRADY
19 Director University Police ... Mr. Michael L. PRESCOTT
46 Dir Sponsored Research/Programs ... Ms. Cheryl HALL
41 Athletic Director ... Mr. Bart BELLAIRS
18 Director Facility Planning ... Mr. Ken D. HOWE
92 Director Honors Program ... Dr. Kent NEUERBURG
23 Director Health Services ... Ms. Vera A. WILLIAMS
38 Director Counseling Center ... Dr. Barbara B. HEBERT
07 Director Admissions ... Mr. Richard BEAUGH
37 Director Financial Aid ... Ms. Mary LACOUR
09 Director Inst Research/Assessment ... Dr. Michelle HALL
26 Director Public Information ... Mr. Rene G. ABADIE
96 Dir Purchasing/Property Control ... Mr. Ed E. GAUTIER
85 Dir Multicultural/Intl Stdnt Affs ... Mr. Eric J. SUMMERS
22 Coordinator EEO/ADA ... Mr. Gene E. PREGEANT
49 Int Dn Col Arts/Human/Soc Sciences ... Dr. Karen FONTENOT
50 Dean of College of Business ... Dr. Randy P. SETTOON
53 Dean College Education & Human Dev ... Dr. John FISCHETTI
66 Dean Col of Nursing & Health Sci ... Dr. Ann CARRUTH
72 Dean Col of Science & Technology ... Dr. Daniel MCCARTHY
56 Asst VP Extended Studies ... Ms. Joan GUNTER

*University of Louisiana at Lafayette (D)

104 University Circle, Lafayette LA 70503-0001
County: Lafayette FICE Identification: 002031
Unit ID: 160658
Telephone: (337) 482-1000 Carnegie Class: RU/H
FAX Number: (337) 482-6195 Calendar System: Semester
URL: www.louisiana.edu
Established: 1898 Annual Undergrad Tuition & Fees (In-State): $4,857
Enrollment: 16,885 Coed
Affiliation or Control: State IRS Status: 501(c)3
Highest Offering: Doctorate
Program: Liberal Arts And General; Teacher Preparatory; Professional
Accreditation: SC, ART, BUS, BUSA, CIDA, CS, DIETD, DIETI, ENG, JOUR, MUS, NAIT, NURSE, SP, TED

02 President ... Dr. E. Joseph SAVOIE
05 Provost and VP for Academic Affairs ... Dr. Carolyn BRUDER
10 VP Administration & Finance ... Mr. Jerry L. LEBLANC
32 Interim VP for Student Affairs ... Ms. Patricia COTTONHAM
30 Vice Pres University Advancement ... Mr. Ken ARDOIN
46 Vice Pres for Research/Grad Studies ... Dr. Robert TWILLEY
84 VP for Enrollment Mgmt ... Dr. DeWayne BOWIE
13 Chief Information Officer ... Mr. Gene FIELDS
11 Director of Administrative Services ... Ms. Lisa C. LANDRY
21 Asst Vice Pres Financial Services ... Mr. Ronald P. LAJAUNIE
21 Comptroller ... Ms. Debra CALAIS
45 Asst VP Institutional Planning ... Dr. Paula P. CARSON
108 Asst VP Institutional Plng & Effect ... Dr. Paula CARSON
20 Asst VP Academic Affairs ... Ms. Ellen D. COOK
35 Dean of Students ... Ms. Patricia F. COTTONHAM
25 Director Research/Sponsored Pgms ... Ms. Ruth LANDRY
91 Director of Information Systems ... Mr. Sam F. BULLARD
14 Director Computing Support Services ... Mr. Patrick LANDRY
08 Dean of University Libraries ... Dr. Charles W. TRICHE, III
07 Dir of UN Admissions & Recruitment ... Mr. Andy BENOIT
88 Director Information Networks ... Mr. Stephen J. MAHLER
09 Director of Institutional Research ... Ms. Lisa LORD
55 Director University College ... Ms. Amanda DOYLE
37 Director of Financial Aid ... Ms. Cindy SHOWS-PEREZ
96 Assistant Director Purchasing ... Ms. Lark CHARTIER
27 Assoc Director Publications ... Ms. Kathleen A. THAMES
36 Director Career Services ... Ms. Kim A. BILLEAUDEAU
19 Chief of Police ... Chief Joey STURM
23 Director Student Health Svcs ... Dr. Marelle YONGUE
49 Dean Liberal Arts ... Dr. A. David BARRY
54 Dean of Engineering ... Dr. Mark E. ZAPPI
53 Dean of Education ... Dr. Gerald P. CARLSON
66 Dean of Nursing ... Dr. Gail P. POIRRIER
58 Dean of Graduate School ... Dr. C. Eddie PALMER
50 Dean of Business Administration ... Dr. Joby JOHN
81 Dean of Sciences ... Dr. Bradd CLARK
97 Dean of General Studies ... Dr. Phebe A. HAYES
57 Dean College of the Arts ... Mr. H. Gordon BROOKS, II
77 Director Ctr Adv Computer Studies ... Dr. Magdy A. BAYOUMI
18 Director Physical Plant ... Mr. William J. CRIST
22 Director Operational Review/EEO Off ... Ms. Christine BRASHER
39 Director Housing ... Ms. Lisa L. LANDRY
40 Manager Bookstore ... Mr. Robert RICHARD
24 Director Univ Media/Printing Svcs ... Mr. Steve MAHLER
41 Athletic Director ... Mr. Scott FARMER
85 Director Office of Intl Affairs ... Dr. Rose HONEGGER
51 Director of Continuing Education ... Ms. Elaine D. LIVERS
31 Dean of Community Service ... Mr. David YARBROUGH
86 Coordinator Governmental Relations ... Vacant
26 Dir of Communication and Marketing ... Mr. Aaron MARTIN
29 Exec Director Alumni Affairs ... Mr. Dan W. HARE
44 Planned Giving Officer ... Mr. David P. COMEAUX
38 Director Counseling and Testing ... Mr. Brian FREDERICK
16 Human Resources Coordinator ... Ms. Charlene HAMILTON
06 Registrar ... Mr. Chip JACKSON

*University of Louisiana at Monroe (E)

700 University Avenue, Monroe LA 71209-0001
County: Ouachita FICE Identification: 002020
Unit ID: 159993
Telephone: (318) 342-1000 Carnegie Class: Master's L
FAX Number: (318) 342-5161 Calendar System: Semester
URL: www.ulm.edu
Established: 1931 Annual Undergrad Tuition & Fees (In-State): $5,101
Enrollment: 8,583 Coed
Affiliation or Control: State IRS Status: 501(c)3
Highest Offering: Doctorate
Program: 2-Year Principally Bachelor's Creditable; Liberal Arts And General; Teacher Preparatory; Professional; Business Emphasis
Accreditation: SC, AAB, BUS, BUSA, CACREP, CONST, CS, DH, EXSC, MFCD, MT, MUS, NURSE, OTA, PHAR, RAD, SP, SW, TED

02 President ... Dr. Nick J. BRUNO
04 Executive Assistant to President ... Dr. Richard J. HOOD
03 Executive VP ... Dr. Stephen P. RICHTERS
10 Chief Business Officer ... Mr. William T. GRAVES
32 Vice President for Student Affairs ... Dr. Wendell W. BRUMFIELD
35 Asst VP for Student Affairs ... Dr. Camile W. CURRIER
05 Academic Affairs VP ... Dr. Eric A. PANI
84 Asst VP for Enrollment Mgmt ... Mrs. Lisa R. MILLER
07 Director of Admissions ... Ms. Jennifer MALONE
29 Exec Director Alumni ... Mr. Keith A. BROWN
41 Director of Athletics ... Mr. Robert H. STAUB
27 Director Media Relations ... Mrs. Laura J. WOODARD
88 Director Internal Audit ... Mr. Kirby D. CAMPBELL
49 Dean College of Arts & Sciences ... Dr. Michael CAMILLE
97 Director Program General Studies ... Dr. Richard B. CHARDKOFF
50 Dean Col Business Administration ... Dr. Ronald BERRY
88 Dir Ctr Business/Economic Research ... Dr. Robert C. EISENSTADT
53 Dean Col of Education/Human Devel ... Dr. Sandra M. LEMOINE
53 Dir of Graduate Studies/Col of Ed ... Dr. Jack PALMER
76 Dean College of Health Sciences ... Dr. Denny G. RYMAN
67 Dean College of Pharmacy ... Dr. Benny BLAYLOCK
58 Interim Dean of Graduate Programs ... Dr. William MCCOWN
92 Director Honors Program ... Dr. Christian RUBIO
108 Director Assessment and Evaluation ... Mrs. Allison L. THOMPSON
09 Exec Dir Univ Planning/Analysis ... Mr. Justin P. ROY
08 Dean of the Library ... Mr. Donald R. SMITH
51 Director Continuing Education ... Ms. Paula THORNHILL
26 Director of Marketing ... Ms. Lauren BROWNELL
06 Registrar ... Mr. Anthony MALTA
37 Interim Director of Financial Aid ... Ms. Cori SMIT
88 Director Testing ... Ms. Denise M. DUPLECHIN
85 Dir Intl Student Program and Svcs ... Dr. Mara C. LOEB

88 Director of University Retention .... Mrs. Barbara MICHAELIDES
39 Director Residential Life .... Ms. Tresea L. BUCKHAULTS
45 Budget Officer .... Ms. Gail C. PARKER
21 Controller .... Ms. Sandra WALKER
15 Director Human Resources .... Mr. Larry M. ESTESS
96 Director Purchasing .... Mr. Larry M. ESTESS
14 Int Director Computer Center .... Mr. Chance W. EPPINETTE
88 Exec Dir Auxiliary Enterprises .... Mr. Michael R. TREVATHAN
40 Manager University Bookstore .... Ms. Rebecca BOOTHBY
18 Director Physical Plant Admin .... Mr. Lawrence B. THORN
88 Dir Facilities Mgmt & Ehs .... Mr. Jason S. ROUBIQUE
35 Director of Student Services .... Ms. Pamela JACKSON
88 Asst Dean Student Life/Leadership .... Mr. Nathan HALL
38 Director Counseling Center .... Ms. Karen FOSTER
23 Director Student Health Services ....Ms. Yolanda CAMPER
19 Director University Police ....Mr. Larry M. ELLERMAN
36 Director Career Connections/Exp ....Ms. Roslynn POGUE
88 Dir Recreational Svcs/Facilities .... Ms. Treina LANDRUM
88 Director of Development ....Ms. Anne A. LOCKHART
105 Director of Web Services .... Mr. Lindsey S. WILKERSON
102 Chief Finan Ofcr Univ Foundations .... Mr. Mark S. LABUDE
29 Associate Director Alumni Relations ...... Mr. Tommy A. WALPOLE

Xavier University of Louisiana (A)

One Drexel Drive, New Orleans LA 70125-1098
County: Orleans　FICE Identification: 002032
Unit ID: 160904
Telephone: (504) 486-7411　Carnegie Class: Bac/A&S
FAX Number: (504) 520-7904　Calendar System: Semester
URL: www.xula.edu
Established: 1925　Annual Undergrad Tuition & Fees: $17,700
Enrollment: 3,399　Coed
Affiliation or Control: Roman Catholic　IRS Status: 501(c)3
Highest Offering: Doctorate
Program: Liberal Arts And General; Teacher Preparatory; Professional
Accreditation: SC, ACBSP, MUS, PHAR, TED

01 President .... Dr. Norman C. FRANCIS
11 Sr Vice Pres for Administration .... Mr. Calvin S. TREGRE
05 Sr Vice Pres for Academic Affairs .... Dr. Loren BLANCHARD
30 Sr VP for Resource Development ....Dr. Gene D'AMOUR
32 Vice President for Student Services ....Mr. Joseph K. BYRD
30 Vice President for Inst Advancement .....Dr. Kenneth ST.CHARLES
10 Vice President for Finance .... Mr. Edward PHILLIPS
13 Interim VP for Office of Technology .... Mrs. Melva WILLIAMS
45 Vice Pres Planning & Inst Research .....Dr. Ronald R. DURNFORD
18 Vice President Facilities Planning .... Mr. Marion BRACY
26 Assoc VP Public Affairs/Comm .... Vacant
20 Assoc VP for Academic Affairs .... Dr. Marguerite GIGUETTE
31 Assoc Vice Pres Auxiliary Services .... Mr. William JEFFRION
07 Dean of Admissions ....Mr. Winston D. BROWN
06 Registrar .... Ms. Avis STUARD
42 Director of Campus Ministry .... Mrs. Lisa L. MCCLAIN
21 Director of Accounting .... Ms. Joyce SANDIFER
21 Director of Operations .... Ms. Lori GIE
21 Dir Fin Reporting & External Audit .... Mrs. Ingenue S. SCHEXNIDER-FIELDS
15 Director of Human Resources .... Mr. Larry CALVIN
49 Dean of Arts & Sciences .... Dr. Anil KUKREJA
67 Dean of College of Pharmacy .... Dr. Kathleen KENNEDY
89 Director of Freshmen Studies ....Sr. Monica LOUGHLIN
09 Dir of Inst Effectiv & Assessment ....Dr. Danielle DUFFOURC
09 Director of Institutional Research ....Dr. Treva A. LEE
08 Director of the Library ....Mr. Robert E. SKINNER
36 Director of Career Services ....Mrs. Carolyn D. THOMAS
37 Director of Financial Aid ....Ms. Emily LONDON-JONES
19 Director of Campus Police .... Mr. Duane CARKUM
23 Director Student Health Services ....Ms. Brenda MEDLEY
38 Director of Counseling Services ....Ms. Eloise DOXIE-DIXON
29 Director of Alumni Relations .... Ms. Kimberly REESE
40 Manager Bookstore .... Ms. Rose NAQUIN
41 Athletic Director .... Mr. Dennis COUSIN

MAINE

Bangor Theological Seminary (B)

PO Box 411, Bangor ME 04402-0411
County: Penobscot　FICE Identification: 002035
Unit ID: 160968
Telephone: (207) 942-6781　Carnegie Class: Spec/Faith
FAX Number: (207) 990-1267　Calendar System: Semester
URL: www.bts.edu
Established: 1814　Annual Graduate Tuition & Fees: $11,760
Enrollment: 85　Coed
Affiliation or Control: United Church Of Christ　IRS Status: 501(c)3
Highest Offering: Doctorate; No Undergraduates
Program: Professional; Religious Emphasis
Accreditation: EH, THEOL

01 President .... Rev Dr. Robert GROVE-MARKWOOD
05 Academic Dean .... Rev Dr. Steven LEWIS
04 Exec Asst to the President .... Ms. Adrea JAEHNIG
06 Registrar ....Ms. Danielle R. LAVINE
08 Librarian ....Ms. Laurie MCQUARRIE
10 Controller ....Mrs. Caroline HAMMOND
04 Assistant to the President ....Mrs. Patricia O. ANNIS

Bates College (C)

2 Andrews Road, Lewiston ME 04240-6047
County: Androscoggin　FICE Identification: 002036
Unit ID: 160977
Telephone: (207) 786-6255　Carnegie Class: Bac/A&S
FAX Number: (207) 786-6123　Calendar System: Other
URL: www.bates.edu
Established: 1855　Annual Undergrad Tuition & Fees: $57,235
Enrollment: 1,754　Coed
Affiliation or Control: Independent Non-Profit　IRS Status: 501(c)3
Highest Offering: Baccalaureate
Program: Liberal Arts And General
Accreditation: EH

01 President ....Dr. A. Clayton SPENCER
05 VP Academic Affairs/Dean of Faculty ....Dr. Pamela J. BAKER
10 VP Finance & Admin/Treasurer .... Ms. Terry J. BECKMANN
86 VP and Sr Advisor to the President ....Dr. Nancy J. CABLE
08 VP Info & Libr Services/Librarian ....Dr. Eugene L. WIEMERS
30 VP Advancement ....Ms. Sarah R. PEARSON
32 Dean of Students .... Mr. Tedd GOUNDIE
21 Asst Vice Pres Financial Planning ....Mr. Douglas W. GINEVAN
20 Associate Dean of Faculty .... Dr. Kathryn G. LOW
31 Director of Community Partnerships ....Ms. Darby K. RAY
06 Registrar .... Ms. Mary MESERVE
09 Acting Dir Inst Rsch/Assessment .... Ms. Sarah J. BERNARD
15 Dir Human Resources ....Ms. Mary MAIN
18 Dir Physical Plant Operations ....Mr. Daniel F. NEIN
88 Dir Capital Planning/Construction ......Ms. Pamela J. WICHROSKI
07 Dean of Admissions & Financial Aid .... Ms. Leigh WEISENBURGER
29 Dir Alumni & Parent Engagement .... Ms. Marianne COWAN
19 Dir Security & Campus Safety .... Mr. Thomas P. CAREY
23 Dir Health Services .... Ms. Christy TISDALE
26 Asst VP Communications/Media Rels .... Ms. Margaret KIMMEL
37 Dir Student Financial Services .... Ms. Wendy G. GLASS
40 Dir Bookstore/Contract Officer ....Ms. Sarah POTTER
36 Dir of Career Services ....Mr. David MCDONOUGH
91 Dir Sys Development & Integration ... Ms. Eileen P. ZIMMERMAN
24 Dir of Academic Technology Services .... Mr. Andrew W. WHITE
41 Athletic Director .... Mr. Kevin MCHUGH
42 College Chaplain ....Mr. William BLAINE-WALLACE
39 Asst Dean of Students/Housing ....Ms. Erin FOSTER ZSIGA
102 Dir of the Office for External Grnt ....Mr. Philip WALSH
104 Assoc Dean of Students/Study Abroad .... Mr. Stephen SAWYER

† Tuition figure is a comprehensive fees figure.

Beal College (D)

99 Farm Road, Bangor ME 04401-6831
County: Penobscot　FICE Identification: 005204
Unit ID: 160995
Telephone: (207) 947-4591　Carnegie Class: Assoc/PrivFP
FAX Number: (207) 947-0208　Calendar System: Other
URL: www.bealcollege.edu
Established: 1891　Annual Undergrad Tuition & Fees: $7,080
Enrollment: 550　Coed
Affiliation or Control: Proprietary　IRS Status: Proprietary
Highest Offering: Associate Degree
Program: 2-Year Principally Bachelor's Creditable
Accreditation: ACICS, MAC

01 President .... Mr. Allen T. STEHLE
05 Director of Education .... Ms. Deborah CROCKETT
08 Chief Librarian ....Mrs. Ann W. REA
37 Director Student Financial Aid ....Ms. Maggie MAGEE
18 Superintendent Physical Plant .... Mr. Kevin HARDY
10 Associate Business Officer ....Ms. Pollyanne HEWES
88 Dir Early Child Ed/Hospitality Svcs .... Ms. Susan XIRINACHS
76 Director Allied Health .... Ms. Barbara MARCHELLETTA
88 Director Criminal Justice .... Mr. Roger GUAY
40 Director Bookstore .... Ms. Lisa PORTER
36 Director Student Placement ....Ms. Donna GILLETTE
06 Registrar ....Ms. Ellen EDWARDS
07 Director of Admissions .... Ms. Erin LEIGHTON
32 Director of Student Affairs .... Ms. Debbie LEBLANC
88 Director Accounting ....Ms. Joan TUKEY
88 Director Social & Human Svcs Asst ....Ms. Susan POLYOT

Bowdoin College (E)

5700 College Station, Brunswick ME 04011-8448
County: Cumberland　FICE Identification: 002038
Unit ID: 161004
Telephone: (207) 725-3000　Carnegie Class: Bac/A&S
FAX Number: (207) 725-3123　Calendar System: Semester
URL: www.bowdoin.edu
Established: 1794　Annual Undergrad Tuition & Fees: $43,676
Enrollment: 1,778　Coed
Affiliation or Control: Independent Non-Profit　IRS Status: 501(c)3
Highest Offering: Master's
Program: Liberal Arts And General
Accreditation: EH

01 President ....Dr. Barry MILLS
10 Sr VP Finance/Admin & Treasurer ..... Ms. S. Catherine LONGLEY
46 Sr VP Devel & Alumni Relations .... Mr. Kelly K. KERNER
32 Dean of Student Affairs ....Mr. Timothy W. FOSTER
05 Dean for Academic Affairs ....Dr. Cristle Collins JUDD
07 Dean of Admissions ....Mr. Scott A. MEIKLEJOHN
26 VP/Dir Comm/Public Affairs ....Mr. Scott W. HOOD
09 VP Institutional Planning & Assess ....Mrs. Becky BRODIGAN
30 Sr VP for Devel & Alumni Relations ....Mr. Kelly KERNER
20 Assoc Dean for Academic Affairs .... Dr. Barry LOGAN
35 Sr Associate Dean Student Affairs ....Ms. Margaret L. HAZLETT
29 Director Alumni Relations ....Ms. Rodie F. LLOYD
08 Acting Librarian .... Ms. Judith R. MONTGOMERY
37 Director of Student Aid .... Mr. Michael D. BARTINI
21 Controller .... Mr. Matthew ORLANDO
06 Registrar ....MS. Jan BRACKETT
15 Director of Human Resources .... Ms. Tamara D. SPOERRI
19 Director of Security .... Mr. Randall NICHOLS
36 Director of Career Planning ....Mr. Timothy DIEHL
38 Director of Counseling Service .... Dr. Bernie HERSHBERGER
41 Interim Director of Athletics ....Mr. Timothy M. RYAN
13 Chief Information Officer .... Mr. Mitchel W. DAVIS
23 Director of Health Services ....Ms. Sandra J. HAYES
18 Director Facilities Ops/Maintenance ....Mr. Theodore R. STAM
24 Instructional Media Librarian ....Ms. Carmen M. GREENLEE
21 Director of Finance & Campus Svcs ....Mr. Delwin C. WILSON
39 Director of Residential Life ....Ms. Mary Pat MCMAHON
40 Dir Dining & Bookstore Services ....Ms. Mary M. KENNEDY
35 Director of Student Activities ....Dr. Allen W. DELONG
88 Dir of the Museum of Art ....Vacant
18 Director of Capital Projects ....Mr. Donald V. BORKOWSKI

Central Maine Medical Center College of Nursing and Health Professions (F)

70 Middle Street, Lewiston ME 04240-7027
County: Androscoggin　FICE Identification: 006305
Unit ID: 161022
Telephone: (207) 795-2840　Carnegie Class: Assoc/PrivNFP
FAX Number: (207) 795-2849　Calendar System: Semester
URL: www.cmmccollege.edu
Established: 1891　Annual Undergrad Tuition & Fees: $8,895
Enrollment: 217　Coed
Affiliation or Control: Independent Non-Profit　IRS Status: 501(c)3
Highest Offering: Associate Degree
Program: Occupational; 2-Year Principally Bachelor's Creditable; Nursing Emphasis
Accreditation: EH, ADNUR, NMT, RAD

01 President .... Mrs. Susan C. BALTRUS
05 Director .... Ms. Nancy J. ROSS
07 Chair Admissions ....Mrs. Jacqueline F. COLLINS
06 Registrar ....Mrs. Kathleen C. JACQUES
37 Student Financial Aid Specialist .... Mrs. Jenna ROCQUE
24 Educational Media Coordinator ....Vacant

Colby College (G)

4000 Mayflower Hill, Waterville ME 04901-8840
County: Kennebec　FICE Identification: 002039
Unit ID: 161086
Telephone: (207) 859-4000　Carnegie Class: Bac/A&S
FAX Number: (207) 859-4603　Calendar System: 4/1/4
URL: www.colby.edu
Established: 1813　Annual Undergrad Tuition & Fees: $55,700
Enrollment: 1,815　Coed
Affiliation or Control: Independent Non-Profit　IRS Status: 501(c)3
Highest Offering: Baccalaureate
Program: Liberal Arts And General
Accreditation: EH

01 President .... Dr. William D. ADAMS
05 Vice Pres Acad Affs/Dean of Faculty ....Dr. Lori G. KLETZER
10 Vice President Admin & Treasurer .... Mr. Douglas C. TERP
30 Vice Pres Development & Alumni Rels .... Vacant
03 Vice President/Secy of the Corp ....Ms. Sally A. BAKER
32 VP Student Affairs/Dean of Students ....Mr. James S. TERHUNE
27 Vice President Communications .... Mr. Michael D. KISER
07 Vice Pres/Dean Admiss & Fin Aid ....Dr. Terry E. COWDREY
88 Assoc Vice President Investments .... Vacant
20 Assoc VP Acad Affs/Assoc Dn Faculty . Dr. Paul G. GREENWOOD
35 Senior Associate Dean of Students ....Mr. Paul E. JOHNSTON
06 Registrar ....Ms. Elizabeth N. SCHILLER
08 Director of Libraries .... Mr. Clement P. GUTHRO
36 Director of Career Center .... Mr. Roger W. WOOLSEY
88 Director of Special Programs .... Mr. Jacques MOORE
37 Director of Financial Aid ....Vacant
29 Director of Alumni Relations .... Ms. Margaret M. BOYD
35 Assoc Dean Stdnts/Dir Campus Life ....Mr. Jed W. WARTMAN
16 Director Human Resources .... Mr. Mark CROSBY
19 Director of Security ....Mr. Peter S. CHENEVERT
13 Director of Info-Tech Services ....Dr. Raymond B. PHILLIPS
18 Director of Physical Plant .... Ms. Patricia C. WHITNEY
23 Medical Director .... Dr. Paul D. BERKNER
38 Director of Counseling Services ....Ms. Patricia N. NEWMEN
41 Director of Athletics .... Ms. Marcella K. ZALOT
09 Dir Instnl Research & Assessment ....Dr. William P. WILSON
21 Controller ....Mr. Ruben L. RIVERA
40 Director of the Bookstore .... Ms. Barbara C. SHUTT
104 Director of Off-Campus Study .... Dr. Nancy DOWNEY
102 Dir Corp/Found/Govt Relations ....Ms. Marcella J. BERNARD

College of the Atlantic (H)

105 Eden Street, Bar Harbor ME 04609-1198
County: Hancock　FICE Identification: 011385
Unit ID: 160959
Telephone: (207) 288-5015　Carnegie Class: Bac/A&S

FAX Number: (207) 288-3780 Calendar System: Trimester
URL: www.coa.edu
Established: 1969 Annual Undergrad Tuition & Fees: $37,701
Enrollment: 363 Coed
Affiliation or Control: Independent Non-Profit IRS Status: 501(c)3
Highest Offering: Master's
Program: Liberal Arts And General; Teacher Preparatory
Accreditation: EH

01 President ... Dr. Darron COLLINS
05 Academic Dean ... Dr. Ken HILL
10 Administrative Dean ... Mr. Andy GRIFFITHS
32 Dean for Student Life ... Ms. Sarah LUKE
06 Registrar ... Ms. Judy ALLEN
08 Library Director ... Ms. Jane HULTBERG
07 Dean of Admission ... Ms. Sarah BAKER
21 Comptroller ... Mrs. Melissa COOK
37 Director of Financial Aid ... Mr. Bruce HAZAM
30 Dean of Development ... Ms. Lynn BOULGER
26 Director Public Relations ... Ms. Donna GOLD
36 Internship Director ... Ms. Jill BARLOW-KELLEY

Husson University (A)

1 College Circle, Bangor ME 04401-2929
County: Penobscot FICE Identification: 002043
Unit ID: 161165
Telephone: (207) 941-7000 Carnegie Class: Master's M
FAX Number: (207) 941-7139 Calendar System: Semester
URL: www.husson.edu
Established: 1898 Annual Undergrad Tuition & Fees: $15,013
Enrollment: 3,157 Coed
Affiliation or Control: Independent Non-Profit IRS Status: 501(c)3
Highest Offering: Doctorate
Program: Liberal Arts And General; Professional
Accreditation: EH, IACBE, NURSE, OT, @PHAR, PTA

01 President ... Dr. Robert A. CLARK
05 Provost ... Dr. Lynne COY-OGAN
10 Vice Pres for Finance & Treasurer ... Craig HADLEY
30 Vice President for Advancement ... Thomas MARTZ
11 VP of Administration ... John RUBINO
32 Dean of Students ... Sharon WILSON-BARKER
50 Dean School of Business ... Ronald NYKIEL
67 Dean School of Pharmacy ... Rodney LARSON
66 Dean College of Health & Education ... Barbara HIGGINS
58 Dean of Graduate Studies ... Vacant
53 Director School of Education ... Barbara MOODY
07 Director of Admissions ... Carlena BEAN
37 Director of Financial Aid ... Linda HILL
08 Librarian ... Amy AVERRE
06 Registrar ... Nancy FENDERS
49 Dean Science/Humanities ... Francis HUBBARD
29 Director of Alumni Affairs ... Vacant
36 Director Career Services ... James WESTHOFF
41 Director of Athletics ... Robert REASSO
26 Dir of Public Affs/Govt Relations ... Julia GREEN
39 Director of Student Life ... Pamela KROPP-ANDERSON
16 Human Resources Director ... Mary DEMERS
14 Director of Institutional Research ... Gail TUDOR
18 Director of Maintenance ... Vacant
13 Exec Dir of Information Resources ... Kevin CASEY
44 Director of Advancement Services ... Christina CARON

Institute for Doctoral Studies in the Visual Arts (B)

130 Neal Street, Portland ME 04102
County: Cumberland FICE Identification: 041888
Unit ID: 462044
Telephone: (207) 879-8757 Carnegie Class: Not Classified
FAX Number: N/A Calendar System: Semester
URL: www.idsva.org
Established: 2007 Annual Graduate Tuition & Fees: $26,000
Enrollment: 40 Coed
Affiliation or Control: Independent Non-Profit IRS Status: 501(c)3
Highest Offering: Doctorate; No Undergraduates
Program: Professional
Accreditation: @EH

01 President ... George SMITH
03 Executive Vice President ... Amy CURTIS

Kaplan University-Maine (C)

265 Western Avenue, South Portland ME 04106
County: Cumberland FICE Identification: 009292
Unit ID: 160940
Telephone: (207) 774-6126 Carnegie Class: Assoc/PrivFP
FAX Number: (207) 774-1715 Calendar System: Other
URL: www.kucampus.edu
Established: 1966 Annual Undergrad Tuition & Fees: $11,115
Enrollment: 973 Coed
Affiliation or Control: Proprietary IRS Status: Proprietary
Highest Offering: Baccalaureate
Program: Occupational; 2-Year Principally Bachelor's Creditable; Business Emphasis
Accreditation: &NH

01 President ... Dr. Christopher QUINN
12 Lewiston Campus Director ... Matthew COTE
11 Director of Operations ... Lyndsey ERICKSON
05 Academic Dean ... Melanie BAAK
20 Associate Academic Dean-Lewiston ... Erin CONNOR
20 Associate Academic Dean-SoPortland ... Anne RYAN
32 Dean of Student Affairs-SoPortland ... Geraldine NEY
35 Director of Student Services-Lewist ... Karyn ESTES-LEWIS
08 Director of Library Services ... Martha OTT
14 KHE Team Leader/TS New England ... Stephen J. HORR
36 Director Career Services ... Robert KLAIBER
07 Director of Admissions-SoPortland ... Craig MACMUNN
07 Director of Admissions-Lewiston ... Kashina BRYANT
06 Registrar ... Lynsey WOOD
50 Director Business Administration ... Dr. Deborah WYMAN
88 Director of Criminal Justice ... Vacant
61 Director of Paralegal Studies ... Darren DEFOE
49 Director of Arts & Sciences ... Kevin KELLY
76 Director of Medical Assisting ... Dr. Peter NICKLESS
37 Director of Financial Aid ... Kelly KNIGHT
88 Director of Early Childhood Educ ... Lori LEVESQUE
88 Director of Travel & Hospitality ... Miriam GOUGH
40 Bookstore Manager ... Barbara VASSALLO
10 Business Office Manager ... Carol A. GAGNON

† Regional accreditation is carried under the parent institution in Davenport, IA.

The Landing School (D)

286 River Road, Arundel ME 04046
County: York FICE Identification: 023613
Telephone: (207) 985-7976 Carnegie Class: Not Classified
FAX Number: (207) 985-7942 Calendar System: Other
URL: www.landingschool.edu
Established: 1978 Annual Undergrad Tuition & Fees: $19,000
Enrollment: 68 Coed
Affiliation or Control: Independent Non-Profit IRS Status: 501(c)3
Highest Offering: Associate Degree
Program: Occupational
Accreditation: ACCSC

01 President ... Mr. Robert DECOLFMACKER
05 Director of Education ... Mr. Ken RUSINEK

Maine College of Art (E)

522 Congress St, Portland ME 04101
County: Cumberland FICE Identification: 011673
Unit ID: 161509
Telephone: (207) 775-3052 Carnegie Class: Spec/Arts
FAX Number: (207) 775-5087 Calendar System: Semester
URL: www.meca.edu
Established: 1882 Annual Undergrad Tuition & Fees: $30,062
Enrollment: 382 Coed
Affiliation or Control: Independent Non-Profit IRS Status: 501(c)3
Highest Offering: Master's
Program: Liberal Arts And General; Professional; Fine Arts Emphasis
Accreditation: EH, ART

01 President ... Mr. Donald TUSKI
03 Executive Vice President ... Ms. Beth ELICKER
05 Dean/Vice Pres Academic Affairs ... Mr. Ian ANDERSON
30 VP for Institutional Advancement ... Ms. Rebecca CONRAD
06 Registrar ... Ms. Anne DENNISON
32 Interim Director Student Engagement ... Ms. Anna SCHWARTZ
07 Interim Director of Admissions ... Ms. Shannon COTE
14 Director Technology ... Mr. David BRANSON
26 Dir Public Relations & Publications ... Ms. Jessica J. TOMLINSON
10 Director of Business Services ... Mr. Phil STEVENS
37 Director of Financial Aid ... Ms. Adrienne AMARI
51 Director Continuing Studies ... Ms. Sara GIBSON
18 Chief Facilities/Physical Plant ... Mr. Douglas DOERING
08 Librarian ... Ms. Moira STEVENS

*Maine Community College System (F)

323 State Street, Augusta ME 04330-7131
County: Kennebec Identification: 666092
Unit ID: 409713
Telephone: (207) 629-4000 Carnegie Class: N/A
FAX Number: (207) 629-4048
URL: www.mccs.me.edu

01 President ... Dr. John FITZSIMMONS

*Central Maine Community College (G)

1250 Turner Street, Auburn ME 04210-6498
County: Androscoggin FICE Identification: 005276
Unit ID: 161077
Telephone: (207) 755-5100 Carnegie Class: Assoc/Pub-R-M
FAX Number: (207) 755-5491 Calendar System: Semester
URL: www.cmcc.edu
Established: 1964 Annual Undergrad Tuition & Fees (In-State): $3,324
Enrollment: 2,913 Coed
Affiliation or Control: State IRS Status: 501(c)3
Highest Offering: Associate Degree
Program: Occupational; 2-Year Principally Bachelor's Creditable; Technical Emphasis
Accreditation: EH, ADNUR, ENGT

02 President ... Dr. Scott E. KNAPP
05 Dean Academic Affairs ... Dr. Judy WILDER
06 Registrar ... Ms. Sonya SAMPSON
10 Dean of Finance and General Service ... Ms. Pamela REMIERES-MORIN
37 Director of Financial Aid ... Mr. John BOWIE
16 Dean Corporate/Community Services ... Ms. Diane DOSTIE
32 Dean of Student Services/Admissions ... Ms. Betsy LIBBY
26 Dean Planning/Development/PR ... Mr. Roger PHILIPPON
72 Director of Technology/Prep ... Mr. Walter RIDLON
08 Head Librarian ... Ms. Judith FROST
18 Chief Physical Plant ... Mr. Raymond MASSE
22 Affirmative Action Officer ... Ms. Barbara OWEN
39 Director of Housing/Athletic Dir ... Mr. David GONYEA
40 Director of Bookstore ... Ms. Christine MORIN
15 Director of Human Resources ... Ms. Barbara OWEN
30 Director of Development ... Mr. Marc GOSSELIN

*Eastern Maine Community College (H)

354 Hogan Road, Bangor ME 04401-4280
County: Penobscot FICE Identification: 005277
Unit ID: 161138
Telephone: (207) 974-4600 Carnegie Class: Assoc/Pub-R-M
FAX Number: (207) 974-4608 Calendar System: Semester
URL: www.emcc.edu
Established: 1966 Annual Undergrad Tuition & Fees (In-State): $3,720
Enrollment: 2,233 Coed
Affiliation or Control: State IRS Status: 501(c)3
Highest Offering: Associate Degree
Program: Occupational; 2-Year Principally Bachelor's Creditable; Liberal Arts And General
Accreditation: EH, ADNUR, MAC, RAD, SURGT

02 President ... Dr. Lawrence M. BARRETT
05 Academic Dean ... Dr. Pamela PROULX-CURRY
10 Dir Finance & Auxiliary Services ... Mr. Eric MACDONALD
09 Dean Inst Research/Enrollment Mgmt ... Mr. Daniel CROCKER
88 Dean Professional/Industry Services ... Mr. E. Michael BALLESTEROS
07 Director of Admissions ... Ms. Elizabeth RUSSELL
15 Director of Human Resources ... Ms. Jody BOYD
08 Librarian ... Ms. Janet BLOOD
37 Director of Financial Aid ... Ms. Candace WARD
13 Dean of Communication/Info Tech ... Mr. Timothy CONROY
18 Dir Facilities Mgmt/Student Life ... Mr. Daniel BELYEA
20 Assistant Academic Dean ... Ms. Merlene SANBORN
30 Dir of Institutional Advancement ... Ms. CarolAnne DUBE

*Kennebec Valley Community College (I)

92 Western Avenue, Fairfield ME 04937-1367
County: Somerset FICE Identification: 009826
Unit ID: 161192
Telephone: (207) 453-5000 Carnegie Class: Assoc/Pub-R-M
FAX Number: (207) 453-5010 Calendar System: Semester
URL: www.kvcc.me.edu
Established: 1970 Annual Undergrad Tuition & Fees (In-State): $3,315
Enrollment: 2,529 Coed
Affiliation or Control: State IRS Status: 501(c)3
Highest Offering: Associate Degree
Program: Occupational; 2-Year Principally Bachelor's Creditable
Accreditation: EH, ACBSP, ADNUR, DMS, MAC, OTA, PTAA, RAD

02 President ... Dr. Barbara W. WOODLEE
05 Academic Dean/Vice President ... Mrs. Karen WHITE
13 Dean of Information Technology ... Mr. Ryan CONNON
32 Dean of Student Affairs ... Ms. Karen NORMANDIN
10 Dean of Finance & Administration ... Mr. John DELILE
06 Registrar ... Mrs. Lisa YORK-LEMELIN
30 Director of Development ... Ms. Michelle WEBB
07 Director of Admissions ... Mr. Jim BOURGOIN
37 Director Student Financial Aid ... Ms. Anne CONNORS

*Northern Maine Community College (J)

33 Edgemont Drive, Presque Isle ME 04769-2099
County: Aroostook FICE Identification: 005760
Unit ID: 161484
Telephone: (207) 768-2700 Carnegie Class: Assoc/Pub-R-S
FAX Number: (207) 768-2831 Calendar System: Semester
URL: www.nmcc.edu
Established: 1961 Annual Undergrad Tuition & Fees (In-State): $3,343
Enrollment: 1,033 Coed
Affiliation or Control: State IRS Status: 501(c)3
Highest Offering: Associate Degree
Program: Occupational; 2-Year Principally Bachelor's Creditable
Accreditation: EH, ACBSP, ADNUR

02 President ... Mr. Timothy D. CROWLEY
05 Academic Dean ... Dr. Dorothy MARTIN
32 Dean of Students ... Dr. William G. EGELER
10 Director of Finance ... Mr. Larry LAPLANTE
51 Dean of Continuing Education ... Ms. Sue BERNARD
30 Director Development & College Rels ... Ms. Jason PARENT
07 Director of Admissions ... Mr. Eugene MCCLUSKEY
06 Registrar ... Ms. Betsy A. HARRIS
37 Asst Director for Financial Aid ... Ms. Norma M. SMITH
39 Director of Housing & Resident Life ... Mr. Thomas J. RICHARD
38 Director of Counseling ... Ms. Tammy NELSON

18 Director of Facilities .... Mr. Barry INGRAHAM
21 Business Manager .... Mr. Philip R. BROWN
15 Human Resource Manager .... Mr. Thomas J. RICHARD
40 Bookstore Manager .... Ms. Rebecca A. MAYNARD
88 Tech Prep Coordinator .... Ms. Elizabeth M. MORGAN

*Southern Maine Community College (A)

Fort Road, South Portland ME 04106-1698
County: Cumberland FICE Identification: 005525
Unit ID: 161545
Telephone: (207) 741-5500 Carnegie Class: Assoc/Pub-R-M
FAX Number: (207) 741-5751 Calendar System: Semester
URL: www.smccme.edu
Established: 1946 Annual Undergrad Tuition & Fees (In-State): $4,199
Enrollment: 7,482 Coed
Affiliation or Control: State IRS Status: 501(c)3
Highest Offering: Associate Degree
Program: Occupational; 2-Year Principally Bachelor's Creditable; Liberal Arts And General
Accreditation: EH, ACFEI, ADNUR, DIETT, RAD, RTT

02 President/CEO .... Ronald G. CANTOR
05 Vice President/Academic Dean .... Janet M. SORTOR
32 Dean of Student Affairs .... Diane M. VICKREY
26 Dean of Communications .... Vacant
84 Associate Dean of Enrollment .... Staci GRASKY
35 Associate Dean of Student Services .... Mark A. KROGMAN
04 Exec Assistant to the President .... Laura E. LIBBY
12 Asst to Vice Pres/Dir Bath Campus .... Vacant
10 Dean of Finance .... Robert COOMBS
11 Dean of Administration .... Scott BEATTY
30 Dean of Advancement .... Kaylene WAINDLE
37 Director of Financial Aid .... Michel LUSSIER
36 Director of Student Development .... Shane LONG
09 Director of Institutional Research .... Diane VICKREY
19 Director Campus Security .... Joseph MANHARDT
41 Director of Athletics .... Matthew RICHARDS
72 Computer Technology Chair .... Howard BURPEE
18 Plant Maintenance Engineer III .... James RENY
88 Learning Assistance Chair .... Joyce LESLIE
40 Manager Campus Store .... Cherie BRYANT
21 Manager of Financial Services .... Shaun GRAY
21 Business Manager of Student Billing .... Irene FINCH
15 HR & Benefits Manager .... Denise RENY

*Washington County Community College (B)

One College Drive, Calais ME 04619-9704
County: Washington FICE Identification: 009231
Unit ID: 161581
Telephone: (207) 454-1000 Carnegie Class: Assoc/Pub-R-S
FAX Number: (207) 454-1092 Calendar System: Semester
URL: www.wccc.me.edu
Established: 1969 Annual Undergrad Tuition & Fees (In-State): $3,400
Enrollment: 509 Coed
Affiliation or Control: State IRS Status: 501(c)3
Highest Offering: Associate Degree
Program: Occupational; 2-Year Principally Bachelor's Creditable
Accreditation: EH, MAC

02 President .... Dr. Joyce B. HEDLUND
05 Dean of Academic & Student Affairs .... Vacant
10 Dean of Finance & Admin Services .... Ms. Desiree THOMPSON
15 Director of HR and Public Relations .... Ms. Tina ERSKINE
84 Assoc Dean Enroll/Retention Svcs .... Ms. Susan MINGO
31 Dean of Community Education .... Mr. Scott HARRIMAN
07 Director of Admissions .... Ms. Susan MINGO

*York County Community College (C)

112 College Drive, Wells ME 04090-0529
County: York FICE Identification: 031229
Unit ID: 420440
Telephone: (207) 646-9282 Carnegie Class: Assoc/Pub-R-S
FAX Number: (207) 646-9675 Calendar System: Semester
URL: www.yccc.edu
Established: 1994 Annual Undergrad Tuition & Fees (In-State): $3,315
Enrollment: 1,361 Coed
Affiliation or Control: State IRS Status: 501(c)3
Highest Offering: Associate Degree
Program: Occupational; 2-Year Principally Bachelor's Creditable
Accreditation: EH

02 President .... Vacant
05 Vice President/Academic Dean .... Ms. Paula GAGNON
30 Dean of Institutional Advancement .... Dr. John J. RAINONE
32 Dean of Students .... Dr. Corinne KOWPAK
10 Dean of Finance & Administration .... Ms. Nancy DROUIN
26 Coord Marketing & Public Relations .... Ms. Stacy CHILICKI
51 Director of Continuing Education .... Ms. Paulette MILLETTE
04 Admin Assistant to the President .... Ms. Erin HAYE
20 Associate Academic Dean .... Ms. Doreen ROGAN
08 Director Library/Learning Resources .... Ms. Amber TATNALL
88 Faculty Development Coordinator .... Ms. Stefanie FORSTER
07 Director of Admissions .... Mr. Fred QUISTGARD
84 Director of Enrollment Services .... Ms. Jessica MASI
37 Director Financial Aid .... Mr. David DAIGLE

13 Director of Technology .... Mr. Tim DUNNE
21 Business Manager .... Mr. Samuel ELLIS
15 Human Resources & Benefits Manager .... Ms. Ellen HARFORD
18 Manager of Facilities .... Mr. Dana PETERSEN
09 Institutional Research Coordinator .... Mr. Nicholas GILL

Maine Maritime Academy (D)

Castine ME 04420-0001
County: Hancock FICE Identification: 002044
Unit ID: 161299
Telephone: (207) 326-4311 Carnegie Class: Bac/Diverse
FAX Number: (207) 326-2218 Calendar System: Semester
URL: www.mma.edu
Established: 1941 Annual Undergrad Tuition & Fees (In-State): $15,925
Enrollment: 927 Coed
Affiliation or Control: State IRS Status: 501(c)3
Highest Offering: Master's
Program: Professional
Accreditation: EH, ENG, ENGT

01 President .... Dr. William J. BRENNAN
05 Academic Dean .... Dr. John BARLOW
11 Vice Pres Administration & Finance .... Mr. Richard R. ERICSON
84 Vice Pres of Enrollment Management .... Mr. Jeffrey LOUSTAUNAU
30 Vice President for Advancement .... Ms. Ellie WILLMANN
15 Human Resource Officer .... Mr. James SOUCIE
32 Chief Student Life Officer .... Ms. Kristen WENTWORTH
35 Dean of Student Services .... Ms. Deidra DAVIS
36 Placement Director .... Mr. Timothy LEACH
07 Director of Admissions .... Mr. Jeffrey WRIGHT
06 Registrar .... Ms. Christina STEPHENS
29 Director Alumni Relations .... Mr. Paul MERCER
37 Director Student Financial Aid .... Ms. Kathy HEATH
38 Director Student Counseling .... Mr. Paul FERREIRA
08 Head Librarian .... Ms. Wendy GIRVEN
10 Chief Business Officer .... Ms. Diana SNAPP
18 Chief Facilities/Physical Plant .... Vacant
20 Associate Academic Dean .... Dr. Joceline BOUCHER
26 Chief Public Relations Officer .... Mr. Michael WHETSTON
09 Director of Institutional Research .... Dr. Darrell DONOHUE

New England School of Communications (E)

One College Circle, Bangor ME 04401-2999
County: Penobscot FICE Identification: 023471
Unit ID: 373827
Telephone: (207) 941-7176 Carnegie Class: Spec/Other
FAX Number: (207) 941-7139 Calendar System: Semester
URL: www.nescom.edu
Established: 1981 Annual Undergrad Tuition & Fees: $13,482
Enrollment: 531 Coed
Affiliation or Control: Independent Non-Profit IRS Status: 501(c)3
Highest Offering: Baccalaureate
Program: Occupational
Accreditation: ACCSC

01 President .... Mr. Thomas C. JOHNSTON
03 Exec Vice President/Academic Dean .... Mr. Benjamin E. HASKELL
07 Director of Admissions .... Mrs. Louise G. GRANT
84 Dir of Enrollment Mgmt/Registrar .... Ms. Anne E. REED
37 Director of Student Financial Aid .... Ms. Nicole VACHON
29 Director Alumni Relations .... Mr. Mark NASON

Saint Joseph's College of Maine (F)

278 Whites Bridge Road, Standish ME 04084-5236
County: Cumberland FICE Identification: 002051
Unit ID: 161518
Telephone: (207) 892-6766 Carnegie Class: Master's M
FAX Number: (207) 893-7861 Calendar System: Semester
URL: www.sjcme.edu
Established: 1912 Annual Undergrad Tuition & Fees: $30,030
Enrollment: 3,129 Coed
Affiliation or Control: Roman Catholic IRS Status: 501(c)3
Highest Offering: Master's
Program: Liberal Arts And General; Teacher Preparatory; Professional
Accreditation: EH, NURSE

01 President .... Dr. James S. DLUGOS
03 Executive Vice President .... Mr. John ZERILLO
05 Vice President for Academic Affairs .... Dr. Randall KRIEG
30 VP Institutional Advancement .... Mr. Michael DEMPSEY
84 Vice Pres Enrollment Management .... Ms. Kathleen DAVIS
88 Vice Pres for Sponsorship & Mission .... Sr. Kathleen SULLIVAN
58 Dean Graduate/Prof Studies .... Ms. Lynn OLSON
07 Dean of Admission .... Vacant
37 Director of Financial Aid .... Ms. Andrea CROSS
32 Dean of Student Life .... Ms. Lynn BROWN
06 Director of Academic Records .... Mr. Kevin PAQUETTE
08 Director of the Library .... Ms. Shelly DAVIS
29 Dir Alumni & Parent Communications .... Ms. Kristina GREEN
44 Director of Annual Giving .... Ms. Heather PLATI
18 Chief Facilities/Physical Plant .... Mr. Charles DAWES
41 Athletic Director .... Mr. Brian CURTIN
26 Chief Public Relations Officer .... Vacant
38 Director Student Counseling .... Dr. Elizabeth WIESEN
13 Director Information Systems .... Ms. Gayle LANGIS
23 Director Health Services .... Dr. Sue-Anne HAMMOND
36 Director Career Services .... Mr. Thomas NOVAK

96 Director of Purchasing .... Ms. Carlene P. LEMIEUX
39 Director Student Housing .... Mr. Jon BLANCHARD
11 Chief Administration Officer .... Ms. Janet LAFLAMME
20 Associate Dean .... Mrs. Elaine TRUMBLE
09 Director of Institutional Research .... Dr. Paul J. WOODWARD

Thomas College (G)

180 W River Road, Waterville ME 04901-5097
County: Kennebec FICE Identification: 002052
Unit ID: 161563
Telephone: (207) 859-1111 Carnegie Class: Bac/Diverse
FAX Number: (207) 859-1114 Calendar System: Semester
URL: www.thomas.edu
Established: 1894 Annual Undergrad Tuition & Fees: $22,160
Enrollment: 1,005 Coed
Affiliation or Control: Independent Non-Profit IRS Status: 501(c)3
Highest Offering: Master's
Program: Liberal Arts And General; Teacher Preparatory; Professional
Accreditation: EH

01 President .... Ms. Laurie G. LACHANCE
05 Provost .... Dr. Thomas EDWARDS
10 Senior Vice President/CFO/Treasurer .... Ms. Beth B. GIBBS
13 Vice President Information Services .... Mr. Christopher RHODA
84 Vice Pres Enrollment Management .... Vacant
32 Vice President Student Affairs .. Ms. Lisa DESAUTELS-POLIQUIN
30 Vice Pres Advancement .... Mr. Robert M. MOORE
20 Assistant Academic Dean .... Ms. Jamie BALLINGER
07 Dean of Admissions .... Ms. Wendy MARTIN
37 Director Student Financial Services .... Ms. Jeannine BOSSE
36 Director Career Services .... Mr. Richard GRANT
35 Assistant Dean of Students .... Ms. Hannah GLADSTONE
18 Director Physical Plant .... Mr. James PARSONS
15 Director Human Resources .... Ms. Michelle JOLER-LABBE
26 Director Public Relations .... Ms. Jennifer BUKER
08 Director Library Services .... Ms. Lisa AURIEMMA
06 Registrar .... Ms. Meghan REITCHEL
29 Director Alumni Relations .... Ms. Cathy DUMONT
40 Manager of Bookstore .... Ms. Katie THOMAS

Unity College (H)

90 Quaker Hill Road, Unity ME 04988-9502
County: Waldo FICE Identification: 006858
Unit ID: 161572
Telephone: (207) 948-9100 Carnegie Class: Bac/Diverse
FAX Number: (207) 948-9771 Calendar System: Semester
URL: www.unity.edu
Established: 1965 Annual Undergrad Tuition & Fees: $24,100
Enrollment: 581 Coed
Affiliation or Control: Independent Non-Profit IRS Status: 501(c)3
Highest Offering: Baccalaureate
Program: Occupational; 2-Year Principally Bachelor's Creditable; Liberal Arts And General; Teacher Preparatory
Accreditation: EH

01 President .... Dr. Stephen MULKEY
101 Exec Asst to President/Sec to Board .... Ms. Chris MELANSON
05 Sr VP for Academic Affairs .... Dr. William TRUMBLE
10 Vice Pres Finance & Administration .... Ms. Deborah CRONIN
30 Interim VP for College Advancement .... Mr. Joseph GALLI
84 Dean of Enrollment Management .... Ms. Alisa JOHNSON
32 Dean for Student Affairs .... Mr. Gary ZANE
06 Registrar .... Ms. Holly A. HEIN
07 Sr Associate Director Admissions .. Mr. Joseph SALTALAMACHIA
88 Director Outdoor Adventure Center .... Ms. Jessica STEELE
41 Director of Athletics .... Mr. Chris KEIN
88 Director Dining Services .... Ms. Sandy DONAHUE
18 Director Facilities & Public Safety .... Mr. Daniel LAFORGE
37 Director Financial Aid .... Mr. Rand E. NEWELL
23 Director Health & Wellness Center .... Ms. Anna MCGALLIARD
16 Director Human Resources .... Mrs. Kathleen HALE
13 Director Information Technology .... Mr. Bert AUDETTE
24 Director Learning Resource Center .... Mr. James J. HORAN
08 Director Quimby Library .... Mrs. Melora NORMAN
39 Director Residence Life .... Mr. Stephen S. NASON
35 Director Student Accounts .... Ms. Jeri ROBERTS
88 Director Writing Center .... Ms. Judy WILLIAMS
88 Sustainability Coordinator .... Mr. Jesse PYLES
29 Alumni/Parent Relations Coordinator .... Ms. Debora NOONE
26 Assoc Dir College Communications .... Mr. Mark TARDIF
88 Community-Based Learning Coord .... Ms. Jen OLIN
36 Career Consultant/Internship Coord .... Ms. Nicole COLLINS
53 Co-Director of Teacher Education .... Ms. Angela HARDY
19 Chief Public Safety Officer .... Mr. Dean BESSEY
40 Manager Bookstore .... Ms. Leigh JUSKEVICE

† The 2011-2012 tuition should have been lited as $23,540.

*University of Maine System Office (I)

16 Central Street, Bangor ME 04401-5106
County: Penobscot FICE Identification: 008012
Unit ID: 161280
Telephone: (207) 973-3200 Carnegie Class: N/A
FAX Number: (207) 973-3296
URL: www.maine.edu

01 Chancellor .... Dr. James H. PAGE
10 CFO & Treasurer .... Ms. Rebecca WYKE
43 University Counsel/Clerk of Board .... Mr. J. Kelley WILTBANK

86 Asst to Chanc Governmental Rels ... Mr. Ryan LOW
15 Exec Director of Human Resources ... Ms. Tracy BIGNEY
32 Chief Student Affairs Officer ... Ms. Rosa REDONNETT
27 Chief Information Officer ... Mr. Dick THOMPSON
18 Director of Facilities ... Mr. M. F. Chip GAVIN

*University of Maine (A)

Orono ME 04469-0001
County: Penobscot FICE Identification: 002053
Unit ID: 161253
Telephone: (207) 581-1110 Carnegie Class: RU/H
FAX Number: (207) 581-1604 Calendar System: Semester
URL: www.umaine.edu
Established: 1865 Annual Undergrad Tuition & Fees (In-State): $10,588
Enrollment: 11,168 Coed
Affiliation or Control: State IRS Status: 501(c)3
Highest Offering: Doctorate
Program: Liberal Arts And General; Teacher Preparatory; Professional
Accreditation: EH, BUS, CLPSY, CS, DIETD, DIETI, ENG, ENGT, FOR, IPSY, MUS, NURSE, SP, SPAA, SW, TED

02 President ... Dr. Paul W. FERGUSON
05 Sr VP for Academic Affairs/Provost ... Dr. Susan J. HUNTER
10 Vice Pres Administration & Finance ... Ms. Janet E. WALDRON
30 Vice President for Development ... Mr. Eric F. ROLFSON
32 VP Student Affs/Dean of Students ... Dr. Robert Q. DANA
46 Vice President for Research ... Dr. Michael J. ECKARDT
15 Assoc VP Human Res/Administration ... Ms. Judith S. RYAN
20 Assoc Provost/Dean Undergrad Educ ... Dr. Stuart L. MARRS
04 Senior Advisor to the President ... Ms. Julie D. HOPWOOD
08 Dean of Libraries ... Ms. Joyce V. RUMERY
13 Exec Dir of Information Technology ... Dr. John H. GREGORY
18 Int Dir of Facilities Management ... Mr. Stewart A. HARVEY
26 Int Director University Relations ... Ms. Margaret A. NAGLE
39 Int Director of Auxiliary Services ... Mr. Daniel H. STURRUP
25 Director Research & Sponsor Program ... Mr. Michael M. HASTINGS
06 Int Director Student Records ... Ms. Linda S. REID
07 Director of Admissions ... Ms. Sharon M. OLIVER
37 Int Director of Financial Aid ... Ms. Gianna F. MARRS
36 Director of Career Center ... Ms. Patricia B. COUNIHAN
09 Director Institutional Studies ... Mr. Ted T. COLADARCI
85 Director International Pgms ... Ms. Karen BOUCIAS
41 Athletic Director ... Mr. Steven W. ABBOTT
28 Director Equal Employment Diversity ... Ms. Karen D. KEMBLE
19 Dir of Public Safety/Transportation ... Chief Roland J. LACROIX
29 Director Alumni Relations ... Mr. Todd SAUCIER
40 Interim Director of Bookstore ... Mr. Richard YOUNG
96 Dir Purchasing/Resource Efficiency ... Ms. June BALDACCI
21 Dir of Budget & Business Services ... Mrs. Claire I. STRICKLAND
38 Director Student Counseling ... Mr. Douglas P. JOHNSON
49 Dean Liberal Arts & Sciences ... Dr. Jeffrey E. HECKER
50 Int Dean Bus/Public Policy/Health ... Dr. Ivan M. MANEV
53 Dean Education/Human Development ... Dr. William D. NICHOLS
54 Dean Engineering ... Dr. Dana N. HUMPHREY
65 Dean Natural Science/Forestry/Agric ... Dr. Edward N. ASHWORTH
51 Interim Dean Lifelong Learning ... Dr. Lucille A. ZEPH
58 Dean Graduate School ... Dr. Daniel H. SANDWEISS

*University of Maine at Augusta (B)

46 University Drive, Augusta ME 04330-9410
County: Kennebec FICE Identification: 006760
Unit ID: 161217
Telephone: (207) 621-3000 Carnegie Class: Bac/Assoc
FAX Number: (207) 621-3116 Calendar System: Semester
URL: www.uma.edu
Established: 1965 Annual Undergrad Tuition & Fees (In-State): $7,448
Enrollment: 4,974 Coed
Affiliation or Control: State IRS Status: 501(c)3
Highest Offering: Baccalaureate
Program: 2-Year Principally Bachelor's Creditable; Liberal Arts And General; Professional
Accreditation: EH, ADNUR, DA, DH, MLTAD

02 President ... Dr. Allyson HUGHES HANDLEY
05 Executive Vice President/Provost ... Dr. Joe S. SZAKAS
10 Vice President of Finance and Admin ... Ms. Ellen SCHNEITER
84 Vice President Enrollment Services ... Mr. Jon HENRY
11 Exec Director of Admin Services ... Ms. Sheri R. STEVENS
04 Executive Assistant to President ... Ms. Joyce BLANCHARD
08 Dean of Libraries ... Dr. Thomas E. ABBOTT
12 Dean Bangor Campus ... Ms. Gillian JORDAN
32 Dean of Students ... Ms. Kathleen A. DEXTER
107 Interim Dean Prof Studies ... Ms. Brenda MCALEER
37 Director of Financial Aid ... Ms. Sherry MCCOLLETT
06 Registrar ... Ms. Ann CORBETT
15 Director Personnel Services ... Mr. David LANE
18 Chief Facilities/Physical Plant ... Mr. Peter ST. MICHEL
38 Dir of Cornerstone & Counseling ... Mr. William STONE
88 Director of Advising ... Ms. Sheri C. FRASER
35 Director of Student Life ... Mr. Warren NEWTON
40 Director Bookstore ... Mr. Jerry GARTHOFF
26 Exec Director of External Relations ... Mr. Bob STEIN
30 Director of University Advancement ... Ms. Joyce BLANCHARD
09 Exec Director of IR & Planning ... Mr. Gregory LAPOINTE

*University of Maine at Farmington (C)

224 Main Street, Farmington ME 04938-1911
County: Franklin FICE Identification: 002040
Unit ID: 161226
Telephone: (207) 778-7000 Carnegie Class: Bac/Diverse
FAX Number: (207) 778-7247 Calendar System: Semester
URL: www.umf.maine.edu
Established: 1864 Annual Undergrad Tuition & Fees (In-State): $9,367
Enrollment: 2,269 Coed
Affiliation or Control: State IRS Status: 501(c)3
Highest Offering: Master's
Program: Liberal Arts And General; Teacher Preparatory
Accreditation: EH, TED

02 President ... Dr. Kathryn A. FOSTER
05 Interim VP Academic Affairs/Provost ... Dr. Daniel P. GUNN
11 Exec Dir Finance & Administration ... Ms. Laurie A. GARDNER
32 Vice Pres Student & Community Svcs ... Ms. Celeste BRANHAM
07 Director of Admissions ... Mr. Jamie E. MARCUS
84 Vice Pres Enrollmt Mgmt & Mktg ... Mr. Roberto NOYA
88 Sustainability Coordinator ... Dr. Lucas C. KELLETT
53 Assoc Provost & Dean of Education ... Dr. Katherine W. YARDLEY
20 Assoc Provost & Dean of Acad Svcs ... Dr. Robert L. LIVELY
89 Asst to Dean First Yr Experience ... Mr. Douglas H. RAWLINGS
92 Director of Honors Program ... Dr. Mellisa A. CLAWSON
88 Dir of Learning Assistance Center ... Ms. Claire N. NELSON
08 Director of Library ... Mr. Franklin D. ROBERTS
37 Financial Aid Director ... Mr. Ronald P. MILLIKEN
15 Dir Human Resources & Finance ... Ms. Kathleen P. FALCO
06 Director Adm Sys/Student Records ... Ms. Sharon L. NADEAU
88 Dir Admin Svcs Stdnt Health Ctr ... Mr. Robert A. PEDERSON
44 Dir Gift Planning & Stewardship ... Ms. Patricia A. CARPENTER
27 Director of Media Relations ... Ms. April C. MULHERIN
14 Ex Dir Information Technolog Svcs ... Mr. Frederick L. BRITTAIN
41 Dir Athletics/Fitness & Recreation ... Ms. Julie A. DAVIS
88 Dir Fitness & Recreation Center ... Mr. James D. TONER
88 Coordinator of Outdoor Recreation ... Ms. Elizabeth E. BREIDENBACH
39 Director Residential Life ... Mr. Brian K. UFFORD
35 Dir Center for Stdnt Involvement ... Ms. Kirsten SWAN
23 Dir Clinical Svcs Stdnt Health Ctr ... Dr. Susan E. COCHRAN
18 Director of Facilities Management ... Mr. Bernard PRATT
19 Director of Public Safety ... Mr. Edward J. BLAIS
29 Director of Alumni Relations ... Ms. Jennifer A. ERIKSEN
88 Director of Dining Services ... Mr. Patrick ANDERSON

*University of Maine at Fort Kent (D)

23 University Drive, Fort Kent ME 04743-1292
County: Aroostook FICE Identification: 002041
Unit ID: 161235
Telephone: (207) 834-7500 Carnegie Class: Bac/Diverse
FAX Number: (207) 834-7503 Calendar System: Semester
URL: www.umfk.maine.edu
Established: 1878 Annual Undergrad Tuition & Fees (In-State): $7,575
Enrollment: 1,080 Coed
Affiliation or Control: State IRS Status: 501(c)3
Highest Offering: Baccalaureate
Program: Occupational; 2-Year Principally Bachelor's Creditable; Liberal Arts And General; Teacher Preparatory; Professional; Nursing Emphasis
Accreditation: EH, IACBE, NURSE

02 President ... Mr. Wilson G. HESS
05 Vice President Academic Affairs ... Dr. Rachel E. ALBERT
11 Vice President for Administration ... Mr. John D. MURPHY
31 Dean of Community Education ... Mr. Scott A. VOISINE
36 Assistant Dean of Student Success ... Ms. Eleanor B. HESS
06 Registrar ... Mr. Humberto PORTELLEZ
15 Director of Human Resources ... Mr. James E. BRIMBERRY
66 Nursing Division Director ... Ms. Erin SOUCY
08 Dir of Information Svcs/Library ... Ms. Leslie E. KELLY
07 Director of Admissions ... Ms. Jill CAIRNS
37 Director of Financial Aid ... Mr. Michael HUDDY
26 Dir University Relations/Alum Affs ... Mr. Terence KELLY
18 Director of Facilities Management ... Mr. Andrew C. JACOBS
28 Assoc Dir Res Life & Diversity Pgms ... Mr. Raymond R. PHINNEY
09 Assoc Dir of Institutional Research ... Mr. Joseph R. BJERKLIE
21 Director of Business Systems ... Ms. Leslie R. GUERRETTE

*University of Maine at Machias (E)

116 O'Brien Avenue, Machias ME 04654-1397
County: Washington FICE Identification: 002055
Unit ID: 161244
Telephone: (207) 255-1200 Carnegie Class: Bac/A&S
FAX Number: (207) 255-4864 Calendar System: Semester
URL: www.umm.maine.edu
Established: 1909 Annual Undergrad Tuition & Fees (In-State): $7,480
Enrollment: 863 Coed
Affiliation or Control: State IRS Status: 501(c)3
Highest Offering: Baccalaureate
Program: Liberal Arts And General; Teacher Preparatory
Accreditation: EH, NRPA

02 President ... Dr. Cynthia E. HUGGINS
05 Vice Pres Academic Affairs/Provost ... Mr. Stuart G. SWAIN
10 Vice Pres Finance/Administration ... Mr. Thomas L. POTTER
32 Director Student Life ... Mr. Paul LAMANTIA
06 Registrar ... Ms. Mary STOVER
08 Director Library ... Ms. Angelynn KING
07 Director Admissions ... Mr. Michael MATTISON
15 Director Human Resources ... Ms. Kim PAGE
37 Director Student Financial Aid ... Mrs. Stephanie D. LARRABEE
18 Director Physical Facilities ... Mr. Robert FARRIS
26 Director Public Relations ... Mr. Erik SMITH
13 Director Information Technology ... Mr. Michael MATIS
41 Director Athletics ... Mr. Brac BRADY

*University of Maine at Presque Isle (F)

181 Main Street, Presque Isle ME 04769-2888
County: Aroostook FICE Identification: 002033
Unit ID: 161341
Telephone: (207) 768-9400 Carnegie Class: Bac/Diverse
FAX Number: (207) 768-9608 Calendar System: Semester
URL: www.umpi.edu
Established: 1903 Annual Undergrad Tuition & Fees (In-State): $7,435
Enrollment: 1,453 Coed
Affiliation or Control: State IRS Status: 501(c)3
Highest Offering: Baccalaureate
Program: Liberal Arts And General; Teacher Preparatory; Professional
Accreditation: EH, MLTAD, @PTAA, SW

02 President ... Dr. Linda K. SCHOTT
05 Vice President Academic Affairs ... Dr. Michael E. SONNTAG
11 Vice Pres Administration & Finance ... Mr. Charles G. BONIN
35 Dean of Students ... Vacant
07 Director of Admissions ... Ms. Erin V. BENSON
15 Asst Director of Human Resources ... Ms. Jennie R. SAVAGE
38 Director of Counseling Services ... Mr. John D. HARRINGTON
27 Director of Information Services ... Ms. JoAnne L. WALLINGFORD
06 Director of Student Records ... Ms. Kathy K. DAVIS
37 Director of Financial Aid ... Mr. Christopher A R. BELL
36 Director Student Placement ... Ms. Barbara J. DEVANEY
39 Director Residence Life ... Mr. James D. STEPP
41 Director of Athletics ... Vacant
26 Director of Media Relations ... Ms. Rachel RICE
29 Director of Alumni Relations ... Mr. Keith L. MADORE
40 Bookstore Manager ... Mr. Greg DOAK
18 Manager of Physical Facilities ... Mr. David L. ST. PETER

*University of Southern Maine (G)

96 Falmouth Street, PO Box 9300,
Portland ME 04101-9300
County: Cumberland FICE Identification: 002054
Unit ID: 161554
Telephone: (207) 780-4141 Carnegie Class: Master's L
FAX Number: (207) 780-4933 Calendar System: Semester
URL: www.usm.maine.edu
Established: 1878 Annual Undergrad Tuition & Fees (In-State): $7,590
Enrollment: 9,301 Coed
Affiliation or Control: State IRS Status: 501(c)3
Highest Offering: Doctorate
Program: Liberal Arts And General; Teacher Preparatory; Professional
Accreditation: EH, ART, BUS, CACREP, CORE, CS, ENG, EXSC, HSA, LAW, MUS, NAIT, NURSE, OT, SW, TEAC

02 President ... Dr. Selma BOTMAN
04 Special Asst to the President ... Dr. Timothy STEVENS
11 Chief Operating Officer ... Ms. Katherine GREENLEAF
05 Provost/VPAA ... Dr. Michael STEVENSON
10 Chief Financial Officer/VP Admin ... Mr. Richard CAMPBELL
27 Chief Information Officer ... Mr. William WELLS
32 Chief Student Affairs Officer ... Mr. Craig HUTCHINSON
88 Chief Student Success Officer ... Dr. Susan CAMPBELL
30 Vice President for Advancement ... Vacant
09 Assoc Dir Institutional Research ... Ms. Patricia DAVIS
18 Exec Director Facilities Management ... Mr. Bob BERTRAM
21 Director of Business Services ... Mr. Gregg N. ALLEN
24 University Librarian/Director ITMS ... Mr. David NUTTY
88 Director Academic Assessment Ctr ... Ms. Susan L. KING
38 Director of Health & Counseling ... Dr. Kristine BERTINI
15 Chief Human Resources Office ... Ms. Martha FREEMAN
26 Executive Director Public Affairs ... Mr. Robert S. CASWELL
37 Director of Financial Aid ... Mr. Keith DUBOIS
88 Executive Director Student Success ... Ms. Elizabeth HIGGINS
07 Sr Assoc Director Admissions ... Ms. Deborah DAERIS
06 Registrar ... Mr. Steven RAND
22 Director of Equity and Compliance ... Mr. Daryl MCLLWAIN
72 Interim Director CTEL ... Ms. Barbara STEBBINS
25 Dir of Office of Sponsored Programs ... Mr. Lawrence WAXLER
31 Director of Community Standards ... Mr. Stephen NELSON
30 Director of Development ... Mr. David HUGHES
41 Director of Athletics & Rec Sports ... Mr. Al BEAN
51 Director of Continued Education ... Ms. Monique LAROCQUE
39 Director of Residential Life ... Ms. Denise NELSON
40 Director of USM Bookstore ... Ms. Nicole PIAGET
61 Dean School of Law ... Mr. Peter PITEGOFF
50 Dean College of Mgmt & Human Svcs ... Dr. Joseph MCDONNELL
88 Dean College of Sci/Tech & Health ... Dr. Andrew ANDERSON
88 Dean of Arts/Humanities & Soc Sci ... Dr. Lynn KUZMA
12 Dean Lewiston-Auburn College ... Dr. Joyce GIBSON
58 Dean for Graduate Studies ... Vacant
35 Executive Director Student Success ... Mr. Joseph M. AUSTIN
88 Manager Audiovisual/Media Services ... Ms. Angela COOK
94 Director of Women's Studies ... Dr. Wendy CHAPKIS
09 Director of Institutional Research ... Dr. Cristi CARSON
20 Associate Provost Academic Affairs ... Dr. Dahlia LYNN
88 Coordinator Multicultural Affairs ... Mr. Reza JALALI
29 Director of Alumni Relations ... Ms. Peggy SCHICK
88 Director of Marketing ... Ms. Traci ST. PIERRE
42 Director of Interfaith Chaplaincy ... Ms. Andrea THOMPSON-MCCALL
102 President USM Foundation ... Vacant
108 Dir Inst Research/Assessment ... Ms. Cristi CARSON
46 Associate VP for Research ... Dr. Samantha LANGLETY-TURNBAUGH

University of New England (A)

11 Hills Beach Road, Biddeford ME 04005-9988
County: York FICE Identification: 002050
Unit ID: 161457
Telephone: (207) 283-0171 Carnegie Class: Master's L
FAX Number: (207) 282-6379 Calendar System: Semester
URL: www.une.edu
Established: 1831 Annual Undergrad Tuition & Fees: $30,750
Enrollment: 5,587 Coed
Affiliation or Control: Independent Non-Profit IRS Status: 501(c)3
Highest Offering: Doctorate
Program: Occupational; 2-Year Principally Bachelor's Creditable; Liberal Arts And General; Teacher Preparatory; Professional
Accreditation: EH, ACBSP, ADNUR, ANEST, ARCPA, DENT, DH, NUR, OSTEO, OT, PH, @PHAR, PTA, SW

01 President ... Dr. Danielle RIPICH
04 Executive Asst to the President ... Ms. MaryLou KADLIK
05 Vice Pres Academic Affairs/ Provost ... Dr. Williams JACK
23 Sr Vice Pres for Health Affairs ... Vacant
18 Vice Pres of Operations ... Mr. William BOLA
88 Vice President Clinical Affairs ... Dr. Dora MILLS
10 Vice Pres Fiscal Services ... Ms. Nicole TRUFANT
30 Vice Pres Institutional Advancement ... Vacant
63 Director School of Nurse Anesthesia ... Ms. Maribeth MASSIE
32 Vice Pres Student Affairs ... Dr. Cynthia FORREST
26 VP of Communications ... Mr. Thomas WHITE
102 Asst VP Institutional Advancement ... Mr. Scott MARCHILDON
15 Assoc VP Human Resources ... Vacant
30 Assoc VP Institutional Advancement ... Mr. William CHANCE
88 Assoc Provost Global Initiatives ... Dr. Anouar MAJID
88 Assoc Provost for Research & Dev ... Mr. Edward BILSKY
106 Assoc Provost of On Line Education ... Dr. Martha WILSON
49 Dean College Arts & Sciences ... Dr. Jeanne HEY
17 Dean College Health Professions ... Dr. David WARD
63 Dean College Osteopathic Medicine ... Dr. Marc HAHN
67 Dean College of Pharmacy ... Dr. Gayle BRAZEAU
52 Dean College of Dental Medicine ... Dr. James KOELBL
58 Dean Graduate Studies ... Dr. Timothy FORD
62 Dean Library Services ... Mr. Andrew GOLUB
35 Dean of Students ... Mr. Mark NAHORNEY
88 Asst Dean Student Support Svcs ... Mr. John LANGEVIN
17 Assoc Dean College Health Prof ... Mrs. Karen PARDUE
66 Assoc Director of Nursing ... Ms. Patricia MORGAN
49 Assoc Dean College Arts & Sciences ... Ms. Paulette ST. OURS
76 Assoc Dean Health Professions ... Dr. Clay GRAYBEAL
29 Director Alumni Relations ... Ms. Amy HAIL
39 Asst Dean of Students Res Life ... Ms. Jennifer DEBURRO
41 Interim Director of Athletics ... Mr. Curt SMYTH
09 Director for Institutional Research ... Mr. Kuldeep PUPPALA
88 Director Campus Planning ... Mr. Alan THIBEAULT
19 Director Campus Safety & Security ... Mr. Donald CLARK
52 Director of Dental Hygiene ... Ms. Bernice MILLS
88 Dirctor Exercise & Sport Perf ... Mr. Wayne LAMARRE
66 Director of Nursing HSM ... Ms. Bonnie DAVIS
63 Director Occupational Therapy ... Mr. Regi ROBNETT
63 Director of Physical Therapy ... Mr. Michael SHELDON
96 Director Purch/Risk Mgmt/Contract ... Mr. William BOLA
62 Director Reference Services ... Ms. Barbara SWARTZLANDER
28 Director Multi-Cultural Affairs ... Ms. Donna GASPAR JARVIS
70 Interim Director Social Work ... Dr. Clay GRAYBEAL
88 Director Sponsored Programs ... Mr. Nicholas GERE
38 Director Student Counseling ... Dr. John LANGEVIN
37 Exec Director Student Fiscal Svcs ... Mr. Paul HENDERSON
07 Exec Director for U Admissions ... Mrs. Stacy GATO

MARYLAND

Allegany College of Maryland (B)

12401 Willowbrook Road, SE,
Cumberland MD 21502-2596
County: Allegany FICE Identification: 002057
Unit ID: 161688
Telephone: (301) 784-5000 Carnegie Class: Assoc/Pub-R-M
FAX Number: (301) 784-5050 Calendar System: Semester
URL: www.allegany.edu
Established: 1961 Annual Undergrad Tuition & Fees (In-District): $3,990
Enrollment: 3,770 Coed
Affiliation or Control: Local IRS Status: 501(c)3
Highest Offering: Associate Degree
Program: Occupational; 2-Year Principally Bachelor's Creditable
Accreditation: M, ADNUR, COMTA, DH, MAC, MLTAD, OTA, PTAA, RAD

01 President ... Dr. Cynthia S. BAMBARA
05 Int Vice Pres Instructional Affairs ... Mrs. Fran LEIBFREID
10 Vice President Finance ... Mr. David DEWITT
30 VP Col Advancement/Enroll Mgmt ... Mrs. Linda A. PRICE
11 VP Administrative Services ... Mrs. Mona CLITES
32 VP Student Services ... Dr. B. Renee CONNER
51 VP of Continuing Education ... Dr. Barbara R. BEEBE
14 Assoc Dean Computer Services ... Mr. Tim PELESKY
21 Associate Dean of Finance ... Vacant
30 Director Fundraising/Grant Writing ... Mr. David R. JONES
37 Director Student Financial Aid ... Mrs. Vicki SMITH
07 Director Admissions/Registration ... Mrs. Cathy M. NOLAN
18 Director of Physical Plant ... Mr. Adam PHIPPS
08 Director of Learning Resources ... Mr. Robert D. BALDWIN
26 Public Relations/Dir Recruitment ... Ms. Shauna N. MCQUADE
41 Interim Athletic Director ... Mr. Steve BAZARNIC
29 Secretary Alumni Association ... Mrs. Gail ROTRUCK
50 Director of Business/Indus Training ... Vacant
51 Director Professional Cont Educ ... Mrs. Becky L. HADRA
09 Director of Institutional Research ... Mr. Scott HARRAH
69 Director Health Prof Cont Education ... Ms. Linda ATKINSON
38 Director Student Counseling ... Vacant
15 Director Personnel ... Mrs. Rhonda WILES

Anne Arundel Community College (C)

101 College Parkway, Arnold MD 21012-1895
County: Anne Arundel FICE Identification: 002058
Unit ID: 161767
Telephone: (410) 777-2222 Carnegie Class: Assoc/Pub-S-SC
FAX Number: (410) 777-2489 Calendar System: Semester
URL: www.aacc.edu
Established: 1961 Annual Undergrad Tuition & Fees (In-District): $3,750
Enrollment: 17,957 Coed
Affiliation or Control: State/Local IRS Status: 501(c)3
Highest Offering: Associate Degree
Program: Occupational; 2-Year Principally Bachelor's Creditable
Accreditation: M, ACFEI, ADNUR, ARCPA, EMT, MAC, MLTAD, PTAA, RAD

01 President ... Dr. Dawn LINDSAY
05 Interim Vice President for Learning ... Ms. Patricia A. CASEY-WHITEMAN
10 VP Learning Resources Management ... Ms. Melissa A. BEARDMORE
03 VP for Learner Support Services ... Ms. Felicia L. PATTERSON
106 Dean of Virtual Campus ... Ms. Jean M. RUNYON
30 Exec Dir Institutional Advancement ... Vacant
30 Director of Development ... Vacant
32 Dean of Student Services ... Dr. Ivan L. HARRELL
76 Dean School Health/Wellness/Phys Ed ... Dr. Claire L. SMITH
66 Director of Nursing ... Ms. Beth Anne BATTURS
49 Dean School Arts & Sciences ... Dr. Daniel F. SYMANCYK
72 Dean Sch Bus/Computing/Tech Stds ... Ms. Kelly A. KOERMER
51 Dean Sch of Continuing/Prof Studies ... Dr. Faith A. HARLAND-WHITE
103 Dean of Workforce Development ... Dr. Laura E. WEIDNER
22 Controller ... Ms. Martha D. ROTHSCHILD
21 Executive Director of Finance ... Mr. Andrew P. LITTLE
14 Chief Technology Officer/Info Svcs ... Ms. Shirin M. GOODARZI
08 Director of Library ... Ms. Cynthia K. STEINHOFF
06 Registrar ... Ms. Nancy A. BEIER
09 Dean Plng/Rsrch/Inst Assess ... Dr. Ricka K. FINE
15 Exec Director of Human Resources ... Ms. Suzanne L. BOYER
26 Exec Director PR & Marketing ... Mr. Daniel B. BAUM
37 Director of Financial Aid ... Mr. Richard C. HEATH
07 Dir Admissions/Enroll Development .. Mr. Thomas J. MCGINN, III
11 Exec Dir of Administrative Services ... Mr. Maury L. CHAPUT, JR.
35 Asst Dean Student Devel & Success ... Ms. Terry M. CLAY
84 Asst Dean Enrollment Services ... Dr. John F. GRABOWSKI
36 Dir Counseling/Advising/Reten Svcs ... Ms. Bonnie J. GARRETT
35 Director of Student Life ... Ms. Christine M. STORCK
22 Federal Compliance Officer ... Ms. Karen L. COOK
40 College Bookstore Manager ... Mr. Steven M. PEGG
19 Director Public Safety ... Mr. J. Gary LYLE
96 Director Purchasing/Contracting ... Ms. Debbie E. JACKSON
29 Coordinator Alumni Relations ... Ms. Leslie H. SALVAIL
23 Coordinator Health Services ... Ms. Beth A. MAYS
41 Intercollegiate Athletics Coordntor ... Mr. D. Bruce SPRINGER
28 Coordinator of Minority Recruitment ... Mr. James T. JACKSON, JR.
94 Coordinator of Women's Studies ... Dr. Suzanne J. SPOOR
88 Director of Environmental Center ... Dr. M. Stephen AILSTOCK
88 Director Center Study Local Issues ... Dr. Daniel D. NATAF
88 Dir Homeland Sec/Crim Justice Inst ... Dr. Tyrone POWERS
53 Director TEACH Institute ... Ms. Colleen K. EISENBEISER
88 Director Hosp/Cul Arts/Tourism Inst ... Ms. Mary Ellen MASON
38 Coordinator Inst for the Future ... Mr. Steven T. HENICK
88 Dir Sarbanes Center/Pub & Cmty Svc ... Ms. Cathleen H. DOYLE

Bais HaMedrash & Mesivta of Baltimore (D)

6823 Old Pimlico Road, Baltimore MD 21209
County: Baltimore Identification: 667075
Telephone: (410) 486-0006 Carnegie Class: Not Classified
FAX Number: (410) 602-9738 Calendar System: Semester
Established: 1997 Annual Undergrad Tuition & Fees: $16,200
Enrollment: 63 Male
Affiliation or Control: Independent Non-Profit IRS Status: 501(c)3
Highest Offering: First Talmudic Degree
Program: Professional
Accreditation: RABN

01 Rosh Yeshiva ... Rabbi Zvi Dov SLANGER

Baltimore City Community College (E)

2901 Liberty Heights Avenue, Baltimore MD 21215-7893
County: Baltimore City FICE Identification: 002061
Unit ID: 161864
Telephone: (410) 462-8300 Carnegie Class: Assoc/Pub-U-MC
FAX Number: (410) 462-7795 Calendar System: Semester
URL: www.bccc.edu
Established: 1947 Annual Undergrad Tuition & Fees (In-District): $7,190
Enrollment: 7,086 Coed
Affiliation or Control: State/Local IRS Status: 501(c)3
Highest Offering: Associate Degree
Program: Occupational; 2-Year Principally Bachelor's Creditable
Accreditation: M, ACBSP, ADNUR, DH, DIETT, #PTAA, SURGT

01 President ... Dr. Carolane WILLIAMS
10 Vice President Business & Finance ... Ms. Susan NIEHOFF
32 Vice President for Student Affairs ... Dr. Alicia B. HARVEY-SMITH
05 Interim Vice Pres Academic Affairs ... Dr. Peggy BRADFORD
51 Vice Pres Business & Cont Educ ... Mr. Lucious ANDERSON
84 Dean of Enrollment Management ... Ms. Julia PITTMAN
30 Vice Pres of Institutional Advance ... Ms. Deidre SOILEAU
18 Int Dir Facilities/Plng/Operations ... Mr. Kevin SEAWRIGHT
21 Controller/Chief of Accounting ... Ms. Linda WEAVER
37 Director Student Financial Aid ... Ms. Vera BROOKS
13 Chief Information Tech Officer ... Mr. Antonio HERRERA
08 Director Library/Media Services ... Ms. Stephanie REIDY
06 Exec Director Records/Registrar ... Ms. Kathleen STYLES
15 Exec Director of Human Resources ... Mr. Tony WARNER
09 Director Institutional Research ... Mr. Gerard REICHENBERG
102 Exec Director of Foundation ... Ms. Leslie REED
96 Chief Procurement Officer ... Mr. Dan COLMAN

Capitol College (F)

11301 Springfield Road, Laurel MD 20708-9759
County: Prince Georges FICE Identification: 001436
Unit ID: 162061
Telephone: (301) 369-2800 Carnegie Class: Spec/Engg
FAX Number: (301) 953-1442 Calendar System: Semester
URL: www.capitol-college.edu
Established: 1927 Annual Undergrad Tuition & Fees: $20,972
Enrollment: 816 Coed
Affiliation or Control: Independent Non-Profit IRS Status: 501(c)3
Highest Offering: Doctorate
Program: Technical Emphasis
Accreditation: M, ENG, ENGT, IACBE

01 President ... Dr. Michael T. WOOD
05 Vice President for Academic Affairs ... Dr. W. Vic MACONACHY
10 Vice Pres Finance/Administration ... Derick A. VEENSTRA
46 Vice Pres for Planning/Assessment ... Dianne M. VEENSTRA
30 Vice President Advancement ... Dr. Michael GIBBS
20 Academic Dean ... Vacant
32 Dean Student Life & Retention ... Melinda A. BUNNELL-RHYNE
54 Dean Engineering/Computer Sci/Tech ... Dr. Robert WEILER
06 Director of Registration & Records ... Sallie MCKEVITT
08 Dir Library/Information Literacy ... Rick A. SAMPLE
11 Dir Administration/Human Resources ... Jacquelyn K. ENRIGHT
07 Director of Graduate Admissions ... Anthony G. MILLER
26 Director Marketing Communications ... Megan CAMPBELL
29 Dir Alumni Relations & Advancement ... Jason COPLEY
07 Dir Undergrad Recruiting/Admissions ... George WALLS
37 Director of Financial Aid ... Suzanne THOMPSON
21 Director of Finance ... Kathleen WERNER
51 Director of Continuing Education ... Vacant
91 Director Administrative Computing ... Allen EXNER
18 Director of Maintenance ... Harry TRAPP

Carroll Community College (G)

1601 Washington Road, Westminster MD 21157-6913
County: Carroll FICE Identification: 031007
Unit ID: 405872
Telephone: (410) 386-8000 Carnegie Class: Assoc/Pub-S-SC
FAX Number: (410) 386-8181 Calendar System: Semester
URL: www.carrollcc.edu
Established: 1993 Annual Undergrad Tuition & Fees (In-District): $3,589
Enrollment: 4,041 Coed
Affiliation or Control: Local IRS Status: 501(c)3
Highest Offering: Associate Degree
Program: Occupational; 2-Year Principally Bachelor's Creditable
Accreditation: M, PTAA

01 President ... Dr. Faye PAPPALARDO
11 Exec Vice Pres Administration ... Mr. Alan M. SCHUMAN
05 VP of Academic & Student Affairs ... Dr. James D. BALL
45 VP Planning Marketing & Assessment ... Dr. Craig A. CLAGETT
51 VP Continuing Education/Training ... Ms. Karen L. MERKLE
04 Executive Assistant to President ... Ms. Sylvia BLAIR
30 Exec Dir Inst Devel/College Found ... Mr. Steven WANTZ
88 Integrity & Judicial Affairs Advoca ... Mr. Joel M. HOSKOWITZ
88 Director Transfer ... Ms. Toyette SULLIVAN
35 Dean of Student Affairs ... Dr. Michael KIPHART
50 Dean of Business/Math/Sciences ... Mr. Robert BROWN
49 Dean of Arts/Letters & Soc Sci ... Mr. Steve GEPPI
38 Director of Advising/Counseling ... Ms. Janenne CORCORAN
07 Director of Admissions ... Ms. Candace EDWARDS
89 Dir Student Life/1st Yr Pgm/Honor ... Ms. Kristie CRUMLEY
06 Registrar ... Ms. Lauren SHIELDS
37 Director of Financial Aid ... Mr. John GAY
66 Director of Nursing ... Ms. Nancy PERRY
08 Sr Dir Library/Media/Dist Lrn ... Mr. Alan BOGAGE
106 Director Distance Lrng Programs ... Dr. Susan BIRO
26 Director Publications/Comm Design ... Ms. Eleni SWENGLER
09 Director Institutional Research ... Ms. Janet NICKELS
103 Sr Dir Cont Ed/Workforce/Bus Devel .Ms. Kathleen T. MENASCHE
31 Sr Dir Lifelong Lrng/Pgm Support ... Ms. Sally LONG
105 Director of Network & Tech Services ... Ms. Patti DAVIS
21 Director Fiscal Affairs ... Mr. Timothy LEAGUE
15 Director Human Resources ... Ms. Bridget S. LEIMBACH
18 Director Facilities Management ... Ms. Terry BOWEN

Cecil College (A)

One Seahawk Drive, North East MD 21901-1999

County: Cecil FICE Identification: 008308
Unit ID: 162104
Telephone: (410) 287-6060 Carnegie Class: Assoc/Pub-S-SC
FAX Number: (410) 287-1026 Calendar System: Semester
URL: www.cecil.edu
Established: 1968 Annual Undergrad Tuition & Fees (In-District): $3,240
Enrollment: 2,606 Coed
Affiliation or Control: State/Local IRS Status: 501(c)3
Highest Offering: Associate Degree
Program: Occupational; 2-Year Principally Bachelor's Creditable
Accreditation: M, ADNUR, MAC

01 President ....Dr. W. Stephen PANNILL
05 Vice President Academic Programs ....Dr. Mary WAY BOLT
11 Vice Pres Administrative Services ....Dr. Christine A. VALUCKAS
32 VP Students/Instit Effectiveness ....Dr. Diane C. LANE
13 VP/Chief Information Officer ....Mr. Steve DIFILIPO
30 Vice Pres Institutional Advancement ....Ms. Chris Ann SZEP
18 Director of Facilities ....Mr. James PETTUS
09 Director of Institutional Research ....Mr. Dan STOICESCU
06 Registrar/Dir Admiss & Registration ....Ms. S. Tomeka SWAN
37 Director of Financial Aid Services ....Mr. Stephen AMPERSAND
08 Director of Library Services ....Ms. Lorraine MARTORANA
15 Director Human Resources ....Dr. Jim WILBURN
26 Director of Marketing ....Ms. Charlene CONOLLY
29 Coordinator Alumni Relations ....Ms. Mary MOORE
93 Director Minority Student Services ....Ms. Laney HOXTER
66 Dean Nursing Ed/Alld Hlth/Hlth Sci ....Dr. Christy DRYER
20 Dean of Academic Programs ....Dr. David LINTHICUM
31 Dean of Career/Community Education ....Ms. Debbie KLENK
41 Director Athletics ....Mr. Ed DURHAM
04 Assistant to the President ....Ms. Dawn KISNER

Chesapeake College (B)

PO Box 8, 1000 College Circle, Wye Mills MD 21679-0008

County: Queen Annes FICE Identification: 004650
Unit ID: 162168
Telephone: (410) 822-5400 Carnegie Class: Assoc/Pub-R-M
FAX Number: (410) 827-5875 Calendar System: Semester
URL: www.chesapeake.edu
Established: 1965 Annual Undergrad Tuition & Fees (In-District): $3,950
Enrollment: 2,982 Coed
Affiliation or Control: State/Local IRS Status: 501(c)3
Highest Offering: Associate Degree
Program: Occupational; 2-Year Principally Bachelor's Creditable
Accreditation: M, ADNUR, PTAA, RAD, SURGT

01 President ....Dr. Barbara A. VINIAR
05 VP Academic Affairs & Econ Develop ....Dr. Kathryn A. BARBOUR
11 Vice Pres for Administrative Svcs ....Mr. Michael D. KILGUS
32 VP Student Success/Enrollment Svcs ....Dr. Richard D. MIDCAP
18 Director of Facilities ....Mr. Monte W. GARRETTSON
51 Continuing Education Dean ....Vacant
49 Dean for Liberal Arts & Sciences ....Vacant
107 Dean for Career & Professional Stds ....Ms. Maureen A. GILMARTIN
72 VP Technology & Academic Support ....Mr. Douglass P. GRAY
08 Dean Lrng Res/Acad Sppt Svcs ....Ms. Chandra M. GIGLIOTTI-GURIDI
15 Director of Human Resources ....Ms. Susan A. CIANCHETTA
37 Director of Financial Aid ....Ms. Mindy M. SCHAFFER
30 Director Resource Development ....Ms. Lauren C. HALTERMAN
09 Dir Inst Planning/Research & Assmnt ....Ms. Kimberly A. MILLER
07 Dean for Recruitment Services ....Ms. Kathleen J. PETRICHENKO
26 Director of Public Information ....Ms. Marcie A. MOLLOY
06 Registrar ....Mr. James A. DAVIDSON
20 Dean for Retention Services ....Ms. Joan M. SEITZER

College of Southern Maryland (C)

PO Box 910, La Plata MD 20646-0910

County: Charles FICE Identification: 002064
Unit ID: 162122
Telephone: (301) 934-2251 Carnegie Class: Assoc/Pub-S-MC
FAX Number: (301) 934-7698 Calendar System: Semester
URL: www.csmd.edu
Established: 1958 Annual Undergrad Tuition & Fees (In-District): $4,096
Enrollment: 9,166 Coed
Affiliation or Control: Local IRS Status: 501(c)3
Highest Offering: Associate Degree
Program: Occupational; 2-Year Principally Bachelor's Creditable
Accreditation: M, ACBSP, ADNUR, PNUR, PTAA

01 President ....Dr. Bradley GOTTFRIED
05 Interim Vice Pres Academic Affairs ....Dr. Sue SUBOCZ
12 Vice President Leonardtown Campus ....Dr. Tracy HARRIS
12 VP Prince Frederick Campus ....Dr. Richard FLEMING
102 VP Corporate/Cmty Training Inst ....Dr. Daniel MOSSER
10 VP Financial & Admin Services ....Mr. Tony JERNIGAN
32 VP Student/Instruc Support Svcs ....Dr. William COMEY
30 Vice President for Advancement ....Ms. Michelle GOODWIN
43 Vice President/General Counsel ....Mr. Craig PATENAUDE
20 Associate VP Academic Affairs ....Dr. Sue SUBOCZ
09 Assoc VP Plng/Inst Effective/Rsrch ....Dr. Kelly MCMURRAY
84 Assoc VP Enrollment Mgmt Team ....Ms. Joan MIDDLETON
18 Director of Facilities ....Mr. Adam POTTER
15 Exec Director Human Resources ....Ms. Denise BAILEY CLARK
26 Exec Director Community Relations ....Ms. Karen SMITH-HUPP
37 Director Financial Assistance ....Mr. Christian ZIMMERMANN
06 Registrar ....Ms. Carol HARRISON
08 Director of Library ....Mr. Thomas REPENNING
66 Chair Nursing Dept ....Dr. Laura POLK
35 Director of Athletics/Student Life ....Ms. Michelle RUBLE
40 General Mgr College Store ....Ms. Marcy GANNON
07 Int Director Admissions Department ....Ms. Joan MIDDLETON
38 Director Advisement/Career Services ....Ms. Susan STRAUS
96 Director of Procurement ....Mr. Tom KELLEY
28 Ex Dir Diversity/Equal Opportunity ....Ms. Makeba CLAY

The Community College of Baltimore County (D)

7200 Sollers Point Road, Baltimore MD 21222-4649

County: Baltimore FICE Identification: 002063
Unit ID: 434672
Telephone: (443) 840-3700 Carnegie Class: Assoc/Pub-S-MC
FAX Number: (443) 840-1100 Calendar System: Semester
URL: www.ccbcmd.edu
Established: N/A Annual Undergrad Tuition & Fees (In-District): $3,922
Enrollment: 26,271 Coed
Affiliation or Control: Local IRS Status: 501(c)3
Highest Offering: Associate Degree
Program: Occupational; 2-Year Principally Bachelor's Creditable
Accreditation: M, ACBSP, ADNUR, COMTA, DH, EMT, FUSER, MLTAD, MUS, OTA, POLYT, RAD, RTT, SURGT, THEA

01 President ....Dr. Sandra L. KURTINITIS
30 Vice Pres Institutional Advancement ....Mr. Kenneth WESTARY
10 Vice Pres Finance/Administration ....Ms. Melissa HOPP
05 Vice Pres Instruction ....Dr. Mark MCCOLLOCH
84 VP Enrollment & Student Services ....Dr. Richard LILLEY
26 Sr Director for Public Relations ....Ms. Mary DELUCA
16 Senior Director Human Resources ....Ms. Penny MILSOM
51 Int Assoc VP Learning/Dean CE & WD ....Ms. Karen REILLY
88 Assoc VP Teaching & Learning ....Dr. Christine HELFRICH
35 Assoc VP/Dean of Students ....Dr. Irvin T. CLARK, III
20 Assoc VP Lrng/Dean Academic & Prof ....Dr. Gerald L. BOYD
18 Exec Dir Facilities Planning ....Mr. Sam YOUNG
08 Exec Dir Library ....Mr. Mick O'LEARY
09 Exec Dir Outcome Assess/Plng/Res ....Dr. Gohar FARAHANI
19 Exec Dir Risk Mgmt/Public Services ....Mr. Walter SMITH
26 Exec Dir Marketing/Public Relations . Mr. Michael H. PRITCHARD
38 Exec Dir Advising & Counseling ....Ms. Rachel NACHLAS
37 Exec Dir Financial Aid ....Ms. Brenda DAYHOFF
88 Exec Dir Academic Ops & Ext Lng ....Ms. Michelle HALL
04 Exec Asst to the President & Board ....Ms. Diane MORTON
88 Director Monroe Center ....Mr. James HARTSOCK
14 Director of Software Development ....Mr. Adam RENO
41 Director of Athletics ....Dr. Tom JANDOVITZ
88 Director Children's Center ....Ms. Teri BICKEL
88 Director Learning Technologies ....Mr. Alberto RAMIREZ
106 Director Distance Learning ....Mr. Jurgen HILKE
35 Dir Student Engagement/Student Life ....Ms. Jeanni WINSTON-MUIR
88 Dir Multicultural Student Services ....Mr. Chad ADERO
88 Int Dir Office of Adult Services ....Ms. Janice BROWN
88 Dir Svcs for Students w/ Disbilities ....Ms. Kate KRAMER-JEFFERSON
07 Director of Admissions ....Ms. Lisa FREEL
88 Dir Career & Transfer Services ....Ms. Lorraine DODSON
28 Director of Diversity ....Ms. Beverly HENDRIX
18 Director Plant Operations ....Mr. Curt SANDUSKY
14 Dir Network Info Security & Telecom ....Mr. Joe MARSHALL
105 Director Web Services ....Ms. Cindy OSBON
88 Dir Inst & Admin Support Services ....Vacant
96 Director of Purchasing ....Mr. Robert GILL
31 Exec Director Auxillary Services ....Mr. Frederick HOCKENBERRY
88 Dir Business Systems & Compliance ....Ms. Karen REILLY
88 Manager Food Services ....Ms. Donna S. SOWERS
29 Coord Annual Giving/Alumni Relation ....Vacant

DeVry University - Bethesda Center (E)

4550 Montgomery Avenue, Suite 100 N, Bethesda MD 20814-3304

County: Montgomery Identification: 666210
Unit ID: 439330
Telephone: (301) 652-8477 Carnegie Class: Spec/Bus
FAX Number: (301) 652-8577 Calendar System: Semester
URL: www.devry.edu
Established: 2001 Annual Undergrad Tuition & Fees: $16,156
Enrollment: 256 Coed
Affiliation or Control: Proprietary IRS Status: Proprietary
Highest Offering: Master's
Program: Occupational; Professional; Business Emphasis
Accreditation: &NH

01 Center Dean ....Mary Kay PORTER

† Regional accreditation is carried under the parent institution in Downers Grove, IL.

Faith Theological Seminary (F)

529 Walker Avenue, Baltimore MD 21212

County: Baltimore City Identification: 667016
Telephone: (410) 323-6211 Carnegie Class: Not Classified
FAX Number: (410) 323-6331 Calendar System: Semester
URL: www.faiththeological.org
Established: 1937 Annual Undergrad Tuition & Fees: $5,080
Enrollment: 147 Coed
Affiliation or Control: Non-denominational IRS Status: 501(c)3
Highest Offering: Doctorate; No Lower Division
Program: Religious Emphasis
Accreditation: @TRACS

01 President ....Dr. Norman J. MANOHAR
05 Academic Dean ....Dr. Stephen T. HAGUE

Frederick Community College (G)

7932 Opossumtown Pike, Frederick MD 21702-2097

County: Frederick FICE Identification: 002071
Unit ID: 162557
Telephone: (301) 846-2400 Carnegie Class: Assoc/Pub-S-SC
FAX Number: (301) 846-2498 Calendar System: Semester
URL: www.frederick.edu
Established: 1957 Annual Undergrad Tuition & Fees (In-District): $3,161
Enrollment: 7,404 Coed
Affiliation or Control: State/Local IRS Status: 501(c)3
Highest Offering: Associate Degree
Program: Occupational; 2-Year Principally Bachelor's Creditable
Accreditation: M, ADNUR, NMT, SURGT

01 President ....Dr. Frederico J. TALLEY
05 Interim Vice Pres for Learning ....Mr. David CROGHAN
11 Vice Pres for Administration ....Mr. Douglas D. BROWNING
32 Vice Pres for Learning Support ....Dr. Debralee MCCLELLAN
30 Chief Development Officer ....Mr. Christopher A. MASSI
13 Chief Technology Officer ....Ms. Lori ROUNDS
84 Assoc VP Enrollment Management ....Ms. Laura MEARS
15 Assoc VP Human Resources ....Mr. Donald FRANCIS
10 Assoc VP for Fiscal & Aux Services ....Ms. Dana MCDONALD
06 Assoc VP Stdnt Operations/Registrar ....Ms. Kathy FRAWLEY

Garrett College (H)

687 Mosser Road, McHenry MD 21541-1265

County: Garrett FICE Identification: 010014
Unit ID: 162609
Telephone: (301) 387-3000 Carnegie Class: Assoc/Pub-R-S
FAX Number: (301) 387-3038 Calendar System: Semester
URL: www.garrettcollege.edu
Established: 1966 Annual Undergrad Tuition & Fees (In-District): $3,222
Enrollment: 902 Coed
Affiliation or Control: State/Local IRS Status: 501(c)3
Highest Offering: Associate Degree
Program: Occupational; 2-Year Principally Bachelor's Creditable
Accreditation: M

01 President ....Dr. Richard MACLENNAN
04 Executive Assistant to President ....Ms. Marcia KNEPP
10 Dean of Administration & Finance ....Ms. Josephine GILMAN
05 Interim Dean of Instruction ....Mr. James ALLEN, JR.
51 Dean of Cont Educ/Workforce Devel ....Ms. Julie YODER
13 Interim Director of IT ....Ms. Jami REYNOLDS
26 Dean of Marketing & Enrollment Mgmt ....Ms. Ann WELLHAM
32 Dean of Student Life ....Dr. George BRELSFORD
30 Dir Develop/Exec Dir Foundation ....Mr. Fred LEAREY
06 Director of Records & Registration ....Ms. Kim DEGIOVANNI
37 Director of Financial Aid ....Ms. Cissy VANSICKLE
08 Interim Library Director ....Ms. Ellen SHEAFFER
21 Director of Business Office ....Ms. Katherine BROWNING
18 Plant Manager ....Mr. Hugh SCHRIER
15 Director of Human Resources ....Ms. Linda K. FIKE
65 Dir of Natural Res/Wildlife Tech ....Mr. Kevin DODGE
41 Director of Athletics ....Mr. Shawn NOEL
50 Director of Business/Info Tech ....Dr. Qing YUAN
36 Dir Acad Career & Trans Advising ....Ms. Judy CARBONE
96 Purchasing/Accounts Payable ....Ms. Bonnie BROADWATER
09 Institutional Research Analyst ....Ms. Kalie ASHBY
40 Bookstore Manager ....Ms. Margi L. PERFETTI
07 Director of Admissions ....Ms. Rachelle DAVIS
38 Coordinator of Counseling Services ....Ms. Madonna POOL
17 Coordinator of Health Services ....Ms. Jamie RESH-KAMP
39 Coordinator of Residential Services ....Ms. Tracy BARCUS
45 Director of Institutional Planning ....Mr. James ALLEN, JR.
105 Webmaster ....Ms. Linda STEVANUS
79 Dir of Humanities & Social Sciences ....Mr. Ron SKIDMORE
88 Director of Adventure Sports ....Mr. Michael LOGSDON
81 Dir of Math/Science & Teacher Educ ....Mr. Alexander TUEL

Goucher College (I)

1021 Dulaney Valley Road, Towson MD 21204-2780

County: Baltimore FICE Identification: 002073
Unit ID: 162654
Telephone: (410) 337-6000 Carnegie Class: Bac/A&S
FAX Number: (410) 337-6123 Calendar System: Semester
URL: www.goucher.edu
Established: 1885 Annual Undergrad Tuition & Fees: $37,072
Enrollment: 2,173 Coed
Affiliation or Control: Independent Non-Profit IRS Status: 501(c)3
Highest Offering: Master's
Program: Liberal Arts And General; Teacher Preparatory
Accreditation: M

01 President ....Mr. Sanford J. UNGAR
05 Provost & Chief Academic Officer ....Dr. Marc ROY

32 Vice Pres/Dean of Students .... Dr. Gail N. EDMONDS
30 Actg Vice Pres Devel/Alumni Affs .... Ms. Janet WILEY
84 Vice President Enrollment Mgmt .... Mr. Michael O'LEARY
26 Vice President Communications .... Vacant
13 VP for Technology and Planning .... Mr. Bill LEIMBACH
43 General Counsel .... Ms. Laura BURTON-GRAHAM
20 Associate Dean Academic Affairs .... Ms. Janine BOWEN
82 Assoc Dean International Studies .... Mr. Daniel NORTON
35 Assoc Dean for Student Engagement .... Ms. Emily PERL
15 Asst VP Finance/Dir Human Resources .... Ms. Deborah LUPTON
21 Controller .... Mr. Alex ANTKOWIAK
07 Director of Admissions .... Mr. Carlton E. SURBECK, III
08 Librarian .... Ms. Nancy MAGNUSON
29 Exec Director of Alumnae/i .... Ms. Margaret-Ann RADFORD-WEDEMEYER
36 Director of Career Development .... Ms. Traci MARTIN
58 Director Grad Program in Education .... Ms. Phyllis SUNSHINE
06 Registrar .... Mr. Andrew WESTFALL
09 Asst Dir of Institutional Research .... Ms. Pallabi ROY
10 Dir Business/Auxiliary Services .... Mr. Calvin GLADDEN
18 Dir Facilities Management Services .... Mr. Harold TINSLEY
37 Director Financial Aid .... Ms. Ellen OSTENDORF
93 Asst Dean for Multicultural Stds .... Ms. Mary TANDIA

Hagerstown Community College (A)

11400 Robinwood Drive, Hagerstown MD 21742-6590
County: Washington FICE Identification: 002074
Unit ID: 162690
Telephone: (240) 500-2000 Carnegie Class: Assoc/Pub-R-M
FAX Number: (301) 393-3682 Calendar System: Semester
URL: www.hagerstowncc.edu
Established: 1946 Annual Undergrad Tuition & Fees (In-District): $2,958
Enrollment: 5,075 Coed
Affiliation or Control: State/Local IRS Status: 501(c)3
Highest Offering: Associate Degree
Program: Occupational; 2-Year Principally Bachelor's Creditable
Accreditation: M, DA, EMT, RAD

01 President .... Dr. Guy ALTIERI
05 Vice President of Academic Affairs .... Dr. David WARNER
11 Vice Pres Administration/Finance .... Ms. Anna M. BARKER
32 Dean of Students .... Dr. Donna RUDY
09 Dean of Plng/Instl Effectiveness .... Ms. Barbara E. MACHT
18 Dir Facilities Management & Plng .... Dr. Robert SPONG
07 Dir Admissions/Records/Registration .... Dr. Jennifer A. HAUGHIE
30 Exec Director College Advancement .... Ms. Stacey L. LOWMAN
26 Director Marketing/Public Info .... Ms. Elizabeth K. STULL
37 Director of Financial Aid .... Ms. Carolyn S. COX
14 Dir Technology/Computer Studies .... Ms. Margaret C. SPIVEY
51 Dean Continuing Educ/Extension Svcs .... Ms. Theresa SHANK
21 Director of Business Services .... Ms. Lita ORNER
66 Director of Nursing .... Ms. Karen HAMMOND
15 Director of Human Resources .... Ms. Donna MARRIOTT
41 Dir Athletics/Phys Ed/Leisure Stds .... Mr. Robert MYERS
20 Director of Instruction .... Mr. Gerald C. HAINES
13 Director of Information Technology .... Mr. Craig M. FENTRESS
21 Director of Finance .... Mr. David C. BITTORF
88 Dir Organization Devel/Special Proj .... Vacant
76 Director of Health Sciences .... Ms. Angela STOOPS

Harford Community College (B)

401 Thomas Run Road, Bel Air MD 21015-1698
County: Harford FICE Identification: 002075
Unit ID: 162706
Telephone: (443) 412-2000 Carnegie Class: Assoc/Pub-S-SC
FAX Number: (443) 412-2120 Calendar System: Semester
URL: www.harford.edu
Established: 1957 Annual Undergrad Tuition & Fees (In-District): $2,923
Enrollment: 7,132 Coed
Affiliation or Control: Local IRS Status: 501(c)3
Highest Offering: Associate Degree
Program: Occupational; 2-Year Principally Bachelor's Creditable
Accreditation: M, ADNUR, HT, MAC

01 President .... Dr. Dennis GOLLADAY
05 Vice President Academic Affairs .... Dr. M. Annette HAGGRAY
10 Vice President Finance & Operations ... Mr. Fredrick P. JOHNSON
45 VP Student Dev & Inst Effectiveness .... Dr. Deborah J. CRUISE
31 VP Mkting/Dev/Community Relations . Ms. Brenda M. MORRISON
13 VP Information Technology .... Ms. Annie PAGURA
84 Assoc VP Enrollment Services .... Ms. Amanda A. KASTERN
32 Assoc VP Student Development .... Dr. Diane L. RESIDES
21 Assoc VP Finance & Budget .... Mr. Stephen S. PHILLIPS
51 Assoc VP Continuing Educ & Training .... Vacant
18 Assoc VP Campus Operations .... Dr. Gregory A. DEAL
37 Director Financial Aid .... Ms. D. Lynn LEE
06 Registrar .... Ms. Sandra G. CLARK
96 Director for Procurement .... Mr. Victor H. DODSON
26 Dir Marketing & Public Relations .... Ms. Nancy J. DYSARD
15 Dir Human Resources/Employee Dev .... Ms. Cheryl E. HICKSON
29 Director College/Alumni Development .... Ms. Denise M. DREGIER
08 Director Library & Info Resources .... Ms. Carol M. ALLEN
106 Dir eLearning & Info Resources .... Mr. LeRoy A. TRUSTY
09 Dir Inst Research/Plng/Effective .... Mr. William M. EKEY
38 Dir Advising/Career/Transfer Svcs .... Ms. J. Bonnie SULZBACH
40 Coordinator College Store .... Ms. Linda L. FIFE
07 Coordinator for Admissions .... Mr. Brian J. HAMMOND
81 Dean Science/Tech/Engr/Math .... Ms. Deborah R. WROBEL
83 Dean Behavioral & Social Sciences .... Mr. Avery W. WARD
79 Dean Humanities .... Dr. Karry L. HATHAWAY
57 Dean Visual/Performing/Applied Arts .... Mr. Paul E. LABE
50 Dean Bus/Computing/Applied Tech .... Mr. John F. MAYHORNE
88 Dean Educ & Transitional Studies .... Mr. Carl E. HENDERSON
66 Dean Nursing & Allied Health Profs .... Ms. Laura C. PRESTON

Hood College (C)

401 Rosemont Avenue, Frederick MD 21701-8575
County: Frederick FICE Identification: 002076
Unit ID: 162760
Telephone: (301) 663-3131 Carnegie Class: Master's M
FAX Number: (301) 694-7653 Calendar System: Semester
URL: www.hood.edu
Established: 1893 Annual Undergrad Tuition & Fees: $32,300
Enrollment: 2,435 Coed
Affiliation or Control: Independent Non-Profit IRS Status: 501(c)3
Highest Offering: Master's
Program: Liberal Arts And General; Teacher Preparatory; Fine Arts Emphasis
Accreditation: M, ACBSP, SW, TED

01 President .... Dr. Ronald J. VOLPE
05 Provost/Dean of Faculty .... Dr. Katherine CONWAY-TURNER
10 Vice Pres Finance .... Mr. Charles G. MANN
30 VP for Institutional Advancement .... Ms. Nancy E. GILLECE
32 VP Student Life/Dean of Students .... Dr. Olivia G. WHITE
84 VP Undergrad/Grad Enrollment .... Dr. Kathleen BANDS
07 Director of Admissions .... Mr. David ADAMS
58 Dean of Graduate School .... Dr. Allen FLORA
20 Director CAAR .... Mr. Herbert ENGLISH
26 Exec Dir Marketing/Communications .... Mr. Dave DIEHL
29 Director of Alumnae/i Programs .... Ms. Linda ROTH
06 Registrar .... Mrs. Nanette MARKEY
08 Librarian .... Mrs. Jan SAMET
37 Director of Financial Aid .... Ms. Carol SCHROYER
15 Director of Human Resources .... Ms. Carol M. WUENSCHEL
18 Director of Facilities .... Mr. John WICHSER
13 Chief Technology Officer .... Mr. Cornelius R. FAY, III
09 Director of Institutional Research .... Ms. Cynthia EMORY

Howard Community College (D)

10901 Little Patuxent Parkway, Columbia MD 21044-3197
County: Howard FICE Identification: 008175
Unit ID: 162779
Telephone: (443) 518-1000 Carnegie Class: Assoc/Pub-S-SC
FAX Number: N/A Calendar System: Semester
URL: www.howardcc.edu
Established: 1966 Annual Undergrad Tuition & Fees (In-District): $4,343
Enrollment: 10,081 Coed
Affiliation or Control: State/Local IRS Status: 501(c)3
Highest Offering: Associate Degree
Program: Occupational; 2-Year Principally Bachelor's Creditable
Accreditation: M, ADNUR, CVT, EMT, MUS, PNUR, RAD

01 President .... Dr. Kathleen B. HETHERINGTON
32 Vice President of Student Services .... Dr. Cynthia J. PETERKA
05 Vice President of Academic Affairs .... Dr. Sharon PIERCE
10 Vice Pres of Administration/Finance .... Ms. Lynn C. COLEMAN
13 Vice President for Information Tech .... Mr. Thomas J. GLASER
51 Assoc Vice Pres Cont Education .... Ms. JoAnn HAWKINS
84 Assoc Vice Pres for Enroll Svcs .... Ms. Alison BUCKLEY
35 Assoc Vice Pres for Student Devel .... Ms. Janice L. MARKS
15 Associate Vice Pres Human Resources .... Mr. Dave JORDAN
21 Associate VP of Finance .... Ms. Janet L. CULLISON
09 Exec Dir Plng/Research & Org Dev .... Ms. Zoe A. IRVIN
18 Exec Dir Capital Proj/Facilities .... Mr. Charles NIGHTINGALE
101 Executive Associate to President .... Ms. Linda EMMERICH
27 Director of Mktg & Communications .... Mr. Randall R. BENGFORT
37 Director Financial Aid Services .... Ms. Stephanie BENDER
30 Exec Director of Development .... Ms. Melissa MATTEY
40 Director Auxiliary Services .... Ms. Arla J. WEBB
19 Director of Security Services .... Mr. Ken MCGLYNN
35 Director Student Life .... Ms. Llatetra D. BROWN
04 Exec Assistant to the President .... Ms. Farida GUZDAR
26 Executive Dir of PR & Marketing .... Ms. Nancy S. GAINER
36 Director of Testing .... Mr. Eli STAV
96 Director of Purchasing .... Ms. Elizabeth H. MOSS

ITT Technical Institute (E)

11301 Red Run Boulevard, Owings Mills MD 21117-3246
County: Baltimore Identification: 666377
Unit ID: 446914
Telephone: (443) 394-7115 Carnegie Class: Assoc/PrivFP4
FAX Number: N/A Calendar System: Quarter
URL: www.itt-tech.edu
Established: N/A Annual Undergrad Tuition & Fees: N/A
Enrollment: 1,190 Coed
Affiliation or Control: Proprietary IRS Status: Proprietary
Highest Offering: Baccalaureate
Program: Technical Emphasis
Accreditation: ACICS

† Branch campus of ITT Technical Institute, Indianapolis, IN..

Johns Hopkins University (F)

Charles and 34th Streets, Baltimore MD 21218-2680
County: Independent City FICE Identification: 002077
Unit ID: 162928
Telephone: (410) 516-8000 Carnegie Class: RU/VH
FAX Number: N/A Calendar System: Semester
URL: www.jhu.edu
Established: 1876 Annual Undergrad Tuition & Fees: $43,930
Enrollment: 21,410 Coed
Affiliation or Control: Independent Non-Profit IRS Status: 501(c)3
Highest Offering: Doctorate
Program: Liberal Arts And General; Teacher Preparatory; Professional
Accreditation: M, BBT, CACREP, CS, DENT, DIETC, DIETI, DMS, ENG, ENGR, HSA, IPSY, MED, MIL, NMT, NURSE, PH, TED

01 President .... Mr. Ronald J. DANIELS
100 Sr Vice President/Chief of Staff .... Ms. Jacqueline MOK
05 Interim Provost & Sr VP Acad Affs .... Dr. Jonathan BAGGER
17 CEO Johns Hopkins Medicine .... Dr. Paul D. ROTHMAN
10 Sr VP Finance & Administration .... Mr. Daniel G. ENNIS
30 Sr VP for External Affairs/Develop .... Vacant
29 VP for Development & Alum Relations .... Mr. Fritz SCHROEDER
45 Vice Pres Strategic Initiatives .... Mr. Phillip SPECTOR
26 Vice Pres Comm/Public Affairs .... Mr. Glenn M. BIELER
43 Vice Pres/General Counsel .... Mr. Frederick G. SAVAGE
86 Vice Pres Govt/Community Affairs .... Mr. Thomas LEWIS
18 Vice Pres Real Estate/Campus Svcs .... Mr. Alan FISH
16 Vice Pres Human Resources .... Ms. Charlene M. HAYES
21 Vice Pres Finance & CFO .... Vacant
21 Vice Pres Chief Investment Officer .... Dr. Kathryn J. CRECELIUS
20 Vice Provost for Student Affairs .... Dr. Sarah STEINBERG
20 Vice Provost Faculty Affairs .... Dr. Barbara LANDAU
20 Asst Vice Provost Accred/Acad Svcs .... Mr. Philip TANG
84 Vice Provost for Admiss & Fin Aid .... Mr. David PHILLIPS
58 Vice Provost Grad/Post-Doc Programs .. Dr. Jonathan A. BAGGER
88 Vice Provost International Programs .... Dr. Pam CRANSTON
27 Vice Provost Info Technology/CIO .... Ms. Stephanie REEL
22 Vice Provost Institutional Equity .... Ms. Caroline LAGUERRE-BROWN
46 Vice Provost Research .... Dr. Scott L. ZEGER
09 Asst Provost Institutional Research .... Dr. Cathy J. LEBO
82 Dean Nitze School Adv Intl Studies .... Dr. Vali NASR
49 Dean Krieger School Arts & Sciences .... Dr. Kathleen NEWMAN
50 Dean Carey Business School .... Dr. Bernard FERRARI
53 Dean School of Education .... Dr. David W. ANDREWS
54 Dean Whiting School of Engineering .... Dr. Nicholas P. JONES
63 Dean School of Medicine .... Dr. Paul ROTHMAN
66 Dean School of Nursing .... Dr. Martha N. HILL
69 Dean Bloomberg School Public Health .... Dr. Michael J. KLAG
08 Dean Sheridan Libraries and Museums .... Mr. Winston G. TABB
64 Director Peabody Institute .... Mr. Jeffrey SHARKEY
81 Director Applied Physics Lab .... Mr. Ralph SEMMEL
96 Director Purchasing .... Mr. Paul N. BEYER
21 Controller .... Mr. Gregory S. OLER
19 Exec Director Safety & Security .... Mr. Edmund SKRODZKI
21 Exec Director Internal Audits .... Mr. Francis X. BOSSLE
27 Exec Director Comm & Public Affairs .... Mr. Dennis O'SHEA
88 Exec Director JH Real Estate .... Mr. Brian B. DEMBECK

Kaplan University (G)

18618 Crestwood Drive, Hagerstown MD 21742-2797
County: Washington FICE Identification: 007946
Unit ID: 162681
Telephone: (301) 766-3600 Carnegie Class: Assoc/PrivFP4
FAX Number: (301) 791-7661 Calendar System: Quarter
URL: www.hagerstown.kaplanuniversity.edu
Established: 1938 Annual Undergrad Tuition & Fees: $16,695
Enrollment: 731 Coed
Affiliation or Control: Proprietary IRS Status: Proprietary
Highest Offering: Baccalaureate
Program: Occupational; 2-Year Principally Bachelor's Creditable
Accreditation: &NH, MAC

01 President .... Mr. W. Christopher MOTZ
05 Academic Dean .... Dr. Samuel T. CROCKETT
32 Dean of Students .... Ms. Lisa A. COPENHAVER
06 Registrar .... Ms. Sheila R. GATES
37 Director of Student Financial Aid .... Ms. Kristin D. BREZLER
07 Director of Admissions .... Mr. James W. KLEIN
36 Director of Career Services .... Ms. Shannon N. CIANELLI
08 Director of Library Services .... Mr. Thomas M. STATTON
10 Business Manager .... Ms. Barbara A. KEESECKER

† Regional accreditation is carried under the parent institution in Davenport, IA.

Lincoln College of Technology (H)

9325 Snowden River Parkway, Columbia MD 21046
County: Howard FICE Identification: 007936
Unit ID: 163028
Telephone: (410) 290-7100 Carnegie Class: Assoc/PrivFP
FAX Number: (410) 290-7880 Calendar System: Quarter
URL: www.lincolntech.com
Established: 1978 Annual Undergrad Tuition & Fees: $27,958
Enrollment: 1,095 Coed
Affiliation or Control: Proprietary IRS Status: Proprietary
Highest Offering: Associate Degree
Program: Occupational
Accreditation: ACCSC

01 Director .... Vacant

Loyola University Maryland (I)

4501 N Charles Street, Baltimore MD 21210-2694
County: Independent City FICE Identification: 002078
Unit ID: 163046
Telephone: (410) 617-2000 Carnegie Class: Master's L

FAX Number: (410) 322-2768 Calendar System: Semester
URL: www.loyola.edu
Established: 1852 Annual Undergrad Tuition & Fees: $51,810
Enrollment: 6,080 Coed
Affiliation or Control: Roman Catholic IRS Status: 501(c)3
Highest Offering: Doctorate
Program: Liberal Arts And General; Teacher Preparatory
Accreditation: M, BUS, BUSA, CACREP, CLPSY, CS, ENG, SP, TED

01 President .... Rev. Brian F. LINNANE, SJ
03 Executive Vice President .... Dr. Susan DONOVAN
04 Assistant to the President .... Ms. Vicki WELLER
05 Vice President for Academic Affairs .... Dr. Timothy L. SNYDER
10 Vice Pres for Finance & Treasurer .... Mr. Randall GENTZLER
11 Vice President for Administration .... Mr. Terrence M. SAWYER
30 Vice President Advancement .... Ms. Megan GILLICK
32 VP Student Devel/Dean of Students . Dr. Sheilah SHAW HORTON
84 Vice Pres Enrollment Management .... Mr. Marc CAMILLE
20 Assoc Vice Pres Academic Affairs .... Ms. Jenny LOWRY
28 Asst VP Academic Affrs/Diversity .... Dr. Martha L. WHARTON
37 Asst Vice Pres of Financial Aid .... Mr. Mark L. LINDENMEYER
09 Asst VP of Institutional Research .... Ms. Terra SCHEHR
18 Assoc VP Facilities/Campus Services .... Ms. Helen SCHNEIDER
13 Asst VP of Technology Services/CIO .... Ms. Louise FINN
26 Director Public Relations .... Ms. Courtney JOLLEY
35 Asst Vice Pres Student Development .... Mr. Xavier COLE
15 Asst Vice Pres for Human Resources .... Ms. Kathleen PARNELL
21 Asst Vice Pres for Administration .... Ms. Joan FLYNN
26 Asst VP Marketing/Communications .... Ms. Sharon HIGGINS
41 Asst VP/Director of Athletics .... Mr. James PAQUETTE
38 Dir Counsel Ctr/Ast VP Student Dev .... Dr. Donelda COOK
102 Dir Corporation & Foundation Rels .... Ms. Beth SCHRODER
07 Director Undergraduate Admissions .... Ms. Elena HICKS
07 Director of Graduate Admissions .... Ms. Maureen FAUX
06 Director of Records .... Ms. Rita L. STEINER
85 Director of International Programs .... Dr. Andre COLOMBAT
08 Director of Library .... Mr. John MCGINTY
42 Director of Campus Ministry .... Mr. Jack DENNIS
88 Dir Center Community Svc/ Justice .... Sr. Catherine GUGERTY, SSND
36 Dir Career Devel/Placement Center .... Dr. CreSaundra Y. SILLS
88 Dir Alcohol/Drug Ed/Support Svcs .... Mr. Jan WILLIAMS
88 Director Recreational Sports .... Ms. Pamela WETHERBEE-METCALF
88 Dir Leadership/New Student Program .... Mr. Jeffrey KNIPLE
35 Director Student Activities .... Mr. Mark C. BRODERICK
88 Director Alana Services .... Mr. Rodney PARKER
21 Controller .... Ms. Kelly NELSON
45 Director of Resource Management .... Mr. David DAUGHADAY
31 Director Event Svcs/Auxiliary Mgmt .... Mr. Joseph BRADLEY
18 Dir Project Mgmt/Facilities Maint .... Mr. Laszlo PELY
88 Director Environment Health/Safety .... Mr. Thomas HETTLEMAN
19 Dir of Public Safety/Campus Police .... Mr. Timothy FOX
29 Director Alumni Relations .... Mr. Brian OAKES
44 Director of Annual Giving .... Ms. Jane Curley HOGGE
27 Director of Creative Services .... Mr. Brian HATCHER
88 Director Advancement Communications .... Mr. Carl LUTY
89 Dean First Yr Stdnts/Academic Svcs .... Dr. Ilona MCGUINESS
49 Dean College of Arts & Sciences .... Rev. James F. MIRACKY, SJ
50 Dean Sellinger Sch Business & Mgmt .... Ms. Karyl LEGGIO
49 Assistant Dean Arts & Sciences .... Dr. Suzanne KEILSON
50 Assistant Dean for Business Program .... Ms. Ann ATTANASIO
88 Associate Dean of Students .... Ms. Michelle CHEATEM

Maple Springs Baptist Bible College & Seminary (A)

4130 Belt Road, Capitol Heights MD 20743-5712
County: Prince Georges FICE Identification: 038224
Unit ID: 446394
Telephone: (301) 736-3631 Carnegie Class: Spec/Faith
FAX Number: (301) 735-6507 Calendar System: Semester
URL: www.msbbcs.edu
Established: 1986 Annual Undergrad Tuition & Fees: $4,590
Enrollment: 110 Coed
Affiliation or Control: Baptist IRS Status: 501(c)3
Highest Offering: Doctorate
Program: Religious Emphasis
Accreditation: TRACS

01 President .... Dr. Larry W. JORDAN
04 Executive Assistant to President .... Dr. Jerome S. TARVER
03 Executive Vice President .... Dr. Vivian E. BESS
05 Vice President Academic Affairs .... Mr. Lewis ANTHONY
11 Vice Pres Administration & Finance .... Dr. Jerrye B. FELICIANA
73 Dean Chr Dept Church Vocations .... Dr. Carl KEELS
88 Academic Dean Seminary Div .... Dr. Daryl WATSON
06 Director Records/Admissions .... Ms. Esther BIRCH
09 Dir Institutional Plng/Assessment .... Ms. Veronica GRAVES
10 Director Business Affairs .... Mrs. Fannie G. THOMPSON
32 Director Student Affairs .... Dr. James THOMPSON
08 Dir Library/Instrnl Resource Center .... Mr. Darren JONES
37 Financial Aid Coordinator .... Ms. Patricia JONES

Maryland Institute College of Art (B)

1300 Mount Royal Avenue, Baltimore MD 21217-4191
County: Independent City FICE Identification: 002080
Unit ID: 163295
Telephone: (410) 669-9200 Carnegie Class: Spec/Arts
FAX Number: (410) 669-9206 Calendar System: Semester
URL: www.mica.edu
Established: 1826 Annual Undergrad Tuition & Fees: $37,900
Enrollment: 2,044 Coed
Affiliation or Control: Independent Non-Profit IRS Status: 501(c)3
Highest Offering: Master's
Program: Fine Arts Emphasis
Accreditation: M, ART

01 President .... Mr. Fred LAZARUS, IV
05 Vice Pres Academic Affairs/Provost .... Mr. Ray ALLEN
10 Vice Pres Fiscal Affairs .... Mr. Douglas MANN
30 Vice Pres Advancement .... Mr. Michael R. FRANCO
32 Vice Pres/Dean Student Affairs .. Mr. J. Davidson (Dusty) PORTER
84 Vice Pres/Dean Admiss/Finan Aid .... Ms. Theresa BEDOYA
13 Vice Pres Technology Systems & Svcs .... Mr. Tom HYATT
11 Vice Pres Operations .... Mr. Mike MOLLA
20 Vice Prov Ugrad Studies & Faculty .... Ms. Jan STINCHCOMB
46 Vice Provost Research .... Vacant
04 Executive Assistant to President .... Ms. Marian SMITH
37 Assoc VP Financial Aid .... Ms. Diane PRENGAMAN
44 Assoc VP Dev Constituent Rels .... Ms. Alison DAVITT
27 Assoc VP Institutnal Communication .... Mr. Cedric MOBLEY
44 Assoc VP Advancement/Plan/Sp Projct . Ms. Mary Ann LAMBROS
14 Assoc VP Technology .... Ms. Susan MILTENBERGER
18 Assoc VP Facilities Management .... Mr. Timothy MILLNER
16 Assoc VP Human Resources .... Vacant
20 Dean Academic Services .... Ms. Cynthia BARTH
58 Interim Dean Graduate Studies .... Mr. Robert MERRILL
53 Dean Art Education .... Ms. Karen CARROLL
51 Dean Continuing & Professnl Studies .... Mr. David GRACYALNY
35 Assoc Dean Stdnt Life/Judicial Affs .... Mr. Michael PATTERSON
88 Assoc Dean Student Health Wellness .... Mr. Bryant FORD
07 Assoc Dean Undergraduate Admissions .... Ms. Christine SEESE
88 Assoc Dean Graduate Admission .... Mr. Scott KELLY
88 Assoc Dean Continuing Studies .... Mr. Peter DUBEAU
06 Assoc Dean Enrollment Svs/Registrar .... Ms. Christine PETERSON
28 Asst Dean Diversity Intercultur Dev .... Mr. Clyde JOHNSON, JR.
21 Director Accounting .... Ms. Jessica RURKA
88 Director Budget .... Ms. Brigitte SULLIVAN
88 Director Student Accounts .... Vacant
39 Director Residence Life .... Mr. Scott STONE
36 Director Career Development .... Ms. Megan MILLER
31 Director Community Engagement .... Ms. Karen STULTS
31 Director Community Art Partnerships .... Ms. Agnes MOON
38 Director Counseling Center .... Ms. Pat FARRELL
88 Director Student Activities .... Ms. Karol MARTINEZ
88 Director Admissions Operations .... Ms. Cheryl ISSOD
08 Director & Head Librarian .... Mr. Anthony WHITE
88 Director Annual Fund .... Ms. Carolyn STRATFORD-YOUNCE
88 Director Advancement Services .... Ms. Dana COSTELLO
88 Director Stewardships .... Ms. Erin CHREST
26 Director Public Relations .... Ms. Jessica WEGLEIN
88 Director Exhibitions .... Mr. Gerald ROSS
85 Director International Affairs .... Ms. Petra VISSCHER
88 Director Writing St/Learn Res Cnt .... Mr. Daniel GUTSTEIN
88 Dir Data Mgmt/Registration Cont Std .... Ms. Kathy GREENBLATT
88 Director Marketing & Enrollment Svs .... Ms. Tracy JACOBS
09 Director Student Records & Research .... Mr. Hadley GARBART
19 Director of Campus Safety .... Mr. Stephen DAVIS
88 Director Events .... Ms. Anne SOUTH
88 Director Operation Services .... Mr. Chris BOHASKA
29 Dir Alumni & Parent Rels .... Mr. David HART
102 Director Corp/Found/Govt Relations .... Ms. Sara WARREN
105 Director of Web Communications .... Mr. Gregory RAGO
24 Director Technical Support Services .... Mr. John RHODES
91 Director Administrative Systems .... Mr. Ted SIMPSON
88 Director Network Services .... Mr. David APAW
90 Dir Instructional Advance & Tech .... Mr. Paul IWANCIO
40 Manager College Store .... Ms. Kerri LITZ

McDaniel College (C)

2 College Hill, Westminster MD 21157-4390
County: Carroll FICE Identification: 002109
Unit ID: 164270
Telephone: (410) 848-7000 Carnegie Class: Bac/A&S
FAX Number: (410) 857-2279 Calendar System: Semester
URL: www.mcdaniel.edu
Established: 1867 Annual Undergrad Tuition & Fees: $35,800
Enrollment: 3,374 Coed
Affiliation or Control: Independent Non-Profit IRS Status: 501(c)3
Highest Offering: Master's
Program: Liberal Arts And General; Teacher Preparatory
Accreditation: M, SW, TED

01 President .... Dr. Roger N. CASEY
05 Provost/Dean of Faculty .... Dr. Thomas M. FALKNER
10 Vice Pres Administration & Finance .... Dr. Ethan A. SEIDEL
44 Vice Pres Institutional Advancement .... Ms. Lori LEWIS
32 Vice Pres/Dean of Student Affairs .... Ms. Beth R. GERL
84 VP Enroll Mgt/Dean of Admissions .... Ms. Florence W. HINES
30 Assoc Vice Pres/Director Devel .... Mr. Lawrence JUNKIN
29 Assoc Vice Pres of Alumni Relations .... Ms. Robin A. BRENTON
27 Assoc Vice Pres Comm/Marketing .... Ms. Joyce D. MULLER
04 Exec Assistant to the President .... Ms. Tamara BOWEN
58 Dean Graduate/Professional Stds .... Dr. Henry B. REIFF
20 Associate Dean of Academic Affairs .... Dr. Debora JOHNSON-ROSS
88 Assoc Dean Student Acad Life .... Ms. Lisa BRESLIN
102 Dir Corp & Foundation Relations .... Ms. Kathleen M. CURTIN
08 Director of Library .... Ms. Jessame E. FERGUSON
37 Director Financial Aid .... Ms. Patricia M. WILLIAMS
06 Registrar .... Ms. Jan A. KIPHART
41 Director Athletics .... Mr. Paul MOYER
36 Director Career Advising .... Vacant
38 Director Counseling .... Ms. Susan J. GLORE
35 Director Student Engagement .... Ms. Christine WORKMAN
25 Director Financial Services/Treas .... Mr. Arthur S. WISNER
15 Director Human Resources .... Mr. Thomas G. STEBACK
45 Dir Facility Plng/Capital Projects .... Mr. Edgar S. SELL, JR.
18 Director Physical Plant .... Mr. George W. BRENTON
19 Director of Campus Safety .... Mr. Michael N. WEBSTER
40 Manager Bookstore .... Mr. Kyle MELOCHE
18 Director Conferences/Auxil Svcs .... Ms. Mary J. COLBERT
13 Chief Information Officer .... Dr. Esther IGLICH
28 Director of Multicultural Services .... Ms. Mahlia JOYCE
92 Director of Honors Program .... Dr. Stephanie D. MADSEN
96 Director of Purchasing/Receiving .... Ms. Margaret G. BELL
88 Coord of Deaf Education Program .... Dr. Mark M. RUST
09 Director Institutional Research .... Dr. Brian AULT
101 Secretary of the Board of Trustees .... Ms. Tamara BOWEN
86 Director of Government Relations .... Dr. Herbert C. SMITH

Montgomery College (D)

900 Hungerford Drive, Rockville MD 20850-1733
County: Montgomery FICE Identification: 006911
Unit ID: 163426
Telephone: (240) 567-5000 Carnegie Class: Assoc/Pub-S-MC
FAX Number: (240) 567-6397 Calendar System: Semester
URL: www.montgomerycollege.edu
Established: 1946 Annual Undergrad Tuition & Fees (In-District): $4,452
Enrollment: 26,996 Coed
Affiliation or Control: Local IRS Status: 501(c)3
Highest Offering: Associate Degree
Program: Occupational; 2-Year Principally Bachelor's Creditable
Accreditation: M, ADNUR, DMS, MUS, POLYT, #PTAA, RAD, SURGT

01 President .... Dr. DeRionne P. POLLARD
05 Sr VP for Academic Affairs .... Dr. Donald PEARL
32 Sr VP for Student Services .... Dr. Beverly WALKER-GRIFFEA
11 Sr VP Admin & Fiscal Services .... Ms. Cathy JONES
88 Int Assoc SVP for Adm & Fiscal Svcs .... Dr. Janet WORMACK
12 Vice Pres/Provost Rockville Campus .... Dr. Judy ACKERMAN
12 Vice Pres/Provost Germantown Campus .... Dr. Sanjay RAI
12 Vice Pres/Prov Takoma Park Campus .... Dr. Brad J. STEWART
103 VP for Workforce Dev & Contuing Ed .... Mr. George M. PAYNE
100 Chief of Staff/Chief Strategy Ofcr .... Dr. Stephen D. CAIN
30 Vice Pres of Advancement .... Mr. David SEARS
45 VP for Planning and Inst Effective .... Ms. Kathleen WESSMAN
13 Acting VP of Instructional & IT/CIO .... Ms. Donna SCHENA
09 Dir Institutional Rsrch & Analysis .... Dr. Robert LYNCH
86 Chief Government Relations Officer .... Ms. Susan MADDEN
43 General Counsel .... Mr. Clyde H. SORRELL
15 VP of Human Res/Dev & Engagement .... Ms. Sarah ESPINOSA
18 Acting VP of Facilities & Security .... Ms. Janet CUBAR
28 Chief Diversity Officer .... Dr. Michelle T. SCOTT
37 College Dir Student Financial Aid .... Ms. Melissa GREGORY
07 Dir of Admissions/Enrollment Mgmt .... Vacant
21 Director of Budget .... Ms. Donna L. DIMON
31 Director of Auxiliary Services .... Dr. Kathi CAREY-FLETCHER
26 Director of Communications .... Ms. Elizabeth HOMAN
29 Alumni Coordinator .... Mr. John LIBBY
96 Acting VP of Procurement .... Mr. Patrick JOHNSON
10 Interim VP of Finance/CFO .... Ms. Ruby SHERMAN
10 Interim VP of Finance/CFO .... Mr. Robert PRESTON

Morgan State University (E)

1700 East Cold Spring Lane, Baltimore MD 21251-0001
County: Independent City FICE Identification: 002083
Unit ID: 163453
Telephone: (443) 885-3333 Carnegie Class: DRU
FAX Number: (443) 885-3698 Calendar System: Semester
URL: www.morgan.edu
Established: 1867 Annual Undergrad Tuition & Fees (In-State): $7,042
Enrollment: 8,000 Coed
Affiliation or Control: State IRS Status: 501(c)3
Highest Offering: Doctorate
Program: Liberal Arts And General; Teacher Preparatory; Professional
Accreditation: M, BUS, BUSA, DIETD, ENG, LSAR, MT, MUS, PH, PLNG, SW, TED

01 President .... Dr. David WILSON
05 Provost/Vice Pres Academic Affairs .... Dr. T. Joan ROBINSON
88 VP Academic Outreach and Engagement .... Dr. Maurice TAYLOR
10 Vice President Finance & Management ... Mr. Raymond VOLLMER
45 Vice President Planning .... Dr. Joseph POPOVICH
32 Vice Pres Student Affairs .... Dr. Kevin BANKS
30 Vice Pres Institutional Advancement .... Ms. Cheryl Y. HITCHCOCK
20 Assoc VP for Academic Affairs .... Dr. Kara TURNER
21 Asst Vice President for Finance .... Mr. Bickram JANAK
35 Associate VP Student Affairs .... Ms. Tanya RUSH
100 Chief of Staff .... Dr. Willie LARKIN
49 Acting Dean College of Liberal Arts .... Dr. Mbare NGOM
50 Dean School Busines & Management .... Dr. Otis THOMAS
53 Dean School of Education .... Dr. Patricia WELCH
54 Dean School of Engineering .... Dr. Eugene DELOATCH
58 Acting Dean of the Graduate School .... Dr. Mark GARRISON
48 Dean School of Architecture .... Dr. Mary Anne AKERS
70 Dean School of Social Work .... Dr. Anna MCPHATTER
69 Act Dean School of Community Health .... Dr. Kim SYDNOR
37 Director of Financial Aid .... Ms. Tanya WILKERSON
38 Director of Counseling Services .... Ms. Nina DOBSON-HOPKINS
08 Director of Library .... Dr. Richard BRADBERRY
06 Director of Records/Registration .... Mr. Paul THOMPSON
07 Director of Admissions .... Ms. Shonda GRAY
36 Director of Placement .... Mr. William CARSON

15 Director Human Resources ..... Mrs. Armada GRANT
29 Director Alumni Association ..... Mrs. Joyce BROWN
14 Director Computer Center ..... Mr. Gilbert MORGAN
86 Director State Relations ..... Mr. Claude E. HITCHCOCK
09 Director of Institutional Research ..... Ms. Cheryl ROLLINS
18 Director Physical Plant ..... Mr. Kenneth ELLIS
26 Director Public Relations ..... Mr. Clinton R. COLEMAN
84 Director Enrollment Management ..... Mr. Joseph C. BOZEMAN
96 Director of Purchasing ..... Mr. Churchill B. WORTHERLY
28 Director of Diversity ..... Vacant

Mount St. Mary's University (A)

16300 Old Emmitsburg Road,
Emmitsburg MD 21727-7799
County: Frederick FICE Identification: 002086
Unit ID: 163462
Telephone: (301) 447-6122 Carnegie Class: Master's M
FAX Number: (301) 447-5634 Calendar System: Semester
URL: www.msmary.edu
Established: 1808 Annual Undergrad Tuition & Fees: $32,954
Enrollment: 2,305 Coed
Affiliation or Control: Roman Catholic IRS Status: 501(c)3
Highest Offering: Master's
Program: Liberal Arts And General; Teacher Preparatory; Professional; Religious Emphasis
Accreditation: M, IACBE, TED, THEOL

01 President ..... Dr. Thomas H. POWELL
03 Vice President/Rector ..... Msgr. Steven ROHLFS
03 Executive Vice President ..... Mr. Dan SOLLER
88 Vice President University Affairs ..... Ms. Pauline ENGLESTATTER
05 Provost ..... Dr. David B. REHM
10 Vice Pres for Business & Finance ..... Vacant
30 Vice President for Advancement ..... Mr. Robert J. BRENNAN
84 Vice Pres Enrollment Management ..... Mr. Michael POST
20 Assoc Provost ..... Dr. Leona SEVICK
50 Dean Richard J Bolte Sr Sch of Bus ..... Dr. Karl W. EINOLF
53 Dean Sch Education & Human Services ..... Dr. Barbara MARTIN PALMER
81 Dean School Natural Science & Math ..... Dr. David BUSHMAN
79 Dean College of Liberal Arts ..... Dr. Joshua HOCHSCHILD
41 Director of Athletics ..... Ms. Lynne P. ROBINSON
42 Chaplain ..... Fr. Brian NOLAN
32 Dean of Students ..... Mr. Michael TABERSKI
51 Director Professional/Cont Studies ..... Mr. Joe LEBHERZ
08 Dean of the Library ..... Mr. Charles KUHN
09 Director Institutional Research ..... Ms. Linda K. JUNKER
06 Registrar ..... Ms. Margot RHOADES
50 Director of Grad/Adult Business Pgm ..... Ms. Deborah POWELL
88 Director Conferences/Special Pgms ..... Ms. Marianne DEMPSEY
23 Director of Health Services ..... Dr. Bonnie PORTIER
24 Director of the Media Center ..... Mr. John B. BREWER, JR.
37 Director of Financial Aid ..... Mr. David C. REEDER
36 Director Career Center ..... Ms. Claire TAURIELLO
13 Chief Information Officer ..... Mr. Bobby L. FLACK
26 Director of Communications ..... Mr. Duffy ROSS
44 Director of Annual Giving ..... Ms. Marie CACACE
16 Director of Human Resources ..... Ms. Barbara R. MILLER
19 Director of Public Safety ..... Mr. R. Barry TITLER
29 Director of Alumni Relations ..... Ms. Maureen C. PLANT
18 Director of Physical Plant ..... Mr. Bruce NORMAN
88 Director Community Services ..... Mr. Jeff ABEL
28 Director Ctr for Student Diversity ..... Ms. Chianti BLACKMON
35 Dir Campus Activ/Student Ldrshp ..... Mr. Kenneth MCVEARRY
92 Director of the Honors Program ..... Dr. Caroline EICK
40 Manager of College Store ..... Mr. Joseph KNORR
96 Purchasing Agent ..... Ms. Maria L. TOPPER

National Labor College (B)

10000 New Hampshire Avenue,
Silver Spring MD 20903-1706
County: Montgomery FICE Identification: 034555
Unit ID: 434034
Telephone: (301) 431-6400 Carnegie Class: Spec/Bus
FAX Number: (301) 434-5411 Calendar System: Semester
URL: www.nlc.edu
Established: 1997 Annual Undergrad Tuition & Fees: $4,830
Enrollment: 686 Coed
Affiliation or Control: Independent Non-Profit IRS Status: 501(c)3
Highest Offering: Baccalaureate
Program: Liberal Arts And General
Accreditation: M

01 President & CEO ..... Dr. Paula PEINOVICH
04 Executive Asst to the President ..... Laura BARRANTES
05 Interim Provost ..... Dr. Paula PEINOVICH
49 Dean Labor Studies ..... Dr. Daniel KATZ
107 Interim Dean Professional Studies ..... Dr. Daniel KATZ
10 VP for Finance & CFO ..... Bruce PANKEY
86 VP Govt Rels/Legal Cous/HR Dir ..... James GENTILE
30 Advancement Officer ..... Beth SHANNON
26 VP for Marketing & Communications ..... Lara MANZIONE
09 Institutional Research Director ..... Dr. Ann STEHNEY
06 Interim Registrar ..... Jeff BRIA
07 Admissions Director ..... Carol RODGERS
37 Financial Aid Director ..... Tracie SUMNER
10 Interim Controller ..... Patricia SOCKWELL

Ner Israel Rabbinical College (C)

400 Mount Wilson Lane, Baltimore MD 21208-1198
County: Baltimore FICE Identification: 002087
Unit ID: 163532
Telephone: (410) 484-7200 Carnegie Class: Spec/Faith
FAX Number: (410) 484-3060 Calendar System: Semester
Established: 1933 Annual Undergrad Tuition & Fees: $9,700
Enrollment: 604 Male
Affiliation or Control: Independent Non-Profit IRS Status: 501(c)3
Highest Offering: Doctorate
Program: Teacher Preparatory; Professional; Religious Emphasis
Accreditation: RABN

01 President ..... Rabbi Sheftel M. NEUBERGER
05 Chief Academic Officer ..... Rabbi Aharon FELDMAN
03 Executive Director ..... Mr. Jerome H. KADDEN
04 Assistant to the President ..... Rabbi Boruch NEUBERGER
07 Director of Admissions ..... Rabbi Beryl WEISBORD
13 Director of Administrative Services ..... Mr. Larry RIBAKOW
06 Registrar ..... Rabbi Chaim D. LAPIDUS
37 Director Student Financial Aid ..... Rabbi Shmuel SCHACHTER
85 Foreign Student Advisor ..... Rabbi Eliyahu HAKKAKIAN
30 Director of Development ..... Rabbi Louis HOFFMAN
45 Director of Planning ..... Rabbi Leonard OBERSTEIN
26 Director Community Relations ..... Rabbi Jonathan SEIDEMANN
18 Chief Physical Plant ..... Mr. David FRIEDMAN
08 Head Librarian ..... Rabbi Avrohom SHNIDMAN
39 Director of Student Housing ..... Rabbi Emanuel GOLDFEIZ
29 Associate Director Alumni Relations ..... Rabbi Eli GREENGART

Notre Dame of Maryland University (D)

4701 N Charles Street, Baltimore MD 21210-2404
County: Independent City FICE Identification: 002065
Unit ID: 163578
Telephone: (410) 435-0100 Carnegie Class: Master's L
FAX Number: (410) 532-5791 Calendar System: Semester
URL: www.ndm.edu
Established: 1873 Annual Undergrad Tuition & Fees: $30,850
Enrollment: 2,929 Female
Affiliation or Control: Roman Catholic IRS Status: 501(c)3
Highest Offering: Doctorate
Program: Liberal Arts And General; Teacher Preparatory; Professional
Accreditation: M, NUR, @PHAR, TED

01 President ..... Dr. James CONNEELY
05 Vice President Academic Affairs ..... Sr. Christine DE VINNE
32 Vice President Student Development ..... Dr. Patricia SWATFAGER-HANEY
30 Vice Pres Institutional Advancement ..... Ms. Patricia A. BOSSE
84 Vice Pres Enrollment Management ..... Ms. Heidi L. FLETCHER
10 Vice Pres Finance & Administration ..... Mr. Thomas MAHER
20 Associate VP Academic Affairs ..... Dr. Anne HENDERSON
35 Dean of Students ..... Ms. Pauline WILLIAMSON
04 Special Assistant to the President ..... Ms. Candace CARACO
06 Assoc VP Enrollment/Registrar ..... Ms. Sharon BOGDAN
37 Director of Financial Aid ..... Ms. Zhanna GOLTSER
36 Dir Academic & Career Enrichment ..... Ms. Diane MCCANN
13 Director Information Technology ..... Mr. Warren SZELISTOWSKI
29 Director of Alumnae Relations ..... Ms. Emilia POITER
08 Librarian ..... Mr. John W. MCGINTY
85 Director International Program ..... Vacant
07 Director of Admissions ..... Mr. Lucas J. SIFUENTES
09 Sr Dir Inst Research/Effectiveness ..... Mr. Shuang LIU
15 Director of Human Resources ..... Ms. Geri LARSEN
18 Director of Facility Management ..... Mr. Mario CANDIELLO
21 Controller ..... Ms. Barbara MORRIS
38 Director Counseling Center ..... Ms. Amy PROVAN
19 Director of Public Safety ..... Mr. Jeff MUNCHEL
40 Bookstore Manager ..... Ms. Ashley ROENIGK
41 Athletic Director ..... Ms. Erin FOLEY
42 Director Campus Ministry ..... Ms. Melissa LEES
67 Dean School of Pharmacy ..... Dr. Anne LIN
07 Director Pharmacy Admissions ..... Mr. Larry SHATTUCK

Peabody Institute of Johns Hopkins University (E)

1 E Mount Vernon Place, Baltimore MD 21202-2397
County: Independent City FICE Identification: 002088
Unit ID: 163611
Telephone: (410) 234-4500 Carnegie Class: Not Classified
FAX Number: (410) 659-8129 Calendar System: Semester
URL: www.peabody.jhu.edu
Established: 1857 Annual Undergrad Tuition & Fees: $38,450
Enrollment: 769 Coed
Affiliation or Control: Independent Non-Profit IRS Status: 501(c)3
Highest Offering: Doctorate
Program: Teacher Preparatory; Professional; Music Emphasis
Accreditation: &M, MUS

01 Director of the Institute ..... Mr. Jeffrey SHARKEY
05 Dean of Conservatory/Deputy Dir ..... Dr. Mellasenah MORRIS
20 Assoc Dean Academic Affairs ..... Dr. Paul MATHEWS
32 Assoc Dean Student Affairs ..... Ms. Katsura KURITA
11 Assoc Dean for Administration ..... Ms. Maureen HARRIGAN
26 Assoc Dean External Relations ..... Ms. Andrea TRISCIUZZI
27 Director of Communications ..... Mr. Richard SELDEN
06 Registrar ..... Mr. James DOBSON
07 Director of Admissions ..... Mr. David H. LANE
08 Head Librarian ..... Ms. Jennifer OTTERVIK
37 Director of Financial Aid ..... Ms. Rebecca POLGAR
88 Director of Constituent Engagement ..... Ms. Debbie KENNISON
18 Director Facilities Management ..... Mr. Joseph BRANT
15 Manager Human Resources & Payroll ..... Ms. Laura BROOKS
36 Dir Mus Entrepreneurship/Career Ctr ..... Mr. Gerald KLICKSTEIN

† Regional accreditation is carried under the parent institution, Johns Hopkins University, MD.

Prince George's Community College (F)

301 Largo Road, Largo MD 20774-2199
County: Prince Georges FICE Identification: 002089
Unit ID: 163657
Telephone: (301) 336-6000 Carnegie Class: Assoc/Pub-S-SC
FAX Number: (301) 808-0960 Calendar System: Semester
URL: www.pgcc.edu
Established: 1958 Annual Undergrad Tuition & Fees (In-District): $3,290
Enrollment: 14,647 Coed
Affiliation or Control: Local IRS Status: 501(c)3
Highest Offering: Associate Degree
Program: Occupational; 2-Year Principally Bachelor's Creditable
Accreditation: M, ADNUR, NMT, RAD

01 President ..... Dr. Charlene M. DUKES
05 Vice Pres Academic Affairs ..... Dr. Sandra F. DUNNINGTON
32 Vice Pres Student Services ..... Dr. Tyjaun A. LEE
10 Vice Pres Administrative Services ..... Mr. Tom E. KNAPP
103 Interim VP Workforce Devel/Cont Ed . Mr. Joseph L. MARTINELLI
72 Vice Pres Technology Services ..... Dr. Joseph G. ROSSMEIER
20 Sr Acad Admin to VP for Acad Affs ..... Ms. Catherine LAPALOMBARA
38 Dean Student Development Svcs ... Dr. Scheherazade W. FORMAN
84 Dean of Enrollment Services ..... Dr. Tracy A. HARRIS
09 Dean Planning/Institutional Rsrch ..... Dr. Andrea A. LEX
51 Dean Wrkfrce Dev/Cont Educ Pgms ... Mr. Joseph I. MARTINELLI
15 Dean Human Resources ..... Ms. Lark T. DOBSON
88 Dean of Learning Foundations ..... Dr. Beverly S. REED
21 Dean Financial Affairs ..... Ms. Nancy E. BURGESS
100 Chief of Staff ..... Ms. Alonia C. SHARPS
08 Dir Library/Learning Resources ..... Ms. Priscilla C. THOMPSON
06 Director Admissions & Records ..... Ms. Vera L. BAGLEY
07 Director Recruitment ..... Ms. Jennifer M. PRICE
18 Dean Facilities Management ..... Dr. David C. MOSBY
88 Director Physical Facilities ..... Mr. Gilberto HINOJOSA
86 Dir Community & Government Affairs ... Dr. Jacqueline L. BROWN
30 Exec Dir Institutional Advancement ..... Ms. Brenda S. MITCHELL
26 Director Marketing & Creative Svcs ..... Dr. Deidra W. HILL
13 Chief Technology Officer ..... Mr. William L. ANDERSON
96 Procurement Officer ..... Vacant
37 Director Financial Aid ..... Ms. Sharon E. HASSAN
36 Manager Career & Job Services ..... Ms. Stephanie S. PAIR-CUNNINGHAM
79 Dean of Liberal Arts ..... Dr. Carolyn F. HOFFMAN
35 Dean College Life Services ..... Mr. Malverse A. NICHOLSON, JR.
76 Dean of Health Science ..... Ms. Angela D. ANDERSON
81 Dean Science/Tech/Engr/Math ..... Dr. Christine E. BARROW
83 Int Dean Soc Sci/Bus Studies Div ..... Dr. Lorraine P. BASSETTE

St. John's College (G)

PO Box 2800, Annapolis MD 21404-2800
County: Anne Arundel FICE Identification: 002092
Unit ID: 163976
Telephone: (410) 263-2371 Carnegie Class: Bac/A&S
FAX Number: (410) 626-2886 Calendar System: Semester
URL: www.sjca.edu
Established: 1784 Annual Undergrad Tuition & Fees: $45,004
Enrollment: 549 Coed
Affiliation or Control: Independent Non-Profit IRS Status: 501(c)3
Highest Offering: Master's
Program: Liberal Arts And General
Accreditation: M

01 President ..... Mr. Christopher B. NELSON
30 Vice Pres Advancement Annapolis ..... Ms. Barbara GOYETTE
05 Dean ..... Ms. Pamela KRAUS
10 Treasurer ..... Ms. Bronte JONES
06 Registrar ..... Mr. Daniel CROWE
07 Director of Admissions ..... Ms. Sarah MORSE
102 Director Corporate/Foundation Rels ..... Ms. Susan BORDEN
37 Director of Financial Aid ..... Ms. Dana KENNEDY
08 Librarian ..... Ms. Cathy DIXON
15 Director of Personnel ..... Ms. Deborah ANAWALT
18 Supt of Buildings & Grounds ..... Mr. Sid PHIPPS
19 Chief of Security ..... Mr. Timon LINN
23 Director of Student Health ..... Ms. Nancy CALABRESE
27 Director of Communications ..... Ms. Patricia DEMPSEY
32 Director of Student Services ..... Ms. Taylor WATERS
20 Assistant Dean ..... Ms. Susan PAALMAN
36 Director of Career Services ..... Ms. Jaime DUNN
40 Bookstore Manager ..... Mr. Robin DUNN
41 Director of Athletics ..... Mr. Michael MCQUARRIE
58 Director of Graduate Institute ..... Mr. Jeff BLACK
21 Controller ..... Ms. Diane SAWYER
29 Director of Alumni Relations ..... Mr. Leo PICKENS

† See Affiliate: St. John's College at Santa Fe, NM.

St. Mary's College of Maryland (A)

18952 E Fisher Road, Saint Mary's City MD 20686-3001
County: Saint Mary's FICE Identification: 002095
Unit ID: 163912
Telephone: (240) 895-2000 Carnegie Class: Bac/A&S
FAX Number: (240) 895-4462 Calendar System: Semester
URL: www.smcm.edu
Established: 1840 Annual Undergrad Tuition & Fees (In-State): $14,773
Enrollment: 1,992 Coed
Affiliation or Control: State IRS Status: 501(c)3
Highest Offering: Master's
Program: Liberal Arts And General
Accreditation: M

01 President .... Dr. Joseph R. URGO
05 Dean of Faculty/VP for Acad Affairs .... Dr. Beth RUSHING
10 VP Business & Finance .... Dr. Thomas J. BOTZMAN
30 Vice President for Advancement .... Dr. Maureen C. SILVA
44 Asst Vice Pres for Development .... Vacant
26 Assoc VP for Marketing/Public Rels .... Vacant
29 Director Alumni Relations .... Mr. David M. SUSHINSKY
09 Assoc Dir Institutional Research .... Vacant
06 Registrar .... Ms. Susan A. BENNETT
20 Assoc Dean of Faculty .... Dr. Rich PLATT
20 Dean of the Core Curric/1st-yr Exp .... Dr. Elizabeth N. WILLIAMS
07 VP Dean Admissions/Financial Aid .... Ms. Patricia GOLDSMITH
37 Director of Financial Aid .... Ms. Caroline O. BRIGHT
88 Asst VP for Academic Administration .... Mr. Mark W. HEIDRICH
35 Interim Dean of Students .... Dr. Roberto IFILL
38 Director of Counseling Services .... Dr. Mary-Jeanne RALEIGH
41 Director of Athletics/Recreation .... Mr. Scott W. DEVINE
83 Chair Anthropology .... Dr. William C. ROBERTS
57 Chair of Arts & Art History .... Ms. Carrie C. PATTERSON
88 Chair of Biology .... Dr. Holly GORTON
88 Chair of Chemistry .... Dr. Randolph K. LARSEN, III
88 Chair of Economics .... Dr. Michael H. YE
83 Chair Educational Studies .... Dr. Lois T. STOVER
79 Chair of English .... Dr. Ben A. CLICK
83 Acting Chair of History .... Dr. Christine M. ADAMS
79 Chair of Intl Languages/Cultures .... Dr. Laine DOGGETT
81 Chair of Math/Computer Science .... Dr. Susan GOLDSTINE
64 Chair of Music .... Dr. David FROOM
79 Chair Philosophy/Religious Studies .... Dr. Michael S. TABER
77 Acting Chair of Physics .... Dr. Joshua M. GROSSMAN
82 Chair of Political Science .... Dr. Sahar SHAFQAT
83 Chair of Psychology .... Dr. Aileen M. BAILEY
83 Chair of Sociology .... Dr. Curt RANEY
57 Chair of Theatre/Film/Media Stds .... Dr. Joanne R. KLEIN
51 Asst Vice Pres Lifelong Learning .... Vacant
20 Asst Vice Pres Academic Services .... Dr. William L. HOWARD
18 Assoc Vice President of Facilities .... Mr. Charles C. JACKSON
19 Director of Public Safety .... Vacant
40 Director of the Campus Store .... Mr. Richard T. WAGNER
15 Associate Vice President of HR .... Ms. Sally A. MERCER
23 Director of Health Services .... Ms. Linda WALLACE
35 Associate Dean of Students .... Ms. Joanne A. GOLDWATER
13 Asst VP of Information Technology .... Dr. C. Michael GASS
44 Senior Development Officer .... Ms. Karen C. RALEY
08 Director of the Library/Media Svcs .... Dr. Celia E. RABINOWITZ
102 Director of Development & Campaigns .... Ms. Liisa E. FRANZEN
21 Comptroller/Director of Accounting .... Mr. Gabriel A. MBOMEH
43 Assistant Attorney General .... Ms. Sara SLAFF
22 Affirm Act/Equal Opportunity Office .... Mr. Melvin A. MCCLINTOCK
25 Director of Sponsored Research .... Mrs. Sabine DILLINGHAM
28 Fair Practices Officer .... Ms. Sally A. MERCER
84 Director Enrollment Management .... Vacant
96 Procurement Officer .... Mr. Patrick G. HUNT

Saint Mary's Seminary and University (B)

5400 Roland Avenue, Baltimore MD 21210-1994
County: Independent City FICE Identification: 002096
Unit ID: 163842
Telephone: (410) 864-4000 Carnegie Class: Spec/Faith
FAX Number: (410) 864-4278 Calendar System: Semester
URL: www.stmarys.edu
Established: 1791 Annual Undergrad Tuition & Fees: $29,450
Enrollment: 375 Coed
Affiliation or Control: Roman Catholic IRS Status: 501(c)3
Highest Offering: First Professional Degree
Program: Liberal Arts And General; Professional; Religious Emphasis
Accreditation: M, THEOL

01 President/Rector .... Rev. Thomas R. HURST
30 Vice Pres Institutional Advancement .... Mrs. Elizabeth L. VISCONAGE
05 Dean School Theology .... Rev. Timothy A. KULBICKI, OFM CONV
73 Dean Ecumenical Institute Theology .... Dr. Brent LAYTHAM
73 Dean Ecclesiastical Faculty .... Rev. Timothy A. KULBICKI, OFM CONV
10 University Treasurer .... Mr. Richard G. CHILDS
06 University Registrar .... Ms. Paula M. THIGPEN
37 Director Financial Aid .... Mrs. Victoria F. GAUNT
08 Director of Library .... Mr. Thomas RASZEWSKI

The SANS Technology Institute (C)

8120 Woodmont Avenue, Suite 205, Bethesda MD 20814
County: Montgomery Identification: 667006
Telephone: (301) 654-7267 Carnegie Class: Not Classified
FAX Number: (301) 951-0140 Calendar System: Semester
URL: www.sans.edu
Established: N/A Annual Graduate Tuition & Fees: $17,800
Enrollment: N/A Coed
Affiliation or Control: Independent Non-Profit IRS Status: 501(c)3
Highest Offering: Master's; No Undergraduates
Program: Professional
Accreditation: @M

01 President .... Mr. Stephen NORTHCUTT
05 Dean of the Faculty .... Dr. Johannes ULLRICH
07 Dean of Admissions/Student Svcs .... Dr. Debbie SVOBODA

Sojourner-Douglass College (D)

200 North Central Avenue, Baltimore MD 21202
County: Baltimore FICE Identification: 021279
Unit ID: 163921
Telephone: (410) 276-0306 Carnegie Class: Bac/Diverse
FAX Number: (410) 675-1810 Calendar System: Trimester
URL: www.sdc.edu
Established: 1980 Annual Undergrad Tuition & Fees: $12,540
Enrollment: 1,315 Coed
Affiliation or Control: Independent Non-Profit IRS Status: 501(c)3
Highest Offering: Master's
Program: Liberal Arts And General
Accreditation: M, @SW

01 President .... Dr. Charles W. SIMMONS
03 Executive Vice President .... Dr. Howard L. SIMMONS
05 Provost/Vice Pres Academic Affairs .... Dr. Marian STANTON
10 Vice Pres for Admin & Fiscal Affs .... Mr. Donald L. HUTCHINS
44 Ex Asst to Pres/Spon Pgms/Appld Res .... Dr. Alice THOMAS
04 Special Assistant to the President .... Ms. Carolyn J. ECHOLS
15 Department Chair Human Services .... Ms. Kelly TRIBBLE-SPENCER
36 Dept Chair Human Growth/Development .... Mr. Donald WILLIAMS
20 Dean of Academic Affairs .... Ms. Shirley EVANS
12 Dean of Lanham Campus .... Dr. Bernard M. GROSS
12 Dean of Annapolis Campus .... Dr. Charlestine FAIRLEY
12 Dean of Salisbury Campus .... Ms. Constance STEWART
12 Dean of Cambridge Campus .... Dr. Vivian FULLER
12 Dean of Nassau Bahamas Campus .... Hon. Theresa MOXEY-INGRAHAM
12 Dean of Owings Mills Campus .... Ms. Doris W. CARROLL
06 Registrar .... Ms. Mary ROBINSON
51 Director of Continuing Education .... Dr. Ann BOSTIC
37 Director of Financial Aid .... Ms. Rebecca CHALK
04 Spec Asst to Pres Institution .... Mr. Benjamin MASON
31 Director Community Outreach .... Mr. Jamal MUBDI-BEY
18 Director Facilities/Physical Plant .... Mr. Gilbert RAWLINGS
08 Director of Library .... Mr. Omowali ALI
19 Director Security/Safety .... Col. Mahdi EL-HAQQ
21 Bursar .... Mr. Bert LEE
29 Director Alumni Relations .... Ms. Marshear MARSH
58 Director of Graduate Studies .... Dr. Linda FASSETT
09 Dir of Institutional Research/Plng .... Mr. Kareem AZIZ
35 Chief Admin Stdt Dev/Stdt Sppt Svcs .... Dr. John BARBER
38 Director Student Counseling .... Ms. Chantaye HAUGHTON
07 Director of Admissions .... Ms. Diana SAMUELS
13 Director Information Technology .... Mr. Tacuma SIMMONS

Stevenson University (E)

1525 Greenspring Valley Road,
Stevenson MD 21153-0641
County: Baltimore FICE Identification: 002107
Unit ID: 164173
Telephone: (410) 486-7000 Carnegie Class: Master's S
FAX Number: (410) 486-3552 Calendar System: Semester
URL: www.stevenson.edu
Established: 1947 Annual Undergrad Tuition & Fees: $25,311
Enrollment: 4,317 Coed
Affiliation or Control: Independent Non-Profit IRS Status: 501(c)3
Highest Offering: Master's
Program: Liberal Arts And General; Teacher Preparatory
Accreditation: M, MT, NUR, NURSE, TED

01 President .... Dr. Kevin J. MANNING
04 Assistant to President .... Ms. Ruth HUBBARD
03 Exec Vice President/Academic Dean .... Dr. Paul D. LACK
10 Exec Vice Pres/Chief Financial Ofcr .... Mr. Timothy M. CAMPBELL
05 Chief Academic Officer .... Dr. Paul D. LACK
30 Vice Pres University Advancement .... Mr. Steve CLOSE
84 Vice Pres Enrollment Management .... Mr. Mark J. HERGAN
32 Vice Pres Student Affairs .... Ms. Claire E. MOORE
27 VP Marketing & Public Relations .... Ms. Glenda G. LE GENDRE
15 Vice Pres for Human Resources .... Ms. Brenda BALZER
100 Chief of Staff .... Ms. Sue KENNEY
20 Asst Vice Pres for Academic Affairs .... Dr. Jo-Ellen ASBURY
88 Asst Vice Pres for Exp Learning/Ca .... Ms. Christine A. NOYA
58 Dean Graduate/Professional Studies .... Ms. Joyce K. BECKER
50 Dean School of Business .... Dr. Norman A. ENDLICH
81 Dean School of Science .... Dr. Susan GORMAN
83 Dean Sch of Humanities/Social Sci .... Dr. James SALVUCCI
88 Dean School of Design .... Mr. Keith KUTCH
53 Interim Dean School of Education .... Dr. Deborah KRAFT
18 Asst VP Fac & Campus Svcs .... Mr. Leland BEITEL
21 Asst VP Finan Affs/Controller .... Ms. Melanie M. EDMONDSON
07 Asst VP Enrollment Management .... Vacant
37 Director of Financial Aid .... Ms. Barbara MILLER
35 Associate VP and Dean of Students .... Dr. Jeffrey M. KELLY
14 Chief Information Officer/Asst VP .... Mr. Tom ALLEN
88 Assistant VP for Acad Supp Svcs .... Dr. Virginia N. IANNONE
09 Assoc Dean Inst Rsrch & Assess .... Ms. Nicole C. MARANO
23 Assoc Dean/Dir of Wellness Center .... Ms. Linda REYMANN
88 Associate Dean GPS UG Programs .... Ms. Patricia ELLIS
66 Associate Dean GPS Nursing .... Dr. Judith FEUSTLE
66 Associate Dean for Nursing Educ .... Dr. Denise SEIGART
106 Associate Dean Distance Education .... Dr. Barbara ZIRKIN
08 Director of Library Services .... Ms. Maureen A. BECK
36 Exec Director of Career HQ .... Ms. Anne E. SCHOLL-FIEDLER
06 Registrar .... Ms. Tracy L. BOLT
19 Director of Safety & Security .... Mr. Timothy OSTENDARP
41 Athletic Director .... Mr. Brett C. ADAMS
40 Director Auxiliary Services .... Mr. Robert REED
28 Director of Multicultural Affairs .... Ms. Cheryl HINTON
29 Director Alumni Rels .... Mr. James MYERS
88 Director Acad Link and PASS .... Ms. Christine FLAX
88 Director of Developmental Studies .... Ms. Esther ROSENSTOCK

Tai Sophia Institute (F)

7750 Montpelier Road, Laurel MD 20723-6010
County: Howard FICE Identification: 025784
Unit ID: 164085
Telephone: (410) 888-9048 Carnegie Class: Master's S
FAX Number: (410) 888-9004 Calendar System: Trimester
URL: www.tai.edu
Established: 1981 Annual Graduate Tuition & Fees: $26,500
Enrollment: 469 Coed
Affiliation or Control: Independent Non-Profit IRS Status: 501(c)3
Highest Offering: Master's; No Undergraduates
Program: Professional
Accreditation: M, ACUP

01 President & CEO .... Mr. Frank VITALE
05 Provost/Vice Pres Academic Affairs .... Dr. Judith BROIDA
11 VP Administration/General Counsel .... Ms. Louise GUSSIN
30 Vice Pres Institutional Advancement .... Mr. Marc LEVIN
26 VP Marketing/Enrollment Mgmt .... Ms. Gail DOERR
10 Vice Pres Business/Financial Svcs .... Mr. Marc LEVIN
04 Assistant to the President .... Ms. Robin REEL
06 Assoc VP Student Svcs/Registrar .... Mr. Reginald GARCON
07 Director of Graduate Admissions .... Ms. Gabrielle JULIEN-MOLINEAUX
37 Director Student Financial Aid .... Ms. Christa DEAN
08 Director of Library Services and IT .... Ms. Jenifer KIRIN
29 Coordinator Alumni Relations .... Ms. Patricia DELORENZO
32 Academic & Student Affairs Advisor .... Vacant

TESST College of Technology (G)

1520 S Caton Avenue, Baltimore MD 21227-1063
County: Baltimore City FICE Identification: 007491
Unit ID: 163736
Telephone: (410) 644-6400 Carnegie Class: Assoc/PrivFP
FAX Number: (410) 644-6481 Calendar System: Quarter
URL: www.tesst.com
Established: 1956 Annual Undergrad Tuition & Fees: N/A
Enrollment: 732 Coed
Affiliation or Control: Proprietary IRS Status: Proprietary
Highest Offering: Associate Degree
Program: Occupational
Accreditation: ACCSC

01 President .... Ms. Amy BEAUREGARD
11 Director of Operations .... Vacant

TESST College of Technology (H)

4600 Powder Mill Road, Suite 500,
Beltsville MD 20705-2649
County: Prince Georges FICE Identification: 020836
Unit ID: 164058
Telephone: (301) 937-8448 Carnegie Class: Assoc/PrivFP
FAX Number: (301) 937-5327 Calendar System: Quarter
URL: www.tesst.com
Established: 1956 Annual Undergrad Tuition & Fees: N/A
Enrollment: 447 Coed
Affiliation or Control: Proprietary IRS Status: Proprietary
Highest Offering: Associate Degree
Program: Occupational
Accreditation: ACCSC

01 President .... Ms. Shartoyea SCOTT DIXON
06 Registrar .... Mrs. LaDonna DAVIS
07 Director of Admissions .... Ms. Cathy MCKINNEY
36 Director of Career Services .... Ms. Marsha D. HUNT
37 Director of Financial Aid .... Ms. Carmenita Renee CLARK
35 Director of Student Service .... Vacant
10 Finance Manager .... Vacant
05 Director of Education .... Vacant

TESST College of Technology (I)

803 Glen Eagles Court, Towson MD 21286-2201
County: Baltimore FICE Identification: 010410
Unit ID: 161776
Telephone: (410) 296-5350 Carnegie Class: Assoc/PrivFP
FAX Number: (410) 296-5356 Calendar System: Quarter
URL: www.tesst.com
Established: 1956 Annual Undergrad Tuition & Fees: $14,722
Enrollment: 361 Coed
Affiliation or Control: Proprietary IRS Status: Proprietary
Highest Offering: Associate Degree

Program: Occupational
Accreditation: ACCSC

01 President ... Mr. Chris CATHCART
07 Director of Admissions ... Mr. Nicholas BUIZZARD

*The University System of Maryland Office (A)

3300 Metzerott Road, Adelphi MD 20783-1690
County: Prince Georges FICE Identification: 007959
Unit ID: 164146
Telephone: (301) 445-1901 Carnegie Class: N/A
FAX Number: (301) 445-1931
URL: www.usmd.edu

01 Chancellor ... Dr. William KIRWAN
12 Pres Univ of Md Ctr Environment Sci ... Dr. Donald F. BOESCH
05 Sr VC Academic Affairs ... Dr. Joann BOUGHMAN
11 COO/Vice Chanc Admin & Finance ... Mr. Joseph F. VIVONA
30 Vice Chancellor Advancement ... Mr. Leonard R. RALEY
100 USM Chief of Staff ... Ms. Janice B. DOYLE
10 Assoc VC Financial Affairs ... Vacant
86 VC Governmental Relations ... Mr. Patrick J. HOGAN
20 Assoc Vice Chanc Academic Affairs ... Ms. Teri HOLLANDER
26 VC for Communications ... Ms. Anne MOULTRIE
13 Assoc VC Information Technology ... Mr. Donald Z. SPICER
21 Asst VC Administration & Finance ... Ms. JoAnn GOEDERT
21 Director Internal Audit ... Mr. David MOSCA
21 Director Budget Analysis ... Ms. Monica WEST

*University of Maryland College Park (B)

College Park MD 20742-0001
County: Prince Georges FICE Identification: 002103
Unit ID: 163286
Telephone: (301) 405-1000 Carnegie Class: RU/VH
FAX Number: (301) 314-9560 Calendar System: Semester
URL: www.umd.edu
Established: 1856 Annual Undergrad Tuition & Fees (In-State): $8,909
Enrollment: 37,200 Coed
Affiliation or Control: State IRS Status: 501(c)3
Highest Offering: Doctorate
Program: Liberal Arts And General; Teacher Preparatory; Professional
Accreditation: M, AUD, BUS, CACREP, CEA, CLPSY, COPSY, DIETD, DIETI, ENG, IACBE, IPSY, JOUR, LIB, LSAR, MFCD, MUS, PH, PLNG, SCPSY, SP, SPAA, TED

02 President ... Dr. Wallace D. LOH
05 Sr Vice Pres and Provost ... Dr. Ann G. WYLIE
11 Vice President Administrative Affs ... Mr. Robert M. SPECTER
43 General Counsel ... Mr. J. Terrance ROACH
26 Vice President University Relations ... Mr. Peter B. WEILER
32 Vice President Student Affairs ... Dr. Linda M. CLEMENT
13 Vice President & CIO ... Mr. Brian D. VOSS
46 Vice President Research ... Dr. Patrick G. O'SHEA
47 Dean Col Agric/Natural Resources ... Dr. Cheng-I WEI
48 Dean Sch Architecture/Plng/Preserv ... Mr. David CRONRATH
79 Dean College Arts & Humanities ... Dr. Bonnie T. DILL
83 Dean Col Behavioral/Social Sciences ... Dr. John R. TOWNSHEND
50 Dean Smith School of Business ... Dr. G. Anand ANANDALINGAM
81 Dean Computer/Math/Natural Science ... Dr. Jayanth R. BANAVAR
53 Dean of College of Education ... Dr. Donna WISEMAN
54 Dean Clark School of Engineering ... Dr. Darryll J. PINES
69 Dean School of Public Health ... Dr. Jane E. CLARK
60 Dean Merrill College of Journalism ... Ms. Lucy DALGLISH
62 Dean College Info Studies ... Dr. Jennifer J. PREECE
80 Dean School Public Policy ... Dr. Donald F. KETTL
20 Dean Undergraduate Studies ... Dr. Donna B. HAMILTON
58 Dean Graduate School ... Dr. Charles A. CARAMELLO
08 Dean of Libraries ... Dr. Patricia A. STEELE
88 Assoc Provost International Affairs ... Dr. Ross LEWIN
20 Professor/Assoc Prov Faculty Affs ... Dr. Juan URIAGEREKA
09 Assoc VP/Inst Research & Planning ... Dr. Mona LEVINE
18 Associate VP Facilities/Management ... Mr. Carlo COLELLA
28 Assoc VP & Chief Diversity Officer ... Dr. Kumea SHORTER-GOODEN
39 Asst VP/Director Resident Life ... Dr. Deborah F. GRANDNER
25 Assoc VP/Dir Research Adv & Admin ... Ms. Denise CLARK
35 Asst Vice Pres Student Affairs ... Mr. John ZACKER
07 Asst VP Admissions ... Ms. Barbara A. GILL
06 Asst VP Records/Registration ... Mr. Chuck A. WILSON
29 Asst VP Alumni Relation/Devel ... Vacant
37 Asst VP Student Financial Aid ... Ms. Sarah J. BAUDER
27 Asst VP Marketing & Communications ... Mr. Brian ULLMANN
36 Executive Director Career Center ... Mr. Rick HEARIN
64 Director School of Music ... Dr. Robert L. GIBSON
85 Int Dir International Services ... Ms. Barbara VARSA
41 Director Athletics ... Mr. Kevin ANDERSON
40 Director University Book Center ... Mr. Mike GORE
23 Director Health Center ... Dr. Sacared A. BODISON
38 Director Counseling Center ... Dr. Sharon E. KIRKLAND-GORDON
19 Chief Campus Police ... Mr. David B. MITCHELL
15 Director University Human Resources ... Mr. Dale O. ANDERSON
92 Director University Honors Program ... Dr. William DORLAND
96 Director Procurement & Supply ... Mr. James S. STIRLING
31 Asst Director Community Service ... Mr. Craig SLACK

*University of Maryland Baltimore (C)

620 W. Lexington Street, Baltimore MD 21201-1508
County: Independent City FICE Identification: 002104
Unit ID: 163259
Telephone: (410) 706-7004 Carnegie Class: Spec/Med
FAX Number: (410) 706-0500 Calendar System: 4/1/4
URL: www.umaryland.edu
Established: 1807 Annual Undergrad Tuition & Fees (In-State): $9,173
Enrollment: 6,395 Coed
Affiliation or Control: State IRS Status: 501(c)3
Highest Offering: Doctorate
Program: Professional
Accreditation: M, ANEST, DENT, DH, DIETI, IPSY, LAW, MED, MT, NURSE, PA, PH, PHAR, PTA, RADDOS, SW

02 President ... Dr. Jay A. PERMAN
05 Sr VP/Chief Acad & Research Officer ... Dr. Bruce E. JARRELL
11 Sr VP/Chief Operating Officer ... Mr. Peter N. GILBERT
17 Vice President Medical Affairs/Dean ... Dr. E. Albert REECE
10 Chief Admin & Finance Officer/VP ... Ms. Kathleen M. BYINGTON
13 Vice President and CIO ... Dr. Peter J. MURRAY
46 Chief Enterprise & Econ Dev Ofcr/VP ... Mr. James L. HUGHES
26 Int Chief Communications Ofcr /VP ... Ms. Jennifer B. LITCHMAN
30 Int Chief Development Officer/VP ... Mr. Thomas F. HOFSTETTER
43 Chief University Counsel ... Ms. Susan GILLETTE
20 Assoc VP AA/Ch Accountability Ofc ... Dr. Roger J. WARD
18 Assoc VP Facilities & Operations ... Mr. Robert M. ROWAN
16 Assoc VP Human Resource Services ... Ms. Marjorie L. POWELL
86 Assoc VP Govt & Community Affairs ... Ms. Barbara A. KLEIN
45 Asst VP Resource Management ... Dr. Judith S. BLACKBURN
21 Asst Vice Pres Budget & Finance ... Vacant
25 AVP Research & Global Health Init ... Ms. Marjorie FORSTER
14 Asst VP Information Technology ... Mr. Christopher G. PHILLIPS
24 Asst VP Technology Svcs & Support ... Mr. Paul S. PETROSKI
22 Asst Vice President for Compliance ... Mr. Joseph J. GIFFELS
09 Asst VP Institutional Research ... Mr. Gregory C. SPENGLER
37 Asst VP Student Financial Assist ... Ms. Patricia A. SCOTT
27 Asst VP Communications & Ext Aff ... Ms. Laura A. KOZAK
32 AVP Student Affairs & Wellness ... Mr. Flavius R. LILLY
19 Chief of Police/AVP Public Safety ... Mr. Antonio WILLIAMS
08 Exec Dir Health Sci/Human Svc Libr ... Ms. Mary J. TOOEY
06 Director Records & Registration ... Mr. Thomas C. DAY
41 Dir Univ Recreation & Fitness ... Mr. William P. CROCKETT
88 Director Auxiliary Services ... Ms. Marion A. LIPINSKI
88 Director Benefits & Compensation ... Ms. Patricia ILOWITE
31 Coordinator Community Affairs ... Mr. Brian C. STURDIVANT
15 Exec Dir Human Resource Services ... Mr. Joseph T. SMITH
38 Director Counseling ... Ms. Emilia K. PETRILLO
35 Director Student Services ... Ms. Cynthia E. RICE
88 Director of Financial Services ... Ms. Susan E. MCKECHNIE
96 Director of Procurement Services ... Mr. Joseph EVANS
52 Dean Dental School ... Dr. Christian S. STOHLER
58 Dean Graduate School ... Dr. Bruce E. JARRELL
61 Dean School of Law ... Ms. Phoebe A. HADDON
63 Dean School of Medicine ... Dr. E. Albert REECE
66 Dean School of Nursing ... Dr. Janet D. ALLAN
67 Dean School of Pharmacy ... Dr. Natalie D. EDDINGTON
70 Dean School of Social Work ... Dr. Richard P. BARTH
84 Asst Dean Grad Admin/Enrollment Mgt ... Mr. Keith BROOKS

*University of Maryland Baltimore County (D)

1000 Hilltop Circle, Baltimore MD 21250-0001
County: Baltimore FICE Identification: 002105
Unit ID: 163268
Telephone: (410) 455-1000 Carnegie Class: RU/H
FAX Number: (410) 455-1210 Calendar System: 4/1/4
URL: www.umbc.edu
Established: 1966 Annual Undergrad Tuition & Fees (In-State): $9,467
Enrollment: 13,199 Coed
Affiliation or Control: State IRS Status: 501(c)3
Highest Offering: Doctorate
Program: Liberal Arts And General; Teacher Preparatory
Accreditation: M, CLPSY, CS, DMS, EMT, ENG, SPAA, SW, TED

02 President ... Dr. Freeman A. HRABOWSKI
05 Int Provost/Sr Vice Pres Acad Affs ... Dr. Philip ROUS
10 Vice Pres Finance/Administration ... Ms. Lynne SCHAEFER
32 Vice President Student Affairs ... Dr. Nancy YOUNG
30 Vice Pres Institutional Advancement ... Mr. Gregory SIMMONS
27 Vice Pres Information Technology ... Mr. Jack J. SUESS
46 Vice President of Research ... Dr. Geoffrey P. SUMMERS
49 Dean Col of Arts/Humanities/Soc Sci ... Dr. John JEFFRIES
81 Int Dean Col Natural/Math Sciences ... Dr. William LACOURSE
54 Dean College of Engr/Info Tech ... Dr. Warren R. DEVRIES
84 Asst Dean Graduate Enrollment Mgmt ... Ms. K. Jill BARR
20 Vice Provost/Dean Undergrad Educ ... Dr. Diane M. LEE
51 VP Cont/Prf Std/Ex Dir Shriver Ctr ... Dr. John S. MARTELLO
20 Vice Provost Academic Affairs ... Dr. Antonio R. MOREIRA
58 Dean/Vice Provost for Graduate Educ ... Dr. Janet RUTLEDGE
15 Vice Provost Faculty Affairs ... Dr. Patrice MCDERMOTT
84 Assistant Provost Enrollment Mgmt ... Dr. Yvette MOZIE-ROSS
21 Assoc VP Financial Services ... Mr. Benjamin LOWENTHAL
26 Assistant to Pres/Assoc VP Mktg/PR ... Ms. Lisa G. AKCHIN
11 Assoc VP Administrative Services ... Ms. Terry COOK
15 Associate VP for Human Resources ... Ms. Valerie A. THOMAS
29 Asst VP for Alumni Relations/Devel ... Ms. Susan EMFINGER
88 Asst VP New Media/Instruction Tech ... Mr. John FRITZ
18 Asst VP Facilities Management ... Mr. Rusty POSTLEWATE
04 Assistant to the President ... Mr. Douglas R. PEAR
96 Director of Procurement ... Ms. Sharon QUINN
92 Acting Director Honors College ... Dr. Simon STACEY
41 Director Physical Educ & Athletics ... Dr. Charles R. BROWN
19 Director University Police ... Mr. Mark SPARKS
36 Director Career Services Cntr ... Ms. Anne SCHOLL-FIEDLER
23 Director Health Services ... Ms. Jennifer LEPUS
37 Director Financial Aid ... Ms. Stephanie JOHNSON
27 Director of Communications ... Ms. Elyse ASHBURN
28 Director of Human Relations ... Vacant
25 Director Sponsored Programs ... Ms. Jocelyn CHASIS
40 Director of UMBC Bookstore ... Mr. Robert J. SOMERS
85 Director International Educ Svcs ... Dr. Arlene V. WERGIN
08 Director Library ... Dr. Larry M. WILT
06 Registrar ... Mr. Steven SMITH
35 Director Student Life ... Ms. Lee CALIZO
43 General Counsel ... Mr. David GLEASON
07 Dir Undergrd Admissions ... Mr. Dale BITTINGER
39 Director Residential Life ... Ms. Katherine B. BOONE
09 Director of Institutional Research ... Dr. Michael DILLON
38 Director Student Counseling ... Dr. J. LaVelle INGRAM

*University of Maryland Eastern Shore (E)

Princess Anne MD 21853-1299
County: Somerset FICE Identification: 002106
Unit ID: 163338
Telephone: (410) 651-2200 Carnegie Class: Master's S
FAX Number: (410) 651-6105 Calendar System: Semester
URL: www.umes.edu
Established: 1886 Annual Undergrad Tuition & Fees (In-State): $6,713
Enrollment: 4,509 Coed
Affiliation or Control: State IRS Status: 501(c)3
Highest Offering: Doctorate
Program: Liberal Arts And General; Teacher Preparatory; Professional
Accreditation: M, ARCPA, BUS, CONST, CORE, DIETD, DIETI, @PHAR, PTA, TED

02 President ... Dr. Juliette B. BELL
04 Executive Assistant to President ... Vacant
05 Acting Provost/VP Academic Affairs ... Dr. Retia S. WALKER
10 Vice Pres Administrative Affairs ... Dr. Ronnie E. HOLDEN
30 Vice President Inst Advancement ... Vacant
32 Vice President Student Affairs ... Dr. Anthony L. JENKINS
88 Vice Pres Tech/Commercialization ... Dr. Ronald G. FORSYTHE, JR.
20 Asst Vice Pres Academic Affairs ... Vacant
20 Assoc Vice Pres Academic Affairs ... Dr. Bernita M. SIMS-TUCKER
11 Asst Vice President Admin Affairs ... Mr. Alverne W. CHESTERFIELD
88 Asst to VP Administrative Affairs ... Dr. Maurice C. NGWABA
21 Asst VP Admin Affs/Budget Director ... Ms. Nelva G. COLLIER-WHITE
84 Assoc VP Student Life/Enroll Mgt ... Dr. James M. WHITE
04 Special Assistant to the President ... Ms. Rolanda C. BURNEY
91 Director Administrative Computing ... Mr. Kenneth GASTON
56 Assoc Dir Cooperative Extension ... Dr. Henry M. BROOKS
29 Director Alumni Affairs ... Dr. Kimberly C. DUMPSON
15 Director Human Resources ... Ms. Marie H. BILLIE
08 Dean Library Services ... Dr. Ellis B. BETECK
37 Director Financial Aid ... Mr. James W. KELLAM
23 Director Student Health Services ... Ms. Sharone V. GRANT
96 Director Procurement ... Ms. Jacqueline M. COLLINS
88 Director Univ Dining Services ... Mr. David SCOTT
07 Director Admissions ... Mr. Tyrone YOUNG
06 Registrar ... Ms. Cheryl HOLDEN-DUFFY
12 Director Richard A Henson Center ... Dr. Corey J. BOWEN
36 Director Career Services ... Dr. Theresa QUEENAN
09 Director Inst Research/Plng/Assess. ... Dr. Stanley M. NYIRENDA
19 Director Public Safety ... Mr. Warner I. SUMPTER
18 Director Physical Plant ... Mr. Leon J. BIVENS
39 Director Residence Life ... Mr. Marvin L. JONES
41 Athletic Director ... Mr. Keith S. DAVIDSON
21 Comptroller ... Ms. Bonita E. BYRD
46 Director Sponsored Research ... Ms. Catherine BOLEK
88 Director Student Retention & Svcs ... Dr. Johnny D. JONES
88 Director Rural Development ... Mr. Daniel S. KUENNEN
88 Director Upward Bound ... Dr. Nicole L. GALE
35 Director Student Activities ... Mr. James G. LUNNERMON, JR.
88 Director Title III Program ... Dr. Frances H. MCKINNEY
26 Director Public Relations ... Mr. William ROBINSON
44 Director Development ... Dr. Veronique L. DIRIKER
88 Director Advancement Services ... Mrs. Chenita R. KOLLOCK
51 Coordinator Continuing Education ... Ms. Gretchen M. BOGGS
38 Coordinator Counseling Services ... Dr. Patricia E. TILGHMAN
58 Dean Graduate Studies ... Dr. Jennifer M. KEANE-DAWES
47 Int Dean Sch Agric/Natural Sciences ... Dr. Jurgen G. SCHWARZ
49 Dean School of Arts & Professions ... Dr. Ray J. DAVIS
50 Dean School Business & Technology ... Dr. Ayodele J. ALADE
67 Dean Sch Pharmacy/Health Profession ... Dr. Nicholas R. BLANCHARD

*University of Maryland University College (F)

3501 University Boulevard East, Adelphi MD 20783-7998
County: Prince Georges FICE Identification: 011644
Unit ID: 163204
Telephone: (301) 985-7000 Carnegie Class: Master's L
FAX Number: (301) 985-7678 Calendar System: Semester
URL: www.umuc.edu
Established: 1947 Annual Undergrad Tuition & Fees (In-State): $6,168
Enrollment: 42,713 Coed
Affiliation or Control: State IRS Status: 501(c)3
Highest Offering: Doctorate
Program: Liberal Arts And General; Professional
Accreditation: M

02 Acting President ... Mr. Javier MIYARES
03 Chief Operating Officer ... Mr. George SHOENBERGER
10 Vice Pres Chief Financial Officer ... Mr. Eugene D. LOCKETT, JR.
05 Acting Provost Academic Officer ... Dr. Marie CINI
15 Vice President Human Resources ... Ms. Nadine PORTER
26 Sr Vice President Communications ... Mr. Michael FREEDMAN
45 Sr VP Institutional Effectiveness ... Vacant
86 Sr VP Partnerships Mktg Enroll Mgmt ... Mr. James H. SELBE
43 Vice President & General Counsel ... Ms. Nancy WILLIAMSON
49 Acting Dean The Undergrad School ... Ms. Cynthia DAVIS
58 Interim Dean The Graduate School ... Mr. Robert GOODWIN
13 Vice Pres & CIO ... Mr. Peter C. YOUNG
84 Vice Pres Enrollment Management ... Mr. Sean CHUNG
08 Assoc Provost of Library Services ... Mr. Stephen MILLER
18 Associate Vice President Facilities ... Mr. George TRUJILLO
88 Associate VP Government Relations ... Mr. Benjamin BIRGE
37 AVP Student Financial Aid ... Ms. Cheryl STORIE
09 Director Institutional Research ... Wei ZHOU
06 Int Assoc Provost/Univ Registrar ... Ms. Michelle SAMUELS-JONES
28 Director of Diversity Initiatives ... Dr. Blair HAYES
07 Director of Admissions ... Ms. Insiya JIWANJI

*Bowie State University (A)

14000 Jericho Park Road, Bowie MD 20715-3318
County: Prince Georges | FICE Identification: 002062
Unit ID: 162007
Telephone: (301) 860-4000 | Carnegie Class: DRU
FAX Number: (301) 860-3510 | Calendar System: Semester
URL: www.bowiestate.edu
Established: 1865 | Annual Undergrad Tuition & Fees (In-State): $6,639
Enrollment: 5,608 | Coed
Affiliation or Control: State | IRS Status: 501(c)3
Highest Offering: Doctorate
Program: Liberal Arts And General; Teacher Preparatory
Accreditation: M, ACBSP, CS, NUR, SW, TED

02 President ... Dr. Mickey L. BURNIM
05 Provost/Vice Pres Academic Affs ... Dr. Weldon JACKSON
10 Vice Pres Finance & Administration ... Dr. Karl B. BROCKENBROUGH
30 Vice Pres Institutional Advancement ... Dr. Richard LUCAS, JR.
32 VP Student Affairs/Campus Life ... Dr. Artie L. TRAVIS
43 Vice Pres & General Counsel ... Ms. Karen JOHNSON-SHAHEED
35 Student Code of Conduct ... Mrs. Thomaice BOARDLEY
13 VP Office of Information Technology ... Vacant
84 Asst VP Enrollment Management ... Mr. Donald L. KIAH
88 Asst to Prov Institutional Effec ... Ms. Gayle M. FINK
06 University Registrar ... Ms. Patricia MITCHELL
08 Assoc Library Dir/Interim Dean ... Ms. Marian RUCKER-SHAMU
36 Director Career Services ... Ms. April JOHNOSON
15 Sr Director of Human Resources ... Ms. Sheila HOBSON
19 Chief of Campus Police ... Mr. Ernest WAITERS
58 Int Dean Sch of Grad Stds/Research ... Dr. Cosmos NWOKEAFOR
49 Dean School of Arts & Sciences ... Dr. George ACQUAAH
50 Dean School of Business ... Dr. Anthony NELSON
53 Dean Sch of Education ... Dr. Traki TAYLOR-WEBB
107 Dean School of Professional Studies ... Dr. Jerome H. SCHIELE
92 Director UCE Honors Program ... Dr. Monika GROSS
23 Director University Wellness Center ... Dr. Rita WUTHO
41 Director Athletics ... Mr. Anton GOFF
26 Dir University Relations/ Marketing ... Ms. Cassandra M. ROBINSON
88 Director University Wiseman Centre ... Mr. Frank WALLER
37 Director Financial Aid ... Ms. Deborah STANLEY
18 Director Facilities ... Mr. Darryl WILLIFORD
07 Director Undergraduate Admissions ... Mr. Lonnie MORRIS
29 Director of Alumni Relations ... Ms. Anette WEDDERBURN
88 Dir of Model Inst for Excellence ... Vacant
96 Director of Purchasing ... Mr. Steve A. JOST
09 Director of Institutional Research ... Dr. Doug NUTTER

*Coppin State University (B)

2500 W North Avenue, Baltimore MD 21216-3698
County: Baltimore City | FICE Identification: 002068
Unit ID: 162283
Telephone: (410) 951-3000 | Carnegie Class: Master's S
FAX Number: (410) 523-7238 | Calendar System: Semester
URL: www.coppin.edu
Established: 1900 | Annual Undergrad Tuition & Fees (In-State): $5,732
Enrollment: 3,813 | Coed
Affiliation or Control: State | IRS Status: 501(c)3
Highest Offering: Doctorate
Program: Liberal Arts And General; Teacher Preparatory; Professional
Accreditation: M, CORE, NUR, NURSE, SW, TED

02 President ... Dr. Reginald S. AVERY
05 Interim Provost/VP Academic Affairs ... Dr. Ronnie L. COLLINS, SR.
30 VP Institutional Advancement ... Mr. Douglas DALZELL
10 VP Administration & Finance ... Mr. Richard SIEMER
32 Vice Pres Student Affairs ... Dr. Franklin D. CHAMBERS
13 VP Information Systems/CIO ... Dr. Ahmed EL-HAGGAN
84 Acting VP Enrollment Management ... Dr. Monica RANDALL
45 Assoc VP Planning/Assessment ... Dr. Scott J. DANTLEY
20 Actg Assoc Vice Pres Academic Affs ... Dr. Habtu BRAHA
21 Assoc Vice Pres Admin/Finance ... Vacant
32 Associate VP Student Affairs ... Dr. Joann CHRISTOPHER-HICKS
18 Assoc VP Capital Plng/Constr & Cont ... Mr. Maqbool PATEL
86 Assoc VP of Pub Policy & Govt Rel ... Dr. Monica E. RANDALL
07 Director of Admissions ... Ms. Michelle R. GROSS
06 Registrar ... Dr. Margaret W. TURNER
21 Controller ... Mrs. Crystal MOSLEY
08 Director of the Library ... Dr. Mary WANZA
09 Director of Institutional Research ... Dr. Oyebanjo LAJUBUTU
37 Director of Financial Aid ... Mr. Mose CARTIER
36 Director of Career Services Center ... Mrs. Linda BOWIE
15 Director of Human Resorces ... Mrs. Lisa EARLY
19 Chief of Public Safety ... Chief Leonard HAMM
39 Director of Housing/Residence Life ... Mrs. Vallyn MERRICK
41 Director of Athletics ... Mr. Derrick RAMSEY
35 Director Student Support Services ... Ms. Leila WASHINGTON
88 Director Academic Resource Center ... Vacant
88 Director of Academic Advisement ... Vacant
29 Director Alumni Relations ... Ms. Tara TURNER
96 Director of Purchasing ... Mr. Thomas E. DAWSON, JR.
26 Director of University Relations ... Vacant
88 Director Client Computing Services ... Mr. Emmanuel OWUSU-SEKYERE
88 Director Coppin Academy ... Mr. Frank WHORLEY
35 Director of Student Activities ... Mrs. Jocelyn BRYANT-WEBB
27 Director Telecommunications ... Mr. Claude K. RADER
105 Director Web & Multimedia ... Mr. Andrew C. BAIN
31 Exec Dir of Community Partnerships ... Mr. Albert ROBINSON
88 Exec Dir Local to Global Engagement ... Dr. York BRADSHAW
49 Interim Dean Arts & Sciences ... Dr. Alcott S. ARTHUR
92 Dean Honors College & McNair Pgms ... Mr. Ronnie L. COLLINS, SR.
58 Dean Graduate School ... Dr. Mary E. OWENS-SOUTHHALL
66 Dean of Nursing ... Dr. Marcella COPES
53 Interim Dean of Education ... Dr. Edna SIMMONS
04 Executive Assistant to President ... Mrs. Sherie JOHNSON
88 Chair Interdisciplinary Studies ... Ms. Tondelaya BLACKSTONE
97 Chair General & Adult Education ... Dr. Jacqueline H. WILLIAMS
88 Int Chr Applied Psych/Rehab Counsel ... Mr. James STEWART
61 Chair Crim Justice/Law Enforcement ... Dr. Dilip DAS
53 Chair Curriculum & Instruction ... Dr. Glynis BARBER
57 Chair Fine Arts ... Dr. Garey HYATT
82 Chair History Geography/Global Stds ... Dr. Katherine BANKOLE-MEDINA
79 Interim Chair Humanities ... Dr. Seth FORREST
50 Chr Mgmt Sci & Economics (Business) ... Dr. Habtu BRAHA
77 Int Chair Math & Computer Science ... Dr. Sean BROOKS
65 Chair Natural Sciences ... Dr. Gilbert OGONJI
83 Chair Social Sciences ... Dr. John L. HUDGINS
70 Chair Social Work ... Dr. Errol BOLDEN
68 Chair Health/Physical Education ... Dr. Edna SIMMONS
88 Chair Special Education ... Dr. Daniel P. JOSEPH

*Frostburg State University (C)

101 Braddock Road, Frostburg MD 21532-2303
County: Allegany | FICE Identification: 002072
Unit ID: 162584
Telephone: (301) 687-4000 | Carnegie Class: Master's L
FAX Number: (301) 687-4737 | Calendar System: Semester
URL: www.frostburg.edu
Established: 1898 | Annual Undergrad Tuition & Fees (In-State): $7,436
Enrollment: 5,429 | Coed
Affiliation or Control: State | IRS Status: 501(c)3
Highest Offering: Doctorate
Program: Liberal Arts And General; Teacher Preparatory
Accreditation: M, BUS, NRPA, NURSE, SW, TED

02 President ... Dr. Jonathan GIBRALTER
05 Provost & Vice Pres Acad Affs ... Dr. Stephen J. SIMPSON
32 Vice Pres Student/Education Svcs ... Dr. Thomas L. BOWLING
10 Vice President for Admin & Finance ... Mr. David C. ROSE
30 Interim Vice Pres Univ Advancement ... Ms. Colleen C. STUMP
84 Assoc VP for Enrollment Management ... Mr. Wray BLAIR
86 Chief of Staff/VP for Govt Relation ... Mr. Steven SPAHR
15 Vice President Human Resources ... Ms. Katherine SNYDER
43 University Counsel ... Ms. Karen A. TREBER
20 Interim Associate Provost ... Dr. Randall RHODES
21 Assoc VP Finance & Controller ... Mr. Richard A. REPAC
35 Asst VP Student Svcs/Dean of Stdnts ... Dr. Jesse KETTERMAN
35 Asst Vice Pres Student Services ... Mr. Bernard WYNDER
45 Assoc Director Budget & Planning ... Ms. Denise MURPHY
20 Vice Provost ... Dr. John BOWMAN
49 Dean Col Liberal Arts & Science ... Dr. Joseph M. HOFFMAN
50 Dean College of Business ... Dr. Ahmad TOOTOONCHI
53 Dean College of Education ... Dr. Clarence GOLDEN
08 Director of the Library ... Dr. David M. GILLESPIE
37 Director of Financial Aid ... Mrs. Angela L. HOVATTER
108 Asst Vice Pres Planning and Assess ... Mr. Robert E. SMITH
09 Director of Institutional Research ... Vacant
58 Director of Graduate Services ... Ms. Vickie MAZER
18 Director Facilities/Physical Plant ... Mr. Robert BOYCE
27 Director News & Media Services ... Ms. Elizabeth MEDCALF
36 Director Career Services ... Dr. Robbie L. CORDLE
38 Director Counseling & Psyc Svcs ... Dr. Spencer F. DEAKIN
40 Director Bookstore & ID Services ... Ms. Melissa HILLER
41 Athletic Director ... Mr. Troy DELL
19 Chief University Police ... Col. Cynthia SMITH
90 Director of Academic Computing ... Ms. Beth KENNEY
91 Director of Admin Computing ... Mr. Bruce LEHMAN
44 Director Annual Giving ... Ms. Shannon L. GRIBBLE
22 Director of AA/EEO ... Mrs. Beth HOFFMAN
25 Dir Research/Sponsored Programs ... Mr. Aaron HOEL
07 Director of Admissions ... Ms. Trisha GREGORY
28 Director of Diversity ... Ms. Robin WYNDER
29 Director Alumni Programs ... Vacant
13 Dir Networking/Telecommunications ... Vacant
96 Coord Procurement/Material Handling ... Mr. Alan R. SNYDER
23 Director Health Services ... Ms. Mary A. TOLA
39 Director Residence Life ... Mr. Dana A. SEVERANCE

*Salisbury University (D)

1101 Camden Avenue, Salisbury MD 21801-6860
County: Wicomico | FICE Identification: 002091
Unit ID: 163851
Telephone: (410) 543-6000 | Carnegie Class: Master's L
FAX Number: (410) 548-2587 | Calendar System: Semester
URL: www.salisbury.edu
Established: 1925 | Annual Undergrad Tuition & Fees (In-State): $7,700
Enrollment: 8,606 | Coed
Affiliation or Control: State | IRS Status: 501(c)3
Highest Offering: Doctorate
Program: Liberal Arts And General; Teacher Preparatory; Professional
Accreditation: M, BUS, EXSC, MT, MUS, NURSE, SW, TED

02 President ... Dr. Janet E. DUDLEY-ESHBACH
05 Provost/VPAA ... Dr. Diane D. ALLEN
100 Chief of Staff ... Ms. Amy S. HASSON
10 Vice Pres Administration/Finance ... Mrs. Betty P. CROCKETT
32 Vice Pres of Student Affairs ... Dr. Dane R. FOUST
30 Vice Pres Institutional Advancement ... Vacant
84 VP of Enrollment Management ... Mr. Aaron M. BASKO
28 Chief Diversity Officer ... Vacant
35 Associate VP of Student Affairs ... Vacant
20 Associate Provost ... Dr. Melanie L. PERREAULT
20 Asst Vice Pres Academic Affairs ... Ms. Melissa M. BOOG
21 Asst VP of Admin/Fin Fac & Cap Mgmt ... Mr. Eric J. BERKHEIMER
35 Dean of Students ... Mr. Edwin A. COWELL
27 Int Chief Information Officer ... Mr. Ken F. KUNDELL
26 Director of Public Relations ... Mr. Richard W. CULVER
31 Director of Auxiliary Services ... Mr. Paul W. LAND
41 Athletics Director ... Dr. Michael P. VIENNA
92 Int Director Honors Program ... Dr. Jay R. CARLANDER
06 Registrar ... Ms. Jacqueline M. MAISEL
07 Director of Admissions ... Ms. Elizabeth A. SKOGLUND
09 Special Asst to Pres/IARA ... Dr. Kara O. SIEGERT
08 Dean of Library & Info Resources ... Dr. Beatriz B. HARDY
38 Director of Counseling Center ... Dr. Kathleen J. SCOTT
36 Director of Career Services ... Dr. Rebecca A. EMERY
37 Director of Financial Aid ... Ms. Barri ZIMMERMAN
15 Assoc VP of Admin & Finance for HR ... Mr. Marvin L. PYLES
29 Int Dir Alumni Rels/Annual Giving ... Mr. Jayme E. BLOCK
23 Director of Student Health Services ... Ms. Jennifer R. BERKMAN
35 Director of Student Activities ... Vacant
43 General Counsel ... Ms. Jen PALANCIA SHIPP
86 Dir Of Government Relations ... Mr. Robert J. SHEEHAN
39 Director Housing/Residence Life ... Mr. David P. GUTOSKEY
19 Director of Public Safety ... Mr. Edwin L. LASHLEY
40 Director of Bookstore ... Ms. Lisa G. GRAY
18 Director Facilities/Physical Plant ... Mr. Kevin J. MANN
96 Director of Purchasing ... Vacant
75 Dean Henson Sch Science/Tech ... Dr. Karen L. OLMSTEAD
50 Dean Perdue School of Business ... Dr. Bob G. WOOD
49 Dean Fulton School of Liberal Arts ... Dr. Maarten L. PEREBOOM
53 Int Dean Seidel Sch Ed/Prof Studies ... Dr. Carol A. WOOD
58 Dean Graduate Studies/Research ... Dr. Clifton P. GRIFFIN
88 Dir Ctr for Student Achievement ... Dr. Heather W. HOLMES

*Towson University (E)

8000 York Road, Baltimore MD 21252-0001
County: Baltimore | FICE Identification: 002099
Unit ID: 164076
Telephone: (410) 704-2000 | Carnegie Class: Master's L
FAX Number: N/A | Calendar System: 4/1/4
URL: www.towson.edu
Established: 1866 | Annual Undergrad Tuition & Fees (In-State): $8,132
Enrollment: 21,464 | Coed
Affiliation or Control: State | IRS Status: 501(c)3
Highest Offering: Doctorate
Program: Liberal Arts And General; Teacher Preparatory; Professional
Accreditation: M, ARCPA, AUD, BUS, BUSA, CS, DANCE, IPSY, MUS, NURSE, OT, SP, TED, THEA

02 President ... Dr. Maravene S. LOESCHKE
05 Interim Provost ... Dr. James DILISIO
10 Interim Vice Pres Admin & Finance ... Mr. Mark E. BEHM
30 Vice Pres University Advancement ... Dr. Gary N. RUBIN
32 Vice President Student Affairs ... Dr. Debra MORIARTY
31 VP Economic/Community Outreach ... Ms. Dyan L. BRASINGTON
100 Interim Chief of Staff ... Ms. Jennifer GAJEWSKI
100 Deputy Chief of Staff ... Ms. Marina COOPER
04 Spec Asst to the Pres Div & Equ Opp ... Ms. Debra SEEBERGER
20 Interim Associate Provost ... Dr. Jane NEAPOLITAN
84 Interim Sr Assoc VP Enrollment Mgmt ... Mr. Robert GIORDANI
44 Assoc Vice President Development ... Vacant
26 Assoc VP University Marketing ... Ms. Ellen E. STOKES
29 Assoc Vice Pres Alumni Relations ... Ms. Lori B. ARMSTRONG
13 Assoc Vice President OTS/CIO ... Mr. Jeffrey SCHMIDT
31 Assoc Vice Pres Auxiliary Services ... Mr. Joseph OSTER
18 Int Assoc Vice Pres Facilities Mgmt ... Mr. Roger HAYDEN
21 Assoc VP Fiscal Planning & Svcs ... Vacant
15 Associate Vice Pres Human Resources ... Mr. Phillip ROSS, III
35 Assoc Vice Pres Student Affairs ... Dr. Jana VARWIG
45 Assoc Prov Academic Res & Plng ... Dr. Gary LEVY
88 Assoc Vice President Campus Life ... Dr. Teresa HALL
28 Asst VP Ctr for Student Diversity ... Mr. L. Victor COLLINS

39 Asst VP/Dir Housing/Residence Life ... Mr. Jerome T. DIERINGER
37 AVP Cmty College Rels/Financial Aid ... Mr. Vincent C. PECORA
25 Asst VP University Research Svcs ... Ms. Amy TAYLOR
07 Asst VP & Director of Admissions ... Mr. Brian HAZLETT
19 Asst VP Public Sfty/Chief of Police ... Chief Bernard GERST
53 Dean College of Education ... Dr. Raymond LORION
50 Dean College of Business/Economics ... Dr. Shohreh KAYNAMA
49 Dean College of Liberal Arts ... Dr. Terry COONEY
81 Dean J&M Fisher Col of Science/Math ... Dr. David VANKO
57 Dean Col Fine Arts/Communications ... Ms. Susan PICINICH
76 Dean College of Health Professions ... Dr. Charlotte E. EXNER
92 Dean Honors College ... Dr. Joseph MCGINN
43 University Counsel ... Mr. Michael A. AMSELMI
08 Dean of University Libraries ... Ms. Deborah NOLAN
104 Director Study Abroad ... Dr. Rebecca L. PISANO
94 Chair Women's Studies ... Dr. Karen DUGGER
09 Director Institutional Research ... Ms. Laura BAGEANT
26 Director University Relations ... Ms. Carol DUNSWORTH
41 Director of Athletics ... Mr. Michael WADDELL
23 Director of Health Services ... Dr. Jane L. HALPERN
40 Director of University Bookstore ... Ms. Stacey ELOFIR
96 Director of Procurement ... Ms. Lucy SLAICH
88 Exec Dir Technology Support Svcs ... Vacant
38 Director Counseling Center ... Dr. James SPIVACK
36 Director of Career Services ... Ms. Lorie LOGAN-BENNETT

*University of Baltimore (A)

1420 N Charles Street, Baltimore MD 21201-5779
County: Independent City　FICE Identification: 002102
Unit ID: 161873
Telephone: (410) 837-4200　Carnegie Class: Master's L
FAX Number: N/A　Calendar System: Semester
URL: www.ubalt.edu
Established: 1925　Annual Undergrad Tuition & Fees (In-State): $7,664
Enrollment: 6,406　Coed
Affiliation or Control: State　IRS Status: 501(c)3
Highest Offering: Doctorate
Program: Liberal Arts And General; Professional
Accreditation: M, BUS, LAW, SPAA

02 President ... Mr. Robert L. BOGOMOLNY
05 Provost & Sr VP Academic Affiars ... Dr. Joseph S. WOOD
10 Sr VP Admin & Finance ... Mr. Harry SCHUCKEL
100 Exec Dir Pres Operations & Projects ... Ms. Susan SCHUBERT
84 Sr Vice Pres Enrollment Management ... Ms. Miriam E. KING
30 Vice Pres Institutional Advancement ... Ms. Theresa SILANSKIS
45 Vice Pres Planning/External Affairs ... Mr. Peter TORAN
86 VP Government & Community Relations ... Ms. Anita THOMAS
18 VP Facil Mgmt/Capital Planning ... Mr. Steve CASSARD
13 Vice Pres Technology/CIO ... Mr. David BOBART
15 Asst Vice Pres Human Resources ... Ms. Mary MAHER
20 Associate Provost ... Dr. Beverly SCHNELLER
09 AVP for Institutional Research ... Mr. Paul MONIODIS
35 Assoc Vice Pres Student Affairs ... Ms. Shelia BURKHALTER
32 Dean of Students ... Ms. Kathleen ANDERSON
35 Director Center Student Involvement ... Ms. Kari OSBORNE
28 Dir Diversity and Culture Center ... Ms. Karla M. SHEPHERD
07 Actg Executive Director Admissions ... Ms. Janet WHELAN
08 Director of Library ... Ms. Lucy HOLMAN
19 Chief of Police ... Mr. Samuel D. TRESS
07 AVP for Enrollment Services ... Ms. Anne HAMILL
96 Director of Procurement & Supply ... Mr. Blair BLANKINSHIP
44 Dir Annual Giving/Alumni Relations ... Ms. Kate CRIMMINS
38 Director Counseling Services ... Dr. Myra WATERS
36 Director Career & Professional Dev ... Mr. Ray MCCREE
06 Registrar ... Mr. Michael DRISCOLL
09 Director Institutional Research ... Mr. Merrill R. PRITCHETT
27 Manager Public Information ... Mr. Chris HART
80 Dean College of Public Affairs ... Dr. Steve PERCY
49 Interim Dean College of Arts & Sci ... Dr. Jeffery SAWYER
61 Dean of the School of Law ... Dr. Ronald WEICH
50 Dean School of Business ... Dr. Darlene SMITH
88 Dir Center for Education Access ... Ms. Karyn SCHULZ
21 AVP Admin & University Budget Dir ... Ms. Barbara AUGHENBAUGH
07 AVP Admissions ... Mr. David WAGGONER

Washington Adventist University (B)

7600 Flower Avenue, Takoma Park MD 20912-7794
County: Montgomery　FICE Identification: 002067
Unit ID: 162210
Telephone: (301) 891-4000　Carnegie Class: Bac/Diverse
FAX Number: (301) 270-1618　Calendar System: Semester
URL: www.wau.edu
Established: 1904　Annual Undergrad Tuition & Fees: $18,900
Enrollment: 1,493　Coed
Affiliation or Control: Seventh-day Adventist　IRS Status: 501(c)3
Highest Offering: Master's
Program: Liberal Arts And General; Teacher Preparatory; Professional
Accreditation: M, NUR

01 President ... Dr. Weymouth SPENCE
10 Exec VP Financial Administration ... Mr. Patrick FARLEY
32 Vice Pres Student Life ... Ms. Jean WARDEN
13 Assoc VP for Info Tech Systems ... Mr. Gregory INGRAM
58 Dean Sch Grad/Professional Studies ... Dr. Jude EDWARDS
33 Dean of Men ... Mr. Tim NELSON
34 Dean of Women ... Ms. Adrienne MATTHEWS
08 Librarian ... Ms. Lee Marie WISEL
30 Director of Development ... Vacant
06 Director of Records/Admissions ... Vacant
19 Director Safety & Security ... Vacant
42 Chaplain ... Pastor Gary WIMBISH
41 Athletic Director ... Vacant
84 Director of Student Recruiting ... Vacant
29 Director of Alumni ... Vacant
15 Director of Human Resources ... Ms. Estevanny JIMENEZ
21 Comptroller ... Vacant
27 Director Marketing & Communications ... Mr. William JACKSON
78 Dir Coop Educ/Acad Support & Test ... Mr. Fitzroy THOMAS
18 Chief Facilities/Physical Plant ... Mr. Steve LAPHAM
37 Director Student Financial Aid ... Ms. Sharon CONWAY
38 Director Student Counseling ... Ms. Lauri PRESTON
09 Director of Institutional Research ... Ms. Janette NEUFVILLE
40 Manager the College Bookstore ... Mr. Lloyd YUTUC

Washington Bible College/Capital Bible Seminary (C)

6511 Princess Garden Parkway, Lanham MD 20706-3599
County: Prince Georges　FICE Identification: 001462
Unit ID: 164207
Telephone: (301) 552-1400　Carnegie Class: Spec/Faith
FAX Number: (301) 552-2775　Calendar System: Semester
URL: www.bible.edu
Established: 1938　Annual Undergrad Tuition & Fees: $14,220
Enrollment: 502　Coed
Affiliation or Control: Independent Non-Profit　IRS Status: 501(c)3
Highest Offering: First Professional Degree
Program: Teacher Preparatory; Religious Emphasis
Accreditation: M, #BI, THEOL

01 President ... Dr. George HARTON
05 Academic Dean Wash Bible College ... Dr. Ed CURTIS
05 Academic Dean Capital Bible College ... Dr. Neil HOLLIKER
32 Dean of Students ... Rev. Brian SMITH
37 Director of Financial Aid ... Ms. Hie Ju SEUNG
08 Librarian ... Ms. Sue KOLODZEJSKI
41 Athletic Director ... Rev. Brian P. SMITH
07 Director of Admissions ... Mr. B.J WALBERT
15 Human Resource Director ... Ms. Lorraine HEIGH
10 Chief Financial Officer ... Mr. Doug CROW
30 Development Director ... Ms. Brenda ULMAN
18 Maintenance Manager ... Mr. Brian SHIELDS

Washington College (D)

300 Washington Avenue, Chestertown MD 21620-1197
County: Kent　FICE Identification: 002108
Unit ID: 164216
Telephone: (410) 778-2800　Carnegie Class: Bac/A&S
FAX Number: (410) 778-7850　Calendar System: Semester
URL: www.washcoll.edu
Established: 1782　Annual Undergrad Tuition & Fees: $39,208
Enrollment: 1,515　Coed
Affiliation or Control: Independent Non-Profit　IRS Status: 501(c)3
Highest Offering: Master's
Program: Liberal Arts And General; Teacher Preparatory; Fine Arts Emphasis
Accreditation: M

01 President ... Dr. Mitchell B. REISS
05 Provost/Dean of College ... Dr. Emily CHAMLEE-WRIGHT
100 Chief of Staff ... Mr. Joseph L. HOLT
10 Senior Vice Pres Finance & Mgmt ... Mr. James V. MANARO
30 Sr Vice Pres College Advancement ... Mrs. Barbara H. HECK
44 Vice Pres for College Advancement ... Mrs. Gretchen V. DWYER
07 Vice Pres Admiss/Enrollment Mgmt ... Mr. Kevin C. COVENEY
26 VP College Relations/ Marketing ... Ms. Meredith DAVIES HADAWAY
32 Vice President & Dean of Students ... Dr. Mela DUTKA
29 Dir Alumni Rels/Ldrship Annual Gvng ... Ms. Rebekah L. HARDY
46 Asst Provost/Instl Research & Assmt ... Mr. Dale W. TRUSHEIM
20 Asst Dean Academic Initiatives ... Dr. Andrea G. LANGE
31 Director of Campus Special Events ... Mrs. Laura J. WILSON
41 Director of Athletics ... Dr. Bryan L. MATTHEWS
06 Registrar ... Mr. James A. THIEMANN
08 Director of Miller Library ... Dr. Ruth C. SHOGE
27 Chief Information Officer ... Mrs. Billie S. DODGE
91 Director of Admin Computing ... Mr. Kenneth W. SUTTON
58 Director of Graduate Program ... Dr. Christopher AMES
21 Controller ... Ms. Penelope L. FARLEY
18 Director of Physical Plant ... Mr. Reid C. RAUDENBUSH
15 Director of Human Resources ... Dr. Alan P. CHESNEY
19 Director of Public Safety ... Mr. Gerald K. RODERICK
37 Director of Financial Aid ... Ms. Jeani M. NARCUM
35 Dir of Student Development Programs ... Dr. Sarah R. FEYERHERM
39 Dir Resid Life/Assoc Dean of Stdnts ... Mr. Carl CROWE
85 Director International Programs ... Ms. Kathryn S. MCCLEARY
23 Clinical Director Health Services ... Vacant
38 Director of Counseling Center ... Dr. Bonnie MICHAELSON FISHER
36 Director of Career Development ... Mr. James M. ALLISON, JR.
28 Director of Multi-Cultural Affairs ... Mr. Darnell PARKER
27 Director of Media Relations ... Mrs. Kay H. MACINTOSH
40 Bookstore Manager ... Ms. Shannon WYBLE

Wor-Wic Community College (E)

32000 Campus Drive, Salisbury MD 21804-1486
County: Wicomico　FICE Identification: 020739
Unit ID: 164313
Telephone: (410) 334-2800　Carnegie Class: Assoc/Pub-R-M
FAX Number: (410) 334-2951　Calendar System: Semester
URL: www.worwic.edu
Established: 1975　Annual Undergrad Tuition & Fees (In-District): $3,002
Enrollment: 4,063　Coed
Affiliation or Control: Local　IRS Status: 501(c)3
Highest Offering: Associate Degree
Program: Occupational; 2-Year Principally Bachelor's Creditable
Accreditation: M, ACFEI, RAD

01 President ... Dr. Murray K. HOY
05 Vice Pres Academic & Student Affs ... Dr. Stephen L. CAPELLI
11 Vice Pres Administrative Services ... Ms. Jennifer A. SANDT
26 Vice Pres Institutional Affairs ... Dr. Reenie MCCORMICK
32 Dean Student Development ... Dr. Lynn M. WILJANEN
51 Dean Continuing Education ... Mrs. Ruth E. BAKER
97 Dean General Education ... Dr. Colleen C. DALLAM
75 Dean Occupational Education ... Dr. Trevor H. JONES
07 Director Admissions ... Mr. Richard C. WEBSTER
14 Director Information Technology ... Ms. Ruth GILL
36 Director Career Services ... Ms. Lori SMOOT
37 Director Financial Aid ... Ms. Deborah D. JENKINS
21 Director Accounting ... Mr. Thomas N. TYSON
15 Director Human Resources ... Vacant
38 Director Counseling ... Ms. Suzanne T. ALEXANDER
27 Director Marketing ... Ms. Janet S. KENNINGTON
09 Director Institutional Research ... Ms. Carol A. MENZEL
30 Director Development ... Ms. Janice MURPHY
06 Registrar ... Ms. Kelly HEWETT
88 Dir Retention & Student Success ... Ms. Deirdra G. JOHNSON
35 Director Student Activities ... Ms. Tricia G. SMITH
08 Media Center Director ... Ms. Cheryl MICHAEL
18 Director Plant Management ... Mr. Paul MACE
96 Director Purchasing & Auxiliary Svc ... Ms. Allison M. CANADA
105 Webmaster ... Mr. Joshua W. TOWNSEND

Yeshiva College of the Nation's Capital (F)

1216 Arcola Avenue, Silver Spring MD 20902-3408
County: Montgomery　FICE Identification: 039373
Unit ID: 434937
Telephone: (301) 593-2534　Carnegie Class: Spec/Faith
FAX Number: (301) 593-2534　Calendar System: Semester
Established: 1995　Annual Undergrad Tuition & Fees: $9,300
Enrollment: 46　Male
Affiliation or Control: Independent Non-Profit　IRS Status: 501(c)3
Highest Offering: Second Talmudic Degree
Program: Teacher Preparatory; Professional; Religious Emphasis
Accreditation: RABN

01 President ... Rabbi Yitzchok MERKIN
05 Rosh Yeshiva ... Rabbi Aaron LOPIANSKY
37 Financial Aid Director ... Ms. Irene LAWSON

MASSACHUSETTS

American International College (G)

1000 State Street, Springfield MA 01109-3155
County: Hampden　FICE Identification: 002114
Unit ID: 164447
Telephone: (413) 737-7000　Carnegie Class: Master's L
FAX Number: (413) 205-3943　Calendar System: Semester
URL: www.aic.edu
Established: 1885　Annual Undergrad Tuition & Fees: $29,158
Enrollment: 3,449　Coed
Affiliation or Control: Independent Non-Profit　IRS Status: 501(c)3
Highest Offering: Doctorate
Program: Liberal Arts And General; Teacher Preparatory; Professional; Nursing Emphasis
Accreditation: EH, IACBE, NURSE, OT, PTA

01 President ... Dr. Vincent M. MANIACI
05 Provost ... Dr. Todd G. FRITCH
11 Exec VP Administration ... Mr. Mark R. BERMAN
41 Executive VP for Athletics ... Mr. Richard F. BEDARD
27 Chief Information Officer ... Mr. Bill SERETTA
16 Vice President forf Human Resources ... Ms. Nicolle M. CESTERO
32 VP Student Affairs ... Dr. Blaine K. STEVENS
09 VP for Institutional Effectiveness ... Dr. Gregory T. SCHMUTTE
30 Exec Dir for Institutional Advance ... Ms. Heather CAHILL
84 VP Enrollment Managemt ... Ms. Linda DAGRADI
10 Vice President for Finance ... Mr. Thomas DYBICK
18 Assoc VP for Facilities ... Mr. Richard LINIO
51 Assoc VP Educational Enterprise ... Ms. Ellen R. NOONAN
88 Dean of Academic Success ... Dr. Carol SITTERLY
76 Dean Health Sciences ... Dr. Cesarina THOMPSON
49 Dean Arts/Education & Sciences ... Dr. Vickie HESS
06 Registrar ... Ms. Diane H. FURTEK
08 Director of Library ... Ms. Estelle H. SPENCER
38 Director Counseling Center ... Dr. Rose L. ANDREJCZYK
36 Dir Career Dev/Placement/Employment ... Ms. Abby MAHONEY
76 Director Occupational Therapy Pgm ... Dr. Cathy A. DOW-ROYER
76 Director Physical Therapy Program ... Dr. Gail STERN
66 Director Division of Nursing ... Ms. Karen S. ROUSSEAU
96 Director Auxiliary Svcs/Purchasing ... Ms. Katherine M. TOOHEY
60 Director Communications Center ... Vacant
21 Comptroller ... Vacant

Amherst College (A)

PO Box 5000, Amherst MA 01002-5000
County: Hampshire FICE Identification: 002115
Unit ID: 164465
Telephone: (413) 542-2000 Carnegie Class: Bac/A&S
FAX Number: (413) 542-2621 Calendar System: Semester
URL: www.amherst.edu
Established: 1821 Annual Undergrad Tuition & Fees: $44,610
Enrollment: 1,791 Coed
Affiliation or Control: Independent Non-Profit IRS Status: 501(c)3
Highest Offering: Baccalaureate
Program: Liberal Arts And General
Accreditation: EH

01 President ... Dr. Carolyn (Biddy) A. MARTIN
100 Chief of Staff ... Ms. Susan PIKOR
05 Dean of the Faculty ... Dr. Gregory S. CALL
32 Dean of Students ... Dr. Allen HART
07 Dean Admission/Financial Aid ... Mr. Thomas H. PARKER
20 Associate Dean of the Faculty ... Dr. John CHENEY
20 Associate Dean of the Faculty ... Dr. Fredrick GRIFFITHS
21 Interim Treasurer/Dir of the Budget ... Ms. Shannon D. GUREK
30 Chief Advancement Officer ... Ms. Megan MOREY
43 Legal & Admin Counsel/AAO ... Mr. Paul MURPHY
29 Exec Director Alumni/Parent Pgms ... Ms. Elizabeth CANNON SMITH
06 Registrar ... Ms. Kathleen GOFF
37 Director of Financial Aid ... Mr. Joe P. CASE
15 Director of Human Resources ... Ms. Maria-Judith RODRIGUEZ
21 Comptroller ... Mr. Stephen M. NIGRO
09 Director of Institutional Research ... Ms. Marian F. MATHESON
26 Director of Public Affairs ... Mr. Peter J. ROONEY
08 College Librarian ... Mr. Bryn GEFFERT
13 Chief Information Officer ... Ms. Gayle BARTON
23 Director of Student Health Services ... Dr. Warren H. MORGAN
38 Director of Counseling Center ... Dr. Jacqueline S. BEARCE
36 Director of the Career Center ... Ms. Ursula J. OLENDER
39 Director of Resident Life ... Mr. Torin Y. MOORE
41 Director of Athletics ... Dr. Suzanne R. COFFEY
18 Director Facilities/Planning/Mgmt ... Mr. James D. BRASSORD
19 Chief of Campus Police ... Mr. John B. CARTER
88 Director of Dining Services ... Mr. Charles G. THOMPSON

Andover Newton Theological School (B)

210 Herrick Road, Newton Centre MA 02459-2243
County: Middlesex FICE Identification: 002116
Unit ID: 164474
Telephone: (617) 964-1100 Carnegie Class: Spec/Faith
FAX Number: (617) 965-9756 Calendar System: Semester
URL: www.ants.edu
Established: 1807 Annual Graduate Tuition & Fees: $15,470
Enrollment: 282 Coed
Affiliation or Control: Independent Non-Profit IRS Status: 501(c)3
Highest Offering: Doctorate; No Undergraduates
Program: Professional; Religious Emphasis
Accreditation: EH, THEOL

01 President ... Dr. Nick CARTER
05 Dean of the Faculty ... Dr. Sarah B. DRUMMOND
10 Vice President for Finance ... Mr. Peter CHINETTI
30 Vice Pres Institutional Advance ... Ms. Jennifer CRAIG
29 Director of the Annual Fund ... Rev. Ruth EDENS
06 Registrar ... Ms. Nayda G. AGUILA
84 Director of Recruitment ... Ms. Alison MCCARTY
08 Co-Director of the Library ... Ms. Diana YOUNT
08 Co-Director of the Library ... Mr. Jeffrey BRIGHAM
32 Dean of Students ... Dr. Nancy E. NIENHUIS
04 Assistant to the President ... Ms. Marjorie BELL
18 Director Physical Plant ... Mr. Frank CAVACO
27 Interim Director Information Office ... Mr. Brian ASSELIN
37 Coordinator Financial Aid ... Ms. Rosemary TURANO
39 Director Housing & Events Planning ... Mr. Frank NOVO

Anna Maria College (C)

50 Sunset Lane, Paxton MA 01612-1198
County: Worcester FICE Identification: 002117
Unit ID: 164492
Telephone: (508) 849-3300 Carnegie Class: Master's M
FAX Number: (508) 849-3334 Calendar System: 4/1/4
URL: www.annamaria.edu
Established: 1946 Annual Undergrad Tuition & Fees: $30,676
Enrollment: 1,422 Coed
Affiliation or Control: Roman Catholic IRS Status: 501(c)3
Highest Offering: Beyond Master's But Less Than Doctorate
Program: Liberal Arts And General; Teacher Preparatory; Professional
Accreditation: EH, ADNUR, MUS, NUR, SW

01 President ... Dr. Jack P. CALARESO
03 Executive Vice President ... Ms. Mary Louise RETELLE
10 COO Finance/Administration ... Mr. Lloyd L. HAMM, JR.
21 Controller ... Ms. Yvonnie MALCOLM
05 Vice President for Academic Affairs ... Dr. Billye W. AUCLAIR
32 Vice President for Student Affairs ... Mr. Andrew O. KLEIN
84 VP for Marketing & College Relation ... Ms. Paula L. GREEN
09 Director of Institutional Research ... Ms. Irene IRUDAYAM
06 Registrar ... Ms. Barbara ZAWALICH
30 Director Institutional Advancement ... Ms. Susan A. WOJTAS
38 Director Counseling Services ... Mr. Dennis VANASSE
23 Director of Health Services ... Ms. Linda ARONSON
08 Director of Library ... Ms. Ruth PYNE
29 Director Alumni Relations ... Ms. Ann E. THOMPSON
26 VP of Marketing/College Relations ... Ms. Paula L. GREEN
36 Director Career Counsel/Placement ... Ms. Judith M. SPARANGES
37 Director Financial Aid ... Ms. Sandra PEREIRA
13 Director of Information Technology ... Mr. Michael MIERS
04 Administrative Assistant ... Ms. Renee J. MARKIEWICZ
04 Executive Asst to the President ... Mrs. Kay PRENTISS
18 Director Physical Plant ... Mr. Mark COLLETTE
66 Director of Nursing Program ... Dr. Carol GABRIELE
39 Assoc Dean of Campus Life ... Ms. Elizabeth BONNEAU
41 Athletic Director ... Mr. Stanley VIEIRA
42 Director Campus Ministry ... Ms. Maria BARI
15 Director of Human Resources ... Ms. Lisa DRISCOLL
44 Director of Annual Fund ... Ms. Jodi WALSH
88 Dean of Mission Effectiveness ... Sr. Rollande QUINTAL

Assumption College (D)

500 Salisbury Street, Worcester MA 01609-1296
County: Worcester FICE Identification: 002118
Unit ID: 164562
Telephone: (508) 767-7000 Carnegie Class: Master's M
FAX Number: (508) 756-1780 Calendar System: Semester
URL: www.assumption.edu
Established: 1904 Annual Undergrad Tuition & Fees: $33,805
Enrollment: 2,787 Coed
Affiliation or Control: Roman Catholic IRS Status: 501(c)3
Highest Offering: Beyond Master's But Less Than Doctorate
Program: Liberal Arts And General; Teacher Preparatory; Professional
Accreditation: EH, CORE

01 President ... Dr. Francesco C. CESAREO
03 Executive Vice President ... Mr. Christian MCCARTHY
05 Provost/Academic Vice Pres ... Dr. Francis M. LAZARUS
32 Vice President for Student Affairs ... Dr. Catherine M. WOODBROOKS
30 Vice Pres Institutional Advancement ... Vacant
42 Vice President Mission ... Rev. Dennis M. GALLAGHER, AA
84 Vice Pres for Enrollment Management ... Mr. Evan E. LIPP
43 General Counsel ... Dr. Michael H. RUBINO
20 Associate Provost ... Dr. Louise CARROLL KEELEY
51 Dir of Career and Continuing Ed ... Mr. Dennis BRAUN
07 Dean of Admissions ... Ms. Kathleen M. MURPHY
20 Dean of Undergraduate Studies ... Dr. Eloise KNOWLTON
58 Dean of Graduate Studies ... Vacant
89 Associate Dean for the First Year ... Dr. Jennifer K. MORRISON
42 Director of Campus Ministry ... Mr. James RIZZA
35 Dean of Student Development ... Dr. Neil R. CASTRONOVO
08 Director of Library Services ... Ms. Doris Ann SWEET
10 Director of Finance ... Mr. John F. KOMPEL
21 Dir of Facilities Planning & Projs ... Vacant
09 Director Inst Research and Ac Asst ... Mr. Stuart J. MUNRO
58 Director Grad Enrollment/Mgmt/Svcs ... Ms. Barbara Z. BENOIT
06 Registrar ... Mr. David W. AALTO
13 Exec Dir Info Tech & Media Svcs ... Dr. Dawn M. THISTLE
15 Director of Human Resources/AAO ... Ms. Grace BLUNT
26 Director of Public Affairs ... Ms. Renee BUISSON
29 Director of Alumni Relations ... Ms. Diane LASKA-NIXON
44 Director of Annual Giving ... Mr. Timothy R. MARTIN
88 Director of Academic Support Center ... Dr. Allen A. BRUEHL
35 Dean of Campus Life ... Ms. Nancy P. CRIMMIN
39 Assoc Dean Campus Life/Dir Res Life ... Mr. Conway CAMPBELL
41 Director of Athletics ... Mr. Nichloas A. SMITH
19 Director of Public Safety ... Mr. Robert MURPHY
23 Director of Health Services ... Ms. Christine ZANFINI-PARKER
24 Director of Media Services ... Mr. Ted HALEY
37 Director of Financial Aid ... Ms. Linda MULARCZYK
88 Director of Auxiliary Services ... Mr. John LANGLOIS
25 Director of Grant Development ... Dr. Landy C. JOHNSON
35 Dean of Students ... Mr. Robert G. RAVENELLE
28 Director of Multicultural Affairs ... Vacant
96 Director of Purchasing ... Ms. Gail M. RACINE
86 Exec Asst for Govt/Cmty Relations ... Mr. Paul BELSITO

Babson College (E)

231 Forest Street, Babson Park MA 02457-0310
County: Norfolk FICE Identification: 002121
Unit ID: 164580
Telephone: (781) 235-1200 Carnegie Class: Spec/Bus
FAX Number: (781) 239-5231 Calendar System: Semester
URL: www.babson.edu
Established: 1919 Annual Undergrad Tuition & Fees: $41,888
Enrollment: 3,380 Coed
Affiliation or Control: Independent Non-Profit IRS Status: 501(c)3
Highest Offering: Master's
Program: Professional; Business Emphasis
Accreditation: EH, BUS

01 President ... Dr. Leonard A. SCHLESINGER
05 Provost ... Dr. Shahid ANSARI
11 VP of Administration ... Ms. Mary ROSE
29 VP Alumni and Friends Network ... Ms. Carol J. HACKER
30 Executive Director Development ... Ms. Diana P. ZAIS
10 VP for Finance and CFO ... Mr. Philip SHAPIRO
15 VP Human Resources ... Ms. Donna BONAPARTE
43 VP and General Counsel ... Mr. Jonathan MOLL
07 VP Enrollment & Dean of Admissions ... Mr. Grant GOSSELIN
58 Vice Provost & Dean Graduate School ... Dr. Dennis HANNO
18 Assoc VP Facilities/Services ... Mr. Shelley KAPLAN
13 Chief Information Officer ... Mr. Samuel DUNN
26 Chief Marketing Officer ... Ms. Sarah SYKORA
32 VP Student Affairs/Program Strategy ... Ms. Elizabeth NEWMAN
35 Dean of Student Affairs ... Dr. Shannon FINNING
20 Dean of Faculty ... Ms. Carolyn HOTCHKISS
100 Chief of Staff ... Ms. Tracee PETRILLO
50 Interim Dean/Undergraduate School ... Dr. Robert HALSEY
51 Dean of Babson Exec Education ... Ms. Elaine EISENMAN
37 Assoc Dean UG Sch/Dir Std Fin Svcs ... Ms. Melissa J. SHAAK
06 Registrar ... Ms. Linda KEAN
88 Exec Dir Ctr for Women's Leadership ... Dr. Susan DUFFY
07 Director Graduate Admissions ... Ms. Barbara J. SELMO
36 Dir Graduate Career Svcs ... Ms. Cheri PAULSON
36 Dir Undergraduate Career Services ... Ms. Megan HOULKER
09 Director of Institutional Research ... Ms. Anne Marie DELANEY
26 Sr Dir Institutional Communications ... Ms. Kelly LYNCH
72 Digital Marketing Director ... Mr. Gene BEGIN
26 Director Public Relations ... Mr. Michael CHMURA
21 Assoc VP Fin Services/Controller ... Mr. Richard BOWMAN
96 Director of Business Services ... Ms. Teresa PITARO
28 Chief Diversity & Inclusion Officer ... Dr. Sadie BURTON-GOSS

Bard College at Simon's Rock (F)

84 Alford Road, Great Barrington MA 01230-9702
County: Berkshire FICE Identification: 009645
Unit ID: 167792
Telephone: (413) 644-4400 Carnegie Class: Bac/Assoc
FAX Number: (413) 528-7365 Calendar System: Semester
URL: www.simons-rock.edu
Established: 1964 Annual Undergrad Tuition & Fees: $44,075
Enrollment: 349 Coed
Affiliation or Control: Independent Non-Profit IRS Status: 501(c)3
Highest Offering: Baccalaureate
Program: Liberal Arts And General
Accreditation: EH

01 President ... Dr. Leon BOTSTEIN
03 Executive Vice President ... Mr. Dimitri PAPADIMITRIOU
05 Vice President/Provost ... Dr. Peter LAIPSON
04 Asst to Vice President & Provost ... Vacant
84 VP Early College Policies/Programs ... Mr. U. Ba WIN
32 Dean of the College ... Ms. Leslie DAVIDSON
20 Dean of Academic Affairs ... Dr. Anne O'DWYER
35 Dean of Students ... Mr. Robert GRAVES
27 Director of College Relations ... Mr. Christopher SINK
06 Registrar ... Ms. Heidi ROTHBERG
08 Library Director ... Mr. Brian MIKESELL
37 Director of Financial Aid ... Ms. Ann MURTAGH GITTO
18 Director Physical Plant ... Mr. Steven CARIGNAN
10 Dir of Finance/Administration/HR ... Mr. Darwin FLINN
38 Dir Counseling Services ... Dr. Judith WIN
23 Director of Student Health Services ... Ms. Jodi TULLER, RN
90 Director of ITS ... Ms. Janice GILDAWIE
19 Director of Security ... Mr. Kenneth GEREMIA
44 Director of Annual Fund ... Mr. Richard MONTONE
41 Athletic Center Manager ... Mr. David COLLOPY
57 Division Head Arts ... Ms. Karen BEAUMONT
81 Division Head Science/Math/Computer ... Dr. Eric KRAMER
83 Division Head Social Studies ... Dr. Asma ABBAS
79 Division Head Language & Literature ... Dr. Colette VAN KERCKVOORDE

Bay Path College (G)

588 Longmeadow Street, Longmeadow MA 01106-2292
County: Hampden FICE Identification: 002122
Unit ID: 164632
Telephone: (413) 565-1000 Carnegie Class: Bac/A&S
FAX Number: (413) 565-1105 Calendar System: Semester
URL: www.baypath.edu
Established: 1897 Annual Undergrad Tuition & Fees: $28,532
Enrollment: 2,191 Female
Affiliation or Control: Independent Non-Profit IRS Status: 501(c)3
Highest Offering: Master's
Program: Liberal Arts And General; Teacher Preparatory; Professional
Accreditation: EH, #ARCPA, OT

01 President ... Dr. Carol A. LEARY
05 Vice Pres Academic Affairs/Provost ... Dr. Melissa MORRISS-OLSON
10 VP Finance/Administrative Services ... Mr. Michael GIAMPIETRO
30 VP for Institutional Advancement ... Ms. Kathleen BOURQUE
45 Vice Pres Plng/Student Development ... Ms. Caron T. HOBIN
88 VP Academic & Adminstrative Tech ... Dr. David DEMERS
04 Assistant to the President ... Ms. Barbara KOCHON
21 Associate Vice President Finance ... Ms. Donna GUERTIN
20 Founding Dean of Research ... Ms. Ann DOBMEYER
12 Director of the Burlington Campus ... Dr. Cristy SUGARMAN
12 Director CMC Campus ... Ms. Kathy JARRETT
26 Director of Communications ... Ms. Kathleen WROBLEWSKI
37 Director of Student Financial Svcs ... Ms. Stephanie KING
36 Exec Dir Career & Life Planning ... Ms. Laureen CIRILLO
07 Director of Graduate Admissions ... Ms. Lisa ADAMS
08 Director of the Library ... Mr. Michael MORAN
06 Registrar ... Ms. Laura LANDER
36 Director Career Services ... Ms. Sally J. SCHIRMER-SMITH
29 Dir of Alumni Relations ... Ms. Kathleen COTNOIR
23 Director of Health Services ... Ms. Margaret ANDERSON
19 Campus Public Safety Officer ... Mr. Vincent ROSSI
15 Director Human Resources ... Ms. Kathleen HALPIN-ROBBINS

14 Information Systems Administrator .... Mrs. Linda A. SIMONDS
18 Director Facilities/Campus Svcs .... Mr. Paul E. STANTON
41 Director of Athletics .... Mr. Steven J. SMITH
88 Dir Masters of Sci Commun/Info Mgmt .... Dr. Elizabeth RIVET
32 Director of Student Life .... Mr. Peter AXTMANN
88 Dir Business Pgms for One-Day Pgm .... Dr. Sandi COYNE
88 Dir MBA Entrepr Thnkg/Innov Practic .... Mr. Mo SATTAR
88 Dir Grad Pgms Nonprofit Mgmt/Philan .... Mr. Jeffrey GREIM
09 Dir Institutional Research & Data .... Ms. Amanda GOULD
88 Director of Life Skills Program .... Ms. Katie JONES
88 Dir Center for Teaching & Learning .... Vacant
17 Director of Clinical Education .... Mr. Anthony PELLEGRINO
96 Director of Purchasing/Office Svcs .... Mr. Ted LETH-STEENSEN
102 Dir Foundation/Corporate Relations .... Ms. Janine MCVAY
49 Dean College of Arts & Sciences .... Dr. Michael KONIG
53 Dean School of Education .... Dr. Elizabeth FLEMING
88 Dean School of Mgmt/Social Justice .... Dr. Geofrey MILLS
107 Fndng Dean Sch Adult & Profess Stds .... Dr. Gina JOSEPH-COLLINS
88 Dean of Student Success .... Mr. Dave YELLE
83 Fndg Dean Sch Health Sci/Hum Behav .... Vacant
50 Chair Business Department .... Ms. Lauren WAY
88 Chair Criminal Justice Department .... Atty. Elizabeth DINEEN
88 Chair Occupational Therapy Dept .... Dr. Lori VAUGHN
88 Chair Psychology Department .... Ms. Kathy WIEZBICKI-STEVENS
61 Chair Legal Studies Department .... Atty. John WOODRUFF
51 Dean Cont Educ & Grad Recruitment .... Ms. Diane RANALDI
79 Chair Liberal Studies .... Dr. Thomas SCHORLE
81 Chair Science .... Dr. Gina SEMPREBON
81 Chair Math & Information Systems .... Dr. Farrokh SABA
88 Chair Creative and Performing Arts .... Vacant
88 Director PA Program .... Dr. Jennifer HIXON

Bay State College (A)

122 Commonwealth Avenue, Boston MA 02116-2975
County: Suffolk FICE Identification: 003965
Unit ID: 164641
Telephone: (617) 217-9000 Carnegie Class: Assoc/PrivFP4
FAX Number: (617) 249-0400 Calendar System: Semester
URL: www.baystate.edu
Established: 1946 Annual Undergrad Tuition & Fees: $23,040
Enrollment: 1,225 Coed
Affiliation or Control: Proprietary IRS Status: Proprietary
Highest Offering: Baccalaureate
Program: Occupational; 2-Year Principally Bachelor's Creditable
Accreditation: EH, ADNUR, MAAB, PTAA

01 President .... Craig PFANNENSTIEHL
05 Vice President of Academic Affairs .... Dr. William CARROLL
32 Vice President of Student Services .... Sylvia REIFLER
10 Vice Pres Administration & Finance .... Meg TRANT
37 Director of Financial Aid .... Jeani DEVANI
84 Vice Pres of Enrollment & Marketing .... Chip BERGSTROM
06 Registrar .... Lynn DUNHAM
08 Librarian .... Jessica NEAVE
32 Chief Student Life Officer .... Michelle BROKAW
35 Director Student Affairs .... Kate ACKERMAN
07 Director of Admissions .... Kim OLDS
18 Chief Facilities/Physical Plant .... Kate AKERMAN
21 Bursar .... Jeff MCMASTER
36 Director Student Placement .... Tom CORRIGAN
38 Director Student Counseling .... Cheryl RAICHE

Becker College-Worcester (B)

61 Sever Street, Worcester MA 01609-2165
County: Worcester FICE Identification: 002123
Unit ID: 164720
Telephone: (508) 791-9241 Carnegie Class: Bac/Diverse
FAX Number: (508) 831-7505 Calendar System: Semester
URL: www.becker.edu
Established: 1887 Annual Undergrad Tuition & Fees: $30,340
Enrollment: 1,784 Coed
Affiliation or Control: Independent Non-Profit IRS Status: 501(c)3
Highest Offering: Baccalaureate
Program: 2-Year Principally Bachelor's Creditable; Liberal Arts And General
Accreditation: EH, ADNUR

01 President .... Dr. Robert E. JOHNSON
10 Senior Vice President & CFO .... Mr. David A. ELLIS
30 Vice President Advancement .... Mr. Dean HICKEY
32 Vice President of Student Affairs .... Mr. Ken CAMERON
84 Vice Pres of Enrollment Management .... Mr. Kevin MAYNE
15 Assoc Vice Pres of Human Resources . Mrs. Kathleen M. GARVEY
05 Dean of Academic Affairs .... Ms. Elizabeth FULLER
66 Dean of Nursing/Health Stds .... Ms. Linda ESPER
08 Director of the Libraries .... Mr. Garrett EASTMAN
27 Chief Information officer .... Ms. Patty PATRIA
06 Registrar .... Ms. Nikki ANDREWS
29 Assistant Director Alumni Affairs .... Ms. Caitlin VISSCHER
35 Dir of Student Services - Leicester .... Ms. Michelle FATCHERIC
38 Director of Counseling .... Ms. Wendy MILES
20 Dir Center for Academic Success .... Ms. Dolores RADLO
88 Director for BA in Design .... Mr. Paul COTNOIR
41 Director of Athletics .... Mr. Frank MILLERICK
74 Director Animal Science Programs .... Dr. James KNIGHT
27 Communications Director .... Ms. Sandy LASHIN-CUREWITZ
96 Director of Business Services .... Mr. Mike MONGEON
26 Director Marketing/Strategic Comm .... Ms. Amy DEAN
21 Controller .... Mr. Richard NAYLOR
19 Campus Police Chief .... Mr. David BOUSQUET
36 Director of Career Services .... Mr. Eric SACZAWA

Benjamin Franklin Institute of Technology (C)

41 Berkeley Street, Boston MA 02116-6296
County: Suffolk FICE Identification: 002151
Unit ID: 165884
Telephone: (617) 423-4630 Carnegie Class: Spec/Tech
FAX Number: (617) 482-3706 Calendar System: Semester
URL: www.bfit.edu
Established: 1908 Annual Undergrad Tuition & Fees: $16,950
Enrollment: 478 Coed
Affiliation or Control: Independent Non-Profit IRS Status: 501(c)3
Highest Offering: Baccalaureate
Program: Occupational; 2-Year Principally Bachelor's Creditable; Technical Emphasis
Accreditation: EH

01 President .... George C. CHRYSSIS
05 Dean of Academic Affairs .... Anthony BENOIT
32 Dean of Students .... Brian BICKNELL
10 Chief Financial Officer .... Keith DROPKIN
11 Chief Operating Officer .... Stephen LOZEN
06 Registrar .... James KLASEN
08 Librarian .... Sharon B. BONK
84 Dean of Enrollment Management .... Mike BOSCO
07 Director of Admissions .... Marvin LOISEAU
30 Chief Advancement Officer .... Vacant
20 Director of Advising .... Rachel ARNO
09 Director of Institutional Research .... James KLASEN
15 Director Human Resources .... Shelley DROPKIN
19 Director of Facilities .... Myftar MYRTAJ
36 Director Student Placement .... Phyllis MOLTA
37 Director Student Financial Aid .... Tatjana HASKAJ

Bentley University (D)

175 Forest Street, Waltham MA 02452-4705
County: Middlesex FICE Identification: 002124
Unit ID: 164739
Telephone: (781) 891-2000 Carnegie Class: Master's L
FAX Number: (781) 891-2569 Calendar System: Semester
URL: www.bentley.edu
Established: 1917 Annual Undergrad Tuition & Fees: $38,130
Enrollment: 5,565 Coed
Affiliation or Control: Independent Non-Profit IRS Status: 501(c)3
Highest Offering: Doctorate
Program: Liberal Arts And General; Professional; Business Emphasis
Accreditation: EH, BUS, BUSA

01 President .... Ms. Gloria C. LARSON
43 General Counsel .... Ms. Judith A. MALONE
102 Director Foundation Relations .... Mr. Paul K. CARBERRY
05 VP Academic Affairs/Provost .... Dr. Michael J. PAGE
10 VP Business/Finance/Treas .... Vacant
30 VP University Advancement .... Mr. John PINI
32 VP Student Affairs .... Dr. Andrew J. SHEPARDSON
13 COO & VP for Information Technology .... Ms. Traci A. LOGAN
84 VP Enrollment Management .... Ms. Joann C. MCKENNA
49 Dean of Arts and Sciences .... Dr. Daniel L. EVERETT
50 Dean of Business/McCallum Grad Sch .... Dr. Michael J. PAGE
09 Reporting Specialist/Inst Research .... Ms. Lindsey C. LEWIS
49 Assoc Dean of Arts and Sciences ...... Dr. Juliet GAINSBOROUGH
44 Senior Director of Special Gifts .... Mr. John A. PINI
29 Mng Dir Alumni/Parents & Friends .... Ms. Leigh GASPAR
27 Exec Director Mktg/Communication .... Ms. Katherine H. BLAKE
16 Exec Director of Human Resources .... Ms. Ann DEXTER
11 Assoc Dean of Administration .... Ms. Judy KAMM
21 Exec Dir Financial Operations .... Ms. Marianne F. CWALINA
06 Registrar .... Ms. Patricia A. ROGERS
22 Pres Assistant Equal Opportunity .... Dr. Earl L. AVERY
38 Assoc Dean/Dir Couns & Student Dev ..... Dr. Roger A. DANCHISE
41 Director of Athletics .... Mr. Robert A. DEFELICE
37 Exec Dir Enroll Mgmt & Fin Assist .... Ms. Donna M. KENDALL
39 Dir Housing & Student Systems .... Mr. Ronald M. ARDIZZONE
90 Dir Academic Tech/Library/Rsch Svcs .... Dr. Phillip G. KNUTEL
31 Director Service-Learning Center ...... Mr. Franklyn P. SALIMBENE
19 Executive Director of Public Safety .... Mr. Ernest H. LEFFLER
26 Director Public & Media Relations .... Ms. Michele M. WALSH
88 Mng Dir Corp Fin & Sponsored Pgms .. Mr. Leonard MORRISON
23 Asst Dean/Dir Health & Wellness .... Ms. Geraldine S. TAYLOR
25 Director of Sponsored Programs .... Ms. Mary Louise PAULI
88 Director of Conference Services .... Mr. Robert L. WEBB
07 Asst Dean/Dir of Grad Admission .... Ms. Sharon F. HILL
58 Director of MBA Programs .... Vacant
88 Senior Associate Dir Reunion Pgms .... Mr. Gary E. KELLY
18 Director Facilities Management .... Mr. Thomas W. KANE
96 Director Purchasing/Contract Svcs .... Ms. Julianne BRITT
28 Director of Diversity .... Vacant
35 Dean of Student Affairs .... Dr. J. Andrew SHEPARDSON

Berklee College of Music (E)

1140 Boylston Street, Boston MA 02215-3693
County: Suffolk FICE Identification: 002126
Unit ID: 164748
Telephone: (617) 266-1400 Carnegie Class: Spec/Arts
FAX Number: (617) 247-6878 Calendar System: Semester
URL: www.berklee.edu
Established: 1945 Annual Undergrad Tuition & Fees: $34,680
Enrollment: 4,307 Coed
Affiliation or Control: Independent Non-Profit IRS Status: 501(c)3
Highest Offering: Master's
Program: Music Emphasis
Accreditation: EH

01 President .... Roger H. BROWN
05 Sr Vice Pres Academic Affs/Provost .... Lawrence J. SIMPSON
32 Vice Pres Student Affs/Dean Stdnts .... Lawrence E. BETHUNE
102 Sr VP Institutional Advancement .... Cindy ALBERT LINK
10 Chief Financial Officer .... Richard M. HISEY
11 Vice President Administration .... John ELDERT
21 Vice President Finance .... Amelia KOCH
30 Vice Pres Institutional Advancement .... David MCKAY
13 Vice Pres Technology/Educ Outreach .... David MASH
28 Vice Pres for Cultural Diversity .... Myra HINDUS
88 Assoc VP for Administration .... Nancy EAGEN
84 Vice President Enrollment .... Mark CAMPBELL
14 Assoc VP Information Technology .... Scott V. STREET
15 Vice Pres Human Res/Diversity/Incl .... Christine M. CONNORS
88 Assoc Ed Outreach/Ex Dir BC Music .... J. Curtis WARNER, JR.
82 Asst Vice Pres Intl Programs .... Greg BADOLATO
35 Asst VP Student Affs/Student Devel .... Steven LIPMAN
20 Assoc VP Academic Affs/Assoc Prov .... Jay S. KENNEDY
27 Asst VP for Public Information .... Rob HAYES
88 Asst VP Academic Technology .... Matt MARVUGLIO
88 Dean Prof Writing Div/Music Tech .... Kari JUUSELA
53 Dean of Prof Education Division .... Darla S. HANLEY
08 Dean of Learning Resources .... Gary HAGGERTY
09 Director Inst Reseach & Assessment .... Susan Coia GAILEY
91 Director Telecom/Networking Svcs .... Norman E. SILVER
06 Registrar .... Michael HAGERTY
39 Director of Housing .... William M. MACKAY
37 Director of Financial Aid .... Julie POORMAN
38 Director of Counseling .... Sara REGAN
07 Director of Admissions .... Damien S. BRACKEN
29 Director Alumni Relations .... Karen BELL
36 Director Career Development Center .... Peter SPELLMAN
18 Assoc Director of Physical Plant .... George O'MEARA

Blessed John XXIII National Seminary (F)

558 South Avenue, Weston MA 02493-2699
County: Middlesex FICE Identification: 002202
Unit ID: 167464
Telephone: (781) 899-5500 Carnegie Class: Spec/Faith
FAX Number: (781) 899-9057 Calendar System: Semester
URL: www.blessedjohnxxiii.edu
Established: 1964 Annual Graduate Tuition & Fees: $25,500
Enrollment: 65 Male
Affiliation or Control: Roman Catholic IRS Status: 501(c)3
Highest Offering: Master's; No Undergraduates
Program: Professional
Accreditation: THEOL

01 Rector and President .... Rev. William B. PALARDY
05 Academic Dean/Registrar .... Dr. Anthony KEATY
08 Librarian .... Sr. Jacqueline MILLER
10 Business Manager .... Mrs. Kyle RYAN

Boston Architectural College (G)

320 Newbury Street, Boston MA 02115-2795
County: Suffolk FICE Identification: 003966
Unit ID: 164872
Telephone: (617) 262-5000 Carnegie Class: Spec/Arts
FAX Number: (617) 585-0111 Calendar System: Semester
URL: www.the-bac.edu
Established: 1889 Annual Undergrad Tuition & Fees: $17,330
Enrollment: 1,113 Coed
Affiliation or Control: Independent Non-Profit IRS Status: 501(c)3
Highest Offering: Master's
Program: Professional
Accreditation: EH, CIDA, LSAR

01 President/CEO .... Dr. Theodore C. LANDSMARK
03 Executive Vice President .... Mr. James DUNN
04 Assistant to the President .... Ms. Kristin KOCHANCZYK
04 Assistant to the Exec VP & Board .... Ms. Amyjo HOFNER
05 Provost .... Ms. Julia HALEVY
10 Vice President for Finance/Admin .... Ms. Kathleen C. ROOD
30 VP Institutional Advancement .... Mr. Christopher COX
107 VP of Prof & Cont Education .... Ms. Karen MUNCASTER
88 Head School of Interior Design .... Mr. Crandon GUSTAFSON
88 Head School of Landscape Architect .... Ms. Maria BELLALTA
88 Head School of Design Studies .... Mr. Donald HUNSICKER
51 Head Continuing Ed Pgms/Curriculum .... Ms. Jane TOLAND
88 Head of Practice .... Mr. Len CHARNEY
46 Dean Research and Assessment .... Mr. Herb CHILDRESS
32 Assoc Provost/Dean of Students .... Mr. Richard M. GRISWOLD
51 Director of Continuing Education .... Mr. Adam MAGUIRE
88 Director of Technical Operations .... Mr. Timothy OGAWA
88 Dir of Master's Thesis Arch .... Mr. Ian TABERNER
88 Director of Design Computing .... Mr. Diego L. MATHO
88 Director of Media Arts .... Mr. Luis MONTALVO
88 Director of Distance M Arch .... Mr. Tom PARKS
08 Library Director .... Ms. Susan A. LEWIS
06 Registrar .... Ms. Ann ROYALL
07 Director Admissions .... Mr. Richard MOYER
37 Dean Enrollment & Student Fin Svcs .... Mr. James RYAN
86 Director of External/Gov Relations .... Ms. Janet OBERTO
35 Director of Student Development .... Ms. Kara PEET
18 Director of Facilities .... Mr. Arthur BYERS
11 Dir of Administrative Operations .... Ms. Patti VAUGHN
88 Director of Academic Services .... Mr. Joshua WHITE

88 Director of Faculty Development .... Ms. Tina BLYTHE
20 Director of Educational Services .... Mr. Christopher RAICHLE
88 Director of Foundation Education .... Ms. Chala J. HADIMI
88 Head School of Architecture .... Ms. Karen L. NELSON
88 Director of Foundation Studies .... Mr. Lee PETERS
106 Director of Distance M. Arch .... Mr. Michael WOLFSON
88 Director of Practice Instruction .... Mr. David ECCLESTON
88 Director of Sustainable Design Inst .... Mr. Lance FLETCHER
88 Director of the Landscape Institute .... Ms. Heather HEIMARCK
88 Director of Global Initiatives .... Ms. Sharon MATTHEWS
88 Dir of Historic Preservation Stds .... Mr. Robert OGLE
88 Director of Liberal Studies .... Ms. Diana RAMIREZ-JASSO

Boston Baptist College (A)

950 Metropolitan Avenue, Boston MA 02136-4000
County: Suffolk FICE Identification: 032483
Unit ID: 164614
Telephone: (617) 364-3510 Carnegie Class: Spec/Faith
FAX Number: (775) 245-1498 Calendar System: Semester
URL: www.boston.edu
Established: 1976 Annual Undergrad Tuition & Fees: $14,945
Enrollment: 103 Coed
Affiliation or Control: Baptist IRS Status: 501(c)3
Highest Offering: Baccalaureate
Program: Religious Emphasis
Accreditation: TRACS

01 President .... Rev. David V. MELTON
05 Vice President for Academics .... Rev. Kenneth D. GILLMING
32 Vice President for Student Affairs .... Vacant
11 Vice President for Operations .... Mr. Randall WARD
84 Director of Enrollment Services .... Mr. Noah FOX
07 Director of Admissions .... Mrs. Karen FOX
08 Head Librarian .... Mr. Fred TATRO
31 Community Relations Officer .... Vacant

Boston College (B)

140 Commonwealth Avenue, Chestnut Hill MA 02467-3934
County: Middlesex FICE Identification: 002128
Unit ID: 164924
Telephone: (617) 552-8000 Carnegie Class: RU/H
FAX Number: (617) 552-8828 Calendar System: Semester
URL: www.bc.edu
Established: 1863 Annual Undergrad Tuition & Fees: $43,878
Enrollment: 14,640 Coed
Affiliation or Control: Roman Catholic IRS Status: 501(c)3
Highest Offering: Doctorate
Program: Liberal Arts And General; Teacher Preparatory; Professional
Accreditation: EH, THEOL, ANEST, BUS, COPSY, LAW, NURSE, SW, TEAC

01 President .... Rev. William P. LEAHY, SJ
00 Chancellor .... Rev. J. Donald MONAN, SJ
05 Provost/Dean of Faculties .... Dr. Cutberto GARZA
03 Executive Vice President .... Dr. Patrick J. KEATING
26 Senior Vice President .... Dr. James P. MCINTYRE
30 Sr Vice Pres University Advancement .... Mr. James J. HUSSON
04 Executive Assistant to President .... Mr. Kevin J. SHEA
100 Chief of Staff Provost's Office .... Dr. Anita TIEN
10 Financial Vice President/Treasurer .... Mr. Peter C. MCKENZIE
101 Vice President/University Secretary .... Mrs. Mary Lou DELONG
32 Vice Pres Student Affairs .... Dr. Patrick H. ROMBALSKI
16 Vice President for Human Resources .... Mr. Leo V. SULLIVAN
44 Vice Pres for Development .... Mr. Thomas P. LOCKERBY
13 Vice Pres Information Technology .... Mr. Michael J. BOURQUE
88 Vice Pres Univ Mission & Ministry .... Rev. John T. BUTLER, SJ
86 Vice Pres Govt/Community Affairs .... Mr. Thomas J. KEADY
18 Vice Pres Facilities Management .... Mr. Daniel F. BOURQUE
04 Vice Pres/Special Asst to President .. Rev. William B. NEENAN, SJ
45 Vice Pres Planning & Assessment .... Dr. Kelli J. ARMSTRONG
20 Vice Provost for Undergrad Affairs .... Dr. Donald L. HAFNER
58 Vice Provost Graduate Education .... Dr. Gilda MORELLI
46 Vice Provost for Research .... Dr. Larry MCLAUGHLIN
20 Vice Provost for Faculties .... Dr. Patricia DE LEEUW
14 Assoc VP Information Technology .... Mrs. Mary C. CORCORAN
44 Assoc VP Capital Giving/Development .... Mr. Matthew EYNON
20 Assoc Vice Provost Undergrad Acad .... Dr. J. Joseph BURNS
18 Assoc VP Capital Projects .... Ms. Mary S. NARDONE
29 Associate VP for Alumni Relations .... Mr. John A. FEUDO
49 Dean College Arts & Sciences .... Dr. David QUIGLEY
87 Dean Col Adv Stds/Summer Session .... Rev. James R. BURNS
53 Interim Dean School of Education .... Ms. Maureen E. KENNY
61 Dean Law School .... Mr. Vincent D. ROUGEAU
50 Dean School of Management .... Dr. Andrew C. BOYNTON
66 Dean of School of Nursing .... Dr. Susan GENNARO
70 Dean Grad School of Social Work .... Dr. Alberto A. GODENZI
84 Dean of Enrollment Management .... Mr. Robert S. LAY
35 Sr Assoc Dean Student Development .... Mr. Paul J. CHEBATOR
08 University Librarian Emeritus .... Dr. Thomas WALL
90 Exec Director Academic Technology .... Mrs. Rita OWENS
28 Exec Dir Institutional Diversity .... Mr. Richard P. JEFFERSON
06 Exec Director Student Services .... Dr. Louise M. LONABOCKER
07 Director of Admission .... Mr. John L. MAHONEY, JR.
26 Exec Dir/Special Asst to Pres/Mktg .... Mr. Ben BIRNBAUM
27 Dir Office of News & Public Affairs .... Mr. John B. DUNN
102 Director Corp & Foundation Rels .... Mrs. Ginger K. SAARIAHO
41 Director Athletic Department .... Mr. Eugene B. DEFILIPPO
36 Director of Career Center .... Ms. Theresa A. HARRIGAN
42 Director Campus Ministry .... Rev. Anthony PENNA
31 Director of Community Affairs .... Mr. William R. MILLS
38 Director Univ Counseling Services . Dr. Thomas P. MCGUINNESS
37 Director Financial Aid .... Mrs. Mary S. MCGRANAHAN
23 Director Health Services .... Dr. Thomas I. NARY
39 Director of Residential Life .... Mr. George A. AREY
25 Dir Pre-Award Admin Sponsored Pgms .... Mrs. Sharon COMVALIUS-GODDARD
25 Dir Post-Award Admin Sponsored Pgms .... Ms. Susan ZIPKIN
19 Dir Public Safety/Chief of Police .... Mr. John M. KING
40 Director Bookstore .... Mr. Robert STEWART
43 General Counsel .... Mr. Joseph M. HERLIHY
24 Director Media Technology Services .... Mr. David CORKUM
85 Director International Programs .... Dr. Bernd WIDDIG
92 Director Honors Program A & S .... Dr. Mark F. O'CONNOR
93 Director AHANA Student Programs .... Dr. Ines MATURANA SENDOYA
86 Director Governmental Relations .... Ms. Jeanne LEVESQUE
94 Director of Women's Studies .... Dr. Sharlene HESSE-BIBER
96 Director Procurement Services .... Mr. Paul MCGOWAN
09 Director Institutional Research .... Dr. Jessica A. GREENE

The Boston Conservatory (C)

8 The Fenway, Boston MA 02215-4006
County: Suffolk FICE Identification: 002129
Unit ID: 164933
Telephone: (617) 536-6340 Carnegie Class: Spec/Arts
FAX Number: (617) 912-9101 Calendar System: Semester
URL: www.bostonconservatory.edu
Established: 1867 Annual Undergrad Tuition & Fees: $39,660
Enrollment: 730 Coed
Affiliation or Control: Independent Non-Profit IRS Status: 501(c)3
Highest Offering: Master's
Program: Teacher Preparatory; Professional; Music Emphasis
Accreditation: EH, MUS

01 President .... Mr. Richard ORTNER
05 VP Academic Affairs/Dean/CAO .... Dr. Patricia HOY
10 Chief Financial Officer .... Mr. Charles P. PETIT
11 VP for Finance and Planning .... Mr. Eric NORMAN
32 Vice Pres Stdnt Affs/Dean Students .... Dr. Carmen S. GRIGGS
20 Assoc Dean Academic Operations .... Mr. James O'DELL
07 Director of Admissions .... Ms. Meghan CADWALLADER
30 Director of Development .... Ms. Eileen M. MENY
64 Director Music Division .... Dr. Karl PAULNACK
88 Director Dance Division .... Ms. Cathy YOUNG
57 Director Theater Division .... Mr. Neil DONOHOE
06 Registrar .... Mr. Gregory KARAS
37 Director Student Financial Aid .... Ms. Nicole BRENNAN
08 Director of the Library .... Ms. Jennifer HUNT
13 Director of Information Technology .... Mr. Bob XAVIER
18 Director Facilities & Plant .... Mr. Dan CORSETTI
39 Asst Dean Housing & Resident Life .... Ms. Kim RUSSELL
26 Director Marketing & Communications .... Ms. Karen FOGERTY
85 Director International Student Svcs .... Mr. Gordon HOMANN
15 Director Human Resources .... Mr. Rob ELKIN
29 Dir of Alumni and Parent Relations .... Ms. Tracy SMITH
35 Dir of Student & Community Programs .... Ms. Kim HAACK
38 Director of Counseling .... Ms. Melanie DUARTE

Boston Graduate School of Psychoanalysis (D)

1581 Beacon Street, Brookline MA 02446-4602
County: Norfolk FICE Identification: 031943
Unit ID: 164915
Telephone: (617) 277-3915 Carnegie Class: Spec/Health
FAX Number: (617) 277-0312 Calendar System: Semester
URL: www.bgsp.edu
Established: 1973 Annual Graduate Tuition & Fees: $13,920
Enrollment: 179 Coed
Affiliation or Control: Independent Non-Profit IRS Status: 501(c)3
Highest Offering: Doctorate; No Undergraduates
Program: Professional
Accreditation: EH

01 President .... Dr. Jane SYNDER
05 Vice President/Provost .... Dr. Jane SNYDER
10 Vice President Finance .... Dr. Carol PANETTA
58 Dean of Graduate Studies .... Dr. Lynn PERLMAN
07 Director of Admissions .... Ms. Jill SOLOMON
26 Director of Marketing .... Ms. Paula BERMAN
06 Registrar .... Ms. Allison WILLIAMS
37 Director of Financial Aid .... Ms. Stephanie WOOLBERT
21 Controller .... Ms. Gayle DOLAN

Boston University (E)

One Silber Way, Boston MA 02215-1700
County: Suffolk FICE Identification: 002130
Unit ID: 164988
Telephone: (617) 353-2000 Carnegie Class: RU/VH
FAX Number: (617) 353-2053 Calendar System: Semester
URL: www.bu.edu
Established: 1839 Annual Undergrad Tuition & Fees: $42,994
Enrollment: 33,116 Coed
Affiliation or Control: Independent Non-Profit IRS Status: 501(c)3
Highest Offering: Doctorate
Program: Liberal Arts And General; Teacher Preparatory; Professional
Accreditation: EH, BUS, CEA, CLPSY, DENT, DIETD, DIETI, ENG, HSA, IPSY, LAW, MED, MUS, OT, PH, PTA, SP, SW, THEOL

01 President .... Robert A. BROWN
05 University Provost .... Jean MORRISON
17 Provost Medical Campus .... Karen H. ANTMAN
11 Vice Pres Administrative Services .... Peter FIEDLER
10 Senior Vice Pres/CFO & Treasurer .... Martin J. HOWARD
88 VP/Assoc Provost Global Programs .... Willis G. WANG
30 Senior VP Devel/Alumni Relations .... Scott G. NICHOLS
84 VP Enrollment & Student Affairs .... Laurie POHL
86 Vice Pres Government & Cmty Affairs .... Edward M. KING
18 Senior Vice President Operations .... Gary W. NICKSA
43 Sr VP/General Counsel & Board Secy .... Todd L C. KLIPP
90 VP Information Systems & Technology .... Tracy SCHROEDER
26 Senior VP Marketing & Comm .... Stephen P. BURGAY
88 Assoc VP BUMC Fin & Business Affs .... William GASPER
21 Vice President Administration .... Peter SMOKOWSKI
21 Sr Assoc Vice Pres Financial Affs .... John IMBERGAMO
18 Sr Assoc VP Real Estate Management .... Michael DONOVAN
29 VP Development & Alumni Rels .... Steven A. HALL
18 Assoc VP Facilities Mgmt & Planning .... Thomas DALEY
25 Assoc Provost Sponsored Programs .... Joan KIRKENDALL
46 VP & Assoc Provost Research .... Andrei E. RUCKENSTEIN
88 Assoc VP Global Leadership .... Christopher J. MENARD
44 Assoc VP Sch-based Dev & Alum Rels .... Adam K. WISE
15 Chief Human Resouce Officer .... Diane P. TUCKER
32 Dean of Students .... Kenneth ELMORE
42 Dean of Marsh Chapel .... Robert A. HILL
55 Dean Metropolitan Col/Extended Educ .... Jay HALFOND
73 Dean School of Theology .... Mary E. MOORE
49 Dean Col/Grad Sch Arts & Sciences .... Virginia SAPIRO
61 Dean of School of Law .... Maureen A. O'ROURKE
63 Dean School of Medicine .... Karen H. ANTMAN
52 Dean Sch of Dental Medicine .... Jeffery W. HUTTER
54 Dean College of Engineering .... Kenneth R. LUTCHEN
70 Dean School of Social Work .... Gail STEKETEE
60 Dean College of Communication .... Thomas FIEDLER
53 Dean School of Education .... Hardin COLEMAN
57 Dean College of Fine Arts .... Benjamin JUAREZ
76 Dean Health & Rehab Science .... Gloria S. WATERS
50 Dean School Management .... Kenneth FREEMAN
97 Dean College General Studies .... Linda S. WELLS
69 Dean School of Public Health .... Robert F. MEENAN
88 Dean School of Hospitality Admin .... Christopher MULLER
87 Assistant Dean Summer Term .... Donna SHEA
88 Dir University Professors Program .... Sir Hans KORNBERG
06 Assistant VP & Registrar .... Jeffrey VON MUNKWITZ-SMITH
68 Exec Director Physical Education .... Timothy MOORE
41 Exec Dir Department of Athletics .... Jack PARKER
08 Director Mugar Library .... Robert HUDSON
37 Director Financial Assistance .... Christine MCGUIRE
39 Director of Housing .... Marc ROBILLARD
07 Exec Dir Undergraduate Admissions .... Kelly WALTER
23 Director Student Health Services .... David R. MCBRIDE
09 Exec Dir of Institutional Research .... Melanie MADAIO-O'BRIEN
10 Chief Investment Officer .... Lila HUNNEWELL
27 Asst VP Strategic Communication .... Amy HOOK
44 Director of Annual Giving .... Daniel ALLENBY
85 Director Intl Student/Scholars Ofc .... Jeanne KELLEY
19 Chief of Police .... Thomas G. ROBBINS
36 Director Career Planning Services .... Kimberley DELGIZZO
35 Director of Student Activities .... Melinda STROH
96 Director Sourcing and Procurement .... Richard STACK
28 Director Thurman Center .... Katherine KENNEDY
88 Asst Dean/Director Judicial Affairs .... Daryl DELUCA
39 Asst Dean/Director Residence Life .... David ZAMOJSKI
88 Director of Stewardship DAR .... Maureen D. DONNELLY
38 Asst Dir Wellness & Residential Ed .... Laura A. DEVEAU
100 VP & Chief of Staff to President .... Douglas SEARS
45 VP Budget and Planning .... Derek HOWE
20 Assoc Provost Strategic Initiatives .... Nicole HAWKS
20 Assoc Provost for Faculty Affairs .... Julie SANDELL
20 Assoc Provost Budget & Planning .... Christopher GOSS
20 Assoc Provost Undergraduate Affairs .... Elizabeth BERGMANN LOIZECEUX

Brandeis University (F)

415 South Street, Waltham MA 02454-9110
County: Middlesex FICE Identification: 002133
Unit ID: 165015
Telephone: (781) 736-2000 Carnegie Class: RU/VH
FAX Number: (781) 736-8699 Calendar System: Semester
URL: www.brandeis.edu
Established: 1948 Annual Undergrad Tuition & Fees: $44,294
Enrollment: 5,828 Coed
Affiliation or Control: Independent Non-Profit IRS Status: 501(c)3
Highest Offering: Doctorate
Program: Liberal Arts And General; Professional
Accreditation: EH, BUS

00 Chairman of the Board .... Mr. Malcolm SHERMAN
01 President .... Mr. Frederick M. LAWRENCE
04 Executive Asst to the President .... Ms. Celia D. HARRIS
05 Provost/Sr Vice Pres for Acad Affs .... Dr. Steve GOLDSTEIN
20 Vice Provost for Academic Affairs .... Dr. Michaele WHELAN
30 Sr Vice Pres Inst Advancement .... Ms. Nancy K. WINSHIP
29 Vice President of Development .... Mr. Myles E. WEISENBERG
102 Sr Director Corporate & Foundations .... Mr. Robert SILK
84 Sr Vice Pres for Students/Enroll .... Mr. Andrew FLAGEL
26 Sr VP Communication & External Affs .... Vacant
43 Sr VP and General Counsel .... Ms. Judith R. SIZER
100 Chief of Staff .... Mr. David A. BUNIS
88 Chief Investment Officer .... Mr. Nicholas WARREN
10 Sr VP for Finance and CFO .... Ms. Frances DROLETTE
90 VP for IT/Vice Provost for Library .... Mr. John UNSWORTH

11 Senior VP for Administration Mr. Mark COLLINS
18 Associate VP for Facilities Mr. Peter C. SHIELDS
19 Director of Public Safety Mr. Edward CALLAHAN
15 Vice Pres Human Resources Mr. Scot R. BEMIS
18 VP for Planning & Inst Research Mr. Dan FELDMAN
58 Exec Director Div Grad Prof Studies Ms. Sybil SMITH
49 Dean of Arts & Sciences Dr. Susan J. BIREN
58 Dean Grad School/Arts & Sciences Dr. Malcolm W. WATSON
70 Dean Heller School Social Pol & Mgt Dr. Lisa LYNCH
50 Dean International Business School Dr. Bruce R. MAGID
32 Assoc VP & Dean of Student Life Mr. Rick SAWYER
35 Associate Dean of Student Life Mr. Jamele ADAMS
35 Associate Dean of Student Life Ms. Maggie BALCH
41 Director of Athletics Ms. Sheryl A. SOUSA
07 Director of Admissions Mr. Mark SPENCER
37 Dean of Student Financial Svcs Mr. Peter M. GIUMETTE
08 Chief University Librarian Vacant
06 University Registrar Dr. Mark S. HEWITT
88 Asst Provost for Research Admin Mr. Paul O'KEEFE
36 Director Hiatt Career Center Mr. Joseph DUPONT
38 Director Psych Counseling Center Mr. Robert Y. BERLIN
96 Director of Procurement Mr. Edward PERKINS
42 Coordinator Interfaith Chaplaincy Fr. Walter CUENIN
104 Asst Dean/Director of Study Abroad Mr. J. Scott VAN DER MEID

Cambridge College (A)

1000 Massachusetts Avenue, Cambridge MA 02138-5304
County: Middlesex FICE Identification: 021829
Unit ID: 165167
Telephone: (617) 868-1000 Carnegie Class: Master's L
FAX Number: (617) 349-3545 Calendar System: Trimester
URL: www.cambridgecollege.edu
Established: 1971 Annual Undergrad Tuition & Fees: $13,140
Enrollment: 4,732 Coed
Affiliation or Control: Independent Non-Profit IRS Status: 501(c)3
Highest Offering: Doctorate
Program: Liberal Arts And General; Professional
Accreditation: EH, @TEAC

01 President Deborah JACKSON
05 Provost Dr. Elwood ROBINSON
10 Interim CFO/VP of Finance Helen OULETTE
43 General Counsel R. Yvette CLARK
30 Vice Pres Institutional Advancement Vacant
16 Director of Human Resources Laura GEORGE
37 Director of Financial Aid Frank LAUDER
21 Controller Lynn WOOD
06 Registrar Mark SLAWSON
84 Dean of Enrollment Management Elaine LAPOMARDO
90 Director of Information Technology Richard PAPAZIAN
18 Director of Business Operations Michael PIERCE
12 Director Chesapeake VA Reg Ctr Dr. Ella BENSON
12 Director of Merrimack Valley Center Linda RICHELSON
12 Director Springfield Center Teresa (Terrie) FORTE
12 Director Inland Empire Center Dr. Ellie KAUCHER
12 Director Puerto Rico Center Dr. Jose R. IRIZARRY
12 Director Memphis Regional Center Karen STREETER
12 Director Augusta Regional Center Sharlotte EVANS
56 Exec Dir Regional Centers/NITE Dr. Kristin POPPO

Clark University (B)

950 Main Street, Worcester MA 01610-1477
County: Worcester FICE Identification: 002139
Unit ID: 165334
Telephone: (508) 793-7711 Carnegie Class: RU/H
FAX Number: (508) 793-7780 Calendar System: Semester
URL: www.clarku.edu
Established: 1887 Annual Undergrad Tuition & Fees: $38,100
Enrollment: 3,462 Coed
Affiliation or Control: Independent Non-Profit IRS Status: 501(c)3
Highest Offering: Doctorate
Program: Liberal Arts And General; Teacher Preparatory; Professional
Accreditation: EH, BUS, CLPSY

01 President Dr. David P. ANGEL
03 Executive Vice President Mr. James E. COLLINS
05 Provost & Vice Pres Academic Affs Dr. Davis BAIRD
30 Vice Pres University Advancement Mr. C. Andrew MCGADNEY
26 Vice Pres Marketing & Communication Ms. Paula DAVID
10 Vice President Budget & Planning Ms. Andrea P. MICHAELS
13 Vice Pres for Information Tech/CIO Ms. Pennie TURGEON
86 VP Government/Cmty Affs/Campus Svcs Mr. John FOLEY
32 VP Student Affairs/Dean of Students Ms. Denise M. DARRIGRAND
46 Assoc Provost/Dean of Research Dr. Nancy BUDWIG
58 Assoc Provost/Dean Graduate Studies Dr. William FISHER
49 Assoc Provost/Dean of College Dr. Mary-Ellen BOYLE
35 Associate Dean of Students Mr. Jason ZELESKY
38 Associate Dean Academic Advising Dr. Kevin M. MCKENNA
50 Dean Graduate School Mgmt Dr. Catherine USOFF
51 Dean Col Profess & Cont Education Dr. Thomas P. MASSEY
07 Dean of Admissions & Financial Aid Mr. Donald HONEMAN
37 Director of Financial Aid Ms. Mary Ellen SEVERANCE
08 University Librarian Dr. Gwendolynne ARTHUR
21 Controller Ms. Katherine CANNON
36 Director of Career Services Mr. David MCDONOUGH
29 Dir of Stewardship/Alumni Affairs Ms. Aixa L. KIDD
06 Registrar Ms. Rebecca HUNTER
15 Dir of Human Resources/Affirm Act Ms. Lynn F. OLSON
18 Director of Physical Plant Mr. Michael DAWLEY

41 Director of Athletics Mr. Sean SULLIVAN
19 Chief of Campus Police Mr. Stephen P. GOULET
23 Director of Health Service Ms. Robin MCNALLY
04 Assistant to the President Ms. Joanne MILLER
21 Business Manager Mr. Paul WYKES

College of the Holy Cross (C)

1 College Street, Worcester MA 01610-2322
County: Worcester FICE Identification: 002141
Unit ID: 166124
Telephone: (508) 793-2011 Carnegie Class: Bac/A&S
FAX Number: (508) 793-3030 Calendar System: Semester
URL: www.holycross.edu
Established: 1843 Annual Undergrad Tuition & Fees: $43,400
Enrollment: 2,872 Coed
Affiliation or Control: Roman Catholic IRS Status: 501(c)3
Highest Offering: Baccalaureate
Program: Liberal Arts And General
Accreditation: EH, THEA

01 President Rev. Philip L. BOROUGHS, SJ
03 Senior Vice President Dr. Frank VELLACCIO
10 Treasurer/VP Admin & Finance Mr. Michael LOCHHEAD
10 Chief Investment Officer Mr. Timothy JARRY
88 Dir of Finance/Asst Treasurer Ms. Dottie HAUVER
32 VP Student Affairs/Dean of Students Ms. Jacqueline D. PETERSON
30 VP for Development/Alumni Relations Ms. Tracy BARLOK
05 VP Academic Affairs/Dean of College Dr. Timothy R. AUSTIN
88 Vice President for Mission Rev. Paul F. HARMAN, SJ
20 Associate Dean of the College Ms. Margaret FREIJE
20 Associate Dean of the College Dr. Amy WOLFSON
06 Registrar Ms. Patricia RING
07 Director of Admissions Ms. Ann B. MCDERMOTT
08 Director of Library Services Ms. Kathleen CARNEY
37 Director of Financial Aid Ms. Lynne M. MYERS
25 Director Grants/Found & Corp Giving Dr. Charles S. WEISS
42 Director Ofc of College Chaplains Ms. Marybeth KEARNS-BARRETT
71 Director Ctr Interdisc/Spec Studies Dr. Richard E. MATLAK
36 Director of Career Planning Ms. Amy MURPHY
13 Director Information Tech Services Ms. Ellen J. KEOHANE
26 Director of Public Affairs Ms. Ellen RYDER
29 Director of Alumni Relations Ms. Kristyn M. DYER
19 Director of Public Safety Mr. Robert HART
35 Director of Campus Center Mr. Jeremiah O'CONNOR
16 Human Resources Director Ms. Donna C. WRENN
18 Director of Physical Plant Mr. Scott M. MERRILL
41 Director of Athletics Mr. Richard M. REGAN
21 Controller Mr. Charles F. ESTAPHAN
45 Director of Planning Ms. Judy A. HANNUM
38 Director Counseling Center Dr. Paul GALVINHILL
23 Director Student Health Services Ms. Martha SULLIVAN
11 Director Administrative Services Mr. William J. CONLEY
96 Manager of Purchasing Ms. Joan E. ANDERSON
09 Ofc of Assessment/Research Ms. Denise BELL
86 Dir of Government/Cmty Relations Mr. Edward AUGUSTUS

College of Our Lady of the Elms (D)

291 Springfield Street, Chicopee MA 01013-2839
County: Hampden FICE Identification: 002140
Unit ID: 167394
Telephone: (413) 594-2761 Carnegie Class: Bac/Diverse
FAX Number: (413) 592-4871 Calendar System: Semester
URL: www.elms.edu
Established: 1928 Annual Undergrad Tuition & Fees: $29,112
Enrollment: 1,469 Coed
Affiliation or Control: Roman Catholic IRS Status: 501(c)3
Highest Offering: Master's
Program: Liberal Arts And General; Teacher Preparatory; Professional
Accreditation: EH, IACBE, NURSE, SW

01 President Dr. Mary REAP
05 Vice President of Academic Affairs Dr. Walter C. BREAU
10 Vice Pres Finance/Administration Mr. Brian E. DOHERTY
32 Vice Pres of Student Affairs Mr. John KELLER
30 Vice Pres of Instl Advancement Mr. Kevin M. EDWARDS
35 Associate Dean of Students Ms. Teresa WINTERS-DUNN
20 Assoc Acad Dean Grad Studies/CE Dr. Elizabeth HUKOWICZ
44 Director of Development Ms. Bernadette NOWAKOWSKI
07 Director of Admissions Mr. Joseph WAGNER
42 Director of Campus Ministry Sr. Carol ALLAN
06 Registrar Ms. Frances BLISS
08 Director of Library Vacant
18 Director of Campus Operations Mr. Michael SULLIVAN
19 Director of Public Safety Mr. Michael SULLIVAN
26 Director of Institutional Marketing Ms. Nancy FARRELL
37 Director of Financial Aid Ms. Heidi SHAW
36 Director of Career Services Ms. Nancy DAVIS
14 Director Information Technology Mr. Tom MANLEY
38 Director Student Counseling Svcs Mr. John COAN
41 Director of Athletics Vacant
15 Director Human Resources/Personnel Ms. Marie PHILLIPS
35 Director of Student Activities Vacant
85 Dir of ESL/International Program Ms. Joyce HAMPTON

Conway School of Landscape Design (E)

332 S Deerfield Road, PO Box 179,
Conway MA 01341-0179
County: Franklin FICE Identification: 022743
Unit ID: 165495
Telephone: (413) 369-4044 Carnegie Class: Spec/Arts
FAX Number: (413) 369-4032 Calendar System: Trimester
URL: www.csld.edu
Established: 1972 Annual Graduate Tuition & Fees: $31,450
Enrollment: 12 Coed
Affiliation or Control: Independent Non-Profit IRS Status: 501(c)3
Highest Offering: Master's; No Undergraduates
Program: Professional
Accreditation: EH

01 President/Director Mr. Paul C. HELLMUND
32 Assoc Dir Student Svcs/Fin/Fac Mr. David NORDSTROM
07 Assoc Dir Admissions/Comm Ms. Mollie BABIZE
30 Director of Development Ms. Lynn BARCLAY

Curry College (F)

1071 Blue Hill Avenue, Milton MA 02186-2395
County: Norfolk FICE Identification: 002143
Unit ID: 165529
Telephone: (617) 333-0500 Carnegie Class: Master's M
FAX Number: (617) 979-3540 Calendar System: Semester
URL: www.curry.edu
Established: 1879 Annual Undergrad Tuition & Fees: $33,465
Enrollment: 2,959 Coed
Affiliation or Control: Independent Non-Profit IRS Status: 501(c)3
Highest Offering: Master's
Program: Liberal Arts And General; Professional
Accreditation: EH, NURSE

01 President Mr. Kenneth K. QUIGLEY, JR.
05 Chief Academic Officer Dr. David POTASH
30 Vice Pres Institutional Advancement Mr. Christopher LAWSON
10 Chief Financial Officer Mr. Richard F. SULLIVAN, JR.
07 Dean of Admission Ms. Jane P. FIDLER
32 Dean of Student Affairs Ms. Maryellen M. KILEY
45 Dean for Institutional Planning Dr. Susan W. PENNINI
04 Assistant to the President Ms. Amy M. BIANCHI
08 Librarian Mr. Edward TALLENT
14 Chief Information Officer Mr. Dennis THIBEAULT
15 Director of Human Resources Ms. Mary E. DUNN
20 Associate Dean Academic Affairs Vacant
84 Asst Dean Enrollment Mgt/Registrar Ms. Sally A. BUCKLEY
18 Chief Facilities/Physical Plant Mr. Robert G. O'CONNELL
26 Chief Public Relations Officer Ms. Frances L. JACKSON
29 Director of Alumni Relations Vacant
36 Director of Student Placement Ms. Maureen A. ASHBURN
37 Dir of Student Financial Services Ms. Stephanny J. ELIAS
38 Director of Student Counseling Dr. Alison W. MARKSON
51 Dean of Continuing Ed/Graduate Stds Dr. Ruth D. SHERMAN

Dean College (G)

99 Main Street, Franklin MA 02038-1994
County: Norfolk FICE Identification: 002144
Unit ID: 165574
Telephone: (508) 541-1508 Carnegie Class: Assoc/PrivNFP4
FAX Number: (508) 541-8726 Calendar System: Semester
URL: www.dean.edu
Established: 1865 Annual Undergrad Tuition & Fees: $31,950
Enrollment: 1,396 Coed
Affiliation or Control: Independent Non-Profit IRS Status: 501(c)3
Highest Offering: Baccalaureate
Program: 2-Year Principally Bachelor's Creditable; Liberal Arts And General
Accreditation: EH

01 President Dr. Paula M. ROONEY
04 Assistant to the President Ms. Sandra CAIN
05 Vice President Academic Affairs Dr. Linda RAGOSTA
84 VP Enrollment Services/Marketing Mr. John MARCUS
10 Vice Pres Financial Svcs/Treasurer Mr. Dan MODELANE
32 VP Student Development & Retention Ms. Cindy T. KOZIL
15 Vice President Human Resources Mr. Peter MARTEL
30 Vice Pres Institutional Advancement Ms. Coleen RESNICK
27 VP/Chief Information Officer Mr. Darrell KULESZA
44 Assoc Vice Pres Leadership Gifts Mr. Peter MOLLO
21 Assoc VP/Controller/Asst Treasurer Ms. Kathleen MCGUIRE
07 Asst VP Enrollment/Dean Admission Mr. James FOWLER
20 Asst VP Acad Supp Svcs/Career Plng Ms. Wendy ADLER
20 Asst Vice Pres Academic Affairs Ms. Melissa P. READ
45 Asst VP Capital Planning/Facilities Mr. Brian KELLY
29 Asst VP Alumni Pgms/Camp Spec Event Ms. Maureen RIDINGS
35 Dean of Students Mr. David DRUCKER
51 Assoc Dean Professional/Cont Stds Ms. Ida M. LAMOTHE
26 Director Marketing/Communications Mr. Gregg CHALK
06 Registrar Mr. Daniel O'DRISCOLL
19 Dir Public Safety/Risk Management Mr. Kenneth F. CORKRAN
08 Director of the Library Mr. Ted BURKE
41 Athletic Director Mr. John A. JACKSON
39 Director Residence Life Ms. Shannon OVERCASH
35 Dir Student Activities/Orientation Ms. Jennifer BOTHWELL
40 Director of Bookstore Ms. Kathleen EKBOLM
37 Director of Financial Aid Ms. Jenny AGUIAR
84 Director Enrollment Operations Ms. Kathleen RYAN

Eastern Nazarene College (A)

23 E Elm Avenue, Quincy MA 02170-2999
County: Norfolk FICE Identification: 002145
Unit ID: 165644
Telephone: (617) 745-3000 Carnegie Class: Bac/A&S
FAX Number: (617) 745-3907 Calendar System: 4/1/4
URL: www.enc.edu
Established: 1918 Annual Undergrad Tuition & Fees: $25,300
Enrollment: 1,036 Coed
Affiliation or Control: Church Of The Nazarene IRS Status: 501(c)3
Highest Offering: Master's
Program: Liberal Arts And General; Teacher Preparatory
Accreditation: EH, SW

01 President .... Dr. Corlis A. MCGEE
05 Provost & Dean of the College .... Dr. Timothy T. WOOSTER
10 Vice President Financial Affairs .... Mr. Jan G. WEISEN
32 Vice Pres Student Devel & Retention .... Dr. Vernon L. WESLEY
07 VP of Admissions/Financial Aid .... Dr. Timothy T. WOOSTER
30 Vice President Inst Advancement .... Dr. Scott TURCOTT
32 Assoc Dean Students/Residence Life .... Vacant
06 Registrar .... Mrs. Margaret BALLARD
37 Director Financial Aid .... Mr. Lerick FANFANX
08 Director of Library Services .... Ms. Susan J. WATKINS
19 Director Safety/Security/Risk Mgmt .... Mr. Jan G. WEISEN
38 Dir Counseling & Career Services .... Mr. Bradford E. THORNE
58 Dean of Div of Graduate/Prof Stds .... Vacant
41 Athletic Director .... Dr. Nancy DETWILER
18 Director of Facilities .... Mr. Jim HARDING
45 Director of Instructional Resources .... Ms. Patricia VASQUEZ
21 Controller .... Mrs. Myrna GIBERTSON
42 Chaplain/VP Spiritual Development .... Dr. Corey MACPHERSON
22 Director Human Resources .... Mrs. Francine WRIGHT
40 Director Bookstore .... Vacant
13 Director of Information Technology .... Mr. Charles BURT
58 Director Adult/Graduate Studies .... Dr. William DRISCOLL
04 Admin Assistant to the President .... Mrs. Sheryl WEISEN
39 Dir Resident Life/Multicultural Aff .... Mr. Robert BENJAMIN

Emerson College (B)

120 Boylston Street, Boston MA 02116-4624
County: Suffolk FICE Identification: 002146
Unit ID: 165662
Telephone: (617) 824-8500 Carnegie Class: Master's L
FAX Number: (617) 824-8511 Calendar System: Semester
URL: www.emerson.edu
Established: 1880 Annual Undergrad Tuition & Fees: $33,568
Enrollment: 4,037 Coed
Affiliation or Control: Independent Non-Profit IRS Status: 501(c)3
Highest Offering: Doctorate
Program: Liberal Arts And General; Professional
Accreditation: EH, SP

01 President .... Mr. M. Lee PELTON
43 Vice President & General Counsel .... Ms. Christine HUGHES
11 Vice President for Admin & Finance .... Ms. Maureen MURPHY
05 Vice President for Academic Affairs .... Dr. Linda MOORE
13 VP for Information Technology .... Dr. William GILLIGAN
26 Vice Pres Communications/Marketing .... Mr. Andrew TIEDEMANN
28 VP Diversity & Inclusion .... Ms. Sylvia SPEARS
10 AVP for Finance/Int Chf Fin Ofcr .... Mr. John DONOHOE
15 Assoc Vice Pres for Human Resources .... Ms. Alexa JACKSON
29 AVP Inst Advance/Dir Alumni Affrs .... Ms. Barbara RUTBERG
86 Assoc Vice Pres Govt/Community Rels .... Ms. Margaret Ann INGS
58 Dean Grad Studies/AVP Acad Affairs .... Dr. Richard ZAUFT
32 Dean of Students .... Dr. Ronald LUDMAN
107 Exec Director Professional Studies .... Mr. Henry W. ZAPPALA
08 Exec Director of Library Services .... Mr. Robert FLEMING
07 Director of Graduate Admission .... Ms. Kristin BURKE
36 Director of Career Services .... Ms. Carol SPECTOR
38 Director Counseling Center .... Dr. Cheryl ROSENTHAL
19 Director of Public Safety .... Mr. Robert SMITH
41 Int Director Athletics/Head Coach .... Mr. Stan NANCE
85 Director International Student Affs .... Ms. Virga MOHSINI
96 Director Purchasing/Risk Management .... Ms. Margaret ROGAN
39 Assoc Dean Housing/Residence Life .... Mr. David W. HADEN
21 Controller .... Vacant
06 Registrar .... Mr. William DEWOLF
42 Chair Center for Spiritual Life .... Mr. Albert S. AXELRAD
101 Exec Asst to the Board of Trustees .... Ms. Anne SHAUGHNESSY
18 Int Assoc Director of Facilities .... Mr. Joseph KNOLL
37 Director Financial Aid .... Ms. Kerri JACOBS
07 Sr Assoc Director of Admissions .... Ms. Sara CUMMINGS
09 Director of Institutional Research .... Mr. Eric SYKES

Emmanuel College (C)

400 The Fenway, Boston MA 02115-5798
County: Suffolk FICE Identification: 002147
Unit ID: 165671
Telephone: (617) 277-9340 Carnegie Class: Master's S
FAX Number: (617) 735-9877 Calendar System: Semester
URL: www.emmanuel.edu
Established: 1919 Annual Undergrad Tuition & Fees: $33,650
Enrollment: 2,832 Coed
Affiliation or Control: Roman Catholic IRS Status: 501(c)3
Highest Offering: Master's
Program: Liberal Arts And General; Teacher Preparatory; Professional
Accreditation: EH, NURSE

01 President .... Sr. Janet EISNER, SND
03 Exec Asst to the President .... Ms. Michelle H. ERICKSON
04 Senior Assistant to President .... Ms. Lori SULLIVAN
05 Vice President Academic Affairs .... Dr. Joyce DE LEO
10 Exec Vice Pres & Chief Oper Ofcr .... Mr. Neil G. BUCKLEY
26 Vice President Govt/Cmty Relations .... Ms. Sarah WELSH
32 Vice President of Student Affairs .... Dr. Patricia RISSMEYER
37 Assoc VP Student Financial Services .... Ms. Jennifer C. PORTER
26 Assoc Vice President of Mktg/Comm .... Ms. Molly HONAN
07 Dean of Enrollment .... Ms. Sandra ROBBINS
35 Dean of Students .... Dr. Joseph ONOFRIETTI
49 Dean of Arts & Sciences .... Dr. William LEONARD
06 Associate Dean & Registrar .... Ms. Elizabeth ROSS
38 Director of Academic Advising .... Sr. Susan THORNELL
08 Director of Library .... Ms. Susan VON DAUM THOLL
15 Director Human Resources .... Ms. Erin FARMER NOONAN
41 Director of Athletics .... Ms. Pamela ROECKER
42 Director of Campus Ministry .... Fr. John SPENCER
24 Director Academic Program Support .... Ms. Cindy O'CALLAGHAN
38 Director Counseling Services .... Dr. Linda JURGELA
90 Director Academic Resource Ctr .... Ms. Wendy LABRON
89 Asst Dean & Dir Student Ctr Svcs .... Ms. Mary Beth THOMAS

Endicott College (D)

376 Hale Street, Beverly MA 01915-2098
County: Essex FICE Identification: 002148
Unit ID: 165699
Telephone: (978) 927-0585 Carnegie Class: Master's M
FAX Number: (978) 927-0084 Calendar System: 4/1/4
URL: www.endicott.edu
Established: 1939 Annual Undergrad Tuition & Fees: $28,166
Enrollment: 4,245 Coed
Affiliation or Control: Independent Non-Profit IRS Status: 501(c)3
Highest Offering: Doctorate
Program: Liberal Arts And General; Professional
Accreditation: EH, CIDA, NUR

01 President .... Dr. Richard E. WYLIE
05 Vice President & Academic Dean .... Dr. Laura ROSSI-LE
03 Executive VP/Vice President Finance .... Ms. Lynne B. O'TOOLE
84 Vice Pres Admissions/Financial Aid .... Mr. Thomas J. REDMAN
58 VP/Dean Graduate & Prof Stds .... Dr. Mary HUEGEL
32 Vice President Student Affairs .... Ms. Beverly DOLINSKY
30 Vice Pres Institutional Advancement .... Mr. David VIGNERON
11 Vice Pres Special Proj/Omudsperson .... Ms. Denise BILODEAU
04 Assistant to the President .... Ms. Joanne L. WALDNER
90 Assoc Dean of Academic Technology .... Mr. Kent BARCLAY
07 Associate Dean of Admission .... Mr. George M. SHERMAN
45 Executive Director of Research .... Mr. Peter L. HART
15 Director Human Resources .... Ms. Sally ARNOLD
21 Treasurer .... Ms. Donna L. COUTURE
06 Registrar .... Ms. Rosa CADENA
08 Library Director .... Mr. Brian COURTEMANCHE
29 Director Alumni Relations .... Ms. Sarah EARNEST
37 Director Financial Aid .... Ms. Marcia D. TOOMEY
41 Athletic Director .... Mr. Brian WYLIE
91 Chief Information Systems Officer .... Mr. Gary F. KELLEY
19 Director Campus Safety .... Mr. Gary DERICKSON
38 Senior Counselor .... Mr. Scott RUSSELL
39 Director of Residence Life .... Ms. Erica HEDRICK
18 Director of Physical Plant .... Mr. Dennis MONACO
26 Director Communications .... Ms. Carol RAICHE
36 Director of Career Services .... Ms. Dale MCLENNAN
09 Assoc Dir of Institutional Research .... Mr. Donald FEMINO
96 Purchasing Agent .... Mr. Terry SCHWENK
85 Dean of Undergrad International Ed .... Dr. Warren JAFERIAN
20 Dean of Academic Resources .... Dr. Kathleen BARNES
49 Dean of Arts & Sciences .... Dr. Gene WONG
53 Dean of Education .... Dr. Sara QUAY
57 Dean of Art & Design .... Mr. Mark TOWNER
59 Dean of Hospitality Management .... Dr. William H. SAMENFINK
68 Dean of Sports Science .... Dr. Deborah SWANTON
66 Dean of Nursing .... Dr. Kelly FISHER
50 Dean of Business & Technology .... Dr. Michael PAIGE
60 Dean of Communication .... Dr. Laurel HELLERSTEIN

Episcopal Divinity School (E)

99 Brattle Street, Cambridge MA 02138-3494
County: Middlesex FICE Identification: 002149
Unit ID: 165705
Telephone: (617) 868-3450 Carnegie Class: Spec/Faith
FAX Number: (617) 864-5385 Calendar System: Semester
URL: www.eds.edu
Established: 1857 Annual Graduate Tuition & Fees: $13,781
Enrollment: 88 Coed
Affiliation or Control: Protestant Episcopal IRS Status: 501(c)3
Highest Offering: Doctorate; No Undergraduates
Program: Professional; Religious Emphasis
Accreditation: THEOL

01 President and Dean .... Rev. Katherine H. RAGSDALE
05 Academic Dean .... Dr. Angela BAUER-LEVESQUE
100 Dean of Student & Community Life .... Rev. Miriam GELFER
30 Int Dir Institutional Advancement .... Mr. Christopher HARTLEY
08 Director of the Library .... Ms. Pat PAYNE
27 Dir of Communications & Marketing .... Mr. Jeffrey PERKINS
10 Chief Financial and Planning Office .... Mr. William JUDGE
21 Comptroller .... Ms. Joanne MANNING
07 Director of Recruitment .... Ms. Rachel SHELTON
06 Registrar/Manager Academic Affairs .... Ms. Cecelia CULL
88 Director Congregational Studies .... Vacant
88 Director Field Education .... Dr. William KONDRATH
18 Superintendent Buildings & Grounds .... Mr. Gustavo VILLATORO
04 Exec Assistant to President & Dean .... Ms. Jane WAGNER
37 Director Student Financial Aid .... Ms. Valeria PATERSON
15 Director of Human Resources .... Ms. Samaria WILSON-STALLINGS

FINE Mortuary College (F)

150 Kerry Place, Norwood MA 02062
County: Norfolk FICE Identification: 033164
Unit ID: 436599
Telephone: (781) 762-1211 Carnegie Class: Assoc/PrivFP
FAX Number: (781) 762-7177 Calendar System: Quarter
URL: www.fine-ne.com
Established: 1996 Annual Undergrad Tuition & Fees: $22,890
Enrollment: 75 Coed
Affiliation or Control: Proprietary IRS Status: Proprietary
Highest Offering: Associate Degree
Program: Occupational; Business Emphasis
Accreditation: FUSER

01 President .... Dr. Louis MISANTONE
03 Executive Vice President .... Dr. Jocelyn PRENDERGAST
37 Director Financial Aid .... Ms. Brenda SWANSON

Fisher College (G)

118 Beacon Street, Boston MA 02116-1500
County: Suffolk FICE Identification: 002150
Unit ID: 165802
Telephone: (617) 236-8800 Carnegie Class: Bac/Assoc
FAX Number: (617) 236-8858 Calendar System: Semester
URL: www.fisher.edu
Established: 1903 Annual Undergrad Tuition & Fees: $26,775
Enrollment: 1,821 Coed
Affiliation or Control: Independent Non-Profit IRS Status: 501(c)3
Highest Offering: Baccalaureate
Program: Occupational; 2-Year Principally Bachelor's Creditable; Liberal Arts And General; Business Emphasis
Accreditation: EH

01 President .... Dr. Thomas MCGOVERN
05 Vice President Academic Affairs .... Ms. Janet KUSER
10 VP for Finance .... Mr. Steven RICH
11 VP for Administration .... Ms. Rhonda PIERONI
30 VP for Development and Outreach .... Ms. Janet HARRINGTON
07 Dean of Admissions .... Mr. Robert MELARAGNI
32 Dean of Students .... Ms. Shiela LALLY
88 Dean Intl Acad Oper/Curriculum Dev .... Ms. Nancy PITHIS
49 Chairman Div of Arts & Sciences .... Dr. Dean WALTON
06 College Registrar .... Mr. Gregory KARAS
41 Director of Athletics .... Mr. Scott DULIN
21 Director of Accounting .... Mr. Jeffrey CONRAD
13 Director of Information Services .... Mr. Jonathan BARTSCH
18 Director of Facilities .... Mr. Paul MCBRINE
37 Director of Financial Aid .... Ms. Anne SYLVAIN
66 Director of Nursing Services .... Ms. Bonnie CHUK
100 Chief of Staff .... Ms. Melinda COOK
88 Dir of Acad Center for Enrichment .... Mrs. Jennifer MANDOLESE
35 Director of Student Activities .... Ms. Margarita ASCENCIO
42 Director of Spiritual Life .... Dr. Ann CLARKE
19 Chief of Campus Police .... Mr. Timothy CALLAHAN
26 Dir Communications/Special Projects .... Ms. Jennie MOORE
36 Director of Career Services .... Ms. Heather CARPENTER
88 Director of Accessibility Service .... Ms. Michele ALMEIDA
15 Director of Human Resources .... Mr. Gary PARNHAM
21 College Bursar .... Ms. Joy NELSON
08 College Librarian .... Mr. Joshua MCKAIN
29 Director Alumni Relations .... Ms. Kristen SHERMAN
51 Dean Div Cont Ed/Sch Hlth Professn .... Dr. Neil TROTTA
88 Project Dir Office of the President .... Ms. Nadia ALAM

Franklin W. Olin College of Engineering (H)

Olin Way, Needham MA 02492-1200
County: Norfolk FICE Identification: 039463
Unit ID: 441982
Telephone: (781) 292-2300 Carnegie Class: Spec/Engg
FAX Number: (781) 292-2210 Calendar System: Semester
URL: www.olin.edu
Established: 2002 Annual Undergrad Tuition & Fees: $40,000
Enrollment: 344 Coed
Affiliation or Control: Independent Non-Profit IRS Status: 501(c)3
Highest Offering: Baccalaureate
Program: Professional
Accreditation: EH, ENG

01 President .... Dr. Richard K. MILLER
04 Asst to President .... Ms. Nancy SULLIVAN
10 Executive Vice President/Treasurer .... Mr. Stephen P. HANNABURY
07 VP External Rels/Dean of Admission .... Dr. Charles S. NOLAN
05 Provost/Dean of Faculty .... Dr. Vincent P. MANNO
11 VP Operations/Chief Info Officer .... Ms. Joanne KOSSUTH
32 Dean of Student Life .... Dr. Roger C. CRAFTS, JR.
27 AVP Ext Relations/Dir Communication .... Mr. Joseph A. HUNTER
29 Director Family & Alumni Relations .... Ms. Kristina RAPOSA
30 VP Development/Family & Alumni Rel .... Mr. J. Thomas KRIMMEL

09 Dir Inst Research & Eval ....Mr. Jeremy GOODMAN

† All admitted students who enroll at Olin College receive an Olin Scholarship covering half tuition during the eight semesters of the baccalaureate program.

Gordon College (A)

255 Grapevine Road, Wenham MA 01984-1899

County: Essex
FICE Identification: 002153
Unit ID: 165936
Telephone: (978) 927-2300
Carnegie Class: Bac/A&S
FAX Number: (978) 867-4659
Calendar System: Semester
URL: www.gordon.edu
Established: 1889
Annual Undergrad Tuition & Fees: $32,100
Enrollment: 1,573
Coed
Affiliation or Control: Independent Non-Profit
IRS Status: 501(c)3
Highest Offering: Master's
Program: Liberal Arts And General
Accreditation: EH, MUS, SW

01 President ....Dr. D. Michael LINDSAY
05 Provost ....Dr. Janel CURRY
10 Vice President for Finance/CFO ....Mr. Michael J. AHEARN
27 EVP Advancement/Communications/Tech ....Mr. Daniel TYMANN
84 Vice President Enrollment ....Ms. June BODONI
32 Vice President/Dean of Students ....Mr. Barry J. LOY
26 VP of Marketing and Communications ....Mr. Rick SWEENEY
20 Academic Dean ....Dr. Daniel RUSS
45 Dean College Planning/Legal Counsel ..Dr. Stephen C. MACLEOD
42 Dean of the Chapel ....Dr. Gregory W. CARMER
08 Director Library ....Mr. Myron SCHIRER-SUTER
06 Registrar ....Ms. Carol A. HERRICK
13 Dir of Ctr for Education Technology ....Mr. Christopher JONES
37 Dir of Student Financial Services ....Mr. Daniel O'CONNELL
15 Director Human Resources ....Ms. Nancy ANDERSON
18 Chief Facilities/Physical Plant ....Mr. Paul HELGESEN
21 Controller ....Ms. Kim MATHER
26 Assoc Dir of College Communications ....Ms. Cyndi MCMAHON
29 Director Alumni & Parent Relations ....Ms. Adrienne COOK
36 Director Student Placement ....Ms. Pam LAZARAKIS
96 Director of Purchasing ....Mr. Ken EBERSOLE

Gordon-Conwell Theological Seminary (B)

130 Essex Street, South Hamilton MA 01982-2317

County: Essex
FICE Identification: 009747
Unit ID: 165945
Telephone: (978) 468-7111
Carnegie Class: Spec/Faith
FAX Number: (978) 468-6691
Calendar System: Semester
URL: www.gordonconwell.edu
Established: 1884
Annual Graduate Tuition & Fees: $17,100
Enrollment: 2,005
Coed
Affiliation or Control: Independent Non-Profit
IRS Status: 501(c)3
Highest Offering: Doctorate; No Undergraduates
Program: Professional; Religious Emphasis
Accreditation: EH, THEOL

01 President ....Dr. Dennis HOLLINGER
10 Executive Vice President & CFO ....Mr. Robert S. LANDREBE
30 Vice President of Advancement ....Mr. Kurt W. DRESCHER
12 VP for Academic Affairs ....Dr. Richard LINTS
12 Dean of Boston Campus ....Dr. Mark HARDEN
12 Academic Dean - Charlotte ....Dr. Timothy S. LANIAK
32 Dean of Students/Dir Stdnt Life Svc ....Mrs. Lita SCHLUETER
16 Director of Human Resources ....Ms. Susan M. BESSE
13 Chief Information Officer ....Mrs. Amy E. DONOVAN
84 Dean Enrollment Mgmt ....Mr. Scott B. POBLENZ
18 Director of Physical Plant ....Mr. Timothy INGRAHAM
08 Director of Goddard Library ....Mr. Meredith KLINE
88 Director of the Ockenga Institute ....Dr. David G. HORN
37 Director of Financial Aid ....Mr. Stacey T. GLIDDEN
40 Director of Support Services ....Mr. David SHOREY
19 Director of Campus Safety ....Mr. Cabot W. DODGE
26 Dir of Communications & Marketing ....Mr. Michael L. COLARERI
07 Director of Admissions & Marketing ....Ms. Jill M. BARLOW
21 Controller & Dir Financial Svcs ....Mr. Gregg HANSEN
30 Chief Advancement Ofcr Charlotte ....Dr. Neely GASTON
42 Sr Administrator Mentored Ministry ..Mrs. Katherine K. HORVATH

Hampshire College (C)

893 West Street, Amherst MA 01002-3372

County: Hampshire
FICE Identification: 004661
Unit ID: 166018
Telephone: (413) 549-4600
Carnegie Class: Bac/A&S
FAX Number: (413) 559-5584
Calendar System: 4/1/4
URL: www.hampshire.edu
Established: 1965
Annual Undergrad Tuition & Fees: $44,700
Enrollment: 1,549
Coed
Affiliation or Control: Independent Non-Profit
IRS Status: 501(c)3
Highest Offering: Baccalaureate
Program: Liberal Arts And General
Accreditation: EH

01 President ....Dr. Jonathan LASH
101 Secretary of the College ....Ms. Beth I. WARD
05 Vice President & Dean of Faculty ....Dr. Eva RUESCHMANN
32 Dean of Student Services ....Ms. Diana FERNANDEZ
10 Vice Pres for Finance & Admin ....Mr. Mark SPIRO
15 Assoc Vice Pres Human Resources .....Ms. Ann Michele RUOCCO
30 Chief Advancement Officer ....Mr. Clay BALLANTINE
07 Dean of Admissions & Financial Aid ......Ms. Julie RICHARDSON
08 Director of Library/Info Services ....Ms. Jennifer KING
06 Director of Central Records ....Ms. Roberta P. STUART
37 Director of Financial Aid ....Ms. Jennifer G. LAWTON
09 Director of Institutional Research ....Ms. Carol TROSSET
18 Director of Facilities and Grounds ....Mr. Larry ARCHEY
20 Associate Dean of Faculty ....Ms. Yaniris FERNANDEZ
26 Chief Public Relations Officer ....Ms. B. Elaine THOMAS
29 Director Alumni Relations ....Ms. Killara BURN
36 Director Student Placement ....Ms. Carin RANK
38 Director Student Counseling ....Dr. Eliza MCARDLE
100 Chief of Staff ....Ms. Joanna OLIN
28 Director of Diversity ....Mr. Jaime DAVILA

Harvard University (D)

1350 Massachusetts Ave, Cambridge MA 02138-3800

County: Middlesex
FICE Identification: 002155
Unit ID: 166027
Telephone: (617) 495-1000
Carnegie Class: RU/VH
FAX Number: (617) 495-0500
Calendar System: Semester
URL: www.harvard.edu
Established: 1636
Annual Undergrad Tuition & Fees: $39,851
Enrollment: 27,392
Coed
Affiliation or Control: Independent Non-Profit
IRS Status: 501(c)3
Highest Offering: Doctorate
Program: Liberal Arts And General; Teacher Preparatory; Professional
Accreditation: EH, BUS, CLPSY, DENT, ENG, IPSY, LAW, LSAR, MED, PH, PLNG, SPAA, THEOL

01 President ....Drew G. FAUST
05 Provost ....Alan M. GARBER
03 Executive Vice President ....Katherine N. LAPP
88 Treasurer ....James ROTHENBERG
49 Dean Faculty Arts & Sciences ....Michael D. SMITH
20 Dean of Harvard College ....Evelynn M. HAMMONDS
58 Dean Grad School of Arts & Science ....Allan M. BRANDT
54 Dean of Engineering/Applied Science ....Cherry A. MURRAY
50 Dean of Harvard Business School ....Nitin NOHRIA
52 Dean of Dental Medicine ....R. Bruce DONOFF
48 Dean Graduate School of Design ....Mohsen MOSTAFAVI
73 Dean of the Divinity School ....William A. GRAHAM
51 Dean of Continuing Education ....Michael SHINAGEL
53 Dean Graduate School of Education ....Kathleen MCCARTNEY
61 Dean of the Law School ....Martha MINOW
63 Dean of the Medical School ....Dr. Jeffrey S. FLIER
80 Dean of Government ....David ELLWOOD
69 Dean of Public Health ....Julio FRENK
88 Int Dean Radcliffe Inst Advance Std ....Lizabeth COHEN
88 Vice President for Policy ....Vacant
10 Vice President for Finance and CFO ....Daniel SHORE
11 Vice President for Campus Services ....Lisa HOGARTY
43 Vice President & General Counsel ....Robert W. IULIANO
26 Vice Pres Public Aff/Communications ....Christine HEENAN
29 Vice Pres Alumni Affs & Development ....Tamara E. ROGERS
15 Vice President for Human Resources ......Marilyn HAUSAMMANN
28 Sr Vice Prov Fac Devel & Diversity ....Judith SINGER
18 Vice President for Campus Services ....Lisa HOGARTY
25 Director Sponsored Programs ....Catherine BREEN
28 Chief Diversity Ofc/Sp Asst to Pres ....Lisa M. COLEMAN
13 Univ Chief Information Officer ....Anne MARGULIES
07 Dean of Admissions/Financial Aid ....William R. FITZSIMMONS
06 Registrar/Faculty Arts & Sciences ....Michael P. BURKE
08 Exec Director for Harvard Library ....Helen SHENTON
23 Director Health Services ....David S. ROSENTHAL
19 Dir Police/Security/Chief of Police ....Francis D. RILEY
09 Director of Institutional Research ....Erin DRIVER-LINN
37 Director Student Financial Aid ....Sally C. DONAHUE

Hebrew College (E)

160 Herrick Road, Newton Centre MA 02459-2237

County: Middlesex
FICE Identification: 002157
Unit ID: 166045
Telephone: (617) 559-8600
Carnegie Class: Spec/Faith
FAX Number: (617) 559-8601
Calendar System: Semester
URL: www.hebrewcollege.edu
Established: 1921
Annual Undergrad Tuition & Fees: $18,240
Enrollment: 200
Coed
Affiliation or Control: Independent Non-Profit
IRS Status: 501(c)3
Highest Offering: Beyond Master's But Less Than Doctorate
Program: Professional; Religious Emphasis
Accreditation: EH

01 President ....Rabbi Daniel LEHMANN
10 Vice Pres Finance & Administration ....Mr. Leon ZAIMES
05 Provost ....Dr. Barry MESCH
84 Director of Enrollment Management ....Ms. Sara SHALVA
06 Registrar/Financial Aid Services ....Ms. Marilyn JAYE
30 Director of Development ....Mr. Paul ROSENSTEIN
15 Director Personnel Services ....Ms. Steffi BOBBIN
04 Assistant to the President ....Ms. Annette ASHIN

Hellenic College-Holy Cross Greek Orthodox School of Theology (F)

50 Goddard Avenue, Brookline MA 02445-7496

County: Norfolk
FICE Identification: 002154
Unit ID: 166054
Telephone: (617) 731-3500
Carnegie Class: Spec/Faith
FAX Number: (617) 850-1460
Calendar System: Semester
URL: www.hchc.edu
Established: 1937
Annual Undergrad Tuition & Fees: $21,268
Enrollment: 206
Coed
Affiliation or Control: Greek Orthodox
IRS Status: 501(c)3
Highest Offering: Master's
Program: Teacher Preparatory; Professional
Accreditation: EH, THEOL

01 President ....Rev. Nicholas C. TRIANTAFILOU
73 Dean School of Theology ....Rev Dr. Thomas FITZGERALD
05 Dean Hellenic College ....Dr. Demetrios KATOS
32 Dean of Students ....Dean Nicholas BELCHER
11 Chief Operating Officer ....Mr. James D. KARLOUTSOS
10 Chief Financial Officer ....Mr. Charles KROLL
07 Director of Admissions & Records ....Mr. Gregory FLOOR
08 Director Library ....Rev. Joachim COTSONIS
37 Financial Aid Officer ....Mr. George GEORGENES
06 Registrar ....Ms. Alba PAGAN
13 Director Computing/Information Mgmt ....Mr. Mugur ROZ
42 Chaplain ....Rev. Peter CHAMBERAS
38 Director Student Counseling ....Ms. Athina-Eleni MAVROUDHIS
30 Director Institutional Advancement ....Rev. James KATINAS
29 Director of Alumni Office ....Mr. Gregory FLOOR
40 Bookstore Manager ....Ms. Tanya CONTOS
04 Administrator of President's Office ....Mrs. Joanna BAKAS

Hult International Business School (G)

One Education Street, Cambridge MA 02141-1805

County: Middlesex
FICE Identification: 020727
Unit ID: 164368
Telephone: (617) 746-1990
Carnegie Class: Not Classified
FAX Number: (617) 746-1991
Calendar System: Other
URL: www.hult.edu
Established: 1964
Annual Undergrad Tuition & Fees: $64,500
Enrollment: 1,519
Coed
Affiliation or Control: Proprietary
IRS Status: Proprietary
Highest Offering: Master's
Program: Professional; Business Emphasis
Accreditation: EH

01 President ....Dr. Stephen HODGES
05 Chief Academic Officer ....Dr. Mukul KUMAR
20 Vice President for Academic Affairs ....Dr. Richard JOSEPH
12 Dean Boston Campus ....Mr. Henrik TOTTERMAN
12 Acting Dean San Francisco Campus ....Mr. Larry LOUIE
84 Dir of Recruiting ....Mr. Steve WYNN
36 Dir of Career Services Boston ....Mr. James MORRISON
36 Dir of Career Services San Franciso ....Ms. Christina FOX
35 Dir Student Services Boston ....Mr. David HIETT
06 Registrar Boston Campus ....Ms. Nicole GREGOIRE
06 Asst Registrar San Francisco Campus ....Ms. Caroline CONNOR

ITT Technical Institute (H)

333 Providence Highway, Norwood MA 02062

County: Norfolk
Identification: 666541
Unit ID: 366580
Telephone: (781) 278-7200
Carnegie Class: Spec/Tech
FAX Number: (781) 278-0766
Calendar System: Quarter
URL: www.itt-tech.edu
Established: 1990
Annual Undergrad Tuition & Fees: N/A
Enrollment: 552
Coed
Affiliation or Control: Proprietary
IRS Status: Proprietary
Highest Offering: Baccalaureate
Program: Technical Emphasis
Accreditation: ACICS

† Branch campus of ITT Technical Institute, Indianapolis, IN.

ITT Technical Institute (I)

200 Ballardvale Street, Suite 200, Wilmington MA 01887

County: Middlesex
Identification: 666119
Unit ID: 439136
Telephone: (978) 658-2636
Carnegie Class: Assoc/PrivFP
FAX Number: (781) 937-3402
Calendar System: Quarter
URL: www.itt-tech.edu
Established: 2000
Annual Undergrad Tuition & Fees: N/A
Enrollment: 488
Coed
Affiliation or Control: Proprietary
IRS Status: Proprietary
Highest Offering: Baccalaureate
Program: Technical Emphasis
Accreditation: ACICS

† Branch campus of ITT Technical Institute, Indianapolis, IN.

Laboure College (J)

2120 Dorchester Avenue, Boston MA 02124-5698

County: Suffolk
FICE Identification: 006324
Unit ID: 165264
Telephone: (617) 296-8300
Carnegie Class: Assoc/PrivNFP
FAX Number: (617) 296-7947
Calendar System: Semester
URL: www.laboure.edu
Established: 1892
Annual Undergrad Tuition & Fees: $30,430
Enrollment: 726
Coed
Affiliation or Control: Roman Catholic
IRS Status: 501(c)3
Highest Offering: Baccalaureate
Program: Occupational; 2-Year Principally Bachelor's Creditable

Accreditation: EH, ADNUR, DIETT, NDT, RTT

01 President ... Ms. Maureen A. SMITH
10 Chief Financial Officer ... Mr. Mark VIRELLO
05 Dean Academic Affairs ... Ms. Paula VOSBURGH
32 Vice Pres/Dean Student Affairs ... Mrs. Karen MASTERS
08 Director Learning Resources Center ... Mr. Andrew CALO
06 Registrar ... Mr. John SACCO
84 Director of Enrollment Services ... Vacant
30 VP Institutional Advancement ... Ms. Catherine PHILBIN
26 Director Public Relations/Marketing ... Ms. Katelyn DWYER
37 Director Student Financial Aid ... Ms. Erin HANLON
66 Int Dir Nursing Division ... Ms. Denise EDINGER
88 Chair of Dietetic Division ... Mrs. Anne MANION
76 Div Chair Health Info Tech ... Ms. Elise BELANGER
88 Div Chair Radiation Technology ... Mrs. Pauline CLANCY
88 Div Chair Electroneuro Technology ... Mrs. Jean FARLEY

Lasell College (A)

1844 Commonwealth Avenue, Newton MA 02466-2716
County: Middlesex FICE Identification: 002158
Unit ID: 166391
Telephone: (617) 243-2000 Carnegie Class: Bac/Diverse
FAX Number: (617) 243-2389 Calendar System: Semester
URL: www.lasell.edu
Established: 1851 Annual Undergrad Tuition & Fees: $29,000
Enrollment: 1,647 Coed
Affiliation or Control: Independent Non-Profit IRS Status: 501(c)3
Highest Offering: Master's
Program: Liberal Arts And General
Accreditation: EH, EXSC

01 President ... Michael B. ALEXANDER
04 Exec Assistant to the President ... Pamela FARIA
05 VP Academic Affairs ... James OSTROW
10 VP Business & Finance ... Michael HOYLE
84 VP Enrollment Management ... Kathleen O'CONNOR
88 VP Lasell Village ... Paula PANCHUCK
32 VP of Student Affairs ... Diane AUSTIN
30 Dean of Institutional Advancement ... Ruth SHUMAN
07 Dean of Undergraduate Admission ... James TWEED
20 Assoc VP/Dean Undergraduate Educ ... Steven BLOOM
58 Dean of Grad & Prof Studies ... Joan DOLAMORE
89 Dean of Advis & First Year Programs ... Helena SANTOS
35 Dean of Student Affairs ... David HENNESSEY
21 Asst VP for Finance ... Diane PARKER
37 Dir Student Financial Planning ... Michele KOSBOTH
09 Dir of Institutional Research ... Vacant
06 Registrar ... Dianne POLIZZI
44 Dir of Annual Giving/Const Rel ... Haegan FORREST
18 Int Dir Plant Opers/Sustainability ... Marc FOURNIER
27 Dir of Communications ... Michelle GASSEAU
30 Dir of Development ... Mark LAFRANCE
30 Senior Advancement Officer ... Katharine URNER-JONES
29 Assoc Dir of Alumni Relations ... Lauren MCCAUSLIN
35 Dir of Student Act & Orientation ... Jennifer GRANGER
23 Dir of Health Services ... Ann SHERMAN
08 Dir of Library ... Marilyn NEGIP
41 Dir of Athletics ... Kristy WALTER
15 Dir of Human Resources ... Kathryn BRYNE
38 Dir of Counseling Center ... Janice FLETCHER
07 Dir of Graduate Admission ... Adrienne FRANCIOSI
42 Dir of Center for Spirtual Life ... Thomas SULLIVAN
13 Chief Information Officer ... Deborah GELCH
39 Dir of Residential Life ... Scott LAMPHERE

Lesley University (B)

29 Everett Street, Cambridge MA 02138-2790
County: Middlesex FICE Identification: 002160
Unit ID: 166452
Telephone: (617) 868-9600 Carnegie Class: Master's L
FAX Number: (617) 349-8717 Calendar System: Semester
URL: www.lesley.edu
Established: 1909 Annual Undergrad Tuition & Fees: $31,200
Enrollment: 5,899 Coed
Affiliation or Control: Independent Non-Profit IRS Status: 501(c)3
Highest Offering: Doctorate
Program: Liberal Arts And General; Teacher Preparatory; Professional
Accreditation: EH, ART, TEAC

01 President ... Dr. Joseph B. MOORE
05 Provost ... Dr. Selase W. WILLIAMS
11 Vice President for Administration ... Ms. Marylou BATT
10 Vice President/CFO ... Ms. Bernice BRADIN
30 Vice President of Advancement ... Mr. Randy STABILE
84 VP Enrollment Mgmt ... Vacant
21 VP for Budgeting & Fin Planning ... Ms. M. L. DYMSKI
43 General Counsel ... Ms. Shirin PHILIPP
100 Chief of Staff ... Dr. MaryPat LOHSE
20 Associate Provost ... Ms. Lisa IJIRI
22 Dir Equal Opportunity & Inclusion ... Dr. Barbara ADDISON REID
58 Dean Grad Sch Arts & Social Sci ... Dr. Catherine KOVEROLA
53 Dean School of Education ... Dr. Jack GILLETTE
32 Dean of Student Life & Academic Dev ... Dr. Nathaniel MAYS
88 Dean Art Institute of Boston ... Mr. Stan TRECKER
88 Dean Lesley College ... Dr. Mary COLEMAN
18 Dir Operations & Campus Planning ... Mr. George SMITH
13 Chief Information Officer ... Mr. Daryl FORD
07 Director of Graduate Admissions ... Ms. Martha SHEEHAN
91 Director Admin Applications UT ... Mr. Scott BOULET
90 Assoc VP Acad Tech/Program Planning ... Vacant
15 Director of Human Resources ... Ms. Jane JOYCE
37 Director of Financial Aid ... Mr. Scott JEWELL
19 Captain of Security ... Ms. Nicole O'LEARY
88 Budget Director ... Ms. Anne GROGAN
88 Director Student Accounts ... Ms. Heather CLANG
21 Controller ... Ms. Karen BAYTCH
40 Manager of Bookstore/Campus Shop ... Ms. Lee-Ann LANZILLO
44 Dir of Annual Giving & Alumni Rels ... Ms. Pattyanne LYONS
08 Director of Libraries ... Ms. Patricia PAYNE
06 Registrar ... Ms. Melissa JANOT
36 Assoc Dean Career/Community Service ... Ms. Alice DIAMOND
41 Director of Athletics ... Mrs. Jennifer BENWAY
07 Dir Undergrad Admissions Lesley Col ... Ms. Deb KOCAR
88 Director of Admissions AIB ... Mr. Robert GIELOW
39 Director Residence Life ... Ms. Nancy GALVIN
38 Director Counseling Center ... Ms. Magi MCKINNIES
85 Dir International Student Services ... Ms. Janie BESS
09 Dir of Assessment/Inst Research ... Dr. Linda PURSLEY
26 Director Public Affairs ... Mr. Bill DONCASTER
88 Director of Marketing Comm ... Mr. Leo RICE
27 Dir of Advancement Communications ... Ms. Anya WOODS
96 Director of Purchasing ... Mr. William HOYT

Marian Court College (C)

35 Littles Point Road, Swampscott MA 01907-2896
County: Essex FICE Identification: 006873
Unit ID: 166601
Telephone: (781) 595-6768 Carnegie Class: Assoc/PrivNFP
FAX Number: (781) 595-3560 Calendar System: Semester
URL: www.mariancourt.edu
Established: 1964 Annual Undergrad Tuition & Fees: $16,400
Enrollment: 233 Coed
Affiliation or Control: Roman Catholic IRS Status: 501(c)3
Highest Offering: Associate Degree
Program: Occupational; 2-Year Principally Bachelor's Creditable
Accreditation: EH

01 Interim President ... Dr. Denise HAMMON
10 Chief Financial Officer ... Ms. Maribeth FORBES
30 VP Development and Marketing ... Ms. Michele L. AHOUSE
05 Dean of Academic & Student Affairs ... Dr. Denise HAMMON
06 Registrar ... Ms. Linda LUNDSTROM
07 Sr Assoc Director of Admissions ... Mr. Peter SCHILLING
08 Librarian & Career Info Specialist ... Ms. Mia MORGAN
38 Dir of Academic & Career Services ... Ms. Megan PENYACK
37 Director of Financial Aid ... Ms. Stacy BONSANG
50 Chair Business Dept ... Ms. Joan THOMPSON
79 Chair Liberal Studies ... Dr. Tom HALLORAN
13 Director of Information Technology ... Mr. Jorge CORREIA
88 Chair Criminal Justice ... Mr. Fran BRENNAN

*Massachusetts Board of Higher Education (D)

One Ashburton Place, Room 1401,
Boston MA 02108-1696
County: Suffolk FICE Identification: 029283
Unit ID: 166531
Telephone: (617) 994-6950 Carnegie Class: N/A
FAX Number: (617) 727-6397
URL: www.mass.edu

01 Commissioner ... Dr. Richard M. FREELAND
103 Assoc Comm of Workforce Development . Mr. David C. CEDRONE
05 Deputy Comm Academic Policy ... Ms. Aundrea KELLEY
43 General Counsel ... Ms. Constantia PAPANIKOLAOU
10 Dep Comm Administration and Finance .... Mr. Steven LENHARDT
09 Assoc Comm Institutional Research ... Dr. Jonathan KELLER
37 Sr Dep Comm Student Financial Aid ... Dr. Clantha MCCURDY

*University of Massachusetts Central Office (E)

225 Franklin Street, 33rd Floor, Boston MA 02110
County: Suffolk FICE Identification: 008017
Unit ID: 166665
Telephone: (617) 287-7050 Carnegie Class: N/A
FAX Number: (617) 287-7167
URL: www.massachusetts.edu

01 President ... Dr. Robert L. CARET
03 Exec VP/Chief Operating Officer ... Mr. James R. JULIAN
05 Sr VP Acad Affs/Stdnt & Intl Affs ... Dr. Marcellette WILLIAMS
11 VP Administration & Finance ... Vacant
102 Exec VP UMass Foundation ... Mr. Robert M. GOODHUE
46 Vice President Economic Development .... Mr. Thomas J. CHMURA
26 VP Strategic Comm/Univ Spokesperson ... Mr. Robert P. CONNOLLY
104 Asst VP International Relations ... Ms. Susan M. KELLY
86 Special Asst to Pres Govt Rels ... Mr. David MCDERMOTT
43 General Counsel ... Ms. Deirdre HEATWOLE
27 Assoc VP and Chief Info Officer ... Mr. Robert SOLIS
101 Secretary to Board of Trustees ... Ms. Barbara F. DEVICO
21 Director for University Auditing ... Mr. Kyle DAVID
15 Dir of Human Resources & Labor Rels ... Mr. Mark PREBLE
106 Interim CEO UMass Online ... Dr. John CUNNINGHAM

*University of Massachusetts (F)

Amherst MA 01003-0001
County: Hampshire FICE Identification: 002221
Unit ID: 166629
Telephone: (413) 545-0111 Carnegie Class: RU/VH
FAX Number: N/A Calendar System: Semester
URL: www.umass.edu
Established: 1863 Annual Undergrad Tuition & Fees (In-State): $13,230
Enrollment: 28,084 Coed
Affiliation or Control: State IRS Status: 501(c)3
Highest Offering: Doctorate
Program: Liberal Arts And General; Teacher Preparatory; Professional
Accreditation: EH, AUD, BUS, BUSA, CLPSY, DIETD, DIETI, ENG, FOR, IPSY, LSAR, MUS, NURSE, PH, #PLNG, SCPSY, SP, TED

02 Chancellor ... Dr. Kumble R. SUBBASWAMY
05 Provost/Sr Vice Chancellor ... Dr. James V. STAROS
10 Vice Chancellor Admin/Finance ... Mr. James P. SHEEHAN
30 Vice Chancellor Univ Advancement ... Mr. Michael A. LETO
46 Vice Chancellor Research ... Dr. Michael F. MALONE
32 VC Student Affairs & Campus Life ... Dr. Jean KIM
31 Vice Chanc University Relations ... Mr. John KENNEDY
41 Director of Athletics ... Mr. John F. MCCUTCHEON
43 Senior Counsel ... Mr. Brian W. BURKE
13 Special Asst to Chancellor & CIO ... Dr. John F. DUBACH
88 Associate Chancellor ... Ms. Susan PEARSON
22 Assoc Chanc Equal Oppty/Diversity ... Ms. Debora D. FERREIRA
04 Asst to the Chancellor ... Ms. Becky DEAN
20 Vice Provost Undegrad & Cont Educ ... Dr. Carol A. BARR
58 Vice Provost/Dean of Grad School ... Dr. John J. MCCARTHY
88 Vice Provost/Dean of Faculty ... Dr. Joel W. MARTIN
85 Assoc Provost Intl Programs ... Dr. Jack AHERN
84 Assoc Provost Enrollment Management ... Dr. James ROCHE
45 Assoc Provost Academic Plng/Assess ... Dr. Bryan C. HARVEY
20 Asst Provost Advising/Acad Support ... Dr. Pamela R. MARSH-WILLIAMS
09 Asst Provost Institutional Research ... Dr. Marilyn H. BLAUSTEIN
108 Asst Provost Assessment/Educ Effect ... Dr. Martha L. STASSEN
87 Assistant Provost Summer Programs ... Dr. Ed FERSZT
51 Exec Director Continuing Education ... Mr. William S. MCCLURE
07 Director Undergraduate Admissions ... Mr. Kevin KELLY
37 Director Financial Aid Services ... Ms. Suzanne PETERS
06 University Registrar ... Mr. John LENZI
92 Dean Commonwealth Honors College ... Dr. Priscilla M. CLARKSON
79 Dean Col Humanities & Fine Arts ... Dr. Julie C. HAYES
81 Dean Col Natural Science ... Dr. Steve GOODWIN
83 Dean Col Social & Behavioral Sci ... Dr. Robert S. FELDMAN
53 Dean School of Education ... Dr. Christine B. MCCORMICK
54 Dean College of Engineering ... Dr. Theodore E. DJAFERIS
50 Dean School of Management ... Dr. Mark A. FULLER
66 Dean School of Nursing ... Dr. Stephen CAVANAGH
69 Dean Sch Public Health/Health Sci ... Dr. C. Marjorie AELION
08 Director of Libraries ... Mr. Jay SCHAFER
56 Director of Extension ... Ms. Nancy GARRABRANTS
47 Dir Stockbridge School Agriculture ... Mr. William MITCHELL
15 Asst Vice Chanc Human Resources ... Mr. Juan A. JARRETT
21 Assoc VC/Budget Director/Controller .... Mr. Andrew P. MANGELS
18 Assoc VC Facilities Planning ... Ms. Juanita M. HOLLER
19 Director Public Safety/Chief Police ... Mr. Patrick ARCHBALD
96 Director of Purchasing ... Mr. John O. MARTIN
40 Manager Univ Store/Retail Services ... Mr. Ken KAHLER
35 Dean Student Affairs ... Ms. Enku GELAYE
39 Exec Director Housing & Res Life ... Mr. Edward C. HULL
23 Director of Medical Care ... Dr. Alan CALHOUN
38 Director Mental Health/Health Svcs ... Dr. Harry S. ROCKLAND-MILLER
36 Director Career Services ... Mr. Jeffrey I. SILVER
29 Exec Director Alumni Relations ... Mr. JC SCHNABL
44 Director Annual Giving ... Ms. Sarah SLIGO
27 Exec Director News & Media ... Mr. Edward F. BLAGUSZEWSKI
26 Assoc VC University Relations ... Ms. Amy C. GLYNN
86 Dir Public/Constituent Relations ... Mr. Christopher DUNN
102 Director Corporate/Foundation Rels ... Ms. Linda SOPP
31 Dir Cmty Relations/Special Events ... Dr. Nancy BUFFONE
25 Director Grant & Contract Admin ... Ms. Carol SPRAGUE
91 Associate CIO/Dir Admin Applics ... Ms. Heidi DOLLARD
90 Director OIT Academic Computing ... Ms. Copper F. GILOTH
24 Director Educational Media ... Mr. Stephen PIELOCK
105 Web Manager ... Ms. Nina SOSSEN

*University of Massachusetts Boston (G)

100 Morrissey Boulevard, Boston MA 02125-3393
County: Suffolk FICE Identification: 002222
Unit ID: 166638
Telephone: (617) 287-5000 Carnegie Class: RU/H
FAX Number: (617) 265-7173 Calendar System: Semester
URL: www.umb.edu
Established: 1964 Annual Undergrad Tuition & Fees (In-State): $12,463
Enrollment: 15,741 Coed
Affiliation or Control: State IRS Status: 501(c)3
Highest Offering: Doctorate
Program: Liberal Arts And General; Teacher Preparatory; Professional; Business Emphasis
Accreditation: EH, BUS, CLPSY, CORE, CS, MFCD, NURSE, @TEAC

02 Chancellor ... Dr. J. Keith MOTLEY
88 Assistant Chancellor ... Dr. Theresa MORTIMER
100 Chief of Staff ... Mr. Christopher HOGAN
05 Provost ... Dr. Winston LANGLEY
10 Vice Chanc for Admin & Finance ... Ms. Ellen O'CONNOR
30 VC Chanc for Univ Advancement ... Ms. Gina CAPPELLO
84 Vice Chanc Enrollment Management ... Ms. Kathleen TEEHAN
32 Vice Chancellor Student Affairs ... Mr. Patrick K. DAY

41 VC for Athletics & Special Projects ....Mr. Charlie TITUS
86 VC for Govt Rel/Public Aff ....Mr. John CICCARELLI
14 Vice Provost Information Tech/CIO ....Ms. Anne S. AGEE
84 Assoc Vice Chanc Enrollment Mgmt ....Dr. Lisa JOHNSON
15 Asst Vice Chanc for Human Resources ....Mr. Jeff MCCUE
29 Asst VC Family & Alumni Relations ....Vacant
31 Asst Vice Chanc Community Relations ....Ms. Gail HOBIN
23 Ast VC Std Aff/Ex Dir Univ Hlth Svc ....Dr. Kathleen GOLDEN MCANDREW
20 Associate Provost ....Ms. Kristine ALSTER
20 Assoc Provost Assess and Planning ....Dr. Peter LANGER
53 Int Dean Col of Educ & Human Dev ....Ms. Felicia WILCZENSKI
51 Dean of University College ....Dr. Philip DISALVIO
81 Dean of Math & Science ....Dr. Andrew GROSOVSKY
79 Int Dean of Liberal Arts ....Dr. Emily MCDERMOTT
50 Dean College of Management ....Dr. Philip L. QUAGLIERI
66 Int Dean College of Nursing ....Dr. Marion WINFREY
80 Int Dean of CPCS ....Dr. Anna MADISON
35 Dean of Students ....Vacant
43 Interim General Counsel ....Ms. Deirdre HEATWOLE
26 Director of Communications ....Mr. DeWayne LEHMAN
38 Director Univ Advising Center ....Ms. Gail STUBBS
09 Director Institutional Research ....Dr. Jennifer A. BROWN
06 Director of Registration & Records ....Mr. David R. CESARIO
07 Director of Undergrad Admissions ....Mr. John DREW
37 Director Financial Aid Services ....Ms. Judy KEYES
08 Director of Libraries ....Dr. Daniel ORTIZ
22 Chief Diversity Officer-ODI ....Mr. Juan NUNEZ
18 Director of Facilities Devel & Mgmt ....Ms. Dorothy RENAGHAN
19 Director of Public Safety ....Mr. James OVERTON
40 Director of Campus Services ....Ms. Diane D'ARRIGO
41 Senior Assoc Director of Athletics ....Ms. Terry CONDON
36 Director of Career Services ....Mr. Len KONARSKI
24 Media Services Manager ....Mr. John POTTER
96 Director of Procurement ....Mr. Darryl MAYERS
92 Director of Honors Programs ....Ms. Rajini SRIKANTH
20 Asst Vice Provost Undergrad Studies ....Ms. Maura MAST

*University of Massachusetts Dartmouth (A)

285 Old Westport Road, North Dartmouth MA 02747-2300
County: Bristol | FICE Identification: 002210
Unit ID: 167987
Telephone: (508) 999-8000 | Carnegie Class: Master's L
FAX Number: (508) 999-8901 | Calendar System: Semester
URL: www.umassd.edu
Established: 1895 | Annual Undergrad Tuition & Fees (In-State): $11,681
Enrollment: 9,225 | Coed
Affiliation or Control: State | IRS Status: 501(c)3
Highest Offering: Doctorate
Program: Liberal Arts And General; Teacher Preparatory; Professional
Accreditation: EH, ART, BUS, CS, ENG, #LAW, MT, NUR

02 Chancellor ....Dr. Divina GROSSMAN
05 Int Provost/VC Acad & Stdnt Affs ....Dr. John FARRINGTON
10 Vice Chanc Admin/Fiscal Services ....Ms. Deborah MCLAUGHLIN
30 Interim Asst Chancellor Advancement ....Mr. Michael EATOUGH
04 Executive Office Director ....Ms. Clare POIRIER
51 Asst VC/Director of PCE ....Dr. Joy MCGUIRL-HADLEY
09 Asst Chanc Inst Rsrch & Assessment ....Vacant
20 Assoc Provost Undergrad Studies ....Dr. Magali CARRERA
20 Assoc Provost Grad Studies/Research ....Dr. Alex FOWLER
84 Assc VC Enrollment Management ....Ms. Teresa MAUK
21 Associate Vice Chancellor Finance ....Mr. William A. MITCHELL
11 Assoc VC Admin & Fiscal Services ....Mr. Salvatore FILARDI
58 Dir Graduate Studies/Admissions ....Mr. Scott WEBSTER
22 Asst Chanc Eq Oppty/Divers/Outrch ....Vacant
31 Asst Chanc Economic Development ....Mr. Paul VIGEANT
88 Assistant VC Academic Affairs ....Dr. Bruce ROSE
35 Assoc Vice Chanc Student Affairs ....Dr. David M. MILSTONE
13 CIO & Assoc VC IT ....Ms. Donna R. MASSANO
91 Asst VC IT System & Planning ....Ms. Carolyn HAMEL
25 Director Research Administration ....Ms. Joanne ZANELLA-LITKE
49 Interim Dean College Arts & Science ....Dr. Jeannette RILEY
50 Int Dean Charlton Col of Business ....Dr. Richard PEGNETTER
54 Dean College of Engineering ....Dr. Robert PECK
66 Dean College of Nursing ....Dr. James FAIN
57 Dean College Visual Perform Arts ....Mr. Adrian TIO
88 Dean School Marine Science/Tech ....Dr. Steven LOHRENZ
53 Dean Sch Educ/Pub Pol & Civic ....Dr. Ismael RAMIREZ-SOTO
96 Asst VC for Administrative Services ....Mr. Michael LAGRASSA
21 Controller ....Vacant
92 Director Honors Program ....Dr. Robert DARST
94 Dir Women & Gender Studies Program ..Dr. Catherine GARNDER
88 Assoc Dir Academic Advising Center ....Ms. Suzanne MELLONI
06 University Registrar ....Dr. Carnell JONES, JR.
07 Director of Admissions ....Mr. Michael LYNCH
09 Director of Institutional Research ....Ms. Tammy A. SILVA
08 Dean Library Services ....Mr. Terrance BURTON
19 Dir Public Safety/Chief of Police ....Col. Emil FIORAVANTI
36 Director Career Development Center ....Dr. Gail L. BERMAN-MARTIN
37 Director Financial Aid ....Mr. Bruce H. PALMER
38 Dir Counseling/Stdnt Develop Ctr ....Dr. D. Christine FRIZZELL
90 Exec Dir IT Service Assurance ....Ms. Margaret S. DIAS
29 AVC Alumni Relations ....Ms. Lori JACQUES
29 Director of Alumni Relations ....Mr. C. Chad ARGOSINGER
15 Asst VC Human Resources ....Ms. Carol SANTOS
18 Director Facilities/Physical Plant ....Mr. Jeffrey LOURO
41 Director of Athletics ....Mr. Ian DAY
23 Director of Health Services ....Ms. Sheila DORGAN
39 Director of Housing/Residence Life ....Ms. Lucinda POUDRIER-AARONSON
40 Director Campus Store ....Ms. Catherine M. HICKEY
44 Director Annual Giving/Development ....Ms. Jen RAXTER
26 Asst Chancellor/Public Info ....Mr. John T. HOEY
88 Bursar ....Ms. Kathleen L. EUBANKS
35 Asst VC Student Affairs ....Ms. Cynthia CUMMINGS
35 Associate Dean of Students ....Ms. Shelly METIVIER SCOTT
104 Dir Intl Exch/Study Abroad Programs ....Ms. Kristen KALBRENER
85 Dir International Student Center ....Ms. Christina M. BRUEN
93 Dir FD Unity House/Asst Dean Stdnts ....Mr. Keith WILDER
88 Director Academic Resource Center ....Mr. Thomas DAIGLE
88 Ombudsman ....Mr. William KING
105 Webmaster ....Mr. Don KING
108 Dir Learning Outcomes & Assessment ....Ms. Barika L. BARBOZA

*University of Massachusetts Lowell (B)

1 University Avenue, Lowell MA 01854-2881
County: Middlesex | FICE Identification: 002161
Unit ID: 166513
Telephone: (978) 934-4000 | Carnegie Class: RU/H
FAX Number: (978) 934-3000 | Calendar System: Semester
URL: www.uml.edu
Established: 1894 | Annual Undergrad Tuition & Fees (In-State): $11,847
Enrollment: 15,431 | Coed
Affiliation or Control: State | IRS Status: 501(c)3
Highest Offering: Doctorate
Program: 2-Year Principally Bachelor's Creditable; Liberal Arts And General; Teacher Preparatory; Professional
Accreditation: EH, ART, BUS, ENG, ENGR, ENGT, MT, MUS, NURSE, PTA, TED

02 Chancellor ....Mr. Martin T. MEEHAN
03 Executive Vice Chancellor ....Dr. Jacqueline MOLONEY
05 Provost ....Dr. Ahmed ABDELAL
20 Vice Provost Undergrad Education ....Dr. Charlotte MANDELL
58 Vice Provost Graduate Education ....Dr. Donald PIERSON
10 Vice Chancellor Finance & Operation ...Ms. Joanne YESTRAMSKI
30 Vice Chancellor for Advancement ....Mr. Edward CHIU
46 Vice Provost for Research ....Dr. Julie CHEN
18 Assoc VC Facilities Mgmt ....Mr. Thomas DREYER
88 Assoc VC Entrepreneurship Econ Dev ....Mr. Steven TELLO
31 Asst VC Community Outreach ....Mr. Paul MARION
49 Dean Col Fine Arts/Hum/Soc Sci ....Dr. Luis FALCON
81 Dean College of Sciences ....Dr. Mark HINES
53 Dean of Education ....Dr. Anita GREENWOOD
51 Exec Dir Academic Svcs/Cont Educ ....Ms. Pauline CARROLL
54 Dean College of Engineering ....Dr. John TING
76 Dean School of Health & Environment ....Dr. Shortie MCKINNEY
50 Dean Manning School of Business ....Dr. Kathryn CARTER
88 Dean School of Marine Sci & Tech ....Dr. Robert GAMACHE
13 Exec Dir Information Technology ....Mr. Richard ZERA
09 Director of Institutional Research ....Dr. Julie ALIG
08 Director of Libraries ....Mr. George HART
06 Registrar ....Ms. Patricia DUFF
37 Director of Financial Aid ....Ms. Joyce MCLAUGHLIN
35 Dean of Students ....Mr. Larry SIEGEL
38 Director of Counseling Svcs ....Dr. John PAKSTIS
36 Director of Career Services ....Ms. Patricia A. YATES
41 Director of Athletics ....Mr. Dana SKINNER
44 Associate Director of Development ....Vacant
29 Dir of Alumni Relations ....Ms. Heather MAKREZ
15 Assoc VC Human Resources and EOO ....Ms. Lauren TURNER
19 Chief Univ Police Dir Public Safe ....Mr. Randolph BRASCHERS
23 Exec Director Health Services ....Ms. Nancy QUATTROCCHI
88 Dir Graduate Admissions ....Ms. Linda SOUTHWORTH
96 Dir Purchasing & Campus Services ....Mr. Thomas HOOLE
88 Dir Outreach & Recruitment ....Mr. Michael BELCHER
07 Director of Undergrad Admissions ....Ms. Kerrie JOHNSTON
88 Associate Dir U Card Services ....Mr. John VICTORINE
28 Dir Equal Opportunity & Outreach ....Ms. Oneida BLAGG
84 Dean Enrollment & Student Success ....Mr. Thomas TAYLOR
26 VC University Relations ....Ms. Patricia MCCAFFERTY
21 Assoc Vice Chancellor for Finance ....Mr. Steven O'RIORDAN
88 Director Student Disability Svcs ....Ms. Jody GOLDSTEIN
39 Dir of Student Residence Life ....Mr. John KOHL
88 Director Graduate Administration ....Ms. Deborah WHITE

*University of Massachusetts Medical School (C)

55 Lake Avenue N, Worcester MA 01655-0001
County: Worcester | FICE Identification: 009756
Unit ID: 166708
Telephone: (508) 856-8989 | Carnegie Class: Spec/Med
FAX Number: (508) 856-8181 | Calendar System: Semester
URL: www.umassmed.edu
Established: 1962 | Annual Graduate Tuition & Fees: $18,593
Enrollment: 1,189 | Coed
Affiliation or Control: State | IRS Status: 501(c)3
Highest Offering: Doctorate; No Undergraduates
Program: Professional
Accreditation: EH, DENT, IPSY, MED, NMT, NURSE, PDPSY, RTT

02 Chancellor & SVP Health Sciences ....Dr. Michael F. COLLINS
05 Exec Dep Chanc Provost & Dean ....Dr. Terence R. FLOTTE
10 VC Administration & Finance ....Mr. Robert E. JENAL
30 Vice Chancellor for Development ....Mr. Charles J. PAGNAM
88 Exec Vice Chance UMass Biologics ....Dr. Mark D. KLEMPNER
11 Exec Vice Chancellor & Commwlth Med ..Ms. Joyce A. MURPHY
16 Vice Chanc Human Res/Diversity ....Dr. Deborah L. PLUMMER
86 Vice Chanc Government/Cmty Relation ....Mr. James LEARY
26 Vice Chancellor of Communications ....Mr. Edward J. KEOHANE
18 Assoc Vice Chanc Facilities Mgmt ....Mr. John T. BAKER
88 Vice Provost Faculty Affairs ....Dr. Luanne THORNDYKE
88 Vice Provost School Services ....Dr. Deborah-Harmon HINES
43 General Counsel/AVP Management ....Mr. James HEALY
46 Vice Provost for Research ....Dr. John L. SULLIVAN
53 Sr Assoc Dean Educational Affairs ....Dr. Michele P. PUGNAIRE
63 Sr Assc Dean Clin Aff/Assc Dean GME ... Dr. Deborah DEMARCO
66 Dean Graduate School of Nursing ....Dr. Paulette SEYMOUR-ROUTE
32 Associate Dean Student Affairs ....Dr. Mai-Lan A. ROGOFF
58 Dean Grad School Biomedical Science ....Dr. Anthony CARRUTHERS
06 Registrar ....Mr. Michael F. BAKER
13 Chief Information Officer ....Mr. Robert P. PETERSON
07 Assoc Dean for Admissions ....Dr. John A. PARASKOS
37 Director Financial Aid ....Ms. Betsy A. GROVES
08 Director of Library ....Ms. Elaine R. MARTIN
100 Chief of Staff ....Mr. Brendan H. CHISHOLM
04 Exec Assistant to the Chancellor ....Ms. Jill ALMY
17 Sr Assoc Dean UMass Medical Group ....Dr. Eric DICKSON
88 Assoc Provost for Global Health ....Dr. Katherine LUZURIAGA
88 Asst Dean for Admin/Chief of Staff ....Ms. Lisa B. BEITTEL
09 Institutional Research Officer ....Dr. Mary L. ZANETTI

*Bridgewater State University (D)

Bridgewater MA 02325-0001
County: Plymouth | FICE Identification: 002183
Unit ID: 165024
Telephone: (508) 531-1000 | Carnegie Class: Master's L
FAX Number: N/A | Calendar System: Semester
URL: www.bridgew.edu
Established: 1840 | Annual Undergrad Tuition & Fees (In-State): $8,052
Enrollment: 11,294 | Coed
Affiliation or Control: State | IRS Status: 501(c)3
Highest Offering: Master's
Program: Liberal Arts And General; Teacher Preparatory; Professional
Accreditation: EH, ART, CACREP, MUS, SPAA, SW, TED

02 President ....Dr. Dana MOHLER-FARIA
03 Exec VP/VP for External Affairs ....Mr. Fred CLARK
05 Provost & VP Academic Affairs ....Dr. Howard LONDON
11 Vice Pres Administration/Finance ....Mr. Miguel GOMES
32 Vice President Student Affairs ....Dr. Jason PINA
30 VP Univ Advance/Strategic Planning ....Mr. Bryan BALDWIN
10 Assoc Vice Pres Finance ....Dr. Darlene COSTA-BROWN
15 Assoc Vice Pres Human Resources ....Ms. Keri POWERS
22 Asst to Pres Affirmative Action ....Dr. Alan COMEDY
32 Asst Vice Pres Student Affairs ....Mr. Brian SALVAGGIO
35 Assoc Vice Pres Student Affairs ....Dr. Catherine HOLBROOK
84 Assoc Vice Pres for Enrollment Svcs ....Dr. Heather SMITH
88 Acting Assoc Provost Faculty Affs ....Dr. Ann BRUNJES
45 Assoc Provost Academic Plng/Admin ....Dr. Michael YOUNG
79 Dean Col of Humanities/Social Sci ....Dr. Paula KREBS
53 Actg Dean Col Education/Allied Stds ....Dr. Lisa BATTAGLINO
50 Dean College of Business ....Dr. Marian EXTEJT
100 Chief of Staff ....Dr. Brenda MOLIFE
07 Dean of University Admissions ....Mr. Gregg MEYER
13 Chief Information Officer ....Mr. Patrick CRONIN
06 Director Student Records/Registrar ....Ms. Irene C. CHECKOVICH
38 Director Academic Achievement Ctr ....Ms. Alicia D'OYLEY
29 Director Alumni Relations ....Ms. Shana MURRELL
30 Director of Development ....Mr. Todd AUDYATIS
41 Director Athletics ....Vacant
21 Director Admin Support Svcs ....Mrs. Margarida VIEIRA
19 Chief Campus Police ....Mr. David H. TILLINGHAST
36 Director Career Services ....Mr. John PAGANELLI
88 Director Day Care Center ....Ms. Judith RITACCO
18 Director Facilities ....Mr. Keith MACDONALD
37 Director of Financial Aid ....Ms. Janet GUMBRIS
23 Director Counseling/Health Services ....Ms. Mary Lou FRIAS
08 Director Library Services ....Mr. Michael SOMERS
51 Dir Continuing/Distance Education ....Dr. Mary W. FULLER
22 Director Multicultural Affairs ....Ms. Andrea GARR-BARNES
27 Acting Director of Publications ....Ms. Marie MURPHY
25 Director Grants/Sponsored Projects ....Ms. Mia ENRIGHT
96 Director of Purchasing ....Vacant
28 Director of Institutional Diversity ..Dr. Sabrina GENTLEWARRIOR

*Fitchburg State University (E)

160 Pearl Street, Fitchburg MA 01420-2697
County: Worcester | FICE Identification: 002184
Unit ID: 165820
Telephone: (978) 345-2151 | Carnegie Class: Master's L
FAX Number: (978) 665-3693 | Calendar System: Semester
URL: www.fitchburgstate.edu
Established: 1894 | Annual Undergrad Tuition & Fees (In-State): $8,710
Enrollment: 6,891 | Coed
Affiliation or Control: State | IRS Status: 501(c)3
Highest Offering: Master's
Program: Liberal Arts And General; Teacher Preparatory; Professional
Accreditation: EH, CS, IACBE, NURSE, TED

02 President ....Dr. Robert V. ANTONUCCI
05 Vice President Academic Affairs ....Dr. Robin E. BOWEN
10 Vice Pres Finance & Administration ....Mr. Jay BRY
20 Associate VP Academic Affairs ....Dr. Paul WEIZER
11 Chief Operating Officer ....Mr. Jay D. BRY

26 Exec Asst to Pres for External Affs .... Mr. Michael V. SHANLEY
32 Dean of Student & Academic Life .... Dr. Stanley BUCHOLC
84 Dean Enrollment Mgmt .... Ms. Pamela MCCAFFERTY
51 Dean of Graduate Cont Educ ....Ms. Catherine E. CANNEY
53 Interim Dean of Education ....Dr. Pamela HILL
30 Vice President of Inst Advancement ....Mr. Christopher HENDRY
35 Assistant Dean for Student Devel ...Dr. Henry C. PARKINSON, III
06 Registrar ....Ms. Linda DUPELL
09 Director of Institutional Research ....Vacant
08 Director Library ....Mr. Robert A. FOLEY
41 Director Athletics ....Ms. Sue M. LAUDER
07 Director of Admissions ....Ms. Kay REYNOLDS
36 Director of Career Services ....Ms. Erin C. KELLEHER
38 Director Counseling ....Dr. Robert HYNES
23 Director Student Health Services ....Ms. Martha FAVRE
29 Asst Director of Alumni Relations ....Mr. Michael KUSHMEREK
19 Director of Campus Police ....Chief James HAMEL
44 Director of Annual Fund ....Vacant
96 Director of Procurement ....Ms. Doreen ARES
15 Asst VP of Human Resources/Payroll .... Ms. Jessica MURDOCH
18 Dir Capital Planning/Maintenance ....Mr. Eric HANSEN

*Framingham State University (A)

100 State Street, PO Box 9101,
Framingham MA 01701-9101
County: Middlesex FICE Identification: 002185
Unit ID: 165866
Telephone: (508) 620-1220 Carnegie Class: Master's L
FAX Number: (508) 626-4592 Calendar System: Semester
URL: www.framingham.edu
Established: 1839 Annual Undergrad Tuition & Fees (In-State): $8,080
Enrollment: 6,415 Coed
Affiliation or Control: State IRS Status: 501(c)3
Highest Offering: Master's
Program: Liberal Arts And General; Teacher Preparatory
Accreditation: EH, DIETC, DIETD, NURSE

02 President ....Dr. Timothy J. FLANAGAN
03 Executive VP Admin/Finance/Tech ....Dr. Dale M. HAMEL
05 VP Academic Affairs ....Dr. Linda VADEN-GOAD
84 VP Enrollment & Student Development ... Dr. Susanne H. CONLEY
100 VP Chief of Staff & General Counsel ....Ms. Rita COLUCCI
20 Associate VP Academic Affairs ....Dr. Ellen ZIMMERMAN
20 Associate VP DGCE ....Dr. Scott B. GREENBERG
13 Associate VP Technology and CITO ....Mr. Patrick LAUGHRAN
18 Assistant VP Capital Planning .... Mr. Warren FAIRBANKS
07 Dean of Admissions ....Mr. Jeremy SPENCER
32 Dean of Student Affairs ....Dr. Melinda K. STOOPS
39 Associate Dean Residence Life ....Mr. Glenn COCHRAN
28 Assistant Dean Multicultural Affair .... Mr. David N. BALDWIN
88 Assistant Dean Advising ....Dr. Christopher GREGORY
15 Associate Director HR .... Ms. Erin NECHIPURENKO
09 Associate Director IR ....Ms. Ann CASO
19 Chief Public Safety Police Services ....Mr. Brad MEDEIROS
88 Director of Academic Support ....Ms. LaDonna BRIDGES
108 Director of Assessment ....Dr. Susan CHANG
91 Director Student Info Systems ....Ms. Marsha BRYAN
41 Director of Athletics ....Mr. Thomas KELLEY
36 Director Career Services ....Mr. Rich DAVINO
106 Director of Education Technology .... Ms. Robin ROBINSON
37 Director Financial Aid ....Ms. Susan LANZILLO
21 Director Financial Services ....Mr. Joseph P. CALAPA
89 Director First Year Programs .... Mr. Benjamin J. TRAPANICK
23 Director of Health Services .... Ms. Ilene HOFRENNING
104 Director International Education .... Ms. Jane DECATUR
90 Director of User Services ....Ms. Deborah MOSCHELLA
08 Director of Library Services ....Mrs. Bonnie MITCHELL
38 Director Counseling Center ....Dr. Paul WELCH
35 Director Student Involvement ....Ms. Rachel LUCKING
06 Registrar ....Mr. Mark R. POWERS
88 Director of Student Accounts ....Ms. Deborah DALTON
04 Special Assistant to the President .... Ms. Kathleen BROSNIHAN
88 Network and Telecom ....Mr. Michael ZINKUS
30 Director Development ....Mr. Eric GUSTAFSON

*Massachusetts College of Art and Design (B)

621 Huntington Avenue, Boston MA 02115-5882
County: Suffolk FICE Identification: 002180
Unit ID: 166674
Telephone: (617) 879-7000 Carnegie Class: Spec/Arts
FAX Number: (617) 566-4034 Calendar System: Semester
URL: www.massart.edu
Established: 1873 Annual Undergrad Tuition & Fees (In-State): $10,400
Enrollment: 2,014 Coed
Affiliation or Control: State IRS Status: 501(c)3
Highest Offering: Master's
Program: Teacher Preparatory; Professional
Accreditation: EH, ART

02 President .... Ms. Dawn BARRETT
03 Executive Vice President .... Mr. Kurt STEINBERG
05 Senior Vice Pres Academic Affairs .... Dr. Maureen KELLY
32 Vice President Student Development ....Dr. Maureen KEEFE
30 Vice Pres Institutional Advancement .... Mr. Hunter O'HANIAN
09 Assoc VP of Planning/Research ....Ms. Kathleen KEENAN
20 Associate VP Academic Affairs ....Ms. Michele FURST
21 Asst Vice Pres of Fiscal Affairs .... Mr. Donald ARPINO
100 Chief of Staff President's Office ....Ms. Julianne WALSH
86 Asst to Pres Government/Cmty Rels .... Mr. Robert CHAMBERS
07 Dean of Admissions ....Ms. Karen TOWNSEND
35 Dean Students/Multi-Cultural Affrs ....Dr. Jamie COSTELLO
58 Dean Graduate Programs ....Mr. George CREAMER
06 Registrar .... Mr. Frank CALLAHAN
37 Director of Financial Aid .... Mr. Aurelio RAMIREZ
88 Dir Curatorial Pgms/Prof Galleries ....Ms. Lisa TUNG
08 Director Library ....Mr. Paul DOBBS
15 Director Human Resources .... Ms. Elaine O'SULLIVAN
22 Dir Civil Rights Compliance/Dvrsty ....Ms. Mercedes EVANS
18 Director Facilities/Physical Plant ....Mr. Howie LAROSEE
11 Director of Administrative Services ....Mr. James MCDAID
27 Chief Information Officer ....Mr. Eric BIRD
29 Director of Alumni Relations ....Ms. Emily FOSTER-DAY
26 Exec Dir Marketing/Communications .... Ms. Ana DAVIS

*Massachusetts College of Liberal Arts (C)

375 Church Street, North Adams MA 01247-4100
County: Berkshire FICE Identification: 002187
Unit ID: 167288
Telephone: (413) 662-5000 Carnegie Class: Bac/A&S
FAX Number: (413) 662-5010 Calendar System: Semester
URL: www.mcla.edu
Established: 1894 Annual Undergrad Tuition & Fees (In-State): $8,525
Enrollment: 1,866 Coed
Affiliation or Control: State IRS Status: 501(c)3
Highest Offering: Master's
Program: Liberal Arts And General; Teacher Preparatory; Professional
Accreditation: EH

02 President ....Dr. Mary K. GRANT
05 VP Academic Affairs ....Dr. Cynthia F. BROWN
10 VP Administration & Finance .... Dr. James M. STAKENAS
84 VP Enrollment & External Relations ... Ms. Denise RICHARDELLO
30 Chief Advancement Officer .... Ms. Marianne DRAKE
32 Dean of Students ....Ms. Charlotte DEGEN
20 Dean Academic Affairs ....Dr. Monica JOSLIN
04 Executive Assistant to President .... Mr. Thomas BERNARD
26 Coord of Marketing & Communications ....Ms. Bernadette LUPO
27 Chief Information Officer ....Mr. Curt KING
21 Treasurer .... Mr. Gerald DESMARAIS
07 Dean Admissions and Enrollment ....Ms. Annette S. JEFFES
108 Assoc Dean Assessment & Planning ....Dr. Kristina BENDIKAS
08 Assoc Dean Library Services .... Ms. Maureen HORAK
90 Assoc Dean Information Technology .... Mr. Peter ALLMAKER
35 Asst Dean of Students .... Ms. Theresa M. O'BRYANT
06 Asst Dean Enrollment Services .... Mr. Steven KING
37 Director Financial Aid ....Ms. Elizabeth PETRI
39 Director Residential Programs ....Ms. Dianne M. MANNING
41 Director Athletics .... Mr. Scott NICHOLS
18 Director Facilities Management ....Mr. Charles L. KIMBERLING
44 Dir Annual Fund & Alumni Relations ....Ms. Jocelyn MERRICK
21 Director Student Accounts/
Bursar ....Ms. Jennifer MACKSEY-ETHIER
23 Director Health Services ....Ms. JoAnn TIERNEY
15 Director Human Resources ....Ms. Marilyn C. TRUSKOWSKI
19 Director Public Safety ....Mr. Joseph CHARON
38 Director Counseling Services ....Ms. Heidi A. RIELLO
09 Staff Assoc Institutional Research ....Mr. Jason G. CANALES
36 Coordinator Career Services .... Ms. Janine DESGRES

*Massachusetts Maritime Academy (D)

101 Academy Drive, Buzzards Bay MA 02532-3400
County: Barnstable FICE Identification: 002181
Unit ID: 166692
Telephone: (508) 830-5000 Carnegie Class: Bac/Diverse
FAX Number: (508) 830-5004 Calendar System: Semester
URL: www.maritime.edu
Established: 1891 Annual Undergrad Tuition & Fees (In-State): $7,203
Enrollment: 1,305 Coed
Affiliation or Control: State IRS Status: 501(c)3
Highest Offering: Master's
Program: Professional
Accreditation: EH

02 President ....RADM. R. G. GURNON
05 Vice President/Dean ....CAPT. Brad LIMA
26 Vice Pres External Relations ....Mr. Michael A. JOYCE
30 Vice Pres Advancement ....Ms. Holly KNIGHT
32 Dean of Students ....CAPT. Edward ROZAK
36 Assoc Dir Career/Professional Svcs .... CDR. Maryanne RICHARDS
84 Vice Pres Enrollment Management .. CAPT. Elizabeth STEVENSON
06 Director Student Records/Registrar .... Mr. Michael CUFF
08 Director Library ....Ms. Susan BERTEAUX
15 Director Personnel Services ....Mrs. Elizabeth BENWAY
18 Chief Facilities/Physical Plant ....Mr. Paul O'KEEFE
21 Associate Business Officer ....Mrs. Rose CASS
26 Chief Public Relations Officer ....Mr. Christopher RYAN
29 Director Alumni Relations ....Mr. Ian MACLEOD
37 Director Student Financial Aid ....Mrs. Cathy KEDSKI
96 Director of Purchasing ....Mr. Brian CHURCHILL

*Salem State University (E)

352 Lafayette Street, Salem MA 01970-5353
County: Essex FICE Identification: 002188
Unit ID: 167729
Telephone: (978) 542-6000 Carnegie Class: Master's L
FAX Number: (978) 542-6970 Calendar System: Semester
URL: www.salemstate.edu
Established: 1854 Annual Undergrad Tuition & Fees (In-State): $8,110
Enrollment: 9,646 Coed
Affiliation or Control: State IRS Status: 501(c)3
Highest Offering: Master's
Program: Liberal Arts And General; Teacher Preparatory; Professional
Accreditation: EH, ART, CS, MUS, NMT, NURSE, OT, SW, TED, THEA

02 President ....Dr. Patricia M. MESERVEY
03 Executive Vice President ....Dr. Stanley P. CAHILL
05 Provost & Academic VP .... Dr. Kristin G. ESTERBERG
10 VP Finance & Facilities ....Mr. Andrew SOLL
30 VP Institutional Advancement .... Ms. Cynthia MCGURREN
08 Dean Library & Instr/Learning Supp ....Dr. Susan E. CIRILLO
70 Dean School of Human Services ....Dr. Neal DECHILLO
50 Dean School of Business ....Dr. K. Brewer DORAN
58 Dean Graduate School ....Dr. Carol A. GLOD
51 Dean Continuing Education ....Dr. Arlene T. GREENSTEIN
49 Dean School of Arts & Sciences ....Dr. Jude NIXON
26 Assoc VP Marketing & Communications .... Ms. Karen CADY
21 Assoc VP Financial Svcs ....Mr. Joseph DONOVAN
84 Assoc VP Enrollment Management ....Dr. Scott JAMES
32 Assoc VP & Dean of Student Life ....Dr. James G. STOLL
15 Assistant VP for HR & EEO ....Ms. Beth A. MARSHALL
44 Asst VP Alumni Affairs/Annual Giv ....Ms. Eileen M. O'BRIEN
13 CIO Information Technology Svcs .... Mrs. Patricia AINSWORTH
19 Director Public Safety ....Mr. Gene R. LABONTE
100 Chief of Staff ....Ms. Beth A. BOWER
101 Exec Asst to President/Secy to BOT ....Ms. Jean FLEISCHMAN
41 Director Athletics ....Mr. Timothy P. SHEA
09 Dir Inst Effectiveness & Planning ....Dr. Neal FOGG

*Westfield State University (F)

577 Western Avenue, Westfield MA 01086-1630
County: Hampden FICE Identification: 002189
Unit ID: 168263
Telephone: (413) 572-5300 Carnegie Class: Master's M
FAX Number: (413) 572-8147 Calendar System: Semester
URL: www.westfield.ma.edu
Established: 1838 Annual Undergrad Tuition & Fees (In-State): $8,297
Enrollment: 6,092 Coed
Affiliation or Control: State IRS Status: 501(c)3
Highest Offering: Beyond Master's But Less Than Doctorate
Program: Liberal Arts And General; Teacher Preparatory
Accreditation: EH, MUS, CS, EXSC, SW, TED

02 President ....Dr. Evan S. DOBELLE
05 Vice Pres Academic Affairs ....Dr. Elizabeth PRESTON
32 Vice Pres Student Affairs ....Dr. Carlton PICKRON
84 Vice Pres Enrollment Management .... Dr. Carol PERSSON
10 Vice Pres Administration & Finance ....Mr. Jerry HAYES
30 Vice Pres Advancement/Univ Rels ....Ms. Nanci SALVIDIO
20 Dean of Faculty ....Dr. Andrew BONACCI
49 Dean of Undergraduate Programs .... Dr. Marsha MAROTTA
51 Dean Graduate/Continuing Educ .... Dr. Kimberly TOBIN
53 Dean of Education .... Dr. Cheryl STANLEY
35 Dean Student Affairs .... Ms. Susan LAMONTAGNE
06 Registrar ....Mr. John OHOTNICKY
09 Assoc Dean Institutional Reseach ....Dr. Lisa PLANTEFABER
22 Director Multicult Affairs/AA/EO .... Ms. Waleska LUGO-DEJESUS
08 Director Library .... Mr. Thomas RAFFENSPERGER
11 Asst Vice Pres Administration ....Dr. Curt D. ROBIE
39 Exec Director Residential Life .... Dr. Jon CONLOGUE
19 Interim Director Public Safety .... Mr. Michael NOCKUNAS
27 Asst to President Communications .... Mr. Robert PLASSE
36 Director Career Services ....Mr. Junior DELGADO
13 Exec Dir Information Technology .... Mr. Christopher HIRTLE
91 Director Admin Systems ....Mr. Rudolph HEBERT
44 Associate VP Advancement/College ....Mr. Don BOWMAN
18 Asst Dir Facilities/Physical Plant ....Mr. Terry FENSTAD
41 Director Athletics ....Mr. Richard LENFEST
24 Director Media Services ....Mr. Robert MAILLOUX
38 Director Counseling Center ....Ms. Tammy BRINGAZE
23 Director Health Services ....Ms. Patricia BERUBE
37 Director of Financial Aid ....Ms. Catherine RYAN
07 Director of Admissions ....Dr. Kelly HART
21 Director Administrative Services .... Ms. Elizabeth MOKRZECKI
21 Director of Finance ....Ms. Lisa FREEMAN
29 Assoc VP Alumni Relations ....Ms. Nanci SALVIDIO
96 Director of Purchasing ....Mr. Chris RAYMOND
16 Director of Human Resources ....Mr. Rafael BONES
102 Director of Corporate Relations .... Mr. Olen BIELSKI
25 Director Faculty Grants Spons Rsrch ....Ms. Louann D'ANGELO

*Worcester State University (G)

486 Chandler Street, Worcester MA 01602-2597
County: Worcester FICE Identification: 002190
Unit ID: 168430
Telephone: (508) 929-8000 Carnegie Class: Master's M
FAX Number: (508) 929-8191 Calendar System: Semester
URL: www.worcester.edu
Established: 1874 Annual Undergrad Tuition & Fees (In-State): $8,229
Enrollment: 6,204 Coed
Affiliation or Control: State IRS Status: 501(c)3
Highest Offering: Master's
Program: Occupational; Liberal Arts And General; Teacher Preparatory; Professional
Accreditation: EH, NMT, NURSE, OT, SP, @TEAC

02 President ....Mr. Barry M. MALONEY
05 Provost/Vice President Academic Aff ....Dr. Charles CULLUM
10 Vice President of Fiscal Affairs .... Ms. Kathleen EICHELROTH

32 Vice President Student Affairs ... Dr. Sibyl M. BROWNLEE
30 Vice Pres Institutional Advancement ... Mr. Thomas MCNAMARA
04 Exec Assistant to the President ... Ms. Judith A. ST. AMAND
58 Assoc VP CE/Out & Dean Grad Stds ... Dr. William H. WHITE
93 Asst Dean/Dir Multicultural Affairs ... Ms. Marcela A. URIBE-JENNINGS
55 Assoc Dean of Graduate/Cont Educ ... Dr. Roberta KYLE
22 Director of Affirmative Action ... Dr. Calvin HILL
13 Interim Chief Information Officer ... Mr. Eihab JABOR
20 Asst VP for Assessment & Planning ... Dr. Carol LERCH
20 Assoc Vice President for Academics ... Dr. Maureen SHAMGOCHIAN
35 Associate VP/Dean of Students ... Ms. Julie KAZARIAN
21 Assoc VP for Fiscal Affairs ... Ms. Robin QUILL
17 Exec Dir Center for Health Profess ... Vacant
07 Interim Director of Admissions ... Mr. Jeremy KRAUSS
26 Asst VP of PR/Marketing ... Ms. Lea Ann ERICKSON
37 Director of Financial Aid ... Ms. Jayne MCGINN
08 Director Library ... Vacant
18 Director of Facilities ... Ms. Sandra OLSON
15 Director Human Resources ... Mr. Russell E. VICKSTROM
19 Chief of Campus Police ... Ms. Rosemary NAUGHTON
88 Operations/Production Manager ... Ms. Mary Ellen THORPE
36 Director Career Services ... Ms. Marcia EAGLESON
06 Registrar ... Ms. Julie CHAFEE
41 Director Athletics & Rec Sports ... Ms. Susan E. CHAPMAN
39 Assistant Director of Life/Housing ... Mr. Adrian GAGE
35 Dir Student Center/Stdnt Activities ... Mr. Timothy J. SULLIVAN
38 Director Student Counseling ... Ms. Laura MURPHY
42 Chaplain ... Fr. Robert LOFTUS
85 Int Dir of International Students ... Ms. Katey PALUMBO
96 Director of Procurement/Bus Mgr ... Ms. Brenda BUSSEY
88 Manager of Student Accounts ... Ms. Julie CARMEL
09 Director of Institutional Research ... Mr. Kenneth SMITH
29 Director Alumni Relation ... Ms. Tara HANCOCK
84 Interim Director Enrollment Mgmt ... Dr. Donald VESCIO

*Berkshire Community College (A)

1350 West Street, Pittsfield MA 01201-5786

County: Berkshire FICE Identification: 002167
Unit ID: 164775
Telephone: (413) 499-4660 Carnegie Class: Assoc/Pub-R-M
FAX Number: (413) 447-7840 Calendar System: Semester
URL: www.berkshirecc.edu
Established: 1960 Annual Undergrad Tuition & Fees (In-State): $5,965
Enrollment: 2,566 Coed
Affiliation or Control: State IRS Status: 501(c)3
Highest Offering: Associate Degree
Program: Occupational; 2-Year Principally Bachelor's Creditable
Accreditation: EH, ADNUR, PTAA

02 President ... Ms. Ellen KENNEDY
05 Vice President for Academic Affairs ... Dr. Frances FEINERMAN
10 Vice President Admin/Finance ... Ms. Ellen KENNEDY
32 Vice Pres Student Affs/Enroll Svcs ... Mr. Michael BULLOCK
30 Vice Pres Institutional Advancement ... Mr. Jeffrey DOSCHER
79 Dean Humanities ... Mr. Thomas CURLEY
54 Dean Engineering/Sciences ... Dr. Charles KAMINSKI
66 Dean Nursing/Allied Hlth ... Ms. Anna FOSS
103 VP Lifelong Lrng/Workforce Dev ... Mr. William MULHOLLAND
37 Director Student Financial Aid ... Ms. Anne MOORE
13 Director Information Technology ... Mr. Richard WIXSOM
06 Registrar ... Mr. Donald PFEIFER
08 Director of Library ... Ms. Nancy WALKER
15 VP Human Res/Affirm Action Officer ... Ms. Deborah COTE
88 Student Advisor Transfer ... Mr. Geoff TABOR
26 Director Public Relations ... Ms. Christina BARRETT
12 Director of So County Center ... Ms. Phylene FARRELL
18 Director of Facilities ... Mr. Scott RICHARDS
40 Manager Bookstore ... Ms. Kristen SCALA
32 Director of Student Life ... Mr. Dane WESTED
24 Dir of Instructional Technology ... Vacant
09 Dir Institutional Rsrch/Plng/Grants ... Mr. John PASKUS
31 Dir Development/Community Outreach ... Ms. Jennifer KERWOOD

*Bristol Community College (B)

777 Elsbree Street, Fall River MA 02720-7395

County: Bristol FICE Identification: 002176
Unit ID: 165033
Telephone: (508) 678-2811 Carnegie Class: Assoc/Pub-U-MC
FAX Number: (508) 730-3270 Calendar System: Semester
URL: www.bristolcc.edu
Established: 1965 Annual Undergrad Tuition & Fees (In-State): $4,178
Enrollment: 9,000 Coed
Affiliation or Control: State IRS Status: 501(c)3
Highest Offering: Associate Degree
Program: Occupational; 2-Year Principally Bachelor's Creditable
Accreditation: EH, ADNUR, COMTA, DH, MAC, MLTAD, OTA

02 President ... Dr. John J. SBREGA
03 Executive Vice President ... Mr. David F. FEENEY
05 Acting VP of Academic Affairs ... Mr. Greg SETHARES
50 Dean of Business & Info Tech ... Mr. William BERARDI
79 Dean of Humanities & Education ... Ms. Joanne PRESTON
83 Dean of Behavioral & Soc Sciences ... Dr. Vernon HARLAN
76 Dean of Health Sciences ... Ms. Patricia DENT
81 Dean of Math/Science & Engineering ... Dr. Peter SCHUYLER
10 VP of Administration & Finance ... Mr. Steven KENYON
30 VP of Resource Development ... Ms. Elizabeth K. MCCARTHY
84 VP of Students and Enrollment Mgt ... Mr. Steve OZUG
91 VP of Information Technology ... Ms. Jo-Ann M. PELLETIER
32 Director Student Engagement ... Ms. Kathleen BURNS
07 Dean of Admissions ... Ms. Shilo HENRIQUES
12 Dean of New Bedford Campus ... Ms. Theresa ROMANOVITCH
12 Dean of Attleboro Center ... Mr. Rodney CLARK
06 Acting Registrar ... Mr. Benjamin BAUMANN
08 Assistant Dean of the Library ... Mr. Sainath CHINNASWAMY
25 Dean of Grant Development ... Ms. Marianne TAYLOR
37 Director Student Financial Aid ... Mr. David ALLEN
38 Director Counseling Services ... Mr. Michael BENSINK
15 VP of Human Resources/Affirm Action ... Mr. Tafa AWOLAJU
18 Director of Facilities Management ... Mr. Leo RACINE
19 Director of Public Safety ... Mr. Wayne WOOD
21 Comptroller ... Mr. Keith TONI
11 Associate VP of Administration ... Ms. Linda DANZELL
20 Assoc VP Academic Affairs ... Dr. Michael VIEIRA
20 Acting Assoc VP of Academic Affairs ... Mr. Anthony UCCI
84 Assoc VP Enrollment Services ... Ms. Kathleen TORPEY GARGANTA
27 VP College Communications ... Ms. Sally C. CAMERON
29 Dir Alumni Relations/Special Events ... Ms. Jane L H. ASH
88 Dean Disability Svcs & Student Engm ... Ms. Susan BOISSONEAULT
78 Director Coop Education ... Ms. Margaret (Peg) CURRO
50 Dean Center for Business & Industry ... Ms. Carmen AGUILAR
23 Health Services Coordinator ... Ms. Carol CONSTANTINE
56 Asst Dean Instructional Lrng Tech ... Ms. April BELLAFIORE
09 VP Inst Research/Plng & Assesssment ... Ms. Rhonda GABOVITCH
92 Director Honors Program ... Mr. J. Thomas GRADY
96 Director of Purchasing ... Ms. Philicia PACHECO
36 Career Services - Sr Acad Counselor ... Ms. Patricia CONDON
41 Athletic Director ... Mr. Derek VIVEIROS
04 Executive Assistant to President ... Ms. Karen L. GIGLIO
88 Dean Developmental Educ ... Ms. Sarah MORRELL

*Bunker Hill Community College (C)

250 New Rutherford Avenue, Boston MA 02129-2925

County: Suffolk FICE Identification: 011210
Unit ID: 165112
Telephone: (617) 228-2000 Carnegie Class: Assoc/Pub-U-MC
FAX Number: (617) 228-2082 Calendar System: Semester
URL: www.bhcc.mass.edu
Established: 1973 Annual Undergrad Tuition & Fees (In-State): $3,384
Enrollment: 12,934 Coed
Affiliation or Control: State IRS Status: 501(c)3
Highest Offering: Associate Degree
Program: Occupational; 2-Year Principally Bachelor's Creditable
Accreditation: EH, ADNUR, DMS, MLTAD, RAD, SURGT

02 President ... Dr. Mary L. FIFIELD
03 Executive Vice President & CFO ... Mr. Jesse M. THOMPSON
05 VP Academic Affairs/Student Service ... Dr. James F. CANNIFF
28 Director Diversity & Inclusion ... Mr. Thomas L. SALTONSTALL
09 Exec Dean Inst Effectiveness ... Dr. Emily DIBBLE
20 Associate Academic Dean ... Ms. Judith GRAHAM-ROBEY
35 Dean of Students ... Ms. Janice M. BONANNO
26 Exec Director of Communications ... Dr. Colleen ROACH
18 Director Facilities Management ... Mr. Paul A. RIGHI
81 Dean of Mathematics/Behav Sciences ... Dr. Valerie T. SMITH
79 Dean of Humanities ... Ms. Lori A. CATALLOZZI
54 Dean Science/Engineering ... Dr. Laurie K. MCCORRY
107 Dean of Professional Studies ... Dr. Bogusia WOJCIECHOWSKA
66 Interim Dean Nurse Education ... Dr. Patti-Ann COLLINS
12 Dean Chelsea Campus ... Ms. MaryAnne MILLER
21 Comptroller ... Mr. Weusi A. TAFAWA
25 Director of Grants Development ... Mr. Steven A. ROLLER
06 Registrar ... Ms. Debra A. BOYER
08 Director Library/Info Center ... Dr. Vivica D. PIERRE
27 Chief Information Officer ... Mr. Bret MOELLER
15 Dir Human Resources/Labor Relations ... Ms. Molly B. AMBROSE
19 Director of Public Safety ... Mr. Robert BARROWS
37 Director of Financial Aid ... Ms. Melissa HOLSTER
96 Director of Purchasing ... Mr. Richard J. PISHKIN
38 Dir Advising/Counseling/Assessment ... Ms. Anne BROWN
30 Executive Director of Development ... Ms. Anne HYDE

*Cape Cod Community College (D)

2240 Iyannough Road, West Barnstable MA 02668-1599

County: Barnstable FICE Identification: 002168
Unit ID: 165194
Telephone: (508) 362-2131 Carnegie Class: Assoc/Pub-R-M
FAX Number: (508) 362-3988 Calendar System: Semester
URL: www.capecod.edu
Established: 1960 Annual Undergrad Tuition & Fees (In-State): $4,792
Enrollment: 4,371 Coed
Affiliation or Control: State IRS Status: 501(c)3
Highest Offering: Associate Degree
Program: Occupational; 2-Year Principally Bachelor's Creditable
Accreditation: EH, ADNUR, DH, MAC

02 President ... Dr. John L. COX
05 Vice Pres Academic/Student Affairs ... Ms. Susan MILLER
10 Vice President Admin & Finance ... Ms. Dixie K. NORRIS
21 Asst VP Administration & Finance ... Ms. Cynthia CROSSMAN
18 Asst VP Sustainability/Facil Mgmt ... Mr. John LEBICA
13 Asst VP Information Technology ... Mr. Gregory BANWARTH
49 Dean Arts & Humanities ... Dr. Lore DEBOWER
81 Dean Science/Tech/Math/Business ... Dr. Robert CODY
08 Dean Learning Res & Student Success ... Mr. David ZIEMBA
84 Dean Enroll Mgmt/Advising Services ... Ms. Roseanna PENA-WARFIELD
83 Dean Health/Social Sci/Human Svcs ... Ms. Susan MADDIGAN
15 Dean Human Resources & Admin ... Mr. Chester W. YACEK
08 Assoc Dean Learning Resources ... Ms. Jeanmarie FRASER
07 Director Admissions ... Vacant
37 Director of Financial Aid ... Ms. Sherry ANDERSEN
27 Director College Communications ... Mr. Michael GROSS
06 Registrar ... Ms. Sandra BRITO
19 Director Public Safety ... Mr. Philip RYAN
04 Staff Assoc to President ... Ms. Linda HOULE
36 Coord Career Plng & Placement ... Ms. Kristina IERARDI
09 Dir Institutional Research & Effec ... Dr. Elizabeth O'CONNOR-JOHNSTON

*Greenfield Community College (E)

1 College Drive, Greenfield MA 01301-9739

County: Franklin FICE Identification: 002169
Unit ID: 165981
Telephone: (413) 775-1000 Carnegie Class: Assoc/Pub-S-SC
FAX Number: (413) 774-4676 Calendar System: Semester
URL: www.gcc.mass.edu
Established: 1962 Annual Undergrad Tuition & Fees (In-State): $5,357
Enrollment: 2,510 Coed
Affiliation or Control: State IRS Status: 501(c)3
Highest Offering: Associate Degree
Program: Occupational; 2-Year Principally Bachelor's Creditable
Accreditation: EH, ADNUR

02 President ... Dr. Robert L. PURA
05 Chief Academic/Student Affairs Ofcr ... Dr. Sheryl HRUSKA
10 Chief Financial Officer ... Mr. Barry BRAIM
31 Dean of Community Education ... Mr. Robert BARBA
84 Dean Enrollment Services ... Mr. Shane HAMMOND
20 Dean Learning Resources ... Ms. Judi GREENE-CORVEE
79 Dean Humanities ... Mr. Leo HWANG-CARLOS
81 Dean Soc & Nat Sci/Math/Bus/Tech ... Dr. Peter ROSNIK
107 Dean Professional Studies ... Mr. Terence LYNN
15 Executive Dir of Human Resources ... Dr. Rita HARDIMAN
30 Exec Director Resource Development ... Ms. Regina CURTIS
13 Chief Information Officer ... Mr. Michael ASSAF
28 Chief Diversity Officer ... Dr. Rita HARDIMAN
18 Director Physical Plant ... Mr. Jeffrey MARQUES
07 Director Admissions ... Mr. Herbert E. HENTZ
37 Director Financial Aid ... Ms. Linda DESJARDINS
19 Director Public Safety ... Mr. William MAYROSE
96 Director of Purchasing ... Mr. Ryan AIKEN
08 Director Library ... Ms. Deborah CHOWN
21 Comptroller ... Ms. Karen PHILLIPS
06 Registrar ... Ms. Jennifer DUZINSKI
38 Co-Coord Learning Asst Programs ... Ms. Mary Ellen KELLY
38 Co-Coord Learning Asst Programs ... Mr. Norman BEEBE
36 Coordinator of Student Assessment ... Ms. Jean BOUCIAS
08 Coordinator Library ... Mr. Eric POULIN
35 Coordinator of Student Life ... Ms. Melissa EICH

*Holyoke Community College (F)

303 Homestead Avenue, Holyoke MA 01040-1099

County: Hampden FICE Identification: 002170
Unit ID: 166133
Telephone: (413) 538-7000 Carnegie Class: Assoc/Pub-S-SC
FAX Number: (413) 552-2045 Calendar System: Semester
URL: www.hcc.edu
Established: 1946 Annual Undergrad Tuition & Fees (In-State): $236
Enrollment: 7,228 Coed
Affiliation or Control: State IRS Status: 501(c)3
Highest Offering: Associate Degree
Program: Occupational; 2-Year Principally Bachelor's Creditable
Accreditation: EH, ACFEI, ADNUR, MUS, RAD

02 President ... Dr. William F. MESSNER
11 Vice Pres Administration & Finance ... Mr. William FOGARTY
05 Vice President Academic Affairs ... Dr. Matthew REED
32 Vice President Student Affairs ... Ms. Yanina VARGAS
30 Vice Pres Institutional Development ... Ms. Erica BROMAN
28 Assistant Vice Pres of Diversity ... Ms. Idelia SMITH
08 Dean Library ... Ms. Kathleen MCDONOUGH
15 Dean Human Resources ... Ms. Clara ELLIOTT
36 Dean Coop Education & Career Svcs ... Ms. Christine HOLBROOK
06 Registrar ... Mr. Anthony SBALBI
07 Director of Admissions ... Ms. Marcia ROSBURY-HENNE
37 Director of Financial Aid ... Ms. Karen DEROUIN
91 Director Administrative Computing ... Vacant
18 Director of Facilities ... Mr. Dan CAMPBELL
10 Comptroller ... Mr. John O'ROURKE
13 Chief Information Officer ... Ms. Linda SZALANKIEWICZ
21 Dir Business Services/Purchasing ... Ms. Tara WOLMAN
09 Director Institutional Research ... Ms. Michelle RIBERDY
26 Dir of Marketing/Public Relations ... Ms. JoAnne ROME
29 Director of Alumni Relations ... Ms. Joanna BROWN
35 Dean of Student Services ... Vacant
20 Director of Academic Administration ... Ms. Idelia SMITH
38 Dir Retention & Adult Support Svcs ... Vacant

*Massachusetts Bay Community College (G)

50 Oakland Street, Wellesley Hills MA 02481-5357

County: Norfolk FICE Identification: 002171
Unit ID: 166647
Telephone: (781) 239-3000 Carnegie Class: Assoc/Pub-S-MC

FAX Number: (781) 237-1061 Calendar System: Semester
URL: www.massbay.edu
Established: 1961 Annual Undergrad Tuition & Fees (In-State): $4,600
Enrollment: 5,276 Coed
Affiliation or Control: State IRS Status: 501(c)3
Highest Offering: Associate Degree
Program: Occupational; 2-Year Principally Bachelor's Creditable
Accreditation: EH, ADNUR, RAD, SURGT

02 President ... Dr. John O'DONNELL
05 Provost/Chief Academic Officer ... Dr. Francesca PURCELL
10 VP Admin & Finance/CFO ... Mr. Richard HASKELL
26 Associate VP for Marketing ... Mr. Jeremy SOLOMON
84 Asst VP Enrol Mgmt/Student Affairs ... Ms. Marva PERRY
15 Assistant VP of Human Resources ... Ms. Robin NELSON-BAILEY
30 Director Institutional Advancement ... Vacant
106 Dean of eLearning ... Dr. Lynn HUNTER
09 Dean Inst Planning Res & Assessment ... Dr. Yves SALOMON-FERNÁNDEZ
32 Project Director Title III ... Dr. Craig MACK
76 Dean Health Sciences Division ... Dr. JoAnn MACKEY
107 Dean Social Sci & Profess Studies ... Dr. Jane O'BRIEN FRIEDERICHS
81 Interim Dean STEM Division ... Ms. Carol STAFFIER
88 Dean Transportation & Energy ... Mr. Howard FERRIS
55 Dean Evening & Weekend Programming ... Ms. Carol STAFFIER
51 Dean Corporate/Community Education ... Vacant
32 Dean of Students (Wellesley Hills) ... Dr. Elizabeth BLUMBERG
20 Dean Academic Advancement ... Dr. David COLEMAN
07 Director of Admissions ... Ms. Donna RAPOSA
37 Director of Financial Aid ... Ms. Elizabeth ENOS
06 Registrar ... Mr. Ali GUVENDIREN
88 Interim Dir Acad Achievement Ctr ... Ms. Barbara HATCH
20 Director of Academic Advising ... Ms. Sarah READING
38 Director of Counseling ... Mr. Jon EDWARDS
36 Director of Career Services ... Ms. Julie KOMACK
90 Dir Ctr for Teaching & Learning ... Dr. Linda GRISHAM
85 Director of International Education ... Ms. Marie Lourdes ELGIRUS
41 Dir Athletics Recreation & Wellness ... Mr. Bill RAYNOR
35 Coordinator of Student Activities ... Ms. Julie SCHLEICHER
21 Controller ... Ms. Linda FAZIO
96 Budget Analyst/Purchasing Manager ... Mr. Kevin FLYNN
96 Purchasing Supervisor ... Ms. Lauren CURLEY
88 Director of Grants Development ... Dr. Cheryl WEST
13 Chief Information Officer ... Mr. Michael LYONS
91 Director Administrative Computing ... Mr. Terry KRAMER
08 Director of Learning Services ... Mr. Timothy RIVARD
18 Director of Facilities ... Mr. Marco BRANCATO
19 Manager of Public Safety ... Mr. John MCCUNE
04 Exec Assistant to the President ... Ms. Vivian ORTIZ

*Massasoit Community College (A)

1 Massasoit Boulevard, Brockton MA 02302-3996
County: Plymouth FICE Identification: 002177
Unit ID: 166823
Telephone: (508) 588-9100 Carnegie Class: Assoc/Pub-R-L
FAX Number: (508) 427-1202 Calendar System: Semester
URL: www.massasoit.mass.edu
Established: 1966 Annual Undergrad Tuition & Fees (In-State): $5,070
Enrollment: 8,263 Coed
Affiliation or Control: State IRS Status: 501(c)3
Highest Offering: Associate Degree
Program: Occupational; 2-Year Principally Bachelor's Creditable
Accreditation: EH, ADNUR, DA, MAC, RAD

02 President ... Dr. Charles WALL
05 Sr Vice Pres/VP Faculty & Instruct ... Dr. Barbara E. FINKELSTEIN
10 Chief Financial Officer ... Ms. Betty Ann LEARNED
32 Vice Pres Student Svcs/Enroll Mgmt ... Mr. David TRACY
12 Vice Pres/Dean of Canton Campus ... Mr. Nicholas PALANTZAS
15 VP & Director of Human Resources ... Mr. Peter AKEKE
04 Exec Dir Extrnl Affs/Asst to Pres ... Mr. Phillip SHEPPARD
26 Public Relations Director ... Ms. Laurie MAKER
84 Dean of Enrollment Management ... Ms. Nancy SULLIVAN
35 Dean Student Affairs ... Ms. Maureen THAYER
07 Director of Admissions ... Ms. Michelle HUGHES
37 Director Student Financial Aid ... Ms. Mary Beth COURTRIGHT
06 Registrar ... Ms. Elizabeth COLLINS
09 Director of Institutional Research ... Ms. Mary GOODHUE LYNCH
38 Director Student Counseling ... Ms. Christine DYMENT
28 Director of Diversity ... Ms. Joyce ZYMARIS
13 CIO ... Mr. Albert B. AYERS
21 Comptroller ... Ms. Sophie LEE
36 Director of Career Placement ... Ms. Kathyrn PRYLES
18 Director Facilities/Physical Plant ... Vacant
41 Director of Athletics ... Ms. Julie MULVEY
29 Director Alumni Relations ... Ms. Sheryl SAVAGE
25 Director of Grants ... Ms. Hollyce STATES
50 Acting Dean Business & Technology ... Ms. Lynda THOMPSON
79 Dean Humanities/Social Science ... Ms. Deanna YAMEEN
76 Dean Allied Health ... Dr. Anne SCALZO-MCNEIL
83 Dean Public Svc/Social Science ... Ms. Karyn BOUTIN
81 Acting Dean Science & Math ... Ms. Fran MCCUTCHEON
72 Dean of Emergent Technologies ... Mr. Felix DEVITO
88 Dean of Academic Advising ... Mr. Peter JOHNSTON

*Middlesex Community College (B)

591 Springs Road, Bedford MA 01730-1197
County: Middlesex FICE Identification: 009936
Unit ID: 166887
Telephone: (781) 280-3200 Carnegie Class: Assoc/Pub-S-MC
FAX Number: (781) 275-0741 Calendar System: Semester
URL: www.middlesex.mass.edu
Established: 1969 Annual Undergrad Tuition & Fees (In-State): $4,274
Enrollment: 9,840 Coed
Affiliation or Control: State IRS Status: 501(c)3
Highest Offering: Associate Degree
Program: Occupational; 2-Year Principally Bachelor's Creditable
Accreditation: EH, ADNUR, DA, DH, DMS, DT, MAC, RAD

02 President ... Dr. Carole A. COWAN
05 Provost/VP of Academic Affairs ... Mr. Philip SISSON
03 Executive Vice President ... Mr. James F. LINNEHAN, JR.
84 VP Enrollment Svcs/Rsrch & Plng ... Dr. Lois A. ALVES
04 Assistant to the President ... Ms. Lura SMITH
20 Associate Provost ... Ms. Clea ANDREADIS
32 Dean of Students ... Ms. Pamela FLAHERTY
88 Dean of International Arts ... Mr. Kent H. MITCHELL
79 Dean Humanities and Social Sciences ... Mr. Matthew OLSON
72 Dean of Business/Education & Publi ... Ms. Judith HOGAN
17 Dean of Health and STEM ... Ms. Kathleen J. SWEENEY
88 Dean Professional/Instructional Dev ... Ms. Mary Anne DEAN
22 Asst Dir HR/Affirm Action Officer ... Ms. Darcy ORELLANA
12 Dean of Lowell Campus ... Dr. Molly H. SHEEHY
12 Dean Fac Mgmt/Bedford Campus Mgr ... Mr. Matt SEPE
84 Dean of Enrollment Services ... Ms. Eileen M. FAGAN
26 Dean External Affs/Col Advancement ... Mr. Dennis MALVERS
07 Dean of Admissions ... Ms. Marilynn GALLAGAN
26 Director Marketing Communication ... Ms. Jennifer C. ARADHYA
35 Associate Dean of Students ... Ms. Susan WOODS
09 Assoc Dean Institutional Planning ... Vacant
27 Exec Director Public Affairs ... Mr. Patrick COOK
10 Director of Budget & Financial Svcs ... Ms. Gina SPAZIANI
16 Director Human Resources ... Mr. Gary R. MCPHEE
37 Director of Financial Aid ... Mr. Robert BAUMAL
21 Comptroller ... Ms. Kathy RICH
21 Bursar ... Mr. Christopher FIORI
08 Director Library Services ... Ms. Maryann NILES
23 Director of Health Services ... Vacant
15 Director Human Resources ... Mr. Gary MCPHEE
06 Registrar ... Mr. Kevin GATELY
96 Coordinator of Purchasing ... Ms. Maureen HUDSON

*Mount Wachusett Community College (C)

444 Green Street, Gardner MA 01440-1000
County: Worcester FICE Identification: 002172
Unit ID: 166957
Telephone: (978) 632-6600 Carnegie Class: Assoc/Pub-R-M
FAX Number: (978) 632-6155 Calendar System: Semester
URL: www.mwcc.mass.edu
Established: 1963 Annual Undergrad Tuition & Fees (In-State): $5,840
Enrollment: 4,893 Coed
Affiliation or Control: State IRS Status: 501(c)3
Highest Offering: Associate Degree
Program: Occupational; 2-Year Principally Bachelor's Creditable; Business Emphasis
Accreditation: EH, ADNUR, DH, MAC, MLTAD, PNUR, PTAA

02 President ... Dr. Daniel M. ASQUINO
03 Exec VP & VP of Enrollment Services ... Ms. Ann M. MCDONALD
05 Vice Pres of Academic Affairs ... Dr. Melissa FAMA
51 VP Lifelong Learning/Workforce Dev ... Ms. Jacqueline FELDMAN
88 Sr VP Transition & Development ... Ms. Sharyn RICE
30 Assoc VP Institutional Advancement ... Mr. Joseph STISO
11 VP Finance & Administration ... Mr. Robert LABONTE
15 VP HR/Affirmative Action Officer ... Ms. Diane RUKSNAITIS
12 Dean Leominster Campus ... Mr. John WALSH
72 Dean Academic & Inst Technology ... Mr. Vincent IALENTI
76 Dean School of Health Sciences ... Ms. Eileen COSTELLO
08 Dean Library and Academic Support ... Ms. Heidi MCCANN
36 Dir North Central Career Services ... Ms. Cynthia KRUSEN
27 Director of Marketing ... Ms. Nichole CARTER
07 Director of Admissions ... Vacant
18 Director Maintenance/Mechanical Sys ... Mr. William SWIFT
09 Dir Institutional Research ... Ms. Veena DHANKHER
37 Dir Student Records/Financial Mgmt ... Vacant
68 Director Fitness & Wellness Center ... Mr. Stephen WASHKEVICH
19 Chief Public Safety & Security ... Ms. Karen KOLIMAGA
35 Assistant Dean of Student Services ... Mr. Gregory CLEMENT
38 Director of Counseling ... Vacant
84 Assoc Dean Enrollment Services ... Mr. Glenn ROBERTS
29 Dir Alumni Affairs/Annual Giving ... Vacant
06 Registrar ... Ms. Rebecca FOREST

*North Shore Community College (D)

1 Ferncroft Road, PO Box 3340, Danvers MA 01923-0840
County: Essex FICE Identification: 002173
Unit ID: 167312
Telephone: (978) 762-4000 Carnegie Class: Assoc/Pub-S-MC
FAX Number: (978) 762-4020 Calendar System: Semester
URL: www.northshore.edu
Established: 1965 Annual Undergrad Tuition & Fees (In-State): $5,070
Enrollment: 7,974 Coed
Affiliation or Control: State IRS Status: 501(c)3
Highest Offering: Associate Degree
Program: Occupational; 2-Year Principally Bachelor's Creditable
Accreditation: EH, AAB, ADNUR, MAC, OTA, PTAA, RAD, SURGT

02 President ... Dr. Wayne M. BURTON
05 Vice President of Academic Affairs ... Mr. Paul M. FRYDRYCH
84 Vice Pres Enrollment Mgmt/Students ... Dr. Donna L. RICHEMOND
30 Vice Pres Institutional Advancement ... Dr. Sandra B. EDWARDS
11 Vice President of Administration ... Ms. Janice M. FORSSTROM
15 Vice President Human Res/Affirm Act ... Ms. Madeline WALLIS
31 Dean of Community Svcs/Corp Ed ... Ms. Dianne PALTER-GILL
90 Dean Academic Technology ... Mr. Michael BADOLATO
84 Dean of Enrollment ... Dr. Joanne LIGHT
32 Dean of Students ... Dr. Lloyd A. HOLMES
20 Assistant Dean Academic Affairs ... Dr. Laura VENTIMIGLIA
08 Director of Learning Resources ... Ms. Karen PANGALLO
14 Dir of Networking/Info Services ... Mr. Gary HAM
37 Dean of Financial Aid ... Mr. Stephen CREAMER
09 Director Inst Research/Planning ... Ms. Laurie LACHAPELLE
18 Director of Facilities Mgmt ... Mr. Richard RENEY
19 Campus Police Chief ... Mr. Douglas P. PUSKA
21 Comptroller ... Ms. Patricia CALLAHAN
26 Director Public Relations/Marketing ... Ms. Linda BRANTLY
29 Director Alumni Relations ... Ms. Sandra ROCHON
35 Chief Student Life Officer ... Ms. Lisa MILSO
36 Director Student Placement ... Ms. Lynn MARCUS
07 Director of Recruitment ... Ms. Jennifer KIRK
38 Director Student Support Center ... Mr. Daniel O'NEILL
40 Bookstore Manager ... Mr. Shawn CRONIN

*Northern Essex Community College (E)

100 Elliott Street, Haverhill MA 01830-2399
County: Essex FICE Identification: 002174
Unit ID: 167376
Telephone: (978) 556-3000 Carnegie Class: Assoc/Pub-S-MC
FAX Number: (978) 556-3723 Calendar System: Semester
URL: www.necc.mass.edu
Established: 1960 Annual Undergrad Tuition & Fees (In-State): $4,860
Enrollment: 7,036 Coed
Affiliation or Control: State IRS Status: 501(c)3
Highest Offering: Associate Degree
Program: Occupational; 2-Year Principally Bachelor's Creditable; Fine Arts Emphasis
Accreditation: EH, ADNUR, DA, MAC, PNUR, POLYT, RAD

02 President ... Dr. Lane A. GLENN
05 Vice President of Academic Affairs ... Dr. William HEINEMAN
30 Vice Pres Institutional Advancement ... Ms. Jean C. POTH
84 Exec VP Enroll Mgmt/Student Svcs ... Ms. Mary Ellen ASHLEY
11 Vice President of Administration ... Mr. David GINGERELLA
15 Vice President of Human Resources . Mr. Stephen W. FABBRUCCI
07 Assoc VP Enroll Svcs/Admissions ... Ms. Nora SHERIDAN
103 Dean Workforce Devel/Continuing Ed ... Vacant
12 Dean of Lawrence Campus ... Ms. Mary Ellen ASHLEY
09 Dean of Institutional Research ... Mr. Thomas FALLON
44 Assistant Dean of Development ... Ms. Wendy SHAFFER
38 Asst Dean/Dir Counseling Center ... Vacant
27 Chief Information Officer ... Mr. Jeffrey BICKFORD
06 Registrar ... Ms. Sue SHAIN
37 Director of Financial Aid ... Ms. Alexis FISHBONE
26 Director of Public Relations ... Ms. Ernestine GREENSLADE
29 Director Alumni Relations ... Ms. Lindsey MAYO
32 Chief Student Life Officer ... Ms. Nita LAMBORGHINI
35 Director Student Affairs ... Ms. Dina BROWN
18 Chief Facilities/Physical Plant ... Mr. Richard GOULET
96 Director of Purchasing ... Vacant

*Quinsigamond Community College (F)

670 W Boylston Street, Worcester MA 01606-2092
County: Worcester FICE Identification: 002175
Unit ID: 167534
Telephone: (508) 853-2300 Carnegie Class: Assoc/Pub-U-SC
FAX Number: (508) 852-6943 Calendar System: Semester
URL: www.qcc.mass.edu
Established: 1963 Annual Undergrad Tuition & Fees (In-State): $5,430
Enrollment: 9,130 Coed
Affiliation or Control: State IRS Status: 501(c)3
Highest Offering: Associate Degree
Program: Occupational; 2-Year Principally Bachelor's Creditable; Business Emphasis
Accreditation: EH, ADNUR, DA, DH, MAC, OTA, PNUR, RAD, SURGT

02 President ... Dr. Gail E. CARBERRY
05 Vice President of Academic Affairs ... Ms. Patricia A. TONEY
11 Interim VP of Administration ... Mr. Stephen T. MARINI
32 Vice Pres Enrollment/Student Svcs ... Mr. Stephen B. SULLIVAN
26 Vice Pres of Community Engagement ... Mr. Dale ALLEN
88 Asst VP to the President & Trustees ... Ms. Susan LAPRADE
20 Assistant VP Academic Affairs ... Ms. Jane SHEA
04 Executive Assistant to President ... Ms. Patricia A. SOLITRO
21 Comptroller ... Ms. Debra A. LAFLASH
81 Dean Instruction Math/Social Sci ... Mr. James BROWN
79 Dean Humanities ... Vacant
76 Dn Instruction Health Care/Hum Svcs ... Dr. Jane JUNE
84 Assoc VP of Enrollment Management ... Ms. Iris GODES
15 Assoc VP of Human Resources ... Mr. William DARING
06 Associate Dean/Registrar ... Ms. Tara F. JENKINS
62 Dean of Library Services ... Ms. Andrea MACRITCHIE
09 Director of Institutional Research ... Dr. Ingrid SKADBERG
07 Director of Admissions ... Ms. Michelle TUFAU-AFRIYIE
13 Chief Technology Officer ... Mr. Ken DWYER
26 Director of Public Affs ... Mr. Victor SOMMA
35 Director Student Life ... Mr. Jonathan MILLER
18 Director of Facilities ... Mr. Donny HALL
37 Director Student Financial Aid ... Ms. Paula OGDEN
96 Director of Purchasing ... Ms. Paula CAREY

19 Director Of Public Safety ... Mr. Kevin RITACCO
88 Director of Institutuinal Communica ... Mr. Joshua MARTIN
22 Director Affirm Action/Equal Opp ... Ms. Anita BOWDEN
38 Coordinator Student Counseling ... Ms. Karen COX

*Roxbury Community College (A)

1234 Columbus Avenue,
Roxbury Crossing MA 02120-3423
County: Suffolk FICE Identification: 011930
Unit ID: 167631
Telephone: (617) 427-0060 Carnegie Class: Assoc/Pub-S-MC
FAX Number: (617) 541-5351 Calendar System: Semester
URL: rcc.mass.edu
Established: 1973 Annual Undergrad Tuition & Fees (In-State): $3,962
Enrollment: 2,744 Coed
Affiliation or Control: State IRS Status: 501(c)3
Highest Offering: Associate Degree
Program: Occupational; 2-Year Principally Bachelor's Creditable
Accreditation: EH, ADNUR, RAD

02 President ... Dr. Linda E. TURNER
04 Executive Asst to the President ... Ms. Shirley Y. LESLIE
05 Vice President of Academic Affairs ... Dr. Brenda W. MERCOMES
10 Vice President of Admin & Finance ... Mr. Chuks OKOLI
84 VP Enrollment Mgmt/Student Affairs ... Dr. Stephanie C. JANEY
13 Chief Information Tech Officer ... Mr. Patrick JEAN-LOUIS
81 Dean of Science/Tech/Eng/Math ... Dr. Tala KHUDAIRI
66 Dean of Health Sciences ... Dr. Gloria H. CATER
49 Dean of Liberal Arts ... Dr. Nancy A. TEEL
09 Dean of Inst Research & Planning ... Mr. Mike WALKER
90 Dean of Academic Technology ... Ms. Jenene COOK
07 Dean of Enroll Mgmt/Stdnt Jud Affs ... Mr. Charles DIGGS
88 Dean of Student Success ... Mr. Mark GARTH
51 Asst Dean Continuing Education ... Mr. Morisset ST. PREUX
20 Assoc Dean of Academic Affairs ... Dr. Jose ALICEA
41 Director of RLTAC & Athletics ... Mr. A. Keith MCDERMOTT
29 Director of Alumni Affairs ... Ms. Carol BLISS-FURR
21 Comptroller ... Ms. Florence CRAIG
21 Budget Director ... Mr. Gib PORNKITTICHOTCHAROEN
88 Bursar ... Ms. Nicole V. KULIG
37 Director Financial Aid ... Mr. Raymond O'ROURKE
08 Director of Library ... Mr. Mark LAWRENCE
23 Director of Health Services ... Ms. Ruth HINES
06 Registrar ... Vacant
88 Associate Registrar ... Vacant
35 Director of Student Life ... Ms. Elizabeth CLARK
18 Director of Facilities ... Mr. Thomas GALVIN
15 Director of Human Resources/AA ... Mr. P. Paul ALEXANDER
26 Director Marketing/Communications ... Mr. Milton SAMUELS
36 Director Testing & Assessment ... Ms. Colleen SPENCE
25 Director of Grants Development ... Ms. Theresa BREWER
103 Dir of Corp & Community Education ... Mr. Freddy GONZALES
57 Dir of Visual/Performing/Media Arts ... Mr. Marshall HUGHES
88 Director of the Writing Center Lab ... Ms. Judith KAHALAS
88 Director of Academic Advising ... Ms. Lisa CARTER
88 Director of Upward Bound ... Mr. Mark JACKSON

*Springfield Technical Community College (B)

Armory Square, Springfield MA 01105-1296
County: Hampden FICE Identification: 008078
Unit ID: 167905
Telephone: (413) 781-7822 Carnegie Class: Assoc/Pub-U-SC
FAX Number: (413) 755-6309 Calendar System: Semester
URL: www.stcc.edu
Established: 1967 Annual Undergrad Tuition & Fees (In-State): $5,106
Enrollment: 6,888 Coed
Affiliation or Control: State IRS Status: 501(c)3
Highest Offering: Associate Degree
Program: Occupational; 2-Year Principally Bachelor's Creditable; Technical Emphasis
Accreditation: EH, ADNUR, COMTA, DA, DH, DMS, ENGT, MAC, MLTAD, NMT, OTA, PTAA, RAD, SURGT

02 President ... Dr. Ira H. RUBENZAHL
05 Exec Vice Pres Academic Affairs ... Mr. Stephen H. KELLER
10 VP of Finance/CFO ... Mr. Joseph DASILVA
84 Vice Pres Enroll Mgmt/Student Affs ... Dr. Patrick TIGUE
20 Dean of Curriculum ... Mr. Matthew GRAVEL
15 VP Human Res/Multi-Cultural Affairs ... Mrs. Myra D. SMITH
04 Assistant to the President ... Mr. Michael J. SUZOR
50 Dean Business ... Dr. Leona R. ITTLEMAN
66 Dean of Nursing ... Ms. Mary TARBELL
72 Dean Engineering Technologies ... Ms. Adrienne SMITH
76 Dean School of Health ... Mr. Michael C. FOSS
79 Dean Arts/Humanities/Social Sci ... Dr. Arlene RODRIGUEZ
81 Dean Math/Science/Engineering ... Dr. Robert DICKERMAN
51 Dean School Continuing Education ... Dr. Debbie BELLUCCI
32 Dean of Student Affairs ... Mr. Ray BLAIR
07 Dean of Admissions ... Ms. Louisa M. DAVIS FREEMAN
09 Dean of Institutional Effectiveness ... Dr. Barb CHALFONTE
06 Registrar ... Mrs. Theresa REMILLARD
41 Director of Athletics ... Mr. J. Vincent GRASSETTI
102 Int Dir STCC Foundation/Alumni Svcs ... Mr. Bob LEPAGE
19 Director of Public Safety ... Ms. Wendy MASIUK
18 Sr Director of Facilities ... Mrs. Maureen SOCHA
88 Sr Director Enterprise Applications ... Mrs. Eileen CUSICK
38 Director of Academic Advising ... Mr. Kamari COLLINS
23 Director of Health Services ... Mr. Jonathan L. MILLER

26 Director of Marketing ... Mrs. Joan THOMAS
36 Director of Coop/Career Placement ... Ms. Pamela WHITE
15 Director of Human Resources ... Ms. Michelle CAPDEVILLE
37 Director Student Financial Aid ... Mr. Jeremy GREENHOUSE
21 Bursar ... Mr. Jason COHEN
96 Asst Dir Purchasing/Business Svcs ... Ms. Francene CLINTON
35 Coord Student Activities/Devel ... Ms. Andrea TARPEY
27 Coordinator of Media Relations ... Ms. Carla POTTS

Massachusetts College of Pharmacy and Health Sciences (C)

179 Longwood Avenue, Boston MA 02115-5896
County: Suffolk FICE Identification: 002165
Unit ID: 166656
Telephone: (617) 732-2800 Carnegie Class: Spec/Health
FAX Number: (617) 732-2801 Calendar System: Semester
URL: www.mcphs.edu
Established: 1823 Annual Undergrad Tuition & Fees: $26,600
Enrollment: 5,327 Coed
Affiliation or Control: Independent Non-Profit IRS Status: 501(c)3
Highest Offering: Doctorate
Program: Professional
Accreditation: EH, ARCPA, DH, NMT, NURSE, @OPT, PHAR, @PTA, RAD, RTT

01 President ... Mr. Charles F. MONAHAN, JR.
05 VP Academic Affairs/Provost ... Dr. George E. HUMPHREY
10 Exec Vice Pres Finance & Admin/COO ... Mr. Richard J. LESSARD
30 VP for Development & Chief of Staff ... Ms. Marguerite JOHNSON
12 Vice President Wor/Manch Campuses ... Vacant
20 Assoc Provost for Academic Affairs ... Dr. Lily HSU
20 Assoc Provost for Undergraduate Ed ... Dr. David TANNER
106 Assoc Provost Online Education/CEO ... Dr. Barbara MACAULAY
43 Legal Counsel ... Ms. Deborah A. O'MALLEY
32 Dean of Students-Boston ... Dr. Jean JOYCE-BRADY
32 Dean of Students-W/M ... Dr. Shuli XU
67 Dean Pharmacy Boston ... Dr. Douglas J. PISANO
67 Dean Pharmacy Worcester ... Dr. Michael J. MALLOY
08 Dean Library & Learning Resources ... Mr. Richard KAPLAN
49 Dean School of Arts and Sciences ... Dr. Delia C. ANDERSON
66 Dean School of Nursing ... Dr. Carol ELIADI
52 Dean Forsyth School for Dental Hyg ... Dr. Linda D. BOYD
88 Dean School of Phys Asst Studies ... Dr. Michael MILNER
88 Dean School of Physicial Therapy ... Dr. Linda J. TSOUMAS
88 Dean Sch Medical Imaging & Therap ... Vacant
37 Exec Dir Student Enrollment Svcs ... Ms. Carrie GLASS
15 Director of Human Resources ... Ms. Mary LILLY
06 Registrar ... Ms. Stacey TAYLOR
13 Director of Information Services ... Mr. Tom SCANLON
21 Chief Business Officer ... Mr. Keith BELLUCCI
12 Exec Director Manchester Campus ... Mr. Seth P. WALL
29 Exec Director Alumni Relations ... Ms. Dawn BALLOU
07 Executive Director of Admissions ... Ms. Kathleen RYAN
96 Director of Purchasing ... Ms. Margaret EATON-CRAWFORD
38 Director Counseling Services ... Ms. Molly PAYNE
27 Director of Communications ... Mr. Michael RATTY
39 Director of Residence Life ... Ms. Jennifer KOSSES
35 Asst Dean Campus Life & Leadership ... Ms. Jennifer MICHAEL
18 Director of Facilities ... Mr. Michael O'NEIL
19 Chief of Public Safety ... Mr. Jack KELLY
105 Director of Web Services ... Ms. Linda DANGELO
21 Dean of Optometry ... Dr. Lesley WALLS
09 Dir Institutional Res & Assessment ... Mr. Rajiv MALHOTRA

Massachusetts Institute of Technology (D)

77 Massachusetts Avenue, Cambridge MA 02139-4307
County: Middlesex FICE Identification: 002178
Unit ID: 166683
Telephone: (617) 253-1000 Carnegie Class: RU/VH
FAX Number: N/A Calendar System: 4/1/4
URL: web.mit.edu
Established: 1861 Annual Undergrad Tuition & Fees: $42,050
Enrollment: 10,894 Coed
Affiliation or Control: Independent Non-Profit IRS Status: 501(c)3
Highest Offering: Doctorate
Program: Technical Emphasis
Accreditation: EH, BUS, CS, ENG, PLNG

01 President ... Dr. L. Rafael REIF
00 Chairman of the Corporation ... Mr. John REED
05 Provost ... Dr. Chris A. KAISER
88 Chancellor ... Prof. W. Eric L. GRIMSON
03 Exec Vice President & Treasurer ... Mr. Israel RUIZ
101 VP Institute Affairs & Secy of Corp . Dr. Kirk D. KOLENBRANDER
30 Vice Pres for Resource Development ... Mr. Jeffrey L. NEWTON
43 Vice President & General Counsel ... Mr. R. Gregory MORGAN
10 Vice President for Finance ... Mr. Michael W. HOWARD
15 Vice President for Human Resources ... Dr. Alison ALDEN
46 VP for Research & Associate Provost ... Prof. Claude R. CANIZARES
29 Exec VP & CEO Alumni Association ... Ms. Judith M. COLE
88 President MIT Investment Mgmt Co ... Mr. Seth ALEXANDER
20 Associate Provost ... Prof. Martin A. SCHMIDT
20 Associate Provost ... Prof. Philip S. KHOURY
20 Associate Provost Faculty Equity ... Prof. Barbara LISKOV
20 Associate Provost Faculty Equity ... Prof. Wesley L. HARRIS
48 Dean Sch of Architecture & Planning .. Prof. Adele Naude SANTOS
54 Dean School of Engineering ... Prof. Ian A. WAITZ
79 Dean Sch Hum/Arts/Soc Sciences . Prof. Deborah K. FITZGERALD
50 Dean Sloan School of Management ... Prof. David C. SCHMITTLEIN
81 Dean School of Science ... Prof. Marc A. KASTNER
58 Dean Graduate for Education ... Dr. Christine ORTIZ
88 Dean for Undergraduate Education ... Prof. Daniel E. HASTINGS
32 Dean for Student Life ... Mr. Chris COLOMBO
08 Director of Libraries ... Ms. Ann J. WOLPERT
88 Director Lincoln Laboratory ... Dr. Eric D. EVANS
86 Director MIT Washington Office ... Mr. William B. BONVILLIAN
27 Dir of MIT Communications ... Mr. Nate NICKERSON
07 Dean of Admissions ... Mr. Stuart SCHMILL
37 Exec Dir Student Financial Services ... Ms. Elizabeth M. HICKS
23 Medical Dir & Head MIT Medical ... Dr. William M. KETTYLE
13 Head of Info Services & Technology ... Ms. Marilyn T. SMITH
18 Dir Facilities Operations&Security ... Chief John DI FAVA
45 Director Campus Planning & Design ... Ms. Pamela DELPHENICH
102 Director Foundation Relations ... Ms. Lindley HUEY
25 Dir Office of Sponsored Programs ... Ms. Michelle D. CHRISTY
96 Asst Dir of Strategic Sourcing ... Ms. Sara MALCONIAN
41 Director of Athletics ... Ms. Julie SORIERO
09 Director of Institutional Research ... Mrs. Lydia S. SNOVER
85 Dir International Students Office ... Ms. Danielle GUICHARD-ASHBROOK
36 Exec Dir Global Educ/Career Dev Ctr ... Ms. Melanie L. PARKER
93 Associate Dean and Director OME ... Ms. DiOnetta JONES
06 Registrar ... Ms. Mary CALLAHAN
40 Director MIT Press ... Ms. Ellen W. FARAN
39 Director of Housing ... Mr. Dennis COLLINS
42 Chaplain to the Institute ... Dr. Robert M. RANDOLPH
38 Assoc Dean Student Support Services ... Mr. David RANDALL
94 Women's and Gender Studies Director ... Prof. Sally HASLANGER
104 Associate Dean Global Education ... Ms. Malgorzata HEDDERICK
105 Web Manager ... Mr. Patrick GILLOOLY
24 Manager Audio Visual ... Mr. Louis W. GRAHAM, JR.

Massachusetts School of Law at Andover (E)

500 Federal Street, Andover MA 01810-1094
County: Essex FICE Identification: 032353
Unit ID: 369002
Telephone: (978) 681-0800 Carnegie Class: Spec/Law
FAX Number: (978) 681-6330 Calendar System: Semester
URL: www.mslaw.edu
Established: 1988 Annual Graduate Tuition & Fees: $16,990
Enrollment: 650 Coed
Affiliation or Control: Independent Non-Profit IRS Status: 501(c)3
Highest Offering: Doctorate; No Undergraduates
Program: Professional
Accreditation: EH

01 Dean ... Mr. Lawrence R. VELVEL
05 Chief Acad Ofcr/Dir Personnel Svc ... Prof. Michael COYNE
10 Chief Business Officer ... Prof. Paula KALDIS
37 Director Student Financial Aid ... Ms. Lynn BOWAB
06 Registrar ... Ms. Louise ROSE
07 Director of Admissions ... Ms. Paula COLBY CLEMENTS
26 Chief Public Relations Officer ... Vacant
29 Director Alumni Relations ... Vacant

Massachusetts School of Professional Psychology (F)

221 Rivermoor Street, Boston MA 02132-4935
County: Suffolk FICE Identification: 021636
Unit ID: 166717
Telephone: (617) 327-6777 Carnegie Class: Spec/Health
FAX Number: (617) 327-4447 Calendar System: Semester
URL: www.mspp.edu
Established: 1974 Annual Graduate Tuition & Fees: $34,867
Enrollment: 550 Coed
Affiliation or Control: Independent Non-Profit IRS Status: 501(c)3
Highest Offering: Doctorate; No Undergraduates
Program: Professional
Accreditation: EH, CLPSY, IPSY

01 President ... Dr. Nicholas COVINO
04 Executive Asst to the President ... Mrs. Julie M. ROWLINGS
05 Provost ... Dr. Dan KING
10 VP Finance and Operations ... Mr. Patrick CAPOBIANCO
21 Assoc VP Finance ... Mr. Daniel BRENT
46 Assoc VP for Research ... Dr. Edward DEVOS
06 Director of Student Services ... Ms. Eileen O'DONNELL
28 Dir Diversity Educ & Inclusion ... Dr. Stacey LAMBERT
37 Director Financial Aid ... Mrs. Elaine TOOMEY
32 Dean of Students ... Dr. Frances MERVYN
88 Director of Multicultural Affairs ... Mrs. Gretchen NASH
07 Director of Admissions ... Mr. Mario MURGA
51 Director Continuing Prof Education ... Mr. Dean ABBY
36 Director Career Services ... Mrs. Tricia KRZYWICKI
27 Director of Marketing ... Mrs. Katie O'HARE
13 Dir Information Technology ... Mr. Jeff CHOO
78 Assoc Dir Community Education ... Mrs. Beth BASNIGHT
24 Manager of Classroom/Media Support ... Ms. Tracy CHEN
08 Head Librarian ... Mr. Matt KRAMER
15 Human Resource Manager ... Mrs. Ellen COLLINS
18 Facilities Manager ... Mr. Kevin COSTELLO
26 Chief Public Relations Officer ... Ms. Patti JACOBS
96 Director of Purchasing ... Ms. Marice NICHOLS

Merrimack College (A)

315 Turnpike Street, North Andover MA 01845-5800
County: Essex FICE Identification: 002120
Unit ID: 166850
Telephone: (978) 837-5000 Carnegie Class: Bac/Diverse
FAX Number: (978) 837-5222 Calendar System: Semester
URL: www.merrimack.edu
Established: 1947 Annual Undergrad Tuition & Fees: $33,920
Enrollment: 2,447 Coed
Affiliation or Control: Roman Catholic IRS Status: 501(c)3
Highest Offering: Master's
Program: Liberal Arts And General; Teacher Preparatory; Professional
Accreditation: EH, ENG

Code	Title	Name
01	President	Dr. Christopher E. HOPEY
100	Chief of Staff	Mr. Jeffrey DOGGETT
04	Director Office of the President	Ms. Lisa JEBALI
43	Vice President Admin & Gen Counsel	Ms. Alexa ABOWITZ
05	Provost	Dr. Josephine MODICA-NAPOLITANO
20	Vice Provost	Dr. Raymond SHAW
84	Vice Pres for Enrollment Management	Vacant
88	Vice Pres Mission/Student Affairs	Rev. Raymond DLUGOS, OSA
13	Interim Chief Information Officer	Mr. Chip STILES
10	Vice Pres Finance/CFO	Mr. Mark VADALA
30	Interim VP for Advancement	Ms. Heather STACCHI
09	Asst VP Inst Research & Planning	Ms. Kim BRIDGEO
15	Asst VP of Personnel & Payroll Svs	Ms. Linda MURPHY
88	Asst VP Prof Grad & Intl Enrollment	Mr. Mark GOULD
88	AVP & Ex Dir Bus Strategy & Res Dev	Mr. Michael ACCARDI
88	AVP Bus Processes & Project Mgmt	Mr. Doug BERMAN
88	Asst VP for Marketing	Ms. Zoe COHEN
06	Registrar	Ms. Elaine GRELLE
07	Dean of Admissions	Mr. Mark BARRETT
50	Dean Girard Sch Business/Intl Comm	Dr. Mark CORDANO
54	Interim Dean Science & Engineering	Ms. Mary NOONAN
49	Dean of Liberal Arts	Dr. Michael J. ROSSI
53	Dean School of Education	Dr. Dan BUTIN
08	Interim Director of the Library	Ms. Kathryn GEOFFRION-SCANNELL
18	Director of Physical Plant	Mr. Robert COPPOLA
19	Director of Police Services	Mr. Ronald GUILMETTE
26	VP Communications and Marketing	Vacant
29	Director of Alumni Relations	Vacant
32	Dean of Campus Life	Dr. Donna L. SWARTWOUT
23	Director Counseling & Health Svcs	Vacant
41	Director of Athletics	Mr. Glenn HOFMANN
42	Director of Campus Ministry	Rev. Keith HOLLIS
37	Director of Student Financial Aid	Ms. Adrienne MONTGOMERY
36	Director Career Services/Co-op Educ	Dr. Heather MAIETTA
28	Director Diversity Education	Mr. J. Scott GAGE
24	Dir of Media Instructional Services	Mr. Kevin SALEMME
35	Assistant Dean of Campus Life	Ms. Allison GILL
104	Director of International Programs	Ms. Lauren BENT
39	Associate Director of Res Life	Ms. Sara HICKS

MGH Institute of Health Professions (B)

36 1st Avenue, Boston MA 02129-4557
County: Suffolk FICE Identification: 022316
Unit ID: 166869
Telephone: (617) 726-2947 Carnegie Class: Spec/Health
FAX Number: (617) 726-3716 Calendar System: Semester
URL: www.mghihp.edu
Established: 1977 Annual Graduate Tuition & Fees: $1,092
Enrollment: 1,111 Coed
Affiliation or Control: Independent Non-Profit IRS Status: 501(c)3
Highest Offering: Doctorate; No Undergraduates
Program: Professional
Accreditation: EH, NURSE, PTA, RAD, SP

Code	Title	Name
01	President	Dr. Janis P. BELLACK
05	Provost/VP of Academic Affairs	Dr. Alex F. JOHNSON
10	VP for Finance & Administration	Mr. Atlas D. EVANS
26	Chief Information Officer	Mr. Denis G. STRATFORD
30	Chief Development Officer	Ms. Harriet S. KORNFELD
32	Dean of Student Affairs	Ms. Carolyn LOCKE
66	Dean of Nursing	Dr. Laurie LAUZON CLABO
76	Int Dean School of Hlth & Rehab Sci	Dr. Leslie PORTNEY
88	Chair Comm Sciences & Disorders	Dr. Gregory LOF
20	Assoc Provost for Acad Affairs	Dr. Peter CAHN
06	Asst Dean of Students/Registrar	Mr. James V. VITAGLIANO
04	Executive Assistant to President	Ms. Elizabeth M. PIPES
37	Director Student Financial Aid	Mrs. Kathy ANDERSON
09	Director of Inst Effectiveness	Ms. Cynthia P. KING
88	Assistant Director of Admissions	Mr. Anthony MICELI
21	Student Accounts Manager	Ms. Joyce DESANCTIS
07	Director of Admissions	Ms. Maureen JUDD
27	Director of Communications	Mr. Paul W. MURPHY

Montserrat College of Art (C)

23 Essex Street, Box 26, Beverly MA 01915-4508
County: Essex FICE Identification: 020630
Unit ID: 166911
Telephone: (978) 922-8222 Carnegie Class: Spec/Arts
FAX Number: (978) 922-4268 Calendar System: Semester
URL: www.montserrat.edu
Established: 1970 Annual Undergrad Tuition & Fees: $25,290
Enrollment: 378 Coed
Affiliation or Control: Independent Non-Profit IRS Status: 501(c)3
Highest Offering: Baccalaureate
Program: Liberal Arts And General
Accreditation: EH, ART

Code	Title	Name
01	President	Dr. Stephen D. IMMERMAN
05	Dean Faculty/Academic Affairs	Ms. Laura TONELLI
84	Dean Admissions/Enrollment Mgmt	Mr. Rick LONGO
32	Dean of Students	Ms. Maureen WARK
30	Dean of Development	Mr. Howard AMIDON
26	Dean College Rels/Spec Asst to Pres	Ms. Jo BRODERICK
10	Chief Financial Officer	Mr. James MACDONALD
21	Controller	Ms. Susan JACOBS
13	Director of Information Technology	Mr. Jake SYNDER
08	Library Director	Ms. Cheri COE
06	Registrar	Mrs. Theresa SKELLY
37	Director of Financial Aid	Vacant
15	Human Resources Director	Ms. Jennifer THOMAS TROUPE

Mount Holyoke College (D)

50 College Street, South Hadley MA 01075-1424
County: Hampshire FICE Identification: 002192
Unit ID: 166939
Telephone: (413) 538-2000 Carnegie Class: Bac/A&S
FAX Number: (413) 538-2391 Calendar System: Semester
URL: www.mtholyoke.edu
Established: 1837 Annual Undergrad Tuition & Fees: $41,270
Enrollment: 2,362 Female
Affiliation or Control: Independent Non-Profit IRS Status: 501(c)3
Highest Offering: Master's
Program: Liberal Arts And General; Teacher Preparatory
Accreditation: EH

Code	Title	Name
01	President	Lynn PASQUERELLA
05	Dean of Faculty/Vice Pres Acad Affs	Christopher BENFEY
10	Vice Pres Finance/Administration	Ben HAMMOND
84	Vice Pres Enrollment	Diane ANCI
30	Vice President for Development	MaryAnne YOUNG
32	Dean of the College/VP Student Affs	Cerri BANKS
04	Chief of Staff	Jennifer SANBORN
26	Dir Comm and Marketing	Patricia VANDENBERG
06	Registrar	Elizabeth PYLE
36	Dir of Career Development Center	Steve KOPPI
37	Director of Financial Assistance	Kathryn BLAISDELL
29	Exec Director Alumnae Association	Jane E. ZACHARY
15	Director of Human Resources	Chris ABBUHL
08	Executive Director Library & IT	Charlotte PATRIQUIN
09	Director of Institutional Research	Alison K. DONTA-VENMAN

Mount Ida College (E)

777 Dedham Street, Newton MA 02459
County: Middlesex FICE Identification: 002193
Unit ID: 166948
Telephone: (617) 928-4500 Carnegie Class: Bac/Diverse
FAX Number: (617) 928-4746 Calendar System: Semester
URL: www.mountida.edu
Established: 1899 Annual Undergrad Tuition & Fees: $26,644
Enrollment: 1,434 Coed
Affiliation or Control: Independent Non-Profit IRS Status: 501(c)3
Highest Offering: Master's
Program: Liberal Arts And General; Professional
Accreditation: EH, ART, CIDA, DH, FUSER

Code	Title	Name
01	President	Mr. Barry BROWN
05	Vice Pres Academic Affairs	Dr. Ellen BEAULIEU
30	Vice President for Development	Dr. Deborah HIRSCH
10	Vice Pres Finance/Administration	Ms. Cheryl ST. PIERRE-SLEBODA
84	Vice Pres Enrollment Mgmt/Marketing	Ms. Maureen MORIARTY
32	Vice President of Student Affairs	Dr. Elizabeth TRUE
21	Assoc Vice Pres for Finance	Mr. Edward MOLLER
35	Associate Dean of Students	Mr. William CRIBBY
06	Registrar	Ms. Kathy POSEY
08	Director of Learning Resources	Vacant
29	Dir Alumni Relations/Annual Giving	Ms. Candace CRABTREE
37	Director Financial Aid	Ms. Dyan TEEHAN
36	Director of Career Services	Mr. Robert BROOKS
15	Director of Human Resources	Ms. Omaira ROY
26	Director of Mkting & Communications	Ms. Annmarie FARRETTA
85	Director of Intl Student Affairs	Vacant
41	Athletic Director	Mr. Matthew BURKE
19	Director Campus Security	Mr. Ben KATZ
18	Director of Facilities	Ms. Donna LEMIERE
09	Director of Institutional Research	Mr. Jerome DEAN
88	Dean of College Academic Services	Ms. Alyce CURTIS
24	Director of Educational Media	Mr. Manouche MADANIPOUR
96	Director of Business Services	Ms. Leah WEBBER
28	Director of Multicultural Affairs	Ms. Roxanne LONGORIA
42	College Chaplain	Vacant
14	Director Network Services	Mr. David VALENTINE
23	Director Health Services	Ms. Marsha WELBURN
35	Director Student Activities	Ms. Adebimpe DARE
58	Dean Graduate Studies/Cont Educ	Ms. Lois NUNEZ

The National Graduate School of Quality Systems Management (F)

186 Jones Road, Falmouth MA 02540-2908
County: Barnstable FICE Identification: 035043
Unit ID: 441478
Telephone: (508) 457-1313 Carnegie Class: Spec/Bus
FAX Number: (508) 457-5347 Calendar System: Other
URL: www.ngs.edu
Established: 1993 Annual Undergrad Tuition & Fees: $20,100
Enrollment: 234 Coed
Affiliation or Control: Independent Non-Profit IRS Status: 501(c)3
Highest Offering: Doctorate
Program: Business Emphasis
Accreditation: EH

Code	Title	Name
01	President	Dr. John H. BRIDGES
84	Vice Pres Enrollment Management	Ms. Virginia C. PETISCE
88	Director Regulatory Affairs	Ms. Maureen REARDON
06	Registrar	Ms. Lee Anita O'ROURKE
10	Comptroller	Ms. Mary ORLANDO

New England College of Business and Finance (G)

10 High Street, Suite 204, Boston MA 02110
County: Suffolk FICE Identification: 039653
Unit ID: 164438
Telephone: (617) 951-2350 Carnegie Class: Assoc/PrivFP4
FAX Number: (617) 951-2533 Calendar System: Other
URL: www.necb.edu
Established: 1909 Annual Undergrad Tuition & Fees: $9,875
Enrollment: 1,319 Coed
Affiliation or Control: Proprietary IRS Status: Proprietary
Highest Offering: Master's
Program: 2-Year Principally Bachelor's Creditable; Business Emphasis
Accreditation: EH

Code	Title	Name
01	President	Mr. Howard E. HORTON
05	Vice President Academic Affairs	Dr. Sharon FROSS
32	Sr Vice Pres of Student Services	Ms. Paula BRAMANTE
84	Vice Pres of Student Enrollment	Mr. Richard KRATOCHVIL
10	Controller	Mr. William MCDONALD
04	Asst to the President/Office Mgr	Ms. Kathy CANTALUPA
06	Registrar	Mr. Robert WAGSTAFF
37	Director of Financial Aid	Ms. Jennifer ROBINSON
88	Asst Dean E-Learning & Instr Des	Mr. Jonathan SMALL
97	Department Chair General Education	Dr. Christian BROCATO
50	Department Chair Business/Finance	Dr. Christopher WEIR

The New England College of Optometry (H)

424 Beacon Street, Boston MA 02115-1129
County: Suffolk FICE Identification: 002164
Unit ID: 167093
Telephone: (617) 266-2030 Carnegie Class: Spec/Health
FAX Number: (617) 424-9202 Calendar System: Semester
URL: www.neco.edu
Established: 1894 Annual Undergrad Tuition & Fees: $37,399
Enrollment: 475 Coed
Affiliation or Control: Independent Non-Profit IRS Status: 501(c)3
Highest Offering: Doctorate
Program: Professional
Accreditation: EH, OPT, OPTR

Code	Title	Name
01	President	Dr. Clifford SCOTT
05	VP & Dean of Academic Affairs	Dr. Barry FISCH
10	VP Business Development	Mr. Robert GORDON
17	VP Clinical Affairs & CEO of NEEI	Ms. Jody FLEIT
30	VP of Philanthropy	Ms. Nancy BROUDE
32	Assoc Dean Students/Dir Stdnt Svcs	Ms. Barbara MCGINLEY
07	Assoc Dean of Admissions	Dr. Taline FARRA
37	Director Student Financial Aid	Ms. Carol RUBEL
15	Director of Human Resources	Ms. Patricia DAHILL
06	Registrar	Ms. Glenda UNDERWOOD
08	Director of Library Services	Ms. Kristin MOTTE
04	Executive Asst to the President	Ms. Marie HILL

New England Conservatory of Music (I)

290 Huntington Avenue, Boston MA 02115-5018
County: Suffolk FICE Identification: 002194
Unit ID: 167057
Telephone: (617) 585-1100 Carnegie Class: Spec/Arts
FAX Number: (617) 262-0500 Calendar System: Semester
URL: www.necmusic.edu
Established: 1867 Annual Undergrad Tuition & Fees: $36,700
Enrollment: 775 Coed
Affiliation or Control: Independent Non-Profit IRS Status: 501(c)3
Highest Offering: Doctorate
Program: Liberal Arts And General; Teacher Preparatory; Professional
Accreditation: EH, MUS

Code	Title	Name
01	President	Mr. Tony WOODCOCK
05	Dean of the College	Mr. Thomas NOVAK
10	Sr Vice Pres Finance/Operations	Mr. Edward R. LESSER
30	Exec Vice Pres Institutional Advanc	Mr. Don JONES
26	Vice Pres Marketing/Public Rel	Ms. Carol PHELAN
100	Chief of Staff	Ms. Suzanne WILSON
56	Dean of Extension Division	Mr. Mark CHURCHILL
32	Dean of Students	Mr. Tom HANDEL
07	Asst Dean for Admissions	Ms. Christina DALY
11	Head of Operations/Inst Planning	Ms. Hilary FIELD
21	Controller	Ms. Amanda GATES
18	Exec Dir Facilities/Engrng/Constr	Mr. Michael RYAN
06	Registrar	Mr. Robert WINKLEY
08	Director of Libraries	Ms. Jean MORROW
37	Director Financial Aid	Ms. Lauren URBANEK

35 Director Student Activities ... Ms. Colleen PALMER
36 Director of Career Services ... Dr. Angela Myles BEECHING
29 Director of Alumni Relations ... Ms. Cheryl WEBER
15 Director of Human Resources ... Ms. Elise COMEAU
13 Director ITS ... Mr. Charles MEMBRINO
09 Director of Institutional Research ... Ms. Sarah DOW
20 Asst Dean of Academic Studies ... Vacant
38 Director Student Counseling ... Ms. Jan LERBINGER
51 Director of Continuing Education ... Mr. Sean P. HAGON

The New England Institute of Art (A)

10 Brookline Place W, Brookline MA 02445-7295
County: Norfolk FICE Identification: 007486
Unit ID: 167321
Telephone: (617) 739-1700 Carnegie Class: Spec/Arts
FAX Number: (617) 582-4500 Calendar System: Semester
URL: www.artinstitutes.edu/boston
Established: 1952 Annual Undergrad Tuition & Fees: $25,740
Enrollment: 1,248 Coed
Affiliation or Control: Proprietary IRS Status: Proprietary
Highest Offering: Baccalaureate
Program: Occupational; Fine Arts Emphasis
Accreditation: EH

01 President ... Dr. David WARREN
05 Dean of Academic Affairs ... Dr. Rick KETTNER-POLLEY
32 Dean of Student Affairs ... Ms. Michele TRACIA
06 Registrar ... Ms. Dawn NORRIS
07 Senior Director of Admissions ... Ms. Mary BURNE
10 Director of Admin & Financial Svcs ... Mr. Ross SORACI
13 Campus Technology Manager ... Ms. Connie BURKE
15 Human Resources Generalist ... Ms. Ashley JENKINS
36 Director of Career Services ... Mr. John LAY
37 Director Student Financial Services ... Mr. Michael CARDENAS
40 Bookstore Manager ... Ms. Stephanie VINCENT

New England Law | Boston (B)

154 Stuart Street, Boston MA 02116-5687
County: Suffolk FICE Identification: 008916
Unit ID: 167215
Telephone: (617) 451-0010 Carnegie Class: Spec/Law
FAX Number: (617) 422-7333 Calendar System: Semester
URL: www.nesl.edu
Established: 1908 Annual Undergrad Tuition & Fees: $42,490
Enrollment: 1,104 Coed
Affiliation or Control: Independent Non-Profit IRS Status: 501(c)3
Highest Offering: First Professional Degree
Program: Professional
Accreditation: LAW

01 Dean ... Mr. John F. O'BRIEN
05 Associate Dean ... Ms. Judith G. GREENBERG
11 Associate Dean of Administration ... Ms. Susan S. CALAMARE
07 Director of Admission ... Ms. Michelle L'ETOILE
10 Chief Financial Officer ... Mr. Fred COVELLE
08 Librarian ... Ms. Anne ACTON
36 Director Career Services ... Ms. Mandie A. LEBEAU
37 Director of Financial Aid ... Mr. Eric A. KRUPSKI
06 Registrar ... Mr. David M. BERTI
18 Director of Facilities/Security ... Mr. Anthony GIORDANO
35 Director of Student Services ... Ms. Jacqueline PILGRIM

New England School of Acupuncture (C)

150 California Street, Newton MA 02458-1005
County: Middlesex FICE Identification: 025798
Unit ID: 167181
Telephone: (617) 558-1788 Carnegie Class: Spec/Health
FAX Number: (617) 558-1789 Calendar System: Trimester
URL: www.nesa.edu
Established: 1975 Annual Undergrad Tuition & Fees: $19,885
Enrollment: 174 Coed
Affiliation or Control: Independent Non-Profit IRS Status: 501(c)3
Highest Offering: Master's; No Lower Division
Program: Professional
Accreditation: ACUP

01 President/Executive Dean ... Susan L. GORMAN
05 Academic Dean ... Meredith ST. JOHN
07 Admissions Director ... Vacant

Newbury College (D)

129 Fisher Avenue, Brookline MA 02445-5796
County: Norfolk FICE Identification: 007484
Unit ID: 167251
Telephone: (617) 730-7000 Carnegie Class: Bac/Diverse
FAX Number: (617) 731-9618 Calendar System: Semester
URL: www.newbury.edu
Established: 1962 Annual Undergrad Tuition & Fees: $27,850
Enrollment: 1,025 Coed
Affiliation or Control: Independent Non-Profit IRS Status: 501(c)3
Highest Offering: Baccalaureate
Program: Liberal Arts And General
Accreditation: EH, CIDA

01 President ... Ms. Hannah M. MCCARTHY
05 VP Academic Affairs/Dean of the Col ... Dr. Hannah LEVERTOV
10 Vice President Finance/CFO ... Ms. Joyce HANLON
03 Executive Vice President ... Mr. Joseph CHILLO
32 Vice President of Student Affairs ... Mr. Paul MARTIN
30 VP for Development ... Ms. Clare MCCULLY
35 Dean of Student Affairs ... Ms. Amy SHIRLEY
20 Assoc Dean for Academic Services ... Ms. Sara D'ANJOU
08 Director of Library Services ... Mr. Peter G. OBUCHAN
37 Exec Director of Financial Services ... Mr. Elreo CAMPBELL
06 Registrar ... Ms. Rachelle E. MAZZA
27 Chief Information Officer ... Mr. Gary HAMMON
15 Director Human Resources ... Ms. Amy DOWNING
36 Director of Career Services ... Ms. Sara SHECKELLS
38 Director Counseling/Health Educ ... Ms. Susan CHAMANDY
18 Director of Facilities ... Mr. Ron MINERVINI
88 Asst VP for Adult Enrollment ... Ms. Eileen SHERIDAN
41 Director of Athletics ... Ms. Jessica GOULD

Nichols College (E)

Center Road, PO Box 5000, Dudley MA 01571-5000
County: Worcester FICE Identification: 002197
Unit ID: 167260
Telephone: (508) 213-1560 Carnegie Class: Bac/Diverse
FAX Number: N/A Calendar System: Semester
URL: www.nichols.edu
Established: 1815 Annual Undergrad Tuition & Fees: $31,740
Enrollment: 1,069 Coed
Affiliation or Control: Independent Non-Profit IRS Status: 501(c)3
Highest Offering: Master's
Program: Liberal Arts And General; Teacher Preparatory; Professional; Business Emphasis
Accreditation: EH, IACBE

01 President ... Susan WEST ENGELKEMEYER
05 Provost and Senior Vice President ... Alan J. REINHARDT
10 Vice President Administration ... Michael J. STANTON
30 Vice President for Advancement ... William C. PIECZYNSKI
84 Vice Pres Enrollment & Marketing ... Thomas R. CAFARO
32 Vice Pres Student Affairs & Dean ... Brian T. MCCOY
13 Vice Pres for Information Services ... Kevin F. BRASSARD
58 Assoc VP Graduate & Prof Studies ... Kevin F. BRASSARD
21 Assoc Vice Pres for Finance ... Patricia A. HERTZFELD
04 Exec Assistant to the President ... Cynthia L. BROWN
09 Assoc Dean Academic Admin/Records ... Peter M. ENGH
41 Assoc Dn Stdt Svcs/Dir Athletics ... Charlyn A. ROBERT
07 Director Admissions ... Paul O. BROWER
06 Registrar ... Betin ROBICHAUD
08 Director of Library ... Jim DOUGLAS
15 Director of Human Resources ... Rick WOODS
29 Director of Alumni Relations ... Brianne S. CALLAHAN
35 Dir Student Activities/Orientation ... Brian QUINLAN
36 Director of Career Services ... Elizabeth HORGAN
37 Director of Financial Aid ... Denise BRINDLE
38 Director Mental Health Services . Monica GOODRICH PELLETIER
26 Director of Communications ... Ronald SCHACHTER
18 Assoc VP for Facilities Management ... Robert W. LAVIGNE
07 Associate Director of Admissions ... Paul A. MAY
96 Director Procurement & Contract Svc ... Kay F. YOUNG
19 Director Public Safety ... Jack CAULFIELD
23 Director Health Services ... Katherine NICOLETTI
39 Dir Res Life & Judicial Affairs ... P. J. BOGGIO
42 Director Spiritual Life & Chaplain ... Wayne-Daniel S. BERARD

Northeastern University (F)

360 Huntington Avenue, Boston MA 02115-0195
County: Suffolk FICE Identification: 002199
Unit ID: 167358
Telephone: (617) 373-2000 Carnegie Class: RU/H
FAX Number: N/A Calendar System: Semester
URL: www.northeastern.edu
Established: 1898 Annual Undergrad Tuition & Fees: $39,856
Enrollment: 31,066 Coed
Affiliation or Control: Independent Non-Profit IRS Status: 501(c)3
Highest Offering: Doctorate
Program: Liberal Arts And General; Teacher Preparatory; Professional
Accreditation: EH, ANEST, ARCPA, AUD, BUS, CS, ENG, ENGT, LAW, NURSE, PH, PHAR, PSPSY, PTA, SP, SPAA

01 President ... Dr. Joseph E. AOUN
04 Exec Assistant to the President ... Ms. Susie C. GUSZCZA
05 Sr Vice Pres Academic Affs/Provost ... Dr. Stephen W. DIRECTOR
100 Chief of Staff ... Ms. Elisabeth A. WERBY
84 Sr VP Enroll Mgmt & Student Life .. Dr. Philomena V. MANTELLA
11 Sr Vice Pres Admin & Finance ... Mr. John H. MCCARTHY
43 Sr Vice Pres and General Counsel ... Mr. Ralph C. MARTIN II
26 Sr Vice Pres External Affairs ... Mr. Michael A. ARMINI
30 Sr Vice President Advancement ... Ms. Diane N. MACGILLIVRAY
88 Vice President & University Counsel ... Mr. Vincent J. LEMBO
10 Vice President & Chief Fin Ofc ... Mr. Thomas NEDELL
32 Vice Pres Student Affairs ... Dr. Laura A. WANKEL
84 Vice President Enrollment Mgmt ... Ms. Jane B. BROWN
23 AVP Student Affairs ... Ms. Madeleine A. ESTABROOK
18 Vice President Facilities ... Ms. Nancy S. MAY
16 Vice President Human Resources ... Ms. Katherine N. PENDERGAST
29 Vice President Alumni Relations ... Mr. Jack MOYNIHAN
88 Vice Pres Public Affairs ... Mr. Robert P. GITTENS
86 Vice President Government Relations ... Mr. Tim E. LESHAN
27 Vice President Information Systems ... Mr. Rehan KHAN
31 Vice Pres City & Community Affairs ... Mr. John M. TOBIN
46 Sr Vice Prov Rsch & Grad Education ... Dr. Melvin BERNSTEIN
20 Vice Provost for Undergrad Educ ... Dr. Bruce E. RONKIN
20 Vice Provost Academic Affairs ... Dr. Mary LOEFFELHOLZ
21 Vice Provost Budget/Planning/Admin ... Dr. Anthony RINI
92 Vice Provost Honors & FY Programs ... Dr. Susan G. POWERS-LEE
104 Vice Provost International Affairs ... Dr. Robert P. LOWNDES
88 Vice Provost Health Research ... Dr. Stephen ZOLOTH
107 Dean Col Prof Studies/VP Prof Educ ... Dr. John G. LABRIE
76 Dean Bouve Col Health Science ... Dr. Terry FULMER
77 Dean Col Computer and Info Science .. Dr. Larry A. FINKELSTEIN
54 Dean College of Engineering ... Dr. Allen SOYSTER
81 Dean College of Science ... Dr. J. Murray GIBSON
50 Dean College of Business Admin ... Dr. Hugh COURTNEY
61 Dean School of Law ... Vacant
49 Dean College of Arts/Media & Design ... Dr. Xavier COSTA
83 Dean Col of Soc Sci & Humanities ... Dr. Georges VAN DEN ABBEELE
08 Dean University Libraries ... Mr. William M. WAKELING
07 AVP Enrollment ... Ms. Ronne PATRICK-TURNER
88 VP Bus Affs Regional Campuses ... Mr. M. Seamus HARREYS
39 Assoc Dean Cultural & Res Life ... Mr. Robert O. JOSE
06 University Registrar ... Ms. Linda D. ALLEN
09 AVP Inst Rsch & Data Administration ... Dr. Nancy M. LUDWIG
22 Dir Inst Diversity & Equity ... Vacant
42 Director Spiritual Life ... Ms. Shelli M. JANKOWSKI-SMITH
92 Director Honors Program ... Dr. Maureen E. KELLEHER
36 Director Career Services ... Ms. Maria K. STEIN
21 Director of Finance & Treasurer ... Mr. Samuel B. SOLOMON
19 Director Public Safety ... Mr. D. Joseph GRIFFIN
60 Director of Communications ... Ms. Renata NYUL
41 Director Athletics ... Mr. Peter P. ROBY

Pine Manor College (G)

400 Heath Street, Chestnut Hill MA 02467-2332
County: Norfolk FICE Identification: 002201
Unit ID: 167455
Telephone: (617) 731-7000 Carnegie Class: Bac/A&S
FAX Number: (617) 731-7199 Calendar System: Semester
URL: www.pmc.edu
Established: 1911 Annual Undergrad Tuition & Fees: $23,744
Enrollment: 338 Female
Affiliation or Control: Independent Non-Profit IRS Status: 501(c)3
Highest Offering: Master's
Program: Liberal Arts And General; Teacher Preparatory
Accreditation: #EH

01 President ... Dr. Alane K. SHANKS
05 Dean of College ... Dr. William VOGELE
100 Chief of Staff ... Ms. Lisa KAMISHER
11 Chief Operating Officer ... Ms. Anna TRASK
30 Chief Development Officer ... Ms. Susan FUGLIESE
32 Dean Student Affs/Cmty Engagement ... Ms. Jamica LOVE
84 Director of Enrollment ... Vacant
10 Director of Finance ... Mr. Timothy JOHNSON
15 Director of Human Resources ... Mr. Jerry SAUNDERS
06 Registrar ... Mr. Jeffrey MEI
26 Dir Publications/Media Relations ... Ms. Efrat ZINNAR-SHAVIT
08 Interim Library Director ... Ms. Sarah WOOLF

Quincy College (H)

1250 Hancock Street, Quincy MA 02169-4324
County: Norfolk FICE Identification: 002205
Unit ID: 167525
Telephone: (617) 984-1700 Carnegie Class: Assoc/Pub-S-MC
FAX Number: (617) 984-1779 Calendar System: Semester
URL: www.quincycollege.edu
Established: 1956 Annual Undergrad Tuition & Fees (In-District): $5,395
Enrollment: 4,674 Coed
Affiliation or Control: Local IRS Status: 501(c)3
Highest Offering: Associate Degree
Program: Occupational; 2-Year Principally Bachelor's Creditable
Accreditation: EH, ADNUR, MLTAD, PNUR, SURGT

01 President ... Mr. Peter H. TSAFFARAS
05 Vice Pres Academic Affairs ... Dr. Anna WILLIAMS-COTE
11 Vice Pres Administration/Finance ... Mr. Pushap R. KAPOOR
100 Assistant to the President ... Dr. Robert BAKER
10 Chief Financial Officer ... Vacant
04 Admin Asst to President ... Ms. Donna M. BRUGMAN
84 Assoc VP/Enroll Svcs & Registrar ... Ms. Paula M. SMITH
66 Dean of Nursing ... Vacant
49 Dean Liberal Arts ... Dr. Henry RUBIN
50 Dean Business & Public Service ... Dr. Sandra SMALES
81 Dean of Natural & Health Sciences ... Dr. Laura CORINA
21 Director of Finance ... Mr. Martin AHERN
13 Assoc VP/Comm & Info Technology ... Mr. Tom C. PHAM
12 Dean of Plymouth Campus ... Ms. Mary BURKE
37 Assoc VP for Financial Aid ... Ms. Rose M. DE VITO
88 Director of Administrative Services ... Mr. William C. HALL
32 Assoc VP for Student Development ... Ms. Susan G. BOSSA
15 Vice Pres for Human Resources ... Ms. Mary SCOTT
26 Dir Strategic Mktg/Brand Mgmt ... Mr. Taggart BOYLE
07 Director of Enrollment Services ... Ms. Lisa J. STACK
85 Assoc Dir of Int'l Student Services ... Ms. Ela KIJOWSKA
103 Dir of Workforce Development ... Mr. Gary G. WALLRAPP
09 Assoc VP for Inst Research & Assess ... Dr. Kimberly PUHALA
35 Director of Student Development ... Ms. Kathi SCHAEFFER

Regis College (A)

235 Wellesley Street, Weston MA 02493-1571
County: Middlesex FICE Identification: 002206
Unit ID: 167598
Telephone: (781) 768-7000 Carnegie Class: Spec/Health
FAX Number: (781) 768-8339 Calendar System: Semester
URL: www.regiscollege.edu
Established: 1927 Annual Undergrad Tuition & Fees: $33,060
Enrollment: 1,833 Coed
Affiliation or Control: Independent Non-Profit IRS Status: 501(c)3
Highest Offering: Doctorate
Program: Liberal Arts And General; Teacher Preparatory; Professional
Accreditation: EH, ADNUR, NMT, NUR, RAD, SW

01 President ... Dr. Antoinette M. HAYS
10 Vice President Finance/Business ... Mr. Thomas G. PISTORINO
84 Vice Pres Enrollment & Marketing ... Mr. Paul VACCARO
20 Assoc Vice Pres Academic Affairs ... Ms. Sarah BARRETT
07 Director of Admission ... Ms. Wanda SURIEL
37 Director of Financial Aid ... Ms. Bonnie QUINN
06 Registrar ... Ms. Esther A. GHAZARIAN
09 Dean of Institutional Research ... Ms. Susan TAMMARO
15 Director of Human Resources ... Ms. Joan D. SULLIVAN
18 Director of Physical Plant ... Mr. Joseph SHAUGHNESSY
21 Director Finance & Business ... Mr. Steven SAVAS
29 Director of Alumni Relations ... Mrs. Christina DUGGAN
32 Dean of Students ... Ms. Kara KOLOMITZ
23 Director of Health Services ... Ms. Dianna JONES
04 Special Assistant to President ... Ms. Mary Jane DOHERTY
08 Director of Library ... Ms. Lynn TRIPLETT
13 Director ITS ... Ms. Marla BOTELHO
41 Director Athletics & Physical Ed ... Ms. Marybeth LAMB
42 Director Campus Ministry ... Sr. Rosemary MULVIHILL
96 Director of Purchasing ... Ms. Diep SHEEHAN
31 Director of Community Living ... Mr. Shawn EDIE
44 Director Annual Fund ... Ms. Tara BRADY
35 Director of Student Programs ... Ms. Jessica HOMER
30 Chief Development Officer ... Ms. Miriam FINN-SHERMAN

Saint John's Seminary (B)

127 Lake Street, Brighton MA 02135-3898
County: Suffolk FICE Identification: 002214
Unit ID: 167677
Telephone: (617) 254-2610 Carnegie Class: Spec/Faith
FAX Number: (617) 787-2336 Calendar System: Semester
URL: www.sjs.edu
Established: 1884 Annual Undergrad Tuition & Fees: $23,000
Enrollment: 300 Male
Affiliation or Control: Roman Catholic IRS Status: 501(c)3
Highest Offering: Master's
Program: Professional; Religious Emphasis
Accreditation: EH, THEOL

01 Rector ... Msgr. James MORONEY
03 Vice Rector ... Rev. Christopher K. O'CONNOR
05 Dean of Faculty ... Rev. Raymond VAN DE MOORTELL
32 Dean of Students ... Rev. Edward RILEY
07 Director of Admissions & Records ... Mrs. Maureen DEBERNARDI
08 Librarian ... Rev. Raymond VAN DE MOORTELL
10 Director Finance and Operations ... Mr. Richard A. FLAHERTY
73 Director Pre-Theology Program ... Rev. Joseph SCORZELLO
21 Associate Business Officer ... Ms. Susan MOLNAR

Salter College (C)

184 West Boylston Street, West Boylston MA 01583
County: Worcester FICE Identification: 004666
Unit ID: 167738
Telephone: (508) 853-1074 Carnegie Class: Assoc/PrivFP
FAX Number: (508) 853-1674 Calendar System: Semester
URL: www.saltercollege-us.com
Established: 1937 Annual Undergrad Tuition & Fees: N/A
Enrollment: 813 Coed
Affiliation or Control: Proprietary IRS Status: Proprietary
Highest Offering: Associate Degree
Program: Occupational; 2-Year Principally Bachelor's Creditable
Accreditation: ACICS, ACFEI, #COMTA, DA, MAC

01 Campus Director ... Ms. Karen SPRINGER

Sanford-Brown College of Boston, Inc. (D)

126 Newbury Street, Boston MA 02116-2904
County: Suffolk FICE Identification: 007481
Unit ID: 166276
Telephone: (617) 578-7100 Carnegie Class: Assoc/PrivFP
FAX Number: (617) 262-6210 Calendar System: Other
URL: www.sanfordbrown.edu/boston
Established: 1917 Annual Undergrad Tuition & Fees: $24,066
Enrollment: 303 Coed
Affiliation or Control: Proprietary IRS Status: Proprietary
Highest Offering: Associate Degree
Program: Occupational; 2-Year Principally Bachelor's Creditable; Technical Emphasis
Accreditation: ACICS, MAAB

01 President ... Dr. Richard FARMER
05 Academic Dean ... Ms. Debra HESSELL
08 Librarian ... Mr. William GREALISH
07 Director of Admissions ... Ms. Jaimee TYLER
37 Director of Financial Aid ... Mr. Jay BEIRNE
06 Registrar ... Ms. Elisa ADAMS
36 Director Career Services ... Ms. Laura MEYER

School of the Museum of Fine Arts-Boston (E)

230 The Fenway, Boston MA 02115-5518
County: Suffolk FICE Identification: 004667
Unit ID: 166984
Telephone: (617) 267-6100 Carnegie Class: Spec/Arts
FAX Number: (617) 424-6271 Calendar System: Semester
URL: www.smfa.edu
Established: 1876 Annual Undergrad Tuition & Fees: $38,028
Enrollment: 765 Coed
Affiliation or Control: Independent Non-Profit IRS Status: 501(c)3
Highest Offering: Master's
Program: Liberal Arts And General; Teacher Preparatory; Fine Arts Emphasis
Accreditation: ART

01 President ... Chris BRATTON
04 Executive Assistant ... Christine WILLIS
05 Senior VP for Academic Affairs/Dean ... Sarah MCKINNON
06 Registrar ... Vacant
30 VP for Development & Ext Relations ... Anne COWIE
84 VP for Enrollment ... Eric THOMPSON
10 Chief Financial Officer ... Mark KERWIN
21 Director of Business Operations ... Barbara DONNELLAN
09 Assoc VP Operations and Research ... Mary ROETZEL
32 Dean of Students ... Claudia BELL
45 Budget and Planning Officer ... Christopher FOX
51 Director Artist's Res Ctr/Cont Educ ... Debra SAMDPERIL
20 Assoc VP Academic Administration ... Greg D'ANGELO
58 Assoc Dean Graduate Studies ... David BROWN
37 Director of Financial Aid ... Beth GOREHAM
20 Assoc Dean Undergraduate Studies ... Susan LUSH
88 Bursar ... Kelly LANE
07 Associate Dean of Admissions ... Robyn REED
27 Dir of Marketing & Communications ... Vacant
44 Senior Development Officer ... Alexandra HUFF
26 Press Coordinator ... Brooke DANIELS
29 Dir Alum Relations/Special Projects ... Stephanie BOYE'
08 Librarian ... Darin MURPHY
90 Mgr of Instructional Technology ... Matthew GIRARD
40 School Store Manager ... Terri NORDONE
88 Asst Dir Artist Resource Center ... Catherine TUTTER
35 Asst Director of Student Life ... Ryan O'CONNELL
39 Asst Dir of Residential Housing ... Holly GOULD
18 Director of Facilities ... David GELDART
15 Director Human Resources ... Jane O'REILLY
96 Director of Purchasing ... Brendan MULLIGAN
19 Director of Protective Services ... Craig MCQUATE
88 Curator ... Joanna SOLTAN

Simmons College (F)

300 The Fenway, Boston MA 02115-5898
County: Suffolk FICE Identification: 002208
Unit ID: 167783
Telephone: (617) 521-2000 Carnegie Class: Master's L
FAX Number: (617) 521-3199 Calendar System: Semester
URL: www.simmons.edu
Established: 1899 Annual Undergrad Tuition & Fees: $33,350
Enrollment: 4,881 Coordinate
Affiliation or Control: Independent Non-Profit IRS Status: 501(c)3
Highest Offering: Doctorate
Program: Liberal Arts And General; Teacher Preparatory; Professional
Accreditation: EH, BUS, DIETD, DIETI, HSA, LIB, NURSE, #PTA, SW

01 President ... Helen G. DRINAN
05 Provost ... Charlena SEYMOUR
76 Dean Sch Nursing & Health Sciences ... Judy BEAL
62 Dean Grad Sch Library/Info Science ... Michele CLOONAN
70 Dean School of Social Work ... Stefan KRUG
50 Dean School of Management ... Cathy MINEHAN
49 Dean College of Arts & Sciences ... Renee WHITE
104 Program Manager Study Abroad ... Laura BEY
06 Asst VP Acad Operations & Registrar ... Donna M. DOLAN
108 Director Assessment ... Susan GRACIA
08 Director Library ... Daphne HARRINGTON
25 Director Sponsored Programs ... Jon KIMBALL
09 Director Institutional Research ... Heather S. ROSCOE
36 Director Career Education Center ... Andrea WOLF
10 Sr VP Finance/Admin/Treasurer ... Stefano FALCONI
21 Asst VP Finance ... Patricia C. FALLON
11 Asst VP Administration ... Janet FISHSTEIN
37 Director Student Financial Services ... Daniel FORSTER
13 Executive Director Technology CIO ... Debra ORR
96 Director Purchasing & Procurement ... Kathy PERONI-CALLAHAN
19 Director Public Safety ... Sean COLLINS
26 VP Marketing & Admissions ... Cheryl HOWARD
07 Assoc VP Mktg and Grad Admissions ... Jacob BERRY
07 Asst VP Undergrad Admission & Mktg ... Catherine CAPULUPO
26 Director Marketing Communications ... Allyson IRISH
30 VP Advancement ... Marianne E. LORD
30 Assoc VP Capital Giving ... Laura BRINK
102 Director Corp/Foundation Relations ... Amy FISHER
44 Asst VP Annual Fund and Alumnae/i ... Janice TAYLOR
32 Dean Student Life ... Sarah NEILL
39 Director Residence Life ... Jessica FAULK
41 Director Athletics ... Ali KANTOR
35 Assoc Dean Office for Student Life ... Lisa SMITH-MCQUEENIE
43 VP & General Counsel ... Kathleen R. ROGERS
15 VP Talent & Human Capital Mgmt ... Regina SHERWOOD

Smith College (G)

Northampton MA 01063-0001
County: Hampshire FICE Identification: 002209
Unit ID: 167835
Telephone: (413) 584-2700 Carnegie Class: Bac/A&S
FAX Number: (413) 585-2123 Calendar System: Semester
URL: www.smith.edu
Established: 1871 Annual Undergrad Tuition & Fees: $41,460
Enrollment: 3,162 Female
Affiliation or Control: Independent Non-Profit IRS Status: 501(c)3
Highest Offering: Doctorate
Program: Liberal Arts And General; Teacher Preparatory; Professional
Accreditation: EH, ENG, SW

01 President ... Carol T. CHRIST
04 Secretary to the President ... Jackie SCALZO
10 Vice Pres Finance & Administration ... Ruth H. CONSTANTINE
05 Provost & Dean of the Faculty ... Marilyn R. SCHUSTER
20 Dean for Academic Development ... John DAVIS
32 Dean of the College ... Maureen A. MAHONEY
35 Dean of Students ... Julianne OHOTNICKY
70 Dean School for Social Work ... Carolyn JACOBS
39 Director of Residence Life ... Becky SHAW
85 Assoc Dean International Students ... Lisa D. JOHNSON
30 Associate VP for Development ... Sandra DOUCETT
38 Assoc Dir Health Svcs/Stdnt Counsel ... Pamela MCCARTHY
26 VP for Public Affairs ... Laurie FENLASON
29 Exec Director Alumnae Association ... Carrie S. CADWELL BROWN
13 Exec Director Info Technology Svcs ... David D. GREGORY
09 Dir Inst Research and Edu Assess ... Cate ROWEN
08 Director of Libraries ... Christopher LORING
15 Assoc VP for Human Resources ... Lawrence HUNT
07 Director of Admission ... Debra D. SHAVER
58 Director of Graduate Study ... Danielle D. RAMDATH
37 Dir Student Financial Services ... David J. BELANGER
06 Registrar ... Patricia A. O'NEIL
36 Director Career Development Office ... Stacie HAGENBAUGH
28 Dir for Inst Diversity and Equity ... Pamela NOLAN YOUNG
28 Associate Dean of the Faculty ... Danielle D. RAMDATH
18 Assoc VP for Facilities Management ... John SHENETTE
23 Director of Health Services ... Leslie R. JAFFE
41 Director of Athletics ... Lynn OBERBILLIG
42 Dean of Religious Life ... Jennifer L. WALTERS
43 Office of General Counsel ... Vacant
84 Assoc VP for Enrollment ... Audrey Y. SMITH
96 Procurement Manager ... Linda HIESIGER

Springfield College (H)

263 Alden Street, Springfield MA 01109-3788
County: Hampden FICE Identification: 002211
Unit ID: 167899
Telephone: (413) 748-3000 Carnegie Class: Master's L
FAX Number: (413) 748-3746 Calendar System: Semester
URL: www.spfldcol.edu
Established: 1885 Annual Undergrad Tuition & Fees: $31,690
Enrollment: 5,390 Coed
Affiliation or Control: Independent Non-Profit IRS Status: 501(c)3
Highest Offering: Doctorate
Program: Liberal Arts And General; Professional
Accreditation: EH, ARCPA, CORE, EXSC, IACBE, NRPA, OT, PTA, SW

01 President ... Dr. Richard B. FLYNN
45 Executive Vice President ... Dr. Jill F. RUSSELL
04 Special Assistant to President ... Ms. Mary Lou DYJAK
05 Vice President Academic Affairs ... Dr. Jean A. WYLD
29 Vice President Devel & Alumni Rels ... Mr. John A. WHITE
10 VP for Administration/Finance ... Mr. John MAILHOT
32 VP Student Affairs/Dean of Students ... Dr. David BRAVERMAN
20 Assistant VP Academic Affairs ... Dr. Mary Ann COUGHLIN
84 Dir Enrollment Management ... Ms. Mary DEANGELO
15 Asst Vice President Admin/Finance ... Ms. Rosanne CAPTAIN
21 Treasurer ... Mr. Michael DOBISE
30 Associate VP Development ... Mr. Scott M. BERG
06 Registrar ... Mr. Keith INGALLS
07 Dir Undergrad Admission ... Mr. Richard VERES
08 Director Library ... Ms. Andrea S. TAUPIER
29 Director Alumni Programs ... Ms. Tamie KIDESS LUCEY
37 Director of Financial Aid ... Mr. Edward CIOSEK
36 Director Career Services ... Ms. Barbara K. KAUTZ
13 Chief Information Officer ... Mr. Danny DAVIS
90 Director Academic Computer Center ... Mr. Thomas F. LARKIN
26 Director of Marketing/Communication ... Mr. Stephen ROULIER
38 Director of Counseling Center ... Vacant
19 Director Campus Police Department ... Ms. L. Judy JACKSON
88 Director YMCA Programs ... Mr. Harry ROCK
85 Director of International Center ... Dr. Deborah ALM
42 Director Campus Ministry ... Mr. David MCMAHON
18 Director of Facilities & Campus Svc ... Mr. Stephen LEFEVER
39 Director of Residence Life ... Mr. Tarome ALFORD
41 Director of Athletics ... Dr. Cathie SCHWEITZER
96 Director of Purchasing ... Ms. Lita ADAMS
28 Director Multicultural Affairs ... Mr. John WILSON

Stonehill College (A)

320 Washington Street, Easton MA 02357-6110
County: Bristol　FICE Identification: 002217
Unit ID: 167996
Telephone: (508) 565-1000　Carnegie Class: Bac/A&S
FAX Number: (508) 565-1500　Calendar System: Semester
URL: www.stonehill.edu
Established: 1948　Annual Undergrad Tuition & Fees: $48,420
Enrollment: 2,456　Coed
Affiliation or Control: Roman Catholic　IRS Status: 501(c)3
Highest Offering: Master's
Program: Liberal Arts And General; Teacher Preparatory; Professional
Accreditation: EH, BUS

01 President .... Rev. Mark T. CREGAN, CSC
05 Interim Provost/VP for Acad Affairs .... Dr. Joseph FAVAZZA
10 Vice Pres for Finance & Treasurer .... Ms. Jeanne FINLAYSON
30 Vice President for Advancement .... Mr. Francis X. DILLON
32 Vice President for Student Affairs .... Rev. John DENNING, CSC
88 Vice President for Mission .... Rev. James LIES, CSC
84 VP for Enrollment Mgmt & Marketing .... Mr. Christopher LYDON
21 AVP for Finance & Operations .... Mr. Craig BINNEY
35 Assoc VP for Students Affairs .... Ms. Pauline DOBROWSKI
20 Assoc VP for Academic Affairs .... Dr. Joseph FAVAZZA
18 Assoc VP for Operations .... Vacant
37 Asst VP/Dir of Student Aid/Finance .... Mrs. Eileen K. O'LEARY
04 Sr Executive Asst to the President .... Mrs. Jessica L. GRACIA
43 General Counsel .... Mr. Thomas V. FLYNN
21 Controller .... Ms. Jennifer MATHEWS
07 Dean of Admissions .... Mr. Daniel MONAHAN
06 Registrar .... Mr. John PESTANA
09 Director Planning/Inst Research .... Ms. Laura J. UERLING
08 Director of College Library .... Ms. Cheryl MCGRATH
26 Dir of Media Rels & Communications .... Mr. Martin P. MCGOVERN
29 Director of Alumni Affairs .... Ms. Anne M. SANT
15 Director of Human Resources .... Ms. Maryann B. PERRY
38 Dir of Counseling & Testing Center ... Ms. Maria A. KAVANAUGH
27 Chief Information Officer .... Ms. Tamara ANDERSON
19 Chief of Police .... Mr. Peter CARNES
42 Director Campus Ministry .... Rev. Hugh CLEARY, CSC
90 Manager of Instructional Technology .... Ms. Janice HARRISON
45 Director of Academic Development .... Ms. Bonnie L. TROUPE
88 Dir of Enterprise Infrastructure .... Mr. Thomas MCGRATH
23 Director of Health Services .... Ms. Diane LEARY
36 Director of Career Services .... Ms. Heather HEERMAN
41 Dir of Intercollegiate Athletics .... Mr. Brendan SULLIVAN
92 Director of Honors Program .... Rev. George PIGGFORD, CSC
44 Director of Development .... Mr. Douglas J. SMITH
20 Asst Dean for Academic Services .... Mr. Kevin PISKADLO
96 Director of Purchasing .... Mr. Gregory WOLFE
45 Asst VP for Planning & Budgeting .... Mr. Stephen BEAUREGARD
39 Director of Residence Life .... Ms. Ali HICKS
24 Dir of Media/Videography Services .... Mr. Michael PIETROWSKI
40 Manager of College Bookstore .... Ms. Mary CULLINANE
88 Dean of Academic Achievement .... Dr. Craig ALMEIDA
97 Dir Gen Educ/First Year Experience .... Dr. Todd S. GERNES
18 Dir of Facilities Management .... Mr. Bruce BOYER
88 Dir of Ctr for Teaching & Learning .... Ms. Stacy GROOTERS
104 Director International Programs .... Ms. Alice CRONIN
31 Campus Minister for Community Svc .... Ms. Mary Anne CAPPELLERI
88 Dir Ctr for Academic Achievement .... Dr. Martha UCCI
28 Director of Intercultural Affairs .... Ms. Liza TALUSAN

Suffolk University (B)

8 Ashburton Place, Boston MA 02108-2770
County: Suffolk　FICE Identification: 002218
Unit ID: 168005
Telephone: (617) 573-8000　Carnegie Class: Master's L
FAX Number: (617) 573-8353　Calendar System: Semester
URL: www.suffolk.edu
Established: 1906　Annual Undergrad Tuition & Fees: $30,672
Enrollment: 9,292　Coed
Affiliation or Control: Independent Non-Profit　IRS Status: 501(c)3
Highest Offering: Doctorate
Program: Liberal Arts And General; Teacher Preparatory; Professional
Accreditation: EH, ART, BUS, BUSA, CIDA, CLPSY, ENG, IPSY, LAW, RTT, SPAA

01 President .... Dr. James MCCARTHY
05 Interim Provost .... Dr. Michael BELL
10 Vice President/Treasurer .... Ms. Danielle MANNING
84 Vice Pres Enrollment Plng/Mgmt .... Mr. Walter CAFFEY
20 Vice Pres Academic Affairs .... Vacant
26 VP Marketing/Communications .... Mr. Greg GATLIN
86 VP External Affairs .... Mr. John A. NUCCI
30 Assoc Vice Pres of Advancement ...... Ms. Madelyne CUDDEBACK
32 Dean of Student Affairs .... Dr. Nancy C. STOLL
13 CIO .... Vacant
50 Dean Sawyer Business School .... Mr. William J. O'NEILL
61 Dean of the Law School .... Ms. Camile NELSON
49 Dean College Arts & Science .... Dr. Kenneth S. GREENBERG
37 AVP/Dir of Financial Aid .... Ms. Christine M. PERRY
93 Asst to Pres/Dir Minority Affairs .... Dr. Eric LEE
07 Director Undergraduate Admission .... Mr. John HAMEL
07 Director Graduate Admission .... Ms. Judith L. REYNOLDS
08 Director of Sawyer Library .... Mr. Robert E. DUGAN
06 College Registrar .... Miss Mary LALLY
36 Director Career Plng & Placement .... Mr. Paul TANKLEFSKY
15 Director of Human Resources .... Ms. Judy MINARDI
29 Director of Alumni Affairs/Law Sch .... Ms. Diane SCHOENFELD
13 Chief Information Officer .... Mr. Fouad YATIM
19 Captain University Police .... Mr. John PAGLIARULO
35 Director of Student Activities .... Mr. John SILVERIA
41 Director of Athletics .... Mr. James E. NELSON
18 Sr Dir Facilites Plng & Mgmt .... Mr. Gordon B. KING
07 Director of Law School Admission .... Ms. Gail ELLIS
06 Law School Registrar .... Ms. Lorraine D. COVE
36 Director of Law School Placement .... Mr. David JAMES
08 Law Librarian .... Ms. Elizabeth MCKENZIE
09 Director of Institutional Research .... Mr. Michael B. DUGGAN
38 Director of Student Counseling .... Dr. Kenneth F. GARNI
21 Associate Business Officer .... Mr. Gregory HARRIS

Tufts University (C)

Medford MA 02155-5555
County: Middlesex　FICE Identification: 002219
Unit ID: 168148
Telephone: (617) 628-5000　Carnegie Class: RU/VH
FAX Number: N/A　Calendar System: Semester
URL: www.tufts.edu
Established: 1852　Annual Undergrad Tuition & Fees: $44,666
Enrollment: 10,777　Coed
Affiliation or Control: Independent Non-Profit　IRS Status: 501(c)3
Highest Offering: Doctorate
Program: Liberal Arts And General; Teacher Preparatory; Professional
Accreditation: EH, CS, DENT, DIETI, ENG, IPSY, MED, OT, PH, PLNG, VET

01 President .... Dr. Anthony P. MONACO
100 Chief of Staff .... Mr. Michael BAENEN
03 Executive Vice President .... Ms. Patricia CAMPBELL
05 Sr Vice President/Provost .... Mr. David R. HARRIS
26 Sr Vice Pres University Relations .... Ms. Mary R. JEKA
30 Vice Pres University Advancement .... Mr. Eric C. JOHNSON
11 Vice President for Operations .... Mr. Richard REYNOLDS
10 Vice President Finance/Treasurer .... Mr. Thomas S. MCGURTY
16 Vice President Human Resources .... Ms. Kathe CRONIN
13 VP & Chief Information Officer .... Mr. David J. KAHLE
20 Vice Provost .... Ms. Peggy NEWELL
09 Assoc Provost Inst Res & Eval .... Dr. Dawn G. TERKLA
20 Associate Provost .... Dr. Mary Y. LEE
20 Assistant Provost .... Mr. Gary ROBERTS
21 Assistant Provost for Admin/Finance .... Ms. Suna K. GRASSI
29 Exec Director Alumni Relations .... Mr. Tim BROOKS
45 Exec Dir Planning & Administration .... Ms. Martha POKRAS
22 Exec Director Inst Diversity .... Vacant
15 Sr Director Human Res & Talent Mgmt .... Ms. Alison A. BLACKBURN
23 Sr Director Health/Wellness Svcs .... Ms. Michelle D. BOWDLER
43 Senior Legal Counsel .... Mr. Martin OPPENHEIMER
43 Senior Legal Counsel .... Mr. Dickens MATHIEU
37 Director of Financial Aid .... Ms. Patricia REILLY
26 Director Public Relations .... Ms. Kimberly M. THURLER
36 Director Career Services .... Ms. Jean M. PAPALIA
08 Director Tisch Library .... Ms. Laura WOOD
18 Director of Facilities Services .... Mr. Bob BURNS
28 Director Equal Opportunity .... Ms. Jill A. ZELLMER
38 Director Mental Health Services .... Dr. Julie S. ROSS
19 Director Public & Env Safety .... Mr. Kevin C. MAGUIRE
49 Dean Arts & Sciences .... Dr. Joanne E. BERGER-SWEENEY
54 Dean of Engineering .... Dr. Linda ABRIOLA
58 Dean Grad School of Arts & Science .... Dr. Lynne PEPALL
82 Dean Fletcher Law & Diplomacy .... Mr. Stephen BOSWORTH
52 Dean of Dental Medicine .... Dr. Huw F. THOMAS
74 Dean Cummings Sch of Veterinary Med . Dr. Deborah KOCHEVAR
63 Dean Medical School .... Dr. Harris BERMAN
88 Dean Sackler School .... Dr. Naomi ROSENBERG
88 Interim Dean Friedman School Nutri .... Dr. Robin KANAREK
88 Interim Dean Tisch College .... Ms. Nancy WILSON
53 Dean Undergrad & Grad Educ .... Mr. John BARKER
88 Dean Academic Adv & Undergrad Study .... Dr. Carmen LOWE
88 Dean of Student Services/Art & Sci .... Mr. Paul STANTON
32 Dean of Student Affairs .... Mr. Bruce REITMAN
07 Dean Undergrad Admiss/Enroll Mgt .... Mr. Lee A. COFFIN
06 Registrar ASE & Stdnt Svcs Desk Mgr .... Ms. Jo Ann JACK
96 Purchasing Director .... Ms. Diane M. DEVLIN
94 Director Women's Center .... Ms. Steph L. GAUCHEL
41 Director Athletics .... Mr. William GEHLING
42 Interim Chaplain .... Rev. Patricia BUDD KEPLER

Urban College of Boston (D)

178 Tremont Street, Boston MA 02111-1093
County: Suffolk　FICE Identification: 031305
Unit ID: 429128
Telephone: (617) 348-6359　Carnegie Class: Assoc/PrivNFP
FAX Number: (617) 423-4758　Calendar System: Semester
URL: www.urbancollege.edu
Established: 1993　Annual Undergrad Tuition & Fees: $8,880
Enrollment: 563　Coed
Affiliation or Control: Independent Non-Profit　IRS Status: 501(c)3
Highest Offering: Associate Degree
Program: 2-Year Principally Bachelor's Creditable
Accreditation: EH

01 President .... Dr. Robert A. REGAN
05 Academic Dean .... Vacant
84 Dean Enrollment Svcs & Registrar .... Dr. Henry J. JOHNSON
08 Dir of Learning Resource Center .... Ms. Nancy DANIEL
10 Business Manager .... Ms. Denise HARGAN
37 Director of Financial Aid .... Ms. Mia TAYLOR
20 Director Academic Support Services .... Mr. Josie HATUEY
30 Director Institutional Advancement .... Ms. Christa JONES

Wellesley College (E)

106 Central Street, Wellesley MA 02481-8203
County: Norfolk　FICE Identification: 002224
Unit ID: 168218
Telephone: (781) 283-1000　Carnegie Class: Bac/A&S
FAX Number: (781) 283-3639　Calendar System: Semester
URL: www.wellesley.edu
Established: 1875　Annual Undergrad Tuition & Fees: $55,114
Enrollment: 2,362　Female
Affiliation or Control: Independent Non-Profit　IRS Status: 501(c)3
Highest Offering: Baccalaureate
Program: Liberal Arts And General
Accreditation: EH

01 President .... Kim BOTTOMLY
05 Provost & Dean of the College .... Andrew SHENNAN
30 VP for Resources & Public Affairs .... Cameran MASON
10 Vice President Finance & Treasurer .... Andrew EVANS
18 Asst VP Facilities Management/Plng .... Peter ZURAW
27 Chief Information Officer .... Ganesan RAVISHANKER
07 Dean of Admission .... Jennifer DESJARLAIS
32 Dean of Students .... Debra DEMEIS
42 Dn Intercult Educ/Relig/Spirit Life .... Victor H. KAZANJIAN
20 Dean of Academic Affairs .... Richard G. FRENCH
20 Dean of Faculty Affairs .... Kathryn LYNCH
09 Asc Prov Institutional Plng/Assess .... Elena BERNAL
06 Registrar .... Carol SHANMUGARATNAM
29 Executive Director Alumnae Assn .... Susan CHALLENGER
37 Director of Student Financial Svcs .... Scott JUEDES
15 Acting Co-Director Human Resources .... Carolyn SLABODEN
15 Acting Co-Director Human Resources .... Kathryn STEWART
36 Director Center for Work & Service .... Joanne S. MURRAY
26 Chief Public Relations Officer .... Elizabeth T. GILDERSLEEVE
35 Assoc Director Student Involvement .... Megan K. JORDAN
38 Administrative Counseling Svcs .... Robin COOK-NOBLES
101 Clerk Board of Trustees .... Marianne B. COOLEY
96 Purchasing Manager .... Tina M. DOLAN

Wentworth Institute of Technology (F)

550 Huntington Avenue, Boston MA 02115-5998
County: Suffolk　FICE Identification: 002225
Unit ID: 168227
Telephone: (617) 989-4590　Carnegie Class: Bac/Diverse
FAX Number: (617) 989-4591　Calendar System: Semester
URL: www.wit.edu
Established: 1904　Annual Undergrad Tuition & Fees: $25,900
Enrollment: 3,541　Coed
Affiliation or Control: Independent Non-Profit　IRS Status: 501(c)3
Highest Offering: Master's
Program: Professional; Technical Emphasis
Accreditation: EH, ART, CIDA, CONST, CS, ENG, ENGT, IACBE

01 President .... Dr. Zorica PANTIC
100 Chief of Staff .... Ms. Amy INTILLE
05 Sr VP Academic Affairs/Provost .... Dr. Russell PINIZZOTTO
10 Vice Pres Finance .... Mr. Robert TOTINO
21 Vice President Business .... Mr. David A. WAHLSTROM
30 Vice Pres Institutional Advancement .... Ms. Brenda CROSS-SANCHEZ
32 VP Enrollment Mgmt/Student Affairs ...... Ms. Keiko BROOMHEAD
15 Vice Pres Human Resources .... Ms. Anne M. GILL
13 VP of Information Technology .... Mr. Mark STAPLES
04 Exec Assistant to the President .... Ms. Nancy BANDOIAN
20 Assoc Provost .... Mr. Charles HOTCHKISS
35 Assoc Vice Pres of Student Affairs .... Ms. Annamaria WENNER
21 Assoc Vice President Finance .... Mr. Peter MADDOCKS
84 Assoc VP of Enrollment Management .... Ms. Dianne PLUMMER
31 Assoc VP Community Affairs .... Ms. Sandra E. PASCAL
91 Assoc VP Information Technology .... Mr. Leslie VAUGHAN
90 Assoc VP Learning & Development .... Ms. Monique FUCHS
20 Assoc Provost for Acad Operations .... Ms. Susan PARIS
51 Dean of College of Prof & Cont Educ .... Mr. Larry CARR
07 Executive Director of Admissions .... Ms. Maureen DISCHINO
06 Registrar .... Ms. Nichole MANCONE
08 Director of Library .... Mr. Walter PUNCH
35 Dir Student Financial Services .... Ms. Wen-Hsin CHEN
18 Associate VP Physical Facilities .... Mr. Michael PANKIEVICH
29 Director of Alumni Programs .... Vacant
27 Director of Publications .... Mr. Daniel MORRELL
35 Associate Dean of Students .... Mr. Peter FOWLER
102 Director of Corporate Relations .... Mr. Jonathan CARROLL
37 Director Financial Aid .... Ms. Anne-Marie CARUSO
38 Director of Counseling .... Ms. Maura MULLIGAN
26 Associate Vice Pres Public Affairs .... Mr. Jamie KELLY
19 Director of Public Safety .... Mr. Charlie NOYES
41 Associate Athletic Director .... Mr. William P. GORMAN
36 Director of Career Services .... Mr. Gregory DENON
39 Director Housing & Residential Life .... Mr. Philip BERNARD
41 Director of Athletics .... Ms. Angel AYRES
09 Director of Institutional Research .... Mr. Bradford WILD
96 Director of Purchasing .... Mr. Gerald INMAN
09 Institutional Researcher .... Mr. Alan T. WHITEMORE
49 Dean for Arts & Sciences .... Mr. Patrick HAFFORD
48 Dean for Arch/Design & Const Mgmt .... Dr. Glenn WIGGINS
54 Dean for Engineering & Technology .... Mr. Frederick DRISCOLL
88 Director of Marketing & Comm .... Mr. Robert YEE

18 Director of Physical Plant .... Mr. Robert FERRO
88 Dir of Stdnt Lead Pgm & Camp Ctr .... Ms. Carissa DURFEE
88 Assistant Provost .... Ms. Tracy RUSCH

Western New England University (A)

1215 Wilbraham Road, Springfield MA 01119-2684
County: Hampden FICE Identification: 002226
Unit ID: 168254
Telephone: (413) 782-3111 Carnegie Class: Master's M
FAX Number: (413) 782-1746 Calendar System: Semester
URL: www.wne.edu
Established: 1919 Annual Undergrad Tuition & Fees: $31,912
Enrollment: 3,729 Coed
Affiliation or Control: Independent Non-Profit IRS Status: 501(c)3
Highest Offering: Doctorate
Program: Liberal Arts And General; Professional; Fine Arts Emphasis
Accreditation: EH, BUS, ENG, LAW, @PHAR, SW

01 President .... Dr. Anthony S. CAPRIO
05 Provost/Vice Pres Academic Affairs .... Dr. Jerry A. HIRSCH
26 Vice Pres Marketing & External Affs .... Mrs. Barbara A. CAMPANELLA
10 Vice Pres Finance & Administration .... Mr. William J. KELLEHER
84 Vice President for Enrollment Mgmt .... Dr. Charles R. POLLOCK
32 VP Student Affairs/Dean of Students .... Dr. Jeanne S. STEFFES
30 Vice President Advancement .... Ms. Beverly J. DWIGHT
14 Asst Vice Pres Information Tech .... Mr. Scott J. COOPEE
88 Vice Pres for Strategic Initiatives .... Dr. Richard S. KEATING
61 Dean of Law .... Prof. Arthur R. GAUDIO
54 Dean of Engineering .... Dr. S. Hossein CHERAGHI
50 Dean School of Business .... Dr. Julie SICILIANO
49 Dean of Arts & Sciences .... Dr. Saeed GHAHRAMANI
89 Dean Freshmen/Transfer Students .... Ms. Kerri P. JARZABSKI
39 Assistant Dean for Residence Life .... Mr. Thomas P. WOZNIAK
15 Exec Dir Human Res/Career Ctr .... Ms. Joanne OLLSON
09 Director Inst Research & Planning .... Dr. Richard A. WAGNER
29 Dir Alumni Relations/Annual Giving .... Ms. Kathrine PAPPAS
20 Academic Schdl Contr/Info Analyst .... Ms. Linda M. CHOJNICKI
08 Director of D'Amour Library .... Mrs. Priscilla L. PERKINS
37 Director of Student Admin Services .... Mr. Rodney W. PEASE
38 Director of Counseling Services .... Dr. Wayne D. CARPENTER
18 Director of Facilities Management .... Mr. Michael C. DUNCAN
41 Director of Athletics .... Dr. Michael THEULEN
31 Cultural Liaison Coordinator .... Rabbi Jerome S. GURLAND
08 Assoc Dean Library/Info Resources .... Ms. Pat NEWCOMBE
23 Director of Health Services .... Mrs. Kathleen A. REID
19 Director of Public Safety .... Mr. Adam WOODROW
28 Director of Diversity Programs .... Mrs. Yvonne BOGLE
11 Director Administrative Services .... Ms. Arlene M. ROCK

Wheaton College (B)

26 E Main Street, Norton MA 02766-2322
County: Bristol FICE Identification: 002227
Unit ID: 168281
Telephone: (508) 285-7722 Carnegie Class: Bac/A&S
FAX Number: (508) 286-8270 Calendar System: Semester
URL: www.wheatonma.edu
Established: 1834 Annual Undergrad Tuition & Fees: $43,774
Enrollment: 1,622 Coed
Affiliation or Control: Independent Non-Profit IRS Status: 501(c)3
Highest Offering: Baccalaureate
Program: Liberal Arts And General
Accreditation: EH

01 President .... Dr. Ronald A. CRUTCHER
05 Provost .... Dr. Linda EISENMANN
10 Vice Pres Finance/Administration .... Mr. Brian DOUGLAS
30 Vice President College Advancement .... Ms. Mary M. CASEY
84 Vice President Enrollment/Marketing .... Ms. Gail BERSON
32 VP Student Affairs/Dean of Students .... Ms. Lee B. WILLIAMS
37 Asst VP Enroll/Stdnt Finan Svcs .... Ms. Robin RANDALL
26 Asst Vice Pres for Communications .... Mr. Michael GRACA
06 Registrar/Dean Academic Systems .... Ms. Patricia SANTILLI
29 Dir Alumni Rels/Annual Giving .... Ms. Jill LAWLOR
105 Director College Web Strategy .... Mr. David CALDWELL
15 Asst VP/Director Human Resources .... Ms. Barbara LEMA
38 Director College Counseling .... Ms. Martha LAMB
07 Director of Admissions .... Ms. Lynne STACK
18 Asst VP Business Svcs/Phys Plant .... Mr. John M. SULLIVAN
96 Director of Purchasing .... Vacant
26 Director Public Affairs .... Vacant
09 Director of Institutional Research .... Ms. Audrey ADAM
39 Assoc Dean Stdnt Affs/Dir Res Life .... Ms. Kathryn E. MCCAFFREY
19 Director Public Safety .... Mr. Charles A. FURGAL

Wheelock College (C)

200 The Riverway, Boston MA 02215-4176
County: Suffolk FICE Identification: 002228
Unit ID: 168290
Telephone: (617) 879-2000 Carnegie Class: Master's M
FAX Number: (617) 566-7369 Calendar System: Semester
URL: www.wheelock.edu
Established: 1888 Annual Undergrad Tuition & Fees: $30,055
Enrollment: 1,285 Coed
Affiliation or Control: Independent Non-Profit IRS Status: 501(c)3
Highest Offering: Beyond Master's But Less Than Doctorate
Program: Liberal Arts And General; Teacher Preparatory
Accreditation: EH, SW, TED

01 President .... Ms. Jackie JENKINS-SCOTT
04 Executive Assistant to President .... Ms. Valerie THORNHILL-HUDSON
32 VP Campus Life/Information Svcs .... Mr. Roy SCHIFILLITI
05 Vice Pres for Academic Affairs .... Dr. Joan GALLOS
30 Vice Pres for Inst Advancement .... Ms. Linda Allaire WELTER
10 Vice Pres/Chief Financial Officer .... Ms. Anne Marie MARTORANA
84 VP Enrollment Mgt/Student Success .... Dr. Adrian K. HAUGABROOK
35 Dean of Students .... Ms. Barbara MORGAN
49 Dean of Arts & Sciences .... Dr. Shirley MALONE-FENNER
104 Dean International Pgms/Prtrnshp .... Dr. Linda DAVIS
53 Int Dean of Education/Social Work .... Dr. Donna MCKIBBENS
07 Senior Dir of Undergrad Admissions .... Ms. Kristen HARRINGTON
07 Director of Graduate Admissions .... Mr. Brian MINCHELLO
06 Interim Registrar .... Ms. Michelle ORMEROD
08 Director of Academic Resc & Library .... Ms. Brenda ECSEDY
15 Director of Human Resources .... Ms. Michele CREWS
13 Director of Information Technology .... Mr. Jonathan LAPIERRE
37 Director Financial Aid .... Ms. Roxanne DUMAS
36 Dir Center for Career Development .... Vacant
85 Int Director Center for Intl Educ .... Dr. Linda DAVIS
18 Chief Facilities/Physical Plant .... Mr. Ed JACQUES
38 Director Counseling Center .... Ms. Eileen THOMPSON
26 Interim Director of Marketing Comm .... Mr. Stephen DILL
86 Dir of Government and Ext Affairs .... Ms. Marta ROSA
29 Dir of Development/Alumni Relations .... Ms. Lauren MARQUIS
41 Athletic Director .... Ms. Diana CUTAIA

Williams College (D)

Williamstown MA 01267
County: Berkshire FICE Identification: 002229
Unit ID: 168342
Telephone: (413) 597-3131 Carnegie Class: Bac/A&S
FAX Number: N/A Calendar System: 4/1/4
URL: www.williams.edu
Established: 1793 Annual Undergrad Tuition & Fees: $44,660
Enrollment: 2,109 Coed
Affiliation or Control: Independent Non-Profit IRS Status: 501(c)3
Highest Offering: Master's
Program: Liberal Arts And General
Accreditation: EH

01 President .... Adam F. FALK
05 Dean of Faculty .... Peter T. MURPHY
45 Provost .... William C. DUDLEY
10 VP for Fin & Admin and Treasurer .... Frederick W. PUDDESTER
32 Vice President for Campus Life .... Stephen P. KLASS
30 Vice Pres for College Relations .... John M. MALCOLM
28 VP Strategic Plng/Inst Diversity .... Michael E. REED
04 Asst to Pres/Secretary of the Col .... Keli A. KAEGI
20 Dean of the College .... Sarah R. BOLTON
26 Asst to Pres for Public Affairs .... James G. KOLESAR
18 Assoc VP for Facilities .... Diana E. PRIDEAUX-BRUNE
06 Interim Registrar .... Barbara A. CASEY
07 Director of Admission .... Richard L. NESBITT
37 Director of Financial Aid .... Paul J. BOYER
08 Librarian .... David M. PILACHOWSKI
21 Controller .... Susan S. HOGAN
29 Director Alumni Relations .... Brooks L. FOEHL
15 Director of Human Resources .... Martha R. TETRAULT
36 Director of Career Counseling .... John H. NOBLE
88 Director of Dining Services .... Robert P. VOLPI
14 Chief Technology Officer .... Dinny S. TAYLOR
09 Director of Institutional Research .... Courtney WADE
23 Director of Health Services .... Ruth G. HARRISON
35 Director Office of Student Life .... Douglas J. SCHIAZZA
41 Director of Athletics/PE .... Lisa M. MELENDY
42 Chaplain .... Richard E. SPALDING

Woods Hole Oceanographic Institution (E)

266 Woods Hole Road, Woods Hole MA 02543-1535
County: Barnstable FICE Identification: 002230
Unit ID: 166610
Telephone: (508) 289-2252 Carnegie Class: Not Classified
FAX Number: N/A Calendar System: 4/1/4
URL: www.whoi.edu
Established: 1930 Annual Graduate Tuition & Fees: $55,970
Enrollment: 130 Coed
Affiliation or Control: Independent Non-Profit IRS Status: 501(c)3
Highest Offering: Doctorate; No Undergraduates
Program: Professional
Accreditation: EH

01 President and Director .... Dr. Susan AVERY
09 Director of Research .... Dr. Laurence P. MADIN
05 VP of Academic Programs and Dean .... Dr. James A. YODER
10 Vice Pres of Finance & Admin/CFO .... Mr. Jeffrey FERNANDEZ
20 Associate Dean .... Dr. Margaret K. TIVEY
06 Registrar .... Ms. Julia WESTWATER
08 Research Librarian .... Ms. Holly N. MILLER

Worcester Polytechnic Institute (F)

100 Institute Road, Worcester MA 01609-2280
County: Worcester FICE Identification: 002233
Unit ID: 168421
Telephone: (508) 831-5000 Carnegie Class: DRU
FAX Number: (508) 831-5753 Calendar System: Semester
URL: www.wpi.edu
Established: 1865 Annual Undergrad Tuition & Fees: $41,380
Enrollment: 5,778 Coed
Affiliation or Control: Independent Non-Profit IRS Status: 501(c)3
Highest Offering: Doctorate
Program: Liberal Arts And General; Professional; Technical Emphasis
Accreditation: EH, BUS, CS, ENG

01 President .... Dr. Dennis D. BERKEY
05 Provost .... Dr. Eric OVERSTROM
10 Executive Vice President & CFO .... Mr. Jeffrey S. SOLOMON
30 Vice Pres Devel & Alumni Relations .... Mr. William MCAVOY
32 VP Student Affairs/Campus Life .... Ms. Janet BEGIN-RICHARDSON
26 Exec Director Mktg & Communication .... Ms. Amy M. MORTON
13 CIO .... Ms. Deborah C. SCOTT
84 Sr VP Enrollment & Instnl Strategy .... Ms. Kristin R. TICHENOR
18 Asst Vice President for Facilities .... Mr. Alfred DIMAURO, JR.
15 Vice President of Human Resources .... Ms. A. Tracy HASSETT
20 VP Acad & Corp Devel .... Mr. Stephen P. FLAVIN
35 Dean of Students .... Mr. Philip N. CLAY
22 University Compliance Officer .... Mr. Michael J. CURLEY
36 Director of Career Devel Services .... Ms. Jeanette M. DOYLE
08 Dean of Library Services .... Dr. Tracey LEGER-HORNBY
100 Chief of Staff/Sec of the Corp .... Ms. Stephanie PASHA
07 Dean of Admissions .... Mr. Edward J. CONNOR
06 Registrar .... Ms. Heather JACKSON
27 Director of Research/Communications .... Mr. Michael W. DORSEY
96 Manager of Procurement Services .... Ms. Laurie COLELLA
21 University Controller .... Ms. Charlene M. BELLOWS
09 Assistant VP of Budget Planning .... Ms. Judith L. TRAINOR
38 Asst Dean of Stdnt Dev/Dir SDCC .... Mr. Charles C. MORSE
88 Director Life Sciences Center .... Mr. Donald D. EASSON
37 Director Student Financial Aid .... Ms. Monica M. BLONDIN
19 Mgr Env Occupational Safety .... Mr. David H. MESSIER
28 Director of Diversity .... Ms. NaTonia TRAMMELL
29 Exec Director of Alumni Relations .... Mr. Peter A. THOMAS

Zion Bible College (G)

320 South Main Street, Haverhill MA 01835
County: Essex FICE Identification: 035705
Unit ID: 217606
Telephone: (978) 478-3400 Carnegie Class: Spec/Faith
FAX Number: (978) 478-3406 Calendar System: Semester
URL: www.zbc.edu
Established: 1924 Annual Undergrad Tuition & Fees: $10,093
Enrollment: 350 Coed
Affiliation or Control: Assemblies Of God Church IRS Status: 501(c)3
Highest Offering: Baccalaureate
Program: Religious Emphasis
Accreditation: BI

01 President .... Rev Dr. Charles CRABTREE
03 Executive Vice President .... Rev Dr. Patrick G. GALLAGHER
32 Vice President of Student Affairs .... Ms. Donna Jo SCRUGGS
10 Director of Finance .... Mr. Ed LAUGHLIN
07 Director of Admissions .... Rev. David HODGE
08 Head Librarian .... Miss Ginger MCDONALD
37 Director of Financial Aid .... Miss Patricia STAUFFER

MICHIGAN

Adrian College (H)

110 S Madison Street, Adrian MI 49221-2575
County: Lenawee FICE Identification: 002234
Unit ID: 168528
Telephone: (517) 265-5161 Carnegie Class: Bac/Diverse
FAX Number: (517) 264-3331 Calendar System: Semester
URL: www.adrian.edu
Established: 1859 Annual Undergrad Tuition & Fees: $27,440
Enrollment: 1,677 Coed
Affiliation or Control: United Methodist IRS Status: 501(c)3
Highest Offering: Master's
Program: Liberal Arts And General; Teacher Preparatory
Accreditation: NH, SW, @TEAC

01 President .... Dr. Jeffrey R. DOCKING
03 Executive Vice President .... Vacant
05 Vice Pres/Dean for Academic Affairs .... Dr. Agnes CALDWELL
30 Vice Pres Institutional Advancement .... Mr. Ron REEVES
84 Vice President of Enrollment .... Mr. Frank J. HRIBAR
10 Vice Pres Business Affairs/CFO .... Mr. Jerry WRIGHT
32 Dean of Student Affairs .... Mr. Troy SCHMIDLI
20 Asst Dean of Academic Affairs .... Dr. Keith MCCLEARY
21 Asst Vice Pres of Business Affairs .... Mr. David DREWS
44 Asst Vice President for Development .... Mr. James A. MAHONY
07 Associate Director of Admissions .... Ms. Mallory FRAILING
42 Chaplain/Director Church Relations .... Dr. Christopher P. MOMANY
26 Director of Public Relations .... Ms. Jennifer COMPTON
06 Registrar .... Ms. Bridgette WINSLOW
35 Associate Dean for Student Life .... Vacant
21 Controller .... Ms. Nicole MEGALE
86 Dir of Govt & Foundation Relations .... Ms. Katie F. HAMMOND
15 Director of Human Resources .... Mrs. Ann FORRISTER
40 Bookstore Manager .... Ms. Rachelle M. DUFFY
93 Dir Multicultural Cultural Programs .... Ms. Idali FELICIANO
29 Director Alumni Relations .... Mrs. Marsha FIELDER
41 Director of Athletics .... Mr. Michael DUFFY
19 Director of Campus Safety .... Mr. Charley DECKER
36 Director of Career Planning .... Mrs. Janna D'AMICO
88 Director of Conferences .... Ms. Lesley CARSON

38 Director of Counseling ... Ms. Monique J. SAVAGE
08 Head Librarian ... Mr. David CRUSE
23 Director of Health Center ... Ms. Dawn MARSH
96 Director of Purchasing ... Ms. Heather HOLSOPPLE
37 Director of Financial Aid ... Mr. Andy SPOHN
18 Director of Facilities ... Mr. John E. JOHNSTON
09 Director of Institutional Research ... Dr. Jason M. HARTZ
88 Director of Academic Services ... Ms. Linda JACOBS
88 Assoc Director of Academic Services ... Ms. Carolyn QUINLAN
27 Asst Dir of Information Services ... Mr. Bradley MAGGARD

Albion College (A)

611 E Porter Street, Albion MI 49224-1831

County: Calhoun — FICE Identification: 002235
Unit ID: 168546
Telephone: (517) 629-1000 — Carnegie Class: Bac/A&S
FAX Number: (517) 629-0509 — Calendar System: Semester
URL: www.albion.edu
Established: 1835 — Annual Undergrad Tuition & Fees: $33,600
Enrollment: 1,501 — Coed
Affiliation or Control: United Methodist — IRS Status: 501(c)3
Highest Offering: Baccalaureate
Program: Liberal Arts And General; Teacher Preparatory
Accreditation: NH, MUS, TEAC

01 President ... Dr. Donna M. RANDALL
10 Int Vice Pres Business & Finance ... Mr. Michael FRANDSEN
05 Provost ... Dr. Susan CONNER
30 Vice Pres Institutional Advancement ... Mr. Joshua MERCHANT
84 Int Vice Pres Enrollment Mgmt ... Mr. Joshua D. MERCHANT
32 Vice Pres & Dean Student Affairs ... Dr. Sally J. WALKER
13 Assoc Vice Pres Info Svcs/CIO ... Mr. Scott STEPHAN
07 Director of Admissions ... Ms. Mandy DUBIEL
39 Director Residential Life ... Mr. Michael WADSWORTH
08 Director of Libraries ... Dr. Michael VAN HOUTEN
26 Director of Communications ... Ms. Sarah F. BRIGGS
29 Director of Alumni Engagement ... Ms. Elinor MARSH
38 Director of Counseling ... Dr. Frank KELEMAN
37 Director of Financial Aid ... Ms. Ann WHITMER
06 Registrar ... Dr. Andrew DUNHAM
88 Director Dining & Hospitality Svcs ... Mr. Todd TEKIELE
18 Director of Facilities Operations ... Mr. Donald MASTERNAK
19 Director of Campus Safety ... Mr. Kenneth SNYDER
41 Athletic Director ... Mr. Matthew AREND
42 College Chaplain ... Rev. Daniel MCQUOWN
15 Director of Human Resources ... Mrs. Lisa LOCKE
09 Director of Institutional Research ... Dr. Andrew DUNHAM
20 Associate Academic Officer ... Dr. John WOELL
28 Assoc Director Multicultural Affs ... Vacant
40 Manager of Bookstore ... Mr. Nick ANGLE

Alma College (B)

614 W Superior, Alma MI 48801-1599

County: Gratiot — FICE Identification: 002236
Unit ID: 168591
Telephone: (989) 463-7111 — Carnegie Class: Bac/A&S
FAX Number: (989) 463-7277 — Calendar System: Other
URL: www.alma.edu
Established: 1886 — Annual Undergrad Tuition & Fees: $30,960
Enrollment: 1,417 — Coed
Affiliation or Control: Independent Non-Profit — IRS Status: 501(c)3
Highest Offering: Baccalaureate
Program: Liberal Arts And General; Teacher Preparatory
Accreditation: NH, MUS, @TEAC

01 President ... Dr. Jeff ABERNATHY
05 Provost & Vice Pres for Acad Affs ... Dr. Michael L. SELMON
10 Vice Pres for Business Affairs ... Mr. David V. BUHL
30 Vice President for Advancement ... Ms. Carol F. HYBLE
84 Int Vice President for Enrollment ... Mr. Bob GARCIA
32 Vice President for Student Life ... Dr. Nicholas A. PICCOLO
26 Vice Pres Communication/Marketing ... Ms. Ann HALL
04 Executive Asst to the President ... Ms. Sandee A. GADDE
20 Assistant Provost ... Ms. Julie WILLIAMS
06 Registrar ... Ms. Susan M. DEEL
42 Chaplain ... Dr. Carol M. GREGG
37 Director of Financial Aid ... Ms. Michelle MCNIER
08 Director of Library ... Ms. Carol ZEILE
26 Director of College Communications ... Mr. Mike SILVERTHORN
14 Chief Technology Officer ... Dr. Keith R. NELSON
18 Director Facilities & Service Mgmt ... Mr. Douglas DICE
15 Director Human Resources ... Mr. Kenneth L. BORGMAN
21 Controller ... Mr. Dan HENRIS
29 Director Alumni Relations ... Ms. Lou ECKEN
35 Director Campus Life ... Mr. David K. BLANDFORD
38 Director Counseling & Wellness ... Ms. Anne K. LAMBRECHT
07 Director Admissions ... Mr. Bob GARCIA
09 Director of Institutional Research ... Mr. Robert ROE

Alpena Community College (C)

665 Johnson Street, Alpena MI 49707-1495

County: Alpena — FICE Identification: 002237
Unit ID: 168607
Telephone: (989) 356-9021 — Carnegie Class: Assoc/Pub-R-M
FAX Number: (989) 358-7553 — Calendar System: Semester
URL: www.alpenacc.edu
Established: 1952 — Annual Undergrad Tuition & Fees (In-District): $3,720
Enrollment: 1,987 — Coed
Affiliation or Control: Local — IRS Status: 501(c)3
Highest Offering: Associate Degree
Program: Occupational; 2-Year Principally Bachelor's Creditable
Accreditation: NH, MAC

01 President ... Dr. Olin JOYNTON
10 Vice President Admin & Finance ... Mr. Richard SUTHERLAND
21 Controller ... Ms. Lyn KOWALEWSKY
20 Dean Learning Resource Center ... Ms. Wendy BROOKS
103 Dean Workplace Partnership Program ... Mr. Donald MACMASTER
13 Co-Director Computing/Info Mgmt ... Ms. Vicky KROPP
13 Co-Director Computing/Info Mgmt ... Mr. Mark GRUNDER
26 Director Public Information ... Mr. Jay WALTERREIT
40 Director Bookstore ... Mr. William MATZKE
102 Foundation Director ... Ms. Penny BOLDREY
18 Director Buildings & Grounds ... Mr. Thomas LUDWIG
88 Director Volunteer Center ... Ms. Kathleen BRUSKI
06 Registrar ... Ms. Lori DZIESINSKI
15 Director Personnel Services ... Ms. Carolyn THOMAS
07 Director of Admissions ... Mr. Mike KOLLIEN
37 Director Student Financial Aid ... Mr. Robert ROOSE

Andrews University (D)

Berrien Springs MI 49104-0001

County: Berrien — FICE Identification: 002238
Unit ID: 168740
Telephone: (269) 471-7771 — Carnegie Class: DRU
FAX Number: (269) 471-6900 — Calendar System: Semester
URL: www.andrews.edu
Established: 1874 — Annual Undergrad Tuition & Fees: $24,478
Enrollment: 3,547 — Coed
Affiliation or Control: Seventh-day Adventist — IRS Status: 501(c)3
Highest Offering: Doctorate
Program: Liberal Arts And General; Teacher Preparatory; Professional
Accreditation: NH, CACREP, DIETD, DIETI, ENG, IACBE, MT, MUS, NUR, PTA, SW, TED, THEOL

01 President ... Dr. Niels-Erik A. ANDREASEN
05 Provost ... Dr. Andrea T. LUXTON
20 Associate Provost ... Dr. Emilio GARCIA-MARENKO
10 Vice President for Financial Admin ... Mr. Lawrence E. SCHALK
32 Vice President for Student Life ... Dr. Frances M. FAEHNER
26 Vice Pres Marketing & Communication ... Mr. Stephen D. PAYNE
84 Vice Pres for Enrollment Management ... Mr. Randy K. GRAVES
30 Vice President for Advancement ... Dr. David A. FAEHNER
43 General Counsel ... Mr. Brent G T. GERATY
06 Registrar ... Dr. Emilio GARCIA-MARENKO
49 Dean College Arts & Sciences ... Dr. Keith E. MATTINGLY
76 Dean School of Health Professions ... Dr. Emmanuel RUDATSIKIRA
50 Dean School of Business Admin ... Dr. Allen F. STEMBRIDGE
53 Dean School of Education ... Dr. James R. JEFFERY
48 Dean Sch Architecture/Art & Design ... Mr. Carey CARSCALLEN
73 Dean of Theological Seminary ... Dr. Denis FORTIN
58 Dean School of Grad Studies ... Dr. Christon ARTHUR
106 Dean School of Distance Education ... Dr. Alayne THORPE
08 Dean of Libraries ... Mr. Lawrence W. ONSAGER
21 Associate Business Officer ... Mr. Glenn A. MEEKMA
90 Chief Information Officer ... Ms. Lorena L. BIDWELL
39 Dir of University Apartment Life ... Mr. Alfredo RUIZ
34 Dir of the Women's Residence Halls ... Ms. Jennifer R. BURRILL
33 Dir of the Men's Residence Halls ... Mr. Spencer D. CARTER
85 Dir of International Student Svcs ... Dr. Najeeb W. NAKHLE
92 Director of Honors Program ... Dr. L. Monique PITTMAN
15 Director of Human Resources ... Mr. Daniel E. AGNETTA
37 Director Student Financial Aid ... Ms. Elynda A. BEDNEY
88 Media Relations Specialist ... Ms. Keri SUAREZ
29 Director of Alumni Services ... Ms. Tami CONDON
38 Dir of Counseling/Testing Center ... Dr. Judith FISHER
40 Manager of Bookstore ... Ms. Cheryl KEAN
19 Director of Campus Safety ... Mr. Dale B. HODGES
23 Director of Medical Services ... Dr. Dan REICHERT
42 University Chaplain ... Mr. Japhet DE OLIVEIRA
09 Director Institutional Research ... Mr. James R. MASSENA
18 Director of Facilities Management ... Mr. Richard L. SCOTT

Aquinas College (E)

1607 Robinson Road, SE, Grand Rapids MI 49506-1799

County: Kent — FICE Identification: 002239
Unit ID: 168786
Telephone: (616) 632-8900 — Carnegie Class: Master's M
FAX Number: (616) 732-4469 — Calendar System: Semester
URL: www.aquinas.edu
Established: 1886 — Annual Undergrad Tuition & Fees: $25,070
Enrollment: 2,142 — Coed
Affiliation or Control: Roman Catholic — IRS Status: 501(c)3
Highest Offering: Master's
Program: Liberal Arts And General; Teacher Preparatory; Professional
Accreditation: NH, @TEAC

01 President ... Dr. Juan OLIVAREZ
05 Provost/Dean of Faculty ... Dr. Charles GUNNOE, JR.
30 Vice Pres Institutional Advancement ... Mr. Greg MCALEENAN
10 Vice President Finance ... Mr. Stephen WONCH
84 Vice Pres Enrollment Management ... Ms. Paula T. MEEHAN
04 Assistant to President ... Ms. Jan SOMMERVILLE
102 Assoc VP for Inst Advancement ... Mr. Gregory MEYER
26 Assoc VP Marketing & Communication ... Ms. Meg DERRER
06 Registrar ... Mrs. Cecelia MESLER
07 Dean of Admissions ... Mr. Thomas MIKOWSKI
32 Dean of Student Services ... Mr. Brian MATZKE
20 Associate Provost ... Ms. Nanette CLATTERBUCK
35 Associate Dean of Student Affairs ... Dr. Jennifer DAWSON
38 Director of Career/Counseling Svcs ... Ms. Sharon E. SMITH
104 Dir International Education Pgms ... Ms. Joelle BALDWIN
94 Director of Women's Studies ... Dr. Susan HAWORTH-HOEPPNER
92 Director of Honors Program ... Dr. Michelle DEROSE
58 Director of Graduate Management ... Mr. Brian DIVITA
08 Co-Director Woodhouse Library ... Ms. Shellie JEFFRIES
08 Co-Director Woodhouse Library ... Ms. Francine PAOLINI
21 Controller ... Ms. Cathy LUCK
15 Director of Human Resources ... Mr. Stephen WOLF
14 Director College Computing ... Ms. Joyce L. LAFLEUR
18 Director of Maintenance ... Mr. Dale HAISMA
39 Director Residence Life ... Vacant
07 Director of Admissions ... Ms. Angela SCHLOSSER-BACON
37 Director of Financial Aid ... Mr. David J. STEFFEE
41 Director Athletics ... Mr. Terry M. BOCIAN
42 Director Campus Ministry ... Ms. Mary CLARK-KAISER
13 Dir Information Technology & Svcs ... Ms. Joyce LAFLEUR
29 Director of Alumni Relations ... Ms. Brigid AVERY
35 Director of Campus Life ... Ms. Heather HALL
44 Director of Major Gifts ... Ms. Cecelia CUNNINGHAM
44 Director of Corporate Giving ... Dr. Ali ERHAN
20 Director of Academic Advising ... Ms. Cecelia MESLER
28 Director of Diversity ... Ms. Marnika BROWN
40 Director Bookstore ... Ms. Marian TODISH
23 Manager of Health and Wellness ... Ms. Veronica BEITNER
24 Media Coordinator ... Ms. Francine PAOLINI

The Art Institute of Michigan (F)

28125 Cabot Drive, Novi MI 48377

County: Oakland — Identification: 666692
Unit ID: 451796
Telephone: (248) 675-3800 — Carnegie Class: Spec/Arts
FAX Number: (248) 489-3961 — Calendar System: Semester
URL: www.artinstitutes.edu/detroit
Established: 2007 — Annual Undergrad Tuition & Fees: $43,470
Enrollment: 799 — Coed
Affiliation or Control: Proprietary — IRS Status: Proprietary
Highest Offering: Baccalaureate
Program: Fine Arts Emphasis
Accreditation: &NH, ACFEI

01 President ... Dr. Ted BLASHAK

† Regional accreditation is carried under the parent institution The Illinois Institute of Art, Chicago, IL.

*Baker College System (G)

1050 W Bristol Road, Flint MI 48507-5508

County: Genesee — Identification: 666923
Unit ID: 419572
Telephone: (810) 766-4280 — Carnegie Class: N/A
FAX Number: (810) 766-4279
URL: www.baker.edu

00 Chairman of the Board ... Mr. Edward J. KURTZ
01 CEO/President of System ... Mr. F. James CUMMINS
05 Vice President for Academics ... Dr. Denise A. BANNAN
13 Vice President for Computer Systems ... Ms. Jacqueline SPICER
32 Vice President for Student Services ... Mr. Ellis P. SALIM
15 Vice President of Human Resources ... Ms. Rosemary ZAWACKI
26 Vice Pres Marketing/Admissions/PR ... Mr. Richard DELONG
10 Vice President for Finance ... Ms. Tiffany DAVIS
12 Campus Director-Cass City ... Ms. Karen EASTERLING
07 System Director for Admissions ... Mr. Bruce LUNDEEN
35 Director of Student Life ... Vacant
45 Director of Assessment ... Ms. Debra BILLINGS
20 Director Curriculum ... Ms. Kim L. LUTZ
36 Director of Career Services ... Ms. Beth NUCCIO
13 Director Computer Programming ... Vacant
14 Director Computer Operations ... Mrs. Sheryl L. DEAN
08 Director of Library Services ... Mr. Eric PALMER
58 President Graduate Studies ... Dr. Michael HEBERLING

*Baker College of Allen Park (H)

4500 Enterprise Drive, Allen Park MI 48101-3033

Identification: 666996
Unit ID: 444167
Telephone: (313) 425-3700 — Carnegie Class: Bac/Assoc
FAX Number: (313) 425-3777 — Calendar System: Quarter
URL: www.baker.edu
Established: 2003 — Annual Undergrad Tuition & Fees: $7,740
Enrollment: 3,954 — Coed
Affiliation or Control: Independent Non-Profit — IRS Status: 501(c)3
Highest Offering: Baccalaureate
Program: Occupational; 2-Year Principally Bachelor's Creditable; Liberal Arts And General
Accreditation: &NH, IACBE, MAC, MLTAD, OTA, PTAA, SURGT

02 Campus President ... Mr. Aaron J. MAIKE
05 Chief Academic Officer ... Dr. Karen BRATUS
07 Vice President of Admissions ... Mr. Steven PETERSON
10 Vice President of Finance ... Ms. Kristine BARANN
06 Registrar ... Ms. Michelle MAXFIELD
37 Director Student Financial Aid ... Ms. Candi RUFFNER

*Baker College of Auburn Hills (I)

1500 University Drive, Auburn Hills MI 48326-2642

County: Oakland — Identification: 666940
Unit ID: 404073
Telephone: (248) 340-0600 — Carnegie Class: Bac/Assoc

FAX Number: (248) 340-0608 Calendar System: Quarter
URL: www.baker.edu
Established: 1992 Annual Undergrad Tuition & Fees: $7,740
Enrollment: 3,803 Coed
Affiliation or Control: Independent Non-Profit IRS Status: 501(c)3
Highest Offering: Baccalaureate
Program: Occupational; 2-Year Principally Bachelor's Creditable; Liberal Arts And General
Accreditation: &NH, DA, DH, DMS, IACBE, MAC

02 President .... Mr. Jeffrey M. LOVE
05 Vice President of Academics .... Dr. Susan D. CATHCART
10 Vice President of Finance .... Mr. Jim MARTIN
07 Director of Admissions .... Ms. Nicole CHIRCO
06 Registrar/Student Counseling .... Mr. Tim M. YOUNT
18 Director of Facilities .... Mr. Jim OMLOR
36 Director of Career Services .... Ms. Melissa RODIC
37 Director of Financial Aid .... Mr. Greg LITTLE

*Baker College of Cadillac (A)

9600 E 13th Street, Cadillac MI 49601-9600
County: Wexford Identification: 666941
Unit ID: 404648
Telephone: (231) 876-3100 Carnegie Class: Bac/Assoc
FAX Number: (231) 775-8505 Calendar System: Quarter
URL: www.baker.edu
Established: 1986 Annual Undergrad Tuition & Fees: $7,740
Enrollment: 1,639 Coed
Affiliation or Control: Independent Non-Profit IRS Status: 501(c)3
Highest Offering: Baccalaureate
Program: Occupational; 2-Year Principally Bachelor's Creditable; Technical Emphasis
Accreditation: &NH, IACBE, MAC, SURGT

02 Campus President .... Dr. Kelly SMITH
05 Chief Academic Officer .... Ms. Nancy FOSTER
07 Director of Admissions .... Ms. Audrey CHARMOLI
06 Registrar/Academic Advisor .... Mr. Cliff REDES
10 Business Manager .... Ms. Ami MCBRIDE
36 Director of Career Services .... Mrs. Matt WHETSTANE
37 Director of Financial Aid .... Mrs. Kristin HATHAWAY
08 Librarian .... Ms. Laurie ARRICK
53 Dean of Education .... Vacant
76 Dean of Health .... Ms. Gail BALLARD
97 Dean of General Education .... Mr. David DARROW
13 Dean Computer Info Systems/Tech .... Vacant

*Baker College of Clinton Township (B)

34950 Little Mack Avenue,
Clinton Township MI 48035-4701
County: Macomb Identification: 666942
Unit ID: 404082
Telephone: (586) 791-6610 Carnegie Class: Bac/Assoc
FAX Number: (586) 791-6611 Calendar System: Quarter
URL: www.baker.edu
Established: 1990 Annual Undergrad Tuition & Fees: $7,740
Enrollment: 5,712 Coed
Affiliation or Control: Independent Non-Profit IRS Status: 501(c)3
Highest Offering: Baccalaureate
Program: Occupational; 2-Year Principally Bachelor's Creditable; Liberal Arts And General
Accreditation: &NH, IACBE, MAC, RAD, SURGT

02 President .... Mr. Donald R. TORLINE
07 Vice President of Admissions .... Ms. Annette LOOSER
32 Vice President of Student Services .... Ms. Lisa HARVENER
10 Vice President of Finance .... Ms. Marsha ADAMKIEWICZ
05 Vice President of Academics .... Dr. Laura TREANOR
50 Dean of Business .... Mr. Joseph PEPOY
72 Dean of CIS/Technology .... Ms. Pauline DUEWEKE
76 Dean of Allied Health Sciences .... Ms. Anna CZUBATYJ
06 Registrar .... Mr. Shaun STEVENS
38 Director Student Counseling .... Ms. Barbara KRYGEL
08 Head Librarian .... Ms. Kathy HARGER
36 Director Student Placement .... Ms. Marilyn WOODS
19 Director Security/Safety .... Mr. Dan OSBORN

*Baker College of Flint (C)

1050 W Bristol Road, Flint MI 48507-5508
County: Genesee FICE Identification: 004673
Unit ID: 168847
Telephone: (810) 766-4000 Carnegie Class: Bac/Assoc
FAX Number: (810) 766-4293 Calendar System: Quarter
URL: www.baker.edu
Established: 1911 Annual Undergrad Tuition & Fees: $7,740
Enrollment: 6,329 Coed
Affiliation or Control: Independent Non-Profit IRS Status: 501(c)3
Highest Offering: Doctorate
Program: Occupational; 2-Year Principally Bachelor's Creditable; Liberal Arts And General; Business Emphasis
Accreditation: NH, ENG, ENGT, IACBE, MAC, OT, POLYT, PTAA, SURGT, TEAC

02 President .... Dr. Julianne T. PRINCINSKY
05 Vice President of Academics .... Dr. Candace JOHNSON
07 Vice President of Admissions .... Ms. Jodi CUNEAZ
15 Vice President of Human Resources .... Ms. Rosemary ZAWACKI
32 Vice President of Student Services .... Mr. Gerald MCCARTY, II
88 Dean of Developmental Education .... Mrs. Connie WARNER
50 Dean of Business Administration .... Dr. John C. COTE
97 Dean of General Education .... Dr. Mary Ann THAYER
76 Dean of Health/Human Services .... Ms. Clementine RICE
72 Dean of Technical Division .... Mrs. Anca SALA
08 Director of Library Services .... Mr. Eric PALMER
06 Registrar .... Mr. Robert MARTIN
13 Director of Computer Operations .... Mr. Michael MEYERS
18 Director of Facilities .... Mr. Marvin DEAN
38 Director of Counseling/Assessment .... Mr. Paul ZANG
19 Director of Safety/Security .... Mr. Thomas POKORA
40 Director of Bookstore .... Mr. James ROTTA
54 Dir Engineering/Computer Science .... Mrs. Anca SALA
26 Actg Director Community Relations .. Dr. Julianne T. PRINCINSKY
10 Business Officer .... Mrs. Rebecca AYRE-BOGGS
36 Director of Career Services .... Mrs. Janie STEWART
37 Director Student Financial Aid .... Ms. Veta NORRIS
31 Director Corporate/Community Svcs .... Ms. Karen EASTERLING
23 Director of Health and Fitness .... Ms. Maureen PARMANN
39 Housing Coordinator .... Mr. Leon CARTER

*Baker College of Jackson (D)

2800 Springport Road, Jackson MI 49202-1290
County: Jackson FICE Identification: 004680
Unit ID: 414160
Telephone: (517) 788-7800 Carnegie Class: Bac/Assoc
FAX Number: (517) 789-7331 Calendar System: Quarter
URL: www.baker.edu
Established: 1994 Annual Undergrad Tuition & Fees: $7,740
Enrollment: 2,730 Coed
Affiliation or Control: Independent Non-Profit IRS Status: 501(c)3
Highest Offering: Baccalaureate
Program: Occupational; 2-Year Principally Bachelor's Creditable; Technical Emphasis
Accreditation: &NH, IACBE, MAC, MLTAD, OPD, RTT, SURGT

02 President .... Dr. Patty KAUFMAN
05 Chief Academic Officer .... Dr. Dana CLARK
07 Vice President of Admissions .... Mr. Kevin M. PNACEK
10 Vice President of Finance .... Vacant
32 VP Student Affs/Dir Stdnt Placment .... Ms. Michelle SHIELDS
20 Dean of Developmental Education .... Ms. Cindy VAN GIESON
15 Dean of Education/Human Services .... Mr. Blaine GOODRICH
37 Financial Aid Director .... Ms. Jenni SAMONS
06 Registrar .... Ms. Jill M. DUTTON
18 Director Facilities/Physical Plant .... Mr. Ryan SMITHSOM
50 Dean Business & Technology .... Mr. Jack JORDAN
76 Dean Allied Health .... Ms. Marie BONKOWSKI
97 Dean General Education .... Ms. Nancy HILL
38 Director of Student Counseling .... Vacant
21 Business Officer & Personnel Svcs .... Ms. Lisa GOWDY

*Baker College of Muskegon (E)

1903 Marquette Avenue, Muskegon MI 49442-1490
County: Muskegon FICE Identification: 002296
Unit ID: 171298
Telephone: (231) 777-5200 Carnegie Class: Bac/Assoc
FAX Number: (231) 777-5265 Calendar System: Quarter
URL: www.baker.edu
Established: 1911 Annual Undergrad Tuition & Fees: $7,740
Enrollment: 5,000 Coed
Affiliation or Control: Independent Non-Profit IRS Status: 501(c)3
Highest Offering: Baccalaureate
Program: Occupational; 2-Year Principally Bachelor's Creditable; Liberal Arts And General
Accreditation: &NH, ACFEI, IACBE, MAC, OTA, PTAA, RAD, SURGT

02 President .... Dr. Lee COGGIN
05 Vice President for Academics .... Dr. DeAnna BURT
10 Vice President for Finance .... Ms. Manifa DENNISON
32 Vice President for Student Services .... Mr. Michael L. HELSEN
07 Vice President Admissions .... Ms. Kathy JACOBSON
06 Registrar .... Ms. Christine FOGG
50 Dean for Business & Office Admin .... Vacant
97 Dean for General Education .... Ms. Kijm PILIECI
77 Dean for CIS Technical .... Mr. Gary VERSALLE
15 Dean for Health .... Mr. Eric SURGE
37 Financial Aid Director .... Mrs. Leslie JOLMAN
08 Director of Library Services .... Ms. Gail POWERS-SCHAUB
18 Director of Facilities .... Mr. David STURGEON
19 Director of Campus Safety .... Mr. Joe STAPEL
38 Director of Counseling & Assessment .... Ms. Christine BULTEMA

*Baker College of Owosso (F)

1020 S Washington Street, Owosso MI 48867-4400
County: Shiawassee Identification: 666937
Unit ID: 168838
Telephone: (989) 729-3370 Carnegie Class: Bac/Assoc
FAX Number: (989) 729-3429 Calendar System: Quarter
URL: www.baker.edu
Established: 1983 Annual Undergrad Tuition & Fees: $7,740
Enrollment: 3,078 Coed
Affiliation or Control: Independent Non-Profit IRS Status: 501(c)3
Highest Offering: Baccalaureate
Program: Occupational; 2-Year Principally Bachelor's Creditable; Liberal Arts And General
Accreditation: &NH, ADNUR, DMS, IACBE, MAC, MLTAD, RAD

02 President .... Mr. Peter KARSTEN
05 Vice President of Academics .... Dr. Carol DOWSETT
32 Vice President of Student Services .... Mrs. Lisa A. LYNCH
10 Vice President of Finance .... Mr. Michael MOORE
07 Vice President of Admissions .... Mr. Michael KONOPACKE
37 Director of Financial Aid .... Ms. Nicole BOELK
06 Registrar .... Ms. Christy VERITY
18 Chief Facilities/Physical Plant .... Mr. Pat PRASKI
26 Chief Public Relations Officer .... Vacant
38 Director Student Counseling .... Mr. James BAUER

*Baker College of Port Huron (G)

3403 Lapeer Road, Port Huron MI 48060-2597
County: Saint Clair Identification: 666943
Unit ID: 381617
Telephone: (810) 985-7000 Carnegie Class: Bac/Assoc
FAX Number: (810) 985-7066 Calendar System: Quarter
URL: www.baker.edu
Established: 1990 Annual Undergrad Tuition & Fees: $7,740
Enrollment: 1,453 Coed
Affiliation or Control: Independent Non-Profit IRS Status: 501(c)3
Highest Offering: Baccalaureate
Program: Occupational; 2-Year Principally Bachelor's Creditable; Liberal Arts And General
Accreditation: &NH, DA, DH, IACBE, MAC, MLTAD, SURGT

02 President .... Dr. Connie HARRISON
05 Chief Academic Officer .... Dr. Iris LANE
07 Vice President of Admissions .... Mr. Dan KENNY
32 Vice President of Student Services .... Ms. Betsy WHITE
06 Registrar .... Ms. Judi LANGOLF
97 Dean General Education .... Ms. Louise WANG-WELDON
76 Dean Health Science .... Dr. Pamela GOLL
53 Dean Education & Human Services .... Dr. Janelle MCGUIRE
08 Director of Library .... Ms. Dora MARSHALL-TURNER
37 Senior Officer of Financial Aid .... Ms. Barbara MALCOLM
38 Director Academic Counseling .... Mr. Greg RUMPZ
18 Director of Facilities .... Mr. Shane HENSLEY
10 Business Manager .... Mr. Charles DECKER

Bay Mills Community College (H)

12214 W Lakeshore Drive, Brimley MI 49715-9750
County: Chippewa FICE Identification: 030666
Unit ID: 380359
Telephone: (906) 248-3354 Carnegie Class: Tribal
FAX Number: (906) 248-3351 Calendar System: Semester
URL: www.bmcc.edu
Established: 1984 Annual Undergrad Tuition & Fees: $2,880
Enrollment: 575 Coed
Affiliation or Control: Tribal Control IRS Status: 501(c)3
Highest Offering: Associate Degree
Program: Occupational; 2-Year Principally Bachelor's Creditable; Business Emphasis
Accreditation: NH

01 President .... Michael C. PARISH
05 Vice President of Academic Affairs .... Samantha CAMERON
10 VP of Business & Finance .... Laura POSTMA
32 Dean of Student Services .... Debra J. WILSON
13 Technology Director .... Chet KASPER
06 Registrar .... Sherri SCHOFIELD
37 Director Student Financial Aid .... Tina MILLER
07 Director of Admissions .... Elaine LEHRE

Bay Noc Community College (I)

2001 N Lincoln Road, Escanaba MI 49829-2510
County: Delta FICE Identification: 002240
Unit ID: 168883
Telephone: (906) 786-5802 Carnegie Class: Assoc/Pub-R-M
FAX Number: (906) 789-6952 Calendar System: Semester
URL: www.baycollege.edu
Established: 1962 Annual Undergrad Tuition & Fees (In-District): $3,430
Enrollment: 2,742 Coed
Affiliation or Control: Local IRS Status: 501(c)3
Highest Offering: Associate Degree
Program: Occupational; 2-Year Principally Bachelor's Creditable
Accreditation: NH, ADNUR

01 President .... Dr. Laura L. COLEMAN
05 VP Instructional/Student Lrng .... Dr. Wendolyn E. TETLOW
10 VP Administrative Svcs .... Vacant
12 Vice President West Campus .... Dr. Patrick KENNEDY
32 Exec Dean of Student Services .... Mr. Matthew R. SOUCY
49 Dean of Arts and Sciences .... Dr. Deborah ANDERSON
72 Dean of Business and Tech .... Mr. Mark KINNEY
30 Exec Dir Institutional Advancement .... Ms. Kim CARNE
13 Chief Info Research and Effect Ofc .... Ms. Christine WILLIAMS
37 Director of Financial Aid .... Ms. Laurie SPANGENBERG
07 Director of Admissions .... Ms. Cynthia A. CARTER
15 Director of Human Resources .... Mr. Thomas J. GRIGGS
18 Superintendent Buildings/Grounds .... Mr. Ralph W. CURRY
76 Dean Allied Health/Wellness .... Ms. Patti HENNING
51 Manager Continuing Educ & Prof Dev .... Ms. Lori L. SHEA
36 Career/Academic Advisor .... Ms. Annette M. JOHNSON
38 Director Student Counseling .... Mr. Douglas S. KENDRICK
103 Director of Workforce Development .... Mr. Mark KINNEY

Calvin College (A)

3201 Burton Street, SE, Grand Rapids MI 49546-4388
County: Kent　　FICE Identification: 002241
Unit ID: 169080
Telephone: (616) 526-6000　　Carnegie Class: Bac/A&S
FAX Number: (616) 526-8551　　Calendar System: 4/1/4
URL: www.calvin.edu
Established: 1876　　Annual Undergrad Tuition & Fees: $26,480
Enrollment: 3,967　　Coed
Affiliation or Control: Christian Reformed Church　　IRS Status: 501(c)3
Highest Offering: Master's
Program: Liberal Arts And General; Teacher Preparatory
Accreditation: NH, CS, ENG, MUS, NURSE, @SP, SW, @TEAC

01 President ... Dr. Michael K. LE ROY
04 Senior Executive Associate ... Mr. Robert A. BERKHOF
04 Executive Associate ... Ms. Darlene K. MEYERING
05 Provost ... Dr. Claudia BEVERSLUIS
10 Vice Pres Admin/Finance/Info Tech ... Dr. Henry E. DEVRIES, II
30 Vice President for Advancement ... Mr. Kenneth ERFFMEYER
84 Vice Pres Enrollment Management ... Mr. Russell J. BLOEM
32 Vice President Student Life ... Dr. Shirley VOGELZANG HOOGSTRA
21 Director of Finance ... Mr. Samuel L. WANNER
08 Director of the Library ... Mr. Glenn A. REMELTS
29 Director Alumni/Parent Relations ... Mr. Michael J. VAN DENEND
06 Director Academic Svcs/Registrar ... Mr. Thomas L. STEENWYK
39 Dean of Residence Life ... Mr. John WITTE
35 Dean of Student Development ... Mr. C. Robert CROW
88 Dean of Students for Judicial Affs ... Ms. Jane E. HENDRIKSMA
46 Dean of Research & Scholarship ... Dr. Matthew WALHOUT
108 Dean Institutional Effectiveness ... Dr. Michael STOB
83 Academic Dean Soc Sci/Context Disc ... Dr. Cheryl BRANDSEN
79 Acad Dean Arts/Language/Education ... Dr. Mark WILLIAMS
81 Academic Dean Natural Science/Math ... Dr. Stanley L. HAAN
28 Dean of Multicultural Academic Affs ... Dr. Michelle LOYD-PAIGE
15 Director of Human Resources ... Mr. Todd K. HUBERS
36 Director of Career Development ... Mr. Glenn E. TRIEZENBERG
09 Dir Institutional/Enroll Research ... Mr. Thomas A. VAN ECK
31 Director Conferences/Campus Events ... Mr. Jeffrey A. STOB
26 Director of Communic & Marketing ... Mr. Timothy L. ELLENS
88 Director Social Research Center ... Dr. Neil CARLSON
19 Director of Campus Safety ... Mr. William T. CORNER
18 Director Physical Plant ... Mr. Philip D. BEEZHOLD
24 Director Instruc Resources Center ... Mr. Randal G. NIEUWSMA
38 Director Broene Counseling Center ... Dr. Cynthia KOK
23 Director Health Services ... Dr. Laura CHAMPION
92 Director Honors Program ... Dr. Kenneth D. BRATT
42 College Chaplain ... Dr. Mary HULST
40 Manager of the College Store ... Mr. Thomas J. VAN WINGERDEN
41 Athletic Director Men ... Dr. James TIMMER, JR.
41 Athletic Director Women ... Dr. Nancy L. MEYER

Calvin Theological Seminary (B)

3233 Burton Street, SE, Grand Rapids MI 49546-4387
County: Kent　　FICE Identification: 002242
Unit ID: 169099
Telephone: (616) 957-6036　　Carnegie Class: Spec/Faith
FAX Number: (616) 957-8621　　Calendar System: Semester
URL: www.calvinseminary.edu
Established: 1876　　Annual Graduate Tuition & Fees: $13,548
Enrollment: 286　　Coed
Affiliation or Control: Christian Reformed Church　　IRS Status: 501(c)3
Highest Offering: Doctorate; No Undergraduates
Program: Professional; Religious Emphasis
Accreditation: THEOL

01 President ... Rev. Julius T. MEDENBLIK
05 Dean of Academic Programs ... Dr. Ronald J. FEENSTRA
20 Dean of the Faculty ... Dr. Lyle D. BIERMA
06 Registrar ... Ms. Joan BEELEN
32 Dean of Students ... Rev. Jeff SAJDAK
08 Theological Librarian ... Rev. Lugene L. SCHEMPER
10 Chief Financial Officer ... Mr. Jim LUYK
30 Director of Development ... Mr. Robert KNOOR
36 Director of Mentored Ministries ... Rev. Alvern GELDER
07 Director of Admissions ... Mr. Matthew COOKE
37 Director of Financial Aid ... Mrs. Jennifer SETTERGREN

Central Michigan University (C)

Mount Pleasant MI 48859-0001
County: Isabella　　FICE Identification: 002243
Unit ID: 169248
Telephone: (989) 774-4000　　Carnegie Class: DRU
FAX Number: (989) 774-3537　　Calendar System: Semester
URL: www.cmich.edu
Established: 1892　　Annual Undergrad Tuition & Fees (In-State): $10,950
Enrollment: 28,194　　Coed
Affiliation or Control: State　　IRS Status: 501(c)3
Highest Offering: Doctorate
Program: Liberal Arts And General; Teacher Preparatory; Professional
Accreditation: NH, ART, ACAE, ARCPA, AUD, BUS, BUSA, CIDA, CLPSY, DIETD, DIETI, ENG, JOUR, #MED, MUS, NAIT, NRPA, PTA, SCPSY, SP, SPAA, SW, TEAC

01 President ... Dr. George E. ROSS
05 Executive VP/Provost ... Dr. E. Gary SHAPIRO
10 Vice Pres Finance/Admin Svcs ... Mr. David A. BURDETTE
30 Vice Pres Development/Ext Relations ... Ms. Kathleen M. WILBUR
84 Vice Pres Enroll Mgmt/Stdnt Svcs ... Mr. Steven JOHNSON
107 VP/Executive Director Prof Educ ... Dr. Merodie A. HANCOCK
14 Vice President Information Tech/CIO ... Dr. Roger E. REHM
21 AVP Fin Svcs & Reporting/Controller ... Mr. Barrie J. WILKES
26 AVP University Communications ... Ms. Sherry KNIGHT
18 Assoc Vice Pres Facilities Mgmt ... Mr. Stephen P. LAWRENCE
39 Assoc VP Residence/Auxiliary Svcs ... Mr. John S. FISHER
88 Assoc VP Faculty Personnel Svcs ... Mr. Matthew SERRA
28 Assoc VP Institutional Diversity ... Dr. Denise O. GREEN
15 Assoc VP Human Resources ... Ms. Lori L. HELLA
88 Assoc VP Academic Pgm/Global Campus ... Mr. Peter G. ROSS
20 Interim Vice Provost Acad Affairs ... Dr. Claudia B. DOUGLASS
88 Vice Provost Academic Admin ... Dr. Ray L. CHRISTIE
46 Interim Vice Provost Research ... Dr. James H. HAGEMAN
44 Asst VP Major/Planned Giving Pgm ... Mr. Edward A. TOLCHER
08 Dean of Libraries ... Mr. Thomas J. MOORE
32 Interim Assoc VP Student Affairs ... Mr. Tony A. VOISIN
35 Asst Dean/Director Student Life ... Mr. Tony A. VOISIN
88 Exec Dir Acad Advis/Assistance ... Ms. Michelle L. HOWARD
29 Exec Dir of Alumni Relations ... Ms. Marcie OTTEMAN
09 Director Institutional Research ... Dr. Wei ZHOU
22 Director Civil Rights/Inst Equity ... Ms. Jeannie JACKSON
07 Interim Director of Admissions ... Mr. Kevin L. WILLIAMS
43 General Counsel ... Dr. Manuel R. RUPE
06 Registrar ... Ms. Karen E. HUTSLAR
37 Director Scholarships/Financial Aid ... Mr. Kirk M. YATS
36 Director Career Services ... Ms. Julia B. SHERLOCK
41 Assoc VP/Athletics Director ... Mr. David HEEKE, JR.
38 Director Counseling Center ... Mr. Ross J. RAPAPORT
45 Director Financial Plan & Budgets ... Ms. Carol A. HAAS
88 Director MI Special Olympics ... Ms. Lois ARNOLD
88 Director Internal Audit ... Mr. Michael J. ROETHLISBERGER
27 Director Public Relations ... Mr. Steven F. SMITH
19 Chief of Police ... Mr. William YEAGLEY
40 Director CMU Bookstore ... Mr. Barry D. WATERS
72 Dean College of Sci & Tech ... Dr. Ian R. DAVISON
76 Dean Col of Health Professions ... Dr. Chris INGERSOLL
63 Dean College of Medicine ... Dr. Ernest YODER
79 Dean Col Hum/Soc/Behav Sci ... Dr. Pamela S. GATES
57 Dean College Comm/Fine Arts ... Dr. Salma I. GHANEM
50 Dean College of Business Admin ... Dr. Charles T. CRESPY
53 Dean College Education/Human Svcs ... Dr. Dale-Elizabeth PEHRSSON
58 Interim Dean Graduate Studies ... Dr. Roger L. COLES
04 Executive Assistant to President ... Ms. Mary Jane FLANAGAN
88 General Manager Public Broadcasting ... Dr. Edward B. GRANT
85 Exec Dir International Affairs ... Vacant
88 Asst VP Univ Rec/Events & Confs ... Mr. Stan L. SHINGLES
96 Dir Contract & Purch Svcs/Hlth Svcs ... Mr. Thomas P. TRIONFI
92 Dir University Honors/Centralis ... Dr. Phame M. CAMARENA
93 Director of Minority Students Svcs ... Ms. Traci L. GUINN
88 Associate Dean Libraries ... Dr. Richard M. COCHRAN
88 Assoc Dean/Administration & Finance ... Deborah L. BIGGS
88 Assoc Dean Educ/Human Svcs ... Dr. Kathryn KOCK
88 Assoc Dean Science & Technology ... Dr. Pete VERMEIRE
88 Assoc Dean Clin Affairs & Hosp Rel ... Sean K. KESTERSON
88 Sr Assoc Dean Educ Pgms-Med ... Joel LANPHEAR
88 Assoc Dean Medical Education ... Linda PERKOWSKI
88 Assoc Dean Science & Technology ... Dr. Jane M. MATTY
88 Assoc Dean Health Professions ... Dr. Thomas J. MASTERSON
88 Assoc Dean Human/Soc/Behav Sci ... Dr. Rick S. KURTZ
88 Associate Dean Comm/Fine Arts ... Dr. Shelly S. HINCK
88 Sr Assoc Dean Business Admin ... Dr. Daniel E. VETTER
31 Exec Asst to Pres-Detroit Outreach ... Mr. Tyrone JORDAN
86 Director Government Relations ... Mr. Toby ROTH

Cleary University (D)

3601 Plymouth Road, Ann Arbor MI 48105-2659
County: Washtenaw　　FICE Identification: 002246
Unit ID: 169327
Telephone: (800) 686-1886　　Carnegie Class: Spec/Bus
FAX Number: (734) 332-4646　　Calendar System: Quarter
URL: www.cleary.edu
Established: 1883　　Annual Undergrad Tuition & Fees: $385
Enrollment: 711　　Coed
Affiliation or Control: Independent Non-Profit　　IRS Status: 501(c)3
Highest Offering: Master's
Program: Occupational; Professional; Business Emphasis
Accreditation: NH

01 President & CEO ... Mr. Thomas P. SULLIVAN
05 Provost & VP Academic Affairs ... Dr. Vincent P. LINDER
10 VP Finance & Administration ... Ms. Judy WALKER
06 Asst VP Academic Svcs/Registrar ... Ms. Dawn M. FISER
04 Exec Asst to Pres/Board of Trustees ... Ms. Linda T. RENTZ
72 Dn Col Bus Innovation/Applied Tech ... Ms. Dawn MARKELL
20 Academic Dean ... Ms. Sadhana ALANGAR
13 Exec Director/Chief Info Officer ... Mr. David G. BOWERS
09 Dir Institutional Research/Analysis ... Mr. Tim VEENSTRA
18 Director Facilities ... Mr. Gary BACHMAN
30 Exec Dir Development/Alumni Rel ... Mr. Dennis PURDY
37 Director Financial Aid ... Ms. Vesta SMITH-CAMPBELL
36 Dir Career Services & Placement ... Ms. Corrie WILLIAMS
40 Director Bookstore Services ... Ms. Sheila THOMPSON
07 Director of Admissions ... Ms. Carrie BONOFIGLIO
26 Chief Public Relations Officer ... Ms. Amanda HOLDSWORTH

College for Creative Studies (E)

201 E Kirby, Detroit MI 48202-4034
County: Wayne　　FICE Identification: 006771
Unit ID: 169442
Telephone: (313) 664-7400　　Carnegie Class: Spec/Arts
FAX Number: (313) 872-8377　　Calendar System: Semester
URL: www.collegeforcreativestudies.edu
Established: 1906　　Annual Undergrad Tuition & Fees: $34,375
Enrollment: 1,382　　Coed
Affiliation or Control: Independent Non-Profit　　IRS Status: 501(c)3
Highest Offering: Master's
Program: Teacher Preparatory; Professional; Fine Arts Emphasis
Accreditation: NH, ART, CIDA

01 President ... Mr. Richard L. ROGERS
100 Executive Assistant/Chief of Staff ... Ms. Sandra BRADEN
04 Admin Assistant to the President ... Ms. Brigette NEAL
10 Vice Pres Administration & Finance ... Ms. Anne D. BECK
30 Vice Pres Institutional Advancement ... Ms. Nina HOLDEN
05 Dean of the College ... Mr. Imre MOLNAR
84 Dean of Enrollmnt and Student Svcs ... Ms. Julie HINGELBERG
07 Director of Admissions ... Ms. Lori WATSON
28 Director of Multicultural Affairs ... Mr. Cliff HARRIS
20 Assoc Dean Academic Affairs ... Ms. Sharon PROCTER
51 Director Continuing Education ... Ms. Carla GONZALEZ
31 Dir Community Arts Partnerships ... Mr. Mikel BRESEE
13 Director Information Technology ... Mr. Greg FRASER
90 Director of Academic Technologies ... Ms. Laurie EVANS
08 Director Library ... Ms. Beth WALKER
21 Director Business Services ... Ms. Kerri MCKAY
32 Director Student Life ... Mr. Michael COLEMAN
85 Director Intl Student Services ... Ms. Jennifer DICKEY
37 Director Financial Aid ... Ms. Kristin MOSKOVITZ
15 Director Human Resources ... Mr. Gregory KNOFF
18 Director Facilities & Admin Svcs ... Mr. Geoffrey SLEEMAN
26 Director Marketing & Communications ... Mr. Marcus POPIOLEK
29 Alumni Coordinator ... Ms. Ingrida KAMIS
06 Registrar & Acad Advising Director ... Ms. Nadine ASHTON
102 Director Corp/Foundation Relations ... Ms. Shannon MCPARTLON
44 Dir Annual Giving/Donor Services ... Ms. Elizabeth KLOS
38 Personal Counselor ... Mr. James BAUER
36 Director Career Services ... Ms. Cathy KARRY
40 Manager Bookstore ... Ms. Sara WORSHAM
35 Assistant Director Student Life ... Mr. Daniel LONG
19 Director of Security ... Mr. Garrett OCHALEK

Compass College of Cinematic Arts (F)

41 Sheldon Blvd, SE, Grand Rapids MI 49503
County: Kent　　FICE Identification: 041633
Unit ID: 459417
Telephone: (616) 988-1000　　Carnegie Class: Not Classified
FAX Number: (616) 458-4676　　Calendar System: Other
URL: www.compass.edu
Established: 2003　　Annual Undergrad Tuition & Fees: $20,405
Enrollment: 61　　Coed
Affiliation or Control: Independent Non-Profit　　IRS Status: 501(c)3
Highest Offering: Associate Degree
Program: Occupational
Accreditation: ACCSC

01 President ... Keri LOWE
11 Vice President Administration ... Jill POSTMA
32 Student Svcs Coord/Acad Advising ... Phil WORFEL
07 Admissions/Marketing Coordinator ... Stephanie BERGMAN

Concordia University (G)

4090 Geddes Road, Ann Arbor MI 48105-2797
County: Washtenaw　　FICE Identification: 002247
Unit ID: 169363
Telephone: (734) 995-7300　　Carnegie Class: Bac/Diverse
FAX Number: (734) 995-4610　　Calendar System: Semester
URL: www.cuaa.edu
Established: 1962　　Annual Undergrad Tuition & Fees: $22,464
Enrollment: 711　　Coed
Affiliation or Control: Lutheran Church - Missouri Synod
IRS Status: 501(c)3
Highest Offering: Master's
Program: Liberal Arts And General; Teacher Preparatory
Accreditation: NH, TED

01 Acting President/CFO ... Mr. Randall LUECKE
05 Int Vice President Academic Affairs ... Dr. Ross STUEBER
10 Vice Pres/Chief Operating Officer ... Mr. Randall LUECKE
07 Director of Admissions ... Mr. Benjamin LIMBACK
13 Chief Information Ofcr/Dir IT Svcs ... Mr. Woodrow HOLBERT
06 Registrar ... Ms. Colleen CLELAND
32 Executive Director Student Services ... Mr. Eric CHAMBERS
08 Librarian ... Mrs. Brenda BURROUGHS
37 Director Financial Aid ... Mrs. Karen NEUENDORF
42 Director of Spiritual Life ... Mr. Robert MCKINNEY
30 Director of Development ... Mr. Martin MORO
19 Director Security/Safety ... Mr. Kevin TANNER
26 Director Marketing & Communication ... Mr. Joel IVERSON
38 Director Student Counseling ... Mrs. Gina VERSEMAN
29 Director of Alumni Relations ... Mrs. Shannon MACLELLAN
39 Director Residence Life ... Ms. Elizabeth HENKE
41 Director of Athletics ... Ms. Andrea GORSKI
18 Chief Facilities/Physical Plant ... Mr. Jerry NOVAK
21 Controller ... Mr. Rocky MAZZARO
36 Director Student Placement ... Mrs. Susan GRESE
96 Director of Purchasing ... Mr. Dean ROE
09 Director of Institutional Research ... Vacant
15 Director Personnel Services ... Mrs. Barb WALTHER

Cornerstone University (A)

1001 E Beltline Avenue, NE, Grand Rapids MI 49525-5897
County: Kent FICE Identification: 002266
Unit ID: 170037
Telephone: (616) 949-5300 Carnegie Class: Master's L
FAX Number: (616) 222-1540 Calendar System: Semester
URL: www.cornerstone.edu
Established: 1941 Annual Undergrad Tuition & Fees: $22,690
Enrollment: 3,009 Coed
Affiliation or Control: Independent Non-Profit IRS Status: 501(c)3
Highest Offering: Master's
Program: Liberal Arts And General; Teacher Preparatory; Professional
Accreditation: NH, MUS, SW, @TEAC, THEOL

01 President ....Dr. Joseph M. STOWELL
03 Executive Vice President ....Mr. Marc FOWLER
05 Provost ....Dr. Richard OSTRANDER
30 Exec Vice President Advancement ....Mr. William KNOTT
88 Vice President of Broadcasting ....Mr. Chris LEMKE
42 Vice Pres Spiritual Formation ....Mr. Gerald LONGJOHN
58 Assoc Prov/Professional & Grad Stds ....Dr. Robert SIMPSON
97 Dean of Undergraduate Education ....Dr. Martin HUGHES
73 Dean Grand Rpds Theol Seminary ....Mr. John VER BERKMOES
32 Dean of Student Engagement ....Mr. Chip HUBER
09 Dean Institutional Effectiveness ....Dr. Tim DETWILER
35 Director of Student Services ....Mr. Keith DEBOER
08 Director of Miller Library ....Mr. Fred SWEET
37 Director Financial Services ....Mr. Scott STEWART
21 Controller ....Mr. Scott STEWART
88 Director of Retention ....Mrs. Kay LANDRUM
41 Athletic Director ....Mr. Dave GRUBE
15 Director of Human Resources ....Mrs. Emilie AZKOUL
18 Director of Campus Services ....Vacant
19 Director of Campus Safety ....Mr. Richard HONHOLT
36 Director of Career Services ....Mr. John WARREN
29 Director of Alumni ....Mrs. Darci IRWIN
06 Registrar ....Mrs. Gail DUHON
24 Director of Technical Support ....Mr. Dan MILLS
38 Director of the Counseling Center ....Vacant
92 Director of Honors Program ....Mr. Michael STEVENS
07 Director of Admissions ....Mrs. Lisa LINK
10 Chief Financial Officer ....Mrs. Nancy SCHOONMAKER
26 Chief Public Relations Officer ....Mr. Bob SACK

Cranbrook Academy of Art (B)

39221 Woodward Avenue, PO Box 801,
Bloomfield Hills MI 48303-0801
County: Oakland FICE Identification: 002248
Unit ID: 169424
Telephone: (248) 645-3300 Carnegie Class: Spec/Arts
FAX Number: (248) 645-3591 Calendar System: Semester
URL: www.cranbrook.edu
Established: 1932 Annual Graduate Tuition & Fees: $31,225
Enrollment: 160 Coed
Affiliation or Control: Independent Non-Profit IRS Status: 501(c)3
Highest Offering: Master's; No Undergraduates
Program: Professional
Accreditation: NH, ART

01 Director ....Mr. Reed KROLOFF
07 Dean of Admissions ....Mrs. Katharine WILLMAN

Davenport University (C)

6191 Kraft Avenue, S.E., Grand Rapids MI 49512
County: Kent FICE Identification: 002249
Unit ID: 169479
Telephone: (616) 698-7111 Carnegie Class: Master's M
FAX Number: N/A Calendar System: Semester
URL: www.davenport.edu
Established: 1866 Annual Undergrad Tuition & Fees: $13,142
Enrollment: 12,401 Coed
Affiliation or Control: Independent Non-Profit IRS Status: 501(c)3
Highest Offering: Master's
Program: Professional; Business Emphasis
Accreditation: NH, ADNUR, IACBE, MAC, NUR, PNUR

01 President ....Dr. Richard J. PAPPAS
30 Exec VP Advancement ....Vacant
26 Exec VP Univ Relations & Communic ....Ms. Kimberly A. BRUYN
46 Exec VP of Quality & Effectiveness ....Dr. Scott EPSTEIN
15 Exec VP Human/Organizational Devel ....Mr. Dave VENEKLASE
07 Exec VP Admission & Student Svcs ....Dr. Larry POLSELLI
10 Exec Vice President for Finance/CFO ....Mr. Michael S. VOLK
05 Exec VP Academics/Provost ....Dr. Linda RINKER
13 Vice Pres Information Technology ....Mr. Brian MILLER
09 VP for Institutional Research ....Dr. Kathy ABOUFADEL
18 Vice President for Plant & Security ....Mr. Duane TERPSTRA
32 Vice President Student Services ....Vacant
50 Dean College of Business ....Vacant
72 Dean College of Technology ....Mr. Michael CLANCY
76 Dean College of Health Professions ....Dr. Karen DALEY
49 Dean College of Arts and Sciences ....Dr. Thomas LONERGAN
106 Dean Online ....Dr. Christine WALLACE
37 Exec Director Financial Aid ....Mr. David DE BOER
29 Director of Alumni Relations ....Ms. Cathie ROGG
21 Controller ....Mr. Michael SLEVA
06 University Registrar ....Ms. Donna MILHAM
96 Director of Purchasing ....Mr. Bruce RENTZ
41 Director of Athletics ....Mr. Paul LOWDEN
26 Executive Dir of Communications ....Mr. Robyn LUYMES

Delta College (D)

1961 Delta Rd., University Center MI 48710-0001
County: Bay FICE Identification: 002251
Unit ID: 169521
Telephone: (989) 686-9000 Carnegie Class: Assoc/Pub-R-L
FAX Number: (989) 667-0620 Calendar System: Semester
URL: www.delta.edu
Established: 1961 Annual Undergrad Tuition & Fees (In-District): $3,494
Enrollment: 11,498 Coed
Affiliation or Control: Local IRS Status: 501(c)3
Highest Offering: Associate Degree
Program: Occupational; 2-Year Principally Bachelor's Creditable
Accreditation: NH, ADNUR, DA, DH, DMS, PTAA, RAD, SURGT

01 President ....Dr. Jean GOODNOW
10 Vice President Finance/Treasurer ....Ms. Debra K. LUTZ
32 Vice President Student & Educ Svcs ....Vacant
05 Vice Pres Instruction/Learning Svcs ....Dr. Thomas LANE
20 Dean of Teaching & Learning ....Dr. Gail HOFFMAN-JOHNSON
20 Dean of Student and Acad Services ....Ms. Judy MILLER
36 Dean Career Educ/Learning Part ....Ms. Ginny PRZYGOCKI
26 Marketing & Public Info Director ....Ms. Leanne GOVITZ
24 Dir Broadcasting/General Mgr ....Mr. Barry BAKER
30 Ex Dir Delta Col Found/Inst Advance ....Ms. Pam CLARK
11 Asst to Pres/Dir Strat Plng/Bd Secy ....Ms. Andrea L. URSUY
25 Exec Dir Corp Services & Res Devel ....Dr. Patricia A. GRAVES
43 General Counsel ....Vacant
13 Chief Information Officer ....Mr. Jason STAHL
37 Director of Student Financial Aid ....Mr. David URBANIAK
15 Director of Human Resources ....Ms. Tamie L. GRUNOW
18 Director of Facilities Management ....Mr. Larry E. RAMSEYER
35 Dean Stdnt & Educ Svc Interim VPSES ....Ms. Margaret MOSQUEDA
40 Bookstore Manager ....Ms. Barbara POWERS
07 Director of Admissions ....Mr. Gary BRASSEUR
06 Registrar ....Mr. Keith MALKOWSKI
19 Director Law Enforce & Training Ctr ....Mr. Mike WILTSE
08 Library Learning Info Center Dir ....Mr. Jack WOOD
38 Dir Counseling Advising/Career Svcs ....Ms. Diana GUTIERREZ
21 Business Services Director ....Ms. Barbara WEBB
09 Director of Institutional Research ....Mr. Wm. Michael WOOD
44 Coordinator of Development ....Ms. Mary HARDING
31 Assoc Dean of Community Develop ....Ms. Teresa STITT

DeVry University - Southfield (E)

26999 Central Park Blvd, Suite 125,
Southfield MI 48076-4174
County: Oakland Identification: 666557
Unit ID: 450508
Telephone: (248) 213-1610 Carnegie Class: Bac/Assoc
FAX Number: (248) 353-1804 Calendar System: Semester
URL: www.devry.edu
Established: 1931 Annual Undergrad Tuition & Fees: $16,156
Enrollment: 267 Coed
Affiliation or Control: Proprietary IRS Status: Proprietary
Highest Offering: Master's
Program: Professional; Business Emphasis
Accreditation: &NH

01 Campus Director ....Georgianna BAILEY

† Regional accreditation is carried under the parent institution in Downers Grove, IL.

Eastern Michigan University (F)

Ypsilanti MI 48197-2207
County: Washtenaw FICE Identification: 002259
Unit ID: 169798
Telephone: (734) 487-1849 Carnegie Class: Master's L
FAX Number: (734) 481-1095 Calendar System: Semester
URL: www.emich.edu
Established: 1849 Annual Undergrad Tuition & Fees (In-State): $9,026
Enrollment: 23,441 Coed
Affiliation or Control: State IRS Status: 501(c)3
Highest Offering: Doctorate
Program: Liberal Arts And General; Teacher Preparatory; Professional
Accreditation: NH, BUS, CACREP, CIDA, CLPSY, CONST, DIETC, MT, MUS, NURSE, OPE, OT, PLNG, SP, SPAA, SW, TED

01 President ....Dr. Susan MARTIN
05 Provost and Vice President ....Dr. Kim SCHATZEL
10 Chief Financial Officer ....Mr. John LUMM
26 Vice President Communications ....Mr. Walter KRAFT
30 Vice President Advancement ....Mr. Thomas STEVICK
32 Vice President Student Affairs ....Ms. Bernice LINDKE
101 VP & Secretary Board of Regents ....Ms. Vicki REAUME
20 Interim Associate Provost ....Dr. James CARROLL
58 Interim Director Graduate Programs ....Dr. Deborah DE LASKI-SMITH
26 Assoc VP Marketing & Communication ....Mr. Theodore G. COUTILISH
15 Chief Human Resources Officer ....Dr. James GALLAHER
35 Assoc Vice Pres Enrollment Mgmt ....Mr. Kevin KUCERA
21 Associate Vice President Finance ....Ms. Andrea JAECKEL
86 Exec Dir Gov & Community Relations ....Mr. Leigh GREDEN
21 Dir Financial Svcs/Controller ....Ms. Doris CELIAN
18 Chief of Operations ....Mr. John P. DONEGAN
69 Dean Col Health & Human Svcs ....Dr. Murali NAIR
51 Director Extended Programs ....Ms. Julie KNUTSON
49 Dean of Art & Sciences ....Dr. Thomas VENNER
50 Dean of Business ....Dr. Michael TIDWELL
53 Dean of Education ....Dr. Jann JOSEPH
72 Interim Dean of Technology ....Dr. Wade TOURNQUIST
43 University Attorney ....Ms. Gloria HAGE
13 Chief Information Officer ....Dr. Carl POWELL
09 Asst VP & Exec Dir IRIM ....Dr. Bin NING
102 Exec Dir Foundation Operations/CFO ....Ms. Laura WILBANKS
07 Director of Admissions ....Ms. Kathryn B. ORSCHELN
36 Director Career Dev & Outreach ....Ms. Sarah KERSEY OTTO
88 Ombudsman ....Mr. Gregory A. PEOPLES
46 Int Dir Research Development Office ....Ms. Caryn CHARTER
29 Interim Exec Dir Alumni Relations ....Mr. Daniel MATHIS
19 Exec Director Public Safety ....Mr. Robert HEIGHES
28 Director of Diversity/Affirm Action ....Ms. Sharon ABRAHAM
23 Exec Director Student Wellbeing ....Ms. Ellen GOLD
39 Interim Director Residence Life ....Ms. Marney BUSS
41 Director Intercollegiate Athletics ....Dr. Derrick L. GRAGG, JR.
85 Director International Students Ofc ....Ms. Esther L. GUNEL
27 Executive Director Media Relations ....Mr. Geoffrey LARCOM
96 Director Purchasing ....Mr. Dean BACKOS
38 Director Counseling Services ....Dr. Lisa LAUTERBACH
06 Registrar ....Ms. Christina SHELL
37 Director Financial Aid ....Ms. Cynthia VAN PELT
88 Director Special Events ....Ms. Andrea CHICKONOSKI

Ecumenical Theological Seminary (G)

2930 Woodward Avenue, Detroit MI 48201-3035
County: Wayne FICE Identification: 040024
Unit ID: 247102
Telephone: (313) 831-5200 Carnegie Class: Spec/Faith
FAX Number: (313) 831-1353 Calendar System: Quarter
URL: www.etseminary.edu
Established: 1980 Annual Undergrad Tuition & Fees: $12,300
Enrollment: 142 Coed
Affiliation or Control: Independent Non-Profit IRS Status: 501(c)3
Highest Offering: Doctorate
Program: Professional; Religious Emphasis
Accreditation: THEOL

01 President ....Dr. Marsha FOSTER BOYD
05 Vice Pres Academic Affs/Acad Dean ....Dr. Anneliese SINNOTT
11 Vice President of Administration ....Rev. Margaret PRIEST
30 Director of Advancement ....Ms. Cathy MAHER
06 Registrar ....Ms. Jean D. MURPHY
08 Head Librarian ....Rev. Dianne VAN MARTER

Ferris State University (H)

1201 S. State Street, Big Rapids MI 49307-2295
County: Mecosta FICE Identification: 002260
Unit ID: 169910
Telephone: (231) 591-2000 Carnegie Class: Master's L
FAX Number: (231) 591-2990 Calendar System: Semester
URL: www.ferris.edu
Established: 1884 Annual Undergrad Tuition & Fees (In-State): $10,710
Enrollment: 14,560 Coed
Affiliation or Control: State IRS Status: 501(c)3
Highest Offering: First Professional Degree
Program: Occupational; 2-Year Principally Bachelor's Creditable; Liberal Arts And General; Teacher Preparatory; Professional
Accreditation: NH, ACBSP, ART, CIDA, CONST, DH, DMS, ENG, ENGT, MLTAD, MT, NMT, NRPA, NUR, OPT, OPTR, PHAR, RAD, SW, @TEAC

01 President ....Dr. David L. EISLER
05 Provost & VP for Academic Affairs ....Dr. Fritz J. ERICKSON
43 Vice President & General Counsel ....Mr. Miles J. POSTEMA
10 VP of Administration & Finance ....Mr. Jerry L. SCOBY
30 Interim VP of Advancement & Mktg ....Ms. Shelly ARMSTRONG
32 Vice President Student Affairs ....Dr. Daniel BURCHAM
12 President/Vice Chancellor KCAD ....Dr. David ROSEN
88 Vice Chancellor Admin & Fin KCAD ....Ms. Sandra DAVISON-WILSON
12 VP for Extended and Intl Operations ....Dr. Donald GREEN
28 VP for Diversity and Inclusion ....Dr. David PILGRIM
20 Associate Provost ....Dr. Roberta TEAHEN
20 Associate Provost ....Dr. Paul BLAKE
20 Associate Provost ....Dr. William POTTER
21 Assoc Vice President Finance ....Mr. Richard CHRISTNER
35 Assoc Vice Pres Student Affairs ....Dr. Michael A. CAIRNS
16 Assoc Vice Pres Human Resources ....Vacant
30 Assoc Vice Pres for Advancement ....Ms. Carla MILLER
18 Assoc Vice Pres Plant Management ....Mr. Mike HUGHES
84 Associate Dean Enrollment Services ....Ms. Kathy LAKE
06 Dean Enroll Svc/Dir Admiss & Rec ....Dr. Kristen SALOMONSON
88 Associate VP Auxiliary Enterprises ....Mr. James HESSLER
45 Director Budget Planning/Analysis ....Ms. Sally DEPEW
14 Chief Technology Officer ....Mr. John URBANICK
22 Director of Equal Opportunity ....Vacant
19 Director of Public Safety ....Mr. Martin BLEDSOE
36 Mgr Stdnt Employment & Career Svcs ....Mr. John RANDLE
88 Director Rankin Student Center ....Mr. Mark SCHUELKE
23 Interim Director Counseling Center ....Ms. Renee DOUGLAS
23 Interim Director Health Center ....Ms. Renee DOUGLAS
35 Dean of Student Life ....Mr. Leroy WRIGHT
88 Dir Multicultural Student Svcs ....Dr. Matthew CHANEY
88 Dir Student Leadership/Activities ....Vacant
88 Director University Recreation ....Ms. Cindy HORN

29 Dir Alumni Relations/Annual Giving ... Mr. Jeremy MISHLER
09 Director of Institutional Research ... Dr. Kristen SALOMANSON
39 Director Residential Life ... Mr. Jon SHAFFER
40 Director Bookstore ... Ms. Karen BOHREN
41 Director of Athletics ... Mr. Perk WEISENBURGER
44 Director Planned Giving ... Mr. Todd JACOBS
96 Director Purchasing ... Mr. Michael PETHICK
49 Dean of Arts & Sciences ... Dr. Rick KURTZ
50 Dean of Business ... Dr. David NICOL
51 Dean of Professional & Tech Studies ... Dr. Donald GREEN
53 Dean of Education & Human Services ... Dr. Michelle JOHNSTON
67 Dean of Pharmacy ... Dr. Steve DURST
76 Dean of Health Professions ... Dr. Matthew ADEYANJU
63 Dean Michigan College Optometry ... Dr. Michael CRON
72 Dean of Engineering Technology ... Dr. JK YATES
92 Dean Retention & Student Success ... Dr. William POTTER
08 Dean of FLITE ... Dr. Scott GARRISON

Finlandia University (A)

601 Quincy Street, Hancock MI 49930-1882
County: Houghton FICE Identification: 002322
Unit ID: 172440
Telephone: (906) 482-5300 Carnegie Class: Bac/Diverse
FAX Number: (906) 487-7366 Calendar System: Semester
URL: www.finlandia.edu
Established: 1896 Annual Undergrad Tuition & Fees: $20,480
Enrollment: 602 Coed
Affiliation or Control: Evangelical Lutheran Church In America
IRS Status: 501(c)3
Highest Offering: Baccalaureate
Program: Liberal Arts And General; Professional
Accreditation: NH, NURSE, PTAA

01 President ... Dr. Philip JOHNSON
10 Exec Vice Pres Business/Finance ... Mr. Nick STEVENS
05 Executive Vice Pres/Provost ... Ms. TyAnn LINDELL
26 Exec VP External Relations/CAO ... Mr. Duane AHO
04 Executive Administrative Assistant ... Ms. Doreen KORPELA
27 Executive Director Communications ... Ms. Karen JOHNSON
20 Assistant Provost ... Ms. Carol BATES
102 Director Foundation Relations ... Ms. Robin BONINI
08 Librarian ... Ms. Elizabeth MARTIN
32 Director of Living and Learning ... Mr. Michael BAILY
42 University Chaplain ... Mr. Soren SCHMIDT
06 Registrar ... Ms. Evelyn GOKE
29 Director Alumni Relations ... Ms. Cheryl RIES
38 Director Student Support Services ... Vacant
13 Director Information Technology ... Mr. Scott BLAKE
41 Athletic Director ... Mr. Chris SALANI
44 Advancement Officer ... Vacant
18 Director of Plant and Facilities ... Mr. Curt HAHKA
21 Controller ... Vacant
37 Director Student Financial Aid ... Ms. Sandra TURNQUIST
36 Career Services Manager ... Mr. Mark CAVIS
09 Institutional Research Analyst ... Mr. Hannu LEPPANEN
40 Bookstore Manager ... Ms. Alana EVANS
96 Purchaser ... Ms. Janine NOTTKE
15 Director of Human Resources ... Ms. Ann TESTINI
07 Director of Admissions ... Ms. Julie JENNERJOHN
19 Director of Campus Safety/Security ... Mr. Jim HARDEN
39 Residence Life Coordinator ... Vacant
49 Dean College of Arts & Sciences ... Dr. Christine O'NEIL
57 Dean Intl School of Art & Design ... Ms. Denise VANDEVILLE
76 Dean College of Health Science ... Dr. Fredi DE YAMPERT
104 Dean Intl School of Business ... Dr. Terry MONSON

Glen Oaks Community College (B)

62249 Shimmel Road, Centreville MI 49032-9719
County: Saint Joseph FICE Identification: 002263
Unit ID: 169974
Telephone: (269) 467-9945 Carnegie Class: Assoc/Pub-R-S
FAX Number: (269) 467-4114 Calendar System: Semester
URL: www.glenoaks.edu
Established: 1965 Annual Undergrad Tuition & Fees (In-District): $3,756
Enrollment: 1,334 Coed
Affiliation or Control: Local IRS Status: 501(c)3
Highest Offering: Associate Degree
Program: Occupational; 2-Year Principally Bachelor's Creditable
Accreditation: NH, MAC

01 President ... Dr. Gary WHEELER
05 Dean of Teaching & Learning ... Dr. Ana GAILLAT
10 Dean of Finance/Administrative Svcs ... Ms. Marilyn WIESCHOWSKI
32 Dean of Students ... Dr. Margaret HALE-SMITH
66 Asst Dean of Nursing ... Ms. Karen GANGER
84 Asst Dean Enrollment Svcs/Registrar ... Ms. Beverly ANDREWS
20 Assoc Dean Extend Lrng/Wrkfce Devel ... Ms. Patricia MORGENSTERN
08 Director Learning Resources Center ... Ms. Betsy S. MORGAN
21 Accountant ... Ms. Jennifer DODSON
18 Director of Buildings/Grounds ... Mr. Nick MILLIMAN
07 Director of Admissions ... Ms. Tonya HOWDEN
06 Registrar ... Ms. Bev ANDREWS
37 Dir of Financial Aid/Scholarships ... Ms. Jean ZIMMERMAN
09 Dir Grants/Institutional Research ... Vacant
41 Director of Athletics ... Mr. Steve PROEFROCK
15 Personnel Coordinator ... Ms. Candy BOHACZ
26 Public Relations/Marketing ... Mr. Lon HUFFMAN

Gogebic Community College (C)

E4946 Jackson Road, Ironwood MI 49938-1366
County: Gogebic FICE Identification: 002264
Unit ID: 169992
Telephone: (906) 932-4231 Carnegie Class: Assoc/Pub-R-S
FAX Number: (906) 932-5541 Calendar System: Semester
URL: www.gogebic.edu
Established: 1931 Annual Undergrad Tuition & Fees (In-District): $4,033
Enrollment: 1,149 Coed
Affiliation or Control: Local IRS Status: 501(c)3
Highest Offering: Associate Degree
Program: Occupational; 2-Year Principally Bachelor's Creditable
Accreditation: NH

01 President ... Mr. James A. LORENSON
05 Dean of Instruction/Dir Exten Pgm ... Mr. Ken J. TRZASKA
10 Dean of Business Services ... Mr. Erik M. GUENARD
32 Interim Dean Student Services ... Ms. Jeanne GRAHAM
37 Dir Financial Aid/Veterans Svcs ... Ms. Suzetta R. FORBES
76 Director of Allied Health Program ... Ms. Dawn MCPHERSON
18 Director of Buildings & Grounds ... Vacant
88 Director of Ski Area Management ... Mr. James VANDERSPOEL
08 Dir Learning Resource/Instruct Tech ... Mr. Walter LESSUN
14 Director of Computer Services ... Ms. Kathie A. MUNN
07 Dir of Admission/Public Information ... Ms. Kim ZECKOVICH
30 Dir of Institutional Development ... Ms. Kelly MARZCAK
88 Transfer Coordinator ... Ms. Therese PAWLAK

Grace Bible College (D)

1011 Aldon Street, SW, Grand Rapids MI 49509-1998
County: Kent FICE Identification: 002265
Unit ID: 170000
Telephone: (616) 538-2330 Carnegie Class: Bac/Diverse
FAX Number: (616) 538-0599 Calendar System: Semester
URL: www.gbcol.edu
Established: 1939 Annual Undergrad Tuition & Fees: $15,300
Enrollment: 234 Coed
Affiliation or Control: Independent Non-Profit IRS Status: 501(c)3
Highest Offering: Baccalaureate
Program: Liberal Arts And General; Teacher Preparatory; Religious Emphasis
Accreditation: NH, BI

01 President ... Dr. Kenneth B. KEMPER
05 Vice President/Academic Dean ... Mr. Paul R. SWEET
10 Financial Controller/Dir Bus Svcs ... Mrs. Laura WRIGHT
30 Vice Pres Institutional Advancement ... Mr. Gregory HEATH
32 Vice Pres Cmty Life/Student Svcs ... Mr. Brian P. SHERSTAD
106 Vice Pres Adult & Online Education ... Mr. Mike STOWELL
44 Fund Development Director ... Mr. Steve HILBRANDS
04 Admin Assistant to President ... Mrs. Joyce A. STORMS
06 Registrar ... Ms. Linda K. SILER
08 Librarian ... Mrs. Kathy L. MOLENKAMP
37 Director of Financial Aid ... Mr. Kurt POSTMA
84 Director of Enrollment ... Mr. Kevin E. GILLIAM
13 Information Technology Director ... Mr. James PETERS
18 Director of Maintenance ... Mr. Nathan JOHNSON
41 Sports Information Director ... Mr. Gary BAILEY
42 Director of Campus Ministries ... Mr. John SPOONER
39 Director of Residence Life ... Vacant
88 Dir Recruitment Online & Adult Stds ... Mr. Zak SORENSEN

Grand Rapids Community College (E)

143 Bostwick Avenue, NE, Grand Rapids MI 49503-3295
County: Kent FICE Identification: 002267
Unit ID: 170055
Telephone: (616) 234-4000 Carnegie Class: Assoc/Pub-U-SC
FAX Number: (616) 234-4005 Calendar System: Semester
URL: www.grcc.edu
Established: 1914 Annual Undergrad Tuition & Fees (In-District): $2,778
Enrollment: 17,575 Coed
Affiliation or Control: Local IRS Status: 501(c)3
Highest Offering: Associate Degree
Program: Occupational; 2-Year Principally Bachelor's Creditable
Accreditation: NH, ACFEI, ADNUR, ART, DA, DH, MUS, OTA, PNUR, RAD

01 President ... Dr. Steven C. ENDER
05 Exec Vice Pres Academic Affairs ... Dr. Gilda G. GELY
10 Exec VP Business/Financial Services ... Ms. Lisa FREIBURGER
13 VP & CIO Lrng Res/Tech Solutions ... Mr. Kevin O'HALLA
30 Assoc VP College Advancement ... Mr. Andy BOWNE
88 Dean of Adult & Developmental Educ ... Ms. Cindy MARTIN
103 Director Workforce Training ... Ms. Julie PARKS
21 Exec Director Financial Services ... Mr. James PETERSON
75 Dean Sch Workforce Development ... Ms. Fiona HERT
32 Dean Student Affairs ... Ms. Tina OEN-HOXIE
09 Dean Inst Research & Planning ... Ms. Donna KRAGT
49 Dean School of Arts & Science ... Dr. Laurie CHESLEY
72 Dean Instruct Design/Info Tech ... Ms. Patti TREPKOWSKI
07 Assoc Dean Admiss/Enrollment Mgmt ... Ms. Diane D. PATRICK
26 Director of Communications ... Mr. Raul ALVAREZ, JR.
37 Exec Dir Student Financial Services ... Ms. Jill M. NUTT
16 Executive Director Human Resources ... Ms. Cathy WILSON
06 Registrar ... Ms. Diane PATRICK
35 Director Student Activities ... Mr. Eric MULLEN
36 Assoc Director Student Employment ... Ms. Luann WEDGE
08 Director of Library Services ... Ms. Pat INGERSOLL
18 Executive Director of Facilities ... Mr. Thomas J. SMITH
88 Director MTEC/Employment Training ... Mr. George WAITE
19 Chief of Campus Police ... Ms. Rebecca R. WHITMAN
43 General Counsel ... Ms. Kathy KEATING
96 Director Purchasing ... Mr. Mansfield MATTHEWSON
12 Dean of Lakeshore Campus & Outreach ... Mr. Daniel CLARK
22 Exec Dir Equity/Community/Legis ... Mr. Eric WILLIAMS
28 Dir Diversity Learning Center ... Ms. Christina ARNOLD

Grand Valley State University (F)

1 Campus Drive, Allendale MI 49401-9403
County: Ottawa FICE Identification: 002268
Unit ID: 170082
Telephone: (616) 331-5000 Carnegie Class: Master's L
FAX Number: (616) 331-3503 Calendar System: Semester
URL: www.gvsu.edu
Established: 1960 Annual Undergrad Tuition & Fees (In-State): $10,078
Enrollment: 24,662 Coed
Affiliation or Control: State IRS Status: 501(c)3
Highest Offering: Doctorate
Program: Liberal Arts And General; Teacher Preparatory; Professional
Accreditation: NH, ARCPA, ART, BUS, BUSA, CS, DMS, ENG, IPSY, MT, MUS, NURSE, OT, PTA, RTT, SPAA, SW, TED

01 President ... Dr. Thomas J. HAAS
05 Provost & Vice Pres Academic Affs ... Dr. Gayle R. DAVIS
10 Vice President Finance/Admin ... Mr. James BACHMEIER
26 Vice President University Relations ... Mr. Matthew E. MCLOGAN
30 Vice President of Development ... Ms. Karen M. LOTH
22 VP Inclusion and Equity ... Dr. Jeanne J. ARNOLD
04 Special Assistant to President ... Ms. Teri L. LOSEY
32 Vice Provost/Dean Student Services ... Dr. H. Bart MERKLE
20 Vice Provost/Dean Academic Svcs ... Ms. Lynn BLUE
20 Assoc Vice Pres Academic Affairs ... Mr. Jon A. JELLEMA
20 Assoc Vice Pres Academic Affairs ... Dr. Joseph H. GODWIN
20 Asst Vice Pres Academic Affairs ... Dr. Nancy GIARDINA
20 Asst Vice Pres Academic Affairs ... Dr. Julia GUEVARA
21 Associate VP Business/Finance ... Mr. Brian COPELAND
21 Asst VP for University Budgets ... Mr. Jeff MUSSER
15 Assoc Vice Pres Human Resources ... Mr. D. Scott RICHARDSON
26 Assoc VP Institutional Marketing ... Ms. Rhonda LUBBERTS
27 Assoc VP News & Information Svcs ... Ms. Mary Eilleen LYON
18 Assoc Vice Pres Facilities Services ... Mr. Timothy THIMMESCH
88 Assoc VP for Facilities Planning ... Mr. James MOYER
88 Asst VP for Pew Campus Operations ... Ms. Lisa HAYNES
49 Dean Col of Liberal Arts & Sciences ... Dr. Frederick ANTCZAK
50 Dean Seidman College of Business ... Dr. H. James WILLIAMS
70 Dean College of Cmty/Public Service ... Dr. George GRANT
53 Dean College of Education ... Dr. Elaine COLLINS
54 Dean Padnos Col Engr & Computing ... Dr. Paul PLOTKOWSKI
76 Dean College of Health Professions ... Dr. Roy OLSSON
66 Dean Kirkhof College of Nursing ... Dr. Cynthia MCCURREN
58 Dean Graduate Studies ... Dr. Jeffrey POTTEIGER
25 Dir Grants Administration ... Ms. Christine CHAMBERLAIN
07 Director of Admissions ... Ms. Jodi CHYCINSKI
08 Dean University Libraries ... Dr. Lee VAN ORSDEL
43 University Counsel ... Mr. Thomas A. BUTCHER
37 Director of Financial Aid ... Ms. Michelle RHODES
06 Interim Registrar ... Dr. Sherril SOMAN
36 Director Career Services ... Mr. Troy FARLEY
14 Director of Information Technology ... Ms. Sue KORZINEK
29 Director Alumni Relations ... Mr. Chris W. BARBEE
09 Director of Institutional Analysis ... Dr. Philip BATTY
39 Dir of Housing and Residence Life ... Dr. Andrew J. BEACHNAU
85 Exec Dir International Educ ... Dr. Mark SCHAUB
28 Director Multicultural Affairs ... Ms. Connie DANG
19 Director of Public Safety Services ... Ms. Barbara BERGERS
88 Exec Dir Van Andel Global Trade Ctr ... Ms. Sonja JOHNSON
88 Dir Pew Faculty Teaching/Lrng Ctr ... Dr. Christine RENER
88 Dir Sm Business/Technology Dev Ctr ... Ms. Carol LOPUCKI
96 Director of Procurement Services ... Mr. Kim PATRICK
41 Athletic Director ... Mr. Tim SELGO
40 Bookstore Manager ... Mr. Jerrod NICKELS
88 General Manager WGVU TV & Radio ... Mr. Michael WALENTA
88 Spec Asst for Charter Schools ... Mr. Tim WOOD
88 Dean College Interdisciplin Studies ... Dr. Anne HISKES
88 Director Annis Water Resources Inst ... Dr. Alan STEINMAN
88 Dir Michigan Alt/Renwble Energy Ctr ... Mr. Arn BOEZAART
88 Int Dir W MI Sci/Tech Initiative ... Mr. Rich COOK
38 Interim Dir Counseling/Career Dev ... Dr. Amber ROBERTS
88 Director of Hauenstein Center ... Mr. Gleaves WHITNEY
22 Asst VP for Affirmative Action ... Mr. Dwight HAMILTON

Great Lakes Christian College (G)

6211 Willow Highway, Lansing MI 48917-1299
County: Eaton FICE Identification: 002269
Unit ID: 170091
Telephone: (517) 321-0242 Carnegie Class: Spec/Faith
FAX Number: (517) 321-5902 Calendar System: Semester
URL: www.glcc.edu
Established: 1949 Annual Undergrad Tuition & Fees: $15,000
Enrollment: 250 Coed
Affiliation or Control: Christian Churches And Churches of Christ
IRS Status: 501(c)3
Highest Offering: Baccalaureate
Program: Professional; Religious Emphasis
Accreditation: NH, BI

01 President ... Mr. Lawrence L. CARTER
10 Vice President Finance/Operations ... Mr. William D. BROSSMANN
05 Vice President of Academic Affairs ... Mr. David J. RICHARDS

30 Vice Pres Institutional Advancement .... Mr. Philip E. BEAVERS
84 Vice Pres of Enrollment Management .... Mr. Lloyd S. SCHARER
32 Dean of Student Affairs .... Mrs. Betsy L. CARTER
06 Registrar .... Mr. Brian SLENSKI
08 Director of Library Services .... Mr. James ORME
37 Financial Aid Director .... Mr. Tedd C. KEES
35 Director of Student Life .... Mr. Ryan BUSHNELL
41 Athletic Director .... Mr. John PIERCEFIELD
88 Director of Outreach Ministries .... Mrs. Judy BEAVERS
18 Maintenance Supervisor .... Mr. Brian SMITH
27 Publications Coordinator .... Mrs. Robyn ORME

Griggs University (A)

8903 N US Highway 31, Suite 2,
Berrien Springs MI 49104-1900

County: Berrien FICE Identification: 009454
Telephone: (800) 782-4769 Carnegie Class: Not Classified
FAX Number: (269) 471-2804 Calendar System: Semester
URL: www.griggs.edu
Established: 1990 Annual Undergrad Tuition & Fees: $11,190
Enrollment: 2,756 Coed
Affiliation or Control: Seventh-day Adventist IRS Status: 501(c)3
Highest Offering: Master's
Program: Religious Emphasis
Accreditation: DETC

01 President .... Dr. Alayne D. THORPE
03 Vice President .... Dr. Janine LIM
32 Director of Student Services .... Dr. Glynis BRADFIELD
07 Director of Admissions/Registrar .. Dr. Emilio GARCIA-MARENKO
10 Chief Financial Officer .... Mr. Nantoo BANERJEE
07 Graduate Admissions .... Ms. M. Angelica MUNOZ
21 Administrative Services Manager .... Vacant
15 Human Resources Manager .... Mr. Daniel AGNETTA
05 Chief Academic Officer .... Dr. Janine LIM
09 Director of Institutional Research .... Ms. Charlotte CONWAY
26 Chief Public Relations Officer .... Mr. Stephen D. PAYNE

Henry Ford Community College (B)

5101 Evergreen Road, Dearborn MI 48128-1495

County: Wayne FICE Identification: 002270
Unit ID: 170240
Telephone: (313) 845-9615 Carnegie Class: Assoc/Pub-S-MC
FAX Number: (313) 845-9658 Calendar System: Semester
URL: www.hfcc.edu
Established: 1938 Annual Undergrad Tuition & Fees (In-District): $2,772
Enrollment: 17,650 Coed
Affiliation or Control: Local IRS Status: 501(c)3
Highest Offering: Associate Degree
Program: Occupational; 2-Year Principally Bachelor's Creditable
Accreditation: NH, ACFEI, ADNUR, MAC, PTAA, RAD, SURGT

01 President .... Dr. Gail C. MEE
10 Vice President/Controller .... Ms. Marjorie SWAN
32 Vice Pres/Dean Student Service .... Dr. Lisa JONES-HARRIS
05 Vice Pres/Dean Academic Education .... Dr. Reg GERLICA
75 Vice Pres/Dean Career Education .... Dr. Charles JACOBS
30 Exec Director of Development .... Mr. John LEWANDOWSKI
18 Director Buildings & Grounds .... Mr. T. Allen GIGLIOTTI
06 Director of Registration and Record .... Ms. Holly DIAMOND
38 Division Director Counseling .... Mr. Imad NOURI
51 Director Corporate Training .... Mr. Gary SAGANSKI
52 Director of Nursing .... Ms. Katherine HOWE
08 Director Library .... Ms. Barbara LUKASIEWICZ
13 Director Data & Voice .... Mr. Sandro SILVESTRI
84 Director of Enrollment Development .... Mr. Douglas A. FREED
21 Director Financial Services .... Dr. David CUNNINGHAM
26 Communications Director .... Mr. Gary ERWIN
37 Director Student Financial Aid .... Mr. Kevin J. CULLER
15 Director Human Resources .... Dr. Cynthia ESCHENBURG
92 Director Honors Program .... Dr. Nabeel ABRAHAM
94 Director Women's Studies .... Vacant
96 Director Purchasing .... Mr. Fred STEINER
09 Director Research Planning Effectiv .... Ms. Becky J. CHADWICK
40 Manager of College Store .... Ms. Pamela HALL
24 Instructional Technologist .... Dr. Vivian BEATY
19 Coordinator of Security .... Mr. Gary MCBAIN

Hillsdale College (C)

33 East College Street, Hillsdale MI 49242-1298

County: Hillsdale FICE Identification: 002272
Unit ID: 170286
Telephone: (517) 437-7341 Carnegie Class: Bac/A&S
FAX Number: (517) 437-3923 Calendar System: Semester
URL: www.hillsdale.edu
Established: 1844 Annual Undergrad Tuition & Fees: $20,950
Enrollment: 1,377 Coed
Affiliation or Control: Independent Non-Profit IRS Status: 501(c)3
Highest Offering: Baccalaureate
Program: Liberal Arts And General; Teacher Preparatory
Accreditation: NH

01 President .... Dr. Larry P. ARNN, III
05 Provost .... Dr. David WHALEN
30 Vice Pres Institutional Advancement .... Mr. John CERVINI
10 Chf Admin Ofcr/VP Fin Affs & Treas .... Mr. Patrick FLANNERY
11 VP Admin & Sec of Board of Trustees .... Mr. Richard P. PEWE
26 VP of External Affairs .... Mr. Douglas JEFFREY
32 VP Student Affairs/Dean of Women .... Mrs. Diane PHILIPP
88 Vice Pres for Dow Leadership Center .... Mr. Jack OXENRIDER
100 Chief of Staff/Asst to President .... Mr. Mike HARNER
20 Associate Provost .... Dr. Mark MAIER
33 Dean of Men .... Mr. Aaron PETERSEN
07 Director of Admissions .... Mr. Jeffrey S. LANTIS
27 Exec Director of Media Relations .... Mr. Douglas JEFFREY
37 Director of Financial Aid .... Mr. Richard MOEGGENBERG
41 Athletic Director .... Mr. Don BRUBACHER
06 Registrar .... Mr. Douglas MCARTHUR
29 Director of Alumni Affairs .... Mr. Grigor HASTED
36 Director Career Planning .... Mr. Michael MURRAY
08 Librarian .... Mr. Daniel L. KNOCH
40 Bookstore Manager .... Mrs. Vicki NASH
42 Chaplain .... R.Rev. Peter BECKWITCH
18 Physical Plant Director .... Mr. Todd CLOW
90 Director of Academic Computing .... Mr. David M. ZENZ
15 Director Personnel Services .... Ms. Janet MARSH

Hope College (D)

141 E 12th Street, Holland MI 49423-3607

County: Ottawa FICE Identification: 002273
Unit ID: 170301
Telephone: (616) 395-7000 Carnegie Class: Bac/A&S
FAX Number: (616) 395-7922 Calendar System: Semester
URL: www.hope.edu
Established: 1866 Annual Undergrad Tuition & Fees: $27,810
Enrollment: 3,249 Coed
Affiliation or Control: Reformed Church In America IRS Status: 501(c)3
Highest Offering: Baccalaureate
Program: Liberal Arts And General; Teacher Preparatory; Professional
Accreditation: NH, ART, DANCE, ENG, MUS, NURSE, SW, @TEAC, THEA

01 President .... Dr. James E. BULTMAN
05 Provost .... Dr. R. Richard RAY, JR.
10 Vice Pres and Chief Fiscal Officer .... Mr. Thomas W. BYLSMA
07 Vice President for Admissions .... Mr. William VANDERBILT
30 Interim VP for College Advancement .... Mr. David VANDERWEL
32 VP Student Devel/Dean of Students .... Dr. Richard A. FROST
20 Associate Provost .... Mr. Alfredo M. GONZALES
26 Assoc VP Public & Community Rels .... Mr. Tom L. RENNER
08 Librarian .... Ms. Kelly G. JACOBSMA
39 Dir of Residential Life & Housing .... Dr. John E. JOBSON
22 Director of Multicultural Life .... Ms. Vanessa GREENE
94 Director of Women's Studies .... Dr. Jeanne D. PETIT
81 Dean for Natural Sciences .... Dr. Moses LEE
79 Dean for Arts & Humanities .... Dr. William D. REYNOLDS
83 Dean for Social Sciences .... Dr. Scott D. VANDER STOEP
88 Dean of the Chapel .... Rev. Trygve D. JOHNSON
06 Registrar .... Ms. Carol DEJONG
37 Director of Financial Aid .... Ms. Jill NUTT
36 Director Career Services .... Mr. Dale F. AUSTIN
21 Director of Finance & Business Svcs .... Mr. Douglas VAN DYKEN
13 Director of Operations & Technology .... Mr. Greg MAYBURY
14 Director of Computing & Info Tech .... Mr. Carl E. HEIDEMAN
15 Director Human Resources .... Mrs. Lori MULDER
18 Director Physical Plant .... Mr. Greg MAYBURY
40 Manager of Bookstore .... Mr. Mark COOK
29 Dir of Parent & Alumni Relations .... Mr. Scott TRAVIS
41 Co-Director of Athletics .... Mr. Tim SCHOONVELD
41 Co-Director of Athletics .... Mrs. Eva Dean FOLKERT
42 Senior Chaplain .... Rev. Paul H. BOERSMA
42 Chaplain .... Rev. Kate DAVELAAR
38 Asst Dean/Director Counseling Ctr .... Dr. Kristen GRAY

International Academy of Design and Technology (E)

1850 Research Drive, Troy MI 48083

County: Oakland Identification: 666632
Unit ID: 445124
Telephone: (248) 457-2700 Carnegie Class: Spec/Arts
FAX Number: (248) 526-1710 Calendar System: Quarter
URL: www.iadt.edu/detroit
Established: 2003 Annual Undergrad Tuition & Fees: $16,200
Enrollment: 750 Coed
Affiliation or Control: Proprietary IRS Status: Proprietary
Highest Offering: Baccalaureate
Program: Liberal Arts And General; Fine Arts Emphasis
Accreditation: ACICS, CIDA

01 President .... Ms. Cynthia BECHILL
05 Director of Education .... Dr. Julia SMETANKA
07 Director of Admissions .... Ms. Roslyn WHITE
10 Regional Controller .... Mr. Michael THAYER
37 Director of Student Finance .... Mr. Donald STEVENS
32 Student Services Manager .... Mr. Giovannie THOMAS
36 Director Career Services .... Ms. Cheryl HARVEY-PATE
13 IT Manager .... Mr. Jordan KOTUBEY

† Branch campus of International Academy of Design and Technology, Chicago, IL.

ITT Technical Institute (F)

1905 S Haggerty Road, Canton MI 48188-2025

County: Wayne Identification: 666323
Unit ID: 442338
Telephone: (734) 397-7800 Carnegie Class: Assoc/PrivFP
FAX Number: (734) 397-1945 Calendar System: Quarter
URL: www.itt-tech.edu
Established: 2003 Annual Undergrad Tuition & Fees: N/A
Enrollment: 659 Coed
Affiliation or Control: Proprietary IRS Status: Proprietary
Highest Offering: Baccalaureate
Program: Technical Emphasis
Accreditation: ACICS

† Branch campus of ITT Technical Institute, Indianapolis, IN.

ITT Technical Institute (G)

6359 Miller Road, Swartz Creek MI 48473-1520

County: Genesee Identification: 666146
Unit ID: 448479
Telephone: (810) 628-2500 Carnegie Class: Assoc/PrivFP
FAX Number: N/A Calendar System: Quarter
URL: www.itt-tech.edu
Established: 2006 Annual Undergrad Tuition & Fees: N/A
Enrollment: 760 Coed
Affiliation or Control: Proprietary IRS Status: Proprietary
Highest Offering: Baccalaureate
Program: Technical Emphasis
Accreditation: ACICS

† Branch campus of ITT Technical Institute, Indianapolis, IN.

ITT Technical Institute (H)

1522 E Big Beaver Road, Troy MI 48083-1905

County: Oakland Identification: 666542
Unit ID: 261472
Telephone: (248) 524-1800 Carnegie Class: Assoc/PrivFP
FAX Number: (248) 524-1965 Calendar System: Quarter
URL: www.itt-tech.edu
Established: 1987 Annual Undergrad Tuition & Fees: N/A
Enrollment: 1,251 Coed
Affiliation or Control: Proprietary IRS Status: Proprietary
Highest Offering: Baccalaureate
Program: Technical Emphasis
Accreditation: ACICS

† Branch campus of ITT Technical Institute, Indianapolis, IN.

ITT Technical Institute (I)

1980 Metro Court S.W., Wyoming MI 49519

County: Kent FICE Identification: 010627
Unit ID: 170417
Telephone: (616) 406-1200 Carnegie Class: Spec/Tech
FAX Number: (616) 956-5606 Calendar System: Quarter
URL: www.itt-tech.edu
Established: 1968 Annual Undergrad Tuition & Fees: N/A
Enrollment: 694 Coed
Affiliation or Control: Proprietary IRS Status: Proprietary
Highest Offering: Baccalaureate
Program: Technical Emphasis
Accreditation: ACICS

† Branch campus of ITT Technical Institute, Indianapolis, IN.

Jackson Community College (J)

2111 Emmons Road, Jackson MI 49201-8399

County: Jackson FICE Identification: 002274
Unit ID: 170444
Telephone: (517) 787-0800 Carnegie Class: Assoc/Pub-R-L
FAX Number: (517) 789-1623 Calendar System: Semester
URL: www.jccmi.edu
Established: 1928 Annual Undergrad Tuition & Fees (In-District): $3,312
Enrollment: 6,988 Coed
Affiliation or Control: Local IRS Status: 501(c)3
Highest Offering: Associate Degree
Program: Occupational; 2-Year Principally Bachelor's Creditable
Accreditation: NH, ACBSP, DMS, MAC, RAD

01 President / CEO .... Dr. Daniel J. PHELAN
11 Vice Pres Finance & College Opers .... Vacant
32 Executive Dean of Students .... Mrs. Nancy MILLER
05 Provost .... Dr. Rebekah WOODS
31 Vice Pres of Administration .... Ms. Cindy ALLEN
102 President of JCC Foundation .... Mr. Jason VALENTE
15 Exec Director of HR & Org Develop .... Mr. William HENDRY

Kalamazoo College (K)

1200 Academy Street, Kalamazoo MI 49006-3295

County: Kalamazoo FICE Identification: 002275
Unit ID: 170532
Telephone: (269) 337-7000 Carnegie Class: Bac/A&S
FAX Number: (269) 337-7251 Calendar System: Quarter
URL: www.kzoo.edu
Established: 1833 Annual Undergrad Tuition & Fees: $45,984
Enrollment: 1,403 Coed
Affiliation or Control: Independent Non-Profit IRS Status: 501(c)3
Highest Offering: Baccalaureate
Program: Liberal Arts And General
Accreditation: NH

01 President .... Dr. Eileen B. WILSON-OYELARAN
05 Provost .... Dr. Michael A. MCDONALD
10 Vice President Business & Finance .... Mr. James E. PRINCE
30 Vice President College Advancement .... Mr. Albert J. DESIMONE

32 VP Student Devel & Dean of Students ... Dr. Sarah B. WESTFALL
20 Associate Provost ... Dr. Paul R. SOTHERLAND
85 Associate Provost for Intl Pgms ... Dr. Joseph L. BROCKINGTON
13 Associate Provost for Info Services ... Mr. Gregory S. DIMENT
09 Asst Provost Inst Support/Research ... Ms. Anne T. DUEWEKE
89 Dean of First Year & Advising ... Dr. Zaide E. PIXLEY
06 Registrar ... Mr. Ted WITRYK
15 Human Resources Manager ... Ms. Laura A. ANDERSEN
07 Dean of Admission and Financial Aid ... Mr. Eric P. STAAB
37 Director of Financial Aid ... Ms. Marian STOWERS
27 Director of College Communication ... Mr. James A. VANSWEDEN
18 Director of Facilities Management ... Mr. Paul W. MANSTROM
40 Director Bookstore ... Ms. Deborah L. THOMPSON
29 Director of Alumni Relations ... Ms. Kimberly J. ALDRICH
38 Director of Student Counseling ... Dr. Patricia A. PONTO
36 Dir Ctr Career/Professional Devel ... Ms. Joan HAWXHURST
20 Associate Provost ... Dr. Amy L. SMITH

Kalamazoo Valley Community College (A)

6767 West O Avenue, PO Box 4070,
Kalamazoo MI 49003-4070
County: Kalamazoo FICE Identification: 006949
Unit ID: 170541
Telephone: (269) 488-4400 Carnegie Class: Assoc/Pub-R-L
FAX Number: (269) 488-4555 Calendar System: Semester
URL: www.kvcc.edu
Established: 1966 Annual Undergrad Tuition & Fees (In-District): $2,540
Enrollment: 13,500 Coed
Affiliation or Control: Local IRS Status: 501(c)3
Highest Offering: Associate Degree
Program: Occupational; 2-Year Principally Bachelor's Creditable
Accreditation: NH, DH, EMT, MAC

01 President ... Dr. Marilyn J. SCHLACK
05 Vice President Academic Services ... Dr. Bruce KOCHER
10 Vice President Financial Services ... Ms. Louise ANDERSON
32 VP for College & Student Relations ... Mr. Michael COLLINS
15 Vice President of Human Resources ... Ms. Sandra BOHNET
13 Vice Pres Information Technologies ... Mr. Terrel F. HUTCHINS
50 VP Econ & Business Development ... Mr. James DEHAVEN
20 Asst VP for Academic Services ... Mr. Dennis BERTCH
86 Exec Dir of Governmental Relations ... Ms. Kathy JOHNSON
12 Dean Arcadia Commons Campus ... Mr. Grant CHANDLER
19 Director of Public Safety ... Mr. Ken COLBY
08 Director of Libraries ... Ms. Janet ALM
07 Dir Admissions/Records/Registrar ... Mr. Michael MCCALL
09 Director of Institutional Research ... Mr. Stephen CANNELL
30 Director Development ... Mr. Steve DOHERTY
37 Director Financial Aid ... Mr. Roger MILLER
49 Dean Liberal Arts & Business ... Dr. Nora EVERS
76 Dean Health/Science & Technology ... Mr. James W. TAYLOR
18 Chief Facilities/Physical Plant ... Mr. Daniel MALEY
96 Director of Purchasing ... Ms. Kathy CAMPBELL
21 Business Manager ... Ms. Muriel HICE
35 Director of Student Success ... Ms. Laura COSBY
101 Asst to President and Plng Coord ... Ms. Patricia NIEWOONDER
66 Director of Nursing ... Ms. Susan MOTT

Kellogg Community College (B)

450 North Avenue, Battle Creek MI 49017-3397
County: Calhoun FICE Identification: 002276
Unit ID: 170550
Telephone: (269) 965-3931 Carnegie Class: Assoc/Pub-R-L
FAX Number: (269) 962-4260 Calendar System: Semester
URL: www.kellogg.edu
Established: 1956 Annual Undergrad Tuition & Fees (In-District): $2,713
Enrollment: 6,071 Coed
Affiliation or Control: Local IRS Status: 501(c)3
Highest Offering: Associate Degree
Program: Occupational; 2-Year Principally Bachelor's Creditable
Accreditation: NH, DH, MLTAD, PTAA, RAD

01 President ... Dr. Dennis BONA
05 Vice President Instruction ... Ms. Catherine HENDLER
11 Vice Pres Administration/Finance ... Mr. Mark O'CONNELL
32 Vice President Student Services ... Dr. Kay KECK
10 Chief Financial Officer ... Mr. Richard SCOTT
13 Chief Information Officer ... Mr. Robert REYNOLDS
57 Chair Arts & Communication Dept ... Ms. Barbara SUDEIKIS
81 Chair Math & Science Dept ... Mr. Bob WESTDORP
49 Dean Arts/Sciences/Regional Educ ... Dr. Kevin RABINEAU
102 Executive Director KCC Foundation ... Ms. Ginger CUTSINGER
96 Director Purchasing ... Ms. Angela COCHRAN
06 Registrar ... Dr. Kay KECK
08 Director Library Services ... Ms. Martha STILWELL
41 Director Athletics & PE ... Mr. Tom SHAW
12 Director of Grahl Center ... Ms. Roberta GAGNON
12 Director Fehsenfeld Center ... Mr. Timothy SLEEVI
12 Director Eastern Academic Center ... Mr. Colin MCCALEB
15 Director Human Resources ... Ms. Ali ROBERTSON
18 Dir Inst Facilities/Public Safety ... Mr. John DIPIERRO
51 Director Lifelong Learning ... Ms. Mary GREEN
09 Director Institutional Research ... Ms. Doris LEWIS
21 Director of Finance ... Ms. Tracy BEATTY
84 Director Enrollment Services ... Vacant
12 Dir Reg Manufacturing Tech Center ... Vacant
38 Dir Academic Advising/Student Life ... Ms. Terah ZAREMBA
26 Dir Public Information & Marketing ... Vacant
07 Director of Admissions ... Ms. Meredith STRAVERS
40 Bookstore Manager ... Ms. Catherine JAMES

Kettering University (C)

1700 University Avenue, Flint MI 48504-6214
County: Genesee FICE Identification: 002262
Unit ID: 169983
Telephone: (810) 762-9500 Carnegie Class: Master's M
FAX Number: (810) 762-9837 Calendar System: Semester
URL: www.kettering.edu
Established: 1919 Annual Undergrad Tuition & Fees: $33,946
Enrollment: 2,079 Coed
Affiliation or Control: Independent Non-Profit IRS Status: 501(c)3
Highest Offering: Master's
Program: Professional
Accreditation: NH, ACBSP, CS, ENG

01 President ... Dr. Robert K. MCMAHAN
04 Executive Assistant to President ... Ms. Susan M. FLECKENSTEIN
04 Assistant to President ... Ms. Tabitha BOURASSA
05 Provost & VP Academic Affairs ... Dr. Robert L. SIMPSON
10 VP Administration & Finance ... Mr. Tom AYERS
84 VP Enrollment Services ... Mr. Kip DARCY
32 VP Student Life & Dean of Students ... Ms. Betsy E. HOMSHER
30 VP Univ Advancement/Ext Relations ... Ms. Susan DAVIES
13 VP Instruct/Admin & Info Technology ... Ms. Viola SPRAGUE
11 Dir Special Projects President Ofc ... Mr. Robert NICHOLS
20 Vice Provost/Assoc VP Acad Services ... Dr. Jacqueline A. EL-SAYED
26 Chief Public Relations Officer ... Ms. Pat A. MROCZEK
15 Director Human Resources ... Ms. Beth EWALD
102 Dir of Philanthropy Corp/Found ... Ms. Eve VITALE
44 Dir of Philanthropy Planned Giving ... Ms. Sue WEISS
88 Dir of Philanthropy Indiv Giving ... Mr. Jack P. STOCK
19 Chief Campus Safety ... Mr. James R. BENFORD
37 Director Student Financial Aid ... Ms. Diane K. BICE
21 Controller ... Ms. Beth A. COVERS
09 Director Institution Effectiveness ... Dr. Edwin IMASUEN
58 Director Grad Ops & Corp Activities ... Mr. Todd J. STEELE
18 Director Physical Plant ... Ms. Patricia A. ENGLE
08 Director Library Services ... Dr. Charles D. HANSON
07 Director Intl & Undergrad Admiss ... Ms. Karen A. FULL
41 Director Athletics/Rec Service ... Mr. Michael L. SCHAAL
93 Director Minority Student Affairs ... Mr. Dwight L. TAVADA
104 Director International Office ... Dr. Basem ALZAHABI
88 Director Environment Health/Safety ... Ms. Nadine L. THOR
27 Director of Marketing ... Ms. Julie A. ULSETH
06 Registrar ... Ms. Sheila R. RUPP
23 Director Wellness Center ... Ms. Cristina REED
39 Director Residence Life ... Ms. Katherine BOSIO
78 Director Coop Educ & Career Svcs ... Ms. Venetia S. PETTEWAY
88 MI SBTDC Regional Director ... Ms. Marsha J. LYTTLE
96 Purchasing Manager ... Ms. Kathleen A. REMENDER
44 Director of Annual Giving ... Ms. Michelle D. LOPER
88 Director Adv Technology Incubator ... Mr. Neil G. SHERIDAN
14 Director of IT Operations ... Mr. Daniel GARCIA
25 Contract/Grant Specialist ... Ms. Jodi L. DORR
105 Webmaster ... Ms. Donna WICKS
88 Dir Center Excellence Teach & Learn ... Dr. Terri LYNCH-CARIS

Keweenaw Bay Ojibwa Community College (D)

111 Beartown Rd, PO Box 519, Baraga MI 49908
County: Baraga Identification: 667037
Telephone: (906) 353-4600 Carnegie Class: Not Classified
FAX Number: N/A Calendar System: Semester
URL: www.kbocc.org
Established: 1975 Annual Undergrad Tuition & Fees (In-District): $1,055
Enrollment: N/A Coed
Affiliation or Control: Local IRS Status: 501(c)3
Highest Offering: Associate Degree
Program: Occupational; 2-Year Principally Bachelor's Creditable
Accreditation: @NH

01 President ... Ms. Debra J. PARRISH
05 Dean of Instruction ... Ms. Kristin TEPSA
07 Interim Admissions Officer ... Mr. Patrick RACETTE
10 Business Officer ... Ms. Megan SHANAHAN
32 Dean of Student Services ... Ms. Cherie DAKOTA
37 Director Financial Aid/Enroll Coord ... Ms. Elizabeth JULIO
88 Cultural Advisor ... Ms. Liz JULIO

Kirtland Community College (E)

10775 N Saint Helen Road, Roscommon MI 48653-9721
County: Roscommon FICE Identification: 007171
Unit ID: 170587
Telephone: (989) 275-5000 Carnegie Class: Assoc/Pub-R-M
FAX Number: (989) 275-8210 Calendar System: Semester
URL: www.kirtland.edu
Established: 1966 Annual Undergrad Tuition & Fees (In-District): $3,235
Enrollment: 2,051 Coed
Affiliation or Control: Local IRS Status: 501(c)3
Highest Offering: Associate Degree
Program: Occupational; 2-Year Principally Bachelor's Creditable
Accreditation: NH

01 President ... Dr. Thomas QUINN
05 Dean of Instruction ... Ms. Kathy MARSH
32 Dean of Student Services ... Ms. Michelle VYSKOCIL
76 Associate Dean Health Sciences ... Ms. Julie LAVENDER
20 Associate Dean Instruction ... Vacant

08 Director of Library ... Ms. Deb SHUMAKER
37 Director of Financial Aid ... Ms. Christin HORNDT
10 Chief Financial Officer ... Mr. Jason BROGE
26 Director of Institutional Services ... Mr. Tim SCHERER
18 Director of Physical Plant ... Ms. Evelyn SCHENK
06 Registrar ... Ms. Michelle VYSKOCIL
15 Director of Human Resources ... Mr. Dale SHANTZ
09 Director of Institutional Research ... Mr. Nick BAKER
102 Foundation Director ... Mr. Don BASSETT
07 Admissions Coordinator ... Ms. Michelle DEVINE

Kuyper College (F)

3333 East Beltline Avenue, NE,
Grand Rapids MI 49525-9749
County: Kent FICE Identification: 002311
Unit ID: 171881
Telephone: (616) 222-3000 Carnegie Class: Bac/Diverse
FAX Number: (616) 988-3608 Calendar System: Semester
URL: www.kuyper.edu
Established: 1939 Annual Undergrad Tuition & Fees: $17,950
Enrollment: 318 Coed
Affiliation or Control: Independent Non-Profit IRS Status: 501(c)3
Highest Offering: Baccalaureate
Program: Professional; Religious Emphasis
Accreditation: NH, BI, SW

01 President ... Dr. Nicholas V. KROEZE
05 Provost ... Dr. Melvin J. FLIKKEMA
30 Vice President College Advancement ... Mr. Ken CAPISCIOLTO
10 Vice Pres Business Administration ... Mr. Duane BRAS
04 Assistant to the President ... Ms. Dawn A. LYNEMA
20 Dean for Academic Programs ... Vacant
08 Librarian ... Ms. Dianne V. ZANDBERGEN
06 Registrar ... Ms. Joy MILANO
07 Director of Admissions ... Ms. Sung-Ae REED
35 Director of Student Life ... Mr. Cisco GONZALEZ
37 Financial Aid Director ... Ms. Agnes M. RUSSELL
29 Director of Alumni/Public Relations ... Vacant
39 Resident Director ... Mr. Curt ESSENBURG
13 Director Computing/Info Management ... Mr. Keith TORNO
19 Supervisor of Physical Plant ... Mr. Lance EBENSTEIN
18 Director of Plant ... Mr. Tim CHUPP
40 Bookstore Manager ... Vacant

Lake Michigan College (G)

2755 E Napier, Benton Harbor MI 49022-1899
County: Berrien FICE Identification: 002277
Unit ID: 170620
Telephone: (269) 927-3571 Carnegie Class: Assoc/Pub-R-M
FAX Number: (269) 927-6656 Calendar System: Semester
URL: www.lakemichigancollege.edu
Established: 1946 Annual Undergrad Tuition & Fees (In-District): $1,464
Enrollment: 4,654 Coed
Affiliation or Control: Local IRS Status: 501(c)3
Highest Offering: Associate Degree
Program: Occupational; 2-Year Principally Bachelor's Creditable
Accreditation: NH, ADNUR, DA, RAD

01 President ... Dr. Robert HARRISON
05 Vice President of Instruction ... Ms. Sarah DEMPSEY
11 VP Admin Svcs/Special Asst to Pres ... Ms. Anne C. ERDMAN
30 VP Institutional Advance/Planning ... Mr. Greg A. KOROCH
10 Vice President Financial Services ... Ms. Kelli HAHN
04 Exec Assistant to the President ... Ms. Kerri LEROUX
49 Exec Dean Arts & Sciences ... Mr. Chris RODDY
50 Dean Tech/Health Sciences/Business ... Ms. Leslie KELLOGG
12 Exec Dean South Haven Campus ... Ms. Janice VARNEY
12 Exec Dean Bertrand Crossing ... Mrs. Barbara CRAIG
32 Vice President Student Services ... Dr. Clinton GABBARD
88 Manager Mainstage Services ... Ms. Deedy FOWLER
18 Director Facilities Management ... Mr. Lee H. VAN GINHOVEN
13 Exec Dir Info Tech/Inst Rsrch ... Mr. Randall MELTON
26 Director Marketing Services ... Ms. Laura KRAKLAU
37 Director of Financial Aid ... Ms. Anne TEWS
06 Associate Registrar ... Mr. Tezuko HIROKO
51 Dir Cmty Outreach/Continuing Educ ... Vacant
102 Director Foundations & Grants ... Ms. Mary FOWLER
96 Dir Purchasing and Support Services ... Ms. Linda MARUTZ
88 Dir Conference and Event Services ... Vacant
91 Network Systems/Database Admin ... Ms. Alecia LIN
90 Activity Dir/Instruction Technology ... Mr. Mark KELLY
09 Director Institutional Research ... Ms. Alissa SHEFTIC

Lake Superior State University (H)

650 W Easterday Avenue,
Sault Sainte Marie MI 49783-1699
County: Chippewa FICE Identification: 002293
Unit ID: 170639
Telephone: (906) 632-6841 Carnegie Class: Bac/Diverse
FAX Number: (906) 635-2111 Calendar System: Semester
URL: www.lssu.edu
Established: 1946 Annual Undergrad Tuition & Fees (In-State): $9,715
Enrollment: 2,805 Coed
Affiliation or Control: State IRS Status: 501(c)3
Highest Offering: Master's
Program: Liberal Arts And General; Teacher Preparatory; Professional
Accreditation: NH, ENG, ENGT, IFSAC, NUR, @TEAC

01 President .... Dr. Tony L. MCLAIN
05 Vice President/Provost .... Mr. Maurice WALWORTH
32 Vice President Student Affairs .... Dr. Kenneth PERESS
10 Vice President Finance .... Ms. Sherry L. BROOKS
84 Vice President Enrollment Services .... Mr. William EILOLA
49 Int Dean Arts/Letters/Social Sci .... Dr. Paige GORDIER
20 Dean Academic Services .... Vacant
13 Act Director Information Technology .... Mr. Scott OLSON
18 Director Physical Plant .... Ms. Sherry BROOKS
06 Registrar .... Ms. Nancy NEVE
07 Director of Admissions .... Ms. Susan K. CAMP
16 Director Human Resources .... Vacant
36 Director of Career Services .... Ms. Theresa WEAVER
37 Director of Financial Aid .... Ms. Deborah FAUST
38 Director of Counseling .... Ms. Theresa H. WEAVER
39 Director Housing/Residential Life .... Mr. Scott M. KORB
26 Director of Public Affairs .... Mr. Thomas A. PINK
29 Director Alumni Relations .... Ms. Susan FITZPATRICK
102 Director of Foundation .... Mr. Tom COATES
96 Director of Purchasing .... Ms. Colleen RYE
23 Director Health Services .... Ms. Karen STOREY
28 Dir Native American Ctr/Diversity .... Ms. Stephanie SABATINE
41 Athletic Director .... Ms. Kristin DUNBAR
35 Director Student Life .... Mr. Scott KORB
40 Bookstore Manager .... Ms. Amber MCLEAN
09 Institutional Research Analyst .... Ms. Cynthia F. MERKEL

Lansing Community College (A)

419 N Capitol Avenue, Lansing MI 48901-7211
County: Ingham FICE Identification: 002278
Unit ID: 170657
Telephone: (517) 483-1957 Carnegie Class: Assoc/Pub-R-L
FAX Number: (517) 483-1845 Calendar System: Semester
URL: www.lcc.edu
Established: 1957 Annual Undergrad Tuition & Fees (In-District): $2,511
Enrollment: 20,857 Coed
Affiliation or Control: Local IRS Status: 501(c)3
Highest Offering: Associate Degree
Program: Occupational; 2-Year Principally Bachelor's Creditable
Accreditation: NH, ADNUR, COMTA, DH, DMS, EMT, HT, IFSAC, RAD, SURGT

01 President .... Dr. Brent KNIGHT
05 Provost .... Dr. Stephanie SHANBLATT
10 Sr VP Finance/Admin & Advancement .. Ms. Lisa WEBB SHARPE
21 Chief Financial Officer .... Ms. Catherine FISHER
13 Chief Information Officer .... Mr. Kevin BUBB
11 Exec Dir Administrative Services .. Mr. Chris STRUGAR-FRITSCH
20 Associate VP Academic Affairs .... Mr. Jack BERGERON
30 Assoc VP External Affs/Development .... Ms. Elva REVILLA
56 Dean Ext Learning & Prof Studies .... Dr. Jean MORCIGLIO
88 Dean Health & Human Services .... Ms. Margie CLARK
49 Dean Arts & Sciences .... Dr. Michael NEALON
32 Dean Student Services .... Dr. Evan MONTAGUE
72 Dean Technical Careers .... Mr. George BERGHORN
15 Exec Director Human Resources .... Ms. Ann KRONEMAN
26 Director Public Affairs .... Ms. Ellen JONES
27 Director Strategic Communications .... Ms. Kristan TETENS

Lawrence Technological University (B)

21000 W Ten Mile Road, Southfield MI 48075-1058
County: Oakland FICE Identification: 002279
Unit ID: 170675
Telephone: (248) 204-4000 Carnegie Class: Master's L
FAX Number: (248) 204-3727 Calendar System: Semester
URL: www.ltu.edu
Established: 1932 Annual Undergrad Tuition & Fees: $27,870
Enrollment: 4,257 Coed
Affiliation or Control: Independent Non-Profit IRS Status: 501(c)3
Highest Offering: Doctorate
Program: Liberal Arts And General; Professional
Accreditation: NH, ACBSP, ART, CIDA, ENG, IACBE

01 President .... Dr. Virinder K. MOUDGIL
04 Exec Assistant to the President .... Ms. Louise M. GARRETT
05 Provost .... Dr. Maria J. VAZ
10 Vice Pres Finance/Admin .... Ms. Linda L. HEIGHT
30 VP of University Advancement .... Mr. Stephen E. BROWN
88 Assoc VP Advance/Chief Dev Officer .... Mr. Dennis J. HOWIE
58 Assoc Provost/Dean Grad Program .... Dr. S. Alan MCCORD
84 Asst Provost Enrollment Management .... Ms. Lisa R. KUJAWA
48 Dean of Architecture & Design .... Mr. Glen S. LEROY
49 Dean of Arts & Sciences .... Dr. Hsiao-Ping H. MOORE
54 Dean of Engineering .... Dr. Nabil F. GRACE
50 Dean of Management .... Dr. Bahman MIRSHAB
32 Dean of Students .... Mr. Kevin FINN
26 Exec Dir Marketing & Public Affs .... Mr. Bruce J. ANNETT, JR.
10 Director Business Services .... Vacant
07 Director Admissions .... Ms. Jane T. ROHRBACK
06 Interim Registrar .... Ms. Noreen FERGUSON
08 Director Library .... Mr. Gary R. COCOZZOLI
18 Director Campus Facilities .... Mr. Carey G. VALENTINE
14 Ex Dir IT Svc Delivery Organization .... Mr. Tim CHAVIS
37 Int Dir Financial Aid & Vet Affs .... Ms. Dee KING
35 Dir Stdnt Rec/Athletics & Wellness .... Mr. Scott TRUDEAU
36 Director of Career Services .... Ms. Peg PIERCE
44 Asst Vice Pres/Campaign Director .... Mr. Dino M. HERNANDEZ
85 Director of International Programs .... Ms. Cyndi MCMICHAEL
24 Director Audio Visual Media Svcs .... Mr. Walter G. BIZON
39 Director Residence Life .... Ms. Kimberly OSANTOWSKI

86 Exec Dir Econ Dev & Govt Relations .... Mr. Mark J. BRUCKI
102 Dir of Corp & Foundation Relations .... Mr. Howard DAVIS
44 Director Major Gifts .... Ms. Julie VULAJ
13 Director Help Desk/Services .... Ms. Charlene RAMOS
28 Director of Diversity .... Mr. Kevin FINN
89 Director of Freshman Studies .... Vacant
15 Human Resources Director .... Ms. Deshawn JOHNSON
40 Manager Campus Bookstore .... Mr. Carl CAMPANELLA
88 Manager Dining Services .... Ms. Nancy THOMAS
27 Managing Editor News Bureau .... Mr. Eric POPE
19 Director of Campus Safety .... Mr. Harry P. BUTLER
29 Manager Alumni Rels/Alumni Giving .... Ms. Mary RANDAZZO
31 Dir of University Special Events .... Ms. Robin LECLERC
26 Dir Univ Comm & Academic Editor .... Ms. Anne M G. ADAMUS
44 Mgr Advancement Svcs/Annual Giving .... Vacant
88 University Architect .... Mr. Joseph C. VERYSER
88 Director of Student Engagement .... Vacant
88 Dir of Academic Achievement Center .... Dr. Gladys M. AVILES
09 Dir of Inst Research/Academic Plng .... Vacant
96 Purchasing Agent .... Ms. Michelle BUTKOVICH

Macomb Community College (C)

14500 Twelve Mile Road, Warren MI 48088-9838
County: Macomb FICE Identification: 008906
Unit ID: 170790
Telephone: (586) 445-7999 Carnegie Class: Assoc/Pub-S-MC
FAX Number: (586) 445-7886 Calendar System: Semester
URL: www.macomb.edu
Established: 1954 Annual Undergrad Tuition & Fees (In-District): $2,680
Enrollment: 24,325 Coed
Affiliation or Control: Local IRS Status: 501(c)3
Highest Offering: Associate Degree
Program: Occupational; 2-Year Principally Bachelor's Creditable
Accreditation: NH, ACFEI, ADNUR, MAC, MLTAD, NMT, OTA, PTAA, SURGT

01 President .... Dr. James JACOBS
05 Vice Pres/Provost Learning Unit .... Dr. James SAWYER
10 Vice President for Business .... Ms. Elizabeth ARGIRI
16 Vice President for Human Resources .... Vacant
26 VP College Adv/Community Relations .... Ms. Casandra ULBRICH
18 Vice President Facilities/Operation .... Ms. Libby ARGIRI
88 Director University Relations .... Ms. Donna PETRAS
32 Vice President for Student Services .... Ms. Jill M. LITTLE
49 Dean Arts & Sciences .... Ms. Katherine GRENDA
49 Dean Arts & Sciences .... Ms. Carole A. DEYER
76 Dean Health/Human Services .... Ms. Charlene MCPEAK
54 Dean Engineering & Adv Tech .... Mr. Joseph PETROSKY
50 Dean Info/Technology/Business .... Mr. David CORBA
35 Dean of Student Success .... Ms. Susan BOYD
31 Dean Student & Cmty Services .... Mr. Geary MAIURI
45 Exec Director Planning & Research .... Ms. Gerri Lynn PAVONE
21 Director Finance & Investments .... Ms. Roberta REMIAS
19 Captain College Police .... Mr. Thomas WILK
88 Director Public Service Institute .... Mr. Carl SEITZ
26 Director Marketing & Recruitment .... Ms. Audrey TAKACS
09 Director Institutional Research .... Mr. Randall HICKMAN
06 Registrar/Dir Enrollment Services .... Mr. Ronald HUGHES
29 Director Alumni Rels/Foundation .... Ms. Dawn MAGRETTA
38 Dir Counseling & Academic Advising .... Mr. Gerald KNESEK
96 Director of Purchasing .... Mr. Dennis COSTELLO
41 Dir Athletics/Sports Clubs .... Mr. Brent BIEBUYCK
18 Director of Plant Operations .... Mr. Stevan ALTON
37 Director of Financial Aid .... Mr. Douglas LEVY
36 Dir Student Dev/Career Services .... Mr. Robert PENKALA
51 Dir Workforce Continuing Education .... Ms. Elise JOHNSON
27 Chief Information Officer .... Mr. Michael ZIMMERMAN
08 Dean Libraries/Learning Resources .... Mr. Michael BALSAMO
43 General Counsel .... Mr. Hunter WENDT

Madonna University (D)

36600 Schoolcraft Road, Livonia MI 48150-1176
County: Wayne FICE Identification: 002282
Unit ID: 170806
Telephone: (734) 432-5300 Carnegie Class: Master's M
FAX Number: (734) 432-5333 Calendar System: Semester
URL: www.madonna.edu
Established: 1947 Annual Undergrad Tuition & Fees: $15,300
Enrollment: 4,458 Coed
Affiliation or Control: Roman Catholic IRS Status: 501(c)3
Highest Offering: Doctorate
Program: Liberal Arts And General; Teacher Preparatory; Professional
Accreditation: NH, DIETD, NURSE, SW, TED

01 President .... Sr. Rose Marie KUJAWA
30 Vice President for Advancement .... Ms. Andrea NODGE
05 Provost and VP for Academic Admin .... Dr. Ernest NOLAN
10 Vice Pres for Finance/Operations .... Mr. Leonard WILHELM
32 Vice President for Student Affairs ... Dr. Connie TINGSON-GATUZ
84 Vice Pres Planning/Enrollment Mgmt .... Mr. Michael KENNEY
12 Dean Outreach and Distance Learning .... Dr. James NOVAK
42 Director of Campus Ministry .... Sr. Anita Marie TADDONIO
06 Registrar .... Ms. Dina DUBUIS
07 Director of Admissions .... Mr. Mike QUATTRO
28 Director Diversity/Multicultural .... Vacant
08 Director of Library Services .... Ms. Joanne LUMETTA
37 Director of Financial Aid .... Mr. Chris ZIEGLER
13 Director Information Systems .... Sr. Serafina Marie DIXON
15 Director of Human Resources .... Ms. Tracey DURDEN
36 Director of Career Services .... Ms. Christine BRANT
30 Director Corp Devel/Special Events .... Ms. Ashley FREDRICK

19 Director Public Safety .... Mr. David HAMMERSCHMIDT
41 Director Athletics .... Mr. Bryan RIZZO
40 Bookstore Manager .... Ms. Debbie MITCHELL
39 Director Residence Hall .... Ms. Tanisha MCINTOSH
24 Director Media Services .... Ms. Patricia DERRY
23 Director Instruction Center .... Dr. Patricia VINT
09 Director of Institutional Research .... Dr. Edith RALEIGH
18 Chief Facilities/Physical Plant .... Mr. Craig FLICKINGER
29 Director Alumni Relations .... Ms. Carole BOOMS
26 Director of Marketing .... Ms. Karen SANBORN
79 Dean Arts & Humanities .... Dr. Kathleen O'DOWD
50 Dean Business .... Dr. Stuart ARENDS
58 Dean Graduate Studies .... Dr. Edith RALEIGH
66 Dean Nursing & Health .... Dr. Teresa THOMPSON
72 Dean Science & Mathematics .... Dr. Theodore BIERMANN
83 Dean Social Sciences .... Dr. Karen ROSS
53 Dean Education .... Dr. Karen OBSNIUK

Marygrove College (E)

8425 W McNichols Road, Detroit MI 48221-2599
County: Wayne FICE Identification: 002284
Unit ID: 170842
Telephone: (313) 927-1200 Carnegie Class: Master's L
FAX Number: (313) 927-1345 Calendar System: Semester
URL: www.marygrove.edu
Established: 1905 Annual Undergrad Tuition & Fees: $18,900
Enrollment: 2,327 Coed
Affiliation or Control: Roman Catholic IRS Status: 501(c)3
Highest Offering: Master's
Program: 2-Year Principally Bachelor's Creditable; Liberal Arts And General; Teacher Preparatory; Professional
Accreditation: NH, SW, @TEAC

01 President .... Dr. David J. FIKE
05 VP Academic Affairs .... Ms. Jane HAMMANG-BUHL
32 VP Student Affs & Enrollment Svcs .... Dr. Juliana MOSLEY
30 Vice Pres Institutional Advancement .... Mr. Kenneth MALECKE
10 VP Finance/Admin & CFO .... Mr. William L. JOHNSON
53 Dean of Education .... Dr. Chris KOENIG SEGUIN
49 Dean of Arts and Sciences .... Dr. Judith HEINEN
31 Dean of Community Based Learning .... Dr. Brenda BRYANT
57 Dean of Visual & Performing Arts .... Ms. Rose DESLOOVER
51 Asst Dean of Continuing Education .... Ms. Sherry LEFTON
06 Registrar .... Ms. Gladys SMITH
07 Dir of Grad & Undergrad Admissions .... Vacant
09 Director of Institutional Research .... Mr. John SENKO
29 Director of Alumni Relations .... Ms. Diane PUHL
84 Dir Enrollment Svcs & Financial Aid .... Ms. Patricia CHAPLIN
41 Athletic Director .... Mr. David SICHTERMAN
42 Director of Campus Ministry .... Mr. Jesse COX
15 Director of Human Resources .... Ms. Anne JOHNSON
38 Director of Student Counseling .... Dr. Carolyn ROBERTS
39 Director Housing & Residence Life .... Mr. Timothy JOHNSTON
104 Director of International Programs .... Ms. Michelle CADE
19 Dir of Campus Security & Services .... Mr. Horace DANDRIDGE
35 Director of Student Life .... Mr. Garth HOWARD

Michigan Jewish Institute (F)

6890 West Maple, West Bloomfield MI 48322
County: Oakland FICE Identification: 032843
Unit ID: 434414
Telephone: (248) 414-6900 Carnegie Class: Bac/A&S
FAX Number: (248) 414-6907 Calendar System: Semester
URL: www.mji.edu
Established: 1994 Annual Undergrad Tuition & Fees: $10,900
Enrollment: 1,352 Coed
Affiliation or Control: Independent Non-Profit IRS Status: 501(c)3
Highest Offering: Baccalaureate
Program: Business Emphasis
Accreditation: ACICS

01 President/CFO/VP Financial Affs .... Rabbi Kasriel SHEMTOV
05 VP Inst Adv & Dean Academic Admin .... Dr. T. Hershel GARDIN
06 Registrar .... Ms. Alicia JAMES
20 Director of Academics .... Mr. Dov STEIN
37 Financial Aid Administrator .... Ms. Fran HERMAN
105 Web & Lan Services .... Mr. Philip KLUMP

Michigan School of Professional Psychology (G)

26811 Orchard Lake Road,
Farmington Hills MI 48334-4512
County: Oakland FICE Identification: 021989
Unit ID: 169220
Telephone: (248) 476-1122 Carnegie Class: Spec/Health
FAX Number: (248) 476-1125 Calendar System: Semester
URL: www.mispp.edu
Established: 1981 Annual Graduate Tuition & Fees: $26,963
Enrollment: 149 Coed
Affiliation or Control: Independent Non-Profit IRS Status: 501(c)3
Highest Offering: Doctorate; No Undergraduates
Program: Professional
Accreditation: NH

01 President/Chief Academic Officer .... Dr. Kerry MOUSTAKAS
03 Vice President .... Ms. Diane ZALAPI
10 Chief Financial/Business Officer .... Mr. Tom HRZEK
58 Academic Program Chair .... Dr. Lee BACH

88 Director of Clinical Training .... Dr. Fran BROWN
13 Information Systems Coordinator .... Mr. Jeffrey CROSS
37 Director of Financial Aid .... Ms. Sandra BUTTERWORTH
08 Head Academic Librarian .... Ms. Michelle WHEELER
06 Registrar .... Ms. Heather RIGBY
07 Admissions/Recruitment Coordinator .... Ms. Amanda MING
04 Special Assistant .... Ms. Laura LANE

Michigan State University (A)

East Lansing MI 48824-1046
County: Ingham　FICE Identification: 002290
Unit ID: 171100
Telephone: (517) 355-1855　Carnegie Class: RU/VH
FAX Number: N/A　Calendar System: Semester
URL: www.msu.edu
Established: 1855　Annual Undergrad Tuition & Fees (In-State): $13,211
Enrollment: 47,954　Coed
Affiliation or Control: State　IRS Status: 501(c)3
Highest Offering: Doctorate
Program: Liberal Arts And General; Teacher Preparatory; Professional
Accreditation: NH, ANEST, BUS, BUSA, CEA, CIDA, CLPSY, CONST, CORE, CS, DIETD, DIETI, DMOLS, ENG, FOR, IPSY, JOUR, LAW, LSAR, MED, MFCD, MT, MUS, NURSE, OSTEO, #PLNG, SCPSY, SP, SW, TEAC, VET

01 President .... Dr. Lou Anna K. SIMON
05 Provost/Vice Pres Academic Affairs .... Dr. Kim A. WILCOX
10 Vice Pres Finance Opers/Treasurer .... Dr. Fred L. POSTON
32 Interim VP Student Affairs & Svcs .... Dr. Denise B. MAYBANK
46 Vice President Research & Grad Stds .... Dr. J. Ian GRAY
86 Vice President Governmental Affairs .... Mr. Mark A. BURNHAM
30 Vice Pres Univ Advancement .... Mr. Robert GROVES
26 Interim Vice Pres Comm Brand Strat .... Ms. Heather C. SWAIN
43 General Counsel/VP Legal Affairs .... Mr. Robert A. NOTO
13 Assoc VP Research/Graduate Studies .... Dr. Paul M. HUNT
35 Sr Assoc VP and Dir Student Life .... Vacant
101 Secy Board Trust/Exec Asst to Pres .... Mr. William R. BEEKMAN
20 Senior Associate Provost .... Dr. June P. YOUATT
51 Assoc Prov Univ Outreach/ Engagement .... Dr. Hiram E. FITZGERALD
88 Assoc Prov Academic Student Svcs .... Vacant
88 Assoc Provost Academic Svcs .... Dr. Linda O. STANFORD
58 Assoc Prov Grad Stds/Dean Grad Sch .... Dr. Karen L. KLOMPARENS
88 Asc Prov Ugrad Educ/Dn Ugrad Stds .... Dr. Douglas ESTRY
17 Assoc Provost Human Health Affairs .... Vacant
15 Assoc Prov/VP Academic Human Res .... Mr. Theodore H. CURRY, II
88 Vice Prov Libraries Info Tech Svcs .... Mr. David GIFT
21 Asst Vice Pres Finance/Operations .... Ms. Kathryn E. LINDAHL
45 Asst VP & Director of Plng/Budgets .... Mr. David S. BYELICH
18 Asst Vice Pres Physical Plant Admin .... Mr. Ronald T. FLINN
39 Asst VP Housing & Food Service .... Mr. Vennie GORE
21 Asst VP for Business and CFO .... Mr. Mark P. HAAS
16 Asst Vice Pres for Human Resources .... Ms. Sharon BUTLER
88 Asst VP Ofc of Sponsored Programs .... Dr. Twila REIGHLEY
21 Controller .... Mr. Greg DEPPONG
91 Director Admin Information Services .... Vacant
07 Director of Admissions .... Mr. James W. COTTER
22 Dir Incl/Intrcult Init/Sr Adv P Dvr .... Ms. Paulette GRANBERRY-RUSSELL
29 Assoc VP University Advancement .... Mr. W. Scott WESTERMAN, III
36 Int Dir Career Services/Placement .... Ms. Theda RUDD
90 Dir Academic Technology Services .... Mr. Thomas D. DAVIS
25 Director Contract & Grant Admin .... Mr. Daniel T. EVON
38 Director Counseling Center .... Dr. Jan T. COLLINS-EAGLIN
88 Dir Michigan AGR Experiment Stn .... Dr. Steven G. PUEPPKE
56 Director MSU Extension .... Dr. Thomas G. COON
37 Director of Financial Aid .... Mr. Richard SHIPMAN
06 Registrar .... Dr. Nicole ROVIG
85 Director Intl Students/Scholars .... Mr. Peter F. BRIGGS
23 Director MSU Student Health Ctr .... Dr. Glynda M. MOORER
92 Dean Honors College .... Dr. Cynthia JACKSON-ELMOORE
41 Director Intercollegiate Athletics .... Mr. Mark J. HOLLIS
08 Director of Libraries .... Mr. Clifford H. HAKA
88 Director National Cyclotron Lab .... Dr. Konrad GELBKE
19 Police Chf/Dir Police & Pub Safety .... Mr. James H. DUNLAP
88 Director Undergraduate Univ Div .... Dr. Bonita P. CURRY
96 Actg Dir University Svc/Purchasing .... Mr. Nathan MAHER
47 Interim Dean Col Ag & Nat Resources .... Dr. Douglas BUHLER
79 Dean College Arts & Letters .... Dr. Karin A. WURST
79 Dean Res Col Arts/Humanities .... Dr. Stephen L. ESQUITH
50 Dean Eli Broad Col of Business .... Dr. Stefanie A. LENWAY
60 Dean Col Commun Arts & Science .... Dr. Pamela WHITTEN
53 Dean College of Education .... Dr. Donald E. HELLER
54 Dean College of Engineering .... Dr. Satish S. UDPA
63 Dean College Human Medicine .... Dr. Marsha D. RAPPLEY
82 Dean James Madison College .... Dr. Sherman W. GARNETT
61 Dean College of Law .... Ms. Joan W. HOWARTH
81 Dean Lyman Briggs College .... Dr. Elizabeth H. SIMMONS
64 Dean College of Music .... Mr. James FORGER
81 Dean College Natural Science .... Dr. R. James KIRKPATRICK
66 Dean College of Nursing .... Dr. Mary H. MUNDT
63 Dean College Osteopathic Medicine .... Dr. William D. STRAMPEL
83 Dean College of Social Science .... Dr. Marietta BABA
74 Dean College Veterinary Medicine .... Dr. Christopher M. BROWN
82 Dean Intl Studies & Programs .... Dr. Jeffrey M. RIEDINGER

Michigan Technological University (B)

1400 Townsend Drive, Houghton MI 49931-1295
County: Houghton　FICE Identification: 002292
Unit ID: 171128
Telephone: (906) 487-1885　Carnegie Class: RU/H
FAX Number: (906) 487-2935　Calendar System: Semester
URL: www.mtu.edu
Established: 1885　Annual Undergrad Tuition & Fees (In-State): $14,448
Enrollment: 7,031　Coed
Affiliation or Control: State　IRS Status: 501(c)3
Highest Offering: Doctorate
Program: Liberal Arts And General; Teacher Preparatory; Professional
Accreditation: NH, BUS, ENG, ENGT, FOR, TEAC

01 President .... Dr. Glenn D. MROZ
05 Provost/Vice Pres Academic Affairs .... Dr. Max SEEL
86 Vice Pres Governmental Relations .... Dr. Dale R. TAHTINEN
11 Vice President for Administration .... Ms. Ellen S. HORSCH
46 Vice President for Research .... Dr. David D. REED
32 Vice President for Student Affairs .... Dr. Les P. COOK
30 Vice President Michigan Tech Fund .... Mr. Shea MCGREW
84 Asst VP for Enrollment Services .... Mr. John B. LEHMAN
35 Dean of Students .... Ms. Bonnie GORMAN
10 Chief Financial Officer .... Mr. Daniel D. GREENLEE
26 Director Marketing/Communications .... Ms. Linda BAKER
08 Director of the Library .... Ms. Ellen MARKS
09 Institutional Analysis .... Mr. Richard ELENICH
29 Director Alumni Association .... Ms. Brenda RUDIGER
06 Registrar .... Ms. Theresa K. JACQUES
07 Director Undergraduate Recruitment .... Ms. Allison A. CARTER
15 Director Human Resources .... Ms. Anita QUINN
37 Director of Financial Aid .... Mr. William R. ROBERTS
36 Director University Career Center .... Mr. James TURNQUIST
18 Int Dir Facilities/Physical Plant .... Mr. George BUTVILAS
21 Director Planning & Budgeting .... Ms. Deborah L. LASSILA
38 Director Counseling Services .... Mr. Donald S. WILLIAMS
19 Director Public Safety .... Mr. Daniel P. BENNETT
22 Director Affirmative Programs .... Dr. Jill HODGES
28 Director Institutional Diversity .... Ms. Chris S. ANDERSON
96 Director of Purchasing .... Mr. Raymond E. LASANEN
58 Dean Graduate School .... Dr. Jacqueline E. HUNTOON
50 Dean Business & Economics .... Dr. Darrell RADSON
54 Dean of Engineering .... Dr. William WOREK
65 Dean of Forestry .... Dr. Terry SHARIK
49 Dean Sciences/Arts .... Dr. Bruce E. SEELY
72 Dean of Technology .... Dr. James FRENDEWEY, JR.

Mid Michigan Community College (C)

1375 S Clare Avenue, Harrison MI 48625-9447
County: Clare　FICE Identification: 006768
Unit ID: 171155
Telephone: (989) 386-6622　Carnegie Class: Assoc/Pub-R-M
FAX Number: (989) 386-2411　Calendar System: Semester
URL: www.midmich.edu
Established: 1965　Annual Undergrad Tuition & Fees (In-District): $3,213
Enrollment: 4,885　Coed
Affiliation or Control: State/Local　IRS Status: 501(c)3
Highest Offering: Associate Degree
Program: Occupational; 2-Year Principally Bachelor's Creditable
Accreditation: NH, MAC, PTAA, RAD

01 President .... Ms. Carol A. CHURCHILL
05 Vice President of Academic Services . Dr. Michael W. JANKOVIAK
32 VP Community/Student Relations .... Mr. Matt MILLER
10 Vice President for Admin & Finance .... Ms. Lillian K. FRICK
04 Executive Assistant to President .... Ms. Sherry L. KYLE
15 Exec Director of Human Resources .... Ms. Gail NUNAMAKER
13 Director IT .... Mr. Kirk A. LEHR
81 Dean of Math & Science .... Mr. Peter VELGUTH
09 Dir of Inst Research/Grants Mgr .... Ms. Carol DARLINGTON
07 Director of Admissions .... Mr. Scott MERTES
21 Director of Accounting .... Mr. Gene SCHMIDT
96 Purchasing Manager .... Mr. Jeffery PUNCHES
84 General/Occupational Recruiter .... Mr. Chris PELLERITO
88 SBTDC Director .... Mr. Anthony FOX
26 Director of Marketing .... Ms. Jessica GORDON
08 Dir Library/Learning Services .... Mr. Corey GOETHE
37 Director of Financial Aid .... Mr. Gale M. CRANDELL
40 Director Auxiliary Services .... Ms. Kelly KOCH
18 Director of Facilities .... Mr. William D. WHITMAN
88 Hospitality Services Manager .... Ms. Cathy STARKWEATHER
76 Director Radiology .... Mr. John B. SKINNER
25 Title III Coordinator .... Ms. Lori CORTEZ
88 Radiology Tech Clinical Coordinator .... Mr. Galen P. MILLER
27 College Info/Org Dev Officer .... Mr. Anthony FREDS
14 Systems Programmer .... Mr. Chris KLIEWONEIT
66 Dean of Academics .... Mr. Chris GOFFNETT
50 Associate Dean Business .... Mr. Shawn TROY
103 Exec Dir Econ/Workforce Dev .... Mr. Scott GOVITZ
35 Exec Dean of Student Services .... Ms. Kimberly BARNES

Monroe County Community College (D)

1555 S Raisinville Road, Monroe MI 48161-9746
County: Monroe　FICE Identification: 002294
Unit ID: 171225
Telephone: (734) 242-7300　Carnegie Class: Assoc/Pub-S-SC
FAX Number: (734) 242-9711　Calendar System: Semester
URL: www.monroeccc.edu
Established: 1964　Annual Undergrad Tuition & Fees (In-District): $2,910
Enrollment: 4,440　Coed
Affiliation or Control: Local　IRS Status: 170(c)1
Highest Offering: Associate Degree
Program: Occupational; 2-Year Principally Bachelor's Creditable
Accreditation: NH, ADNUR

01 President .... Dr. David E. NIXON
05 Vice President of Instruction .... Dr. Grace B. YACKEE
10 Vice Pres of Admin & Exec Dir Fdn .... Ms. Suzanne M. WETZEL
32 Vice Pres Student & Information Svc .... Mr. Randell W. DANIELS
50 Dean of Business .... Mr. Paul L. KNOLLMAN
76 Dean of Health Sciences .... Ms. Kimberly LINDQUIST
79 Dean of Humanities/Social Science .... Dr. Paul HEDEEN
72 Dean of Industrial Technology .... Mr. Parmeshwar COOMAR
81 Dean of Science/Mathematics .... Mr. Vincent MALTESE
31 Dean of Corporate/Cmty Svcs .... Mr. John A. JOY
08 Director Learning Resources .... Ms. Barbara MCNAMEE
06 Registrar .... Ms. Tracy VOGT
07 Director of Admissions/Guidance .... Mr. Mark HALL
88 Director of Upward Bound .... Mr. Anthony QUINN
88 Director of Respiratory Therapy .... Ms. Bonnie B. BOGGS
21 Director of Financial Services .... Ms. Deborah BEAGLE
18 Director Physical Plant .... Mr. James J. BLUMBERG
96 Dir Auxiliary Services/Purchasing .... Ms. Jean FORD
14 Director Data Processing Services .... Mr. James A. ROSS
37 Director of Financial Aid .... Ms. Valerie CULLER
36 Dir Business Devel/Employment Svcs .... Mr. Barry C. KINSEY
56 Director of Extension Centers .... Vacant
88 Director of Lifelong Learning .... Ms. Tina PILLARELLI
13 Manager Information Services .... Mr. Brian K. LAY
27 Director of Marketing .... Mr. Joseph VERKENNES
15 Director of Human Resources .... Ms. Molly M. MCCUTCHAN

Montcalm Community College (E)

2800 College Drive, Sidney MI 48885-9723
County: Montcalm　FICE Identification: 002295
Unit ID: 171234
Telephone: (989) 328-2111　Carnegie Class: Assoc/Pub-R-M
FAX Number: (989) 328-2950　Calendar System: Semester
URL: www.montcalm.edu
Established: 1965　Annual Undergrad Tuition & Fees (In-District): $3,030
Enrollment: 2,063　Coed
Affiliation or Control: Local　IRS Status: 501(c)3
Highest Offering: Associate Degree
Program: Occupational; 2-Year Principally Bachelor's Creditable; Liberal Arts And General
Accreditation: NH, MAC

01 President .... Mr. Robert C. FERRENTINO
11 Vice Pres Administrative Services .... Mr. James D. LANTZ
05 Vice Pres for Academic Affairs .... Mr. Robert SPOHR
32 Dean of Student Services .... Ms. Denise NEWMAN
31 Dean of Community Outreach .... Ms. Susan HATTO
37 Director of Financial Aid .... Ms. Traci NICHOLS
21 Director of Accounting .... Ms. Margery E. FORIST
18 Director of Facilities .... Mr. George F. GERMAIN
13 Information Systems Director .... Mr. Rodney C. MIDDLETON
66 Director of Nursing & Allied Health .... Ms. Beth MOWATT
103 Dir of Workforce Training Solutions .... Vacant
84 Director of Enrollment Services .... Ms. Denise E. EDWARDS
30 Dir of Institutional Advancement .... Ms. Therese A. SMITH
07 Dir Admissions/Asc Dn Student Svcs .... Ms. Debra ALEXANDER
09 Dir of Assessment & Inst Research .... Ms. Lisa LUND
26 Public Information Coordinator .... Ms. Shelly STRAUTZ-SPRINGBORN
20 Dean of Instruction & Faculty .... Mr. Gary HAUCK
06 Registrar .... Ms. Denise E. EDWARDS
10 Chief Business Officer .... Mr. James D. LANTZ
15 Director of Human Resources .... Ms. Connie STEWART

Moody Theological Seminary-Michigan (F)

41550 E Ann Arbor Trail, Plymouth MI 48170-4308
County: Wayne　FICE Identification: 031353
Unit ID: 429076
Telephone: (734) 207-9581　Carnegie Class: Spec/Faith
FAX Number: (734) 207-9582　Calendar System: Trimester
URL: www.mts.edu
Established: 1993　Annual Graduate Tuition & Fees: $13,680
Enrollment: 171　Coed
Affiliation or Control: Independent Non-Profit　IRS Status: 501(c)3
Highest Offering: Master's; No Undergraduates
Program: Religious Emphasis
Accreditation: &NH, THEOL

01 President .... Dr. Paul NYQUIST
05 Associate Academic Dean .... Dr. John RESTUM
11 Director of Operations .... Mr. Brian MOLLENKAMP
06 Registrar .... Mr. George MOSHER
08 Director of Library Services .... Mr. Micah JELINAK
42 Chaplain .... Dr. Paul WILSON
18 Facilities Operations .... Mr. Brian L. MOLLENKAMP

† Regional accreditation is carried under the parent institution Moody Bible Institute, Chicago, IL.

Mott Community College (G)

1401 E Court Street, Flint MI 48503-2089
County: Genesee　FICE Identification: 002261
Unit ID: 169275
Telephone: (810) 762-0200　Carnegie Class: Assoc/Pub-R-L
FAX Number: (810) 762-0257　Calendar System: Semester
URL: www.mcc.edu
Established: 1923　Annual Undergrad Tuition & Fees (In-District): $3,400
Enrollment: 11,000　Coed
Affiliation or Control: Local　IRS Status: 501(c)3

Highest Offering: Associate Degree
Program: Occupational; 2-Year Principally Bachelor's Creditable; Business Emphasis
Accreditation: NH, ACBSP, ADNUR, DA, DH, OTA, PTAA

01 President .... Dr. Dick SHAINK
30 Exec Dir Inst Developmnt/Foundation .... Ms. Lennetta CONEY
05 Vice Pres Academic Affairs .... Dr. Amy FUGATE
11 VP Student & Administrative Svcs .... Mr. Scott JENKINS
10 Chief Financial Officer .... Mr. Larry GAWTHROP
16 Chief Human Resources Officer .... Mr. Mark KENNEDY
88 Exec Dean Regional Tech Ctr Project .... Mr. Tom CRAMPTON
51 Exec Dir Corporate Svcs & Cont Educ .... Mr. Chuck THIEL
32 Interim Exec Dean Student Services .... Mr. Troy BOQUETTE
37 Exec Dir Student Fin Svcs .... Ms. Jennifer DOW-MCDONALD
81 Dean of Math & Science .... Dr. Johanna BROWN
38 Dean Counseling & Student Devlop .... Vacant
83 Dean Social Sciences & Fine Arts .... Ms. Mary CUSACK
50 Dean of Business .... Mr. Chuck HAYES
72 Dean of Technology .... Mr. Clark HARRIS
26 Exec Director Marketing & PR .... Mr. Michael KELLY
27 Chief Technology Officer .... Ms. Cheryl BASSETT
06 Registrar .... Mr. Chris ENGLE
36 Exec Dir Career Ctr/Job Placement .... Mrs. Cindy MCDANIEL
62 Executive Director Library .... Mrs. Kathy IRWIN
18 Exec Dir Physical Plant/Architect .... Mr. Larry KOEHLER
41 Director Athletics/Campus Rec .... Mr. Tom HEALEY
09 Exec Dir Institutional Research .... Mrs. Lori HANCOCK
35 Director Student Life .... Ms. Dawn VANNIMAN
96 Director of Purchasing .... Ms. Jody MICHAEL

Muskegon Community College (A)

221 S Quarterline Road, Muskegon MI 49442-1493
County: Muskegon FICE Identification: 002297
Unit ID: 171304
Telephone: (231) 773-9131 Carnegie Class: Assoc/Pub-U-SC
FAX Number: (231) 777-0255 Calendar System: Semester
URL: www.muskegoncc.edu
Established: 1926 Annual Undergrad Tuition & Fees (In-District): $2,850
Enrollment: 5,156 Coed
Affiliation or Control: Local IRS Status: Exempt
Highest Offering: Associate Degree
Program: Occupational; 2-Year Principally Bachelor's Creditable
Accreditation: NH, ADNUR

01 President .... Dr. Dale K. NESBARY
05 Vice President of Academic Affairs .... Ms. Teresa STURRUS
11 Vice Pres Administrative Service .... Ms. Rosemary ZINK
32 Vice President Student Services .... Dr. John SELMON
06 Dean of Academic Svcs/Registrar .... Ms. Jean ROBERTS
20 Dean of Instruction & Assessment .... Mr. Ed BREITENBACH
51 Dean Continuing Ed/Program Outreach .... Ms. Trynette Lottie HARPS
84 Dean of Enrollment Services .... Ms. Cindy RUSS
10 Director of Finance .... Ms. Beth DICK
13 Chief Information Officer .... Mr. Mike ALSTROM
37 Director Financial Aid .... Mr. Bruce WIERDA
09 Director of Institutional Research .... Dr. Adane KASSA
31 Dir Community Relations/Public Info .... Ms. Tina DEE
15 Director of Human Resources .... Mr. Aaron HILLIARD
41 Athletic Director .... Mr. Marty MCDERMOTT

North Central Michigan College (B)

1515 Howard Street, Petoskey MI 49770-8717
County: Emmet FICE Identification: 002299
Unit ID: 171395
Telephone: (231) 348-6600 Carnegie Class: Assoc/Pub-R-M
FAX Number: (231) 348-6628 Calendar System: Semester
URL: www.ncmich.edu
Established: 1958 Annual Undergrad Tuition & Fees (In-District): $1,152
Enrollment: 2,959 Coed
Affiliation or Control: Local IRS Status: 501(c)3
Highest Offering: Associate Degree
Program: Occupational; 2-Year Principally Bachelor's Creditable
Accreditation: NH

01 President .... Dr. Cameron BRUNET-KOCH
05 Dean of Instruction .... Dr. Christine HAMMOND
10 Dean Finance & Facilities .... Mr. Todd MCDONALD
32 Dean of Students .... Mrs. Naomi DEWINTER
102 Executive Director Foundation .... Mr. Sean POLLION
08 Librarian .... Mrs. Eunice TEEL
37 Director of Financial Aid .... Mrs. Virginia PANOFF
18 Director of Physical Plant .... Mr. Jeff GARDNER
84 Dir Enrollment Services/Registrar .... Ms. Renee DEYOUNG
21 Controller .... Mr. Troy SLATER
29 Director Alumni Relations .... Mr. Sean POLLION
35 Dir Student Activities/Camp Housing .... Mr. Josh DEAL
15 Human Resources .... Ms. Diana SOUZA
40 Bookstore Manager .... Ms. Julie WEAVER

Northern Michigan University (C)

1401 Presque Isle Avenue, Marquette MI 49855-5301
County: Marquette FICE Identification: 002301
Unit ID: 171456
Telephone: (906) 227-1000 Carnegie Class: Master's M
FAX Number: (906) 227-2204 Calendar System: Semester
URL: www.nmu.edu
Established: 1899 Annual Undergrad Tuition & Fees (In-State): $8,709
Enrollment: 9,405 Coed
Affiliation or Control: State IRS Status: 501(c)3
Highest Offering: Beyond Master's But Less Than Doctorate
Program: Occupational; 2-Year Principally Bachelor's Creditable; Liberal Arts And General; Teacher Preparatory; Professional
Accreditation: NH, BUS, DMOLS, ENGT, MLTAD, MT, MUS, NURSE, RAD, SURGT, SW, TEAC

01 President .... Dr. David S. HAYNES
10 VP for Finance & Administration .... Mr. R. Gavin LEACH
30 Vice Pres Advancement .... Ms. Martha B. HAYNES
09 Assoc VP for Inst Research .... Dr. Paul B. DUBY
21 Assoc VP Business & Auxiliary Svcs .... Mr. Arthur J. GISCHIA
05 Interim Provost/VP Academic Affairs .... Dr. Paul L. LANG
32 Assoc Prov Student Svcs/Enrollment .... Mr. William A. BERNARD
20 Associate Provost Academic Affairs .... Dr. Terrance L. SEETHOFF
58 Asst Provost Graduate Educ/Research .... Dr. Brian CHERRY
90 Dean Academic Information Services .... Ms. Darlene M. WALCH
35 Dean of Students .... Ms. Christine G. GREER
49 Dean of Arts & Sciences .... Dr. Michael J. BROADWAY
50 Dean Walker L. Cisler Col Bus .... Dr. Jamal A. RASHED
107 Interim Dean College Prof Studies .... Dr. Harvey A. WALLACE
06 Registrar .... Ms. Kim M. ROTUNDO
43 General Counsel .... Ms. Catherine L. DEHLIN
44 Director Major/Planned Giving .... Ms. Amy M. HUBINGER
27 Director Communications & Marketing .... Ms. Cindy L. PAAVOLA
36 Dir of Acad & Career Advisement .... Mr. James G. GADZINSKI
37 Director of Financial Aid .... Mr. Michael R. ROTUNDO
38 Head Counseling Center .... Ms. Marie M. AHO
88 Dir US Olympic Education Center .... Mr. Forrest KARR
88 Director Glenn T. Seaborg Center .... Ms. Debra L. HOMEIER
41 Athletic Director .... Mr. Forrest KARR
19 Interim Dir Public Safety/Pol, Svcs .... Mr. Michael J. BATH
39 Director Housing/Residence Life .... Mr. Carl D. HOLM
07 Director of Admissions .... Ms. Gerri L. DANIELS
23 Chief of Staff/Physician .... Dr. David M. LOUMA
15 Director of Human Resources .... Ms. Ann M. SHERMAN
26 Marketing Director .... Ms. Anne M. STARK
28 Dir Multicult Educ/Resource Center .... Vacant
85 Exec Dir International Programs .... Vacant
92 Director of Honors Program .... Dr. David H. WOOD
88 Director of Support/Consulting Svcs .... Ms. Felecia J. FLACK
24 Director Broadcast & AV Services .... Mr. Eric L. SMITH
29 Director Alumni Operations .... Vacant
40 Bookstore Manager .... Mr. Michael J. KUZAK
18 Associate VP Eng & Plan/Facilities .... Ms. Kathy A. RICHARDS
13 Chief Technology Officer .... Mr. David W. MAKI

Northwestern Michigan College (D)

1701 E Front Street, Traverse City MI 49686-3061
County: Grand Traverse FICE Identification: 002302
Unit ID: 171483
Telephone: (231) 995-1000 Carnegie Class: Assoc/Pub-R-M
FAX Number: (231) 995-1339 Calendar System: Semester
URL: www.nmc.edu
Established: 1951 Annual Undergrad Tuition & Fees (In-District): $2,584
Enrollment: 6,390 Coed
Affiliation or Control: Local IRS Status: 501(c)3
Highest Offering: Associate Degree
Program: 2-Year Principally Bachelor's Creditable
Accreditation: NH, ACFEI, DA

01 President .... Mr. Timothy J. NELSON
05 Vice Pres for Educational Services .... Dr. Stephen N. SICILIANO
88 VP Lifelong/Professional Learning .... Ms. Marguerite C. COTTO
10 Interim VP of Fin & Administration .... Ms. Vicki COOK
04 Exec Assistant to President & Board .... Ms. Holly J. GORTON
08 Exec Director Lrng Res/Technologies .... Mr. Craig A. MULDER
15 Director of Human Resources .... Mr. Aaron T. BEACH
88 Exec Dir of Dennos Museum Center .... Mr. Eugene A. JENNEMAN
32 Dean for Enrollment & Student Svcs .... Dr. Chris WEBER
24 Director Educational Media Tech .... Ms. Janet W. OLIVER
12 Supt Great Lakes Maritime Academy .... RAdm. Gerard ACHENBACH, USMS
20 Dir Academic Affairs/Business Div .... Ms. Susan DECAMILLIS
31 Director Extended Educ Services .... Ms. Carol A. EVANS
06 Registrar .... Ms. Carol J. TABERSKI
23 Director of Health Services .... Ms. Renee R. JACOBSON
09 Dir Research Planning Effectiveness .... Dr. Darby L. HILLER-FREUND
18 Director of Campus Services .... Mr. Paul PERRY
26 Exec Dir of Communications & PR .... Mr. Andrew B. DOLAN
44 Exec Dir of Resource Dev & Found .... Ms. Rebecca M. TEAHEN
62 Director of Library Services .... Ms. Tina J. ULRICH
88 Director Great Lakes Culinary Inst .... Mr. Frederick L. LAUGHLIN
88 Director Upward Bound .... Ms. Patty ROTH
88 Director Training & Research .... Mr. Richard R. WOLIN
21 Controller .... Ms. Cheryl SULLIVAN
96 Purchasing Manager .... Mr. Stephen A. WESTPHAL
19 Asst Dir Campus Safety & Security .... Mr. Jim WHITE
07 Director of Admissions .... Mr. James S. BENSLEY
37 Director of Financial Aid .... Ms. Pam PALERMO
36 Director of Learning Services .... Ms. Kari L. KAHLER
68 Coordinator Physical Education .... Mr. Peter W. LACOURSE
60 Communications Chair .... Ms. Deirdre M. MAHONEY
75 Director of Technical Division .... Mr. Ed BAILEY
88 Director of Aviation .... Mr. Aaron COOK
79 Humanities Chair .... Mr. Jim PRESS
81 Science & Math Chair .... Mr. Ernie L. EAST
76 Health Occupations Chair .... Ms. Jean M. ROKOS

Northwood University (E)

4000 Whiting Drive, Midland MI 48640-2398
County: Midland FICE Identification: 004072
Unit ID: 171492
Telephone: (989) 837-4200 Carnegie Class: Spec/Bus
FAX Number: (989) 837-4111 Calendar System: Semester
URL: www.northwood.edu
Established: 1959 Annual Undergrad Tuition & Fees: $21,118
Enrollment: 6,496 Coed
Affiliation or Control: Independent Non-Profit IRS Status: 501(c)3
Highest Offering: Master's
Program: Liberal Arts And General; Business Emphasis
Accreditation: NH

01 President & Chief Executive Officer .... Dr. Keith A. PRETTY
05 EVP/CAO/COO .... Dr. Kristin STEHOUWER
10 Vice President Finance & Treasurer .... Mr. W. Karl STEPHAN
30 Vice President Alumni & Advancement .... Mr. Arnold D'AMBROSIO
88 VP Strategic/Corporate Alliances .... Dr. Timothy G. NASH
84 VP Marketing/Communications/PR .... Mr. John O. YOUNG
12 President Michigan Campus .... Dr. William K. BATEMAN
12 President Northwood Florida .... Dr. Tom L. DUNCAN
12 President Northwood Texas .... Dr. Kevin G. FEGAN
51 Associate Dean Adult Degree Program .... Ms. Rhonda C. ANDERSON
07 Dean of Admissions .... Vacant
32 Dean of Students .... Mr. Larry J. LINDSEY
85 Interim Dean International Programs .... Ms. Mamiko REEVES
45 Director of Asset Management .... Mr. David L. BENDER
26 Director of Communications .... Mr. Michael D. CURRY
06 Registrar .... Ms. Marisa L. TOSCHKOFF
09 Dir of Institutional Effectiveness .... Vacant
37 System Financial Aid Director .... Mr. Mark A. MARTIN
15 Director of Human Resources .... Ms. Pamela L. CHRISTIE
21 System Bussines Officer .... Ms. Susan M. RIDGWAY
29 Executive Director Alumni Relations .... Ms. Julie L. FELSKE

Oakland Community College (F)

2480 Opdyke Road, Bloomfield Hills MI 48304-2266
County: Oakland FICE Identification: 002303
Unit ID: 171535
Telephone: (248) 341-2000 Carnegie Class: Assoc/Pub-S-MC
FAX Number: (248) 341-2118 Calendar System: Semester
URL: www.oaklandcc.edu
Established: 1964 Annual Undergrad Tuition & Fees (In-District): $2,373
Enrollment: 29,262 Coed
Affiliation or Control: State/Local IRS Status: 501(c)3
Highest Offering: Associate Degree
Program: Occupational; 2-Year Principally Bachelor's Creditable
Accreditation: NH, ACFEI, ADNUR, DH, DMS, MAC, RAD, SURGT

01 Chancellor .... Dr. Timothy R. MEYER
05 Vice Chanc Academic Affairs .... Dr. Richard E. HOLCOMB
45 Vice Chanc for Planning & Devel .... Vacant
11 Vice Chanc Administrative Services .... Mr. Clarence E. BRANTLEY
26 Vice Chancellor External Affairs .... Ms. Sharon MILLER
04 Exec Assistant to Chancellor .... Ms. Cherie A. FOSTER
12 President Highland Lakes Campus .... Dr. Gordon F. MAY
12 President Royal Oak/Southfield Camp .... Dr. Steven J. REIF
12 President Auburn Hills Campus .... Dr. Patricia A. DOLLY
12 President Orchard Ridge Campus .... Dr. Jacqueline SHADKO
16 Chief Human Resources Officer .... Vacant
27 Director College Communication .... Mr. George A. CARTSONIS
13 Chief Information Officer .... Vacant
84 Dean Enrollment Services .... Mrs. Carla R. MATHEWS
76 Dean Allied Health .... Dr. Cynthia ROMAN
26 Executive Director Marketing .... Ms. Janet ROBERTS
72 Exec Director Tech Infrastructure .... Mr. Robert J. MONTGOMERY
88 Director of Training .... Ms. Pamela L. DORRIS
20 Dean Academic Services .... Vacant
06 Registrar .... Mr. Stephen M. LINDEN
18 Director Physical Facilities .... Mr. Daniel P. CHEREWICK
14 Exec Director Tech Applications .... Mr. David M. DUNSHEE
19 Director Public Safety .... Mr. Terry L. MCCAULEY
30 Chief Strategic Devel Officer .... Vacant
21 Controller .... Mrs. Gail S. PITTS
22 Director Employee Relations .... Mr. Gary S. CASEY
102 Director of OCC Foundation .... Ms. Cynthia A. TANNER
36 Director Placement/Coop Education .... Mr. Willie L. LLOYD
41 Athletic Director .... Ms. Laurie G. HUBER
96 Director Purchasing/Auxiliary Svcs .... Ms. Gheretta R. HARRIS
09 Director Assessment & Effectiveness .... Mr. Martin A. ORLOWSKI
21 Director Financial Services .... Ms. Sharon K. CONVERSE
37 Director Financial Res/Scholarships .... Mrs. Wilma B. PORTER
15 Director of Personnel Services .... Mrs. Margaret R. CARROLL
35 Exec Director Student Services .... Vacant
29 Coordinator Alumni Association .... Vacant

Oakland University (G)

2200 N. Squirrel Road, Rochester MI 48309-4401
County: Oakland FICE Identification: 002307
Unit ID: 171571
Telephone: (248) 370-2100 Carnegie Class: DRU
FAX Number: N/A Calendar System: Semester
URL: www.oakland.edu
Established: 1957 Annual Undergrad Tuition & Fees (In-State): $10,398
Enrollment: 19,379 Coed
Affiliation or Control: State IRS Status: 501(c)3
Highest Offering: Doctorate
Program: Liberal Arts And General; Teacher Preparatory; Professional
Accreditation: NH, ANEST, BUS, BUSA, CACREP, CS, DANCE, ENG, ENGR, #MED, MUS, NURSE, PTA, SPAA, SW, TEAC, THEA

01 President .... Dr. Gary D. RUSSI

04 Executive Asst to the President ......Ms. Karen S. KUKUK
05 Int Sr VP Academic Affairs/Provost ......Dr. Susan M. AWBREY
32 VP Student Affs & Enrollment Mgmt ......Dr. Mary Beth SNYDER
30 VP Dev Alumni Community Engagement ......Mr. Eric D. BARRITT
10 VP Finance & Administration ......Mr. John W. BEAGHAN
43 VP Legal Affairs & General Counsel ......Mr. Victor A. ZAMBARDI
86 VP Government Relations ......Ms. Rochelle A. BLACK
12 AVP Outreach/Exec Dir OU Macomb .. Dr. Betty J. YOUNGBLOOD
66 Dean of Nursing ......Dr. Kerri D. SCHUILING
54 Dean Engineer & Computer Science ......Dr. Louay M. CHAMRA
76 Dean School Health Sciences ......Dr. Kenneth R. HIGHTOWER
53 Dean Educ & Human Services ......Dr. Louis B. GALLIEN
49 Dean College Arts & Sciences ......Dr. Ronald A. SUDOL
50 Dean School of Business Admin ......Dr. Mohan R. TANNIRU
63 Dean School of Medicine ......Dr. Robert FOLBERG
62 Dean of the Library ......Ms. Adriene I. LIM
20 Senior Associate Provost ......Dr. Susan M. AWBREY
46 Vice Provost Research ......Dr. Dorothy A. NELSON
27 Chief Information Officer ......Ms. Theresa M. ROWE
09 Dir Inst Research & Assessment ......Ms. Laura A. SCHARTMAN
24 Asst VP Classrm Spprt/Instruct Tech ......Mr. George T. PREISINGER
90 Asst VP E-Learning/Instr Support ......Dr. Catheryn L. CHEAL
20 Asst VP Academic Affairs ......Ms. Peggy S. COOKE
88 Dir Ctr Excellence Tchg Lrng ......Dr. Judith ABLESER
88 Dir Eye Research Institute ......Dr. Frank GIBLIN
88 Director FAJRI ......Dr. Sayed NASSAR
21 Asst VP Finance & Administration ......Mr. Stephen W. ROBERTS
18 Assoc VP Facilities Mgmt ......Mr. Terry STOLLSTEIMER
15 Asst VP University Human Resources ......Mr. Ronald P. WATSON
102 Asst VP & Campaign Director ......Ms. Bernice LOPATA
07 Asst VP Student Affs Admissions ......Ms. Eleanor L. REYNOLDS
35 Asst VP & Dean Student Life ......Mr. Glenn MCINTOSH
19 Chief of Police ......Mr. Samuel C. LUCIDO
06 Registrar ......Mr. Steven J. SHABLIN
44 Director Annual Giving Programs ......Ms. Starr CORNELL
37 Director of Financial Aid ......Ms. Cindy L. HERMSEN
29 Director of Alumni Relations ......Vacant
27 Director Communications & Marketing ......Vacant
41 Director of Athletics ......Mr. Tracy A. HUTH
28 Dir Inclus Intercu Initiatives/Atty ......Ms. Joi M. CUNNINGHAM
39 Director of University Housing ......Mr. James R. ZENTMEYER
36 Director Career Services ......Mr. Wayne J. THIBODEAU
38 Director Counseling Center ......Dr. David J. SCHWARTZ
85 Director International Students ......Mr. David John J. ARCHBOLD
88 Director Disability Support Svcs ......Ms. Linda G. SISSON
96 Purchasing Manager ......Ms. Maria E. EBNER-SMITH

Olivet College (A)

320 S Main Street, Olivet MI 49076-9406
County: Eaton FICE Identification: 002308
Unit ID: 171599
Telephone: (269) 749-7000 Carnegie Class: Bac/Diverse
FAX Number: (269) 749-7600 Calendar System: Semester
URL: www.olivetcollege.edu
Established: 1844 Annual Undergrad Tuition & Fees: $21,971
Enrollment: 1,128 Coed
Affiliation or Control: Independent Non-Profit IRS Status: 501(c)3
Highest Offering: Master's
Program: Liberal Arts And General; Teacher Preparatory
Accreditation: NH, @TEAC

01 President ......Dr. Steven M. COREY
05 Provost and Dean of the College ......Dr. Maria DAVIS
10 Sr Vice Pres/Chief Financial Ofcr ......Mr. William KURTZ
11 Vice President Admin/Physical Plant ......Mr. Larry COLVIN
84 Vice Pres Enrollment Management ......Vacant
32 Vice President/Dean Student Life ......Dr. Linda LOGAN
30 Vice Pres Development/Inst Advance ......Vacant
06 Registrar ......Ms. Leslie SULLIVAN
41 Athletic Director ......Ms. Heather BATEMAN
42 Director of Church Relations ......Mr. Michael F. FALES
36 Int Dir Career Services Network ......Ms. Joanne WILLIAMS
37 Director of Student Financial Aid ......Ms. Libby JEAN
07 Director of Admissions ......Ms. Melissa CASAREZ
94 Director of Women's Resource Center ......Ms. Dianne THOMAS
39 Student Housing ......Ms. Tamyra WALTERS
13 Information & Technology Manager ......Mr. Suresh ACHARYA
15 Human Resources Specialist ......Mrs. Therese WOOD
29 Alumni Relations Coordinator ......Ms. Martha MASON JENNINGS

Puritan Reformed Theological Seminary (B)

2965 Leonard St NE, Grand Rapids MI 49525
County: Kent Identification: 667099
Telephone: (616) 977-0599 Carnegie Class: Not Classified
FAX Number: (616) 285-3246 Calendar System: Semester
URL: puritanseminary.org
Established: 1995 Annual Graduate Tuition & Fees: N/A
Enrollment: N/A Coed
Affiliation or Control: Independent Non-Profit IRS Status: 501(c)3
Highest Offering: Master's; No Undergraduates
Program: Religious Emphasis
Accreditation: @BI

01 President ......Dr. Joel R. BEEKE

Robert B. Miller College (C)

450 North Avenue, Battle Creek MI 49017-3397
County: Calhoun FICE Identification: 040943
Unit ID: 448804
Telephone: (269) 660-8021 Carnegie Class: Bac/Diverse
FAX Number: (269) 565-2180 Calendar System: Semester
URL: www.millercollege.edu
Established: 2002 Annual Undergrad Tuition & Fees: $10,590
Enrollment: 367 Coed
Affiliation or Control: Independent Non-Profit IRS Status: 501(c)3
Highest Offering: Baccalaureate
Program: Liberal Arts And General; Teacher Preparatory; Business Emphasis
Accreditation: NH, NURSE, @TEAC

01 President ......Dr. David J. HARRIS
11 Director of Administrative Services ......Ms. Lorene E. FRISBIE
05 Provost ......Ms. Gloria ROBERTSON
32 Vice President of Student Services ......Mr. Chad DANIELSON
37 Dean Student Svcs & Financial Aid ..Ms. Kimberly F. CVITKOVIC

Rochester College (D)

800 W Avon Road, Rochester Hills MI 48307-2764
County: Oakland FICE Identification: 002288
Unit ID: 170967
Telephone: (248) 218-2000 Carnegie Class: Bac/Diverse
FAX Number: (248) 218-2025 Calendar System: Semester
URL: www.rc.edu
Established: 1959 Annual Undergrad Tuition & Fees: $17,976
Enrollment: 1,045 Coed
Affiliation or Control: Independent Non-Profit IRS Status: 501(c)3
Highest Offering: Master's
Program: Liberal Arts And General
Accreditation: NH, NURSE, @TEAC

01 President ......Dr. Thomas R. SHELLY
05 Vice President Academic Affairs ......Dr. John D. BARTON
84 Vice President Enrollment ......Mr. Klint PLEASANT
10 Chief Financial Officer ......Mr. Mark VANRHEENEN
30 Assoc Vice Pres Inst Advancement ......Mr. Scott SAMUELS
20 Academic Dean ......Dr. Katrina VANDERWOUDE
21 Controller ......Ms. Kim WILLIAMS
14 Director Operational Support ......Mr. Mark JOHNSON
50 Chair Div Col of Bus/Prof Studies ......Mr. Larry NORMAN
49 Chair Div Col of Arts & Sciences ......Dr. David KELLER
15 Director of Human Resources ......Ms. Lindsey M. DUNFEE
26 Director of Mktg & Design ......Mr. Elliot JONES
32 Dean of Students ......Mr. Brian COLE
37 Director of Student Financial Svcs ......Ms. Jessica BRISTOW
08 Director of Library Services ......Ms. Alison KELLER
06 Registrar ......Ms. Rebekah PINCHBACK
108 Director of Assessment ......Mr. J. Mark MANRY
29 Director of Alumni/Bookstore Mgr ......Mr. Larry STEWART
35 Assoc Dean of Students/Campus Life ......Mr. Terrill HALL
41 Director of Athletics ......Mr. Klint PLEASANT
42 Campus Minister ......Mr. Chris SHIELDS
19 Director of Safety & Security ......Mr. Shawn WESTAWAY
04 Assistant to the President ......Ms. Karen HART

Sacred Heart Major Seminary (E)

2701 Chicago Boulevard, Detroit MI 48206-1799
County: Wayne FICE Identification: 002313
Unit ID: 172033
Telephone: (313) 883-8500 Carnegie Class: Spec/Faith
FAX Number: (313) 868-6440 Calendar System: Semester
URL: www.shms.edu
Established: 1919 Annual Undergrad Tuition & Fees: $16,505
Enrollment: 466 Coed
Affiliation or Control: Roman Catholic IRS Status: 501(c)3
Highest Offering: Master's
Program: Liberal Arts And General; Professional
Accreditation: NH, THEOL

01 Rector & President ......Msgr. Todd LAJINESS
32 Vice Rector/Dean of Seminarians ......Rev. Gerard BATTERSBY
05 Dean of Studies ......Rev. Timothy LABOE
73 Dean of the Institute for Ministry ......Mrs. Janet DIAZ
10 Director Finance/Treasurer ......Ms. Ann Marie CONNOLLY
06 Registrar ......Mr. John MELDRUM
35 Director Undergraduate Seminarians ......Rev. Stephen BURR
38 Graduate Spiritual Director ......Rev. Daniel TRAPP
08 Library Director ......Mr. Christopher SPILKER
38 Undergraduate Spiritual Director ......Rev. Robert SPEZIA
58 Dir Graduate Pastoral Formation ......Rev. John VANDENAKKER

Saginaw Chippewa Tribal College (F)

2274 Enterprise Drive, Mount Pleasant MI 48858-2335
County: Isabella FICE Identification: 037723
Unit ID: 441070
Telephone: (989) 775-4123 Carnegie Class: Tribal
FAX Number: (989) 775-4528 Calendar System: Semester
URL: www.sagchip.edu
Established: 1998 Annual Undergrad Tuition & Fees: $2,040
Enrollment: 133 Coed
Affiliation or Control: Tribal Control IRS Status: 501(c)3
Highest Offering: Associate Degree
Program: 2-Year Principally Bachelor's Creditable
Accreditation: NH

01 President ......Ms. Carla SINEWAY
05 Dean of Instruction ......Vacant
32 Dean of Student Services ......Ms. Kathryn DENHEETEN
07 Admissions Officer/Registrar ......Ms. Patricia ALONZO
37 Financial Aid Officer ......Ms. Tracy REED

Saginaw Valley State University (G)

7400 Bay Road, University Center MI 48710-0001
County: Saginaw FICE Identification: 002314
Unit ID: 172051
Telephone: (989) 964-4000 Carnegie Class: Master's L
FAX Number: (989) 964-0180 Calendar System: Semester
URL: www.svsu.edu
Established: 1963 Annual Undergrad Tuition & Fees (In-State): $8,120
Enrollment: 10,790 Coed
Affiliation or Control: State IRS Status: 501(c)3
Highest Offering: Master's
Program: Liberal Arts And General; Teacher Preparatory; Professional
Accreditation: NH, BUS, ENG, MT, MUS, NURSE, OT, SW, TED

01 President ......Dr. Eric R. GILBERTSON
05 Provost/VP Academic Affairs ......Dr. Donald J. BACHAND
10 Exec VP Admin & Business Affairs ......Mr. James G. MULADORE
84 Vice Pres Enrollment Management ......Mr. James P. DWYER
32 VP Student Affairs/Dean of Students ......Ms. Merry Jo BRANDIMORE
86 Spec Asst to Pres/Government Rels ......Dr. Eugene J. HAMILTON
28 Spec Asst to Pres/Diversity Pgms ......Dr. Mamie T. THORNS
04 Exec Asst Pres/Dir Public Affairs ......Dr. Carlos RAMET
45 Assoc Provost ......Dr. Marc PERETZ
09 Assoc VP Institutional Research ......Dr. Clifford DORNE
21 Assoc VP Admin & Business Affairs ....Mr. Ronald E. PORTWINE
18 Asst Vice Pres Campus Facilities ......Mr. Stephen L. HOCQUARD
13 Exec Dir Information Tech Svcs ......Vacant
85 Director International Programs ......Ms. Stephanie SIEGGREEN
07 Director Admissions ......Ms. Jennifer PAHL
88 Director Integrated Marketing ......Ms. Jan R. POPPE
36 Dir Career Planning & Placement ......Mr. Michael MAJOR
21 University Controller ......Ms. Susan L. CRANE
21 Director Business Services ......Ms. Connie J. SCHWEITZER
88 University Ombudsman ......Mr. Richard P. THOMPSON
29 Director Alumni ......Mr. Kevin J. SCHULTZ
14 Director Information Tech Svcs ......Mr. Patrick C. SAMOLEWSKI
31 Dir Media & Community Relations ......Mr. J. J. BOEHM
08 Director Library/Learning Resources ......Ms. Linda J. FARYNK
25 Director Spnsrd/Acad Pgms Support ......Ms. Janet D. RENTSCH
15 Director Human Resources ......Dr. Jack VANHOORELBEKE
19 Chief University Police ......Mr. Ronald E. TREPKOWSKI
37 Director Scholarships/Financial Aid ......Mr. Robert L. LEMUEL
51 Director Continuing Education ......Ms. Monica B. REYES
38 Dir Student Counseling Center ......Ms. Jennifer N. ORDWAY
41 Director of Athletics ......Mr. Michael E. WATSON
44 Director Annual & Planned Giving ......Mr. Joseph A. VOGL
88 Dir Sch & University Partnerships ......Mr. Joseph ROUSSEAU
88 Dir Enviornmental Health & Safety ......Mr. Robert J. TUTSOCK
06 Registrar ......Mr. Chris LOONEY
88 Exec Dir Ctr for Business/Econ Dev ......Mr. Harold L. LEAVER
93 Director Multicultural Services ......Mr. Shawn WILSON
20 Associate Provost ......Dr. Marc H. PERETZ
26 Dir Media & Community Relations ......Mr. J. J. BOEHM
102 Executive Director SVSU Foundation ......Mr. Andrew J. BETHUNE
40 Bookstore Manager ......Mr. Chris J. PAWLOSKI
96 Purchasing Manager ......Mr. Joshua M. WEBB
35 Asst Dean Student Life ......Mr. Tony THOMSON
49 Dean Arts & Behavioral Science ......Dr. Joni BOYE-BEAMAN
50 Dean Business & Management ......Dr. Jill WETMORE
53 Int Dean College of Education ......Dr. Susie EMOND
76 Dean of Health & Human Services ......Dr. Judith RULAND
54 Dean Science Engr & Technology ......Dr. Deborah HUNTLEY

St. Clair County Community College (H)

323 Erie Street, PO Box 5015, Port Huron MI 48061-5015
County: St. Clair FICE Identification: 002310
Unit ID: 172291
Telephone: (810) 984-3881 Carnegie Class: Assoc/Pub-S-SC
FAX Number: (810) 984-4730 Calendar System: Semester
URL: www.sc4.edu
Established: 1923 Annual Undergrad Tuition & Fees (In-District): $3,253
Enrollment: 4,740 Coed
Affiliation or Control: Local IRS Status: 501(c)3
Highest Offering: Associate Degree
Program: Occupational; 2-Year Principally Bachelor's Creditable
Accreditation: NH, ADNUR, RAD

01 President ......Dr. Kevin A. POLLOCK
04 Executive Assistant to President ......Ms. Mary L. HAWTIN
10 Vice Pres Administrative Services ......Mr. Kirk A. KRAMER
05 Vice President Academic Services ......Mrs. Denise M. MCNEIL
32 Vice President Student Services ......Mr. Pete LACEY
15 Exec Director Human Resources/LR ......Mr. Kenneth M. LORD
35 Dean of Students & Grants ......Dr. Patricia Y. LEONARD
23 Director of Health/Human Services ......Ms. Cindy NICHOLSON
37 Dir of Financial Assistance/Svcs ......Ms. Josephine R. CASSAR
06 Registrar ......Ms. Carrie BEARSS
18 Director of Physical Plant ......Mr. Thomas R. DONOVAN
21 Controller ......Ms. Mary K. BRUNNER
26 Exec Dir PR/Mktg/Legis Affairs ......Mr. Shawn M. STARKEY
41 Dir Campus Activities/Athletics ......Mr. Dale R. VOS
106 Dean of eLearning/Instr Technology ......Ms. Linda DAVIS
30 Dir Advancement/Alumni Relations ......Mr. David GOETZE
20 Associate Dean of Instruction ......Dr. Suzanne O'BRIEN
08 Director of Library Services ......Mr. Christopher RENNIE

Schoolcraft College (A)

18600 Haggerty Road, Livonia MI 48152-2696
County: Wayne FICE Identification: 002315
Unit ID: 172200
Telephone: (734) 462-4400 Carnegie Class: Assoc/Pub-S-SC
FAX Number: (734) 462-4507 Calendar System: Semester
URL: www.schoolcraft.edu
Established: 1961 Annual Undergrad Tuition & Fees (In-District): $3,056
Enrollment: 12,770 Coed
Affiliation or Control: Local IRS Status: 501(c)3
Highest Offering: Associate Degree
Program: Occupational; 2-Year Principally Bachelor's Creditable
Accreditation: NH, ACFEI, MAC

01 President .... Dr. Conway A. JEFFRESS
10 Vice Pres/Chief Financial Officer .... Mr. Glenn CERNY
05 Vice Pres of Instruction .... Mr. Richard WEINKAUF
46 VP Planning/Information Management .... Ms. Susan LUPO
32 Dean of Student Services .... Ms. Cheryl M. HAGEN
49 Dean Liberal Arts & Sciences .... Ms. Cheryl HAWKINS
75 Dean Occupational Prog/Econ Dev .... Mr. William DUNBAR
45 Assoc Dean Learning Support Svcs .... Dr. Deborah DAIEK
88 Assoc Dean College Centers .... Dr. Todd SCOTT
56 Assoc Dean Distance Learning .... Ms. Cheri HOLMAN
51 Assoc Dean Cont Educ/Prof Develop .... Dr. Leslie PETTY
35 Assoc Dean Student Services .... Ms. Michelle KOSS
72 Asst Dean Occupational Programs .... Dr. Mark POGLIANO
30 Exec Director Devel/Govt Relations .... Dr. James RYAN
15 Exec Director of Human Resources .... Ms. Cindy J. KOENIGSKNECHT
21 Exec Dir Business Services/Risk Mgt .... Mr. James R. POLKOWSKI
12 Director of College Centers .... Dr. Bonnie HECKARD
09 Director of Business Intelligence .... Mr. Rob STIRTON
84 Dir of Enrollment Svcs/Registrar .... Ms. Nicole WILSON-FENNELL
37 Director of Financial Aid .... Ms. Regina MOSLEY
26 Director of Marketing .... Mr. Martin HEATOR
19 Director of Campus Security Police .... Mr. Steven KAUFMAN
21 Director of Finance .... Mr. Jeffrey LILLEY
96 Director of Purchasing .... Mr. Matthew WILSON

Siena Heights University (B)

1247 Siena Heights Drive, Adrian MI 49221-1796
County: Lenawee FICE Identification: 002316
Unit ID: 172264
Telephone: (517) 263-0731 Carnegie Class: Master's M
FAX Number: (517) 264-7704 Calendar System: Semester
URL: www.sienaheights.edu
Established: 1919 Annual Undergrad Tuition & Fees: $21,152
Enrollment: 2,690 Coed
Affiliation or Control: Roman Catholic IRS Status: 501(c)3
Highest Offering: Beyond Master's But Less Than Doctorate
Program: Occupational; Liberal Arts And General; Teacher Preparatory; Professional
Accreditation: NH, ART, NURSE, SW, @TEAC

01 President .... Dr. Peg ALBERT, OP
10 Sr Vice Pres for Business/Finance .... Dr. J. Lee JOHNSON
30 Vice President for Advancement .... Mr. Mitchell P. BLONDE
05 Vice President for Academic Affairs .... Dr. Sharon R. WEBER, OP
84 Vice Pres of Enrollment Mgmt Svcs .... Mr. C. Patrick PALMER
26 Assoc Vice Pres Advancement .... Mrs. Jennifer H. CHURCH
58 Dean of Graduate Studies .... Mrs. Anne HOOGHART
107 Dean College Professional Studies .... Mrs. Deborah CARTER
32 Dean for Students .... Mr. Michael ORLANDO
06 Registrar .... Mrs. Brenda K. DOREMUS
08 Library Director .... Dr. Robert W. GORDON
13 Director Computer Systems/Services .... Mr. Robert C. METZ
41 Director of Athletics .... Mr. Frederick M. SMITH
15 Human Resource Director .... Mr. Michael L. KARABETSOS
42 Director of Campus Ministry .... Mr. Thomas PUSZCZEWICZ
38 Director of Counseling Services .... Mrs. Sandy MORLEY
20 Director of Academic Advising .... Ms. Wiona PORATH
18 Supt of Buildings & Grounds .... Mr. Brian BERTRAM
39 Director of Residence Life .... Mr. Justin LANDIS
19 Director of Campus Security .... Mrs. Cindy A. BIRDWELL
23 Director of Health Services .... Ms. Marlene WALDVOGEL
29 Director of Alumni Relations .... Mrs. Jennifer H. CHURCH
36 Director of Career Services .... Mrs. Melissa A. GROWDEN
44 Director of Donor Relations .... Mrs. Jenn BROOKET
88 Dir of Integrated Univ Marketing .... Mr. Doug GOODNOUGH
37 Director Student Financial Aid .... Mr. Christian HOWARD
21 Controller .... Ms. Mary KRUSE
07 Director of Admissions .... Ms. Sara JOHNSON
44 Coordinator of Annual Fund .... Mrs. Kate HAMILTON
49 Dean College of Arts and Science .... Dr. Mark SCHERSTEN

Southwestern Michigan College (C)

58900 Cherry Grove Road, Dowagiac MI 49047-9793
County: Cass FICE Identification: 002317
Unit ID: 172307
Telephone: (269) 782-1000 Carnegie Class: Assoc/Pub-R-M
FAX Number: (269) 782-8414 Calendar System: Semester
URL: www.swmich.edu
Established: 1964 Annual Undergrad Tuition & Fees (In-District): $4,537
Enrollment: 3,029 Coed
Affiliation or Control: State/Local IRS Status: 501(c)3
Highest Offering: Associate Degree
Program: Occupational; 2-Year Principally Bachelor's Creditable
Accreditation: NH

01 President .... Dr. David MATHEWS
100 Chief of Staff .... Mr. John FANNIN
03 Exec Vice Pres/Chief Operating Ofcr .... Dr. Diane CHADDOCK
10 Vice President Chief Business Ofcr .... Ms. Susan COULSTON
27 Chief Information Officer .... Mr. Ronald YOUNG
05 Vice President of Instruction .... Dr. David FLEMING
26 Exec Dir of Mktg Enrollment Mgmt .... Mr. Gregory DERUE
32 Exec Dir Student Housing/Camp Life .... Ms. Eileen CROUSE
88 Director of Developmental Studies .... Dr. Naomi LUDMAN
88 Dean of Academic Studies .... Dr. Scott TOPPING
66 Dean School Nursing/Human Services .... Ms. Rebecca JELLISON
103 Dean of Workforce Ed/Bus Solutions .... Mr. Thomas BUSZEK
09 Director of Institutional Research .... Dr. Angela CARRICO
18 Director of Buildings & Grounds .... Mr. George DIERICKX
37 Director of Financial Aid .... Vacant
15 Director of Human Resources .... Ms. Diana CLARK
88 Senior Budget Analyst .... Ms. Breighan BROWN
88 Manager of Accounting .... Ms. Christy MANGUS
44 Director of Development .... Ms. Eileen TONEY
103 Director of Workforce Training .... Mr. Tim CHILDS
35 Dean of Students .... Ms. Angela PALSAK
88 Assistant Dean of Academic Support .... Mr. Shane VARGA
08 Director of Library Services .... Ms. Colleen WELSCH
06 Director of Records/Registrar .... Ms. Kathy PETERSON
35 Director Student Support Services .... Ms. Laura SKILLINGS
88 Dir of Educational Talent Srch Prgm .... Ms. Amy ANDERSON
88 Dir of Acad Assess & Testing Svcs .... Ms. Charlotte MCGOWAN
84 Director of Enrollment Management .... Mr. Brent BREWER
39 Director of Student Housing .... Mr. Jason WILT
35 Director of Student Activity Center .... Mr. Shawn RAWSON

Spring Arbor University (D)

106 E Main Street, Spring Arbor MI 49283-9799
County: Jackson FICE Identification: 002318
Unit ID: 172334
Telephone: (517) 750-1200 Carnegie Class: Master's L
FAX Number: (517) 750-6620 Calendar System: Semester
URL: www.arbor.edu
Established: 1873 Annual Undergrad Tuition & Fees: $22,538
Enrollment: 4,271 Coed
Affiliation or Control: Free Methodist IRS Status: 501(c)3
Highest Offering: Master's
Program: Liberal Arts And General
Accreditation: NH, NURSE, SW, TEAC

01 President .... Dr. Charles H. WEBB
05 Provost/Chief Academic Officer .... Dr. Betty J. OVERTON-ADKINS
10 Vice Pres Finance & Administration .... Mr. Jerry L. WHITE
30 Vice Pres University Advancement .... Dr. Brent ELLIS
32 VP Student Development/Learning .... Mrs. Kimberly K. HAYWORTH
84 VP for Enrollment Services .... Mr. Matthew S. OSBORNE
13 VP Technology Services/CIO .... Mr. Jeff E. EDWARDS
20 Assoc VP for Academic Affairs .... Mr. Rod S. STEWART
100 Chief of Staff .... Mr. Damon M. SEACOTT
58 Interim Dean Sch Grad/Prof Studies .... Mrs. Natalie GIANETTI
58 Associate Dean Graduate Programs .... Dr. Carl E. PAVEY
107 Associate Dean Professional Studies .... Mrs. Tamara L. DINDOFFER
49 Int Dean School Arts & Sciences .... Mr. Roger M. VARLAND
50 Int Dean Gainey School of Business .... Dr. Caleb K. CHAN
53 Dean School of Education .... Dr. Linda G. SHERRILL
106 Dean SAU Online .... Mr. Todd MARSHALL
06 Registrar .... Mr. Tim WIEGERT
21 Controller .... Mrs. Dawn I. SCHNITKEY
41 Athletic Director .... Mr. John S. RIGGLEMAN
91 Asst VP Technology Services .... Mr. Michael K. DEVER
26 Asst VP for Univ Communications .... Mrs. Robyn L. FLORIAN
105 Director of Web Development .... Vacant
88 Director of Support Services .... Mrs. Christina E. RANDALL
106 Director Content and eLearning .... Mr. John R. MEREDITH
44 Executive Director of Development .... Mrs. Linda SCHAUB
07 Executive Director of Admissions .... Mr. Randy C. COMFORT
15 Assistant VP for Human Resources .... Mr. Randy S. ROSSMAN
08 Director Library .... Mr. Roy MEADOR
37 Director Student Financial Aid .... Mr. Geoff A. MARSH
29 Director Alumni Relations .... Mrs. Irene L. PRICE
09 Director Institutional Research .... Mr. Thomas P. KORMAN
18 Director of Physical Plant .... Mr. Larry OUSLEY
35 Asst VP Student Development .... Mr. Dan VANDERHILL
39 Asst Dean Students/Dir of Housing .... Mr. Robert C. PRATT
31 Asst Dean Students/Dir of Outreach .... Mr. Steven D. NEWTON
89 Director Retention & Fresh Programs .... Mrs. Robin R. SMITH
36 Director Career Svcs/Acad Advising .... Mr. John BECK
42 Chaplain .... Mr. Ronald L. KOPICKO
19 Director Campus Safety .... Mr. Tom D. FIERO
104 Director Cross Cultural Studies .... Mrs. Diane L. KURTZ
23 Director Student Health Services .... Mrs. Mary A. RICK
40 Bookstore Supervisor .... Vacant

SS. Cyril and Methodius Seminary (E)

3535 Indian Trail, Orchard Lake MI 48324-1623
County: Oakland FICE Identification: 037384
Unit ID: 260211
Telephone: (248) 683-0310 Carnegie Class: Not Classified
FAX Number: (248) 738-6735 Calendar System: Semester
URL: www.sscms.edu
Established: 1885 Annual Graduate Tuition & Fees: $15,350
Enrollment: 30 Coed
Affiliation or Control: Roman Catholic IRS Status: 501(c)3
Highest Offering: Master's; No Undergraduates
Program: Professional
Accreditation: THEOL

01 Rector/President .... RevCan. Thomas MACHALSKI
05 Academic Dean .... Rev. Leonard OBLOY

Thomas M. Cooley Law School (F)

300 S Capitol Avenue, Lansing MI 48933
County: Ingham FICE Identification: 012627
Unit ID: 172477
Telephone: (517) 371-5140 Carnegie Class: Spec/Law
FAX Number: (517) 334-5718 Calendar System: Semester
URL: www.cooley.edu
Established: 1972 Annual Graduate Tuition & Fees: $37,140
Enrollment: 3,745 Coed
Affiliation or Control: Independent Non-Profit IRS Status: 501(c)3
Highest Offering: First Professional Degree; No Undergraduates
Program: Professional
Accreditation: NH, LAW

01 President .... Don LEDUC
04 Executive Asst to the President .... Cherie BECK
05 Dean .... Don LEDUC
10 Chief Financial Officer .... Kathleen CONKLIN
11 Chief Operating Officer .... William SCHOETTLE
07 Dean Admissions .... Paul ZELENSKI
08 Associate Dean Library/Info Svcs .... Duane STROJNY
20 Associate Dean for Faculty .... Charles CERCONE
45 Associate Dean Planning/Programs .... M. Ann WOOD
36 Assoc Dean Career Prof Development .... Charles TOY
32 Assoc Dean Students/Professionalism .... Amy TIMMER
30 Associate Dean for Development .... James ROBB
13 Associate Dean for Information Tech .... Charles MICKENS
84 Assoc Dean for Enrollment Services .... Paul ZELENSKI
26 Assoc Dean for Community Relations .... Helen MICKENS
12 Associate Dean Auburn Hills .... John NUSSBAUMER
12 Associate Dean Grand Rapids .... Nelson MILLER
12 Asst Dean Tampa Bay .... Jeffre MARTLEW
23 Assoc Dean Ann Arbor .... Joan VESTRAND
104 Assoc Dean International Programs .... William WEINER
88 Assistant Dean Auburn HIlls .... Lisa HALUSHKA
88 Assistant Dean Ann Arbor .... Martha MOORE
88 Assistant Dean Grand Rapids .... Tracey BRAME
06 Registrar & Assistant Dean .... Sherida WYSOCKI
37 Director Financial Aid .... Richard BORUSZEWSKI
40 Director Bookstore .... Joelle TOPP
21 Controller .... Ronda BECK
29 Director Alumni Donor Relations .... Pamela HEOS
27 Director Communications .... Terry CARELLA
15 Director Human Resources .... Scott HARRISON
96 Purchasing Manager .... Theresa ISKRA
35 Director Student Services .... Christopher LEWIS

University of Detroit Mercy (G)

4001 W McNichols Road, Detroit MI 48221-3038
County: Wayne FICE Identification: 002323
Unit ID: 169716
Telephone: (313) 993-1000 Carnegie Class: Master's L
FAX Number: (313) 993-1229 Calendar System: Semester
URL: www.udmercy.edu
Established: 1877 Annual Undergrad Tuition & Fees: $34,530
Enrollment: 5,335 Coed
Affiliation or Control: Roman Catholic IRS Status: 501(c)3
Highest Offering: Doctorate
Program: Liberal Arts And General; Teacher Preparatory; Professional
Accreditation: NH, ANEST, ARCPA, BUS, CACREP, CLPSY, DENT, DH, ENG, LAW, NURSE, SW, @TEAC

01 President .... Dr. Antoine M. GARIBALDI
05 Provost and VP for Academic Affairs .... Ms. Pamela ZARKOWSKI
10 VP for Business & Finance and CFO .... Mr. Vincent ABATEMARCO
44 VP Dev/Major/Plan Gift Campn .... Mr. Gregory CASCIONE
07 Vice President Enrollment/Admission .... Ms. Denise WILLIAMS MALLETT
101 Corporate Council/Univ Secretary .... Ms. Monica BARBOUR
11 Assoc Vice Pres Facil Management .... Ms. Tamara BATCHELLER
15 Associate Vice Pres Human Resources .... Mr. Steven J. NELSON
27 Assoc VP Marketing & Public Affairs .... Ms. Liz PATTERSON
14 Associate Vice President ITS .... Mr. Edward TRACY, II
06 Associate VP/Registrar .... Ms. Diane M. PRAET
29 Assoc VP Annual Giving & Alumni Rel .... Vacant
32 Dean of Students .... Ms. Monica WILLIAMS
08 Dean of Libraries .... Ms. Margaret AUER
09 Director Institutional Research .... Ms. Elaine BELL
37 Director Scholarships & Aid .... Ms. Jenny MCALONAN
35 Director of Student Life .... Ms. Dorothy STEWART
41 Director of Athletics .... Ms. Karen L. GAITHER
42 Director University Ministry .... Mr. David NANTAIS
49 Interim Dean Col Lib Arts/Education .... Dr. Roy FINKENBINE
61 Dean School of Law .... Mr. Lloyd SEMPLE
54 Dean College Engineering & Science .... Vacant
48 Dean School of Architecture .... Mr. William WITTIG
50 Dean Col Business Admin .... Dr. Joseph EISENHAUER
52 Dean School of Dentistry .... Dr. Mert AKSU
76 Dean CHP/Nursing .... Dr. Christine PACINI
88 Dean Coop Education/Career Ctr .... Ms. Sheryl MCGRIFF
39 Director Residence Life .... Ms. Lanae GILL
04 Exec Asst to the President .... Ms. Lisa MACDONNELL
88 Executive Assistant to the Acad VP .... Vacant
85 Director International Students .... Vacant
36 Director Student Placement .... Vacant
38 Director Student Counseling .... Ms. Natalie WICKS
92 Director of Honors Program .... Mr. Jason ROCHE

96 Director of Purchasing ..... Ms. Tina A. MAITLAND
18 Director of Facility Ops/Const Mgmt .... Mr. David VANDELINDER
30 Coordinator of Advancement ..... Ms. Stephanie LANDERS

University of Michigan-Ann Arbor (A)

Ann Arbor MI 48109-1318
County: Washtenaw FICE Identification: 002325
Unit ID: 170976
Telephone: (734) 764-1817 Carnegie Class: RU/VH
FAX Number: N/A Calendar System: Trimester
URL: www.umich.edu
Established: 1817 Annual Undergrad Tuition & Fees (In-State): $12,994
Enrollment: 42,716 Coed
Affiliation or Control: State IRS Status: 501(c)3
Highest Offering: Doctorate
Program: Liberal Arts And General; Teacher Preparatory; Professional
Accreditation: NH, DANCE, ART, BUS, CLPSY, CS, DENT, DH, DIETD, DIETI, ENG, ENGR, HSA, IPSY, LAW, LIB, LSAR, MED, MIDWF, MUS, NURSE, PDPSY, PH, PHAR, PLNG, SW, TEAC

01 President ..... Dr. Mary Sue COLEMAN
05 Provost/Exec VP Academic Affs ..... Dr. Philip J. HANLON
10 Exec VP/Chief Financial Officer ..... Mr. Timothy P. SLOTTOW
17 Exec VP for Medical Affairs ..... Dr. Ora H. PESCOVITZ
30 Vice President Development ..... Mr. Jerry A. MAY
32 Vice President Student Affairs ..... Dr. E. Royster HARPER
46 Vice President for Research ..... Dr. Stephen R. FORREST
86 Vice Pres Governmental Relations ..... Ms. Cynthia H. WILBANKS
26 Vice Pres Global Communications ..... Ms. Lisa M. RUDGERS
43 Int Vice Pres/General Counsel ..... Ms. Debra A. KOWICH
101 Vice Pres/Sec of the University ..... Ms. Sally J. CHURCHILL
20 Sr Vice Provost Academic Affairs ..... Dr. Lester P. MONTS
04 Deputy Asst to the President ..... Ms. Erika J. HRABEC
100 Chief of Staff ..... Ms. Stephanie L. RIEGLE
20 Vice Provost Acad/Budget Affairs ..... Dr. Martha E. POLLACK
20 Vice Provost Acad & Faculty Affairs ..... Dr. Lori J. PIERCE
20 Vice Provost Acad & Faculty Affairs ..... Dr. Chris WHITMAN
58 Vice Provost Acad Affs Grad Stds ..... Dr. Janet A. WEISS
104 Vice Provost Intl Affairs ..... Dr. Mark A. TESSLER
09 Assoc Vice Provost & Exec Dir OBP ..... Ms. Glenna L. SCHWEITZER
07 Assoc VP/Exec Dir UG Admissions ..... Mr. Theodore L. SPENCER
88 Assoc Vice Provost/Exec Dir OAMI ..... Dr. John H. MATLOCK
88 Assoc Vice Provost/Exec Dir CRLT ..... Dr. Constance E. COOK
15 Assoc VP & Sr Dr Acad HR ..... Mr. Jeffery R. FRUMKIN
22 Assoc VP/Sr Dir Ofc Inst Equity ..... Mr. Anthony J. WALESBY
18 Assoc VP Facilities/Operations ..... Mr. Henry D. BAIER
21 Assoc VP Finance ..... Dr. Rowan A. MIRANDA
88 Chief Investment Officer ..... Mr. Erik LUNDBERG
30 Assoc VP for Development ..... Mr. Jefferson PORTER
30 Assoc VP for Development ..... Mr. Dondi L. CUPP
17 Assoc VP for Medical Affairs ..... Dr. John E. BILLI
46 Assoc VP for Research ..... Dr. Mark M. BANASZAK HOLL
46 Assoc VP for Research ..... Dr. Jeffrey B. FOWLKES
46 Assoc VP for Research ..... Dr. Toni C. ANTONUCCI
46 Assoc VP for Research ..... Mr. Marvin G. PARNES
35 Assoc VP Student Affs/Dean Stdnts ..... Ms. Laura B. JONES
35 Assoc VP Student Affairs ..... Ms. Anjali N. ANTURKAR
35 Assoc VP Student Affairs ..... Dr. Simone HIMBEAULT-TAYLOR
35 Assoc VP Student Affairs ..... Mr. Loren J. RULLMAN
16 Assoc VP for Human Resources ..... Ms. Laurita E. THOMAS
13 Assoc VP Info Tech /Chief Info Ofcr ... Ms. Laura M. PATTERSON
06 University Registrar ..... Mr. Paul A. ROBINSON
96 Director Procurement Services ..... Ms. Nancy A. HOBBS
38 Director Counseling & Psych Service ..... Dr. Todd D. SEVIG
39 Director University Housing ..... Ms. Linda L. NEWMAN
23 Director University Health Service ..... Dr. Robert A. WINFIELD
19 Interim Exec Dir Pub Safety/Secur ..... Mr. Joseph G. PIERSANTE
37 Exec Director Financial Aid ..... Ms. Pamela W. FOWLER
18 Executive Director Plant Operations ..... Mr. Richard W. ROBBEN
41 Athletic Director ..... Mr. David A. BRANDON
48 Dean Col Architecture & Urban Plng ..... Ms. Monica PONCE DE LEON
49 Dean Col Literature/Science/Arts ..... Dr. Terrence J. MCDONALD
54 Dean College of Engineering ..... Dr. David C. MUNSON
61 Dean Law School ..... Mr. Evan H. CAMINKER
63 Dean Medical School ..... Dr. James O. WOOLLISCROFT
67 Dean College of Pharmacy ..... Dr. Frank J. ASCIONE
65 Dean Sch Natural Resrc/Environ ..... Dr. Marie L. MIRANDA
64 Dean School Music Theatre & Dance ..... Mr. Christopher W. KENDALL
57 Dean School of Art & Design ..... Dr. Gunalan L. NADARAJAN
50 Dean School of Business ..... Dr. Alison DAVIS-BLAKE
52 Dean School of Dentistry ..... Dr. Peter J. POLVERINI
53 Dean School of Education ..... Dr. Deborah L. BALL
62 Dean School of Information ..... Dr. Jeffrey K. MACKIE-MASON
68 Dean School of Kinesiology ..... Dr. Ronald F. ZERNICKE
66 Dean School of Nursing ..... Dr. Kathleen M. POTEMPA
80 Dean School of Public Policy ..... Dr. Susan M. COLLINS
70 Dean School of Social Work ..... Dr. Laura LEIN
69 Dean School of Public Health ..... Dr. Martin A. PHILBERT
29 President Alumni Association ..... Mr. Steve C. GRAFTON

University of Michigan-Dearborn (B)

4901 Evergreen Road, Dearborn MI 48128-1491
County: Wayne FICE Identification: 002326
Unit ID: 171137
Telephone: (313) 593-5000 Carnegie Class: Master's L
FAX Number: (313) 593-5452 Calendar System: Trimester
URL: www.umd.umich.edu
Established: 1959 Annual Undergrad Tuition & Fees (In-State): $10,250
Enrollment: 8,955 Coed
Affiliation or Control: State IRS Status: 501(c)3
Highest Offering: Doctorate
Program: Liberal Arts And General; Teacher Preparatory; Professional
Accreditation: NH, BUS, CS, ENG, TEAC

01 Chancellor ..... Dr. Daniel LITTLE
05 Prov/Vice Chanc Academic Affs ..... Dr. Catherine A. DAVY
10 Vice Chancellor Business Affairs ..... Mr. Jeffrey L. EVANS
84 Vice Chanc Enrollment Management . Mr. Stanley E. HENDERSON
30 Vice Chanc Inst Advancement ..... Ms. Mallory M. SIMPSON
86 Vice Chanc for Govt Relations ..... Mr. Edward J. BAGALE
21 Assoc Vice Chancellor Finance ..... Mr. Robert K. GASSEL
06 Registrar ..... Ms. Janice LEWIS-BOYD
100 Chief of Staff ..... Mr. Ray METZ
26 Director of Communications ..... Mr. Ken KETTENBEIL
15 Director of Human Resources ..... Ms. Ginny ZARRAS
29 Alumni Engagement ..... Ms. Peggy PATTISON
20 Associate Provost ..... Mr. Ismael AHMED
20 Associate Provost ..... Dr. Malayppan SHRIDHAR
20 Associate Provost ..... Dr. Martin HERSHOCK
13 Interim Chief Technology Officer ..... Dr. Francine ALEXANDER
08 Director of Library ..... Ms. Elaine LOGAN
09 Director of Institutional Research ..... Ms. Roma E. HEANEY
84 Asst VC for Enrollment Management ..... Mr. Christopher W. TREMBLAY
07 Director of Admissions ..... Ms. Deb PEFFER
37 Director of Financial Aid ..... Ms. Katherine ALLEN
38 Director of Counseling ..... Dr. David SCHROAT
36 Director of Career Services ..... Ms. Regina M. STORRS
35 Interim Director Student Activities ..... Dr. Ann LAMPKIN-WILLIAMS
18 Director of Facilities Management ..... Mr. Lawrence HICKS
19 Director of Campus Safety ..... Mr. Richard GORDON
22 Institutional Equity Officer ..... Ms. Anita GREEN
28 Multicultural Affairs ..... Dr. Ann LAMPKIN-WILLIAMS
49 Dean Col Arts/Science/Letters ..... Dr. Jerold HALE
54 Interim Dean Col of Engr/Comp Sci ..... Dr. A. W. ENGLAND
50 Interim Dean College of Business ..... Dr. Lee REDDING
53 Dean School of Education ..... Dr. Edward SILVER

University of Michigan-Flint (C)

303 E Kearsley Street, Flint MI 48502-1950
County: Genesee FICE Identification: 002327
Unit ID: 171146
Telephone: (810) 762-3000 Carnegie Class: Master's L
FAX Number: (810) 762-5725 Calendar System: Semester
URL: www.umflint.edu
Established: 1956 Annual Undergrad Tuition & Fees (In-State): $9,028
Enrollment: 8,262 Coed
Affiliation or Control: State IRS Status: 501(c)3
Highest Offering: Doctorate
Program: Liberal Arts And General; Teacher Preparatory; Professional
Accreditation: NH, ANEST, BUS, MUS, NURSE, PTA, RTT, SW

01 Chancellor ..... Dr. Ruth J. PERSON
05 Provost/VC Academic Affairs ..... Dr. Gerard VOLAND
32 Vice Chancellor for Student Affairs ..... Dr. Mary Jo S. SEKELSKY
11 Vice Chanc for Business and Finance ... Mr. David BARTHELMES
35 Asst VC for Student Affairs ..... Vacant
21 Asst Vice Chanc Business & Finance .. Mr. William C. WEBB, JR.
58 Assoc Provost/Dean Grad Pgms ..... Dr. Vahid LOTFI
20 Asst Prov/Dean Undergrad Studies ..... Ms. Christine WATERS
26 Exec Director University Relations ..... Ms. Jennifer HOGAN
86 Director Government Relations ..... Mr. David E. LOSSING
28 Exec Director Educational Oppty ..... Mr. Tendaji W. GANGES
08 Director of Library ..... Mr. Robert L. HOUBECK, JR.
06 Registrar ..... Ms. Karen A. ARNOULD
07 Interim Admissions Director ..... Mr. Jon DAVIDSON
37 Director Financial Aid ..... Ms. Lori VEDDER
15 Director Human Res/Affirm Action ..... Ms. Diana T. CURRAN
49 Dean College Arts & Sciences ..... Dr. D. J. TRELA
50 Interim Dean School of Management ..... Dr. Vahid LOTFI
66 Director Nursing Program ..... Dr. Margaret ANDREWS
76 Dean Sch Health Prof & Studies ..... Dr. David GORDON
53 Int Dean Sch Education & Human Svcs ..... Dr. Robert BARNETT
51 Director of Extended Learning ..... Ms. Deborah WHITE
19 Director of Public Safety ..... Mr. Raymond D. HALL
18 Director Facilities Mgmt/Auxil Svcs ..... Mr. George HAKIM
14 Director Info Technology Services ..... Mr. Scott ARNST
36 Director Acad Advis & Career Center ..... Ms. Aimi MOSS
46 Director of Research ..... Dr. Terry VAN ALLEN
21 Director of Financial Svcs & Budget ..... Mr. Gerald GLASCO
88 Int Director University Outreach ..... Mr. Jonathan JAROSZ
29 Exec Dir of Dev and Alumni Relation ..... Vacant
96 Director of Purchasing ..... Mr. Gregory J. SNYDER
09 Director of Institutional Analysis ..... Ms. Fawn SKARSTEN

Van Andel Institute Graduate School (D)

333 Bostwick Avenue NE, Grand Rapids MI 49503
County: Kent Identification: 667085
Telephone: (616) 234-5708 Carnegie Class: Not Classified
FAX Number: (616) 234-5709 Calendar System: Other
URL: www.vai.org/education/graduateschool.aspx
Established: 1996 Annual Graduate Tuition & Fees: $25,000
Enrollment: N/A Coed
Affiliation or Control: Independent Non-Profit IRS Status: 501(c)3
Highest Offering: Doctorate; No Undergraduates
Program: Professional
Accreditation: @NH

01 President/Dean of the Graduate Sch . Dr. Steven J. TREIZENBERG

Walsh College of Accountancy and Business Administration (E)

3838 Livernois Road, Box 7006, Troy MI 48007-7006
County: Oakland FICE Identification: 004071
Unit ID: 172608
Telephone: (248) 689-8282 Carnegie Class: Spec/Bus
FAX Number: (248) 689-9066 Calendar System: Semester
URL: www.walshcollege.edu
Established: 1922 Annual Undergrad Tuition & Fees: $11,175
Enrollment: 3,189 Coed
Affiliation or Control: Independent Non-Profit IRS Status: 501(c)3
Highest Offering: Doctorate
Program: Professional; Business Emphasis
Accreditation: NH, ACBSP, IACBE

01 President & CEO ..... Ms. Stephanie W. BERGERON
05 Exec VP/Chief Academic Officer ..... Dr. David SHIELDS
10 Vice President/CFO/Treasurer . Ms. Helen C. KIEBA-TOLKSDORF
84 VP/Chief Mktg & Enrollment Mgt Ofcr ..... Vacant
16 VP/Chief Human Resources/Admin Ofcr ..... Ms. Elizabeth A. BARNES
30 Vice President/Chief Devel Officer ..... Ms. Audrey OLMSTEAD
04 Exec Assistant to the President ..... Ms. Rosemarie E. ZOOK
08 Assoc VP Acad Admin/Librarian ..... Vacant
32 Asst VP Student Services/Marketing ..... Ms. Victoria R. SCAVONE
20 Asst VP Academic Administration ..... Ms. Terri WASHBURN
106 Dean Office of Online Learning ..... Vacant
20 Director Academic Administration ..... Ms. Monique CARDENAS
37 Director Financial Aid ..... Mr. Howard THOMAS
18 Director Facilities/Auxiliary Svcs ..... Ms. Chris STOUT
21 Director Accounting/Business Ofcr ..... Mr. Brant WRIGHT
07 Director Admissions/Acad Advising ..... Mr. Jeremy GUC
06 Director of Records/Registrar ..... Ms. Karen HILLEBRAND
13 Exec Dir Ofc of Info Technology ..... Mr. Joseph ESDALE
12 Director Novi Campus ..... Mr. Ed BATAYEH
36 Director Career Services ..... Ms. Laurie SIEBERT
88 Director of MBA/MSM Program ..... Dr. Sheila R. RONIS
88 Director Doctoral Program ..... Dr. Linda HAGAN
88 Director Undergrad Business Program ..... Dr. Michael LEVENS
88 Director Corporate Rel/BLI ..... Ms. Janet HUBBARD
88 Director Information Assurance ..... Ms. Nanette POULIOS
88 Dir Center for Entrepreneurship ..... Ms. Tara MICELI
29 Manager of Alumni Relations ..... Ms. Duc ABRAHAMSON
26 Public Relations Coordinator ..... Ms. Donna MIRABITO
72 Int Chair Business Info Tech/IA ..... Ms. Terri WASHBURN
88 Chair Accounting ..... Mr. Richard BERSCHBACK
88 Chair Taxation & Business Law ..... Mr. Mark R. SOLOMON
88 Chair Economics & Finance ..... Dr. Linda WIECHOWSKI

Washtenaw Community College (F)

4800 E Huron River Dr, Ann Arbor MI 48105-4800
County: Washtenaw FICE Identification: 002328
Unit ID: 172617
Telephone: (734) 973-3300 Carnegie Class: Assoc/Pub-U-SC
FAX Number: (734) 677-5413 Calendar System: Semester
URL: www.wccnet.edu
Established: 1965 Annual Undergrad Tuition & Fees (In-District): $2,900
Enrollment: 13,400 Coed
Affiliation or Control: Local IRS Status: 501(c)3
Highest Offering: Associate Degree
Program: Occupational; 2-Year Principally Bachelor's Creditable
Accreditation: NH, ACFEI, ADNUR, DA, PTAA, RAD

01 President ..... Dr. Rose BELLANCA
11 Vice President Admin & Finance ..... Mr. Steven HARDY
05 Vice President for Instruction ..... Dr. Stuart BLACKLAW
16 Assoc VP Human Resources Mgmt ..... Mr. Douglas KRUZEL
32 VP Student & Academic Services ..... Ms. Linda S. BLAKEY
18 Assoc VP Facilities Devel & Opers ..... Mr. Damon FLOWERS
30 Vice Pres of College Advancement ..... Ms. Wendy LAWSON
88 Assoc VP Econ Devel/Cmty/Corp ..... Ms. Michelle MUELLER
45 Exec Associate to the President ..... Ms. Julie MORRISON
79 Dean Humanities & Social Science ..... Dr. William ABERNETHY
20 Dean Supp Svcs & Student Advocacy ..... Dr. Patricia TAYLOR
62 Dean Learning Resources ..... Mr. Victor LIU
50 Dean Business & Computer Tech ..... Ms. Rosemary WILSON
81 Dean Math/Natural & Behavioral Sci ..... Ms. Martha SHOWALTER
88 Dean Adv Manuf Trades/Publ Svcs ..... Ms. Marilyn DONHAM
106 Dean Distance Learning ..... Mr. James EGAN
07 Dean Admissions & Student Life ..... Mr. Arnett CHISHOLM
13 Chief Information Officer ..... Mr. Amin LADHA
10 Controller ..... Ms. Lynn MARTIN
21 Dir Budget Purchasing Aux Svcs ..... Ms. Barbara FILLINGER
15 Director Compensation/Benefits ..... Ms. Christine MIHALY
37 Director Financial Aid ..... Ms. Lori TRAPP
09 Director Institutional Research ..... Dr. Roger MOURAD
20 Director Educational Services ..... Ms. Kathleen A. STADTFELD
19 Director Safety & Security ..... Mr. Jacque DESROSIERS
26 Director Public Relations & Mktg ..... Ms. Catherine SMILLIE
43 General Counsel ..... Ms. Sarah STITT
35 Dir Student Development/Activities ..... Mr. Pete LESHKEVICH
84 Dean of Enrollment Mgmt/Ombudsman ..... Mr. Larry AEILTS
88 Enrollment Svcs Info Officer ..... Ms. Kathryn STAFFORD

Wayne County Community College District (G)

801 W Fort Street, Detroit MI 48226-3010
County: Wayne FICE Identification: 009230
Unit ID: 172635
Telephone: (313) 496-2600 Carnegie Class: Assoc/Pub-U-MC

FAX Number: (313) 961-9439 Calendar System: Semester
URL: www.wcccd.edu
Established: 1967 Annual Undergrad Tuition & Fees (In-District): $1,882
Enrollment: 20,440 Coed
Affiliation or Control: State/Local IRS Status: 501(c)3
Highest Offering: Associate Degree
Program: Occupational; 2-Year Principally Bachelor's Creditable
Accreditation: NH, DA, DH, DIETT, SURGA, SURGT

01 Chancellor .... Dr. Curtis L. IVERY
03 Executive Vice Chancellor Dist Ofc .... Mr. John BOLDEN
05 Vice Chanc Educational Affairs .... Dr. Stephanie BULGER
26 Vice Chanc External Affairs .... Dr. George W. SWAN, III
32 Vice Chanc Student Services .... Mr. Brian SINGLETON
51 Vice Chanc Sch Cont Ed/Wrkforce Dev .... Ms. Shawna FORBES
10 Vice Chanc Admin/Finance .... Ms. Kim DICARO
15 Vice Chanc HR/Accountability .... Mr. Mirza F. AHMED
09 District VC IE/Info Management .... Ms. Johnesa HODGE
35 Dist Assoc Vice Chanc Student Svcs .... Mr. Adrian PHILLIPS
12 Campus President Downriver .... Mr. Anthony ARMINIAK
12 Campus President Downtown .... Ms. Annette BLACK
12 Campus President Western .... Mr. Michael P. DOTSON
12 Campus Pres NW/Exec Prov Hlth Sci .... Dr. Debraha WATSON
12 Campus President Eastern/Corp Col .... Dr. Sandra T. ROBINSON
88 Asst to Chanc Instruct/Stdnt Succes .... Dr. Patrick MCNALLY

Wayne State University (A)

656 W. Kirby, Room # 4070, Detroit MI 48202-4095
County: Wayne FICE Identification: 002329
Unit ID: 172644
Telephone: (313) 577-2424 Carnegie Class: RU/VH
FAX Number: (313) 577-8154 Calendar System: Semester
URL: www.wayne.edu
Established: 1868 Annual Undergrad Tuition & Fees (In-State): $10,189
Enrollment: 30,765 Coed
Affiliation or Control: State IRS Status: 501(c)3
Highest Offering: Doctorate
Program: Occupational; Liberal Arts And General; Teacher Preparatory; Professional
Accreditation: NH, ANEST, ARCPA, AUD, BUS, CACREP, CLPSY, CORE, DANCE, DIETC, ENG, ENGR, ENGT, #FUSER, IPSY, LAW, LIB, MED, MIDWF, MT, MUS, NURSE, OT, PA, PH, PHAR, PLNG, PTA, RAD, RTT, SP, SPAA, SW, @TEAC, THEA

01 President .... Mr. Allan GILMOUR
100 Chief of Staff/VP Marketing & Comm .... Mr. Michael G. WRIGHT
05 Sr Vice Pres Acad Affairs & Provost .... Dr. Ronald T. BROWN
10 VP Finance & Business/Treasurer/CFO .... Mr. Rick NORK
43 Vice President & General Counsel .... Mr. Louis A. LESSEM
46 Vice Pres Res/Dean Grad School .... Dr. Hilary H. RATNER
30 Vice Pres Devel/Alumni Affairs .... Mr. David RIPPLE
86 Vice Pres Govt & Community Affairs .... Mr. Patrick O. LINDSEY
20 Assoc VP Academic Affairs .... Dr. Howard N. SHAPIRO
84 Assoc Vice President Enrollment .... Mrs. Corinne M. WEBB
101 Sec to the BOG & Exec Asst to Pres .... Ms. Julie H. MILLER
04 Assistant to the President .... Ms. Allison GUILLIOM
29 Asst Vice Pres Alumni Relations .... Ms. Marguerite S. RIGBY
15 Interim Assoc VP Human Resources .... Mr. Paul SUNDBERG
18 Assoc VP Facilities/Planning/Mgmt .... Mr. James R. SEARS
21 Assoc Vice Pres University Budget .... Mr. Robert KOHRMAN
32 Dean of Students .... Dr. David J. STRAUSS
07 Sr Dir of UG Admiss/New Stdnt Ornt .... Ms. Judy B. TATUM
26 Director Corporate/Public Affairs .... Ms. Francine WUNDER
25 Asst VP Sponsored Programs Admin .... Ms. Gail L. RYAN
37 Sr Director Student Financial Aid .... Mr. Albert G. HERMSEN
38 Director Career Services .... Dr. Ronald H. KENT
08 Dean University Libraries .... Dr. Sandra G. YEE
06 Sr Director Registrar .... Ms. Linda K. FALKIEWICZ
09 Asst VP for Institutional Research .... Mr. Mark A. BYRD
49 Dean Liberal Arts & Sciences .... Dr. Wayne RASKIND
61 Dean of the Law School .... Mr. Robert M. ACKERMAN
63 Dean School of Medicine .... Dr. Valarie M. PARISI
66 Dean College of Nursing .... Dr. Barbara K. REDMAN
54 Dean College of Engineering .... Dr. Farshad FOTOUHI
50 Dean Sch Business Administration .... Dr. Margaret WILLIAMS
70 Dean School of Social Work .... Dr. Cheryl WAITES
67 Dean Pharmacy & Health Sciences .... Dr. Lloyd Y. YOUNG
53 Dean College of Education .... Dr. Carolyn C. SHIELDS
57 Dean Col Fine/Performing/Comm Arts .... Mr. Matthew SEEGER
92 Dean Honors College .... Dr. Jerry HERRON
96 Asst VP Purchasing .... Mr. Kenneth DOHERTY

West Shore Community College (B)

3000 N. Stiles Rd., Scottville MI 49454-0277
County: Mason FICE Identification: 007950
Unit ID: 172671
Telephone: (231) 845-6211 Carnegie Class: Assoc/Pub-R-S
FAX Number: (231) 845-0207 Calendar System: Semester
URL: www.westshore.edu
Established: 1967 Annual Undergrad Tuition & Fees (In-District): $2,250
Enrollment: 1,617 Coed
Affiliation or Control: Local IRS Status: 501(c)3
Highest Offering: Associate Degree
Program: Occupational; 2-Year Principally Bachelor's Creditable
Accreditation: NH

01 President .... Dr. Charles T. DILLON
11 VP of Administrative Services .... Mr. Scott WARD
05 VP of Academic and Student Services .... Ms. Lisa STICH
32 Dean of Student Services .... Mr. Chad E. INABINET
40 Director of Bookstore & Food Svcs .... Ms. Cheryl HOGAN
04 Executive Assistant to President .... Ms. Lisa STANKOWSKI
37 Director Financial Aid .... Ms. Juliann MURPHY
91 Manager of Adm Computing Systems .... Mr. Stephen VON PFAHL
88 Director of Criminal Justice .... Mr. Dan DELLAR
88 Director of Recreational Services .... Mr. Michael A. MOORE
15 Director of Human Resources .... Ms. Debbie CAMPBELL
88 Director of Women's Resource Center .... Ms. Carla E. SHAY
26 Director of College Relations .... Mr. Thomas A. HAWLEY
23 Director of Wellness Center .... Ms. Julie PAGE-SMITH
10 Director of Accounting .... Ms. Kristen BIGGS
106 Director Distance Learning & Info .... Mr. John GERTS

Western Michigan University (C)

1903 W Michigan Avenue, Kalamazoo MI 49008-5202
County: Kalamazoo FICE Identification: 002330
Unit ID: 172699
Telephone: (269) 387-1000 Carnegie Class: RU/H
FAX Number: (269) 387-0958 Calendar System: Semester
URL: www.wmich.edu
Established: 1903 Annual Undergrad Tuition & Fees (In-State): $9,982
Enrollment: 25,086 Coed
Affiliation or Control: State IRS Status: 501(c)3
Highest Offering: Doctorate
Program: Liberal Arts And General; Teacher Preparatory; Professional
Accreditation: NH, AAB, ARCPA, ART, AUD, BUS, BUSA, CACREP, CEA, CIDA, CLPSY, COPSY, CORE, CS, DANCE, DIETD, DIETI, ENG, ENGT, IPSY, MUS, NURSE, OT, SP, SPAA, SW, TED, THEA

01 President .... Dr. John M. DUNN
05 Provost/Vice Pres Academic Affairs .... Dr. Timothy J. GREENE
10 Vice Pres Business & Finance/CFO .... Ms. Jan VAN DER KLEY
32 VP Student Affairs/Dean of Students .... Dr. Diane K. ANDERSON
46 Vice President for Research .... Dr. Daniel M. LITYNSKI
30 VP Development & Alumni Relations .... Mr. James THOMAS
43 VP Legal Affairs/General Counsel .... Ms. Carol L J. HUSTOLES
86 VP Governmental Affs/University Rel .... Mr. Greg J. ROSINE
28 Vice Pres Diversity/Inclusion .... Dr. Martha B. WARFIELD
27 Vice Provost Budget Personnel/CIO .... Dr. James A. GILCHRIST
84 Vice Provost for Enrollment Mgmt .... Dr. Keith M. HEARIT
09 Assoc Provost Inst Effectiveness .... Dr. Jody BRYLINSKY
108 Assoc VP Assessment/Undergrad Stdnt .... Dr. David REINHOLD
51 Assoc Prov Extended Univ Pgms .... Dr. Dawn GAYMER
82 Assoc VP Haenicke Inst Global Ed .... Vacant
21 Assoc Vice President of Finance .... Ms. Sandra STEINBACH
15 Assoc Vice Pres Human Resource .... Mr. Warren HILLS
18 Assoc Vice Pres Facilities Mgmt .... Mr. Peter J. STRAZDAS
35 Assoc Vice Pres Student Affairs .... Ms. Suzie NAGEL
35 Assoc VP for Student Affairs .... Mr. Vernon PAYNE
45 Assoc VP Budget and Planning .... Mr. Dean HONSBERGER
88 Assoc VP Institutional Equity .... Mr. David GLENN
31 Assoc VP Community Outreach .... Mr. Robert MILLER
101 Secretary Board of Trustees .... Ms. Betty A. KOCHER
58 Dean Graduate College .... Dr. Susan STAPLETON
49 Dean of Arts & Sciences .... Dr. Alexander ENYEDI
88 Dean of Aviation .... Capt. Dave POWELL
50 Dean of Business .... Dr. Kay PALAN
53 Int Dean of Educ & Human Dev .... Dr. Van COOLEY
54 Dean of Engr & Applied Sciences .... Dr. Anthony J. VIZZINI
57 Dean of Fine Arts .... Dr. Margaret M. MERRION
76 Dean Health & Human Services .... Dr. Earlie WASHINGTON
63 Dean School of Medicine .... Dr. Hal B. JENSON
92 Dean of Honors College .... Dr. Nicholas ANDREADIS
08 Dean of Libraries .... Dr. Joseph G. REISH
26 Exec Dir of University Relations .... Ms. Cheryl ROLAND
29 Executive Director Alumni Relations .... Ms. M. Jamie JEREMY
36 Exec Dir Career & Employment Svcs .... Ms. Lynn KELLY-ALBERTSON
06 Interim Registrar .... Ms. Carrie CUMMING
07 Director Admissions/Orientation .... Ms. Penny BUNDY
37 Director Student Financial Aid .... Mr. Mark J. DELOREY
38 Dir Counseling Services .... Dr. Geniene M. GERSH
41 Dir Intercollegiate Athletics .... Ms. Kathy BEAUREGARD
96 Dir Logistical Svcs (Purchasing) .... Mr. Donald PENSKAR

Western Theological Seminary (D)

101 E 13th Street, Holland MI 49423-3622
County: Ottawa FICE Identification: 002331
Unit ID: 172705
Telephone: (616) 392-8555 Carnegie Class: Spec/Faith
FAX Number: (616) 392-7717 Calendar System: Semester
URL: www.westernsem.edu
Established: 1866 Annual Graduate Tuition & Fees: $12,256
Enrollment: 251 Coed
Affiliation or Control: Reformed Church In America IRS Status: 501(c)3
Highest Offering: Doctorate; No Undergraduates
Program: Professional; Religious Emphasis
Accreditation: THEOL

01 President .... Dr. Timothy BROWN
05 Dean/Vice Pres Academic Affairs .... Dr. Leanne VAN DYK
30 Vice President Advancement/Comm .... Rev. Jeffrey MUNROE
10 Vice President of Finance .... Mr. Norman DONKERSLOOT
08 Director of the Library .... Rev. Paul M. SMITH

Yeshiva Beth Yehuda - Yeshiva Gedolah of Greater Detroit (E)

24600 Greenfield, Oak Park MI 48237-1544
County: Oakland FICE Identification: 023638
Unit ID: 247773
Telephone: (248) 968-3360 Carnegie Class: Spec/Faith
FAX Number: (248) 968-8613 Calendar System: Semester
Established: 1985 Annual Undergrad Tuition & Fees: $6,100
Enrollment: 80 Male
Affiliation or Control: Independent Non-Profit IRS Status: 501(c)3
Highest Offering: Doctorate
Program: Professional
Accreditation: RABN

01 Dean .... Rabbi Y. BAKST
05 Assistant Dean .... Rabbi M. S. BAKST
11 Executive Administrator .... Rabbi P. RUSHNAWITZ
37 Director of Financial Aid .... Rabbi Y. BLITZ

MINNESOTA

Academy College (F)

1101 E 78th Street, Suite 100, Minneapolis MN 55420-1402
County: Hennepin FICE Identification: 020503
Unit ID: 172866
Telephone: (952) 851-0066 Carnegie Class: Bac/Assoc
FAX Number: (952) 851-0094 Calendar System: Quarter
URL: www.academycollege.edu
Established: 1936 Annual Undergrad Tuition & Fees: $19,533
Enrollment: 191 Coed
Affiliation or Control: Proprietary IRS Status: Proprietary
Highest Offering: Baccalaureate
Program: 2-Year Principally Bachelor's Creditable
Accreditation: ACICS, MAC

01 Director .... Ms. Mary ERICKSON

Adler Graduate School (G)

1550 E 78th Street, Richfield MN 55423
County: Hennepin FICE Identification: 030519
Unit ID: 374024
Telephone: (612) 861-7554 Carnegie Class: Spec/Health
FAX Number: (612) 861-7559 Calendar System: Quarter
URL: www.alfredadler.edu
Established: 1969 Annual Graduate Tuition & Fees: $9,150
Enrollment: 359 Coed
Affiliation or Control: Independent Non-Profit IRS Status: 501(c)3
Highest Offering: Master's; No Undergraduates
Program: Professional
Accreditation: NH

01 President .... Dr. Daniel HAUGEN
05 Academic Vice President .... Dr. David MATHIEU
10 Vice President for Finance .... Ms. Leslie ROHDE
07 Director of Admissions/Student Svcs .... Ms. Evelyn HAAS
37 Director of Student Financial Aid .... Ms. Jeanette MAYNARD NELSON

American Academy of Acupuncture and Oriental Medicine (H)

1925 W County Road B2, Roseville MN 55113-2703
County: Ramsey FICE Identification: 038333
Unit ID: 446002
Telephone: (651) 631-0204 Carnegie Class: Spec/Health
FAX Number: (651) 631-0361 Calendar System: Trimester
URL: www.aaaom.org
Established: 1997 Annual Graduate Tuition & Fees: $11,212
Enrollment: 106 Coed
Affiliation or Control: Proprietary IRS Status: Proprietary
Highest Offering: Master's; No Undergraduates
Program: Professional
Accreditation: ACUP

01 President .... Dr. Changzhen GONG
05 Academic Dean .... Dr. Yubin LU
11 Administrative Director .... Leila NIELSEN
37 Financial Aid Officer .... Lillian CHEUNG

Argosy University, Twin Cities (I)

1515 Central Parkway, Eagan MN 55121-1756
County: Dakota FICE Identification: 007619
Unit ID: 173984
Telephone: (888) 844-2004 Carnegie Class: Master's S
FAX Number: (651) 994-0895 Calendar System: Semester
URL: www.argosy.edu/twincities
Established: 1961 Annual Undergrad Tuition & Fees: $13,224
Enrollment: 2,143 Coed
Affiliation or Control: Proprietary IRS Status: Proprietary
Highest Offering: Doctorate
Program: Professional
Accreditation: &WC, CLPSY, DH, DMS, HT, MAC, MFCD, MLTAD, #RAD, RTT

01 Campus President .... Dr. Scott TJADEN
05 Vice President of Academic Affairs .... Dr. Kristin BENSON
07 Senior Director of Admissions .... Janet ZIMPRICH
32 Director of Student Services .... Aprile EICH
15 Human Resources .... Crystal BUSCH

06 Registrar ... Amy SUDBECK
37 Director of Student Finances ... Larry WERNER
11 Dir of Admin & Financial Services ... Jeff SWENSON
36 Director of Career Services ... Andrew SYKES

† Regional accreditation is carried under the parent institution in Orange, CA.

The Art Institutes International Minnesota (A)

15 S 9th Street, Minneapolis MN 55402-2808
County: Hennepin FICE Identification: 010248
Unit ID: 173887
Telephone: (612) 332-3361 Carnegie Class: Spec/Arts
FAX Number: (612) 904-1541 Calendar System: Quarter
URL: www.artinstitutes.edu/minneapolis
Established: 1964 Annual Undergrad Tuition & Fees: $17,616
Enrollment: 1,804 Coed
Affiliation or Control: Proprietary IRS Status: Proprietary
Highest Offering: Baccalaureate
Program: Occupational
Accreditation: ⊕NH, ACICS, ACFEI

01 President ... Dr. Jeffrey ALLEN
05 Dean of Academic Affairs ... Dr. Susan TARNOWSKI
32 Dean of Student Affairs ... Pam BOERSIG
36 Director of Career Services ... Becky BATES
07 Director of Admissions ... Mary STRAND
26 Director of Communications ... Anj KOZEL

Augsburg College (B)

2211 Riverside Avenue, Minneapolis MN 55454-1398
County: Hennepin FICE Identification: 002334
Unit ID: 173045
Telephone: (612) 330-1000 Carnegie Class: Master's L
FAX Number: (612) 330-1649 Calendar System: Semester
URL: www.augsburg.edu
Established: 1869 Annual Undergrad Tuition & Fees: $31,902
Enrollment: 3,908 Coed
Affiliation or Control: Evangelical Lutheran Church In America
IRS Status: 501(c)3
Highest Offering: Doctorate
Program: Liberal Arts And General; Teacher Preparatory; Professional
Accreditation: NH, ARCPA, MUS, NURSE, SW, TED

01 President ... Dr. Paul C. PRIBBENOW
88 Exec Dir Center Faith & Learning ... Dr. Thomas F. MORGAN
05 VP Academic Affs/Dean of College ... Dr. Barbara FARLEY
10 CFO/Vice Pres Finance/Admin ... Ms. Tammy MCGEE
44 Vice President Advancement ... Vacant
84 Vice Pres Enrollment Management ... Ms. Julie A. EDSTROM
32 Vice President Student Affairs ... Ms. Anne L. GARVEY
30 Asst Vice President Development ... Ms. Cassidy TITCOMB
58 Asst VP/Dean of Grad & Prof Stds ... Dr. Lori PETERSON
12 Director Rochester Program ... Dr. Karl WOLFE
26 Vice President of Marketing/Comm ... Ms. Rebecca JOHN
42 Campus Pastor ... Rev. David T. WOLD
37 Director Student Financial Services ... Mr. Paul L. TERRIO
06 Registrar ... Vacant
07 Asst VP for Admissions ... Ms. Carrie M. CARROLL
09 Dir Enrollment Plng/Systems Devel ... Mr. James C. ERCHUL
18 Director Facilities Management ... Mr. David A. DRAUS
25 Director Sponsored Programs ... Ms. Carol M. FORBES
29 Director Alum & Constituent Rels ... Ms. Kim STONE
36 Director Ctr Service/Work/Learning ... Ms. Lois A. OLSON
13 VP & Chief Information Officer ... Mr. Leif B. ANDERSON
38 Director Counseling & Health Promo ... Ms. Nancy G. GUILBEAULT
15 Asst VP for Human Resources ... Ms. Andrea TURNER
35 Dean of Students ... Dr. Sarah GRIESSE
35 Dir Campus Activities/Orientation ... Ms. Joanne REECK-IRBY
08 Director Library Services ... Ms. Jane A. NELSON
86 Dir Government Relations ... Mr. Jay BENANAV
19 Director Public Safety ... Mr. Jesse CASHMAN
102 Dir Corporate/Foundation Relations ... Ms. Laura ROLLER
31 Director Community Relations ... Mr. Steve PEACOCK
88 Director Parent/Family Relations ... Ms. Sally DANIELS
55 Dir Augsburg for Adults ... Vacant
88 Director StepUp Program ... Ms. Patrice SALMERI
88 Director Advancement Services ... Mr. Kevin HEALY
88 Dir Center for Teaching/Learning ... Ms. Velma J. LASHBROOK
40 Bookstore Manager ... Ms. Laura FORGEY
96 Director Purchasing/Central Support ... Mr. Matthew RUMPZA
85 Asst Vice Pres Intl Programs ... Mr. Orval J. GINGERICH
49 Asst Vice Pres/Dean of Arts & Sci ... Dr. Amy GORT
41 Athletic Director ... Mr. Jeffrey F. SWENSON

Bethany Lutheran College (C)

700 Luther Drive, Mankato MN 56001-6163
County: Blue Earth FICE Identification: 002337
Unit ID: 173142
Telephone: (507) 344-7000 Carnegie Class: Bac/A&S
FAX Number: (507) 344-7376 Calendar System: Semester
URL: www.blc.edu
Established: 1911 Annual Undergrad Tuition & Fees: $23,270
Enrollment: 634 Coed
Affiliation or Control: Evangelical Lutheran Synod IRS Status: 501(c)3
Highest Offering: Baccalaureate
Program: Liberal Arts And General
Accreditation: NH

01 President ... Dr. Dan R. BRUSS
42 Dir Campus Spiritual Life/Chaplain ... Rev. Donald L. MOLDSTAD
05 Dean of Academic Affairs ... Dr. Eric K. WOLLER
32 Vice President for Student Affairs ... Mr. Steven C. JAEGER
10 Chief Financial/Administrative Ofcr ... Mr. Daniel L. MUNDAHL
30 Chief Advancement Officer ... Mr. Arthur P. WESTPHAL
35 Dean of Student Services ... Dr. Theodore E. MANTHE
37 Director of Financial Aid ... Mr. Jeffrey W. YOUNGE
06 Registrar ... Ms. Mary Jo H. STARKSON
07 Dean of Admissions ... Mr. Donald M. WESTPHAL
16 Manager of Employee Relations ... Mrs. Paulette L. TONN BOOKER
08 Director of Library Services ... Mr. Orrin J. AUSEN
13 Director of Information Technology ... Mr. John M. SEHLOFF
26 Director of Marketing/Public Rels ... Mr. Lance W. SCHWARTZ
57 Director of Fine Arts ... Mrs. Lois A. JAEGER
41 Director of Athletics ... Mr. Karl E. FAGER
29 Manager of Alumni Relations ... Mr. Jacob C. KRIER
19 Manager of Security Services ... Mr. Jonathan L. MOLDSTAD
91 Manager of Administrative Computing ... Ms. Lisa A. SHUBERT
90 Manager of Academic Computing ... Mr. Mark S. MEYER
40 Bookstore Manager ... Mr. Paul G. WOLD
21 Controller ... Mr. Gregory W. COSTELLO
28 Coord Ctr for Intercultural Develop ... Mr. Thomas G. FLUNKER
36 Coord Career Svcs & Internships ... Ms. Brittany D. NASH
38 Coord of Student Counseling ... Mrs. Patricia J. REAGLES
18 Director of Facilities ... Mr. Juel O. MERSETH

Bethel University (D)

3900 Bethel Drive, Saint Paul MN 55112-6999
County: Ramsey FICE Identification: 009058
Unit ID: 173160
Telephone: (651) 638-6400 Carnegie Class: Master's L
FAX Number: (651) 638-6001 Calendar System: Semester
URL: www.bethel.edu
Established: 1871 Annual Undergrad Tuition & Fees: $30,840
Enrollment: 5,438 Coed
Affiliation or Control: Baptist IRS Status: 501(c)3
Highest Offering: Doctorate
Program: Liberal Arts And General; Teacher Preparatory
Accreditation: NH, MFCD, NURSE, SW, TEAC, THEOL

01 President ... Dr. James H. BARNES, III
100 Executive Assistant to President ... Dr. Richard J. SHERRY
05 Executive Vice Pres and Provost ... Dr. David K. CLARK
10 Sr Vice Pres Business Affs ... Ms. Kathleen J. NELSON
46 Sr VP Strategic Plng & Opers Effect ... Mr. Joseph LALUZERNE
26 Sr VP Communications/Marketing ... Ms. Sherie J. LINDVALL
30 Sr VP University Relations ... Mr. Patrick MAZOROL
44 Vice President Development ... Mr. Bruce W. ANDERSON
07 VP for Admiss/Fin Aid & Retention ... Mr. Daniel NELSON
90 Vice President Information Tech ... Mr. Mark POSNER
29 Vice Pres Constituent Relations ... Mr. Ralph GUSTAFSON
32 Vice President Student Life ... Dr. Edee SCHULZE
49 Vice Pres/Dean of Arts & Sciences ... Dr. Debra HARLESS
58 Vice Pres Dean Cont Stds/Grad Pgm ... Mr. Richard CROMBIE
51 Dean Acad of Cont Studies/Grad Pgm ... Dr. Lori JASS
73 Interim VP and Dean BSSP ... Dr. David CLARK
20 Associate Dean Arts and Sciences ... Dr. Barrett FISHER
20 Assoc Dean Gen Educ & Fac Develop ... Dr. Deborah SULLIVAN-TRAINOR
46 Actg Assoc Dean Inst Assess Accred ... Dr. Joel FREDERICKSON
81 Acting Assoc Dean Nat Behav Sci ... Dr. Jeffrey L. PORT
107 Assoc Dean of Prof Programs ... Dr. Pamela ERWIN
104 Assoc Dean Off-Campus Programs ... Mr. Vincent PETERS
12 Dean/Exec Ofcr Bethel Sem San Diego ... Dr. John R. LILLIS
12 Dean/Exec Ofcr Bethel Sem East ... Dr. Douglas W. FOMBELLE
35 Dean of Students ... Mr. James A. FEREIRA
35 Dean of Students ... Dr. Marie WISNER
08 Director of Libraries ... Mr. David R. STEWART
15 Director of Human Resources ... Mr. William L. GOODMAN
41 Athletic Director ... Mr. Robert B. BJORKLUND
37 Financial Aid Officer ... Mr. Jeffery D. OLSON
42 Dean Campus Ministrs/Campus Pastor ... Ms. Laurel BUNKER
07 Director of CAS Admissions ... Mr. Jay T. FEDJE
07 Director of Seminary Admissions ... Mr. Joseph V. DWORAK
07 Director of CAPS/GS Admissions ... Mr. Paul IVES
06 University Registrar ... Ms. Katrina CHAPMAN
36 Acting Dir Career Counsel/Placement ... Mr. Dave BROZA
19 Chief of Security and Safety ... Mr. Andrew LUCHSINGER
40 Director Campus Stores ... Ms. Jill SONSTEBY
23 Director of Health Services ... Mrs. Elizabeth K. MILLER
96 Director of Purchasing ... Mr. Bill KIDDER
21 Associate Business Officer ... Mr. John BERGESON
38 Director Student Counseling ... Dr. James KOCH
18 Director of Facilities Mgmt ... Mr. Tom TRAINOR
28 Chief Diversity Officer ... Dr. Leon RODRIGUES

† The marriage and family therapy master's program at Bethel Seminary San Diego is accredited by the Commission on Accreditation for Marriage and Family Therapy Education (COAMFTE) of the American Association for Marriage and Family Therapy (AAMFT)

Brown College (E)

1340 Mendota Heights Road, Mendota Heights MN 55120
County: Dakota FICE Identification: 007351
Unit ID: 174394
Telephone: (651) 905-3400 Carnegie Class: Bac/Assoc
FAX Number: (651) 905-3550 Calendar System: Other
URL: www.browncollege.edu
Established: 1946 Annual Undergrad Tuition & Fees: $19,850
Enrollment: 700 Coed
Affiliation or Control: Proprietary IRS Status: Proprietary
Highest Offering: Baccalaureate
Program: Occupational; 2-Year Principally Bachelor's Creditable; Professional; Business Emphasis
Accreditation: ACCSC, ACICS, MAAB

01 President ... Dr. Michelle ERNST
05 Dean of Education ... Ms. Lisa THOMAS
07 Director of Admissions ... Ms. May THAO-SCHUCK
12 Director of Brooklyn Center Campus ... Mr. Timothy PETERSON
36 Director of Career Services ... Mr. Paul KRAIMER
13 Director of Information Technology ... Mr. John HANS
06 Registrar ... Ms. Debra NEWGARD
08 Librarian ... Mr. Philip DUDAS
10 Business Office Manager ... Ms. Jennifer BOLISH
29 Director of Alumni Affairs ... Vacant

Capella University (F)

225 S 6th Street, 9th Floor, Minneapolis MN 55402-4319
County: Hennepin FICE Identification: 032673
Unit ID: 413413
Telephone: (888) 227-3552 Carnegie Class: DRU
FAX Number: (612) 977-5066 Calendar System: Other
URL: www.capella.edu
Established: 1993 Annual Undergrad Tuition & Fees: $11,700
Enrollment: 36,375 Coed
Affiliation or Control: Proprietary IRS Status: Proprietary
Highest Offering: Doctorate
Program: Professional
Accreditation: NH, CACREP, NURSE, TED

01 President ... Mr. Scott KINNEY
05 Chief Academic Officer ... Dr. Amy DONOVAN
04 Executive Asst Supervisor ... Ms. Cristy SIEDE
27 Vice President/Chief Info Officer ... Mr. Scott HENKEL
84 Vice President Enrollment Services ... Ms. Leslie BRONK
15 Vice President Human Resources ... Ms. Sally CHIAL
43 VP Govt Affs/Gen Counsel/Secretary ... Mr. Greg THOM
79 Dean School of Human Services ... Dr. Deborah BUSHWAY
72 Act Dean School of Business/Tech ... Dr. William REED
53 Dean School of Education ... Dr. Barbara BUTTS WILLIAMS
88 Dean School of Psychology ... Dr. Deb BUSHWAY
09 Assessment & Inst Rsch Director ... Ms. Kim PEARCE
06 Registrar ... Ms. Nancy PENNA
10 Chief Financial Officer ... Ms. Lois MARTIN
21 Corporate Controller ... Ms. Amy DRIFKA
21 Director of Finance ... Mr. Andy WATT
88 Director Next Generation Learning ... Mr. Keith KOCH
27 Director Marketing/Communications ... Mr. Brad FRANK
31 Director Events & Outreach ... Mr. Tom CLEMENS
26 Director of Public Relations ... Ms. Irene SILBER
46 Director Academic Research ... Dr. Tsuey-Hwa CHEN
18 Director of Facilities ... Ms. Carla BUSTROM
08 Manager Library Services ... Ms. Kathe PELLETIER
88 Licensing Specialist ... Mr. Dick BUTALA
07 Asst Reg/Mgr Operational Strategies ... Ms. Debra NEWGARD
43 Corp Attorney/Govt Affs/Compliance ... Ms. Priscilla MCNULTY

Carleton College (G)

1 N College Street, Northfield MN 55057-4001
County: Rice FICE Identification: 002340
Unit ID: 173258
Telephone: (507) 222-4000 Carnegie Class: Bac/A&S
FAX Number: (507) 222-4204 Calendar System: Trimester
URL: www.carleton.edu
Established: 1866 Annual Undergrad Tuition & Fees: $44,445
Enrollment: 2,000 Coed
Affiliation or Control: Independent Non-Profit IRS Status: 501(c)3
Highest Offering: Baccalaureate
Program: Liberal Arts And General; Teacher Preparatory
Accreditation: NH

01 President ... Mr. Steven G. POSKANZER, JR.
05 Dean of the College ... Ms. Beverly NAGEL
10 VP Business & Finance/Treasurer ... Mr. Fred A. ROGERS
30 Vice President External Relations ... Mr. Donald HASSELTINE
32 VP for Student Dev/Dean of Students ... Ms. Hudlin WAGNER
84 Dean of Admissions ... Mr. Paul THIBOUTOT
100 Assoc Vice President/Chief of Staff ... Ms. Elise ESLINGER
26 Assoc VP Ext Relations/Dir Develop ... Ms. Gayle MCJUNKIN
26 Assoc VP Ext Relations/Dir Col Rels ... Mr. Joe HARGIS
20 Associate Dean of the College ... Mr. Fernan JARAMILLO
20 Associate Dean of the College ... Mr. Arjendu PATTANAYAK
35 Associate Dean of Students ... Ms. Julie THORNTON
35 Associate Dean of Students ... Mr. Joseph BAGGOT
35 Associate Dean of Students ... Ms. Cathy CARLSON
37 Assoc Dean Admiss/Dir Stdnt Fin Svc ... Mr. Rod M. OTO
42 Chaplain ... Rev. Carolyn FURE-SLOCUM
06 Registrar ... Mr. Roger LASLEY
08 College Librarian ... Mr. Bradley SCHAFFNER
09 Dir of Inst Research and Assessment ... Mr. James FERGERSON
44 Asst VP Alum/Par Rel/Dir Annual Fnd ... Ms. Becky ZRIMSEK
29 Director of Alumni Relations ... Vacant
13 Interim Dir Information Tech Svc ... Mr. Sam PATTERSON
91 Assoc Dir InformationTechnology Svc ... Ms. Sue TRAXLER
105 Dir Web Communications/Development ... Ms. Jaye LAWRENCE
27 Director of Media/Public Relations ... Mr. Eric SIEGER
15 Director of Human Resources ... Ms. Kerstin CARDENAS
39 Director of Residential Life ... Vacant
88 Dir Intercult/International Life ... Ms. Joy KLUTTZ

85 Assoc Dir Intercult/Internatnl Life .... Mr. Luyen PHAN
104 Director of Off-Campus Studies .... Ms. Helena KAUFMAN
36 Director Career Center .... Vacant
23 Dir Student Health and Counseling .... Ms. Marit LYSNE
18 Dir of Facilities/Capital Planning .... Mr. Steven SPEHN
21 Comptroller .... Ms. Linda THORNTON
102 Dir Corporate/Foundation Relations .... Mr. Mark GLEASON
88 Dir of Curricular/Research Support .... Ms. Andrea NIXON
88 Director of Auxiliary Services .... Mr. Daniel BERGESON
40 Director of Carleton Bookstore .... Mr. David SCHLOSSER
41 Athletic Director .... Mr. Gerald YOUNG
19 Director of Security Services .... Mr. Wayne EISENHUTH

Central Baptist Theological Seminary of Minneapolis (A)

900 Forestview Lane N, Plymouth MN 55441-5934

County: Hennepin — Identification: 666050
Telephone: (763) 417-8250 — Carnegie Class: Not Classified
FAX Number: (763) 417-8258 — Calendar System: Semester
URL: www.centralseminary.edu
Established: 1956 — Annual Undergrad Tuition & Fees: $6,800
Enrollment: 90 — Coed
Affiliation or Control: Baptist — IRS Status: 501(c)3
Highest Offering: Doctorate
Program: Religious Emphasis
Accreditation: TRACS

01 President .... Dr. Samuel E. HORN
05 VP of Academic Affairs .... Dr. Jonathan R. PRATT
06 Registrar .... Jason STAMPER

*College of Medicine, Mayo Clinic (B)

200 First Street, Rochester MN 55905-3712

County: Olmsted — Identification: 666719
Telephone: (507) 284-2511 — Carnegie Class: N/A
FAX Number: (507) 284-0999
URL: www.mayo.edu

01 Chief Executive Officer .... Dr. John H. NOSEWORTHY
05 Exec Dean for Education Mayo Clinic .... Dr. Terrence CASCINO
46 Exec Dean for Research Mayo Clinic .... Dr. Robert A. RIZZA
22 Affirmative Action Administrator .... Mr. Kenneth J. SCHNEIDER
27 Chief Public Affairs Officer .... Mr. John LAFORGIA
43 Immigration Attorney .... Mr. Bruce R. LARSON
37 Financial Aid Officer .... Mr. David L. DAHLEN
08 Director of Libraries .... Mr. J. Michael HOMAN
29 Director Mayo Clinic Alumni Center .... Ms. Karen D. HERMAN
30 Director of Development .... Dr. Michael CAMILLERI
86 Director Government Relations .... Vacant

*Mayo Clinic College of Medicine-Mayo Graduate School (C)

200 First Street, SW, Rochester MN 55905-0001

County: Olmsted — FICE Identification: 011516
Unit ID: 365426
Telephone: (507) 538-1160 — Carnegie Class: DRU
FAX Number: (507) 293-0838 — Calendar System: Quarter
URL: www.mayo.edu/mgs/
Established: 1915 — Annual Graduate Tuition & Fees: $24,500
Enrollment: 177 — Coed
Affiliation or Control: Independent Non-Profit — IRS Status: 501(c)3
Highest Offering: Doctorate; No Undergraduates
Program: Professional
Accreditation: &NH

02 Dean .... Dr. L. James MAHER
05 Associate Dean Academic Affairs .... Vacant
32 Assoc Dean Student Affairs .... Dr. Bruce F. HORAZDOVSKY
20 Assistant Dean .... Ms. Kim WOLFGRAM SALZ

† Regional accreditation is carried under College of Medicine, Mayo Clinic.

*Mayo Medical School (D)

200 1st Street, SW, Rochester MN 55905-0001

County: Olmsted — FICE Identification: 011732
Unit ID: 173957
Telephone: (507) 538-4897 — Carnegie Class: Spec/Med
FAX Number: (507) 284-2634 — Calendar System: Other
URL: www.mayo.edu/mms
Established: 1971 — Annual Undergrad Tuition & Fees: $29,355
Enrollment: 192 — Coed
Affiliation or Control: Independent Non-Profit — IRS Status: 501(c)3
Highest Offering: First Professional Degree
Program: Professional
Accreditation: &NH, MED

02 Dean .... Dr. Terrence CASCINO
05 Assoc Dean Academic Affairs .... Dr. Joseph GRANDE
32 Assoc Dean Student Affairs .... Dr. Alexandra A. WOLANSKYJ
20 Assoc Dean Faculty Affairs .... Dr. Thomas R. VIGGIANO
11 Administrator for Mayo Med School .... Mr. Jonathan TORRENS-BURTON
22 Chief Human Resources .... Ms. Jill RAGSDALE
26 Chief Mrktng Ofcr/Chair Public Affs .... Mr. John W. LAFORGIA
85 International Personnel Advisor .... Ms. Ann H. LANCE
37 Financial Aid Officer .... Mr. David L. DAHLEN
08 Head Librarian .... Mr. J. Michael HOMAN

† Regional accreditation is carried under College of Medicine, Mayo Clinic.

*Mayo School of Health Sciences (E)

200 First St. SW, Siebens Bldg 11, Rochester MN 55905-0001

County: Olmsted — FICE Identification: 008182
Unit ID: 173966
Telephone: (507) 284-3678 — Carnegie Class: Spec/Health
FAX Number: (507) 284-0656 — Calendar System: Semester
URL: www.mayo.edu/mshs/
Established: 1973 — Annual Undergrad Tuition & Fees: N/A
Enrollment: 1,500 — Coed
Affiliation or Control: Independent Non-Profit — IRS Status: 501(c)3
Highest Offering: Doctorate
Program: Occupational; Professional
Accreditation: &NH, ANEST, CYTO, DENT, DIETI, DMS, HT, MT, NDT, NMT, PDPSY, PTA, RAD, RTT

02 Dean .... Dr. Claire E. BENDER
05 Associate Dean .... Dr. Michael H. SILBER
05 Associate Dean .... Dr. David C. AGERTER
20 Associate Dean Jacksonville .... Dr. Galen PERDIKIS
20 Associate Dean Scottsdale .... Dr. Catherine C. ROBERTS
88 Administrator/Assistant Dean .... Ms. Bethany KROM
12 Operations Manager Jacksonville .... Ms. Kate RAY
12 Operations Manager Scottsdale .... Ms. Nancy GRAY
11 Operations Manager Rochester .... Mr. Troy TYNSKY
11 Operations Manager Rochester .... Ms. Virginia WRIGHT-PETERSON
32 Operations Manager/Student Svcs .... Mr. Troy KEACH
06 Director of Financial Aid/Registrar .... Mr. David DAHLEN
37 Asst Director Financial Aid .... Ms. Marcy LANSWERK

† Regional accreditation is carried under College of Medicine, Mayo Clinic.

College of Saint Benedict (F)

37 S College Avenue, Saint Joseph MN 56374-2099

County: Stearns — FICE Identification: 002341
Unit ID: 174747
Telephone: (320) 363-5011 — Carnegie Class: Bac/A&S
FAX Number: (320) 363-6099 — Calendar System: Semester
URL: www.csbsju.edu
Established: 1913 — Annual Undergrad Tuition & Fees: $36,218
Enrollment: 2,041 — Coordinate
Affiliation or Control: Roman Catholic — IRS Status: 501(c)3
Highest Offering: Baccalaureate
Program: Liberal Arts And General; Teacher Preparatory
Accreditation: NH, DIETD, MUS, NURSE, TED

01 President .... Dr. MaryAnn BAENNINGER
05 Provost Academic Affairs .... Dr. Rita KNUESEL
32 Vice President Student Development .... Ms. Mary A. GELLER
30 Vice Pres Institutional Advancement .... Ms. Kimberly FERLAAK MOTES
84 VP Planning and Public Affairs .... Mr. Jon D. MCGEE
10 Vice Pres Finance/Administration .... Ms. Susan M. PALMER
07 VP Admission & Financial Aid .... Dr. Calvin MOSLEY
18 Exec Director Facilities .... Mr. Brad SINN
20 Vice Provost .... Dr. Joseph DESJARDINS
20 Academic Dean .... Dr. Richard ICE
27 Exec Dir Comm & Marketing Svcs .... Mr. Greg A. HOYE
34 Dean of Students .... Ms. Jody L. TERHAAR
06 Registrar .... Ms. Julie E. GRUSKA
08 Director Library .... Ms. Kathleen PARKER
37 Exec Director Financial Aid .... Mr. Stuart PERRY
15 Director Human Resources .... Ms. Carol ABELL
38 Director of Counseling .... Dr. Mike J. EWING
42 Director of Campus Ministry .... Sr. Sharon NOHNER, OSB
41 Athletic Director .... Ms. Carol L. HOWE-VEENSTRA
13 Director of Info Technology Svc .... Mr. Jim J. KOENIG
19 Director of Security .... Mr. Darren SWANSON
21 Controller .... Ms. Anne OBERMAN
44 Director of Planned Giving .... Mr. Bill HICKEY
36 Director of Career Services .... Dr. Heidi HARLANDER
09 Assoc Dir of Institutional Research .... Ms. Karen KNUTSON
40 Director of Bookstores .... Mr. Don L. FORBES
100 Chief of Staff/Exec Asst to Pres .... Ms. Kathryn ENKE
44 Director of Annual Giving .... Ms. Heather PIEPER-OLSON
28 Director Intercultural Center .... Ms. BernaDette W. SUWAREH
29 Director Alumnae Relations .... Ms. Jessie SANDOVAL
22 Human Resources Coordinator .... Ms. Marlene ERGEN
96 Purchasing Coordinator .... Ms. Briana WENTLAND

The College of Saint Scholastica (G)

1200 Kenwood Avenue, Duluth MN 55811-4199

County: Saint Louis — FICE Identification: 002343
Unit ID: 174899
Telephone: (218) 723-6000 — Carnegie Class: Master's M
FAX Number: (218) 723-6290 — Calendar System: Semester
URL: www.css.edu
Established: 1912 — Annual Undergrad Tuition & Fees: $30,208
Enrollment: 4,014 — Coed
Affiliation or Control: Roman Catholic — IRS Status: 501(c)3
Highest Offering: Doctorate
Program: Liberal Arts And General; Teacher Preparatory; Professional
Accreditation: NH, NURSE, OT, PTA, SW, TEAC

01 President .... Dr. Larry GOODWIN
10 Vice President Finance .... Mr. Patrick FLATTERY
05 Vice Pres Academic Affairs .... Dr. Elizabeth DOMHOLDT
30 Vice Pres College Advancement .... Ms. Margot ZELENZ
32 Vice President for Student Affairs .... Mr. Steve LYONS
84 Vice Pres for Enrollment Management .... Mr. Eric BERG
15 Vice President for Human Resources .... Vacant
88 Assoc Vice Pres College Advancement .... Ms. Janet S. ROSEN
06 Registrar .... Mr. George A. BEATTIE
26 Exec Dir Public & Media Relations .... Mr. Robert J. ASHENMACHER
13 Chief Information Officer .... Dr. Lynne HAMRE
08 Director of Library .... Mr. Kevin MCGREW
09 Director of Institutional Research .... Dr. Iwalani ELSE
18 Director of Facilities Services .... Mr. Tom BREKKE
88 Director OneStop Student Service .... Ms. Linda ROGENTINE
29 Director Alumni Relations .... Ms. Lisa ROSETH
07 Director of Freshman Admissions .... Mr. Joe WICKLUND
07 Director of Transfer Admissions .... Mr. Clarence SHARPE
41 Athletic Director .... Mr. Don OLSON
42 Director of Campus Ministry .... Mr. Nathan LANGER
37 Director Student Financial Aid .... Mr. Jon ERICKSON
38 Dir Stdnt Ctr Health/Well-Being .... Mr. Tad SEARS
96 Purchasing Manager .... Ms. Lisa ANDERSON
79 Dean School of Arts & Letters .... Dr. Tammy OSTRANDER
50 Dean Sch of Business & Technology .... Mr. Kurt LINBERG
53 Dean School of Education .... Dr. Jo OLSEN
76 Dean School of Health Sciences .... Dr. Rondell BERKELAND
66 Dean School of Nursing .... Dr. Marty WITRAK
81 Dean School of Sciences .... Dr. Aileen BEARD
85 International Student Advisor .... Ms. Alison CHAMPEAUX
104 Director of International Eduction .... Mr. Thomas HOMAN
45 Vice Pres for Strategic Initiatives .... Mr. Donald WORTHAM
04 Exec Admin Asst to President .... Ms. Joan HOLTER
19 Safety and Security Manager .... Mr. Michael TURNER
39 Asst Dean of Students-Campus Life .... Ms. Elizabeth KNEEPKENS
92 Director Honors Program .... Dr. Debra SCHROEDER
44 Exec Dir of Dev/Planned Giving .... Mr. Gary GARLIE
40 Bookstore Manager .... Ms. Ksenia OLSON
97 Director of General Education .... Dr. Darryl DIETRICH
88 Assoc Vice Pres of Mission Integrat .... Sr. Mary ROCHEFORT
88 Exec Dir Ctr for Healthcare Innovat .... Ms. Tami LICHTENBERG
88 Virtual Campus Director .... Mr. Craig BRIDGES
35 Dean of Students .... Ms. Megan PERRY-SPEARS
88 Asst Dean Advising & Retention .... Mr. David BAUMAN
28 Director of Institutional Diversity .... Ms. Emily SEGAR-JOHNSON

College of Visual Arts (H)

344 Summit Avenue, Saint Paul MN 55102-2199

County: Ramsey — FICE Identification: 007462
Unit ID: 174932
Telephone: (651) 757-4000 — Carnegie Class: Spec/Arts
FAX Number: (651) 757-4010 — Calendar System: Semester
URL: www.cva.edu
Established: 1924 — Annual Undergrad Tuition & Fees: $25,761
Enrollment: 210 — Coed
Affiliation or Control: Independent Non-Profit — IRS Status: 501(c)3
Highest Offering: Baccalaureate
Program: Fine Arts Emphasis
Accreditation: NH, ART

01 President & Academic Dean .... Ms. Ann LEDY
09 Vice President Inst Research/COO .... Dr. Susan SHORT
37 Director of Financial Aid .... Mr. David WOODWARD
13 Exec Director of Technology Support .... Ms. Barbara SZUREK
26 Director of External Relations .... Ms. Demeri C. MULLIKIN
06 Registrar .... Ms. Lois CANEDAY
10 Controller .... Ms. Sibyl ROCHE
08 Library Director .... Ms. Kathy HEUER

Concordia College (I)

901 8th Street S, Moorhead MN 56562-0001

County: Clay — FICE Identification: 002346
Unit ID: 173300
Telephone: (218) 299-4000 — Carnegie Class: Bac/A&S
FAX Number: (218) 299-3947 — Calendar System: Semester
URL: www.cord.edu
Established: 1891 — Annual Undergrad Tuition & Fees: $30,650
Enrollment: 2,772 — Coed
Affiliation or Control: Evangelical Lutheran Church In America
IRS Status: 501(c)3
Highest Offering: Master's
Program: Liberal Arts And General; Teacher Preparatory
Accreditation: NH, DIETD, DIETI, MUS, NURSE, SW, @TEAC

01 President .... Dr. William J. CRAFT
05 Provost and Dean of the College .... Dr. Mark J. KREJCI
10 Vice Pres Finance/Treasurer .... Ms. Linda J. BROWN
84 Vice President for Enrollment .... Mr. Steven M. SCHUETZ
88 VP Concordia Language Villages .... Dr. Christine L. SCHULZE
30 Vice Pres Advancement .... Ms. Teresa L. HARLAND
32 VP Student Affairs/Dean of Students .... Dr. Jennifer S. OATEY
04 Senior Associate to the President .... Ms. Tracey A. MOORHEAD
07 Director of Admissions .... Mr. Scott D. ELLINGSON
06 Interim Registrar .... Ms. Ericka HAUG
37 Director Financial Aid .... Mr. Eric ADDINGTON
08 Librarian .... Mrs. Sharon R. HOVERSON
36 Director of Career Center .... Mr. Jay H. THORESON
15 Director Human Resources .... Ms. Peggy L. TORRANCE
29 Director Alumni Relations .... Ms. Karen A. CARLSON

27 Sr Dir of Communications/Marketing ....Mr. Roger E. DEGERMAN
13 Chief Information Ofcr/Asc Provost ....Mr. Bruce W. VIEWEG
09 Director of Institutional Research ....Dr. Polly A. FASSINGER
18 Director of Facilities Management ....Mr. Wayne R. FLACK
38 Director of Student Counseling ....Ms. Monica R. KERSTING
41 Athletic Director ....Mr. Rich GLAS
42 Campus Pastor ....Rev. Timothy M. MEGORDEN
85 Director Intercultural Affairs .... Dr. Per ANDERSON

Concordia University, St. Paul (A)

275 Syndicate Street N, Saint Paul MN 55104-5494

County: Ramsey FICE Identification: 002347
Unit ID: 173328
Telephone: (651) 641-8278 Carnegie Class: Master's L
FAX Number: (651) 659-0207 Calendar System: Semester
URL: www.csp.edu
Established: 1893 Annual Undergrad Tuition & Fees: $29,700
Enrollment: 2,800 Coed
Affiliation or Control: Lutheran Church - Missouri Synod
IRS Status: 501(c)3
Highest Offering: Master's
Program: Liberal Arts And General; Teacher Preparatory
Accreditation: NH, ACBSP, TED

01 President ....Rev. Thomas Karl RIES
03 Executive Vice President .... Dr. Cheryl T. CHATMAN
05 Vice President Academic Affairs .... Mr. Lonn D. MALY
10 Vice President for Finance .... Rev. Michael H. DORNER
30 Vice President for Advancement ....Mr. Paul SELTZ
11 Sr Vice Pres for Administration ....Dr. Eric E. LAMOTT
20 Assoc Vice Pres Academic Affairs ....Dr. Miriam E. LUEBKE
32 Assoc VP Student Life/Dn of Stdnts .... Mr. Jason M. RAHN
53 Dean College of Education .... Dr. Donald W. HELMSTETTER
49 Dean College of Arts & Sciences ....Dr. David A. LUMPP
58 Dean of Graduate School ....Dr. Michael WALCHESKI
73 Dean College of Vocation/Ministry ....Dr. David A. LUMPP
50 Dean College of Bus/Org Leadership ....Dr. Bruce P. CORRIE
28 Dean of Diversity .... Dr. Cheryl T. CHATMAN
39 Associate Dean of Residence Life ....Ms. Sharon R. SCHEWE
06 Registrar ....Mrs. Toni SQUIRES
23 Director Health Services ....Mrs. Cher A. RAFFTERY
08 Director of Library Services .... Dr. Charlotte M. KNOCHE
07 Director Undergraduate Admission .... Mrs. Kristin M. SCHOON
27 Director University Communications ....Mr. Jason DEBOER-MORAN
102 Dir Foundation/Corporate Relations ..... Dr. Alan D. WINEGARDEN
15 Director of Human Resources ....Mrs. Mary M. ARNOLD
37 Director of Financial Aid ....Ms. Jeanie PECK
04 Executive Assistant to President ....Mrs. Jill K. SIMON
42 Interim Campus Chaplain ....Rev. Richard CARTER
88 Director of Traditional Advising ....Ms. Renee L. RERKO
09 Director of Institutional Research ....Ms. Beth C. PETER
29 Director of Alumni Relations ....Mrs. Rhonda K. BEHM
41 Director of Athletics ....Mr. Thomas J. RUBBELKE
18 Director of Operations ....Mr. James P. ORCHARD
36 Director of Placement/Prof ....Ms. Mary LEWIS
40 Bookstore Manager .... Mr. Anthony J. ROSS
90 Director of Computer Services .... Mr. Jonathan S. BREITBARTH
91 Director Administrative Computing ....Ms. Beth C. PETER
38 Director of Counseling Services ....Vacant
19 Risk Manager ....Mrs. Sara K. MULSO
24 Help Desk Coordinator .... Mr. Jason T. DEBOER-MORAN

Crossroads College (B)

920 Mayowood Road, SW, Rochester MN 55902-2382

County: Olmsted FICE Identification: 002366
Unit ID: 174206
Telephone: (507) 288-4563 Carnegie Class: Spec/Faith
FAX Number: (507) 288-9046 Calendar System: Semester
URL: www.crossroadscollege.edu
Established: 1913 Annual Undergrad Tuition & Fees: $15,280
Enrollment: 160 Coed
Affiliation or Control: Christian Churches And Churches of Christ
IRS Status: 501(c)3
Highest Offering: Baccalaureate
Program: 2-Year Principally Bachelor's Creditable; Religious Emphasis
Accreditation: BI

01 President ....Michael KILGALLIN
05 Vice President of Academics .... Claudio DIVINO
11 Vice Pres Administration & Finance ....Roger LANGSETH
32 Vice President Student Development ....Tim MCKINNEY
30 VP of Institutional Advancement ....Vacant
06 Registrar .... Robert DAMON
08 Director of the Library ....Jim GODSEY
07 Director of Admissions .... Christopher WILLIAMS
37 Director of Financial Aid .... Polly KELLOGG-BRADLEY
10 Business Manager ....Roger W. LANGSETH

Crown College (C)

8700 College View Drive, Saint Bonifacius MN 55375-9001

County: Carver FICE Identification: 002383
Unit ID: 174862
Telephone: (952) 446-4100 Carnegie Class: Bac/Diverse
FAX Number: (952) 446-4149 Calendar System: Semester
URL: www.crown.edu
Established: 1916 Annual Undergrad Tuition & Fees: $29,580
Enrollment: 1,198 Coed
Affiliation or Control: The Christian And Missionary Alliance
IRS Status: 501(c)3
Highest Offering: Master's
Program: Liberal Arts And General; Teacher Preparatory
Accreditation: NH, NURSE

01 President ....Dr. Richard P. MANN
04 Exec Assistant to the President .... Mrs. Shirley M. GRANLUND
10 VP Finance .... Mr. David TARRANT
05 VP Academic Affairs .... Dr. Scott MOATS
32 VP Student Development .... Mr. Michael SOHM
84 VP Enrollment & Marketing Services ....Mr. Mike PRICE
30 VP Advancement ....Mrs. Wendy EDGAR
11 Director of Operations .... Mr. Benjamin WAURMS
20 Dean for Undergraduate Pgms .... Dr. Scott MOATS
66 Director of Nursing .... Mrs. Teresa NEWBY
21 Controller .... Mr. Ronald STRAKA
41 Athletic Director .... Mr. Joshua DUNWOODY
08 Director of Media Services .... Dr. Dennis INGOLFSLAND
06 Registrar ....Mrs. Cheryl FISK
37 Director of Financial Aid .... Mrs. Shannon SCHAAF
35 Dir Leadership Dev/Student Activit ....Mr. Matt KORTUS
84 Director of Enrollment Services ....Ms. Maggie UNGER
18 Director of Facilities Services ....Mr. Rick LARSON
40 Director of Bookstore Services .... Mr. Leroy JAURIGUI
58 Director/Adult & Graduate Studies ....Mr. Jim HUNTER
44 Director of Development ....Mrs. Karen ROSE
42 Chaplain .... Mr. Bill KUHN
07 Director Undergraduate Admissions ....Mr. Bret HYDER
15 Director of Human Resources ....Mrs. Amy LUESSE
36 Dir Career Svcs/Academic Advising .... Mr. Donald TALBERT
13 Director of Technology Services .... Mr. Jeff AUNE
26 Director of Marketing .... Mr. Brian WRIGHT
29 Director Alumni Relations ....Mr. Michael WOOD

DeVry University - Edina (D)

7700 France Avenue South, Suite 575, Edina MN 55435-5876

County: Hennepin Identification: 666558
Unit ID: 445407
Telephone: (952) 838-1860 Carnegie Class: Spec/Bus
FAX Number: (952) 838-3737 Calendar System: Semester
URL: www.devry.edu
Established: 1931 Annual Undergrad Tuition & Fees: $16,156
Enrollment: 262 Coed
Affiliation or Control: Proprietary IRS Status: Proprietary
Highest Offering: Master's
Program: Liberal Arts And General; Professional; Business Emphasis
Accreditation: &NH

01 Campus Director .... Stephanie GRGURICH

† Regional accreditation is carried under the parent institution in Downers Grove, IL.

Duluth Business University, Inc. (E)

4724 Mike Colalillo Drive, Duluth MN 55807-2723

County: Saint Louis FICE Identification: 009892
Unit ID: 173489
Telephone: (218) 722-4000 Carnegie Class: Assoc/PrivFP
FAX Number: (218) 628-2127 Calendar System: Quarter
URL: www.dbumn.edu
Established: 1891 Annual Undergrad Tuition & Fees: $15,785
Enrollment: 329 Coed
Affiliation or Control: Proprietary IRS Status: Proprietary
Highest Offering: Baccalaureate
Program: Occupational; 2-Year Principally Bachelor's Creditable; Technical Emphasis
Accreditation: ACICS, MAC

01 President ....Mr. James R. GESSNER
03 Campus Director ....Mrs. Bonnie L. KUPCZYNSKI
05 Director of Education ....Mrs. LaVonne R. TUCCI
91 Dir Info Technology/Dist Educ Oper ....Mr. David R. LUTZKA
06 Registrar ....Ms. Lisa E. NAGURSKI
08 Librarian ....Ms. Joyce C. PETERSON
36 Career Services Manager ....Mr. David E. COOK
37 Financial Aid Advisor .... Mrs. Gloria G. COOLE

Dunwoody College of Technology (F)

818 Dunwoody Boulevard, Minneapolis MN 55403-1192

County: Hennepin FICE Identification: 004641
Unit ID: 175227
Telephone: (612) 374-5800 Carnegie Class: Assoc/PrivNFP4
FAX Number: (612) 381-9620 Calendar System: Quarter
URL: www.dunwoody.edu
Established: 1914 Annual Undergrad Tuition & Fees: $18,000
Enrollment: 1,052 Coed
Affiliation or Control: Independent Non-Profit IRS Status: 501(c)3
Highest Offering: Baccalaureate
Program: Occupational; Technical Emphasis
Accreditation: NH, RAD

01 President .... Mr. Rich WAGNER
05 Provost ....Mr. Jeff YLINEN
03 Associate Provost ....Ms. Ann IVERSON
10 Chief Financial Officer ....Ms. Nancy J. FUCHS
84 Vice President Enrollment Mgmt ....Ms. Collette GARRITY
15 Director of Human Resources ....Ms. Patricia EDMAN

Globe University (G)

8089 Globe Drive, Woodbury MN 55125-3388

County: Washington FICE Identification: 004642
Unit ID: 173629
Telephone: (651) 730-5100 Carnegie Class: Bac/Assoc
FAX Number: (651) 730-5151 Calendar System: Quarter
URL: www.globeuniversity.edu
Established: 1885 Annual Undergrad Tuition & Fees: $15,300
Enrollment: 1,284 Coed
Affiliation or Control: Proprietary IRS Status: Proprietary
Highest Offering: Master's
Program: Occupational
Accreditation: ACICS, MAAB

01 Campus Director .... Ms. Lisa PALERMO
05 Dean of Faculty .... Ms. Denise RADCLIFFE
32 Dean of Students ....Mr. Brian RAICHE
37 Director of Financial Aid ....Mr. Ben FLIKEID
07 Director of Admissions ....Ms. Sonia SULTAN
36 Director of Career Services ....Ms. Teresa DYE

Globe University/Minnesota School of Business (H)

5910 Shingle Creek Parkway, #200, Brooklyn Center MN 55430-2319

County: Hennepin Identification: 666453
Unit ID: 407285
Telephone: (763) 566-7777 Carnegie Class: Bac/Assoc
FAX Number: (763) 566-7030 Calendar System: Quarter
URL: www.msbcollege.edu
Established: 1877 Annual Undergrad Tuition & Fees: $15,660
Enrollment: 442 Coed
Affiliation or Control: Proprietary IRS Status: Proprietary
Highest Offering: Baccalaureate
Program: Occupational
Accreditation: ACICS, MAAB

01 Director .... Ms. Jana GYMER-KOCH

† Branch campus of Minnesota School of Business, Richfield, MN.

Globe University Northwest Technical Institute (I)

950 Blue Gentian Road, Suite 500, Eagan MN 55121-1626

County: Dakota FICE Identification: 008267
Unit ID: 174482
Telephone: (952) 944-0080 Carnegie Class: Assoc/PrivFP
FAX Number: (952) 944-9274 Calendar System: Semester
URL: www.nti.edu
Established: 1957 Annual Undergrad Tuition & Fees: N/A
Enrollment: N/A Coed
Affiliation or Control: Proprietary IRS Status: Proprietary
Highest Offering: Associate Degree
Program: Occupational; 2-Year Principally Bachelor's Creditable; Technical Emphasis
Accreditation: ACCSC

00 Chairman of the Board ....Mr. Norris J. NELSON
36 Placement ....Mrs. Theres HEIMEL

† In Teach-out mode, will close in February 2013.

Gustavus Adolphus College (J)

800 W College Avenue, Saint Peter MN 56082-1498

County: Nicollet FICE Identification: 002353
Unit ID: 173647
Telephone: (507) 933-8000 Carnegie Class: Bac/A&S
FAX Number: (507) 933-7041 Calendar System: Semester
URL: www.gustavus.edu
Established: 1862 Annual Undergrad Tuition & Fees: $37,210
Enrollment: 2,471 Coed
Affiliation or Control: Evangelical Lutheran Church In America
IRS Status: 501(c)3
Highest Offering: Baccalaureate
Program: Liberal Arts And General; Teacher Preparatory
Accreditation: NH, MUS, NURSE, TED

01 President .... Mr. Jack R. OHLE
05 Provost and Dean of the College .... Dr. Mark J. BRAUN
10 VP for Finance and Treasurer ....Mr. Kenneth C. WESTPHAL
07 VP for Enrollment Management ....Dr. Thomas M. CRADY
30 VP for Institutional Advancement .... Mr. Thomas W. YOUNG
32 VP for Student Life ....Dr. JoNes R. VANHECKE
26 VP Marketing & Communication ....Mr. Timothy R. KENNEDY
28 Dir Multicult Pgm/Asst Dean Stdnts ....Mr. Virgil E. JONES
09 Director Institutional Research ....Dr. David A. MENK
08 Head Librarian ....Ms. Barbara R. FISTER
88 Director Church Relations .... Rev. Grady I. ST. DENNIS
29 Director Alumni Relations ....Mr. Randall M. STUCKEY
36 Director Career Development ....Ms. Cynthia L. FAVRE
06 Registrar ....Ms. Kristianne R. WESTPHAL
13 Dir Gustavus Technology Services .... Mr. Bruce N. AARSVOLD
18 Director Physical Plant .... Mr. Warren P. WUNDERLICH
37 Director Student Financial Aid ....Mr. Doug O. MINTER
39 Director Residential Life ....Mr. Lawrence C. POTTS
42 Chaplain .... Rev. Rachel S. LARSON

35 Associate Dean of Students ... Mr. Stephen R. BENNETT
41 Athletics Director ... Mr. Thomas W. BROWN
15 Director Human Resources ... Dr. Kirk D. BEYER
19 Director Campus Security ... Mr. Raymond H. THROWER
40 Manager Book Mark ... Ms. Molly L. YONKERS
27 Director Media Relations ... Mr. Matthew D. THOMAS
04 Asst to the Pres & Sec of the Board ... Ms. Jolene D. CHRISTENSEN

Hamline University (A)

1536 Hewitt Avenue, MS-C1914,
Saint Paul MN 55104-1284

County: Ramsey FICE Identification: 002354
Unit ID: 173665
Telephone: (651) 523-2800 Carnegie Class: Master's L
FAX Number: (651) 523-2899 Calendar System: 4/1/4
URL: www.hamline.edu
Established: 1854 Annual Undergrad Tuition & Fees: $33,236
Enrollment: 4,852 Coed
Affiliation or Control: United Methodist IRS Status: 501(c)3
Highest Offering: Doctorate
Program: Liberal Arts And General; Teacher Preparatory; Professional
Accreditation: NH, LAW, MUS, TED

01 President ... Dr. Linda N. HANSON
05 Provost ... Dr. Eric JENSEN
10 Vice President Finance ... Mr. Douglas P. ANDERSON
26 Vice Pres Marketing/Enrollment Mgmt ... Mr. Jeffrey RICH
30 VP Development & Alumni Relations .. Mr. Tony GRUNDHAUSER
32 Dean of Students ... Dr. Alan A. SICKBERT
43 VP HR/General Counsel ... Ms. Catherine WASSBERG
13 Assoc VP/Dir IT ... Mr. Mark KONDRAK
26 Assoc VP Marketing Communications ... Ms. Breanne HANSON HEGG
84 Assoc VP of Enrollment Services ... Ms. Pamela JOHNSON
28 Dir Multicult and Div Initiatives ... Dr. Veena DEO
18 Assoc VP Facilities/Physical Plant ... Mr. Lowell BROMANDER
61 Dean School of Law ... Mr. Donald M. LEWIS
50 Dean School of Business ... Ms. Anne MCCARTHY
53 Dean School of Education ... Dr. Nancy SORENSON
49 Dean College Liberal Arts ... Dr. John MATACHEK
28 Ast Dn/Dir Multicult/Intl Stdt Affs ... Mr. Carlos SNEED
06 Registrar Undergrad/Grad Schools ... Mr. Tim TRAFFIE
29 Exec Director Assoc of Hamline Alum .... Ms. Elizabeth L. RADTKE
37 Director Financial Aid ... Ms. Lynette WAHL
06 Registrar Law School ... Ms. Colleen CLISH
07 Director Law School Admissions ... Ms. Robin C. INGLI
07 Director of Admissions ... Mr. Milyon TRULOVE
15 Director Human Resources ... Ms. Dorcas M. MICHAELSON
36 Interim Dir Career Development ... Mr. Terry MIDDENDORF
41 Athletic Director ... Mr. Robert BEEMAN
19 Director of Safety & Security ... Mr. James SCHUMANN
23 Director Counseling & Health Center ... Ms. Barbara BESTER
35 Dir Student Leadership & Activities ... Ms. Wendy BURNS
42 Chaplain & Director ... Ms. Nancy M. VICTORIN-VANGERUD
96 Director of Purchasing ... Ms. Susan BORNUS
04 Exec Assistant to the President ... Ms. Jane A. TELLEEN

Hazelden Graduate School of Addiction Studies (B)

PO Box 11 (CO9), Center City MN 55012-0011

County: Chisago FICE Identification: 040443
Unit ID: 173683
Telephone: (651) 213-4175 Carnegie Class: Spec/Health
FAX Number: (651) 213-4710 Calendar System: Semester
URL: www.hazelden.edu
Established: 1999 Annual Graduate Tuition & Fees: $28,702
Enrollment: 109 Coed
Affiliation or Control: Independent Non-Profit IRS Status: 501(c)3
Highest Offering: Master's; No Undergraduates
Program: Professional
Accreditation: NH

01 President and CEO ... Mr. Mark MISHEK
05 Chief Academic Officer & Provost ... Dr. Valerie SLAYMAKER
88 Asst to the Chief Academic Officer ... Ms. Heidi SOLOMONSON
20 Dean ... Dr. Daniel FRIGO
07 Admissions Specialist ... Ms. Nancy KAMINSKI
06 Registrar ... Ms. Debra MATTISON
09 Dir of Institutional Effectiveness ... Dr. Timothy SHEEHAN
06 Registrar of Administrative Service ... Ms. Twyla RAMSDELL

Herzing University (C)

5700 West Broadway, Minneapolis MN 55428

County: Hennepin FICE Identification: 011017
Unit ID: 174154
Telephone: (763) 535-3000 Carnegie Class: Spec/Health
FAX Number: (763) 535-9205 Calendar System: Semester
URL: www.herzing.edu
Established: 1961 Annual Undergrad Tuition & Fees: $15,490
Enrollment: 376 Coed
Affiliation or Control: Proprietary IRS Status: Proprietary
Highest Offering: Baccalaureate
Program: Professional
Accreditation: &NH, DA, DH, MAC, NURSE, OTA

01 Chief Executive Officer ... Mr. John SLAMA
05 Academic Dean ... Mr. Larry DOTY
07 Director of Admissions ... Ms. Jennifer SEKULA
10 Dir Financial Svcs/Financial Aid ... Ms. Heather BOES

† Regional accreditation is carried under the parent institution in Madison, WI.

Institute of Production and Recording (D)

312 Washington Avenue North, Minneapolis MN 55401

County: Hennepin FICE Identification: 041302
Unit ID: 454616
Telephone: (612) 375-1900 Carnegie Class: Assoc/PrivFP
FAX Number: (612) 375-1919 Calendar System: Other
URL: www.ipr.edu
Established: 2002 Annual Undergrad Tuition & Fees: $24,300
Enrollment: 373 Coed
Affiliation or Control: Proprietary IRS Status: Proprietary
Highest Offering: Associate Degree
Program: Occupational
Accreditation: ACCSC

01 Campus Director ... Brian JACOBY
03 Vice President ... Lance SABIN
05 Dean of Faculty ... Madeline HENGEL
07 Director of Admissions ... Suzanne FERKINGSTAD
32 Director of Student Services ... Erica WEST
08 Librarian ... Tina HALFMANN

ITT Technical Institute (E)

8911 Columbine Road, Eden Prairie MN 55347-4143

County: Hennepin Identification: 666319
Unit ID: 445081
Telephone: (952) 914-5300 Carnegie Class: Spec/Tech
FAX Number: (952) 914-5350 Calendar System: Quarter
URL: www.itt-tech.edu
Established: 2004 Annual Undergrad Tuition & Fees: N/A
Enrollment: 523 Coed
Affiliation or Control: Proprietary IRS Status: Proprietary
Highest Offering: Baccalaureate
Program: Technical Emphasis
Accreditation: ACICS

† Branch campus of ITT Technical Institute, Indianapolis, IN.

Le Cordon Bleu College of Culinary Arts in Minneapolis/St Paul (F)

1315 Mendota Heights Road,
Mendota Heights MN 55120-1129

County: Dakota Identification: 666370
Unit ID: 446844
Telephone: (651) 675-4700 Carnegie Class: Assoc/PrivFP
FAX Number: (651) 452-5282 Calendar System: Quarter
URL: www.chefs.edu/minneapolis-st-paul
Established: 1999 Annual Undergrad Tuition & Fees: $20,550
Enrollment: 750 Coed
Affiliation or Control: Proprietary IRS Status: Proprietary
Highest Offering: Associate Degree
Program: Occupational; Technical Emphasis
Accreditation: ACICS, ACFEI

01 President ... Mr. Kevin L. SANDERSON
10 Business Operations Manager ... Ms. Pamela TRANDAHL
05 Executive Chef ... Mr. Steven SHAPLEY
07 Senior Director of Admissions ... Mr. David PETERSON
36 Director of Career Services ... Ms. Kianna RAMOS
22 Director of Compliance ... Vacant
88 Lead Instructor Patisserie-Baking ... Ms. Amy SHIPSHOCK
88 Lead Instructor Culinary Arts ... Ms. Farley KAISER
06 Associate Registrar ... Ms. Cindy THOMPSON

† Branch campus of Le Cordon Bleu College of Culinary Arts, Portland, OR.

Leech Lake Tribal College (G)

P.O. Box 180, Cass Lake MN 56633-0180

County: Cass FICE Identification: 030964
Unit ID: 413626
Telephone: (218) 335-4200 Carnegie Class: Tribal
FAX Number: (218) 335-4282 Calendar System: Semester
URL: www.lltc.edu
Established: 1990 Annual Undergrad Tuition & Fees: $4,432
Enrollment: 206 Coed
Affiliation or Control: Tribal Control IRS Status: 501(c)3
Highest Offering: Associate Degree
Program: Occupational; 2-Year Principally Bachelor's Creditable
Accreditation: NH

01 President ... Dr. Ginny CARNEY
03 Vice President ... Dr. Beverly RODGERS
05 Dean of Academics ... Dr. Sharon MARCOTTE
10 Chief Financial Officer ... Rochelle PEMBERTON
30 Director Institutional Advancement ... Kyle ERICKSON

Luther Seminary (H)

2481 Como Avenue, Saint Paul MN 55108-1496

County: Ramsey FICE Identification: 002357
Unit ID: 173896
Telephone: (651) 641-3456 Carnegie Class: Spec/Faith
FAX Number: (651) 641-3425 Calendar System: Semester
URL: www.luthersem.edu
Established: 1869 Annual Graduate Tuition & Fees: $15,000
Enrollment: 806 Coed
Affiliation or Control: Evangelical Lutheran Church In America
IRS Status: 501(c)3
Highest Offering: Doctorate; No Undergraduates
Program: Professional; Religious Emphasis
Accreditation: NH, THEOL

01 President ... Dr. Richard BLIESE
05 Dean of Academic Affairs ... Dr. Roland MARTINSON
11 VP Admininstration & Finance ... Mr. Donald LEWIS
26 VP Seminary Relations ... Mr. Thomas JOLIVETTE
32 VP Student Affairs & Enrollment ... Ms. Carrie CARROLL
15 VP Human Resources ... Ms. Sandra MIDDENDORF
42 Seminary Pastor ... Rev. Paul HARRINGTON
07 Director of Admissions ... Vacant
06 Registrar ... Ms. Diane DONCITS

Lutheran Brethren Seminary (I)

815 West Vernon Avenue, Fergus Falls MN 56537-2676

County: Otter Tail Identification: 666644
Telephone: (218) 739-3375 Carnegie Class: Not Classified
FAX Number: (218) 739-1259 Calendar System: Semester
URL: www.lbs.edu
Established: 1903 Annual Undergrad Tuition & Fees: $10,206
Enrollment: 20 Coed
Affiliation or Control: Other IRS Status: 501(c)3
Highest Offering: Master's
Program: Liberal Arts And General; Religious Emphasis
Accreditation: @TRACS

01 President ... Dr. David VEUM
05 Dean ... Dr. Eugene BOE
06 Registrar ... Dr. Gaylan MATHIESEN

Macalester College (J)

1600 Grand Avenue, Saint Paul MN 55105-1801

County: Ramsey FICE Identification: 002358
Unit ID: 173902
Telephone: (651) 696-6000 Carnegie Class: Bac/A&S
FAX Number: (651) 696-6689 Calendar System: Semester
URL: www.macalester.edu
Established: 1874 Annual Undergrad Tuition & Fees: $43,693
Enrollment: 2,005 Coed
Affiliation or Control: Presbyterian Church (U.S.A.) IRS Status: 501(c)3
Highest Offering: Baccalaureate
Program: Liberal Arts And General
Accreditation: NH

01 President ... Dr. Brian C. ROSENBERG
05 Dean of the Faculty & Provost ... Dr. Kathleen M. MURRAY
88 Chief Investment Officer ... Mr. Mansco PERRY
30 Vice President College Advancement ... Mr. Thomas P. BONNER
32 Vice President Student Affairs ... Ms. Laurie B. HAMRE
11 Vice President for Admin/Finance ... Mr. David M. WHEATON
08 Associate Vice President ITS ... Mr. Jerry R. SANDERS
07 Dean of Admissions/Financial Aid ... Mr. Lorne T. ROBINSON
85 Inst for Global Citizenship ... Ms. Christy L. HANSON
20 Director of Academic Programs ... Ms. Ann M. MINNICK
28 Dean of Multicultural Life ... Mr. Chris A. MACDONALD-DENNIS
09 Assoc Provost/Inst Research ... Mr. Daniel J. BALIK
35 Dean of Students ... Mr. Jim HOPPE
37 Director Student Financial Aid ... Mr. Brian LINDEMAN
06 Registrar ... Ms. Jayne L. NIEMI
36 Assoc Dean for Student Services ... Ms. Denise WARD
15 Director Human Resources ... Mr. Bob GRAF
18 Director Facilities Management ... Mr. Mark D. DICKINSON
41 Athletic Director ... Ms. Kim CHANDLER
04 Assistant to the President ... Ms. Cynthia L. HENDRICKS
21 Assistant Vice President Finance ... Ms. Kate WALKER
26 Director Communications and PR ... Mr. David P. WARCH
29 Director Alumni Relations ... Ms. Gabrielle S. LAWRENCE
38 Director Health and Wellness Center ... Ms. Denise WARD
96 Dir Purchasing/Accounts Payable ... Ms. Kathleen L. JOHNSON

Martin Luther College (K)

1995 Luther Court, New Ulm MN 56073-3300

County: Brown FICE Identification: 002361
Unit ID: 173452
Telephone: (507) 354-8221 Carnegie Class: Bac/Diverse
FAX Number: (507) 354-8225 Calendar System: Semester
URL: www.mlc-wels.edu
Established: 1995 Annual Undergrad Tuition & Fees: $11,770
Enrollment: 777 Coed
Affiliation or Control: Wisconsin Evangelical Lutheran Synod
IRS Status: 501(c)3
Highest Offering: Master's
Program: Liberal Arts And General; Teacher Preparatory
Accreditation: NH

01	President	Rev. Mark G. ZARLING
05	Vice President for Academics	Dr. David O. WENDLER
11	Vice President for Administration	Prof. Steven R. THIESFELDT
84	Vice President for Enrollment Mgmt	Vacant
32	Vice President Student Life	Prof. Jeffrey L. SCHONE
53	Academic Dean Educational Ministry	Vacant
73	Academic Dean Pastoral Ministry	Prof. Daniel N. BALGE
10	Director of Finance	Mrs. Carla J. HULKE
08	Librarian	Prof. David M. GOSDECK
37	Director of Financial Aid	Mr. Gene A. SLETTEDAHL
07	Director of Admissions	Prof. Mark A. STEIN
58	Director Graduates Studies/Cont Edu	Prof. John E. MEYER
88	Director of Clinical Experiences	Prof. Paul A. TESS
41	Director of Athletics	Prof. James M. UNKE
42	Campus Pastor	Rev. John C. BOEDER
14	Director of Technology	Mr. James A. RATHJE
26	Director of Public Relations	Prof. William A. PEKRUL
40	Bookstore Manager	Mrs. Valerie J. BOVEE
90	Director of Academic Computing	Dr. James R. GRUNWALD
29	Director Alumni Relations	Mr. Stephen J. BALZA

McNally Smith College of Music (A)

19 Exchange Street, Saint Paul MN 55101-2220
County: Ramsey FICE Identification: 030012
Unit ID: 367194
Telephone: (651) 291-0177 Carnegie Class: Spec/Arts
FAX Number: (651) 291-0366 Calendar System: Semester
URL: www.mcnallysmith.edu
Established: 1985 Annual Undergrad Tuition & Fees: $23,520
Enrollment: 674 Coed
Affiliation or Control: Proprietary IRS Status: Proprietary
Highest Offering: Baccalaureate
Program: Occupational; Liberal Arts And General; Professional; Music Emphasis
Accreditation: MUS

01	President	Harry CHALMIERS
37	Financial Aid Director	Jeffrey R. AALBERS
07	Admissions Director	Kathy HAWKS

Minneapolis Business College (B)

1711 W County Road B, Roseville MN 55113-4056
County: Ramsey FICE Identification: 004645
Unit ID: 174118
Telephone: (651) 636-7406 Carnegie Class: Assoc/PrivFP
FAX Number: (651) 636-8185 Calendar System: Semester
URL: www.minneapolisbusinesscollege.edu
Established: 1874 Annual Undergrad Tuition & Fees: $14,500
Enrollment: 275 Coed
Affiliation or Control: Proprietary IRS Status: Proprietary
Highest Offering: Associate Degree
Program: Occupational; 2-Year Principally Bachelor's Creditable; Business Emphasis
Accreditation: ACICS, MAC

01	President	Mr. David WHITMAN
05	Director of Education	Mr. Jon BLUMENTHAL
32	Director of Student Services	Mrs. Marie MARTIN
36	Placement Coordinator	Mrs. Suzanne ERICKSON

Minneapolis College of Art Design (C)

2501 Stevens Avenue, Minneapolis MN 55404-4343
County: Hennepin FICE Identification: 002365
Unit ID: 174127
Telephone: (612) 874-3700 Carnegie Class: Spec/Arts
FAX Number: (612) 874-3704 Calendar System: Semester
URL: www.mcad.edu
Established: 1886 Annual Undergrad Tuition & Fees: $31,550
Enrollment: 678 Coed
Affiliation or Control: Independent Non-Profit IRS Status: 501(c)3
Highest Offering: Master's
Program: Liberal Arts And General; Professional; Fine Arts Emphasis
Accreditation: NH, ART

01	President	Mr. Jay COOGAN
04	Executive Assistant to President	Ms. Kate MOHN
05	Vice President Academic Affairs	Ms. Karen WIRTH
30	Vice Pres Institutional Advancement	Ms. Joan G. OLSON
11	Vice President Administration	Ms. Pam NEWSOME
32	Vice President Student Affairs	Ms. Susan P. CALMENSON
84	Vice Pres Enrollment Management	Mr. William MULLEN
18	Assoc VP Facilities/Public Safety	Mr. Brock RASMUSSEN
13	Assoc Vice President Technology	Mr. R. Hal WELLS
10	Chief Financial Officer/Treasurer	Mr. Dan SJOQUIST
06	Registrar	Ms. Jacki L. CHESTNUT
51	Director of Continuing Studies	Ms. Lara ROY
08	Interim Library Director	Ms. Amy NAUGHTON
24	Director of Media Center	Mr. Scott BOWMAN
36	Director of Career Services	Ms. Christine DAVES
29	Director Major and Alumni Giving	Mr. Brian GIOIELLI
39	Director Student Housing	Mr. Nate K. LUTZ
26	Director Communications	Mr. Rob DAVIS
37	Director Student Financial Aid	Ms. Laura LINK
40	Manager of Bookstore	Ms. Allyson R. HARPER

Minnesota School of Business (D)

1401 W 76th Street, Suite 500, Richfield MN 55423-3846
County: Hennepin FICE Identification: 004646
Unit ID: 174279
Telephone: (612) 861-2000 Carnegie Class: Master's S
FAX Number: (612) 861-5548 Calendar System: Quarter
URL: www.msbcollege.edu
Established: 1877 Annual Undergrad Tuition & Fees: $15,300
Enrollment: 1,504 Coed
Affiliation or Control: Proprietary IRS Status: Proprietary
Highest Offering: Master's
Program: Occupational
Accreditation: ACICS, MAAB, NURSE

01	Campus Director	Mrs. Stacy SEVERSON
05	Dean of Faculty	Vacant
32	Dean of Students	Ms. Shelby NAFUS
07	Director of Admissions	Mr. Chad PETERSON
36	Director of Career Services	Ms. Sara SHORE
37	Director of Financial Aid	Ms. Nicole PAULSON

*Minnesota State Colleges and Universities System Office (E)

WellsFargo Pl, Ste 350, 30 7th St,E, Saint Paul MN 55101-4901
County: Ramsey FICE Identification: 009346
Unit ID: 428453
Telephone: (651) 201-1800 Carnegie Class: N/A
FAX Number: (651) 297-5550
URL: www.mnscu.edu

01	Chancellor	Steven J. ROSENSTONE
05	Vice Chanc Academic/Student Affairs	Douglas D. KNOWLTON
10	Vice Chancellor Finance/CFO	Laura M. KING
16	Int Vice Chancellor Human Resources	Sheila REGER
13	Vice Chanc/Chief Information Ofcr	Darrel S. HUISH
30	Vice Chanc Advancement	Michael I. DOUGHERTY
18	Assoc Vice Chancellor Facilities	Brian D. YOLITZ
46	Assoc Vice Chanc Research/Planning	Leslie K. MERCER
35	Assoc Vice Chanc Student Affairs	Mike LOPEZ
22	Exec Dir Diversity/Multiculturalism	Whitney Stewart HARRIS
102	Exec Dir System/Foundation Rels	Maria R. MCLEMORE
43	General Counsel	Gail M. OLSON
09	System Director for Research	Craig V. SCHOENECKER
21	Director of Internal Auditing	Beth H. BUSE

*Alexandria Technical & Community College (F)

1601 Jefferson Street, Alexandria MN 56308-2796
County: Douglas FICE Identification: 005544
Unit ID: 172918
Telephone: (320) 762-0221 Carnegie Class: Assoc/Pub-R-M
FAX Number: (320) 762-4501 Calendar System: Semester
URL: www.alextech.edu
Established: 1961 Annual Undergrad Tuition & Fees (In-State): $6,453
Enrollment: 2,589 Coed
Affiliation or Control: State IRS Status: 501(c)3
Highest Offering: Associate Degree
Program: Occupational; 2-Year Principally Bachelor's Creditable; Technical Emphasis
Accreditation: NH, MLTAD

02	President	Dr. Kevin KOPISCHKE
05	Exec VP Academic/Student Affairs	Dr. Jan DOEBBERT
41	Vice Pres/Athletic Director	Vacant
51	Vice Pres Custom Services	Dr. Chad COAUETTE
10	Chief Financial Officer	Mr. David BJELLAND
05	Dean of Academic Affairs	Mr. Gregg RAISANEN
32	Dean of Student Affairs	Vacant
72	Dean of Technology	Mr. Steve RICHARDS
20	Associate Dean of Academic Affairs	Ms. Kellie TATGE
19	Associate Dean of Law Enforcement	Mr. Scott BERGER
37	Financial Aid Director	Mr. Steve RICHARDS
22	Human Rights Officer	Ms. Tamzin BUKOWSKI
36	Director Student Placement	Mr. Patrick RUNNING
30	Exec Dir Advancement/Foundation	Ms. Kathy NOHRE
06	Registrar	Ms. Debra LE DOUX
18	Director of Facilities	Mr. Tim TOUGAS
15	Chief Human Resources Officer	Ms. Shari MALONEY
09	Director Institutional Research	Ms. Rebekah SUMMER
07	Director of Admissions/Diversity	Mr. Charles (Tex) CLAYMORE
35	Director of Student Activities	Ms. Michelle AHLQUIST
38	Dir Testing Center/PSEO Specialist	Ms. Mary LENZ
04	Asst to Pres/Dir of Office Services	Ms. Annette PAVEK
21	Accounting Supervisor	Ms. Joan STICH
40	Bookstore Manager	Ms. Karen SLACK
29	Alumni Coordinator	Ms. Linda DOLAN
88	Support Services Coordinator	Ms. Mary ACKERMAN

*Anoka-Ramsey Community College (G)

11200 Mississippi Boulevard NW, Coon Rapids MN 55433-3499
County: Anoka FICE Identification: 002332
Unit ID: 172963
Telephone: (763) 433-1100 Carnegie Class: Assoc/Pub-S-MC
FAX Number: (763) 433-1121 Calendar System: Semester
URL: www.anokaramsey.edu
Established: 1965 Annual Undergrad Tuition & Fees (In-State): $4,906
Enrollment: 9,221 Coed
Affiliation or Control: State IRS Status: 501(c)3
Highest Offering: Associate Degree
Program: Occupational; 2-Year Principally Bachelor's Creditable
Accreditation: NH, ADNUR, MUS, PTAA

02	Interim President	Dr. Jessica STUMPF
10	VP Finance & Administration	Vacant
05	VP Academic/Student Affairs	Ms. Deidra PEASLEE
32	Dean/Chief Student Affairs Officer	Dr. Mary RAEKER-REBEK
18	Physical Plant Manager	Mr. Roger FREEMAN
16	Chief HR Director	Mr. Darren HOFF
57	Dean of Arts & Letters	Ms. Dana IRGENS
88	Dean CE/CT/Bus/Tech/Wellness	Ms. Luanne KANE
35	Interim Dean Student Life	Ms. Lisa HARRIS
76	Dean of Allied Health	Ms. Natasha BAER
21	Director Fiscal & Auxillary Svcs	Ms. Marilyn SMITH
46	Dean of Innovative Teaching	Vacant
09	Dean of Research & Assessment	Ms. Nora MORRIS
28	Director of Multicultural Affairs	Mr. Marcellus DAVIS
102	Director of Foundations	Mr. Marc JOHNSON
26	Director of Mktg/Public Relations	Ms. Mary JACOBSON
19	Director of Safety & Security	Mr. Orrin NYHUS
35	Director of Student Life	Ms. Joyce TRACZYK
13	Interim Director of Technology	Mr. Tim ZONDLO
21	Business Manager	Ms. Kim BIENFANG

*Anoka Technical College (H)

1355 W Highway 10, Anoka MN 55303-1590
County: Anoka FICE Identification: 007350
Unit ID: 172954
Telephone: (763) 576-4700 Carnegie Class: Assoc/Pub-S-MC
FAX Number: (763) 576-4715 Calendar System: Semester
URL: www.anokatech.edu
Established: 1967 Annual Undergrad Tuition & Fees (In-District): $5,430
Enrollment: 2,389 Coed
Affiliation or Control: State/Local IRS Status: 501(c)3
Highest Offering: Associate Degree
Program: Occupational; 2-Year Principally Bachelor's Creditable
Accreditation: NH, MAC, OTA, SURGT

02	Interim President	Jessica STUMPF
05	Int Vice Pres of Acad/Student Affs	Chad COAUETTE
13	Chief Information/Facilities Ofcr	David JEFFREY
10	Chief Business Ofcr/Facil/Phys Plnt	Wendy MEYER
20	Academic Dean	James CLARK
04	Assistant to the President	Carol LARSON
15	Chief Human Res Ofcr/Dir Diversity	Marybeth CHRISTENSON-JONES
26	Director of Marketing/Diversity	Bobbie DAHLKE
06	Registrar	Kimberly ROAN
07	Admissions Director	LeAnn BROWN
37	Financial Aid Director	Lucy ROSS

*Bemidji State University (I)

1500 Birchmont Drive NE, Bemidji MN 56601-2699
County: Beltrami FICE Identification: 002336
Unit ID: 173124
Telephone: (218) 755-2001 Carnegie Class: Master's S
FAX Number: (218) 755-2749 Calendar System: Semester
URL: www.bemidjistate.edu
Established: 1919 Annual Undergrad Tuition & Fees (In-State): $8,043
Enrollment: 5,360 Coed
Affiliation or Control: State IRS Status: 501(c)3
Highest Offering: Master's
Program: Liberal Arts And General; Teacher Preparatory
Accreditation: NH, IACBE, MUS, NAIT, NURSE, SW

02	President	Dr. Richard A. HANSON
05	Provost & VP for Academic Affairs	Dr. Martin TADLOCK
10	VP for Finance & Administration	Mr. William D. MAKI
84	Int VP Student Development	Dr. Mary WARD
20	VP for Innovation & Extended Lrng	Mr. Robert J. GRIGGS
50	Int Dean Col Business/Tech/Commun	Ms. Carol NIELSEN
49	Int Dean of Arts & Sciences	Dr. Colleen GREER
76	Dean Col Health Sci/Human Ecology	Dr. Patricia L. ROGERS
20	Int Assoc VP for Academic Affairs	Dr. Patrick G. GUILFOILE
07	Int Director of Admissions	Ms. MaryJo CHIRPICH
06	Registrar	Ms. Michelle FRENZEL
37	Director Financial Aid	Mr. Paul G. LINDSETH
09	Director Inst Rsrch/Effectiveness	Dr. Douglas P. OLNEY
26	Dir of Communications & Marketing	Mr. Scott FAUST
36	Director of Career Services	Ms. Margie T. GIAUQUE
29	Int Director Alumni Relations	Ms. Molly AITKEN-JULIN
92	Director Honors Program	Dr. Marsha DRISCOLL
88	Dir American Indian Resource Ctr	Dr. Donald R. DAY
94	Director Women's Studies	Vacant
96	Director of Logistical Services	Ms. Belinda S. LINDELL
15	Dir Human Resources/Affirm Action	Ms. Linda J. GILSRUD
21	Business Manager	Ms. Diane ILLIES
18	Physical Plant Director	Mr. Jeff A. SANDE
19	Director of Security/Safety	Mr. Casey J. MCCARTHY
41	Athletic Director	Dr. Rick A. GOEB
39	Director of Residential Life	Vacant
30	Exec Dir for University Advancement	Mr. Robert D. BOLLINGER
27	Int Chief Information Officer	Mr. Tim GILSRUD

*Central Lakes College (J)

501 W College Drive, Brainerd MN 56401-3900
County: Crow Wing FICE Identification: 002339
Unit ID: 173203
Telephone: (218) 855-8000 Carnegie Class: Assoc/Pub-R-M
FAX Number: (218) 855-8057 Calendar System: Semester
URL: www.clcmn.edu
Established: 1938 Annual Undergrad Tuition & Fees (In-State): $5,745

Enrollment: 4,746 Coed
Affiliation or Control: State IRS Status: 501(c)3
Highest Offering: Associate Degree
Program: Occupational; 2-Year Principally Bachelor's Creditable
Accreditation: NH, DA

02 President ... Dr. Larry A. LUNDBLAD
05 Int Vice Pres Academic/Student Affs ... Dr. Kelly MCCALLA
11 VP Administrative Svcs/Facilities ... Ms. Kari CHRISTIANSEN
103 Dean Workforce/Econ & Regional Dev ... Ms. Rebecca BEST
12 Dean Technical Pgms/Staples Campus ... Mr. Jeff WIG
32 Dean of Students ... Ms. Beth ADAMS
13 Dean of Academic/Technology Svcs ... Mr. Michael AMICK
49 Dean of Liberal Arts ... Mr. Kelly MCCALLA
30 Dir Resource Development/CLC Fndtn ... Ms. Pamela THOMSEN
15 Director of Human Resources ... Ms. Nancy PAULSON
07 Director of Admissions & Advising ... Mr. Nick HEISSERER
06 Registrar ... Mr. Nick HEISSERER
08 Librarian ... Vacant
37 Director Financial Aid ... Mr. Mike BARNABY
27 Public Information Officer ... Mr. Steve WALLER
21 Director of Business Services ... Ms. Christina VOPATEK
18 Physical Plant Director ... Mr. Rick OTTESON
28 Director of Diversity ... Ms. Mary SAM

*Century College (A)

3300 Century Avenue N, White Bear Lake MN 55110-1894
County: Ramsey FICE Identification: 010546
Unit ID: 175315
Telephone: (651) 779-3200 Carnegie Class: Assoc/Pub-S-SC
FAX Number: (651) 779-3417 Calendar System: Semester
URL: www.century.edu
Established: 1967 Annual Undergrad Tuition & Fees (In-State): $5,357
Enrollment: 10,707 Coed
Affiliation or Control: State IRS Status: 501(c)3
Highest Offering: Associate Degree
Program: Occupational; 2-Year Principally Bachelor's Creditable
Accreditation: NH, ADNUR, DA, DH, EMT, MAC, OPE, RAD

02 President ... Dr. Ron ANDERSON
05 VP Academic Affairs/CAO ... Dr. Suresh TIWARI
32 VP Student Services ... Dr. Michael BRUNER
51 VP Continuing Educ/Customized Train ... Ms. Jeralyn JARGO
10 VP Finance & Administration ... Dr. Patrick OPATZ
96 Purchasing & Auxiliary Svcs Suprvr ... Mr. Todd OSEBY
21 Director of Finance ... Ms. Bonnie MEYERS
13 Assoc VP Information Tech/Admn Svcs ... Mr. John ROHLEDER
102 Executive Director Foundation ... Ms. Jill GREENHALGH
06 Registrar ... Ms. Susan DICKENS
15 Director of Human Resources ... Ms. Mary NIENABER
07 Director of Admissions ... Ms. Christine PAULOS
45 Director of Resource Development ... Mr. Donald LONG
37 Director of Financial Aid ... Ms. Pam ENGEBRETSON
18 Mgr of Physical Plant/Super of Bld ... Mr. Michael HOUFER
28 Director of Diversity ... Mr. Herbert KING
26 Dir Cmty Rels/College Advanc/Alumni ... Ms. Nancy LIVINGSTON
66 Dean Nursing/Allied Health ... Ms. Kathleen BELL
75 Dean Trades/Public Safety/Svcs ... Ms. Jane NICHOLSON
72 Dean Science/Technology ... Ms. Brenda LYSENG
81 Dean English/ESOL/Reading/Math ... Dr. Susan EHLERS
83 Dean Social & Behav Sci/Lang/Com ... Ms. Pakou VANG
35 Dean of Student Services ... Mr. Jason CARDINAL
35 Dean of Student Services ... Ms. Andrea RYSTROM
35 Dean of Student Services ... Ms. Kristin HAGEMAN
09 Dean of Institutional Effectiveness ... Ms. Lisa SCHLOTTERHAUSEN
19 Director of Public Safety ... Mr. Mark HOLPER

*Dakota County Technical College (B)

145th Street E, Rosemount MN 55068-2999
County: Dakota FICE Identification: 010402
Unit ID: 173416
Telephone: (651) 423-8000 Carnegie Class: Assoc/Pub-S-SC
FAX Number: (651) 423-8775 Calendar System: Semester
URL: www.dctc.edu
Established: 1970 Annual Undergrad Tuition & Fees (In-District): $5,850
Enrollment: 3,774 Coed
Affiliation or Control: State/Local IRS Status: 501(c)3
Highest Offering: Associate Degree
Program: Occupational; 2-Year Principally Bachelor's Creditable; Technical Emphasis
Accreditation: NH, DA, MAC

02 President ... Dr. Ron THOMAS
05 VP Academic & Student Affairs ... Dr. Kelly MURTAUGH
88 Dean Transportation Indust Careers ... Dr. Mike OPP
50 Dean of Business/Technology and GE ... Ms. Gayle LARSON
32 Dean of Student Affairs ... Mr. Greg MCCALLEY
06 Registrar ... Ms. Jodie SWEARINGEN
15 Human Resources Director ... Ms. Susan RADDATZ
18 Chief Facilities/Physical Plant ... Mr. Paul DEMUTH
32 Chief Student Life Officer ... Ms. Nicole MEULEMANS
103 Dean of Customized Training ... Mr. Pat MCQUILLAN
07 Admissions Coordinator ... Mr. Patrick LAIR
30 Director Institutional Advancement ... Ms. Erin LARSEN
37 Financial Aid Coordinator ... Mr. Scott ROELKE
09 Director of Institutional Research ... Ms. Carrie SCHNEIDER

*Fond du Lac Tribal and Community College (C)

2101 14th Street, Cloquet MN 55720-2984
County: Carlton FICE Identification: 031291
Unit ID: 380368
Telephone: (218) 879-0800 Carnegie Class: Tribal
FAX Number: (218) 879-0814 Calendar System: Semester
URL: www.fdltcc.edu
Established: 1987 Annual Undergrad Tuition & Fees (In-State): $5,256
Enrollment: 2,345 Coed
Affiliation or Control: State IRS Status: 501(c)3
Highest Offering: Associate Degree
Program: Occupational; 2-Year Principally Bachelor's Creditable; Liberal Arts And General
Accreditation: NH

02 President ... Mr. Larry ANDERSON
05 Vice President of Instruction ... Dr. Anna FELLEGY
10 Director of Fiscal Operations ... Ms. Stephanie HAMMITT
27 Director of Public Information ... Mr. Tom URBANSKI
06 Registrar ... Ms. Leah LENO
88 Disability Services Student Service ... Ms. Patricia GRACE
13 Information Technology Specialist ... Mr. Loran WAPPES
37 Director of Financial Aid ... Mr. David SUTHERLAND
07 Director of Admissions ... Ms. Kathie JUBIE
09 Director of Institutional Research ... Vacant
32 Dir of Student Support Services ... Ms. Roberta TORGERSON
62 Library Services ... Ms. Nancy BROUGHTON
30 Director of Development ... Mr. Larry ANDERSON
39 Director of Housing ... Mr. Jesse STIREWALT
15 Director of Human Resources ... Ms. Louise LIND
18 Chief Facilities/Physical Plant ... Mr. Mark BERNHARDSON
40 Bookstore Coordinator ... Ms. Bonnie BERNHARDSON
04 Executive Assistant to President ... Ms. Mary SOYRING

*Hennepin Technical College (D)

9000 Brooklyn Boulevard, Brooklyn Park MN 55445-2399
County: Hennepin FICE Identification: 010491
Unit ID: 173708
Telephone: (952) 995-1300 Carnegie Class: Assoc/Pub-S-MC
FAX Number: (763) 488-2956 Calendar System: Semester
URL: www.hennepintech.edu
Established: 1972 Annual Undergrad Tuition & Fees (In-District): $4,701
Enrollment: 6,745 Coed
Affiliation or Control: State/Local IRS Status: 501(c)3
Highest Offering: Associate Degree
Program: Occupational
Accreditation: NH, ACFEI, DA, IFSAC

02 President ... Dr. Cecillia Y M. CERVANTES
05 Vice President Academic Affairs ... Dr. Lisa LARSON
11 Vice Pres Administrative Services ... Ms. Dawn REIMER
32 Vice President Student Affairs ... Dr. Lisa LARSON
06 Registrar ... Ms. Julie HIGDEM
15 Chief Human Resources Officer ... Ms. Sharon MOHR
30 Dir Development/Alumni Relations ... Ms. Jeanne MORPHEW
28 Director of Diversity ... Ms. Jean MAIERHOFER
07 Director of Admissions ... Ms. Monir JOHNSON
09 Director of Institutional Research ... Ms. Donna S. STATZELL
26 Exe Dir Inst Adv and Marketing ... Ms. Annette ROTH
37 Director of Financial Aid ... Mr. Tim JACOBSON

*Hibbing Community College, A Technical and Community College (E)

1515 E 25th Street, Hibbing MN 55746-3300
County: Saint Louis FICE Identification: 002355
Unit ID: 173735
Telephone: (218) 262-7200 Carnegie Class: Assoc/Pub-R-S
FAX Number: (218) 262-6717 Calendar System: Semester
URL: www.hibbing.edu
Established: 1916 Annual Undergrad Tuition & Fees (In-State): $5,293
Enrollment: 1,484 Coed
Affiliation or Control: State IRS Status: 501(c)3
Highest Offering: Associate Degree
Program: Occupational; 2-Year Principally Bachelor's Creditable
Accreditation: NH, ADNUR, DA, MLTAD

02 President ... Dr. M. Sue COLLINS
03 Provost ... Dr. Ken SIMBERG
05 Dean of Acad Affairs & Student Svcs ... Mr. Mike RAICH
32 Associate Dean of Student Services ... Vacant
10 Chief Fiscal Officer ... Mr. Bill MANNEY
09 Institutional Research ... Ms. Tracey ROY
37 Director Student Financial Aid ... Mr. Paul HATCH
18 Plant Maintenance Engineer ... Mr. Jimmer HODGE
26 Director of Public Information ... Ms. Susan DEGNAN

*Inver Hills Community College (F)

2500 80th Street E, Inver Grove Heights MN 55076-3224
County: Dakota FICE Identification: 009740
Unit ID: 173799
Telephone: (651) 450-3000 Carnegie Class: Assoc/Pub-S-SC
FAX Number: (651) 450-3679 Calendar System: Semester
URL: www.inverhills.edu
Established: 1970 Annual Undergrad Tuition & Fees (In-State): $6,182
Enrollment: 6,106 Coed
Affiliation or Control: State IRS Status: 501(c)3
Highest Offering: Associate Degree
Program: Occupational; 2-Year Principally Bachelor's Creditable
Accreditation: NH, ACBSP, ADNUR, EMT

02 President ... Mr. Timothy WYNES
05 Prov/VP Academic Affs & Student Dev ... Dr. Joan COSTELLO
10 Vice Pres Administrative Services ... Ms. Dee BERNARD
32 Vice Pres for Student Affairs ... Mr. Jason HOSENEY
35 Dean of Student/Enroll Svcs ... Mr. Tom WILLIAMSON
50 Dean of Business & Social Sciences ... Ms. Anne JOHNSON
76 Dean of Allied Health Sciences ... Dr. Doris HILL
79 Dean of Fine Arts and Humanities ... Dr. Douglas BINSFELD
81 Dean of STEM ... Dr. Kevin GYOLAI
30 Exec Dir of Foundation & Advancemnt ... Mrs. Gail MORRISON
15 Director of Human Resources ... Ms. Elizabeth NEWBERRY
51 Dean of Continuing Education ... Mr. Pat MCQUILLAN
08 Librarian ... Ms. Julie BENOLKEN
84 Director of Enrollment Services ... Mr. Matt TRAXLER
88 Dir Paralegal Pgm/Ofc Sys-Legal ... Ms. Sally DAHLQUIST
90 Director Acad Tech/Computing Svcs ... Mr. Mark PETERSON
18 Director Facilities Plng/Management ... Mr. Pat BUHL
88 Interim Dir of Emerg Health Svcs ... Ms. Tia RADANT
28 Director of Access & Opportunity ... Mr. Tadael EMIRU
37 Director of Financial Aid ... Mr. Steve YANG
09 Director of Institutional Research ... Ms. Wendy MARSON
26 Director of Marketing ... Ms. Marie MARCOGLIESE
28 Director of Diversity ... Ms. Sarah NAPOLI-RANGEL
45 Interim Assoc Dean of Acad Affair ... Mr. Matt SIMONEAU
88 Director of TRIO/SSS ... Ms. Sarah DOMAN-FLYGARE

*Itasca Community College (G)

1851 E Highway 169, Grand Rapids MN 55744-3397
County: Itasca FICE Identification: 002356
Unit ID: 173805
Telephone: (800) 996-6422 Carnegie Class: Assoc/Pub-R-S
FAX Number: (218) 322-2332 Calendar System: Semester
URL: www.itascacc.edu
Established: 1922 Annual Undergrad Tuition & Fees (In-State): $5,306
Enrollment: 1,296 Coed
Affiliation or Control: State IRS Status: 501(c)3
Highest Offering: Associate Degree
Program: 2-Year Principally Bachelor's Creditable
Accreditation: NH

02 Provost ... Dr. Michael JOHNSON
05 Academic Dean ... Dr. Barbara MCDONALD
10 Director of Finance & Facilities ... Ms. Patricia LEISTIKOW
84 Dir of Enrollment Mgmt/Admissions ... Ms. Candace PERRY
06 Registrar ... Ms. Gwen LITCHKE
29 Director of Alumni Relations ... Ms. Beth ANDERSON
30 Director of College Development ... Vacant
37 Director of Student Financial Aid ... Mr. Nathan WRIGHT
08 Head Librarian ... Mr. Steve BEAN
18 Chief Facilities/Physical Plant ... Mr. Chad HAATVEDT
40 Director of Bookstore ... Ms. Cheryl BENNETT
28 Director of Diversity ... Mr. Harold ANNETTE

*Lake Superior College (H)

2101 Trinity Road, Duluth MN 55811-3399
County: Saint Louis FICE Identification: 005757
Unit ID: 173461
Telephone: (218) 733-7600 Carnegie Class: Assoc/Pub-R-L
FAX Number: (218) 733-4921 Calendar System: Semester
URL: www.lsc.edu
Established: 1995 Annual Undergrad Tuition & Fees (In-State): $4,872
Enrollment: 5,221 Coed
Affiliation or Control: State IRS Status: 501(c)3
Highest Offering: Associate Degree
Program: Occupational; 2-Year Principally Bachelor's Creditable
Accreditation: NH, DH, MAC, MLTAD, PTAA, RAD, SURGT

02 President ... Dr. Patrick JOHNS
05 Vice Pres Academic/Student Affairs ... Mr. Mark MAGNUSON
10 Vice President of Administration ... Mr. Al FINLAYSON
49 Dean of Liberal Arts & Sciences ... Ms. Hanna ERPESTAD
75 Dean of Business/Industry Division ... Ms. Jenni SWENSON
76 Dean of Allied Health & Nursing ... Ms. Pamela ELSTAD
103 Exec Dir Workforce/Cmty Develop ... Mr. Steve WAGNER
09 Dir IR/Accred Assessment/Research ... Mr. Kent RICHARDS
15 Director of Human Resources ... Ms. Mary Kay NIENABER
26 Dir of Public Affairs/Advancement ... Mr. Gary KRUCHOWSKI
06 Registrar ... Ms. Jean STOJEVICH
07 Director of Admissions ... Ms. Melissa LENO
18 Director Physical Plant ... Mr. Gary ADAMS
28 Dir Diversity & Stdnt Support Svcs ... Mr. Wade GORDON
36 Director Student Placement ... Ms. Betsy JACOBSON
37 Director Student Financial Aid ... Ms. LaNita ROBINSON
29 Director Alumni Relations ... Ms. LuAnne ANDERSON
35 Director Student Life ... Mr. Roger JOHNSON
96 Director of Purchasing ... Ms. Joyce CLOCK
21 Director Business Services ... Ms. Kathy DUGDALE
102 Foundation Director ... Mr. Paul DAMBERG
105 Dir of Web & Information Services ... Mr. Steve FUDALLY

*Mesabi Range Community & Technical College (I)

1001 Chestnut Street West, Virginia MN 55792-3401
County: Saint Louis FICE Identification: 005739
Unit ID: 173993
Telephone: (218) 741-3095 Carnegie Class: Assoc/Pub-R-S
FAX Number: (218) 748-2419 Calendar System: Semester
URL: www.mesabirange.edu

Established: 1963 Annual Undergrad Tuition & Fees (In-State): $2,556
Enrollment: 2,556 Coed
Affiliation or Control: State IRS Status: Exempt
Highest Offering: Associate Degree
Program: Occupational; 2-Year Principally Bachelor's Creditable; Fine Arts Emphasis
Accreditation: NH, EMT

02	President	Dr. Sue COLLINS
05	Provost	Ms. Kathy BURLINGAME
32	Dean of Students	Mr. David DAILEY
10	Chief Finance and Facilities Office	Mr. Keith HARVEY
15	Director Human Resources	Ms. Carmen BRADACH
37	Director Student Financial Aid	Ms. Jodi PONTINEN
06	Registrar	Vacant
07	Director of Admissions	Ms. Brenda KOCHEVAR
09	Director of Institutional Research	Ms. Tracey ROY
26	Chief Public Relations Officer	Ms. Brenda KOCHEVAR
38	Director Student Counseling	Ms. Kelly BAKK
36	Director Student Placement	Mr. Toby ANDERSON
84	Director Enrollment Management	Ms. Brenda KOCHEVAR

*Metropolitan State University (A)

700 E 7th Street, Saint Paul MN 55106-5000
County: Ramsey FICE Identification: 010374
Unit ID: 174020
Telephone: (651) 793-1300 Carnegie Class: Master's M
FAX Number: (651) 793-1235 Calendar System: Semester
URL: www.metrostate.edu
Established: 1971 Annual Undergrad Tuition & Fees (In-State): $6,340
Enrollment: 8,170 Coed
Affiliation or Control: State IRS Status: 501(c)3
Highest Offering: Doctorate
Program: Liberal Arts And General; Teacher Preparatory; Professional
Accreditation: NH, NURSE, SW

02	President	Dr. Sue K. HAMMERSMITH
05	Provost/Vice Pres Academic Affs	Ms. Virginia ARTHUR
11	Vice Pres Administrative Affairs	Mr. Martuza SIDDIQUI
32	Vice President Student Affairs	Dr. Trenda BOYUM-BREEN
30	Vice Pres University Advancement	Mr. Jesse BETHKE-GOMEZ
35	Dean of Students	Ms. Cecilia STANTON
18	Assoc Vice Pres Admin Affairs	Mr. Daniel HAMBROCK
13	Assoc VP Info/Telecom/Tech/CIO	Vacant
10	Assoc VP Financial Management	Mr. Ronald BECKSTROM
15	Director Human Resources	Ms. Stephanie MILLER
06	Registrar	Mr. Daryl JOHNSON
37	Director Financial Aid	Ms. Lois LARSON
26	Dir of Communications and Marketing	Vacant
27	Publication/News Services Director	Ms. Susan M. AMOS PALMER
29	Director Alumni Relations	Ms. Vicki LOFQUIST
22	Director Affirmative Action	Ms. Truly WEBB
09	Director Institutional Research	Ms. Cynthia DEVORE
07	Director of Admissions	Mr. Daryl JOHNSON
49	Dean College of Arts & Sciences	Dr. Becky OMDAHL
58	Dean of College of Management	Vacant
107	Int Dean Col Professional Studies	Dr. Leah HARVEY
88	Interim Dean First College	Dr. Leah HARVEY
66	Interim Dean School of Nursing	Dr. Ann LEJA
88	Dean Sch Law Enforce/Crim Justice	Dr. Everett DOOLITTLE

*Minneapolis Community and Technical College (B)

1501 Hennepin Avenue, Minneapolis MN 55403-9810
County: Hennepin FICE Identification: 002362
Unit ID: 174136
Telephone: (612) 659-6000 Carnegie Class: Assoc/Pub-U-SC
FAX Number: (612) 659-6210 Calendar System: Semester
URL: www.minneapolis.edu
Established: 1996 Annual Undergrad Tuition & Fees (In-State): $5,342
Enrollment: 10,232 Coed
Affiliation or Control: State IRS Status: 501(c)3
Highest Offering: Associate Degree
Program: Occupational; 2-Year Principally Bachelor's Creditable
Accreditation: NH, ADNUR, DA, NDT, PNUR, POLYT

02	President	Mr. Phillip L. DAVIS
05	Vice Pres Academic/Student Affairs	Dr. Lois BOLLMAN
10	Vice President Finance/Operations	Mr. Scott ERICKSON
32	Vice President Student Affairs	Dr. Joi LEWIS
09	Assoc VP Strat/Plng/Accountability	Dr. Gail O'KANE
103	Assoc VP Workforce Development	Mr. Mike CHRISTENSON
84	Dean of Enrollment Management	Ms. Laura FEDOCK
49	Dean of Liberal Arts	Dr. Linnea STENSON
81	Dean of Science & Math	Mr. Chuck PAULSON
51	Dean of Continuing Education	Ms. Jess NIEBUHR
66	Dean of Nursing & Allied Health	Mr. Robert MUSTER
72	Dean of Technical Programs	Mr. Mick COLEMAN
35	Dean of Students	Mr. Robert REESE
20	Interim Dean Academic Development	Ms. Melissa O'CONNOR
30	Dean of College Advancement	Mr. Reede O. WEBSTER
43	Director Legal Affairs	Ms. Dianna CUSICK
16	Director of Human Resources	Mr. Keith BALASKI
13	Chief Information Officer	Mr. Jim DILLEMUTH
07	Director of Admissions	Ms. Kerri CARLSON
06	Interim Registrar	Ms. Jeanne MAANUM
08	Librarian	Mr. Tom ELAND
37	Financial Aid Director	Ms. Angela CHRISTENSEN
09	Director of Institutional Research	Ms. Katie DEBOER
18	Director Facilities	Mr. Roger BROZ
19	Director of Public Safety	Mr. Curt SCHMIDT
26	Chief Public Relations Officer	Ms. Dawn SKELLY
32	Chief Student Life Officer	Ms. Tara MARTINEZ

*Minnesota State College - Southeast Technical (C)

1250 Homer Road, PO Box 409, Winona MN 55987-4897
County: Winona FICE Identification: 002393
Unit ID: 175263
Telephone: (507) 453-2700 Carnegie Class: Assoc/Pub-R-M
FAX Number: (507) 453-2795 Calendar System: Semester
URL: www.southeastmn.edu
Established: 1949 Annual Undergrad Tuition & Fees (In-District): $4,575
Enrollment: 2,976 Coed
Affiliation or Control: State/Local IRS Status: 501(c)3
Highest Offering: Associate Degree
Program: Occupational; 2-Year Principally Bachelor's Creditable
Accreditation: NH, RAD

02	President	Mr. James J. JOHNSON
04	Assistant to President	Ms. Casie JOHNSON
05	Vice President Academic Affairs	Mr. Ron SELLNAN
32	Vice Pres Student Affs/Inst Rsrch	Mr. Nate EMERSON
20	Dean of Academic Affairs	Dr. Nancee WOZNEY
49	Dean of Liberal Arts & Sciences	Ms. Jolene PONCELET
10	Chief Finance Officer/Purchasing	Mr. Mike KROENING
15	Chief Human Resource Officer	Ms. Deanna VOTH
26	Director of Public Relations	Ms. Erin LATTEN
13	Chief Information Officer	Mr. Rick NAHRGANG
06	Registrar	Ms. Mary JOHNSON
37	Director Financial Aid	Ms. Anne DAHLEN
09	Director of Institutional Research	Mr. Josh BUBLITZ
84	Dir of Enrollment Svcs/Stdnt Plcmt	Vacant
30	Exec Dir Institutional Advancement	Ms. Cheryl HANCOCK
84	Director Student Enrollment	Ms. Jackie BRIGGS
07	Admissions Counselor	Ms. Melissa CARRINGTON-IRWIN
07	Admissions Counselor	Mr. Gale LANNING
18	Chief Facilities/Physical Plant	Mr. Thomas HOFFMAN
51	Dir Continuing/Workforce Education	Ms. Cheryl HANCOCK

*Minnesota State Community and Technical College (D)

1414 College Way, Fergus Falls MN 56537-1000
County: Otter Tail FICE Identification: 005541
Unit ID: 173559
Telephone: (218) 736-1500 Carnegie Class: Assoc/Pub-R-L
FAX Number: (218) 736-1510 Calendar System: Semester
URL: www.minnesota.edu
Established: 1960 Annual Undergrad Tuition & Fees (In-State): $5,824
Enrollment: 6,948 Coed
Affiliation or Control: State IRS Status: 501(c)3
Highest Offering: Associate Degree
Program: Occupational; 2-Year Principally Bachelor's Creditable; Liberal Arts And General
Accreditation: NH, DA, MLTAD, RAD

02	President	Dr. Peggy KENNEDY
05	Chief Academic Officer	Ms. Kathy BROCK
16	Director of Human Resources	Mrs. Dacia JOHNSON
13	Chief Information Officer	Mr. Dave OVERBY
10	Chief Financial Officer	Mr. Pat NORDICK
84	Interim Dean of Enrollment	Mr. Anthony SCHAFFHAUSER
26	Dir of Communications & Marketing	Ms. Mary DEVINE
32	Assoc VP of Acad & Student Affairs	Mrs. Carrie BRIMHALL
18	Supt of Buildings & Grounds	Mr. Matt SHEPPARD
88	Dean for Student Success	Mr. Shawn ANDERSON
12	Provost - Wadena and CSSO	Dr. Peter WIELINSKI
20	eCampus Dean	Dr. Jill ABBOTT
20	Academic Dean - Detroit Lakes	Mr. Tom WHELIHAN
20	Academic Dean - Fergus Falls	Dr. Gary HENRICKSON
20	Academic Dean - Wadena	Mr. Monty JOHNSON
88	Dean of CTS/BES	Mr. G.L TUCKER
66	Dean of Nursing	Mrs. Kathy BURLINGAME

*Minnesota State University, Mankato (E)

309 Wigley Administration Center,
Mankato MN 56001-6062
County: Blue Earth FICE Identification: 002360
Unit ID: 173920
Telephone: (507) 389-1111 Carnegie Class: Master's L
FAX Number: (507) 389-6200 Calendar System: Semester
URL: www.mnsu.edu
Established: 1868 Annual Undergrad Tuition & Fees (In-State): $10,709
Enrollment: 14,955 Coed
Affiliation or Control: State IRS Status: Exempt
Highest Offering: Doctorate
Program: Liberal Arts And General; Teacher Preparatory; Professional
Accreditation: NH, ART, BUS, CACREP, CONST, CORE, DH, DIETD, ENG, ENGT, MUS, NRPA, NURSE, SP, SW, TED

02	President	Dr. Richard DAVENPORT
05	VP Academic & Student Affairs	Vacant
10	Vice Pres Finance & Administration	Mr. Richard STRAKA
30	VP Univ Advance/Chief Dev Ofcr	Mr. Douglas MAYO
13	VP Technology/CIO	Mr. Ed CLARK
88	VP Strategic/Busnss/Ed/Reg Prtrshps	Dr. Robert HOFFMAN
28	Interm Dean Institutional Diversity	Mr. Henry MORRIS
32	Assoc VP for Student Affairs	Dr. David JONES
20	Asso Vice Pres for Academic Affairs	Dr. Warren SANDMANN
04	Assistant to the President	Ms. Carol STALLKAMP
20	Asst VP for Undergrad Stds Intl Ed	Dr. Maria-Claudia TOMANY
27	Asst VP Integrated Marketing/Comm	Mr. Jeff ISEMINGER
18	Int Asst Vice Pres Facilities Mgmt	Mr. David COWAN
06	University Registrar	Mr. Marcius BROCK
07	Director of Admissions	Mr. Brian JONES
08	Dean Library Services	Dr. Joan ROCA
15	Director of Human Resources	Ms. Becky BARKMEIER
36	Director Career Development	Ms. Pamela WELLER-DENGEL
26	Director Media Relations	Mr. Daniel BENSON
41	Dir of Intercollegiate Athletics	Mr. Kevin BUISMAN
29	Director of Alumni Relations	Ms. Jennifer GUYER- WOOD
22	Director Affirmative Action	Ms. Linda HANSON
37	Director Student Financial Services	Ms. Jan MARBLE
58	Int Dean Graduate Studies/Research	Dr. Barry RIES
79	Dean of Arts & Humanities	Dr. Walter ZAKAHI
53	Dean of Education	Dr. Jean HAAR
50	Dean of Business	Dr. Brenda FLANNERY
76	Interim Dean Allied Health/Nursing	Dr. Harry KRAMPF
81	Dean Science/Engineering/Technology	Dr. Vijendra AGARWAL
83	Dean Social/Behavioral Science	Dr. Kimberly GREER
38	Director Student Counseling	Ms. Kari MUCH

*Minnesota State University Moorhead (F)

1104 7th Avenue S, Moorhead MN 56563-2996
County: Clay FICE Identification: 002367
Unit ID: 174358
Telephone: (218) 477-4000 Carnegie Class: Master's M
FAX Number: (218) 477-2168 Calendar System: Semester
URL: www.mnstate.edu
Established: 1887 Annual Undergrad Tuition & Fees (In-State): $7,834
Enrollment: 7,254 Coed
Affiliation or Control: State IRS Status: 501(c)3
Highest Offering: Doctorate
Program: Liberal Arts And General; Teacher Preparatory; Professional
Accreditation: NH, ART, BUS, CACREP, CONST, DH, MUS, NAIT, NURSE, SP, SW, TED

02	President	Dr. Edna M. SZYMANSKI
05	Provost & Sr VP Academic Affairs	Dr. Anne E. BLACKHURST
10	VP Finance & Administration	Ms. Janet L. MAHONEY
32	VP Student Affairs	Vacant
29	VP Alumni Foundation	Ms. Laura L. HUTH
84	VP Enrollment Management	Ms. Diane P. SOLINGER
45	AVP F&A/Univ Plng & Budget Ofcr	Ms. Jean R. HOLLAAR
04	Assistant to the President	Ms. Kathleen J. MCNABB
20	AVP Acad Affairs	Ms. Ginny V. BAIR
41	Director of Athletics	Mr. Doug D. PETERS
14	Chief Information Officer	Mr. Daniel A. HECKAMAN
21	Comptroller	Mr. Mark P. RICE
28	AVP Student Affairs for Diversity	Dr. Donna L. BROWN
50	Dean Business & Industry	Dr. Marsha L. WEBER
79	Dean Arts & Humanities	Dr. Timothy A. BORCHERS
53	Dean Education & Human Services	Dr. Boyd L. BRADBURY
83	Dean Social & Natural Sciences	Dr. Michelle L. MALOTT
08	Dean Instructional Resources	Ms. Brittney G. GOODMAN
89	Dean University College	Ms. Denise M. GORSLINE
15	Director Human Resources	Mr. Mark A. YURAN
06	AVP Records & Inst Effectiveness	Dr. Russell L. CURLEY
22	Affirmative Action Officer	Dr. Donna L. BROWN
26	Director Marketing/Communications	Mr. David C. WAHLBERG
19	Director of Security	Mr. Gregory J. LEMKE
37	Dir Financial Aid & Scholarships	Ms. Carolyn F. ZEHREN
23	Dir Health/Wellness/Counseling Ctrs	Ms. Carol M. GRIMM
38	Dir Disabilities & Career Services	Mr. Greg A. TOUTGES
07	Int Director of Admissions	Ms. Sarah J. NISSEN
44	AVP Fundraising	Vacant
35	Exec Dir Student Union	Ms. Karen B. MEHNERT-MELAND
39	Dir Housing & Residential Life	Ms. Heather PHILLIPS
40	Bookstore Supervisor	Ms. Kim M. SAMSON
18	Director Physical Plant	Mr. Jeffrey D. GOEBEL
85	Director International Student Affs	Ms. Janet M. HOHENSTEIN

*Minnesota West Community and Technical College (G)

1450 Collegeway, Worthington MN 56187
County: Nobles FICE Identification: 005263
Unit ID: 173638
Telephone: (507) 372-3400 Carnegie Class: Assoc/Pub-R-M
FAX Number: (507) 372-5801 Calendar System: Semester
URL: www.mnwest.edu
Established: 1985 Annual Undergrad Tuition & Fees (In-State): $5,660
Enrollment: 3,364 Coed
Affiliation or Control: State IRS Status: 501(c)3
Highest Offering: Associate Degree
Program: Occupational; 2-Year Principally Bachelor's Creditable
Accreditation: NH, ADNUR, DA, MAC, MLTAD, RAD, SURGT

02	President	Dr. Richard SHRUBB
05	College Provost	Dr. Jeff WILLIAMSON
11	Vice President of Administration	Ms. Lori VOSS
106	Dean Technology/Distance Learning	Ms. Kayla WESTRA
84	Director of Enrollment Management	Vacant
37	Director of Student Financial Aid	Ms. Jodi LANDGAARD

18 Chief Facilities/Physical Plant ... Mr. Jeff HARMS
06 Registrar ... Ms. Crystal STROUTH
15 Director Human Resources ... Ms. Karen MILLER
102 Foundation Director ... Mr. James SMALLEY

*Normandale Community College (A)

9700 France Avenue S, Bloomington MN 55431-4399
County: Hennepin FICE Identification: 007954
Unit ID: 174428
Telephone: (952) 358-8200 Carnegie Class: Assoc/Pub-S-SC
FAX Number: (952) 358-8101 Calendar System: Semester
URL: www.normandale.mnscu.edu
Established: 1968 Annual Undergrad Tuition & Fees (In-State): $5,694
Enrollment: 9,904 Coed
Affiliation or Control: State IRS Status: 501(c)3
Highest Offering: Associate Degree
Program: Occupational; 2-Year Principally Bachelor's Creditable
Accreditation: NH, ACBSP, ADNUR, ART, DH, DIETT, MUS, THEA

02 President ... Dr. Joe OPATZ
10 Vice Pres Finance & Operations ... Mr. Ed WINES
05 Vice President Academic Affairs ... Ms. Julie GUELICH
32 Vice President Student Affairs ... Dr. Lisa WHEELER
35 Dean of Students ... Dr. Orinthia MONTAGUE
50 Dean Bus/Tech/Library/Social Sci ... Vacant
79 Dean of Humanities/Col Readiness ... Mr. Jeff JUDGE
81 Dean Natural Science/Mathematics ... Mr. Cary KOMOTO
76 Dean of Health Sciences ... Dr. Colleen BRICKLE
10 Director Fiscal Services ... Mr. Craig ERICKSON
15 Director Human Resources ... Ms. Michelle THOM
35 Associate Dean of Students ... Ms. Catherine L. BREUER
13 Director of Information Tech Svcs ... Ms. Andrea KODNER-WENZEL
18 Director of Building Services ... Mr. Michael KOREEN
102 Director of Foundation Office ... Mr. Chuck WALETZKO
84 Dean of Enroll/Marketing/Multicul ... Mr. Matt CRAWFORD
26 Chief Public Relations Officer ... Mr. Geoffrey JONES
06 Registrar ... Ms. Tonya HANSON HUBER
07 Director of Admissions ... Vacant
09 Assoc VP Planning & Inst Research ... Mr. Michael BERNDT

*North Hennepin Community College (B)

7411 85th Avenue N, Brooklyn Park MN 55445-2299
County: Hennepin FICE Identification: 002370
Unit ID: 174376
Telephone: (763) 424-0702 Carnegie Class: Assoc/Pub-S-SC
FAX Number: (763) 424-0929 Calendar System: Semester
URL: www.nhcc.edu
Established: 1966 Annual Undergrad Tuition & Fees (In-State): $5,447
Enrollment: 7,432 Coed
Affiliation or Control: State IRS Status: 501(c)3
Highest Offering: Associate Degree
Program: Occupational; 2-Year Principally Bachelor's Creditable
Accreditation: NH, ACBSP, ADNUR, HT, MLTAD

02 President ... Dr. John O'BRIEN
05 Vice Pres Academic Affairs ... Ms. Jane REINKE
32 Vice Pres of Student Affairs ... Dr. Landon PIRIUS
10 Vice Pres of Finance & Facilities ... Mr. Daniel HILL
72 Int Dean Academics/Technology Svcs ... Ms. Kristine BOIKE
35 Assoc Dean Student Affairs ... Mr. Jim BORER
37 Assoc Dean Financial Aid ... Ms. Jackie OLSSON
08 Librarian ... Mr. Craig LARSON
06 Director Records & Registration ... Ms. Lori KIRKEBY
07 Director Admissions & Outreach ... Ms. Melissa LEIMBEK
15 Chief Human Resources Officer ... Ms. Sue APPELQUIST
45 Director Planning & Research ... Ms. Sheryl OLSON
18 Director of Plant Services ... Mr. Larry MEYERS
30 Director of Development ... Ms. Jennifer LAMBRECHT
28 Director Diversity/Multiculturalism ... Mr. Michael BIRCHARD
26 Director of Communications ... Ms. Carmen SHIELDS
21 Business Manager ... Ms. Dawn BELKO
49 Dean Liberal Arts ... Ms. Suellen RUNDQUIST
50 Dean Business & Career Programs ... Ms. Renae FRY
76 Dean Health Careers/Science ... Dr. Elaina BLEIFIELD
51 Dean of Cont Educ/Custom Trng ... Vacant

*Northland Community and Technical College (C)

1101 Highway 1 E, Thief River Falls MN 56701-2598
County: Pennington FICE Identification: 002385
Unit ID: 174473
Telephone: (218) 683-8800 Carnegie Class: Assoc/Pub-R-M
FAX Number: (218) 683-8980 Calendar System: Semester
URL: www.northlandcollege.edu
Established: 1965 Annual Undergrad Tuition & Fees (In-State): $5,291
Enrollment: 5,244 Coed
Affiliation or Control: State IRS Status: 501(c)3
Highest Offering: Associate Degree
Program: Occupational; 2-Year Principally Bachelor's Creditable; Technical Emphasis
Accreditation: NH, ADNUR, CVT, EMT, OTA, PTAA, RAD, SURGT

02 President ... Dr. Anne T. TEMTE
05 VP Academic Affairs/Student Svcs ... Dr. Kent HANSON
04 Assistant to the President ... Ms. Cindy CEDERGREN
20 Dean of Academic Affairs ... Ms. Norma KONSCHAK
20 Dean of Academic Affairs ... Mr. Brian HUSCHLE
32 Dean of Student Development ... Mr. Steve CRITTENDEN
32 Dean of Students East Grand Forks ... Ms. Mary FONTES
103 Dean Workforce & Econ Development ... Mr. James RETKA
08 Learning Center Director ... Mr. Dean DALEN
10 Chief Finance Officer ... Ms. Shannon JESME
38 Counselor ... Ms. Kelsy BLOWERS
38 Counselor ... Ms. Kate SCHMALENBERG
66 Dean of Nursing ... Ms. Jodi STASSEN
66 Director of Nursing ... Ms. Barb FORREST
84 Director of Enrollment Management ... Mr. Gene KLINKE
37 Director Student Financial Aid ... Mr. Gerald SCHULTE
09 Director of Institutional Research ... Mr. Rocky AMMERMAN
15 Director Personnel Services ... Ms. Becky LINDSETH
18 Chief Facilities/Physical Plant ... Mr. Clinton CASTLE
26 Director Marketing/Communication ... Mr. Jason TRAINER
44 Dir Annual Giving/Alumni Relations ... Mr. Lars DYRUD
06 Registrar ... Mr. Rocky AMMERMAN
07 Director of Admissions ... Mr. Gene KLINKE
28 Director of Diversity ... Vacant
30 Chief Development Officer ... Mr. Dan KLUG
13 Director Computing/Information Mgmt ... Ms. Stacey HRON
27 Chief Information Officer ... Ms. Becky LINDSETH
41 Athletic Director ... Mr. Paul PETERSON

*Northwest Technical College (D)

905 Grant Avenue, SE, Bemidji MN 56601-4907
County: Beltrami FICE Identification: 005759
Unit ID: 173115
Telephone: (218) 333-6600 Carnegie Class: Assoc/Pub-R-S
FAX Number: (218) 333-6694 Calendar System: Semester
URL: www.ntcmn.edu
Established: 1966 Annual Undergrad Tuition & Fees (In-State): $5,481
Enrollment: 1,411 Coed
Affiliation or Control: State IRS Status: 501(c)3
Highest Offering: Associate Degree
Program: Occupational; 2-Year Principally Bachelor's Creditable
Accreditation: NH, DA

05 Provost/Vice President ... Mr. John CENTKO

*Pine Technical College (E)

900 Fourth Street, SE, Pine City MN 55063-2198
County: Pine FICE Identification: 005535
Unit ID: 174570
Telephone: (320) 629-5100 Carnegie Class: Assoc/Pub-R-S
FAX Number: (320) 629-5101 Calendar System: Semester
URL: www.pinetech.edu
Established: 1965 Annual Undergrad Tuition & Fees (In-State): $5,080
Enrollment: 1,155 Coed
Affiliation or Control: State IRS Status: 501(c)3
Highest Offering: Associate Degree
Program: Occupational; 2-Year Principally Bachelor's Creditable; Business Emphasis
Accreditation: NH

02 President ... Dr. Robert MUSGROVE
05 Chief Academic Officer ... Dr. Joan BLOEMENDAAL-GRUETT
13 Chief Information Officer ... Mr. Kenneth RIES
10 Chief Financial Officer ... Ms. Janis WEGNER
32 Interim Dean Student Affairs ... Ms. Paula HOFFMAN
51 Dean of Continuing Edu/Custom Trng ... Mr. Jason SPAETH
88 Dir Johnson Center for Simulation ... Ms. Cynthia GALBRAITH
46 Director Strategic Initiatives ... Ms. Stephanie SCHROEDER
36 Exec Dir Employment/Training Ctr ... Mr. Tony GANTENBEIN
06 Registrar ... Mr. Robert BAKER
15 Int Chief Human Resources Officer . Ms. Marybeth CHRISTENSON
07 Director of Admissions ... Mr. James STUMNE
37 Director Student Financial Aid ... Ms. Susan PIXLEY
18 Physical Plant Supervisor ... Mr. Steven LANGE

*Rainy River Community College (F)

1501 Highway 71, International Falls MN 56649-2187
County: Koochiching FICE Identification: 006775
Unit ID: 174604
Telephone: (218) 285-7722 Carnegie Class: Assoc/Pub-R-S
FAX Number: (218) 285-2239 Calendar System: Semester
URL: www.rrcc.mnscu.edu
Established: 1967 Annual Undergrad Tuition & Fees (In-State): $5,323
Enrollment: 307 Coed
Affiliation or Control: State IRS Status: 501(c)3
Highest Offering: Associate Degree
Program: Occupational; 2-Year Principally Bachelor's Creditable
Accreditation: NH

02 Provost ... Dr. Kenneth SIMBERG
06 Registrar ... Ms. Berta HAGEN
37 Dir of Financial Aid/Housing ... Mr. Scott T. RILEY
13 Dir Information Technology ... Mr. James BUJOLD

*Ridgewater College (G)

PO Box 1097, 2101 15th Ave NW, Willmar MN 56201-1097
County: Kandiyohi FICE Identification: 005252
Unit ID: 175236
Telephone: (320) 222-5200 Carnegie Class: Assoc/Pub-R-M
FAX Number: (320) 222-5212 Calendar System: Semester
URL: www.ridgewater.edu
Established: 1961 Annual Undergrad Tuition & Fees (In-State): $5,375
Enrollment: 4,147 Coed
Affiliation or Control: State IRS Status: 501(c)3
Highest Offering: Associate Degree
Program: Occupational; 2-Year Principally Bachelor's Creditable
Accreditation: NH, ADNUR, EMT, MAC

02 President ... Dr. Douglas W. ALLEN
05 Vice Pres Acad Affs/Student Svcs ... Ms. Betty J. STREHLOW
10 Vice President Finance & Operations ... Mr. Daniel F. HOLTZ
51 Dean of Cust Trng & Cont Education ... Ms. Kathy M. SCHWANTES
20 Dean of Instruction ... Mr. Michael J. BOEHME
20 Dean of Instruction ... Dr. Carl E. POLDING
20 Dean of Instruction ... Dr. Ronald L. PRIBBLE
32 Dean of Student Services ... Ms. Heidi L. OLSON
21 Director of Business Services ... Ms. Cheryl A. NORLIEN
15 Chief Human Resource Officer ... Ms. Jodi L. KNAUS
66 Director of Nursing ... Ms. C. Lynn JOHNSON
37 Director of Financial Aid ... Mr. James W. RICE
07 Director of Admissions ... Ms. Sally KERFELD
41 Athletic Director ... Mr. Todd M. THORSTAD
06 Registrar ... Ms. Kelli S. KIENITZ
13 Chief Information Officer ... Mr. Timothy L. FURR
26 Director of Communication/Marketing ... Mr. Samuel J. BOWEN
102 Foundation Executive Director ... Ms. Kelly J. MAGNUSON
47 Director of Management Programs ... Mr. James H. MOLENAAR
09 Director of Institutional Research ... Dr. Mary L. MYERS
28 Director of Multicultural Affairs ... Mr. Edelgard FERNANDEZ MEJIA
18 Physical Plant Director ... Mr. Kip R. OVESON

*Riverland Community College (H)

1900 8th Avenue, NW, Austin MN 55912-1473
County: Mower FICE Identification: 002335
Unit ID: 173063
Telephone: (507) 433-0600 Carnegie Class: Assoc/Pub-R-M
FAX Number: (507) 433-0665 Calendar System: Semester
URL: www.riverland.edu
Established: 1940 Annual Undergrad Tuition & Fees (In-State): $2,554
Enrollment: 3,717 Coed
Affiliation or Control: State IRS Status: 501(c)3
Highest Offering: Associate Degree
Program: Occupational; 2-Year Principally Bachelor's Creditable; Liberal Arts And General
Accreditation: NH, ACBSP, ADNUR, RAD

02 Interim President ... Dr. Kent HANSON
05 Interim VP of Acad & Stdnt Affs ... Dr. Mary DAVENPORT
10 Chief Financial Officer ... Mr. Brad DOSS
16 VP of Employee & Student Affairs ... Ms. Celeste RUBLE
56 Dean of Extended Learning ... Mr. David HIETALA
76 Interim Assoc Dean of Allied Hlth ... Ms. Danyel HELGESON
49 Dean for Liberal Arts & Sciences ... Ms. Jan WALLER
103 Dean for Workforce Education ... Mr. Scott WILLIAMS
32 Dean of Student Affairs ... Vacant
30 Dean for Institutional Advancement ... Mr. Steve BOWRON
06 Dir of Enrollment Svcs/Registrar ... Ms. Sue JECH
07 Director of Admissions ... Vacant
26 Director of Communications ... Mr. James DOUGLASS
37 Director of Financial Aid ... Ms. Judy ROBECK
36 Director of Placement & Grad Svcs ... Ms. Tricia WHALEN
04 Executive Assist to the President ... Ms. Marijo ALEXANDER
13 Director of Technology ... Mr. Dan HARBER
18 Facilities Supervisor ... Ms. Judy ENRIGHT
96 Purchasing Agent ... Ms. Page PETERSEN
28 Regional Diversty Trainer/Investgtr ... Ms. Ricki WALTERS

*Rochester Community and Technical College (I)

851 30th Avenue, SE, Rochester MN 55904-4999
County: Olmsted FICE Identification: 002373
Unit ID: 174738
Telephone: (507) 285-7210 Carnegie Class: Assoc/Pub-R-M
FAX Number: (507) 285-7496 Calendar System: Semester
URL: www.rctc.edu
Established: 1915 Annual Undergrad Tuition & Fees (In-State): $5,736
Enrollment: 6,049 Coed
Affiliation or Control: State IRS Status: 501(c)3
Highest Offering: Associate Degree
Program: Occupational; 2-Year Principally Bachelor's Creditable; Liberal Arts And General
Accreditation: NH, ADNUR, DA, DH, EMT, PNUR, SURGT

02 President ... Mr. Don D. SUPALLA
05 Vice President Academic Affairs ... Dr. Jim GROSS
10 Vice Pres Finance and Facilities ... Mr. Steve SCHMALL
76 Dean Allied Health ... Dr. Nirmala KOTAGAL
49 Dean ... Dr. Barbara J. MOLLBERG
75 Dean ... Ms. Michelle PYFFEROEN
15 Chief Human Resources Officer ... Mrs. Renee ENGELMEYER
13 Chief Information Technology Ofcr ... Mr. Scott SAHS
45 Chief Student Affairs Officer ... Mr. Dave N. WEBER
51 Dir of Business/Econ Development ... Ms. Michelle PYFFEROEN
32 Student Life Coordinator ... Mr. Scott KROOK
06 Registrar ... Ms. Nancy SHUMAKER
07 Director Admissions ... Ms. Holly BIGELOW
37 Director Financial Aid ... Ms. Beth DIEKMANN
09 Director of Institutional Research ... Ms. Christine MILLER
04 Assistant to President ... Mrs. Judy K. KINGSBURY

21	Business Office Supervisor	Ms. Ruth SIEFERT
26	Chief Public Relations Officer	Mr. Dave WEBER
19	Security Officer	Mr. Andrew HAMANN
40	Bookstore Coordinator	Ms. Michelle PETERSON
96	Director of Purchasing	Ms. June MEITZNER
29	Dir Alumni Rels/Found Exec Dir	Ms. Lisa BALDUS

*St. Cloud State University (A)

720 4th Avenue S, Saint Cloud MN 56301-4498
County: Stearns FICE Identification: 002377
Unit ID: 174783
Telephone: (320) 308-0121 Carnegie Class: Master's L
FAX Number: N/A Calendar System: Semester
URL: www.stcloudstate.edu
Established: 1869 Annual Undergrad Tuition & Fees (In-State): $7,833
Enrollment: 17,231 Coed
Affiliation or Control: State IRS Status: 501(c)3
Highest Offering: Doctorate
Program: Occupational; 2-Year Principally Bachelor's Creditable; Liberal Arts And General; Teacher Preparatory; Professional
Accreditation: NH, AAB, ART, BUS, CACREP, CORE, CS, ENG, ENGR, #JOUR, MFCD, MT, MUS, NAIT, NURSE, SP, SW, TED, THEA

02	President	Dr. Earl H. POTTER, III
05	Provost/Vice Pres Academic Affairs	Dr. Devinder MALHOTRA
88	Assoc Provost for Organizat	Dr. John PALMER
46	Assoc Provost for Research	Dr. Dan GREGORY
20	Assoc Provost Undergraduate Ed	Dr. Miguel SAENZ
88	Interim Asst Provost Student Supp	Ms. Nancy MILLS
32	Vice Pres Student Life Development	Dr. Wanda OVERLAND
11	Interim Vice Pres Finance/Admin	Mr. Len SIPPEL
30	Vice Pres University Advancement	Mr. Craig WRUCK
85	Assoc VP International Studies	Dr. Ann B. RADWAN
10	Assoc VP Finance/Admin	Vacant
45	Assoc VP Strategy/Planning/Effectiv	Ms. Lisa FOSS
27	Asst VP Marketing & Communications	Mr. Loren BOONE
43	Special Advisor to the President	Dr. Judith P. SIMINOE
50	Dean Herberger Business School	Dr. Diana LAWSON
51	Dean of Continuing Studies	Dr. John BURGESON
53	Dean School of Education	Dr. Osman ALAWIYE
57	Dean Liberal Arts	Dr. Mark SPRINGER
72	Dean Science & Engineering	Dr. David K. DEGROOTE
83	Int Dean School of Public Affairs	Dr. Orn BODVARSSON
76	Int Dean Health/Human Service	Dr. Monica DEVERS
08	Interim Dean Learning Resources	Mr. Keith EWING
07	Director of Admissions	Mr. Richard SHEARER
22	Equity and Affirmative Action Ofc	Ms. Ellyn BARTGES
06	Registrar	Ms. Sue BAYERL
29	Director of Constituent Engagement	Ms. Terri MISCHE
41	Athletic Director	Ms. Heather WEEMS
18	Facilities Management Director	Mr. Tim NORTON
36	Director Career Services	Ms. Addie TURKOWSKI
91	Dir Info Technology Services	Mr. Phil THORSON
38	Director of Counseling	Dr. John M. EGGERS
37	Director of Financial Aid	Mr. Mike T. URAN
39	Director of Student Housing	Mr. Daniel T. PEDERSEN
09	Institutional Research	Mr. Brent DONNAY
15	Director Human Resources	Ms. Holly SCHOENHERR
19	Director Public Safety	Mr. Miles J. HECKENDORN
40	Bookstore Manager	Mr. Ted MEARS

*Saint Cloud Technical and Community College (B)

1540 Northway Drive, Saint Cloud MN 56303-1240
County: Stearns FICE Identification: 005534
Unit ID: 174756
Telephone: (320) 308-5000 Carnegie Class: Assoc/Pub-R-M
FAX Number: (320) 308-5981 Calendar System: Semester
URL: www.sctcc.edu
Established: 1948 Annual Undergrad Tuition & Fees (In-State): $5,159
Enrollment: 3,437 Coed
Affiliation or Control: State IRS Status: 501(c)3
Highest Offering: Associate Degree
Program: 2-Year Principally Bachelor's Creditable; Technical Emphasis
Accreditation: NH, CVT, DA, DH, DMS, EMT, SURGT

02	President	Ms. Joyce M. HELENS
05	VP of Academic Affairs	Ms. Margaret (Peg) SHROYER
04	Assistant to the President	Ms. Karen A. HIEMENZ
32	Vice President of Student Affairs	Mr. Phillip SCHROEDER
10	Vice Pres Admin/Chief Finan Officer	Ms. Lori KLOOS
75	Dean Trade/Industry	Mr. Bruce A. PETERSON
76	Dean Health/Human Services	Ms. Janet STEINKAMP
49	Dean of Liberal Arts & Sciences	Mr. Jason TETZLOFF
50	Dean of Business/Comp Science	Ms. Kristina KELLER
66	Dean of Nursing	Ms. Carolyn OLSON
06	Registrar	Ms. Lana L. FEDDEMA
15	Dir Personnel Services/Aff Action	Ms. Deb A. HOLSTAD
84	Dir of Enroll Management/Admissions	Ms. Jodi M. ELNESS
08	Head Librarian	Ms. Patricia AKERMAN
19	Security/Safety Officer	Ms. Joni AKERSON
37	Director Student Financial Aid	Ms. Anita G. BAUGH
20	Curriculum/Faculty Development	Ms. Margaret (Peg) SHROYER
36	Director Student Placement	Ms. Jackie BAUER
40	Director Bookstore	Mr. James SCHOLLA
38	Director Student Counseling	Ms. Judy JACOBSON-BERG
35	Activ Dir/Chief Student Life Ofcr	Mr. John R. HALLER
18	Chief Facilities/Physical Plant	Mr. Jason THEISEN
27	Chief Information Officer	Vacant
09	Director of Institutional Research	Vacant

21	Associate Business Officer	Mr. Duane DAHLSTROM
96	Director of Purchasing	Ms. Susan MEYER
13	Director Library & Info Technology	Ms. Viola BERGQUIST
22	Director Affirm Action/Equal Oppty	Ms. Deb HOLSTAD
30	Chief Devel/Dir Annual/Planned Giv	Ms. Shannon WIGER

*Saint Paul College-A Community & Technical College (C)

235 Marshall Avenue, Saint Paul MN 55102-1800
County: Ramsey FICE Identification: 005533
Unit ID: 175041
Telephone: (651) 846-1600 Carnegie Class: Assoc/Pub-U-SC
FAX Number: (651) 846-1451 Calendar System: Semester
URL: www.saintpaul.edu
Established: 1910 Annual Undergrad Tuition & Fees (In-State): $5,198
Enrollment: 5,780 Coed
Affiliation or Control: State IRS Status: 501(c)3
Highest Offering: Associate Degree
Program: Occupational; 2-Year Principally Bachelor's Creditable
Accreditation: NH, ACBSP, ACFEI, MLTAD, PNUR

02	President	Dr. Rassoul DASTMOZD
05	Int Sr VP Academic Affs/Student Dev	Dr. Marilyn KRASOWSKI
10	Vice President Finance & Operations	Mr. Shaan HAMILTON
35	Assoc VP Student Development/Svcs	Mr. Thomas MATOS
103	Dean Workforce Trng/Continuing Educ	Ms. Heather MCGANNON
46	Dean Research/Planning/Effective	Dr. Margie TOMSIC
07	Assc Dean Admissions/Enrollment Mgt	Ms. Sarah CARRICO
90	Assoc Dean of Academic Services	Ms. Shelley BIBEAU
20	Assoc Dean Student Develop/Svcs	Ms. Molly BAHNEMAN
15	Chief Human Resources Officer	Ms. Rachelle M. SCHMIDT
06	Registrar	Ms. Katie YEP
18	Director Facilities/Physical Plant	Mr. Tom DOODY
21	Business Manager	Mr. John PALMER
26	Director of Marketing	Ms. Allison FRIEDLY
36	Director of Student Placement	Mr. Brian MOGREN
37	Director of Student Financial Aid	Ms. Susan PIXLEY
102	Exec Dir of Foundation/Alumni Rels	Ms. Laura SAVIN
13	Chief Information Officer	Mr. Najam SAEED
32	Chief Student Life Officer	Mr. Andrew CLEVELAND
17	Interim Dean of Health & Services	Dr. Mary DAVENPORT
49	Dean of Liberal Arts & Sciences	Dr. Linda KINGSTON
50	Int Dean Business/Career Tech Educ	Ms. Susan SENGER

*South Central College (D)

1920 Lee Boulevard, PO Box 1920,
North Mankato MN 56002-1920
County: Nicollet FICE Identification: 005537
Unit ID: 173911
Telephone: (507) 389-7200 Carnegie Class: Assoc/Pub-R-M
FAX Number: (507) 388-9951 Calendar System: Semester
URL: www.southcentral.edu
Established: 1946 Annual Undergrad Tuition & Fees (In-District): $5,355
Enrollment: 4,110 Coed
Affiliation or Control: State/Local IRS Status: 501(c)3
Highest Offering: Associate Degree
Program: Occupational; 2-Year Principally Bachelor's Creditable
Accreditation: NH, DA, EMT, MLTAD

02	President	Mr. Keith STOVER
04	Exec Assistant to the President	Ms. Carol FREED
05	Vice President of Academic Affairs	Dr. Nancy GENELIN
10	Vice President Finance & Operations	Ms. Karen SNOREK
45	Director of Research & Planning	Ms. Dena COLEMER
32	Dean of Student Affairs	Ms. Linda BEER
20	Dean of Academic Affairs	Dr. Suzanne NORDBLOM
20	Dean of Academic Affairs	Mr. W. C. SANDERS
20	Interim Dean of Academic Affairs	Dr. Jane GREATHOUSE
27	Public Information Officer	Ms. Ann SPLINTER
06	Registrar/Dir Enrollment Management	Ms. Donna MARZOLF
09	Director of Institutional Research	Ms. Dena COLEMER
28	Interim Director of Diversity	Dr. Jane GREATHOUSE
15	Dir Human Resource/Personnel Svcs	Ms. Laural KUBAT
37	Director Student Financial Aid	Ms. Jayne DINSE
18	Chief Facilities/Physical Plant	Ms. Karen SNOREK
07	Director of Admissions	Mr. David MILLER
08	Director of Library/Media Services	Ms. Johnna HORTON
13	Dean of Technology	Mr. Wes TAYLOR
18	Director of Safety	Mr. Al KLUEVER

*Southwest Minnesota State University (E)

1501 State Street, Marshall MN 56258-1598
County: Lyon FICE Identification: 002375
Unit ID: 175078
Telephone: (507) 537-7678 Carnegie Class: Master's M
FAX Number: (507) 537-7154 Calendar System: Semester
URL: www.smsu.edu
Established: 1963 Annual Undergrad Tuition & Fees (In-State): $8,074
Enrollment: 6,771 Coed
Affiliation or Control: State IRS Status: 501(c)3
Highest Offering: Master's
Program: Liberal Arts And General; Teacher Preparatory; Professional
Accreditation: NH, MUS, SW

02	Interim President	Dr. Ronald A. WOOD
05	Provost	Dr. Beth WEATHERBY
10	VP Finance and Admin	Ms. Debra KERKAERT
32	AVP Stdnt Affairs/Dean of Students	Mr. Scott CROWELL
102	AVP Advance/Dir Devel/Foundation	Mr. William MULSO
49	Interim Dean Arts/Letters/Sciences	Dr. Jan LOFT
50	Interim Dean Bus/Ed/Grad/Prof Stud	Dr. Raphael ONYEAGHALA
20	Assoc Dean Academics/Student Svcs	Mr. Scott CROWELL
41	Athletic Director	Mr. Christopher HMIELEWSKI
27	Chief Information Officer	Mr. Dan BAUN
07	Director Admissions	Mr. Gary GILLIN
14	Director of Computer Services	Mr. Shawn HEDMAN
06	Registrar	Ms. Patricia CARMODY
19	Director University Public Safety	Mr. Michael MUNFORD
28	Director Cultural Diversity	Mr. Don ROBERTSON
15	Director Human Resources	Ms. Deb ALMER
29	Interim Director of Alumni	Mr. Michael VANDREHLE
18	Director of Facilities	Ms. Cyndi HOLM
36	Director of Career Services	Ms. Sheila RISACHER
35	Director of Student Center	Mr. Scott CROWELL
37	Director of Student Financial Aid	Mr. David VIKANDER
38	Director of Student Counseling	Mr. Robert LARSEN
96	Director of Purchasing	Mr. Jeff KUIPER
21	Business Manager	Mr. Eric RUNESTAD

*Vermilion Community College (F)

1900 E Camp Street, Ely MN 55731-1998
County: Saint Louis FICE Identification: 002350
Unit ID: 175157
Telephone: (218) 235-2101 Carnegie Class: Assoc/Pub-R-S
FAX Number: (218) 235-2173 Calendar System: Semester
URL: www.vcc.edu
Established: 1922 Annual Undergrad Tuition & Fees (In-State): $4,729
Enrollment: 780 Coed
Affiliation or Control: State IRS Status: 501(c)3
Highest Offering: Associate Degree
Program: Occupational; 2-Year Principally Bachelor's Creditable
Accreditation: NH

02	Provost/Chief Academic Officer	Mr. Shawn BINA
06	Registrar	Ms. Nadine FORSMAN
07	Director of Admissions/Student Affs	Mr. Jeff NELSON
09	Director of Institutional Research	Ms. Tracey ROY
10	Business Manager	Ms. Nicole SQUIRES
15	Director of Personnel Services	Ms. Carmen BRADACH
32	Dir Student Life/Facil/Phy Plant	Mr. Dave MARSHALL
36	Director of Student Placement	Mr. Doug FURNSTAHL
37	Director of Student Financial Aid	Ms. Kristi L'ALLIER
38	Director of Student Counseling	Ms. Cindy ANDERSON-BINA
29	Director Alumni Relations	Ms. Patti ZUPANCICH
28	Director of Diversity	Ms. Donna PRICHARD
26	Chief Public Relations Officer	Mr. Jeff NELSON

*Winona State University (G)

PO Box 5838, Winona MN 55987-0838
County: Winona FICE Identification: 002394
Unit ID: 175272
Telephone: (507) 457-5000 Carnegie Class: Master's M
FAX Number: (507) 457-5586 Calendar System: Quarter
URL: www.winona.edu
Established: 1858 Annual Undergrad Tuition & Fees (In-State): $8,400
Enrollment: 8,896 Coed
Affiliation or Control: State IRS Status: 501(c)3
Highest Offering: Doctorate
Program: Liberal Arts And General; Teacher Preparatory; Professional
Accreditation: NH, BUS, CACREP, ENG, MUS, NURSE, SW, TED, THEA

02	President	Dr. Scott R. OLSON
05	Interim VP Academic Affairs	Dr. Nancy JANNIK
10	Interim VP Finance & Administration	Mr. Scott ELLINGHUYSEN
30	Vice Pres University Advancement	Dr. James SCHMIDT
32	Vice President Student Life & Dev	Dr. Connie GORES
13	Assoc Vice Pres/CIO Tech Svcs	Mr. Kenneth JANZ
21	Assoc VP for Finance/Admin Svcs/CFO	Mr. Scott ELLINGHUYSEN
20	Assoc Vice Pres Academic Affairs	Dr. Nancy JANNIK
26	Asst VP Marketing & Communications	Ms. Cristeen CUSTER
38	Chairperson of Counseling Services	Ms. Patricia FERDEN
54	Interim Dean Col of Science/Engr	Dr. Charla MIERTSCHIN
49	Dean Liberal Arts	Dr. Ralph TOWNSEND
50	Dean of Business	Dr. Bill MURPHY
53	Dean of Education	Vacant
66	Dean Nursing/Health Science	Dr. William MCBREEN
35	Dean of Students	Ms. Karen JOHNSON
06	Registrar	Mr. Glenn PETERSEN
09	Director Institutional Research	Vacant
37	Director of Financial Aid	Mr. Greg PETERSON
36	Associate Director Career Services	Ms. Deanna GODDARD
07	Director of Admissions	Mr. Carl STANGE
39	Residential College Program Coord	Ms. Sarah OLCOTT
31	Director of Auxiliary Services	Vacant
29	Director of Alumni Relations	Mr. Michael SWENSON
40	Bookstore Manager	Ms. Karen KRAUSE
44	Director Major Gifts	Ms. Mary ROHRER
88	Director of International Svcs	Mr. Jay SKRANKA
19	Director of Security	Mr. Don WALSKI
41	Athletic Director	Mr. Eric SCHOH
18	Facilities Manager	Mr. Richard LANDE
27	Director University Communications	Ms. Andrea MIKKELSEN
94	Director of Women's Studies	Dr. Tamara BERG
96	Director of Purchasing	Ms. Deborah BENZ
28	Director of Cultural Diversity	Mr. Alexander HINES
15	Director of Human Resources	Ms. Lori REED

North Central University (A)

910 Elliot Avenue, Minneapolis MN 55404-1391

County: Hennepin FICE Identification: 002369
Unit ID: 174437
Telephone: (612) 343-4400 Carnegie Class: Bac/Diverse
FAX Number: (612) 343-4778 Calendar System: Semester
URL: www.northcentral.edu
Established: 1930 Annual Undergrad Tuition & Fees: $18,610
Enrollment: 1,388 Coed
Affiliation or Control: Assemblies Of God Church IRS Status: 501(c)3
Highest Offering: Baccalaureate
Program: Liberal Arts And General
Accreditation: NH, @SW

01 President .... Dr. Gordon L. ANDERSON
04 Executive Assistant of President .... Mrs. Beth Ann ROCKETT
10 Vice President Finance .... Mrs. Cheryl A. BOOK
05 Vice Pres Academic Affs/Acad Dean .... Dr. Tom A. BURKMAN
30 Vice President Advancement .... Dr. Paul A. FREITAG
32 Vice President Student Development .... Mr. Mike A. NOSSER
26 VP University Rels/Enrollment .... Mr. Nate P. RUCH
57 Executive Director Fine Arts .... Dr. Larry C. BACH
84 Exec Director Enrollment .... Mr. Troy PEARSON
21 Exec Director of Accounting .... Mr. Bruce JENSEN
39 Dean of Residence Life .... Mr. Juice MONTEZON
31 Dean of Community Life .... Mr. Greg J. LEEPER
41 Athletic Director .... Mr. Jon HIGH
37 Director of Financial Aid .... Ms. Donna JAGER
08 Library Director .... Ms. Melody REEDY
13 Director of Information Technology .... Mr. Michael CAPPELLI
06 Registrar .... Mr. Cody SCHMITZ
18 Director of Plant/Operations .... Mr. Marv LANGMADE
44 Director Plannned Giving .... Mr. Wes BOOK
09 Director of Institutional Research .... Mr. Casey ROZOWSKI
07 Director of Admissions .... Mr. Joshua MARTIN
38 Director of Student Success .... Mr. Todd MONGER

Northwestern College (B)

3003 Snelling Avenue N, Saint Paul MN 55113-1598

County: Ramsey FICE Identification: 002371
Unit ID: 174491
Telephone: (651) 631-5100 Carnegie Class: Bac/Diverse
FAX Number: (651) 628-3339 Calendar System: Semester
URL: www.nwc.edu
Established: 1902 Annual Undergrad Tuition & Fees: $26,740
Enrollment: 3,069 Coed
Affiliation or Control: Independent Non-Profit IRS Status: 501(c)3
Highest Offering: Master's
Program: Liberal Arts And General; Teacher Preparatory
Accreditation: NH, MUS

01 President .... Dr. Alan S. CURETON
05 Senior Vice Pres Academic Affairs .... Dr. Janet B. SOMMERS
30 Vice President Advancement .... Mrs. Amy B. CAREY
10 Vice President Finance/CFO .... Mr. Douglas R. SCHROEDER
27 Senior Vice President Media .... Dr. Paul H. VIRTS
32 Vice Pres Student Life & Athletics .... Dr. Mathew B. HILL
00 President Emeritus .... Dr. Donald O. ERICKSEN
21 Director of Business Services .... Mrs. Marla K. DENNISON
20 Interim Dean of Faculty .... Dr. Richard C. THOMAN
88 Dean of Retention .... Ms. Monica R. GROVES
35 Dean of Student Development .... Mr. Paul A. BRADLEY
35 Assoc Dean Student Development .... Dr. Katie J. SMITH
06 Registrar .... Mr. Andrew L. SIMPSON
09 Institutional Researcher Rprt Spec .... Mr. Russell E. ERICKSON
29 Dir of Alumni & Parent Relations .... Mr. James E. BENDER
37 Director of Financial Aid .... Mr. Richard L. BLATCHLEY
58 Asst Dean Acad Pgm/Grad Cont Educ .... Dr. Erin L. HEATH
13 Vice Pres for Campus Technology/CIO .... Vacant
88 Controller .... Mr. Bryon D. KRUEGER
08 Director of Library Services .... Mrs. Ruth A. MCGUIRE
15 Director of Human Resources .... Mr. Timothy A. RICH
24 Director of Academic Technology .... Vacant
23 Director of Health Services .... Mrs. Cynthia P. REEDSTROM
42 Senior Dir of Campus Ministries .... Mr. James K. JOHNSON
18 Assoc VP Facility Ops & Planning .... Mr. Brian L. HUMPHRIES
36 Dir Center for Calling & Career .... Ms. Linda F. MAYES
26 Dir of Mktg & Communications .... Ms. Marita K. MEINERTS
40 Manager Campus Store .... Ms. Andrea R. HALVERSON
19 Director of Public Safety .... Mr. Peter L. SOLA
38 Director of Counseling/Student Svcs .... Ms. Dannette C. WILFAHRT
44 Director of Planned Giving .... Mr. David D. DANIELSON
96 Purchasing Manager .... Mrs. Lindy J. STANKEY
07 Senior Director of Admissions .... Mr. Ken K. FAFFLER
88 Asst to Pres for ADA Initiatives .... Dr. Yvonne R. BANKS
88 Assoc Dean Commuter Life/Transition .... Mr. Jeff B. SNYDER
102 Senior Director Development .... Mr. Brian J. MOLOHON
101 Exec Secy to Pres & Bd of Trustees .... Ms. Mona S. GRELLSON
39 Associate Dean for Residence Life .... Mr. Jerod L. CORNELIUS

Northwestern Health Sciences University (C)

2501 W 84th Street, Bloomington MN 55431-1599

County: Hennepin FICE Identification: 012328
Unit ID: 174507
Telephone: (952) 888-4777 Carnegie Class: Spec/Health
FAX Number: (952) 888-6713 Calendar System: Trimester
URL: www.nwhealth.edu
Established: 1941 Annual Undergrad Tuition & Fees: $13,620
Enrollment: 859 Coed
Affiliation or Control: Independent Non-Profit IRS Status: 501(c)3
Highest Offering: First Professional Degree
Program: Professional
Accreditation: NH, ACUP, CHIRO, COMTA

01 Interim President .... Dr. Michael WILES
03 Senior Vice President .... Dr. Charles E. SAWYER
05 Provost .... Dr. Michael WILES
11 VP Administrative Affairs/CFO .... Mr. Ross B. DUGAS
46 Vice President for Research .... Dr. Gert BRONFORT
32 Dean Student Affs/Enrollment Mgmt .... Dr. Emily J. TWEED
07 Director of Admissions .... Ms. Kate DIANA
08 Director of Library Services .... Ms. Della SHUPE
29 Dir Alumni Relations/Career Svcs .... Ms. Deborah A. PETERSON
06 Chief Records Officer & Registrar .... Ms. RuthAnn MARKS
15 Director of Human Resources .... Ms. Deborah HOGENSON
37 Director of Financial Aid .... Ms. Ruth Ann MARKS
51 Director Continuing Education .... Ms. Diana BERG
26 Director of Marketing .... Ms. Kathryn GRIMES
30 Chief Development Officer .... Mr. Scott PALMER
13 Chief Information Systems Officer .... Mr. Steve HIDY
09 Dir Institutional Research/Planning .... Ms. Deborah HOGENSON
38 University Counselor .... Ms. Becky LAWYER
18 Director Facilities Management .... Mr. Kevin WOLPERN
96 Director Bookstore & Purchasing .... Ms. Jan HALLEEN

Oak Hills Christian College (D)

1600 Oak Hills Road, SW, Bemidji MN 56601-8826

County: Beltrami FICE Identification: 009992
Unit ID: 174525
Telephone: (218) 751-8670 Carnegie Class: Spec/Faith
FAX Number: (218) 751-8825 Calendar System: Semester
URL: www.oakhills.edu
Established: 1946 Annual Undergrad Tuition & Fees: $14,670
Enrollment: 126 Coed
Affiliation or Control: Interdenominational IRS Status: 501(c)3
Highest Offering: Baccalaureate
Program: Liberal Arts And General; Religious Emphasis
Accreditation: BI

01 President .... Dr. Steve J. HOSTETTER
05 Dean of the College .... Dr. Steven J. WARE
30 Vice President for Advancement .... Mrs. Joan L. BERNTSON
10 Business Manager .... Mrs. Carol NELSON
06 Registrar .... Mrs. Mary HANNAH
08 Library Director .... Mr. Keith BUSH
07 Dean of Student Enrollment .... Mr. John ENGQUIST
37 Director of Financial Aid .... Mr. Daniel HOVESTOL

*Rasmussen College - Lake Elmo/ Woodbury (E)

8550 Hudson Blvd, Suite 110, Lake Elmo MN 55042

County: Washington Identification: 667034
Unit ID: 17501405
Telephone: (651) 636-3305 Carnegie Class: N/A
FAX Number: (651) 636-3375
URL: www.rasmussen.edu

01 Campus Director .... Mr. Phillip KAGOL

*Rasmussen College - Blaine (F)

3629 95th Avenue Northeast, Blaine MN 55014

County: Anoka Identification: 667061
Unit ID: 17501406
Telephone: (763) 795-4720 Carnegie Class: Not Classified
FAX Number: (763) 795-4721 Calendar System: Quarter
URL: www.rasmussen.edu
Established: 1900 Annual Undergrad Tuition & Fees: $16,340
Enrollment: 204 Coed
Affiliation or Control: Proprietary IRS Status: Proprietary
Highest Offering: Baccalaureate
Program: Occupational; 2-Year Principally Bachelor's Creditable
Accreditation: &NH, MAAB

02 Campus Director .... Patty SAGERT

† Regional accreditation is carried under the parent institution in Lake Elmo, MN.

*Rasmussen College - Bloomington (G)

4400 W 78th St, 6th Floor, Bloomington MN 55435

County: Hennepin FICE Identification: 011686
Unit ID: 174464
Telephone: (952) 545-2000 Carnegie Class: Assoc/PrivFP4
FAX Number: (952) 545-7038 Calendar System: Quarter
URL: www.Rasmussen.edu
Established: 1963 Annual Undergrad Tuition & Fees: $16,340
Enrollment: 701 Coed
Affiliation or Control: Proprietary IRS Status: Proprietary
Highest Offering: Baccalaureate
Program: Occupational; 2-Year Principally Bachelor's Creditable
Accreditation: &NH, MAC

02 Campus Director .... Mr. Jeff BROSZ

† Regional accreditation carried under the parent institution in Lake Elmo, MN.

*Rasmussen College - Brooklyn Park (H)

8301 93rd Avenue North, Brooklyn Park MN 55445-1512

County: Hennepin Identification: 666769
Unit ID: 17501404
Telephone: (763) 493-4500 Carnegie Class: Not Classified
FAX Number: N/A Calendar System: Semester
URL: www.rasmussen.edu
Established: N/A Annual Undergrad Tuition & Fees: $16,340
Enrollment: 1,203 Coed
Affiliation or Control: Proprietary IRS Status: Proprietary
Highest Offering: Baccalaureate
Program: Occupational; 2-Year Principally Bachelor's Creditable
Accreditation: &NH, MAC

02 Campus Director .... Ms. Naomi MOGARD

† Regional accreditation carried under the parent institution in Lake Elmo, MN.

*Rasmussen College - Eagan (I)

3500 Federal Drive, Eagan MN 55122-1346

County: Dakota FICE Identification: 004648
Unit ID: 174622
Telephone: (651) 687-9000 Carnegie Class: Bac/Assoc
FAX Number: (651) 687-0507 Calendar System: Quarter
URL: www.Rasmussen.edu
Established: 1900 Annual Undergrad Tuition & Fees: $16,340
Enrollment: 1,016 Coed
Affiliation or Control: Proprietary IRS Status: Proprietary
Highest Offering: Baccalaureate
Program: Occupational; 2-Year Principally Bachelor's Creditable
Accreditation: &NH, MAC

02 Campus Director .... Ms. Tammy JACKSON

† Regional accreditation carried under the parent institution in Lake Elmo, MN.

*Rasmussen College - Mankato (J)

130 Saint Andrews Drive, Mankato MN 56001

County: Blue Earth FICE Identification: 025033
Unit ID: 174631
Telephone: (507) 625-6556 Carnegie Class: Bac/Assoc
FAX Number: (507) 625-6557 Calendar System: Quarter
URL: www.Rasmussen.edu
Established: 1900 Annual Undergrad Tuition & Fees: $16,340
Enrollment: 935 Coed
Affiliation or Control: Proprietary IRS Status: Proprietary
Highest Offering: Baccalaureate
Program: Occupational; 2-Year Principally Bachelor's Creditable
Accreditation: &NH, MAC, MLTAD

02 Campus Director .... Ms. Kathy SANGER

† Regional accreditation carried under the parent institution in Lake Elmo, MN.

*Rasmussen College - St. Cloud (K)

226 Park Avenue South, Saint Cloud MN 56301-3713

County: Stearns FICE Identification: 008694
Unit ID: 175014
Telephone: (320) 251-5600 Carnegie Class: Assoc/PrivFP4
FAX Number: (320) 251-3702 Calendar System: Quarter
URL: www.Rasmussen.edu
Established: 1902 Annual Undergrad Tuition & Fees: $16,340
Enrollment: 1,251 Coed
Affiliation or Control: Proprietary IRS Status: Proprietary
Highest Offering: Baccalaureate
Program: Occupational; 2-Year Principally Bachelor's Creditable
Accreditation: &NH, MAC, MLTAD, SURGT

02 Campus Director .... Mr. John SMITH-COPPES

† Regional accreditation carried under the parent institution in Lake Elmo, MN.

St. Catherine University (L)

2004 Randolph Avenue, Saint Paul MN 55105-1789

County: Ramsey FICE Identification: 002342
Unit ID: 175005
Telephone: (651) 690-6000 Carnegie Class: Master's L
FAX Number: (651) 690-6024 Calendar System: 4/1/4
URL: www.stkate.edu
Established: 1905 Annual Undergrad Tuition & Fees: $33,176
Enrollment: 5,227 Female
Affiliation or Control: Roman Catholic IRS Status: 501(c)3
Highest Offering: Doctorate
Program: Liberal Arts And General; Teacher Preparatory; Professional
Accreditation: NH, ADNUR, #ARCPA, DIETD, DMS, EXSC, LIB, MACTE, NUR, OT, OTA, PTA, PTAA, RAD, SW

01 President .... Dr. Andrea J. LEE, IHM
03 Senior Vice President .... Ms. Colleen HEGRANES
10 Vice Pres Finance/Administration .... Mr. Thomas ROONEY

26 Vice Pres for External Relations ..... Ms. Marjorie MATHISON HANCE
84 VP Enrollment Mgmt/Student Affairs ..... Dr. Brian BRUESS
35 Dean of Student Affairs ..... Mr. Curt GALLOWAY
05 Chief Academic Officer ..... Ms. Colleen HEGRANES
06 Registrar ..... Ms. Cynthia EGENESS
08 Library Director ..... Ms. Carol JOHNSON
30 Chief Development ..... Ms. Elizabeth RIEDEL CARNEY
32 Chief Student Life Officer ..... Dr. Brian BRUESS
29 Director of Alumnae Relations ..... Ms. Karen G. JOTHEN
26 Dir of Marketing & Communications ..... Ms. Amy GAGE
37 Director of Financial Aid ..... Ms. Elizabeth STEVENS
36 Director of Career Development ..... Ms. Kimberly BETZ
14 Director of Computing Services ..... Mr. John JERIES
21 Business Manager ..... Ms. Tracey GRAN
04 Exec Assistant to the President ..... Ms. Stacy JACOBSON
15 Director of Personnel Services ..... Ms. Susan SEXTON
38 Director of Student Counseling ..... Ms. Heide MALAT
92 Director of Honors Program ..... Dr. Gayle GASKILL
94 Director of Women's Studies ..... Dr. Sharon DOHERTY
96 Director of Purchasing ..... Ms. Gail BLIVEN
09 Dir Instl Rsrch/Plng/ Assessment ..... Dr. Jennifer ROBINSON KLOOS
18 Chief Facilities/Physical Plant ..... Mr. James MANSHIP
49 AVP/Dean Sch Humanities/Arts/Sci ..... Dr. Alan SILVA
76 Dean Hen Schmoll Sch Hlth/Grad Col ..... Dr. Penelope MOYERS
07 Associate Dean of Admissions ..... Ms. Marlene MOHS
27 Assoc Dean Admiss/Market Devel ..... Mr. Greg STEENSON
50 Dean School Business & Leadership ..... Dr. Paula KING
20 Associate Dean Academic Affairs ..... Ms. Bonnie LADUCA
20 Associate Dean of Academic Affairs ..... Dr. Lynda SZYMANSKI

Saint John's University (A)

Box 2000, Collegeville MN 56321-2000
County: Stearns FICE Identification: 002379
Unit ID: 174792
Telephone: (320) 363-2011 Carnegie Class: Bac/A&S
FAX Number: (320) 363-2504 Calendar System: Semester
URL: www.csbsju.edu
Established: 1857 Annual Undergrad Tuition & Fees: $35,486
Enrollment: 1,865 Coordinate
Affiliation or Control: Roman Catholic IRS Status: 501(c)3
Highest Offering: Master's
Program: Liberal Arts And General; Teacher Preparatory; Professional
Accreditation: NH, DIETD, MUS, NURSE, TED, THEOL

01 President ..... Dr. Michael HEMESATH
05 Provost Academic Affairs ..... Dr. Rita KNUESEL
20 Vice Provost ..... Dr. Joseph DESJARDINS
20 Academic Dean ..... Dr. Richard ICE
30 Vice President for Inst Advancement ..... Mr. Rob CULLIGAN
32 Vice President Student Development ... Fr. Douglas MULLIN, OSB
10 Vice Pres Finance/Admin Services ..... Mr. Richard ADAMSON
46 VP Inst Plng/Research/Communication ..... Mr. Jon MCGEE
07 Vice Pres Admissions/Financial Aid ..... Dr. Cal MOSLEY
73 Dean School Theology ..... Dr. William CAHOY
88 Dir of Center for Global Educ ..... Mr. Joseph ROGERS
35 Dean of Students ..... Mr. Michael CONNOLLY
45 Associate Dean Planning/Budget ..... Mr. David LYNDGAARD
26 Exec Director of Comm & Marketing ..... Mr. Greg HOYE
08 Director of Library ..... Ms. Kathleen PARKER
06 Registrar ..... Ms. Julie GRUSKA
38 Director of Career Services ..... Ms. Heidi HARLANDER
37 Exec Director of Financial Aid ..... Mr. Stuart PERRY
13 Director of Info Technology Svcs ..... Mr. Jim KOENIG
29 Director of Alumni Relations ..... Mr. Adam HERBST
15 Director Human Resources ..... Ms. Carol ABELL
41 Athletic Director ..... Mr. Tom STOCK
19 Director Life Safety Services ..... Mr. Shawn VIERZBA
42 Director of Campus Ministry ..... Fr. William SCHIPPER, OSB
18 Director Facilities/Physical Plant ..... Mr. Bill BOOM
40 Director Bookstore ..... Mr. Donald FORBES
09 Assoc Director Inst Research ..... Ms. Karen G. KNUTSON

Saint Mary's University of Minnesota (B)

700 Terrace Heights, Winona MN 55987-1399
County: Winona FICE Identification: 002380
Unit ID: 174817
Telephone: (507) 452-4430 Carnegie Class: DRU
FAX Number: (507) 457-1633 Calendar System: Semester
URL: www.smumn.edu
Established: 1912 Annual Undergrad Tuition & Fees: $28,320
Enrollment: 5,688 Coed
Affiliation or Control: Roman Catholic IRS Status: 501(c)3
Highest Offering: Doctorate
Program: Liberal Arts And General; Teacher Preparatory
Accreditation: NH, ANEST, IACBE, MFCD, MUS, NMT, NURSE, SURGT

01 President ..... Bro. William MANN, FSC
03 Vice President of the College ..... Mr. James BEDTKE
07 Director of Admission ..... Ms. Brandi DEFRIES
30 Sr Vice Pres University Advancement ..... Dr. Steve TITUS
32 Vice President Student Development ..... Mr. Chris KENDALL
10 Vice President Financial Affairs ..... Ms. Cynthia MAREK
43 Exec Vice Pres/General Counsel ..... Ms. Ann E. MERCHLEWITZ
05 Vice President for Academic Affairs ..... Dr. Donna ARONSON
58 VP Schs of Graduate/Professnl Pgms ..... Dr. Marcel DUMESTRE
26 Assoc VP Marketing & Communications ..... Mr. Nick LEMMER
20 Academic Dean/Assoc Vice President ..... Ms. Linka HOLEY
35 Dean of Students/Dir Resident Life ..... Mr. Tim GOSSEN
04 Assistant to the President ..... Ms. Mary BECKER
06 Registrar ..... Ms. Lori TURNER
13 Chief Information Officer ..... Mr. Scott COWDREY
37 Director of Financial Aid ..... Ms. Jayne WOBIG
88 Director of Toner Student Center ..... Ms. Terrie LUECK
36 Dir Career Services & Internships ..... Ms. Jackie BAKER
38 Director of Counseling Center ..... Dr. Ruth MATTHEWS
08 Director of Library ..... Ms. Laura OANES
22 Affirmative Action Officer ..... Ms. Ann E. MERCHLEWITZ
21 Assistant Controller ..... Mr. Paul J. WILDENBORG
19 Director of Security ..... Mr. Phil GADDIS
18 Director of Buildings/Grounds ..... Mr. John SCHOLLMEIER
23 Director of Health Services ..... Ms. Angela WEISBROD
29 Director Alumni Relations ..... Ms. Margaret RICHTMAN
41 Director of Athletics ..... Ms. Nicole FENNERN
15 Director of Human Resources ..... Ms. Genelle GROH BECK
09 Institutional Researcher ..... Ms. Kara WENER
53 Dean School Education ..... Dr. Scott SORVAAG
79 Dean School of the Arts ..... Mr. Michael CHARRON

St. Olaf College (C)

1520 St. Olaf Avenue, Northfield MN 55057-1098
County: Rice FICE Identification: 002382
Unit ID: 174844
Telephone: (507) 786-2222 Carnegie Class: Bac/A&S
FAX Number: (507) 786-3549 Calendar System: 4/1/4
URL: www.stolaf.edu
Established: 1874 Annual Undergrad Tuition & Fees: $48,650
Enrollment: 3,113 Coed
Affiliation or Control: Evangelical Lutheran Church In America
IRS Status: 501(c)3
Highest Offering: Baccalaureate
Program: Liberal Arts And General; Teacher Preparatory; Professional
Accreditation: NH, DANCE, MUS, NURSE, SW, TED, THEA

01 President ..... Dr. David R. ANDERSON
05 Provost & Dean of the College ..... Dr. Marci J. SORTOR
10 Vice President & Treasurer ..... Dr. Alan J. NORTON
30 Vice Pres for Advancement ..... Mr. Enoch BLAZIS
32 Vice Pres of Student Life ..... Mr. Greg KNESER
84 Vice Pres Enrollment/Col Relations ..... Mr. Michael KYLE
88 Vice President for Mission ..... Dr. Paula J. CARLSON
18 Asst Vice President for Facilities ..... Mr. Peter SANDBERG
31 Asst to the Pres for Inst Diversity ..... Mr. Bruce KING
20 Assistant Provost ..... Dr. Phyllis LARSON
06 Asst VP Registrar ..... Dr. Mary CISAR
89 Assoc Dean Interdisciplin/Gen Stds ..... Dr. Phyllis LARSON
81 Assoc Dean Natural Sciences & Math ..... Dr. Matthew RICHEY
79 Assoc Dean Humanities ..... Dr. Corliss SWAIN
57 Assoc Dean Fine Arts ..... Dr. Dan DRESSEN
83 Assoc Dean Social Sciences ..... Dr. Dan HOFRENNING
21 Asst VP/Chief Investment Officer ..... Mr. Mark GELLE
07 Dean of Admissions & Financial Aid ..... Vacant
35 Dean of Students ..... Ms. Rosalyn EATON-NEEB
35 Assoc Dean of Students ..... Mr. Timothy SCHROER
35 Assoc Dean of Students ..... Mr. Justin FLEMING
42 Campus Pastor ..... Dr. Matthew MAROHL
36 Sr Assoc Dir of Career Connections ..... Ms. Kirsten CAHOON
13 Director of IT and Libraries ..... Ms. Roberta LEMBKE
08 Director of IT and Libraries ..... Ms. Roberta LEMBKE
44 Director Annual Giving ..... Ms. Tracy FOSSUM
29 Director of Alumni Parent Relations ..... Mr. Nathan SOLAND
15 Director of Human Resources ..... Mr. Roger LOFTUS
19 Director of Public Safety ..... Mr. Fred C. BEHR
41 Director of Athletics ..... Mr. Matt C. MCDONALD
38 Director of Counseling ..... Dr. Stephen O'NEILL
26 Dir of Marketing & Communications ..... Mr. Steve BLODGETT
75 Dir Center for Vocation and Career ..... Mr. Branden GRIMMETT
09 Director of Institutional Research ..... Ms. Susan CANON
108 Director of Evaluation & Assessment ..... Dr. Jo M. BELD
39 Director of Residence Life ..... Ms. Pamela MCDOWELL
40 Bookstore Director ..... Ms. Victoria BEUSSMAN
96 Director of Auxiliary Operations ..... Mr. Steve ABBOTT
37 Director of Student Financial Aid ..... Ms. Sandra SUNDSTROM
102 Dir of Govt & Foundation Relations ..... Ms. Patricia MARTIN
104 Dir of Intl & Off Campus Studies ..... Dr. Eric LUND
85 International Student Advisor ..... Ms. Christy HALL-HOLT
04 Exec Assistant to the President ..... Ms. Pat HESS

United Theological Seminary of the Twin Cities (D)

3000 Fifth Street, NW, New Brighton MN 55112-2598
County: Ramsey FICE Identification: 002386
Unit ID: 175139
Telephone: (651) 633-4311 Carnegie Class: Spec/Faith
FAX Number: (651) 633-4315 Calendar System: 4/1/4
URL: www.unitedseminary.edu
Established: 1962 Annual Graduate Tuition & Fees: $15,180
Enrollment: 179 Coed
Affiliation or Control: United Church Of Christ IRS Status: 501(c)3
Highest Offering: Doctorate; No Undergraduates
Program: Professional; Religious Emphasis
Accreditation: NH, THEOL

01 President ..... Rev. Barbara A. HOLMES
05 Dean of the Seminary ..... Ms. Susan EBBERS
10 VP for Finance and Administration ..... Mr. Tom LOCKHART
30 VP for Development ..... Mr. Jim OLSEN
44 Director of Development ..... Ms. Julie BROWN
07 Director of Admissions ..... Rev. Glen HERRINGTON-HALL
04 Admin Assistant to the President ..... Ms. Gretchen MILLOY
06 Registrar ..... Ms. Susan HASTINGS
37 Director Student Financial Aid ..... Ms. Michelle TURNAU
08 Librarian ..... Ms. Susan EBBERS
51 Director Continuing Education ..... Dr. Cindi Beth JOHNSON
42 Chaplain/Assc Prof Spirit Formation ..... Rev. Martha POSTLETHWAITE
18 Director Physical Plant ..... Mr. Brandon KROSCH

University of Minnesota-Crookston (E)

2900 University Avenue, Crookston MN 56716-5001
County: Polk FICE Identification: 004069
Unit ID: 174075
Telephone: (218) 281-6510 Carnegie Class: Bac/Diverse
FAX Number: (218) 281-8040 Calendar System: Semester
URL: www.crk.umn.edu
Established: 1965 Annual Undergrad Tuition & Fees (In-State): $11,465
Enrollment: 1,600 Coed
Affiliation or Control: State IRS Status: 501(c)3
Highest Offering: Baccalaureate
Program: Occupational; Business Emphasis
Accreditation: NH

01 Chancellor ..... Dr. Fred WOOD
05 Sr VC Academic/Student Affairs ..... Dr. Thomas BALDWIN
32 Assoc VC Student Affs/Enrollment ..... Dr. Peter PHAIAH
18 Director Facilities/Operations ..... Vacant
10 Dir of Finance/University Services ..... Ms. Tricia SANDERS
15 Director Human Resources ..... Mr. Les JOHNSON
37 Director Financial Aid ..... Ms. Melissa DINGMANN
26 Director of Communications ..... Mr. Andrew SVEC
30 Dir Development/Alumni Relations ..... Mr. Corby KEMMER
08 Director Library ..... Mr. Owen WILLIAMS
36 Director Career/Counseling ..... Mr. Donald R. CAVALIER
49 Head of Arts/Humanities/Soc Sci ..... Dr. Jack GELLER
47 Head Agriculture & Nat Resources ..... Dr. Ron DEL VECCHIO
72 Head Math/Science/Technology ..... Dr. Adel ALI
50 Head Business ..... Dr. Susan BRORSON
51 Director Center for Adult Learning ..... Ms. Michelle CHRISTOPHERSON
06 Registrar ..... Dr. Bob NELSON
07 Director of Admissions ..... Ms. Amber EVANS-DAILEY
28 Director of Diversity ..... Mr. Thomas WILLIAMS
85 Dir of International Programs ..... Dr. Kimberly GILLETTE

University of Minnesota Duluth (F)

1049 University Drive, Duluth MN 55812-3011
County: Saint Louis FICE Identification: 002388
Unit ID: 174233
Telephone: (218) 726-8000 Carnegie Class: Master's M
FAX Number: (218) 726-6254 Calendar System: Semester
URL: www.d.umn.edu
Established: 1947 Annual Undergrad Tuition & Fees (In-State): $12,756
Enrollment: 11,806 Coed
Affiliation or Control: State IRS Status: 501(c)3
Highest Offering: Doctorate
Program: Liberal Arts And General; Teacher Preparatory; Professional
Accreditation: NH, BUS, CS, ENG, MUS, SP, SW, TED

01 Chancellor ..... Dr. Lendley C. BLACK
05 Exec Vice Chanc Academic Affairs ..... Dr. Andrea SCHOKKER
32 Vice Chancellor Student Life ..... Dr. Lisa ERWIN
10 Vice Chanc Finance/Operations ..... Mr. Michael SEYMOUR
26 Vice Chanc University Relations ..... Mr. William WADE
06 Registrar ..... Ms. Carla L. BOYD
08 Director of Library ..... Mr. Basil W. SOZANSKY, JR.
37 Director Financial Aid ..... Ms. Brenda H. HERZIG
36 Director Career Services ..... Ms. Julie A. WESTLUND
13 Director Info Tech Systems/Services ..... Dr. Linda DENEEN
09 Director Institutional Research ..... Dr. Giljae LEE
25 Senior Grant Administrator ..... Vacant
51 Director Continuing Education ..... Dr. Robert KRUMWIEDE
41 Athletic Director ..... Mr. Robert NIELSON
15 Director Personnel Services ..... Ms. Judith S. KARON
07 Director Admissions ..... Ms. Beth ESSELSTROM
18 Director Facilities/Physical Plant ..... Mr. John KING
29 Director Alumni Relations ..... Ms. Lisa PRATT
30 Director Development ..... Ms. Tricia BUNTEN
63 Associate Dean School of Medicine ..... Dr. Gary DAVIS
81 Interim Dean Col Science/Engr ..... Dr. Penny MORTON
49 Dean College Liberal Arts ..... Dr. Susan MAHER
53 Dean Col Education/Human Svc Prof ..... Dr. Paul DEPUTY
50 Dean School of Business & Economics ..... Dr. Kjell KNUDSEN
57 Dean School Fine Arts ..... Mr. William PAYNE
58 Director of Graduate Programs ..... Dr. Tim HOLST

University of Minnesota-Morris (G)

600 E 4th Street, Morris MN 56267-2132
County: Stevens FICE Identification: 002389
Unit ID: 174251
Telephone: (320) 589-2211 Carnegie Class: Bac/A&S
FAX Number: (320) 589-6399 Calendar System: Semester
URL: www.morris.umn.edu
Established: 1959 Annual Undergrad Tuition & Fees (In-State): $12,547
Enrollment: 1,932 Coed
Affiliation or Control: State IRS Status: 501(c)3
Highest Offering: Baccalaureate
Program: Liberal Arts And General; Teacher Preparatory

Accreditation: NH, TED

01 Chancellor .... Dr. Jacqueline JOHNSON
05 Int Vice Chanc Academic Affs/Dean .... Dr. Bart FINZEL
32 Vice Chanc for Student Affairs .... Ms. Sandra OLSON-LOY
30 Assoc VC for External Relations .... Ms. Maddy MAXEINER
18 Assoc VC Physical Plant/Master Plng .... Mr. Lowell C. RASMUSSEN
10 Director for Finance .... Ms. Colleen MILLER
08 Head Librarian .... Ms. LeAnn DEAN
06 Registrar .... Ms. Clare DINGLEY
26 Interim Director of Communications .... Ms. Melissa WEBER
29 Director of Alumni Relations .... Ms. Carla RILEY
09 Director of Institutional Research .... Ms. Nancy HELSPER
36 Director Career Center .... Mr. Gary L. DONOVAN
14 Director of Information Technology .... Mr. James HALL
38 Director of Counseling .... Dr. Henry FULDA
37 Director of Financial Aid .... Ms. Jill BEAUREGARD
93 Dir Multi Ethnic Student Program .... Ms. Hilda LADNER
24 Director Educational Media .... Mr. Roger P. BOLEMAN
07 Director of Admissions .... Mr. Bryan HERRMANN
53 Chair of Education Division .... Dr. Gwen RUDNEY
81 Chair of Science/Math Division .... Dr. Peh Peh NG
79 Chair of Humanities Division .... Dr. Pieranno GARAVASO
83 Chair of Social Science Division .... Dr. Leslie MEEK

University of Minnesota-Twin Cities (A)

100 Church Street, SE, Minneapolis MN 55455-0213
County: Hennepin — FICE Identification: 003969
Unit ID: 174066
Telephone: (612) 625-5000 — Carnegie Class: RU/VH
FAX Number: (612) 624-6369 — Calendar System: Semester
URL: www.umn.edu
Established: 1851 — Annual Undergrad Tuition & Fees (In-State): $13,309
Enrollment: 52,557 — Coed
Affiliation or Control: State — IRS Status: 501(c)3
Highest Offering: Doctorate
Program: Occupational; Liberal Arts And General; Teacher Preparatory; Professional
Accreditation: NH, ANEST, AUD, BUS, CIDA, CLPSY, COPSY, DANCE, DENT, DH, DIETC, DIETD, DIETI, ENG, ENGR, FOR, FUSER, HSA, IPSY, JOUR, LAW, LSAR, MED, MFCD, MIDWF, MT, MUS, NURSE, OT, PH, PHAR, PLNG, PTA, RTT, #SCPSY, SP, SPAA, SW, TED, THEA, VET

01 President .... Dr. Eric W. KALER
100 Chief of Staff .... Ms. Amy PHENIX
05 Sr VP for Academic Affairs/Provost .... Dr. Karen HANSON
17 Vice President for Health Sciences .... Dr. Aaron FRIEDMAN
11 Sr Vice Pres for Acad Admin .... Dr. Robert J. JONES
10 Vice President/Chief Financial Ofcr .... Mr. Richard H. PFUTZENREUTER
46 Vice President for Research .... Dr. R. Timothy MULCAHY
58 Vice Prov/Dean Graduate Education .... Dr. Henning SCHROEDER
20 Vice Prov/Dean Undergrad Education .... Dr. Robert MCMASTER
15 Vice President Human Resources .... Ms. Kathryn F. BROWN
88 Vice Pres for University Services .... Ms. Pam WHEELOCK
28 Acting VP for Equity and Diversity .... Ms. Kristin LOCKHART
43 General Counsel .... Mr. Mark B. ROTENBERG
27 Vice President/Chief Info Officer .... Mr. Scott STUDHAM
102 President Univ Minnesota Foundation .... Mr. L. Steven GOLDSTEIN
25 Assoc VP Sponsored Projects Admin .... Ms. Frances LAWRENZ
86 Assoc Vice Pres for Govt Relations .... Mr. Jason ROHLOF
18 Associate VP/Chief of Facilities .... Mr. Mike BERTHELSEN
32 Vice Provost for Student Affairs .... Mr. Gerald D. RINEHART
19 Asst VP Pub Safety/Chief of Police .... Mr. Gregory S. HESTNESS
08 University Librarian .... Dr. Wendy P. LOUGEE
06 Registrar .... Ms. Sue N. VAN VOORHIS
07 Director of Admissions .... Vacant
09 Director of Institutional Research .... Dr. John KELLOGG
22 Director Equal Oppty/Affirm Action .... Ms. Kimberly HEWITT BOYD
37 Director of Student Finance .... Ms. Kristine A. WRIGHT
40 Director of the U of M Bookstores .... Mr. Robert J. CRABB
39 Dir of Housing & Residential Life .... Ms. Laurie L. MCLAUGHLIN
48 Dean of the College of Design .... Dr. Thomas R. FISHER
86 Director of Federal Relations .... Ms. Channing RIGGS
29 CEO Alumni Association .... Dr. Phil L. ESTEN
38 Dir of Counseling & Consulting Srvc .... Dr. Glenn HIRSCH
87 Director of the Summer Session .... Michelle KOKER
21 Associate VP for Budget/Finance .... Ms. Julie A. TONNESON
36 Director of Student Placement .... Vacant
96 Interim Director of Purchasing .... Mr. Tim BRAY
35 Chief Student Life Officer .... Mr. Gerald D. RINEHART
49 Dean of the College of Liberal Arts .... Mr. James A. PARENTE, JR.
51 Dean College of Continuing Educ .... Dr. Mary L. NICHOLS
61 Dean of the Law School .... Mr. David WIPPMAN
74 Dean College of Veterinary Medicine .... Dr. Trevor R. AMES
63 Dean of the Medical School .... Dr. Aaron FRIEDMAN
66 Dean of the School of Nursing .... Dr. Connie J. DELANEY
53 Dean College Education/Human Devel .... Dr. Jean K. QUAM
52 Dean of the School of Dentistry .... Dr. Leon ASSAEL
69 Dean of the School Public Health .... Dr. John FINNEGAN
72 Dean College of Science/Engineering .... Dr. Steven CROUCH
67 Dean of the College Pharmacy .... Dr. Marilyn K. SPEEDIE
50 Dean Carlson School of Management .... Dr. Srilata A. ZAHEER
80 Int Dean Humphrey Sch of Pub Aff .... Dr. Greg LINDSEY
81 Dean College of Biological Science .... Dr. Robert P. ELDE
47 Dean Col Food/Agric/Nat Resourc Sci .... Dr. Allen LEVINE
41 Director Intercollegiate Athletics .... Mr. Norwood TEAGUE

University of Saint Thomas (B)

2115 Summit Avenue, Saint Paul MN 55105-1096
County: Ramsey — FICE Identification: 002345
Unit ID: 174914
Telephone: (651) 962-5000 — Carnegie Class: DRU
FAX Number: (651) 962-6360 — Calendar System: 4/1/4
URL: www.stthomas.edu
Established: 1885 — Annual Undergrad Tuition & Fees: $33,040
Enrollment: 10,534 — Coed
Affiliation or Control: Roman Catholic — IRS Status: 501(c)3
Highest Offering: Doctorate
Program: Liberal Arts And General; Teacher Preparatory; Professional
Accreditation: NH, BUS, COPSY, ENG, HSA, IPSY, LAW, MUS, SW, TED, THEOL

01 President .... Rev. Dennis J. DEASE
04 Executive Advisor to President .... Dr. Susan L. ALEXANDER
03 Exec Vice Pres/Chief Admin Officer .... Dr. Mark C. DIENHART
05 Int Exec VP/Chief Academic Officer .... Dr. Susan J. HUBER
88 Rector/Vice Pres School of Divinity .... Msgr. Aloysius R. CALLAGHAN
88 Vice President for Mission .... Fr. John MALONE
32 Vice President for Student Affairs .... Ms. Jane W. CANNEY
10 Vice Pres for Business Affairs/CFO .... Mr. Mark D. VANGSGARD
26 Vice President University Relations .... Mr. Doug E. HENNES
13 VP Information Resources & Tech .... Dr. Samuel J. LEVY
20 Assoc Vice Pres Academic Affairs .... Dr. Joseph L. KREITZER
20 Assoc Vice Pres Academic Affs .... Dr. Eleni ROULIS
84 Assoc VP Enrollment Services .... Ms. Marla J. FRIEDERICHS
15 Assoc VP Human Res/General Counsel .... Ms. Sara E. GROSS METHNER
21 Assoc VP/Finance & Controller .... Mr. Gary L. THYEN
18 Associate Vice Pres Facilities .... Mr. Gerald M. ANDERLEY
88 Associate VP for Auxiliary Services .... Mr. Bruce VAN DEN BERGHE
49 Dean College Arts & Sciences .... Dr. Terrence G. LANGAN
50 Dean Opus College of Business .... Dr. Christopher P. PUTO
53 Int Dean of School of Education .... Dr. Bruce H. KRAMER
83 Dean of School of Social Work .... Dr. Barbara W. SHANK
73 Dean St Paul Seminary School of Div .... Dr. Christopher J. THOMPSON
61 Int Dean School of Law .... Mr. Neil W. HAMILTON
35 Dean of Student Life .... Ms. Karen M. LANGE
88 Assoc Dean Grad Prof Psychology .... Dr. Christopher VYE
58 Dir Graduate Programs/Business Comm .... Dr. Michael PORTER
88 Sr Assoc Dean College of Business .... Dr. Michael GARRISON
54 Dean School of Engineering .... Dr. Donald H. WEINKAUF
30 Executive Director for Development .... Mr. Stephen A. HOEPPNER
06 Registrar .... Mr. Paul M. SIMMONS
07 Director Admissions & Financial Aid .... Ms. Kris A. GETTING
09 Director of Institutional Research .... Dr. Michael F. COGAN
35 Executive Director Campus Life .... Ms. Mary A. RYAN
36 Director of Career Services .... Ms. Diane G. CRIST
27 Director of the News Service .... Mr. James C. WINTERER
29 Exec Dir Alumni/Constituent Rels .... Ms. Rachel A. WOBSCHALL
41 Athletic Director .... Mr. Stephen J. FRITZ
40 Director Bookstore .... Mr. Tony W. ERICKSON
42 Director Campus Ministry .... Fr. Erich RUTTEN
19 Director Safety/Security .... Mr. Daniel J. MEUWISSEN
39 Director Campus Life .... Ms. Margaret D. CAHILL
38 Director Student Counseling .... Dr. Jeri M. ROCKETT
96 Director Purchasing Services .... Ms. Karen M. HARTHORN
88 Director Recruit/Admis MBA Pgms .... Dr. William WOODSON
28 Director of Diversity .... Dr. MariAnn GRAHAM

Walden University (C)

100 Washington Ave S, Suite 900, Minneapolis MN 55401
County: Hennepin — FICE Identification: 025042
Unit ID: 125231
Telephone: (612) 338-7224 — Carnegie Class: DRU
FAX Number: (612) 338-5092 — Calendar System: Other
URL: www.waldenu.edu
Established: 1970 — Annual Undergrad Tuition & Fees: $10,725
Enrollment: 48,982 — Coed
Affiliation or Control: Proprietary — IRS Status: Proprietary
Highest Offering: Doctorate
Program: Teacher Preparatory
Accreditation: NH, ACBSP, CACREP, NURSE

00 Chief Executive Officer .... Mr. Jonathan A. KAPLAN
01 President .... Dr. Cynthia G. BAUM
05 Interim Chief Academic Officer .... Dr. Eric RIEDEL
69 Int VP College Health Sciences .... Dr. Cynthia G. BAUM
53 VP RWR College of Education .... Ms. Debra TERVALA
83 VP College Soc & Behav Sciences .... Dr. Melanie STORMS
50 VP College of Mgmt & Tech .... Mr. Paul THOMAS
26 VP Marketing .... Mr. Christian SCHINDLER
43 VP and Assistant General Counsel .... Ms. Deborah L. ZIMIC
20 VP of Undergraduate Programs .... Ms. Susan B. DREIFUSS
88 Div VP for Inst Quality & Integrity .... Dr. John A. SABATINI, JR.
10 COO and CFO .... Mr. Rick PATRO
53 Dean RWR College of Education .... Dr. Kate STEFFENS
46 Exec Dir Office of IR & Assesment .... Dr. Eric RIEDEL
32 Exec Dir Ctr for Student Success .... Ms. Susanna DAVIDSEN
45 Int Dir Ctr for Fac Exc .... Dr. Kimberlee BONURA
88 Exec Dir Center for UG Studies .... Vacant
88 Exec Dir Ctr for Research Support .... Dr. Laura LYNN
88 Exec Dir International Programs .... Ms. Victoria REID
15 Director of Human Resources .... Ms. Sherine HIGH
13 IT Director .... Mr. Jason ROWLEY

07 Director of Admissions .... Ms. Devon LOETZ
21 Bursar .... Ms. Linda ANTHONY
37 Director of Financial Aid .... Ms. Teresa DRZEWIECKI
06 Registrar .... Ms. Eve DAUER

White Earth Tribal and Community College (D)

PO Box 478, Mahnomen MN 56557-0478
County: Mahnomen — FICE Identification: 039214
Unit ID: 434751
Telephone: (218) 935-0417 — Carnegie Class: Tribal
FAX Number: (218) 936-5814 — Calendar System: Semester
URL: www.wetcc.edu
Established: 1997 — Annual Undergrad Tuition & Fees: $3,285
Enrollment: 85 — Coed
Affiliation or Control: Tribal Control — IRS Status: 501(c)3
Highest Offering: Associate Degree
Program: 2-Year Principally Bachelor's Creditable; Liberal Arts And General
Accreditation: NH

01 Interim President .... Deborah MCARTHUR
05 Academic Dean .... Michael PRICE
32 Dean of Recruitment & Retention .... Vacant
10 Director of Finance .... Denise WARREN
45 Director of Special Projects .... Deborah MCARTHUR
37 Director Student Financial Aid .... Doreen STONE
56 Director of Extension .... Steve DAHLBERG
06 Registrar .... Angel STANHOPE

William Mitchell College of Law (E)

875 Summit Avenue, Saint Paul MN 55105-3076
County: Ramsey — FICE Identification: 002391
Unit ID: 175281
Telephone: (651) 227-9171 — Carnegie Class: Spec/Law
FAX Number: (651) 290-6414 — Calendar System: Semester
URL: www.wmitchell.edu
Established: 1900 — Annual Graduate Tuition & Fees: $36,230
Enrollment: 1,004 — Coed
Affiliation or Control: Independent Non-Profit — IRS Status: 501(c)3
Highest Offering: First Professional Degree; No Undergraduates
Program: Professional
Accreditation: LAW

01 President & Dean .... Mr. Eric S. JANUS
04 Exec Asst to President & Board .... Ms. Deb CALVERT
11 Assoc Dean for Administration .... Ms. Mary Pat BYRN
05 Assoc Dean for Academic Programs .... Ms. Nancy M. VER STEEGH
30 VP of Institutional Advancement .... Ms. Linda K. BERG
16 Vice President Human Resources .... Ms. Mary E. GALE
13 Vice Pres Information Technology .... Mr. James VILLARS
10 Vice President Finance .... Ms. Kathy PANCIERA
32 Vice President of Student Affairs .... Mr. Daniel J. THOMPSON
08 Assoc Dean of Info Resources .... Mr. Simon CANICK
28 Assoc Dean/Multicultural Affairs .... Hon. Edward TOUSSAINT
28 Asst Dean/Dir Multicultural Affairs .... Ms. Lawrencina ORAMALU
36 Asst Dean for Career Development .... Ms. Karen VANDER SANDEN
07 Asst Dean/Director of Admissions .... Ms. Kendra DANE
06 Registrar .... Mr. Jim STEVENS
26 Director of Marketing/Alumni Rels .... Ms. Louise COPELAND
37 Director of Financial Aid .... Ms. Patty HARRIS
18 Director of Facilities .... Mr. Larry EVELAND
30 Director of Development .... Mr. Brian NELSON
96 Purchasing Manager .... Ms. Paula B. MERTH

MISSISSIPPI

Alcorn State University (F)

1000 ASU Drive, #359, Alcorn State MS 39096-7500
County: Claiborne — FICE Identification: 002396
Unit ID: 175342
Telephone: (601) 877-6100 — Carnegie Class: Master's M
FAX Number: (601) 877-2975 — Calendar System: Semester
URL: www.alcorn.edu
Established: 1871 — Annual Undergrad Tuition & Fees (In-State): $5,712
Enrollment: 4,018 — Coed
Affiliation or Control: State — IRS Status: 501(c)3
Highest Offering: Beyond Master's But Less Than Doctorate
Program: 2-Year Principally Bachelor's Creditable; Liberal Arts And General; Teacher Preparatory; Professional
Accreditation: SC, AAFCS, ADNUR, DIETD, MUS, NAIT, NUR, NURSE, SW, TED

01 President .... Dr. M.Christopher BROWN, II
05 Exec VP/Provost for Academic Affair .... Dr. Samuel L. WHITE
46 Chief Research Officer .... Dr. Babu P. PATLOLLA
04 Exec Asst to the President .... Mrs. Karen R. SHEDRICK
88 Special Asst to the President .... Mr. Gralon JOHNSON
88 Director of Internal Audit .... Mr. Permy K. THUHA
10 Sr VP for Admin and Finance/CFO .... Dr. Betty ROBERTS
21 VP for Fiscal Affairs .... Ms. Carolyn DUPRE
32 VP for Student Affairs .... Ms. E. Cheryl PONDER
30 VP Institutional Affairs .... Mr. Marcus D. WARD
20 Assoc VP for Academic Affs .... Dr. Donzell LEE
35 Assoc VP of Student Affairs .... Vacant
18 Assoc VP for Facilities Management .... Mr. Jessie STEPHNEY
39 Director Housing .... Ms. Jessica L. FOXWORTH
21 Director of Accounting .... Mrs. Cassandra B. LEWIS

96	Purchasing Agent	Ms. Mertha V. GEORGE
07	Director of Admissions/Recruiting	Mr. Emanuel BARNES
37	Director Student Financial Aid	Mrs. Juanita RUSSELL
06	Registrar	Mr. Jimmy L. SMITH
08	Dean University Libraries	Dr. Blanche SANDERS
47	Dean School of Agriculture	Dr. Barry BEQUETTE
49	Actg Dean School of Arts & Science	Dr. Norris EDNEY
50	Int Dean School of Business	Dr. Vivek BHARGAVA
53	Dean School of Education	Dr. Robert CARR
66	Dean School of Nursing	Dr. Linda GODLEY
88	Dir Academic Support Services	Dr. Edward L. VAUGHN
13	CIO for Ctr for Info Tech Svcs	Ms. Donna G. HAYDEN
27	Assoc VP for University Relations	Ms. Clara R. STAMPS
15	Director of Human Resources	Ms. Carla WILLIAMS
36	Director Career Services	Vacant
23	Director of Health Services	Ms. Dorothy G. JACKSON
41	Interm Director of Athletics	Mr. Dwayne WHITE
40	Bookstore Manager	Mrs. Classie O. JOHNSON
38	Director of Counseling & Testing	Mrs. Dyann W. MOSES
09	Director Institutional Res/Assess	Dr. Ramesh MADDALI
88	Dir Institutional Effectiveness	Dr. Latoya HART
19	Chief of Campus Police	Mr. Melvin MAXWELL
88	General Manager Sodexo	Mr. Corey D. YOUNG
102	Exec Dir ASU Foundation	Vacant
31	Dir Ctr Rural Life/Econ Dev	Dr. Samuel L. WHITE
92	Director of Pre-Prof/Honors Program	Dr. Thomas C. STURGIS
58	Dean Graduate Studies	Dr. Donzell LEE
25	Grants/Contract Administrator	Ms. Sallie GRIFFIN
28	Dir of Diversity/Equity Engagement	Dr. Derek GREENFIELD
88	Senior Dir Community Outreach	Dr. Ruth R. NICHOLS
12	Exec Director Vicksburg Campus	Dr. Cheryl KARIUKI

Antonelli College (A)

1500 N 31st Avenue, Hattiesburg MS 39401-3056

County: Forrest | Identification: 666517 | Unit ID: 383950

Telephone: (601) 583-4100 | Carnegie Class: Assoc/PrivFP

FAX Number: (601) 583-0839 | Calendar System: Quarter

URL: www.antonellicollege.edu

Established: 1996 | Annual Undergrad Tuition & Fees: $15,550

Enrollment: 368 | Coed

Affiliation or Control: Proprietary | IRS Status: Proprietary

Highest Offering: Associate Degree

Program: Occupational

Accreditation: ACCSC

01	President	Mr. Steve BRYANT

† Branch campus of Antonelli College, OH.

Antonelli College (B)

2323 Lakeland Drive, Jackson MS 39208-9549

County: Rankin | Identification: 666518 | Unit ID: 175528

Telephone: (601) 362-9991 | Carnegie Class: Assoc/PrivFP

FAX Number: (601) 362-2333 | Calendar System: Quarter

URL: www.antonellicollege.edu

Established: 1996 | Annual Undergrad Tuition & Fees: $14,850

Enrollment: 632 | Coed

Affiliation or Control: Proprietary | IRS Status: Proprietary

Highest Offering: Associate Degree

Program: Occupational

Accreditation: ACCSC

01	Director	Ms. Debra J. MOORE

† Branch campus of Antonelli College, OH.

Belhaven University (C)

1500 Peachtree, Jackson MS 39202-1798

County: Hinds | FICE Identification: 002397 | Unit ID: 175421

Telephone: (601) 968-5919 | Carnegie Class: Master's M

FAX Number: (601) 968-9998 | Calendar System: Semester

URL: www.belhaven.edu

Established: 1883 | Annual Undergrad Tuition & Fees: $19,200

Enrollment: 3,103 | Coed

Affiliation or Control: Presbyterian Church (U.S.A.) | IRS Status: 501(c)3

Highest Offering: Master's

Program: Liberal Arts And General; Teacher Preparatory; Professional

Accreditation: SC, ART, DANCE, IACBE, MUS, THEA

01	President	Dr. Roger PARROTT
05	Exec Vice President & Provost	Dr. Dan FREDERICKS
30	Vice Pres Institutional Advancement	Mr. Kevin RUSSELL
03	VP of Adult & Graduate Marketing	Dr. Audrey KELLEHER
10	Chief Financial Officer	Mrs. Virginia HENDERSON
32	VP for Student Affairs and Athletic	Mr. Scott LITTLE
11	Asst Vice Pres Campus Operations	Mr. David POTVIN
51	Asst Vice Pres of Adult Studies	Dr. Richard HARRIS
88	Dean of Academic Enhancement	Dr. Lee SKINKLE
12	Academic Dean/Texas	Dr. Marguerite P. JOYCE
12	Academic Dean/Mississippi	Dr. Kay OWEN
12	Academic Dean/Tennessee	Vacant
12	Academic Dean/Chattanooga-Atlanta	Vacant
53	Dean of the School of Education	Dr. Sandra RASBERRY
50	Dean of the School of Business	Dr. Chip MASON
08	Librarian	Mr. Chris CULLNANE
07	Asst VP Trad & Online Admissions	Mrs. Suzanne SULLIVAN
06	Registrar	Mrs. Donna WEEKS
27	Director of Integrated Marketing	Mr. Bryant BUTLER
35	Director of Student Leadership	Ms. JoBeth PETTY
29	Director Alumni Relations	Mr. Michael DUKES
13	Director Institutional Technology	Mr. Bo MILLER
19	Director Security/Safety	Mr. Steve FARMER
40	Bookstore Manager	Ms. Sheila LYONS
36	Dean of Student Development	Mr. Ron PIRTLE
35	Dean of Student Life	Mr. Greg HAWKINS

Blue Cliff College (D)

12251 Bernard Parkway, Gulfport MS 39503-5086

County: Harrison | FICE Identification: 035253 | Unit ID: 441502

Telephone: (228) 896-9727 | Carnegie Class: Assoc/PrivFP

FAX Number: (228) 896-7238 | Calendar System: Quarter

URL: www.bluecliffcollege.com

Established: 1987 | Annual Undergrad Tuition & Fees: $15,468

Enrollment: 335 | Coed

Affiliation or Control: Proprietary | IRS Status: Proprietary

Highest Offering: Associate Degree

Program: Occupational

Accreditation: ACCSC

01	Director	Ms. Sharon L. ANSLEY

Blue Mountain College (E)

201 W Main Street, PO Box 160, Blue Mountain MS 38610-0160

County: Tippah | FICE Identification: 002398 | Unit ID: 175430

Telephone: (662) 685-4771 | Carnegie Class: Bac/Diverse

FAX Number: (662) 685-4776 | Calendar System: Semester

URL: www.bmc.edu

Established: 1873 | Annual Undergrad Tuition & Fees: $9,230

Enrollment: 555 | Coed

Affiliation or Control: Southern Baptist | IRS Status: 501(c)3

Highest Offering: Master's

Program: Liberal Arts And General; Teacher Preparatory; Fine Arts Emphasis

Accreditation: SC

01	President	Dr. Bettye R. COWARD
05	Vice President for Academic Affairs	Dr. Sharon B. ENZOR
32	Executive VP Stdnt Affs/Graduate	Dr. Janice I. NICHOLSON
04	Admin Assistant to the President	Mrs. Pam BOWMAN
06	Registrar	Mrs. Sheila D. FREEMAN
08	Librarian for Collection Management	Miss Sherry N. DIXON
37	Director of Financial Aid	Mrs. Michelle HALL
07	Director of Admissions	Miss Maria TEEL
40	Director Bookstore	Mrs. Dot M. LOCKE
41	Athletic Director	Mr. Lavon DRISKELL
42	Director Baptist Student Union	Mrs. Tracy S. MOSER
09	Director of Institutional Research	Mr. Robert E. RUCKER
36	Director Career Services	Dr. Teresa R. ARRINGTON
13	Director of Information Services	Mr. Kevin BAREFIELD
26	Dir of PR/Publications	Ms. Emma L. AINSWORTH
29	Director of Alumni Affairs	Mrs. Lea S. BENNETT
10	Chief Financial Officer	Mrs. Joyce PETERS

Coahoma Community College (F)

3240 Friars Point Road, Clarksdale MS 38614-9700

County: Coahoma | FICE Identification: 002401 | Unit ID: 175519

Telephone: (662) 627-2571 | Carnegie Class: Assoc/Pub-R-S

FAX Number: (662) 627-9451 | Calendar System: Semester

URL: www.ccc.cc.ms.us

Established: 1949 | Annual Undergrad Tuition & Fees (In-District): $2,060

Enrollment: 3,006 | Coed

Affiliation or Control: State/Local | IRS Status: 501(c)3

Highest Offering: Associate Degree

Program: Occupational; 2-Year Principally Bachelor's Creditable

Accreditation: SC, POLYT

01	President	Dr. Vivian M. PRESLEY
05	Vice President for Academic Affairs	Dr. Rosetta HOWARD
10	Vice Pres for Finance & Operations	Ms. Deborah MCNEAL
32	Vice Pres Student Affs/Support Svcs	Dr. Gregory HUDSON
09	VP Inst Effectiveness/SACS Liaison	Ms. Rosemary DILL
30	VP Instnl Advance/Federal Programs	Mrs. Marilyn STARKS
75	VP Career & Technical Education	Mrs. Anne SHELTON-CLARK
07	Dean of Admissions	Mrs. Delores RICHARD
08	Dean Library/Instructionl Resources	Mrs. Yvonne STANFORD
14	Director Computer Service	Mr. Leandrew PRESLEY
19	Director of Safety/Transportation	Mr. William HOUSTON
26	Director of Public Relations	Ms. Panny MAYFIELD
37	Director of Financial Aid	Mrs. Patricia BROOKS
15	Director Human Resources	Mrs. Wanda HOLMES
18	Chief Facilities/Physical Plant	Mr. Jerone SHAW
51	Director of Educational Outreach	Ms. Cynthia WILLIAMS
06	Registrar	Mrs. Delores RICHARD
29	Director Alumni Relations	Mrs. Rita HANFOR
36	Director Student Placement	Mr. Orlando PADEN
38	Director Student Counseling	Vacant
96	Director of Purchasing	Mrs. Deborah MCNEAL

Copiah-Lincoln Community College (G)

PO Box 649, Wesson MS 39191-0649

County: Copiah | FICE Identification: 002402 | Unit ID: 175573

Telephone: (601) 643-5101 | Carnegie Class: Assoc/Pub-R-M

FAX Number: (601) 643-8212 | Calendar System: Semester

URL: www.colin.edu

Established: 1928 | Annual Undergrad Tuition & Fees (In-State): $5,000

Enrollment: 3,707 | Coed

Affiliation or Control: State | IRS Status: 501(c)3

Highest Offering: Associate Degree

Program: Occupational; 2-Year Principally Bachelor's Creditable

Accreditation: SC, ADNUR, MLTAD, RAD

01	President	Dr. Ronald E. NETTLES
04	Assistant to the President	Mrs. Brenda J. PARRETT
10	Vice President Business Affairs	Mr. Michael TANNER
05	Vice Pres of Instructional Services	Dr. Jane HULON
12	VP of the Simpson County Center	Dr. John DICKERSON
12	Vice Pres of the Natchez Campus	Ms. Teresa BUSBY
32	Dean of Student Services	Mrs. Brenda SMITH
75	Dean Career &Technical Educ	Dr. Gail BALDWIN
41	Athletic Director	Mr. Gwyn YOUNG
38	Director of Counseling/Recruitment	Mrs. Lea Ann KNIGHT
35	Assistant Dean of Students	Mr. Bryan NOBILE
37	Director Student Financial Aid	Mrs. Leslie SMITH
40	Director Bookstore	Mr. Charles HART
08	Director of Library Resources	Mr. Kendall P. CHAPMAN
26	Director of Public Relations	Mrs. Natalie DAVIS
14	Director of Computer Center	Mr. Danny DYKES
19	Director of Security	Mr. Wayne ROBERTS
09	Director of Institutional Research	Mr. Jeff POSEY
07	Director of Admissions	Mr. Chris WARREN
102	Executive Dir Foundation/Alumni	Mr. David CAMPBELL
18	Director of Physical Plant	Mr. Daniel CASE
66	Director of Assoc Degree Nursing	Mrs. Mary Ann CANTERBURY
06	Student Records Manager	Mrs. Gay LANGHAM
57	Chair Fine Arts Division	Mrs. Janet SMITH
50	Chair Business Division	Mr. Michael MCINTYRE
68	Chair Physical Education Division	Dr. Stephanie DUGUID
81	Chair Math/Computer Science Div	Mrs. Carol FORD
79	Chair Humanities Division	Mrs. Pam REID
82	Chair Social Science Division	Mr. David HIGGS
88	Chair Science Division	Dr. Kevin MCKONE
96	Director of Purchasing	Mrs. Erin LIKENS

Delta State University (H)

1003 W. Sunflower Rd., Cleveland MS 38733

County: Bolivar | FICE Identification: 002403 | Unit ID: 175616

Telephone: (662) 846-3000 | Carnegie Class: Master's L

FAX Number: (662) 846-4014 | Calendar System: Semester

URL: www.deltastate.edu

Established: 1924 | Annual Undergrad Tuition & Fees (In-State): $5,724

Enrollment: 4,624 | Coed

Affiliation or Control: State | IRS Status: 501(c)3

Highest Offering: Doctorate

Program: Liberal Arts And General; Teacher Preparatory; Professional

Accreditation: SC, AAFCS, ACBSP, ART, CACREP, DIETC, MUS, NURSE, SW, TED

01	President	Dr. John M. HILPERT
05	Provost/VP Academic Affairs	Dr. Ann C. LOTVEN
32	Vice President for Student Affairs	Dr. H. Wayne BLANSETT
10	Vice President for Finance	Mr. Greg REDLIN
11	Vice President University Relations	Dr. Michelle A. ROBERTS
21	Assoc Vice President for Finance	Dr. Myrtis TABB
41	Director of Athletics	Mr. Jeremy MCCLAIN
29	Exec Dir of Alumni/Foundation	Mr. D. Keith FULCHER
04	Exec Assistant to the President	Ms. Leigh S. KORB
49	Dean College of Arts & Sciences	Dr. Paul HANKINS
50	Dean College of Business	Dr. Billy MOORE
53	Dean College of Education	Dr. Leslie GRIFFIN
66	Dean School of Nursing	Dr. Libby L. CARLSON
08	Dean Library Services	Mr. Jeff SLAGELL
58	Dean Graduate/Continuing Studies	Vacant
07	Dean Enrollment Management	Dr. Debbie S. HESLEP
46	Dean Research/Assessment/Planning	Dr. Beverly MOON
88	Internal Auditor	Ms. Vicki WILLIAMS
88	Associate Dean Delta Regional Devel	Dr. Luther BROWN
13	Chief Information Officer	Mr. Edwin CRAFT
20	Director Academic Support Services	Vacant
25	Director Institutional Grants	Ms. Robin BOYLES
09	Director Institutional Research	Ms. Suzanne SIMPSON
06	Registrar	Vacant
106	Director of E-Learning	Vacant
31	Director Ctr for Community/Econ Dev	Dr. Paulette MEIKLE
88	Director Coahoma County Higher Educ	Ms. Jennifer WALLER
88	Director Small Bus Devel Center	Vacant
88	Director Field Experiences	Dr. Cheryl CUMMINS
21	Comptroller	Mr. James RUTLEDGE
18	Director of Facilities Management	Ms. Linda SMITH
88	Director Student Business Services	Ms. Teresa HOUSTON
96	Manager Procurement & Accts Payable	Ms. Beverly LINDSEY
35	Ast to VP Stdnt Affs/Dir Stdnt Life	Ms. Elsie L. ERVIN
38	Director Counsel/Stdnt Health Svcs	Dr. Richard HOUSTON
37	Director Student Financial Assist	Ms. Ann M. MULLINS
19	Director of Police Department	Mr. N. Lynn BUFORD
36	Director Career Services/Placement	Ms. Christy MONTESI

39 Director of Housing .... Ms. Julie JACKSON
30 Director of Development .... Ms. Sarah D. AYLWARD
29 Director of Alumni Affairs .... Mr. Jeffery FARRIS
26 Director of Communications & Mktg .... Mr. Michael GANN
88 Executive Director BPAC .... Vacant
40 Manager of Bookstore .... Ms. Tina GLADDEN

East Central Community College (A)

PO Box 129, Decatur MS 39327-0129
County: Newton FICE Identification: 002404
Unit ID: 175643
Telephone: (601) 635-2111 Carnegie Class: Assoc/Pub-R-M
FAX Number: (601) 635-4011 Calendar System: Semester
URL: www.eccc.edu
Established: 1928 Annual Undergrad Tuition & Fees (In-District): $2,070
Enrollment: 2,832 Coed
Affiliation or Control: Local IRS Status: 501(c)3
Highest Offering: Associate Degree
Program: Occupational; 2-Year Principally Bachelor's Creditable
Accreditation: SC, ADNUR, EMT, SURGT

01 President .... Dr. Billy W. STEWART
05 Vice President for Instruction .... Dr. Teresa L. HOUSTON
10 Vice Pres for Business Operations .... Mr. Mickey VANCE
32 Vice President for Student Services .... Dr. Randall LEE
102 Vice Pres Foundation/Alumni Rels .... Vacant
26 Vice Pres for Public Information .... Mr. E. Bubby JOHNSTON
51 Director of ABE/GED .... Mr. Ryan CLARKE
75 Director of Career Tech Instruction .... Mr. Wayne EASON
07 Dean Admission/Records/Research .... Mr. David CASE
41 Athletic Dir/Dir of Personnel Svcs .... Mr. Chris HARRIS
18 Director of Physical Plant .... Mr. Artie FOREMAN
103 Dean Workforce Educ & Development .... Mr. Roger WHITLOCK
72 Director for Technology Management .... Mr. Derek PACE
38 Academic Counselor .... Mr. Michael D. ALEXANDER
37 Director of Financial Aid .... Mrs. Brenda B. CARSON
08 Library Director .... Mr. Leslie HUGHES
13 Assoc Director for Technology Mgmt .... Mrs. Regena BOYKIN
19 Chief of Police .... Mr. Mitch MCCLEON
35 Director of Student Activities .... Mr. Scott HILL
29 Director Alumni Relations .... Dr. Stacey HOLLINGSWORTH
57 Chairperson Fine Arts Division .... Mrs. Vicki BLAYLOCK
83 Chairperson Social Sciences .... Mrs. Wanda HURLEY
81 Chrpn Mathematics/Computer Science .... Dr. Lisa MCMILLIN
76 Dean of Healthcare Education .... Mrs. Denita THOMAS
81 Chairperson Science .... Mr. Curt SKIPPER
60 Chairperson Communications/ Language .... Mrs. Carol SHACKELFORD

East Mississippi Community College (B)

PO Box 158, Scooba MS 39358-0158
County: Kemper FICE Identification: 002405
Unit ID: 175652
Telephone: (662) 476-8442 Carnegie Class: Assoc/Pub-R-M
FAX Number: (662) 476-5058 Calendar System: Semester
URL: www.eastms.edu
Established: 1927 Annual Undergrad Tuition & Fees (In-District): $2,450
Enrollment: 4,851 Coed
Affiliation or Control: State/Local IRS Status: 501(c)3
Highest Offering: Associate Degree
Program: Occupational; 2-Year Principally Bachelor's Creditable
Accreditation: SC, ADNUR, EMT, FUSER

01 President .... Dr. F. Rick YOUNG
05 Vice Pres for Instruction .... Dr. Thomas WARE
12 Vice President for GT Campus .... Dr. Paul MILLER
12 Vice President for Scooba Campus .... Dr. Andrea MAYFIELD
10 Chief Financial Officer .... Ms. Melissa MOSLEY
32 VP for SC Student Affs & Athletics .... Mr. Mickey E. STOKES
30 VP Institutional Advanc/Alumni Affs .... Mr. Nick CLARK
103 VP of Workforce & Cmty Services .... Dr. Raj SHAUNAK
37 Vice Pres for Financial Aid .... Mr. James GIBSON
04 Administrative Asst to President .... Mrs. Doreen BRYAN
09 Dist Dir Instl Research/Effective .... Mrs. Diana PRUETT
08 District Librarian .... Ms. Donna BALLARD
13 Dist Director of Info Technology .... Mr. Michael TVARKUNAS
18 Physical Plant Director-Scooba .... Mr. Bobby JONES
37 Director of Financial Aid GT .... Mr. Garry JONES
06 Registrar-Scooba .... Mrs. Melinda SCIPLE
07 Director of Admissions-SC .... Mrs. Karen BRIGGS
56 Director of MNAS Extension .... Mr. James MCMULLAN
40 District Bookstore Manager .... Ms. Vickie TURNER
27 Director of Public Information .... Ms. Suzanne MONK
35 Director Student Affairs .... Mr. Tony MONTGOMERY

Hinds Community College (C)

PO Box 1100, Raymond MS 39154-1100
County: Hinds FICE Identification: 002407
Unit ID: 175786
Telephone: (601) 857-5261 Carnegie Class: Assoc/Pub-R-L
FAX Number: (601) 857-3392 Calendar System: Semester
URL: www.hindscc.edu
Established: 1917 Annual Undergrad Tuition & Fees (In-District): $2,060
Enrollment: 18,174 Coed
Affiliation or Control: State/Local IRS Status: 501(c)3
Highest Offering: Associate Degree
Program: Occupational; 2-Year Principally Bachelor's Creditable
Accreditation: SC, ADNUR, DA, DMS, EMT, MAC, MLTAD, PTAA, RAD, SURGT

01 President .... Dr. Clyde MUSE
11 VP Admin Svcs/VP Utica/Vicksburg .... Dr. George BARNES
10 Vice President Business Services .... Mr. Russell SHAW
12 VP Raymond/NSG/AH/Parallel Pgm .... Dr. Theresa HAMILTON
12 VP Rankin/Jackson/Dir Occup Pgm .... Dr. Sue POWELL
31 Vice Pres Community Relations .... Ms. Colleen C. HARTFORD
88 VP for Economic Dev & Training .... Mr. John J. WOODS
18 VP Physical Plant & Aux Services .... Mr. Thomas WASSON
30 Vice Pres Institutional Advancement .... Ms. Jacqueline M. GRANBERRY
84 Director of Enrollment Services .... Ms. Kathryn B. COLE
32 Dean of Student Affairs .... Dr. Barbara BLANKENSHIP
07 Dean of Admissions & Records .... Mr. Randall HARRIS
08 Dean of Learning Resources .... Ms. Mary Beth APPLIN
20 Academic Dean .... Dr. Thomas KELLY
15 Director of Human Resources .... Ms. Gay Lynn CASTON
37 Dir of Financial Aid & VA Affairs .... Ms. Joy WILLIS
38 Director of Counseling Services .... Ms. Mary Lee MCDANIEL
41 Athletic Director .... Mr. Gene MURPHY
09 Director of Institutional Research .... Ms. Carley DEAR
26 Public Relations Director .... Ms. Cathy C. HAYDEN
96 Director of Purchasing .... Mr. Samuel LEMONIS

Holmes Community College (D)

Hill Street, PO Box 369, Goodman MS 39079-0369
County: Holmes FICE Identification: 002408
Unit ID: 175810
Telephone: (662) 472-2312 Carnegie Class: Assoc/Pub-R-L
FAX Number: (662) 472-9152 Calendar System: Semester
URL: www.holmescc.edu
Established: 1925 Annual Undergrad Tuition & Fees (In-District): $5,010
Enrollment: 6,420 Coed
Affiliation or Control: Local IRS Status: 501(c)3
Highest Offering: Associate Degree
Program: Occupational; 2-Year Principally Bachelor's Creditable
Accreditation: SC, ADNUR, EMT, FUSER, NAIT, OTA, SURGT

01 President .... Dr. Glenn F. BOYCE
04 Asst to President/Dir Inst Rsch .... Dr. Lindy MCCAIN
05 Vice Pres for Academic Programs .... Dr. Fran COX
12 Vice President Ridgeland Campus .... Dr. Don BURNHAM
12 Vice President Grenada Center .... Dr. Jim HAFFEY
07 Vice Pres of Admissions & Records .... Mr. Joshua GUEST
72 Vice Pres Career/Technical Educ .... Mrs. Sherrie CHEEK
10 Director of Financial Services .... Mr. Sonny SPARKS
08 Librarian .... Mrs. Joan TIERCE
26 District Director of Communications .... Mr. Steve DIFFEY
32 Dn Goodman Cam/Dist Coord Stdt Svcs .... Mr. Andy WOOD
31 Director Community/Workforce Devel .... Mr. Mike BLANKENSHIP
37 Director Student Financial Aid .... Mrs. Gail MUSE
15 Director Personnel Services .... Ms. Julia BROWN
09 Director of Institutional Research .... Dr. Lindy MCCAIN
27 Dir Communications & Publications .... Mr. Steve DIFFEY
18 Chief Facilities/Physical Plant .... Vacant
96 Director of Purchasing .... Ms. Roxanne CHISOLM
21 Business Manager .... Mr. Matt SURRELL

Itawamba Community College (E)

602 W Hill Street, Fulton MS 38843-1022
County: Itawamba FICE Identification: 002409
Unit ID: 175829
Telephone: (662) 862-8000 Carnegie Class: Assoc/Pub-R-M
FAX Number: (662) 862-8036 Calendar System: Semester
URL: www.icc.cc.ms.us
Established: 1948 Annual Undergrad Tuition & Fees (In-District): $1,900
Enrollment: 9,010 Coed
Affiliation or Control: Local IRS Status: 501(c)3
Highest Offering: Associate Degree
Program: Occupational; 2-Year Principally Bachelor's Creditable
Accreditation: SC, ADNUR, EMT, OTA, PTAA, RAD, SURGT

01 President .... Dr. David C. COLE
05 Vice President of Instruction .... Dr. Sara JOHNSON
10 Vice President of Business Services .... Mr. Jerry SENTER
32 Vice President of Student Services .... Mr. Buddy COLLINS
30 Vice Pres Dev/Plng/Telecom/Info Svc .... Mr. Wayne SULLIVAN
07 Dir Admiss/Registration .... Ms. Cay LOLLAR
26 Dir Pub Rel/Mktg/Sports Info .... Mr. Will KOLLMEYER
37 Director of Financial Aid .... Mr. Robert WALKER
24 Director of Learning Resources .... Dr. Glenda SEGARS
08 Librarian/Tupelo .... Ms. Janet Y. ARMOUR
51 Director of Adult & Continuing Educ .... Vacant
41 Athletic Director .... Ms. Carrie BALL-WILLIAMSON
44 Dir of Institutional Advancement .... Mr. Jim INGRAM
18 Chief Facilities/Physical Plant .... Mr. Thomas BONDS
35 Director Stdnt Affs/Counseling .... Mr. Larry BOGGS
09 Director of Institutional Research .... Mrs. Elizabeth EDWARDS
15 Director Personnel Services .... Mr. Timothy C. SENTER

ITT Technical Institute (F)

382 Galleria Parkway, Suite 100, Madison MS 39110
County: Madison Identification: 666701
Unit ID: 456393
Telephone: (601) 607-4500 Carnegie Class: Assoc/PrivFP4
FAX Number: (601) 607-4550 Calendar System: Quarter
URL: www.itt-tech.edu
Established: N/A Annual Undergrad Tuition & Fees: N/A
Enrollment: 197 Coed
Affiliation or Control: Proprietary IRS Status: Proprietary
Highest Offering: Baccalaureate
Program: Technical Emphasis
Accreditation: ACICS

† Branch campus of ITT Technical Institute, Indianapolis, IN.

Jackson State University (G)

1400 J. R. Lynch Street, Jackson MS 39217
County: Hinds FICE Identification: 002410
Unit ID: 175856
Telephone: (601) 979-2100 Carnegie Class: RU/H
FAX Number: (601) 979-2358 Calendar System: Semester
URL: www.jsums.edu
Established: 1877 Annual Undergrad Tuition & Fees (In-State): $5,988
Enrollment: 8,903 Coed
Affiliation or Control: State IRS Status: 501(c)3
Highest Offering: Doctorate
Program: Liberal Arts And General; Teacher Preparatory; Professional
Accreditation: SC, ART, BUS, CACREP, CLPSY, CORE, CS, ENG, JOUR, MUS, NAIT, PH, PLNG, SP, SPAA, SW, TED

01 President .... Dr. Carolyn MEYERS
100 Exec Assistant to the President .... Dr. James RENICK
05 Provost/VP Academic Affairs .... Dr. Mark G. HARDY
10 VP for Business & Finance .... Mr. Michael THOMAS
46 VP for Federally Funded Research .... Dr. Felix A. OKOJIE
30 VP Institutional Advancement .... Mr. David HOARD
13 VP for Information & Process Mgmt .... Vacant
43 Legal Counsel .... Mr. David BUFORD
21 Internal Auditor .... Ms. Ella HOLMES
18 Assoc VP for Facil/Construct/ Mgmt .... Mr. Wayne GOODWIN
21 Assoc VP for Business & Finance .... Ms. Sherry WILSON
20 Assoc Provost for Academic Affairs .... Dr. James MADDIRALA
106 Executive Dir of Distance Learning .... Dr. Della POSEY
32 VP for Student Life .... Dr. Marcus A. CHANAY
84 Assoc VP for Process Management .... Dr. Bettye GRAVES
09 Assoc VP Inst Research/Plng/ Effect .... Dr. Nicole EDWARDS- EVANS
13 Assoc VP for Information Technology .... Vacant
46 Assoc VP for Research & Development .... Ms. Ethel R. PRESLEY
53 Dean College Educ/Human Devel .... Dr. Daniel WATKINS
58 Dean Division of Graduate Studies .... Dr. Dorris R. ROBINSON-GARDNER
20 Dean Division Undergrad Studies .... Dr. Evelyn LEGGETTE
49 Int Dean College of Liberal Arts .... Dr. Thomas CALHOUN
88 Dean Division of Internat Studies .... Vacant
50 Dean College of Business .... Dr. Glenda B. GLOVER
80 Int Dean College of Public Service .... Dr. Mario AZEVEDO
72 Int Dean College of Sci/Engr/Tech .... Dr. Paul B. TCHOUNWOU
51 Asst Provost for Div of Extend Lrng .... Dr. Johnnie MILLS-JONES
08 Int Dean Div of Library & Info Res .... Dr. Melissa DRUCKREY
20 Assoc Dean University College .... Dr. Marie O'BANNER-JACKSON
92 Assoc Dean Div of Honors College .... Dr. Maria HARVEY
46 Dir of JSU RTRNDTCC/Prof Chem .... Dr. Jim PERKINS
88 Director Testing & Assessment .... Dr. Arthur JEFFERSON
31 Exe Dir Ctr Svc & Comm/Eng Learning .... Dr. Valerie J. SHELBY
29 Int Dir Alumni/Constituency Rels .... Mrs. Tabatha TERRELL-BROOKS
15 Executive Director Human Resources .... Mrs. Sandra SELLERS
07 Recruitment Manager .... Ms. Uriia HAMBRICH
88 Asst VP of Development .... Mrs. Patricia MITCHELL
39 Director of Residence Life .... Ms. Vera JACKSON
18 Director of Facilities Operations .... Ms. Jennie GRIFFIN
37 Director of Financial Aid .... Mrs. Betty MONCURE
21 Dir Budget & Financial Analysis .... Mrs. Tammiko HARRISON
06 Registrar .... Mr. Alfred B. JACKSON
23 Dir/Head Nurse Student Hlth Center .... Mrs. Ollie HARPER
88 Dir Mississippi Learning Inst .... Mrs. Nikisha GREEN WARE
20 Executive Dir of Univ Scholar Ctr .... Dr. Alisa MOSLEY
89 Director of First Year Experience .... Mrs. Patricia SHERIFF-TAYLOR
07 Enr Mgr/Dir Undergraduate Admission .... Mrs. Stephanie CHATMAN
41 Director of Athletics .... Ms. Vivian L. FULLER
88 Director of Title III .... Dr. Mary MYLES
96 Dir Univ Strategic Sourcing Svcs .... Vacant
88 Director MS Urban Research Ctr .... Dr. Melvin DAVIS
19 Interim Director Public Safety .... Mr. Thomas ALBRIGHT
26 Director University Communications .... Vacant
22 ADA Coordinator .... Vacant
88 Exec Dir Auxiliary Enterprises .... Mr. Alfred CARTER
88 Director Human Capital Development .... Ms. Angela GOBAR
13 Director of Process Management .... Mr. Jerry DANNER
88 Director of Capital Improvement .... Mr. Walter JOHNSON
35 Assoc Director of Campus Life .... Mrs. Lori STEWART
40 Manager Bookstore .... Mr. Mark PERSON

Jones County Junior College (H)

900 S Court Street, Ellisville MS 39437-3999
County: Jones FICE Identification: 002411
Unit ID: 175883
Telephone: (601) 477-4000 Carnegie Class: Assoc/Pub-R-M
FAX Number: (601) 477-4017 Calendar System: Semester
URL: www.jcjc.edu
Established: 1927 Annual Undergrad Tuition & Fees (In-District): $2,520
Enrollment: 5,079 Coed
Affiliation or Control: State/Local IRS Status: Exempt
Highest Offering: Associate Degree
Program: Occupational; 2-Year Principally Bachelor's Creditable
Accreditation: SC, ACBSP, ADNUR, EMT, RAD

01 President .... Dr. Jesse R. SMITH
05 VP Instructional Affrs/Assessment .... Dr. Laverne ULMER

10 Vice President of Business Affairs ... Mr. Rick YOUNGBLOOD
32 Vice President of Student Affairs ... Mr. Ed SMITH
88 Vice President of External Affairs ... Mr. Jim WALLEY
30 VP of Institutional Advancement ... Ms. Caroline RAMAGOS
13 VP of Information Technology ... Mr. Casey MERCIER
26 Vice President of Marketing ... Ms. Marlo DORSEY
04 Assistant to the President ... Ms. Gwen MAGEE
04 Assistant to the President ... Mr. John M. CARTER
20 Academic Dean ... Dr. Shannon CAMPBELL
35 Dean of Student Affairs ... Dr. Sam JONES
88 Director of the Adv Tech Center ... Mr. Greg BUTLER
09 Dir of Inst Effectiveness/Planning ... Dr. Laverne ULMER
92 Dean of Honors College/Campus Life ... Dr. Mark TAYLOR
07 Director of Admissions & Records ... Mr. Rick HAMILTON
38 Dir of Student Success Center ... Mr. Andrew SHARP
37 Director of Student Financial Aid ... Ms. Jennifer SUBER
75 Dean Career/Technical Education ... Ms. Candace WEAVER
39 Director of Housing-Women ... Ms. Ashley HILL
39 Director of Housing-Men ... Mr. Van TUGGLE
40 Bookstore Manager ... Mr. Kevin KUHN
41 Athletic Director ... Ms. Katie HERRINGTON
18 Chief Physical Plant ... Mr. Michael BRADSHAW
25 Director of Grants ... Mr. Jason DEDWYLDER
15 Director of Human Resources ... Ms. Christy HILBUN
96 Director of Purchasing ... Ms. LeAnne NIXON
106 eLearning Coordinator ... Ms. Jennifer POWELL

Meridian Community College (A)

910 Highway 19 N, Meridian MS 39307-5890
County: Lauderdale FICE Identification: 002413
Unit ID: 175935
Telephone: (601) 483-8241 Carnegie Class: Assoc/Pub-R-M
FAX Number: (601) 481-1305 Calendar System: Semester
URL: www.meridiancc.edu
Established: 1937 Annual Undergrad Tuition & Fees (In-District): $2,140
Enrollment: 4,189 Coed
Affiliation or Control: Local IRS Status: 501(c)3
Highest Offering: Associate Degree
Program: Occupational; 2-Year Principally Bachelor's Creditable
Accreditation: SC, ADNUR, DA, DH, MLTAD, PNUR, PTAA, RAD, SURGT

01 President ... Dr. Scott D. ELLIOTT
10 Assoc Vice President for Finance ... Mrs. Amy BRAND
03 Vice President of Operations ... Mrs. Barbara JONES
07 Director of Admissions ... Mrs. Angela PAYNE
09 Dir Institutional Effectiveness ... Mrs. Cathy PARKER
32 Dean of Students ... Mrs. Soraya WELDEN
05 Dean of Academic Affs/General Educ ... Mr. Michael THOMPSON
62 Dean of Learning Resources ... Mr. Billy BEAL
30 Dir Institutional Advancement ... Mrs. Kathy BROOKSHIRE
18 Director Physical Plant ... Mr. Terry WILLIAMS
37 Director Financial Aid ... Ms. Nedra BRADLEY
15 Director Human Resources ... Ms. Shellye ESPEY
41 Athletic Director ... Mr. Hilary ALLEN
19 Chief of Security ... Mr. Shane WILLIAMS
40 Bookstore Manager ... Mrs. Martha WILLIAMS
27 College Promotions Coordinator ... Mrs. Kay THOMAS
36 Career Center Development Director ... Ms. Darlene MAYATT
75 Assoc Vice Pres for Workforce Educ ... Dr. Richie MCALISTER

Millsaps College (B)

1701 N State Street, Jackson MS 39210-0001
County: Hinds FICE Identification: 002414
Unit ID: 175980
Telephone: (601) 974-1000 Carnegie Class: Bac/A&S
FAX Number: (601) 974-1059 Calendar System: Semester
URL: www.millsaps.edu
Established: 1890 Annual Undergrad Tuition & Fees: $30,974
Enrollment: 985 Coed
Affiliation or Control: United Methodist IRS Status: 501(c)3
Highest Offering: Master's
Program: Liberal Arts And General; Teacher Preparatory
Accreditation: SC, BUS, TED

01 President ... Dr. Rob PEARIGEN
05 VP/Dean of the College ... Dr. Keith DUNN
10 Vice President for Finance ... Ms. Louise BURNEY
30 VP for Institutional Advancement ... Vacant
32 VP Student Life/Dean Students ... Dr. Brit KATZ
50 Dean of the School of Management ... Dr. Kimberly G. BURKE
84 Dean of Enrollment ... Vacant
79 Assoc Dean Arts & Letters ... Dr. David DAVIS
81 Associate Dean Sciences Division ... Dr. Timothy J. WARD
82 Assoc Dean International Education ... Dr. George J. BEY
26 Dir of Communications & Marketing ... Ms. Patti P. WADE
37 Director of Financial Aid ... Mr. Patrick JAMES
20 Director Academic Support Services ... Ms. Janet R. LANGLEY
51 Director of Continuing Education ... Dr. Nola R. GIBSON
08 College Librarian ... Mr. Thomas W. HENDERSON
36 Director of Career Center ... Ms. Tonya CRAFT
41 Director of Athletics ... Mr. Tim WISE
15 Dir of Payroll & Employee Services ... Ms. Patricia S. BRUCE
42 Chaplain ... Rev. Rwth ASHTON
28 Director of Multicultural Affairs ... Ms. Sherryl E. WILBURN
21 Assistant Controller ... Ms. Allison ROOKER
06 Coordinator of Records ... Ms. Katherine ADAMS
09 Institutional Research Analyst ... Ms. Katherine S. LANDRUM
18 Director of Physical Plant ... Mr. W. David WILKINSON

Mississippi College (C)

200 W College Street, Clinton MS 39058-0001
County: Hinds FICE Identification: 002415
Unit ID: 176053
Telephone: (601) 925-3000 Carnegie Class: Master's L
FAX Number: (601) 925-3276 Calendar System: Semester
URL: www.mc.edu
Established: 1826 Annual Undergrad Tuition & Fees: $14,430
Enrollment: 5,218 Coed
Affiliation or Control: Southern Baptist IRS Status: 501(c)3
Highest Offering: Doctorate
Program: Liberal Arts And General; Teacher Preparatory; Professional
Accreditation: SC, ACBSP, #ARCPA, CACREP, CIDA, LAW, MUS, NURSE, SW, TED

01 President ... Dr. Lee G. ROYCE
04 Sr Exec Assistant to President ... Ms. Patty TADLOCK
10 Chief Financial Officer ... Ms. Donna LEWIS
05 Vice President Academic Affairs ... Dr. Ronald HOWARD
32 VP Enrollment Mgmt/ Student Affairs ... Dr. Jim TURCOTTE
45 Vice President Planning/Assessment ... Dr. Debbie NORRIS
42 Vice Pres Christian Development ... Dr. Eric PRATT
30 VP Inst Advan/Alum/Leg Coun to Pres ... Dr. Bill TOWNSEND
11 Vice Pres Admin/Government Rels ... Dr. Steve STANFORD
84 Director Enrollment Services ... Mr. Mark HUGHES
06 Registrar ... Ms. Ginger ROBBINS
09 Director of Institutional Research ... Ms. Cassandra SESSUMS
08 Librarian ... Ms. Kathleen HUTCHISON
21 Comptroller ... Ms. Cheryl MOBLEY
27 Chief Information Officer ... Mr. Bill CRANFORD
38 Director Counseling/Testing Center ... Dr. Morgan BRYANT
15 Director Human Resources ... Ms. Donna SMITH
29 Director Alumni Affairs ... Vacant
26 Director Public Relations ... Ms. Tracey HARRISON
18 Director of Physical Plant ... Mr. Billy THORNTON
39 Director of Residence Life ... Mr. Joseph ODENWALD
37 Director Student Financial Aid ... Ms. Karon MCMILLAN
07 Director of Admissions ... Mr. Kyle BRANTLEY
35 Assistant Director Student Affairs ... Ms. Dannie WOODS
19 Director of Public Safety ... Mr. Steven MCCRANEY
41 Director of Athletics ... Mr. Mike JONES
96 Director of Purchasing ... Ms. Dana ELMORE
40 Manager Bookstore ... Ms. Karen BARNES
36 Coordinator of Career Services ... Ms. Karen LINDSEY-LLOYD
81 Dean School of Science/Mathematics ... Dr. Stan BALDWIN
50 Dean School of Business Admin ... Dr. Marcelo EDUARDO
79 Dean School of Humanities ... Dr. Gary MAYFIELD
53 Dean School of Education ... Dr. Don LOCKE
73 Dean Sch Christian Studies/Fine Art ... Dr. Wayne VAN HORN
61 Dean School of Law ... Dr. Jim ROSENBLATT
58 Dean Grad School/Special Programs ... Dr. Debbie NORRIS
66 Dean School of Nursing ... Dr. Mary Jean PADGETT

Mississippi Delta Community College (D)

PO Box 668, Moorhead MS 38761-0668
County: Sunflower FICE Identification: 002416
Unit ID: 176008
Telephone: (662) 246-6322 Carnegie Class: Assoc/Pub-R-M
FAX Number: (662) 246-6321 Calendar System: Semester
URL: www.msdelta.edu
Established: 1926 Annual Undergrad Tuition & Fees (In-District): $2,330
Enrollment: 3,360 Coed
Affiliation or Control: Local IRS Status: 501(c)3
Highest Offering: Associate Degree
Program: Occupational; 2-Year Principally Bachelor's Creditable
Accreditation: SC, ADNUR, DH, MLTAD, PNUR, RAD

01 Interim President ... Dr. Lynda A. STEELE
11 VP of GHEC Administration ... Dr. Mary Jean LUSH
05 Vice President of Instruction ... Ms. Magdalene ABRAHAM
10 Vice President of Business Services ... Mr. Don GARRETT
32 Vice President of Student Services ... Dr. Edward RICE
21 Associate VP of Business Services ... Mrs. Marsha LEE
88 Assoc VP GHEC Operations ... Dr. MaryAnne BROCATO
84 Associate Vice Pres of Enrollment ... Dr. Brent GREGORY
102 Assoc VP College Rels/Development ... Mr. Reed ABRAHAM
04 Admin Asst to President/Coord of HR ... Ms. Brenda VANLANDINGHAM
37 Director of Financial Aid ... Mrs. Mary P. RODGERS
07 Director of Admissions ... Mr. Joe F. RAY
13 Director Computer & Info Tech Svcs ... Mr. Jimmy H. FREE
08 Director of Library Services ... Mrs. Kristi BARIOLA
07 Director Counseling/Recruiting ... Mrs. Stacy UPTON
18 Director of Maintenance ... Mr. Rick DAVIS
26 Director of Public Relations ... Mrs. Corey SMITH
09 Director of Institutional Research ... Dr. Sharon FREEMAN

Mississippi Gulf Coast Community College (E)

PO Box 609, Perkinston MS 39573-0012
County: Stone FICE Identification: 002417
Unit ID: 176071
Telephone: (601) 928-5211 Carnegie Class: Assoc/Pub-R-L
FAX Number: (601) 928-6386 Calendar System: Semester
URL: www.mgccc.edu
Established: 1911 Annual Undergrad Tuition & Fees (In-District): $2,712
Enrollment: 9,957 Coed
Affiliation or Control: Local IRS Status: 501(c)3
Highest Offering: Associate Degree
Program: Occupational; 2-Year Principally Bachelor's Creditable
Accreditation: SC, ADNUR, EMT, FUSER, MLTAD, PNUR, RAD, SURGT

01 President ... Dr. Mary S. GRAHAM
05 Vice Pres Instruction/Student Svcs ... Dr. Jason PUGH
10 Vice Pres Administration/Finance ... Dr. Michael J. HEINDL
12 Vice President Perkinston Campus ... Dr. Jay ALLEN
12 Vice Pres Jefferson Davis Campus ... Dr. Susan SCAGGS
12 Vice President Community Campus ... Ms. Anna Faye KELLEY-WINDERS
12 Vice Pres Jackson County Campus ... Vacant
30 Assoc Vice Pres for Development ... Mr. F. Russell YOUNG
09 Director Inst Research & Planning ... Ms. Angela BRYAN
14 Director of Information Technology ... Mr. David BESANCON
41 College Dean for Athletics ... Mr. Ladd TAYLOR
106 Director of E-Learning ... Ms. Jennifer LEIMER
103 Director Workforce Dev JD Campus ... Mr. Wayne KUNTZ
103 Director Workforce Dev JC Campus ... Mr. Mark LANDRY
21 Comptroller ... Ms. Shelly FORD
06 Records Clerk Perkinston Campus ... Ms. Latrice MCDONALD
06 Records Clerk Jackson Co Campus ... Ms. Linda OTIS
06 Records Clerk Jeff Davis Campus ... Ms. Mary JOYCE
20 Dean Instruct Jackson Co Campus ... Mr. Jonathan WOODWARD
05 Dean of Instruction Jeff Davis Camp ... Mr. Larry MILLER
05 Dean of Instruction Perkinston Camp ... Dr. Jan MOODY
21 Dn Business Svcs Perkinston Campus ... Ms. Tracy WILSON
21 Dn Business Svcs Jackson Co Campus ... Ms. Tammy FRANKS
21 Dn Business Svcs Jeff Davis Campus ... Ms. Stacy CARMICHAEL
75 Asst Dean Vo-Tec Instruc Perk Camp ... Dr. Dean BELTON
75 Asst Dean Vo-Tec Instruc JD Camp ... Dr. Beverly CLARK
75 Asst Dean Vo-Tec Instruc JC Camp ... Mr. Brock CLARK
08 Librarian Perkinston Campus ... Dr. Brenda RIVERO
08 Librarian Jackson County Campus ... Dr. Pam LADNER
08 Librarian Jefferson Davis Campus ... Mr. Charles CLARK
32 Dean Student Svcs Perkinston Campus ... Ms. Michelle SEKUL
32 Dean Student Svcs Jackson Co Campus ... Dr. Bill YATES
32 Dean Student Svcs Jeff Davis Campus ... Dr. Tyrone JACKSON
07 Dir Admissions Perkinston Campus ... Ms. Nichol GREEN
07 Dir Admissions Jack County Campus ... Ms. Kay ROSONET
07 Dir Admissions Jeff Davis Campus ... Mr. Bruce LAYTON
29 Alumni Relations Coordinator ... Ms. Jenifer FRERIDGE
75 Dean of Career/Technical Education ... Mr. John SHOWS
37 Financial Aid Director Jeff Davis ... Dr. Stephanie MESSER-ROY
37 Financial Aid Director Perkinston ... Ms. LeighAnn HUSSEY
37 Financial Aid Dir Jackson County ... Ms. LaShanda CHAMBERLAIN
15 Director Human Resources ... Mr. Glen MOORE
96 Dir Purchasing/Property Control ... Ms. Lynn DEEGEN
18 Construction Manager ... Mr. Jason BRELAND
26 Coord Institutional Development ... Ms. Brenda DAVIS
88 Admin Dean George County Center ... Ms. Cheryl BOND
04 Special Assistant to the President ... Ms. Monica M. MARLOWE

Mississippi State University (F)

Mississippi State MS 39762-5708
County: Oktibbeha FICE Identification: 002423
Unit ID: 176080
Telephone: (662) 325-2323 Carnegie Class: RU/VH
FAX Number: (662) 325-7455 Calendar System: Semester
URL: www.msstate.edu
Established: 1878 Annual Undergrad Tuition & Fees (In-State): $6,264
Enrollment: 20,424 Coed
Affiliation or Control: State IRS Status: 501(c)3
Highest Offering: Doctorate
Program: Liberal Arts And General; Teacher Preparatory; Professional
Accreditation: SC, AAFCS, ART, BUS, BUSA, CACREP, CIDA, CORE, CS, DIETD, DIETI, ENG, FOR, LSAR, MUS, SCPSY, SPAA, SW, TED, VET

01 President ... Dr. Mark E. KEENUM
05 Provost/Executive Vice President ... Dr. Jerome A. GILBERT
32 Vice President for Student Affairs ... Dr. William L. KIBLER
30 VP for Development and Alumni ... Mr. John P. RUSH
10 VP for Budget and Planning ... Mr. Don ZANT
46 Vice Pres Research & Economic Devel ... Dr. David SHAW
47 Vice Pres Agricult/Forestry/Vet Med ... Dr. Gregory BOHACH
41 Athletic Director ... Mr. Scott STRICKLIN
18 VP for Campus Services ... Ms. Amy TUCK
04 Assistant to the President ... Mr. Joe R. FARRIS
43 General Counsel ... Ms. Joan LUCAS
28 Dir Diversity/Equity Programs ... Dr. Tommy STEVENSON, JR.
21 Director Internal Audit ... Ms. Leisa BRYANT
26 Exec Dir External Affairs ... Mr. Kyle STEWARD
20 Assoc Provost Academic Affairs ... Dr. Peter RYAN
13 Chief Information Officer ... Mr. J. Mike RACKLEY
48 Dean of Architecture/Art/Design ... Mr. James L. WEST
49 Int Dean College Arts & Sciences ... Dr. Greg DUNAWAY
50 Dean College Business ... Dr. Sharon OSWALD
53 Dean of Education ... Dr. Richard L. BLACKBOURN
58 Dean of Graduate Studies ... Dr. Louis D'ABRAMO
54 Dean College of Engineering ... Dr. Sarah A. RAJALA
65 Dean of Forest Resources ... Dr. George M. HOPPER
47 Dean College Agriculture & Life Sci ... Dr. George M. HOPPER
74 Dean of Veterinary Medicine ... Dr. Kent H. HOBLET
12 Dean/Assoc VP Meridian Campus ... Dr. Steven F. BROWN
08 Dean of Libraries ... Ms. Frances N. COLEMAN
92 Dean Honors College ... Dr. Christopher SNYDER
35 Dean of Students ... Dr. Thomas BOURGEOIS
51 Int Dir Acad Outreach/Cont Ed ... Dr. Steve TAYLOR
35 Asst Vice Pres of Student Affairs ... Vacant
09 Director Institutional Research ... Dr. Tim CHAMBLEE
06 Interim Registrar ... Dr. Lynn REINSCHMIEDT

07 Exec Director Enrollment ... Dr. Philip BONFANTI
38 Director of Counseling Center ... Dr. Leigh JENSEN
37 Director Student Financial Aid ... Mr. Paul MCKINNEY
39 Director Housing/Residence Life ... Dr. Ann BAILEY
36 Director Career Services/Coop Educ ... Mr. Scott MAYNARD
85 Asst Dir International Services ... Mr. Stephen E. COTTRELL
35 Assoc Dean of Students ... Dr. Edwin M. KEITH
14 Dir Enterprise Information Systems ... Ms. Rene HUNT
23 Director Student Health Center ... Dr. Robert K. COLLINS
16 Director Human Resources Mgmt ... Ms. Judith SPENCER
29 Director of Alumni Association ... Dr. Jimmy ABRAHAM
26 Director University Relations ... Ms. Maridith W. GEUDER
44 Director of Planned Giving ... Mr. Vance BRISTOW
86 Director Government Relations ... Mr. John A. TOMLINSON
25 Director Sponsored Programs ... Mr. Richard SWANN
24 Director of Television Center ... Mr. Michael R. GODWIN
19 Police Chief ... Ms. Georgia LINDLEY
56 Dir Univ Extension Service ... Dr. Gary JACKSON
88 Dir Agricultural Experiment Station ... Dr. George M. HOPPER
96 Director Procurement/Contracts ... Mr. Don BUFFUM

Mississippi University for Women (A)

1100 College Street, Columbus MS 39701-5800
County: Lowndes — FICE Identification: 002422
Unit ID: 176035
Telephone: (877) 462-8439 — Carnegie Class: Master's S
FAX Number: (662) 329-7297 — Calendar System: Semester
URL: www.muw.edu
Established: 1884 — Annual Undergrad Tuition & Fees (In-State): $5,316
Enrollment: 2,661 — Coed
Affiliation or Control: State — IRS Status: 501(c)3
Highest Offering: Master's
Program: Liberal Arts And General; Teacher Preparatory; Professional
Accreditation: SC, ACBSP, ADNUR, ART, MUS, NURSE, SP, TED

01 President ... Dr. Jim BORSIG
05 Provost/VP Academic Affairs ... Dr. Dan HEIMMERMANN
10 Vice President for Finance & Admin ... Ms. Nora R. MILLER
30 VP University Relations/Advancement ... Ms. Allegra BRIGHAM
32 Vice Pres for Student Affairs ... Dr. Jennifer MILES
20 Assoc Vice Pres Academic Affairs ... Dr. Martin HATTON
04 Assistant to the President ... Mr. Perry SANSING
49 Dean College Arts/Sciences ... Dr. Thomas C. RICHARDSON
107 Dean Business/Professional Studies ... Dr. Scott TOLLISON
53 Dean College Educ/Human Sciences ... Dr. Sue JOLLY-SMITH
66 Dean College Nursing/Speech ... Dr. Sheila V. ADAMS
08 Dean of Library Services ... Ms. Gail P. GUNTER
58 Director Graduate Studies ... Dr. Martin HATTON
51 Director Continuing Education ... Dr. Barbara MOORE
06 Registrar ... Ms. Tammy PRATHER
88 Dir Center for Academic Excellence ... Ms. Kimberly GATHINGS
88 Director Advising ... Ms. Rhonda THOMAS
92 Dir Honors College/Study Abroad ... Dr. Thomas VELEK
88 Director Sponsored Programs ... Mr. James DENNEY
29 Director Alumni Relations ... Ms. Mary Margaret ROBERTS
30 Executive Director Development ... Ms. Andrea N. STEVENS
44 Director Annual Giving ... Ms. Brandy WILLIAMS
26 Director Public Affairs ... Ms. Anika M. PERKINS
105 Director Web Development ... Vacant
21 Director University Accounting ... Ms. Susan SOBLEY
88 Director Internal Audit ... Vacant
13 Director Information Tech Services ... Mr. Larry W. JONES
07 Director Admissions ... Ms. Cassie DERDEN
37 Director Financial Aid ... Mr. Dan MILLER
15 Director Human Resources ... Ms. Melanie H. FREEMAN
09 Director Institutional Research ... Ms. Carla LOWERY
19 Interim Chief of Police ... Ms. Mary SLATER
18 Director of Facilities Management ... Mr. Dewey BLANSETT
96 Director Resources Management ... Ms. Angie S. ATKINS
28 Director Student Life ... Mr. Phillip COCKRELL
39 Director Community Living ... Ms. Sirena PARKER
41 Exec Director Campus Recreation ... Ms. Lindsey SHELNUT
40 Director Bookstore ... Ms. Lana ALLEN
85 Coord of International Programs ... Mr. Kevin PATRICK

Mississippi Valley State University (B)

14000 Highway 82 W, Itta Bena MS 38941-1400
County: Leflore — FICE Identification: 002424
Unit ID: 176044
Telephone: (662) 254-9041 — Carnegie Class: Master's M
FAX Number: (662) 254-6709 — Calendar System: Semester
URL: www.mvsu.edu
Established: 1950 — Annual Undergrad Tuition & Fees (In-State): $5,914
Enrollment: 2,452 — Coed
Affiliation or Control: State — IRS Status: 501(c)3
Highest Offering: Master's
Program: Liberal Arts And General; Teacher Preparatory; Professional
Accreditation: SC, ACBSP, ART, CS, MUS, SW, TED

01 President ... Dr. Donna H. OLIVER
05 Executive Vice President/Provost ... Dr. Anna HAMMOND
10 Vice Pres for Business and Finance ... Mr. James B. WASHBURN
32 Vice Pres for Student Affairs ... Dr. Jerald ADLEY
35 Assoc VP for Student Affairs ... Dr. Yvette U. MURPH
20 Assoc Provost for Academic Affairs ... Dr. John JONES
20 Asst Provost Academic Affairs ... Vacant
35 Asst VP for Student & Enroll Svcs ... Vacant
21 Asst Vice Pres Business & Finance ... Ms. Joyce DIXON
100 Chief of Staff/Spec Asst to Pres ... Dr. A. Zachary FAISON, JR.
30 Vice Pres for Univ Advancement ... Ms. Angela GETTER
12 Director Greenwood Center ... Vacant
53 Int Dean Professionanl Stds/Educ ... Vacant
51 Director of Continuing Education ... Dr. Ronald LOVE
88 Coordinator Renaissance Programs ... Ms. Gladys FLAGGS
58 Dean of Graduate College ... Vacant
41 Interim Director of Athletics ... Mr. Donald R. SIMS
06 Acting Director of Student Records ... Mr. Jeff LOGGINS
07 Actg Asst Dir Admission/Recruitment ... Ms. Ann WILLIAMS
08 Head Librarian ... Ms. Mantra HENDERSON
15 Director of Human Resources ... Mr. Frank SOWELL
14 Director of Computer Center ... Mr. Steven L. PITCHFORD
37 Interim Director of Financial Aid ... Mrs. Deborah BANKS
29 Director of Alumni Relations ... Vacant
26 Acting Dir of University Relations ... Ms. Maxine BOWEN
19 Director University Police ... Mr. Robert SANDERS
18 Director Facilities/Physical Plant ... Mr. Tommy VERDELL
39 Director Residential Life ... Mr. Byrce LOWE
36 Director Career Development ... Ms. Tiffany WALLACE
38 Director Student Counseling ... Ms. Yolanda JONES
50 Chair of Business Department ... Dr. Lawrence GULLEY
53 Int Chair of Education Department ... Vacant
65 Int Chair Nat Sci/Env Health Dept ... Dr. Louis J. HALL
49 Dean College of Arts & Sciences ... Vacant
88 Chair English/Foreign Language ... Dr. John ZHENG
57 Chair Fine Arts Department ... Dr. Alphonso SANDERS
68 Actg Chair Health/Phys Ed/Rec Dept ... Mr. James WILKINSON
81 Chair of Math/Computer Science Dept ... Dr. Constance BLAND
54 Actg Chair of Industrial Tech Dept ... Dr. Richard MAXWELL
60 Chair Mass Communication Dept ... Dr. Samuel OSUNDE
70 Chair Criminal Justice ... Dr. Arthur MOGHALU
70 Chair Social Work Department ... Dr. Vincent VENTURINI
96 Director of Purchasing ... Mr. Billy SCOTT
28 Director of Cultural Diversity ... Vacant
84 Director Enrollment Management ... Vacant

Northeast Mississippi Community College (C)

101 Cunningham Boulevard, Booneville MS 38829-1731
County: Prentiss — FICE Identification: 002426
Unit ID: 176169
Telephone: (662) 728-7751 — Carnegie Class: Assoc/Pub-R-M
FAX Number: (662) 728-1165 — Calendar System: Semester
URL: www.nemcc.edu
Established: 1948 — Annual Undergrad Tuition & Fees (In-District): $1,920
Enrollment: 3,733 — Coed
Affiliation or Control: State/Local — IRS Status: 501(c)3
Highest Offering: Associate Degree
Program: Occupational; 2-Year Principally Bachelor's Creditable
Accreditation: SC, ADNUR, DH, MAC, MLTAD, RAD

01 President ... Johnny L. ALLEN
03 Executive Vice President ... Larry J. NABORS
103 Vice Pres Wrkfrce Training/Econ Dev ... Nadara L. COLE
26 Assoc Vice Pres of Public Info ... Tony FINCH
09 Assoc Vice Pres Planning/Research ... Rilla C. JONES
05 Dean of Instruction ... Charlie BARNETT
35 Assoc Dean of Student Activities ... Angie LANGLEY
08 Director Learning Resources ... Glenice STONE
96 Director of Purchasing ... Sheila OWENS
37 Director of Financial Aid ... Greg WINDHAM
38 Director Student Counseling ... Joey WILLIFORD
14 Director Computer Center ... Gregory SMITH
18 Director Facilities/Maintenance ... Mark HATFIELD
39 Director Residential Housing ... Rod COGGIN
32 Dean of Students/Athletic Director ... Ricky FORD
75 Director of Vocational Tech Educ ... Ritchie WILLIAMS
84 Dir of Enrollment Svcs/Registrar ... Lynn GIBSON
15 Human Resources Officer ... Tammie HARDIN

Northwest Mississippi Community College (D)

4975 Highway 51 N, Senatobia MS 38668-1703
County: Tate — FICE Identification: 002427
Unit ID: 176178
Telephone: (662) 562-3200 — Carnegie Class: Assoc/Pub-R-L
FAX Number: (662) 562-3911 — Calendar System: Semester
URL: www.northwestms.edu
Established: 1927 — Annual Undergrad Tuition & Fees (In-State): $1,125
Enrollment: 8,800 — Coed
Affiliation or Control: State — IRS Status: 501(c)3
Highest Offering: Associate Degree
Program: Occupational; 2-Year Principally Bachelor's Creditable
Accreditation: SC, ADNUR, EMT, #FUSER

01 President ... Dr. Gary Lee SPEARS
10 Vice President for Fiscal Affairs ... Mr. Gary MOSLEY
32 VP Student Affairs/Chief of Staff ... Mr. Dan SMITH
05 Vice Pres for Educational Affairs ... Dr. Chuck STRONG
20 Academic Dean ... Dr. Matthew S. DOMAS
103 Dean Career Tech Ed/Wrkfce Dev Trng ... Mr. Jerry NICHOLS
51 Dir Division of Continuing Educ ... Ms. Pam WOOTEN
84 Dean Enrollment Mgmt & Registrar ... Mr. Larry SIMPSON
35 Director of Student Personnel ... Mr. Mike DOTTOREY
27 Director of Communications ... Mrs. Sarah SAPP
37 Director of Financial Aid ... Mr. Terry BLAND
36 Dir Student Development Center ... Ms. Meg ROSS
08 Director of Learning Resources ... Mrs. Maggie MORAN
13 Director Management Information Sys ... Mrs. Amy LATHAM
07 Director of Recruiting ... Mrs. Jere HERRINGTON
09 Director Planning/Inst Research ... Dr. Carolyn WARREN
18 Director of Physical Plant Building ... Mr. Mike ROBISON
19 Chief of Campus Security ... Mr. Al DODSON
30 Director of Development/Alumni Rels ... Mrs. Sybil CANON
39 Director of Campus Life and Housing ... Mrs. Aime ANDERSON
40 Director Bookstore ... Mr. Joel BOYLES
41 Director of Athletics/Intramurals ... Mr. Cameron BLOUNT
96 Director of Purchasing ... Mrs. Barbara YOUNG
15 Personnel Officer ... Mrs. Rita DOWDLE
29 Director Alumni Relations ... Mrs. Dolores WOOTEN
21 Business Manager ... Ms. Ruthie CASTLE

Pearl River Community College (E)

101 Highway 11 N, Poplarville MS 39470-2298
County: Pearl River — FICE Identification: 002430
Unit ID: 176239
Telephone: (601) 403-1000 — Carnegie Class: Assoc/Pub-R-M
FAX Number: (601) 403-1129 — Calendar System: Semester
URL: www.prcc.edu
Established: 1909 — Annual Undergrad Tuition & Fees (In-District): $2,200
Enrollment: 4,986 — Coed
Affiliation or Control: State/Local — IRS Status: 501(c)3
Highest Offering: Associate Degree
Program: Occupational; 2-Year Principally Bachelor's Creditable
Accreditation: SC, ADNUR, DA, DH, MLTAD, OTA, PTAA, RAD, SURGT

01 President ... Dr. William A. LEWIS
05 VP for General Education ... Dr. Martha L. SMITH
32 VP Poplarville Campus/Hancock Ctr ... Dr. Adam BREERWOOD
10 VP for Business/Admn Services ... Mr. Roger A. KNIGHT
08 Director of College Libraries ... Vacant
26 Director of Public Relations ... Mr. Chuck ABADIE
84 VP for Enrollment Management ... Mr. Dow FORD
12 VP of Forrest County Operations ... Dr. Cecil BURT
14 Chief Technology Officer ... Mr. Steve HOWARD
18 Director of Physical Plant ... Mr. Craig TYNES
30 Director Development/Alumni Rels ... Mr. Ernest L. LOVELL, JR.
37 Director Student Financial Aid ... Ms. Valerie HORNE
41 Director of Athletics ... Vacant
07 Director of Recruitment/Orientation ... Ms. Casey RAWLS
09 VP for Planning & Research ... Dr. Rebecca ASKEW
36 Dir Student Placement/Counselor ... Dr. Ann MOORE
31 VP Econ/Comm Development ... Dr. David S. ALSOBROOKS

Reformed Theological Seminary (F)

5422 Clinton Boulevard, Jackson MS 39209-3099
County: Hinds — FICE Identification: 009193
Unit ID: 176284
Telephone: (601) 923-1600 — Carnegie Class: Not Classified
FAX Number: (601) 923-1654 — Calendar System: 4/1/4
URL: www.rts.edu
Established: 1965 — Annual Graduate Tuition & Fees: $14,150
Enrollment: 329 — Coed
Affiliation or Control: Independent Non-Profit — IRS Status: 501(c)3
Highest Offering: Doctorate; No Undergraduates
Program: Professional
Accreditation: SC, MFCD, THEOL

00 Chancellor Emeritus ... Dr. Robert C. CANNADA, JR.
01 Chancellor & CEO ... Dr. Michael MILTON
100 Chief of Staff/Chf Operations Ofcr ... Mr. Steve WALLACE
10 Chief Financial Officer ... Mr. Bradley TISDALE
05 Chief Academic Officer ... Dr. Robert CARA
30 Chief Development Officer ... Dr. Lynwood C. PEREZ
12 President Charlotte Campus ... Dr. Mike MILTON
12 President Orlando Campus ... Dr. Don SWEETING
12 President Jackson Campus ... Dr. Guy L. RICHARDSON
12 President RTS Virtual Campus ... Dr. Andrew J. PETERSON
12 President Atlanta Campus ... Mr. John T. SOWELL
12 President Washington DC ... Mr. Scott REDD
84 Senior VP Enrollment Management ... Vacant
44 Vice President for Development ... Mr. Robert PENNY
06 Registrar Jackson Campus ... Ms. Kim LEE
08 Library Director ... Mr. John MUETHER
32 Dean of Student Affairs/Admissions ... Mr. Brian C. GAULT
29 Dir Alum Rels/Dev/Supt Svcs Jackson ... Mrs. Stephanie J. HARTLEY
04 Assistant to Pres Jackson Campus ... Mrs. Wanda RUSHING
88 Dir Marriage & Fam Ther Jackson ... Dr. James B. HURLEY
18 Maintenance Director Jackson Campus ... Mr. Joe MORRIS
26 Dir of Institutional Communications ... Dr. Lynwood C. PEREZ
09 Director of Institutional Research ... Ms. Polly STONE
15 Director Personnel Svcs Jackson ... Ms. Linda COCHRAN

Rust College (G)

150 Rust Avenue, Holly Springs MS 38635-2328
County: Marshall — FICE Identification: 002433
Unit ID: 176318
Telephone: (662) 252-8000 — Carnegie Class: Bac/A&S
FAX Number: (662) 252-6107 — Calendar System: Semester
URL: www.rustcollege.edu
Established: 1866 — Annual Undergrad Tuition & Fees: $8,300
Enrollment: 922 — Coed
Affiliation or Control: United Methodist — IRS Status: 501(c)3
Highest Offering: Baccalaureate
Program: Liberal Arts And General
Accreditation: SC, SW, @TEAC

01 President .... Dr. David L. BECKLEY
30 Vice President for College Relation .... Dr. Ishmell H. EDWARDS
10 Vice President for Finance .... Mr. Donald MANNING-MILLER
09 Interim Asst to the Pres for Assess .... Dr. Sandra VAUGHN
05 VP for Academic Affairs .... Dr. Paul C. LAMPLEY
06 Registrar .... Mr. Clarence E. SMITH
08 Head Librarian .... Mrs. Anita W. MOORE
14 Director Computer Center .... Ms. Barbara NAYLOR MOORE
32 Dean of Student Affairs .... Mrs. Carolyn HYMON
35 Director Student Activities .... Mrs. Priscilla FISHER
37 Director of Financial Aid .... Mrs. Helen STREET
25 Director Contracts & Grants .... Mrs. Christine L. RATCLIFF
27 Director of Public Information .... Ms. Adrienne PHILLIPS
29 Director Alumni Development .... Ms. Jo Ann SCOTT
89 Chair First Year Experience .... Dr. Kenneth E. JONES
26 Director of Public Relations .... Vacant
21 Comptroller .... Vacant
84 Director Enrollment Services .... Mr. Johnny MCDONALD
23 Director Student Health Services .... Dr. Dianna HUGHES
39 Director Student Housing .... Mrs. Dorothy DONNELL
36 Director of Career Development .... Mr. John PEACHES
18 Director Physical Plant .... Mr. Robert CURRY
83 Division Chair Social Science .... Dr. Alfred J. STOVALL
15 Director Personnel Services .... Ms. Patricia PEGUES
19 Chief of Security .... Mr. Claude GLEETON
30 Director of Development .... Ms. Jo Ann SCOTT
40 Bookstore Manager .... Mrs. Patricia HARRIS
42 College Chaplain .... Rev. Annie TRAVIS
96 Director of Purchasing .... Ms. Ollie BOWENS
28 Director of Diversity .... Miss Patricia PEGUES
50 Division Chair Business .... Mr. Richard FREDERICK
53 Division Chair Education .... Dr. Leon HOWARD
79 Division Chair Humanities .... Dr. Sylvester W. OLIVER
81 Chair Division Science & Math .... Dr. Frank YEH
70 Chair Department of Social Work .... Dr. Gemma BECKLEY

Southeastern Baptist College (A)

4229 Highway 15 N, Laurel MS 39440-1096
County: Jones | FICE Identification: 002435
Unit ID: 176336
Telephone: (601) 426-6346 | Carnegie Class: Spec/Faith
FAX Number: (601) 426-6347 | Calendar System: Semester
URL: www.southeasternbaptist.edu
Established: 1948 | Annual Undergrad Tuition & Fees: $4,000
Enrollment: 65 | Coed
Affiliation or Control: Baptist | IRS Status: 501(c)3
Highest Offering: Baccalaureate
Program: 2-Year Principally Bachelor's Creditable; Liberal Arts And General; Religious Emphasis
Accreditation: BI

01 Interim President .... Mr. Joseph HARRIS
03 Executive Vice President .... Mr. Joseph HARRIS
05 Academic Dean .... Dr. Aaron L. PARKER
32 Dean of Student Services .... Mr. Greg HILLMAN
13 Director Information Technology .... Mr. Hubert DYESS
07 Director of Admissions/Recruitment .... Mr. Ronnie KITCHENS
06 Registrar .... Mrs. Emma BOND
37 Financial Aid Administrator .... Ms. Ginny SINGLETON
08 Director of Library .... Mrs. Amy E. HINTON
38 Director of Student Counseling .... Mr. Greg HILLMAN

Southwest Mississippi Community College (B)

1156 College Drive, Summit MS 39666-9029
County: Pike | FICE Identification: 002436
Unit ID: 176354
Telephone: (601) 276-2000 | Carnegie Class: Assoc/Pub-R-S
FAX Number: (601) 276-3888 | Calendar System: Semester
URL: www.smcc.edu
Established: 1918 | Annual Undergrad Tuition & Fees (In-District): $2,090
Enrollment: 2,128 | Coed
Affiliation or Control: Local | IRS Status: 501(c)3
Highest Offering: Associate Degree
Program: Occupational; 2-Year Principally Bachelor's Creditable
Accreditation: SC, ADNUR

01 President .... Dr. Steve BISHOP
05 Vice President of Academic Affairs .... Ms. Alicia SHOWS
10 Vice President of Financial Affairs .... Mr. Grady SMITH
32 Vice President of Student Affairs .... Mr. Bill ASHLEY
06 Registrar/Vice President Admissions .... Mr. Matthew CALHOUN
75 Vice Pres Career & Tech Education .... Mr. Jeremy SMITH
37 Director Student Financial Aid .... Mrs. Stacey HODGES
09 Director of Institutional Research .... Dr. Bill TUCKER
08 Librarian .... Mrs. Natalie MCMAHON

Tougaloo College (C)

500 West County Line Road, Tougaloo MS 39174-9999
County: Madison | FICE Identification: 002439
Unit ID: 176406
Telephone: (601) 977-7730 | Carnegie Class: Bac/A&S
FAX Number: (601) 977-7739 | Calendar System: Semester
URL: www.tougaloo.edu
Established: 1869 | Annual Undergrad Tuition & Fees: $9,740
Enrollment: 945 | Coed
Affiliation or Control: United Church Of Christ | IRS Status: 501(c)3
Highest Offering: Baccalaureate
Program: Liberal Arts And General
Accreditation: SC

01 President .... Dr. Beverly W. HOGAN
05 Provost/Vice Pres Academic Affairs .... Dr. Bettye Parker SMITH
32 Vice President for Student Affairs .... Mr. Fred ALEXANDER
30 Act Vice Pres Institutional Advance .. Dr. Delores Bolden STAMPS
10 Vice Pres Finance Administration .... Dr. Cynthia MELVIN
18 Vice Pres for Facilities Management .... Mr. Kelle MENOGAN
20 Asst Provost/VP Academic Affairs .... Vacant
84 Asst VP for Enrollment Management .... Mr. Steven SMITH
35 Asst Vice Pres for Student Affairs .... Mrs. Gladys J. JONES
88 Ex Dir Ntnl Transp Sec Ctr of Excel .... Mr. Eduardo MARTINEZ
08 Director of Library Services .... Mrs. Orthella P. MOMAN
13 Chief Information Officer .... Mr. Terry J. JORDAN
37 Director of Student Financial Aid .... Ms. Maria THOMAS
09 Director Inst Research/Assess/Plng .... Dr. Larry JOHNSON
06 Registrar .... Ms. Carolyn L. EVANS
15 Director Human Resources .... Ms. Doretha PRESLEY
26 Dir Communications/Public Affairs .... Mr. Danny L. JONES
29 Director of Alumni Affairs .... Mrs. Doris BRIDGEMAN
07 Director of Admissions .... Ms. Junoesque JACOBS
36 Director of Career Services .... Mrs. Gladys J. JONES
44 Director of Advancement Services .... Mrs. Sanette LANGSTON-SMITH
46 Dir of Sponsored Programs/Research .... Vacant
88 Director of TRiO .... Dr. Valvia WILSON
38 Director of Counseling Services .... Dr. Rosie HARPER
96 Purchasing Agent .... Ms. Easter COMMON
102 Dir Corporation & Foundation Rels .... Vacant

University of Mississippi (D)

University MS 38677-9999
County: Lafayette | FICE Identification: 002440
Unit ID: 176017
Telephone: (662) 915-7211 | Carnegie Class: RU/H
FAX Number: (662) 915-7010 | Calendar System: Semester
URL: www.olemiss.edu
Established: 1844 | Annual Undergrad Tuition & Fees (In-State): $6,282
Enrollment: 18,224 | Coed
Affiliation or Control: State | IRS Status: 501(c)3
Highest Offering: Doctorate
Program: Liberal Arts And General; Teacher Preparatory; Professional
Accreditation: SC, ART, BUS, BUSA, CACREP, CLPSY, CS, @DIETC, DIETD, ENG, JOUR, LAW, MUS, NRPA, PHAR, SP, SW, TED, THEA

01 Chancellor .... Dr. Daniel W. JONES
26 Chief Communications Officer .... Mr. Thomas E. EPPES
05 Provost/Vice Chanc Academic Affairs .... Dr. Morris H. STOCKS
10 Vice Chanc Finance & Administration .... Mr. Larry D. SPARKS
32 Vice Chancellor Student Life .... Dr. Brandi HEPHNER-LABANC
46 Vice Chanc Research/Sponsored Pgms .... Dr. Alice M. CLARK
35 Asst Vice Chanc Student Affairs .... Dr. Thomas J. REARDON
87 Int Asst Prov Summer Sch/Outreach .... Dr. Linda CHITWOOD
20 Asst VC Academic Affairs/Registrar .... Dr. Charlotte FANT
20 Associate Provost .... Dr. Maurice R. EFTINK
20 Associate Provost .... Dr. Noel E. WILKIN
85 Ast Prov/Ast to Chanc Multicul Affs .... Dr. Donald R. COLE
08 Dean of Libraries .... Ms. Julia RHOLES
13 Chief Information Officer .... Dr. Kathryn F. GATES
30 Sr Executive Dir of Development .... Ms. Deborah S. VAUGHN
29 Exec Director of Alumni Affairs .... Mr. Timothy L. WALSH
37 Director of Financial Aid .... Ms. Laura DIVEN-BROWN
36 Director Career Center .... Ms. Toni D. AVANT
41 Director Intercollegiate Athletics .... Mr. Ross BJORK
15 Director of Human Resources .... Mr. Clayton H. JONES
18 Director of Physical Plant .... Mr. Ashton PEARSON
19 Director Univ Police/Campus Safety .... Chief Calvin SELLERS
38 Director of Counseling Center .... Dr. Marc K. SHOWALTER
23 Director University Health Service .... Ms. Barbara COLLIER
39 Dir of Student Housing/Res Life .... Mr. Lionel MATEN
09 Director Institutional Research .... Ms. Mary M. HARRINGTON
22 Exec Dir Equal Oppty/Reg Compliance .... Ms. Wilma F. WEBBER-COLBERT
100 Chief of Staff to the Chancellor .... Dr. Andrew P. MULLINS
04 Assistant to the Chancellor .... Ms. Sue T. KEISER
43 Univ Attorney/Spec Asst to Chanc .... Dr. Lee TYNER
96 Director of Procurement Services .... Mr. James R. WINDHAM
06 Associate Registrar .... Mrs. Denise KNIGHTON
21 Controller .... Mr. Sam THOMAS
84 Director of Enrollment Services .... Mr. Whitman SMITH
50 Dean School of Business Admin .... Dr. Kendall B. CYREE
49 Dean College of Liberal Arts .... Dr. Glenn W. HOPKINS
81 Dean School of Applied Sciences .... Dr. Velmer S. BURTON, JR.
53 Dean School of Education .... Dr. David ROCK
54 Dean School of Engineering .... Dr. Alex CHENG
61 Dean School of Law .... Dr. I. Richard GERSHON
67 Dean of the School of Pharmacy .... Dr. David D. ALLEN
88 Dean School of Accountancy .... Dr. W. Mark WILDER
60 Dean Journalism & New Media .... Dr. H. Will NORTON

University of Mississippi Medical Center (E)

2500 N State Street, Jackson MS 39216-4505
County: Hinds | FICE Identification: 004688
Unit ID: 176026
Telephone: (601) 984-1000 | Carnegie Class: Spec/Med
FAX Number: (601) 984-1013 | Calendar System: Semester
URL: www.umc.edu
Established: 1955 | Annual Undergrad Tuition & Fees (In-State): $6,282
Enrollment: 2,620 | Coed
Affiliation or Control: State | IRS Status: 501(c)3
Highest Offering: Doctorate
Program: Professional; Nursing Emphasis
Accreditation: SC, CYTO, DENT, DH, IPSY, MED, MT, NMT, NURSE, OT, PTA, RAD

01 Vice Chancellor Health Affairs .... Dr. James E. KEETON
63 Assoc VC Health Affs/Vice Dean SOM .. Dr. LouAnn WOODWARD
100 Chief of Staff to Vice Chancellor .... Mr. Brian RUTLEDGE
10 Chief Financial Officer .... Mr. James WENTZ
21 Comptroller .... Mr. Sam E. SMITH
11 Chief Administrative Officer .... Dr. David L. POWE
46 Associate Vice Chanc Research .... Dr. John E. HALL
05 Interim Assoc VC Acadamic Affairs .... Dr. LouAnn WOODWARD
20 Deputy Chief Academic Officer .... Dr. Robin ROCKHOLD
28 Assoc Vice Chanc Multicultural Affs .... Dr. Jasmine P. TAYLOR
23 Assoc Vice Chanc Clinical Affairs .... Vacant
17 Interim CEO Univ Hosp & Clinics .... Ms. Janet Y. HARRIS
43 Chief Legal Officer .... Mr. John T. NEWSOME
26 Chief Public Affs & Comm Officer .... Mr. Tom FORTNER
27 Chief Information Officer .... Vacant
15 Chief Human Resources Officer .... Mr. Michael ESTES
66 Dean School of Nursing .... Dr. Kim HOOVER
58 Dean Sch Grad Stds Health Sciences .... Dr. Joey GRANGER
76 Interim Dean Sch Health Relate Prof .... Dr. Jessica H. BAILEY
52 Dean of School of Dentistry .... Dr. Gary W. REEVES
63 Assoc Dean-Graduate Medical Educ .. Dr. Shirley SCHLESSINGER
09 Director Institutional Research .... Dr. David G. FOWLER
19 Director Police & Logistical Svcs .... Mr. Arty E. GIROD
18 Director Physical Facilities .... Mr. Ivory BOGAN
30 Director Development .... Ms. Sara MERRICK
88 Director of Accreditation .... Dr. Mitzi NORRIS
96 Director Supply Chain .... Mr. Edward SMITH
29 Assoc Director Alumni Affairs .... Mr. Geoffrey MITCHELL
38 Director Academic Counseling .... Dr. Natalie W. GAUGHF
37 Director Student Financial Aid .... Ms. Carrie COOPER
32 Chief Student Affairs Officer .... Dr. Jerry CLARK
06 Dir Student Records & Registrar . Ms. Barbara M. WESTERFIELD
08 Director Rowland Medical Library .... Ms. Susan B. CLARK

University of Southern Mississippi (F)

118 College Drive, #5001, Hattiesburg MS 39406-0001
County: Forrest | FICE Identification: 002441
Unit ID: 176372
Telephone: (601) 266-1000 | Carnegie Class: RU/H
FAX Number: (601) 266-5756 | Calendar System: Semester
URL: www.usm.edu
Established: 1910 | Annual Undergrad Tuition & Fees (In-State): $6,336
Enrollment: 16,604 | Coed
Affiliation or Control: State | IRS Status: 501(c)3
Highest Offering: Doctorate
Program: Liberal Arts And General; Teacher Preparatory; Professional
Accreditation: SC, AAFCS, ART, AUD, BUS, BUSA, CIDA, CLPSY, CONST, COPSY, CS, DANCE, DIETD, DIETI, ENGT, JOUR, KIN, LIB, MFCD, MT, MUS, NRPA, NURSE, PH, SCPSY, SP, SW, TED, THEA

01 Interim President .... Dr. Aubrey LUCAS
04 Assistant to the President .... Ms. Mary D. GREGG
05 Provost .... Dr. Denis WIESENBURG
10 Int VP Finance & Administration .... Dr. Thomas ESTES
12 Vice Pres for Gulf Coast Campus .... Dr. Frances LUCAS
32 Vice President for Student Affairs .... Dr. Joseph S. PAUL
30 Vice President Advancement .... Mr. Bob PIERCE
20 Associate Provost Academic Affairs .... Dr. William W. POWELL
20 Assoc Provost Academic Affairs .... Dr. Cynthia EASTERLING
46 Vice Provost Research .... Dr. Gordon CANNON
37 Asst VP Student Affs & Finan Aid .... Dr. Kristi MOTTER
35 Asc Vice President Student Affairs .... Mr. Sid GONSOULIN
53 Dean College Education/Psychology .... Dr. Ann BLACKWELL
49 Int Dean College Arts & Letters .... Dr. Steven MOSER
50 Dean College Business .... Dr. Lance NAIL
72 Dean College Science/Technology .... Dr. Joe WHITEHEAD
92 Dean of Honors College .... Dr. David DAVIES
76 Dean College Health .... Dr. Michael FORSTER
58 Dean Graduate School .... Dr. Susan SILTANEN
08 Dean/University Librarian .... Dr. Carole KIEHL
18 Director Physical Plant .... Mr. Chris CRENSHAW
14 Int Chf Information Technology Ofcr .... Mr. David SLIMAN
41 Athletic Director .... Mr. Jeff HAMMOND
06 Registrar .... Mr. Greg PIERCE
25 Dir Research & Sponsored Programs .... Ms. Constance V. WYLDMON
09 Director of Institutional Research .... Mrs. Michelle ARRINGTON
45 Dir of Institutional Effectiveness .... Mrs. Kathryn LOWERY
29 Alumni Activities/Exec Director .... Mr. Jerry DEFATTA
36 Director Career Planning/Placement .... Mr. Russell ANDERSON
21 Controller .... Ms. Allyson EASTERWOOD
22 Director of Affirmative Action .... Ms. Rebecca WOODRICK
38 Director of Counseling Center .... Dr. Deena CRAWFORD
23 Director of Health Services .... Dr. Virginia CRAWFORD
39 Director of Residence Life .... Dr. Scott BLACKWELL
15 Director of Human Resources .... Mrs. Linda RASMUSSEN
94 Director of Women's Studies .... Dr. Kay HARRIS
96 Director Purchasing/Procuremnt Svcs .... Mr. Michael HERNDON
07 Int Director of Admissions .... Ms. Amanda KING

Virginia College (G)

920 Cedar Lake Road, Biloxi MS 39532-2107
County: Harrison | Identification: 666073
Unit ID: 450191
Telephone: (228) 546-9100 | Carnegie Class: Assoc/PrivFP
FAX Number: (228) 392-2039 | Calendar System: Quarter
URL: www.vc.edu
Established: 2005 | Annual Undergrad Tuition & Fees: $15,616

Enrollment: 470 Coed
Affiliation or Control: Proprietary IRS Status: Proprietary
Highest Offering: Associate Degree
Program: Occupational
Accreditation: ACICS

01 Campus President ....Ms. Kimberly NICHOLS
05 Academic Dean ....Mr. Richard SCHNORBUS
06 Registrar ....Ms. Nancy J. WEBSTER
07 Director of Admissions ....Ms. Betina D. YURKUS

† Branch campus of Virginia College, Birmingham, AL.

Virginia College (A)

4795 I-55 North, Jackson MS 39206
County: Hinds Identification: 666032
Unit ID: 441919
Telephone: (601) 977-0960 Carnegie Class: Assoc/PrivFP
FAX Number: (601) 956-4325 Calendar System: Quarter
URL: www.vc.edu
Established: 1999 Annual Undergrad Tuition & Fees: $19,258
Enrollment: 958 Coed
Affiliation or Control: Proprietary IRS Status: Proprietary
Highest Offering: Associate Degree
Program: Occupational
Accreditation: ACICS

01 Campus President ....Mr. Milton ANDERSON
05 Academic Dean ....Mr. William M. BRANCAMP
07 Director of Admissions ....Ms. Ellie DENMAN
06 Registrar ....Ms. Gina S. PHELPS

† Branch campus of Virginia College, Birmingham, AL.

Wesley Biblical Seminary (B)

787 E Northside Drive, Jackson MS 39206-4945
County: Hinds FICE Identification: 025162
Unit ID: 176451
Telephone: (601) 366-8880 Carnegie Class: Spec/Faith
FAX Number: (601) 366-8832 Calendar System: Semester
URL: www.wbs.edu
Established: 1974 Annual Graduate Tuition & Fees: $11,500
Enrollment: 107 Coed
Affiliation or Control: Interdenominational IRS Status: 501(c)3
Highest Offering: Master's; No Undergraduates
Program: Professional; Religious Emphasis
Accreditation: THEOL

01 President ....Dr. James L. PORTER
05 Vice President Academic Affairs ....Dr. Daniel L. BURNETT
32 VP of Business/Student Development ....Rev. Tom HALFORD
08 Director of Library Services ....Dr. Daniel L. BURNETT
10 Business Officer ....Mrs. Leigh THOMAS
18 Director of Operations ....Mr. Ken MONEY

William Carey University (C)

498 Tuscan Avenue, Hattiesburg MS 39401-5461
County: Forrest FICE Identification: 002447
Unit ID: 176479
Telephone: (601) 318-6051 Carnegie Class: Master's L
FAX Number: (601) 318-6494 Calendar System: Trimester
URL: www.wmcarey.edu
Established: 1892 Annual Undergrad Tuition & Fees: $10,350
Enrollment: 3,751 Coed
Affiliation or Control: Southern Baptist IRS Status: 501(c)3
Highest Offering: Doctorate
Program: Liberal Arts And General; Teacher Preparatory; Professional
Accreditation: SC, MUS, NURSE, @OSTEO, TED

01 President/Chief Executive Officer ....Dr. Tommy KING
05 Vice President of Academic Affairs ....Dr. Garry M. BRELAND
10 Vice Pres Business Affs/CFO ....Mr. Grant GUTHRIE
32 Vice President Student Services ....Ms. Brenda WALDRIP
46 Vice President Inst Effectiveness ....Dr. Bennie R. CROCKETT
30 VP Advancement/Church Relations ....Dr. Scott HUMMEL
63 Dean College Osteopathic Medicine ....Dr. Darrell LOVINS
12 Admin Dean Tradition Campus ....Mr. Gerald BRACEY
04 Executive Assistant to President ....Ms. Barbara HAMILTON
50 Dean School of Business ....Dr. Cheryl DALE
53 Dean School of Education ....Dr. Barry MORRIS
83 Dean Sch Natural/Behavioral Science ....Dr. Frank BAUGH
66 Dean School of Nursing ....Dr. Janet WILLIAMS
49 Dean School of Arts & Letters ....Dr. Myron NOONKESTER
64 Dean Winters School of Music ....Dr. Don ODOM
73 Dean School of Missions ....Dr. Daniel CALDWELL
84 Dean of Enrollment Management ....Mr. William N. CURRY
58 Dean of Graduate Studies ....Dr. Frank BAUGH
20 Assoc Dean of Academic Services ....Dr. Les STEVERSON
09 Director Institutional Research ....Dr. William T. RIVERO
06 Registrar ....Mrs. Gayle KNIGHT
08 Director of Libraries ....Mrs. Sherry LAUGHLIN
29 Alumni Director ....Mrs. Cindy COFIELD
26 Chief Public Relations Officer ....Vacant
13 Director of Information Technology ....Mr. Jeff ANDREWS
92 Director of Honors Program ....Dr. Scott HUMMEL
21 Director of Budget Management ....Mr. Grant GUTHRIE
41 Athletic Director ....Mr. Steven H. KNIGHT
18 Dir Facilities/Grounds/Maintenance ....Mr. Robert BLEVINS
32 Dir Student Svcs Tradition Campus ....Mr. James M. HARRISON
66 Associate Dean Nursing NO Campus ....Dr. Marilyn COOKSEY
21 Dir Business Svcs Tradition Campus ....Mr. Gerald BRACEY
12 Director of Keesler Center ....Ms. Amanda KNESAL
15 Director Personnel Services ....Ms. Deidre SHOWS
19 Director Campus Security ....Vacant
88 Coord of Instructional Technology ....Mr. David J. BROCKWAY
12 Coordinator New Orleans Campus ....Mr. LaRue HATTEN

MISSOURI

A. T. Still University of Health Sciences (D)

800 W Jefferson Street, Kirksville MO 63501-1497
County: Adair FICE Identification: 002477
Unit ID: 177834
Telephone: (660) 626-2391 Carnegie Class: Spec/Med
FAX Number: (660) 626-2672 Calendar System: Quarter
URL: www.atsu.edu
Established: 1892 Annual Graduate Tuition & Fees: N/A
Enrollment: 3,293 Coed
Affiliation or Control: Independent Non-Profit IRS Status: 501(c)3
Highest Offering: First Professional Degree; No Undergraduates
Program: Professional
Accreditation: NH, OSTEO

01 President ....Dr. Craig PHELPS
05 Interim Sr VP Academic Affairs ....Dr. Michael MCMANIS
63 Dean of KCOM ....Dr. Margaret WILSON
32 VP Student & Alumni Affairs ....Mrs. Lori HAXTON
30 VP for Institutional Advancement ....Mr. Robert BASHAM
43 General Counsel ....Mr. Matthew HEEREN
46 Vice Pres Inst Research & Grants ....Dr. John HEARD
26 Interim VP Comm & Marketing ....Jacqueline FORSYTHE
52 Dean MO Sch of Dentistry/Oral Hlth ....Dr. Chris HALLIDAY
58 Dean School of Health Managemnt ....Dr. Kimberly O'REILLY
52 Dean AZ Sch of Dentistry/Oral Hlth ....Dr. Jack DILLENBERG
76 Dean Arizona Sch of Health Sciences ....Dr. Randy DANIELSEN
63 Dean School of Osteo Med in Arizona ....Dr. Kay KALOUSEK
10 Vice President for Finance/CFO ....Mrs. Monnie HARRISON
07 Assoc VP Admissions & Alumni Svcs ....Mrs. Beth POPPRE
13 Asst VP Info Technologies/Services ....Mr. Bryan KRUSNIAK
20 Associate Dean Academic Affairs ....Dr. Stephen LAIRD
20 Assoc Dean Clinical Regional Affs ....Dr. Jeff SUZEWITS
51 Asst Dean/Cont Osteopathic Med Educ ....Dr. Lloyd CLEAVER
04 Assistant to the President ....Mrs. Norine EITEL
06 Registrar ....Dr. Deanna HUNSAKER
08 Director of Library ....Mr. Michael KRONENFIELD
15 Director of Human Resources ....Mrs. Donna BROWN
18 Director Facilities/Plant Operation ....Mr. Robert EHRLICH
22 Affirmative Action Officer ....Mrs. Donna BROWN
37 Dir Student Financial Assistance ....Mr. Steven JORDEN
38 Director of Student Counseling ....Mr. Thomas VAN VLECK
96 Director of Purchasing ....Mr. Corey LOUDER

† Arizona campus accreditation includes ARPCA, AUD, DENT, OSTEO, OT, PTA.

American College of Technology (E)

2300 Frederick Avenue, Saint Joseph MO 64506
County: Buchanan FICE Identification: 041187
Unit ID: 457688
Telephone: (816) 279-7000 Carnegie Class: Not Classified
FAX Number: (888) 890-8190 Calendar System: Other
URL: www.acot.edu
Established: 2001 Annual Undergrad Tuition & Fees: $19,000
Enrollment: 200 Coed
Affiliation or Control: Proprietary IRS Status: Proprietary
Highest Offering: Master's
Program: Occupational; 2-Year Principally Bachelor's Creditable; Technical Emphasis
Accreditation: DETC

01 President ....Mr. Sam ATIEH
11 Director of Operations ....Mr. Lute ATIEH
37 Financial Aid Administrator ....Mr. Calvin HAYNES

Anthem College (F)

13723 Riverport Drive, Suite 103,
Maryland Heights MO 63043-4819
County: Saint Louis FICE Identification: 022392
Unit ID: 176549
Telephone: (314) 595-3400 Carnegie Class: Assoc/PrivFP
FAX Number: (314) 739-5133 Calendar System: Other
URL: www.anthemcollege.edu
Established: 1981 Annual Undergrad Tuition & Fees: $31,343
Enrollment: 267 Coed
Affiliation or Control: Proprietary IRS Status: Proprietary
Highest Offering: Associate Degree
Program: Occupational
Accreditation: ABHES, SURTEC

01 Executive Director ....Ms. Barbara HALOMAN

Aquinas Institute of Theology (G)

23 S Spring Avenue, Saint Louis MO 63108-3323
County: City of Saint Louis FICE Identification: 001632
Unit ID: 176600
Telephone: (314) 256-8800 Carnegie Class: Spec/Faith
FAX Number: (314) 256-8888 Calendar System: Semester
URL: www.ai.edu
Established: 1951 Annual Graduate Tuition & Fees: $16,230
Enrollment: 192 Coed
Affiliation or Control: Roman Catholic IRS Status: 501(c)3
Highest Offering: Doctorate; No Undergraduates
Program: Professional; Religious Emphasis
Accreditation: NH, THEOL

01 President ....Rev. Richard A. PEDDICORD
05 Academic Dean ....Rev. Gregory HEILLE
10 Director of Finance ....Mr. Thomas BARBARAK
06 Registrar ....Ms. Julie QUINT
30 Director of Inst Advancement ....Mrs. Barbara MAYNARD
32 Dean of Students ....Rev. George BOUDREAU
07 Director Admissions/Financial Aid ....Mr. David WERTHMANN
26 Director of Marketing ....Mr. Thomas BARBARAK

Assemblies of God Theological Seminary (H)

1435 N Glenstone Avenue, Springfield MO 65802-2131
County: Greene FICE Identification: 012120
Unit ID: 176619
Telephone: (417) 268-1000 Carnegie Class: Spec/Faith
FAX Number: (417) 268-1001 Calendar System: Semester
URL: www.agts.edu
Established: 1972 Annual Graduate Tuition & Fees: $13,032
Enrollment: 425 Coed
Affiliation or Control: Assemblies Of God Church IRS Status: 501(c)3
Highest Offering: Doctorate; No Undergraduates
Program: Professional; Religious Emphasis
Accreditation: NH, THEOL

01 President ....Dr. Byron D. KLAUS
05 Academic Dean ....Dr. Stephen LIM
58 Dir Intercultural Doctoral Studies ....Dr. DeLonn L. RANCE
58 Director DMin Program ....Dr. Cheryl A. TAYLOR
10 Director of Business ....Rev. David W. WILLEMSEN
26 Director of Institutional Relations ....Mrs. Dorothea J. LOTTER
08 Director of Library Services ....Mr. Joseph F. MARICS
30 Director of Development ....Dr. Byron D. KLAUS
27 Promotions Coordinator ....Mrs. Jennifer S. HALL
73 Chair Bible/Theology Department ....Dr. Roger D. COTTON
88 Chair Global Missions Department ....Dr. DeLonn L. RANCE
88 Chair Prac Theology Department ....Dr. Jay P. TAYLOR
42 Director of Spiritual Formation ....Dr. Jay P. TAYLOR
51 Director of Continuing Education ....Dr. Randy C. WALLS
84 Director of Enrollment Management ....Dr. Mario H. GUERREIRO

Avila University (I)

11901 Wornall Road, Kansas City MO 64145-9990
County: Jackson FICE Identification: 002449
Unit ID: 176628
Telephone: (816) 942-8400 Carnegie Class: Master's M
FAX Number: (816) 942-3362 Calendar System: Semester
URL: www.avila.edu
Established: 1916 Annual Undergrad Tuition & Fees: $23,950
Enrollment: 1,818 Coed
Affiliation or Control: Roman Catholic IRS Status: 501(c)3
Highest Offering: Master's
Program: Liberal Arts And General; Teacher Preparatory; Professional
Accreditation: NH, IACBE, NURSE, RAD, SW

01 President ....Dr. Ron SLEPITZA
05 Provost/Vice Pres Academic Affairs ....Sr. Marie Joan HARRIS
20 Vice Provost for Academic Affairs ....Dr. Sue KING
10 Vice Pres for Finance/Admin Svcs ....Mr. Paul G. BOOKMEYER
30 Chief Development Officer ....Ms. Angela HEER
32 Dean of Students ....Ms. Darby GOUGH
07 Director of Admission ....Mr. Brandon JOHNSON
06 Registrar ....Mrs. Dana R. SHIRLEY
08 Librarian ....Ms. Kathleen FINEGAN
37 Director of Financial Aid ....Ms. Crystal BRUNTZ
42 Dir Mission Effect & Campus Ministr ....Mr. David M. ARMSTRONG
21 Controller ....Mr. Joseph H. SJUTS
29 Director Alumni & Donor Relations ....Mrs. Susan RANDOLPH
41 Athletic Director ....Mr. Gary GALLUP
15 Director of Human Resources ....Ms. Janet MCMANUS
18 Chief Facilities/Physical Plant ....Mr. Mike STUCKEY
40 Bookstore Manager ....Mr. John A. TARANTO
38 Coord Counseling & Career Services ....Ms. Susan WULFF

Baptist Bible College (J)

628 E Kearney St, Springfield MO 65803-3498
County: Greene FICE Identification: 013208
Unit ID: 176664
Telephone: (417) 268-6013 Carnegie Class: Spec/Faith
FAX Number: (417) 268-6694 Calendar System: Semester
URL: www.gobbc.edu
Established: 1950 Annual Undergrad Tuition & Fees: $6,500
Enrollment: 498 Coed
Affiliation or Control: Baptist IRS Status: 501(c)3
Highest Offering: First Professional Degree
Program: Teacher Preparatory; Professional; Religious Emphasis
Accreditation: NH, BI

01 President ....Mr. Mark L. MILIONI

05 Vice President of Academic Affairs ..... Dr. Greg T. CHRISTOPHER
10 Chief Financial Officer .... Mrs. Krista L. CORCORAN
32 Senior Director of Student Life .... Mr. John L. SLAYDEN
18 Chief Facilities/Physical Plant .... Mr. Chris C. WILLIAMS
20 Director of Academic Advising .... Dr. Joseph K. GLEASON
06 Registrar/Dir Enrollment Svcs .... Mr. Terry A. ALLCORN
37 Director of Financial Aid .... Mr. Bob L. KOTULSKI
38 Campus Counselor .... Mr. Bill A. PIATT
39 Director of Resident Life .... Mr. Bill J. LEVERGOOD
15 Director of Human Resources .... Mrs. Angel M. SARVER
19 Director Security/Safety .... Mr. James C. CLATWORTHY
41 Athletic Director .... Mr. Mark HEDGER
40 Bookstore .... Mrs. Julie BECK
08 Director of Library Services .... Mr. Jon JONES
09 Director of Institutional Research .... Mrs. Lesa M. CHASTAIN
106 Dean of Online Education .... Ms. Cheryl PAGE
72 Director of Technology .... Mr. Landon GHAN
108 Director of Campus Assessment .... Mrs. Lesa M. CHASTAIN

Bolivar Technical College (A)

2001 W Broadway Street, PO Box 592,
Bolivar MO 65613-1861

County: Polk — Identification: 667033
Telephone: (417) 777-5062 — Carnegie Class: Not Classified
FAX Number: (417) 777-8908 — Calendar System: Semester
URL: www.bolivarcollege.org
Established: 1996 — Annual Undergrad Tuition & Fees: N/A
Enrollment: 153 — Coed
Affiliation or Control: Independent Non-Profit — IRS Status: 501(c)3
Highest Offering: Associate Degree
Program: Occupational; 2-Year Principally Bachelor's Creditable
Accreditation: ACICS

01 President/Campus Director .... Ms. Charlotte GRAY
03 Vice President .... Dr. William GRAY
05 Academic Director .... Mr. Dave THOMPSON

Brown Mackie College-St. Louis (B)

2 Soccer Park Road, Fenton MO 63026-2564

County: St. Louis — Identification: 666793
Unit ID: 460048
Telephone: (636) 651-3290 — Carnegie Class: Not Classified
FAX Number: (636) 651-3349 — Calendar System: Other
URL: www.brownmackie.edu
Established: N/A — Annual Undergrad Tuition & Fees: $10,188
Enrollment: 511 — Coed
Affiliation or Control: Proprietary — IRS Status: Proprietary
Highest Offering: Baccalaureate
Program: Occupational; 2-Year Principally Bachelor's Creditable; Business Emphasis
Accreditation: ACICS, OTA, SURTEC

01 President .... Terri LEAP
07 Senior Director of Admissions .... Phyllis HUTTO
05 Dean of Academic Affairs .... Lisa CASIMERE

† Branch campus of Brown Mackie College, Tucson, AZ.

Bryan College (C)

4255 Nature Center Way, Springfield MO 65804

County: Greene — FICE Identification: 030663
Unit ID: 369516
Telephone: (417) 862-5700 — Carnegie Class: Assoc/PrivFP
FAX Number: (417) 865-7144 — Calendar System: Other
URL: www.bryancolleges.edu
Established: 1982 — Annual Undergrad Tuition & Fees: $17,500
Enrollment: 472 — Coed
Affiliation or Control: Proprietary — IRS Status: Proprietary
Highest Offering: Associate Degree
Program: Occupational; 2-Year Principally Bachelor's Creditable; Business Emphasis
Accreditation: ACICS

01 Executive Director .... Mr. Scott HAAR

Calvary Bible College and Theological Seminary (D)

15800 Calvary Road, Kansas City MO 64147-1341

County: Cass — FICE Identification: 002450
Unit ID: 176789
Telephone: (816) 322-0110 — Carnegie Class: Spec/Faith
FAX Number: (816) 331-4474 — Calendar System: Semester
URL: www.calvary.edu
Established: 1932 — Annual Undergrad Tuition & Fees: $10,116
Enrollment: 370 — Coed
Affiliation or Control: Independent Non-Profit — IRS Status: 501(c)3
Highest Offering: First Professional Degree
Program: Teacher Preparatory; Religious Emphasis
Accreditation: NH, BI

01 President .... Dr. James L. CLARK
11 Vice President of Operations .... Mr. Randy GRIMM
05 Academic Dean of the College .... Dr. Teddy BITNER
20 Seminary Academic Dean .... Dr. Thomas S. BAURAIN
32 Dean of Students .... Mr. Corey D. TROWBRIDGE
34 Dean of Women .... Mrs. Kim BAILEY
06 Dean Enrollment Mgmt/Registrar .... Mr. Larry SPRY
08 Head Librarian .... Miss Hannah BITNER
29 Director of Alumni .... Miss Dorothy JEFFREY
07 Director Admissions .... Mr. Robert CRANK
18 Director Buildings & Grounds .... Mr. Caleb ARNETT
41 Athletic Director .... Miss Jeanette REGIER
91 Director Administrative Computing .... Mr. Aaron HEATH
38 Director Biblical Counsel/Educ Ctr .... Mrs. Patricia A. MILLER
30 Director of Development .... Mr. Jeff CAMPA
19 Director of Security .... Mr. Cory D. TROWBRIDGE
37 Director of Financial Aid .... Mr. Robert CRANK
26 Coordinator of Public Relations .... Vacant
09 Institutional Research Coordinator .... Mr. Jesse A. RIGGS
15 Human Resources Coordinator .... Mrs. Jolayne ROGERS

Central Bible College (E)

3000 N Grant, Springfield MO 65803-1096

County: Greene — FICE Identification: 002452
Unit ID: 176938
Telephone: (417) 833-2551 — Carnegie Class: Spec/Faith
FAX Number: (417) 833-5141 — Calendar System: Semester
URL: www.cbcag.edu
Established: 1922 — Annual Undergrad Tuition & Fees: $13,010
Enrollment: 665 — Coed
Affiliation or Control: Assemblies Of God Church — IRS Status: 501(c)3
Highest Offering: Baccalaureate
Program: Liberal Arts And General; Religious Emphasis
Accreditation: NH, BI

01 President .... Dr. Gary A. DENBOW
05 Vice President Academic Affairs .... Dr. David ARNETT
32 Vice President Student Development .... Dr. Jim VIGIL
10 Chief Financial Officer .... Rev. David WILLEMSEN
08 Librarian .... Mr. Lynn ANDERSON
06 Registrar/Dir Student Records .... Dr. Leo THERIOT
18 Chief Facilities/Physical Plant .... Mr. Dwayne HUFF
29 Director Alumni Relations .... Mrs. Kathy ARNETT
36 Director Student Placement .... Rev. Philip GOCKE
37 Director Student Financial Services .... Mr. William A. TATE
38 Director Student Counseling .... Rev. Deonna CRABTREE
84 Director Enrollment Services .... Mrs. Lisa DRECKMAN
15 Director Human Resources .... Mr. Nathan HALL

Central Christian College of the Bible (F)

911 E Urbandale Drive, Moberly MO 65270-1997

County: Randolph — FICE Identification: 022664
Unit ID: 176910
Telephone: (660) 263-3900 — Carnegie Class: Spec/Faith
FAX Number: (660) 263-3936 — Calendar System: Semester
URL: www.cccb.edu
Established: 1957 — Annual Undergrad Tuition & Fees: $8,950
Enrollment: 318 — Coed
Affiliation or Control: Christian Churches And Churches of Christ — IRS Status: 501(c)3
Highest Offering: Baccalaureate
Program: 2-Year Principally Bachelor's Creditable; Liberal Arts And General; Professional; Religious Emphasis
Accreditation: BI

01 President .... Dr. Ronald L. OAKES
05 Vice President of Academics .... Dr. David B. FINCHER
32 Vice President Student Development .... Mr. Richard R. REXRODE
30 VP of Institutional Advancement .... Mr. Phillip MARLEY
10 Chief Financial Officer .... Mrs. Lara LAWRENCE
108 Associate Dean of Assessment .... Mr. Richard A. FORDYCE
07 Associate Director of Admissions .... Mr. Michael BUTRUM
07 Director of Admissions Services .... Mr. Rocky CHRISTENSEN
44 Asst Director of Development .... Mr. Alan G. WILSON
04 Executive Asst to the President .... Mrs. Loretta L. KELCHNER
33 Dean of Men .... Mr. Jason LYKINS
34 Dean of Women .... Ms. Anne P. MENEAR
41 Athletic Director .... Ms. Anne P. MENEAR
08 Head Librarian .... Mrs. Patty A. AGEE
06 Registrar .... Mrs. Faith M. AXTON
37 Director of Financial Aid .... Mrs. Rhonda J. DUNHAM
13 Director of Information Systems .... Mr. David ROSADO
18 Physical Plant Manager .... Mr. Mark E. DUNHAM
40 Bookstore Manager .... Mrs. Kelly HARDING
29 Alumni Relations & Event Coord .... Mrs. Sherry WALLIS
35 Director of Student Services .... Mrs. Lori PETER
39 Residence Director - Women .... Mrs. April CHRISTENSEN
39 Residence Director - Men .... Mr. Rocky CHRISTENSEN
21 Accounting Manager .... Mrs. Theresa BARTHOLMEY
102 Foundation & Corporate Relations .... Mrs. Veronica HAMBLIN
04 Administrative Executive Assistant .... Mrs. Cindy MEYER

Central Methodist University (G)

411 Central Methodist Square, Fayette MO 65248-1198

County: Howard — FICE Identification: 002453
Unit ID: 445267
Telephone: (660) 248-3391 — Carnegie Class: Bac/Diverse
FAX Number: (660) 248-2287 — Calendar System: 4/1/4
URL: www.centralmethodist.edu
Established: 1854 — Annual Undergrad Tuition & Fees: $20,720
Enrollment: 5,222 — Coed
Affiliation or Control: United Methodist — IRS Status: 501(c)3
Highest Offering: Master's
Program: Liberal Arts And General; Teacher Preparatory
Accreditation: NH, MUS, NURSE

01 President .... Dr. Marianne E. INMAN
05 Vice Pres & Dean of the University .... Dr. Rita GULSTAD
10 Vice Pres Finance & Administration .... Ms. Julee SHERMAN
30 Vice Pres Advancement/Alumni Rels .... Ms. Donna MERRELL
32 VP Instl Growth/Student Engagement .... Mr. Kenneth R. OLIVER
20 Assoc Dean for Academics .... Dr. Barbara ANDERSON
27 Vice President Information Services .... Mr. Chad GAINES
09 Asst Dean Inst Research/Assessment .... Ms. Amy DYKENS
07 Director of Admission .... Mr. Larry ANDERSON
41 Athletic Director .... Mr. Kenneth R. OLIVER
29 Dir Development/Alumni Programs .... Mr. Alan G. MARSHALL
06 Registrar .... Ms. Kathryn WINEGARD
37 Director of Financial Assistance .... Ms. Kristen GIBBS
18 Chief Facilities/Physical Plant .... Mr. Derry WISWALL
26 Exec Dir Marketing Communications .... Mr. Kent PROPST
36 Director Student Placement .... Ms. Nicolette YERICH

Chamberlain College of Nursing - St. Louis (H)

11830 Westline Industrial Dr, #106, Saint Louis MO 63146

County: Saint Louis — FICE Identification: 006385
Unit ID: 466921
Telephone: (314) 991-6200 — Carnegie Class: Spec/Health
FAX Number: (314) 991-6283 — Calendar System: Semester
URL: www.chamberlain.edu
Established: 1889 — Annual Undergrad Tuition & Fees: $16,360
Enrollment: 7,952 — Coed
Affiliation or Control: Proprietary — IRS Status: Proprietary
Highest Offering: Baccalaureate
Program: Nursing Emphasis
Accreditation: NH

01 President .... Ms. Susan L. GROENWALD
02 Campus President .... Dr. Janice DEMASTERS
05 Vice President of Academic Affairs .... Dr. William Richard COWLING
106 Dean Online Programs .... Ms. Margaret WHEELER
88 Director Accreditation .... Ms. Kathleen R. MODENE
32 Senior Director Student Services .... Ms. June MARLOWE
26 Director of Marketing .... Ms. Stephanie L. GALLO

† Part of DeVry University, IL.

City Vision College (I)

712 E 31st Street, Kansas City MO 64109

County: Jackson — FICE Identification: 041191
Unit ID: 457697
Telephone: (816) 960-2008 — Carnegie Class: Not Classified
FAX Number: (617) 825-0313 — Calendar System: Other
URL: www.cityvision.edu
Established: 1998 — Annual Undergrad Tuition & Fees: $6,000
Enrollment: 68 — Coed
Affiliation or Control: Other — IRS Status: 501(c)3
Highest Offering: Baccalaureate
Program: Professional; Religious Emphasis
Accreditation: DETC

01 Executive Director/President .... Mr. Andrew SEARS
05 Chief Academic Officer .... Rev. Michael K. LIIMATTA
10 Business Office Manager .... Mrs. Harriet HODGE-HENRY

College of the Ozarks (J)

PO Box 17, Point Lookout MO 65726-0017

County: Taney — FICE Identification: 002500
Unit ID: 178697
Telephone: (417) 334-6411 — Carnegie Class: Bac/Diverse
FAX Number: (417) 335-2618 — Calendar System: Semester
URL: www.cofo.edu
Established: 1906 — Annual Undergrad Tuition & Fees: $430
Enrollment: 1,377 — Coed
Affiliation or Control: Independent Non-Profit — IRS Status: 501(c)3
Highest Offering: Baccalaureate
Program: Liberal Arts And General
Accreditation: NH, DIETD, NURSE

01 President .... Dr. Jerry C. DAVIS
03 Vice President .... Dr. Howell W. KEETER
05 Dean of the College .... Dr. Eric BOLGER
30 Dean of Development .... Mr. Timothy HUDDLESTON
10 Treasurer .... Mr. Charles F. HUGHES
11 Dean of Administration .... Dr. Marvin SCHOENECKE
88 Dean of the Work Program .... Dr. Chris LARSEN
32 Dean of Student Services .... Mr. Nick SHARP
07 Dean Director of Admissions .... Dr. Marci LINSON
06 Registrar .... Mrs. Fran FORMAN
29 Director of Alumni Affairs .... Mrs. Angela WILLIAMSON
36 Director of Career Placement .... Mr. Ron MARTIN
37 Director Student Financial Aid .... Mrs. Kyla MCCARTY
26 Director Public Relations .... Mrs. Elizabeth B. HUGHES
96 Director of Purchasing .... Mr. Kurt MCDONALD
38 Student Counseling .... Mrs. Pat MCLEAN

Colorado Technical University, Kansas City (K)

520 E 19th Avenue, North Kansas City MO 64116-3614

County: Clay — Identification: 666457
Unit ID: 409838

Telephone: (816) 303-7799 Carnegie Class: Bac/Assoc
FAX Number: (816) 472-0688 Calendar System: Quarter
URL: www.ctukansascity.com
Established: 1965 Annual Undergrad Tuition & Fees: $25,800
Enrollment: 218 Coed
Affiliation or Control: Proprietary IRS Status: Proprietary
Highest Offering: Baccalaureate
Program: Occupational; 2-Year Principally Bachelor's Creditable; Business Emphasis
Accreditation: &NH, MAAB, RAD, SURGT

11 Director of Operations ... Ms. Nancy BRAMLETT

† Regional accreditation is carried under the parent institution in Colorado Springs, CO.

Columbia College (A)

1001 Rogers Street, Columbia MO 65216-0001
County: Boone FICE Identification: 002456
Unit ID: 177065
Telephone: (573) 875-8700 Carnegie Class: Master's M
FAX Number: (573) 875-7209 Calendar System: Semester
URL: www.ccis.edu
Established: 1851 Annual Undergrad Tuition & Fees: $17,950
Enrollment: 1,050 Coed
Affiliation or Control: Christian Church (Disciples Of Christ)
IRS Status: 501(c)3
Highest Offering: Master's
Program: Liberal Arts And General; Teacher Preparatory; Professional
Accreditation: NH

01 President ... Dr. Gerald T. BROUDER
04 Exec Assistant to the President ... Ms. Lori K. EWING
05 Exec Vice Pres/Dean Academic Affs ... Dr. Terry B. SMITH
56 Vice Pres of Adult Higher Education ... Mr. Mike RANDERSON
84 Assistant VP for Enrollment Mgmt ... Mr. Tery DONELSON
32 Dean for Student Affairs ... Ms. Faye C. BURCHARD
10 Controller/Chief Financial Officer ... Mr. Bruce E. BOYER
30 Exec Director of Devel/Alumni Svcs ... Mr. Mike KATEMAN
18 Exec Director of Admin Services ... Mr. Bob C. HUTTON
88 Executive Director of Marketing ... Ms. Lana POOLE
27 Chief Information Officer ... Mr. Kevin PALMER
07 Director of Admissions ... Ms. Samantha WHITE
06 Registrar ... Ms. Sue M. KOOPMANS
29 Senior Director of Alumni Services ... Ms. Susan Y. DAVIS
26 Senior Director of Public Relations ... Ms. Joanne TEDESCO
37 Director of Financial Aid ... Ms. Sharon A. ABERNATHY
08 Director of Stafford Library ... Ms. Janet CARUTHERS
35 Director of Student Activities ... Ms. Elizabeth BALL
36 Director Career Services Center ... Mr. Don G. MALSON
16 Director Human Resources ... Ms. Patty FISCHER
23 Director of Wellness Center ... Ms. Kim J. KINYON
13 Deputy Chief Information Officer ... Mr. Gary STANOWSKI
55 Assoc Dean Adult Higher Education ... Mr. Eric CUNNINGHAM
58 Associate Dean Graduate Studies ... Dr. Steve C. WIEGENSTEIN
41 Athletic Director ... Mr. Bob P. BURCHARD
09 Institutional Research Analyst ... Ms. Misty HASKAMP
19 Director of Campus Safety ... Mr. Robert KLAUSMEYER
21 Associate Controller ... Mr. Randal SCHENEWERK
51 Dean for Adult Higher Education ... Mr. Gary MASSEY

Conception Seminary College (B)

37174 State Highway VV, PO Box 502,
Conception MO 64433-0502
County: Nodaway FICE Identification: 002467
Unit ID: 177083
Telephone: (660) 944-3105 Carnegie Class: Spec/Faith
FAX Number: (660) 944-2829 Calendar System: Semester
URL: www.conception.edu
Established: 1883 Annual Undergrad Tuition & Fees: $17,534
Enrollment: 110 Male
Affiliation or Control: Roman Catholic IRS Status: 501(c)3
Highest Offering: Baccalaureate
Program: Liberal Arts And General; Religious Emphasis
Accreditation: NH

01 Rector & President ... Rev. Samuel J. RUSSELL
11 Director of Administration ... Mrs. Amy K. SCHIEBER
32 Dean of Students ... Rev. Ralph O'DONNELL
05 Dean of Academic Affairs ... Dr. William BROWNSBERGER
10 Business Manager/Dir Auxiliary Svcs ... Rev. Benedict T. NEENAN
30 Development Director ... Rev. Adam RYAN
07 Director of Admissions ... Bro. Etienne HUARD
37 Director of Student Financial Aid ... Bro. Justin J. HERNANDEZ
06 Registrar ... Mrs. Jeanette SCHIEBER
29 Director of Alumni ... Rev. Daniel PETSCHE
08 Librarian ... Bro. Thomas SULLIVAN
26 Director of Communications ... Mrs. Jenny HUARD
13 Director of Information Technology ... Mr. Tony MEISTER
38 Director of Counseling Services ... Rev. Duane REINERT
41 Director of Wellness Program ... Mr. Skip SHEAR

Concorde Career College (C)

3239 Broadway Boulevard, Kansas City MO 64111-2407
County: Jackson FICE Identification: 023616
Unit ID: 155283
Telephone: (816) 531-5223 Carnegie Class: Assoc/PrivFP
FAX Number: (816) 756-3231 Calendar System: Other
URL: www.concordecareers.com/kansas/
Established: 1986 Annual Undergrad Tuition & Fees: $26,085
Enrollment: 735 Coed
Affiliation or Control: Proprietary IRS Status: Proprietary
Highest Offering: Associate Degree
Program: Occupational
Accreditation: ACCSC, DA, DH, @PTAA

01 President ... Debra CROW
05 Academic Dean ... James KRALICEK
07 Director Student Recruitment ... Aaron GRAY

Concordia Seminary (D)

801 Seminary Place, Saint Louis MO 63105-3168
County: Saint Louis FICE Identification: 002457
Unit ID: 177092
Telephone: (314) 505-7000 Carnegie Class: Spec/Faith
FAX Number: (314) 505-7001 Calendar System: Quarter
URL: www.csl.edu
Established: 1839 Annual Graduate Tuition & Fees: $25,200
Enrollment: 634 Coed
Affiliation or Control: Lutheran Church - Missouri Synod
IRS Status: 501(c)3
Highest Offering: Doctorate; No Undergraduates
Program: Professional; Religious Emphasis
Accreditation: NH, THEOL

01 President ... Dr. Dale A. MEYER
03 Provost ... Dr. Arthur D. BACON
05 Vice President for Academic Affairs ... Dr. Andrew H. BARTELT
10 Sr VP for Financial Planning/Admin ... Mr. Michael A. LOUIS
84 Sr VP of Enrollment Management ... Rev. Michael REDEKER
30 Senior VP for Advancement ... Mr. Fred BLEEKE
21 VP of Financial Planning/Admin ... Mr. Chad CATTOOR
58 Dean of Advanced Studies ... Dr. Bruce G. SCHUCHARD
06 Registrar ... Mrs. Beth R. MENNEKE
08 Director of Library Services ... Rev. Daniel MATSON
51 Director Continuing Education ... Dr. Jeffrey KLOHA
26 Director of Communications ... Dr. Paul DEVANTIER
88 Director Center for Hispanic Study ... Dr. Leopoldo A. SANCHEZ
15 Director of Human Resources ... Mr. Thomas MYERS
18 Director Facilities/Physical Plant ... Mr. Stephen B. MUDD
36 Dir Student Placement/Alumni Activ ... Rev. Robert HOEHNER
37 Director of Student Financial Aid ... Mrs. Kerry R. HALLAHAN
27 Chief Information Officer ... Mr. John KLINGER

Cottey College (E)

1000 W Austin Boulevard, Nevada MO 64772-2763
County: Vernon FICE Identification: 002458
Unit ID: 177117
Telephone: (417) 667-8181 Carnegie Class: Assoc/PrivNFP
FAX Number: (417) 667-8103 Calendar System: Semester
URL: www.cottey.edu
Established: 1884 Annual Undergrad Tuition & Fees: $17,410
Enrollment: 319 Female
Affiliation or Control: Independent Non-Profit IRS Status: 501(c)3
Highest Offering: Baccalaureate
Program: 2-Year Principally Bachelor's Creditable; Liberal Arts And General
Accreditation: NH, MUS

01 President ... Dr. Judy R. ROGERS
05 Vice President for Academic Affairs ... Dr. Cathryn PRIDAL
88 Exec Dir Women's Leadership ... Ms. Sonia COWEN
36 Student Success Coordinator ... Ms. Renee HAMPTON
04 Assistant to the President ... Mrs. Tricia BOBBETT
10 VP for Administration & Finance ... Mrs. Mary S. HAGGANS
26 VP for Inst Advancement ... Ms. Judyth WIER
32 VP for Student Life ... Dr. Mari Anne PHILLIPS
42 Dir Spiritual Life & Diversity ... Ms. Erica SIGAUKE
84 VP for Enrollment Management ... Vacant
07 Director of Admissions ... Ms. Judi STEEGE
06 Registrar ... Ms. Marcia MORTON
21 Controller ... Ms. Amy RUETTEN
08 Library Director ... Ms. Rebecca J. KIEL
18 Director Physical Plant/Security ... Mr. Neal R. SWARNES
27 Director of Public Information ... Mr. Steve E. REED
15 Director of Human Resources ... Ms. Betsy A. MCREYNOLDS
91 Director Administratrive Computing ... Mr. Keith J. SPENCER
37 Director of Financial Aid ... Mrs. Sherry R. PENNINGTON
90 Director Academic Computing ... Mr. Adam S. DEAN
88 Director Center Women's Leadership ... Ms. Denise C. HEDGES
39 Director of Student Housing ... Ms. Helen LODGE
41 Director of Athletics ... Mr. Dave V. KETTERMAN
30 Director of Development ... Ms. Terri FALLIN
21 Asst to VP Admin & Finance ... Ms. Tina BUCKNER
40 Bookstore Manager ... Mrs. Lois J. WITTE
09 Coordinator Institutional Research ... Mrs. Nancy KERBS
29 Coordinator Alumnae Relations ... Ms. Courtney MAJORS
38 Coordinator of Counseling ... Ms. Jeanna BRAUER
88 Campaign Manager ... Ms. Carla FARMER
88 Director of Food Service ... Mr. Michael RICHARDSON
88 Coordinator of PEO Relations ... Ms. Tracy H. CORDOVA

Covenant Theological Seminary (F)

12330 Conway Road, Saint Louis MO 63141-8697
County: Saint Louis FICE Identification: 004707
Unit ID: 177126
Telephone: (314) 434-4044 Carnegie Class: Spec/Faith
FAX Number: (314) 434-4819 Calendar System: 4/1/4
URL: www.covenantseminary.edu
Established: 1956 Annual Graduate Tuition & Fees: $14,400
Enrollment: 698 Coed
Affiliation or Control: Presbyterian Church In America IRS Status: 501(c)3
Highest Offering: Doctorate; No Undergraduates
Program: Professional; Religious Emphasis
Accreditation: NH, THEOL

01 Interim President ... Dr. Mark DALBEY
03 Executive Vice President ... Vacant
05 Vice President of Academics ... Dr. Mark DALBEY
10 Vice President of Business Admin ... Mr. Al LI
32 Dean of Students ... Rev. Michael HIGGINS
20 Dean of Academic Administration ... Rev. Christopher FLORENCE
30 Sr Director of Development ... Mr. John RANHEIM
07 Sr Director of Admissions ... Mr. Jeremy KICKLIGHTER
21 Controller ... Miss Jean LEHMKUHL
13 Director of Information Technology ... Mr. Richard HIERS
18 Director Facilities & Operations ... Mr. David BROWN
08 Library Director ... Rev. James C. PAKALA
37 Director of Financial Aid ... Miss Melinda CONN
29 Dir Alumni Relations/Career Svcs ... Mr. Joel HATHAWAY
06 Registrar ... Miss Betsy GASOSKE

Cox College (G)

1423 N Jefferson Avenue, Springfield MO 65802-1917
County: Greene FICE Identification: 020682
Unit ID: 176770
Telephone: (417) 269-3401 Carnegie Class: Spec/Health
FAX Number: (417) 269-3581 Calendar System: Semester
URL: www.coxcollege.edu
Established: 1995 Annual Undergrad Tuition & Fees: $11,935
Enrollment: 894 Coed
Affiliation or Control: Independent Non-Profit IRS Status: 501(c)3
Highest Offering: Master's
Program: Occupational; 2-Year Principally Bachelor's Creditable; Professional
Accreditation: NH, ADNUR, DIETI, NURSE, RAD

01 President ... Dr. Anne BRETT
05 Vice President of Academic Affairs ... Dr. Dennis EDWARDS
32 Vice President Student Services ... Mr. David SCHOOLFIELD
08 Director Library Services ... Wilma C. BUNCH
66 Dean Department of Nursing ... Dr. Tricia WAGNER
76 Dean Health Sciences Department ... Sonya HAYTER
09 Director of Institutional Research ... Vacant
10 Comptroller ... Deborah ADKINS
37 Director of Financial Aid ... Steve NICHOLS
07 Director of Admissions ... Lindy BIGLIENI
29 Director of Alumni Relations & Mktg ... Todd RUTLEDGE

Crowder College (H)

601 Laclede Avenue, Neosho MO 64850-9165
County: Newton FICE Identification: 002459
Unit ID: 177135
Telephone: (417) 451-3223 Carnegie Class: Assoc/Pub-R-M
FAX Number: (417) 455-5702 Calendar System: Semester
URL: www.crowder.edu
Established: 1963 Annual Undergrad Tuition & Fees (In-District): $2,670
Enrollment: 5,410 Coed
Affiliation or Control: Local IRS Status: 501(c)3
Highest Offering: Associate Degree
Program: Occupational; 2-Year Principally Bachelor's Creditable
Accreditation: NH

01 President ... Dr. Alan D. MARBLE
10 Vice President of Finance ... Dr. Jim CUMMINS
05 Vice President of Academic Affairs ... Dr. Glenn COLTHARP
06 Vice President of Student Affairs ... Dr. Nicole STRIEGEL
20 Assoc VP of Academic Affairs ... Mrs. Amy RAND
75 Assoc VP of Careers & Tech Ed ... Mr. Ken RHUEMS
07 Director of Admissions ... Mr. Jim RIGGS
09 Director of Institutional Research ... Mrs. Mickie MAHAN
08 Director of Lee Library ... Mr. Eric DEATHERAGE
27 Director of Public Information ... Mrs. Cindy BROWN
41 Athletic Director ... Mrs. Millie GILION
37 Director of Financial Aid ... Mrs. Michelle PAUL
15 Director of Human Resources ... Mrs. Gale MARSH
25 Director of Grants & Development ... Mrs. Pam HUDSON
40 Bookstore Manager ... Ms. Colleen HOLLAND
36 Career Svcs Coordinator ... Ms. Casey OWENS
13 Director of Information Technology ... Mr. Chris WOITOWITZ

Culver-Stockton College (I)

1 College Hill, Canton MO 63435-1257
County: Lewis FICE Identification: 002460
Unit ID: 177144
Telephone: (573) 288-6000 Carnegie Class: Bac/Diverse
FAX Number: (573) 288-6611 Calendar System: Semester
URL: www.culver.edu
Established: 1853 Annual Undergrad Tuition & Fees: $22,550
Enrollment: 752 Coed
Affiliation or Control: Christian Church (Disciples Of Christ)
IRS Status: 501(c)3
Highest Offering: Baccalaureate
Program: Liberal Arts And General; Teacher Preparatory; Professional
Accreditation: NH, IACBE, MUS

01 President ... Mr. Richard D. VALENTINE
05 Vice Pres Academic Affs/Dean of Col ... Dr. Daniel K. SILBER
32 Dean of Student Life ... Mr. D. Christopher GILL

07 Director of Admission .... Mrs. Misty MCBEE
30 Director of Advancement/Alumni Pgm .... Mr. Eric BARKLEY
06 Registrar/Director Inst Research .... Mrs. Chris HUEBOTTER
08 Librarian .... Mrs. Sharon K. UPCHURCH
26 Director of College Communications .... Mr. Kyle TRUDELL
37 Director Financial Aid .... Mrs. Tina WISEMAN
29 Director of Alumni Programs .... Mr. Jeffrey MCREYNOLDS
91 Exec Dir Admin Systems & Service .... Mr. Joseph LIESEN
10 Chief Financial Officer/Controller .... Mrs. Diane BOZARTH
15 Director of Human Resources .... Mrs. Amy BAKER
35 Coordinator of Student Activities .... Mr. Devon OSSORIO
42 Chaplain .... Vacant
41 Athletic Director .... Mr. Greg MCVEY
40 Logo Shop Manager .... Mrs. Sharon FARR
04 Assistant to the President .... Mrs. Doris BRISCOE
19 Director Campus Security & Facil .... Mr. Michael BRINGER
81 Chair Natural & Math Sciences Div .... Dr. Lauren SCHELLENBERGER
50 Chair Business Division .... Dr. Kimberly GAITHER
53 Chair Education/Applied Arts Div .... Ms. Ann E. HAMMER
57 Chair Fine Arts Division .... Mr. Kent MILLER
79 Chair Humanities Division .... Dr. P. Ronald STORMER
83 Chair Social/Behavior Sciences Div .... Dr. Chad DEWAARD
88 Assoc Dean/Experiential Learning .... Dr. Dell Ann JANNEY
92 Director of Honors Program .... Vacant
93 Director of Minority Students .... Dr. Mohamed EL-BERMAWY
24 Media Coordinator .... Mrs. Julie WRIGHT
44 Director of the Annual Fund .... Mr. Scott MCGAUGHEY
36 Coord of Career Services/Internship .... Vacant
39 Director of Residential Life .... Ms. Heather KELLER
20 Director of Advising/Retention/FY .. Ms. Holly ANDRESS-MARTIN
38 Dir Counseling/Student Wellness .... Ms. Susan MOON
09 Director of Institutional Research .... Mrs. Karla MCREYNOLDS
88 Director of Advancement Operations .... Mrs. Marjorie ELLISON

DeVry University - Kansas City Campus (A)

11224 Holmes Road, Kansas City MO 64131-3626

County: Jackson | FICE Identification: 002455 | Unit ID: 177162

Telephone: (816) 943-7300 | Carnegie Class: Master's S

FAX Number: N/A | Calendar System: Semester

URL: www.devry.edu

Established: 1931 | Annual Undergrad Tuition & Fees: $16,156

Enrollment: 1,168 | Coed

Affiliation or Control: Proprietary | IRS Status: Proprietary

Highest Offering: Master's

Program: Occupational; Professional; Business Emphasis

Accreditation: &NH, ENGT

01 Metro President .... Mr. Ken ROSS
06 Registrar .... Mr. Ryan MEADOR
05 Dean Academic Affairs .... Ms. Cathleen PETERSON
08 Director of Library Services .... Ms. Beth CALDARELLO
31 Director Community Outreach .... Ms. Adele LISKO
15 Human Resources Business Partner .... Ms. Maria LEVIT
36 Director of Career Services .... Mr. Gerald ELLIS
07 Senior Director of Admissions .... Ms. Kena WOLF
54 Dean of Engineering .... Mr. Don WEISS

† Regional accreditation is carried under the parent institution in Downers Grove, IL.

DeVry University - Kansas City Downtown Center (B)

1100 Main Street, Suite 118, Kansas City MO 64105-2112

County: Jackson | Identification: 666211 | Unit ID: 437370

Telephone: (816) 221-1300 | Carnegie Class: Not Classified

FAX Number: (816) 474-0318 | Calendar System: Semester

URL: www.devry.edu

Established: 2003 | Annual Undergrad Tuition & Fees: $16,156

Enrollment: 261 | Coed

Affiliation or Control: Proprietary | IRS Status: Proprietary

Highest Offering: Master's

Program: Occupational; Professional; Business Emphasis

Accreditation: &NH

01 Center Dean .... Cass BUTLER

† Regional accreditation is carried under the parent institution in Downers Grove, IL.

DeVry University - St. Louis (C)

11830 Westline Industrial Dr., Saint Louis MO 63146-4157

County: Saint Louis | Identification: 666214 | Unit ID: 432180

Telephone: (314) 991-6400 | Carnegie Class: Not Classified

FAX Number: N/A | Calendar System: Semester

URL: www.devry.edu

Established: 1993 | Annual Undergrad Tuition & Fees: $16,156

Enrollment: 437 | Coed

Affiliation or Control: Proprietary | IRS Status: Proprietary

Highest Offering: Master's

Program: Occupational; Professional; Business Emphasis

Accreditation: &NH

01 Campus Dean .... Vacant

† Regional accreditation is carried under the parent institution in Downers Grove, IL.

Drury University (D)

900 N Benton Avenue, Springfield MO 65802-3791

County: Greene | FICE Identification: 002461 | Unit ID: 177214

Telephone: (417) 873-7879 | Carnegie Class: Master's M

FAX Number: (417) 873-7529 | Calendar System: Semester

URL: www.drury.edu

Established: 1873 | Annual Undergrad Tuition & Fees: $21,000

Enrollment: 5,371 | Coed

Affiliation or Control: Independent Non-Profit | IRS Status: 501(c)3

Highest Offering: Master's

Program: Liberal Arts And General; Teacher Preparatory; Professional

Accreditation: NH, ACBSP, BUS, MUS, TED

01 President .... Mr. Todd PARNELL
10 Chief Financial Officer .... Mr. Rob FRIDGE
11 Vice President for Administration .... Mr. Bill SCORSE
32 Vice President for Student Services .... Dr. Tijuana S. JULIAN
18 VP Campus Oper/Sustainability .... Mr. Pete RADECKI
05 Vice President for Academic Affairs .... Dr. Charles TAYLOR
30 Vice Pres Alumni & Development .... Dr. Krystal MCCULLOCH
84 Vice Pres of Enrollment Management .... Ms. Dawn HILES
58 Interim Dean Grad & Cont Studies .... Mr. Aaron JONES
20 Associate Dean of College .... Dr. Bruce CALLEN
06 Registrar .... Mrs. Gale M. BOUTWELL
26 Dir of Marketing & Communications .... Ms. Jann HOLLAND
37 Director of Financial Aid .... Mrs. Annette AVERY
88 Director of Facilities Services .... Mr. Ron CUSHMAN
08 Director of Library/Info Services .... Ms. Polly BORUFF-JONES
36 Director of Career Development .... Ms. Jill WIGGINS
15 Director of Human Resources .... Ms. Scotti SIEBERT
29 Director Alumni Relations .... Ms. Meleah SPENCER
09 Director of Institutional Research .... Vacant
38 Dir of Counseling/Student Devel .... Mr. Ed DERR
19 Director Safety/Security .... Ms. Sarene DEEDS
28 Director of Diversity .... Mr. L. A. ANDERSON
35 Director Student Affairs .... Ms. Emily GIVENS

East Central College (E)

1964 Prairie Dell Road, Union MO 63084-0529

County: Franklin | FICE Identification: 008862 | Unit ID: 177250

Telephone: (636) 583-5193 | Carnegie Class: Assoc/Pub-S-MC

FAX Number: (636) 583-1897 | Calendar System: Semester

URL: www.eastcentral.edu

Established: 1968 | Annual Undergrad Tuition & Fees (In-District): $2,430

Enrollment: 4,127 | Coed

Affiliation or Control: Local | IRS Status: 501(c)3

Highest Offering: Associate Degree

Program: Occupational; 2-Year Principally Bachelor's Creditable

Accreditation: NH, ACFEI, NAIT, OTA

01 President .... Dr. C. Jon BAUER
10 Vice Pres Finance/Administration .... Vacant
05 Vice President Instruction .... Ms. Jean A. MCCANN
32 Vice President Student Development .... Ms. Ina R. HAYS
75 VP Career and Outreach Education .... Ms. Brenda A. BOUSE
12 Director of Rolla Campus .... Ms. Christina M. AYRES
30 Dir of Institutional Development .... Ms. Shannon M. GRUS
18 Director Facilities & Grounds .... Mr. Mark A. EATON
08 Director of Library Services .... Ms. Lisa M. FARRELL
96 Purchasing Manager .... Ms. Melissa D. POPP
83 Div Chair Educ/Business/Soc Science .... Ms. Mary B. HUXEL
57 Div Chair Fine & Performing Arts .... Mr. Vincent T. NIEHAUS
79 Div Chair English/For Language .... Mr. John M. HARDECKE
81 Div Chair Science .... Ms. Fatemeh NICHOLS
15 Director Human Resources .... Ms. Wendy HARTMANN
66 Director of Nursing/Allied Health .... Ms. Robyn C. WALTER
37 Director Financial Aid .... Ms. Karen KOENIG-GRIFFIN
06 Registrar .... Ms. Karen S. WIEDA
21 Director Financial Svcs/Comptroller . Ms. Shirley A. HOFSTETTER
09 Director of Institutional Research .... Ms. Bethany L. LOHDEN
26 Director of Public Relations .... Ms. Dorothy A. SCHOWE
13 Director Information Technology .... Mr. Brian A. RUDOLPH
40 Bookstore/Mail/Imaging Coordinator .... Mr. Doug A. AGEE
36 Coordinator Advisement Services .... Ms. Tammy A. WEINHOLD
103 Executive Director Workforce Devel .... Ms. Gretchen A. PETTIT
51 Coordinator Adult Educ & Literacy .... Ms. Micki D. HOFFMAN
24 Coordinator Instructional Design .... Mr. R. Chad BALDWIN
35 Coordinator Student Activities .... Vacant

Eden Theological Seminary (F)

475 E Lockwood Avenue,
Webster Groves MO 63119-3192

County: Saint Louis | FICE Identification: 002462 | Unit ID: 177278

Telephone: (314) 961-3627 | Carnegie Class: Spec/Faith

FAX Number: (314) 918-2626 | Calendar System: 4/1/4

URL: www.eden.edu

Established: 1850 | Annual Graduate Tuition & Fees: $14,470

Enrollment: 191 | Coed

Affiliation or Control: United Church Of Christ | IRS Status: 501(c)3

Highest Offering: Doctorate; No Undergraduates

Program: Professional; Religious Emphasis

Accreditation: NH, THEOL

01 President .... Dr. David M. GREENHAW
03 Executive Vice President .... Mr. Richard WALTERS
30 Vice Pres Institutional Advancement .... Mr. Bryce KRUG
05 Academic Dean .... Dr. Deborah KRAUSE
44 Director of Development .... Ms. Jackie HAMILTON
06 Registrar .... Ms. Michelle WOBBE
08 Director Eden Library .... Mr. Michael BODDY
07 Director of Recruitment/Admissions .... Rev. Carol SHANKS
40 Director Eden Bookstore .... Ms. Hannah RICE
10 Director of Finance .... Mr. Richard WALTERS
04 Executive Asst to the President .... Ms. Denise STAUFFER

Evangel University (G)

1111 N Glenstone, Springfield MO 65802-2191

County: Greene | FICE Identification: 002463 | Unit ID: 177339

Telephone: (417) 865-2811 | Carnegie Class: Bac/Diverse

FAX Number: (417) 865-9599 | Calendar System: Semester

URL: www.evangel.edu

Established: 1955 | Annual Undergrad Tuition & Fees: $19,050

Enrollment: 2,168 | Coed

Affiliation or Control: Assemblies Of God Church | IRS Status: 501(c)3

Highest Offering: Master's

Program: Liberal Arts And General; Teacher Preparatory

Accreditation: NH, MUS, SW, TED

01 President .... Dr. Robert H. SPENCE
10 Vice President for Business/Finance .... Mr. George F. CRAWFORD
32 Vice Pres for Student Development .... Dr. David R. BUNDRICK
30 Vice Pres Institutional Advancement .... Mr. James WILLIAMS
05 Vice President for Academic Affairs .... Dr. Glenn H. BERNET
84 Vice Pres Enrollment Management .... Dr. Andy DENTON
18 Director of Physical Plant .... Mr. Tom KELTNER
41 Director of Athletics .... Dr. David L. STAIR
06 Registrar .... Mrs. Cathy WILLIAMS
14 Director Computer Svcs/Acad Comput .... Mr. Brett WEIMER
08 Librarian .... Mr. Dale JENSEN
19 Director of Security .... Mr. Gene THOMLINSON
38 Director of Counseling Services .... Mr. Brian UPTON
29 Director Alumni Relations .... Mr. Chuck COX
37 Dir of Student Financial Services .... Mrs. Dorynda CARPENTER
36 Career Development/Placement .... Mrs. Sheri PHILLIPS
42 Campus Pastor .... Rev. John PLAKE
26 Director of Public Relations .... Mr. Paul LOGSDON
07 Director Grad & Prof Admissions .... Mr. Jeff BURNETT
07 Director Undergraduate Admissions .... Ms. Julie LYONS
23 Director of Health Services .... Mrs. Susan BRYAN
21 Controller .... Mr. John KRAUS
35 Director Student Life .... Miss Gina RENTSCHLER
15 Supervisor Human Resources .... Mrs. Ocki HAAS
39 Housing Coordinator .... Mrs. Pamela SMALLWOOD
09 Director of Institutional Research .... Dr. Linda WELLBORN

Everest College (H)

1010 W Sunshine, Springfield MO 65807-2488

County: Greene | FICE Identification: 022506 | Unit ID: 179070

Telephone: (417) 864-7220 | Carnegie Class: Bac/Assoc

FAX Number: (417) 864-5697 | Calendar System: Quarter

URL: www.everestcollege.com

Established: 1976 | Annual Undergrad Tuition & Fees: $12,798

Enrollment: 380 | Coed

Affiliation or Control: Proprietary | IRS Status: Proprietary

Highest Offering: Baccalaureate

Program: Occupational; 2-Year Principally Bachelor's Creditable; Business Emphasis

Accreditation: ACICS, MAC

01 President .... Mr. Brian J. HARVEY
05 Academic Dean .... Ms. Pam HELVEY
07 Director of Admissions .... Ms. Wendy WOOSLEY
06 Registrar .... Ms. Annette THOMAS
37 Financial Aid Director .... Ms. Brenda GROOVER
10 Director of Student Accounts .... Ms. Jennifer RUMLEY
07 High School Director of Admissions .... Mr. Kevin ASBERRY
08 Librarian .... Mr. Trenton TUBBS

Fontbonne University (I)

6800 Wydown Boulevard, Saint Louis MO 63105-3098

County: Saint Louis | FICE Identification: 002464 | Unit ID: 177418

Telephone: (314) 862-3456 | Carnegie Class: Master's L

FAX Number: (314) 889-1451 | Calendar System: Semester

URL: www.fontbonne.edu

Established: 1923 | Annual Undergrad Tuition & Fees: $20,860

Enrollment: 2,293 | Coed

Affiliation or Control: Roman Catholic | IRS Status: 501(c)3

Highest Offering: Master's

Program: Liberal Arts And General; Teacher Preparatory; Professional

Accreditation: NH, ACBSP, DIETD, SP, @SW, TED

01 President .... Dr. Dennis C. GOLDEN
03 Executive Vice Pres Strat/Oper .... Mr. Gregory TAYLOR
05 Vice Pres/Dean Academic Affairs .... Vacant
30 Vice President Inst Advancement .... Ms. Sandra LEHRER
32 Vice President Student Affairs .... Ms. Randi WILSON
10 Vice President Finance & Admin/CFO .... Dr. Gary L. ZACK

84 Vice President Enrollment Mgt — Vacant
13 Vice Pres Information Technology — Mr. Mark FRANZ
35 Associate Vice Pres Student Affairs — Ms. Carla HICKMAN
20 Interim Assoc Dean/Dir Grad Studies — Dr. Heather NORTON
97 Dean of Undergraduate Studies — Vacant
58 Director of Graduate Studies/MAED — Vacant
53 Dean of Education — Dr. William FREEMAN
50 Dean of Global Business & Prof Stds — Ms. Linda MAURER
88 Asst to the Pres for Mission Integ — Dr. Mary Beth GALLAGHER
06 Registrar — Ms. Mazie MOORE
15 Director of Human Resources — Ms. Linda PIPITONE
08 University Librarian — Ms. Sharon MCCASLIN
45 Director of Academic Resources — Mr. Mark POUSSON
09 Dir of Inst Research & Assessment — Dr. Laurie A. RODGERS
26 Director Communications/Marketing — Mr. Mark JOHNSON
106 Director of Online Program — Vacant
37 Director of Financial Aid — Ms. Nicole MOORE
88 Director of Academic Advising — Ms. Lee DELAET
85 Director of International Affairs — Ms. Rebecca GRANT BAHAN
29 Director of Alumni Relations — Ms. Carrie WENBERG
41 Interim Director of Athletics — Ms. Maria EFTINK
28 Director of Multicultural Affairs — Ms. Leslie DOYLE
88 Dir Ldrshp Educ & Stdnt Activities — Dr. Janelle DENSBERGER
42 Director of Campus Ministry — Ms. Sarah BOUL
19 Director of Public Safety — Mr. Bob KRAEUCHI
21 Controller — Mr. Dennis JOHNSON
07 Director of Admissions — Ms. Dorothy DAVIS
18 Director Physical Plant — Mr. Brent SPIES

Global University (A)

1211 South Glenstone Avenue, Springfield MO 65804-1894
County: Greene — Identification: 666687
Unit ID: 247296
Telephone: (800) 443-1083 — Carnegie Class: Not Classified
FAX Number: (417) 865-7167 — Calendar System: Other
URL: www.globaluniversity.edu
Established: 1948 — Annual Undergrad Tuition & Fees: $3,750
Enrollment: 5,597 — Coed
Affiliation or Control: Assemblies Of God Church — IRS Status: 501(c)3
Highest Offering: Doctorate
Program: Occupational; 2-Year Principally Bachelor's Creditable; Liberal Arts And General; Professional; Religious Emphasis
Accreditation: NH, DETC

01 President — Dr. Gary SEEVERS, JR.
03 Executive Vice President — Rev. Keith HEERMANN
05 Provost — Dr. Jack NILL
20 Vice Provost — Dr. Robert LOVE
58 Graduate School Dean — Dr. Carl CHRISNER
88 Berean School of the Bible Dean — Dr. Randy HEDLUN
73 UG School of Bible & Theology — Dr. Willard TEAGUE
13 VP Info Tech/Media Dept — Dr. Mark BARCLIFT
09 Director Research/Evaluation — Rev. Brad AUSBURY
07 Director of Enrollment Services — Rev. Todd WAGGONER
06 Registrar — Mrs. Lynne KROH
10 Chief Financial Officer — Mr. Mark PERRY
15 Director of Human Resources — Rev. Bob ARMONT

Goldfarb School of Nursing at Barnes-Jewish College (B)

4483 Duncan Avenue, Saint Louis MO 63110-1111
County: Saint Louis — FICE Identification: 006389
Unit ID: 177719
Telephone: (314) 454-7055 — Carnegie Class: Spec/Health
FAX Number: (314) 362-9250 — Calendar System: Semester
URL: www.barnesjewishcollege.edu
Established: 1902 — Annual Undergrad Tuition & Fees: $27,000
Enrollment: 850 — Coed
Affiliation or Control: Independent Non-Profit — IRS Status: 501(c)3
Highest Offering: Doctorate
Program: Professional; Nursing Emphasis
Accreditation: NH, ANEST, NURSE

01 Interim Dean — Dr. Connie KOCH
05 Associate Dean of Academic Programs — Dr. Connie KOCH
11 Assoc Dean for Administration — Mr. Thomas EDLER
20 Assoc Dean for Student Programs — Dr. Michael WARD
46 Associate Dean for Research — Dr. Donna TALIAFERRO
88 Asst Dean Post-Licensure Programs — Dr. Gretchen DRINKARD
88 Asst Dean Pre-Licensure Programs — Dr. Gail REA
08 Library & Info Services Director — Ms. Renee GORRELL
13 Information System Director — Mr. Wade LEHDE
37 Financial Aid Director — Mr. Jason CROWE
32 Student & Support Services Director — Ms. June COWELL-OATES
84 Enrollment Manager — Ms. Margaret O'CONNOR

Graceland University (C)

1401 West Truman Road, Independence MO 64050-3434
County: Jackson — Identification: 666262
Unit ID: 15336601
Telephone: (816) 833-0524 — Carnegie Class: Not Classified
FAX Number: (816) 833-2990 — Calendar System: 4/1/4
URL: www.graceland.edu
Established: 1895 — Annual Undergrad Tuition & Fees: $21,950
Enrollment: 884 — Coed
Affiliation or Control: Other — IRS Status: 501(c)3
Highest Offering: Master's
Program: Liberal Arts And General; Professional
Accreditation: &NH, NURSE

01 President — Dr. John D. SELLARS
05 Vice Pres Acad Affairs/Dean of Fac — Dr. Parris R. WATTS
51 Exec Dir for Grad & Continuing Educ — Dr. Paul BINNICKER
66 Dean of Nursing — Dr. Claudia D. HORTON

† Regional accreditation is carried under the parent institution in Lamoni, IA.

Grantham University (D)

7200 NW 86th Street, Kansas City MO 64153-2262
FICE Identification: 004283
Unit ID: 442569
Telephone: (800) 955-2527 — Carnegie Class: Master's S
FAX Number: (816) 595-5757 — Calendar System: Other
URL: www.grantham.edu
Established: 1951 — Annual Undergrad Tuition & Fees: $6,390
Enrollment: 9,323 — Coed
Affiliation or Control: Proprietary — IRS Status: Proprietary
Highest Offering: Master's
Program: Occupational; Professional; Technical Emphasis
Accreditation: DETC

01 President — Joseph C. MCGRATH
05 Provost/Chief Academic Officer — Dr. Marilyn BARTELS
06 Registrar — Russell PERKINS
26 Chief Marketing Officer — Lori TUREC
07 Vice President of Admissions — Les HYDE
10 Vice President of Finance — Ed SAMMARCO
30 Vice Pres of Strategic Initiatives — Dr. Jeffrey CROPSEY
15 Vice President of Human Resources — Kip ESRY
13 Chief Information Officer — Jeff BRAMBLETT
37 Vice President of Financial Aid — Roman YAGNITINSKY
20 Associate Provost — Cheryl HAYEK
38 Director of Student Advising — Lisa WACHTER
103 Exec Dir, Education Outreach — George COLON
22 Vice President of Compliance — Karan KRNA

Hannibal-La Grange University (E)

2800 Palmyra Road, Hannibal MO 63401-1999
County: Marion — FICE Identification: 009089
Unit ID: 177542
Telephone: (573) 221-3675 — Carnegie Class: Bac/Diverse
FAX Number: (573) 221-6594 — Calendar System: Semester
URL: www.hlg.edu
Established: 1858 — Annual Undergrad Tuition & Fees: $17,800
Enrollment: 1,164 — Coed
Affiliation or Control: Southern Baptist — IRS Status: 501(c)3
Highest Offering: Master's
Program: Liberal Arts And General
Accreditation: NH, ADNUR

01 President — Dr. Anthony W. ALLEN
05 VP for Academic Affairs — Dr. David J. PELLETIER
84 VP for Enrollment Management — Dr. Raymond W. CARTY
30 VP for Institutional Advancement — Mr. Steve T. MILLER
32 Dean of Student Development — Mr. Kyle R. BRENNEMANN
10 Dean of Business & Finance — Mrs. Betty L. ANDERSON
26 Director Public Relations — Mrs. Carolyn A. CARPENTER
06 Director of Records/Student Accts — Mrs. Mary E. FORD
37 Director of Financial Aid — Mr. Brice D. BAUMGARDNER
29 Director Alumni Services — Ms. Lauren YOUSE
35 Director Student Affairs — Ms. Margaret F. STREET
36 Director Student Placement — Dr. Karry D. RICHARDSON
08 Librarian — Mrs. Julie A. ANDRESEN
18 Chief Facilities/Physical Plant — Mr. James P. MILLER
19 Director Security/Safety — Mr. Lucas R. HIRTZEL
39 Director Student Housing — Mrs. Sara E. KECK
40 Director Bookstore — Mrs. Susan A. BOOTH
41 Athletic Director — Mr. Jason D. NICHOLS
42 Director Campus Ministry — Dr. Jeffrey D. BROWN

Harris-Stowe State University (F)

3026 Laclede Avenue, Saint Louis MO 63103-2199
County: Independent City — FICE Identification: 002466
Unit ID: 177551
Telephone: (314) 340-3366 — Carnegie Class: Bac/Diverse
FAX Number: (314) 340-3399 — Calendar System: Semester
URL: www.hssu.edu
Established: 1857 — Annual Undergrad Tuition & Fees (In-State): $5,110
Enrollment: 1,584 — Coed
Affiliation or Control: State — IRS Status: 501(c)3
Highest Offering: Baccalaureate
Program: Teacher Preparatory; Professional; Business Emphasis
Accreditation: NH, ACBSP, IACBE, TED

01 President — Dr. Albert WALKER
05 Vice President Academic Affairs — Dr. Dwayne SMITH
10 Exec VP Business/Financial Affairs — Mrs. Constance G. GULLY
21 Asst VP Business/Financial Affairs — Vacant
26 Asst VP Comm/Mktg/Alumni Affs/Dev — Ms. Courtney MCCALL
06 Registrar — Ms. Chauvette MCELMURRY
07 Exec Dir Admissions/Enrollment Mgmt — Ms. LaShanda R. BOONE
88 Director of Academic Advisement — Ms. Carla LEE
08 Director Library Services — Mrs. Barbara NOBLE
37 Director of Financial Aid — Ms. Regina BLACKSHEAR
15 Director Human Resources — Mrs. Virginia J. MALONE
38 Director Counseling Services — Mrs. Vicki BERNARD
56 Exec Dir Title III/Sponsored Pgms — Mrs. Heather BOSTIC
20 Director Special Acad Support Pgms — Vacant
41 Director of Athletics — Mr. Don KAVERMAN
18 Director of Physical Plant — Mr. Paul KENNON
30 Dir Development & Alumni Affairs — Vacant
88 Director of Business Services — Ms. Barbara A. MORROW
09 Director of Institutional Research — Vacant
36 Director of Career Services — Mrs. Wanda MCNEIL
21 Comptroller/Grants Officer — Mrs. Andrea DAVIS
38 Coord Student Counseling/Wellness — Vacant
53 Dean College of Education — Dr. LaTisha T. SMITH
50 Dean Busch School of Business — Ms. Fatemeh ZAKERY
32 Dean Student Affairs — Mr. Charles H. GOODEN
88 Chair Urban Specializations — Vacant
49 Dean College of Arts & Sciences — Dr. Lateef ADELANI

Heartland Christian College (G)

500 New Creation Rd, Newark MO 63458
County: Knox — Identification: 667091
Telephone: (660) 284-4800 — Carnegie Class: Not Classified
FAX Number: (680) 284-4098 — Calendar System: Semester
URL: www.heartlandcollege.org
Established: 1992 — Annual Undergrad Tuition & Fees: N/A
Enrollment: N/A — Coed
Affiliation or Control: Non-denominational — IRS Status: 501(c)3
Highest Offering: Associate Degree
Program: Religious Emphasis
Accreditation: @BI

01 President — Kris R. PALMER
05 Chief Academic Officer — Martha PALMER
10 CFO — David BARTON
06 Registrar — Heather TORO

Heritage College (H)

1200 E 104th Street, Suite 300, Kansas City MO 64131-4557
County: Jackson — Identification: 666155
Unit ID: 445814
Telephone: (816) 942-5474 — Carnegie Class: Assoc/PrivFP
FAX Number: (816) 942-5405 — Calendar System: Other
URL: www.heritage-education.com
Established: 2002 — Annual Undergrad Tuition & Fees: $23,388
Enrollment: 796 — Coed
Affiliation or Control: Proprietary — IRS Status: Proprietary
Highest Offering: Associate Degree
Program: Occupational
Accreditation: ABHES

01 Director — Mr. Larry CARTMILL

† Branch campus of Heritage College, Denver, CO.

Hickey College (I)

940 W Port Plaza, Suite 101, Saint Louis MO 63146-3127
County: Saint Louis — FICE Identification: 010279
Unit ID: 177579
Telephone: (314) 434-2212 — Carnegie Class: Bac/Assoc
FAX Number: (314) 434-1974 — Calendar System: Other
URL: www.hickeycollege.edu
Established: 1933 — Annual Undergrad Tuition & Fees: $13,560
Enrollment: 393 — Coed
Affiliation or Control: Proprietary — IRS Status: Proprietary
Highest Offering: Baccalaureate
Program: Business Emphasis
Accreditation: ACICS, ACFEI

01 President — Mr. Christopher A. GEARIN
11 Director of Operations — Mr. Patrick M. GLYNN
05 Director of Education — Ms. Connie L. SCOTT
32 Director of Student Services — Ms. Deanna L. PECORONI
07 Director of Admissions — Mr. Bill E. LEWIS

IHM Academy of EMS (J)

2500 Abbott Place, Saint Louis MO 63143
County: Saint Louis — Identification: 667021
Telephone: (314) 768-1234 — Carnegie Class: Not Classified
FAX Number: (314) 768-1595 — Calendar System: Other
URL: www.ihmacademyofems.net
Established: N/A — Annual Undergrad Tuition & Fees: N/A
Enrollment: N/A — Coed
Affiliation or Control: Proprietary — IRS Status: Proprietary
Highest Offering: Associate Degree
Program: Occupational
Accreditation: EMT

01 Chief Administrator — Vacant
05 Dean — Charlene CORLEY

ITT Technical Institute (K)

1930 Meyer Drury Drive, Arnold MO 63010-6004
County: Jefferson — Identification: 666033
Unit ID: 434548
Telephone: (636) 464-6600 — Carnegie Class: Spec/Tech
FAX Number: (636) 464-6611 — Calendar System: Quarter
URL: www.itt-tech.edu
Established: 1997 — Annual Undergrad Tuition & Fees: N/A

Enrollment: 638 Coed
Affiliation or Control: Proprietary IRS Status: Proprietary
Highest Offering: Baccalaureate
Program: Technical Emphasis
Accreditation: ACICS

† Branch campus of ITT Technical Institute, Indianapolis, IN.

ITT Technical Institute (A)

3640 Corporate Trail Drive, Earth City MO 63045-1122
County: St. Louis FICE Identification: 007557
Unit ID: 176637
Telephone: (314) 298-7800 Carnegie Class: Spec/Tech
FAX Number: (314) 298-0559 Calendar System: Quarter
URL: www.itt-tech.edu
Established: 1936 Annual Undergrad Tuition & Fees: N/A
Enrollment: 889 Coed
Affiliation or Control: Proprietary IRS Status: Proprietary
Highest Offering: Baccalaureate
Program: Technical Emphasis
Accreditation: ACICS

† Branch campus of ITT Technical Institute, Indianapolis, IN.

ITT Technical Institute (B)

9150 East 41st Terrace, Kansas City MO 64133-1448
County: Jackson Identification: 666380
Unit ID: 446899
Telephone: (816) 276-1400 Carnegie Class: Spec/Tech
FAX Number: N/A Calendar System: Quarter
URL: www.itt-tech.edu
Established: N/A Annual Undergrad Tuition & Fees: N/A
Enrollment: 642 Coed
Affiliation or Control: Proprietary IRS Status: Proprietary
Highest Offering: Baccalaureate
Program: Technical Emphasis
Accreditation: ACICS

† Branch campus of ITT Technical Institute, Indianapolis, IN.

ITT Technical Institute (C)

3216 South National Avenue, Springfield MO 65807
County: Greene Identification: 666702
Unit ID: 456409
Telephone: (417) 877-4800 Carnegie Class: Assoc/PrivFP4
FAX Number: (417) 877-4800 Calendar System: Quarter
URL: www.itt-tech.edu
Established: N/A Annual Undergrad Tuition & Fees: N/A
Enrollment: 259 Coed
Affiliation or Control: Proprietary IRS Status: Proprietary
Highest Offering: Baccalaureate
Program: Technical Emphasis
Accreditation: ACICS

† Branch campus of ITT Technical Institute, Indianapolis, IN.

Jefferson College (D)

1000 Viking Drive, Hillsboro MO 63050-2441
County: Jefferson FICE Identification: 002468
Unit ID: 177676
Telephone: (636) 797-3000 Carnegie Class: Assoc/Pub-S-MC
FAX Number: (636) 789-4012 Calendar System: Semester
URL: www.jeffco.edu
Established: 1963 Annual Undergrad Tuition & Fees (In-District): $2,850
Enrollment: 6,089 Coed
Affiliation or Control: State/Local IRS Status: 501(c)3
Highest Offering: Associate Degree
Program: Occupational; 2-Year Principally Bachelor's Creditable
Accreditation: NH

01 President ... Dr. Raymond V. CUMMISKEY
05 VP Instruction ... Dr. Melinda K. SELSOR
10 VP Finance & Administration ... Dr. Richard T. TURLEY
32 Associate VP Student Services ... Ms. Julie FRASER
49 Dean of Arts & Sciences ... Ms. Shirley DAVENPORT
75 Interim Dean Career/Technical Ed ... Dr. Dena MCCAFFREY
30 Executive Director of Advancement ... Vacant
15 Director of Human Resources ... Ms. Tasha D. WELSH
26 Director of PR & Marketing ... Mr. Roger A. BARRENTINE
09 Director Research & Planning ... Vacant
81 Division Chair Math/Sci/Business ... Ms. Linda ABERNATHY
83 Division Chair Social Sciences ... Ms. Sandy FREY
60 Division Chair Comm/Fine Arts ... Vacant
75 Div Chair Business/Technical Educ ... Dr. Marybeth OTTINGER
35 Director Student Support Services ... Ms. Diane ARNZEN
21 Controller ... Mr. Richard H. HARDIN
41 Director Athletics ... Mr. Doug STOTLER
31 Director Business & Community Devel ... Mr. Bryan D. HERRICK
12 Director Outreach/Educational Sites ... Vacant
08 Director Library Services ... Ms. Lisa C. WOLFE
90 Dir Online Learning/Inst Tech ... Mr. Allan A. WAMSLEY
18 Director Buildings & Grounds ... Mr. Ed TOMASZKIEWICZ
96 Procurement Coordinator ... Ms. Sheree BELL
13 Director Information Technology ... Mr. Tracy JAMES
74 Director Veterinary Technology ... Ms. Dana A. NEVOIS
88 Director Child Care Center ... Ms. Sandra K. BASLER
76 Director Health Occupation Programs ... Mr. Kenny WILSON

06 Director Admissions/Student Records ... Dr. Kim M. HARVEY
37 Director Student Financial Services ... Ms. Sarah BRIGHT
66 Director of Nursing ... Ms. Linda BOEVINGLOH
38 Director Advising & Retention ... Ms. Kathy JOHNSTON
39 Director Residential & Student Life ... Ms. Anna FABATZ

Kansas City Art Institute (E)

4415 Warwick Boulevard, Kansas City MO 64111-1874
County: Jackson FICE Identification: 002473
Unit ID: 177746
Telephone: (816) 472-4852 Carnegie Class: Spec/Arts
FAX Number: (816) 472-3439 Calendar System: Semester
URL: www.kcai.edu
Established: 1885 Annual Undergrad Tuition & Fees: $31,992
Enrollment: 777 Coed
Affiliation or Control: Independent Non-Profit IRS Status: 501(c)3
Highest Offering: Baccalaureate
Program: Fine Arts Emphasis
Accreditation: NH, ART

01 President ... Ms. Jacqueline CHANDA
11 Executive Vice Pres Administration ... Mr. Ronald E. CATTELINO
05 Vice President for Academic Affairs ... Ms. Bambi BURGARD
30 Vice President for Advancement ... Vacant
84 VP Enroll Mgt & Student Achievement ... Mr. Michael GRAVITT
26 Vice President for Communications ... Ms. Anne CANFIELD
13 Vice Pres/Chief Information Officer ... Mr. Larry DICKERSON
20 Associate Academic Officer ... Mr. Milton KATZ
51 Dir Continuing/Professional Studies ... Ms. Tabitha SCHMIDT
06 Registrar ... Ms. Andrea KHAN
15 Director of Human Resources ... Ms. Barbara FINKE
18 Facilities Director/Plant Services ... Mr. Larry STUCKEY
29 Director of Alumni Relations ... Mr. Eric DOBBINS
37 Executive Director of Financial Aid ... Ms. Christal D. WILLIAMS
21 Controller ... Ms. Suzette NAYLOR
36 Director of Career Services ... Ms. Julie METZLER
08 Director of Library ... Ms. M. J. POEHLER
39 Dir Residence Life/Campus Activity ... Ms. Gina GOLBA
24 Director of Media Center ... Mr. Aldo BACCHETTA
19 Director of Safety & Security ... Mr. Robert BAYLESS
40 Director of Auxiliary Services ... Mr. Ed RODRIGUEZ
88 Director of Block Artspace Gallery ... Ms. Raechell SMITH
104 Study Abroad Coordinator ... Ms. Emily BRATTIN
04 Exec Admin Asst to the President ... Ms. Susan KLEIN

Kansas City University of Medicine & Biosciences (F)

1750 East Independence Avenue, Kansas City MO 64119
County: Jackson FICE Identification: 002474
Unit ID: 179812
Telephone: (816) 654-7000 Carnegie Class: Spec/Med
FAX Number: (816) 654-7101 Calendar System: Semester
URL: www.kcumb.edu
Established: 1916 Annual Graduate Tuition & Fees: $42,039
Enrollment: 1,033 Coed
Affiliation or Control: Independent Non-Profit IRS Status: 501(c)3
Highest Offering: First Professional Degree; No Undergraduates
Program: Professional
Accreditation: NH, OSTEO

01 President & CEO ... Dr. H. Danny WEAVER
05 Exec VP Acad & Med Affairs/Dean COM ... Dr. Marc B. HAHN
10 Chief Financial Officer ... Mr. Joseph MASSMAN
30 Vice Pres for Advancement ... Ms. Beth DOLLASE
10 Vice President Finance & Admin ... Mr. James E. PARK
43 Interim EVP Adm & Legal Affairs ... Mr. Nelson T. MANN
20 Assoc Dean for Clin Educ & Med Affs ... Dr. John DOUGHERTY
20 Assoc Dean for Curriculum Affairs ... Ms. Linda ADKISON
32 Assoc Dean for Student Affairs ... Dr. Maurice OELKLAUS
35 Asst Dean for Student Affairs ... Ms. LeAnn K. CARLTON
88 Exec Director University Events ... Ms. Nancy A. JONES
26 Vice Pres Marketing/Univ Relations ... Ms. Natalie LUTZ
08 Director of Libraries ... Miss Marilyn J. DEGEUS
15 Vice Pres Human Resources ... Ms. Dawn M. ROHRS
18 Director Physical Facilities ... Mr. Walter W. SNYDER
96 Director of Purchasing ... Ms. Carrie L. SIMSHEUSER
88 Director Clinical Research ... Dr. Patrick G. CLAY
27 Chief Information Officer ... Ms. Rebecca G. TALKEN
37 Director of Financial Aid ... Ms. Sharon S. HERMAN
30 Director of Development ... Ms. Christine A. WAHLERT
84 VP Enrollment & Registrar ... Ms. Heidi TERRY
88 Adm Dir Community Clin Educ ... Ms. Valorie L. MILLICAN
19 Director Security ... Mr. Freddy D. POINDEXTER
28 Director Learning Enhancement ... Mr. Stan VIEBROCK
44 Dir Alumni & Major Gift Development ... Mr. Ted P. PLACE
35 Exec Dir Comm of Student Affairs ... Ms. Sara E. SELKIRK
76 Dean of College of Biosciences ... Dr. Douglas R. RUSHING
63 Assoc Dean Basic Medical Sciences ... Dr. Alan G. GLAROS
20 Asst Dean Curricular Affairs ... Dr. Gary O. BALLAM
76 Assoc Dean College of Biosciences ... Dr. Robert E. STEPHENS
24 Instructional Tech Media Technician ... Mr. Wade W. GLOSSER
04 Assistant to the President ... Mr. Brian T. REESE
07 Director Admissions ... Ms. Patricia HARPER
36 Coordinator Placement ... Ms. Allison O. MOORE

Kenrick-Glennon Seminary-Kenrick School of Theology (G)

5200 Glennon Drive, Saint Louis MO 63119-4399
County: Saint Louis FICE Identification: 002476
Unit ID: 177816
Telephone: (314) 792-6100 Carnegie Class: Spec/Faith
FAX Number: (314) 768-1755 Calendar System: Semester
URL: www.kenrick.edu
Established: 1893 Annual Undergrad Tuition & Fees: $21,963
Enrollment: 112 Male
Affiliation or Control: Roman Catholic IRS Status: 501(c)3
Highest Offering: Master's
Program: Professional; Religious Emphasis
Accreditation: NH, THEOL

01 President/Rector ... Rev. John P. HORN, SJ
42 Dir Pre-Theology/Vice Rector ... Msgr. Gregory MIKESCH
05 Academic Dean ... Dr. John GRESHAM
32 Dean of Students ... Rev. Paul ROTHSCHILD
08 Director of Library ... Ms. Mary Ann AUBIN
88 Director of Spiritual Formation ... Rev. Peter RYAN, SJ
88 Director of Worship ... Rev. James SWIFT, CM
30 Director of Development ... Ms. Kate GUYOL
06 Registrar/Financial Aid ... Deacon Joseph MEIERGERD
18 Chief Facilities/Physical Plant ... Mr. Tracy LATO

L'Ecole Culinaire (H)

9811 South Outer Forty Drive, Saint Louis MO 63124
Identification: 666275
Unit ID: 445726
Telephone: (314) 587-2433 Carnegie Class: Assoc/PrivFP
FAX Number: (314) 587-2430 Calendar System: Semester
URL: www.lecoleculinaire.com
Established: 2004 Annual Undergrad Tuition & Fees: $13,782
Enrollment: 477 Coed
Affiliation or Control: Proprietary IRS Status: Proprietary
Highest Offering: Associate Degree
Program: Occupational
Accreditation: ACCSC, ACFEI

01 President ... Ms. Pamela BELL
05 Director ... Ms. Jane MCNAMEE

† Branch campus of Vatterott College, Des Moines, IA.

Lincoln University (I)

820 Chestnut Street, Jefferson City MO 65101-3537
County: Cole FICE Identification: 002479
Unit ID: 177940
Telephone: (573) 681-5000 Carnegie Class: Master's S
FAX Number: (573) 681-5566 Calendar System: Semester
URL: www.lincolnu.edu
Established: 1866 Annual Undergrad Tuition & Fees (In-State): $6,725
Enrollment: 3,388 Coed
Affiliation or Control: State IRS Status: 501(c)3
Highest Offering: Beyond Master's But Less Than Doctorate
Program: 2-Year Principally Bachelor's Creditable; Liberal Arts And General; Teacher Preparatory; Professional; Music Emphasis
Accreditation: NH, ACBSP, ADNUR, MUS, NUR, SURGT, TED

01 President ... Dr. Carolyn R. MAHONEY
05 Interim VP Academic Affairs/Provost ... Dr. Ann HARRIS
32 Vice President Student Affairs ... Mrs. Theressa FERGUSON
30 VP University Advancement ... Mrs. Benecia R. WILLIAMS
10 Vice President Administration ... Mr. Curtis CREAGH
83 Dean Col Behavioral\Technical Sci ... Dr. Ruthie STURDEVANT
107 Dean Col of Professional Studies ... Dr. Linda S. BICKEL
49 Interim Dean College of Art/Letters ... Dr. Ruthie STURDEVANT
47 Dean College of Ag/Natural Sciences ... Dr. Steven MEREDITH
08 University Librarian ... Mr. Jerome OFFORD, JR.
21 Controller ... Mrs. Sandy KOETTING
51 Director Continuing Education ... Ms. Kathy PABST
15 Director Human Resources ... Mr. James MARCANTONIO
88 Director Design and Construction ... Mrs. Sheila GASSNER
19 Director Police Department ... Mr. Bill NELSON
41 Director of Athletics ... Mrs. Betty KEMNA
29 Director Alumni Affairs ... Mrs. Benecia WILLIAMS
26 Director Public Info/Univ Relations ... Ms. Misty YOUNG
06 Director of Records/Registrar ... Ms. Liz MORROW
38 Director Counseling/Career Services ... Dr. Cheryl AVANT
07 Director of Admissions ... Ms. Annette CROWDER
09 Director Ctr Assess/Inst Rsrch ... Mrs. Beth NOLTE
23 Director Student Health Services ... Mrs. Latoya DUCKWORTH
35 Director of Student Activities ... Ms. Tammy NOBLES
43 Director Legal Svcs/Genl Counsel ... Mr. Kent BROWN
37 Dir Financial Aid/Stdnt Employment ... Mr. Alfred L. ROBINSON
96 Director of Purchasing ... Ms. Debra KIDWELL
18 Director of Buildings and Grounds ... Mr. Mark FRIEDMAN
13 Chief Information Officer ... Mrs. Ruth CAMPBELL
39 Director of Student Housing ... Mr. Carlos GRAHAM
12 Director Fort Leonard Wood Site ... Mrs. Barbara LANE
86 Director of Government Relations ... Mr. Ken FERGUSON
24 Director of Innovative Instruction ... Dr. Rachel SALE
40 Manager LU Bookstore ... Mr. James HOWARD
101 Exec Asst to President & Curators ... Ms. Rose Ann ORTMEYER
85 International Student Advisor ... Mrs. Mary BEZA
105 Web Content Manager ... Ms. Cherryl JONES

Lindenwood University (J)

209 S Kingshighway, Saint Charles MO 63301-1695
County: Saint Charles FICE Identification: 002480
Unit ID: 177968
Telephone: (636) 949-2000 Carnegie Class: Master's L
FAX Number: (636) 949-4910 Calendar System: Semester
URL: www.lindenwood.edu
Established: 1827 Annual Undergrad Tuition & Fees: $14,670

Enrollment: 17,850 Coed
Affiliation or Control: Independent Non-Profit IRS Status: 501(c)3
Highest Offering: Doctorate
Program: Liberal Arts And General; Teacher Preparatory; Professional
Accreditation: NH, ACBSP, SW, @TEAC

01 President Dr. James D. EVANS
04 Executive Assistant Ms. Judy SHANAHAN
05 Provost & Vice Pres Acad Affairs Dr. Jann RUDD WEITZEL
11 Vice Pres Operations/Finance & COO Ms. Julie MUELLER
30 Vice Pres Institutional Advancement Dr. Lucy S. MORROS
32 Vice President Student Development Dr. John OLDANI
16 Vice Pres Human Res/Dean Faculty Dr. Richard A. BOYLE
09 Dean of Institutional Research Dr. Jeannie THIES
06 Registrar Ms. Christine HANNAR
10 Chief Financial Officer Mr. David KANDEL
29 Director Alumni Relations Ms. Elizabeth KING
26 Dir Communications/Public Relations Mr. Scott QUEEN
31 Director Community Development Ms. Charlsie FLOYD
13 Director of Information Services Mr. Shawn HAGHIGHI
08 Director of Library Services Ms. Elizabeth MACDONALD
37 Director of Financial Aid Ms. Lori BODE
35 Director of Student Activites Ms. Angela ROYAL
39 Director of Residential Operations Mr. Terry RUSSELL
39 Director of Residential Life Ms. Michelle GIESSMAN
92 Director of Honors Program Dr. Michael WHALEY
44 Dir Planned Giving/Internal Counsel Mr. Eric STUHLER
102 Dir Corporate/Foundation Relations Vacant
86 Dir of Outreach & Govt Relations Vacant
85 Director International Programs Dr. Ryan GUFFEY
40 Director of Auxiliary Services Mr. David DICKHERBER
22 Director of Compliance Ms. Christine REBORI
84 Dean of Enrollment Management Ms. Christie RODGERS
07 Dean of Undergraduate Admissions Dr. Joseph PARISI
89 Dean First Year Programs Dr. Shane WILLIAMSON
51 Dean Distance Learning Dr. Ed PERANTONI
12 Dean of Boone Campus Dr. David KNOTTS
20 Dean of Academic Services Mr. Barry FINNEGAN
55 Dean Evening/Ext Campus Admissions Mr. Brett BARGER
36 Director of Student Placement Ms. Dana WEHRLI
41 Athletic Director Mr. John CREER
42 Chaplain Dr. Michael MASON
15 Personnel Officer Ms. Joyce TOWNSEND
79 School Dean Humanities Dr. Michael WHALEY
81 School Dean Sciences Dr. Ricardo DELGADO
53 School Dean Education Dr. Cynthia BICE
57 School Dean Arts Mr. Joe ALSOBROOK
50 Sch Dean Business/Entrepreneurship Dr. Roger ELLIS
60 School Dean Communications Mr. Mike WALL
88 School Dean Human Services Dr. Carla MUELLER
51 School Dean LCIE(Adult Learning) Mr. Dan KEMPER

Linn State Technical College (A)

One Technology Drive, Linn MO 65051-0479
County: Osage FICE Identification: 004711
Unit ID: 177977
Telephone: (573) 897-5000 Carnegie Class: Assoc/Pub-R-S
FAX Number: (573) 897-4656 Calendar System: Semester
URL: www.linnstate.edu
Established: 1961 Annual Undergrad Tuition & Fees (In-State): $4,584
Enrollment: 1,168 Coed
Affiliation or Control: State IRS Status: 501(c)3
Highest Offering: Associate Degree
Program: Occupational; 2-Year Principally Bachelor's Creditable
Accreditation: NH, ENGT, NAIT, PTAA

01 President Dr. Donald M. CLAYCOMB
05 Dean Academic Affairs/Student Svcs Victoria SCHWINKE
13 Dean Information Technology Don LLOYD
09 Dean Institutional Research/Plng Dr. Rick MIHALEVICH
30 Actg Executive Director Development Scott PETERS
08 Int College Librarian Fran STUMPF
37 Director Student Financial Aid Becky WHITHAUS
06 Registrar Elaine BRANDT
07 Director Admissions/Enroll Mgmt Kathy SCHEULEN
11 Dir of Administrative Services Jeff FLETCHER
20 Associate Academic Officer Janet CLANTON
21 Director of Business Affairs Kim STALEY
29 Dir Alumni Relations/Chief PR Ofcr Scott PETERS
35 Director Student Affairs Richard PEMBERTON
36 Director Student Placement Glenda WHITNEY
28 Director of Diversity Richard PEMBERTON
18 Chief Facilities/Physical Plant Dennis SALLIN
38 Student Counselor Ronda THOMPSON

Logan College of Chiropractic (B)

1851 Schoettler Road, PO Box 1065,
Chesterfield MO 63006-1065
County: Saint Louis FICE Identification: 004703
Unit ID: 177986
Telephone: (636) 227-2100 Carnegie Class: Spec/Health
FAX Number: (636) 207-2424 Calendar System: Trimester
URL: www.logan.edu
Established: 1935 Annual Undergrad Tuition & Fees: $6,690
Enrollment: 997 Coed
Affiliation or Control: Independent Non-Profit IRS Status: 501(c)3
Highest Offering: First Professional Degree
Program: Professional
Accreditation: NH, CHIRO

01 President Dr. George A. GOODMAN
05 VP Academic Affairs Dr. Carl W. SAUBERT, IV
10 Chief Financial Officer Ms. Pat MARCELLA
11 VP Administrative Affairs Ms. Sharon K. KEHRER
84 VP Enrollment Management Dr. Boyd BRADSHAW
30 VP Institutional Advancement Ms. Patricia C. JONES
17 VP Chiropractic Affairs/PostGrad Ed Dr. Ralph BARALLE
43 General Counsel Ms. Laura MCLAUGHLIN
27 Chief Information Officer Dr. Bradley HOUGH
26 Associate VP Public Relations Mr. Thomas KELLER
20 Associate VP Academic Affairs Dr. Angela R. MCCALL
23 Chief of Clinical Services Dr. Michael WITTMER
24 Associate VP for Educational Tech Mr. Vince MCGEE
49 Dean University Programs Dr. Elizabeth A. GOODMAN
46 Dean of Research and Development Dr. Rodger E. TEPE
32 Dean of Student Services Mr. James PAINE
88 Director of Assessment Center Dr. Martha KAESER
106 Associate Dean Educational Tech Dr. Nicholas FARHA
07 Director of Admissions Mr. Steve HELD
06 Registrar Mr. John-Herbert JAFFRY
37 Director Student Financial Aid Ms. Linda HAMAN
08 Director Learning Resource Center Ms. Chabha TEPE
15 Director of Human Resources Mr. Les LEXOW
13 Director Information Systems Ms. Ginger JACKSON
96 Director of Purchasing Mr. Charles FELTMANN
18 Physical Plant Superintendent Mr. Bill WHARTON
29 Executive Alumni Director Dr. Kimberly HARTMANN
28 Multicultural Advisor Mr. James PAINE

Maryville University of Saint Louis (C)

650 Maryville University Drive,
Saint Louis MO 63141-7299
County: Saint Louis FICE Identification: 002482
Unit ID: 178059
Telephone: (314) 529-9300 Carnegie Class: DRU
FAX Number: (314) 542-9085 Calendar System: Semester
URL: www.maryville.edu
Established: 1872 Annual Undergrad Tuition & Fees: $22,786
Enrollment: 3,846 Coed
Affiliation or Control: Independent Non-Profit IRS Status: 501(c)3
Highest Offering: Doctorate
Program: Liberal Arts And General; Teacher Preparatory; Professional
Accreditation: NH, ACBSP, ART, CIDA, CORE, MUS, NURSE, OT, PTA, TED

01 President Dr. Mark LOMBARDI
05 Vice Pres Academic Affairs Dr. Mary Ellen FINCH
45 Exec Dir of Planning/Research/Tech Mr. Jerry BRISSON
10 Vice Pres Administration & Finance Dr. Larry HAYS
84 Vice President Enrollment Mr. Jeffrey MILLER
30 VP Inst Advancemnt & Chief Dev Ofcr Mr. Thomas ESCHEN
32 VP for Student Life & Dn of Stdnts Dr. Nina CALDWELL
107 VP for Adult & Online Education Dr. Donna PAYNE
20 Associate VP Academic Affairs Dr. Tammy GOCIAL
100 Chief of Staff Ms. Kathy LUNAN
50 Dean School of Business Dr. Pamela HORWITZ
53 Dean School of Education Dr. Sam HAUSFATHER
76 Dean School Health Professions Dr. Charles GULAS
49 Dean College of Arts & Sciences Dr. Candace CHAMBERS
08 Dean University Library Dr. Eugenia MCKEE
06 Exec Dir Student Svcs Ctr/Registrar Ms. Stephanie ELFRINK
88 Assoc Dir Acad Success & FYE Ms. Kelly MOCK
07 Assoc VP Enrollment Ms. Shani LENORE-JENKINS
29 Director of Alumni Affairs Ms. Erin VERRY
41 Director of Athletics Mr. Marcus MANNING
42 Dir Campus Ministry & Comm Service Mr. Stephen DISALVO
35 Assoc Dean of Students Ms. Kathy QUINN
36 Director Career Education Ms. Lynn WILLITS
35 Director Student Involvement Mr. Brian GARDNER
21 Controller/Dir Finance & Aux Entrpr Mr. Steven MANDEVILLE
102 Director of Development Ms. Megan OVER
37 Dir Student Svcs Ctr/Financial Aid Ms. Martha HARBAUGH
23 Director of Health & Wellness Ms. Pamela CULLITON
15 Dir HR/Affirm Action Officer Ms. Jackie PLUNKETT
14 Director Technology Services Mr. Richard KUBB
91 Dir Enterprise Information Systems Mr. David SCHULTE
09 Director Institutional Research Ms. Mary MERRIFIELD
90 Dir Learning Design & Technology Ms. Julie BERGFELD
26 Exec Dir Marketing & Community Rel Ms. Susan DAVIS
28 Asst Dean & Dir Multicultural Pgm Ms. Christie CRUISE-HARPER
18 Director of Physical Plant Mr. Tom BENNING
44 Director of Planned Gifts Mr. Mark ROOCK
102 Dir Foundation/Corp Relations Ms. Peggy MICHELSON
19 Director of Public Safety Mr. Michael PARKINSON
39 Director of Residential Life Ms. Kimberly WATSON
88 Assoc VP/Dir Acad Success & FYE Dr. Jennifer MCCLUSKEY
104 Assoc VP/Dir Ctr for Global Educ Dr. James HARF
44 Exec Dir Advancement Services Ms. Beth ALBES
88 Asst Athletic Dir-Communications Mr. Charles YAHNG
53 Asst Dean & Dir Teacher Education Dr. Nancy WILLIAMS
21 Dir Student Svcs Ctr/Student Accts Ms. Karen SCHOLBE
88 Director Fresh Ideas Food Services Ms. Linda THACKER
38 Director Personal Counseling Ms. Jennifer HENRY
44 Director of Development Ms. Fay FETICK
105 Mgr Interactive Media Group Ms. Ronnie GAUBATZ
88 Assoc VP Ctr for Civic Engage & Dem Dr. Alden CRADDOCK

Messenger College (D)

300 E 50th Street, Joplin MO 64804-4909
County: Newton FICE Identification: 030926
Unit ID: 417752
Telephone: (417) 624-7070 Carnegie Class: Spec/Faith
FAX Number: (417) 624-5070 Calendar System: Semester
URL: www.messengercollege.edu
Established: 1987 Annual Undergrad Tuition & Fees: $8,390
Enrollment: 60 Coed
Affiliation or Control: Pentecostal Church of God IRS Status: 501(c)3
Highest Offering: Baccalaureate
Program: Liberal Arts And General; Religious Emphasis
Accreditation: TRACS

01 President Dr. Daniel P. DAVIS
05 Vice President Academic Affairs Dr. Vernell INGLE
10 Vice President Business Affairs Ms. Angela HEPPNER
32 Vice President of Student Life Ms. Rhonda DAVIS
07 Dir of Admissions/Recruitment Coord Ms. Kayli PRICE
08 Director of Library Services Ms. Pam INGLE
06 Registrar Mr. Jose MARTINEZ

Metro Business College (E)

1732 N Kingshighway, Cape Girardeau MO 63701-2122
County: Cape FICE Identification: 021802
Unit ID: 178110
Telephone: (573) 334-9181 Carnegie Class: Assoc/PrivFP
FAX Number: (573) 334-0617 Calendar System: Quarter
URL: www.metrobusinesscollege.edu
Established: 1981 Annual Undergrad Tuition & Fees: $10,000
Enrollment: 168 Coed
Affiliation or Control: Proprietary IRS Status: Proprietary
Highest Offering: Associate Degree
Program: Occupational; 2-Year Principally Bachelor's Creditable; Business Emphasis
Accreditation: ACICS

01 President Ms. Mary BUCKLEY
12 Campus Director Mrs. Jan REIMANN
05 Education Director Mr. Shannon BUFORD
37 Financial Aid Director Mrs. Janie WARNE
36 Career Services Coordinator Ms. Diane JORDAN

Metro Business College (F)

210 El Mercado Plaza, Jefferson City MO 65109
County: Cole Identification: 666454
Unit ID: 245430
Telephone: (573) 635-6600 Carnegie Class: Not Classified
FAX Number: (573) 635-6999 Calendar System: Quarter
URL: www.metrobusinesscollege.edu
Established: 1979 Annual Undergrad Tuition & Fees: $9,875
Enrollment: 231 Coed
Affiliation or Control: Proprietary IRS Status: Proprietary
Highest Offering: Associate Degree
Program: Occupational
Accreditation: ACICS

01 Director Mrs. Cheri CHOCKLEY
36 Career Services Coordinator Mr. Daniel NICHOLS
14 IT Coordinator Mr. Randy CHOCKLEY

† Branch campus of Metro Business College, Cape Girardeau, MO.

Metro Business College (G)

1202 E Highway 72, Rolla MO 65401-3938
County: Phelps Identification: 666455
Unit ID: 245421
Telephone: (573) 364-8464 Carnegie Class: Not Classified
FAX Number: (573) 364-8077 Calendar System: Quarter
URL: www.metrobusinesscollege.edu
Established: 1984 Annual Undergrad Tuition & Fees: $9,875
Enrollment: 91 Coed
Affiliation or Control: Proprietary IRS Status: Proprietary
Highest Offering: Associate Degree
Program: Occupational
Accreditation: ACICS

01 Director Ms. Mary GACSEH

† Branch campus of Metro Business College, Cape Girardeau, MO.

*Metropolitan Community College - Kansas City Administrative Center (H)

3200 Broadway, Kansas City MO 64111-2429
County: Jackson FICE Identification: 009137
Unit ID: 178129
Telephone: (816) 604-1000 Carnegie Class: N/A
FAX Number: (816) 759-1158
URL: www.mcckc.edu

01 Chancellor Mr. Mark S. JAMES
101 Chancellor's Asst/Board Secretary Ms. Cindy K. JOHNSON
05 Vice Chanc Acad Affairs/Technology Mr. Paul D. LONG
10 Vice Chanc Admin Svcs/Student Dev Dr. Tuesday L. STANLEY
100 Chief of Staff Ms. Kathy WALTER-MACK
27 Assoc VC College/Cmty Relations Dr. Tom M. VANSAGHI
15 Assoc VC Human Resources Ms. Carolyn R. BASKETT
88 Performance Director Resource Dev Ms. Carolyn S. BROWN
45 Director Budget and Planning Mr. Reinhard WEGLARZ
14 Director Computer Services Mr. Gary W. SCHIEBER
102 Director MCC Foundation Mr. Vincent M. ANCH
96 Director Purchasing Ms. Dorothy A. MILLER
18 Director Physical Facilities Mr. Darrel W. MEYER

103 Exec Dir Workforce Dev/HSI ....Ms. Margaret E. BOYD
88 Director Community Engagement ....Mr. Juan M. RANGEL
88 Director Educational Services ....Ms. Fran A. PADOW
106 Director Distance Education ....Dr. Leo J. HIRNER
88 Director Educ Progams/Employee Dev ....Dr. Rich HIGGASON
09 Director Inst Research/Assessment ....Dr. Kristy A. BISHOP
88 Director of Student Success ....Vacant
37 Director Student Financial Services ....Ms. Dena NORRIS
84 Director of Enrollment Services ....Ms. Kathy M. HALE
21 Director of Accounting ....Mr. Steve FROMMELT
88 Director Adm Sys & Mngment Svcs ....Ms. Patricia A. AMICK
19 Assoc Director Public Safety ....Mr. Domenick R. BROUILLETTE
88 Chief of Campus Police ....Mr. Bill HUDSON
88 Director Tech Prep ....Ms. Teresa A. LONEY
88 Director Business Development ....Mr. Stan D. FIELDS
21 Director Finance & Business Service ....Mr. Mark A. BURNS

*Metropolitan Community College - Blue River (A)

20301 E 78 Highway, Independence MO 64057-2053
County: Jackson FICE Identification: 032613
Unit ID: 440305
Telephone: (816) 604-6550 Carnegie Class: Assoc/Pub-U-MC
FAX Number: (816) 759-6582 Calendar System: Semester
URL: www.mcckc.edu
Established: 1997 Annual Undergrad Tuition & Fees (In-District): $2,580
Enrollment: 3,945 Coed
Affiliation or Control: State/Local IRS Status: 501(c)3
Highest Offering: Associate Degree
Program: Occupational; 2-Year Principally Bachelor's Creditable
Accreditation: &NH

02 President ....Dr. Michael BANKS
04 Assistant to the President ....Mrs. Kimberly A. MORICONI
05 Dean of Instruction ....Dr. Cheryl CARPENTER-DAVIS
32 Dean of Student Development ....Dr. Jonathan L. BURKE
51 Assoc Dean of Instruction ....Mr. Basil M. LISTER
88 Director Western Missouri PSTI ....Mr. Mike W. HENDERSHOT
08 Head Librarian ....Mr. Jared RINCK
35 Assoc Dean of Student Development ....Mrs. Karen GOOS
18 Facilities Superintendent ....Mr. Bob L. SHRAUNER
38 Lead Counselor ....Mr. Jeff WILT
84 Enrollment Manager ....Mr. Rowdy PYLE
13 Campus Network Coordinator ....Mr. Jeffrey M. EUBANK
19 Campus Police Captain ....Mr. Booker S. ARMSTRONG
26 Marketing Coordinator ....Mr. Bob K. FLORENCE

*Metropolitan Community College - Business and Technology (B)

1775 Universal Avenue, Kansas City MO 64120-2429
Identification: 666295
Unit ID: 442000
Telephone: (816) 604-5200 Carnegie Class: Assoc/Pub-U-MC
FAX Number: (816) 482-5256 Calendar System: Semester
URL: www.mcckc.edu/btc
Established: 1995 Annual Undergrad Tuition & Fees (In-District): $2,208
Enrollment: 1,092 Coed
Affiliation or Control: Local IRS Status: 501(c)3
Highest Offering: Associate Degree
Program: Occupational; 2-Year Principally Bachelor's Creditable; Technical Emphasis
Accreditation: &NH

02 President ....Ms. Debbie GOODALL
05 Dean of Instruction ....Dr. Thomas WHEELER
32 Dean of Student Development ....Ms. Karen MOORE
84 Enrollment Manager ....Ms. Rene BENNETT
04 Assistant to the President ....Vacant

*Metropolitan Community College - Longview (C)

500 SW Longview Road, Lee's Summit MO 64081-2105
County: Jackson FICE Identification: 009140
Unit ID: 177995
Telephone: (816) 604-2000 Carnegie Class: Assoc/Pub-U-MC
FAX Number: (816) 672-2025 Calendar System: Semester
URL: www.mcckc.edu
Established: 1969 Annual Undergrad Tuition & Fees (In-District): $2,760
Enrollment: 7,647 Coed
Affiliation or Control: Local IRS Status: 501(c)3
Highest Offering: Associate Degree
Program: Occupational; 2-Year Principally Bachelor's Creditable
Accreditation: &NH

02 President ....Dr. Fred L. GROGAN
05 Dean of Instruction ....Mrs. Nancy L. RUSSELL
32 Dean Student Devel/Support Services ....Vacant
20 Associate Dean Instruction ....Ms. Karen B. DEXTER
35 Assoc Dean Student Dev/Support Svcs ....Dr. Marvin R. AARON
07 Director of Admissions/Registrar ....Mr. David A. FRITZ
37 Manager of Student Financial Aid ....Ms. Lisa L. FANNAN
10 Business Office Supervisor ....Ms. Dianna M. CARPENTER
18 Physical Facilities Superintendent ....Mr. Steve B. GREIFE
36 Coordinator Student Employment Svcs . Ms. Linda S. ANDERSON
38 Director Student Counseling ....Mrs. Gretchen S. BLYTHE

*Metropolitan Community College - Maple Woods (D)

2601 NE Barry Road, Kansas City MO 64156-1299
County: Clay FICE Identification: 009139
Unit ID: 178022
Telephone: (816) 604-3000 Carnegie Class: Assoc/Pub-U-MC
FAX Number: (816) 437-3049 Calendar System: Semester
URL: www.mcckc.edu
Established: 1968 Annual Undergrad Tuition & Fees (In-District): $2,760
Enrollment: 7,186 Coed
Affiliation or Control: Local IRS Status: 501(c)3
Highest Offering: Associate Degree
Program: Occupational; 2-Year Principally Bachelor's Creditable
Accreditation: &NH

02 President ....Dr. Merna S. SALIMAN
05 Dean Instruction ....Dr. Arminda MCCALLUM
32 Dean Student Services ....Ms. Shelli ALLEN
20 Associate Dean ....Mrs. Dawn K. HATTERMAN
20 Associate Dean ....Dr. Brian BECHTEL
08 Librarian ....Mrs. Linda CARTER
41 Athletic Director ....Dr. Brian BECHTEL
37 Manager Student Financial Aid ....Mrs. Robin STIMAC
40 College Bookstore Manager ....Ms. Beth AUSTIN
18 Physical Facilities Superintendent ....Mr. Jeff ALLEN
10 Business Office Supervisor ....Ms. Emily THOMPSON
31 Community Relations Coordinator ....Mrs. Heather K. PEREZ
36 Student Employment Service Coord ....Ms. Mary Lynn MUNGER
38 Lead Counselor ....Ms. Barbara COOKE

*Metropolitan Community College - Penn Valley (E)

3201 Southwest Trafficway, Kansas City MO 64111-2764
County: Jackson FICE Identification: 002484
Unit ID: 178785
Telephone: (816) 604-4000 Carnegie Class: Assoc/Pub-U-MC
FAX Number: (816) 759-4010 Calendar System: Semester
URL: www.mcckc.edu
Established: 1915 Annual Undergrad Tuition & Fees (In-District): $2,610
Enrollment: 5,409 Coed
Affiliation or Control: Local IRS Status: 501(c)3
Highest Offering: Associate Degree
Program: Occupational; 2-Year Principally Bachelor's Creditable; Nursing Emphasis
Accreditation: &NH, ADNUR, DA, OTA, PNUR, PTAA, RAD, SURGT

02 President ....Dr. Joe SEABROOKS
05 Dean of Instruction ....Dr. Al DIMMITT
32 Dean of Student Services ....Dr. Elizabeth MINIS
35 Associate Dean of Student Services ....Mrs. Mindy JOHNSON
23 Director of Health Sciences ....Ms. Sandy MCILNAY
06 Registrar/Director of Admissions ....Mr. Carlton FOWLER
14 NUS Department Dir ....Ms. Marsha LERENBERG
18 Maintenance Supervisor ....Vacant
19 Campus Police Captain ....Cpt. Gary WILSON
41 Athletic Programs Manager ....Mr. Marcus HARVEY
37 Student Financial Aid Manager ....Ms. Rossann DOWNING
40 College Bookstore Manager ....Ms. Selin GAONA
10 Business Office Supervisor ....Ms. Michele ALLEN
08 Librarian ....Ms. Gloria MAXWELL
27 Community & Public Relations Coord ....Ms. Kimberly RILEY
36 Career Coordinator ....Ms. Melanie BOWMAN

Midwest Institute (F)

964 S. Highway Drive, Fenton MO 63026
County: St. Louis FICE Identification: 021211
Unit ID: 178183
Telephone: (314) 965-8363 Carnegie Class: Assoc/PrivFP
FAX Number: (636) 326-1059 Calendar System: Other
URL: www.midwestinstitute.com
Established: 1965 Annual Undergrad Tuition & Fees: $14,680
Enrollment: 226 Coed
Affiliation or Control: Proprietary IRS Status: Proprietary
Highest Offering: Associate Degree
Program: Occupational
Accreditation: ABHES

01 Director ....Dr. Adam EPSTEIN

Midwest Institute-Earth City (G)

4260 Shoreline Drive Suite 100, Earth City MO 63045
County: Saint Louis Identification: 667074
Telephone: (314) 344-4440 Carnegie Class: Not Classified
FAX Number: (314) 344-0495 Calendar System: Other
URL: www.midwestinstitute.com
Established: 1970 Annual Undergrad Tuition & Fees: N/A
Enrollment: N/A Coed
Affiliation or Control: Proprietary IRS Status: Proprietary
Highest Offering: Associate Degree
Program: Occupational
Accreditation: ABHES

01 President ....Ms. Christine SHREFFLER

Midwestern Baptist Theological Seminary (H)

5001 N Oak Trafficway, Kansas City MO 64118-4697
County: Clay FICE Identification: 002485
Unit ID: 178208
Telephone: (816) 414-3700 Carnegie Class: Spec/Faith
FAX Number: (816) 414-3724 Calendar System: Semester
URL: www.mbts.edu
Established: 1957 Annual Undergrad Tuition & Fees: $6,680
Enrollment: 1,177 Coed
Affiliation or Control: Southern Baptist IRS Status: 501(c)3
Highest Offering: Doctorate
Program: Professional; Religious Emphasis
Accreditation: NH, THEOL

01 Interim President ....Dr. Robin HADAWAY
10 Vice President for Business Svcs ....Vacant
05 VP Academic Dev & Academic Dean ....Dr. Jerry SUTTON
09 Vice President Inst Effectiveness ....Dr. Rodney A. HARRISON
32 Vice President Student Development ....Dr. David M. MCALPIN
30 VP of Institutional Advancement ....Vacant
13 Vice President Info Technology ....Mr. Terry JOHNSON
06 Registrar ....Dr. Mike HAWKINS
08 Librarian ....Dr. Craig KUBIC
73 Director of Doctoral Studies ....Dr. Rodney A. HARRISON
21 Director Financial Services ....Mrs. Cheryl HICKS
15 Human Resources ....Mr. Gary CRUTCHER
04 Exec Assistant to the President ....Mrs. Rhonda NICHOLS
18 Director of Campus Operations ....Mr. Larry HEADLEY
37 Financial Aid Director ....Mrs. Raschelle JOHNSTON
84 Dir Student Recruitment & Admission ....Vacant
20 Associate Dean ....Dr. Rustin UMSTATTD
26 Director Communications/Public Rels ....Mr. Pat HUDSON

Mineral Area College (I)

5270 Flat River Drive, Park Hills MO 63601-2224
County: Saint Francois FICE Identification: 002486
Unit ID: 178217
Telephone: (573) 431-4593 Carnegie Class: Assoc/Pub-R-M
FAX Number: (573) 518-2164 Calendar System: Semester
URL: www.mineralarea.edu
Established: 1922 Annual Undergrad Tuition & Fees (In-District): $2,760
Enrollment: 4,065 Coed
Affiliation or Control: Local IRS Status: 501(c)3
Highest Offering: Associate Degree
Program: Occupational; 2-Year Principally Bachelor's Creditable
Accreditation: NH, @PTAA, RAD

01 President ....Dr. Steve KURTZ
03 Vice Pres/Dean Career/Tech Educ ....Mr. John (Gil) KENNON
49 Dean of Arts & Sciences ....Ms. Carolyn CRECELIUS
32 Dean Student Services ....Ms. Jean MERRILL-DOSS
10 Business Manager ....Mr. Rusty STRAUGHAN
13 Director of Computer Services ....Vacant
06 Registrar ....Ms. Linda HUFFMAN
07 Director of Admissions ....Ms. Julie SHEETS
09 Director of Institutional Research ....Ms. Lisa EDBURG
18 Chief Facil/Phys Plnt/Purchasing ....Mr. Rusty STRAUGHAN
26 Chief Public Relations Officer ....Ms. Sarah HAAS
29 Director Alumni Relations ....Ms. Julia DILL
15 Chief Human Resource Officer ....Ms. Kathryn NEFF
37 Director Student Financial Aid ....Ms. Denise SEBASTIAN
38 Director Student Counseling ....Mr. Michael EASTER
88 General Services Supervisor ....Mr. Tom BOWYER
21 Director Payroll ....Ms. Lisa CLAUSER

Missouri Baptist University (J)

One College Park Drive, Saint Louis MO 63141-8698
County: Saint Louis FICE Identification: 007540
Unit ID: 178244
Telephone: (314) 434-1115 Carnegie Class: Master's L
FAX Number: (314) 434-7596 Calendar System: Semester
URL: www.mobap.edu
Established: 1964 Annual Undergrad Tuition & Fees: $20,764
Enrollment: 5,068 Coed
Affiliation or Control: Baptist IRS Status: 501(c)3
Highest Offering: Doctorate
Program: Liberal Arts And General; Teacher Preparatory
Accreditation: NH, EXSC, MUS, TED

01 President ....Dr. R. Alton LACEY
04 Assistant to the President ....Mrs. Susan RUTLEDGE
05 Senior VP of Academic Affs/Provost ....Dr. Arlen R. DYKSTRA
30 Senior VP of Inst Advancement ....Mr. Keith ROSS
32 Senior VP of Student Development ....Dr. Andy CHAMBERS
10 Senior VP for Business Affairs ....Mr. Ken REVENAUGH
58 VP of Grad Stds/Academic Pgm Review ....Dr. Clark TRIPLETT
84 VP of Enrollment Services ....Mr. Terry Dale CRUSE
29 Director for Alumni Relations ....Ms. Abigail LESLIE
85 Director of International Services ....Mrs. Kari SAUNDERS
09 Director Institutional Research ....Mrs. Heather BRASE
08 Librarian ....Ms. Nitsa HINDELEH
37 Director Financial Services ....Vacant
26 Director University Communications ....Mr. Bryce CHAPMAN
36 Dir Career Svcs/Assoc Dean Students ....Ms. Kimberly GREY
41 Athletic Director ....Dr. Thomas SMITH
20 Associate Academic Dean ....Vacant
18 Director Campus Operations ....Mr. Stu LINDLEY

06 Director of Records ....Mrs. Linda CHRISOPE
15 Director Personnel Services ....Mrs. Barb BURNS
14 Director of Information Systems ....Mr. Chris SANDERS
19 Director Public Safety ....Mr. Stephen HEIDKE
35 Director Student Activities ....Mrs. Lara HINES
21 Associate Business Officer ....Mr. Mike BASLER
30 Director of Development ....Mr. Jon VESTAL
07 Director of Admissions ....Mr. Aaron BLACK

Missouri College (A)

1405 South Hanley Road, Brentwood MO 63144-2902

County: St. Louis FICE Identification: 009795
Unit ID: 178305
Telephone: (314) 768-7800 Carnegie Class: Bac/Assoc
FAX Number: (314) 768-7900 Calendar System: Semester
URL: www.missouricollege.com
Established: 1963 Annual Undergrad Tuition & Fees: $11,100
Enrollment: 934 Coed
Affiliation or Control: Proprietary IRS Status: Proprietary
Highest Offering: Baccalaureate
Program: Occupational; 2-Year Principally Bachelor's Creditable
Accreditation: **ACICS**, DA, DH, MAAB

01 President ....Mr. Karl PETERSEN
05 Dean of Academics ....Mrs. Nicole GRAMLICH
07 Admissions Director ....Ms. Heidi HOLMES
06 Registrar ....Ms. Katie FERRY

Missouri Southern State University (B)

3950 E Newman Road, Joplin MO 64801-1595

County: Jasper FICE Identification: 002488
Unit ID: 178341
Telephone: (417) 625-9300 Carnegie Class: Bac/Diverse
FAX Number: (417) 625-3121 Calendar System: Semester
URL: www.mssu.edu
Established: 1965 Annual Undergrad Tuition & Fees (In-State): $5,271
Enrollment: 5,591 Coed
Affiliation or Control: State IRS Status: 501(c)3
Highest Offering: Master's
Program: Liberal Arts And General; Teacher Preparatory; Professional
Accreditation: **NH**, ACBSP, DH, ENGT, NUR, NURSE, RAD, TED

01 President ....Dr. Bruce SPECK
05 Interim Vice Pres Academic Affairs ....Dr. Pat LIPIRA
32 Vice President for Student Affairs ....Mr. Darren S. FULLERTON
10 Vice President Business Affairs ....Mr. Rob YUST
13 Dir of Information Technology Svcs ....Mr. Albert (Al) STADLER
09 Asst VP Assessment/Inst Research ....Dr. Delores HONEY
20 Int Asst Vice Pres Academic Affairs ....Dr. Crystal LEMMONS
35 Dean of Students ....Dr. Ronald S. MITCHELL
06 Registrar ....Ms. Cheryl DOBSON
84 Director of Admissions ....Mr. Derek S. SKAGGS
92 Director of Honors Program ....Dr. Michael HOWARTH
08 Library Director ....Mrs. Wendy MCGRANE
30 Vice Pres for Development ....Mrs. JoAnn K. GRAFFAM
27 Director Univ Relations & Marketing ....Ms. Cassie M. MATHES
36 Director of Career Services ....Ms. Nicole R. BROWN
29 Director Alumni Association ....Mrs. Lee Eliff POUND
37 Director Student Financial Aid ....Ms. Becca L. DISKIN
38 Director of ACTS ....Mrs. Kelly WILSON
39 Director Student Housing ....Mr. Josh DOAK
21 Treasurer ....Mrs. Linda EIS
15 Director Human Resources ....Ms. Debbie D. KELLEY
18 Director Facilities/Physical Plant ....Mr. Robert HARRINGTON
32 Director of Student Activities ....Ms. Malorie CASHEL
96 Director of Purchasing ....Ms. Hiedi CARLIN
72 Dean School Technology ....Dr. Tia STRAIT
49 Dean School of Arts & Sciences ....Dr. Richard B. MILLER
53 Dean School Education ....Dr. Alfred CADE
50 Dean School of Business Admin ....Dr. John GROESBECK

Missouri State University (C)

901 S National Avenue, Springfield MO 65897-0027

County: Greene FICE Identification: 002503
Unit ID: 179566
Telephone: (417) 836-8500 Carnegie Class: Master's L
FAX Number: (417) 836-7669 Calendar System: Semester
URL: www.missouristate.edu
Established: 1905 Annual Undergrad Tuition & Fees (In-State): $6,793
Enrollment: 20,802 Coed
Affiliation or Control: State IRS Status: 501(c)3
Highest Offering: Doctorate
Program: Liberal Arts And General; Teacher Preparatory; Professional
Accreditation: **NH**, ADNUR, ANEST, ARCPA, AUD, BUS, BUSA, CEA, CONST, CS, DIETD, @DIETI, MUS, NRPA, NURSE, PLNG, PTA, SP, SPAA, SW, TED, THEA

01 President ....Mr. Clifton M. SMART, III
05 Provost ....Dr. Frank E. EINHELLIG
12 Chancellor West Plains Campus ....Dr. Drew A. BENNETT
46 VP for Research/Economic Devel ....Dr. James P. BAKER
11 Vice Pres Administrative/Info Svcs ....Mr. Ken MCCLURE
30 Vice Pres University Advancement ....Mr. W. Brent DUNN
32 VP Student Affairs & Dean of Stdts ....Dr. Earle F. DOMAN
28 Vice Pres Diversity/Inclusion ....Dr. Kenneth COOPWOOD, SR.
20 Associate Provost ....Dr. Christopher J. CRAIG
20 Associate Provost ....Dr. Rachelle DARABI
20 Associate Provost ....Dr. Joye NORRIS
58 Dean of Grad College ....Dr. Pawan KAHOL
10 Chief Financial Officer ....Mr. Steve FOUCART
84 Asst VP Stdnt Affs/Enrollment Svcs ....Mr. Donald E. SIMPSON
08 Dean Library Services ....Mr. Thomas A. PETERS
09 Director of Institutional Research ....Dr. Katherine C. COY
29 Exec Dir of Alumni Relations ....Ms. Julie A. EBERSOLD
15 Director of Human Resources ....Mr. Edward CHOATE
37 Director of Student Financial Aid ....Ms. Vicki S. MATTOCKS
19 Director of Safety & Transportation ....Mr. Donald A. CLARK
36 Director of the Career Center ....Mr. Jack M. HUNTER
14 Director of Computer Services ....Mr. Jeff P. MORRISSEY
22 Equal Opportunity Officer ....Mr. Harold W. PRATT
100 Chief of Staff ....Mr. Paul K. KINCAID
23 Director of Health & Wellness Svcs ....Mr. Burnie L. SNODGRASS
92 Director Honors College ....Dr. John F. CHUCHIAK
18 Director Facilities Management ....Mr. Robert T. ECKELS
96 Director of Procurement ....Mr. Mike WILLS
07 Director of Admissions ....Mr. Andrew WRIGHT
06 Enrollment Services Systems Coord ....Mr. Rob HORNBERGER
49 Dean College Arts & Letters ....Vacant
79 Dean Col Humanities/Public Affairs ....Dr. Victor MATTHEWS
76 Dean Col Health/Human Services ....Dr. Helen C. REID
81 Dean Col Natural/Applied Science ....Dr. Tamera S. JAHNKE
53 Dean College of Education ....Dr. Dennis J. KEAR
50 Dean Col of Business Administration ....Dr. Stephanie BRYANT
51 Asst Provost Extended Campus ....Mr. Stephen H. ROBINETTE
105 Director of Web Services ....Ms. Sara M. CLARK

Missouri State University - West Plains (D)

128 Garfield, West Plains MO 65775-2715

County: Howell FICE Identification: 031060
Unit ID: 179344
Telephone: (417) 255-7255 Carnegie Class: Assoc/Pub2in4
FAX Number: (417) 255-7962 Calendar System: Semester
URL: www.wp.missouristate.edu
Established: 1963 Annual Undergrad Tuition & Fees (In-State): $3,624
Enrollment: 2,142 Coed
Affiliation or Control: State IRS Status: 501(c)3
Highest Offering: Associate Degree
Program: Occupational; 2-Year Principally Bachelor's Creditable
Accreditation: **NH**

05 Chief Academic Officer ....Dr. Chris DYER
32 Dean of Student Services ....Dr. Herbert LUNDAY
10 Director of Business Services ....Vacant
30 Director of Development ....Mrs. Elizabeth GRISHAM
27 Director of Univ Communications ....Mrs. Cheryl CALDWELL
31 Director of Univ/Community Pgms ....Mrs. Brenda MALKOWSKI
14 Director of Computer Services ....Mrs. Sue INGRAM
06 Registrar ....Mrs. Shanna DALE
07 Coordinator of Admissions ....Mrs. Melissa JETT
09 Coord of Institutional Research ....Mrs. Patricia J. WALSH
26 Chief Public Relations Officer ....Mrs. Cheryl CALDWELL
36 Coordinator of Student Placement ....Mrs. Pam TATE
37 Coord of Student Financial Aid ....Mrs. Donna BASSHAM
84 Director Enrollment Management ....Dr. Herbert LUNDAY
18 Chief Facilities/Physical Plant ....Mr. Ron HENSLEY

Missouri Tech (E)

1690 Country Club Plaza Drive, Saint Charles MO 63303

County: Saint Louis FICE Identification: 023040
Unit ID: 178350
Telephone: (636) 573-9300 Carnegie Class: Spec/Tech
FAX Number: (636) 573-9398 Calendar System: Semester
URL: www.motech.edu
Established: 1932 Annual Undergrad Tuition & Fees: $14,330
Enrollment: 129 Coed
Affiliation or Control: Proprietary IRS Status: Proprietary
Highest Offering: Baccalaureate
Program: Technical Emphasis
Accreditation: **ACCSC**

01 President ....Ms. Cynthia DODGE
05 Dean of Education ....Dr. Mark STINSON
37 Director Financial Aid ....Ms. Cindy Ann SINNOTT

Missouri Valley College (F)

500 E College, Marshall MO 65340-3197

County: Saline FICE Identification: 002489
Unit ID: 178369
Telephone: (660) 831-4000 Carnegie Class: Bac/Diverse
FAX Number: (660) 831-4039 Calendar System: Semester
URL: www.moval.edu
Established: 1889 Annual Undergrad Tuition & Fees: $18,080
Enrollment: 1,459 Coed
Affiliation or Control: Presbyterian Church (U.S.A.) IRS Status: 501(c)3
Highest Offering: Master's
Program: Liberal Arts And General; Teacher Preparatory
Accreditation: **NH**

01 President ....Dr. Bonnie HUMPHREY
00 Chancellor Emeritus ....Dr. Earl J. REEVES
10 Chief Financial Officer ....Mr. Greg SILVEY
30 Vice Pres Institutional Advancement ....Mr. Eric SAPPINGTON
05 Chief Academic Officer ....Dr. Sharon WEISER
07 Dean of Admissions ....Ms. Tennille LANGDON
06 Registrar ....Ms. Marsha LASHLEY
21 Business Officer ....Mrs. Tonia BARTEL
08 Head Librarian ....Mrs. Pamela K. REEDER
41 Athletic Director/Dir of Operations ....Mr. Tom FIFER
42 Director Campus Ministry ....Rev. Pam SEBASTIAN
18 Director Maintenance ....Mr. Tim SCHULTE
32 Dean of Students ....Mr. Heath MORGAN
09 Director of Institutional Research ....Ms. Marilyn BELWOOD
15 Dir Personnel Svcs/Dir Purchasing ....Mr. Greg SILVEY
37 Director Student Financial Aid ....Mr. Buddy MAYFIELD
38 Director Student Counseling ....Mrs. Rachel MAYFIELD
13 Director of Systems Administration ....Mr. Jason RINNE
29 Director Alumni Relations ....Mr. Eric SAPPINGTON
26 Dir of Marketing & Media Relations ....Mr. Chad JAECQUES

Missouri Western State University (G)

4525 Downs Drive, Saint Joseph MO 64507-2294

County: Buchanan FICE Identification: 002490
Unit ID: 178387
Telephone: (816) 271-4200 Carnegie Class: Bac/Diverse
FAX Number: N/A Calendar System: Semester
URL: www.missouriwestern.edu
Established: 1915 Annual Undergrad Tuition & Fees (In-State): $5,252
Enrollment: 6,296 Coed
Affiliation or Control: State IRS Status: 501(c)3
Highest Offering: Master's
Program: Liberal Arts And General; Teacher Preparatory
Accreditation: **NH**, BUS, ENGT, MUS, NURSE, PTAA, SW, TED

01 President ....Dr. Robert A. VARTABEDIAN
05 Provost/VP Academic Affairs ....Dr. Jeanne DAFFRON
30 Vice Pres University Advancement ....Dr. Jonathan YORDY
10 Int VP Financial Plng and Admin ....Mr. Rick GILMORE
32 Int Vice Pres for Student Affairs ....Dr. Judy GRIMES
20 Assoc Vice Pres Academic Affairs ....Dr. Cindy HEIDER
21 Assoc VP Financial Plng/Admin ....Mr. Rick GILMORE
35 Dean of Students ....Dr. Judith GRIMES
49 Dean Liberal Arts & Science ....Dr. Murray NABORS
75 Dean Professional Studies ....Vacant
51 Dean of Western Institute ....Dr. Gordon MAPLEY
06 Registrar ....Ms. Susan BRACCIANO
07 Director of Admissions ....Mr. Howard MCCAULEY
08 Director of Library ....Ms. Julia SCHNEIDER
37 Director Student Financial Aid ....Ms. Marilyn BAKER
13 Director of Information Technology ....Mr. Mark MABE
38 Director Student Counsel & Testing ....Mr. H. David BROWN
18 Director Physical Plant ....Mr. Lonnie JOHNSON
41 Director of Athletics ....Mr. Kurt MCGUFFIN
15 Director of Human Resources ....Ms. Sally SANDERS
24 Director of Instructional Media ....Vacant
26 Dir of Public Relations & Marketing ....Vacant
29 Director of Alumni Services ....Ms. Colleen KOWICH
44 Director of Development ....Mr. Jerry PICKMAN
96 Director of Purchasing ....Ms. Carey MCMILLIAN

Moberly Area Community College (H)

101 College Avenue, Moberly MO 65270-1304

County: Randolph FICE Identification: 002491
Unit ID: 178448
Telephone: (660) 263-4110 Carnegie Class: Assoc/Pub-R-M
FAX Number: (660) 263-6252 Calendar System: Semester
URL: www.macc.edu
Established: 1927 Annual Undergrad Tuition & Fees (In-District): $2,640
Enrollment: 5,662 Coed
Affiliation or Control: State/Local IRS Status: 501(c)3
Highest Offering: Associate Degree
Program: Occupational; 2-Year Principally Bachelor's Creditable
Accreditation: **NH**, MLTAD, OTA

01 President ....Dr. Evelyn E. JORGENSON
05 Vice President for Instruction ....Dr. Jeffery LASHLEY
10 Vice President for Finance ....Mr. Gary STEFFES
75 Dean of Career/Technical Educ ....Vacant
32 Dean of Student Services ....Dr. James GRANT
12 Dean Off-Camp Pgms/Instr Tech ....Ms. Michele MCCALL
20 Dean of Academic Affairs ....Ms. Paula GLOVER
09 Director Inst Effectiveness/Plng ....Mrs. Deanne K. FESSLER
21 Director Business/Accounting Svcs ....Ms. Sandra MAREK
26 Dir of Mktg and Public Relations ....Mrs. Jaime MORGANS
18 Director of Plant Operations ....Mr. Eric ROSS
14 Chief Information Officer ....Mr. Lloyd MARCHANT
08 Director of Library Services ....Ms. Valerie DARST
15 Director of Human Resources ....Ms. Ann PARKS
40 Director of Inst Svcs/Bookstore Mgr ....Ms. Virginia GEBHARDT
37 Director of Financial Aid ....Mrs. Amy HAGER
06 Registrar ....Ms. Lynn WALKER
29 Director Alumni Services ....Mr. Scott MCGARVEY
36 Dir of Career and Technical Pgms ....Ms. Susan BROUK
88 Dir of Academic Services ....Ms. Meghan HOLLERAN

Nazarene Theological Seminary (I)

1700 E Meyer Boulevard, Kansas City MO 64131-1263

County: Jackson FICE Identification: 002494
Unit ID: 178518
Telephone: (816) 268-5400 Carnegie Class: Spec/Faith
FAX Number: (816) 268-5500 Calendar System: Semester
URL: www.nts.edu
Established: 1945 Annual Graduate Tuition & Fees: $8,020
Enrollment: 265 Coed
Affiliation or Control: Church Of The Nazarene IRS Status: 501(c)3
Highest Offering: Doctorate; No Undergraduates

Program: Professional
Accreditation: THEOL

01	President	Dr. David BUSIC
05	Dean of the Faculty	Dr. Roger HAHN
11	Dean for Administration	Dr. D. Martin BUTLER
08	Director Library Service	Mrs. Debra BRADSHAW
06	Registrar & Director of Admissions	Mrs. Pamela ASHER
37	Financial Aid Coordinator	Mr. Derek DAVIS

North Central Missouri College (A)

1301 Main Street, Trenton MO 64683-1824
County: Grundy — FICE Identification: 002514
Unit ID: 179715
Telephone: (660) 359-3948 — Carnegie Class: Assoc/Pub-R-S
FAX Number: (660) 359-2211 — Calendar System: Semester
URL: www.ncmissouri.edu
Established: 1925 — Annual Undergrad Tuition & Fees (In-District): $3,024
Enrollment: 1,802 — Coed
Affiliation or Control: Local — IRS Status: 501(c)3
Highest Offering: Associate Degree
Program: Occupational; 2-Year Principally Bachelor's Creditable
Accreditation: NH, DH, OTA

01	President	Dr. Neil NUTTALL
05	VP Instruction/Student Services	Dr. James GARDNER
11	Vice Pres Administrative Services	Ms. Sharon BARNETT
32	Dean of Student Services	Dr. Kristen ALLEY
20	Dean of Instruction	Dr. Jamie HOOYMAN
76	Dean Allied Health Sciences	Ms. Janet VANDERPOOL
06	Registrar	Ms. Linda BROWN
27	Chief Information Officer	Mr. Alan BARNETT
08	Librarian	Ms. Ann SAMPSON
37	Director of Financial Aid	Ms. Melissa GUESS
30	Director Development	Mr. Steve MAXEY
40	Director Bookstore	Ms. Cecilia MARSH
39	Director Student Housing	Mr. Donnie HILLERMAN
41	Athletic Director	Mr. Steve RICHMAN
18	Director of Facilities	Mr. Randy YOUNG
15	Director Human Resources	Ms. Donna CALLIHAN
101	Sec of Inst/Board of Governors	Ms. Vicki WEAVER
105	Director Web Services	Mr. Anthony ALEXANDER
09	Director of Institutional Research	Ms. Tara NOAH

Northwest Missouri State University (B)

800 University Drive, Maryville MO 64468-6015
County: Nodaway — FICE Identification: 002496
Unit ID: 178624
Telephone: (660) 562-1212 — Carnegie Class: Master's L
FAX Number: (660) 562-1900 — Calendar System: Trimester
URL: www.nwmissouri.edu
Established: 1905 — Annual Undergrad Tuition & Fees (In-State): $7,719
Enrollment: 7,225 — Coed
Affiliation or Control: State — IRS Status: 501(c)3
Highest Offering: Beyond Master's But Less Than Doctorate
Program: Liberal Arts And General; Teacher Preparatory
Accreditation: NH, AAFCS, ACBSP, DIETD, MUS, NRPA, TED

01	President	Dr. John JASINSKI
05	Provost	Dr. Doug DUNHAM
10	Vice Pres for Finance	Ms. Stacy CARRICK
32	Vice President for Student Affairs	Dr. Matt BAKER
13	Interim VP for Information Systems	Ms. Kyra MILLS
26	Vice President University Relations	Ms. Mitzi LUTZ
15	Interim VP of Human Resources	Mr. Clarence GREEN, JR.
30	VP University Advancement	Mr. Michael JOHNSON
35	Dean of Students	Dr. Matthew BAKER
84	Dean Enrollment Management	Ms. Beverly S. SCHENKEL
09	Assoc Dir Institutional Research	Ms. Mary Ann PENNISTON
08	Dir of Academic & Library Services	Dr. Leslie GALBREATH
06	Registrar	Ms. Terri VOGEL
37	Director Financial Aid	Mr. Del MORLEY
36	Director of Career Services	Ms. Joan SCHNEIDER
29	Director Alumni Relations	Mr. Steve SUTTON
19	Chief University Police Department	Mr. Clarence GREEN
41	Director Athletics/HPERD	Mr. Wren BAKER
23	Director Wellness Services	Dr. Gerald WILMES
96	Director of Purchasing	Ms. Ann MARTIN
18	Director Facility Services	Mr. David BRIDGE
58	Dean of Graduate School	Dr. Gregory HADDOCK
53	Dean Col of Education & Human Svcs	Dr. Joyce PIVERAL
49	Dean Col of Arts & Sciences	Dr. Charles MCADAMS
50	Int Dean Col of Business/Prof Stds	Dr. Greg HADDOCK
38	Director Student Counseling Center	Vacant

Ozark Christian College (C)

1111 N Main Street, Joplin MO 64801-4804
County: Jasper — FICE Identification: 022027
Unit ID: 178679
Telephone: (417) 626-1234 — Carnegie Class: Spec/Faith
FAX Number: (417) 624-0090 — Calendar System: Semester
URL: www.occ.edu
Established: 1942 — Annual Undergrad Tuition & Fees: $9,900
Enrollment: 660 — Coed
Affiliation or Control: Independent Non-Profit — IRS Status: 501(c)3
Highest Offering: Baccalaureate
Program: Religious Emphasis
Accreditation: BI

01	President	Matt PROCTOR
03	Executive Vice President	Greg HAFER
04	Assistant to the President	Kathy BOWERS
05	Academic Dean	Doug ALDRIDGE
06	Registrar	Jennifer MCMILLIN
32	Exec Director of Student Devel	Monte SHOEMAKE
10	Exec Dir of Business Operations	David MCMILLIN
07	Executive Director Admissions	Troy NELSON
09	Exec Dir Inst Research/Gen Counsel	Doug MILLER
29	Exec Director Alumni	Dru ASHWELL
30	Exec Director of Development	David DUNCAN
20	Assistant Academic Dean	Chad RAGSDALE
26	Dir Alumni/Publications/Conventions	Meredith WILLIAMS
37	Director of Student Financial Aid	Kim BALENTINE
90	Director Academic Computing	David FISH
07	Director of Recruitment	Joe BANKER
88	Director of Church Relations	Travis HURLEY
08	Director of Library Services	John HUNTER
106	Associate Dean Online Learning	Shawn LINDSAY
88	Coordinator College Relations/Event	Lisa WITTE
64	Coordinator of Music Department	Scott HANDLEY
38	Student Counselor	Sharon ENGELBRECHT
88	Director of Food Services	Rita PEABODY
23	Campus Nurse	Alecia CHAFFEE
34	Dean of Women	Lisa WHITE
42	Director Campus Ministry	Kevin GREER
88	Director of Christian Services	Doug WELCH
88	Director Youth Minister Relations	Bob WITTE
40	Director of Bookstore	Bob HEATH
41	Director Athletics	Chris LAHM
18	Director Physical Plant	Bob RASMUSSEN
13	Director of College Technology Dept	Mitchell PIERCY
105	Web Developer/Network Admin	Matt DICKEY
14	Coordinator of Data Processing	Gary WHEAT

Ozarks Technical Community College (D)

1001 E Chestnut Expressway, Springfield MO 65802-3625
County: Greene — FICE Identification: 030830
Unit ID: 177472
Telephone: (417) 447-7500 — Carnegie Class: Assoc/Pub-R-L
FAX Number: N/A — Calendar System: Semester
URL: www.otc.edu
Established: 1990 — Annual Undergrad Tuition & Fees (In-District): $3,330
Enrollment: 15,179 — Coed
Affiliation or Control: State/Local — IRS Status: 501(c)3
Highest Offering: Associate Degree
Program: Occupational; 2-Year Principally Bachelor's Creditable
Accreditation: NH, ACFEI, ADNUR, DA, DH, EMT, IFSAC, MLTAD, OTA, PTAA, SURGT

01	Chancellor	Dr. Hal L. HIGDON
04	Exec Secretary to Chancellor	Ms. Karen CREIGHTON
05	Vice Chancellor Academic Affairs	Dr. Steve BISHOP
11	Vice Chancellor Admin Services	Mr. Rob RECTOR
13	Vice Chancellor IT	Mr. Joel LAREAU
30	Vice Chancellor Inst Advancement	Mr. Cliff DAVIS
10	Vice Chancellor Finance	Ms. Marla MOODY
12	President Richwood Valley Campus	Dr. Jeff JOCHEMS
32	Assoc Chancellor Student Services	Ms. Joan BARRETT
20	Dean of Academic Services	Dr. Kathy PERKINS
76	Dean of Allied Health Programs	Dr. Sherry TAYLOR
97	Interim Dean of General Education	Mr. Richard TURNER
56	Dean Extended Campus/Col Outreach	Mr. Steve BIERMAN
72	Dean of Technical Education	Mr. Layton CHILDRESS
08	Dean of Learning Resources	Mr. Mike MADDEN
103	Dir Ctr Workforce Development	Ms. Sherry COKER
38	Director of Counseling & Advising	Ms. Joyce THOMAS
26	College Dir Comm & Marketing	Mr. Joel DOEPKER
18	Director of College Facilities	Mr. Rick TAYLOR
13	Asst Vice Chancellor IT	Mr. Gerald BRYANT
14	Director of Computer Services	Mr. Jack DOZIER
28	Asst Dean Disabilities Support Svcs	Ms. Julie EDWARDS
37	College Director of Financial Aid	Mr. Jeff FORD
15	College Director of Human Resources	Ms. Alice RAMEY
88	Director of Learning Resources Ctr	Mr. Corky MCCORMACK
36	Director of Career Employment Svcs	Ms. Kathy CHRISTY
102	Exec Director of OTC Foundation	Mr. Cliff DAVIS
09	Dir Research/Strategic Planning	Mr. John CLAYTON
19	Director of Safety & Security	Mr. Peter ROTHROCK
35	Dean of Students	Ms. Karla GREGG
29	Director of Alumni Relations	Ms. Stephanie BROWN
56	Coord Dual Credit/Tech Prep Program	Ms. Cindy PHILLIPS

Park University (E)

8700 River Park Drive, Parkville MO 64152-3795
County: Platte — FICE Identification: 002498
Unit ID: 178721
Telephone: (816) 741-2000 — Carnegie Class: Master's M
FAX Number: (816) 746-6423 — Calendar System: Semester
URL: www.park.edu
Established: 1875 — Annual Undergrad Tuition & Fees: $10,380
Enrollment: 11,759 — Coed
Affiliation or Control: Independent Non-Profit — IRS Status: 501(c)3
Highest Offering: Master's
Program: Liberal Arts And General; Teacher Preparatory; Professional
Accreditation: NH, ADNUR, SW

01	President	Dr. Michael DROGE
03	Provost	Dr. Jerry JORGENSEN
10	Vice President for Finance & Admin	Ms. Dorla WATKINS
30	Vice Pres University Advancement	Ms. Laurie MCCORMACK
84	VP Enrollment Mgt/Student Services	Mr. Alan J. LIEBRECHT
27	Vice President for Communication	Ms. Rita WEIGHILL
05	Associate VP for Academic Affairs	Dr. Dan DONALDSON
11	Assoc VP for Administration	Mr. Brian DAVIS
32	Associate VP for Student Services	Ms. Clarinda CREIGHTON
31	Assoc VP for Constituent Engagement	Mr. Erik BERGRUD
35	Dean of Student Life	Dr. Diana MCELROY
58	Dean School of Grad & Prof Studies	Dr. Laurie DIPADOVA-STOCKS
06	Registrar	Ms. Jody MANCHION
07	Assoc Dean Admissions and SFS	Ms. Cathy COLAPIETRO
08	Director of Library Systems	Ms. Ann SCHULTIS
12	Director Park Accelerated Programs	Mr. S. L. SARTAIN
88	Director of Advancement Services	Mrs. Sandra SANDERS
15	Director of Human Resources	Mr. Roger DUSING
29	Director of Alumni Relations	Ms. Julie MCCOLLUM
96	Dir or Budget and Purchasing	Ms. Donna BAKER
18	Director of Environmental Services	Mr. Brian SLENKER
41	Director of Athletics	Mr. Claude ENGLISH
66	Director of Nursing Program	Ms. Gerry WALKER
85	Director of Foreign Students	Mr. Michael HERNANDEZ
37	Director Student Financial Services	Ms. Carla BOREN
13	CIO Technical Services	Mr. David MONCHUSIE
09	Director Inst Research & Assessment	Dr. John TEW, JR.
50	Director MBA Program	Dr. Nick KOUDOU
96	Asst Director Purchasing Services	Ms. Alicia THIESSEN
04	Exec Asst to the President	Ms. Laure CHRISTENSEN
26	Director of Marketing	Vacant
25	Director Sponsored Programs	Mr. Edmund BRACKETT
50	Dean School of Business/Mgmt	Dr. Brad KLEINDL
106	Assoc VP Park Distance Learning	Dr. Charles KATER
49	Dean Liberal Arts & Sciences	Dr. Jane WOOD
53	Dean School for Education	Dr. Michelle MYERS
80	Associate Dean HSPA	Dr. Rebekkah STUTEVILLE

Pinnacle Career Institute (F)

1001 E 101st Terrace, Suite 325,
Kansas City MO 64131-3368
County: Jackson — FICE Identification: 010405
Unit ID: 177302
Telephone: (816) 331-5700 — Carnegie Class: Assoc/PrivFP
FAX Number: (816) 331-2026 — Calendar System: Quarter
URL: www.pcitraining.edu
Established: 1952 — Annual Undergrad Tuition & Fees: $13,470
Enrollment: 1,105 — Coed
Affiliation or Control: Proprietary — IRS Status: Proprietary
Highest Offering: Associate Degree
Program: Occupational
Accreditation: ACICS

01	Executive Director	Ms. Maggie FRANZ
05	Director of Education	Dr. Rene HEWITT
20	Academic Dean	Mr. Larry FAJEN
36	Director Student Placement	Ms. Bri WARDRIP
07	Director of Admissions	Mr. Nick LAUBER

Ranken Technical College (G)

4431 Finney Avenue, Saint Louis MO 63113-2898
County: Saint Louis — FICE Identification: 012500
Unit ID: 178891
Telephone: (314) 371-0236 — Carnegie Class: Assoc/PrivNFP4
FAX Number: (314) 371-0241 — Calendar System: Semester
URL: www.ranken.edu
Established: 1907 — Annual Undergrad Tuition & Fees: $13,944
Enrollment: 1,950 — Coed
Affiliation or Control: Independent Non-Profit — IRS Status: 501(c)3
Highest Offering: Baccalaureate
Program: Occupational; 2-Year Principally Bachelor's Creditable; Technical Emphasis
Accreditation: NH

01	President	Mr. Stan SHOUN
10	Vice President for Finance & Admin	Mr. Peter T. MURTAUGH
05	Vice President for Education	Mr. Don POHL
30	Vice President for Development	Mr. Timothy J. WILLARD
32	Vice President for Student Success	Mr. John WOOD
51	Dean of Continuing Education	Mr. Keyvan GERAMI
20	Dean Academic Affairs	Ms. Crystal HERRON
07	Admissions Director	Mr. Michael E. HAWLEY
06	Registrar	Ms. Carol J. WINKLER
08	Head Librarian	Ms. Barbara EDWARDS
18	Director Buildings & Grounds	Mr. Steve P. HARTGE
29	Director of Alumni Relations	Ms. Kathy T. FERN
37	Director Financial Aid	Ms. Michelle L. WILLIAMS
21	Business Office Manager	Ms. Seletha R. CURTIS
36	Career Services Coordinator	Ms. Janie K. SUMMERS
15	Human Resources Coordinator	Ms. Janice A. BOLLMANN

Research College of Nursing (H)

2525 E Meyer Boulevard, Kansas City MO 64132-1133
County: Jackson — FICE Identification: 006392
Unit ID: 178989
Telephone: (816) 995-2800 — Carnegie Class: Spec/Health
FAX Number: (816) 995-2817 — Calendar System: Semester
URL: www.researchcollege.edu
Established: 1980 — Annual Undergrad Tuition & Fees: $30,050
Enrollment: 434 — Coed
Affiliation or Control: Proprietary — IRS Status: Proprietary

Highest Offering: Master's
Program: Liberal Arts And General; Professional; Nursing Emphasis
Accreditation: NH, NURSE

01 President/Dean ..... Dr. Nancy O. DEBASIO
05 Assoc Dean Academic Programs ..... Vacant
07 Director Admissions ..... Ms. Leslie MENDENHALL
28 Director Diversity ..... Ms. Victoria HAYNES
37 Director Financial Aid ..... Ms. Stacie WITHERS
24 Director LRC ..... Ms. Tobey STOSBERG
32 Director Student Affairs ..... Ms. Lori VITALE
105 Director Web Based Education ..... Ms. Sheryl MAX
09 Senior Technology Analyst ..... Mr. Will GIVENS

Rockhurst University (A)

1100 Rockhurst Road, Kansas City MO 64110-2561
County: Jackson FICE Identification: 002499
Unit ID: 179043
Telephone: (816) 501-4000 Carnegie Class: Master's L
FAX Number: (816) 501-4588 Calendar System: Semester
URL: www.rockhurst.edu
Established: 1910 Annual Undergrad Tuition & Fees: $29,100
Enrollment: 2,801 Coed
Affiliation or Control: Roman Catholic IRS Status: 501(c)3
Highest Offering: Doctorate
Program: Liberal Arts And General; Teacher Preparatory; Professional; Business Emphasis
Accreditation: NH, BUS, OT, PTA, SP, TEAC

01 President ..... Rev. Thomas B. CURRAN, OSFS
30 Vice Pres University Advancement ..... Mr. Robert GRANT
10 Vice Pres Finance & Administration ..... Mr. Guy SWANSON
05 Int Vice Pres for Academic Affairs ..... Dr. Jeffrey BREESE
88 Vice Pres for Mission & Ministry ..... Vacant
32 VP Student Developmnt/Athletics ..... Dr. Matthew D. QUICK
11 Assoc VP Facilities & Technology ..... Mr. Matt W. HEINRICH
84 Associate Vice Pres Enrollment ..... Mr. Lane RAMEY
35 Director of Student Life ..... Ms. Angie CARR ROBINETT
88 Assistant Dean of Students ..... Mrs. Sandy WADDELL
39 Assistant Dean of Students ..... Mr. Sean GRUBE
04 Assistant to the President ..... Ms. Kathy J. SOLODUCHA
50 Int Dean Helzberg Sch of Management ..... Dr. Cheryl M. MCCONNELL
49 Dean Arts & Sciences ..... Dr. Timothy MCDONALD
58 Int Dean Sch Graduate/Prof Studies ..... Dr. James MILLARD
66 Pres/Dean Research Col of Nursing ..... Dr. Nancy DEBASIO
08 Director Library ..... Ms. Laurie E. HATHMAN
06 Registrar ..... Ms. Minda THROWER
37 Int Director Student Financial Aid ..... Ms. Maureen MCKINNON
41 Director of Athletics ..... Mr. Richard KONZEM
15 Director of Human Resources ..... Ms. Mary R. BURNETT
14 Director of Infrastructure Services ..... Mr. Michael CRAIG
36 Director of Career Center ..... Mr. Michael J. THEOBALD
26 Director of Public Relations ..... Ms. Katherine FROHOFF
88 Director of Marketing ..... Ms. Lauren DEBIAK
29 Director Alumni Rels & Constituent ..... Mrs. Mary LANDERS
42 Director of Campus Ministry ..... Ms. Maureen E. HENDERSON
19 Director Security/Safety ..... Mr. William G. EVANS
38 Director of Student Counseling ..... Dr. Rick D. HANSON
44 Director of Gift Planning ..... Mr. Ed FREDENBERG
31 Director Community Relations ..... Ms. Alicia R. DOUGLAS
40 Director Bookstore ..... Mr. James GARBARINO
92 Director Honors Program ..... Dr. Mindy WALKER
45 Assessment Coordinator ..... Ms. Keli BRAITMAN
44 Senior Development Officer ..... Ms. Amy DROUIN
09 Institutional Research Coordinator ..... Ms. Wendy PICKEL
28 Area & Diversity Coordinator ..... Ms. Emily J. KEMPF
24 Coordinator AV and Media ..... Mr. Darnell JONES
88 Controller ..... Ms. Rachel LIERZ

St. Charles Community College (B)

4601 Mid Rivers Mall Drive, Cottleville MO 63376-2865
County: Saint Charles FICE Identification: 025306
Unit ID: 262031
Telephone: (636) 922-8000 Carnegie Class: Assoc/Pub-S-SC
FAX Number: (636) 922-8352 Calendar System: Semester
URL: www.stchas.edu
Established: 1986 Annual Undergrad Tuition & Fees (In-District): $2,700
Enrollment: 8,260 Coed
Affiliation or Control: State/Local IRS Status: 501(c)3
Highest Offering: Associate Degree
Program: Occupational; 2-Year Principally Bachelor's Creditable
Accreditation: NH, ADNUR, OTA

01 President ..... Dr. Ronald CHESBROUGH
05 Vice Pres Academic/Student Affairs ..... Mr. Chris BREITMEYER
11 Vice Pres for Administrative Svcs ..... Mr. Todd GALBIERZ
45 Vice Pres for IT/Research/Planning ..... Dr. Barbara KEIM
15 Vice President for Human Resources ..... Ms. Donna DAVIS
20 Asst Vice Pres for Academic Affairs ..... Dr. Michael B. DOMPIERRE
26 Vice President for Marketing & Comm ..... Ms. Heather MCDORMAN
57 Dean Arts & Humanities ..... Dr. Denise KING
50 Dean Business & Social Science ..... Mr. Bill STRECKER
81 Dean Mathematics/Science/Health ..... Mr. Chris BREITMEYER
31 Dean Corporate & Community Dev ..... Ms. Yvonne WILLS
08 Dean Learning Resources ..... Dr. Stephanie TOLSON
04 Exec Assistant to the President ..... Ms. Julie PARCEL
30 Vice Pres for College Advancement ..... Ms. Kasey MCKEE
21 Director of Financial Services ..... Ms. Susan RUBEMEYER
06 Registrar/Director of Admissions ..... Ms. Kathy BROCKGREITENS
40 Director of Bookstore ..... Ms. Patricia A. HAYNES
91 Director of Admin Computing ..... Ms. Floretha J. JOHNSON
07 Director of Admissions ..... Ms. Kathy BROCKGREITENS
09 Director of Institutional Research ..... Dr. Ronald PENNINGTON
96 Director of Purchasing ..... Ms. Christine E. ROMER
41 Athletic Director ..... Mr. Chris G. GOBER
38 Dean of Student Development ..... Ms. Yvette M. SWEENEY
51 Assoc Dean Continuing Education ..... Ms. Tina SIEKER
103 Director of Workforce Development ..... Ms. Amanda SIZEMORE
36 Job Placement Coordinator ..... Ms. Martha A. TOEBBEN
18 Director of Facilities ..... Mr. Al KOEHLER
37 Director Student Financial Aid ..... Ms. Kathy BROCKGREITENS
35 Student Activities Coordinator ..... Ms. Kelley PFEIFFER
84 Dean of Enrollment Services ..... Ms. Kathy BROCKGREITENS
91 Manager of Academic Computing ..... Ms. Lisa MOUSER
19 Director of Public Safety ..... Mr. Bob RONKOSKI

Saint Louis Christian College (C)

1360 Grandview Drive, Florissant MO 63033-6499
County: Saint Louis FICE Identification: 012580
Unit ID: 179256
Telephone: (314) 837-6777 Carnegie Class: Spec/Faith
FAX Number: (314) 837-8291 Calendar System: Semester
URL: www.slcconline.edu
Established: 1956 Annual Undergrad Tuition & Fees: $1,300
Enrollment: 292 Coed
Affiliation or Control: Other Protestant IRS Status: 501(c)3
Highest Offering: Baccalaureate
Program: 2-Year Principally Bachelor's Creditable; Religious Emphasis
Accreditation: BI

00 Chancellor ..... Mr. Thomas W. MCGEE
01 President ..... Dr. Guthrie VEECH
05 Academic Dean ..... Dr. Michael CHAMBERS
10 Vice Pres of Finance/Operations ..... Dr. Judy LINCOLN
32 Dean of Students ..... Ms. Christine CABLE
08 Library Manager ..... Mr. Matt DEWITT
41 Athletic Director ..... Mr. John-Michael BROWN
06 Registrar ..... Ms. Cindy BINGAMON
07 Director of Admissions ..... Ms. Carrie CHAPMAN
37 Financial Aid Director ..... Ms. Cathy WILHOIT
40 Bookstore Co-Manager ..... Ms. Dawn OTTWELL
40 Bookstore Co-Manager ..... Ms. Melissa RABIDEAU

Saint Louis College of Health Careers-Fenton Campus (D)

1297 N Highway Drive, Fenton MO 63026-1909
County: Saint Louis Identification: 666274
Unit ID: 442426
Telephone: (636) 529-0000 Carnegie Class: Assoc/PrivFP
FAX Number: (636) 529-0430 Calendar System: Semester
URL: www.slchc.com
Established: 1981 Annual Undergrad Tuition & Fees: $24,300
Enrollment: 282 Coed
Affiliation or Control: Proprietary IRS Status: Proprietary
Highest Offering: Associate Degree
Program: Occupational
Accreditation: ABHES, OTA

01 Chief Executive Officer ..... Mr. Steven N. BARSAM
05 Dean of Nursing & Allied Health ..... Ms. Nancy K. KAUFMANN

† Branch campus of Saint Louis College of Health Careers-South Taylor, Saint Louis, MO.

Saint Louis College of Health Careers-South Taylor (E)

909 S Taylor Avenue, Saint Louis MO 63110-1511
County: Saint Louis FICE Identification: 023405
Unit ID: 179511
Telephone: (314) 652-0300 Carnegie Class: Assoc/PrivFP
FAX Number: (314) 652-2125 Calendar System: Semester
URL: www.slchc.com
Established: 1981 Annual Undergrad Tuition & Fees: $19,650
Enrollment: 384 Coed
Affiliation or Control: Proprietary IRS Status: Proprietary
Highest Offering: Associate Degree
Program: Occupational
Accreditation: ABHES

01 Associate Dean ..... Lou VIDOVIC
05 Director of Education ..... Michelle YEAGER

St. Louis College of Pharmacy (F)

4588 Parkview Place, Saint Louis MO 63110-1088
County: Independent City FICE Identification: 002504
Unit ID: 179265
Telephone: (314) 367-8700 Carnegie Class: Spec/Health
FAX Number: (314) 446-8304 Calendar System: Semester
URL: www.stlcop.edu
Established: 1864 Annual Undergrad Tuition & Fees: $26,966
Enrollment: 1,261 Coed
Affiliation or Control: Independent Non-Profit IRS Status: 501(c)3
Highest Offering: First Professional Degree
Program: Professional
Accreditation: NH, PHAR

01 President ..... Dr. John A. PIEPER
30 Vice Pres Devel/Alumni Relations ..... Mr. Brett T. SCHOTT
10 VP Finance/Administration/CFO ..... Mr. Gary G. TORRENCE
07 Vice Pres of Enrollment Services ..... Ms. Gloria J. VERTREES
90 Vice Pres Info Technology & CIO ..... Mr. Chad SHEPHERD
49 Dean Arts & Science/Student Affairs ..... Dr. Kimberly J. KILGORE
67 Dean of Pharmacy ..... Dr. Wendy DUNCAN
15 Director of Human Resources ..... Mr. Daniel C. BAUER
06 Registrar ..... Ms. Penny J. BRYANT
08 Library Director ..... Ms. Jill NISSEN
37 Director of Financial Aid ..... Mr. Daniel J. STIFFLER
36 Director of Placement Services ..... Vacant
18 Chief Facilities/Physical Plant ..... Mr. Al FARROW
26 Vice President Mktg/Communications ..... Mr. Marcus LONG
29 Director Devel/Alumni Relations ..... Ms. Necole POWELL
41 Director of Athletics ..... Ms. Jill JOKERST-HARTER
04 Special Assistant to the President ..... Sr. Mary Louise DEGENHART

*Saint Louis Community College Center (G)

300 S Broadway, Saint Louis MO 63102-2820
County: Saint Louis FICE Identification: 002469
Unit ID: 179283
Telephone: (314) 539-5000 Carnegie Class: N/A
FAX Number: (314) 539-5170
URL: www.stlcc.edu

01 Chancellor ..... Dr. Myrtle E B. DORSEY
05 Vice Chanc Academic & Stdnt Affairs ..... Dr. Donna DARE
10 Vice Chanc Finance/Administration ..... Mr. Kent KAY
13 Vice Chancellor Technology ..... Dr. Craig KLIMCZAK
103 Vice Chanc Workforce & Cmty Develop ..... Mr. Rod NUNN
102 Executive Director Foundation ..... Ms. Jo-Ann DIGMAN
84 Director Enrollment Management ..... Dr. Joanie FRIEND
21 Controller ..... Mr. Bruce VOGELGESANG
15 Acting Director Human Resources ..... Mr. Roy SHANEBERGER
26 Director Communications ..... Mr. DeLancey SMITH
09 Director of Institutional Research ..... Mr. John J. COSGROVE
20 Director Instructional Resources ..... Vacant
30 Director Institutional Development ..... Ms. Castella HENDERSON
06 Manager Central Student Records ..... Ms. Lauren ROBERDS

*Saint Louis Community College at Florissant Valley (H)

3400 Pershall Road, Saint Louis MO 63135-1499
County: Saint Louis FICE Identification: 002470
Unit ID: 179292
Telephone: (314) 513-4200 Carnegie Class: Assoc/Pub-U-MC
FAX Number: N/A Calendar System: Semester
URL: www.stlcc.edu
Established: 1962 Annual Undergrad Tuition & Fees (In-District): $1,992
Enrollment: 7,440 Coed
Affiliation or Control: Local IRS Status: 501(c)3
Highest Offering: Associate Degree
Program: Occupational; 2-Year Principally Bachelor's Creditable
Accreditation: &NH, ADNUR, ART, DIETT, ENGT

02 President ..... Dr. Marcia F. PFEIFFER
05 Vice President Academic Affairs ..... Mr. Ashok AGRAWAL
32 Act Vice President Student Affairs ..... Dr. Joseph B. WORTH
50 Dean Business/Human Development ..... Ms. Ruby CURRY
49 Dean Liberal Arts ..... Dr. Nancy LINZY
81 Acting Dean Math/Sci/Engineering ..... Dr. Eilene LYONS
04 Executive Assistant to President ..... Ms. Adria WERNER
31 Community Relations Director ..... Ms. Kedra TOLSON
06 Registrar ..... Ms. Brenda DAVENPORT
21 Manager Business Services ..... Mr. Douglas MAHONEY
18 Manager Facilities/Physical Plant ..... Mr. John FERLISI
37 Manager of Student Aid ..... Ms. Khaneetah CUNNINGHAM
35 Manager Campus Life ..... Ms. Gwen NIXON
36 Coordinator Career & Employment ..... Ms. Michela WALSH
84 Coordinator Enrollment Management ..... Ms. Janice FITZGERALD
29 Coordinator Alumni Relations ..... Vacant
38 Acting Department Chair Counseling ..... Mr. Troy HANSEN

*Saint Louis Community College at Forest Park (I)

5600 Oakland Avenue, Saint Louis MO 63110-1393
County: Independent City FICE Identification: 002471
Unit ID: 179308
Telephone: (314) 644-9100 Carnegie Class: Assoc/Pub-U-MC
FAX Number: (314) 644-9752 Calendar System: Semester
URL: www.stlcc.edu
Established: 1962 Annual Undergrad Tuition & Fees (In-District): $2,112
Enrollment: 8,863 Coed
Affiliation or Control: Local IRS Status: 501(c)3
Highest Offering: Associate Degree
Program: Occupational; 2-Year Principally Bachelor's Creditable
Accreditation: &NH, ACFEI, ADNUR, DA, DH, DMS, FUSER, MLTAD, RAD, SURGT

02 President ..... Dr. Cindy K. HESS
05 Vice President Academic Affairs ..... Dr. Tracy HALL
32 Vice President Student Affairs ..... Dr. Thomas WALKER, JR.
83 Dean Hum/Social Sci/Soc Pgms ..... Mrs. Amanda MEAD-ROACH
76 Dean Allied Health/Natural Science ..... Mr. Vincent FEATHERSON
50 Dean Business/Math/Technology ..... Ms. Elizabeth WILCOXSON
38 Chair of Counseling ..... Ms. Marlene RHODES

27 Manager Campus Community Relations .... Ms. Claudia PERRY
19 College Police Chief .... Mr. Richard BANAHAN
10 Manager Campus Business Office .... Ms. Chitra SUBRAMANIAN
36 Manager Career & Employment Svcs .... Mr. Davis MOORE
37 Manager of Student Aid .... Ms. Paulette JOHNSON
51 Manager Continuing Education .... Ms. Kim PORTER

*Saint Louis Community College at Meramec (A)

11333 Big Bend Rd., Kirkwood MO 63122-5799
County: Saint Louis FICE Identification: 002472
Unit ID: 179113
Telephone: (314) 984-7500 Carnegie Class: Assoc/Pub-U-MC
FAX Number: (314) 984-7006 Calendar System: Semester
URL: www.stlcc.edu
Established: 1962 Annual Undergrad Tuition & Fees (In-District): $2,232
Enrollment: 11,353 Coed
Affiliation or Control: Local IRS Status: 501(c)3
Highest Offering: Associate Degree
Program: Occupational; 2-Year Principally Bachelor's Creditable
Accreditation: &NH, ADNUR, ART, OTA, PTAA

02 President .... Mr. George WASSON
05 VP Academic Affairs .... Dr. Andrew LANGREHR
32 VP Student Affairs .... Ms. Linden G. CRAWFORD
50 Dean Business Administration .... Ms. Donna SNEED
81 Dean Communications & Math .... Dr. Vernon KAYS
79 Dean Humanities/Social Sciences .... Dr. Yvonne J. JOHNSON
72 Acting Dean Science & Technology .... Ms. Janet WALSH
26 Coordinator Community Relations .... Ms. Toni L. OPLT
21 Manager Business Office .... Ms. Vicki KETTENACKER
37 Manager Financial Aid .... Mr. Michael T. SMITH
08 Sr Mgr Library/Instruct Resources .... Vacant
12 Manager South County Educ Center .... Ms. Claudia J. POTTS
35 Manager Student Activities .... Mr. Steven D. BRADY
19 Campus Police Chief .... Mr. Paul J. BANTA
40 Manager Auxiliary Services .... Mr. Kevin P. METZLER
36 Manager Career/Employ Services .... Ms. Jacqueline D. MEADERS-BOOTH
18 Manager Buildings & Grounds .... Mr. Willie WRIGHT
06 Manager Admissions/Registration .... Dr. Michael CUNDIFF
38 Chair Dept of Counseling .... Ms. Donna ZUMWINKEL
91 Mgr Technology Support Svcs .... Ms. Sharon K. SWAN

*Saint Louis Community College at Wildwood (B)

2645 Generations Drive, Wildwood MO 63040-1168
County: Saint Louis Identification: 667084
Unit ID: 450137
Telephone: (636) 422-2000 Carnegie Class: Assoc/Pub-U-MC
FAX Number: (636) 422-2020 Calendar System: Semester
URL: www.stlcc.edu
Established: 1962 Annual Undergrad Tuition & Fees (In-District): $2,232
Enrollment: 2,100 Coed
Affiliation or Control: Local IRS Status: 501(c)3
Highest Offering: Associate Degree
Program: Occupational; 2-Year Principally Bachelor's Creditable
Accreditation: &NH

02 President .... Ms. Pam MCINTYRE
05 Vice President Academic Affairs .... Dr. Patrick VAUGHN
32 Director of Student Affairs .... Ms. Marilyn TARAS
26 Coordinator of Community Relations .... Ms. Trish AUMANN
18 Manager of Physical Facilities .... Mr. John TETSTILL
40 Manager of Campus Auxiliary Svcs .... Ms. Ellen GOUGH
04 Executive Asst to the President .... Ms. Judy BROUK

Saint Louis University (C)

One Grand Boulevard, Saint Louis MO 63103-2097
County: Independent City FICE Identification: 002506
Unit ID: 179159
Telephone: (314) 977-2500 Carnegie Class: RU/H
FAX Number: (314) 977-3874 Calendar System: Semester
URL: www.slu.edu
Established: 1818 Annual Undergrad Tuition & Fees: $34,740
Enrollment: 14,073 Coed
Affiliation or Control: Roman Catholic IRS Status: 501(c)3
Highest Offering: Doctorate
Program: Liberal Arts And General; Teacher Preparatory; Professional
Accreditation: NH, AAB, ARCPA, ART, BUS, CLPSY, CYTO, DENT, DIETD, DIETI, ENG, HSA, LAW, MED, MFCD, MT, NMT, NURSE, OT, PH, PTA, RTT, SP, SPAA, SW, TED

01 President .... Rev. Lawrence BIONDI, SJ
05 Vice President for Academic Affairs .... Dr. Manoj PATANKAR
10 Vice Pres/Chief Financial Officer .... Mr. David HEIMBURGER
18 Vice Pres Facilities Management .... Ms. Kathleen BRADY
12 Director Madrid Campus .... Dr. Paul VITA
16 Vice Pres Human Resources .... Mr. Kenneth FLEISCHMANN
30 VP Advancement/Univ Relations .... Mr. Jeffrey FOWLER
43 Vice President/General Counsel .... Mr. William R. KAUFFMAN
32 Vice President Student Development .... Dr. Kent PORTERFIELD
42 Vice President Mission & Ministry .... Rev. Paul STARK, SJ
13 Vice Pres Information Tech Svcs/CIO .... Mr. Keith HACKE
23 Vice President for Medical Affairs .... Dr. Philip O. ALDERSON
26 Asst VP for Marketing & Creat Svcs .... Ms. Laura GEISER
29 Assoc VP for Alumni Relations .... Ms. Meg CONNOLLY
21 Controller .... Mr. David HELMBURGER
35 Associate VP and Dean of Students .... Dr. Ramona HICKS
54 Assoc Dean Parks Col Engr/Aviation ... Dr. Theodore ALEXANDER
76 Dean Doisy College of Health Scis .... Dr. Lisa DORSEY
49 Dean Arts & Sciences .... Rev. Michael BARBER, SJ
50 Dean Cook School of Business .... Dr. Ellen F. HARSHMAN
61 Dean of Law .... Vacant
63 Dean of Medical School .... Dr. Philip O. ALDERSON
79 Dean Philosophy & Letters .... Bro. William REHG, SJ
69 Dean of Public Health .... Dr. Ed TREVATHAN
53 Dean Col of Educ & Public Svc .... Dr. Donald LINHOST
08 University Librarian .... David CASSENS
88 Exec Dir Ctr for Health Care Ethics .... Dr. Jeffrey BISHOP
52 Exec Dir Ctr Advanced Dental Educ .... Dr. John HATTON
46 Vice President for Research .... Dr. Raymond TAIT
19 Director Public Safety & Security .... Mr. Roland CORVINGTON
06 University Registrar .... Mr. Jay HAUGEN
07 Dean of Undergraduate Admission .... Ms. Jean GILMAN
37 Director Financial Aid .... Ms. Cari S. WICKLIFFE
39 Director Housing & Res Life .... Mr. Joshua WALEHWA
41 Athletics Director .... Mr. Christopher V. MAY
36 Director Career Services .... Ms. Kim REITTER
28 Dir Diversity/Affirmative Action .... Mr. Chad MARTINEZ
85 Director International Center .... Mr. Tim HERCULES
92 Director Honors Program .... Dr. Elizabeth WHITT
23 Director Student Health Center .... Ms. Deborah M. SCHEFF
31 Pgm Mgr Leadership Community Svcs .... Mr. Robert WASSEL
88 Director Internal Audit .... Ms. Elizabeth A. WINCHESTER
04 Assistant to the President .... Ms. Bridget FLETCHER
88 Director Univ Museums/Galleries .... Dr. Petruta LIPAN
44 Director Planned Giving .... Mr. Kent G. LEVAN
40 Manager Bookstore .... Ms. Debbie SCHNEIDER
09 Assistant Vice President .... Dr. Steven SANCHEZ

Saint Luke's College of Health Sciences (D)

624 Westport Road, Kansas City MO 64111
County: Jackson FICE Identification: 009782
Unit ID: 179450
Telephone: (816) 932-6700 Carnegie Class: Spec/Health
FAX Number: (816) 932-6761 Calendar System: Semester
URL: www.saintlukescollege.edu
Established: 1903 Annual Undergrad Tuition & Fees: $13,620
Enrollment: 131 Coed
Affiliation or Control: Independent Non-Profit IRS Status: 501(c)3
Highest Offering: Master's
Program: Nursing Emphasis
Accreditation: NH, NURSE

01 President .... Dr. Dean L. HUBBARD
10 Exec Dir Bus Operations/Stdnt Svcs .... Ms. Marcia LADAGE
09 Exec Asst to Pres/Dir Inst Research .... Ms. Tere E. NAYLOR
05 Academic Dean .... Dr. Jim HAUSCHILDT
07 Director Admissions .... Mr. Josh RICHARDS
06 Registrar .... Ms. Jean SUMMERS

Saint Paul School of Theology (E)

5123 E. Truman Road, Kansas City MO 64127-2499
County: Jackson FICE Identification: 002509
Unit ID: 179317
Telephone: (816) 483-9600 Carnegie Class: Spec/Faith
FAX Number: (816) 483-9605 Calendar System: Other
URL: www.spst.edu
Established: 1958 Annual Graduate Tuition & Fees: $17,400
Enrollment: 184 Coed
Affiliation or Control: United Methodist IRS Status: 501(c)3
Highest Offering: Doctorate; No Undergraduates
Program: Professional; Religious Emphasis
Accreditation: NH, THEOL

01 President .... Dr. Myron F. MCCOY
05 VP Academic Affairs/Dean .... Dr. Harold WASHINGTON
20 Associate Dean .... Dr. Suzanne MCLAUGHLIN
30 Vice President for Advancement .... Rev. Jim OMAN
10 Chief Financial Officer .... Ms. Laura SNOW
12 Academic Dean for OCU Extens Site .... Dr. Elaine ROBINSON
08 Librarian .... Dr. Logan S. WRIGHT
07 Director of Admissions .... Rev. Lee JOHNSON
04 Executive Assistant to President .... Ms. Leigh PRECISE
26 Director of Communications .... Ms. Heather CHAMBERLIN

Sanford-Brown College (F)

1345 Smizer Mill Road, Fenton MO 63026-3400
County: Saint Louis FICE Identification: 022052
Unit ID: 179201
Telephone: (636) 651-1600 Carnegie Class: Bac/Assoc
FAX Number: (636) 651-1732 Calendar System: Quarter
URL: www.sanfordbrown.edu/Fenton
Established: 1866 Annual Undergrad Tuition & Fees: $11,833
Enrollment: 1,089 Coed
Affiliation or Control: Proprietary IRS Status: Proprietary
Highest Offering: Baccalaureate
Program: Occupational; 2-Year Principally Bachelor's Creditable; Liberal Arts And General
Accreditation: ACICS, DMS, MAAB, POLYT, RAD

01 Campus President .... Ms. Melissa MANGOLD
10 Vice President of Finance .... Mr. Jim REICH
12 Campus President-Hazelwood .... Ms. Phyllis FORNEY
12 Campus President-St. Peters .... Ms. Julia LEEMAN
27 Information Technology Manager .... Mr. Wade THURMOND
07 Director of Admissions .... Mr. Henry GAMEL
37 Director Student Financial Aid .... Ms. Amy KETTS

Sanford-Brown College (G)

75 Village Square, Hazelwood MO 63042-1817
County: Saint Louis Identification: 666456
Unit ID: 406264
Telephone: (314) 687-2900 Carnegie Class: Assoc/PrivFP
FAX Number: (314) 731-0550 Calendar System: Quarter
URL: www.sanfordbrown.edu/Hazelwood
Established: 1982 Annual Undergrad Tuition & Fees: $10,269
Enrollment: 782 Coed
Affiliation or Control: Proprietary IRS Status: Proprietary
Highest Offering: Associate Degree
Program: Occupational
Accreditation: ACICS, MAAB, OTA

01 Director .... Ms. Julia LEEMAN

Sanford-Brown College (H)

100 Richmond Center Boulevard,
Saint Peters MO 63376-5950
County: Saint Charles Identification: 666458
Unit ID: 409829
Telephone: (636) 696-2300 Carnegie Class: Spec/Health
FAX Number: (636) 696-2067 Calendar System: Quarter
URL: www.sanfordbrown.edu/St-Peters
Established: 1982 Annual Undergrad Tuition & Fees: $11,386
Enrollment: 526 Coed
Affiliation or Control: Proprietary IRS Status: Proprietary
Highest Offering: Baccalaureate
Program: Occupational
Accreditation: ACICS, MAAB, SURTEC

01 Campus President .... Ms. Julia LEEMAN

† Branch campus of Sanford-Brown College, Fenton, MO.

The School of Professional Psychology at Forest Institute (I)

2885 West Battlefield Road, Springfield MO 65807-1445
County: Greene FICE Identification: 021642
Unit ID: 177427
Telephone: (800) 424-7793 Carnegie Class: Spec/Health
FAX Number: (417) 823-3442 Calendar System: Semester
URL: www.forest.edu
Established: 1979 Annual Graduate Tuition & Fees: $26,000
Enrollment: 308 Coed
Affiliation or Control: Independent Non-Profit IRS Status: 501(c)3
Highest Offering: Doctorate; No Undergraduates
Program: Professional
Accreditation: NH, #CLPSY, IPSY, MFCD

01 President .... Dr. Mark SKRADE
05 Vice President of Academic Affairs .... Dr. Gerald PORTER
17 Vice Pres of Innovation/Cmty Health .... Ms. Jennifer BAKER
10 Chief Financial Officer .... Mr. Bob DAVIS
58 Dean of Doctoral Program .... Dr. Michael LEFTWICH
12 Exec Dir Forest Institute-St Louis .... Mr. Brian NEDWEK
17 Director of Clinical Training .... Mr. David MRAD
37 Director of Financial Aid .... Ms. Carolyn BURROS
06 Registrar .... Ms. Beth BENNETT
08 Library Services Manager .... Ms. Renee MCHENRY

Southeast Missouri Hospital College of Nursing and Health Sciences (J)

2001 William Street, 2nd Floor,
Cape Girardeau MO 63703-5815
County: Cape Girardeau FICE Identification: 030709
Unit ID: 417734
Telephone: (573) 334-6825 Carnegie Class: Assoc/PrivNFP
FAX Number: (573) 339-7805 Calendar System: Other
URL: www.southeastmissourihospitalcollege.edu
Established: 1990 Annual Undergrad Tuition & Fees: $13,800
Enrollment: 186 Coed
Affiliation or Control: Independent Non-Profit IRS Status: 501(c)3
Highest Offering: Associate Degree
Program: 2-Year Principally Bachelor's Creditable; Nursing Emphasis
Accreditation: NH, ADNUR, MT, RAD

01 President .... Dr. Tonya BUTTRY
06 Registrar .... Mr. Don PUGH

Southeast Missouri State University (K)

One University Plaza, Cape Girardeau MO 63701-4799
County: Cape Girardeau FICE Identification: 002501
Unit ID: 179557
Telephone: (573) 651-2000 Carnegie Class: Master's L
FAX Number: (573) 651-2200 Calendar System: Semester
URL: www.semo.edu

Established: 1873 Annual Undergrad Tuition & Fees (In-State): $6,750
Enrollment: 11,510 Coed
Affiliation or Control: State IRS Status: 501(c)3
Highest Offering: Beyond Master's But Less Than Doctorate
Program: Liberal Arts And General; Teacher Preparatory; Professional
Accreditation: NH, BUS, CACREP, CS, DIETD, DIETI, ENG, ENGT, #JOUR, MUS, NAIT, NRPA, NURSE, SP, SW, TED

01 President ... Dr. Kenneth W. DOBBINS
05 Provost ... Dr. Ronald ROSATI
10 VP Finance & Administration ... Mrs. Kathy M. MANGELS
84 VP Enrollment Mgmt & Stdnt Success ... Dr. Dennis HOLT
30 Vice Pres University Advancement ... Mr. Bill HOLLAND
20 Vice Provost ... Dr. Bill EDDLEMAN
04 Assistant to the President ... Ms. Diane O. SIDES
13 Asst Vice Pres Information Tech ... Mr. Archie SPRENGEL
56 Assoc Provost for Extend/Online Lrn ... Dr. Gerald MCDOUGALL
106 Associate Dean Online Lrng ... Dr. Allen GATHMAN
58 Dean Sch of Grad Studies ... Dr. Bill EDDLEMAN
89 Dean of University Studies ... Dr. Francisco BARRIOS
50 Dean DL Harrison College Business ... Dr. Gerald S. MCDOUGALL
53 Dean College of Education ... Dr. Diana ROGERS-ADKINSON
76 Int Dean College Health & Human Svc ... Dr. Diana BRUNS
79 Dean College of Liberal Arts ... Dr. Francisco BARRIOS
72 Dean College of Science/Tech & Ag ... Dr. Chris MCGOWAN
32 Dean of Students ... Dr. Dennis HOLT
88 Dean Academic Information Svcs ... Dr. David STARRETT
07 Assoc VP of Enrl Mgmt & Dir of Adm ... Dr. Debbie BELOW
35 Director of Campus Life ... Ms. Michele IRBY
26 Director Marketing & Univ Relations ... Ms. Karen GREBING
41 Director of Athletics ... Mr. Mark ALNUTT
29 Director Alumni Services ... Mr. Jay WOLZ
85 Exec Dir Intl Education & Svcs ... Mr. Zahir AHMED
51 Dir Extended & Continuing Education ... Ms. Joyce D. BECKER
12 Director Malden Campus ... Dr. Nicholas THIELE
12 Director Kennett Campus ... Ms. Marsha L. BLANCHARD
12 Director Sikeston Campus ... Mr. Stephen BORGSMILLER
18 Director of Facilities Management ... Ms. Angela MEYER
37 Director of Financial Aid ... Ms. Karen WALKER
09 Director of Institutional Research ... Dr. Patricia C. RYAN
27 Director of News Bureau ... Ms. Ann K. HAYES
15 Director of Human Resources ... Mr. Jim COOK
19 Director of Public Safety/Transit ... Mr. Doug RICHARDS
06 Registrar ... Ms. Sandy L. HINKLE
39 Director of Residence Life ... Dr. Bruce SKINNER
88 Int Director of Show Me Center ... Mr. Bob CERCHIO
21 Director of Business Operations ... Ms. Laura D. STOCK
92 Director University Honors Program ... Dr. Craig W. ROBERTS
38 Dir Counseling & Disability Svcs ... Mr. Bob LEFEBVRE
96 Director of Purchasing ... Ms. Sarah STEINNERD

Southwest Baptist University (A)

1600 University Avenue, Bolivar MO 65613-2597
County: Polk FICE Identification: 002502
Unit ID: 179326
Telephone: (417) 328-5281 Carnegie Class: Master's L
FAX Number: (417) 328-1514 Calendar System: Semester
URL: www.sbuniv.edu
Established: 1878 Annual Undergrad Tuition & Fees: $19,150
Enrollment: 3,579 Coed
Affiliation or Control: Southern Baptist IRS Status: 501(c)3
Highest Offering: Doctorate
Program: Liberal Arts And General; Teacher Preparatory; Professional
Accreditation: NH, ACBSP, ADNUR, MUS, NUR, PTA, @SW

01 President ... Dr. Pat TAYLOR
05 Provost ... Dr. Bill BROWN
11 Vice President Administration ... Mr. Ron MAUPIN
30 Vice President University Relations ... Vacant
84 Vice Pres Enrollment Management ... Dr. Stephanie MILLER
13 Vice Pres Computer/Info Services ... Dr. Robert MCGLASSON
20 Associate Provost ... Dr. Allison LANGFORD
44 Director Estate Planning ... Vacant
29 Director Alumni & Church Relations ... Mrs. Lindsay SCHINDLER
07 Director Admissions ... Mr. Darren CROWDER
41 Athletic Director ... Mr. Mike PITTS
06 Registrar ... Mr. John CREDILLE
32 Dean Student Development ... Mr. Rob HARRIS
35 Director Student Activities ... Mr. Nathan PENLAND
39 Director Residence Life ... Ms. Landee NEVILLS
42 Director University Ministries ... Mr. Kurt CADDY
15 Director of Human Resources ... Mr. David PIERCE
18 Director Physical Plant ... Mr. Bob GLIDWELL
19 Director Campus Security ... Mr. Mark GRABOWSKI
08 Director of Library Services ... Mr. Ed WALTON
50 Dean College Business/Computer Sci ... Vacant
73 Dean College Theology/Ministry ... Dr. Rodney REEVES
53 Dean Education/Social Sciences ... Dr. Linda WOODERSON
57 Dean Music/Arts/Letters ... Dr. Jeff WATERS
81 Dean Science/Math ... Dr. Perry TOMPKINS
36 Director of Career Services ... Mrs. Suzanne POWERS
14 Director Computer Services ... Mr. Kevin KELLEY
90 Director Institutional Computing ... Mr. Jeffery H. HOGUE
91 Director Administrative Computing ... Mr. David BOLTON
38 Director Counseling Services ... Mrs. Pearlene BRESHEARS
37 Director Student Financial Planning ... Mr. Brad GAMBLE
26 Chief Public Relations Officer ... Mrs. Sharina SMITH
09 Director of Institutional Research ... Mr. Jason VAUGHN
96 Director of Purchasing ... Vacant
40 Book Store Manager ... Ms. Carol SHOEMAKER

State Fair Community College (B)

3201 W 16th Street, Sedalia MO 65301-2199
County: Pettis FICE Identification: 008080
Unit ID: 179539
Telephone: (660) 530-5800 Carnegie Class: Assoc/Pub-R-M
FAX Number: (660) 530-5820 Calendar System: Semester
URL: www.sfccmo.edu
Established: 1966 Annual Undergrad Tuition & Fees (In-District): $2,700
Enrollment: 5,073 Coed
Affiliation or Control: Local IRS Status: 501(c)3
Highest Offering: Associate Degree
Program: Occupational; 2-Year Principally Bachelor's Creditable
Accreditation: NH, CONST, DH, OTA, RAD

01 President ... Dr. Marsha K. DRENNON
05 VP for Educ/Student Support Svcs ... Dr. Brent BATES
10 VP for Finance/Administration & HR ... Mr. Garry SORRELL
13 CIO Information Systems & Tech ... Mr. Mark HAVERLY
20 Dean of Academic Affairs ... Mr. Steve SCHEINER
75 Dean Vocational/Technical Studies ... Mr. Mark KELCHNER
38 Dean Student Support ... Dr. Joe GILGOUR
30 Exec Director for Development ... Ms. Jackie ALMQUIST
09 Director Institutional Planning ... Mrs. Patricia GILLMAN
06 Registrar ... Mrs. Jennifer WILBANKS
37 Director of Financial Aid ... Mr. John MATTHEWS
18 Chief Facilities/Physical Plant ... Mr. Steve KUCYNDA
21 Associate Business Officer ... Mrs. Diane BROCKMAN
26 Director of Marketing/Communication ... Mrs. Dana KELCHNER
07 Director of Admissions ... Mr. Mark CARTER

Stephens College (C)

1200 E Broadway, Columbia MO 65215-0001
County: Boone FICE Identification: 002512
Unit ID: 179548
Telephone: (573) 442-2211 Carnegie Class: Bac/Diverse
FAX Number: (573) 876-7248 Calendar System: Semester
URL: www.stephens.edu
Established: 1833 Annual Undergrad Tuition & Fees: $27,210
Enrollment: 1,029 Female
Affiliation or Control: Independent Non-Profit IRS Status: 501(c)3
Highest Offering: Master's
Program: Liberal Arts And General; Teacher Preparatory; Professional; Fine Arts Emphasis
Accreditation: NH, IACBE

01 President ... Dr. Dianne LYNCH
10 Vice Pres Finance/Business/CFO ... Dr. Lindi OVERTON
05 Vice President Academic Affairs ... Dr. Annette DIGBY
30 Vice President of Philanthropy ... Ms. Shannon WALLS
32 Vice President for Student Services ... Ms. Deborah DUREN
26 VP of Marketing/Public Relations ... Ms. Amy GIPSON
84 Vice Pres Enrollment Management ... Ms. Suzanne SHARP
49 Dean of Liberal Arts ... Ms. Mimi HEDGES
51 Dean of Grad & Continuing Studies ... Vacant
29 Director of Alumnae Relations/Phila ... Ms. Marissa TODD
06 Registrar ... Ms. Linda SHARP
13 IT Director ... Mr. Mark BRUNNER
16 Director Human Resources ... Mr. Richard ENYARD
36 Director Career Development ... Ms. Amanda ROBERTS
41 Athletic Director ... Ms. Deborah DUREN
44 Director Annual/Planned Giving ... Vacant
07 Director of Recruitment ... Vacant
21 Director of Accounting ... Mr. Josh HENGGLER
37 Financial Aid Coordinator ... Ms. Gena BOLING
09 Dir of Institutional Research ... Mr. Isaac TUTTLE
39 Director of Residence Life ... Mr. Ryan SMITH
23 Director of Health Services ... Vacant
08 Library Dir/Tech Svcs Librarian ... Ms. Corrie HUTCHINSON

Stevens Institute of Business & Arts (D)

1521 Washington Avenue, Saint Louis MO 63103
County: Saint Louis FICE Identification: 008552
Unit ID: 178767
Telephone: (314) 421-0949 Carnegie Class: Bac/Diverse
FAX Number: (314) 421-0304 Calendar System: Quarter
URL: www.siba.edu
Established: 1947 Annual Undergrad Tuition & Fees: $16,200
Enrollment: 195 Coed
Affiliation or Control: Proprietary IRS Status: Proprietary
Highest Offering: Baccalaureate
Program: Occupational
Accreditation: ACICS

01 President ... Ms. Cynthia A. MUSTERMAN
05 Academic Dean & Registrar ... Ms. Ruth Ann HOLTMANN
37 Director of Financial Aid ... Mr. Gregory M. ELSENRATH
07 Director of Admissions ... Mr. J.D SOSNOFF

Texas County Technical College (E)

6915 S Highway 63 PO Box 314, Houston MO 65483
County: Texas FICE Identification: 035793
Unit ID: 441487
Telephone: (417) 967-5466 Carnegie Class: Assoc/PrivNFP
FAX Number: (417) 967-4604 Calendar System: Semester
URL: www.texascountytech.edu
Established: 1986 Annual Undergrad Tuition & Fees: $16,979
Enrollment: 110 Coed
Affiliation or Control: Independent Non-Profit IRS Status: 501(c)3
Highest Offering: Associate Degree
Program: Occupational; 2-Year Principally Bachelor's Creditable
Accreditation: ACICS

01 President ... Ms. Charlotte GRAY
07 Director of Admissions/Registrar ... Ms. Clarice CASEBEER
37 Acting Financial Aid Director ... Ms. Clarice CASEBEER

Three Rivers Community College (F)

2080 Three Rivers Boulevard,
Poplar Bluff MO 63901-2350
County: Butler FICE Identification: 004713
Unit ID: 179645
Telephone: (573) 840-9600 Carnegie Class: Assoc/Pub-R-M
FAX Number: (573) 840-9604 Calendar System: Semester
URL: www.trcc.edu
Established: 1966 Annual Undergrad Tuition & Fees (In-State): $3,204
Enrollment: 4,234 Coed
Affiliation or Control: State IRS Status: 501(c)3
Highest Offering: Associate Degree
Program: Occupational; 2-Year Principally Bachelor's Creditable
Accreditation: NH, ACBSP, ADNUR, MLTAD, OTA

01 President ... Dr. Devin STEPHENSON
10 Chief Financial Officer ... Ms. Charlotte EUBANK
32 Vice President for Student Success ... Mr. Jason HOSENEY
05 Vice President for Learning ... Dr. Wesley A. PAYNE
08 Director Library Services ... Mr. Gordon T. JOHNSTON
37 Director Financial Aid ... Ms. Laura MILLIGAN
06 Registrar ... Ms. Marcia C. FIELDS
35 Director of Student Services ... Ms. Marcia C. FIELDS
09 Director of Institutional Research ... Ms. Melanie HAMANN
18 Chief Facilities/Physical Plant ... Mr. Derick A. ALLEN
15 Director Human Resources ... Ms. Kristina D. MCDANIEL

Truman State University (G)

100 E Normal, Kirksville MO 63501-4221
County: Adair FICE Identification: 002495
Unit ID: 178615
Telephone: (660) 785-4000 Carnegie Class: Master's M
FAX Number: (660) 785-4030 Calendar System: Semester
URL: www.truman.edu
Established: 1867 Annual Undergrad Tuition & Fees (In-State): $7,216
Enrollment: 6,070 Coed
Affiliation or Control: State IRS Status: 501(c)3
Highest Offering: Master's
Program: Liberal Arts And General; Teacher Preparatory; Professional
Accreditation: NH, BUS, BUSA, MUS, NURSE, SP, TED

01 President ... Dr. Troy D. PAINO
05 Provost/VP for Academic Affairs ... Dr. Joan POOR
30 Vice Pres University Advancement ... Mr. Mark GAMBAIANA
11 VP for Admin Finance & Planning ... Mr. David RECTOR
84 Assoc VP for Enrollment Management ... Mrs. Regina MORIN
32 Dean of Student Affairs ... Dr. Lou Ann GILCHRIST
43 General Counsel ... Mr. Warren WELLS
21 Comptroller ... Mrs. Judy MULLINS
41 Athletic Director ... Mr. Jerry WOLLMERING
15 Exec Dir HR/EEO Compliance Ofcr ... Ms. Sally DETWEILER
07 Director of Admissions ... Mrs. Melody CHAMBERS
37 Financial Aid Director ... Mrs. Kathy ELSEA
06 Registrar ... Mrs. Margaret HERRON
13 Director Information Technology ... Mrs. Donna LISS
26 Director of Public Relations ... Mrs. Heidi TEMPLETON
88 Director of Truman Institute ... Dr. Kevin MINCH
38 Dir Student Health/Counseling Svcs ... Dr. Brenda HIGGINS
88 Dean of Social & Cultural Studies ... Dr. Douglas DAVENPORT
49 Int Dean School of Arts & Letters ... Dr. Marty EISENBERG
81 Dean Sch of Science & Mathematics ... Dr. Jon GERING
53 Dean Sch of Health Sciences & Educ ... Dr. Janet GOOCH
08 Dean of Libraries & Museums ... Mr. Richard COUGHLIN
50 Dean School of Business ... Dr. Debra KERBY

University of Central Missouri (H)

Administration Building, room 101,
Warrensburg MO 64093-5299
County: Johnson FICE Identification: 002454
Unit ID: 176965
Telephone: (660) 543-4255 Carnegie Class: Master's L
FAX Number: (660) 543-4200 Calendar System: Semester
URL: www.ucmo.edu
Established: 1871 Annual Undergrad Tuition & Fees (In-State): $7,146
Enrollment: 11,637 Coed
Affiliation or Control: State IRS Status: 501(c)3
Highest Offering: Beyond Master's But Less Than Doctorate
Program: Liberal Arts And General; Teacher Preparatory; Professional
Accreditation: NH, AAB, AAFCS, ART, BUS, BUSA, CACREP, CEA, CONST, DIETD, ENGR, MUS, NAIT, NURSE, SP, SW, TED

01 President ... Dr. Charles M. AMBROSE
101 Spec Asst to Pres for Board Affs ... Ms. Monica R. HUFFMAN
05 Provost and Chief Learning Officer ... Dr. Deborah J. CURTIS
32 Vice Prov Student Experience/Engage ... Dr. Sharlene GARBER BAX
45 Vice Provost Institutional Effectiv ... Dr. Michael GRELLE
35 Asst Vice Pres Student Affairs ... Dr. Corey L. BOWMAN
84 Vice Provost Enrollment Management ... Dr. Richard D. SLUDER
30 Vice President Advancement ... Mr. Jason S. DRUMMOND

08 Dean of Library Services .... Ms. Mollie D. DINWIDDIE
58 Dean Graduate and Extended Studies .... Dr. Joseph VAUGHN
49 Dean College of Arts/Humanities/Sci .... Dr. Gersham NELSON
72 Dean College of Health/Science/Tech .... Dr. Alice L. GREIFE
50 Dean Harmon Col Business/Prof Stds .... Dr. Roger J. BEST
92 Dean of the Honors College .... Dr. Joseph D. LEWANDOWSKI
53 Dean of College of Education .... Dr. Michael D. WRIGHT
10 Vice Pres Finance/Chief Ops Ofcr .... Mr. John MERRIGAN
30 University Director Development .... Vacant
13 Vice Provost for Technology .... Dr. James F. GRAHAM
43 General Counsel .... Mr. Henry R. SETSER
41 Athletic Director .... Mr. Jerry M. HUGHES
06 Director of Registrar .... Ms. Teri A. BOWMAN
26 University Director Communications .... Vacant
09 Director Testing & Assess Services .... Vacant
36 Director Career Services .... Ms. Teresa Fine ALEWEL
37 Dir Student Financial Assistance .... Ms. Angela L. KARLIN
19 Director of Public Safety .... Ms. Kimberly J. VANSELL
39 Sr Dir Univ Housing/Res Dining Svcs ..... Mr. Patrick J. BRADLEY
21 Director Accounting Services .... Ms. Toni L. KREKE
18 Dir Facilities & Planning Op .... Mr. Christopher WELLMAN
96 Director Purchasing .... Vacant
15 Director Human Resources .... Mr. Rick L. DIXON
40 Director of Univ Store & Textbooks .... Mr. Charles D. RUTT
85 Director of International Center .... Dr. Adalynn J. STEVENSON
88 Director User Services .... Vacant
88 Accreditation Coordinator .... Ms. Carole E. NIMMER
07 Director Admissions .... Ms. Ann A. NORDYKE
15 Asst Director of Human Resources .... Ms. Cheryl D. TRELOW
29 Asst VP Resources Development ... Ms. Jennifer L. VANDERBOUT
38 Director Counseling Center .... Dr. Paul D. POLYCHRONIS
44 Manager Annual Fund .... Mr. Scott ALVESTED
24 Coord of Academic Media Services .... Ms. Mary E. GRIFFIS

*University of Missouri System Administration (A)

321 University Hall, Columbia MO 65211-3020

County: Boone　FICE Identification: 002515

Unit ID: 178439

Telephone: (573) 882-2011　Carnegie Class: N/A

FAX Number: (573) 882-2721

URL: www.umsystem.edu

01 President .... Mr. Timothy M. WOLFE
100 Chief of Staff .... Dr. Robert W. SCHWARTZ
10 Vice Pres Finance & Administration .... Ms. Natalie KRAWITZ
05 Sr Assoc Vice Pres Academic Affairs .... Dr. Steven W. GRAHAM
13 Vice President Info Technology .... Dr. Gary K. ALLEN
86 Vice President Government Relations .... Mr. Stephen C. KNORR
15 Vice Pres Human Resource Services ... Ms. Elizabeth RODRIGUEZ
46 Vice President Research & Econ Dev ..... Mr. Michael F. NICHOLS
43 Acting General Counsel .... Mr. Phillip J. HOSKINS
26 Chief Communications Officer .... Ms. Jennifer HOLLINGSHEAD
17 Executive Director UM Health Care .... Mr. James H. ROSS
23 Vice Chancellor for Health Sciences .. Dr. Harold A. WILLIAMSON
21 Treasurer .... Mr. Thomas RICHARDS
21 Controller .... Ms. Jane E. CLOSTERMAN

*University of Missouri - Columbia (B)

Columbia MO 65211-0001

County: Boone　FICE Identification: 002516

Unit ID: 178396

Telephone: (573) 882-2121　Carnegie Class: RU/VH

FAX Number: (573) 882-9907　Calendar System: Semester

URL: www.missouri.edu

Established: 1839　Annual Undergrad Tuition & Fees (In-State): $9,257

Enrollment: 33,805　Coed

Affiliation or Control: State　IRS Status: 501(c)3

Highest Offering: Doctorate

Program: Liberal Arts And General; Teacher Preparatory; Professional

Accreditation: NH, BUS, BUSA, CIDA, CLPSY, COPSY, DIETC, DMS, ENG, FOR, HSA, IPSY, JOUR, LAW, #LIB, MED, MUS, NMT, NRPA, NURSE, OT, PH, PTA, RAD, #SCPSY, SP, SPAA, SW, @TEAC, VET

02 Chancellor .... Dr. Brady J. DEATON
03 Deputy Chancellor .... Mr. Michael A. MIDDLETON
05 Provost .... Dr. Brian L. FOSTER
20 Deputy Provost .... Mr. Kenneth D. DEAN
20 Vice Provost Undergrad Studies .... Dr. James SPAIN
32 Vice Chancellor Student Affairs .... Dr. Catherine C. SCROGGS
11 VC Administrative Services .... Ms. Jacquelyn K. JONES
58 VP Adv Studies/Dean Grad Sch .... Mr. George JUSTICE
58 Associate Graduate Dean .... Dr. Sheryl TUCKER
04 Asst to Chanc for University Affs .... Ms. Christine H. KOUKOLA
30 VC Development/Alumni Relations .... Mr. David P. HOUSH
29 Assoc VC Alumni Relations/Devel .... Mr. Todd A. MCCUBBIN
17 Vice Chancellor for Health Sciences .... Dr. Harold A. WILLIAMSON, JR.
57 Director School of Music .... Dr. Robert SHAY
84 Vice Provost for Enrollment Mgmt .... Dr. Ann J. KORSCHGEN
56 Vice Provost for Extension .... Dr. Michael D. OUART
85 Vice Provost International Pgms .... Dr. Handy WILLIAMSON
46 Vice Chancellor for Research .... Mr. Robert DUNCAN
88 Director of Budget .... Mr. Timothy R. ROONEY
13 Chief Information Officer .... Dr. Gary K. ALLEN
15 Asst Vice Chanc Human Resources .... Ms. Karen E. TOUZEAU
18 Assoc Vice Chanc Campus Facilities .... Mr. Gary L. WARD
46 Spec Asst to Vice Chanc of Research .... Dr. Michael WARNOCK
35 Asst Vice Chanc Student Affairs .... Dr. Jeffrey ZEILENGA
06 University Registrar .... Ms. Brenda V. SELMAN
09 Director Institutional Research .... Dr. Mardy T. EIMERS
08 Director of Libraries .... Mr. James A. COGSWELL
37 Assoc Dir Student Financial Aid .... Mr. Nick PREWETT
47 Vice Chan & Dean Agric/Food/Nat Res .... Dr. Thomas L. PAYNE
49 Dean Arts & Science .... Dr. Michael J. O'BRIEN
50 Dean of Business .... Ms. Joan GABEL
88 Director School of Accountancy .... Dr. Vairam ARUNACHALAM
53 Dean of Education .... Dr. Daniel CLAY
54 Dean of Engineering .... Dr. James E. THOMPSON
65 Dir School of Natural Resources .... Dr. Mark R. RYAN
76 Dean School of Health Professions .... Dr. Richard E. OLIVER
59 Dean Human Environmental Science . Dr. Stephen R. JORGENSEN
60 Dean of Journalism .... Dr. R. Dean MILLS
61 Dean of Law .... Dr. R. Lawrence DESSEM
63 Dean of Medicine .... Dr. Robert CHURCHILL
66 Dean of Nursing .... Dr. Judith FITZGERALD MILLER
70 Director School of Social Work .... Dr. Marjorie SABLE
74 Dean of Veterinary Medicine .... Dr. Neil OLSON
19 Director of University Police .... Mr. Jack W. WATRING
27 Director News Services .... Ms. Mary Jo BANKEN
41 Intercollegiate Athletic Director .... Mr. Michael F. ALDEN
39 Director Residential Life .... Mr. Frankie D. MINOR
25 Director Sponsored Program Admin .... Ms. Jennifer DUNCAN
40 Regional Director Retail Operations .... Ms. Sherry POLLARD
38 Director Counseling Services .... Dr. David WALLACE
88 Assoc Vice Provost Intl Initiatives .... Dr. James K. SCOTT
36 Director Career Services .... Dr. Matthew REISKE
23 Director Student Health Services .... Dr. Susan E. EVEN
92 Director Honors College .... Dr. Stuart B. PALONSKY
94 Director Women's/Gender Studies .... Dr. Jacquelyn S. LITT
88 Director Info Science Learning Tech .... Dr. John WEDMAN
80 Director Truman Schl Public Affairs ...... Dr. Barton J. WECHSLER
07 Director of Admissions .... Ms. Barbara A. RUPP
26 Assistant to Chancellor Univ Affs .... Ms. Christine H. KOUKOLA
35 Director Student Life .... Dr. Mark L. LUCAS
28 Chief Diversity Officer .... Dr. Roger L. WORTHINGTON
96 Manager of Campus Procurement .... Ms. Sherri L. WOOD

*University of Missouri - Kansas City (C)

5100 Rockhill Road, Kansas City MO 64110-2499

County: Jackson　FICE Identification: 002518

Unit ID: 178402

Telephone: (816) 235-1000　Carnegie Class: RU/H

FAX Number: (816) 235-1717　Calendar System: Semester

URL: www.umkc.edu

Established: 1929　Annual Undergrad Tuition & Fees (In-State): $7,626

Enrollment: 15,492　Coed

Affiliation or Control: State　IRS Status: 501(c)3

Highest Offering: Doctorate

Program: Liberal Arts And General; Teacher Preparatory; Professional

Accreditation: NH, AA, ANEST, BUS, CLPSY, COPSY, CS, DANCE, DENT, DH, ENG, IPSY, LAW, MED, MUS, NURSE, OTA, PHAR, SPAA, SW, TED, THEA

02 Chancellor .... Mr. Leo E. MORTON
28 Deputy Chancellor for Diversity .... Dr. Karen L. DACE
05 Exec Vice Chanc and Provost .... Dr. Gail HACKETT
32 Vice Chanc Stdnt Affs/Enroll Mgmt .... Mr. Melvin C. TYLER
11 Vice Chanc for Admin Services .... Ms. Sharon LINDENBAUM
21 Director Budgeting and Planning .... Ms. Karen D. WILKERSON
30 Vice Chanc for Univ Advancement .... Mr. Curt J. CRESPINO
41 Athletic Director .... Mr. Timothy W. HALL
20 CIO & Vice Prov for Acad Pgms . Dr. Mary Lou A. HINES-FRITTS
20 Vice Prov for Academic Affairs .... Dr. Cynthia L. PEMBERTON
20 Vice Prov for Faculty Affairs .... Dr. Denis M. MEDEIROS
49 Dean College of Arts & Sciences .... Dr. Wayne VAUGHT
50 Dean Bloch School Bus Public Admin .... Dr. Teng-Kee TAN
81 Dean School Biological Sciences .... Dr. Lawrence A. DREYFUS
64 Dean Conservatory of Music & Dance .... Mr. Peter T. WITTE
52 Dean School of Dentistry .... Dr. Marsha A. PYLE
53 Dean School of Education .... Dr. Wanda J. BLANCHETT
54 Dean Sch of Computing/Engineering .... Dr. Kevin Z. TRUMAN
61 Dean School of Law .... Ms. Ellen Y. SUNI
63 Dean School of Medicine .... Dr. Betty M. DREES
66 Dean School of Nursing .... Dr. Lora LACEY-HAUN
67 Dean School of Pharmacy .... Dr. Russell B. MELCHERT
62 Dean University Libraries .... Dr. Sharon L. BOSTICK
58 Dean of School of Graduate Studies ...... Dr. Denis M. MEDEIROS
09 Director Institutional Research .... Dr. Larry BUNCE
16 Asst Vice Chanc Human Resources .... Ms. Carol HINTZ
84 Assoc Vice Chanc Enrollment Mgmt ... Ms. Jennifer DEHAEMERS
35 Assistant Dean of Students .... Dr. Eric GROSPITCH
35 Assistant Dean of Students .... Dr. Jeff TRAIGER
35 Director Student Involvement .... Dr. Angela COTTRELL
88 Asst VC Univ Communications .... Ms. Sarah L. MORRIS
26 Associate Director Public Relations .... Ms. Wandra B. GREEN
102 Asst VC for Development .... Ms. Jenea OLIVER
29 Asst VC AlumniConstituent Relations .... Ms. Lisen TAMMEUS
44 Director Planned Giving .... Mr. Phil WATSON
86 Legislative Liaison .... Mr. Troy LILLEBO
22 Director Affirmative Action .... Mr. Michael D. BATES
88 Dir Center for Academic Develop .... Dr. Marion STONE
07 Director of Admissions .... Ms. Tammy CLOUTIER BYLAND
85 Director Internatl Student Affairs .... Ms. Sandra GAULT
28 Director Multicultural Affairs .... Ms. Tiffany S. WILLIAMS
37 Director Student Financial Aid .... Ms. Nancy MERZ
06 Registrar .... Mr. Doug SWINK
19 Chief Campus Police .... Mr. Michael BONGARTZ
40 Director Bookstore .... Mr. Pete EISENTRAGER
38 Director Counseling/Health Test Ctr .... Dr. Marita BARKIS
88 Director Womens Center .... Dr. Brenda BETHMAN
36 Director Career Services .... Mr. Greg HAYES
39 Director Residential Life .... Ms. Kristen ABELL
96 Manager Campus Procurement .... Ms. Catherine A. BARKER
25 Asst to VC for Admin Services .... Mr. Colin C. GAGE
18 Director Campus Facilities .... Mr. Robert A. SIMMONS
104 Director International Acad Pgms .... Dr. Linna F. PLACE

*University of Missouri - Saint Louis (D)

One University Boulevard, Saint Louis MO 63121-4400

County: Saint Louis　FICE Identification: 002519

Unit ID: 178420

Telephone: (314) 516-5000　Carnegie Class: RU/H

FAX Number: (314) 516-5378　Calendar System: Semester

URL: www.umsl.edu

Established: 1963　Annual Undergrad Tuition & Fees (In-State): $9,314

Enrollment: 12,689　Coed

Affiliation or Control: State　IRS Status: 501(c)3

Highest Offering: Doctorate

Program: Liberal Arts And General; Teacher Preparatory; Professional

Accreditation: NH, BUS, BUSA, CACREP, CLPSY, ENG, IPSY, MUS, NURSE, OPT, OPTR, SPAA, SW, TED

02 Chancellor .... Dr. Thomas F. GEORGE
05 Provost/Vice Chanc Academic Affairs .... Dr. Glen H. COPE
10 Vice Chanc Managerial/Tech Svcs .... Dr. James M. KRUEGER
30 Vice Chancellor Univ Advancement .... Mr. Martin F. LEIFELD
22 Dir of Equal Opportunity/Diversity .... Ms. Deborah J. BURRIS
46 Vice Provost Research Admin .... Dr. Nasser ARSHADI
32 Vice Provost Student Affairs .... Mr. Curtis C. COONROD
58 Vice Prov Acad Affs/Dean Grad Sch .... Dr. Judith WALKER DE FELIX
13 Assoc VC Information Technology/ CIO .... Mr. Lawrence W. FREDERICK
88 Dir Center for Teaching & Learning .... Dr. Margaret W. COHEN
85 Director International Studies .... Dr. Joel N. GLASSMAN
49 Dean College Arts & Sciences .... Dr. Ronald YASBIN
50 Dean College of Business Admin .... Dr. N. Keith WOMER
53 Dean College of Education .... Dr. Carole G. BASILE
57 Int Dean College of Fine Arts/Comm ..... Dr. James E. RICHARDS
66 Dean College of Nursing .... Dr. Susan DEAN-BAAR
92 Dean Honors College .... Dr. Robert M. BLISS
88 Dean College of Optometry .... Dr. Larry J. DAVIS
08 Dean of Libraries .... Mr. Christopher DAMES
54 Dean Engineering Program .... Dr. Joseph O'SULLIVAN
51 Dean Continuing Education .... Dr. Wm Thomas WALKER
88 Assistant to Provost Public Affairs .... Ms. Elizabeth VAN UUM
23 Asst Vice Provost Hlth/Wellness .... Dr. Nancy M. MAGNUSON
88 Asst Dean of Students/Stdnt Conduct .... Mr. D'Andre BRADDIX
93 Asst Dean of Stdnts/MultiCultural .... Ms. Natissia SMALL
35 Asst Dean of Students/Student Life .... Ms. Miriam I. ROCCIA
41 Director of Athletics .... Ms. Lori FLANAGAN
07 Dean of Enrollment .... Mr. Alan BYRD
40 Manager Bookstore .... Ms. Stephanie EATON
36 Director Career Services .... Ms. Teresa A. BALESTRERI
38 Director Counseling Services .... Dr. M. Sharon BIEGEN
06 Registrar .... Ms. Linda C. SILMAN
39 Director Residential Life .... Mr. Jonathan A. LIDGUS
37 Director Student Financial Aid .... Dr. Anthony C. GEORGES
88 Vice Pres Ctr Emerging Technologies .. Ms. Barbara A. ENNEKING
88 Director Ctr Nanoscience .... Dr. George W. GOKEL
88 Director Center Neurodynamics .... Dr. Sonya BAHAR
88 Dir Scientific & Computing/ITE .... Mr. William J. LEMON
88 Dir MO Institute of Mental Health .... Mr. Joseph PARKS
25 Manager Bus/Fiscal/Research Admin .... Ms. Karen O. BOYD
88 Director Business Services .... Ms. Gloria J. LEONARD
18 Director Engr/Planning & Const .... Mr. H. Sam DARANDARI
18 Director Facilities Services .... Mr. Frank S. KOCHIN
21 Director of Finance .... Mr. Ernest A. CORNFORD
15 Assoc VC Human Resources .... Mr. Peter A. HEITHAUS
19 Director Institutional Safety .... Mr. Forrest L. VAN NESS
09 Director Institutional Research .... Mr. Lawrence W. WESTERMEYER
26 Chief Marketing Officer .... Mr. Ronald H. GOSSEN
102 Assoc VC Dev Corporation/Foundation ... Dr. Brenda M. MCPHAIL
88 Sr Dir Development Colleges/Units .... Mr. Dan C. DIEDRIECH
88 Sr Dir University Campaigns .... Mr. Mark A. BERLYN
88 Director KWMU-FM Radio/Gen Mgr .... Mr. Tim J. EBY
29 Dir Alumni Relations/Annual Giving ...... Ms. Deborah L. GRAHAM
27 Chief Information Officer .... Mr. Robert D. SAMPLES
44 Director of Planned Giving .... Mr. Kent KROBER
94 Director Women's & Gender Studies .... Dr. Kathy J. GENTILE
70 Director Social Work .... Dr. Lois PIERCE
79 Director Center for the Humanities .... Dr. Diane H. TOULIATOS-MILES
88 Dir Gateway Writing Project .... Dr. Nancy SINGER
88 Dir Public Policy Administration .... Dr. Deborah B. BALSER
88 Director Public Policy Research Ctr .... Dr. Mark TRANEL
88 Dir Women in Public Life .... Ms. Vivian EVELOFF
31 Director Community College Relation .... Ms. Melissa HATTMAN
88 Managing Dir Performing Arts Center ... Mr. John R. CATTANACH
88 Dir Des Lee Collaborative Vision .... Ms. Patricia ZAHN

*Missouri University of Science & Technology (E)

300 W 13th Street, Rolla MO 65409-0001

County: Phelps　FICE Identification: 002517

Unit ID: 178411

Telephone: (573) 341-4111　Carnegie Class: RU/H

FAX Number: (573) 341-4307　Calendar System: Semester

URL: www.mst.edu

Established: 1870　Annual Undergrad Tuition & Fees (In-State): $9,350

Enrollment: 7,522 Coed
Affiliation or Control: State IRS Status: 501(c)3
Highest Offering: Doctorate
Program: Professional; Technical Emphasis
Accreditation: NH, CS, ENG

02 Chancellor .... Dr. Cheryl B. SCHRADER
05 Provost/Exec Vice Chanc Acad Affs .... Dr. Warren K. WRAY
11 Vice Chanc Administrative Services .... Mr. F. Stephen MALOTT
30 Vice Chance University Advancement .... Ms. Joan M. NESBITT
32 Vice Chancellor Student Affairs .... Dr. Debra A G. ROBINSON
46 Vice Provost for Research Services .... Dr. K. KRISHNAMURTHY
20 Interim Vice Provost Acad Affairs .... Dr. Philip D. WHITEFIELD
20 Vice Prov Undergrad Studies .... Dr. Harvest L. COLLIER
58 Vice Provost Graduate Studies .... Dr. Venkata ALLADA
56 Vice Provost of Global Learning .... Dr. Henry A. WIEBE
84 Vice Prov & Dean of Enrollment Mgmt .... Ms. Laura K. STOLL
08 Director of Library .... Mr. J. Andrew STEWART
13 Interim Chief Info Ofcr/Assoc VP .... Mr. John BAX
06 Registrar .... Ms. Deanne JACKSON
38 Asst Vice Chanc Stdnt Affs/Supp Svc .... Dr. Carl F. BURNS
41 Director of Athletics .... Mr. Mark E. MULLIN
15 Dir Human Resource/Affirm Action .... Ms. Shenethia MANUEL
36 Dir Career Opportunities Center .... Dr. Edna GROVER-BISKER
85 Director Intl/Cultural Affairs .... Ms. Jeanie H. HOFER
35 Director Student Life/Univ Center-R .... Mr. Mark POTRAFKA
39 Director Residential Life .... Ms. Tina F. SHEPPARD
09 Director Inst Research & Assessment .... Dr. Thulasi KUMAR
07 Interim Director of Admissions .... Ms. Lynn STICHNOTE
29 Director Alumni/Constit Relations .... Ms. Marianne A. WARD
37 Interim Dir Student Financial Aid .... Ms. Bridget K. BETZ
26 Director of Communications .... Mr. Andrew P. CAREAGA
18 Director of Physical Facilities .... Mr. James PACKARD
28 Dir Ctr Pre-College Pgms/Stdnt Divr .... Mr. Will PERKINS
88 Dir of Womens Leadership Institute .... Ms. Cecilia ELMORE
40 Asst Director of Univ Bookstore .... Mr. Mark GALLARDO

Urshan Graduate School of Theology (A)

704 Howdershell Road, Florissant MO 63031-7526
County: St. Louis FICE Identification: 041461
Unit ID: 455099
Telephone: (314) 921-9290 Carnegie Class: Spec/Faith
FAX Number: (314) 921-9203 Calendar System: Semester
URL: www.ugst.edu
Established: 2001 Annual Undergrad Tuition & Fees: $9,775
Enrollment: 73 Coed
Affiliation or Control: Other Protestant IRS Status: 501(c)3
Highest Offering: Master's
Program: Professional; Religious Emphasis
Accreditation: THEOL

01 President .... Dr. David K. BERNARD
03 Vice President .... Dr. Bobbi MOREHEAD
05 Academic Dean .... Dr. James A. LITTLES

Vatterott College-Joplin (B)

809 Illinois, Joplin MO 64801-9538
County: Jasper Identification: 666060
Unit ID: 404374
Telephone: (417) 781-5633 Carnegie Class: Assoc/PrivFP
FAX Number: (417) 781-6437 Calendar System: Other
URL: www.vatterott-college.edu
Established: 1969 Annual Undergrad Tuition & Fees: $11,583
Enrollment: 297 Coed
Affiliation or Control: Proprietary IRS Status: Proprietary
Highest Offering: Associate Degree
Program: Occupational; Business Emphasis
Accreditation: ACCSC

01 CEO & President .... Ms. Pam BELL
05 Vice President Academic Affairs .... Mr. Brandon SHEDRON
10 Chief Financial Officer .... Mr. Dennis BEAVERS
43 Associate Counsel .... Mr. Mike HODGE
12 Campus Director .... Ms. Jacqueline O'DELL

† Branch campus of Vatterott College-North Park, Berkeley, MO.

Vatterott College-Kansas City (C)

8955 East 38th Terrace, Kansas City MO 64129-1692
County: Jackson Identification: 666519
Unit ID: 404383
Telephone: (816) 861-1000 Carnegie Class: Assoc/PrivFP
FAX Number: (816) 861-1400 Calendar System: Other
URL: www.vatterott-college.edu
Established: 1969 Annual Undergrad Tuition & Fees: $12,259
Enrollment: 761 Coed
Affiliation or Control: Proprietary IRS Status: Proprietary
Highest Offering: Associate Degree
Program: Occupational; Technical Emphasis
Accreditation: ACCSC

01 CEO & President .... Ms. Pam BELL
10 Chief Financial Officer .... Mr. Dennis BEAVERS
05 Chief Academic Officer .... Dr. John TUCKER
11 Chief Administrative Officer .... Mr. Erio COMICI
12 Campus Director .... Mr. Brian SCHUMANN

† Branch campus of Vatterott College-North Park, Berkeley, MO.

Vatterott College-NorthPark (D)

8580 Evans Avenue, Berkeley MO 63134-2900
County: Saint Louis FICE Identification: 025997
Unit ID: 245342
Telephone: (314) 264-1000 Carnegie Class: Assoc/PrivFP4
FAX Number: (314) 522-6174 Calendar System: Other
URL: www.vatterott-college.edu
Established: 1969 Annual Undergrad Tuition & Fees: $11,834
Enrollment: 1,534 Coed
Affiliation or Control: Proprietary IRS Status: Proprietary
Highest Offering: Baccalaureate
Program: Occupational; 2-Year Principally Bachelor's Creditable; Technical Emphasis
Accreditation: ACCSC

01 Campus Director .... Robert DONNELL
10 Chief Financial Officer .... Dennis BEAVERS
05 Director of Education .... Al WASHINGTON
05 Director of Education .... Samuel BOYD, III
06 Registrar .... Brenda LINCOLN-PENZEL
07 Director of Admissions .... Harvey CHAMBERLAIN

Vatterott College-O'Fallon (E)

3550 West Clay Street, St. Charles MO 63301
County: Saint Charles Identification: 666584
Unit ID: 445559
Telephone: (636) 978-7488 Carnegie Class: Assoc/PrivFP
FAX Number: (636) 978-5121 Calendar System: Semester
URL: www.vatterott.edu
Established: 1969 Annual Undergrad Tuition & Fees: N/A
Enrollment: 323 Coed
Affiliation or Control: Proprietary IRS Status: Proprietary
Highest Offering: Associate Degree
Program: Occupational
Accreditation: ACCSC

01 Campus Director .... Mr. James GROVER

† Branch campus of Vatterott College-North Park, Berkeley, MO.

Vatterott College-Saint Joseph (F)

3131 Frederick Avenue, Saint Joseph MO 64506
County: Buchanan Identification: 666520
Unit ID: 436182
Telephone: (816) 364-5399 Carnegie Class: Assoc/PrivFP
FAX Number: (816) 364-1593 Calendar System: Other
URL: www.vatterott-college.edu
Established: 1969 Annual Undergrad Tuition & Fees: $12,033
Enrollment: 314 Coed
Affiliation or Control: Proprietary IRS Status: Proprietary
Highest Offering: Associate Degree
Program: Occupational; Technical Emphasis
Accreditation: ACCSC

01 CEO & President .... Ms. Pam BELL
10 Chief Financial Officer .... Mr. Dennis BEAVERS
05 Vice President Academic Affairs .... Dr. Brandon SHEDRON
30 VP Regulatory Affs/Strategic Devel .... Mr. Aaron LACEY
43 General Counsel/Chief Administrator .... Mr. Scott CASANOVER
12 Campus Director .... Ms. Shawn RIGGINS

† Branch campus of Vatterott College-Des Moines, Des Moines, IA.

Vatterott College-Springfield (G)

3850 S Campbell Avenue, Springfield MO 65807-5340
County: Greene Identification: 666521
Unit ID: 404365
Telephone: (417) 831-8116 Carnegie Class: Assoc/PrivFP
FAX Number: (417) 831-5099 Calendar System: Other
URL: www.vatterott-college.edu
Established: 1969 Annual Undergrad Tuition & Fees: $11,863
Enrollment: 364 Coed
Affiliation or Control: Proprietary IRS Status: Proprietary
Highest Offering: Associate Degree
Program: Occupational; Technical Emphasis
Accreditation: ACCSC

01 CEO & President .... Ms. Pam BELL
43 Vice Pres of HR/General Counsel .... Mr. D. Scott CASANOVER
10 Chief Financial Officer .... Mr. Dennis BEAVERS
05 Chief Academic Officer .... Mr. Brandon SHEDRON
12 Campus Director .... Ms. Rebecca MATNEY

† Branch campus of Vatterott College-North Park, Berkeley, MO.

Vatterott College-Sunset Hills (H)

12970 Maurer Industrial Drive,
Sunset Hills MO 63127-1516
County: Saint Louis Identification: 666522
Unit ID: 436191
Telephone: (314) 843-4200 Carnegie Class: Bac/Assoc
FAX Number: (314) 843-1709 Calendar System: Other
URL: www.vatterott-college.com
Established: 1969 Annual Undergrad Tuition & Fees: $11,973
Enrollment: 734 Coed
Affiliation or Control: Proprietary IRS Status: Proprietary
Highest Offering: Baccalaureate
Program: Occupational; Technical Emphasis
Accreditation: ACCSC

01 CEO & President .... Ms. Pam BELL
10 Chief Financial Officer .... Mr. Dennis BEAVERS
05 Vice President Academic Affairs .... Dr. Brandon SHEDRON
45 VP Regulatory Affs/Strategic Devel .... Mr. Aaron LACEY
43 General Counsel/Chief Administrator .... Mr. Scott CASANOVER
12 Campus Director .... Ms. Leanne EDWARDS
106 Online Director .... Mr. Darrell JOY

† Branch campus of Vatterott College-North Park, Berkeley, MO.

Washington University in St. Louis (I)

One Brookings Drive, Saint Louis MO 63130-4899
County: Saint Louis FICE Identification: 002520
Unit ID: 179867
Telephone: (314) 935-5000 Carnegie Class: RU/VH
FAX Number: N/A Calendar System: Semester
URL: www.wustl.edu
Established: 1853 Annual Undergrad Tuition & Fees: $43,705
Enrollment: 14,067 Coed
Affiliation or Control: Independent Non-Profit IRS Status: 501(c)3
Highest Offering: Doctorate
Program: Liberal Arts And General; Professional
Accreditation: NH, ACAE, ART, AUD, BUS, CLPSY, ENG, LAW, MED, OT, PH, PTA, SW

01 Chancellor .... Prof. Mark S. WRIGHTON
05 Exec VC Academic Affairs/Provost .... Prof. Edward S. MACIAS
11 Exec VC Administration .... Mr. Henry S. WEBBER
63 Exec Vice Chanc/Dean of Medicine .... Dr. Larry J. SHAPIRO
43 Exec Vice Chanc/General Counsel .... Mr. Michael R. CANNON
30 Exec VC Alumni & Development .... Mr. David T. BLASINGAME
10 Vice Chancellor for Finance/CFO .... Ms. Barbara A. FEINER
46 VC for Research .... Prof. Evan D. KHARASCH
16 Vice Chanc for Human Resources .... Ms. Ann B. PRENATT
32 Vice Chanc for Students .... Dr. Sharon STAHL
26 Vice Chanc for Public Affairs .... Ms. Jill D. FRIEDMAN
86 VC Government & Community Relations . Ms. Pamela S. LOKKEN
88 Chief Investment Officer .... Ms. Kimberly G. WALKER
21 Assoc VC for Finance and Treasurer .... Ms. Amy B. KWESKIN
49 Dean of Faculty of Arts & Sciences .... Prof. Gary S. WIHL
61 Dean School of Law .... Prof. Kent D. SYVERUD
54 Dean Engineering & Applied Science .... Dr. Ralph S. QUATRANO
57 Dean Sam Fox Sch Design Visual Arts .... Prof. Carmon COLANGELO
57 Dean College & Graduate Sch of Art .... Prof. Franklin SPECTOR
50 Dean Olin Business School .... Prof. Mahendra R. GUPTA
58 Dean Graduate School of A & S .... Prof. Richard J. SMITH
70 Dean Brown School of Social Work .... Prof. Edward F. LAWLOR
55 Dean University College .... Prof. Robert E. WILTENBURG
48 Dean Architecture .... Prof. Bruce M. LINDSEY
04 Assistant to Chancellor .... Dr. Robert M. WILD
101 Secretary to the Board of Trustees .... Ms. Ida H. EARLY
84 Assoc VC Undergraduate Admissions .... Mr. John A. BERG
20 Assoc VC Spec Asst Academic Affs .... Prof. Gerhild S. WILLIAMS
88 Assoc VC for Development .... Mr. William S. STOLL
29 Assoc VC Alumni & Development Pgm .. Ms. Pamella A. HENSON
26 Assoc VC/Exec Dir Med Public Affs .... Mr. Donald E. CLAYTON
28 Vice Provost/Diversity .... Prof. Adrienne D. DAVIS
85 Assoc VC International Affairs .... Prof. James V. WERTSCH
08 Dean of Libraries .... Mr. Jeffrey G. TRZECIAK
39 Assoc VC Students/Dean Students .... Mr. Justin X. CARROLL
35 Assoc VC Students/Dean Campus Life .... Dr. Jill E. CARNAGHI
13 Assoc VC Info Services & Tech .... Mr. Andrew D. ORTSTADT
27 Assoc VC for Public Affairs/U News .... Mr. Steven J. GIVENS
85 Asst VC/Dir International Students .... Ms. Kathy STEINER-LANG
96 Asst Vice Chanc Resource Management .... Mr. Alan S. KUEBLER
36 Asst VC/Dir Career Planning & Plcmt .... Mr. Mark W. SMITH
18 Asst VC Facilities Planning/Mgmt .... Mr. Arthur J. ACKERMANN
88 Asst VC Environ Health & Safety .... Mr. Bruce D. BACKUS
88 Asst VC Real Estate .... Ms. Mary B. CAMPBELL
72 Asst VC/Co-Dir Tech Management .... Dr. Bradley J. CASTANHO
72 Asst VC/Co-Dir Tech Management .... Mr. Michael T. MARRAH
14 Asst VC App Development & Support .... Ms. Denise R. HIRSCHBECK
23 Asst VC/Dir Student Health Services .... Dr. Alan I. GLASS
37 Director of Student Financial Svcs .... Mr. William H. WITBRODT
41 Director of Athletics .... Mr. John M. SCHAEL
19 Director of Campus Police .... Mr. Donald STROM
07 Director of Admissions .... Ms. Julie SHIMABUKURO
06 Director Student Records/Registrar .... Ms. Susan E. HOSACK
38 Assoc Director of Student Health .... Dr. Thomas M. BROUNK

Webster University (J)

470 E Lockwood, Webster Groves MO 63119-3141
County: Saint Louis FICE Identification: 002521
Unit ID: 179894
Telephone: (314) 968-6900 Carnegie Class: Master's L
FAX Number: (314) 968-7112 Calendar System: Semester
URL: www.webster.edu
Established: 1915 Annual Undergrad Tuition & Fees: $23,010
Enrollment: 21,278 Coed
Affiliation or Control: Independent Non-Profit IRS Status: 501(c)3
Highest Offering: Doctorate
Program: Liberal Arts And General
Accreditation: NH, ANEST, MUS, NUR, TED

01 President .... Dr. Elizabeth J. STROBLE
04 Special Assistant to President .... Dr. Oren YAGIL

05 Provost ....Dr. Julian Z. SCHUSTER
30 Vice Pres Development/Alumni Pgms ....Ms. Faith D. MADDY
32 VP Student Affairs/Enrollment Mgmt ....Dr. Paul CARNEY
10 VP Finance & Administration ....Dr. Greg GUNDERSON
13 Interim VP Information Technology ....Mr. Kenneth FREEMAN
20 AVP Academic Affairs ....Dr. Carol J. ADAMS
20 AVP Academic Affairs ....Dr. Elizabeth RUSSELL
20 AVP Academic Affairs ....Mr. Randy WRIGHT
21 AVP Resource Planning & Budget ....Mr. Dan HITCHELL
44 AVP Development/Alumni Pgms ....Mr. Matt ANDREW
32 Associate VP/Dean of Students ....Dr. Ted HOEF
106 AVP Acad Affs/Dir OnLine Learning ....Mr. Dan VIELE
82 AVP Academic Affairs/Dir Intl Pgms ....Dr. Grant CHAPMAN
15 AVP Human Resources ....Ms. Betsy SCHMUTZ
84 AVP for Enrollment Management ....Ms. Anne EDMUNDS
29 AVP Alumni Programs ....Ms. Jennifer JEZEK-TAUSSIG
86 VP Military & Government Programs ....Mr. Mike CALLAN
46 AVP & Chief Strategic Initiatives ....Mr. Tom JOHNSON
20 Associate Provost ....Ms. Nancy HELLERUD
50 Dean School Business & Technology ....Dr. Benjamin O. AKANDE
53 Dean School of Education ....Dr. Brenda S. FYFE
57 Dean Leigh Gerdine Col of Fine Arts ....Mr. Peter E. SARGENT
49 Dean Col of Arts & Sciences ....Dr. David C. WILSON
60 Dean School of Communications ....Mr. Eric ROTHENBUHLER
08 Act Dean of University Library ....Ms. Eileen CONDON
39 Assoc Dean Stdts/Housing/Res Life ....Dr. John BUCK
20 Director of Academic Advising ....Dr. Tom NICKOLAI
19 Director Public Safety ....Mr. Dan PESOLD
06 Registrar ....Mr. Don MORRIS
27 Director News & Public Information ....Ms. Polly BURTCH
24 Director of Media Services ....Mr. Dewey MARTIN
88 Director International Recruitment ....Mr. Calvin SMITH
41 Director Athletics ....Mr. Tom HART
36 Director Career Center ....Ms. Tamara GEGG-LAPLUME
23 Director Student Health Svcs ....Ms. Ann BROPHY
35 Director Student Activities ....Mr. John GINSBURG
37 Director Financial Aid ....Mr. Jon GRUETT
38 Director Counsel & Life Development ....Dr. Patrick STACK
96 Director of Procurement Services ....Mr. Kenneth CREEHAN
09 Director Institutional Effectivenes ....Dr. Julie WEISSMAN
88 Senior Project Manager ....Mr. Steven STRANG
18 Project Manager ....Mr. Craig MILLER

Wentworth Military Academy and Junior College (A)

1880 Washington Avenue, Lexington MO 64067-1799
County: Lafayette FICE Identification: 002522
Unit ID: 179919
Telephone: (800) 962-7682 Carnegie Class: Assoc/PrivNFP
FAX Number: (660) 259-2677 Calendar System: Semester
URL: www.wma.edu
Established: 1880 Annual Undergrad Tuition & Fees: $5,335
Enrollment: 858 Coed
Affiliation or Control: Independent Non-Profit IRS Status: 501(c)3
Highest Offering: Associate Degree
Program: Occupational; 2-Year Principally Bachelor's Creditable
Accreditation: NH

01 President ....Col. William W. SELLERS
03 Superintendent ....Col. Michael LIERMAN
05 Chief Academic Officer ....Col. Timothy CASEY
11 Chief of Operations/Admin ....Col. Rick COTTRELL
30 Chief Development ....Mr. Dan RYAN
32 Commandant of Cadets ....1Sgt. Gary WILLIS
84 Director Enrollment Managment ....LtCol. Bob HARMON
41 Athletic Director ....LtCol. Tom HUGHES
10 CFO ....LtCol. Glenn MILLER
21 Director of Business Services ....Maj. Jacque FRITCH
81 Professor of Military Science ....LtCol. Jeff PERRY
29 Alumni Director ....LtCol. Al MCCORMICK
04 Executive Assistant ....Ms. Rebecca MARKLEY
06 Registrar ....Ms. Melissa SCOTT
08 Librarian ....Capt. Linda CHRISTIAN
37 Director Student Financial Aid ....Capt. Brad FULLER
13 Director Information Technology ....Maj. Logan SEALS
85 Director Foreign Students ....Maj. Christhina STARKE
23 Director Health Services ....Capt. Carol LAJAUNIE
42 Chaplain ....Vacant
19 Director Safety and Security ....Maj. Fred FAILING
40 Director Bookstore ....Capt. Chris FIORA
35 Director Student Affairs ....Capt. Lindsey MESNER

Westminster College (B)

501 Westminster Avenue, Fulton MO 65251-1230
County: Callaway FICE Identification: 002523
Unit ID: 179946
Telephone: (573) 642-3361 Carnegie Class: Bac/A&S
FAX Number: (573) 592-5227 Calendar System: Semester
URL: www.westminster-mo.edu
Established: 1851 Annual Undergrad Tuition & Fees: $20,850
Enrollment: 1,076 Coed
Affiliation or Control: Independent Non-Profit IRS Status: 501(c)3
Highest Offering: Baccalaureate
Program: Liberal Arts And General; Teacher Preparatory
Accreditation: NH

01 President ....Dr. George B. FORSYTHE
05 VP Academic Affairs/Dean of Faculty ....Dr. Carolyn J. PERRY
30 VP for Advancement ....Dr. John COMERFORD
10 VP for Business and CFO ....Mr. Phil DANIELS
26 Director of College Relations ....Mr. Robert CROUSE
84 Dean of Enrollment Services ....Mr. George WOLF
32 VP & Dean of Student Life ....Dr. Stephanie KRAUTH
20 Associate Dean ....Dr. Linda WEBSTER
08 Director of Library Services ....Ms. Angela GERLING
06 Registrar ....Mrs. Phyllis J. MASEK
13 Executive Director of IT ....Mr. Bill LOUCKS
37 Director of Financial Aid ....Ms. Aimee BRISTOW
15 Director of Human Resources ....Ms. Marcia TWENTER
39 Director of Residential/Greek Life ....Ms. Jacqueline J. WEBER
41 Athletic Director ....Mr. Matt MITCHELL
38 Asst Director Counseling Services ....Ms. Kate HARRISON
23 Exec Director Wellness Center ....Dr. Kasi HOWARD
88 Exec Dir Marketing/Communications ....Ms. Kris LENSMEYER
29 Dir Alumni Engagement/Events ....Ms. Melanie BARGER
36 Director of Career Services ....Ms. Meg LANGLAND
18 Exec Dir Plant Ops/Auxiliary Svcs ....Mr. Daniel HASLAG
07 Director of Admissions ....Ms. Kelle SILVEY
09 Director of Institutional Research ....Dr. Ray BROWN
19 Dir Campus Safety & Security ....Mr. Jack BENKE
42 Chaplain ....Ms. Jamie HASKINS

William Jewell College (C)

500 College Hill, Liberty MO 64068-1896
County: Clay FICE Identification: 002524
Unit ID: 179955
Telephone: (816) 781-7700 Carnegie Class: Bac/A&S
FAX Number: (816) 415-5027 Calendar System: Semester
URL: www.jewell.edu
Established: 1849 Annual Undergrad Tuition & Fees: $30,200
Enrollment: 1,060 Coed
Affiliation or Control: Independent Non-Profit IRS Status: 501(c)3
Highest Offering: Baccalaureate
Program: Liberal Arts And General; Teacher Preparatory; Professional
Accreditation: NH, MUS, NURSE

01 President ....Dr. David L. SALLEE
05 Provost ....Dr. Anne C. DEMA
10 Vice Pres for Finance & Operations ....Mr. Brian CLEMONS
30 Vice Pres Institutional Advancement ....Mr. Clark MORRIS
84 Vice Pres for Enrollment ....Mr. Gary BRACKEN
42 Chaplain/Vice Pres Rel Ministries ....Dr. Andrew L. PRATT
32 Dean of Student Affairs ....Ms. Shelly KING
07 Dean of Admissions ....Mr. Clint CHAPMAN
06 Registrar ....Dr. Edwin H. LANE
08 Director of the Library ....Ms. Stephanie DECLUE
21 Controller ....Mr. Ron DEMPSEY
13 Manager of Information Services ....Ms. Lan GUO
97 Assoc Dean Core Curriculum ....Dr. Ron WITZKE
37 Director of Financial Aid ....Ms. Susan J. KARNES
15 Assoc Director of Human Resources ....Ms. Penny OWENS
18 Director of Facilities Mgmt ....Mr. Steve ANDERSON
57 Executive Director Harriman-Jewell ....Mr. Clark W. MORRIS
41 Director of Athletics ....Dr. Darlene BAILEY
36 Director of Career Services ....Ms. Judith A. RYCHLEWSKI
38 Director of Counseling Services ....Dr. Beth GENTRY-EPLEY
29 Director of Alumni Relations ....Ms. Andrea MELOAN
104 Director of International Study ....Ms. Sara ROUND

William Woods University (D)

One University Avenue, Fulton MO 65251-1098
County: Callaway FICE Identification: 002525
Unit ID: 179964
Telephone: (573) 642-2251 Carnegie Class: Master's L
FAX Number: (573) 592-1146 Calendar System: Other
URL: www.williamwoods.edu
Established: 1870 Annual Undergrad Tuition & Fees: $19,200
Enrollment: 1,699 Coed
Affiliation or Control: Christian Church (Disciples Of Christ)
IRS Status: 501(c)3
Highest Offering: Beyond Master's But Less Than Doctorate
Program: Liberal Arts And General; Teacher Preparatory; Professional
Accreditation: NH, SW, TEAC

01 President ....Dr. Jahnae H. BARNETT
03 Vice President ....Scott GALLAGHER
05 Vice President & Academic Dean ....Dr. Sherry MCCARTHY
11 Vice President Administration ....Dr. Robert FESSLER
04 Executive Assistant to President ....Kenda E G. SHINDLER
07 Dean of Admissions ....Sarah MUNNS
58 VP and Dean of Grad Studies ....Dr. Michael W. WESTERFIELD
32 Dean of Student Life ....Venita MITCHELL
41 Director of Athletics ....Jason VITTONE
10 Chief Financial Officer ....Cale FESSLER
20 Assoc Dean Academic Services ....Tom FRANKMAN
88 Assoc Dean Assessment ....Dr. Susan JONES
44 Assoc VP of Advancement ....D. Scott MINIEA
08 Director Libraries ....Erlene DUDLEY
26 Director of Marketing ....Kristina BRIGHT
18 Director of Buildings & Grounds ....Mike DILLON
06 Director of Records/Registrar ....Tara DEIERLING
15 Director Human Resources & Benefits ....Kathy GROVES
21 Controller ....Marie BEAVER
37 Director Student Financial Services ....Deana READY
27 Director of University Relations ....Mary Ann BEAHON
29 Director of Alumni Activities ....Becky STINSON
50 Chair Business & Economics Division ....David FORSTER
53 Chair Education Division ....Dr. Betty R. TUTT
49 Chair Art Division ....Dr. Aimee SAPP
88 Chair Equestrian Studies Division ....Claudia STARR
88 Chair Human Performance Division ....Anthony LUNGSTRUM
83 Chair Behavioral/Soc Sciences Div ....Shawn HULL
88 Director Graduate Education Pgms ....Dr. E. Douglas EBERSOLD
39 Dir Residential Life/Campus Safety ....Mike WILLS
13 Director of Technology ....Jim LONG
09 Director of Institutional Research ....Dr. Erin M. HANSMAN
36 Dir Career Svcs/Student Success ....Amy DITTMER
35 Coord Greek Life/Student Involvemnt ....Neil STANGLEIN
42 Chaplain/Faith & Service Director ....Travis TAMERIUS
88 ADA Coordinator/Interpreter ....Margie COATNEY
28 Coordinator Multicultural Affairs ....Tamara CARTER
38 Counselor ....Rebecca SEITZ

MONTANA

Aaniiih Nakoda College (E)

PO Box 159, Harlem MT 59526-0159
County: Blaine FICE Identification: 025175
Unit ID: 180203
Telephone: (406) 353-2607 Carnegie Class: Tribal
FAX Number: (406) 353-2898 Calendar System: Semester
URL: www.fbcc.edu
Established: 1984 Annual Undergrad Tuition & Fees: $2,410
Enrollment: 229 Coed
Affiliation or Control: Tribal Control IRS Status: 501(c)3
Highest Offering: Associate Degree
Program: Occupational; 2-Year Principally Bachelor's Creditable
Accreditation: NW

01 President ....Dr. Carole FALCON-CHANDLER
05 Dean of Academic Affairs ....Ms. Carmen CORNELIUS TAYLOR
32 Dean of Student Affairs ....Ms. Clarena BROCKIE
10 Comptroller ....Ms. Debra EVE
06 Registrar/Admissions Officer ....Mrs. Dixie BROCKIE
37 Financial Aid Director ....Ms. Toma CAMPBELL-RAMONE
08 Director of Library Services ....Ms. Eva ENGLISH
25 Director Sponsored Programs ....Mr. Scott FRISKICS
13 Information Systems Manager ....Mr. Harold H. HEPPNER
40 Bookstore Manager ....Ms. Kimberly BROCKIE
04 Assistant to the President ....Ms. Michele LEWIS

Blackfeet Community College (F)

Box 819, Browning MT 59417-0819
County: Glacier FICE Identification: 025106
Unit ID: 180054
Telephone: (406) 338-5441 Carnegie Class: Tribal
FAX Number: (406) 338-3272 Calendar System: Semester
URL: www.bfcc.edu
Established: 1976 Annual Undergrad Tuition & Fees: $2,350
Enrollment: 480 Coed
Affiliation or Control: Independent Non-Profit IRS Status: 501(c)3
Highest Offering: Associate Degree
Program: Occupational; 2-Year Principally Bachelor's Creditable
Accreditation: NW

01 President ....Dr. Billie Jo KIPP
05 Int Dean of Academic Affairs ....Ms. Anne RACINE
32 Dean Student Services ....Mr. Robert TAILFEATHERS
10 Chief Financial Officer ....Ms. Natalie JACKSON
37 Director of Financial Aid ....Ms. Gaylene DUCHARME
06 Registrar/Admissions Officer ....Ms. Deana M. MCNABB
15 Director Human Resources ....Ms. Dana L. PEMBERTON
07 Director of Admissions ....Ms. Deana M. MCNABB
09 Director of Institutional Research ....Ms. Cheri KICKING WOMAN
18 Chief Facilities/Physical Plant ....Mr. Smokey HENRIKSEN

Carroll College (G)

1601 N Benton Avenue, Helena MT 59625-0002
County: Lewis And Clark FICE Identification: 002526
Unit ID: 180106
Telephone: (406) 447-4300 Carnegie Class: Bac/Diverse
FAX Number: (406) 447-4533 Calendar System: Semester
URL: www.carroll.edu
Established: 1909 Annual Undergrad Tuition & Fees: $26,558
Enrollment: 1,502 Coed
Affiliation or Control: Roman Catholic IRS Status: 501(c)3
Highest Offering: Baccalaureate
Program: Occupational; Liberal Arts And General; Teacher Preparatory; Professional
Accreditation: NW, ENG, NURSE

01 President ....Dr. Thomas EVANS
05 Sr Vice President Academic Affairs ....Dr. Paula MCNUTT
10 VP for Finance & Administration ....Ms. Lori PETERSON
30 VP Institutional Advanc/Cmty Rels ....Mr. Thomas J. MCCARVEL
32 Vice President for Student Life ....Dr. James D. HARDWICK
84 Assoc Vice Pres of Enrollment Mgmt ....Ms. Nina LOCOCO
42 Chaplain/Director ....Rev. Marc LENNEMAN
26 Dir of Communications ....Ms. Ashley OLIVERIO
26 Director of Marketing ....Ms. Patty WHITE
06 Registrar ....Ms. Catherine D. DAY
08 Director of Library ....Mr. Christian FRAZZA
37 Financial Aid Director ....Ms. Janet RIIS
36 Dir of Career Services/Testing ....Ms. Rosalie K. WALSH
07 Director Admissions/Enrollment Ops ....Ms. Cynthia J. THORNQUIST
15 Director of Human Res & Adm Svcs ....Ms. Renee M. MCMAHON

18 Director of Facilities ....Mr. Walter H. BISKUPIAK
39 Director of Community Living ....Mr. Bennett MACINTYRE
35 Dir Student Activities/Ldrshp ....Mr. Patrick HARRIS
38 Director of Counseling ....Mr. K. Mike FRANKLIN
21 Controller ....Ms. Lori LADAS
13 Director Information Technology ....Ms. Loretta ANDREWS
29 Director Alumni Relations ....Ms. Kathy RAMIREZ
09 Dir Research/Planing/Assess ....Dr. Dawn GALLINGER

Chief Dull Knife College (A)

PO Box 98, Lame Deer MT 59043-0098
County: Rosebud FICE Identification: 025452
Unit ID: 180160
Telephone: (406) 477-6215 Carnegie Class: Tribal
FAX Number: (406) 477-6219 Calendar System: Semester
URL: www.cdkc.edu
Established: 1975 Annual Undergrad Tuition & Fees: $2,260
Enrollment: 374 Coed
Affiliation or Control: Independent Non-Profit IRS Status: 501(c)3
Highest Offering: Associate Degree
Program: Occupational; 2-Year Principally Bachelor's Creditable
Accreditation: NW

01 President ....Dr. Richard LITTLEBEAR
03 Vice President ....Mr. William WERTMAN
05 Dean Academic Affairs ....Ms. Michelle CURLEE
32 Dean Student Affairs ....Mr. Zane SPANG
37 Director Student Financial Aid ....Mr. Devin WERTMAN
08 Head Librarian ....Mrs. Joan HANTZ

Dawson Community College (B)

Box 421, Glendive MT 59330-0421
County: Dawson FICE Identification: 002529
Unit ID: 180151
Telephone: (406) 377-3396 Carnegie Class: Assoc/Pub-R-S
FAX Number: (406) 377-8132 Calendar System: Semester
URL: www.dawson.edu
Established: 1940 Annual Undergrad Tuition & Fees (In-District): $3,050
Enrollment: 1,209 Coed
Affiliation or Control: State/Local IRS Status: 501(c)3
Highest Offering: Associate Degree
Program: Occupational; 2-Year Principally Bachelor's Creditable
Accreditation: NW

01 President ....Dr. Jim A. CARGILL
05 Dean of Instructional Services ....Dr. Jackie SCHULTZ
32 Dean of Student Services ....Ms. Joyce AYRE
11 Dean of Administrative Services ....Mr. Justin CROSS
06 Registrar ....Ms. Virginia BERUBE
88 Director Special Services ....Mr. Kent DION
08 Librarian ....Mr. Todd KNISPEL
07 Director Admissions/Financial Aid ....Ms. Jolene MYERS
13 Dir Technology/Computer Svcs ....Mr. Shane BISHOP
26 Chief Public Relations Officer ....Ms. Jane WYNNE
41 Athletic Director ....Ms. Joyce AYRE

Flathead Valley Community College (C)

777 Grandview Drive, Kalispell MT 59901
County: Flathead FICE Identification: 006777
Unit ID: 180197
Telephone: (406) 756-3822 Carnegie Class: Assoc/Pub-R-M
FAX Number: (406) 756-3815 Calendar System: Semester
URL: www.fvcc.edu
Established: 1967 Annual Undergrad Tuition & Fees (In-District): $3,730
Enrollment: 2,495 Coed
Affiliation or Control: Local IRS Status: 501(c)3
Highest Offering: Associate Degree
Program: Occupational; 2-Year Principally Bachelor's Creditable
Accreditation: NW, MAC, @PTAA, SURGT

01 President ....Dr. Jane A. KARAS
05 Vice President Instruction ....Dr. Kristen JONES
10 Vice Pres Administration & Finance ....Mr. Chuck JENSEN
12 Director Lincoln County Campus ....Mr. Patrick PEZZELLE
20 Director Educational Services ....Ms. Mary JORDT
32 Dean of Students ....Ms. Brenda HANSON
06 Registrar/Coord/Admissions/Records ....Ms. Marlene STOLTZ
51 Director Economic Dev/Continuing Ed ....Ms. Susan BURCH
20 Director TRIO ....Ms. Lynn L. FARRIS
13 Director Mgmt Information Services ....Mr. Bill E. BOND
37 Director Student Financial Aid ....Ms. Cindy KIEFER
15 Director of Human Resources ....Mr. Warren D. TOLLEY
88 Director of Adult Basic Education ....Ms. Margaret L. GIRKINS
18 Director Maintenance Service ....Mr. Jack ROARK
21 Controller ....Mr. Kirk ZANDER
26 Asst Dir Marketing/Communications ....Ms. Tara E. ROTH
24 Coord Instructional Media Services ....Ms. Malinda CRAWFORD
36 Director Student Placement ....Ms. Karen DARROW
96 Director of Purchasing ....Mr. Steve LARSON
30 Director Institutional Advancement ....Ms. Coleen UNTERREINER
09 Director of Institutional Research ....Dr. Brad ELDREDGE

Fort Peck Community College (D)

PO Box 398, Poplar MT 59255-0398
County: Roosevelt FICE Identification: 023430
Unit ID: 180212
Telephone: (406) 768-6300 Carnegie Class: Tribal
FAX Number: (406) 768-6301 Calendar System: Semester
URL: www.fpcc.edu
Established: 1978 Annual Undergrad Tuition & Fees: $2,250
Enrollment: 513 Coed
Affiliation or Control: Tribal Control IRS Status: 501(c)3
Highest Offering: Associate Degree
Program: Occupational; 2-Year Principally Bachelor's Creditable; Business Emphasis
Accreditation: NW

01 President ....Dr. Florence GARCIA
05 Academic Vice President ....Mr. Wayne TWO BULLS
32 Vice President Student Services ....Ms. Haven GOURNEAU
09 Vice Pres Institutional Research ....Mr. Craig SMITH
31 Vice President Community Services ....Mr. Larry WETSIT
10 Business Manager ....Ms. Rose ATKINSON
06 Registrar/Admissions ....Ms. Linda L. HANSEN
37 Financial Aid Officer ....Ms. Lanette CLARKE
40 Bookstore Manager ....Ms. Jackie AZURE
08 Head Librarian ....Mrs. Anita A. SCHEETZ

Little Big Horn College (E)

PO Box 370, Crow Agency MT 59022-0370
County: Big Horn FICE Identification: 022866
Unit ID: 180328
Telephone: (406) 638-3104 Carnegie Class: Tribal
FAX Number: (406) 638-3169 Calendar System: Semester
URL: www.lbhc.edu
Established: 1980 Annual Undergrad Tuition & Fees: $2,760
Enrollment: 387 Coed
Affiliation or Control: Tribal Control IRS Status: 501(c)3
Highest Offering: Associate Degree
Program: Occupational; 2-Year Principally Bachelor's Creditable; Business Emphasis
Accreditation: NW

01 President ....Dr. David YARLOTT, JR.
05 Academic Dean ....Miss Frederica LEFT HAND
32 Dean of Student Services ....Miss Te-Atta OLD BEAR
11 Dean of Administration ....Mr. David SMALL
08 Director of Library ....Mr. Tim BERNARDIS
13 Chief Information Officer ....Mr. Franklin COOPER
10 Chief Finance Officer ....Ms. Aldean GOOD LUCK
15 Director Human Resources ....Ms. Natalie COLLIFLOWER
97 Dept Head/General Stds/Crow Stds ....Dr. Tim MCCLEARY
81 Dept Head/Math/Science/Technology ....Dr. Dianna HOOKER

Miles Community College (F)

2715 Dickinson, Miles City MT 59301-4799
County: Custer FICE Identification: 002528
Unit ID: 180373
Telephone: (406) 874-6100 Carnegie Class: Assoc/Pub-R-S
FAX Number: (406) 874-6282 Calendar System: Semester
URL: www.milescc.edu
Established: 1939 Annual Undergrad Tuition & Fees (In-District): $3,720
Enrollment: 491 Coed
Affiliation or Control: State/Local IRS Status: 501(c)3
Highest Offering: Associate Degree
Program: Occupational; 2-Year Principally Bachelor's Creditable
Accreditation: NW, ADNUR

01 President ....Dr. Stefani G. HICSWA
11 VP Administration & Finance ....Ms. Lisa WATSON
05 Vice Pres of Academic Affairs ....Ms. Shelly WEIGHT
32 VP Student Success/Inst Research ....Ms. Jessie DUFNER
08 Director of Library ....Ms. Ann O. RUTHERFORD
13 Director Information Technology ....Mr. Donald D. WARNER
37 Director Student Financial Aid ....Mr. Loren LANCASTER
18 Chief Facilities/Physical Plant ....Mr. Ross LAWRENCE
21 Controller ....Vacant
06 Registrar ....Ms. Lisa BLUNT
09 Dir Institutional Rsrch/Pub Rels ....Vacant
15 Director Human Resources ....Ms. Kylene PHIPPS
66 Director Nursing ....Ms. Karla LUND
20 Associate Academic Officer ....Mr. Garth SLEIGHT
40 Manager Bookstore ....Mrs. Judy STROBEL

Montana Bible College (G)

3625 South 19th Avenue, Bozeman MT 59718-9108
County: Gallatin FICE Identification: 041403
Telephone: (406) 586-3585 Carnegie Class: Not Classified
FAX Number: (406) 586-3585 Calendar System: Semester
URL: www.montanabiblecollege.edu
Established: 1987 Annual Undergrad Tuition & Fees: $6,240
Enrollment: 120 Coed
Affiliation or Control: Independent Non-Profit IRS Status: 501(c)3
Highest Offering: Baccalaureate
Program: Religious Emphasis
Accreditation: BI

01 President ....Mr. Jim CARLSON
05 Academic Dean ....Dr. Gale HEIDE
06 Registrar ....Mrs. Louise TURNER
07 Admissions Coordinator ....Mrs. Susan JACKSON
08 Head Librarian ....Mr. Micah FORSYTHE
32 Dean of Students ....Mr. Scott MORNINGSTAR
10 Business Manager ....Mrs. Leota FRED
21 Office Manager ....Mrs. Jeanie TYPOLT
18 Facilities Manager ....Mr. Ty TYPOLT

30 Advancement ....Ms. Barbara HANNO
26 Recruitment ....Mr. Ryan WARD

*Montana University System Office (H)

2500 Broadway, Helena MT 59601-3201
County: Lewis And Clark FICE Identification: 029072
Unit ID: 180470
Telephone: (406) 444-6570 Carnegie Class: N/A
FAX Number: (406) 444-1469
URL: www.mus.edu

01 Commissioner Higher Education ....Mr. Clayton T. CHRISTIAN
05 Deputy Comm Academic/Student Affs ....Dr. Sylvia MOORE
10 Assoc Comm for Fiscal Affairs ....Mr. Mick ROBINSON
45 Assoc Comm for Plng & Public Policy ....Mr. Tyler TREVOR
43 Chief Legal Counsel ....Ms. Catherine SWIFT
15 Director Labor Relations/Personnel ....Mr. Kevin MCRAE
88 Director of Benefits ....Mrs. Connie WELSH
37 Director Guaranteed Student Loans ....Vacant
21 Director Accounting & Budget ....Ms. Frieda HOUSER
88 Director of Work Comp Risk Mgmt ....Ms. Leah Jo TIETZ
88 Dir of Distance Learning/Bus Devel ....Dr. Tom GIBSON
103 Deputy Comm Two-Year Educ ....Mr. John CECH
93 Dir Minority/Amer Ind Achievement ....Ms. Brandi FOSTER
88 Gear UP Director ....Vacant
88 IT Manager ....Ms. Edwina MORRISON

*The University of Montana - Missoula (I)

32 Campus Drive, Missoula MT 59812-0001
County: Missoula FICE Identification: 002536
Unit ID: 180489
Telephone: (406) 243-0211 Carnegie Class: RU/H
FAX Number: (406) 243-2797 Calendar System: Semester
URL: www.umt.edu
Established: 1893 Annual Undergrad Tuition & Fees (In-State): $5,985
Enrollment: 15,669 Coed
Affiliation or Control: State IRS Status: 501(c)3
Highest Offering: Doctorate
Program: 2-Year Principally Bachelor's Creditable; Liberal Arts And General; Teacher Preparatory; Professional
Accreditation: NW, ART, BUS, BUSA, CACREP, CLPSY, CS, FOR, JOUR, LAW, MUS, PH, PHAR, PTA, @SP, SW, TED, THEA

02 President ....Dr. Royce C. ENGSTROM
88 Interim VP for Integrated Comm ....Ms. Peggy KUHR
05 Interim Provost/VP Academic Affairs ....Dr. Perry BROWN
10 Vice President Finance/Admin ....Mr. Robert A. DURINGER
32 Vice President for Student Affairs ....Dr. Teresa S. BRANCH
46 Interim VP Research/Development ....Dr. David FORBES
84 Asst Vice Pres Enrollment Services ....Mr. Jed LISTON
45 AVP for Plng/Budget Analysis ....Ms. Dawn RESSEL
20 Associate Provost ....Dr. Arlene WALKER-ANDREWS
104 Interim International Pgms Director ....Dr. Gerald FETZ
58 Dean of the Graduate School ....Dr. Sandy ROSS
35 Dean of Students ....Ms. Rhondie VOORHEES
43 Legal Counsel ....Vacant
12 Interim Director Mansfield Center ....Dr. Daniel SMITH
88 Director Broadcast Media Center ....Mr. William MARCUS
22 Dir Equal Opportunity/Affirm Action ....Ms. Lucy FRANCE
15 AVP Human Resource Services ....Ms. Terri PHILLIPS
06 Registrar ....Mr. Edwin JOHNSON
18 Director Facilities Services ....Mr. Hugh A. JESSE
13 Interim CIO ....Dr. Loey KNAPP
38 Interim Director Counseling ....Mr. Mike FROST
36 Director Career Services ....Mr. Michael HEURING
37 Director of Financial Aid ....Mr. Kent MCGOWAN
26 Director University Relations ....Vacant
29 Director of Alumni Relations ....Mr. William S. JOHNSTON
102 President & CEO/UM Foundation ....Ms. Laura BREHM
19 Director of Public Safety ....Mr. Gary TAYLOR
23 Int Director Curry Health Center ....Dr. Rick CURTIS
24 Director Presentation Tech Services ....Mr. Randy GOTTFRIED
39 Director Residence Life ....Ms. Sandra SCHOONOVER
40 General Manager Univ Bookstore ....Mr. Bryan C. THORNTON
41 Interim Athletic Director ....Ms. Jean GEE
85 Dir Foreign Student & Scholar Svcs ....Ms. Effie F. KOEHN
21 Director Business Services ....Mr. Mark H. PULLIUM
07 Director Marketing Recruitment ....Ms. Juana J. ALCALA
62 Dean Library Services ....Dr. Sha Li ZHANG
51 Dean Continuing Education ....Dr. Roger MACLEAN
49 Dean College Arts & Sciences ....Dr. Christopher COMER
61 Dean School of Law ....Dr. Irma RUSSELL
65 Dean Col Forestry/Conservation ....Dr. James BURCHFIELD
50 Dean School of Business Admin ....Dr. Larry D. GIANCHETTA
76 Int Dean Col Hlth Prof & Biomed Sci ....Dr. Vernon GRUND
60 Interim Dean School of Journalism ....Ms. Denise DOWLING
53 Dean College of Educ & Human Svcs ....Dr. Roberta EVANS
57 Dean College Visual Performing Arts ....Mr. Stephen KALM
75 Dean Missoula College ....Dr. Barry GOOD
92 Dean Honors College ....Dr. James MCKUSICK

*The University of Montana Western (J)

710 S Atlantic St, Dillon MT 59725-3598
County: Beaverhead FICE Identification: 002537
Unit ID: 180692
Telephone: (406) 683-7011 Carnegie Class: Bac/Diverse
FAX Number: (406) 683-7493 Calendar System: Other
URL: www.umwestern.edu
Established: 1893 Annual Undergrad Tuition & Fees (In-State): $2,054
Enrollment: 1,379 Coed

Affiliation or Control: State IRS Status: 501(c)3
Highest Offering: Baccalaureate
Program: 2-Year Principally Bachelor's Creditable; Liberal Arts And General; Teacher Preparatory
Accreditation: NW, IACBE, TED

02 Chancellor .... Dr. Richard D. STOREY
05 Provost/Vice Chanc Academic Affairs .... Dr. Karl ULRICH
10 Vice Chanc Administration/Finance .... Ms. Susan BRIGGS
26 Director Marketing/Univ Relations .... Mr. Kent J. ORD
06 Interim Registrar .... Ms. Jeannette PITTMAN
07 Director of Admissions .... Ms. Catherine REDHEAD
08 Librarian .... Mr. Michael SCHULZ
36 Director of Field Learning .... Mr. Michael MILLER
24 Director of Media Relations .... Mr. David NOLT
41 Interim Director of Athletics .... Ms. Janelle HANDLOS
14 Director of Computer Center .... Mr. Scott WADE
18 Director of Facilities Services .... Mr. Dan PAYNE
32 Dean of Students .... Ms. Nicole HAZELBAKER
09 Director of Institutional Research .... Ms. Anneliese RIPLEY
30 Director of Devel/Alumni Relations .... Ms. Roxanne ENGELLANT
37 Director Student Financial Aid .... Ms. Erica JONES
38 Director Student Counseling .... Ms. Lynn MEIER WELTZIEN
15 Director Personnel Services .... Ms. Susan BRIGGS

*The University of Montana - Helena College of Technology (A)

1115 N Roberts, Helena MT 59601-3098
County: Lewis and Clark FICE Identification: 007570
Unit ID: 180276
Telephone: (406) 447-6900 Carnegie Class: Assoc/Pub2in4
FAX Number: (406) 444-6892 Calendar System: Semester
URL: www.umhelena.edu
Established: 1939 Annual Undergrad Tuition & Fees (In-State): $3,030
Enrollment: 1,709 Coed
Affiliation or Control: State IRS Status: 501(c)3
Highest Offering: Associate Degree
Program: Occupational; 2-Year Principally Bachelor's Creditable; Technical Emphasis
Accreditation: NW, ADNUR

02 Dean/CEO .... Dr. Daniel BINGHAM
04 Assistant to the Dean/CEO .... Ms. Gigi BOTTENFIELD
05 Associate Dean of Academic Affairs .... Vacant
06 Director of Admissions and Records .... Ms. Sarah DELLWO
08 Director of Library Services .... Vacant
51 Director of Continuing Education .... Ms. Mary LANNERT
18 Assistant Dean of Fiscal & Plant .... Mr. Russ FILLNER
13 Director of IT Services .... Mr. Jeff BLOCK
40 Retail Services Manager .... Mr. Josh BENNETT
32 Assistant Dean of Student Services .... Ms. Elizabeth STEARNS-SIMS
26 Marketing & Comm Coordinator .... Ms. Barb MCALMOND
37 Director Student Financial Aid .... Ms. Valerie CURTIN
32 Director of Student Success .... Ms. Suzanne HUNGER
88 Dir Disability & Veterans Services .... Ms. Cindy YARBERRY
15 Director of Human Resources .... Vacant
36 Career Services Coordinator .... Mr. Alan THOMPSON

*The University of Montana - College of Technology (B)

909 South Avenue W, Missoula MT 59801-7910
County: Missoula FICE Identification: 007561
Unit ID: 180382
Telephone: (406) 243-7811 Carnegie Class: Not Classified
FAX Number: (406) 243-7899 Calendar System: Semester
URL: www.cte.umt.edu
Established: 1994 Annual Undergrad Tuition & Fees (In-State): $3,400
Enrollment: 2,803 Coed
Affiliation or Control: State IRS Status: 501(c)3
Highest Offering: Associate Degree
Program: Occupational; 2-Year Principally Bachelor's Creditable; Professional; Technical Emphasis
Accreditation: &NW, ACFEI, ADNUR, SURGT

02 Dean .... Dr. Barry GOOD
05 Associate Dean .... Ms. Lynn STOCKING
05 Associate Dean .... Mr. Kevin BROCKBANK
11 Administrative Officer .... Ms. Jacqueline HOFMANN

† Regional accreditation is carried under the parent institution The University of Montana-Missoula, Missoula, MT.

*Montana State University (C)

PO Box 172190, Bozeman MT 59717-2190
County: Gallatin FICE Identification: 002532
Unit ID: 180461
Telephone: (406) 994-2452 Carnegie Class: RU/VH
FAX Number: (406) 994-1923 Calendar System: Semester
URL: www.montana.edu
Established: 1893 Annual Undergrad Tuition & Fees (In-State): $6,705
Enrollment: 14,153 Coed
Affiliation or Control: State IRS Status: 501(c)3
Highest Offering: Doctorate
Program: Occupational; 2-Year Principally Bachelor's Creditable; Liberal Arts And General; Teacher Preparatory; Professional
Accreditation: NW, ART, BUS, CACREP, CS, DIETD, @DIETI, ENG, ENGT, IPSY, MT, MUS, NURSE, TEAC

02 President .... Dr. Waded CRUZADO
05 Provost/Vice Pres Academic Affairs .... Dr. Martha POTVIN
20 Assoc Provost .... Dr. David SINGEL
88 Assoc Provost Accreditation .... Dr. Ron LARSEN
10 Vice Pres Admin/Finance .... Mr. Terry LEIST
32 Vice Pres Student Success .... Dr. Jim RIMPAU
86 Vice Pres Ext Rels/Dir Extension .... Dr. Douglas STEELE
46 VP Rsrch/Creativity/Tech Transfer .... Dr. Thomas MCCOY
04 Special Assistant to the President .... Dr. Henrietta MANN
18 Assoc Vice Pres University Services .... Mr. Robert V. LASHAWAY
88 Assoc VP Res/Creativity/Tch Trnsfer .... Dr. Lee SPANGLER
15 Chief Human Resources Officer .... Mr. Dennis DEFA
21 Asst Vice Pres Financial Services .... Ms. Laura HUMBERGER
102 President/CEO MSU Foundation .... Mr. Michael STEVENSON
104 Exec Dir International Education .... Dr. Norman PETERSON
27 Exec Director Univ Communications .... Mr. Thomas CALCAGNI
88 Exec Director Museum of the Rockies .... Ms. Sheldon MCKAMEY
50 Interim Dean Business .... Dr. Susan DANA
53 Dean Education/Health/Human Dev .... Dr. Larry BAKER
54 Acting Dean Engineering .... Dr. Brett GUNNINK
49 Dean Letters & Science .... Dr. Paula LUTZ
66 Dean Nursing .... Dr. Helen MELLAND
08 Acting Dean Libraries .... Mr. Brian ROSSMANN
88 Dean Students .... Dr. Matthew CAIRES
58 Dean Graduate School .... Dr. Carl FOX
47 Dean Agriculture .... Dr. Jeffrey JACOBSEN
48 Dean Arts/Architecture .... Dr. Nancy CORNWELL
70 Dean Gallatin College Programs .... Mr. Robert HIETALA
07 Director Admissions .... Ms. Ronda RUSSELL
22 Interim Dir Affirmative Action/HR .... Ms. Diane LETENDRE
29 Pres/CEO Alumni Relations .... Ms. Jaynee GROSETH
41 Director Athletics .... Mr. Peter FIELDS
88 Director Auxiliary Services .... Mr. Tom STUMP
36 Director Career Services .... Dr. Carina BECK
38 Director Counseling/Psych Services .... Dr. Patrick DONAHOE
88 Dir Disability/Re-ent/Veteran Svcs .... Ms. Brenda YORK
56 Exec Director Extended University .... Dr. Kim OBBINK
37 Director Financial Aid .... Ms. Brandi PAYNE
43 Legal Counsel .... Dr. Leslie TAYLOR
45 Director Planning & Analysis .... Dr. Chris FASTNOW
96 Director Purchasing .... Mr. Brian O'CONNOR
06 Registrar .... Ms. Bonnie ASHLEY
26 Director Marketing/Creative Service .... Ms. Julie KIPFER
19 Director University Police .... Mr. Robert PUTZKE

*Montana State University - Billings (D)

1500 University Drive, Billings MT 59101-0245
County: Yellowstone FICE Identification: 002530
Unit ID: 180179
Telephone: (406) 657-2011 Carnegie Class: Master's M
FAX Number: (406) 657-2302 Calendar System: Semester
URL: www.msubillings.edu
Established: 1927 Annual Undergrad Tuition & Fees (In-State): $5,711
Enrollment: 5,274 Coed
Affiliation or Control: State IRS Status: 501(c)3
Highest Offering: Master's
Program: Occupational; Liberal Arts And General; Teacher Preparatory; Business Emphasis
Accreditation: NW, ART, BUS, CORE, EMT, MUS, TED

02 Chancellor .... Dr. Rolf S. GROSETH
11 Administrative Vice Chancellor .... Ms. Terrie IVERSON
05 Academic Vice Chancellor & Provost .... Dr. Mark PAGANO
32 Vice Chancellor for Student Affairs .... Dr. Stacy KLIPPENSTEIN
102 President/CEO Foundation .... Ms. Marilynn MILLER
08 Director Library Services .... Mr. Brent ROBERTS
84 Director Enrollment Management .... Dr. Stacy KLIPPENSTEIN
07 Director Admiss/Records/Registrar .... Ms. Cheri JOHANNES
15 Director Human Resources/EEO AA .... Ms. Janet SIMON
36 Director Career Services .... Ms. Patricia B. REUSS
27 Chief Information Officer .... Dr. Michael J. BARBER
25 Assoc Dir Grants & Sponsored Pgms .... Mr. John WALSH
25 Assoc Dir Grants & Sponsored Pgms .... Ms. Deborah PETERS
26 Director University Relations .... Mr. Dan CARTER
09 Office Institutional Planning .... Vacant
18 Director Facility Services .... Mr. Eakle BARFIELD
58 Director Graduate Programs .... Dr. Mark PAGANO
41 Athletic Director .... Dr. Gary GRAY
19 Chief of Campus Police .... Mr. Scott FORSHEE
29 Interim Director Alumni Relations .... Ms. Krista MONTAGUE
37 Director Student Financial Aid .... Ms. Leslie WELDON
40 Director Bookstore .... Mr. Chad SCHREIER
39 Dir Stdnt Union/Housing/Res Life .... Ms. Jeannie MCISAAC-TRACY
31 Director of Community Involvement .... Ms. Kathy KOTECKI
35 Dir Student Svcs/Assoc Registrar .... Dr. Rita KRATKY
21 University Budget Director .... Ms. Trudy COLLINS
96 Director of Business Services .... Mr. Jim NIELSEN
20 Dir Academic Support Center .... Mr. Benjamin BARCKHOLTZ
20 Dir Ctr for Applied Econ Research .... Dr. Scott RICKARD
28 Dir Montana Center on Disabilities .... Ms. Marsha SAMPSON
89 Int Assoc Dir New Student Services .... Ms. Julie HRUBES
38 Director of Advising .... Ms. Becky LYONS
88 Director American Indian Outreach .... Ms. Reno CHARETTE
85 Int Director International Studies .... Dr. Tom RUST
106 Director eLearning Services .... Dr. Michael BARBER
92 Director of Honors Program .... Ms. Tami HAALAND
104 Program Mgr Intl Studies & Outreach .... Ms. Janese CARSTENS
12 Executive Director MSUB Downtown .... Mr. John WALSH
49 Dean of Arts & Sciences .... Dr. Tasneem KHALEEL
53 Dean of Education .... Dr. Mary Susan FISHBAUGH
50 Int Dean College of Business .... Dr. Tim WILKINSON
12 Dean City College @ MSU Billings .... Dr. Marsha RILEY
76 Dean Col of Allied Health Prof .... Dr. Diane DUIN
88 Assoc Dean City Col @ MSU Billings .... Ms. Tammi MILLER

*Montana State University - Northern (E)

PO Box 7751, Havre MT 59501-7751
County: Hill FICE Identification: 002533
Unit ID: 180522
Telephone: (406) 265-3700 Carnegie Class: Bac/Diverse
FAX Number: N/A Calendar System: Semester
URL: www.msun.edu
Established: 1929 Annual Undergrad Tuition & Fees (In-State): $4,818
Enrollment: 1,273 Coed
Affiliation or Control: State IRS Status: 501(c)3
Highest Offering: Master's
Program: Liberal Arts And General; Teacher Preparatory; Professional; Music Emphasis
Accreditation: NW, ADNUR, ENGT, NUR

02 Chancellor .... Dr. James LIMBAUGH
05 Provost/Vice Chanc Academic Affairs .... Dr. Rosalyn TEMPLETON
10 Director of Business Services .... Ms. Sue OST
102 Executive Director of Foundation .... Ms. Shauna ALBRECHT
72 Dean College Technical Sciences .... Mr. Gregory KEGEL
32 Assistant Dean of Students .... Mr. William LANIER
53 Int Dn Col Educ/Arts & Sci/Nursing .... Dr. Carol REIFSCHNEIDER
06 Dean of Students/Registrar .... Ms. Lindsey BROWN
66 Director of Nursing .... Dr. Lisa O'NEIL
41 Athletic Director .... Mr. Christian OBERQUELL
36 Director Career Planning/Placement .... Ms. Tracey JETTE
13 Dir Information Technology Svcs .... Mr. Rock BROWN
37 Director of Financial Aid .... Ms. Cindy SMALL
26 Director of University Relations .... Mr. James POTTER
08 Interim Director of Library .... Ms. Vicki GIST
38 Director Student Support Services .... Mr. John A. DONALDSON
15 Director Human Resources .... Ms. Kathy JAYNES
35 Director Student Success .... Ms. Tracey JETTE
18 Interim Facilities Manager .... Mr. Dan ULMEN
29 Alumni Coordinator .... Ms. Autumn ELLIOT

*City College at Montana State University Billings (F)

3803 Central Avenue, Billings MT 59102-4398
County: Yellowstone FICE Identification: 010166
Unit ID: 180045
Telephone: (406) 247-3000 Carnegie Class: Assoc/Pub2in4
FAX Number: (406) 247-3014 Calendar System: Semester
URL: www.msubillings.edu/cot/
Established: 1969 Annual Undergrad Tuition & Fees (In-State): $3,747
Enrollment: 1,391 Coed
Affiliation or Control: State IRS Status: 501(c)3
Highest Offering: Associate Degree
Program: Occupational
Accreditation: &NW

02 Dean COT .... Dr. Marsha RILEY
05 Associate Dean .... Ms. Tammi MILLER
10 Chief Business Officer .... Ms. Susan STEWART
07 Admissions and Registrar .... Dr. Rita KRATKY
08 Co-Librarian .... Ms. Shelly LOVELESS
08 Co-Librarian .... Ms. Gail BINFORD
20 Associate Academic Officer .... Vacant

† Regional accreditation is carried under the parent institution Montana State University-Billings, Billings, MT.

*Great Falls College Montana State University (G)

2100 16th Avenue South, Great Falls MT 59405-4909
County: Cascade FICE Identification: 009314
Unit ID: 180249
Telephone: (406) 771-4300 Carnegie Class: Assoc/Pub2in4
FAX Number: (406) 771-4317 Calendar System: Semester
URL: www.msugf.edu
Established: 1969 Annual Undergrad Tuition & Fees (In-State): $3,077
Enrollment: 1,861 Coed
Affiliation or Control: State IRS Status: 501(c)3
Highest Offering: Associate Degree
Program: Occupational; 2-Year Principally Bachelor's Creditable
Accreditation: NW, DA, DH, @DIETT, EMT, MAC, PTAA, SURGT

02 CEO/Dean .... Dr. Susan J. WOLFF
04 Executive Assistant to the Dean .... Ms. Lorene JAYNES
05 Assoc Dean Academic Affairs .... Dr. Heidi PASEK
10 Assoc Dean Administration & Finance .... Vacant
14 CTO .... Mr. Ken WARDINSKY
26 Exec Director Community Relations .... Ms. Pamela PARSONS
06 Registrar .... Ms. Dena WAGNER-FOSSEN
07 Dir of Admissions/New Student Svcs .... Ms. Dana FRESHLY
15 Exec Director Human Resources .... Ms. Mary Kay BONILLA
30 Director of Development .... Mr. Thomas FIGARELLE
37 Director Student Financial Aid .... Ms. Leah HABEL
36 Director Advising & Career Center .... Ms. Courtney JOHNSRUD
35 Assistant Dean Student Services .... Dr. Judy HAY
40 Bookstore Manager .... Mr. Steve HALSTED
96 Budget & Purchasing Officer .... Ms. Deby GUNTER

18 Director of Facilities Services .... Mr. Dennis DEVINE
08 Director of Weaver Library .... Ms. Laura WIGHT
09 Director of Institutional Research .... Ms. Wendy DOVE

*Highlands College of Montana Tech (A)

25 Basin Creek Road, Butte MT 59701-9704
County: Silver Bow FICE Identification: 009282
Unit ID: 180081
Telephone: (406) 496-3701 Carnegie Class: Assoc/Pub-R-S
FAX Number: (406) 496-3710 Calendar System: Semester
URL: www.mtech.edu
Established: 1969 Annual Undergrad Tuition & Fees (In-State): $3,155
Enrollment: 726 Coed
Affiliation or Control: State IRS Status: Exempt
Highest Offering: Associate Degree
Program: Occupational; 2-Year Principally Bachelor's Creditable
Accreditation: &NW

02 Dean .... Dr. John M. GARIC
05 Vice Chancellor of Academic Affairs .... Dr. Douglas ABBOTT
10 Vice Chancellor Admin & Finance .... Mrs. Margaret PETERSON
32 Assoc Vice Chancellor Student Svcs .... Mr. Paul BEATTY
37 Financial Aid Officer .... Mr. Michael W. RICHARDSON
08 Director of Library .... Ms. Ann ST CLAIR
38 Counselor .... Ms. Joyce O'NEIL
38 Counselor .... Ms. Cricket PIETSCH
09 Director of Institutional Research .... Ms. Melissa HARRINGTON
18 Director of Physical Facilities .... Mr. Arthur ANDERSON
21 Controller .... Mr. John BADOVINAC
26 Director of Public Relations .... Mrs. Amanda BADOVINAC
29 Director of Alumni Affairs .... Ms. Peggy MCCOY
84 Director of Enrollment Services .... Ms. Kathy WILLIAMS
96 Associate Director Budgets .... Mr. Daniel FAUGHT

*Montana Tech of The University of Montana (B)

1300 W Park Street, Butte MT 59701-8997
County: Silver Bow FICE Identification: 002531
Unit ID: 180416
Telephone: (406) 496-4101 Carnegie Class: Bac/Diverse
FAX Number: (406) 496-4133 Calendar System: Semester
URL: www.mtech.edu
Established: 1893 Annual Undergrad Tuition & Fees (In-State): $6,693
Enrollment: 2,803 Coed
Affiliation or Control: State IRS Status: 501(c)3
Highest Offering: Master's
Program: 2-Year Principally Bachelor's Creditable; Liberal Arts And General; Professional; Technical Emphasis
Accreditation: NW, ADNUR, CS, ENG, ENGR

02 Chancellor .... Dr. Donald M. BLACKKETTER
05 Vice Chanc Acad Affs/Research .... Dr. Douglas M. ABBOTT
10 Business Officer/Controller .... Mr. John C. BADOVINAC
11 VC for Administration & Finance .... Ms. Maggie PETERSON
30 Vice Chanc Dev/Alumni Aff .... Vacant
32 Assoc VC for Student Affairs .... Mr. Paul V. BEATTY
20 Assoc VC AA/Research/Dean Grad Sch .... Vacant
65 Director Bureau of Mines & Geology .... Dr. John J. METESH
84 Director of Enrollment Management .... Ms. Kathy WILLIAMS
31 Dir Inst of Educational Opportunity .... Ms. Amy VERLANIC
36 Director Career Services .... Ms. Sarah RAYMOND
08 Director Library .... Ms. Ann F. ST. CLAIR
37 Director of Financial Aid .... Mr. Michael W. RICHARDSON
18 Director of Physical Facilities .... Mr. Art ANDERSON
29 Director Alumni Affairs .... Ms. Peggy S. MCCOY
41 Athletic Director .... Mr. Joe MCCLAFFERTY
21 Dir Financial Planning/Analysis .... Mr. Daniel FAUGHT
72 Dean College of Technology .... Mr. John GARIC
81 Dean Col Letters/Sci/Prof Studies .... Dr. Douglas A. COE
88 Dean School of Mines & Engineering .... Dr. H. Peter KNUDSEN
44 Director of Development .... Mr. Michael BARTH
39 Director Residence Life .... Mr. Scott FORTHOFER
26 Director Public Relations .... Ms. Amanda BADOVINAC
40 Bookstore Director .... Ms. Jeni L. LUFT
09 Director Institutional Research .... Ms. Melissa HARRINGTON

Rocky Mountain College (C)

1511 Poly Drive, Billings MT 59102-1796
County: Yellowstone FICE Identification: 002534
Unit ID: 180595
Telephone: (406) 657-1000 Carnegie Class: Bac/Diverse
FAX Number: (406) 259-9751 Calendar System: Semester
URL: www.rocky.edu
Established: 1878 Annual Undergrad Tuition & Fees: $22,892
Enrollment: 1,013 Coed
Affiliation or Control: Interdenominational IRS Status: 501(c)3
Highest Offering: Master's
Program: Liberal Arts And General; Teacher Preparatory
Accreditation: NW, AAB, ARCPA

01 President .... Mr. Michael R. MACE
05 Academic Vice President/Provost .... Mr. Anthony PILTZ
32 Vice President of Student Services .... Mr. Bradley A. NASON
84 Vice Pres Enrol Svcs/Dir Admissions .... Ms. Kelly EDWARDS
10 Chief Financial Officer .... Ms. Carol JENSEN
35 Associate Dean of Students .... Ms. Katie CARPENTER
16 Director of Human Resources .... Mr. Gregory N. KOHN
88 Director of Educational Leadership .... Ms. Stevie SCHMITZ
08 Director of the Library .... Mr. Bill KEHLER
44 Director of Planned Giving .... Mr. Obert UNDEM
26 Director News and Information .... Mr. Dan BURKHART
91 Dir of Administrative Computing .... Ms. Kellee PIERCE
18 Director of Facilities Management .... Mr. Terry STEINER
41 Director of Athletics .... Mr. Robert BEERS
30 Director of Advancement .... Ms. Vickie DAVISON
09 Institutional Research Analyst .... Mr. Erik WILLBORG
06 Registrar .... Dr. Leslie G. EDWARDS
37 Director of Financial Assistance .... Ms. Jessica FRANCISCHETTI
39 Director of Residence Life .... Ms. Lindsay ROSSMILLER
04 Executive Assistant to the Pres .... Ms. Pam ERICKSON
29 Dir of Parent Relations and Alumni .... Ms. Kristin MULLANEY

Salish Kootenai College (D)

PO Box 70, Pablo MT 59855-0070
County: Lake FICE Identification: 021434
Unit ID: 180647
Telephone: (406) 275-4800 Carnegie Class: Tribal
FAX Number: (406) 275-4801 Calendar System: Quarter
URL: www.skc.edu
Established: 1977 Annual Undergrad Tuition & Fees: $6,549
Enrollment: 1,112 Coed
Affiliation or Control: Independent Non-Profit IRS Status: 501(c)3
Highest Offering: Baccalaureate
Program: Occupational; 2-Year Principally Bachelor's Creditable; Liberal Arts And General
Accreditation: NW, ADNUR, DA, NUR, SW

01 President .... Dr. Luana ROSS
05 Interim Academic Vice President .... Dr. Elaine FRANK
10 Vice Pres Finance/Business/Admin .... Ms. Kathleen HICKS
06 Registrar .... Ms. Cleo KENMILLE
37 Financial Aid Director .... Ms. Jackie SWAIN
09 Director of Institutional Research .... Dr. Robert PEREGOY
15 Director Personnel Services .... Mrs. Dawn BENSON
30 Development Director .... Mrs. Lois SLATER
32 Chief Student Life Officer .... Mr. Juan PEREZ
13 Director of Information Technology .... Mr. Al ANDERSON
18 Facilities/Physical Plant Manager .... Mr. Mike BIGCRANE
35 Interim Campus Coordinator .... Mr. Corky CLAIRMONT

Stone Child College (E)

8294 Upper Box Elder Road, Box Elder MT 59521-9796
County: Hill FICE Identification: 026109
Unit ID: 366340
Telephone: (406) 395-4313 Carnegie Class: Tribal
FAX Number: (406) 395-4836 Calendar System: Semester
URL: www.stonechild.edu/
Established: 1984 Annual Undergrad Tuition & Fees: $2,450
Enrollment: 1,222 Coed
Affiliation or Control: Tribal Control IRS Status: 501(c)3
Highest Offering: Associate Degree
Program: 2-Year Principally Bachelor's Creditable; Business Emphasis
Accreditation: NW

01 President .... Ms. Melody HENRY
05 Dean of Instruction .... Ms. Cory SANGREY-BILLY
32 Dean of Student Services .... Ms. Clarice MORSETTE
10 Business Manager .... Ms. Jewel L. WHITFORD
04 Admin Asst to the President .... Ms. Wanda ST. MARKS
06 Registrar .... Mrs. Gaile TORRES
13 Management Information Specialist .... Mr. Jeffery HENRY
40 Bookstore Manager .... Ms. Shannon MONTEAU
37 Financial Aid Officer .... Ms. Tiffany GALBAVY
18 Plant Manager .... Mr. Frank HENRY
08 Head Librarian .... Ms. Helen WINDY BOY

University of Great Falls (F)

1301 Twentieth Street S, Great Falls MT 59405-4996
County: Cascade FICE Identification: 002527
Unit ID: 180258
Telephone: (800) 856-9544 Carnegie Class: Bac/Diverse
FAX Number: (406) 791-5209 Calendar System: Semester
URL: www.ugf.edu
Established: 1932 Annual Undergrad Tuition & Fees: $20,288
Enrollment: 1,074 Coed
Affiliation or Control: Roman Catholic IRS Status: 501(c)3
Highest Offering: Master's
Program: Liberal Arts And General; Teacher Preparatory; Professional
Accreditation: NW, NURSE

01 President .... Dr. Eugene J. MCALLISTER
05 VP for Academic Affairs .... Dr. Timothy LAURENT
10 Vice President for Finance .... Ms. Stacey EVE
32 Dean of Student Development .... Ms. Twila CROFT
30 VP for Philanthropy .... Mr. Tenis TENNYSON
84 VP for Enrollment Management .... Ms. Charlene BROWN
20 Academic Dean .... Fr. James SIKORA
37 Director Financial Aid .... Ms. Kelli ENGELHARDT
06 Registrar .... Ms. Kerri KOTESKEY
14 Director Administrative Computing .... Ms. Kathryn CARBIS
26 Director of Marketing and PR .... Ms. Tara TANNER
18 Director Physical Plant .... Mr. Chet PIETRYKOWSKI
38 Director Student Counseling .... Ms. Linda FAGENSTROM
41 Director of Athletics .... Mr. Gary EHNES
21 Director of the Business Office .... Ms. Amber OBRESLEY
51 Director of Continuing Education .... Ms. Sonja BICKFORD
106 Director of Distance Learning .... Mr. Jim GRETCH
15 Director of Human Resources .... Ms. Kristen RANTZ
09 Director of Institutional Research .... Mr. Greg MADSON
40 Campus Store Manger .... Ms. Cheryl DORN
88 Director of Mission Integration .... Sr. Mary Kaye NEALEN
13 Operations Manager/IT Services .... Mr. John KOEHLER
88 Director Student Support Services .... Ms. LaTosha WILLIAMS
88 Community Relations Fund Raiser .... Ms. Liz PINION

NEBRASKA

Alegent Health School of Radiologic Technology (G)

7500 Mercy Road, Omaha NE 68124
County: Douglas FICE Identification: 008492
Unit ID: 181145
Telephone: (402) 398-5527 Carnegie Class: Assoc/PrivNFP
FAX Number: (402) 398-6650 Calendar System: Semester
URL: www.alegent.com
Established: 1953 Annual Undergrad Tuition & Fees: $5,050
Enrollment: 19 Coed
Affiliation or Control: Independent Non-Profit IRS Status: 501(c)3
Highest Offering: Associate Degree
Program: Occupational; 2-Year Principally Bachelor's Creditable
Accreditation: RAD

01 Program Director .... Robert A. HUGHES

Bellevue University (H)

1000 Galvin Road S, Bellevue NE 68005-3098
County: Sarpy FICE Identification: 009743
Unit ID: 180814
Telephone: (402) 293-2000 Carnegie Class: Master's L
FAX Number: (402) 293-2020 Calendar System: Other
URL: www.bellevue.edu
Established: 1966 Annual Undergrad Tuition & Fees: $7,800
Enrollment: 10,304 Coed
Affiliation or Control: Independent Non-Profit IRS Status: 501(c)3
Highest Offering: Doctorate
Program: Liberal Arts And General
Accreditation: NH, IACBE

01 President .... Dr. Mary B. HAWKINS
00 Chancellor .... Dr. John B. MULLER
11 Vice President Administration .... Mr. Jerry A. BLASIG
88 VP Enterprise Services .... Ms. Martyne HALLGREN
10 VP Finance .... Mr. Russ ANDERSEN
05 Vice President Academic Affairs .... Ms. Donna N. MCDANIEL
45 Exec VP Strategic Initiatives .... Dr. Mike ECHOLS
07 VP Mktg/Sales/Enrollmnt Mgmt .... Mr. Matthew DAVIS
106 Dean Ctr Learning Innovation .... Ms. Cathy ERION
72 Dean of College of Information Tech .... Ms. Mary DOBRANSKY
50 Dean College of Business .... Dr. Rod HEWLETT
108 Dean Center for Academic Excellence .... Dr. Linda WILD
51 Dean of Continuing and Profess Educ .... Ms. Michelle EPPLER
14 Asst VP of Information Technology .... Mr. James S. VEREBELY
04 Exec Assistant to the President .... Ms. Christine DOOCY
35 Assoc VP Student Services .... Mr. Russ LANE
37 Director Student Financial Svcs .... Ms. Janet YALE
08 Sr Dir Library Services .... Ms. Robin BERNSTEIN
102 Foundation CEO .... Mr. Russ RUPIPER
41 Director of Athletics .... Mr. Ed LEHOTAK
40 Director Bookstore .... Mr. Mark RIGGERT
18 Director of Facilities .... Mr. Ralph (Sam) J. BORER
30 VP Development Programs .... Ms. Dorothy MORROW
21 Asst VP Financial Strategies .... Ms. Lori PIRSCH
15 Sr Director Human Resources .... Ms. Lora IOSSI
19 Director of Security/Safety .... Mr. Greg ALLEN
88 Quality Assurance Programs Director .... Mr. Pete HEINEMAN
85 Director International Admissions .... Mr. Todd BETTS
26 Associate Dir Public Relations .... Mr. Jim MAXWELL
105 Director Web Services .... Mr. Terry SEVERSON
49 Dean College Arts & Sciences .... Dr. Therese MICHELS

Bryan LGH College of Health Sciences (I)

5035 Everett Street, Lincoln NE 68506-1315
County: Lancaster FICE Identification: 006399
Unit ID: 180878
Telephone: (402) 481-8697 Carnegie Class: Spec/Health
FAX Number: N/A Calendar System: Semester
URL: www.bryanlghcollege.edu
Established: 2001 Annual Undergrad Tuition & Fees: $11,421
Enrollment: 528 Coed
Affiliation or Control: Independent Non-Profit IRS Status: 501(c)3
Highest Offering: Master's
Program: Professional; Nursing Emphasis
Accreditation: NH, ANEST, DMS, NUR

01 President .... Dr. Marilyn MOORE
05 Provost .... Dr. Kay MAIZE
97 Dean of General Studies .... Vacant
11 Dean of Operations .... Dr. June SMITH
66 Dean of Nursing .... Dr. Theresa DELAHOYDE
76 Dean of Health Professions .... Ms. Diane KATHOL

58 Dean of Graduate Studies .... Dr. Sharon HADENFELDT
32 Dean of Students .... Ms. Debra BORDER
08 Director of Library Services .... Ms. Anne HEIMANN
84 Director of Enrollment Management .... Ms. Kelli BACKMAN
06 Registrar .... Ms. Pam MCMASTER

Central Community College (A)

PO Box 4903, Grand Island NE 68802-4903

County: Hall | FICE Identification: 020995 | Unit ID: 180902

Telephone: (308) 398-4222 | Carnegie Class: Assoc/Pub-R-L

FAX Number: (308) 398-7398 | Calendar System: Semester

URL: www.cccneb.edu

Established: 1966 | Annual Undergrad Tuition & Fees (In-District): $2,640

Enrollment: 7,521 | Coed

Affiliation or Control: Local | IRS Status: 501(c)3

Highest Offering: Associate Degree

Program: Occupational; 2-Year Principally Bachelor's Creditable

Accreditation: NH, ADNUR, DA, DH, EMT, MAC, MLTAD, OTA

01 College President .... Dr. Greg P. SMITH
05 Exec Vice Pres/Chief Academic Ofcr .... Dr. Deb BRENNAN
12 Columbus Campus President .... Dr. Matt R. GOTSCHALL
12 Grand Island Campus President .... Dr. Lynn C. BLACK
12 Hastings Campus President .... Mr. Bill HITESMAN
26 Public Relations/Marketing Director .... Mr. James E. STRAYER
10 College Business Officer .... Mr. Larry C. GLAZIER
13 Dir Information Technology Services .... Mr. Tom D. PETERS
102 Foundation Director .... Mr. Dean MOORS
15 Human Resource Manager .... Dr. Chris WADDLE
06 Registrar .... Ms. Barb LARSON
29 Director Alumni Relations .... Mr. Dean MOORS
37 Director Student Financial Aid .... Mr. Steve MILLNITZ
84 Director Enrollment Management .... Mr. Ken REZAC
09 Director Institutional Research .... Mr. Brian MCDERMOTT
28 Director Diversity .... Dr. Chris WADDLE
32 Director Student Affairs .... Mr. Ken REZAC
96 Director of Purchasing .... Ms. Alicia HAUSSLER
29 Alumni Coordinator .... Ms. Pat STANGE

Clarkson College (B)

101 S 42nd Street, Omaha NE 68131-2739

County: Douglas | FICE Identification: 009862 | Unit ID: 180832

Telephone: (402) 552-3100 | Carnegie Class: Spec/Health

FAX Number: (402) 552-3369 | Calendar System: Semester

URL: www.clarksoncollege.edu

Established: 1888 | Annual Undergrad Tuition & Fees: $13,890

Enrollment: 1,114 | Coed

Affiliation or Control: Independent Non-Profit | IRS Status: 501(c)3

Highest Offering: Master's

Program: Liberal Arts And General; Professional; Nursing Emphasis

Accreditation: NH, ANEST, IACBE, NUR, PTAA, RAD

01 President .... Dr. Louis W. BURGHER
05 VP of Academic Affairs .... Dr. Jody WOODWORTH
84 VP of Enroll Mgt/Campus Life Ops .... Tony M. DAMEWOOD
10 Controller .... Megan WICKLESS
06 Registrar .... Michele D. STIRTZ
15 Director Human Resources .... Deb TOMEK
13 Director Technology .... Larry J. VINSON
26 Director of Marketing .... Jina PAUL
28 Director Diversity Services .... Aubray D. ORDUNA
37 Director Student Financial Services .... Margie R. HARRIS
08 Director Library Services .... Nancy M. RALSTON
38 Director Success Center .... Chuck C. MACDONELL
97 Director General Education .... Lori BACHLE
66 Dean Nursing/Dir BS & Grad Nursing .... Dr. Aubray ORDUNA
50 Dir of Business & HIM .... Carla DIRKSCHNEIDER
76 Dir Medical Imaging/Radiologic Tech .... Ellen COLLINS
76 Dir Physical Therapist Asst Pgm .... Andreia NEBEL
07 Director Admissions .... Denise WORK
51 Director of Professional Dev .... Judi B. DUNN
29 Director Alumni Relations .... Rita VANFLEET
88 Dir Basic and Advanced Life Support .... Liz A. SVATOS
106 Coordinator Online Education .... Linda A. NIETO
88 Dir Center of Teaching Excellence .... Mark WHITE

College of Saint Mary (C)

7000 Mercy Road, Omaha NE 68106-2606

County: Douglas | FICE Identification: 002540 | Unit ID: 181604

Telephone: (402) 399-2400 | Carnegie Class: Master's S

FAX Number: (402) 399-2647 | Calendar System: Semester

URL: www.csm.edu

Established: 1923 | Annual Undergrad Tuition & Fees: $25,310

Enrollment: 1,063 | Female

Affiliation or Control: Roman Catholic | IRS Status: 501(c)3

Highest Offering: Doctorate

Program: Liberal Arts And General; Teacher Preparatory; Professional

Accreditation: NH, ADNUR, IACBE, NUR, OT

01 President .... Dr. Maryanne STEVENS, RSM
32 Vice President Student Development .... Dr. Tara KNUDSON-CARL
05 Vice Pres Academic Affairs/Dean .... Dr. Christine PHARR
30 Vice Pres Institutional Advancement .... Verlyn SCHUELER
07 Vice President Enrollment .... Mr. Greg FRITZ
10 Vice Pres Financial Services/CFO .... Ms. Sarah KOTTICH
04 Executive Asst to the President .... Ms. Shirley GUNDERSON
06 Registrar .... Mrs. Deb NUGEN
08 Director of Library .... Ms. Sara WILLIAMS
14 Director of Computer Center .... Mr. Jason DEGN
29 Director of Alumnae .... Ms. Diane PROULX
37 Director Student Financial Aid .... Ms. Beth SISK
26 Public Relations Director .... Mr. Brittney LONG
35 Director Student Affairs .... Mrs. Katty PETAK
39 Director Student Housing .... Vacant
40 Director Bookstore .... Mr. Steve WESTENBROEK
41 Athletic Director .... Mr. Jim KRUEGER
42 Director Campus Ministry .... Ms. Vicki ZOBRIST
85 Director Foreign Students .... Ms. Jennifer WITTSTOCK
18 Director Physical Plant .... Mr. Dan SPARGEN
44 Director Annual Giving .... Ms. Keli OFFERMAN
21 Associate Business Officer .... Ms. Bridgette RENBARGER
15 Director Personnel Services .... Ms. Sarah M. LIVINGSTON

Concordia University (D)

800 N Columbia Avenue, Seward NE 68434-1599

County: Seward | FICE Identification: 002541 | Unit ID: 180984

Telephone: (402) 643-3651 | Carnegie Class: Master's S

FAX Number: (402) 643-4073 | Calendar System: Other

URL: www.cune.edu

Established: 1894 | Annual Undergrad Tuition & Fees: $23,800

Enrollment: 2,197 | Coed

Affiliation or Control: Lutheran Church - Missouri Synod | IRS Status: 501(c)3

Highest Offering: Master's

Program: Liberal Arts And General; Teacher Preparatory

Accreditation: NH, IACBE, MUS, TED

01 President .... Rev Dr. Brian L. FRIEDRICH
05 Provost .... Dr. Jenny MUELLER-ROEBKE
30 Vice President Inst Advancement .... Rev. Richard MADDOX
84 VP Enroll Mgt/Stdnt Svcs/Athletics .... Mr. Scott SEEVERS
20 Associate Provost .... Vacant
10 Chief Financial Officer .... Mr. David KUMM
53 Dean of College of Education .... Dr. Ronald BORK
49 Dean of Arts & Sciences .... Dr. Brent ROYUK
13 Co-Dean Information Technology .... Dr. Donald SYLWESTER
13 Co-Dean Information Technology .... Dr. Kent EINSPAHR
58 Dean College Grad Studies/Adult Ed .... Dr. Thad WARREN
08 Director of Library Services .... Mr. Philip HENDRICKSON
06 University Registrar .... Mr. Ed SIFFRING
36 Synodical & Education Placement Dir .... Mr. William SCHRANZ
29 Director Alumni/University Rels .... Mrs. Jan KOOPMAN
35 Director Student Life .... Mr. Charles GEBHARDT
36 Career Counselor .... Mr. Corey GRAY
41 Athletic Director .... Mr. Devin SMITH
42 Campus Pastor .... Rev. Ryan MATTHIAS
37 Director of Financial Aid .... Mrs. Gloria HENNIG
18 Chief Facilities/Physical Plant .... Mr. Rick IHDE
15 Director of Human Resources .... Mrs. Connie BUTLER
07 Director Undergraduate Admissions .... Mr. Aaron ROBERTS
26 Director of Marketing .... Mr. Andrew SWENSON
21 Dir Invest/Student Admin Svcs .... Mr. Curt SHERMAN
44 Coord of Resource Devel Ops .... Mrs. Janet TONJES
38 Director of Counseling .... Ms. Dina CRITEL-RATHJE

The Creative Center (E)

10850 Emmet Street, Omaha NE 68164-2911

County: Douglas | FICE Identification: 031643 | Unit ID: 430485

Telephone: (402) 898-1000 | Carnegie Class: Spec/Arts

FAX Number: (402) 898-1301 | Calendar System: Semester

URL: www.creativecenter.edu

Established: 1993 | Annual Undergrad Tuition & Fees: N/A

Enrollment: 119 | Coed

Affiliation or Control: Proprietary | IRS Status: Proprietary

Highest Offering: Baccalaureate

Program: Occupational; 2-Year Principally Bachelor's Creditable; Fine Arts Emphasis

Accreditation: ACCSC

01 President .... Mr. Ray DOTZLER
05 Director .... Ms. Kim GUYER

Creighton University (F)

2500 California Plaza, Omaha NE 68178-0001

County: Douglas | FICE Identification: 002542 | Unit ID: 181002

Telephone: (402) 280-2700 | Carnegie Class: Master's L

FAX Number: N/A | Calendar System: Semester

URL: www.creighton.edu

Established: 1878 | Annual Undergrad Tuition & Fees: $33,330

Enrollment: 7,730 | Coed

Affiliation or Control: Roman Catholic | IRS Status: 501(c)3

Highest Offering: Doctorate

Program: Liberal Arts And General; Teacher Preparatory; Professional

Accreditation: NH, BUS, BUSA, DENT, EMT, LAW, MED, NURSE, OT, PHAR, PTA, SW, TED

01 President .... Rev. Timothy R. LANNON, SJ
05 Vice President Academic Affairs .... Mr. Patrick J. BORCHERS
32 Vice President for Student Services .... Dr. John C. CERNECH
11 Vice President for Administration .... Mr. John L. WILHELM
17 Vice President Health Sciences .... Dr. Donald FREY
03 Sr Vice President for Operations .... Mr. Daniel E. BURKEY
26 Vice Pres for University Relations .... Vacant
13 Vice President Information Systems .... Mr. Brian A. YOUNG
42 Vice President University Ministry .... Rev. Andrew F. ALEXANDER, SJ
43 VP and General Legal Counsel .... Mr. James S. JANSEN
30 Sr Assoc VP Devel/Campaign Dir .... Vacant
39 Assoc Vice President Resident Life .... Dr. Richard E. ROSSI
22 Assoc VP Affirm Act/Divrsty Outrch .... Mr. John E. PIERCE
84 Assoc VP Enrollment Management .... Ms. Mary E. CHASE
20 Assoc VP Academic Affairs .... Ms. Tricia A. BRUNDO-SHARRAR
20 Assoc VP for Acad Excel .... Dr. Mary Ann DANIELSON
35 Assoc VP Student Services .... Vacant
27 Asst VP Marketing/Public Relations .... Ms. Kim B. MANNING
90 Assoc VP Information Technology .... Vacant
30 Asst VP Advancement .... Vacant
46 Assoc VP for Research/Compliance .... Mrs. Kathleen J. TAGGART
29 Assistant VP for Alumni Relations .... Ms. Anna NUBEL
15 Exec Director Human Resources .... Mr. Jeffrey C. BRANSTETTER
10 Chief Business Officer .... Ms. Jan D. MADSEN
06 Registrar .... Ms. Patricia HALL
07 Director Admissions/Scholarships .... Ms. Sarah RICHARDSON
08 Director Reinert Alumni Library .... Mr. Michael J. LACROIX
85 Director International Programs .... Dr. Maria C. KRANE
18 Director Facility Planning/Mgmt .... Mr. Lennis D. PEDERSON
19 Director of Public Safety .... Mr. Richard J. MCAULIFFE
38 Director of Univ Counseling Center .... Dr. Michael KELLEY
37 Director Student Financial Aid .... Mr. Robert D. WALKER
36 Director Career Services .... Mr. Jim BRETL
41 Director Athletics .... Mr. Bruce D. RASMUSSEN
27 Director Public Relations .... Ms. Deborah DALEY
21 Budget Director .... Ms. Tara MCGUIRE
92 Director Honors Program .... Dr. Jeffrey HAUSE
96 Director of Purchasing .... Mr. Joseph J. ZABOROWSKI
87 Director of the Summer Session .... Ms. Debra DALY
28 Director of Multicultural Affairs .... Mr. Ricardo ARIZA
40 Bookstore Manager .... Mr. Calvin PETERSEN
09 Sr Analyst Institutional Research .... Dr. Stephanie WERNIG
49 Dean Arts & Sciences .... Dr. Robert LUEGER
58 Dean of Graduate School .... Dr. Gail JENSEN
61 Dean of Law .... Ms. Marianne B. CULHANE
63 Dean of Medicine .... Dr. Rowen ZETTERMAN
52 Interim Dean of Dentistry .... Dr. Mark A. LATTA
50 Dean Business Administration .... Dr. Anthony HENDRICKSON
67 Dean Pharm/Allied Health Profession .... Dr. J. Chris BRADBERRY
66 Dean of Nursing .... Dr. Eleanor V. HOWELL
51 Dean of University College .... Dr. Gail JENSEN

Doane College (G)

1014 Boswell Avenue, Crete NE 68333

County: Saline | FICE Identification: 002544 | Unit ID: 181020

Telephone: (402) 826-2161 | Carnegie Class: Bac/A&S

FAX Number: (402) 826-8600 | Calendar System: 4/1/4

URL: www.doane.edu

Established: 1872 | Annual Undergrad Tuition & Fees: $25,080

Enrollment: 2,701 | Coed

Affiliation or Control: United Church Of Christ | IRS Status: 501(c)3

Highest Offering: Master's

Program: Liberal Arts And General; Teacher Preparatory

Accreditation: NH, TED

01 President .... Dr. Jacque CARTER
05 Vice President Academic Affairs .... Dr. John BURNEY
10 Vice President Financial Affairs .... Ms. Julie SCHMIDT
30 Vice Pres Institutional Advancement .... Dr. Jerry WOOD
32 Vice President Student Leadership .... Ms. Kim JACOBS
13 VP for Information Technology .... Mr. Mike CARPENTER
07 VP for Enrollment Svcs & Marketing .... Mr. Joel WEYAND
88 Dean of Educational Leadership .... Dr. Jed JOHNSTON
20 Dean of Curriculum & Instruction .... Dr. Lyn FORESTER
58 Dean of Grad Studies in Mgmt .... Ms. Janice M. HADFIELD
51 Dean Adult Undergraduate Studies .... Ms. Janice M. HADFIELD
88 Director of Hansen Leadership Pgm .... Ms. Carrie PETR
06 Registrar .... Ms. Denise ELLIS
37 Director of Financial Aid .... Ms. Peggy TVRDY
08 Director of the Library .... Ms. Julie PINNELL
21 Controller .... Mr. Ned TUCKER
36 Director Career Development .... Ms. Carolyn ERSLAND
26 Assoc VP of Marketing Communication .... Ms. Jacque POMAJZL
29 Director of Alumni Relation .... Ms. Anne GOLDEN
29 Director of Advancement Operation .... Ms. Jennifer JORGENSEN
15 Director of Human Resources .... Ms. Laura SEARS
18 Dir of Facilities & Constr Proj .... Mr. Wayne SPARY
58 Dean of Grad Studies in Counseling .... Dr. Thomas J. GILLIGAN
41 Athletic Director .... Mr. Greg HEIER
42 Chaplain .... Ms. Karla COOPER
40 Bookstore Manager .... Ms. Lynette NEWTON
28 Director of Multicultural Pgm & Edu .... Ms. Wilma JACKSON
23 Director of Health and Wellness .... Ms. Kelly JIROVEC
35 Director of Student Support Service .... Ms. Sherri HANIGAN
09 Director of Institutional Research .... Ms. Raja TAYEH
19 Dir of Campus Safety/Assoc Dean .... Mr. Russ HEWITT

Grace University (H)

1311 S 9th Street, Omaha NE 68108-3629

County: Douglas | FICE Identification: 002547 | Unit ID: 181093

Telephone: (402) 449-2800 | Carnegie Class: Bac/Diverse

FAX Number: (402) 341-9587 | Calendar System: Semester

URL: www.graceu.edu

Established: 1943 | Annual Undergrad Tuition & Fees: $17,366

Enrollment: 459 Coed
Affiliation or Control: Independent Non-Profit IRS Status: 501(c)3
Highest Offering: Master's
Program: Liberal Arts And General; Teacher Preparatory; Religious Emphasis
Accreditation: NH, BI

01 President Dr. David M. BARNES
03 Executive Vice President Mr. Michael F. JAMES
05 Academic Dean Dr. John D. HOLMES
32 Student Services Dean Mrs. Deb OSMANSON
84 Enrollment Management Dean Mr. Chris PRUITT
10 Director of Finance Ms. Anita RODRIGUEZ
06 Registrar Mr. Kris J. UDD
88 Director of Adult Education Dr. Martin (Dick) R. DAHLQUIST
07 Manager TUG Admissions Ms. Tara KOTH
09 Dir of Assessment & Inst Research Dr. Ronald J. SHOPE
37 Director of Financial Aid Mr. Ray MILLER
15 Director Human Resources Mr. Steve R. WIEMEYER
26 Development & Marketing Officer Vacant
08 Librarian Mr. Harold (Ben) B. BRICK, III
04 Admin Assistant to the President Ms. Joanne R. FAST
11 Director of Operations Mrs. Deb OSMANSON
33 Dean of Men Mr. Jon T. MCNEEL
34 Dean of Women Ms. Marilyn AMSTUTZ
41 Athletic Director Mr. Jon HOOD
13 Director Information Services Vacant
88 Director Christian Formation & SLT Mr. Wesley WILMER

Hastings College (A)

710 N Turner Avenue, Box 269, Hastings NE 68902-0269
County: Adams FICE Identification: 002548
Unit ID: 181127
Telephone: (402) 463-2402 Carnegie Class: Bac/Diverse
FAX Number: (402) 461-7490 Calendar System: 4/1/4
URL: www.hastings.edu
Established: 1882 Annual Undergrad Tuition & Fees: $22,784
Enrollment: 1,193 Coed
Affiliation or Control: Presbyterian Church (U.S.A.) IRS Status: 501(c)3
Highest Offering: Master's
Program: Liberal Arts And General; Teacher Preparatory
Accreditation: NH, MUS, TED

01 President of the College Mr. Dennis C. TROTTER
00 Chairman of the Board Mr. Harold "Hal" E. DITTMER
30 Interim Pres of the Foundation Mr. Bill ASBURY
10 Vice Pres Finance/Administration Ms. Kay LANGSETH
84 VP for Enrollment Management Ms. Maryjo "MJ" HUEBNER
05 Vice Pres Acad Affs/Dean Faculty Dr. W. Clark HENDLEY
32 Interim VP Student Affairs Rev. Joan MCCARTHY
26 Assoc VP for Mkting/Communications Ms. Susan MEESKE
20 Assoc VP for Academic Affairs Dr. Anne FAIRBANKS
41 Athletic Director Mr. Jerry SCHMUTTE
35 Assoc VP for Student Affairs Rev. Joan MCCARTHY
07 Assoc VP Admissions & Enrollment Ms. Mary MOLLICONI
44 VP for Planned & Major Gifts Mr. Michael KARLOFF
88 VP of Scholarship Development Ms. Patty SITORIUS
00 Development President Emeritus Dr. Phillip L. DUDLEY, JR.
102 Assoc VP for Development Ms. Judee L. KONEN
06 Registrar Mr. Daniel J. PETERS
37 Director of Financial Aid Ms. Terri GRAHAM
39 Director of Housing Mrs. Lori HERGOTT
15 Director of Human Resources Ms. Margo BUSBOOM
105 Web Content Manager Mr. Christopher FRUEHLING
08 Director of Libraries Mr. Robert M. NEDDERMAN
24 Director Educ Media/Librarian Ms. Susan FRANKLIN
29 Director of Alumni Relations Ms. Hauli SABATKA
13 Director Computing & Info Mgmt Vacant
105 Network Administrator Mr. Jim MACKIN
90 Acad Computer Support Specialist Mr. Erik NIELSEN
18 Director Physical Plant Services Mr. James RUZICKA
93 Minority Students Dr. Moses DOGBEVIA
28 International Studies/Diversity Pgm Dr. Anne FAIRBANKS
36 Director of Career Services Ms. Kimberly K. GRAVIETTE
23 Director Campus Health Services Ms. Beth LITTRELL
42 Chaplain Rev Dr. David B. MCCARTHY
21 Director of Accounting Mr. Dan LAUX
35 Director Student Activities Mr. Pat MCCAULEY
19 Director of Security/Safety Mr. John SILVESTER
38 Director of Counseling Services Mr. Jon LOETTERLE
40 Bookstore Manager Mrs. Monica LLOYD
27 News Service/Writer/Editor Ms. Amber MEDINA
88 Graphic Designer/Publisher Ms. Camille KIRCHHOFF
85 Foreign Students/Student Life Dr. Antje ANDERSON

ITT Technical Institute (B)

1120 North 103rd Plaza, Ste. 200, Omaha NE 68114
County: Douglas Identification: 666543
Unit ID: 407319
Telephone: (402) 331-2900 Carnegie Class: Spec/Tech
FAX Number: (402) 331-9495 Calendar System: Quarter
URL: www.itt-tech.edu
Established: 1991 Annual Undergrad Tuition & Fees: N/A
Enrollment: 735 Coed
Affiliation or Control: Proprietary IRS Status: Proprietary
Highest Offering: Baccalaureate
Program: Technical Emphasis
Accreditation: ACICS

† Branch campus of ITT Technical Institute, Indianapolis, IN.

Kaplan University (C)

1821 K Street, PO Box 82826, Lincoln NE 68501-2826
County: Lancaster FICE Identification: 004721
Unit ID: 181242
Telephone: (402) 474-5315 Carnegie Class: Assoc/PrivFP4
FAX Number: (402) 474-0896 Calendar System: Quarter
URL: www.lincoln.kaplanuniversity.edu
Established: 1884 Annual Undergrad Tuition & Fees: $21,300
Enrollment: 469 Coed
Affiliation or Control: Proprietary IRS Status: Proprietary
Highest Offering: Baccalaureate
Program: Occupational; 2-Year Principally Bachelor's Creditable; Professional
Accreditation: &NH, MAC

01 Campus President Ms. Kate NOBLE
05 Dean of Education Mr. Timothy SCHOLL
07 Director of Admissions Mr. Michael KLACIK
10 Director of Finance Ms. Valerie STANDEVEN
36 Director of Career Services Mr. Jason LEMON
06 Registrar Ms. Christina RUHGE
32 Director of Student Services Ms. Jill MATHERS
08 Director Library/Bookstore Services Ms. Kathleen KELLER

† Regional accreditation is carried under the parent institution in Davenport, IA.

Kaplan University (D)

5425 N. 103rd Street, Omaha NE 68134-1002
County: Douglas FICE Identification: 008491
Unit ID: 181400
Telephone: (402) 431-6100 Carnegie Class: Assoc/PrivFP4
FAX Number: (402) 573-1341 Calendar System: Other
URL: www.omaha.kaplanuniversity.edu
Established: 1891 Annual Undergrad Tuition & Fees: $20,750
Enrollment: 650 Coed
Affiliation or Control: Proprietary IRS Status: Proprietary
Highest Offering: Associate Degree
Program: Occupational; 2-Year Principally Bachelor's Creditable
Accreditation: &NH, DA, MAC

01 President Mr. Jeremy BRUNSSEN
05 Campus Academic Dean Ms. Kara STEFFEY
06 Registrar Ms. Linda SMITH
07 Director of Admissions Mr. Zac LORENZEN
36 Director Student Placement Mr. Robert GIDDINGS
37 Director of Financial Aid Ms. Crystal FAXON

† Regional accreditation is carried under the parent institution in Davenport, IA.

Little Priest Tribal College (E)

PO Box 270, Winnebago NE 68071-0270
County: Thurston FICE Identification: 033233
Unit ID: 434016
Telephone: (402) 878-2380 Carnegie Class: Tribal
FAX Number: (402) 878-2355 Calendar System: Semester
URL: www.littlepriest.edu
Established: 1996 Annual Undergrad Tuition & Fees: $2,985
Enrollment: 334 Coed
Affiliation or Control: Independent Non-Profit IRS Status: 501(c)3
Highest Offering: Associate Degree
Program: Occupational; 2-Year Principally Bachelor's Creditable
Accreditation: NH

01 President Mr. Paul ROBERTSON
05 Academic Dean Ms. Brigid QUINN
10 Controller Mr. Robert BAXTER
37 Director of Financial Aid Ms. Jennifer BARTA
13 IT Director Mr. Brandon STOUT
31 Coordinator of Community Education Ms. Sharon REDHORN-CHAMBERLAIN
06 Registrar Ms. Janet NIELSEN

Mary Lanning Healthcare School of Radiology (F)

715 North St. Joseph Avenue, Hastings NE 68901
County: Adams FICE Identification: 004431
Unit ID: 181251
Telephone: (402) 461-5177 Carnegie Class: Not Classified
FAX Number: (402) 460-5059 Calendar System: Other
URL: www.marylanning.org
Established: 1952 Annual Undergrad Tuition & Fees: $3,375
Enrollment: 28 Coed
Affiliation or Control: Independent Non-Profit IRS Status: 501(c)3
Highest Offering: Associate Degree
Program: Occupational
Accreditation: RAD

01 Program Director Cristi L. ENGEL

Metropolitan Community College (G)

PO Box 3777, Omaha NE 68103-0777
County: Douglas FICE Identification: 012586
Unit ID: 181303
Telephone: (402) 457-2400 Carnegie Class: Assoc/Pub-U-MC
FAX Number: (402) 457-2395 Calendar System: Quarter
URL: www.mccneb.edu
Established: 1974 Annual Undergrad Tuition & Fees (In-District): $2,520
Enrollment: 18,518 Coed
Affiliation or Control: Local IRS Status: 501(c)3
Highest Offering: Associate Degree
Program: Occupational; 2-Year Principally Bachelor's Creditable
Accreditation: NH, ACBSP, ACFEI, ADNUR, DA, EMT, MAC

01 President Mr. Randy SCHMAILZL
03 Executive Vice President Mr. James GROTRIAN
05 Vice President Academic Affairs Mr. David HO
11 VP Technology/Administrative Svcs Dr. Mary K. WISE
32 VP of Campuses/Student Affairs Dr. Arthur RICH
28 Assoc Vice Pres Equity/Diversity Dr. Cynthia GOOCH
16 Assoc Vice Pres of Human Resources Ms. Maureen MOEGLIN
30 Assoc Vice Pres of Development Ms. Pat CRISLER
20 Associate VP of Academic Affairs Mr. William OWEN
84 Asst Vice Pres for Student Affairs Ms. Marie VAZQUEZ
10 Executive College Business Officer Mr. Dave KOEBEL
26 Exec Director of Public Affairs Ms. Sheila O'CONNOR
18 Director Facilities Management Mr. Bernard SEDLACEK
37 Director of Financial Aid Ms. Wilma HJELLUM
13 Dir Management Information Svcs Mr. Mick GAHAN
96 Director Administrative Management Mr. Richard HANNEMAN
19 Chief of Police/Dir Emergency Mgmt Mr. David FRIEND

Mid-Plains Community College (H)

601 W State Farm Road, North Platte NE 69101-9491
County: Lincoln FICE Identification: 002557
Unit ID: 181312
Telephone: (308) 535-3600 Carnegie Class: Assoc/Pub-R-M
FAX Number: (308) 535-3790 Calendar System: Semester
URL: www.mpcc.edu
Established: 1926 Annual Undergrad Tuition & Fees (In-District): $2,760
Enrollment: 2,623 Coed
Affiliation or Control: State/Local IRS Status: 501(c)3
Highest Offering: Associate Degree
Program: Occupational; 2-Year Principally Bachelor's Creditable; Technical Emphasis
Accreditation: NH, ADNUR, DA, MLTAD

01 President Mr. Ryan PURDY
12 VP North Platte Community College Mr. Marcus GARSTECKI
12 Interim VP McCook Community College Ms. Michele GILL
11 Assoc VP Administrative Services Vacant
32 Area VP Educ Svcs/Student Devel Dr. Jody TOMANEK
09 Area Dir Instl Research & Planning Mr. Tad PFEIFER
32 Area Dean of Student Life Ms. Michele GILL
56 Dean of Outreach & Training Mr. Bruce DOWSE
36 Area Dean of Career Services Mr. Bill EAKINS
84 Area Dean of Enrollment Management Ms. Kelly RIPPEN
06 Area Registrar Ms. Mari Jo WIDGER
26 Area Dir Public Inform/Marketing Mr. Charles SALESTROM
15 Area Director of Human Resources Mr. Bruce BERGMAN
21 Area Accounting Director Mr. Bruce BERGMAN
13 Area Director of Info Technology Mr. Tim HALL
37 Area Dir of Student Financial Aid Mr. Dale BROWN

Midland University (I)

900 N Clarkson, Fremont NE 68025-4395
County: Dodge FICE Identification: 002553
Unit ID: 181330
Telephone: (402) 721-5480 Carnegie Class: Bac/Diverse
FAX Number: (402) 721-0250 Calendar System: 4/1/4
URL: www.midlandu.edu
Established: 1883 Annual Undergrad Tuition & Fees: $24,810
Enrollment: 1,030 Coed
Affiliation or Control: Evangelical Lutheran Church In America
IRS Status: 501(c)3
Highest Offering: Master's
Program: Occupational; Liberal Arts And General; Teacher Preparatory; Professional; Business Emphasis
Accreditation: NH, NUR

01 President Dr. Benjamin E. SASSE
32 Vice Pres Student Development Mr. Greg FRITZ
05 Chief Academic Officer Dr. Steven BULLOCK
10 Vice Pres for Administration & CFO Ms. Jodi BENJAMIN
07 Admissions Director Ms. Eliza FERZELY
26 Director of Communications Mr. Nate NEUFIND
06 Registrar & Institutional Research Ms. Jenifer JOST
37 Director of Financial Aid Mr. Doug WATSON
21 Controller Ms. Jessie COMBS
36 Dir of Career Resource Devel Ctr Ms. Connie M. BOTTGER
41 Director of Athletic Operations Mr. Jason DANNELLY
66 Chair of Nursing Ms. Linda QUINN
14 Director Information Technology Mr. Ken CLIPPERTON
18 Director of Physical Plant Mr. Gary STRONG
30 Director of Advancement Ms. Kari RIDDER
84 Director of Student Recruitment Mr. Jason BLOHM
53 Education Department Chair Dr. Keith ROHWER

Myotherapy Institute (J)

4001 Pioneer Woods Drive, Lincoln NE 68506-7547
County: Lancaster FICE Identification: 032793
Unit ID: 434432
Telephone: (402) 421-7410 Carnegie Class: Assoc/PrivFP
FAX Number: (402) 421-6736 Calendar System: Other
URL: www.myotherapy.edu
Established: 1992 Annual Undergrad Tuition & Fees: $12,300

Enrollment: 38 Coed
Affiliation or Control: Proprietary IRS Status: Proprietary
Highest Offering: Associate Degree
Program: Occupational
Accreditation: ACCSC

01 Director ..... Ms. Sue KOZISEK

Nebraska Christian College (A)

12550 S 114th Street, Papillion NE 68046-4256
County: Sarpy FICE Identification: 012976
Unit ID: 181376
Telephone: (402) 935-9400 Carnegie Class: Spec/Faith
FAX Number: (402) 935-9500 Calendar System: Semester
URL: www.nechristian.edu
Established: 1945 Annual Undergrad Tuition & Fees: $10,900
Enrollment: 130 Coed
Affiliation or Control: Christian Churches And Churches of Christ
IRS Status: 501(c)3
Highest Offering: Baccalaureate
Program: Religious Emphasis
Accreditation: BI

01 President ..... Mr. Richard MILLIKEN
05 Vice Pres Academics ..... Dr. Mark KRAUSE
10 Vice Pres Operations ..... Mr. Tony CLARK
30 Director of Development ..... Mr. James HARDY
32 Dean of Students/Chief Stdnt Ofcr ..... Vacant
07 Director of Admissions ..... Mr. Brian TAYLOR
26 Director of Marketing ..... Mr. J. D KING
18 Director of Facilities ..... Mr. Paul MILLER
08 Head Librarian ..... Ms. Linda LLOYD
37 Financial Aid Officer ..... Mrs. Tina LARSEN
34 Dean of Women ..... Mrs. Leslie STEVENS

Nebraska Indian Community College (B)

1111 Hwy 75 - PO Box 428, Macy NE 68039-0428
County: Thurston FICE Identification: 025508
Unit ID: 181419
Telephone: (402) 494-2311 Carnegie Class: Tribal
FAX Number: (402) 837-4183 Calendar System: Semester
URL: www.thenicc.edu
Established: 1973 Annual Undergrad Tuition & Fees: $4,080
Enrollment: 140 Coed
Affiliation or Control: Tribal Control IRS Status: Exempt
Highest Offering: Associate Degree
Program: Occupational; 2-Year Principally Bachelor's Creditable
Accreditation: NH

01 President ..... Dr. Michael OLTROGGE
05 Academic Dean ..... Don TORGERSON
10 Business Office Director ..... Tiffany SPARKS
32 Student Support Services ..... Dawne PRICE
30 Director of Development ..... Mark GORDON
27 Chief Information Officer ..... Justin KOCIAN

Nebraska Methodist College (C)

720 N 87th Street, Omaha NE 68114-2852
County: Douglas FICE Identification: 006404
Unit ID: 181297
Telephone: (402) 354-7000 Carnegie Class: Spec/Health
FAX Number: (402) 354-7090 Calendar System: Semester
URL: www.methodistcollege.edu
Established: 1891 Annual Undergrad Tuition & Fees: $11,989
Enrollment: 867 Coed
Affiliation or Control: Independent Non-Profit IRS Status: 501(c)3
Highest Offering: Master's
Program: Professional; Nursing Emphasis
Accreditation: NH, DMS, MAC, NURSE, PTAA, RAD, SURGT

01 President ..... Dr. Dennis A. JOSLIN
05 Vice President Academic Affairs ..... Dr. Paul A. SAVORY
32 Vice President Student Affairs ..... Dr. Kristine M. HESS
26 VP Business Dev & Communication ..... Ms. Danielle DUBUC-PEDERSEN
45 VP Organizational Development ..... Dr. Deborah CARLSON
35 Dean of Students ..... Dr. Melissa HOFFMAN
66 Dean Nursing ..... Dr. Linda HUGHES
58 Program Director Master's Nursing ..... Dr. Linda FOLEY
66 Pgm Director Undergrad Nursing ..... Dr. Karen JOHNSON
88 Director of Special Pgms Nursing ..... Dr. Susie WARD
76 Dean Health Professions ..... Dr. Patricia SULLIVAN
97 Dean General Education ..... Dr. Mary Lee LUSBY
76 Pgm Director Phys Therapist Asst ..... Ms. Shannon STRUBY
76 Program Director Respiratory Care ..... Dr. John JAROSZ
88 Program Director Radiography ..... Ms. Jane SIMS
88 Program Director Sonography ..... Ms. Rebecca MATHIASEN
88 Pgm Director Surgical Technology ..... Ms. Christy GRANT
08 Director of Library Services ..... Ms. Beverly SEDLACEK
42 Dir Spiritual Dev/Campus Ministry ..... Rev. Daniel JOHNSTON
29 Director Alumni Relations ..... Ms. Denise M. CARLSON
07 Director Enrollment Services ..... Ms. Sara HANSON
06 Director Registration & Records ..... Ms. Melinda STONER
37 Director Financial Aid ..... Ms. Penny JAMES
88 Exec Dir Professional Development ..... Ms. Candy HOABY
10 Director Business Office ..... Ms. Beth FRIEDMAN
88 Educational Compliance Officer ..... Mr. Ryan PORTWOOD

*Nebraska State College System (D)

PO Box 94605, Lincoln NE 68509-4605
County: Lancaster FICE Identification: 033441
Telephone: (402) 471-2505 Carnegie Class: N/A
FAX Number: (402) 471-2669
URL: www.nscs.edu

01 Chancellor ..... Mr. Stan CARPENTER
43 General Counsel & VC for Emp Rel ..... Ms. Kristin PETERSEN
10 Vice Chancellor Finance/Admin ..... Ms. Carolyn MURPHY
32 VC for Stdnt Aff/Mkt/Enrol/Pub Info ..... Ms. Korinne TANDE
18 Vice Chanc Facil/Plng/Info Tech ..... Mr. Ed HOFFMAN
05 Assoc VC Acad Planning/Partnerships ..... Ms. Lois PODOBNIK
13 Network Specialist/Accountant ..... Ms. Becky KOHRS
88 Director of Systemwide Accounting ..... Ms. Amy HOCK

*Chadron State College (E)

1000 Main Street, Chadron NE 69337-2690
County: Dawes FICE Identification: 002539
Unit ID: 180948
Telephone: (308) 432-6000 Carnegie Class: Bac/Diverse
FAX Number: (308) 432-6464 Calendar System: Semester
URL: www.csc.edu
Established: 1911 Annual Undergrad Tuition & Fees (In-State): $5,576
Enrollment: 2,932 Coed
Affiliation or Control: State IRS Status: 501(c)3
Highest Offering: Master's
Program: Liberal Arts And General; Teacher Preparatory; Professional
Accreditation: NH, ACBSP, SW, TED

02 Interim President ..... Dr. Randy RHINE
30 Executive Director CS Foundation ... Ms. Connie A. RASMUSSEN
05 Vice President Academic Affairs ..... Dr. Charles SNARE
32 Interim Exec Dir of Student Life ..... Mr. Aaron PRESTWICH
11 Vice Pres Administration & Finance ..... Mr. Dale E. GRANT
09 Asst VP Enroll Mgmt/Inst Research ..... Ms. Theresa R. DAWSON
26 Assoc VP for Market Development ..... Mr. Steve M. TAYLOR
06 Director of Records ..... Ms. Melissa MITCHELL
07 Director of Admissions ..... Ms. Tena COOK
10 Comptroller ..... Ms. Julie GOODMAN
88 Dean of Professional Licensure ..... Dr. Margaret CROUSE
49 Dean of Teaching and Learning ..... Dr. Katharine FORSTROM
20 Dean of Curriculum & Academic Advmt ..... Dr. Joel HYER
08 Director Library/Learning Resources ..... Mr. Milton WOLF
14 Chief Information Officer ..... Ms. Ann M. BURK
35 Interim Exec Dir Student Services ..... Ms. Sherry L. DOUGLAS
16 Director Human Resources ..... Ms. Kara VOGT
39 Director of Housing ..... Ms. Sherri J. SIMONS
41 Director of Athletics ..... Mr. Bradley R. SMITH
12 Director Extended Campus Sites ..... Ms. Deann BAYNE
36 Director of Internships/Career Svcs ..... Ms. Deena KENNELL
21 Budget Director ..... Ms. Melany HUGHES
26 Marketing Coordinator ..... Mr. Justin HAAG
18 Coordinator of Physical Facilities ..... Mr. Blair BRENNAN

*Peru State College (F)

PO Box 10, Peru NE 68421-0010
County: Nemaha FICE Identification: 002559
Unit ID: 181534
Telephone: (402) 872-3815 Carnegie Class: Master's L
FAX Number: (402) 872-2375 Calendar System: Semester
URL: www.peru.edu
Established: 1867 Annual Undergrad Tuition & Fees (In-State): $5,656
Enrollment: 2,368 Coed
Affiliation or Control: State IRS Status: 501(c)3
Highest Offering: Master's
Program: Liberal Arts And General; Teacher Preparatory
Accreditation: NH, TED

02 President ..... Dr. Daniel HANSON
05 Vice Pres Academic Affairs ..... Dr. Todd DREW
10 Vice Pres Administration & Finance ..... Mr. Bruce BATTERSON
84 VP Enrollment Mgmt/Student Services ..... Ms. Michaela WILLIS
32 Dean of Student Life ..... Ms. Karla FRASER
102 Executive Director Foundation ..... Mr. Todd SIMPSON
41 Athletic Director ..... Mr. Steve SCHNEIDER
26 Dir of Marketing & Media Services ..... Ms. Regan ANSON
06 Registrar ..... Ms. Dixie TETEN
37 Director of Financial Aid ..... Ms. Janice VOLKER
08 Director of Library ..... Mr. Roger BECKER
15 Human Resources Director ..... Ms. Eulanda CADE
18 Director Campus Services ..... Mr. Richard HARRISON
09 Dir Student Assess & Success Svcs ..... Dr. Ursula WALN
21 Director of Business Services ..... Ms. Kathy TYNON

*Wayne State College (G)

1111 Main Street, Wayne NE 68787-1172
County: Wayne FICE Identification: 002566
Unit ID: 181783
Telephone: (402) 375-7000 Carnegie Class: Master's L
FAX Number: (402) 375-7204 Calendar System: Semester
URL: www.wsc.edu
Established: 1909 Annual Undergrad Tuition & Fees (In-State): $5,520
Enrollment: 3,517 Coed
Affiliation or Control: State IRS Status: 501(c)3
Highest Offering: Beyond Master's But Less Than Doctorate
Program: Liberal Arts And General; Teacher Preparatory; Professional; Business Emphasis
Accreditation: NH, ART, IACBE, MUS, TED

02 President ..... Mr. Curt FRYE
05 Vice President Academic Affairs ..... Dr. Michael ANDERSON
10 Vice Pres Admin/Finance ..... Ms. Jean DALE
30 Vice Pres Institutional Advancement ..... Ms. Phyllis CONNER
32 Vice President & Dean Students ..... Dr. Jeffrey CARSTENS
37 Director Financial Aid ..... Ms. Kyle ROSE
07 Director of Admissions ..... Mr. Kevin HALLE
38 Director of Counseling ..... Ms. Lin BRUMMELS
39 Director Housing/Residence Life ..... Mr. Matt WEEKLEY
36 Director of Career Services ..... Ms. Jason BARELMAN
14 Director of Computer Center ..... Ms. Janell SCARDINO
26 Director College Relations ..... Mr. Jay COLLIER
41 Director of Athletics ..... Vacant
18 Director of Physical Plant ..... Mr. Chad ALTWINE
08 Director of Library Services ..... Mr. David GRABER
06 Registrar ..... Ms. Lynette LENTZ
29 Dir Development & Alumni Relations ..... Ms. Deb LUNDAHL
15 Director Personnel Services ..... Dr. Cheryl WADDINGTON
79 Dean School of Arts & Humanities ..... Dr. James O'DONNELL
50 Dean Sch of Business & Technology ..... Dr. Vaughn BENSON
53 Int Dean Sch of Educ & Couns ..... Dr. Jean BLOMENKAMP
83 Dean School of Natural/Social Sci ..... Dr. Jon DALAGER
28 Director of Multicultural Affairs ..... Dr. Osaro AIREN
09 Institutional Research Analyst ..... Ms. Jeannette BARRY
27 Chief Information Officer ..... Mr. John DUNNING

Nebraska Wesleyan University (H)

5000 St. Paul Avenue, Lincoln NE 68504-2794
County: Lancaster FICE Identification: 002555
Unit ID: 181446
Telephone: (402) 466-2371 Carnegie Class: Bac/A&S
FAX Number: (402) 465-2179 Calendar System: Semester
URL: www.nebrwesleyan.edu
Established: 1887 Annual Undergrad Tuition & Fees: $25,918
Enrollment: 2,077 Coed
Affiliation or Control: United Methodist IRS Status: 501(c)3
Highest Offering: Master's
Program: Liberal Arts And General
Accreditation: NH, ACBSP, MUS, NUR, SW, TED

01 President ..... Dr. Frederik OHLES
05 Provost ..... Dr. Judy A. MUYSKENS
10 Vice Pres Finance/Administration ..... Mr. Clark T. CHANDLER
26 Vice President External Relations ..... Ms. Patricia F. KARTHAUSER
30 Vice President Advancement ..... Mr. John GREVING
58 Dean of University College ..... Dr. Jack E. SIEMSEN
32 Dean of Students ..... Mr. Peter ARMSTRONG
49 Dean College of Lib Arts & Sciences ..... Dr. Katherine J. WOLFE
88 Asst Provost Experiential Learning ..... Dr. Kelly E. EATON
06 Interim Registrar ..... Ms. Nancy SCHILZ
35 Asst Dean of Students ..... Ms. Geri E. COTTER
09 Asst Dean Inst Effectiveness ..... Ms. Bette OLSON
15 Asst Vice Pres for Human Resources ..... Ms. Nancy B. COOKSON
18 Asst Vice Pres for Physical Plant ..... Mr. Matthew T. KADAVY
07 Director of Admissions ..... Mr. David B. DUZIK
27 Director of Public Relations ..... Ms. Sara M. OLSON
08 Director of Media Services ..... Ms. Margaret L. EMONS
37 Director of Financial Aid ..... Mr. Tom J. OCHSNER
29 Director of Alumni Relations ..... Ms. Shelley MCHUGH
41 Athletic Director ..... Dr. Ira A. ZEFF
13 Director of Computer Services ..... Mr. Steven R. DOW
26 Director of Marketing ..... Ms. Peggy S. HAIN
36 Director Career & Counseling Ctr ..... Ms. Janelle S. ANDREINI
39 Director Residential Education ..... Ms. Brandi SESTAK
104 Director of Global Engagement ..... Ms. Sarah BARR
92 Director Wesleyan Honors Academy ..... Dr. Marian BORGMANN-INGWERSEN
102 Director of Foundation Relations ..... Ms. Nancy WEHRBEIN
23 Director Student Health Services ..... Ms. Nancy J. NEWMAN
88 Asst to President Church Relations ..... Rev. Mel LUETCHENS
42 University Minister ..... Rev. Mara Z. BAILEY

Northeast Community College (I)

801 E Benjamin, PO Box 469, Norfolk NE 68702-0469
County: Madison FICE Identification: 011667
Unit ID: 181491
Telephone: (402) 371-2020 Carnegie Class: Assoc/Pub-R-M
FAX Number: (402) 844-7400 Calendar System: Semester
URL: www.northeast.edu
Established: 1973 Annual Undergrad Tuition & Fees (In-District): $2,837
Enrollment: 5,161 Coed
Affiliation or Control: Local IRS Status: 501(c)3
Highest Offering: Associate Degree
Program: Occupational; 2-Year Principally Bachelor's Creditable; Technical Emphasis
Accreditation: NH, ADNUR, EMT, PTAA

01 President ..... Dr. Michael R. CHIPPS
03 Executive Vice President ..... Ms. Mary J. HONKE
05 Vice President Educational Services ..... Mr. John V. BLAYLOCK
10 Vice Pres of Administrative Svcs ..... Ms. Lynne D. KOSKI
15 Vice President of Human Resources ..... Mr. David H. PTAK
32 Vice President of Student Services ..... Dr. Karen J. SEVERSON
75 Dean of Applied Technology ..... Mr. Lyle J. KATHOL
47 Interim Dean Ag/Health/Sciences ..... Mrs. Corinne MORRIS
51 Dean of Cont Educ/Distance Lrng ..... Mr. Wayne ERICKSON
49 Dean Humanities/Arts/Social Sci ..... Mrs. Donna A. NIEMEYER
50 Dean of Business/Math/Tech ..... Mr. Eric JOHNSON
11 Dean of Administrative Services ..... Mrs. Coleen BRESSLER

Code	Title	Name
30	Assoc VP of Development & External	Vacant
84	Director of Enrollment Management	Mrs. Amanda NIPP
21	Director of Business Services	Mrs. Mary J. MEYER
06	Registrar	Mrs. Kathy J. STOVER
37	Financial Aid Director	Ms. Stacy DIECKMAN
12	Dean of College Center	Mrs. Pamela MILLER
18	Director of Physical Plant	Mr. Brandon MCLEAN
36	Director of Career Services	Mrs. Terri HEGGEMEYER
24	Director of Technology Support	Mr. Tom A. LARSEN
66	Director of Nursing Programs	Mrs. Karen K. WEIDNER
21	Director of Accounting Services	Mr. John ROBERTSON
15	Human Resources Coordinator	Mrs. Jennifer HAPPOLD
96	Director of Purchasing	Mrs. Nell VOTRUBA
41	Athletic Director	Mr. Kurt PYTLESKI
07	Advisor/Recruiter	Mrs. Shelley LAMMERS
105	Web Development Manager	Mr. Derek BIERMAN
14	Communications Supervisor	Mrs. Janet HEBERER
26	Director of Media Relations	Mrs. Janelle GERHARTER
29	Alumni & Resource Development Coord	Mrs. Connie L. SIXTA
13	Director of Information Services	Ms. Karen I. GUY
38	Advisor/Recruiter	Mr. Anthony FAUST
39	Director Residence & Student Life	Mr. Pete RIZZO
35	Student Activities Coordinator	Ms. Carissa KOLLATH
08	Director of Library Services	Mrs. Mary Louise FOSTER
50	Director Econ Dev/Business Industry	Mr. Joe C. FERGUSON
40	Bookstore Manager	Vacant
09	Director of Institutional Research	Ms. Julie MELNICK
35	Dean of Students	Mrs. Maureen BAKER
76	Director of Allied Health Services	Mrs. Heather CLAUSEN

Saint Gregory the Great Seminary (A)

800 Fletcher Road, Seward NE 68434-8145

County: Seward — Identification: 667027

Telephone: (402) 643-4052 — Carnegie Class: Not Classified

FAX Number: (402) 643-6964 — Calendar System: Semester

URL: www.stgregoryseminary.edu

Established: 1998 — Annual Undergrad Tuition & Fees: $8,000

Enrollment: 44 — Male

Affiliation or Control: Roman Catholic — IRS Status: 501(c)3

Highest Offering: Baccalaureate

Program: Liberal Arts And General; Religious Emphasis

Accreditation: **NH**

Code	Title	Name
01	Rector/President	Msgr. John T. FOLDA

Southeast Community College (B)

301 S 68 Street Place, Lincoln NE 68510-2449

County: Lancaster — FICE Identification: 025083

Unit ID: 181640

Telephone: (402) 323-3400 — Carnegie Class: Assoc/Pub-R-L

FAX Number: (402) 323-3420 — Calendar System: Quarter

URL: www.southeast.edu

Established: 1973 — Annual Undergrad Tuition & Fees (In-District): $2,486

Enrollment: 11,479 — Coed

Affiliation or Control: State/Local — IRS Status: 501(c)3

Highest Offering: Associate Degree

Program: Occupational; 2-Year Principally Bachelor's Creditable

Accreditation: **NH**, ACBSP, ACFEI, ADNUR, DA, DIETT, MAC, MLTAD, PNUR, POLYT, PTAA, RAD, SURGT

Code	Title	Name
01	President	Dr. Jack J. HUCK
05	Vice President Instruction	Dr. Dennis HEADRICK
22	Vice Pres Access/Equity/Diversity	Mr. Jose SOTO
11	Vice Pres Administrative Services	Mr. Theodore G. SUHR
12	VP Student Svcs/Campus Director	Ms. Jeanette VOLKER
12	VP Technology/Campus Director	Mr. Lyle NEAL
15	Vice President for Human Resources	Mr. Bruce TANGEMAN
37	Dean Student Svcs/Dir Financial Aid	Mr. Dave SONENBERG
35	Dean Student Svcs/Dir Stdnt Support	Dr. Thomas CARDWELL
84	Dean Student Svcs/Dir Enrollment	Ms. Robin MOORE
26	Dir of Public Information/Marketing	Mr. Stu OSTERTHUN
90	Information Services Manager	Mr. Alan BRUNKOW

Union College (C)

3800 S 48th, Lincoln NE 68506-4300

County: Lancaster — FICE Identification: 002563

Unit ID: 181738

Telephone: (402) 486-2600 — Carnegie Class: Bac/Diverse

FAX Number: (402) 486-2895 — Calendar System: Semester

URL: www.ucollege.edu

Established: 1891 — Annual Undergrad Tuition & Fees: $21,850

Enrollment: 886 — Coed

Affiliation or Control: Seventh-day Adventist — IRS Status: 501(c)3

Highest Offering: Master's

Program: Liberal Arts And General; Teacher Preparatory; Professional

Accreditation: **NH**, ARCPA, NURSE, SW, TED

Code	Title	Name
01	President	Dr. John WAGNER
05	Vice President for Academic Admin	Dr. Malcolm RUSSELL
10	Vice President for Financial Admin	Mr. Gary BOLLINGER
32	Vice President Student Services	Dr. Linda BECKER
30	Vice President for Advancement	Ms. LuAnn DAVIS
07	Vice President Enrollment Services	Ms. Nadine NELSON
42	Vice President for Spiritual Life	Dr. Rich CARLSON
08	Library Director	Ms. Sabrina RILEY
14	Director of Information Systems	Mr. Tom BECKER
34	Dean of Women	Ms. LeAnn MERTH
33	Dean of Men	Mr. Doug TALLMAN
06	Dir Records/Registrar	Ms. Michelle YOUNKIN
26	Director of Public Relations	Mr. Ryan TELLER
29	Director Alumni Relations	Ms. Kenna Lee CARLSON
37	Director Student Financial Aid	Ms. Elina CAMARINA
15	Director for Human Resources	Mr. Jonathan SHIELDS
18	Director of Plant Services	Mr. Paul JENKS
18	Director of New Construction	Mr. Don MURRAY
21	Associate Business Officer	Mr. Harvey MEIER
36	Career Center Coordinator	Ms. Teresa EDGERTON
38	Director Student Counseling	Dr. Linda BECKER

Universal College of Healing Arts (D)

8702 N 30th Street, Omaha NE 68112-1810

County: Douglas — FICE Identification: 038214

Unit ID: 446598

Telephone: (402) 556-4456 — Carnegie Class: Assoc/PrivFP

FAX Number: (402) 561-0635 — Calendar System: Semester

URL: www.ucha.com

Established: 1995 — Annual Undergrad Tuition & Fees: $15,010

Enrollment: 46 — Coed

Affiliation or Control: Proprietary — IRS Status: Proprietary

Highest Offering: Associate Degree

Program: Occupational

Accreditation: **ABHES**

Code	Title	Name
01	Director	Ms. Paulette GENTHON

*University of Nebraska Central Administration (E)

3835 Holdrege, Lincoln NE 68583-0745

County: Lancaster — FICE Identification: 008025

Unit ID: 181747

Telephone: (402) 472-2111 — Carnegie Class: N/A

FAX Number: (402) 472-1237

URL: www.nebraska.edu

Code	Title	Name
01	President	Mr. James B. MILLIKEN
05	Exec Vice President & Provost	Dr. Linda R. PRATT
10	Vice President Business & Finance	Mr. David LECHNER
43	Vice President General Counsel	Mr. Joel D. PEDERSEN
47	VP Agriculture/Natural Resources	Dr. Ronnie GREEN
88	Vice Provost for Global Engagement	Mr. Thomas FARRELL
100	Chief of Staff	Ms. Dara L. TROUTMAN
13	Chief Information Officer	Mr. Walter G. WEIR
101	Corporation Secretary	Ms. Carmen K. MAURER
86	Assoc VP/Director Govt Relations	Mr. Ron WITHEM
16	Asst VP/Dir HR/Acad Affs/Diversity	Mr. Edward D. WIMES
88	Sr Assoc to Pres Innov/Econ Compet	Dr. Jim LINDER
18	Asst VP/Dir Facility Plng/Mgmt	Ms. Rebecca H. KOLLER
26	Vice President External Affairs	Ms. Sharon R. STEPHAN
09	Asst VP/Dir Inst Research/Planning	Dr. Kristin YATES

*University of Nebraska at Kearney (F)

905 W 25th Street, Kearney NE 68849

County: Buffalo — FICE Identification: 002551

Unit ID: 181215

Telephone: (308) 865-8208 — Carnegie Class: Master's L

FAX Number: (308) 865-8665 — Calendar System: Semester

URL: www.unk.edu

Established: 1903 — Annual Undergrad Tuition & Fees (In-State): $6,506

Enrollment: 7,100 — Coed

Affiliation or Control: State — IRS Status: 501(c)3

Highest Offering: Beyond Master's But Less Than Doctorate

Program: Liberal Arts And General; Teacher Preparatory; Professional

Accreditation: **NH**, BUS, CACREP, CIDA, MUS, NAIT, SP, SW, TED

Code	Title	Name
02	Chancellor	Dr. Douglas A. KRISTENSEN
05	Sr VC Academic & Student Affairs	Dr. Charles J. BICAK
10	Vice Chanc Business & Finance	Ms. Barbara L. JOHNSON
26	Vice Chanc University Relations	Mr. Curtis K. CARLSON
30	Vice President Development	Mr. Peter KOTSIOPULOS
13	Asst Vice Chanc Info Technology	Ms. Debbie SCHROEDER
21	Assistant Vice Chancellor Business	Mr. John LAKEY
83	Dean Natural/Social Science	Dr. John C. LA DUKE
50	Dean Business/Technology	Dr. Timothy J. BURKINK
53	Dean of Education	Dr. Edgar (Ed) L. SCANTLING
57	Dean Fine Arts & Humanities	Dr. William JURMA
58	Dean Graduate Studies & Research	Dr. Kenya S. TAYLOR
32	Dean of Student Affairs	Dr. Joseph A. ORAVECZ
04	Exec Assistant to the Chancellor	Mr. Neal H. SCHNOOR
06	Registrar	Ms. Kim SCHIPPOREIT
08	Dean of the Library	Ms. Janet S. WILKE
15	Director Human Resources	Ms. Cheryl BRESSINGTON
36	Director Academic & Career Services	Ms. Mary DAAKE
07	Director of Admissions	Mr. Dusty NEWTON
18	Director Facilities	Mr. Lee MCQUEEN
19	Director Police & Parking Services	Ms. Michelle HAMAKER
22	Dir Affirm Action/Equal Opportunity	Ms. Cheryl BRESSINGTON
09	Director Institutional Research	Ms. Kathy LIVINGSTON
27	Director University Communications	Ms. Glennis NAGEL
29	Director Alumni Services	Mr. Peter KOTSIOPULOS
88	Director Student Union	Ms. Sharon PELC
38	Director Counseling Center	Dr. LeAnn OBRECHT
39	Director Residential Life	Dr. C. Anthony EARLS
40	Director Bookstore	Mr. Len J. FANGMEYER
41	Athletic Director	Mr. Jon MCBRIDE
21	Director Finance	Mr. Larry RIESSLAND
23	Director Student Health Service	Dr. LeAnn OBRECHT
104	Director International Education	Dr. Keith (Dallas) KENNY
21	Budget Director	Mrs. Jean MATTSON
96	Director Business Services	Mrs. Jane SHELDON
37	Director Financial Aid	Ms. Mary SOMMERS
28	Director of Diversity	Mr. Juan GUZMAN

*University of Nebraska - Lincoln (G)

14th and R Streets, Lincoln NE 68588-0002

County: Lancaster — FICE Identification: 002565

Unit ID: 181464

Telephone: (402) 472-7211 — Carnegie Class: RU/VH

FAX Number: (402) 472-2410 — Calendar System: Semester

URL: www.unl.edu

Established: 1869 — Annual Undergrad Tuition & Fees (In-State): $7,896

Enrollment: 24,593 — Coed

Affiliation or Control: State — IRS Status: 501(c)3

Highest Offering: Doctorate

Program: Liberal Arts And General; Teacher Preparatory; Professional

Accreditation: **NH**, ART, AUD, BUS, BUSA, CIDA, CLPSY, CONST, COPSY, CS, DANCE, DIETD, DIETI, ENG, IPSY, JOUR, LAW, MFCD, MUS, PLNG, SCPSY, SP, TEAC, THEA

Code	Title	Name
02	Chancellor	Mr. Harvey PERLMAN
05	Senior Vice Chanc Academic Affairs	Ms. Ellen WEISSINGER
10	Vice Chanc Business & Finance	Ms. Christine JACKSON
32	Vice Chancellor Student Affairs	Dr. Juan FRANCO
65	Vice Chanc Agric/Nat Resources	Dr. Ronnie D. GREEN
46	VC Research & Economic Development	Dr. Prem S. PAUL
13	Chief Information Officer	Mr. Mark ASKREN
04	Associate to Chancellor	Mr. William NUNEZ
31	Asst to Chanc Community Relations	Ms. Michelle WAITE
15	Asst Vice Chanc for Human Resources	Mr. Bruce A. CURRIN
18	Asst VC Facilities Mgt/Planning	Dr. Ted WEIDNER
07	Director Admissions	Ms. Amber S. HUNTER
08	Dean University Libraries	Dr. Joan R. GIESECKE
58	Dean Graduate Studies	Dr. Lance C. PEREZ
49	Dean Arts & Sciences	Dr. David C. MANDERSCHEID
54	Dean Engineering	Dr. Timothy WEI
61	Dean of Law	Dr. Susan POSER
47	Dean Agric Scienc/Nat Resources	Dr. Steven WALLER
50	Dean Business Administration	Dr. Donde PLOWMAN
60	Interim Dean Journ/Mass Communic	Dr. James P. O'HANLON
53	Dean Education & Human Sciences	Dr. Marjorie KOSTELNIK
48	Interim Dean College Architecture	Dr. Kim L. WILSON
47	Dean Agricultural Research Division	Dr. Archie CLUTTER
56	Dean & Dir Cooperative Extens	Dr. Elbert C. DICKEY
93	Director Educ Access & TRIO Pgms	Ms. Catherine YAMAMOTO
57	Dean Fine & Performing Arts	Dr. Charles D. O'CONNOR
37	Director Scholarships/Financial Aid	Mr. Craig D. MUNIER
09	Director Inst Research & Planning	Dr. William J. NUNEZ
92	Director Honors Program	Dr. Patrice BERGER
94	Director Women's Studies	Dr. Marie-Chantal KALISA
06	Director Registrar & Records	Dr. Earl W. HAWKEY
36	Director Career Services Center	Dr. Larry R. ROUTH
19	Chief University Police Services	Mr. Owen YARDLEY
22	Director Affirm Action/Diversity	Ms. Linda CRUMP
23	Director University Health Center	Dr. James GUEST
39	Director Housing Office	Ms. Susan M. GILDERSLEEVE
41	Director of Athletics	Dr. Tom OSBORNE
55	Dir Distance Education Services	Dr. Nancy ADEN-FOX
29	Exec Director Alumni Association	Ms. Diane MENDENHALL
26	Director University Communications	Dr. Meg LAUERMAN
20	Associate Academic Officer	Dr. Lance C. PEREZ
30	Interim Chief Development	Mr. John GOTTSCHALK
38	Director Student Counseling	Dr. Robert N. PORTNOY
84	Dean Enrollment Management	Dr. Alan CERVENY
96	Director of Purchasing	Mr. Gary L. KRAFT
28	Director of Diversity	Ms. Linda CRUMP

*University of Nebraska Medical Center (H)

987020 Nebraska Medical Center, Omaha NE 68198-7020

County: Douglas — FICE Identification: 006895

Unit ID: 181428

Telephone: (402) 559-4000 — Carnegie Class: Spec/Med

FAX Number: (402) 559-4396 — Calendar System: Semester

URL: www.unmc.edu

Established: 1869 — Annual Undergrad Tuition & Fees (In-State): $8,338

Enrollment: 3,626 — Coed

Affiliation or Control: State — IRS Status: 501(c)3

Highest Offering: Doctorate

Program: Professional

Accreditation: **NH**, ARCPA, CYTO, DENT, DH, DIETI, DMS, MED, MT, NMT, NURSE, PERF, PH, PHAR, PTA, RAD, RADMAG, RTT

Code	Title	Name
02	Chancellor	Dr. Harold M. MAURER
05	Vice Chancellor Acad Affairs	Dr. Herbert O. DAVIES
10	Vice Chanc Business & Finance	Mr. Donald LEUENBERGER
46	Vice Chancellor for Research	Dr. Jennifer LARSEN
86	Vice Chanc for External Affairs	Mr. Robert D. BARTEE
20	Assoc Vice Chanc Academic Affairs	Dr. James TURPEN
20	Asst Vice Chanc Acad Affairs	Dr. Cheryl THOMPSON
20	Assoc Vice Chanc Acad Affs/Reg Comp	Dr. Ernest D. PRENTICE
45	Assoc Vice Chanc for Basic Rsch	Dr. Kenneth BAYLES
45	Assoc Vice Chanc for Clinical Rsch	Dr. Christopher KRATOCHVIL
21	Assoc Vice Chanc Business/Finance	Ms. Deborah THOMAS
13	Assoc Vice Chanc Bus Dev/CIO	Dr. Rodney MARKIN
18	Assistant Vice Chancellor for FMP	Mr. Kenneth HANSEN
21	Asst VC for Budget & Plng	Ms. Pamela BATAILLON
14	Exec Dir Information Tech Services	Ms. Yvette A. HOLLY

58 Dean Graduate Studies .... Dr. Herbert O. DAVIES
52 Dean College of Dentistry .... Dr. John W. REINHARDT
63 Dean College of Medicine .... Dr. Bradley E. BRITIGAN
66 Dean College of Nursing .... Dr. Juliann SEBASTIAN
67 Dean College of Pharmacy .... Dr. Courtney FLETCHER
69 Dean College of Public Health .... Dr. Ayman EL MOHANDES
76 Assoc Dean Allied Health Profession .... Dr. Kyle MEYER
88 Dir Eppley Cancer Research Inst .... Dr. Kenneth H. COWAN
88 Director Munroe-Meyer Inst .... Dr. J. Michael LEIBOWITZ
08 Director Library of Medicine .... Dr. Nancy N. WOELFL
37 Dir Financial Aid Office .... Ms. Judith D. WALKER
26 Director of Public Relations .... Mr. William O'NEILL
15 Exec Director Human Resources .... Mr. John P. RUSSELL
29 Director Alumni Affairs .... Ms. Roxana JOKELA
38 Director Student Counseling .... Dr. David S. CARVER
28 Director of Diversity .... Vacant
96 Director of Purchasing .... Mr. Jeffrey ELLIOTT
09 Director Institutional Research .... Ms. Jeanne FERBRACHE

*University of Nebraska at Omaha (A)

6001 Dodge Street, Omaha NE 68182-0001
County: Douglas FICE Identification: 002554
Unit ID: 181394
Telephone: (402) 554-2200 Carnegie Class: DRU
FAX Number: (402) 554-3555 Calendar System: Semester
URL: www.unomaha.edu
Established: 1908 Annual Undergrad Tuition & Fees (In-State): $6,510
Enrollment: 14,712 Coed
Affiliation or Control: State IRS Status: 501(c)3
Highest Offering: Doctorate
Program: Liberal Arts And General; Teacher Preparatory; Professional
Accreditation: **NH**, AAB, ART, BUS, CACREP, CS, MUS, SP, SPAA, SW, TED

02 Chancellor .... Dr. John E. CHRISTENSEN
05 Sr Vice Chanc Acad/Student Affs .... Dr. Burton J. REED
10 Vice Chanc Business & Finance .... Mr. Bill CONLEY
04 Exec Assistant to the Chancellor .... Ms. Nancy CASTILOW
20 Assoc Vice Chanc Acad Affs-Tech .... Mr. John L. FIENE
21 Assoc Vice Chanc Business & Finance .... Ms. Julie TOTTEN
32 Assoc Vice Chanc Student Affairs .... Dr. Daniel SHIPP
84 Asst Vice Chanc Enroll Mgmt Svcs .... Dr. Pelema I. MORRICE
58 Dean Graduate Studies .... Dr. Deb SMITH-HOWELL
57 Dean Fine Arts/Communication/Media .... Dr. Gail BAKER
53 Dean of Education .... Dr. Nancy EDICK
50 Dean of Business Administration .... Dr. Lou POL
49 Dean of Arts & Sciences .... Dr. David BOOCKER
82 Dean of International Studies .... Mr. Thomas E. GOUTTIERRE
72 Dean Info Science/Technology .... Dr. Hesham ALI
80 Int Dean Public Affairs/Community .... Dr. John R. BARTLE
62 Dean of Library Services .... Mr. Stephen SHORB
09 Dir Institutional Effectiveness .... Dr. Russell SMITH
35 Chief Student Life Officer .... Ms. Rita HENRY
15 Director Human Resources .... Ms. Molllie ANDERSON
18 Director Facilities Mgmt/Planning .... Mr. John AMEND
06 Registrar .... Mr. Mark GOLDSBERRY
07 Director of Admissions .... Vacant
37 Director Financial Aid .... Mr. Randall L. SELL
88 Director Student Testing Center .... Ms. Marion FORTIN-WAVRA
41 Director of Athletics .... Mr. Trev ALBERTS
29 Director of Alumni Association .... Mr. Lee DENKER
26 Director Communications .... Mr. Tim KALDAHL
96 Director of Purchasing .... Mr. Ken HULTMAN
40 Manager Book Store .... Mr. Michael E. SCHMIDT
19 Manager Campus Security .... Mr. Paul KOSEL

*University of Nebraska - Nebraska College of Technical Agriculture (B)

404 E 7th Street, Curtis NE 69025-9502
County: Frontier FICE Identification: 007358
Unit ID: 181765
Telephone: (308) 367-4124 Carnegie Class: Assoc/Pub2in4
FAX Number: (308) 367-5203 Calendar System: Semester
URL: www.ncta.unl.edu
Established: 1912 Annual Undergrad Tuition & Fees (In-State): $3,912
Enrollment: 333 Coed
Affiliation or Control: State IRS Status: 501(c)3
Highest Offering: Associate Degree
Program: Occupational; 2-Year Principally Bachelor's Creditable; Technical Emphasis
Accreditation: **NH**

02 Dean .... Dr. Weldon SLEIGHT
03 Associate Dean .... Dr. Scott R. MICKELSEN
10 Business Officer .... Ms. Jan GILBERT

Vatterott College-Omaha (C)

11818 I Street, Omaha NE 68137-1237
County: Douglas FICE Identification: 030233
Unit ID: 181756
Telephone: (402) 891-9411 Carnegie Class: Assoc/PrivFP
FAX Number: (402) 891-9413 Calendar System: Quarter
URL: www.vatterott-college.edu
Established: 1996 Annual Undergrad Tuition & Fees: $11,849
Enrollment: 587 Coed
Affiliation or Control: Proprietary IRS Status: Proprietary
Highest Offering: Associate Degree
Program: Occupational; 2-Year Principally Bachelor's Creditable; Technical Emphasis
Accreditation: **ACCSC**, DA, MAAB

01 CEO & President .... Ms. Pam BELL
10 Chief Financial Officer .... Mr. Dennis BEAVERS
05 Vice President Academic Affairs .... Dr. Brandon SHEDRON
45 VP Regulatory Affs/Strategic Devel .... Mr. Aaron LACEY
43 General Counsel/Chief Administrator .... Mr. Scott CASANOVER
12 Campus Director .... Vacant

Western Nebraska Community College (D)

1601 E 27th Street, Scottsbluff NE 69361-1815
County: Scotts Bluff FICE Identification: 002560
Unit ID: 181817
Telephone: (308) 635-3606 Carnegie Class: Assoc/Pub-R-L
FAX Number: (308) 635-6100 Calendar System: Semester
URL: www.wncc.edu
Established: 1926 Annual Undergrad Tuition & Fees (In-District): $2,895
Enrollment: 2,280 Coed
Affiliation or Control: State/Local IRS Status: 501(c)3
Highest Offering: Associate Degree
Program: Occupational; 2-Year Principally Bachelor's Creditable
Accreditation: **NH**, PNUR

01 President .... Dr. Todd R. HOLCOMB
05 Vice President Educational Services .... Mr. Terry B. GAALSWYK
16 Vice President Human Resources .... Mr. David E. GROSHANS
32 Vice President Student Services .... Ms. Susan K. YOWELL
11 Vice Pres Administrative Services .... Mr. William D. KNAPPER
20 Dean of Instruction .... Mr. Garry R. ALKIRE
103 Dean of Workforce Development .... Mr. Jason L. STRATMAN
50 Dean Business & Individual Training .... Ms. Judith L. AMOO
35 Int Dean Stdnt Svcs/Dir of College .... Dr. James I. SCHMUCKER
12 Sidney Campus Director .... Ms. Paula J. ABBOTT
12 Alliance Campus Director .... Vacant
102 Foundation Executive Director .... Ms. Dayle L. WALLIEN
06 Registrar .... Mr. Roger S. HOVEY
37 Financial Aid Director .... Ms. Sheila R. JOHNS
26 College Relations Director .... Ms. Erin STINNER
38 Counseling Director .... Mr. Norman J. STEPHENSON
08 Library Services Director .... Mr. Curtis T. BRUNDY
21 Accounting Services Director .... Mr. David KOEHLER
41 Athletic Director .... Mr. Ryan C. BURGNER
88 Bus & Individual Training Director .... Ms. Lori S. STROMBERG
07 Admissions Director .... Ms. Gretchen K. FOSTER
39 Residence Life Director .... Mr. Mario J. CHAVEZ
13 Exec Dir Information Technology .... Dr. Paul G. JACOBSEN
40 Bookstore Operations Director .... Ms. Suzane KARBOWSKI
19 Safety/Environmental Mgmt Director .... Mr. Robert L. HESSLER
09 Director of Institutional Research .... Mrs. Mary E. BARKELOO
88 ILAC Coordinator .... Ms. Tammie KLEICH
39 Residence Life/Activities Coord .... Mr. Yahosh BONNER
39 Residence Life/Activities Coord .... Ms. Molly A. BONUCHI
50 Division Chair Business .... Mr. Tom ROBINSON
81 Division Chair Math/Sciences/PE .... Ms. Judy SCHNELL
83 Division Chair Social Sciences .... Ms. Hallie L. FEIL
88 Division Chair Language & Arts .... Vacant
72 Division Chair Applied Technology .... Mr. Willie QUINDT
76 Div Chair Health/Acad Enrichment .... Vacant

York College (E)

1125 E 8th Street, York NE 68467-2699
County: York FICE Identification: 002567
Unit ID: 181853
Telephone: (402) 363-5600 Carnegie Class: Bac/Diverse
FAX Number: (402) 363-5623 Calendar System: Semester
URL: www.york.edu
Established: 1890 Annual Undergrad Tuition & Fees: $15,600
Enrollment: 508 Coed
Affiliation or Control: Churches Of Christ IRS Status: 501(c)3
Highest Offering: Master's
Program: Liberal Arts And General; Business Emphasis
Accreditation: **NH**, TED

01 President .... Dr. Steven W. ECKMAN
05 Academic Dean .... Dr. Tracey L. WYATT
10 Vice President Finance & Operations .... Mr. Todd SHELDON
30 Vice Pres Advancement .... Mr. Brent MAGNER
32 Vice Pres for Student Development .... Dr. Shane MOUNTJOY
21 Business Manager .... Mr. Dan COLE
06 Registrar .... Mr. Tod J. MARTIN
07 Vice President of Admissions .... Mr. Willie SANCHEZ
08 Director of Library .... Mrs. Ruth CARLOCK
26 Director of Publications .... Mr. Steddon L. SIKES
37 Financial Aid Director .... Mr. Brien ALLEY
40 Bookstore Director .... Mr. Ronald SHIELDS
41 Athletic Director .... Mr. Jared A. STARK
18 Supervisor Buildings & Grounds .... Mr. Bob GAVER
91 Director Administrative Computing .... Mr. Joel COEHOORN
36 Director Student Placement .... Vacant
42 Campus Minister .... Mr. Tim D. LEWIS
50 Chair Business .... Dr. Mark MOORE
53 Chair Education .... Mr. Robert DEHART
73 Chair Bible .... Dr. Frank E. WHEELER
88 Chair History .... Mr. Tim D. MCNEESE
50 Chair English .... Mr. Joshua FULLMAN
81 Chair Math/Sciences .... Dr. Ray MILLER
57 Chair Performing Arts/Communication .... Dr. Clark A. ROUSH
29 Dir Alumni & Community Relations .... Mrs. Sue ROUSH

NEVADA

The Art Institute of Las Vegas (F)

2350 Corporate Circle, Henderson NV 89074-7737
County: Clark FICE Identification: 030846
Unit ID: 182111
Telephone: (702) 369-9944 Carnegie Class: Spec/Arts
FAX Number: (702) 992-8564 Calendar System: Quarter
URL: www.ailv.artinstitutes.edu
Established: 1983 Annual Undergrad Tuition & Fees: $17,616
Enrollment: 1,232 Coed
Affiliation or Control: Proprietary IRS Status: Proprietary
Highest Offering: Baccalaureate
Program: Occupational; 2-Year Principally Bachelor's Creditable; Liberal Arts And General
Accreditation: **ACICS**, ACFEI, CIDA

01 Interim President .... Mr. Daniel KLAAS
32 Dean of Student Affairs .... Ms. Sallie PALMER
05 Dean of Academic Affairs .... Mr. Dave NOFFINGER

† Branch campus of The Art Institute of Phoenix, AZ.

Career College of Northern Nevada (G)

1421 Pullman Drive, Sparks NV 89434
County: Washoe FICE Identification: 026215
Unit ID: 181941
Telephone: (775) 856-2266 Carnegie Class: Assoc/PrivFP
FAX Number: (775) 856-0935 Calendar System: Quarter
URL: www.ccnn.edu
Established: 1984 Annual Undergrad Tuition & Fees: $23,973
Enrollment: 602 Coed
Affiliation or Control: Proprietary IRS Status: Proprietary
Highest Offering: Associate Degree
Program: Occupational
Accreditation: **ACCSC**

01 President .... Mr. L. Nathan N. CLARK

DeVry University - Henderson (H)

2490 Paseo Verde Parkway, Suite 150, Henderson NV 89074-7120
County: Clark Identification: 666560
Unit ID: 443997
Telephone: (702) 933-9700 Carnegie Class: Bac/Diverse
FAX Number: (803) 933-9717 Calendar System: Semester
URL: www.devry.edu
Established: 1931 Annual Undergrad Tuition & Fees: $16,156
Enrollment: 552 Coed
Affiliation or Control: Proprietary IRS Status: Proprietary
Highest Offering: Master's
Program: Professional; Business Emphasis
Accreditation: **&NH**

01 Campus Director .... Lori BRYANT

† Regional accreditation is carried under the parent institution in Downers Grove, IL.

Everest College (I)

170 North Stephanie Street, Henderson NV 89074
FICE Identification: 022375
Unit ID: 182148
Telephone: (702) 567-1920 Carnegie Class: Assoc/PrivFP
FAX Number: (702) 566-9725 Calendar System: Semester
URL: www.everest.edu
Established: 2004 Annual Undergrad Tuition & Fees: N/A
Enrollment: 800 Coed
Affiliation or Control: Proprietary IRS Status: Proprietary
Highest Offering: Associate Degree
Program: Occupational
Accreditation: **ACICS**, MAAB

01 President .... Mr. Dave FRITZ

ITT Technical Institute (J)

168 N Gibson Road, Henderson NV 89014-6712
County: Clark Identification: 666544
Unit ID: 429599
Telephone: (702) 558-5404 Carnegie Class: Spec/Tech
FAX Number: (702) 558-5412 Calendar System: Quarter
URL: www.itt-tech.edu
Established: 1997 Annual Undergrad Tuition & Fees: N/A
Enrollment: 816 Coed
Affiliation or Control: Proprietary IRS Status: Proprietary
Highest Offering: Baccalaureate
Program: Technical Emphasis
Accreditation: **ACICS**

† Branch campus of ITT Technical Institute, Indianapolis, IN.

Kaplan College (A)

3535 West Sahara Ave, Las Vegas NV 89102
County: Clark FICE Identification: 030432
Unit ID: 374875
Telephone: (702) 368-2338 Carnegie Class: Assoc/PrivFP
FAX Number: (702) 368-3853 Calendar System: Other
URL: www.kaplancollege.com
Established: 1991 Annual Undergrad Tuition & Fees: $14,945
Enrollment: 765 Coed
Affiliation or Control: Proprietary IRS Status: Proprietary
Highest Offering: Associate Degree
Program: Occupational; 2-Year Principally Bachelor's Creditable; Technical Emphasis
Accreditation: ACCSC, MAAB, PNUR

01 Campus President .... Mr. Jake ELSEN
05 Director of Education .... Ms. Pam LIVINGSTON
07 Director of Admissions .... Mr. Derrick PERRY
06 Registrar .... Ms. Kassy PINDAR
10 Director of Finance .... Ms. Carmen TORRES
36 Director of Career Services .... Mr. Ryan GUNDERSEN
20 Assistant Director of Education .... Mr. Jeffrey FOUNTAIN
66 Director of Nursing .... Ms. Catherine CYLKE
61 Dept Chair Criminal Justice .... Mr. John NORTON
76 Dept Chr Med Coder & Biller .... Mrs. Phyllis ECKERT
67 Dept Chair Pharmacy Technician .... Mr. Mark BRUNTON
88 Dept Chair Medical Assistant .... Mrs. Renee CANAS

Le Cordon Bleu College of Culinary Arts in Las Vegas (B)

1451 Center Crossing Road, Las Vegas NV 89144-7047
County: Clark Identification: 666303
Unit ID: 445115
Telephone: (702) 365-7690 Carnegie Class: Assoc/PrivFP
FAX Number: (702) 365-7911 Calendar System: Other
URL: www.chefs.edu/las-vegas
Established: 2003 Annual Undergrad Tuition & Fees: $14,114
Enrollment: 803 Coed
Affiliation or Control: Proprietary IRS Status: Proprietary
Highest Offering: Associate Degree
Program: Occupational
Accreditation: ACCSC, ACFEI, ACICS

01 President .... Mr. Anthony WILLIAMS

† Branch campus of Le Cordon Bleu College of Culinary Arts, Scottsdale, AZ.

Morrison University (C)

10315 Professional Circle, Ste 201, Reno NV 89521-4826
County: Washoe FICE Identification: 010098
Unit ID: 182430
Telephone: (775) 850-0700 Carnegie Class: Bac/Diverse
FAX Number: (775) 850-0711 Calendar System: Quarter
URL: www.morrisonuniversity.com
Established: 1902 Annual Undergrad Tuition & Fees: $9,975
Enrollment: 332 Coed
Affiliation or Control: Proprietary IRS Status: Proprietary
Highest Offering: Master's
Program: Occupational; Liberal Arts And General; Professional
Accreditation: ACICS

01 Campus Director .... Mr. Dave HECKELER
05 Director of Education .... Mr. Joel NELSON
08 Library Director .... Ms. Usha MEHTA
37 Director Financial Aid .... Mr. Jim HADWICK
06 Registrar .... Ms. Nancy GANS
36 Director Career Services .... Ms. Donna TILLMAN

*Nevada System of Higher Education (D)

2601 Enterprise Road, Reno NV 89512-1666
County: Washoe FICE Identification: 008026
Unit ID: 182519
Telephone: (775) 784-4901 Carnegie Class: N/A
FAX Number: (775) 784-1127
URL: www.nevada.edu

01 Chancellor .... Mr. Daniel J. KLAICH
05 VC Academic & Student Affairs .... Ms. Crystal ABBA
10 Asst Vice Chancellor of Finance .... Mr. Larry EARDLEY
88 Chief Exec Ofcr Board of Regents .... Mr. Scott WASSERMAN

*College of Southern Nevada (E)

6375 W Charleston Boulevard, Las Vegas NV 89146-1139
County: Clark FICE Identification: 010362
Unit ID: 182005
Telephone: (702) 651-5000 Carnegie Class: Assoc/Pub4
FAX Number: (702) 651-4835 Calendar System: Semester
URL: www.csn.edu
Established: 1971 Annual Undergrad Tuition & Fees (In-State): $2,160
Enrollment: 37,717 Coed
Affiliation or Control: State IRS Status: 501(c)3
Highest Offering: Baccalaureate
Program: Occupational; 2-Year Principally Bachelor's Creditable
Accreditation: NW, ACBSP, ACFEI, ADNUR, CEA, DA, DH, DMS, EMT, ENGT, MAC, MLTAD, OPD, #OTA, PNUR, PTAA, SURGT

02 President .... Dr. Michael D. RICHARDS
04 Exec Assistant to the President .... Ms. Francine WOODHOUSE
10 Sr Vice Pres Finance & Facilities .... Ms. Patricia A. CHARLTON
05 Vice Pres Academic Affairs .... Dr. Darren D. DIVINE
32 Vice Pres for Student Affairs .... Dr. Santos MARTINEZ
12 Sr Advsr to Pres/Chf Admin-Cheyenne .... Mr. Thomas BROWN
12 Campus Manager Charleston .... Dr. Joan MCGEE
12 Campus Manager Henderson .... Vacant
20 Assoc VP Academic Affairs .... Dr. Hyla WINTERS
21 Asst Vice Pres Fin Svcs/Controller .... Ms. Mary Kaye BAILEY
18 Assoc VP Facilities/Oper/Maint .... Ms. Sherri PAYNE
43 Legal Counsel .... Mr. Richard HINCKLEY
88 Interim Dean Charleston Campus .... Dr. Bradley W. GRUNER
06 Registrar .... Ms. Pat ZOZAYA
21 Exec Director Business Services .... Mr. Dan MORRIS
75 Exec Dir Apprenticeship Studies .... Mr. Dan GOUKER
36 Director Student Services .... Ms. Kelly WUEST
102 Exec Dir CSN Foundation .... Ms. Jacque MATTHEWS
30 Operations Manager CSN Foundation .... Ms. Shirley CARTON
72 Dean Adv & Applied Technologies .... Dr. Michael SPANGLER
81 Dean Science & Mathematics .... Ms. Sally JOHNSTON
83 Dean Social Sciences & Education .... Dr. Charles OKEKE
88 Dean Arts & Letters .... Dr. Wendy WEINER
76 Dean Health Sciences .... Dr. Patricia CASTRO
103 Exec Dir Workforce/Economic Devel .... Ms. Rebecca METTY-BURNS
96 Int Director of Purchasing .... Mr. Mark CAHILL
41 Director of Athletics .... Mr. Marc MORSE
27 Director of Communications & Events .. Ms. Kathryn C. BREKKEN
35 Director of Student Activities .... Ms. Stephanie C. HILL
45 Director Resource Development .... Ms. Rosemary W. WEST
88 Director of Budget Services .... Ms. Lisa BAKKE
09 Director of Institutional Research .... Mr. John BEARCE
62 Director Library Services .... Ms. Clarissa ERWIN
88 Director of Scheduling .... Dr. Joe WEST
37 Asst Director Student Financial Aid .... Ms. Katharyn VAN DE CAR
19 Chief of Police .... Mr. Darryl CARABALLO
85 Director International Student Ctr .... Ms. Tammy SILVER
13 Technology CIO .... Mr. Mugunth VAITHYLINGAM
105 Webmaster .... Mr. Taylor C. GRAY
88 Assistant General Counsel .... Ms. Diane L. WELCH

*Great Basin College (F)

1500 College Parkway, Elko NV 89801-5032
County: Elko FICE Identification: 006977
Unit ID: 182306
Telephone: (775) 738-8493 Carnegie Class: Bac/Assoc
FAX Number: (775) 738-8771 Calendar System: Semester
URL: www.gbcnv.edu
Established: 1967 Annual Undergrad Tuition & Fees (In-State): $2,700
Enrollment: 3,324 Coed
Affiliation or Control: State IRS Status: 501(c)3
Highest Offering: Baccalaureate
Program: Occupational; 2-Year Principally Bachelor's Creditable
Accreditation: NW, ADNUR, NUR, RAD

02 President .... Dr. Mark CURTIS
32 Vice President Student Services .... Mrs. Lynn M. MAHLBERG
05 Vice President Academic Affairs .... Dr. Mike MCFARLANE
04 Assistant to the President .... Ms. Mardell WILKINS
07 Director of Admissions .... Ms. Janice KING
09 Dir Institutional Rsrch/Effective .... Ms. Cathy FULKERSON
30 Chief Development Officer .... Dr. John RICE
08 Library Director .... Mr. David ELLEFSEN
37 Dir Student Financial Svcs & VA .... Mr. Scott NIELSEN
10 Chief Business Officer .... Ms. Sonja SIBERT
26 Public Information Officer .... Dr. John RICE
84 Director Enrollment Management .... Ms. Julie BYRNES
75 Dean of Applied Science .... Mr. Bret MURPHY
76 Dir of Health Sciences & Human Svcs .... Dr. Kris MILLER
12 Director Ely Center .... Ms. Mary SWETICH
12 Director Winnemucca Center .... Ms. Lisa CAMPBELL
12 Manager Pahrump Valley Center .... Ms. Diane WRIGHTMAN
21 Controller .... Mr. Wayne OLMSTEAD
51 Director Continuing Education .... Mrs. Angie DEBRAGA
56 Dean of Extended Studies .... Vacant
06 Registrar .... Ms. Janice KING
88 Director Child & Family Center .... Vacant
102 Director Foundation .... Dr. John RICE
19 Director Safety and Security .... Ms. Patricia ANDERSON

*Nevada State College (G)

1125 Nevada State Drive, Henderson NV 89002-9455
County: Clark FICE Identification: 041143
Unit ID: 441900
Telephone: (702) 992-2000 Carnegie Class: Bac/Diverse
FAX Number: (702) 992-2226 Calendar System: Semester
URL: www.nsc.edu
Established: 2002 Annual Undergrad Tuition & Fees (In-District): $3,570
Enrollment: 3,192 Coed
Affiliation or Control: State/Local IRS Status: 501(c)3
Highest Offering: Master's
Program: Liberal Arts And General; Teacher Preparatory; Professional; Nursing Emphasis
Accreditation: NW, NURSE

02 President .... Mr. Bart PATTERSON
05 Provost .... Dr. Erika BECK
10 VP Finance and Administration .... Mr. Buster NEEL
26 Assoc VP for College Relations .... Dr. Spencer STEWART
06 Registrar .... Ms. Adelfa SULLIVAN
29 Exec Coordinator Alumni Relations .... Ms. Danielle JOHNSTON
30 Assoc Vice Pres Development .... Dr. Russell RAKER
100 Exec Assistant to the President .... Ms. Jennifer HAFT

*Truckee Meadows Community College (H)

7000 Dandini Boulevard, Reno NV 89512-3999
County: Washoe FICE Identification: 021077
Unit ID: 182500
Telephone: (775) 673-7000 Carnegie Class: Assoc/Pub-R-L
FAX Number: (775) 673-7108 Calendar System: Semester
URL: www.tmcc.edu
Established: 1971 Annual Undergrad Tuition & Fees (In-State): $2,513
Enrollment: 11,616 Coed
Affiliation or Control: State IRS Status: 501(c)3
Highest Offering: Associate Degree
Program: Occupational; 2-Year Principally Bachelor's Creditable
Accreditation: NW, ACFEI, ADNUR, DA, DH, DIETT

02 President .... Dr. Maria C. SHEEHAN
04 Executive Assistant to President .... Ms. Nadine J. WINSLOW
05 Vice President Academic Affairs .... Dr. John TUTHILL
10 Vice Pres Finance & Admin Services .... Dr. Rachel SOLEMSAAS
32 Dean of Student Services .... Vacant
72 Dean of Sciences .... Mr. Ted PLAGGEMEYER
50 Dean of Liberal Arts .... Dr. Armida FRUZZETTI
79 Arts & Humanities Chair .... Mr. Wade HAMPTON
51 Dean Workforce Devel/Cont Education .... Vacant
20 Assoc Dean Office of the President .... Ms. Pat SLAVIN
102 Exec Dir Institutional Advancement .... Ms. Paula Lee HOBSON
07 Director Admissions & Records .... Ms. Mona CONCHA-BUCKHEART
21 Controller .... Vacant
37 Director Financial Aid .... Ms. Sharon WURM
08 Director Learning Resources Center .... Ms. Michelle NOEL
15 Director Human Resources .... Ms. Michele MEADOR
18 Director Facilities Services .... Mr. Dave ROBERTS
26 Dir Institutional Advancement .... Dr. J. Kyle DALPE
103 Dir Workforce Devel/Cont Education .... Ms. Deb O'GORMAN
38 Director Counseling .... Ms. Estela LEVARIO-GUTIERREZ
45 Budget & Planning Technician .... Vacant
13 Exec Director Information Tech Ops ... Mr. Christopher WINSLOW
19 Chief of Police/Campus Police .... Mr. Randy FLOCCHINI
09 Director Institutional Research .... Ms. Elena BUBNOVA
28 Director of Equity & Inclusion .... Dr. Barbara WRIGHT-SANDERS
29 Donor & Alumni Coordinator .... Ms. Tara HAWKINS

*University of Nevada, Las Vegas (I)

4505 S Maryland Parkway, Las Vegas NV 89154-1001
County: Clark FICE Identification: 002569
Unit ID: 182281
Telephone: (702) 895-3201 Carnegie Class: RU/H
FAX Number: (702) 895-1088 Calendar System: Semester
URL: www.unlv.edu
Established: 1957 Annual Undergrad Tuition & Fees (In-State): $6,428
Enrollment: 27,364 Coed
Affiliation or Control: State IRS Status: 501(c)3
Highest Offering: Doctorate
Program: Liberal Arts And General; Teacher Preparatory; Professional
Accreditation: NW, ART, BUS, BUSA, CACREP, CIDA, CLPSY, CONST, CS, DENT, DIETD, DIETI, ENG, ENGR, LAW, LSAR, MFCD, MT, MUS, NMT, NURSE, PTA, RAD, SPAA, SW, THEA

02 President .... Dr. Neal SMATRESK
100 Chief of Staff .... Dr. Fred TREDUP
05 Executive Vice President & Provost .... Mr. John V. WHITE
10 Senior Vice Pres Finance & Business .... Mr. Gerry BOMOTTI
41 Dir Intercollegiate Athletics .... Mr. Jim LIVENGOOD
32 Vice President for Student Affairs .... Dr. Juanita FAIN
58 Int VP Research & Graduate Studies .... Dr. Thomas C. PIECHOTA
88 Senior Advisor to President .... Vacant
30 VP Advancement .... Dr. William BOLDT
86 VP Diversity & Govt Relations .... Mr. Luis VALERA
43 General Counsel .... Mrs. Elda SIDHU
11 Assoc Vice Pres for Administration .... Dr. Mike SAUER
35 Assoc VP for Student Affairs .... Ms. Karen STRONG
31 Assoc VP Alumni Relations .... Mr. Jim RATIGAN
26 Assoc Vice Pres Community Relations .... Ms. Lucy KLINKHAMMER
15 Chief Human Resources Officer .... Mr. Larry HAMILTON
87 Int Vice Prov Educational Outreach .... Dr. Margaret REES
13 Vice Provost Info Technology .... Dr. Lori TEMPLE
50 Dean Business .... Dr. Percy POON
49 Dean Liberal Arts .... Dr. Chris HUDGINS
53 Interim Dean of Education .... Dr. William SPEER
54 Dean of Engineering .... Dr. Rama VENKAT
52 Dean School of Dental Medicine .... Dr. Karen P. WEST
61 Dean School of Law .... Ms. Nancy RAPOPORT
81 Dean of Sciences .... Dr. Timothy PORTER
88 Dean Hotel Administration .... Dr. Donald SNYDER
57 Dean Fine Arts .... Dr. Jeffrey KOEP
08 Dean of Libraries .... Ms. Patricia IANNUZZI
88 Interim Dean Urban Affairs .... Dr. Lee BERNICK
92 Dean Honors College .... Dr. Marta MEANA
88 Dean Academic Success Ctr .... Dr. Ann MCDONOUGH
88 Founding Dean Community Health .... Dr. Mary GUINAN

76 Dean Sch Allied Health Sciences ..... Dr. Carolyn YUCHA
06 Exec Dir of Admissions & Recruiting ..... Vacant
37 Financial Aid & Scholarships ..... Mr. Norm BEDFORD
27 Assoc VP Univ Communications ..... Mr. Earnest PHILLIPS
19 Director Public Safety ..... Mr. Jose ELIQUE
09 Director Inst Analysis/Planning ..... Mrs. Kari C. COBURN
39 Exec Dir Residential Life ..... Mr. Richard CLARK
38 AVP Student Wellness ..... Dr. Jamie DAVIDSON
23 Director Student Health ..... Ms. Kathy A. UNDERWOOD
96 Director Purchasing ..... Ms. Sharrie MAYDEN
85 Director Intl Students & Scholars ..... Ms. Kristen YOUNG
25 Director Sponsored Programs ..... Ms. Rochelle ATHEY
46 AVP for Research ..... Dr. Stan SMITH
102 Sr Assoc VP & Exec Dir UNLV Found ..... Ms. Nancy STROUSE
44 Assoc VP Development ..... Mr. Scott ROBERTS

*University of Nevada, Reno (A)

Reno NV 89557-0095
County: Washoe — FICE Identification: 002568
Unit ID: 182290
Telephone: (775) 784-1110 — Carnegie Class: RU/H
FAX Number: (775) 784-1300 — Calendar System: Semester
URL: www.unr.edu
Established: 1874 — Annual Undergrad Tuition & Fees (In-State): $6,296
Enrollment: 18,004 — Coed
Affiliation or Control: State — IRS Status: 501(c)3
Highest Offering: Doctorate
Program: Liberal Arts And General; Teacher Preparatory; Professional
Accreditation: NW, BUS, BUSA, CACREP, CLPSY, CS, DIETD, DIETI, ENG, JOUR, MED, MUS, NURSE, PH, SP, SW, TED

02 President ..... Dr. Marc JOHNSON
05 Interim Exec Vice Pres & Provost ..... Dr. Heather HARDY
11 Vice Pres Administration & Finance ..... Mr. Ronald M. ZUREK
63 VP Health Sci/Dean Sch of Medicine ..... Dr. Thomas L. SCHWENK
30 Vice President Devel/Alumni Rels ..... Mr. John CAROTHERS
32 Vice President for Student Services ..... Dr. Shannon ELLIS
46 Vice President for Research ..... Dr. Marsha READ
08 Dean of Libraries ..... Dr. Kathlin D. RAY
20 Vice Prov Instr/Undergrad Programs ..... Dr. Joseph CLINE
20 Vice Provost/Sec of Univ ..... Dr. Jannet VREELAND
51 Vice Provost for Extended Studies ..... Dr. Fred B. HOLMAN
10 Assoc VP Business & Finance ..... Mr. Thomas L. JUDY
84 Assoc VP Enrollment Services ..... Dr. Melisa N. CHOROSZY
38 Assoc VP Student Success Services ..... Dr. Jerry MARCZYNSKI
45 Asst VP Planning/Budget/Analysis ..... Mr. Bruce L. SHIVELY
18 Int Asst Vice Pres Facilities Svcs ..... Mr. John WALSH
21 Controller ..... Ms. Philomena MCCAFFREY
41 Director Athletics ..... Ms. Cary GROTH
96 Director Purchasing ..... Mr. Garth KWIECHIEN
19 Director University Police Svcs ..... Mr. Adam GARCIA
22 Dir Equal Opportunity & Title IX ..... Ms. Denise CORDOVA
37 Director Student Financial Svcs ..... Mr. Timothy WOLFF
39 Director Resident Life & Housing . Mr. Rodney L. AESCHLIMANN
23 Director Student Health Svcs ..... Dr. Cheryl HUG-ENGLISH
09 Director Institutional Analysis ..... Dr. Serge HERZOG
86 Dir Govt Relations & Economic Dev ..... Dr. Robert E. DICKENS
65 Dir Mackay Sch Mines/Earth Science ..... Dr. Russell FIELDS
66 Director of Nursing ..... Dr. Patsy L. RUCHALA
57 Director School of the Arts ..... Dr. David AKE
25 Int Director Sponsored Projects ..... Dr. Richard BJUR
40 Director Wolf Shop ..... Mr. Steve DUBEY
49 Interim Dean Liberal Arts ..... Dr. Scott CASPER
47 Dean Agriculture/Biotech/Nat Res ..... Dr. Ron PARDINI
50 Dean Business Admininistration ..... Dr. Gregory MOSIER
53 Dean of Education ..... Dr. Christine CHENEY
54 Dean Engineering ..... Dr. Emmanuel MARAGAKIS
60 Dean School of Journalism ..... Mr. Alan STAVITSKY
81 Dean College of Science ..... Dr. Jeffrey S. THOMPSON
65 Director Academy for Environment ..... Dr. Jen HUNTLEY-SMITH
07 Director of Admissions ..... Dr. Stephen MAPLES
29 Director Alumni Relations ..... Ms. Amy CAROTHERS

*Western Nevada College (B)

2201 W College Parkway, Carson City NV 89703-7316
County: Carson — FICE Identification: 010363
Unit ID: 182564
Telephone: (775) 445-3000 — Carnegie Class: Assoc/Pub4
FAX Number: (775) 887-3051 — Calendar System: Semester
URL: www.wnc.edu
Established: 1971 — Annual Undergrad Tuition & Fees (In-State): $2,700
Enrollment: 4,278 — Coed
Affiliation or Control: State — IRS Status: 501(c)3
Highest Offering: Baccalaureate
Program: Occupational; 2-Year Principally Bachelor's Creditable
Accreditation: NW, ADNUR

02 President ..... Dr. Carol A. LUCEY
04 Assistant to the President ..... Ms. Bonnie M. BERTOCCHI
05 Vice Pres Academic/Student Affairs ..... Ms. Connie CAPURRO
15 VP Human Resources/Dir Diversity ..... Mr. Mark GHAN
20 Dean of Instruction ..... Vacant
32 Dean Student Services ..... Mr. John KINKELLA
10 Controller ..... Ms. Coral LOPEZ
88 Director Child Development Center ..... Ms. Andrea DORAN
38 Director of Counseling/Advising ..... Ms. Deborah CASE
18 Director Facilities Mgmt/Planning ..... Mr. Dave ROLLINGS
37 Director Financial Aid ..... Ms. Lori TIEDE
27 Director Information & Marketing ..... Ms. Anne P. HANSEN
08 Director Library & Media Services ..... Mr. Kenneth A. SULLIVAN

06 Registrar/Director of Admissions ..... Ms. Dianne HILLIARD
30 Director of Development ..... Ms. Amy GINDER
13 Director of Computing Services ..... Ms. Susan SCHOEFFLER
21 Budget Officer ..... Ms. Darla DODGE
15 Asst Director Human Resources ..... Ms. Irene TUCKER
51 Outreach Coordinator ..... Ms. Katie LEAO
35 Student Life Coordinator ..... Ms. Katie LEAO
81 Div Chair Science Math/Engr ..... Dr. Brigette DILLET
83 Div Chair Soc Sci/Educ/Hum/Publ Svc ..... Dr. Robert MORIN
57 Div Chair Communications/Fine Arts ..... Ms. Maxine CIRAC
76 Div Chair Nursing/Allied Health ..... Dr. Judith CORDIA
72 Division Chair Technology ..... Mr. Edward MARTIN

Pima Medical Institute-Las Vegas (C)

3333 E Flamingo Road, Las Vegas NV 89121-4329
County: Clark — Identification: 666273
Unit ID: 445230
Telephone: (702) 458-9650 — Carnegie Class: Assoc/PrivFP
FAX Number: (702) 458-9653 — Calendar System: Quarter
URL: www.pmi.edu
Established: 2003 — Annual Undergrad Tuition & Fees: $10,550
Enrollment: 1,167 — Coed
Affiliation or Control: Proprietary — IRS Status: Proprietary
Highest Offering: Associate Degree
Program: Occupational
Accreditation: ABHES, @PTAA, RAD

01 Director ..... Mr. Sam A. GENTILE

† Branch campus of Pima Medical Institute, Tucson, AZ.

Roseman University of Health Sciences (D)

11 Sunset Way, Henderson NV 89014-2333
County: Clark — FICE Identification: 040653
Unit ID: 445735
Telephone: (702) 990-4433 — Carnegie Class: Spec/Health
FAX Number: (702) 990-4435 — Calendar System: Other
URL: www.roseman.edu
Established: 1999 — Annual Undergrad Tuition & Fees: $31,400
Enrollment: 1,096 — Coed
Affiliation or Control: Independent Non-Profit — IRS Status: 501(c)3
Highest Offering: Doctorate
Program: Professional
Accreditation: NW, DENT, IACBE, NUR, PHAR

01 President ..... Dr. Harry ROSENBERG
03 Executive VP Quality Assurance ..... Dr. Renee COFFMAN
12 Chancellor South Jordan Campus ..... Dr. Mark A. PENN
12 Chancellor Henderson Campus ..... Dr. Eucharia E. NNADI
10 VP for Fiscal Affairs & Treasurer ..... Mr. Stuart A. WIENER
18 Vice President Facilities & Mgmt ..... Ms. Marlene R. MILLER
13 Vice President Info Technologies ..... Mr. Raymond PEREZ
03 Vice President Executive Affairs ..... Dr. Charles F. LACY
26 Vice President Communications & PR ..... Mr. Jason ROTH
67 Dean College of Pharmacy ..... Dr. Scott STOLTE
67 Campus Dean College of Pharmacy UT ..... Dr. Larry FANNIN
66 Dean College of Nursing Henderson ..... Dr. Mable H. SMITH
66 Dean College of Nursing UT ..... Dr. Marlene LUNA
52 Dean College of Dental Medicine ..... Dr. Richard BUCHANAN
52 Dean College of Dental Medicine Hen ..... Dr. Jaleh POURHAMIDI
50 Director MBA Program ..... Dr. Okeleke NZEOGWU
09 Dir of Inst Research/Assessment ..... Dr. Thomas METZGER
88 Assoc Dean Admissions Pharmacy ..... Dr. Michael DEYOUNG
37 Director of Financial Aid ..... Mr. Jesse STASHER
88 Assoc Dean Clinical Programs Pharm ..... Dr. Gary M. LEVIN
51 Director of Continuing Education ..... Dr. Katherine SMITH
52 Assoc Dean Academic Affairs Dental ..... Dr. Victor A. SANDOVAL
52 Assoc Dean Clinical Affairs ..... Dr. Leslie KARNS
07 Assoc Dean Admissions/Student Svcs ..... Dr. William HARMAN
15 Director of Human Resources ..... Dr. G. Benjamin WILLS
62 Director of Library Services ..... Ms. Karen CANEPI
30 Director of University Relations ..... Ms. Barbara WOOD
44 Director of Development ..... Ms. Brenda GRIEGO
06 Registrar/Director of Student Svcs ..... Ms. Angela D. BIGBY
88 Marketing Director South Jordan ..... Ms. Tracy HERNANDEZ
66 Assoc Dean Nursing ..... Dr. Catherine D'AMICO

Sierra Nevada College (E)

999 Tahoe Boulevard, Incline Village NV 89451-9500
County: Washoe — FICE Identification: 009192
Unit ID: 182458
Telephone: (775) 831-1314 — Carnegie Class: Master's M
FAX Number: (775) 832-1696 — Calendar System: Semester
URL: www.sierranevada.edu
Established: 1969 — Annual Undergrad Tuition & Fees: $27,272
Enrollment: 1,025 — Coed
Affiliation or Control: Independent Non-Profit — IRS Status: 501(c)3
Highest Offering: Master's
Program: Liberal Arts And General
Accreditation: NW

00 Chairman Board of Trustees ..... Dr. Barry MUNITZ
01 President ..... Dr. Lynn GILLETTE
05 Executive Vice President/Provost ..... Dr. Shannon BEETS
30 VP Development & College Relations ..... Dr. Deborah PROUT
84 Dean Enrollment Services & Student ..... Ms. Julie FOSTER
20 Associate Provost ..... Mr. Dan O'BRYAN

37 Director of Financial Aid ..... Ms. Nicole FERGUSON
07 Director of Admissions ..... Ms. Amye COLE
08 Director of Library ..... Dr. Elizabeth MARKLE
06 Registrar ..... Ms. Rose BEENK
53 Statewide Dir Teacher Education ..... Ms. Beth BOUCHARD
13 Director Information Technology ..... Ms. Nicole FERGERSON
10 Chief Financial Officer ..... Mr. Dan RUSHIN
15 Director Human Resources ..... Mr. David WEBB
21 Controller ..... Ms. Lynda ODELL
04 Executive Asst to the President ..... Ms. Kristine YOUNG

NEW HAMPSHIRE

Antioch University New England (F)

40 Avon Street, Keene NH 03431-3516
County: Cheshire — Identification: 666992
Unit ID: 245865
Telephone: (800) 553-8920 — Carnegie Class: Master's L
FAX Number: (603) 357-0718 — Calendar System: Other
URL: www.antioch.edu
Established: 1964 — Annual Graduate Tuition & Fees: $21,775
Enrollment: 944 — Coed
Affiliation or Control: Independent Non-Profit — IRS Status: 501(c)3
Highest Offering: Doctorate; No Undergraduates
Program: Professional
Accreditation: &NH, CACREP, CLPSY, MFCD

01 President ..... Dr. David A. CARUSO
05 Vice Pres Academic Affairs ..... Dr. Stephen NEUN
30 Vice Pres Institutional Advancement ..... Ms. Tracey THOMPSON
10 Vice Pres Finance/Administration ..... Mr. Timothy G. JORDAN
06 Registrar ..... Ms. Susan CHAMBERLIN
07 Director of Admissions ..... Ms. Laura B. ANDREWS
21 Controller ..... Ms. Kathleen M. CURTISS
29 Int Dir of Development/Alumni Rels ..... Ms. Faith LINSKY
37 Director Student Financial Aid ..... Ms. Susan L. HOWARD
18 Director Facilities/Security/Safety ..... Mr. Paul R. WHICKER
15 Director of Human Resources ..... Ms. Andrea HODSON
27 Dir of Marketing & Communications ..... Ms. Janet FIDERIO
96 Director of Purchasing ..... Ms. Joan A. NELSON
20 Assoc Acad Ofcr/Chf Stdnt Svcs Ofcr ..... Ms. Leatrice ORAM

† Regional accreditation is carried under the parent institution in Yellow Springs, OH.

Colby-Sawyer College (G)

541 Main Street, New London NH 03257-7835
County: Merrimack — FICE Identification: 002572
Unit ID: 182634
Telephone: (603) 526-3000 — Carnegie Class: Bac/Diverse
FAX Number: (603) 526-2135 — Calendar System: Semester
URL: www.colby-sawyer.edu
Established: 1837 — Annual Undergrad Tuition & Fees: $35,810
Enrollment: 1,257 — Coed
Affiliation or Control: Independent Non-Profit — IRS Status: 501(c)3
Highest Offering: Baccalaureate
Program: Liberal Arts And General; Teacher Preparatory
Accreditation: EH, NURSE

01 President ..... Mr. Thomas C. GALLIGAN
05 Academic Vice Pres/Dean of Faculty ..... Dr. Deborah A. TAYLOR
11 Vice President Administration ..... Mr. Douglas G. ATKINS
10 Vice Pres for Finance & Treasurer ..... Mr. Todd C. EMMONS
32 VP Stdnt Devel/Dean of Students ..... Mr. David A. SAUERWEIN
30 Vice President Advancement ..... Ms. Elizabeth A. CAHILL
84 Vice Pres Enrollment Management ..... Mr. Gregory W. MATTHEWS
101 Secretary of the College ..... Ms. Linda J. VARNUM
04 Assistant to the President ..... Ms. Lisa F. TEDESCHI
20 Academic Dean ..... Dr. Elizabeth C. CROCKFORD
35 Assoc Dean Stdnt/Dir Citizenship Ed ..... Ms. Robin BURROUGHS-DAVIS
39 Director Residential Education ..... Ms. Mary MCLAUGHLIN
37 Director of Financial Aid ..... Mr. Ted W. CRAIGIE
30 Director of Development ..... Ms. Kathleen A. CARROLL
08 College Librarian ..... Ms. Carrie THOMAS
06 Registrar ..... Ms. Carole H. PARSONS
07 Director of Admission Counseling ..... Ms. Tracey G. PERKINS
13 Director Information Resources ..... Mr. Kenneth G. KOCHIEN
41 Director of Athletics ..... Ms. Deborah F. MCGRATH
18 Director of Facilities ..... Mr. Robert MORSE
23 Director of Health & Counseling ..... Ms. Jacqueline F. WEBB
27 Exec Director of Publications ..... Vacant
36 Director of Career Development ..... Ms. Kathy J. TAYLOR
88 Asst Dir Acad Development Ctr ..... Ms. Caren BALDWIN-DIMEO
85 Dir English Lang/Amer Culture Pgm ..... Mr. David ELLIOTT
44 Dir Annual Giving ..... Mr. Christopher S. REED
29 Dir Alumni Relations ..... Ms. Tracey M. AUSTIN
19 Director of Campus Safety ..... Mr. Peter L. BERTHIAUME
15 Director of Human Resources ..... Ms. Sharon L. BEAUDRY
35 Director of Campus Activities ..... Ms. Sharon WILLIAMSON
09 Director Institutional Research ..... Dr. Yi NI
21 Controller ..... Ms. Karen I. BONEWALD
26 Director of Communications ..... Ms. Kimberly S. SLOVER
40 Bookstore Manager ..... Ms. Mairim KILMISTER
92 Coordinator of the Honors Program ..... Ms. Ann Page STECKER
28 Associate Dean of Intl & Diversity ..... Dr. Pamela SEROTA COTE

*Community College System of New Hampshire (A)

26 College Drive, Concord NH 03301-7407
County: Merrimack Identification: 666462
Telephone: (603) 271-2722 Carnegie Class: N/A
FAX Number: (603) 271-2725
URL: www.ccsnh.edu

01	Chancellor	Dr. Ross GITTELL
03	Vice Chancellor	Vacant
10	Director of Financial Management	Michael MARR
15	Director of Human Resources	Sara SAWYER
27	Director of Communications	Shannon REID

*Great Bay Community College (B)

320 Corporate Drive, Portsmouth NH 03801-2879
County: Rockingham FICE Identification: 002583
Unit ID: 183150
Telephone: (603) 427-7600 Carnegie Class: Assoc/Pub-R-M
FAX Number: (603) 334-6308 Calendar System: Semester
URL: www.greatbay.edu
Established: N/A Annual Undergrad Tuition & Fees (In-State): $7,008
Enrollment: 1,941 Coed
Affiliation or Control: State IRS Status: 501(c)3
Highest Offering: Associate Degree
Program: Occupational; 2-Year Principally Bachelor's Creditable
Accreditation: EH, ACBSP, ADNUR, SURGT

02	President	Mr. Wildolfo ARVELO
05	Vice President Academic Affairs	Ms. Diane KING
84	Vice Pres Enrollment Mgmt/Students	Dr. Bruce BAKER
06	Registrar	Ms. Sandra HO
10	Chief Financial Officer	Ms. Joanne BERRY

*Lakes Region Community College (C)

379 Belmont Road, Laconia NH 03246-1364
County: Belknap FICE Identification: 007555
Unit ID: 183123
Telephone: (603) 524-3207 Carnegie Class: Assoc/Pub-R-S
FAX Number: (603) 527-2042 Calendar System: Semester
URL: www.lrcc.edu
Established: 1967 Annual Undergrad Tuition & Fees (In-District): $6,840
Enrollment: 1,684 Coed
Affiliation or Control: State/Local IRS Status: 501(c)3
Highest Offering: Associate Degree
Program: Occupational; 2-Year Principally Bachelor's Creditable
Accreditation: EH

02	President	Dr. Scott KALICKI
05	VP of Academic & Community Affairs	Mr. Thomas GOULETTE
32	VP of Student Services & Enrollment	Dr. Larissa BAIA
10	Chief Financial Officer	Ms. Alice MOWERY

*Manchester Community College (D)

1066 Front Street, Manchester NH 03102-8518
County: Hillsborough FICE Identification: 002582
Unit ID: 183132
Telephone: (603) 206-8000 Carnegie Class: Assoc/Pub-R-M
FAX Number: (603) 668-5354 Calendar System: Semester
URL: www.mccnh.edu
Established: 1945 Annual Undergrad Tuition & Fees (In-State): $5,226
Enrollment: 2,856 Coed
Affiliation or Control: State IRS Status: 501(c)3
Highest Offering: Associate Degree
Program: Occupational; 2-Year Principally Bachelor's Creditable
Accreditation: EH, ACBSP, ADNUR, MAC

02	President	Dr. Susan D. HUARD
05	Vice President Academic Affairs	John COOK
32	VP Students/Community Development	Kim KEEGAN
20	Associate VP Academic Affairs	Joan ACORACE
84	Assoc VP Enrollment Management	Vacant
26	Director of Communications	Janet PHELPS
37	Financial Aid Officer	Stephanie J. WELDON
06	Registrar	Evelyn R. PERRON
08	Librarian	Mary MARKS
09	Director Institutional Research	Dr. Jere TURNER
10	Chief Financial Officer	Sarah DIVERSI
22	Human Resources Officer	Alicia CUTTING
40	Bookstore Manager	Vacant
66	Nursing Director	Charlene WOLFE-STEPRO
21	Accountant I	Carol DESPATHY
13	Director Information Technology	Naim SYED
35	Director Student Life	Aileen CLAY

*Nashua Community College (E)

505 Amherst Street, Nashua NH 03063-1092
County: Hillsborough FICE Identification: 009236
Unit ID: 183141
Telephone: (603) 882-6923 Carnegie Class: Assoc/Pub-R-M
FAX Number: (603) 882-8690 Calendar System: Semester
URL: www.nashuacc.edu
Established: 1967 Annual Undergrad Tuition & Fees (In-State): $7,232
Enrollment: 2,229 Coed
Affiliation or Control: State IRS Status: 501(c)3
Highest Offering: Associate Degree
Program: Occupational; 2-Year Principally Bachelor's Creditable
Accreditation: EH, ADNUR, ENGT

02	President	Ms. Lucille A. JORDAN
32	Vice Pres Student Services	Ms. Patricia GOODMAN
10	Chief Financial Officer	Ms. Amber WHEELER
06	Registrar-Nashua	Ms. Jennifer LEITNER
08	Librarian-Nashua	Mr. William A. MCINTYRE
37	Financial Aid Officer	Ms. Lizbeth GONZALEZ

*NHTI-Concord's Community College (F)

31 College Drive, Concord NH 03301-7412
County: Merrimack FICE Identification: 002581
Unit ID: 183099
Telephone: (603) 271-6484 Carnegie Class: Assoc/Pub-R-M
FAX Number: (603) 271-7734 Calendar System: Semester
URL: www.nhti.edu
Established: 1965 Annual Undergrad Tuition & Fees (In-State): $6,890
Enrollment: 4,568 Coed
Affiliation or Control: State IRS Status: 501(c)3
Highest Offering: Associate Degree
Program: Occupational; 2-Year Principally Bachelor's Creditable
Accreditation: EH, ACBSP, ADNUR, DA, DH, DMS, EMT, ENGT, PNUR, RAD, RTT

02	President	Ms. Lynn KILCHENSTEIN
32	Vice President Student Affairs	Mr. Stephen P. CACCIA
05	Vice President Academic Affairs	Ms. Pamela LANGLEY
51	Vice Pres Continuing/Corp Education	Vacant
20	Assoc Vice Pres of Academic Affairs	Vacant
09	Assoc VP of Acad Affairs/Inst Rsrch	Ms. Beth BLANKENSTEIN
84	Assoc VP of Enrollment Management	Vacant
10	Chief Financial Officer	Ms. Melanie KIRBY
08	Director Learning Resources	Mr. Stephen AMBRA
07	Director of Admissions	Mr. Francis P. MEYER
06	Registrar	Ms. Michele KARWOCKI
13	Director of Computer Services	Mr. Thomas TOWLE
18	Director of Facilities Maintenance	Mr. Michael THERRIEN
27	Director of Communications	Mr. Alan BLAKE
36	Dir Residence Life/Career Counsel	Ms. Trish GODINO
38	Director Student Counseling	Ms. Donna DOOLEY
37	Financial Aid Director	Ms. Sheri GONTHIER
19	Chief of Campus Safety	Ms. Anne L. BREEN
41	Athletic Director	Mr. Paul HOGAN
15	Director Human Resources	Ms. Alyssa LABELLE
28	Dir Cross-Cultural Education/ESOL	Ms. Dawn HIGGINS
96	Director of Purchasing	Ms. Irene AUBUT
21	Bursar	Ms. Jessica BRYAN
105	Website Coordinator	Ms. Christine METCALF
35	Coordinator of Campus Activities	Mr. Chuck LLOYD

*River Valley Community College (G)

1 College Place, Claremont NH 03743-9707
County: Sullivan FICE Identification: 007560
Unit ID: 183114
Telephone: (603) 542-7744 Carnegie Class: Assoc/Pub-R-S
FAX Number: (603) 543-1844 Calendar System: Semester
URL: www.rivervalley.edu
Established: 1968 Annual Undergrad Tuition & Fees (In-State): $5,455
Enrollment: 1,035 Coed
Affiliation or Control: State IRS Status: 501(c)3
Highest Offering: Associate Degree
Program: Occupational; 2-Year Principally Bachelor's Creditable
Accreditation: EH, ACBSP, ADNUR, MAC, MLTAD, OTA, PTAA

02	President	Mr. Harvey D. HILL
05	Vice President Academic Affairs	Ms. Andrea GORDON
32	VP Student Svcs/Cmty Relations	Ms. Valerie MAHAR
20	Assoc Vice Pres Academic Affairs	Dr. Lisa HAYWARD-WYZIK
37	Financial Aid Officer	Ms. Julia DOWER
06	Registrar	Ms. Sharon GILBERT
10	Chief Financial Officer	Ms. Marie MARCUM

*White Mountains Community College (H)

2020 Riverside Drive, Berlin NH 03570-3799
County: Coos FICE Identification: 005291
Unit ID: 183105
Telephone: (603) 752-1113 Carnegie Class: Assoc/Pub-R-S
FAX Number: (603) 752-6335 Calendar System: Semester
URL: www.wmcc.edu
Established: 1966 Annual Undergrad Tuition & Fees (In-State): $7,374
Enrollment: 926 Coed
Affiliation or Control: State IRS Status: 501(c)3
Highest Offering: Associate Degree
Program: Occupational; 2-Year Principally Bachelor's Creditable
Accreditation: EH, MAC

02	President	Katharine ENEGUESS
05	Vice Pres Academic Affairs	Frank CLULOW
32	Vice President Student Affairs	Martha LAFLAMME
37	Financial Aid Officer	Tyler BERGMEIER
10	Business Administrator	Lynn MOORE
06	Registrar	Marie BLY
08	Librarian	Katherine DOHERTY
18	Chief Facilities/Physical Plant	Stephen DEROSIER
14	Director Computer Center	Jeffrey SCHALL
91	Director Administrative Computing	Donald WEEKS
38	Director Student Counseling	Emily ELLIOTT
22	Dir Affirmative Action/Equal Oppty	Donna BRIERE
40	Director Bookstore	Karen SEVIER
07	Director of Admissions	Mark DESMARAIS

Daniel Webster College (I)

20 University Drive, Nashua NH 03063-1300
County: Hillsborough FICE Identification: 004731
Unit ID: 182661
Telephone: (603) 577-6000 Carnegie Class: Bac/Diverse
FAX Number: (603) 577-6001 Calendar System: Semester
URL: www.dwc.edu
Established: 1965 Annual Undergrad Tuition & Fees: $15,090
Enrollment: 667 Coed
Affiliation or Control: Proprietary IRS Status: Proprietary
Highest Offering: Master's
Program: Liberal Arts And General; Technical Emphasis
Accreditation: EH, AAB, ENG

01	President	Dr. Michael E. DIFFILY
05	VP Academic Affairs	Dr. Ben LATIGO
10	Director of Finance & Operations	Ms. Darla AMMIDOWN
32	Vice President Student Services	Ms. Susan C. ELSASS
09	Director of Institutional Research	Ms. Heidi CROWELL
106	Director of Online Operations	Dr. Jeremy OWENS
04	Exec Assistant to the President	Mrs. Dee KOUMARIANOS
49	Dean School of Arts and Sciences	Dr. Kathleen HIPP
88	Dean School of Aviation Science	Mr. Jonathan PROHASKA
20	Dean of Academic Affairs Online	Dr. Deborah JAMESON
50	Dean School of Business Management	Dr. Roland LIVINGSTON
54	Dean School Engnieering & Comp Sci	Mr. Nicholas BERTOZZI
07	Director of Admissions	Mr. Stephen WALTZ
88	Director of Flight Operations	Vacant
08	Library Director	Ms. Susan WAGNER
06	Registrar	Ms. Mariyn NIEUWEBOER
06	Registrar Online	Ms. Laura CLEAVES
35	Dean of Students	Ms. Michelle O'MALLEY
20	Dean Acad Support & Faculty Affairs	Vacant
36	Director Career Planning/Placement	Ms. Shelia MURPH
41	Director of Athletics	Mr. Robin SEIDMAN
19	Director of Campus Safety	Mr. John CLARK
21	Director of Finance	Mrs. Sandra MCINTOSH
15	Human Resources Generalist	Ms. Donna BAILEY

Dartmouth College (J)

Hanover NH 03755-4030
County: Grafton FICE Identification: 002573
Unit ID: 182670
Telephone: (603) 646-1110 Carnegie Class: RU/VH
FAX Number: N/A Calendar System: Quarter
URL: www.dartmouth.edu
Established: 1769 Annual Undergrad Tuition & Fees: $42,996
Enrollment: 6,144 Coed
Affiliation or Control: Independent Non-Profit IRS Status: 501(c)3
Highest Offering: Doctorate
Program: Liberal Arts And General; Professional
Accreditation: EH, BUS, ENG, IPSY, MED, PH

01	Interim President	Dr. Carol L. FOLT
03	Executive Vice President and CFO	Mr. Steven N. KADISH
101	Secretary to Board of Trustees	Ms. Marcia J. KELLY
05	Interim Provost	Dr. Martin N. WYBOURNE
30	Sr Vice President for Advancement	Vacant
46	Interim Vice Provost for Research	Dr. Lindsay J. WHALEY
10	Vice Pres Finance	Mr. Michael F. WAGNER
26	Vice Pres for Communications	Vacant
28	Vice Pres for Inst Diversity/Equity	Dr. Evelynn ELLIS
15	Vice Pres Human Resources	Mr. Myron S. MCCOO
29	Vice President Alumni Relations	Ms. Martha J. BEATTIE
63	VP Hlth Affs/Dean Geisel Sch of Med	Dr. Wiley W. SOUBA, JR.
18	VP Campus Planning and Facilities	Ms. Linda L. SNYDER
100	Chief of Staff	Mr. David P. SPALDING
43	General Counsel	Mr. Robert B. DONIN
20	Dean of the College	Ms. Charlotte H. JOHNSON
06	Registrar	Ms. Meredith BRAZ
07	Dean Admiss/Finan Aid/Assoc Provost	Ms. Maria LASKARIS
37	Director of Financial Aid	Ms. Virginia S. HAZEN
13	Chief Information Officer	Ms. Ellen J. WAITE-FRANZEN
08	Dean of Libraries/Librarian of Col	Mr. Jeffrey L. HORRELL
49	Dean of Faculty of Arts & Sciences	Dr. Michael MASTANDUNO
50	Dean of Amos Tuck School	Dr. Paul DANOS
54	Dean of the Thayer School	Dr. Joseph HELBLE
58	Dean of Graduate Studies	Dr. Brian W. POGUE
88	Dean of Tucker Foundation	Dr. Richard R. CROCKER
41	Director of Athletics	Mr. Harry SHEEHY
21	Director Integrated Risk Mgmt/Insur	Ms. Catherine LARK
23	Director of Health Services	Dr. John H. TURCO
36	Acting Co-Director Career Services	Ms. Kathryn DOUGHTY
36	Acting Co-Director Career Services	Ms. Monica WILSON
25	Dir Office of Sponsored Projects	Ms. Jill M. MORTALI
35	Assoc Dean Student Acad Spprt Svcs	Dr. Inge-Lise AMEER
19	Director Safety & Security	Mr. Harry C. KINNE, III
09	Actg Dir of Institutional Research	Ms. Lynn FOSTER-JOHNSON
38	Dir Counseling/Human Development	Dr. Mark H. REED
22	Dir Equal Opportunity/Affirm Action	Dr. Evelynn ELLIS
96	Director of Procurement	Ms. Tammy L. MOFFATT
88	Chief Investment Officer	Ms. Pamela L. PEEDIN

Franklin Pierce University (A)

40 University Drive, Rindge NH 03461-5046
County: Cheshire FICE Identification: 002575
Unit ID: 182795
Telephone: (603) 899-4000 Carnegie Class: Master's S
FAX Number: (603) 899-6448 Calendar System: Semester
URL: www.franklinpierce.edu
Established: 1962 Annual Undergrad Tuition & Fees: $29,950
Enrollment: 2,110 Coed
Affiliation or Control: Independent Non-Profit IRS Status: 501(c)3
Highest Offering: Doctorate
Program: 2-Year Principally Bachelor's Creditable; Liberal Arts And General; Teacher Preparatory; Professional
Accreditation: EH, #ARCPA, NUR, PTA

01 President Dr. James F. BIRGE
05 VP Academic Affairs/Provost Dr. Kim MOONEY
41 Vice President/Athletic Director Mr. Bruce M. KIRSH
10 Vice Pres Finance & Planning Mr. Richard MARSHALL
32 Vice President for Student Affairs Dr. James P. EARLE
84 Vice Pres Enrollment Management Ms. Lisa BUNDERS
11 Vice Pres Student Admin Svcs/CIO Vacant
26 Vice Pres for College Relations Mr. Ahmad BOURA
58 Dean Grad/Professional Studies Dr. Thomas SABBAGH
35 Dean Student Affairs Mr. Jules TETREAULT
07 Director of Admissions Ms. Linda QUIMBY
09 Director of Institutional Research Vacant
15 Director of Human Resources Ms. Sharon T. BURKE
06 Registrar Ms. Tonya B. LABROSSE
08 Director of Library Resource Center Ms. Carissa DELIZIO
37 Director of Financial Aid Mr. Ken FERREIRA
29 Director of Alumni Affairs Mrs. Shirley ENGLISH-WHITMAN
12 Academic Dean Rindge Campus Dr. Paul M. KOTILA
12 Director Concord Center Mrs. Paula SMYKIL
12 Director Portsmouth Center Ms. Heather THIBODEAU
12 Director Manchester Campus Mr. Brian EGO
12 Asst Dean Goodyear (AZ) Campus Mrs. Andrea M. BRODE
27 Dir of Marketing & Communication Ms. Patricia GARRITY
36 Director of Career Development Ms. Rosemary NICHOLS
20 Dir Center for Academic Excellence Ms. Teresa DOWNING
42 Chaplain Rev. Bill BEARDSLEE
23 Director Health Services Ms. Aletha E. POTTER
19 Director Campus Safety Vacant
39 Director Residential Life Mr. Kenneth ERVIN
85 Director Int'l Student Services Ms. Susan OEHLSCHLAEGER
18 Chief Facilities/Physical Plant Mr. Doug LEAR
21 Director of Financial Services Ms. Sandra QUAYE
96 Director of Purchasing Mr. Robert ST. JEAN
104 Director Study Abroad Mrs. Stella WALLING
40 Manager Follett's Bookstore Ms. Kate BROWN

Hesser College (B)

3 Sundial Avenue, Manchester NH 03103-7245
County: Hillsborough FICE Identification: 004729
Unit ID: 182865
Telephone: (603) 668-6660 Carnegie Class: Bac/Assoc
FAX Number: (603) 666-4722 Calendar System: Semester
URL: www.hesser.edu
Established: 1900 Annual Undergrad Tuition & Fees: $9,870
Enrollment: 3,283 Coed
Affiliation or Control: Proprietary IRS Status: Proprietary
Highest Offering: Baccalaureate
Program: Occupational; 2-Year Principally Bachelor's Creditable
Accreditation: EH, MAC, PTAA

01 President Dr. Jacquelyn ARMITAGE
05 Int Vice Pres for Academic Affairs Dr. Carol FAGAN
20 Academic Dean Dr. Jan WYATT
32 Dean of Student Services Vacant
10 Director of Finance Ms. Tana PEREZCASTANEDA
37 Director Financial Aid Ms. Elizabeth NILSSON
06 Registrar Ms. Susan PROVENCHER
08 Director of Library Services Ms. Ada KEMP
18 Director of Operations/Security Vacant
36 Director of Career Services Mr. Rudy RACINE
37 Director Student Financial Aid Vacant
04 Assistant to the President Mrs. Carol DEWALT

Lebanon College (C)

15 Hanover Street, Lebanon NH 03766-1312
County: Grafton FICE Identification: 007025
Unit ID: 182908
Telephone: (603) 448-2445 Carnegie Class: Assoc/PrivNFP
FAX Number: (603) 448-2491 Calendar System: Trimester
URL: www.lebanoncollege.edu
Established: 1956 Annual Undergrad Tuition & Fees: $6,600
Enrollment: 246 Coed
Affiliation or Control: Independent Non-Profit IRS Status: 501(c)3
Highest Offering: Associate Degree
Program: Occupational; 2-Year Principally Bachelor's Creditable
Accreditation: ACICS, RAD

01 President Vacant
05 Academic Dean Dr. Dan WHITAKER
06 Registrar Ms. Jennifer THODY
88 Chair Management Committee Arthur Z. GARDINER

New England College (D)

98 Bridge Street, Henniker NH 03242-3244
County: Merrimack FICE Identification: 002579
Unit ID: 182980
Telephone: (603) 428-2211 Carnegie Class: Master's M
FAX Number: (603) 428-7230 Calendar System: Semester
URL: www.nec.edu
Established: 1946 Annual Undergrad Tuition & Fees: $31,744
Enrollment: 1,902 Coed
Affiliation or Control: Independent Non-Profit IRS Status: 501(c)3
Highest Offering: Doctorate
Program: Liberal Arts And General; Teacher Preparatory; Professional
Accreditation: EH

01 President Dr. Michele D. PERKINS
05 Int VP for Academic Affairs Mr. Mark WATMAN
84 VP of Enrollment and Marketing Dr. Barbara LAYNE
10 VP for Finance and Administration Ms. Paula A. AMATO
30 Int Vice President Advancement Mr. Morgan SMITH
08 Director of Danforth Library Ms. Kathy VAN WEELDEN
32 Dean of Students Ms. Laura PANTANO
58 Dean Graduate School Dr. Nelly LEJTER
07 Dean of Admissions Ms. Diane RAYMOND
20 Associate Dean of Academic Services Mr. Mark WATMAN
04 Admin Assistant to President Ms. Melissa K. STEPHENSON
91 Director of Information Technology Mr. Greg SCHOLZ
06 Registrar Mr. Frank L. HALL
37 Director Student Financial Svcs Ms. Kristen BLASE
21 Controller Ms. Betty FARR
18 Dir Campus Facilities/Planning Mr. Jay BURGESS
41 Athletic Director Ms. Lori RUNKSMEIER
26 Director of Public Information Ms. Kathleen WILLIAMS
15 Human Resources Manager Ms. Holly COLE

New Hampshire Institute of Art (E)

148 Concord Street, Manchester NH 03104-4858
County: Hillsborough FICE Identification: 031823
Unit ID: 430810
Telephone: (603) 623-0313 Carnegie Class: Spec/Arts
FAX Number: (603) 641-1832 Calendar System: Semester
URL: www.nhia.edu
Established: 1898 Annual Undergrad Tuition & Fees: $22,050
Enrollment: 464 Coed
Affiliation or Control: Independent Non-Profit IRS Status: 501(c)3
Highest Offering: Master's
Program: Fine Arts Emphasis
Accreditation: EH, ART

01 President Mr. Roger WILLIAMS
03 Executive Vice President Mr. Richard STRAWBRIDGE
10 Vice President for Finance Mr. Jim CHATTERTON
30 Vice President of Development Ms. Suzanne LENZ
84 Vice President of Enrollment Mr. Liam SULLIVAN
04 Executive Assistant to President Vacant
05 Dean of Academic Affairs Vacant
08 Library Director Ms. Betsy HOLMES
88 Director of Advising Vacant
06 Registrar Ms. Gail SORA
20 Academic Affairs Administrator Ms. Melissa SULLIVAN
88 Bursar Ms. Mary Anne LABRIE
32 Director of Student Affairs Ms. Paulette CHAPLIN
37 Director Financial Aid Ms. Cami CZOHARA
51 Continuing Education Director Ms. Karen FRANCIS
15 Director of Human Resources Vacant
21 Accounting Manager Ms. Mary Anne LA BRIE
21 Business Services Manager Ms. Kelly LEVIS
18 Facilities Manager Mr. Jonathan WOODCOCK
40 Retail Manager Mr. Joe VIVILECCHIA
13 Manager of Information Technologies Mr. Drew ROYER
88 IT Specialist Mr. Erwan DE BECKERS
38 Counselor Ms. Tanya POPOLOSKI
88 Academic Support Center Coordinator Ms. Liza OPPENHEIM

Rivier College (F)

420 S Main Street, Nashua NH 03060-5086
County: Hillsborough FICE Identification: 002586
Unit ID: 183211
Telephone: (603) 888-1311 Carnegie Class: Master's L
FAX Number: (603) 897-8811 Calendar System: Semester
URL: www.rivier.edu
Established: 1933 Annual Undergrad Tuition & Fees: $26,430
Enrollment: 924 Coed
Affiliation or Control: Roman Catholic IRS Status: 501(c)3
Highest Offering: Doctorate
Program: Liberal Arts And General; Teacher Preparatory; Professional; Nursing Emphasis
Accreditation: EH, ADNUR, NUR

01 President Sr. Paula Marie BULEY
05 Vice President for Academic Affairs Sr. Therese LAROCHELLE
10 Vice Pres Finance & Administration Mr. Brent WINIGER
32 Vice President Student Development Ms. Linda JANSKY
84 Vice Pres Enrollment Management Mr. David BOISVERT
35 Asst Vice Pres Student Development Ms. Paula RANDAZZA
13 Exec Director Info Technologies Mr. H. William SCHLEIFER
30 Exec Director Development/Marketing Ms. Karen COOPER
21 Controller Ms. Jennifer YEOMANS
06 Registrar Mr. Kevin GATELY
08 Library Director Mr. Daniel SPEIDEL
36 Director Career Placement Ms. Marie SULLIVAN
37 Director Student Financial Aid Ms. Valerie PATNAUDE
15 Director Human Resources Ms. Diana STRANO
18 Director Facilities Management Mr. Richard PERRINE
14 Director Instructional Computing Sr. Martha VILLENEUVE
41 Athletic Director Ms. Joanne MERRILL
42 Chaplain Campus Ministry Bro. Paul DEMERS
28 Director Multicultural Affairs Ms. Sharron ROWLETT
29 Asst Director Alumni Relations Ms. Mary BOLLINGER

Saint Anselm College (G)

100 Saint Anselm Drive, Manchester NH 03102-1310
County: Hillsborough FICE Identification: 002587
Unit ID: 183239
Telephone: (603) 641-7000 Carnegie Class: Bac/A&S
FAX Number: (603) 641-7116 Calendar System: Semester
URL: www.anselm.edu
Established: 1889 Annual Undergrad Tuition & Fees: $34,205
Enrollment: 1,899 Coed
Affiliation or Control: Roman Catholic IRS Status: 501(c)3
Highest Offering: Baccalaureate
Program: Liberal Arts And General; Teacher Preparatory
Accreditation: EH, NURSE

01 President Rev. Jonathan P. DEFELICE, OSB
03 Executive Vice President Dr. Suzanne K. MELLON
30 Vice President College Advancement Mr. James P. FLANAGAN
11 Vice President for Administration Ms. Patricia SHUSTER
84 VP College Mktg & Enrollment Mgmt Mr. Brad F. POZNANSKI
32 Vice President Student Affairs Dr. Joseph M. HORTON
26 Asst VP of College Comm & Mktg Ms. Barbara LEBLANC
05 Dean of the College Rev. Augustine KELLY, OSB
10 Treasurer Dr. Harry E. DUMAY
06 Registrar Ms. MaryAnn ERICSON
07 Dean of Admissions Vacant
08 Librarian Vacant
37 Director of Financial Aid Ms. Elizabeth KEUFFEL
35 Dean of Students Dr. Alicia A. FINN
36 Director of Career Planning Mr. Samuel ALLEN, JR.
20 Director of Academic Advisement Ms. Anne E. HARRINGTON
87 Director Summer Sessions Dr. Dennis SWEETLAND
66 Dean of Nursing Dr. Sharon A. GEORGE
04 Assistant to the President Ms. Janet L. POIRIER
18 Director of Maintenance Mr. Donald MOREAU
23 Director of Health Services Ms. Maura MARSHALL
29 Asst VP of Alum/Advanc Programming Ms. Patricia GUANCI-THERRIEN
41 Director of Athletics Dr. Kelly HIGGINS
42 Director of Campus Ministry Ms. Susan S. GABERT
09 Director of Institutional Research Dr. Hui-Ling CHEN
27 Chief Information Officer Mr. Adam R. ALBINA
15 Director Human Resources Mr. David HARRINGTON
19 Director Security/Safety Mr. Donald DAVIDSON
53 Director Education Planning Dr. Laura WASIELEWSKI
28 Director Multicultural Center Ms. Oluyemi MAHONEY
39 Director Student Housing Ms. Susan WEINTRAUB

St. Joseph School of Nursing (H)

5 Woodward Avenue, Nashua NH 03060
County: Hillsborough FICE Identification: 021404
Unit ID: 183248
Telephone: (603) 594-2567 Carnegie Class: Not Classified
FAX Number: (603) 578-5028 Calendar System: Semester
URL: www.sjhacademiccenter.org
Established: 1964 Annual Undergrad Tuition & Fees: $28,293
Enrollment: 94 Coed
Affiliation or Control: Independent Non-Profit IRS Status: 501(c)3
Highest Offering: Associate Degree
Program: Occupational; 2-Year Principally Bachelor's Creditable; Nursing Emphasis
Accreditation: ACCSC, PNUR

01 Director Dr. Camilie TWISS

Southern New Hampshire University (I)

2500 N River Road, Manchester NH 03106-1045
County: Hillsborough FICE Identification: 002580
Unit ID: 183026
Telephone: (603) 668-2211 Carnegie Class: Master's L
FAX Number: (603) 645-9665 Calendar System: Semester
URL: www.snhu.edu
Established: 1932 Annual Undergrad Tuition & Fees: $28,050
Enrollment: 11,851 Coed
Affiliation or Control: Independent Non-Profit IRS Status: 501(c)3
Highest Offering: Doctorate
Program: Liberal Arts And General; Teacher Preparatory; Professional
Accreditation: EH, ACBSP, ACFEI

01 President Dr. Paul LEBLANC
04 Exec Asst to the President Ms. Nancy RICHARDSON
05 Provost/Sr VP Academic Affairs Dr. Patricia LYNOTT
51 CEO College of Online & Cont Educ Mr. Stephen HODOWNES
10 Sr VP Finance & Administration Mr. William D. MCGARRY
88 Sr VP Innovation Lab Ms. Yvonne SIMON
30 VP Institutional Advancement Mr. Donald BREZINSKI
20 VP Academic Administration COCE Dr. Gregory FOWLER

15 VP Human Resources & Development .... Ms. Pamela HOGAN
13 Chief Information Officer .... Mr. John HOLLINGER
43 General Counsel/Secretary to Board .... Ms. Karen D. ABBOTT
50 Dean School of Business .... Mr. William GILLETT
08 Dean of the Library .... Ms. Kathy GROWNEY
49 Dean School of Arts & Sciences .... Dr. Karen ERICKSON
53 Dean School of Education .... Dr. Mark MCQUILLAN
32 Dean of Students .... Ms. Heather LORENZ
20 Assoc VP Academic Affairs .... Dr. Nicholas HUNT-BULL
26 Assoc VP Marketing & Communications .. Mr. Gregory MAZZOLA
21 Assoc VP and Controller .... Mr. Darrell KROOK
37 Assoc VP Enrolled Student Services .... Ms. Beverly COTTON
18 Assoc VP Facilities/Physical Plant .... Mr. Robert VACHON
07 Asst VP/Director of UG Admissions .... Mr. Steven SOBA
06 Registrar .... Ms. Jennifer DISTEFANO
09 Director of Institutional Research .... Mr. Thomas F. BERALDI, JR.
07 Director of Intl Admissions .... Dr. Steven HARVEY
07 Director of Transfer Admissions .... Ms. Bethany PERKINS
28 Dir Cultural Outreach & Involvement .... Ms. Louisa MARTIN
19 Director of Public Safety .... Mr. James WINN
29 Director of Alumni Relations .... Ms. Kristi DURETTE
23 Director Wellness Center .... Ms. Jeanette GOLDBERG
36 Director of Career Development .... Ms. Jennifer LANDON
35 Director of Student Life .... Mr. Scott TIERNO
39 Director of Residence Life .... Mr. Robert SCHIAVONI
41 Director of Athletics .... Mr. Joseph (Chip) POLAK
42 Director of Campus Ministry .... Rev. Bruce COLLARD
92 Director of Univ Honors Program .... Dr. Andrew MARTINO
85 Director of Intl Student Services .... Ms. Dawn SEDUTTO
96 Director of Purchasing & Risk Mgmt .... Mr. Frank EATON
102 Director of Foundation & Corp Rel .... Ms. Catherine LAFORGE
14 Director of Computing Resources .... Mr. Daryl A. DREFFS
105 Director of Web Services .... Mr. Curtis KIMBALL
88 Director of Academic Advising .... Ms. Carey GLINES
88 Director of the Learning Center .... Ms. Lori DECONINCK
88 Director of Disability Services .... Ms. Hyla JAFFE
31 Asst Dean Cmty Engaged Learning .... Ms. Sarah JACOBS
90 Assoc Dir of Academic Computing .... Mr. Aaron FLINT
24 AV Services Manager .... Mr. Thomas HELM

The Thomas More College of Liberal Arts (A)

6 Manchester Street, Merrimack NH 03054-4805
County: Hillsborough FICE Identification: 030431
Unit ID: 183275
Telephone: (603) 880-8308 Carnegie Class: Bac/A&S
FAX Number: (603) 880-9280 Calendar System: Semester
URL: www.thomasmorecollege.edu
Established: 1978 Annual Undergrad Tuition & Fees: $17,600
Enrollment: 80 Coed
Affiliation or Control: Independent Non-Profit IRS Status: 501(c)3
Highest Offering: Baccalaureate
Program: Liberal Arts And General; Religious Emphasis
Accreditation: EH

01 President .... Dr. William E. FAHEY
11 Vice President Administration .... Mr. Clint HANSON
30 Vice Pres Institutional Advancement .... Mr. Charlie MCKINNEY
05 Academic Dean .... Dr. Christopher BLUM
32 Dean of Students .... Mr. Walter J. THOMPSON
07 Director of Admission .... Mr. Mark SCHWERDT
06 Registrar .... Ms. Pamela BERNSTEIN
35 Direct Student Life .... Ms. Gwen ADAMS
04 Executive Asst President's Office .... Ms. Valerie BURGESS

*University System of New Hampshire (B)

Dunlap Center, 25 Concord Road, Durham NH 03824-3545
County: Strafford FICE Identification: 008027
Unit ID: 183327
Telephone: (603) 862-1800 Carnegie Class: N/A
FAX Number: (603) 862-0908
URL: usnh.edu

01 Chancellor .... Dr. Edward R. MACKAY
03 Vice Chancellor & Treasurer .... Mr. Ken CODY
15 Director Human Resource Services .... Ms. Joan M. TAMBLING
43 General Counsel .... Mr. Ronald F. RODGERS
04 USNH Secretary .... Mr. Ronald F. RODGERS
86 Assoc Vice Chanc Government Affs ..... Ms. Kathleen SALISBURY
26 Assoc Vice Chanc for External Affs .... Vacant
05 Assoc Vice Chanc Academic & Student .... Vacant

*University of New Hampshire (C)

Durham NH 03824
County: Strafford FICE Identification: 002589
Unit ID: 183044
Telephone: (603) 862-1234 Carnegie Class: RU/H
FAX Number: N/A Calendar System: Semester
URL: www.unh.edu
Established: 1866 Annual Undergrad Tuition & Fees (In-State): $16,422
Enrollment: 14,596 Coed
Affiliation or Control: State IRS Status: 501(c)3
Highest Offering: Doctorate
Program: Occupational; 2-Year Principally Bachelor's Creditable; Liberal Arts And General; Teacher Preparatory; Professional
Accreditation: EH, BUS, CS, DIETD, DIETI, DIETT, ENG, ENGT, FOR, IPSY, MFCD, MT, MUS, NRPA, NURSE, OT, PH, SP, SW, TEAC

02 President .... Dr. Mark W. HUDDLESTON
100 Chief of Staff .... Ms. Megan W. DAVIS
05 Prov & VP Academic Affairs .... Dr. John D. ABER
10 VP Finance/Administration .... Mr. Richard J. CANNON
46 Sr Vice Provost Research .... Dr. Jane A. NISBET
32 VP Student & Academic Services .... Dr. Mark RUBINSTEIN
26 Assoc VP Univ Communications .... Mr. Justin HARMON
43 General Counsel .... Mr. Ronald F. RODGERS
88 Assoc Prov Academic Administration .... Ms. Leigh Anne MELANSON
28 Vice Prov & Chief Diversity Officer .... Vacant
20 Sr Vice Prov Academic Affairs .... Dr. Lisa MACFARLANE
20 Asst Prov AcadAff/MPA Program Dir .... Mr. James S. VARN
88 Sr VP Rsrch & Outreach Scholar .... Dr. Julie E. WILLIAMS
21 Int Assoc VP for Finance .... Ms. Joanna YOUNG
13 Assoc VP Computing/Info Svcs .... Ms. Joanna C. YOUNG
16 Asst VP Human Resources .... Ms. Sari M. BENNETT
21 Assoc VP Business Affairs .... Mr. David J. MAY
18 Asst VP Energy & Campus Development .... Mr. Paul D. CHAMBERLIN
35 Dean of Students .... Dr. Martha A. LAWING
35 Asst VP Stdnt/Acad Svc/Dir Res Life .... Mr. Scott CHESNEY
23 Asst VP SAS/Exec Dir Health Svcs .... Dr. Kevin E. CHARLES
36 Assoc Prov Acad Achievement/Support .... Dr. Judith SPILLER
25 Dir Sponsored Programs .... Mr. Victor SOSA
30 VP Advancement .... Vacant
47 Dean Life Sciences/Agriculture .... Dr. Jon M. WRAITH
49 Dean Liberal Arts .... Dr. Kenneth FULD
50 Dean Whittemore Sch Business/Econ .... Dr. Daniel E. INNIS
58 Dean Graduate School .... Dr. Harry J. RICHARDS
76 Dean Health & Human Services .... Dr. Neil B. VROMAN
54 Dean Engineering/Physical Sciences .... Dr. Samuel MUKASA
12 Dean UNH at Manchester .... Dr. Ali RAFIEYMEHR
08 Dean of the University Library .... Dr. Sherry VELLUCCI
56 Dean/Dir Cooperative Extension .... Dr. John E. PIKE
88 Dir Thompson School Appl Science .... Dr. Regina A. SMICK-ATTISANO
22 Dir Affirmative Action & Equity ... Ms. Donna Marie SORRENTINO
07 Asst VP Stdnt & Acad Svc/Dir Admiss .... Mr. Robert P H. MCGANN
06 Registrar .... Ms. Kathryn P. FORBES
37 Dir Financial Aid .... Ms. Susan K. ALLEN
41 Dir Intercollegiate Athletics .... Mr. Martin SCARANO
38 Dir Counseling Center .... Dr. David CROSS
29 Assoc VP Advance/Exec Dir Alum Assn .... Mr. Stephen J. DONOVAN
39 Dir Housing/Conf Services .... Ms. Kathy IRLA-CHESNEY
19 Exec Dir Public Safety .... Chief Paul M. DEAN
85 Dir Intl Students & Scholars .... Ms. Leila L. PAJE-MANALO
42 University Chaplain .... Pastor Larry BRICKNER-WOOD
96 Dir Purchasing & Contract Svcs .... Ms. Denise M. SMITH
92 Dir Honors Program .... Dr. Sean MOORE
09 Dir Inst Research & Assessment .... Dr. John D. KRAUS
88 Dir Writing Program .... Dr. Edward A. MUELLER
18 Director of Facility Operations .... Ms. Michelle HAYES
104 Dir Center International Education .... Dr. Claire L. MALARTE-FELDMAN
94 Coord Women's Studies Program .... Dr. Marla B. BRETTSCHNEIDER
40 Manager of UNH Bookstore .... Ms. Sarah HUTZ

*University of New Hampshire at Manchester (D)

400 Commerical Street, Manchester NH 03101-1113
County: Hillsborough FICE Identification: 009009
Unit ID: 183071
Telephone: (603) 641-4321 Carnegie Class: Bac/A&S
FAX Number: (603) 641-4305 Calendar System: Semester
URL: www.manchester.unh.edu
Established: 1967 Annual Undergrad Tuition & Fees (In-State): $12,060
Enrollment: 1,368 Coed
Affiliation or Control: State IRS Status: 501(c)3
Highest Offering: Master's
Program: Liberal Arts And General
Accreditation: &EH

02 Dean .... Dr. Ali RAFIEYMEHR
05 Associate Dean Academic Affairs .... Dr. Daniel W. REAGAN
10 Director of Administration & Financ .... Ms. Kathy E. BRAUN
32 Asst Dean of Academic Student Svcs .. Ms. Regina K. MCCARTHY
91 Dir of UNHM Information Technology .... Mr. Sean P. EMBREE
19 Supervisor of Security Services .... Mr. Gary W. SEARS
62 Director Library Services .... Dr. Ann E. DONAHUE
28 Director Center Academic Enrichment .... Ms. Jennifer JEFFERSON
26 Dir of Marketing & Cmty Relations .... Dr. Virginia H. LEVER
37 Associate Director Financial Aid .... Ms. Jodi A. ABAD
07 Assistant Director of Admissions .... Ms. Miho S. BEAN
06 Associate Registrar .... Ms. Doreen E. PALMER
38 Director of Academic Counseling .... Ms. Carol A. SWIECH
15 Human Resources Partner .... Ms. Stacey J. SILVA

*University of New Hampshire School of Law (E)

Two White Street, Concord NH 03301-4197
County: Merrimack FICE Identification: 020979
Unit ID: 182829
Telephone: (603) 228-1541 Carnegie Class: Spec/Law
FAX Number: (603) 228-1074 Calendar System: Semester
URL: www.law.unh.edu
Established: 1973 Annual Graduate Tuition & Fees: $41,190
Enrollment: 424 Coed
Affiliation or Control: Independent Non-Profit IRS Status: 501(c)3
Highest Offering: First Professional Degree; No Undergraduates
Program: Professional
Accreditation: EH, LAW

02 Dean/President .... Mr. John T. BRODERICK, JR.
04 Executive Assistant to The Dean .... Ms. Linda L. LUGG
05 Associate Dean .... Prof. Jordan BUDD
00 Chairman of the Board .... Ms. Cathy GREEN
10 Vice President Financial Affairs .... Ms. Yvonne BERRY
32 Assistant Dean for Student Affairs .... Ms. Fran CANNING
06 Assistant Dean Registration/Records .... Ms. Lory ATTALLA
84 Chair Admissions Committee .... Prof. Albert SCHERR
08 Director Law Librarian .... Ms. Susan ZAGO
88 Director of Accreditation .... Prof. Margaret S. MCCAPE
88 Director of Clinical Programs .... Prof. Peter WRIGHT
88 Director Inst for Health/Law/Ethics .... Prof. Tom BUNNELL
36 Assistant Dean for Career Services .... Ms. Donna MILLER
58 Director of Graduate Programs .... Ms. Debbie BEAUREGARD
07 Assistant Dean for Admissions .... Ms. Katie MCDONALD
30 VP for Institutional Development .... Ms. Karen BORGSTROM
29 Director of Alumni Relations .... Ms. Mary SHEFFER
37 Director of Financial Aid .... Ms. Susan AHERN
26 Director of Communications .... Mr. Peter DAVIES

*Granite State College (F)

25 Hall Street, Concord NH 03301-7317
County: Merrimack FICE Identification: 031013
Unit ID: 183257
Telephone: (603) 228-3000 Carnegie Class: Bac/A&S
FAX Number: (603) 513-1389 Calendar System: Trimester
URL: www.granite.edu
Established: 1972 Annual Undergrad Tuition & Fees (In-State): $7,065
Enrollment: 1,919 Coed
Affiliation or Control: State IRS Status: 501(c)3
Highest Offering: Master's
Program: Liberal Arts And General; Teacher Preparatory; Professional
Accreditation: EH

02 President .... Dr. Todd LEACH
100 Chief of Staff .... Dr. Kathi MULLIN
05 Dean of Academic Affairs .... Dr. Sheila TAYLOR-KING
11 Dean/Integrated Technologies/Svcs .... Mr. Mike MOROUKIAN
10 Dean of Finance Affairs .... Ms. Lisa SHAWNEY
35 Dean of Students/External Engage .... Ms. Teresa H. MCDONNELL
53 Dean of the School of Education .... Dr. Mary FORD
20 Dean of Undergraduate Studies .... Dr. Laurie QUINN
58 Dean of Graduate Studies .... Dr. Scott STANLEY
31 Dean/Campus Develop/New Initiative .... Dr. Elaine MILLEN
84 Dean of Enrollment Management .... Ms. Mary Beth LUFKIN
06 Registrar .... Ms. Kristin MULLANEY
13 Chief Technical Officer .... Mr. Marty CHANG
24 Director of Educational Technology .... Ms. Reta CHAFFEE
14 Director of Information Technology .... Mr. Charles LIPORTO
26 Director of Public Affairs .... Ms. Kate YERKES
37 Actg Director of Financial Aid .... Ms. Nancy SABIN
15 Director of Human Resources .... Ms. Beth DALZELL
09 Director of Institutional Research .... Mr. Jim MILLER
18 Dir of Facilities/Safety/Sustain .... Mr. Peter CONKLIN
08 College Librarian/Senior Lecturer ..... Ms. Patricia ERWIN-PLOOG
07 Associate Director of Admissions .... Ms. Ruth NAWN
21 Director of Financial Operations .... Mr. Steve PERROTTA
21 Bursar .... Ms. Jodi WOLBERT
04 Exec Assistant to the President .... Ms. Mary YOUNG

*Keene State College (G)

229 Main Street, Keene NH 03435-0001
County: Cheshire FICE Identification: 002590
Unit ID: 183062
Telephone: (603) 352-1909 Carnegie Class: Master's S
FAX Number: (603) 358-2257 Calendar System: Semester
URL: www.keene.edu
Established: 1909 Annual Undergrad Tuition & Fees (In-State): $12,776
Enrollment: 5,247 Coed
Affiliation or Control: State IRS Status: 501(c)3
Highest Offering: Master's
Program: Liberal Arts And General; Teacher Preparatory; Professional
Accreditation: EH, DIETD, DIETI, MUS, TED

02 Interim President .... Dr. Jay V. KAHN
05 Interim Provost/VP Academic Affairs ..... Dr. Melinda TREADWELL
32 Vice President Student Affairs .... Dr. Andrew ROBINSON
10 Interim VP Finance & Planning .... Ms. Karen HOUSE
30 Vice President Advancement .... Ms. Maryann LINDBERG
04 Interim Special Asst to the Pres .... Ms. Barbara HALL
04 Executive Asst to the President .... Ms. Ann M. GAGNON
20 Assoc Provost Academic Affairs .... Dr. Ann RANCOURT
35 Dean of Students .... Dr. Gail ZIMMERMAN
08 Dean of Library .... Dr. Irene HEROLD
07 Director of Admissions .... Ms. Margaret RICHMOND
06 Registrar .... Mr. Thomas RICHARD
27 Chief Information Officer .... Ms. Laura SERAICHICK
30 Director of Development .... Mr. Ken GOEBEL
15 Human Resources Director .... Ms. Kim HARKNESS
26 Director of Marketing & Comm .... Ms. Kathleen WILLIAMS
37 Director Financial Aid .... Ms. Patricia A. BLODGETT
18 Director Physical Plant .... Mr. Frank MAZZOLA
39 Director of Residential Life .... Mr. Kent DRAKE-DEESE

09 Director of Institutional Research .... Ms. Cathryn TURRENTINE
29 Director of Alumni Relations .... Ms. Patricia FARMER
38 Director Student Counseling .... Dr. Brian QUIGLEY
21 Associate Business Officer .... Vacant
96 Purchasing Agent .... Mr. James DRAPER
81 Dean of Sciences .... Dr. Gordon LEVERSEE
58 Dean Professional/Graduate Studies .... Mr. Wayne HARTZ
79 Dean Arts & Humanities .... Dr. Andrew HARRIS
28 Chief Officer Diversity/Multicult .... Dr. Dottie MORRIS

*Plymouth State University (A)

17 High Street, Plymouth NH 03264-1595
County: Grafton FICE Identification: 002591
Unit ID: 183080
Telephone: (603) 535-5000 Carnegie Class: Master's L
FAX Number: (603) 535-2654 Calendar System: Semester
URL: www.plymouth.edu
Established: 1871 Annual Undergrad Tuition & Fees (In-State): $12,560
Enrollment: 5,686 Coed
Affiliation or Control: State IRS Status: 501(c)3
Highest Offering: Doctorate
Program: Liberal Arts And General; Teacher Preparatory; Business Emphasis
Accreditation: EH, ACBSP, CACREP, SW, TED

02 President .... Dr. Sara Jayne STEEN
05 Vice Pres Academic Affairs/Provost .... Dr. Julie N. BERNIER
10 VP for Finance & Administration .... Mr. Stephen TAKSAR
32 Vice President for Student Affairs .... Dr. James HUNDRIESER
20 VP for Undergraduate Studies .... Dr. David ZEHR
30 VP for University Advancement .... Ms. Sally C. HOLLAND
20 Vice Provost Research & Engagement .... Dr. Thad GULDBRANDSEN
58 Associate VP Graduate Studies .... Dr. George F. TUTHILL
13 AVP Info Tech Svcs/Chief Info Ofcr .. Mr. Richard G. GROSSMAN
35 Dean of Students .... Mr. Timothy C. KEEFE
09 Interim Dir IR & Effectiveness .... Ms. Joyce LARSON
06 Registrar .... Mr. George GILMORE
08 Dean of Library & Academic Support .... Dr. David BERONA
07 Senior Assoc Director of Admissions .... Mr. Eugene D. FAHEY
26 Exec Director University Relations .... Mr. Steve BARBA
29 Director of Alumni Relations .... Mr. Rodney EKSTROM
36 Director Career Services .... Vacant
37 Director of Financial Aid .... Ms. June SCHLABACH
15 Director of Human Resources .... Ms. Elaine DOELL
19 Chief of Campus Police .... Mr. Creig DOYLE
41 Athletic Director .... Mr. John P. CLARK
18 Director of Physical Plant .... Ms. Ellen SHIPPEE
38 Director of Counseling .... Dr. Michael L. FISCHLER
40 Bookstore Manager .... Mr. Steve RHEAUME
39 AVP Student Affairs - Res Life .... Mr. Frank L. COCCHIARELLA
88 AVP Student Affairs - HUB .... Ms. Terri L. POTTER
96 Manager of Purchasing .... Ms. Heather HUCKINS

NEW JERSEY

Assumption College for Sisters (B)

350 Bernardsville Road, Mendham NJ 07945-2923
County: Morris FICE Identification: 002595
Unit ID: 183600
Telephone: (973) 543-6528 Carnegie Class: Assoc/PrivNFP
FAX Number: (973) 543-1738 Calendar System: Semester
URL: www.acs350.org
Established: 1953 Annual Undergrad Tuition & Fees: $10,300
Enrollment: 43 Female
Affiliation or Control: Roman Catholic IRS Status: 501(c)3
Highest Offering: Associate Degree
Program: 2-Year Principally Bachelor's Creditable; Religious Emphasis
Accreditation: M

01 President/Chief of Development .... Sr. Joseph SPRING, SCC
05 Dean/Registrar/Admissions .... Sr. Gerardine TANTSITS, SCC
10 Treasurer .... Mrs. Patricia MCGRADY
32 Chief Student Life Officer .... Sr. Marie Cecelia LANDIS, SCC
08 Librarian/Technology .... Sr. Theresa BOWER, SCC

Atlantic Cape Community College (C)

5100 Black Horse Pike, Mays Landing NJ 08330-2699
County: Atlantic FICE Identification: 002596
Unit ID: 183655
Telephone: (609) 343-4900 Carnegie Class: Assoc/Pub-R-L
FAX Number: (609) 343-4917 Calendar System: Semester
URL: www.atlantic.edu
Established: 1964 Annual Undergrad Tuition & Fees (In-District): $3,735
Enrollment: 7,592 Coed
Affiliation or Control: State/Local IRS Status: 501(c)3
Highest Offering: Associate Degree
Program: Occupational; 2-Year Principally Bachelor's Creditable
Accreditation: M, ACFEI, ADNUR, SURGT

01 President .... Dr. Peter L. MORA
05 Vice President Academic Affairs .... Dr. Arthur WEXLER
51 Dean Cape May Camp/Cont Ed/Res Dev .... Dr. Patricia GENTILE
46 Dean Facilities/Planning/Research .... Dr. Richard PERNICIARO
10 Dean Finance and Administration .... Ms. Catherine SKINNER
35 Dean of Students .... Ms. Carmen ROYAL
14 Dean Information Tech Services .... Mr. Douglas HEDGES
15 Dean Human Resources & Compliance ... Ms. Eileen CURRISTINE
20 Dean of Instruction .... Dr. Ronald MCARTHUR
88 Dean Academy of Culinary Arts .... Ms. Kelly MCCLAY
32 Dir of Stdnt Dev & Judical Officer .... Ms. Nancy PORFIDO
88 Assoc Dean Academic Support Svcs .... Mr. Grant WILINSKI
88 Assoc Dean Aviation/Tech Inst & GIS .... Mr. Otto HERNANDEZ
09 Asst Dean Research & Assessment .... Ms. Paula PITCHER
101 Exec Asst to Pres/Dir of Board Svcs .... Mr. Sean FISCHER
21 Exec Director Business Services .... Ms. Therese SAMPSON
84 Director Enrollment Services .... Ms. Heather PETERSON
26 Exec Director College Relations .... Ms. Kathleen J. CORBALIS
37 Director Financial Aid .... Ms. Linda DESANTIS
06 Registrar .... Ms. Heather PETERSON
07 Director of Admissions .... Ms. Regina SKINNER
18 Director Facil Plng & Capital Proj .... Mr. Mark STRECKENBEIN
38 Director of Student Counseling .... Ms. Paula DAVIS

Bais Medrash Toras Chesed (D)

910 Monmouth Avenue, Lakewood NJ 08701-1921
County: Ocean FICE Identification: 040813
Unit ID: 449658
Telephone: (732) 364-1220 Carnegie Class: Spec/Faith
FAX Number: (732) 886-2323 Calendar System: Semester
Established: 1999 Annual Undergrad Tuition & Fees: $8,700
Enrollment: 109 Male
Affiliation or Control: Independent Non-Profit IRS Status: 501(c)3
Highest Offering: Baccalaureate
Program: Professional
Accreditation: RABN

01 Dean .... Rabbi N. STEIN
37 Director of Financial Aid .... Mrs. A. R. STEIN
10 Bursar .... Rabbi M. GELFAND

Bergen Community College (E)

400 Paramus Road, Paramus NJ 07652-1595
County: Bergen FICE Identification: 004736
Unit ID: 183743
Telephone: (201) 447-7100 Carnegie Class: Assoc/Pub-S-SC
FAX Number: (201) 444-7036 Calendar System: Semester
URL: www.bergen.edu
Established: 1965 Annual Undergrad Tuition & Fees (In-District): $5,034
Enrollment: 17,271 Coed
Affiliation or Control: State/Local IRS Status: 501(c)3
Highest Offering: Associate Degree
Program: Occupational; 2-Year Principally Bachelor's Creditable
Accreditation: M, ADNUR, DH, DMS, MAC, RAD, RTT, SURGT

01 Interim President .... Dr. Jose A. ADAMES
05 Interim Academic Vice President .... Dr. Bonnie MACDOUGALL
32 Vice President Student Services .... Vacant
11 Int Chief of Admin Services .... Ms. Deborah SOUSA
10 Senior Financial Officer .... Ms. Diane MANDRAFINA
09 Int Coord Institutional Assessment .... Ms. Joann MARZOCCO
81 Dean Business/Social Sci/Pub Svc .... Mr. Andrew TOMKO
79 Dean Arts/Humanities & Wellness .... Prof. Amparo CODDING
17 Dean Health Professions .... Dr. Susan BARNARD
57 Dean English .... Dr. Carol MIELE
106 Int Dean School of Virtual Studies .... Mr. Thomas JEWELL
81 Dean Math & Science .... Mr. Pascal J. RICATTO
51 Int Dean Cont Ed/Corp/Pub Sect Trng .... Ms. Sandra SROKA
08 Dean Library Services .... Ms. Amy BETH
35 Dean of Student Svcs/Retention Svcs .... Dr. Denise JERMAN LIGUORI
32 Int Asst Dean Ctr Student Success .... Ms. Jennifer REYES
15 Chief Human Resources Officer .... Mr. James MILLER
18 Director Physical Plant .... Mr. Norman SHAPIRO
19 Director Public Safety .... Mr. William CORCORAN
13 Chief Information Officer .... Mr. Evan KOBOLAKIS
06 Dir Student Records & Registration .... Ms. Jacqueline OTTEY
88 Director Community/Cultural Affairs .... Mr. Peter LEDONNE
101 Secretary to Board of Trustees .... Ms. Wendy DODGE
29 Director Alumni Relations .... Ms. Laurie FRANCIS
51 Dir Inst of Learning in Retirement .... Ms. Ilene KLEINMAN
37 Dir Financial Ops/Stdnt Assistance .... Ms. Caroline OFODILE
102 Director Foundation/Development .... Ms. Laurie FRANCIS
25 Director of Grants .... Dr. William YAKOWICZ
96 Director of Purchasing & Services .... Ms. Barbara HAMILTON-GOLDEN
26 Asst Director Public Relations .... Mr. Joseph CAVALUZZI
04 Int Exec Assistant to the President .... Dr. Ursula DANIELS

Berkeley College (F)

44 Rifle Camp Road, Woodland Park NJ 07424-3367
County: Passaic FICE Identification: 007502
Unit ID: 183789
Telephone: (973) 278-5400 Carnegie Class: Spec/Bus
FAX Number: (973) 278-0080 Calendar System: Quarter
URL: www.berkeleycollege.edu
Established: 1931 Annual Undergrad Tuition & Fees: $21,750
Enrollment: 3,363 Coed
Affiliation or Control: Proprietary IRS Status: Proprietary
Highest Offering: Baccalaureate
Program: Business Emphasis
Accreditation: M

00 Chairman of the Board .... Mr. Kevin L. LUING
01 President .... Dr. Dario A. CORTES
100 Chief of Staff & Assoc VP Planning .... Ms. Linda LUCIANO
04 Special Assistant to the President .... Dr. Rose Mary HEALY
05 Provost .... Dr. Glen ZEITZER
10 Sr Vice President Finance & Admin .... Ms. Lee S. MIARA
36 Vice President Advisement .... Dr. Beth COYLE
84 Sr Vice Pres Enrollment Mgmt .... Ms. Diane RECINOS
26 Senior Vice President Marketing .... Mr. Don CHALLIS
20 Assoc Provost for Faculty Affairs .... Dr. Marianne VAKALIS
20 Assoc Provost Academic Admin .... Dr. Troy ADAIR
32 VP Stdnt Development & Campus Life .... Dr. Edwin HUGHES
20 Vice President Academic Admin .... Ms. Tia DELOUISE
07 Vice President Enrollment .... Ms. Christine G. RICHARD
07 VP International Enrollment Svcs .... Ms. Cynthia C. MARCHESE
22 Vice Pres & Compliance Officer .... Mr. William BRANDT
08 Vice President Library Services .... Ms. Marlene DOTY
12 Garret Mountain Campus Oper Ofcr .... Ms. Linda PINSKY
12 Middlesex Campus Operating Officer . Ms. Debra L. MALLAMACE
12 Newark Campus Operating Officer .... Mr. W. Stan HOLLAND
12 Paramus Campus Operating Officer .... Mr. Evan MILLER
12 Online Campus Operating Officer .... Ms. Sharon GOLDSTEIN
09 Asst VP Assessment & Inst Research .... Dr. Ross MILLER
50 Dean School of Business .... Dr. John RAPANOS
49 Dean School Liberal Arts .... Dr. Don KIEFFER
107 Dean School Professional Studies .... Dr. Judith KORNBERG
51 Dean School Continuing Education .... Mr. Ricardo ORTEGON
106 Assistant Provost & Dean of Online .... Ms. Carol SMITH
86 Senior Vice Pres External Affairs .... Ms. Teri DUDA
84 Assoc Vice President Enrollment .... Ms. Carol ALLEN-COVINO
38 Sr Director Personal Counseling .... Ms. Sandra COPPOLA
35 Director Student Devel/Campus Life .... Ms. Amy YOUNG
21 Assoc VP Student Accounts .... Ms. Ursula BISCONTI
37 Senior Director Financial Aid .... Ms. Barbara SYLVESTER
09 Director Institutional Research .... Mr. Christopher J. VINGER
26 Director Media Relations .... Ms. Ilene LUMPKIN
36 VP Advisement .... Ms. Gail OKUN
41 Athletic Director .... Mr. Brian MAHER

Beth Medrash Govoha (G)

617 Sixth Street, Lakewood NJ 08701-2797
County: Ocean FICE Identification: 007947
Unit ID: 183804
Telephone: (732) 367-1060 Carnegie Class: Spec/Faith
FAX Number: (732) 367-7487 Calendar System: Semester
URL: www.bmg.edu
Established: 1943 Annual Undergrad Tuition & Fees: $16,816
Enrollment: 6,374 Male
Affiliation or Control: Independent Non-Profit IRS Status: 501(c)3
Highest Offering: Beyond Master's But Less Than Doctorate
Program: Teacher Preparatory; Professional
Accreditation: RABN

00 President .... Rabbi A. Malkiel KOTLER
01 Chief Executive Officer .... Rabbi Aaron KOTLER
10 VP Finance/Technology Compliance .... Mr. Isaac LEVINE
43 VP Finance/Corporate/Legal Affairs .... Rabbi Eli KUPERMAN
11 Vice President Admin/Campus Life .... Rabbi Yitzchok S. KOTLER
33 Dean of Students .... Rabbi Mattisyahu SALOMON
58 Dean of Graduate Studies .... Rabbi Yisroel NEUMAN
05 Executive Administrator .... Rabbi Mordechai HERSKOWITZ
86 Director Government Affairs .... Mrs. Chanie JACOBOWITZ
06 Registrar .... Rabbi Jacob BURSZTYN
07 Director of Admissions .... Rabbi Avraham FEUER
08 Director Library/Research Programs .... Rabbi Benjamin SPIEGEL
36 Director of Field Services .... Rabbi Jacob SHULMAN
39 Director Residence Halls .... Rabbi Yosef SLOMOVITS

Bloomfield College (H)

467 Franklin Street, Bloomfield NJ 07003-3425
County: Essex FICE Identification: 002597
Unit ID: 183822
Telephone: (973) 748-9000 Carnegie Class: Bac/A&S
FAX Number: (973) 743-3998 Calendar System: Semester
URL: www.bloomfield.edu
Established: 1868 Annual Undergrad Tuition & Fees: $23,850
Enrollment: 2,145 Coed
Affiliation or Control: Presbyterian Church (U.S.A.) IRS Status: 501(c)3
Highest Offering: Master's
Program: Liberal Arts And General; Teacher Preparatory; Professional
Accreditation: M, NURSE, TEAC

01 President .... Richard A. LEVAO
10 Senior Vice Pres of Admin/Finance .... Howard BUXBAUM
04 Administrative Asst to President .... Christina NOLAN
05 Vice President Academic Affairs .... Marion TERENZIO
07 Interim VP Enroll Mgmt/Admission .... Adam CASTRO
32 VP Student Affairs/Dean of Students .... Patrick J. LAMY
30 VP for Advancement .... Kwi BRENNAN
72 VP Inst of Tech & Prof Studies .... Peter JEONG
21 AVP for Finance and Administration .... William A. MCDONALD
20 AVP for Academic Development .... Josephine COHN
06 Registrar and Director of Advising .... Eileen M. POLAZZI
09 Director Instnl Research/Assessment .... Eugene W. MULLER
20 Associate Dean for Faculty .... Carolyn I. SPIES
79 Chair Div of Humanities .... Paul GENEGA
83 Chair Div Social/Behavioral Science .... Denise DENNIS
66 Chair Div of Nursing .... Neddie SERRA
81 Chair Div of Natural Science/Math .... Jim MURPHY
57 Chair Div Creative Arts Technology .... Nancy BACCI
50 Chair Div Accounting/Business/CIS .... Robert COLLMIER
53 Chair Div of Education .... Nora KRIEGER
88 Assoc Dean Inst Educ Support Svcs .... Leonard ROBERTS

08 Library Director Danilo H. FIGUEREDO
13 Director of Information Services Erzsebet FELSOVALYI
36 Director of Career Services Carol RUIZ
37 Director of Financial Aid Stacy SALINAS
31 Director Center for Adult Learning John MWAURA
06 Associate Registrar Annette RAYMOND
35 Associate Dean Student Development Rose MITCHELL
15 Assoc Director Human Resources Janice CECERE
18 Super of Buildings & Grounds Jack V. MCGRANE
07 Coordinator of Intl Admissions Ninah PRETTO
44 Director Annual Giving/Alumni Rels Carrie BENNETT
38 Director Personal Counseling Jessica DISLA
26 Director Public Rels/Advancemnt Mkt Jill ALEXANDER
42 Dir Spirtual Life/Col Chaplain Cynthia BETZ-BOGOLY
88 Director Teacher Education Dayna HASSELL
41 Director of Athletics Sheila WOOTEN
88 Director Center Academic Develop Patricia ARTEAGA
19 Director of Security Jack CORTEZ
39 Director Res Educ & Housing Rochelle GABRIEL
105 Webmaster Rob KRIEGER
24 Director of Media Center Barbara ISACSON
88 Director Office for Instnl Tech Yifeng BAI
40 Store Manager Roberta STEVENSON

Brookdale Community College (A)

Newman Springs Road, Lincroft NJ 07738-1597
County: Monmouth FICE Identification: 008404
Unit ID: 183859
Telephone: (732) 842-1900 Carnegie Class: Assoc/Pub-S-SC
FAX Number: (732) 224-2242 Calendar System: Other
URL: www.brookdalecc.edu
Established: 1967 Annual Undergrad Tuition & Fees (In-District): $4,297
Enrollment: 14,952 Coed
Affiliation or Control: State/Local IRS Status: 501(c)3
Highest Offering: Associate Degree
Program: Occupational; 2-Year Principally Bachelor's Creditable
Accreditation: M, ADNUR, MLTAD, RAD

01 President Dr. Maureen MURPHY
03 Executive Vice President Dr. Dianna PHILLIPS
10 Vice Pres Business & Finance Ms. Maureen LAWRENCE
11 Exec VP Admin/Oprtns/Info Tech Svcs Dr. James SULTON
04 Executive Assistant to President Ms. Louise M. HORGAN
46 Vice Pres Plng/Dev/Govt & Comm Rels Dr. Webster B. TRAMMELL
31 Vice Pres Outreach Bus & Cmty Devel Dr. Linda MILSTEIN
13 Executive Director/OIT Dr. Patricia KAHN
84 Int Dean Enroll Dev/Student Affrs Mr. Richard PFEFFER
05 Dean of Academic Affairs Dr. Nancy KEGELMAN
15 Dean Human Resources Ms. Patricia SENSI
08 Executive Director Library Mr. David MURRAY
45 Exec Dir Planning/Assessment/Rsrch Mr. Arnold J. GELFMAN
27 Dir Communications & Public Rels Ms. Avis MCMILLON
102 Exec Dir Foundation/Alumni Affs Mr. Timothy ZEISS
18 Exec Dir Facilities Plng/Engnrng Mr. Richard FRANK
32 Director Stdnt Affs/Support Svcs Mr. Richard J. PFEFFER
88 Assoc Director/Creative Services Ms. Barbara PETERSON
37 Director of Financial Aid Ms. Stephanie FITZSIMMONS
25 Director Grants & Institutional Dev Ms. Laura V. QAISSAUNEE
38 Director Student Development Svcs Dr. Stephen A. CURTO
06 Registrar Ms. Kimberly TOOMEY
09 Dir of Institutional Research/Evalu Ms. Laura HEUSER
26 Dir of Marketing/Creative Services Ms. Laurie BENDER
96 Director Material & Printing Svcs Mr. Raimondi OTTO
28 Mgr Diversity/Inclusion/Compliance Ms. Sondra CANNON

Burlington County College (B)

601 Pemberton-Browns Mills Road,
Pemberton NJ 08068-1599
County: Burlington FICE Identification: 007730
Unit ID: 183877
Telephone: (609) 894-9311 Carnegie Class: Assoc/Pub-S-MC
FAX Number: (609) 894-0183 Calendar System: Semester
URL: www.bcc.edu
Established: 1966 Annual Undergrad Tuition & Fees (In-District): $3,615
Enrollment: 10,278 Coed
Affiliation or Control: State/Local IRS Status: 501(c)3
Highest Offering: Associate Degree
Program: Occupational; 2-Year Principally Bachelor's Creditable
Accreditation: M, ADNUR, DH, ENGT, RAD

01 Acting President Mr. Ronald BRAND
05 Vice President Academic Programs Dr. David SPANG
10 Vice Pres Finance/Admin Services Mr. Ronald BRAND
32 VP Student Svcs/Dean Cmty Enrich Dr. Kris DIXON
30 Interim VP College Advancement Dr. Beverly A. RICHARDSON
16 VP of Human Resources Mr. Dennis HAGGERTY
26 Dir of Marketing and Col Relations Ms. Valerie WINTER
09 Exec Dir of Institutional Research Mr. Max SLUSHER
14 Chief Information Technology Mr. Mark MEARA
81 Dean Science Math & Technology Dr. Victor BROWN
79 Dean of Liberal Arts Vacant
07 Director of Student Recruitment Ms. Dotti PURSLEY
88 Dean of Corporate College Mr. Ketan GANDHI
08 Director of the Library Ms. Michelle MARTIN
37 Financial Aid Director Mr. Michael CIOCE
38 Director Academic Advising/Transfer Dr. Robert ARIOSTO
25 Director of Grants Administration Ms. Barbara WITKOWSKI
06 Registrar Ms. Nyambura M. PHILLIPS
35 Dir of Stdnt Activities/Campus Pgms Ms. Catherine BRIGGS

19 Director of Security & Safety Mr. Hector GONZALEZ
66 Dean of Nursing/Allied Health Ms. Charlotte MCCARRAHER
21 Director Admin & Auxilliary Svcs Mr. Matthew FARR
24 Educational Tech Spec Distance Lrng Mr. Martin HOFFMAN
88 Director Construction Management Mr. Donald HUDSON
84 Exec Dir of Enroll Mgmt/Resrch/ Plng Ms. Mary Louise MASCARIN
18 Manager of Physical Plant Mr. John FRITSCH
103 Assoc Dean Business Development Ms. Sharon ROGERS
30 Exec Dir Development/Foundation Ms. Rebecca CORBIN
41 Director of Athletics Ms. Heather CONGER
96 Asst Director of Purchasing Mr. Chester HEINLEIN

Caldwell College (C)

120 Bloomfield Avenue, Caldwell NJ 07006-5310
County: Essex FICE Identification: 002598
Unit ID: 183910
Telephone: (973) 618-3000 Carnegie Class: Master's M
FAX Number: (973) 618-3300 Calendar System: Semester
URL: www.caldwell.edu
Established: 1939 Annual Undergrad Tuition & Fees: $27,890
Enrollment: 2,253 Coed
Affiliation or Control: Roman Catholic IRS Status: 501(c)3
Highest Offering: Doctorate
Program: Liberal Arts And General; Teacher Preparatory
Accreditation: M, ACBSP, CACREP, NURSE, TEAC

01 President Dr. Nancy BLATTNER
05 Vice President for Academic Affairs Dr. Patrick R. PROGAR
10 Vice President for Finance & Admin Mr. Jack T. RAINEY
16 VP Institutional Effectiveness Mrs. Sheila N. O'ROURKE
32 Vice President for Student Affairs Sr. Kathleen TUITE
84 Vice President for Enrollment Mgmt Mr. Joseph J. POSILLICO
30 Vice Pres Development/Alumni Affs Mr. Kevin BOYLE
50 Associate Dean Business Division Dr. Bernard C. O'ROURKE
53 Associate Dean Education Division Dr. Janice STEWART
35 Director International Student Svcs Mr. Andrew BRACKETT
88 Exec Director Student Success Ms. Joann GONZALEZ-GENERALS
44 Director Development Ms. Beth GORAB
29 Director of Gift Planning Ms. Kathleen BUSE
06 Registrar & Director Inst Research Mr. Michael E. MAYSILLES
08 College Librarian Vacant
07 Executive Director Admissions Mr. Stephen QUINN
58 Director Graduate Studies Ms. Vilma MUELLER
88 Assoc Dean External Partnerships Dr. Lisa DIBISCEGLIE
38 Director of Counseling Ms. Robin DAVENPORT
39 Director Residence Life Ms. Sandra GILOT
13 Exec Director Information Techn Vacant
36 Dir Career Plng & Development Ms. Geraldine PERRET
37 Director Financial Aid Mr. Hayato SUZUKI
42 Chaplain Fr. Albert J. BERNER
41 Executive Director of Athletics Mr. Mark A. CORINO
88 Director Technical Support Services Ms. Roselle LAZA-SCHMITZ
27 Dir Media Relations and Advertising Ms. Colette LIDDY
19 Director Campus Safety Mr. William B. ORTMAN
91 Director Administrative Technology Mr. David BOHNY
15 Dir Recruitment and Development Mrs. Michelle STAUSS
35 Director Student Activities Ms. Michele DEVOE

Camden County College (D)

PO Box 200, Blackwood NJ 08012-0200
County: Camden FICE Identification: 006865
Unit ID: 183938
Telephone: (856) 227-7200 Carnegie Class: Assoc/Pub-S-MC
FAX Number: (856) 374-4894 Calendar System: Semester
URL: www.camdencc.edu
Established: 1967 Annual Undergrad Tuition & Fees (In-District): $4,050
Enrollment: 14,613 Coed
Affiliation or Control: State/Local IRS Status: 501(c)3
Highest Offering: Associate Degree
Program: Occupational; 2-Year Principally Bachelor's Creditable
Accreditation: M, DA, DH, DIETT, MLTAD, OPD

01 President Dr. Raymond YANNUZZI
05 Vice Pres Academic Affairs Dr. Margaret HAMILTON
30 VP for Institutional Advancement Mr. William THOMPSON
41 Athletic Director Mr. Peter DILORENZO
15 Executive Director Human Resources Ms. Rose COSTON-MCHUGH
26 Dean Communications/Enroll Dev Ms. Rosemary SCHAMP
32 Actg Dean Student Support Services Ms. Jackie BALDWIN
96 Executive Director of Finance Mr. Steve BLATHERWICK
21 Acting Director Business Office Mr. Maris KUKAINIS
08 Library Refer & Instr Coordinator Ms. Miriam MLYNARSKI
10 Chief Fiscal Officer Ms. Patricia MEEHAN
37 Director of Financial Aid Ms. Felicia BRYANT
09 Dean Inst Research/Planning/Grants Dr. Marilyn FEINGOLD
18 Exec Dir Safety and Facilities Mr. Edward CARNEY
84 Exec Dean Enrollment/Student Svcs Dr. James CANONICA
07 Dir Admissions/Registration Svcs Ms. Danielle POWERS
12 Exec Dean William G Rohrer Center Dr. Robert KACZOROWSKI
81 Dean of Math & Science Dr. Susan CHOI
66 Dean Nursing/Health Sci/Human Svcs Dr. Anne M. MCGINLEY
50 Dean Div Business/Comptr/Tech Stds Dr. Melvin ROBERTS
12 Exec Dean Camden City Campus Mr. Gary DIVENS
36 Director Testing/Assessment Ms. Eve HIGHSTREET

Centenary College (E)

400 Jefferson Street, Hackettstown NJ 07840-2100
County: Warren FICE Identification: 002599
Unit ID: 183974
Telephone: (908) 852-1400 Carnegie Class: Master's M
FAX Number: (908) 850-9508 Calendar System: Semester
URL: www.centenarycollege.edu
Established: 1867 Annual Undergrad Tuition & Fees: $28,890
Enrollment: 2,644 Coed
Affiliation or Control: Independent Non-Profit IRS Status: 501(c)3
Highest Offering: Master's
Program: Liberal Arts And General; Teacher Preparatory
Accreditation: M, IACBE, SW, TEAC

01 President Dr. Barbara-Jayne LEWTHWAITE
05 Provost & Chief Academic Officer Dr. James PATTERSON
10 Chief Operating Officer Mr. Roger ANDERSON
26 Sr VP College Relations/Marketing Ms. Diane P. FINNAN
32 VP Student Engagement/Service Rev. David JONES
18 Assoc Vice Pres of Facilities Mr. Todd MILLER
31 Dean Community & College Affairs Ms. Nancy PAFFENDORF
07 Dean of Admissions/Financial Aid Ms. Glenna WARREN
09 Dean of Institutional Research Mr. Robert MILLER
06 Registrar/Academic Dean Mr. Thomas BRUNNER
08 Director Learning Services Ms. Suzanne MCCARTHY
36 Director Career Services Mr. Michael IRIS
15 Exec Director of Human Resources Ms. Virginia GALDIERI
23 Director of Health Services Ms. Jean ROBERT
41 Director of Athletics Ms. Billie Jo BLACKWELL
42 Chaplain Rev. David JONES
44 Exec Director Strategic Alliances Ms. Francine ANDREA
19 Director of Security Mr. Leonard CUNZ
38 Director of Counseling Center Ms. Lorna FARMER
29 Director of Alumni Ms. Deana CYNAR
13 Director Technology Services Mr. Matthew KELLY
40 Manager of the Bookstore Ms. Heidi MCDONNELL

The College of New Jersey (F)

2000 Pennington Road, Ewing NJ 08628-1104
County: Mercer FICE Identification: 002642
Unit ID: 187134
Telephone: (609) 771-1855 Carnegie Class: Master's L
FAX Number: (609) 637-5191 Calendar System: Semester
URL: www.tcnj.edu
Established: 1855 Annual Undergrad Tuition & Fees (In-State): $14,358
Enrollment: 6,927 Coed
Affiliation or Control: State IRS Status: 501(c)3
Highest Offering: Master's
Program: Liberal Arts And General; Teacher Preparatory; Professional
Accreditation: M, BUS, CACREP, CS, ENG, MUS, NURSE, TED

01 President Dr. R. Barbara GITENSTEIN
05 Interim Provost Dr. Susan BAKEWELL-SACHS
11 Vice Pres for Administration Mr. Curt HEURING
10 Treasurer Mr. Lloyd RICKETTS
43 General Counsel Mr. Thomas MAHONEY
30 Interim Vice Pres Advancement Mr. Peter MANETAS
32 Int Vice President Student Affairs Dr. Vicky TRIPONEY
15 Vice Pres Human Resources Dr. Gregory POGUE
84 Vice Pres Enrollment Management Ms. Lisa ANGELONI
101 Exec Asst to Pres/Secy to Board Ms. Heather FEHN
18 Assoc VP Facilities & Admin Svcs Ms. Kathryn LEVERTON
44 Assoc Vice President of Development Vacant
35 Assoc VP Student Affs/Dn Students Ms. Magda MANETAS
38 AVP Stdnt Affs/Dir Couns/Psych Svc Dr. Marc CELENTANA
20 Interim Vice Provost Dr. William BEHRE
57 Dean School of The Arts & Comm Dr. John LAUGHTON
50 Dean School of Business Dr. John KEEP
79 Dean Sch Humanities/Social Sciences Dr. Benjamin RIFKIN
53 Int Dean School of Education Dr. Mark KISELICA
54 Dean School of Engineering Dr. Steven SCHREINER
66 Int Dean Nursing/Hlth/Exercise Sci Dr. Marcia BLICHARZ
81 Dean School of Science Dr. Jeffrey OSBORN
58 Dir Grad & Intersession Programs Dr. Susan HYDRO
21 Assistant Treasurer Ms. Amy MERCOGLIANO
37 Dir of Student Financial Services Ms. Anne MACMORRIS
09 Asst Dir Ctr for Inst Effectiveness Dr. Debra FRANK
41 Director of Athletics Mr. John CASTALDO
35 Asst Vice Pres Student Affairs Ms. Cecelia O'CALLAGHAN
29 Director Alumni Affairs Ms. Lisa MCCARTHY
102 Dir Corp & Foundation Relations Mr. Gregory CAIOLA
18 Director of Campus Construction Mr. William RUDEAU
23 Assoc Director for Health Services Ms. Janice VERMEYCHUK
06 Exec Director Records/Registration Mr. Frank COOPER
19 Chief of Police/Dir Campus Police Chief John COLLINS
21 Director of Budgets & Purchasing Mr. Mark MEHLER
26 Exec Director College Relations Ms. Stacy SCHUSTER
28 Director of EEO/AA/Diversity Ms. Kerry TILLETT
07 Director of Admissions Ms. Grecia MONTERO

College of Saint Elizabeth (G)

2 Convent Road, Morristown NJ 07960-6989
County: Morris FICE Identification: 002600
Unit ID: 186618
Telephone: (973) 290-4000 Carnegie Class: Master's L
FAX Number: (973) 290-4488 Calendar System: Semester
URL: www.cse.edu
Established: 1899 Annual Undergrad Tuition & Fees: $29,901
Enrollment: 1,874 Coed
Affiliation or Control: Roman Catholic IRS Status: 501(c)3
Highest Offering: Doctorate

Program: Liberal Arts And General; Teacher Preparatory
Accreditation: M, DIETD, DIETI, NUR, TEAC

01 President .... Sr. Francis RAFTERY
05 VP Academic Affairs/Dean of Studies .... Vacant
32 VP Student Affairs/Dean of Students .... Ms. Katherine BUCK
10 VP Finance/Administration/Treasurer . Ms. Maria R. CAMMARATA
30 Vice Pres Institutional Advancement .... Ms. Deborah M. MCCREERY
07 Dean of Admission .... Ms. Donna TATARKA
58 Dean of Graduate Programs .... Dr. Jacqueline MCGLADE
20 Dean Women's College/Undergrad Stds .... Dr. Carol STROBECK
06 Registrar .... Ms. Laura Lee BOWENS GELLMAN
21 Controller .... Mr. Anthony COLABRARO
13 Chief Technology Officer .... Mr. Brad MORTON
09 Director Institutional Research .... Dr. Louise MURRAY
73 Act Dir Ctr Theol/Spiritual Devel .... Ms. Carol PISANI
08 Director of Library .... Ms. Amira UNVER
42 Campus Minister .... Ms. Marie NOEL
18 Director of Facilities .... Mr. Frank A. NEGLIA
37 Director of Financial Aid .... Ms. Debra WULFF
27 Director Marketing/ Communications .... Ms. Donna M. LINDEMEYER
22 Director EOF Program .... Ms. Carolina E. GONZALEZ
36 Director Career Services .... Ms. Teri CORSO
39 Director of Residence Life .... Ms. Meredith NOVKOVIC
38 Director of Counseling .... Ms. Sharon MCNULTY
88 Director of Volunteer Services .... Ms. Nanette SPEDDEN
35 Director of Student Activities .... Ms. Leigh Anne WALTERS
41 Director of Athletics .... Ms. Juliene SIMPSON
90 Director of Academic Computing .... Ms. Kathy MARINO
91 Dir Application Devel & Support .... Ms. Ana M. FIGUEROA
44 Director of Annual Fund .... Ms. Tanya SORCE
51 Asst Director Continuing Studies .... Sr. Gabriel M. DONAHUE
24 Director Media Services .... Mr. Ronald LONEKER
29 Exec Director Alumnae Association .... Ms. Debbie MARTIN
15 Director Human Resources .... Ms. Dianna SOFO
84 Director of Recruitment .... Vacant
85 Director Intl/Multicultural Affairs .... Ms. Lenee WOODSON
28 Asst Dir Intl/Multicultural Affairs .... Ms. Maya BLEY
19 Securitas Site Manager .... Mr. Donald GREEN
40 College Store Manager .... Ms. Amy HAUSMAN
04 Spec Asst to Pres Mission/Values .... Ms. Carol PISANI

County College of Morris (A)

214 Center Grove Road, Randolph NJ 07869-2086
County: Morris FICE Identification: 007729
Unit ID: 184180
Telephone: (973) 328-5000 Carnegie Class: Assoc/Pub-S-SC
FAX Number: (973) 328-1282 Calendar System: Semester
URL: www.ccm.edu
Established: 1965 Annual Undergrad Tuition & Fees (In-District): $4,155
Enrollment: 8,554 Coed
Affiliation or Control: State/Local IRS Status: 501(c)3
Highest Offering: Associate Degree
Program: Occupational; 2-Year Principally Bachelor's Creditable
Accreditation: M, ACBSP, ADNUR, ENGT, RAD

01 President .... Dr. Edward J. YAW
05 Vice President of Academic Affairs .... Dr. Dwight L. SMITH
10 Vice President of Business/Finance .... Ms. Karen VANDERHOOF
32 VP of Student Dev/Enrollment Mgmt .... Dr. Bette M. SIMMONS
30 Exec Dir Col Advancement/Planning .... Mr. Joseph VITALE
15 Dir Human Resources & Labor Rels .... Mr. Thomas BURK
09 Director Inst Research & Planning .... Dr. Charles SECOLSKY
21 Director Budget & Business Services .... Mr. John YOUNG
25 Director Resource Development .... Dr. Kevin KEEFE
07 Admissions Officer .... Ms. Jessica CHAMBERS
37 Director Financial Aid .... Mr. Harvey WILLIS
06 Associate Registrar .... Ms. Karen WHITMORE
06 Registrar .... Ms. Michelle DUNN
26 Chief Public Relations Officer .... Ms. Kathleen BRUNET EAGAN
29 Director Alumni Office .... Ms. Barbara CAPSOURAS
13 Director Information Systems .... Mr. Roger FLAHIVE
08 Director of Library Services .... Ms. Heather CRAVEN
36 Director Career Svcs/Coop Education .... Ms. Denise SCHMIDT
38 Counseling Services Coordinator .... Dr. Lorna JOASIL
79 Dean Liberal Arts .... Dr. Keith SMITH
76 Dean Health/Natural Sciences .... Ms. Joan CUNNINGHAM
81 Dean Business/Math/Engr/Technology .... Mr. Patrick ENRIGHT
31 Dean Corp & Community Programs .... Dr. Jane ARMSTRONG
19 Director Security & Safety .... Mr. Harvey JACKSON
41 Director Athletics .... Mr. Jack SULLIVAN
23 Health Services Coordinator .... Ms. Elizabeth HOBAN
18 Director of Plant & Maintenance .... Mr. Joseph PONTURO
96 Director of Purchasing .... Ms. Joanne KEARNS
40 Bookstore Manager .... Mr. Abdelilan ENNASSEF

Cumberland County College (B)

3322 College Drive, PO Box 1500,
Vineland NJ 08362-1500
County: Cumberland FICE Identification: 002601
Unit ID: 184205
Telephone: (856) 691-8600 Carnegie Class: Assoc/Pub-R-M
FAX Number: (856) 691-3876 Calendar System: Semester
URL: www.cccnj.edu
Established: 1963 Annual Undergrad Tuition & Fees (In-District): $4,170
Enrollment: 4,188 Coed
Affiliation or Control: State/Local IRS Status: 501(c)3
Highest Offering: Associate Degree
Program: Occupational; 2-Year Principally Bachelor's Creditable
Accreditation: M, ADNUR, RAD

01 President .... Dr. Thomas A. ISEKENEGBE
05 VP Academic Affairs/Enrollment Svcs .... Dr. Jacqueline GALBIATI
10 Vice President Finance & Admin Svcs .... Mr. John K. PITCHER
30 Exec Dir Grant Develop/Trustee Rels .... Ms. Anne M. BERGAMO
21 Director Finance & Budget .... Ms. Sherri L. WELCH
07 Director of Admissions .... Ms. Anne M. DALY-EIMER
32 Exec Dir Student Life/Campus Svcs .... Mr. Joseph L. HIBBS
08 Director Library Services .... Ms. Patti A. SCHMID
88 Ex Dir Ctr for Acad & Student Succ .... Dr. Maud FRIED-GOODNIGHT
26 Director Public Relations .... Mr. John S. NICHOLS
29 Exec Dir Foundation & Alumni .... Ms. Sue A. PERRY
35 Director Student Affairs .... Mr. Joseph L. HIBBS
37 Director Student Financial Aid .... Ms. Kim HENRY-MITCHELL
88 Dean University Ctr .... Dr. Terrence HARDEE
50 Dean Business/Educ/Social Sciences .... Dr. Charles KOCHER
51 Exec Dir Prof & Community Education .... Ms. Vicki SIMEK
76 Dean STEM/Health .... Ms. MaryAnn WESTERFIELD
57 Dean Arts & Humanities .... Mr. James PICCONE
100 Assistant to the President .... Ms. Anne M. BERGAMO
15 Executive Director Human Resources .... Ms. Patricia N. BRINING
72 Chief Technology Officer .... Mr. Douglas WHITE
18 Director Facilities & Grounds .... Mr. Brian EWAN
96 Purchasing Agent .... Ms. Cynthia OSTER
09 Exec Dir Plng/Research/Inst Effect .... Dr. Sandra D. VADEN
108 Director of Assessment .... Ms. Rebecca SHEPPARD
38 Director Adv/Trans & Career Svcs .... Dr. Steven M. STOLAR

DeVry University - North Brunswick Campus (C)

630 US Highway One, North Brunswick NJ 08902-3362
County: Middlesex FICE Identification: 009228
Unit ID: 184269
Telephone: (732) 729-3532 Carnegie Class: Bac/Assoc
FAX Number: (732) 729-3806 Calendar System: Semester
URL: www.devry.edu
Established: 1931 Annual Undergrad Tuition & Fees: $16,156
Enrollment: 1,796 Coed
Affiliation or Control: Proprietary IRS Status: Proprietary
Highest Offering: Baccalaureate
Program: Occupational; Professional; Business Emphasis
Accreditation: &NH, ENGT, NDT

01 Metro President .... Mr. Chris GREVESEN
05 Dean of Academic Affairs .... Mr. Joseph KONOPKA
07 Director of Admissions .... Ms. Lisa DOUGHERTY
36 Director of Career Services .... Ms. Laura PAKHMANOV
37 Director of Student Finance .... Mr. Albert CAMA
15 Human Resources Business Partner .... Ms. Wendy CHARLAP
72 Dean Technology Programs .... Mr. Tom KIST
06 Registrar .... Ms. Janine EMMA
08 Director of Library Services .... Mr. Joseph LOUDERBACK
38 Student Services Manager .... Ms. Lisa LYLE

† Regional accreditation is carried under the parent institution in Downers Grove, IL.

DeVry University - Paramus (D)

81 East State Route 4, Suite 102,
Paramus NJ 07652-2634
County: Bergen Identification: 666561
Telephone: (201) 556-2840 Carnegie Class: Not Classified
FAX Number: (201) 556-2863 Calendar System: Semester
URL: www.devry.edu
Established: 1931 Annual Undergrad Tuition & Fees: $16,176
Enrollment: 503 Coed
Affiliation or Control: Proprietary IRS Status: Proprietary
Highest Offering: Master's
Program: Liberal Arts And General; Business Emphasis
Accreditation: &NH

01 Center Dean .... Pavi JALLOH

† Regional accreditation is carried under the parent institution in Downers Grove, IL.

Drew University (E)

36 Madison Avenue, Madison NJ 07940-1493
County: Morris FICE Identification: 002603
Unit ID: 184348
Telephone: (973) 408-3000 Carnegie Class: Bac/A&S
FAX Number: N/A Calendar System: 4/1/4
URL: www.drew.edu
Established: 1866 Annual Undergrad Tuition & Fees: $41,688
Enrollment: 2,632 Coed
Affiliation or Control: Independent Non-Profit IRS Status: 501(c)3
Highest Offering: Doctorate
Program: Liberal Arts And General; Professional
Accreditation: M, @TEAC, THEOL

01 Interim President .... Dr. Vivian BULL
05 Provost & Academic Vice President .... Dr. Pamela J. GUNTER-SMITH
11 Vice President Admin/Univ Relations .... Mrs. Margaret HOWARD
30 Vice Pres Devel/Alumni Affairs .... Vacant
10 Vice Pres Finance/Business Affairs .... Vacant
20 Vice President & Dean of College .... Dr. Jonathan LEVIN
73 Vice Pres/Dean Theological School .... Dr. Jeffrey KUAN
29 Assoc VP Devel/Alumni/ae Affs .... Mr. Kenneth ALEXO
13 Asst VP University Technology .... Dr. Alan CANDIOTTI
07 Dean Col Admissions/Financial Asst .... Vacant
08 Dean of the Libraries .... Dr. Andrew SCRIMGEOUR
32 Dean Campus Life & Student Affs .... Dr. Sara WALDRON
26 Chief Communications Officer .... Mr. David MUHA
29 Director Alumni Affairs .... Ms. Melissa FUEST
15 Director of Human Resources .... Ms. Deborah RAIKES-COLBERT
22 Affirmative Action Officer .... Dr. George-Harold JENNINGS
90 Dir Instructional Technology Svcs .... Ms. Gamin BARTLE
91 Director Administrative Computing .... Vacant
21 Controller .... Mr. Frank MALTINO
96 Director Purchasing .... Mr. Harry C. SCARPA
18 Director Facilities Operations .... Mr. Michael KOPAS
37 Dir Finan Assistance/Col Admissions .... Ms. Renee VOLAK
19 Director Public Safety .... Mr. Thomas EVANS
23 Director Health Services .... Ms. Joyce MAGLION
39 Director Housing/Conf/Hospitality .... Ms. Patricia NAYLOR
35 Director Student Activities .... Ms. Michelle BRISSON
38 Director Counseling Services .... Dr. Jim MANDALA
36 Director Career Planning/Placement .... Ms. Patricia LAPREY
07 Director Theological Admissions .... Mr. Kevin D. MILLER
07 Director Graduate Admissions .... Ms. Carla BURNS
58 Dean of Casperson Sch Grad Stdy .... Dr. Richard GREENWALD
42 University Chaplain .... Rev. Tanya Lynn BENNETT
09 Director Institutional Research .... Dr. John MUCCIGROSSO
41 Director Athletics .... Mr. Jason FEIN
06 Registrar .... Mr. Horace TATE
28 Special Asst to Prov for Diversity .... Dr. Carlos YORDAN
40 Manager Bookstore .... Ms. Liz GALLO

Eastern International College (F)

3000 Kennedy Blvd, Ste 310, Jersey City NJ 07306
County: Hudson FICE Identification: 031226
Unit ID: 421878
Telephone: (201) 216-9901 Carnegie Class: Assoc/PrivFP
FAX Number: (201) 216-9225 Calendar System: Semester
URL: www.eicollege.edu
Established: 1990 Annual Undergrad Tuition & Fees: $22,500
Enrollment: 7,500 Coed
Affiliation or Control: Proprietary IRS Status: Proprietary
Highest Offering: Associate Degree
Program: Occupational
Accreditation: ACCSC

01 President .... Mr. Bashir MOHSEN
05 Vice President of Academic Affairs .... Dr. Mustafa MUSTAFA

Eastwick College (G)

10 South Franklin Turnpike, Ramsey NJ 07446
FICE Identification: 020537
Unit ID: 184959
Telephone: (201) 327-8877 Carnegie Class: Assoc/PrivFP
FAX Number: (201) 327-9054 Calendar System: Other
URL: www.eastwick.edu
Established: 1968 Annual Undergrad Tuition & Fees: $17,624
Enrollment: 953 Coed
Affiliation or Control: Proprietary IRS Status: Proprietary
Highest Offering: Associate Degree
Program: Occupational; 2-Year Principally Bachelor's Creditable; Nursing Emphasis
Accreditation: ACICS, SURGT

01 Corporate Systems Administrator .... Antonio JEREZ
05 Vice President Academic Affairs .... Rafael CASTILLA
32 Dean of Students .... Bobby DAVIES
37 Director of Financial Aid .... Christy DELAGUERRA

Essex County College (H)

303 University Avenue, Newark NJ 07102-1798
County: Essex FICE Identification: 007107
Unit ID: 184481
Telephone: (973) 877-3000 Carnegie Class: Assoc/Pub-U-MC
FAX Number: (973) 877-3044 Calendar System: Other
URL: www.essex.edu
Established: 1966 Annual Undergrad Tuition & Fees (In-District): $3,384
Enrollment: 12,532 Coed
Affiliation or Control: State/Local IRS Status: 501(c)3
Highest Offering: Associate Degree
Program: Occupational; 2-Year Principally Bachelor's Creditable
Accreditation: M, ADNUR, ENGT, OPD, PTAA, RAD

01 President .... Dr. Edythe M. ABDULLAH
05 Sr Vice Pres for Academic Affairs .... Dr. Gale E. GIBSON
101 Asst to Pres/Director Board Affairs .... Ms. June PERSAUD
10 Vice Pres & Chief Financial Ofcr .... Dr. Sherry HAWN
21 Comptroller .... Mr. Louis GENOVESE, JR.
45 Dean Planning/Inst Research .... Dr. Stephen KIESTER
20 Dean of Faculty .... Dr. Ladylease WHITE
20 Dean of Educational Services .... Dr. Felix LINFANTE
51 Dean Community & Cont Education .... Mr. Charles G. LOVALLO
13 Dean Information Technology/CIO .... Mr. Mohamed SEDDIKI
32 Dean of Student Affairs .... Dr. Susan C. MULLIGAN
09 Assoc Dean Plng/Research/Assessment .... Dr. J. Scott DRAKULICH
35 Asst Dean Student Affs/Enroll Svcs .... Ms. Marva MACK
12 Assoc Dean West Essex Campus .... Ms. Elvira VIEIRA
08 Director Learning Resource Center .... Mrs. Gwendolyn SLATON

35 Director Student Life & Activities .... Ms. Patricia SLADE
18 Asst to Vice Pres Facilities Mgmt .... Mr. Jeff SHAPIRO
19 Asst to Exec VP Public Safety .... Mr. Cromartie ANTHONY
26 Director of Public Relations .... Ms. Karen TINEBRA
30 Director of Development .... Ms. Annette WEIS
15 Director of Human Resources ....Ms. Jeannette ROBINSON
96 Director Purchasing ....Ms. Marylyn RUTHERFORD
37 Director Financial Aid ....Mrs. Mildred COFER
84 Asst Dean Student Affs/Enroll Svcs .... Ms. Zewdnesh KASSA
21 Director Office of Bursar .... Ms. Darlene MILLER
36 Director Career Resource Center ....Ms. Pamela MAYNARD
88 Director Child Development Center .... Ms. Deloris GRIMSLEY
41 Director Athletics ....Mr. Melvin KNIGHT
24 Dir Media Prod Technology (MPT) .... Ms. Nadine SHAW
78 Director Cooperative Education ....Ms. Marcia HOSPEDALES
55 Director of Evening/Weekend Svcs ....Mr. Ronald ROSS

Fairleigh Dickinson University (A)

1000 River Road, Teaneck NJ 07666-1996

County: Bergen | FICE Identification: 002607
Unit ID: 184603
Telephone: (201) 692-2000 | Carnegie Class: Master's L
FAX Number: N/A | Calendar System: Semester
URL: www.fdu.edu
Established: 1942 | Annual Undergrad Tuition & Fees: $32,852
Enrollment: 9,107 | Coed
Affiliation or Control: Independent Non-Profit | IRS Status: 501(c)3
Highest Offering: Doctorate
Program: Occupational; 2-Year Principally Bachelor's Creditable; Liberal Arts And General; Teacher Preparatory; Professional
Accreditation: M, BUS, CACREP, CLPSY, CS, ENG, ENGT, NURSE, @PHAR, TEAC

01 Interim President ....Mr. Sheldon DRUCKER
43 University Counsel/Secretary .... Mr. Wayne M. RICHARDSON
05 Univ Provost/VPAA ....Dr. Christopher CAPUANO
30 Sr Vice Pres University Advancement ....Mr. Richard REISS
03 Senior Vice President & CEO ....Mr. Sheldon DRUCKER
10 Vice Pres for Finance & Treasurer ....Ms. Hania FERRARA
11 Vice President for Administration .... Mr. Richard A. RICCIO
84 Vice Pres for Enrollment Management ....Mr. Jon WEXLER
13 VP/Chief Information Officer ....Mr. Neal M. STURM
26 Assistant VP for University Advance ....Mr. Angelo CARFAGNA
16 Univ Director for Human Resources .... Ms. Rose D'AMBROSIO
29 Director Alumni Affairs .... Mr. Okang MCBRIDE
12 Dean Petrocelli Col of Cont Stds ....Mr. Kenneth T. VEHRKENS
49 Dean Becton Col of Arts & Sci ....Dr. Geoffrey WEINMAN
50 Dean College Business Admin ....Dr. William MOORE
20 Dean University College ....Dr. Patti MILLS
32 Dean of Students-Teaneck
Campus .... Ms. Michelle MCCROY-HEINS
32 Dean of Students-Madison Campus ....Dr. Brian MAURO
08 Assoc University Librarian-Florham ....Ms. Maria WEBB
08 Associate University Librarian-Met .... Ms. Kathy STEIN-SMITH
51 Director Continuing Education ....Dr. Thomas SWANZEY
26 Dir Public Administration Institute ....Dr. William ROBERTS
38 Director Psychology ....Dr. Ronald DUMONT
21 Director Internal Audit ....Mr. Peter FORMAN
53 Director School of Education ....Dr. Vicki COHEN
66 Director Sch of Nurs/Allied Health .... Dr. Minerva GUTTMAN
88 Director Sch Hotel/Restaurant Mgmt ....Dr. Richard WISCH
41 Director of Athletics-Teaneck .... Mr. David LANGFORD
41 Director of Athletics-Madison ....Mr. William KLIKA
07 Univ Dir of Undergrad Admissions ....Mr. Andrew IPPOLITO
09 Director of Institutional Research .... Ms. Indira GOVINDAN
37 University Director Financial Aid ....Mr. Vincent TUNSTALL
19 Campus Dir Public Safety/F/M Campus .....Ms. Willie THORNTON
20 Provost Metropolitan Campus ....Dr. Joseph KIERNAN
12 Provost Florham/Madison Campus ....Dr. Kenneth GREENE
19 Univ Dir Public Safety/T/H Campus ....Mr. David A. MILES
96 Director of Purchasing .... Ms. Juliette BROOKS

Felician College (B)

262 S Main Street, Lodi NJ 07644-2198

County: Bergen | FICE Identification: 002610
Unit ID: 184612
Telephone: (201) 559-6000 | Carnegie Class: Master's S
FAX Number: (201) 559-6188 | Calendar System: Semester
URL: www.felician.edu
Established: 1942 | Annual Undergrad Tuition & Fees: $29,400
Enrollment: 2,361 | Coed
Affiliation or Control: Roman Catholic | IRS Status: 501(c)3
Highest Offering: Master's
Program: Liberal Arts And General; Teacher Preparatory; Professional
Accreditation: M, IACBE, NURSE, TEAC

01 President .... Dr. Anne PRISCO
03 Senior Exec Vice President ....Dr. Charles J. ROONEY
05 Provost/Vice Pres Acad Affairs ....Sr. Mary Rosita BRENNAN
20 Asst VP Academic Support Services ....Dr. Ann V. GUILLORY
30 Vice Pres Institutional Advancement ... Ms. Celeste A. ORANCHAK
10 Exec Vice Pres for Admin & Finance ....Mr. Marc J. CHALFIN
21 Vice President for Finance ....Mr. Michael FESCOE
32 Vice President for Student Affairs ...Sr. Tarcilia M. JUCHNIEWICZ
32 VP Stdnt Svcs/Admin Ruth Campus ....Ms. Susan M. CHALFIN
11 Interim VP for Admin Operations .... Mr. Arthur D. GOON
04 Admin Assistant to the President ....Vacant
06 Registrar .... Ms. June FINN
07 Assoc VP Undergrad Enroll Services ....Vacant
07 Assoc VP Adult/Grad & Intl Enroll ....Mr. Michael SZAREK

08 Director of the Library ....Mr. Paul GLASSMAN
09 Director Institutional Research ....Dr. Jerry TROMBELLA
15 Coordinator Human Resources ....Ms. Diane DEPADOVA
31 Director Community Svc Facilities .... Ms. Maria MALLIA
37 Director Student Financial Aid .... Ms. Janet MERLI
29 Director of Alumni Relations .... Ms. Lori WALKER
42 Director Campus Ministry/Chaplain .... Rev. Damian COLICCHIO
39 Director of Residence Life ....Ms. Laura BARRY
36 Director of Career Counseling .... Ms. Melissa FAULKNER
11 Director of Administrative Services .... Ms. Meggan O'NEILL
13 Director of Information Technology .... Mr. Christopher FINCH
24 Director A-V Center ....Mr. Anthony KLYMENKO
88 Assoc Director Center for Learning .... Mr. Hamdi SHAHIN
26 Director of Public Relations ....Ms. Angela DAIDONE
26 Dir Inst Marketing & Publications . Ms. Barbara PURDUE-LYNCH
40 Manager College Bookstore ....Ms. Beth LIGNOWSKI
76 Dean Div Nurs/Health Mgmt Sciences ....Dr. Muriel SHORE
53 Dean Division of Teacher Educ ....Dr. Rose RUDNITSKI
49 Dean Division of Arts & Science ....Dr. Edward KUBERSKY
50 Dean Div of Business Mgmt Sciences ....Dr. Beth CASTIGLIA
88 Dean Assessment/Fac Excellence ....Dr. Dolores HENCHY
88 Director EOF Program ....Ms. Dinelia GARDNER
104 Director Study Abroad Program .... Mr. Carlo COLECCHIA
85 Director of International Programs .... Ms. Corinne SPRING
23 Director Health Services .... Ms. Carolyn LEWIS
41 Director of Athletics .... Mr. Benjamin DI NALLO
92 Director Honors Program .... Dr. Maria VECCHIO
91 Director Administrative Computing ......Mr. John PANNEGGIANTE

Georgian Court University (C)

900 Lakewood Avenue, Lakewood NJ 08701-2697

County: Ocean | FICE Identification: 002608
Unit ID: 184773
Telephone: (732) 987-2200 | Carnegie Class: Master's L
FAX Number: N/A | Calendar System: Semester
URL: www.georgian.edu
Established: 1908 | Annual Undergrad Tuition & Fees: $28,460
Enrollment: 2,555 | Female
Affiliation or Control: Roman Catholic | IRS Status: 501(c)3
Highest Offering: Master's
Program: Liberal Arts And General; Teacher Preparatory; Professional
Accreditation: M, ACBSP, SW, TEAC

01 President .... Sr. Rosemary JEFFRIES
05 Provost .... Ms. Evelyn QUINN
10 Chief Financial Officer ....Mr. Robert KENNY
30 Spec Asst to Pres for Advancement .... Ms. Cynthia WHITNEY
20 Assoc Provost Academic Pgm Devel .... Dr. Michael GROSS
84 VP of Enrollment Management .... Mr. John MCAULIFFE
32 Dean of Students .... Ms. Karen GOFF
88 Director of Advising ....Mrs. Carol A. LIPPIN
42 Director of Campus Ministry ....Sr. Mariann MAHON
41 Director Athletics/Recreation ....Ms. Laura LIESMAN
88 Dir Academic Development Center ....Vacant
50 Dean School of Business ....Dr. Janice WARNER
53 Dean of School of Education .... Dr. Jacqueline KRESS
49 Dean School of Arts & Sciences ....Dr. Rita KIPP
09 Director of Institutional Research ....Mr. Wayne S. ARNDT
08 Director of Library Services .... Ms. Laura GEWISSLER
06 Registrar ....Vacant
21 Controller .... Mrs. Maureen RYAN-HOFFMAN
15 Director of Human Resources .... Dr. Lisa BIAGAS
13 Chief Information Officer ....Ms. Christine MEHOLIC
07 Asst Dir Undergraduate Admissions ....Ms. Maria COLON
37 Director of Student Financial Svcs ....Ms. Linda PAGAN
26 Dir Public Rels/Col Communications ....Ms. Gail TOWNS
31 Dir Conferences & Special Events ....Ms. Mary E. CRANWELL
29 Director of Alumni Engagement ....Ms. Lauren TRAYLOR
36 Director Career Development ....Mrs. Catherine MOORE
38 Director of Counseling ....Dr. Robin SOLBACH
23 Director Student Health Services ....Vacant
22 Affirmative Action Officer .... Dr. Lisa BIAGAS
18 Director of Facilities .... Mr. Mark BIANCHI
96 Director of Purchasing ....Mr. Thomas BARANOWSKI
19 Director of Security .... Mr. Thomas ZAMBRANO
09 Dir Ofc Assessment/Intl Research .... Dr. Pamela SCHNEIDER
07 Director Graduate Admissions .... Mr. Patrick GIVENS
44 Director of Annual Giving ....Ms. Jennifer LOYSEN
39 Coordinator Residence Life .... Ms. Crystal LOPEZ

Gloucester County College (D)

1400 Tanyard Road, Sewell NJ 08080-9518

County: Gloucester | FICE Identification: 006901
Unit ID: 184791
Telephone: (856) 468-5000 | Carnegie Class: Assoc/Pub-S-SC
FAX Number: N/A | Calendar System: 4/1/4
URL: www.gccnj.edu
Established: 1966 | Annual Undergrad Tuition & Fees (In-District): $3,570
Enrollment: 6,829 | Coed
Affiliation or Control: State/Local | IRS Status: 501(c)3
Highest Offering: Associate Degree
Program: Occupational; 2-Year Principally Bachelor's Creditable
Accreditation: M, ADNUR, DMS, NMT

01 President .... Mr. Frederick KEATING
05 Provost and VP Academic Svcs ....Mr. John HENZY
03 Vice President & COO .... Mr. Dominick BURZICHELLI
32 Vice President Student Svcs .... Ms. Judith ATKINSON
10 Exec Director Financial Services ....Mrs. Elizabeth HALL
16 Exec Director Human Resource .... Ms. Danielle MORGANTI

04 Exec Assistant to the President ....Mrs. Karen SITARSKI
22 Exec Dir Diversity and Equity ....Mrs. Almarie JONES
09 Exec Dir Inst Research & Assessment ....Ms. Karen DURKIN
13 Chief Information Officer ....Mr. Josh R. PIDDINGTON
66 Dean Nursing & Allied Health ....Dr. Susan HALL
49 Dean Liberal Arts ....Dr. Paul RUFINO
81 Dean STEM ....Ms. Barbara TURNER
05 Dean Curriculum & Instruction .... Ms. Barbara NIENSTEDT
68 Dean Health/Physical Educ/Rec ....Mr. Ron CASE
88 Dean Public Safety & Security ....Mr. Fred H. MADDEN
50 Dean Business Studies & CE ....Ms. Patricia CLAGHORN
07 Director Admissions/Registrar .... Ms. Sandra HOFFMAN
36 Director Advising ....Mr. Richard BROWN
35 Director Student Affairs ....Ms. Hilda SANTIAGO
08 Director Library Services ....Mrs. Jane S. CROCKER

Hudson County Community College (E)

25 Journal Square, 14th Floor, Jersey City NJ 07306-4301

County: Hudson | FICE Identification: 012954
Unit ID: 184995
Telephone: (201) 714-7100 | Carnegie Class: Assoc/Pub-U-SC
FAX Number: (201) 656-1799 | Calendar System: Semester
URL: www.hccc.edu
Established: 1974 | Annual Undergrad Tuition & Fees (In-District): $4,530
Enrollment: 9,414 | Coed
Affiliation or Control: State/Local | IRS Status: 501(c)3
Highest Offering: Associate Degree
Program: Occupational; 2-Year Principally Bachelor's Creditable
Accreditation: M, ACFEI

01 President ....Dr. Glen E. GABERT
05 Vice President Academic Affairs ....Dr. Eric FRIEDMAN
10 Vice President for Finance ....Mr. John SOMMER
30 VP Development/Asst to President ....Mr. Joseph SANSONE
11 Vice President College Operations .... Mr. Frank MERCADO
32 VP North Hudson Ctr/Student Affairs ....Ms. Paula PANDO
88 Dean for Non Traditional Programs ....Dr. Jennifer DUDLEY
09 Assoc Dean Institutional Rsrch/Plng .... Mr. Kris KRISHNAN
20 Assistant Dean Academic Affairs .... Dr. Chanida KATKANANT
84 Assoc Dean Enrollment Services ....Mr. Peter VIDA
50 Assoc Dean Business and
Science .... Ms. Catherine SIRANGELO-ELBADAWY
79 Associate Dean English/Humanities .... Ms. Linda RODRIQUES
37 Assoc Dean Student Financial
Asst .... Ms. Pamela F. NORRIS-LITTLES
35 Associate Dean for Student Services ....Mr. Michael REIMER
88 Assoc Dean ESL/Bilingual & Dev Educ ....Vacant
06 Registrar .... Ms. Victoria ORELLANA
13 Chief Information Officer ....Mr. Vincent ZICOLELLO
07 Director of Admissions ....Mr. Jose OLIVARES
20 Dean of Arts and Sciences .... Mr. Chris WAHL
88 Director Testing & Assessment ....Ms. Darlery FRANCO
88 Director EOF .... Ms. Sabrina MAGLIULO
88 Executive Director Culinary Arts ....Mr. Paul DILLON
76 Director Health Related Programs ....Ms. Susanne SANSEVERE
88 Ex Dir Ctr Bus/Industry/Cntrct Trng ....Vacant
45 Director Academic Foundations ....Vacant
18 Director of Facilities .... Mr. Joseph TORTURELLI
21 Controller ....Mr. Robert CRUZ
25 Director of Grants .... Mr. Ryan MARTIN
08 Librarian .... Ms. Cynthia COULTER
35 Director Student Activities .... Ms. Ophelia MORGAN
26 Director of Communications ....Ms. Jennifer CHRISTOPHER
28 Director of Diversity .... Ms. Randi MILLER
29 Director Alumni Relations/Devel ....Mr. Joseph SANSONE
15 Executive Director Human Resources .... Ms. Randi MILLER
38 Director Advisement & Counseling .... Ms. Rose CUNNINGHAM
40 Manager HCCC Bookstore .... Ms. Christine SALZMAN
96 Manager Purchasing .... Mr. Alus GREEN
88 Coordinator Medical Assisting .... Ms. Judith A. BENDER
36 Coordinator Career & Transfer Svc .. Ms. Karine PIERRE-PIERRE

Immaculate Conception Seminary of Seton Hall University (F)

400 S Orange Avenue, South Orange NJ 07079-2646

County: Essex | FICE Identification: 002611
Unit ID: 185004
Telephone: (973) 761-9575 | Carnegie Class: Not Classified
FAX Number: (973) 761-9577 | Calendar System: Semester
URL: www.shu.edu
Established: 1861 | Annual Undergrad Tuition & Fees: $32,230
Enrollment: 283 | Coed
Affiliation or Control: Roman Catholic | IRS Status: 501(c)3
Highest Offering: Master's
Program: Professional
Accreditation: &M, THEOL

01 Rector and Dean ....Msgr. Joseph R. REILLY
10 Vice Rector/Business Manager ....Rev. Robert K. SUSZKO
05 Associate Dean ....Rev. Christopher M. CICCARINO
20 Associate Dean ....Dr. Dianne M. TRAFLET
88 Assoc Dean Undergraduate
Programs .... Rev. Douglas J. MILEWSKI
88 Director of Foundation .... Rev. Renato J. BAUTISTA
42 Spiritual Director .... Msgr. Gerard H. MCCARREN
08 Director of Seminary Library ....Rev. Lawrence B. PORTER
30 Director of Development ....Mrs. Catherine A. CUNNING

07 Academic Svcs & Admissions Coord ... Mrs. Diane M. CARR

† Regional accrediation is carried under the parent institution in South Orange, NJ.

Kean University (A)

1000 Morris Avenue, Union NJ 07083-0411
County: Union FICE Identification: 002622
Unit ID: 185262
Telephone: (908) 737-5326 Carnegie Class: Master's L
FAX Number: (908) 737-4636 Calendar System: Semester
URL: www.kean.edu
Established: 1855 Annual Undergrad Tuition & Fees (In-State): $10,600
Enrollment: 16,187 Coed
Affiliation or Control: State IRS Status: 501(c)3
Highest Offering: Doctorate
Program: Liberal Arts And General; Teacher Preparatory; Professional
Accreditation: #M, ART, CACREP, CIDA, MUS, NUR, OT, SP, SPAA, SW, TED, THEA

01 President ... Dr. Dawood FARAHI
10 Exec VP for Operations ... Mr. Philip CONNELLY
101 Exec Asst Board/Exec Dir Media/Pub ... Ms. Audrey KELLY
05 Vice Pres Academic Affairs ... Dr. Jeffrey TONEY
30 Vice Pres Institutional Advancement ... Dr. Kristie REILLY
32 Vice President for Student Affairs ... Ms. Janice MURRAY-LAURY
20 Assoc VP for Academic Affairs ... Dr. Katerina ANDRIOTIS-BAITINGER
12 Assoc VP/Dean Kean Ocean ... Vacant
58 Dean Nathan Weiss Grad Col ... Vacant
53 Dean Col Education ... Dr. Susan POLIRSTOK
79 Actg Dean Col Humanities/Social Sci ... Dr. Suzanne BOUSQUET
81 Acting Dean Col Nat & Appl Hlth Sci ... Dr. George CHANG
50 Dean Col Business & Public Admin ... Vacant
57 Dean Col Visual & Performing Arts ... Dr. George ARASIMOWICZ
15 Director Human Resources ... Mr. Faruque CHOWDHURY
07 Director for Undergrad Admissions ... Ms. Valerie WINSLOW
06 Registrar ... Mr. Ken WOLPIN
08 University Librarian ... Mr. Luis RODRIGUEZ
27 Dir Media & Publications ... Mr. Matt CARUSO
21 Dir Student Financial Services ... Mr. Charlie XU
25 Director Research & Sponsored Pgms ... Ms. Susan GANNON
09 Director Institutional Research ... Dr. Shiji SHEN
108 Director for Accredit & Assessment ... Dr. Edward BARBONI
37 Acting Director Financial Aid ... Ms. Sherrell WATSON-HALL
39 Director Residence Life ... Ms. Maximina RIVERA
38 Dir Counseling & Disability Servs ... Dr. Andrew LEE
41 Director for Athletics ... Mr. Chris MORGAN
29 Director Alumni Relations ... Ms. Adriana BRENNAN
96 Director for Purchasing ... Mr. George THORN
18 Dir Facilities & Campus Planning ... Ms. Phyllis DUKE
88 Director for Sustainability ... Dr. Nicholas SMITH-SEBASTO
23 Director for Health Services ... Ms. Lori PURWIN
22 Director Affirmative Action ... Dr. Charlie WILLIAMS
14 Dir Office for Computer/Inform Svcs ... Mr. Anthony SANTORA
35 Dir Center for Leadership & Service ... Mr. Scott SNOWDEN
36 Dir Career Development & Adv ... Dr. Steven KUBOW
104 Dir Center International Studies ... Dr. Stephen FERST
88 Veterans Affairs ... Ms. Lilliam BANNER
19 Acting Director of Campus Police ... Mr. Adam SHUBSDA
43 University Counsel ... Mr. Michael TRIPODI
42 Chaplain for Campus Ministry ... Vacant

Mercer County Community College (B)

1200 Old Trenton Road, PO Box 17202, Trenton NJ 08690-1099
County: Mercer FICE Identification: 004740
Unit ID: 185509
Telephone: (609) 586-4800 Carnegie Class: Assoc/Pub-R-L
FAX Number: (609) 570-3870 Calendar System: Semester
URL: www.mccc.edu
Established: 1966 Annual Undergrad Tuition & Fees (In-District): $4,140
Enrollment: 9,304 Coed
Affiliation or Control: State/Local IRS Status: 501(c)3
Highest Offering: Associate Degree
Program: Occupational; 2-Year Principally Bachelor's Creditable
Accreditation: M, AAB, ADNUR, FUSER, MLTAD, PTAA, RAD

01 President ... Dr. Patricia C. DONOHUE
30 Vice President College Advancement ... Dr. Mellissia ZANJANI
05 Vice President Academic Affairs ... Dr. Donald GENERALS
11 Vice President for Admin & CBO ... Mr. Jacob EAPEN
32 Exec Dean for Student Affairs ... Dr. Diane CAMPBELL
76 Dean Sciences/Health Professions ... Dr. Linda MARTIN
49 Dean Liberal Arts ... Dr. Robin SCHORE
50 Dean Business and Technology ... Ms. Judith A. EHRESMAN
31 Ast Dean-JKC-Acad Pgm/Evening Svcs ... Mr. Edward W. FREDERICK
35 Asst Dean Student Services ... Mr. John SIMONE
13 Exec Dir for Info Technology Svcs ... Ms. Susan BOWEN
21 Exec Dir of Finance ... Mr. Walter BROOKS
26 Dir Marketing/Public Information ... Ms. Lynn HOLL
15 Exec Dir for Compliance & Human Res ... Mr. Jose FERNANDEZ
06 Registrar ... Ms. Joan GUGGENHEIM
37 Director of Financial Aid ... Mr. Jason TAYLOR
09 Director Institutional Research ... Ms. Nina MAY
18 Chief Facilities/Physical Plant ... Mr. Bryon MARSHALL
96 Director of Purchasing ... Mr. Stephen GREGOROWICZ
07 Director of Admissions & Outreach ... Ms. Savita BAMBHROLIA

38 Director Student Counseling ... Ms. Laurene JONES
84 Director Enrollment Management ... Ms. Latonya ASHFORD-LIGON
29 Manager of Alumni Relations ... Ms. Amy FRANGIONE

Mesivta Keser Torah (C)

503 Eleventh Avenue, Belmar NJ 07719-2407
County: Monmouth FICE Identification: 041803
Unit ID: 461847
Telephone: (732) 367-4259 Carnegie Class: Not Classified
FAX Number: (732) 681-7171 Calendar System: Semester
Established: 1991 Annual Undergrad Tuition & Fees: $13,400
Enrollment: 50 Male
Affiliation or Control: Independent Non-Profit IRS Status: 501(c)3
Highest Offering: Baccalaureate
Program: Liberal Arts And General; Professional; Religious Emphasis
Accreditation: RABN

01 President ... Rabbi Dovid HEINEMANN

Middlesex County College (D)

2600 Woodbridge Avenue, Edison NJ 08818-3050
County: Middlesex FICE Identification: 002615
Unit ID: 185536
Telephone: (732) 548-6000 Carnegie Class: Assoc/Pub-S-SC
FAX Number: (732) 494-8244 Calendar System: Semester
URL: www.middlesexcc.edu
Established: 1964 Annual Undergrad Tuition & Fees (In-District): $4,095
Enrollment: 13,078 Coed
Affiliation or Control: State/Local IRS Status: 501(c)3
Highest Offering: Associate Degree
Program: Occupational; 2-Year Principally Bachelor's Creditable
Accreditation: M, ADNUR, DH, DIETT, ENGT, MLTAD, RAD

01 President ... Dr. Joann LA PERLA-MORALES
05 Vice President Academic Affairs ... Dr. Karen HAYS
10 Vice Pres Finance & Administration ... Ms. Susan K. PERKINS
30 VP for Institutional Advancement ... Mr. Patrick MADAMA
84 Dean Enrollment Management ... Ms. Marla BRINSON
107 Dean Professional Studies ... Ms. Marilyn LASKOWSKI-SACHNOFF
49 Dean Arts and Sciences ... Mr. David EDWARDS
31 Dean Corporate & Commuity Education ... Ms. Mary Ann CONNERS
18 Exec Director Facilities Management ... Mr. Donald DROST
14 Exec Director Information Tech ... Mr. Neil SACHNOFF
21 Controller ... Ms. Lori WILKIN
07 Asst Dean of Admissions ... Ms. Aretha WATSON
06 Registrar ... Mr. Richard COLE
36 Director of Counseling/Career Svcs ... Vacant
37 Financial Aid Director ... Vacant
08 Director Learning Resources ... Mr. Mark THOMPSON
26 Chief Public Relations Officer ... Mr. Thomas PETERSON
96 Director of Purchasing ... Mr. David FRICKE

Monmouth University (E)

400 Cedar Avenue, West Long Branch NJ 07764-1898
County: Monmouth FICE Identification: 002616
Unit ID: 185572
Telephone: (732) 571-3400 Carnegie Class: Master's L
FAX Number: (732) 571-3629 Calendar System: Semester
URL: www.monmouth.edu
Established: 1933 Annual Undergrad Tuition & Fees: $29,710
Enrollment: 6,570 Coed
Affiliation or Control: Independent Non-Profit IRS Status: 501(c)3
Highest Offering: Doctorate
Program: 2-Year Principally Bachelor's Creditable; Liberal Arts And General; Teacher Preparatory; Professional
Accreditation: M, BUS, CACREP, ENG, NURSE, SW, TED

01 President ... VADM. Paul G. GAFFNEY, II
04 Executive Assistant to President ... Mrs. Annette GOUGH
101 Special Asst Board of Trustees ... Ms. Janet FELL
05 Vice Pres Academic Affs/Provost ... Dr. Thomas PEARSON
20 Vice Provost/Dean Graduate School ... Dr. Datta V. NAIK
49 Dean Sch Humanities/Social Science ... Dr. Stanton GREEN
50 Dean Leon Hess Business Sch ... Prof. Donald MOLIVER
53 Dean School of Education ... Dr. Lynn ROMEO
81 Dean School of Science ... Dr. Michael PALLADINO
66 Dean School of Nursing/Health Stds ... Dr. Janet MAHONEY
70 Dean School of Social Work ... Dr. Robin MAMA
92 Dean Honors School ... Dr. Kevin DOOLEY
08 Dean of Library ... Dr. Ravindra SHARMA
10 Vice President Finance ... Mr. William G. CRAIG
21 Assoc VP for Finance/Budgets ... Mr. Jack GAVIN
96 Director of Purchasing ... Mr. Mark MIRANDA
43 Vice President & General Counsel ... Mr. Grey DIMENNA
88 Dir of Compliance/Staff Attorney ... Ms. Melissa DALE
22 Dir Equity and Diversity ... Mr. Julian WILLIAMS
11 Vice President Administrative Svcs ... Mrs. Patricia SWANNACK
18 Assoc VP Campus Plng/Construction ... Mr. Robert CORNERO
19 Director/Chief of Police ... Capt. William MCELRATH
15 Director of Human Resources ... Ms. Robyn SALVO
32 VP Student & Community Services ... Mrs. Mary Anne NAGY
35 Assoc VP for Student Services ... Mr. James PILLAR
35 Dir Student Activities/Student Ctr ... Ms. Amy BELLINA
26 Director of Public Affairs ... Ms. Petra LUDWIG
30 Vice Pres University Advancement ... Vacant
29 Director of Alumni Affairs ... Ms. Marilynn PERRY
84 Vice Pres Enrollment Management ... Dr. Robert MC CAIG

37 Assoc VP/Director Financial Aid ... Ms. Claire ALASIO
07 Assistant VP Undergrad Admissions ... Ms. Lauren VENTO-CIFELLI
07 Director Graduate Admission ... Mr. Kevin ROANE
41 Vice Pres & Director of Athletics ... Dr. Marilyn MCNEIL
13 Vice Pres Information Management ... Dr. Edward CHRISTENSEN
108 Assoc VP Acad & Inst Assessment ... Dr. David STROHMETZ
09 Director of Institutional Research ... Dr. Eleanor SWANSON
06 Assoc VP Academic Admin/Registrar ... Ms. Susan O'KEEFE
38 Dean of the Center for Student Succ ... Dr. Mercy AZEKE
36 Assistant Dean for Career Services ... Mr. William HILL
20 Assoc VP for Global Initiatives ... Dr. Saliba SARSAR
86 Dir of Gov & Community Relations ... Mr. Paul DEMENT

Montclair State University (F)

1 Normal Avenue, Montclair NJ 07043-9987
County: Essex and Passaic FICE Identification: 002617
Unit ID: 185590
Telephone: (973) 655-4000 Carnegie Class: Master's L
FAX Number: N/A Calendar System: Semester
URL: www.montclair.edu
Established: 1908 Annual Undergrad Tuition & Fees (In-State): $10,975
Enrollment: 18,498 Coed
Affiliation or Control: State IRS Status: 501(c)3
Highest Offering: Doctorate
Program: Liberal Arts And General; Teacher Preparatory; Professional
Accreditation: M, ART, AUD, BUS, CACREP, CS, DANCE, DIETD, DIETI, MUS, SP, TED, THEA

01 President ... Dr. Susan A. COLE
05 Provost/Vice Pres Academic Affairs ... Dr. Willard P. GINGERICH
10 Vice President Finance & Treasurer ... Mr. Donald D. CIPULLO
32 Vice Pres Student Devel/Campus Life ... Dr. Karen L. PENNINGTON
30 Vice Pres University Advancement ... Mr. John T. SHANNON
16 Vice President Human Resources ... Ms. Judith E. HAIN
18 Vice Pres Univ Facilities ... Mr. Gregory W. BRESSLER
13 VP Information Technology ... Dr. Edward V. CHAPEL
43 University Counsel ... Ms. Valerie L. VAN BAAREN
86 Director Government Relations ... Ms. Shivaun P. GAINES
45 Exec Director Budget and Planning ... Mr. David JOSEPHSON
101 Special Asst to the President ... Dr. Frank J. SCHWARTZ
79 Dean College Humanities/Soc Scis ... Dr. Marietta MORRISSEY
81 Dean College Science & Math ... Dr. Robert S. PREZANT
53 Dean Col Education & Human Svcs ... Dr. Francine PETERMAN
57 Dean College of the Arts ... Dr. Daniel A. GURSKIS
50 Dean School of Business ... Dr. E. LaBrent CHRITE
08 Dean of Library Services ... Dr. Judith L. HUNT
20 Dean of Grad School ... Dr. Joan C. FICKE
35 Dean of Students ... Dr. Rose Mary HOWELL
84 Assoc VP Enrollment/Stdnt Acad Sup ... Dr. Bryan J. TERRY
20 Vice Provost for Learning and Teach ... Vacant
58 Vice Provost for Research ... Vacant
20 Assoc Provost Acad Pgm/Assessment ... Dr. Joanne F. COTE-BONANNO
18 Assoc Vice Pres Facilities Svcs ... Dr. Timothy CAREY
18 Assoc VP Design & Construction ... Mr. Charles SARAJIAN
18 Assoc VP Facilities Maintenance ... Mr. Shawn CONNOLLY
18 Exec Dir Facil Maintnc/Engineering ... Mr. Walter D. EDDY
91 Asso VP Enterprise Software/Dep CIO ... Ms. Carolyn M. ORTEGA
35 Assoc VP Student Dev/Campus Life ... Ms. Kathleen E. RAGAN
15 Asst VP Univ Staffing Services ... Ms. Catherine N. BONGO
15 Asst VP Employee Relations ... Mr. Michael G. OWEN
64 Director School of Music ... Dr. Robert CART
09 Director Institutional Research ... Dr. Steven L. JOHNSON
06 Registrar ... Ms. Denise M. DEBLASIO
07 Director Undergraduate Admissions ... Ms. Lisa A. KASPER
30 Assoc VP Univ Advancement ... Ms. Carol A. BLAZEJOWSKI
30 Assoc VP Univ Advancement ... Ms. Jane M. BOYLE
26 Exec Dir Strategic Communications ... Ms. Deborah GAINES
26 Dir Marketing and Graphic Svcs ... Ms. Claudia BOGRIS
31 Exec Dir Community Rel/Univ Events ... Ms. Julie ADAMS
29 Exec Dir Alumni Relations ... Ms. Jeanne MARANO
19 Chief of University Police ... Mr. Paul M. CELL
22 Dir EO/Affirmative Action/Diversity ... Ms. Barbara J. MILTON
38 Director Counseling/Psych Services ... Dr. Jaclyn FRIEDMAN-LOMBARDO
39 Exec Director Residential Ed/Svcs ... Mr. Dominic A. PETRUZZELLI
40 General Mgr University Bookstore ... Mr. Richard AMMERMAN
41 Director Intercollegiate Athletics ... Ms. Holly P. GERA
37 Director Financial Aid ... Mr. James T. ANDERSON
56 Assoc Dean Extended Learning ... Mr. Jamieson A. BILELLA
36 Exec Dir Ctr Career Svcs/Coop Educ ... Ms. Carolyn D. JONES
96 Dir Procurement/Fin Div Admin ... Ms. Nancy G. CARVER
88 Exec Director Center for Advising ... Ms. Michele CAMPAGNA
92 Director Honors Program ... Dr. Gregory L. WATERS
21 Asst VP for Finance & Controller ... Ms. Catherine A. CORYAT
21 Director of Student Accounts ... Ms. Marion CAGGIANO
23 Director University Health Center ... Ms. Donna M. BARRY
104 Exec Director International Affairs ... Ms. Marina CUNNINGHAM
28 Director Equity and Diversity ... Ms. Esmilda M. ABREU-HORNBOSTEL
25 Dir Research & Sponsored Programs ... Mr. Tedq RUSSO
88 Asst Dean for Student Life ... Ms. Fatima DECARVALHO
105 Dir Web Services ... Ms. Cindy L. MENEGHIN
04 Exec Asst to the President ... Ms. Phyllis L. WOOSTER
42 Chaplain ... Fr. James CHERN
88 Director Fin Systems Administration ... Ms. Catherine I. RUSH
88 Dir Construction Procurement ... Mr. Daniel ROCHE
88 Asst VP Enterprise Tech Services ... Mr. Jeff GIACOBBE
88 Exec Dir Advancement Services ... Ms. Jeanette HANLEIN
88 Dir Campus Planning ... Mr. Michael ZANKO
88 Dir Tech Training and Integration ... Ms. Yanling SUN
88 Dir Environmental Health and Safety ... Ms. Amy FERDINAND

New Brunswick Theological Seminary (A)

17 Seminary Place, New Brunswick NJ 08901-1196
County: Middlesex FICE Identification: 002619
Unit ID: 185758
Telephone: (732) 247-5241 Carnegie Class: Spec/Faith
FAX Number: (732) 249-5412 Calendar System: Semester
URL: www.nbts.edu
Established: 1784 Annual Graduate Tuition & Fees: $10,296
Enrollment: 187 Coed
Affiliation or Control: Reformed Church In America IRS Status: 501(c)3
Highest Offering: Doctorate; No Undergraduates
Program: Professional; Religious Emphasis
Accreditation: THEOL

01 President ... Dr. Gregg A. MAST
04 Assistant to the President ... Ms. Yasha PEOPLE
05 Dean of the Seminary ... Dr. Renee HOUSE
10 Director Finance & Administration ... Mr. Allan BENISH
21 Controller ... Mr. Kenneth TERMOTT
32 Dean of Students ... Dr. Jessica DAVIS
30 Director of Development ... Mrs. Catherine PROCTOR
08 Director of Library ... Mr. Christopher BRENNAN
06 Registrar & Assistant Dean of AA ... Ms. Sharon A. WATTS
07 Admissions Committee Chair ... Dr. Beth L. TANNER

New Jersey City University (B)

2039 Kennedy Boulevard, Jersey City NJ 07305-1597
County: Hudson FICE Identification: 002613
Unit ID: 185129
Telephone: (201) 200-2000 Carnegie Class: Master's L
FAX Number: (201) 200-2352 Calendar System: Semester
URL: www.njcu.edu
Established: 1927 Annual Undergrad Tuition & Fees (In-State): $10,422
Enrollment: 8,328 Coed
Affiliation or Control: State IRS Status: 501(c)3
Highest Offering: Master's
Program: Liberal Arts And General; Teacher Preparatory; Professional
Accreditation: M, ACBSP, ART, MUS, NUR, TEAC, TED

01 President ... Dr. Sue HENDERSON
05 Vice Pres Academic Affairs ... Dr. Joanne Z. BRUNO
32 Vice Pres for Student Affairs ... Dr. John MELENDEZ
11 Vice Pres Administration/Finance ... Dr. Aaron ASKA
30 Interim VP University Advancement ... Mr. William FELLENBERG
21 Controller ... Ms. Mary BOLOWSKI
13 Assoc VP Computer Inform Systems ... Mr. Robert MCBRIDE
18 Assoc VP Facil/Construction Mgmt ... Mr. Andrew CHRIST
25 Assoc VP AA/Director of Grants ... Mr. Ruddys ANDRADE
07 Assoc VP Admissions/Enrollment Mgmt ... Dr. Carmen PANLILIO
20 Asst Vice Pres Academic Affs ... Dr. Deborah WOO
26 Asst VP Pub Info/Community Rel . Ms. Ellen WAYMAN-GORDON
14 Asst VP Information Technology ... Ms. Phyllis SZANI
88 Interim Asst VP Univ Advancement ... Mr. Michael PERNA
35 Asst Vice Pres Student Affairs ... Mr. Demond HARGROVE
101 Exec Asst to Pres/Sec for Board ... Mr. Alfred RAMEY
04 Executive Asst to the President ... Ms. Maria COBARRUBIAS
49 Dean Arts & Sciences ... Dr. Barbara FELDMAN
58 Dean of Graduate Studies ... Vacant
53 Dean Education ... Dr. Allan DE FINA
107 Dean Professional Studies ... Dr. Sandra BLOOMBERG
35 Dean of Students ... Dr. Lyn HAMLIN
08 Director of University Library ... Ms. Grace F. BULAONG
06 Registrar ... Ms. Miriam LARIA
36 Director Career Planning/Placement ... Dr. Jennifer JONES
09 Director Institutional Research ... Dr. Arthur KRAMER
15 Director Human Resources ... Mr. Robert PIASKOWSKY
19 Director Public Safety ... Mr. Bruce HARMAN
41 Director Athletics/Recreation ... Ms. Alice DE FAZIO
22 Dir Affirmative Action/Equal Oppty ... Ms. Lisa NORCIA
29 Director Alumni Relations ... Ms. Jane MCCLELLAN
78 Director Cooperative Education ... Dr. Jennifer JONES
44 Director Annual Giving ... Vacant
38 Director Student Counseling ... Dr. Abisola GALLAGHER
96 Director of Purchasing ... Ms. Edie DELVECCHIO
90 Director of Academic Computing ... Dr. Charles PRATT
85 Foreign Student Advisor ... Mr. Craig KATZ
43 University Counsel ... Vacant
37 Director Student Financial Aid ... Mr. Frank CUOZZO
30 Director of Development ... Ms. Lori SUMMERS
58 Acting Director of Graduate Studies ... Dr. William BAJOR
88 Director of Leadership Gifts ... Mr. Alan GROSSMAN
88 Director Student Fin Svcs/Risk Mgr ... Mr. Peter LJUTIC

New Jersey Institute of Technology (C)

University Heights, Newark NJ 07102-1982
County: Essex FICE Identification: 002621
Unit ID: 185828
Telephone: (973) 596-3000 Carnegie Class: RU/H
FAX Number: (973) 642-4380 Calendar System: Semester
URL: www.njit.edu
Established: 1881 Annual Undergrad Tuition & Fees (In-State): $14,533
Enrollment: 9,558 Coed
Affiliation or Control: State IRS Status: 501(c)3
Highest Offering: Doctorate
Program: Professional
Accreditation: M, BUS, CS, ENG, ENGT, PH

01 President ... Dr. Joel BLOOM
05 Provost/Sr VP for Academic Affairs ... Dr. Ian GATLEY
10 Senior Vice Pres Admin & Treasurer ... Mr. Henry A. MAUERMEYER
30 Vice Pres University Advancement ... Dr. Charles DEES
46 Vice President Research & Devel ... Dr. Donald H. SEBASTIAN
22 VP HR/Ex Dir Cmplnce/Trng/Cmty Rels ... Dr. Theodore T. JOHNSON
48 Dean of Architecture ... Mr. Urs P. GAUCHAT
54 Dean of Engineering ... Dr. Sunil SAIGAL
49 Dean College Science/Liberal Arts ... Dr. Fadi P. DEEK
50 Dean School of Management ... Dr. Pius J. EGBELU
92 Dean Albert Dorman Honors College ... Dr. Atam P. DHAWAN
77 Dean College Computing Science ... Dr. Ian GATLEY
21 Asst Vice Pres Finance & Controller ... Mr. William GARCIA
18 Assoc VP Facilities Management ... Mr. Joseph F. TARTAGLIA
58 Assoc Provost Graduate Studies ... Dr. Marino XANTOS
13 Assoc Provost Information Svcs Tech ... Mr. David F. ULLMAN
51 Assoc VP Cont/Distance Education ... Dr. Gale T. SPAK
07 Assoc VP Enroll Svcs/Dean Admiss ... Ms. Kathryn KELLY
88 Asst Vice Pres Pre-College Programs ... Dr. Howard S. KIMMEL
32 Dean Student Services ... Dr. Jack GENTUL
89 Assoc Dean/Ctr for First Yr Stdnts ... Dr. Sharon E. MORGAN
27 Executive Director Communications ... Ms. Jean M. LLEWELLYN
29 Exec Director of Alumni Affairs ... Mr. Robert A. BOYNTON
04 Executive Assistant to President ... Ms. Mary Jane POHERO
78 Exec Director Career Devel Svcs ... Mr. Gregory MASS
26 Director of Public Relations ... Ms. Sheryl M. WEINSTEIN
105 University Webmaster ... Mr. Andrew E. SCHERER
09 Director Inst Research/Planning ... Dr. Eugene P. DEESS
08 University Librarian ... Mr. Richard T. SWEENEY
06 Registrar ... Mr. Joseph F. THOMPSON
37 Director of Financial Aid ... Ms. Ivon NUNEZ
38 Director of Counseling Center ... Dr. Phyllis BOLLING
19 Director of Public Safety ... Mr. Robert G. SABATTIS
24 Dir Instructional Tech/Media Svcs ... Mr. William F. REYNOLDS
41 Sr Admin Physical Educ/Athletics ... Mr. Leonard I. KAPLAN
85 Director International Students/Fac ... Mr. Jeffrey W. GRUNDY
35 Director Student Activities ... Ms. Donna MINNICH
96 Director Purchasing/Office Services ... Ms. Eugenia REGENCIO
43 Office of General Counsel ... Ms. Holly C. STERN

Ocean County College (D)

PO Box 2001, Toms River NJ 08754-2001
County: Ocean FICE Identification: 002624
Unit ID: 185873
Telephone: (732) 255-0400 Carnegie Class: Assoc/Pub-S-SC
FAX Number: (732) 255-0444 Calendar System: Semester
URL: www.ocean.edu
Established: 1964 Annual Undergrad Tuition & Fees (In-District): $3,880
Enrollment: 10,317 Coed
Affiliation or Control: State/Local IRS Status: 501(c)3
Highest Offering: Associate Degree
Program: Occupational; 2-Year Principally Bachelor's Creditable
Accreditation: M, ADNUR

01 President ... Dr. Jon H. LARSON
11 Executive VP Operational ... Dr. James J. MCGINTY
05 Executive VP Instructional ... Mr. Richard STRADA
32 VP Student Affairs ... Mr. Donald DORAN
10 VP of Finance ... Ms. Sara WINCHESTER
26 VP of College Advancement ... Vacant
04 Senior Asst to the President ... Mr. David WOLFE
04 Asst to Pres for Inst Quality ... Ms. Janet HUBBS
20 Assoc VP of Academic Affairs ... Dr. Carolyn LAFFERTY
20 Asst VP for Instructional Services ... Dr. Antoinette M. CLAY
18 Asst VP Facilities/Planning/Constr ... Mr. Kenneth E. OLSEN
57 Actg Dean Language and the Arts ... Mr. Kleinschmidt ROBERT
81 Acting Dean Math/Science & Tech ... Dr. Yehia ELMOGZHZY
66 Dean for the School of Nursing ... Vacant
106 Dean of E-learning and Adj Faculty ... Dr. Maysa HAYWARD
83 Actg Dean Soc Sci & Off Campus Svc ... Ms. Eileen SCHILLING
102 Exec Dir OCC Foundation ... Ms. Sandy S. BROUGHTON
106 Exec Director of E-learning ... Ms. Patricia FENN
51 Director of Cont & Prof Educ ... Vacant
08 Director of Library Services ... Mr. Joseph TOTH
13 CIO ... Vacant
37 Director of Financial Aid ... Dr. Norma BETZ
88 Director of Academic Planning ... Ms. Mary KELLER
19 Director of Security Operations ... Mr. Robert KUMPF
88 Dir Broadcast/Instructional Tech ... Mr. Lee KOBUS
88 Director of College Relations ... Ms. Jan KIRSTEN
15 Director of Human Resourses ... Ms. Karen BLYSKAL
06 Dir of Recruitment & Admissions ... Ms. Jaclyn RODEMANN
93 Director of EOF & OMS ... Ms. Laura RICKARDS
18 Dir of Facilities/Engr & Ops ... Mr. Fulvio CESCO-CANCIAN
41 Director of Athletics ... Ms. Ilene COHEN
09 Acting Director of Inst Research ... Dr. Mary MORLEY
40 Dir of Auxiliary Svcs ... Ms. Carol KAUNITZ
44 Manager OCC Foundation/Alumni ... Ms. Kathy H. BUFFUM

Passaic County Community College (E)

1 College Boulevard, Paterson NJ 07509-1179
County: Passaic FICE Identification: 009994
Unit ID: 186034
Telephone: (973) 684-6868 Carnegie Class: Assoc/Pub-S-SC
FAX Number: (973) 684-5843 Calendar System: Semester
URL: www.pccc.edu
Established: 1968 Annual Undergrad Tuition & Fees (In-District): $4,034
Enrollment: 10,002 Coed
Affiliation or Control: State/Local IRS Status: 501(c)3
Highest Offering: Associate Degree
Program: Occupational; 2-Year Principally Bachelor's Creditable
Accreditation: M, ADNUR, ENGT, RAD

01 President ... Dr. Steven ROSE
05 Vice Pres Academic/Student Affairs ... Dr. Jacqueline KINEAVY
10 Vice Pres Finance/Administration ... Mr. Maurice FEIGENBAUM
12 Vice Pres Passaic Academic Center . Ms. Josephine HERNANDEZ
13 Vice Pres Information Technology ... Mr. Robert MONDELLI
15 Vice Pres Human Resources ... Mr. Gilbert RIVERA
20 Dean Academic Affairs ... Dr. Bassel STASSIS
08 Associate Dean Learning Resources ... Mr. Greg FALLON
66 Asst Dean Nurse Educ/Health Scis ... Ms. Donna STANKIEWICZ
09 Exec Dir Institutional Rsrch/Plng ... Dr. Gurvinder KHANEJA
88 Ex Dir Cultural Affs/The Poetry Ctr ... Ms. Maria GILLAN
30 Exec Dir of Institutional Devel ... Mr. Todd SORBER
84 Exec Dir of Enrollment Management ... Ms. Betsy MARINACE
18 Exec Dir Facilities Mgmt/Planning ... Mr. Brian EGAN
37 Director Financial Aid ... Ms. Linda GAYTON
06 Registrar ... Ms. Donna FISCHER
19 Director Security ... Mr. John MORGAN
35 Director Student Activities ... Ms. Takem DEAN
41 Athletic Director ... Mr. Bernard JOHNSON
07 Director of Admissions ... Ms. Stephanie DECKER
29 Director Alumni Relations ... Ms. Maria MEDINA
32 Chief Student Life Officer ... Dr. Sharon GOLDSTEIN
36 Director Student Placement ... Vacant
26 Chief Public Relations Officer ... Ms. Betsy MARINACE
96 Director of Purchasing ... Ms. Marge HOLLINGSWORTH
88 Coordinator of Academic Testing ... Mr. Patrick PAJEROWSKI
04 Administrative Asst to President ... Ms. Evelyn DEFEIS

Princeton Theological Seminary (F)

PO Box 821, Princeton NJ 08542-0803
County: Mercer FICE Identification: 002626
Unit ID: 186122
Telephone: (609) 921-8300 Carnegie Class: Spec/Faith
FAX Number: (609) 924-2973 Calendar System: Semester
URL: www.ptsem.edu
Established: 1812 Annual Graduate Tuition & Fees: $11,250
Enrollment: 542 Coed
Affiliation or Control: Presbyterian Church (U.S.A.) IRS Status: 501(c)3
Highest Offering: Doctorate; No Undergraduates
Program: Professional; Religious Emphasis
Accreditation: M, THEOL

01 President ... Dr. Iain R. TORRANCE
10 Sr Vice Pres/Chief Oper Ofcr/Treas ... Mr. John W. GILMORE
45 Vice Pres Strategy ... Dr. Charles F. KALMBACH
26 Vice President Seminary Relations .. Rev. Rosemary C. MITCHELL
13 Vice Pres Information Technology ... Mr. Adrian BACKUS
05 Dean of Academic Affairs ... Dr. James F. KAY
32 Dean of Student Life ... Rev. Lori A. NEFF
20 Associate Dean of Curricula ... Dr. Shawn OLIVER
73 Dir Sch of Christian/Voc/Mission ... Dr. Charles F. KALMBACH
21 Controller ... Mr. Barry L. GRUVER
29 Director Alumni/ae Relations/ Giving ... Rev. W. Robert SHARMAN, III
06 Registrar ... Mr. David H. WALL
07 Director Admissions/Financial Aid ... Mr. Matthew R. SPINA
08 Interim Chief Librarian ... Mr. Donald M. VORP
30 Director Development ... Vacant
35 Director Stdnt Rels/Sr Placement ... Dr. Catherine C. DAVIS
15 Director of Human Resources ... Ms. Sandra J. MALEY
27 Director Communications/Publication ... Rev. Barbara A. CHAAPEL
18 Director of Facilities ... Mr. German MARTINEZ
14 Dir Telecomm/Network/Suport Svcs ... Mr. William R. FRENCH
24 Director Educational Media ... Rev. Joicy BECKER-RICHARDS
39 Director of Housing/Auxiliary Svcs ... Mr. Stephen CARDONE
44 Director of Planned Giving ... Mr. John S. MCANLIS
36 Director of Student Placement ... Dr. Catherine C. DAVIS
38 Director of Student Counseling ... Rev. Nancy L. SCHONGALLA-BOWMAN
42 Minister of the Chapel ... Rev. Janice S. AMMON
28 Director Multicultural Relations ... Rev. Victor ALOYO, JR.
108 Director Accreditation/Advising ... Rev. Lori A. NEFF

Princeton University (G)

Princeton NJ 08544-1098
County: Mercer FICE Identification: 002627
Unit ID: 186131
Telephone: (609) 258-3000 Carnegie Class: RU/VH
FAX Number: N/A Calendar System: Semester
URL: www.princeton.edu
Established: 1746 Annual Undergrad Tuition & Fees: $38,650
Enrollment: 7,859 Coed
Affiliation or Control: Independent Non-Profit IRS Status: 501(c)3
Highest Offering: Doctorate
Program: Liberal Arts And General; Teacher Preparatory; Professional
Accreditation: M, ENG, TEAC

01 President ... Shirley M. TILGHMAN
03 Executive Vice President ... Mark BURSTEIN
05 Provost ... Christopher L. EISGRUBER
04 Vice President & Secretary ... Robert K. DURKEE
10 Vice Pres for Finance & Treasurer ... Carolyn N. AINSLIE
30 Vice President for Development ... Elizabeth B. WOOD
26 Vice President for Public Affairs ... Robert K. DURKEE
32 Vice President of Campus Life ... Cynthia CHERREY
18 Vice President for Facilities ... Michael E. MCKAY
13 Vice President Info Technology/CIO ... Betty LEYDON

16 Vice President for Human Resources ... Lianne C. SULLIVAN-CROWLEY
11 VP for University Services ... Chad L. KLAUS
20 Vice Provost Academic Affairs ... Katherine ROHRER
22 Vice Provost Instl Equity/Diversity ... Michelle MINTER
09 Vice Provost Institutional Research ... Jed MARSH
25 Vice Prov Space Programming/Plan ... Paul LAMARCHE
21 Budget Dir/Vice Provost Finance ... Steven GILL
20 Vice Provost Intl Initiatives ... Diana K. DAVIES
26 Asst Vice President Communications ... Lauren D. UGORJI
29 Asst Vice President Alumni Affairs ... Margaret M. MILLER
44 Asst Vice President Annual Giving ... William M. HARDT
19 Asst VP Safety/Administration ... Charlotte Treby WILLIAMS
88 Asst VP for University Services ... Paul BREITMAN
88 AVP Facilities Design/Construction ... Anne ST. MAURO
18 Asst Vice Pres Facilities Plant ... Roger DEMARESKI
46 Chair Univ Rsrch Bd/Dean Research ... A. J. Stewart SMITH
43 General Counsel ... Peter G. MCDONOUGH
88 President PRINCO ... Andrew K. GOLDEN
88 Dean of the Faculty ... David P. DOBKIN
58 Dean of Graduate School ... William B. RUSSEL
49 Dean of the College ... Valerie SMITH
54 Dean of School of Engineering ... H. Vincent POOR
82 Dean of WW Sch of Public/Intl Affs ... Cecilia ROUSE
48 Dean of School of Architecture ... Stanley T. ALLEN
42 Dean of Religious Life ... Alison BODEN
35 Dean of Undergraduate Students ... Kathleen DEIGNAN
07 Dean of Admission ... Janet L. RAPELYE
17 Exec Director Health Services ... John KOLLIGIAN
08 University Librarian ... Karin TRAINER
06 Registrar ... Polly WINFREY GRIFFIN
37 Dir Undergraduate Financial Aid ... Robin A. MOSCATO
86 Director Government Affairs ... Joyce A. RECHTSCHAFFEN
31 Dir Community & Regional Affairs ... Kristin APPELGET
41 Director of Athletics ... Gary D. WALTERS
96 Director of Purchasing ... Donald E. WESTON, JR.
38 Dir of Counseling & Psych Services ... Anita MCLEAN
15 Director Human Resources ... Claire JACOBS ELSON
85 Director Davis International Center ... Jackie LEIGHTON
36 Director Career Services ... Beverly HAMILTON-CHANDLER
90 Assoc CIO/Dir Academic Services OIT ... Serge J. GOLDSTEIN
14 Assoc CIO/Dir Support Services OIT ... Steven M. SATHER
91 Dir Enterprise Infrastructure OIT ... Donna E. TATRO
27 Director of News and Editorial Svcs ... Daniel DAY
105 Director of Web Communications ... Thomas J. BARTUS
88 Dir of Development Communications ... Ruth STEVENS
44 AVP for Development ... Kerstin LARSEN
104 Sr Asc Dn of Col/Dir Ofc Intl Pgms ... Nancy A. KANACH
39 Director Housing ... Andrew KANE

Rabbi Jacob Joseph School (A)

1 Plainfield Avenue, Edison NJ 08817-4494

County: Middlesex | FICE Identification: 030775 | Unit ID: 384421

Telephone: (732) 985-6533 | Carnegie Class: Spec/Faith

FAX Number: (732) 985-6553 | Calendar System: Semester

URL: www.jfgmc.org/rjjy/htm

Established: 1982 | Annual Undergrad Tuition & Fees: $10,900

Enrollment: 69 | Male

Affiliation or Control: Independent Non-Profit | IRS Status: 501(c)3

Highest Offering: Baccalaureate

Program: Teacher Preparatory; Professional

Accreditation: @RABN

01 President ... Dr. Marvin SCHICK
03 Rosh Yeshiva ... Rabbi Yaakov BUSEL
05 Rosh Yeshiva ... Rabbi Joseph EICHENSTEIN
37 Financial Aid Director ... Rabbi Yitzchok WEINTRAUB

Rabbinical College of America (B)

226 Sussex Avenue, Morristown NJ 07960-3600

County: Morris | FICE Identification: 008609 | Unit ID: 186186

Telephone: (973) 267-9404 | Carnegie Class: Spec/Faith

FAX Number: (973) 267-5208 | Calendar System: Trimester

URL: www.rca.edu

Established: 1956 | Annual Undergrad Tuition & Fees: $10,700

Enrollment: 250 | Male

Affiliation or Control: Independent Non-Profit | IRS Status: 501(c)3

Highest Offering: Baccalaureate

Program: Teacher Preparatory

Accreditation: RABN

00 Chairman of the Board ... David T. CHASE
01 Dean ... Rabbi Moshe HERSON
04 Admin Assistant to the Dean ... Shoshana SOLOMON
26 Public Relations Officer ... Rabbi Mendel SOLOMON
06 Registrar ... Rabbi Yossi WEINGARTEN
20 Director New Direction Program ... Rabbi Zalman DUBINSKY
33 Director Ordination Program ... Rabbi Sholom SPALTER
10 Chief Business Officer ... Rabbi Hershel LIPSKIER
37 Director Student Financial Aid ... Rabbi Moshe WEISBERG
08 Chief Librarian ... Rabbi Sholom SPALTER
51 Dir Continuing Educ/Alumni Rels ... Rabbi Boruch HECHT
88 Director Semicha Program ... Rabbi Chaim SCHAPIRO

Ramapo College of New Jersey (C)

505 Ramapo Valley Road, Mahwah NJ 07430-1680

County: Bergen | FICE Identification: 009344 | Unit ID: 186201

Telephone: (201) 684-7500 | Carnegie Class: Master's M

FAX Number: (201) 684-7508 | Calendar System: Semester

URL: www.ramapo.edu

Established: 1969 | Annual Undergrad Tuition & Fees (In-State): $13,144

Enrollment: 5,926 | Coed

Affiliation or Control: State | IRS Status: 501(c)3

Highest Offering: Master's

Program: Liberal Arts And General; Teacher Preparatory; Professional

Accreditation: M, BUS, NUR, SW, TEAC

01 President ... Dr. Peter P. MERCER
05 Provost/VP Academic Affairs ... Dr. Beth BARNETT
10 Vice Pres Administration & Finance ... Vacant
32 Assoc VP of Student Affairs ... Dr. Miki CAMMARATA
84 Assoc VP of Enrollment Mgmt ... Mr. Christopher ROMANO
46 Chief Planning Officer ... Dr. Dorothy ECHOLS TOBE
20 Vice Provost for Academic Affairs ... Dr. Eric DAFFRON
21 Assoc Vice Pres Admin/Finance ... Mr. Richard ROBERTS
08 College Librarian/Dean ... Ms. Elizabeth SIECKE
102 Exec Director Ramapo Found/VPIA ... Ms. Cathleen DAVEY
06 Registrar ... Ms. Cynthia BRENNAN
07 Director of Admissions ... Mr. Peter RICE
37 Director of Financial Aid ... Mr. Mark SINGER
21 Controller ... Vacant
13 Chief Information Officer ... Mr. George TABBACK
26 Asst VP Marketing & Communications ... Ms. Anna FARNESKI
15 Director of Human Resources ... Mr. Bill STOVALL
78 Dir Exper Learning/Career Svcs ... Ms. Beth RICCA
39 Director Residence Life ... Ms. Linda DIAZ
41 Director of Athletics ... Mr. Charles J. GORDON
18 Director Campus Facilities ... Mr. Ronald MARTUCCI
19 Director Security & Safety ... Mr. Vincent MARKOWSKI
88 Director Educ Opportunity Program ... Mr. Lorne WEEMS
50 Dean Anisfield School of Business ... Dr. Lewis CHAKRIN
82 Dean Salameno Sch Amer Intl Studies ... Dr. Hassan NEJAD
57 Dean Sch of Contemporary Arts ... Mr. Steven PERRY
83 Dean Sch Soc Science & Human Svc ... Dr. Samuel ROSENBERG
81 Actg Dn Sch Theoretical/Applied Sci ... Dr. Edward SAIFF
53 Coordinator of Teacher Education ... Dr. Alexander URBIEL
38 Director Ctr for Health/Counseling ... Dr. Judith GREEN
29 Asst Director Alumni Relations ... Ms. Purvi PAREKH
24 Asst Manager Academic Media Svcs ... Mr. Michael SAVIANESO
04 Executive Assistant to President ... Ms. Patricia KOZAKIEWICZ
25 Dir Grants Admin/Assoc VPIA ... Dr. Ronald KASE
23 Coordinator Health Services ... Ms. Debbie LUKACSKO
09 Asst VP Inst Effect & Plng/Inst Res ... Ms. Babette VARANO
22 Dir Affirm Action/Equal Opportunity ... Ms. Lorraine EDWARDS
35 Assoc VP Student Affairs ... Dr. Patrick CHANG
40 Bookstore Manager ... Ms. Theresa KING
85 Exec Director of Intl Education ... Mr. Ben LEVY
36 Asst Dir Career Dev & Placement ... Ms. Debra STARK
96 Director of Purchasing ... Mr. Stephen SONDEY
04 Special Assistant to President ... Ms. Brittany WILLIAMS-GOLDSTEIN
30 Chief Develop/VP Inst Advancement ... Ms. Cathleen DAVEY

Raritan Valley Community College (D)

118 Lamington Road, Branchgurg NJ 08876

County: Somerset | FICE Identification: 007731 | Unit ID: 186645

Telephone: (908) 526-1200 | Carnegie Class: Assoc/Pub-S-SC

FAX Number: (908) 526-0253 | Calendar System: Semester

URL: www.raritanval.edu

Established: 1966 | Annual Undergrad Tuition & Fees (In-District): $4,454

Enrollment: 8,370 | Coed

Affiliation or Control: State/Local | IRS Status: 501(c)3

Highest Offering: Associate Degree

Program: Occupational; 2-Year Principally Bachelor's Creditable

Accreditation: M, ADNUR, MAC, OPD

01 President ... Dr. Casey CRABILL
05 Sr Vice Pres Academic Affairs ... Dr. Eileen ABEL
10 Vice President Finance/Facilities ... Mr. John TROJAN
13 Vice Pres Technology/Assess/Plng ... Mr. Charles E. CHULVICK
15 VP Human Resources/Labor Relations ... Ms. Nancy MOORE
30 Dean of College Advancement ... Ms. Jackie BELIN
20 Dean of Instruction ... Dr. Maxwell STEVENS
45 Dean Academic Resource Development ... Ms. Nancy E. JORDAN
51 Dean of Corporate & Continuing Educ ... Ms. Janet L. PERANTONI
20 Dean of Faculty ... Mr. Thomas VALASEK
32 Dean Student Services ... Ms. Diane LEMCOE
85 Dean Multicultural Affairs ... Ms. Richeleen DASHIELD
18 Exec Director Facilities/Grounds ... Mr. Brian O'ROURKE
84 Exec Dir of Enrollment Services ... Ms. Mary O'MALLEY
24 Director Media Relations ... Ms. Donna STOLZER
88 Conference Services Director ... Ms. Karen VAUGHAN
72 Executive Director Inst Technology ... Mr. Michael E. MACHNIK
102 Executive Director Foundation ... Vacant
13 Director Management Info Services ... Mr. Warren RUTE
21 Controller/Exec Dir of Finance ... Ms. Violet J. WILLENSKY
57 Director of Theatre ... Mr. Alan C. LIDDELL
09 Dir of Inst Research/Assessment ... Mr. Keith GUERIN
88 Director of Planetarium ... Mr. Jerome VINSKI
88 Director of Child Care Center ... Ms. Cathy GRIFFIN
37 Director of Financial Aid ... Mr. Lenny MESONAS
08 Library Director ... Ms. Julie MAGINN
06 Registrar ... Mr. Dan PALUBNIAK
96 Director of Purchasing ... Mr. Lester MILLER
35 Director of Student Life ... Ms. Mary SULLIVAN
36 Director Transfer/Career Services ... Mr. Paul MICHAUD
26 Executive Director Marketing ... Ms. Janet THOMPSON

The Richard Stockton College of New Jersey (E)

101 Vera King Farris Drive, Galloway NJ 08205-9441

County: Atlantic | FICE Identification: 009345 | Unit ID: 186876

Telephone: (609) 652-1776 | Carnegie Class: Master's M

FAX Number: (609) 652-0275 | Calendar System: Semester

URL: www.stockton.edu

Established: 1969 | Annual Undergrad Tuition & Fees (In-State): $12,322

Enrollment: 8,108 | Coed

Affiliation or Control: State | IRS Status: 501(c)3

Highest Offering: Doctorate

Program: Liberal Arts And General; Teacher Preparatory; Professional

Accreditation: M, NURSE, OT, PTA, @SP, SW, TEAC

01 President ... Dr. Herman J. SAATKAMP, JR.
05 Provost/Exec Vice Pres of Acad Affs ... Dr. Harvey KESSELMAN
100 Chief of Staff ... Mr. Brian K. JACKSON
10 Vice Pres Administration & Finance ... Mr. Charles E. INGRAM
32 Vice President Student Affairs ... Dr. Thomasa GONZALEZ
45 Chief Planning Officer ... Vacant
20 Interim Associate Provost ... Dr. Sonia GONSALVES
20 Assistant Provost ... Dr. Debra DAGAVARIAN
96 Asst Supervisor Purchasing ... Ms. Annette HAMM
13 Assoc Prov Computing/Communication ... Mr. James MCCARTHY
21 Assoc VP Administration & Finance ... Vacant
22 Sp Ast to Pres Affirm Act/Ethcl Std ... Ms. Nancy W. HICKS
26 Spec Asst to Pres for External Affs ... Ms. Sharon SCHULMAN
30 Chief Dev Ofcr/Exec Dir Foundation ... Mr. Philip T. ELLMORE
84 Dean of Enrollment Management ... Mr. John IACOVELLI
07 Associate Dean of Admissions ... Ms. Alison HENRY
35 Dean of Students ... Mr. Pedro SANTANA
06 Assoc Dean Records/Registration ... Mr. Joseph LO SASSO
53 Dean School of Education ... Dr. Claudine KEENAN
97 Dean School of General Studies ... Dr. G. Jan COLIJN
79 Dean School of Arts & Humanities ... Dr. Robert S. GREGG
50 Dean School of Business ... Dr. Janet M. WAGNER
58 Dean School of Graduate Studies ... Dr. Lewis LEITNER
81 Dean School of Natural Science/Math ... Dr. Dennis WEISS
83 Dean Sch Social/Behavioral Sciences ... Dr. Cheryl KAUS
76 Dean School of Health Sciences ... Dr. Brenda STEVENSON-MARSHALL
15 Director Human Resource Management ... Ms. Natalie M. HAVRAN
09 Director Institutional Research ... Dr. Xiangping KONG
08 Int Director of Library Services ... Ms. Mary Ann TRAIL
88 Director South Regional ETTC ... Ms. Patricia WEEKS
37 Director of Financial Aid ... Ms. Jeanne LEWIS
19 Dir Campus Security/Chief of Police ... Chief Glenn MILLER
88 Director Performing Arts Center ... Mr. Michael COOL
41 Dir of Athletics and Recreations ... Mr. Lonnie FOLKS
39 Director of Residential Life ... Dr. Denise O'NEILL
36 Director of Career Services ... Mr. Walter L. TARVER, III
43 General Counsel ... Ms. Melissa HAGER
38 Dir Counseling and Health Services ... Ms. Frances H. BOTTONE
88 Director Academic Advising ... Dr. Peter HAGEN
21 Director Budget & Fiscal Planning ... Mr. Michael WOOD
29 Director Alumni Relations ... Ms. Sara FAUROT-CROWLEY
44 Assoc Chf Devel Ofcr/Campaign Mgr ... Ms. Cindy CRAGER

Rider University (F)

2083 Lawrenceville Road, Lawrenceville NJ 08648-3099

County: Mercer | FICE Identification: 002628 | Unit ID: 186283

Telephone: (609) 896-5000 | Carnegie Class: Master's L

FAX Number: (609) 896-8029 | Calendar System: Semester

URL: www.rider.edu

Established: 1865 | Annual Undergrad Tuition & Fees: $32,820

Enrollment: 5,636 | Coed

Affiliation or Control: Independent Non-Profit | IRS Status: 501(c)3

Highest Offering: Master's

Program: Liberal Arts And General; Teacher Preparatory; Professional

Accreditation: M, BUS, BUSA, CACREP, MUS, TED

01 President ... Dr. Mordechai ROZANSKI
05 Vice Pres Academic Affairs/Provost ... Dr. Donald A. STEVEN
10 Vice President Finance/Treasurer ... Ms. Julie A. KARNS
30 Vice Pres University Advancement ... Mr. Jonathan D. MEER
32 VP Student Affairs/Dean of Students ... Dr. Anthony CAMPBELL
84 Vice Pres Enrollment Management ... Mr. James P. O'HARA
14 Assoc VP Information Technology ... Ms. Carol S. KONDRACH
21 Associate Vice President/Controller ... Mr. William ROELL
09 Assoc Vice Pres Institutional Rsrch ... Mr. Ronald WALKER
18 Associate Vice President ... Mr. Michael F. RECA
45 Associate Vice President Planning ... Ms. Debbie STASOLLA
26 Asst VP for Univ Comm/Marketing ... Mr. William J. AHEARN
20 Associate Provost ... Dr. James O. CASTAGNERA
12 Dean Westminster ... Mr. Robert L. ANNIS
07 Dean of Enrollment ... Ms. Susan C. CHRISTIAN
51 Dean College of Cont Studies ... Mr. Boris VILIC
49 Dean Liberal Arts & Science/Educ ... Dr. Pat MOSTO
53 Dean School of Education ... Dr. Sharon SHERMAN
50 Dean Business Administration ... Dr. Steven J. LORENZET
06 Registrar ... Ms. Susan A. STEFANICK
36 Director of Career Placement ... Ms. Gwendolyn J. TYLER
08 Director of Library Services ... Mr. F. William CHICKERING
15 Dir Human Resources/Affirm Action ... Mr. Robert STOTO
40 Manager College Store ... Mr. Joseph JUDGE
19 Director of Public Safety ... Ms. Vickie L. WEAVER
29 Director of Alumni Relations ... Ms. Natalie M. POLLARD
41 Director of Athletics ... Mr. Donald P. HARNUM

37 Director Student Financial Svcs ... Mr. Drew C. AROMANDO
04 Executive Asst to the President ... Ms. Christine ZELENAK

Rowan University (A)

201 Mullica Hill Road, Glassboro NJ 08028-1700
County: Gloucester FICE Identification: 002609
Unit ID: 184782
Telephone: (856) 256-4000 Carnegie Class: Master's L
FAX Number: (856) 256-4929 Calendar System: Semester
URL: www.rowan.edu
Established: 1923 Annual Undergrad Tuition & Fees (In-State): $12,380
Enrollment: 11,816 Coed
Affiliation or Control: State IRS Status: 501(c)3
Highest Offering: Doctorate
Program: Liberal Arts And General; Teacher Preparatory; Professional
Accreditation: M, ART, BUS, CACREP, CS, ENG, #MED, MUS, NURSE, TED, THEA

01 President ... Dr. Ali A. HOUSHMAND
05 Interim Provost ... Dr. James NEWELL
10 Vice Pres of Finance/CFO ... Mr. Joseph F. SCULLY
30 Vice Pres University Advancement ... Vacant
32 VP Student Life/Dean of Students ... Mr. Richard JONES
86 Vice Pres Civic/Governmental Rels ... Vacant
18 VP for Facilities & Operations ... Mr. Donald MOORE
44 Assoc VP University Advancement ... Mr. Ronald J. TALLARIDA
20 Int Assoc Provost Academic Affairs ... Dr. Roberta HARVEY
16 Assoc VP Employee & Labor Relations ... Mr. Robert ZAZZALI
13 Assoc Provost Information Resources ... Mr. Anthony A. MORDOSKY
46 Assoc Provost Research ... Dr. Shreekanth MANDAYAM
09 Assoc VP Inst Effectiveness/Plng ... Dr. Mira LALOVIC-HAND
26 Interim VP for University Relations ... Dr. Jose CARDONA
84 Assoc Prov Strategic Enroll Mgmt ... Dr. Jeffrey HAND
88 Asst VP Campus Rec/Stdnt Ctr/CES ... Ms. Tina M. PINOCCI
19 Asst VP Public Safety/Emerg Mgmt ... Mr. Michael KANTNER
15 Asst VP Labor Relations ... Mr. Kenneth KUERZI
38 Dir Counseling/Psych Services ... Dr. David RUBENSTEIN
91 Director of EIS ... Mr. James HENDERSON
37 Director of Financial Aid ... Mr. Luis A. TAVAREZ
06 Registrar ... Ms. Muriel FRIERSON
63 Dean of Cooper Medical School of RU ... Dr. Paul KATZ
08 Dean of the Library ... Mr. Bruce WHITHAM
50 Dean Rohrer College of Business ... Dr. Robert BEATTY
81 Dean of Science & Mathematics ... Dr. Parviz ANSARI
53 Dean of Education ... Dr. Carol SHARP
57 Dean of Performing Arts ... Dr. John R. PASTIN
58 Dean Graduate & Continuing Educ ... Dr. Horacio SOSA
54 Interim Dean of Engineering ... Dr. Steven CHIN
60 Dean Communication & Creative Arts ... Dr. Lorin ARNOLD
83 Dean Humanities & Social Sciences ... Dr. Cindy VITTO
12 Asst Provost/Dean Camden Campus ... Dr. Tyrone MCCOMBS
15 Assoc VP Employment/Labor Relations ... Ms. Eileen SCOTT
22 Asst VP for Equity and Diversity ... Dr. Johanna VELEZ-YELIN
41 Director of Athletics ... Mr. Dan GILMORE
29 Director Alumni Relations ... Ms. Kathy ROZANSKI
07 Director of Admissions ... Dr. Albert BETTS
36 Dir Career Management Center ... Ms. Lizziel SULLIVAN-WILLIAMS
96 Sr Dir Contracting & Procurement ... Ms. Christina BRASTETER
27 Director University Publications ... Ms. Lori MARSHALL
105 Director Web Services ... Ms. Jennifer BELL
85 Director International Center ... Mr. Timothy TORRE
28 Assoc Dean Acad Enrich/Dir EOF/MAP ... Dr. Penny MCPHERSON-BARNES
04 Asst to the President ... Dr. Joanne CONNOR

*Rutgers the State University of New Jersey Central Office (B)

83 Somerset Street, New Brunswick NJ 08901-1281
County: Middlesex FICE Identification: 002629
Unit ID: 186362
Telephone: (732) 932-4636 Carnegie Class: N/A
FAX Number: (732) 932-8060
URL: www.rutgers.edu

01 President ... Dr. Robert L. BARCHI
05 Interim Exec VP for Acad Affairs ... Dr. Richard EDWARDS
10 Senior VP for Admin & CFO ... Mr. Bruce C. FEHN
51 Sr VP Lifelng Lrng/Strategic Growth ... Dr. David L. FINEGOLD
21 Vice President Budgeting ... Dr. Nancy S. WINTERBAUER
46 Int VP Research & Econ Development ... Dr. Kenneth J. BRESLAUER
14 Vice President Info Tech ... Mr. Donald E. SMITH
26 Vice President University Relations ... Ms. Kimberly M. MANNING
32 Vice President Student Affairs ... Vacant
18 Vice Pres Univ Facil/Capital Plng ... Mr. Antonio CALCADO
43 Interim Senior VP & General Counsel ... Mr. John W. WOLF
29 Asst VP Alumni Relations ... Mr. Brian R. PERILLO
04 Exec Assistant to the President ... Ms. Carol KONCSOL
20 Acting VP Academic Affairs & Admin ... Dr. Karen R. STUBAUS
15 Vice Pres of Fac & Staff Resources ... Ms. Vivian FERNANDEZ
102 Pres RU Found/Exec VP Dev/Alum Rels ... Ms. Carol P. HERRING
08 VP Info Services & Univ Librarian ... Ms. Marianne I. GAUNT
101 Secretary of the University ... Mrs. Leslie A. FEHRENBACH
19 Vice Pres Admin & Public Safety ... Mr. Jay KOHL
23 Exec Director Student Health Svcs ... Ms. Melodee S. LASKY
06 University Registrar ... Mr. Kenneth J. IUSO
07 Director Grad/Prof Admiss ... Ms. Linda J. COSTA
37 University Dir Financial Aid ... Mr. Jean MCDONALD-RASH
39 Executive Director of Housing ... Mr. Michael C. IMPERIALE
41 Director Intercollegiate Athletics ... Mr. Tim R. PERNETTI
22 Dir Employment Equity ... Ms. Jayne M. GRANDES
36 Acting Dir Career Dev/Placemt Svcs ... Ms. Janet JONES
09 Director Institutional Research ... Dr. Robert J. HEFFERNAN
14 U Dir & Deputy Chief Inform Officer ... Ms. Bernice GINDER
86 Vice President Public Affairs ... Mr. Peter J. MCDONOUGH, JR.
84 Vice President Enrollment Mgmt ... Dr. Courtney MCANUFF
88 VP Undergrad Education ... Dr. Barry V. QUALLS
29 VP Alumni Relations ... Ms. Donna THORNTON
28 Dir Inst Diversity & Equity ... Dr. Karen R. STUBAUS
86 Asst VP Federal Relations ... Ms. Francine PFEIFFER
86 Senior Director State Relations ... Vacant
88 Assc VP Promtg Women Sci Eng Math ... Dr. Joan W. BENNETT
88 VP Health Science Partnerships ... Dr. Kenneth J. BRESLAUER

*Rutgers the State University of New Jersey New Brunswick Campus (C)

85 Somerset Street, New Brunswick NJ 08901-1281
County: Middlesex FICE Identification: 006964
Unit ID: 186380
Telephone: (732) 932-4636 Carnegie Class: RU/VH
FAX Number: (732) 932-8060 Calendar System: Semester
URL: www.rutgers.edu
Established: 1766 Annual Undergrad Tuition & Fees (In-State): $13,073
Enrollment: 39,950 Coed
Affiliation or Control: State IRS Status: 501(c)3
Highest Offering: Doctorate
Program: Liberal Arts And General; Teacher Preparatory; Professional
Accreditation: M, CACREP, CEA, CLPSY, DANCE, DIETD, ENG, LIB, LSAR, MUS, PH, PHAR, PLNG, SCPSY, SPAA, SW, TEAC

02 Dean Graduate School ... Dr. Jerome J. KUKOR
80 Dean EJB School Plng/Public Policy ... Dr. James W. HUGHES
81 Exec Dean Sch Enviro/Biological Sci ... Dr. Robert M. GOODMAN
12 Dean Douglass Residential College ... Dr. Jacquelyn S. LITT
12 Dean Livingston Campus ... Dr. Lea P. STEWART
12 Dean Busch Campus ... Dr. Thomas V. PAPATHOMAS
49 Executive Dean of SAS ... Vacant
12 Dean College Avenue Campus ... Dr. Matthew K. MATSUDA
12 Dean Cook Campus ... Dr. Barbara TURPIN
12 Dean Univ College/Comm/NB ... Dr. Susan J. SCHURMAN
54 Dean School of Engineering ... Dr. Thomas N. FARRIS
67 Acting Dean Ernest Mario Sch Pharm ... Dr. Joseph BARONE
57 Dean Mason Gross School of Art ... Dr. George B. STAUFFER
62 Dean Sch Communication & Info ... Dr. Jorge R. SCHEMENT
83 Dean Grad School Applied/Prof Psych ... Dr. Stanley B. MESSER
53 Dean Grad School of Education ... Dr. Richard DELISI
66 Dean College of Nursing ... Dr. William L. HOLZEMER
70 Act Dean School of Social Work ... Dr. Kathleen J. POTTICK
50 Sr Assoc Dean Sch of Business NB ... Dr. Martin S. MARKOWITZ
88 Dean Sch Mgmt/Labor Relations ... Dr. Susan J. SCHURMAN
06 University Registrar ... Mr. Kenneth J. IUSO
104 Dean Rutgers Study Abroad ... Dr. Stephen L. REINERT

*Rutgers the State University of New Jersey Camden Campus (D)

303 Cooper Street, Camden NJ 08102-1461
County: Camden FICE Identification: 004741
Unit ID: 186371
Telephone: (856) 225-6026 Carnegie Class: Master's M
FAX Number: (856) 225-6495 Calendar System: Semester
URL: www.camden.rutgers.edu
Established: 1927 Annual Undergrad Tuition & Fees (In-State): $12,923
Enrollment: 6,428 Coed
Affiliation or Control: State IRS Status: 501(c)3
Highest Offering: Doctorate
Program: Liberal Arts And General; Teacher Preparatory; Professional
Accreditation: &M, BUS, LAW, NURSE, PTA, SPAA, TEAC

02 Chancellor ... Dr. Wendell E. PRITCHETT
11 Assoc Chancellor Admin & Finance ... Dr. Larry R. GAINES, JR.
32 Assoc Chancellor Student Life ... Dr. Mary Beth B. DAISEY
84 Assoc Chancellor Enrollment Mgmt ... Dr. Rodney MORRISON
88 Director Economic Development ... Mr. Gregory GAMBLE
61 Dean School of Law ... Dr. Rayman L. SOLOMON
58 Dean Grad School ... Dr. Kriste LINDENMEYER
50 Dean School of Business ... Dr. Jaishankar GANESH
49 Dean Fac Arts & Sci/Univ Col ... Dr. Kriste LINDENMEYER
66 Dean School of Nursing ... Dr. Joanne P. ROBINSON
26 Assoc Chancellor for Ext Relations ... Mr. Michael J. SEPANIC
06 Registrar ... Ms. Theresa R. CRISTOFARO
37 Manager Financial Aid ... Ms. Linda J. TAYLOR-BURCH
10 Director Campus Financial Services ... Ms. Rosa M. RIVERA
19 Chief Campus Police ... Chief Guy M. STILL
29 Director Alumni Relations ... Mr. Charles J. MANNELLA
96 Supplier Diversity Manager ... Ms. Pamela Y. WELLS
15 Human Resources Manager ... Mr. Gregory M. O'SHEA
18 Director Facilities Services ... Vacant
21 Business Manager FAS Camden ... Ms. Marlene DRUDING
28 Director of Diversity ... Dr. Nancy G. ROSOFF
41 Dir Athletics & Rec Services ... Mr. Jeffrey L. DEAN
36 Asst Dean/Director Stdnt Career Ctr ... Mr. James MARINO
38 Assoc Director Student Counseling ... Dr. N. Maria SERRA
30 Director of Development/FASC ... Ms. Akua ASIAMAH-ANDRADE
08 Director Paul Robeson Library ... Dr. Gary A. GOLDEN
23 Director Health Services ... Dr. Paul P. BROWN
39 Asst Dean/Dir House & Resident Life ... Dr. Allison A. WISNIEWSKI
87 Director Summer Session ... Dr. Paul C. BUTLER
46 Director Sponsored Research ... Ms. Carberta A. MORRISON
13 Director Information Technology ... Mr. Joseph R. SANDERS
30 Asst Chancellor Development Camden ... Ms. Tracy E. ELLIOTT
31 Director Community Outreach ... Mr. Andrew J. SELIGSOHN

*Rutgers the State University of New Jersey Newark Campus (E)

249 University Avenue, Newark NJ 07102-1897
County: Essex FICE Identification: 002631
Unit ID: 186399
Telephone: (973) 353-5568 Carnegie Class: RU/H
FAX Number: (973) 353-1048 Calendar System: Semester
URL: www.newark.rutgers.edu
Established: 1892 Annual Undergrad Tuition & Fees (In-State): $12,590
Enrollment: 11,804 Coed
Affiliation or Control: State IRS Status: 501(c)3
Highest Offering: Doctorate
Program: Liberal Arts And General; Teacher Preparatory; Professional
Accreditation: &M, BUS, LAW, NURSE, SPAA, SW, TEAC

02 Interim Chancellor ... Dr. Philip L. YEAGLE
10 Exec Vice Chancellor Administration ... Dr. Kemel W. DAWKINS
32 Vice Chancellor Stdnt/Cmty Outreach ... Dr. Marcia W. BROWN
15 Assoc Chancellor Human Resources ... Dr. Carol MARTANCIK
18 Assoc Vice Chancellor Facilities ... Dr. Martin B. RYAN
30 Vice Chancellor for Development ... Dr. Irene O'BRIEN
05 Vice Chancellor Acad Pgms & Svcs ... Dr. John GUNKEL
11 Asst Chanc Admin Services/Budget ... Dr. Mary TAMASCO
35 Asst Chancellor for Student Life ... Dr. Gerald MASSENBURG
06 Registrar ... Dr. Miguel A. ESTREMERA
13 Director Information Technology ... Ms. Marie J. BOTTICELLI
07 Director of Admissions ... Mr. Jason HAND
19 Director Public Safety Newark ... Mr. Michael P. LATTIMORE
27 Director of Communications ... Ms. Helen S. PAXTON
08 Asst Chancellor/Dir Dana Library ... Dr. Mark D. WINSTON
37 Manager of Financial Aid ... Mr. Melvin L. BROWN
49 Acting Dean Faculty Arts & Science ... Dr. Jan Ellen LEWIS
61 Dean of School of Law ... Dr. John J. FARMER, JR.
50 Dean Business Newark/New Bruns ... Dr. Glenn R. SHAFER
66 Dean College of Nursing ... Dr. William L. HOLZEMER
88 Dean School Criminal Justice ... Dr. Todd R. CLEAR
38 Director Student Counseling ... Dr. Pamela K. HEARD
96 Director of Purchasing & Admin Svc ... Mr. Alvin L. COOLEY
88 Dean Sch of Public Affairs & Admin ... Dr. Marc HOLZER
39 Director Housing & Residence Life ... Dr. Angelita BONILLA
23 Director Health Services ... Dr. Sandra SAMUELS
41 Director of Athletics ... Mr. Mark GRIFFIN
82 Director of Global Affairs ... Dr. Jean-Marc COICAUD
58 Dean Graduate School Newark ... Dr. Margaret M. SHIFFRAR
87 Director Summer Session ... Dr. Elizabeth C. ROWE

Saint Peter's College (F)

2641 Kennedy Boulevard, Jersey City NJ 07306-5997
County: Hudson FICE Identification: 002638
Unit ID: 186432
Telephone: (201) 761-6000 Carnegie Class: Master's L
FAX Number: (201) 761-7801 Calendar System: Semester
URL: www.spc.edu
Established: 1872 Annual Undergrad Tuition & Fees: $31,220
Enrollment: 2,986 Coed
Affiliation or Control: Roman Catholic IRS Status: 501(c)3
Highest Offering: Doctorate
Program: Liberal Arts And General; Teacher Preparatory; Professional
Accreditation: M, NURSE, TEAC

01 President ... Dr. Eugene J. CORNACCHIA
05 Provost/Vice Pres Academic Affairs ... Dr. Marylou YAM
10 Vice Pres of Finance & Business ... Mr. Denton L. STARGEL
30 Vice President Advancement ... Mr. Michael A. FAZIO
32 Assoc VP Student Life & Develop ... Ms. Carla THARP
42 Vice Pres for Mission & Ministry ... Fr. Michael L. BRADEN, SJ
84 VP Enrollment Mgmt & Marketing ... Vacant
04 Special Assistant to the President ... Dr. Virginia BENDER
20 Academic Dean Day Session ... Dr. Velda GOLDBERG
51 Assoc Dean & Director of JC SPCS ... Ms. Elizabeth KANE
78 Assoc Dean of Experiential Lrng ... Dr. Peter M. GOTLIEB
88 Associate Dean of Undergraduates ... Dr. Anna CICIRELLI
35 Dean of Students ... Vacant
26 Director of College Communications ... Ms. Sarah MALINOWSKI
84 Director Enrollment/Research/Tech ... Mr. Ben SCHOLZ
07 Director of Admissions ... Mr. David GRIFFEY
08 Director of the Libraries ... Mr. David HARDGROVE
37 Director of Student Fin Aid ... Ms. Jennifer RAGSDALE
06 Registrar & Dir of Student Accounts ... Ms. Irma WILLIAMS
27 Chief Information Officer ... Ms. Dale HOCHSTEIN
09 Director of Institutional Research ... Mr. Lamberto C. NIEVES
66 Director BSN/MSN Nursing Program ... Dr. Ann TRITAK
19 Director of Campus Safety ... Mr. Art YOUMANS
24 Instructional Design Specialist ... Ms. Renee EVANS
15 Director of Human Resources ... Mr. Joseph A. DESCISCIO
29 Director Alumni Relations ... Ms. Gloria MERCURIO
30 Director of Gift/Planning ... Ms. Ana M. CRAVO
38 Director Personal Development ... Mr. Ron BECKER
39 Director of Residence Life ... Ms. Honey MINKOWITZ
41 Director of Athletics ... Mr. Joseph QUINLAN
42 Director of Campus Ministry ... Vacant
36 Director of Career Services ... Mr. Crescenzo FONZO

13	Director of Network Services	Mr. Bert VABRE
85	Foreign Studies Adviser	Mr. Tushar TRIVEDI
18	Manager of College Services	Ms. Anna DE PAULA

Salem Community College (A)

460 Hollywood Avenue, Carneys Point NJ 08069-2799

County: Salem FICE Identification: 005461
Unit ID: 186469
Telephone: (856) 299-2100 Carnegie Class: Assoc/Pub-S-SC
FAX Number: (856) 351-2634 Calendar System: Semester
URL: www.salemcc.edu
Established: 1972 Annual Undergrad Tuition & Fees (In-District): $4,050
Enrollment: 1,321 Coed
Affiliation or Control: State/Local IRS Status: 501(c)3
Highest Offering: Associate Degree
Program: Occupational; 2-Year Principally Bachelor's Creditable
Accreditation: M, ADNUR, PNUR

01	President	Mrs. Joan M. BAILLIE
26	Exec Asst to Pres/Dir Public Rels	Mr. William CLARK
32	Chief Student Affairs Officer	Dr. Joanne DAMMINGER
11	Acting Dean of Admin Services	Mr. John PARDINI
35	Director of Student Succes Programs	Dr. Cherita G. WEATHERSPOON
20	Dean of Academic Affairs/CAO	Mr. Mark MCCORMICK
66	Director Nursing	Mrs. Michelle O'NEAL
41	Athletic Director	Ms. Karen FREED
29	Director Alumni Relations	Mr. William CLARK
84	Director Enrollment Management	Mr. Kevin CATALFAMO
102	Chief Foundation Officer	Ms. Linda P. SMITH
96	Manager of Purchasing	Ms. Janet CROUSE
09	Director Inst Rsrch/Planning/Devel	Ms. Denise DERSCH
21	Manager of Finance	Ms. Catherine PRIEST
37	Director of Financial Aid	Mr. Maurice THOMAS
06	Registrar	Ms. Elizabeth MERCADO

Seton Hall University (B)

400 S Orange Avenue, South Orange NJ 07079-2697

County: Essex FICE Identification: 002632
Unit ID: 186584
Telephone: (973) 761-9000 Carnegie Class: DRU
FAX Number: N/A Calendar System: Semester
URL: www.shu.edu
Established: 1856 Annual Undergrad Tuition & Fees: $34,750
Enrollment: 9,112 Coed
Affiliation or Control: Roman Catholic IRS Status: 501(c)3
Highest Offering: Doctorate
Program: Liberal Arts And General; Teacher Preparatory; Professional
Accreditation: M, ARCPA, BUS, BUSA, COPSY, MFCD, NURSE, OT, PTA, SP, SPAA, SW, TED

01	President	Dr. A. Gabriel ESTEBAN
05	Provost & Executive Vice President	Dr. Larry ROBINSON
10	Vice Pres for Finance/CFO	Mr. Stephen A. GRAHAM
11	Vice President for Administration	Mr. Dennis J. GARBINI
43	Vice President & General Counsel	Ms. Catherine A. KIERNAN
30	Vice Pres Univ Advancement	Mr. David BOHAN
32	Vice President Student Affairs	Dr. Tracy T. GOTTLIEB
84	Vice President of Enrollment Mgmt	Dr. Alyssa MCCLOUD
42	Vice Pres for Mission & Ministry	Msgr. C. Anthony ZICCARDI
16	Assoc Vice Pres Human Resources	Mr. David K. MCNICHOL
29	Assoc VP Alumni/Government Rels	Mr. Matthew BOROWICK
44	Int Assoc Vice Pres Univ Advance	Mr. Joseph GUASCONI
26	Assoc VP Public Relations & Mktg	Mr. Gregory G. TOBIN
18	Assoc VP for Facilities & Operation	Mr. John SIGNORELLO
88	Asst VP Finance & Technology	Mr. David MIDDLETON
35	Asst VP Student Affs/Dir Pub Safety	Mr. Patrick LINFANTE
31	Asc VP/Dean of Students/Cmty Dev	Ms. Karen VAN NORMAN
20	Senior Vice Provost	Dr. Joan GUETTI
88	Assoc Prov Finance/Administration	Dr. Nicholas SNOW
45	Assoc Provost/Dean Rsrch/Grad Stds	Dr. Gregory A. BURTON
104	Asc Prov Intl Pgms/Acad Support Svc	Mrs. Mary K. RAWN
49	Dean of Arts & Sciences	Dr. Michael S. ZAVADA
50	Dean School of Business	Dr. Joyce A. STRAWSER
66	Dean of Nursing	Dr. Phyllis HANSELL
53	Dean College Education Svcs	Dr. Joseph DEPIERRO
73	Dean School of Theology	Msgr. Joseph R. REILLY
63	Dean School of Health & Med Science	Dr. Brian SHULMAN
82	Dean Diplomacy/Intl Relations	Dr. John K. MENZIES
61	Dean of Law School	Mr. Patrick J. HOBBS
08	Dean of University Libraries	Dr. John E. BUSCHMAN
51	Dean Cont Educ/Professional Studies	Ms. Nancy LOW-HOGAN
88	Assoc Dean/Director of EOP	Dr. Hasani CARTER
88	Assoc Dean/Exec Dir of Special Pgms	Ms. Cassandra E. DAVIS
21	Director of Business Affairs	Ms. Theresa L. DEEHAN
13	Chief Information Officer	Dr. Stephen LANDRY
28	Director Compliance & Risk Mgmt	Ms. Lori A. BROWN
37	Director for Financial Aid	Ms. Javonda T. ASSANTE
39	Director of Housing/Residence Life	Ms. Tara HART
06	University Registrar	Ms. Mary Ellen FARRELL
07	Recruitment/Compensation Manager	Ms. Jane JACOBS
36	Director of the Career Center	Ms. Jacquline CHAFFIN
41	Dir Athletics/Recreational Services	Mr. Patrick G. LYONS
46	Director of Grants & Research	Vacant
18	Director of Physical Plant	Mr. Steve KURTYKA
23	Acting Director of Counseling	Dr. Katherine EVANS
42	Director of Campus Ministry	Rev. Stanley GOMES
88	Minister to Priest Community	Msgr. James M. CAFONE
09	Dir Planning Inst Research & Asses	Ms. Connie L. BEALE
07	Dir of Undergraduate Admissions	Dr. Wendy W. LIN-COOK
96	Director of Procurement	Mr. Martin E. KOELLER
38	Director Health Services	Ms. Mary Elizabeth COSTELLO
88	Director Core Curriculum	Dr. Anthony C. SCIGLITANO, JR.
15	Manager Employer & Labor Relations	Vacant

Seton Hall University School of Law (C)

One Newark Center, Newark NJ 07102-5210

County: Essex FICE Identification: 009986
Telephone: (973) 642-8500 Carnegie Class: Not Classified
FAX Number: (973) 642-8031 Calendar System: Semester
URL: law.shu.edu
Established: 1951 Annual Graduate Tuition & Fees: $47,330
Enrollment: 983 Coed
Affiliation or Control: Roman Catholic IRS Status: 501(c)3
Highest Offering: First Professional Degree; No Undergraduates
Program: Professional
Accreditation: &M, LAW

01	Dean	Patrick E. HOBBS
05	Vice Dean	Erik R. LILLQUIST
20	Associate Dean	Claudette L. ST. ROMAIN
84	Dean of Enrollment Management	Gisele JOACHIM
32	Dean of Students	Cara Herrick FOERST
20	Asst Dean Academic Affairs/Policy	Gary S. BAVERO
11	Asst Dean Administration/Finance	Terry DE ALMEIDA
30	Asst Dean Alumni/Development	Vicki FLEISCHER
13	Asst Dean Leg Comp/Info Tech/Comm	Carmelo LUBRANO
88	Asst Dean Special Projects	Rosa ALVES
36	Asst Dean of Career Services	David WEINBERG
36	Director of Career Services	Sonia CUNHA
08	Director Law Library	Charles SULLIVAN
09	Director of Institutional Research	Vacant
96	Director Special Programs	Gina FONDETTO
37	Director of Financial Resource Mgmt	Karen A. SOKOL
37	Associate Director of Financial Aid	Tai GEDEON
42	Chaplain	Rev. Nicholas GENGARO
06	Registrar & Bursar	Jo Ann MALDONADO
18	Facilities Engineer	John FLANAGAN
90	Director PC Support	Michael J. MCBRIDE
90	PC Support Specialist	Vacant
91	Director IT Projects	Eric D. WINCH
19	Security Manager	Gerald LENIHAN
88	Director Legal Educ Oppty Pgms	Christina L. BENNETT
102	Director Corp & Foundation Relation	Denise M. PINNEY
43	Director Center for Social Justice	Lori A. NESSEL
29	Director Alumni Relations	Lori THIMMEL
44	Director of Annual Giving	Anthony BELLUCCI
35	Director Student Affairs	Molly MARMION
44	Director of Major Gift	Vacant
20	Director Academic Services	Gwenda R. DAVIS
26	Director of Communications	Janet LEMONNIER
28	Director of Diversity	Vacant
36	Assoc Director Career Services	Paula EDGAR
36	Assoc Director of Career Services	Erin SCHERZER
07	Assoc Director of Admissions	Katherine VALASEK
07	Assoc Director of Admissions	Mimi HUANG
23	Exec Director Healthcare Compl Pgm	Simone HANDLER-HUTCHINSON
58	Administrator of Graduate Pgm	Helen CUMMINGS
30	Development & Scholarship Coord	Andrea DECHELLIS
30	Development & Reunion Coord	Vacant
105	Webmaster/Web Coordinator	Ana L. SANTOS
36	Career Counselor	Joseph STEINBERG

† Regional accreditation is carried under the parent institution in South Orange, NJ.

Somerset Christian College (D)

60 Park Place, Suite 701, Newark NJ 07102

County: Essex FICE Identification: 036663
Unit ID: 440794
Telephone: (973) 803-5000 Carnegie Class: Spec/Faith
FAX Number: (973) 242-3282 Calendar System: Semester
URL: www.somerset.edu
Established: 1908 Annual Undergrad Tuition & Fees: $15,912
Enrollment: 275 Coed
Affiliation or Control: Wesleyan Church IRS Status: 501(c)3
Highest Offering: Baccalaureate
Program: Liberal Arts And General; Professional; Religious Emphasis
Accreditation: M, BI

01	President	Dr. David E. SCHROEDER
03	Executive Vice President	Mr. Daniel W. WRIGHT
05	VP Academic Affairs	Vacant
26	VP Public Relations	Dr. Ralph T. GRANT
45	VP Strategic Initiatives	Ms. Linda SCHMITT
10	Assistant VP of Financial Services	Mr. Joel DAVIS
06	Assistant Dean & Registrar	Mrs. Amy HUBER
07	Director of Admissions	Ms. Keyla GUZMAN
88	Director of Adult Degree Program	Mr. Gary LOUNSBERRY
37	Director of Financial Aid	Mrs. Betzi SCHROEDER
32	Director of Student Life	Dr. Joanne NOEL

Stevens Institute of Technology (E)

Castle Point on Hudson, Hoboken NJ 07030-5991

County: Hudson FICE Identification: 002639
Unit ID: 186867
Telephone: (201) 216-5000 Carnegie Class: RU/H
FAX Number: (201) 216-8341 Calendar System: Semester
URL: www.stevens.edu
Established: 1870 Annual Undergrad Tuition & Fees: $43,368
Enrollment: 5,541 Coed
Affiliation or Control: Independent Non-Profit IRS Status: 501(c)3
Highest Offering: Doctorate
Program: Liberal Arts And General; Technical Emphasis
Accreditation: M, CS, ENG

01	President	Dr. Nariman FARVARDIN
04	Exec Assistant to the President	Ms. Diana COLOMBO
03	Provost/University Vice President	Dr. George P. KORFIATIS
30	Vice Pres Development	Mr. Edward EICHHORN
10	Vice Pres for Finance/Treasurer	Mr. Randy GREENE
07	VP Univ Enrollment/Administration	Dr. Maureen WEATHERALL
18	VP Facilities/Community Relations	Mr. Henry DOBBELAAR
15	Vice President Human Resources	Mr. Mark SAMOLEWICZ
43	Vice President General Counsel	Ms. Kathy L. SCHULZ
32	Asst VP Stdnt Dev/Dir Coop Educ	Mr. Joseph STAHLEY
13	Asst VP for Information Technology	Vacant
27	AVP Mktg & Univ Communications	Vacant
05	Dean Undergraduate Academics	Dr. Larry RUSS
35	Dean of Student Life	Mr. Kenneth NILSEN
39	Dean of Residence Life	Ms. Trina BALLANTYNE
84	Dean of University Enrollment	Mr. Daniel GALLAGHER
20	Assoc Dean Undergraduate Academics	Dr. Erol CESMEBASI
29	Exec Director Alumni Association	Miss Anita LANG
36	Director of Career Services	Ms. Lynn INSLEY
19	Chief/Director of Security	Mr. Timothy GRIFFIN
41	Athletic Director	Mr. Russell ROGERS
85	Dir of Intl Student/Scholar Svcs	Ms. Doris CLAUSEN
06	Associate Registrar	Ms. Sherra JONES
96	Director of Business Services	Mr. James NEWMAN
37	Director Student Financial Aid	Mr. Shawn O'NEILL
38	Director Student Counseling	Vacant
08	Director of Library	Ms. Ourida OUBRAHAM
40	Manager Campus Bookstore	Ms. Teresa TRIDENTE
25	Director Sponsored Research	Ms. Barbara DEHAVEN
58	Dean of Graduate Academics	Dr. Charles SUFFEL
54	Dean School of Engineering & Scienc	Dr. Michael S. BRUNO
72	Dean Howe Sch of Technology Mgmt	Dr. Gregory PRASTACOS
49	Dean College of Arts & Letters	Dr. Lisa DOLLING
88	Dean School of Systems & Enterprise	Dr. Dinesh VERMA
09	Director of Institutional Research	Ms. Agata WOLFE
26	Chief Public Relations Officer	Ms. Danielle WOODRUFFE

Sussex County Community College (F)

One College Hill Road, Newton NJ 07860-1146

County: Sussex FICE Identification: 025688
Unit ID: 247603
Telephone: (973) 300-2100 Carnegie Class: Assoc/Pub-S-SC
FAX Number: (973) 579-9351 Calendar System: Semester
URL: www.sussex.edu
Established: 1982 Annual Undergrad Tuition & Fees (In-District): $5,010
Enrollment: 3,794 Coed
Affiliation or Control: State/Local IRS Status: 501(c)3
Highest Offering: Associate Degree
Program: Occupational; 2-Year Principally Bachelor's Creditable
Accreditation: M, MAC, SURGT

01	President	Dr. Paul MAZUR
04	Asst to President/Board of Trustees	Wendy FULLEM
05	Sr VP of Academic & Student Affairs	Harold DAMATO
10	VP of Finance and Operations	Frank NOCELLA
16	Exec Dir of Human Res/Legal Matters	Debra CARTER
26	Exec Dir of Marketing/Public Info	Kathleen SCOTT
30	Exec Director of the Foundation	Barbara WORTMANN
20	Sr Dean of Business/Law/Math/Scienc	William WAITE
20	Dean of Lib Arts/Social Sci/Educati	Dr. Marian EBERLY
24	Assoc Dean of Learning Resources	Dr. Kathleen OKAY
20	Asst Dean of Academic Affairs	Alberta JAEGER
103	Asst Dean of Community Ed/Workf Dev	Kathleen NELSON
38	Asst Dean of Counseling/Fin Aid/Reg	Deborah MCFADDEN
41	Asst Dean of Athletics/Student Affs	John KUNTZ
21	Exec Director of Finance	Kristine PERRY
18	Dir Facilities/Campus Security	Kenneth EVANS
13	Dir of Management Info Systems	Craig MACKEY
88	Director of Bursar Office	Catherine WINTERFIELD
106	Dir of Media Services/Distance Educ	Tony SELIMO
08	Director of Library	Stephanie COOPER
07	Director of Admissions	Todd POLTERSDORF
88	Director of Health Sciences	Barbara COOK
88	Director of Instructional Design	Anthony SORRENTO
37	Director of Financial Aid	Michael CORSO
88	Director of Accounting	Patricia NOBLIN
09	Assoc Dir of Institutional Research	Matthew MILLER
06	Assoc Registrar	Solweig DIMINO
35	Assoc Dir of Student Activities	Heidi GREGG

Talmudical Academy of New Jersey (G)

Route 524, Adelphia NJ 07710-9999

County: Monmouth FICE Identification: 011989
Unit ID: 186900
Telephone: (732) 431-1600 Carnegie Class: Spec/Faith
FAX Number: (732) 431-3951 Calendar System: Semester
Established: 1971 Annual Undergrad Tuition & Fees: $11,000
Enrollment: 57 Male
Affiliation or Control: Independent Non-Profit IRS Status: 501(c)3
Highest Offering: Baccalaureate
Program: Teacher Preparatory; Professional

Accreditation: RABN

01 President .... Mr. Charles SEMAH
05 Dean .... Rabbi Yeruchim SHAIN

Thomas Edison State College (A)

101 W State Street, Trenton NJ 08608-1176
County: Mercer FICE Identification: 021922
Unit ID: 187046
Telephone: (609) 984-1100 Carnegie Class: Master's S
FAX Number: (609) 292-9000 Calendar System: Other
URL: www.tesc.edu
Established: 1972 Annual Undergrad Tuition & Fees (In-State): $5,508
Enrollment: 20,642 Coed
Affiliation or Control: State IRS Status: 501(c)3
Highest Offering: Master's
Program: Liberal Arts And General; Professional
Accreditation: M, NUR, NURSE, POLYT, TEAC

01 President .... Dr. George A. PRUITT
05 Vice President & Provost .... Mr. William J. SEATON
10 Vice President & Treasurer .... Mr. Christopher STRINGER
26 Vice President Public Affairs .... Mr. John P. THURBER
45 Vice President Planning & Research .... Mr. Dennis DEVERY
84 VP Enrollment Mgmt/Learner Services .... Dr. Mary Ellen CARO
106 Vice Prov Directed Indp Adult Lrng .... Dr. Henry VAN ZYL
51 Vice Prov/Dean Watson Sch Cont Educ .... Dr. Joseph YOUNGBLOOD
88 AVP Enroll Mgmt/Strategic Partnrshp .... Ms. Sylvia HAMILTON
88 AVP Military & Veteran Education .... Mr. Louis MARTINI
32 Assoc VP and Dean of Learner Svcs .... Dr. Raymond YOUNG
21 Treasurer .... Vacant
35 Asst Vice Prov Learner Services .... Mr. Dave ANDERSON
100 Chief of Staff .... Ms. Linda M. VASBINDER
26 Director Market Assessment .... Ms. Marie R. POWER-BARNES
86 Dir Communications/Govt Affairs .... Ms. Robin WALTON
43 General Counsel .... Ms. Barbara KLEVA
09 Director Inst Res/Outcomes Assess .... Dr. Ann Marie SENIOR
66 Dean School of Nursing .... Dr. Phyllis MARSHALL
49 Dean Heavin Sch of Arts & Sciences .. Dr. Susan C. DAVENPORT
50 Dean School of Business & Mgmt .... Dr. Susan GILBERT
06 Registrar .... Ms. Sharon SMITH
72 Dean School of Applied Sci/Tech .... Vacant
21 Controller .... Ms. Michele EVANCHIK
13 Chief Information Officer .... Mr. Drew W. HOPKINS
88 Dir Center for Acad Program Reviews .... Vacant
07 Director Admissions .... Mr. David HOFTIEZER
16 Director Human Resources .... Ms. Mindi SHALITA
29 Director of Alumni Affairs .... Ms. Roxanne GLOBIS
37 Director of Financial Aid .... Mr. James OWENS
11 Director Administrative Services .... Ms. Mary C. HACK
21 Director Budget and Analysis .... Ms. Diane KOYE
21 Bursar .... Mr. Philip SANDERS
30 Director of Development .... Ms. Misty ISAK
102 Director Corporate/Foundation Rels .... Mr. Frederick BRAND
27 Director of Communications .... Mr. Joseph GUZZARDO
08 State Librarian .... Ms. Mary CHUTE
105 Director Website & Multimedia Produ .... Mr. Jeffery LUSHBAUGH
88 Director of Advancement Services .... Ms. Erica SPIZZIRRRI
44 Asc Dir Annual Fund/Donor Relations .... Ms. Jennifer GUERRERO
88 Executive Director Watson Institute .... Ms. Barbara JOHNSON
88 Director Instr Design & Course Dev .... Mr. Matthew COOPER
88 Director of Outcomes Assessment .... Ms. Cynthia MACMILLAN
88 ADA Coordinator .... Ms. Laura BRENNER-SCOTTI

Union County College (B)

1033 Springfield Avenue, Cranford NJ 07016-1598
County: Union FICE Identification: 002643
Unit ID: 187198
Telephone: (908) 709-7000 Carnegie Class: Assoc/Pub-S-MC
FAX Number: (908) 709-0527 Calendar System: Semester
URL: www.ucc.edu
Established: 1933 Annual Undergrad Tuition & Fees (In-District): $4,535
Enrollment: 12,416 Coed
Affiliation or Control: State/Local IRS Status: 501(c)3
Highest Offering: Associate Degree
Program: Occupational; 2-Year Principally Bachelor's Creditable
Accreditation: M, PNUR, PTAA

01 President .... Dr. Margaret M. MCMENAMIN
05 Vice President Academic Affairs .... Dr. Maris LOWN
10 Vice Pres Financial Affs/Treasurer .... Mr. Bernard LENIHAN
32 Vice President Student Services .... Dr. Ralph FORD
11 Vice Pres Administrative Services .... Dr. Stephen NACCO
12 Provost Elizabeth Campus .... Dr. Barbara GABA
12 Provost Plainfield Campus .... Dr. Negar FARAKISH
84 Dean of Enrollment Management .... Vacant
26 Exec Director College Relations .... Ms. Ellen DOTTO
13 Director of Information Tech .... Mr. Thomas CHERUBINO
06 Dir Admissions/Records/Registrar .... Ms. Nina HERNANDEZ
08 Acting Director Libraries .... Ms. Dena LEITER
38 Director of Counseling .... Ms. Heather KEITH
37 Director of Financial Aid .... Vacant
21 Director of Student Accounts .... Mr. Larry GOLDMAN
51 Dean Continuing Educ/Econ Dev .... Dr. Lisa HISCANO
09 Exec Dir Assessment Plng & Research ...... Dr. Patricia S. BIDDAR
15 Dir Human Res/Purch/Aux Enterpr .... Vacant
18 Director Facilities .... Mr. Henry KEY
45 Director Resource Development ... Ms. Barbara GAVIN-WILLIAMS
102 Executive Director Foundation .... Ms. Beth GORIN
20 Director Academic Testing .... Vacant

28 Director EOF .... Mr. Ruben MELENDEZ
41 Director Athletics .... Ms. Tamalea SMITH
19 Director Public Safety .... Mr. Joseph HINES
24 Director Media Technologies .... Mr. Stephen KATO
20 Director Academic Learning Center .... Ms. Gail HEIN
21 Controller .... Ms. Lynne WELCH
96 Director of Purchasing .... Ms. Sandra AULD
40 Manager Bookstore .... Mr. Carl BRUSS

*University of Medicine and Dentistry of New Jersey (C)

65 Bergen Street, Newark NJ 07101-1709
County: Essex FICE Identification: 010394
Unit ID: 187222
Telephone: (973) 972-4400 Carnegie Class: N/A
FAX Number: (973) 972-4429
URL: www.umdnj.edu

01 Interim President .... Dr. Denise V. RODGERS
05 Exec VP Academic/Clinical Affairs .... Dr. Denise V. RODGERS
43 Senior Vice Pres/General Counsel .... Mr. Lester ARON
10 University Chief Financial Officer .... Ms. Denise MULKERN
13 Chief Information Officer .... Ms. Denise ROMANO
17 Acting Pres/CEO University Hosp .... Mr. James GONZALEZ
11 President & CEO/UBHC .... Mr. Christopher O. KOSSEFF
26 Senior VP Public Affairs .... Ms. Julane MILLER-ARMBRISTER
88 Sr VP Chief Ethics & Compliance .... Mr. Bret S. BISSEY
100 Chief of Staff .... Mr. Steven K. ANDREASSEN, JR.
21 Vice President Finance/Treasurer .... Mr. Francis X. COLFORD
18 Interim VP Administration .... Mr. David C. SCHULZ
15 Interim VP Human Resources .... Mr. Gerard GARCIA
88 Vice Pres Supply Chain Management .... Mr. Thomas W. KENYON, JR.
20 VP for Academic Affairs .... Ms. Freda ZACKIN
46 Vice President Research .... Dr. Kathleen W. SCOTTO
88 VP Investigations Group .... Mr. Neil SCHORR
88 Vice President Internal Audit .... Mr. James ROWAN
102 Vice Chairman/CEO UMDNJ Foundation .... Dr. George F. HEINRICH
102 Pres & COO UMDNJ Foundation ...... Mr. James M. GOLUBIESKI
88 Assoc VP Rsrch/Regulatory Affairs .... Dr. Judith NEUBAUER
22 Assoc VP Workplace Diversity .... Ms. Catherine M. BOLDER
08 Assoc VP Scholarly Resour/Univ Lib .... Ms. Judith S. COHN
51 Assoc VP/CEO Continuing Education .... Vacant
96 Asst VP Supplier Diversity/Vendors .... Ms. Ernestine WATSON
09 Exec Dir Faculty Affairs/Inst Rsch .... Dr. Sheila EDER
06 University Registrar .... Ms. Susan E. NELSON
37 Director University Financial Aid .... Ms. Elaine P. VARAS
19 Director Public Safety .... Mr. Carmelo V. HUERTAS

*UMDNJ-New Jersey Dental School (D)

110 Bergen Street, Room B-830, Newark NJ 07101-1709
County: Essex FICE Identification: 024635
Telephone: (973) 972-4633 Carnegie Class: Not Classified
FAX Number: (973) 972-3689 Calendar System: Semester
URL: dentalschool.umdnj.edu/
Established: 1954 Annual Graduate Tuition & Fees: N/A
Enrollment: 498 Coed
Affiliation or Control: State IRS Status: 501(c)3
Highest Offering: First Professional Degree; No Undergraduates
Program: Professional
Accreditation: &M, DENT

02 Dean .... Dr. Cecile A. FELDMAN
10 Vice President of Finance .... Ms. Jacqueline SCHROEDERS
05 Interim Assoc Dean Academic Affairs .... Dr. Kim FENESY
32 Assoc Dean Student Affairs .... Dr. Kim E. FENESY
46 Acting Associate Dean Research .... Dr. Barbara L. GREENBERG
17 Assoc Dean Clinical Affairs .... Dr. Michael CONTE
07 Acting Dir Predoc Admiss & Recruit .... Dr. Rosa M. CHAVIANO-MORAN

*UMDNJ-Graduate School of Biomedical Sciences (E)

185 South Orange Avenue, MSB C-696, Newark NJ 07107-1709
County: Essex FICE Identification: 011174
Telephone: (973) 972-5332 Carnegie Class: Not Classified
FAX Number: (973) 972-7148 Calendar System: Semester
URL: gsbs.umdnj.edu/
Established: 1970 Annual Undergrad Tuition & Fees (In-State): N/A
Enrollment: 1,319 Coed
Affiliation or Control: State IRS Status: 501(c)3
Highest Offering: Doctorate
Program:
Accreditation: &M

02 Dean .... Dr. Kathleen W. SCOTTO
12 Senior Associate Dean NJMS .... Dr. Andrew P. THOMAS
12 Senior Associate Dean RWJMS .... Dr. Terri G. KINZY
12 Senior Associate Dean SOM .... Dr. Carl E. HOCK
06 Manager .... Ms. Barbara COLEMAN-LEE
04 Exec Asst to the Dean .... Ms. Susan M. LOMANTO

*UMDNJ-New Jersey Medical School (F)

185 S Orange Avenue, Newark NJ 07101-1709
County: Essex FICE Identification: 002620
Telephone: (973) 972-4538 Carnegie Class: Not Classified
FAX Number: (973) 972-7104 Calendar System: Semester
URL: njms.umdnj.edu/
Established: 1954 Annual Undergrad Tuition & Fees (In-State): N/A
Enrollment: 751 Coed
Affiliation or Control: State IRS Status: 501(c)3
Highest Offering: First Professional Degree; No Lower Division
Program: Professional
Accreditation: &M, MED

02 Dean .... Dr. Robert L. JOHNSON
05 Vice Dean .... Dr. Maria L. SOTO-GREENE
17 Sr Assoc Dean Clinical Affairs .... Dr. Kendell R. SPROTT
10 Associate Dean/CFO .... Mr. David L. ROE
46 Senior Associate Dean Research .... Dr. William C. GAUSE
32 Assoc Dean Student Affairs .... Dr. James M. HILL
07 Assoc Dean Admissions/Special Pgms ... Dr. George F. HEINRICH
35 Assistant Dean Student Affairs .... Ms. Julie FERGUSON
21 Business Manager .... Mr. Ronald JENKINS

*UMDNJ-Robert Wood Johnson Medical School (G)

675 Hoes Lane, Piscataway NJ 08854-5635
County: Middlesex FICE Identification: 024549
Telephone: (732) 235-6300 Carnegie Class: Not Classified
FAX Number: (732) 235-6315 Calendar System: Semester
URL: rwjms.umdnj.edu/
Established: 1962 Annual Undergrad Tuition & Fees (In-State): N/A
Enrollment: 638 Coed
Affiliation or Control: State IRS Status: 501(c)3
Highest Offering: First Professional Degree
Program: Professional
Accreditation: &M, IPSY, MED

02 Dean .... Dr. Peter S. AMENTA
05 Interim Sr Assoc Dean Education .... Dr. Carol TERREGINO
88 Senior Assoc Dean Community Health .... Dr. Eric G. JAHN
46 Interim Senior Assoc Dean Research .... Dr. Terri KINZY
17 Sr Assoc Dean Clinical Affairs .... Dr. Anthony T. SCARDELLA
32 Associate Dean Student Affairs .... Dr. Carol TERREGINO
07 Interim Associate Dean Admissions .... Dr. Carol A. TERREGINO
11 Chief Operating Officer .... Ms. Alice LUSTIG
06 Registrar .... Mr. Daniel OSTIN

*UMDNJ-School of Nursing (H)

65 Bergen Street, Room 1126, Newark NJ 07101-1709
County: Essex Identification: 666970
Telephone: (973) 972-4276 Carnegie Class: Not Classified
FAX Number: (973) 972-3225 Calendar System: Semester
URL: sn.umdnj.edu/
Established: 1992 Annual Undergrad Tuition & Fees (In-State): N/A
Enrollment: 1,625 Coed
Affiliation or Control: State IRS Status: 501(c)3
Highest Offering: Doctorate
Program: Nursing Emphasis
Accreditation: &M, ANEST, MIDWF, NURSE

02 Dean .... Dr. Susan W. SALMOND
46 Associate Dean Research .... Vacant
05 Associate Dean For Academic Affairs .... Dr. Marie T. O'TOOLE
31 Assoc Dean Community/Clinical Affs .... Vacant
11 Assistant Dean for Administration .... Ms. Wendy A. RITCH
17 Assistant Dean Clinical Affairs .... Mr. David W. UNKLE
32 Assistant Dean for Student Affairs .... Dr. Donna CILL
58 Assistant Dean Graduate Studies .... Dr. Patricia K. HINDIN
12 Associate Dean Stratford Campus .... Dr. Marie T. O'TOOLE
06 Registrar .... Ms. Bianca THOMPSON

*UMDNJ-School of Osteopathic Medicine (I)

One Medical Center Drive, Stratford NJ 08084-1501
County: Camden FICE Identification: 024540
Telephone: (856) 566-6764 Carnegie Class: Not Classified
FAX Number: (856) 566-6895 Calendar System: Semester
URL: som.umdnj.edu/
Established: 1976 Annual Undergrad Tuition & Fees (In-State): N/A
Enrollment: 549 Coed
Affiliation or Control: State IRS Status: 501(c)3
Highest Offering: First Professional Degree
Program: Professional
Accreditation: &M, OSTEO

02 Dean .... Dr. Thomas A. CAVALIERI
11 Chief Operating Officer .... Ms. Vivian LUBIN
10 Interim Chief Financial Officer .... Mr. Michael RIEKER
05 Assoc Dean Academic Affairs .... Vacant
17 Assoc Dean Clinical Affairs .... Dr. Vincent J. DERISIO
46 Assoc Dean Research .... Dr. Carl E. HOCK
32 Assistant Dean Student Affairs .... Dr. Kathryn C. LAMBERT
06 Associate Registrar .... Ms. Regina WILMES

*UMDNJ-School of Public Health (A)

683 Hoes Lane W, Room 235, Piscataway NJ 08854-8021

County: Middlesex | Identification: 666991
Telephone: (732) 445-9700 | Carnegie Class: Not Classified
FAX Number: (732) 445-9755 | Calendar System: Semester
URL: sph.umdnj.edu/
Established: 1998 | Annual Undergrad Tuition & Fees (In-State): N/A
Enrollment: 376 | Coed
Affiliation or Control: State | IRS Status: 501(c)3
Highest Offering: Doctorate
Program: Professional
Accreditation: &M, PH

02 Interim Dean .... Dr. George RHOADS
12 Associate Dean Pisc/NB .... Dr. Pamela STRICKLAND
12 Associate Dean Newark .... Dr. William E. HALPERIN
12 Asst Dean Stratford/Camden .... Dr. Bernadette WEST
05 Assoc Dean Acad and Faculty Affairs .... Dr. Alan C. MONHEIT
46 Associate Dean Research .... Dr. Patrick CLIFFORD
32 Asst Dean Student/Alumni Affairs .... Dr. Shou-En LU
10 Business Manager .... Mr. Alexander ZAROS
06 Assistant Registrar .... Vacant

*UMDNJ-School of Health Related Professions (B)

65 Bergen Street, Room 149, Newark NJ 07101-1709

County: Essex | FICE Identification: 020668
Telephone: (973) 972-5454 | Carnegie Class: Not Classified
FAX Number: (973) 972-7028 | Calendar System: Semester
URL: shrp.umdnj.edu/
Established: 1976 | Annual Undergrad Tuition & Fees (In-State): N/A
Enrollment: 1,544 | Coed
Affiliation or Control: State | IRS Status: 501(c)3
Highest Offering: Doctorate
Program: Professional
Accreditation: &M, ARCPA, CACREP, CORE, CVT, CYTO, DA, DH, DIETC, DIETI, DMS, MIDWF, MT, NMT, PTA

02 Interim Dean .... Dr. Julie O'SULLIVAN-MAILLET
11 Assoc Dean Administrative Service .... Dr. Gwendolyn MAHON
05 Interim Assoc Dean Academic Affairs .... Dr. Ann W. TUCKER
12 Assoc Dean Southern New Jersey .... Dr. Ann W. TUCKER
12 Administrator Scotch Plains .... Mr. Vernon CABALFIN
32 Assoc Dean Acad & Student Services .... Vacant
46 Interim Associate Dean for Research .... Dr. Robert M. DENMARK
06 Registrar .... Ms. Bianca THOMPSON

Warren County Community College (C)

475 Route 57 W, Washington NJ 07882-4343

County: Warren | FICE Identification: 025039
Unit ID: 245625
Telephone: (908) 835-9222 | Carnegie Class: Assoc/Pub-S-SC
FAX Number: (908) 689-9262 | Calendar System: Semester
URL: www.warren.edu
Established: 1981 | Annual Undergrad Tuition & Fees (In-District): $3,900
Enrollment: 2,304 | Coed
Affiliation or Control: State/Local | IRS Status: 501(c)3
Highest Offering: Associate Degree
Program: Occupational; 2-Year Principally Bachelor's Creditable
Accreditation: M, ADNUR, MAC

01 President .... Dr. William AUSTIN
05 Vice Pres Academics/Student Svcs .... Dr. Lisa SUMMINS
10 Vice Pres Finance & Operations .... Ms. Barbara PRATT
51 Vice Pres Corporate/Continuing Educ .... Ms. Eve AZAR
11 Dean of Administration .... Mr. Dennis FLORENTINE
20 Dean of Academic Affairs .... Mr. David ORENSTEIN
37 Director of Financial Aid .... Ms. Jessica LEEPER
32 Asst Dean of Academic & Stdnt Svcs .... Mr. Jeremy BEELER
15 Director Human Resources .... Ms. Sharon HINTZ
35 Director Student Activities .... Ms. Rose LYNCH
21 Director Business Services .... Mr. Jay ALEXANDER
36 Director Student Success .... Ms. Fae GUERIN

William Paterson University of New Jersey (D)

300 Pompton Road, Wayne NJ 07470-2152

County: Passaic | FICE Identification: 002625
Unit ID: 187444
Telephone: (973) 720-2000 | Carnegie Class: Master's L
FAX Number: (973) 720-2399 | Calendar System: Semester
URL: www.wpunj.edu
Established: 1855 | Annual Undergrad Tuition & Fees (In-State): $11,694
Enrollment: 11,518 | Coed
Affiliation or Control: State | IRS Status: 501(c)3
Highest Offering: Doctorate
Program: Liberal Arts And General; Teacher Preparatory; Professional
Accreditation: M, ART, BUS, CACREP, CS, MUS, NURSE, SP, TED

01 President .... Dr. Kathleen WALDRON
05 Senior Vice President/Provost .... Dr. Edward WEIL
101 Chf of Staff to Pres/Board of Trust .... Dr. Robert SEAL
11 Vice Pres Administration/Finance .... Mr. Stephen BOLYAI
30 Vice Pres Institutional Advancement .... Ms. Pamela FERGUSON
32 Vice President Student Development .... Dr. John MARTONE
84 VP of Enrollment Management .... Ms. Kristin COHEN
58 Assoc VP Acad Affs/Dean Grad Stds .... Dr. Claudia SCHRADER
21 Assoc VP for Administration .... Mr. Richard STOMBER
26 Assoc VP Mkting & Public Relations .... Mr. Stuart GOLDSTEIN
16 Associate Vice Pres Human Resources .... Mr. John POLDING
08 Assoc VP Library Services/Info Tech .... Vacant
35 Associate VP for Campus Life .... Mr. Roland WATTS
19 Dir Public Safety & Univ Police .... Mr. Robert FULLEMAN
35 Asst Vice Pres for Campus Life .... Mr. Francisco DIAZ
35 Assoc VP/Dean Student Development .... Dr. Glen SHERMAN
60 Acting Dean Col Arts/Comm .... Dr. Stephen HAHN
53 Dean College of Education .... Dr. Candace BURNS
66 Dean College of Science & Health .... Dr. Kenneth WOLF
79 Dean Human & Social Science .... Dr. Kara M. RABBITT
50 Interim Dean College of Business .... Dr. Rajiv KASHYAP
08 Dean D & L Cheng Library .... Dr. Anne CILIBERTI
21 Assoc VP Finance & Comptroller .... Ms. Rosemarie GENCO
28 Dir Employment Equity & Diversity .... Mr. John SIMS
46 Exec Director Academic Development .... Ms. Janet DAVIS-DUKES
51 Exec Dir Cont Educ/Distance Lrng .... Ms. Bernadette TIERNAN
20 Associate Provost .... Dr. Stephen HAHN
26 Director External Relations .... Mr. Patrick DEDEO
29 Executive Director Alumni .... Ms. Janis SCHWARTZ
45 Director Inst Research & Assessment .... Dr. Jane ZEFF
43 General Counsel .... Mr. Glenn JONES
13 Chief Information Officer .... Mr. Eric ROSENBERG
15 Director of Human Resources .... Ms. Denise ROBINSON-LEWIS
07 Director of Undergrad Admissions .... Ms. Colleen M. O'CONNOR
37 Director Financial Aid .... Ms. Elizabeth RIQUEZ
06 Registrar .... Ms. Nina TRELISKY
41 Director Athletics .... Ms. Sabrina GRANT
36 Director of Career Dev & Advisement .... Ms. Sharon ROSENGART
39 Director of Residence Life .... Mr. Joseph CAFFARELLI
23 Director Health & Wellness Center .... Dr. Eileen LUBECK
90 Director Instruction/Research Tech .... Dr. Sandra MILLER
09 Dir Institutional Research/Assess .... Dr. Jane ZEFF
40 Director Bookstore .... Mr. Scott DUNLAP
27 Director Public Information .... Ms. Mary Beth ZEMAN
24 Head Audio Visual-Library .... Ms. Jane HUTCHISON
18 Director Capital Plng/Design/Constr .... Vacant
85 Director International Student Svcs .... Ms. Cinzia RICHARDSON
94 Director of Women's Center .... Ms. Librada SANCHEZ
96 Director of Purchasing .... Mr. Lirse JONES
38 Director Student Counseling .... Dr. Eileen LUBECK
89 Director of Freshmen Studies .... Dr. Kim DANIEL-ROBINSON
92 Director of Honors College .... Dr. Susan DINAN

Yeshiva Gedolah Zichron Leyma (E)

1000 Orchard Terrace, Linden NJ 07036

County: Union | Identification: 667078
Telephone: (908) 587-0502 | Carnegie Class: Not Classified
FAX Number: N/A | Calendar System: Semester
Established: 1999 | Annual Undergrad Tuition & Fees: $11,000
Enrollment: 49 | Male
Affiliation or Control: Independent Non-Profit | IRS Status: 501(c)3
Highest Offering: First Talmudic Degree
Program: Professional
Accreditation: RABN

Yeshiva Toras Chaim (F)

1027 Ridge Avenue, Lakewood NJ 08701-2120

County: Ocean | FICE Identification: 041311
Unit ID: 451398
Telephone: (732) 414-2834 | Carnegie Class: Spec/Faith
FAX Number: (732) 358-0220 | Calendar System: Semester
Established: 2000 | Annual Undergrad Tuition & Fees: $11,800
Enrollment: 185 | Male
Affiliation or Control: Independent Non-Profit | IRS Status: 501(c)3
Highest Offering: Baccalaureate
Program: Teacher Preparatory; Professional
Accreditation: RABN

05 Chief Academic Officer .... Rabbi Mendel SLOMOVITS
06 Registrar .... Mrs. Devoiry DURST
21 Bookkeeper .... Mrs. Ruth GROSSMAN

Yeshiva Yesodei Hatorah (G)

2 Yesodei Court, Lakewood NJ 08701

County: Ocean | Identification: 667109
Telephone: (732) 370-3360 | Carnegie Class: Not Classified
FAX Number: (732) 886-2659 | Calendar System: Semester
Established: 1995 | Annual Undergrad Tuition & Fees: $10,800
Enrollment: 44 | Male
Affiliation or Control: Independent Non-Profit | IRS Status: 501(c)3
Highest Offering: First Talmudic Degree
Program: Professional
Accreditation: RABN

05 Dean .... Rabbi Shaya TREFF
10 Chief Financial/Business Officer .... Rabbi Shaya UNGAR
20 Associate Academic Officer .... Rabbi Yisroel Meir TREFF

Yeshivas Be'er Yitzchok (H)

1391 North Avenue, Elizabeth NJ 07208-2480

County: Union | FICE Identification: 041234
Unit ID: 451370
Telephone: (908) 354-6057 | Carnegie Class: Spec/Faith
FAX Number: (908) 820-0431 | Calendar System: Semester
Established: 1999 | Annual Undergrad Tuition & Fees: $12,200
Enrollment: 65 | Male
Affiliation or Control: Independent Non-Profit | IRS Status: 501(c)3
Highest Offering: Baccalaureate
Program: Professional
Accreditation: RABN

01 Chief Executive Officer .... Rabbi Avrohom SCHULMAN
37 Director of Student Financial Aid .... Chani MILLER
11 Chief of Administration .... Shlomo PINES

NEW MEXICO

Brookline College (I)

4201 Central Avenue NW Ste J, Albuquerque NM 87105-1649

County: Bernalillo | Identification: 666724
Unit ID: 444088
Telephone: (505) 880-2877 | Carnegie Class: Assoc/PrivFP
FAX Number: (505) 352-0199 | Calendar System: Other
URL: www.brooklinecollege.edu
Established: 1979 | Annual Undergrad Tuition & Fees: $15,515
Enrollment: 707 | Coed
Affiliation or Control: Proprietary | IRS Status: Proprietary
Highest Offering: Baccalaureate
Program: Occupational; Liberal Arts And General
Accreditation: ACICS, @PTAA

01 Campus Director .... Mr. Andrew WEBB
05 Director of Education .... Mr. David GOULD

† Branch campus of Brookline College, Phoenix, AZ

Carrington College - Albuquerque (J)

1001 Menaul Boulevard NE, Albuquerque NM 87107-1642

County: Bernalillo | Identification: 666014
Unit ID: 442602
Telephone: (505) 254-7777 | Carnegie Class: Not Classified
FAX Number: (505) 254-1101 | Calendar System: Other
URL: www.apollocollege.com
Established: 1976 | Annual Undergrad Tuition & Fees: $44,785
Enrollment: 778 | Coed
Affiliation or Control: Proprietary | IRS Status: Proprietary
Highest Offering: Associate Degree
Program: Occupational; 2-Year Principally Bachelor's Creditable
Accreditation: ACICS, PTAA

01 Executive Campus Director .... Mr. Mark E. LUCERO

† Branch campus of Carrington College, Phoenix, AZ.

Central New Mexico Community College (K)

525 Buena Vista, SE, Albuquerque NM 87106-4096

County: Bernalillo | FICE Identification: 004742
Unit ID: 187532
Telephone: (505) 224-4412 | Carnegie Class: Assoc/Pub-U-MC
FAX Number: (505) 224-4417 | Calendar System: Semester
URL: www.cnm.edu
Established: 1965 | Annual Undergrad Tuition & Fees (In-District): $1,857
Enrollment: 29,180 | Coed
Affiliation or Control: State/Local | IRS Status: 501(c)3
Highest Offering: Associate Degree
Program: 2-Year Principally Bachelor's Creditable
Accreditation: NH, ACBSP, ACFEI, ADNUR, CONST, DA, DMS, EMT, MLTAD, PNUR, SURGT

01 President .... Dr. Katharine W. WINOGRAD
05 Interim Vice Pres for Acad Affairs .... Dr. Sydney D. GUNTHORPE
35 Vice President for Student Services .... Mr. Phillip BUSTOS
10 Vice Pres for Finance & Operations .... Mrs. Katherine ULIBARRI
84 Assoc Vice Pres Enrollment Mgmt .... Mr. Eugene PADILLA
08 Director Learning Resources .... Ms. Poppy JOHNSON RENVALL
23 Director Student Health Center .... Ms. Marti BRITTENHAM
19 Director Security .... Mr. Ernest CHAVEZ
13 Director Info Technology Services .... Mr. Joe GIERI
103 Director Workforce Training Center .... Ms. Evelyn DOW-SIMPSON
36 Director of Job Connection Center .... Ms. Tammy STRICKLER
30 Director of Development .... Mrs. Lisa MCCULLOCH
07 Director Enrollment Services .... Mr. Glenn DAMIANI
26 Dir Marketing & Public Relations .... Mrs. Alexis KERSCHNER-TAPPAN
27 Dir Communications & Media Relation .... Mr. Brad MOORE
37 Director Student Financial Aid .... Mr. Lee CARRILLO
15 Interim Director Human Resources .... Mrs. Rose OROZCO-MONROY
81 Dean School of Math/Sci/Engineering .... Mr. Richard CALABRO
50 Dean School of Bus/Info Technology .... Mr. Sydney GUNTHORPE
72 Dean School of Applied Technologies .... Mr. John BRONISZ
53 Dean School of Adult & General Edu .... Dr. Pam ETRE-PEREZ
83 Dean Comm/Humanities/Soc Sci .... Ms. Erica VOLKERS
76 Interim Dean Health/Well/Pub Safety .... Mr. John BLEWETT
06 Registrar .... Ms. Yvonne MARTINEZ
18 Exec Dir Facilities/Physical Plant .... Mr. Luis CAMPOS
21 Comptroller .... Ms. Loretta MONTOYA
29 Director of Alumni Relations .... Mrs. Anna SANCHEZ
32 Dean of Student Services .... Mr. Rudy GARCIA

38 Director of Student Counseling .... Ms. Tammy STRICKLER
96 Director of Purchasing .... Mrs. Charlotte GENSLER

Clovis Community College (A)

417 Schepps Boulevard, Clovis NM 88101-8381
County: Curry FICE Identification: 004743
Unit ID: 187639
Telephone: (575) 769-2811 Carnegie Class: Assoc/Pub-R-M
FAX Number: (575) 769-4190 Calendar System: Semester
URL: www.clovis.edu
Established: 1971 Annual Undergrad Tuition & Fees (In-State): $936
Enrollment: 3,700 Coed
Affiliation or Control: State IRS Status: 501(c)3
Highest Offering: Associate Degree
Program: Occupational; 2-Year Principally Bachelor's Creditable
Accreditation: NH, ADNUR, RAD

01 President .... Dr. Becky ROWLEY
03 Executive Vice President .... Dr. Robin JONES
10 Chief Financial Officer .... Mrs. Debbie ZURZOLO
05 Chief Academic Officer .... Dr. Robin JONES
13 VP of Information Technology .... Vacant
09 Vice Pres Instl Effectiveness .... Vacant
11 VP Administration/Govt Relations .... Mr. Tom DRAKE
21 Director of Business Affairs .... Ms. Jayne CRAIG
07 Dir Admissions/Records/Registrar .... Ms. Rosie CORRIE
37 Director of Financial Aid .... Ms. April CHAVEZ
08 Director Library/Learning Resources ...... Ms. Deborah ANDERSON
40 Bookstore Manager .... Mrs. Jacque OCHS
35 Dir Center for Student
Success .... Mrs. Mona Lee NORMAN-ARMSTRONG
38 Dir of Counseling/Testing/Advisemnt .... Mrs. Bonnie MILLER
15 Director of Human Resource Services .... Mrs. Rhonda JESKO
88 Director Small Business
Development .... Mrs. Sandra TAYLOR-SAWYER
91 Director of Administrative Info Sys .... Ms. Teresa WHITEHEAD
103 Director Workforce Training Center .... Vacant
56 Director Extended Learning .... Ms. Judith SPILLANE
36 Director Student Placement .... Vacant
30 Chief Development Officer .... Ms. Natalie DAGGETT
18 Director of Physical Plant .... Ms. Brenda DIXON
26 Director of Marketing/Cmty Rels .... Ms. Lisa SPENCER
76 Div Chair Allied Health Programs .... Ms. Shawna MCGILL
83 Div Chair Soc/Behav Sci/Humanities .... Mr. Paul NAGY
50 Div Chair of Business Admin & Tech . Mrs. Becky CARRUTHERS
81 Division Chair of Math/Science .... Mr. Todd KUYKENDALL

Eastern New Mexico University Main Campus (B)

1500 S Avenue K, Portales NM 88130-7400
County: Roosevelt FICE Identification: 002651
Unit ID: 187648
Telephone: (575) 562-1011 Carnegie Class: Master's S
FAX Number: (575) 562-2256 Calendar System: Semester
URL: www.enmu.edu
Established: 1927 Annual Undergrad Tuition & Fees (In-State): $4,350
Enrollment: 5,574 Coed
Affiliation or Control: State IRS Status: 501(c)3
Highest Offering: Master's
Program: Liberal Arts And General; Teacher Preparatory
Accreditation: NH, ACBSP, MUS, NUR, SP, SW, TED

01 President .... Dr. Steven GAMBLE
05 Vice President Academic Affairs .... Dr. Jamie LAURENZ
10 Vice President Business Affairs .... Mr. Scott SMART
32 Vice President for Student Affairs .... Dr. Judith HAISLETT
26 VP University Relations/Enroll Svcs .... Ms. Ronnie BIRDSONG
45 Exec Dir Planning/Analysis/Inst Ren .... Dr. Patrice CALDWELL
20 Asst Vice Pres for Academic Affairs .... Dr. Renee NEELY
20 Asst Vice Pres Academic Affairs .... Dr. John MONTGOMERY
21 Comptroller .... Mrs. Kathy KNOLL
53 Dean Education/Technology .... Dr. Jerry HARMON
50 Interim Dean Business .... Dr. Gene SMITH
57 Dean Fine Arts .... Dr. Joseph KLINE
49 Dean Liberal Arts & Science .... Dr. Mary AYALA
58 Dean Graduate School .... Dr. Linda WEEMS
22 Affirmative Action Officer .... Ms. Tammi GARDNER
08 Director of Library .... Ms. Melveta WALKER
06 Registrar .... Ms. Crystal CREEKMORE
37 Director Student Financial Aid .... Mr. Brent SMALL
07 Director Enrollment Services .... Mr. Cody SPITZ
30 Director Development .... Ms. Noelle BARTL
13 Dir Computing/Information Mgmt .... Mr. Clark ELSWICK
15 Director of Human Resources .... Ms. Julie GAWEHN
88 Director of Broadcasting .... Mr. Duane RYAN
18 Director Physical Plant .... Mr. Ted FARES
41 Athletic Director .... Dr. Jeff GEISER
19 Chief of University Police .... Mr. Brad MAULDIN
23 Director of Health Services .... Ms. Darlene JENKINS
36 Dir Counseling Ctr/Career Svcs .... Ms. Susan LARSON
39 Director Student Housing .... Mr. Steven ESTOCK
09 Assoc Dir Institutional Research .... Ms. Amy HOLT
96 Director of Purchasing .... Ms. Jane BLAKELEY
27 Director of Publications .... Mr. Jim DODSON
29 Coordinator of Alumni .... Vacant
56 Dir of Distance Learning/Outreach .... Ms. Trish MAGUIRE
25 Director Grant Activities .... Ms. Jo LANEY
84 Director Enrollment Management .... Ms. Ronnie BIRDSONG
38 Director Student Counseling .... Ms. Susan LARSON
35 Director Campus Life .... Mr. Draco MILLER

Eastern New Mexico University-Roswell (C)

PO Box 6000, Roswell NM 88202-6000
County: Chaves FICE Identification: 002661
Unit ID: 187666
Telephone: (575) 624-7000 Carnegie Class: Assoc/Pub2in4
FAX Number: (575) 624-7119 Calendar System: Semester
URL: www.roswell.enmu.edu
Established: 1958 Annual Undergrad Tuition & Fees (In-State): $1,506
Enrollment: 4,008 Coed
Affiliation or Control: State IRS Status: 501(c)3
Highest Offering: Associate Degree
Program: Occupational; 2-Year Principally Bachelor's Creditable
Accreditation: NH, ADNUR, DH, EMT, MAC, OTA

01 President .... Dr. John MADDEN
05 Provost Academic/Stdnt Affs .... Vacant
10 VP for Business Affairs .... Mr. Eric JOHNSTON-ORTIZ
32 VP for Student Affairs .... Mr. Robert BOWMAN
20 Asst VP for Academic Affairs .... Vacant
20 Asst VP for Academic Affairs/CTE .... Ms. Dusty LEWIS
21 Controller .... Ms. Karen FRANKLIN
35 Asst VP for Student Affairs .... Mr. Mike MARTINEZ
08 Director Learning Resource Center .... Mr. Rollah ASTON
37 Director Financial Aid .... Ms. Jessie SJUE
30 Director College Development .... Ms. Donna ORACION
07 Director Admissions and Records .... Vacant
13 Director of Computer Services .... Mr. Tillman CROCKER
15 Director of Human Resources .... Dr. Steve CHAMBERS
18 Director of Physical Plant .... Mr. Darryl WARD
19 Director of Security .... Mr. Robert NEWBERRY
96 Director of Purchasing .... Ms. Roberta BRUCE
09 Institutional Research Professional .... Ms. Rhonda CROCKER

Institute of American Indian Arts (D)

83 Avan Nu Po Road, Santa Fe NM 87508-1300
County: Santa Fe FICE Identification: 021464
Unit ID: 187745
Telephone: (505) 424-2300 Carnegie Class: Tribal
FAX Number: (505) 424-3900 Calendar System: Semester
URL: www.iaia.edu
Established: 1962 Annual Undergrad Tuition & Fees: $3,080
Enrollment: 374 Coed
Affiliation or Control: Federal IRS Status: 501(c)3
Highest Offering: Baccalaureate
Program: Fine Arts Emphasis
Accreditation: NH, ART

01 President .... Dr. Robert MARTIN
05 Academic Dean .... Dr. Ann FILEMYR
32 Dean of Student Life .... Ms. Carmen HENAN
08 Director of Library Programs .... Ms. Valerie NYE
10 Dir of Finance & Administration .... Mr. Larry MIRABAL
26 Communications/Marketing Director .... Ms. Kim BACA
84 Dir Admission/Records/Enroll Mgmt .... Mr. Undrell PERSON
30 Dir of Institutional Advancement .... Vacant
37 Director of Financial Aid .... Ms. LaLa GALLEGOS
18 Facilities Management .... Mr. James MASON
15 Human Resources Director .... Ms. Maria HIDALGO

ITT Technical Institute (E)

5100 Masthead Street NE, Albuquerque NM 87109-4366
County: Bernalillo Identification: 666545
Unit ID: 369084
Telephone: (505) 828-1114 Carnegie Class: Spec/Tech
FAX Number: (505) 828-1849 Calendar System: Quarter
URL: www.itt-tech.edu
Established: 1989 Annual Undergrad Tuition & Fees: N/A
Enrollment: 786 Coed
Affiliation or Control: Proprietary IRS Status: Proprietary
Highest Offering: Baccalaureate
Program: Technical Emphasis
Accreditation: ACICS

† Branch campus of ITT Technical Institute, Indianapolis, IN.

Luna Community College (F)

366 Luna Drive, Las Vegas NM 87701-1510
County: San Miguel FICE Identification: 009962
Unit ID: 363633
Telephone: (505) 454-2500 Carnegie Class: Assoc/Pub-R-M
FAX Number: (505) 454-2519 Calendar System: Semester
URL: www.luna.cc.nm.us
Established: 1970 Annual Undergrad Tuition & Fees (In-District): $960
Enrollment: 1,866 Coed
Affiliation or Control: State/Local IRS Status: 501(c)3
Highest Offering: Associate Degree
Program: Occupational; Liberal Arts And General; Teacher Preparatory; Professional
Accreditation: NH, ADNUR, DA

01 President .... Dr. Pete CAMPOS
10 Vice President of Finance .... Ms. Donna FLORES-MEDINA
09 Exec Dir Inst Research/Development .... Dr. Peter MANTHEI
05 Vice Pres Academic/Student Affairs .... Dr. Vidal MARTINEZ
07 Int Director of Admissions .... Mr. Moses MARQUEZ

06 Registrar .... Mr. Johnathan ORTIZ
18 Director Facilities/Physical Plant .... Mr. Ron GONZALES
37 Director Student Financial Aid .... Ms. Regina MADRID
15 Director Human Resources .... Mr. Lawrence QUINTANA
30 Chief Development .... Ms. Mary WARD
13 Director of Computer Services .... Vacant

Mesalands Community College (G)

911 S 10th Street, Tucumcari NM 88401-3352
County: Quay FICE Identification: 032063
Unit ID: 188261
Telephone: (505) 461-4413 Carnegie Class: Assoc/Pub-R-S
FAX Number: (505) 461-1901 Calendar System: Semester
URL: www.mesalands.edu
Established: 1980 Annual Undergrad Tuition & Fees (In-District): $1,740
Enrollment: 990 Coed
Affiliation or Control: State/Local IRS Status: 501(c)3
Highest Offering: Associate Degree
Program: Occupational; 2-Year Principally Bachelor's Creditable
Accreditation: NH

01 President .... Dr. Mildred P. LOVATO
04 Executive Asst to President .... Ms. Connie CHAVEZ
32 Vice President Student Services .... Dr. Aaron KENNEDY
05 Vice President of Academic Affairs .... Ms. Natalie GILLARD
37 Director Financial Aid .... Ms. Amanda HAMMER
26 Director Public Relations .... Ms. Kimberly HANNA
72 Director of NAWRTC .... Mr. Jim MORGAN
84 Director of Enrollment Management .... Ms. Amber MCCLURE
14 Coord of Institutional Computing .... Mr. Larry WICKMAN
09 Dir Inst Research and Development .... Ms. Robin ALDEN

National College of Midwifery (H)

209 State Road 240, Taos NM 87571-6834
County: Taos Identification: 666251
Telephone: (575) 758-8914 Carnegie Class: Not Classified
FAX Number: (575) 758-0302 Calendar System: Other
URL: www.midwiferycollege.org
Established: 1989 Annual Undergrad Tuition & Fees: $5,000
Enrollment: 160 Coed
Affiliation or Control: Independent Non-Profit IRS Status: 501(c)3
Highest Offering: Doctorate
Program: Professional; Nursing Emphasis
Accreditation: MEAC

01 President .... Elizabeth GILMORE

Navajo Technical College (I)

PO Box 849, Crownpoint NM 87313-0849
County: McKinley FICE Identification: 023576
Unit ID: 187596
Telephone: (505) 786-4100 Carnegie Class: Tribal
FAX Number: (505) 786-5644 Calendar System: Semester
URL: www.navajotech.edu
Established: 1979 Annual Undergrad Tuition & Fees: $1,500
Enrollment: 1,173 Coed
Affiliation or Control: Tribal Control IRS Status: 501(c)3
Highest Offering: Baccalaureate
Program: Occupational; 2-Year Principally Bachelor's Creditable; Technical Emphasis
Accreditation: NH, ACFEI

01 President .... Mr. Elmer GUY
05 Provost .... Mr. Tom DAVIS
32 Dean of Student Affairs .... Dr. Delores BECENTI
06 Registrar/Director of Admissions .... Ms. Jerlynn HENRY
09 Data Assessment Director .... Mr. Roy TRACY
25 Contracts & Grant Officer .... Ms. Christine REIDHEAD
37 Director of Student Financial Aid .... Mr. Tyrrell HARDY
15 Director Human Resources .... Mr. Steven BENALLY
18 Director of Operations .... Mr. Lawrence ISAAC, JR.
21 Associate Business Officer .... Vacant

† Tuition figure is for a student enrolled in a federally recognized Indian tribe; for students who are not members of a federally recognized Indian tribe, tuition including fees is $2,280.

New Mexico Highlands University (J)

PO Box 9000, Las Vegas NM 87701-9000
County: San Miguel FICE Identification: 002653
Unit ID: 187897
Telephone: (505) 425-7511 Carnegie Class: Master's L
FAX Number: N/A Calendar System: Semester
URL: www.nmhu.edu
Established: 1893 Annual Undergrad Tuition & Fees (In-State): $3,504
Enrollment: 3,804 Coed
Affiliation or Control: State IRS Status: 501(c)3
Highest Offering: Master's
Program: Liberal Arts And General; Teacher Preparatory
Accreditation: NH, ACBSP, @CORE, NURSE, SW, TED

01 President .... Dr. James FRIES
05 VP for Academic Affairs .... Dr. Gilbert RIVERA
10 VP Finance & Administration .... Vacant
32 Vice Pres of Student Affairs/Dean .... Dr. Fidel J. TRUJILLO
20 Associate VP of Academic Affairs .... Dr. Linda LAGRANGE
07 Registrar/Director of Admissions .... Mr. John COCA

08 Library Director Mr. Ruben ARAGON
09 Dir Inst Effectiveness & Research Dr. Jean HILL
14 Director of Information Technology Mr. Max BACA
15 Director Human Resources Ms. Donna CASTRO
18 Director of Facilities Management Ms. Marisol GREENE
19 Chief Police/Security Mr. Donato SENA
21 Comptroller Vacant
26 Director of University Relations Mr. Sean WEAVER
29 Coordinator of Alumni Affairs Mr. James MANDARINO
30 Executive Dir for Advancement Dr. Sharon CABALLERO
36 Director of Career Services Mr. Ron GARCIA
37 Director of Financial Aid Ms. Eileen SEDILLO
40 Bookstore Manager Vacant
41 Athletic Director Mr. Ed MANZANARES
49 Dean College of Arts & Sci Dr. Kenneth BENTSON
50 Dean School of Business Dr. Margaret YOUNG
70 Dean School of Social Work Dr. Alfredo GARCIA
96 Director of Purchasing Mr. Michael SAAVEDRA

New Mexico Institute of Mining and Technology (A)

801 Leroy Place, Socorro NM 87801-4796
County: Socorro FICE Identification: 002654
Unit ID: 187967
Telephone: (575) 835-5434 Carnegie Class: Master's M
FAX Number: (575) 835-6329 Calendar System: Semester
URL: www.nmt.edu
Established: 1889 Annual Undergrad Tuition & Fees (In-State): $5,488
Enrollment: 2,009 Coed
Affiliation or Control: State IRS Status: 501(c)3
Highest Offering: Doctorate
Program: Professional; Technical Emphasis
Accreditation: NH, CS, ENG

01 President Dr. Daniel H. LOPEZ
10 Vice Pres Administration & Finance Mr. Lonnie G. MARQUEZ
05 Vice President Academic Affairs Dr. Peter F. GERITY
26 VP Student & Univ Rels/Dean Stdnt Ms. Melissa JARAMILLO FLEMING
46 Vice Pres Research/Economic Devel Dr. Van D. ROMERO
20 Assoc Vice Pres Academic Affairs Dr. Mary DEZEMBER
45 Asst VP Research/Econ Development Mr. Richard CERVANTES
08 Librarian Ms. Lisa BEINHOFF
15 Director of Human Resources Ms. Joann SALOME
06 Registrar Ms. Sara GRIJALVA
07 Director of Admission Mr. Michael KLOEPPEL
37 Director of Financial Aid Ms. Annette KAUS
30 Director Office for Advancement Ms. Colleen GUENGERICH
22 Director Affirm Action & Compliance Ms. Joann SALOME
14 Director Computer Center Dr. Michael L. TOPLIFF
13 Director of Information Services Mr. Joseph FRANKLIN
65 Director Bur Geology & Mineral Res Dr. Peter A. SCHOLLE
12 Director Petro Recovery Res Ctr Dr. Robert L. LEE
58 Interim Dean of Graduate Studies Dr. David WESTPFAHL
18 Director Facilities Management Ms. Yvonne MANZANO-BROWN
21 Director of Finance Ms. Arleen VALLES
36 Director Career Services Ms. Chelsea BUFFINGTON
38 Dir Counseling/Disabilities Svcs Ms. Janet WARD
96 Director of Purchasing Ms. Kimela MILLER

New Mexico Junior College (B)

1 Thunderbird Circle, Hobbs NM 88240-9123
County: Lea FICE Identification: 002655
Unit ID: 187903
Telephone: (575) 392-4510 Carnegie Class: Assoc/Pub-R-M
FAX Number: (575) 492-2732 Calendar System: Semester
URL: www.nmjc.edu
Established: 1965 Annual Undergrad Tuition & Fees (In-District): $1,056
Enrollment: 3,603 Coed
Affiliation or Control: Local IRS Status: 501(c)3
Highest Offering: Associate Degree
Program: Occupational; 2-Year Principally Bachelor's Creditable
Accreditation: NH, ADNUR

01 President Dr. Steve MCCLEERY
05 Vice President Instruction Dr. Dennis ATHERTON
10 Vice President Finance Dan HARDIN
32 Vice President Student Services Dr. Regina ORGAN
103 Vice President Training & Outreach Dr. Robert RHODES
84 Dean Enrollment Management Dr. A. Michele CLINGMAN
14 Dir Computer Information System Bill KUNKO
26 Director PR/Marketing Vicki VARDEMAN
04 Executive Asst to the President Jerri SHIELDS
37 Director Financial Aid Vacant
09 Director of Inst Effectiveness Dr. Larry SANDERSON
66 Director of Nursing Delores THOMPSON
18 Chief Facilities/Physical Plant Dr. Charley CARROLL
81 Dean Business/Math & Sciences Kelly HOLLADAY
79 Dean Arts/Humanities & Career Tech Dianne MARQUEZ
40 Director of Bookstore Services Robert ADAMS
106 Dean of Training & Outreach Jeffery MCCOOL
75 Dean of Public Safety & Industry Dr. August FONS
08 Director of Library Services Mary TUYTSCHAEVERS
96 Coordinator of Purchasing Regina CHOATE
41 Director of Athletics Donald WORTH
102 Acct/Controller-NMJC Foundation Christina KUNKO
11 Director of Administrative Services Bill MORRILL
88 Controller Joshua MORGAN
39 Director Student Housing Sandy HARDIN

New Mexico Military Institute (C)

101 W College, Roswell NM 88201-5173
County: Chaves FICE Identification: 002656
Unit ID: 187912
Telephone: (575) 622-6250 Carnegie Class: Assoc/Pub-Spec
FAX Number: (575) 624-8058 Calendar System: Semester
URL: www.nmmi.edu
Established: 1891 Annual Undergrad Tuition & Fees (In-State): $10,805
Enrollment: 463 Coed
Affiliation or Control: State IRS Status: 501(c)3
Highest Offering: Associate Degree
Program: 2-Year Principally Bachelor's Creditable
Accreditation: NH

01 Superintendent/President MGen. Jerry W. GRIZZLE
32 Commandant BGen. Richard V. GERACI
100 Chief of Staff Col. David WEST
10 Chief Financial Officer Col. Judy SCHARMER
21 Asst Chief Financial Officer LtCol. Charles HENDRICKSON
05 Dean BGen. Douglas J. MURRAY
07 Director of Admissions LtCol. Jeffery SAVAGE
41 Athletic Director/Dir Physical Educ Col. Reginald FRANKLIN
30 Director of Development LtCol. Nickie VIGIL-GARCIA
21 Internal Auditor LtCol. David GRAY
88 Professor of Military Science LtCol. Jonathan GRAFF
20 Asst Dean & High School Princ LtCol. George BRICK
35 Associate Dean Leadership Vacant
50 Assoc Dean Social Science/Business Col. Walter T. HITCHCOCK
81 Assoc Dean Science/Mathematics LtCol. John R. MCVAY
79 Associate Dean Humanities Major Joel DYKSTRA
64 Director of Music LtCol. Stephen M. THORP
08 Director of the Library Col. Jerome J. KLOPFER
26 Public Relations Officer CWO3 Carl K. HANSEN
18 Chief Facilities/Physical Plant Mr. Kent TAYLOR
06 Registrar Maj. Edwin G. PREBLE
37 Director Student Financial Aid Maj. Sonya F. RODRIGUEZ
38 Dir College Acad Advising/Placement Maj. Donald HANAK
19 Director Security/Safety Mr. Jerrold LONOWSKI
42 Chaplain/Director Campus Ministry Maj. Dan MUSGRAVE
29 Director Alumni Association LtCol. David ROMERO

New Mexico State University Main Campus (D)

Box 30001, Las Cruces NM 88003-8001
County: Dona Ana FICE Identification: 002657
Unit ID: 188030
Telephone: (575) 646-2035 Carnegie Class: RU/H
FAX Number: (575) 646-6334 Calendar System: Semester
URL: www.nmsu.edu
Established: 1888 Annual Undergrad Tuition & Fees (In-State): $6,041
Enrollment: 18,024 Coed
Affiliation or Control: State IRS Status: 501(c)3
Highest Offering: Doctorate
Program: Liberal Arts And General; Teacher Preparatory; Professional
Accreditation: NH, BUS, BUSA, CACREP, COPSY, DIETD, @DIETI, ENG, ENGT, MUS, NURSE, PH, SP, SPAA, SW, TED

01 President Dr. Barbara COUTURE
05 Provost & Executive Vice President Dr. Wendy K. WILKINS
10 Sr VP Administration/Finance Ms. Angela THRONEBERRY
100 Sr VP External Rel/Chief of Staff Mr. Benjamin E. WOODS
30 VP Univ Advance/Pres NMSU Found Mr. Dennis PRESCOTT
85 Assoc Provost Intl & Border Program Dr. Cornell MENKING
26 Assoc VP Univ Comm/Marketing Ms. Maureen HOWARD
21 Assoc VP Admin & Finance Ms. D'Anne STUART
20 VP Student Affairs/Enroll Mgmt Dr. Bernadette MONTOYA
20 Asst VP/Deputy Provost Dr. Greg FANT
47 Dean College of Agric & Home Econ Dr. Lowell CATLETT
49 Dean College of Arts & Sciences Dr. Christa D. SLATON
50 Dean Business College Dr. Garrey E. CARRUTHERS
53 Dean College of Education Dr. Michael A. MOREHEAD
54 Dean College of Engineering Dr. Ricardo JACQUEZ
58 Dean Graduate School Dr. Linda LACEY
76 Dean Col of Health & Social Svcs Dr. Tilahun ADERA
35 Interim Dean of Students Dr. Susan WALDO
37 Dir Fin Aid/Scholarship Svcs Ms. Janie MERCHANT
27 Chief Information Officer Dr. Shaun COOPER
06 Registrar Mr. Michael ZIMMERMAN
43 General Counsel Mr. Bruce KITE
08 Dean University Library Dr. Elizabeth TITUS
29 Director Alumni Affairs Dr. Tammie CAMPOS
25 Assoc Controller Sponsored Projects Ms. Norma NOEL
39 Director Student Housing Ms. Julie WEBER
09 Asst VP Institutional Analysis Ms. Judy BOSLAND
23 Director Student Health Center Ms. Lori MCKEE
38 Director Counseling Center Dr. Karen D. SCHAEFER
86 Asst VP Government Relations Mr. Ricardo REL
41 Director Athletics Dr. McKinley BOSTON
36 Int Dir Placement/Career Services Dr. Susan WALDO
96 Int Dir Purchasing/Risk Management Ms. Rennette APODACA
28 Dir Institutional Equity/EEO Mr. Gerard NEVAREZ
07 Director Admissions Ms. Valerie PICKETT
15 Int Dir Personnel Services Ms. Dorothy ANDERSON

New Mexico State University at Alamogordo (E)

2400 N Scenic Drive, Alamogordo NM 88310-4239
County: Otero FICE Identification: 002658
Unit ID: 187994
Telephone: (575) 439-3600 Carnegie Class: Assoc/Pub2in4
FAX Number: (575) 439-3643 Calendar System: Semester
URL: www.nmsua.edu
Established: 1958 Annual Undergrad Tuition & Fees (In-State): $1,896
Enrollment: 3,479 Coed
Affiliation or Control: State IRS Status: 501(c)3
Highest Offering: Associate Degree
Program: Occupational; 2-Year Principally Bachelor's Creditable
Accreditation: NH, ADNUR

01 President Dr. Cheri A. JIMENO
05 Vice President for Academic Affairs Dr. Debra TEACHMAN
32 Vice President for Student Services Mr. Juan B. GARCIA
10 Vice President for Business/Finance Mr. Antonio SALINAS
56 Assoc Vice Pres Extended Programs Mrs. Donna L. COOK
26 Campus Public Information Officer Ms. Hope PATTERSON
08 Librarian Dr. Sharon JENKINS
07 Director of Admissions/Registrar Ms. Tina TRUONG
37 Int Director Student Financial Aid Ms. Stefanie LEDESMA
09 Director of Institutional Research Dr. Bruce MARTIN
06 Registrar Ms. Tina TRUONG
36 Director Student Placement Mr. Juan B. GARCIA
15 Director Human Resources Mrs. Brenda W. GARCIA
18 Director Facilities/Physical Plant Mrs. Nancy MONTGOMERY
38 Director Student Counseling Mr. Juan B. GARCIA
96 Buyer Specialist 1 Mr. Lee M. KINNEY

New Mexico State University at Carlsbad (F)

1500 University Drive, Carlsbad NM 88220-3598
County: Eddy FICE Identification: 002659
Unit ID: 188003
Telephone: (575) 234-9200 Carnegie Class: Assoc/Pub2in4
FAX Number: (575) 885-4951 Calendar System: Semester
URL: www.carlsbad.nmsu.edu
Established: 1950 Annual Undergrad Tuition & Fees (In-State): $1,036
Enrollment: 1,747 Coed
Affiliation or Control: State IRS Status: 501(c)3
Highest Offering: Associate Degree
Program: Occupational; 2-Year Principally Bachelor's Creditable
Accreditation: NH, ADNUR

01 Campus President Dr. John GRATTON
05 Interim Chief Academic Officer Dr. Mark BUCKHOLZ
32 Vice Pres Student Services Mr. Michael J. CLEARY
10 Chief Business Officer Mr. Robert KEYES
38 Director Student Counseling Ms. Karla K. THOMPSON
37 Director Financial Aid Ms. Diana CAMPOS
15 Human Resources Specialist Ms. Melinda WILSON
09 Institutional Researcher Dr. Yingchen WANG
26 Director Marketing & Publications Mr. Khushroo GHADIALI
18 Manager Facilities Services Mr. Brian STEPHENS

New Mexico State University Dona Ana Community College (G)

Box 30001, MSC 3DA, Las Cruces NM 88003-8001
County: Dona Ana Identification: 666649
Unit ID: 187620
Telephone: (575) 527-7500 Carnegie Class: Assoc/Pub2in4
FAX Number: (575) 527-7515 Calendar System: Semester
URL: dacc.nmsu.edu
Established: 1973 Annual Undergrad Tuition & Fees (In-State): $1,848
Enrollment: 9,900 Coed
Affiliation or Control: State IRS Status: 501(c)3
Highest Offering: Associate Degree
Program: Occupational; 2-Year Principally Bachelor's Creditable
Accreditation: NH, ACBSP, DA, DH, DMS, EMT, IFSAC, RAD

01 President Dr. Margie C. HUERTA
05 VP for Academic Affairs Vacant
10 VP for Business & Finance Mr. Andrew J. BURKE
32 VP for Student Services Mr. Amadeo LEDESMA
20 Assoc VP for Academic Affairs Dr. John WALKER
50 Division Dean Business/Info Systems Ms. Lydia BAGWELL
97 Division Dean General Studies Dr. Bernard PINA
76 Div Dean Health/Public Services Ms. Evelyn HOBBS
72 Division Dean Technical Studies Vacant
55 Exec Director Adult Basic Education Ms. Sylvia NICKERSON
51 Exec Director Continuing Education Vacant
62 Director Library Services Ms. Tammy WELCH
09 Campus Inst Effectiveness/Plng Ofcr Dr. Fred LILLIBRIDGE
26 Chief Public Relations/Devel Ofcr Vacant
31 Director Community Education Ms. Vickie GALINDO
40 Bookstore Manager Mr. Marvin PAZ
21 Business Manager Ms. Nancy RITTER
15 Human Resources Manager Mr. Mack ADAMS
90 Computer Support Manager Ms. Lori ALLEN
18 Facilities Manager Ms. Kathleen REDDINGTON
07 Coordinator Admissions & Records Ms. Geraldine MARTINEZ
37 Financial Aid Coordinator Ms. Gladys CHAIREZ
28 Coord Disabled Student Services Vacant
78 Coord Cooperative Educ/Placement Ms. Rosa DE LA TORRE-BURMEISTER

New Mexico State University Grants (H)

1500 Third Street, Grants NM 87020-2025
County: Cibola FICE Identification: 008854
Unit ID: 188021
Telephone: (505) 287-6678 Carnegie Class: Assoc/Pub2in4

FAX Number: (505) 287-2329 Calendar System: Semester
URL: www.grants.nmsu.edu
Established: 1968 Annual Undergrad Tuition & Fees (In-State): $1,782
Enrollment: 1,314 Coed
Affiliation or Control: State IRS Status: 501(c)3
Highest Offering: Associate Degree
Program: Occupational; 2-Year Principally Bachelor's Creditable
Accreditation: &NH

01 President .... Ms. Felicia CASADOS
05 Vice Pres Academic Affairs .... Dr. Harry SHESKI
32 Vice Pres Student Services .... Ms. Beth ARMSTEAD
10 Vice Pres Business/Finance .... Ms. Gaylyn YANKE
08 Librarian .... Ms. Cecilia STAFFORD
09 Director of Institutional Research .... Ms. Rose CARLSON
18 Chief Facilities/Physical Plant .... Mr. Dan CHRISTMANN

† Regional accreditation is carried under the parent institution in Las Cruces, NM.

Northern New Mexico College (A)

921 N Paseo de Onate, Espanola NM 87532-2649
County: Rio Arriba FICE Identification: 020839
Unit ID: 188058
Telephone: (505) 747-2100 Carnegie Class: Bac/Assoc
FAX Number: (505) 747-2170 Calendar System: Semester
URL: www.nnmc.edu
Established: 1909 Annual Undergrad Tuition & Fees (In-State): $2,776
Enrollment: 1,861 Coed
Affiliation or Control: State IRS Status: 501(c)3
Highest Offering: Baccalaureate
Program: Occupational; 2-Year Principally Bachelor's Creditable; Liberal Arts And General; Teacher Preparatory
Accreditation: NH, ACBSP, NURSE, RAD

01 President .... Dr. Nancy (Rusty) BARCELO
10 Vice Pres Finance & Administration .... Mr. Domingo SANCHEZ
30 Vice Pres Institutional Advancement .... Mr. Ricky SERNA
05 Provost .... Dr. Anthony SENA
32 Dean of Student Services .... Mr. Frank ORONA
12 Director El Rito Campus .... Ms. Melissa VELASQUEZ
06 Registrar .... Dr. Jan DAWSON
08 Head Librarian .... Ms. Isabel RODARTE
84 Director of Recruitment .... Mr. Frank ORONA
37 Director of Financial Aid .... Mr. Jacob PACHECO
13 Director of Management Info Systems .... Mr. Jorge LUCERO
15 Director of Human Resources .... Ms. Karen DVORAK
18 Director of Facilities .... Mr. David SCHUTZ
26 Director of Public Information .... Vacant
35 Director of TRIO Programs .... Mr. Hilario ROMERO
09 Director of Inst Effectiveness .... Ms. Carmella MARTINEZ
96 Director of Budget & Procurement .... Ms. Connie ROMERO
108 Dir Inst Advise/Coord Stdnt Advise .... Mr. Fidel TORRES
41 Athletic Director/Coach .... Mr. Ryan CORDOVA
51 Coordinator Continuing Education .... Ms. Virginia CATA
53 Dean College of Teacher Education .... Dr. Cathy BERRYHILL
49 Dean College of Arts and Sciences .... Dr. Mellis SCHMIDT
103 Dn Col Cmty Wrkfrce/Career Tech Ed . Dr. Camilla BUSTAMANTE

Pima Medical Institute-Albuquerque (B)

4400 Cutler Avenue NE, Albuquerque NM 87110-3935
County: Bernalillo FICE Identification: 036783
Unit ID: 105543
Telephone: (505) 881-1234 Carnegie Class: Assoc/PrivFP
FAX Number: (505) 881-5329 Calendar System: Other
URL: www.pmi.edu
Established: 1985 Annual Undergrad Tuition & Fees: N/A
Enrollment: 1,064 Coed
Affiliation or Control: Proprietary IRS Status: Proprietary
Highest Offering: Associate Degree
Program: Occupational; 2-Year Principally Bachelor's Creditable
Accreditation: ABHES, DH, PTAA, RAD

01 Campus Director .... Ms. Lisa KNIGGE

St. John's College (C)

1160 Camino de la Cruz Blanca,
Santa Fe NM 87505-4599
County: Santa Fe FICE Identification: 002093
Unit ID: 245652
Telephone: (505) 984-6000 Carnegie Class: Master's S
FAX Number: (505) 984-6003 Calendar System: Semester
URL: www.stjohnscollege.edu
Established: 1964 Annual Undergrad Tuition & Fees: $43,655
Enrollment: 447 Coed
Affiliation or Control: Independent Non-Profit IRS Status: 501(c)3
Highest Offering: Master's
Program: Liberal Arts And General
Accreditation: NH

01 President .... Mr. Michael P. PETERS
05 Dean .... Mr. Walter J. STERLING
30 Vice President for Advancement .... Mr. James OSTERHOLT
10 Treasurer .... Mr. Bryan VALENTINE
06 Registrar .... Mrs. Marline MARQUEZ-SCALLY
08 Library Director .... Ms. Jennifer SPRAGUE
07 Director of Admissions .... Mr. Larry CLENDENIN
58 Director of Graduate Institute .... Mr. David CARL
09 Director of Institutional Research .... Mr. Nick GIACONA
15 Director of Human Resources .... Ms. Lois RAEL
18 Chief Facilities/Physical Plant .... Mr. Pat HOLMAN
26 Dir of Communications/External Rels .... Mr. Gabe GOMEZ
29 Assoc Director Alumni Relations .... Ms. Nancie WINGO
36 Director Student Placement .... Ms. Margaret ODELL
37 Director Student Financial Aid .... Mr. Mike RODRIQUEZ

† Affiliated with St. John's College, Maryland.

San Juan College (D)

4601 College Boulevard, Farmington NM 87402-4699
County: San Juan FICE Identification: 002660
Unit ID: 188100
Telephone: (505) 326-3311 Carnegie Class: Assoc/Pub-R-L
FAX Number: (505) 566-3385 Calendar System: Semester
URL: www.sanjuancollege.edu
Established: 1956 Annual Undergrad Tuition & Fees (In-District): $1,242
Enrollment: 9,470 Coed
Affiliation or Control: Local IRS Status: 501(c)3
Highest Offering: Associate Degree
Program: Occupational; 2-Year Principally Bachelor's Creditable
Accreditation: NH, ACBSP, ADNUR, DH, MLTAD, PTAA, SURGT

01 President .... Dr. Toni PENDERGRASS
05 Vice Pres for Learning .... Vacant
10 Vice Pres Administrative Services .... Mr. Russell LITKE
32 Vice Pres for Student Services .... Mr. David EPPICH
04 Administrative Asst to President .... Ms. MaryAnne FACIO
20 Assoc Vice Pres for Learning .... Dr. Pamela MILLER
102 Executive Director Foundation .... Ms. Gayle DEAN
31 Chief Community Relations Officer .... Ms. Nancy SHEPHERD
21 Controller .... Vacant
26 Director Marketing/Public Relations .... Ms. Rhonda SCHAEFER
88 Dir Ctr for Student Engagement .... Vacant
84 Sr Dir Enrollment Management .... Mr. Jon BETZ
50 Dean Sch Business/Sciences .... Dr. Merrill ADAMS
79 Dean School of Humanities .... Ms. Lisa WILSON
76 Dean School of Health Sciences .... Mr. Oliver BORDEN
65 Dean School of Energy .... Mr. Randy PACHECO
72 Dean School Trades & Technology .... Mr. Bill LEWIS
22 Director Affirmative Action/EEO .... Ms. Stacey ALLEN
88 Director Native American Programs .... Ms. Michele PETERSON
08 Director Library Services .... Mr. Chris SCHIPPER
37 Director of Financial Aid .... Mr. Jerry MCKEEN
18 Director Physical Plant .... Mr. Steve BIERNACKI
19 Director Security/Safety .... Mr. Billy NEWTON
35 Director Student Activities .... Ms. Marcia STERLING
96 Director Purchasing .... Vacant
38 Director Student Advising Center .... Mr. Ken KERNAGIS
74 Director Vet-Tech Program .... Dr. David WRIGHT
36 Dir Quality/Improve/Career Svcs Ctr .... Ms. Tonya NELSON
06 Registrar .... Ms. Sherri GAUGH
09 Director of Institutional Research .... Ms. Candace GILFILLAN

Santa Fe Community College (E)

6401 Richards Avenue, Santa Fe NM 87508-4887
County: Santa Fe FICE Identification: 022781
Unit ID: 188137
Telephone: (505) 428-1000 Carnegie Class: Assoc/Pub-R-L
FAX Number: (505) 428-1296 Calendar System: Semester
URL: www.sfcc.edu
Established: 1983 Annual Undergrad Tuition & Fees (In-State): $1,063
Enrollment: 6,524 Coed
Affiliation or Control: State IRS Status: 501(c)3
Highest Offering: Associate Degree
Program: Occupational; 2-Year Principally Bachelor's Creditable
Accreditation: NH, ADNUR, DA, EMT, MAC

01 President .... Dr. Ana (Cha) GUZMAN
05 VP of Academic & Student Affairs .... Dr. Ron LISS
10 Vice Pres Finance & Administration .... Ms. Meridee WALTERS
09 VP Planning & Inst Effectiveness .... Dr. Jacqueline VIRGINT
21 Associate Vice President Finance .... Ms. Gilda ESPINOZA
20 Asst VP of Student Retention .... Ms. Jill DOUGLASS
84 Asst VP Enrollment & Student Svcs . Dr. Cheryl DRANGMEISTER
51 Asst VP Cont Educ Customized Trng .... Mr. Randy GRISSOM
53 Asst VP for School of Education .... Ms. Michelle STOBNICKE
26 Exec Dir Marketing/Public Rels .... Ms. Janet WISE
30 Grow SFCC Foundation .... Ms. Deborah BOLDT
06 Registrar .... Ms. Barbara TUCCI
13 Chief Information Officer .... Vacant
37 Financial Aid Director .... Mr. Scott WHITAKER
66 Director of Nursing .... Vacant
08 Library Director .... Ms. Peg JOHNSON
15 Director of Human Resources .... Ms. Karla QUINTANA
88 Director Small Business Development .... Mr. Michael MYKRIS
18 Director of Plant Operations .... Mr. Frank JOY
24 Media Technician .... Vacant
49 Dean Sch Liberal Arts/Core Studies .... Vacant
76 Dean Sch Health and Sciences .... Dr. Julie GOOD
57 Int Dean School of Arts and Design .... Dr. Mechele HESBROOK
50 Dean Sch Business & Applied Tech .... Vacant
101 Executive Asst to the President .... Ms. Rosemarie M. GARCIA
96 Director of Purchasing .... Mr. Michael CLOKEY

Santa Fe University of Art and Design (F)

1600 St. Michael's Drive, Santa Fe NM 87505-7634
County: Santa Fe FICE Identification: 002649
Unit ID: 188146
Telephone: (505) 473-6011 Carnegie Class: Spec/Arts
FAX Number: (505) 473-6127 Calendar System: Semester
URL: www.santafeuniversity.edu
Established: 1947 Annual Undergrad Tuition & Fees: $31,836
Enrollment: 485 Coed
Affiliation or Control: Proprietary IRS Status: Proprietary
Highest Offering: Master's
Program: Liberal Arts And General; Professional; Fine Arts Emphasis
Accreditation: NH

01 President .... Mr. Laurence A. HINZ
05 Vice President for Academic Affairs .... Mr. Gerry SNYDER
32 Sr Director of Student Life .... Ms. Laura NUNNELLY
13 Dir Campus Technology Services .... Mr. Jeff PEARCE
06 Registrar .... Ms. Mary ANGELL
88 Director Campus-Based Facilities .... Mr. Thomas OLMSTEAD
18 Dir Facilities & Security .... Mr. Peter ROMERO
15 Director of Human Resources .... Mr. Todd SPILMAN
07 Director of Admissions .... Ms. Christine GUEVARA
39 Director of Campus Life .... Ms. Rachel GANTT
37 Director of Financial Aid .... Ms. Amy KEARNS
88 Dir of International Recruitment .... Mr. Mark ASTROM
85 Dir International Student Support .... Mr. John RODRIGUEZ
88 Marketing Director .... Ms. Betty CESARANO
88 Marketing Manager .... Mr. Daniel MILLER
26 Public Relations Manager .... Ms. Lauren EICHMANN
35 Student Activities Coordinator .... Ms. Anne RITCHIE

Southwest Acupuncture College (G)

1622 Galisteo Street, Santa Fe NM 87505-6351
County: Santa Fe FICE Identification: 026220
Unit ID: 366605
Telephone: (505) 438-8884 Carnegie Class: Spec/Health
FAX Number: (505) 438-8883 Calendar System: Trimester
URL: www.acupuncturecollege.edu
Established: 1980 Annual Undergrad Tuition & Fees: $13,945
Enrollment: 279 Coed
Affiliation or Control: Proprietary IRS Status: Proprietary
Highest Offering: Master's; No Lower Division
Program: Professional
Accreditation: ACUP

01 President .... Dr. Anthony ABBATE
03 Executive Director .... Dr. Skya ABBATE
10 Fiscal Officer .... Ms. Piper KING
12 Campus Director Albuquerque .... Ms. Toni MEEKS
12 Campus Director Boulder .... Dr. Valerie HOBBS
12 Campus Director Santa Fe ... Ms. Latricia GONZALES-MCKOSKY
12 Administrative Director Boulder .... Ms. Heather LANG
17 Clinical Director Santa Fe .... Dr. Mary Ellen MARINO
17 Clinical Director Albuquerque .... Dr. Paul ROSSIGNOL
17 Clinic Director Boulder .... Ms. Joanne NIVELE
05 Academic Dean Santa Fe .... Dr. Maya YU
05 Academic Dean Albuquerque .... Dr. Dawei SHAO
05 Academic Dean Boulder .... Ms. Melanie CRANE
37 Director of Financial Aid .... Ms. Angela ANAYA

Southwest Acupuncture College-Albuquerque (H)

7801 Academy Blvd N Town Bdg #1 NE,
Albuquerque NM 87109
County: Bernalillo Identification: 666666
Unit ID: 413644
Telephone: (505) 888-8898 Carnegie Class: Spec/Health
FAX Number: (505) 888-1380 Calendar System: Other
URL: www.acupuncturecollege.edu
Established: 1980 Annual Graduate Tuition & Fees: $12,893
Enrollment: 84 Coed
Affiliation or Control: Proprietary IRS Status: Proprietary
Highest Offering: Master's; No Undergraduates
Program: Professional
Accreditation: ACUP

01 Campus Director .... Mrs. Toni MEEKS

† Branch campus of Southwest Acupuncture College, Santa Fe, NM.

Southwest University of Visual Arts (I)

5000 Marble Avenue, NE, Albuquerque NM 87110-6344
County: Bernalillo Identification: 666524
Unit ID: 402776
Telephone: (505) 254-7575 Carnegie Class: Spec/Arts
FAX Number: (505) 254-4754 Calendar System: Trimester
URL: www.theartcenter.edu
Established: 1989 Annual Undergrad Tuition & Fees: $18,360
Enrollment: 292 Coed
Affiliation or Control: Proprietary IRS Status: Proprietary
Highest Offering: Baccalaureate
Program: Occupational
Accreditation: &NH, CIDA

01 Assoc Dean of Instruction .... Ms. Amy BOLDT

† Regional accreditation is carried under the parent institution in Tucson, AZ.

Southwestern College (A)

PO Box 4788, Santa Fe NM 87502-4788
County: Santa Fe FICE Identification: 030761
Unit ID: 188207
Telephone: (505) 471-5756 Carnegie Class: Assoc/PrivNFP4
FAX Number: (505) 471-4071 Calendar System: Quarter
URL: www.swc.edu
Established: 1979 Annual Graduate Tuition & Fees: $16,200
Enrollment: 140 Coed
Affiliation or Control: Independent Non-Profit IRS Status: 501(c)3
Highest Offering: Master's; No Undergraduates
Program: Professional
Accreditation: NH

01 President .... Dr. Jim NOLAN
03 Vice Pres/Dir Community Educ Pgms .... Ms. Katherine NINOS
05 Academic Dean .... Dr. Webb GARRISON
07 Director of Admissions .... Ms. Dru PHOENIX
06 Registrar .... Ms. Andrea PACHECO

Southwestern Indian Polytechnic Institute (B)

9169 Coors Blvd., NW, Albuquerque NM 87120
County: Bernalillo FICE Identification: 025110
Unit ID: 188216
Telephone: (505) 346-2347 Carnegie Class: Tribal
FAX Number: (505) 346-2343 Calendar System: Trimester
URL: www.sipi.edu
Established: 1971 Annual Undergrad Tuition & Fees: $280
Enrollment: 500 Coed
Affiliation or Control: Federal IRS Status: 501(c)3
Highest Offering: Associate Degree
Program: Occupational; 2-Year Principally Bachelor's Creditable; Technical Emphasis
Accreditation: @NH, OPD, OPLT

01 President .... Dr. Sherry ALLISON
10 Acting Vice Pres College Operations .... Mr. Monte MONTEITH
05 Vice President Academic Programs .... Ms. Valerie MONTOYA
39 Director of Residential Life .... Mr. Raymond GACHUPIN
07 Director Admissions/Registrar .... Mr. Joseph CARPIO
09 Director of Institutional Research .... Mr. Edward HUMMINGBIRD
15 Human Resources Specialist .... Ms. Bernadine FISHERMAN
18 Facilities Director .... Ms. Karlisa SHOMOUR
37 Director Student Financial Aid .... Mr. Joseph CARPIO

University of New Mexico Main Campus (C)

1 University of New Mexico, Albuquerque NM 87131-0001
County: Bernalillo FICE Identification: 002663
Unit ID: 187985
Telephone: (505) 277-0111 Carnegie Class: RU/VH
FAX Number: (505) 277-6019 Calendar System: Semester
URL: www.unm.edu
Established: 1889 Annual Undergrad Tuition & Fees (In-State): $6,049
Enrollment: 29,056 Coed
Affiliation or Control: State IRS Status: 501(c)3
Highest Offering: Doctorate
Program: Liberal Arts And General; Teacher Preparatory; Professional
Accreditation: NH, ARCPA, BUS, BUSA, CACREP, CLPSY, CONST, CS, DANCE, DENT, DH, DIETD, DIETI, EMT, ENG, IPSY, JOUR, LAW, LSAR, MED, MIDWF, MT, MUS, NURSE, OT, PH, PHAR, PLNG, PTA, SP, SPAA, TED, THEA

01 President .... Dr. Robert G. FRANK
05 Provost/Exec VP Academic Affs .... Dr. Chaouki T. ABDALLAH
17 Chancellor of Health Sciences Ctr .... Dr. Paul B. ROTH
10 Exec Vice Pres Administration .... Dr. David W. HARRIS
100 Chief of Staff .... Dr. Breda BOVA
20 Sr Vice Provost Academic Affairs .... Dr. Michael J. DOUGHER
20 Vice Provost Academic Affairs .... Dr. Wynn M. GOERING
106 Vice Provost Extended University ... Dr. Jeronimo C. DOMINGUEZ
46 Assoc VP for Research Initiatives .... Dr. Johann VAN REENEN
20 Assoc Provost Academic Personnel .... Dr. Jane SLAUGHTER
20 Assoc Provost Curriculum & Instr .... Dr. Gregory HEILEMAN
20 Assoc Provost International Affs .... Dr. Natasha KOLCHEVSKA
32 Vice President Student Affairs .... Dr. Eliseo S. TORRES
28 Vice President Equity & Inclusion .... Dr. Josephine DE LEON
28 Vice President HSC Diversity ...... Dr. Valerie ROMERO-LEGGOTT
84 Assoc VP Enrollment Management .... Dr. Terry BABBITT
15 Vice Pres Human Resources .... Helen GONZALES
41 Vice President for Athletics .... Paul R. KREBS
21 VP HSC/UNM Finance/Controller .... Ava LOVELL
13 Chief Information Officer .... Gilbert GONZALES
43 University Counsel .... K. Lee PEIFER
29 AVP Alumni Relations .... Karen A. ABRAHAM
20 Assoc VP Academic Administration .... Curtis R. PORTER
21 AVP Planning/Budget & Analysis .... Andrew CULLEN
35 AVP Student Life .... Dr. Walter C. MILLER
35 AVP Student Services .... Dr. Tim GUTIERREZ
50 Dean Anderson School of Management .... Doug M. BROWN
48 Dean Sch of Architecture & Planning .... Dr. Geraldine FORBES ISAIS
49 Dean College of Arts & Sciences .... Dr. Mark PECENY
53 Dean College of Education .... Dr. Richard HOWELL
54 Dean School of Engineering .... Dr. Catalin ROMAN
57 Dean College of Fine Arts .... Dr. Kymberly PINDER
61 Dean School of Law .... Kevin WASHBURN
63 Exec Vice Dean School of Medicine .... Dr. Jeffrey GRIFFITH
66 Dean College of Nursing .... Dr. Nancy A. RIDENOUR
67 Dean College of Pharmacy .... Dr. Lynda S. WELAGE
80 Dir School of Public Administration .... Dr. Uday DESAI
97 Dean University College .... Dr. Kate KRAUSE
58 Dean Office of Graduate Studies .... Dr. Gary HARRISON
51 Dean Continuing Education .... Dr. Rita MARTINEZ-PURSON
08 Dean University Libraries .... Dr. Martha BEDARD
12 Int Exec Director UNM West .... Dr. Beth MILLER
45 Consultant for Strategy & Goals .... Carolyn J. THOMPSON
26 University Marketing Director .... Cinnamon BLAIR
27 Director University Communications .... Dianne ANDERSON
86 Director Government Affairs .... Marc SAAVEDRA
09 Director Institutional Research .... Mark P. CHISHOLM
18 University Planning Officer .... Mary W. KENNEY
19 Chief of Police .... Kathy A. GUIMOND
96 Chief Procurement Officer .... Bruce E. CHERRIN
23 Director Student Health Center .... Dr. Beverly KLOEPPEL
22 Acting Dir Ofc Equal Opportunity .... Theresa RAMOS
24 Dir New Media & Extended Learning .... Debby KNOTTS
35 Interim Dean of Students .... Dr. Kimmerly KLOEPPEL
07 Director Admissions and Recruitment .... Matt HULETT
06 Registrar .... Alex GONZALEZ
37 Director Student Financial Aid .... Brian MALONE
36 Director Career Services .... Jenna S. CRABB
39 Director Housing & Food Svcs/Bus .... Vacant
104 Interim Dir International Programs .... Dr. Kenneth CARPENTER
40 Director Bookstore .... Melanie SPARKS
102 UNM Foundation President and CEO .... Henry NEMCIK
30 VP University Development .... Larry RYAN
30 VP Development Health Sciences Ctr .... Bill UHER
88 CEO UNM Hospital .... Steve MCKERNAN

University of New Mexico-Gallup (D)

705 Gurley Avenue, Gallup NM 87301
County: McKinley FICE Identification: 006881
Unit ID: 187958
Telephone: (505) 863-7500 Carnegie Class: Assoc/Pub2in4
FAX Number: (505) 863-7532 Calendar System: Semester
URL: www.gallup.unm.edu
Established: 1968 Annual Undergrad Tuition & Fees (In-State): $1,704
Enrollment: 2,955 Coed
Affiliation or Control: State IRS Status: 501(c)3
Highest Offering: Associate Degree
Program: Occupational; 2-Year Principally Bachelor's Creditable
Accreditation: &NH, DA, MLTAD

01 Executive Director .... Dr. Sylvia R. ANDREW
05 Dean of Instruction .... Dr. Neal MANGHAM
10 Int Director Business Operations .... Dr. Wynn GOERING
32 Director Student Services .... Zeke GARCIA
07 Manager of Admissions Advisor .... Pearl A. MORRIS
26 Sr Public Affairs Representative .... Linda THORNTON
06 Registrar .... Suzette WYACO
13 Manager Information Technology .... Jim BLACKSHEAR
40 Manager Bookstore .... Rose ADAKI
37 Financial Aid Officer .... Precilla BEGAY
18 Facilities Manager .... Ron PETRANOVICH
84 Enrollment Services Manager .... Suzette WYACCO

† Regional accreditation is carried under the parent institution in Albuquerque, NM.

University of New Mexico-Los Alamos (E)

4000 University Drive, Los Alamos NM 87544-2233
County: Los Alamos Identification: 666742
Unit ID: 187976
Telephone: (505) 662-5919 Carnegie Class: Assoc/Pub2in4
FAX Number: (505) 662-0344 Calendar System: Semester
URL: www.unm.edu
Established: 1980 Annual Undergrad Tuition & Fees (In-State): $1,561
Enrollment: 698 Coed
Affiliation or Control: State IRS Status: 501(c)3
Highest Offering: Associate Degree
Program: Occupational; 2-Year Principally Bachelor's Creditable; Liberal Arts And General; Technical Emphasis
Accreditation: &NH

01 Executive Director .... Dr. Cedric D. PAGE
05 Dean of Instruction .... Dr. Kathy MASSENGALE
10 Campus Resources Director .... Ms. Lisa CLOUGH
13 Manager Info Tech/Telecom Svcs .... Mr. William C. GILSON
32 Student Affairs Director .... Dr. Patricia BOYER
06 Branch Registrar .... Ms. Kathryn VIGIL
08 Library Director .... Mr. Dennis DAVIES-WILSON
88 Accountant II/C&G/Personnel .... Ms. Denise SERNA
37 Branch Financial Aid .... Ms. Pat BOYER
40 Manager Branch Bookstore .... Mr. Steve A. CIDDIO
18 Manager Facilities Services .... Mr. Eugene ORTIZ
26 Communications & Marketing Services .... Ms. Bonnie GORDON
09 Institutional Researcher .... Ms. Valida DUSHDUROVA
15 Human Res/Student Housing Coord .... Ms. Betsy ALLANDER
106 Manager UNM Distance Educ Program .... Ms. Cindy LEYBA

† Regional accreditation is carried under the parent institution in Albuquerque, NM.

University of New Mexico-Taos (F)

1157 Country Road 110, Ranchos de Taos NM 87557
County: Taos Identification: 666743
Unit ID: 188225
Telephone: (575) 737-6200 Carnegie Class: Assoc/Pub2in4
FAX Number: (575) 758-5898 Calendar System: Semester
URL: www.taos.unm.edu
Established: 1993 Annual Undergrad Tuition & Fees (In-State): $1,658
Enrollment: 1,447 Coed
Affiliation or Control: State IRS Status: 501(c)3
Highest Offering: Associate Degree
Program: Occupational; 2-Year Principally Bachelor's Creditable
Accreditation: &NH, ADNUR

01 Exec Director/Branch Campus .... Dr. Kate O'NEILL
05 Dean of Instruction .... Randi ARCHULETA
45 Campus Resource Director .... Mario SPUAZO
35 Academic Student Success Director .... Vacant
84 Student Enrollment Director .... Patricia GONZALES

† Regional accreditation is carried under the parent institution in Albuquerque, NM.

University of New Mexico-Valencia (G)

280 La Entrada Road, Los Lunas NM 87031-7633
County: Valencia Identification: 666741
Unit ID: 188049
Telephone: (505) 925-8500 Carnegie Class: Assoc/Pub2in4
FAX Number: (505) 925-8501 Calendar System: Semester
URL: www.unm.edu/~unmvc/
Established: 1981 Annual Undergrad Tuition & Fees (In-State): $1,561
Enrollment: 2,428 Coed
Affiliation or Control: State IRS Status: 501(c)3
Highest Offering: Associate Degree
Program: Occupational; 2-Year Principally Bachelor's Creditable
Accreditation: &NH

01 Executive Director .... Alice V. LETTENEY
05 Dean Instruction/Chief Acad Officer .... Dr. Richard A. SAX
45 Director Campus Resources .... Andrew E. SANCHEZ
32 Associate Director Student Affairs .... Vigil HANK
88 Mgr Small Business Devel Center .... Wayne ABRAHAM
26 Sr Public Affairs Representative .... Chad L. PERRY
15 Human Resources Representative .... Shireen E. MCDONALD
18 Manager Facilities Services .... William BOWDICH
08 Manager Library Operations .... Barbara LOVATO
40 Manager Bookstore .... Tracy PERALTA
21 Business Manager .... Sally HEBERT
30 Mgr Donor Relations/Develop/Grants .... Ann-Mary MACLEOD
06 Branch Registrar .... Frances DURAN
37 Br/Div Mgr Student Financial Aid .... Bill BLOOM

† Regional accreditation is carried under the parent institution in Albuquerque, NM.

University of the Southwest (H)

6610 Lovington Highway, Hobbs NM 88240-9129
County: Lea FICE Identification: 002650
Unit ID: 188182
Telephone: (575) 392-6561 Carnegie Class: Bac/Diverse
FAX Number: (575) 392-6006 Calendar System: Semester
URL: www.usw.edu
Established: 1962 Annual Undergrad Tuition & Fees: $12,240
Enrollment: 630 Coed
Affiliation or Control: Independent Non-Profit IRS Status: 501(c)3
Highest Offering: Master's
Program: Liberal Arts And General; Teacher Preparatory
Accreditation: NH

01 President .... Dr. Gary DILL
05 VP of Academics and Technology .... Dr. James SMITH
10 VP for Administration & CFO .... Dr. Dee MOONEY
07 Dean of Enrollment Mgmt/Student Sup .... Mrs. Jordan BODINE
32 Dean of Students .... Mr. Tom MULKEY
41 Dean of Athletics .... Mr. Michael GALVAN
18 Campus Steward .... Mr. David ARNOLD
49 Dean School of Arts & Sciences .... Dr. Marianne WESTBROOK
50 Dean School of Business .... Dr. Ryan TIPTON
53 Dean School of Education .... Dr. Mary HARRIS
08 Dean of Library Services .... Mr. John MCCANCE
35 Assoc Dean of Campus Life .... Mrs. Evelyn RISING
42 Campus Minister .... Rev. Kenneth REED
15 Director of Personnel Services .... Mrs. Melody ARNOLD
37 Financial Aid Director .... Mrs. Kerrie MITCHELL
06 University Registrar .... Mrs. Rebecca WHITLEY
44 Director Develop/Public Relations .... Ms. Laurie DEAN
88 Maintenance Supervisor .... Mr. Lonnie HARRISON

Western New Mexico University (I)

PO Box 680, Silver City NM 88062-0680
County: Grant FICE Identification: 002664
Unit ID: 188304
Telephone: (505) 538-6011 Carnegie Class: Master's M
FAX Number: (505) 538-6364 Calendar System: Semester
URL: www.wnmu.edu
Established: 1893 Annual Undergrad Tuition & Fees (In-State): $4,149
Enrollment: 3,331 Coed
Affiliation or Control: State IRS Status: 501(c)3
Highest Offering: Master's

Program: Liberal Arts And General; Teacher Preparatory
Accreditation: NH, ACBSP, ADNUR, NURSE, OT, OTA, SW, TED

01 President ... Dr. Joseph SHEPARD
05 Provost/Vice Pres Academic Affairs ... Dr. Faye VOWELL
32 VP Student Affairs/Enrollment Mgmt ... Dr. Isaac BRUNDAGE
10 Vice President Business Affairs ... Ms. Sherri A. BAYS
30 VP Instl Advancement/Economic Devel ... Ms. Linda Kay JONES
20 Assoc Vice Pres Academic Affairs ... Ms. Marcia BOURDETTE
35 Assoc Vice Pres Student Affairs ... Ms. Peggy LANKFORD
06 Registrar ... Ms. Betsy MILLER
08 University Librarian ... Ms. Gilda BAEZA-ORTEGO
37 Director Student Financial Aid ... Ms. Onorina FRANCO
07 Director Admissions ... Mr. Dan TRESSLER
09 Director of Institutional Research ... Mr. Paul LANDRUM
15 Director of Human Resources ... Ms. Charlene ASHBURN
18 Chief Facilities/Physical Plant ... Mr. Stan PENA
26 Chief Public Relations Officer ... Mr. Abe VILLARREAL
29 Director of Alumni Relations ... Ms. Danielle MOFFETT
44 Chief Development Officer ... Mr. Vance REDFERN
36 Director of Career Services ... Mr. Nick GIORDANO
28 Dir Multi-Cultural Affs/Student Act ... Ms. Maria DOMINGUEZ
96 Director of Purchasing ... Ms. Amy BACA

NEW YORK

Adelphi University (A)

1 South Avenue, PO Box 701,
Garden City NY 11530-0701
County: Nassau FICE Identification: 002666
Unit ID: 188429
Telephone: (516) 877-3000 Carnegie Class: DRU
FAX Number: (516) 877-3545 Calendar System: Semester
URL: www.adelphi.edu
Established: 1896 Annual Undergrad Tuition & Fees: $29,320
Enrollment: 7,922 Coed
Affiliation or Control: Independent Non-Profit IRS Status: 501(c)3
Highest Offering: Doctorate
Program: Liberal Arts And General; Teacher Preparatory; Professional
Accreditation: M, AUD, BUS, CLPSY, NURSE, SP, SW, TED

01 President ... Dr. Robert A. SCOTT
03 Provost ... Dr. Gayle D. INSLER
05 Senior Assoc Provost for Acad Affs ... Dr. Audrey S. BLUMBERG
20 Assoc Provost for Academic Affairs ... Dr. Lester BALTIMORE
11 Assoc Provost for Administration ... Dr. Lawrence HOBBIE
88 Assoc Provost for Faculty Affairs ... Dr. Perry GREENE
32 Vice Pres Admin/Student Services ... Mr. Angelo B. PROTO
10 Senior Vice President & Treasurer ... Mr. Timothy P. BURTON
30 Vice Pres University Advancement ... Mr. Chris VAUPEL
26 Vice President for Communications ... Ms. Lori DUGGAN-GOLD
84 Assoc VP Enrollment Mgt/Stdnt Affs ... Ms. Esther GOODCUFF
21 Assoc VP for Finance & Co-Treasurer ... Mr. Robert L. DECARLO
15 Assoc VP Human Resource/Labor Rel ... Ms. Lisa ARAUJO
49 Dean of Arts & Sciences ... Dr. Sam L. GROGG
53 Dean School of Education ... Dr. Jane ASHDOWN
66 Dean School of Nursing ... Dr. Patrick R. COONAN
70 Dean School of Social Work ... Dr. Andrew SAFYER
58 Dean Derner Inst Advanc Psych Std ... Dr. Jacques BARBER
50 Interim Dean School of Business ... Dr. Barbara NEMECEK
92 Dean of Honors College ... Dr. Richard GARNER
88 Exec Dir University Col/Adult Pgms ... Mr. Shawn O'RILEY
35 Dean Student Affairs ... Mr. Jeffrey A. KESSLER
13 Chief Information Officer/CIO ... Mr. Jack CHEN
41 Asst VP/Director of Athletics ... Mr. Robert E. HARTWELL
56 Exec Dir Off-Campus Administration ... Mr. James MCGOWAN
19 Exec Dir Public Safety ... Mr. Eugene PALMA
18 Exec Dir Facilities/Physical Plant ... Mr. James KOSLOSKI
09 Exec Dir Research/Assessment/Plng ... Dr. Nava LERER
37 Exec Director Student Financial Aid ... Ms. Sheryl L. MIHOPULOS
07 Exec Director of Admissions ... Ms. Christine MURPHY
36 Exec Dir Career Plng & Placement ... Mr. Thomas J. WARD
06 Interim Registrar ... Ms. Linda JEAN-LOUIS
104 Director International Education ... Dr. Barry STINSON
23 Director Health Services ... Ms. Jacqueline CARTABUKE
38 Director Student Counseling Center ... Ms. Carol PHELAN
39 Director Residential Life/Housing ... Mr. Guy SENEQUE
29 Interim Director Alumni Relations ... Ms. Mary Ann MEARINI
88 Assoc Treasurer/Budget Director ... Mr. Michael J. MCLEOD
88 Director Business Affairs ... Mr. Russell A. PALMER
12 Director Manhattan Center ... Ms. June TRIZZINO-PECOR
96 Purchasing Manager ... Ms. Elizabeth F. KASH
40 Bookstore Manager ... Vacant

Albany College of Pharmacy and Health Sciences (B)

106 New Scotland Avenue, Albany NY 12208-3492
County: Albany FICE Identification: 002885
Unit ID: 188526
Telephone: (518) 694-7200 Carnegie Class: Spec/Health
FAX Number: (518) 694-7202 Calendar System: Semester
URL: www.acphs.edu
Established: 1881 Annual Undergrad Tuition & Fees: $26,380
Enrollment: 1,641 Coed
Affiliation or Control: Independent Non-Profit IRS Status: 501(c)3
Highest Offering: Doctorate
Program: Professional
Accreditation: M, CYTO, MT, PHAR

01 President ... James GOZZO
05 Provost ... Mehdi BOROUJERDI
46 Vice Provost for Research ... Shaker MOUSA
35 Dean of Students ... John DENIO
12 Associate Dean for Vermont Campus ... Robert HAMILTON
43 General Counsel ... Gerald KATZMAN
10 VP of Finance ... Michele VIEN
30 VP of Institutional Advancement ... Vicki DILORENZO
84 VP of Enrollment Management ... Tiffany GUTIERREZ
32 VP of Campus Life ... Jose RODRIGUEZ
13 Chief Technology Officer ... Pamela SMITH
11 AVP of Administrative Operations ... Packy MCGRAW
09 AVP of Institutional Effectiveness ... Angela DOMINELLI
100 Special Assistant to the President ... Michael SASS
07 Director of Admissions ... Matthew STEVER
06 Registrar ... Judy SCHMONSKY
08 Director of Library Services ... Sue IWANOWICZ
26 Exec Director of Marketing/Comm ... Gil CHORBAJIAN
41 Athletic Director ... Ryan VENTER
15 Director of Human Resources ... Casey DIMARCO

Albany Law School (C)

80 New Scotland Avenue, Albany NY 12208-3494
County: Albany FICE Identification: 002886
Unit ID: 188535
Telephone: (518) 445-2311 Carnegie Class: Spec/Law
FAX Number: (518) 445-2315 Calendar System: Semester
URL: www.albanylaw.edu
Established: 1851 Annual Undergrad Tuition & Fees: $41,820
Enrollment: 690 Coed
Affiliation or Control: Independent Non-Profit IRS Status: 501(c)3
Highest Offering: First Professional Degree
Program: Professional
Accreditation: LAW

01 President & Dean ... Dean Penny ANDREWS
05 Asc Dean Academic Affs/Dir Law Lib ... Prof. Helane DAVIS
10 Vice President Finance & Business ... Mr. Victor E. RAUSCHER
30 Vice Pres Institutional Advancement ... Ms. Helen ADAMS-KEANE
32 Assistant Dean for Student Affairs ... Ms. Alicia OUELLETTE
06 Assistant Dean and Registrar ... Ms. Joanne FITZSIMMONS
36 Assistant Dean Career Planning ... Ms. Sandra MANS
26 Assoc Dean External Affairs ... Ms. Patricia E. SALKIN
09 Assoc Dean for Rsrch & Scholarship ... Mr. James GATHII
27 Director Communications ... Mr. David SINGER
04 Executive Assistant to the Dean ... Ms. Barbara JORDAN-SMITH
20 Assoc Dean Academic Affairs ... Ms. Connie MAYER
07 Assistant Dean of Admissions ... Ms. Nadia CASTRIOTA
88 Director Clinical Program ... Prof. Joseph CONNOR
13 Director Enterprise Tech Services ... Mr. Christopher CASEY
30 Director Development ... Mr. James KELLERHOUSE
29 Director Alumni Affairs ... Ms. Christina SEBASTIAN
15 Director Human Resources ... Ms. Sherri DONNELLY
37 Director Student Financial Aid ... Ms. Andrea WEDLER
28 Director of Diversity ... Ms. Pershia WILKINS
18 Facilities Manager ... Mr. Brian LA PLANTE
44 Annual Giving Coordinator ... Ms. Morgan MORRISSEY
36 Career Services Coordinator ... Mrs. Joanne CASEY

Albany Medical College (D)

47 New Scotland Avenue, Mail #34,
Albany NY 12208-3479
County: Albany FICE Identification: 002887
Unit ID: 188580
Telephone: (518) 262-6008 Carnegie Class: Spec/Med
FAX Number: (518) 262-6515 Calendar System: Other
URL: www.amc.edu
Established: 1839 Annual Graduate Tuition & Fees: $56,874
Enrollment: 816 Coed
Affiliation or Control: Independent Non-Profit IRS Status: 501(c)3
Highest Offering: Doctorate; No Undergraduates
Program: Professional
Accreditation: M, ANEST, ARCPA, IPSY, MED

01 Dean ... Dr. Vincent P. VERDILE
05 Vice Dean for Academic Admin ... Dr. Henry S. POHL
05 Vice Dean Clinical Affairs ... Dr. Ferdinand VENDITTI
32 Assoc Dean for Acad & Student Affs ... Dr. Elizabeth HIGGINS
63 Assoc Dean Graduate Medical Educ ... Dr. Joel BARTFIELD
90 Assoc Dean Info Resources & Tech ... Ms. Enid GEYER
88 Assoc Dean Undergrad Medical Educ ... Dr. Jonathan M. ROSEN
22 Assoc Dean Cmty Outreach/Medical Ed ... Ms. Ingrid ALLARD
08 Asc Dn Info Resrcs/Tech/Dir Library ... Ms. Enid GEYER
88 Asst Dean Undergrad Medical Educ ... Dr. Rebecca KELLER
88 Asst Dean Undergrad Medical Educ ... Dr. Kimberly KILBY
06 Registrar ... Mr. Len SCHLEGEL
63 Director Graduate Medical Education ... Ms. Catherine RIDDLE
76 Director Physician Asst Program ... Mr. David IRVINE
07 Dir Admissions & Student Records ... Ms. Joanne NANOS
29 Executive Director Alumni Relations ... Ms. Maura MACK-HISGEN
26 Director Public Relations ... Mr. Jeffrey GORDON
30 Chief Development ... Ms. Terri CERVENY
51 Director Cont Medical Education ... Ms. Jennifer PRICE
15 Director Human Resources ... Ms. Cathy HALAKAN
37 Director Student Financial Aid ... Ms. Ann LOUGHMAN
96 Director of Purchasing ... Ms. Patricia MARINO

Alfred University (E)

One Saxon Drive, Alfred NY 14802-1205
County: Allegany FICE Identification: 002668
Unit ID: 188641
Telephone: (607) 871-2111 Carnegie Class: Master's L
FAX Number: (607) 871-2339 Calendar System: Semester
URL: www.alfred.edu
Established: 1836 Annual Undergrad Tuition & Fees: $27,794
Enrollment: 2,393 Coed
Affiliation or Control: Independent Non-Profit IRS Status: 501(c)3
Highest Offering: Doctorate
Program: Liberal Arts And General; Teacher Preparatory; Professional
Accreditation: M, ART, BUS, ENG, SCPSY, TEAC

01 President ... Dr. Charles M. EDMONDSON
05 Provost/VP for Academic Affairs ... Dr. William HALL
10 VP for Business & Finance/Treasurer ... Ms. Giovina LLOYD
30 VP for University Relations ... Mr. Stanley A. COLLA, JR.
84 VP for Enrollment Management ... Mr. Earl E. PIERCE, JR.
32 VP for Student Affairs ... Mrs. Kathy WOUGHTER
57 Dean School of Art & Design ... Ms. Leslie BELLAVANCE
49 Dean Col of Lib Arts & Sciences ... Dr. Mary MCGEE
107 Dean College of Prof Studies ... Dr. Nancy EVANGELISTA
54 Dean School of Engineering ... Dr. Doreen EDWARDS
29 Exec Dir Annual Giv/Alum Relations ... Mr. Mark SHARDLOW
37 Director of Student Financial Aid ... Mr. Earl E. PIERCE, JR.
07 Director of Admissions ... Mr. Corry D. UNIS
06 Registrar ... Mr. Lawrence J. CASEY
19 Chief of Public Safety ... Mr. John M. DOUGHERTY
09 Dir Enrollment Operations & Rsch ... Ms. Karen L. JOHNSON
27 Director of Communications ... Mrs. Susan C. GOETSCHIUS
39 Director of Residence Life ... Mrs. Brenda I. PORTER
13 Director Information Tech Svcs ... Mr. Gary O. ROBERTS
36 Director Career Development Ctr ... Mr. Mark MCFADDEN
41 Director of Athletics ... Mr. Paul VECCHIO
23 Dir Counseling & Wellness Center ... Ms. Cathie L. CHESTER
18 Director of Physical Plant ... Mr. Brian R. DODGE
08 Dir Herrick Lib/Dean of Libraries ... Mr. Stephen S. CRANDALL
08 Director of Scholes Library ... Mr. Mark SMITH
16 Director of Human Resources ... Mr. Mark A. GUINAN, JR.
21 Controller ... Mrs. Tammara RAUB
92 Director of the Honors Program ... Dr. Gordan ATLAS
94 Dir of Women's Leadership Center ... Ms. Julia OVERTON-HEALY
35 Director of Student Activities ... Mr. Daniel NAPOLITANO
96 Director of Office Services ... Ms. Susan M. PECK
43 Dir Capital Operations/Leg Affairs ... Mr. Michael A. NEIDERBACH
101 Secretary to the Corporation ... Ms. Laura J. CRAIN
104 Acting Dir International Programs ... Dr. Vicky WESTACOTT
40 Bookstore Manager ... Mrs. Marcy K. BRADLEY
88 Assistant VP for Statutory Affairs ... Dr. Linda E. JONES
88 Dir of Summer/Parent Programs ... Mrs. Melody H. MCLAY

AMDA College and Conservatory of the Performing Arts (F)

211 West 61st Street, New York NY 10023-7832
County: New York FICE Identification: 007572
Unit ID: 188854
Telephone: (212) 787-5300 Carnegie Class: Spec/Arts
FAX Number: (212) 247-0488 Calendar System: Semester
URL: www.amda.edu
Established: 1964 Annual Undergrad Tuition & Fees: $31,308
Enrollment: 1,377 Coed
Affiliation or Control: Independent Non-Profit IRS Status: 501(c)3
Highest Offering: Baccalaureate
Program: Liberal Arts And General; Fine Arts Emphasis
Accreditation: THEA

01 President/Artistic Director ... Mr. David MARTIN
11 Executive Director ... Ms. Jan MARTIN
07 Director of Admissions ... Ms. Bridget QUINN

American Academy of Dramatic Arts (G)

120 Madison Avenue, New York NY 10016-7089
County: New York FICE Identification: 007465
Unit ID: 188678
Telephone: (212) 686-9244 Carnegie Class: Assoc/PrivNFP
FAX Number: (212) 545-7934 Calendar System: Other
URL: www.aada.edu
Established: 1884 Annual Undergrad Tuition & Fees: $29,900
Enrollment: 224 Coed
Affiliation or Control: Independent Non-Profit IRS Status: 501(c)3
Highest Offering: Associate Degree
Program: Occupational; 2-Year Principally Bachelor's Creditable
Accreditation: M, NY, THEA

01 Acting President/COO ... Ms. Susan ZECH
10 Chief Financial Officer ... Mr. John POLSKY
05 Director of Instruction ... Mr. Constantine SCOPAS
07 Director of Admissions ... Ms. Joan ZAROD
37 Director Financial Aid ... Mr. Roberto LOPEZ
08 Librarian ... Ms. Deborah PICONE
21 Controller ... Ms. Linda VIALA
04 Assistant to the President ... Ms. Lynette BELARDO
26 Director External Affairs ... Mrs. Elizabeth LAWSON
18 Superintendent ... Mr. Oliver SULLIVAN

American Academy McAllister Institute of Funeral Service (H)

619 W 54th Street, 6th Floor, New York NY 10019
County: New York FICE Identification: 010813
Unit ID: 188687
Telephone: (212) 757-1190 Carnegie Class: Assoc/PrivNFP

FAX Number: (212) 765-5923 Calendar System: Semester
URL: www.funeraleducation.org
Established: 1926 Annual Undergrad Tuition & Fees: $11,560
Enrollment: 395 Coed
Affiliation or Control: Independent Non-Profit IRS Status: 501(c)3
Highest Offering: Associate Degree
Program: Occupational
Accreditation: FUSER

01 President/CEO ..... Ms. Meg DUNN
05 Director of Student Support ..... Ms. Regina SMITH
43 Legal Counsel ..... Mr. Charles MAURER
10 Bursar ..... Mr. Jay TSO
06 Registrar/Director of Admissions ..... Mr. Andre RAMPAUL
08 Librarian ..... Ms. Mary MOON
37 Financial Aid Administrator ..... Mr. Jaway TSO
20 Academic Advisor ..... Ms. Charlotte RERRICK
20 Academic Advisor ..... Ms. Kerrigann DENHAM
69 Div Chair Public Hlth/Technical ..... Dr. Elissa DEBENEDICTS
50 Division Chair Business/Law/Ethics ..... Mr. Brian KASLER

The Art Institute of New York City (A)

11 Beach Street, New York NY 10013-1917
County: New York FICE Identification: 025256
Unit ID: 365055
Telephone: (212) 625-6000 Carnegie Class: Assoc/PrivFP
FAX Number: (212) 226-5644 Calendar System: Quarter
URL: www.ainyc.aii.edu
Established: 1980 Annual Undergrad Tuition & Fees: $30,282
Enrollment: 1,413 Coed
Affiliation or Control: Proprietary IRS Status: Proprietary
Highest Offering: Associate Degree
Program: 2-Year Principally Bachelor's Creditable; Fine Arts Emphasis
Accreditation: ACICS

01 President ..... Mr. Tad GRAHAM-HANDLEY
05 Dean of Academic Affairs ..... Mr. David MOUGHALIAN
07 Director of Admissions ..... Mrs. Mary Ann GRILLO
10 Director Admin & Financial Svcs ..... Vacant
37 Director of Student Financial Svcs ..... Mr. Fred HAMILTON
36 Director of Career Services ..... Mr. Marc SCOLERI
32 Dean of Student Affairs ..... Mr. Joe PIRRELLO
06 Registrar ..... Mr. Giovanni PALOMO

ASA Institute of Business & Computer Technology (B)

81 Willoughby Street, Brooklyn NY 11201
County: Kings FICE Identification: 030955
Unit ID: 404994
Telephone: (718) 522-9073 Carnegie Class: Assoc/PrivFP
FAX Number: (718) 532-1430 Calendar System: Semester
URL: www.asa.edu
Established: 1994 Annual Undergrad Tuition & Fees: $12,094
Enrollment: 3,135 Coed
Affiliation or Control: Proprietary IRS Status: Proprietary
Highest Offering: Associate Degree
Program: Occupational; 2-Year Principally Bachelor's Creditable
Accreditation: M, MAC

01 President ..... Mr. Alex SHCHEGOL
05 Sr Vice President Academic Affairs ..... Dr. Alexander AGAFONOV
07 Vice President Marketing/Admissions .. Ms. Victoria KOSTYUKOV
36 Vice Pres Placement/Alumni Svcs ..... Ms. Lesia WILLIS
86 Vice Pres Govt & Community Rels ..... Mr. Roberto DUMAUAL

Bank Street College of Education (C)

610 W 112 Street, New York NY 10025-1898
County: New York FICE Identification: 002669
Unit ID: 189015
Telephone: (212) 875-4400 Carnegie Class: Spec/Other
FAX Number: (212) 875-4759 Calendar System: Semester
URL: www.bankstreet.edu
Established: 1916 Annual Graduate Tuition & Fees: $23,510
Enrollment: 1,027 Coed
Affiliation or Control: Independent Non-Profit IRS Status: 501(c)3
Highest Offering: Master's; No Undergraduates
Program: Teacher Preparatory; Professional
Accreditation: M

01 President ..... Elizabeth D. DICKEY
10 Chief Operating Officer ..... Frank NUARA
30 Vice Pres Institutional Advancement ..... John S. BORDEN
05 Dean of the College ..... Jon D. SNYDER
58 Dean of the Graduate School ..... Virginia ROACH
88 Dean of Childrens Programs ..... Alexis S. WRIGHT
88 Associate Dean for IPR ..... Farhad ASGHAR
11 Associate Dean Administration ..... Barbara COLEMAN
20 Associate Dean Academic Affairs ..... Nancy GROPPER
07 Director of Admissions ..... Ann MORGAN
06 Registrar ..... Sandra SCLAFANI
37 Director Student Financial Aid ..... Lou PALEFSKY
29 Director of Alumni Relations ..... Linda REING
15 Director of Human Resources ..... Carol SAMBERG
13 Director Information Services ..... Christina D'AIELLO
18 Interim Director of Facilities ..... Daniel BENCHIMOL
08 Director of Library Services ..... Kristin FREDA
36 Director Student Placement ..... Susan LEVINE
09 Director of Institutional Research ..... Amy KLINE

Bard College (D)

PO Box 5000, Annandale-On-Hudson NY 12504-5000
County: Dutchess FICE Identification: 002671
Unit ID: 189088
Telephone: (845) 758-6822 Carnegie Class: Bac/A&S
FAX Number: (845) 758-4294 Calendar System: Semester
URL: www.bard.edu
Established: 1860 Annual Undergrad Tuition & Fees: $43,306
Enrollment: 2,305 Coed
Affiliation or Control: Independent Non-Profit IRS Status: 501(c)3
Highest Offering: Doctorate
Program: Liberal Arts And General
Accreditation: M, TEAC

01 President ..... Dr. Leon BOTSTEIN
03 Executive Vice President of College ..... Dr. Dimitri B. PAPADIMITRIOU
05 Vice President Academic Affairs ..... Dr. Robert MARTIN
30 Vice Pres Alumni/ae Affairs/Devel ..... Vacant
11 Vice President for Administration ..... Dr. James BRUDVIG
20 Vice President/Dean of the College ..... Dr. Michele DOMINY
32 VP Student Affairs/Dir Admissions ..... Ms. Mary I. BACKLUND
82 AVP/Dn Intl Aff/Civ Engmt/Dir IILE ..... Dr. Jonathan BECKER
58 Dean of Graduate Studies ..... Dr. Norton BATKIN
08 Dean Information Svcs/Dir Libraries ..... Mr. Jeffrey KATZ
39 Dean of Campus Life ..... Ms. Gretchen PERRY
32 Dean of Students ..... Ms. Erin CANNAN
13 CTO/Assoc Dean Information Svcs ..... Mr. Bill TERRY
88 Associate Dean of the College ..... Dr. Mark D. HALSEY
88 Asst Dean College/Asc Dean Std Affs ..... Dr. David SHEIN
35 Assistant Dean of Students ..... Ms. Bethany NOHLGREN
53 Dir Master of Arts in Teaching Pgm ..... Mr. Ric CAMPBELL
57 Dir Milton Avery Grad Sch of Arts ..... Mr. Arthur GIBBONS
88 Dir Bard Grad Ctr Decorative Arts ..... Dr. Susan WEBER
88 Exec Dir Ctr Curatorial Studies ..... Mr. Tom ECCLES
88 Director of Institutional Support ..... Ms. Karen UNGER
88 Director Ctr Environmental Policy ..... Dr. Eban GOODSTEIN
37 Director Financial Aid ..... Ms. Denise ACKERMAN
06 Registrar ..... Mr. Peter GADSBY
26 Director of Communications ..... Mr. Mark PRIMOFF
15 Director of Human Resources ..... Ms. Fiona SMARRITO
21 Controller ..... Mr. Kevin PARKER
88 Director Inst Writing/Thinking ..... Ms. Peg PEOPLES
18 Director of Buildings & Grounds ..... Mr. Chuck SIMMONS
13 Director Mgmt Info Systems ..... Mr. Michael TOMPKINS
29 Director Alumni/ae Affairs ..... Ms. Jane BRIEN
36 Director Career Development ..... Ms. April KINSER
19 Director Safety & Security ..... Mr. Kenneth COOPER
09 Director of Institutional Research ..... Mr. Joseph F. AHERN
24 Audio/Video Engineer Fisher Ctr ..... Mr. Paul LABARBERA
28 Director of Multicultural Affairs ..... Dr. Ann SEATON
41 Director of Athletics ..... Ms. Kristin E. HALL
42 Chaplain ..... Dr. Bruce D. CHILTON
40 Bookstore Manager ..... Ms. Merry MEYER
23 Director Health Services ..... Ms. Marsha DAVIS
38 Director Student Counseling ..... Vacant
96 Director of Purchasing ..... Ms. Julie K. MYERS

Barnard College (E)

3009 Broadway, New York NY 10027-6598
County: New York FICE Identification: 002708
Unit ID: 189097
Telephone: (212) 854-5262 Carnegie Class: Bac/A&S
FAX Number: (212) 854-6220 Calendar System: Semester
URL: www.barnard.edu
Established: 1889 Annual Undergrad Tuition & Fees: $43,502
Enrollment: 2,390 Female
Affiliation or Control: Independent Non-Profit IRS Status: 501(c)3
Highest Offering: Baccalaureate
Program: Liberal Arts And General
Accreditation: M, DANCE, @TEAC

01 President ..... Debora L. SPAR
05 Acting Vice Provost ..... Hilary LINK
11 Vice President Administration ..... Lisa GAMSU
26 Vice Pres Comm/General Counsel ..... Joanne KWONG
30 Vice President Development ..... Bret SILVER
08 Vice Pres Information Technology ..... Carol KATZMAN
10 Chief Operating Officer ..... Gregory N. BROWN
20 Dean of the College ..... Jennifer FONDILLER
32 Dean of Studies ..... Karen J. BLANK
07 Dean of Admissions ..... Jennifer FONDILLER
39 Assoc Dean Residential Life/Housing ..... Ann AVERSA
06 Registrar ..... Constance BROWN
29 Director of Alumnae Affairs ..... Erin FREDRICK
37 Director of Financial Aid ..... Nanette DILAURO
36 Director of Career Development ..... Robert EARL
15 Director of Human Resources ..... Lori MCFARLAND
19 Director of Safety/Security ..... Dianna PENNETTI
23 Director of Health Services ..... Brenda SLADE
96 Director of Purchasing & Stores ..... Douglas MAGET
21 Associate Business Officer ..... Eileen M. DIBENEDETTO
09 Director of Institutional Support ..... Abigail FEDER-KANE

† Affiliated with Columbia University in the City of New York.

Be'er Yaakov Talmudic Seminary (F)

12 Jefferson Avenue, Spring Valley NY 10977
County: Rockland Identification: 667076
Telephone: (845) 362-3053 Carnegie Class: Not Classified
FAX Number: (845) 406-9699 Calendar System: Semester
Established: 1995 Annual Undergrad Tuition & Fees: $7,000
Enrollment: 227 Male
Affiliation or Control: Independent Non-Profit IRS Status: 501(c)3
Highest Offering: First Talmudic Degree
Program: Professional
Accreditation: RABN

01 CEO ..... Mr. Jacob UNGAR
05 Dean ..... Rabbi Yosef Yisioel EISENBERGER
06 Registrar/Administrator ..... Rabbi Yitzchok SOIFER
37 Financial Aid Administrator ..... Rabbi Yosef BRAILOFSKY

Beis Medrash Heichal Dovid (G)

211 Beach 17th Street, Far Rockaway NY 11691-4433
County: Queens FICE Identification: 037133
Unit ID: 444413
Telephone: (718) 868-2300 Carnegie Class: Spec/Faith
FAX Number: (718) 868-0517 Calendar System: Semester
Established: 1999 Annual Undergrad Tuition & Fees: $7,500
Enrollment: 120 Male
Affiliation or Control: Independent Non-Profit IRS Status: 501(c)3
Highest Offering: Second Talmudic Degree
Program: Teacher Preparatory; Professional
Accreditation: RABN

01 Dean ..... Rabbi Yaakov BENDER
05 Rosh Yeshiva ..... Rabbi Shlomo Avidgor ALTUSKY
37 Financial Aid Officer ..... Rabbi Aaron STEINBERG

Berkeley College (H)

3 E 43rd Street, New York NY 10017-4604
County: New York FICE Identification: 007394
Unit ID: 189228
Telephone: (212) 986-4343 Carnegie Class: Spec/Bus
FAX Number: (212) 818-1169 Calendar System: Quarter
URL: www.berkeleycollege.edu
Established: 1931 Annual Undergrad Tuition & Fees: $21,750
Enrollment: 5,358 Coed
Affiliation or Control: Proprietary IRS Status: Proprietary
Highest Offering: Baccalaureate
Program: Business Emphasis
Accreditation: M

00 Chairman of the Board ..... Mr. Kevin L. LUING
01 President ..... Dr. Dario CORTES
100 Chief of Staff & Director Planning ..... Ms. Linda LUCIANO
04 Special Assistant to the President ..... Dr. Rose Mary HEALY
05 Provost ..... Dr. Glen ZEITZER
10 Sr Vice President Finance & Admin ..... Ms. Lee S. MIARA
11 Assoc Provost Acad Support & Admin ..... Dr. Beth COYLE
84 Sr Vice President Enrollment Mgmt ..... Ms. Diane RECINOS
20 Associate Provost Academic Admin ..... Dr. Troy ADAIR
26 Senior Vice President Marketing ..... Mr. Don CHALLIS
20 Assoc Provost Faculty Affairs ..... Dr. Marianne VAKALIS
37 Vice President Financial Aid ..... Mr. Howard LESLIE
32 VP Student Development/Campus Life ..... Dr. Edwin HUGHES
36 Vice President Advisement ..... Ms. Tia DELOUISE
07 Vice President Enrollment ..... Ms. Christine G. RICHARD
07 VP International Enrollment Svcs ..... Ms. Cynthia C. MARCHESE
22 Vice Pres & Compliance Officer ..... Mr. William BRANDT
88 Vice President External Affairs ..... Mr. Kevin HILL
88 Vice President Student Accounts ..... Ms. Eileen LOFTUS-BERLIN
08 Vice President Library Services ..... Ms. Marlene DOTY
12 NYC Campus Operating Officer ..... Ms. Kristin ROWE
12 Westchester Campus Operatng Officer ..... Ms. Cynthia RUBINO
09 Asst VP Assessment & Inst Research ..... Dr. Ross MILLER
50 Dean School of Business ..... Dr. John RAPANOS
49 Dean School of Liberal Arts ..... Dr. Don KIEFFER
107 Dean School of Professional Studies ..... Dr. Judith KORNBERG
51 Dean School of Continuing Education ..... Mr. Ricardo ORTEGON
106 Dean Berkeley College Online ..... Ms. Carol SMITH
35 Dean Student Devel/Campus Life NYC ..... Dr. Dallas F. REED
35 Dean Student Devel/Campus Life NJ ..... Ms. Neddie RAMADAN
88 Associate VP Advisement ..... Ms. Gail OKUN
84 Assoc Vice President Enrollment ..... Ms. Linda PINSKY
38 Asst Dean Dir Personal Counseling ..... Ms. Katherine WU
07 Sr Dir International Division ..... Ms. Nori JAFFER
37 Senior Director Financial Aid ..... Ms. Christine DESOUSA
21 Associate VP Student Accounts ..... Ms. Ursula BISCONTI
09 Director Institutional Research ..... Mr. Christopher J. VINGER
26 Director Media Relations ..... Ms. Ilene GREENFIELD
41 Athletic Director ..... Mr. Brian MAHER

Beth Hamedrash Shaarei Yosher Institute (I)

4102-10 16th Avenue, Brooklyn NY 11204-1099
County: Kings FICE Identification: 011192
Unit ID: 189273
Telephone: (718) 854-2290 Carnegie Class: Spec/Faith
FAX Number: (718) 436-9045 Calendar System: Semester
Established: 1962 Annual Undergrad Tuition & Fees: $7,200
Enrollment: 35 Male
Affiliation or Control: Independent Non-Profit IRS Status: 501(c)3
Highest Offering: Second Talmudic Degree
Program: Teacher Preparatory; Professional; Religious Emphasis
Accreditation: RABN

05 Chief Academic Officer ..... Rabbi Yosef ROSENBLUM

10 Chief Business Officer .... Rabbi Pinches KAFF
29 Director Alumni Association .... Rabbi Chaim ROSENBERG
15 Director Personnel Services .... Rabbi Mordechai MARGULIES
37 Director Student Financial Aid .... Rabbi Aaron ROTTENBERG
06 Registrar .... Rabbi Aron SOLOMON

Beth Hatalmud Rabbinical College (A)

2127 82nd Street, Brooklyn NY 11214-2594
County: Kings FICE Identification: 011922
Unit ID: 189264
Telephone: (718) 259-2525 Carnegie Class: Spec/Faith
FAX Number: (718) 256-5592 Calendar System: Semester
Established: 1950 Annual Undergrad Tuition & Fees: $7,300
Enrollment: 46 Male
Affiliation or Control: Independent Non-Profit IRS Status: 501(c)3
Highest Offering: Second Talmudic Degree
Program: Teacher Preparatory; Professional
Accreditation: RABN

01 President .... Rabbi Chaim STEFANSKY
10 Fiscal Officer .... Rabbi C. L. PERKOWSKI
08 Librarian .... Mr. Shimon HESS

Beth Medrash Meor Yitzchok (B)

65 Dykstra's Way East, Monsey NY 10952
County: Rockland Identification: 667111
Telephone: (845) 426-3488 Carnegie Class: Not Classified
FAX Number: (845) 425-5415 Calendar System: Semester
Established: 2007 Annual Undergrad Tuition & Fees: $8,000
Enrollment: 137 Male
Affiliation or Control: Independent Non-Profit IRS Status: 501(c)3
Highest Offering: First Talmudic Degree
Program: Professional
Accreditation: RABN

Boricua College (C)

3755 Broadway, New York NY 10032-1599
County: New York FICE Identification: 013029
Unit ID: 189413
Telephone: (212) 694-1000 Carnegie Class: Bac/Diverse
FAX Number: (212) 694-1015 Calendar System: Semester
URL: www.boricuacollege.edu
Established: 1974 Annual Undergrad Tuition & Fees: $10,025
Enrollment: 1,262 Coed
Affiliation or Control: Independent Non-Profit IRS Status: 501(c)3
Highest Offering: Master's
Program: Liberal Arts And General; Professional
Accreditation: M

01 President .... Dr. Victor G. ALICEA
04 Admin Assistant to the President .... Ms. Sandra BELLAMY
12 VP/Dean Academic Affairs .... Dr. Maria MONTES-MORALES
05 VP/Dean & Chief Academic Officer .... Dr. Shivaji SENGUPTA
13 VP Information Technology .... Mr. Irving RAMIREZ
43 Legal Counsel .... Mr. Jorge BATISTA
10 Director Finance .... Mr. Elias OYOLA
07 Director Admissions Northside Ctr .... Ms. Miriam PFEFFER
84 VP Enrollment & Managemen Bronx .... Mr. Abraham CRUZ
07 Director Admissions Graham .... Ms. Aurea MORALES
06 Director Registration & Assessment .... Ms. Beatriz AHORRIO
37 Director Financial Aid .... Ms. Rosalia CRUZ
15 Director Personnel/Human Resources .... Ms. Francia L. CASTRO
08 Director Library/Learning Resources .... Ms. Liza RIVERA
18 Director Environmental Services .... Mr. Angel REYES
41 Director of Athletics .... Mr. Robert GUILBE
30 Director of Development .... Vacant

Bramson O R T College (D)

69-30 Austin Street, Forest Hills NY 11375-4239
County: Queens FICE Identification: 021068
Unit ID: 189422
Telephone: (718) 261-5800 Carnegie Class: Assoc/PrivNFP
FAX Number: (718) 575-5119 Calendar System: Semester
URL: www.bramsonort.edu
Established: 1977 Annual Undergrad Tuition & Fees: $10,610
Enrollment: 906 Coed
Affiliation or Control: Independent Non-Profit IRS Status: 501(c)3
Highest Offering: Associate Degree
Program: Occupational; 2-Year Principally Bachelor's Creditable
Accreditation: NY

01 Director .... Dr. Ephraim BUHKS
05 Dean of Academic Services .... Dr. Robert ADELBERG
07 Recruitment/Admissions .... Ms. Dashia SILVA
10 Chief Financial Officer .... Vacant
08 Librarian .... Ms. Rivka BURKOS
21 Bursar .... Ms. Marina SHALAMOV
37 Financial Aid Coordinator .... Ms. Angelina MARRA
60 ESL/English Coordinator .... Ms. Pamela DAMBROSIA
36 Job Development Advisor .... Ms. Beth MORGANLANDER
50 Business Technology & Account Coord .... Mr. Robert ADELBERG
56 Computer Tech/Distance Learn Coord .... Mr. Damindra PERSAUD
56 Coordinator Extension Site .... Mr. Yair ROSENRAUCH
76 Medical Assistant Program Coord .... Dr. Emil ASDURIAN
96 Director of Purchasing .... Ms. Svetlana NISENBOYM
06 Registrar .... Ms. Aleksandra KAGAN
09 Asst Dir Institutional Research .... Vacant
88 Controller .... Ms. Mary C. RICKEY

Briarcliffe College (E)

1055 Stewart Avenue, Bethpage NY 11714-3545
County: Nassau FICE Identification: 020757
Unit ID: 189459
Telephone: (516) 918-3600 Carnegie Class: Bac/Assoc
FAX Number: (516) 470-6020 Calendar System: Semester
URL: www.briarcliffe.edu
Established: 1966 Annual Undergrad Tuition & Fees: $18,360
Enrollment: 2,112 Coed
Affiliation or Control: Proprietary IRS Status: Proprietary
Highest Offering: Baccalaureate
Program: Business Emphasis
Accreditation: M

01 President .... Dr. George SANTIAGO, JR.
10 VP Finance & Oper/Chief Fin Ofcr .... Mr. Louis COMMISSO
07 Vice Pres Admissions .... Mr. C. Gabriel CASTANO
32 Vice President Student Affairs .... Ms. Kathy GENUA
05 Provost .... Dr. Hubert BENITEZ
22 Director Regulatory Operations .... Ms. Helen GALLAGHER
35 Director of Student Management .... Ms. Georgette OSTROSKE
14 Director of Information Systems .... Mr. Hoober ZULUAGA
21 Business Office Manager .... Ms. Cindy ROYS
06 Registrar .... Ms. Christine MARTINEZ
36 Director of Career Services .... Ms. Marieelena VULPIS
41 Athletic Director .... Ms. Gina D'AMARO
08 Librarian .... Ms. Jennifer DEVITO

Brooklyn Law School (F)

250 Joralemon Street, Brooklyn NY 11201-3798
County: Kings FICE Identification: 002677
Unit ID: 189501
Telephone: (718) 625-2200 Carnegie Class: Spec/Law
FAX Number: (718) 780-0393 Calendar System: Semester
URL: www.brooklaw.edu
Established: 1901 Annual Graduate Tuition & Fees: $49,976
Enrollment: 1,376 Coed
Affiliation or Control: Independent Non-Profit IRS Status: 501(c)3
Highest Offering: First Professional Degree; No Undergraduates
Program: Professional
Accreditation: LAW

01 President .... Ms. Joan G. WEXLER
00 Chairman of the Board of Trustees .... Mr. Stuart SUBOTNICK
05 Dean .... Dean Nicholas W. ALLARD
20 Assoc Dean for Academic Affairs .... Dean Michael T. CAHILL
32 Assoc Dean for Student Affairs .... Dean Beryl R. JONES-WOODIN
30 Assoc Dean for Development .... Dean Michael A. GERBER
10 Chief Financial Officer .... Ms. Laurie H. NEWITZ
21 Treasurer .... Ms. Shoshanna M. CAMPBELL
07 Dean of Admissions & Financial Aid .... Dean Henry W. HAVERSTICK, III
08 Director of Library & Assoc Prof .... Prof. Janet SINDER
30 Director of Development .... Ms. Jean SMITH
29 Director of Alumni Relations .... Ms. Caitlin MONCK-MARCELLINO
36 Director of Career Services .... Ms. Camille CHIN KEE FATT
06 Registrar .... Ms. Suzanne DENNIS
37 Director of Financial Aid .... Ms. Nancy L. ZAHZAM
26 Asst Dean of External Affairs .... Ms. Linda HARVEY
39 Director of Residence Life .... Ms. Jennifer LANG
07 Director of Admissions .... Mr. Myron B. CHAITOVSKY
18 Facilities Manager .... Mr. Steven OLEKSIW
15 Human Resources Manager .... Ms. Christina WALLACE

Broome Community College (G)

PO Box 1017, Binghamton NY 13902-1017
County: Broome FICE Identification: 002862
Unit ID: 189547
Telephone: (607) 778-5000 Carnegie Class: Assoc/Pub-R-L
FAX Number: (607) 778-5310 Calendar System: Semester
URL: www.sunybroome.edu
Established: 1946 Annual Undergrad Tuition & Fees (In-District): $4,171
Enrollment: 6,605 Coed
Affiliation or Control: State/Local IRS Status: 501(c)3
Highest Offering: Associate Degree
Program: Occupational; 2-Year Principally Bachelor's Creditable
Accreditation: M, ADNUR, DH, ENGT, MAC, MLTAD, PTAA, RAD

01 President .... Dr. Kevin DRUMM
05 Actg Exec VP/Chief Academic Officer .... Dr. Francis BATTISTI
11 Vice Pres Admin/Financial Affairs .... Ms. Regina LOSINGER
32 Acting VP Student/CommunityAffairs .... Ms. Debra MORELLO
10 Associate Vice Pres & Controller .... Ms. Jeanette TILLOTSON
50 Actg Dean of Business/Public Svcs .... Ms. Elizabeth MOLLEN
76 Dean of Health Sciences .... Dr. Andrea WADE
49 Acting Dean of Liberal Arts .... Dr. Michael KINNEY
51 Acting Dean Continuing Education .... Ms. Janet HERTZOG
81 Dean Science/Tech/Engr/Math .... Dr. Kelli LIGEIKIS
102 Executive Director BCC Foundation .... Dr. Judy U. SIGGINS
08 Director Learning Resource Center .... Ms. Robin PETRUS
07 Director of Admissions .... Ms. Jenae SCHMIDT-NORRIS
15 Human Resources Officer .... Ms. Elizabeth A. WOOD
06 Registrar .... Mr. Martin GUZZI
36 Director of Placement Services .... Mr. Lawrence T. TRUILLO
09 Institutional Effectiveness Officer .... Mr. Jason ZBOCK
18 Campus Operations Director .... Vacant
37 Director of Financial Aid .... Mr. Douglas S. LUKASIK
14 Dir Information Technology Services .... Mr. John PETKASH
23 Director of Health Services .... Ms. Margaret SMITH
25 Director of Sponsored Programs .... Ms. Barbara HEIN
41 Acting Director of Athletics .... Mr. Brett CARTER
19 Dir of Campus Safety & Security .... Mr. Joseph O'CONNOR
29 Director Alumni Affairs .... Ms. Natalie THOMPSON
35 Director Student Activities .... Mr. David R. MASLAR
40 Director Bookstore .... Vacant
88 Dir Educational Opportunity Pgm .... Ms. Claudia CLARKE
96 Director of Purchasing .... Mr. John HASTIE
26 Public Affairs Officer .... Mr. Richard DAVID
85 Ast Dir Intl Admiss/Intl Stdnt Stds .... Ms. Angela LAROSA
104 Coordinator Study Abroad Program .... Ms. Maria BASUALDO
38 Student Counseling .... Ms. Mary MCCARTHY

*Bryant & Stratton College System Office (H)

2410 N. Forest Road, Suite 101, Getzville NY 14068-1224
County: Erie Identification: 666828
Telephone: (716) 250-7500 Carnegie Class: N/A
FAX Number: (716) 250-7510
URL: www.bryantstratton.edu

01 President & CEO .... Mr. John J. STASCHAK
03 Executive Vice President .... Dr. Francis J. FELSER
05 Vice Pres Chief Academic Officer .... Ms. Beth A. TARQUINO
10 VP/Chief Financial Ofcr/Treasurer .... Mr. David VADEN

*Bryant & Stratton College (I)

1259 Central Avenue, Albany NY 12205-5230
County: Albany FICE Identification: 004749
Unit ID: 188517
Telephone: (518) 437-1802 Carnegie Class: Assoc/PrivFP
FAX Number: (518) 437-1048 Calendar System: Semester
URL: www.bryantstratton.edu
Established: 1857 Annual Undergrad Tuition & Fees: $16,050
Enrollment: 769 Coed
Affiliation or Control: Proprietary IRS Status: Proprietary
Highest Offering: Baccalaureate
Program: Occupational; 2-Year Principally Bachelor's Creditable
Accreditation: &M, MAC

02 Campus Director .... Mr. Michael GUTIERREZ
05 Dean of Instruction .... Mr. Ted SYKES
32 Dean of Student Services .... Ms. Amy MORI
07 Director of Admissions .... Mr. Robert FERRELL
36 Director of Career Services .... Ms. Valerie PETTIGRASS

*Bryant & Stratton College (J)

465 Main Street, Suite 400, Buffalo NY 14203-1795
County: Erie FICE Identification: 002678
Unit ID: 189583
Telephone: (716) 884-9120 Carnegie Class: Assoc/PrivFP4
FAX Number: (716) 884-0091 Calendar System: Semester
URL: www.bryantstratton.edu
Established: 1854 Annual Undergrad Tuition & Fees: $16,350
Enrollment: 876 Coed
Affiliation or Control: Proprietary IRS Status: Proprietary
Highest Offering: Associate Degree
Program: 2-Year Principally Bachelor's Creditable; Liberal Arts And General; Business Emphasis
Accreditation: &M, MAC

02 Campus Director .... Dr. Marvel E. ROSS-JONES
05 Dean of Instruction .... Dr. Adiam TSEGAI
07 Director of Admissions .... Mr. Phil J. STRUEBEL
36 Director of Career Services .... Ms. Diane WESTBROOK
10 WNY Business Office Director .... Ms. Kathleen OWCZARCZAK

*Bryant & Stratton College (K)

3650 Millersport Highway, Getzville NY 14068
County: Erie Identification: 666114
Unit ID: 189556
Telephone: (716) 625-6300 Carnegie Class: Bac/Assoc
FAX Number: N/A Calendar System: Semester
URL: www.bryantstratton.edu
Established: 1854 Annual Undergrad Tuition & Fees: $16,350
Enrollment: 507 Coed
Affiliation or Control: Proprietary IRS Status: Proprietary
Highest Offering: Baccalaureate
Program: Liberal Arts And General; Business Emphasis
Accreditation: &M

02 Campus Director .... Mr. Michael A. MARIANI
05 Dean of Instruction .... Ms. Janice Y. FERGUSON
07 Director of Admissions .... Mr. Nathan J. COLE
36 Director of Career Services .... Mr. Stephen G. MAKOSY
10 Western NY Business Office Director .... Ms. Kathleen OWCZARCZAK

*Bryant & Stratton College (L)

8687 Carling Road, Liverpool NY 13090-1315
County: Onondaga Identification: 666115
Unit ID: 189565
Telephone: (315) 652-6500 Carnegie Class: Assoc/PrivFP
FAX Number: (315) 652-5500 Calendar System: Semester
URL: www.bryantstratton.edu
Established: 1854 Annual Undergrad Tuition & Fees: $16,085
Enrollment: 539 Coed

Affiliation or Control: Proprietary IRS Status: Proprietary
Highest Offering: Associate Degree
Program: 2-Year Principally Bachelor's Creditable
Accreditation: &M

02 Campus Director ..... Ms. Susan K. CUMOLETTI
05 Dean of Instruction ..... Ms. Kathleen M. ZAKRI
10 Market Business Director ..... Ms. Mary CLIFTON
07 Director of Admissions ..... Ms. Heather MACKNIK
32 Dean of Student Services ..... Mr. Terry PUDNEY, JR.
36 Director of Career Services ..... Mr. Christopher GODLESKI

*Bryant & Stratton College (A)

Sterling Park 200 Red Tail, Orchard Park NY 14127-1562
County: Erie Identification: 666460
Unit ID: 374972
Telephone: (716) 677-9500 Carnegie Class: Assoc/PrivFP4
FAX Number: (716) 677-9599 Calendar System: Semester
URL: www.bryantstratton.edu
Established: 1854 Annual Undergrad Tuition & Fees: $16,350
Enrollment: 1,898 Coed
Affiliation or Control: Proprietary IRS Status: Proprietary
Highest Offering: Baccalaureate
Program: Occupational; 2-Year Principally Bachelor's Creditable; Liberal Arts And General
Accreditation: &M

02 Campus Director ..... Mr. Paul BAHR
05 Dean of Instruction ..... Mr. James WESOLOWSKI
07 Director of Admissions ..... Mrs. Tracy DOMINIAK
36 Director of Career Services ..... Mr. Steve MAKOSY
10 WNY Business Office Director ..... Ms. Kathleen OWCZARCZAK

*Bryant & Stratton College (B)

150 Bellwood Drive, Rochester NY 14606-4227
County: Monroe FICE Identification: 012470
Unit ID: 189592
Telephone: (585) 720-0660 Carnegie Class: Assoc/PrivFP
FAX Number: (585) 720-9226 Calendar System: Semester
URL: www.bryantstratton.edu
Established: 1973 Annual Undergrad Tuition & Fees: $16,050
Enrollment: 432 Coed
Affiliation or Control: Proprietary IRS Status: Proprietary
Highest Offering: Associate Degree
Program: Occupational; 2-Year Principally Bachelor's Creditable
Accreditation: &M

02 Campus Director ..... Mr. Marc D. AMBROSI
05 Dean of Instruction ..... Mr. Paul PETRITUS
32 Dean of Student Services ..... Mr. John C. SCHIFANO
36 Director of Career Services ..... Ms. Kelly K. HENRY
10 Market Business Director ..... Ms. Marie A. D'ALESSANDRO
07 Director of Admissions ..... Mr. Brandon DINELL

*Bryant & Stratton College (C)

1225 Jefferson Road, Rochester NY 14623-3136
County: Monroe Identification: 666116
Unit ID: 410496
Telephone: (585) 292-5627 Carnegie Class: Assoc/PrivFP
FAX Number: (585) 292-6015 Calendar System: Semester
URL: www.bryantstratton.edu
Established: 1973 Annual Undergrad Tuition & Fees: $16,050
Enrollment: 432 Coed
Affiliation or Control: Proprietary IRS Status: Proprietary
Highest Offering: Associate Degree
Program: Occupational; 2-Year Principally Bachelor's Creditable
Accreditation: &M, MAC

02 Associate Campus Director ..... Vacant
05 Dean of Instruction ..... Mr. Kennan T. BECKSTRAND
32 Dean of Student Services ..... Mr. Robert SLEBODNIK
07 Market Director of Admissions ..... Mr. Kevin M. LEONARD
10 Market Business Director ..... Ms. Marie A. D'ALESSANDRO
36 Market Director of Career Services ..... Ms. Kelly K. HENRY

*Bryant & Stratton College (D)

953 James Street, Syracuse NY 13203-2502
County: Onondaga FICE Identification: 008276
Unit ID: 189574
Telephone: (315) 472-6603 Carnegie Class: Assoc/PrivFP
FAX Number: (315) 474-4383 Calendar System: Semester
URL: www.bryantstratton.edu
Established: 1854 Annual Undergrad Tuition & Fees: $16,050
Enrollment: 772 Coed
Affiliation or Control: Proprietary IRS Status: Proprietary
Highest Offering: Associate Degree
Program: Occupational; 2-Year Principally Bachelor's Creditable
Accreditation: &M, MAC

02 Campus Director ..... Mr. Michael SATTLER
05 Dean of Instruction ..... Mr. Richard FOWLER
32 Dean of Student Services ..... Mrs. Susan SCHILLING
07 Director of Admissions ..... Mr. Jon BRISTOL
26 Market Business Director ..... Ms. Mary CLIFTON

Business Informatics Center, Inc. (E)

134 S Central Avenue, Valley Stream NY 11580-5418
County: Nassau FICE Identification: 025729
Unit ID: 189653
Telephone: (516) 561-0050 Carnegie Class: Assoc/PrivFP
FAX Number: (516) 561-0074 Calendar System: Quarter
URL: www.thecollegeforbusiness.com
Established: 1983 Annual Undergrad Tuition & Fees: $11,250
Enrollment: 180 Coed
Affiliation or Control: Proprietary IRS Status: Proprietary
Highest Offering: Associate Degree
Program: Occupational
Accreditation: ACCSC

01 President ..... Ms. Constance BROWN
05 Academic Dean ..... Dr. Eugene ALEXANDER
07 Admissions Director ..... Mr. Hank MEANEY
37 Financial Aid Director ..... Mr. Salvatore FERRO

Canisius College (F)

2001 Main Street, Buffalo NY 14208-1098
County: Erie FICE Identification: 002681
Unit ID: 189705
Telephone: (716) 883-7000 Carnegie Class: Master's L
FAX Number: (716) 888-2525 Calendar System: Semester
URL: www.canisius.edu
Established: 1870 Annual Undergrad Tuition & Fees: $32,030
Enrollment: 5,148 Coed
Affiliation or Control: Roman Catholic IRS Status: 501(c)3
Highest Offering: Master's
Program: Liberal Arts And General; Teacher Preparatory; Professional; Business Emphasis
Accreditation: M, BUS, CACREP, TED

01 President ..... Mr. John J. HURLEY
43 Special Counsel to President ..... Mr. George M. MARTIN
05 Interim VP Academic Affairs ..... Dr. Richard A. WALL
10 Vice President Business & Finance ..... Mr. Patrick E. RICHEY
32 Vice President Student Affairs ..... Dr. Ellen O. CONLEY
30 VP for Institutional Advancement ..... Mr. Craig T. CHINDEMI
20 Assoc VP for Academic Affairs ..... Dr. Jerome L. NEUNER
13 Assoc VP Libr/Information Svcs ..... Ms. Kristine E. KASBOHM
07 Dean of Admissions ..... Ms. Donna L. SHAFFNER
44 Director of Principal Gifts ..... Mr. J. Patrick GREENWALD
06 Assoc VP of Acad Affairs/Registrar ..... Mr. Blair W. FOSTER
35 Dean of Students ..... Dr. Terri L. MANGIONE
87 Director of Summer Sessions ..... Mr. Blair W. FOSTER
49 Dean College of Arts & Sciences ..... Dr. David W. EWING
50 Dean School of Business ..... Dr. Antone F. ALBER
37 Director of Student Financial Aid ..... Mr. Curtis C. GAUME
36 Director of Career Center ..... Mr. James V. JONES
26 Assoc VP of Public Relations ..... Ms. Debra S. PARK
15 Director of Human Resourses ..... Ms. Deborah J. WINSLOW-SCHABER
53 Dean School Education/Human Svcs ..... Dr. Michael J. PARDALES
107 Exec Dir of Professional Studies ..... Dr. Khalid W. BIBI
25 Director of Sponsored Programs ..... Ms. Mary Ann LANGLOIS
18 Director Facilities Management ..... Mr. Edward P. COGAN
19 Director of Public Safety ..... Mr. Gary M. EVERETT
88 Associate VP of Finance/Controller ..... Mr. Michael J. EADIE
23 Director Student Health Center ..... Ms. Patricia H. CREAHAN
29 Interim Director Alumni Relations ..... Ms. Rachel FLAMMER
38 Director Counseling Center ..... Ms. Eileen A. NILAND
39 Dir Res Life/Assoc Dean of Stdnts ..... Mr. Matthew H. MULVILLE
85 Director Intl/Student Programs ..... Ms. Esther A. NORTHMAN
40 Manager Bookstore ..... Mr. Bhagbat KARKI
41 Director Athletics ..... Mr. William J. MAHER
42 Assoc Director Campus Ministry ..... Fr. Tom COLGAN, SJ
88 Director of Creative Services ..... Ms. Andolyn M. COURTNEY
88 Director of Advancement Services ..... Ms. Francine R. MERGL
90 Director of Academic Computing ..... Ms. Estelle M. SIENER
88 Associate Controller ..... Mr. Ronald J. HABERER
94 Director of Women Studies ..... Dr. Jane E. FISHER
92 Director of All College Honors Pgm ..... Dr. Bruce J. DIERENFIELD
86 Director of Government Relations ..... Mr. Kenneth C. KRULY
09 Director of Institutional Research ..... Dr. Pat MIZAK
88 Director of Multi Cultural Programs ..... Mr. Sababu C. NORRIS
08 Head Librarian ..... Dr. Barbara BOEHNKE
14 Dir Computer Infrastructure/Opers ..... Mr. Frank W. KIRSTEIN
24 Director Media Center ..... Mr. Daniel J. DREW
44 Director Canisius Fund ..... Ms. Jeanmarie O. CIESLICA
27 Interim Chief Information Officer ..... Mr. Walter J. DRABEK
96 Facilities Operations Manager ..... Mr. Gary B. LEW
102 Director Corp/Foundation Relations ..... Dr. Jennifer KOCH
105 Director of Web Services ..... Mr. Chuck PUSTELNIK
04 Assistand to the President ..... Ms. Erica C. SAMMARCO
88 Director of Marketing ..... Mr. Robert R. HILL

Cayuga Community College (G)

197 Franklin Street, Auburn NY 13021-3099
County: Cayuga FICE Identification: 002861
Unit ID: 189839
Telephone: (315) 255-1743 Carnegie Class: Assoc/Pub-S-SC
FAX Number: (315) 255-2117 Calendar System: Semester
URL: www.cayuga-cc.edu
Established: 1953 Annual Undergrad Tuition & Fees (In-District): $3,950
Enrollment: 4,980 Coed
Affiliation or Control: State/Local IRS Status: 501(c)3
Highest Offering: Associate Degree
Program: Occupational; 2-Year Principally Bachelor's Creditable
Accreditation: M, ADNUR

01 President ..... Dr. Daniel P. LARSON
04 Assistant to President/Board ..... Ms. Carolyn L. GUARIGLIA
05 Vice Pres Academic/Student Affairs ..... Dr. Anne HERRON
32 Assoc VP/Academic & Student Affairs ..... Mr. Jeffrey E. ROSENTHAL
10 Vice Pres Administration/Treasurer ..... Ms. Diane L. HUTCHINSON
12 Assoc VP & Dean Fulton Campus ..... Ms. Margaret KILLORAN
30 Executive Director Foundation ..... Mr. Jeffrey L. HOFFMAN
103 Dean Cmty Educ & Workforce Develop ..... Ms. Carla DESHAW
84 Dean Enrollment Management ..... Ms. Cheryl A. ANDERSON
14 Dean Information Technology ..... Mr. John TAYLOR
07 Director of Admissions ..... Mr. Bruce M. BLODGETT
29 Director Alumni Association ..... Ms. Louise B. WILSON
18 Director Buildings & Grounds ..... Mr. Kevin S. DRAYER
21 Dir Business Services & Comptroller ..... Ms. Marie A. NELLENBACK
106 Director Distance Learning ..... Mr. Edward J. KOWALSKI, JR.
37 Director Financial Aid ..... Ms. Judith G. MILADIN
92 Director Honors Program ..... Vacant
09 Director Institutional Research ..... Ms. Carol E. RUNGE
08 Director Library & Learn Resources ..... Vacant
41 Director Athletics ..... Mr. Peter E. LIDDELL
88 Director Center for Acad Success ..... Ms. Terry L. KUPP
88 Director Adult Learning ..... Ms. Janet A. NELSON
66 Director Nursing ..... Ms. Linda L. ALFIERI
15 Director HR & Affirm Action ..... Mr. Scott WHALEN
27 Director Public Rel & Inst Commun ..... Ms. Margaret SPILLETT
06 Registrar ..... Mr. Michael A. PASTORE
32 Director Student Development ..... Vacant
36 Director Career Services ..... Ms. Margaret H. OSBORNE
19 Director Campus Safety and Security ..... Mr. William J. MARVENTANO
108 Director Assessment ..... Ms. Maureen ERICKSON

Cazenovia College (H)

Cazenovia NY 13035-1085
County: Madison FICE Identification: 002685
Unit ID: 189848
Telephone: (800) 654-3210 Carnegie Class: Bac/Diverse
FAX Number: (315) 655-4143 Calendar System: Semester
URL: www.cazenovia.edu
Established: 1824 Annual Undergrad Tuition & Fees: $28,022
Enrollment: 1,000 Coed
Affiliation or Control: Independent Non-Profit IRS Status: 501(c)3
Highest Offering: Baccalaureate
Program: Liberal Arts And General; Professional
Accreditation: M, IACBE, @TEAC

01 President ..... Dr. Mark J. TIERNO
03 Exec Vice Pres/COO/Sec of College ..... Ms. Susan A. BERGER
05 VP Academic Affs/Dean of Faculty ..... Dr. Donald A. MCCRIMMON
10 VP Financial Affs/Chief Fin Officer ..... Mr. Mark H. EDWARDS
84 VP Enrol Mgmt/Dean Admiss/Fin Aid ..... Mr. Robert A. CROOT
30 VP for Institutional Advancement ..... Ms. Carol SATCHWELL
32 VP Student Devel/Dean of Students ..... Mr. C. Joseph BEHAN
20 Assoc Dean Faculty/Dn First Yr Pgm ..... Dr. Timothy G. MCLAUGHLIN
51 Director of Extended Learning ..... Ms. Lesley C. OWENS-PELTON
08 Director of Library Services ..... Mr. Stanley KOZACZKA
37 Director of Financial Aid ..... Ms. Christine MANDEL
26 Director of Communications ..... Mr. Wayne WESTERVELT
15 Director Human Resources ..... Ms. Janice ROMAGNOLI
23 Director Health Services ..... Ms. Susan A. BERGER
36 Dir Career Svcs/Internship Pgms ..... Ms. Christine RICHARDSON
41 Director Athletics ..... Mr. Robert F. KENNA
13 Director of Technology Development ..... Vacant
06 Registrar ..... Mr. Zachary KELLEY
09 Dir Institutional Rsrch/Assessment ..... Ms. Bridget MILLER
18 Dir of Physical Plant Operations ..... Mr. Jeff SLOCUM
29 Director Alumni Relations ..... Ms. Shari WHITAKER
38 Director of Counseling Services ..... Dr. Todd SPANGLER
42 Chaplain ..... Ms. Elizabeth BURLEW

Central Yeshiva Tomchei Tmimim Lubavitch America (I)

841-853 Ocean Parkway, Brooklyn NY 11230-2798
County: Kings FICE Identification: 004776
Unit ID: 189857
Telephone: (718) 434-0784 Carnegie Class: Spec/Faith
FAX Number: (718) 434-1519 Calendar System: Semester
Established: 1941 Annual Undergrad Tuition & Fees: $6,700
Enrollment: 724 Male
Affiliation or Control: Independent Non-Profit IRS Status: 501(c)3
Highest Offering: Second Talmudic Degree
Program: Teacher Preparatory; Professional
Accreditation: RABN

01 President ..... Rabbi Shloime ZARCHI
05 Dean ..... Rabbi Zalman LABKOWSKI
06 Registrar ..... Rabbi Joseph WILMOWSKY
37 Financial Aid Director ..... Rabbi Moshe M. GLUCKOWSKY
26 Director Public Relations ..... Mr. Shaya BOYMELGREEN
10 Treasurer ..... Rabbi Moshe BOGOMILSKY

Christ the King Seminary (J)

711 Knox Road, Box 607, East Aurora NY 14052-0607
County: Erie FICE Identification: 002822
Unit ID: 189981
Telephone: (716) 652-8900 Carnegie Class: Spec/Faith

FAX Number: (716) 652-8903 Calendar System: Semester
URL: www.cks.edu
Established: 1974 Annual Graduate Tuition & Fees: $9,320
Enrollment: 98 Coed
Affiliation or Control: Roman Catholic IRS Status: 501(c)3
Highest Offering: Master's; No Undergraduates
Program: Religious Emphasis
Accreditation: M, THEOL

01	Rector/President	Rev. Peter DRILLING
03	Vice Rector	Rev. Gregory M. FAULHABER
05	Academic Dean	Dr. Dennis A. CASTILLO
10	Comptroller	Mrs. Nancy M. EHLERS
11	Chief of Operations	Mr. Michael SHERRY
30	Director Institutional Advancement	Mr. David J. KERSTEN
18	Director of Facilities	Vacant
08	Library Director	Ms. Teresa LUBIENECKI
38	Director of Ministry Development	Mr. Douglas J. GEORGE
26	Chief Public Relations Officer	Ms. Susan LANKES

Christie's Education, Inc. (A)

11 West 42nd Street, 8th Floor, New York NY 10036
County: New York FICE Identification: 036654
Telephone: (212) 355-1501 Carnegie Class: Not Classified
FAX Number: (212) 355-7370 Calendar System: Other
URL: www.christieseducation.com
Established: N/A Annual Graduate Tuition & Fees: $45,393
Enrollment: 38 Coed
Affiliation or Control: Proprietary IRS Status: Proprietary
Highest Offering: Master's; No Undergraduates
Program: Professional
Accreditation: NY

01	Director of Studies	Dr. Veronique CHAGNON-BURKE
08	Librarian	Ms. Karen MAGUIRE

*City University of New York (B)

535 E 80th Street, New York NY 10075
County: New York FICE Identification: 025061
Unit ID: 190035
Telephone: (212) 794-5555 Carnegie Class: N/A
FAX Number: (212) 794-5549
URL: www.cuny.edu

01	Chancellor	Dr. Matthew GOLDSTEIN
03	Exec Vice Chanc/Chief Oper Officer	Mr. Allan H. DOBRIN
05	Exec VC/University Provost	Dr. Alexandra LOGUE
26	Sr Vice Chanc University Relations	Mr. Jay HERSHENSON
43	Sr Vice Chancellor Legal Affairs	Mr. Frederick P. SCHAFFER
10	Sr Vice Chancellor Budget/Finance	Mr. Marc SHAW
45	Vice Chanc Facility Plng/Constr Mgt	Ms. Iris WEINSHALL
15	Vice Chanc for Human Resources Mgmt	Ms. Gloriana WATERS
88	Vice Chancellor for Labor Relations	Ms. Pamela S. SILVERBLATT
09	Vice Chancellor for Research	Dr. Gillian SMALL
32	Vice Chancellor Student Affairs	Dr. Frank SANCHEZ
88	Vice Chancellor Community Colleges	Dr. Eduardo MARTI
27	Assoc VC/Chief Information Officer	Mr. Brian COHEN
21	Assoc Vice Chanc Budget/Finance	Mr. Matthew SAPIENZA

*Baruch College/City University of New York (C)

One Bernard Baruch Way, New York NY 10010-5526
County: New York FICE Identification: 007273
Unit ID: 190512
Telephone: (646) 312-1000 Carnegie Class: Master's L
FAX Number: N/A Calendar System: Semester
URL: www.baruch.cuny.edu
Established: 1968 Annual Undergrad Tuition & Fees (In-District): $5,430
Enrollment: 18,055 Coed
Affiliation or Control: State/Local IRS Status: 501(c)3
Highest Offering: Master's
Program: Liberal Arts And General; Professional; Business Emphasis
Accreditation: M, BUS, BUSA, HSA, SPAA

02	President	Dr. Mitchel B. WALLERSTEIN
05	Int Provost/SVP Academic Affairs	Dr. John BRENKMAN
11	Vice Pres Administration/Finance	Ms. Katharine COBB
32	Vice Pres Student Affs/Enroll Mgmt	Dr. Ben CORPUS
30	Vice Pres for College Advancement	Mr. Mark GIBBEL
50	Interim Dean Zicklin Sch Business	Dr. Myung-Soo LEE
45	Asst VP Campus Facilities/Ops	Mr. Jim LLOYD
84	Asst VP Enrollment Services	Ms. Leslie SUTTON-SMITH
13	Asst VP Info Tech/Chief Librarian	Mr. Arthur DOWNING
35	Asst Vice President Student Affairs	Dr. Corlisse THOMAS
21	Asst Vice President Finance	Ms. Mary FINNEN
102	President Baruch College Fund	Mr. Joel J. COHEN
49	Dn Sch Arts & Sci/V Prov Glob Strat	Dr. Jeffrey M. PECK
20	Associate Provost	Dr. Barbara LAWRENCE
20	Associate Provost	Dr. Dennis SLAVIN
80	Dean School Public Affairs	Dr. David BIRDSELL
43	Executive Legal Counsel	Ms. Stephanie VULLO
58	Executive Officer Doctoral Program	Dr. Joseph WEINTROP
100	Chief of Staff	Ms. Mary GORMAN
25	Director of Sponsored Programs	Mr. Alan EVELYN
15	Exec Dir of Human Resources	Ms. Monique GEORGE
36	Director Career Development Center	Dr. Patricia IMBIMBO
90	Asst Dir Client Svcs/Fac Liais	Mr. Frank WERBER
85	Director Intl Student Office	Ms. Rosa KELLEY
19	Director Public Safety	Mr. Henry J. MCLAUGHLIN
09	Dir Institutional Rsrch/Pgm Assess	Mr. John CHOONOO
26	Asst VP for Comm/Mktg/Public Affs	Ms. Christina LATOUF
29	Director Alumni Relations	Ms. Lisa POULLARD-BURTON
96	Director of Purchasing	Dr. Diane OQUENDO
22	Acting Director Affirmative Action	Ms. Mona JHA
41	Athletic Director	Mr. Ray RANKIS
86	Dir of Govt and Community Relations	Mr. Eric LUGO

*City University of New York Borough of Manhattan Community College (D)

199 Chambers Street, New York NY 10007-1047
County: New York FICE Identification: 002691
Unit ID: 190521
Telephone: (212) 220-1230 Carnegie Class: Assoc/Pub-U-MC
FAX Number: (212) 220-1244 Calendar System: Semester
URL: www.bmcc.cuny.edu
Established: 1963 Annual Undergrad Tuition & Fees (In-District): $3,900
Enrollment: 24,463 Coed
Affiliation or Control: State/Local IRS Status: 501(c)3
Highest Offering: Associate Degree
Program: Occupational; 2-Year Principally Bachelor's Creditable
Accreditation: M, ADNUR, EMT

02	President	Dr. Antonio PEREZ
05	Senior Vice Pres Academic Affairs	Dr. Sadie BRAGG
11	Vice President Administration/Plng	Mr. G. Scott ANDERSON
43	VP Legal Affs/Faculty & Staff Rels	Mr. Robert DIAZ
32	Vice President of Student Affairs	Dr. Marva CRAIG
30	Int Vice Pres of Development	Mrs. Chris CLOUD
10	Asst Vice Pres of Finance	Ms. Elena SAMUELS
51	Dean Ctr for Cont Ed/ Workforce Dev	Dr. Sunil GUPTA
25	Dean Grants & Development	Mr. John MONTANEZ
20	Dean for Instruction/Curriculum	Dr. Erwin WONG
88	Assoc Dean Academic Support Svcs	Dr. Michael GILLESPIE
37	Deputy Director Financial Aid	Mr. Ralph W. BUXTON
15	Deputy Director Human Resources	Ms. Gloria CHAO
07	Assoc Director of Admissions	Ms. Antoinette MIDDLETON
84	Director Enrollment Management	Mr. Eugenio BARRIOS
06	Senior Registrar	Mr. Gregory WIST
08	Director Learning Resource Center	Mr. James TYNES
09	Director Institutional Research	Dr. Jane Lee DELGADO
22	Affirmative Action Officer	Ms. Iyana TITUS
18	Campus Facilities Officer	Mr. Edward SULLIVAN
26	Public Relations Officer	Mr. Barry ROSEN
41	Director of Athletics	Mr. Stephen KELLY
102	Dir Foundation/Corporate Relations	Mr. Bryan HALLER
36	Dir Acad Advisement/Transfer Ctr	Ms. Freda MCCLEAN
38	Director Counseling Center	Dr. Ardie DEWALT
96	Director of Procurement	Mr. Robert COX

*City University of New York Bronx Community College (E)

2155 University Avenue, Bronx NY 10453-2895
County: Bronx FICE Identification: 002692
Unit ID: 190530
Telephone: (718) 289-5100 Carnegie Class: Assoc/Pub-U-MC
FAX Number: (718) 289-6011 Calendar System: Semester
URL: www.bcc.cuny.edu
Established: 1957 Annual Undergrad Tuition & Fees (In-District): $3,954
Enrollment: 11,450 Coed
Affiliation or Control: State/Local IRS Status: 501(c)3
Highest Offering: Associate Degree
Program: Occupational; 2-Year Principally Bachelor's Creditable
Accreditation: M, ACBSP, ADNUR, ENGT, NMT, RAD

02	President	Dr. Carole M. BEROTTE JOSEPH
05	VP of Academic Affairs	Dr. Howard WACH
11	SVP of Administration & Finance	Ms. Mary E. COLEMAN
26	Special Asst to Pres for Cmty Rels	Vacant
04	Exec Asst to the Pres	Ms. Carmen VAZQUEZ
32	VP of Student Dev & Enroll Mgmt	Vacant
30	Asst Vice Pres of Institutional Dev	Vacant
84	Dean of Enrollment Management	Mr. Bernard GANTT
45	Dean Inst Research & Planning	Dr. Nancy RITZE
20	Dean of Faculty & Academic Affairs	Vacant
10	Chief Business Officer	Mr. Donovan THOMPSON
06	Registrar	Mr. Robert DEMPSEY
14	Exec Dir of Information Technology	Mr. James KENNELLY
37	Director of Financial Aid	Ms. Maria BARLAAM
07	Admissions Officer	Ms. Alba CANCETTY
15	Personnel Officer	Mrs. Shelley LEVY
08	Chief Librarian	Ms. Teresa MCMANUS
19	Director of Security	Mr. James VERDICCHIO
35	Director Student Life	Ms. Melissa KIRK
41	Director of Athletics	Vacant
18	Chief Superintendnt Phys Plant Svcs	Mr. Wayne MURPHY
29	Director of Alumni Relations	Mr. Robert WHELAN
36	Assoc Dir for Career/Transfer Svcs	Dr. Annecy BAEZ
38	Director of Student Counseling	Dr. Jennifer MISICK
43	Labor Designee/Legal Counsel	Ms. Mary T. ROGAN
96	Director of Purchasing	Ms. Sharon LUCKIE

*City University of New York Brooklyn College (F)

2900 Bedford Avenue, Brooklyn NY 11210-2889
County: Kings FICE Identification: 002687
Unit ID: 190549
Telephone: (718) 951-5000 Carnegie Class: Master's L
FAX Number: N/A Calendar System: Semester
URL: www.brooklyn.cuny.edu
Established: 1930 Annual Undergrad Tuition & Fees (In-District): $5,884
Enrollment: 16,835 Coed
Affiliation or Control: State/Local IRS Status: 501(c)3
Highest Offering: Master's
Program: Liberal Arts And General; Teacher Preparatory; Professional
Accreditation: M, AUD, CACREP, DIETD, DIETI, PH, SP, TED

02	President	Dr. Karen L. GOULD
05	Provost/Vice Pres Acad Affairs	Dr. William A. TRAMONTANO
10	Sr VP for Finance & Administration	Mr. Joseph GIOVANNELLI
30	Vice Pres Institutional Advancement	Dr. Andrew SILLEN
84	VP for Enrollment Management	Dr. Stephen E. JOYNER
32	VP for Student Affairs	Dr. Milga MORALES
26	Senior Dir Communicat & Marketing	Mr. Jeremy THOMPSON
100	Acting Chief of Staff to President	Ms. Nicole HOSTEN-HAAS
86	Exec Dir Govt & External Affairs	Mr. Steven SCHECHTER
20	Associate Provost	Dr. Jerrold MIROTZNIK
20	Acting Associate Provost	Dr. Sharona LEVY
45	Assistant Provost	Ms. Colette WAGNER
57	Dean School Visual Media & Perf Art	Dr. Maria A. CONELLI
50	Dean of School of Business	Dr. Willie HOPKINS
83	Dean School Humanities & Social Sci	Dr. Kimberley L. PHILLIPS
81	Dean School Natural & Behav Science	Dr. Kleanthis PSARRIS
53	Dean School of Education	Dr. Deborah A. SHANLEY
18	Asst VP Facilities Plng/Operations	Vacant
21	AVP Finance/Budget & Planning/Compt	Mr. Alan GILBERT
13	Asst VP Information Technology Svcs	Mr. Mark GOLD
16	Asst VP Human Resource Services	Mr. Michael HEWITT
35	Assoc Dean for Student Affairs	Dr. Jacqueline WILLIAMS
88	Asst Dean for School of Education	Dr. Geraldine FARIA
35	Asst Dean Student Development	Ms. Vannessa GREEN
51	Asst Dean Enroll Effica & Adult Lit	Ms. Lillian O'REILLY
08	Chief Librarian	Ms. Stephanie WALKER
88	Deputy Comptroller	Ms. Beatrice GILLING RAYNOR
88	Bursar	Ms. Yasmin ALI
44	Assoc Director Annual Funds	Ms. Patricia ALLEN
09	Dir Inst Plng/Research & Assess	Dr. Michael AYERS
88	Director of Women's Center	Ms. Sau Fong AU
88	Director of Speech & Hearing Center	Mr. Michael BERGEN
104	Sen Dir Int Ed & Global Engagement	Dr. Alice G. BIER
85	Actg Exec Dir Intl Student Services	Mr. Ryan BUCK
25	Dir Research & Sponsored Programs	Ms. Sabrina CEREZO
40	Bookstore Manager	Mr. Michael D'ACIERNO
37	Director Financial Aid	Mr. Ahad FARHANG
06	Registrar	Mr. Richard FELTMAN
41	Dir Rec Intramurals/Intercol Athl	Mr. Bruce FILOSA
88	General Mgr Media/Perform Arts Ctr	Mr. Richard GROSSBERG
88	Dir Scholarships & Honors Recruit	Ms. Evelyn GUZMAN
105	Web Manager	Ms. Leonora KISSIS
38	Director of Personal Counseling	Dr. Gregory KUHLMAN
30	Assoc Exec Director of Development	Ms. Beth F. LEVINE
94	Coordinator of Women's Studies	Dr. Namita MANOHAR
22	Dir Diversity & Equity Programs	Ms. Natalie L. MASON-KINSEY
15	Dir Human Resource Services	Mr. Earl MONK
36	Dir Magner Ctr Career Dev/Intrn	Mr. Robert OLIVA
96	Dir of Purchasing & Contracting	Ms. Diane OQUENDO
88	Dir Academic Advise & Stdnt Success	Mr. Jesus PEREZ
43	Director of Legal Services	Ms. Pamela POLLACK
29	Director Alumni Affairs	Ms. Marla H. SCHREIBMAN
92	Dir Scholars Pgm & Honors Academy	Dr. Lisa SCHWEBEL
90	Dir Acad Computer & Library Systems	Dr. Howard SPIVAK
88	Director of Testing	Ms. Althea STERLING
88	Dir Ctr for Stdnt Disability Svcs	Ms. Valerie M. STEWART-LOVELL
23	Director Health Clinic	Ms. Ilene TANNENBAUM
07	Dir Undergrad Admiss & Recruitment	Ms. Penelope TERRY
19	Director Safety & Security	Mr. Donald A. WENZ

*City University of New York The City College (G)

160 Convent Avenue, New York NY 10031-9198
County: New York FICE Identification: 002688
Unit ID: 190567
Telephone: (212) 650-7000 Carnegie Class: Master's L
FAX Number: (212) 650-7680 Calendar System: Semester
URL: www1.ccny.cuny.edu
Established: 1847 Annual Undergrad Tuition & Fees (In-District): $5,758
Enrollment: 16,089 Coed
Affiliation or Control: State/Local IRS Status: 501(c)3
Highest Offering: Doctorate
Program: Liberal Arts And General; Teacher Preparatory; Professional
Accreditation: M, ARCPA, #CLPSY, CS, ENG, LSAR, TED

02	President	Dr. Lisa STAIANO-COICO
05	Provost	Dr. Martin MOSKOVITS
27	Act Vice Pres Communication/Mrkting	Mr. Ira KRAWITZ
30	Act VP Development/Inst Advancement	Ms. Karen WENDEROFF
10	Vice Pres Finance & Administration	Mr. Jerald POSMAN
84	Act Vice Pres Enrollment Mgmt	Ms. Celia LLOYD
45	VP Campus Planning/Facilities Mgmt	Mr. Robert SANTOS

26 VP Urban & Governmental Affairs ...... Ms. Karen WITHERSPOON
32 Vice Pres for Student Affairs ...... Ms. Juana REINA
13 Vice Pres of Information Technology ...... Mr. Praveen PANCHAL
21 Asst VP of Finance & Management ...... Mr. Felix LAM
100 Sr Advisor to Pres/Chief of Staff ...... Ms. Deborah HARTNETT
63 Dean Sophie Davis Sch of BioMed Ed ...... Dr. Maurizio TREVISAN
54 Dean of Engineering ...... Dr. Barba A. JOSEPH
53 Dean of the School of Education ...... Dr. Mary Erina DRISCOLL
47 Dean School of Architecture ...... Dr. George RANALLI
88 Dean of CWE ...... Dr. Juan Carlos MERCADO
81 Acting Dean of Science ...... Dr. Christine LI
83 Dean of Social Science ...... Dr. Marilyn HOSKIN
79 Dean of Humanities & The Arts ...... Dr. Eric WEITZ
04 Counsel to President ...... Mr. Paul F. OCCHIOGROSSO
15 Int Exec Dir of Human Resources ...... Mr. John SIDERAKIS
29 Executive Director Alumni Affairs ...... Mr. Donald K. JORDAN
35 Exec Dir Student Support Resources ...... Dr. Sarah HAHN
06 Senior Registrar ...... Mr. Daniel MATOS
35 Exec Dir of Student Affairs at CWE ...... Ms. Sophia DEMETRIOU
08 Chief Librarian ...... Ms. Pamela GILLESPIE
46 Director Research Administration ...... Vacant
09 Director of Institutional Research ...... Mr. Edward SILVERMAN
37 Director of Financial Aid ...... Ms. Thelma MASON
26 Director of Public Relations ...... Mr. Ellis SIMON
28 Chief Diversity Officer ...... Dr. Ardie D. WALSER
90 Director of IT & Computer Services ...... Mr. Curtis RIAS
88 Director of Accessability Center ...... Ms. Sarah DAMSKY
36 Director of Career Services ...... Vacant
19 Director Public Safety & Security ...... Mr. John MCKEE
11 Administrative Superintendent ...... Mr. Gerry MILLER
24 Director of Instructional Media ...... Mr. Nana ABEYIE
07 Director of Admissions ...... Mr. Joseph FANTOZZI
38 Director Student Counseling ...... Dr. Jenev CADDELL
21 Director of Business & Finance ...... Mr. Mario CRESCENZO

*City University of New York College of Staten Island (A)

2800 Victory Boulevard, Staten Island NY 10314-6600
County: Richmond — FICE Identification: 002698
Unit ID: 190558
Telephone: (718) 982-2000 — Carnegie Class: Master's L
FAX Number: N/A — Calendar System: Semester
URL: www.csi.cuny.edu
Established: 1955 — Annual Undergrad Tuition & Fees (In-District): $5,858
Enrollment: 14,200 — Coed
Affiliation or Control: State/Local — IRS Status: 501(c)3
Highest Offering: Beyond Master's But Less Than Doctorate
Program: 2-Year Principally Bachelor's Creditable; Liberal Arts And General; Teacher Preparatory; Professional
Accreditation: M, ADNUR, CS, ENG, ENGT, NUR, PTA, @SW, TED

02 Interim President ...... Dr. William J. FRITZ
05 Int Sr VP Acad Affairs/Provost ...... Dr. Fred NAIDER
10 VP for Finance and Administration ...... Mr. Ira PERSKY
32 VP for Student Affairs ...... Ms. A. R. BROWN
30 VP Inst Advance/External Affairs ...... Ms. Barbara R. ESHOO
72 VP for Technology Systems ...... Dr. Michael KRESS
21 AVP for Finance & Business Services ...... Mr. Ed RIOS
88 AVP Inst Advance/External Affairs ...... Dr. Kenneth BOYDEN
100 Deputy to President/Chief of Staff ...... Mr. Kenichi IWAMA
84 Asst VP for Enrollment Management ...... Ms. MaryBeth REILLY
35 Asst VP for Student Affairs ...... Mr. Salvador B. MENA
18 Actg AVP for Campus Plng/Facil Mgmt ...... Mr. Sirio J. FLORES
20 Assoc Provost Inst Effectiveness ...... Dr. Susan L. HOLAK
20 Assoc Provost for Undergrad Studies ...... Dr. Deborah VESS
81 Dean of Science & Technology ...... Dr. Alex CHIGOGIDZE
79 Dean of Humanities & Social Science ...... Dr. Christine FLYNN SAULNIER
08 Chief Librarian ...... Dr. Wilma JONES
43 Special Counsel and Labor Designee ...... Ms. Kathleen GALVEZ
28 Director of Diversity & Compliance ...... Ms. Danielle E. DIMITROV

*City University of New York Graduate Center (B)

365 Fifth Avenue, New York NY 10016-4309
County: New York — FICE Identification: 004765
Unit ID: 190576
Telephone: (212) 817-7000 — Carnegie Class: RU/VH
FAX Number: (212) 817-1624 — Calendar System: Semester
URL: www.gc.cuny.edu
Established: 1961 — Annual Undergrad Tuition & Fees (In-District): $7,770
Enrollment: 4,907 — Coed
Affiliation or Control: State/Local — IRS Status: 501(c)3
Highest Offering: Doctorate
Program: Professional
Accreditation: M, PH, SCPSY

02 President ...... Dr. William P. KELLY
05 Provost/Senior Vice President ...... Dr. Chase F. ROBINSON
10 Sr VP Finance and Administration ...... Dr. Sebastian T. PERSICO
20 Assoc Provost/Dean Human & Soc Sci ...... Dr. Louise LENNIHAN
32 Vice President Student Affairs ...... Mr. Matthew G. SCHOENGOOD
30 Vice Pres Institutional Advancement ...... Dr. Linda MERIANS
13 VP Information Technology ...... Mr. Robert D. CAMPBELL
21 Asst Vice President Finance ...... Mr. Stuart B. SHOR
15 Asst VP for Faculty & Staff Rels ...... Ms. Yosette JONES JOHNSON
88 Assoc Provost/Dean for Sciences ...... Dr. Ann S. HENDERSON
46 Exec Dir Research & Sponsored Pgm ...... Dr. Edith GONZALEZ DE SCOLLARD
25 Director Sponsored Research ...... Ms. Hilry FISHER
26 Exec Dir Communications/Marketing ...... Ms. Jane E. TROMBLEY
08 Chief Librarian ...... Ms. Polly THISTLETHWAITE
07 Director Admissions ...... Mr. Les GRIBBEN
06 Dir Student Svcs/Senior Registrar ...... Mr. Vincent J. DELUCA
09 Assoc Dir Institutional Research ...... Dr. Marie BURRAGE
88 Director Building Design/Exhibits ...... Mr. Ray RING
28 Executive Officer Educ Opp/Div Pgm ...... Dr. Donald ROBOTHAM
85 Director International Students ...... Mr. Douglas EWING
88 Dir Well Ctr/Psy Coun Svc/Adult Dev ...... Dr. Robert HATCHER
23 Director Student Health Services ...... Ms. Adraenne BOWE
37 Director of Financial Aid ...... Mr. John WILLIAMS
22 Affirmative Action Officer ...... Ms. Edith RIVERA
16 Director of Human Resources ...... Ms. Ella KISELYUK
31 Dpty Dir Special Events/Events Plng ...... Mr. Eric BLOMQUIST
18 Director Facilities/Physical Plant ...... Mr. Michael BYERS
96 Director of Purchasing ...... Mr. Ronald PAYNTER
35 Director Student Affairs ...... Ms. Sharon LERNER
19 Dir of Security & Public Safety ...... Mr. John FLAHERTY
94 Coordinator Women's Studies ...... Dr. Victoria PITTS-TAYLOR

*City University of New York Herbert H. Lehman College (C)

250 Bedford Park Boulevard W, Bronx NY 10468-1589
County: Bronx — FICE Identification: 007022
Unit ID: 190637
Telephone: (718) 960-8000 — Carnegie Class: Master's L
FAX Number: N/A — Calendar System: Semester
URL: www.lehman.cuny.edu
Established: 1968 — Annual Undergrad Tuition & Fees (In-District): $2,715
Enrollment: 12,287 — Coed
Affiliation or Control: State/Local — IRS Status: 501(c)3
Highest Offering: Master's
Program: Liberal Arts And General; Teacher Preparatory; Professional
Accreditation: M, CACREP, DIETD, DIETI, NURSE, PH, SP, SW, TED

02 President ...... Dr. Ricardo R. FERNANDEZ
100 Chief of Staff ...... Ms. Dawn EWING-MORGAN
43 Sp Coun to Pres Legal Affs/Lab Rels ...... Vacant
88 Deputy to Pres for HS & Educ Init ...... Ms. Sandra LERNER
05 Provost/Vice Pres Academic Affs ...... Dr. Anny MORROBEL-SOSA
11 Vice President for Administration ...... Mr. Vincent W. CLARK
32 Vice President Student Affairs ...... Mr. Jose MAGDALENO
30 Vice President for Inst Advancement ...... Mr. Mario DELLAPINA
27 Vice Pres/Chief Info Officer ...... Mr. Ronald BERGMANN
84 Assoc Provost/VP Enroll Mgmt ...... Dr. Robert C. TROY
18 Asst VP Campus Planning/Facilities ...... Ms. Rene M. ROTOLO
30 Asst Vice President Inst Advance ...... Mr. Fredrick GILBERT
88 Exec Asst to Vice Pres Student Affs ...... Mr. Vincent ZUCCHETTO
79 Dean School of Arts/Humanities ...... Dr. Deirdre PENNIPIECE
53 Dean School of Education ...... Dr. Harriet FAYNE
83 Acting Dean School of Nat & Soc Sci ...... Dr. Stefan BECKER
51 Dean Adult & Cont Education ...... Dr. Marzie A. JAFARI
35 Dean of Student Affairs ...... Mr. John HOLLOWAY
21 Business Manager ...... Mr. J. Edward ROBINSON
08 Chief Librarian ...... Dr. Kenneth SCHLESINGER
06 Acting Registrar ...... Ms. Yvette ROSARIO
07 Director of Admissions ...... Ms. Laurie AUSTIN
29 Director of Alumni Relations ...... Ms. Cristina NECULA
88 Director of the Art Gallery ...... Ms. Susan HOELTZEL
36 Director Career Services ...... Ms. Nancy A. CINTRON
38 Director Counseling Center ...... Ms. Norma COFRESI
37 Director Financial Aid ...... Mr. David MARTINEZ
89 Director Freshman Year Initiative ...... Dr. Steven WYCKOFF
25 Director of Grants & Contracts ...... Vacant
92 Director of Honors College Program ...... Dr. Gary SCHWARTZ
15 Director of Human Resources ...... Mr. Eric WASHINGTON
14 Director Info Tech Resources ...... Mr. Joseph MIDDLETON
09 Director of Institutional Research ...... Dr. Susanne M. TUMELTY
38 Dir Instruct Support Services Pgm ...... Ms. Althea FORDE
26 Director Media Rels/Publications ...... Ms. Margaret RICE
88 Director Performing Arts Center ...... Ms. Eva BORNSTEIN
19 Director of Public Safety ...... Mr. Domenick LAPERUTA
96 Director of Purchasing ...... Mr. Sunny VIRK
41 Athletic Director ...... Dr. Martin ZWIREN
40 Bookstore Manager ...... Vacant

*Hostos Community College-City University of New York (D)

500 Grand Concourse, Bronx NY 10451-5323
County: Bronx — FICE Identification: 008611
Unit ID: 190585
Telephone: (718) 518-4300 — Carnegie Class: Assoc/Pub-U-MC
FAX Number: (718) 518-4294 — Calendar System: Semester
URL: www.hostos.cuny.edu
Established: 1970 — Annual Undergrad Tuition & Fees (In-District): $3,600
Enrollment: 7,000 — Coed
Affiliation or Control: State/Local — IRS Status: 501(c)3
Highest Offering: Associate Degree
Program: 2-Year Principally Bachelor's Creditable
Accreditation: M, DH, RAD

02 President ...... Dr. Felix MATOS
05 Provost/Sr VP for Academic Affairs ...... Dr. Carmen COBALLES-VEGA
10 Senior Vice Pres for Admin/ Finance ...... Ms. Esther RODRIGUEZ-CHARDAVOYNE
32 Int Vice Pres Student Development ...... Mr. Nathaniel CRUZ
100 Deputy to President ...... Ms. Dolly MARTINEZ
30 Vice Pres Institutional Advancement ...... Ms. Ana M. CARRION-SILVA
13 Asst Vice Pres Info Technology ...... Mr. Varun SEHGAL
04 Associate Dean for Community Rels ...... Ms. Ana I. GARCIA-REYES
88 VP for Cont Educ & Workforce Dev ...... Dr. Carlos MOLINA
21 Assistant Dean Budget & Finance ...... Vacant
18 Assoc Dean Admin/Director Facility ...... Mr. Steve DELGADO
20 Assoc Dean of Academic Support ...... Ms. Christine MANGINO
35 Assistant Dean of Student Life ...... Ms. Johanna GOMEZ
88 Executive Counsel & Labor Designee ...... Ms. Glenda GRACE
27 Dir of Publications Development ...... Mr. Don BRASWELL
38 Director of Counseling ...... Ms. Linda ALEXANDER-WALLACE
15 College Personnel Officer ...... Ms. Shirley SHEVACH
86 Dir Intergovernmental Relations ...... Vacant
06 Registrar ...... Ms. Nelida PASTORIZA
07 Director of Admissions ...... Mr. Roland VELEZ
37 Director of Financial Aid ...... Mr. Joseph ALICEA
19 Director of Campus Security ...... Mr. Arnaldo BERNABE
25 Director Grants & Contracts ...... Ms. Lourdes TORRES
09 Director Institutional Research ...... Dr. Richard GAMPERT
08 Head Librarian ...... Ms. Madeline FORD
22 Affirmative Action Officer ...... Mr. Eugene SOHN
29 Director Alumni Relations ...... Ms. Nydia EDGECOMBE
36 Director Career Services ...... Vacant
35 Director Student Activities ...... Mr. Jerry ROSA
96 Director of Purchasing ...... Mr. Kevin CARMINE

*City University of New York Hunter College (E)

695 Park Avenue, New York NY 10065
County: New York — FICE Identification: 002689
Unit ID: 190594
Telephone: (212) 772-4000 — Carnegie Class: Master's L
FAX Number: N/A — Calendar System: Semester
URL: www.hunter.cuny.edu
Established: 1870 — Annual Undergrad Tuition & Fees (In-District): $5,829
Enrollment: 22,865 — Coed
Affiliation or Control: State/Local — IRS Status: 501(c)3
Highest Offering: Master's
Program: Liberal Arts And General; Teacher Preparatory; Professional
Accreditation: M, AUD, CACREP, CORE, DIETD, DIETI, ENGR, NURSE, PH, PLNG, PTA, SP, SW, TED

02 President ...... Ms. Jennifer J. RAAB
100 Chief of Staff/Exec Asst to Pres ...... Ms. Anne LYTLE
11 Vice Pres Administration/COO ...... Mr. Len ZINNANTI
05 Provost/Vice Pres Academic Affairs ...... Dr. Vita RABINOWITZ
32 VP Student Affs/Dean of Stdnts ...... Ms. Eija AYRAVAINEN
43 Counsel to the President ...... Ms. Gail A. SCOVELL
13 Asst Vice Pres Information Tech ...... Dr. Franklin STEEN
28 Dean Diversity and Compliance ...... Mr. John ROSE
70 Dean School of Social Work ...... Dr. Jacqueline MONDROS
53 Dean School of Education ...... Dr. David STEINER
66 Dean School of Nursing ...... Dr. Gail C. MCCAIN
49 Dean School of Arts & Sciences ...... Dr. Erec KOCH
18 Asst Vice Pres of Facilities ...... Mr. Rick CHANDLER
30 Executive Director Development ...... Ms. Daphne HALPERN
26 Ex Dir Communication/Marketing ...... Ms. Susan KONIG
10 Vice Pres for Administration ...... Ms. Sharon NEILL
08 Chief Librarian ...... Mr. Daniel CHERUBIN
06 Registrar ...... Ms. Marilyn DALY-WESTON
07 Director of Admissions ...... Mr. William ZLATA
09 Director of Institutional Research ...... Ms. Joan LAMBE
15 Director of Human Resources ...... Ms. Serafina RUTIGLIANO
35 Director Student Advising ...... Ms. Angela VAN DIJK
36 Director Student Placement ...... Ms. Susan MCCARTY
37 Director Student Financial Aid ...... Ms. Aristalia RODRIGUEZ
38 Director Student Counseling ...... Ms. Madlyn STOKELY
29 Director Alumni Relations ...... Ms. Deborah DAVIS
96 Director of Purchasing ...... Mr. John ALBIN
19 College Security Director ...... Mr. Louis MADER

*City University of New York John Jay College of Criminal Justice (F)

899 Tenth Avenue, New York NY 10019-1093
County: New York — FICE Identification: 002693
Unit ID: 190600
Telephone: (212) 237-8000 — Carnegie Class: Master's L
FAX Number: (212) 237-8901 — Calendar System: Semester
URL: www.jjay.cuny.edu
Established: 1964 — Annual Undergrad Tuition & Fees (In-District): $2,730
Enrollment: 14,788 — Coed
Affiliation or Control: State/Local — IRS Status: 501(c)3
Highest Offering: Master's
Program: Liberal Arts And General; Professional
Accreditation: M, SPAA

02 President ...... Mr. Jeremy TRAVIS
05 Prov/Sr Vice Pres Academic Affairs ...... Dr. Jane BOWERS
11 Sr Vice Pres Administrative Affairs ...... Mr. Robert PIGNATELLO
32 Int Vice Pres Student Development ...... Dr. Thomas STAFFORD
30 Vice Pres Marketing/Dev ...... Ms. Jayne ROSENGARTEN
84 Vice Pres Enrollment Management ...... Dr. Richard SAULNIER
45 Assoc Provost for Effect/Assessment ...... Dr. James LLANA
04 Executive Associate to President ...... Ms. Nina CONROY
100 Chief of Staff ...... Ms. Rulisa GALLOWAY-PERRY
58 Graduate & Professional Studies ...... Dr. Jannette DOMINGO
46 Int Asc Prov/Dn Rsrch/Strat Partner ...... Dr. Anthony CARPI
32 Dean of Students ...... Dr. Kenneth HOLMES

15 Dean Human Resources ..... Mr. Kevin HAUSS
20 Dean of Undergraduate Studies ..... Dr. Anne LOPES
10 Exec Dir Financial/Business Svcs ..... Ms. Patricia KETTERER
08 Chief Librarian ..... Dr. Lawrence SULLIVAN
37 Director of Financial Aid ..... Ms. Sylvia CRESPO-LOPEZ
44 Director of Development ..... Vacant
35 Interim Director Student Activities ..... Ms. Danielle OFFICER
25 Director of Funded Research ..... Mr. Jacob MARINI
09 Director of Institutional Research ..... Mr. Ricardo ANZALDVA
89 Director of First Year Experience ..... Ms. Katalin SZUR
06 Registrar ..... Mr. Adam STONE
88 Director of CRJ Research & Eval ..... Dr. Jeffrey BUTTS
07 Director of Admissions ..... Ms. Sandra PALLEJA
13 Interim Chief Information Officer ..... Mr. Joe LAUB
19 Director of Public Safety ..... Mr. Stephen HOLLOWELL
90 Director Technology Services ..... Mr. William PANGBURN
22 Affirmative Action Officer ..... Ms. Silvia MONTALBAN
24 Director of Media Services ..... Mr. Paul BRENNER
27 Exec Dir Marketing & Communications ..... Ms. Vivian TODINI
36 Director of Career Development Svcs ..... Mr. Will SIMKINS
38 Director of Counseling ..... Dr. Calvin CHIN
41 Athletic Director ..... Mr. Daniel PALUMBO
21 Associate Business Officer ..... Ms. Emily KARP
29 Director Alumni Relations ..... Ms. Jerylle KEMP
96 Director of Purchasing ..... Mr. Daniel DOLAN
04 Exec Associate to the President ..... Ms. Raeanne DAVIS
18 Director Facilities/Physical Plant ..... Mr. Elmer PHELON
43 Assistant Vice President & Counsel ..... Hon. Rosemarie MALDONADO
86 Exec Dir of External Relations ..... Ms. Mayra NIEVES
88 Director of Academic Advisement ..... Dr. Sumaya VILLANUEVA
88 Int Dir of Accessibility Services ..... Ms. Malanie CLARKE

*City University of New York Kingsborough Community College (A)

2001 Oriental Boulevard, Brooklyn NY 11235-2333
County: Kings FICE Identification: 002694
Unit ID: 190619
Telephone: (718) 368-5000 Carnegie Class: Assoc/Pub-U-MC
FAX Number: (718) 368-5003 Calendar System: Other
URL: www.kbcc.cuny.edu
Established: 1963 Annual Undergrad Tuition & Fees (In-District): $4,300
Enrollment: 19,261 Coed
Affiliation or Control: State/Local IRS Status: 501(c)3
Highest Offering: Associate Degree
Program: Occupational; 2-Year Principally Bachelor's Creditable
Accreditation: M, ADNUR, PTAA, SURGT

02 President ..... Dr. Regina S. PERUGGI
05 Vice Pres Academic Affs/Provost ..... Dr. Stuart SUSS
10 Vice Pres Finance/Administration ..... Mr. Bill KELLER
100 Executive Chief of Staff ..... Mr. Peter POBAT
32 Dean of Student Affairs ..... Mr. Peter COHEN
51 Dean Continuing Educ/Dir Cmty Rels ..... Dr. Saul W. KATZ
35 Dean of Student Life ..... Ms. Tasheka YOUNG
20 Vice Pres Academic Administration ..... Dr. David GOMEZ
84 Dean Enrollment Management ..... Mr. Thomas FRIEBEL
09 Dean Inst Effective/Strategic Plng ..... Dr. Richard FOX
30 Assoc Dean College Advancement ..... Dr. Elizabeth BASILE
15 Director of Human Resources ..... Ms. Micheline DRISCOLL
22 Dir Affirmative Action/EO Offficer ..... Mr. Angel RIVERA
19 Actg Director of Security & Safety ..... Mr. Pat MORENA
08 Chief Librarian ..... Ms. Josephine MURPHY
06 Registrar ..... Mr. Michael KLEIN
18 Campus Facilities Officer ..... Mr. Anthony CORAZZA
37 Financial Aid Officer ..... Mr. Wayne H. HAREWOOD
27 Chief Information Officer ..... Mr. Asif HUSSAIN
36 Dir Career Couns/Placement/Transfer ..... Mr. Brian MITRA
23 Director of Health Services ..... Vacant
24 Director of Educational Media ..... Mr. Michael ROSSON
41 Director of Athletics ..... Mr. Domani THOMAS
26 Chief Public Relations Officer ..... Ms. Ruby RYLES
96 Director of Purchasing ..... Ms. Lyn RELAY
07 Director of Admissions ..... Ms. Rosalie FAYAD
29 Director Alumni Relations ..... Ms. Laura GLAZIER-SMITH
38 Director Student Counseling ..... Ms. Dasha GORINSHTEYN
14 Assoc Director of Computer Center ..... Vacant
21 Business Manager ..... Mr. Anthony IMPERATO
88 Deputy Business Officer ..... Mr. Bill CORRENTI

*La Guardia Community College/ City University of New York (B)

31-10 Thomson Avenue, Long Island City NY 11101-3083
County: Queens FICE Identification: 010051
Unit ID: 190628
Telephone: (718) 482-7200 Carnegie Class: Assoc/Pub-U-SC
FAX Number: (718) 609-2000 Calendar System: Semester
URL: www.lagcc.cuny.edu
Established: 1971 Annual Undergrad Tuition & Fees (In-District): $4,242
Enrollment: 18,623 Coed
Affiliation or Control: State/Local IRS Status: 501(c)3
Highest Offering: Associate Degree
Program: Occupational; 2-Year Principally Bachelor's Creditable
Accreditation: M, ADNUR, DIETT, OTA, PTAA

02 President ..... Dr. Gail O. MELLOW
05 Provost and Senior Vice President ..... Dr. Paul ARCARIO
04 Executive Associate to President ..... Ms. Rosemary TALMADGE
11 Vice President of Administration ..... Mr. Richard ELLIOTT
30 Vice Pres Institutional Advancement ..... Vacant
13 Vice Pres Information Technology ..... Mr. Henry SALTIEL
32 Vice President Student Affairs ..... Dr. Michael BASTON
51 Vice Pres Adult/Continuing Educ ..... Ms. Jane SCHULMAN
20 Dean of Academic Affairs ..... Vacant
84 Asst Dean Enrollment Services ..... Ms. Reine SARMIENTO
18 Exec Dir Facilities Mgmt/Planning ..... Mr. Shahir ERFAN
15 Exec Director of Human Resources ..... Ms. Diane DARCY
10 Exec Director Finance & Business ..... Mr. Thomas HLADEK
86 Government Relations Manager ..... Ms. Claudia CHAN
35 Asst Dean Student Development ..... Ms. Renee BUTLER
08 Chief Librarian ..... Ms. Jane DEVINE
37 Director Student Financial Services ..... Ms. Gail BAKSH-JARRETT
44 Director of Development ..... Ms. Angela WAMBUGU-COBB
25 Director Grants Development ..... Mr. Robert KAHN
38 Dir Ctr Counseling/Advis/Acad Spprt ..... Dr. Mitchell A. LEVY
07 Director of Admissions ..... Ms. LaVora DESVIGNE
26 Dir Marketing/Communications ..... Ms. Susan LYDDON
43 Legal & Labor Relations Officer ..... Ms. Jemma ROBAIN LACAILLE
22 Affirmative Action Specialist ..... Ms. Arlene PETERSON
09 Director of Institutional Research ..... Mr. Nathan DICKMEYER
21 Associate Business Manager ..... Ms. Carmen LUONG
36 Director Employment/Career Svc Ctr ..... Ms. Claudia BALDONEDO
96 Director Procurement & Contracts ..... Mr. Mitchell HENDERSON
06 Registrar ..... Ms. T. Porter BRANNON

*City University of New York Medgar Evers College (C)

1650 Bedford Avenue, Brooklyn NY 11225-2010
County: Kings FICE Identification: 010097
Unit ID: 190646
Telephone: (718) 270-4900 Carnegie Class: Bac/Assoc
FAX Number: (718) 270-5126 Calendar System: Semester
URL: www.mec.cuny.edu
Established: 1970 Annual Undergrad Tuition & Fees (In-District): $5,732
Enrollment: 6,966 Coed
Affiliation or Control: State/Local IRS Status: 501(c)3
Highest Offering: Baccalaureate
Program: Liberal Arts And General; Teacher Preparatory; Professional
Accreditation: M, ACBSP, ADNUR, NUR, @SW, TED

02 President ..... Dr. William L. POLLARD
05 Provost/Senior Vice President ..... Dr. Howard C. JOHNSON
100 Interim Sr VP for Operations ..... Mr. Earl C. CABBELL
32 Interim VP of Student Affairs ..... Dr. Janice M. BORLANDOE
51 Interim Dean Sch Prof & Comm Dev ..... Dr. Simone RODRIGUEZ-DORESTANT
20 Interim Associate Provost ..... Dr. Claudia SCHRADER
18 Asst VP Facilities Management ..... Ms. Lisa K. EDWARDS
50 Dean of the School of Business ..... Dr. Byron PRICE
89 Dean College of Freshman Studies ..... Vacant
49 Interim Dean Sch of Lib Arts & Educ ..... Dr. Carlyle THOMPSON
72 Dean School of Science/Health/Tech ..... Dr. Mohsin PATWARY
09 Exec Dean Accred/Inst Effectiveness ..... Dean Richard JONES
21 Comptroller ..... Mr. Donal CHRISTIAN
43 Counsel to President ..... Ms. Valerie KENNEDY
04 Exec Assistant to the President ..... Ms. Lisa YOUNG
22 Director of Affirmative Action ..... Ms. Sylvia KINARD
06 Registrar ..... Ms. Johana RIVERA
91 Chief Information Officer ..... Ms. Claudia COLBERT
37 Director of Financial Aid ..... Mr. Conley JAMES
38 Director of Counseling ..... Dr. JoAnn JOYNER-GRAHAM
19 Director of Security ..... Mr. Elvert MILLER
41 Director of Athletics ..... Vacant
25 Grants Officer ..... Mr. Chi KOON
89 Dir Freshman Year Program ..... Mr. Jeffrey SIGLER
55 Director Evening/Weekend Programs ..... Ms. Yvette WALL
36 Director of Career Development ..... Ms. Deborah YOUNG
30 Exec Director of Development ..... Vacant
26 Vice Pres of External Relations ..... Dr. Moses NEWSOME
18 Supt of Buildings & Grounds ..... Mr. Cory WRIGHT
07 Director of Admissions ..... Mr. Warren HEUSNER
29 Director of Alumni Relations ..... Mr. Fred PRICE
21 Exec Dir for Risk Mgmt & Int Con ..... Mr. Bruno DEGEN
96 Director of Purchasing ..... Ms. Goldene LEWIS
84 Director Enrollment Management ..... Dr. Vincent BANREY
09 Director of Institutional Research ..... Dr. Eva CHAN
62 Actg Chair Dept of Library Services ..... Ms. Vanrea THOMAS
66 Chair Dept of Nursing ..... Dr. Jean GUMBS
50 Chair Dept of Business Admin ..... Ms. Evelyn MAGGIO
53 Chair Department of Education ..... Dr. Nancy LESTER
60 Interim Chair Dept of Mass Comm ..... Dr. Clinton CRAWFORD
88 Chair Department Accounting ..... Dr. Rosemary WILLIAMS
81 Chair Department of Mathematics ..... Dr. Umesh NAGARKATTE
77 Chair Dept Physical/Computer Sci ..... Dr. Kwesi AMOA
81 Chair Department of Biology ..... Dr. Anthony UDEOGALANYA
83 Chair Dept of Social/Behavioral Sci ..... Dr. Henry DAVIS
88 Chair Department of Psychology ..... Dr. Ethan GOLOGOR
88 Chair Dept of Public Administration ..... Dr. John FLATEAU
13 Chair Computer Info Systems ..... Dr. Christopher CASTILLO
88 Chair Department Economics/Finance ..... Dr. Emmanuel EGBE
88 Chair Department of English ..... Dr. Augustine OKEREKE
88 Chair Dept of Philosophy & Religion ..... Dr. Gary SEAY
88 Chair Dept of Foreign Languages ..... Dr. Jesus BOTTARO
35 Director of Student Life ..... Mr. Kevin ADAMS
15 Director of Human Resources ..... Mr. Oswald E. FRASER
88 Director of Bursar ..... Mr. George SOFTLEIGH

*New York City College of Technology/City University of New York (D)

300 Jay Street, Brooklyn NY 11201-1909
County: Kings FICE Identification: 002696
Unit ID: 190655
Telephone: (718) 260-5000 Carnegie Class: Bac/Assoc
FAX Number: (718) 260-5198 Calendar System: Semester
URL: www.citytech.cuny.edu
Established: 1946 Annual Undergrad Tuition & Fees (In-District): $5,430
Enrollment: 15,963 Coed
Affiliation or Control: State/Local IRS Status: 501(c)3
Highest Offering: Baccalaureate
Program: Professional; Technical Emphasis
Accreditation: M, ADNUR, DH, DT, ENGT, NUR, OPD, RAD, TED

02 President ..... Dr. Russell K. HOTZLER
05 Provost ..... Dr. Bonne AUGUST
10 Vice Pres Finance/Administration ..... Dr. Miguel CAIROL
84 VP Enrollment/Student Affairs ..... Dr. Marcela ARMOZA
22 Counsel/Affirmative Action Officer ..... Ms. Gilen CHAN
07 Director of Admissions ..... Ms. Alexis CHACONIS
06 Registrar ..... Mr. Jerry M. BERROL
37 Director of Financial Aid ..... Ms. Sandra HIGGINS
08 Librarian ..... Mr. Darrow WOOD
14 Director of Computer Center ..... Ms. Rita UDDIN
107 Dean of Professional Studies ..... Dr. Barbara GRUMET
54 Interim Dean of Technology ..... Mr. Kevin HOM
49 Interim Dean of Arts & Science ..... Dr. Pamela BROWN
51 Dean Continuing Education ..... Dr. Carol SONNENBLICK
55 Director Evening Session ..... Mr. James LAP
15 Director of Human Resources ..... Ms. Marie TINSLEY
25 Grants Officer ..... Ms. Barbara BURKE
24 Director of Inst Tech/Media Svcs ..... Ms. Karen LUNDSTREM
09 Director of Assessment ..... Dr. Tammie CUMMING
26 Chief Public Relations Officer ..... Ms. Michele FORSTEN
29 Director Alumni Relations ..... Ms. Jessica MALAVEZ
36 Director Student Placement ..... Mr. Adrian GRIFFIN
38 Director Student Counseling ..... Ms. Cynthia BINK
96 Director of Purchasing ..... Mr. Wayne ROBINSON
18 Chief Facilities/Physical Plant ..... Mr. James VASQUEZ
30 Chief Development/Spec Asst to Pres ..... Dr. Stephen SOIFFER
35 Director Student Life ..... Mr. Daniel FICTUM
35 Administrator Student Affairs ..... Mr. Joseph LENTO
21 Business Manager ..... Mr. Wayne ROBINSON

*City University of New York Queens College (E)

65-30 Kissena Boulevard, Flushing NY 11367-1597
County: Queens FICE Identification: 002690
Unit ID: 190664
Telephone: (718) 997-5000 Carnegie Class: Master's L
FAX Number: (718) 997-5598 Calendar System: Semester
URL: www.qc.cuny.edu
Established: 1937 Annual Undergrad Tuition & Fees (In-District): $5,607
Enrollment: 20,993 Coed
Affiliation or Control: State/Local IRS Status: 501(c)3
Highest Offering: Master's
Program: Liberal Arts And General; Teacher Preparatory; Professional
Accreditation: M, AAFCS, DIETD, DIETI, LAW, #LIB, SP, TED

02 President ..... Dr. James L. MUYSKENS
11 Chief Operating Officer ..... Ms. Sue HENDERSON
05 Provost ..... Dr. James STELLAR
10 Vice Pres Finance/Administration ..... Vacant
32 Vice President for Student Affairs ..... Mr. Adam ROCKMAN
91 Asst Vice Pres Converging Tech ..... Mr. Naveed HUSAIN
20 Assoc Provost Academic Plng/Pgms ..... Dr. Steven SCHWARZ
43 Asst Vice Pres for Labor Relations ..... Ms. Meryl KAYNARD
27 Asst Vice Pres of Communications ..... Vacant
21 Assistant VP Business Affairs ..... Mr. Brian MURPHY
26 Asst VP Institutional Advancement ..... Ms. Laurie DORF
88 Assistant Provost ..... Dr. June BOBB
57 Dean Arts & Humanities ..... Dr. William MCCLURE
81 Dean Math & Natural Sciences ..... Dr. Larry LIEBOVITCH
53 Dean Education ..... Dr. Francine PETERMAN
58 Dean of Research/Grad Studies ..... Dr. Richard BODNAR
83 Dean Social Sciences ..... Dr. Elizabeth HENDREY
15 Director Human Resources/Payroll ..... Ms. Reinalda MEDINA
41 Assistant Vice President Athletics ..... Ms. China JUDE
88 Director of Events ..... Ms. Wendy LEE
07 Executive Director Admissions ..... Mr. Vincent ANGRISANI
38 Dir of Counseling and Advisement ..... Dr. Barbara MOORE
06 Director Registrar's Office ..... Mr. Matthew CASANOVA
09 Director of Institutional Research ..... Dr. Margaret MCAULIFFE
08 Chief Librarian ..... Dr. Robert SHADDY
37 Director Financial Aid Services ..... Ms. Rena SMITH-KIAWU
29 Manager Alumni Affairs ..... Mr. Christopher GREAVES
19 Director Security/Safety ..... Mr. Pedro PINEIRO
22 Director Affirmative Action ..... Ms. Cynthia ROUNTREE
96 Director of Purchasing ..... Ms. Lorraine PRASAD

*City University of New York Queensborough Community College (F)

222-05 56th Avenue, Bayside NY 11364-1497
County: Queens FICE Identification: 002697
Unit ID: 190673
Telephone: (718) 631-6262 Carnegie Class: Assoc/Pub-U-MC

FAX Number: N/A Calendar System: Semester
URL: www.qcc.cuny.edu
Established: 1958 Annual Undergrad Tuition & Fees (In-District): $3,900
Enrollment: 16,837 Coed
Affiliation or Control: State/Local IRS Status: 501(c)3
Highest Offering: Associate Degree
Program: Occupational; 2-Year Principally Bachelor's Creditable
Accreditation: M, ACBSP, ADNUR, ENGT

02 Interim President .... Dr. Diane CALL
05 Vice President Academic Affairs .... Dr. Karen B. STEELE
10 Vice Pres Finance & Administration .... Ms. Sherri NEWCOMB
30 Vice Pres Institutional Advancement .... Ms. Rosemary S. ZINS
32 Vice President Student Affairs .... Ms. Ellen HARTIGAN
15 Dean Human Resource/Labor Rels .... Ms. Liza LARIOS
51 Dean Continuing Ed/Workforce Devel .... Ms. Denise WARD
20 Assoc Dean Acad Affs/Inst Research .... Dr. Paul MARCHESE
35 Assoc Dean of Student Affairs .... Dr. Paul JEAN-PIERRE
20 Assoc Dean for Academic Affairs .... Ms. Michele CUOMO
88 Assoc Dean Accred Assessment .... Dr. Arthur CORRADETTI
21 Assoc Dean Bus Admin/Comptroller .... Mr. William FAULKNER
13 Chief Information Technology Ofcr .... Mr. George SHERMAN
08 Chief Librarian .... Ms. Jeanne GALVIN
06 Registrar .... Ms. Ann TULLIO
37 Financial Aid Director .... Ms. Veronica LUKAS
07 Director Admissions & Recruitment .... Mr. Winston YARDE
09 Director of Institutional Research .... Ms. Elisabeth LACKNER
15 Personnel Officer .... Ms. Ellen ADAMS
26 Director of Marketing .... Mr. Alex BURNETT
19 Director of Safety & Security .... Mr. Edward LOCKE
22 Affirmative Action Officer .... Ms. Mavis HALL
04 Executive Assistant to President .... Ms. Millie CONTE
104 Dir Ctr for Intl Stds/Study Abroad .... Ms. Lampeto (Betty) EFTHYMIOU
90 Exec Dir Academic Computing Center .... Mr. Bruce NAPLES
96 Director of Purchasing .... Mr. MacArthur MARSHALL
18 Chief Facilities/Physical Plant .... Mr. Joseph CARTOLANO
36 Director of Career Services .... Ms. Constance PELUSO
38 Director of Student Counseling .... Dr. Jannette URCIUOLI
30 Chief Devel/Dir Alumni Relations .... Vacant
84 Director Enrollment Management .... Ms. Veronica LUKAS
44 Director Annual Giving/Major Gifts .... Ms. Laura KOTKIN

*City University of New York York College (A)

94-20 Guy Brewer Boulevard, Jamaica NY 11451-0001
County: Queens FICE Identification: 004759
Unit ID: 190691
Telephone: (718) 262-2000 Carnegie Class: Bac/Diverse
FAX Number: (718) 262-2730 Calendar System: Semester
URL: www.york.cuny.edu
Established: 1966 Annual Undergrad Tuition & Fees (In-District): $5,430
Enrollment: 8,242 Coed
Affiliation or Control: State/Local IRS Status: 501(c)3
Highest Offering: Master's
Program: Liberal Arts And General; Teacher Preparatory; Professional
Accreditation: M, ARCPA, MT, NUR, #OT, SW, TED

02 President .... Dr. Marcia V. KEIZS
05 Provost & Sr VP for Academic Affs .... Dr. Ivelaw L. GRIFFITH
10 Senior Vice Pres & COO .... Mr. Ronald C. THOMAS
11 Interim VP Administrative Affairs .... Mr. Ronald C. THOMAS
32 Vice Pres for Student Development .... Dr. Geneva WALKER-JOHNSON
20 Assistant Provost .... Dr. Holger HENKE
100 Dean for the Executive Office .... Dr. William V. DINELLO
49 Dean School of Arts & Sciences .... Dr. Panayiotis MELETIES
83 Dean Sch of Health & Behavioral Sci .... Dr. Lynne CLARK
50 Dean Sch of Business & Info Systems .... Dr. Alfred NTOKO
35 Associate Dean Student Development .... Dr. Thomas GIBSON
43 Exec Dir Compliance & Legal Affairs .... Ms. Olga DAIS
15 Int Assc Exec Dir HR & Labor Design .... Ms. Barbara MANUEL
13 Chief Information Officer .... Mr. Peter TIGHE
09 Director Institutional Research .... Dr. Aghajan MOHAMMADI
06 Registrar .... Ms. Sharon DAVIDSON
08 Chief Librarian .... Mr. John DROBNICKI
90 Director of Academic Computing .... Dr. Che-Tsao HUANG
86 Dir of Govt and Community Relations .... Mr. Earl G. SIMONS
19 Acting Director of Security .... Lt. Tyrone FORTE
37 Director of Financial Aid .... Ms. Cathy MICHAELS
26 Acting Dir Marketing/Communications .... Ms. Linda ZANGO-HALEY
18 Director Campus Planning .... Mr. Noel GAMBOA
35 Director Student Activites .... Dr. Jean PHELPS
36 Director Career Services .... Ms. Linda H. CHESNEY
25 Dir Research/Sponsored Programs .... Ms. Dawn HEWITT
38 Director of Counseling .... Dr. Susan LINDNER
07 Director of Admissions .... Ms. Laura BRUNO
41 Athletic Director .... Mr. Ronald ST. JOHN
10 Confidential Business Manager .... Ms. Jacqueline CLARK
04 Executive Asst to the President .... Ms. Sandra BELL ADAMS
84 Asst VP for Enrollment Management .... Mr. Michel A. HODGE
96 Director of Purchasing .... Mr. Marlon TORRES
29 Dir of Development & Alumni Rels .... Ms. Mondell A. SEALY

Clarkson University (B)

8 Clarkson Ave, Potsdam NY 13699
County: St. Lawrence FICE Identification: 002699
Unit ID: 190044
Telephone: (315) 268-6400 Carnegie Class: RU/H
FAX Number: (315) 268-7647 Calendar System: Semester
URL: www.clarkson.edu
Established: 1896 Annual Undergrad Tuition & Fees: $38,610
Enrollment: 3,539 Coed
Affiliation or Control: Independent Non-Profit IRS Status: 501(c)3
Highest Offering: Doctorate
Program: Liberal Arts And General; Professional
Accreditation: M, #ARCPA, BUS, ENG, PTA

01 President .... Dr. Anthony G. COLLINS
05 Senior Vice President & Provost .... Dr. Charles E. THORPE
26 Vice Pres External Relations .... Mrs. Kelly O. CHEZUM
32 Vice Pres Outreach & Stdnt Affairs .... Ms. Kathryn B. JOHNSON
30 Vice Pres Philanthropy & Alumni .... Mr. Richard W. JOHNSON
29 Assoc VP Alumni Relations .... Mr. Stephen NEWKOFSKY
28 Assoc VP Inst Diversity Initiatives .... Vacant
44 Assoc VP Philanthropy .... Mr. Paul JULIN
88 Assoc VP Student Success .... Mrs. Catherine CLARK
10 Chief Financial Officer .... Mr. James D. FISH
13 Chief Information Officer .... Mr. Kevin P. LYNCH
54 Dean of Engineering .... Dr. Goodarz AHMADI
50 Dean of Business .... Dr. Timothy F. SUGRUE
49 Dean of Arts & Sciences .... Dr. Peter TURNER
07 Dean of Admissions .... Mr. Brian T. GRANT
35 Dean of Students .... Mr. Kurt W. STIMELING
15 Exec Director Human Resources .... Ms. Marilyn ARDITO
21 Controller .... Mrs. Donna MARTELL
41 Director Athletics & Recreation .... Mr. Steven J. YIANOUKOS
45 Director Budget & Planning .... Mrs. Allison S. ALDRICH
19 Director Campus Safety & Security .... Mr. David W. DELISLE
36 Director Career Center .... Mr. Jeffrey D. TAYLOR
102 Director Corp & Foundation Rels .... Ms. Jennifer CLARKE
38 Director Counseling & Health Svcs .... Mr. Timothy J. CORBITT
18 Director Facilities & Services .... Mr. Ian HAZEN
37 Director Financial Aid .... Mrs. Pamela NICHOLS
86 Director Government Relations .... Mr. Robert H. WOOD
92 Director Honors Program .... Mr. Jonathan D. GOSS
20 Director Institutional Assessment .... Mr. Geoffrey BROWN
85 Director Intl Students & Scholars .... Mrs. Tess C. CASLER
08 Director Libraries .... Ms. Michelle L. YOUNG
96 Dir Payroll/Purchasing/Risk Mgmt .... Mr. George GIORDANO
46 Director Research & Tech Transfer .... Mr. Gregory C. SLACK
88 Director Student Administration .... Mrs. Suzanne E. DAVIS
23 Director Student Health Services .... Mrs. Susan KNOWLES
105 Director Web Development .... Mrs. Julie DAVIS
06 Registrar .... Mrs. Karen J. BURKUM
39 Assoc Dean for Residence Life .... Mr. Mark DERITIS
09 Asst Director Institutional Rsrch .... Mrs. Jenna STONE
25 Contract & Grant Administrator .... Ms. Anna Marie DAWLEY
106 Distance Learning Coordinator .... Mrs. Laura PERRY
40 Bookstore Manager .... Ms. Sara JOHNSON

Clinton Community College (C)

136 Clinton Point Drive, Plattsburgh NY 12901-9573
County: Clinton FICE Identification: 006787
Unit ID: 190053
Telephone: (518) 562-4200 Carnegie Class: Assoc/Pub-R-M
FAX Number: (518) 561-4890 Calendar System: Semester
URL: www.clinton.edu
Established: 1966 Annual Undergrad Tuition & Fees (In-District): $3,994
Enrollment: 2,207 Coed
Affiliation or Control: State/Local IRS Status: 501(c)3
Highest Offering: Associate Degree
Program: Occupational; 2-Year Principally Bachelor's Creditable
Accreditation: M, ADNUR

01 President .... Mr. John E. JABLONSKI
05 Vice President for Academic Affairs .... Dr. Cheryl REAGAN
10 Vice Pres for Admin/Business Affs .... Mr. Thomas MOFFETT
32 Vice President for Student Affairs .... Dr. Steven ST. ONGE
30 Assoc Vice Pres Inst Advancement .... Mr. Steven G. FREDERICK
08 Dean Learning Resource Center .... Vacant
84 Assoc Dean Student Retention Svcs .... Vacant
09 Assoc Dean Inst Research/Planning .... Ms. Victoria DULEY
37 Director of Financial Aid .... Mrs. Cheryl SEYMOUR
07 Director Admissions .... Mrs. Tobi MAY
06 Registrar .... Mr. Sean DERMODY
13 Mgmt Information Systems Director .... Mr. Rick BATCHELDER
15 Human Resource/Affirm Act Officer .... Vacant
26 Director of College Relations .... Ms. Jaime KAZLO WATSON
18 Chief Facilities/Physical Plant .... Mr. John CONLEY

Cochran School of Nursing (D)

967 North Broadway, Yonkers NY 10701-1399
County: Westchester FICE Identification: 006443
Unit ID: 190071
Telephone: (914) 964-4296 Carnegie Class: Assoc/PrivNFP
FAX Number: (914) 964-4266 Calendar System: Semester
URL: www.cochranschoolofnursing.us
Established: N/A Annual Undergrad Tuition & Fees: $14,907
Enrollment: 269 Coed
Affiliation or Control: Independent Non-Profit IRS Status: 501(c)3
Highest Offering: Associate Degree
Program: 2-Year Principally Bachelor's Creditable; Nursing Emphasis
Accreditation: ADNUR

05 Dean .... Dr. Karen DAVENPORT
08 Learning Resources Director .... Ms. Wanda LAMONT
06 Registrar .... Ms. Janee MCCOY

Cold Spring Harbor Laboratory/ Watson School of Biological Sciences (E)

PO Box 100, One Bungtown Road, Cold Spring Harbor NY 11724-0100
County: Suffolk FICE Identification: 034563
Unit ID: 436377
Telephone: (516) 367-6890 Carnegie Class: Not Classified
FAX Number: (516) 367-6919 Calendar System: Other
URL: www.cshl.edu
Established: 1890 Annual Graduate Tuition & Fees: N/A
Enrollment: 10 Coed
Affiliation or Control: Independent Non-Profit IRS Status: 501(c)3
Highest Offering: Doctorate; No Undergraduates
Program: Professional
Accreditation: NY

00 Chancellor Emeritis .... Dr. James D. WATSON
01 President .... Dr. Bruce STILLMAN
05 Dean .... Dr. Alexander GANN

Colgate Rochester Crozer Divinity School (F)

1100 S Goodman Street, Rochester NY 14620-2589
County: Monroe FICE Identification: 002700
Unit ID: 190080
Telephone: (585) 271-1320 Carnegie Class: Spec/Faith
FAX Number: (585) 271-8013 Calendar System: Semester
URL: www.crcds.edu
Established: 1817 Annual Graduate Tuition & Fees: $10,075
Enrollment: 103 Coed
Affiliation or Control: Independent Non-Profit IRS Status: 501(c)3
Highest Offering: Doctorate; No Undergraduates
Program: Religious Emphasis
Accreditation: THEOL

01 President .... Dr. Marvin A. MCMICKLE
05 VP Academic Life & Dean of Faculty .... Prof. Stephanie L. SAUVE
10 Chief Financial Officer .... Mr. Gerald E. VANSTRYDONCK
84 Vice Pres of Enrollment Services .... Ms. Melissa MORRAL
94 Dean of Women & Gender Studies .... Dr. Barbara MOORE
06 Registrar .... Ms. Andrea MASON
18 Director of Facilities .... Mr. Mark DEVINCENTIS
08 Librarian .... Vacant
73 Dean Black Church Studies .... Vacant
40 Director Bookstore .... Ms. Margaret A. NEAD
37 Director of Financial Aid .... Ms. Andrea MASON
44 VP Institutional Advancement .... Mr. W. Thomas MCDADE-CLAY

Colgate University (G)

13 Oak Drive, Hamilton NY 13346-1386
County: Madison FICE Identification: 002701
Unit ID: 190099
Telephone: (315) 228-1000 Carnegie Class: Bac/A&S
FAX Number: (315) 228-7798 Calendar System: Semester
URL: www.colgate.edu
Established: 1819 Annual Undergrad Tuition & Fees: $44,640
Enrollment: 2,934 Coed
Affiliation or Control: Independent Non-Profit IRS Status: 501(c)3
Highest Offering: Master's
Program: Liberal Arts And General
Accreditation: M, TEAC

01 President .... Jeffrey HERBST
101 VP/Sr Advisor/Sec Board of Trustees .... Robert L. TYBURSKI
05 Provost & Dean of Faculty .... Douglas HICKS
10 Vice President Finance & Admin .... David HALE
26 VP Communications/Public Relations .... Debra TOWNSEND
30 Vice President Inst Advancement .... Murray DECOCK
07 Vice President & Dean of Admissions .... Gary L. ROSS
20 Vice Pres & Dean of the College .... Suzy NELSON
21 Associate Vice Pres/Controller .... Thomas O'NEILL
18 Assoc Vice Pres for Facilities .... Paul FICK
21 Assoc VP for Finance/Asst Treasurer .... Carolee WHITE
15 Assoc VP for Human Resources .... Vacant
89 Dean of First Year Students .... Beverly LOW
20 Associate Dean of the Faculty .... Nancy PRUITT
06 Registrar .... Gretchen HERRINGER
08 University Librarian .... Joanne SCHNEIDER
13 Chief Information Technology Offcr .... Vacant
29 Director of Alumni Affairs .... Tim MANSFIELD
37 Director of Financial Aid .... Marcelle TYBURSKI
19 Director of Campus Safety .... William FERGUSON
36 Int Director of Career Services .... Teresa OLSEN
41 Director of Athletics .... David ROACH
40 Director of Bookstore .... Victoria BONDUM
42 University Chaplain .... Mark SHINER
44 Director of Planned Giving .... Andrew CODDINGTON
38 Director Counseling/Psych Services .... Mark THOMPSON
96 Director of Purchasing .... Art PUNSONI
23 Director Student Health Services .... Merrill MILLER
94 Director Women's Studies .... Meika LOE
44 Director Annual Fund Operations .... Sara GROH
39 Director of Residential Life .... Brenda ICE
09 Dir Institutional Planning/Research .... Brendt SIMPSON

College of Mount Saint Vincent (A)

6301 Riverdale Avenue, Riverdale NY 10471-1093

County: Bronx
FICE Identification: 002703
Unit ID: 193399
Telephone: (718) 405-3200
Carnegie Class: Master's S
FAX Number: (718) 601-6392
Calendar System: Semester
URL: www.mountsaintvincent.edu
Established: 1847
Annual Undergrad Tuition & Fees: $29,110
Enrollment: 1,889
Coed
Affiliation or Control: Independent Non-Profit
IRS Status: 501(c)3
Highest Offering: Master's
Program: Liberal Arts And General; Teacher Preparatory; Professional
Accreditation: M, ACBSP, NURSE, TEAC

01 President .... Dr. Charles L. FLYNN
05 Provost/Dean of Faculty .... Dr. Guy LOMETTI
20 Dean Undergraduate College .... Dr. Paul DOUILLARD
30 VP Inst Advancement/External Rels . Mrs. Madeleine MELKONIAN
10 Executive VP/Treasurer .... Mr. Abed ELKESHK
10 VP for Business .... Mr. Kevin DEGROAT
32 VP Student Affs/Dean of Students .... Dr. Dianna DALE
88 Executive Director/Mission .... Dr. Jean FLANNELY, SC
108 Executive Director of Assessmant .... Vacant
88 Assoc VP Institutional Advancement ...... Sr. Kathleen TRACEY, SC
84 VP for Admissions/Financial Aid .... Mr. Timothy NASH
51 Dean School Professional/Cont Stds .... Dr. Edward MEYER
06 Registrar .... Mrs. Jeanette PICHARDO
20 Director of Academic Advisement .... Ms. Sandra JENNINGS
08 Director of Library .... Mr. Sebastian DERRY
13 VP Information Technology/CIO .... Mr. Adam WICHERN
09 Director of Institutional Research .... Sr. Carol M. FINEGAN, SC
36 Director Internships/Career Devel .... Mrs. Diane MACHADO
37 Director of Financial Aid .... Mrs. Monica SIMOTAS
42 Director of Campus Ministry .... Sr. Cecilia HARRIENDORF, SC
39 Director of Residence Life .... Vacant
41 Director of Athletics .... Mr. Jay BUTLER
38 Director Counseling Services .... Ms. Vicki HALLAS
23 Director of Health Services .... Mrs. Eileen MCCABE
29 Director Alumnae Relations .... Ms. Christina WESOLEK
26 Director College Relations .... Ms. Erin WALSH
31 Director Campus Events/Admin Svcs .... Vacant
19 Dir Campus Safety/Security .... Mr. Paul RUNG
66 Director of Nursing .... Dr. Justine TADDEO
44 Director of Annual Giving .... Ms. Nancy TOTINO
15 Director of Human Resources .... Ms. Annette PIECORA
21 Controller .... Ms. Barbara HURLEIGH
04 Assistant to the President .... Ms. Catherine MCKENNA
18 Director of Facilities .... Mr. Timothy DRURY
07 Director of Admissions .... Ms. Brenda NELSON
92 Director of Honors Program .... Dr. Daniel OPLER
97 Director of Core Curriculum .... Dr. Sarah STEVENSON

The College of New Rochelle (B)

29 Castle Place, New Rochelle NY 10805-2338

County: Westchester
FICE Identification: 002704
Unit ID: 193645
Telephone: (914) 654-5000
Carnegie Class: Master's L
FAX Number: (914) 654-5554
Calendar System: Semester
URL: www.cnr.edu
Established: 1904
Annual Undergrad Tuition & Fees: $29,330
Enrollment: 4,397
Coed
Affiliation or Control: Independent Non-Profit
IRS Status: 501(c)3
Highest Offering: Master's
Program: Liberal Arts And General; Teacher Preparatory; Professional
Accreditation: M, NURSE, SW, @TEAC

01 President .... Mrs. Judith HUNTINGTON
03 Executive Vice President .... Dr. Ellen R. CURRY DAMATO
05 Sr Vice Pres Acad Affairs & Provost ..Dr. Dorothy A. ESCRIBANO
10 Vice President Financial Affairs .... Mr. Keith BORGE
32 Vice President Student Services .... Dr. Colette GEARY
30 Vice President College Advancement .... Ms. Brenna S. MAYER
84 Associate VP for Enrollment Mgmt .... Ms. Ellen LOCKAMY
49 Dean School of Arts & Sciences .... Dr. Richard H. THOMPSON
58 Dean of the Graduate School .... Dr. Marie RIBARICH
51 Dean School of New Resources .... Dr. Darryl JONES
66 Dean School of Nursing .... Dr. Mary Alice DONIUS
06 Registrar .... Ms. Tania QUINN
08 Dean of the Library .... Ms. Ana FONTOURA
37 Director of Financial Aid .... Ms. Anne C. PELAK
36 Dir Counseling & Career Services .... Vacant
29 Director Alumnae/i Relations .... Dr. Kelly BRENNAN
44 Exec Director of Capital Campaigns .... Ms. Linda V. DAVID
15 Director of Human Resources .... Ms. JoEllen L. VAVASOUR
18 Director of Facilities Management .... Mr. Fred SULLO
09 Coordinator Institutional Research ... Mr. Lambros G. STAMOULIS
21 Controller .... Mr. Stephen J. WALKER

The College of Saint Rose (C)

432 Western Avenue, Albany NY 12203-1490

County: Albany
FICE Identification: 002705
Unit ID: 195234
Telephone: (518) 454-5111
Carnegie Class: Master's L
FAX Number: (518) 438-3293
Calendar System: Semester
URL: www.strose.edu
Established: 1920
Annual Undergrad Tuition & Fees: $25,722
Enrollment: 4,863
Coed
Affiliation or Control: Independent Non-Profit
IRS Status: 501(c)3
Highest Offering: Master's
Program: Liberal Arts And General; Teacher Preparatory
Accreditation: M, ACBSP, ART, MUS, SP, SW, TED

01 President .... Dr. David SZCZERBACKI
04 Assistant to President .... Ms. Debra LIBERATORE
05 Interim Provost/VP Academic Affairs .... Dr. Margaret KIRWIN
10 Vice Pres Finance/Administration .... Mr. Marcus BUCKLEY
30 Vice President for Inst Advancement .... Ms. Karin CARR
32 Vice President Student Services .... Mr. Dennis MCDONALD
84 Vice Pres of Enroll Mgmt/Admissions . Mrs. Mary M. GRONDAHL
15 Asst Vice Pres Human Res/Risk Mgt .... Mr. Jeffrey KNAPP
07 Asst VP of Undergrad Admissions .... Mr. Jeremy BOGAN
07 Asst VP of Graduate Admissions .... Ms. Susan PATTERSON
37 Asst VP of Financial Aid .... Mr. Steven W. DWIRE
27 Asst VP of Public Information .... Mrs. Lisa HALEY-THOMSON
35 Assoc Dn Stdnt Affs/Dir Stdnt Life ... Ms. Mary R. MCLAUGHLIN
42 Dean of Spiritual Life .... Rev. Christopher DEGIOVINE
86 Exec Dir of Govt Community Affairs .... Mr. Michael D'ATTILIO
90 Exec Dir of Info Technology Service .... Mr. John ELLIS
44 Director Development/Annual Fund .... Ms. Lisa MCKENZIE
21 Comptroller .... Ms. Debra Lee POLLEY
06 Registrar .... Ms. Judith KELLY
08 Director of Library .... Mr. Peter KOONZ
39 Director Residence Life .... Ms. Jennifer RICHARDSON
36 Director Career Development Center .... Ms. Michelle OSBORNE
38 Director Counsel/Psychological Svcs .... Mr. Ronald J. HAMER
41 Director Athletics & Recreation .... Ms. Catherine A. HAKER
91 Director Administrative Info Sys .... Mr. William TRAVER
29 Dir Alumni Relations/Annual Giving .... Mr. Jason MANNING
31 Director Community Services .... Mr. Kenneth SCOTT
42 Director of Campus Ministry .... Ms. Joan HORGAN
23 Director of Health Services .... Ms. Sandra FREHSE
19 Director of Safety/Security .... Mr. Steven STELLA
09 Exec Dir Budget & Inst Research .... Ms. Gail A. GARDNER
28 Director of Diversity .... Ms. Shai BUTLER
38 Director of Advisement .... Dr. Kelly MEYER
88 Art Gallery Director .... Ms. Jeanne FLANAGAN
23 Director of Clinical Services .... Ms. Kimberly LAMPARELLI
96 Director Purchasing/Auxiliary Svcs .... Ms. Patricia BUCKLEY
26 Assoc Dir Media Relations .... Mr. Benjamin MARVIN
18 Dir of Facilities Planning & Mgmt .... Ms. Nancy MACDONALD
09 Manager of Institutional Research .... Mr. Patrick CONNELL
40 Manager of Campus Store .... Mr. Chris WILSON
24 Coord of Academic Media Technology .... Mr. Michael STRATTON

The College of Westchester (D)

PO Box 710, White Plains NY 10602-0710

County: Westchester
FICE Identification: 005208
Unit ID: 197285
Telephone: (914) 948-4442
Carnegie Class: Assoc/PrivFP4
FAX Number: (914) 948-5441
Calendar System: Semester
URL: www.cw.edu
Established: 1915
Annual Undergrad Tuition & Fees: $20,610
Enrollment: 1,078
Coed
Affiliation or Control: Proprietary
IRS Status: Proprietary
Highest Offering: Baccalaureate
Program: Business Emphasis
Accreditation: M

00 Chairman Emeritus .... Mr. Ernest H. SUTKOWSKI
01 President .... Mrs. Karen J. SMITH
03 Vice President .... Mrs. Mary Beth DEL BALZO
26 Vice President Marketing .... Mr. Dale T. SMITH
05 Chief Academic Officer .... Dr. Joann MULQUEEN
20 Dean of Student Academic Services .... Ms. Jean CARLSON
07 Director of Admissions .... Mr. Matt CURTIS
36 Director of Career Services .... Ms. Joann SONDEY
88 Dir of Student Success/Retention .... Dr. Judith LILLESTON
37 Dir of Student Financial Services .... Mrs. Dianne PEPITONE

Columbia-Greene Community College (E)

4400 Route 23, Hudson NY 12534-9543

County: Columbia
FICE Identification: 006789
Unit ID: 190169
Telephone: (518) 828-4181
Carnegie Class: Assoc/Pub-R-S
FAX Number: (518) 828-8543
Calendar System: Semester
URL: www.sunycgcc.edu
Established: 1966
Annual Undergrad Tuition & Fees (In-District): $4,122
Enrollment: 2,098
Coed
Affiliation or Control: State/Local
IRS Status: 501(c)3
Highest Offering: Associate Degree
Program: Occupational; 2-Year Principally Bachelor's Creditable
Accreditation: M, ADNUR

01 President .... Mr. James R. CAMPION
05 VP & Dean of Academic Affairs .... Ms. Phyllis CARITO
11 Vice Pres & Dean of Administration .... Mr. A. Joseph MATTIES
32 VP/Dean of Students/Enrollment Mgmt .... Dr. Joseph WATSON
38 Counselor .... Ms. Diane JOHNSON
18 Director Building & Grounds .... Mr. James FOLZ
26 Director Public Information .... Mr. Allen KOVLER
37 Dir Stndt Fin Aid/Asst Dean Stdnts .... Mr. Richard SABBIA
21 Assistant Dean of Administration .... Ms. Dianne TOPPLE
06 Acting Registrar .... Ms. Gail SHADER
14 Director Information Systems .... Mr. Gino RIZZI
15 Director of Human Resources .... Ms. Melissa FANDOZZI
22 Affirmative Action Officer .... Ms. Melissa FANDOZZI
09 Director of Institutional Research .... Ms. Joanna DEMURANT
31 Director of Community Services .... Mr. Robert BODRATTI
41 Athletic Director .... Mr. Walter RICKARD
88 Director Academic Support Center .... Dr. Mary-Teresa HEATH
103 Director of Workforce Development .... Ms. Mary Alane WILTSE
07 Director of Admissions .... Vacant
30 Dir of Development & Alumni Svcs .... Ms. Joan KOWEEK
20 Assistant Dean of Academic Affairs .... Ms. Carol DOERFER
21 Bursar .... Ms. Christy DECKER
19 Director of Security .... Mr. Raymond TROWBRIDGE
96 Purchasing Officer .... Ms. Patricia DAY
62 Department Chair Library Services .... Ms. Geralynn DEMAREST
83 Div Chair Behavioral/Social Science .... Mr. Thomas GERRY
81 Div Chair Math & Science .... Ms. Siri CARLISLE
57 Division Chair Arts & Humanities .... Mr. Michael ALLARD
66 Division Chair Nursing .... Ms. Dawn WRIGLEY
72 Division Chair Technology .... Vacant

Columbia University in the City of New York (F)

615 West 131st Street, New York NY 10027-6902

County: New York
FICE Identification: 002707
Unit ID: 190150
Telephone: (212) 851-0627
Carnegie Class: RU/VH
FAX Number: (212) 851-7022
Calendar System: Semester
URL: www.columbia.edu
Established: 1754
Annual Undergrad Tuition & Fees: $47,246
Enrollment: 26,050
Coed
Affiliation or Control: Independent Non-Profit
IRS Status: 501(c)3
Highest Offering: Doctorate
Program: Liberal Arts And General; Professional; Business Emphasis
Accreditation: M, ANEST, BUS, DENT, ENG, HSA, IPSY, JOUR, LAW, MED, MIDWF, NURSE, OT, PH, PLNG, PTA, SW

01 President .... Mr. Lee C. BOLLINGER
05 Provost .... Dr. John COATSWORTH
03 Senior Exec Vice President .... Mr. Robert KASDIN
10 Exec Vice President for Finance .... Ms. Anne R. SULLIVAN
76 Exec VP Health/Biomed Sciences .... Dr. Lee GOLDMAN
30 Exec VP Univ Devel/Alumni Rels ... Mr. Frederick M. VAN SICKLE
88 Special Advisor to the President .... Ms. Susan K. FEAGIN
18 Exec Vice Pres Univ Facilities .... Mr. Joe A. IENUSO
32 Exec Vice Pres Student/Admin Svcs .... Mr. Jeffrey F. SCOTT
27 Exec Vice Pres Communications .... Mr. David M. STONE
09 Exec Vice President Research .... Dr. G. Michael PURDY
26 Exec Vice Pres Govt & Cmty Affairs .... Ms. Maxine F. GRIFFITH
49 Exec Vice President Arts & Sciences .... Mr. Nicholas B. DIRKS
08 Vice Pres Info Svcs Univ Libraries .... Dr. James G. NEAL
88 Pres IMC Ofc of Univ Investments .... Mr. Nirmal P. NARVEKAR
15 Vice President Human Resources .... Mr. Louis BELLARDINE
37 Vice Pres Student Financial Svcs .... Ms. Cheryl A. ROSS
29 Vice Pres Alumni Relations .... Ms. Donna H. MACPHEE
96 Vice President Procurement Svcs .... Mr. Joseph M. HARNEY
43 General Counsel .... Ms. Jane E. BOOTH
06 Assoc Vice Pres & Registrar .... Mr. Barry S. KANE
20 Vice Provost Acad Administration .... Mr. Stephen A. RITTENBERG
88 Vice Provost for Academic Planning .... Dr. Andrew R. DAVIDSON
101 University Secretary .... Mr. Jerome DAVIS
07 Dean of Undergraduate Admissions ...... Ms. Jessica MARINACCIO
21 Treasurer .... Ms. Gail HOFFMAN
38 Exec Director Student Counseling .... Dr. Richard EICHLER
48 Dean Grad School Arch/Plng/Preserv .... Dr. Mark A. WIGLEY
57 Dean School of the Arts .... Dr. Carol BECKER
50 Dean Graduate School of Business .... Dr. R. Glenn HUBBARD
49 Dean Columbia College .... Dr. James J. VALENTINI
52 Int Dean Sch Dental & Oral Surgery .... Dr. Ronnie MYERS
54 Int Dean Sch Engr/Applied Science .... Dr. Donald GOLDFARB
97 Dean School General Studies .... Dr. Peter AWN
49 Dean Grad School of Arts & Science .... Dr. Carlos J. ALONSO
82 Int Dean School Intl/Public Affairs ...... Dr. Robert C. LIEBERMAN
60 Dean Graduate School Journalism .... Mr. Nicholas LEMANN
61 Dean School of Law .... Mr. David M. SCHIZER
63 Dean Faculty of Medicine .... Dr. Lee GOLDMAN
66 Dean School of Nursing .... Dr. Bobbie BERKOWITZ
69 Dean School of Public Health .... Dr. Linda P. FRIED
70 Dean School of Social Work .... Dr. Jeanette C. TAKAMURA

† Parent institution of Barnard College and Teachers College, Columbia University.

Concordia College (G)

171 White Plains Road, Bronxville NY 10708-1923

County: Westchester
FICE Identification: 002709
Unit ID: 190248
Telephone: (914) 337-9300
Carnegie Class: Bac/Diverse
FAX Number: (914) 395-4500
Calendar System: Semester
URL: www.concordia-ny.edu
Established: 1881
Annual Undergrad Tuition & Fees: $27,990
Enrollment: 189
Coed
Affiliation or Control: Lutheran Church - Missouri Synod
IRS Status: 501(c)3
Highest Offering: Master's
Program: Liberal Arts And General; Teacher Preparatory; Professional
Accreditation: M, NURSE, SW, TED

01 President .... Dr. Viji D. GEORGE
10 Chief Financial Officer .... Mr. William W. ZAMBELLI
11 Vice Pres Administration .... Mr. Lloyd WARDLEY
30 Vice Pres Advancement .... Mr. Paul D. GRAND PRE
04 Special Assistant to the President .... Ms. Eloise L. MORGAN
05 VP/Dean of the College .... Prof. Sherry J. FRASER
20 Dean of Undergraduate Programs .... Dr. Mandana NAKHAI
66 Dean of Health & Human Services .... Dr. Susan M. APOLD

88 Dean of Adult Education ... Dr. William M. SALVA
42 Campus Pastor ... Rev. Roy MINNIX
32 Assc Dean of Student Development ... Mr. Christopher S. KOUTSOVITIS
06 Registrar ... Mr. Mark E. BLANCO
08 Library Director ... Mr. William L. PERRENOD
38 Director of Counseling ... Ms. Betty C. GEILING
41 Athletic Director ... Mr. Ivan MARQUEZ
23 Director Health Services ... Ms. Susan CRANE
37 Director Financial Aid ... Mr. Kenneth T. FICK
18 Director Support Services ... Mr. Paul A. SCHULZ
26 Senior Director of Marketing ... Mr. North CALLAHAN
42 Director of Church Relations ... Ms. Lorilee JOERZ
07 Director of Admissions ... Mr. Robert C. PIUROWSKI
31 Dir of Cmty Life & Judicial Affairs ... Mr. Michael KUSH
92 Director of Honors Program ... Dr. Kate E. BEHR
15 Director of Human Resources ... Ms. Kathleen D. CLARKE
13 Manager of Information Services ... Mr. Aaron J. MEYER
21 Business Manager ... Mr. Edward J. MCPARTLAN
44 Manager Annual Giving ... Ms. Nancy PETRIE
35 Coord Student Support/Career Devel ... Ms. Johanna L. PERRY
36 Director Student Placement ... Ms. Lois DIERLAM

Cooper Union (A)

30 Cooper Square, New York NY 10003-7120
County: New York FICE Identification: 002710
Unit ID: 190372
Telephone: (212) 353-4100 Carnegie Class: Bac/Diverse
FAX Number: (212) 353-4244 Calendar System: Semester
URL: www.cooper.edu
Established: 1859 Annual Undergrad Tuition & Fees: $38,550
Enrollment: 990 Coed
Affiliation or Control: Independent Non-Profit IRS Status: 501(c)3
Highest Offering: Master's
Program: Liberal Arts And General; Professional
Accreditation: M, ART, ENG

01 President ... Jamshed BHARUCHA
10 Vice President Finance and Admin ... Theresa C. WESTCOTT
26 Vice President of External Affairs ... Vacant
30 Vice President Development ... Derek WITTNER
101 Chf of Staff/Secy Board of Trustees ... Lawrence CACCIATORE
07 Dean Admissions/Records/Registrar ... Mitchell LIPTON
32 Dean of Students ... Linda LEMIESZ
57 Dean of Art ... Saskia BOS
48 Dean of Architecture ... Anthony VIDLER
54 Dean of Engineering ... Vacant
79 Dean Human & Social Sciences ... William GERMANO
08 Acting Head Librarian ... Carol SALOMON
21 Dir Budget/Personnel/Inst Research ... Vacant
44 Dir Major Gifts & Donor Relations ... Jeanne LUNIN
29 Director Alumni Affairs ... Caitlin TRAMEL
44 Director of Institutional Giving ... Vacant
37 Director Financial Aid ... Mary RUOKONEN
06 Registrar ... Ellen DORSEY
46 Director of Research ... Vacant
26 Director of Public Affairs ... Claire H. MCCARTHY
14 Chief Technology Officer ... Robert P. HOPKINS
09 Director Assessment & Innovation ... Gerardo DEL CERRO
88 Director of Off Campus Programming ... Margaret MORTON
18 Director of Facilities Management ... Jody GRAPES
51 Director of Continuing Education ... David GREENSTEIN
41 Director of Athletics ... Stephen BAKER
36 Director of Career Services ... Robert THILL
24 Director of Audiovisual/Media ... Paul TUMMOLO
39 Residence Hall Manager ... Natasha CORNELL-POKU
91 Director of Administrative Database ... Sue MCCOY

† Every student receives a full-tuition scholarship.

Cornell University (B)

Ithaca NY 14853-2801
County: Tompkins FICE Identification: 002711
Unit ID: 190415
Telephone: (607) 255-2000 Carnegie Class: RU/VH
FAX Number: (607) 255-5396 Calendar System: Semester
URL: www.cornell.edu
Established: 1865 Annual Undergrad Tuition & Fees: $43,413
Enrollment: 21,131 Coed
Affiliation or Control: Independent Non-Profit IRS Status: 501(c)3
Highest Offering: Doctorate
Program: Liberal Arts And General; Professional
Accreditation: M, BUS, CIDA, DIETD, DIETI, ENG, HSA, LAW, LSAR, PLNG, @TEAC, VET

01 President ... David J. SKORTON
05 Provost ... W. Kent FUCHS
63 Prov Medical Affairs/Dean Med Col ... Laurie GLIMCHER
20 Sr Vice Provost Academic Affairs ... John A. SILICIANO
20 Vice Provost Undergrad Educ ... Laura S. BROWN
46 Senior Vice Provost Research ... Robert A. BUHRMAN
58 Vice Prov & Dean Graduate School ... Barbara A. KNUTH
88 Vice Prov International Relations ... Alice N. PELL
88 Sr Vice Provost Land Grant Affairs ... Ronald SEEBER
88 Vice Provost Cornell NYC Tech ... Daniel P. HUTTENLOCHER
45 Vice Pres Planning & Budget ... Elmira MANGUM
30 VP Alumni Affairs & Development ... Charles D. PHLEGAR
16 Vice President Human Resources ... Mary George OPPERMAN
32 VP Student & Academic Services ... Susan H. MURPHY
26 Vice Pres for University Relations ... Glenn C. ALTSCHULER
86 VP Government & Community Rels ... Stephen P. JOHNSON
27 Vice President Univ Communications ... Thomas W. BRUCE
88 Vice Pres Cornell NYC Tech ... Cathy S. DOVE
43 University Counsel & Secretary Corp ... James J. MINGLE
10 VP Financial Affs/CFO ... Joanne M. DESTEFANO
13 CIO and VP for Info Technology ... Thomas E. DODDS
18 Vice President Facilities/Services ... Kyu-Jung WHANG
21 University Controller ... Anne SHAPIRO
21 Assoc Vice President/Treasurer ... Patricia A. JOHNSON
21 University Auditor ... Michael B. DICKINSON
20 Dean of Faculty ... Joseph A. BURNS
47 Dean Col Agriculture/Life Sciences ... Kathryn J. BOOR
48 Dean College Arch/Art/Planning ... Kent KLEINMAN
49 Dean College Arts & Science ... G. Peter LEPAGE
54 Dean College of Engineering ... Lance R. COLLINS
88 Dean School Hotel Administration ... Michael D. JOHNSON
59 Dean College Human Ecology ... Alan D. MATHIOS
50 Dean Johnson Graduate School Mgmt ... Soumitra DUTTA
50 Dean School Industrial/Labor Rels ... Harry C. KATZ
61 Dean Law School ... Stewart J. SCHWAB
74 Dean College Veterinary Medicine ... Michael I. KOTLIKOFF
77 Dean Faculty of Computing and Info .. Daniel P. HUTTENLOCHER
51 Dean Cont Education/Summer Session ... Glenn C. ALTSCHULER
08 University Librarian ... Anne R. KENNEY
88 Director Africana Studies/Research ... Gerard ACHING
07 Director Undergraduate Admissions ... Jason C. LOCKE
37 Dir Financial Aid/Student Employ ... Susan HITCHCOCK
35 Dean of Students ... Kent L. HUBBELL
06 University Registrar ... Cassandra C. DEMBOSKY
41 Director Athletics/Physical Educ ... J. Andrew NOEL, JR.
36 Director of Cornell Career Services ... Rebecca M. SPARROW
22 Assoc VP Wrkfrce Dvrsty & Inclusion ... Lynette CHAPPELL-WILLIAMS
23 Assoc Vice Pres Gannett Health Svcs . Janet L. CORSON-RIKERT
28 Assoc Vice Provost Acad Diversity ... Andrew T. MILLER
93 Assoc Dean Intercultural Programs ... Renee T. ALEXANDER
42 Dir Cornell United Religious Works ... Kenneth J. CLARKE
25 Assoc Vice Pres Research Admin ... Catherine E. LONG
25 Sr Director Sponsored Programs Svcs ... Jeffrey A. SILBER
19 Chief Cornell Police ... Kathy R. ZONER
96 Sr Dir Supply Channel Management ... Thomas W. ROMANTIC
44 Sr Assoc VP University Development ... Patricia A. WATSON
29 Assoc Vice Pres Alumni Affairs ... Christopher V. MARSHALL
09 Director Inst Research/Planning ... Marin E. CLARKBERG

† Parent institution of Weill Medical College of Cornell University.

Corning Community College (C)

One Academic Drive, Corning NY 14830-3297
County: Steuben FICE Identification: 002863
Unit ID: 190442
Telephone: (607) 962-9011 Carnegie Class: Assoc/Pub-R-M
FAX Number: (607) 962-9456 Calendar System: Semester
URL: www.corning-cc.edu
Established: 1956 Annual Undergrad Tuition & Fees (In-District): $4,750
Enrollment: 5,295 Coed
Affiliation or Control: State/Local IRS Status: 501(c)3
Highest Offering: Associate Degree
Program: Occupational; 2-Year Principally Bachelor's Creditable
Accreditation: M, ADNUR

01 President ... Dr. Katherine P. DOUGLAS
11 Vice President Administrative Svcs ... Mr. Thomas F. CARR
32 Vice Pres & Dean of Student Devel ... Mr. Donald HEINS
30 Exec Dir Institutional Advancement ... Mr. William LITTLE
08 Director Learning Resources Center ... Ms. Sarah WEISMAN
06 Registrar ... Ms. Karen BOULAS
07 Director of Admissions ... Ms. Karen BROWN
15 Director Human Resources ... Ms. Nannette NICHOLAS
10 Chief Business Officer ... Mr. Thomas F. CARR
18 Chief Facilities/Physical Plant ... Mr. Calvin WILLIAMS
37 Director Student Financial Aid ... Mrs. Barbara SNOW
09 Research Analyst ... Ms. Monica DEFENDORF

Crouse Hospital College of Nursing (D)

736 Irving Avenue, Syracuse NY 13210
County: Onondaga FICE Identification: 006445
Unit ID: 190451
Telephone: (315) 470-7481 Carnegie Class: Assoc/PrivNFP
FAX Number: (315) 470-5774 Calendar System: Semester
URL: www.crouse.org/nursing
Established: 1913 Annual Undergrad Tuition & Fees: $9,546
Enrollment: 281 Coed
Affiliation or Control: Independent Non-Profit IRS Status: 501(c)3
Highest Offering: Associate Degree
Program: 2-Year Principally Bachelor's Creditable; Nursing Emphasis
Accreditation: ADNUR

01 Director ... Dr. Ann SEDORE

Culinary Institute of America (E)

1946 Campus Drive, Hyde Park NY 12538-1499
County: Dutchess FICE Identification: 007304
Unit ID: 190503
Telephone: (845) 452-9600 Carnegie Class: Spec/Other
FAX Number: (845) 452-0165 Calendar System: Semester
URL: www.ciachef.edu
Established: 1946 Annual Undergrad Tuition & Fees: $27,130
Enrollment: 2,807 Coed
Affiliation or Control: Independent Non-Profit IRS Status: 501(c)3
Highest Offering: Baccalaureate
Program: Occupational; 2-Year Principally Bachelor's Creditable; Technical Emphasis
Accreditation: M

01 President ... Dr. Tim RYAN
10 Senior VP Finance/Administration ... Mr. Charles A. O'MARA
30 VP Advancement & Business Develop ... Dr. Victor GIELISSE
05 Provost ... Mr. Mark ERICKSON
88 VP Admissions & Marketing ... Mr. Bruce HILLENBRAND
11 VP Administration & Shared Svcs ... Mr. Richard MIGNAULT
88 VP Strategic Initiatives & Industry ... Mr. Greg DRESCHER
108 Director Academic Assessment & Accr ... Ms. Sharon ZRALY
49 Dean of Liberal Arts & Business Mgt ... Dr. Kathleen MERGET
32 Assoc VP & Dean of Student Affairs ... Ms. Alice-Ann SCHUSTER
35 Assoc Dean Student Activities ... Mr. David WHALEN
12 Assoc VP Branch Campuses ... Ms. Susan CUSSEN
45 Assoc VP Planning & Operations Sup ... Mr. Rick TIETJEN
13 Assoc VP Information Technology ... Mr. Inder SINGH
06 Registrar ... Mr. Chester KOULIK
07 Director Admissions ... Ms. Rachel BIRCHWOOD
19 Director Safety ... Mr. Richard T. CULLEN
08 Library Director ... Ms. Eileen A. DEVRIES
36 Director Career Services ... Mrs. Wendy HIGGINS
37 Director Financial Aid ... Ms. Kathleen GAILOR
18 Director Facilities ... Mr. Thomas M. HIRST
29 Senior Alumni Relations Officer ... Ms. Patti HAMILTON
21 Director Finance & Accounting ... Mr. Steven STROM
38 Director Counseling Services ... Dr. Daria PAPALIA
96 Director Purchasing ... Mr. Brad MATTHEWS

Daemen College (F)

4380 Main Street, Amherst NY 14226-3592
County: Erie FICE Identification: 002808
Unit ID: 190725
Telephone: (716) 839-3600 Carnegie Class: Master's L
FAX Number: (716) 839-8516 Calendar System: Semester
URL: www.daemen.edu
Established: 1947 Annual Undergrad Tuition & Fees: $23,130
Enrollment: 3,054 Coed
Affiliation or Control: Independent Non-Profit IRS Status: 501(c)3
Highest Offering: Doctorate
Program: Liberal Arts And General; Teacher Preparatory; Professional
Accreditation: M, ARCPA, IACBE, NUR, PTA, SW, @TEAC

01 President ... Dr. Edwin G. CLAUSEN
05 Vice Pres Academic Affairs/Dean ... Dr. Michael S. BROGAN
10 VP for Business Affairs & Treasurer ... Mr. Robert C. BEISWANGER
30 Vice President External Relations ... Dr. David A. CRISTANTELLO
84 VP of Enrollment Management ... Dr. Patricia R. BROWN
32 VP Student Affairs/Dean of Students ... Dr. Richanne C. MANKEY
20 Assoc VP Academic Affairs ... Dr. Kathleen C. BOONE
07 Dean of Admissions ... Mr. Frank WILLIAMS
21 Controller & Assistant Treasurer ... Mr. Michael E. LOOKER
91 Director Information Resources Mgmt ... Mr. Brian J. WILKINS
90 Director Academic Computing Service ... Ms. Kelly DURAN
09 Director of Institutional Research ... Dr. Patricia L. BEAMAN
88 Dir of Institutional Assessment ... Dr. Mimi H. STEADMAN
08 Head Librarian ... Mr. Francis J. CAREY
06 Registrar ... Ms. Paulette A. ANZELONE
88 Exec Dir for Academic Support Svcs ... Ms. Sabrina FENNELL
37 Director Financial Aid ... Mr. Jeffrey M. PAGANO
15 Director of Human Resources ... Mrs. Pamela R. NEUMANN
07 Director Grad Admissions ... Mr. Joseph PAGANO
26 Director of College Relations ... Mr. Michael G. ANDREI
44 Dir Annual Giving/Alumni Relations ... Ms. Lauren JAEGER
78 Director of Career Services ... Ms. Maureen MILLANE
39 Director of Residence Life ... Ms. Sara C. ALEXANDERSON
35 Director of Student Activities ... Mr. Christopher P. MALIK
24 Director Instruct Technology Svcs ... Mr. James J. BACHRATY
18 Director of Physical Plant ... Mr. Frank X. SWEITZER, JR.
19 Director Security & Fire Safety ... Mr. Craig HUGHES
42 Director Campus Ministry ... Rev. Cassandra L. SALTER-SMITH
41 Director of Athletics ... Mr. Donald V. SILVERI
96 Dir of Purchasing/Central Services ... Ms. Gwendolyn M. WALKER
92 Director of Honors Program ... Dr. Matthew WARD
40 Bookstore Manager ... Mrs. Julie MILLER
31 Coordinator Service Learning ... Ms. Susan M. MARCHIONE

Davis College (G)

400 Riverside Drive, Johnson City NY 13790-2714
County: Broome FICE Identification: 021691
Unit ID: 194569
Telephone: (607) 729-1581 Carnegie Class: Spec/Faith
FAX Number: (607) 729-2962 Calendar System: Semester
URL: www.davisny.edu
Established: 1900 Annual Undergrad Tuition & Fees: $11,940
Enrollment: 355 Coed
Affiliation or Control: Independent Non-Profit IRS Status: 501(c)3
Highest Offering: Baccalaureate
Program: Professional; Religious Emphasis
Accreditation: M, BI

01 President ... Dr. Dino J. PEDRONE
05 Chief Academic Officer ... Dr. Gilbert A. PARKER
84 Director of Enrollment Management ... Mr. Rick CRAMER
32 Director of Student Development ... Mrs. Nichole POST
11 Chief Operating Officer ... Rev. Jerry TRAISTER
10 Chief Financial Officer ... Mr. Larry ELLIS

04 Assistant to the President ... Mr. Daniel RATHMELL
06 Registrar ... Mr. Spencer KEY
08 Library Manager ... Mrs. Shelley BYRON
37 Director Financial Aid ... Mrs. Sandra CONKLIN
04 Executive Assistant ... Ms. Jenny GREEN

DeVry College of New York (A)

180 Madison Avenue, Suite 900,
New York NY 10016-5267

County: New York — Identification: 666979
Unit ID: 432199
Telephone: (212) 312-4301 — Carnegie Class: Master's M
FAX Number: N/A — Calendar System: Semester
URL: www.devry.edu
Established: 1931 — Annual Undergrad Tuition & Fees: $16,156
Enrollment: 1,279 — Coed
Affiliation or Control: Proprietary — IRS Status: Proprietary
Highest Offering: Master's
Program: Occupational; Professional; Business Emphasis
Accreditation: &NH, ENGT

01 Metro President ... Anthony STANZIANI
10 Sr Director Finance & Admin ... Helen FIALKOFF
05 Dean of Academic Affairs ... Vacant
08 Director of Library Services ... Emily TURNER
15 Human Resources Manager ... Rita TURCIOS
07 Senior Director of Admissions ... Joshua GRINSTEAD
36 Director of Career Services ... Hassan AKMAL

† Regional accreditation is carried under the parent institution in Downers Grove, IL.

Dominican College of Blauvelt (B)

470 Western Highway, Orangeburg NY 10962-1210

County: Rockland — FICE Identification: 002713
Unit ID: 190761
Telephone: (845) 848-7800 — Carnegie Class: Master's S
FAX Number: (845) 359-2313 — Calendar System: Semester
URL: www.dc.edu
Established: 1952 — Annual Undergrad Tuition & Fees: $23,970
Enrollment: 2,058 — Coed
Affiliation or Control: Independent Non-Profit — IRS Status: 501(c)3
Highest Offering: Doctorate
Program: Liberal Arts And General; Teacher Preparatory; Professional
Accreditation: M, IACBE, NURSE, OT, PTA, SW, TEAC

01 President ... Sr Dr. Mary Eileen O'BRIEN
00 Chancellor ... Sr. Kathleen SULLIVAN
05 Vice Pres/Dean Academic Affairs ... Dr. Thomas S. NOWAK
84 Vice Pres of Enrollment Management ... Mr. Brian FERNANDES
32 Dean of Students ... Mr. John BURKE
10 Director of Fiscal Affairs ... Mr. Anthony CIPOLLA
06 Registrar ... Ms. Mary MCFADDEN
07 Director of Admissions ... Ms. Joyce ELBE
08 Librarian ... Mr. John BARRIE
30 Director of Inst Advancement ... Ms. Dorothy FILORAMO
15 Director Human Resources ... Ms. Marybeth BRODERICK
26 Chief Public Relations Officer ... Mr. Brett BEKRITSKY
29 Director Alumni Relations ... Ms. Samira ALLEN
35 Director Student Activities ... Ms. Katrina REDMOND
09 Inst Research/Plng/Assessment Ofcr . Dr. William J. STEGMAYER
37 Director Student Financial Aid ... Mr. Daniel SHIELDS
36 Director Student Placement ... Ms. Evelyn FISKAA
38 Director Student Couseling ... Ms. Alise COHEN
21 Controller ... Ms. Joanne PORETTE
13 Director Information Technology ... Mr. Russell DIAZ
18 Chief Facilities/Physical Plant ... Mr. Michael DEMPSEY
20 Associate Academic Officer ... Ms. Ann VAVOLIZZA
39 Director Student Housing ... Mr. Ryan O'GORMAN
41 Athletic Director ... Mr. Joseph CLINTON
42 Director Campus Ministry ... Sr. Barbara MCENEANY
96 Director of Purchasing ... Ms. Amy BIANCO
28 Director of Diversity ... Vacant
19 Director of Security/Safety ... Mr. John LENNON
42 Chaplain ... Fr. Ronald STANLEY, OP

Dowling College (C)

Idle Hour Boulevard, Oakdale NY 11769-1999

County: Suffolk — FICE Identification: 002667
Unit ID: 190770
Telephone: (631) 244-3000 — Carnegie Class: Master's L
FAX Number: (631) 563-7831 — Calendar System: Semester
URL: www.dowling.edu
Established: 1959 — Annual Undergrad Tuition & Fees: $26,224
Enrollment: 4,636 — Coed
Affiliation or Control: Independent Non-Profit — IRS Status: 501(c)3
Highest Offering: Doctorate
Program: Liberal Arts And General; Teacher Preparatory; Professional
Accreditation: M, IACBE, TED

01 President ... Dr. Jeremy D. BROWN
05 Interim Provost ... Dr. Elana ZOLFO
11 VP Col Administration/Student Svcs ... Dr. David RING
32 VP Enrollment and Student Services ... Ms. Ronnie MACDONALD
26 VP for Marketing & Communications ... Ms. Amy NEIL
51 VP Corporate Programs/Cont Educ ... Dr. Elana ZOLFO
10 CFO and Treasurer ... Vacant
29 Associate VP of Alumni Relations ... Vacant
21 Associate VP Business and Finance ... Ms. Lisa DIIORIO
84 Asst VP for Enrollment/Student Svcs ... Ms. Jennifer A. KUHL
07 Dean of Admissions ... Vacant
26 Dir Communications/Public Relations ... Ms. Heather SHIVOKEVICH
41 Director of Athletics ... Mr. Richard COLE
09 VP Inst Research/Effectiveness ... Mr. Donald RESNICK
15 Exec Director Human Resources ... Ms. Anne DIMOLA
18 Director of Facilities Services ... Vacant
06 Registrar ... Ms. Jennifer A. KUHL
37 Director of Student Financial Svcs ... Ms. Denise SCALZO
96 Director of Purchasing ... Ms. Stephanie SWEET
13 Dir of Information Technology Svcs ... Mr. Thomas FRANZA

Dutchess Community College (D)

53 Pendell Road, Poughkeepsie NY 12601-1595

County: Dutchess — FICE Identification: 002864
Unit ID: 190840
Telephone: (845) 431-8000 — Carnegie Class: Assoc/Pub-R-L
FAX Number: (845) 431-8984 — Calendar System: Semester
URL: www.sunydutchess.edu
Established: 1957 — Annual Undergrad Tuition & Fees (In-District): $3,520
Enrollment: 10,335 — Coed
Affiliation or Control: State/Local — IRS Status: 501(c)3
Highest Offering: Associate Degree
Program: Occupational; 2-Year Principally Bachelor's Creditable; Business Emphasis
Accreditation: M, ADNUR, EMT, MLTAD

01 President ... Dr. D. David CONKLIN
05 Dean of Academic Affairs ... Vacant
20 Associate Dean of Academic Affairs ... Ms. Ellen GAMBINO
20 Associate Dean of Academic Affairs ... Mr. Michael BODEN
32 Dean Student Svcs/Enroll Mgmt ... Dr. Carol STEVENS
11 Dean of Administration ... Mr. William ANDERSON
31 Dean Community Svcs/Special Pgms ... Ms. Virginia STOEFFEL
21 Associate Dean Administration ... Ms. Donna ROCAP
06 Registrar ... Mr. William BENEDETTO
07 Director of Admissions ... Mr. Michael ROE
08 Director of the Library ... Ms. Cathy CARL
14 Director Information Systems ... Mr. Patrick GRIFFIN
30 Director Institutional Advancement ... Ms. Patricia PRUNTY
09 Director Planning/Inst Research ... Ms. Donna JOHNSON
24 Director Telecomm/Instructnl Media ... Vacant
37 Director Financial Aid ... Ms. Susan MEAD
36 Director Counseling/Career Svcs ... Mr. Michael BALABAN
15 Director Human Resources Mgmt ... Vacant
18 Assoc Dean of Admin Facilities Mgmt . Ms. Bridgette ANDERSON
19 Interim Director Campus Security ... Mr. Ed COX
13 Assoc Dean Admin Info Technology ... Mr. Klaus GESSLER
35 Director of Student Activities ... Mr. Michael WEIDA
26 Chief Public Relations Officer ... Ms. Judi STOKES
88 Assoc Dir Teaching Learning Center ... Ms. Chrisie MITCHELL
88 Director of Scheduling ... Ms. Virginia CARRIG
12 Director DCC South Branch ... Mr. Timothy DECKER
04 Admin Assistant to the President ... Ms. Linda M. BEASIMER

D'Youville College (E)

320 Porter Avenue, Buffalo NY 14201-1084

County: Erie — FICE Identification: 002712
Unit ID: 190716
Telephone: (716) 829-8000 — Carnegie Class: Master's L
FAX Number: (716) 829-7820 — Calendar System: Semester
URL: www.dyc.edu
Established: 1908 — Annual Undergrad Tuition & Fees: $21,930
Enrollment: 3,145 — Coed
Affiliation or Control: Independent Non-Profit — IRS Status: 501(c)3
Highest Offering: Doctorate
Program: Liberal Arts And General; Teacher Preparatory; Professional; Nursing Emphasis
Accreditation: M, CHIRO, ARCPA, DIETC, IACBE, NURSE, OT, @PHAR, PTA

01 President ... Sr. Denise A. ROCHE
05 Vice President for Academic Affairs ... Dr. Arup SEN
10 Vice President Financal Affairs ... Mr. Edward JOHNSON
32 VP Student Affairs & Enroll Mgmt ... Mr. Robert P. MURPHY
30 Vice Pres Institutional Advancement ... Mr. Timothy G. BRENNAN
11 Vice President Operations ... Mr. Donald G. KELLER
88 VP Admin Svcs & External Relations ... Dr. William MARIANI
06 Registrar ... Mr. Daryl SMITH
66 Dean School of Nursing ... Dr. Judith LEWIS
53 Dean School of Arts, Sci and Edu ... Vacant
50 Dean School of Management ... Vacant
67 Dean School of Pharmacy ... Dr. Gary STOEHR
76 Dean School of Health Professions ... Dr. Anthony BILLITTIER
88 Artistic Director Kavinoky Theater ... Mr. David LAMB
35 Associate VP for Student Affairs ... Mr. Jeffrey PLATT
35 Assistant VP for Student Affairs ... Mr. Anthony SPINA
21 Bursar ... Mrs. Lisa HIGGINS
18 Director of Facilities ... Mr. Leonard OSEEKEY
21 Controller ... Ms. Laurie HALL
09 Dir Inst Rsrch & Assessment Support ... Mr. Mark ECKSTEIN
90 Director Academic Computing ... Dr. John T. MURPHY
91 Director Administrative Computing ... Mr. Robert HALL
29 Director Alumni Relations ... Ms. Mary PFEIFFER
44 Director Annual Giving ... Mrs. Aimee PEARSON
41 Director Athletics ... Mr. Brian CAVANAUGH
42 Director Campus Ministry ... Fr. Paterick O'KEEFE
36 Director Career Services Center ... Ms. Christine DEMCIE
88 Director College Center ... Ms. Deborah E. OWENS
13 Director Computer & Network Svcs ... Ms. Mary SPENCE
102 Director Foundation Relations ... Mr. William P. MCKEEVER
25 Director Government Grants ... Mrs. Colleen BRENNAN
23 Director Health Center ... Mrs. Susan NIERENBERG
15 Director Human Resources ... Ms. Linda MORETTI
85 Director International Stdnt Svcs ... Mrs. Laryssa PETRYSHYN
88 Director Learning Center ... Mrs. Dorothy BELLANTI
08 Director Library Services ... Mr. Rand BELLAVIA
44 Director Major & Planned Gifts ... Ms. Patricia VAN DYKE
28 Director Multicultural Affairs ... Mrs. Yolanda WOOD
38 Director Personal Counseling ... Ms. Kimberly ZITTEL
26 Director Public Relations ... Mr. D. John BRAY
19 Director Security ... Mr. Mark GRIFFITH
37 Director Student Financial Aid ... Ms. Lorraine METZ
07 Director Undergraduate Admissions ... Dr. Steve SMITH
07 Director Graduate Admissions ... Ms. Linda FISHER
07 Director Intl Admiss & Marketing ... CMDR. Ronald DANNECKER
88 Director Veterans Affairs Office ... Mr. Benjamin RANDLE
27 Chief Information Officer ... Mr. Roozbeh TAVAKOLI
51 Director Prof Development Center ... Mr. Timothy CRAIG

Ellis School of Nursing (F)

1101 Nott Street, Schenectady NY 12308

County: Schenectady — FICE Identification: 006448
Unit ID: 190956
Telephone: (518) 243-4471 — Carnegie Class: Assoc/PrivNFP
FAX Number: (518) 243-4470 — Calendar System: Other
URL: www.ellisschoolofnursing.org
Established: 1903 — Annual Undergrad Tuition & Fees: $8,771
Enrollment: 120 — Coed
Affiliation or Control: Independent Non-Profit — IRS Status: 501(c)3
Highest Offering: Associate Degree
Program: Nursing Emphasis
Accreditation: ADNUR

01 Director ... Dr. Marilyn STAPLETON

The Elmezzi Graduate School of Molecular Medicine (G)

350 Community Drive, Manhasset NY 11030-3828

County: Nassau — Identification: 666671
Telephone: (516) 562-3467 — Carnegie Class: Not Classified
FAX Number: (516) 562-1022 — Calendar System: Other
URL: www.elmezzigraduateschool.org
Established: 2008 — Annual Graduate Tuition & Fees: N/A
Enrollment: N/A — Coed
Affiliation or Control: Independent Non-Profit — IRS Status: 501(c)3
Highest Offering: Doctorate; No Undergraduates
Program: Professional
Accreditation: NY

01 President ... Dr. Kevin J. TRACEY
05 Dean ... Dr. Bettie STEINBERG

Elmira Business Institute (H)

Langdon Plaza, 303 N Main Street, Elmira NY 14901-3086

County: Chemung — FICE Identification: 009043
Unit ID: 190974
Telephone: (607) 733-7177 — Carnegie Class: Assoc/PrivFP
FAX Number: (607) 733-7178 — Calendar System: Semester
URL: www.ebi-college.com
Established: 1858 — Annual Undergrad Tuition & Fees: $11,800
Enrollment: 434 — Coed
Affiliation or Control: Proprietary — IRS Status: Proprietary
Highest Offering: Associate Degree
Program: Occupational
Accreditation: ACICS, MAC

01 President ... Mr. Brad C. PHILLIPS
03 Vice President ... Mrs. Kathleen M. HAMILTON
32 Director of Student Services ... Mrs. Lisa A. ROAN
37 Financial Aid Director ... Mrs. Sue REINBOLD

Elmira College (I)

One Park Place, Elmira NY 14901-2099

County: Chemung — FICE Identification: 002718
Unit ID: 190983
Telephone: (607) 735-1800 — Carnegie Class: Bac/Diverse
FAX Number: (607) 735-1758 — Calendar System: Other
URL: www.elmira.edu
Established: 1855 — Annual Undergrad Tuition & Fees: $36,600
Enrollment: 1,785 — Coed
Affiliation or Control: Independent Non-Profit — IRS Status: 501(c)3
Highest Offering: Master's
Program: Liberal Arts And General; Teacher Preparatory; Professional; Business Emphasis
Accreditation: M, NUR, @TEAC

01 President ... Dr. Ronald O. CHAMPAGNE
10 Vice President & Treasurer ... Dr. Robert W. RUBLE
05 Academic Vice President ... Dr. Stephen F. COLEMAN
30 Vice President of Development ... Ms. Sherry M. TROCINO
32 Vice Pres/Dean of Student Life ... Ms. Julianne D. BAUMANN
26 Vice President Public Relations ... Mr. Michael B. ROGERS
41 Vice President Athletics ... Ms. Patricia A. THOMPSON
51 Dean of Continuing Education ... Ms. Elizabeth A. LAMBERT
07 Dean of Admissions ... Mr. Brett C. MOORE

37 Dean of Financial Aid ... Ms. Kathleen L. COHEN
06 Registrar ... Mr. Michael HALPERIN
08 Dean of Library & IT ... Ms. Elizabeth M. WAVLE
36 Director Counsel/Career Services ... Dr. William D. COUCHON
50 Chair Business Programs ... Dr. Mariam KHAWAR
57 Chair Fine Arts Program ... Prof. George DEFALUSSY
79 Chair of Humanities ... Dr. Heidi DIERCKX
81 Chair Math/Natural Sciences ... Dr. Christine BEZOTTE
83 Chair Social/Behavioral Sciences ... Dr. Charles MITCHELL
88 Chair of Professional Programs .. Dr. Maureen DONOHUE-SMITH
29 Director of Alumni Relations ... Ms. Adriana F. GIANCOLI
66 Director Nursing Program ... Prof. Lois SCHOENER
18 Superintendent of B&G ... Mr. Donald L. BRIMMER
27 Director of Communications ... Mr. Daniel A. BAROODY
39 Director of Campus Life ... Mr. Benjamin J. CURTIS
40 Director Business Operations ... Mrs. Shannon MOYLAN
15 Director Personnel Services ... Ms. Carey L. IPPINECA
09 Director of Development Research ... Ms. Ellen BURKE

Erie Community College City Campus (A)

121 Ellicott Street, Buffalo NY 14203-2698

County: Erie | FICE Identification: 010684
Unit ID: 191083
Telephone: (716) 842-2770 | Carnegie Class: Assoc/Pub-U-MC
FAX Number: (716) 851-1129 | Calendar System: Semester
URL: www.ecc.edu
Established: 1971 | Annual Undergrad Tuition & Fees (In-District): $4,470
Enrollment: 3,519 | Coed
Affiliation or Control: State/Local | IRS Status: 501(c)3
Highest Offering: Associate Degree
Program: Occupational; 2-Year Principally Bachelor's Creditable
Accreditation: M, ADNUR, RTT

01 President ... Mr. Jack F. QUINN
05 Associate Vice President Academics ... Dr. Edward J. HOLMES
88 Assoc VP Academic Transition Pgms ... Vacant
32 Associate VP Student Services ... Dr. Marsha D. JACKSON
19 Assoc Vice President Security ... Mr. John MCDONNELL
102 Associate Vice Pres Foundation ... Mr. Jeffrey BAGEL
10 Chief Admin & Financial Officer ... Mr. William D. REUTER
35 Dean of Students ... Ms. Petrina HILL-CHEATOM
103 Exec Dean Workforce Dev/Cmty Svcs ... Ms. Carrie W. KAHN
49 Asst Academic Dean Liberal Arts ... Dr. Marcia A. GELLIN
50 Asst Academic Dean Business ... Dr. Kenneth J. BARNES
28 Director of Equity & Diversity ... Ms. Darley WILLIS
06 Registrar ... Ms. Susan I. DUKE
08 Librarian ... Ms. Kathleen MCGRIFF-POWERS
40 Bookstore Manager ... Ms. Teresa KALINOWSKI
23 Health Services Nurse ... Ms. Frances WILLIAMS
26 Director of Public Relations ... Mr. Lance R. KONKLE
27 Public Information Officer ... Mr. Michael FARRELL
41 Director of Athletics ... Mr. Peter J. JEREBKO
37 Financial Aid Coordinator ... Ms. Charlotte M. COSTON
24 Audio Visual Coordinator ... Mr. Gregg S. FILIPPONE
36 Career Resource Center Coordinator ... Ms. Barbara S. HOUSE
92 Coordinator Honors Program ... Vacant
88 Coordinator of Corporate Training ... Mr. John P. SLISZ
29 Coordinator of Alumni Affairs ... Ms. Mary Jo R. DENNEE
55 Asst Coordinator Evening Activities ... Vacant
04 Assistant to the President ... Mr. John FOLEY
07 Admissions Counselor ... Ms. Heather A. CRUZ
07 Admissions Counselor ... Ms. Deborah M. MEDINA

Erie Community College North Campus (B)

6205 Main Street, Williamsville NY 14221-7095

County: Erie | FICE Identification: 002865
Unit ID: 191065
Telephone: (716) 634-0800 | Carnegie Class: Not Classified
FAX Number: (716) 851-1429 | Calendar System: Semester
URL: www.ecc.edu
Established: 1946 | Annual Undergrad Tuition & Fees (In-District): $4,470
Enrollment: 6,475 | Coed
Affiliation or Control: State/Local | IRS Status: 501(c)3
Highest Offering: Associate Degree
Program: Occupational; 2-Year Principally Bachelor's Creditable
Accreditation: &M, ADNUR, DH, DIETT, ENGT, MAC, MLTAD, OPD, OTA

01 President ... Mr. Jack F. QUINN
05 Exec Vice Pres Academic Affairs .... Mr. Richard C. WASHOUSKY
84 Asst VP Enrollment Mgmt/Marketing ... Vacant
23 Associate Vice Pres Health Sciences ... Mr. Patrick J. WILES
32 Dean of Students ... Ms. Barbara M. RIEMAN
45 Director Assessment/Accreditation ... Dr. Marilou C. BLAIR
09 Director of Institutional Research ... Ms. Marlene ARNO
14 Director of ERP Sys & Info Svcs ... Mr. David L. ARLINGTON
50 Assistant Academic Dean-Business ... Vacant
49 Assistant Academic Dean-Lib Arts ... Ms. Mary A. BEARD
06 Director of Registration ... Mr. Paul A. LAMANNA
08 Librarian ... Ms. Jane E. ASHWILL
07 Director of Admissions/Call Center ... Dr. Erik D'AQUINO
36 Career Resource Center Coordinator ... Mr. Joseph P. ABBARNO
25 Grants Coordinator ... Dr. William G. FALKOWSKI
37 Financial Aid Assistant Coordinator ... Ms. Sarah E. IZZO
24 Audio Visual Coordinator ... Mr. Ryan NOGLE
23 Health Services Nurse ... Ms. Rita A. BELZER
11 Coordinator Institutional Services ... Mr. Joel J. DAMIANI
41 Assistant Director Athletics ... Mr. Steve L. MULLEN
85 Foreign Student Advisor ... Mr. John DANNA
88 Advanced Studies Coordinator ... Ms. Deborah F. SCHMITT
40 Bookstore Manager ... Ms. Teresa KALINOWSKI
92 Coordinator Honors Program ... Vacant
55 Asst Coordinator Evening Services ... Vacant
25 Grants Coordinator ... Mr. Michael J. BIGGANE
19 Coordinator of Public Safety ... Vacant
37 Financial Aid Asst Coordinator ... Ms. Robin FILIPPONE

† Regional accreditation is carried under the parent institution in Buffalo, NY.

Erie Community College-South Campus (C)

4041 Southwestern Boulevard, Orchard Park NY 14127-2199

County: Erie | FICE Identification: 012427
Unit ID: 191074
Telephone: (716) 648-5400 | Carnegie Class: Not Classified
FAX Number: (716) 851-1629 | Calendar System: Semester
URL: www.ecc.edu
Established: 1974 | Annual Undergrad Tuition & Fees (In-District): $4,470
Enrollment: 4,284 | Coed
Affiliation or Control: State/Local | IRS Status: 501(c)3
Highest Offering: Associate Degree
Program: Occupational; 2-Year Principally Bachelor's Creditable
Accreditation: &M, DT

01 President ... Mr. Jack F. QUINN
32 Exec Vice President Student Affairs ... Ms. Monica RASCOE
43 Exec Vice Pres Legal Affairs ... Ms. Kristin KLEIN-WHEATON
05 Assoc Vice Pres Academic Affairs ... Mr. Edward HOLMES
13 Assoc Vice Pres/Chief Info Officer ... Mr. Joseph W. STEWART
10 Associate VP Finance/Controller ... Mr. Richard G. SCHOTT
35 Dean of Students ... Vacant
15 Human Resources Director ... Ms. Eileen P. FLAHERTY
37 Director of Financial Aid ... Mr. Scott WELTJEN
08 Librarian ... Ms. Melissa E. PETERSON
18 Director Buildings & Grounds ... Mr. Anthony NESCI
49 Assistant Academic Dean-Lib Arts ... Mr. Richard D. WOLCOTT
56 Asst Acad Dean/Distance Learning ... Ms. Martha J. DIXON
72 Assistant Academic Dean-Technology ... Mr. Mark S. HOEBER
06 Registrar ... Mr. Samuel P. PALUMBO
07 Admissions Counselor ... Ms. Kathleen E. SAKO
07 Admissions Counselor ... Ms. Roslyn M. JONES
21 Business Manager ... Mr. Paul F. DANIEU
24 Audio Visual Coordinator ... Mr. David G. MALLORY
88 Coordinator Special Services ... Ms. Kathy S. HOFFMAN
23 Health Services Nurse ... Ms. Sally STEPHENSON
36 Career Resource Center Director .. Mr. Michael M. GOLEBIEWSKI
55 Asst Coordinator Evening Services ... Vacant
92 Coordinator of Honors Program ... Vacant
40 Bookstore Supervisor ... Mr. Ryan SNYDER
15 Assistant Director Human Resources ... Mr. John FORD
78 Coordinator Internships/Coop ... Ms. Margaret ARCADI

† Regional accreditation is carried under the parent institution in Buffalo, NY.

Everest Institute (D)

1630 Portland Avenue, Rochester NY 14521-3007

County: Monroe | FICE Identification: 004811
Unit ID: 194967
Telephone: (585) 266-0430 | Carnegie Class: Assoc/PrivFP
FAX Number: (585) 266-8243 | Calendar System: Quarter
URL: www.everest.edu
Established: 1863 | Annual Undergrad Tuition & Fees: $16,992
Enrollment: 696 | Coed
Affiliation or Control: Proprietary | IRS Status: Proprietary
Highest Offering: Associate Degree
Program: Occupational; 2-Year Principally Bachelor's Creditable; Business Emphasis
Accreditation: ACICS, MAC

01 President ... Mr. Carl A. SILVIO
05 Academic Dean ... Ms. Eva WILCOX
07 Director of Admissions ... Ms. Deanna PFLUKE
37 Director Student Finance ... Mrs. Kandace REID
10 Director of Student Accounts ... Ms. Maureen GILMORE
36 Director of Career Services ... Ms. Annette PERRIN
04 Admin Asst to the President ... Ms. Karen M. BAFFORD-BUBEL
08 Librarian ... Mr. Kyle DANIELS
06 Registrar ... Ms. Gail BRUENGINSEN

Excelsior College (E)

7 Columbia Circle, Albany NY 12203-5156

County: Albany | FICE Identification: 002834
Unit ID: 196680
Telephone: (518) 464-8500 | Carnegie Class: Master's M
FAX Number: (518) 464-8777 | Calendar System: Other
URL: www.excelsior.edu
Established: 1971 | Annual Undergrad Tuition & Fees: N/A
Enrollment: 35,608 | Coed
Affiliation or Control: Independent Non-Profit | IRS Status: 501(c)3
Highest Offering: Master's
Program: Liberal Arts And General; Professional
Accreditation: M, ADNUR, ENGT, IACBE, NUR

01 President ... Dr. John F. EBERSOLE
100 Chief of Staff ... Dr. Murray BLOCK
05 Chief Academic Officer/Provost ... Dr. Mary Beth HANNER
20 Vice Provost ... Dr. Patrick JONES
10 VP Finance & Administration ... Mr. John M. PONTIUS, JR.
43 VP and General Counsel ... Mr. Joseph B. PORTER
26 VP Institutional Advancement ... Ms. Cathy KUSHNER
16 VP Human Resources & Facilities ... Mr. Edmund MCTERNAN
84 VP Enrollment Management ... Mr. Craig MASLOWSKY
13 VP Information Technology ... Ms. Susan O'HERN
07 AVP for Enrollment Management ... Mr. Thomas DALTON
30 AVP Institutional Advancement ... Mr. William M. STEWART
15 AVP for Human Resources ... Ms. Anita BURNS
86 AVP for Government Relations ... Dr. Paul SHIFFMAN
21 AVP and Controller ... Ms. Michele AURICCHIO
106 Dean Online Education/Learning Svcs ... Dr. George TIMMONS
21 AVP/Dir Budgets/Financial Analysis ... Mr. Todd S. THOMAS
13 AVP Information Technology ... Mr. Ronald MARZITELLI
88 AVP Outcomes Assessment & Inst ... Dr. Lisa DANIELS
07 Exec Director of Admissions ... Mr. Roberto FIGUEROA
88 Exec Director of Outreach/Access ... Ms. Lisa LAVIGNA
88 Exec Director of Outreach ... Ms. Lynda HOLT
88 Exec Director of CEM ... Dr. Mika HOFFMAN
88 Exec Director of Marketing ... Ms. Shannon EASTON
88 Exec Director of CME ... Ms. Sue DEWAN
102 Director of Grants and Research ... Ms. Patricia CROOP
37 Director of Financial Aid ... Ms. Donna COOPER
108 Director of Outcomes Assessment ... Dr. Mohua BOSE
88 Director of Faculty Development ... Dr. Joan MIKALSON
88 Director of Advising Services ... Ms. Betsy DEPERSIS
88 Director of Academic Operations ... Ms. Emilsen HOLGUIN
30 Director of Development ... Ms. Marcy STRYKER
06 Registrar ... Ms. Lori MORANO
88 Bursar ... Mr. John LEWIS
66 Dean of Nursing ... Dr. Mary Lee POLLARD
50 Dean of Business & Technology ... Dr. Jane LECLAIR
49 Dean of Liberal Arts ... Dr. Scott DALRYMPLE
76 Dean of Health Sciences ... Dr. Debbie SOPCZYK

Fashion Institute of Technology (F)

Seventh Avenue at 27 Street, New York NY 10001-5992

County: New York | FICE Identification: 002866
Unit ID: 191126
Telephone: (212) 217-7999 | Carnegie Class: Master's S
FAX Number: N/A | Calendar System: Semester
URL: www.fitnyc.edu
Established: 1944 | Annual Undergrad Tuition & Fees (In-District): $5,768
Enrollment: 10,223 | Coed
Affiliation or Control: State/Local | IRS Status: 501(c)3
Highest Offering: Master's
Program: 2-Year Principally Bachelor's Creditable; Professional
Accreditation: M, ART, CIDA

01 President ... Dr. Joyce F. BROWN
10 Treas/VP Finance/Administration ... Ms. Sherry F. BRABHAM
101 Secy of College/General Counsel ... Dr. Stephen TUTTLE
05 Vice President Academic Affairs ... Dr. Giacomo OLIVA
26 Vice Pres Comm/External Rels ... Ms. Loretta LAWRENCE KEANE
84 VP Enrollment Mgmt/Student Success ... Ms. Marybeth MURPHY
84 Assistant VP Enrollment Services ... Dr. Kelly BRENNAN
15 Vice President Human Res/Labor Rels ... Mr. Arthur E. BROWN
13 VP for Information Technology/CIO ... Mr. Gregg CHOTTINER
30 Vice Pres Development & Exec Dir ... Ms. Dawn B. DUNCAN
20 Assoc Vice Pres Academic Affairs ... Mr. Howard DILLON
88 Asst Vice Pres Human Res/Labor Rels ... Ms. Laura SOLOMON
21 Asst Vice Pres Finance ... Mr. Mark BLAIFEDER
21 Assistant VP of Administration ... Ms. Rebecca CORRADO
88 Asst VP Software Svcs/Info Access ... Mr. Van Buren WINSTON
27 Asst Vice Pres for Communications ... Ms. Carol LEVEN
04 Exec Asst to the President ... Ms. Shari PRUSSIN
20 Dean Curriculum/Instruction ... Dr. Dympna BOWLES
32 Asst VP/Dean of Students ... Mr. Erik KNEUBUEHL
51 Dean Continuing & Prof Studies ... Vacant
57 Dean Art & Design ... Ms. Joanne ARBUCKLE
58 Dean School of Graduate Studies ... Dr. Mary DAVIS
49 Dean Liberal Arts ... Dr. Scott F. STODDART
50 Dean Business & Technology ... Dr. Steven FRUMKIN
07 Dir of Admissions/Strat Recruiting ... Ms. Laura ARBOGAST
88 Director Special Events ... Ms. Vicki GURANOWSKI
11 Director Operational Services ... Mr. John WILSON
18 Executive Director of Facilities ... Mr. George JEFREMOW
22 Affirm Action Ofcr/Dir Compliance ... Ms. Griselda GONZALEZ
38 Director of the Counseling Center ... Ms. Terry GINDER
37 Director of Financial Aid ... Ms. Mina FRIEDMANN
08 Dir of the Gladys Marcus Library ... Mr. NJ WOLFE
06 Director of Registration & Records ... Ms. Rita ARMENIA
39 Director of Residental Life ... Ms. Ann Marie GRAPPO
36 Director Career & Internship ... Mr. Andrew CRONAN
35 Director of Student Life ... Ms. Michelle VAN-ESS
23 Director of Health Services ... Ms. Anne MILLER
19 Director of Security ... Mr. Curtis DIXON
88 Director of The Museum at FIT ... Dr. Valerie STEELE
09 Director of Institutional Research ... Vacant
86 Dir Government/Community Relations ... Ms. Lisa WAGER
27 Exec Director of Public & Media Rel ... Ms. Cheri FEIN
104 Director of International Programs ... Dr. Georgianna APPIGNANI
41 Director of Athletics & Recreation ... Ms. Kerri-Ann MCTIERNAN
96 Director of Budget ... Ms. Nancy SU
88 Dir of Education Opportunity Pgms ... Ms. Taur D. ORANGE
21 Controller/Assistant Treas ... Mr. John JOHNSTON
88 Dir Envir Health/Safety Compliance ... Mr. Joseph J. ARCOLEO
92 Coord Presidential Scholars Pgm ... Dr. Irene BUCHMAN

96 Director of Purchasing ... Dr. Robert OTTO
105 Manager of Web Communications ... Ms. Donna LEHMANN
55 Dir Evening/Weekend/Pre-College ... Ms. Michele NAGEL
29 Director of Alumni Relations ... Ms. Allison OLDEHOFF
44 Director of Development ... Mr. Terry CULVER
102 Dir of Corporate & Foundation Rels ... Mr. Kevin HERVAS

Finger Lakes Community College (A)

3325 Marvin Sands Drive, Canandaigua NY 14424-8405
County: Ontario   FICE Identification: 007532
Unit ID: 191199
Telephone: (585) 394-3500   Carnegie Class: Assoc/Pub-S-SC
FAX Number: (585) 394-5005   Calendar System: Semester
URL: www.flcc.edu
Established: 1965   Annual Undergrad Tuition & Fees (In-District): $3,654
Enrollment: 6,811   Coed
Affiliation or Control: State/Local   IRS Status: 501(c)3
Highest Offering: Associate Degree
Program: Occupational; 2-Year Principally Bachelor's Creditable
Accreditation: M, ADNUR

01 President ... Dr. Barbara G. RISSER
05 Vice Pres Academic/Student Affairs ... Dr. Thomas E. TOPPING
10 Vice President of Admin/Treasurer ... Mr. James R. FISHER
84 Vice Pres Enrollment Management ... Ms. Carol S. URBAITIS
32 Assoc Vice Pres of Student Affairs ... Dr. Kerry L. LEVETT
20 Assoc VP Instruction & Assessment ... Dr. Karen TAYLOR
20 Assoc VP Academic Initiatives ... Ms. Nancy H. PURDY
16 Director of Human Resources ... Ms. Grace H. LOOMIS
30 Development Officer ... Ms. Amy I. PAULEY
19 Campus Safety Officer ... Mr. Jason R. MAITLAND
21 Controller ... Mr. Joseph L. DELFORTE
18 Director of Building & Grounds ... Ms. Jan J. JUNE
07 Director of Admissions ... Ms. Bonnie B. RITTS
15 Director Personnel Services ... Ms. Kathryn A. BOLLEN
25 Director of Grants Development ... Ms. Karen A. VAN KEUREN
37 Director of Financial Aid ... Ms. Susan M. ROMANO
35 Director of Student Life ... Ms. Sarah E. WHIFFEN
13 Director Information Technology ... Dr. Richard W. EVANS
38 Director Career Services ... Ms. Corrine M. CANOUGH
36 Career Services Coordinator ... Ms. Laura A. RAKOCZY
08 Director of Library ... Mr. Frank R. QUEENER
26 Director of Marketing ... Ms. Heidi C. MARCIN
23 Director of Student Health ... Ms. Karen P Z. STEIN
24 Director of Educational Technology ... Mr. Daniel P. FARSACI
29 Director of Alumni Relations ... Ms. Susan P. MORGAN
96 Director of Business Services ... Mr. Bruce J. TREAT
72 Chair Science & Technology ... Dr. Melissa A. MILLER
50 Chair Business ... Ms. Mary M. WILSEY
65 Chair Environment Conservation Hort ... Ms. Ann B. SCHNELL
57 Chair Visual/Performing Arts ... Dr. Inez DRASKOVIC
66 Chair Nursing ... Ms. Nancy E. CLARKSON
68 Chair Physical Education ... Mr. Dennis T. MOORE
81 Chair Computer Science ... Ms. April A. DEVAUX
79 Chair Humanities ... Mr. Jon A. PALZER
83 Chair Social Science ... Mr. Joshua W. HELLER
81 Chair Mathematics ... Mr. Jacob E. AMIDON

Five Towns College (B)

305 North Service Road, Dix Hills NY 11746-6055
County: Suffolk   FICE Identification: 012561
Unit ID: 191205
Telephone: (631) 656-2157   Carnegie Class: Bac/Diverse
FAX Number: (631) 656-2172   Calendar System: Semester
URL: www.ftc.edu
Established: 1972   Annual Undergrad Tuition & Fees: $20,170
Enrollment: 1,129   Coed
Affiliation or Control: Proprietary   IRS Status: Proprietary
Highest Offering: Doctorate
Program: Fine Arts Emphasis
Accreditation: M, TED

01 President ... Dr. Stanley G. COHEN
05 Dean of Academic Affairs/Provost ... Dr. Roger H. SHERMAN
11 Dean of Administration ... Dr. Martin L. COHEN
84 Dean of Enrollment ... Mr. Jerry L. COHEN
88 Assoc Dean of Administration ... Mr. Jerome KOHN
06 Registrar ... Ms. Mara MALTZ
21 Business Officer ... Mr. Robert A. SHERMAN
07 Director of Recruitment Services ... Ms. Kelly HAYES
08 Head Librarian ... Mr. John VANSTEEN
38 College Counselor ... Ms. Carolyn NEWMAN
64 Chair of Music Division ... Prof. Jeffrey LIPTON
50 Chair of Business Division ... Ms. Darlene DECICCO
49 Chair of Liberal Arts Division ... Dr. Richard D. KELLEY
53 Chair of Education Division ... Dr. Patricia SCHMIDT
88 Chair of Film/Video ... Mr. Robert DIGIACOMO
88 Chair of Theatre Arts ... Prof. Jeffrey LIPTON

Fordham University (C)

441 East Fordham Road, Bronx NY 10458-9993
County: Bronx   FICE Identification: 002722
Unit ID: 191241
Telephone: (718) 817-1000   Carnegie Class: RU/H
FAX Number: (718) 817-4925   Calendar System: Semester
URL: www.fordham.edu
Established: 1841   Annual Undergrad Tuition & Fees: $41,000
Enrollment: 15,189   Coed
Affiliation or Control: Independent Non-Profit   IRS Status: 501(c)3
Highest Offering: Doctorate
Program: Liberal Arts And General; Teacher Preparatory; Professional
Accreditation: M, BUS, CLPSY, COPSY, DANCE, LAW, SCPSY, SW, TED

01 President ... Rev. Joseph M. MCSHANE, SJ
04 Exec Assistant to the President ... Ms. Dorothy MARINUCCI
04 Assistant to the President ... Dr. Rosemary A. DEJULIO
05 Provost ... Dr. Stephen FREEDMAN
10 Sr VP & Chief Financial Officer ... Mr. John J. LORDAN
21 Vice President for Finance ... Mr. Frank SIMIO
32 Vice President Student Affairs ... Mr. Jeffrey L. GRAY
13 VP for Information Technology ... Dr. Frank SIRIANNI
84 Vice President for Enrollment ... Dr. Peter A. STACE
12 Vice President for Lincoln Center ... Dr. Brian J. BYRNE
30 Vice President for Development ... Mr. Roger MILICI
88 Vice President for Mission/Ministry ... Msgr. Joseph G. QUINN
86 Vice President for Government Rels ... Mr. Thomas A. DUNNE
18 VP Facilities/Physical Plant ... Mr. Marc VALERA
11 Vice President for Administration ... Mr. Thomas A. DUNNE
20 Assoc Vice Pres Academic Affairs ... Dr. Benjamin CROOKER
20 Assoc Vice Pres Academic Affairs ... Dr. Ron JACOBSON
26 AVP Univ Marketing Communications ... Ms. Catherine SPENCER
29 AVP/Director of Alumni Relations ... Mr. Michael GRIFFIN
07 Asst Vice Pres Undgrad Enrollment ... Mr. John W. BUCKLEY
06 Asst Vice Pres Enrollment/Registrar ... Dr. Gene FEIN
37 Asst VP Student Financial Services ... Ms. Angela VAN DEKKER
86 Assoc Vice Pres for Government Rels ... Mr. Joseph P. MURIANA
101 Secretary of the University ... Ms. Margaret T. BALL
43 General Counsel ... Mr. Thomas E. DEJULIO
35 Dean of Students ... Mr. Christopher RODGERS
35 Dean of Student Services ... Mr. Gregory J. PAPPAS
12 Dean Fordham College at Rose Hill ... Dr. Michael LATHAM
58 Dean Graduate Arts & Science ... Dr. Nancy BUSCH
73 Dean Graduate Religious Education ... Dr. C. Colt ANDERSON
50 Dean College Business Admin ... Dr. Donna RAPACCIOLI
107 Dean Fordham Col of Prof Studies ... Dr. Isabel FRANK
12 Dean Fordham College Lincoln Center ... Rev. Robert GRIMES
88 Dean Graduate Business Admin LC ... Dr. David GAUTSCHI
53 Dean Graduate Education LC ... Dr. James HENNESSY
61 Dean School of Law LC ... Mr. Michael MARTIN
70 Dean Graduate Social Service LC ... Dr. Peter VAUGHAN
15 Exec Director of Human Resources ... Mr. Michael MINEO
09 Director Institutional Research ... Dr. Donald A. GILLESPIE
42 AVP Campus Ministry ... Rev. Philip J. FLORIO, SJ
21 Controller ... Mr. Anthony GRONO
19 Director of Security ... Mr. John CARROLL
22 Administrative Policies Monitor ... Vacant
46 Dir Research/Sponsored Programs ... Dr. Nancy BUSCH
08 Director of University Libraries ... Vacant
24 Director Media Center ... Mr. Jerry GREEN
23 Director of Health Center ... Ms. Kathleen MALARA
35 Assistant Dean of Students ... Dr. Greer JASON
41 AVP of Athletic Alumni Relations ... Mr. Francis X. MCLAUGHLIN
96 Director of Procurement ... Mr. Frank A. DEORIO
38 Director of Psychological Svcs ... Dr. Jennifer NEUHOF
28 Director of Multicultural Programs ... Ms. Sofia BAUSTISTA PERTUZ
36 Director Career Services ... Ms. Stefany FATTOR

Fulton-Montgomery Community College (D)

2805 State Highway 67, Johnstown NY 12095-3790
County: Montgomery   FICE Identification: 002867
Unit ID: 191302
Telephone: (518) 762-4651   Carnegie Class: Assoc/Pub-R-M
FAX Number: (518) 762-4334   Calendar System: Semester
URL: www.fmcc.suny.edu
Established: 1963   Annual Undergrad Tuition & Fees (In-District): $3,739
Enrollment: 2,842   Coed
Affiliation or Control: State/Local   IRS Status: 501(c)3
Highest Offering: Associate Degree
Program: Occupational; 2-Year Principally Bachelor's Creditable
Accreditation: M

01 President ... Dr. Dustin SWANGER
05 Provost/Vice Pres Academic Affairs ... Dr. Greg TRUCKENMILLER
10 Vice Pres Finance & Administration ... Mr. David M. MORROW
32 Vice President of Student Affairs ... Ms. Jane KELLEY
49 Dean of Arts & Sciences ... Dr. Shirlee DUFORT
75 Dean Business/Tech/Health Prof ... Ms. Diana PUTNAM
21 Controller ... Vacant
14 Director of Computer Center ... Mr. Paul PUTMAN
18 Superintendent Building & Grounds ... Mr. Joshua FLEMMING
07 Director of Admissions ... Ms. Laura LAPORTE
06 Registrar ... Mrs. Susan CHRISTIANO
08 Librarian ... Mrs. Mary DONOHUE
103 Director Workforce Development ... Vacant
36 Director of Career Planning ... Ms. Andrea SCRIBNER
38 Director Advisement/Counseling/Test ... Ms. Mary-Jo FERRAUILO-DAVIS
30 Chief Development ... Ms. Lesley LANZI
09 Director of Institutional Research ... Mr. Eric KIMMELMAN
37 Coordinator Financial Aid ... Ms. Rebecca COZZOCREA

General Theological Seminary (E)

440 West 21st Street, New York NY 10011-2981
County: New York   FICE Identification: 002726
Unit ID: 191320
Telephone: (212) 243-5150   Carnegie Class: Spec/Faith
FAX Number: (212) 727-3907   Calendar System: Semester
URL: www.gts.edu
Established: 1817   Annual Graduate Tuition & Fees: $15,200
Enrollment: 123   Coed
Affiliation or Control: Protestant Episcopal   IRS Status: 501(c)3
Highest Offering: Doctorate; No Undergraduates
Program: Professional; Religious Emphasis
Accreditation: THEOL

01 President ... Rev. Lang LOWREY
05 Associate Dean ... Rev. Patrick MALLOY
10 Executive VP and CFO ... Ms. Sandra JOHNSON
11 Vice President of Operations ... Mr. Anthony KHANI
30 VP for Institutional Advancement ... Ms. Donna ASHLEY
08 Head Librarian ... Rev. Andrew KADEL
07 Director of Admissions ... Mr. William C. WEBSTER
27 Exec Director of Communications ... Mr. Bruce PARKER
06 Registrar ... Ms. Emily BEEKMAN
04 Exec Asst to the President & Dean ... Vacant

Genesee Community College (F)

One College Road, Batavia NY 14020-9704
County: Genesee   FICE Identification: 006782
Unit ID: 191339
Telephone: (585) 343-0055   Carnegie Class: Assoc/Pub-R-M
FAX Number: (585) 343-4541   Calendar System: Semester
URL: www.genesee.edu
Established: 1966   Annual Undergrad Tuition & Fees (In-District): $3,550
Enrollment: 7,200   Coed
Affiliation or Control: State/Local   IRS Status: 501(c)3
Highest Offering: Associate Degree
Program: Occupational; 2-Year Principally Bachelor's Creditable
Accreditation: M, ADNUR, POLYT, PTAA

01 President ... Dr. James SUNSER
05 Interim Exec VP Academic Affairs ... Mr. Michael STOLL
10 Vice Pres for Finance & Operations ... Mr. Kevin HAMILTON
32 VP for Student & Enrollment Svcs ... Dr. Virginia TAYLOR
45 Exec VP for Planning/Inst Effectiv ... Mr. William T. EMM
103 Assoc VP for Workforce Development ... Mr. Jerry A. KOZLOWSKI
15 Assoc VP for Human Resources ... Ms. Gina WEAVER
20 Asc Dean Accelerated Col Enrol Pgms ... Mr. Edward LEVINSTEIN
81 Dean Math/Science/Career Education ... Dr. Rafael ALICEA-MALDONADO
83 Dean Human Communication/Behavior ... Dr. Katharina E. KOVACH-ALLEN
56 Dean Educ Tech/Distance Learning ... Mr. Robert G. KNIPE
35 Dean of Students ... Ms. Jennifer M. NEWELL
06 Registrar ... Mr. Terrence REDING
07 Director of Admissions ... Ms. Tanya LANE-MARTIN
14 Director of Computer Services ... Ms. Cindy DELMAR
37 Director of Financial Aid ... Mr. Joseph A. BAILEY
26 Director Devel & External Affairs ... Mr. Richard G. ENSMAN, JR.
88 Director of Student Activities ... Mr. Clifford M. SCUTELLA
21 Controller ... Ms. Kristin L. YUNKER
41 Director of Athletics ... Vacant
18 Director of Buildings & Grounds ... Mr. Timothy M. LANDERS
88 Director Business Skills Training ... Mr. Ramon C. CHAYA
09 Assoc Dean Inst Rsrch & Assessment ... Ms. Carol MARRIOTT
57 Director Fine & Performing Arts ... Ms. Maryanne ARENA
90 Manager of Academic Computing ... Mrs. Mary Jane HEIDER
91 Manager of Administrative Computing ... Vacant
40 Manager of Bookstore ... Mr. Christopher SACKETT
35 Assoc Dean for Student Development ... Ms. Margaret HEATER
88 Director of Health and Phys Ed ... Ms. Rebecca DZIEKAN
88 Director Business Skills Training ... Ms. Lina LAMATTINA

Globe Institute of Technology (G)

500 Seventh Avenue, New York NY 10018
County: New York   FICE Identification: 025408
Unit ID: 188465
Telephone: (212) 349-4330   Carnegie Class: Spec/Bus
FAX Number: (212) 227-5920   Calendar System: Semester
URL: www.globe.edu
Established: 1985   Annual Undergrad Tuition & Fees: $11,120
Enrollment: 657   Coed
Affiliation or Control: Proprietary   IRS Status: Proprietary
Highest Offering: Baccalaureate
Program: Occupational
Accreditation: NY

01 President ... Mr. Martin OLINER
05 Academic Dean ... Ms. Elena ESTRIN
11 Dean of Administrative Services ... Mr. Alex OLINER
32 Dean of Student Services ... Ms. Andrea MOSLEY
27 Director of Information Services ... Mr. Boris KAMENETSKIY
13 Director of Information Technology ... Mr. Jacob KUPERSHTEYN
07 Director of Admissions ... Mr. Al GARCIA
37 Director of Financial Aid ... Ms. Tatiana NUSENBAUM
06 Registrar ... Ms. Vivian PAGAN
41 Athletic Director ... Mr. Mark MORSE
38 Coord Student Counseling/Placement ... Ms. Nellie CHEN

Hamilton College (H)

198 College Hill Road, Clinton NY 13323-1218
County: Oneida   FICE Identification: 002728
Unit ID: 191515
Telephone: (315) 859-4011   Carnegie Class: Bac/A&S
FAX Number: (315) 859-4991   Calendar System: Semester
URL: www.hamilton.edu
Established: 1812   Annual Undergrad Tuition & Fees: $44,350
Enrollment: 1,837   Coed
Affiliation or Control: Independent Non-Profit   IRS Status: 501(c)3
Highest Offering: Baccalaureate

Program: Liberal Arts And General
Accreditation: M

01 President .... Joan H. STEWART
05 VPAA/Dean of Faculty .... Patrick D. REYNOLDS
11 Vice Pres Administration/Finance .... Karen L. LEACH
30 Vice President Commun/Development .... Richard C. TANTILLO
13 Vice Pres Information Technology .... David L. SMALLEN
07 VP/Dean Admission & Financial Aid .... Monica C. INZER
32 Dean of Students .... Nancy R. THOMPSON
20 Associate Dean of Faculty .... Margaret GENTRY
41 Athletic Director .... Jonathan T. HIND
39 Director Residential Life .... Travis R. HILL
10 Controller .... Shari K. WHITING
08 Interim Director of the Library .... David L. SMALLEN
27 Director Strategic Communications .... Stacey J. HIMMELBERGER
37 Director of Financial Aid .... Melissa ROSE
36 Exec Director Career Center .... Mary EVANS
06 Registrar .... Kristin M. FRIEDEL
15 Director of Human Resources .... Stephen STEMKOSKI
23 Director Student Health Services .... Christine C. MERRITT
18 Director Physical Plant .... Steven J. BELLONA
19 Director of Campus Safety .... Francis A. MANFREDO
38 Director Counseling/Psych Services .... Robert KAZIN
42 Newman Chaplain .... John CROGHAN
24 Director Audiovisual Services .... Timothy J. HICKS
09 Director of Institutional Research .... Gordon J. HEWITT
27 Exec Director of Communications .... Michael J. DEBRAGGIO
28 Chief Diversity Officer .... Donald M. CARTER
29 Director Alumni Relations .... Sharon T. RIPPEY
96 Director of Purchasing .... Irene K. CORNISH
40 Manager College Store .... Jennifer PHILLIPS

Hartwick College (A)

One Hartwick Drive, Oneonta NY 13820-1790
County: Otsego FICE Identification: 002729
Unit ID: 191533
Telephone: (607) 431-4000 Carnegie Class: Bac/A&S
FAX Number: (607) 431-4206 Calendar System: 4/1/4
URL: www.hartwick.edu
Established: 1797 Annual Undergrad Tuition & Fees: $37,460
Enrollment: 1,578 Coed
Affiliation or Control: Independent Non-Profit IRS Status: 501(c)3
Highest Offering: Baccalaureate
Program: Liberal Arts And General; Teacher Preparatory; Professional
Accreditation: M, ART, MUS, NURSE, TEAC

01 President .... Dr. Margaret L. DRUGOVICH
05 Executive Vice President & Provost .... Dr. Michael TANNENBAUM
10 Vice President Finance/CFO .... Mr. George J. ELSBECK
30 Vice Pres Institutional Advancement .... Mr. Jim BROSCHART
32 Vice President for Student Life .... Dr. Meg NOWAK
84 Vice Pres for Enrollment Management .... Mr. David CONWAY
04 Exec Assistant to the President .... Ms. Ashley MCCARTHY
15 Director Human Resources .... Ms. Suzanne JANITZ
39 Director Residence Life .... Mr. Zachary BROWN
06 Registrar .... Mr. Matthew SANFORD
20 Dean of Academic Affairs .... Dr. Gerald HUNSBERGER
37 Director of Financial Aid .... Ms. Melissa ALLEN
08 Director of Libraries .... Mr. F. Paul COLEMAN
88 Coord Yager Museum of Art & Culture .... Ms. Donna ANDERSON
85 Director International Pgms .... Vacant
46 Exec Dir of Info Technology .... Mr. Davis B. CONLEY
13 Director Inst Info Systems Services .... Ms. Deb B. HILTS
91 Director Technologies Services .... Ms. Suzanne GAYNOR
18 Director of Facilities Services .... Mr. Joseph MACK
41 Director of Athletics .... Dr. Kimberly FIERKE
38 Director of Counseling Services .... Mr. Gary ROBINSON
23 Director of Student Health Center .... Ms. Elizabeth MORLEY
27 Exec Dir Marketing & Communications .... Mr. James JOLLY
26 Director of Donor Relations .... Ms. Alicia FISH
07 Director Admissions .... Mr. Jonathan KENT
12 Director Pine Lake Campus .... Dr. Brian HAGENBUCH
21 Director Financial Svcs/Controller .... Ms. Nancy LEHTONEN
09 Director of Institutional Research .... Ms. Minghui WANG
29 Director of Alumni Relations .... Mr. Duncan MACDONALD
19 Director of Security .... Mr. Thomas KELLY
40 Manager of Bookstore .... Mr. Frank WERDANN
96 Manager of Purchasing .... Ms. Marilyn NIENART
44 Major Gifts Officer .... Ms. Kathryn GIBSON

Hebrew Union College-Jewish Institute of Religion (B)

1 West 4th Street, New York NY 10012-1186
County: New York FICE Identification: 004054
Unit ID: 203067
Telephone: (212) 674-5300 Carnegie Class: Spec/Faith
FAX Number: (212) 388-1720 Calendar System: Semester
URL: www.huc.edu
Established: 1875 Annual Graduate Tuition & Fees: $21,000
Enrollment: 362 Coed
Affiliation or Control: Jewish IRS Status: 501(c)3
Highest Offering: Doctorate; No Undergraduates
Program: Professional; Religious Emphasis
Accreditation: M

01 President .... Rabbi David ELLENSON
30 Vice President Inst Advancement .... Dr. Jane KARLIN
10 Chief Financial Officer .... Ms. Sandra M. MILLS
05 Vice President for Academic Affairs .... Rabbi Michael MARMUR
101 Admin Exec to Board of Governors .... Ms. Sylvia POSNER
26 National Dir Public Affs/Inst Plng .... Ms. Jean B. ROSENSAFT
44 Natl Dir of Institutional Giving .... Dr. Andrew GRANT
08 Director of Libraries .... Dr. David GILNER
79 Director American Jewish Archives .... Dr. Gary ZOLA
09 Director if IR/Assessment .... Dr. David DIRLAM
29 Director of Alumni Relations .... Ms. Joy WASSERMAN
06 Interim National Registrar .... Mr. Adrian RICE
13 Director of Information Systems .... Mr. John H. BRUGGEMAN
106 Director of eLearning .... Mr. Gregg ALPERT
16 Director of Human Resources .... Mr. Jeremy PERLIN
07 Director of Admissions .... Ms. Deborah SHAPIRO
37 Director of Financial Aid .... Ms. Roseanne ACKERLEY

Helene Fuld College of Nursing (C)

24 East 120th Street, New York NY 10035
County: New York FICE Identification: 010153
Unit ID: 191597
Telephone: (212) 616-7200 Carnegie Class: Assoc/PrivNFP
FAX Number: (212) 427-2453 Calendar System: Quarter
URL: www.helenefuld.edu
Established: 1945 Annual Undergrad Tuition & Fees: $16,693
Enrollment: 402 Coed
Affiliation or Control: Independent Non-Profit IRS Status: 501(c)3
Highest Offering: Baccalaureate
Program: Occupational; 2-Year Principally Bachelor's Creditable
Accreditation: M, ADNUR

01 President .... Dr. Margaret WINES
10 Chief Financial Officer .... Mrs. Adenike ABOYADE-COLE
05 Vice President Academic Affairs .... Ms. Wendy ROBINSON
11 Director of Administration .... Ms. Celeste WALLIN
32 Director Student Services .... Mrs. Sandra SENIOR
08 Director of Learning Center .... Mr. Indrajeet SINGH CHAUHAN
35 Associate Director Student Services .... Ms. Gladys PINEDA
26 Director of External Affairs .... Ms. Michelle HERNANDEZ

Herkimer County Community College (D)

100 Reservoir Road, Herkimer NY 13350-1598
County: Herkimer FICE Identification: 004788
Unit ID: 191612
Telephone: (315) 866-0300 Carnegie Class: Assoc/Pub-R-M
FAX Number: (315) 866-7253 Calendar System: Semester
URL: www.herkimer.edu
Established: 1966 Annual Undergrad Tuition & Fees (In-District): $4,240
Enrollment: 3,679 Coed
Affiliation or Control: State/Local IRS Status: 501(c)3
Highest Offering: Associate Degree
Program: Occupational; 2-Year Principally Bachelor's Creditable
Accreditation: M, EMT, PTAA

01 President .... Dr. Ann Marie MURRAY
11 Vice Pres Administration & Finance .... Mr. Nicholas LAINO
05 Dean of Academic Affairs .... Mr. Michael ORIOLO
32 Dean of Students .... Dr. Matthew HAWES
30 Director of Development .... Ms. Lucia BLISS
20 Associate Dean Academic Affairs BH .... Mr. Henry TESTA
27 Director of Information Services .... Mrs. AnneMarie AMBROSE
84 Assoc Dean for Enrollment .... Mr. Robert PALMIERI
83 Assoc Dean Academic Affairs Soc Sci .... Vacant
51 Assoc Dean of Continuing Education .... Mrs. Linda LAMB
35 Assoc Dean of Student Services .... Ms. Janet TAMBURRINO
20 Asst Dean of Academic Affairs .... Mrs. Jackie SNYDER
15 Director of Human Resources .... Mr. James SALAMY
41 Director of Athletics .... Mr. Donald DUTCHER
08 Director of Library Services .... Mr. Andrew URBANEK
09 Director Institutional Research .... Ms. Marie MIKNAVICH
31 Director of Community Education .... Mr. William MCDONALD
18 Director of Facilities Operations .... Mr. Tom STOCK
37 Director Student Financial Aid .... Mrs. Susan TRIPP
26 Director of Public Relations .... Ms. Rebecca RUFFING
06 Registrar .... Mr. Craig DEWAN
36 Career Services Counselor .... Mrs. Suzanne PADDOCK
36 Transfer Counselor .... Mrs. Katie SCHWABACH
40 Bookstore Manager .... Mr. Brian MARHAVER
96 Purchasing Agent .... Mr. Robert NEARY

Hilbert College (E)

5200 S Park Avenue, Hamburg NY 14075-1597
County: Erie FICE Identification: 002735
Unit ID: 191621
Telephone: (716) 649-7900 Carnegie Class: Bac/Diverse
FAX Number: (716) 649-0702 Calendar System: Semester
URL: www.hilbert.edu
Established: 1957 Annual Undergrad Tuition & Fees: $19,400
Enrollment: 1,117 Coed
Affiliation or Control: Independent Non-Profit IRS Status: 501(c)3
Highest Offering: Master's
Program: Liberal Arts And General; Professional
Accreditation: M

01 President .... Dr. Cynthia A. ZANE
05 Provost/Vice Pres Academic Affairs .... Dr. Christopher L. HOLOMAN
30 Vice Pres Institutional Advancement .... Mr. Gregg FORT
10 Vice President Business/ Finance .... Mr. Richard J. PINKOWSKI, JR.
27 Vice President Information Services .... Mr. Michael MURRIN
84 VP Enrollment Mgmt/Dean of Students .... Mr. Peter S. BURNS
32 Vice Prov Leadership Development .... Mr. James P. STURM
49 Chair Arts & Sciences .... Dr. Amy E. SMITH
26 Director Public Relations .... Ms. Paula WITHERELL
92 Director Honors Program .... Dr. Amy E. SMITH
39 Dir Residence Life/Judicial Affairs .... Mr. Jason LANKER
41 Athletic Director .... Ms. Susan VISCOMI
19 Director Security/Safety .... Mr. Matthew SCHAMANN
30 Director of Development .... Mr. Craig HARRIS
42 Dir Mission Intgrtn/Campus Ministry .... Ms. Barbara BONANNO
08 Director of McGrath Library .... Mr. Wilson PROUT
07 Director of Admissions .... Dr. Timothy LEE
36 Director Placement/Career Services .... Ms. Denise HARRIS
37 Director Financial Aid .... Ms. Beverly CHUDY
06 Director of Student Records .... Vacant
38 Director Student Counseling .... Ms. Phyllis K. DEWEY
09 Director of Institutional Research .... Dr. Ron ESKEW
15 Director of Human Resources .... Ms. Maura FLYNN
28 Director of Multicultural Affairs .... Ms. Tara JABBAAR-GYAMBRAH
35 Director of Student Activities .... Ms. Jean MACDONALD
96 Director of Purchasing .... Mr. Gary DILLSWORTH
21 Associate Business Officer .... Mr. Anthony WIERTEL
18 Chief Facilities/Physical Plant .... Mr. Gary DILLSWORTH

Hobart and William Smith Colleges (F)

300 Pulteney Street, Geneva NY 14456-3397
County: Ontario FICE Identification: 002731
Unit ID: 191630
Telephone: (315) 781-3000 Carnegie Class: Bac/A&S
FAX Number: (315) 781-3654 Calendar System: Semester
URL: www.hws.edu
Established: 1822 Annual Undergrad Tuition & Fees: $44,438
Enrollment: 2,171 Coordinate
Affiliation or Control: Independent Non-Profit IRS Status: 501(c)3
Highest Offering: Master's
Program: Liberal Arts And General; Teacher Preparatory; Fine Arts Emphasis
Accreditation: M, @TEAC

01 President .... Mr. Mark D. GEARAN
05 Provost and Dean of Faculty .... Dr. Titilayo UFOMATA
84 VP for Enrollment/Dean of Admission .... Mr. Robert MURPHY
32 Vice President for Student Affairs .... Mr. Robert FLOWERS
30 Vice President for Advancement .... Mr. Robert O'CONNOR
10 Vice President for Finance .... Mr. Peter POLINAK
27 VP for Strategic Initiatives/CIO .... Mr. Fred DAMIANO
16 Vice President for Human Resources .... Ms. Sandra BISSELL
26 Vice President for Communicatons .... Ms. Cathy WILLIAMS
33 Dean of Hobart College .... Dr. Eugen BAER
34 Dean of William Smith College .... Dr. Susanne MCNALLY
42 Chaplain .... Rev. Lesley ADAMS
04 Exec Assistant to the President .... Ms. Valerie VISTOCCO
20 Associate Dean of Faculty .... Dr. Paul KEHLE
20 Associate Provost .... Dr. Christine DE DENUS
35 Assistant VP for Student Affairs .... Dr. Montrose STREETER
35 Assistant VP for Student Affairs .... Mr. Jeffrey VANLONE
07 Director of Admissions .... Mr. John YOUNG
41 Director of Hobart Athletics .... Mr. Michael HANNA
41 Director of William Smith Athletics .... Ms. Deborah STEWARD
08 Director of the Library .... Mr. Vincent BOISSELLE
06 Registrar .... Mr. Peter SARRATORI
21 Controller .... Mr. Michael PAPARO
39 Director of Residential Education .... Ms. Stacey PIERCE
104 Associate Dean Global Education .... Dr. Thomas D'AGOSTINO
09 Assoc Dean Inst Research/Retent .... Mr. Don EMMONS
19 Director of Campus Safety .... Mr. Martin CORBETT
24 Director of Digital Learning .... Mr. Jeffrey WETHERILL
38 Dir Counseling Ctr/Student Wellness .... Ms. Shelly LEAR
85 Director of International Students .... Mr. David GAGE
37 Director of Financial Aid .... Ms. Beth TURNER
36 Director Center for Career Services .... Ms. Brandi FERRARA
25 Director of Grants .... Ms. Martha BOND
29 Director of Alumni Relations .... Mr. Jared WEEDEN
29 Director of Alumnae Relations .... Ms. Kathleen REGAN
40 Director of the College Store .... Ms. Lucille SMART
15 Associate Director Human Resources .... Ms. Peggy FERRAN
44 Director of Annual & Parent Appeals .... Ms. Kristen EINSTEIN
23 Coordinator Health Services/NP .... Ms. Betti GREEN

Hofstra University (G)

Hempstead NY 11549-1000
County: Nassau FICE Identification: 002732
Unit ID: 191649
Telephone: (516) 463-6600 Carnegie Class: DRU
FAX Number: (516) 463-4848 Calendar System: Semester
URL: www.hofstra.edu
Established: 1935 Annual Undergrad Tuition & Fees: $35,950
Enrollment: 11,404 Coed
Affiliation or Control: Independent Non-Profit IRS Status: 501(c)3
Highest Offering: Doctorate
Program: Liberal Arts And General; Teacher Preparatory; Professional
Accreditation: M, ARCPA, AUD, BUS, BUSA, CLPSY, CORE, ENG, JOUR, LAW, #MED, SCPSY, SP, TEAC

01 President .... Mr. Stuart RABINOWITZ
05 Provost/Sr VP for Academic Affairs .... Dr. Herman A. BERLINER
45 Sr VP for Planning and Admin .... Ms. M. Patricia ADAMSKI
10 VP Financial Affairs/Treasurer .... Ms. Catherine HENNESSY
32 Vice President for Student Affairs .... Ms. Sandra JOHNSON
30 Vice President for Development .... Mr. Alan J. KELLY

26 Vice President University Relations ... Ms. Melissa A. CONNOLLY
43 VP Legal Affairs & General Counsel ... Ms. Dolores FREDRICH
13 Vice Pres Information Technology ... Mr. Robert W. JUCKIEWICZ
18 VP for Facilities and Operations ... Mr. Joseph BARKWILL
84 Vice Pres Enrollment Management ... Ms. Jessica L. EADS
86 Vice President Business Dev Ctr ... Mr. Richard V. GUARDINO
91 Asst VP for Information Technology ... Ms. Linda J. HANTZSCHEL
09 VP Inst Research/Admin Assess ... Ms. Stephanie BUSHEY
20 Vice Provost for Academic Affairs ... Dr. Liora P. SCHMELKIN
21 Assoc Provost Budget & Planning ... Mr. Richard M. APOLLO
25 Assoc Provost Rsrch/Sponsored Pgms ... Ms. Sofia KAKOULIDIS
07 Dean Admissions & Financial Aid ... Ms. Jessica L. EADS
50 Dean Frank G Zarb Sch of Business ... Dr. Patrick J. SOCCI
60 Dean School of Communication ... Dr. Evan W. CORNOG
53 Dean School of Education ... Dr. Nancy E. HALLIDAY
49 Dean College Liberal Arts/Science ... Dr. Bernard J. FIRESTONE
08 Acting Dean Library & Info Services ... Dr. Bernard J. FIRESTONE
88 Dean for University Advisement ... Ms. Anne M. MONGILLO
07 Dean Graduate Admissions ... Ms. Carol J. DRUMMER
61 Interim Dean of Law School ... Mr. Eric LANE
63 Dean Medical School ... Dr. Lawrence SMITH
35 Dean of Students ... Mr. Peter LIBMAN
84 Asst Dean Law Sch Enrollment Mgmt ... Mr. John CHALMERS
29 Senior Director Alumni Affairs ... Mr. Robert SALTZMAN
39 Assoc Director Residential Programs ... Ms. Novia P. WHYTE
38 Dir Student Counseling Services ... Dr. John C. GUTHMAN
22 Equal Rights/Opportunity Ofcr ... Ms. Jennifer MONE
23 Director Health & Wellness Center ... Ms. Maureen B. HOUCK
41 Director Intercollegiate Athletics ... Mr. Jeffrey HATHAWAY
15 Director of Human Resources ... Ms. Evelyn V. MILLER-SUBER
90 Director Faculty Computing Services ... Ms. Judith L. TABRON
40 Manager Bookstore ... Mr. Steven BABBITT
19 Director Public Safety ... Ms. Karen O'CALLAGHAN
96 Director of Purchasing ... Mr. Richard FRANCOS
92 Dean Honors College ... Dr. Warren FRISINA
06 Registrar ... Ms. Lynne DOUGHERTY
04 Admin Assistant to the President ... Ms. Isabel D. FREY
37 Director Student Financial Aid ... Ms. Sandra FILBRY

Holy Trinity Orthodox Seminary (A)

PO Box 36, Jordanville NY 13361-0036
County: Herkimer — FICE Identification: 002733
Unit ID: 191658
Telephone: (315) 858-0945 — Carnegie Class: Not Classified
FAX Number: (315) 858-0945 — Calendar System: Semester
URL: www.hts.edu
Established: 1948 — Annual Undergrad Tuition & Fees: $3,000
Enrollment: 30 — Male
Affiliation or Control: Russian Orthodox — IRS Status: 501(c)3
Highest Offering: Baccalaureate
Program: Professional; Religious Emphasis
Accreditation: NY

01 Rector and Dean ... V.Rev. Luke MURIANKA
06 Registrar ... Rev. Theophylact CLAPPER-DEWELL
32 Dean of Students ... Rev. Cyprian ALEXANDROU
04 Administrative Assistant ... RevDcn. Ephraim WILLMARTH

Houghton College (B)

One Willard Avenue, Houghton NY 14744-0128
County: Allegany — FICE Identification: 002734
Unit ID: 191676
Telephone: (585) 567-9200 — Carnegie Class: Bac/A&S
FAX Number: (585) 567-9572 — Calendar System: Semester
URL: www.houghton.edu
Established: 1883 — Annual Undergrad Tuition & Fees: $26,774
Enrollment: 1,264 — Coed
Affiliation or Control: Wesleyan Church — IRS Status: 501(c)3
Highest Offering: Master's
Program: Liberal Arts And General; Teacher Preparatory
Accreditation: M, MUS, TEAC

01 President ... Dr. Shirley A. MULLEN
05 Interim Dean of the College ... Dr. Linda MILLS WOOLSEY
32 Int Vice President of Student Life ... Mr. Dennis STACK
10 Chief Business Officer ... Mr. Dale F. WRIGHT
30 Interim Vice President Advancement ... Mr. Kent STROMAN
06 Registrar ... Ms. Margery L. AVERY
37 Director of Financial Aid ... Ms. Marianne LOPER
08 Director of the Library ... Mr. David STEVICK
29 Executive Director Alumni Relations ... Mr. Daniel NOYES
07 Dean of Admissions ... Mr. Jeff KIRKSEY
09 Assoc Dean Institutional Research ... Dr. Daryl H. STEVENSON
20 Associate Academic Dean ... Dr. Mark HIJLEH
36 Coordinator of Career Services ... Mr. Brian REITNOUR
15 Director of Human Resources ... Mr. Dale F. WRIGHT
26 Dir Marketing & Communications ... Mr. Jeff BABBITT
14 Director of Technology ... Mr. Donald HAINGRAY
18 Director of Facilities ... Mr. Chad PLYMALE
19 Chief Security Officer ... Mr. Ray M. PARLETT
23 Director of Health Services ... Dr. David BRUBAKER
41 Executive Director of Athletics ... Mr. Harold W. LORD
21 Controller ... Mr. David M. MERCER
39 Director Residence Life ... Mr. Gabriel JACOBSON
38 Director Student Counseling ... Dr. Michael D. LASTORIA
92 Director of Honors Program ... Dr. Benjamin LIPSCOMB
31 Director Community Relations ... Mrs. Phyllis E. GAERTE
35 Dean of Students ... Mr. Dennis STACK

Hudson Valley Community College (C)

80 Vandenburgh Avenue, Troy NY 12180-6096
County: Rensselaer — FICE Identification: 002868
Unit ID: 191719
Telephone: (518) 629-4822 — Carnegie Class: Assoc/Pub-U-SC
FAX Number: (518) 629-4576 — Calendar System: Semester
URL: www.hvcc.edu
Established: 1953 — Annual Undergrad Tuition & Fees (In-District): $4,476
Enrollment: 13,594 — Coed
Affiliation or Control: State/Local — IRS Status: 501(c)3
Highest Offering: Associate Degree
Program: Occupational; 2-Year Principally Bachelor's Creditable
Accreditation: M, ADNUR, DH, DMS, EMT, ENGT, FUSER

01 President ... Dr. Andrew J. MATONAK
04 Exec Assistant to the President ... Dr. Michael S. GREEN
04 Assistant to the President ... Ms. Suzanne K. KALKBRENNER
11 Int Vice Pres for Administration ... Mr. James J. LAGATTA
05 Vice President for Academic Affairs ... Dr. Carolyn G. CURTIS
32 VP Enrol Mgmt/Stdnt Development ... Dr. Alexander J. POPOVICS
10 Vice President for Finance ... Mr. Joel R. FATATO
49 Dean Sch Liberal Arts/Health Sci ... Dr. Margaret M. GEEHAN
72 Dean Engr/Indus Tech/Business ... Mr. P. Phillip WHITE
51 Assoc Dean Cmty/Professional Pgms ... Ms. Christine A. HELWIG
08 Director of Learning Resources Ctr ... Mr. David CLICKNER
07 Director of Admissions ... Ms. Mary Claire BAUER
06 Registrar ... Ms. Kathleen PETLEY
14 Chief Information Officer ... Dr. Steve CHEN
18 Director Physical Plant ... Ms. Karen SEWARD
38 Director Student Development ... Dr. Kathleen SWEENER
37 Director of Financial Aid ... Ms. Lisa VAN WIE
36 Dir Center For Careers/Employment ... Ms. Gayle HEALY
15 Director of Human Resources ... Mr. John TIBBETTS
19 Director of Public Safety ... Mr. Fred ALIBERTI
23 Coordinator Health Services ... Ms. Claudine POTVIN-GIORDANO
88 Director of Disability Resources ... Mr. Pablo E. NEGRON
09 Director Planning & Research ... Mr. James F. MACKLIN
35 Director of Student Life ... Mr. Louis COPLIN
85 International Student Advisor ... Mr. Jay DEITCHMAN
40 Director of Bookstore ... Mr. Stephen J. STEGMAN
41 Director of Athletics ... Ms. Kristan M. PELLETIER
72 Assistant to VP of Academics ... Dr. Sondra E. VALLE
88 Asoc Dean Instruct Spprt Svcs/Reten ... Ms. Karen FERRER-MUNIZ
50 Director of Business Services ... Ms. Mary Ellen LAJEUNESSE
21 Comptroller ... Ms. Debra D. STORY
26 Exec Dir Communications/Marketing ... Mr. Dennis KENNEDY
29 Dir Annual Giving/Donor Rels ... Ms. Kimberley PEABODY
44 Dir Advancement Operations ... Vacant
102 Exec Director Foundation ... Ms. Rachel KIMMELBLATT

Institute of Design and Construction (D)

141 Willoughby Street, Brooklyn NY 11201-5317
County: Kings — FICE Identification: 012107
Unit ID: 191764
Telephone: (718) 855-3661 — Carnegie Class: Assoc/PrivNFP
FAX Number: (718) 852-5889 — Calendar System: Semester
URL: www.idc.edu
Established: 1947 — Annual Undergrad Tuition & Fees: $8,775
Enrollment: 145 — Coed
Affiliation or Control: Independent Non-Profit — IRS Status: 501(c)3
Highest Offering: Associate Degree
Program: 2-Year Principally Bachelor's Creditable; Technical Emphasis
Accreditation: NY

01 Executive Director ... Mr. Vincent C. BATTISTA
11 Administrator ... Ms. Ruth DAVIS
18 Chairman Building Construction ... Mr. Richard L. MITCHELL
07 Director of Admissions ... Mr. Kevin GIANNETTI
27 Dir Communications/Inst Development ... Ms. Elizabeth BATTISTA
08 Head Librarian ... Mrs. Eleanor J. BROWN

Iona College (E)

715 North Avenue, New Rochelle NY 10801-1890
County: Westchester — FICE Identification: 002737
Unit ID: 191931
Telephone: (914) 633-2000 — Carnegie Class: Master's L
FAX Number: (914) 633-2642 — Calendar System: Semester
URL: www.iona.edu
Established: 1940 — Annual Undergrad Tuition & Fees: $31,490
Enrollment: 4,065 — Coed
Affiliation or Control: Independent Non-Profit — IRS Status: 501(c)3
Highest Offering: Master's
Program: Liberal Arts And General; Teacher Preparatory; Professional
Accreditation: M, BUS, CS, JOUR, MFCD, SW, TED

01 President ... Dr. Joseph E. NYRE
05 Provost ... Dr. Brian J. NICKERSON
07 Assistant VP for College Admissions ... Vacant
10 Sr Vice President Finance & Admin ... Mr. Jonathan C. IVEC
30 Sr VP Advance/External Affairs ... Mr. Paul J. SUTERA
13 Vice Provost Info Technology/CIO ... Ms. Joanne STEELE
32 Vice Provost Student Development ... Mr. Charles CARLSON
37 Asst VP Student Financial Services ... Ms. Eileen DOYLE
91 Asst Vice Provost for Info Tech ... Mr. Dimitris HALARIS
20 Assistant VP Academic Affairs ... Dr. Tresmaine GRIMES
29 Asst VP Advancement & Spec Projects ... Ms. Nancy PATOTA
39 Asst Vice Provost Residential Life ... Vacant
35 Asst Vice Provost Student Develop ... Ms. Elizabeth OLIVIERI-LENAHAN
49 Int Dean School Arts & Sciences ... Dr. Jeanne ZAINO
50 Dean Hagan School of Business ... Dr. Vincent CALLUZZO
04 Sr Policy Advisor & Board Secretary ... Sr. Patricia MCGINLEY
18 Director of Facilities Management ... Mr. Mark MURPHY
15 Director of Human Resources ... Ms. Mary Ellen CALLAGHAN
38 Director of Counseling Center ... Dr. Ingrid GRIEGER
36 Director of Career Development ... Ms. Christina BARBERO
08 Director of Libraries ... Mr. Richard PALLADINO
42 Director of Campus Ministries ... Mr. Carl PROCARIO-FOLEY
06 Registrar ... Ms. Nancy MILLS
41 Director of Athletics ... Mr. Eugene MARSHALL
86 Director of Govt Relations/Grants ... Mr. Daniel KONOPKA
12 Director of Rockland Campus ... Sr. Patricia MCGINLEY
09 Dir of Inst Effectiveness/Planning ... Dr. Joseph WYCOFF
21 Director of Business Services ... Ms. Joan CLARK
26 Director of Public Relations ... Ms. Dawn INSANALLI
19 Dir Campus Safety and Security ... Mr. Dominic LOCATELLI
23 Director of Health Services ... Ms. Jacqueline AGNELLO-VAZQUEZ
44 Director of Annual Giving ... Ms. Kara BRENNAN
96 Purchasing Coordinator ... Ms. Kimberly MONTEMURRO
92 Director of Honors Program ... Dr. James STILLWAGGON

Island Drafting and Technical Institute (F)

128 Broadway, Amityville NY 11701-2704
County: Suffolk — FICE Identification: 007375
Unit ID: 191959
Telephone: (631) 691-8733 — Carnegie Class: Assoc/PrivFP
FAX Number: (631) 691-8738 — Calendar System: Semester
URL: www.idti.edu
Established: 1957 — Annual Undergrad Tuition & Fees: $15,200
Enrollment: 136 — Coed
Affiliation or Control: Proprietary — IRS Status: Proprietary
Highest Offering: Associate Degree
Program: Occupational
Accreditation: ACCSC

01 President ... Mr. James G. DILIBERTO
03 Vice President ... Mr. John G. DILIBERTO

Ithaca College (G)

953 Danby Road, Ithaca NY 14850-7001
County: Tompkins — FICE Identification: 002739
Unit ID: 191968
Telephone: (607) 274-3011 — Carnegie Class: Master's L
FAX Number: N/A — Calendar System: Semester
URL: www.ithaca.edu
Established: 1892 — Annual Undergrad Tuition & Fees: $37,000
Enrollment: 6,760 — Coed
Affiliation or Control: Independent Non-Profit — IRS Status: 501(c)3
Highest Offering: Doctorate
Program: Liberal Arts And General; Teacher Preparatory; Professional
Accreditation: M, BUS, MUS, NRPA, OT, PTA, SP, THEA

01 President ... Dr. Thomas R. ROCHON
04 Exec Assistant to President ... Ms. Diane VERONEAU
05 Provost/Vice Pres Academic Affairs ... Ms. Marisa KELLY
10 VP of Finance & Administration ... Mr. Carl E. SGRECCI
32 VP Student Affairs/Campus Life ... Mr. Brian J. MCAREE
43 Vice President & General Counsel ... Ms. Nancy E. PRINGLE
84 VP Enrollment Management ... Mr. Eric MAGUIRE
30 Vice Pres Institutional Advancement ... Mr. Christopher BIEHN
20 Asst Prov/Dean Interdis/Intl Stds ... Dr. Tanya R. SAUNDERS
13 Assoc VP for Info Tech Svcs ... Mr. Edwin W. FULLER
15 Assoc VP for Human Resources ... Mr. Mark COLDREN
18 Assoc VP for Facilities Management ... Mr. Richard COUTURE
35 Assoc Vice Pres Student Affairs ... Dr. Roger RICHARDSON
35 Assoc Vice Pres Student Affairs ... Mr. Rory ROTHMAN
20 Associate Provost ... Ms. Carol HENDERSON
58 Dean of Grad & Prof Studies ... Mr. Rob GEARHART
49 Dean School Humanities/Science ... Dr. Leslie LEWIS
64 Dean of School of Music ... Vacant
76 Dean Sch Health Sciences/Human Perf ... Mr. John SIGG
50 Dean School of Business ... Mr. Mark CORDANO
60 Dean School of Communications ... Ms. Diane GAYESKI
29 Director Alumni Relations ... Ms. Gretchen VAN VALEN
44 Executive Director of Development ... Ms. Kate LARRABEE
27 Int Dir Marketing Communications ... Ms. Laurie WARD
06 Registrar ... Mr. Brian SCHOLTEN
22 Asst Counsel & Dir EO Compliance ... Ms. Traevena BYRD
09 Director Institutional Research ... Ms. Martha D. GRAY
07 Director of Admission ... Mr. Gerard TURBIDE
12 Director London Center ... Mr. William SHEASGREEN
51 Program Dir/Graduate & Prof Studies ... Ms. Madelyn WILLIAMS
35 Dir Std Engagement/Multicult Affair ... Ms. Terry MARTINEZ
36 Director Career Services ... Mr. John P. BRADAC
38 Director for Counseling Svcs ... Dr. Deborah HARPER
37 Dir of Student Financial Services ... Mrs. Lisa HOSKEY
23 Director Health Center ... Dr. David E. NEWMAN
39 Dir Res Life/Judicial Affairs ... Ms. Bonnie S. PRUNTY
08 College Librarian ... Ms. Lisabeth CHABOT
41 Dir Intercol Athletics/Rec Sports ... Mr. Ken KUTLER
21 Director of Budget ... Ms. Sally DIETZ
90 Dir Technology/Inst Support Svcs ... Mr. Michael E. TAVES
91 Director Information Systems/Svcs ... Mr. Michael E. TAVES
19 Director Public Safety ... Ms. Terri STEWART
88 Director of Academic Funding ... Dr. Paul J. HAMILL
96 Director of Purchasing ... Vacant

27 Assoc Dir for Campus Communication .... Mr. David C. MALEY
40 Manager of College Stores .... Mr. Rick WATSON
42 Coordinator of Chaplains .... Rev. Meredith ELLIS

ITT Technical Institute (A)

13 Airline Drive, Albany NY 12205-1003
County: Albany Identification: 666138
Unit ID: 434566
Telephone: (518) 452-9300 Carnegie Class: Assoc/PrivFP
FAX Number: (518) 452-9393 Calendar System: Quarter
URL: www.itt-tech.edu
Established: 1998 Annual Undergrad Tuition & Fees: N/A
Enrollment: 366 Coed
Affiliation or Control: Proprietary IRS Status: Proprietary
Highest Offering: Associate Degree
Program: Technical Emphasis
Accreditation: ACICS

† Branch campus of ITT Technical Institute, Indianapolis, IN.

ITT Technical Institute (B)

2295 Millersport Hwy, PO Box 327,
Getzville NY 14068-1219
County: Erie Identification: 666609
Unit ID: 420404
Telephone: (716) 689-2200 Carnegie Class: Assoc/PrivFP
FAX Number: (716) 689-2828 Calendar System: Quarter
URL: www.itt-tech.edu
Established: 1995 Annual Undergrad Tuition & Fees: N/A
Enrollment: 586 Coed
Affiliation or Control: Proprietary IRS Status: Proprietary
Highest Offering: Associate Degree
Program: Technical Emphasis
Accreditation: ACICS

† Branch campus of ITT Technical Institute, Indianapolis, IN.

ITT Technical Institute (C)

235 Greenfield Parkway, Liverpool NY 13088-6653
County: Onondaga Identification: 666137
Unit ID: 434575
Telephone: (315) 461-8000 Carnegie Class: Assoc/PrivFP
FAX Number: (315) 461-8008 Calendar System: Quarter
URL: www.itt-tech.edu
Established: 1998 Annual Undergrad Tuition & Fees: N/A
Enrollment: 337 Coed
Affiliation or Control: Proprietary IRS Status: Proprietary
Highest Offering: Associate Degree
Program: Technical Emphasis
Accreditation: ACICS

† Branch campus of ITT Technical Institute, Indianapolis, IN.

Jamestown Business College (D)

7 Fairmount Avenue, Box 429, Jamestown NY 14702-0429
County: Chautauqua FICE Identification: 008495
Unit ID: 192004
Telephone: (716) 664-5100 Carnegie Class: Assoc/PrivFP4
FAX Number: (716) 664-3144 Calendar System: Quarter
URL: www.jamestownbusinesscollege.edu
Established: 1886 Annual Undergrad Tuition & Fees: $11,400
Enrollment: 317 Coed
Affiliation or Control: Proprietary IRS Status: Proprietary
Highest Offering: Baccalaureate
Program: Occupational; 2-Year Principally Bachelor's Creditable
Accreditation: M

01 President/Academic Dean .... Mr. David CONKLIN
32 Vice Pres/Dean of Student Affairs .... Ms. Rosanne JOHANSON
07 Director Admissions .... Ms. Brenda SALEMME
37 Director of Financial Aid .... Mrs. Diane STURZENBECKER
26 Director of Communications .... Ms. Jessica GOLLEY
04 Assistant to Academic Dean .... Ms. Cindy CARTWRIGHT

Jamestown Community College (E)

525 Falconer Street, Jamestown NY 14701
County: Chautauqua FICE Identification: 002869
Unit ID: 191986
Telephone: (716) 338-1000 Carnegie Class: Assoc/Pub-R-M
FAX Number: (716) 338-1466 Calendar System: Semester
URL: www.sunyjcc.edu
Established: 1950 Annual Undergrad Tuition & Fees (In-District): $4,495
Enrollment: 3,926 Coed
Affiliation or Control: State/Local IRS Status: 501(c)3
Highest Offering: Associate Degree
Program: 2-Year Principally Bachelor's Creditable
Accreditation: M, ADNUR, OTA

01 President .... Dr. Gregory T. DECINQUE
05 VP/Dean of Academic Affairs .... Dr. Marilyn A. ZAGORA
32 VP/Dean of Student Development .... Dr. Eileen J. GOODLING
12 VP/Dean Catt County Campus .... Mr. Jean J. SAYEGH
11 VP/Dean of Administration .... Mr. John R. GARFOOT
06 Registrar .... Mr. Kreig ELICKER
07 Director Admission .... Ms. Wendy PRESENT
26 Executive Director of Marketing .... Mr. Nelson J. GARIFI
08 Library Director .... Ms. Linda LARKIN
36 Placement Coordinator .... Mr. Ronald A. TURAK
37 Director of Financial Aid .... Ms. Laurie A. VORP
15 Director Human Resources .... Ms. Susan BRONSTEIN
09 Director Institutional Research .... Ms. Barbara RUSSELL
41 Athletic Director .... Mr. Keith MARTIN
43 Legal Counsel .... Mr. Stephen ABDELLA
18 Director Facilities/Physical Plant .... Mr. David JOHNSON

Jefferson Community College (F)

1220 Coffeen Street, Watertown NY 13601-1897
County: Jefferson FICE Identification: 002870
Unit ID: 192022
Telephone: (315) 786-2200 Carnegie Class: Assoc/Pub-R-M
FAX Number: (315) 786-0158 Calendar System: Semester
URL: www.sunyjefferson.edu
Established: 1961 Annual Undergrad Tuition & Fees (In-District): $4,277
Enrollment: 3,815 Coed
Affiliation or Control: State/Local IRS Status: 501(c)3
Highest Offering: Associate Degree
Program: Occupational; 2-Year Principally Bachelor's Creditable
Accreditation: M, ADNUR

01 President .... Dr. Carole A. MCCOY
05 Vice President Academic Affairs .... Mr. Thomas FINCH
10 Vice President Admin/Finance .... Mr. Daniel DUPEE
32 Vice President of Students .... Ms. Betsy S. PENROSE
20 Dean Curriculum/Instruction .... Ms. Jerilyn FAIRMAN
51 Dean for Continuing Education .... Ms. Jill PIPPIN
21 Dean for Business .... Ms. Vicki QUIGLEY
04 Assistant to the President .... Ms. Karen A. CARR
08 Library Director .... Ms. Connie HOLBERG
07 Director of Admissions .... Ms. Roseanne N. WEIR
37 Director Financial Aid .... Mr. James AMBROSE
06 Registrar .... Ms. Natalie M. SPOONER
88 Director Small Business Center .... Mr. Eric F. CONSTANCE
09 Director of Institutional Research .... Ms. Mary A. PERRINE
18 Chief Facilities/Physical Plant .... Mr. Mark STRADER
29 Director Alumni Relations .... Ms. Mary KINNE
35 Director Student Devel/Activities .... Mr. Frank DOLDO
36 Director Student Placement .... Ms. Michele D. GEFELL
38 Director Student Counseling .... Mr. Matthew LAMBERT
26 Chief Public Relations Officer .... Ms. Karen J. FREEMAN
15 Exec Dir Finance/Human Resources .... Ms. Kerry A. YOUNG
30 College Development Officer .... Ms. Christine RIZZO
31 Coordinator Community Services .... Ms. Andrea PEDRICK

Jewish Theological Seminary of America (G)

3080 Broadway, New York NY 10027-4649
County: New York FICE Identification: 002740
Unit ID: 192040
Telephone: (212) 678-8023 Carnegie Class: Spec/Faith
FAX Number: (212) 678-8947 Calendar System: Semester
URL: www.jtsa.edu
Established: 1886 Annual Undergrad Tuition & Fees: $17,600
Enrollment: 472 Coed
Affiliation or Control: Independent Non-Profit IRS Status: 501(c)3
Highest Offering: Doctorate
Program: Liberal Arts And General; Teacher Preparatory; Professional; Religious Emphasis
Accreditation: M

01 Chancellor .... Dr. Arnold M. EISEN
03 Exec VC/Chief Operating Officer .... Mr. Marc GARY
30 Vice Chanc/Chief Development Office .... Ms. Marilyn F. KOHN
05 Provost .... Dr. Alan COOPER
88 Senior Advisor to the Chancellor . Rabbi Michael B. GREENBAUM
88 Vice Chancellor .... Rabbi Marc WOLF
10 Chief Financial Officer .... Mr. Fred SCHNUR
43 Counsel .... Ms. Ann H. APPELBAUM
49 Dean List College Jewish Studies .... Dr. Shuly SCHWARTZ
53 Dean Davidson School of Education .... Dr. Barry HOLTZ
58 Dean The Graduate School .... Dr. Shuly SCHWARTZ
64 Director Miller Cantorial School .... Cantor Nancy ABRAMSON
73 Dean of Religious Leadership .... Rabbi Daniel NEVINS
32 Dean of Student Life .... Ms. Sara HOROWITZ
08 Librarian .... Dr. David KRAEMER
09 Director Institutional Research .... Miss Girija V. GHOLKAR
15 Director of Human Resources .... Ms. Diana TORRES-PETRILLI
18 Director of Operations .... Mr. James ESPOSITO
13 Director Information Technology .... Mr. Hal POLLENZ
27 Chief Communications Officer .... Ms. Elise DOWELL
06 Registrar/Director Financial Aid .... Ms. Linda LEVINE
84 Director of Enrollment Management .... Ms. Dana EVANS
39 Director of Residence Life .... Mr. Bradley MOOT
07 Director List College Admissions .... Mrs. Melissa PRESENT
35 Director of Student Life .... Ms. Ruth DECALO
38 Director Student Counseling .... Dr. David DAVAR
29 Director of Alumni Affairs .... Mrs. Melissa FRIEDMAN
20 Associate Provost .... Dr. Stephen GARFINKEL
26 Chief Communications Officer .... Ms. Elise DOWELL
37 Director of Financial Aid .... Ms. Linda LEVINE

The Juilliard School (H)

60 Lincoln Center Plaza, New York NY 10023-6588
County: New York FICE Identification: 002742
Unit ID: 192110
Telephone: (212) 799-5000 Carnegie Class: Spec/Arts
FAX Number: (212) 724-0263 Calendar System: Semester
URL: www.juilliard.edu
Established: 1905 Annual Undergrad Tuition & Fees: $35,140
Enrollment: 844 Coed
Affiliation or Control: Independent Non-Profit IRS Status: 501(c)3
Highest Offering: Doctorate
Program: Professional
Accreditation: M

01 President .... Dr. Joseph W. POLISI
05 Provost & Dean .... Mr. Ara GUZELIMIAN
10 Vice Pres/Chief Operating Officer .... Mr. Jon ROSENHEIN
30 Vice Pres for Dev/Public Affairs .... Mr. Riccardo SALMONA
20 Vice Pres/Dean Academic Affairs .... Ms. Karen WAGNER
43 Vice President & General Counsel .... Ms. Laurie A. CARTER
08 VP for Library/Info Resources .... Ms. Jane GOTTLIEB
18 Vice Pres for Facilities Management .... Mr. Joseph MASTRANGELO
21 Vice Pres for Finance & Controller .... Ms. Christine TODD
84 Vice Pres for Enrollment Management .... Ms. Joan D. WARREN
88 Vice Pres for Global Initiatives .... Mr. Christopher MOSSEY
27 Associate VP for Communications .... Ms. Janet KESSIN
28 Asc VP for Diversity & Campus Life .... Ms. Alison SCOTT-WILLIAMS
88 Assoc VP for Special Projects .... Ms. Tricia ROSS
07 Associate Dean for Admissions .... Ms. Lee CIOPPA
11 Assoc Dean for Administration .... Mr. Adam MEYER
64 Asst Dean/Dir of Chamber Music .... Ms. Barli NUGENT
57 Director Richard Rodgers Drama Div .... Mr. James HOUGHTON
57 Artistic Director of Dance Division .... Mr. Lawrence RHODES
88 Artistic Director of Vocal Arts .... Mr. Brian ZEGER
88 Artist in Residence/Artistic Advise .... Ms. Monica HUGGETT
88 Director of Historical Performance .... Mr. Robert MEALY
88 Artistic Dir Pre-College Division .... Ms. Yoheved KAPLINSKY
06 Registrar .... Ms. Katherine GERTSON
16 Director of Human Resources .... Ms. Caryn G. DOKTOR
32 Director of Student Affairs .... Ms. Sabrina TANBARA
38 Director of Counseling Services .... Mr. William BUSE
37 Director Student Financial Aid .... Ms. Tina GONZALEZ
29 Dir of Natl Advance/Alumni Rels .... Ms. Jamee ARD
88 Artistic Director of Jazz Studies .... Mr. Carl ALLEN
96 Director of Office Services .... Mr. Scott A. HOLDEN
36 Director Career Services .... Ms. Courtney BLACKWELL
13 Director Information Technology .... Mr. Tunde GIWA

Kehilath Yakov Rabbinical Seminary (I)

638 Bedford Avenue, Brooklyn NY 11211-8007
County: Kings FICE Identification: 010549
Unit ID: 192165
Telephone: (718) 963-1212 Carnegie Class: Spec/Faith
FAX Number: (718) 387-8586 Calendar System: Semester
Established: 1948 Annual Undergrad Tuition & Fees: $7,800
Enrollment: 110 Male
Affiliation or Control: Independent Non-Profit IRS Status: 501(c)3
Highest Offering: First Talmudic Degree
Program: Teacher Preparatory; Professional
Accreditation: RABN

01 President .... Mr. Sandor SCHWARTZ

Keller Graduate School of Management (J)

120 W 45th Street, 6th Floor, New York NY 10036-4041
County: New York Identification: 666258
Telephone: (212) 556-0002 Carnegie Class: Not Classified
FAX Number: (212) 556-0040 Calendar System: Semester
URL: www.keller.edu
Established: 2003 Annual Graduate Tuition & Fees: $26,355
Enrollment: 175 Coed
Affiliation or Control: Proprietary IRS Status: Proprietary
Highest Offering: Master's; No Undergraduates
Program: Occupational; Business Emphasis
Accreditation: &NH

01 Campus Dean .... Ms. Patricia CAPALDO

† Regional accreditation is carried under the parent institution, DeVry University, Downers Grove, IL.

Keuka College (K)

Keuka Park NY 14478-0098
County: Yates FICE Identification: 002744
Unit ID: 192192
Telephone: (315) 279-5000 Carnegie Class: Master's S
FAX Number: (315) 279-5216 Calendar System: Semester
URL: www.keuka.edu
Established: 1890 Annual Undergrad Tuition & Fees: $25,235
Enrollment: 1,947 Coed
Affiliation or Control: Independent Non-Profit IRS Status: 501(c)3
Highest Offering: Master's
Program: Liberal Arts And General; Teacher Preparatory; Professional
Accreditation: M, IACBE, NURSE, OT, SW, @TEAC

01 President .... Dr. Jorge L. DIAZ-HERRERA
05 Vice President Academic Affairs .... Dr. Anne WEED
32 Vice Pres of Student Development .... Dr. James BLACKBURN
20 Asc Vice Pres of Academic Programs .... Dr. Timothy SELLERS

10 VP Finance/Chief Financial Officer ..... Mr. Jerry HILLER
08 Director of Library ..... Ms. Linda PARK
29 Director of Alumni/Family Relations ..... Ms. Kathy WAYE
27 Exec Director of Communications ..... Mr. Doug LIPPINCOTT
30 Asc Vice Pres for Devlopment ..... Mr. Larry LELNER
37 Director Financial Aid ..... Ms. Jennifer BATES
84 Dir of Enrollment Management ..... Mr. Jack FARRELL
09 Director of Institutional Research ..... Mr. Mark PALMIERI
14 Director of Computer Services ..... Mr. Brad TURNER
18 Director of Facilities ..... Mr. Dennis HOINS
21 Controller ..... Ms. Carol N. GROVER
19 Director of Security ..... Mr. Kevin TIERNEY
23 Director of Health Services ..... Ms. Martha RICH
38 Director of Counseling Services ..... Ms. Claudia WELBOURNE
35 Director of Student Life Activities ..... Ms. Jennifer FURNER
07 Director of Admissions ..... Mr. Gary BOYER
41 Director of Athletics ..... Mr. David M. SWEET
36 Asst Dean for Experiential Educ ..... Dr. Anne Marie GUTHRIE
58 Assoc VP for Prof & Intl Programs ..... Mr. Gary SMITH
88 Dir Administrative/Adult Learning ..... Ms. Anne KILLEN
42 Chaplain ..... Mr. Eric DETAR
06 Registrar ..... Ms. Linda M. FLEISCHMAN
88 Marketing Manager Adult Learning ..... Mr. Jack FARRELL
96 Purchasing Agent ..... Ms. Audrey FAULKNER
15 Personnel Coordinator ..... Ms. Susan DELYSER
76 Div Chair OT & Dir OT Grad Studies ..... Ms. Victoria SMITH
83 Div Chrm Basic Social & Applied Sci ..... Dr. Steve HALLAM
50 Div Chrm Business & Management ..... Mr. Neil SEIBENHAR
53 Div Chrm Ed & Dir Ed Grad Studies ..... Ms. Diane M. BURKE
79 Div Chrm Humanities/Fine Arts ..... Dr. Alexis HAYNES
81 Div Chrm Natural Sciences/Math/PE ..... Dr. Michael KECK
75 Division Chairman OT ..... Ms. Vicki SMITH
44 Asst Director Dev/Donor Relations ..... Ms. Billie Jo JAYNE
44 Asst Dir Devel/Annual Giving Pgms ..... Ms. Andi LIPPINCOTT

The King's College (A)

350 Fifth Avenue, Suite 1500, New York NY 10118-1500
County: New York — FICE Identification: 040953
Unit ID: 454184
Telephone: (212) 659-7200 — Carnegie Class: Bac/A&S
FAX Number: (212) 659-7210 — Calendar System: Semester
URL: www.tkc.edu
Established: 1938 — Annual Undergrad Tuition & Fees: $29,240
Enrollment: 465 — Coed
Affiliation or Control: Independent Non-Profit — IRS Status: 501(c)3
Highest Offering: Baccalaureate
Program: Liberal Arts And General; Business Emphasis
Accreditation: M

00 Chairman of the Board of Trustees ..... Mr. Andrew MILLS
01 President ..... Mr. Dinesh J. D'SOUZA
07 Vice President of Admissions ..... Mr. Brian PARKER
32 Vice President Student Development ..... Mr. Eric BENNETT
30 Vice President of Advancement ..... Mr. Jamey NORDBY
05 Vice President Academic Affairs ..... Dr. Marvin OLASKY
35 Dean of Students ..... Mr. David LEEDY
10 Chief Financial Officer ..... Vacant
21 Controller ..... Ms. Judy BARRINGER
06 Registrar ..... Ms. Paula THIGPEN
37 Director of Financial Services ..... Ms. Anna PETERS

Le Moyne College (B)

1419 Salt Springs Road, Syracuse NY 13214-1301
County: Onondaga — FICE Identification: 002748
Unit ID: 192323
Telephone: (315) 445-4100 — Carnegie Class: Master's L
FAX Number: (315) 445-4540 — Calendar System: Semester
URL: www.lemoyne.edu
Established: 1946 — Annual Undergrad Tuition & Fees: $29,460
Enrollment: 3,204 — Coed
Affiliation or Control: Independent Non-Profit — IRS Status: 501(c)3
Highest Offering: Master's
Program: Liberal Arts And General; Teacher Preparatory; Professional; Business Emphasis
Accreditation: M, ARCPA, BUS, NURSE, TEAC

01 President ..... Dr. Fred P. PESTELLO
05 Provost & VP for Academic Affairs ..... Dr. Linda M. LEMURA
84 Vice Pres Enrollment Management ..... Dr. Dennis R. DEPERRO
10 Vice Pres Finance & Administration . Mr. Roger W. STACKPOOLE
30 Vice Pres Institutional Advancement ..... Ms. Mary L. COTTER
32 Vice Pres Student Development ... Dr. Deborah M. CADY MELZER
88 Director of Mission & Identity ..... Rev. David C. MCCALLUM, SJ
88 Rector of the Jesuit Community ..... Rev. John P. BUCKI, SJ
22 EEO/Affirmative Action Officer ..... Mr. Jack MATSON
49 Dean of Arts & Sciences ..... Vacant
50 Dean of Madden School of Business ..... Dr. Wally J. ELMER
20 Assoc Provost New Program Develop ..... Dr. Mary K. COLLINS
08 Director of the Library ..... Dr. Robert C. JOHNSTON
07 Dean of Admission ..... Mr. Dennis J. NICHOLSON
07 Director of Graduate Admission ..... Ms. Kristen P. TRAPASSO
07 Director of Transfer Admission ..... Ms. Cathleen R. ANDERSON
26 Director of Communications ..... Mr. Joseph B. DELLA POSTA
51 Director of Continuing Education ..... Ms. Patricia J. BLISS
37 Director of Financial Aid ..... Mr. William C. CHEETHAM
06 Registrar ..... Ms. Mary M. CHANDLER
21 Assoc VP for Finance & Controller ..... Mr. Brian M. LOUCY
41 Asst VP & Director of Athletics ..... Mr. Matthew D. BASSETT
18 Asst VP Facilities Mgmt & Planning ..... Mr. Jed S. SCHNEIDER
15 Assoc VP for Human Resources ..... Mr. Jack MATSON
13 Acting Director of Info Technology ..... Mr. Shaun C. BLACK
09 Director of Institutional Research ..... Dr. Daniel L. SKIDMORE
40 Bookstore Manager ..... Ms. Jessica L. HAMMOND
88 Director of Advancement Services ..... Mr. Paul F. LYNCH
29 Director Alumni & Parent Programs ... Ms. Kimberly B. MCAULIFF
44 Dir of Annual Giving/Stewardship ..... Ms. Katherine COGSWELL
86 Director Govt/Foundation Relations ..... Mr. Steven W. KULICK
44 Director of Major & Planned Giving ..... Mr. Philip J. GEORGE
88 Asst VP for Student Development ..... Ms. Barbara M. KARPER
88 Asst Dean for Academic Advising ..... Ms. Susan E. AMES
35 Asst Dean for Student Development ..... Mr. Mark G. GODLESKI
88 Director Campus Life & Leadership ..... Mr. John R. HALEY
42 Director of Campus Ministry ..... Rev. John P. BUCKI, SJ
36 Director Career Advising/Devpment ..... Vacant
38 Director Health/Counseling Center ..... Ms. Anne E. KEARNEY
19 Director of Security ..... Mr. John P. O BRIEN
88 Director of Service Learning ..... Ms. Gloria C. HEFFERNAN

LIM College (C)

12 E 53rd Street, New York NY 10022-5268
County: New York — FICE Identification: 007466
Unit ID: 192271
Telephone: (212) 752-1530 — Carnegie Class: Spec/Bus
FAX Number: (212) 832-6109 — Calendar System: Semester
URL: www.limcollege.edu
Established: 1939 — Annual Undergrad Tuition & Fees: $22,995
Enrollment: 1,595 — Coed
Affiliation or Control: Proprietary — IRS Status: Proprietary
Highest Offering: Master's
Program: Professional; Business Emphasis
Accreditation: M, ACBSP

01 President ..... Elizabeth S. MARCUSE
04 Special Assistant to the President ..... Linda HARRIS PAOLILLO
03 Executive Vice President ..... Christopher J. CYPHERS
10 Senior Vice Pres Finance/Operations ..... Michael DONOHUE
88 Vice Pres for Student Development ..... Michael FERRY
108 VP Planning & Assessment ..... Jacqueline LEBLANC
32 VP for Student Affairs ..... Michael SACHS
07 Assistant Dean of Admissions ..... Kristina ORTIZ
88 Asst Dean of Stdnt Academic Affairs ..... Patricia FITZMAURICE
37 Asst VP Stndt Fin/Chief Compl Ofcr ..... Christopher T. BARTO
21 Controller ..... Hubert STACHURA
96 Purchasing Agent ..... Eric MARTIN
08 Director of Library Services ..... Lou ACIERNO
26 Director of Communications ..... Meredith FINNIN
15 Director of HR ..... Andrea L. GRANVILLE
88 Sr Dir of Strategic Initiatives ..... Pamela LINTON
13 Chief Technology Officer ..... Maurice MORENCY
88 President Emeritus ..... Adrian G. MARCUSE
06 College Registrar ..... Carolyn DISNEW
18 Manager of Facilities ..... Jonathan ABREU
30 Sr Dir Institutional Advancement ..... Gail NARDIN
58 Vice President for Graduate Studies ..... Milan MILASINOVIC
04 Assistant to the President ..... Paula HOWELL
39 Dir of Housing & Residence Life ..... Jennifer K. LUCIANO
105 Web Content Manager/Administrator ..... Lola REPHANN
09 Assoc Dean Recruit/Inst Research ..... William IMBRIALE
35 Assoc Dean Student Affairs ..... Charles PRYOR
51 Assoc Dean Continuing Education ..... Lisa M. DECKER
36 Assoc Dean Experien Ed & Career Mgt ..... Dudley BLOSSOM
05 Dean of Academic Affairs ..... Rick LESTER
35 Director of Student Life ..... Michael PALLADINO
07 Graduate Admissions Coordinator ..... Paul MUCCIARONE
106 Program Dir of Distance Learning ..... Holly DAVENPORT
38 Director Counseling & Wellness Svcs ..... Jodi N. LICHT

Long Island Business Institute (D)

136-18 39th Avenue, Flushing NY 11354
County: Queens — FICE Identification: 020937
Unit ID: 192509
Telephone: (718) 939-5100 — Carnegie Class: Assoc/PrivFP
FAX Number: (718) 939-9235 — Calendar System: Semester
URL: www.libi.edu
Established: 1968 — Annual Undergrad Tuition & Fees: $14,073
Enrollment: 1,036 — Coed
Affiliation or Control: Proprietary — IRS Status: Proprietary
Highest Offering: Associate Degree
Program: Occupational; 2-Year Principally Bachelor's Creditable; Business Emphasis
Accreditation: ACICS

01 President ..... Ms. Monica W. FOOTE
12 Asst Campus Program Director ..... Ms. Michelle HOUSTON
11 Dean of Administration ..... Mr. Enos CHEUNG
37 Financial Aid Director ..... Mr. Nazaret KIREGIAN
08 Librarian Commack Campus ..... Ms. Terry CANAVAN
08 Librarian Flushing Campus ..... Ms. Adrianna ARGUELLES
05 Chief Academic/Student Svcs Officer ..... Ms. Stacey JOHNSON

*Long Island University (E)

700 Northern Boulevard, Brookville NY 11548-1326
County: Nassau — FICE Identification: 002751
Unit ID: 192457
Telephone: (516) 299-1926 — Carnegie Class: N/A
FAX Number: (516) 299-2072
URL: www.liu.edu

01 President ..... Dr. David J. STEINBERG
05 Vice President Academic Affairs ..... Dr. Jeffrey KANE
88 Academic Budget Officer ..... Ms. M. Peggy RIGGS
10 Vice President Finance & Treasurer ..... Mr. Robert N. ALTHOLZ
20 Exec Asst to VP Acad Affairs ..... Ms. Gabrielle TOBIN
45 VP Planning & Human Resources ..... Dr. Daniel J. RODAS
29 VP For Alumni Relations ..... Mr. Richard GORMAN
43 Vice Pres Legal Svcs/Univ Counsel ..... Ms. Lynette PHILLIPS
88 Sr Advisor & Teasurer Emerita ..... Mrs. Mary M. LAI
04 Exec Assistant to the President ..... Ms. Kathy CAMPO
20 Deputy VP Academic Affairs ..... Dr. Lori KNAPP
13 VP for Information Technology & CIO ..... Mr. George BAROUDI
18 Assoc VP for Capital Projects ..... Mr. Peter TYMUS
21 Assoc Vice Pres/Controller ..... Mr. Mark SCHMOTZER
29 Assoc VP Delevop/Alumni Relations ..... Ms. Jennifer GOODWIN
30 Assoc Vice Pres Development ..... Ms. Melodee GANDIA
20 Asst VP Instr Tech/Faculty Develop ..... Dr. Elizabeth CIABOCCHI
100 Asst Vice Pres Office of President ..... Ms. Heather GIBBS
25 Asst Vice Pres Sponsored Research ..... Ms. Kathryn S. ROCKETT
86 Assoc VP Public Policy/Govt/Found ... Mr. Christopher WILLIAMS
16 Assoc Vice Pres Human Resources ..... Ms. Lisa CONZA
22 Asst VP for Employee Relations ..... Ms. Gail WEINER
14 Assoc VP Information Systems ..... Mr. Sal GRECO
62 Dean of University Libraries ..... Ms. Valeda DENT
26 Assistant VP for Public Relations ..... Mrs. Kimberly VOLPE-CASALINO
21 Assoc VP Finance and Budget Dir ..... Mr. Christopher FEVOLA
88 Assoc Controller Accounting Svcs ..... Mr. Joseph PELIO, JR.
88 Associate Counsel ..... Ms. Catherine MURPHY
88 Assoc Controller Comp Operations ..... Ms. Linda NOYES
21 Dir of Student Financial Services ..... Ms. Lorraine CELLI
88 Director Devel Svcs/Campaign Assoc ..... Ms. Susan SHEBAR
16 Senior Dir of Employee Benefits ..... Mr. John DORAN
15 Director Univ Fringe Benefits Pgm ..... Mrs. Nancy SISSONS
09 Director of Institutional Research ..... Mr. Claude CHEEK
88 Univ Director Network Services ..... Mr. Carlos SIVERIO
96 Director of Purchasing ..... Ms. Margaret NATALIE
37 Univ Director Financial Aid ..... Mr. David MAINENTI

*Long Island University Brentwood Campus (F)

100 Second Avenue, Brentwood NY 11717-5300
County: Suffolk — Identification: 666076
Unit ID: 192563
Telephone: (631) 273-5112 — Carnegie Class: Master's L
FAX Number: (631) 952-0809 — Calendar System: Semester
URL: www.liu.edu
Established: 1959 — Annual Undergrad Tuition & Fees: $30,046
Enrollment: 391 — Coed
Affiliation or Control: Independent Non-Profit — IRS Status: 501(c)3
Highest Offering: Master's
Program: Liberal Arts And General; Teacher Preparatory; Professional
Accreditation: &M

02 Assoc Campus Dir/Admissions/Mktg ..... Ms. Christina SEISERT
05 Provost ..... Ms. Jen BROWN

*Long Island University Brooklyn Campus (G)

1 University Plaza, Brooklyn NY 11201-5301
County: Kings — FICE Identification: 004779
Unit ID: 192439
Telephone: (718) 488-1000 — Carnegie Class: Master's L
FAX Number: (718) 780-4045 — Calendar System: Semester
URL: www.liu.edu
Established: 1926 — Annual Undergrad Tuition & Fees: $28,922
Enrollment: 8,619 — Coed
Affiliation or Control: Independent Non-Profit — IRS Status: 501(c)3
Highest Offering: Doctorate
Program: Occupational; Liberal Arts And General; Teacher Preparatory; Professional
Accreditation: &M, ARCPA, CLPSY, DMS, NURSE, OT, PHAR, PTA, SP, SPAA, SURGT, SW, TEAC

02 Provost ..... Ms. Gale STEVENS HAYNES
05 Associate Provost ..... Dr. Gladys SCHRYNEMAKERS
20 Assistant Provost ..... Ms. Hazel SEIVWRIGHT
11 Associate Provost Campus Services ..... Mr. Brad COHEN
06 Registrar ..... Mr. Thomas CASTIGLIONE
37 Associate Provost Student Fin Svcs ..... Ms. Patricia CONNORS
84 Dean of Enrollment ..... Mr. Alexander SCOTT
49 Dean Conolly Col Arts & Science ..... Dr. David COHEN
67 Dean Col Pharmacy/Sch Health Prof ..... Dr. David TAFT
62 Dean of the Library ..... Ms. Valeda DENT
66 Dean School of Nursing ..... Dr. Shirley GIROUARD
72 Dean of IT/Deputy CIO ..... Dr. Kamel LECHEHEB
46 Dean of Research ..... Dr. Carol MAGAI
53 Dean School of Education ..... Dr. Cecelia TRAUGH
50 Dean Business/Public Admin/Info Sci ..... Dr. Mohammed GHRIGA
30 Dean Inst Advance & Student Affairs ..... Ms. Kimberly WILLIAMS
23 University Health Manager ..... Ms. Virginia SMALL
85 Director International Students ..... Mr. Steve CHIN
88 Director Academic Reinforcement Ctr ..... Mr. Courtney FREDERICK
26 Director of Public Relations ..... Mr. Brian HARMON
36 Asst Dean Career Dev & Coop Educ ... Ms. Stephanie STEINBERG
39 Director Residence Life & Housing ..... Dr. Rodney PINK
09 Director of Institutional Research ..... Mr. Claude CHEEK
29 AVP Development/Alumni Relations ..... Mr. Drew KAIDEN
41 Director of Athletics ..... Mr. John SUAREZ

35 Director Student Life & Leader Dev ... Ms. Karlene JACKSON THOMPSON
18 Director Public Safety ... Mr. Selvin LIVINGSTON
88 Dir Spec Svcs & Achievement Studies ... Vacant
88 Co-Director Higher Educ Oppty Pgms ... Ms. Diana VOELKER
88 Co-Director Higher Educ Oppty Pgms ... Ms. Okarita STEVENS
86 Director Comm Outreach & Arts Prom ... Ms. Fatima KAFELE
15 Human Resources Officer ... Ms. Raquel COLLADO
92 Co-Director of Honors Program ... Ms. Cris GLEICHER
92 Co-Director of Honors Program ... Dr. James CLARKE

*Long Island University C.W. Post Campus (A)

720 Northern Boulevard, Brookville NY 11548-1300
County: Nassau FICE Identification: 002754
Unit ID: 192448
Telephone: (516) 299-2000 Carnegie Class: Master's L
FAX Number: (516) 299-4020 Calendar System: Semester
URL: www.liu.edu/cwpost
Established: 1954 Annual Undergrad Tuition & Fees: $31,646
Enrollment: 11,287 Coed
Affiliation or Control: Independent Non-Profit IRS Status: 501(c)3
Highest Offering: Doctorate
Program: Occupational; Liberal Arts And General; Teacher Preparatory; Professional; Business Emphasis
Accreditation: M, BUS, CACREP, CLPSY, DIETD, DIETI, LIB, MT, NURSE, PERF, RAD, SP, SPAA, SW, TEAC

02 Provost/COO ... Dr. Paul FORESTELL
04 Executive Asst to the Provost ... Ms. Stephanie ARCHER
10 Sr Asst Prov Budget Mgmt/Aux Svcs ... Ms. Dana WEISS
27 Assoc Provost/Director Public Rels ... Ms. Rita LANGDON
84 Assoc Provost Enrollment Services ... Vacant
51 Asst Provost Continuing Ed ... Dr. Kay SATO
32 Asst Provost for Student Affairs ... Ms. Amy URQUHART
36 Associate Provost Student Success ... Mr. William GUSTAFSON
07 Assist Prov/Exec Dir Admiss/Recruit ... Ms. Joanne GRAZIANO
29 Assoc VP of Development/Alumni Rels ... Ms. Lisa MULVEY
06 Registrar ... Ms. Beth CARSON
21 Bursar ... Mr. Edward A. BOSS, JR.
66 Dean School Health Prof/Nursing ... Dr. MaryAnn CLARK
57 Dean School Visual/Performing Arts ... Dr. Noel ZAHLER
53 Dean Col Education & Info Sciences ... Dr. Robert HANNAFIN
50 Dean College of Management ... Mr. Francis BONSIGNORE
49 Dean College Arts & Sci ... Dr. Katherine HILL-MILLER
15 Human Resources Officer ... Mr. Ronald EDWARDS
88 Dir Higher Educ Opportunity Pgms ... Mr. William CLYDE, JR.
92 Director Honors Program ... Dr. Joan DIGBY
88 Director of Conference Services ... Ms. Theresa DUGGAN
88 Dir Life Leadership Development ... Ms. Alerie TIRSCH
90 Deputy Chief Information Officer ... Ms. Nancy MARKSBURY
88 Director NonTraditional Students ... Ms. Rita JORGENSEN
18 Director of Facilities ... Mr. William KIRKER
19 Director of Public Safety ... Mr. Paul RAPESS
38 Dir Student Health & Counseling ... Mr. William MILFORD
41 Director of Athletics ... Mr. Bryan COLLINS
85 Asst Provost Intl Student Services ... Dr. Jessica HAYES
37 Director Student Financial Aid ... Ms. Karen URDAHL
88 Director of Athletic Fundraising ... Vacant
88 Director of SCALE/ACE Programs ... Ms. Ann WALSH
88 Director of English Lang Programs ... Mr. Joseph GRANITTO
42 Director of Religious Life ... Fr. Ted BROWN
88 Dir Student Conduct & Community Ed ... Mr. Adam GROHMAN
45 Assistant Provost Inst Effectiv ... Mr. John MCLOUGHLIN
88 Director Student Information Center ... Vacant
88 Director Recreational Sports ... Ms. Mary NIGRO
88 Director Learning Support Center ... Ms. Susan ROCK
30 Assoc Director of Development ... Ms. Jennifer GREISOFE
36 Exec Dir Prof Exper & Placement ... Vacant
39 Associate Provost - ISS ... Dr. Jessica HAYES
29 Director Alumni Relations ... Ms. Katherine HOWLETT
07 Director of Graduate Admission ... Ms. Carol ZERAH
88 Director of Academic & Career Plng ... Mr. John MCLOUGHLIN
07 Director of Freshman Admissions ... Mr. David FOLLICK
07 Director of Transfer Admissions ... Ms. Denise SEIGEL
88 Director of Admissions Mktg ... Ms. Catherine CALAME
88 Director Veteran Services ... Mr. Adam GROHMAN

*LIU Riverhead (B)

121 Speonk-Riverhead Road - LIU Bld, Riverhead NY 11901-3499
County: Suffolk Identification: 666174
Unit ID: 450766
Telephone: (631) 287-8010 Carnegie Class: Master's S
FAX Number: (631) 287-8253 Calendar System: Semester
URL: www.liu.edu/riverhead
Established: 2007 Annual Undergrad Tuition & Fees: $31,202
Enrollment: 300 Coed
Affiliation or Control: Independent Non-Profit IRS Status: 501(c)3
Highest Offering: Master's
Program: Liberal Arts And General; Teacher Preparatory
Accreditation: &M, TEAC

02 Associate Provost ... Ms. Jennifer BROWNE
07 Director of Admissions ... Ms. Andrea BORRA

*Long Island University Hudson Graduate Center at Rockland (C)

70 Route 340, Orangeburg NY 10962-2219
County: Rockland Identification: 666077
Unit ID: 192554
Telephone: (845) 359-7200 Carnegie Class: Spec/Other
FAX Number: (845) 359-7248 Calendar System: Semester
URL: www.liu.edu
Established: 1980 Annual Graduate Tuition & Fees: $19,224
Enrollment: 350 Coed
Affiliation or Control: Independent Non-Profit IRS Status: 501(c)3
Highest Offering: Master's; No Undergraduates
Program: Teacher Preparatory; Professional
Accreditation: &M

02 CEO/Dean of Education ... Dr. Sylvia BLAKE

*Long Island University Hudson Graduate Center at Westchester (D)

735 Anderson Hill Road, Purchase NY 10577-1400
County: Westchester Identification: 666078
Unit ID: 432357
Telephone: (914) 831-2700 Carnegie Class: Spec/Other
FAX Number: (914) 251-5959 Calendar System: Semester
URL: www.liu.edu/westchester
Established: 1975 Annual Graduate Tuition & Fees: $24,672
Enrollment: 225 Coed
Affiliation or Control: Independent Non-Profit IRS Status: 501(c)3
Highest Offering: Master's; No Undergraduates
Program: Liberal Arts And General; Teacher Preparatory; Professional
Accreditation: &M, TEAC

02 Dean and Chief Operating Officer ... Dr. Sylvia BLAKE
07 Director of Marketing & Enrollment ... Ms. Cindy PAGNOTTA

Louis V. Gerstner Jr. Graduate School of Biomedical Sciences at Memorial Sloan-Kettering Cancer Ctr (E)

1275 York Avenue, P.O. Box 441, New York NY 10065
County: New York Identification: 666643
Telephone: (646) 888-6639 Carnegie Class: Not Classified
FAX Number: N/A Calendar System: Other
URL: www.sloankettering.edu
Established: 2004 Annual Graduate Tuition & Fees: $34,786
Enrollment: 52 Coed
Affiliation or Control: Independent Non-Profit IRS Status: 501(c)3
Highest Offering: Doctorate; No Undergraduates
Program: Professional
Accreditation: NY

01 President ... Dr. Craig THOMPSON
05 Provost ... Dr. Thomas J. KELLY
20 Dean ... Dr. Kenneth J. MARIANS
88 Associate Dean ... Dr. Linda BURNLEY

Machzikei Hadath Rabbinical College (F)

5407 16th Avenue, Brooklyn NY 11204-1805
County: Kings FICE Identification: 013026
Unit ID: 192624
Telephone: (718) 854-8777 Carnegie Class: Spec/Faith
FAX Number: (718) 851-1265 Calendar System: Semester
Established: 1956 Annual Undergrad Tuition & Fees: $9,100
Enrollment: 139 Male
Affiliation or Control: Independent Non-Profit IRS Status: 501(c)3
Highest Offering: Second Talmudic Degree
Program: Teacher Preparatory
Accreditation: RABN

01 President ... Mr. Alexander SCHAECHTER

Mandl School (G)

254 W 54th Street, 9th Floor, New York NY 10019
County: New York FICE Identification: 007401
Unit ID: 192688
Telephone: (212) 247-3434 Carnegie Class: Assoc/PrivFP
FAX Number: (212) 247-3617 Calendar System: Semester
URL: www.mandl.edu
Established: 1924 Annual Undergrad Tuition & Fees: $24,675
Enrollment: 882 Coed
Affiliation or Control: Proprietary IRS Status: Proprietary
Highest Offering: Associate Degree
Program: Occupational; 2-Year Principally Bachelor's Creditable
Accreditation: ABHES, SURTEC

01 President ... Mr. Melvyn P. WEINER
05 Vice President of Academic Affairs ... Ms. Shanthi KONKOTH
37 VP/Director of Financial Aid ... Mr. Stuart WEINER
88 Director of Compliance ... Ms. Maritza E M. MERCADO
15 Director of Human Resources ... Ms. Phylis STAGNO
55 Academic Dean ... Ms. Allison WRIGHT

36 Director of Career Services ... Mr. James FLANAGAN
06 Dean of Records & Registration ... Mr. Marc WEINER
84 Director of Enrollment Management ... Ms. Randie SENSER
06 Registrar ... Ms. Yana DJIN
07 Director of Recruitment ... Ms. Racquel GARCIA
08 Head Librarian ... Ms. Clover STEELE

Manhattan College (H)

Manhattan College Parkway, Bronx NY 10471-4099
County: Bronx FICE Identification: 002758
Unit ID: 192703
Telephone: (718) 862-8000 Carnegie Class: Master's M
FAX Number: (718) 862-8014 Calendar System: Semester
URL: www.manhattan.edu
Established: 1853 Annual Undergrad Tuition & Fees: $32,625
Enrollment: 3,237 Coed
Affiliation or Control: Independent Non-Profit IRS Status: 501(c)3
Highest Offering: Master's
Program: Liberal Arts And General; Teacher Preparatory; Professional
Accreditation: M, BUS, ENG, TEAC

01 President ... Dr. Brennan O'DONNELL
05 Executive Vice President & Provost ... Dr. William CLYDE
10 VP for Finance & Capital Projects ... Mr. Thomas J. RYAN
32 Vice President Student Life ... Dr. Richard SATTERLEE
30 Vice President College Advancement ... Mr. Thomas MAURIELLO
15 Vice President for Human Resources ... Ms. Barbara A. FABE
18 Vice President for Facilities ... Mr. Andrew RYAN
84 Vice President Enrollment Mgmt ... Mr. William J. BISSET
88 Vice President for Mission ... Br. James WALLACE
20 Assoc Prov Res/Fac/Computer System .. Mr. Walter F. MATYSTIK
35 Assistant VP of Student Life ... Dr. Emmanuel AGO
35 Dean of Students ... Dr. Michael CAREY
39 Director Residence Life ... Mr. Jack GORMLEY
06 Registrar ... Mrs. Luz TORRES
07 Director of Admissions ... Ms. Dana ROSE
35 Director Student Development ... Vacant
08 Director of Libraries ... Ms. Maire I. DUCHON
13 Director of Information Tech Svcs ... Mr. Jake HOLMQUIST
19 Director of Public Safety ... Mr. Juan E. CEREZO
29 Director of Alumni Relations ... Mr. Thomas MCCARTHY
26 Director of Mktg & Communications ... Mrs. Lydia E. GRAY
36 Director Career Svcs/Coop Education ... Vacant
38 Dir of Counseling & Health Services ... Dr. Terence HANNIGAN
41 Director of Athletics ... Mr. Robert J. BYRNES
42 Director of Campus Ministry ... Ms. Lois HARR
44 Director of Development/Advancement ... Mr. Stephen WHITE
78 Director Academic Support Services ... Ms. Marilyn CARTER-STEVENS
40 Director of Campus Bookstore ... Mr. Paul QUILLIN
22 Dir of Personnel/Affirm Action Ofcr ... Ms. Vickie M. COWAN
09 Director of Assessment ... Ms. Judith SLISZ
21 Controller ... Mr. Dennis LONERGAN
21 Business Manager ... Mr. George KUZMA
85 International Student Advisor ... Ms. Debra L. DAMICO
37 Director of Student Financial Svcs ... Mr. Edward KEOUGH
49 Dean of Arts ... Dr. Richard K. EMMERSON
50 Dean of Business ... Dr. Salwa AMMAR
53 Dean of Education ... Dr. William J. MERRIMAN
54 Dean of Engineering ... Dr. Tim WARD
51 Exec Dir Sch Cont & Prof Studies ... Dr. Cheryl HARRISON
88 Director Ctr for Academic Success ... Ms. Marisa PASSAFIUME
81 Dean of Science ... Dr. Constantine THEODOSIOU
88 Dir of Specialized Resource Center ... Ms. Anne VACCARO

Manhattan School of Music (I)

120 Claremont Avenue, New York NY 10027-4698
County: New York FICE Identification: 002759
Unit ID: 192712
Telephone: (212) 749-2802 Carnegie Class: Spec/Arts
FAX Number: (212) 749-5471 Calendar System: Semester
URL: www.msmnyc.edu
Established: 1917 Annual Undergrad Tuition & Fees: $35,140
Enrollment: 959 Coed
Affiliation or Control: Independent Non-Profit IRS Status: 501(c)3
Highest Offering: Doctorate
Program: Professional; Music Emphasis
Accreditation: M

01 President ... Dr. Robert SIROTA
00 Vice President Emeritis ... Mr. Richard E. ADAMS
10 VP Finance & Administration ... Mr. Paul D. KELLEHER
30 Vice Pres External Affairs ... Ms. Susan EBERSOLE
05 Vice Pres Academics & Performance ... Dr. Marjorie MERRYMAN
64 Vice Pres Instrument Performance ... Mr. David GEBER
32 Dean of Students ... Ms. Elsa Jean DAVIDSON
07 Associate Dean for Enrollment Mgt ... Ms. Amy A. ANDERSON
26 Dir Public Rel/Mrktng/Publications ... Ms. Debra KINZLER
15 Director Admin & Human Relations ... Ms. Carol MATOS
06 Registrar ... Mr. David MCDONAGH
39 Dir of Student & Residential Life ... Mr. Wadner AUGUSTE
31 Director of Educational Outreach ... Ms. Rebecca CHARNOW
37 Assoc Dir Student Financial Aid ... Ms. Angela PASQUINI
18 Director of Facilities ... Mr. Frank GRAUPE
29 Director Alumni Affairs ... Mr. John BLANCHARD
08 Director of Library Services ... Mr. Peter CALEB

Manhattanville College (J)

2900 Purchase Street, Purchase NY 10577-2132
County: Westchester FICE Identification: 002760
Unit ID: 192749

Telephone: (914) 694-2200 Carnegie Class: Master's L
FAX Number: (914) 694-2386 Calendar System: Semester
URL: www.mville.edu
Established: 1841 Annual Undergrad Tuition & Fees: $49,886
Enrollment: 1,731 Coed
Affiliation or Control: Independent Non-Profit IRS Status: 501(c)3
Highest Offering: Doctorate
Program: Liberal Arts And General; Teacher Preparatory
Accreditation: M, IACBE, TED

01 President Mr. Jon C. STRAUSS
04 Special Asst to the President Ms. Laura PROSTANO
04 Exec Admin Asst to the President Ms. Deborah A. FALLONE
05 Provost/VP of Academic Affairs Dr. Gail SIMMONS
10 Int VP Finance/Administration Ms. Marina VASARHELYI
84 Vice Pres Enrollment Management Ms. Kathy FITZGERALD
30 Vice Pres Institutional Advancement Mr. Jose GONZALEZ
32 Vice President for Student Life Vacant
11 Vice President of Operations Mr. Gregory PALMER
58 Dean Graduate/Professional Studies Dr. Anthony DAVIDSON
53 Dean School of Education Dr. Shelley WEPNER
26 Mng Dir Media/PR/ Communications Ms. Jennifer JAMES PRYOR
06 Registrar Mr. Thomas MURASSO
85 Director of English Lang Institute Ms. Judith H. LEWIS
08 Director of the Library Mr. Jeff ROSEDALE
37 Director of Financial Aid Mr. Robert GILMORE
23 Exec Dir Hlth Svcs/Counseling Svcs Dr. Pamela DUNCAN
35 Dean of Students Mr. Brandon DAWSON
41 Director of Athletics Mr. Keith LEVINTHAL
42 Int Catholic Chpln/Interfaith Coord Fr. Wil TYRRELL
36 Director Center for Career Devel Ms. Rosalie SHEMMER
29 Dir Alumni Relations/Annual Giving Ms. Teresa WEBER
19 Director of Security Mr. Anthony HERRMANN
30 Director of Development Ms. Nancy KINGSTON
07 Director of Undergrad Admissions Mr. Kevin O'SULLIVAN
09 Director of Institutional Research Ms. Noreen O'HARA
15 Director of Human Resources Mr. Don DEAN
35 Director of Student Activities Ms. Pascha MCTYSON
18 Chief Facilities/Physical Plant Mr. Gregory PALMER
96 Director of Purchasing Ms. Cheryl DOBSON

Maria College of Albany (A)

700 New Scotland Avenue, Albany NY 12208-1798
County: Albany FICE Identification: 002763
Unit ID: 192785
Telephone: (518) 438-3111 Carnegie Class: Assoc/PrivNFP
FAX Number: (518) 438-7170 Calendar System: 4/1/4
URL: www.mariacollege.edu
Established: 1958 Annual Undergrad Tuition & Fees: $10,200
Enrollment: 905 Coed
Affiliation or Control: Independent Non-Profit IRS Status: 501(c)3
Highest Offering: Baccalaureate
Program: Occupational; 2-Year Principally Bachelor's Creditable
Accreditation: M, ADNUR, OTA

01 President Dr. Lea JOHNSON
05 Vice President for Academic Affairs Dr. Margie L. BYRD
10 Director of Business Affairs Mrs. Frances BERNARD
51 Director of Continuing Education Sr. Ellen BOYLE
06 Director of Student Records Dr. Kenneth CLOUGH
07 Director of Admissions Ms. Laurie A. GILMORE
08 Librarian Sr. Rose HOBBS
32 Dean of Student Services Ms. Deborah CORRIGAN
13 Director of Academic Computing Mr. Stephen F. DELORENZO
18 Chief Physical Plant Mr. Andrew PEREZ
36 Director Placement/Alumni Sr. Renee M. CUDHEA
30 Chief Development Mrs. Martha FASHOUER

Marist College (B)

3399 North Road, Poughkeepsie NY 12601-1387
County: Dutchess FICE Identification: 002765
Unit ID: 192819
Telephone: (845) 575-3000 Carnegie Class: Master's L
FAX Number: (845) 471-6213 Calendar System: Semester
URL: www.marist.edu
Established: 1929 Annual Undergrad Tuition & Fees: $29,500
Enrollment: 6,303 Coed
Affiliation or Control: Independent Non-Profit IRS Status: 501(c)3
Highest Offering: Master's
Program: Liberal Arts And General; Teacher Preparatory; Professional
Accreditation: M, BUS, MT, SW

01 President Dr. Dennis J. MURRAY
03 Executive Vice President Dr. Geoffrey L. BRACKETT
05 Vice President for Academic Affairs Dr. Thomas S. WERMUTH
84 VP Admission & Enrollment Planning Mr. Sean P. KAYLOR
30 Vice President College Advancement Mr. Christopher M. DELGIORNO
13 VP Information Technology/ CIO Mr. William T. THIRSK
32 VP/Dean of Student Affairs Mrs. Deborah A. DICAPRIO
10 Vice President Business Affairs/CFO Mr. John P. PECCHIA
20 Assoc VP/ Dean Academic Affairs Dr. John RITSCHDORFF
07 Dean of Undergraduate Admission Mr. Kenton W. RINEHART
88 Dean of Grad and Adult Enrollment Mr. Sean-Michael GREEN
35 Assoc Dean of Student Affairs Mr. Steve SANSOLA
29 Executive Director Alumni Relations Ms. Amy K. WOODS
09 Director Inst Research & Planning Mrs. Susan H. DUNCAN
20 Assoc Dean of Academic Affairs Mrs. Judith IVANKOVIC
37 Exec Dir Student Financial Services Mr. Joseph R. WEGLARZ
08 Director Library Mr. Verne NEWTON
38 Director Counseling Services Ms. Naomi A. FERLEGER
90 Director Academic Technology Mr. Joshua D. BARON
18 Director of Physical Plant Mr. Justin BUTWELL
26 Chief Public Affairs Officer Mr. Gregory CANNON
15 Asst VP for Human Resources Vacant
96 Director of Purchasing Mr. Stephen J. KOCHIS
36 Director Career Services Mr. Stephen W. COLE

Marymount Manhattan College (C)

221 E 71st Street, New York NY 10021-4597
County: New York FICE Identification: 002769
Unit ID: 192864
Telephone: (212) 517-0400 Carnegie Class: Bac/A&S
FAX Number: (212) 517-0541 Calendar System: Semester
URL: www.mmm.edu
Established: 1936 Annual Undergrad Tuition & Fees: $25,688
Enrollment: 1,953 Coed
Affiliation or Control: Independent Non-Profit IRS Status: 501(c)3
Highest Offering: Baccalaureate
Program: Liberal Arts And General
Accreditation: M

01 President Dr. Judson R. SHAVER
88 Assoc to the Pres for Operations Ms. Melissa G. RICHMAN
05 VP Acad Affairs/Dean of Faculty Dr. David PODELL
10 Exec Vice Pres Admin & Finance Mr. Paul CIRAULO
30 VP Institutional Advancement Ms. Marilyn L. WILKIE
32 VP Student Affairs/Dean of Students Dr. Carol JACKSON
21 Associate Vice Pres & Controller Mr. Wayne SANTUCCI
07 Dean of Admissions Mr. James ROGERS
20 Associate Dean for Academic Affairs Dr. Kathleen LEBESCO
06 Registrar Ms. Regina CHAN
15 Director of Human Resources Ms. Bree BULLINGHAM
08 Librarian Ms. Donna HURWITZ
13 Director Information Technology Ms. Patricia HANSEN
37 Director Student Financial Svcs Ms. Maria DEINNOCENTIIS
38 Dir Counseling & Psychological Svcs Dr. Paul GRAYSON
18 Director of Facilities Mr. Pete ROMAIN
35 Asst Dean/Dir Student Activities Ms. Rosemary AMPUERO
36 Director Career Svcs & Internships Ms. Melissa BENCA
96 Director of Purchasing Ms. Maria MARZANO
88 Asst Controller Ms. Melissa SAVINO
29 Dir of Annual and Alumni Programs Ms. Carolyn BOLT

Medaille College (D)

Agassiz Circle, Buffalo NY 14214-2695
County: Erie FICE Identification: 002777
Unit ID: 192925
Telephone: (716) 880-2000 Carnegie Class: Master's L
FAX Number: (716) 884-0291 Calendar System: Semester
URL: www.medaille.edu
Established: 1875 Annual Undergrad Tuition & Fees: $22,678
Enrollment: 2,679 Coed
Affiliation or Control: Independent Non-Profit IRS Status: 501(c)3
Highest Offering: Doctorate
Program: Liberal Arts And General; Teacher Preparatory
Accreditation: M, IACBE, TEAC

01 President Dr. Richard T. JURASEK
05 Vice President for Academic Affairs Dr. Douglas W. HOWARD
10 Vice President Business/Finance Mr. Matthew J. CARVER
30 Vice Pres for College Relations Mr. John P. CRAWFORD
84 VP Enroll Mgmt/Sch Adult & Grad Ed Vacant
07 VP Enroll Mgmt/Undergrad Admissions Mr. Gregory P. FLORCZAK
32 Dean for Student Affairs Ms. Amy M. DEKAY
44 Dir of Major Gifts & Planned Giving Vacant
41 Athletic Director Mr. Peter E. LONERGAN
36 Director Career Planning/Placement Ms. Carol CULLINAN
27 Chief Information Officer Mr. Robert D. CHYKA
06 Registrar Mrs. Kathleen LAZAR
09 Dir of Institutional Research Mr. Patrick S. MCDONALD
08 Library Director Ms. Pamela R. JONES
37 Director Financial Aid Ms. Catherine BUZANSKI
15 Director of Human Resources Ms. Barbara J. BILOTTA
20 Sr Dir Special Academic Services Vacant
18 Director Facilities/Physical Plant Mr. Nate R. MARTON
29 Coordinator of Alumni Relations Vacant
35 Director Ofc of Student Involvement Ms. Melisa L. WILLIAMS
38 Director Counseling Services Ms. Jeannine D. SUK
96 Manager of Purchasing Vacant
26 Director of Communications Ms. Kara M. KANE
19 Director of Campus Public Safety Mr. Ronald J. CHRISTOPHER

Memorial Hospital School of Nursing (E)

600 Northern Boulevard, Albany NY 12204-1004
County: Albany FICE Identification: 012203
Unit ID: 192961
Telephone: (518) 471-3260 Carnegie Class: Assoc/PrivNFP
FAX Number: N/A Calendar System: Semester
URL: www.nehealth.com
Established: N/A Annual Undergrad Tuition & Fees: $7,350
Enrollment: 115 Coed
Affiliation or Control: Independent Non-Profit IRS Status: 501(c)3
Highest Offering: Associate Degree
Program: Nursing Emphasis
Accreditation: NY

01 Executive Director Ms. Linda D'ARCANGELIS

Mercy College (F)

555 Broadway, Dobbs Ferry NY 10522-1189
County: Westchester FICE Identification: 002772
Unit ID: 193016
Telephone: (800) 637-2969 Carnegie Class: Master's L
FAX Number: N/A Calendar System: Semester
URL: www.mercy.edu
Established: 1950 Annual Undergrad Tuition & Fees: $17,556
Enrollment: 11,539 Coed
Affiliation or Control: Independent Non-Profit IRS Status: 501(c)3
Highest Offering: Doctorate
Program: 2-Year Principally Bachelor's Creditable; Liberal Arts And General; Teacher Preparatory; Professional
Accreditation: M, ART, ARCPA, NURSE, OT, OTA, PTA, SP, SW

01 President Dr. Kimberly R. CLINE
05 Provost & Vice Pres Acad Affairs Dr. Concetta STEWART
20 Vice Provost Dr. Graham GLYNN
50 Dean School of Business Dr. Ed WEIS
53 Dean School of Education Dr. Alfred POSAMENTIER
83 Act Dean School Soc/Behavioral Sci Dr. Mary Knopp KELLY
76 Act Dean School Health/Natural Sci Dr. Joan TOGLIA
79 Dean School Liberal Arts Dr. Miriam GOGOL
19 Director of Security Mr. Daniel BRACCIA
11 Chief Operating Officer Mr. Joseph SCHAEFER
84 Vice Pres for Enrollment Management Ms. Deirdre WHITMAN
10 Vice President for Finance Ms. Jeanne PLECENIK
37 AVP for Student Financial Services Ms. Margaret MCGRAIL
30 Exec Dir Institutional Advancement Mr. William MARTINOV
100 Chief of Staff Ms. Irene BUCKLEY
04 Staff Assistant Ms. Grace CREIGHTON
108 Chief Assessment Officer Dr. Nancy PAWLYSHYN
88 Chief Compliance Officer Mr. James MCCUE
43 General Counsel Mr. John GALGANO
15 Associate Dir of Human Resources Mr. David VERNON
07 Senior Director of Admissions Ms. Tara FAY-REILLY
09 Dir Institutional Research/Planning Ms. Victoria TYLER
32 Student Success and Engagement Mr. Andy PERSON
39 Deputy Director PACT/Residence Life Ms. Patricia CHRISTIANO
36 Exec Dir Student Life & Career Svcs Mr. Kevin JOYCE
13 Director of Information Technology Mr. Todd PRATTELLA
06 Exec Director of Registrar Ms. Debra KENNEY
88 Exec Dir Student Svcs Inst Eff Ms. Jessica HABER
21 Director of Business Operations Vacant
21 Controller Ms. Narda ROMERO
45 Director Budget & Planning Mr. Domimick BUMBACO
96 Director of Purchasing Ms. Patricia SABATINO
08 Dean of Libraries/Acad Tech & OL Dr. BRADDLEE
41 Director of Athletics Ms. Patricia KENNEDY
26 Associate Director Public Relations Ms. Lauren GELOSO
29 Director of Alumni Relations Mr. Drew BROWN
44 Advancement Services Officer Ms. Brigette PEREZ
31 Dir Community/Govt/Legal Affairs Ms. Carolyn COTTINGHAM
102 Director of Corporate & Foundations Mr. Terrence HENRY
25 Dir Sponsored Programs Ms. Monique CAUBERE
104 Director Center Global Engagement Dr. Sheila GERCH
106 Mercy Online Director Dr. Mary LOZINA
18 Director of Facilities Ms. Elaine TREFFILETTI

Mesivta of Eastern Parkway Rabbinical Seminary (G)

510 Dahill Road, Brooklyn NY 11218-5559
County: Kings FICE Identification: 009335
Unit ID: 193061
Telephone: (718) 438-1002 Carnegie Class: Spec/Faith
FAX Number: (718) 438-2591 Calendar System: Semester
Established: 1947 Annual Undergrad Tuition & Fees: $11,825
Enrollment: 46 Male
Affiliation or Control: Independent Non-Profit IRS Status: 501(c)3
Highest Offering: Second Talmudic Degree
Program: Teacher Preparatory; Professional
Accreditation: RABN

01 President Rabbi Issac HEIMOVITZ
32 Dean of Students Rabbi Chaim L. EPSTEIN
37 Director of Student Financial Aid Rabbi Ira LIBERMAN
46 Director of Research Rabbi Hersch BASCH
10 Chief Fiscal Officer Rabbi Joseph HALBERSTADT

Mesivta Tifereth Jerusalem of America (H)

141-7 E Broadway, New York NY 10002-6301
County: New York FICE Identification: 003974
Unit ID: 193070
Telephone: (212) 964-2830 Carnegie Class: Spec/Faith
FAX Number: (212) 349-5213 Calendar System: Semester
Established: 1907 Annual Undergrad Tuition & Fees: $12,600
Enrollment: 79 Male
Affiliation or Control: Independent Non-Profit IRS Status: 501(c)3
Highest Offering: Second Talmudic Degree
Program: Teacher Preparatory; Professional
Accreditation: RABN

01 President & Dean Faculties Rabbi David FEINSTEIN

Mesivta Torah Vodaath Seminary (A)

425 E Ninth Street, Brooklyn NY 11218-5299
County: Kings | FICE Identification: 007264
Unit ID: 193052
Telephone: (718) 941-8000 | Carnegie Class: Spec/Faith
FAX Number: (718) 941-8032 | Calendar System: Semester
Established: 1918 | Annual Undergrad Tuition & Fees: $9,250
Enrollment: 192 | Male
Affiliation or Control: Independent Non-Profit | IRS Status: 501(c)3
Highest Offering: Second Talmudic Degree
Program: Teacher Preparatory; Professional
Accreditation: RABN

01 Dean ..... Rabbi Moshe WOLFSON
03 Executive Director ..... Rabbi Yitzchok GOTTDIENER
06 Registrar ..... Rabbi Yonason SHAPIRO
33 Dean of Men ..... Rabbi Elya KATZ
31 Director Community Services ..... Mr. Shraga WERNER

Metropolitan College of New York (B)

431 Canal Street, New York NY 10013-1919
County: New York | FICE Identification: 009769
Unit ID: 190114
Telephone: (212) 343-1234 | Carnegie Class: Master's L
FAX Number: (212) 343-7399 | Calendar System: Semester
URL: www.metropolitan.edu
Established: 1964 | Annual Undergrad Tuition & Fees: $17,230
Enrollment: 1,200 | Coed
Affiliation or Control: Independent Non-Profit | IRS Status: 501(c)3
Highest Offering: Master's
Program: Professional
Accreditation: M, TED

01 President ..... Dr. Vinton THOMPSON
10 EVP Finance & Admininstration/CFO ..... Ms. Sherry HAWN
84 EVP for Enrollment Management ..... Mr. Terence PEAVY
07 Director of Admissions ..... Ms. Patricia RAMOS
58 Dean School Public Affairs & Admin ..... Dr. Humphrey CROOKENDALE
50 Dean School of Business ..... Dr. Tilokie DEPOO
88 Dean Audrey Cohen School Human Svcs ..... Dr. Ruth E. LUGO
35 Dean of Students ..... Ms. Dona SOSA
37 Director of Financial Aid ..... Ms. Andrea DAMAR
06 Registrar ..... Ms. Noreen SMITH
08 Director of Library Services ..... Mr. Jay DATEMA
09 Dir Institutional Rsrch/Assessment ..... Dr. Stephen CHEMSAK
15 Director Human Resources ..... Ms. Judith SANTIAGO
18 Chief Facilities/Physical Plant ..... Ms. Mercedes MELENDEZ
30 Chief Development Officer ..... Ms. Beth DUNPHE
26 Chief Public Relations Officer ..... Ms. Tina GEORGIOU
13 Information Systems Manager ..... Mr. Naftaly KLEINMAN

Mildred Elley (C)

855 Central Avenue, Albany NY 12206
County: Albany | FICE Identification: 022195
Unit ID: 193201
Telephone: (518) 786-0855 | Carnegie Class: Assoc/PrivFP
FAX Number: (518) 786-0890 | Calendar System: Other
URL: www.mildred-elley.edu
Established: 1917 | Annual Undergrad Tuition & Fees: $12,900
Enrollment: 861 | Coed
Affiliation or Control: Proprietary | IRS Status: Proprietary
Highest Offering: Associate Degree
Program: Occupational
Accreditation: ACICS

01 President ..... Ms. Faith A. TAKES

Mirrer Yeshiva Central Institute (D)

1795 Ocean Parkway, Brooklyn NY 11223-2010
County: Kings | FICE Identification: 004798
Unit ID: 193247
Telephone: (718) 645-0536 | Carnegie Class: Spec/Faith
FAX Number: (718) 645-9251 | Calendar System: Semester
Established: 1947 | Annual Undergrad Tuition & Fees: $5,125
Enrollment: 273 | Male
Affiliation or Control: Independent Non-Profit | IRS Status: 501(c)3
Highest Offering: Second Talmudic Degree
Program: Teacher Preparatory; Professional
Accreditation: RABN

00 Chancellor ..... Rabbi Avrohom Yaakov NELKENBAUM
01 President and Dean ..... Rabbi Osher KALMANOWITZ
05 Vice President & Dean ..... Rabbi Osher BERENBAUM
33 Dean of Men ..... Rabbi Esrael ERLANGER
03 Executive Director ..... Rabbi Pinchas HECHT
06 Registrar-Administrator ..... Mrs. Devorah BERENBAUM
08 Director of the Library ..... Rabbi Jacob FELDMANN
38 Director of Guidance ..... Rabbi Yisroel FISHMAN
37 Financial Aid Director ..... Mrs. Rachel BERENBAUM

Mohawk Valley Community College (E)

1101 Sherman Drive, Utica NY 13501-5394
County: Oneida | FICE Identification: 002871
Unit ID: 193283
Telephone: (315) 792-5400 | Carnegie Class: Assoc/Pub-R-L
FAX Number: (315) 792-5666 | Calendar System: Semester
URL: www.mvcc.edu
Established: 1946 | Annual Undergrad Tuition & Fees (In-District): $4,130
Enrollment: 7,643 | Coed
Affiliation or Control: State/Local | IRS Status: 501(c)3
Highest Offering: Associate Degree
Program: Occupational; 2-Year Principally Bachelor's Creditable
Accreditation: M, ADNUR, ENGT

01 President ..... Dr. Randall J. VAN WAGONER
04 Assistant to the President ..... Ms. Jill HEINTZ
88 Exec Dir Organizational Development ..... Mr. John BULLIS
88 Director of Strategic Initiatives ..... Vacant
09 Dir Institutional Research/Analysis ..... Mr. Mark E. RADLOWSKI
05 Vice Pres Learning/Academic Affairs ..... Dr. Maryrose EANNACE
20 Director of Academic Systems ..... Mr. Richard PUCINE
79 Dean of Arts & Humanities ..... Mr. Lewis KAHLER
88 Dean of Language & Learn Design ..... Dr. Jennifer BOULANGER
76 Dean of Life & Health Sciences ..... Dr. Terry SCHWANER
88 Dean of STEM ..... Vacant
50 Dean of Business/Soc Sci & Info Sci ..... Ms. Marianne BUTTENSCHON
08 Director College Libraries ..... Mr. Stephen FRISBEE
24 Dir of Educational Technologies ..... Mr. James LYNCH
11 Vice Pres Administrative Services ..... Mr. Ralph J. FEOLA
32 VP Student Affairs ..... Ms. Stephanie C. REYNOLDS
84 Assoc Dean Enrollment & Advisement ..... Mrs. Jennifer DEWEERTH
36 Assoc Dean Development & Transition ..... Mr. James MAIO
39 Assoc Dean Student & Residence Life ..... Mr. Dennis GIBBONS
12 Dean Rome Campus ..... Dr. Richard QUEST
30 Exec Dir Institutional Advancement ..... Mr. Frank DUROSS
44 Dir of Donor & Resource Development ..... Ms. Deanna FERRO
96 Coord Expend/Fixed Asset Procure ..... Ms. Joyce PALMER
13 Exec Dir of Information Technology ..... Mr. Paul KATCHMAR
31 Exec Dir Ctr Community/Economic Dev ..... Ms. Franca ARMSTRONG
15 Director of Human Resources ..... Mrs. Kimberly EVANS-DAME
26 Director Marketing/Communications ..... Mr. Matthew SNYDER
07 Director of Admissions ..... Mr. Daniel IANNO
37 Director of Financial Aid ..... Mrs. Annette BROSKI
06 Dir of Student Records/Registrar ..... Mrs. Rosemary V. SPETKA
18 Dir of Facilities and Operations ..... Mr. Michael MCHARRIS
19 Director Campus Safety & Security ..... Mr. Joseph PALMER
21 Business Office Controller ..... Mr. Brian MOLINARO
29 Coord Annual Funds/Alumni Relations ..... Ms. Marie KOHL

Molloy College (F)

1000 Hempstead Avenue, PO Box 5002,
Rockville Centre NY 11571-5002
County: Nassau | FICE Identification: 002775
Unit ID: 193292
Telephone: (516) 678-5000 | Carnegie Class: Master's L
FAX Number: (516) 256-2247 | Calendar System: 4/1/4
URL: www.molloy.edu
Established: 1955 | Annual Undergrad Tuition & Fees: $24,420
Enrollment: 4,434 | Coed
Affiliation or Control: Independent Non-Profit | IRS Status: 501(c)3
Highest Offering: Doctorate
Program: Liberal Arts And General; Teacher Preparatory; Professional
Accreditation: M, CVT, MUS, NMT, NURSE, @SP, SW, TED

01 President ..... Dr. Drew BOGNER
05 VP Academic Affairs/Dean of Faculty ..... Dr. Valerie COLLINS
10 Vice Pres for Finance & Treasurer ..... Mr. Michael MC GOVERN
84 Vice Pres Enrollment Management ..... Ms. Linda ALBANESE
30 Vice President for Advancement ..... Mr. Edward J. THOMPSON
32 Vice President Student Affairs ..... Mr. Robert HOULIHAN
45 VP Info Tech/Planning/Research ..... Dr. Robert PATERSON
88 Vice President for Mission ..... Sr. Dorothy FITZGIBBONS
42 Director of Campus Ministries ..... Mr. Scott SALVATO
37 Director Student Financial Services ..... Ms. Sharion SCOTT
36 Director of Career Services Center ..... Ms. June HINTON-DOYLE
41 Director of Athletics ..... Ms. Susan CASSIDY
07 Director of Admissions ..... Ms. Marguerite LANE
37 Director of Financial Aid ..... Mrs. Ana C. LOCKWARD
21 Assistant Treasurer ..... Mr. Anthony PERFETTI
44 Director of Development ..... Ms. Catherine MUSCENTE
06 Registrar ..... Ms. Susan FORTMAN
09 Director of Institutional Research ..... Mr. Michael TORRES
15 Director of Human Resources ..... Ms. Lisa MILLER
18 Director of Facilities ..... Mr. James MULTARI
26 Director Public Relations ..... Mr. Ken YOUNG
96 Director Purchasing & Admin Service ..... Ms. Lorraine JACKSON
35 Director of Campus Life ..... Ms. Janine MCELROY
29 Alumni Relations Officer ..... Dr. Marion FLOMENHAFT
19 Director of Public Safety ..... Mr. Harry HERMAN
85 Director of International Education ..... Ms. Kathleen REBA
105 Director Web Technologies ..... Mr. Keith REDO
24 Director Client Services ..... Mr. Nick SIMONE
20 Director Academic Support Services ..... Ms. Nicolette CEO
88 Director St Thomas Aquinas Program ..... Ms. Pamela BRANHAM
13 Dir Info Tech/Planning/Research ..... Mr. Vincent VENTURA
88 Network Manager ..... Mr. Sean LAURIE

Monroe College (G)

2501 Jerome Avenue, Bronx NY 10468-5407
County: Bronx | FICE Identification: 004799
Unit ID: 193308
Telephone: (718) 933-6700 | Carnegie Class: Master's S
FAX Number: (718) 295-5861 | Calendar System: Semester
URL: www.monroecollege.edu
Established: 1933 | Annual Undergrad Tuition & Fees: $12,848
Enrollment: 7,021 | Coed
Affiliation or Control: Proprietary | IRS Status: Proprietary
Highest Offering: Master's
Program: Liberal Arts And General; Teacher Preparatory; Business Emphasis
Accreditation: M, ACFEI

01 President ..... Stephen J. JEROME
12 Exec VP/Director of Branch Campus ..... Marc M. JEROME
03 Sr Vice Pres Student Financial Svcs ..... James GATHARD
05 Vice President Academics ..... Dr. W. Jeff WALLIS
11 Vice President Administration ..... David DIMOND
10 Sr Vice President for Finance ..... Alan E. MINTZ
84 Vice Pres Enroll Mgmt/Campus Dean ..... Anthony ALLEN
32 Vice President Student Affairs ..... Roberta GREENBERG
58 Dean of Graduate Programs ..... Alex CANALS
20 Assoc Vice President for Academics ..... Dr. Karenann CARTY
20 Dean of Academics New Rochelle Camp ..... Dr. Janice GIRARDI
86 Asst Vice Pres Governmental Affairs ..... Dr. Donald E. SIMON
09 Dean Institutional Research ..... Dr. Edward S. SCHNEIDERMAN
55 Director of Evening Division ..... Allen JENKINS
106 Exec Dir of Online Learning ..... Craig PATRICK
06 Registrar ..... Dr. Edward S. SCHNEIDERMAN
09 Dir Institutional Research ..... Peter NWAKEZE
21 Bursar/Branch Campus ..... Michael NIEDZWIECKI
21 Bursar/Branch ..... Daniel SHARON
35 Dean of Student Services - Branch ..... Stephen SCHULTHEIS
21 Bursar ..... Villan CRUZ
88 Assistant Dean for Student Services ..... Mark SONNENSTEIN
31 Director Auxilliary Services ..... Nivia CAMARA
07 Dean of Admissions Branch ..... Gersom LOPEZ
07 Vice President Admissions ..... Evan JEROME
88 Director Student Fin Aid Compliance ..... Erdene KIMS
36 Assoc VP Ofc of Career Advancement ..... Carol GENESE
36 Dir Ofc of Career Advancement-NR ..... Hillary SULLIVAN
08 Director of Library Services ..... Christine ARTIS
08 Director of Library Services/Branch ..... Angela LAURETANO
24 Director of Learning Center ..... Marie LOFTUS
39 Exec Director of Residential Life ..... Walter EDDIE
29 Director of Alumni Relations ..... Leslie JEROME

Monroe Community College (H)

1000 E Henrietta Road, Rochester NY 14623-5780
County: Monroe | FICE Identification: 002872
Unit ID: 193326
Telephone: (585) 292-2000 | Carnegie Class: Assoc/Pub-U-MC
FAX Number: (585) 427-2749 | Calendar System: Semester
URL: www.monroecc.edu
Established: 1961 | Annual Undergrad Tuition & Fees (In-District): $3,140
Enrollment: 17,699 | Coed
Affiliation or Control: State/Local | IRS Status: 501(c)3
Highest Offering: Associate Degree
Program: Occupational; 2-Year Principally Bachelor's Creditable
Accreditation: M, ADNUR, DA, DH, EMT, ENGT, RAD

01 President ..... Dr. Anne M. KRESS
05 Provost & VP Academic Services ..... Dr. Michael J. MCDONOUGH
72 Vice President Educational Tech Svc ..... Dr. Jeffrey P. BARTKOVICH
32 Vice President Student Services ..... Dr. Susan M. SALVADOR
10 CFO and VP Administrative Svcs ..... Mr. Hezekiah N. SIMMONS
103 VP Econ Dev/Workforce Svc ..... Mr. Todd M. OLDHAM
102 Exec Director MCC Foundation ..... Ms. Diane L. SHOGER
35 Assoc Vice Pres Student Services ..... Mr. Richard H. RYTHER
12 Exec Dean Damon City Campus ..... Dr. Emeterio M. OTERO
26 Asst to the Pres College Relations ..... Ms. Cynthia L. COOPER
35 Asst Vice Pres Student Services ..... Dr. Susan D. BAKER
88 Asst VP Educational Technology Svcs ..... Mr. Dale E. MALLORY
18 Assistant Vice President Facilities ..... Mr. David A. SCHOTTLER
20 Dean Curriculum/Program Devel ..... Mrs. Charlotte M. DOWNING
37 Director Financial Aid ..... Mr. Jerome S. ST. CROIX
09 Director Research ..... Mr. Angel E. ANDREU
08 Interim Director ETS Libraries ..... Ms. Alice E. HARRINGTON WILSON
36 Director Career Center ..... Mr. G. Christopher BELLE-ISLE
21 Asst Vice President Admin Svcs ..... Mr. Darrell K. JACHIM-MOORE
06 Director Registration and Records ..... Ms. Elizabeth R. RIPTON
30 Director of Development ..... Mr. Mark J. PASTORELLA
38 Dir Counseling & Advising ..... Ms. Peggy A. HARVEY-LEE
19 Director Public Safety ..... Mr. David T. MOORE
41 Director Athletics ..... Mr. Dudley (Skip) L. BAILEY
25 Director Grants ..... Ms. Patricia R. WILLIAMS
35 Director of Student Life ..... Ms. Elizabeth J. STEWART
23 Director of Health Services ..... Ms. Donna G. MUELLER
21 Controller ..... Mr. Michael G. QUINN
79 Dean Liberal Arts ..... Ms. Kristen M. FRAGNOLI
50 Dean Science/Health/Business ..... Ms. Laurel T. SANGER
75 Dean Career Technical Education ..... Dr. Javier I. AYALA
88 Interim Dean Interdisc Programs ..... Ms. Catherine E. SMITH
19 Dean Public Safety Training Ctr ..... Mr. Michael S. KARNES
32 Dean Student Services-DCC ..... Dr. Ann V. TOPPING
88 Dean Acad Svcs DCC ..... Dr. Kate M. SCHIEFEN
13 Assoc Dean/Director ETS Computing ..... Mr. Robert G. BERTRAM
16 Asst to President Human Resources ..... Ms. Alberta G. LEE
40 Manager Bookstore ..... Ms. Carol M. FISHER
22 Affirmative Action Officer ..... Ms. Diane M. CECERO
07 Director of Admissions ..... Vacant
88 Director Educ Opportunity Program ..... Ms. Brenda A. SMITH
32 Assoc Director Student Svcs-DCC ..... Mr. Rick F. SADWICK
78 Director Adult/Experiential Lrng ..... Mr. William D. SIGISMOND
43 Legal Counsel ..... Ms. Diane M. CECERO
88 Assoc Director Master Scheduling ..... Ms. Kimberley D. WILLIS
96 Director of Purchasing ..... Mr. Patrick M. BATES

39 Director Housing/Residence Life .... Ms. Shelitha W. WILLIAMS
88 Director of Planning .... Ms. Valarie L. AVALONE
28 Chief Diversity Officer .... Ms. Diane M. CECERO

Mount Saint Mary College (A)

330 Powell Avenue, Newburgh NY 12550-3412
County: Orange FICE Identification: 002778
Unit ID: 193353
Telephone: (845) 561-0800 Carnegie Class: Master's L
FAX Number: (845) 562-6762 Calendar System: Semester
URL: www.msmc.edu
Established: 1959 Annual Undergrad Tuition & Fees: $25,300
Enrollment: 2,710 Coed
Affiliation or Control: Independent Non-Profit IRS Status: 501(c)3
Highest Offering: Master's
Program: Liberal Arts And General; Teacher Preparatory; Professional; Nursing Emphasis
Accreditation: M, NURSE, TED

01 President .... Fr. Kevin MACKIN, OFM
05 Vice President Academic Affairs .... Dr. Iris TURKENKOPF
10 Vice Pres Finance & Admin/Treasurer .... Mrs. Cathleen KENNY
30 Vice Pres for College Advancement .... Mr. Joseph VALENTI
45 Vice Pres for Planning & Assessment .... Dr. Mary HINTON
18 Vice Pres Facilities .... Mr. James RAIMO
32 Vice President for Student Affairs .... Mr. Harry R. STEINWAY
84 VP for Enrollment Management .... Mr. Art CRISS
38 Dir Counseling/Coord Prsns w/Disab .... Dr. Orin STRAUCHLER
20 Associate Dean for Academic Affairs .... Dr. Alice WALTERS
06 Registrar .... Mr. Carlos TONCHE, JR.
07 Acting Director of Admissions ..... Mrs. Nancy SCAFFIDI CLARKE
08 Director of the Library .... Mrs. Barbara W. PETRUZZELLI
37 Director of Financial Aid .... Ms. Barbra WINCHELL
09 Director of Planning and Researach .... Mr. Ryan WILLIAMS
15 Director of Human Resources .... Mr. Lee ZAWISTOWSKI
42 Chaplain .... Fr. Francis AMODIO
35 Director of Student Activities .... Ms. Sandra HENDERSON
39 Exec Dir of Operations and Housing .... Mrs. Elaine O'GRADY
29 Director of Alumni Affairs .... Ms. Michelle A. IACUESSA
41 Director of Athletics & Recreation .... Mr. John WRIGHT
36 Exec Director of the Career Center .... Mrs. Janet ZEMAN
27 Chief Information Officer .... Mr. Dennis RUSH
96 Purchasing Manager .... Mr. Brian MOORE

Mount Sinai School of Medicine (B)

One Gustave L. Levy Place, New York NY 10029-6500
County: New York FICE Identification: 007026
Unit ID: 193405
Telephone: (212) 241-6500 Carnegie Class: Spec/Med
FAX Number: (212) 241-7146 Calendar System: Other
URL: www.mountsinai.org/education
Established: N/A Annual Graduate Tuition & Fees: $35,750
Enrollment: 1,187 Coed
Affiliation or Control: Independent Non-Profit IRS Status: 501(c)3
Highest Offering: Doctorate; No Undergraduates
Program: Professional
Accreditation: M, DENT, IPSY, MED, PH

01 President & CEO .... Dr. Kenneth DAVIS
63 Exec Vice Pres/Dean Sch of Medicine .... Dr. Dennis S. CHARNEY
05 Dean for Medical Education .... Dr. David MULLER

Nassau Community College (C)

1 Education Drive, Garden City NY 11530-6793
County: Nassau FICE Identification: 002873
Unit ID: 193478
Telephone: (516) 572-7501 Carnegie Class: Assoc/Pub-S-SC
FAX Number: (516) 572-7750 Calendar System: Semester
URL: www.ncc.edu
Established: 1959 Annual Undergrad Tuition & Fees (In-District): $4,300
Enrollment: 23,769 Coed
Affiliation or Control: State/Local IRS Status: 501(c)3
Highest Offering: Associate Degree
Program: Occupational; 2-Year Principally Bachelor's Creditable
Accreditation: M, ADNUR, ENGT, FUSER, MLTAD, MUS, PTAA, RTT, SURGT

01 President .... Vacant
03 Exec Vice Pres/Officer in Charge .... Dr. Kenneth K. SAUNDERS
05 Vice President Academic Affairs .... Vacant
11 Vice Pres Facilities Management .... Dr. Joseph MUSCARELLA
10 Vice President Finance .... Mr. James BEHRENS
32 Vice Pres Academic/Student Svcs .... Ms. Maria CONZATTI
22 AVP Equity & Inclusion/AA Officer .... Mr. Craig J. WRIGHT
43 Spec Asst to Pres/College Counsel .... Ms. Donna M. HAUGEN
103 Asst Vice Pres Workforce Devel .... Ms. Janet CARUSO
21 Comptroller .... Ms. Inna REZNIK
13 Dean Management Info Svcs .... Mr. Dennis E. GAI
18 Asst VP Maintenance/Operations .... Mr. Masoom ALI
15 Asst Vice Pres Human Resources . Ms. Deborah REED-SEGRETTI
96 Asst Vice President Procurement .... Mr. Gary HOMKOW
35 Dean of Students .... Ms. Charmian SMITH
09 Assc VP Institutional Effectiveness .... Mr. Frank BILLINGS
37 Dean Financial Aid .... Ms. Patricia NOREN
07 Dean of Admissions .... Ms. Tika ESLER
25 Resource Devel/Grants Fiscal Mgr .... Mr. Edmund KOEPPEL
86 General Counsel for Govt Relations .... Mr. Chuck CUTOLO
26 Director Marketing/Communications .... Ms. Alicia STEGER
08 Director of Library .... Ms. Nancy WILLIAMSON
41 Director Special Pgm Athletics/PED .... Mr. Michael C. PELLICCIA
06 Registrar .... Mr. Chester BARKAN
19 Director of Public Safety .... Mr. Martin RODDINI
23 Director Health Services .... Ms. Ethel FRITZ
36 Director of Placement Testing .... Ms. Noreen WADE
38 Dir Advisement/Special Programs .... Mr. John SPIEGEL
27 Chief Information Officer .... Mr. Richard LAWLESS
102 Exec Director Nassau CC Foundation .... Ms. Dawn DISTEFANO

Nazareth College of Rochester (D)

4245 East Avenue, Rochester NY 14618-3790
County: Monroe FICE Identification: 002779
Unit ID: 193584
Telephone: (585) 389-2525 Carnegie Class: Master's L
FAX Number: (585) 586-2452 Calendar System: Semester
URL: www.naz.edu
Established: 1924 Annual Undergrad Tuition & Fees: $28,330
Enrollment: 3,102 Coed
Affiliation or Control: Independent Non-Profit IRS Status: 501(c)3
Highest Offering: Doctorate
Program: Liberal Arts And General; Teacher Preparatory; Professional
Accreditation: M, MUS, NURSE, PTA, SP, SW, TEAC

01 President .... Dr. Daan BRAVEMAN
04 Assistant to President .... Ms. Patricia GENTHNER
04 Executive Secretary to President .... Ms. Cathleen M. STEVENS
05 Vice President Academic Affairs .... Dr. Sara VARHUS
30 Vice Pres Institutional Advancement .... Ms. Kelly GAGAN
10 Vice President Finance & Treasurer ..... Ms. Maragaret C. FERBER
32 Vice President Student Development .... Mr. Kevin WORTHEN
07 Vice Pres Enrollment Management .... Mr. Thomas R. DARIN
29 Director of Alumni Relations .... Ms. Donna BORGUS
22 Director Multicultural Affairs .... Ms. Gaynelle WETHERS
15 Assoc VP Human Resources .... Mrs. JoEllen PINKHAM
20 Asst VP Academic Affairs .... Dr. Robert MARINO
06 Registrar .... Mr. Andrew MORRIS
37 Director Student Financial Aid .... Ms. Samantha VEEDER
26 Director Marketing & Communications .... Ms. Kathleen PHILBIN
13 Director Information Tech Svcs .... Ms. Karen KUPPINGER
08 Director of Library .... Ms. Catherine DOYLE
19 Director of Security .... Mr. Robert MALDONADO
39 Director of Campus Life .... Ms. Jane KELLY
41 Director of Athletics .... Mr. Peter G. BOTHNER
38 Director of Counseling .... Dr. Malika KAPADIA
42 Director Center for Spirituality .... Ms. Lynne BOUCHER
36 Director of Career Services .... Mr. Michael D. KAHL
18 Director Buildings/Grounds .... Mr. Peter LANA
09 Director of Institutional Research .... Ms. Nancy C. GREAR
23 Director of Health Services .... Ms. Donna WILLOME
20 Director of Academic Advisement .... Ms. Linda SEARING
88 Director of the Arts Center .... Ms. Susan C. LUSIGNAN
21 Bursar .... Mr. John GARBE
88 Dir Patricia Carter Child Care Ctr .... Ms. Mimi BERRY
35 Director of Student Affairs .... Vacant
92 Director Honors Program .... Dr. Susan NOWAK
94 Director Women's Studies Program ..... Dr. Rachel BAILEY-JONES
49 Dean of Col of Arts and Sciences .... Dr. Deborah DOOLEY
76 Dean School of Health & Human Svcs ...... Dr. Shirley SZEKERES
53 Dean School of Education .... Dr. Craig HILL
88 Dean School of Management .... Mr. Gerard ZAPPIA
88 Director of the Casa Italiana ..... Dr. Stella PLUTINO-CALABRESE
88 Exec Dir of Ctr International Educ .... Dr. George EISEN
88 Dir the Ctr for Teaching Excellence .... Vacant
88 Dir of Center for Service Learning .... Dr. Marie WATKINS
89 Dir Stdnt Transition/First Year Ctr .... Ms. Marrlee BURGESS
96 Director of Purchasing .... Ms. Tracy MORAN
88 Exec Dir Center 4 Civic Engagement .... Ms. Nuala BOYLE

The New School (E)

66 W 12th Street, New York NY 10011-8603
County: New York FICE Identification: 020662
Unit ID: 193654
Telephone: (212) 229-5600 Carnegie Class: DRU
FAX Number: (212) 229-5330 Calendar System: Semester
URL: www.newschool.edu
Established: 1919 Annual Undergrad Tuition & Fees: $40,140
Enrollment: 10,797 Coed
Affiliation or Control: Independent Non-Profit IRS Status: 501(c)3
Highest Offering: Doctorate
Program: 2-Year Principally Bachelor's Creditable; Liberal Arts And General
Accreditation: M, ART, CLPSY, SPAA

01 President .... Dr. David VAN ZANDT
05 Provost and Chief Academic Officer .... Mr. Tim MARSHALL
10 CFO & Sr VP for Finance & Business .... Mr. Frank BARLETTA
20 Vice Provost Academic Services .... Dr. Elizabeth ROSS
13 Sr VP for Information Technology .... Ms. Shelley REED
30 VP of Development & Alumni .... Ms. Pamela BESNARD
32 Sr Vice President Student Services .... Ms. Linda REIMER
84 VP of Enrollment Management .... Mr. Bob GAY
26 VP Comm/External Affs .... Mr. Peter TABACK
43 VP/General Counsel & Sec of Corp .... Mr. Roy P. MOSKOWITZ
49 Dean Eugene Lang College .... Ms. Stephanie BROWNER
51 Exec Dean School for Public Engage .... Mr. David SCOBEY
57 Exec Dean Parsons School for Design .... Mr. Joel TOWERS
58 Dean New School for Social Research .... Dr. Michael SCHOBER
64 Dean Mannes College of Music .... Mr. Richard KESSLER
20 Dep Provost & Sr VP Academic Affs .... Dr. Bryna SANGER
88 Sr VP for Distributed & Global Lrng .... Ms. Rosemary MATTHEWSON
88 VP Design/Construction & Facilities .... Ms. Lia GARTNER
20 Vice Provost Acad Planning .... Ms. Pat BAXTER
88 Director The New School for Drama .... Mr. Pippin PARKER
88 Exec Dir Jazz & Contemp Music .... Mr. Martin MUELLER
58 Dean Milano School of Intl Affairs .... Dr. Neil GRABOIS
15 Sr VP for HR & Labor Relations .... Ms. Carol CANTRELL
35 Asst VP for Student & Campus Life .... Mr. Tom MCDONALD
21 VP & Treasurer .... Mr. Steve STABILE
46 Assoc Provost Research Sp Projects .... Dr. Ronald KASSIMIR
21 Asst VP & Controller .... Ms. Natalie PRESSEY
07 Asst VP of Enrollment Systems .... Ms. Lisa MURRAY
37 Director Financial Aid .... Ms. Lisa SHAHEEN
96 Sr Director of Business Operations .... Mr. Ed VERDI
18 Director Facilities Management .... Mr. Thomas WHALEN
08 University Librarian .... Mr. Ed SCARCELLE
09 Assoc Provost Inst Rsrch/Effectiv .... Dr. Paula MAAS
106 Director The New School Online .... Mr. James O'CONNOR
06 Asst VP & University Registrar .... Mr. William KIMMEL
23 LCSW/Asst VP Student Health .... Ms. Tracy ROBIN
36 Director Student Development .... Ms. Shannon LOGAN
28 Director of Intercultural Support .... Ms. Keisha DAVENPORT-RAMIREZ
29 Director Alumni Relations .... Ms. Amy GARAWITZ
39 Asst VP Student Housing & Res Life .... Mr. Robert LUTOMSKI
88 Director of Student Disability Svcs .... Mr. Jason LUCHS
85 Sr Dir International Student Svcs .... Ms. Monique N. NRI

New York Academy of Art (F)

111 Franklin Street, New York NY 10013-2911
County: New York FICE Identification: 026001
Unit ID: 366368
Telephone: (212) 966-0300 Carnegie Class: Spec/Arts
FAX Number: (212) 966-3217 Calendar System: Semester
URL: www.nyaa.edu
Established: 1982 Annual Graduate Tuition & Fees: $30,600
Enrollment: 105 Coed
Affiliation or Control: Independent Non-Profit IRS Status: 501(c)3
Highest Offering: Master's; No Undergraduates
Program: Professional; Fine Arts Emphasis
Accreditation: NY

01 President .... Mr. David KRATZ
05 Dean of Academic Affairs .... Mr. Peter DRAKE
37 Director of Student Financial Aid .... Mr. Andrew MUELLER
32 Director of Student Affairs .... Mr. Elvin R. FREYTES
08 Librarian & Archivist .... Ms. Holly FRISBEE

New York Career Institute (G)

11 Park Place, 4th Floor, New York NY 10007
County: New York FICE Identification: 021634
Unit ID: 195845
Telephone: (212) 962-0002 Carnegie Class: Assoc/PrivFP
FAX Number: (212) 385-7574 Calendar System: Trimester
URL: www.nyci.edu
Established: 1941 Annual Undergrad Tuition & Fees: $13,050
Enrollment: 800 Coed
Affiliation or Control: Proprietary IRS Status: Proprietary
Highest Offering: Associate Degree
Program: Occupational; 2-Year Principally Bachelor's Creditable
Accreditation: NY

01 CEO .... Ivan LONDA
05 Chief Academic Officer .... Al RAGUCCI
32 Director of Student Services .... Cindy MCMAHON
37 Director Financial Aid .... Brenda SORIANO

New York Chiropractic College (H)

2360 State Route 89, Seneca Falls NY 13148-0800
County: Seneca FICE Identification: 012277
Unit ID: 193751
Telephone: (315) 568-3000 Carnegie Class: Spec/Health
FAX Number: (315) 568-3012 Calendar System: Trimester
URL: www.nycc.edu
Established: 1919 Annual Undergrad Tuition & Fees: N/A
Enrollment: 838 Coed
Affiliation or Control: Independent Non-Profit IRS Status: 501(c)3
Highest Offering: First Professional Degree
Program: Professional
Accreditation: M, ACUP, CHIRO

01 President .... Dr. Frank J. NICCHI
05 Exec Vice President & Provost .... Dr. Michael A. MESTAN
10 Vice Pres of Finance/Admin Svcs .... Mr. Sean ANGLIM
20 Dean Academic Affairs .... Dr. J. Nicolas POIRIER
20 Dean of Chiropractic Education .... Dr. Karen A. BOBAK
20 Dean Chiropractic Clinical Educ .... Dr. Wendy L. MANERI
88 Vice Pres Inst Quality/Assessment .... Dr. David R. ODIORNE
06 Registrar .... Mr. Kevin MCCARTHY
84 Vice Pres Enrollment Management .... Ms. Diane DIXON
07 Director of Admissions .... Mr. Michael LYNCH
37 Director Financial Aid .... Mr. Darrin ROOKER
88 Director of Bachelor Prof Studies .... Dr. Kristina L. PETROCCO-NAPULI
46 Dean of Research .... Dr. Jeanmarie R. BURKE
12 Depew Health Center Administrator .... Dr. Michael FLYNN
12 Levittown Health Ctr Chief of Staff .... Dr. Charles HEMSEY
17 Seneca Falls Hlth Ctr Chf of Staff .... Dr. Wendy L. MANERI
51 Dean Post Grad & Cont Educ .... Dr. Thomas VENTIMIGLIA

- 08 Director of the Library ... Ms. Bethyn BONI
- 38 Assoc Director Counseling Services ... Ms. Eve ABRAMS
- 88 Dir Academy Admc Excl Stdnt Success ... Vacant
- 39 Secretary Housing ... Mrs. Janette ELSTER
- 41 Dir Health & Fitness Education ... Mr. Anthony M. PETROCCIA
- 35 Director Student Life ... Ms. Holly Anne WAYE
- 36 Director of Career Development Ctr ... Ms. Susan D. PITTENGER
- 30 Exec Director Devel & Govt Rels ... Vacant
- 29 Director of Alumni Relations ... Ms. Diane ZINK
- 30 Vice President of Inst Advancement ... Mr. Peter R. VANTYLE
- 45 Director Accreditation ... Dr. Beth DONOHUE
- 09 Quality Engineer ... Ms. Patricia MERKLE
- 15 Human Resources Manager ... Ms. Christine MCDERMOTT
- 91 Network Administrator ... Mr. Shane SHOWERS
- 19 Director Facilities/Security ... Mr. William WAYNE
- 96 Assoc VP Admin Svcs/Dir Purchasing ... Mr. Richard B. WORDEN
- 40 Bookstore Manager ... Mrs. Helen STUCK
- 63 Dir MS Clinical Anatomy Pgm ... Dr. Karen GANA
- 76 Dir Applied Clinical Nutrition Pgm ... Vacant
- 88 Dean of FL Sch Acup/Oriental Med ... Mr. Jason WRIGHT
- 88 Dir MS Diagnostic Imaging Program ... Dr. Chad WARSHEL
- 88 Dir Academy for Teaching Excellence ... Dr. Kristina L. PETROCCO-NAPULI
- 12 Campus Health Ctr Chief of Staff ... Dr. Jonathon EGAN
- 12 Rochester Hlth Ctr Chf of Staff ... Dr. Wendy L. MANERI
- 90 Systems Administrator ... Ms. Shelly STUCK
- 24 Educational Tech Administrator ... Mr. Bernard CECCHINI
- 23 Executive Dir of the Hlth Ctrs ... Ms. Jennifer VONHAHMANN
- 21 Controller ... Ms. Karen QUEST
- 88 Director Academy for Prof Success ... Dr. Theresa M. HOBAN
- 88 Dir MS Hum Anat Phys Instructn Pgm ... Dr. Robert A. CROCKER

New York College of Health Professions (A)

6801 Jericho Turnpike, Syosset NY 11791-4413

County: Nassau | FICE Identification: 025994 | Unit ID: 418126
Telephone: (516) 364-0808 | Carnegie Class: Spec/Health
FAX Number: (516) 364-6645 | Calendar System: Trimester
URL: www.nycollege.edu
Established: 1981 | Annual Undergrad Tuition & Fees: $11,880
Enrollment: 736 | Coed
Affiliation or Control: Independent Non-Profit | IRS Status: 501(c)3
Highest Offering: Master's
Program: Professional; Technical Emphasis
Accreditation: NY, ACUP

- 01 President ... Ms. Lisa PAMINTUAN
- 04 Executive Assistant to President ... Ms. Jin WU
- 26 Sr VP Mktg/Comm/Business Oper ... Ms. Barbara CARVER
- 10 Chief Financial Officer ... Mr. Errol VIRASAWMI
- 63 Dean Grad Sch Oriental Medicine ... Dr. A. Li SONG
- 05 Chief Academic Officer ... Dr. Mohammad HASHEMIPOUR
- 88 Dean Sch of Massage Therapy ... Dr. Barry NEWMAN
- 06 Registrar ... Ms. Evelyn LOPEZ
- 88 Senior Admissions Counselor ... Ms. Mary RODAS
- 07 Director Admissions ... Ms. Lucy LUO
- 08 Dir Library/Information Services ... Ms. Cynthia CAYEA
- 21 Bursar ... Ms. Jacqueline MCINTYRE
- 13 Manager Information Technology ... Mr. Vicente CALDAS
- 36 Director of Student Career Services ... Mr. Brian JERAN
- 37 Director Student Financial Aid ... Mr. Ashraf MOURAD
- 88 Dean Sch of Massage Therapy NYC ... Dr. Claire CASSEUS
- 88 Bursar ... Ms. Jacqueline MCINTYRE

New York College of Podiatric Medicine (B)

53 E 124th Street, New York NY 10035-1815

County: New York | FICE Identification: 002749 | Unit ID: 194073
Telephone: (212) 410-8000 | Carnegie Class: Spec/Health
FAX Number: (212) 876-7670 | Calendar System: Semester
URL: www.nycpm.edu
Established: 1911 | Annual Undergrad Tuition & Fees: $27,530
Enrollment: 380 | Coed
Affiliation or Control: Independent Non-Profit | IRS Status: 501(c)3
Highest Offering: First Professional Degree
Program: Professional
Accreditation: POD

- 01 President ... Mr. Louis L. LEVINE
- 05 Dean/Chief Academic Officer ... Dr. Michael J. TREPAL
- 11 Chief Operating Officer ... Mr. Joel STURM
- 10 Chief Financial Officer ... Mr. Greg ONAIFO
- 13 Vice Pres Info Systems & Technology ... Vacant
- 32 Dean Student Affairs ... Dr. Laurence LOWY
- 63 Dean Medical Education/Medical Dir ... Dr. Mark SWARTZ
- 81 Dean Basic Sciences ... Dr. Eileen CHUSID
- 51 Dean Post-Doctorate Education ... Dr. Robert ECKLES
- 20 Dean Clinical Educ/Dir Res Pgms ... Dr. Robert ECKLES
- 09 Dean Institutional Research ... Dr. Eileen CHUSID
- 07 Assoc Dean Admissions/Student Svcs ... Ms. Lisa LEE
- 30 VP of Development & Operations ... Mr. Desander MAS
- 26 Director Public Affairs/Development ... Mr. Roger GREENE
- 15 Dir Human Resources/Risk Management ... Mr. Joel STURM
- 08 Director of Library ... Mr. Thomas WALKER
- 18 Director Safety ... Mr. James WARREN
- 37 Director Financial Aid ... Ms. Eve TRAUBE
- 06 Registrar ... Ms. Vernese PANNELL

New York College of Traditional Chinese Medicine (C)

155 First Street, Mineola NY 11501-4005

County: Nassau | FICE Identification: 034433 | Unit ID: 439783
Telephone: (516) 739-1545 | Carnegie Class: Spec/Health
FAX Number: (516) 873-9622 | Calendar System: Trimester
URL: www.nyctcm.edu
Established: 1996 | Annual Undergrad Tuition & Fees: $15,315
Enrollment: 150 | Coed
Affiliation or Control: Independent Non-Profit | IRS Status: 501(c)3
Highest Offering: Master's
Program: Professional
Accreditation: ACUP

- 01 President ... Dr. Yemeng CHEN
- 11 Administrative Dean ... Dr. James S. BARE
- 05 Academic Dean ... Dr. Sunny SHEN
- 07 Admissions Manager ... Ms. Gail AURICCHIO

New York Institute of Technology (D)

Northern Boulevard, Old Westbury NY 11568-8000

County: Nassau | FICE Identification: 004804 | Unit ID: 194091
Telephone: (516) 686-7516 | Carnegie Class: Master's L
FAX Number: (516) 686-7613 | Calendar System: Semester
URL: www.nyit.edu
Established: 1955 | Annual Undergrad Tuition & Fees: $28,020
Enrollment: 8,306 | Coed
Affiliation or Control: Independent Non-Profit | IRS Status: 501(c)3
Highest Offering: Doctorate
Program: Liberal Arts And General; Teacher Preparatory; Professional
Accreditation: M, ARCPA, CIDA, ENG, ENGT, NURSE, OSTEO, OT, PTA, TED

- 01 President ... Dr. Edward GUILIANO
- 05 Provost/Vice Pres Academic Affairs ... Dr. Rahmat SHOURESHI
- 100 Chief of Staff ... Mr. Peter KINNEY
- 20 Associate Provost Global Programs ... Dr. Jonathan HOGGARD
- 30 Vice President for Development ... Mr. John ELIZANDRO
- 17 Vice Pres Health Sci & Medical Affs ... Dr. Barbara ROSS-LEE
- 32 VP Stdnt Affs/Chief Stdnt Affs Ofcr ... Vacant
- 11 Vice Pres of IT & Infrastructure ... Dr. Niyazi BODUR
- 45 Vice Pres for Planning/Assessment ... Dr. Harriet ARNONE
- 84 Vice Pres Enrollment/Comm & Mktg ... Dr. Jacquelyn NEALON
- 10 CFO & Treasurer ... Mr. Leonard AUBREY
- 21 Comptroller ... Mr. Daniel MCGOVERN
- 43 General Counsel ... Ms. Catherine FLICKINGER
- 06 Registrar ... Ms. Kristen SMITH
- 76 Dean School of Health Professions ... Dr. Patricia CHUTE
- 48 Dean Sch Architecture & Design ... Ms. Judith DIMAIO
- 53 Dean School of Education ... Dr. Satasha GREEN
- 54 Dean School of Engr & Comp Sciences ... Dr. Nada ANID
- 49 Dean School Arts & Sciences ... Dr. Roger YU
- 50 Dean School of Management ... Dr. Jess BORONICO
- 88 Vice Pres Health Affairs ... Dr. Barbara ROSS-LEE
- 35 Dean for Campus Life ... Ms. Francy MAGEE
- 36 Dean of Career Services ... Mr. John HYDE
- 75 Dean Voc Independence Program ... Dr. Ernst VANBERGEIJK
- 09 Director Inst Research & Assessment ... Dr. Carol DEVICTORIA
- 07 Associate Dean of UG Admissions ... Mr. Troy MILLER
- 07 Associate Dean of Admissions ... Ms. Celia PRIETO
- 84 Associate Dean Acad Sppt/Enroll ... Dr. Alexander OTT
- 88 Director Branch Services ... Dr. Gerri FLANZRAICH
- 27 Director Publications & Advertising ... Ms. Susan WARNER
- 29 Director of Alumni Relations ... Ms. Jennifer KELLY
- 18 Director of Facilities Operations ... Mr. William MARCHAND
- 37 Associate Dean of Financial Aid ... Ms. Rosemary FERRUCCI
- 37 Senior Director of Financial Aid ... Ms. Karyn WRIGHT-MOORE
- 19 Director Security ... Mr. Denis MCGUCKIN
- 41 Director Athletics & Recreation ... Mr. Clyde DOUGHTY, JR.
- 25 Asst Provost Spnsrd Pgms & Research ... Dr. Allison ANDORS
- 13 Director Plng & Business Affairs ... Ms. Ajisa DERVISEVIC
- 96 Director Purchasing ... Mr. David UDKOW
- 88 Director of Internal Audit ... Ms. Jessica JONES-NAGLE
- 38 Director Counseling & Wellness Svcs ... Ms. Alice HERON-BURKE
- 88 Dir Advising & Enrichment Pgms ... Ms. Monika SCHUEREN
- 15 Director of Human Resources ... Ms. Carol JABLONSKY
- 90 Director Client Services ... Ms. Laurie HARVEY
- 91 Director Systems & Network ... Mr. Brian MAROLDO
- 91 Director Enterprise Systems & Svcs ... Ms. Chuqian ZHANG
- 35 Assoc Dean Student Development ... Ms. Zennabelle SEWELL
- 40 Bookstore Manager ... Ms. Jayne MO
- 88 Dir Events Planning & Hospitality ... Mr. Jerry LIMONCELLI
- 27 Director of Communications/Edit ... Ms. Bobbie DELL'AQUILO

New York Law School (E)

185 West Broadway, New York NY 10013-2959

County: New York | FICE Identification: 002783 | Unit ID: 193821
Telephone: (212) 431-2100 | Carnegie Class: Spec/Law
FAX Number: (212) 965-8838 | Calendar System: Semester
URL: www.nyls.edu
Established: 1891 | Annual Graduate Tuition & Fees: $49,240
Enrollment: 1,765 | Coed
Affiliation or Control: Independent Non-Profit | IRS Status: 501(c)3
Highest Offering: Doctorate; No Undergraduates
Program: Professional
Accreditation: LAW

- 01 Dean and President ... Dean Anthony CROWELL
- 03 Executive VP & Chief Strategy Ofcr ... Ms. Carole POST
- 05 Assoc Dean for Academic Affairs ... Dean Carol BUCKLER
- 10 Vice President for Finance & Admin ... Dean Fred DEJOHN
- 45 Assoc Dean for Special Projects ... Dean Joan R. FISHMAN
- 45 Assoc Dean for Special Projects ... Dean Harry ALTHAUS
- 26 Vice Pres Communications/Mrktng ... Ms. Nancy J. GUIDA
- 30 Assc Dean/Vice Pres Devel/Alum Rels ... Dean Suzanne DAVIDSON
- 08 Director of Law Library/Assoc Dean ... Prof. Camille BROUSSARD
- 32 Assoc Dean Professional Devel ... Dean Marianna HOGAN
- 88 Director Academic Publishing ... Prof. Jethro K. LIEBERMAN
- 07 Sr Dir Admissions/Financial Aid ... Ms. Susan GROSS
- 21 Asst VP Financial Planning & Mgmt ... Ms. Susan REDLER
- 18 Chief of Maintenance/Operations ... Mr. Donald BLANCHARD
- 15 Associate Director Human Resources ... Ms. Jody PARIANTE
- 19 Assist Vice Pres Security & Safety ... Mr. George HAYES
- 21 Asst Vice Pres Business Operations ... Ms. Catherine MACLEOD
- 09 Asst VP Institutional Research ... Dr. Joanne INGHAM
- 44 Assistant Vice Pres Development ... Ms. Tara REGIST-TOMLINSON
- 29 Assistant Vice Pres Alumni Relation ... Mr. Travis FRASER
- 20 Assistant Dean Academic Affairs ... Ms. Victoria EASTUS
- 06 Assistant Dean and Registrar ... Mr. Oral HOPE
- 58 Assistant Dean of Academic Programs ... Ms. Tracey PARR
- 13 AVP for Information Technology ... Mr. John SOUTHARAD
- 32 Assistant Dean for Student Services ... Ms. Helena PRIGAL
- 36 Asst Dean for Career Planning ... Vacant
- 35 Sr Director of Student Life ... Ms. Sally HARDING
- 20 Assoc Director Academic Affairs ... Ms. Haley MEADE
- 20 Assoc Director Academic Affairs ... Ms. Danielle FRIEDMAN
- 96 Purchasing Coordinator ... Mr. Norman DAWKINS

New York Medical College (F)

Valhalla NY 10595-1690

County: Westchester | FICE Identification: 002784 | Unit ID: 193830
Telephone: (914) 594-4900 | Carnegie Class: Spec/Med
FAX Number: (914) 594-4145 | Calendar System: Other
URL: www.nymc.edu
Established: 1860 | Annual Graduate Tuition & Fees: $47,670
Enrollment: 1,455 | Coed
Affiliation or Control: Independent Non-Profit | IRS Status: 501(c)3
Highest Offering: Doctorate; No Undergraduates
Program: Professional
Accreditation: M, DENT, MED, PH, PTA, SP

- 01 CEO/Exec Dean/Chanc Health Affairs ... Dr. Edward C. HALPERIN
- 10 Sr VP/CFO/Vice Prov Admin & Finance ... Mr. Stephen PICCOLO, JR.
- 58 Dean Grad Sch Basic Medical Science ... Dr. Francis L. BELLONI
- 43 Vice President/General Counsel ... Mr. Waldemar A. COMAS
- 30 Vice President Univ Dev/Alumni Rels ... Ms. Julie KUBASKA
- 86 Vice President Government Affairs ... Dr. Robert W. AMLER
- 15 Assoc Vice Pres Human Resources ... Mr. Peter M. BROWN
- 21 Assoc Vice Pres/Controller ... Mr. George NESTLER
- 43 Assoc Vice Pres Legal Affairs ... Ms. Dana LEE
- 26 Assoc Vice Pres Communications ... Ms. Donna E. MORIARTY
- 11 Vice Prov/Sr Assoc Dean Acad Admin ... Mr. William A. STEADMAN, II
- 27 Chief Information Officer ... Dr. Sandra SHIVERS
- 76 Dean Sch Health Sciences & Practice ... Dr. Robert W. AMLER
- 63 Vice Dean Grad Med Ed/Affiliations ... Dr. Richard G. MCCARRICK
- 09 Assoc Dean Research Administration ... Ms. Catharine CREA
- 32 Sr Assoc Dean Student Affairs ... Dr. Gladys M. AYALA
- 37 Asc Dn Stdnt Affs/Dir Finan Plng ... Mr. Anthony M. SOZZO
- 88 Sr Assoc Dean Pre-Internship Pgm ... Dr. Saverio S. BENTIVEGNA
- 07 Sr Associate Dean Admissions ... Dr. Fern R. JUSTER
- 51 Assoc Dean Continuing Med Education ... Dr. Joseph F. DURSI
- 08 Assoc Dean/Dir Health Sci Library ... Ms. Diana J. CUNNINGHAM
- 07 Director of Admissions ... Ms. Robin BAUM
- 06 University Registrar/Assoc Provost ... Ms. Judith A. EHREN
- 39 Director Student Housing ... Ms. Amy SCHACK
- 18 Director Facilities Management ... Mr. Michael J. SHALLO
- 19 Director of Security ... Mr. William ALLISON
- 85 Intl Student/Scholar Advisor ... Ms. Elizabeth WARD
- 51 Director of Continuing Medical Educ ... Ms. Kathy J. KAVANAGH
- 04 Asst to Pres & Board of Trustees ... Ms. Patricia J. TRAVIS
- 23 Director Health Services ... Dr. Joseph F. DURSI
- 38 Director Student Counseling ... Dr. Mark SINGER
- 105 Director Web Services ... Mr. Kevin R. CUMMINGS
- 40 Director Bookstore ... Ms. Liz REYNOLDS
- 24 Head Educational Media ... Mr. Michael COTTER
- 13 Coord of Instruct Computing Tech ... Mr. Jason DI NARDI
- 96 Purchasing Manager ... Mr. John STEIN

New York School of Interior Design (G)

170 East 70th Street, New York NY 10021-5110

County: New York | FICE Identification: 020690 | Unit ID: 194116
Telephone: (212) 472-1500 | Carnegie Class: Spec/Arts
FAX Number: (212) 472-3800 | Calendar System: 4/1/4
URL: www.nysid.edu
Established: 1916 | Annual Undergrad Tuition & Fees: $27,300
Enrollment: 700 | Coed
Affiliation or Control: Independent Non-Profit | IRS Status: 501(c)3
Highest Offering: Master's
Program: Professional
Accreditation: @M, ART, CIDA

- 01 Acting President/Executive VP ... Mr. David SPROULS

05 Dean ... Dr. Ellen FISHER
10 VP for Finance & Administration ... Ms. Jane CHEN
32 Dean of Students ... Ms. Karen HIGGINBOTHAM
04 Assistant to the President ... Ms. Jeanne KO
36 Academic Advisor/Dir Career Place ... Ms. Patricia ZIEGLER
06 Registrar ... Ms. Susan LOVELL
08 Director of the Library ... Ms. Sarah FALLS
07 Director of Admissions ... Ms. Celeste COLLINS
37 Financial Aid Administrator ... Ms. Rashmi WADHVANI
15 Director of Personnel Services ... Ms. Balbina CALO
18 Chief Facilities/Physical Plant ... Mr. Zeke KOLENOVIC
26 Director of External Relations ... Ms. Samantha HOOVER
30 Chief Development/Dir Alumni Rels ... Vacant
20 Associate Dean ... Ms. Veronica WHITLOCK
29 Director Alumni Relations ... Vacant
13 Dir Computing/Information Mgmt ... Mr. Tomasz SOWINSKI
90 Director Academic Computing ... Mr. Richard T. CLASS
40 Director Bookstore ... Mr. Daniel TERCHEK
38 Director Student Counseling ... Dr. Penny MORGANSTEIN
09 Director of Institutional Research ... Mr. Greg LINCOLN

New York Theological Seminary (A)

475 Riverside Drive, Suite 500, New York NY 10115-0083
County: New York FICE Identification: 002674
Unit ID: 193894
Telephone: (212) 870-1211 Carnegie Class: Not Classified
FAX Number: (212) 870-1236 Calendar System: Semester
URL: www.nyts.edu
Established: 1900 Annual Graduate Tuition & Fees: $13,430
Enrollment: 400 Coed
Affiliation or Control: Independent Non-Profit IRS Status: 501(c)3
Highest Offering: Doctorate; No Undergraduates
Program: Professional
Accreditation: THEOL

01 President ... Dr. Dale T. IRVIN
30 VP Development/Institutional Advanc ... Vacant
05 Academic Dean ... Dr. Eleanor MOODY-SHEPHERD
08 Librarian ... Mr. Jerry REISIG
06 Registrar ... Ms. Lydia R. BUMGARDNER
37 Director Financial Aid ... Ms. Tamisia WHITE

New York University (B)

70 Washington Square S, New York NY 10012-1092
County: New York FICE Identification: 002785
Unit ID: 193900
Telephone: (212) 998-1212 Carnegie Class: RU/VH
FAX Number: N/A Calendar System: Semester
URL: www.nyu.edu
Established: 1831 Annual Undergrad Tuition & Fees: $43,204
Enrollment: 43,911 Coed
Affiliation or Control: Independent Non-Profit IRS Status: 501(c)3
Highest Offering: Doctorate
Program: Occupational; 2-Year Principally Bachelor's Creditable; Liberal Arts And General; Teacher Preparatory; Professional
Accreditation: M, BUS, COPSY, DENT, DH, DIETD, DIETI, DMS, HSA, IPSY, JOUR, LAW, MED, MIDWF, NURSE, OT, PH, PLNG, PTA, SCPSY, SP, SPAA, SURGT, SW, TEAC

01 President ... Dr. John SEXTON
05 Provost ... Dr. David MCLAUGHLIN
03 Executive VP ... Dr. Michael ALFANO
17 Executive VP for Health ... Dr. Robert BERNE
100 Chief of Staff/Deputy to President ... Ms. Diane YU
43 Sr VP General Counsel & Secretary ... Ms. Bonnie BRIER
26 Sr VP for Univ Rels/Pub Affairs ... Dr. Lynne BROWN
10 Sr VP for Finance & Budget ... Dr. Martin DORPH
20 Sr Vice Provost Academic Policies ... Dr. Pierre HOHENBERG
46 Sr Vice Provost for Research ... Dr. Paul HORN
30 Sr VP Development/Alumni Relations ... Ms. Debra LAMORTE
18 Sr VP for Operations ... Ms. Alison LEARY
32 Sr Vice Provost Ugrad Ed/Univ Life ... Dr. Linda MILLS
20 Provost Polytech Inst at NYU ... Dr. Katepalli SREENIVASAN
18 VP Construction Management ... Mr. David ALONSO
26 VP for Public Affairs ... Mr. John BECKMAN
45 VP Public Resource Admin & Devel ... Dr. Richard BING
15 VP for Human Resources ... Ms. Catherine CASEY
84 VP Enrollment Management ... Dr. Randall DEIKE
13 VP for Global Technology ... Mr. Thomas DELANEY
11 VP for Admin/Chief of Staff ... Mr. A. Steven DONOFRIO
86 VP Gov Affairs/Community Engagement ... Dr. Alicia HURLEY
21 VP Budget & Planning ... Mr. Anthony JIGA
40 VP for Auxiliary Services ... Dr. Robert KIVETZ
21 VP Finance Operations ... Ms. Stephanie PIANKA
19 VP Global Security & Crisis Mgmt ... Mr. Jules MARTIN
13 VP IT and CITO for NYU NY Campus ... Ms. Marilyn MCMILLAN
06 University Registrar ... Dr. Roger PRINTUP
21 Chief Investment Officer ... Ms. Tina SURH
35 VP for Student Affairs ... Dr. Marc WAIS
88 VP Acad/Fac/Rsrch Affairs ... Ms. C. Cybele RAVER
26 Assoc VP for Marketing Comm ... Ms. Deborah BRODERICK
21 Assoc VP for Finance ... Vacant
88 Assoc Vice Provost Rsrch Compliance ... Dr. Martha DUNNE
96 Assoc VP Administrative Services ... Mr. Charles SCHOTT
88 Assoc VP Planning and Design ... Ms. Lori MAZOR
20 Assoc Vice Provost Acad Initiatives ... Dr. Nancy MORRISON
20 Assoc Provost Academic Operations ... Dr. Carol KLAPERMAN MORROW
88 Assoc VP Real Estate Services ... Mr. David SOLES
07 Asst VP for Undergrad Admissions ... Mr. Shawn ABBOTT
20 Asst Provost Academic Pgm Review ... Mr. Barnett HAMBERGER
28 Asst VP Diversity/Stdnt Comm Devel ... Mr. Allen MCFARLANE
21 Asst Treasurer/Bursar ... Vacant
21 Asst VP/Controller ... Ms. Kerri TRICARICO
41 Dir Athletics/Recreation/Intr Sport ... Mr. Christopher BLEDSOE
23 Deputy Exec Dir & Medical Dir ... Dr. Carlo CIOTOLI
09 Dir Institutional Research ... Dr. Randall DEIKE
37 Dir Financial Aid ... Ms. Lynn HIGINBOTHAM
102 Dir Office of Sponsored Programs ... Mr. Richard LOUTH
88 Dir Internal Audit ... Mr. Eugene PAWLOWSKI
22 Exec Dir Ofc of Equal Opportunity ... Ms. Mary SIGNOR
36 Exec Dir Career Services ... Ms. Trudy STEINFELD

Niagara County Community College (C)

3111 Saunders Settlement Road, Sanborn NY 14132-9460
County: Niagara FICE Identification: 002874
Unit ID: 193946
Telephone: (716) 614-6200 Carnegie Class: Assoc/Pub-S-SC
FAX Number: (716) 614-6700 Calendar System: Semester
URL: www.niagaracc.suny.edu
Established: 1962 Annual Undergrad Tuition & Fees (In-District): $3,958
Enrollment: 7,177 Coed
Affiliation or Control: State/Local IRS Status: 501(c)3
Highest Offering: Associate Degree
Program: Occupational; 2-Year Principally Bachelor's Creditable
Accreditation: M, ADNUR, MAC, PTAA, RAD, SURGT

01 President ... Dr. James KLYCZEK
05 Vice President Academic Affairs ... Dr. Gregory LAMONTAGNE
103 VP Workforce Development ... Vacant
10 Vice President of Finance/Info Tech ... Mr. William SCHICKLING
32 Vice President of Student Services ... Dr. Bassam DEEB
11 Vice President of Operations ... Mr. Michael DOMBROWSKI
09 Director Planning and Research ... Dr. Mary Jane FELDMAN
20 Associate Dean ... Vacant
15 Interim Director of Human Resources ... Mr. Donald ARMSTRONG
07 Director of Admissions ... Ms. Kathy SAUNDERS
21 Director of Business Services ... Ms. Theresa DIGREGORIO
04 Assistant to President ... Ms. Barbara WALCK
06 Registrar ... Ms. Julie SPEER
35 Director of Student Development ... Mrs. Allison ARMUSEWICZ
30 Chief Development Officer ... Ms. Deborah BREWER
37 Director of Financial Aid ... Mr. James TRIMBOLI
26 Director Public Relations ... Ms. Paula SANDY
18 Assistant Director of Facilities ... Mr. James LOBDELL
28 Interim Director of Diversity ... Mr. Donald ARMSTRONG

Niagara University (D)

Niagara University NY 14109-9999
County: Niagara FICE Identification: 002788
Unit ID: 193973
Telephone: (716) 285-1212 Carnegie Class: Master's L
FAX Number: (716) 286-8710 Calendar System: Semester
URL: www.niagara.edu
Established: 1856 Annual Undergrad Tuition & Fees: $27,230
Enrollment: 4,182 Coed
Affiliation or Control: Independent Non-Profit IRS Status: 501(c)3
Highest Offering: Doctorate
Program: Liberal Arts And General; Teacher Preparatory; Professional
Accreditation: M, BUS, NURSE, SW, TED

01 President ... Rev. Joseph LEVESQUE, CM
03 Exec Vice President ... Dr. Bonnie ROSE
05 Vice President for Academic Affairs ... Dr. Timothy M. DOWNS
32 Vice President for Student Affairs ... Dr. Kevin HEARN
10 Vice Pres Business Aff & Treasurer ... Mr. Michael S. JASZKA
30 Vice Pres Institutional Advancement ... Mr. Donald P. BIELECKI
20 Asc VP Academic Affs/Pgms & Policy ... Dr. Marilynn P. FLECKENSTEIN
20 Assoc VP Acad Affs/Ops/Outreach ... Ms. Mary E. BORGOGNONI
44 Assoc VP for Institutional Advance ... Mr. J. Patrick HULSMAN
45 Asst to the President for Planning ... Dr. Judith A. WILLARD
43 General Counsel ... Ms. Stephanie A. COLE
06 Registrar/Dean of Enrollment Mgmt ... Mr. Michael J. KONOPSKI
09 Director Institutional Research ... Ms. Catherine E. SERIANNI
07 Director of Admissions ... Mr. Harry GONG
08 Director of Libraries ... Mr. David SCHOEN
19 Director of Campus Safety ... Mr. John F. BARKER
35 Dean of Student Affairs ... Ms. Carrie MCLAUGHLIN
37 Director Student Financial Aid ... Ms. Maureen SALFI
39 Director of Residence Life ... Vacant
26 Assoc VP of Comm/Public Relations ... Mr. Thomas BURNS
29 Director of Alumni Association ... Mr. Arthur V. CARDELLA
13 Director Information Technology ... Mr. Richard P. KERNIN
49 Dean College of Arts & Science ... Dr. Nancy E. MCGLEN
53 Dean College of Education ... Dr. Debra A. COLLEY
50 Dean College Business Admin ... Dr. Shawn p. DALY
88 Dean Col Hospitality/Tourism Mgmt ... Dr. Gary D. PRAETZEL
57 Director of Art Museum ... Ms. Kate KOPERSKI
15 Director of Human Resources ... Mr. Robert PFEIL
23 Director of Health Services ... Ms. Lori SOOS
41 Director of Athletics ... Mr. Ed MCLAUGHLIN
18 Director of Facility Services ... Mr. Daniel M. GUARIGLIA
44 Director Annual Fund ... Ms. Christine S. O'HARA
42 Assoc VP of Campus Ministry ... Rev. Kevin KREAGH, CM
88 Director of Academic Support ... Mrs. Diane STOELTING
51 Dir Continuing/Community Education ... Mr. Jon Jay STOCKSLADER
38 Director Counseling Services ... Monica ROMEO
21 Controller ... Mr. Donald E. SMITH
96 Director of Business Services ... Ms. Christy FERGUSON
88 Assoc Dean for Graduate Recruitment ... Mr. Carlos TEJADA
88 Assoc Dean for Transfer Recruitment ... Mr. Mark WOJNOWSKI
88 Exec Dir Division of Academic Svcs ... Ms. Antonia KNIGHT
88 Director of Instructional Support ... Dr. Jennifer HERMAN
85 Dir Multicultural & Intl Stdnt Affs ... Mr. David BLACKBURN
06 Director of Records & Operations ... Ms. Lenora ANDREWS
88 Director of Student Accounts ... Ms. Martie HOWELL
25 Dir of Sponsored Programs & Rsrch ... Ms. Adrienne LEIBOWITZ
102 Dir Corporate & Foundations ... Ms. Denise Z. RIVERS
36 Director of Career Services ... Mr. Robert P. SWANSON
88 Director of Academic Exploration ... Ms. Stephanie CURRIE
88 Director of Lean and Serve ... Ms. Fran BOLTZ

North Country Community College (E)

23 Santanoni Avenue, PO Box 89,
Saranac Lake NY 12983-0089
County: Essex FICE Identification: 007111
Unit ID: 194028
Telephone: (518) 891-2915 Carnegie Class: Assoc/Pub-R-S
FAX Number: (518) 891-2915 Calendar System: Semester
URL: www.nccc.edu
Established: 1967 Annual Undergrad Tuition & Fees (In-District): $4,700
Enrollment: 2,454 Coed
Affiliation or Control: State/Local IRS Status: 501(c)3
Highest Offering: Associate Degree
Program: Occupational; 2-Year Principally Bachelor's Creditable
Accreditation: M, RAD

01 President ... Dr. Steve J. TYRELL
05 Vice Pres of Academic Affairs ... Dr. Carole RICHARDSON
10 Vice Pres for Fiscal Operations/CFO ... Mr. William CHAPIN
84 VP Enroll/Stdnt Svcs/Asst to Pres ... Mr. Edwin TRATHEN
06 Registrar/Records Officer ... Ms. Erika SWAIN
09 Asst Dean Inst Research/Support ... Mr. Scott HARWOOD
18 Asst Dean Facilities/Spec Projects ... Mr. Jim JACKSON
07 Dir Admiss/Alumni Rels/Chf PR Ofcr ... Mr. Edwin TRATHEN
35 Director of Campus & Student Life ... Mrs. Roberta KARP

Northeastern Seminary (F)

2265 Westside Drive, Rochester NY 14624-1932
County: Monroe FICE Identification: 034194
Unit ID: 439817
Telephone: (585) 594-6800 Carnegie Class: Spec/Faith
FAX Number: (585) 594-6801 Calendar System: Semester
URL: www.nes.edu
Established: 1998 Annual Graduate Tuition & Fees: $8,234
Enrollment: 153 Coed
Affiliation or Control: Independent Non-Profit IRS Status: 501(c)3
Highest Offering: Doctorate; No Undergraduates
Program: Professional; Religious Emphasis
Accreditation: M, NY, THEOL

01 President ... Dr. John A. MARTIN
05 Academic Vice President and Dean ... Dr. Douglas CULLUM

† The Seminary is affiliated with Roberts Wesleyan College.

Nyack College (G)

1 South Boulevard, Nyack NY 10960-3698
County: Rockland FICE Identification: 002790
Unit ID: 194161
Telephone: (845) 675-4400 Carnegie Class: Master's L
FAX Number: (845) 358-1751 Calendar System: Semester
URL: www.nyack.edu
Established: 1882 Annual Undergrad Tuition & Fees: $22,500
Enrollment: 3,140 Coed
Affiliation or Control: The Christian And Missionary Alliance
IRS Status: 501(c)3
Highest Offering: Doctorate
Program: 2-Year Principally Bachelor's Creditable; Liberal Arts And General; Teacher Preparatory; Professional
Accreditation: M, MUS, SW, TED, THEOL

01 President ... Dr. Michael G. SCALES
04 Assistant to the President ... Mrs. Carol Ann FREEMAN
05 Provost/VP for Academic Affairs ... Dr. David F. TURK
10 Exec Vice President & Treasurer ... Mr. David C. JENNINGS
84 Vice President for Enrollment ... Dr. Andrea HENNESSY
30 Vice President of Advancement ... Mr. Jeff CORY
20 Assistant Provost ... Dr. Bennett SCHEPENS
73 Dean Seminary ... Dr. Ronald WALBORN
50 Dean School of Business & Ldrshp ... Dr. Anita UNDERWOOD
64 Dean School of Music ... Dr. Glenn KOPONEN
53 Dean School of Education ... Dr. JoAnn LOONEY
49 Assoc Dean College of Arts & Sci ... Dr. Fernando ARZOLA
04 Asst to Pres/Dean of NCDC ... Dr. Richard GATHRO
08 Dean of Library Services ... Mrs. Linda K. POSTON
89 Assoc Dean Student Success ... Dr. Gwen PARKER AMES
73 Assoc Dean Seminary (NYC) ... Dr. Luis CARLO
73 Asst Dean Seminary (Puerto Rico) ... Dr. Julio APONTE
32 Dean of Students ... Mrs. Wanda VELEZ
06 Undergraduate Registrar ... Ms. Evangeline COUCHEY
06 Graduate Registrar ... Ms. Rebecca NOSS
07 Dir of Admissions Undergrad ... Mr. Dinesh MAHTANI
07 Dir of Admissions Undergrad (NYC) ... Mrs. Leslie ROSADO
07 Dir of Admissions Seminary ... Mrs. Traci PIESCKI

21 Assistant Treasurer ... Mrs. Dona P. SCHEPENS
37 Dir of Fin Svcs Undergrad ... Mr. Steve PHILLIPS
37 Dir of Fin Svcs Undergrad (NYC) ... Mr. Isaac FOSTER
31 Executive Director of Community Rel ... Mr. Earl MILLER
41 Director of Athletics ... Mr. Keith A. DAVIE
36 Director of Career Services ... Ms. Tiffany AUSTIN
15 Director of Human Resources ... Mrs. Karen DAVIE
13 Director of Information Technology ... Mr. Kevin A. BUEL
09 Director of Institutional Research ... Mr. Greg BEEMAN
18 Director of Operations/Aramark ... Mr. Douglas WALKER
26 Director of Pub & Media Relations ... Ms. Deborah WALKER
42 Director of Spiritual Formation ... Mrs. Wanda F. WALBORN
38 Director of Wellness Services ... Mrs. Drusila F. NIEVES
29 Coordinator of Alumni Services ... Mrs. Melissa HICKEY
105 Webmaster ... Mr. Joshua WAY

Ohr Hameir Theological Seminary (A)

141 Furnace Woods Road,
Cortlandt Manor NY 10567-6112

County: Westchester FICE Identification: 011984
Unit ID: 194189
Telephone: (914) 736-1500 Carnegie Class: Spec/Faith
FAX Number: (914) 736-1055 Calendar System: Semester
Established: 1962 Annual Undergrad Tuition & Fees: $8,300
Enrollment: 119 Male
Affiliation or Control: Independent Non-Profit IRS Status: 501(c)3
Highest Offering: Second Talmudic Degree
Program: Teacher Preparatory; Professional
Accreditation: RABN

01 President ... Rabbi E. KANAREK
30 Chief Devel Ofcr/Dir Financial Aid ... Mr. Naftoly KEMPLER
06 Registrar ... Rabbi Berel KANAREK

Ohr Somayach Tanenbaum Educational Center (B)

244 Route 306, Monsey NY 10952-0334

County: Rockland FICE Identification: 023201
Unit ID: 243805
Telephone: (845) 425-1370 Carnegie Class: Not Classified
FAX Number: (845) 425-8865 Calendar System: Trimester
URL: www.os.edu
Established: 1979 Annual Undergrad Tuition & Fees: $7,250
Enrollment: 50 Coordinate
Affiliation or Control: Independent Non-Profit IRS Status: 501(c)3
Highest Offering: First Professional Degree
Program: Professional
Accreditation: RABN

01 Director ... Rabbi Abraham BRAUN
05 Dean ... Rabbi Israel ROKOWSKY
06 Registrar ... Mrs. Miriam GROSSMAN
10 Chief Business Officer ... Rabbi Eli ROKOWSKY

Olean Business Institute (C)

301 N Union Street, Olean NY 14760-2691

County: Cattaraugus FICE Identification: 009003
Unit ID: 194204
Telephone: (716) 372-7978 Carnegie Class: Assoc/PrivFP
FAX Number: (716) 372-2120 Calendar System: Semester
URL: www.obi.edu
Established: 1961 Annual Undergrad Tuition & Fees: $11,800
Enrollment: 75 Coed
Affiliation or Control: Proprietary IRS Status: Proprietary
Highest Offering: Associate Degree
Program: Occupational; 2-Year Principally Bachelor's Creditable; Business Emphasis
Accreditation: ACICS

01 President/Academic Dean ... Mrs. Jennifer L. MADISON
37 Director of Financial Aid ... Mrs. Valerie A. GOODWIN
07 Director of Admissions & Placement ... Mr. Carl J. ENGLISH
08 Librarian ... Ms. Charlotte STOUGHTON
10 Business Manager ... Mrs. Debra J. RALSTON

Onondaga Community College (D)

4585 West Seneca Turnpike, Syracuse NY 13215-4585

County: Onondaga FICE Identification: 002875
Unit ID: 194222
Telephone: (315) 498-2622 Carnegie Class: Assoc/Pub-U-MC
FAX Number: (315) 492-9208 Calendar System: Semester
URL: www.sunyocc.edu
Established: 1962 Annual Undergrad Tuition & Fees (In-District): $4,634
Enrollment: 12,746 Coed
Affiliation or Control: State/Local IRS Status: 501(c)3
Highest Offering: Associate Degree
Program: Occupational; 2-Year Principally Bachelor's Creditable
Accreditation: M, ADNUR, ENGT, PTAA, SURGT

01 Interim President ... Ms. Margaret M. O'CONNELL
05 Provost and SVP Educational Svcs ... Dr. Cathleen C. MCCOLGIN
10 SVP College-affltd Ent & Asset Mgmt ... Mr. David W. MURPHY
30 Vice President Development ... Mr. John ZACHAREK
26 VP HR & External Affairs ... Ms. Amy KREMENEK
09 Chief Inst Plng/Assess/Resrch Ofcr ... Dr. Agatha AWUAH
14 Chief Information Officer ... Ms. Andrea VENUTI
20 Int VP Academic Services ... Dr. Emmanuel AWUAH
84 VP Enrollment Mgmt & Student Dev ... Dr. Kristine DUFFY
28 Int VP Curr & Instr Supp Diversity ... Ms. Eunice WILLIAMS
18 VP Facilities Management ... Mr. John PADDOCK
37 Director of Student Finance ... Ms. Kate BELLEFEUILLE
41 Athletic Director ... Mr. Rob EDSON
88 Director Student Svcs Initiatives ... Ms. Nancy J. HAZZARD
08 Chair Library ... Ms. Pauline SHOSTACK
38 Chair Counseling Department ... Mr. Timothy SINGER
19 VP Campus Safety & Security ... Mr. Douglas KINNEY
88 Disability Services Specialist ... Ms. Nancy CARR
06 Dir Student Certification/Records ... Ms. Tracey GREEN
21 Bursar ... Ms. Shawn GILLEN-CARYL
36 Director Student Life & Development ... Ms. Lysa SIMMONS
96 Director Management Services ... Mr. Michael MCMULLEN
39 Residence Life Director ... Ms. Cathy DOTTERER
35 Director of Student Activities ... Mr. Monty FLYNN
07 Director of Admissions ... Ms. Katherine PERRY

Orange County Community College (E)

115 South Street, Middletown NY 10940-6437

County: Orange FICE Identification: 002876
Unit ID: 194240
Telephone: (845) 344-6222 Carnegie Class: Assoc/Pub-R-L
FAX Number: (845) 343-1228 Calendar System: Semester
URL: www.sunyorange.edu
Established: 1950 Annual Undergrad Tuition & Fees (In-District): $4,336
Enrollment: 7,304 Coed
Affiliation or Control: State/Local IRS Status: 501(c)3
Highest Offering: Associate Degree
Program: Occupational; 2-Year Principally Bachelor's Creditable
Accreditation: M, ACBSP, ADNUR, DH, MLTAD, OTA, PTAA, RAD

01 President ... Dr. William RICHARDS
05 Vice President Academic Affairs ... Ms. Heather PERFETTI
32 Vice President Student Services ... Mr. Paul BROADIE, II
10 Vice Pres Administration/Finance ... Ms. Roslyn SMITH
30 Vice Pres Institutional Advancement ... Mr. Vinnie CAZZETTA
12 Vice President Newburgh Campus ... Ms. Mindy ROSS
84 Assoc VP for Enrollment Management ... Ms. Gerianne BRUSATI
76 Assoc VP Health Professions ... Mr. Michael GAWRONSKI, JR.
49 Int Assoc Vice Pres of Liberal Arts ... Ms. Mary WARRENER
50 Assoc VP Business/Math/Sci/Tech ... Ms. Stacey MOEGENBURG
88 Assoc Vice Pres Newburgh Campus ... Ms. Rosana REYES-ROSELLO
15 Assoc Vice Pres Human Resources ... Ms. Wendy HOLMES
13 Dir Info Svcs/Network Infrastruct ... Ms. Sharyne A. MILLER
08 Director Learning Resource ... Ms. Susan PARRY
20 Director Academic Services ... Mr. Neil FOLEY
51 Dir Continuing/Professional Educ ... Mr. David KOHN
19 Director Campus Security/Safety ... Mr. John AHERNE
09 Inst Plng/Assessment/Research Ofcr ... Ms. Christine WORK
18 Dir Facilities Administrative Svcs ... Mr. Michael WORDEN
21 Comptroller ... Ms. Jo Ann HAMBURG
37 Director of Financial Aid ... Mr. John IVANKOVIC
06 Registrar ... Mr. Neil FOLEY
27 Director of Communications ... Mr. Mike ALBRIGHT
38 Director Advising and Counseling ... Ms. Crystal SCHACHTER
07 Director of Admissions/Recruitment ... Mr. Michael ROE
35 Director Student Activities ... Mr. Steve HARPST
37 Asst Director of Financial Aid ... Ms. Rosemary BARRETT

Pace University (F)

1 Pace Plaza, New York NY 10038-1598

County: New York FICE Identification: 002791
Unit ID: 194310
Telephone: (212) 346-1200 Carnegie Class: DRU
FAX Number: (212) 346-1933 Calendar System: Semester
URL: www.pace.edu
Established: 1906 Annual Undergrad Tuition & Fees: $35,032
Enrollment: 12,593 Coed
Affiliation or Control: Independent Non-Profit IRS Status: 501(c)3
Highest Offering: Doctorate
Program: Liberal Arts And General; Teacher Preparatory; Professional
Accreditation: M, ARCPA, BUS, BUSA, CS, IPSY, LAW, NURSE, PSPSY, TED

01 President ... Mr. Stephen J. FRIEDMAN
10 Exec Vice Pres/CFO/Treasurer ... Mr. Toby R. WINER
05 Provost/Exec VP Academic Affairs ... Dr. Uday SUKHATME
11 Sr Vice Pres/Chief Admin Ofcr ... Mr. William MCGRATH
84 Vice Pres Enrollment Management ... Ms. Robina C. SCHEPP
30 VP Development/Alumni Relations ... Ms. Christine MEOLA
13 VP Information Tech/Chief Info Ofcr ... Mr. Thomas A. HULL
26 Vice Pres for University Relations ... Mr. Tom TORELLO
15 Int Vice Pres Human Resources ... Mr. Matt RENNA
09 Asst Vice Pres Plng/Assess/Inst Res . Ms. Barbara S. PENNIPEDE
86 Asst Vice Pres Govt/Community Rels ... Ms. Meghan Q. FRENCH
32 AVP Ofc Student Assistance ... Mr. Matthew F. BONILLA
27 Asst VP Marketing/Communications ... Ms. Susan W. KAYNE
21 Assoc VP Finance/Asst Treasurer ... Mr. Ronald NAHUM
19 Associate VP General Services ... Mr. Frank MCDONALD
35 Assoc Provost for Student Success ... Dr. Mark Allen POISEL
20 Associate Provost for Academic Affs ... Dr. Sheying CHEN
50 Dean Lubin School of Business ... Mr. Neil BRAUN
49 Dean Dyson College Arts/Sci ... Dr. Nira HERRMANN
53 Dean School of Education ... Dr. Andrea M. SPENCER
66 Int Dean Lienhard School of Nursing ... Dr. Geraldine COLOMBRARO
77 Dean School of CSIS ... Dr. Susan M. MERRITT
32 Dean of Students New York ... Dr. Marijo RUSSELL O'GRADY
32 Dean of Students Westchester ... Dr. Lisa BARDILL MOSCARITOLO
61 Dean School of Law ... Ms. Michelle S. SIMON
06 Assoc VP Stdnt Svcs/Univ Registrar ... Mr. Steven L. JOHNSON
06 Graduate Registrar ... Ms. Margaret JONES
06 Registrar Pleasantville ... Ms. Annmarie MCGRAIL
06 Law School Registrar ... Ms. Nilda RODRIGUEZ
88 Associate University Registrar ... Ms. Barbara MCCARTHY
36 Exec Director Career Svcs/Coop Educ ... Ms. Jody QUEEN-HUBERT
88 Asst Director Adult Education NY ... Ms. Nicola FOSTER
21 Interim Comptroller ... Mr. William VOLL
44 Manager Annual Fund ... Ms. Nicole L. SOUZA
29 Director of Alumni Relations ... Ms. Sheri GIBSON
43 University Counsel ... Mr. Stephen BRODSKY
08 Associate Director Library ... Mr. Melvin ISAACSON
21 University Bursar ... Ms. Susan WEYGANT
37 Director Financial Aid ... Mr. Steven JOHNSON
07 Dir of Admissions NY/Westchester ... Ms. Joanna BRODA
45 Director Budget/Planning/Analysis ... Mr. Len CERTA
22 Affirmative Action Officer ... Ms. Arletha MILES
14 Univ Director Computer Systems ... Mr. Gerard TARPEY
24 Univ Director Educational Media Svc ... Mr. Frank MANNLE
84 Director Adult Enroll Svcs/New York ... Ms. Janet KIRTMAN
23 Assoc Director Health Care Unit ... Ms. Jamesetta NEWLAND
27 Director of Media Relations ... Mr. Christopher CORY
88 Director Pace Adult Resource Center ... Ms. Tamra PLOTNICK
35 Director of Student Devel New York ... Dr. David CLARK
38 Director Counseling Services ... Dr. Richard SHADICK
39 Director of Residential Life ... Mr. A. Patrick ROGER-GORDON
40 Executive Director Bookstore ... Ms. Mary LIETO
85 Assoc Dir Intl Pgms & Services ... Mr. Kraig WALKUP
96 Director of Purchasing - Contracts ... Ms. Alice SEIFERT
18 Director Facilities/Physical Plant ... Mr. Abdul JABAR
28 Director of Diversity ... Ms. Shanelle HENRY ROBINSON

Pacific College of Oriental Medicine (G)

915 Broadway, Second Floor, New York NY 10107-8243

County: New York Identification: 666139
Unit ID: 414595
Telephone: (212) 982-3456 Carnegie Class: Spec/Health
FAX Number: (212) 982-6514 Calendar System: Semester
URL: www.pacificcollege.edu/
Established: 1993 Annual Undergrad Tuition & Fees: $20,488
Enrollment: 646 Coed
Affiliation or Control: Proprietary IRS Status: Proprietary
Highest Offering: Master's
Program: Professional
Accreditation: ACCSC, ACUP

01 Dean/Chief Operating Officer ... Mr. Malcolm YOUNGREN
06 Head Registrar/Dean of Admin ... Ms. Shana GARWOOD
05 Academic Dean ... Dr. Belinda ANDERSEN

† Branch campus of Pacific College of Oriental Medicine, San Diego CA.

Paul Smith's College (H)

PO Box 265, Paul Smiths NY 12970-0265

County: Franklin FICE Identification: 002795
Unit ID: 194392
Telephone: (518) 327-6000 Carnegie Class: Bac/Diverse
FAX Number: (518) 327-6060 Calendar System: Trimester
URL: www.paulsmiths.edu
Established: 1937 Annual Undergrad Tuition & Fees: $23,630
Enrollment: 1,055 Coed
Affiliation or Control: Independent Non-Profit IRS Status: 501(c)3
Highest Offering: Baccalaureate
Program: 2-Year Principally Bachelor's Creditable; Technical Emphasis
Accreditation: M, ACFEI, ENGT, FOR

01 President ... Dr. John W. MILLS
04 Assistant to the President ... Ms. Kathleen A. KECK
05 Provost ... Dr. Richard NELSON
10 Vice President Business/Finance ... Ms. Ann Marie SOMMA
30 Vice President Inst Advancement ... Mr. F. Raymond AGNEW
84 Vice Pres Enrollment Management ... Mr. Eric FELVER
18 VP Facilities Mgmt/Capital Project ... Mr. Steven W. MCFARLAND
13 Vice Pres Information Services ... Mr. James BUYEA
29 Director of Alumni Relations ... Ms. Heather TUTTLE
38 Director of Student Development ... Ms. Cheryl C. CULOTTA
37 Director of Financial Aid ... Ms. Mary Ellen M. CHAMBERLAIN
23 Director of Health Services ... Ms. Reiko REXILIUS-TUTHILL
24 Director Education Support Services ... Mr. Neil SURPRENANT
26 Director of Communications ... Mr. Kenneth AARON
06 Registrar ... Dr. Loralyn TAYLOR
07 Director of Admissions ... Mr. Charles RENNELL
19 Lead Campus Safety Officer ... Mr. Phil FIACCO
09 Director Institutional Research ... Dr. Loralyn TAYLOR
22 Director HEOP ... Ms. Kate MULLEN
41 Int Dir of Athletics/Physical Educ ... Mr. James TUCKER
21 Comptroller ... Ms. Laura ROZELL
32 Chief Student Affairs Officer ... Mr. Matthew SETON-SCHUR
40 Manager of College Store ... Ms. Diana L. LYNG-GLIDDI
15 Human Resources Generalist ... Ms. Amanda DURYEA
96 Purchasing Coordinator ... Ms. Cynthia LEMERY
36 Career Coordinator ... Ms. Debra DUTCHER
49 Dean Commercial/Applied/Lib Arts ... Dr. Phillip TAYLOR
65 Dean Natural Resource Mgmt/Ecology ... Dr. Jeffrey T. WALTON

Phillips Beth Israel School of Nursing (A)

776 Sixth Avenue, 4th Floor, New York NY 10001-6354
County: New York FICE Identification: 006438
Unit ID: 189282
Telephone: (212) 614-6110 Carnegie Class: Assoc/PrivNFP
FAX Number: (212) 614-6109 Calendar System: Semester
URL: www.futurenursebi.org
Established: 1904 Annual Undergrad Tuition & Fees: $20,590
Enrollment: 285 Coed
Affiliation or Control: Independent Non-Profit IRS Status: 501(c)3
Highest Offering: Associate Degree
Program: Occupational; 2-Year Principally Bachelor's Creditable; Nursing Emphasis
Accreditation: NY, ADNUR

01 Dean .... Dr. Janet MACKIN
05 Assistant Dean .... Mrs. Bernice PASS-STERN
32 Director Student Services .... Ms. Linda FABRIZIO

Plaza College (B)

74-09 37th Avenue, Jackson Heights NY 11372-6391
County: Queens FICE Identification: 012358
Unit ID: 194499
Telephone: (718) 779-1430 Carnegie Class: Bac/Assoc
FAX Number: (718) 779-7423 Calendar System: Semester
URL: www.plazacollege.edu
Established: 1916 Annual Undergrad Tuition & Fees: $12,350
Enrollment: 756 Coed
Affiliation or Control: Proprietary IRS Status: Proprietary
Highest Offering: Baccalaureate
Program: Occupational; 2-Year Principally Bachelor's Creditable
Accreditation: M, MAC

01 President .... Charles E. CALLAHAN, SR.
03 Provost .... Charles E. CALLAHAN, III
10 Vice Pres of Financial Services .... Elizabeth K. CALLAHAN
05 Academic Dean .... Marie DOLLA
06 Registrar .... Carol GARCIA
21 Comptroller .... Linda ROCKHILL
07 Dean of Admissions .... Rose Ann BLACK
20 Dean Curriculum Development .... Marianne C. ZIPF
08 College Librarian .... Eva BABALIS
23 Director Health Services .... Candice CALLAHAN
37 Financial Aid Coord/Dir Fin Svcs .... Peggy CHUNG
29 Alumni Relations/Internship Coord .... Jonathan HOWLE
100 Chief of Staff/HR Officer/Placement .... Correne CAVALIERI
09 Assoc Dean Institutional Research .... Edward DEE
27 Chief Information Officer .... Dean DEBEER
32 Director of Student Services .... Dawn VETRANO
62 Director of Library/LRC .... Kathleen D'APRIX
13 Director Information Technology .... Norman ALVARADO
45 Director Strategic Initiatives .... Charles CALLAHAN, IV
76 Program Director Medical Assisting .... Daryl ANDERSON

Polytechnic Institute of New York University (C)

6 Metrotech Center, Brooklyn NY 11201-3840
County: Kings FICE Identification: 002796
Unit ID: 194541
Telephone: (718) 260-3600 Carnegie Class: RU/H
FAX Number: (718) 260-3136 Calendar System: Semester
URL: www.poly.edu
Established: 1854 Annual Undergrad Tuition & Fees: $38,336
Enrollment: 4,487 Coed
Affiliation or Control: Independent Non-Profit IRS Status: 501(c)3
Highest Offering: Doctorate
Program: Liberal Arts And General; Professional
Accreditation: M, ENG

01 President .... Mr. Jerry M. HULTIN
05 Provost .... Dr. Katepalli SREENIVASAN
10 VP Finance & Business Affairs .... Mr. Dennis DINTINO
30 Interim VP Devel & Alumni Relations .... Ms. Erica MARKS
27 VP of Marketing and Communications .... Vacant
88 VP of Enterprise Learning .... Mr. Robert N. UBELL
100 Chief of Staff/VP Strat Initiatives .... Ms. Elizabeth LUSSKIN
88 Assc Prov Research/Tech Initiatives .... Dr. Kurt BECKER
84 Assoc Provost Enrollment Services .... Ms. Barbara HALL
45 Assc Provost Pgms/Plng/Development .... Dr. Mary COWMAN
54 Assoc Provost Abu Dhabi Engineering .... Dr. Sunil KUMAR
58 Assoc Provost Graduate Academics .... Dr. Walter ZURAWSKY
20 Assoc Provost Undergrad Academics .... Dr. Iraj KALKHORAN
32 Dean of Student Affairs .... Ms. Anita FARRINGTON
26 Director Marketing & Communications .... Ms. Kathleen HAMILTON
08 Director of Libraries .... Ms. Jana STEVENS-RICHMAN
06 Registrar .... Ms. Beth KIENLE-GRANZO
36 Director of Career Services .... Mr. James SILLCOX
88 Director of Special Services .... Vacant
37 Director Financial Aid .... Ms. Christine FALZERANO
15 Director Human Resources .... Mr. Suong IVES
29 Director Alumni Relations .... Ms. Valerie CABRAL
46 Director Sponsored Research .... Ms. Christine VILLANI
18 Director Facilities .... Ms. Annie CARINO
41 Director of Athletics .... Ms. Maureen BRAZIEL
88 Director Student Financial Services .... Mr. Anthony BONANO
09 Director of Institutional Research .... Mr. Michael A. MAINIERO
84 Director Grad Enrollment Mgmt .... Mr. J. C BONILLA
88 Director K-12 Stem Education .... Mr. Ben ESNER

Pratt Institute (D)

200 Willoughby Avenue, Brooklyn NY 11205-3899
County: Kings FICE Identification: 002798
Unit ID: 194578
Telephone: (718) 636-3600 Carnegie Class: Master's L
FAX Number: (718) 636-3670 Calendar System: Semester
URL: www.pratt.edu
Established: 1887 Annual Undergrad Tuition & Fees: $41,092
Enrollment: 4,722 Coed
Affiliation or Control: Independent Non-Profit IRS Status: 501(c)3
Highest Offering: Master's
Program: 2-Year Principally Bachelor's Creditable; Liberal Arts And General; Teacher Preparatory; Professional
Accreditation: M, ART, CIDA, LIB, PLNG, @TEAC

01 President .... Dr. Thomas F. SCHUTTE
05 Provost .... Mr. Peter BARNA
32 Vice President for Student Life .... Dr. Helen MATUSOW-AYRES
10 Vice Pres Finance/Administration .... Mr. Edmund RUTKOWSKI
30 Vice President Development .... Mr. Todd GALITZ
84 Vice President for Enrollment .... Ms. Judith AARON
11 Assistant to Pres Administration .... Ms. Josie CAPORUSCIO
06 Registrar .... Mr. Lisle HENDERSON
08 Acting Director of the Library .... Mr. Russ ABELL
20 Associate Provost .... Dr. Marianthi ZIKOPOULOS
15 Director Human Resources .... Mr. Tom GREENE
51 Dir Ctr for Continuing & Prof Stds .... Mr. Charles MUNSTER
21 Comptroller .... Ms. Sylvia ACUESTA
26 Executive Director Public Relations .... Ms. Mara MCGINNIS
29 Director Alumni Relations .... Mr. Michael SCLAFANI
36 Director Student Placement .... Ms. Judith NYLEN
37 Interim Dir Student Financial Aid .... Ms. Korinne BARNES
09 Exec Dir Institutional Research .... Mr. Vladimir BRILLER
07 Director of Undergraduate Admission .... Mr. William SWAN
96 Director of Purchasing .... Vacant
57 Acting Dean Art & Design .... Mr. Leighton PIERCE
49 Dean Liberal Arts/Science .... Dr. Andrew BARNES
48 Dean School of Architecture .... Mr. Thomas HANRAHAN
62 Dean Information/Library Sci .... Dr. Tula GIANNINI

Professional Business College (E)

408 Broadway, New York NY 10013
County: New York FICE Identification: 023065
Unit ID: 194611
Telephone: (212) 226-7300 Carnegie Class: Assoc/PrivNFP
FAX Number: (212) 431-8294 Calendar System: Semester
URL: www.pbcny.edu
Established: 2004 Annual Undergrad Tuition & Fees: $15,943
Enrollment: 847 Coed
Affiliation or Control: Independent Non-Profit IRS Status: 501(c)3
Highest Offering: Associate Degree
Program: Occupational; 2-Year Principally Bachelor's Creditable; Business Emphasis
Accreditation: ACICS

01 President .... Mr. Leon LEE
05 Academic Vice President .... Mr. Richard SLUSARCZYK
88 Chief Compliance Officer .... Mr. Nick POLISENO
36 Placement Director .... Ms. Judith RODRIGUEZ
06 Registrar .... Mr. Ken CHANG
08 Head Librarian .... Ms. Murielle LOUIS
07 Admissions Director .... Mr. David WANG
37 Financial Aid Director .... Ms. Cheryl ZHANG
10 Director of Advising .... Ms. Taryn SHUHY

Rabbi Isaac Elchanan Theological Seminary (F)

2540 Amsterdam Avenue, New York NY 10033-9986
County: New York FICE Identification: 033104
Unit ID: 194727
Telephone: (212) 960-5310 Carnegie Class: Not Classified
FAX Number: (212) 960-0055 Calendar System: Semester
URL: riets.edu
Established: 1886 Annual Graduate Tuition & Fees: $15,200
Enrollment: 320 Male
Affiliation or Control: Jewish IRS Status: 501(c)3
Highest Offering: Beyond Master's But Less Than Doctorate; No Undergraduates
Program: Professional
Accreditation: NY

01 Chancellor .... Rabbi Norman LAMM
05 Max & Marion Grill Dean .... Rabbi Yonah REESE
64 Director Belz School Jewish Music .... Cantor Bernard BEER
06 Interim Registrar .... Ms. Diana BENMERGUI
07 Director of Admissions .... Mr. Michael KRANZLER
37 Director of Student Finances .... Mr. Robert FRIEDMAN
08 Librarian .... Ms. Pearl BERGER
11 Administrator .... Rabbi Chaim BRONSTEIN
30 Director Institutional Advancement .... Mr. Dan FORMAN

Rabbinical Academy Mesivta Rabbi Chaim Berlin (G)

1605 Coney Island Avenue, Brooklyn NY 11230-4715
County: Kings FICE Identification: 003976
Unit ID: 194657
Telephone: (718) 377-0777 Carnegie Class: Spec/Faith
FAX Number: (718) 338-5578 Calendar System: Semester
Established: 1939 Annual Undergrad Tuition & Fees: $11,400
Enrollment: 315 Male
Affiliation or Control: Independent Non-Profit IRS Status: 501(c)3
Highest Offering: Second Talmudic Degree
Program: Teacher Preparatory; Professional
Accreditation: RABN

01 Provost .... Rabbi Abraham H. FRUCHTHANDLER
05 President of the Faculty .... Rabbi Aaron M. SCHECHTER
03 Executive Director .... Rabbi Y. Mayer LASKER
29 Director of Alumni Association .... Mendel SCHECHTER
45 Chief Planning Officer .... Rabbi Tuvia M. OBERMEISTER
20 Associate Director .... Eli RABINOWITZ
37 Financial Aid Administrator .... Michael A. REISS

Rabbinical College Beth Shraga (H)

28 Saddle River Road, Monsey NY 10952-3035
County: Rockland FICE Identification: 010943
Unit ID: 194693
Telephone: (845) 356-1980 Carnegie Class: Spec/Faith
FAX Number: (845) 425-2604 Calendar System: Semester
Established: 1965 Annual Undergrad Tuition & Fees: $10,550
Enrollment: 39 Male
Affiliation or Control: Independent Non-Profit IRS Status: 501(c)3
Highest Offering: Second Talmudic Degree
Program: Teacher Preparatory; Professional
Accreditation: RABN

01 President .... Rabbi Sidney SCHIFF

Rabbinical College Bobover Yeshiva B'nei Zion (I)

1577 48th Street, Brooklyn NY 11219-3293
County: Kings FICE Identification: 008614
Unit ID: 194666
Telephone: (718) 438-2018 Carnegie Class: Spec/Faith
FAX Number: (718) 871-9031 Calendar System: Semester
Established: 1947 Annual Undergrad Tuition & Fees: $8,960
Enrollment: 323 Male
Affiliation or Control: Independent Non-Profit IRS Status: 501(c)3
Highest Offering: Second Talmudic Degree
Program: Teacher Preparatory; Professional
Accreditation: RABN

01 President .... Rabbi Boruch Avrohom HOROWITZ

Rabbinical College Ch'san Sofer (J)

1876 50th Street, Brooklyn NY 11204-0304
County: Kings FICE Identification: 003977
Unit ID: 194675
Telephone: (718) 236-1171 Carnegie Class: Spec/Faith
FAX Number: (718) 236-1119 Calendar System: Semester
Established: 1940 Annual Undergrad Tuition & Fees: $8,500
Enrollment: 46 Male
Affiliation or Control: Independent Non-Profit IRS Status: 501(c)3
Highest Offering: Second Talmudic Degree
Program: Teacher Preparatory; Professional
Accreditation: RABN

01 Executive Vice President .... Rabbi A. EHRENFELD
05 Dean of the College .... Rabbi S. B. EHRENFELD
10 Treasurer .... Mr. Mordechai STUHL
06 Registrar .... Rabbi Meyer WEINBERGER

Rabbinical College of Long Island (K)

205 W Beech Street, Long Beach NY 11561-0630
County: Nassau FICE Identification: 010378
Unit ID: 194736
Telephone: (516) 255-4700 Carnegie Class: Spec/Faith
FAX Number: (516) 255-4701 Calendar System: Semester
Established: 1965 Annual Undergrad Tuition & Fees: $14,050
Enrollment: 132 Male
Affiliation or Control: Independent Non-Profit IRS Status: 501(c)3
Highest Offering: First Talmudic Degree
Program: Teacher Preparatory; Professional
Accreditation: RABN

01 President .... Rabbi Yitzchok FEIGELSTOCK
06 Registrar .... Rabbi Dovid N. ROTHSCHILD
32 Dean of Students .... Rabbi Yeruchem PITTER
07 Director of Admissions .... Rabbi Chaim HOBERMAN
37 Financial Aid Administrator .... Rabbi Shlomo TEICHMAN

Rabbinical College Ohr Shimon Yisroel (L)

215-217 Hewes Street, Brooklyn NY 11211-8102
County: Kings FICE Identification: 031292
Unit ID: 405854

Telephone: (718) 855-4092 Carnegie Class: Spec/Faith
FAX Number: (718) 855-8479 Calendar System: Semester
Established: N/A Annual Undergrad Tuition & Fees: $10,500
Enrollment: 118 Male
Affiliation or Control: Independent Non-Profit IRS Status: 501(c)3
Highest Offering: First Talmudic Degree
Program: Professional
Accreditation: @RABN

01	President	Rabbi Shulem WALTER

Rabbinical Seminary of America (A)

76-01 147th Street, Flushing NY 11367-3148
County: Queens FICE Identification: 003978
Unit ID: 194763
Telephone: (718) 268-4700 Carnegie Class: Spec/Faith
FAX Number: (718) 268-4684 Calendar System: Semester
Established: 1933 Annual Undergrad Tuition & Fees: $8,000
Enrollment: 501 Male
Affiliation or Control: Independent Non-Profit IRS Status: 501(c)3
Highest Offering: Second Talmudic Degree
Program: Teacher Preparatory; Professional
Accreditation: RABN

01	Executive Director	Rabbi Meir GLAZER
03	Executive Vice President	Rabbi Hayim SCHWARTZ
05	Vice President	Rabbi David HARRIS
20	Vice President	Rabbi Akiva GRUNBLATT
06	Registrar	Rabbi Abraham SEMMEL
30	Director Development	Rabbi Yossi SINGER
37	Director of Financial Aid	Mrs. Laya EISENSTEIN
18	Chief Physical Plant	Mr. David COHEN
88	Director of Special Projects	Vacant
91	Director of Admin Computing	Mr. Jonathan PLATOVSKY
39	Director Student Housing	Rabbi Aryeh GOLDMAN
46	Director Research & Development	Vacant

Rabbinical Seminary M'kor Chaim (B)

1571 55th Street, Brooklyn NY 11219-4300
County: Kings FICE Identification: 008617
Unit ID: 194718
Telephone: (718) 851-0183 Carnegie Class: Spec/Faith
FAX Number: (718) 853-2967 Calendar System: Semester
Established: 1965 Annual Undergrad Tuition & Fees: $6,800
Enrollment: 39 Male
Affiliation or Control: Independent Non-Profit IRS Status: 501(c)3
Highest Offering: Second Talmudic Degree
Program: Teacher Preparatory; Professional
Accreditation: RABN

01	President	Rabbi Benjamin LEDERER

Relay Graduate School of Education (C)

40 West 20th St, 6th Floor, New York NY 10011
County: New York Identification: 667117
Telephone: (212) 228-1888 Carnegie Class: Not Classified
FAX Number: (212) 228-1855 Calendar System: Other
URL: www.relayschool.org
Established: 2011 Annual Graduate Tuition & Fees: $17,500
Enrollment: 220 Coed
Affiliation or Control: Independent Non-Profit IRS Status: 501(c)3
Highest Offering: Master's; No Undergraduates
Program: Teacher Preparatory
Accreditation: @M, TED

01	CEO	Mr. Norman ATKINS
05	Provost	Dr. Brent MADDIN

Rensselaer Polytechnic Institute (D)

110 8th Street, Troy NY 12180-3590
County: Rensselaer FICE Identification: 002803
Unit ID: 194824
Telephone: (518) 276-6000 Carnegie Class: RU/VH
FAX Number: N/A Calendar System: Semester
URL: www.rpi.edu
Established: 1824 Annual Undergrad Tuition & Fees: $42,704
Enrollment: 6,538 Coed
Affiliation or Control: Independent Non-Profit IRS Status: 501(c)3
Highest Offering: Doctorate
Program: Liberal Arts And General; Professional
Accreditation: M, BUS, ENG

01	President	Dr. Shirley A. JACKSON
05	Provost	Dr. Prabhat HAJELA
11	Vice President for Administration	Mr. Claude ROUNDS
22	Vice Pres Strat Comm/External Rels	Mr. William WALKER
10	Vice President for Finance	Ms. Virginia GREGG
30	Vice Pres Institute Advancement	Vacant
32	Vice President Student Life	Dr. Timothy E. SAMS
15	VP Human Resources/Inst Diversity	Mr. Curtis N. POWELL
45	Vice Pres for Research	Vacant
13	Vice Pres for Info Services & CIO	Mr. John E. KOLB
84	Vice Pres Enrollment/Dean Admiss	Dr. Paul MARTHERS
21	Asst Vice Pres for Administration	Mr. Paul MARTIN
26	Asst VP for Govt & Ext Relations	Ms. Allison NEWMAN
29	Asst Vice Pres Alumni Relations	Mr. Jeff SCHANZ
54	Dean School of Engineering	Dr. David ROSOWSKY
81	Dean School of Science	Dr. Laurie LESHIN
79	Dean Sch of Humanities/Social Sci	Dr. Mary SIMONI
50	Dean Lally School of Mgmt/Tech	Dr. Thomas BEGLEY
48	Dean School of Architecture	Mr. Evan DOUGLIS
43	Secy of the Inst/General Counsel	Mr. Charles F. CARLETTA
20	Associate Dean for Information Tech	Mr. David SPOONER
32	Dean of Students	Mr. Mark SMITH
06	Dir Stdnt Records/Fin Svcs/Registr	Ms. Sharon L. KUNKEL
37	Director Financial Aid	Mr. Larry CHAMBERS
09	Director of Institutional Research	Mr. Jack MAHONEY
08	Acting Director of Libraries	Mr. Bob MAYO
25	Director Office Contracts & Grants	Mr. Richard E. SCAMMELL
36	Director Career Development Center	Mr. Thomas L. TARANTELLI
07	Director of Graduate Admissions	Mr. George ROBBINS
100	Chief of Staff	Vacant
18	Director Physical Plant	Mr. Mark FROST
86	Director of Federal Relations	Ms. Deborah E. ALTENBURG
23	Director Student Health Center	Dr. Leslie LAWRENCE
38	Director Student Counseling	Dr. Benjamin MARTE
96	Manager Purchasing Systems	Mr. Craig MCINTOSH

Richard Gilder Graduate School at the American Museum of Natural History (E)

Central Park West at 79th Street, New York NY 10024
County: New York Identification: 667003
Unit ID: 458548
Telephone: (212) 769-5055 Carnegie Class: Not Classified
FAX Number: N/A Calendar System: Other
URL: rggs.amnh.org
Established: 2006 Annual Graduate Tuition & Fees: N/A
Enrollment: 13 Coed
Affiliation or Control: Independent Non-Profit IRS Status: 501(c)3
Highest Offering: Doctorate; No Undergraduates
Program: Professional
Accreditation: NY

01	Dean	Dr. John J. FLYNN

Roberts Wesleyan College (F)

2301 Westside Drive, Rochester NY 14624-1997
County: Monroe FICE Identification: 002805
Unit ID: 194958
Telephone: (585) 594-6000 Carnegie Class: Master's L
FAX Number: (585) 594-6371 Calendar System: Semester
URL: www.roberts.edu
Established: 1866 Annual Undergrad Tuition & Fees: $26,324
Enrollment: 1,823 Coed
Affiliation or Control: Independent Non-Profit IRS Status: 501(c)3
Highest Offering: Master's
Program: Liberal Arts And General; Teacher Preparatory; Professional
Accreditation: M, ART, IACBE, MUS, NURSE, SW, @TEAC

01	President	Dr. John A. MARTIN
03	Sr VP & Provost	Dr. Robert ZWIER
45	Sr VP Advancement & External Rels	Dr. S. Jack CONNELL
10	Sr Vice President & Treasurer	Mr. James E. CUTHBERT
05	VP for Academic & Student Support	Dr. Nelson W. HILL
11	Vice President for Administration	Mrs. Ruth LOGAN
07	Assoc VP for UG Admissions	Mrs. Linda HOFFMAN
44	Assoc VP for Major Gifts	Mr. Maurice (Max) MCGINNIS
40	Director of Bookstore Services	Mr. Arnoldo DEJESUS
41	Director of Athletics	Mr. Michael E. FARO
37	Director of Student Financial Svcs	Mr. Stephen G. FIELD
09	Dir Institutional Research/Assess	Dr. Paul W. KENNEDY
42	Chaplain	Rev. Jonathan BRATT
06	Registrar	Mrs. Lesa J. KOHR
08	Director of Library Services	Mr. Alfred C. KROBER
27	Chief Information Officer	Mr. Pradeep SAXENA

† Parent institution of Northeastern Seminary.

Rochester Institute of Technology (G)

1 Lomb Memorial Drive, Rochester NY 14623-5604
County: Monroe FICE Identification: 002806
Unit ID: 195003
Telephone: (585) 475-2411 Carnegie Class: Master's L
FAX Number: (585) 475-7049 Calendar System: Quarter
URL: www.rit.edu
Established: 1829 Annual Undergrad Tuition & Fees: $33,258
Enrollment: 17,652 Coed
Affiliation or Control: Independent Non-Profit IRS Status: 501(c)3
Highest Offering: Doctorate
Program: Liberal Arts And General; Teacher Preparatory; Professional; Technical Emphasis
Accreditation: M, ARCPA, ART, BUS, CIDA, CS, DIETD, DMS, ENG, ENGR, ENGT, TEAC

01	President	Dr. William W. DESTLER
05	Provost & Sr VP for Acad Affs	Dr. Jeremy A. HAEFNER
100	Chief of Staff	Mrs. Karen A. BARROWS
10	Sr Vice Pres Finance/Administration	Dr. James H. WATTERS
84	Sr VP Enroll Mgmt/Career Svcs	Dr. James G. MILLER
32	Sr Vice President Student Affairs	Dr. Mary-Beth COOPER
12	President NTID/RIT Vice Pres & Dean	Dr. Gerard BUCKLEY
12	Interim President RIT Dubai	Dr. Luther TROELL
30	VP for Development & Alumni Rels	Ms. Lisa CAUDA
86	Vice President Govt/Cmty Relations	Ms. Deborah M. STENDARDI
46	Vice President Research	Dr. Ryne RAFFAELLE
28	VP for Diversity & Inclusion	Mr. Kevin MCDONALD
12	VP AUK/Academic Dir RIT Pgms Kosovo	Dr. Brian BOWEN
20	Senior Assoc Provost	Dr. Christine M. LICATA
36	Assoc VP/Dir Coop Ed/Career Svcs	Dr. Emanuel CONTOMANOLIS
27	Chief Communications Officer	Mr. Robert FINNERTY
20	Asst Provost and Director CIMS	Dr. Nabil NASR
08	Director of RIT Libraries	Ms. Shirley BOWER
20	Assoc Provost for Faculty Success	Dr. Lynn A. WILD
12	Pres/Dean Amer Col Mgt/Tech RIT	Mr. Donald HUDSPETH
29	Asst VP Alumni Relations	Ms. Kelly REDDER
21	Asst VP/Controller/Asst Treasurer	Ms. Lyn KELLY
18	Asst VP of Facilities Management	Mr. John MOORE
35	Ast VP Stdnt Aff/Dir Counseling Ctr	Mr. John WEAS
06	Asst VP/Registrar	Mr. Joe LOFFREDO
07	Asst VP/Dir Undergrad Admissions	Dr. Daniel SHELLEY
37	Asst VP & Dir Fin Aid & Scholarship	Ms. Verna J. HAZEN
88	Asst VP and Dir Grad/PT Enroll Svc	Ms. Diane ELLISON
44	Asst VP for Principal/Planned Gift	Ms. Heather ENGEL
09	Asst VP Inst Rsrch/Policy Studies	Dr. Joan E. GRAHAM
15	Asst VP/Director Human Resources	Ms. Judy BENDER
44	Exec Dir Fund for RIT	Ms. Marisa PSAILA
88	Sr Director Center for Campus Life	Ms. Karey PINE
88	Sr Director Academic Support Center	Ms. Phillippa POWERS
85	Director International Student Svcs	Mr. Jeffrey W. COX
96	Exec Director Procurement Services	Ms. Debra KUSSE
102	Exec Director Foundation Relations	Ms. Susan WATSON MOLINE
102	Dir Corporate Relations	Mr. Paul HARRIS
26	Chief Communications Officer	Mr. Robert FINNERTY
101	Secretary of the Institution	Mrs. Karen A. BARROWS
50	Dean of Business	Dr. dt OGILVIE
54	Dean of Engineering	Dr. Harvey J. PALMER
72	Dean Applied Science/Technology	Dr. H. Fred WALKER
49	Dean of Liberal Arts	Dr. James J. WINEBRAKE
81	Dean of Science	Dr. Sophia MAGGELAKIS
57	Dean College Imaging Arts/Sci	Ms. Lorraine JUSTICE
77	Dean B Golisano Col Comp/Info Sci	Dr. Andrew L. SEARS
58	Dean Graduate Studies	Dr. Hector FLORES
76	Dean College Health Sciences/Tech	Dr. Daniel B. ORNT

Rockefeller University (H)

1230 York Avenue, New York NY 10065-6399
County: New York FICE Identification: 002807
Unit ID: 195049
Telephone: (212) 327-8000 Carnegie Class: RU/VH
FAX Number: (212) 327-8699 Calendar System: Other
URL: www.rockefeller.edu
Established: 1901 Annual Graduate Tuition & Fees: N/A
Enrollment: 207 Coed
Affiliation or Control: Independent Non-Profit IRS Status: 501(c)3
Highest Offering: Doctorate; No Undergraduates
Program: Professional
Accreditation: NY

01	President	Dr. Marc TESSIER-LAVIGNE
43	Vice President & General Counsel	Ms. Harriet RABB
05	Vice President Academic Affairs	Mr. Michael W. YOUNG
10	Vice President Finance	Mr. James H. LAPPLE
30	Vice President Development	Ms. Maren E. IMHOFF
17	Vice President for Medical Affairs	Dr. Barry S. COLLER
20	Dean & Vice Pres of Educ Affairs	Dr. Sidney STRICKLAND
88	Vice Pres Scientific/Fac Oper	Dr. John TOOZE
15	Vice President Human Resources	Ms. Virginia A. HUFFMAN
18	Assoc Vice Pres Plant Operations	Mr. Alexander KOGAN
45	Assoc Vice Pres Plng & Constr	Mr. George B. CANDLER
13	Chief Information Officer	Mr. Gerald LATTER
25	Dir Pgm Dev & Sponsored Research	Dr. Gila BUDESCU
08	University Librarian	Ms. Carol FELTES
19	Director Security	Mr. James ROGERS

Rockland Community College (I)

145 College Road, Suffern NY 10901-3699
County: Rockland FICE Identification: 002877
Unit ID: 195058
Telephone: (845) 574-4000 Carnegie Class: Assoc/Pub-S-SC
FAX Number: (845) 574-4463 Calendar System: Semester
URL: www.sunyrockland.edu
Established: 1959 Annual Undergrad Tuition & Fees (In-District): $4,025
Enrollment: 8,020 Coed
Affiliation or Control: State/Local IRS Status: 501(c)3
Highest Offering: Associate Degree
Program: Occupational; 2-Year Principally Bachelor's Creditable
Accreditation: M, ADNUR, OTA

01	President	Dr. Cliff L. WOOD
03	Interim VP Finance/Administration	Mr. Rondell WALKER
05	Vice President Academic Affairs	Dr. Susan DEER
32	Vice Pres Student Services	Ms. Karen GUALTIERI
10	Assoc VP Finance/Administration	Mr. Larry FERRIER
88	Dean CTR Personal/Prof Development	Mr. Richard SYREK
35	Dean of Student Development	Dr. James SIEGEL
84	Dean of Enrollment Management	Ms. Dana STILLEY
37	Director Financial Aid	Ms. Debra BOUABIDI
06	Registrar	Ms. Robin CONKLIN

14 Director of Information Services .... Dr. Steven FERRES
08 Director of Library/Learning Res .... Vacant
38 Director Student Counseling .... Vacant
18 Chief Facilities/Physical Plant .... Vacant
28 Dir Equity/Compliance/Affirm Act .... Ms. Melissa ROY
09 Director of Institutional Research .... Mr. Michael LIPKIN
20 Asst to Vice Pres Academic Affairs .... Ms. Patricia KOBES
26 Chief Public Relations Officer .... Ms. Tzipora REITMAN

The Sage Colleges (A)

65 First Street, Troy NY 12180-4199
County: Rensselaer FICE Identification: 002810
Unit ID: 195128
Telephone: (518) 244-2000 Carnegie Class: Master's L
FAX Number: (518) 244-2460 Calendar System: Semester
URL: www.sage.edu
Established: 1916 Annual Undergrad Tuition & Fees: $28,000
Enrollment: 2,942 Coed
Affiliation or Control: Independent Non-Profit IRS Status: 501(c)3
Highest Offering: Doctorate
Program: Liberal Arts And General; Teacher Preparatory; Professional
Accreditation: M, ART, DIETD, DIETI, NURSE, OT, PTA, TED

01 President .... Dr. Susan C. SCRIMSHAW
05 Provost .... Dr. Terry WEINER
30 VP for Institutional Advancement .... Ms. Melissa KOMORA
12 Dean Sage College of Albany .... Ms. Sarolta TAKACS
12 Dean Russell Sage College .... Dr. Sharon ROBINSON
10 VP for Finance & Treasurer .... Mr. Peter D. HUGHES
84 VP Marketing/Enrollment Mgmt .... Mr. Daniel LUNDQUIST
32 Vice Pres for Campus Life .... Ms. Patricia CELLEMME
13 VP Administration & Planning .... Ms. Deirdre ZARRILLO
35 Dean of Students - RSC .... Mr. Michael BAUMGARDNER
35 Dean of Students - SCA .... Ms. Sharon MURRAY
76 Dean of Health Sciences .... Dr. Esther HASKVITZ
06 Registrar .... Ms. Andrea DEMAYO
07 Director of Admissions .... Mr. Andrew PALUMBO
88 Dean of School of Management .... Dr. Dan ROBESON
53 Dean School of Education .... Dr. Lori QUIGLEY
29 Director of Alumni Relations .... Ms. Alicia PEPE
29 Director Alumnae Relations .... Ms. Joan CLIFFORD
07 Director of Graduate & Adult Admiss .... Ms. Wendy DIEFENDORF
37 Assoc Director of Financial Aid .... Ms. Kelley ROBINSON
38 Director Student Counseling .... Vacant
15 Director of Human Resources .... Ms. Caryn KENT
09 Director of Institutional Research .... Ms. Lori PIZER
18 Director Facilities Management .... Mr. John ZAJACESKOWSKI
28 Dir Cultural Enrichment/Diversity .... Ms. Sabrina MC GINTY
36 Director of Advising .... Ms. Karen SCHELL
36 Director of Advising .... Ms. Stacy GONZALEZ
26 Dir of Communications & Marketing .... Ms. Shannon BALLARD GORMAN
92 Director of Honors Programs .... Dr. Julie MCINTYRE
21 Senior Director of Finance .... Mr. Thomas GIAQUINTO
96 Dir of Purchasing/Accts Payable .... Ms. Paula SELMER

Saint Bernard's School of Theology & Ministry (B)

120 French Road, Rochester NY 14618-3822
County: Monroe FICE Identification: 002815
Unit ID: 195155
Telephone: (585) 271-3657 Carnegie Class: Spec/Faith
FAX Number: (585) 271-2045 Calendar System: Semester
URL: www.stbernards.edu
Established: 1893 Annual Graduate Tuition & Fees: $3,220
Enrollment: 108 Coed
Affiliation or Control: Roman Catholic IRS Status: 501(c)3
Highest Offering: Master's; No Undergraduates
Program: Professional
Accreditation: THEOL

01 President .... Sr. Patricia A. SCHOELLES, SSJ
05 Academic Dean .... Dr. Devadasan N. PREMNATH
06 Registrar .... Mrs. Ellen MORNINGSTAR
21 Accounting/Computer Operations .... Ms. Mary MUGGLETON
07 Admissions Director .... Ms. Christina SCHMIDT
51 Director Continuing Education .... Rev. George HEYMAN
08 Librarian .... Ms. Sheila SMITH
30 Director of Advancement .... Ms. Laura HAMILTON

St. Bonaventure University (C)

St. Bonaventure NY 14778-9999
County: Cattaraugus FICE Identification: 002817
Unit ID: 195164
Telephone: (716) 375-2000 Carnegie Class: Master's L
FAX Number: (716) 375-2005 Calendar System: Semester
URL: www.sbu.edu
Established: 1858 Annual Undergrad Tuition & Fees: $28,727
Enrollment: 2,460 Coed
Affiliation or Control: Roman Catholic IRS Status: 501(c)3
Highest Offering: Master's
Program: Liberal Arts And General; Teacher Preparatory; Professional
Accreditation: M, BUS, CACREP, TED

01 President .... Dr. Margaret CARNEY, OSF
05 Provost and VP for Academic Affairs .... Dr. Michael J. FISCHER
32 Vice Provost for Student Life .... Mr. Richard C. TRIETLEY, JR.
10 Senior VP Finance & Administration .... Ms. Brenda MCGEE
26 Vice Pres University Relations .... Dr. Emily F. SINSABAUGH
42 Exec Director of Faith Formation .. Fr. Francis J. DISPIGNO, OFM
88 Vice Pres for Franciscan Mission .... Bro. F. Edward COUGHLIN, OFM
30 Vice Pres for Advancement .... Mrs. Mary C. DRISCOLL
30 Assoc VP Development .... Mr. Matthew J. TORNAMBE
84 Associate VP for Enrollment .... Ms. Kate DILLON HOGAN
25 Assc VP Ofc Grants Admn/Lflng Lrng ..... Mr. Lawrence SOROKES
57 Interim Exec Dir of Q Arts Center .... Mr. Ludwig BRUNNER
20 Assoc Provost Academic Affairs .... Dr. Peggy Y. BURKE
04 Director of Operations Ofc of Pres .... Mr. Thomas BUTTAFARRO, JR.
15 Interim Director Human Resources ..... Ms. Francine Z. SCHAEFER
07 Director of Admissions .... Ms. Monica EMERY
37 Director of Financial Aid .... Mr. Troy MARTIN
39 Exec Dir Res Living/Chief Judicial .... Ms. Nichole GONZALEZ
14 Director Technology Services .... Mr. Michael HOFFMAN
08 Director of Friedsam Mem Library .... Mr. Paul J. SPAETH
38 Director Counseling .... Dr. Roger E. KEENER
41 Director of Athletics .... Mr. Steve WATSON
06 Registrar & Dir of Inst Research .... Ms. Ann LEHMAN
29 Director of Alumni Services .... Mr. Joseph V. FLANAGAN
36 Director of Career Services .... Ms. Connie F. WHITCOMB
43 University Counsel .... Mr. J. Michael SHANE
23 Director of the Student Infirmary .... Vacant
18 Director Physical Plant .... Mr. Philip G. WINGER
21 Controller .... Mrs. Nancy K. TAYLOR
19 Director of Safety and Security .... Mr. Vito CZYZ
40 Manager Bookstore .... Ms. Annette MCGRAW
44 Director Annual Giving Program .... Ms. Julie CUNNINGHAM
92 Director of Honors Program .... Vacant
96 Dir of Budget & Purchasing .... Ms. Lorraine SMITH
88 Director Franciscan Institute ...... Bro. F. Edward COUGHLIN, OFM
49 Dean School of Arts & Sci .... Dr. Wolfgang NATTER
50 Dean School of Business .... Dr. Pierre BALTHAZARD
58 Assc Provost/Dean Sch Graduate Stds .... Dr. Peggy Y. BURKE
53 Dean School of Education .... Dr. Joseph ZIMMER
60 Dean Jandoli Sch Journ/Mass Comm ...... Dr. Pauline HOFFMANN

St. Elizabeth College of Nursing (D)

2215 Genesee Street, Utica NY 13501-5998
County: Oneida FICE Identification: 006461
Unit ID: 195687
Telephone: (315) 798-8144 Carnegie Class: Assoc/PrivNFP
FAX Number: (315) 798-8271 Calendar System: Semester
URL: www.secon.edu
Established: 1904 Annual Undergrad Tuition & Fees: $15,250
Enrollment: 209 Coed
Affiliation or Control: Independent Non-Profit IRS Status: 501(c)3
Highest Offering: Associate Degree
Program: 2-Year Principally Bachelor's Creditable
Accreditation: M, ADNUR

01 President .... Mrs. Marian KOVATCHITCH

St. Francis College (E)

180 Remsen Street, Brooklyn NY 11201-4398
County: Kings FICE Identification: 002820
Unit ID: 195173
Telephone: (718) 522-2300 Carnegie Class: Bac/Diverse
FAX Number: (718) 522-1274 Calendar System: Semester
URL: www.sfc.edu
Established: 1859 Annual Undergrad Tuition & Fees: $19,200
Enrollment: 2,697 Coed
Affiliation or Control: Independent Non-Profit IRS Status: 501(c)3
Highest Offering: Master's
Program: Liberal Arts And General; Teacher Preparatory; Nursing Emphasis
Accreditation: M, NURSE, @TEAC

01 President .... Mr. Brendan J. DUGAN
03 Executive Vice President .... Ms. June MCGRISKEN
05 Provost/Vice Pres for Academic Affs .... Dr. Timothy J. HOULIHAN
26 Vice Pres Govt/Community Relations .... Ms. Linda WERBEL DASHEFSKY
30 Vice President of Development .... Mr. Thomas FLOOD
84 Asst Vice Pres Enrollment Mgmt .... Mr. Joseph CUMMINGS
15 Asst Vice Pres Human Resources .... Mr. Richard COLADARCI
18 Asst Vice Pres Facilities Mgmt .... Mr. Kevin O'ROURKE
21 Asst Vice President for Finance .... Mr. John RAGNO
88 Assoc Dean Academic Program Develop ... Dr. Allen BURDOWSKI
20 Asst Dean of Academic Affairs .... Dr. Michele HIRSCH
35 Asst Dn Freshmen Stds/Acad Support .... Ms. Monica MICHALSKI
27 Chief Information Officer .... Mr. Guy F. CARLSEN
06 Registrar .... Ms. Roxanne PERSAUD
32 Dean of Students .... Dr. Cheryl A. HOWELL
08 Director Library .... Dr. James SMITH
36 Director of Career Placement Center .... Ms. Naomi KINLEY
29 Director of Alumni Relations .... Mr. Dennis MCDERMOTT
41 Director of Athletics .... Ms. Irma GARCIA
42 Director Campus Ministry .... Bro. Thomas GRADY, OSF
09 Director of Institutional Research .... Mr. Steven CATALANO

St. John Fisher College (F)

3690 East Avenue, Rochester NY 14618-3597
County: Monroe FICE Identification: 002821
Unit ID: 195720
Telephone: (585) 385-8000 Carnegie Class: DRU
FAX Number: (585) 899-3870 Calendar System: Semester
URL: www.sjfc.edu
Established: 1948 Annual Undergrad Tuition & Fees: $26,810
Enrollment: 3,987 Coed
Affiliation or Control: Independent Non-Profit IRS Status: 501(c)3
Highest Offering: Doctorate
Program: Liberal Arts And General; Teacher Preparatory; Business Emphasis
Accreditation: M, BUS, CACREP, NURSE, PHAR, TED

01 President .... Dr. Donald E. BAIN
04 Exec Asst to Pres/Secy to Board .... Ms. Joan R. BENULIS
05 Interim Provost/Dean of College .... Dr. Eileen LYND-BALTA
84 Sr VP Enrollment Mgmt & Planning .... Dr. Gerard J. ROONEY
10 Vice President for Finance/CFO .... Mr. Thomas E. O'NEIL
32 VP Student Affairs & Diversity .... Dr. Richard DEJESUS-RUEFF
49 Assoc VP Acad Affs/Dean Arts & Sci .... Dr. David S. PATE
50 Dean School of Business .... Dr. David G. MARTIN
53 Interim Dean School of Education .... Dr. Michael WISCHNOWSKI
66 Dean School of Nursing .... Dr. Dianne C. COONEY MINER
67 Dean School of Pharmacy .... Dr. Scott A. SWIGART
28 Director Multicultural Affairs .... Mr. Yantee SLOBERT
06 Registrar .... Ms. Julia M. THOMAS
16 Assistant Vice Pres Human Resources .. Mr. Douglas J. STEWART
27 Director Marketing & Communications .... Ms. Anne R. GEER
06 Associate Registrar .... Ms. Cheryl O. EVANS
08 Director of the Library .... Ms. Melissa JADLOS
14 Chief Information/Computing Officer .... Mr. Stacy S. SLOCUM
15 Director of Payroll & Benefits .... Ms. Mary R. POWLEY
29 Director Alumni Relations .... Mr. Christopher B. SULLIVAN
37 Director Student Financial Aid .... Mrs. Angela B. MONNAT
42 Chaplain/Director Campus Ministry . Rev. Joseph M. LANZALACO
19 Director of Safety & Security .... Mr. Michael E. MCCARTHY
41 Athletic Director .... Mr. Robert A. WARD
18 Director of Physical Plant .... Mr. Larry P. JACOBSON
21 Controller .... Ms. Linda M. STEINKIRCHNER
23 Director of Wellness Center .... Ms. Maureen A. NICHE
31 Director of Community Service .... Mrs. Sally J. VAUGHAN
07 Director of Freshman Admissions .... Ms. Stacy A. LEDERMANN
07 Dir of Transfer/Graduate Admissions .... Mr. Jose PERALES
09 Director of Institutional Research .... Ms. Elizabeth A. LACHANCE
35 Director Student Affairs .... Mr. Thomas C. RODGERS
36 Director Career Services .... Mr. Matt CARDIN
105 Webmaster .... Ms. Jody C. BENEDICT

St. John's University (G)

8000 Utopia Parkway, Queens NY 11439-0001
County: Queens FICE Identification: 002823
Unit ID: 195809
Telephone: (718) 990-6161 Carnegie Class: DRU
FAX Number: (718) 990-5723 Calendar System: Semester
URL: www.stjohns.edu
Established: 1870 Annual Undergrad Tuition & Fees: $35,520
Enrollment: 17,065 Coed
Affiliation or Control: Roman Catholic IRS Status: 501(c)3
Highest Offering: Doctorate
Program: Liberal Arts And General; Teacher Preparatory; Professional
Accreditation: M, ARCPA, ART, AUD, BUS, BUSA, CACREP, CLPSY, EMT, LAW, LIB, MT, PHAR, RAD, SCPSY, SP, TEAC

01 President .... Rev. Donald J. HARRINGTON, CM
10 Sr VP Operations and Treasurer .... Ms. Martha K. HIRST
05 Provost .... Dr. Julia A. UPTON, RSM
03 Exec VP Mission & Student Services . Rev. James J. MAHER, CM
16 Sr VP Human Res/Strategic Plan/ IR .... Ms. Mary T. HARPER HAGAN
100 Sr VP/Chief of Staff to Pres .... Mr. Robert D. WILE
101 Vice Pres & Secretary of University .... Dr. Dorothy E. HABBEN
20 Vice Pres Academic Support Services ...... Dr. Andre A. MCKENZIE
31 Vice President Community Relations .... Mr. Joseph A. SCIAME
09 VP Institutional Research/Acad Plng .... Dr. Clover W. HALL
84 Vice President Enrollment Mgmt .... Ms. Beth EVANS
18 VP Facilities/Branch Campus/Conf Sv .... Mr. Brij B. ANAND
19 Vice President Public Safety .... Mr. Thomas J. LAWRENCE
26 VP Marketing and Communications . Dr. Hallie G. SAMMARTINO
104 Vice President Global Programs .... Mr. Anthony R. PACHECO
13 Vice Pres of Info Technology/CIO .... Mr. Joseph J. TUFANO
21 VP for Business Affairs & CFO .... Vacant
42 VP University Ministry and Events .... Dr. Pamela G. SHEA-BYRNES
32 VP Student Affairs .... Dr. Kathryn T. HUTCHINSON
37 Assoc VP Student Financial Svcs .... Mr. Jorge L. RODRIGUEZ
20 Vice Provost .... Dr. Derek V. OWENS
49 Dean St. John's College .... Dr. Jeffrey W. FAGEN
53 Dean Sch of Edu/Academic VP SI Camp .... Dr. Jerrold ROSS
50 Dean Tobin Col of Business .... Dr. Victoria L. SHOAF
67 Dean Pharmacy/Health Sciences .... Dr. Robert MANGIONE
107 Dean Col of Professional Studies .... Dr. Kathleen VOUTE MACDONALD
61 Dean School of Law .... Mr. Michael A. SIMONS
08 Dean University Libraries .... Ms. Theresa M. MAYLONE
20 Assoc Provost Administration .... Ms. Linda A. SHANNON
20 Associate Provost Planning/Res Mgmt .... Dr. Diane S. HERGENROTHER
35 Assoc VP & Dean of Students .... Dr. Daniel A. TRUJILLO
35 Assoc VP Student Affairs .... Dr. Darren M. MORTON
104 Assoc VP Global Studies .... Mr. Matthew G. PUCCIARELLI
14 Asssoc VP Information Technology .... Ms. Maura A. WOODS
86 Asst VP Government Relations .... Mr. Brian BROWNE
26 Asst VP Media Relations .... Mr. Dominic SCIANNA
21 Asst VP and Exec Dir - SI Campus .. Mr. Gerard A. MCENERNEY
43 General Counsel .... Mr. Joseph E. OLIVA
21 Controller .... Mr. Anthony MACALUSO
06 University Registrar .... Ms. Joanne A. LLERANDI
90 Exec Director User Services .... Mr. Kenneth J. MAHLMEISTER
88 Exec Director Vincentian Center .... Sr. Margaret J. KELLY, DC

88 Exec Dir Aux & Conf Services .... Ms. Bernadette GROGAN LAVIN
36 Exec Director Career Center .... Ms. Denise C. HOPKINS
15 Director Human Resources Svcs .... Ms. Cynthia F. SIMPSON
29 Director Alumni Relations .... Mr. William G. SCHAEFFER
07 Director Admissions .... Ms. Karen A. VAHEY
38 Dir Ctr Counseling & Consultation .... Dr. Edward A. HATTAUER
37 Dir Financial Aid Staten Isl Campus .... Ms. Theresa C. CANTARELLA
39 Director Residence Life .... Mr. Eric M. FINKELSTEIN
44 Director Gift Planning .... Ms. Susan M. DAMIANI
23 Director Queens Health Services .... Mrs. Pauline TUMMINO
23 Director SI Health Services .... Mrs. Margaret A. TIERNEY
96 Director Purchasing .... Mr. Jeffery I. WEISS
41 Athletic Director .... Mr. Chris P. MONASCH
92 Director Honors Program .... Dr. Robert FORMAN
56 Director Special Programs .... Mrs. Cecilia M. RUSSO
88 Director Ctr for Teaching/Learning .... Dr. Maura C. FLANNERY
85 Dir Internatl Students/Scholar Svcs .... Ms. Krista L. GARD
21 Director Internal Audit .... Mr. Alex J. HOEHN
25 Director Grants & Research .... Mr. Jared E. LITTMAN
20 Acad Asst VP - SI Campus .... Dr. Christopher CUCCIA
36 Assoc Dir Career Ctr Staten Island .... Ms. Roseann T. SORENSEN
35 Assoc Dean Student Life - SI Campus .... Ms. Kimberly J. PALMIERI-MOUDED
40 Manager of Bookstore .... Mrs. Denise SERVIDIO

Saint Joseph's College, New York (A)

245 Clinton Avenue, Brooklyn NY 11205-3688
County: Kings FICE Identification: 002825
Unit ID: 195544
Telephone: (718) 940-5300 Carnegie Class: Master's M
FAX Number: (718) 636-7245 Calendar System: Semester
URL: www.sjcny.edu
Established: 1916 Annual Undergrad Tuition & Fees: $19,807
Enrollment: 1,478 Coed
Affiliation or Control: Independent Non-Profit IRS Status: 501(c)3
Highest Offering: Master's
Program: Liberal Arts And General; Teacher Preparatory; Professional
Accreditation: M, ADNUR, NUR, @TEAC

01 President .... Sr. Elizabeth A. HILL
05 Provost .... Sr. Loretta A. MCGRANN
30 VP Institutional Advancement .... Ms. Nancy J. CONNORS
107 VP/Dean Professional/Grad Studies .... Dr. Thomas G. TRAVIS
84 VP Enrollment Management .... Mrs. Theresa LAROCCA MEYER
49 Academic Dean Arts & Sciences .... Dr. Richard GREENWALD
32 Dean of Students .... Dr. Susan HUDEC
10 Chief Financial Officer .... Mr. John C. ROTH
13 Chief Information Officer .... Mr. Kenneth MCCOLLUM
08 Director of Library .... Dr. William MENG
06 Registrar .... Mr. Robert PERGOLIS
37 Director of Financial Aid .... Ms. Amy THOMPSON
38 Exec Director Career Development .... Mr. Frank LATERRA BELLINO
35 Assistant to Dean of Students .... Mrs. Sherrie VAN ARNAM
29 AVP Alumni Relations/Stewardship .... Ms. Mary Jo B. CHIARA
21 Controller .... Mr. Matthew BRELLIS
88 Director of Child Study Center .... Dr. Susan STRAUT COLLARD
18 Director Physical Plant .... Mr. Alvin DORTA
44 Assoc VP Grants/Major Gifts .... Ms. Clare KEHOE
15 Exec Director of Human Resources .... Ms. D'adra CRUMP
28 Director of Diversity .... Mr. Rupert CAMPBELL
26 Director of Public Affairs .... Mr. Michael BANACH
13 Exec Director Network Operations .... Mr. Ted DEC
14 Exec Director Enterprise Systems .... Ms. Michelle PAPAJOHN
90 Exec Director Client Services .... Ms. Lichele ABEAR
41 Director of Athletics .... Mr. Frank CARBONE

Saint Joseph's College, New York - Suffolk Campus (B)

155 W Roe Boulevard, Patchogue NY 11772-2399
County: Suffolk FICE Identification: 029081
Unit ID: 195562
Telephone: (631) 687-5100 Carnegie Class: Master's M
FAX Number: (631) 654-1782 Calendar System: Semester
URL: www.sjcny.edu
Established: 1916 Annual Undergrad Tuition & Fees: $19,807
Enrollment: 4,241 Coed
Affiliation or Control: Independent Non-Profit IRS Status: 501(c)3
Highest Offering: Master's
Program: Liberal Arts And General; Teacher Preparatory; Professional
Accreditation: &M, NRPA

01 President .... Sr. Elizabeth A. HILL
05 Provost .... Sr. Loretta A. MCGRANN
30 VP Institutional Advancement .... Ms. Nancy J. CONNORS
107 VP/Dean Professional/Grad Studies .... Dr. Thomas TRAVIS
84 VP for Enrollment Management . Mrs. Theresa LAROCCA MEYER
07 Assoc VP Enrollment Management .... Ms. Georgia-Lynn LAMENS
44 Assoc VP for Grants & Major Gifts .... Ms. Clare KEHOE
49 Academic Dean Arts & Sciences .... Dr. Christopher FROST
10 Chief Financial Officer .... Mr. John C. ROTH
32 Dean of Students .... Dr. Susan HUDEC
06 Registrar .... Mr. Robert PERGOLIS
08 Director of Library .... Dr. Elizabeth POLLICINO MURPHY
37 Director of Financial Aid .... Ms. Amy THOMPSON
35 Director Student Activities .... Ms. Marian RUSSO
36 Exec Director Career Development .... Mr. Frank LATERRA BELLINO
18 Director Physical Plant .... Ms. Linda VIGNATO
41 Director of Athletics .... Mr. Donald LIZAK
27 Chief Information Officer .... Dr. Kenneth MCCOLLUM
15 Exec Director of Human Resources .... Ms. D'adra CRUMP
21 Controller .... Mr. Matthew BRELLIS
29 Director of Alumni Relations .... Ms. Paige CARBONE
09 Director of Institutional Research .... Ms. Lillian ZHU
28 Director of Diversity .... Mr. Rupert CAMPBELL
26 Director of Public Relations .... Ms. Jessica MCALEER
13 Exec Director Network Operations .... Mr. Ted DEC
14 Exec Director Enterprise Solutions .... Ms. Michelle PAPAJOHN
88 Exec Director Client Services .... Ms. Lichele ABEAR

† Regional accreditation is carried under the parent institution in Brooklyn, NY.

St. Joseph's College of Nursing (C)

206 Prospect Avenue, Syracuse NY 13203-1806
County: Onondaga FICE Identification: 006467
Unit ID: 195191
Telephone: (315) 448-5040 Carnegie Class: Assoc/PrivNFP
FAX Number: (315) 448-5745 Calendar System: Semester
URL: www.sjhsyr.org/sjhhc/sjhcon
Established: 1898 Annual Undergrad Tuition & Fees: N/A
Enrollment: 301 Coed
Affiliation or Control: Independent Non-Profit IRS Status: 501(c)3
Highest Offering: Associate Degree
Program: Occupational; 2-Year Principally Bachelor's Creditable; Nursing Emphasis
Accreditation: @M

01 Dean .... Mrs. Marianne MARKOWITZ

Saint Joseph's Seminary (D)

Dunwoodie, #201 Seminary Avenue,
Yonkers NY 10704-1852
County: Westchester FICE Identification: 002826
Unit ID: 195571
Telephone: (914) 968-6200 Carnegie Class: Spec/Faith
FAX Number: (914) 376-2019 Calendar System: Quarter
URL: www.dunwoodie.edu
Established: 1896 Annual Graduate Tuition & Fees: $12,900
Enrollment: 45 Male
Affiliation or Control: Roman Catholic IRS Status: 501(c)3
Highest Offering: Master's; No Undergraduates
Program: Professional; Religious Emphasis
Accreditation: M, THEOL

01 Rector .... Msgr. Peter I. VACCARI
05 Academic Dean .... Rev. Kevin P. O'REILLY
32 Dean of Students/Admissions .... Rev. Andrew R. KING
08 Director Library Services .... Vacant
10 Director Finance .... Mr. Ronald TUTTLE
30 Director of Development .... Vacant
42 Director Campus Ministry .... Vacant
06 Registrar .... Vacant
38 Director of Psychological Services .... Dr. Richard GALLAGHER
18 Director of Buildings & Grounds .... Mr. Joseph DI LELLO

St. Lawrence University (E)

23 Romoda Drive, Canton NY 13617-1423
County: St. Lawrence FICE Identification: 002829
Unit ID: 195216
Telephone: (315) 229-5011 Carnegie Class: Bac/A&S
FAX Number: (315) 229-5502 Calendar System: Other
URL: www.stlawu.edu
Established: 1856 Annual Undergrad Tuition & Fees: $44,075
Enrollment: 2,457 Coed
Affiliation or Control: Independent Non-Profit IRS Status: 501(c)3
Highest Offering: Master's
Program: Liberal Arts And General; Teacher Preparatory
Accreditation: M, TEAC

01 President .... Dr. William FOX
05 Vice Pres/Dean Academic Affairs .... Dr. Valerie D. LEHR
30 Vice Pres University Advancement .... Dr. Laura ELLIS
10 Vice President Finance & Treasurer ... Ms. Kathryn L. MULLANEY
32 Vice Pres/Dean Student Life .... Dr. Joseph TOLLIVER
07 Vice Pres/Dean Admissions/Fin Aid .... Mr. Jeffrey RICKEY
26 VP for Employee/Community Relations .... Mrs. Lisa M. CANIA
21 Assoc Vice President for Finance .... Ms. Carol GABLE
89 Associate Dean of the First-Year .... Dr. Rebecca DANIELS
35 Associate Dean of Student Life .... Mr. Rance DAVIS
06 Registrar .... Ms. Carolyn FILLIPPI
37 Director of Financial Aid .... Mrs. Patricia J B. FARMER
08 Librarian .... Vacant
36 Director of Career Planning .... Dr. Carol BATE
09 Director of Institutional Research .... Ms. Christine ZIMMERMAN
18 Chief Facilities/Physical Plant .... Mr. Daniel B. SEAMAN
20 Asst Dean of Academic Affairs .... Ms. Lorie MACKENZIE
29 Director Alumni Relations .... Ms. Kimberly HISSONG
35 Director Residence Life .... Mr. Christopher MARQUARDT
23 Director of Health & Counseling .... Ms. Pat ELLIS
84 Director Enrollment Management .... Vacant
96 Director of Purchasing .... Ms. Ruta OZOLS

St. Paul's School of Nursing (F)

30-50 Whitestone Expressway, 4th Fl, Flushing NY 11354
County: Queens FICE Identification: 012364
Unit ID: 189811
Telephone: (718) 357-0500 Carnegie Class: Assoc/PrivFP
FAX Number: (718) 357-4683 Calendar System: Semester
URL: www.stpaulsschoolofnursing.com
Established: 1969 Annual Undergrad Tuition & Fees: $20,000
Enrollment: 433 Coed
Affiliation or Control: Proprietary IRS Status: Proprietary
Highest Offering: Associate Degree
Program: Occupational; 2-Year Principally Bachelor's Creditable; Nursing Emphasis
Accreditation: ABHES

01 President .... Dr. Carol S. ZAJAC
66 Regional Dean of Nursing Schools .... Genevieve M. JENSEN
37 Financial Aid Director .... Jennifer OSORIO
07 Asst Director of Admissions .... Lisa CLARKE
08 Head Librarian .... Chris SCHNUPP
10 Chief Financial/Business Officer .... Eric SEDA
06 Registrar .... Claudia MENJIVAR

Saint Paul's School of Nursing-Staten Island (G)

2 Teleport Dr Ste 203, 2 Corp Comm,
Staten Island NY 10311
County: Richmond FICE Identification: 009479
Unit ID: 195784
Telephone: (718) 818-6470 Carnegie Class: Assoc/PrivFP
FAX Number: (718) 818-6020 Calendar System: Semester
URL: www.stpaulsschoolofnursing.com
Established: 1904 Annual Undergrad Tuition & Fees: $20,580
Enrollment: 547 Coed
Affiliation or Control: Proprietary IRS Status: Proprietary
Highest Offering: Associate Degree
Program: Occupational; 2-Year Principally Bachelor's Creditable; Nursing Emphasis
Accreditation: ABHES

01 President .... Mr. Oleg RABINOVICH
05 Director of Education .... Dr. Ann LUBRANO
66 Director of Nursing .... Ms. Elizabeth BRAUN
06 Registrar .... Ms. Sandra HETZEL
10 Bursar .... Ms. Olga FORINA
07 Director of Admissions .... Ms. Kimberly WEINSTEIN
32 Director of Career Services .... Mr. Jordan ZOLTOWSKY
37 Director of Financial Aid .... Ms. Nayamka WARD

St. Thomas Aquinas College (H)

125 Route 340, Sparkill NY 10976-1050
County: Rockland FICE Identification: 002832
Unit ID: 195243
Telephone: (845) 398-4000 Carnegie Class: Master's S
FAX Number: (845) 359-8136 Calendar System: 4/1/4
URL: www.stac.edu
Established: 1952 Annual Undergrad Tuition & Fees: $25,110
Enrollment: 2,000 Coed
Affiliation or Control: Independent Non-Profit IRS Status: 501(c)3
Highest Offering: Master's
Program: Liberal Arts And General; Teacher Preparatory; Professional
Accreditation: M, IACBE, TED

01 President .... Dr. Margaret M. FITZPATRICK, SC
11 Vice Pres Administration & Finance .... Mr. Joseph DONINI
05 Provost/Vice Pres Academic Affairs .... Dr. L. John DURNEY
32 Vice Pres/Dean Student Development .... Dr. Kirk MANNING
84 Vice Pres Enrollment Mgmt/ Marketing .... Mr. Vincent CRAPANZANO
30 Vice Pres Institutional Advancement .... Mr. Kevin DUIGNAN
15 Sr Exec Director Human Resources .... Ms. Patricia PACCHIANA
07 Director Admissions .... Ms. Danielle MACKAY
09 Dir Inst Research/Program Develop .... Dr. Renee QUINTYNE
21 Controller .... Ms. Jennifer MAZZA
44 Dir Annual Giving & Alumni Affairs .... Mrs. Joanne FAVATA
35 Director Student Activities .... Ms. Anne MOORE
38 Director Student Counseling .... Dr. Louis MUGGEP
08 Librarian .... Vacant
06 Registrar .... Mrs. Mildred ALEXIOU
36 Director Placement Services .... Ms. Rachel JACKIEWICZ
37 Director Financial Aid .... Mrs. Jean Marie MOHR
90 Director of Computing Services .... Mr. Sunny ANTHWAL
18 Dir Facilities & Construction .... Mr. Patrick LAMBERT
26 Associate Director Communications .... Mrs. Bridget CLARK
50 Dean School of Business .... Mr. Michael MURPHY
53 Dean School of Education .... Dr. Meenakshi GAJRIA
49 Dean School of Arts & Sciences .... Dr. Robert MURRAY

Saint Vladimir's Orthodox Theological Seminary (I)

575 Scarsdale Road, Crestwood NY 10707-1699
County: Westchester FICE Identification: 002833
Unit ID: 195580
Telephone: (914) 961-8313 Carnegie Class: Spec/Faith
FAX Number: (914) 961-4507 Calendar System: Semester
URL: www.svots.edu
Established: 1938 Annual Graduate Tuition & Fees: $10,822
Enrollment: 53 Coed
Affiliation or Control: Independent Non-Profit IRS Status: 501(c)3
Highest Offering: Master's; No Undergraduates
Program: Religious Emphasis

Accreditation: THEOL

01 Interim President .... H.E. Most Reverend NATHIEL
00 Chancellor .... V.Rev. Chad HATFIELD
05 Dean .... Rev. John BEHR
10 Assoc Chanc for Finance .... Ms. Melanie RINGA
30 Assoc Chanc for Advancement .... Mr. Theodore BAZIL
20 Assoc Dean Academic Affairs .... Dr. John BARNET
32 Assoc Dean for Student Affairs .... Rev. David MEZYNSKI
08 Librarian/Circulation .... Ms. Eleana SILK
13 Director of Computer Systems .... Mr. Georgios KOKONAS
35 Student Affairs Administrator .... Mrs. Ann SANCHEZ
07 Director Recruitment/Outreach .... Pdn. Joseph MATUSIAK
21 Business Manager .... Mr. Ted BAZIL
40 Bookstore/Operations Manager .... Rev Dn. Gregory HATRAK

Salvation Army School for Officer Training (A)

201 Lafayette Avenue, Suffern NY 10901-4707
County: Rockland Identification: 666020
Telephone: (845) 368-7200 Carnegie Class: Not Classified
FAX Number: (845) 357-6644 Calendar System: Other
URL: www.use.salvationarmy.org
Established: N/A Annual Undergrad Tuition & Fees: $1,070
Enrollment: 94 Coed
Affiliation or Control: Independent Non-Profit IRS Status: 501(c)3
Highest Offering: Associate Degree
Program: Professional
Accreditation: NY

01 Principal .... Major Ronald R. FOREMAN
03 Associate Principal .... Major Dorine M. FOREMAN
11 Asst Principal for Administration .... Major James B. COCKER
05 Director of Curriculum .... Major Eva R. GEDDES
06 Registrar .... Ms. Victoria DESANTIS
09 Director of Institutional Research .... Dr. Dennis VANDER WEELE
10 Chief Business Officer .... Major Wesley GEDDES
15 Director Personnel Services .... Major David B. DAVIS
20 Associate Academic Officer .... Major James GUEST
21 Associate Business Officer .... Mrs. Robin FRASER
35 Director Student Affairs .... Capt. Margaret DAVIS

Samaritan Hospital School of Nursing (B)

2215 Burdett Avenue, Troy NY 12065
County: Rensselaer FICE Identification: 009248
Unit ID: 196289
Telephone: (518) 271-3285 Carnegie Class: Not Classified
FAX Number: (518) 271-3303 Calendar System: Semester
URL: www.nehealth.com
Established: 1903 Annual Undergrad Tuition & Fees: $9,000
Enrollment: 155 Coed
Affiliation or Control: Independent Non-Profit IRS Status: 501(c)3
Highest Offering: Associate Degree
Program: 2-Year Principally Bachelor's Creditable; Nursing Emphasis
Accreditation: NY

01 Executive Director .... Ms. Linda D'ARCANGELIS

Sarah Lawrence College (C)

1 Meadway, Bronxville NY 10708-5999
County: Westchester FICE Identification: 002813
Unit ID: 195304
Telephone: (914) 337-0700 Carnegie Class: Bac/A&S
FAX Number: (914) 395-2668 Calendar System: Semester
URL: www.slc.edu
Established: 1926 Annual Undergrad Tuition & Fees: $45,212
Enrollment: 1,744 Coed
Affiliation or Control: Independent Non-Profit IRS Status: 501(c)3
Highest Offering: Master's
Program: Liberal Arts And General
Accreditation: M, @TEAC

01 President .... Dr. Karen R. LAWRENCE
05 Dean of the College .... Dr. Jerrilynn D. DODDS
10 Int Vice Pres Finance/Operations .... Mr. Vincent MASSARO
30 Vice President for Advancement .... Mr. Charles J. RASBERRY
26 Vice Pres Communication & Marketing .... Dr. Gerald A. SCHORIN
11 Vice President for Administration .... Thomas L. BLUM
15 VP Human Resources/Legal Affairs .... Julie AUSTER
88 Assoc VP for Advancement .... Ellen REYNOLDS
20 Associate Dean of the College .... Dr. Kanwal SINGH
32 Dean of Studies & Student Life .... Dr. Allen GREEN
35 Dean of Student Affairs .... Dr. Paige CRANDALL
07 Dean of Admission & Financial Aid .... Amy ABRAMS
58 Dean Graduate Studies .... Susan GUMA
06 Registrar .... Daniel LICHT
08 Librarian .... Charling FAGAN
13 Director Information Systems .... Sean JAMESON
29 Director of Alumni Relations .... Cheryl CIPRO
36 Director Career Counseling .... Angela CHERUBINI
44 Major Gifts Officer .... Adele CONNOR
28 Director of Diversity .... Natalie GROSS
18 Director of Facilities .... Maureen GALLAGHER
19 Director of Public Safety .... Larry HOFFMAN

SBI Campus-An Affiliate of Sanford-Brown (D)

320 S Service Road, Melville NY 11747-3201
County: Suffolk FICE Identification: 011647
Unit ID: 192156
Telephone: (631) 370-3300 Carnegie Class: Assoc/PrivFP
FAX Number: (631) 293-5872 Calendar System: Quarter
URL: www.sbmelville.com
Established: 2008 Annual Undergrad Tuition & Fees: $10,030
Enrollment: 500 Coed
Affiliation or Control: Proprietary IRS Status: Proprietary
Highest Offering: Associate Degree
Program: Occupational; 2-Year Principally Bachelor's Creditable
Accreditation: ACICS, MAAB

01 President .... Dr. Eric RICIOPPO
05 Director of Education .... Dr. Ajith CHERIYAN
06 Registrar .... Mr. Michael KLEIN
07 Director of Admissions .... Mr. Nicholas FERLISI

Schenectady County Community College (E)

78 Washington Avenue, Schenectady NY 12305
County: Schenectady FICE Identification: 006785
Unit ID: 195322
Telephone: (518) 381-1200 Carnegie Class: Assoc/Pub-U-SC
FAX Number: (518) 346-0379 Calendar System: Semester
URL: www.sunysccc.edu
Established: 1967 Annual Undergrad Tuition & Fees (In-District): $3,384
Enrollment: 7,130 Coed
Affiliation or Control: State/Local IRS Status: 501(c)3
Highest Offering: Associate Degree
Program: Occupational; 2-Year Principally Bachelor's Creditable
Accreditation: M, ACFEI, MUS

01 President .... Dr. Quintin B. BULLOCK
05 Vice President of Academic Affairs .... Dr. Penny A. HAYNES
10 Vice President of Administration .... Mr. Charles J. RICHARDSON
32 Vice President of Student Affairs .... Dr. Martha J. ASSELIN
103 Exec Dir of Workforce Development .... Mr. Matthew GRATTAN
37 Director of Financial Aid .... Mr. Brian F. MCGARVEY
20 Assistant VP Academic Affairs .... Ms. Angela M. PRESTIACOMO
11 Assistant VP of Administration .... Ms. Susan BEAUDOIN
108 Assistant Dean for Assessment & Int .... Dr. Leonard GAINES, JR.
45 Asst Dean for Planning/Acct/Effect .... Mr. Darren JOHNSON
30 Executive Director of Development .... Ms. Carmel PATRICK
06 Registrar .... Ms. Laurie A. HEMPSTEAD
07 Director of Admissions .... Mr. David G. SAMPSON
08 Director Library Services .... Ms. Lynne O. KING
90 Director of Academic Computing .... Mr. Nicholas G. LTAIF
18 Director of Campus Maintenance .... Mr. Alan J. YAUNEY
27 Chief Information Officer .... Mr. Dan NICOLAESCU
44 Coordinator of Development .... Ms. Jennifer VAN ORT
91 Manager of Administrative Computing .... Mr. Arthur PAOLELLI
26 Public Rels/Publications Specialist .... Ms. Heather L. MEANEY
36 Coordinator Career/Employment Svcs .... Mr. Robert FREDERICK
15 Coordinator Personnel Services/AAO .... Ms. Carolyn PINN
09 Coordinator Institutional Research .... Ms. Brandie DINGMAN
28 Coord Multicult/Educ/Oppty Pgms .... Ms. Angela WEST-DAVIS
21 Coordinator for Financial Services .... Ms. Aimee S. WARFIELD
04 Assistant to the President/BOT .... Ms. Paula OHLHOUS
15 Exec Director of Human Resources .... Ms. Jeanette GLIHA

School of Visual Arts (F)

209 E 23rd Street, New York NY 10010-3994
County: New York FICE Identification: 007468
Unit ID: 197151
Telephone: (212) 592-2000 Carnegie Class: Spec/Arts
FAX Number: (212) 725-3587 Calendar System: Semester
URL: www.sva.edu
Established: 1947 Annual Undergrad Tuition & Fees: $29,500
Enrollment: 4,296 Coed
Affiliation or Control: Proprietary IRS Status: Proprietary
Highest Offering: Master's
Program: Fine Arts Emphasis
Accreditation: M, ART, CIDA

00 Acting Chairman .... Milton GLASER
01 President .... David J. RHODES
03 Executive Vice President .... Anthony P. RHODES
05 Provost .... Jeffrey NESIN
10 Chief Financial Officer .... Gary SHILLET
32 Exec Dir of Student Affairs/Admiss .... Javier VEGA
26 Exec Director of External Relations .... Susan MODENSTEIN
13 Chief Information Officer .... Cosmin TOMESCU
06 Registrar .... Jon TODD
07 Director Admission .... Adam ROGERS
35 Director of Student Affairs .... Megan MANNATO
08 Director Visual Arts Library .... Robert LOBE
37 Director Financial Aid .... William BERRIOS
36 Director Career Development .... Jennifer PHILLIPS
30 Director Development/Alumni Affairs .... Carrie LINCOURT
19 Director Security .... Nick AGJMURATI
15 Director of Human Resources .... Frank AGOSTA
09 Director of Institutional Research .... Jerold DAVIS
27 Director of Communications .... Michael GRANT

Seminary of the Immaculate Conception (G)

440 W Neck Road, Huntington NY 11743-1696
County: Suffolk FICE Identification: 002683
Unit ID: 195429
Telephone: (631) 423-0483 Carnegie Class: Spec/Faith
FAX Number: (631) 423-2346 Calendar System: Semester
URL: www.icseminary.edu
Established: 1926 Annual Graduate Tuition & Fees: $20,300
Enrollment: 111 Coed
Affiliation or Control: Roman Catholic IRS Status: 501(c)3
Highest Offering: Doctorate; No Undergraduates
Program: Professional; Religious Emphasis
Accreditation: M, THEOL

01 Rector .... Msgr. Richard HENNING
03 Vice Rector .... Vacant
32 Dean of Seminarians .... Rev. Nicholas ZIENTARSKI
05 Assoc Academic Dean .... Mr. Ryan WILLIAMS
38 Director of Spiritual Formation .... Rev. Charles R. FINK
08 Librarian .... Ms. Elyse BAUM-HAYES
10 Director Finance & Business .... Mr. Dennis J. SCHLOSSER
06 Registrar .... Deacon William F. CASEY

Sh'or Yoshuv Rabbinical College (H)

1 Cedar Lawn Avenue, Lawrence NY 11559-1714
County: Nassau FICE Identification: 025059
Unit ID: 195438
Telephone: (516) 239-9002 Carnegie Class: Spec/Faith
FAX Number: (516) 239-9003 Calendar System: Semester
URL: www.shoryoshuv.org
Established: 1963 Annual Undergrad Tuition & Fees: $9,000
Enrollment: 242 Male
Affiliation or Control: Independent Non-Profit IRS Status: 501(c)3
Highest Offering: Second Talmudic Degree
Program: Teacher Preparatory; Professional
Accreditation: RABN

01 Dean .... Rabbi Naftalie JAEGER
05 Director .... Rabbi Avrohom HALPERN
32 Director of Student Affairs .... Rabbi Moshe GREENE
06 Registrar .... Mrs. Sharon JACOBOWITZ
37 Director SFA .... Mr. Moshe RUBIN

Siena College (I)

515 Loudon Road, Loudonville NY 12211-1462
County: Albany FICE Identification: 002816
Unit ID: 195474
Telephone: (518) 783-2300 Carnegie Class: Bac/A&S
FAX Number: (518) 783-4293 Calendar System: Semester
URL: www.siena.edu
Established: 1937 Annual Undergrad Tuition & Fees: $29,950
Enrollment: 3,342 Coed
Affiliation or Control: Independent Non-Profit IRS Status: 501(c)3
Highest Offering: Master's
Program: Liberal Arts And General; Teacher Preparatory
Accreditation: M, BUS, SW, TED

01 President .... Fr. Kevin J. MULLEN, OFM
05 Vice President for Academic Affairs .... Dr. Linda L. RICHARDSON
32 Vice President for Student Affairs .... Dr. Maryellen GILROY
10 Vice President for Finance & Admin .... Mr. Paul T. STEC
84 VP for Enrollment Management .... Mr. Ned J. JONES
30 VP for Development & External Affs .... Mr. David B. SMITH
100 Chief of Staff .... Fr. Kenneth P. PAULLI, OFM
13 Chief Information Officer .... Mr. Mark A. BERMAN
49 Dean of Liberal Arts .... Dr. Janet L. SHIDELER
50 Dean of Business .... Dr. Jeffrey A. MELLO
81 Dean of Science .... Dr. Allan WEATHERWAX
20 Assoc VP Acad Affs/Student Success .... Dr. Peter C. ELLARD
45 Assoc VP Acad Affs/Inst Effectivns .... Dr. Mary Lou D'ALLEGRO
15 Asst VP for Human Resources .... Ms. Cynthia B. KING-LEROY
07 Asst VP Admissions/Dir Admissions .... Ms. Heather M. RENAULT
21 Asst VP for Finance & Admin .... Ms. Mary C. STRUNK
18 Asst VP for Facilities Management .... Mr. Mark FROST
19 Asst VP Stdnt Aff/Dir Public Safety .... Mr. Michael PAPADOPOULOS
86 Asst VP Acad Affs/Govt & Found Rels .... Mr. Alfredo MEDINA, JR.
06 Registrar .... Mr. James SERBALIK
37 Asst Vice Pres Financial Aid .... Ms. Mary K. LAWYER
08 Dir of Library/Audio Visual Svcs .... Mr. Gary B. THOMPSON
43 College Counsel .... Ms. Sandra M. CASEY
92 Director of Honors Program .... Dr. Lois K. DALY
35 Dean of Students .... Mr. John R. FELIO
39 Director of Residence Life .... Ms. Kathleen BRANNOCK
41 Director of Athletics .... Mr. John D'ARGENIO
36 Director of Career Center .... Ms. Debra DELBELSO
88 Director of ITS .... Mr. Rad W. TAYLOR
42 Chaplain of the College .... Fr. Gregory JAKUBOWICZ, OFM
88 Dir Franciscan Ctr/Svc & Advocacy .... Fr. Russel MURRAY, OFM
26 Dir Strategic Comm/Integrated Mktg .... Ms. Delcy FOX
38 Director of Counseling Center .... Dr. Wally B. BZBELL
29 Director of Alumni Relations .... Ms. Mary Beth FINNERTY
09 Dir of Institutional Research .... Mr. Lee ALLARD
88 Dir of Risk Analysis/Project Mgmt .... Ms. Sandy SERBALIK
94 Dir Sr Thea Bowman Ctr for Women .... Dr. Shannon O'NEILL
23 Director of Health Services .... Ms. Carrie HOGAN
40 Bookstore Manager .... Mr. Richard IVES

88 Director of Development ... Mr. Bob P. KLEIN
44 Director of Planned Giving ... Mr. Jack R. SISE
28 Dir of Damietta Cross-Cultural Ctr ... Mr. Oscar J. MAYORGA
104 Director of Study Abroad/Intl Pgms ... Bro. Brian C. BELANGER, OFM
96 Dir of Auxiliary Svcs & Procurement ... Ms. Laura S. PARRY
09 Institutional Research Analyst ... Ms. Kai ZHOU

Simmons Institute of Funeral Service, Inc. (A)

1828 South Avenue at W Brighton, Syracuse NY 13207-2098
County: Onondaga FICE Identification: 010837
Unit ID: 195492
Telephone: (315) 475-5142 Carnegie Class: Assoc/PrivFP
FAX Number: (315) 475-3817 Calendar System: Semester
URL: www.simmonsinstitute.com
Established: 1900 Annual Undergrad Tuition & Fees: $11,000
Enrollment: 31 Coed
Affiliation or Control: Proprietary IRS Status: Proprietary
Highest Offering: Associate Degree
Program: 2-Year Principally Bachelor's Creditable; Technical Emphasis
Accreditation: FUSER

01 President/CEO ... Maurice C. WIGHTMAN

Skidmore College (B)

815 N Broadway, Saratoga Springs NY 12866-1632
County: Saratoga FICE Identification: 002814
Unit ID: 195526
Telephone: (518) 580-5000 Carnegie Class: Bac/A&S
FAX Number: (518) 580-5936 Calendar System: Semester
URL: www.skidmore.edu
Established: 1911 Annual Undergrad Tuition & Fees: $43,020
Enrollment: 2,696 Coed
Affiliation or Control: Independent Non-Profit IRS Status: 501(c)3
Highest Offering: Master's
Program: Liberal Arts And General; Teacher Preparatory; Professional
Accreditation: M, ART, SW, @TEAC

01 President ... Dr. Philip A. GLOTZBACH
05 Int Vice President Academic Affairs ... Dr. Beau BRESLIN
10 Vice President Finance/Treasurer ... Mr. Michael D. WEST
30 Vice President for Advancement ... Mr. Michael T. CASEY
16 Assoc VP Bus Aff/Dir Human Res ... Ms. Barbara E. BECK
20 Dean of Faculty ... Vacant
32 Dean of Student Affairs ... Ms. W. Rochelle CALHOUN
07 Dean of Admissions & Financial Aid ... Ms. Mary Lou W. BATES
71 Int Dean of Special Programs ... Mr. Paul CALHOUN
06 Registrar ... Mr. David DECONNO
20 Associate Dean Academic Advising ... Dr. Corey FREEMAN-GALLANT
20 Associate Dean of Faculty ... Dr. Paty RUBIO
89 Assoc Dean/Dir of First Year Exper ... Ms. Janet CASEY
35 Int Assoc Dean Student Affairs ... Mr. David KARP
39 Asst Dean Stdnt Affs/Dir Resid Life ... Mr. Donald B. HASTINGS
88 Assoc Dean Higher Ed Oppty Pgm ... Ms. Susan LAYDEN
45 Exec Dir Strategic Initiatives ... Ms. Barbara L. KRAUSE
26 Executive Director Communications ... Mr. Dan FORBUSH
09 Director of Institutional Research ... Mr. Joseph STANKOVICH
102 Dir Foundations & Corporate Rels ... Mr. Barry PRITZKER
46 Director of Sponsored Research ... Mr. Bill TOMLINSON
13 Director Center Info Tech Services ... Vacant
105 Director of Web Development ... Mr. Andy CAMP
31 Director Community Education ... Ms. Sharon A. ARPEY
87 Dir Summer Sessions/Summer Pgms ... Dr. Auden THOMAS
41 Athletic Director ... Dr. Gail L. CUMMINGS-DANSON
28 Director for Intercultural Studies ... Vacant
22 Asst Dir EEO & Workforce Diversity ... Mr. Herb CROSSMAN
91 Director of MIS ... Mr. Jeffrey A. CLARK
104 Dir of Off-Campus Study & Exchanges ... Ms. Cori FILSON
26 Director of Community Relations ... Mr. Robert S. KIMMERLE
44 Director Donor Relations ... Ms. Mary L. SOLOMONS
30 Director of Development ... Ms. Lori EASTMAN
29 Director of Alumni Affairs/Events ... Mr. Michael SPOSILI
36 Director of Career Services ... Ms. Deborah LOFFREDO
37 Director of Financial Aid ... Ms. Beth POST-LUNDQUIST
38 Director Counseling Center ... Dr. Julia C. ROUTBORT
21 Director of Business Services ... Ms. Christine KACZMAREK
23 Director of Health Services ... Ms. Pamela HOULE
18 Director of Facilities Services ... Mr. Daniel RODECKER
19 Director of Campus Safety ... Mr. Dennis S. CONWAY
08 College Librarian ... Ms. Ruth S. COPANS
28 Director Student Diversity Programs ... Ms. Mariel L. MARTIN
96 Director of Purchasing ... Mrs. Carol N. SCHNITZER
42 Dir of Religious & Spiritual Life ... Mr. Rick CHRISMAN
24 Director of Media Services ... Mr. T. Hunt CONARD
40 Manager Skidmore Shop ... Mr. Jon NEIL
101 Coordinator of Trustee Affairs ... Ms. Jeanne M. SISSON
04 Special Asst to the President ... Ms. Elizabeth B. BOURQUE

Sotheby's Institute of Art (C)

570 Lexington Ave, 6th Floor, New York NY 10022
County: New York Identification: 667007
Telephone: (212) 517-3929 Carnegie Class: Not Classified
FAX Number: (212) 517-6568 Calendar System: Semester
URL: www.sothebysinstitute.com
Established: N/A Annual Graduate Tuition & Fees: $53,140
Enrollment: 150 Coed
Affiliation or Control: Proprietary IRS Status: Proprietary
Highest Offering: First Professional Degree; No Undergraduates
Program: Professional; Fine Arts Emphasis
Accreditation: ART

01 Director ... Ms. Lesley A. CADMAN

*State University of New York System Office (D)

State University Plaza, Albany NY 12246-0001
County: Albany FICE Identification: 008788
Unit ID: 195827
Telephone: (518) 320-1100 Carnegie Class: N/A
FAX Number: (518) 320-1561
URL: www.suny.edu

01 Chancellor ... Dr. Nancy L. ZIMPHER
05 Provost and Sr Vice Chancellor ... Dr. David LAVALLEE
88 Chanc's Dpty to Ed Pipeline of SUNY ... Ms. Johanna DUNCAN-POITIER
10 Chief Financial Officer ... Mr. Brian HUTZLEY
102 Senior VP Research Foundation ... Vacant
101 V Chanc for Rsrch/Pres Rsrch Found ... Dr. Timothy KILLEEN
20 Vice Chanc Academic Programs ... Dr. Elizabeth BRINGSJORD
15 Vice Chancellor Human Resources ... Mr. Curtis LLOYD
20 Associate Provost ... Dr. Robert KRAUSHAAR
18 Vice Chanc for Capital Facilities ... Mr. Robert HAELEN
86 Vice Chanc Government Relations ... Vacant
85 Vice Chancellor for Global Affairs ... Dr. Mitchel LEVENTHAL
28 Vice Provost Diversity/Educ Equity ... Vacant
43 Vice Chancellor & General Counsel ... Mr. William F. HOWARD
88 VP/General Counsel Charter Sch Inst ... Mr. Ralph ROSSI
20 Deputy Provost ... Vacant
09 Assc Provost Inst Research/Analysis ... Dr. John PORTER
35 Assoc Provost Opportunity Programs ... Vacant
19 Asst VC for University Police ... Vacant
32 Assoc VC for Student Life ... Dr. Edward ENGELBRIDE
21 University Auditor ... Mr. Michael ABBOTT
26 Asst Vice Chanc/Communications ... Mr. Morgan HOOK
86 Asst Vice Chanc/Govt Relations ... Ms. Stacey HENGSTERMAN

*University at Albany, SUNY (E)

1400 Washington Avenue, Albany NY 12222-1000
County: Albany FICE Identification: 002835
Unit ID: 196060
Telephone: (518) 442-3300 Carnegie Class: RU/VH
FAX Number: N/A Calendar System: Semester
URL: www.albany.edu
Established: 1844 Annual Undergrad Tuition & Fees (In-State): $7,472
Enrollment: 15,501 Coed
Affiliation or Control: State IRS Status: 501(c)3
Highest Offering: Doctorate
Program: Liberal Arts And General; Teacher Preparatory; Professional
Accreditation: M, BUS, BUSA, CLPSY, COPSY, LIB, PH, PLNG, SCPSY, SPAA, SW, TEAC

02 President ... George M. PHILIP
05 Provost/Vice Pres for Academic Affs ... Susan D. PHILLIPS
46 Vice President for Research ... James DIAS
10 Int Vice Pres Finance & Business ... Stephen BEDITZ
32 Vice President Student Success ... Christine A. BOUCHARD
30 Vice Pres University Development ... Fardin SANAI
26 Vice Pres Communications/Marketing ... Catherine HERMAN
54 Sr VP/CEO Col of Nanoscale Sci/Eng ... Alain KALOYEROS
41 VP Athletic Adm/Dir Intercol Athl ... Lee MCELROY
21 Assoc Vice President & Controller ... Kevin WILCOX
35 Assoc Vice Pres for Student Affairs ... John MURPHY
45 Assoc Vice President for Research ... Robert O. WEBSTER
09 Asst VP Inst Rsrch/Plng/Efftvnss ... Bruce SZELEST
18 Assistant Vice President Facilities ... John GIARRUSSO
07 Dir Admiss/Enrol/Assoc Vice Provost ... Robert ANDREA
28 Asst VP Diversity/Inclusion ... Tamra MINOR
84 Vice Provost Enrollment Management ... Vacant
97 Vice Prov Undergraduate Education ... Sue S. FAERMAN
49 Dean of Arts & Sciences ... Edelgard WULFERT
53 Dean School of Education ... Robert BANGERT-DROWNS
50 Dean School of Business ... Donald S. SIEGEL
69 Dean School of Public Health ... Philip NASCA
61 Dean of Criminal Justice ... Alan J. LIZOTTE
80 Interim Dean Rockefeller College ... David ROUSSEAU
70 Dean of Social Welfare ... Katharine BRIAR-LAWSON
77 Dean Col of Computing & Information ... Peter BLONIARZ
58 Dean of Graduate Studies ... Kevin WILLIAMS
08 Dean/Director of Libraries ... Mary F. CASSERLY
13 Chief Information Officer ... Christine E. HAILE
29 Exec Director Alumni Association ... Lee SERRAVILLO, JR.
90 Director Academic Computing ... Felix WU
100 Chief of Staff ... Vincent DELIO
38 Director Advisement Services Center ... Suzanne K. FREED
43 Senior Counsel ... John H. REILLY
38 Director of Health/Counseling Svcs ... Estela RIVERO
36 Director Career Development ... Philippe J. ABRAHAM
96 Director of Administrative Svcs ... Edward KANE, JR.

*State University of New York at Binghamton (F)

Vestal Parkway E, Box 6000, Binghamton NY 13902-6000
County: Broome FICE Identification: 002836
Unit ID: 196079
Telephone: (607) 777-2000 Carnegie Class: RU/H
FAX Number: (607) 777-4000 Calendar System: Semester
URL: www.binghamton.edu
Established: 1946 Annual Undergrad Tuition & Fees (In-State): $7,570
Enrollment: 14,746 Coed
Affiliation or Control: State IRS Status: 501(c)3
Highest Offering: Doctorate
Program: Liberal Arts And General; Professional
Accreditation: M, BUS, CLPSY, CS, ENG, MUS, NURSE, SPAA, SW, TEAC

02 President ... Dr. Harvey G. STENGER, JR.
88 University Ombudsman ... Ms. Dawn OSBORNE-ADAMS
100 Chief of Staff ... Dr. Terrence DEAK
05 Vice Pres Academic Affs/Provost ... Dr. Donald NIEMAN
10 Vice President Administration ... Mr. James R. VANVOORST
32 Vice Pres Student Affairs ... Mr. Brian T. ROSE
26 Vice President External Affairs ... Ms. Marcia R. CRANER
09 Vice President for Research ... Dr. Bahgat SAMMAKIA
104 Vice Prov International Education ... Dr. Katharine KREBS
45 Vice Prov Strat/Fiscal Plng & UG Ed ... Dr. Michael F. MCGOFF
84 Vice Prov Enrollment Management ... Ms. Sandra STARKE
58 Vice Prov/Dean of Graduate School ... Dr. Nancy E. STAMP
18 Assoc VP Facilities Management ... Mr. Lawrence J. ROMA
35 Dean of Students ... Dr. April THOMPSON
25 Assoc Vice President Research ... Mr. Stephen A. GILJE
29 Assoc VP for External Affairs ... Ms. Sheila DOYLE
26 Asst Vice Pres Univ Comm/Mktg ... Mr. Gregory DELVISCIO
21 Assoc VP Computing Services ... Mr. Mark V. REED
35 Asst Vice Pres Student Life ... Mr. Terry WEBB
04 Exec Assistant to the President ... Ms. Laura L. O'NEIL
11 Assoc Vice Pres Admin Services ... Ms. JoAnn NAVARRO
15 Asst Vice Pres for Human Resources ... Mr. Joseph P. SCHULTZ
30 Chief Development Officer ... Ms. Marcia R. CRANER
07 Int Dir Undergraduate Admissions ... Ms. Sandra STARKE
08 Dean of Libraries ... Mr. John M. MEADOR, JR.
85 Director Intl Students/Scholar Svcs ... Ms. Ellen H. BADGER
86 Director of State Relations ... Mr. Terrence KANE
37 Int Dir Stdnt Financial Aid/Employ ... Mr. Dennis J. CHAVEZ
06 University Registrar ... Vacant
38 Director Health & Counseling ... Ms. Johann FIORE CONTE
36 Director Career Development Center ... Ms. Nancy A. PAUL
19 Director Public Safety ... Mr. Timothy FAUGHANAN
41 Director Athletics ... Mr. Patrick ELLIOTT
71 Director EOP/Spec Programs ... Mr. Randall EDOUARD
22 Director of Affirmative Action/EEO ... Ms. Valerie J. HAMPTON
28 Director Multi-Cultural Res Ctr ... Ms. Nicole SIRJU-JOHNSON
92 Director Binghamton Univ Scholars ... Mr. George CATALANO
94 Exec Director of Women's Studies ... Ms. Dara J. SILBERSTEIN
96 Director of Purchasing ... Mr. Kenneth G. WASKIE
09 Actg Dir Inst Rsrch & Assessment ... Mr. Daniel JARDINE
49 Int Dean Arts & Science Harpur Col ... Dr. Wayne E. JONES
53 Dean School of Education ... Dr. S. G GRANT
50 Dean School of Management ... Dr. Upinder S. DHILLON
54 Dn Watson Sch Engr/Applied Science ... Dr. Hari SRIHARI
66 Dean Decker School of Nursing ... Dr. Joyce A. FERRARIO
31 Dean Community and Public Affairs ... Dr. Patricia INGRAHAM
106 Director Continuing Educ/Outreach ... Mr. Thomas KOWALIK

*University at Buffalo-SUNY (G)

3435 Main Street, Buffalo NY 14214
County: Erie FICE Identification: 002837
Unit ID: 196088
Telephone: (716) 645-2000 Carnegie Class: RU/VH
FAX Number: N/A Calendar System: Semester
URL: www.buffalo.edu
Established: 1846 Annual Undergrad Tuition & Fees (In-State): $7,989
Enrollment: 28,069 Coed
Affiliation or Control: State IRS Status: 501(c)3
Highest Offering: Doctorate
Program: Liberal Arts And General; Professional
Accreditation: M, ANEST, AUD, BUS, BUSA, CEA, CLPSY, CORE, DA, DENT, DIETI, ENG, IPSY, LAW, #LIB, MED, MT, NMT, NURSE, OT, PH, PHAR, PLNG, PSPSY, PTA, SP, SW, TEAC

02 President ... Dr. Satish K. TRIPATHI
05 Provost/Exec VP Academic Affs ... Dr. Charles F. ZUKOSKI
10 Vice Pres Finance & Administration ... Ms. Laura E. HUBBARD
32 Vice President Student Affairs ... Mr. Dennis R. BLACK
17 Vice President Health Sciences ... Dr. Michael CAIN
30 Vice Pres Development & Alumni Rels ... Ms. Nancy L. WELLS
46 Vice President for Research/EcoDev . Dr. Alexander CARTWRIGHT
15 Asst VP Human Resources ... Ms. Susan KRZYSTOFIAK
58 Vice Provost Graduate Education ... Mr. John T. HO
20 Vice Provost/Dean Undergraduate Ed ... Dr. Scott WEBER
20 Vice Provost for Faculty Affairs ... Ms. Lucinda M. FINLEY
104 Vice Provost for International Educ ... Dr. Stephen C. DUNNETT
45 Assoc VP Academic Planning & Budget ... Mr. Sean P. SULLIVAN
21 Assoc Vice President & Controller ... Mr. Michael F. LEVINE
18 Assoc Vice Pres Univ Facilities ... Mr. Michael F. DUPRE
08 Assoc VP for Univ Libraries ... Mr. Austin BOOTH
27 Int Assoc VP Information Technology ... Mr. Thomas FURLANI
37 Interim Director Financial Aid ... Ms. Jennifer A. POLLARD
09 Sr Asst VP/Dir Inst Analysis ... Mr. Craig W. ABBEY
96 Asst Vice Pres Procurement Services ... Mr. Daniel VIVIAN
27 Assoc VP Univ Communications ... Mr. Joseph A. BRENNAN
22 Dir Equity/Diversity/Inclusion ... Ms. Sharon E. NOLAN-WEISS
41 Director of Athletics ... Mr. Danny WHITE
20 Director Academic Services CIT ... Vacant
91 Director Enterprise Application Svc ... Ms. Susan A. HUSTON
07 Director of Admissions ... Ms. Patricia G. ARMSTRONG
19 Chief of Police ... Mr. Gerald W. SCHOENLE, JR.
39 Director of Campus Living ... Ms. Andrea COSTANTINO
38 Director of Counseling Services ... Dr. Sharon L. MITCHELL
23 Dir Hlth Svcs/Stdnt Wellness Coord ... Ms. Susan M. SNYDER
36 Director Career Services ... Ms. Arlene F. KAUKUS

85 Director Intl Students/Scholar Svc Ms. Ellen A. DUSSOURD
40 Director University Bookstores Mr. Gregory NEUMANN
92 Admin Dir Univ Honors College Ms. Krista L. HANYPSIAK
29 Sr Assoc Director Alumni Relations Mr. Jay R. FRIEDMAN
48 Dean School Arch & Planning Dr. Robert SHIBLEY
49 Dean College of Arts/Sciences Dr. Bruce PITMAN
52 Dean School Dental Medicine Dr. Michael L. GLICK
53 Dean Graduate Sch of Education Dr. Mary H. GRESHAM
54 Act Dean School Engr/Applied Sci Dr. Rajan BATTA
61 Dean School of Law Prof. Makau W. MUTUA
50 Dean School of Management Dr. Arjang A. ASSAD
63 Dean School Medicine/Biomed Sci Dr. Michael E. CAIN
66 Dean School of Nursing Dr. Marsha L. LEWIS
67 Dean School Pharmacy/Pharm Sciences Dr. Wayne K. ANDERSON
76 Dean Sch Public Hlth/Hlth Prof Dr. Lynn T. KOZLOWSKI
70 Dean School of Social Work Dr. Nancy J. SMYTH

*State University of New York at Fredonia (A)

138 Fenton Hall, Fredonia NY 14063-1136
County: Chautauqua FICE Identification: 002844
Unit ID: 196158
Telephone: (716) 673-3111 Carnegie Class: Master's M
FAX Number: N/A Calendar System: Semester
URL: www.fredonia.edu
Established: 1826 Annual Undergrad Tuition & Fees (In-State): $7,058
Enrollment: 5,730 Coed
Affiliation or Control: State IRS Status: 501(c)3
Highest Offering: Master's
Program: Liberal Arts And General; Teacher Preparatory; Professional
Accreditation: M, MUS, SP, SW, TED, THEA

02 President Dr. Virginia S. HORVATH
05 Int Provost & VP for Acad Affairs Dr. Kevin P. KEARNS
11 Interim VP for Administration Mrs. Karen R. PORPIGLIA
32 Vice President for Student Affairs Dr. David E. HERMAN
35 Asst Vice Pres for Student Affairs Ms. Monica J. WHITE
30 Vice Pres University Advancement Dr. David M. TIFFANY
20 Assoc VP Curriculum & Acad Support Dr. Melinda Ann KARNES
79 Dean Arts & Humanities Dr. John L. KIJINSKI
58 AVP Graduate Studies & Research Vacant
83 Dean Natural & Social Sciences Vacant
88 Int Asst Provost Spec Initiatives Dr. Ingrid JOHNSTON-ROBLEDO
50 Dean School of Business Dr. Russell P. BOISJOLY
53 Dean College of Education Dr. Christine E. GIVNER
102 Director Corp/Univ Advancement Dr. David M. TIFFANY
49 Assoc Dean College Arts & Science Dr. Roger A. BYRNE
18 Director Facilities Services Mr. Kevin P. CLOOS
06 Registrar Mr. Scott D. SAUNDERS
07 Director of Admissions Mr. John C. DEARTH
37 Director Financial Aid Mr. Daniel M. TRAMUTA
08 Director Library Services Mr. Randolph Lee GADIKIAN
09 Dir Institutional Research/Planning Dr. Xiao Y. ZHANG
36 Director of Career Development Ms. Tracy COLLINGWOOD
84 Assoc Vice Pres for Enrollment Mgmt Mr. Daniel M. TRAMUTA
19 Chief University Police Ms. Ann K. MCCARRON-BURNS
25 Director of Sponsored Programs Ms. Maggie BRYAN-PETERSON
39 Director Residence Life Mr. Gary L. BICE, JR.
41 Athletic Director Mr. Gregory D. PRECHTL
23 Director of Health Services Ms. Patricia A. BORIS
38 Director Counseling Dr. Sally J. TURNER
49 Coord of Acad Advising/Liberal Arts Vacant
90 Academic Information Technology Mr. John MCCUNE
15 Director of Human Resources Mr. Michael D. DALEY
26 Director of Public Relations Mr. Michael BARONE
85 Director of Multicultural Affairs Vacant
92 Director of Honors Program Dr. David KINKELA
94 Director of Women's Studies Dr. Adrienne MCCORMICK
96 Director of Purchasing Mrs. Shari K. MILLER
28 Interim Dir of Affirmative Action Dr. Saundra K. LIGGINS
29 Director Alumni Affairs Ms. Patricia A. FERALDI

*State University of New York at New Paltz (B)

1 Hawk Drive, New Paltz NY 12561-2443
County: Ulster FICE Identification: 002846
Unit ID: 196176
Telephone: (845) 257-7869 Carnegie Class: Master's L
FAX Number: (845) 257-3009 Calendar System: Semester
URL: www.newpaltz.edu
Established: 1823 Annual Undergrad Tuition & Fees (In-State): $6,758
Enrollment: 7,972 Coed
Affiliation or Control: State IRS Status: 501(c)3
Highest Offering: Beyond Master's But Less Than Doctorate
Program: Liberal Arts And General; Teacher Preparatory; Professional
Accreditation: M, ART, ENG, MUS, SP, TED, THEA

02 President Dr. Donald P. CHRISTIAN
100 Chief of Staff/AVP Communication Ms. Shelly A. WRIGHT
05 Provost Dr. Philip MAUCERI
11 Vice Pres Administration & Finance Ms. Jacqueline DISTEFANO
32 Student Affairs Vice President Dr. L. David ROONEY
84 Vice Pres Enrollment Management Mr. L. David EATON
13 Asst Vice Pres Tech/Info Systems Mr. Jonathan D. LEWIT
21 Asst Vice President Administration Ms. Michele HALSTEAD
09 Asst VP Inst Research/Planning Dr. Jacqueline ANDREWS
18 Asst VP Facilities Management Mr. John SHUPE
07 Dean of Admissions Ms. Lisa JONES
08 Dean Sojourner Truth Library Mr. W. Mark COLVSON
07 Asst Dean/Dir Freshmen Admissions Ms. Kimberly STRANO
30 Director of Development Ms. Sally CROSS
36 Director Career Resource Center Ms. Tonda S. HIGHLEY
15 Director Human Resources Ms. Dawn BLADES
37 Director of Financial Aid Mr. Daniel SISTARENIK
06 Registrar Ms. Bernadette MORRIS
29 Director Alumni Affairs Vacant
38 Director Student Counseling Dr. Gweneth LLOYD
26 Dir Communication & Marketing Ms. Suzanne GRADY
96 Director of Purchasing/Procurement Mr. David FARBANIEC
19 Director Security/Safety Mr. David DUGATKIN
86 Ex Dir Compliance/Camp Clm/Title IX Ms. Tanhena PACHECO DUNN
53 Dean of Education Dr. Michael ROSENBERG
57 Dean Fine & Performing Arts Dr. Mary HAFELI
49 Dean Liberal Arts & Sciences Dr. James SCHIFFER
54 Dean Science and Engineering Dr. Daniel FREEDMAN
50 Dean School of Business Dr. Hadi SALAVITABAR
58 Assoc Provost/Dean Graduate School Dr. Laurel GARRICK DUHANEY

*State University of New York at Stony Brook (C)

310 Administration Building, Stony Brook NY 11794-0701
County: Suffolk FICE Identification: 002838
Unit ID: 196097
Telephone: (631) 632-6265 Carnegie Class: RU/VH
FAX Number: (631) 632-6621 Calendar System: Semester
URL: www.stonybrook.edu
Established: 1957 Annual Undergrad Tuition & Fees (In-State): $7,560
Enrollment: 24,208 Coed
Affiliation or Control: State IRS Status: 501(c)3
Highest Offering: Doctorate
Program: Liberal Arts And General; Teacher Preparatory; Professional
Accreditation: M, ARCPA, CLPSY, CS, DENT, DIETI, ENG, IPSY, MED, MIDWF, MT, NURSE, OT, PH, POLYT, PTA, RADDOS, SW, TED

02 President Dr. Samuel L. STANLEY
05 Provost & Sr Vice Pres Acad Affairs Dr. Dennis N. ASSANIS
63 Sr VP HSC/Dean School of Medicine Dr. Kenneth KAUSHANSKY
46 Vice President Research Vacant
32 Vice President Student Affairs Dr. Peter M. BAIGENT
10 Interim VP Finance Mr. Lyle GOMES
30 Vice Pres University Advancement Mr. Dexter BAILEY
88 VP Econ Devel/Dean Engr/Applied Sci Dr. Yacov SHAMASH
100 Chief Deputy to President Dr. Tonjanita JOHNSON
45 Asst VP for Budget Mr. Mark MACIULAITIS
11 Sr VP for Administration Ms. Barbara CHERNOW
26 Asst Vice Pres Communications Ms. Yvette ST. JACQUES
39 Asst Vice Pres Campus Residences Dr. Dallas BAUMAN
17 CEO University Hospital Dr. Reuven PASTERNAK
84 Assoc Prov Enrollment/Retent Mgmt Dr. Peter BAIGENT
13 Interim Chief Information Officer Mr. Chuck POWELL
43 Associate Counsel Ms. Susan BLUM
49 Dean College Arts & Sciences Dr. Nancy SQUIRES
54 Dean Col of Engr & Applied Science Dr. Yacov SHAMASH
88 Dean School of Marine & Atmos Sci Dr. Minghua ZHANG
52 Dean School of Dental Medicine Dr. Ray WILLIAMS
68 Dean Div Physical Educ & Athletics Mr. James FIORE
58 Interim Dean Graduate School Dr. Charles TABLE
51 Dean Sch Profess Devel & Cont Educ Dr. Paul EDELSON
07 Asst Provost Admission & Fin Aid Dr. Matthew WHELAN
76 Dean School Health Technology Mgmt Dr. Craig LEHMANN
35 Dean of Students Dr. Jerrold STEIN
66 Dean School of Nursing Dr. Lee XIPPOLITOS
70 Dean School of Social Welfare Dr. Frances L. BRISBANE
08 Director & Dean of Libraries Mr. Andrew WHITE
86 Vice President External Relations Ms. Elaine CROSSON
88 Exec Dir LI State Vets Home Mr. Fred SGANGA
19 Chief of Police Mr. Robert LENAHAN
15 VP Human Resource Svcs Ms. Lynn JOHNSON
28 Dir Diversity/AA/Equal Employ Oppty Ms. Christina LAW
09 Director Planning & Inst Research Vacant
85 Dean International Programs Dr. William ARENS
102 Exec Dir of Stony Brook Foundation Vacant
29 Director Alumni Relations Mr. Matthew COLSON
23 Director University Health Services Dr. Rachel BERGESON
38 Director Counseling Center Dr. Jenny HWANG
36 Director Career Placement Center Ms. Marianna SAVOCA
06 Interim Registrar Ms. Diane BELLO
37 Financial Aid/Scholarships Ms. Jacqueline PASCARIELLO
50 Dean College of Business Dr. Manuel LONDON
08 Director Health Sciences Library Mr. Spencer MARSH
27 University Media Relations Officer Ms. Lauren SHEPROW
96 Director of Purchasing/Procurement Mr. James FABIAN
60 Dean School of Journalism Mr. Howard SCHNEIDER

*State University of New York Health Science Center at Brooklyn (D)

450 Clarkson Avenue, Brooklyn NY 11203-2098
County: Kings FICE Identification: 002839
Unit ID: 196255
Telephone: (718) 270-1000 Carnegie Class: Spec/Med
FAX Number: (718) 270-4092 Calendar System: Semester
URL: www.downstate.edu
Established: 1860 Annual Undergrad Tuition & Fees (In-State): $5,270
Enrollment: 1,738 Coed
Affiliation or Control: State IRS Status: 501(c)3
Highest Offering: Doctorate
Program: Occupational; Liberal Arts And General; Professional
Accreditation: M, ANEST, ARCPA, DMS, MED, MIDWF, NURSE, OT, PH, PTA, RAD

02 Interim President Dr. John F. WILLIAMS
03 Chief Executive Officer Ms. Debra CAREY
10 Chief Financial Officer Mr. Alan DZIJA
11 COO/Exec Vice Pres Administration Vacant
63 Sr VP Biomed Research/Dean Col Med Dr. Ian L. TAYLOR
18 Interim Vice President Facilities Dr. Alvin BERK
17 SVP Inst Dev/Phylthrpy/VP Acad Affs Dr. JoAnn BRADLEY
32 Assoc VP Student Aff/Dean of Stdnts Dr. Lorraine TERRACINA
45 Asst Vice Pres for Planning Ms. Dorothy R. FYFE
39 Asst Vice Pres Stdnt Life/Housing Ms. Meg O'SULLIVAN
16 AVP Labor Relations Mr. Leonzo CUIMAN
15 AVP for Personnel Ms. Hendrina GOELOE-ALSTON
46 Asst Provost Scientific Affairs Mr. John M. ALLEN
58 Dean School Graduate Studies Dr. Mark STEWART
66 Dean College of Nursing Dr. Daisy CRUZ-RICHMAN
20 Asst Dean Academic Development Vacant
30 Director Institutional Advancement Ms. Ellen WATSON
13 Interim Chief Information Officer Mr. Ernest WEBER
17 Interim Medical Director Dr. Michael LUCCHESI
08 Director of Libraries Dr. Richard M. WINANT
90 Dir Scientific/Acad Computer Ctr Dr. Mathew AVITABLE
07 Director of Admissions Ms. Shushawana DEOLIVEIRA
06 Registrar Ms. Anne SHONBRUN
37 Director Student Financial Aid Mr. James NEWELL
21 Bursar Mr. Charles CONWAY
51 Director of CME Ms. Edeline MITTEN
23 Actg Director of Student Health Svc Dr. Sigrid ULRICH
28 Director Ofc Opportunity/Diversity Mr. Kevin ANTOINE
29 Exec Dir Alumni Assn Col Medicine Ms. Jill DITCHIK
38 Director of Student Counseling Dr. Christine V. SAUNDERS-FIELDS
19 Chief of Police Mr. Thomas F. DUGAN
09 Director of Institutional Research Ms. Barbara LAWRENCE
26 Chief Public Relations Officer Ms. Ellen WATSON
96 Director of Purchasing Mr. Carter LARD

*State University of New York Upstate Medical University (E)

750 E Adams Street, Syracuse NY 13210-2375
County: Onondaga FICE Identification: 002840
Unit ID: 196307
Telephone: (315) 464-5540 Carnegie Class: Spec/Med
FAX Number: (315) 464-8823 Calendar System: Semester
URL: www.upstate.edu
Established: 1834 Annual Undergrad Tuition & Fees (In-State): $5,845
Enrollment: 1,590 Coed
Affiliation or Control: State IRS Status: 501(c)3
Highest Offering: Doctorate
Program: Professional
Accreditation: M, #ARCPA, DENT, DMOLS, IPSY, #MED, MT, NURSE, PERF, PTA, RAD, RTT

02 President Dr. David R. SMITH
63 Dean College of Medicine Dr. Steven J. SCHEINMAN
17 CEO University Hospital Dr. John MCCABE
10 Vice President Finance & Management Mr. Steven BRADY
05 Vice President Academic Affairs Dr. Lynn CLEARY
46 VP Research/Dean Col Grad Studies Dr. Steven GOODMAN
32 Dean Student Affairs Dr. Julie R. WHITE
102 Exec Director HSC Foundation Ms. Eileen PEZZI
26 Dir Marketing/Communic/Public Rels Ms. Melanie M. RICH
66 Dean College of Nursing Dr. Elvira SZIGETI
76 Dean College Health Profession Dr. Hugh W. BONNER
06 Registrar/Dir Inst Research Ms. Jennifer MARTIN TSE
25 Director Research Administration Mr. David W. TEMPLE
29 Director of Medical Alumni Affairs Mr. Vincent KUSS
15 Assoc VP Human Resources Mr. Eric FROST
13 Chief Information Officer Ms. Teresa J. WAGNER
08 Director of Libraries Ms. Christina POPE
28 Dir Diversity & Affirmative Action Ms. Maxine THOMPSON
07 Director of Admissions Ms. Jennifer C. WELCH
18 Chief Facilities/Physical Plant Mr. Gary KITTELL
21 Assistant Vice President Finance Mr. Eric SMITH
37 Director Student Financial Aid Mr. Michael PEDE

*State University of New York, The College at Brockport (F)

350 New Campus Drive, Brockport NY 14420-2914
County: Monroe FICE Identification: 002841
Unit ID: 196121
Telephone: (585) 395-2211 Carnegie Class: Master's L
FAX Number: (585) 395-2401 Calendar System: Semester
URL: www.brockport.edu
Established: 1867 Annual Undergrad Tuition & Fees (In-State): $6,881
Enrollment: 8,413 Coed
Affiliation or Control: State IRS Status: 501(c)3
Highest Offering: Master's
Program: Liberal Arts And General; Teacher Preparatory; Professional
Accreditation: M, BUS, CACREP, CS, DANCE, NRPA, NURSE, SPAA, SW, TED, THEA

02 President Dr. John R. HALSTEAD
05 Provost & VP Academic Affairs Dr. Anne E. HUOT

10 VP Administration & Finance ... Dr. James A. WILLIS
32 VP Enrollment Mgmt/Student Affairs ... Dr. Kathryn WILSON
30 VP Advancement ... Ms. Roxanne JOHNSTON
20 Vice Provost ... Dr. P. Michael FOX
58 Asst Provost Research/Dean Grad Sch ... Dr. James SPILLER
28 Asst Provost for Diversity ... Dr. Joel FRATER
84 Asst VP Enroll Mgmt ... Mr. Randall LANGSTON
35 Asst VP Student Affairs ... Ms. Leah A. BARRETT
18 Int Asst VP Facilities & Planning ... Mr. Jerry DESANTIS
21 Asst VP Finance & Management ... Ms. Karen M. RIOTTO
13 Assoc Provost & CIO ... Mr. Frank WOJCIK
49 Dean Arts/Humanities & Social Sci ... Dr. Darwin PRIOLEAU
50 Dean Business ... Dr. Daniel PETREE
53 Dean Education & Human Services ... Dr. Douglas SCHEIDT
68 Dean Health & Human Performance ... Dr. Frank SHORT
81 Dean Science & Mathematics ... Dr. Jose MALIEKAL
13 Director of Info Tech System ... Mr. David R. STRASENBURGH
07 Director of Undergrad Admissions ... Mr. Bernard VALENTO
44 Exec Dir of Advancement ... Mr. Michael ANDRIATCH
56 Exec Dir Brockport Metro Center ... Dr. Karen SCHUHLE-WILLIAMS
44 Exec Dir of Dev & Alumni Relations ... Mr. Bradley C. SCHREIBER
51 Exec Dir Continuing Professional Ed ... Ms. Kathleen H. GROVES
104 Exec Dir International Education ... Dr. Ralph R. TRECARTIN
26 Chief Communications Officer ... Mr. David MIHALYOV
37 Dir Financial Aid & Enrollment Svcs ... Mr. J. Scott ATKINSON
36 Director of Career Services ... Dr. Claire VANDENBERGHE
19 Chief of University Police ... Mr. Robert J. KEHOE
06 College Registrar ... Mr. Peter DOWE
16 Director of Human Resources ... Ms. Amy KAHN
22 Affirmative Action Officer ... Ms. Adrienne COLLIER
23 Director Student Health/Counseling ... Ms. Elizabeth S. CARUSO
39 Dir Residential Life/Learning Comm ... Mr. David K. BAGLEY
41 Director of Athletics ... Mr. Erick HART
25 Director of Grants Development ... Ms. Colleen DONALDSON
92 Director of Honors Program ... Dr. Donna M. KOWAL
09 Director of Inst Effectiveness ... Dr. Jeffrey T. LASHBROOK
96 Director of Procurement & Payment ... Mr. Mark W. STACY
94 Dir of Women and Gender Studies ... Dr. Barbara LESAVOY
29 Director Alumni Relations ... Mr. Kerry GOTHAM

*State University of New York College at Buffalo (A)

1300 Elmwood Avenue, Buffalo NY 14222-1091
County: Erie | FICE Identification: 002842
Unit ID: 196130
Telephone: (716) 878-4000 | Carnegie Class: Master's L
FAX Number: (716) 878-3039 | Calendar System: Semester
URL: www.buffalostate.edu
Established: 1871 | Annual Undergrad Tuition & Fees (In-State): $6,653
Enrollment: 12,204 | Coed
Affiliation or Control: State | IRS Status: 501(c)3
Highest Offering: Master's
Program: Liberal Arts And General; Teacher Preparatory; Professional
Accreditation: M, ART, CIDA, DIETC, DIETD, ENGT, JOUR, MUS, NAIT, SP, SW, TED, THEA

02 President ... Dr. Aaron M. PODOLEFSKY
100 Chief of Staff ... Dr. Bonita R. DURAND
05 Provost ... Dr. Dennis K. PONTON
10 Vice President Finance & Management ... Mr. Michael F. LEVINE
32 Vice President Student Affairs ... Dr. Hal D. PAYNE
30 Vice Pres Inst Advancement & Devel ... Dr. Susanne P. BAIR
28 Chief Diversity Officer ... Dr. Karen A. CLINTON-JONES
20 Interim Assoc VP Teacher Education ... Dr. John F. SISKAR
21 Assoc VP Budget & Planning ... Vacant
84 Associate Vice Pres Enrollment Mgmt ... Mr. Mark J. PETRIE
21 Assoc Vice President & Comptroller ... Mr. James A. THOR
102 Director College & Foundation ... Mr. Robert L. BAUMET
35 Assoc Vice President Campus Life ... Dr. Timothy R. ECKLUND
35 Asc VP Student Affs/Dean Students ... Dr. Charles B. KENYON
14 Assoc Vice Pres Computing Services ... Ms. Judith B. BASINSKI
09 Assoc VP Curriculum/Assessment ... Dr. Rosalyn A. LINDNER
26 Assoc VP College Relations ... Mr. Timothy J. WALSH
08 Assoc VP Library/Instr Technology ... Ms. Maryruth F. GLOGOWSKI
44 Assoc VP Development ... Ms. Jane A. ARMBRUSTER
86 Assoc VP Government Relations ... Mr. William J. BENFANTI
51 Assoc VP Continuing Prof Studies ... Dr. Margaret A. SHAW-BURNETT
20 Dean Univ Col/AVP Undergrad Ed ... Dr. Scott L. JOHNSON
53 Dean School of Education ... Dr. Wendy A. PATERSON
49 Dean School of Arts & Humanities ... Mr. Benjamin C. CHRISTY
83 Dean Natural & Social Science ... Dr. Mark W. SEVERSON
50 Interim Dean Professions ... Dr. Kevin F. MULCAHY
58 Dean Graduate School ... Dr. Kevin J. RAILEY
36 Director of Career Development ... Ms. Stephanie B. ZUCKERMAN-AVILES
07 Director Admissions ... Dr. Carmela THOMPSON
06 Registrar ... Mr. Mark T. BAUSILI
37 Director of Financial Aid ... Ms. Connie F. COOKE
88 Director of Student Accounts ... Ms. Susan F. WRIGHT
38 Director Counseling Center ... Dr. Joan L. MCCOOL
41 Director Intercollegiate Athletics ... Mr. Jerry S. BOYES
39 Director of Residence Life ... Mr. Kris A. KAUFMAN
23 Director Student Health Center ... Dr. Theresa R. STEPHAN HAINS
85 Director Intl Student Affairs ... Dr. Jean F. GOUNARD
15 Assoc VP Human Resource Management ... Ms. Susan J. EARSHEN
26 Director Public Relations ... Mr. Jerod T. DAHLGREN
29 Director of Alumni Affairs ... Vacant
88 Director Research Admin/Svcs ... Vacant
88 Director Special Events & Protocol ... Ms. Pamela B. VOYER
88 Director Campus Services ... Mr. Terry M. HARDING
88 Director Events Management ... Mr. Thomas E. COATES
21 Director Budget & Internal Controls ... Ms. Rebecca J. SCHENK
09 Director Institutional Research ... Mr. Yves M. GACHETTE
19 Chief University Police ... Mr. Peter M. CAREY
88 Director Parking Services ... Ms. Jayme S. RITER
96 Purchasing Manager ... Vacant
40 Manager BSC Bookstore ... Ms. Lynn M. PUMA
88 Director Student Life ... Ms. Gail V. WELLS
88 Interim Director Disability Service ... Dr. Amy ROSEN-BRAND
43 Director Judicial Affairs ... Dr. Latonia D. GASTON-MARSH

*State University of New York College at Cortland (B)

PO Box 2000, Cortland NY 13045-0900
County: Cortland | FICE Identification: 002843
Unit ID: 196149
Telephone: (607) 753-2011 | Carnegie Class: Master's L
FAX Number: (607) 753-5999 | Calendar System: Semester
URL: www.cortland.edu
Established: 1868 | Annual Undergrad Tuition & Fees (In-State): $6,972
Enrollment: 7,331 | Coed
Affiliation or Control: State | IRS Status: 501(c)3
Highest Offering: Master's
Program: Liberal Arts And General; Teacher Preparatory; Professional
Accreditation: M, NRPA, TED

02 President ... Dr. Erik J. BITTERBAUM
05 Provost ... Dr. Mark PRUS
32 Vice Pres Student Affairs ... Mr. C. Gregory SHARER
30 Vice Pres Institutional Advancement ... Ms. Kimberly PIETRO
10 Vice President Business/Finance ... Dr. William SHAUT
21 VP/Assoc Finance & Management ... Ms. Mary K. MURPHY
27 Assoc Provost for Info Resources ... Ms. Amy BERG
18 Assoc VP Facilities Management ... Ms. Nasrin PARVIZI
20 Assoc Prov for Academic Affairs ... Dr. Carol VAN DER KARR
04 Exec Assistant to the President ... Dr. Virginia LEVINE
07 Director of Admissions ... Mr. Mark YACAVONE
09 Assoc Dir Inst Rsrch/Assessment ... Dr. Merle CANFIELD
08 Director of Libraries ... Ms. Gail WOOD
06 Interim Registrar ... Mr. Thomas HANFORD
36 Director of Career Services ... Mr. John SHIRLEY
15 Director of Human Resources ... Ms. Joanne BARRY
29 Interim Director Alumni Affairs ... Ms. Erin BOYLAN
38 Dir Counseling/Student Devel ... Dr. Carolyn BERSHAD
37 Dir of Student Financial Aid ... Ms. Karen GALLAGHER
19 Chief of University Police ... Mr. Steven DANGLER
91 Director Admin Computing Svcs ... Mr. Daniel SIDEBOTTOM
90 Director Campus Technology Services ... Ms. Lisa KAHLE
107 Dean Professional Studies ... Dr. John COTTONE
49 Dean Arts & Sciences ... Dr. Bruce MATTINGLY
26 Chief Public Relations Officer ... Mr. Frederic PIERCE
53 Dean of Education ... Dr. Andrea LACHANCE
93 Director Educational Oppty Program ... Dr. Lewis ROSENGARTEN
92 Director of Honors Program ... Dr. Lisi KRALL
94 Director of Women's Studies ... Dr. Caroline KALTEFLEITER
96 Director of Purchasing ... Mr. Samuel COLOMBO
22 Affirmative Action Officer ... Ms. Wendy M. CRANMER
28 Dir Multicultural Life/Diversity ... Ms. Noelle PALEY
41 Athletic Director ... Mr. Mike URTZ

*State University of New York College at Geneseo (C)

1 College Circle, Geneseo NY 14454-1401
County: Livingston | FICE Identification: 002845
Unit ID: 196167
Telephone: (585) 245-5000 | Carnegie Class: Master's S
FAX Number: (585) 245-5005 | Calendar System: Semester
URL: www.geneseo.edu
Established: 1871 | Annual Undergrad Tuition & Fees (In-State): $7,093
Enrollment: 5,683 | Coed
Affiliation or Control: State | IRS Status: 501(c)3
Highest Offering: Master's
Program: Liberal Arts And General; Teacher Preparatory; Professional
Accreditation: M, BUS, SP, TED

02 President ... Dr. Christopher C. DAHL
05 Provost ... Dr. Carol S. LONG
20 Associate Provost ... Dr. David F. GORDON
11 Vice President Administration ... Dr. James B. MILROY
32 Vice Pres for Student & Campus Life ... Dr. Robert A. BONFIGLIO
30 Vice President College Advancement ... Mr. Michael J. CATILLAZ
84 Assoc Vice Pres Enrollment Mgmt ... Dr. William L. CAREN
10 Assoc VP Administration/Controller ... Mr. Brice M. WEIGMAN
27 Asst Vice Pres Communications ... Mr. Anthony T. HOPPA
86 Asst Prov of International Affairs ... Dr. Rebecca LEWIS
15 Asst Vice Pres Human Resources ... Ms. Julie A. BRIGGS
26 Asst VP for College Advancement ... Ms. Deborah G. HILL
29 Asst VP for Alumni Relations ... Ms. Rose ANDERSON
58 Dean of College ... Vacant
35 Dean of Students ... Dr. Leonard SANCILIO
07 Director of Admissions ... Ms. Kristine M. SHAY
08 Interim Director College Libraries ... Mr. Cyril OBERLANDER
13 Director Computing/Info Technology ... Ms. Susan E. CHICHESTER
37 Director of Financial Aid ... Mr. Archie L. CURETON
25 Director of Sponsored Research ... Dr. Anne E. BALDWIN
09 Director of Institutional Research ... Dr. Julie M. RAO
06 Registrar ... Mr. Delbert W. BROWN
36 Interim Director Career Services ... Ms. Elizabeth M. SEAGER
22 Affirmative Action Officer ... Ms. Gloria LOPEZ
88 Director of Multicultural Affairs ... Ms. Fatima R. JOHNSON
19 Chief of University Police ... Mr. Salvatore J. SIMONETTI
17 Director Counseling & Health Svcs ... Ms. Melinda C. DUBOIS
18 Chief Facilities/Physical Plant ... Mr. George F. STOOKS
21 Director Budget/Financial Analysis ... Vacant
38 Clinical Dir Counseling Services ... Dr. Beth K. CHOLETTE
96 Director of Purchasing ... Ms. Rebecca E. ANCHOR

*State University of New York College at Old Westbury (D)

P.O. Box 210, 223 Store Hill Road, Old Westbury NY 11568-0210
County: Nassau | FICE Identification: 007109
Unit ID: 196237
Telephone: (516) 876-3000 | Carnegie Class: Bac/A&S
FAX Number: (516) 876-3209 | Calendar System: Semester
URL: www.oldwestbury.edu
Established: 1965 | Annual Undergrad Tuition & Fees (In-State): $6,624
Enrollment: 4,340 | Coed
Affiliation or Control: State | IRS Status: 501(c)3
Highest Offering: Master's
Program: Liberal Arts And General; Teacher Preparatory; Professional
Accreditation: M, TED

02 President ... Dr. Calvin O. BUTTS, III
03 Executive Vice President ... Ms. Mona G. RANKIN
05 Provost/Vice Pres Academic Affairs ... Dr. Patrick O'SULLIVAN
84 Vice President Enrollment Services ... Ms. Mary MARQUEZ BELL
32 Vice President Student Affairs ... Dr. Mary L. LANGLIE
10 VP Div of Business & Finance/CFO ... Mr. Len L. DAVIS
16 Asst to Pres for Admin/Dir HR ... Mr. William P. KIMMINS
30 Asst to President for Advancement ... Mr. Michael G. KINANE
53 Dean School of Education ... Dr. Ruben L. GONZALEZ
21 Assoc Vice Pres/Business Affairs ... Ms. Deirdre M. DOWD
21 Assoc VP of Business Compliance ... Mr. Arthur H. ANGST, JR.
20 Asst Vice Pres Academic Affairs ... Mr. Ronald J. WELTON
20 Asst Vice Pres Academic Affairs ... Mr. Anthony BARBERA
35 Dean of Students ... Mr. Rollie O. BUCHANAN
49 Interim Dean School of Arts & Sci ... Dr. Barbara HILLERY
19 Chief of Police ... Mr. Michael C. YANNIELLO
26 Director Public & Media Relations ... Mr. Michael G. KINANE
13 Chief Information Officer ... Mr. Marc P. SEYBOLD
06 Registrar ... Ms. Patricia A. SMITH
96 Director of Purchasing ... Mr. Patrick ADAMS
89 Director First-Year Experience ... Dr. Laura M. ANKER
31 Director of Community Relations ... Ms. Carolyn BENNETT
38 Dir Counseling/Psych Wellness Svcs ... Dr. Trisha BILLARD
29 Director of Alumni Affairs ... Ms. Penny J. CHIN
88 Environmental Health & Safety Ofcr ... Ms. Michelle GLOVER-BROWN
88 Coordinator of Scholarships ... Ms. Pritpal KAINTH
09 Director of Institutional Research ... Ms. Sandra KAUFMANN
08 Library Director ... Mr. Stephen KIRKPATRICK
88 Dir Educational Opportunity Program ... Mr. Alonzo L. MCCOLLUM
18 Director of Facilities ... Mr. Timothy MCGARRY
88 Director of Student Activities ... Ms. Suzanne MCLOUGHLIN
23 Director of Student Health Services ... Ms. Susan R. MUNDY
88 Director of Sponsored Programs ... Mr. Thomas MURPHY
37 Director Financial Aid ... Ms. Mildred O'KEEFE
39 Director of Residential Life ... Mr. Usama SHAIKH
50 Dean School of Business ... Vacant
102 Dir Corp & Foundation Relations ... Vacant
41 Director of Athletics ... Vacant

*State University of New York College at Oneonta (E)

108 Ravine Parkway, Oneonta NY 13820-4015
County: Otsego | FICE Identification: 002847
Unit ID: 196185
Telephone: (607) 436-3500 | Carnegie Class: Master's S
FAX Number: N/A | Calendar System: Semester
URL: www.oneonta.edu
Established: 1889 | Annual Undergrad Tuition & Fees (In-State): $6,867
Enrollment: 6,000 | Coed
Affiliation or Control: State | IRS Status: 501(c)3
Highest Offering: Master's
Program: Liberal Arts And General; Teacher Preparatory; Professional
Accreditation: M, AAFCS, BUS, DIETD, DIETI, MUS, TED

02 President ... Dr. Nancy KLENIEWSKI
04 Senior Assistant to the President ... Ms. Colleen E. BRANNAN
05 Provost/Vice Pres Academic Affairs ... Dr. E. Maria THOMPSON
32 Vice President Student Development ... Dr. Steven R. PERRY
10 Vice Pres Finance/Administration ... Mr. Todd D. FOREMAN
30 Vice President College Advancement ... Mr. Paul J. ADAMO
09 Assoc Prov Inst Assessment & Eff ... Dr. Patricia L. FRANCIS
83 Int Dean Behavioral/Applied Science ... Dr. Alexander THOMAS
83 Int Dean Science/Social Science ... Dr. James EBERT
58 Director of Graduate Studies ... Mr. Patrick J. MENTE
50 Assoc Dean Economics/Business ... Dr. Wade L. THOMAS
53 Associate Dean Education ... Dr. Joanne M. CURRAN
84 Assoc Vice Pres Enrollment Mgmt ... Mr. Roger B. SULLIVAN
35 Assoc Vice President Student Life ... Dr. Jeanne C. MILLER
19 Interim Chief of Police ... Mr. Daniel P. CHAMBERS
15 Sr Exec Employee Services Officer ... Ms. Lisa M. WENCK
18 Assoc Vice Pres Facilities/Safety ... Mr. Thomas M. RATHBONE
90 Dir Academic Info Tech Services ... Mr. Steven J. MANISCALCO
07 Director of Admissions ... Ms. Karen A. BROWN
29 Director of Alumni Affairs ... Ms. Laura MADELONE

44 Director Annual Giving .... Mr. Mark A. PIEKARSKI
41 Athletic Director .... Ms. Tracey M. RANIERI
21 Budget Control Officer/Budget Dir .... Ms. Julie ROSEBOOM
25 Director Business Services .... Ms. Betty M. TIRADO
36 Dir Career Dev/Student Emp Svcs .... Dr. Amy BENEDICT-AUGUSTINE
13 Dir Computing Ctr/Chief Info Ofcr .... Dr. Karlis KAUGARS
38 Director Counseling Services .... Dr. Melissa A. FALLON
24 Director Creative Media Services .... Mr. David W. GEASEY
37 Director Financial Aid .... Mr. Bill GOODHUE
09 Senior Staff Assoc Inst Research .... Dr. Steven D. JOHNSON
85 Director of International Education .... Ms. Carol I. MANDZIK
89 Director Orientation/First Year Exp .... Ms. Monica C. GRAU
96 Purchasing Manager .... Ms. Cynthia L. MERES
06 College Registrar .... Ms. Maureen P. ARTALE
39 Director Residential Community Life .... Ms. Michele LUETTGER
93 Director Special Programs/EOP .... Ms. Lynda D. BASSETTE
23 Director Student Health Services .... Ms. Ricky O' DONNELL
26 Director of Communications .... Mr. Hal S. LEGG
28 Dir of Office of Equity & Incl .... Vacant
88 Affirmative Action Officer .... Mr. Andrew STAMMEL

*State University of New York College at Oswego (A)

7060 State Route 104, Oswego NY 13126-3501

County: Oswego FICE Identification: 002848
Unit ID: 196194
Telephone: (315) 312-2500 Carnegie Class: Master's L
FAX Number: (315) 312-5799 Calendar System: Semester
URL: www.oswego.edu
Established: 1861 Annual Undergrad Tuition & Fees (In-State): $6,841
Enrollment: 8,216 Coed
Affiliation or Control: State IRS Status: 501(c)3
Highest Offering: Master's
Program: Liberal Arts And General; Teacher Preparatory; Professional
Accreditation: M, ART, BUS, MUS, TED, THEA

02 President .... Dr. Deborah F. STANLEY
05 Interim VP Academic Affairs/Provost .... Dr. Lorrie A. CLEMO
10 Vice President Admin/Finance .... Mr. Nicholas A. LYONS
84 Vice Pres Student Affs/Enroll Mgmt .... Vacant
30 Vice Pres Devel/Alumni Relations .... Ms. Kerry DORSEY
32 Assoc VP/Dean of Students Affs .. Dr. James SCHARFENBERGER
18 Asst VP for Facilities Services .... Mr. Thomas SIMMONDS
21 Asst Vice Pres for Finance & Budget .... Mr. Byron SMITH
20 Associate Provost .... Dr. Rameen MOHAMMADI
04 Ex Asst to Pres/Spec Ast Soc Equity .... Mr. Howard GORDON
26 Director of Public Affairs .... Ms. Julie H. BLISSERT
25 Dir Research/Sponsored Pgms .... Dr. Jack GELFAND
94 Director Women's Studies .... Vacant
06 Registrar .... Mr. Jerret LEMAY
08 Director of Libraries .... Ms. Barbara SHAFFER
91 Director Admin Computer Center .... Mr. Michael C. PISA
37 Director of Financial Aid .... Mr. Mark HUMBERT
09 Director Inst Research & Assessment .... Dr. Mehran NOJAN
36 Director Career Services .... Mr. Gary MORRIS
38 Director Counseling Services Center .... Dr. Maria GRIMSHAW-CLARK
15 Dir Human Resources/Affirm Act Ofcr .... Ms. Marta SANTIAGO
19 University Police Chief .... Ms. Cynthia ADAM
23 Director of Student Health Center .... Ms. Elizabeth BURNS
56 Asst Prov Distance Lrng/Info Resour .... Dr. Michael AMEIGH
28 Assoc Prov Multicltrl Pgms & Opps .... Ms. Catherine SANTOS
39 Dir Residence Life/Housing .... Dr. Richard KOLENDA
41 Athletic Director .... Mr. Timothy HALE
96 Director Purchasing .... Mr. Mark COLE
13 Interim Chief Technology Officer .... Mr. Michael PISA
29 Director Alumni Relations .... Mr. Michael SGRO
07 Director of Admissions/Enroll Mgmt .... Vacant
40 College Store Manager .... Ms. Susan RABY
49 Interim Dean Col Lib Arts & Science .... Dr. Richard BACK
53 Interim Dean School of Education .... Dr. Pamela MICHAEL
58 Dean Graduate Studies/Research .... Dr. David KING
50 Dean School of Business .... Dr. Richard J. SKOLNIK
51 Dean of Extended Learning .... Ms. Yvonne PETRELLA
88 Dean of Comm/Media & the Arts .... Mr. Fritz MESSERE

*State University of New York College at Plattsburgh (B)

101 Broad Street, Plattsburgh NY 12901-2637

County: Clinton FICE Identification: 002849
Unit ID: 196246
Telephone: (518) 564-2000 Carnegie Class: Master's L
FAX Number: (518) 564-7827 Calendar System: Semester
URL: www.plattsburgh.edu
Established: 1889 Annual Undergrad Tuition & Fees (In-State): $8,695
Enrollment: 6,350 Coed
Affiliation or Control: State IRS Status: 501(c)3
Highest Offering: Master's
Program: Liberal Arts And General; Teacher Preparatory; Professional
Accreditation: M, BUS, CACREP, DIETD, NURSE, SP, SW, TEAC

02 President .... Dr. John ETTLING
04 Exec Assistant to the President .... Mr. Keith D. TYO
05 Provost/Vice Pres Academic Affairs .... Dr. James LISZKA
10 Vice President for Administration .... Mr. John R. HOMBURGER
30 Vice Pres Institutional Advancement .... Ms. Anne WHITMORE-HANSEN
32 Vice President for Student Affairs .... Mr. William D. LAUNDRY
20 Assistant Provost .... Ms. Diane MERKEL
21 Assoc Vice Pres Administration .... Ms. Diana M. LAPORTE
15 Director of Human Resource Svces .... Ms. Susan T. WELCH
39 Assoc Vice Pres/Dir Residence Life .... Mr. Bryan G. HARTMAN
07 Assoc VP Enroll Mgmt/Admissions .... Mr. Richard J. HIGGINS
06 Registrar .... Mr. Michael J. WALSH
49 Dean of Arts & Science .... Dr. Kathleen H. LAVOIE
53 Dean Educ/Health/Human Services .... Dr. Michael D. MORGAN
50 Dean of Business/Economics .... Dr. Raymond M. GUYDOSH
08 Interim Dean Library/Info Services .... Ms. Holly HELLER-ROSS
12 Dean Branch Campus at ACC .... Mr. Stephen DANNA
35 Dean of Students .... Mr. Stephen P. MATTHEWS
26 Exec Dir of Marketing & Commun .... Mr. Bryce T. HOFFMAN
27 Dir for Public Rel & Publications .... Ms. Michelle M. OUELLETTE
29 Director of Alumni Relations .... Ms. Joanne E. NELSON
88 Dir of Advancement Services .... Mr. David P. GREGOIRE
30 Director of Development .... Ms. Faith LONG
44 Director of Annual Giving .... Mr. Paul D. LEDUC
37 Director of Financial Aid .... Mr. Todd A. MORAVEC
18 Director of Facilities .... Mr. Kevin W. ROBERTS
23 College Physician .... Dr. Kathleen M. CAMELO
19 Chief University Police .... Ms. Arlene SABO
41 Director of Athletics .... Mr. Bruce W. DELVENTHAL
22 Director of Affirmative Action .... Dr. Lynda J. AMES
09 Director of Institutional Research .... Mr. Robert M. KARP
36 Director Career Development .... Vacant
22 Budget Officer .... Mr. Clark M. FOSTER
11 Controller .... Ms. Diane A. WYAND
96 Director of Purchasing .... Mr. Joseph P. TESORIERE
88 Exec Dr/College Aux Services .... Mr. Wayne A. DUPREY
40 Director of College Store .... Mr. Jerry L. DECELLE
46 Dir Sponsored Research/Programs .... Mr. Michael E. SIMPSON
91 Programming Manager .... Mr. Thomas J. HIGGINS

*State University of New York College at Potsdam (C)

44 Pierrepont Avenue, Potsdam NY 13676-2294

County: Saint Lawrence FICE Identification: 002850
Unit ID: 196200
Telephone: (315) 267-2000 Carnegie Class: Master's L
FAX Number: (315) 267-2496 Calendar System: Semester
URL: www.potsdam.edu
Established: 1816 Annual Undergrad Tuition & Fees (In-State): $6,842
Enrollment: 4,402 Coed
Affiliation or Control: State IRS Status: 501(c)3
Highest Offering: Master's
Program: Liberal Arts And General; Teacher Preparatory; Professional; Fine Arts Emphasis
Accreditation: M, IACBE, MUS, TED

02 President .... Dr. John F. SCHWALLER
05 Provost .... Dr. Margaret E. MADDEN
10 Vice President for Business Affairs .... Ms. Natalie L. HIGLEY
32 Vice President for Student Affairs .... Vacant
30 Vice President College Advancement .... Ms. Vicki L. TEMPLETON-CORNELL
09 Interim VP Inst Effect/Enroll Mgmt .... Mr. Bruce BRYDGES
09 VP Inst Effect/Enrollment Mgmt .... Vacant
04 Assistant to the President .... Ms. Carol M. ROURKE
90 Associate VP for Academic Affairs .... Dr. Gerald L. RATLIFF
20 Assistant Provost .... Dr. Jill R. PEARON
18 Asst Vice Pres for Facilities .... Mr. Anthony DITULLIO
88 Director of Special Programs .... Mr. Shailindar SINGH
90 Asst Vice Pres for Information Tech .... Mr. Andy A. HARRADINE
53 Dean Education & Prof Studies .... Dr. Peter S. BROUWER
49 Dean of Arts and Sciences .... Dr. Steven J. MARQUSEE
64 Dean of Music .... Dr. Michael R. SITTON
35 Dean of Students .... Mr. William G. MORRIS
51 Director of Extended Education .... Dr. Thomas W. FUHR
15 Asst VP for Human Resources .... Ms. Mary K. DOLAN
08 Director of Libraries .... Ms. Jenica P. ROGERS
06 Registrar .... Dr. Ramona M. RALSTON
07 Director of Admissions .... Mr. Thomas W. NESBITT
37 Director of Financial Aid .... Ms. Susan C. ALDRICH
36 Director of Career Planning .... Ms. Karen L. HAM
38 Director of Counseling Center .... Mrs. Gena C. NELSON
19 Chief of University Police .... Mr. John A. KAPLAN
29 Director of Alumni Relations .... Ms. Mona O. VROMAN
31 Executive Dir of Auxiliary Corp .... Mr. Daniel J. HAYES
23 Director of Health Services .... Dr. Richard E. MOOSE
39 Director of Residence Life .... Mr. Eric D. DUCHSCHERER
40 Director of College Bookstore .... Ms. Constance V. ROBINSON
41 Athletic Director .... Mr. James A. ZALACCA
25 Director Research & Sponsored Pgms .... Dr. Nancy M. DODGE-REYOME
21 Assistant VP Business Affairs .... Vacant
28 Director of Diversity Center .... Ms. Sheila M. MARSHALL
92 Director of Honors Program .... Dr. Thomas N. BAKER
94 Director of Women's Studies .... Dr. Jacqueline K. GOODMAN
26 Asst VP Marketing/Communications .... Ms. Deborah L. DUDLEY
86 Community and Gov Rel Associate .... Ms. Alexandra M. JACOBS

*Purchase College, State University of New York (D)

735 Anderson Hill Road, Purchase NY 10577-1402

County: Westchester FICE Identification: 006791
Unit ID: 196219
Telephone: (914) 251-6000 Carnegie Class: Bac/A&S
FAX Number: (914) 251-6014 Calendar System: Semester
URL: www.purchase.edu
Established: 1967 Annual Undergrad Tuition & Fees (In-State): $6,829
Enrollment: 4,267 Coed
Affiliation or Control: State IRS Status: 501(c)3
Highest Offering: Master's
Program: Liberal Arts And General; Professional
Accreditation: M, ART

02 President .... Mr. Thomas J. SCHWARZ
19 Chief of University Police .... Mr. Joseph OLENIK
10 CFO/VP Operations .... Ms. Judy NOLAN
05 Provost/Exec VP Academic Affairs .... Dr. Barbara DIXON
32 Vice President Student Affairs .... Mr. Ernie PALMIERI
84 VP Enroll Mgmt/Integrated Mktg .... Mr. Dennis CRAIG
57 Director Conservatory Theatre Arts .... Dr. Gregory TAYLOR
51 Exec Dir Liberal Stds/Cont Educ .... Ms. Danielle D'AGOSTO
81 Dean Sch Natural/Social Sciences .... Dr. Suzanne KESSLER
79 Chair School of Humanities .... Dr. Louise YELIN
20 Associate Provost .... Dr. William BASKIN
88 Artistic Dir Performing Arts Center .... Mr. Wiley HAUSAM
88 Interim Dir Neuberger Museum of Art .... Ms. Lea EMERY
08 Director of the Library .... Mr. Patrick F. CALLAHAN
64 Director Conservatory of Music .... Dr. Suzanne FARRIN
88 Director School of Art & Design .... Mr. Ravi RAJAN
13 Director Campus Technology Services .... Mr. Bill JUNOR
37 Director Student Financial Services .... Ms. Corey YORK
38 Director of Counseling Center .... Dr. Glenn POLLACK
36 Director Career Development .... Ms. Wendy MOROSOFF
15 Director of Human Resources .... Ms. Kathleen FARRELL
41 Inter Collegiate Athletic Director .... Mr. Ernie PALMIERI
39 Dir Residence & Camp Life/Stdnt Dev .... Mr. John DELATE
96 Director of Purchasing .... Mr. Nikolaus LENTNER
06 Exec Dir Enroll Svcs/Assoc Dean Ac .... Ms. Patricia BICE
09 Director of Institutional Research .... Ms. Barbara MOORE
18 Dir Capital Facilities Planning .... Mr. Christopher GAVLICK
29 Director Alumni Affairs .... Vacant
22 Acting Affirmative Action Officer .... Mr. Ricardo ESPINALES
88 Environmental Health/Safety Officer .... Mr. Edward MUSAL
44 Director Annual Giving .... Ms. Carla WEILAND-ZALEZNAK
27 Interim Dir Commun & Creative Svcs .... Ms. Sandy DYLAK

*State University of New York College of Agriculture and Technology at Cobleskill (E)

Route 7, Knapp Hall, Cobleskill NY 12043

County: Schoharie FICE Identification: 002856
Unit ID: 196033
Telephone: (518) 255-5011 Carnegie Class: Bac/Assoc
FAX Number: (518) 255-5333 Calendar System: Semester
URL: www.cobleskill.edu
Established: 1911 Annual Undergrad Tuition & Fees (In-State): $6,519
Enrollment: 2,516 Coed
Affiliation or Control: State IRS Status: 501(c)3
Highest Offering: Baccalaureate
Program: Occupational; 2-Year Principally Bachelor's Creditable; Liberal Arts And General; Technical Emphasis
Accreditation: M, ACFEI, EMT, HT

02 President .... Dr. Candace VANCKO
05 Provost & Vice Pres Academic Affs .... Dr. Deb THATCHER
04 Assistant to President .... Ms. Amy HEALY
32 VP for Student Develop/Student Life .... Mr. Steven M. ACKERKNECHT
10 Vice Pres Business & Finance .... Ms. Carol BISHOP
11 Vice Pres Administration .... Mr. Patrick WIATER
30 VP for Institutional Advancement .... Ms. Regina LAGATTA
35 Asst VP for Student Devel/Col Life .... Mr. Edward ASSELIN
47 Dean Agriculture/Natural Res .... Dr. Timothy MOORE
50 Dean Business & Computer Tech .... Mr. Michael J. MCCASKEY
49 Dean Liberal Arts & Sciences .... Dr. Susan ZIMMERMAN
08 Dean Library/Information Svcs .... Ms. Elizabeth ORGERON
27 Director of Communications .... Mr. Scott SILVERSTEN
06 Registrar .... Ms. Tara WINTER
21 Chief Business Officer .... Ms. Carol VOSATKA
07 Director of Admissions .... Vacant
39 Director of Residential Life .... Mr. Edward E. ASSELIN
36 Int Director of Student Success Ctr .... Ms. Donna PESTA
30 Director Development/Alumni Affairs .... Mrs. Lois E. GOBLET
23 Director Wellness Center .... Ms. Mary RADLIFF
37 Director of Financial Aid .... Mr. Brian D. SMITH
35 Director Student Union .... Mr. Jeffrey C. FOOTE
41 Director of Athletics .... Mr. Kevin MCCARTHY
13 Director Information Tech Services .... Mr. James DUTCHER
19 Director University Police Dept .... Mr. Frank LAWRENCE
09 Dir of IR and Assessment .... Ms. Jennifer L. GRAY
15 Director Human Resources .... Mr. R. Erik SEASTEDT
18 Director Facilities/Physical Plant .... Mr. Philip M. ARNOLD
40 Manager Bookstore .... Mr. Darrin LYONS
21 Associate Business Officer .... Ms. Louise BIRON
38 Director Student Counseling .... Ms. Lynn ONTL
85 Director of International Programs .... Ms. Susan JAGENDORF
96 Director of Purchasing .... Ms. Laura GROSS
25 Dir of Grants and Sponsored Program .... Mr. Barry GELL
88 Director of EOP .... Mr. Derwin BENNETT
88 Dir of Student Accounts .... Ms. Margaret GRIPPIN

*State University of New York College of Agriculture and Technology at Morrisville (F)

PO Box 901, Morrisville NY 13408-0901

County: Madison FICE Identification: 002859
Unit ID: 196051
Telephone: (315) 684-6000 Carnegie Class: Bac/Assoc

FAX Number: (315) 684-6116 Calendar System: Semester
URL: www.morrisville.edu
Established: 1908 Annual Undergrad Tuition & Fees (In-State): $6,945
Enrollment: 3,219 Coed
Affiliation or Control: State IRS Status: 501(c)3
Highest Offering: Baccalaureate
Program: Occupational; 2-Year Principally Bachelor's Creditable; Technical Emphasis
Accreditation: M, ACBSP, ADNUR, DIETT, ENGT

02 Officer-in-Charge ... Dr. Bjong W. YEIGH
05 Provost and Chief Operating Officer ... Dr. David E. ROGERS
11 Vice Pres for Administration ... Mr. Bruce E. REICHEL
32 Dean of Students ... Mr. Geoffrey S. ISABELLE
47 Dean School Agric/Natural Resource .. Dr. Christopher L. NYBERG
50 Interim Dean School Business ... Dr. Christopher L. NYBERG
81 Dean School Science/Technology ... Ms. Christine A. CRING
49 Dean School of Liberal Arts ... Dr. Paul F. GRIFFIN
97 Dean School of General Studies ... Ms. Jeannette H. EVANS
30 Exec Dir Inst Advancement ... Ms. Sara A. WAY
26 Dir Public Relations/Govt Affairs ... Ms. Amy L. CORNUE
06 College Registrar ... Ms. Marian D. WHITNEY
07 Director of Admissions ... Ms. Leslie V. CROSLEY
37 Director of Financial Aid ... Ms. Dacia L. BANKS
08 Director of Library ... Ms. Christine A. RUDECOFF
18 Director Physical Plant ... Mr. Carson SORRELL
38 Director Student Health Center ... Ms. Nancy S. ZLOMEK
10 Director Business Affairs ... Ms. Mary Ellen BURDICK
15 Dir Human Svcs/Affirmative Action . Mr. Anthony F. PANEBIANCO
29 Coordinator of Alumni Relations ... Ms. Kelly E. GARDNER
96 Purchasing Assistant ... Ms. Karen H. PITTS

*State University of New York College of Environmental Science and Forestry (A)

1 Forestry Drive, Syracuse NY 13210-2778
County: Onondaga FICE Identification: 002851
Unit ID: 196103
Telephone: (315) 470-6500 Carnegie Class: DRU
FAX Number: (315) 470-6779 Calendar System: Semester
URL: www.esf.edu
Established: 1911 Annual Undergrad Tuition & Fees (In-State): $6,593
Enrollment: 2,680 Coed
Affiliation or Control: State IRS Status: 501(c)3
Highest Offering: Doctorate
Program: Liberal Arts And General; Professional
Accreditation: M, ENG, ENGT, FOR, LSAR

02 President ... Dr. Cornelius B. MURPHY, JR.
05 Vice Pres Academic Affairs/Provost ..... Dr. Bruce C. BONGARTEN
11 Vice President for Administration ... Mr. Joseph RUFO
84 Vice Pres Enrollment Mgmt/Marketing ... Dr. Robert C. FRENCH
46 Vice Provost for Research ... Dr. Neil H. RINGLER
20 Assoc Prov for Instruction ... Mr. Scott S. SHANNON
32 Dean Student Life/Experiential Lrng ... Dr. Anne E. LOMBARD
10 Director of Business Affairs ... Mr. David R. DZWONKOWSKI
13 Director of Info Tech ... Mr. Yuming TUNG
15 Director Human Resources ... Ms. Marcia A. BARBER
27 Director of Communications ... Mrs. Claire B. DUNN
30 Director of Development ... Ms. Brenda T. GREENFIELD
19 Director of University Police ... Mr. Scott M. BECKSTED
08 Director of College Libraries ... Mr. Stephen WEITER
07 Director of Admissions ... Mrs. Susan H. SANFORD
06 Registrar ... Vacant
37 Director of Financial Aid ... Mr. John E. VIEW
29 Director Alumni Affairs ... Mr. Justin F. CULKOWSKI
09 Director of Institutional Planning ... Dr. Maureen O. FELLOWS
28 Director of Multicultural Affairs ... Dr. Raydora S. DRUMMER FRANCIS
18 Chief Facilities/Physical Plant ... Vacant
21 Associate Business Officer ... Ms. Danette J. DESIMONE
36 Career Planning & Devel Officer ... Mr. John TURBEVILLE
86 Director Government Relations ... Dr. Maureen O. FELLOWS
35 Director Student Activities ... Mrs. Laura CRANDALL

*State University of New York College of Optometry (B)

33 W 42nd Street, New York NY 10036-8003
County: New York FICE Identification: 009929
Unit ID: 196228
Telephone: (212) 938-4000 Carnegie Class: Spec/Health
FAX Number: (212) 938-5696 Calendar System: Semester
URL: www.sunyopt.edu
Established: 1971 Annual Graduate Tuition & Fees: $20,365
Enrollment: 317 Coed
Affiliation or Control: State IRS Status: 501(c)3
Highest Offering: Doctorate; No Undergraduates
Program: Professional
Accreditation: M, OPT, OPTR

02 President ... Dr. David A. HEATH
05 VP Academic Affs/Academic Dean ... Dr. David TROILO
11 VP For Administration and Finance ... Mr. David A. BOWERS
32 Vice President Student Affairs ... Dr. Jeffrey L. PHILPOTT
17 Int Vice Pres for Clinical Affairs ... Dr. Richard SODEN
30 Vice President Advance/Public Rels ... Ms. Ann WARWICK
04 Assistant to the President ... Ms. Karen DEGAZON
09 Director Policy/Planning/Evaluation ... Dr. Steven SCHWARTZ
08 Librarian ... Ms. Elaine WELLS
16 Director of Personnel Services ... Mr. Douglas SCHADING
37 Financial Aid Officer ... Mr. Vito CAVALLARO
06 Registrar ... Mrs. Jacqueline ESTEVEZ MARTINEZ
20 Dir Inst Vision Research/Assoc Dean .... Dr. Stewart BLOOMFIELD

*Alfred State College (C)

10 Upper College Drive, Alfred NY 14802-1196
County: Allegany FICE Identification: 002854
Unit ID: 196006
Telephone: (607) 587-4010 Carnegie Class: Bac/Assoc
FAX Number: N/A Calendar System: Semester
URL: www.alfredstate.edu
Established: 1908 Annual Undergrad Tuition & Fees (In-State): $6,874
Enrollment: 3,614 Coed
Affiliation or Control: State IRS Status: 501(c)3
Highest Offering: Baccalaureate
Program: 2-Year Principally Bachelor's Creditable; Nursing Emphasis
Accreditation: M, ADNUR, CONST, ENGT

02 President ... Dr. John M. ANDERSON
05 Vice Pres Academic Affairs ... Dr. Stephen J. HAVLOVIC
32 Int Vice President Student Affairs ... Mr. Gregory S. SAMMONS
11 VP Administration & Enrollment ... Mrs. Valerie B. NIXON
30 Vice Pres Institutional Advancement ... Dr. Derek M. WESLEY
84 Assoc VP Enrollment Management ..... Ms. Deborah J. GOODRICH
20 Assoc Vice Pres Academic Affairs ... Mr. Charles V. NEAL
35 Associate VP for Student Life ... Mr. Neil F. BENEDICT
09 Dean of Research Services ... Mrs. Nancy B. SHEARER
13 Director Computer Services ... Mr. Michael A. CASE
15 Director Human Res/Affirm Action ... Ms. Wendy DRESSER-RECKTENWALD
37 Sr Dir Student Financial Services ... Mrs. Jane A. GILLILAND
29 Director Alumni Relations ... Ms. Colleen ARGENTIERI
18 Director of Physical Plant ... Mr. Glenn R. BRUBAKER
14 Asst Director of Computing Services ... Mr. Carl H. RAHR, JR.
23 Int Sr Dir Health Svcs/Wellness ... Ms. Hollie M. HALL
38 Director Learning Center ... Ms. Janette B. THOMAS
19 Chief University Police ... Mr. Gregory S. SAMMONS
96 Director of Purchasing ... Mr. Glen E. CLINE
10 Controller ... Ms. Lisa M. PORTER
26 Sr Dir Marketing/Communications ... Ms. Debra ROOT
36 Director of Career Services ... Ms. Elaine MORSMAN
88 Chief Sustainability Officer ...... Mr. Julian DAUTREMONT-SMITH
49 Dean School of Arts & Sciences ... Dr. Terry W. TUCKER
54 Dean School of Mgmt & Engr Tech ... Dr. John WILLIAMS
75 Dean School of Applied Technology ... Mr. Craig R. CLARK

*SUNY Adirondack (D)

640 Bay Road, Queensbury NY 12804-1498
County: Warren FICE Identification: 002860
Unit ID: 188438
Telephone: (518) 743-2200 Carnegie Class: Assoc/Pub-R-M
FAX Number: (518) 745-1433 Calendar System: Semester
URL: www.sunyacc.edu
Established: 1960 Annual Undergrad Tuition & Fees (In-District): $3,664
Enrollment: 4,025 Coed
Affiliation or Control: State/Local IRS Status: 501(c)3
Highest Offering: Associate Degree
Program: Occupational; 2-Year Principally Bachelor's Creditable
Accreditation: M, ADNUR

01 President ... Dr. Ronald C. HEACOCK
04 Assistant to the President ... Ms. Dari L. NORMAN
05 Vice Pres Academic/Student Affairs ... Mr. Brian DURANT
11 Vice Pres Admin Services/Treasurer ... Mr. William LONG, III
30 Exec Dir Dev/Alumni Rels/ACC Fndtn ... Ms. Rachael HUNSINGER PATTEN
51 Dean of Cont & External Stds ... Ms. Denise BRUCKER
20 Dean for Special Academic Svcs ... Ms. Diane DALTO
32 Dean for Student Affairs ... Vacant
26 Director Marketing & Cmty Rels ... Mr. Mark PARFITT
09 Director of Inst Research/Planning ... Mr. David SMITH
27 Chief Information Officer ... Ms. Susan A. TRUMPICK
15 Director of Human Resources ... Ms. Marjorie KELLY
40 Director Bookstore ... Mr. Tom KENT
10 Chief Financial Officer ... Mr. Dan SILVEY
21 Director of Business Affairs ... Ms. Lisa DESTER
18 Director Facilities ... Mr. Anthony PALANGI
37 Director Student Financial Aid ... Ms. Maureen REILLY
06 Director of Records ... Vacant
84 Director of Enrollment Management ... Ms. Sarah J. LINEHAN
90 Director Academic Computer Services ... Ms. Roseann ANZALONE
08 Director of Library Services ... Ms. Teresa RONNING
35 Coordinator of Student Activities ... Ms. Heather CHARPENTIER
41 Athletic Director ... Vacant

*SUNY Canton-College of Technology (E)

Canton NY 13617-1098
County: Saint Lawrence FICE Identification: 002855
Unit ID: 196015
Telephone: (315) 386-7011 Carnegie Class: Bac/Assoc
FAX Number: (315) 386-7930 Calendar System: Semester
URL: www.canton.edu
Established: 1906 Annual Undergrad Tuition & Fees (In-State): $6,829
Enrollment: 3,825 Coed
Affiliation or Control: State IRS Status: 501(c)3
Highest Offering: Baccalaureate
Program: Occupational; 2-Year Principally Bachelor's Creditable; Technical Emphasis
Accreditation: M, ADNUR, DH, ENGT, PTAA

02 President ... Dr. John F. SCHWALLER
05 Interim Provost ... Ms. Karen M. SPELLACY
11 Vice Pres Business Affairs/Admin ... Ms. Natalie HIGLEY
30 Vice President for Advancement ... Mr. David M. GERLACH
32 Vice Pres of Student Affairs ... Dr. Molly A. MOTT
35 Dean of Students ... Ms. Courtney D. BISH
72 Dean Canino Sch Engineer Technology ... Dr. David J. WELLS
76 Dean Sch Sci/Health/Crim Justice ... Dr. Kenneth M. ERICKSON
50 Int Dean Sch Business/Liberal Arts ... Dr. Maureen F. MAIOCCO
30 Asst VP Advancement/Dir Athletics ... Mr. Randy B. SIEMINSKI
100 Chief of Staff ... Mr. Ryan P. DEUEL
101 Secretary to the College Council ... Ms. Stacey L. BASFORD
04 Executive Asst to President ... Ms. Stacey L. BASFORD
35 Interim Director Student Activities ... Mr. Michael J. PERRY
28 Director of Diversity ... Ms. Lashawanda T. INGRAM
96 Director of Purchasing ... Ms. Bethany A. MARTIN
37 Director of Financial Aid ... Ms. Kerrie L. COOPER
15 Director of Human Resources ... Ms. Elizabeth A. CONNOLLY
36 Director of Career Services ... Mr. David F. NORENBERG
06 Registrar ... Ms. Pamela E. ENSER
08 Librarian ... Ms. Michelle L. CURRIER
18 Asst Director of Physical Plant ... Mr. Bruce F. ALEXANDER
19 Chief of University Police ... Ms. Lisa E. COLBERT
23 Director of Health Services ... Ms. Patricia A. TODD
26 Dir Public Rels/Asst VP Advancement .... Mr. Randy B. SIEMINSKI
40 Manager Campus Store ... Mr. Corey JORDAN
39 Director of Residence Life ... Mr. John M. KENNEDY
09 Director of Institutional Research ... Ms. Sarah E. TODD
13 Chief Information Officer ... Mr. Kyle BROWN
22 Director of Affirmative Action ... Ms. Elizabeth A. CONNOLLY
29 Director of Alumni Affairs ... Ms. Peggy S. LEVATO
38 Director of Counseling ... Ms. Melinda A. MILLER
07 Director Admissions ... Ms. Nicole A. CAMPBELL
18 Dir Facilities/Capital Improvement ... Mr. Michael R. MCCORMICK
44 Director of Development ... Ms. Peggy S. LEVATO
88 User Support Services Manager ... Ms. Theresa C. CORBINE
104 Director International Programs ... Ms. Marela FIACCO
105 Web Designer/Coordinator ... Mr. Travis G. SMITH
25 Grants Coordinator ... Ms. JoAnne M. FASSINGER

*State University of New York College of Technology at Delhi (F)

2 Main Street, Delhi NY 13753
County: Delaware FICE Identification: 002857
Unit ID: 196024
Telephone: (607) 746-4000 Carnegie Class: Bac/Assoc
FAX Number: (607) 746-4208 Calendar System: Semester
URL: www.delhi.edu
Established: 1913 Annual Undergrad Tuition & Fees (In-State): $7,170
Enrollment: 3,353 Coed
Affiliation or Control: State IRS Status: 501(c)3
Highest Offering: Baccalaureate
Program: Occupational; 2-Year Principally Bachelor's Creditable; Liberal Arts And General
Accreditation: M, ACFEI, ADNUR, CONST, NUR

02 President ... Dr. Candace S. VANCKO
05 Provost ... Dr. John S. NADER
32 Vice President for Student Life ... Ms. Barbara E. JONES
10 Vice Pres for Business & Finance ... Ms. Carol M. BISHOP
26 Vice Pres for College Relations ... Mr. Joel M. SMITH
30 Vice Pres for College Advancement ... Ms. Regina M. LAGATTA
15 Vice Pres for Operations ... Ms. Bonnie G. MARTIN
36 Coordinator Career & Transfer Svcs ... Ms. Kristin A. DEFOREST
08 Director of the Resnick Library ... Ms. Pamela J. PETERS
27 Communications & New Media Manager ... Ms. Kimberly M. MACLEOD
51 Dir Training & Business Recruitment ... Ms. Glenda V. ROBERTS
19 Chief of University Police ... Mr. Perri D. DEFREECE
20 Director of Resnick Learning Center ... Ms. Michele T. DEFREECE
18 Director of Physical Plant ... Mr. David A. LOVELAND
41 Director of Athletics ... Mr. Robert H. BACKUS
06 Registrar/Dir of Inst Research ... Ms. Nancy L. SMITH
29 Alumni/Annual Giving Coordinator ... Ms. Lucinda C. BRYDON
37 Director of Financial Aid ... Ms. Nancy B. HUGHES
38 Director Counseling & Health Svcs ... Ms. Lori B. OSTERHOUDT
07 Director of Admissions ... Mr. Robert W. MAZZEI
21 Controller ... Ms. Amy L. BROWN
39 Director of Residence Life ... Mr. John J. PADOVANI
13 Chief Information Officer ... Mr. Jonathan R. BRENNAN

*State University of New York Empire State College (G)

2 Union Avenue, Saratoga Springs NY 12866-4390
County: Saratoga FICE Identification: 010286
Unit ID: 196264
Telephone: (518) 587-2100 Carnegie Class: Master's M
FAX Number: (518) 587-2886 Calendar System: Other
URL: www.esc.edu
Established: 1971 Annual Undergrad Tuition & Fees (In-State): $5,570
Enrollment: 11,827 Coed
Affiliation or Control: State IRS Status: 501(c)3
Highest Offering: Master's
Program: Liberal Arts And General; Professional
Accreditation: M, NURSE, TEAC

02 Acting President ... Dr. Meg BENKE
100 Chief of Staff ... Ms. Patrice DECOSTER

05 Acting Provost/Vice Pres AA ..... Dr. Deborah AMORY
10 Vice President for Administration ..... Mr. Paul TUCCI
86 VP for Communications & Govt Rels ..... Ms. Mary Caroline VAN DER VEER
32 Int VP Enroll Mgmt & Stdnt Svcs ..... Dr. Mitchell S. NESLER
30 VP for External Affairs ..... Dr. Hugh B. HAMMETT
13 VP for Integrated Technologies ..... Mr. David O'NEILL
09 VP for Plng & Inst Effectiveness ..... Dr. Mitchell S. NESLER
20 Vice Prov for Academic Development ..... Dr. Marjorie W. LAVIN
106 Int Vice Prov Global/Online Lrng ..... Dr. Robert CLOUGHERTY
88 Vice Prov for Reg Ctrs & Ntd Lrng ..... Vacant
12 Dean Central New York Center ..... Dr. Nikki SHRIMPTON
12 Dean Genesee Valley Center ..... Dr. Jonathan R. FRANZ
88 Dean HVA Center for Labor Studies ..... Dr. Michael MERRILL
12 Dean Hudson Valley Center ..... Dr. Gary LACY
12 Dean Long Island Center ..... Dr. Michael SPITZER
12 Dean Metropolitan Center ..... Dr. Cynthia L. WARD
12 Dean Niagara Frontier Center ..... Dr. Nan M. DIBELLO
12 Dean Northeast Center ..... Dr. Gerald F. LORENTZ
106 Dean Center for Distance Lng ..... Dr. Thomas MACKEY
58 Actg Dean Ctr for Graduate Programs ..... Dr. Tai ARNOLD
20 Asst Vice Pres for Academic Pgms ..... Vacant
21 Asst Vice Pres for Adminstration ..... Mr. Frederick BARTHELMAS
30 Asst Vice Pres for Development ..... Vacant
84 Interim Asst VP for Enrollment Mgmt ..... Ms. Jennifer D'AGOSTINO
14 Asst VP for Integrated Tech Infras ..... Vacant
07 Asst Director Admissions ..... Ms. Tina MASSA
72 Director Academic Technology ..... Ms. Suzanne HAYES
91 Director Admin Applications ..... Mr. Mark CLAVERIE
88 Director Advancement Services ..... Ms. Vicki SCHAAKE
29 Dir Alumni and Student Relations ..... Ms. Maureen WINNEY
44 Director Annual Giving ..... Ms. Diane THOMPSON
21 Director Business Affairs ..... Ms. Becky PALMIERI
88 Director Capital Projects ..... Vacant
88 Dir Center for Mentoring & Learning ..... Dr. Katherine JELLY
20 Dir Col Acad Sppt/H V Arsdale Labor ..... Ms. Sophia MAVOGIANNIS
20 Dir Col Acad Sppt/Long Island Ctr ..... Ms. Mildred VAN BERGEN
20 Dir Collegewide Academic Review ..... Dr. Nan TRAVERS
35 Dir Collegewide Student Services ..... Ms. Patricia MYERS
27 Director of Communications ..... Mr. David HENAHAN
88 Dir Cmty College Partnerships ..... Mr. Brian GOODALE
88 Dir Corp & Community Partnerships ..... Ms. Lisa SAX
88 Dir Environmental Sustainability ..... Ms. Sadie ROSS
18 Director Facilities and Maintenance ..... Mr. Rick REIMANN
37 Director Financial Aid ..... Ms. Kristina DELBRIDGE
44 Director Gift Planning ..... Vacant
30 Director of Development ..... Mr. Toby TOBROCKE
86 Director Government Relations ..... Vacant
25 Director Grants & Contracts ..... Ms. Lorraine ANTHONY
16 Asst VP for Human Resources ..... Ms. Mary Ellen R. KEENEY
88 Director Marketing ..... Ms. Renelle SHAMPENY
88 Director Outcomes Asessment ..... Vacant
88 Director Project Management ..... Mr. Walter LEWIS
96 Director Procurement ..... Mr. Charley SUMMERSELL
88 Director Publications ..... Mr. Kirk STARCZEWSKI
19 Director Campus Safety & Security ..... Mr. Thomas VUMBACO
21 Director Student Accounts ..... Ms. Pamela MALONE
88 Dir Veteran & Military Education ..... Ms. Linda FRANK
26 Senior Director of Marketing ..... Dr. John MCKENNA
22 Affirmative Action Officer ..... Ms. Mary MORTON
06 Registrar ..... Ms. Mary EDINBURGH

*Farmingdale State College (A)

2350 Broadhollow Road, Farmingdale NY 11735-1021
County: Suffolk — FICE Identification: 002858
Unit ID: 196042
Telephone: (631) 420-2000 — Carnegie Class: Bac/Diverse
FAX Number: N/A — Calendar System: Semester
URL: www.farmingdale.edu
Established: 1912 — Annual Undergrad Tuition & Fees (In-State): $6,444
Enrollment: 7,600 — Coed
Affiliation or Control: State — IRS Status: 501(c)3
Highest Offering: Baccalaureate
Program: Liberal Arts And General; Professional
Accreditation: M, ADNUR, DH, ENGT, MLTAD, NAIT, NUR, PNUR

02 President ..... Dr. Hubert KEEN
05 Provost/Vice Pres for Academic Affs ..... Dr. Lucia CEPRIANO
10 Senior Vice President & CFO ..... Mr. George P. LAROSA
32 VP Student Affairs ..... Dr. Tom CORTI
26 Vice Pres Institutional Advancement ..... Mr. Patrick CALABRIA
30 Chief Development Officer ..... Dr. Henry SIKORSKI
20 Assistant VP Academic Affairs ..... Dr. Marie HAYDEN-MILES
11 Asst Vice President Admin Services ..... Vacant
35 Dean of Students ..... Ms. Theresa ESNES-JOHNSON
07 Director of Admissions ..... Mr. Jim HALL
19 Chief University Police ..... Mr. Marvin FISCHER
18 Director of Physical Plant ..... Mr. John S. DZINANKA
27 Director of Communications ..... Ms. Kathryn S. COLEY
06 Registrar ..... Ms. Cindy MCCUE
08 Head Librarian ..... Mr. Michael KNAUTH
15 Director Human Resources ..... Ms. Marybeth INCANDELA
36 Director Career Development ..... Ms. Dolores CIACCIO
37 Director Financial Aid ..... Ms. Diane KAZANECKI-KEMPTER
09 Institutional Research Associate ..... Ms. Patricia LIND-GONZALEZ
23 Director Student Health Services ..... Ms. Audrey KRAPF
41 Director Athletics ..... Mr. Michael HARRINGTON
39 Director of Residence Life ..... Ms. Andela JASUR
102 President Farmingdale Foundation ..... Mr. Richard OVERTON
24 Director Media Resources ..... Mr. Martin BRANDT
29 Director Alumni Affairs ..... Ms. Eileen HASSON

28 Director of Diversity ..... Ms. Veronica HENRY
38 Director Student Success Center ..... Ms. Marguerite FAGELLA-D'ALOSIO
40 Manager Bookstore ..... Ms. Roberta MIRRO
21 Controller ..... Mr. Richard HUME
96 Purchasing Assistant ..... Ms. Lisa HILTONSMITH
75 Director LI Educ Oppty Center ..... Mr. Brian MAHER
50 Dean School of Business ..... Dr. Richard VOGEL
76 Dean School Health Sciences ..... Dr. Marie HAYDEN-MILES
49 Dean Sch of Arts & Sciences ..... Dr. Tony GIFFONE
54 Dean Sch Engineer Technology ..... Dr. Kamal SHAHRABI

*State University of New York Institute of Technology at Utica-Rome (B)

100 Seymour Road, Utica NY 13502
County: Oneida — FICE Identification: 011678
Unit ID: 196112
Telephone: (315) 792-7100 — Carnegie Class: Master's M
FAX Number: (315) 792-7222 — Calendar System: Semester
URL: www.sunyit.edu
Established: 1966 — Annual Undergrad Tuition & Fees (In-State): $6,764
Enrollment: 2,516 — Coed
Affiliation or Control: State — IRS Status: 501(c)3
Highest Offering: Master's
Program: Liberal Arts And General; Professional; Technical Emphasis
Accreditation: M, BUS, ENGT, NURSE

02 President ..... Dr. Bjong W. YEIGH
04 Assistant to the President ..... Ms. Laurie HARTMAN
05 Provost/Vice Pres Academic Affairs ..... Dr. William DURGIN
11 Vice President Administration ..... Mr. Bruce E. REICHEL
15 Associate VP Human Resources ..... Mr. Anthony F. PANEBIANCO
84 Assoc Provost for Student Affairs ..... Ms. Marybeth LYONS
79 Chair Communications/Humanities ..... Dr. Mary PERRONE
83 Chair Social & Behavioral Sci ..... Dr. Paul SCHULMAN
77 Chair Computer Info Sciences ..... Dr. John MARSH
54 Chair Engineering Technologies ..... Dr. Daniel JONES
81 Chair Engineering Science & Math ..... Dr. Andrew WOLFE
66 Chair Nursing & Health Profess ..... Dr. Louise DEAN-KELLY
07 Director Admissions ..... Ms. Jennifer PHELAN-NINH
41 Director Athletics ..... Mr. Kevin M. GRIMMER
21 Director Business Affairs ..... Ms. MaryEllen BURDICK
35 Director Campus Life ..... Mr. John BORNER
36 Director Career Services ..... Vacant
38 Dir Counseling & Special Pgms ..... Mr. David GARRETT
30 Director Development ..... Mr. Peter PERKINS
18 Director Facilities ..... Mr. Carson SORRELL
23 Director Health & Wellness Center ..... Ms. Jo RUFFRAGE
09 Assistant VP Institutional Research ..... Ms. Valerie FUSCO
26 Director Public Relations ..... Mr. John SWANN
19 Director Public Safety ..... Mr. Gary BEAN
39 Director Residential Life & Housing ..... Mrs. Jennifer ADAMS
46 Assoc Prov Spons Rsrch/Cont Prof Ed ..... Ms. Deborah TYKSINSKI
37 Director Student Financial Aid ..... Vacant
06 Registrar ..... Mr. John LASHER
58 Coordinator Graduate Center ..... Ms. Maryrose RAAB
29 Alumni & Advancement Services ..... Mr. Nick GRIMMER
96 Purchasing ..... Mr. Michael DURR

*State University of New York Maritime College (C)

6 Pennyfield Avenue, Throggs Neck NY 10465-4198
County: Bronx — FICE Identification: 002853
Unit ID: 196291
Telephone: (718) 409-7200 — Carnegie Class: Bac/Diverse
FAX Number: (718) 409-7392 — Calendar System: Semester
URL: www.sunymaritime.edu
Established: 1874 — Annual Undergrad Tuition & Fees (In-State): $6,457
Enrollment: 1,823 — Coed
Affiliation or Control: State — IRS Status: 501(c)3
Highest Offering: Master's
Program: Liberal Arts And General; Professional
Accreditation: M, ENG

02 President ..... RADM. Wendi B. CARPENTER
04 Executive Assistant to President ..... Ms. Desiree MARTIN
05 Provost/Vice Pres Academic Affairs ..... Dr. Michael CAPPETO
11 Vice President Operations ..... Ms. Elizabeth PRAETORIUS
32 Commandant of Cadets/Master TSES ..... CAPT. Richard S. SMITH
26 Vice President University Relations ..... Ms. Aimee BERNSTEIN
20 Academic Dean ..... Dr. Gilbert TRAUB
07 Dean of Admissions ..... Ms. Yamiley SAINTVIL
32 Assoc Provost/Dean of Students ..... Dr. Irene R. DELGADO
10 Dir of Business Affairs/CBO ..... Mr. Keith MURPHY
30 Director of Development/CDO ..... Mr. John CONNOLLY
26 Exec Director of External Affairs ..... Ms. Mary MUECKE
27 Director of Communications/PR ..... Ms. Jane BARTNETT
15 Director Human Resources ..... Ms. LuAnn AUGUSTINE-PLAISANCE
18 Exec Dir Phys Plant/Plant Superin ..... Mr. William RUEGER
88 Company Security Officer/Maritime ..... MajGen. Robert WOLF
19 Chief University Police ..... Mr. Myron PRYJMAK
84 Exec Dir Enroll Svcs/Financial Aid ..... Mr. Paul BAMONTE
41 Director of Athletics ..... Ms. Heather MACCULLOCH
88 Director of the Waterfront ..... Mr. Robert CRAFA
09 Dir of Institutional Rsrch/Asses ..... Dr. Michael CAPPETO
88 Coord Institutional Effectiveness ..... Ms. Iris VANKERCKHOVE
06 Registrar ..... Ms. Sarah GRADY

08 Head of Library ..... Ms. Constantia CONSTANTINOU
107 Chair of Prof Education/Training ..... CAPT. Ernest FINK
07 Director of Graduate Admissions ..... MajGen. Robert WOLF
07 Assoc Dir Undergrad Admissions ..... Mr. Matthew GAROFALOW
88 Director of Conference Services ..... Ms. Nancy RUEGER
21 Director of Student Accounts ..... Ms. Denise ALBERTELLI
36 Director Career Services ..... Ms. Michele BERISH
13 Chief Information Officer ..... Mr. Brian CORNELL
22 Affirmative Action Officer ..... Ms. Lu-Ann AUGUSTINE-PLAISANCE
96 Manager of Purchasing/Contracts ..... Vacant
40 Director of Ship's Store ..... Ms. Florence MANDRACHIA
38 EOP/University Counselor ..... Ms. Cortney WORRELL
88 Construction/Capital Programs Mgr ..... Mr. William HERRMANN
85 Coord Intl Student Svcs ..... Ms. Devon SWITZER

*Suffolk County Community College Central Administration (D)

533 College Road, Selden NY 11784-2899
County: Suffolk — Identification: 666658
Unit ID: 366395
Telephone: (631) 451-4000 — Carnegie Class: N/A
FAX Number: (631) 451-4715
URL: www.sunysuffolk.edu

01 President ..... Dr. Shaun L. MCKAY
04 Exec Assistant to the President ..... Dr. Christopher J. ADAMS
03 Executive Vice President ..... Mr. George GATTA
43 College General Counsel ..... Mr. Louis S. PETRIZZO
05 Vice Pres Academic/Student Affairs ..... Dr. Carla MAZZARELLI
10 VP Business/Financial Affairs ..... Mr. Charles K. STEIN
30 Vice Pres Institutional Advancement ..... Ms. Mary Lou ARANEO
45 VP Planning/Inst Effectiveness ..... Dr. Nathaniel PUGH
20 Assoc VP Academic Affairs ..... Dr. Maria DELONGORIA
32 Assoc VP of Student Affs/Dean Col ..... Vacant
103 Assoc VP Workforce/Econ Development ..... Mr. John LOMBARDO
16 Assistant VP Employee Resources ..... Mr. Jeffrey L. TEMPERA
07 College Dean Enroll/Mgt ..... Ms. Joanne E. BRAXTON
06 College Registrar ..... Ms. Anna FLACK
37 Director of Financial Aid ..... Vacant
88 Director of Publications ..... Ms. Mary FEDER

*Suffolk County Community College Ammerman Campus (E)

533 College Road, Selden NY 11784-2899
County: Suffolk — FICE Identification: 002878
Unit ID: 195951
Telephone: (631) 451-4000 — Carnegie Class: Not Classified
FAX Number: (631) 451-4015 — Calendar System: Semester
URL: www.sunysuffolk.edu
Established: 1959 — Annual Undergrad Tuition & Fees (In-District): $4,670
Enrollment: 26,787 — Coed
Affiliation or Control: State/Local — IRS Status: 501(c)3
Highest Offering: Associate Degree
Program: Occupational; 2-Year Principally Bachelor's Creditable
Accreditation: M, ADNUR, PNUR, PTAA

02 Executive Dean/Campus CEO ..... Dr. James SHERWOOD
32 Assoc Dean of Student Services ..... Mr. Charles BARTOLOTTA

*Suffolk County Community College Eastern Campus (F)

121 Speonk-Riverhead Road, Riverhead NY 11901-3499
County: Suffolk — FICE Identification: 004816
Unit ID: 195942
Telephone: (631) 548-2500 — Carnegie Class: Not Classified
FAX Number: (631) 369-2641 — Calendar System: Semester
URL: www.sunysuffolk.edu
Established: 1977 — Annual Undergrad Tuition & Fees (In-District): $4,670
Enrollment: 26,787 — Coed
Affiliation or Control: State/Local — IRS Status: 501(c)3
Highest Offering: Associate Degree
Program: Occupational; 2-Year Principally Bachelor's Creditable
Accreditation: &M, DIETT

02 Executive Dean & Campus CEO ..... Dr. Evon W. WALTERS
32 Assoc Dean of Student Services ..... Dr. Robert BEODEKER

*Suffolk County Community College Grant Campus (G)

1001 Crooked Hill Road, Brentwood NY 11717-1091
County: Suffolk — FICE Identification: 013204
Unit ID: 195960
Telephone: (631) 851-6700 — Carnegie Class: Not Classified
FAX Number: (631) 851-6509 — Calendar System: Semester
URL: www.sunysuffolk.edu
Established: 1974 — Annual Undergrad Tuition & Fees (In-District): $4,670
Enrollment: 26,787 — Coed
Affiliation or Control: State/Local — IRS Status: 501(c)3
Highest Offering: Associate Degree
Program: Occupational; 2-Year Principally Bachelor's Creditable
Accreditation: &M, ADNUR, OTA

02 Exec Dean & Campus CEO ..... Dr. James KEANE
32 Assoc Dean of Student Services ..... Dr. Meryl ROGERS

Sullivan County Community College (A)

112 College Road, Loch Sheldrake NY 12759-5721
County: Sullivan FICE Identification: 002879
Unit ID: 195988
Telephone: (845) 434-5750 Carnegie Class: Assoc/Pub-R-S
FAX Number: (845) 434-4806 Calendar System: Semester
URL: www.sullivan.suny.edu
Established: 1962 Annual Undergrad Tuition & Fees (In-District): $4,474
Enrollment: 1,704 Coed
Affiliation or Control: State/Local IRS Status: 501(c)3
Highest Offering: Associate Degree
Program: Occupational; 2-Year Principally Bachelor's Creditable
Accreditation: M, ACBSP, ADNUR

01 Interim President .... Dr. William J. MURABITO
05 Vice Pres Academic & Student Affs .... Dr. Robert SCHULTZ
11 Vice Pres Administrative Affairs .... Vacant
20 Asst VP Academic/Student Affairs .... Ms. Iman ELGINBEHI
32 Dean Student Services .... Ms. Sara THOMPSON-TWEEDY
51 Dean Workforce Devel/Cont Educ .... Dr. Stephen MITCHELL
39 Asst Dean Student Life & Housing .... Mr. James GOLDFARB
31 Dir Spec Events/Campus Activities .... Ms. Hillary EGELAND
10 Chief Business Officer .... Ms. Susan HORTON
18 Chief Facilities/Physical Plant .... Mr. Tracy HALL
07 Director Admissions/Registration .... Ms. Sari ROSENHECK
21 Controller .... Ms. Susan HORTON
30 Director Inst Development/Outreach .... Ms. Maria INGRASSIA
37 Director of Financial Aid .... Mr. James WINDERL
08 Director of Library Services .... Mr. Jon GRENNAN
35 Director Student Activities .... Ms. Adrianna MAYSON
88 Director Early Childhood .... Ms. Deborah BOGORAD
41 Director of Athletics .... Mr. Chris DEPEW
15 Director of Human Resources .... Ms. Sharon SAND
09 Director Institutional Research .... Dr. Ronald STEVENS
25 Grants Writer .... Vacant
38 Director Student Counseling .... Ms. Rose HANOFEE
96 Purchasing Agent .... Ms. Lorry IRWIN
13 Int Dir Campus Computer Services .... Ms. Cheryl WELSCH
06 Coord of Registration Services .... Dr. Laura SAMPSON
26 Coord of Public & Alumni Relations .... Vacant
50 Chair Business/Information Tech .... Ms. Mary SUDOL
79 Chair Liberal Arts & Humanities .... Dr. Paul REIFENHEISER
107 Chair Professional Studies .... Mr. Michael FISHER
83 Chair Health/Social/Behavioral Sci .... Dr. Beverly MOORE
81 Chair Mathematics/Natural Sciences .... Ms. Debra LEWKIEWICZ

Swedish Institute--College of Health Sciences (B)

226 W 26th Street, New York NY 10001-6700
County: New York FICE Identification: 021700
Unit ID: 196389
Telephone: (212) 924-5900 Carnegie Class: Spec/Health
FAX Number: (212) 924-7600 Calendar System: Semester
URL: www.swedishinstitute.edu
Established: 1916 Annual Undergrad Tuition & Fees: $14,000
Enrollment: 500 Coed
Affiliation or Control: Proprietary IRS Status: Proprietary
Highest Offering: Master's
Program: Occupational; 2-Year Principally Bachelor's Creditable; Professional
Accreditation: ACCSC, ACUP

01 President .... Mr. Peter NEIGLER
03 Senior Vice President .... Ms. Paula J. ECKARDT
10 Chief Financial Officer .... Mr. Bill BERNARD
29 Dean of Alumni Services .... Ms. Meg DARNELL
07 Director of Admissions .... Ms. Tony PELUSO
88 Dean for Massage Therapy .... Ms. Lucy LIBEN
13 Director of Information Technology .... Mr. Benn LI
32 Director of Student Services .... Ms. Jessica FERRANTE
26 Director of Public Relations .... Ms. Barbara GOLDSCHMIDT
37 Financial Aid Director .... Mr. Alex ORMENO
08 Director of Library Services .... Ms. Jill GOLDSTEIN
06 Registrar .... Mr. Jeff NAMIAN
21 Bursar .... Ms. Beatriz ACEVEDO
51 Manager of Continuing Education .... Ms. Meg DARNELL
40 Bookstore Manager .... Mr. Dan YUEN

Syracuse University Main Campus (C)

Syracuse NY 13244-1100
County: Onondaga FICE Identification: 002882
Unit ID: 196413
Telephone: (315) 443-1870 Carnegie Class: RU/H
FAX Number: (315) 443-3503 Calendar System: Semester
URL: www.syr.edu
Established: 1870 Annual Undergrad Tuition & Fees: $39,004
Enrollment: 20,829 Coed
Affiliation or Control: Independent Non-Profit IRS Status: 501(c)3
Highest Offering: Doctorate
Program: Liberal Arts And General; Teacher Preparatory; Professional
Accreditation: M, ART, AUD, BUS, CACREP, CIDA, CLPSY, CS, DIETD, DIETI, ENG, JOUR, LAW, LIB, MFCD, MUS, SCPSY, SP, SPAA, SW, TED

01 Chancellor & President .... Dr. Nancy CANTOR
05 Vice Chanc/Prov Academic Affs .... Dr. Eric F. SPINA
03 Executive Vice President & CFO .... Dr. Louis G. MARCOCCIA
43 Sr Vice Pres General Counsel .... Mr. Thomas S. EVANS
30 Exec VP Advancement/External Affs .... Mr. Thomas J. WALSH
32 Sr Vice Pres/Dean Student Affairs .... Rev. Thomas V. WOLFE
46 Vice Pres Research .... Dr. Gina LEE-GLAUSER
41 Athletic Director .... Dr. Daryl J. GROSS
26 Sr Vice Pres Public Affairs .... Mr. Kevin C. QUINN
84 Vice Pres Enrollment Management .... Mr. Donald A. SALEH
10 Vice President Business Operations .... Ms. Jena P. MCWHA
21 Comptroller .... Ms. Rebecca L. FOOTE
20 Assoc Prov International Education .... Dr. Margaret R. HIMLEY
13 Assc Vice Chanc/Academic Operations .... Mr. Christopher M. SEDORE
08 Dean of University Libraries .... Dr. Suzanne E. THORIN
88 Senior VP Human Capital Development .... Dr. Karen ALSTON
20 Assc Provost Academic Programs .... Ms. Sandra N. HURD
88 Assc Provost Entrep Innovation .... Dr. Bruce KINGMA
48 Dean School of Architecture .... Dr. Mark ROBBINS
49 Dean Col of Arts & Sciences .... Dr. George M. LANGFORD
53 Dean School of Education .... Dr. Douglas P. BIKLEN
76 Dean Col of Sport & Human Dynamics .... Dr. Diane Lyden MURPHY
54 Dean Col Engineering & Computer Sci .... Dr. Laura J. STEINBERG
62 Dean School of Information Studies .... Dr. Elizabeth D. LIDDY
61 Dean College of Law .... Dr. Hannah ARTERIAN
50 Dean Whitman School of Management .... Dr. Melvin T. STITH
80 Dean Maxwell Sch of Citizenship .... Dr. James B. STEINBERG
60 Dean Newhouse School of Public Comm .... Ms. Lorraine BRANHAM
57 Dean Col Visual & Performing Arts .... Ms. Ann CLARKE
58 Dean Graduate Studies .... Dr. Ben R. WARE
51 Dean University College .... Ms. Bethaida GONZALEZ
101 Secretary Board of Trustees .... Ms. Elizabeth B. O'ROURKE

Talmudical Institute of Upstate New York (D)

769 Park Avenue, Rochester NY 14607-3046
County: Monroe FICE Identification: 025506
Unit ID: 196440
Telephone: (585) 473-2810 Carnegie Class: Spec/Faith
FAX Number: (585) 442-0417 Calendar System: Semester
Established: 1974 Annual Undergrad Tuition & Fees: $5,000
Enrollment: 30 Male
Affiliation or Control: Independent Non-Profit IRS Status: 501(c)3
Highest Offering: Second Talmudic Degree
Program: Professional
Accreditation: RABN

01 Dean .... Rabbi Menachem DAVIDOWITZ
03 Executive Vice President .... Rabbi Shlomo NOBLE

Talmudical Seminary of Bobov (E)

5120 New Utrecht Avenue, Brooklyn NY 11204-1108
County: Kings FICE Identification: 041155
Unit ID: 451404
Telephone: (718) 854-8700 Carnegie Class: Spec/Faith
FAX Number: (718) 854-8707 Calendar System: Semester
Established: 2005 Annual Undergrad Tuition & Fees: $6,750
Enrollment: 229 Male
Affiliation or Control: Independent Non-Profit IRS Status: 501(c)3
Highest Offering: First Talmudic Degree
Program: Teacher Preparatory; Professional; Religious Emphasis
Accreditation: RABN

01 Dean .... Rabbi Joshua RUBIN

Talmudical Seminary Oholei Torah (F)

667 Eastern Parkway, Brooklyn NY 11213-3397
County: Kings FICE Identification: 012011
Unit ID: 196431
Telephone: (718) 774-5050 Carnegie Class: Spec/Faith
FAX Number: (718) 778-0784 Calendar System: Semester
Established: 1956 Annual Undergrad Tuition & Fees: $11,000
Enrollment: 375 Male
Affiliation or Control: Independent Non-Profit IRS Status: 501(c)3
Highest Offering: First Talmudic Degree
Program: Teacher Preparatory
Accreditation: RABN

01 Chief Executive Officer .... Mendel MARSOW
05 Dean .... Elchonon LESCHES
10 Business Officer .... Gary SUSSKIND
37 Financial Aid Officer .... Sholom ROSENFELD

Teachers College, Columbia University (G)

525 West 120th Street, New York NY 10027
County: New York FICE Identification: 003979
Unit ID: 196468
Telephone: (212) 678-3000 Carnegie Class: RU/H
FAX Number: (212) 678-4048 Calendar System: Semester
URL: www.tc.columbia.edu
Established: 1887 Annual Graduate Tuition & Fees: $36,930
Enrollment: 5,329 Coed
Affiliation or Control: Independent Non-Profit IRS Status: 501(c)3
Highest Offering: Doctorate; No Undergraduates
Program: Teacher Preparatory; Professional
Accreditation: M, CLPSY, COPSY, DIETI, SCPSY, SP, TED

01 President .... Dr. Susan H. FUHRMAN
05 Provost & VP for Academic Affairs .... Dr. Thomas JAMES
100 Secretary to College/Chief of Staff .... Mr. Scott FAHEY
10 Vice Pres Finance & Administration .... Mr. Harvey SPECTOR
30 Vice Pres Devel/External Affairs .... Ms. Suzanne MURPHY
22 Vice Pres/Dir Diversity/Cmty Affs .... Ms. Janice S. ROBINSON
20 Vice Provost .... Dr. William BALDWIN
21 Assoc Vice Pres/Controller .... Mr. Henry PERKOWSKI
31 Assoc Vice Pres Auxiliary Services .... Mr. James MITCHELL
88 Asc VP/Sch/Cmty Partnshp/Spec Advis .... Dr. Nancy STREIM
20 Associate Vice Provost .... Dr. Katie EMBREE
06 Registrar .... Ms. Diana MAUL
14 Director Computing/Information Svcs .... Ms. Ena HAINES
90 Manager Academic Computing .... Mr. George SCHUESSLER
08 Library Director .... Dr. Gary NATRIELLO
09 Director of Institutional Studies .... Mr. Scott SCHNACKENBERG
36 Director Career Services/Stdnt Life .... Ms. Marianne TRAMELLI
15 Director Human Resources .... Mr. Randy GLAZER
19 Chief of Campus Safety/Security .... Mr. John DE ANGELIS
43 General Counsel .... Ms. Lori FOX
25 Director Grants/Sponsored Programs .... Mr. Paul KRAN
25 Director Contracts & Grants .... Mr. John HERNANDEZ
26 Exec Director of External Affairs .... Mr. Joe LEVINE
29 Asst Director Alumni Relations .... Ms. Lindsey BRENAN
07 Director of Admissions .... Dr. Thomas ROCK
18 Director of Facilities .... Ms. Suzanne JABLONSKI
32 Dir Student Activities/Programs .... Ms. Maria HATAIER
84 Assoc Dean Enrollment/Student Svcs .... Dr. Thomas ROCK
11 Manager Administrative Services .... Ms. Patricia WALKER
37 Director Student Financial Aid .. Ms. Melanie WILLIAMS-BETHEA
39 Director of Resident Life .... Mr. Dewayne WHITE
85 Director of International Affairs .... Dr. Portia WILLIAMS

† Affiliated with Columbia University in the City of New York.

Technical Career Institutes (H)

320 W 31st Street, New York NY 10001-2789
County: New York FICE Identification: 011031
Unit ID: 196477
Telephone: (212) 594-4000 Carnegie Class: Assoc/PrivFP
FAX Number: (212) 330-0898 Calendar System: Semester
URL: www.tcicollege.edu
Established: 1909 Annual Undergrad Tuition & Fees: $13,340
Enrollment: 4,202 Coed
Affiliation or Control: Proprietary IRS Status: Proprietary
Highest Offering: Associate Degree
Program: Occupational; 2-Year Principally Bachelor's Creditable; Technical Emphasis
Accreditation: M, NY, ENGT, OPD

00 Chief Executive Officer .... Dr. John MCGRATH
01 President .... Mr. William TALBOT
05 Provost & VP for Academic Affairs .... Dr. Peter SLATER
11 Exec Vice Pres Administration .... Mr. Felix PRETTO
07 Vice Pres for Admissions .... Mr. Ted HAVELKA
37 Vice President Financial Aid .... Ms. Cynthia FEKARIS
09 Vice Pres for Research and Planning .... Ms. Susanna KUNG
10 Vice President/CFO .... Mr. Richard GOLDENBERG
20 Dean of Academic Administration .... Ms. Pansy JAMES
49 Dean of Arts & Sciences .... Dr. John LUUKKONEN
88 Dean of Environmental Control .... Ms. Regina CAHILL
50 Dean of Business and New Media Tech .... Ms. Clotilde DILLON
72 Dean of Technology .... Vacant
76 Dean of Health Sciences and Tech .... Dr. Michael MEIR

Tompkins Cortland Community College (I)

170 North Street, PO Box 139, Dryden NY 13053-8504
County: Tompkins FICE Identification: 006788
Unit ID: 196565
Telephone: (607) 844-8211 Carnegie Class: Assoc/Pub-R-M
FAX Number: (607) 844-9665 Calendar System: Semester
URL: www.tc3.edu
Established: 1968 Annual Undergrad Tuition & Fees (In-District): $4,700
Enrollment: 3,482 Coed
Affiliation or Control: State/Local IRS Status: 501(c)3
Highest Offering: Associate Degree
Program: Occupational; 2-Year Principally Bachelor's Creditable
Accreditation: M, ADNUR

01 President .... Dr. Carl E. HAYNES
03 Provost and VP of College .... Dr. John R. CONNERS
32 Dean of Student Life .... Ms. Amy TRUEMAN
05 Dean of Instruction .... Mr. Carl PENZIUL
08 Library Director .... Mr. Gregg KIEHL
84 Dean Operations & Enrollment Mgmt .... Ms. Blixy K. TAETZSCH
20 Assoc Dean Curriculum & Acad Record . Ms. Jane F. HAMMOND
14 Director of Technology Support .... Mr. Brian ACKLEY
88 Dean Org Success & Learning .... Ms. Kathryn WUNDERLICH
09 Assoc Dean IR and Org Learning .... Dr. Kristine ALTUCHER
38 Coordinator/Counseling & Career Svc .... Ms. Meg GARVEY
37 Director of Financial Aid .... Ms. Sharon KARWOWSKI
26 Dean of External Relations .... Dr. Bruce RYAN
15 Human Resources Administrator .... Ms. Sharon DOVI
07 Director of Admissions .... Mr. Sandy DRUMLUK
21 Director of Budget & Finance .... Ms. Susan DEWEY
13 Dean of Campus Technology ... Mr. Martin G. CHRISTOFFERSON
19 Director of Safety & Security .... Mr. J. Beau SAUL
41 Athletic Director .... Mr. Mick R. MCDANIEL
39 Director Residence Life .... Ms. Darese DOSKAL-SCAFFIDO

36 Coordinator Counseling/Career Svcs .... Ms. Joan DONOVAN
91 Manager Academic Computer Services .... Mr. Dino LEOPARDI
18 Director of Facilities .... Mr. James TURNER
23 Director of Health Services .... Ms. Shari SHAPLEIGH
28 Director of Multicultural Services .... Mr. Seth THOMPSON
101 Asst to President/Clerk of Board .... Ms. Cathy NORTHROP

Torah Temimah Talmudical Seminary (A)

507 Ocean Parkway, Brooklyn NY 11218-5913
County: Kings FICE Identification: 021916
Unit ID: 196583
Telephone: (718) 853-8500 Carnegie Class: Spec/Faith
FAX Number: (718) 438-5779 Calendar System: Semester
Established: 1978 Annual Undergrad Tuition & Fees: $10,150
Enrollment: 221 Male
Affiliation or Control: Independent Non-Profit IRS Status: 501(c)3
Highest Offering: Second Talmudic Degree
Program: Teacher Preparatory; Professional
Accreditation: RABN

01 President & Dean .... Rabbi L. MARGULIES
03 Executive Director .... Rabbi Yaakov APPLEGRAD
05 Chief Academic Officer .... Rabbi Lipa GELDWORTH
37 Financial Aid Administrator .... Mr. Mendel ROCHLITZ
38 Director of Guidance .... Rabbi Yirmiya GUGENHEIMER
11 Administrator .... Rabbi Yisroel KLEINMAN

Touro College (B)

27 W 23rd Street, 5th Floor, New York NY 10010
County: New York FICE Identification: 010142
Unit ID: 196592
Telephone: (212) 463-0400 Carnegie Class: Master's L
FAX Number: (212) 627-9144 Calendar System: Semester
URL: www.touro.edu
Established: 1970 Annual Undergrad Tuition & Fees: $14,850
Enrollment: 14,530 Coordinate
Affiliation or Control: Independent Non-Profit IRS Status: 501(c)3
Highest Offering: Doctorate
Program: Liberal Arts And General; Professional
Accreditation: M, ARCPA, LAW, OSTEO, OT, #OTA, PHAR, PTA, SP, SW, @TEAC

01 President .... Dr. Alan KADISH
100 Chief of Staff to President .... Mr. David RAAB
10 Senior Vice President & CFO .... Mr. Melvin M. NESS
11 Sr Vice Pres/Chief Admin Officer .... Mr. Alan SCHOOR
03 Senior VP for College Affairs .... Mr. Moshe KRUPKA
30 Vice Pres Institutional Advancement .... Dr. Eric LEVINE
20 VP Undergrad Acad Affs/Dean of Facu .... Dr. Stanley L. BOYLAN
58 Vice Pres of Graduate Studies .... Dr. Anthony POLEMENI
88 Vice Pres for National Programs .... Dr. Jay SEXTER
56 Vice President Com Ed/Ex Dn NYSCAS .... Ms. Eva SPINELLI-SEXTER
32 VP Plng & Assessment/Dean of Stdnts .... Mr. Robert GOLDSCHMIDT
106 VP Online Edu/Dean Women's Division .... Dr. Marion STOLTZ-LOIKE
09 Dean Inst Rsrch/Review/Enroll Mgmt .... Mr. Ira TYSZLER
43 General Counsel/Chief Comp Off .... Mr. Michael NEWMAN
61 Dean Jacob D Fuchsberg Law Center .... Dr. Patricia SALKIN
63 Dean Col of Osteopathic Medicine .... Dr. Robert GOLDBERG
67 Dean College of Pharmacy .... Dr. Stuart FELDMAN
70 Dean School of Social Work .... Dr. Steven HUBERMAN
76 Dean of School of Health Sciences ...... Dr. Louis H. PRIMAVERA
58 Dean Grad School Jewish Studies ...... Dr. Michael A. SHMIDMAN
90 Dn Grad Sch of Tech/Dir Acad Comp ...... Dr. Issac HERSKOWITZ
12 Dean Lander College for Men .... Dr. Moshe Z. SOKOL
50 Acting Dean Grad School of Business .... Dr. Sabra BROCK
38 Dean of Advising & Counseling .... Dr. Avery HOROWITZ
51 Asst Dean School Lifelong Education .... Dr. Charlotte HOLZER
06 Asst Dean Enroll Mgmt/Registrar .... Mr. Vladmir ROZIN
37 Exec Dir Financial Aid/Compliance .... Mrs. Carol ROSENBAUM
08 Director of Libraries .... Ms. Bashe SIMON
07 Director of Admissions .... Mr. Arthur WIGFALL
76 Director Physician Asst Program .... Dr. Joseph TOMMASINO
75 Director of Occupational Therapy .... Dr. Stephanie DAPICE-WONG
76 Director of Physical Therapy .... Ms. Jill HORBACEWICZ
88 Pgm Dir Speech Lang Path/Grad Pgm .... Ms. Hindy LUBINSKY
13 Director of OIT .... Mr. Mark SHOR
13 Chief Info Security Officer .... Ms. Patricia CIUFFO
19 Director of Security .... Ms. Lydia PEREZ
19 Dir of Emergency Preparedness .... Ms. Shoshana YEHUDAH
15 Director of Human Resources .... Ms. Roberta JACKSON
96 Director of Purchasing .... Ms. Wanda HERNANDEZ
18 Dir of Facilities/Real Estate .... Vacant
21 Controller .... Mr. Stuart LIPPMAN
26 Dir of Communication/External Rels .... Ms. Hedy SHULMAN
29 Director Alumni Relations .... Vacant
36 Director Student Placement .... Mr. Stuart ANSEL
09 Director of Assessment .... Dr. Eric LINDEN

Tri-State College of Acupuncture (C)

80 Eighth Avenue, #400, New York NY 10011-0890
County: New York FICE Identification: 025460
Unit ID: 130581
Telephone: (212) 242-2255 Carnegie Class: Spec/Health
FAX Number: (212) 242-2920 Calendar System: Semester
URL: www.tsca.edu
Established: 1982 Annual Graduate Tuition & Fees: $20,850
Enrollment: 158 Coed
Affiliation or Control: Proprietary IRS Status: Proprietary
Highest Offering: Master's; No Undergraduates
Program: Professional
Accreditation: ACUP

01 President .... Ruthann RUSSO
05 Director of Education .... Dr. Mark D. SEEM
11 Director of Operations .... Vacant
06 Registrar .... Sandra TURNER

Trocaire College (D)

360 Choate Avenue, Buffalo NY 14220-2094
County: Erie FICE Identification: 002812
Unit ID: 196653
Telephone: (716) 826-1200 Carnegie Class: Assoc/PrivNFP
FAX Number: (716) 828-6109 Calendar System: Semester
URL: www.trocaire.edu
Established: 1958 Annual Undergrad Tuition & Fees: $14,720
Enrollment: 1,420 Coed
Affiliation or Control: Independent Non-Profit IRS Status: 501(c)3
Highest Offering: Baccalaureate
Program: Occupational; 2-Year Principally Bachelor's Creditable
Accreditation: M, ADNUR, DIETT, MAC, PNUR, RAD, SURGT

01 President .... Dr. Bassam M. DEEB
05 Vice President of Academic Affairs .... Mr. Thomas J. MITCHELL
10 VP for Finance/Administration .... Mr. Richard BERNECKI
30 Vice Pres Institutional Advancement .... Mr. John VECCHIO
32 Dean Student Affairs .... Mr. Tony FUNIGIELLO
76 Academic Dean Health/Human Svcs .... Rev. Robert M. MOCK
46 Dean Research/Planning/Assessment .... Dr. Richard T. LINN
84 Dean Program Devel/Enrollment Mgt .... Dr. Michael LAFEVER
66 Academic Dean for Nursing .... Dr. Marian MEYERS
15 Exec Dir Human Resources/Col Sppt .... Mrs. Rebecca BOYLE
35 Student Activities Coordinator .... Mr. Jon HUDACK
14 Sr InformationTechnology Specialist .... Ms. Robin LOOMIS
103 Sr Director Workforce Development .... Mr. Hal KINGSLEY
105 Director Data Administration .... Ms. Michele PETERS
37 Director of Financial Aid .... Ms. Janet MCGRATH
25 Director of Grants/Govt Relations .... Ms. Sandra MILLER
16 Payroll/Benefits/Human Res Coord .... Ms. Linda SANSONE
06 Registrar .... Mrs. Theresa HORNER
36 Director Career Center .... Mrs. Maureen PERNICK HUBER
42 Campus Ministry .... Sr. Marie Andre MAIN
18 Facilities Director .... Mrs. Margaret ANDRZEJEWSKI
66 Director of Nursing .... Dr. Carol FANUTTI
30 Dir Development/Alumni Relations .... Mrs. Joan P. WILLIAMS
07 Director of Admissions .... Mrs. Maria POVLACK
105 Dir College Communications/Web Mgr ...... Mrs. Kathy POPIELSKI
38 Director Student Counseling .... Ms. Joyce KAISER
40 Manager Bookstore .... Ms. Debbie CAMMARATA
88 Web/Social Media Editor .... Mrs. Jackie HAUSLER

Ulster County Community College (E)

491 Cottekill Road, PO Box 557, Stone Ridge NY 12484
County: Ulster FICE Identification: 002880
Unit ID: 196699
Telephone: (845) 687-5000 Carnegie Class: Assoc/Pub-R-M
FAX Number: (845) 687-5083 Calendar System: Semester
URL: www.sunyulster.edu
Established: 1961 Annual Undergrad Tuition & Fees (In-District): $4,260
Enrollment: 2,246 Coed
Affiliation or Control: State/Local IRS Status: 501(c)3
Highest Offering: Associate Degree
Program: Occupational; 2-Year Principally Bachelor's Creditable
Accreditation: M, ADNUR

01 President .... Dr. Donald C. KATT
84 Vice Pres & Dean Enrollment Mgmt .... Ms. Ann MARROTT
05 Dean of Academic Affairs .... Dr. John GANIO
30 Dean of Advancement/Continuing Educ .... Ms. Marianne COLLINS
10 Dean of Admin/Chief Business Ofcr .... Mr. Mark KOMDAT
04 Executive Assistant to President .... Ms. Jean ROSE
20 Assoc Dean of Academic Affairs .... Ms. Cornelia DENVIR
32 Assoc Dean for Student Services .... Mr. John FRAMPTON
08 Director of Library Services .... Ms. Kari MACK
37 Director of Financial Aid .... Mr. Christopher CHANG
06 Registrar .... Ms. Marion GOSS
41 Athletic Director .... Mr. James DELMAR
19 Director of Safety & Security .... Mr. Wayne FREER
07 Director of Admissions .... Mr. Matthew GREEN
26 Chief Public Relations Officer .... Ms. Ann MARROTT
36 Dir Student Plcmnt/Acad Sppt Svcs .... Ms. Jane KITHCART
35 Director Student Affairs .... Ms. Ann MARROTT
18 Director of Plant Operations .... Mr. Steven FREER
09 Director of Institutional Research ...... Mr. Clarence (Hank) MILLER
103 Workforce Development .... Mr. Christopher MARX
15 Coordinator of Personnel Services .... Mrs. Debra DELANOY
21 Coordinator of Accounting .... Ms. Amy WINTERS
96 Coord Procurement/General Services .... Mr. Stephen GALLART

Unification Theological Seminary (F)

30 Seminary Drive, Barrytown NY 12507-5021
County: Dutchess FICE Identification: 032163
Unit ID: 246789
Telephone: (845) 752-3000 Carnegie Class: Spec/Faith
FAX Number: (845) 758-2156 Calendar System: Semester
URL: www.uts.edu
Established: 1975 Annual Graduate Tuition & Fees: $11,040
Enrollment: 92 Coed
Affiliation or Control: Unification Church IRS Status: 501(c)3
Highest Offering: Doctorate; No Undergraduates
Program: Professional; Religious Emphasis
Accreditation: M

01 President .... Dr. Richard PANZER
05 Academic Dean .... Dr. Kathy WININGS
88 Director of Field Education .... Dr. Jacob DAVID
06 Registrar .... Mrs. Ute DELANEY
07 Admissions Officer .... Ms. Davetta Ann OGUNLOLA
08 Library Director .... Dr. Keisuke NODA
32 Director of Student Life .... Mr. Paul G. RAJAN
11 COO .... Mr. Paul STUPPLE
18 Plant Director .... Mr. Carl VERDERBER
10 Chief Financial Officer .... Mr. John REDMOND

Union College (G)

807 Union Street, Schenectady NY 12308-3181
County: Schenectady FICE Identification: 002889
Unit ID: 196866
Telephone: (518) 388-6000 Carnegie Class: Bac/A&S
FAX Number: (518) 388-6800 Calendar System: Trimester
URL: www.union.edu
Established: 1795 Annual Undergrad Tuition & Fees: $45,219
Enrollment: 2,170 Coed
Affiliation or Control: Independent Non-Profit IRS Status: 501(c)3
Highest Offering: Baccalaureate
Program: Liberal Arts And General; Professional
Accreditation: M, ENG

01 President .... Dr. Stephen C. AINLAY
05 Dean Faculty/VP Academic Affs .... Dr. Therese A. MCCARTY
30 Vice President College Relations .... Mr. Stephen A. DARE
10 Vice President for Finance & Admin .... Ms. Diane T. BLAKE
07 Vice President of Admissions/FA ...... Mr. Matthew J. MALATESTA
100 Chief of Staff .... Mr. Edward SUMMERS
32 Vice President of Student Affairs .... Dr. Stephen C. LEAVITT
20 Dean of Academic Depts/Pgms .... Dr. David M. HAYES
88 Dean of Studies .... Dr. Mark E. WUNDERLICH
13 Chief Information Officer .... Ms. Ellen Y. BORKOWSKI
06 Registrar .... Ms. Penelope S. ADEY
29 Director Alumni Relations .... Mr. Dominick F. FAMULARE
08 College Librarian .... Ms. Frances J. MALOY
26 Director of Media and Public Rels .... Mr. Phillip J. WAJDA
37 Director of Financial Aid .... Ms. Linda M. PARKER
38 Director of Student Counseling .... Mr. Marcus S. HOTALING
36 Director of Career Center .... Mr. Robert C. SOULES
15 Director of Human Resources .... Mr. Eric NOLL
41 Director of Athletics .... Mr. James MCLAUGHLIN
22 Sr Director Campus Diversity/AA .... Dr. Gretchel L. HATHAWAY
19 Director Campus Safety .... Mr. Christopher HAYEN
39 Director Residence Life .... Ms. Molly MACELROY

† Tuition figure is a comprehensive fees figure.

Union Graduate College (H)

80 Nott Terrace, Schenectady NY 12308-3131
County: Schenectady FICE Identification: 038813
Unit ID: 446932
Telephone: (518) 631-9900 Carnegie Class: Master's M
FAX Number: (518) 631-9901 Calendar System: Trimester
URL: www.uniongraduatecollege.edu
Established: 2003 Annual Graduate Tuition & Fees: $2,690
Enrollment: 450 Coed
Affiliation or Control: Independent Non-Profit IRS Status: 501(c)3
Highest Offering: Master's; No Undergraduates
Program: Professional
Accreditation: M, NY, BUS, HSA, TEAC

01 President .... Dr. Laura SCHWEITZER
10 Vice President of Finance/Operation .... Joseph MCDONALD
84 VP Enrollment Mgmt/Student Svcs .... Joanne FITZGERALD
30 VP Institutional Advancement .... Dan CHRISTOPHER
06 Registrar/Director of Admissions .... Rhonda SHEEHAN
50 Dean School of Management .... Dr. Alan BOWMAN
54 Dean School of Engineering .... Bob KOZIK
53 Dean School of Education .... Dr. Patrick ALLEN
76 Director Center for Bioethics .... Dr. Robert BAKER
07 Director Student Recruitment .... Erin WHEELER
36 Coordinator of Career Services .... Jane FLEURY
09 Director Institutional Research .... Amy NEVIN
29 Coordinator of Alumni Relations .... Kim PERRONE
13 Director of Information Technology .... Robert KEENAN
37 Director Financial Aid .... Nikki GALLUCCI

Union Theological Seminary (I)

3041 Broadway, New York NY 10027-5792
County: New York FICE Identification: 002890
Unit ID: 196884
Telephone: (212) 662-7100 Carnegie Class: Spec/Faith
FAX Number: (212) 280-1416 Calendar System: Semester
URL: www.utsnyc.edu
Established: 1836 Annual Graduate Tuition & Fees: $21,890
Enrollment: 248 Coed
Affiliation or Control: Independent Non-Profit IRS Status: 501(c)3
Highest Offering: Doctorate; No Undergraduates
Program: Religious Emphasis
Accreditation: M, THEOL

01 President .... Dr. Serene JONES
10 VP Finance & Operations .... Mr. Richard A. MADONNA, JR.
30 VP for Institutional Advancement .... Mr. Bob BOMERSBACH
05 Dean of Academic Affairs .... Dr. Daisy L. MACHADO
32 Associate Dean Student Life .... Ms. Yvette WILSON
08 Director Library .... Vacant
04 Special Assistant to the President ...... Ms. Tania BRUNO
06 Registrar .... Ms. Edith T. HUNTER
18 Director Facilities/Physical Plant ...... Mr. Michael MALONEY
39 Director Student Housing .... Mr. Michael ORZECHOWSKI
07 Admissions Director .... Ms. Jennifer THOMPSON

United Talmudical Seminary (A)

191 Rodney Street, Brooklyn NY 11211-7900

County: Kings FICE Identification: 011189
Unit ID: 197018
Telephone: (718) 963-9770 Carnegie Class: Spec/Faith
FAX Number: (718) 963-9775 Calendar System: Semester
Established: 1949 Annual Undergrad Tuition & Fees: $10,800
Enrollment: 1,674 Male
Affiliation or Control: Independent Non-Profit IRS Status: 501(c)3
Highest Offering: Second Talmudic Degree
Program: Teacher Preparatory; Professional
Accreditation: RABN

01 Dean .... Rabbi Zalman TEITLBAUM
05 Assoc Dean Scholastic Services .... Rabbi Yeruchem DEUTSCH
37 Financial Aid Administrator .... Mr. Bernard KATZ
10 Business Officer .... Mr. Shia GREENFELD

University of Rochester (B)

Rochester NY 14627-0033

County: Monroe FICE Identification: 002894
Unit ID: 195030
Telephone: (585) 275-2121 Carnegie Class: RU/VH
FAX Number: (585) 275-0359 Calendar System: Semester
URL: www.rochester.edu
Established: 1850 Annual Undergrad Tuition & Fees: $43,636
Enrollment: 10,290 Coed
Affiliation or Control: Independent Non-Profit IRS Status: 501(c)3
Highest Offering: Doctorate
Program: Liberal Arts And General; Teacher Preparatory; Professional
Accreditation: M, BUS, CACREP, CLPSY, DENT, ENG, IPSY, MED, MFCD, MUS, NURSE, PDPSY, PH, TED

01 President .... Mr. Joel SELIGMAN
05 Provost and Dean of Arts/Sci & Engr ..... Mr. Peter LENNIE
10 Sr VP Administration & Fin/CFO .... Mr. Ronald J. PAPROCKI
03 VP/University Dean .... Mr. Paul J. BURGETT
17 Sr VP Health Sciences/Med Ctr CEO .... Dr. Bradford C. BERK
45 Sr VP for Institutional Resources .... Mr. Douglas PHILLIPS
30 Sr VP/Chief Advancement Officer .... Mr. Jim THOMPSON
43 Sr VP/General Counsel .... Ms. Sue STEWART
46 Sr VP for Research .... Vacant
26 VP for Communications .... Mr. Bill MURPHY
13 Vice President/Chief Info Officer .... Mr. David E. LEWIS
15 Assoc VP Human Resources .... Mr. Charles J. MURPHY
58 Vice Provost/Univ Dean Grad Studies ..... Ms. Margaret KEARNEY
100 General Sect/Pres Chief of Staff .... Ms. Lamar R. MURPHY
28 Vice Provost Fac Devel & Diversity ...... Dr. Vivian LEWIS
08 Dean River Campus Libraries .... Ms. Mary Ann MAVRINAC
88 Vice President/Laser Lab Director .... Mr. Robert L. MCCRORY
49 Dean of Arts & Sciences .... Ms. Joanna OLMSTED
54 Dean of Hajim Engineering .... Mr. Rob CLARK
84 Dean AS&E Undergrad Admis & Fin Aid ..... Mr. Jonathan BURDICK
21 Assoc VP for Budgets & Planning .... Ms. Holly CRAWFORD
32 Dean of Students Arts/Sci & Engr .... Mr. Matthew BURNS
63 Dean School of Medicine & Dent .... Dr. Mark B. TAUBMAN
64 Dean Eastman School of Music .... Mr. Douglas LOWRY
66 Interim Dean School of Nursing .... Ms. Kathy RIDEOUT
50 Dean Simon Grad Sch Business Admin ...... Mr. Mark ZUPAN
53 Dean Warner Grad Sch Educ & Hum Dev ..... Ms. Raffaella BORASI
89 Dean of Freshmen Arts/Sci & Engr .... Ms. Marcy KRAUS
88 Dean of Sophmores Arts/Sci & Engr .... Mr. Sean HANNA
37 Assoc Dean Enroll & Fin Aid A/S&E .... Mr. Charles PULS
35 Assoc Dean Students Arts/Sci & Engr ..... Ms. Anne-Marie ALGIER
23 Strong Health Chief Medical Officer ..... Dr. Raymond MAYEWSKI
52 Director Eastman Dental Center .... Dr. Cyril MEYEROWITZ
25 Assoc VP Research & Project Admin .... Ms. Gunta LIDERS
18 Assoc VP Facilities & Services .... Mr. Richard PIFER
86 Executive Director Govt Relations .... Mr. Peter J. ROBINSON
106 Asst Provost for Academic Affairs ...... Mr. Jason ADSIT
96 Director Corporate Purchasing .... Mr. Philip S. PROFETA
04 Executive Asst to the President .... Ms. Susan NIGGLI
06 Registrar .... Ms. Nancy SPECK
19 Director of University Security .... Mr. Walter MAULDIN
57 Director Memorial Art Gallery .... Mr. Grant HOLCOMB
29 Exec Director Alumni Relations .... Mr. Kevin P. WESLEY
41 Director of Athletics & Recreation ...... Mr. George VANDERZWAAG
39 Dir Res Life & Housing Services .... Ms. Laurel CONTOMANOLIS
36 Asst Dean/Director Career Center .... Mr. Burton NADLER
101 Administrator to Board of Trustees ..... Ms. Jackie E. KING

USC The Business College (C)

201 Bleecker Street, Utica NY 13501-2200

County: Oneida FICE Identification: 009077
Unit ID: 197081
Telephone: (315) 733-2300 Carnegie Class: Assoc/PrivFP
FAX Number: (315) 733-9281 Calendar System: Semester
URL: www.uscny.edu
Established: 1896 Annual Undergrad Tuition & Fees: $12,470
Enrollment: 330 Coed
Affiliation or Control: Proprietary IRS Status: Proprietary
Highest Offering: Associate Degree
Program: Occupational; 2-Year Principally Bachelor's Creditable; Business Emphasis
Accreditation: NY

01 President & Treasurer .... Mr. Philip M. WILLIAMS
03 Exec Vice Pres/Asst to President .... Mr. Scott K. WILLIAMS
11 Exec Vice President Administration ...... Mr. John L. CROSSLEY
05 Exec Vice President for Academics .... Mr. Daniel MURPHY
103 VP Corp/Workforce Develop .... Mr. Don REESE
10 Vice President of Finance .... Mr. Richard H. HILTON
43 General Counsel .... Mr. John H. STORY, JR.
12 Director Canastota Branch .... Mrs. Wendy M. CARY
06 Registrar/Bursar .... Mrs. Marian J. NIELSON
30 Director of Development .... Mr. John CROSSLEY
08 Head Librarian .... Ms. Anne NASSAR
37 Director of Student Financial Aid .... Mr. Fred P. ZUCALLA
12 Int Dir Oneonta Campus/Dn Students ...... Mr. Jeffrey HELD
07 Interim Director of Admissions .... Mrs. Rosanne BALASKA
13 Director Information Technology .... Mr. CJ AMAROSA
36 Director of Career Services .... Mrs. Susan SHEAFFER
18 Facilities Manager Physical Plant .... Mr. Joel B. NOLAN

U.T.A. Mesivta of Kiryas Joel (D)

PO Box 2009, Monroe NY 10949-8509

County: Orange FICE Identification: 038023
Unit ID: 446604
Telephone: (845) 783-9901 Carnegie Class: Spec/Faith
FAX Number: (845) 782-3620 Calendar System: Semester
Established: 1999 Annual Undergrad Tuition & Fees: $8,500
Enrollment: 1,410 Male
Affiliation or Control: Independent Non-Profit IRS Status: 501(c)3
Highest Offering: First Talmudic Degree
Program: Teacher Preparatory; Professional
Accreditation: RABN

01 President .... Elias HOROWITZ
05 Rosh Yeshiva .... Rabbi Aharon TEITELBAUM
37 Financial Aid Director .... David SCHWARTZ

Utica College (E)

1600 Burrstone Road, Utica NY 13502-4892

County: Oneida FICE Identification: 002883
Unit ID: 197045
Telephone: (315) 792-3111 Carnegie Class: Master's M
FAX Number: (315) 792-3292 Calendar System: Semester
URL: www.utica.edu
Established: 1946 Annual Undergrad Tuition & Fees: $31,410
Enrollment: 3,717 Coed
Affiliation or Control: Independent Non-Profit IRS Status: 501(c)3
Highest Offering: Doctorate
Program: Liberal Arts And General; Teacher Preparatory; Professional
Accreditation: M, NURSE, OT, PTA, TEAC

01 President .... Dr. Todd S. HUTTON
05 Provost & Vice Pres Academic Aff .... Dr. Judith A. KIRKPATRICK
10 Vice Pres Financial Affs/Treasurer ...... Mr. R. Barry WHITE
32 Vice Pres Stdnt Affs/Dean of Stdnts ..... Mr. Stephen PATTARINI
04 Executive Assistant to President .... Ms. Kim D. LAMBERT
30 Senior VP & Chief Advanc Officer .... Ms. Laura CASAMENTO
09 Vice Pres for Planning & Analysis .... Ms. Carol MACKINTOSH
84 Vice President for Enrollment Mgmt ...... Mr. Patrick A. QUINN
88 Vice President for Strategic Initiv ..... Dr. James C. BROWN
20 Associate Provost .... Dr. Robert M. HALLIDAY
26 Asst VP Marketing/Communication .... Mr. Kelly L. ADAMS
76 Dean for Health Professions/Educ .... Dr. Richard RAFES
49 Dean for Arts & Sciences .... Dr. John H. JOHNSEN
50 Dean for Business & Justice Studies ..... Ms. Patricia SWANN
35 Associate Dean of Students .... Ms. Alane P. VARGA
21 Director of Student Acct Operation ...... Ms. Gail TUTTLE
29 Director Alumni & Parent Relations ...... Mr. Mark C. KOVACS
08 Asst VP for Library & IITS .... Ms. Beverly J. MARCOLINE
36 Director Career Services .... Mr. Edward PULASKI
37 Exec Dir of Student Financial Svcs ...... Ms. Laura BEDFORD
06 Registrar .... Mr. Dominic PASSALACQUA
44 Director of Development .... Mr. Athony VILLANTI
41 Director of Physical Educ/Athletics ..... Mr. David FONTAINE
39 Interim Director of Residence Life ...... Ms. Stephanie WEISHAUPT
13 Infrastructure Manager .... Mr. John KAFTAN
16 Director of Human Resources .... Ms. Lisa GREEN
38 Dean Stdnt Success/Dir Stdnt Devel ...... Mr. Stephen M. PATTARINI
14 Dir College Info & Application Svcs ..... Mr. Scott HUMPHREY
24 Dir Multimedia & Computer User Svcs ..... Ms. Kathleen RANDALL
31 Exec Dir Corp/Professional Pgms .... Ms. Joni L. PULLIAM
51 Director of Credit Programs .... Ms. Evelyn FAZEKAS
85 Dean of International Education .... Dr. Laurence W. ROBERTS, II
07 Director of Enrollment Management .... Ms. Lisa BRONK
18 Director Facilities Management .... Mr. Donald L. HARTER
19 Director of Campus Safety .... Mr. Wayne SULLIVAN
92 Director Honors Program .... Dr. Diane MATZA
28 Dir Office of Opportunity Programs ...... Ms. Johnni F. MAHDI
96 Manager of Purchasing .... Ms. Bobbie H. SMOROL

† Utica College maintains an academic tie with Syracuse University that allows undergraduates to receive a Syracuse University degree.

Vassar College (F)

124 Raymond Avenue, Poughkeepsie NY 12604-0001

County: Dutchess FICE Identification: 002895
Unit ID: 197133
Telephone: (845) 437-7000 Carnegie Class: Bac/A&S
FAX Number: (845) 437-7187 Calendar System: Semester
URL: www.vassar.edu
Established: 1861 Annual Undergrad Tuition & Fees: $57,070
Enrollment: 2,400 Coed
Affiliation or Control: Independent Non-Profit IRS Status: 501(c)3
Highest Offering: Master's
Program: Liberal Arts And General
Accreditation: M, @TEAC

01 President .... Dr. Catharine B. HILL
05 Dean of the Faculty .... Dr. Jonathan CHENETTE
20 Dean of the College .... Dr. Christopher ROELLKE
10 Vice President for Finance & Admin ...... Ms. Elizabeth A. EISMEIER
30 Vice President for Development .... Ms. Catherine E. BAER
26 Vice Pres for College Relations .... Ms. Susan DEKREY
90 Vice Pres for Computing/Info Svcs .... Vacant
32 Dean of Students .... Dr. David H. BROWN
07 Dean Admission/Financial Aid .... Mr. David M. BORUS
49 Dean of Studies .... Dr. Joanne LONG
20 Associate Dean College .... Mr. Edward L. PITTMAN
35 Assoc Dean Col/Dir Campus Activit .... Ms. Teresa QUINN
06 Registrar .... Ms. Colleen MALLET
08 Director of the Libraries .... Ms. Sabrina PAPE
37 Director of Financial Aid .... Mr. Michael P. FRAHER
36 Director Career Development Center ...... Vacant
87 Director Conferences/Summer Pgms .... Ms. Katherine BUSH
39 Director Residential Life .... Mr. Luis INOA
09 Director of Institutional Research ...... Mr. David DAVIS-VAN ATTA
15 Director Human Resources .... Ms. Ruth SPENCER
18 Exec Dir Buildings & Grounds .... Mr. Thomas ALLEN
38 Director of Psychological Services ...... Dr. Sylvia BALDERRAMA
96 Director of Purchasing .... Ms. Rosaleen CARDILLO

Vaughn College of Aeronautics and Technology (G)

86-01 23rd Avenue, Flushing NY 11369

County: Queens FICE Identification: 002665
Unit ID: 188340
Telephone: (718) 429-6600 Carnegie Class: Bac/Assoc
FAX Number: (718) 429-0256 Calendar System: Semester
URL: www.vaughn.edu
Established: 1932 Annual Undergrad Tuition & Fees: $19,300
Enrollment: 1,680 Coed
Affiliation or Control: Independent Non-Profit IRS Status: 501(c)3
Highest Offering: Master's
Program: 2-Year Principally Bachelor's Creditable; Liberal Arts And General; Professional
Accreditation: M, ENGT, IACBE

01 President .... Dr. John C. FITZPATRICK
05 Sr Vice Pres Academic/Student Affs ...... Dr. Sharon B. DEVIVO
10 Vice Pres for Business & Finance .... Mr. Robert G. WALDMANN
84 Vice President Enrollment Services ...... Mr. Ernie SHEPELSKY
11 Asst VP College Services/Human Res ...... Mr. Paul MIRANDA
20 Asst Vice Pres of Academic Affairs ...... Vacant
45 Asst VP Academic Support Svcs .... Mr. Said LAMHAOUAR
35 Asst Vice Pres Student Affairs .... Vacant
84 Asst Vice Pres Enrollment Mgmt .... Mr. Vincent PAPANDREA
37 Director of Financial Aid .... Ms. Dorothy MARTIN
06 Registrar .... Mrs. Beatriz CRUZ
08 Librarian .... Ms. Joanne JAYNE
102 Exec Dir Corp/Foundation Relations ..... Ms. Kalli KOUTSOUTIS
26 Director of Public Affairs .... Vacant
96 Director of Purchasing .... Vacant
09 Director of Institutional Research ...... Vacant
13 Asst Director Computer Operations .... Mr. Hamwant (Neil) SINGH

Villa Maria College of Buffalo (H)

240 Pine Ridge Road, Buffalo NY 14225-3999

County: Erie FICE Identification: 002896
Unit ID: 197142
Telephone: (716) 896-0700 Carnegie Class: Assoc/PrivNFP4
FAX Number: (716) 896-0705 Calendar System: Semester
URL: www.villa.edu
Established: 1960 Annual Undergrad Tuition & Fees: $16,800
Enrollment: 455 Coed
Affiliation or Control: Independent Non-Profit IRS Status: 501(c)3
Highest Offering: Baccalaureate
Program: Liberal Arts And General; Fine Arts Emphasis
Accreditation: M, CIDA, MUS, PTAA

01 President .... Sr. Marcella Marie GARUS
05 Vice President for Academic Affairs ..... Dr. Janet REOHR
10 Vice President for Business Affairs ..... Mr. Vincent GRIZANTI
30 Vice President for Development .... Sr. Mary Marcine BOROWIAK
32 Vice President for Student Affairs ...... Sr. Mary Louis RUSTOWICZ
44 Asst to Vice Pres for Development .... Ms. Kathy SEIBOLD
20 Asst to Vice Pres for Academic Affs ..... Ms. Janice HERCHMER
06 Registrar .... Ms. Melany SHIELDS
84 Director of Enrollment Management .... Mr. Kevin DONOVAN
08 Director of Library .... Sr. Mary Anna FALBO
37 Director of Financial Aid .... Ms. Laura FITZGERALD

09 Director of Institutional Research ..... Sr. Mary Albertine STACHOWSKI
38 Director Student Counseling ..... Ms. Palma M. ZANGHI
13 Director of Computer Services ..... Ms. Christine E. PALCZEWSKI
88 Systems Analyst ..... Mr. Robert STRUBLE
18 Plant & Grounds Manager ..... Mr. David WISNER
23 Director of Health Services ..... Mrs. Minerva MONTIJO
25 Director of Grants ..... Mrs. Mary ROBINSON
51 Instructional Design & Program Dev ..... Mr. Fredrick RODGERS
36 Director of Career Development ..... Ms. Deborah HANDZLIK
42 Director of Campus Ministry ..... Mr. Frank ANTONUCCI
85 Director of Foreign Students ..... Ms. Palma ZANGHI
27 Cooridinator of Communications ..... Vacant
35 Director of Student Life ..... Ms. Ceceile PAWLOWSKI
88 Archivist ..... Sr. Anita BENECKI
22 Affirmative Action Officer ..... Ms. Diane M. HANDZLIK
29 Director of Alumni Relations ..... Ms. Mary MERIGOLD
24 Coordinator of Educational Media ..... Mrs. Barbara WETZEL
88 Coord Academic Success Center ..... Dr. Aimee WOZNICK
76 Business/Educ/Health Science Dept ..... Mr. Todd BAKER
77 Director of Computer Services ..... Ms. Christine PALCZEWSKI
57 Art Department Chair ..... Ms. Sandra REICIS
64 Music Department Chair ..... Sr. Barbara AMROZOWICZ
49 Liberal Arts Department Chair ..... Dr. Matthew GIORDANO

Wagner College (A)

1 Campus Road, Staten Island NY 10301-4479

County: Richmond FICE Identification: 002899
Unit ID: 197197
Telephone: (718) 390-3100 Carnegie Class: Master's M
FAX Number: (718) 390-3467 Calendar System: Semester
URL: www.wagner.edu
Established: 1883 Annual Undergrad Tuition & Fees: $37,240
Enrollment: 1,854 Coed
Affiliation or Control: Independent Non-Profit IRS Status: 501(c)3
Highest Offering: Master's
Program: Liberal Arts And General; Teacher Preparatory; Professional
Accreditation: M, ACBSP, ARCPA, NUR, TED

01 President ..... Dr. Richard GUARASCI
11 Vice President for Administration ..... Mr. David MARTIN
05 Provost/Vice Pres Academic Affairs ..... Dr. Lily D. MCNAIR
10 Vice Pres Business & Finance ..... Mr. William MEA
84 Vice Pres Enrollment Management ..... Mr. Angelo ARAIMO
09 Int VP Instititutional Research ..... Ms. Myra GARCIA
26 Chief of Staff/VP Communications ..... Mr. Joseph ROMANO
04 Assistant to the President ..... Ms. Pat FITZPATRICK
32 Vice Pres and Dean of Campus Life ..... Ms. Ruta SHAH-GORDON
21 Asst Vice Pres/Controller ..... Mr. John CARRESCIA
88 Dean of Assessment ..... Dr. Anne LOVE
20 Associate Provost ..... Dr. Jeffrey KRAUS
06 Registrar ..... Mr. Jeffrey KRAUS
13 Director of Information Technology ..... Mr. Dilawar GREWAL
42 Chaplain ..... Rev. James SMITH
29 Director Alumni Relations ..... Mr. Kenneth LAM
39 Director Housing ..... Mr. Matthew HOLLINGSHEAD
30 Director of Development ..... Vacant
18 Chief Facilities/Physical Plant ..... Mr. Dominick FONTANO
41 Director of Athletics ..... Mr. Walter HAMELINE
23 Director of Health Services ..... Ms. Kathleen OBERFELDT
19 Director Security/Safety ..... Mr. Anthony MARTINESI
15 Director Personnel Services ..... Ms. Tania ROSSINI
37 Director Student Financial Aid ..... Ms. Theresa WEIMER
58 Coordinator of Graduate Studies ..... Dr. Jeffrey KRAUS

Webb Institute (B)

298 Crescent Beach Road, Glen Cove NY 11542-1398

County: Nassau FICE Identification: 002900
Unit ID: 197221
Telephone: (516) 671-2213 Carnegie Class: Spec/Engg
FAX Number: (516) 674-9838 Calendar System: Semester
URL: www.webb-institute.edu
Established: 1889 Annual Undergrad Tuition & Fees: N/A
Enrollment: 81 Coed
Affiliation or Control: Independent Non-Profit IRS Status: 501(c)3
Highest Offering: Baccalaureate
Program: Professional; Technical Emphasis
Accreditation: M, ENG

01 President ..... RADM. Robert C. OLSEN, JR.
05 Dean ..... Prof. Richard P. NEILSON
20 Assistant Dean ..... Prof. Richard C. HARRIS
08 Librarian ..... Ms. Patricia M. PRESCOTT
30 Chief Development ..... Mr. Rick PARADIS
10 Director of Financial Affairs ..... Mr. Andrew BERKO
32 Director of Student Affairs ..... Mr. David BYRNES
18 Director of Facilities ..... Mr. John FERRANTE
84 Director of Enrollment Management ..... Mr. William G. MURRAY
29 Director of Alumni Relations ..... Ms. Gailmarie SUJECKI
26 Chief Public Relations Officer ..... Mr. Rick PARADIS
90 Computer Systems Manager ..... Ms. Erica L. HANSEN
06 Registrar ..... Ms. Jocelyn M. WILSON
37 Director Student Financial Aid ..... Ms. Lauri D'AMBRA

Weill Cornell Medical College (C)

1300 York Avenue, F-113, New York NY 10065-4805

County: New York FICE Identification: 004762
Unit ID: 190424
Telephone: (212) 746-5454 Carnegie Class: Spec/Med
FAX Number: (212) 746-8424 Calendar System: Quarter
URL: www.med.cornell.edu
Established: 1898 Annual Graduate Tuition & Fees: $47,150
Enrollment: 417 Coed
Affiliation or Control: Independent Non-Profit IRS Status: 501(c)3
Highest Offering: Doctorate; No Undergraduates
Program: Professional
Accreditation: &M, ARCPA, DENT, IPSY, MED

01 Provost Med Affs/Dean of College ..... Dr. Laurie H. GLIMCHER
100 Exec Administrator/Dean's Office ..... Ms. Edie SPINELLI
30 Vice Provost Development ..... Mr. Larry SCHAFER
26 Vice Prov Public/Govt/Cmty Affairs ..... Ms. Myrna MANNERS
03 Exec Vice Provost/Sr Exec Vice Dean ..... Dr. David P. HAJJAR
11 Exec Vice Provost ..... Mr. Stephen M. COHEN
09 Assistant Provost Research Admin ..... Dr. Harry M. LANDER
43 Deputy Univ Counsel/Sec of Med Col ..... Mr. James R. KAHN
05 Senior Assoc Dean Education ..... Dr. Carol STOREY-JOHNSON
20 Sr Assoc Dean Clinical Affairs ..... Dr. Michael G. STEWART
88 Chief Medical Officer Phys Org ..... Dr. Daniel M. KNOWLES
17 Associate Dean Burke Hospital ..... Dr. Mary Beth WALSH
20 Associate Dean Curricular Affairs ..... Dr. Peter M. MARZUK
17 Associate Dean Affiliations ..... Dr. Oliver T. FEIN
22 Assoc Dean Student Affs/EO Pgms ..... Dr. Carlyle H. MILLER
07 Associate Dean Admissions ..... Dr. Charles BARDES
51 Assoc Dean Continuing Medical Educ ..... Dr. Scott J. GOLDSMITH
20 Associate Dean Academic Affairs ..... Dr. Shari R. MIDONECK
53 Assistant Dean Departmental Assoc ..... Dr. Marcus M. REIDENBERG
10 Associate Dean Billing Compliance ..... Dr. Stephen J. THOMAS
88 Associate Dean Clinical Research ..... Dr. Ralph L. NACHMAN
58 Assoc Dean Grad School Med Sciences ..... Dr. Randi B. SILVER
23 Associate Dean Healthcare System ..... Dr. Eliot J. LAZAR
12 Associate Dean Intercampus Affairs ..... Dr. Caren A. HELLER
58 Associate Dean MSK Cancer Center ..... Dr. Thomas J. FAHEY, JR.
53 Associate Dean Pre-Med Educ Qatar ..... Dr. Michael D. JOHNSON
07 Assistant Dean of Admissions ..... Ms. Lori NICOLAYSEN
88 Assoc Dean Research Strategy Qatar ..... Mr. Eelco A. SLAGTER
88 Assoc Dean Translational Research ..... Dr. Julianne IMPERATO-MCGINLEY
20 Assistant Dean Faculty Affairs ..... Dr. Mark A. ALBANO
32 Assistant Dean Student Affairs ..... Dr. Elizabeth A. WILSON-ANSTEY
08 Librarian of Medicine ..... Ms. Colleen CUDDY

† Regional accreditation is carried under the parent institution Cornell University, Ithaca, NY.

Wells College (D)

170 Main Street, Aurora NY 13026-0500

County: Cayuga FICE Identification: 002901
Unit ID: 197230
Telephone: (315) 364-3266 Carnegie Class: Bac/A&S
FAX Number: (315) 364-3227 Calendar System: Semester
URL: www.wells.edu
Established: 1868 Annual Undergrad Tuition & Fees: $33,200
Enrollment: 525 Coed
Affiliation or Control: Independent Non-Profit IRS Status: 501(c)3
Highest Offering: Baccalaureate
Program: Liberal Arts And General; Teacher Preparatory
Accreditation: M, @TEAC

01 President ..... Ms. Lisa Marsh RYERSON
05 Provost and Dean of the College ..... Dr. Cindy SPEAKER
11 Chief Operating Officer ..... Mr. Terry NEWCOMB
10 Treasurer and Controller ..... Mr. John DENTES
30 Vice President for Advancement ..... Mr. Michael MCGREEVEY
04 Assistant to the President ..... Ms. Kristen PHILLIPS
32 Dean of Students ..... Ms. Jennifer MICHAEL
07 Dir of Admissions/Financial Aid ..... Ms. Susan SLOAN
06 Registrar ..... Mr. Andre SIAMUNDELE
08 Library Director ..... Ms. Muriel GODBOUT
37 Director Financial Aid ..... Ms. Cathleen PATELLA
44 Director of Annual Giving ..... Ms. Pamela SHERADIN
26 Dir of Communications/Marketing ..... Ms. Ann ROLLO
29 Director Alumni Relations ..... Ms. Laura SANDERS
19 Director of Security ..... Mr. David GARDNER
18 Chief Facilities/Physical Plant ..... Mr. Brian BROWN
15 Manager of Human Resources ..... Ms. Kit VAN ORMAN

Westchester Community College (E)

75 Grasslands Road, Valhalla NY 10595-1636

County: Westchester FICE Identification: 002881
Unit ID: 197294
Telephone: (914) 606-6600 Carnegie Class: Assoc/Pub-S-SC
FAX Number: (914) 606-6780 Calendar System: Semester
URL: www.sunywcc.edu
Established: 1946 Annual Undergrad Tuition & Fees (In-District): $4,512
Enrollment: 13,969 Coed
Affiliation or Control: State/Local IRS Status: 501(c)3
Highest Offering: Associate Degree
Program: Occupational; 2-Year Principally Bachelor's Creditable
Accreditation: M, DIETT, RAD

01 President ..... Dr. Joseph N. HANKIN
05 Vice President Academic Affairs ..... Mr. Jeffrey CONTE
32 Vice Pres Student Personnel Svcs ..... Mr. Donald WEIGAND
11 Vice Pres Administrative Services ..... Mr. Pat D'IMPERIO
102 VP Ext Affs/Exec Dir Found for WCC ..... Mrs. Eve LARNER
51 Dean Community/Adult/Cont Educ ..... Dr. Marjorie GLUSKER
81 Assoc Dean Math/Phys Engr/Tech ..... Mr. Ted NYGREEN
76 Assoc Dean Natural/Health Sciences ..... Mr. Michael OLIVETTE
83 Assoc Dean Bus/Behav/Soc Sci Svcs ..... Mr. Jeffrey A. CONTE
79 Assoc Dean Arts/Humanities/Lrng Res ..... Dr. Jianping WANG
22 Associate Dean of EOC ..... Ms. Renee GUY
35 Assoc Dean Student Personnel Svcs ..... Mr. Kevin B. SLAVIN
08 Asc Dn Lrng Res/Dist Lrng/Inst Tech ..... Ms. Pamela POLLARD
26 Director of College/Cmty Relations ..... Mr. Patrick HENNESSEY
06 Registrar ..... Ms. Susan S. STANTON
37 Dir of Student Financial Assistance ..... Mr. Alikhan MORGAN
13 Vice President of IT ..... Mr. Anthony SCORDINO
07 Director of Admissions ..... Ms. Gloria LEON
38 Acting Director of Counseling ..... Mr. Ruben BARATO
16 Director Human Resources ..... Ms. Sabrina J. CHANDLER
88 Director Faculty Student Assoc ..... Mr. John BOYLE
09 Director Inst Research & Planning ..... Ms. Nancy M. DERIGGI
19 Director of Security ..... Mr. Brian P. DOLANSKY
24 Director Media Services ..... Mr. Thomas GALA
41 Athletic Director ..... Mr. Larry MASSARONI
21 Assoc Business Officer/Controller ..... Mr. Mario CAVALLI
18 Director Physical Plant ..... Mr. Kevin GARVEY
96 Deputy Purchasing Agent ..... Mr. Richard CASHMAN
27 Publications Manager ..... Mr. Craig FISCHER
23 Coordinator Student Health Services ..... Ms. Janice GILROY
75 Coord of Transfer & Career Service ..... Dr. Gwen D. ROUNDTREE

Wood Tobé-Coburn School (F)

Eight E 40th Street, New York NY 10016

County: New York FICE Identification: 007405
Unit ID: 197522
Telephone: (212) 686-9040 Carnegie Class: Assoc/PrivFP
FAX Number: (212) 686-9171 Calendar System: Semester
URL: www.woodtobecoburn.edu
Established: 1879 Annual Undergrad Tuition & Fees: $16,640
Enrollment: 617 Coed
Affiliation or Control: Proprietary IRS Status: Proprietary
Highest Offering: Associate Degree
Program: Occupational; 2-Year Principally Bachelor's Creditable
Accreditation: NY, MAC

01 President ..... Ms. Sandra GRUNINGER
05 Director of Education ..... Ms. Arlette BALRAM
07 Director of Admissions ..... Ms. Sandra ANDUJAR-WENDLAND
32 Student Services Director ..... Ms. Yessika GARCIA
37 Financial Aid Administrator ..... Ms. Linda WALTERS
36 Placement Director ..... Ms. Lisa RINI

Yeshiva Derech Chaim (G)

1573 39th Street, Brooklyn NY 11218-4413

County: Kings FICE Identification: 022651
Unit ID: 197647
Telephone: (718) 438-5476 Carnegie Class: Spec/Faith
FAX Number: (718) 435-9285 Calendar System: Semester
Established: 1975 Annual Undergrad Tuition & Fees: $10,200
Enrollment: 165 Male
Affiliation or Control: Independent Non-Profit IRS Status: 501(c)3
Highest Offering: Second Talmudic Degree
Program: Professional; Religious Emphasis
Accreditation: RABN

01 President ..... Rabbi Mordechai RENNERT
01 President ..... Rabbi Yisroel PLUTCHOK

Yeshiva D'Monsey Rabbinical College (H)

2 Roman Boulevard, Monsey NY 10952-3106

County: Rockland FICE Identification: 031473
Unit ID: 420325
Telephone: (845) 426-3276 Carnegie Class: Spec/Faith
FAX Number: (845) 352-1119 Calendar System: Semester
Established: 1984 Annual Undergrad Tuition & Fees: $4,350
Enrollment: 74 Male
Affiliation or Control: Independent Non-Profit IRS Status: 501(c)3
Highest Offering: Second Talmudic Degree
Program: Teacher Preparatory; Professional
Accreditation: RABN

01 Rosh Yeshiva ..... Rabbi Moishe GREEN
05 Rosh Yeshiva ..... Rabbi Ruvain GREEN
37 Financial Aid Director ..... Rabbi Aron BERGER

Yeshiva of Far Rockaway (I)

802 Hicksville Road, Far Rockaway NY 11691-5219

County: Queens FICE Identification: 041196
Telephone: (718) 327-7600 Carnegie Class: Not Classified
FAX Number: (718) 327-1430 Calendar System: Semester
Established: 1969 Annual Undergrad Tuition & Fees: $9,500
Enrollment: 65 Male
Affiliation or Control: Independent Non-Profit IRS Status: 501(c)3
Highest Offering: First Talmudic Degree
Program: Professional; Religious Emphasis
Accreditation: RABN

01 President ..... Rabbi Yechiel I. PERR
03 Executive Director ..... Rabbi Shayeh KOHN
32 Dean of Students ..... Rabbi Dovid KLEINKAUFMAN

Yeshiva Gedolah Imrei Yosef D'Spinka (A)

1466 56th Street, Brooklyn NY 11219-4696
County: Kings FICE Identification: 030001
Unit ID: 375230
Telephone: (718) 851-8721 Carnegie Class: Spec/Faith
FAX Number: (718) 686-8849 Calendar System: Semester
Established: 1987 Annual Undergrad Tuition & Fees: $7,500
Enrollment: 124 Male
Affiliation or Control: Independent Non-Profit IRS Status: 501(c)3
Highest Offering: First Talmudic Degree
Program: Teacher Preparatory; Religious Emphasis
Accreditation: @RABN

01 President .... Mordechai MAJEROWITZ

Yeshiva Gedolah Kesser Torah (B)

28 Cedar Lane, Monsey NY 10952
County: Rockland Identification: 667112
Telephone: (845) 406-4308 Carnegie Class: Not Classified
FAX Number: (845) 406-4199 Calendar System: Semester
Established: 2004 Annual Undergrad Tuition & Fees: $9,200
Enrollment: 67 Male
Affiliation or Control: Independent Non-Profit IRS Status: 501(c)3
Highest Offering: First Talmudic Degree
Program: Teacher Preparatory; Professional
Accreditation: RABN

00 CEO .... Rabbi David FISHMAN
01 President .... David BERNSTEIN

Yeshiva Gedolah Ohr Yisrael (C)

2899 Nostrand Avenue, Brooklyn NY 11229
County: Kings Identification: 667077
Telephone: (718) 382-8702 Carnegie Class: Not Classified
FAX Number: (718) 382-8703 Calendar System: Semester
Established: 1999 Annual Undergrad Tuition & Fees: $6,500
Enrollment: 78 Male
Affiliation or Control: Independent Non-Profit IRS Status: 501(c)3
Highest Offering: First Talmudic Degree
Program: Professional
Accreditation: RABN

01 Rosh Yeshiva .... Avraham ZUCKER
10 Treasurer .... Avi KAHN

Yeshiva Karlin Stolin Beth Aaron V'Israel Rabbinical Institute (D)

1818 54th Street, Brooklyn NY 11204-1545
County: Kings FICE Identification: 025058
Unit ID: 197601
Telephone: (718) 232-7800 Carnegie Class: Spec/Faith
FAX Number: (718) 331-4833 Calendar System: Semester
Established: 1948 Annual Undergrad Tuition & Fees: $7,600
Enrollment: 93 Male
Affiliation or Control: Independent Non-Profit IRS Status: 501(c)3
Highest Offering: Second Talmudic Degree
Program: Teacher Preparatory; Professional
Accreditation: RABN

01 Chief Executive Officer .... Rabbi Yochanan PILCHICK
05 Dean Theology/Chief Acad Officer .... Rabbi Chaim WOLPIN
06 Registrar .... Rabbi Aryeh WOLPIN
08 Librarian .... Rabbi Yochanan GOLDHABER
10 Fiscal Officer .... Rabbi Irving PERRES
37 Financial Aid Director .... Rabbi Mayer PILCHICK
33 Dean of Men .... Rabbi Gedelyah MACHLIS

Yeshiva and Kolel Bais Medrash Elyon (E)

73 Main Street, Monsey NY 10952-3013
County: Rockland Identification: 666707
Unit ID: 245777
Telephone: (845) 356-7064 Carnegie Class: Spec/Faith
FAX Number: (845) 356-7065 Calendar System: Semester
Established: 1945 Annual Undergrad Tuition & Fees: $10,575
Enrollment: 47 Male
Affiliation or Control: Independent Non-Profit IRS Status: 501(c)3
Highest Offering: Second Talmudic Degree
Program: Professional
Accreditation: @RABN

01 President .... Rabbi Yerachmiel CENSOR
05 Dean .... Rabbi Israel FALK

Yeshiva and Kollel Harbotzas Torah (F)

1049 E 15th Street, Brooklyn NY 11230-4462
County: Kings FICE Identification: 023506
Unit ID: 245731
Telephone: (718) 692-0208 Carnegie Class: Spec/Faith
FAX Number: (718) 692-0363 Calendar System: Semester
Established: 1969 Annual Undergrad Tuition & Fees: $7,100
Enrollment: 42 Male
Affiliation or Control: Independent Non-Profit IRS Status: 501(c)3
Highest Offering: Second Talmudic Degree
Program: Professional
Accreditation: @RABN

01 President .... Rabbi Y. BITTERSFELD

Yeshiva of Machzikai Hadas (G)

1301 47th Street, Brooklyn NY 11219
County: Kings FICE Identification: 041381
Unit ID: 455257
Telephone: (718) 853-2442 Carnegie Class: Spec/Faith
FAX Number: (718) 853-2504 Calendar System: Semester
Established: 2001 Annual Undergrad Tuition & Fees: $7,000
Enrollment: 289 Male
Affiliation or Control: Independent Non-Profit IRS Status: 501(c)3
Highest Offering: First Talmudic Degree
Program: Professional
Accreditation: RABN

01 Rosh Yeshiva .... Rabbi Yidel MONHEIT

Yeshiva Mikdash Melech (H)

1326 Ocean Parkway, Brooklyn NY 11230-5655
County: Kings FICE Identification: 025068
Unit ID: 197610
Telephone: (718) 339-1090 Carnegie Class: Spec/Faith
FAX Number: (718) 998-9321 Calendar System: Semester
URL: www.mikdashmelech.org
Established: 1972 Annual Undergrad Tuition & Fees: $10,000
Enrollment: 109 Male
Affiliation or Control: Independent Non-Profit IRS Status: 501(c)3
Highest Offering: Second Talmudic Degree
Program: Teacher Preparatory; Professional; Religious Emphasis
Accreditation: RABN

01 Dean .... Rabbi Haim BENOLIEL
05 Dean of Faculty .... Rabbi David LOPIAN
06 Registrar .... Rabbi Josh SANANES
10 Chief Business Officer .... Rabbi Avraham BENOLIEL
11 Administrator .... Rabbi Amram SANANES

Yeshiva of Nitra Rabbinical College (I)

194 Division Avenue, Brooklyn NY 11211-7199
County: Kings FICE Identification: 011670
Unit ID: 197674
Telephone: (718) 387-0422 Carnegie Class: Spec/Faith
FAX Number: (718) 387-9400 Calendar System: Semester
Established: 1946 Annual Undergrad Tuition & Fees: $7,600
Enrollment: 223 Male
Affiliation or Control: Independent Non-Profit IRS Status: 501(c)3
Highest Offering: Second Talmudic Degree
Program: Professional
Accreditation: RABN

01 President .... Mr. Alexander FISCHER
03 Vice President .... Mr. Mendel KLEIN
05 Dean .... Rabbi Samuel D. UNGAR
11 Administrative Officer .... Mr. Ernest SCHWARTZ

Yeshiva Shaar HaTorah-Grodno (J)

83-96 117th Street, Kew Gardens NY 11415
County: Queens FICE Identification: 021520
Unit ID: 197692
Telephone: (718) 846-1940 Carnegie Class: Spec/Faith
FAX Number: (718) 850-7916 Calendar System: Semester
Established: 1976 Annual Undergrad Tuition & Fees: $15,750
Enrollment: 100 Male
Affiliation or Control: Independent Non-Profit IRS Status: 501(c)3
Highest Offering: Second Talmudic Degree
Program: Professional
Accreditation: RABN

01 Administrator .... Rabbi Yoel YANKELEWITZ

Yeshiva Shaarei Torah of Rockland (K)

91 W Carlton Road, Suffern NY 10901-4013
County: Rockland FICE Identification: 034963
Unit ID: 441609
Telephone: (845) 352-3431 Carnegie Class: Spec/Faith
FAX Number: (845) 352-3433 Calendar System: Semester
Established: 1977 Annual Undergrad Tuition & Fees: $12,750
Enrollment: 70 Male
Affiliation or Control: Independent Non-Profit IRS Status: 501(c)3
Highest Offering: First Talmudic Degree
Program: Professional
Accreditation: RABN

01 President .... Rabbi Mordechai WOLMARK
30 Chief Devel Officer/Financial Aid .... Mrs. Teri SCHILLER
06 Registrar .... Rabbi Neil RATNER

Yeshiva of the Telshe Alumni (L)

4904 Independence Avenue, Riverdale NY 10471
County: Bronx FICE Identification: 025463
Unit ID: 431983
Telephone: (718) 601-3523 Carnegie Class: Spec/Faith
FAX Number: (718) 601-2141 Calendar System: Semester
Established: 1981 Annual Undergrad Tuition & Fees: $8,800
Enrollment: 97 Male
Affiliation or Control: Independent Non-Profit IRS Status: 501(c)3
Highest Offering: First Talmudic Degree
Program: Teacher Preparatory; Professional
Accreditation: RABN

01 President .... Rabbi Avrohom AUSBAND
03 Executive Director .... Rabbi Noson JOSEPH
29 Director Alumni Relations .... Rabbi Yosef FREILICH

Yeshiva University (M)

500 W 185th Street, New York NY 10033-3201
County: New York FICE Identification: 002903
Unit ID: 197708
Telephone: (212) 960-5400 Carnegie Class: RU/VH
FAX Number: (212) 960-0055 Calendar System: Semester
URL: www.yu.edu
Established: 1886 Annual Undergrad Tuition & Fees: $35,200
Enrollment: 6,563 Coordinate
Affiliation or Control: Independent Non-Profit IRS Status: 501(c)3
Highest Offering: Doctorate
Program: Liberal Arts And General; Professional
Accreditation: M, CLPSY, DENT, IPSY, LAW, MED, PSPSY, SW, @TEAC

01 President .... Mr. Richard M. JOEL
05 Provost/Sr VP Academic Affairs .... Dr. Morton LOWENGRUB
17 Vice President Medical Affairs .... Dr. Allen M. SPIEGEL
10 Vice President Business Affairs/CFO .... Mr. J. Michael GOWER
30 Vice Pres Institutional Advancement .... Mr. Daniel T. FORMAN
11 Vice President University Affairs .... Dr. Herbert C. DOBRINSKY
13 VP Information Technology/CIO .... Mr. Marc MILSTEIN
43 VP Legal Affs/Secretary/Gen Counsel .... Mr. Andrew J. LAUER
32 Vice President University Life .... Dr. Hillel DAVIS
26 Vice Pres Communications/Pub Affs .... Mrs. Georgia B. POLLAK
18 Vice Pres Administrative Services .... Mr. Jeffrey ROSENGARTEN
100 Vice Pres/Chief of Staff .... Mr. Josh JOSEPH
04 Assistant to President .... Ms. Cynthia PHELPS
08 Dean of University Libraries .... Mrs. Pearl BERGER
35 Senior Univ Dean of Students .... Dr. Victor SCHWARTZ
88 Dean of Students .... Mr. David HIMBER
49 Dean Yeshiva College .... Dr. Barry EICHLER
49 Dean Undergrd Jewish Stds/Mazer Sch .... Rabbi Yona REISS
49 Dean Stern College for Women .... Dr. Karen BACON
50 Dean Sy Syms School of Business .... Dr. Michael J. GINZBERG
63 Dean Albert Einstein Col Medicine .... Dr. Allen M. SPIEGEL
58 Dean Ferkauf Graduate School .... Dr. Lawrence J. SIEGEL
58 Dean Bernard Revel Graduate School .... Dr. David BERGER
58 Dean Azrieli Graduate School .... Dr. David SCHNALL
58 Director Sue Golding Grad Program .... Dr. Victoria FREEDMAN
70 Dean Wurzweiler School Social Work .... Dr. Sheldon R. GELMAN
84 Director Enrollment Management .... Ms. Diana BENMERGUI
37 Director of Student Finances .... Mr. Robert FRIEDMAN
07 Director Undergraduate Admissions .... Mr. Michael KRANZLER
29 Director University Alumni Affairs .... Ms. Barbara BIRCH
06 Interim University Registrar .... Ms. Diana BENMERGUI
09 Director of Institutional Research .... Dr. Ariel FISHMAN
96 Director of Purchasing .... Mr. Jack ZENCHECK
15 Director Human Resources .... Ms. Yvonne RAMIREZ
38 Director Student Counseling .... Dr. Chaim NISSEL

Yeshiva Zidvon Aryeh (N)

2242 Baysumter Avenue, Far Rockaway NY 11691
County: Queens Identification: 667110
Telephone: (516) 295-5700 Carnegie Class: Not Classified
FAX Number: (516) 295-5737 Calendar System: Semester
Established: 1992 Annual Undergrad Tuition & Fees: $8,750
Enrollment: 36 Male
Affiliation or Control: Independent Non-Profit IRS Status: 501(c)3
Highest Offering: Second Talmudic Degree
Program: Teacher Preparatory; Religious Emphasis
Accreditation: RABN

03 Executive Vice President .... Rabbi Shaya COHEN
06 Registrar .... Rabbi Yosef AMSTER
07 Dir of Admiss/Financial Aid Admin .... Rabbi Avrohom BURGER
11 Chief of Operations .... Mr. Ezra PACHT
18 Chief Facilities .... Mr. Danny SCHUSTER

Yeshivas Novominsk (O)

1690 60th Street, Brooklyn NY 11204-2138
County: Kings FICE Identification: 031271
Unit ID: 405058
Telephone: (718) 438-2727 Carnegie Class: Spec/Faith
FAX Number: (718) 438-2472 Calendar System: Semester
Established: 1988 Annual Undergrad Tuition & Fees: $9,000
Enrollment: 123 Male
Affiliation or Control: Independent Non-Profit IRS Status: 501(c)3
Highest Offering: First Talmudic Degree
Program: Teacher Preparatory; Professional
Accreditation: RABN

01 Administrative Director ..... Rabbi Lipa BRENNAN
32 Dean of Students ..... Rabbi Yaakov PERLOW

Yeshivath Viznitz (A)

PO Box 446, Monsey NY 10952-0446
County: Rockland FICE Identification: 013027
Unit ID: 197735
Telephone: (845) 731-3700 Carnegie Class: Spec/Faith
FAX Number: (845) 356-7359 Calendar System: Semester
Established: 1946 Annual Undergrad Tuition & Fees: $6,400
Enrollment: 565 Male
Affiliation or Control: Independent Non-Profit IRS Status: 501(c)3
Highest Offering: Second Talmudic Degree
Program: Teacher Preparatory; Professional
Accreditation: RABN

01 President ..... Gershon NEIMAN
10 Chief Fiscal Officer ..... Rabbi J. LURIA

Yeshivath Zichron Moshe (B)

PO Box 580, South Fallsburg NY 12779-0580
County: Sullivan FICE Identification: 011821
Unit ID: 197744
Telephone: (845) 434-5240 Carnegie Class: Spec/Faith
FAX Number: (845) 434-1009 Calendar System: Semester
Established: 1969 Annual Undergrad Tuition & Fees: $10,700
Enrollment: 176 Male
Affiliation or Control: Independent Non-Profit IRS Status: 501(c)3
Highest Offering: Second Talmudic Degree
Program: Professional
Accreditation: RABN

01 President ..... Rabbi Ephraim Y. SHER
37 Director Student Financial Aid ..... Rabbi Dov PERECMAN
06 Registrar ..... Mrs. Miryom R. MILLER

NORTH CAROLINA

Apex School of Theology (C)

2945 S Miami Boulevard, Ste 114-115,
Durham NC 27703-8024
County: Durham FICE Identification: 035134
Unit ID: 441511
Telephone: (919) 572-1625 Carnegie Class: Spec/Faith
FAX Number: (919) 572-1762 Calendar System: Other
URL: www.apexsot.edu
Established: 1995 Annual Undergrad Tuition & Fees: $6,200
Enrollment: 725 Coed
Affiliation or Control: Independent Non-Profit IRS Status: 501(c)3
Highest Offering: Doctorate
Program: Religious Emphasis
Accreditation: TRACS

01 President ..... Dr. Joseph E. PERKINS
03 Executive Vice President ..... Dr. Herbert R. DAVIS
05 Academic Dean/Graduate Dean ..... Dr. Lafayette MAXWELL
06 Registrar ..... Ms. Juretta RUFFIN
08 Head Librarian ..... Ms. Cynthia RUFFIN
106 Director of E-Learning ..... Dr. John CHAPMAN
88 Director Doctor of Ministry Program ..... Dr. Terry THOMAS
10 Director of Finance ..... Mr. Dexter PERRY
20 Undergraduate Dean ..... Dr. Gladys LONG
88 Dean Master of Arts Christian Couns ..... Dr. John F. BRADSHAW
73 Dean Doctor of Ministry ..... Dr. Sherman TRIBBLE
32 Director Student Affairs ..... Dr. Clarence BURKE
09 Dir of Institutional Effectiveness ..... Dr. Henry D. WELLS, JR.

The Art Institute of Charlotte (D)

2110 Water Ridge Parkway, Charlotte NC 28217-4536
County: Mecklenburg FICE Identification: 021105
Unit ID: 197832
Telephone: (704) 357-8020 Carnegie Class: Spec/Arts
FAX Number: (704) 357-1133 Calendar System: Quarter
URL: www.aich.artinstitutes.edu
Established: 1973 Annual Undergrad Tuition & Fees: $23,004
Enrollment: 986 Coed
Affiliation or Control: Proprietary IRS Status: Proprietary
Highest Offering: Baccalaureate
Program: Occupational
Accreditation: ACICS, ACFEI

01 President ..... Mr. Maurice LEE
04 Exec Assistant to the President ..... Mrs. Melanie BRANNON
05 Dean of Academic Affairs ..... Dr. Diana LAWRENCE
32 Dean of Student Affairs ..... Mrs. Janice SUMNER
07 Senior Director of Admissions ..... Mrs. Michelle L. LAING-IDLE
10 Dir of Admin & Finance Services ..... Mr. Richard L. WALKER
06 Registrar ..... Mrs. Cheryl COYLE
08 Librarian ..... Ms. Elaine WOOD
36 Director Career Services ..... Mrs. Jen READ
40 Supply Store Manager ..... Ms. Debra SULLIVAN
21 Accounting Supervisor ..... Miss Lauren BROWN
91 Technology Support Supervisor ..... Mr. Stephen FULLER
15 Human Resources Generalist ..... Ms. Jacki WISLER

Barton College (E)

704-A College Street, PO Box 5000,
Wilson NC 27893-7000
County: Wilson FICE Identification: 002908
Unit ID: 197911
Telephone: (252) 399-6300 Carnegie Class: Bac/Diverse
FAX Number: (252) 399-6571 Calendar System: Semester
URL: www.barton.edu
Established: 1902 Annual Undergrad Tuition & Fees: $24,180
Enrollment: 1,194 Coed
Affiliation or Control: Christian Church (Disciples Of Christ)
IRS Status: 501(c)3
Highest Offering: Master's
Program: Liberal Arts And General; Teacher Preparatory
Accreditation: SC, NUR, SW, TED

01 President ..... Dr. Norval C. KNETEN
10 Vice Pres Finance & Aministration ..... Mr. Kris LYNCH
05 Vice President Academic Affairs ..... Dr. John MARSDEN
100 Senior Advisor to President ..... Mrs. Carolyn H. BROWN
31 Vice President External Relations ..... Dr. Kelly M. THOMPSON
32 Vice President Student Life ..... Mr. George SOLAN
30 Asst VP Inst Advancement ..... Vacant
35 Asst Vice Pres for Student Affairs ..... Ms. Holly ZACHARIAS
21 Comptroller ..... Vacant
06 Registrar ..... Ms. Sheila MILNE
08 Librarian ..... Mr. Rodney U. LIPPARD
42 Chaplain ..... Rev. Hollie E. WOODRUFF
36 Director of Career Services ..... Mr. Lance W. KAHN
23 Director of Health Services ..... Mrs. Amy BRIDGERS
26 Director of Public Relations ..... Mrs. Kathy DAUGHETY
29 Director of Alumni Affairs ..... Ms. Summer BROCK
07 Director of Admissions ..... Ms. Amanda METTS
15 Director Human Resources ..... Mrs. Linda TYSON
37 Director Student Financial Aid ..... Ms. Bridget ELLIS
87 Director Summer Sch/Cont Education ..... Dr. Deborah KING
14 Director Computer Center ..... Mr. Kent WHEELESS
40 Bookstore Manager ..... Ms. Brenda DAVIDSON
41 Athletic Director ..... Mr. Gary HALL
13 Director of Information Technology ..... Ms. Callie BISSETTE
35 Director of Student Activities ..... Mr. Jared TICE
18 Director of Physical Plant ..... Mr. Phil BEHE
09 Director of Institutional Research ..... Mr. Robert HUDSON
50 Interim Dean School of Business ..... Ms. Patricia BURRUS
53 Dean School of Education ..... Dr. Jackie ENNIS
66 Dean School of Nursing ..... Dr. Sharon SARVEY
88 Dean School of Behavioral Sciences ..... Dr. Barbara CONKLIN

Belmont Abbey College (F)

100 Belmont Mount Holly Road, Belmont NC 28012-1802
County: Gaston FICE Identification: 002910
Unit ID: 197984
Telephone: (704) 461-6700 Carnegie Class: Bac/Diverse
FAX Number: (704) 461-6670 Calendar System: Semester
URL: www.bac.edu
Established: 1876 Annual Undergrad Tuition & Fees: $27,622
Enrollment: 1,628 Coed
Affiliation or Control: Roman Catholic IRS Status: 501(c)3
Highest Offering: Baccalaureate
Program: Liberal Arts And General; Teacher Preparatory
Accreditation: SC

01 President ..... Dr. William K. THIERFELDER
05 VP Academic Affs/Dean of Faculty ..... Dr. Carson DALY
84 Vice Pres Enrollment & Student Affs ..... Dr. Lucas LAMADRID
11 Vice Pres Administration & Finance ..... Mr. Wayne SCROGGINS
26 Int Vice Pres College Relations ..... Mr. Dave TARGONSKI
04 Assistant to the President ..... Ms. Rita F. LEWIS
29 Director of Alumni Relations ..... Ms. Chris Goff PEELER
08 Director of the Library ..... Mr. Donald BEAGLE
06 Registrar ..... Fr. David BROWN, OSB
09 Director of Institutional Research ..... Dr. Sandra NICKS
36 Director Career Counseling/Placemnt ..... Ms. Stephannie MILES
27 Director Marketing ..... Mr. Edward JONES
37 Director of Student Financial Aid ..... Mrs. Anne A. STEVENS
38 Director Counseling Services ..... Vacant
41 Athletic Director ..... Mr. Quin MONAHAN
21 Staff Accountant ..... Ms. Patti PIZZANO
19 Chief of Campus Police ..... Mr. Shane STARNES
42 Director of Campus Ministry ..... Ms. Tricia STEVENSON
30 Dir Stewardship & Strategic Plng ..... Mr. David TARGONSKI
15 Director of Human Resources ..... Ms. Cheryl TROTTER
18 Chief Facilities/Physical Plant ..... Mr. J. R. MARR
07 Director of Admissions ..... Mr. Roger JONES

Bennett College (G)

900 E Washington Street, Greensboro NC 27401-3239
County: Guilford FICE Identification: 002911
Unit ID: 197993
Telephone: (336) 273-4431 Carnegie Class: Bac/A&S
FAX Number: (336) 370-8688 Calendar System: Semester
URL: www.bennett.edu
Established: 1873 Annual Undergrad Tuition & Fees: $16,794
Enrollment: 736 Female
Affiliation or Control: United Methodist IRS Status: 501(c)3
Highest Offering: Baccalaureate
Program: Liberal Arts And General; Teacher Preparatory; Business Emphasis
Accreditation: SC, SW, TED

01 Interim President ..... Dr. Esther TERRY
05 Provost/Academic VP ..... Dr. Millicent RAINEY
100 Exec VP/Chief of Staff ..... Dr. James DIXON
10 Vice President for Fiscal Affairs ..... Ms. LaTonya FLAMER
39 Director of Residence Life ..... Ms. Ruth DENNIS-PHILLIPS
30 Interim Vice Pres Inst Advancement ..... Ms. Iris RAMEY
26 Dir Public Relations & Publication ..... Ms. Wanda MOBLEY
09 Dir Institutional Effective/Rsrch ..... Ms. Xiaowen QIN
20 Assoc Provost of Academic Affs ..... Dr. Joyce BLACKWELL
84 Vice Pres Enrollment Mgmt ..... Mr. Les FERRIER
06 Registrar ..... Ms. Karen GREEN
08 Director of Holgate Library ..... Ms. Joan WILLIAMS
07 Interim Director of Admissions ..... Ms. Taunya N. MONROE
37 Director of Financial Aid ..... Ms. Keisha RAGSDALE
29 Director Alumnae Affairs ..... Ms. Audrey FRANKLIN
36 Director Career Services ..... Ms. Ilona MCGRIFF
38 Director of Counseling Services ..... Ms. Robin CAMPBELL
23 Director of Health Services ..... Ms. Shaina CRUDUP
15 Director of Human Resources ..... Ms. Linda MACK
42 Chaplain/Director Campus Ministry ..... Rev. Natalie MCLEAN
83 Chair Social Sciences/Educ Division ..... Dr. Rhonda WHITE
79 Chair Humanities/Fine Arts Division ..... Mr. Steven WILLIS
81 Chair Natural & Behavioral Sciences ..... Dr. Susan CURTIS
97 Dean of Academic Support ..... Dr. Audrey WARD

Brevard College (H)

One Brevard College Drive, Brevard NC 28712-3306
County: Transylvania FICE Identification: 002912
Unit ID: 198066
Telephone: (828) 883-8292 Carnegie Class: Bac/A&S
FAX Number: (828) 884-3790 Calendar System: Semester
URL: www.brevard.edu
Established: 1853 Annual Undergrad Tuition & Fees: $24,070
Enrollment: 627 Coed
Affiliation or Control: United Methodist IRS Status: 501(c)3
Highest Offering: Baccalaureate
Program: Liberal Arts And General
Accreditation: SC, MUS, TEAC

01 President ..... Dr. David C. JOYCE
05 VP Academic Affairs/Dean of Faculty ..... Dr. John S. HARDT
10 Vice President for Business/Finance ..... Ms. Deborah P. HALL
30 Vice Pres Institutional Advancement ..... Mrs. Susan L. COTHERN
07 Vice Pres Admissions/Financial Aid ..... Mr. Matthew COX
04 Assistant to the President ..... Ms. Cheryl K. TINSLEY
32 Dean of Students ..... Mrs. Debora D'ANNA
44 Director of Development ..... Ms. Huldah WARREN
13 Int Dir of Information Technology ..... Mr. Jay TRUSSELL
06 Registrar ..... Mrs. Amy HERTZ
37 Director of Financial Aid ..... Mrs. Beth POCOCK
26 Dir of Marketing/Donor Relations ..... Ms. Carole FUTRELLE
08 Director of Library ..... Mr. Michael M. MCCABE
29 Director of Alumni Affairs ..... Mrs. Rebecca GILL
19 Dir of Safety/Security/Risk Mgmt ..... Mr. Stan JACOBSEN
41 Director of Athletics ..... Mr. Juan MASCARO
18 Director of Facilities/Grounds ..... Mr. William ELFERDINK
24 Director Academic Enrichment Ctr ..... Ms. Shirley E. ARNOLD
36 Dir Ofc Career Exploration/Devel ..... Vacant
92 Director of Honors Program ..... Dr. Laura L. FRANKLIN
21 Controller ..... Mr. Thomas Ove ANDERSEN
38 Coordinator of Counseling Services ..... Ms. Deanne DASBURG
57 Chair Division of Fine Arts ..... Dr. Laura FRANKLIN
79 Chair Division of Humanities ..... Dr. Mary L. BRINGLE
83 Chair Div of Social Studies ..... Dr. Helen C. GIFT
81 Chair Div Env Stds/Math/Nat Science ..... Dr. Kenneth DUKE

Cabarrus College of Health Sciences (I)

401 Medical Park Drive, Concord NC 28025-3959
County: Cabarrus FICE Identification: 006477
Unit ID: 198109
Telephone: (704) 403-1555 Carnegie Class: Spec/Health
FAX Number: (704) 403-2077 Calendar System: Semester
URL: www.cabarruscollege.edu
Established: 1942 Annual Undergrad Tuition & Fees: $11,010
Enrollment: 477 Coed
Affiliation or Control: Independent Non-Profit IRS Status: 501(c)3
Highest Offering: Baccalaureate
Program: Occupational; 2-Year Principally Bachelor's Creditable; Nursing Emphasis
Accreditation: SC, ADNUR, MAC, NURSE, OTA, SURGT

01 Chancellor ..... Dr. Dianne O. SNYDER
05 Provost ..... Dr. Margaret B. PATCHETT
11 Dean for Admin & Financial Svcs ..... Mr. Mark E. COLEMAN
32 Dean of Student Svcs/Enrollment Mgt ..... Ms. Chris L. CORSELLO
66 ADN Program Chair ..... Ms. Kim PLEMMONS
66 BSN Program Chair ..... Ms. Molly PATTON
07 Director of Admissions ..... Dr. Mark A. ELLISON
32 Director of Student Affairs ..... Mrs. Angela M. FERGUSON
37 Director of Financial Aid ..... Ms. Valerie RICHARD
06 Registrar ..... Mr. Michael P. SMITH

Campbell University (J)

PO Box 97, Buies Creek NC 27506-0097
County: Harnett FICE Identification: 002913
Unit ID: 198136
Telephone: (910) 893-1200 Carnegie Class: Master's L
FAX Number: (910) 893-1424 Calendar System: Semester
URL: www.campbell.edu

Established: 1887 Annual Undergrad Tuition & Fees: $25,000
Enrollment: 6,637 Coed
Affiliation or Control: Baptist IRS Status: 501(c)3
Highest Offering: Doctorate
Program: Liberal Arts And General; Teacher Preparatory; Professional
Accreditation: SC, ACBSP, #ARCPA, LAW, @OSTEO, PHAR, SW, TED, THEOL

01 President .... Dr. Jerry M. WALLACE
05 Vice Pres Academic Affs & Provost .... Dr. M. Dwaine GREENE
10 Vice President Business/Treasurer .... Mr. Jim O. ROBERTS
30 Vice President for Advancement .... Mr. Britt DAVIS
32 Vice President for Student Life .... Dr. Dennis BAZEMORE
84 Vice Pres Enrollment Management .... Dr. John ROBERSON
07 Asst Vice Pres of Admissions .... Mr. Jason HALL
49 Dean of College of Arts & Science .... Dr. Mark L. HAMMOND
61 Dean of the Law School .... Mr. B. Keith FAULKNER
50 Dean Lundy-Fetterman Sch Business .... Dr. Ben HAWKINS
53 Dean School of Education .... Dr. Karen NERY
67 VP of Health Sciences and Dean .... Dr. Ronald W. MADDOX
63 Dean of Osteopathic Medical School .... Dr. John M. KAUFFMAN, JR.
35 Dean of Students .... Dr. Sherry L. HAEHL
51 Director Continuing Education .... Mr. Thomas G. HARRIS
06 Registrar .... Mr. David MCGIRT
21 Assistant Treasurer .... Mr. Win QUAKENBUSH
29 Director of Alumni Relations .... Rev. Doug JONES
89 Director of Freshman Experience .... Dr. Jennifer A. LATINO
08 Librarian .... Mrs. Borree KWOK
37 Director of Financial Aid .... Mrs. Michelle DAY
14 Director of Computing Services .... Mr. Chris BUCKLEY
26 Director of Public Information .... Ms. Haven HOTTEL
15 Human Resources Director .... Mr. Bob COGSWELL
18 Chief Facilities/Physical Plant .... Mr. David MARTIN
38 Director Student Counseling .... Mrs. Laura RICH
96 Director of Purchasing .... Vacant
92 Director of Honors Program .... Dr. Ann ORTIZ
09 Director of Institutional Research .... Dr. Timothy D. METZ

Carolina Bible College (A)

817 S. McPherson Church Road, Fayetteville NC 28303
County: Cumberland FICE Identification: 041542
Unit ID: 461032
Telephone: (910) 323-5614 Carnegie Class: Not Classified
FAX Number: (910) 323-0425 Calendar System: Semester
URL: www.carolinabiblecollege.org
Established: 1973 Annual Undergrad Tuition & Fees: $5,300
Enrollment: 105 Coed
Affiliation or Control: Non-denominational IRS Status: 501(c)3
Highest Offering: Baccalaureate
Program: Religious Emphasis
Accreditation: @BI

01 President .... Dr. Bill KORVER
05 Academic Dean .... Dr. Harry GHEE
30 Vice Pres Strategic Development .... Dr. Bill BOYD
06 Registrar .... Ms. Kathy SCHULTINGKEMPER
07 Director of Admissions .... Ms. Pamela RECOD

Carolina Christian College (B)

PO Box 777, Winston-Salem NC 27102
County: Forsyth FICE Identification: 035703
Unit ID: 199971
Telephone: (336) 744-0900 Carnegie Class: Spec/Faith
FAX Number: (336) 744-0901 Calendar System: Semester
URL: www.carolina.edu
Established: 1945 Annual Undergrad Tuition & Fees: $3,785
Enrollment: 72 Coed
Affiliation or Control: Independent Non-Profit IRS Status: 501(c)3
Highest Offering: Baccalaureate
Program: Liberal Arts And General; Religious Emphasis
Accreditation: BI

01 President .... Dr. Donald R. YOUNG
05 Academic Dean .... Ms. LaTanya V. LUCAS
32 Dean of Students .... Vacant
08 Library Director .... Ms. Laura RHODEN
37 Financial Aid Director .... Vacant

Carolina Graduate School of Divinity (C)

2400 Old Chapman St., Greensboro NC 27403
County: Guilford FICE Identification: 039395
Telephone: (336) 315-8660 Carnegie Class: Not Classified
FAX Number: (336) 315-8660 Calendar System: Semester
URL: www.carolinagrad.edu
Established: 2003 Annual Graduate Tuition & Fees: $10,000
Enrollment: 54 Coed
Affiliation or Control: Interdenominational IRS Status: 501(c)3
Highest Offering: Doctorate; No Undergraduates
Program: Professional; Religious Emphasis
Accreditation: THEOL

01 President .... Dr. Frank P. SCURRY
05 Vice President for Academics .... Dr. Terry W. EDDINGER
32 Director of Student Life .... Dr. Darryl A. BODIE
06 Director of Student Records .... Mrs. Cindy H. BODIE
37 Director of Financial Aid .... Ms. Shirley P. CARTER
10 Business Manager .... Mrs. Rosalie CARR

Carolinas College of Health Sciences (D)

PO Box 32861, 1200 Blythe Boulevard, Charlotte NC 28232-2861
County: Mecklenburg FICE Identification: 031042
Unit ID: 433174
Telephone: (704) 355-5043 Carnegie Class: Assoc/Pub-Spec
FAX Number: (704) 355-5967 Calendar System: Semester
URL: www.CarolinasCollege.edu
Established: 1990 Annual Undergrad Tuition & Fees (In-District): $11,475
Enrollment: 524 Coed
Affiliation or Control: Local IRS Status: 501(c)3
Highest Offering: Associate Degree
Program: 2-Year Principally Bachelor's Creditable
Accreditation: SC, ADNUR, MT, RAD, SURGT

01 President .... Dr. Ellen SHEPPARD
05 Provost .... Dr. Janice TERRELL
10 Dean of Business/Finance/Technology .... Ms. Kim BRADSHAW
32 Dean Student Svcs/Enrollment Mgmt .... Dr. T. Hampton HOPKINS
66 Dean of Nursing .... Dr. Deborah BLACKWELL
97 Dean Assessment/Gen Ed/Pre-Nursing .... Dr. Lori BEQUETTE
76 Director Surgical Technology .... Ms. Kali SIMIEN
76 Director Radiologic Technology .... Mr. Doug FRANKENBURG
76 Director Radiation Therapy .... Mr. Lee BRASWELL
76 Director Medical Technology .... Ms. Kelly SHIRLEY
06 Registrar .... Ms. Sue ROUX
07 Admissions Coordinator .... Ms. Rhoda RILLORTA
37 Financial Aid Coordinator .... Ms. Jill POWELL
29 Director Alumni Relations .... Dr. Ruthie MIHAL
90 Instructional Tech Coordinator .... Mr. Larry TURNER
26 Chief Public Relations Officer .... Mr. Kevin MCCARTHY
36 Director Student Placement .... Ms. Nancy WATKINS
51 Director Continuing Education .... Ms. Susan THOMASSON
09 Director of Institutional Research .... Dr. Lori BEQUETTE
18 Chief Facilities/Physical Plant .... Ms. Kim BRADSHAW
30 Chief Development .... Dr. Ellen SHEPPARD
96 Director of Purchasing .... Ms. Kim BRADSHAW

Catawba College (E)

2300 W Innes Street, Salisbury NC 28144-2488
County: Rowan FICE Identification: 002914
Unit ID: 198215
Telephone: (704) 637-4111 Carnegie Class: Bac/Diverse
FAX Number: (704) 637-4444 Calendar System: Semester
URL: www.catawba.edu
Established: 1851 Annual Undergrad Tuition & Fees: $26,140
Enrollment: 1,325 Coed
Affiliation or Control: United Church Of Christ IRS Status: 501(c)3
Highest Offering: Master's
Program: Liberal Arts And General; Teacher Preparatory
Accreditation: SC, TED

01 President .... Mr. Brien LEWIS
03 Senior Vice President/Chaplain .... Dr. Kenneth W. CLAPP
30 Sr Vice Pres/Chief of Development .... Mr. Thomas C. CHILDRESS
05 Provost .... Dr. Richard STEPHENS
04 Assistant to President .... Mrs. Amy H. WILLIAMS
09 Assoc Provost/Dir Instl Research .... Dr. Steven J. COGGIN
10 Chief Financial Officer .... Mr. Charles F. WILLIAMS
84 Vice Pres of Enrollment Management .... Ms. Lois H. WILLIAMS
15 Chief Human Resources Officer .... Mr. Larry G. FARMER
26 Chief Public Relations Officer .... Mrs. Tonia BLACK-GOLD
32 Dean of Students .... Mr. G. Ben SMITH
08 Head Librarian .... Dr. Steve MCKINZIE
06 Registrar .... Ms. Carol GAMBLE
07 Sr Director of Admissions .... Ms. Elaine P. HOLDEN
37 Director of Financial Assistance .... Ms. Dawn SNOOK
36 Director of Placement .... Ms. Robin PERRY
88 Director Sports Info & Promotion .... Mr. Jim D. LEWIS
40 Director Bookstore .... Mrs. Stephanie TAYLOR
41 Athletic Director .... Mr. Dennis W. DAVIDSON
18 Chief Facilities/Physical Plant .... Mr. Eric NIANOURIS
29 Director Alumni Relations .... Ms. Margaret FAUST
38 Director Student Counseling .... Dr. Nancy ZIMMERMAN
39 Director of Residence Life .... Ms. Sarah ROSSINI

Charlotte School of Law (F)

2145 Suttle Avenue, Charlotte NC 28208
County: Mecklenburg FICE Identification: 041435
Unit ID: 455169
Telephone: (704) 971-8500 Carnegie Class: Spec/Law
FAX Number: (704) 971-8599 Calendar System: Semester
URL: www.charlottelaw.org
Established: 2008 Annual Graduate Tuition & Fees: $38,604
Enrollment: 409 Coed
Affiliation or Control: Proprietary IRS Status: Proprietary
Highest Offering: First Professional Degree; No Undergraduates
Program: Professional
Accreditation: LAW

01 President .... Mr. Dennis STONE
05 Interim Dean .... Ms. Denise SPRIGGS
20 Interim Assoc Dean for Academics .... Mr. Daniel PIAR
32 Assistant Dean for Student Services .... Mr. Michael FARLEY
07 Associate Dean of Admissions .... Vacant
08 Assoc Dean for Library/Info Svcs .... Vacant
10 Associate Dean for Business/Finance .... Mr. Frank TOLIVER
06 Dir of Academic Svcs/Registration .... Ms. Traci FLEURY
37 Director of Financial Aid .... Ms. Lauren MACK

Chowan University (G)

One University Place, Murfreesboro NC 27855-1844
County: Hertford FICE Identification: 002916
Unit ID: 198303
Telephone: (252) 398-6500 Carnegie Class: Bac/Diverse
FAX Number: (252) 398-1190 Calendar System: Semester
URL: www.chowan.edu
Established: 1848 Annual Undergrad Tuition & Fees: $26,630
Enrollment: 1,324 Coed
Affiliation or Control: Baptist IRS Status: 501(c)3
Highest Offering: Master's
Program: Liberal Arts And General
Accreditation: SC, MUS, TED

01 President .... Dr. M. Chrisopher WHITE
05 Vice President Academic Affairs .... Dr. Danny B. MOORE
10 Vice President Business Affairs .... Mr. Donnie O. CLARY
32 Vice President Student Affairs .... Mr. P. Randy HARRELL
30 Vice President Advancement .... Mr. John TAYLOE
15 Vice President Human Resources .... Mr. John A. HINTON
07 Vice President Admissions .... Mr. Chad HOLT
13 Exec Dir Info Tech/Network Svcs .... Mr. James R. HOWELL
06 Registrar .... Ms. Donna WOODARD
26 Director of Public Relations .... Mr. Joshua BARKER
08 Head Librarian .... Mrs. Georgia E. WILLIAMS
37 Director of Financial Aid .... Mrs. Sharon ROSE
42 Campus Minister .... Ms. Mari E. WILES
18 Director Physical Plant .... Mr. Bob ROWE
19 Chief of Security .... Mr. Derek A. BURKE
35 Director Student Life .... Ms. Laurica YANCEY
38 Director Counseling/Career Services .... Mrs. Frances E. COLE
39 Director Housing & Residence Life .... Mr. Brandon ZOCH
41 Athletics Director .... Mr. Dennis HELSEL
09 Director Institutional Research .... Mr. Daniel MCCAMISH
88 Director Upward Bound .... Mr. E. Frank STEPHENSON
21 Director Business Services .... Mrs. Julie W. EMORY
29 Director Alumni Services .... Mr. Michael P. TEMPLE
49 Dean Liberal Arts .... Dr. John DILUSTRO
50 Dean Business .... Dr. Linda MILES
53 Dean Education .... Dr. Brenda S. TINKHAM
40 Bookstore Manager .... Vacant

Daoist Traditions College of Chinese Medical Arts (H)

382 Montford Ave, Asheville NC 28801
County: Buncombe FICE Identification: 041464
Unit ID: 455178
Telephone: (828) 225-3993 Carnegie Class: Not Classified
FAX Number: (828) 255-3306 Calendar System: Semester
URL: www.daoisttraditions.edu
Established: 2003 Annual Undergrad Tuition & Fees: $15,500
Enrollment: 67 Coed
Affiliation or Control: Proprietary IRS Status: Proprietary
Highest Offering: Master's
Program: Professional
Accreditation: ACUP

01 President .... Dr. Mary Cissy MAJEBE

Davidson College (I)

PO Box 5000, Davidson NC 28035-5000
County: Mecklenburg FICE Identification: 002918
Unit ID: 198385
Telephone: (704) 894-2000 Carnegie Class: Bac/A&S
FAX Number: (704) 894-2005 Calendar System: Semester
URL: www.davidson.edu
Established: 1837 Annual Undergrad Tuition & Fees: $40,809
Enrollment: 1,756 Coed
Affiliation or Control: Presbyterian Church (U.S.A.) IRS Status: 501(c)3
Highest Offering: Baccalaureate
Program: Liberal Arts And General
Accreditation: SC

01 President .... Dr. Carol E. QUILLEN
05 Vice Pres Acad Affs/Dean of Faculty .... Dr. Clark G. ROSS
26 Vice President College Relations .... Ms. Eileen M. KEELEY
10 Vice Pres Finance & Administration .... Mr. Edward A. KANIA
32 VP Student Life/Dean of Students .... Dr. Thomas C. SHANDLEY
07 VP & Dean Admissions/Financial Aid .... Mr. Christopher J. GRUBER
27 Assoc VP College Communications .... Ms. Stacey SCHMEIDEL
09 VP Planning/Institutional Research .... Ms. Linda M. LEFAUVE
20 Assoc Dean Academic Administration .... Ms. Leslie M. MARSICANO
20 Assoc Dean for Curriculum .... Dr. Patrick J. SELLERS
20 Assoc Dean Teaching/Lrng/Rsrch .... Dr. Verna M. CASE
06 Registrar .... Ms. Angela B. DEWBERRY
13 Exec Director Information Tecnology .... Mr. Mur K. MUCHANE
37 Director Financial Aid .... Mr. David GELINAS
15 Director of Human Resources .... Dr. Kim BALL
41 Director of Athletics .... Mr. James E. MURPHY, III
08 Director of the Library .... Ms. Gillian (Jill) S. GREMMELS
29 Director Alumni Relations .... Ms. Marya L. HOWELL
21 Controller/Director Business Svcs .... Ms. Lori GASTON
18 Director Facilities & Engineering .... Mr. David M. HOLTHOUSER

19 Director of Public Safety & Police .... Ms. Adrienne M. MURRAY
36 Director Career Services .... Mr. Nathan J. ELTON
35 Director of College Union .... Mr. William H. BROWN
39 Dir Resid Life/Assoc Dean Students .... Mr. Jason S. SHAFFER
42 College Chaplain .... Dr. Robert C. SPACH
71 Dir Cntr for Interdisciplinary Stds .... Dr. Scott D. DENHAM
82 Assoc Dean Int'l Programs/ Studies .... Dr. M. Christopher ALEXANDER
25 Director of Grants & Contracts .... Dr. Mary W. MUCHANE
24 Director Instructional Support .... Ms. Diane S. STIRLING
38 Director Student Counseling Center .... Dr. Trish MURRAY
44 Director of Annual Fund .... Ms. Maria ALDRICH
96 Director of Purchasing .... Ms. Elizabeth S. CHRISTENBURY
40 Bookstore Manager .... Ms. Gwendolyn S. GARDNER

DeVry University - Charlotte Center (A)

2015 Ayrsley Town Blvd, Suite 109,
Charlotte NC 28273-4068

County: Mecklenburg — Identification: 666215
Unit ID: 442365
Telephone: (704) 362-2345 — Carnegie Class: Spec/Bus
FAX Number: (704) 362-2668 — Calendar System: Semester
URL: www.devry.edu
Established: 2001 — Annual Undergrad Tuition & Fees: $16,156
Enrollment: 714 — Coed
Affiliation or Control: Proprietary — IRS Status: Proprietary
Highest Offering: Master's
Program: Occupational; Professional; Business Emphasis
Accreditation: &NH

01 Campus Dean .... Ms. Regina CAMPBELL

† Regional accreditation is carried under the parent institution in Downers Grove, IL.

DeVry University - Raleigh/Durham (B)

1600 Perimeter Park Drive, Ste 100,
Morrisville NC 27560-8421

County: Durham — Identification: 666562
Telephone: (919) 463-1380 — Carnegie Class: Not Classified
FAX Number: (919) 468-5688 — Calendar System: Semester
URL: www.devry.edu
Established: 1931 — Annual Undergrad Tuition & Fees: $16,156
Enrollment: 446 — Coed
Affiliation or Control: Proprietary — IRS Status: Proprietary
Highest Offering: Master's
Program: Professional; Business Emphasis
Accreditation: &NH

01 Campus Director .... Sandy GARETON

† Regional accreditation is carried under the parent institution in Downers Grove, IL.

Duke University (C)

Durham NC 27706-8001

County: Durham — FICE Identification: 002920
Unit ID: 198419
Telephone: (919) 684-8111 — Carnegie Class: RU/VH
FAX Number: (919) 684-3200 — Calendar System: Semester
URL: www.duke.edu
Established: 1838 — Annual Undergrad Tuition & Fees: $42,308
Enrollment: 15,231 — Coed
Affiliation or Control: Independent Non-Profit — IRS Status: 501(c)3
Highest Offering: Doctorate
Program: Liberal Arts And General; Teacher Preparatory; Professional
Accreditation: SC, ANEST, ARCPA, BUS, CLPSY, ENG, #FOR, IPSY, LAW, MED, NURSE, PA, PTA, TED, THEOL

01 President .... Richard H. BRODHEAD
05 Provost .... Peter LANGE
11 Exec Vice Pres for Administration .... Tallman TRASK, III
26 Vice President Public Affairs .... Michael J. SCHOENFELD
45 President/Duke Management Company .... Neal TRIPLETT
30 Vice Pres Alumni Affs/Development .... Robert S. SHEPARD
23 VP Admin Duke Univ Health Systems .... Monte BROWN
32 Vice President for Student Affairs .... Larry MONETA
22 Vice Pres for Institutional Equity .... Benjamin D. REESE
10 Vice President Financial Services .... Timothy WALSH
17 Chief Exec Officer Duke Univ Hosp .. William J. FULKERSON, JR.
88 Vice Pres - Chief Medical Officer .... Karen FRUSH
15 Vice President for Administration .... Kyle CAVANAUGH
41 Vice Pres & Director of Athletics .... Kevin WHITE
101 Vice Pres & University Secretary .... Richard RIDDELL
17 Chancellor for Health Affairs .... Victor DZAU
30 VP Duke Med Devel/Alumni Affairs .... Ellen MEDEARIS
72 Vice Chanc Science & Technology .... Vacant
31 Assoc VP Community Affairs DUHS .... Maryann BLACK
35 Asst VP Student Affs/Dean Students .... Sue WASIOLEK
19 Assoc VP Campus Safety and Security .... Aaron GRAVES
07 Dean Undergraduate Admissions .... Christoph O. GUTTENTAG
21 Exec Vice Provost Finance & Admin .... James S. ROBERTS
13 Vice Prov Information Technology .... Tracy FUTHEY
88 Vice Provost Interdisciplin Studies .... Susan ROTH
20 Vice Provost for Academic Affairs .... Keith WHITFIELD
88 Director Intl Area Studies .... Gilbert MERKX
88 Vice Prov Faculty Diversity & Dev .... Nancy ALLEN
88 Vice Provost for the Arts .... Scott A. LINDTORTH
46 Vice Provost for Research .... James N. SIEDOW
29 Executive Director Alumni Affairs .... Sterly WILDER
36 Executive Director Career Devel Ctr .... William WRIGHT-SWADEL
21 Exec Director of Internal Audits .... Michael L. SOMICH
23 Exec Dir Student Health Service .... William PURDY
38 Exec Director of Student Counseling .... Kathy R. HOLLINGSWORTH
06 Registrar .... Bruce W. CUNNINGHAM
08 Librarian/Vice Prov Library Affairs .... Deborah JAKUBS
43 University Counsel .... Pamela BERNARD
09 Director of Institutional Research .... David JAMIESON-DRAKE
37 Asst Vice Provost/Dir Financial Aid .... Alison RABIL
87 Director of Summer Session .... Paula E. GILBERT
61 Dean of Law School .... David F. LEVI
63 Dn Sch Med/Sr Vice Chanc Acad Affs .... Nancy ANDREWS
50 Dean Fuqua School of Business .... William BOULDING
65 Dean School of the Environment .... William L. CHAMEIDES
73 Dean of the Divinity School .... Richard HAYS
58 Dean Grad School/Vice Prov Grad Ed .... Paula D. MCCLAIN
49 Dean Faculty Arts/Science .... Laurie PATTON
88 Dean of the Natural Sciences .... Robert CALDERBANK
49 Dean Acad Affs Trinity Col Arts/Sci .... Lee D. BAKER
66 Dean School of Nursing .... Catherine GILLISS
54 Dean of Engineering .... Thomas KATSOULEAS
83 Dean of the Humanities .... Srinivas ARAVAMUDAN
83 Dean of the Social Sciences .... Angela M. O'RAND
53 Dean and Vice Provost Undergrad Ed .... Stephen NOWICKI
94 Director of Women's Studies .... Ranjana KHANNA
93 Director Ofc of Intercultural Affs .... Julian SANCHEZ
88 Director Duke University Press .... Stephen A. COHN
18 Vice President for Facilities .... John NOONAN
27 Chief Info Ofcr/Vice Pres Duke Med .... Art GLASGOW
88 Vice Chanc for Clinical Research .... Robert M. CALIFF
88 Chief Med Ofcr .... Thomas OWENS
88 Exec Vice Dean Admin Sch Med .... Scott GIBSON
88 Vice Pres/Vice Prov Global Strategy .... Michael H. MERSON
88 Vice Chanc Corp and Venture Devel .... Robert L. TABER
45 VP Bus Devel & Chf Strat Plng Ofcr .... Mollie O'NEILL

Elon University (D)

2700 Campus Box, Elon NC 27244-2010

County: Alamance — FICE Identification: 002927
Unit ID: 198516
Telephone: (336) 278-2000 — Carnegie Class: Master's S
FAX Number: N/A — Calendar System: 4/1/4
URL: www.elon.edu
Established: 1889 — Annual Undergrad Tuition & Fees: $28,980
Enrollment: 5,916 — Coed
Affiliation or Control: Independent Non-Profit — IRS Status: 501(c)3
Highest Offering: Doctorate
Program: Liberal Arts And General; Teacher Preparatory; Professional
Accreditation: SC, BUS, JOUR, LAW, PTA, TED

01 President .... Dr. Leo M. LAMBERT
03 Executive Vice President .... Dr. Gerald L. FRANCIS
100 Chief of Staff/Sec to the Board .... Mr. Jeff STEIN
05 Provost/Vice Pres Academic Affairs .... Dr. Steven D. HOUSE
07 VP of Admissions/Financial Planning .... Mr. Greg ZAISER
10 Senior VP for Business/Finance/ Tech .... Mr. Gerald O. WHITTINGTON
30 Vice Pres Institutional Advancement .... Mr. James B. PIATT
32 Vice Pres/Dean of Student Life .... Dr. G. Smith JACKSON
27 Vice Pres University Communications ... Mr. Daniel J. ANDERSON
20 Associate VP of Academic Affairs .... Dr. Mary B. WISE
20 Associate Provost for Academic Affs .... Dr. Connie BOOK
88 Associate Provost for Faculty Affs .... Dr. Tim PEEPLES
21 Asst VP for Finance .... Ms. Susan M. KIRKLAND
49 Dean College of Arts & Sci ..... Dr. Alison MORRISON-SHETLAR
50 Dean Love School of Business .... Dr. Raghu TADEPALLI
60 Dean of School of Communications .... Dr. Paul F. PARSONS
53 Dean of School of Education .... Dr. David H. COOPER
61 Dean of School of Law .... Mr. George JOHNSON
76 Dean of School of Health Sciences .... Dr. Elizabeth A. ROGERS
85 Dean of International Programs .... Mr. Woody PELTON
35 Assistant VP of Student Life .... Mrs. Jana Lynn F. PATTERSON
08 Dean and University Librarian .... Ms. Joan RUELLE
41 Director of Athletics .... Mr. Dave L. BLANK
06 Registrar/Assistant to the Provost .... Mr. Mark R. ALBERTSON
42 University Chaplain .... Dr. Janet FULLER
37 Director of Financial Planning .... Dr. M. Patrick MURPHY
29 Director Alumni Relations .... Ms. Sallie HUTTON
88 Assoc Dean of Academic Support .... Dr. Becky OLIVE-TAYLOR
36 Exec Director of Career Services .... Dr. Tom VECCHIONE
88 Dir of Planning/Design/Construction .... Mr. Brad D. MOORE
18 Director of Physical Plant .... Mr. Robert BUCHHOLZ
15 Director of Human Resources .... Mr. Ronald A. KLEPCYK
31 Director of Auxiliary Services .... Ms. Vickie L. SOMERS
19 Director of Campus Safety & Police .... Mr. Dennis FRANKS
23 Director of Health Services .... Vacant
38 Director Counseling Services .... Mr. Bruce F. NELSON
27 Assistant VP of Technology/CIO . Mr. Christopher D. FULKERSON
09 Director Institutional Research .... Dr. Robert I. SPRINGER
13 Assistant CIO .... Mr. Christopher C. WATERS
25 Director of Sponsored Programs .... Ms. Bonnie BRUNO
93 Director of Multicultural Center .... Mr. Leon T. WILLIAMS
92 Director of Honors Program .... Dr. Maureen VANDERMAAS-PEELER
94 Director Women's Stds/Gender Stds .... Dr. Mandy GALLAGHER
96 Director of Purchasing .... Mr. Jeff HENDRICKS
88 Sustainability Coordinator .... Ms. Elaine DURR

Gardner-Webb University (E)

PO Box 897 (110 South Main Street),
Boiling Springs NC 28017-0897

County: Cleveland — FICE Identification: 002929
Unit ID: 198561
Telephone: (704) 406-2361 — Carnegie Class: Master's L
FAX Number: (704) 406-4329 — Calendar System: Semester
URL: www.gardner-webb.edu
Established: 1905 — Annual Undergrad Tuition & Fees: $24,250
Enrollment: 4,768 — Coed
Affiliation or Control: Baptist — IRS Status: 501(c)3
Highest Offering: Doctorate
Program: 2-Year Principally Bachelor's Creditable; Liberal Arts And General; Teacher Preparatory; Professional; Business Emphasis
Accreditation: SC, ACBSP, ADNUR, CACREP, MUS, NUR, TED, THEOL

01 President .... Dr. A. Frank BONNER
05 Provost & Senior Vice President .... Dr. Benjamin C. LESLIE
04 Sr Assistant to the President .... Mrs. Glenda S. CROTTS
10 Vice President for Business/Finance .... Mr. Mike W. HARDIN
26 Sr VP University Rels Marketing .... Mr. Ralph W. DIXON, JR.
30 Vice President for Advancement .... Mr. Monte WALKER
32 Vice Pres/Dean Student Development .... Dr. Delores HUNT
84 Vice Pres Enrollment Management .... Mrs. Debra HINTZ
41 Vice President for Athletics .... Mr. Chuck S. BURCH
09 VP Distance Learning/Inst Research .... Dr. Jeffrey L. TUBBS
18 Assoc Vice Pres for Operations .... Mr. Wayne E. JOHNSON
91 Assoc VP for Technology Services .... Mr. Joey BRIDGES
20 Associate Provost for Schools .... Dr. Franki BURCH
49 Assoc Provost for Arts & Sciences .... Dr. Earl LEININGER
21 Asst Vice President Business .... Mr. Jeff S. INGLE
51 Asst Provost for Distance Learning .... Dr. Bobbie COX
07 Dir of Undergraduate Admissions .... Ms. Kristen SETZER
37 Director of Financial Planning .... Ms. Summer ROBERTSON
06 Registrar .... Mrs. LouAnn P. SCATES
35 Director of Academic Advising .... Dr. Doug BRYAN
19 Chief of University Police .... Mr. Barry JOHNSON
27 Dir of University & Media Relations .... Mr. Noel T. MANNING
08 Director of the Library .... Ms. Mary ROBY
38 Dir of Counseling & Career Svcs .... Ms. Cindy WALLACE
89 Director of Freshmen Programs .... Vacant
58 Dean of Graduate School .... Vacant
73 Dean of Divinity School .... Dr. Robert W. CANOY
66 Dean of Nursing School .... Dr. Rebecca BECK-LITTLE
50 Director of School Management .... Dr. Sue C. CAMP
92 Director of Honors Program .... Dr. Thomas H. JONES
88 Director Program for Blind/Deaf .... Mrs. Cheryl J. POTTER
21 Comptroller .... Mrs. Robin G. HAMRICK
35 Director Student Activities .... Ms. Karissa L. WEIR
42 Minister to the University .... Dr. Tracy C. JESSUP
39 Director of Residence Life .... Ms. Sherry INGRAM
50 Dean of Business School .... Dr. Anthony I. NEGBENEBOR
15 Director Human Resources .... Mr. W. Scott WHITE
29 Director Alumni Relations .... Ms. Meghan DALTON
44 Director of Annual Campaign .... Ms. Rebecca GUNN
24 Asst Dir University Media Relations .... Ms. Kathy MARTIN
40 Bookstore Manager .... Mr. Wayne MERRITT
96 Director of Operations Support .... Vacant

Grace College of Divinity (F)

5117 Cliffdale Road, Fayetteville NC 28314

County: Cumberland — FICE Identification: 041737
Unit ID: 461528
Telephone: (910) 221-2224 — Carnegie Class: Not Classified
FAX Number: (910) 221-2226 — Calendar System: Semester
URL: www.gcdivinity.org
Established: 2000 — Annual Undergrad Tuition & Fees: $3,435
Enrollment: 94 — Coed
Affiliation or Control: Other Protestant — IRS Status: 501(c)3
Highest Offering: Baccalaureate
Program: Religious Emphasis
Accreditation: BI

01 President .... Dr. Steven CROWTHER
05 Academic Dean .... Dr. Ron CREWS
84 Dean of Enrollment Management .... Mr. David CHOI
32 Dean of Students .... Mr. Tom JOHNSON
11 Vice President of Administration .... Mr. Dick GAFFNEY
10 Chief Financial Officer .... Ms. Omayra COON
08 Librarian .... Mr. David ASPINALL
108 Director of Assessment & Planning .... Ms. Sharyn J. TEAGUE
06 Assistant Registar .... Ms. Shaila BERMUDEZ

Greensboro College (G)

815 W Market Street, Greensboro NC 27401-1875

County: Guilford — FICE Identification: 002930
Unit ID: 198598
Telephone: (336) 272-7102 — Carnegie Class: Bac/Diverse
FAX Number: (336) 217-6634 — Calendar System: Semester
URL: www.greensboro.edu
Established: 1838 — Annual Undergrad Tuition & Fees: $25,600
Enrollment: 1,200 — Coed
Affiliation or Control: United Methodist — IRS Status: 501(c)3
Highest Offering: Master's
Program: Liberal Arts And General; Teacher Preparatory
Accreditation: #SC, ACBSP, MUS, TED

01 President .... Dr. Lawrence D. CZARDA

10 VP for Administration and Finance ... Ms. Marci H. PEACE
05 VP Academic Affairs/Dean of Faculty ... Dr. Paul L. LESLIE
11 Vice President for Operations ... Dr. Robin L. DANIEL
84 Vice Pres Enrollment Mgmt & Mktg ... Ms. Colleen F. MURPHY
21 Assoc Vice President for Finance ... Mr. Chris ELMORE
13 Assoc Vice President for Technology ... Ms. Pamela R. MCKIRDY
20 Asst Vice President Academic Admin ... Mrs. Martha M. BUNCH
30 Acting Exec Dir Inst Advancement ... Ms. Joan M. GLYNN
37 Interim Exec Dir of Financial Aid ... Ms. Ann CAMPBELL
27 Dir of External Communications ... Mr. Lex ALEXANDER
06 Registrar ... Ms. Carol G. WILLIAMS
35 Dean of Students ... Ms. Ilona T. OWENS
07 Director of Admissions ... Ms. Julianne SCHATZ
36 Director Career Exploration & Dev ... Mr. Brent ATWATER
09 Director Institutional Rsrch & SIS ... Ms. Phyllis P. CHAMBERS
88 Director Academic Success Program ... Ms. Christy OXENDINE
15 Director of Human Resources ... Mrs. Sharon P. HUNT
18 Director of Facilities ... Mr. Richard SMITH
19 Director of Campus Security ... Mr. Calvin L. GILMORE
23 Director of Student Health ... Ms. Lauren T. CHILDREY
53 Director of Teacher Education ... Vacant
38 Director of Counseling Services ... Ms. Shahnaz KHAWAJA
92 Interim Dir George Ctr/Honors Stds ... Dr. Jessica G. SHARPE
44 Dir of Annual Giving/Alumni Engage ... Ms. Kristen C. BROWN
08 Director of Library Services ... Ms. Christine A. WHITTINGTON
41 Athletic Director ... Mr. Daniel P. CERONE
42 Campus Chaplin ... Rev. Robert W. BREWER
40 Bookstore Manager ... Mr. Cliff BRALY, JR.
21 Budget and Finance Analyst ... Mr. Peter O. EVENSON

Guilford College (A)

5800 W Friendly Avenue, Greensboro NC 27410-4173
County: Guilford FICE Identification: 002931
Unit ID: 198613
Telephone: (336) 316-2000 Carnegie Class: Bac/A&S
FAX Number: (336) 316-2950 Calendar System: Semester
URL: www.guilford.edu
Established: 1837 Annual Undergrad Tuition & Fees: $31,000
Enrollment: 2,739 Coed
Affiliation or Control: Friends IRS Status: 501(c)3
Highest Offering: Baccalaureate
Program: Liberal Arts And General; Teacher Preparatory
Accreditation: SC

01 President ... Dr. Kent J. CHABOTAR
05 Vice President & Academic Dean ... Dr. Adrienne M. ISRAEL
04 Executive Asst to the President ... Mrs. Joyce A. EATON
45 Asst to President for Planning ... Mr. Jeff E. FAVOLISE
11 Vice President Administration ... Mr. Jonathan P. VARNELL
10 Vice President Finance ... Mr. Gregory F. BURSAVICH
30 Vice Pres Institutional Advancement ... Mr. Michael J. POSTON
84 Vice Pres for Enrollment Services ... Mr. B. Randy DOSS
32 Vice President Student Affairs ... Mr. Aaron L. FETROW
26 Assoc VP Communications & Marketing ... Mr. R. Ty BUCKNER
29 Assoc Vice Pres Alumni Relations ... Mr. Jerry W. HARRELSON
21 Associate Vice President Finance ... Mr. James WILSON
51 Assoc VP/Dean Continuing Education ... Dr. Rita S. SEROTKIN
31 Director Community Learning ... Mr. Alan C. MUELLER
20 Assistant Academic Dean ... Ms. Erin B. DELL
20 Assistant Academic Dean ... Dr. Barbara G. BOYETTE
37 Director Student Financial Svcs ... Mr. Paul COSCIA
06 Registrar ... Mrs. Norma L. MIDDLETON
18 Director Facilities Engineering ... Mr. Dan YOUNG
08 Director of the Library ... Vacant
41 Director of Athletics ... Mr. Tom J. PALOMBO
19 Director of Public Safety ... Mr. Ron M. STOWE
15 Director Human Resources ... Mr. Frederick R. DEVINE
09 Dir Institutional Research/Assess ... Dr. Owen Kent GRUMBLES
90 Director Info Technology & Services ... Mr. Craig GRAY
42 Campus Ministry Coordinator ... Rev. Max L. CARTER
87 Director of Summer School ... Dr. Rita S. SEROTKIN
38 Director Student Counseling ... Ms. Gaither M. TERRELL
28 Director Multicultural Education ... Vacant
92 Director Honors Program ... Dr. Heather HAYTON
89 Director of First Year Program ... Dr. James HOOD
96 Director of Purchasing ... Ms. Tracy A. HALL
104 Director Study Abroad ... Dr. Jack ZERBE

Heritage Bible College (B)

PO Box 1628, Dunn NC 28335-1628
County: Harnett FICE Identification: 030893
Unit ID: 198677
Telephone: (910) 892-3178 Carnegie Class: Spec/Faith
FAX Number: (910) 891-1809 Calendar System: Semester
URL: www.heritagebiblecollege.edu
Established: 1971 Annual Undergrad Tuition & Fees: $9,120
Enrollment: 71 Coed
Affiliation or Control: Other IRS Status: 501(c)3
Highest Offering: Baccalaureate
Program: Occupational; 2-Year Principally Bachelor's Creditable; Religious Emphasis
Accreditation: TRACS

01 President ... Dr. Elvin BUTTS
05 Academic Dean ... Dr. Herbert CARTER
32 Dean Student Services ... Mr. Angel PADILLA
06 Registrar ... Ms. Traci NEWTON
07 Admissions ... Ms. Peggy PARKER
08 Librarian ... Ms. Janet PARKER
10 Business Administrator ... Ms. Sandra FRAZIER
37 Director Financial Aid ... Ms. Traci NEWTON
09 Director of Inst Effectiveness ... Ms. Hazel KING
20 Associate Academic Officer ... Mr. Stephen RZONCA
29 Director Alumni Relations ... Ms. Traci NEWTON
30 Director of Advancement ... Vacant

High Point University (C)

833 Montlieu Avenue, High Point NC 27262-3598
County: Guilford FICE Identification: 002933
Unit ID: 198695
Telephone: (336) 841-9000 Carnegie Class: Bac/Diverse
FAX Number: (336) 841-4599 Calendar System: Semester
URL: www.highpoint.edu
Established: 1924 Annual Undergrad Tuition & Fees: $39,800
Enrollment: 4,205 Coed
Affiliation or Control: United Methodist IRS Status: 501(c)3
Highest Offering: Doctorate
Program: Liberal Arts And General; Teacher Preparatory; Professional
Accreditation: SC, CIDA, TED

01 President ... Dr. Nido R. QUBEIN
05 Provost ... Dr. Dennis G. CARROLL
10 VP of Business Affairs ... Dr. Denny G. BOLTON
13 VP of Strategic Business Planning ... Mr. Wellington O. DESOUZA
31 VP of Community Relations ... Dr. Donald A. SCARBOROUGH
100 VP and Chief of Staff ... Mr. Christopher H. DUDLEY
32 VP of Student Life ... Mrs. Gail C. TUTTLE
84 VP of Enrollment ... Mr. Andy BILLS
41 Director of Athletics ... Mr. Craig D. KEILITZ
88 Assoc VP of Inst Effectiveness ... Dr. Alberta H. HERRON
88 Asst VP of Inst Effectiveness ... Dr. Jeffrey M. ADAMS
27 Assoc VP of Communication & Culture ... Mr. Roger D. CLODFELTER, JR.
49 Dean of College of Arts & Science ... Dr. Carole B. STONEKING
76 Dean of School of Health Sciences ... Dr. Daniel E. ERB
67 Dean of School of Pharmacy ... Dr. Ronald E. RAGAN
57 Dean of School of Art and Design ... Dr. John C. TURPIN
50 Dean of School of Business ... Dr. James B. WEHRLEY
53 Dean of School of Education ... Dr. Mariann W. TILLERY
35 Dean of Students ... Mr. Paul KITTLE
58 Assoc Dean of Graduate Admissions ... Mrs. Tracy L. COLLUM
20 Assoc Dean Academic Development ... Dr. Allen GOEDEKE
88 Bishop in Residence ... Bishop Thomas B. STOCKTON
23 Medical Director ... Dr. Danielle MAHAFFEY
19 Chief of Security ... Mr. Jeff A. KARPOVICH
08 Director of Library Services ... Mr. David L. BRYDEN
06 Registrar ... Ms. Diana L. ESTEY
07 Director of Admissions ... Mr. Kevin M. SELLERS
29 Director of Alumni Relations ... Ms. Jill THOMPSON
21 Director of Accounting Services ... Mr. James H. SPESSARD
15 Director of Human Resources ... Mrs. Kathy S. SMITH
37 Director of Student Accounts ... Mrs. Teresa L. KANE
38 Director of Student Counseling ... Ms. Lynda D. NOFFSINGER
18 Dir of Construction and Renovation ... Mr. Ron GUERRA
18 Director of Facility Operations ... Mr. Stephen L. POTTER
88 Dir Stdnt Activities & Engagement ... Ms. Hillary C. KOKAJKO
88 Director of Judicial Affairs ... Ms. Heather P. BEATTY
88 Director of University Events ... Ms. Melissa L. ANDERSON
09 Coordinator of Inst Assessment ... Ms. Andrea KENNEDY
44 Major Gifts Officer ... Ms. Jan H. KNOX
88 Director of Campus Enhancement ... Mr. Troy J. THOMPSON
88 Dir Athletic Facilities/Operations ... Mr. Ryan TRESSEL
06 Associate Registrar ... Ms. Ann M. MILLER
40 Manager Bookstore ... Mr. William HOLSTON
85 Director of International Education ... Ms. Judy DANLEY
36 Director of Career Services ... Mr. Eric J. MELNICZEK
104 Director of Study Abroad ... Ms. Heidi FISCHER
88 Director of Service Learning ... Dr. Joseph D. BLOSSER
88 Director of Undergraduate Research ... Dr. Joanne D. ALTMAN
27 Media Relations Coordinator ... Ms. Pamela J. HAYNES
04 Admin Assistant to President ... Ms. Judy K. RAY
88 Manager of University Mail Center ... Mr. Michael R. HALL

Hood Theological Seminary (D)

1810 Lutheran Synod Drive, Salisbury NC 28144-5768
County: Rowan FICE Identification: 036633
Unit ID: 443076
Telephone: (704) 636-7611 Carnegie Class: Spec/Faith
FAX Number: (704) 636-7699 Calendar System: Semester
URL: www.hoodseminary.edu
Established: 1904 Annual Undergrad Tuition & Fees: $12,960
Enrollment: 274 Coed
Affiliation or Control: African Methodist Episcopal Zion Church
IRS Status: 501(c)3
Highest Offering: Doctorate
Program: Professional; Religious Emphasis
Accreditation: THEOL

01 President ... Dr. Albert AYMER
05 VP for Academic Affairs ... Dr. Vergel L. LATTIMORE
20 Associate Academic Dean ... Dr. Trevor EPPEHIMER
32 Dean of Students ... Dr. Dora R. MBUWAYESANGO
10 Fiscal Officer ... Dr. Regina M. DANCY
30 Development Officer ... Mrs. Margaret KLUTTZ
06 Registrar ... Ms. Nancy BAKER

ITT Technical Institute (E)

5520 Dillard Drive, Suite 100, Cary NC 27518
County: Wake Identification: 666704
Unit ID: 451936
Telephone: (919) 233-2520 Carnegie Class: Assoc/PrivFP4
FAX Number: (919) 463-5850 Calendar System: Quarter
URL: www.itt-tech.edu
Established: N/A Annual Undergrad Tuition & Fees: N/A
Enrollment: 390 Coed
Affiliation or Control: Proprietary IRS Status: Proprietary
Highest Offering: Baccalaureate
Program: Technical Emphasis
Accreditation: ACICS

† Branch campus of ITT Technical Institute, Indianapolis, IN.

ITT Technical Institute (F)

4135 S Stream Boulevard, Suite 200, Charlotte NC 28217-4555
County: Mecklenburg Identification: 666161
Unit ID: 448442
Telephone: (704) 423-3100 Carnegie Class: Assoc/PrivFP4
FAX Number: N/A Calendar System: Quarter
URL: www.itt-tech.edu
Established: 2006 Annual Undergrad Tuition & Fees: N/A
Enrollment: 636 Coed
Affiliation or Control: Proprietary IRS Status: Proprietary
Highest Offering: Baccalaureate
Program: Technical Emphasis
Accreditation: ACICS

† Branch campus of ITT Technical Institute, Indianapolis, IN.

ITT Technical Institute (G)

10926 David Taylor Drive, Suite 100, Charlotte NC 28262
County: Mecklenburg Identification: 666705
Unit ID: 456445
Telephone: (704) 548-2300 Carnegie Class: Assoc/PrivFP4
FAX Number: N/A Calendar System: Quarter
URL: www.itt-tech.edu
Established: N/A Annual Undergrad Tuition & Fees: N/A
Enrollment: 418 Coed
Affiliation or Control: Proprietary IRS Status: Proprietary
Highest Offering: Baccalaureate
Program: Technical Emphasis
Accreditation: ACICS

† Branch campus of ITT Technical Institute, Indianapolis, IN.

ITT Technical Institute (H)

4050 Piedmont Parkway, Suite 110, High Point NC 27265
County: Guilford Identification: 666703
Unit ID: 451990
Telephone: (336) 819-5900 Carnegie Class: Assoc/PrivFP4
FAX Number: (336) 819-5950 Calendar System: Quarter
URL: www.itt-tech.edu
Established: N/A Annual Undergrad Tuition & Fees: N/A
Enrollment: 401 Coed
Affiliation or Control: Proprietary IRS Status: Proprietary
Highest Offering: Baccalaureate
Program: Technical Emphasis
Accreditation: ACICS

† Branch campus of ITT Technical Institute, Indianapolis, IN.

Johnson & Wales University-Charlotte (I)

801 W Trade Street, Charlotte NC 28202-1122
County: Mecklenburg Identification: 666375
Unit ID: 445708
Telephone: (980) 598-1000 Carnegie Class: Bac/Assoc
FAX Number: (980) 598-1111 Calendar System: Quarter
URL: www.jwu.edu
Established: 2004 Annual Undergrad Tuition & Fees: $26,112
Enrollment: 2,537 Coed
Affiliation or Control: Independent Non-Profit IRS Status: 501(c)3
Highest Offering: Baccalaureate
Program: Occupational; 2-Year Principally Bachelor's Creditable
Accreditation: &EH

01 President ... Mr. Arthur J. GALLAGHER
05 Vice Pres & Dean of Acad Affairs ... Mr. Tarun MALIK
20 Assoc Dean of Academic Affairs ... Mr. Peter LEHMULLER
07 Director of Admissions ... Mr. Joseph CAMPOS
11 Exec Director of Operations ... Mr. Mark NORMAN
08 Director of Library Services ... Dr. Richard MONIZ
19 Safe & Sec Operations Lieutenant ... Mr. Robert BOYD
23 Director of Health/Counseling Svcs ... Ms. Karen HINEY
26 Comm & Media Relations Manager ... Ms. Melinda LAW
36 Dir Experiential Educ & Career Svcs ... Ms. Deborah LANGENSTEIN
29 Manager of Alumni Relations ... Ms. Sara GUERRY
32 Dean of Students ... Ms. Tanaya WALTERS
06 Asst Dir of Student Academic Svcs ... Ms. Laurie HASLAM
18 Director of Facilities Management ... Mr. Glenn HAMILTON
39 Director of Residential Life ... Mr. James MINTON
96 Purchasing Director ... Mr. Evan NASH
85 International Student Advisor ... Ms. Karyn MONIZ
10 Campus Controller ... Ms. Allison DIAZ
13 Director of Campus Services ... Mr. Chesley BLACK
15 Human Resources Team Leader ... Ms. Tracy SMITH

88 Dean of Culinary Education ... Mr. Mark ALLISON
50 Dept Chair College of Business ... Dr. Roland SPARKS
88 Dept Chair Hospitality College ... Ms. Ann-Marie WELDON
49 Dept Chair School of Arts & Science ... Mr. David JEWELL
88 Dept Chair College of Culinary Arts ... Mr. Jerry LANUZZA

† Regional accreditation is carried under the parent institution in Providence, RI.

Johnson C. Smith University (A)

100 Beatties Ford Road, Charlotte NC 28216-5398
County: Mecklenburg FICE Identification: 002936
Unit ID: 198756
Telephone: (704) 378-1000 Carnegie Class: Bac/A&S
FAX Number: (704) 372-1242 Calendar System: Semester
URL: www.jcsu.edu
Established: 1867 Annual Undergrad Tuition & Fees: $18,236
Enrollment: 1,541 Coed
Affiliation or Control: Independent Non-Profit IRS Status: 501(c)3
Highest Offering: Baccalaureate
Program: Liberal Arts And General; Teacher Preparatory
Accreditation: SC, SW, TED

01 President ... Dr. Ronald L. CARTER
03 Exec Vice Pres/Chief Operating Ofcr ... Dr. Elfred A. PINKARD
10 Vice Pres for Finance ... Mr. Gerald HECTOR
30 Vice President for Inst Advancement ... Ms. Joy PAIGE
86 VP Government Sponsored Pgms ... Dr. Diane BOWLES
15 Asst VP for Human Resources ... Ms. Latrelle P. MCALLISTER
30 Asst VP for Institutional Advancmnt ... Ms. Sharon HARRINGTON
05 Council of Deans Chair/Dean of STEM ... Dr. Magdy ATTIA
49 Dean of Arts and Letters ... Dr. Joseph TURNER
107 Dean of Professional Studies ... Dr. Helen CALDWELL
84 Dean of Enrollment Services ... Ms. Cathy HURD
32 Dean of Student Development ... Mrs. Cathy JONES
51 Dean of Metropolitan College ... Dr. Zenobia EDWARDS
08 Director of the Library ... Ms. Monika RHUE
07 Director of Admissions ... Vacant
14 Director Information Technology ... Mr. John NORRIS
31 Dir of App Leadership/Comm Dev ... Ms. Sherill HAMPTON
09 Dir Plng/Assess/Effect/Rsrch ... Ms. Kelli RAINEY
26 Director of Comm and Marketing ... Ms. Sherri BELFIELD
29 Director Alumni Affairs ... Mr. Ron MATTHEWS
37 Director Financial Aid ... Vacant
38 Director Counseling and Testing ... Vacant
19 Director of Campus Police ... Mr. Gregory C. HARRIS
41 Athletic Director ... Mr. Stephen JOYNER, SR.
06 Registrar ... Mrs. Keisha WILSON
85 Mgr of Multi/International Stud Aff ... Mr. Rixon CAMPBELL
44 Major Gift Officer ... Mr. Alvin AUSTIN
102 Director Foundations Rel/Priv Grant ... Ms. Jenene SEYMOUR
102 Director of Corporate Relations ... Ms. Angela MAULDIN
36 Director Career Services ... Mrs. Barbara WILKS
39 Director Residence Life ... Mr. Terry MCPHERSON
40 Manager of Bookstore ... Ms. Robin SORENSEN
96 Purchasing Manager ... Mr. Joe MAJORS
16 Manager Risk Management ... Mrs. Debra HOLLIS
88 Coordinator of Retention ... Ms. Lisa DURHAM
23 Health Center Coordinator ... Ms. Marian JONES

King's College (B)

322 Lamar Avenue, Charlotte NC 28204-2493
County: Mecklenburg FICE Identification: 002937
Unit ID: 382504
Telephone: (704) 372-0266 Carnegie Class: Assoc/PrivFP
FAX Number: (704) 348-2029 Calendar System: Semester
URL: www.kingscollege.org
Established: 1901 Annual Undergrad Tuition & Fees: $14,280
Enrollment: 529 Coed
Affiliation or Control: Proprietary IRS Status: Proprietary
Highest Offering: Associate Degree
Program: Occupational; 2-Year Principally Bachelor's Creditable
Accreditation: ACICS, MAC

01 School Director ... Mrs. Diane RYON
05 Chief Academic Officer ... Ms. Barbara ROCKECHARLIE

Laurel University (C)

1215 Eastchester Drive, High Point NC 27265-3115
County: Guilford FICE Identification: 002935
Unit ID: 198747
Telephone: (336) 887-3000 Carnegie Class: Spec/Faith
FAX Number: (336) 889-2261 Calendar System: Semester
URL: www.laureluniversity.edu
Established: 1903 Annual Undergrad Tuition & Fees: $10,930
Enrollment: 465 Coed
Affiliation or Control: Independent Non-Profit IRS Status: 501(c)3
Highest Offering: Doctorate
Program: Professional; Religious Emphasis
Accreditation: BI

01 President ... Dr. Larry D. MCCULLOUGH
05 Undergraduate Academic Dean ... Dr. John LINDSEY
06 Registrar ... Mr. Greg WORKMAN
84 Director of Enrollment Management ... Mr. Jeremy REESE
37 Director of Financial Aid ... Mrs. Shirley CARTER
18 Director of Facilities and Grounds ... Mr. Eugene ALBERTSON
08 Librarian ... Mrs. April LINDSEY
10 Chief Financial Officer ... Mr. David WHITE
38 Director of Human Resources ... Mrs. Kathy CUTRELL
32 Director of Student Life ... Mr. Kevin DUNOVANT
03 Dean School of Mgt & Exec Vice Pres ... Dr. Owen ALLEN
106 Director of Distance Education ... Mr. Marty HILL
26 Public Relations Director ... Ms. Wanda CLARK
29 Alumni Coordinator ... Mrs. April LINDSEY

Lees-McRae College (D)

PO Box 128, 191 Main Street, Banner Elk NC 28604-0128
County: Avery FICE Identification: 002939
Unit ID: 198808
Telephone: (828) 898-5241 Carnegie Class: Bac/Diverse
FAX Number: (828) 898-8814 Calendar System: Semester
URL: www.lmc.edu
Established: 1900 Annual Undergrad Tuition & Fees: $23,175
Enrollment: 890 Coed
Affiliation or Control: Presbyterian Church (U.S.A.) IRS Status: 501(c)3
Highest Offering: Baccalaureate
Program: Liberal Arts And General; Teacher Preparatory
Accreditation: SC, NURSE, @TEAC, THEA

01 President ... Dr. Barry M. BUXTON
05 Provost/Dean Faculty ... Dr. Kacy CRABTREE
10 VP Finance & Business Affairs ... Vacant
30 Vice Pres Institutional Advancement ... Ms. Caroline HART
84 Vice Pres Enrollment Management ... Ms. Ginger HANSEN
18 Vice Pres Facilities Management ... Mr. Bill MCGOWAN
32 Dean of Students ... Mrs. Allison M. NORRIS
29 Director of Alumni Relations ... Vacant
08 Director of Libraries ... Mr. Russell TAYLOR
06 Registrar ... Ms. Lynn HINSHAW
04 Secretary to the President ... Ms. Darcy VASILIS
37 Financial Aid Director ... Ms. Cathy SHELL
44 Director of Prospect Research ... Mrs. Frankie NEEDHAM
21 Business Affairs Liaison ... Ms. Meghan WRIGHT
15 Director Human Resources/Telecomm ... Mrs. Carolyn WARD
38 Director Student Counseling ... Ms. Jan HALL
96 Dir Col Post Ofc/Purchasing Clerk ... Ms. Sandy RAMSEY
41 Athletic Director ... Mr. Craig MCPHAIL

Lenoir-Rhyne University (E)

625 7th Avenue NE, Hickory NC 28601-3984
County: Catawba FICE Identification: 002941
Unit ID: 198835
Telephone: (828) 328-1741 Carnegie Class: Bac/Diverse
FAX Number: (828) 328-7368 Calendar System: Semester
URL: www.lr.edu
Established: 1891 Annual Undergrad Tuition & Fees: $26,524
Enrollment: 1,860 Coed
Affiliation or Control: Evangelical Lutheran Church In America
IRS Status: 501(c)3
Highest Offering: Master's
Program: Liberal Arts And General; Teacher Preparatory; Professional
Accreditation: SC, ACBSP, @DIETI, NURSE, OT, TED

01 President ... Dr. Wayne POWELL
05 Provost ... Dr. Larry HALL
10 Vice President Finance/Admin ... Mr. Peter KENDALL
30 Vice Pres Institutional Advancement ... Mr. Drew VAN HORN
84 Vice President for Enrollment Mgmt ... Ms. Rachel NICHOLS
32 Dean of Students ... Dr. Katie FISHER
104 Assoc Dean Global Learning ... Ms. Charlotte WILLIAMS
58 Dean Grad Studies/Lifelong Learning ... Dr. Amy WOOD
97 Assoc Dean Co-Curricular Programs ... Mr. Leonard GEDDES
06 Registrar ... Ms. Kathy HAHN
08 Librarian ... Ms. Rita JOHNSON
15 Director of Human Resources ... Mr. Rick NICHOLS
40 Director of Bookstore ... Ms. Leslie SKAFF
18 Director of Facilities/Plant ... Mr. Otis PITTS
41 Athletic Director ... Mr. Neill MCGEACHY
42 Campus Pastor ... Rev. Andrew WEISNER
19 Director of Security ... Mr. Norris YODER
92 Director of Honors Program ... Dr. Joshua RING
13 Chief Information Officer ... Ms. Melissa MULLINAX
26 Director of Marketing/Communication ... Mr. Mike LANGFORD
88 Director of Conferences & Events ... Ms. Janet MATTHEWS
29 Director of Alumni Relations ... Ms. Suzanne JACKSON
07 Director of Admissions ... Ms. Karen FEEZOR
09 Director of Institutional Research ... Dr. Ginger BISHOP
37 Director Student Financial Aid ... Mr. Eric BRANDON
38 Dir Student Counseling/Placement ... Ms. Jenny SMITH
88 Dir Liberal Arts/Visiting Writers ... Dr. Rand BRANDES
88 Dir of Deaf/Hard-of-Hearing Svcs ... Ms. Shawn FRANK
88 Institute on Obesity ... Ms. Michelle RIMER
65 Institute on Conservation ... Dr. John BRZORAD
85 Coord of International Programs ... Dr. Duane KIRKMAN
53 College of Education/Human Services ... Dr. Hank WEDDINGTON
76 College of Health Sciences ... Dr. Katherine PASOUR
49 College of Arts & Sciences ... Dr. Dan KISER
81 Int Col Professional/Math Studies ... Mr. Dick HALL

Living Arts College @ School of Communication Arts (F)

3000 Wakefield Crossing Drive, Raleigh NC 27614-7076
County: Wake FICE Identification: 031090
Unit ID: 421832
Telephone: (919) 488-8500 Carnegie Class: Assoc/PrivFP
FAX Number: (919) 488-8490 Calendar System: Quarter
URL: www.living-arts-college.edu
Established: 1992 Annual Undergrad Tuition & Fees: $25,680
Enrollment: 540 Coed
Affiliation or Control: Proprietary IRS Status: Proprietary
Highest Offering: Baccalaureate
Program: Occupational; Technical Emphasis
Accreditation: ACICS, MAC

01 Director ... Ms. Debra A. HOOPER

Livingstone College (G)

701 W Monroe Street, Salisbury NC 28144-5298
County: Rowan FICE Identification: 002942
Unit ID: 198862
Telephone: (704) 216-6000 Carnegie Class: Bac/Diverse
FAX Number: (704) 216-6217 Calendar System: Semester
URL: www.livingstone.edu
Established: 1879 Annual Undergrad Tuition & Fees: $15,708
Enrollment: 1,137 Coed
Affiliation or Control: African Methodist Episcopal Zion Church
IRS Status: 501(c)3
Highest Offering: Baccalaureate
Program: Liberal Arts And General; Teacher Preparatory; Professional
Accreditation: SC, SW, TED

01 President ... Dr. Jimmy R. JENKINS, SR.
04 Exec Asst to the President ... Mr. State ALEXANDER
05 Vice Pres Academic Affairs ... Dr. Lelia VICKERS
10 Int VP Business & Finance/Ops ... Mr. Roger MCLEAN
32 Vice President Student Affairs ... Vacant
30 Vice Pres Inst Advance/College Rels ... Dr. Herman FELTON
35 Assoc Vice Pres of Student Affairs ... Vacant
20 Asst Vice Pres Academic Affairs ... Dr. Tom COAXUM
38 Dean of Counseling Services . Mrs. Elizabeth ALSTON-PINCKNEY
06 Registrar ... Mrs. Wendy JACKSON
08 Director Library Services ... Dr. Gwendolyn PEART
26 Director of Public Relations ... Mr. State W. ALEXANDER
37 Director of Financial Aid ... Ms. Sheri JEFFERSON
36 Dir Career Counseling/Placement ... Mrs. Vicki MCMOORE-GRAY
13 Director of Computer Info Systems ... Vacant
15 Director of Human Resources ... Ms. Sharon THOMPSON
29 Director Alumni Affairs ... Ms. Carmen C. WILDER
09 Director of Institutional Research ... Mr. Robert L. MCINNIS
84 Dir Enrollment Mgmt & Admissions ... Vacant
40 Bookstore Director ... Mr. Jerome FUNDERBURK
41 Athletic Director ... Vacant
96 Director of Purchasing ... Ms. Debra WOOD
18 Director of Physical Plant ... Mr. Russell SMYRE
23 Health Services Manager ... Vacant
07 Director of Admissions ... Ms. Jocelyn BIGGS

Louisburg College (H)

501 N Main Street, Louisburg NC 27549-7705
County: Franklin FICE Identification: 002943
Unit ID: 198871
Telephone: (919) 496-2521 Carnegie Class: Assoc/PrivNFP
FAX Number: (919) 496-7141 Calendar System: Semester
URL: www.louisburg.edu
Established: 1787 Annual Undergrad Tuition & Fees: $14,944
Enrollment: 687 Coed
Affiliation or Control: United Methodist IRS Status: 501(c)3
Highest Offering: Associate Degree
Program: 2-Year Principally Bachelor's Creditable
Accreditation: SC

01 President ... Rev Dr. Mark D. LA BRANCHE
05 VP of Academic Life ... Dr. James C. ECK
11 VP of Administration/Inst Effect ... Vacant
30 Vice Pres Institutional Advancement ... Mr. Kurt CARLSON
32 Vice President of Student Life ... Mr. Jason E. MODLIN
10 Vice President of Finance ... Ms. Belinda FAULKNER
84 Vice Pres of Enrollment Management . Ms. Stephanie B. TOLBERT
29 Alumni Director ... Ms. Jamie PATRICK
06 Registrar/Dir of Inst Research ... Ms. Catherine ZIENCIK
08 Librarian ... Ms. Candace L. JONES
38 Director of Counseling Services ... Ms. Fonda PORTER
37 Director of Financial Aid ... Ms. Vickie FLEMING
26 Director of College Communications ... Ms. Amy MCMANUS
18 Chief Facilities/Physical Plant ... Mr. Steve SPARKS

Mars Hill College (I)

PO Box 370, Mars Hill NC 28754-0370
County: Madison FICE Identification: 002944
Unit ID: 198899
Telephone: (828) 689-1307 Carnegie Class: Bac/Diverse
FAX Number: (828) 689-1478 Calendar System: Semester
URL: www.mhc.edu
Established: 1856 Annual Undergrad Tuition & Fees: $24,536
Enrollment: 1,295 Coed
Affiliation or Control: Other Protestant IRS Status: 501(c)3
Highest Offering: Master's
Program: Liberal Arts And General; Teacher Preparatory
Accreditation: SC, MUS, SW, TED, THEA

01 President ... Dr. Dan G. LUNSFORD
30 Vice President for Inst Advancement ... Mr. Harold (Bud) G. CHRISTMAN
05 Exec Vice Pres Acad & Student Affs ... Dr. John W. WELLS
32 Asst Vice Pres for Student Life ... Ms. Laura WHITAKER-LEA
07 Dean of Admissions/Financial Aid ... Dr. Craig GOFORTH

06 Dean Academic Records/Resource .... Ms. Edith L. WHITT
08 Director of Library Services .... Ms. Beverly ROBERTSON
26 Director of Public Information .... Mr. Mike D. THORNHILL
10 Vice Pres for Finance .... Mr. Neil TILLEY
42 Campus Chaplain .... Rev. Stephanie MCLESKEY
41 Director of Athletics .... Mr. David W. RIGGINS
37 Director of Financial Aid .... Ms. Nichole THOMAS
29 Director of Alumni Relations .... Ms. Elizabeth HARDIN
85 Director International Education .... Mr. Gordon HINNERS
09 Director Institutional Research .... Dr. Suzanne C. KLONIS
38 Director Student Counseling .... Ms. Cassandra PAVONE
15 Director of Human Resources .... Ms. Deana K. HOLLAND
13 Director Information Technology Svc .... Mr. Gerald D. BALL
18 Director of Facilities .... Mr. Donald EDWARDS
40 Director of Bookstore .... Mr. Darryl R. NORTON
51 Dean of Adult & Graduate Studies .... Ms. Marie NICHOLSON
97 Chair of General Studies .... Ms. Cathy L. ADKINS

Meredith College (A)

3800 Hillsborough Street, Raleigh NC 27607-5298
County: Wake FICE Identification: 002945
Unit ID: 198950
Telephone: (919) 760-8600 Carnegie Class: Bac/Diverse
FAX Number: (919) 760-2828 Calendar System: Semester
URL: www.meredith.edu
Established: 1891 Annual Undergrad Tuition & Fees: $29,186
Enrollment: 1,980 Female
Affiliation or Control: Independent Non-Profit IRS Status: 501(c)3
Highest Offering: Master's
Program: Liberal Arts And General; Teacher Preparatory; Professional
Accreditation: SC, BUS, CIDA, DIETD, DIETI, MUS, SW, TED

01 President .... Dr. Jo ALLEN
05 Sr Vice Pres Academic Admin .... Dr. Denise ROTONDO
45 VP for Academic Planning/Programs .... Dr. Elizabeth WOLFINGER
30 Vice Pres Institutional Advancement .... Dr. Charles "Lennie" BARTON
10 Vice Pres for Business & Finance .... Mr. Craig BARFIELD
32 Vice President for College Programs .... Dr. Jean JACKSON
84 Assoc VP Enrollment Management .... Dr. Danny GREEN
35 Dean of Students .... Ms. Ann C. GLEASON
06 Registrar .... Ms. Amanda STEELE-MIDDLETON
09 Dir of Assessment & Inst Research .... Ms. Dianne RAUBENHEIMER
08 Director Library Info Services .... Ms. Laura DAVIDSON
07 Director of Admissions .... Ms. Jen MILLER-HOGG
37 Director of Financial Assistance .... Mr. Kevin MICHAELSEN
26 Director of Marketing/Col Commun .... Ms. Kristi EAVES-MCLENNAN
35 Dir Student Activ/Leadership Devel .... Ms. Cheryl S. JENKINS
28 Dir Commuter Life/Diversity Pgms .... Ms. Tomecca SLOANE
36 Director of Career Planning .... Dr. Marie B. SUMEREL
29 Dir of Alumnae & Parent Relations .... Ms. Hilary ALLEN
38 Director of Counseling Center .... Ms. Beth A. MEIER
58 Director of Graduate Studies .... Dr. Denise ROTONDO
39 Director Resident Life/Housing .... Ms. Heidi LECOUNT
88 Dir Undergrad Degree Pgm Women 23+ .... Dr. Susan ADAMS
20 Director of Academic Advising .... Ms. Amy HITLIN
31 Dir Cmty Outreach & Campus Events .... Mr. Bill BROWN
23 Director Health Services .... Ms. Sherri HENDERSON
42 Campus Minister .... Rev. Stacy PARDUE
13 Chief Information Officer .... Mr. Jeffrey HOWLETT
19 Chief Campus Police .... Mr. David KENNEDY
15 Director of Human Resources .... Ms. Pamela DAVIS
18 Chief Facilities/Physical Plant .... Ms. Sharon CAMPBELL
21 Controller .... Ms. Lori DUKE

Methodist University (B)

5400 Ramsey Street, Fayetteville NC 28311-1498
County: Cumberland FICE Identification: 002946
Unit ID: 198969
Telephone: (910) 630-7000 Carnegie Class: Bac/Diverse
FAX Number: (910) 630-7317 Calendar System: Semester
URL: www.methodist.edu
Established: 1956 Annual Undergrad Tuition & Fees: $27,042
Enrollment: 2,476 Coed
Affiliation or Control: United Methodist IRS Status: 501(c)3
Highest Offering: Master's
Program: Liberal Arts And General; Teacher Preparatory
Accreditation: SC, ACBSP, ARCPA, SW, TED

01 President .... Dr. Ben E. HANCOCK, JR.
05 Vice Pres for Academic Affairs .... Dr. Delmas S. CRISP, JR.
10 Vice President for Business Affairs .... Mr. Gene T. CLAYTON
32 Vice President for Student Affairs .... Mr. William WALKER
30 Vice President for Development .... Mrs. Robin DAVENPORT
09 VP of Institutional Research .... Dr. Donald L. LASSITER
20 Associate VP for Academic Affairs .... Ms. Jane W. GARDINER
35 Assoc Dean Student Services .... Mr. Todd D. HARRIS
84 Director Enrollment Management .... Mr. Rick D. LOWE
42 Chaplain/Director Campus Ministry .... Rev. Michael W. SAFLEY
26 Director of Public Relations .... Mrs. Pam MCEVOY
41 Director of Athletics .... Mr. Robert T. MCEVOY
29 Director of Alumni Affairs .... Ms. Lauren C. WIKE
07 Dean of Admissions .... Mr. Jamie W. LEGG
37 Director of Financial Aid .... Ms. Bonnie J. ADAMSON
06 Registrar .... Ms. Jasmin K. BROWN
08 Head Librarian .... Ms. Tracey PEARSON
85 Director Foreign Students .... Ms. Lyle SHEPPARD
19 Director Security/Safety .... Mr. James K. PHILLIPS
15 Director Personnel Services .... Mrs. Debra YEATTS
18 Chief Facilities/Physical Plant .... Mr. Thomas W. DAUGHTREY, III
21 Associate Business Officer .... Ms. Dawn AUSBORN
36 Director Student Placement .... Ms. Antoinette P. BELLAMY
38 Director Student Counseling .... Ms. Darlene HOPKINS
96 Director of Purchasing .... Ms. Deborah DEMBOSKY
14 Director Institutional Computing .... Mr. Samuel J. CLARK, III

Mid-Atlantic Christian University (C)

715 N Poindexter, Elizabeth City NC 27909-4054
County: Pasquotank FICE Identification: 022809
Unit ID: 199458
Telephone: (252) 334-2000 Carnegie Class: Bac/Diverse
FAX Number: (252) 334-2071 Calendar System: Semester
URL: www.macuniversity.edu
Established: 1948 Annual Undergrad Tuition & Fees: $11,680
Enrollment: 169 Coed
Affiliation or Control: Churches Of Christ IRS Status: 501(c)3
Highest Offering: Baccalaureate
Program: Liberal Arts And General; Religious Emphasis
Accreditation: SC

01 President .... Dr. D. Clay PERKINS
05 Vice President Academic Affairs .... Dr. Kevin W. LARSEN
10 Vice President Finance .... Mr. Kurtis L. KIGHT
84 Vice President Enrollment Services .... Dr. Ken S. GREENE
30 Vice President Development .... Mr. W. Keith WOOD
09 Director of Institutional Research .... Dr. Kevin W. LARSEN
06 Registrar .... Miss Yolanda TESKE
08 Director of Library .... Vacant
38 Counselor .... Mr. Donald W. MCKINNEY
37 Financial Aid Administrator .... Mrs. Lisa W. PIPKIN
18 Superintendent Buildings & Grounds .... Mr. Phillip N. ALLIGOOD
21 Assistant Vice President Finance .... Mrs. Carol M. STUART
42 Campus Minister .... Mr. Chris STANLEY
49 Chair of Arts and Sciences .... Dr. Robert W. SMITH
73 Chair of Biblical Studies .... Dr. Lee M. FIELDS
88 Chair of Christian Ministry .... Dr. Robert B. REESE
88 Chair of Marketplace Ministry .... Mr. Donald W. MCKINNEY

Miller-Motte Technical College (D)

5000 Market Street, Wilmington NC 28405-3430
County: New Hanover FICE Identification: 030632
Unit ID: 198978
Telephone: (910) 392-4660 Carnegie Class: Spec/Health
FAX Number: (910) 799-6224 Calendar System: Quarter
URL: www.miller-motte.com
Established: 1916 Annual Undergrad Tuition & Fees: $10,485
Enrollment: 1,662 Coed
Affiliation or Control: Proprietary IRS Status: Proprietary
Highest Offering: Baccalaureate
Program: Occupational
Accreditation: ACICS, DA, MAC, SURGT

01 Campus Director .... Mr. Ned SNYDER
07 Director of Admissions .... Mr. Adam MERRITT

† Branch campus of Miller-Motte Technical College, TN.

Montreat College (E)

PO Box 1267, 310 Gaither Circle, Montreat NC 28757-1267
County: Buncombe FICE Identification: 002948
Unit ID: 199032
Telephone: (828) 669-8012 Carnegie Class: Master's S
FAX Number: (828) 669-9554 Calendar System: Semester
URL: www.montreat.edu
Established: 1916 Annual Undergrad Tuition & Fees: $22,784
Enrollment: 785 Coed
Affiliation or Control: Non-denominational IRS Status: 501(c)3
Highest Offering: Master's
Program: Liberal Arts And General; Teacher Preparatory
Accreditation: SC, IACBE, TED

01 President .... Dr. Dan STRUBLE
04 Interim Assistant to the President .... Ms. Kate LEDBETTER
05 Senior Vice President and Provost .... Dr. Marshall FLOWERS
10 Vice President for Finance .... Mr. Geoff BREMER
84 VP for Enrollment and Marketing .... Mr. Jonathan SHORES
32 Vice President for Student Services .... Mr. Charles A. LANCE
30 Vice President for Advancement .... Mr. Joe KIRKLAND
13 Vice President for Technology .... Vacant
42 Interim Chaplain .... Dr. John ELLINGTON
08 Library Director .... Ms. Elizabeth R. PEARSON
06 Registrar .... Vacant
37 Director of Financial Aid .... Mr. Jeff HOLLIDAY
26 Director of Communications .... Ms. Annie CARLSON
38 Director of Counseling .... Ms. Jane CARTER
41 Athletic Director .... Mr. Craig JACKSON
35 Director of Student Activities .... Mr. Jim DAHLIN
40 Bookstore Manager .... Ms. Carly BRAENDEL
09 Assoc Dean of Academics & Inst Eff .... Ms. Becky FRAWLEY
19 Chief of Campus Police .... Dr. N. Scott ADAMS
07 Director of Admissions and Outreach .... Mr. Tony ROBINSON

Mount Olive College (F)

634 Henderson Street, Mount Olive NC 28365-1263
County: Wayne FICE Identification: 002949
Unit ID: 199069
Telephone: (919) 658-2502 Carnegie Class: Bac/Diverse
FAX Number: (919) 658-7180 Calendar System: Semester
URL: www.moc.edu
Established: 1951 Annual Undergrad Tuition & Fees: $16,800
Enrollment: 3,825 Coed
Affiliation or Control: Original Free Will Baptist Church IRS Status: 501(c)3
Highest Offering: Baccalaureate
Program: Liberal Arts And General
Accreditation: SC, ACBSP

01 President .... Dr. Philip P. KERSTETTER
03 Executive Vice President .... Dr. Carol G. CARRERE
05 VP for Academic Affairs .... Dr. Ellen S. JORDAN
88 VP for Special Services .... Dr. Opey D. JEANES
10 Interim VP Finance & Treasurer .... Ms. Debra SMITH
84 VP for Enrollment .... Dr. Barbara R. KORNEGAY
32 VP for Student Affairs .... Dr. Dan SULLIVAN
30 VP for Institutional Advancement .... Mr. Kevin J. JEAN
50 Interim Dean School of Business .... Dr. Ellen JORDAN
49 Dean School of Arts and Sciences .... Dr. Kenneth D. HINES
08 Director of Library Services .... Ms. Pamela R. WOOD
12 Director of MOC New Bern .... Mr. Guy BRADBURY
12 Director of MOC Jacksonville .... Mr. Guy BRADBURY
12 Director of MOC Goldsboro .... Dr. Opey JEANES
12 Director of MOC Evening College .... Mr. Stanley J. ELLIOTT
12 Director of MOC Wilmington .... Dr. Marna R. MCMURRY
12 Director MOC Research Triangle Park .... Ms. Lisa NUESELL
07 Director of Admissions .... Mr. Timothy E. WOODARD
06 Registrar .... Mr. David L. BOURGEOIS
36 Director of Career Center .... Vacant
27 Director of Public Relations .... Ms. Rhonda E. JESSUP
102 Dir Foundations & Sponsored Program .... Vacant
29 Dir Young Alumni Relations .... Ms. Vickie S. ROBINSON
44 Director of Annual Fund .... Mr. Yeeka YAU
37 Director of Financial Aid .... Ms. Katrina K. LEE
15 Director of Human Resources .... Mr. Stephen A. SWEET
23 Student Health Services .... Ms. Jonnie L. MORGAN
42 Campus Chaplain .... Ms. Carla WILLIAMSON
04 Assistant to the President .... Ms. Katherine B. GARDNER
18 Superintendent Building & Grounds .... Mr. Jeff D. BROGDEN
40 Bookstore Manager .... Mr. Brian GRIFFIN
41 Athletics Director .... Mr. Jeffrey M. EISEN
13 Director Technology Support .... Mr. Robert R. PRUETT
88 Director Technology Services .... Mr. Kenneth M. DAVIS, JR.
92 Director Honors Program .... Dr. Ellen JORDAN
09 Director Inst Research & Planning .... Vacant

Native American Bible College (G)

PO Box 248, Shannon NC 28386
County: Robeson Identification: 667092
Telephone: (910) 843-5304 Carnegie Class: Not Classified
FAX Number: N/A Calendar System: Semester
URL: nativeamericanbiblecollege.org
Established: 1968 Annual Undergrad Tuition & Fees: $1,590
Enrollment: N/A Coed
Affiliation or Control: Assemblies Of God Church IRS Status: 501(c)3
Highest Offering: Baccalaureate
Program: Religious Emphasis
Accreditation: @BI

01 President .... James A. KEYS
05 Chief Academic Officer .... Dossie MORRIS WOOD, JR.
32 Chief Student Development Officer .... Larry GILMER
10 CFO .... Michael GRIFFES
08 Chief Librarian .... T. Liisa KELLY
06 Registrar .... Michelle Rae GRIFFES

New Life Theological Seminary (H)

3117 Whting Avenue / PO Box 790106, Charlotte NC 28206-4910
County: Mecklenburg FICE Identification: 038273
Unit ID: 444778
Telephone: (704) 334-6882 Carnegie Class: Spec/Faith
FAX Number: (704) 334-6885 Calendar System: Semester
URL: www.nlts.edu
Established: 1996 Annual Undergrad Tuition & Fees: $7,700
Enrollment: 141 Coed
Affiliation or Control: Independent Non-Profit IRS Status: 501(c)3
Highest Offering: Master's
Program: 2-Year Principally Bachelor's Creditable; Professional; Religious Emphasis
Accreditation: TRACS

01 President .... Dr. Eddie G. GRIGG
04 Executive Asst to the President .... Mr. Travis JOHNSON
05 Vice President of Academic Affairs .... Dr. Robert A. YOST
32 Vice President of Student Affairs .... Dr. Nathaniel PEARCE
30 Director of Advancement .... Mr. Michael ANDRUS
06 Registrar/Dir International Student .... Ms. Anne WITT
08 Head Librarian .... Mr. Robert MCINNES
07 Director of Admissions .... Ms. Constance HEMPHILL
10 Chief Finance Officer .... Mr. Al WITT, JR.
37 Financial Aid Officer .... Mr. Kenneth ROACH

*North Carolina Community College System (I)

200 W Jones Street, 5001 MSC, Raleigh NC 27699-5001
County: Wake FICE Identification: 033445
Unit ID: 199166
Telephone: (919) 807-7100 Carnegie Class: N/A

FAX Number: (919) 807-7164
URL: www.nccommunitycolleges.edu

01 President ... Dr. R. Scott RALLS
03 Exec Vice President/Chief of Staff ... Mr. Kennon BRIGGS
103 Sr VP Tech & Workforce Development ... Dr. Saundra WILLIAMS
05 Vice Pres Academic & Student Svcs ... Dr. Sharron MORRISSEY
10 Vice President Business & Finance ... Ms. Jennifer HAYGOOD
101 Director State Board Affairs ... Mr. Bryan JENKINS
04 Special Assistant to the President ... Ms. Pia MCKENZIE
46 VP Engagement/Strategic Innovation ... Ms. Linda WEINER

*Alamance Community College (A)

1247 Jimmie Kerr Road/PO Box 8000,
Graham NC 27253-8000
County: Alamance FICE Identification: 005463
Unit ID: 199786
Telephone: (336) 578-2002 Carnegie Class: Assoc/Pub-S-MC
FAX Number: (336) 578-1987 Calendar System: Semester
URL: www.alamancecc.edu
Established: 1958 Annual Undergrad Tuition & Fees (In-District): $1,686
Enrollment: 5,222 Coed
Affiliation or Control: State/Local IRS Status: 501(c)3
Highest Offering: Associate Degree
Program: Occupational; 2-Year Principally Bachelor's Creditable
Accreditation: SC, ACFEI, DA, MAC, MLTAD

02 President ... Dr. Martin H. NADELMAN
05 Executive Vice President ... Dr. Gene C. COUCH, JR.
10 Vice Pres Admin & Fiscal Svcs ... Mr. Mark NEWSOME
30 VP Institutional Advancement ... Ms. Carolyn RHODE
20 Dean of Curriculum Programs ... Dr. William T. MCNEILL
51 Dean of Continuing Education ... Vacant
32 Dean of Student Development ... Dr. Carol DISQUE
50 Assoc Dean Business Technologies ... Mr. Scott QUEEN
72 Assoc Dean Industrial/Graphics Tech ... Mr. Wally M. SHEARIN
49 Assoc Dean Arts & Sciences ... Ms. Catherine W. JOHNSON
69 Assoc Dean Health & Public Svcs ... Ms. Connie STACK
21 Controller ... Ms. Cynthia COLLIE
11 Director Administrative Services ... Mr. Erik CONTI
16 Director Human Resources ... Ms. Lorri ALLISON
08 Director Learning Resources Center ... Ms. Sheila STREET
26 Director Public Information/Mktg ... Mr. Edward WILLIAMS
56 Director Occupational Ext Program ... Mr. David PARKER
84 Director Enrollment Management ... Ms. Elizabeth BREHLER
37 Director Financial Aid ... Ms. Sabrina DEGAIN
36 Director Counseling & Career Svcs ... Mr. Steven C. REINHARTSEN
38 Special Needs/Counseling Svcs Coord ... Ms. Monica ISBELL
88 Academic Support Specialist ... Ms. Jennifer BROWNELL
09 Institutional Researcher ... Ms. Teresa WALKER

*Asheville - Buncombe Technical Community College (B)

340 Victoria Road, Asheville NC 28801-4897
County: Buncombe FICE Identification: 004033
Unit ID: 197887
Telephone: (828) 254-1921 Carnegie Class: Assoc/Pub-R-L
FAX Number: (828) 251-6355 Calendar System: Semester
URL: www.abtech.edu
Established: 1959 Annual Undergrad Tuition & Fees (In-District): $1,998
Enrollment: 8,056 Coed
Affiliation or Control: State/Local IRS Status: 501(c)3
Highest Offering: Associate Degree
Program: Occupational; 2-Year Principally Bachelor's Creditable
Accreditation: SC, ACFEI, DA, DH, DMS, MAC, MLTAD, RAD, SURGT

02 President ... Dr. Hank DUNN
10 VP Business & Finance/CFO ... Mr. Scott MCKINNEY
13 Vice Pres Information Technology ... Mr. Brian WILLIS
05 VP Instructional Services ... Ms. Melissa QUINLEY
20 Associate VP Instructional Services ... Dr. Gene LOFLIN
32 Interim VP Student Services ... Dr. Debby HARMON
100 Special Asst to President ... Ms. Sara SMITH
103 Sr Exec Dir Econ Wrkfrc Dev/Cont Ed ... Ms. Shelley WHITE
04 Executive Administrative Assistant ... Ms. Martha SHANKS
49 Dean Arts & Sciences ... Dr. Beth STEWART
30 Exec Director/College Advancement ... Ms. Sana EFIRD
50 Dean Business & Hospitality Educ ... Mr. Philip LEFTWICH
54 Dean Engineering & Applied Tech ... Mr. Vernon D. DAUGHERTY
91 Director Info Systems Technology ... Mr. David C. MCKINNEY
84 Dir Recruitment/Student Activities ... Ms. Michele HATHCOCK
61 Director Law Enforcement Academy ... Ms. Dianne L. DAVIS
21 Director Business Services ... Ms. Lisa EVANS
37 Director of Financial Aid ... Ms. Donna TURNER
06 Registrar ... Mr. Scott C. DOUGLAS
07 Director of Admissions ... Ms. Lisa F. BUSH
24 Director Library Services ... Ms. Carol FLEMING
12 Director Madison County Campus ... Dr. Connie S. BUCKNER
18 Director Plant Operations ... Mr. Benny R. SMITH
19 Director Security ... Ms. Kara KELLER
31 Director Community Services ... Ms. Brinda W. CALDWELL
08 Librarian ... Ms. Martha DICKENS
09 Director Research & Planning ... Mr. David B. WHITE
15 Vice President Human Resources & OD ... Ms. Kaye N. WAUGH
27 Dir Community Relns & Marketing ... Ms. Mona L. CORNWELL
28 Director of Diversity ... Vacant
40 Bookstore Manager ... Mr. Tom BENOIT
96 Coordinator of Purchasing ... Ms. Rebecca R. WATKINS
72 Coordinator Technology Services ... Mr. Cris HARSHMAN

*Beaufort County Community College (C)

Box 1069, Washington NC 27889-1069
County: Beaufort FICE Identification: 008558
Unit ID: 197966
Telephone: (252) 946-6194 Carnegie Class: Assoc/Pub-R-S
FAX Number: (252) 946-0271 Calendar System: Semester
URL: www.beaufortccc.edu
Established: 1967 Annual Undergrad Tuition & Fees (In-District): $2,272
Enrollment: 1,925 Coed
Affiliation or Control: State/Local IRS Status: 501(c)3
Highest Offering: Associate Degree
Program: Occupational; 2-Year Principally Bachelor's Creditable
Accreditation: SC, MLTAD

02 President ... Dr. Barbara TANSEY
05 Dean of Instruction ... Mr. Wesley BEDDARD
11 Dean of Administrative Services ... Dr. Phillip PRICE
32 Dean of Student Services ... Dr. Crystal ANGE
51 Dean of Continuing Education ... Mr. Chet JARMAN
45 Dir of Planning/Inst Effectiveness ... Vacant
26 Director of Public Relations ... Mrs. Judy JENNETTE
55 Dir of Evening/Off Campus Svcs ... Mr. Clay CARTER
76 Chairperson Allied Health ... Ms. Erica SCHATZ
49 Chairperson Arts & Sciences ... Mr. Dixon BOYLES
50 Chairperson Business ... Mrs. Donna DUNN
72 Chairperson Industrial Technology ... Mr. Ben MORRIS
08 Dir Learning Resources Center ... Mrs. Penny SERMONS
88 Network Administrator ... Mr. Brown MCFADDEN
91 System Administrator ... Mr. Chuck HAUSER
15 Director of Human Resources ... Mrs. Emily WOOLARD
19 Director of Campus Police ... Mr. Hal SWINDELL
06 Registrar ... Mrs. Camille RICHARDSON
37 Director of Financial Aid ... Mr. Harold SMITH
07 Director of Admissions ... Mr. Daniel WILSON
38 Director of Counseling ... Vacant
88 Director of Retention Services ... Mrs. Sue BROOKSHIRE
36 Director of Career Center ... Mrs. Sandy MCFADDEN
103 Dir of Business & Industry Svcs ... Mr. Lentz STOWE

*Bladen Community College (D)

PO Box 266, Dublin NC 28332-0266
County: Bladen FICE Identification: 007987
Unit ID: 198011
Telephone: (910) 879-5500 Carnegie Class: Assoc/Pub-R-S
FAX Number: (910) 879-5564 Calendar System: Semester
URL: www.bladencc.edu
Established: 1967 Annual Undergrad Tuition & Fees (In-State): $2,281
Enrollment: 1,556 Coed
Affiliation or Control: State IRS Status: 501(c)3
Highest Offering: Associate Degree
Program: Occupational; 2-Year Principally Bachelor's Creditable; Technical Emphasis
Accreditation: SC

02 President ... Dr. William FINDT
10 Vice President for Finance ... Mr. Jay STANLEY
05 VP for Instruction & Student Svcs ... Mr. Jeffrey KORNEGAY
32 Dean of Students ... Ms. Marva DINKINS
08 Director Learning Resource Ctr ... Ms. Sherwin RICE
55 Dean Distance & Evening Programs ... Ms. Ann RUSSELL
84 Dean of Enrollment Management ... Mr. Barry PRIEST
09 Dir Institutional Effect & Planning ... Ms. Harriet HOBBS
18 Director of Facilities ... Mr. Bradley TAYLOR
20 Assoc to VP Instruct & Student Svcs ... Mr. Lynn KING
21 Director of Budgeting ... Ms. Sheila DOCKERY
37 Director of Financial Aid ... Ms. Samantha BENSON
15 Human Resources Officer ... Ms. Tiina MUNDY
26 Public Information Officer ... Mr. Jack MCDUFFIE
30 Foundation Specialist ... Ms. Linda BURNEY

*Blue Ridge Community College (E)

180 W Campus Drive, Flat Rock NC 28731-4728
County: Henderson FICE Identification: 009684
Unit ID: 198039
Telephone: (828) 694-1700 Carnegie Class: Assoc/Pub-R-M
FAX Number: (828) 694-1690 Calendar System: Semester
URL: www.blueridge.edu
Established: 1969 Annual Undergrad Tuition & Fees (In-District): $2,292
Enrollment: 2,480 Coed
Affiliation or Control: State/Local IRS Status: 501(c)3
Highest Offering: Associate Degree
Program: Occupational; 2-Year Principally Bachelor's Creditable
Accreditation: SC, EMT, SURGT

05 VP for Instruction ... Dr. Alan H. STEPHENSON
10 VP for Finance and Operations ... Ms. Rhonda K. DEVAN
32 VP for Student Services ... Ms. Marcia L. STONEMAN
13 VP for Technology ... Vacant
51 VP for Continuing Education ... Ms. Julie G. THOMPSON
30 Chief Inst Advancement Officer ... Dr. Chad MERRILL
49 Dean for Arts and Sciences ... Mr. David H. DAVIS
72 Dean for Applied Technology ... Mr. Chris ENGLISH
76 Dean for Allied Health ... Ms. Rita D. CONNER
97 Dean for Basic Skills ... Mr. Rick MARSHALL
50 Dean for Business/Service Careers ... Ms. Celeste P. OPREAN
102 Exec Dir Educational Foundation ... Ms. Ann F. GREEN
44 Institutional Advance/Rsrch Coord ... Ms. Carol Ann LYDON
06 Registrar ... Ms. Kirsten H. BUNCH
07 Director of Admissions ... Ms. Marcia L. STONEMAN
08 Librarian ... Ms. Susan D. WILLIAMS
21 Director Financial Services ... Ms. Shannon BISHOP
37 Financial Aid Officer ... Ms. Lisanne MASTERSON
38 Director for Counseling ... Vacant
91 Director of Network Services ... Mr. Steve YOUNG
18 Facilities Director ... Mr. Peter HEMANS
26 Director of Public Relations ... Ms. Lee Anna HANEY
35 Student Activities Coordinator ... Ms. April KILLOUGH
84 Director Enrollment Management ... Ms. Cathy STEPHENSON
96 Director of Purchasing ... Ms. Carolyn ALLEY
15 Director Human Resources ... Mr. Tommy OAKMAN

*Brunswick Community College (F)

PO Box 30, Supply NC 28462-0030
County: Brunswick FICE Identification: 021707
Unit ID: 198084
Telephone: (910) 755-7300 Carnegie Class: Assoc/Pub-R-S
FAX Number: (910) 754-7805 Calendar System: Semester
URL: www.brunswickcc.edu
Established: 1979 Annual Undergrad Tuition & Fees (In-State): $1,700
Enrollment: 1,540 Coed
Affiliation or Control: State IRS Status: 501(c)3
Highest Offering: Associate Degree
Program: Occupational; 2-Year Principally Bachelor's Creditable; Business Emphasis
Accreditation: SC

02 President ... Dr. Susanne H. ADAMS
05 VP Academic Svcs & Student Affairs ... Dr. Sharon THOMPSON
10 Vice President Budget and Finance ... Dr. Benjamin A. DEBLOIS
32 Assoc VP Student Svcs & Enrollment ... Vacant
11 Vice President Operations ... Mr. Jerry L. THRIFT
09 Coordinator Inst Effectiveness ... Ms. Pamela FEDERLINE
08 Director Library ... Ms. Carmen BLANTON
06 Registrar ... Mr. Lawrence PAKOWSKI
15 Director Human Resources ... Ms. Nicole WILLIAMS
19 Public Safety/Police Director ... Mr. Lindsay WALTON
18 Physical Plant Director ... Ms. Donna BAXTER
102 Executive Director Foundation ... Mrs. Susan LAWING
26 Director of Marketing & Public Info ... Vacant
37 Financial Aid/Veterans Affs Coord ... Ms. Paula ALMOND
72 Dean Professional Technical Service ... Ms. Gina ROBINSON
49 Dean Arts & Sciences ... Ms. Jennifer WOODHEAD

*Caldwell Community College and Technical Institute (G)

2855 Hickory Boulevard, Hudson NC 28638-1399
County: Caldwell FICE Identification: 004835
Unit ID: 198118
Telephone: (828) 726-2200 Carnegie Class: Assoc/Pub-R-M
FAX Number: (828) 726-2216 Calendar System: Semester
URL: www.cccti.edu
Established: 1964 Annual Undergrad Tuition & Fees (In-District): $2,284
Enrollment: 4,971 Coed
Affiliation or Control: State/Local IRS Status: 501(c)3
Highest Offering: Associate Degree
Program: Occupational; 2-Year Principally Bachelor's Creditable
Accreditation: SC, DMS, NMT, PTAA, RAD

02 President ... Dr. Kenneth A. BOHAM
03 Executive Vice President ... Mr. Mark POARCH
18 Vice President Facility Services ... Mr. Donnie BASSINGER
32 Vice President Student Services ... Mrs. Dena HOLMAN
51 VP Adult/Corp/Continuing Education ... Mrs. Elaine LOCKHART
12 Executive Director Watauga Campus ... Mr. Steve MELTON
84 Dir Enrollment Mgmt Services ... Ms. LaTosha HICKS
08 Director Learning Resources Center ... Vacant
37 Director Financial Aid ... Mrs. Eva HARMON
36 Dir Career Planning/Job Placement ... Mr. Rick SHEW
15 Director Human Resources ... Mrs. Kathy SEITZ
26 Director Marketing & Communications ... Mrs. Sherry WILSON
10 Controller ... Mr. Scott ROGERS
09 Director Inst Effectiveness/Rsrch ... Mrs. Kate BENOIT
26 Public Relations Officer ... Mr. Edward TERRY
102 Director Foundation Office ... Mrs. Marla CHRISTIE
28 Director of Diversity ... Mrs. Alice LENTZ
38 Director Student Counseling ... Mr. Shannon BROWN
96 Director of Purchasing ... Mrs. Pam ROUSE
40 Manager Bookstore ... Mr. Michael PHILYAW

*Cape Fear Community College (H)

411 N Front Street, Wilmington NC 28401-3993
County: New Hanover FICE Identification: 005320
Unit ID: 198154
Telephone: (910) 362-7000 Carnegie Class: Assoc/Pub-R-L
FAX Number: (910) 763-2279 Calendar System: Semester
URL: www.cfcc.edu
Established: 1958 Annual Undergrad Tuition & Fees (In-District): $2,344
Enrollment: 9,173 Coed
Affiliation or Control: State/Local IRS Status: 501(c)3
Highest Offering: Associate Degree
Program: Occupational; 2-Year Principally Bachelor's Creditable
Accreditation: SC, ADNUR, DA, DH, DMS, OTA, RAD, SURGT

02 President ... Dr. Ted SPRING
05 Vice President of Instruction ... Dr. Amanda LEE

10 Vice Pres of Business & Inst Svcs .... Ms. Camellia N. RICE
32 Vice Pres of Student Development .... Ms. Carol J. CULLUM
09 Vice Pres of Inst Effectiveness .... Ms. Kim LAWING
18 Director of Institutional Services .... Mr. Kenneth D. PEARCE
06 Registrar .... Mr. Phil FARINHOLT
102 Exec Director of the CFCC Found Inc ...... Ms. Margaret ROBISON
84 Director of Enrollment Management .... Ms. Linda KASYAN
08 Director Learning Resources Center .... Ms. Catherine LEE
37 Director of Financial Aid .... Ms. Jo-Ann CRAIG
36 Director of Career & Testing .... Mr. Patrick PITTMAN
26 Public Information Officer .... Mr. David M. HARDIN
13 Director Info Technology Services .... Mr. David CHAPPELL
15 Director Personnel .... Mr. John UPTON
41 Dir Student Activities/Athletics .... Mr. Robert MCGEE
96 Director of Purchasing & Inventory .... Mr. Brooke MESEROLE
38 Director Student Counseling .... Ms. Jacqueline FOSTER
21 Assoc Business Officer/Controller ..... Mr. Ravi VELAUTHAPILLAI
28 Director of Diversity .... Mr. David HARDIN
07 Director of Admissions .... Ms. Linda KASYAN
44 Annual Giving Director .... Ms. Dana MCKOY
30 Chief Development Officer .... Ms. Margaret ROBISON
51 Dean of Continuing Education .... Mr. Clarence L. SMITH
75 Dean Vocational/Technical Education .... Mr. Pat HOGAN
49 Dean Arts & Sciences .... Ms. Orangel J. DANIELS
105 Web Services Analyst .... Ms. Christina HEIKKILA

*Carteret Community College (A)

3505 Arendell Street, Morehead City NC 28557-2989

County: Carteret FICE Identification: 008081
Unit ID: 198206
Telephone: (252) 222-6000 Carnegie Class: Assoc/Pub-R-S
FAX Number: (252) 222-2514 Calendar System: Semester
URL: www.carteret.edu
Established: 1963 Annual Undergrad Tuition & Fees (In-District): $2,261
Enrollment: 1,744 Coed
Affiliation or Control: State/Local IRS Status: 501(c)3
Highest Offering: Associate Degree
Program: Occupational; 2-Year Principally Bachelor's Creditable
Accreditation: SC, ADNUR, MAC, RAD

02 President .... Dr. Kerry L. YOUNGBLOOD
05 VP for Instruction/Student Support .... Dr. Fran EMORY
11 Vice Pres Administrative Services .... Ms. Madelene BROOKS
31 Vice Pres Corporate & Community .... Mr. Perry L. HARKER
30 VP College Advance/Ex Dir CCC Found .... Vacant
04 Executive Assistant to President .... Ms. Brenda REASH
08 Director LRC .... Ms. Elizabeth BAKER
32 Senior Director Student Services .... Ms. Robie MCFARLAND
55 Director of Evening Programs .... Vacant
13 Director Information Technology .... Vacant
15 Director of Human Resources .... Ms. Barbara I. COOPER
49 Div Director Arts & Sciences .... Ms. Doree EVANS
76 Div Director Health Sciences .... Ms. Laurie A. FRESHWATER
75 Div Director Service Technology .... Ms. Evanglene REELS
50 Div Director Business Technologies .... Vacant
61 Div Director Legal & Community Svcs . Ms. Susan H. MCINTYRE
37 Financial Aid Officer .... Ms. Brenda J. LONG
06 Registrar .... Ms. Tammi COBLE
07 Admissions Officer .... Mr. Martin NICHOLS
09 Dir of Institutional Effectiveness .... Ms. Jennifer A. ULZ
18 Dir Operations/Auxiliary Services .... Ms. Pam OLSSON
26 Director of Public Affairs .... Mr. Morgan SMITH
40 Bookstore Manager .... Vacant
96 Purchasing Officer .... Ms. Donna L. CUMBIE
106 Director Distance Learning .... Mr. Patrick J. KEOUGH

*Catawba Valley Community College (B)

2550 Highway 70, SE, Hickory NC 28602-9699

County: Catawba FICE Identification: 005318
Unit ID: 198233
Telephone: (828) 327-7000 Carnegie Class: Assoc/Pub-R-M
FAX Number: (828) 327-7276 Calendar System: Semester
URL: www.cvcc.edu
Established: 1960 Annual Undergrad Tuition & Fees (In-District): $1,560
Enrollment: 5,529 Coed
Affiliation or Control: State/Local IRS Status: 501(c)3
Highest Offering: Associate Degree
Program: Occupational; 2-Year Principally Bachelor's Creditable
Accreditation: SC, ADNUR, DH, EMT, NDT, POLYT, RAD, SURGT

02 President .... Dr. Garrett D. HINSHAW
05 Vice President of Instruction .... Dr. Keith MACKIE
10 Vice President of Fiscal Affairs .... Mr. Wes BUNCH
32 Vice Pres Student Svcs/Technology .... Mr. Bill DULIN
35 CEO of of Student Services .... Mrs. Cindy COULTER
15 Director Human Resources .... Mr. Mike KIDD
06 Director of Admissions/Records .... Ms. Paula HOLLAR
21 Controller .... Ms. Robyn F. CHAPMAN
37 Director Scholarships/Financial Aid .... Ms. Debbie BARGER
09 Ofc Accountability/Efficienc/Effect .... Mr. Kevin ROUSE
88 Director Industrial Training .... Ms. Crystal GLENN
88 Director Small Business Center .... Mr. Jeff NEUVILLE
50 Director Business/Technolgy Ext .... Ms. Susan KILLIAN
88 Director Hosiery Technology Center .... Mr. Daniel C. ST. LOUIS
13 Director Information Technologies .... Mr. Ken ELLIOTT
19 Director Campus Safety/Security .... Mr. Bill DULIN
27 Director Community Relations .... Ms. Mary K. MILLER
31 Director Community Education .... Ms. Louise GARRISON
36 Counselor/Job Placement Svcs Coord .... Ms. Kathy CAREY
16 Coordinator Health/Human Services .... Ms. Donna TRADO

*Central Carolina Community College (C)

1105 Kelly Drive, Sanford NC 27330-9000

County: Lee FICE Identification: 005449
Unit ID: 198251
Telephone: (919) 775-5401 Carnegie Class: Assoc/Pub-R-M
FAX Number: (919) 718-7380 Calendar System: Semester
URL: www.cccc.edu
Established: 1958 Annual Undergrad Tuition & Fees (In-District): $2,296
Enrollment: 4,773 Coed
Affiliation or Control: State/Local IRS Status: 501(c)3
Highest Offering: Associate Degree
Program: Occupational; 2-Year Principally Bachelor's Creditable
Accreditation: SC, DA, DH, MAC, POLYT

02 President .... Dr. T. Eston MARCHANT
05 Exec Vice Pres of Instruction .... Dr. Lisa M. CHAPMAN
11 Vice Pres for Administrative Svcs .... Mr. Wayne G. ROBINSON
32 Vice President Student Services .... Mr. Ken R. HOYLE
51 VP Economic & Community Development .. Ms. Pamela SENEGAL
30 VP of Institutional Advancement .... Mrs. Celia HURLEY
12 Provost Chatham Campus .... Dr. Karen H. ALLEN
12 Provost Harnett Campus .... Mr. William R. TYSON
08 Director of Library Services .... Ms. Tara GUTHRIE
15 Exec Human Resources Director .... Ms. Stacey CARTER-COLEY
102 Foundation Executive Director .... Ms. Diane F. GLOVER
06 Registrar .... Ms. Jamie CHILDRESS
07 Director of Admissions .... Ms. Jamee STIFFLER
26 Director Marketing & Public Affairs .... Ms. Marcie DISHMAN
37 Director Student Financial Aid .... Ms. Ann PEACOCK
96 Director of Purchasing .... Mrs. Starlene JACKSON
18 Physical Plant Manager .... Mr. Ronnie MEASAMER
75 Dean Vocational/Technical Programs .... Dr. Stephan ATHANS
50 Dean Business/Media Tech/Publ Srvs .... Mrs. Joni P. PAVLIK
36 Dean of College & Career Readiness .... Ms. Dawn TUCKER

*Central Piedmont Community College (D)

PO Box 35009, Charlotte NC 28235-5009

County: Mecklenburg FICE Identification: 002915
Unit ID: 198260
Telephone: (704) 330-2722 Carnegie Class: Assoc/Pub-U-MC
FAX Number: (704) 330-5045 Calendar System: Semester
URL: www.cpcc.edu
Established: 1963 Annual Undergrad Tuition & Fees (In-District): $2,617
Enrollment: 19,840 Coed
Affiliation or Control: State/Local IRS Status: 501(c)3
Highest Offering: Associate Degree
Program: Occupational; 2-Year Principally Bachelor's Creditable
Accreditation: SC, ACFEI, CVT, CYTO, DA, DH, ENGT, MAC, MLTAD, PTAA, SURGT

02 President .... Dr. P. Anthony ZEISS
03 Executive Vice President .... Dr. Kathy DRUMM
05 Vice President for Learning .... Mr. Richard ZOLLINGER
84 VP Enrollment & Student Services .... Dr. Marcia CONSTON
10 VP Finance/Administrative Services .... Mr. Michael MOSS
04 Exec Assistant to the President .... Ms. Susan OLESON-BRIGGS
30 VP for Inst Advancement .... Dr. Kevin MCCARTHY
13 Assoc VP for Technology .... Mr. David KIM
11 Assoc VP Financial Svcs .... Ms. Diep TONG
20 Assoc VP Learning .... Dr. Deborah BOUTON
18 Assoc VP Facilities & Construction .... Mr. Rich ROSENTHAL
09 Assoc VP Institutional Research .... Dr. Terri MANNING
88 Assoc VP Compliance and Audit .... Dr. Brenda LEONARD
15 Assoc VP of Human Resources .... Mr. Paul SANTOS
25 Assoc VP Government Rels & Grants .... Mr. Michael HORN
26 PIO & Asst to Pres Cmty Rels/Mktg .... Mr. Jeffrey LOWRANCE
12 Dean Levine Campus .... Dr. Edith MCELROY
12 Dean Merancas Campus .... Ms. Beverly DICKSON
12 Dean Central Campus .... Mr. Paul KOEHNKE
12 Dean Cato Campus .... Ms. Janet MALKEMES
12 Dean Harris Campus .... Ms. Mary VICKERS-KOCH
12 Dean Harper Campus .... Mr. Jay POTTER
54 Dean STEM .... Mr. Chad RAY
88 Dean Retention Services .... Dr. Clint MCELROY
35 Dean Student Life/Service Learning .... Mr. Mark HELMS
38 Dean Student Success Services .... Ms. Rita DAWKINS
84 Dean Enrollment Management .... Mr. Daniel MCEACHERN
08 Dean Libraries .... Ms. Gloria KELLEY
88 Dean Community Development .... Ms. Kathi POLIS
07 Dean Enrollment Services .... Ms. April JONES

*Cleveland Community College (E)

137 S Post Road, Shelby NC 28152-6296

County: Cleveland FICE Identification: 008082
Unit ID: 198321
Telephone: (704) 669-6000 Carnegie Class: Assoc/Pub-R-M
FAX Number: (704) 669-4202 Calendar System: Semester
URL: www.clevelandcc.edu
Established: 1965 Annual Undergrad Tuition & Fees (In-District): $1,742
Enrollment: 3,445 Coed
Affiliation or Control: State/Local IRS Status: 501(c)3
Highest Offering: Associate Degree
Program: Occupational; 2-Year Principally Bachelor's Creditable
Accreditation: SC, RAD, SURGT

02 President .... Dr. L. Steve THORNBURG
05 Vice President of Academic Programs .... Dr. Becky SAIN
32 Vice President of Student Services .... Mr. Andy GARDNER
10 Senior VP Finance/Admin Svcs .... Mr. Tommy GREENE
51 Vice Pres of Continuing Education .... Dr. Barbara GREENE
26 Senior Dean Cmty Relations/Devel .... Mr. Eddie HOLBROOK
84 Dean of Enrollment Management .... Vacant
20 Executive VP of Instr & Student Dev ...... Mrs. Shannon KENNEDY
102 Executive Director Foundation .... Mr. U. L. PATTERSON, III
09 Dir Planning/Inst Effectiveness .... Mrs. Laura BOWEN
40 Bookstore Manager .... Vacant
06 Registrar .... Vacant
07 Director of Enrollment Services .... Ms. Nedra MADDOX
37 Financial Aid Coordinator .... Vacant
08 Dean of Learning Resources .... Mrs. Barbara MCKIBBIN
96 Director of Purchasing .... Mrs. Kathy EVERETT
18 Director of Physical Plant .... Mr. Mark FOX
19 Director of Campus Security .... Mr. Bill NEAL
15 Human Resources & Safety Manager .... Vacant
24 Coord of Audiovisual Services .... Mr. Danny MORTON
14 Systems Administrator .... Mr. Mike FALLS
90 Computer Network Administrator .... Mr. Robin DYER
49 Dean Arts/Sciences/Public Service .... Mrs. Barbara ROMICH
50 Dean Business Technologies .... Dr. John LATTIMORE
75 Dean Vocation Engineering Tech .... Mr. Michael MCSWAIN
88 Dean Basic Skills .... Dr. Chris NANNEY

*Coastal Carolina Community College (F)

444 Western Boulevard, Jacksonville NC 28546-6816

County: Onslow FICE Identification: 005316
Unit ID: 198330
Telephone: (910) 455-1221 Carnegie Class: Assoc/Pub-R-M
FAX Number: (910) 455-7027 Calendar System: Semester
URL: www.coastalcarolina.edu
Established: 1963 Annual Undergrad Tuition & Fees (In-District): $2,529
Enrollment: 4,766 Coed
Affiliation or Control: State/Local IRS Status: 501(c)3
Highest Offering: Associate Degree
Program: Occupational; 2-Year Principally Bachelor's Creditable
Accreditation: SC, DA, DH, MLTAD, SURGT

02 President .... Dr. Ronald K. LINGLE
03 Executive Vice President .... Mr. David L. HEATHERLY
05 VP Instruction/Info Resources .... Mr. Dewey H. LEWIS
51 Vice Pres for Inst Effect & Cont Ed ...... Ms. Sharon R. MCGINNIS
32 Division Chair for Student Services .... Dr. Donald R. HERRING
16 Personnel Officer .... Ms. Renita G. LOGAN
26 Pub Info Ofcr/Ex Dir Col Foundation ...... Ms. Colette B. TEACHEY
06 Dir Admin/Data Mgmt Svc/Registrar .... Ms. Sue FLAHARTY
18 Dir Physical Plant & Aux Services .... Ms. Carol PHILLIPS
37 Director for Financial Aid Services .... Ms. Tammy LYON
88 Director for Veterans Services .... Mr. Christopher P. SABIN
88 Director Economic Development .... Ms. Anne C. SHAW

*College of the Albemarle (G)

1208 North Road Street, Elizabeth City NC 27906-2327

County: Pasquotank FICE Identification: 002917
Unit ID: 197814
Telephone: (252) 335-0821 Carnegie Class: Assoc/Pub-R-M
FAX Number: (252) 335-2011 Calendar System: Semester
URL: www.albemarle.edu
Established: 1960 Annual Undergrad Tuition & Fees (In-District): $2,128
Enrollment: 2,913 Coed
Affiliation or Control: State/Local IRS Status: 501(c)3
Highest Offering: Associate Degree
Program: Occupational; 2-Year Principally Bachelor's Creditable
Accreditation: SC, ADNUR, MAC, MLTAD, SURGT

02 President .... Dr. Kandi W. DEITEMEYER
10 VP Business & Admin Services .... Mr. James TURDICI
05 Vice President for Learning .... Vacant
32 VP for Student Suc & Enr Mgnt .... Mr. Steven WOODBURN
51 VP Workforce Dev & Cont Edu .... Ms. Suzanne ROHRBAUGH
12 Dean Dare County Campus .... Mr. Joseph T. TURNER
35 Assistant Dean SSEM .... Ms. Martha JOHNSON
26 Director Marketing & Communications ..... Mrs. Lisa A. JOHNSON
07 Director Admissions & Testing .... Mr. Kenneth L. KRENTZ
37 Director Scholarship/Student Aid .... Ms. Angela R. GODFREY-DAWSON
88 Director Student Activities .... Mrs. Maenecia COLE
06 Registrar .... Ms. Andrea DANCE
88 Director Small Business Center .... Ms. Ginger H. O'NEAL
78 Director Coop Educ/Job Placement .... Mr. Charles K. CARTER
04 Exec Assistant to the President .... Ms. Sandra W. STRICKLAND
08 Director Learning Resources Center .... Mr. Robert B. SCHENCK
12 Dean Edenton-Chowan Campus .... Ms. B. Lynn HURDLE-WINSLOW
13 Director Mgmt Information Services .... Mr. Wayman WHITE
15 Director Human Resources .... Ms. Wendy W. BRICKHOUSE
18 Director Physical Facilities .... Mr. Richard R. SEYMOUR
21 Controller .... Ms. Susan GENTRY
40 Director Admin Support Services .... Ms. Deborah R. HOLLAND
08 Dir Learning Resources Ctr-Dare .... Mr. George STRAWLEY
36 Director Counseling & Career Devel .... Mr. John M. WELLS
09 Director of Inst Effectiveness .... Dr. Eric LOVIK
88 Coord Prison Education Programs .... Mr. Cecil PHILPOTT
24 Coord Learning Lab & Learning Ctr .... Dr. Ann PARKINSON
88 Director Secondary Education .... Ms. Rita O. JENNINGS
49 Division Chair Arts and Sciences .... Mr. Bobby ADAMS

50 Dept Chair Business and Office Tech .... Vacant
76 Divison Chair Health & Wellness .... Mr. Mark FAITHFUL
83 Department Chair Social Sciences .... Mr. Rodger ROSSMAN
76 Department Chair Health Sciences .... Ms. Robin HARRIS
60 Dept Chair Language & Literature .... Mr. Dean ROUGHTON
75 Dept Chair Const & Industrial Tech .... Mr. Charles PURSER
88 Director Business & Economic Devel .... Vacant
77 Dept Chair Computer Systems & Elect .... Vacant
103 Dir Workforce & Cont Educ .... Ms. Lynda HESTER
57 Department Chair Fine Arts .... Mrs. Patricia STERRITT
50 Int Div Chair Business Applied Tech .....Ms. Robin ZINSMEISTER
88 Dept Chair Developmental Studies .... Ms. Ruth WARREN
88 Department Chair Public Services .... Vacant
88 Div Chair Foundational Studies .... Ms. Michelle WATERS
19 Director Public Safety & Preparedns .... Mr. Joe DESTEFANO
25 Director of Institutional Grants .... Vacant
88 Dir Basic Skills/Workforce Reading .... Mr. Timothy SWEENEY

*Craven Community College (A)

800 College Court, New Bern NC 28562-4984
County: Craven FICE Identification: 006799
Unit ID: 198367
Telephone: (252) 638-7200 Carnegie Class: Assoc/Pub-R-M
FAX Number: (252) 638-4232 Calendar System: Semester
URL: www.cravencc.edu
Established: 1965 Annual Undergrad Tuition & Fees (In-District): $1,064
Enrollment: 3,609 Coed
Affiliation or Control: State/Local IRS Status: 501(c)3
Highest Offering: Associate Degree
Program: Occupational; 2-Year Principally Bachelor's Creditable
Accreditation: SC, MAC, PTAA

02 President .... Dr. Catherine CHEW
05 Exec VP Learning/Student Success .... Dr. Daryl MINUS
12 VP Hvlck-Chry Pt/Mil Affs/Wrkfc Dev .... Mr. Layne HARPINE
11 Vice Pres of Administrative Svcs .... Ms. Karla (Page) JONES-VARNELL
49 Dean Liberal Arts & Univ Transfer .... Ms. Betty K. HATCHER
76 Dean Health Pgms/Spec Asst to EVP .... Ms. Kathleen GALLMAN
36 Dean Career Programs .... Mr. James R. MILLARD
09 Dean Instl Effective/Learning Spprt .... Dr. Jill FEGLEY
06 Registrar .... Mr. John A. FONVILLE
102 Exec Dir Craven Cmty Col Foundation .... Ms. Suzanne GIFFORD
103 Ex Dir Ops Wrkfc Dev/Mil Aff-New Bn .... Mr. Eddie D. FOSTER
88 Ex Dir Oper Wrkfc Dev/Mil Affs-Hvlk .... Mr. Walter CALABRESE
37 Director Financial Aid .... Ms. Kathryn M. BANKS
103 Dir Workforce Readiness & Spec Pgms .... Mr. Mark W. BEST
88 Director Basic Skills Programs .... Ms. Zeledith BLAKELY
84 Director Enrollment Services .... Mr. John F. SMITH
88 Director Academic Skills Center .... Mr. Frederick E. COOZE
32 Director Student Services-Havelock .... Ms. Amy DERCK
08 Director Library Services .... Mrs. Catherine C. CAMPBELL
10 Director Financial Svcs/Purchasing .Mrs. Cynthia A. PATTERSON
35 Director TRIO Student Support Svcs .Ms. LaRhonda K. JOHNSON
15 Director Human Resources .... Mrs. Vickie MOSELEY-JONES
88 Dir Workforce Develop/Military Pgms .... Mr. Robin MATTHEWS
106 Dir Distance Learning/Prof Devel .... Dr. Autumn GRUBB
18 Director Facilities/Security .... Mr. Larry HENDERSON
13 Director Technology Services .... Ms. Bambi EDWARDS
19 Chief Campus Security .... Mr. H. Steve CARTER
96 Procurement & Fixed Assets Officer .... Mr. Hiram Todd MURPHREY

*Davidson County Community College (B)

PO Box 1287, Lexington NC 27293-1287
County: Davidson FICE Identification: 002919
Unit ID: 198376
Telephone: (336) 249-8186 Carnegie Class: Assoc/Pub-S-SC
FAX Number: (336) 249-0379 Calendar System: Semester
URL: www.davidsonccc.edu
Established: 1958 Annual Undergrad Tuition & Fees (In-District): $1,786
Enrollment: 4,386 Coed
Affiliation or Control: State/Local IRS Status: 501(c)3
Highest Offering: Associate Degree
Program: Occupational; 2-Year Principally Bachelor's Creditable
Accreditation: SC, ADNUR, HT, MAC, MLTAD

02 President .... Dr. Mary E. RITTLING
05 VP Academic Programs & Services .... Ms. Jeannine WOODY
32 VP Student Affairs .... Ms. Kim W. SEPICH
10 VP Financial/Administrative Svcs .... Mr. Rusty HUNT
30 VP Ext Affairs & Foundation .... Ms. Jenny M. VARNER
09 Exec Dir Rsrch Planning Innovation .... Ms. Susan BURLESON
51 Dean Cmty Educ/Wrkfrce Dev/Entship .... Mr. Jim DONNELLY
76 Dean Health/Wellness/Pub Safety .... Ms. Frankie LYONS
49 Dean Arts/Sciences/Education .... Dr. Mark BRANSON
88 Dean Foundational Stdnt/Acad Supp .... Ms. Christy FORREST
50 Dean Business Engineering Technical .... Mr. Randy LEDFORD
12 Dean Davie Campus .... Ms. Teresa KINES
35 Dean Student Support & Campus Life .... Mr. Stephen CAMP
21 Dean Financial/Admin Svcs .... Ms. Laura L. YARBROUGH
06 Int Dir Stdnt Records/Registration .... Ms. Julie OCEL
07 Director Admissions & Financial Aid .... Ms. Lori BLEVINS
36 Director Career Development .... Mr. Charles MAYER
18 Director Physical Plant Services .... Mr. Skip EDWARDS
26 Exec Dir Marketing & Communications .... Ms. Terri SMITH

*Durham Technical Community College (C)

1637 Lawson Street, Durham NC 27703-5023
County: Durham FICE Identification: 005448
Unit ID: 198455
Telephone: (919) 536-7200 Carnegie Class: Assoc/Pub-U-SC
FAX Number: (919) 686-3601 Calendar System: Semester
URL: www.durhamtech.edu
Established: 1961 Annual Undergrad Tuition & Fees (In-District): $1,748
Enrollment: 5,098 Coed
Affiliation or Control: State/Local IRS Status: 501(c)3
Highest Offering: Associate Degree
Program: Occupational; 2-Year Principally Bachelor's Creditable
Accreditation: SC, ADNUR, DT, MAC, OPD, OTA, PNUR, SURGT

02 President .... Dr. William G. INGRAM
03 Senior Vice President .... Ms. Wanda S. MAGGART
05 VP Student Learning/Devel & Support .... Dr. Valarie J. EVANS
10 VP Finance and Administration .... Mr. Robert KEENEY
51 VP Corporate & Continuing Education .... Vacant
88 Exec Dir Center for Global Learner .... Ms. Constanza GOMEZ-JOINS
04 Assistant to the President .... Vacant
04 Executive Secy to the President .... Ms. Angela G. PERRY
09 Director Institutional Research .... Dr. Teri L. KAASA
07 Director of Admissions .... Ms. Iesha M. CLEVELAND
30 Director Resource Development .... Ms. Gayle SIMS
14 Executive Director Info Tech Svcs .... Ms. Beverly S. MCCOMB
15 Director Human Resources .... Ms. Kathy MCKINLEY
08 Director Library & Media Services .... Ms. Irene H. LAUBE
55 Coordinator Evening College .... Mr. Felix M. DRYE
18 Director Facility Services .... Mr. Richard A. MCKOWN
37 Director Financial Aid .... Mr. Everett M. JETER
96 Director Auxiliary Services .... Ms. Yolanda V. MOORE-JONES
20 Exec Dean Student Learning & Assess .... Dr. Peter W. WOOLDRIDGE
49 Dean Arts & Sciences .... Dr. Thomas E. GOULD
76 Dean Health Technologies .... Ms. Melissa OAKLEY OCKERT
88 Asst Dean Applied & Public Svc .... Mr. Randall J. EGSEGIAN
38 Executive Dean Student Development .... Mr. D. Thomas JAYNES
75 Dean Career and Technical Programs ....Ms. Pamela G. SENEGAL
77 Assoc Dean Info Systems Technology .... Ms. Charlene C. WEST
06 Dean Student Services .... Vacant
19 Director Campus Police & Safety .... Ms. Sarah L. MINNIS

*Edgecombe Community College (D)

2009 W Wilson Street, Tarboro NC 27886-9399
County: Edgecombe FICE Identification: 008855
Unit ID: 198491
Telephone: (252) 823-5166 Carnegie Class: Assoc/Pub-R-M
FAX Number: (252) 823-6817 Calendar System: Semester
URL: www.edgecombe.edu
Established: 1967 Annual Undergrad Tuition & Fees (In-District): $2,200
Enrollment: 3,395 Coed
Affiliation or Control: State/Local IRS Status: 501(c)3
Highest Offering: Associate Degree
Program: Occupational; 2-Year Principally Bachelor's Creditable
Accreditation: SC, MAC, RAD, SURGT

02 President .... Dr. Deborah L. LAMM
05 Vice President of Instruction .... Dr. Kristi L. SNUGGS
11 Vice Pres Administrative Services .... Mr. Charlie R. HARRELL
32 Vice President Student Services .... Mr. Michael J. JORDAN
20 Asc VP Instruct/Curriculum/Cont Ed .... Mr. Lynn CALE
51 Dean Continuing Education .... Ms. Helen CLARK
84 Dean Enrollment Management .... Ms. Ginny MCLENDON
45 Director of Inst Effectiveness .... Ms. Sheila HOSKINS
26 Director of Public Information .... Ms. Mary T. BASS
08 Director of Library Services .... Ms. Rejeanor SCOTT
06 Registrar .... Ms. Cathy P. DUPREE
15 Director Personnel Services .... Ms. Janice TOLSON
18 Chief Facilities/Physical Plant .... Mr. Donald R. CAUDLE
37 Director Student Financial Aid .... Mr. Henry ANDERSON

*Fayetteville Technical Community College (E)

PO Box 35236, 2201 Hull Road,
Fayetteville NC 28303-0236
County: Cumberland FICE Identification: 007640
Unit ID: 198534
Telephone: (910) 678-8400 Carnegie Class: Assoc/Pub-R-L
FAX Number: (910) 678-8269 Calendar System: Semester
URL: www.faytechcc.edu
Established: 1961 Annual Undergrad Tuition & Fees (In-State): $2,298
Enrollment: 11,438 Coed
Affiliation or Control: State IRS Status: 501(c)3
Highest Offering: Associate Degree
Program: Occupational; 2-Year Principally Bachelor's Creditable
Accreditation: SC, ADNUR, DA, DH, FUSER, PTAA, RAD, SURGT

02 President .... Dr. Larry KEEN
11 Vice Pres for Administrative Svcs ..Mr. Joseph W. LEVISTER, JR.
05 Vice Pres for Academic/Student Svcs .... Dr. David BRAND
15 VP Human Res/Inst Effect/Assessment .... Mr. Carl MITCHELL
10 Vice Pres for Business and Finance .... Mrs. Betty J. SMITH
30 Vice Pres Institutional Advancement .... Mr. Brent MICHAELS
72 Vice Pres Learning Technologies .... Mr. Bob J. ERVIN
51 Assoc Vice Pres for Continuing Educ .... Dr. Joe W. MULLIS
32 Assoc Vice Pres Student Services .... Dr. Rosemary KELLY
56 Assoc Vice Pres Off-Campus Programs .... Mr. Phillip JACKSON
84 Dean of Enrollment Management .... Mr. Harper SHACKELFORD
06 Registrar .... Ms. Melissa A. JONES
21 Controller .... Mrs. Robin DEAVER
07 Director of Admissions .... Vacant
13 Director Management Information Svc .... Mr. Roderick BROWER
38 Director of Counseling Services ..... Ms. DeSandra WASHINGTON
37 Int Financial Aid Director .... Ms. Christine PORCHIA
18 Director of Facility Services .... Mr. Harold WYCKOFF
96 Purchasing Agent .... Ms. Amy SAMPERTON
50 Dean of Business Programs .... Mr. William GRIFFIN
49 Dean College Transfer/Gen Educ Pgms .... Dr. Anthony HUBERT
76 Dean of Health Programs .... Ms. Mary JOHNSON
54 Dean Engr/Pub Svs/Applied Tech Pgms .... Mr. Daryle NOBLES

*Forsyth Technical Community College (F)

2100 Silas Creek Parkway,
Winston-Salem NC 27103-5197
County: Forsyth FICE Identification: 005317
Unit ID: 198552
Telephone: (336) 723-0371 Carnegie Class: Assoc/Pub-U-SC
FAX Number: (336) 761-2399 Calendar System: Semester
URL: www.forsythtech.edu
Established: 1960 Annual Undergrad Tuition & Fees (In-State): $1,955
Enrollment: 10,606 Coed
Affiliation or Control: State IRS Status: 501(c)3
Highest Offering: Associate Degree
Program: Occupational; 2-Year Principally Bachelor's Creditable
Accreditation: SC, DA, DH, DMS, ENGT, MAC, NMT, RAD, RTT

02 President .... Dr. Gary M. GREEN
05 Vice Pres Instructional Services .... Dr. Conley F. WINEBARGER
13 Vice Pres of Planning & Info Svcs .... Ms. Rachel M. DESMARAIS
32 Vice President Student Services .... Ms. Jewel B. CHERRY
30 VP Inst Advancement/Exec Dir Found .... Vacant
10 Vice President Business Services .... Ms. Wendy R. EMERSON
103 Vice Pres Economic & Workforce Dev .... Mr. Alan K. MURDOCK
04 Exec Assistant to the President .... Ms. Sherri W. BOWEN
50 Dean Business Info Tech Div .... Mr. G. Bernard YEVIN
79 Dean of Humanities/Social Sci Div .... Ms. Yolanda S. WILSON
81 Dean Math/Science & Technologies .... Mr. Michael V. AYERS
54 Dean of Engineering Tech Div .... Mr. Leonard R. KISER
17 Dean of Health Technologies .... Dr. Bonnie G. POPE
31 Dean Community/Economic Development .... Ms. Sharon D. ANDERSON
08 Dean Learning Resources .... Mr. J. Randel CANDELARIA
88 Dean Adult Literacy .... Mr. Michael E. HARRIS
66 Director Nursing .... Ms. Linda H. LATHAM
76 Director Imaging .... Ms. Deborah D. TAYLOR
76 Director Health Services .... Ms. Jean E. MIDDLESWARTH
84 Dean Enrollment & Student Svcs .... Vacant
21 Dean Financial Services .... Ms. Melanie L. NUCKOLS
38 Dir Student Success Ctr/Counseling .... Mr. Joe E. MCINTOSH
15 Director Human Resources .... Mr. Gregory M. CHASE
09 Dir Institutional Effectiveness .... Ms. Dana L. DALTON
14 Director Information Systems .... Mr. Randall A. ROBERTSON
88 Dir Recruiting/Student Support Svcs .... Mr. Edwin B. WADDELL
37 Director Student Financial Services .... Mr. Ricky C. HODGES
06 Director Records/Registrar .... Ms. Gwen D. WHITAKER
07 Director of Admissions .... Ms. Jean M. GROOME
18 Director Physical Plant Services .... Mr. Scot R. QUESENBERRY
19 Director Campus Police .... Mr. Renarde D. EARL
88 Coordinator Small Business Center .... Vacant
35 Director Student Activities .... Ms. Beverly N. LEWIS
96 Director Purchasing/Equipment .... Mr. Philip L. MCCLUNG
40 Director Auxiliary Svcs/Bookstore .... Mr. Brian A. HICKS
12 Director Grady Swisher Center .... Ms. Mary B. KING
12 Director Mazie Woodruff Center .... Mr. TerCraig D. EDWARDS
12 Director Northwest Forsyth Center .... Ms. Kristie F. BAITY
12 Sr Dir Off-Campus/Stokes Cty Op .... Ms. Ann B. WATTS
88 Dean Educational Partnerships .... Dr. Susan Q. PHELPS
88 Dean Business and Industry .... Ms. Jennifer B. COULOMBE
88 Dean Health and Emergency Programs .... Mr. Wesley D. HUTCHINS

*Gaston College (G)

201 Highway 321 S, Dallas NC 28034-1499
County: Gaston FICE Identification: 002973
Unit ID: 198570
Telephone: (704) 922-6200 Carnegie Class: Assoc/Pub-S-SC
FAX Number: (704) 922-2323 Calendar System: Semester
URL: www.gaston.edu
Established: 1964 Annual Undergrad Tuition & Fees (In-District): $2,480
Enrollment: 5,606 Coed
Affiliation or Control: State/Local IRS Status: 501(c)3
Highest Offering: Associate Degree
Program: Occupational; 2-Year Principally Bachelor's Creditable
Accreditation: SC, ACBSP, ADNUR, DIETT, ENGT, MAC, PNUR

02 President .... Dr. Patricia A. SKINNER
10 VP Finance/Facilities/Operations .... Ms. Cynthia MCCRORY
05 Vice President of Academic Affairs .... Dr. Don AMMONS
20 Associate VP Academic Affairs .... Dr. Dewey DELLINGER
32 VP Student Services/Enrollment Mgmt .... Dr. Silvia Patricia RIOS-HUSAIN
35 Assistant VP for Student Services .... Ms. Audrey SHERRILL
103 VP Econ Workforce & Marketing/PR .... Dr. Linda L. GREER

04 Exec Admin Assistant to the Pres .... Ms. Sylvia DIXON
09 Director Insti Effectiveness .... Dr. Rex J. CLAY
08 Director Libraries .... Dr. Harry COOKE
13 Chief Technology Services Officer .... Ms. Savonne MCNEILL
38 Director of Counseling .... Ms. Jennifer NICHOLS
84 Director Enrollment Mgmt/Admission .... Dr. Terry BRASIER
06 Director of Registration/Records .... Ms. Alisa ROY
37 Director of Financial Aid .... Ms. Judy SCHNEIDER
19 Chief of Campus Police .... Mr. Billy LYTTON
15 Director Human Resources and Safety .... Mr. Todd BANEY
18 Director Facilities Management .... Mr. Wes LANDRUM
26 Director of Marketing/PR .... Ms. Stephanie MICHAEL-PICKETT
30 Chief Development Officer .... Vacant
96 Director Purchasing/Receiv/Shipping .... Mr. Chuck WRAY
21 Controller .... Mr. Bruce COLE
40 Director Bookstore .... Mr. Charles WILSON
49 Dean of Liberal Arts & Science .... Ms. Heather WOODSON
72 Dean Engr/Industrial Technologies .... Mr. Virgil COX
66 Dean Health Education .... Dr. Sharon STARR
50 Dean Business & Information Tech .... Ms. Michelle BYRD
51 Dean Cont Educ and Public Safety .... Dr. Karen LESS
12 Dean Lincoln Campus .... Dr. John MCHUGH
12 Dean Kimbrell Campus/Textile Ctr .... Dr. Joe KEITH
78 Dir Co-op Educ/Student Employ .... Ms. Brenda KINCAID

*Guilford Technical Community College (A)

PO Box 309, Jamestown NC 27282-0309
County: Guilford FICE Identification: 004838
Unit ID: 198622
Telephone: (336) 334-4822 Carnegie Class: Assoc/Pub-S-MC
FAX Number: (336) 819-2007 Calendar System: Semester
URL: www.gtcc.edu
Established: 1958 Annual Undergrad Tuition & Fees (In-State): $2,314
Enrollment: 15,134 Coed
Affiliation or Control: State IRS Status: 501(c)3
Highest Offering: Associate Degree
Program: Occupational; 2-Year Principally Bachelor's Creditable
Accreditation: SC, ACFEI, DA, DH, MAC, PTAA, RAD, SURGT

02 President .... Dr. Randy PARKER
03 Executive Vice President .... Mrs. Rae Marie SMITH
05 Vice President of Instruction .... Dr. Beth PITONZO
32 Vice Pres Student Support Services .... Dr. Quentin JOHHSON
11 Assoc Vice Pres Administrative Svcs .... Mr. Mitchell JOHNSON
10 Assoc VP of Business & Finance .... Ms. Nancy B. SOLLOSI
20 Assoc VP Student Support Services .... Dr. Alison WIERS
51 VP Corporate & Continuing Educ .... Mr. Leroy STOKES
30 Exec Dir Institutional Advancement .... Mr. Alan PIKE
12 Dean Greensboro Campus .... Mr. Manuel DUDLEY
12 Dean High Point Campus .... Ms. Janette N. MCNEILL
50 Dir Business & Industry Training .... Mr. Stephen CASTELLOE
30 Director of Development .... Vacant
15 Director of Human Resources .... Ms. Jean R. JACKSON
13 Chief Information Officer .... Ms. Sandie I. KIRKLAND
18 Director of Construction .... Mr. Dan J. SITKO
09 Director of Institutional Research .... Ms. Stephanie WRIGHT
07 Director of Admissions .... Mr. Jesse CROSS
35 Director of Student Life .... Ms. Berri V. CROSS
37 Director Financial Aid .... Ms. Lisa A. KORETOFF
19 Chief of Campus Police .... Ms. Dawn TEVEPAUGH
06 Registrar .... Mr. Sanjay RAMDATH
21 Controller .... Ms. Angela M. CARTER
40 Bookstore Manager .... Mr. Shawn G. DEE
36 Coordinator Career Services .... Mr. Daniel J. GRIGG
38 Director Counseling & Assessment .... Ms. Angela LEAK
29 Coord Resource Dev/Alumni Affairs .... Vacant
08 Dir of Library Services .... Ms. Mary LANE

*Halifax Community College (B)

PO Drawer 809, Weldon NC 27890-0809
County: Halifax FICE Identification: 007986
Unit ID: 198640
Telephone: (252) 536-4221 Carnegie Class: Assoc/Pub-R-S
FAX Number: (252) 536-4144 Calendar System: Semester
URL: www.halifaxcc.edu
Established: 1967 Annual Undergrad Tuition & Fees (In-District): $2,187
Enrollment: 1,560 Coed
Affiliation or Control: State/Local IRS Status: 501(c)3
Highest Offering: Associate Degree
Program: Occupational; 2-Year Principally Bachelor's Creditable; Business Emphasis
Accreditation: SC, DH, MLTAD

02 President .... Dr. Ervin V. GRIFFIN, SR.
04 Exec Assistant to the President .... Ms. Kimberly J. MACK
05 Vice Pres Academic Affairs .... Dr. Erica HOLMES
10 Vice President Admin Services .... Mr. Robert HOWARD
30 Vice Pres Institutional Advancement .... Dr. Dianne RHOADES
32 Dean Student Svcs & Enrollment Mgmt .... Dr. Barbara BRADLEY-HASTY
20 Dean of Curriculum Programs .... Ms. B. T. BROWN
06 Registrar .... Ms. Veliky DAWN
07 Director of Admissions .... Mr. James Bernard WASHINGTON
08 Director Learning Resources .... Ms. Laura M. SMITH
09 Dir of Institutional Effectiveness .... Vacant
40 Bookstore Manager .... Mrs. Doris GARNER
38 Director Counseling Services .... Ms. Teresa MAYLER
18 Chief Facilities/Physical Plant .... Mr. Ray HESTER
84 Director Enrollment Management .... Mrs. Julia HORSLEY
37 Director of Financial Aid .... Mrs. Tara KEETER
96 Purchasing Agent .... Mrs. Tina CURRY
15 Personnel Officer .... Mrs. Delois BATTLE-MERCER
13 Computer Network Manager .... Mr. Jerry THOMPSON
49 Div Chair Arts & Sciences .... Mr. Calvin STANSBURY
50 Div Chair Business/Commercial Tech .... Mr. Lateef BALOGUN
76 Division Chair Health Sciences .... Mrs. Kelly HARVEY
88 Div Chair Public Service Technology .... Ms. Precious VINES
75 Div Chair Vocation/Industrial Tech .... Mr. Hunter TAYLOR

*Haywood Community College (C)

185 Freedlander Drive, Clyde NC 28721-9453
County: Haywood FICE Identification: 008083
Unit ID: 198668
Telephone: (828) 627-2821 Carnegie Class: Assoc/Pub-R-M
FAX Number: (828) 627-3606 Calendar System: Semester
URL: www.haywood.edu
Established: 1965 Annual Undergrad Tuition & Fees (In-State): $2,208
Enrollment: 2,522 Coed
Affiliation or Control: State IRS Status: 501(c)3
Highest Offering: Associate Degree
Program: Occupational; 2-Year Principally Bachelor's Creditable; Technical Emphasis
Accreditation: SC, MAC

02 President .... Dr. Rose JOHNSON
05 Interim Vice Pres of Academic Svcs .... Dr. Buddy TIGNOR
32 VP Student/Workforce Development .... Dr. Laura LEATHERWOOD
10 Exec Director Business Operations .... Mrs. Karen DENNEY
13 Exec Dir Tech/Instruct Support Svcs .... Dr. Annemarie TIMMERMAN
18 Director of Campus Development .... Mr. Bill DECHANT
30 Dir of Institutional Advancement .... Mrs. Sherri MYERS
26 Director Marketing & Communications .... Ms. Debbie DAVIS
15 Director of Human Resources .... Mrs. Marsha STINES
84 Director of Enrollment Management .... Mrs. Jennifer HERRERA
37 Director of Financial Aid .... Ms. Sayward CABE
36 Career Devel Specialist/Recruiter .... Mrs. Meg CONNER
09 Data Manager Institutional Research .... Vacant

*Isothermal Community College (D)

PO Box 804, Spindale NC 28160-0804
County: Rutherford FICE Identification: 002934
Unit ID: 198710
Telephone: (828) 286-3636 Carnegie Class: Assoc/Pub-R-M
FAX Number: (828) 286-1120 Calendar System: Semester
URL: www.isothermal.edu
Established: 1964 Annual Undergrad Tuition & Fees (In-District): $2,566
Enrollment: 2,512 Coed
Affiliation or Control: State/Local IRS Status: 501(c)3
Highest Offering: Associate Degree
Program: Occupational; 2-Year Principally Bachelor's Creditable
Accreditation: SC

02 President .... Dr. Myra B. JOHNSON
11 Vice Pres Administrative Services .... Mr. Stephen MATHENY
05 VP Academic/Stdnt Svcs/Instl Assess .... Dr. Kim GOLD
103 VP Cmty/Workforce Educ/Inst Advance .... Mr. Thad HARRILL
32 Dean of Student Affairs .... Dr. Karen JONES
50 Dean of Business Sciences .... Ms. Kim ALEXANDER
49 Dean of Arts & Sciences .... Dr. Kathy ACKERMAN
75 Dean of Applied Science/Technology .... Ms. Amber THOMPSON
51 Dean of Continuing Education .... Mrs. Donna HOOD
12 Director of Polk Campus .... Mrs. Kate BARKSCHAT
20 Director Academic Development .... Mrs. Debbie PUETT
08 Director Library Services .... Mr. Charles WIGGINS
10 Controller .... Mrs. Amy M. PENSON
37 Financial Aid Officer .... Mr. Jeff BOYLE
26 Dir Marketing/Community Relations .... Mr. Mike GAVIN
18 Dir Plant Operations/Maintenance .... Mr. Rick EDWARDS
38 Director Student Counseling Testing .... Mr. Johnny SMITH
84 Director of Enrollment Management .... Ms. Alice MCCLUNEY
06 Registrar .... Ms. Kelly METCALF
96 Director of Purchasing .... Ms. Trish HUNTSINGER
13 Director of Information Technology .... Mr. Robby WALTERS
40 Bookstore Manager .... Mr. Nathan COLE

*James Sprunt Community College (E)

PO Box 398, Kenansville NC 28349-0398
County: Duplin FICE Identification: 007687
Unit ID: 198729
Telephone: (910) 296-2400 Carnegie Class: Assoc/Pub-R-S
FAX Number: (910) 296-1636 Calendar System: Semester
URL: www.jamessprunt.edu
Established: 1964 Annual Undergrad Tuition & Fees (In-State): $2,208
Enrollment: 1,563 Coed
Affiliation or Control: State IRS Status: 501(c)3
Highest Offering: Associate Degree
Program: Occupational; 2-Year Principally Bachelor's Creditable; Technical Emphasis
Accreditation: SC, MAC

02 Chief Executive Officer/President .... Dr. Lawrence L. ROUSE
05 VP of Curriculum Services .... Ms. June DAVIS
51 VP of Continuing Education .... Dr. Unita KNIGHT
10 VP of Admin & Fiscal Services .... Mr. John HARDISON
32 VP of Student Services .... Mr. Toney BOND
30 VP Coll Advance/Inst Effectiveness .... Mr. Robert TURNER
06 Registrar .... Ms. Patricia NORRIS
07 Admissions Specialist .... Ms. Lea W. MATTHEWS
37 Director Financial Aid/Vet Affairs .... Vacant
38 Director of Student Counseling .... Vacant
08 Director Library Services .... Ms. Patricia KLIMSCHOT
15 Dir Human Resources/Campus Safety .... Ms. Kristy BRINSON
51 Director Continuing Education .... Vacant
97 Director of General Education .... Mr. Andy CAVENAUGH
09 Dir Research/Plng/Instl Effective .... Mr. William (Bill) CANUETTE, JR.
18 Chief Facilities/Physical Plant .... Mr. Arthur KORNEGAY
96 Director of Purchasing .... Ms. Toni HENDERSON
55 Instr/Coord Evening/Weekend Svcs .... Mr. James THOMAS

*Johnston Community College (F)

PO Box 2350, 245 College Road, Smithfield NC 27577-2350
County: Johnston FICE Identification: 009336
Unit ID: 198774
Telephone: (919) 934-3051 Carnegie Class: Assoc/Pub-S-SC
FAX Number: (919) 209-2142 Calendar System: Semester
URL: www.johnstoncc.edu
Established: 1969 Annual Undergrad Tuition & Fees (In-District): $1,690
Enrollment: 5,635 Coed
Affiliation or Control: State/Local IRS Status: 501(c)3
Highest Offering: Associate Degree
Program: Occupational; 2-Year Principally Bachelor's Creditable
Accreditation: SC, DMS, MAC, RAD

02 President .... Dr. David N. JOHNSON
10 VP Finance & Administrative Svcs .... Mr. Michael CROSS
05 Vice Pres Curriculum Programs .... Mrs. Dee Dee D. DAUGHTRY
32 Vice Pres of Student Services .... Dr. Pamela J. HARRELL
30 VP Institutional Effectiveness .... Mrs. Dale A. O'NEILL
102 Executive Director of Foundation .... Ms. Twyla C. WELLS
13 Executive Director Info Technology .... Mr. Hal MURY
08 Director Learning Resources Center .... Ms. Christine B. ROBERTS
105 Internet Info Systems Coordinator .... Ms. Lisa H. MCLAURIN
06 Registrar .... Ms. Deena H. HENRY
37 Financial Aid Officer .... Mrs. Betty C. WOODALL
88 Director of Auditorium .... Mr. Ken H. MITCHELL
07 Director of Admissions/Counseling .... Mrs. Joan S. MCLENDON
103 Director Workforce Development .... Mrs. Joy T. CALLAHAN
26 Chief Public Relations Officer .... Mrs. Traci D. ASHLEY
18 Manager Facilities/Physical Plant .... Mr. Michael MASSEY
96 Coordinator of Purchasing .... Mr. Doug PATE

*Lenoir Community College (G)

231 Highway 58 South, Kinston NC 28502-0188
County: Lenoir FICE Identification: 002940
Unit ID: 198817
Telephone: (252) 527-6223 Carnegie Class: Assoc/Pub-R-M
FAX Number: (252) 233-6879 Calendar System: Semester
URL: www.lenoircc.edu
Established: 1958 Annual Undergrad Tuition & Fees (In-District): $2,327
Enrollment: 3,496 Coed
Affiliation or Control: State/Local IRS Status: 501(c)3
Highest Offering: Associate Degree
Program: Occupational; 2-Year Principally Bachelor's Creditable
Accreditation: SC, ACFEI, MAC, POLYT, RAD, SURGT

02 President .... Dr. Brantley BRILEY
51 VP Continuing Education .... Dr. Jay CARRAWAY
11 VP of Administrative Services .... Ms. Deborah SUTTON
05 VP Academic & Student Services .... Dr. Deborah GRIMES
10 Chief Financial Officer .... Ms. Deborah S. SUTTON
06 Registrar .... Mrs. Emily SMITH
84 Director Enrollment Mgmt/Admissions .... Ms. Pam MAZINGO
32 Dean of Student Services .... Mr. Levy BROWN
37 Director of Student Financial Aid .... Mrs. Reekitta DEAVER
27 Director of Information Services .... Mr. Lee WETHERINGTON
09 Dir Planning Rsch/Inst Effective .... Mrs. Karen HILL
15 Director Human Resources .... Ms. Lisa BARROW
18 Director of Maintenance .... Mr. Reed LOVICK
41 Dir Student Center/Athletic Pgms .... Mr. Stony WINE
21 Director of Financial Services .... Ms. Jessica MCMAHON
96 Director of Purchasing .... Mrs. Rhonda REEDER
26 Director of Mktg/Recruiting/Comm .... Mrs. Richy HUNEYCUTT
30 Director Institutional Advancement .... Mrs. Jeanne KENNEDY
36 Director Coop Ed/Job Dev/Placement .... Mrs. Frances GASKINS
08 Director of Learning Resources .... Mr. Carenado DAVIS
50 Dean of Business/Industrial/Technol .... Mr. Gary CLEMENTS
49 Dean of Arts & Sciences .... Dr. John Paul BLACK
76 Dean of Health Sciences & Nursing .... Dr. Alexis WELCH
89 Director of Freshman Studies .... Mrs. Evelyn KELLY
92 Dean/Director of Honors Program .... Dr. John Paul BLACK
93 Dean/Director of Minority Students .... Mr. Levy BROWN
94 Dean/Director of Women's Studies .... Dr. Deborah GRIMES
35 Director Student Activities .... Ms. Samara TAFT

*Martin Community College (H)

1161 Kehukee Park Road, Williamston NC 27892-9988
County: Martin FICE Identification: 007988
Unit ID: 198905
Telephone: (252) 792-1521 Carnegie Class: Assoc/Pub-R-S
FAX Number: (252) 792-0826 Calendar System: Semester
URL: www.martin.cc.nc.us
Established: 1967 Annual Undergrad Tuition & Fees (In-State): $1,836
Enrollment: 762 Coed
Affiliation or Control: State IRS Status: 501(c)3

Highest Offering: Associate Degree
Program: Occupational; 2-Year Principally Bachelor's Creditable
Accreditation: SC, DA, MAC, PTAA

02 President ... Dr. Ann R. BRITT
05 Dean Curriculum Pgm/Dean Stdnt Svcs ... Dr. Phyllis J. BROUGHTON
11 Dean of Administrative Services ... Ms. Cynthia MODLIN
04 Asst to Pres for Business/Industry ... Mr. Billy BARBER
37 Financial Aid Director ... Ms. Michelle LANE COBB
38 Counselor ... Dr. Thomas POWELL
06 Registrar ... Ms. Jennifer BALLS
07 Admissions Officer ... Mr. Michael CURRY
51 Int Exec Dir Continuing Education ... Mr. Walter V. WHITFIELD
75 Department Chair Technology ... Ms. Barbara M. DALY
50 Department Chair Business ... Ms. Bess L. PATTON
97 Department Chair General Studies ... Vacant
14 Systems Administrator ... Ms. Donna ROGERS
18 Director of Facilities ... Mr. Jackie F. HAISLIP
15 Human Resource Officer ... Ms. Rebecca P. WOOLARD
88 Telecommunication/Network Manager ... Mr. Elijah T. FREEMAN
09 Director of Institutional Research ... Ms. Catherine CURRIN

*Mayland Community College (A)

PO Box 547, Spruce Pine NC 28777-0547
County: Avery FICE Identification: 011197
Unit ID: 198914
Telephone: (828) 765-7351 Carnegie Class: Assoc/Pub-R-S
FAX Number: (828) 765-0728 Calendar System: Semester
URL: www.mayland.edu
Established: 1971 Annual Undergrad Tuition & Fees (In-District): $1,817
Enrollment: 1,327 Coed
Affiliation or Control: State/Local IRS Status: 501(c)3
Highest Offering: Associate Degree
Program: Occupational; 2-Year Principally Bachelor's Creditable; Technical Emphasis
Accreditation: SC, MAC

02 President ... Dr. John C. BOYD
04 Assistant to the President ... Ms. Kristabell KENNEDY
05 Vice Pres Instructional Services ... Mrs. Rhia CRAWFORD
10 Vice President Administrative Svcs ... Mr. Gerald HYDE
51 Assoc VP Cont Ed Programs/Workforce ... Mrs. Rita EARLEY
32 Dean of Students ... Mrs. Michelle MUSICH
66 Dean of Nursing Program ... Mrs. Sheryl YOUNG
49 Dean of Arts & Sciences ... Mrs. Beth MITCHELL
08 Dean Learning Resources Center ... Mr. Jon WILMESHERR
09 Institutional Effectiveness ... Mrs. Liz SILVERS
06 Registrar ... Mrs. Tracy E. WEBBER
88 Director of Basic Skills Programs ... Mr. Steve GUNTER
12 Director Avery County Programs ... Mrs. Melissa C. PHILLIPS
12 Director of Mitchell County Cont Ed ... Mr. Chris HELMS
12 Dean of Yancey County Cont Ed ... Dr. Monica S. CARPENTER
37 Director Student Financial Aid ... Mrs. Cassie FORBES
18 Director Facilities/Physical Plant ... Mr. Lee WHITTINGTON
13 Director Mgt Information Systems ... Mr. Tommy R. LEDFORD
105 Webmaster ... Mr. Greg LEDFORD
15 Interim Director Personnel Services ... Mrs. Anne CASTRO
26 Chief Public Relations Officer ... Mrs. Beth MORRIS
96 Coordinator of Purchasing/Equipment ... Mr. Sam PRESNELL

*McDowell Technical Community College (B)

54 College Drive, Marion NC 28752-8728
County: McDowell FICE Identification: 008085
Unit ID: 198923
Telephone: (828) 652-6021 Carnegie Class: Assoc/Pub-R-S
FAX Number: (828) 652-1014 Calendar System: Semester
URL: www.mcdowelltech.edu
Established: 1964 Annual Undergrad Tuition & Fees (In-District): $2,070
Enrollment: 1,264 Coed
Affiliation or Control: State/Local IRS Status: 501(c)3
Highest Offering: Associate Degree
Program: Occupational; 2-Year Principally Bachelor's Creditable
Accreditation: SC

02 President ... Dr. Bryan W. WILSON
05 Vice President for Learning ... Mrs. Shirley F. BROWN
20 Dean Academic Programs ... Dr. James BENTON
09 Director of Inst Effectiveness ... Mr. Ladelle HARMON
26 Director of External Relations ... Mr. Michael K. LAVENDER
13 Director of Technology/Info Systems ... Mr. Elmer R. MACOPSON
08 Director of Library Services ... Ms. Sharon P. SMITH
88 Director of Correctional Programs ... Mr. Frank D. SILVER
88 Director of Industrial Training ... Mr. Eddie SHUFORD
76 Director of Health Sciences ... Ms. Penny CROSS
06 Registrar ... Ms. Kelly HAMLIN
37 Dir Student Financial Aid/Counselor ... Ms. Kim M. LEDBETTER
36 Director of Student Enrichment Ctr ... Ms. Donna SHORT
88 Director of Adult Basic Skills ... Mrs. Teresa VALENTINO
88 Counselor/VA Director ... Mrs. Donna SHORT
51 Director of Continuing Education ... Mr. William B. LEDBETTER
88 Director Basic Law Enforcement Trng ... Mr. Stacy BUFF
07 Director of Admissions ... Mr. Wingate CAIN
30 Resource Development ... Ms. Susan BERLEY
106 Coordinator of Distance Education ... Mrs. Joan WEILER
16 Coord of Human Resources Devel ... Mrs. Mary L. LEDBETTER
18 Coord Maintenance/Custodial Svcs ... Mr. Carl COSTNER
88 Coord of Small Business Center ... Mr. H. Dean KANIPE
04 Exec Assistant to the President ... Mrs. Rhonda SILVER

*Mitchell Community College (C)

500 W Broad Street, Statesville NC 28677-5293
County: Iredell FICE Identification: 002947
Unit ID: 198987
Telephone: (704) 878-3200 Carnegie Class: Assoc/Pub-R-M
FAX Number: (704) 878-0872 Calendar System: Semester
URL: www.mitchellcc.edu
Established: 1852 Annual Undergrad Tuition & Fees (In-State): $2,201
Enrollment: 3,811 Coed
Affiliation or Control: State IRS Status: 501(c)3
Highest Offering: Associate Degree
Program: Occupational; 2-Year Principally Bachelor's Creditable
Accreditation: SC, ADNUR, MAC

02 President ... Dr. Tim BREWER
05 Vice President of Instruction ... Dr. Camille REESE
10 Vice Pres of Finance/Administration ... Mr. Richard J. LEFEVRE
103 Vice Pres Workforce Development/CEC ... Ms. Carol JOHNSON
32 Vice Pres Student Services ... Mr. Dan MANNING
09 Director Inst Effectiveness ... Ms. Mary Ellen GOLDSTEIN
08 Int Director of Learning Resources ... Ms. Vicki CALDWELL
37 Director of Financial Aid ... Ms. Candace COOPER
18 Exec Dir Facilities/Auxiliary Svcs ... Mr. Gary JOHNSON
29 Director Alumni Relations ... Vacant
26 Chief Public Relations Officer ... Ms. Kathy HOLLAND
30 Dir Development/College Relations ... Mr. Harry STILLERMAN

*Montgomery Community College (D)

1011 Page Street, Troy NC 27371-0787
County: Montgomery FICE Identification: 008087
Unit ID: 199023
Telephone: (910) 576-6222 Carnegie Class: Assoc/Pub-R-S
FAX Number: (910) 576-2176 Calendar System: Semester
URL: www.montgomery.edu
Established: 1967 Annual Undergrad Tuition & Fees (In-District): $1,830
Enrollment: 775 Coed
Affiliation or Control: State/Local IRS Status: 501(c)3
Highest Offering: Associate Degree
Program: Occupational; 2-Year Principally Bachelor's Creditable
Accreditation: SC, DA, MAC

02 President ... Dr. Mary P. KIRK
05 VP of Instruction/Continuing Ed ... Dr. Jeff HAMILTON
11 VP of Administrative Services ... Jeanette MCBRIDE
32 VP of Student Services ... Beth SMITH
97 Dean of Curriculum Programs ... Randy GUNTER
51 Dean of Continuing Education ... Gary SAUNDERS
102 Executive Director Foundation/Grant ... Gay ROATCH
26 Public Information Officer ... Michele HAYWOOD
106 Dir of Distance Learning/Prof Dev ... Julie M. KENNEDY
09 Dir Institutional Effectiveness ... Tim KENNEDY
13 Dir of Information Technology ... Mitch WALKER
04 Assistant to the President ... Korrie ERVIN
38 Director of Counseling Services ... Margo H. GADDY
07 Admissions Officer ... Karen FRYE
37 Director of Financial Aid ... Doni S. CODY
15 Coordinator Of Human Resources ... Susan MCLEOD
10 Accountant ... Anita PRESNELL
18 Director of Facilities ... Kevin MCNEILL
35 Student Activities Coordinator ... Riley BEAMAN

*Nash Community College (E)

522 N Old Carriage Road, Rocky Mount NC 27804-0488
County: Nash FICE Identification: 008557
Unit ID: 199087
Telephone: (252) 443-4011 Carnegie Class: Assoc/Pub-R-M
FAX Number: (252) 451-8201 Calendar System: Semester
URL: www.nashcc.edu
Established: 1967 Annual Undergrad Tuition & Fees (In-District): $1,776
Enrollment: 3,442 Coed
Affiliation or Control: State/Local IRS Status: 501(c)3
Highest Offering: Associate Degree
Program: Occupational; 2-Year Principally Bachelor's Creditable; Business Emphasis
Accreditation: SC, MAC, PTAA

02 President ... Dr. William S. CARVER, II
05 Vice President for Instruction ... Dr. Trent L. MOHRBUTTER
10 Executive Vice President and CFO ... Ms. Annette H. DISHNER
30 Assoc VP Institutional Advancement ... Ms. Pat E. DANIELS
08 Director of Library Services ... Ms. Deana GUIDO
88 Director Small Business Center ... Mr. Fred BROOKS
86 Assoc VP Community & Govt Affairs ... Dr. Keith SMITH
32 VP Student & Enrollment Svcs ... Mr. Larry K. MITCHELL
21 Assoc VP Finance ... Ms. Stephanie B. FISHER
14 Director Institutional Technology ... Mr. Jonathan VESTER
07 Director of Admissions ... Ms. Dorothy GARDNER
06 Registrar ... Ms. Kathy S. ADCOX
37 Director of Financial Aid ... Ms. Tammy LESTER
15 Director Human Resources ... Ms. Susan L. BARKALOW
04 Executive Asst to the President ... Ms. Susan H. NIPPER
31 Director Institutional Services ... Mr. James M. QUIGLEY
18 Director of Facilities ... Mr. C. Ted KENNEDY

*Pamlico Community College (F)

PO Box 185, Grantsboro NC 28529-0185
County: Pamlico FICE Identification: 007031
Unit ID: 199263
Telephone: (252) 249-1851 Carnegie Class: Assoc/Pub-R-S
FAX Number: (252) 249-2377 Calendar System: Semester
URL: www.pamlicocc.edu
Established: 1962 Annual Undergrad Tuition & Fees (In-District): $2,128
Enrollment: 500 Coed
Affiliation or Control: State/Local IRS Status: 501(c)3
Highest Offering: Associate Degree
Program: Occupational; 2-Year Principally Bachelor's Creditable; Technical Emphasis
Accreditation: SC, MAC, NDT

02 President ... Dr. Cleve H. COX
11 Vice Pres Administrative Svcs ... Mr. James CURRY
05 Vice Pres Instructional Svcs ... Dr. Larry W. GRACIE
32 Vice Pres of Student Services ... Mr. Jamie GIBBS

*Piedmont Community College (G)

PO Box 1197, 1715 College Drive, Roxboro NC 27573-1197
County: Person FICE Identification: 009646
Unit ID: 199324
Telephone: (336) 599-1181 Carnegie Class: Assoc/Pub-R-M
FAX Number: (336) 597-3817 Calendar System: Semester
URL: www.piedmontcc.edu
Established: 1970 Annual Undergrad Tuition & Fees (In-District): $2,221
Enrollment: 2,663 Coed
Affiliation or Control: State/Local IRS Status: 501(c)3
Highest Offering: Associate Degree
Program: Occupational; 2-Year Principally Bachelor's Creditable; Technical Emphasis
Accreditation: SC, EMT, MAC

02 President ... Dr. Walter C. BARTLETT
05 Vice Pres Instruction/Student Devel ... Mr. Michael S. DOSSETT
51 Vice President Continuing Education ... Dr. Doris W. CARVER
11 Vice Pres Administrative Services ... Mr. Robert E. SIMONS
12 Executive Director Caswell Campus ... Vacant
20 Dean Caswell Curriculum Programs ... Ms. Shelly T. STONE
32 Dean Student Development ... Mr. R. Leland PROCTOR
08 Dean Learning Resources Center ... Ms. Gretchen M. BELL
06 Coordinator Student Records ... Vacant
13 Director Mgmt Information Services ... Mr. William P. HILLE
09 Dir Research/Inst Effectiveness ... Dr. Jeff PATON
15 Director Personnel/Payroll ... Ms. Pamelia C. HOBBS
102 Director PCC Foundation Inc ... Ms. Elizabeth R. TOWNSEND
26 Director Public Information ... Ms. Bonnie H. DAVIS
37 Dir Financial Aid/Veterans Affairs ... Ms. Frances M. LUNSFORD
40 Manager Bookstore ... Ms. Tammy H. MORRIS
25 Director Grants ... Dr. Karen BOWEN
07 Coordinator Admissions ... Ms. Sheila D. WILLIAMSON
18 Coordinator Buildings and Grounds ... Mr. Bruce CHISHOLM
97 Dean General Educ/Devel Studies ... Dr. Dawn LANGLEY
75 Dean Technical/Occupational Pgms ... Ms. Judy S. BRADSHER
50 Dean Business Studies and Tech ... Dr. Sherry L. STOUT-STEWART
76 Dean Health Sciences and Human Svcs ... Ms. Kelly H. HOLDER

*Pitt Community College (H)

PO Drawer 7007, Greenville NC 27835-7007
County: Pitt FICE Identification: 004062
Unit ID: 199333
Telephone: (252) 493-7200 Carnegie Class: Assoc/Pub-R-L
FAX Number: (252) 321-4458 Calendar System: Semester
URL: www.pittcc.edu
Established: 1961 Annual Undergrad Tuition & Fees (In-State): $2,294
Enrollment: 8,544 Coed
Affiliation or Control: State IRS Status: 501(c)3
Highest Offering: Associate Degree
Program: Occupational; 2-Year Principally Bachelor's Creditable
Accreditation: SC, ADNUR, DMS, MAC, OTA, POLYT, RAD, RADDOS, RTT

02 President ... Dr. Dennis MASSEY
05 Vice President Academic Affairs ... Dr. Pamela HILBERT
11 Vice Pres Administrative Services ... Ms. Susan EVERETT
32 Vice President Student Development ... Dr. Donald R. SPELL
30 Vice Pres Institutional Advancement ... Mrs. Susan Q. NOBLES
20 Asst Vice Pres Academic Affairs ... Ms. Maria PHARR
35 Asst Vice Pres Student Development ... Mrs. Leslie D. ROGERS
13 AVP Information Technology/Services ... Mr. Rick OWENS
04 Administrative Asst to President ... Mrs. Kathy M. CARNES
31 Dean Economic & Cmty Development ... Dr. David LUSK
08 Dean Learning Resources ... Mr. Xudong JIN
09 Dean of Planning & Research ... Dr. Larry C. DENDY
46 Resource Development Director ... Vacant
15 Director of Human Resources ... Mr. Donald HEISEY
91 Director of Admin Computing ... Mrs. Janet MINTERN
06 Registrar ... Ms. Joanne T. CERES
38 Director of Counseling ... Dr. Kimberly WILLIAMSON
88 Director Basic Skills Program ... Ms. Marilyn BEAUMONT
18 Director of Facilities ... Mr. Walter Ashley DAIL
103 Director of JobLink Career Center ... Vacant
84 Director of Admiss & Enroll Mgmt ... Ms. Joanne T. CERES
41 Athletic Director ... Mr. William BAILEY
29 Director of Alumni Relations ... Mrs. Ashley SMITH
36 Director of Student Placement ... Ms. Sharon CERES
96 Director of Purchasing ... Mr. Wade QUINN
19 Chief-Public Safety/Campus Police ... Mr. Alan T. EDWARDS
88 Director Business & Industry Svcs ... Mrs. Mary PARAMORE
104 Director Study Abroad ... Mrs. Darlene SMITH-WORTHINGTON
09 Dir Institutional Effectiveness ... Dr. Brian MILLER
37 Director Financial Aid ... Mrs. Lisa M. REICHSTEIN

10 Business Manager Mr. Ricky BROWN
40 Manager of College Store Mrs. Judy HARRIS
106 Coord Instructional Tech/Dist Ed Mr. Mike CLENDENEN
55 Coord/Counselor Evening Programs Mr. Kendrick PRICE
50 Division Dean of Business Dr. Donald E. LEE
76 Division Dean Health Sciences Ms. Donna V. NEAL
49 Division Dean of Art & Sciences Dr. Stephanie MANLEY-ROOK
75 Div Dean Construct/Indus Tech Dr. Van MADRAY
61 Div Dean Legal Sci/Public Svc Dr. Dan MAYO

*Randolph Community College (A)

629 Industrial Park Avenue, Asheboro NC 27205
County: Randolph FICE Identification: 005447
Unit ID: 199421
Telephone: (336) 633-0200 Carnegie Class: Assoc/Pub-S-SC
FAX Number: (336) 629-4695 Calendar System: Semester
URL: www.randolph.edu
Established: 1962 Annual Undergrad Tuition & Fees (In-District): $2,296
Enrollment: 2,967 Coed
Affiliation or Control: State/Local IRS Status: 501(c)3
Highest Offering: Associate Degree
Program: Occupational; 2-Year Principally Bachelor's Creditable
Accreditation: SC, ADNUR

02 President Dr. Robert S. SHACKLEFORD, JR.
11 Vice Pres Administrative Services Ms. Daffie H. MATTHEWS
05 Vice Pres Instructional Services Ms. Anne B. HOCKETT
32 Vice President Student Services Mr. James W. KELLEY
101 Exec Asst to Pres/Board of Trustees Ms. Wanda C. BROWN
88 Dean of Basic Skills Ms. Amanda P. BYRD
62 Dean Library Services Ms. Deborah S. LUCK
106 Director Distance Education Mr. Devin A. SOVA
09 Director Planning & Assessment Ms. Karen R. RITTER
30 Assoc VP Institutional Advancement Ms. Susan V. MILNER
27 Director Communications Ms. Cathy D. HEFFERIN
15 Director of Human Resources Ms. Nancy BULLINS
37 Director Student Financial Aid Mr. Chad WILLIAMS
06 Director Enrollment Mgmt/Registrar Ms. Brandi F. HAGERMAN
18 Facilities Director Ms. Cindi J. GOODWIN
96 Purchasing Agent Ms. Sharon P. REYNOLDS
21 Controller Ms. Susan I. RICE
51 Dean Corporate & Continuing Educ Mr. Robert LESLIE
26 Senior Director Marketing Ms. Shelley W. GREENE
12 Director Archdale Center Ms. Lisa L. BOCK
88 Director ESTC/Coord Fire Services Mr. Brian C. CAUSEY

*Richmond Community College (B)

Box 1189, Hamlet NC 28345-1189
County: Richmond FICE Identification: 005464
Unit ID: 199449
Telephone: (910) 410-1700 Carnegie Class: Assoc/Pub-R-S
FAX Number: (910) 582-7028 Calendar System: Semester
URL: www.richmondcc.edu
Established: 1964 Annual Undergrad Tuition & Fees (In-District): $2,276
Enrollment: 2,455 Coed
Affiliation or Control: State/Local IRS Status: 501(c)3
Highest Offering: Associate Degree
Program: Occupational; 2-Year Principally Bachelor's Creditable; Technical Emphasis
Accreditation: SC, MAC

02 President Dr. W. Dale MCINNIS
32 Vice President for Student Services Ms. Saundra RICHARDSON
05 Vice President for Instruction/CAO Dr. Anthony CLARKE
10 VP Admin Svcs/Chief Financial Ofcr Mr. Brent BARBEE
51 VP for Workforce & Economic Develop Mr. Steve SMITH
08 Dean of Learning Resources Ms. Carolyn BITTLE
88 Director of Basic Skills Ms. Sherry BYRD
30 Dean of Inst Effectiveness & Acct Mr. William COUNCIL
06 Registrar Mr. John CURTIS
09 Director of Institutional Research Ms. Lucinda COLE
15 Director of Human Resources Ms. Gaye CLARK
26 Public Information Officer Ms. Anne MORRIS
21 Controller Ms. Debbie CASHWELL
37 Director Student Financial Aid Mr. Bruce BLACKMON
96 Purchasing Officer Mr. Martin BRIDGES
18 Director of Facility Services Mr. Glenn SIMS
38 Director Student Counseling Ms. Sharon GOODMAN
07 Director of Admissions Ms. Daphne STANCIL

*Roanoke-Chowan Community College (C)

109 Community College Road, Ahoskie NC 27910-9522
County: Hertford FICE Identification: 008613
Unit ID: 199467
Telephone: (252) 862-1200 Carnegie Class: Assoc/Pub-R-S
FAX Number: (252) 862-1358 Calendar System: Semester
URL: www.roanokechowan.edu
Established: 1967 Annual Undergrad Tuition & Fees (In-District): $2,229
Enrollment: 963 Coed
Affiliation or Control: State/Local IRS Status: 501(c)3
Highest Offering: Associate Degree
Program: Occupational; 2-Year Principally Bachelor's Creditable
Accreditation: SC

02 President Dr. Ralph G. SONEY
05 Dean of Curriculum Programs/CAO Dr. Pocahantas JONES
103 Dean Workforce & Student Devel Ms. Myra POOLE
88 Dean Basic Skills Mrs. Michelle MEISCHEID
32 Dean of Student Services Mrs. Wendy VANN
10 Controller Ms. Sheena SUGGS
08 Dean Learning Res/Info Systems Mrs. Monique MITCHELL
06 Registrar Mrs. Belinda SMITH
18 Int Dir Facilities/Physical Plant Mr. Charles STRICKLAND
38 Director Student Counseling Ms. Sandra COPELAND
106 Director Distance Learning Ms. Rita ROGERS
37 Director Financial Aid Mrs. Trisha SAWYER
09 Compliance & Data Director Mr. Juan E. VAUGHAN, II
07 Director of Admissions Mrs. Amy F. WIGGINS
35 Director Student Support Services Ms. Lorraine C. MITCHELL
15 Human Resource Coordinator Ms. Kathleen TOURE

*Robeson Community College (D)

PO Box 1420, Lumberton NC 28359-1420
County: Robeson FICE Identification: 008612
Unit ID: 199476
Telephone: (910) 272-3700 Carnegie Class: Assoc/Pub-R-M
FAX Number: (910) 272-3328 Calendar System: Semester
URL: www.robeson.edu
Established: 1965 Annual Undergrad Tuition & Fees (In-District): $2,305
Enrollment: 2,705 Coed
Affiliation or Control: State/Local IRS Status: 501(c)3
Highest Offering: Associate Degree
Program: Occupational; 2-Year Principally Bachelor's Creditable
Accreditation: SC, SURGT

02 President Dr. Charles V. CHRESTMAN
05 Vice Pres Instruction/Support Svcs Dr. Mark O. KINLAW
51 Vice Pres Adult & Continuing Educ Mr. R. Channing JONES
10 Vice President Business Services Mrs. Tami B. GEORGE
11 VP for Institutional Services Mr. Alphonzo MCRAE
55 Asst VP Public Svc/Appl Tech Pgms Mr. William L. LOCKLEAR
88 Asst VP Univ Transfer/Bus/Hlth Pgms Ms. Sheila A. REGAN
32 Asst Vice Pres Student Services Mr. Billy L. MAUNEY
07 Director of Admissions Ms. Judith A. REVELS
22 Director Affirm Action/Equal Oppty Mr. Alphonzo MCRAE
08 Director of Library Mrs. Maryellen CLARKE
38 Director Counseling & Testing Mr. Danford F. GROVES
06 Registrar Mrs. Beth CARMICAL
37 Director Financial Aid Ms. Teresa TUBBS
09 Director of Institutional Research Mrs. Lisa O. HUNT
18 Chief Facilities/Physical Plant Mr. Alphonzo MCRAE
102 Director College Foundation Ms. Rebekah R. LOWRY
36 Director Student Placement Mr. Danford F. GROVES
29 Director Alumni Relations Ms. Rebekah LOWRY
84 Director Enrollment Management Mrs. Beth CARMICAL
13 Systems Administrator Mr. James TAGLIARENI
15 Personnel Services Specialist Ms. Pam ROMANO
96 Purchasing Specialist Mr. Jason O. LEVISTER

*Rockingham Community College (E)

PO Box 38, Wentworth NC 27375-0038
County: Rockingham FICE Identification: 002958
Unit ID: 199485
Telephone: (336) 342-4261 Carnegie Class: Assoc/Pub-R-M
FAX Number: (336) 349-9986 Calendar System: Semester
URL: www.rockinghamcc.edu
Established: 1963 Annual Undergrad Tuition & Fees (In-District): $2,202
Enrollment: 2,408 Coed
Affiliation or Control: State/Local IRS Status: 501(c)3
Highest Offering: Associate Degree
Program: Occupational; 2-Year Principally Bachelor's Creditable
Accreditation: SC, SURGT

02 President Dr. Michael S. HELMICK
05 Vice President Instruction Dr. Jan G. OVERMAN
11 VP of Administrative Services Mr. Steven W. WOODRUFF
32 Vice Pres for Student Development Dr. Robert S. LOWDERMILK
88 Assoc VP Administrative Services Dr. E. Anthony GUNN
51 Dean of Continuing Education Ms. Laura F. COFFEE
50 Dean of Business Technologies Ms. Sandra K. GANN
75 Dean Industrial Technologies Mr. C. M. FRAZIER
79 Dean of Humanities/Social Sciences Ms. Joyce W. RUSSELL
81 Dean of Sciences & Math Ms. Celeste H. ALLIS
76 Dean of Health Sciences Ms. Tiffany D. MORRIS
08 Director of Library Services Ms. Kimberly SHIREMAN
09 Director Inst Research/Planning Mr. Kevin OSBORNE
30 Director Development/Foundation Ms. Gaye B. CLIFTON
14 Dir Technology Support Services Ms. Gretchen PARRISH
37 Director of Financial Aid Ms. Coe Ann TRENT
84 Director of Enrollment Services Mr. Derick SATTERFIELD
35 Director Student Life Mr. Dean MYRICK
40 Bookstore Manager Ms. Della J. GASTON
15 Director Human Resources Ms. Dana K. HUSKEY
27 Director Public Information Ms. Kim A. PRYOR
96 Director of Purchasing Mr. John PARRISH

*Rowan-Cabarrus Community College (F)

1333 Jake Alexander Blvd., South, Salisbury NC 28145
County: Rowan FICE Identification: 005754
Unit ID: 199494
Telephone: (704) 216-7222 Carnegie Class: Assoc/Pub-S-MC
FAX Number: N/A Calendar System: Semester
URL: www.rccc.edu
Established: 1963 Annual Undergrad Tuition & Fees (In-State): $2,192
Enrollment: 6,800 Coed
Affiliation or Control: State IRS Status: 501(c)3
Highest Offering: Associate Degree
Program: Occupational; 2-Year Principally Bachelor's Creditable
Accreditation: SC, ADNUR, DA, PNUR, RAD

02 President Dr. Carol SPALDING
05 Academic Vice President Dr. Rod TOWNLEY
10 Chief Financial Officer Ms. Janet SPRIGGS
32 Vice President Student Services Ms. Gaye MCCONNELL
51 Vice Pres Advancement & Cont Educ Mrs. Jeanie MOORE
27 Chief Information Officer Mr. Jeremy CAMPBELL
55 Director Evening & Weekend Oper Mr. Mike HENSLEY
20 Assoc Academic Vice President Mr. Ron SCOZZARI
13 Assoc Dean Information Technology Mr. Ian STEVENS
50 Dean Science Bus Math & Info Tech Dr. Marcy CORJAY
49 Dean Liberal Arts & General Educ Dr. Carolyn HOLBERT
88 Assoc VP Cont Educ Pre-College Stds Mrs. Cheryl MARSH
08 Director Learning Resource Center Mr. Rodney LIPPARD
103 Dean Corporate Programs Mrs. Ann MORRIS
72 Dean Eductional Resource Services Ms. Debra NEESMITH
71 Dean Spec Pgm/Coord Cosmetology Ctr Mrs. Lou DORTON-SHUE
18 Director Facilities Services Mr. Gayle PHIPPS
06 Director Registration & Records Mrs. Joan CREEGER
07 Director Admissions & Enrollment Mr. Rob DUNNAM
15 Director Human Resources Ms. Tina HAYNES
38 Director Counseling and Career Svs Mrs. Misty MOLER
37 Director Fin Aid & VA Benefit Mrs. Lisa LEDBETTER
26 Dir College Relations Mktg & Comm Ms. Paula DIBLEY
35 Director Student Life & Leadership Ms. Natasha LIPSCOMB
37 Dir Scholarships & Job Placement Vacant
21 Controller Mrs. Debbie HOPKINS
46 Director Curriculum Development Vacant
102 Executive Director RCCC Foundation Mrs. Celeste A. GRUNER
25 Director Grants Development Mrs. Daphne LEWIS
18 Chief of Facilities Mr. Jonathan CHAMBERLIN

*Sampson Community College (G)

PO Box 318, Clinton NC 28329-0318
County: Sampson FICE Identification: 007892
Unit ID: 199625
Telephone: (910) 592-8081 Carnegie Class: Assoc/Pub-R-S
FAX Number: (910) 592-8048 Calendar System: Semester
URL: www.sampsoncc.edu
Established: 1967 Annual Undergrad Tuition & Fees (In-District): $2,285
Enrollment: 1,650 Coed
Affiliation or Control: State/Local IRS Status: 501(c)3
Highest Offering: Associate Degree
Program: Occupational; 2-Year Principally Bachelor's Creditable
Accreditation: SC

02 President Dr. Paul C. HUTCHINS
05 Vice President of Academic Affairs Vacant
10 Vice President of Finance Mrs. Virginia S. LUCAS
11 Vice President of Administration Dr. William J. STARLING
32 Dean of Student Services Ms. Amy NOEL
07 Director of Admissions Mr. Oscar RODRIGUEZ
06 Registrar Mrs. Denise Q. RACKLEY
27 Public Information Office Ms. Erica JONES
37 Director Financial Aid Ms. Judye TART
08 Director Library Services Mr. Mark RUSHING
30 Resource Development Officer Mrs. Lisa TURLINGTON
15 Personnel Officer Mrs. Frankie K. SUTTER
35 Director Student Support Services Ms. Lisa DOBSON
51 Dean of Continuing Education Mrs. Ann BUTLER

*Sandhills Community College (H)

3395 Airport Road, Pinehurst NC 28374-8283
County: Moore FICE Identification: 002961
Unit ID: 199634
Telephone: (910) 692-6185 Carnegie Class: Assoc/Pub-R-M
FAX Number: (910) 695-1823 Calendar System: Semester
URL: www.sandhills.edu
Established: 1963 Annual Undergrad Tuition & Fees (In-State): $2,208
Enrollment: 4,547 Coed
Affiliation or Control: State IRS Status: 501(c)3
Highest Offering: Associate Degree
Program: Occupational; 2-Year Principally Bachelor's Creditable
Accreditation: SC, MLTAD, POLYT, RAD, SURGT

02 President Dr. John R. DEMPSEY
05 Provost Dr. John T. TURNER
10 Exec VP Business/Admin Svcs Dr. Richard GOUGH
09 Dean of Institutional Plng/Rsrch Mrs. Kristie SULLIVAN
32 Dean of Student Services Mrs. Kellie SHOEMAKE
35 Dean of Student LIfe Mr. David FARMER
04 Exec Assistant to the President Mrs. Wendy B. DODSON
10 Chief Business Officer Mrs. Brenda JACKSON
20 Dean of Instruction Dr. Rebecca ROUSH
51 Dean Continuing Education Ms. Andi KORTE
30 Dean of Institutional Advancement Mr. Rick H. SMITH
08 Dean of Learning Resources Dr. John STACEY
06 Director of Records & Registration Ms. Phyllis DOWDY
37 Financial Aid Officer Ms. Lindsey FARMER
106 Director of Distance Learning Ms. Wendy KAUFFMAN
14 Director of Computer Center Ms. Dorothy SYKES
19 Director of Security/Safety Mr. David REECE
18 Physical Plant Manager Mr. Melvin RITTER
15 Director Human Resources Ms. Wendy B. DODSON
21 Assistant Business Officer Mr. Joseph BROWN
26 Director of Marketing and PR Ms. Karen MANNING
40 Bookstore Manager Ms. Sandra DALES

*South Piedmont Community College (A)

PO Box 126, Polkton NC 28135-0126

County: Anson/Union — FICE Identification: 007985
Unit ID: 197850
Telephone: (704) 272-5300 — Carnegie Class: Assoc/Pub-R-M
FAX Number: (704) 272-5350 — Calendar System: Semester
URL: www.spcc.edu
Established: 1999 — Annual Undergrad Tuition & Fees (In-District): $2,356
Enrollment: 2,596 — Coed
Affiliation or Control: State/Local — IRS Status: 501(c)3
Highest Offering: Associate Degree
Program: Occupational; 2-Year Principally Bachelor's Creditable; Business Emphasis
Accreditation: SC, DMS, MAC, SURGT

02 President ... Dr. Stanley M. SIDOR
49 Interim VP School of Arts & Scis ... Mrs. Hayne WHITE
10 VP of Finance & Administration Svcs ... Mr. John DEVITTO
32 VP Student Success ... Mrs. Elaine CLODFELTER
04 Exec Assistant to President ... Ms. Rita ADAMS
72 VP School of Applied Science/Tech ... Mr. Stuart WASILOWSKI
13 VP Information Services ... Mr. Ernest SIMONS
08 Dean Learning Assessment & Resource ... Ms. Lynn GAMBON
06 Director of Records/Registrar ... Ms. Cathy HORNE
07 Director of Admissions/Enrollment ... Ms. Tracie BOONE
09 Director of Institutional Research ... Mr. Mark LUPTON
21 Director of Financial Services ... Ms. Michelle BROCK
26 Chief Public Information Officer ... Ms. Rosemary BRITT
15 Director Human Resources ... Ms. Susan R. FLAKE
18 Director Facility & Property Svcs ... Mr. William M. TRUETT
37 Director of Financial Aid ... Mr. John RATLIFF
84 Director Student Recruitment ... Mr. Scott COLLIER
96 Director of Purchasing ... Mr. Joe CAMERON
102 Exec Dir of Foundation & Cmty Rels ... Ms. Charlene BROOME
49 Dean Arts & Science ... Ms. Valerie JONES
76 Assoc Dean Allied Health ... Ms. Alice BRADLEY
88 Dean Learning Tech & Accountability ... Ms. Jill MILLARD
97 Dean Applied Science & Technology ... Dr. Maria LANDER
66 Associate Dean Nursing ... Ms. Joyce LONG
107 Associate Dean Professional Pgms ... Ms. Geri DUNCAN
88 Chair Academic Development ... Ms. Sharon CELLEMME
38 Director Counseling ... Ms. Serena JOHNSON
88 Director Adult Basic Skills Program ... Ms. Denise WILSON

*Southeastern Community College (B)

4564 Chadbourn Highway, PO Box 151,
Whiteville NC 28472-0151

County: Columbus — FICE Identification: 002964
Unit ID: 199722
Telephone: (910) 642-7141 — Carnegie Class: Assoc/Pub-R-M
FAX Number: (910) 642-5658 — Calendar System: Semester
URL: www.sccnc.edu
Established: 1964 — Annual Undergrad Tuition & Fees (In-State): $2,227
Enrollment: 1,923 — Coed
Affiliation or Control: State — IRS Status: 501(c)3
Highest Offering: Associate Degree
Program: Occupational; 2-Year Principally Bachelor's Creditable
Accreditation: SC, MLTAD

02 President ... Dr. Kathy MATLOCK
10 Vice President Operations/Finance ... Ms. Betty Jo RAMSEY
05 Vice Pres Academic/Student Affairs ... Dr. Morgan PHILLIPS
103 VP Workforce & Cmty Development ... Mrs. Beverlee S. NANCE
30 Exec Dean Institutional Advancement ... Mrs. Sue W. HAWKS
32 Dean of Students ... Ms. Kelly KINGRY
06 Dir of Student Records/Registrar ... Mrs. Sylvia MCQUEEN
08 Librarian ... Mrs. Kay HOUSER
07 Admissions/Records Assistant ... Ms. Shirley FLOYD
37 Director of Financial Aid ... Mr. Glenn HANSON
09 Director of Research & Assessment ... Vacant
15 Director Personnel Services ... Ms. Betty Jo RAMSEY
26 Director Marketing & Public Affairs ... Mr. Justin SMITH
21 Controller/Operations/Finance ... Ms. Donna TURBEVILLE
18 Chief Facilities/Physical Plant ... Ms. Betty Jo RAMSEY

*Southwestern Community College (C)

447 College Drive, Sylva NC 28779-8581

County: Jackson — FICE Identification: 008466
Unit ID: 199731
Telephone: (828) 339-4000 — Carnegie Class: Assoc/Pub-R-M
FAX Number: (828) 586-3129 — Calendar System: Semester
URL: www.southwesterncc.edu
Established: 1964 — Annual Undergrad Tuition & Fees (In-District): $2,224
Enrollment: 2,687 — Coed
Affiliation or Control: State/Local — IRS Status: 501(c)3
Highest Offering: Associate Degree
Program: Occupational; 2-Year Principally Bachelor's Creditable
Accreditation: SC, DMS, EMT, MAC, MLTAD, PTAA, RAD

02 President ... Dr. Don TOMAS
03 Executive Vice President ... Dr. Janet K. BURNETTE
05 Vice Pres Instructional Services ... Dr. Tom BROOKS
11 VP for Administrative Services ... Ms. Janet K. BURNETTE
51 VP Extension/Economic Development ... Ms. Susan MCCASKILL
12 Dean Macon Campus/Inst Dev ... Dr. Cheryl DAVIDS
13 VP Information Technology ... Mr. Ryan SCHWIEBERT
32 Dean of Student Services ... Dr. Phil WEAST
06 Registrar ... Ms. Christy DEAVER
08 Director of Learning Resources ... Mrs. Dianne LINDGREN
09 Inst Research & Planning Officer ... Mr. Delos D. MONTEITH
37 Director of Financial Aid ... Ms. Melody L. LAWRENCE

*Stanly Community College (D)

141 College Drive, Albemarle NC 28001-7458

County: Stanly — FICE Identification: 011194
Unit ID: 199740
Telephone: (704) 982-0121 — Carnegie Class: Assoc/Pub-R-M
FAX Number: (704) 982-0819 — Calendar System: Semester
URL: www.stanly.edu
Established: 1971 — Annual Undergrad Tuition & Fees (In-District): $2,208
Enrollment: 3,009 — Coed
Affiliation or Control: State/Local — IRS Status: 501(c)3
Highest Offering: Associate Degree
Program: Occupational; 2-Year Principally Bachelor's Creditable
Accreditation: SC, MAC, MLTAD

02 President ... Dr. Brenda KAYS
05 Exec VP Student/Academic Affairs ... Mrs. Robin MCCREE
10 Chief Financial Officer ... Mrs. Becky WALL
13 Vice Pres InfoTechnology Services ... Mr. Joel ALLEN
51 VP Cont Ed & Crutchfield Campus ... Vacant
04 Exec Assistant to the President ... Mrs. Gaye WOOD
26 Director Marketing & Communication ... Mrs. Michelle PEIFER
32 Interim Dean of Students ... Mr. Tony OETTINGER
36 Dean Stdnt Outrch/Career Plng/Plcmt ... Mrs. Kathy GARDNER
76 Dean Health & Public Svcs ... Dr. Tammy CRUMP
50 Dean Business & Technology ... Mrs. Merlin AMIRTHARAJ
06 Assoc Dean of Records/Registrar ... Mrs. Kristina EUDY
07 Assoc Dean of Admissions/Counseling ... Mrs. Denise ROSS
20 Assoc Dean of Academic Affairs ... Vacant
21 Controller ... Mrs. Debra HARWOOD
18 Director of Physical Plant ... Mr. David HINSON
88 Director of Learning Technologies ... Dr. Jana ULRICH
102 Foundation Director ... Mrs. Janet SISTARE
37 Associate Dean Financial Aid ... Ms. Petra FIELDS
15 Director Human Resources ... Miss Donna KIMREY
08 Director Library Services ... Mrs. Erin ALLEN
88 Director Basic Skills ... Ms. Dianne COOKER
24 Dir Testing/Media Specialist Svcs ... Mr. Mark SAMPLE
96 Purchasing Agent ... Mrs. Shelley OSBORNE

*Surry Community College (E)

630 S Main Street, Dobson NC 27017-0304

County: Surry — FICE Identification: 002970
Unit ID: 199768
Telephone: (336) 386-8121 — Carnegie Class: Assoc/Pub-R-M
FAX Number: (336) 386-8951 — Calendar System: Semester
URL: www.surry.edu
Established: 1964 — Annual Undergrad Tuition & Fees (In-State): $2,146
Enrollment: 3,497 — Coed
Affiliation or Control: State — IRS Status: 501(c)3
Highest Offering: Associate Degree
Program: Occupational; 2-Year Principally Bachelor's Creditable
Accreditation: SC, MAC, PTAA

02 President ... Dr. David R. SHOCKLEY
05 Vice Pres Curriculum Programs ... Dr. Jami WOODS
10 Vice President for Finance ... Mr. Tony L. MARTIN
32 Vice Pres Student Development ... Mrs. Jamie P. CHILDRESS
45 Vice Pres Planning/Rsrch/Assessment ... Dr. Anne R. HENNIS
51 VP Corporate & Cont Education ... Dr. George O. SAPPENFIELD
11 Vice Pres of Administrative Svcs ... Mrs. Susan PENDERGRAFT
13 Vice President Technology Services ... Dr. Candace HOLDER
49 Dean of Arts & Sciences ... Ms. Connie WOLFE
50 Dean of Business/Tech/Hlth Sciences ... Mr. Mike B. MILLER
55 Assoc Dean Evening Operations ... Ms. Sabra L. RICE
08 Assoc Dean of Learning Resources ... Dr. David WRIGHT
84 Assoc Dean Enrollment Mgmt ... Mr. Brian WEBB
37 Director Financial Aid ... Mrs. Andrea SIMPSON
14 Director Computer Center ... Ms. Rhonda L. HAZELWOOD
18 Director of Physical Facilities ... Mr. Randy ROGERS
31 Director Auxiliary Services ... Ms. Debbie WOLFE
41 Athletic Director ... Mr. Mark TUCKER
07 Director of Admissions ... Mrs. Renita HAZELWOOD
19 Chief Campus Police ... Mr. Martin W. SHROPSHIRE
96 Director of Purchasing ... Mrs. Cindy A. GALLIMORE
35 Director Student Activities ... Mr. Tony V. SEARCY
15 Human Resources Generalist ... Mrs. Melonie WEATHERS

*Tri-County Community College (F)

21 Campus Circle, Murphy NC 28906-7919

County: Cherokee — FICE Identification: 009430
Unit ID: 199795
Telephone: (828) 837-6810 — Carnegie Class: Assoc/Pub-R-S
FAX Number: (828) 837-0028 — Calendar System: Semester
URL: www.tricountycc.edu
Established: 1964 — Annual Undergrad Tuition & Fees (In-State): $2,266
Enrollment: 1,446 — Coed
Affiliation or Control: State — IRS Status: 501(c)3
Highest Offering: Associate Degree
Program: Occupational; 2-Year Principally Bachelor's Creditable; Technical Emphasis
Accreditation: SC, MAC

02 President ... Dr. Donna TIPTON-ROGERS
11 Exec Vice Pres for Operations ... Vacant
05 VP for Instructional Services ... Ms. Linda LOVINGOOD
09 VP for Institutional Effectiveness ... Dr. Steve WOOD
13 Dir of Computing & Information Mgt ... Mr. Jason OUTEN
30 Vice Pres for Resource Development ... Dr. Terrie KELLY
103 Dir of Economic & Workforce Develop ... Mr. Paul WORLEY
45 VP College & Community Initiatives ... Mr. Bo GRAY
12 Asst to Pres Graham Cty Operations ... Ms. Charlene WOOD
88 Dean Plng/Research Student Engage ... Dr. Jason CHAMBERS
10 Chief Financial Officer ... Mr. Bill VESPASIAN
15 Director of Human Resources ... Ms. Sallie BAKER
91 Systems Administrator/Data Base Mgr ... Mr. Wes CHASTAIN
08 Dean Learning Resources & Assessmt ... Ms. Linda KRESSAL
106 Distance Learning Coordinator ... Vacant
38 Coordinator Career/Counseling/Test ... Ms. Linda HOWELL
26 Communications Officer ... Vacant
06 Registrar Curriculum ... Ms. Holly HYDE
37 Director of Financial Aid ... Ms. Diane OWL
96 Purchasing Agent ... Ms. Judy OWENBY
32 Director of Student Affairs ... Vacant

*Vance-Granville Community College (G)

PO Box 917, Henderson NC 27536-0917

County: Vance — FICE Identification: 009903
Unit ID: 199838
Telephone: (252) 492-2061 — Carnegie Class: Assoc/Pub-R-M
FAX Number: (252) 430-0460 — Calendar System: Semester
URL: www.vgcc.edu
Established: 1969 — Annual Undergrad Tuition & Fees (In-State): $1,694
Enrollment: 4,314 — Coed
Affiliation or Control: State Related — IRS Status: 501(c)3
Highest Offering: Associate Degree
Program: Occupational; 2-Year Principally Bachelor's Creditable
Accreditation: SC, MAC, RAD

02 President ... Dr. Stelfanie WILLIAMS
05 Vice President of Instruction ... Dr. Angela BALLENTINE
10 Vice Pres for Finance & Operations ... Mr. Matt WILLIAMS
13 Vice Pres Information Technology ... Dr. Kenneth A. LEWIS, JR.
30 Vice President of Inst Advancement ... Ms. JoAnna JONES
32 Vice President of Student Affairs ... Mr. A. Gene PURVIS
31 Vice Pres Cmty/Economic Development ... Ms. Vanessa JONES
12 Dean South Campus ... Ms. Cecilia B. WHEELER
12 Dean Franklin County Campus ... Ms. Bobbie Jo C. MAY
12 Dean Warren County Campus ... Mr. George A. HENDERSON
08 Director Learning Resources Center ... Mr. Dave TRUDEAU
06 Registrar ... Ms. Kathy KTUL
15 Director of Human Resources ... Ms. Katherine WILLIAMSON
37 Director Financial Aid ... Mr. Frank A. CLARK
18 Director of Plant Operations ... Mr. Jack PUCKETT
27 Director of Marketing ... Ms. Elaine STEM
38 Director Student Counseling ... Vacant
07 Director of Admissions ... Ms. Tonya WADDLE
09 Director of Institutional Research ... Dr. Rodney FOTH
40 Bookstore Manager ... Ms. Sandra NEWTON

*Wake Technical Community College (H)

9101 Fayetteville Road, Raleigh NC 27603-5696

County: Wake — FICE Identification: 004844
Unit ID: 199856
Telephone: (919) 866-5000 — Carnegie Class: Assoc/Pub-U-MC
FAX Number: (919) 779-3360 — Calendar System: Semester
URL: www.waketech.edu
Established: 1958 — Annual Undergrad Tuition & Fees (In-District): $2,380
Enrollment: 19,138 — Coed
Affiliation or Control: State/Local — IRS Status: 501(c)3
Highest Offering: Associate Degree
Program: Occupational; 2-Year Principally Bachelor's Creditable
Accreditation: SC, ACFEI, DA, DH, MAC, MLTAD, RAD, SURGT

02 President ... Dr. Stephen C. SCOTT
03 Executive Vice President ... Mr. Gerald A. MITCHELL
102 SVP College Dev/Exec Dir Foundation ... Mr. O. Mort CONGLETON
43 General Counsel/VP Legal Services ... Ms. Clay T. HINES
26 AVP Communications ... Mrs. Laurie C. CLOWERS
05 Senior VP Curriculum Education Svcs ... Mr. Bryan K. RYAN
32 Senior VP Student Services ... Mrs. Rita H. JERMAN
51 Senior VP Continuing Education Svcs ... Mr. Samuel STRICKLAND
10 SVP of Financial & Business Svcs ... Mr. Arthur W. ANDREWS
18 Facility Engineering Officer ... Mr. Wendell B. GOODWIN
13 Chief Information Officer ... Dr. Darryl D. MCGRAW
12 VP Northern Wake Campus & HR ... Dr. D. Gayle GREENE
20 AVP Arts and Sciences ... Ms. Tonya FORBES
20 AVP Career Programs ... Ms. Sandra DIETRICH
12 AVP Campus Operations ... Mr. Anthony M. CAISON
84 AVP Enrollment Services ... Mr. John W. SAPARILAS
15 Chief Human Resource Officer ... Ms. Benita I. CLARK
21 Chief Accounting Officer ... Ms. Marla L. TART
10 Chief Business Officer ... Mrs. Debra S. WALLACE
46 Dean IE and Accreditation ... Dr. John B. BOONE
30 Director of Development ... Mrs. Stephanie S. LAKE
25 Dean Sponsored Pgms & Fed Relations ... Mrs. Carol C. WHITE
06 Dean Enrollment/Records/Registrar ... Mrs. Amanda T. ROBERTS
06 Dean Records & Reg/Registrar CE ... Ms. Margaret R. ROBERTON
35 Dean of Student Development ... Mr. Mark T. GIBSON
72 Dean Educ Svcs & Technology ... Mr. Ray L. TIMS
37 Dean Financial Aid and Veterans ... Mrs. Regina M. HUGGINS

35 Dean Student Svcs Northen Campus ... Mrs. Karen B. PHINAZEE
88 Sr Dir BioNetwork Learning Center ... Ms. Ana M. MCCLANAHAN
38 Dean Advising/Retention ... Mr. Kevin A. BROWN
07 Dean Admissions/Outreach Services ... Ms. Susan R. BLOOMFIELD
08 Dean Library Services ... Ms. Jackie L. CASE
27 Director Creative Services ... Mrs. Francie W. SANDERSON
36 Dean Career Readiness & Employment ... Mrs. Deborah L. HADLEY
76 Dean Health Sciences Campus ... Mrs. Dianne B. HINSON
81 Dean Mathematics/Sciences Div ... Dr. Cheryl L. KEETON
79 Dean Arts/Humanities/Soc Sci Div ... Dr. Diane E. LODDER
50 Dean Business Technology ... Mr. Walter MARTIN
75 Interim Dean Applied Technologies ... Mr. Samuel E. WELLS
12 Academic Dean Western Wake Campus ... Mr. James A. ROBERSON
55 Dean Evening Division ... Ms. Pamela M. LITTLE
77 Dean Computer & Engineering Tech ... Ms. Angela L. BEQUETTE
88 Dean of Basic Skills ... Mrs. Susan B. PAYNE
50 Dean of Business & Industry ... Mr. Wayne A. LOOTS

*Wayne Community College (A)

3000 Wayne Memorial Drive Box 8002,
Goldsboro NC 27533-8002
County: Wayne
FICE Identification: 002980
Unit ID: 199892
Telephone: (919) 735-5151
Carnegie Class: Assoc/Pub-R-M
FAX Number: (919) 736-9425
Calendar System: Semester
URL: www.waynecc.edu
Established: 1957
Annual Undergrad Tuition & Fees (In-District): $2,300
Enrollment: 3,714
Coed
Affiliation or Control: State/Local
IRS Status: 501(c)3
Highest Offering: Associate Degree
Program: Occupational; 2-Year Principally Bachelor's Creditable
Accreditation: SC, ADNUR, DA, DH, MAC, PNUR

02 President ... Dr. Kay H. ALBERTSON
05 VP Academic and Student Services ... Dr. Peggy S. TEAGUE
32 AVP Academic and Student Services ... Mr. Gene SMITH
51 VP Continuing Education Services ... Mr. Ray BURRELL
30 Assoc VP Institutional Advancement ... Mr. Bill T. THOMPSON
72 Division Head Applied Technologies ... Mr. Ernie WHITE
49 Division Head Arts & Sciences ... Dr. Tracey IVEY
50 Div Head Business & Computer Tech ... Ms. Beth HOOKS
76 Division Head Allied Health ... Mrs. Pattie PFEIFFER
88 Division Head Public Safety ... Ms. Beverly DEANS
62 Head Librarian ... Dr. Aletha ANDREW
12 Coordinator Seymour Johnson AFB ... Mrs. Dori FRASER
92 Honors Program Coordinator ... Mr. Brandon JENKINS
45 Chief Admin Support Services ... Mr. Don MAGOON
106 Coord Distance Education ... Mr. Randall SHEARON
105 Coord Educ Tech Services/Webmaster ... Mr. Brent HOOD
13 Director Information Systems ... Ms. Katherine JONES
18 Chief Facilities/Physical Plant ... Mr. Edward E. FARRIS
19 Chief Security ... Mr. Willie L. BRINSON
40 Director Bookstore ... Mrs. Trellie HERRING
88 Ex Dir Wayne Bus/Indus Ctr & WORKS ... Mrs. Diane IVEY
07 Director Admissions & Records ... Mrs. Susan M. SASSER
37 Director Student Financial Aid ... Mrs. Brenda D. MERCER
84 Dir Student Devel/Enrollment Mgmt ... Mrs. Joanna MORRISETTE
36 Coord Coop Ed and Career Services ... Mrs. Lorie WALLER
78 Director Cooperative Programs ... Mrs. Anne MILLINGTON
35 Student Activities Coordinator ... Ms. Paige HAM
10 Chief Financial Officer ... Mrs. Joy KORNEGAY
96 Accountant/Equipment Coordinator ... Mr. Mark R. JOHNSON
102 Executive Director of Foundation ... Mr. Jack KANNAN
26 Public Information Officer ... Ms. Tara HUMPHRIES
16 Director Personnel ... Mrs. Ina R. RAWLINSON
55 Evening Coord/Security Services ... Mr. James BYNUM

*Western Piedmont Community College (B)

1001 Burkemont Avenue, Morganton NC 28655-4504
County: Burke
FICE Identification: 002982
Unit ID: 199908
Telephone: (828) 438-6000
Carnegie Class: Assoc/Pub-R-M
FAX Number: (828) 438-6015
Calendar System: Semester
URL: www.wpcc.edu
Established: 1964
Annual Undergrad Tuition & Fees (In-State): $2,200
Enrollment: 2,995
Coed
Affiliation or Control: State
IRS Status: 501(c)3
Highest Offering: Associate Degree
Program: Occupational; 2-Year Principally Bachelor's Creditable
Accreditation: SC, ADNUR, DA, MAC, MLTAD

02 President ... Dr. Jim W. BURNETT
10 Exec Vice Pres/Chief Financial Ofcr ... Mr. Malone C. MCNEELY
05 Vice President Academic Affairs ... Dr. Chad BLEDSOE
32 Vice President Student Development ... Mr. Atticus J. SIMPSON
51 Dean of Continuing Education ... Mr. Lee KISER
35 Dean of Student Services ... Ms. Susan WILLIAMS
08 Dean Learning Resources/Technology ... Mr. Daniel R. SMITH
54 Dean Science/Engineering/Math ... Mr. Michael DANIELS
79 Dean Humanities/Social Sciences ... Mrs. Mary C. SAFFORD
76 Dean Health Sciences ... Dr. Linda S. SATEY
50 Dean Business Technologies ... Mrs. Leslie MCKESSON
21 Controller ... Mrs. Sandra K. HOILMAN
06 Registrar ... Mrs. Joan P. HOGAN
15 Director Human Resources ... Ms. Lisa H. SESSIONS
07 Director of Admissions ... Mrs. Jennifer PROPST
37 Director Student Financial Aid ... Mr. Keith A. CONLEY
91 Director Management Info Systems ... Ms. Nancy E. NORRIS
09 Director of Planning & Research ... Mr. William L. LEFEVERS
96 Director of Purchasing ... Ms. Linda CARSWELL
18 Director of Maintenance ... Vacant

*Wilkes Community College (C)

1328 S Collegiate Drive, Wilkesboro NC 28697-0120
County: Wilkes
FICE Identification: 002983
Unit ID: 199926
Telephone: (336) 838-6100
Carnegie Class: Assoc/Pub-R-M
FAX Number: (336) 903-3219
Calendar System: Semester
URL: www.wilkescc.edu
Established: 1965
Annual Undergrad Tuition & Fees (In-State): $2,328
Enrollment: 2,519
Coed
Affiliation or Control: State
IRS Status: 501(c)3
Highest Offering: Associate Degree
Program: Occupational; 2-Year Principally Bachelor's Creditable; Technical Emphasis
Accreditation: SC, DA, MAC

02 President ... Dr. Gordon G. BURNS
05 Sr VP of Instruction ... Dr. Dean E. SPRINKLE
10 Senior VP of Administration ... Mr. D. Morgan FRANCIS, JR.
20 VP of Instr Support/Student Svcs ... Ms. Kim E. FAW
103 VP Adv Industrial & Workforce Dev ... Mr. John HAUSER
13 Assoc VP Information Technology ... Mr. Mike WINGLER
12 Assoc VP Ashe Campus ... Mr. Christopher D. ROBINSON
12 Director Alleghany Center ... Ms. Jayne PHIPPS-BOGER
09 Inst Effectiveness Exec Director ... Mr. J. Kelly PIPES, III
50 Dean Business/Public Svc Tech Div ... Mrs. Robin PHILLIPS-HAUSER
76 Dean Health Sciences Division ... Vacant
49 Dean Arts & Sciences Division ... Ms. Blair M. HANCOCK
18 Exec Director/Facilities Services ... Mr. Ronald DOLLYHITE
30 Exec Director/Endowment ... Ms. Allison PHILLIPS
15 Director of Human Resources ... Mr. Tracy D. MCENTIRE
06 Registrar ... Ms. Melonie KILBY
07 Director of Admissions ... Mr. Scott JOHNSON
37 Director of Financial Aid ... Ms. Vickie G. CALL
38 Director Counseling & Career Svcs ... Dr. Lynda K. BLACK
32 Director Enrollment Mgmt/Stdnt Life ... Ms. Jane BOWMAN
08 Interim Director Learning Resources ... Ms. Christy EARP
38 Director Student Support Services ... Ms. Angela SCHEUERMANN
40 Bookstore Manager ... Ms. Lynn OSBORNE
26 PIO & Relations Officer ... Ms. Amber HERMAN
19 Safety & Security Manager ... Mr. Jamie MCGUIRE

*Wilson Community College (D)

902 Herring Avenue, Wilson NC 27893-3310
County: Wilson
FICE Identification: 004845
Unit ID: 199953
Telephone: (252) 291-1195
Carnegie Class: Assoc/Pub-R-M
FAX Number: (252) 243-7148
Calendar System: Semester
URL: www.wilsoncc.edu
Established: 1958
Annual Undergrad Tuition & Fees (In-State): $2,313
Enrollment: 1,873
Coed
Affiliation or Control: State
IRS Status: 501(c)3
Highest Offering: Associate Degree
Program: Occupational; 2-Year Principally Bachelor's Creditable
Accreditation: SC, SURGT

02 President ... Dr. Rusty STEPHENS
05 Vice Pres Instruction/Student Devel ... Dr. Denise L. SESSOMS
10 Vice Pres for Finance & Admin Svcs ... Mr. Hadie C. HORNE
51 Dean of Cont Educ/Sustainability ... Mr. Robert D. HOLSTEN
32 Dean of Student Development ... Mr. Don L. BOYETTE
76 Associate Dean of Allied Health ... Ms. Glenda P. BONDURANT
88 Assoc Dean Indust Tech/Public Svcs ... Ms. NaDene TUCKER
49 Assoc Dean Arts & Sciences/ Dev Std ... Ms. Debra S. HOLLEY
50 Assoc Dean of Business/Comp Tech ... Vacant
15 Dir of Human Resources/Marketing ... Ms. Denise M. HORNE
08 Head Librarian ... Mr. Gerry J. O'NEILL
45 Planning & Research Director ... Ms. Pat B. PERRY
21 Controller ... Ms. Jessica S. JONES
07 Director of Admissions/Registrar ... Mr. Leonard W. MANSFIELD
18 Director of Facilities ... Mr. Tim H. STRICKLAND
37 Dir of Financial Aid/Vet Affairs ... Ms. Lisa SHEARIN
102 Director of Foundation ... Ms. Lynn WAGNER
13 Director of IT & Audit Services ... Mr. Jarvis MCBRIDE
96 Purchasing Manager ... Ms. Donna A. TURNER
40 Bookstore Manager ... Ms. Kaschia SPELLS

North Carolina Wesleyan College (E)

3400 N Wesleyan Boulevard,
Rocky Mount NC 27804-8630
County: Nash
FICE Identification: 002951
Unit ID: 199209
Telephone: (252) 985-5100
Carnegie Class: Bac/Diverse
FAX Number: (252) 985-5231
Calendar System: 4/1/4
URL: www.ncwc.edu
Established: 1956
Annual Undergrad Tuition & Fees: $25,760
Enrollment: 1,402
Coed
Affiliation or Control: United Methodist
IRS Status: 501(c)3
Highest Offering: Baccalaureate
Program: Liberal Arts And General; Teacher Preparatory
Accreditation: SC, TED

01 President ... Mr. James A. GRAY, III
05 Vice President Academic Affairs ... Dr. Jay STUBBLEFIELD
10 Vice President of Finance ... Mrs. Loren W. LOOMIS-HUBBELL
30 Vice President of Development ... Mr. Michael PRATT
84 Vice President of Enrollment ... Mr. Bill ALLEN
32 VP Student Affairs/Dean of Students ... Mr. Randy WILLIAMS
09 Director of Institutional Research ... Mr. Larry KELLEY
06 Registrar ... Mr. Cliff SULLIVAN
08 Director of Library ... Mrs. Kathy WINSLOW
26 Director of Communications ... Mrs. Diane LEFILES
23 Director Wellness Ctr/College Nurse ... Vacant
36 Director Internship & Career Center ... Ms. Tiffany ALEXANDER
19 Director of Campus Security ... Vacant
41 Director of Athletics ... Mr. John THOMPSON
29 Director Alumni Rels/Annual Fund ... Ms. Cricket MORRIS
21 Controller ... Ms. Robin CHAMP
37 Director of Financial Aid ... Ms. Leah HILL
15 Director of Human Resources ... Mr. Darrell S. WHITLEY
18 Chief Facilities/Physical Plant ... Mr. David KNIGHT
07 Interim Director of Admissions ... Ms. Lori MELTON
38 Director Student Counseling ... Ms. Leslie VEACH
40 Manager College Store ... Ms. Rachel T. DIX

Pfeiffer University (F)

48380 US Highway 52 N / PO Box 960,
Misenheimer NC 28109-0960
County: Stanly
FICE Identification: 002955
Unit ID: 199306
Telephone: (704) 463-1360
Carnegie Class: Master's L
FAX Number: (704) 463-1363
Calendar System: Semester
URL: www.pfeiffer.edu
Established: 1885
Annual Undergrad Tuition & Fees: $22,900
Enrollment: 2,020
Coed
Affiliation or Control: United Methodist
IRS Status: 501(c)3
Highest Offering: Master's
Program: Liberal Arts And General; Teacher Preparatory; Professional
Accreditation: SC, MFCD, MUS, TED

01 President ... Mr. Michael C. MILLER
04 Executive Assistant to President ... Ms. Teena P. MAULDIN
11 Chief Operations Officer ... Vacant
10 Vice President for Finance ... Ms. Robin A. LESLIE
05 Provost/VP Academic Affairs ... Dr. Tracy Y. ESPY
84 VP for Enrollment Mgmt/Marketing ... Vacant
32 VP for Student Development ... Dr. Russell SHARPLES
30 Spec Asst to Pres for Ldrship & Adv ... Mr. Thad HENRY
07 Director of Undergrad Admissions ... Ms. Terry PARKER-JEFFRIES
20 Associate VP for Academic Affairs ... Dr. Alan BELCHER
06 Registrar ... Ms. Lourdes SILVA
15 Director of Human Resources ... Ms. Kathy ODELL
09 Director Institutional Rsrch/Plng ... Ms. Eva EISNAUGLE
26 Director Inst Communications ... Ms. Susan G. MESSINA
38 Director Counseling/Residence Educ ... Ms. Laura HERRICK
08 Acquisitions Librarian ... Mr. John MERCER, JR.
37 Director of Financial Aid ... Ms. Amy BROWN
13 Director of IT ... Mr. William SEWARD, II
07 Associate Director of Admissions ... Ms. Diane MARTIN
20 Dir of Academic Support Services ... Dr. Jim E. GULLEDGE
19 Dir of Campus Safety & Security ... Mr. Erik MCGINNIS
23 Director of Health Services ... Vacant
18 Director of Facilities ... Ms. Sharon K. BARD
41 Athletic Director ... Ms. Mary Ann SUNBURY
42 Minister to the University ... Rev. Dana MCKIM
36 Director of Career Services ... Vacant
35 Dir of Student Involvement ... Mr. Demond HAIRSTON
50 Dean of School of Business ... Dr. Kenneth BANDY
53 Dean of School of Education ... Dr. Dawn LUCAS
79 Dean of School of Humanities ... Dr. David HECKEL
81 Dean Sch of Natural & Health Sci ... Dr. Mark MCCALLUM
83 Dean Sch of Soc & Behav Sciences ... Dr. Donald POE, JR.
51 Director of School of Adult Studies ... Dr. Paulita BROOKER
88 Director of MHA Program ... Ms. Vernease MILLER
88 Exec Director Intl Business Studies ... Vacant
58 Director MS Org Leadership & Change ... Vacant
58 Director of MCE Program ... Rev. Kathleen KILBOURNE
102 Assoc VP Adv/Dir Corp & Found Rels ... Vacant
44 Director of Alumni & Annual Giving ... Vacant
39 Director of Residence Life ... Ms. Rebecca MCQUEEN
40 Bookstore Manager ... Ms. Dechelle ELLIS
12 Director of Triangle Campus ... Mr. Bennie L. FELTS

Piedmont Baptist College and Graduate School (G)

420 S Broad Street, Winston-Salem NC 27101-5197
County: Forsyth
FICE Identification: 002956
Unit ID: 199315
Telephone: (336) 725-8344
Carnegie Class: Spec/Faith
FAX Number: (336) 725-5522
Calendar System: Semester
URL: www.pbc.edu
Established: 1945
Annual Undergrad Tuition & Fees: $12,790
Enrollment: 524
Coed
Affiliation or Control: Independent Non-Profit
IRS Status: 501(c)3
Highest Offering: Doctorate
Program: Liberal Arts And General; Teacher Preparatory; Religious Emphasis
Accreditation: TRACS

01 President ... Dr. Charles W. PETITT
00 Chancellor ... Dr. Howard L. WILBURN
05 Provost ... Dr. Beth D. ASHBURN
11 Vice President of Operations ... Dr. Alan COX
20 Vice President of Academics ... Dr. Jeff MCCANN

58 Vice Pres of Graduate Studies .... Dr. Barkev TRACHIAN
30 Director of Advancement .... Dr. Jeffrey CRUM
06 Registrar .... Mrs. Darlene RICHTER
08 Librarian .... Mrs. Delores FULTON
32 Dean of Students .... Mr. Erich RICHTER
34 Dean of Women .... Mrs. Rebecca BOTTOMS

Queens University of Charlotte (A)

1900 Selwyn Avenue, Charlotte NC 28274-0001
County: Mecklenburg FICE Identification: 002957
Unit ID: 199412
Telephone: (704) 337-2200 Carnegie Class: Master's M
FAX Number: (704) 337-2517 Calendar System: Semester
URL: www.queens.edu
Established: 1857 Annual Undergrad Tuition & Fees: $15,780
Enrollment: 2,600 Coed
Affiliation or Control: Presbyterian Church (U.S.A.) IRS Status: 501(c)3
Highest Offering: Master's
Program: Liberal Arts And General; Teacher Preparatory; Professional; Business Emphasis
Accreditation: SC, ACBSP, ADNUR, BUS, MUS, NURSE, TED

01 President .... Dr. Pamela L. DAVIES
05 VP Academic Affairs & Provost .... Dr. Abiodun GOKE-PARIOLA
30 Vice Pres University Advancement .... Mr. James BULLOCK
84 Vice Pres Enrollment Management .... Dr. Brian RALPH
10 Vice Pres for Finance .... Mrs. Susan GARY
26 Vice Pres Marketing & Cmty Rels .... Mrs. Rebecca ANDERSON
45 VP Campus Planning and Services .... Mr. Bill NICHOLS
11 CFO & VP for Administration .... Mr. Matthew PACKEY
19 AVP Campus Safety & Security .... Mr. Clarence BIRKHEAD
29 Exec Director Alumni Relations .... Ms. Sara BLAKENEY
32 Dean of Students .... Dr. John DOWNEY
06 Registrar .... Mr. Edward ADAMS
07 Dir Tradition Undergrad Admissions .... Mr. Will LEE
09 Director of Inst Research & Assess .... Dr. Jamie SLATER
39 Director Residence Life .... Mr. Edward YOUNG
13 Chief Information Officer .... Mr. John CHAMPION
15 Director of Human Resources .... Ms. Teri ORSINI, SPHR
08 University Librarian .... Dr. Carol W. JORDAN
36 Int Dir Internships/Career Pgm .... Ms. Karen ARNIE
42 Chaplain/Director Campus Ministry .... Rev. J. Diane MOWREY
19 Chief of Campus Police .... Mr. Johnnie RAVENELL
41 Director of Athletics .... Ms. Jeannie KING
20 Asst Prov/Dir International Pgms .... Dr. Eric J. LIEN
04 Exec Director Pres Affairs .... Mrs. Tamara BURRELL
37 AVP Student Financial Services .... Mrs. Christy MAJORS
18 Facilities Manager .... Mr. Tim ESTEP
50 Dean of McColl School of Business .... Mr. Ronald SHIFFLER
49 Dean College of Arts & Sciences .... Dr. Lynn MORTON
53 Dean Cato School of Education .... Dr. Lynn MORTON
76 Dean Blair College of Health .... Dr. Kevin L. BURKE
60 Dean Knight School of Communication .... Dr. Erie FREEDMAN
55 Dean of Hayworth College Adult Stds .... Dr. Kevin BUTLER

Reformed Theological Seminary (B)

2101 Carmel Road, Charlotte NC 28226-6399
County: Mecklenburg Identification: 666785
Unit ID: 405924
Telephone: (704) 366-5066 Carnegie Class: Not Classified
FAX Number: (704) 366-9295 Calendar System: 4/1/4
URL: www.rts.edu
Established: 1992 Annual Graduate Tuition & Fees: $14,655
Enrollment: 306 Coed
Affiliation or Control: Independent Non-Profit IRS Status: 501(c)3
Highest Offering: Doctorate; No Undergraduates
Program: Professional; Religious Emphasis
Accreditation: &SC, &THEOL

00 Chancellor & CEO .... Dr. Robert C. CANNADA, JR.
01 President .... Dr. Michael A. MILTON
05 Academic Dean .... Dr. Michael J. KRUGER
10 Vice Pres Business Administration ... Mr. Stephen J. HALVORSON
30 Vice President Development .... Mr. Charlie DUNN
32 Dean Student Development ...... Dr. Rodney A. CULBERTSON, JR.
34 Dean of Women .... Mrs. Tari WILLIAMSON
07 Director of Admissions .... Mr. Stephane JEANRENAUD
08 Library Director .... Mr. Kenneth J. MCMULLEN
09 Director Institutional Assessment .... Mrs. Pauline M. STONE
06 Registrar .... Mrs. Angela P. QUEEN
13 Director Information Technology .... Mr. Todd WHITING

† Regional accreditation is carried under the parent institution in Jackson, MS.

St. Andrews University (C)

1700 Dogwood Mile, Laurinburg NC 28352-5598
County: Scotland FICE Identification: 002967
Unit ID: 199698
Telephone: (910) 277-5000 Carnegie Class: Bac/Diverse
FAX Number: (910) 277-5020 Calendar System: Semester
URL: www.sapc.edu
Established: 1896 Annual Undergrad Tuition & Fees: $32,050
Enrollment: 458 Coed
Affiliation or Control: Presbyterian Church (U.S.A.) IRS Status: 501(c)3
Highest Offering: Baccalaureate
Program: Liberal Arts And General
Accreditation: &SC, TED

01 President .... Mr. Paul BALDASARE
05 Vice Pres Acad Affs/Dean of College .... Dr. Robert J. HOPKINS
10 Vice Pres Business and Finance .... Ms. Terry LAUGHTER
11 Vice Pres Administration .... Mr. Glenn T. BATTEN
30 Vice Pres Institutional Advancement .... Vacant
84 Vice Pres Enrollment .... Mr. Jeff D. BENNETT
32 Dean of Students/Athletic Director .... Mr. Glenn T. BATTEN
06 Registrar .... Ms. Deborah A. SMITH
08 Director DeTamble Library .... Ms. Mary MCDONALD
14 Director of Computer Services .... Mr. Tony D. INSKEEP
15 Director Personnel Services .... Ms. Millie ENGLISH
18 Chief Facilities/Physical Plant .... Mr. William S. JAMES
29 Director of Alumni Relations .... Vacant
36 Director Career Services .... Ms. Renee P. JONES
37 Director Student Financial Aid .... Ms. Kimberly A. DRIGGERS
09 Director of Institutional Research .... Ms. Deborah A. SMITH
26 Director of Communications .... Ms. Melissa HOPKINS
35 Sr Assoc Dean of Students/Security .... Mr. Lewis STROUD
40 Online Bookstore .... Vacant
20 Associate Academic Officer .... Dr. Edna A. LOFTUS
96 Director of Purchasing .... Mr. William S. JAMES
07 Associate Director of Admissions .... Ms. Debbie BELL

† Regional accreditation is carried under the parent institution, Webber International University, Babson Park, FL.

Saint Augustine's University (D)

1315 Oakwood Avenue, Raleigh NC 27610-2298
County: Wake FICE Identification: 002968
Unit ID: 199582
Telephone: (919) 516-4000 Carnegie Class: Bac/Diverse
FAX Number: (919) 828-0817 Calendar System: Semester
URL: www.st-aug.edu
Established: 1867 Annual Undergrad Tuition & Fees: $17,160
Enrollment: 1,506 Coed
Affiliation or Control: Protestant Episcopal IRS Status: 501(c)3
Highest Offering: Master's
Program: Liberal Arts And General; Teacher Preparatory
Accreditation: SC, TED

01 President .... Dr. Dianne BOARDLEY SUBER
04 Exec Assistant to the President .... Mrs. Gloria T. ROWLAND
89 Special Asst to Pres/FYE Director .... Mr. Michael P. JACKSON
03 ExecVP/VP for Business & Finance .... Mr. Leon L. SCOTT
05 Provost/VP for Academic Affairs .... Dr. B. Connie ALLEN
30 VP for Inst Advancement & Dev .... Mr. Marc A. NEWMAN
32 Vice Pres Student Development & Svc ... Dr. Roland N. BULLARD
45 VP Strategic Initiatives .... Dr. Ronald H. BROWN
21 Asst Vice Pres for Business/Finance .... Ms. Angela N. HAYNES
20 Asst VP Academic Affairs .... Dr. Orlando E. HANKINS
21 Asst Vice President/Comptroller .... Vacant
26 Assoc VP Marketing & Communication .... Mrs. Shelley M. WILLINGHAM-HINTON
09 Asst VP Institutional Research .... Dr. Tammalyn M. THOMAS-GOLDEN
35 Dean of Students & Residential Life .... Vacant
42 Chaplain .... Mr. Colin B. ADAMS
13 Interim Chief Information Officer .... Mr. Harod C. DEMBY
15 Director Human Resources .... Ms. Lottie R. FERRELL
41 Director Athletics .... Mr. George D. WILLIAMS
06 Registrar .... Ms. Crystal G. WILLIAMS
50 Dean Business & Computer Science .... Dr. F. Perna CARTER
83 Dean Social Sciences .... Vacant
81 Dean Natural Sciences/Mathematics .... Dr. Mark A. MELTON
76 Dean Allied Health .... Dr. Hengameh G. ALLEN
49 Interim Dean Liberal Arts & Educ .... Dr. M. Iyailu MOSES
56 Dean Extended Studies .... Mrs. Dekhasta B. ROZIER
07 Director Admissions .... Vacant
37 Director Financial Aid/Scholarships .... Ms. Nadine Y. FORD
08 Dean of Library Services .... Mr. Clevell S. ROSEBORO
36 Director Career Services .... Ms. Nichole R. LEWIS
19 Chief of Police .... Mr. George H. BOYKIN, III
18 Director Physical Plant .... Ms. Sonya Y. CANNADY
29 Director Alumni Affairs .... Ms. Sheryl H. XIMINES
90 Director Academic Computing .... Ms. Carlene J. MORGAN

Salem College (E)

601 South Church Street, Winston-Salem NC 27101
County: Forsyth FICE Identification: 002960
Unit ID: 199607
Telephone: (336) 721-2600 Carnegie Class: Bac/A&S
FAX Number: (336) 917-5339 Calendar System: 4/1/4
URL: www.salem.edu
Established: 1772 Annual Undergrad Tuition & Fees: $23,478
Enrollment: 1,130 Female
Affiliation or Control: Moravian Church IRS Status: 501(c)3
Highest Offering: Master's
Program: Liberal Arts And General; Teacher Preparatory; Professional
Accreditation: SC, MUS, TED

01 President .... Dr. Susan E. PAULY
05 VP Acad & Stdnt Affs/Dn of College .... Dr. Susan CALOVINI
30 VP for Institutional Advancement .... Ms. Vicki SHEPPARD
07 Dean Admissions & Financial Aid .... Ms. Katherine K. WATTS
32 Dean of Students .... Ms. Krispin W. BARR
58 Dean of Graduate Studies .... Dr. Susan GEBHARD
51 Dean of Continuing Studies .... Ms. Suzanne WILLIAMS
20 Dean Undergraduate Studies .... Dr. Richard VINSON
11 Director of Administration .... Ms. Anna GALLIMORE
08 Librarian .... Dr. Rose A. SIMON
44 Director Annual Giving .... Ms. Laura SLAWTER
13 Director Information Technology .... Mr. Paul BENNINGER
15 Director of Payroll & Benefits .... Ms. Cheryl HAMILTON
10 Chief Financial Officer .... Mr. Derek BRYAN
38 Director Counseling Services .... Mr. Jack LOCICERO
37 Director Student Financial Aid .... Ms. Lori LEWIS
27 Director of Communications .... Ms. Michelle MELTON
26 Assistant Director Public Relations .... Ms. Jennifer BRINGLE
36 Director Career Devel/Internships .... Ms. Esther GONZALEZ
06 Registrar/Dir Inst Research .... Ms. Amy CECIL
18 Chief Facilities/Physical Plant .... Mr. George MORALES
29 Director Alumnae Relations .... Ms. Karla GORT
21 Accounts Receivable Manager .... Ms. Nikki BROCK
21 Accounts Payable Manager .... Ms. Judy SIGMON
19 Coordinator Institutional Services .... Mr. Tommy WILLIAMSON

Shaw University (F)

118 E South Street, Raleigh NC 27601
County: Wake FICE Identification: 002962
Unit ID: 199643
Telephone: (919) 546-8200 Carnegie Class: Bac/Diverse
FAX Number: (919) 546-8301 Calendar System: Semester
URL: www.shawuniversity.edu
Established: 1865 Annual Undergrad Tuition & Fees: $14,414
Enrollment: 2,405 Coed
Affiliation or Control: Baptist IRS Status: 501(c)3
Highest Offering: Master's
Program: Liberal Arts And General
Accreditation: SC, KIN, SW, TED, THEOL

01 President .... Dr. Dorothy COWSER YANCY
32 Vice Pres Student Affairs/Admin .... Dr. Jeffrey SMITH
05 Vice Pres Academic Affairs .... Dr. Marilyn SUTTON-HAYWOOD
10 VP for Fiscal Affairs .... Ms. Debra LATIMORE
30 VP for Institutional Advancement .... Ms. Evelyn LEATHERS
20 Int Assoc VP for Academic Affairs .... Dr. Renata DUSENBURY
20 Asst VP for Academic Affairs .... Dr. Cynthia BEAMON
25 Spec Asst/Dir of Special Programs .... Ms. Paula "Tendai" JOHNSON
27 Chief Information Officer .... Mr. Hooshang FOROUDASTAN
21 Controller .... Ms. Gwendolyn WEBB
21 Bursar .... Ms. Shirley FENNELL
06 Registrar .... Ms. Jody HAMILTON-DAVIS
32 Dean of Students .... Mr. Alfonza CARTER
84 Dean of Enrollment Management .... Ms. Rochelle KING
49 Dean Col of Arts and Sciences .... Dr. Renata DUSENBURY
58 Dean Col of Grad/Prof Studies .... Dr. Gaddis FAULCON
73 Dean Shaw Univ Divinity School .... Dr. Bruce GRADY
42 Assoc Dean of Chapel .... Ms. Donna BATTLE
39 Assoc Dean of Students .... Ms. Shannon BENNETT
15 Director of Human Resources .... Ms. Diane CRAWFORD
26 Director of Public Relations .... Ms. Odessa HINES
08 Director of Library Services .... Ms. Carolyn PETERSON
07 Director of Admissions/Recruitment ... Mr. Sherlock MCDOUGALD
37 Director of Financial Aid .... Ms. Rochelle KING
29 Director Alumni Affairs .... Mr. Seddrick HILL
45 Dir of Stratetic Planning/Inst Res .... Dr. Cecil MCMANUS
41 Int Director of Athletics .... Mr. Marcus CLARKE
19 Chief of Campus Police & Security .... Mr. Wayne JOINER
96 Manager of Procurement & Contracts .... Ms. Gwendolyn PERRY
18 Facilities Manager .... Mr. Cleon PIERCE
25 Int Dir Inst for HSC Research .... Dr. Moses GOLDMAN
38 Director of Counseling Center .... Ms. Jerelene CARVER
88 Director of Judicial Affairs .... Ms. Agnes BAXTER
36 Dir Experiential Lrng/Career Devel .... Dr. Denise VAUGHN
50 Chair Dept Business/Public Admin .... Dr. Mma KALU
53 Chair Dept Education .... Dr. Paula MOTEN-TOLSON
81 Chair Dept Natural Science/Math .... Dr. Tashni DUBROY
76 Chair Dept Allied Health .... Dr. James MCCALLUM
79 Chair Dept Humanities .... Dr. Desire' BALOUBI
60 Interm Chair Dept Mass Comm .... Dr. Teri BURNETTE
57 Chair Dept Visual/Performing Arts .... Mr. George HATCHER
83 Interim Chair Dept Social Sciences .... Dr. Elaine YARBOROUGH
77 Chair Dept Computer/Information Sci ..... Dr. Harold RAMCHARAN
88 Int Chair Dept Religion/Philosophy .... Dr. James KIRKLEY

Shepherds Theological Seminary (G)

6051 Tryon Road, Cary NC 27518-9316
County: Wake FICE Identification: 041730
Unit ID: 461485
Telephone: (800) 672-3060 Carnegie Class: Not Classified
FAX Number: (919) 459-0022 Calendar System: Semester
URL: www.shepherds.edu
Established: 2003 Annual Graduate Tuition & Fees: $5,460
Enrollment: 89 Coed
Affiliation or Control: Independent Non-Profit IRS Status: 501(c)3
Highest Offering: Master's; No Undergraduates
Program: Professional; Religious Emphasis
Accreditation: TRACS

01 President .... Dr. Stephen DAVEY
05 Vice President & Dean .... Dr. Larry PETTEGREW
06 Registrar .... Dr. Randall L. MCKINION
07 Director of Recruitment .... Dr. Douglas BOOKMAN
18 Chief Facilities/Physical Plant .... Dr. Samuel WINCHESTER
30 Development .... Dr. William BARBER
37 Financial Aid Officer .... Mrs. Lucy BURGGRAFF

South College (H)

140 Sweeten Creek Road, Asheville NC 28803
County: Buncombe FICE Identification: 010264
Unit ID: 198242

Telephone: (828) 398-2500 Carnegie Class: Assoc/PrivFP4
FAX Number: (828) 277-6151 Calendar System: Quarter
URL: www.southcollegenc.edu
Established: 1905 Annual Undergrad Tuition & Fees: $15,000
Enrollment: 250 Coed
Affiliation or Control: Proprietary IRS Status: Proprietary
Highest Offering: Baccalaureate
Program: Occupational; 2-Year Principally Bachelor's Creditable; Nursing Emphasis
Accreditation: **ACICS**, MAC, PTAA, RAD, SURGT

Code	Title	Name
00	President/Owner	Mr. Stephen A. SOUTH
01	Executive Director	Ms. Trina VAZQUEZ
05	Dean of Academic Affairs	Dr. Susan S. WHISENHUNT
10	Business Manager	Ms. Christine CHANCEY
07	Director of Admissions	Ms. Debra KACEY
37	Financial Aid Officer	Ms. Ronda BLACKMAN
08	Head Librarian	Ms. Jennifer FINLEY

Southeastern Baptist Theological Seminary (A)

Box 1889, Wake Forest NC 27588-1889
County: Wake FICE Identification: 002963
Unit ID: 199759
Telephone: (919) 761-2100 Carnegie Class: Not Classified
FAX Number: N/A Calendar System: Semester
URL: www.sebts.edu
Established: 1950 Annual Undergrad Tuition & Fees: $8,090
Enrollment: 2,340 Coed
Affiliation or Control: Southern Baptist IRS Status: 501(c)3
Highest Offering: Doctorate
Program: Professional
Accreditation: **SC**, THEOL

Code	Title	Name
01	President	Dr. Daniel L. AKIN
05	Academic Vice Pres/Dean of Faculty	Dr. Kenneth KEATHLEY
10	Sr VP for Business Administration	Mr. Ryan HUTCHINSON
20	Associate Academic Officer	Mr. Sheldon H. ALEXANDER
06	Registrar	Mr. Shane BAKER
07	Director of Admissions	Mr. Larry LYON
09	Asst VP Institutional Effectiveness	Dr. Michael E. TRAVERS
29	Director of Alumni Development	Mr. Albie BRICE
30	Vice Pres Institutional Advancement	Mr. Dennis DARVILLE
37	Director of Financial Aid	Dr. Don ALLARD

Southern Evangelical Seminary (B)

3000 Tilley Morris Road, Matthews NC 28105-8635
County: Union FICE Identification: 036115
Unit ID: 438522
Telephone: (704) 847-5600 Carnegie Class: Not Classified
FAX Number: (704) 845-1747 Calendar System: Semester
URL: www.ses.edu
Established: 1992 Annual Undergrad Tuition & Fees: $30,000
Enrollment: 357 Coed
Affiliation or Control: Independent Non-Profit IRS Status: 501(c)3
Highest Offering: Doctorate
Program: Professional; Religious Emphasis
Accreditation: **TRACS**

Code	Title	Name
01	President & COO	Mr. Robert C. WESTRA
07	Director of Admissions/Exec VP	Mr. Duke HALE
10	Business Manager	Mrs. Joan C. SOLHEIM
08	Librarian	Mr. Ronald I. JORDAHL
06	Registrar	Dr. Douglas E. POTTER
29	Director Alumni Rels/Student Svcs	Mrs. Jill JOYNER
30	Director of Development	Mr. Eric T. GUSTAFSON
04	Administrative Asst to President	Mrs. Christina S. WOODSIDE
33	Dean of Men	Mr. Duke HALE
34	Dean of Women	Mrs. Nora M. HALE
40	Director Bookstore	Mr. David S. ONUFER
88	Director Missions	Mr. Simon BRACE
106	Dir Online Education/E-learning	Dr. Daniel JANOSIK

*University of North Carolina General Administration (C)

Box 2688, 910 Raleigh Road, Chapel Hill NC 27515-2688
County: Orange FICE Identification: 002971
Unit ID: 199175
Telephone: (919) 962-1000 Carnegie Class: N/A
FAX Number: (919) 962-2751
URL: www.northcarolina.edu

Code	Title	Name
01	President	Mr. Thomas W. ROSS
100	Chief of Staff	Mr. Jeffrey DAVIES
05	Sr Vice Pres Academic Affairs	Dr. Suzanne ORTEGA
10	Vice President for Finance	Mr. Charles E. PERUSSE
45	Vice Pres for Academic Planning	Vacant
13	Vice Pres Information Resources/CIO	Mr. John LEYDON
43	VP Legal Affairs/General Counsel	Ms. Laura B. FJELD
46	VP Research/Graduate Education	Dr. Christopher BROWN
101	Secretary of the University	Mr. Bart CORGNATI
86	Vice President for Govt Relations	Vacant
86	Vice President for Federal Rels	Ms. Kimrey RHINEHARDT
26	Vice President for Communications	Ms. Joni WORTHINGTON
15	Vice Pres for Human Resources	Mr. William FLEMING

*Appalachian State University (D)

Boone NC 28608-0001
County: Watauga FICE Identification: 002906
Unit ID: 197869
Telephone: (828) 262-2000 Carnegie Class: Master's L
FAX Number: (828) 262-2347 Calendar System: Semester
URL: www.appstate.edu
Established: 1899 Annual Undergrad Tuition & Fees (In-State): $6,059
Enrollment: 17,344 Coed
Affiliation or Control: State IRS Status: 501(c)3
Highest Offering: Doctorate
Program: Liberal Arts And General; Teacher Preparatory; Professional
Accreditation: **SC**, AAFCS, ART, BUS, CACREP, CIDA, CS, DIETD, DIETI, IPSY, MFCD, MUS, NRPA, NURSE, SP, SPAA, SW, TED, THEA

Code	Title	Name
02	Chancellor	Dr. Kenneth E. PEACOCK
05	Provost/Exec Vice Chancellor	Dr. Lori S. GONZALEZ
10	Int Vice Chanc Business Affairs	Mr. Greg M. LOVINS
32	Vice Chanc Student Development	Ms. Cindy A. WALLACE
30	Vice Chanc Univ Advancement	Mrs. Susan H. PETTYJOHN
20	Int Vice Provost for Undergrad Educ	Dr. Mike W. MAYFIELD
45	Vice Provost for Resource Mgmt	Dr. Tim H. BURWELL
26	Assc VC Univ Comm/Cultural Affairs	Mr. Hank T. FOREMAN
84	Assoc VC for Enrollment Management	Mrs. Susan DAVIES
22	Dir of Equity/Diversity/Compliance	Ms. Linda M. FOULSHAM
29	Exec Director of Alumni Affairs	Mr. Patrick K. SETZER
43	University Attorney	Mr. Dayton T. COLE
13	Interim Chief Info Officer/ITS	Mr. David E. HAYLER
06	University Registrar	Ms. Andrea C. WAWRZUSIN
38	Director of Counseling Center	Dr. Dan L. JONES
37	Director of Financial Aid	Ms. Esther M. MANOGIN
15	Director of Human Resource Services	Mr. Patrick J. MCCOY
36	Director of Career Development Ctr	Ms. Marjorie N. ELLIS
09	Director Inst Research & Planning	Dr. Bobby H. SHARP
51	Director of Distance Education	Dr. Mary F. ENGLEBERT
41	Director of Athletics	Mr. Charles G. COBB
49	Dean for College of Arts & Sciences	Dr. Anthony G. CALAMAI
50	Dean for College of Business	Dr. Randy K. EDWARDS
53	Dean for College of Education	Dr. Charles R. DUKE
57	Dean for College Fine/Applied Arts	Dr. Glenda J. TREADAWAY
64	Dean for the School of Music	Dr. Bill L. PELTO
58	Dean of Research/Graduate Studies	Dr. Edelma D. HUNTLEY
08	University Librarian	Dr. Mary L. REICHEL
18	Director of the Physical Plant	Mr. Mike J. O'CONNOR
21	Budget Director	Ms. Betsy P. PAYNE
35	Dean of Students/Assoc VC Stdnt Dev	Mr. J.J BROWN
07	Director of Admissions	Mr. Lloyd M. SCOTT
96	Director of Purchasing	Mr. Jeff D. TALBOT
28	Int Dir Multicultural Student Devel	Mr. Augusto E. PENA

*East Carolina University (E)

1000 East Fifth Street, Greenville NC 27858-4353
County: Pitt FICE Identification: 002923
Unit ID: 198464
Telephone: (252) 328-6212 Carnegie Class: DRU
FAX Number: (252) 328-4155 Calendar System: Semester
URL: www.ecu.edu
Established: 1907 Annual Undergrad Tuition & Fees (In-State): $5,869
Enrollment: 27,386 Coed
Affiliation or Control: State IRS Status: 501(c)3
Highest Offering: Doctorate
Program: Liberal Arts And General; Teacher Preparatory; Professional
Accreditation: **SC**, ANEST, ARCPA, ART, AUD, BUS, CIDA, CLPSY, CONST, CORE, DENT, DIETD, DIETI, ENG, MED, MFCD, MIDWF, MT, MUS, NAIT, NRPA, NURSE, OT, PH, PLNG, PTA, SP, SPAA, SW, TED, THEA

Code	Title	Name
02	Chancellor	Dr. Steve BALLARD
100	Chief of Staff	Mr. Philip ROGERS
05	Provost & Sr Vice Chanc Acad Affs	Dr. Marilyn SHEERER
32	Vice Chancellor for Student Affairs	Dr. Virginia HARDY
17	Vice Chanc Health Sciences	Dr. Phyllis N. HORNS
10	Vice Chanc Administration & Finance	Dr. Frederick NISWANDER
30	Vice Chanc Univ Advancement	Dr. Mickey DOWDY
46	Int VC Research/Graduate Studies	Dr. Ron MITCHELSON
29	Assoc VC for Alumni Relations	Mr. Paul CLIFFORD
39	Assoc VC Camp Liv/Dining	Mr. William L. MCCARTNEY, JR.
38	Assoc Vice Chanc & Dean of Stdnts	Dr. Lynn M. ROEDER
35	Assoc Dean of Students	Dr. Lathan E. TURNER
22	Int Assoc Provost Equity/Diversity	Ms. Lakesha ALSTON
43	University Attorney	Ms. Donna G. PAYNE
09	Associate Provost IPRE	Dr. David WEISMILLER
41	Athletic Director	Mr. Terry HOLLAND
13	Int CIO and Assoc Vice Chanc ITCS	Mr. Don SWEET
15	Assoc Vice Chanc Human Resources	Mr. John TOLLER
18	Assoc VC for Campus Opers	Mr. William BAGNELL
21	Assoc VC for Business Services	Mr. A. Scott BUCK
19	Assoc VC Environ Health & Safety	Mr. Bill KOCH
82	Assoc VC of International Affairs	Dr. Jim GEHLHAR
88	Assoc VC for Academic Outreach	Dr. Elmer POE
20	Assoc VC for Academic Programs	Dr. Linner GRIFFIN
88	Asst VC Recreational/Wellness Svcs	Ms. Nancy MIZE
84	Assoc Provost for Enrollment Svcs	Dr. John FLETCHER
07	Director of Admissions	Mr. Anthony BRITT
06	Registrar	Ms. Angela R. ANDERSON
08	Director Library Services	Dr. Larry BOYER
88	Director Health Sciences Library	Dr. Dorothy A. SPENCER
101	Asst Secretary to Board of Trustees	Mr. John DURHAM
37	Director of Financial Aid	Ms. Julie POORMAN
19	Director/Chief of Police	Mr. Scott SHELTON
51	Director of Continuing Studies	Dr. F. Clayton SESSOMS
27	Director of Publications	Mr. Jimmy ROSTAR
88	Director of Military Programs	Dr. Steve DUNCAN
96	Director of Purchasing	Mr. Kevin CARRAWAY
36	Director Career Center	Ms. Karen S. THOMPSON
26	Director of University Marketing	Mr. Clint BAILEY
21	Director of Internal Audit	Ms. Stacie TRONTO
21	Director for Financial Services	Ms. Anne JENKINS
26	Ex Dir Communication/Pub Affs/Mktg	Ms. Mary C. SHULKEN
49	Dean College of Arts & Sciences	Dr. Alan R. WHITE
76	Dean Sch Allied Health Sciences	Dr. Stephen W. THOMAS
68	Dean Col Health/Human Performance	Dr. Glen G. GILBERT
59	Dean College of Human Ecology	Dr. Judy SIGUAW
66	Dean College of Nursing	Dr. Sylvia BROWN
50	Dean College of Business	Dr. Stanley G. EAKINS
57	Interim Dean Col Fine Arts/Comm	Dr. Michael DORSEY
53	Dean College of Education	Dr. Linda PATRIARCA
72	Dean of Col Tech/Computer Sci	Dr. David WHITE
58	Dean Graduate School	Dr. Paul GEMPERLINE
92	Interim Dean Honors College	Dr. Richard R. EAKIN
63	Dean Brody School of Medicine	Dr. Paul R G. CUNNINGHAM
52	Int Dean School of Dental Medicine	Dr. D. Gregory CHADWICK

*Elizabeth City State University (F)

1704 Weeksville Road, Elizabeth City NC 27909-7806
County: Pasquotank FICE Identification: 002926
Unit ID: 198507
Telephone: (252) 335-3400 Carnegie Class: Bac/Diverse
FAX Number: (252) 335-3731 Calendar System: Semester
URL: www.ecsu.edu
Established: 1891 Annual Undergrad Tuition & Fees (In-State): $4,150
Enrollment: 2,930 Coed
Affiliation or Control: State IRS Status: 501(c)3
Highest Offering: Master's
Program: Liberal Arts And General; Teacher Preparatory; Fine Arts Emphasis
Accreditation: **SC**, BUS, MUS, NAIT, SW, TED

Code	Title	Name
02	Chancellor	Dr. Willie J. GILCHRIST
100	Chief of Staff	Ms. Gwendolyn SANDERS
05	Provost/VC Academic Affairs	Dr. Ali A. KHAN
10	VC for Business & Finance	Mr. Benjamin DURANT
32	VC for Student Affairs	Dr. Anthony BROWN
30	VC for Institutional Advancemnt	Mr. William G. SMITH
43	Asst to Chanc for Legal Affairs	Ms. Bernetta H. BROWN
35	Assoc VC for Student Affairs	Mrs. Deborah G. BRANCH
35	Assoc VC for Student Affairs	Ms. Barbaina M. HOUSTON-BLACK
20	Assoc VC Academic Affs/Acad Support	Dr. W. E. THOMAS
13	Director of Information Systems	Mr. Matthew SIMPSON
38	Dir Counsel/Test Student Affairs	Ms. Felicia BROWN
27	Chief Information Officer	Mr. Anthony K. ADADE
06	Registrar	Mr. Vincent L. BEAMON
84	Director Enrollment Management	Dr. Monette WILLIAMS
09	Dir Institutional Effectiveness/Res	Dr. Damon R. WADE
08	Director of Library Services	Dr. Juanita MIDGETTE
07	Director of Admissions	Mr. Darius EURE
37	Director Student Financial Aid	Mr. Kenneth B. WILSON
36	Director of Career Services	Vacant
15	Director Human Resources	Mrs. Donna JAMES-WHIDBEE
29	Director of Alumni Relations	Ms. Barbara B. SUTTON
18	Director Facilities/Physical Plant	Mr. Dennis LEARY
26	Director of Marketing	Ms. Rhonda M. HAYES
87	Director of Summer School	Mr. Warren E. POOLE
41	Athletic Director	Mr. Thurlis J. LITTLE
21	Director of Budgets	Mrs. Sharnita L. WILSON-PARKER
92	Director of Honors Program	Dr. Velma B. BLACKMON
96	Director of Purchasing	Vacant
53	Dean Sch Education & Psychology	Dr. Charles D. CHERRY
49	Dean Sch of Arts & Humanities	Dr. Murel M. JONES
50	Dean Sch of Business & Economics	Dr. David BEJOU
81	Dean Sch of Math/Science/Technology	Dr. Harry S. BASS

*Fayetteville State University (G)

1200 Murchison Road, Fayetteville NC 28301-4298
County: Cumberland FICE Identification: 002928
Unit ID: 198543
Telephone: (910) 672-1111 Carnegie Class: Master's M
FAX Number: (910) 672-1769 Calendar System: Semester
URL: www.uncfsu.edu
Established: 1867 Annual Undergrad Tuition & Fees (In-State): $6,186
Enrollment: 5,930 Coed
Affiliation or Control: State IRS Status: 501(c)3
Highest Offering: Doctorate
Program: Liberal Arts And General; Teacher Preparatory
Accreditation: **SC**, BUS, CS, MUS, NURSE, SW, TED

Code	Title	Name
02	Chancellor	Dr. James A. ANDERSON
100	Vice Chancellor and Chief of Staff	Dr. Thomas CONWAY
05	Provost & Vice Chanc Academic Affs	Dr. Jon YOUNG
10	Vice Chancellor Business/Finance	Mr. Robert L. BOTLEY
32	Vice Chancellor Student Affairs	Dr. Janice HAYNIE
30	Vice Chancellor Inst Advancement	Mr. Getchel CALDWELL
13	Vice Chanc Info Technology/CIO	Mr. Arasu GANESAN
44	Asst Vice Chanc for Advancement	Ms. Mary H. BAILEY
35	Assoc Vice Chanc Student Affairs	Ms. Juanette COUNCIL
18	Assoc Vice Chanc Facilities Mgmt	Mr. Rudolph CARDENAS
21	Asst VC Business/Financ/Comptroller	Ms. Jolene ELKINS
20	Assoc Vice Chanc Academic Affs	Dr. Curtis CHARLES
15	Assoc Vice Chanc Human Resources	Ms. Denise BROWN-HART
88	AVC Inst Research/Testing/Title III	Vacant

85 Asst VC Acad Affs/Interntl Studies .... Dr. Chen YUNKAI
88 Senior Assoc Vice Chancellor .... Dr. Perry A. MASSEY
45 Assoc VC Pgms/Plng/Assessment .... Vacant
84 Assoc VC for Enrollment Management .... Ms. Roxie SHABAZZ
36 Director Career Svcs & Bus Mgr SA .... Ms. Helene CAMERON
92 Program Director Honors .... Dr. Booker T. ANTHONY
06 Registrar .... Ms. Sarah BAKER
29 Director of Alumni Affairs .... Mrs. Michaela BROWN
26 Director Public Relations .... Mr. Jeff WOMBLE
08 Director of Library Services .... Mr. Bobby C. WYNN
07 Director of Admissions .... Ms. Ulisa BOWLES
90 Director of IT Operations .... Ms. Michelle WHITAKER
09 Director Institutional Research .... Mr. Ivan WALKER
39 Director of Residence Life .... Mr. Greg MOYD
37 Director Student Financial Aid .... Ms. Kamesia EWING
43 General Counsel .... Mrs. Wanda LESSANE JENKINS
41 Athletic Director .... Dr. Edward MCLEAN
96 Director of Purchasing .... Ms. Willie MCINTYRE
38 Dir Center Personal Development .... Mr. Fred SAPP
28 Director of Diversity .... Vacant
88 Dean University College .... Dr. John I. BROOKS
66 Department Chair Nursing .... Dr. Afua ARHIN
50 Dean School Business/Economics .... Dr. Assad TAVAKOLI
53 Dean School of Education .... Dr. Leontye LEWIS
58 Dean Graduate Stds/Sponsored Rsrch .... Dr. LaDelle OLION
49 Dean College of Arts and Sciences .... Dr. David BARLOW

*North Carolina Agricultural and Technical State University (A)

1601 E Market Street, Greensboro NC 27411-0001
County: Guilford FICE Identification: 002905
Unit ID: 199102
Telephone: (336) 334-7500 Carnegie Class: DRU
FAX Number: (336) 334-7136 Calendar System: Semester
URL: www.ncat.edu
Established: 1891 Annual Undergrad Tuition & Fees (In-State): $5,058
Enrollment: 10,881 Coed
Affiliation or Control: State IRS Status: 501(c)3
Highest Offering: Doctorate
Program: Liberal Arts And General; Teacher Preparatory; Professional
Accreditation: SC, AAFCS, BUS, BUSA, CACREP, CONST, @CORE, CS, DIETD, ENG, JOUR, LSAR, MUS, NAIT, NUR, SW, TED, THEA

02 Chancellor .... Dr. Harold L. MARTIN
05 Int Provost/Vice Chanc Academic Aff .. Dr. Winser E. ALEXANDER
10 Vice Chanc Business & Finance .... Mr. Robert POMPEY, JR.
30 Vice Chanc University Advancement .... Ms. Barbara P. MILLER
46 Vice Chanc Research/Economic Dev .... Dr. Barry L. BURKS
32 Vice Chancellor of Student Affairs .... Dr. Melody C. PIERCE
15 Vice Chancellor for Human Resources .... Ms. Linda R. MCABEE
13 Vice Chanc Info Tech & Telecom/CIO .... Ms. Barbara J. ELLIS
43 General Counsel .... Dr. J. Charles WALDRUP
20 Assoc VC for Undergraduate Pgm .... Vacant
27 Assoc Vice Chanc for Univ Relations .... Ms. Nicole PRIDE
21 Asst Vice Chanc Budget & Planning .. Mrs. Akua J. MATHERSON
84 Assoc VC Acad Affs/ Enrollment Mgmt .... Vacant
87 Int Asst Vice Chanc Summer School .... Dr. Sanjiv SARIN
18 Asst VC for Bus/Finance/Facilities .. Mr. Andrew M. PERKINS, JR.
19 Asst VC Police/Public Safety .... Mr. Glen C. NEWELL
08 Dean of Library Services .... Ms. Vicki COLEMAN
47 Dean Agric/Environmental Sci .... Dr. William M. RANDLE
49 Dean Arts & Sciences .... Dr. Goldie S. BYRD
53 Dean School of Education .... Dr. William B. HARVEY
54 Dean of Engineering .... Dr. Robin N. COGER
58 Dean of Graduate School .... Dr. Sanjiv SARIN
66 Dean of Nursing .... Dr. Inez TUCK
50 Dean of Business & Economics .... Dr. Quiester CRAIG
72 Dean School of Technology .... Dr. Benjamin O. UWAKWEH
88 Dean Joint Sch Nanoscience/Nanoengr .... Dr. James G. RYAN
09 Director Inst Research/Planning .... Dr. G. Scott JENKINS
06 University Registrar .... Mr. Lester LUGO
07 Director of Admissions .... Ms. Keyana SCALES
37 Director Financial Aid .... Mrs. Sherri M. AVENT
36 Director Career Services .... Ms. Joyce P. EDWARDS
91 Dir Info Systems/Data Center Ops .... Vacant
29 Director of Alumni Affairs .... Mrs. Leonora C. BRYANT
85 Dir International Student Affairs .... Ms. Loreatha D. GRAVES
88 Dir Multicultural Student Center .... Mr. Gerald SPATES
41 Director of Athletics .... Mr. Earl M. HILTON, III
39 Dir Student Housing/Residence Life .... Ms. Linda D. INMAN
23 Director Student Health Services .... Ms. Linda WILSON
38 Director of Counseling Service .... Dr. Vivian D. BARNETTE
25 Director of Contracts/Grants .... Ms. Lavonne MATTHEWS
92 Director of Honors Program .... Dr. Michael CUNDALL, JR.
96 Director of Purchasing .... Mr. Ted A. LITTLE
26 Director of Media Relations .... Mrs. Nettie ROWLAND
40 Manager of Bookstore .... Mrs. Donna MORRIS-POWELL

*North Carolina Central University (B)

1801 Fayetteville Street, Durham NC 27707-3129
County: Durham FICE Identification: 002950
Unit ID: 199157
Telephone: (919) 530-6100 Carnegie Class: Master's L
FAX Number: (919) 530-5014 Calendar System: Semester
URL: www.nccu.edu
Established: 1910 Annual Undergrad Tuition & Fees (In-State): $5,119
Enrollment: 8,360 Coed
Affiliation or Control: State IRS Status: 501(c)3
Highest Offering: Doctorate
Program: Liberal Arts And General; Teacher Preparatory; Professional
Accreditation: SC, ACBSP, BUS, CACREP, DIETD, DIETI, LAW, LIB, NRPA, NUR, SP, SW, TED, THEA

02 Chancellor .... Dr. Charlie NELMS
05 Provost/Vice Chanc Academic Affairs .... Dr. Debbie THOMAS
100 Vice Chanc/Chief of Staff .... Ms. Susan HESTER
43 General Counsel .... Ms. Melissa JACKSON HOLLOWAY
46 Vice Chanc Research/Economic Devel .... Dr. Hazell REED
11 Vice Chanc Admin & Finance .... Mr. Wendell M. DAVIS
32 Vice Chanc Student Affs/Enroll Mgt .... Dr. Kevin D. ROME
30 Vice Chanc Inst Advancement .... Ms. Lois DELOATCH
20 Assoc Provost/Assoc VC .... Dr. Bernice D. JOHNSON
10 Assoc VC Administration/ Finance .... Ms. Yolanda E. BANKS-DEAVER
20 Assoc Vice Chanc Academic Affairs .... Dr. Frances D. GRAHAM
15 Assoc Vice Chanc Human Resources .... Mr. James C. DOCKERY
88 Asst VC for University Programs .... Dr. Janice A. HARPER
88 Ast Dean of Stdnts/Dir Stdnt Union .... Mr. Kevin M. JONES
45 Director Strategic Planning .... Mr. Johnnie SOUTHERLAND
35 Dir Student Rights/Responsibilities .... Mr. Gary L. BROWN
13 Chief Information Officer .... Mr. John SMITH
07 Admissions Director .... Mr. Anthony M. BROOKS
31 Dir Govt & Community Relations .... Ms. Starla H. TANNER
88 Dir JLC Biomed/Biotech Rsrch Inst .... Dr. K. Sean KIMBRO
44 Director Major Gifts .... Mr. Randal V. CHILDS
88 Dir Biomanfct Rsch Inst/Tech Ent .... Dr. Li-An YEH
44 Director Annual Giving .... Vacant
06 Registrar .... Dr. Jerome GOODWIN
91 Dir Enterprise Information System .... Mr. Donald R. NOLEN
29 Director of Alumni Affairs .... Ms. Anita B. WALTON
26 Director of Public Relations .... Ms. Ayana D. HERNANDEZ
37 Director of Student Financial Aid .... Ms. Sharon J. OLIVER
08 Director Library Services .... Dr. Theodosia T. SHIELDS
19 Chief of Campus Police & Security .... Mr. Timothy R. BELLAMY
88 Director Academic Advising .... Dr. Jennifer SCHUM
88 Director Art Museum .... Dr. Kenneth G. RODGERS
18 Director Facilities Services .... Mr. Phillip POWELL
39 Director Residential Life .... Dr. Jennifer A. WILDER
41 Director Athletics .... Dr. Ingrid L. WICKER-MCCREE
09 Dir Research/Evaluation/Planning .... Mr. Shawn STEWART
96 Director of Purchasing .... Mr. Godfrey B. HERNDON
92 Director of Honors Program .... Dr. Ansel E. BROWN
38 Director of Counseling Center .... Dr. Carolyn D. MOORE-ASSEM
22 Dir Equal Opportunity/Affirm Act .... Vacant
84 Director Enrollment Management .... Ms. Sharon J. OLIVER
88 Asst Dir Greek Life/Special Pgms .... Mrs. Robin FEATHERSTONE-HANES
21 Dir Auxiliaries/Business Services .... Mr. Timothy J. MOORE
40 Manager Bookstore .... Ms. Stephanie L. GETCHELL
58 Dean Sch Grad Stds/Asc VC Grad Rsch .... Dr. Chanta HAYWOOD
61 Dean of the Law School .... Mr. Raymond C. PIERCE
62 Dean School of Library/Info Science .... Dr. Irene OWENS
50 Dean School of Business .... Mr. D. Keith PIGUES
88 Dean of University College .... Dr. Ontario S. WOODEN
49 Dean College of Liberal Arts .... Dr. Carlton E. WILSON
72 Dean College of Science/Technology .. Dr. Abdul K. MOHAMMED
83 Dean College Behavioral/Social Scis .... Vacant
53 Dean School of Education .... Dr. Wynetta LEE

*North Carolina State University (C)

20 Watauga Club Drive, Raleigh NC 27695-0001
County: Wake FICE Identification: 002972
Unit ID: 199193
Telephone: (919) 515-2011 Carnegie Class: RU/VH
FAX Number: (919) 515-7740 Calendar System: Semester
URL: www.ncsu.edu
Established: 1887 Annual Undergrad Tuition & Fees (In-State): $7,644
Enrollment: 34,767 Coed
Affiliation or Control: State IRS Status: 501(c)3
Highest Offering: Doctorate
Program: Occupational; Liberal Arts And General; Teacher Preparatory; Professional
Accreditation: SC, ART, BUS, BUSA, CACREP, CS, ENG, FOR, LSAR, NRPA, SCPSY, SPAA, SW, TED, VET

02 Chancellor .... Dr. William Randy WOODSON
05 Provost/Exec Vice Chancellor .... Dr. Warwick A. ARDEN
43 Vice Chanc & General Counsel .... Ms. Eileen GOLDGEIER
10 Vice Chanc Finance & Business .... Mr. Charles D. LEFFLER
46 Vice Chanc Research/Grad Studies .... Dr. Terri L. LOMAX
32 Vice Chan/Dean Div Acad & Stdnt Aff .... Dr. Michael D. MULLEN
30 Vice Chanc Univ Advancement .... Mr. Nevin E. KESSLER
13 Vice Chanc Information Technology .... Dr. Marc I. HOIT
100 Assistant to the Chancellor .... Ms. P. J. TEAL
26 Asst to Chanc External Affairs .... Mr. Kevin HOWELL
106 Sr Vice Prov Acad Outreach/Entrepre .... Dr. Thomas K. MILLER
08 Vice Provost/Director of Libraries .... Ms. Susan K. NUTTER
22 Vice Prov Inst Equity & Diversity .... Ms. Joanne G. WOODARD
21 Assoc Vice Chanc Finance/Res Mgt .... Mr. Stephen W. KETO
18 Assoc Vice Chanc Facilities .... Mr. Kevin J. MACNAUGHTON
39 Vice Provost for Residential Life .... Dr. Timothy R. LUCKADOO
29 Assoc Vice Chanc Alumni Relations .... Mr. Benny SUGGS
15 Assoc Vice Chanc Human Resources .... Ms. Barbara L. CARROLL
19 Director Public Safety .... Mr. Jack W. MOORMAN
09 Director Univ Planning/Analysis .... Ms. Karen P. HELM
07 Director Undergrad Admissions .... Mr. Thomas H. GRIFFIN
06 Registrar .... Dr. Louis D. HUNT
25 Director Contracts & Grants .... Ms. Julie A. BRASFIELD
27 Director News Services .... Vacant
37 Director of Financial Aid .... Ms. Krista R. DOMNICK
38 Director of Counseling Center .... Dr. Monica OSBURN
41 Director Athletics .... Ms. Deborah YOW

21 Treasurer .... Ms. Mary T. PELOQUIN-DODD
88 Director of Materials Management .... Mrs. Sharon LOOSMAN
79 Dean Humanities/Social Sciences .... Dr. Jeffery P. BRADEN
48 Dean of Design .... Dr. Marvin J. MALECHA
54 Dean of Engineering .... Dr. Louis A. MARTIN-VEGA
47 Dean Agriculture/Life Sciences .... Dr. Johnny C. WYNNE
65 Dean of Natural Resources .... Dr. Mary WATZIN
53 Dean of Education .... Dr. Jayne FLEENER
50 Dean of Management .... Dr. Ira R. WEISS
81 Dean Physical/Mathematical Sciences .... Dr. Daniel L. SOLOMON
88 Dean of Textiles .... Dr. Blanton GODFREY
74 Dean of Veterinary Medicine .... Dr. D. Paul LUNN
58 Interim Dean of Graduate School .... Dr. Rebeca C. RUFTY

*University of North Carolina at Asheville (D)

1 University Heights, Asheville NC 28804-8503
County: Buncombe FICE Identification: 002907
Unit ID: 199111
Telephone: (828) 251-6600 Carnegie Class: Bac/A&S
FAX Number: (828) 251-6495 Calendar System: Semester
URL: www.unca.edu
Established: 1927 Annual Undergrad Tuition & Fees (In-State): $5,916
Enrollment: 3,665 Coed
Affiliation or Control: State IRS Status: 501(c)3
Highest Offering: Master's
Program: Liberal Arts And General; Teacher Preparatory
Accreditation: SC, BUS, ENG, TED

02 Chancellor .... Dr. Anne PONDER
100 Chief of Staff .... Ms. Christine RILEY
05 Provost/VC Academic Affairs .... Dr. Jane K. FERNANDES
10 Vice Chancellor Finance/Operations .... Mr. John PIERCE
30 Interim VC Advancement .... Ms. Elizabeth BAGWELL
32 Vice Chanc for Student Affairs .... Dr. Bill HAGGARD
41 Director of Athletics .... Ms. Janet R. CONE
43 University General Counsel .... Mr. Lucien CAPONE
15 Interim Dir HR/Affirmative Act .... Ms. Christy WILLIAMS
09 Director of Institutional Research .... Dr. Archer R. GRAVELY
20 Asst Provost Academic Admin .... Ms. Patricia MCCLELLAN
81 Dean Natural Science .... Dr. Keith KRUMPE
79 Dean Humanities .... Dr. Gwen ASHBURN
83 Dean Social Science .... Dr. Jeff KONZ
88 Dean University Programs .... Dr. Edward J. KATZ
08 University Librarian .... Ms. Leah DUNN
13 Chief Information Officer .... Mr. Jeff BROWN
07 Dean Admissions .... Vacant
25 Director Contracts & Grants .... Dr. Gerard VOOS
06 Registrar .... Ms. Debbie RACE
21 Assoc Vice Chancellor of Finance .... Ms. Suzanne BRYSON
21 Controller .... Ms. Karen SHAW
19 Director of Public Safety .... Mr. Eric BOYCE
96 Director of Purchasing .... Ms. Betty J. PONDER
29 Dir Alumni Relations & Univ Events .... Ms. Ann MARTIN
26 Director Communication & Mktg .... Ms. Debbie GRIFFITH
27 Director of News Services .... Ms. Merianne MILLER
23 Dir Student Health/Counseling .... Mr. John CUTSPEC
39 Director Residential Education .... Ms. Melanie RHODARMER
39 Director Housing Operations .... Mr. Vollie BARNWELL
36 Director of Career Center .... Vacant
35 Dean of Students .... Ms. Jackie MCHARGUE
37 Assoc Director Financial Aid .... Ms. Beth BARTLETT
04 Exec Asst to Chancellor .... Ms. Lynn SPAIGHT

*University of North Carolina at Chapel Hill (E)

Chapel Hill NC 27599-0001
County: Orange FICE Identification: 002974
Unit ID: 199120
Telephone: (919) 962-2211 Carnegie Class: RU/VH
FAX Number: (919) 962-5604 Calendar System: Semester
URL: www.unc.edu
Established: 1789 Annual Undergrad Tuition & Fees (In-State): $7,694
Enrollment: 29,137 Coed
Affiliation or Control: State IRS Status: 501(c)3
Highest Offering: Doctorate
Program: Occupational; Liberal Arts And General; Teacher Preparatory; Professional
Accreditation: SC, ACAE, AUD, BUS, CACREP, CLPSY, CORE, DA, DENT, DH, DIETC, DMOLS, HSA, IPSY, JOUR, LAW, LIB, MED, MT, NMT, NUR, NURSE, OT, PH, PHAR, PLNG, PTA, RAD, RADDOS, RTT, SCPSY, SP, SPAA, SW, TED

02 Chancellor .... Dr. Holden THORP
03 Exec Vice Chancellor & Provost .... Dr. Bruce CARNEY
05 Exec Vice Provost/Chief Intl Ofcr .... Dr. Ronald STRAUSS
43 Vice Chancellor/General Counsel .... Ms. Leslie C. STROHM
11 Vice Chancellor Finance & Admin .... Ms. Karol GRAY
32 Vice Chancellor Student Affairs .... Mr. Winston B. CRISP
30 Vice Chancellor Univ Advancement .... Mr. Matthew G. KUPEC
16 Vice Chancellor Human Resources .... Ms. Brenda R. MALONE
13 VC Info Technology/Chief Info Ofcr .... Mr. Larry D. CONRAD
04 Secretary of the University .... Vacant
46 Vice Chancellor for Research .... Dr. Barbara ENTWISLE
26 Assoc Vice Chanc Univ Relations .... Ms. Nancy DAVIS
24 Asst Vice Chanc Teaching/Learning .... Ms. Ruth MARINSHAW
08 Assoc Prov/University Librarian .... Ms. Sarah MICHALAK
10 Vice Prov Finance & Acad Planning .... Dr. Dwayne PINKNEY
20 Vice Provost Academic Initiatives .... Dr. Carol TRESOLINI
18 Assoc Vice Chanc Facilities Plng .... Mr. Bruce L. RUNBERG

31	Director Community Relations	Ms. Linda DOUGLAS
28	Vice Prov Diversity/Multicultural	Dr. Taffye B. CLAYTON
09	Asst Prov Inst Research/Assessment	Dr. Lynn E. WILLIFORD
39	Dir Housing & Residential Education	Dr. Larry HICKS
41	Director of Athletics	Mr. Lawrence (Bubba) R. CUNNINGHAM
06	Asst Prov/University Registrar	Mr. Christopher DERICKSON
07	Vice Prov Enrollment & Ugrad Admiss	Dr. Stephen M. FARMER
29	Director General Alumni Association	Mr. Douglas S. DIBBERT
37	Assoc Prov/Dir Scholar/Student Aid	Ms. Shirley A. ORT
36	Director University Career Services	Mr. Ray ANGLE
38	Director Counseling & Wellnes Svc	Dr. Allen H. O'BARR
44	Director of Annual Giving	Ms. Rebecca BRAMLETT
22	Equal Opportunity/ADA Officer	Ms. Ann E. PENN
19	Dir Public Safety/Chief of Police	Chief Jeff B. MCCRACKEN
51	Director Center for Cont Education	Mr. Rob BRUCE
27	Dir Univ Communications	Mr. Mike MCFARLAND
96	Director Procurement Services	Ms. Martha PENDERGRASS
35	Assoc Vice Chanc Student Affairs	Dr. Bettina SHUFORD
87	Dean of the Summer School	Ms. Jan YOPP
49	Dean College Arts & Sciences	Dr. Karen GIL
61	Dean School of Law	Mr. John C. BOGER
17	V Chanc Med Affs/CEO UNC HlthCare	Dr. William L. ROPER
66	Dean School of Nursing	Dr. Kristen M. SWANSON
52	Dean School of Dentistry	Dr. Jane WEINTRAUB
58	Dean of Graduate School	Dr. Steven W. MATSON
50	Dean Kenan-Flagler Business School	Dr. James DEAN
70	Dean School of Social Work	Dr. Jack M. RICHMAN
67	Dean School of Pharmacy	Dr. Robert A. BLOUIN
60	Dean School of Journalism/Mass Comm	Ms. Susan KING
62	Dean School of Info/Library Science	Dr. Gary MARCHIONINI
69	Dean School of Public Health	Dr. Barbara K. RIMER
53	Dean School of Education	Dr. Bill MCDIARMID
80	Dean School of Government	Dr. Michael SMITH
23	Exec Dir Campus Health Services	Dr. Mary COVINGTON
92	Assoc Dean for Honors	Dr. James L. LELOUDIS

*University of North Carolina at Charlotte (A)

9201 University City Boulevard, Charlotte NC 28223-0001

County: Mecklenburg — FICE Identification: 002975
Unit ID: 199139
Telephone: (704) 687-2000 — Carnegie Class: DRU
FAX Number: (704) 687-2144 — Calendar System: Semester
URL: www.uncc.edu
Established: 1946 — Annual Undergrad Tuition & Fees (In-State): $5,873
Enrollment: 25,277 — Coed
Affiliation or Control: State — IRS Status: 501(c)3
Highest Offering: Doctorate
Program: Liberal Arts And General; Teacher Preparatory; Professional
Accreditation: SC, ANEST, BUS, BUSA, CACREP, ENG, ENGT, EXSC, HSA, IPSY, NURSE, PH, SPAA, SW, TED

02	Chancellor	Dr. Philip L. DUBOIS
101	Chief of Staff	Ms. Krista L. NEWKIRK
05	Vice Chanc Academic Affs/Provost	Dr. Joan F. LORDEN
20	Senior Associate Provost	Dr. Jay RAJA
88	Assoc Provost/Academic Services	Dr. Cynthia WOLF JOHNSON
10	Vice Chancellor Business Affairs	Ms. Elizabeth A. HARDIN
30	Vice Chancellor Univ Advancement	Mr. Niles F. SORENSEN
86	Spec Asst for Constituent Relations	Ms. Betty DOSTER
32	Vice Chancellor Student Affairs	Dr. Arthur R. JACKSON
46	Vice Chanc Research/Econ Dev	Dr. Robert W. WILHELM
13	Int Vice Chanc Info Tech Svcs/CIO	Mr. Michael G. CATO
18	Assoc Vice Chanc Facilities Mgmt	Mr. Philip M. JONES, JR.
08	University Librarian	Mr. Stanley J. WILDER
82	Asst Provost for Intl Programs	Mr. Joel A. GALLEGOS
27	Exec Dir Univ Communications	Mr. Stephen P. WARD
51	Exec Dir Extended Acad Programs	Dr. Constance M. MARTIN
26	Director of Public Relations	Mr. John D. BLAND
31	Director Community Affairs	Ms. Jeanette SIMS
39	Assoc Vice Chanc/Dir Residence Life	Ms. Jacklyn A. SIMPSON
21	Assoc Vice Chancellor for Finance	Ms. Susan H. BROOKS
58	Assoc Provost/Dean Graduate School	Dr. Thomas L. REYNOLDS
84	Assoc Provost for Enrollment Mgmt	Ms. Tina M. MCENTIRE
43	General Counsel	Mr. David E. BROOME, JR.
07	Director Undergraduate Admissions	Ms. Claire J. KIRBY
35	Dean of Students/Assoc VC Stdnt Aff	Dr. Michele M. HOWARD
37	Director of Financial Aid	Mr. Anthony D. CARTER
38	Assoc VC Health Programs & Services	Dr. David B. SPANO
36	Director University Career Center	Ms. Denise DWIGHT SMITH
40	Campus Bookstore Manager	Mr. Jimmy E. GRINNELL
29	Exec Director Alumni Affairs	Ms. Jenny JONES
88	Assoc VC Risk Mgmt/Safety/Security	Mr. Henry D. JAMES
19	Chief/Dir Police & Public Safety	Mr. Jeffrey A. BAKER
09	Asst Provost Institutional Reseach	Mr. Stephen A. COPPOLA
41	Director of Athletics	Ms. Judy W. ROSE
96	Director of Purchasing	Mr. Randy DUNCAN
93	Dir Multicultural Academic Services	Dr. Sam T. LOPEZ
23	Admin Director Student Health Svcs	Mr. David ROUSMANIERE
15	Assoc Vice Chanc HumanRes/Aff Act	Mr. Gary W. STINNETT
85	Director Intl Student/Scholar Svcs	Ms. Marian E. BEANE
104	Director Study Abroad	Mr. Brad SEKULICH
48	Dean College of Arts/Architecture	Mr. Kenneth A. LAMBLA
50	Dean College of Business	Dr. Steven H. OTT
54	Dean College of Engineering	Dr. Robert E. JOHNSON
53	Dean College of Education	Dr. Mary Lynne CALHOUN
49	Dean Col of Liberal Arts & Sciences	Dr. Nancy A. GUTIERREZ
88	Dean College Health & Human Svcs	Dr. Nancy FEY-YENSAN
72	Dean College Computing/Informatics	Dr. Yi DENG
97	Dean University College	Dr. John SMAIL
92	Exec Director of Honors College	Dr. Malin PEREIRA
06	University Registrar	Mr. Christopher B. KNAUER

44	Director of Gift Planning	Dr. Carl E. JOHNSON
88	Assoc Provost Metro Studies/Ext Pgm	Dr. Owen J. FURUSETH
88	Exec Dir Institute for Social Cap	Dr. Sharon G. PORTWOOD

*University of North Carolina at Greensboro (B)

PO Box 26170,1000 Spring Garden St, Greensboro NC 27402-6170

County: Guilford — FICE Identification: 002976
Unit ID: 199148
Telephone: (336) 334-5000 — Carnegie Class: RU/H
FAX Number: (336) 256-0408 — Calendar System: Semester
URL: www.uncg.edu
Established: 1891 — Annual Undergrad Tuition & Fees (In-State): $6,136
Enrollment: 18,274 — Coed
Affiliation or Control: State — IRS Status: 501(c)3
Highest Offering: Doctorate
Program: Liberal Arts And General; Teacher Preparatory; Professional
Accreditation: SC, ANEST, BUS, BUSA, CACREP, CEA, CIDA, CLPSY, CS, DANCE, DIETD, DIETI, LIB, MUS, NRPA, NUR, NURSE, PH, SP, SPAA, SW, TED, THEA

02	Chancellor	Dr. Linda P. BRADY
100	Chief of Staff	Ms. Bonita J. BROWN
05	Provost and VC for Academic Affairs	Dr. David H. PERRIN
10	Vice Chancellor Business Affairs	Mr. Reade TAYLOR
11	Vice Chanc Info Tech Services	Dr. James H. CLOTFELTER
32	Vice Chanc for Student Affairs	Dr. Cheryl M. CALLAHAN
30	Sr Assoc Vice Chanc Univ Advncemnt	Ms. Judy PIPER
43	University Counsel	Mr. Steve SERCK
20	Vice Provost	Dr. Alan J. BOYETTE
97	Dean of Undergraduate Studies	Dr. Steve ROBERSON
46	Vice Chanc Research & Econ Devel	Dr. Terri L. SHELTON
104	Assoc Provost Intl Programs	Dr. Penelope J. PYNES
15	Assoc VC Human Resource Services	Dr. Edna CHUN
21	Associate VC Financial Services	Mr. Steven W. RHEW
18	Associate Vice Chanc for Facilities	Mr. Jorge QUINTAL
88	Associate VC for Campus Enterprises	Mr. Michael T. BYERS
09	Director of Institutional Research	Dr. Sarah D. CARRIGAN
26	Associate VC University Relations	Ms. Helen D. HEBERT
91	Associate VC for Administrative Sys	Mr. Joel DUNN
35	Assistant VC for Student Affairs	Dr. Vickie J. MCNEIL
88	Assoc VC for Enterprise Admin Appl	Ms. Laura R. YOUNG
44	Asst VC for Central Develop Pgms	Ms. Lynn BRESKO
88	Asst VC for Foundation Finance	Ms. Jill HILLYER
58	Dean of Graduate School	Dr. William R. WIENER
49	Dean of Arts & Sciences	Dr. Timothy D. JOHNSTON
50	Dean of Business & Economics	Dr. McRae BANKS
53	Dean of Education	Dr. Karen WIXSON
68	Dean of Health & Human Sciences	Dr. Celia R. HOOPER
64	Int Dean of Music/Theatre & Dance	Dr. Susan W. STINSON
66	Dean of Nursing	Dr. Lynne G. PEARCEY
08	Dean of University Libraries	Ms. Rosann V. BAZIJIAN
06	University Registrar	Dr. Kelly A. ROWETT-JAMES
108	Dir Assessment and Accreditation	Dr. Jodi E. PETTAZZONI
07	Director of Admissions	Ms. Lise K. KELLER
29	Director of Alumni Relations	Ms. Linda CARTER
88	Director of Campus Recreation	Ms. Jill BEVILLE
23	Director Student Health Services	Dr. Tresa M. SAXTON
36	Director Career Services Center	Mr. Patrick O. MADSEN
51	Int Dean Division of Continual Lrng	Dr. James M. EDDY
25	Acting Dir Contracts and Grants	Mr. William D. WALTERS
38	Director Counseling/Testing Center	Dr. Bruce G. LYNCH
37	Director of Financial Aid	Ms. Deborah TOLLEFSON
39	Director Housing & Residence Life	Mr. Timothy JOHNSON
41	Director Intercollegiate Athletics	Ms. Kim RECORD
88	Director of Orientation	Dr. Kim SOUSA-PEOPLES
19	Assoc VC for Safety and Emergency	Mr. Rollin DONELSON
28	Director Multicultural Affairs	Ms. Audrey O. LUCAS
96	Dir Purchasing and Warehouse Svcs	Mr. Trace LITTLE
40	University Bookstore Manager	Mr. Brad LIGHT

*University of North Carolina at Pembroke (C)

One University Drive, PO Box 1510, Pembroke NC 28372-1510

County: Robeson — FICE Identification: 002954
Unit ID: 199281
Telephone: (910) 521-6000 — Carnegie Class: Master's M
FAX Number: (910) 521-6176 — Calendar System: Semester
URL: www.uncp.edu
Established: 1887 — Annual Undergrad Tuition & Fees (In-State): $4,867
Enrollment: 6,251 — Coed
Affiliation or Control: State — IRS Status: 501(c)3
Highest Offering: Master's
Program: Liberal Arts And General; Teacher Preparatory; Business Emphasis
Accreditation: SC, ART, MUS, NURSE, SW, TED

02	Chancellor	Dr. Kyle R. CARTER
05	Provost/Vice Chanc Academic Affairs	Dr. Kenneth D. KITTS
10	Vice Chancellor Business Affairs	Vacant
32	Inter Vice Chanc Student Affairs	Dr. Lisa SCHAEFFER
30	Vice Chancellor for Advancement	Ms. Wendy LOWERY
84	Vice Chanc Enrollment Management	Vacant
26	Special Asst for Constituent Rels	Dr. Glen G. BURNETTE, JR.
41	Athletic Director	Mr. Dan KENNEY
20	Assoc Vice Chanc Planning and Acred	Dr. Elizabeth NORMANDY

35	Assoc Vice Chanc Student Affairs	Vacant
13	Int Assoc VC Info Res/Chf Info Ofcr	Mr. Tom JACKSON
85	Assoc Vice Chanc International Pgms	Vacant
43	General Counsel	Mr. Joshua MALCOLM
39	Dir Housing and Resident Life	Mr. R. Preston SWINEY
49	Dean of Arts & Sciences	Dr. Mark CANADA
08	Interim Dean of Library Services	Ms. Susan WHITT
58	Interim Dean of Graduate Studies	Dr. William H. GASH
92	Dean of Honors College	Dr. Mark MILEWICZ
53	Interim Dean of School of Education	Dr. Zoe LOCKLEAR
50	Dean of School of Business	Dr. Ramin MAYSAMI
29	Director Alumni Relations	Ms. Renee STEELE
09	Asst VC Institutional Effectiveness	Dr. Beverly KING
36	Director Career Services Center	Dr. Karen PRUETT
38	Director Counseling/Testing Center	Dr. Monica Z. OSBURN
06	Registrar	Ms. Sharon KISSICK
37	Director Financial Aid	Ms. Jenelle HANDCOX
96	Director of Business Services	Ms. Denise CARROLL
15	Director of Human Resources	Ms. Debbie BURGESS
44	Director of Donor Relations	Vacant
25	Dir for Center Sponsored Research	Dr. Linda LITTLE
88	Director Public Administration Pgm	Dr. Warren S. ELLER
24	Director of Media Center	Vacant
27	Public Communications Specialist	Mr. Scott BIGELOW
21	Asst VC Business Affs/Controller	Mr. George GUTHRIE
40	Director of Bookstore	Ms. Karen SWINEY
88	Sports Information Director	Mr. Todd ANDERSON
07	Director of Admissions	Ms. Lela CLARK
18	Director of Physical Plant	Mr. Larry FREEMAN
28	Dir Multicultural/Minority Affairs	Mr. Robert L. CANIDA, II
88	Dir Fac Plng/Construction/Univ Engr	Mr. Michael CLARK
88	Dir Ctr for Academic Excellence	Mr. Steven HUNT

*University of North Carolina Wilmington (D)

601 S College Road, Wilmington NC 28403-3297

County: New Hanover — FICE Identification: 002984
Unit ID: 199218
Telephone: (910) 962-3000 — Carnegie Class: Master's L
FAX Number: (910) 962-4050 — Calendar System: Semester
URL: www.uncw.edu
Established: 1947 — Annual Undergrad Tuition & Fees (In-State): $6,199
Enrollment: 13,145 — Coed
Affiliation or Control: State — IRS Status: 501(c)3
Highest Offering: Doctorate
Program: Liberal Arts And General; Teacher Preparatory; Professional
Accreditation: SC, BUS, CS, MUS, NRPA, NURSE, SPAA, SW, TED

02	Chancellor	Dr. Gary L. MILLER
05	Provost/Vice Chanc Acad Affs	Dr. Denise BATTLES
10	Vice Chancellor Business Affairs	Dr. Charles MAIMONE
32	Vice Chanc for Student Affairs	Ms. Patricia L. LEONARD
30	Vice Chanc University Advancement	Mrs. Mary M. GORNTO
21	Sr Assoc Vice Chanc Finance	Mr. Rick N. WHITFIELD
20	Assoc Vice Chanc Academic Affairs	Dr. Johnson O. AKINLEYE
44	Assoc Vice Chanc Univ Advancement	Ms. Marla D. RICE-EVANS
20	Vice Provost	Dr. Stephen L. MCFARLAND
21	Assoc Vice Chanc Business Services	Ms. Sharon H. BOYD
21	Int Assoc VC Bus Affs Facilities	Mr. Billy J. GRAVES
28	Assoc Provost/Diversity & Inclusion	Dr. Jose E. HERNANDEZ
26	Exec Dir of University Relations	Vacant
09	Asst VC Institutional Rsrch/Assess	Ms. Lisa CASTELLINO
35	Dean of Students	Dr. Michael A. WALKER
84	Assoc Provost for Enrollment Mgmt	Dr. Terrence M. CURRAN
85	Asst Provost International Programs	Dr. Denise DIPUCCIO
15	Int VC for Human Resources	Ms. Joann MCDOWELL
100	Chief of Staff	Mr. Max ALLEN
22	Int Assoc VC for HR	Ms. Joann MCDOWELL
06	Registrar	Mr. Gilbert C. BOWEN
08	University Librarian	Ms. Sarah WATSTEIN
37	Director Fin Aid/Veterans Svcs	Ms. Emily J. BLISS
18	Director of Physical Plant	Mr. Thomas A. FRESHWATER
19	Director Envir Health & Safety	Mr. Stanley H. HARTS
23	Dir Student Health/Wellness Center	Ms. Katrin WESNER
31	Director of Auxiliary Services	Mr. Brian DAILEY
41	Director of Athletics	Mr. Jimmy BASS
36	Director Career Services	Mr. Thomas D. RAKES
29	Director of Alumni Relations	Mr. Rob MCINTURF
96	Director of Purchasing	Ms. Mary E. FORSYTHE
38	Director Student Counseling Center	Dr. Lynne REEDER
40	Manager Bookstore	Ms. Stephanie GARAY
49	Dean College Arts & Sciences	Dr. David P. CORDLE
50	Dean Cameron School of Business	Dr. Lawrence S. CLARK
53	Dean Watson School of Education	Dr. Kenneth TEITELBAUM
66	Director School of Nursing	Dr. James D. MCCANN
58	Dean of Graduate School	Dr. Robert D. ROER
76	Dean Col Health & Human Svcs	Dr. Charles HARDY

*University of North Carolina School of the Arts (E)

1533 S Main Street, Winston-Salem NC 27127-2738

County: Forsyth — FICE Identification: 003981
Unit ID: 199184
Telephone: (336) 770-3399 — Carnegie Class: Spec/Arts
FAX Number: (336) 770-3375 — Calendar System: Semester
URL: www.uncsa.edu
Established: 1963 — Annual Undergrad Tuition & Fees (In-State): $6,908
Enrollment: 893 — Coed
Affiliation or Control: State — IRS Status: 501(c)3
Highest Offering: Master's
Program: Fine Arts Emphasis

Accreditation: SC

02 Chancellor ... Mr. John MAUCERI
05 Chief Academic Officer ... Dr. David P. NELSON
10 Senior Director of Business Affairs ... Ms. Carin IOANNOU
11 Chief Operating Officer ... Mr. George BURNETTE
31 Director Econ Devel/External Affs ... Mr. James DECRISTO
18 Assoc VC Facilities/Services ... Mr. Chrispher BOYD
09 Director Institutional Research ... Dr. Geri COCHRAN
07 Director of Admissions ... Ms. Sheeler LAWSON
08 Librarian ... Ms. Vicki WEAVIL
26 Director Communications/Marketing ... Ms. Marla CARPENTER
06 Registrar ... Ms. Erin MORIN
15 Director Human Resources ... Mr. James LUCAS
37 Director Financial Aid ... Mrs. Jane KAMIAB
49 Int Dean Grad/Undergrad Studies ... Mr. Dean WILCOX
64 Dean School of Music ... Dr. Wade WEAST
57 Dean School of Dance ... Mr. Ethan STIEFEL
88 Dean School of Design/Production ... Mr. Joseph TILFORD
88 Dean School of Drama ... Mr. Gerald FREEDMAN
13 Chief Information Officer ... Ms. Lisa HARDEN SMITH
19 Director of Campus Police ... Ms. Dorothy CHEESEBRO
38 Director of Student Counseling ... Mr. Thomas MURRAY

*Western Carolina University (A)

65 West University Way, HFR 501,
Cullowhee NC 28723-9646

County: Jackson — FICE Identification: 002981
Unit ID: 200004
Telephone: (828) 227-7211 — Carnegie Class: Master's L
FAX Number: (828) 227-7202 — Calendar System: Semester
URL: www.wcu.edu
Established: 1889 — Annual Undergrad Tuition & Fees (In-State): $7,557
Enrollment: 9,352 — Coed
Affiliation or Control: State — IRS Status: 501(c)3
Highest Offering: Doctorate
Program: Liberal Arts And General; Teacher Preparatory; Professional
Accreditation: SC, ANEST, ART, BUS, CACREP, CIDA, CONST, DIETD, DIETI, EMT, ENG, ENGT, MUS, NURSE, PTA, SP, SW, TED, THEA

02 Chancellor ... Dr. David O. BELCHER
05 Provost ... Dr. Angela BRENTON
10 Vice Chanc/Admin & Finance ... Mr. Robert EDWARDS
30 Vice Chanc Advance/External Affairs ... Mr. Clifton METCALF
32 Vice Chancellor/Student Affairs ... Dr. H. Samuel MILLER
35 Asst Vice Chanc Student Affairs ... Mrs. Jane ADAMS-DUNFORD
35 Asst Vice Chanc/Student Affairs ... Ms. Kellie MONTEITH
30 Assoc Vice Chancellor Development ... Mr. Jim MILLER
20 Interim Associate Provost ... Dr. Mark LORD
18 Assoc VC for Facilities Management ... Mr. Joe WALKER
100 Chief of Staff ... Ms. Dianne LYNCH
04 Executive Asst to the Chancellor ... Ms. Terry WELCH
44 Sr Director Development ... Mr. Brett WOODS
43 Legal Counsel ... Ms. Mary Ann LOCHNER
88 Director Student Support Services ... Mrs. Suzanne BAKER
38 Director of Counseling Services ... Vacant
06 Registrar ... Mr. Larry HAMMER
07 Director of Student Recruitment ... Mr. Phil CAULEY
09 Asst Vice Chancellor for OIPE ... Dr. Melissa WARGO
37 Director of Financial Aid ... Ms. Trina ORR
15 Director of Human Resources ... Ms. Kathy WONG
27 Chief Information Officer ... Mr. Craig FOWLER
29 Director of Alumni Affairs ... Mr. Marty RAMSEY
08 Dean of Library Services ... Dr. Dana SALLY
19 Director University Police ... Mr. Earnest HUDSON
88 Interim Dean Educational Outreach ... Dr. Regis GILMAN
31 Director Auxiliary Services ... Mr. Jeff BEWSEY
41 Athletic Director ... Mr. Randy EATON
23 Director University Health Services ... Ms. Pamela BUCHANAN
28 Director of Intercultural Affairs ... Mr. James FELTON
96 Director of Purchasing ... Mr. Arthur STEPHENS
40 Director Book & Supply Store ... Ms. Pamela DEGRAFFENREID
88 Director of Orientation ... Ms. Tammy HASKETT
38 Director of Undergraduate Advising ... Mr. David GOSS
36 Director of Career Services ... Ms. Mardy ASHE
27 Sr Director Comm & Public Relations ... Mr. Bill STUDENC
57 Dean of Fine & Performing Arts ... Dr. Robert KEHRBERG
58 Interim Dean Grad School & Research ... Dr. Mimi FENTON
49 Interim Dean Arts & Sciences ... Dr. Richard STARNES
72 Int Dn Kimmel Sch Constr Mgmt/Tech ... Dr. James ZHANG
50 Dean College of Business ... Dr. Darrell PARKER
53 Int Dean Educ & Allied Professions ... Dr. Dale CARPENTER
76 Associate Dean Health/Human Science ... Dr. Marie HUFF
76 Dean Health & Human Sciences ... Vacant
92 Dean of Honors College ... Dr. Brian RAILSBACK

*Winston-Salem State University (B)

601 MLK Jr. Drive, 200 Blair Hall,
Winston-Salem NC 27110-0001

County: Forsyth — FICE Identification: 002986
Unit ID: 199999
Telephone: (336) 750-2000 — Carnegie Class: Master's M
FAX Number: (336) 750-2049 — Calendar System: Semester
URL: www.wssu.edu
Established: 1892 — Annual Undergrad Tuition & Fees (In-State): $5,979
Enrollment: 6,400 — Coed
Affiliation or Control: State — IRS Status: 501(c)3
Highest Offering: Doctorate
Program: Liberal Arts And General; Teacher Preparatory; Professional
Accreditation: SC, BUS, CORE, CS, MT, MUS, NRPA, NURSE, OT, PTA, SW, TED

02 Chancellor ... Dr. Donald J. REAVES
05 Provost/VC Academic Affairs ... Dr. Brenda ALLEN
32 Vice Chancellor Student Affairs ... Dr. Trae COTTON
09 Asst Prov Plng/Assessmt/Research ... Dr. Carolynn BERRY
45 Int Asst Prov Administration/Plng ... Ms. Letitia CORNISH
20 Sr Assoc Provost Academic Affairs ... Dr. Merdis J. MCCARTER
10 Vice Chanc Finance & Administration ... Mr. Gerald E. HUNTER
21 Assoc VC Financial Plng & Budget ... Dr. Randy W. MILLS
30 Vice Chanc University Advance ... Mrs. Michelle COOK
18 Assoc Vice Chanc Facilities Mgmt ... Mr. Owen J. COOKS
27 Assoc Provost Info Resources/CIO ... Mr. Justin D. MCKENZIE
51 Assoc Dir Cont Educ/Summer Sessions ... Mr. W. Kenneth BULLS
88 Director Internal Audit/Compliance ... Ms. Shannon B. HENRY
53 Dean Sch Educ/Human Performance ... Dr. Manuel VARGAS
19 Chief of Campus Police ... Mrs. Patricia D. NORRIS
08 Librarian ... Dr. Mae L. RODNEY
39 Int Director Hous/Residence Life ... Mr. Peter BLUTREICH
37 Director of Financial Aid ... Mr. Robert MUHAMMED
15 Asst Vice Chanc Human Resources ... Mr. Ivan V. FOSTER
36 Asst Director of Career Services ... Mrs. LaMonica SINGLETON
27 Director Public & Media Relations ... Ms. Nancy N. YOUNG
26 Director Marketing/Publications ... Ms. Sigrid HALL-PITTSLEY
88 Dir Enrollment Communications ... Ms. Cathy HOOTS
29 Director of Alumni Affairs ... Mr. Gregory G. HAIRSTON
44 Director Institutional Annual Fund ... Mrs. Kimberly REESE
35 Assoc Director Student Activities ... Ms. Heather DAVIS
23 Director of Student Health Center ... Ms. Ether JOE
41 Athletic Director ... Mr. William HAYES
101 Asst to the Chancellor/Sec of Univ ... Mrs. RaVonda DALTON-RANN
07 Asst VC Enrollment Services ... Mrs. Tomikia LEGRANDE
43 General Legal Counsel ... Mrs. Camille KLUTTZ-LEACH
96 Director Purchasing ... Mr. Alan IRELAND
90 Director Academic Computer Center ... Mr. Cuthrell JOHNSON
50 Dean School Business/Economics ... Dr. Jessica M. BAILEY
88 Assoc Provost Life Long Learning ... Dr. Doria K. STITTS
49 Dean College Arts & Sciences ... Vacant
76 Dean School of Health Sciences ... Dr. Peggy VALENTINE
89 Dean of University College ... Dr. Michele RELEFORD
92 Int Director of Honors College ... Dr. Soncerey L. MONTGOMERY
88 Director of Title III ... Dr. Everette L. WITHERSPOON
88 Asst Provost Faculty Affairs ... Dr. Denise PEARSON

Wake Forest University (C)

1834 Wake Forest Road, Winston-Salem NC 27109-8758

County: Forsyth — FICE Identification: 002978
Unit ID: 199847
Telephone: (336) 758-5000 — Carnegie Class: RU/H
FAX Number: (336) 758-6074 — Calendar System: Semester
URL: www.wfu.edu
Established: 1834 — Annual Undergrad Tuition & Fees: $42,700
Enrollment: 7,344 — Coed
Affiliation or Control: Independent Non-Profit — IRS Status: 501(c)3
Highest Offering: Doctorate
Program: Liberal Arts And General; Teacher Preparatory; Professional
Accreditation: SC, ANEST, ARCPA, BUS, BUSA, CACREP, DENT, LAW, MED, MT, TED, THEOL

01 President ... Dr. Nathan O. HATCH
43 VP Gen Counsel/Sec Board of Trust ... Mr. J. Reid MORGAN
03 Sr Vice Pres/Chief Financial Ofcr ... Vacant
05 Provost ... Mr. Rogan KERSH
10 Exec VP Finance/Admin/Chf Oper Ofcr ... Mr. B. Hofler MILAM
17 Sr Vice Pres Health Affairs ... Vacant
11 Vice President for Administration ... Dr. Matthew S. CULLINAN
30 Vice Pres University Advancement ... Mr. Mark A. PETERSEN
32 Vice Pres Student Life ... Mr. Kenneth A. ZICK
88 Vice Pres/Chief Investment Officer ... Mr. James J. DUNN
20 Assoc Provost Academic Initiatives ... Ms. Jennifer COLLINS
04 Senior Advisor to the President ... Ms. Sandra C. BOYETTE
35 Assoc VP/Dean of Student Services ... Mr. Harold R. HOLMES
44 Ast VP/Dir Parent/Donor Relations ... Ms. Minta A. MCNALLY
30 Asst VP/Director of Development ... Mr. Robert T. BAKER
13 Assoc Prov for Information Systems ... Dr. Rick MATTHEWS
46 Vice Provost for Research ... Dr. Mark WELKER
49 Dean of the College ... Dr. Jacquelyn FETROW
63 Dean School Med/Int Health Sci Pres ... Dr. Edward ABRAHAM
58 Dean Graduate School Arts/Sciences ... Dr. Lorna G. MOORE
61 Dean School of Law ... Mr. Blake MORANT
50 Dean of Business ... Mr. Steven REINEMUND
73 Dean of Divinity ... Dr. Gail R. O'DAY
89 Assoc Dean & Dean of Freshmen ... Dr. Paul N. ORSER
09 Dir Inst Research/Academic Admin ... Mr. Ross A. GRIFFITH
08 Dir of the Z Smith Reynolds Library ... Dr. Lynn SUTTON
85 Director of International Studies ... Steven DUKE
07 Director of Admissions ... Ms. Martha B. ALLMAN
37 Director of Financial Aid ... Mr. William T. WELLS
36 VP/Office of Personal & Career Dev ... Mr. Andy CHAN
06 Registrar ... Mr. Harold PACE
41 Director of Athletics ... Mr. Ronald D. WELLMAN
15 Chief Human Resources Officer ... Ms. Carmen I. CANALES
18 Director Facilities Management ... Mr. James ALTY
38 Dir University Counseling Center ... Dr. Marianne A. SCHUBERT
84 Director Enrollment Management ... Vacant
23 Director Student Health Service ... Dr. Cecil D. PRICE
39 Exec Dir of Residential Services ... Vacant
40 Exec Director Business Services ... Mr. Donald J. MOSER
42 Chaplain ... Rev. Timothy L. AUMAN
19 Chief University Police ... Ms. Regina G. LAWSON
22 EEO Mgr/Diversity & Compliance Dir ... Ms. Doris A. MCLAUGHLIN
96 Director Purchasing ... Mr. Phillip E. HENDRIX
94 Director Women's & Gender Studies ... Dr. Wanda BALZANO

Warren Wilson College (D)

PO Box 9000, Asheville NC 28815-9000

County: Buncombe — FICE Identification: 002979
Unit ID: 199865
Telephone: (828) 298-3325 — Carnegie Class: Bac/A&S
FAX Number: (828) 771-7097 — Calendar System: Semester
URL: www.warren-wilson.edu
Established: 1894 — Annual Undergrad Tuition & Fees: $27,740
Enrollment: 903 — Coed
Affiliation or Control: Presbyterian Church (U.S.A.) — IRS Status: 501(c)3
Highest Offering: Master's
Program: Liberal Arts And General; Teacher Preparatory
Accreditation: SC, SW

01 President ... Dr. Steven L. SOLNICK
05 VP Academic Affairs/Dean of College ... Dr. Paula K. GARRETT
11 VP for Administration/Finance ... Mr. Jonathan D. EHRLICH
30 VP for Advancement/Admiss & Mktg ... Mr. Richard BLOMGREN
32 Interim Dean of Students ... Mr. Paul PERRINE
88 Dean of Work ... Mr. Ian ROBERTSON
88 Dean of Service ... Ms. Cathy KRAMER
20 Assoc Dean for Faculty ... Ms. Carol HOWARD
06 Registrar ... Miss Christa L. BRIDGMAN
09 Director Institutional Research ... Ms. Allyson HETTRICK
08 Director Library ... Dr. Christine R. NUGENT
37 Director Financial Aid ... Ms. Kathy P. PACK
21 Controller ... Ms. Mary DAVIS
29 Director Alumni Relations ... Mr. Rodney LYTLE
26 Director of Media Relations ... Mr. Benjamin J. ANDERSON
88 Director Community Relations ... Ms. Ally DONLAN
20 Director Academic Support Service ... Ms. Lyn O'HARE
88 Director of Service Leaning ... Ms. Brooke MILLSAPS
35 Mail Services Manager ... Mr. Andrew L. MERCURIO
38 Director of Counseling ... Mr. Arthur SHUSTER
36 Director Career Services ... Ms. Wendy SELIGMANN
42 Dir of Spiritual Life & Chaplain ... Rev. Brian AMMONS
41 Director of Athletics ... Ms. Stacey ENOS
91 Dir Admin Data Processing ... Ms. Omega HODGES
40 Campus Store Manager ... Ms. Keller Anne KNIGHT
15 Director Human Resources ... Ms. Gail BAYLOR
18 Acting Dir Facil Mgmt/Tech Svcs ... Ms. Deborah ANSTROM
19 Director Public Safety ... Mr. Terry PAYNE
88 Interim Dir Environ Leader Ctr ... Dr. John BROCK
88 Director Swannanoa Gathering ... Mr. Jim MAGILL
104 Director of International Programs ... Ms. Naomi OTTERNESS
42 Minister of WW Pres Church ... Mr. Steve ROHNHOLT
96 Director of Purchasing ... Ms. Deborah ANSTROM
13 Manager Computing Services ... Mr. David HARPER
85 Dir Diversity & International Stds ... Ms. Lorrie JAYNE
88 Conference Coordinator ... Ms. Liz BRACE

William Peace University (formerly Peace College) (E)

15 E Peace Street, Raleigh NC 27604-1194

County: Wake — FICE Identification: 002953
Unit ID: 199272
Telephone: (919) 508-2000 — Carnegie Class: Bac/A&S
FAX Number: (919) 508-2326 — Calendar System: Semester
URL: www.peace.edu
Established: 1857 — Annual Undergrad Tuition & Fees: $23,700
Enrollment: 660 — Coed
Affiliation or Control: Presbyterian Church (U.S.A.) — IRS Status: 501(c)3
Highest Offering: Baccalaureate
Program: Liberal Arts And General
Accreditation: SC

01 President ... Dr. Debra M. TOWNSLEY
04 Executive Secretary to President ... Ms. Patricia L. LUKASZEWSKI
05 Vice President for Academic Affairs ... Dr. Ann DENLINGER
30 Exec Dir of Development & Alumnae ... Ms. Julie E. RICCIARDI
10 Vice Pres Finance & Administration ... Mr. George A. YEARWOOD
15 Asst Vice Pres for Human Resources ... Ms. Amber M. KIMBALL
107 Dean Wm Peace School of Prof Stds ... Ms. Laurie ALBERT
84 Dean of Enrollment & Adult Educ ... Vacant
32 Dean of Student & Academic Services ... Mr. Jerry J. NUESELL
35 Assistant Dean of Students ... Vacant
06 Registrar ... Ms. Carmella CHANEY
08 Director of Library Services ... Mr. Nathan J. HELLMERS
27 Chief Information Officer ... Mr. Larry ESSARY
18 Director of Facilities ... Mr. John B. CRANHAM
19 Director Campus Safety & Security ... Mr. Michael A. JOHN
23 Director of Health Services ... Vacant
35 Director of Student Engagement ... Vacant
36 Director of Career Services ... Ms. Barbara M. EFIRD
37 Director of Financial Aid ... Ms. Angela J. KIRKLEY
41 Director of Athletics ... Mr. P. Kelly JOHNSON, JR.
42 Chaplain ... Rev. R. Lee CARTER
21 Comptroller ... Ms. Susan T. CHILDS
84 Vice Pres Enrollment Mgmt/Admission ... Ms. Amber L. STENBECK
07 Associate Director of Admissions ... Ms. Jenny L. PEACOCK
40 Bookstore Manager ... Ms. Brittany LITTLE
44 Director of Loyalty Fund ... Vacant
39 Assistant Dean for Campus Life ... Ms. Dawn M. DILLON

Wingate University (F)

220 N. Camden Street, Wingate NC 28174-0157

County: Union — FICE Identification: 002985
Unit ID: 199962
Telephone: (704) 233-8000 — Carnegie Class: Master's S
FAX Number: (704) 233-8192 — Calendar System: Semester

URL: www.wingate.edu
Established: 1896 Annual Undergrad Tuition & Fees: $23,845
Enrollment: 2,529 Coed
Affiliation or Control: Southern Baptist IRS Status: 501(c)3
Highest Offering: Doctorate
Program: Liberal Arts And General; Teacher Preparatory; Professional; Business Emphasis
Accreditation: SC, ACBSP, ARCPA, MUS, PHAR, TED

01 President .... Dr. Jerry E. MCGEE
05 Senior VP Academic Affairs .... Dr. Martha S. ASTI
10 VP Business/Chief Financial Ofcr .... Mr. William H. DURHAM
30 Vice President Resource Development .... Mr. E. Vincent TILSON
41 Vice Pres & Director of Athletics .... Mr. R. Stephen POSTON
32 VP for Student Life/Enrollment Mgmt .... Mr. T. Rhett BROWN
58 VP for Grad & Prof Programs .... Dr. Robert B. SUPERNAW
21 Asst VP for Business Operations .... Mr. Scott E. HUNSUCKER
23 Asst VP for Health Sciences Div .... Mr. Roy Lee RAGSDALE, JR.
12 Asst VP Matthews Campus .... Dr. Greg CLEMMER
32 Dean of Student Affairs .... Mrs. Glenda H. BEBBER
49 Dean School Arts & Sciences .... Dr. H. Donald MERRILL
50 Dean School of Business .... Mr. Joe M. GRAHAM
53 Dean School of Education .... Dr. Sarah H. BURNS
08 Director of Library .... Mrs. Arnee M. ODOM
12 Dean of the Metro College .... Dr. Greg R. CLEMMER
35 Director of Involvement .... Ms. Brandy SHOTT
30 Director of Development .... Dr. Wayne D. WIKE
09 Director Inst Research/Registrar .... Mrs. Nicci C. BROWN
37 Director Student Financial Planning ...... Ms. Teresa G. WILLIAMS
26 Dir of Marketing/Communications .... Mr. Jeffrey ATKINSON
91 Director Administrative Computing .... Mr. Timothy D. HERRIN
29 Director of Alumni Development .... Vacant
42 Minstr to Stdnts/Asst Dn Stdnt Affs .... Rev. A. Dane JORDAN
40 Manager of Campus Store .... Mr. Danny KEY
19 Director of Campus Safety .... Mr. Mike EASLEY
44 Director of Annual Giving .... Vacant
44 Dir of Major Gifts & Planned Giving ... Mr. J. Theodore JOHNSON
27 Asst Dir Marketing & Communications .... Vacant
38 Director of Counseling Services .... Ms. Jessica HYLTON
13 Director of Information Technology .... Ms. Jeanette K. BUJAK
36 Dir of Internships and Career Svcs .... Ms. Sharon ROBINSON
15 Human Resources Coordinator .... Mrs. Lisa B. RAGSDALE
39 Dir Resid Life/Asst Dn Stdnt Affs .... Mr. Patrick BIGGERSTAFF
35 Dir of Retention/Asst Dn Stdnt Affs .... Ms. Kristin WHARTON

NORTH DAKOTA

Cankdeska Cikana Community College (A)

PO Box 269, 214 First Avenue, Fort Totten ND 58335-0269
County: Benson FICE Identification: 022365
Unit ID: 200208
Telephone: (701) 766-4415 Carnegie Class: Tribal
FAX Number: (701) 766-4077 Calendar System: Semester
URL: www.littlehoop.edu
Established: 1974 Annual Undergrad Tuition & Fees: $2,525
Enrollment: 203 Coed
Affiliation or Control: Independent Non-Profit IRS Status: 501(c)3
Highest Offering: Associate Degree
Program: Occupational; 2-Year Principally Bachelor's Creditable
Accreditation: NH

01 President .... Dr. Cynthia A. LINDQUIST
05 Vice President Academics .... Dr. Leander MCDONALD
10 Vice President for Finance .... Ms. Chelly MERKEL-VEER
32 Vice Pres Student Services .... Ms. Erica CAVANAUGH
06 Registrar .... Mr. Ermen BROWN, JR.

Ft. Berthold Community College (B)

PO Box 490, New Town ND 58763-0490
County: Mountrail FICE Identification: 025537
Unit ID: 200086
Telephone: (701) 627-4738 Carnegie Class: Tribal
FAX Number: (701) 627-3609 Calendar System: Semester
URL: www.fortbertholdcc.edu
Established: 1973 Annual Undergrad Tuition & Fees: $4,210
Enrollment: 199 Coed
Affiliation or Control: Independent Non-Profit IRS Status: 501(c)3
Highest Offering: Baccalaureate
Program: Occupational; 2-Year Principally Bachelor's Creditable
Accreditation: NH

01 President .... Mr. Russell D. MASON, JR.
05 Academic Dean .... Dr. Stacey MORTENSON
32 Dean of Students .... Ms. Kathy KRAFT
10 Chief Finance Manager .... Mr. Kim CONNOLE
37 Financial Aid Administration .... Ms. Beverly MASON
06 Registrar .... Mr. Garrett TITUS
08 Librarian .... Mrs. Quincee BAKER
38 Counselor .... Vacant
40 Bookstore Manager .... Ms. Iona LITTLE WHITEMAN

Jamestown College (C)

6000 College Lane, Jamestown ND 58405-0001
County: Stutsman FICE Identification: 002990
Unit ID: 200156
Telephone: (701) 252-3467 Carnegie Class: Bac/Diverse
FAX Number: (701) 253-4318 Calendar System: Semester
URL: www.jc.edu
Established: 1883 Annual Undergrad Tuition & Fees: $23,900
Enrollment: 939 Coed
Affiliation or Control: Presbyterian Church (U.S.A.) IRS Status: 501(c)3
Highest Offering: Master's
Program: Liberal Arts And General; Teacher Preparatory; Professional
Accreditation: NH, IACBE, NUR

01 President .... Dr. Robert S. BADAL
05 Vice Pres/Dean Academic Affairs .... Dr. Gary WATTS
32 Dean of Students .... Mr. Gary VAN ZINDEREN
11 VP Planning/Administrative Services .... Mr. Thomas R. HECK
30 VP Inst Advancement/Business Affs .... Ms. Polly J. PETERSON
84 Dean of Enrollment Management .... Ms. Tena LAWRENCE
04 Assistant to the President .... Ms. Liz SCHWARTZ
06 Registrar .... Mr. Michael P. WOODLEY
37 Director of Financial Aid .... Mrs. Marge M. MICHAEL
08 Librarian .... Mrs. Phyllis K. BRATTON
36 Director Experiential Education .... Ms. Pat J. RINDE
27 Director Information Office .... Ms. Donna SCHMITZ
41 Athletic Director .... Mr. Lawrie PAULSON
14 Director Computer Center .... Mr. Tim KACHEL
18 Chief Facilities/Physical Plant .... Mr. Mark KOEPKE
42 Chaplain .... Rev. Darin NAMMINGA
101 Secretary to the Board of Trustees .... Ms. Liz SCHWARTZ

Medcenter One College of Nursing (D)

512 N 7th Street, Bismarck ND 58501-4494
County: Burleigh FICE Identification: 009354
Unit ID: 200244
Telephone: (701) 323-6271 Carnegie Class: Spec/Health
FAX Number: (701) 323-6289 Calendar System: Semester
URL: www.medcenterone.com/collegeofnursing
Established: 1988 Annual Undergrad Tuition & Fees: $11,167
Enrollment: 90 Coed
Affiliation or Control: Independent Non-Profit IRS Status: 501(c)3
Highest Offering: Baccalaureate
Program: Nursing Emphasis
Accreditation: NH, NURSE, RAD

01 Provost/Dean .... Dr. Karen K. LATHAM
20 Associate Dean .... Dr. Wanda F. ROSE
32 Director Student Services .... Ms. Mary J. SMITH
37 Dir Student Financial Aid/Registrar .... Ms. Janell D. THOMAS
08 Head Librarian .... Mr. Travis SCHULTZ
10 Chief Business Officer .... Ms. Candy RIFFEY

*North Dakota University System Office (E)

600 E Boulevard Avenue, Dept 215, Bismarck ND 58505-0230
County: Burleigh FICE Identification: 033434
Telephone: (701) 328-2960 Carnegie Class: N/A
FAX Number: (701) 328-2961
URL: www.ndus.edu

01 Chancellor .... Hamid SHIRVANI
05 Vice Chanc Academic/Student Affairs .... Michel HILLMAN
10 Vice Chanc Administrative Affairs .... Laura GLATT
45 Vice Chancellor Strategic Planning .... Vacant
13 Chief Information Officer .... Randall THURSBY
24 Director Interactive Video Network .... Jerry ROSTAD
37 Director Financial Aid .... Nathan STRATTON
16 Human Resources .... Laura GLATT
20 Academic Affairs Associate .... Aimee COPAS
37 Indn Schlrshp Pgm/Dir St Aprvd Agy .... Rhonda SCHAUER
21 Director of Finance .... Cathy MCDONALD
88 Research Analyst .... Michelle OLSEN
43 General Counsel/Executive Secretary .... H. P. SEAWORTH
26 Public Affairs Director .... Vacant
88 Director Financial Reporting .... Robin PUTNAM
106 Distance Education Coordinator .... Robert LARSON
88 Articulation & Transfer .... Lisa JOHNSON
88 Dir Consortium for Subst Abuse Prev .... Jane VANGSNESS
88 Coord ND Col Access Challenge Pgm .... Tim MUELLER
88 Dir Internal Audit/Risk Assessmen .... Bill EGGERT
NDUS Grant Developer .... Cathleen RUCH

*University of North Dakota Main Campus (F)

264 Centennial Drive, Grand Forks ND 58202
County: Grand Forks FICE Identification: 003005
Unit ID: 200280
Telephone: (701) 777-2011 Carnegie Class: RU/H
FAX Number: (701) 777-2696 Calendar System: Semester
URL: www.und.edu
Established: 1883 Annual Undergrad Tuition & Fees (In-State): $7,254
Enrollment: 14,697 Coed
Affiliation or Control: State IRS Status: 501(c)3
Highest Offering: Doctorate
Program: Liberal Arts And General; Teacher Preparatory; Professional
Accreditation: NH, AAB, ANEST, ARCPA, ART, BUS, CLPSY, COPSY, CS, CYTO, DIETC, ENG, HT, IPSY, LAW, MED, MT, MUS, NAIT, NURSE, OT, PTA, SP, SPAA, SW, TED, THEA

02 President .... Dr. Robert O. KELLEY
29 Exec Vice Pres & CEO Alumni Assoc .... Mr. Tim O'KEEFE
05 Vice Pres Academic Affairs/Provost .... Mr. Paul LEBEL
10 Vice President Operations/Finance .... Ms. Alice BREKKE
32 Vice Pres Student Affairs .... Dr. Lori REESOR
17 Vice President Health Affairs .... Dr. Joshua WYNNE
46 Vice Pres Research/Economic Devel .... Dr. Phyllis E. JOHNSON
26 VP for University & Public Affairs .... Ms. Susan WALTON
26 Exec Assoc VP University Rels .... Mr. Peter B. JOHNSON
35 Associate VP & Dean of Students .... Dr. Cara HALGREN
21 Assoc VP Finance/Operations .... Ms. Peggy LUCKE
21 Assoc VP Finance/Operations .... Ms. Margaret MYERS
45 Assoc Vice Pres Research/Econ Dev .... Dr. Barry MILAVETZ
45 Assoc VP Research/Economic Develop .... Dr. Mark HOFFMANN
25 AVP Intellectual Prop Comm/Econ Dev .... Mr. Michael MOORE
88 Assoc VP for Health & Wellness .... Dr. Laurie BETTING
25 Asst VP Grants/Contracts Admin .... Mr. David O. SCHMIDT
88 Asst VP Student Affairs .... Ms. Lisa BURGER
08 Director of Libraries .... Mr. Wilbur STOLT
27 Chief Information Officer .... Dr. Joshua RIEDY
06 Registrar .... Dr. Suzanne ANDERSON
15 Dir Human Resources/Payroll Svcs .... Ms. Patricia HANSON
19 Chief of University Police .... Vacant
38 Director Counseling Center .... Dr. Myron VEENSTRA
36 Int Dir Career Services/Coop Educ .... Ms. Ilene ODEGARD
87 Director Summer Sessions .... Ms. Diane HADDEN
20 Director Instructional Development .... Dr. Anne KELSCH
22 Affirmative Action Officer .... Ms. Sally J. PAGE
37 Int Director Student Financial Aid .... Ms. Janelle KILGORE
39 Director Residence Services .... Ms. Judy L. SARGENT
23 Director of Student Health .... Ms. Michelle D. ESLINGER
43 General Counsel .... Ms. Julie EVANS
41 Director Athletics .... Mr. Brian FAISON
18 Director of Facilities Management .... Mr. Larry L. ZITZOW
85 Director International Programs .... Mr. Ray LAGASSE
21 Controller .... Ms. Sharon LOILAND
88 Director Judicial Affs/Crisis Pgm .... Vacant
09 Director of Institutional Research .... Ms. Carmen WILLIAMS
94 Director Women's Center .... Ms. Kay MENDICK
96 Director Purchasing .... Mr. Scott SCHREINER
30 Chief Development Officer .... Mr. Tim O'KEEFE
92 Director Honors Program .... Dr. Sally PYLE
28 Dir Multicultural Student Services .... Ms. Malika CARTER
19 Dir Emergency Mgmt & Public Safety .... Vacant
13 Deputy CIO IT Systems & Services .... Mr. Rick ANDERSON
21 Budget Manager .... Ms. Cindy FETSCH
40 Manager University Bookstore .... Ms. Lisa SIMONSON
49 Int Dean of Arts & Sciences .... Dr. Kathleen TIEMANN
58 Int Dean of Graduate School .... Dr. Wayne SWISHER
61 Dean School of Law .... Ms. Kathryn RAND
66 Dean College of Nursing .... Dr. Denise KORNIEWICZ
50 Dean Business/Public Administration .... Dr. Dennis J. ELBERT
54 Dean College of Engr/Mines .... Dr. Hesham EL-REWINI
53 Int Dean Col Education/Human Devel .... Dr. Dennis CAINE
88 Dean of Aerospace Sciences .... Dr. Bruce SMITH
63 Dean Sch Medicine/Health Science .... Dr. Joshua WYNNE

*Dickinson State University (G)

291 Campus Drive, Dickinson ND 58601-4896
County: Stark FICE Identification: 002989
Unit ID: 200059
Telephone: (701) 483-2507 Carnegie Class: Bac/Diverse
FAX Number: (701) 483-2006 Calendar System: Semester
URL: www.dickinsonstate.edu
Established: 1918 Annual Undergrad Tuition & Fees (In-State): $5,717
Enrollment: 2,346 Coed
Affiliation or Control: State IRS Status: 501(c)3
Highest Offering: Baccalaureate
Program: Liberal Arts And General; Teacher Preparatory
Accreditation: NH, IACBE, MUS, NUR, PNUR, TED

02 President .... Dr. D.C COSTON
05 Vice President for Academic Affairs .... Dr. Rich BRAUHN
10 Vice President for Business Affairs .... Mr. Alvin G. BINSTOCK
32 Vice Pres for Student Development .... Mr. Hal HAYNES
49 Dean of Arts & Sciences .... Dr. Kenneth HAUGHT
53 Dean of Educ/Business/Applied Sci .... Vacant
102 Exec Dir Alumni Assoc/Foundation .... Mr. Kevin J. THOMPSON
26 Director of University Relations .... Marie MOE
41 Director of Intercollege Athletics .... Mr. Tim DANIEL
88 Strom Ctr for Entrpshp & Ino .... Josh NICHOLS
56 Director of Extended Learning .... Mr. John HURLIMANN
07 Director of Enrollment Services .... Vacant
06 Director of Academic Records .... Kathy MEYER
08 Director of Library Services .... Ms. Rita ENNEN
13 Director of Computer Services .... Mr. Todd HAUF
37 Director of Financial Aid .... Ms. Sandy L. KLEIN
88 Director Academic Success Center .... Dr. Stacie VARNSON
88 Director of Food Service .... Mr. Charles DORSA
40 Manager University Store .... Ms. Loretta A. HEIDT
21 Controller .... Mr. Mark S. LOWE
36 Director of Career Services .... Ms. Bonnie G. BOHLMAN
09 Coordinator of Institutional Rsrch .... Mr. Scott STAUDINGER
28 Director of Multicultural Center .... Ms. Ronnie WALKER
39 Housing Coordinator .... Ms. Lydia DWORSHAK
15 Coordinator Personnel Services .... Ms. Gail EBELTOFT

*Mayville State University (H)

330 3rd Street, NE, Mayville ND 58257-1299
County: Traill FICE Identification: 002993
Unit ID: 200226
Telephone: (701) 788-2301 Carnegie Class: Bac/Diverse
FAX Number: (701) 788-4748 Calendar System: Semester
URL: www.mayvillestate.edu
Established: 1889 Annual Undergrad Tuition & Fees (In-State): $6,193
Enrollment: 970 Coed

Affiliation or Control: State IRS Status: 501(c)3
Highest Offering: Baccalaureate
Program: 2-Year Principally Bachelor's Creditable; Liberal Arts And General; Teacher Preparatory; Business Emphasis
Accreditation: NH, TED

02 President ....Dr. Gary D. HAGEN
04 Exec Assistant to the President ....Mrs. Shirley K. RUX
05 Vice President for Academic Affairs ....Dr. Keith A. STENEHJEM
10 Vice President for Business Affairs ....Mr. Steven P. BENSEN
32 VP for Student Affairs/Inst Researc ....Dr. Raymond H. GERSZEWSKI
08 Director of Library Services ....Ms. Kelly KORNKVEN
37 Director of Financial Aid ....Mrs. Shirley M. HANSON
06 Registrar ....Mrs. Pamela K. BRAATEN
84 Director of Enrollment Services ....Mr. James MOROWSKI
36 Dir Career Services & Internships ....Mr. Jay A. HENRICKSON
39 Director of Student Housing ....Mr. Richard SMITH
40 Director of Bookstore ....Mrs. Pam B. SOHOLT
41 Athletic Director ....Mr. Mike K. MOORE
18 Physical Plant Director ....Mr. Dennis N. SCHULTZ
26 Chief Public Relations Officer ....Ms. Beth I. SWENSON
18 Director of Facilities Services ....Mr. Bob J. KOZOJED
15 Director of Human Resources ....Ms. Jane GRINDE
13 Director of Information Technology ....Mr. Patrick W. STEELE
14 Director of Computer Center ....Mr. Shawn D. OGBURN
105 Director of Web Services ....Mr. James E. BURMEISTER
07 Director of Admissions & Ext Learn ....Ms. Misti L. WUORI
96 Business Office Accountant ....Mrs. Janice E. JORGENSEN
30 Director of Development ....Mr. John J. KLOCKE

*Minot State University (A)

500 University Avenue W, Minot ND 58707-0001
County: Ward FICE Identification: 002994
Unit ID: 200253
Telephone: (701) 858-3000 Carnegie Class: Master's M
FAX Number: (701) 839-6933 Calendar System: Semester
URL: www.minotstateu.edu
Established: 1913 Annual Undergrad Tuition & Fees (In-State): $5,922
Enrollment: 3,657 Coed
Affiliation or Control: State IRS Status: 501(c)3
Highest Offering: Beyond Master's But Less Than Doctorate
Program: Liberal Arts And General; Teacher Preparatory; Professional; Business Emphasis
Accreditation: NH, IACBE, MUS, NUR, SP, SW, TED

02 President ....Dr. David FULLER
05 VP for Academic Affairs ....Dr. Lenore KOCZON
10 Vice President for Finance/Admin ....Mr. Brian FOISY
30 Vice President for Advancement ....Mr. Marv SEMRAU
32 Vice President for Student Affairs ....Dr. Richard J. JENKINS
21 AVP Business Services/Controller ....Ms. Jonelle WATSON
07 AVP Admissions ....Mr. Kevin HARMON
18 AVP Facilities Management ....Mr. Roger KLUCK
06 Registrar ....Ms. Rebecca PORTER
08 Director of the Library ....Mr. Stephen BANISTER
35 Director of Student Life ....Vacant
37 Director of Financial Aid ....Mr. Dale GEHRING
58 Dean of Graduate School ....Vacant
50 Dean College of Business ....Dr. JoAnn LINRUD
49 Dean College Arts & Science ....Dr. Conrad DAVIDSON
53 Dean Col Education/Health Sci ....Dr. Neil NORDQUIST
51 Dean Continuing Education ....Dr. Kristin WARMOTH
29 Director Alumni Relations ....Ms. Janna MCKECHNIE
14 Director Computer Services ....Ms. Cathy HORVATH
40 Director Bookstore ....Ms. Gerri KUNA
41 Athletic Director ....Mr. Rick HEDBERG
27 Director of Public Information ....Ms. Susan NESS
15 Director of Human Resources ....Mr. Wesley MATTHEWS
12 Dean of Dakota College at Bottineau ....Dr. Kenneth GROSZ
36 Director of Campus Career Services ....Ms. Lynda BERTSCH
38 Director of Student Services ....Ms. Evelyn KLIMPEL
25 Grants & Contracts Accountant ....Vacant
09 Director of Institutional Research ....Ms. Cari OLSON

*North Dakota State University Main Campus (B)

P.O. Box 6050, Fargo ND 58108-6050
County: Cass FICE Identification: 002997
Unit ID: 200332
Telephone: (701) 231-8011 Carnegie Class: RU/VH
FAX Number: (701) 231-8722 Calendar System: Semester
URL: www.ndsu.edu
Established: 1890 Annual Undergrad Tuition & Fees (In-State): $7,782
Enrollment: 14,399 Coed
Affiliation or Control: State IRS Status: 501(c)3
Highest Offering: Doctorate
Program: Liberal Arts And General; Teacher Preparatory; Professional
Accreditation: NH, ART, BUS, CACREP, CIDA, CONST, DIETC, DIETD, ENG, EXSC, #LSAR, MFCD, MUS, NURSE, PHAR, TED, THEA

02 President ....Dr. Dean BRESCIANI
05 Provost/Vice Pres Academic Affairs ....Dr. J. Bruce RAFERT
10 Vice President Business & Finance ....Mr. Bruce BOLLINGER
32 Vice President for Student Affairs ....Mr. Prakash C. MATHEW
46 Vice Pres Research Crea Act & Tech ....Dr. Philip BOUDJOUK
88 Vice President Ag/Univ Extension ....Dr. Ken GRAFTON
30 Exec Dir NDSU Dev Found/Alumni Assn ....Mr. James C. MILLER
13 Interim VP Information Technology ....Mr. Marc WALLMAN
22 VP Equity/Diversity/Global Outreach ....Mrs. Eveadean MYERS
35 Associate Vice Pres Student Affairs ....Dr. Catherine (Kate) HAUGEN
88 Assoc VP Sponsored Programs Admin ....Ms. Valrey V. KETTNER
06 University Registrar ....Dr. Kristi D. WOLD-MCCORMICK
84 Coordinator Enrollment Management ....Mr. Viet DOAN
08 Dean of Libraries ....Dr. Michelle REID
35 Dean Student Life ....Ms. Janna M. STOSKOPF
51 Dir Distance/Continuing Education ....Ms. Lisa NORDICK
37 Director Student Financial Services ....Ms. Jeanette E. ENEBO
36 Director Career Center ....Ms. Jill J. WILKEY
27 Communication Coordinator ....Ms. Ann ROBINSON-PAUL
88 Asst VP University Relations ....Ms. Laura MCDANIEL
56 Director Extension Service ....Mr. Chris BOERBOOM
50 Dean Business Administration ....Dr. Ronald D. JOHNSON
54 Dean Engineering/Architecture ....Dr. Gary R. SMITH
59 Dean Human Development & Education ....Dr. Virginia L. CLARK JOHNSON
49 Dean Arts/Humanities/Social Science ....Dr. Kent SANDSTROM
81 Dean of Science & Math ....Dr. Kevin D. MCCAUL
67 Dean of Pharmacy/Nursing/Allied Sci ....Dr. Charles D. PETERSON
58 Dean Col of Grad/Inter Studies ....Dr. David A. WITTROCK
89 Assoc Dean University Studies ....Dr. Carolyn A. SCHNELL
21 Director of Budget ....Ms. Cynthia ROTT
25 Manager Grant & Contract Acctng ....Ms. Karen HENDRICKSON
18 Director Facilities Management ....Mr. Mike ELLINGSON
19 Dir of Univ Police/Safety Officer ....Mr. Raymond E. BOYER
38 Director Counseling/Disability Svcs ....Dr. William BURNS
23 Director Wellness Center ....Mr. Gary T. FISHER
39 Director of Residence Life ....Mr. Rian NOSTRUM
40 Director Bookstore ....Ms. Carol J. MILLER
41 Director of Athletics ....Mr. Gene F. TAYLOR
43 General Counsel ....Mr. Chris WILSON
57 Director Fine Arts ....Dr. E. John MILLER
09 Director Inst Research/Analysis ....Dr. William D. SLANGER
96 Director of Purchasing ....Ms. Stacey O. WINTER
07 Director of Admissions ....Mr. Jobey L. LICHTBLAU

*Valley City State University (C)

101 College Street, SW, Valley City ND 58072-4098
County: Barnes FICE Identification: 003008
Unit ID: 200572
Telephone: (701) 845-7990 Carnegie Class: Bac/Diverse
FAX Number: (701) 845-7253 Calendar System: Semester
URL: www.vcsu.edu
Established: 1889 Annual Undergrad Tuition & Fees (In-State): $6,334
Enrollment: 1,384 Coed
Affiliation or Control: State IRS Status: 501(c)3
Highest Offering: Master's
Program: Liberal Arts And General; Teacher Preparatory
Accreditation: NH, MUS, TED

02 President ....Dr. Steven W. SHIRLEY
05 Vice President Academic Affairs ....Dr. Margaret DAHLBERG
10 Vice President Business Affairs ....Mr. Doug DAWES
32 Vice President Student Affairs ....Mr. Glen J. SCHMALZ
53 Dean Sch of Educ/Graduate Stds ....Dr. Gary THOMPSON
08 Library Director ....Ms. Donna JAMES
20 Director Student Academic Services ....Ms. Janet M. DRAKE
37 Director Student Financial Aid ....Ms. Betty A. SCHUMACHER
36 Director Career Services ....Ms. Marcia J. FOSS
14 Chief Information Officer ....Mr. Joseph TYKWINSKI
41 Athletic Director ....Mr. Jack DENHOLM
84 Director of Enrollment Services ....Ms. Charlene STENSON
30 Director of University Advancement ....Mr. Larry J. ROBINSON
18 Director of Facilities Services ....Mr. Ron POMMERER
07 Director of Admissions & Records ....Ms. Charlene STENSON
15 Director of Human Resources ....Mr. Derek HUGHES
44 Asst Dir University Advancement ....Ms. Kim HESCH
38 Director of Student Counseling ....Ms. Erin KLINGENBERG
26 Director Marketing/Communications ....Mr. Doug ANDERSON
40 Director Bookstore ....Mr. Todd ROGELSTAD
06 Registrar ....Ms. Jody KLIER

*Bismarck State College (D)

PO Box 5587, Bismarck ND 58506-5587
County: Burleigh FICE Identification: 002988
Unit ID: 200022
Telephone: (701) 224-5400 Carnegie Class: Assoc/Pub4
FAX Number: (701) 224-5550 Calendar System: Semester
URL: www.bismarckstate.edu
Established: 1939 Annual Undergrad Tuition & Fees (In-State): $3,485
Enrollment: 4,392 Coed
Affiliation or Control: State IRS Status: 501(c)3
Highest Offering: Baccalaureate
Program: Occupational; 2-Year Principally Bachelor's Creditable; Liberal Arts And General
Accreditation: NH, EMT, ENGT, MLTAD, SURGT

02 President ....Dr. Larry C. SKOGEN
03 Executive Vice President ....Mr. David CLARK
05 Provost/VP Academic Affairs ....Dr. Drake CARTER
30 VP College Advance/Exec Dir Found ....Mr. Gordy BINEK
88 VP National Energy Ctr of Excellenc ....Ms. Kari KNUDSON
09 AVP Inst Effect/Strategic Planning ....Dr. Jane SCHULZ
32 Associate VP for Student Affairs ....Dr. Donna FISHBECK
10 Assoc VP for Finance & Operations ....Mrs. Tamara BARBER
88 Assoc VP Nat Energy Ctr of Excell ....Mr. Bruce EMMIL
51 Assoc VP Cont Educ/Training & Innov ....Mrs. Carla HIXSON
07 Dir Admissions/Enrollment Services ....Ms. Karen ERICKSON
20 Dean of Academic Affairs ....Dr. Janelle MASTERS
08 Director of Library Services ....Ms. Marlene ANDERSON
26 Director of College Relations ....Mrs. Mary FRIESZ
41 Director of Athletics ....Mr. Buster GILLISS
106 Chief Dist Learning/Military Affair ....Mr. Lane HUBER
37 Director of Financial Aid ....Mr. Jeff JACOBS
51 Dir of Cont Educ/Trng & Innovation ....Ms. Lori HEINSOHN
88 Project Manager NECE ....Mr. Zachery ALLEN
88 Dir Great Plains Energy Corridor ....Ms. Emily MCKAY
88 Program Manager NECE ....Mr. Kevin HOLMSTROM
88 Program Manager NECE ....Mr. Dan SCHMIDT
88 Program Manager NECE ....Mr. Wade VOGEL
46 Dir of Resource Development ....Ms. Julie ERICKSON
35 Director Student & Residence Life ....Ms. Heather SHEEHAN
18 Chief Buildings/Grounds Officer ....Mr. Don ROETHLER
06 Director Academic Records/Registrar ....Mr. Tom LENO
16 Chief Human Resources Officer ....Mrs. Rita LINDGREN
13 Chief Information Services Officer ....Mr. Elmer WEIGEL
40 Bookstore Manager/Purchasing Coord ....Mrs. Tanya FUHER
36 Dir Couseling and Advising Services ....Mr. Jay MEIER
44 Development Manager ....Mrs. Gina BUCHHOLTZ
29 Alumni Coordinator ....Mrs. Rita NODLAND
04 Executive Assistant to President ....Mrs. Debbie VAN BERKOM

*Dakota College at Bottineau (E)

105 Simrall Boulevard, Bottineau ND 58318-1198
County: Bottineau FICE Identification: 002995
Unit ID: 200314
Telephone: (701) 228-2277 Carnegie Class: Assoc/Pub2in4
FAX Number: (701) 228-5468 Calendar System: Semester
URL: www.dakotacollege.edu
Established: 1907 Annual Undergrad Tuition & Fees (In-State): $3,887
Enrollment: 812 Coed
Affiliation or Control: State IRS Status: 501(c)3
Highest Offering: Associate Degree
Program: Occupational; 2-Year Principally Bachelor's Creditable
Accreditation: NH

02 Campus Dean ....Dr. Ken GROSZ
10 Director of Business Affairs ....Ms. Kara BOWEN
32 Assoc Dean for Student Affairs ....Ms. Paula BERG
05 Assoc Dean for Academic Affairs ....Mr. Larry BROOKS
08 Librarian ....Dr. Debra SYVERTSON
07 Director of Admissions ....Ms. Leann WEBER
06 Registrar ....Ms. Paula BERG
37 Director Financial Aid ....Ms. Valerie HEILMAN
41 Athletic Director ....Mr. Scott JOHNSON
29 Director Alumni Relations ....Ms. Brandy SIMPSON
18 Chief Facilities/Physical Plant ....Ms. Kara BOWEN
39 Housing Director ....Mr. Eric KESTER-MABON
28 Director of Diversity ....Ms. Colette SCHIMETZ
40 Bookstore Manager ....Ms. Janeen POLLMAN

*Lake Region State College (F)

1801 College Drive N, Devils Lake ND 58301-1598
County: Ramsey FICE Identification: 002991
Unit ID: 200192
Telephone: (701) 662-1600 Carnegie Class: Assoc/Pub-R-M
FAX Number: (701) 662-1570 Calendar System: Semester
URL: www.lrsc.edu
Established: 1941 Annual Undergrad Tuition & Fees (In-State): $3,908
Enrollment: 2,056 Coed
Affiliation or Control: State IRS Status: 501(c)3
Highest Offering: Associate Degree
Program: Occupational; 2-Year Principally Bachelor's Creditable
Accreditation: NH

02 President ....Dr. Mike BOWER
05 Vice Pres of Instruction Services ....Dr. Douglas D. DARLING
10 Vice Pres Administrative Services ....Mr. Corry G. KENNER
32 Vice Pres Student Services ....Dr. Randall FIXEN
12 Director of Branch Campus ....Mr. John COWGER
30 Vice Pres Advancmnt/Foundation ....Ms. Laurel GOULDING
84 Director of Enrollment Management ....Ms. Stephanie SHOCK
37 Dir Student Finan Aid/Placemnt Svcs ....Ms. Katie NETTELL
88 Director Food Service ....Ms. Myrna UNGER
18 Superintendent Buildings/Grounds ....Mr. Donald JORGENSON
08 Librarian ....Ms. Celeste ERTELT
41 Director Athletics ....Mr. Duane SCHWAB
13 Chief Information Officer ....Ms. Toofawn SIMHAI
15 Chief of Personnel ....Mr. Corry G. KENNER
40 Director of Bookstore ....Ms. Melissa STOTTS
06 Registrar ....Mr. Daniel JOHNSON
26 Director of Public Relations/Mktg ....Ms. Erin WOOD
31 Director Community Education ....Ms. Edith ARMEY
09 Director of Institutional Research ....Ms. Brandi NELSON
28 Director of Diversity ....Mrs. Nicole CLAUSSEN
38 Director Counseling Services ....Ms. Brigitte FRESCHETTE
07 Director of Admissions ....Ms. Stephanie SHOCK
21 Controller ....Ms. Joann KITCHENS

*North Dakota State College of Science (G)

800 N Sixth Street, Wahpeton ND 58076-0002
County: Richland FICE Identification: 002996
Unit ID: 200305
Telephone: (800) 342-4325 Carnegie Class: Assoc/Pub-R-M
FAX Number: (701) 671-2145 Calendar System: Semester
URL: www.ndscs.edu
Established: 1903 Annual Undergrad Tuition & Fees (In-State): $4,177
Enrollment: 3,127 Coed
Affiliation or Control: State IRS Status: 501(c)3

Highest Offering: Associate Degree
Program: Occupational; 2-Year Principally Bachelor's Creditable
Accreditation: NH, DA, DH, EMT, OTA, PNUR

02 President .... Dr. John RICHMAN
05 VP Academic & Student Affairs .... Mr. Harvey LINK
11 Vice Pres Administrative Affairs .... Mr. Mike RENK
09 Assoc Vice Pres Institutional Rsrch .... Mrs. Gloria DOHMAN
32 Assoc Vice Pres Acad/Student Affs .... Mr. Philip PARNELL
84 Dir Enroll Svcs/Finan Aid/Placement .... Mrs. Karen REILLY
08 Director Library .... Ms. Karen M. CHOBOT
26 Dir Marketing/Communications/PR .. Mrs. Barbara SPAETH-BAUM
29 Director of Alumni Foundation .... Mr. Brad BARTH
41 Athletic Director .... Mr. Stuart ENGEN
15 Human Resource Director .... Mrs. Ann HIEDEMAN
18 Director Facilities/Physical Plant .... Mr. Dallas FOSSUM
20 Academic Services Director .... Ms. Maria KADUC
39 Director of Residence Life .... Mrs. Melissa JOHNSON
06 Associate Registrar .... Mrs. Barb MUND
21 Business Manager .... Mr. Keith JOHNSON
24 Instructional Technology Coord .... Mr. Tom HICKMAN
07 Admissions Counselor .... Mr. Dale GROSZ
38 Counseling Center .... Mr. Vince PLUMMER
96 Director of Purchasing .... Mr. David MEYER
49 Dean Arts Sciences/Business .... Mr. Ken KOMPELIEN
72 Dean Technology/Services Division .... Mrs. Barbara BANG
64 Director of Music .... Ms. Laurie LEKANG
56 Dean of Extended Learning .... Mrs. Margaret WALL
88 Dean of College Outreach .... Mrs. Patricia KLINE

*Williston State College (A)

1410 University Avenue, Williston ND 58801-1326
County: Williams FICE Identification: 003007
Unit ID: 200341
Telephone: (701) 774-4200 Carnegie Class: Assoc/Pub-R-S
FAX Number: (701) 774-4275 Calendar System: Semester
URL: www.willistonstate.nodak.edu
Established: 1961 Annual Undergrad Tuition & Fees (In-State): $4,182
Enrollment: 993 Coed
Affiliation or Control: State IRS Status: 501(c)3
Highest Offering: Associate Degree
Program: Occupational; 2-Year Principally Bachelor's Creditable
Accreditation: NH

02 President .... Raymond NADOLNY
05 Provost/VP Instructn & Student Svcs .... Wanda MEYER
103 CEO of Workforce Education Train .... Deanette PIESIK
10 Exec Director for Business Services .... James FOERTSCH
26 VP College Advancement .... Terry OLSON

Rasmussen College - Bismarck (B)

1701 East Century Avenue, Bismarck ND 58503
County: Burleigh Identification: 666301
Unit ID: 20001301
Telephone: (701) 530-9600 Carnegie Class: Bac/Assoc
FAX Number: (701) 530-9604 Calendar System: Quarter
URL: www.rasmussen.edu
Established: 1902 Annual Undergrad Tuition & Fees: $16,340
Enrollment: 463 Coed
Affiliation or Control: Proprietary IRS Status: Proprietary
Highest Offering: Baccalaureate
Program: Occupational; 2-Year Principally Bachelor's Creditable
Accreditation: &NH, MLTAD

01 Campus Director .... Mr. Doug GARDNER

† Regional accreditation carried under the parent institution in Lake Elmo, MN.

Rasmussen College - Fargo/ Moorhead (C)

4012 19th Avenue, SW, Fargo ND 58103-7196
County: Cass FICE Identification: 004846
Unit ID: 200013
Telephone: (701) 277-3889 Carnegie Class: Bac/Assoc
FAX Number: (701) 277-5604 Calendar System: Quarter
URL: www.rasmussen.edu
Established: 1902 Annual Undergrad Tuition & Fees: $16,340
Enrollment: 1,264 Coed
Affiliation or Control: Proprietary IRS Status: Proprietary
Highest Offering: Baccalaureate
Program: Occupational; 2-Year Principally Bachelor's Creditable
Accreditation: &NH, MAC

01 Campus Director .... Ms. Elizabeth LARGENT

† Regional acrreditation is carried under parent institution in Lake Elmo, MN.

Sitting Bull College (D)

9299 Highway 24, Fort Yates ND 58538-9706
County: Sioux FICE Identification: 021882
Unit ID: 200466
Telephone: (701) 854-8000 Carnegie Class: Tribal
FAX Number: (701) 854-8197 Calendar System: Semester
URL: www.sittingbull.edu
Established: 1971 Annual Undergrad Tuition & Fees: $4,410
Enrollment: 313 Coed
Affiliation or Control: Tribal Control IRS Status: 501(c)3
Highest Offering: Baccalaureate
Program: Occupational; 2-Year Principally Bachelor's Creditable
Accreditation: NH

01 President .... Dr. Laurel VERMILLION
05 Vice President of Academic Affairs .... Dr. Koreen RESSLER
10 Vice President of Finance .... Ms. Leonica ALKIRE
37 Director Financial Student Aid .... Ms. Donna SEABOY
06 Registrar .... Ms. Melody SILK
08 Head Librarian .... Mr. Mark HOLMAN
40 Director of Bookstore .... Mrs. Tracy MAHER

Trinity Bible College (E)

50 S 6th Avenue, Ellendale ND 58436-7150
County: Dickey FICE Identification: 012059
Unit ID: 200484
Telephone: (701) 349-3621 Carnegie Class: Spec/Faith
FAX Number: (701) 349-5443 Calendar System: Semester
URL: www.trinitybiblecollege.edu
Established: 1948 Annual Undergrad Tuition & Fees: $13,440
Enrollment: 247 Coed
Affiliation or Control: Assemblies Of God Church IRS Status: 501(c)3
Highest Offering: Baccalaureate
Program: 2-Year Principally Bachelor's Creditable; Liberal Arts And General; Teacher Preparatory; Religious Emphasis
Accreditation: #BI

01 President .... Dr. Paul ALEXANDER
05 Vice President Academic Affairs .... Vacant
10 Director of Administration .... Rev. Winston TITUS
32 Director of Student Life .... Rev. Ian O'BRIEN
06 Academic Registrar .... Ms. Rachelle SPRINGER
84 Director of Enrollment .... Mrs. Jan DRESSANDER
08 Librarian .... Mrs. Diane OLSON
37 Director Student Financial Aid .... Ms. Nicole MCINTOSH
13 Director of Computer Services .... Mr. Matthew JOHNSON

Turtle Mountain Community College (F)

Box 340, Belcourt ND 58316-0340
County: Rolette FICE Identification: 023011
Unit ID: 200527
Telephone: (701) 477-7862 Carnegie Class: Tribal
FAX Number: (701) 477-7807 Calendar System: Semester
URL: www.tm.edu
Established: 1972 Annual Undergrad Tuition & Fees: $1,125
Enrollment: 598 Coed
Affiliation or Control: Independent Non-Profit IRS Status: 501(c)3
Highest Offering: Baccalaureate
Program: Occupational; 2-Year Principally Bachelor's Creditable; Technical Emphasis
Accreditation: NH

01 President .... Jim L. DAVIS
03 Executive Vice President .... Kellie HALL
05 Academic Dean .... Larry HENRY
32 Dean Student Affairs .... Anita FREDERICK
37 Director Financial Aid .... Wanda LADUCER
10 Comptroller .... Tracy AZURE
75 Director Vocational/Education .... Sheila TROTTIER
06 Registrar .... Angel GLADUE
36 Career Ladder Coordinator .... Vacant
31 Dir of Community/Adult Education .... Sandra LAROCQUE
07 Director of Admissions .... Joni LAFONTAINE
15 Director Personnel Services .... Holly CAHILL
37 Financial Aid Officer .... Diane BERCIER
40 Director of Bookstore .... Kathe ZASTE
18 Chief Facilities/Physical Plant .... Wesley DAVIS
30 Chief Development .... Dave RIPLEY
13 Chief Informational Officer .... Vacant
25 Sponsored Programs Officer .... Larretta HALL
35 Student Support Services Coord .... Steve DECOTEAU

United Tribes Technical College (G)

3315 University Drive, Bismarck ND 58504-7596
County: Burleigh FICE Identification: 022429
Unit ID: 200554
Telephone: (701) 255-3285 Carnegie Class: Tribal
FAX Number: (701) 530-0605 Calendar System: Semester
URL: www.uttc.edu
Established: 1969 Annual Undergrad Tuition & Fees: $3,840
Enrollment: 651 Coed
Affiliation or Control: Independent Non-Profit IRS Status: 501(c)3
Highest Offering: Baccalaureate
Program: Occupational; 2-Year Principally Bachelor's Creditable
Accreditation: NH, PNUR

01 President .... Dr. David GIPP
05 Vice Pres Academic Career/Tech Educ .... Dr. Phil BAIRD
32 Vice Pres Student & Campus Services .... Dr. Russell SWAGGER
10 Dean Finance & Business Services .... Vacant
07 Director of Admissions .... Ms. Vivian GILLETTE
06 Registrar .... Ms. Joetta MCLEOD
46 Director Research .... Vacant
15 Director Human Resources .... Ms. Barbara LITTLE OWL
20 Director Academic Support Services .... Vacant
84 Director Enrollment Management .... Mr. Nathan STRATTON
19 Director Security & Safety .... Mr. James REDTOMAHAWK
37 Director Financial Aid .... Vacant
41 Athletic Director .... Mr. Daryl BEARS TAIL
13 Network Manager .... Mr. Brian DECOTEAU

University of Mary (H)

7500 University Drive, Bismarck ND 58504-9652
County: Burleigh FICE Identification: 002992
Unit ID: 200217
Telephone: (701) 255-7500 Carnegie Class: Master's L
FAX Number: (701) 255-7687 Calendar System: Other
URL: www.umary.edu
Established: 1959 Annual Undergrad Tuition & Fees: $13,600
Enrollment: 2,971 Coed
Affiliation or Control: Roman Catholic IRS Status: 501(c)3
Highest Offering: Doctorate
Program: Liberal Arts And General; Professional
Accreditation: NH, EXSC, IACBE, NURSE, OT, PTA, SW

01 President .... Fr. James P. SHEA
05 Vice President for Academic Affairs .... Dr. Diane FLADELAND
10 Vice President Financial Affairs .... Mr. Brent WINIGER
32 Vice President Student Development .... Dr. Timothy SEAWORTH
84 Vice President Enrollment Services .... Mrs. Brenda KASPARI
26 Vice President for Public Affairs .... Mr. Neal KALBERER
06 Registrar .... Mr. Rod SCHEETT
08 Librarian .... Mrs. Cheryl BAILEY
37 Director of Financial Aid .... Mrs. Brenda ZASTOUPIL

OHIO

Akron Institute of Herzing University (I)

1600 S Arlington Street, Suite 100, Akron OH 44306-3958
County: Summit FICE Identification: 020695
Unit ID: 200785
Telephone: (330) 724-1600 Carnegie Class: Assoc/PrivFP
FAX Number: (330) 724-9688 Calendar System: Semester
URL: www.herzing.edu/akron
Established: 1970 Annual Undergrad Tuition & Fees: $10,982
Enrollment: 596 Coed
Affiliation or Control: Proprietary IRS Status: Proprietary
Highest Offering: Associate Degree
Program: Occupational; 2-Year Principally Bachelor's Creditable; Technical Emphasis
Accreditation: &NH, ADNUR, MAC

01 President .... Mr. David LARUE

† Regional accreditation is carried under the parent institution in Madison, WI.

Allegheny Wesleyan College (J)

2161 Woodsdale Road, Salem OH 44460-8920
County: Columbiana FICE Identification: 034573
Unit ID: 200873
Telephone: (330) 337-6403 Carnegie Class: Spec/Faith
FAX Number: (330) 337-6255 Calendar System: Semester
URL: www.awc.edu
Established: 1956 Annual Undergrad Tuition & Fees: $8,400
Enrollment: 52 Coed
Affiliation or Control: Wesleyan Church IRS Status: 501(c)3
Highest Offering: Baccalaureate
Program: Liberal Arts And General; Religious Emphasis
Accreditation: BI

01 President .... Dr. Robert E. ENGLAND
05 Interim Academic Dean .... Dr. Robert E. ENGLAND
10 Business Manager .... Mr. Troy MUIR
32 Dean of Students .... Mrs. Eveline MCHUGH
26 Director of Public Relations .... Mr. Tom SANDERS
06 Registrar & Director Admissions .... Mrs. Jeanne ZVARITCH
08 Head Librarian .... Mrs. Alice WEINGARD
37 Financial Aid Administrator .... Mrs. Esther PHELPS
09 Dir of Institutional Effectiveness .... Mrs. Jeanne ZVARITCH
40 Bookstore Manager .... Dr. Robert E. ENGLAND
33 Dean of Men .... Mr. Stephen TROYER
34 Dean of Women .... Mrs. Eveline MCHUGH
07 Director of Admissions .... Mrs. Jeanne ZVARITCH
18 Chief Facilities/Physical Plant .... Mr. Darrin PATTERSON
21 Associate Business Officer .... Mr. Darrell MONTGOMERY
29 Director Alumni Relations .... Rev. John DYE
35 Director Student Affairs .... Mrs. Eveline MCHUGH
38 Director Student Counseling .... Mrs. Kimberly FORD

American Institute of Alternative Medicine (K)

6685 Doubletree Avenue, Columbus OH 43229-1113
County: Franklin FICE Identification: 035344
Unit ID: 441636
Telephone: (614) 825-6255 Carnegie Class: Not Classified
FAX Number: (614) 825-6279 Calendar System: Other
URL: www.aiam.edu
Established: 1990 Annual Undergrad Tuition & Fees: N/A
Enrollment: 258 Coed
Affiliation or Control: Independent Non-Profit IRS Status: 501(c)3
Highest Offering: Master's
Program: Professional

Accreditation: ACCSC, ACUP

01 President ..... John W. ELAM
05 Director of Education ..... Dennis GRIFFIN

*Antioch University (A)

900 Dayton Street, Yellow Springs OH 45387-1635
County: Greene FICE Identification: 003010
Unit ID: 442392
Telephone: (937) 769-1351 Carnegie Class: N/A
FAX Number: (937) 769-1350
URL: www.antioch.edu

01 Chancellor ..... Ms. Felice NUDELMAN
10 Vice Chanc/Chief Financial Officer ..... Ms. Pari SABETY
05 Vice Chanc Univ Academic Affairs ..... Dr. Laurien ALEXANDRE
13 Vice Chancellor CIO ..... Mr. Bob DEWITT
15 Director HR Systems/Payroll Svcs ..... Ms. Suzette CASTONGUAY
91 Dir Administrative Info Systems ..... Ms. Candice SANTELL
04 Executive Asst to the Chancellor ..... Ms. Leslie BATES

† Parent institution of Antioch University Midwest in OH; Antioch University Seattle in WA; Antioch University New England in NH; and Antioch University Los Angeles and Antioch University Santa Barbara in CA.

*Antioch University Midwest (B)

900 Dayton Street, Yellow Springs OH 45387-1745
County: Greene Identification: 666811
Unit ID: 245892
Telephone: (937) 769-1800 Carnegie Class: Master's M
FAX Number: (937) 769-1805 Calendar System: Quarter
URL: midwest.antioch.edu/
Established: 1988 Annual Undergrad Tuition & Fees: $15,898
Enrollment: 545 Coed
Affiliation or Control: Independent Non-Profit IRS Status: 501(c)3
Highest Offering: Master's
Program: Liberal Arts And General; Teacher Preparatory; Professional
Accreditation: &NH, TED

02 Interim President ..... Dr. Ellen W. HALL
05 Int Vice Pres Academic Affairs ..... Dr. Steve BRZEZINSKI
10 Vice Pres Finance/Administration ..... Ms. Darlene ROBERTSON
100 Chief of Staff ..... Ms. Deena KENT-HUMMEL
13 Director Information Systems ..... Vacant
37 Director Student Financial Aid ..... Ms. Kathy JOHN
15 Director Personnel Services ..... Ms. Suzette CASTONGUAY
21 Associate Business Officer ..... Ms. Deborah CARAWAY
84 Director Enrollment Services ..... Mr. Oscar ROBINSON
49 Assoc Dean Liberal Studies ..... Dr. Joseph CRONIN
18 Director Facility Management ..... Mr. Ray SIMONELLI
06 Registrar ..... Dr. Maureen HEACOCK
30 Dir Development/Alumni Relations ..... Ms. Kimberly HORTON
26 Director Marketing & Communications ..... Mr. Walt ULBRICHT
88 Chair Management Leadership & Chang .. Dr. Richard MCGUIGAN
53 Director School of Education ..... Dr. Marian GLANCY
88 Chair Analysis & Engagement ..... Dr. Richard MCGUIGAN

† Regional accreditation is carried under the parent institution in Yellow Springs, OH.

Antonelli College (C)

124 E Seventh Street, Cincinnati OH 45202-2592
County: Hamilton FICE Identification: 012891
Unit ID: 201016
Telephone: (800) 505-4338 Carnegie Class: Assoc/PrivFP
FAX Number: (513) 241-9396 Calendar System: Quarter
URL: www.antonellicollege.edu
Established: 1947 Annual Undergrad Tuition & Fees: $15,850
Enrollment: 266 Coed
Affiliation or Control: Proprietary IRS Status: Proprietary
Highest Offering: Associate Degree
Program: Occupational
Accreditation: ACCSC

01 Director ..... Vacant
05 Director of Education ..... Ms. Frances CARROLL
32 Director Student Services ..... Ms. Leah ELKINS
06 Registrar ..... Ms. Shawnya AMENDOLA
36 Career Services Coordinator ..... Ms. Betty POLING-BOLLAS

Art Academy of Cincinnati (D)

1212 Jackson Street, Cincinnati OH 45202-7106
County: Hamilton FICE Identification: 003011
Unit ID: 201061
Telephone: (513) 562-6262 Carnegie Class: Spec/Arts
FAX Number: (513) 562-8778 Calendar System: Semester
URL: www.artacademy.edu
Established: 1869 Annual Undergrad Tuition & Fees: $24,330
Enrollment: 230 Coed
Affiliation or Control: Independent Non-Profit IRS Status: 501(c)3
Highest Offering: Master's
Program: Fine Arts Emphasis
Accreditation: NH, ART

01 President ..... John M. SULLIVAN
10 Vice President Finance/Operations ..... Vacant
84 Vice President of Enrollment Mgmt ..... Dr. Gregory STEWART
05 Academic Dean ..... Diane K. SMITH
37 Director of Financial Aid ..... Kristina OLBERDING
06 Registrar ..... Sue HUTCHENS
31 Director of Community Education ..... Jennifer SPURLOCK
18 Director of Facilities ..... Jack HENNEN
32 Director of Student Services ..... Galen CRAWFORD

The Art Institute of Cincinnati (E)

1171 East Kemper Road, Cincinnati OH 45246-3322
County: Hamilton FICE Identification: 021286
Unit ID: 200624
Telephone: (513) 751-1206 Carnegie Class: Assoc/PrivFP
FAX Number: (513) 751-1209 Calendar System: Quarter
URL: www.aic-arts.edu
Established: 1976 Annual Undergrad Tuition & Fees: $17,066
Enrollment: 30 Coed
Affiliation or Control: Proprietary IRS Status: Proprietary
Highest Offering: Associate Degree
Program: Occupational
Accreditation: ACCSC

00 CEO ..... Ms. Marion K. ALLMAN
01 President ..... Mr. Sean M. MENDELL

The Art Institute of Ohio-Cincinnati (F)

8845 Governors Hill Drive, Cincinnati OH 45249
County: Hamilton Identification: 666693
Unit ID: 446668
Telephone: (513) 833-2400 Carnegie Class: Assoc/PrivFP
FAX Number: (513) 833-2411 Calendar System: Quarter
URL: www.artinstitutes.edu/cincinnati
Established: 2004 Annual Undergrad Tuition & Fees: $23,088
Enrollment: 752 Coed
Affiliation or Control: Proprietary IRS Status: Proprietary
Highest Offering: Baccalaureate
Program: Occupational; 2-Year Principally Bachelor's Creditable; Professional; Technical Emphasis
Accreditation: &NH, ACFEI

† Regional accreditation is carried under the parent institution The Illinois Institute of Art, Chicago, IL.

Ashland University (G)

401 College Avenue, Ashland OH 44805-3799
County: Ashland FICE Identification: 003012
Unit ID: 201104
Telephone: (419) 289-4142 Carnegie Class: DRU
FAX Number: (419) 289-5333 Calendar System: Semester
URL: www.ashland.edu
Established: 1878 Annual Undergrad Tuition & Fees: $28,858
Enrollment: 5,901 Coed
Affiliation or Control: Brethren Church IRS Status: 501(c)3
Highest Offering: Doctorate
Program: 2-Year Principally Bachelor's Creditable; Liberal Arts And General; Teacher Preparatory; Professional
Accreditation: NH, ACBSP, @DIETD, MUS, NURSE, SW, TED, THEOL

01 President ..... Dr. Frederick J. FINKS
73 President Theological Seminary ..... Dr. John C. SHULTZ
05 Provost ..... Dr. Frank E. PETTIGREW
32 VP Student Affairs/Dean of Students ..... Mrs. B. Sue HEIMANN
84 Vice Pres Enroll Mgt & Marketing ..... Dr. Scott D. VAN LOO
13 Vice Pres Information Technology ..... Mr. Curtis WHITE
18 Vice Pres Facilities/Mgmt & Plng ..... Mr. Rick M. EWING, II
21 Vice President Business Opers ..... Mr. James L. KIRTLAND
42 Dean of Religious Life ..... Dr. Dan L. LAWSON
06 Registrar ..... Ms. Kathleen HALL
08 Director of the Library ..... Mr. Edward M. KRAKORA
37 Director Student Financial Aid ..... Mr. Stephen C. HOWELL
29 Director Alumni/Parent Relations ..... Mr. Jeff ALIX
15 Director of Human Resources ..... Mr. John R. BRANDON
36 Executive Director Career Services ..... Ms. Karen HAGANS
26 Director of Public Relations ..... Mr. Steven M. HANNAN
41 Director of Athletics ..... Mr. William J. GOLDRING
88 Exec Dir Ashbrook Ctr ..... Dr. Peter W. SCHRAMM
09 Director of Institutional Research ..... Mrs. Karen A. LITTLE
07 Director of Admissions ..... Mr. W.C VANCE
49 Dean College of Arts & Sciences ..... Dr. Dawn WEBER
73 Dean Theological Seminary ..... Dr. Paul CHILCOTE
50 Dean College Business/Econ ..... Dr. Jeffery RUSSELL
53 Dean College of Education ..... Dr. James P. VANKEUREN
58 Dean Graduate School ..... Vacant
66 Dean Col of Nursing & Health Sci ..... Ms. Faye GRUND
51 Dean School of Continuing Educ ..... Mr. Dwight MCELFRESH
28 Director of Diversity ..... Vacant
28 Dir Multicultural Stdnt Svcs & Stds ..... Mr. Jonathan E. LOCUST, JR.
104 Exec Dir International Programs ..... Dr. Nathan D. MYERS
88 Director of Marketing ..... Ms. Jan BOND

Athenaeum of Ohio (H)

6616 Beechmont Avenue, Cincinnati OH 45230-5900
County: Hamilton FICE Identification: 003013
Unit ID: 201140
Telephone: (513) 231-2223 Carnegie Class: Spec/Faith
FAX Number: (513) 231-3254 Calendar System: Quarter
URL: www.athenaeum.edu
Established: 1829 Annual Graduate Tuition & Fees: $20,400
Enrollment: 213 Coed
Affiliation or Control: Roman Catholic IRS Status: 501(c)3
Highest Offering: Master's; No Undergraduates
Program: Professional; Religious Emphasis
Accreditation: NH, THEOL

01 President & Rector ..... Rev. Benedict O'CINNSEALAIGH
03 Vice President ..... Mr. Dennis K. EAGAN
05 Dean of Athenaeum ..... Rev. Earl K. FERNANDES
08 Librarian ..... Mrs. Connie SONG
30 Director of Development ..... Mr. James JACKSON
06 Registrar ..... Mr. Michael E. SWEENEY
88 Dir Lay Pastoral Ministry Program ..... Dr. Susan MCGURGAN
71 Dean Special Studies Division ..... Dr. Terrance D. CALLAN

ATS Institute of Technology (I)

325 Alpha Park, Highland Heights OH 44143-2216
County: Cuyahoga FICE Identification: 034685
Unit ID: 439455
Telephone: (440) 449-1700 Carnegie Class: Assoc/PrivFP
FAX Number: (440) 449-1389 Calendar System: Semester
URL: www.atsinstitute.edu
Established: 1997 Annual Undergrad Tuition & Fees: $22,447
Enrollment: 150 Coed
Affiliation or Control: Proprietary IRS Status: Proprietary
Highest Offering: Associate Degree
Program: Occupational
Accreditation: ACICS

01 Director ..... Ms. Yelena BYKOV
37 Director of Financial Aid ..... Ms. Yelena KSENDZOVSKY
07 Co-Admissions Director ..... Ms. Julia PROTSKY
07 Co-Admissions Director ..... Ms. Debbie LINKOFF

Aultman College of Nursing and Health Sciences (J)

2600 6th Street SW, Canton OH 44710-1702
County: Stark FICE Identification: 006487
Unit ID: 201177
Telephone: (330) 363-6347 Carnegie Class: Assoc/PrivNFP
FAX Number: (330) 580-6654 Calendar System: Semester
URL: www.aultmancollege.edu
Established: 2004 Annual Undergrad Tuition & Fees: $17,424
Enrollment: 314 Coed
Affiliation or Control: Independent Non-Profit IRS Status: 501(c)3
Highest Offering: Associate Degree
Program: 2-Year Principally Bachelor's Creditable; Nursing Emphasis
Accreditation: NH, ADNUR, RAD

01 President ..... Ms. Rebecca R. CROWL
11 Vice President Internal Affairs ..... Ms. Jeannine SHAMBAUGH
26 Vice President External Affairs ..... Ms. Vi LEGGETT
07 Director Administrative Services ..... Ms. Susan B. SHEPHERD
45 Director Student Affairs ..... Ms. Lyn SABINO
05 Interim Chief Academic Officer ..... Dr. Jean PADDOCK
97 Interim Director General Education ..... Dr. Stephen T. GRAEF
76 Director Allied Health ..... Dr. Sherri COLE

Baldwin Wallace University (K)

275 Eastland Road, Berea OH 44017-2088
County: Cuyahoga FICE Identification: 003014
Unit ID: 201195
Telephone: (440) 826-2900 Carnegie Class: Master's L
FAX Number: (440) 826-2329 Calendar System: Semester
URL: www.bw.edu/
Established: 1845 Annual Undergrad Tuition & Fees: $35,940
Enrollment: 4,177 Coed
Affiliation or Control: United Methodist IRS Status: 501(c)3
Highest Offering: Master's
Program: Liberal Arts And General; Teacher Preparatory; Professional
Accreditation: NH, MUS, TED

01 President ..... Dr. Robert C. HELMER
03 Senior Vice President ..... Mr. Richard L. FLETCHER
05 Int Vice Pres Academic Affairs/Dean ..... Mr. Guy FARISH
30 Vice President for Advancement ..... Mr. William J. SPIKER
10 Vice President for Finance & Admin ..... Mr. William M. RENIFF
32 VP Student Affairs/Dean of Students ..... Dr. Trina DOBBERSTEIN
84 Vice Pres of Enrollment Management ..... Ms. Susan DILENO
26 Asst VP/Director College Relations ..... Mr. George RICHARD
20 Associate Academic Dean ..... Ms. Janet STOCKS
35 Director of Student Success ..... Mr. Marc ADKINS
51 Director of Adult Learning ..... Ms. Nancy JIROUSEK
08 Director of Ritter Library ..... Dr. Patrick SCANLAN
13 Chief Information Officer ..... Mr. Greg G. FLANIK
44 Director Annual Giving ..... Ms. Aimee BELL
29 Director Alumni Relations ..... Mr. Terry J. KURTZ
44 Director Development Gift Plng ..... Mr. Thomas H. KONKOLY
37 Director of Financial Aid ..... Dr. George ROLLESTON
15 Asst VP for Human Resources ..... Mr. Sam RAMIREZ
38 Director of Counseling Services ..... Ms. Joy D. WYATT
36 Director of Academic Advising ..... Ms. Margaret STINER
06 Registrar ..... Ms. Linda L. YOUNG
07 Director of Undergraduate Admission ..... Ms. Pattie SKRHA
88 Dir of Adult/Cont Educ Admission ..... Ms. Winifred GERHARDT
18 Director of Buildings & Grounds ..... Mr. William KERBUSCH
88 Director of Intercultural Education ..... Dr. Judith B. KRUTKY
96 Director of Purchasing ..... Ms. Karen STENGER
28 Director Campus Diversity Affairs ..... Mr. Charles HARKNESS

Beckfield College (A)

225 Pictoria Drive Suite 200, Cincinnati OH 45246
Identification: 666673
Unit ID: 452373
Telephone: (513) 671-1920 Carnegie Class: Assoc/PrivFP
FAX Number: (513) 671-1927 Calendar System: Other
URL: www.beckfield.edu
Established: 1984 Annual Undergrad Tuition & Fees: N/A
Enrollment: 492 Coed
Affiliation or Control: Proprietary IRS Status: Proprietary
Highest Offering: Associate Degree
Program: Occupational
Accreditation: ACICS

01 President .... Ms. Diane WOLFER
05 Campus Director .... Mr. Edward RITO

† Branch campus of Beckfield College, Florence, KY.

Belmont College (B)

120 Fox Shannon Place, Saint Clairsville OH 43950-9766
County: Belmont FICE Identification: 009941
Unit ID: 201283
Telephone: (740) 695-9500 Carnegie Class: Assoc/Pub-R-M
FAX Number: (740) 695-2247 Calendar System: Quarter
URL: www.belmontcollege.edu
Established: 1969 Annual Undergrad Tuition & Fees (In-State): $4,310
Enrollment: 2,076 Coed
Affiliation or Control: State IRS Status: 501(c)3
Highest Offering: Associate Degree
Program: Occupational; 2-Year Principally Bachelor's Creditable
Accreditation: NH, MAC

01 President .... Dr. Joseph E. BUKOWSKI
05 VP of Learning & Student Services .... Dr. Rebecca KURTZ
11 Vice Pres of Administrative Affairs .. Mr. John S. KOUCOUMARIS
20 Exec Dean of Academic Affairs .... Dr. Brenda LOHRI-POSEY
09 Dean Institutional Research/Plng .... Dr. Jane EVANS
08 Assoc Dean Lrng/Info Svcs/Tech .... Mrs. Cathy BENNETT
103 Dean Workforce Devel/Econ Devel .... Dr. Holly BENNETT
18 Director of Facilities Management .... Mr. Steve MORGAN
06 Registrar .... Mrs. Colleen SECKMAN
15 Exec Director of HR & Org Dev .... Ms. Marge HAWTHORNE
37 Assoc Dean of Financial Aid .... Mr. Jody PEELER
07 Director of Recruitment .... Mr. Michael STERLING
20 Director of Educational Services .... Mrs. Elayne STUPAK
24 Dir Library/Info/Lrng Commons Svcs .... Ms. Joyce BAKER
54 Faculty Admin Industrial Trades Pgm .... Mr. Dirk DECOY
26 Director of Strategic Comm .... Mrs. Laura DOTY
29 Coordinator of Development .... Ms. Erin NEELY
36 Transfer/Articulat/Academic Advisor .... Ms. Jane BLACK
27 Exec Dir of Information Services .... Mr. Matthew TARBETT
30 Dir of Dev & External Affairs .... Mr. RJ KONKOLESKI

Bexley Hall Seminary (C)

583 Sheridan Avenue, Columbus OH 43209
County: Franklin FICE Identification: 037473
Unit ID: 443702
Telephone: (614) 231-3095 Carnegie Class: Spec/Faith
FAX Number: (614) 231-3236 Calendar System: Semester
URL: www.bexley.edu
Established: N/A Annual Graduate Tuition & Fees: $14,672
Enrollment: 15 Coed
Affiliation or Control: Independent Non-Profit IRS Status: 501(c)3
Highest Offering: Master's; No Undergraduates
Program: Religious Emphasis
Accreditation: THEOL

01 President .... Rev. Roger FERLO
05 Dean .... Mr. Thomas FERGUSON

Bluffton University (D)

1 University Drive, Bluffton OH 45817-2104
County: Allen FICE Identification: 003016
Unit ID: 201371
Telephone: (419) 358-3000 Carnegie Class: Bac/Diverse
FAX Number: (419) 358-3323 Calendar System: Semester
URL: www.bluffton.edu
Established: 1899 Annual Undergrad Tuition & Fees: $27,426
Enrollment: 1,240 Coed
Affiliation or Control: Mennonite Church IRS Status: 501(c)3
Highest Offering: Master's
Program: Liberal Arts And General; Teacher Preparatory; Business Emphasis
Accreditation: NH, DIETD, MUS, SW, TED

01 President .... Dr. James M. HARDER
10 Vice President for Fiscal Affairs .... Mr. Kevin A. NICKEL
30 Vice President for Inst Advancement .... Dr. Hans HOUSHOWER
05 Vice Pres & Dean Academic Affairs .... Dr. Sally W. SOMMER
84 VP for Enrollment Management .... Mr. Ronald HEADINGS
32 VP for Student Life/Dean of Stdnts .... Dr. Julie DEGRAW
21 Chief Business Officer .... Mr. Richard LICHTLE
08 Director of Libraries .... Ms. Mary Jean JOHNSON
06 Registrar .... Ms. Iris NEUFELD
26 Chief Public Relations Officer .... Mrs. Robin BOWLUS
29 Dir of Alumni Relations/Annual Giv .... Mrs. Julia SZABO
37 Director of Student Financial Aid .... Mr. Lawrence MATTHEWS
07 Director of Admissions .... Mr. Chris JEBSEN
18 Director Building/Grounds .... Mr. Mustaq AHMED
15 Director Human Resources .... Vacant

Bowling Green State University (E)

220 McFall Center, Bowling Green OH 43403-0001
County: Wood FICE Identification: 003018
Unit ID: 201441
Telephone: (419) 372-2531 Carnegie Class: RU/H
FAX Number: (419) 372-8446 Calendar System: Semester
URL: www.bgsu.edu
Established: 1910 Annual Undergrad Tuition & Fees (In-State): $10,378
Enrollment: 19,994 Coed
Affiliation or Control: State IRS Status: 501(c)3
Highest Offering: Doctorate
Program: Liberal Arts And General; Teacher Preparatory; Professional
Accreditation: NH, ART, BUS, BUSA, CACREP, CLPSY, CONST, CORE, DIETD, DIETI, IPSY, JOUR, MT, MUS, NAIT, NRPA, NURSE, PH, SP, SW, TED, THEA

01 President .... Dr. Mary Ellen MAZEY
05 Sr VP Academic Affairs/Provost .... Dr. Rodney K. ROGERS
10 CFO/VP Finance & Admin .... Ms. Sherideen S. STOLL
100 Chief of Staff .... Ms. Lisa C. MATTIACE
32 Vice President Student Affairs .... Vacant
04 Asst to President .... Ms. Laurel E. ZAWODNY
30 Interim VP Univ Advancement .... Mr. Tim KODER
84 VP Enrollment Management .... Mr. Albert N. COLOM
20 Vice Provost Undergraduate Educ .... Dr. M. Sue HOUSTON
35 Asst VP Student Affs/Dean of Stdnts .... Ms. Jill CARR
11 Assoc VP for Campus Operations .... Mr. Bruce MEYER
27 Chief Communications Officer .... Ms. Robin GERROW
29 Director Alumni Affairs .... Ms. Montique R. COTTON KELLY
46 VP Research & Econ Dev .... Dr. Michael Y. OGAWA
41 Asst VP Student Affs/Dir Rec Sports .... Dr. Stephen KAMPF
41 Director of Athletics .... Mr. Gregory A. CHRISTOPHER
16 Chief Human Resources Officer .... Ms. Rebecca C. FERGUSON
39 Director of Residence Life .... Ms. Sarah WATERS
88 Assoc VP Capital Planning & Design .... Mr. Steve P. KRAKOFF
13 Chief Information Officer .... Mr. John M. ELLINGER
43 General Counsel .... Mr. Sean P. FITZGERALD
22 Director Equity & Diversity .... Ms. Barbara WADDELL
58 Interim Dean Graduate College .... Dr. Michael OGAWA
49 Dean College Arts/Sciences .... Dr. Simon N. MORGAN-RUSSELL
50 Dean College Business Admin .... Mr. Raymond BRAUN
51 Exec Director Cont & Extended Educ .... Dr. Marcia SALAZAR-VALENTINE
53 Dean College Educ/Human Development .... Dr. Brad COLWELL
12 Dean Firelands College .... Dr. William BALZER
69 Int Dean College Hlth/Human Svcs .... Dr. Chris DUNN
08 Dean University Libraries .... Ms. Sara BUSHONG
64 Dean College of Musical Arts .... Dr. Jeffrey A. SHOWELL
72 Dean College of Technology .... Dr. Faris A. MALHAS
57 Director of School of Art .... Dr. Katerina R. RAY
60 Dir Sch of Media & Communication .... Dr. Terry RENTNER
88 Dir Sch Human Move/Sport/Leisure .... Dr. Philip F. XIE
88 Dir Sch Family & Consumer Sciences .... Dr. Deborah G. WOOLDRIDGE
53 Dir Sch Educ Fnds/Leadership/Policy .... Dr. Margaret BOOTH
53 Dir Sch of Teaching and Learning .... Vacant
92 Director Honors Program .... Dr. Paul A. MOORE
106 Assc VP Acad Technology & eLearning ... Dr. Bruce L. EDWARDS
85 Dir Ctr for International Programs .... Vacant
21 Exec Dir of Business Operations .... Mr. Bradley K. LEIGH
07 Asst VP/Director Admissions .... Mr. Gary D. SWEGAN
21 Dir Budgeting & Resource Planning .... Mr. Geofrey L. TRACY
09 Director of Institutional Research .... Vacant
06 University Registrar .... Mr. Christopher P. COX
40 Director Bookstore .... Mr. Jeffrey D. NELSON
19 Director Public Safety .... Ms. Monica M. MOLL
36 Interim Director Career Center .... Ms. Jessica TUROS
23 Exec Director Center for Health .... Mr. Richard G. SIPP
38 Assoc Director Counseling Center .... Dr. Garrett GILMER
37 Director Student Financial Aid .... Ms. Laura EMCH
23 Assoc Dir Student Health Services .... Ms. Barbara HOFFMAN
44 Director of Annual Giving .... Ms. Shannon SPENCER
101 Secretary to the Board .... Dr. Patrick PAUKEN
88 Co-Gen Manager WBGU Public Media .... Mr. Anthony E. SHORT
88 Co-Gen Manager WBGU Public Media .... Ms. Tina L. SIMON
35 Director TRIO Collegiate Services .... Mr. Sidney CHILDS
21 Internal Auditing & Adv Svcs .... Mr. James LAMBERT
88 Director Women's Center .... Dr. Mary M. KRUEGER
88 Assoc Director Disability Services .... Ms. Peggy DENNIS
88 Dir President's Leadership Acad .... Dr. Julie A. SNYDER
88 Director Dining Services .... Mr. Michael L. PAULUS
96 Director of Business Operations .... Mr. Andrew D. GRANT
88 Director Student Employment .... Ms. Michelle SIMMONS
88 Director Learning Commons .... Mr. Mark NELSON
88 Director Advising Services .... Mr. Dermot M. FORDE
88 Asst VP Non-Trad & Transfer Svcs .... Dr. Barbara L. HENRY
20 Vice Provost Strategic Initiatives .... Dr. Joseph FRIZADO
65 Dir Sch Earth/Environ & Society .... Dr. Charles ONASCH

Bowling Green State University Firelands College (F)

One University Drive, Huron OH 44839-9719
County: Erie FICE Identification: 007856
Unit ID: 201432
Telephone: (419) 433-5560 Carnegie Class: Assoc/Pub-R-S
FAX Number: (419) 433-9696 Calendar System: Semester
URL: www.firelands.bgsu.edu
Established: 1967 Annual Undergrad Tuition & Fees (In-State): $4,834
Enrollment: 2,419 Coed
Affiliation or Control: State IRS Status: 501(c)3
Highest Offering: Baccalaureate
Program: Occupational; 2-Year Principally Bachelor's Creditable
Accreditation: &NH

01 Dean .... Dr. William K. BALZER
05 Assoc Dean Academic & Student Affs .... Dr. Andrew J. KURTZ
09 Asst Dean Institutional Research .... Ms. Patricia J. DAVEY
10 Director Finance & Operations .... Mr. Mark R. CHARVILLE
84 Dir Enroll Mgt/Stdnt Retention Svcs .... Ms. Debralee DIVERS
06 Registrar .... Ms. Vicki B. HILLIS
13 Director Technology Support Svcs .... Ms. Julie A. HAMANN
30 College Development Officer .... Ms. Stacey M. HARTLEY
26 Director Marketing & Communication .... Mr. Dean D. SCHNURR
08 Head Librarian .... Ms. Sharon R. BRITTON
51 Director for Educational Outreach .... Ms. Kelly J. CUSACK
36 Career Services Coordinator .... Mr. John L. CLARK
88 Dir Student Academic Enhancement .... Ms. Penny L. NEMITZ
19 Campus Security .... Mr. Edward E. WIMMER
105 Web Production Manager .... Mr. James A. KIMBLE
40 Sales Manager Bookstore .... Ms. Bonnie G. LINDSLEY
20 Manager Academic Advising .... Ms. Amy L. MCKINLEY
35 Coord Student/Campus Activities .... Ms. Sandra V. DICARLO
24 Audio Visual Specialist .... Mr. Earl B. LISK, III

† Regional accreditation is carried under the parent institution in Bowling Green, OH.

Bradford School (G)

2469 Stelzer Road, Columbus OH 43219-3129
County: Franklin FICE Identification: 004853
Unit ID: 202161
Telephone: (614) 416-6200 Carnegie Class: Assoc/PrivFP
FAX Number: (614) 416-6210 Calendar System: Semester
URL: www.bradfordschoolcolumbus.edu
Established: 1985 Annual Undergrad Tuition & Fees: $13,800
Enrollment: 603 Coed
Affiliation or Control: Proprietary IRS Status: Proprietary
Highest Offering: Associate Degree
Program: Occupational
Accreditation: ACICS, MAC

01 President .... Mr. Dennis BARTELS
05 Director of Education .... Ms. Barbara ELLISON
07 Director of Admissions .... Ms. Raeann LEE

Brown Mackie College-Akron (H)

755 White Pond Drive, Suite 101, Akron OH 44320-4221
County: Summit Identification: 666470
Unit ID: 205647
Telephone: (330) 869-3600 Carnegie Class: Assoc/PrivFP
FAX Number: (330) 869-3650 Calendar System: Other
URL: www.brownmackie.edu
Established: 1927 Annual Undergrad Tuition & Fees: $11,124
Enrollment: 796 Coed
Affiliation or Control: Proprietary IRS Status: Proprietary
Highest Offering: Associate Degree
Program: Occupational; 2-Year Principally Bachelor's Creditable; Business Emphasis
Accreditation: ACICS, OTA, SURGT

01 President .... Ms. Kim AMES
05 Dean of Academic Affairs .... Ms. Judith QUAYLE
06 Registrar .... Ms. Ronnell NOVISKY
07 Senior Director of Admissions .... Mr. Bill HORNSBERGER
36 Director of Career Services .... Ms. Judith SPOONER

† Branch campus of Brown Mackie College-Cincinnati, Cincinnati, OH.

Brown Mackie College-Cincinnati (I)

1011 Glendale-Milford Road, Cincinnati OH 45215-1107
County: Hamilton FICE Identification: 005127
Unit ID: 205610
Telephone: (513) 771-2424 Carnegie Class: Assoc/PrivFP
FAX Number: (513) 771-3413 Calendar System: Other
URL: www.brownmackie.edu
Established: 1927 Annual Undergrad Tuition & Fees: $11,124
Enrollment: 1,143 Coed
Affiliation or Control: Proprietary IRS Status: Proprietary
Highest Offering: Associate Degree
Program: Occupational; 2-Year Principally Bachelor's Creditable; Business Emphasis
Accreditation: ACICS, MAC, SURGT

01 President .... Mrs. Robin KROUT
07 Senior Director of Admissions .... Mr. JP SMITH
06 Registrar .... Ms. Kyla TEUFEL
05 Dean of Academic Affairs .... Ms. Tara DAILEY
36 Director of Career Services .... Ms. Anita JONES

Brown Mackie College-Findlay (J)

1700 Fostoria Avenue, Suite 100, Findlay OH 45840-6857
County: Hancock FICE Identification: 026162
Unit ID: 375489
Telephone: (419) 423-2211 Carnegie Class: Assoc/PrivFP
FAX Number: (419) 423-0725 Calendar System: Other
URL: www.brownmackie.edu
Established: 1986 Annual Undergrad Tuition & Fees: $11,124

Enrollment: 516 Coed

Affiliation or Control: Proprietary IRS Status: Proprietary

Highest Offering: Associate Degree

Program: Occupational; 2-Year Principally Bachelor's Creditable; Business Emphasis

Accreditation: ACICS, OTA, SURGT

01	President	Mr. Wayne KORPICS
05	Dean of Academic Affairs	Ms. Julie BAKER
07	Senior Director of Admissions	Vacant
06	Registrar	Ms. Heather ELLIOTT
36	Director of Career Services	Vacant

Brown Mackie College-North Canton (A)

4300 Munson Street, NW, Canton OH 44718-3674

County: Stark FICE Identification: 030778

Unit ID: 204316

Telephone: (330) 494-1214 Carnegie Class: Assoc/PrivFP

FAX Number: (330) 494-8112 Calendar System: Other

URL: www.brownmackie.edu

Established: 1985 Annual Undergrad Tuition & Fees: $11,124

Enrollment: 615 Coed

Affiliation or Control: Proprietary IRS Status: Proprietary

Highest Offering: Associate Degree

Program: Occupational; 2-Year Principally Bachelor's Creditable; Business Emphasis

Accreditation: ACICS, SURTEC

01	President	Mr. Peter PERKOWSKI
05	Dean of Academic Affairs	Ms. Marcy TREW
06	Registrar	Ms. Christine MONTINI
07	Senior Director of Admissions	Mr. Sanjay KETTY
36	Director of Career Services	Ms. Brenda RAYE

† Branch campus of Brown Mackie College-Tucson, Tucson, AZ.

Bryant & Stratton College (B)

3121 Euclid Avenue, Cleveland OH 44115

County: Cuyahoga FICE Identification: 009343

Unit ID: 202684

Telephone: (216) 771-1700 Carnegie Class: Bac/Assoc

FAX Number: (216) 771-7787 Calendar System: Semester

URL: www.bryantstratton.edu

Established: 1854 Annual Undergrad Tuition & Fees: $15,570

Enrollment: 1,080 Coed

Affiliation or Control: Proprietary IRS Status: Proprietary

Highest Offering: Baccalaureate

Program: Occupational

Accreditation: &M

01	Campus Dir/Dir Cleveland Market	Mr. Jim SMOLKA
32	Dean of Student Services	Mr. Paris LUMPKINS

† Regional accreditation is carried under the parent institution (corporate office) in Buffalo, NY.

Bryant & Stratton College (C)

35350 Curtis Blvd, Eastlake OH 44095

County: Lake Identification: 666466

Unit ID: 369905

Telephone: (440) 510-1112 Carnegie Class: Bac/Assoc

FAX Number: (440) 306-2015 Calendar System: Semester

URL: www.bryantstratton.edu

Established: 1854 Annual Undergrad Tuition & Fees: $16,290

Enrollment: 944 Coed

Affiliation or Control: Proprietary IRS Status: Proprietary

Highest Offering: Associate Degree

Program: 2-Year Principally Bachelor's Creditable; Business Emphasis

Accreditation: &M, ADNUR

01	Campus Director	Dr. Ted P. HANSEN
05	Dean of Instruction	Mr. Rich S. BENARD
10	Business Office Manager	Mr. Ian R. MARKS
36	Career Service Director	Ms. Rhonda BUTLER

† Regional accreditation is carried under the parent institution (corporate office) in Buffalo, NY.

Bryant & Stratton College (D)

12955 Snow Road, Parma OH 44130-1013

County: Cuyahoga FICE Identification: 022744

Unit ID: 201469

Telephone: (216) 265-3151 Carnegie Class: Assoc/PrivFP4

FAX Number: (216) 265-0325 Calendar System: Semester

URL: www.bryantstratton.edu

Established: 1854 Annual Undergrad Tuition & Fees: $15,670

Enrollment: 788 Coed

Affiliation or Control: Proprietary IRS Status: Proprietary

Highest Offering: Baccalaureate

Program: 2-Year Principally Bachelor's Creditable

Accreditation: &M, MAC

01	Campus Director	Mrs. Lisa MASON
05	Dean of Instruction	Ms. Susan JELENIC
36	Director of Career Services	Ms. Deborah JOHNS
10	Business Manager	Ms. Donna GOLDSTEIN

† Regional accreditation is carried under the parent institution (corporate office) in Buffalo, NY.

Capital University (E)

1 College and Main Street, Columbus OH 43209-2394

County: Franklin FICE Identification: 003023

Unit ID: 201548

Telephone: (614) 236-6011 Carnegie Class: Master's M

FAX Number: (614) 236-6820 Calendar System: Semester

URL: www.capital.edu

Established: 1850 Annual Undergrad Tuition & Fees: $31,364

Enrollment: 3,550 Coed

Affiliation or Control: Evangelical Lutheran Church In America

IRS Status: 501(c)3

Highest Offering: First Professional Degree

Program: Liberal Arts And General; Teacher Preparatory; Professional

Accreditation: NH, ACBSP, LAW, MUS, NURSE, SW, TED

01	President	Dr. Denvy A. BOWMAN
05	Vice Pres Academic/Student Affairs	Dr. Richard M. ASHBROOK
10	Vice President Business & Finance	Ms. Susan E. TATE
45	Exec VP Planning & Advancement	Dr. Kevin W. SAYERS
32	Assoc VP for Student Affairs	Dr. Betty M. LOVELACE
84	Assoc VP Enrollment Services	Dr. Amy ADAMS
43	University Counsel	Dr. Tanya J. POTEET
20	Associate Provost	Dr. Terry D. LAHM
26	Asst Vice Pres External Relations	Ms. Patricia CRAMER
21	Assistant VP Business & Finance	Ms. Lori MCKIRNAN
44	Asst Vice President Major Gifts	Ms. April NOVOTNY
100	Dir Pres Ofc/Liaison to Board Trust	Ms. Nona S. MCGUIRE
27	Dir Communications/Media Relations	Ms. D. Nichole JOHNSON
09	Director of Institutional Research	Dr. Larry T. HUNTER
06	Registrar	Mr. Brent KOERBER
37	Director of Financial Aid	Ms. Susan E. KANNENWISCHER
07	Director of Admissions	Ms. Amanda SOHL
29	Director Alumni/Parent Relations	Ms. Diane LOESER
36	Director of Career Services	Mr. Eric R. ANDERSON
08	University Librarian/Director IMC	Ms. Belen FERNANDEZ
87	Director of Summer Programs	Dr. Jerry P. THOMAS
88	Academic Service Coordinator	Mr. Bruce EPPS
26	Director Public Relations	Ms. Denise RUSSELL
41	Interim Athletic Director	Dr. Steve BRUNING
88	Director of Faith Relations	Vacant
42	Campus Pastor	Rev. Amy OEHLSCHLAEGER
13	Int Dir Information Technology	Mr. Jeff GUILER
85	Director Intl Education & ESL Pgm	Ms. Jennifer ADAMS
35	Director Student Activities	Mr. Melvin ADAMS
18	Director Facilities Management	Ms. Beth Anne CARMEN
15	Director of Human Resources	Ms. Theresa FELDMEIER
38	Dir Univ Counseling/Health Svcs	Vacant
28	Dir Diversity/Multicultural Affairs	Ms. Cynthia DUNCAN JOSEPH
92	Honors Program	Dr. Dina LENTSNER
40	Manager Bookstore	Mr. Joseph AMBUSKE
61	Dean of Law School	Mr. Richard SIMPSON
64	Ast Dn Conservtry of Music/Sch Comm	Dr. Lynn ROSEBERRY
49	Dean Unified College	Dr. Cedric ADDERLEY
50	Asst Dean Sch Management/Leadership	Dr. Keirsten MOORE
66	Asst Dean Sch Nat Sci/Nursing/Hlth	Dr. Jens HEMMINGSEN
83	Asst Dean Sch Social Sciences/Educ	Dr. Jody FOURNIER
79	Assistant Dean School of Humanities	Dr. David BELCASTRO

Case Western Reserve University (F)

10900 Euclid Avenue, Cleveland OH 44106-7001

County: Cuyahoga FICE Identification: 003024

Unit ID: 201645

Telephone: (216) 368-2000 Carnegie Class: RU/VH

FAX Number: N/A Calendar System: Semester

URL: www.case.edu

Established: 1826 Annual Undergrad Tuition & Fees: $40,490

Enrollment: 9,636 Coed

Affiliation or Control: Independent Non-Profit IRS Status: 501(c)3

Highest Offering: Doctorate

Program: Liberal Arts And General; Professional

Accreditation: NH, AA, ANEST, BUS, BUSA, CLPSY, CS, DENT, DIETD, DIETI, ENG, LAW, MED, MIDWF, MUS, NUR, NURSE, PH, SP, SW, TEAC

01	President	Ms. Barbara R. SNYDER
05	Provost/Executive Vice President	Dr. William A. BAESLACK, III
20	Deputy Provost/VP Academic Programs	Dr. Lynn T. SINGER
10	Senior Vice Pres for Finance & CFO	Mr. John F. SIDERAS
11	Senior Vice Pres for Administration	Mr. John D. WHEELER
30	Sr VP for Univ Rels & Development	Mr. Bruce A. LOESSIN
17	Vice President Medical Affairs	Dr. Pamela B. DAVIS
46	Vice President for Research	Dr. Robert H. MILLER
13	Vice President Information Services	Dr. Lev S. GONICK
32	Vice President for Student Affairs	Mr. Glenn NICHOLLS
18	VP Campus Planning/Facilities Mgmt	Mr. Stephen CAMPBELL
16	Vice President for Human Resources	Ms. Carolyn GREGORY
43	Vice President/General Counsel	Ms. Elizabeth KEEFER
19	Vice President for Campus Services	Mr. Richard J. JAMIESON
26	Vice Pres for University Relations	Ms. Lara A. KALAFATIS
86	Asso VP Govt & Foundation Relations	Dr. Julie M. REHM
86	Exec Director Government Relations	Ms. Jennifer RUGGLES
31	Dir Center Community Partnerships	Ms. Latisha JAMES
45	Vice Pres for University Planning	Ms. Christine A. ASH
84	Vice Pres for Enrollment Management	Mr. Richard W. BISCHOFF
28	VP Inclusion/Diversity/Equal Opptny	Dr. Marilyn S. MOBLEY
26	VP Univ Marketing/Communications	Ms. Chris SHERIDAN
88	Treasurer	Mr. Robert C. BROWN
88	Chief Investment Officer	Ms. Sally STALEY
20	Vice Provost Undergrad Education	Dr. Donald L. FEKE
88	Assoc Prov for International Affs	Mr. David FLESHLER
100	Chief of Staff	Ms. Jennifer CIMPERMAN
88	Dean of Undergraduate Studies	Mr. Jeffrey WOLCOWITZ
21	Controller	Mr. Bradley W. FRALIC
06	Registrar	Ms. Amy S. HAMMETT
29	Associate VP for Alumni Relations	Mr. Christopher J. VLAHOS
37	Director of Financial Aid	Ms. Venus PULIAFICO
07	Director Undergraduate Admissions	Mr. Robert R. MCCULLOUGH
08	University Librarian	Mr. Arnold HIRSHON
36	Director Career Center	Dr. Thomas MATTHEWS
85	Dir International Student Svcs	Ms. Elise LINDSAY
38	Director University Counseling Svcs	Dr. James E. SELLERS
09	Director of Institutional Research	Ms. Jean E. GUBBINS
96	Dir Procurement/Distribution Svcs	Ms. Melinda BOYKIN
41	Athletic Director	Dr. David DILES
61	Dean of Law	Mr. Lawrence E. MITCHELL
49	Dean of Arts & Sciences	Dr. Cyrus C. TAYLOR
63	Dean of Medicine	Dr. Pamela B. DAVIS
66	Dean of Nursing	Dr. Mary E. KERR
52	Dean of Dental Medicine	Dr. Jerold S. GOLDBERG
50	Dean of Management	Dr. Robert E. WIDING, II
70	Dean Applied Social Science	Dr. Grover C. GILMORE
54	Dean of Engineering	Dr. Jeffrey DUERK
58	Dean of Graduate Studies	Dr. Charles E. ROZEK

Cedarville University (G)

251 N Main Street, Cedarville OH 45314-0601

County: Greene FICE Identification: 003025

Unit ID: 201654

Telephone: (937) 766-2211 Carnegie Class: Bac/Diverse

FAX Number: (937) 766-2760 Calendar System: Semester

URL: www.cedarville.edu

Established: 1887 Annual Undergrad Tuition & Fees: $28,536

Enrollment: 3,220 Coed

Affiliation or Control: Baptist IRS Status: 501(c)3

Highest Offering: Doctorate

Program: Liberal Arts And General; Teacher Preparatory; Professional

Accreditation: NH, ACBSP, CS, ENG, MUS, NURSE, @PHAR, SW, TED

01	President	Dr. William E. BROWN
03	Provost	Dr. John W. GREDY
05	Academic Vice President	Dr. Thomas H. CORNMAN
10	Sr Vice President for Business	Mr. Christopher SOHN
30	Vice President for Advancement	Mr. William L. BIGHAM
32	Vice President for Student Life	Dr. Carl A. RUBY
42	Vice Pres for Christian Ministry	Rev. Robert K. ROHM
84	Vice Pres Enrollment Management	Mrs. Janice SUPPLEE
43	General Counsel	Mr. John HART
11	Assoc VP for Operations	Mr. Rodney JOHNSON
32	Dean of Students	Miss Kirsten GIBBS
07	Director of Admissions	Miss Amy HOLDERBY
06	Registrar	Mrs. Frances CAMPBELL
34	Assoc Dean Women	Miss Rebecca STOWERS
106	Sr Assoc Acad VP Col Extended Lrng	Dr. Andy RUNYAN
16	Assoc VP of Human Resources	Mrs. Lisa TODD
14	Assoc VP for Tech/Computer Services	Dr. David L. ROTMAN
09	Associate VP for Strategic Planning	Mr. David ORMSBEE
69	Assoc VP Col of Health Professions	Dr. Pamela D. JOHNSON
49	Assoc VP Col of Arts & Sciences	Dr. Steven WINTEREGG
107	Assoc VP College of Professions	Dr. Mark MCCLAIN
08	Dean of Library Services	Mr. Lynn A. BROCK
37	Executive Director of Financial Aid	Mr. Kim JENERETTE
67	Dean School of Pharmacy	Dr. Marc SWEENEY
38	Director of Counseling Services	Mr. John M. POTTER
29	Director of Alumni Relations	Mr. Jeff BESTE
36	Director Career Services	Mr. Jeff REEP
87	Director Summer School/Cont Educ	Dr. Jewerl MAXWELL
92	Director Honors Program	Dr. David MILLS
35	Associate Dean/Campus Life	Mr. Brad D. SMITH
96	Director of Purchasing/Inventory	Mr. Tim P. JOHNSON
04	Executive Asst to the President	Mrs. Carol S. GEORGE
41	Athletic Director	Dr. Alan GEIST
26	Exec Director of Public Relations	Mr. Mark WEINSTEIN
19	Director of Campus Safety	Mr. Douglas W. CHISHOLM
40	Manager of Retail Services	Mrs. Tammy L. SLONE

Central Ohio Technical College (H)

1179 University Drive, Newark OH 43055-1767

County: Licking FICE Identification: 011046

Unit ID: 201672

Telephone: (740) 366-1351 Carnegie Class: Assoc/Pub-S-SC

FAX Number: (740) 366-5047 Calendar System: Semester

URL: www.cotc.edu

Established: 1971 Annual Undergrad Tuition & Fees (In-State): $6,300

Enrollment: 4,260 Coed

Affiliation or Control: State IRS Status: 501(c)3

Highest Offering: Associate Degree

Program: Occupational; 2-Year Principally Bachelor's Creditable; Technical Emphasis

Accreditation: NH, ADNUR, DMS, RAD, SURGT

01	President	Dr. Bonnie L. COE
10	Vice President Business & Finance	Mr. David BRILLHART
05	Vice President for Academic Affairs	Vacant
32	Director of Student Life	Dr. John BERRY
15	VP for Instnl Planning & HR Develop	Ms. Jacqueline PARRILL
08	Director of Library	Ms. Susan SCOTT

06 Records Manager/Registrar ... Ms. Veronica RINE
07 Director of Enrollment Management ... Ms. Tara HOUDESHELL
88 Director Child Development Center ... Vacant
27 Director Marketing/Public Relations ... Ms. Alice HUTZEL-BATESON
37 Director Financial Aid/Veteran Affs ... Ms. Faith PHILLIPS
19 Director Public Safety ... Mr. Denny HOLLERN
29 Dir Alumni Rels/Development Officer ... Mr. Matthew KELLY
35 Asst Director of Student Affairs ... Ms. Holly MASON
13 Chief Information Officer ... Mr. Howard IMHOF
38 Program Mgr Learn Asst Ctr Disabled ... Ms. Connie ZANG
11 Director of Operations ... Vacant
96 Manager of Purchasing ... Ms. Kimberley SIBERT
18 Manager Facilities ... Mr. Brian BOEHME
51 Coord of Community Svc/Learning ... Ms. Vorley TAYLOR
36 Dir Career Dev & Experiential Lrng ... Mr. Derek THATCHER
12 Coshocton Campus Administrator ... Ms. Melanie BOLENDER
12 Knox Campus Administrator ... Mr. Joel DANIELS
12 Pataskala Campus Administrator ... Ms. Julie MAURER
93 Minority Recruiter/Counselor ... Vacant
04 Assistant to the President ... Ms. Jan TOMLINSON

Central State University (A)

PO Box 1004, 1400 Brush Row Road,
Wilberforce OH 45384-1004

County: Greene — FICE Identification: 003026
Unit ID: 201690
Telephone: (937) 376-6332 — Carnegie Class: Bac/Diverse
FAX Number: (937) 376-6138 — Calendar System: Semester
URL: www.centralstate.edu
Established: 1887 — Annual Undergrad Tuition & Fees (In-State): $5,870
Enrollment: 2,503 — Coed
Affiliation or Control: State — IRS Status: 501(c)3
Highest Offering: Master's
Program: Liberal Arts And General; Teacher Preparatory; Business Emphasis
Accreditation: NH, ART, ENG, MUS, TED

01 President ... Dr. Cynthia JACKSON-HAMMOND
04 Exec Asst to the President ... Mrs. Wendy HAYES
05 Provost/VP Academic Affairs ... Dr. Patrick LIVERPOOL
10 Vice President Admin & Finance ... Mrs. Daarel BURNETTE
30 Vice Pres Institutional Advancement ... Mr. Anthony FAIRBANKS
11 Asst VP Administration & Finance ... Vacant
32 Vice President for Student Affairs ... Mr. Jerryl BRIGGS
13 Vice Pres/Chief Information Officer ... Dr. Donald STEWARD
20 Assoc Vice Pres Academic Affairs ... Dr. Willie HOUSTON
06 Registrar ... Mrs. LaTonya BRANHAM
07 Director of Admissions ... Ms. Robin RUCKER
08 Director of Hallie Q Brown Library ... Mr. Johnny JACKSON
89 Int Dean Ctr Stdnt Academic Success ... Dr. LaKeysha CATRON
12 Dean CSU Dayton Campus ... Dr. Kaye JETER
09 Director Assessment/Inst Research ... Mr. Mohammad ALI
19 Chief of Police ... Chief Anthony PETTIFORD
26 Director Public Relations ... Dr. Gayle BARGE
23 Medical Director ... Dr. Karen MATHEWS
29 Director Alumni Relations ... Mr. Keith PERKINS
88 Director Career Services ... Ms. Elizabeth BEEMER
37 Director Student Financial Aid ... Ms. Sonia SLOMBIA
39 Director Residence Life ... Mr. Raynaldo GILLUS
41 Athletic Director ... Mr. Jahan CULBREATH
42 Director Campus Ministry ... Rev. Nigel FELDER
46 Director Sponsored Research ... Mr. Morakinyo KUTI
49 Dean Coll of Humanities/Arts & Sci ... Dr. Lovette CHINWAH
50 Dean College Business & Industry ... Dr. Charles SHOWELL, JR.
53 Dean College of Education ... Dr. Reginald NNAZOR
15 Director of Human Resources ... Ms. Kimberly MANIGAULT
21 Director Business Svcs/Capital Dev ... Mr. Harlan HENDERSON
25 Director Grants Accounting ... Vacant
92 Director Honors Program ... Vacant
21 Controller ... Ms. Beth ANDERSON
21 Budget Director ... Mr. Curtis PETTIS
38 Director Student Counseling ... Mr. Frank PORTER

Chancellor University (B)

3921 Chester Avenue, Cleveland OH 44114

County: Cuyahoga — FICE Identification: 003043
Unit ID: 202611
Telephone: (216) 391-6937 — Carnegie Class: Bac/Diverse
FAX Number: (216) 426-9296 — Calendar System: Semester
URL: www.chancelloru.edu
Established: 1848 — Annual Undergrad Tuition & Fees: $12,000
Enrollment: 523 — Coed
Affiliation or Control: Proprietary — IRS Status: Proprietary
Highest Offering: Master's
Program: Business Emphasis
Accreditation: NH, IACBE

01 Chancellor and Interim President ... Mr. Robert C. DAUGHERTY
84 Vice President Enrollment Services ... Ms. Leslie BRUGA
05 Provost/CAO ... Dr. Steven KERR
15 Vice President of Human Resources ... Dr. Theresa HUEFTLE
45 VP of Strategic Planning ... Dr. Trish GORMAN
06 Registrar ... Ms. Miria T. BATIG
08 Manager Student Knowledge Resource ... Mr. Richard D. BRHEL
37 Director Financial Aid ... Ms. Chris TUNEBURG
10 Chief Financial Officer ... Mr. Brian MCELYEA
32 Senior Director Student Services ... Ms. Bethany BATEMAN
24 Assoc Dir of Learning & Acad Tech ... Mr. Daniel TAYLOR
04 Exec Asst to the President ... Ms. Kate HERRNSTEIN

09 Sr Dir of Institutional Research ... Dr. Dmitry SUSPITSIN
18 Director Facilities and IT ... Vacant
21 Controller ... Vacant
58 Exec VP Jack Welch Mgmt Institute ... Dr. Steve KERR
50 Dean College of Business ... Mr. Todd Allyn WILLIAMS
49 Dean College of Arts & Sciences ... Dr. Darius NAVRAN
107 Dean College Professional Studies ... Dr. Darius NAVRAN
108 Director of Assessment ... Mr. Doug CLAY
88 Director of Faculty T&D ... Ms. Janelle COUTURE
102 Sr Dir Corporate Dev Liason ... Mr. Kevan FORD
88 Director Student Info Systems ... Ms. Shauna YOUNG

Chatfield College (C)

20918 State Route 251, Saint Martin OH 45118-9059

County: Brown — FICE Identification: 010880
Unit ID: 201751
Telephone: (513) 875-3344 — Carnegie Class: Assoc/PrivNFP
FAX Number: (513) 875-3912 — Calendar System: Semester
URL: www.chatfield.edu
Established: 1971 — Annual Undergrad Tuition & Fees: $10,515
Enrollment: 433 — Coed
Affiliation or Control: Independent Non-Profit — IRS Status: 501(c)3
Highest Offering: Associate Degree
Program: 2-Year Principally Bachelor's Creditable; Fine Arts Emphasis
Accreditation: NH

01 President ... Mr. John P. TAFARO
05 Chief Academic Officer/Dean ... Mr. Alan SIMMONS
10 Director of Finance ... Ms. Mary R. JACOBS
30 Director of Advancement ... Mr. Steve RANIERI
07 Director of Admissions ... Mr. John PENROSE
20 Associate Dean/Site Director ... Ms. Wanda HILL
20 Associate Dean/Site Director ... Sr. Patricia HOMAN
26 Director of Marketing Communication ... Ms. Pamela SPENCER

The Christ College of Nursing and Health Sciences (D)

2139 Auburn Avenue, Cincinnati OH 45219

County: Hamilton — FICE Identification: 006489
Unit ID: 201821
Telephone: (513) 585-2401 — Carnegie Class: Assoc/PrivNFP
FAX Number: (513) 585-3540 — Calendar System: Semester
URL: www.thechristcollege.edu
Established: 2006 — Annual Undergrad Tuition & Fees: $15,800
Enrollment: 346 — Coed
Affiliation or Control: Independent Non-Profit — IRS Status: 501(c)3
Highest Offering: Associate Degree
Program: 2-Year Principally Bachelor's Creditable; Nursing Emphasis
Accreditation: NH, ADNUR

01 President & Chief Academic Officer ... Dr. Nathan A. LONG
66 Dean Nursing and Health Sciences ... Ms. Kathleen D. CARISSIMI
49 Dean Liberal Arts and Sciences ... Mr. Michael SMITH
09 Dean Inst Planning & Research ... Ms. Carolyn A. HUNTER
30 Major Gifts Director ... Ms. Danielle GENTRY-BARTH
32 Dean Student Affairs ... Ms. Jill A. LOCH
10 Assistant Registrar/Bursar ... Ms. Cathy SILVERMAN
37 Director Financial Aid ... Mr. Timothy RING
06 Registrar ... Mr. Perry CARROLL
07 Director Recruitment & Admissions ... Mr. Bradley JACKSON

Cincinnati Christian University (E)

2700 Glenway Avenue, Cincinnati OH 45204-3200

County: Hamilton — FICE Identification: 003029
Unit ID: 201858
Telephone: (513) 244-8100 — Carnegie Class: Spec/Faith
FAX Number: (513) 244-8140 — Calendar System: Semester
URL: www.ccuniversity.edu
Established: 1924 — Annual Undergrad Tuition & Fees: $14,766
Enrollment: 1,002 — Coed
Affiliation or Control: Christian Churches And Churches of Christ
IRS Status: 501(c)3
Highest Offering: First Professional Degree
Program: Liberal Arts And General; Professional; Religious Emphasis
Accreditation: NH, BI, MUS, TEAC, THEOL

01 President ... Dr. David M. FAUST
05 Vice President Academic Affairs ... Dr. Jon A. WEATHERLY
32 Vice Pres Leadership Development ... Vacant
30 Vice President for Advancement ... Mrs. Barbara RENDEL
10 Vice President Finance & Operations ... Mr. Chuck ABBOTT
20 Dean of Seminary ... Dr. Johnny PRESSLEY
20 Dean of College ... Dr. Jon A. WEATHERLY
51 Director College of Adult Learning ... Ms. Judy PRATT
09 Dean of Dist Educ & Inst Research ... Dr. Paul PENNINGTON
06 Registrar ... Mr. Don A. THOMASON
08 Director of Libraries ... Mr. James H. LLOYD
35 Dean of Students ... Mrs. Kristin MERRILL
33 Dean of Men/Campus Minister ... Mr. Dan BURTON
37 Director of Financial Aid ... Mrs. Linda WAUGH
07 Director Undergraduate Admissions ... Mr. David BRUNNER
29 Director of Alumni Ministries ... Mr. Mark KOERNER
21 Accounting Manager ... Mr. Randy KOEHLER
88 Dir Center for Church Advancement ... Mr. David ROADCUP
41 Director of Athletics ... Mr. Aaron BURGESS
18 Director of Operations ... Vacant
15 Human Resources Director ... Mrs. Nancy HARTMAN
14 Director of Computer Services ... Mr. James MCINTYRE

19 Director of Security ... Mrs. Karen LITTLE
40 Manager of Bookstore ... Miss Beth ROGERS
07 Director of Graduate Admissions ... Mr. Alex EDDY
38 Director Student Counseling ... Dr. Douglas SPEARS
28 Director of CUGO ... Mr. Steve SKAGGS
04 Assistant to the President ... Mrs. Wendy SPALDING

Cincinnati College of Mortuary Science (F)

645 W North Bend Road, Cincinnati OH 45224-1462

County: Hamilton — FICE Identification: 010906
Unit ID: 201867
Telephone: (513) 761-2020 — Carnegie Class: Spec/Other
FAX Number: (513) 761-3333 — Calendar System: Quarter
URL: www.ccms.edu
Established: 1882 — Annual Undergrad Tuition & Fees: $20,250
Enrollment: 126 — Coed
Affiliation or Control: Independent Non-Profit — IRS Status: 501(c)3
Highest Offering: Baccalaureate
Program: Occupational; Liberal Arts And General
Accreditation: NH, FUSER

01 Interim President ... Mr. Jeffrey SHAPIRO
84 Exec Director Enrollment Management ... Ms. Pat SULLIVAN

Cincinnati State Technical and Community College (G)

3520 Central Parkway, Cincinnati OH 45223-2690

County: Hamilton — FICE Identification: 010345
Unit ID: 201928
Telephone: (513) 569-1500 — Carnegie Class: Assoc/Pub-U-SC
FAX Number: (513) 569-1495 — Calendar System: Other
URL: www.cincinnatistate.edu
Established: 1966 — Annual Undergrad Tuition & Fees (In-State): $4,265
Enrollment: 10,581 — Coed
Affiliation or Control: State — IRS Status: 501(c)3
Highest Offering: Associate Degree
Program: Occupational; 2-Year Principally Bachelor's Creditable; Business Emphasis
Accreditation: NH, ACFEI, ADNUR, CONST, DIETT, DMS, ENGT, #MAC, MLTAD, OTA, PNUR, SURGT

01 President ... Dr. O'dell OWENS
03 Executive Vice President ... Ms. Carla CHANCE
05 Academic Vice President ... Dr. Monica POSEY
10 Vice President Finance/Treasurer ... Mr. Michael GEOGHEGAN
26 Vice Pres Marketing/Communications ... Ms. Jean MANNING
72 Dean of Engineering Technology ... Mr. Doug BOWLING
50 Dean of Business Technologies ... Dr. Nick NISSLEY
76 Dean Health Technologies ... Ms. Bessie PITTS
81 Dean Humanities/Sciences ... Dr. Rayma SMITH
84 Dean Enrollment/Student Services ... Dr. Anthony CRUZ
06 Registrar ... Mr. Ryan HUNT
08 Library Director ... Mrs. Cindy SEFTON
41 Dir Athletics/Student Activities ... Mr. Tom HATHAWAY
13 Vice President of IT/CIO ... Dr. David HICKEY
18 Director of Facilities ... Mr. Rob EPLING
103 Director of Workforce Development ... Dr. Dennis ULRICH
09 Director of Institutional Research ... Ms. Anne FOSTER
07 Director of Admissions ... Ms. Gabriele BOECKERMANN
15 Director of Human Resources ... Ms. Lisa EVANS
32 Chief Student Life Officer ... Ms. Brenda MAPLES-STERRY
35 Director of Student Affairs ... Ms. Sharon DAVIS
96 Director of Purchasing ... Mr. Brian FRANK
92 Coordinator Honors Program ... Dr. Andrea LESLIE
30 Director of Development ... Ms. Dawn PERRIN
86 Director of Government Affairs ... Ms. Nan KOHNEN-CAHALL
04 Executive Administrative Associate ... Mrs. Michelle GRIFFIN-DONALDSON
19 Director of Public Safety ... Mr. Michael WYLIE
37 Director of Financial Aid ... Mrs. La Saundra CRAIG
101 Secretary to the Board of Trustees ... Mrs. Nancy STUBBEMAN
88 Director of Student Success ... Mr. Martino HARMON
25 Contract Administrator ... Mrs. Ann JAMES

Clark State Community College (H)

570 E Leffel Lane, PO Box 570,
Springfield OH 45501-0570

County: Clark — FICE Identification: 004852
Unit ID: 201973
Telephone: (937) 325-0691 — Carnegie Class: Assoc/Pub-U-SC
FAX Number: (937) 328-6142 — Calendar System: Quarter
URL: www.clarkstate.edu
Established: 1966 — Annual Undergrad Tuition & Fees (In-State): $5,894
Enrollment: 5,168 — Coed
Affiliation or Control: State — IRS Status: 501(c)3
Highest Offering: Associate Degree
Program: Occupational; 2-Year Principally Bachelor's Creditable
Accreditation: NH, ADNUR, MAC, MLTAD, PTAA

01 President ... Dr. Karen E. RAFINSKI
05 Vice Pres Academic/Student Affairs ... Dr. David H. DEVIER
10 Vice President Business Affairs ... Joseph R. JACKSON
30 Vice President of Advancement ... Kristin J. CULP
21 Controller ... Dixie A. DEPEW
12 Interim Dean Greene Center ... Dr. Edward J. BUSHER
08 Director Library Services ... Beth DEGER

32 Dean of Stdnt Affs/Enrollment Mgmt ....Dr. Edward J. BUSHER
49 Dean Arts & Sciences/Public Svcs ....Martha CRAWMER
50 Dean Business/Applied Technologies ....Jane A. CAPE
76 Dean Health and Human Services ....Kathleen J. WILCOX
37 Financial Aid Director ....Kathy A. KLAY
06 Registrar ....Teresa A. MABRY
07 Director of Admissions ....Corey HOLLIDAY
13 Exec Dir Information Technology ....Barbara DESCHAPELLES
102 Foundation/Executive Director ....Kristin J. CULP
45 Dir of Inst Research and Planning ....Cynthia APPLIN
15 Director of Human Resources ....Marvin NEPHEW
57 Director of Performing Arts Center ....Stuart A. SECTTOR
18 Dir Facilities/Oper/Maintenance ....Randall CONOVER
41 Dir Athletics/Act & Evening Svcs ....Ronald GORDON
51 Program Mgr Continuing Education ....Vacant
09 Institutional Research Technician ....Jennifer J. NICKELL

Cleveland Institute of Art (A)

11141 East Boulevard, Cleveland OH 44106-1710
County: Cuyahoga FICE Identification: 003982
Unit ID: 202046
Telephone: (216) 421-7000 Carnegie Class: Spec/Arts
FAX Number: (216) 421-7438 Calendar System: Semester
URL: www.cia.edu
Established: 1882 Annual Undergrad Tuition & Fees: $35,145
Enrollment: 546 Coed
Affiliation or Control: Independent Non-Profit IRS Status: 501(c)3
Highest Offering: Baccalaureate
Program: Professional; Fine Arts Emphasis
Accreditation: NH, ART

01 President a& CEO ....Mr. Grafton J. NUNES
05 VP Academic & Faculty Affairs ....Mr. Chris WHITTEY
30 Sr Vice Pres Inst Advancement ....Mr. Michael COLE
10 Vice President Business Affairs/CFO ....Mrs. Almut ZVOSEC
26 Vice President Mktg & Communication ....Mr. Mark INGLIS
07 Exec Dir Enrollment & Financial Aid ....Mr. Robert BORDEN
37 Asst Director of Financial Aid ....Ms. Delores HALL
06 Registrar ....Mrs. Karen HUDY
08 Librarian ....Ms. Cristine ROM
07 Director of Admissions ....Ms. Joanne LANDERS
18 Director Safety & Facility Mgmt ....Mr. Howard D. WEINER
29 Director Annual Giving/Alumni Rels ....Mr. Michael KINSELLA
20 Director of Academic Services ....Ms. Anne GATES
44 Director Major Gifts/Planned Giving ....Ms. Margaret GUDBRANSON
15 Exec Dir of HR & Inclusion ....Mr. Raymond SCRAGG
32 Dean of Student Affairs ....Ms. Nancy NEVILLE
37 Director of Financial Aid ....Mr. Martin CARNEY
26 Director of Mktg & Communications ....Ms. Susan ILER
57 Art Director ....Mr. Richard SARIAN
88 Senior Writer ....Ms. Ann MCGUIRE

Cleveland Institute of Electronics (B)

1776 E 17th Street, Cleveland OH 44114-3679
County: Cuyahoga FICE Identification: 005210
Unit ID: 202064
Telephone: (216) 781-9400 Carnegie Class: Assoc/PrivFP
FAX Number: (216) 781-0331 Calendar System: Other
URL: www.cie-wc.edu
Established: 1934 Annual Undergrad Tuition & Fees: $4,150
Enrollment: 1,815 Coed
Affiliation or Control: Proprietary IRS Status: Proprietary
Highest Offering: Associate Degree
Program: Occupational
Accreditation: DETC

01 President ....Mr. J. Randall DRINKO
37 Director of Financial Aid ....Mr. Scott KATZENMEYER
88 Coordinator Veteran Affairs ....Mrs. Marites CAPISTRANO

Cleveland Institute of Music (C)

11021 East Boulevard, Cleveland OH 44106-1776
County: Cuyahoga FICE Identification: 003031
Unit ID: 202073
Telephone: (216) 791-5000 Carnegie Class: Spec/Arts
FAX Number: (216) 791-3063 Calendar System: Semester
URL: www.cim.edu
Established: 1920 Annual Undergrad Tuition & Fees: $42,030
Enrollment: 450 Coed
Affiliation or Control: Independent Non-Profit IRS Status: 501(c)3
Highest Offering: Doctorate
Program: Professional; Music Emphasis
Accreditation: NH, MUS

01 President/CEO ....Mr. Joel SMIRNOFF
03 Vice President/COO/Asst Treasurer ....Mr. Eric BOWER
30 VP for Institutional Advancement ....Ms. Karin STONE
51 Dean Prep/Continuing Education .... Ms. Sandra SHAPIRO
05 Dean of Conservatory ....Dr. Adrian DALY
26 Director Marketing & Communications ....Ms. Lorraine SCHUCHART
13 Director Systems Management ....Ms. Aimee BARTON
07 Associate Director of Admission ....Mr. William FAY
32 Associate Dean of Student Affairs ....Mr. David GILSON
37 Director Financial Aid ....Ms. Kristine GRIPP
21 Chief Financial Office ....Ms. Kristen KOLLAR
06 Registrar ....Mrs. Hallie MOORE
15 Director Human Resources ....Mrs. Megan SWERBINSKY
08 Director of the Library ....Ms. Jean TOOMBS
18 Director Buildings & Grounds ....Mr. Alan VALEK
88 Director of Concerts & Events ....Ms. Lori WRIGHT
40 Bookstore Manager ....Ms. Antoinette MILLER
106 Director of Distance Learning ....Mr. Gregory HOWE

Cleveland State University (D)

2121 Euclid Avenue, Cleveland OH 44115-2214
County: Cuyahoga FICE Identification: 003032
Unit ID: 202134
Telephone: (216) 687-2000 Carnegie Class: RU/H
FAX Number: (216) 687-9366 Calendar System: Semester
URL: www.csuohio.edu
Established: 1964 Annual Undergrad Tuition & Fees (In-State): $9,264
Enrollment: 17,447 Coed
Affiliation or Control: State IRS Status: 501(c)3
Highest Offering: Doctorate
Program: Liberal Arts And General; Teacher Preparatory; Professional
Accreditation: NH, ARCPA, BUS, BUSA, CACREP, COPSY, ENG, ENGT, LAW, MUS, NURSE, OT, PH, PLNG, PTA, SP, SPAA, SW, TED

01 President ....Dr. Ronald M. BERKMAN
100 Chief of Staff ....Mr. Michael ARTBAUER
05 Interim Provost ....Dr. George WALKER
10 Vice President Finance ....Ms. Stephanie MCHENRY
84 VP Enrollment/Student Affairs .....Ms. Carmen ALVAREZ BROWN
09 Actg VP Research & Graduate Studies .... Dr. Jerzy SAWICKI
31 Vice Pres University Engagement ....Dr. Byron WHITE
30 VP Univ Advancement/Exec Dir Found ....Ms. Berinthia LEVINE
45 Vice Provost for Academic Planning ....Dr. Teresa LAGRANGE
20 Vice Provost Academic Affairs ....Dr. Vijaya KONANGI
26 Asst VP University Mktg/Admissions ....Mr. Robert SPADEMAN
15 Asst Vice Pres Human Resources Dev ....Vacant
88 Asst VP Campus Support Services ....Ms. Clare RAHM
21 Controller/Assoc VP Finance ....Ms. Kathleen MURPHY
32 Dean of Student Life ....Dr. James DRNEK
49 Dean Coll Liberal Arts/Soc Sci ....Dr. Gregory M. SADLEK
81 Dean College of Science ....Dr. Meredith R. BOND
50 Dean Ahuja College Business Admin ....Mr. Stephen PERCY
53 Dean College Education ....Dr. Sajit ZACHARIAH
54 Dean Fenn College of Engineering .... Dr. Anette KARLSSON
58 Dean College Graduate Studies ....Dr. Jianping ZHU
61 Dean of College of Law ....Mr. Craig BOISE
80 Dean of College of Urban Affairs ....Dr. Edward HILL
43 General Counsel ....Ms. Sonali B. WILSON
86 Sr Advisor to Pres Government Rels ....Dr. William NAPIER
08 Director of Libraries ....Dr. Glenda THORNTON
22 Affirmative Affairs Officer ....Vacant
07 Director Undergraduate Admissions .... Ms. Heike HEINRICH
09 Director Institutional Research ....Mr. Tom GEAGHAN
85 Director International Programs ....Mr. George BURKE
36 Director Career Services ....Ms. Yolanda BURT
38 Director Counseling Services ....Dr. Janilee B. WHEATON
19 Executive Director of Campus Safety ....Vacant
37 Director Student Financial Aid ....Ms. Rachel SCHMIDT
06 Registrar ....Ms. Janet STIMPLE
41 Director of Athletics ....Mr. John PARRY
29 Director Alumni Affairs .... Ms. Carolyn CHAMPION-SLOAN
18 Chief Facilities/Physical Plant ....Mr. Christopher K. WILSON
96 Director of Purchasing ....Vacant
92 Director Honors Program ....Dr. Peter MEIKSINS
28 Director of Diversity ....Ms. Melodie YATES

College of Mount St. Joseph (E)

5701 Delhi Road, Cincinnati OH 45233-1670
County: Hamilton FICE Identification: 003033
Unit ID: 204200
Telephone: (513) 244-4200 Carnegie Class: Master's M
FAX Number: (513) 244-4654 Calendar System: Semester
URL: www.msj.edu
Established: 1920 Annual Undergrad Tuition & Fees: $24,200
Enrollment: 2,324 Coed
Affiliation or Control: Roman Catholic IRS Status: 501(c)3
Highest Offering: Doctorate
Program: Liberal Arts And General; Teacher Preparatory; Professional
Accreditation: NH, MUS, NURSE, PTA, SW, TEAC

01 President ....Dr. Anthony J. ARETZ
05 Chief Academic Officer/Dean Faculty ....Dr. Alan DECOURCY
30 Vice Pres Institutional Advancement ....Ms. Patricia L. RAGIO
32 Vice President for Student Affairs ....Dr. Douglas K. FRIZZELL
58 Dean of Adult & Graduate Studies ....Dr. Darla VALE
35 Assistant Dean of Students ....Mr. Daniel VAN VECHTEN
10 Chief Financial Officer ....Ms. Anne Marie WAGNER
06 Registrar .... Ms. Irene RICHARDSON
13 Chief Information Officer ....Mr. Keith A. WEBER
29 Director of Alumni Relations ....Ms. Nicki VELDHAUS
37 Director Student Admin Services ....Ms. Kathy KELLY
36 Director Career/Experiential Educ ....Ms. Jan FRANCHAK
25 Director Grants and Research ....Ms. Linda B. LIEBAU
18 Director Buildings & Grounds ....Mr. Dennis YOUNG
09 Director Institutional/Market Rsrch ... Mr. Joseph S. SPORTSMAN
07 Director of Admission ....Ms. Peggy MINNICH
88 Chief Compliance and Risk Officer .... Ms. Linda PANZECA
20 Associate Academic Dean ....Ms. Maggie DAVIS
21 Controller Fiscal Operations ....Ms. Liane SZUCS
38 Director Wellness Center ....Ms. Patsy SCHWAIGER
08 Director Library ....Mr. Paul JENKINS
14 Director Instructional Technology ....Ms. Kim HUNTER
19 Director of Campus Police ....Mr. Tim CARNEY
41 Director of Athletics ....Mr. Steve RADCLIFFE
68 Int Chair/Assoc Prof Athletic Trng ....Dr. Angela WOLFE
88 Director Learning Center ....Dr. Dana FREER
42 Director of Campus Ministry ....Sr. Nancy BRAMLAGE, SC
44 Director of Development ....Ms. Lisa ODENBECK
66 Dean of Health Sciences ....Dr. Susan JOHNSON
40 Manager of Bookstore ....Mr. Brad HOFFMAN
50 Dean of Business ....Dr. Charles KRONCKE
53 Dean of Education ....Dr. Mary WEST
81 Dean Behavioral/Natural Sciences ....Dr. Diana DAVIS
26 Director of Marketing ....Ms. Kathleen LUNDRIGAN
91 Director Administrative Computing ....Mr. Dan LUKAC
105 Webmaster ....Ms. Carolyn BOLAND
102 Director Donor Corporate Relations ....Ms. Carol PIEPER
88 Exec Dir Ethical Leadership Devel ....Dr. Tim BRYANT
44 Coordinator Annual Giving ....Ms. Alissa BECK
89 Coordinator First Year Experience ....Dr. Patty MILLS
23 Coordinator Health Services ....Ms. Linda PRUSS

The College of Wooster (F)

1189 Beall Avenue, Wooster OH 44691-2363
County: Wayne FICE Identification: 003037
Unit ID: 206589
Telephone: (330) 263-2000 Carnegie Class: Bac/A&S
FAX Number: (330) 263-2427 Calendar System: Semester
URL: www.wooster.edu
Established: 1866 Annual Undergrad Tuition & Fees: $39,500
Enrollment: 1,982 Coed
Affiliation or Control: Independent Non-Profit IRS Status: 501(c)3
Highest Offering: Baccalaureate
Program: Liberal Arts And General; Teacher Preparatory
Accreditation: NH, MUS, TED

01 President ....Dr. Grant H. CORNWELL
05 Provost ....Dr. Carolyn NEWTON
10 Vice Pres Finance/Bus/Treasurer .. Ms. Laurie W. STICKELMAIER
30 Vice President for Development ....Ms. Laurie HOUCK
84 Vice Pres Enrollment/College Rels .... Dr. Scott FRIEDHOFF
04 Exec Assistant to the President ....Vacant
26 Assoc VP College Rels & Marketing .... Mr. John HOPKINS
18 Assc VP Facilities & Auxiliaries .... Ms. Jacqueline MIDDLETON
32 Dean of Students ....Mr. Kurt HOLMES
20 Dean Curriculum/Academic Engagement .... Dr. Henry B. KREUZMAN
20 Dean for Faculty Development ....Dr. Heather M. FITZGIBBON
07 Dean of Admissions .... Ms. Jennifer D. WINGE
35 Senior Associate Dean of Students ....Ms. Carolyn BUXTON
35 Assoc Dean of Students ....Robyn LADITKA
35 Assoc Dean of Students .... Ms. Christie KRACKER
28 Asst Dn Stdnts/Co-Dir Ctr for D&GE ....Ms. Susan LEE
85 Dir Office of Intl Student Affairs ....Yorgun MARCEL
09 Chief Information Planning Officer ....Dr. Ellen FALDUTO
06 Registrar ....Ms. Suzanne BATES
08 Director of Libraries ....Mr. Mark A. CHRISTEL
37 Director of Financial Aid ....Dr. David MILLER
27 Director Office Public Information ....Mr. John FINN
29 Dir of Alumni Rels & Wooster Fund ...Ms. Heidi A. MCCORMICK
36 Director Career Services ....Ms. Lisa KASTOR
35 Dir Student Center/Stdnt Activities ....Vacant
41 Dir Phys Educ/Athletics/Recreat ....Dr. Keith BECKETT
18 Director Physical Plant Operations ....Mr. Doug LADITKA
19 Director Security/Protective Svcs ....Mr. Steven GLICK
16 Director of Human Resources ....Ms. Melanie YOUNG
39 Director of Residence Life ....Ms. Krista KRONSTEIN
42 Camp Chaplain/Dir Intfth Camp Mins ....Rev. Linda MORGAN-CLEMENT
101 Secretary of College/Chief Staff .... Ms. Angela JOHNSTON

Columbus College of Art & Design (G)

60 Cleveland Avenue, Columbus OH 43215-1758
County: Franklin FICE Identification: 003039
Unit ID: 202170
Telephone: (614) 224-9101 Carnegie Class: Spec/Arts
FAX Number: (614) 222-4040 Calendar System: Semester
URL: www.ccad.edu
Established: 1879 Annual Undergrad Tuition & Fees: $28,164
Enrollment: 1,347 Coed
Affiliation or Control: Independent Non-Profit IRS Status: 501(c)3
Highest Offering: Master's
Program: Professional; Fine Arts Emphasis
Accreditation: NH, ART, CIDA

01 President .... Mr. Dennison W. GRIFFITH
04 Exec Assistant to the President ....Ms. Sheri LUCAS
05 Vice President for Academic Affairs .... Mr. Kevin J. CONLON
10 Senior Vice President/CFO ....Mr. Jeffrey A. FISHER
30 Vice President for Advancement ....Ms. Laurie Beth SWEENEY
84 VP Enrollment Mgmt & Communications . Mr. Jonathan LINDSAY
32 Vice President for Student Affairs ....Mr. Dwayne TODD
20 Dean of Faculty ....Ms. Char NORMAN
60 Dean School of Design Arts ....Mr. Ron SAKS
57 Dean School of Studio Arts ....Ms. Julie TAGGART
58 Director Graduate Studies ....Mr. Ric PETRY
06 Registrar .... Ms. Michele KIBLER
13 Information Technology Director ....Vacant
15 Director of Human Resources ....Ms. Barbara DAVIS
08 Director of Library Services ....Ms. Gail STORER
19 Director of Safety & Security .... Mr. Wallace TANKSLEY
18 Director of Facilities ....Mr. Joseph SPYBEY

27 Director Communications & Marketing ... Ms. Robin HEPLER
38 Director of Counseling & Wellness ... Ms. Erin VLACH
37 Director Student Financial Aid ... Ms. Anna M. SCHOFIELD
36 Director Career Resources ... Vacant
21 Controller ... Mr. Roger ESCOLAS
35 Dir of Student Involvement ... Vacant
51 Dir Continuing/Professional Study ... Ms. Catherine SHERIDAN
39 Director of Residence Life ... Vacant
88 Director of Special Projects ... Mr. Dave STOCKWELL
40 Supply Store Manager ... Mr. Danny HINTY

Columbus State Community College (A)

Box 1609, Columbus OH 43216-1609

County: Franklin FICE Identification: 006867
Unit ID: 202222
Telephone: (614) 287-5353 Carnegie Class: Assoc/Pub-U-SC
FAX Number: (614) 287-5113 Calendar System: Quarter
URL: www.cscc.edu
Established: 1963 Annual Undergrad Tuition & Fees (In-State): $2,958
Enrollment: 30,921 Coed
Affiliation or Control: State IRS Status: 501(c)3
Highest Offering: Associate Degree
Program: Occupational
Accreditation: NH, ACBSP, ACFEI, ADNUR, CONST, DH, DIETT, EMT, ENGT, MAC, MLTAD, RAD, SURGT

01 President ... Dr. David T. HARRISON
100 Chief of Staff ... Ms. Kimberly HALL
05 Senior Vice Pres Academic Affairs ... Dr. John COOLEY
10 Sr Vice President & CFO ... Ms. Theresa GEHR
26 Vice Pres Marketing/Communications ... Mr. Will KOPP
13 Vice President Info Technology ... Mr. Hamid DANESH
45 Vice Pres for Knowledge Res/Plng ... Dr. Deborah D. COLEMAN
15 Vice President for Human Resources ... Mr. Timothy WAGNER
32 Vice Pres for Student Affairs ... Dr. Janet ROGERS
84 Dean of Enrollment Services ... Mr. Martin MALIWESKY
12 Dean of Delaware Campus ... Mr. Angelo FROLE
49 Interim Dean of Arts & Sciences ... Ms. Karen MUIR
50 Dean of Technical/Career Programs ... Dr. Polly OWEN
35 Dean Student Life ... Ms. Rene HAMPTON
30 Executive Director for Development ... Mr. Matt KELLY
14 Director of Data Center ... Mr. Etienne MARTIN
21 Director of Business Services ... Ms. Aletha SHIPLEY
06 Director of Records & Registration ... Dr. Regina A. PEAL
37 Dir Enroll/Fin Aid/Veterans Svcs ... Mr. David METZ
19 Director of Public Safety ... Dr. John NESTOR
18 Director of Facilities Planning ... Mr. Mark FRENCH
28 Director of Diversity ... Ms. Renee HAMPTON
08 Director Educational Resources Ctr ... Mr. Bruce MASSIS
07 Director of Admissions ... Ms. Tari BLANEY
40 Bookstore Supervisor ... Mr. Phillip SANDERS

Cuyahoga Community College (B)

700 Carnegie Avenue, Cleveland OH 44115-2878

County: Cuyahoga FICE Identification: 003040
Unit ID: 202356
Telephone: (216) 987-4000 Carnegie Class: Assoc/Pub-U-MC
FAX Number: (216) 566-5977 Calendar System: Semester
URL: www.tri-c.edu
Established: 1963 Annual Undergrad Tuition & Fees (In-District): $2,936
Enrollment: 31,261 Coed
Affiliation or Control: State/Local IRS Status: 501(c)3
Highest Offering: Associate Degree
Program: Occupational; 2-Year Principally Bachelor's Creditable
Accreditation: NH, ACFEI, ADNUR, ARCPA, DH, DIETT, DMS, ENGT, MAC, MLTAD, NDT, NMT, OTA, POLYT, PTAA, RAD, SURGT

01 President ... Dr. Jerry Sue THORNTON
05 Provost/EVP Acad & Stdnt Affairs ... Dr. Belinda MILES
10 Exec Vice Pres Admin and Finance ... Dr. Craig FOLTIN
103 Exec Vice Pres Workforce & Econ Dev ... Ms. Susan MUHA
12 Campus President/VP West Shore ... Dr. Michael J. THOMSON
12 Corporate College President ... Vacant
12 Campus President/VP West ... Dr. Patricia ROWELL
12 Campus President/VP Metro ... Dr. Michael SCHOOP
12 Campus President/VP East ... Dr. Paul GASPARRO
21 Vice Pres Finance & Admin ... Mr. Mike ABOUSERHAL
15 Vice President Human Resources ... Ms. Judith MCMULLEN
31 Vice Pres College Pathway Programs ... Mr. Terry BUTLER
30 Vice Pres Development Office ... Ms. Gloria MOOSMANN
27 Vice Pres/Chief Info Officer ... Mr. Gerard HOURIGAN
32 Vice Pres Student Sucess ... Vacant
09 VP Inst Planning/Effectiveness ... Dr. Jennifer SPIELVOGEL
86 Vice Pres Govt Affair/Comm Outreach ... Ms. Claire ROSACCO
18 Vice Pres Facilities Devel & Opers ... Mr. Peter MAC EWAN
84 Vice Pres Enroll Mgmt/Stdnt Affairs ... Ms. Katen MILLER
26 Vice Pres Marketing/Communications ... Mr. Alan MORAN
43 Vice President Legal Services ... Ms. Rebecca MCMAHON
20 Vice Pres Academic Affairs ... Ms. Sandy ROBINSON
103 Vice Pres CC/WEDD ... Dr. Sherry JONES
17 Vice Pres Health Care Educ ... Ms. Patricia REID
88 Associate VP Faculty Affairs & Prof ... Ms. Sandra MCKNIGHT
106 Associate VP eLearning/Innovation ... Ms. Christina ROYAL
19 Vice Pres Public Safety & Security ... Chief Clayton HARRIS
88 Exec Dir Business Continuity ... Mr. Tom SOMERVILLE
88 Exec Director Media Engineering ... Mr. Robert BRYAN
13 Exec Dir Information Technology Svc ... Mr. Edward KLEINERT
07 Executive Director Enrollment Opers ... Ms. Angela JOHNSON
21 Exec Dir Plant Operations ... Mr. Blair BOSWORTH
88 Exec Dir Veteran Services/Programs ... Mr. Richard DE CHANT
26 Exec Dir Marketing ... Ms. Christine JINDRA
88 Exec Dir Campus Svcs & Retail ... Mr. Chris MOIR
51 Executive Dirctor Cmty Cont Educ ... Ms. Sharon STYFFE
88 Exec Dir College Pathway Programs ... Mr. Kenneth HALE
96 Executive Dir Supplier Manage Svcs ... Ms. Cynthia LEITSON
36 Exec Dir Career Dev & Trng Center ... Ms. Treacy CROWLEY
20 Dean Academic Affairs East ... Dr. John W. MARR, JR.
20 Dean Academic Affairs West ... Dr. Amit SINGH
32 Dean Student Affairs West ... Ms. Diana DEL ROSARIO
32 Dean Student Affairs East ... Dr. Mel A. MAY
66 Dean Nursing Metro ... Dr. Marsha ATKINS
88 Dean Creative Arts ... Ms. Amy PARKS
88 Dean & GM Hospitality Mgmt ... Mr. Gregory FORTE
32 Dean Student Affairs West Shore ... Ms. Ann PROUDFIT
76 Assoc Dean Health & Science Metro ... Ms. Barbara MIKUSZEWSKI
76 Assoc Dean Health Careers ... Dr. Donna MOORE-RAMSEY
81 Assoc Dean Math & Applied Tech West ... Dr. Guy HUTT
83 Assoc Dean Social Sciences West ... Dr. Carol FRANKLIN
49 Assoc Dean Liberal Arts East ... Mr. Vince DIMARIA
49 Assoc Dean Liberal Arts Metro ... Dr. Jocelyn LADNER-MATHIS
49 Assoc Dean Liberal Arts West ... Mr. Mark CURTIS-CHAVEZ
50 Assoc Dean Business/Math Tech Metro ... Dr. Pamela ELLISON
72 Assoc Dean Business & Technology ... Dr. Lorraine HARTLEY
54 Assoc Dean Engineering ... Mr. Lam WONG
35 Interim Dean Student Affairs ... Ms. Denise MCCORY
23 Exec Dir Healthcare Ind Solutions ... Mrs. Kimberly BABICH-SPECK
16 Exec Dir HR Ops & Employee Svcs ... Ms. Christine BOARD
50 Assoc Dean Business & IT ... Mr. David FRAZEE
100 Chief of Staff/Spcl Asst President ... Mr. George HALLSMITH

Davis College (C)

4747 Monroe Street, Toledo OH 43623-4389

County: Lucas FICE Identification: 004855
Unit ID: 202435
Telephone: (419) 473-2700 Carnegie Class: Assoc/PrivFP
FAX Number: (419) 473-2472 Calendar System: Quarter
URL: www.daviscollege.edu
Established: 1858 Annual Undergrad Tuition & Fees: $15,738
Enrollment: 386 Coed
Affiliation or Control: Proprietary IRS Status: Proprietary
Highest Offering: Associate Degree
Program: Occupational; 2-Year Principally Bachelor's Creditable; Business Emphasis
Accreditation: NH, MAC

01 President ... Diane BRUNNER
05 Vice President Academic Affairs ... Vicky RYAN
32 Vice President of Student Services ... Mary RYAN
06 Registrar ... Marsha KLINGBEIL
37 Director Student Financial Aid ... Melissa KOSINSKI
07 Director of Admissions ... Dana STERN
36 Director of Student Placement ... Nick NIGRO
04 Assistant to the President ... Jane MULLIKIN
13 Information Services Director ... Ann SHEIDLER
29 Director Alumni Relations ... Mary RYAN
26 Chief Public Relations Officer ... Tim BRUNNER
18 Chief Facilities/Physical Plant ... Greg RIPPKE
08 Librarian ... Peggy PETERSON-SENIUK
96 Purchasing ... Marilyn BOVIA
13 Director of Information Technology ... Aaron COWELL
31 Chief Community Relations Officer ... Dan BRUNNER, JR.
40 Director Bookstore ... Belinda QUINN
108 Director Institutional Assessment ... Marsha KLINGBEIL
50 Business Admin & IT Chair ... Mary DELOE
57 Design Dept Chair ... Janet WEBER
97 General Education Dept Chair ... Kathleen FRANCE
76 Admin Prof & Allied Health Chair ... Terry DIPPMAN

Daymar College-Chillicothe (D)

1410 Industrial Drive, Chillicothe OH 45601-3977

County: Ross FICE Identification: 020568
Unit ID: 205568
Telephone: (740) 774-6300 Carnegie Class: Assoc/PrivFP
FAX Number: (740) 774-6317 Calendar System: Quarter
URL: www.daymarcollege.edu
Established: 1962 Annual Undergrad Tuition & Fees: $16,610
Enrollment: 269 Coed
Affiliation or Control: Proprietary IRS Status: Proprietary
Highest Offering: Associate Degree
Program: Occupational; Technical Emphasis
Accreditation: ACICS

01 President ... Mr. Mark GABIS
12 Campus President ... Ms. Teresa BEESON
07 Senior Director of Admissions ... Ms. Robin RE
36 Dir of Career Svc & Cmty Relations ... Mr. Scott NEFF
37 Director Student Financial Services ... Ms. Lisa REED
06 Registrar ... Ms. Emily BOGGS
32 Director of Student Services ... Mr. Bob ARCHER

Daymar College-Jackson (E)

980 East Main, Jackson OH 45640

County: Jackson Identification: 666468
Unit ID: 205531
Telephone: (740) 286-1554 Carnegie Class: Assoc/PrivFP
FAX Number: (740) 286-4476 Calendar System: Quarter
URL: www.daymarcollege.edu
Established: 1976 Annual Undergrad Tuition & Fees: $16,610
Enrollment: 196 Coed
Affiliation or Control: Proprietary IRS Status: Proprietary
Highest Offering: Associate Degree
Program: Occupational
Accreditation: ACICS

01 Campus Director ... Dr. David SHELPMAN

† Branch campus of Daymar College, Chillicothe, OH.

Daymar College-Lancaster (F)

1522 Sheridan Drive, Lancaster OH 43130-1303

County: Fairfield Identification: 666469
Unit ID: 205559
Telephone: (740) 687-6126 Carnegie Class: Assoc/PrivFP
FAX Number: (740) 687-0431 Calendar System: Quarter
URL: www.daymarcollege.edu
Established: 1984 Annual Undergrad Tuition & Fees: $16,610
Enrollment: 93 Coed
Affiliation or Control: Proprietary IRS Status: Proprietary
Highest Offering: Associate Degree
Program: Occupational; Technical Emphasis
Accreditation: ACICS

07 Director of Admissions ... Ms. Robin RE

† Branch campus of Daymar College, Chillicothe, OH.

Daymar College-New Boston (G)

3879 Rhodes Avenue, Suite A,
New Boston OH 45662-4900

County: Scioto Identification: 667082
Unit ID: 205522
Telephone: (740) 456-4124 Carnegie Class: Assoc/PrivFP
FAX Number: (740) 456-5163 Calendar System: Quarter
URL: www.daymarcollege.edu
Established: N/A Annual Undergrad Tuition & Fees: $15,600
Enrollment: 218 Coed
Affiliation or Control: Proprietary IRS Status: Proprietary
Highest Offering: Baccalaureate
Program: Technical Emphasis
Accreditation: ACICS

01 President ... Mark A. GABIS
12 Campus Director ... Rebecca MOWERY

† Branch campus of Daymar College, Chillicothe, OH.

The Defiance College (H)

701 N Clinton Street, Defiance OH 43512-1695

County: Defiance FICE Identification: 003041
Unit ID: 202514
Telephone: (419) 784-4010 Carnegie Class: Bac/Diverse
FAX Number: (419) 784-0426 Calendar System: Semester
URL: www.defiance.edu
Established: 1850 Annual Undergrad Tuition & Fees: $27,360
Enrollment: 1,084 Coed
Affiliation or Control: United Church Of Christ IRS Status: 501(c)3
Highest Offering: Master's
Program: Liberal Arts And General; Teacher Preparatory
Accreditation: NH, IACBE, NURSE, SW, TED

01 President ... Mr. Mark C. GORDON
05 Provost/VP for Academic Affairs ... Dr. Barbara SCHIRMER
30 Vice Pres Institutional Advancement ... Mrs. Wendy PESTRUE
10 Vice Pres for Finance & Management ... Mrs. Lois N. MCCULLOUGH
32 VP Stdnt Engagement/Dean of Stdnts ... Dr. Kenneth A. WETSTEIN
84 Vice Pres for Enrollment Management ... Mr. Michael SUZO
88 Dean McMaster Sch Adv Hum ... Mrs. Mary Ann STUDER
20 Associate Academic Dean ... Dr. Donald S. KNUEVE
07 Director of Admissions ... Mr. Brad HARSHA
15 Director of Human Resources ... Ms. Mary E. BURKHOLDER
29 Director Alumni and Parent Relation ... Mr. David PLANT
08 Dir of Library and Instr Resource ... Mr. Andrew WHITIS
26 Director Public Relations/Marketing ... Mrs. Kathy M. PUNCHES
14 Director of Computer Services ... Mr. Todd R. HARPEST
06 Registrar ... Mrs. Mariah ORZOLEK
36 Director of Career Development ... Mrs. Lisa MARSALEK
37 Director of Financial Aid ... Mrs. Amy FRANCIS
41 Athletic Director ... Mrs. Jenni MORRISON
42 Campus Minister/Church Relations ... Rev. Janice L. BECHTEL
28 Director Intercultural Relations ... Ms. Mercedes CLAY
58 Dir Center for Adult/Graduate Pgms ... Ms. Sally B. BISSELL
39 Director of Residence Life ... Ms. Kim LAMMERS
18 Director of Physical Plant ... Mr. James CORESSEL
21 Director of Accounting ... Mrs. Kristine BOLAND

Denison University (I)

100 W College Street, Granville OH 43023-1359

County: Licking FICE Identification: 003042
Unit ID: 202523
Telephone: (740) 587-0810 Carnegie Class: Bac/A&S
FAX Number: (740) 587-6417 Calendar System: Semester
URL: www.denison.edu
Established: 1831 Annual Undergrad Tuition & Fees: $42,280
Enrollment: 2,143 Coed
Affiliation or Control: Independent Non-Profit IRS Status: 501(c)3
Highest Offering: Baccalaureate

Program: Liberal Arts And General
Accreditation: NH

01 President .... Dr. Dale T. KNOBEL
05 Provost .... Dr. Bradley W. BATEMAN
20 Associate Provost .... Dr. Susan P. GARCIA
20 Associate Provost .... Dr. Kimberly A. COPLIN
20 Associate Provost .... Dr. Toni C. KING
10 Vice President Finance & Management .... Mr. Seth H. PATTON
30 VP Institutional Advancement .... Ms. Julia BEYER HOUPT
32 Vice President Student Affairs .... Dr. Laurel B. KENNEDY
07 Vice Pres/Director of Admissions .... Mr. Perry H. ROBINSON
89 Dean of First-Year Students .... Dr. Mark MOLLER
35 Dean of Students .... Mr. William A. FOX
06 Registrar .... Ms. Yadigar COLLINS
08 Interim Director of Libraries .... Ms. Mary Webb PROPHET
37 Dir of Financial Aid & Student Empl .... Ms. Nancy Z. HOOVER
14 Dir Information Technology Services .... Ms. Lisa BAZLEY
15 Director of Human Resources .... Mr. Jim ABLES
18 Director of Facilities Services .... Mr. Arthur J. CHONKO
19 Dir Security/Safety/Risk Mgmt .... Mr. Garret MOORE
26 Admin Dir of Univ Communications .... Mr. Jack HIRE
88 Creative Dir of Univ Communications .... Mr. Paul A. PEGHER
29 Director of Alumni Relations .... Mr. Steven R. CRAWFORD
36 Dir Career Exploration & Dev .... Ms. Kathleen I. POWELL
38 Director Health/Counseling Services .... Dr. Sonya M. TURNER-MURRAY
40 Manager of Bookstore/Business Svc .... Mr. Joseph E. WARMKE
42 Chaplain/Director of Religious Life .... Rev. Mark ORTEN
100 Special Asst to Pres/Chief of Staff .... Dr. Joyce MEREDITH
93 Dir Multicultural Stdnt Affs/Ast Dn .... Mr. Erik S. FARLEY
11 Director of Administrative Services .... Ms. Jenna MCDEVITT
09 Director of Institutional Research .... Dr. Todd M. JAMISON
41 Director of Athletics .... Ms. Nan CARNEY-DEBORD
88 Chief Investment Officer .... Ms. Adele N. GORRILLA

DeVry University - Cincinnati (A)

8800 Governors Hill Drive, Ste 100,
Cincinnati OH 45249-1367
County: Hamilton — Identification: 666563
Telephone: (513) 583-5000 — Carnegie Class: Not Classified
FAX Number: (513) 583-5035 — Calendar System: Semester
URL: www.devry.edu
Established: 1931 — Annual Undergrad Tuition & Fees: $16,156
Enrollment: 430 — Coed
Affiliation or Control: Proprietary — IRS Status: Proprietary
Highest Offering: Master's
Program: Professional; Business Emphasis
Accreditation: &NH

01 Campus Director .... Graham IRWIN

† Regional accreditation is carried under the parent institution in Downers Grove, IL.

DeVry University - Columbus Campus (B)

1350 Alum Creek Drive, Columbus OH 43209-2705
County: Franklin — FICE Identification: 003099
Unit ID: 202541
Telephone: (614) 253-7291 — Carnegie Class: Master's M
FAX Number: (614) 258-6773 — Calendar System: Semester
URL: www.devry.edu
Established: 1931 — Annual Undergrad Tuition & Fees: $16,156
Enrollment: 3,061 — Coed
Affiliation or Control: Proprietary — IRS Status: Proprietary
Highest Offering: Master's
Program: Occupational; Professional; Business Emphasis
Accreditation: &NH, ENGT

01 Metro President .... Ms. Scarlett HOWERY
32 Dean Student Central .... Ms. Kathy HOFF
08 Director of Library Services .... Mr. Bruce WEAVER
07 Director of Admissions .... Ms. Rachel DUNPHY
05 Dean of Academic Affairs .... Ms. Marilyn WIGGAM
20 Associate Dean .... Mr. Rasoul ESFAHANI
21 Director of Student Finance .... Vacant
06 Registrar .... Ms. Cynthia PRICE
15 HR Business Partner .... Ms. Amannda MONROE
36 Director of Career Services .... Ms. Amy RAAB

† Regional accreditation is carried under the parent institution in Downers Grove, IL.

DeVry University - Columbus North Center (C)

8800 Lyra Drive, Suite 120, Columbus OH 43240-2100
County: Franklin — Identification: 666217
Unit ID: 441140
Telephone: (614) 854-7500 — Carnegie Class: Not Classified
FAX Number: (614) 846-5780 — Calendar System: Semester
URL: www.devry.edu
Established: 2001 — Annual Undergrad Tuition & Fees: $16,156
Enrollment: 676 — Coed
Affiliation or Control: Proprietary — IRS Status: Proprietary
Highest Offering: Master's
Program: Occupational; Professional; Business Emphasis
Accreditation: &NH

01 Campus Dean .... Vacant

† Regional accreditation is carried under the parent institution in Downers Grove, IL.

DeVry University - Dayton (D)

3610 Pentagon Boulevard, Suite 100,
Dayton OH 45431-1708
County: Greene — Identification: 666564
Telephone: (937) 320-3200 — Carnegie Class: Not Classified
FAX Number: (937) 320-9380 — Calendar System: Semester
URL: www.devry.edu
Established: 1931 — Annual Undergrad Tuition & Fees: $16,156
Enrollment: 490 — Coed
Affiliation or Control: Proprietary — IRS Status: Proprietary
Highest Offering: Master's
Program: Professional; Business Emphasis
Accreditation: &NH

01 Center Dean .... Ken BAKER

† Regional accreditation is carried under the parent institution in Downers Grove, IL.

DeVry University - Seven Hills (E)

4141 Rockside Road, Suite 110,
Seven Hills OH 44131-2537
County: Cuyahoga — Identification: 666565
Telephone: (216) 328-8754 — Carnegie Class: Not Classified
FAX Number: (216) 328-8764 — Calendar System: Semester
URL: www.devry.edu
Established: 1931 — Annual Undergrad Tuition & Fees: $16,156
Enrollment: 630 — Coed
Affiliation or Control: Proprietary — IRS Status: Proprietary
Highest Offering: Master's
Program: Professional; Business Emphasis
Accreditation: &NH

01 Campus Director .... Joe ONORIO

† Regional accreditation is carried under the parent institution in Downers Grove, IL.

Eastern Gateway Community College - Jefferson County Campus (F)

4000 Sunset Boulevard, Steubenville OH 43952-3594
County: Jefferson — FICE Identification: 007275
Unit ID: 203331
Telephone: (740) 264-5591 — Carnegie Class: Assoc/Pub-R-M
FAX Number: (740) 264-1338 — Calendar System: Semester
URL: www.egcc.edu
Established: 1966 — Annual Undergrad Tuition & Fees (In-District): $2,880
Enrollment: 2,440 — Coed
Affiliation or Control: State/Local — IRS Status: 501(c)3
Highest Offering: Associate Degree
Program: Occupational; 2-Year Principally Bachelor's Creditable
Accreditation: NH, DA, MAC, MLTAD, RAD

01 President .... Dr. Laura M. MEEKS
05 Exec Vice Pres Academic/Stdnt Affs .... Dr. James BABER
10 Vice Pres Business Services/Treas .... Mr. James J. MCGRAIL, III
11 Vice Pres Administrative Services .... Ms. Sherri VANTASSEL
46 Vice Pres Strategic Initiatives .... Vacant
84 Dean Enrollment Management .... Ms. Patty Jo STURCH
76 Dean Health & Biological Sciences .... Dr. Robin FLOHR
50 Dean Business/Engineering & Info .... Mr. Jerry KLINESMITH
21 Controller .... Mr. C. Michael PAYNE
07 Director of Admissions .... Vacant
26 Dir Public Information/Web Coord .... Mrs. Ann M. KOON
37 Director Student Info/Financial Aid .... Ms. Kelly WILSON
103 Dir Workforce/Community Outreach .... Vacant
14 Director Technology Services .... Ms. Karen L. TUCCI
36 Director Career Services/Alumni .... Mrs. Judith MILLER
40 Director of Bookstore .... Mrs. Judith LUDE
21 Director Student Billing/Payroll .... Ms. Tonya LOGAN
18 Director Building & Grounds .... Mr. Julius J. DZIEWATKOSKI
08 Int Dean/Library Services .... Mrs. Lois T. REKOWSKI

Edison State Community College (G)

1973 Edison Drive, Piqua OH 45356-9239
County: Miami — FICE Identification: 012750
Unit ID: 202648
Telephone: (937) 778-8600 — Carnegie Class: Assoc/Pub-S-SC
FAX Number: (937) 778-1920 — Calendar System: Semester
URL: www.edisonohio.edu
Established: 1973 — Annual Undergrad Tuition & Fees (In-State): $4,019
Enrollment: 3,442 — Coed
Affiliation or Control: State — IRS Status: 501(c)3
Highest Offering: Associate Degree
Program: Occupational; 2-Year Principally Bachelor's Creditable
Accreditation: NH, ADNUR, MAC, MLTAD, PTAA

01 President .... Dr. Cristobal O. VALDEZ
04 Executive Asst to the President .... Ms. Heather LANHAM
05 Senior VP of Academic Affairs .... Ms. Sharon S. BROWN
11 VP of Administration & Finance .... Mr. Daniel R. REKE
90 VP of Information Technology .... Mr. David GANSZ
30 VP for Institutional Advancement .... Mr. Christopher NORMAN
15 VP of Strategic Human Resources .... Mrs. Linda M. PELTIER
07 Director of Admissions .... Ms. Teresa ROTH
49 Dean of Arts and Science .... Mr. Richard S. BRITTEN
50 Dean of Business/Workforce Develop .... Ms. Shirley MOORE
69 Dean of Health/Public Services .... Ms. Gwendolyn A. STEVENSON
32 Dean of Student Affairs .... Mr. Scott M. BURNAM
09 Director of Institutional Research .... Ms. Rebecca P. TELFORD
38 Dean of Student Success .... Ms. Margaret D. SYKES
72 Dean of IT and Engineering .... Ms. Patricia A. ROSS
21 Controller .... Ms. Debbie A. HIRTZINGER
32 Dir of Student Life and Athletics .... Mr. Chip J. HARE
37 Director of Financial Aid .... Ms. Kathi S. RICHARDS
26 Dir of Mktg/Community Relations .... Mr. Ryan C. HONEYMAN
07 Coord of Admissions .... Mr. Trevor STUTZ

ETI Technical College of Niles (H)

2076-86 Youngstown-Warren Road, Niles OH 44446-4398
County: Trumbull — FICE Identification: 030790
Unit ID: 200590
Telephone: (330) 652-9919 — Carnegie Class: Assoc/PrivFP
FAX Number: (330) 652-4399 — Calendar System: Semester
URL: www.eticollege.edu
Established: 1989 — Annual Undergrad Tuition & Fees: $8,620
Enrollment: 215 — Coed
Affiliation or Control: Proprietary — IRS Status: Proprietary
Highest Offering: Associate Degree
Program: Occupational; 2-Year Principally Bachelor's Creditable
Accreditation: ACCSC

01 Director .... Mrs. Renee ZUZOLO
07 Director of Admissions .... Mrs. Diane MARSTELLER
37 Director Financial Aid .... Ms. Kay MADIGAN

Fortis College (I)

555 E Alex-Bell Road, Centerville OH 45459-6120
County: Montgomery — FICE Identification: 021907
Unit ID: 205179
Telephone: (937) 433-3410 — Carnegie Class: Assoc/PrivFP
FAX Number: (937) 435-6516 — Calendar System: Semester
URL: www.fortiscollege.edu
Established: 1970 — Annual Undergrad Tuition & Fees: $11,210
Enrollment: 1,060 — Coed
Affiliation or Control: Proprietary — IRS Status: Proprietary
Highest Offering: Baccalaureate
Program: Occupational; 2-Year Principally Bachelor's Creditable
Accreditation: ACCSC, ADNUR, EMT, MAC

01 President .... Richard RUCKER
11 Director of Administration .... Terry FARRIS
05 Director Education .... Claude SMITH
07 Director Admissions .... Sean KUHN
37 Director Financial Aid .... Tom BARKER

Fortis College (J)

2545 Bailey Road, Cuyahoga Falls OH 44221-2949
County: Summit — FICE Identification: 009412
Unit ID: 204307
Telephone: (330) 923-9959 — Carnegie Class: Assoc/PrivFP
FAX Number: (330) 923-0886 — Calendar System: Other
URL: www.fortis.edu
Established: 1922 — Annual Undergrad Tuition & Fees: $18,100
Enrollment: 721 — Coed
Affiliation or Control: Proprietary — IRS Status: Proprietary
Highest Offering: Associate Degree
Program: Occupational
Accreditation: ACCSC, DA

01 Director .... Ms. Carson BURKE

Fortis College (K)

653 Enterprise Parkway, Ravenna OH 44266-8058
County: Portage — FICE Identification: 023036
Unit ID: 201399
Telephone: (330) 297-7319 — Carnegie Class: Assoc/PrivFP
FAX Number: (330) 296-2159 — Calendar System: Quarter
URL: www.fortis.edu
Established: 1922 — Annual Undergrad Tuition & Fees: $14,793
Enrollment: 442 — Coed
Affiliation or Control: Proprietary — IRS Status: Proprietary
Highest Offering: Associate Degree
Program: Occupational; Business Emphasis
Accreditation: ACICS

01 Campus Director .... Ms. Sonya HARTBURG

Fortis College (L)

4151 Executive Parkway, Suite 120,
Westerville OH 43081-3860
County: Franklin — Identification: 666602
Unit ID: 450058
Telephone: (614) 882-2551 — Carnegie Class: Assoc/PrivFP
FAX Number: (614) 882-2914 — Calendar System: Other
URL: www.fortis.edu
Established: 2010 — Annual Undergrad Tuition & Fees: $12,315
Enrollment: 826 — Coed

Affiliation or Control: Proprietary IRS Status: Proprietary
Highest Offering: Associate Degree
Program: Occupational; 2-Year Principally Bachelor's Creditable
Accreditation: **ABHES**, RAD, SURGT

01 President .... Mr. Wynn BLANTON

Franciscan University of Steubenville (A)

1235 University Boulevard, Steubenville OH 43952-1763
County: Jefferson FICE Identification: 003036
Unit ID: 205957
Telephone: (740) 283-3771 Carnegie Class: Master's M
FAX Number: (740) 283-6472 Calendar System: Semester
URL: www.franciscan.edu
Established: 1946 Annual Undergrad Tuition & Fees: $21,740
Enrollment: 2,387 Coed
Affiliation or Control: Roman Catholic IRS Status: 501(c)3
Highest Offering: Master's
Program: Liberal Arts And General; Religious Emphasis
Accreditation: **NH**, NUR, SW, TED

01 President .... Rev. Terence HENRY, TOR
00 Chancellor .... Vacant
03 Executive Vice President .... Dr. Robert G. FILBY
05 Vice President for Academic Affairs .... Dr. Daniel KEMPTON
10 Vice President for Finance .... Mr. David M. SKIVIAT
30 Vice President for Advancement .... Mr. Michael HERNON
31 Vice Pres for Community Relations .... Rev. Richard DAVIS, TOR
46 Vice Pres for Mission Effectiveness .... Vacant
15 VP of Human Resources/Legal Counsel .... Mr. Adam SCURTI
32 Vice President of Student Life .... Mr. David A. SCHMIESING
84 Vice Pres of Enrollment Management .... Mr. Joel S. RECZNIK
88 Religious Administrator .... Rev. Richard DAVIS, TOR
42 University Chaplain .... Rev. Dominic SCOTTO, TOR
20 Dir of Advising & Acad Operations .... Ms. Ann DULANY
13 Exec Dir of Information Technology .... Mr. Kevin G. SEBOLT
35 Asst Vice Pres of Student Life .... Ms. Catherine J. HECK
08 Director of Library .... Mr. William JAKUB
88 Exec Director Christian Outreach .... Vacant
44 Director of Planned Giving .... Dr. Mark E. RECZNIK
30 Director of Development .... Mr. Mark NEHRBAS
29 Director of Alumni Relations .... Mr. Timothy J. DELANEY
26 Director of Public Relations .... Miss Lisa M. FERGUSON
07 Director of Admissions .... Mrs. Margaret WEBER
07 Director of Graduate Enrollment .... Mr. Mark T. MCGUIRE
06 Registrar .... Mrs. Kathryn REEHL
37 Dir of Financial Aid/Student Accts .... Mr. John L. HERRMANN
09 Institutional Research Manager .... Mr. Mark A. ERSTE
21 Controller .... Mr. John A. STEITZ
96 Director of Business Services .... Ms. Marlene K. TERPENNING
40 Bookstore Manager .... Mr. John RECZNIK
91 Data Processing Manager .... Mr. Vince E. CARTLEDGE
16 Director of Human Resources .... Mr. Brenan PERGI
18 Director Physical Plant Services .... Mr. Joseph P. MCGURN
88 Director of Missionary Outreach .... Mr. Rhett YOUNG
88 Director of Chapel Ministries .... Mr. Robert PALLADINO
88 Director of JCW Center/Planning .... Mrs. Kathy L. MATTIOLI
104 Dir of Study Abroad/Internatl Pgms .... Miss Mary Beth COEN
38 Director of Counseling .... Mr. Joseph A. LOIZZO
41 Director of Athletics .... Mr. Christopher L. LEDYARD
36 Director Career Planning/Placement .... Mrs. Nancy S. RONEVICH
73 Director MA Theology Program .... Rev. Daniel J. PATTEE, TOR
50 Director MBA Program .... Mr. Joseph ZORIC
83 Director MA Counseling Program .... Dr. Milo C. MILBURN
53 Director MS Education Program .... Dr. Charles JOYCE
88 Director MA Philosophy Program .... Dr. Mark ROBERTS
90 Coord Academic Computer Services .... Ms. Sandy M. RADVANSKY
28 Director of Diversity .... Vacant
66 Director MS Nursing .... Dr. Carolyn MILLER

Franklin University (B)

201 S Grant Avenue, Columbus OH 43215-5399
County: Franklin FICE Identification: 003046
Unit ID: 202806
Telephone: (614) 797-4700 Carnegie Class: Spec/Bus
FAX Number: N/A Calendar System: Trimester
URL: www.franklin.edu
Established: 1902 Annual Undergrad Tuition & Fees: $12,450
Enrollment: 7,465 Coed
Affiliation or Control: Independent Non-Profit IRS Status: 501(c)3
Highest Offering: Master's
Program: Professional; Business Emphasis
Accreditation: **NH**, IACBE

01 President .... Dr. David R. DECKER
11 Sr VP Adminstration/Chief of Staff .... Ms. Jane L. ROBINSON
05 Provost/Sr VP for Academic Affairs .... Dr. Christopher L. WASHINGTON
12 Director Indianapolis Location .... Ms. Marnie GLANNER
45 Sr Vice Pres Planning/Global Pgms .... Mr. Klaus HABERICH
27 VP Marketing .... Ms. Linda M. STEELE
30 Vice Pres University Advancement .... Ms. Bonnie SMITH QUIST
16 VP fo Human Resources & Campus Svcs .... Ms. Christi CABUNGCAL
09 VP Accred/Institutional Effective .... Dr. Pamela SHAY
22 VP for Institutional Compliance .... Ms. Evelyn LEVINO
04 Executive Assistant to President .... Ms. Bonnie MCCANN
32 Dean of Students .... Mr. Billy MOLASSO
108 Asst Dean/Exec Dir of Accreditation .... Mr. Wayne C. MILLER
88 Dir CPTD Operations & Client Rels .... Dr. Terry BOYD
88 Assoc Dean Ctr Professional Trng .... Dr. Garry MCDANIEL
10 Chief Financial Officer .... Mr. Marvin BRISKEY
13 Chief Information Officer .... Mr. Rick SUNDERMAN
20 Dir of Academic Support Services .... Ms. Susanne SMITH
06 Registrar .... Mr. Frank YANCHAK
08 Director of Library Services .... Mr. John CANTER
37 Director of Financial Aid .... Ms. Goldie LANGLEY
46 Director of Strategic Relations .... Ms. Jody NOREEN
35 Dir Undergradute Student Services .... Ms. Wendi ROBINSON
35 Dir Graduate Stdnt Svcs/Operations .... Ms. Leslie GIBBS
88 Exec Dir Planning & Univ Services .... Mr. Patrick BENNETT
84 Exec Director of Enrollment Mgmt .... Mr. Scott BOOTH
12 Exec Dir Domestic Expan/Reg Cmps .... Mr. Bill CHAN
18 Director of Facilities .... Mr. Carl BROWN
26 Director of Public Relations .... Ms. Sherry MERCURIO
29 Director of Alumni Relations .... Ms. Julie BARRY
96 Director of Purchasing .... Mr. Bob DONAHUE
28 Director of Benefits .... Ms. Brenda LISTON
24 Director of Student Learning Center .... Mr. Christopher FIELDS
88 Director of Teaching Effectiveness .... Dr. Fawn WINTERWOOD
49 Dean Arts/Science & Technology .... Dr. Keith GROFF
50 Dean College of Business .... Dr. Ross WIRTH
69 Dean College of Health & Public Adm .... Dr. Robert CURTIS
88 Dean Global Programs .... Dr. Godfrey MENDES
15 Director of Human Resources .... Ms. Randi MOLDOVAN
88 Director of Accounting .... Mr. Jeffrey GERBERRY
88 Exec Dir of Financial Services .... Mr. Randolph SNYDER

Gallipolis Career College (C)

1176 Jackson Pike, Suite 312, Gallipolis OH 45631-2600
County: Gallia FICE Identification: 030079
Unit ID: 205513
Telephone: (740) 446-4367 Carnegie Class: Assoc/PrivFP
FAX Number: (740) 446-4124 Calendar System: Quarter
URL: www.gallipoliscareercollege.edu
Established: 1962 Annual Undergrad Tuition & Fees: $12,320
Enrollment: 152 Coed
Affiliation or Control: Proprietary IRS Status: Proprietary
Highest Offering: Associate Degree
Program: 2-Year Principally Bachelor's Creditable; Business Emphasis
Accreditation: **ACICS**

01 President .... Mr. Robert L. SHIREY, JR.
05 Director of Education .... Mr. Wes YOUNG
07 Director of Admissions .... Mr. Bo SHIREY, III
37 Director Student Financial Aid .... Mrs. Jeanette SHIREY

God's Bible School and College (D)

1810 Young Street, Cincinnati OH 45202-6838
County: Hamilton FICE Identification: 022205
Unit ID: 202903
Telephone: (513) 721-7944 Carnegie Class: Spec/Faith
FAX Number: (513) 763-6649 Calendar System: Semester
URL: www.gbs.edu
Established: 1900 Annual Undergrad Tuition & Fees: $6,770
Enrollment: 321 Coed
Affiliation or Control: Interdenominational IRS Status: 501(c)3
Highest Offering: Baccalaureate
Program: Religious Emphasis
Accreditation: **NH**, BI

01 President .... Dr. Michael R. AVERY
05 Vice President Academic Affairs .... Dr. Ken R. FARMER
32 Vice President Student Development .... Mr. Richard MILES
30 Director Institutional Advancement .... Mrs. Faith AVERY
06 Registrar .... Mr. Christopher LAMBETH
08 Head Librarian .... Mr. Joshua AVERY
10 Director of Finance .... Mr. David FREDERICK
37 Director of Financial Aid .... Mr. Stephen BUCKLAND
18 Campus Administrator .... Mr. Tom BUTCHER
26 Director of Public Relations .... Mr. Don DAVISON
13 Coordinator Information Services .... Mr. Steve HARMS
07 Student Recruiter .... Mr. Adam PROFITT

Good Samaritan College of Nursing and Health Science (E)

375 Dixmyth Avenue, Cincinnati OH 45220-2489
County: Hamilton FICE Identification: 006494
Unit ID: 202912
Telephone: (513) 876-2743 Carnegie Class: Assoc/PrivNFP
FAX Number: (513) 862-3572 Calendar System: Semester
URL: www.gscollege.edu
Established: 2001 Annual Undergrad Tuition & Fees: $19,992
Enrollment: 329 Coed
Affiliation or Control: Independent Non-Profit IRS Status: 501(c)3
Highest Offering: Associate Degree
Program: 2-Year Principally Bachelor's Creditable; Nursing Emphasis
Accreditation: **NH**, ADNUR

01 President .... Mr. Morris COHEN
05 Dean of Academic Affairs .... Ms. Patricia MCMAHON
32 Dean of Students/Alumni .... Ms. Mary Jo KATHMAN
09 Dir of Inst Research/Assessment .... Ms. Sherry DOWNING
84 Dean of Enrollment Management .... Ms. Linda HAYES

Heidelberg University (F)

310 E Market Street, Tiffin OH 44883-2462
County: Seneca FICE Identification: 003048
Unit ID: 203085
Telephone: (419) 448-2000 Carnegie Class: Master's S
FAX Number: (419) 448-2124 Calendar System: Semester
URL: www.heidelberg.edu
Established: 1850 Annual Undergrad Tuition & Fees: $24,000
Enrollment: 1,317 Coed
Affiliation or Control: United Church Of Christ IRS Status: 501(c)3
Highest Offering: Master's
Program: Liberal Arts And General; Teacher Preparatory
Accreditation: **NH**, CACREP, MUS, TED

01 President .... Dr. Robert HUNTINGTON
05 VP for Academic Affairs & Provost .... Dr. David WEININGER
10 VP for Admin & Business Affairs .... Mr. John WILKIN
84 VP for Enrollment Mgmt .... Ms. Lindsay SOOY
30 VP Inst Advancement & Univ Relation .... Dr. James TROHA
20 Assoc VP Acad Affs/Dean Undergr Fac .... Dr. Vicki OHL
44 Assoc VP for Institutional Advance .... Dr. Kathryn VENEMA
13 Assoc VP for Information Resources .... Mr. Kurt HUENEMANN
18 Assoc VP for Facilities & Engrng .... Mr. Rodney MORRISON
50 Dean of the School of Business .... Dr. Haseeb AHMED
06 Registrar .... Ms. Cindy SUTER
88 Director MA in Counseling Pgm .... Dr. Jo-Ann SANDERS
53 Director of School of Education .... Dr. Robert SWANSON
64 Director of School of Music .... Dr. John OWEN
92 Assoc Dean for Honors Program .... Dr. Doug COLLAR
104 Director Intl Affairs & Studies .... Ms. Julie ARNOLD
36 Asst Dean Stdnt Affs for Stdnt Succ .... Ms. Kristen LINDSAY
12 Director of Heidelberg at Arrowhead .... Mr. Allen UNDERWOOD
88 Dir Faculty Student Advising & Supp .... Dr. Ellen NAGY
08 Director of Library .... Ms. Nancy RUBENSTEIN
41 Athletic Director .... Mr. Matt PALM
21 Business Officer .... Ms. Barb GABEL
37 Director Student Financial Aid .... Mrs. Juli WEININGER
30 Director of Development .... Mr. Lee MARTIN
29 Director of Alumni Relations .... Dr. Kathryn VENEMA
32 Dean of Student Affairs .... Mr. Dustin BRENTLINGER
39 Asst Dn Stdnt Affs for Campus Life .... Mr. Mark ZENO
88 Dir Student Engagement .... Ms. Andrea WENSOWITCH
15 Director of Human Resources .... Ms. Jeannine CURNS
21 Controller .... Mr. Mike FEHLEN
04 Exec Assistant to President .... Ms. Monica VERHOFF
40 Director of University Bookstore .... Ms. Gail ROBERTS
42 Director of Campus Ministry .... Rev. Paul STARK

Hiram College (G)

Box 67, Hiram OH 44234-0067
County: Portage FICE Identification: 003049
Unit ID: 203128
Telephone: (330) 569-3211 Carnegie Class: Bac/A&S
FAX Number: (330) 569-5494 Calendar System: Semester
URL: www.hiram.edu
Established: 1850 Annual Undergrad Tuition & Fees: $39,750
Enrollment: 1,336 Coed
Affiliation or Control: Independent Non-Profit IRS Status: 501(c)3
Highest Offering: Master's
Program: Liberal Arts And General; Teacher Preparatory
Accreditation: **NH**, MUS, NURSE, TED

01 President .... Mr. Thomas V. CHEMA
05 Vice President & Dean of College .... Dr. Robert HAAK
10 Vice President Business & Finance .... Mr. Stephen W. JONES
30 Vice Pres Development & Alumni Rels .... Mr. Patrick S. ROBERTS
32 Vice President & Dean of Students .... Mr. Eric R. RIEDEL
07 Vice Pres Admission/Financial Aid .... Mr. James M. ABBUHL
20 Associate Dean of the College .... Ms. Ellen L. WALKER
107 Assc Dean Professional/Grad Studies .... Ms. Jennifer N. MCDONOUGH
06 Registrar .... Ms. Virginia L. TAYLOR
08 Head Librarian .... Mr. David D. EVERETT
29 Director Alumni Relations .... Mr. John B. COYNE
37 Director Student Financial Services .... Ms. Andrea L. CAPUTO
36 Director of Career Services .... Ms. Kathryn M. CRAIG
14 Director of Computer Center .... Mr. Frank J. VENTURA
26 Director of College Relations .... Mr. Tom B. FORD
56 Dean of Extended Learning .... Mr. Paul E. BOWERS
09 Director of Institutional Research .... Dr. Michael A. GRAJEK
41 Director of Athletics .... Mr. Thomas E. MULLIGAN
42 Chaplain .... Ms. Linda M. DAY
15 Director of Human Resources .... Ms. Lynn M. KOSTRAB
18 Director of the Physical Plant .... Mr. Sam V. MORGANO
21 Controller/Director of Accounting .... Ms. Susan A. BOYLE
35 Director of Student Involvement .... Ms. Demetria B. ANDERSON
38 Director Student Counseling .... Dr. Kevin P. FEISTHAMEL
28 Director Ethnic Diversity Affairs .... Ms. Detra E. WEST
96 Director of Purchasing .... Ms. Martha A. SCHETTLER

Hocking College (H)

3301 Hocking Parkway, Nelsonville OH 45764-9704
County: Athens FICE Identification: 007598
Unit ID: 203155
Telephone: (740) 753-3591 Carnegie Class: Assoc/Pub-R-L
FAX Number: (740) 753-7039 Calendar System: Semester
URL: www.hocking.edu
Established: 1968 Annual Undergrad Tuition & Fees (In-State): $6,285
Enrollment: 5,908 Coed
Affiliation or Control: State IRS Status: 501(c)3
Highest Offering: Associate Degree

Program: Occupational; 2-Year Principally Bachelor's Creditable; Technical Emphasis
Accreditation: NH, ACBSP, ACFEI, ADNUR, MAC, PNUR, PTAA

01 President .... Dr. Ron ERICKSON
10 Vice President & Treasurer .... Ms. Gina FETTY
05 Provost/VP Acad & Student Affairs .... Dr. Carl BRIDGES
11 Vice Pres Administrative Services .... Dr. Myriah SHORT
20 Associate Provost .... Mr. Joe WAKEMAN
04 Executive Assistant to President .... Ms. Nancy VANDEMAN
20 Dean of Reg Campuses/Industry Tech .... Mr. Neil HINTON
84 Dean of Enrollment Services .... Dr. Sally LOZADA
88 Dean School of Hospitality .... Mr. Tom LAMBRECHT
66 Dean School of Health & Nursing .... Ms. Sheena FENNELL
13 Chief Technology Officer .... Mr. Ben DALTON
19 Director Public Safety Services .... Ms. Susan WHITE
08 Director Learning Resource Center .... Ms. Carrie ATOR-JAMES
15 Director Human Resources .... Mr. John SANDERS
26 Director Public Relations .... Ms. Laura ALLOWAY
19 Director Campus Safety .... Mr. Al MATTHEWS
06 Registrar .... Ms. Roxana HERDLITZKA
18 Director Building/Grounds .... Mr. Ron MASH
29 Director Alumni Relations .... Ms. Libby VILLAVICENCIO
09 Director of Institutional Research .... Ms. Kensey LOVE
30 Director Marketing & Advancement .... Ms. Laura ALLOWAY
21 Controller/Assistant Treasurer .... Mrs. Anna JOHNSON

Hondros College (A)

4140 Executive Parkway, Westerville OH 43081-3855
County: Franklin FICE Identification: 040743
Unit ID: 203386
Telephone: (614) 508-7277 Carnegie Class: Assoc/PrivFP
FAX Number: (614) 508-7280 Calendar System: Quarter
URL: www.hondros.edu
Established: 1981 Annual Undergrad Tuition & Fees: $20,622
Enrollment: 1,140 Coed
Affiliation or Control: Proprietary IRS Status: Proprietary
Highest Offering: Associate Degree
Program: Occupational; 2-Year Principally Bachelor's Creditable; Nursing Emphasis
Accreditation: ACICS

01 President .... Ms. Linda HONDROS
66 President Nursing Programs .... Ms. Carol THOMAS
07 Director of Admission .... Mr. Josh MOORE
06 Registrar .... Ms. Sarah WILLIAMS

International College of Broadcasting (B)

6 S Smithville Road, Dayton OH 45431-1898
County: Montgomery FICE Identification: 013132
Unit ID: 203289
Telephone: (937) 258-8251 Carnegie Class: Assoc/PrivFP
FAX Number: (937) 258-8714 Calendar System: Semester
URL: www.icbcollege.com
Established: 1968 Annual Undergrad Tuition & Fees: $14,950
Enrollment: 61 Coed
Affiliation or Control: Proprietary IRS Status: Proprietary
Highest Offering: Associate Degree
Program: Occupational
Accreditation: ACCSC

01 President .... J. Michael LEMASTER
05 School Director .... Rhonda HORNE

ITT Technical Institute (C)

4717 Hilton Corporate Drive, Columbus OH 43232
County: Franklin Identification: 666706
Unit ID: 451963
Telephone: (614) 868-2000 Carnegie Class: Assoc/PrivFP4
FAX Number: (614) 868-2050 Calendar System: Quarter
URL: www.itt-tech.edu
Established: N/A Annual Undergrad Tuition & Fees: N/A
Enrollment: 367 Coed
Affiliation or Control: Proprietary IRS Status: Proprietary
Highest Offering: Baccalaureate
Program: Technical Emphasis
Accreditation: ACICS

† Branch campus of ITT Technical Institute, Indianapolis, IN.

ITT Technical Institute (D)

3325 Stop Eight Road, Dayton OH 45414-3456
County: Montgomery FICE Identification: 009088
Unit ID: 203313
Telephone: (937) 264-7700 Carnegie Class: Assoc/PrivFP
FAX Number: N/A Calendar System: Quarter
URL: www.itt-tech.edu
Established: 1935 Annual Undergrad Tuition & Fees: N/A
Enrollment: 436 Coed
Affiliation or Control: Proprietary IRS Status: Proprietary
Highest Offering: Baccalaureate
Program: Technical Emphasis
Accreditation: ACICS

† Branch campus of ITT Technical Institute, Indianapolis, IN.

ITT Technical Institute (E)

3781 Park Mill Run Drive, Hilliard OH 43026-8110
County: Franklin Identification: 666318
Unit ID: 443535
Telephone: (614) 771-4888 Carnegie Class: Assoc/PrivFP
FAX Number: (614) 921-4179 Calendar System: Quarter
URL: www.itt-tech.edu
Established: 2003 Annual Undergrad Tuition & Fees: N/A
Enrollment: 507 Coed
Affiliation or Control: Proprietary IRS Status: Proprietary
Highest Offering: Baccalaureate
Program: Technical Emphasis
Accreditation: ACICS

† Branch campus of ITT Technical Institute, Indianapolis, IN.

ITT Technical Institute (F)

1656 Henthorne Boulevard, Suite B,
Maumee OH 43537-3920
County: Lucas Identification: 666160
Unit ID: 448497
Telephone: (419) 861-6500 Carnegie Class: Assoc/PrivFP
FAX Number: N/A Calendar System: Quarter
URL: www.itt-tech.edu
Established: 2006 Annual Undergrad Tuition & Fees: N/A
Enrollment: 467 Coed
Affiliation or Control: Proprietary IRS Status: Proprietary
Highest Offering: Baccalaureate
Program: Technical Emphasis
Accreditation: ACICS

† Branch campus of ITT Technical Institute, Indianapolis, IN.

ITT Technical Institute (G)

4750 Wesley Avenue, Norwood OH 45212-2244
County: Hamilton Identification: 666546
Unit ID: 430379
Telephone: (513) 531-8300 Carnegie Class: Assoc/PrivFP
FAX Number: (513) 531-8368 Calendar System: Quarter
URL: www.itt-tech.edu
Established: 1995 Annual Undergrad Tuition & Fees: N/A
Enrollment: 558 Coed
Affiliation or Control: Proprietary IRS Status: Proprietary
Highest Offering: Baccalaureate
Program: Technical Emphasis
Accreditation: ACICS

† Branch campus of ITT Technical Institute, Indianapolis, IN.

ITT Technical Institute (H)

14955 Sprague Road, Strongsville OH 44136-1758
County: Cuyahoga Identification: 666547
Unit ID: 430388
Telephone: (440) 234-9091 Carnegie Class: Assoc/PrivFP
FAX Number: (440) 234-7568 Calendar System: Quarter
URL: www.itt-tech.edu
Established: 1994 Annual Undergrad Tuition & Fees: N/A
Enrollment: 450 Coed
Affiliation or Control: Proprietary IRS Status: Proprietary
Highest Offering: Baccalaureate
Program: Technical Emphasis
Accreditation: ACICS

† Branch campus of ITT Technical Institute, Indianapolis, IN.

ITT Technical Institute (I)

4700 Richmond Road,
Warrensville Heights OH 44128-5984
County: Cuyahoga Identification: 666379
Unit ID: 446923
Telephone: (216) 896-6500 Carnegie Class: Assoc/PrivFP
FAX Number: N/A Calendar System: Quarter
URL: www.itt-tech.edu
Established: N/A Annual Undergrad Tuition & Fees: N/A
Enrollment: 474 Coed
Affiliation or Control: Proprietary IRS Status: Proprietary
Highest Offering: Baccalaureate
Program: Technical Emphasis
Accreditation: ACICS

† Branch campus of ITT Technical Institute, Indianapolis, IN.

ITT Technical Institute (J)

1030 N Meridian Road, Youngstown OH 44509-4098
County: Mahoning FICE Identification: 009837
Unit ID: 206631
Telephone: (330) 270-1600 Carnegie Class: Assoc/PrivFP
FAX Number: (330) 270-8333 Calendar System: Quarter
URL: www.itt-tech.edu
Established: 1967 Annual Undergrad Tuition & Fees: N/A
Enrollment: 615 Coed
Affiliation or Control: Proprietary IRS Status: Proprietary
Highest Offering: Baccalaureate
Program: Technical Emphasis
Accreditation: ACICS

† Branch campus of ITT Technical Institute, Indianapolis, IN.

James A. Rhodes State College (K)

4240 Campus Drive, Lima OH 45804-3597
County: Allen FICE Identification: 010027
Unit ID: 203678
Telephone: (419) 995-8200 Carnegie Class: Assoc/Pub-R-M
FAX Number: (419) 221-0450 Calendar System: Quarter
URL: www.rhodesstate.edu
Established: 1971 Annual Undergrad Tuition & Fees (In-State): $4,613
Enrollment: 4,050 Coed
Affiliation or Control: State IRS Status: 501(c)3
Highest Offering: Associate Degree
Program: Occupational; 2-Year Principally Bachelor's Creditable
Accreditation: NH, ACBSP, ADNUR, DH, ENGT, MAC, OTA, PTAA, RAD

01 President .... Dr. Debra L. MCCURDY
10 Vice President Business & Treasurer .... Mr. Chris R. SCHMIDT
32 Associate Dean for Student Services .... Ms. Judi MAZZARELLLI
30 Executitve Director of Development .... Mr. Henry "Tre" M. WALDREN
05 Assoc VP Academic Affairs .... Mr. Richard WOODFIELD
07 Director of Admissions .... Ms. Traci R. COX
37 Director Student Financial Aid .... Ms. Cathy L. KOHLI
09 Director Institutional Research .... Mr. Steve S. MILLER
36 Director of Career Services .... Ms. Krista RICHARDSON
08 Head Librarian .... Ms. Tina SCHNEIDER
103 Exec Dir for Workforce & Econ Dev .... Dr. Matthew J. KINKLEY
15 Director Human Resources .... Mr. Jonathon HORN
50 Dean Div Business & Public Services .... Ms. Brenda RIZOR
54 Dean Div Info Tech/Engr Tech .... Ms. Antoinette BALDIN
49 Dean Division of Arts & Sciences .... Mr. William C. WELLS
66 Dean Division of Nursing .... Ms. Carol SCHMIDT
76 Interim Dean Div of AH/Sciences .... Ms. Tish HATFIELD
45 Vice President Inst Effect/Planning .... Ms. Becky BURRELL
18 Chief Facilities/Physical Plant .... Mr. Chris R. SCHMIDT
21 Assoc Business Officer/Controller .... Mr. Mark RUSSELL
26 Coordinator Public Relations .... Ms. Paula J. SIEBENECK
06 Registrar .... Dr. Rose REINHART

John Carroll University (L)

1 John Carroll Boulevard, Cleveland OH 44118-4581
County: Cuyahoga FICE Identification: 003050
Unit ID: 203368
Telephone: (216) 397-1886 Carnegie Class: Master's L
FAX Number: (216) 397-4256 Calendar System: Semester
URL: www.jcu.edu
Established: 1886 Annual Undergrad Tuition & Fees: $33,180
Enrollment: 3,709 Coed
Affiliation or Control: Roman Catholic IRS Status: 501(c)3
Highest Offering: Master's
Program: Liberal Arts And General; Teacher Preparatory; Professional
Accreditation: NH, BUS, BUSA, CACREP, TED

01 President .... Rev. Robert L. NIEHOFF, SJ
43 General Counsel .... Ms. Maria ALFARO-LOPEZ
04 VP and Exec Asst to the President .... Dr. Jonathan E. SMITH
88 VP for Univ Mission & Identity .... Dr. Paul V. MURPHY
101 Asst to Pres/Sec to Board of Dir .... Ms. Laurie A. FRANTZ
05 Provost & Academic Vice President .... Dr. John T. DAY
32 Vice President for Student Affairs .... Dr. Mark D. MCCARTHY
84 Vice President for Enrollment .... Mr. Brian G. WILLIAMS
10 Vice President for Finance .... Mr. Richard F. MAUSSER
30 Vice President for Univ Advancement .... Ms. Doreen K. RILEY
20 Assoc Academic Vice President .... Dr. James H. KRUKONES
20 Assc Acad VP Acad Pgm/Fac Diversity .... Dr. Lauren L. BOWEN
45 Chief Planning Officer .... Vacant
108 Asst Provost for Inst Effectiveness .... Dr. Kathleen L. DEAN
21 Exec Dir Administrative Finance .... Mr. David W. WONG
49 Dean College of Arts & Sciences .... Dr. Jeanne COLLERAN
50 Dean Boler School of Business .... Dr. Karen SCHUELE
35 Dean of Students .... Dr. Sherri A. CRAHEN
13 Chief Information Officer .... Mr. Michael BESTUL
26 Asst VP Intg Mktg & Communications .... Mr. John CARFAGNA
18 Assoc Vice Pres for Facilities .... Ms. Carol P. DIETZ
16 Director of Human Resources .... Mr. Charles STUPPY
08 Director of the Library .... Ms. Michelle MILLET
36 Director Center for Career Services .... Ms. Hilary FLANAGAN
28 Director Multicultural Affairs .... Ms. Danielle J. CARTER
104 Dir Center for Global Education .... Dr. Andreas SOBISCH
06 Registrar .... Mrs. Kathleen J. DIFRANCO
88 Bursar & Dir of Student Accounts .... Ms. Diane WARD
39 Director of Residence Life .... Ms. Lisa M. BROWN
92 Director Honors Program .... Dr. Julia KAROLLE-BERG
07 Executive Director of Enrollment .... Mr. Steven P. VITATOE
37 Director of Financial Aid .... Ms. Claudia WENZEL
31 Dir Ctr for Service & Social Action .... Dr. Margaret FINUCANE
42 Director of Campus Ministry .... Mr. John SCARANO
38 Director Univ Counseling Center .... Dr. Mary E. JAVOREK
24 Dir Instructional Tech Services .... Dr. Jay TARBY
23 Director Student Health Center .... Ms. Janet M. KREVH
41 Sr Director Athletics & Recreation .... Ms. Laurie MASSA
29 Director Alumni Relations .... Mr. David A. VITATOE
44 Director Planned Giving .... Mr. Peter R. BERNARDO
102 Dir Corp Relations and Major Gifts .... Ms. Christina BEG
25 Director Fdn Rels & Grant Writing .... Ms. Pamela GEORGE
86 Dir Government & Community Rels .... Ms. Dora PRUCE
96 Director Purchasing & Aux Services .... Mr. Andrew F. FRONCZEK
19 Director Campus Safety Services .... Mr. Timothy PEPPARD
105 Dir Marketing Services (Web) .... Mr. Michael RICHWALSKY

Kaplan Career Institute (A)

8720 Brookpark Road, Brooklyn OH 44129

County: Cuyahoga FICE Identification: 025829
Unit ID: 206093
Telephone: (216) 485-0900 Carnegie Class: Assoc/PrivFP
FAX Number: (216) 661-6842 Calendar System: Other
URL: cleveland.kaplancareerinstitute.com
Established: 1980 Annual Undergrad Tuition & Fees: $15,522
Enrollment: 317 Coed
Affiliation or Control: Proprietary IRS Status: Proprietary
Highest Offering: Associate Degree
Program: Occupational; 2-Year Principally Bachelor's Creditable; Technical Emphasis
Accreditation: ACCSC

01 Campus Director .... James ROYSTER

Kaplan College (B)

2745 Winchester Pike, Columbus OH 43232-4827

County: Franklin FICE Identification: 011005
Unit ID: 202189
Telephone: (614) 456-4600 Carnegie Class: Assoc/PrivFP
FAX Number: (614) 456-4640 Calendar System: Semester
URL: www.teccollege.com
Established: 1989 Annual Undergrad Tuition & Fees: $14,799
Enrollment: 335 Coed
Affiliation or Control: Proprietary IRS Status: Proprietary
Highest Offering: Associate Degree
Program: Occupational
Accreditation: ACCSC

01 Director .... Mr. Michael SEAMAN
07 Director of Admissions .... Ms. Angela TURNER
05 Director of Education .... Ms. Diana RANKIN
37 Director of Financial Aid .... Ms. Ashley SOUTH

Kaplan College (C)

2800 East River Road, Dayton OH 45439

County: Montgomery FICE Identification: 020520
Unit ID: 204626
Telephone: (937) 294-6155 Carnegie Class: Assoc/PrivFP
FAX Number: (937) 294-2259 Calendar System: Quarter
URL: dayton.kaplancollege.com
Established: 1971 Annual Undergrad Tuition & Fees: $14,665
Enrollment: 523 Coed
Affiliation or Control: Proprietary IRS Status: Proprietary
Highest Offering: Associate Degree
Program: Occupational; Technical Emphasis
Accreditation: ACCSC, MAC

01 President .... Ms. Karen LARSEN-REUTER
05 Director of Education .... Ms. Carol JACOBS

Kent State University Main Campus (D)

PO Box 5190, Kent OH 44242-0001

County: Portage FICE Identification: 003051
Unit ID: 203517
Telephone: (330) 672-2121 Carnegie Class: RU/H
FAX Number: (330) 672-2190 Calendar System: Semester
URL: www.kent.edu
Established: 1910 Annual Undergrad Tuition & Fees (In-State): $9,672
Enrollment: 27,855 Coed
Affiliation or Control: State IRS Status: 501(c)3
Highest Offering: Doctorate
Program: Liberal Arts And General; Teacher Preparatory; Professional
Accreditation: NH, AAB, ART, AUD, BUS, BUSA, CACREP, CIDA, CLPSY, CORE, DANCE, DIETD, DIETI, EXSC, JOUR, LIB, MUS, NAIT, NRPA, NURSE, POD, SCPSY, SP, SPAA, TED, THEA

01 President .... Dr. Lester A. LEFTON
05 Provost/Sr VP Academic Affairs .... Dr. Todd DIACON
10 Vice Pres Finance & Administration .... Mr. Gregg S. FLOYD
16 Vice Pres Human Resources .... Mr. Willis WALKER
30 Vice Pres Institutional Advancement .... Mr. Eugene J. FINN
26 Vice Pres Univ Relations .... Ms. Iris E. HARVEY
32 VP Student Affairs/Enrollment Mgmt .... Mr. Greg I. JARVIE
46 Vice President Research .... Dr. W. Grant MCGIMPSEY
27 Vice Pres Information Services/CIO .... Mr. Edward G. MAHON
22 VP Diversity/Equity Inclusion .... Dr. Alfreda BROWN
20 Dean Undergraduate Studies .... Dr. Said SEWELL
35 Student Ombuds .... Dr. Jennifer KULICS
45 Sr Assoc Provost .... Dr. Timothy J. CHANDLER
20 Assoc Provost Faculty Affairs .... Ms. Sue AVERILL
44 Assoc VP Univ Rels/Inst Advance .... Mr. Stephen G. SOKANY
84 Assoc Vice Pres Enrollment Managemt .... Mr. David GARCIA
29 Exec Director of Alumni Affairs .... Mrs. Lori RANDORF
07 Director of Admissions .... Ms. Nancy J. DELLAVECCHIA
06 Registrar .... Mr. Glenn DAVIS
43 University Counsel .... Mr. Willis WALKER
100 Sec Bd Trustees/Chief of Staff .... Ms. Charlene K. REED
41 Director Intercollegiate Athletics .... Mr. Joel NIELSON
22 Dir Equal Opportunity/Affirm Action .... Mr. James MCELROY
37 Director Student Financial Aid .... Mr. Mark EVANS
19 Director of Public Safety .... Mr. John PEACH
12 Dean Trumball Campus .... Dr. Wanda THOMAS
09 Director of Institutional Research .... Dr. Sally A. KANDEL
96 Director of Procurement .... Mr. Timothy J. KONCZAL
49 Dean College of Arts & Sciences .... Dr. Timothy J. CHANDLER
50 Int Dean Business Administration .... Dr. Kathryn WILSON
53 Dean of Education .... Dr. Daniel F. MAHONY
57 Dean of the Arts .... Dr. John CRAWFORD
66 Dean College of Nursing .... Dr. Laura DZUREC
51 Exec Director Continuing Studies .... Ms. Deborah C. HUNTSMAN
92 Interim Dean Honors College .... Dr. Donald F. PALMER
08 Dean Library & Media Services .... Dr. James BRACKEN
48 Dean Architect/Environ Design .... Mr. Douglas STEIDL
27 Dean Communication & Information .... Dr. Stanley T. WEARDEN
72 Dean Col of Applied Engr/Tech/Sust .... Dr. Shin-Min (Simon) SONG
58 Dean of Graduate Studies .... Dr. Mary Ann STEPHENS

Kent State University at Ashtabula (E)

3300 Lake Road W, Ashtabula OH 44004-2299

County: Ashtabula FICE Identification: 003052
Unit ID: 203447
Telephone: (440) 964-3322 Carnegie Class: Assoc/Pub4
FAX Number: (440) 964-4269 Calendar System: Semester
URL: www.ashtabula.kent.edu
Established: 1958 Annual Undergrad Tuition & Fees (In-State): $5,472
Enrollment: 2,457 Coed
Affiliation or Control: State IRS Status: 501(c)3
Highest Offering: Baccalaureate
Program: Occupational; 2-Year Principally Bachelor's Creditable
Accreditation: &NH, ADNUR, OTA, PTAA, RAD

01 Dean .... Dr. Susan J. STOCKER
05 Assistant Dean .... Mr. Kevin L. DEEMER
08 Library Director .... Ms. Amy A. THOMAS
20 Senior Academic Program Director .... Ms. Carol K. DRENNEN
10 Director Admin/Business Affairs .... Mr. W. David SCHULTZ
21 Business Manager .... Ms. Amy S. THOMPSON
84 Dir Enrol Mgt/Registrar/Stdnt Svcs .... Dr. Gerald KIEL
13 Network Systems Manager .... Mr. Kevin K. ACIERNO
88 Director PT Asst/Tech Program .... Ms. Kathrine GIFFIN
30 Senior Development Associate .... Ms. Pamela J. PALERMO
88 Director of Radiologic Technology .... Ms. Gail M. SCHROEDER
18 Chief Facilities/Physical Plant .... Mr. W. David SCHULTZ
37 Coordinator Student Financial Aid .... Ms. Robyn M. GIFFORD
88 Dir of Respiratory Therapy Tech .... Mr. David A. GOSWICK
88 Director of Occupational Therapy .... Ms. Julie L. MIRABELL

† Regional accreditation is carried under the parent institution in Kent, OH.

Kent State University East Liverpool Campus (F)

400 E Fourth Street, East Liverpool OH 43920-3497

County: Columbiana FICE Identification: 003056
Unit ID: 203456
Telephone: (330) 385-3805 Carnegie Class: Assoc/Pub2in4
FAX Number: (330) 382-7562 Calendar System: Semester
URL: www.eliv.kent.edu
Established: 1965 Annual Undergrad Tuition & Fees (In-State): $5,150
Enrollment: 1,200 Coed
Affiliation or Control: State IRS Status: 501(c)3
Highest Offering: Associate Degree
Program: Occupational; 2-Year Principally Bachelor's Creditable
Accreditation: &NH, ADNUR, OTA, PTAA

01 Dean .... Dr. Stephen NAMETH
05 Interim Assistant Dean .... Dr. Susan ROSSI
08 Library Director .... Ms. Susan M. WEAVER
88 Director Physical Therapy .... Vacant
66 Director of Nursing .... Dr. Frances Anne FREITAS
88 Director Occupational Therapy .... Ms. Harriett BYNUM
84 Director Enrollment Management .... Ms. Michelle LINGENFELTER
88 Director Justice Studies .... Ms. Lynnette RAWLINGS
13 Network Systems Manager .... Mr. Wallace AIKEN
10 Business Manager .... Mr. Henry TRENKELBACH
07 Admissions Coordinator .... Ms. Lisa FRANK
36 Coordinator Career Planning .... Ms. Deborah WOODS
88 Clin Coord Phys Therapy Asst Pgm .... Vacant
26 Marketing Assistant .... Ms. Bethany GADD ZIRILLO

† Regional accreditation is carried under the parent institution in Kent, OH.

Kent State University Geauga Campus (G)

14111 Claridon-Troy Road,
Burton Township OH 44021-9500

County: Geauga FICE Identification: 003059
Unit ID: 203526
Telephone: (440) 834-4187 Carnegie Class: Assoc/Pub4
FAX Number: (440) 834-8846 Calendar System: Semester
URL: www.geauga.kent.edu
Established: 1964 Annual Undergrad Tuition & Fees (In-State): $5,784
Enrollment: 2,800 Coed
Affiliation or Control: State IRS Status: 501(c)3
Highest Offering: Master's
Program: Occupational; 2-Year Principally Bachelor's Creditable; Liberal Arts And General
Accreditation: &NH

01 Dean .... Dr. David MOHAN
05 Associate Dean .... Dr. Mathew MCINTOSH
10 Chief Business Officer .... Mr. John GRANNY
84 Dir Enrollment Mgmt/Student Svcs .... Mr. Thomas HOILES
20 Dir of Academic Support Svcs .... Mr. Bennett MORRISON
37 Director Student Financial Aid .... Ms. Donna HOLCOMB
30 Director of Development .... Mr. David DAY
32 Director Student Services .... Mr. Thomas HOILES
07 Admissions/Records .... Ms. Reina TAYLOR

† Regional accreditation is carried under the parent institution in Kent, OH.

Kent State University Salem Campus (H)

2491 State Road 45 South, Salem OH 44460-9412

County: Columbiana FICE Identification: 003061
Unit ID: 203492
Telephone: (330) 332-0361 Carnegie Class: Bac/Assoc
FAX Number: (330) 337-4122 Calendar System: Semester
URL: www.salem.kent.edu
Established: 1962 Annual Undergrad Tuition & Fees (In-State): $5,472
Enrollment: 2,023 Coed
Affiliation or Control: State IRS Status: 501(c)3
Highest Offering: Baccalaureate
Program: Occupational; 2-Year Principally Bachelor's Creditable; Liberal Arts And General
Accreditation: &NH, NMT, RAD, RTT

01 Dean .... Dr. Stephen NAMETH
05 Assistant Dean .... Vacant
08 Director Library .... Ms. Lilith R. KUNKEL
84 Director Enrollment Management .... Ms. Shelly LINGENFELTER
30 Development Officer .... Mr. Matthew T. BUTTS
10 Business Administrator .... Mr. Henry TRENKELBACH
07 EMSS Advisor .... Ms. Sarah MOTTS
07 EMSS Advisor .... Ms. Kristin TOOTHMAN

† Regional accreditation is carried under the parent institution in Kent, OH.

Kent State University at Stark (I)

6000 Frank Avenue, NW, Canton OH 44720-9988

County: Stark FICE Identification: 003054
Unit ID: 203465
Telephone: (330) 499-9600 Carnegie Class: Assoc/Pub4
FAX Number: (330) 494-6121 Calendar System: Semester
URL: www.stark.kent.edu
Established: 1946 Annual Undergrad Tuition & Fees (In-State): $5,472
Enrollment: 4,919 Coed
Affiliation or Control: State IRS Status: 501(c)3
Highest Offering: Baccalaureate
Program: Liberal Arts And General; Teacher Preparatory; Professional
Accreditation: &NH

01 Dean & Chief Administrative Officer .... Dr. Walter WAGOR
05 Associate Dean .... Dr. Ruth CAPASSO
10 Dir Business Affairs & Operations .... Vacant
84 Assistant Dean for Enrollment .... Ms. Mary S. SOUTHARDS
26 Dir External Affairs & Cmty Rels .... Ms. Tina BIASELLA
30 Development Officer .... Ms. Linda FERGASON
88 Outreach Program Director .... Vacant
32 Director Student Services .... Ms. Diane WALKER
08 Library Director .... Mr. Rob KAIRIS
88 General Manager Conference Center .... Mr. Joseph FOLK
07 Director of Admissions .... Ms. Deb SPECK
37 Director Student Financial Aid .... Ms. Gail PUKYS
36 Director Student Placement .... Mr. Chris PAVELOI
15 Human Resource Generalist .... Ms. Michelle REID
38 Counseling Specialist .... Ms. Emily RIBNIK
13 Network Services Manager .... Ms. JoEllen KLCO
18 Senior Facilities Manager .... Mr. Brent WOOD
24 Manager Media Services .... Ms. Sue MARKOVICH
21 Business Manager .... Mr. Joseph POLACK
19 Security Supervisor .... Mr. Mark ELLIOTT
88 Special Events Coordinator .... Ms. Jenny HUTH
26 Marketing Coordinator .... Ms. Rachel FIGUEROA
20 Coordinator Academic Services .... Ms. Lisa HART

† Regional accreditation is carried under the parent institution in Kent, OH.

Kent State University Trumbull Campus (J)

4314 Mahoning Avenue, NW, Warren OH 44483-1998

County: Trumbull FICE Identification: 003064
Unit ID: 203474
Telephone: (330) 847-0571 Carnegie Class: Assoc/Pub4
FAX Number: (330) 675-8888 Calendar System: Semester
URL: www.trumbull.kent.edu
Established: 1954 Annual Undergrad Tuition & Fees (In-State): $5,472
Enrollment: 3,207 Coed
Affiliation or Control: State IRS Status: 501(c)3
Highest Offering: Associate Degree
Program: Occupational; 2-Year Principally Bachelor's Creditable
Accreditation: &NH

01 Dean .... Mr. Robert G. SINES
05 Assistant Dean .... Dr. Daniel E. PALMER
11 Director Admin/Business Services .... Ms. Elaine PETROSKY
06 Registrar .... Dr. James RITTER
08 Librarian .... Ms. Rose A. GUERRIERI
84 Assist Dir Enrollment Management .... Ms. Sarah HELMICK

† Regional accreditation is carried under the parent institution in Kent, OH.

Kent State University Tuscarawas Campus (A)

330 University Drive, NE,
New Philadelphia OH 44663-9403
County: Tuscarawas FICE Identification: 003062
Unit ID: 203483
Telephone: (330) 339-3391 Carnegie Class: Assoc/Pub2in4
FAX Number: (330) 339-3321 Calendar System: Semester
URL: www.tusc.kent.edu
Established: 1962 Annual Undergrad Tuition & Fees (In-State): $5,472
Enrollment: 2,696 Coed
Affiliation or Control: State IRS Status: 501(c)3
Highest Offering: Baccalaureate
Program: Occupational; 2-Year Principally Bachelor's Creditable
Accreditation: &NH, ADNUR, ENGT

01 Dean ... Dr. Gregg L. ANDREWS
05 Assistant Dean ... Dr. Fran HALDAR
84 Director Enroll Mgmt & Student Svcs ... Ms. Laurie DONLEY
51 Director Continuing Studies ... Ms. Patricia COMANITZ
10 Director Business & Admin Services ... Mr. Walt GRITZAN
66 Director Nursing ... Ms. Joan LAPPIN
08 Librarian ... Ms. Tollie BANKER
13 Network Systems Manager ... Mr. Shannon BAILEY
21 Business Manager ... Ms. Waliah POTO
26 Coordinator Public Relations ... Ms. Pam PATACCA
88 Coord Small Business Devel Ctr ... Mr. Stephen SCHILLIG
36 Coordinator Career Planning ... Mr. Rob BRINDLEY
37 Financial Aid Coordinator ... Ms. Dawn PLUG
88 Outreach Program Coordinator ... Mr. Joseph BELINSKY
88 Outreach Program Coordinator ... Mr. Timothy LONG
88 Outreach Program Coordinator ... Mr. Terry THEIS
74 Acad Pgm Dir for Veterinary Tech ... Dr. Ronald SOUTHERLAND
54 Acad Pgm Dir for Engineering Tech ... Dr. Kamal BICHARA
14 IT User Support Analyst ... Mr. Jeremy BAILEY
30 Director of Advancement ... Mr. Monte BALL
88 General Manager ... Mr. Michael MORELLI

† Regional accreditation is carried under the parent institution in Kent, OH.

Kent State University College of Podiatric Medicine (B)

6000 Rockside Woods Boulevard,
Independence OH 44131-2330
County: Cuyahoga FICE Identification: 003088
Unit ID: 204547
Telephone: (216) 231-3300 Carnegie Class: Spec/Health
FAX Number: (216) 231-0453 Calendar System: Semester
URL: www.kent.edu/cpm
Established: 1916 Annual Graduate Tuition & Fees: $35,952
Enrollment: 425 Coed
Affiliation or Control: Independent Non-Profit IRS Status: 501(c)3
Highest Offering: First Professional Degree; No Undergraduates
Program: Professional
Accreditation: &NH, POD

01 CEO-CPM ... Dr. Thomas V. MELILLO, SR.
03 Exec Vice President-CPM ... Dr. David R. NICOLANTI
05 Sr Assoc Dean-CPM ... Dr. Vincent J. HETHERINGTON
10 Assoc Vice Pres of Finance-CPM ... Mr. Jon C. CARLSON
32 Asst Dean Student Affairs ... Mrs. Lois LOTT
08 Librarian ... Mrs. Donna M. PERZESKI
15 Human Resources Director-CPM ... Mr. David DIXON
06 Director of Student Academic Svcs ... Mr. David PUTMAN
46 Division Head Research ... Ms. Jill S. CARROLL
30 Sr Advancement Officer ... Mr. Mark SYRONEY
18 Director of Operations ... Mr. Dan RIDGWAY
84 Director of Enrollment Management ... Ms. Carla RONNENBAUM
13 Sr Project Manager-CPM ... Mr. Garrett GASTON
36 Residency Coordinator ... Ms. Heather BLAHA

† Regional accreditation is carried under the parent institution in Kent, OH

Kenyon College (C)

Gambier OH 43022-9623
County: Knox FICE Identification: 003065
Unit ID: 203535
Telephone: (740) 427-5000 Carnegie Class: Bac/A&S
FAX Number: (740) 427-3077 Calendar System: Semester
URL: www.kenyon.edu
Established: 1824 Annual Undergrad Tuition & Fees: $44,420
Enrollment: 1,658 Coed
Affiliation or Control: Independent Non-Profit IRS Status: 501(c)3
Highest Offering: Baccalaureate
Program: Liberal Arts And General
Accreditation: NH

01 President ... Dr. S. Georgia NUGENT
05 Provost ... Dr. Nayef SAMHAT
26 Vice President College Relations ... Ms. Sarah H. KAHRL
10 Vice President for Finance ... Mr. Joseph G. NELSON
13 Vice Pres Library & Info Svcs ... Mr. Ronald K. GRIGGS
100 Advisor to President ... Mr. Jesse E. MATZ
21 Assoc Vice President for Finance ... Ms. Teri L. BLANCHARD
32 Dean of Students ... Dr. Henry P. TOUTAIN
07 Dean of Admissions/Fin Aid ... Ms. Jennifer DELAHUNTY
20 Associate Provost ... Dr. Ric S. SHEFFIELD
08 Director of Information Resources ... Mr. Joseph M. MURPHY
06 Registrar/Dean Academic Support ... Ms. Ellen K. HARBOUT
44 Director Planned Giving ... Mr. Kyle W. HENDERSON
26 Director of Public Affairs ... Mr. Shawn PRESLEY
14 Director Systems Design/Consulting ... Mr. Ronald K. GRIGGS
29 Dir Alumni/Parent Rels ... Mr. Scott R. BAKER
37 Director of Financial Aid ... Mr. Craig A. DAUGHERTY
38 Director of Counseling Services ... Dr. Patrick K. GILLIGAN
15 Director of Human Resources ... Ms. Jennifer G. CABRAL
42 Director Board College Ministries ... Rev. Karl P B. STEVENS
21 Chief Business Officer ... Mr. Mark KOLMAN
22 Equal Opportunity Officer ... Ms. Mariam N. EL-SHAMAA
19 Director of Campus Safety ... Mr. Robert D. HOOPER
09 Director of Institutional Research ... Ms. Erika M. FARFAN
21 Manager of Business Services ... Mr. Frederick S. LINGER
28 Director of Multicultural Affairs ... Mr. A. Chris KENNERLY

Kettering College of Medical Arts (D)

3737 Southern Boulevard, Kettering OH 45429-1299
County: Montgomery FICE Identification: 007035
Unit ID: 203544
Telephone: (937) 395-8601 Carnegie Class: Spec/Health
FAX Number: (937) 395-8106 Calendar System: Semester
URL: www.kcma.edu
Established: 1967 Annual Undergrad Tuition & Fees: $11,460
Enrollment: 938 Coed
Affiliation or Control: Seventh-day Adventist IRS Status: 501(c)3
Highest Offering: Master's
Program: Occupational; 2-Year Principally Bachelor's Creditable; Professional; Nursing Emphasis
Accreditation: NH, ADNUR, ARCPA, DMS, NUR, RAD

00 Chairman of the Board ... Mr. Fred M. MANCHUR
01 President ... Dr. Charles W. SCRIVEN
15 Vice President Human Resources ... Mrs. Beverly MORRIS
05 Dean for Academic Affairs ... Dr. William G. NELSON
102 President Foundation ... Dr. Martin CLARK
84 Dean for Enrollment Services ... Mr. Victor BROWN
10 Chief Business Officer ... Mr. Jack BURDICK
06 Director Academic Info & Records ... Mr. Jim NESBIT
88 Dean Assessment & Learning Support ... Dr. Beverly COBB
37 Director Student Financial Aid ... Mrs. Kim SNELL
40 Manager Bookstore ... Mrs. Stella FREEMAN
42 Chaplain Director Campus Ministry ... Mr. Clive WILSON
32 Director Student Life/Residence ... Ms. Amy MORETTA
26 Public Relations Officer ... Ms. Mindy CLAGGETT
08 Director of Library ... Mrs. Bev ERVIN
29 Director Alumni Relations ... Vacant
07 Director of Enrollment Services ... Mrs. Becky MCDONALD
27 Senior Information Officer ... Mr. Jim NESBIT

Lake Erie College (E)

391 W Washington Street, Painesville OH 44077-3389
County: Lake FICE Identification: 003066
Unit ID: 203580
Telephone: (440) 375-7000 Carnegie Class: Master's S
FAX Number: (440) 375-7005 Calendar System: Semester
URL: www.lec.edu
Established: 1856 Annual Undergrad Tuition & Fees: $27,368
Enrollment: 1,147 Coed
Affiliation or Control: Independent Non-Profit IRS Status: 501(c)3
Highest Offering: Master's
Program: Liberal Arts And General; Teacher Preparatory; Professional; Business Emphasis
Accreditation: NH, IACBE, @TEAC

01 President ... Michael T. VICTOR
05 Vice Pres for Academic Affairs/CAO ... Dr. Jana HOLWICK
10 Vice Pres Administration & Finance ... Rick EPLAWY
84 VP Enroll Mgmt & Student Affairs ... Robin MCDERMOTT
26 Interim VP Institutional Advance ... Dr. M. Sue DREITZLER
20 Assoc VP for Academic Admin ... Dr. Jennifer COLLIS
10 Assoc VP for Finance & CFO ... Brian DIRK
53 Int Dean School of Prof & Innova ... Prof. Dale SHEPTAK
50 Dean School of Business ... Prof. Robert TREBAR
88 Dean School of Equine Studies ... Dr. Pam HESS
88 Dean School of Arts/Human & SS ... Dr. Tom DAVIS
81 Dean School of Natural Sci & Math ... Dr. Steven REYNOLDS, JR.
06 Registrar ... Barbara ARILSON
88 Director Academic Advising & ALC ... Dr. Brent ROBINSON
107 Director Prof Development & ADCP ... Lisa STRAUSBAUGH
58 Director Parker MBA Program ... Donna BARES
88 Director Physician Assistant Pgm ... Joe WEBER
36 Director Career Services ... Erin NUNN
50 Director Entrepreneurship Program ... Dr. Tom LIX
38 Director Student Success Center ... Dr. John SPIESMAN
37 Director Financial Aid ... Patricia PANGONIS
15 Director Human Resources ... Alexis HANNA
13 Director Information Technology ... Jason SPOTZ
32 Dean of Students ... Billie DUNN
07 Dean Admissions/Financial Aid ... Chris HARRIS
18 Director Physical Plant ... Herb DILL
29 Director Alumni & Public Relations ... Vacant
41 Director Athletics ... Griz ZIMMERMANN
08 Director Lincoln Library ... Christopher BENNETT
19 Director Security ... Richard KLINE
39 Director Residence Life ... Megan MCKENNA
09 Institutional Research Specialist ... Amanda ZINNI

Lakeland Community College (F)

7700 Clocktower Drive, Kirtland OH 44094-5198
County: Lake FICE Identification: 006804
Unit ID: 203599
Telephone: (440) 525-7000 Carnegie Class: Assoc/Pub-S-SC
FAX Number: (440) 525-7651 Calendar System: Semester
URL: www.lakelandcc.edu
Established: 1967 Annual Undergrad Tuition & Fees (In-District): $3,087
Enrollment: 9,611 Coed
Affiliation or Control: State/Local IRS Status: 501(c)3
Highest Offering: Associate Degree
Program: Occupational; 2-Year Principally Bachelor's Creditable
Accreditation: NH, ADNUR, DH, ENGT, HT, IFSAC, MAC, MLTAD, RAD, SURGT

01 President ... Dr. Morris W. BEVERAGE, JR.
05 Exec VP & Provost/Dean Faculty ... Dr. Margaret BARTOW
10 Sr Vice Pres Admin Svcs/Treasurer ... Mr. Michael E. MAYHER
100 Chief of Staff/Sr VP Inst Effectiv ... Ms. Mary Ann BLAKELEY
26 Chief Commun Ofcr/VP College Rels ... Ms. Dawn M. PLANTE
38 Assc Provst Teaching/Learning Effct ... Ms. Deborah L. HARDY
84 Assoc Provost for Enrollment Mgmt ... Mr. William KRAUS
20 Assoc VP Student Development ... Mr. Richard J. NOVOTNY
83 Dean Social Science/Public Services ... Dr. Steven OLUIC
76 Dean Science/Health/Math ... Vacant
79 Dean Arts/Humanities ... Dr. Donald KILLEEN
50 Dean Business/Engineering ... Dr. Gary L. EITH
88 Dean of Learning Technologies ... Mr. William KNAPP
21 Assoc VP Bus Svcs/Deputy Treasurer ... Mr. Brian COOK
13 Dir Administrative Technologies ... Mr. Rick PENNY
31 Director Community Learning ... Vacant
21 Controller & Bursar ... Mr. Paul D. HENSCHEL
15 Director Hum Res/Organizational Dev ... Ms. Cathy BUSH
18 Director for Facilities Management ... Mr. Bert DIEHL
19 Chief of Police/Director of Safety ... Mr. Gerald JENKINS
07 Director for Admissions/Registrar ... Ms. Tracey L. COOPER
37 Dir Financial Aid/Enroll Support ... Ms. Melissa A. AMSPAUGH
35 Director of Student Activities ... Mr. Mario PETITTI
30 Dir Development/Alumni Relations ... Dr. Robert CAHEN
96 Director of Purchasing ... Mr. Tom A. KIRCHNER
09 Director of Institutional Research ... Mrs. Kathryn REYNOLDS

Lakewood College (G)

12900 Lake Avenue, Lakewood OH 44107-1558
County: Cuyahoga Identification: 666715
Telephone: (800) 517-0857 Carnegie Class: Not Classified
FAX Number: (216) 803-9899 Calendar System: Other
URL: www.lakewoodcollege.edu
Established: 1998 Annual Undergrad Tuition & Fees: $4,500
Enrollment: N/A Coed
Affiliation or Control: Independent Non-Profit IRS Status: 501(c)3
Highest Offering: Associate Degree
Program: Occupational
Accreditation: DETC

01 President ... Ms. Tanya HAGGINS

Laura and Alvin Siegal College of Judaic Studies (H)

26500 Shaker Boulevard, Beachwood OH 44122-7197
County: Cuyahoga FICE Identification: 012838
Unit ID: 202019
Telephone: (216) 464-4050 Carnegie Class: Not Classified
FAX Number: (216) 464-5827 Calendar System: Semester
URL: www.siegalcollege.edu
Established: 1963 Annual Undergrad Tuition & Fees: $17,990
Enrollment: 125 Coed
Affiliation or Control: Independent Non-Profit IRS Status: 501(c)3
Highest Offering: Master's
Program: Liberal Arts And General; Teacher Preparatory
Accreditation: NH

01 Interim President ... Dr. Seymour KOPELOWITZ
05 Provost ... Dr. Brian D. AMKRAUT
08 Chief Librarian ... Mrs. Jean LETTOFSKY
13 Director Information Technology ... Mr. Eli ASCHKENASY

Lincoln College (I)

149 Northland Boulevard, Cincinnati OH 45246-1116
County: Hamilton Identification: 666472
Unit ID: 205708
Telephone: (513) 874-0432 Carnegie Class: Assoc/PrivFP
FAX Number: (513) 874-0123 Calendar System: Quarter
URL: www.swcollege.net
Established: 1978 Annual Undergrad Tuition & Fees: $13,325
Enrollment: 464 Coed
Affiliation or Control: Proprietary IRS Status: Proprietary
Highest Offering: Associate Degree
Program: Occupational
Accreditation: ACICS, MAAB

01 Executive Director ... Mr. Ron MILLS

† Branch campus of Lincoln College of Technology, Dayton, OH.

Lincoln College of Technology (A)

632 Vine Street, Suite 200, Cincinnati OH 45202-2421
County: Hamilton　Identification: 666471
Unit ID: 205717
Telephone: (513) 421-3212　Carnegie Class: Assoc/PrivFP
FAX Number: (513) 421-8325　Calendar System: Quarter
URL: www.lincolncollegeoftechnology.com
Established: 1973　Annual Undergrad Tuition & Fees: $13,325
Enrollment: 266　Coed
Affiliation or Control: Proprietary　IRS Status: Proprietary
Highest Offering: Associate Degree
Program: Occupational; 2-Year Principally Bachelor's Creditable; Business Emphasis
Accreditation: ACICS, MAAB

01 Executive Director .... Sandra RHODES

† Branch campus of Lincoln College of Technology, Dayton, OH.

Lincoln College of Technology (B)

111 W First Street, Suite 700, Dayton OH 45402-1105
County: Montgomery　FICE Identification: 012128
Unit ID: 205726
Telephone: (937) 224-0061　Carnegie Class: Assoc/PrivFP
FAX Number: (937) 224-0065　Calendar System: Quarter
URL: www.lincolnedu.com
Established: 1978　Annual Undergrad Tuition & Fees: $13,325
Enrollment: 343　Coed
Affiliation or Control: Proprietary　IRS Status: Proprietary
Highest Offering: Associate Degree
Program: Occupational
Accreditation: ACICS, MAAB

01 Director .... Mr. James A. SMOLINSKI
06 Registrar .... Ms. Sara BIELECK
07 Director of Admissions .... Mr. Bill FURLONG
36 Director Student Placement .... Ms. Melanie JOHNSON
37 Director Student Financial Aid .... Ms. Abby PERKINS

Lincoln College of Technology (C)

201 E Second Street, Franklin OH 45005-2267
County: Warren　Identification: 666473
Unit ID: 205692
Telephone: (937) 746-6633　Carnegie Class: Assoc/PrivFP
FAX Number: (937) 746-6754　Calendar System: Quarter
URL: www.lincolnedu.com
Established: 1978　Annual Undergrad Tuition & Fees: $13,325
Enrollment: 200　Coed
Affiliation or Control: Proprietary　IRS Status: Proprietary
Highest Offering: Associate Degree
Program: Occupational; 2-Year Principally Bachelor's Creditable; Technical Emphasis
Accreditation: ACICS, MAAB

01 Director .... Ronald MILLS

† Branch campus of Lincoln College of Technology, Dayton, OH - Campus closing December 2012.

Lorain County Community College (D)

1005 N Abbe Road, Elyria OH 44035-1691
County: Lorain　FICE Identification: 003068
Unit ID: 203748
Telephone: (440) 365-5222　Carnegie Class: Assoc/Pub-U-SC
FAX Number: (440) 365-6519　Calendar System: Semester
URL: www.loraincc.edu
Established: 1963　Annual Undergrad Tuition & Fees (In-District): $2,876
Enrollment: 13,147　Coed
Affiliation or Control: State/Local　IRS Status: 501(c)3
Highest Offering: Associate Degree
Program: Occupational; 2-Year Principally Bachelor's Creditable
Accreditation: NH, ADNUR, ART, DH, DMS, ENGT, MAC, MLTAD, OTA, PNUR, PTAA, RAD, SURGT

01 President .... Dr. Roy A. CHURCH
46 VP Strategic & Institutional Devel .... Vacant
05 Provost/VP for Acad & Student Svcs .... Ms. Marcia BALLINGER
10 Vice President Admin Svcs/Treasurer .... Mr. Quentin J. POTTER
88 Assoc Prov University Partnership .... Dr. John R. CROOKS
08 Int Dean Library/Instruction Media .... Ms. Susan PAUL
84 Dean Enroll Svcs/Fin Aid/Registrar .... Ms. Stephanie SUTTON
14 Int Director Information Systems .... Mr. Lou KOMPARE
15 Director Human Resources .... Mrs. Sydney LANCASTER
88 Dir Entrepreneurship Innov Inst .... Ms. Terri B. SANDU
19 Director of Campus Security .... Mr. Keith BROWN
18 Director of Physical Plant .... Mr. Robert FLYER
51 Director Public Services .... Ms. Shara DAVIS
88 Dean Academic Foundations .... Vacant
57 Dir Stocker Humanit/Fine Arts Ctr .... Ms. Janet HERMAN-BARLOW
09 Director Institutional Effect/Plng .... Ms. Shara DAVIS
96 Dir Purchasing/Facilities Planning .... Ms. Laura K. CARISSIMI
50 Dean of Business .... Dr. Robert B. YOUNG
54 Dean Engineering Tech .... Ms. Kelly ZELESNIK
76 Int Dean Allied Health & Nursing .... Ms. Hope MOON
79 Dean Arts/Humanities .... Dr. Robert A. BECKSTROM
81 Dean Science/Math .... Dr. Rosa HAINAJ
83 Dean Social Science/Human Svc .... Dr. Sunil AHUJA
68 Int Dean Health/PE/Recreation .... Ms. Lisa AUGUSTINE

Lourdes University (E)

6832 Convent Boulevard, Sylvania OH 43560-2898
County: Lucas　FICE Identification: 003069
Unit ID: 203757
Telephone: (419) 885-3211　Carnegie Class: Master's S
FAX Number: (419) 882-3987　Calendar System: Semester
URL: www.lourdes.edu
Established: 1958　Annual Undergrad Tuition & Fees: $16,950
Enrollment: 2,279　Coed
Affiliation or Control: Roman Catholic　IRS Status: 501(c)3
Highest Offering: Master's
Program: Liberal Arts And General; Professional
Accreditation: NH, ANEST, IACBE, NURSE, SW, TEAC

01 Interim President .... Dr. Janet H. ROBINSON
00 President Emerita .... Sr. Ann Francis KLIMKOWSKI
05 Interim Provost .... Dr. Keith SCHLENDER
32 Vice Pres for Student Life .... Ms. Roseanne GILL-JACOBSON
10 Vice Pres Finance & Administration .... Mr. Michael KILLIAN
42 Vice Pres for Mission & Ministry .Sr. Ann Carmen BARONE, OSF
30 Vice President for Inst Advancement .... Ms. Mary ARQUETTE
49 Dean College of Arts & Sciences .... Dr. Geoffrey J. GRUBB
53 Dean Coll of Education & Human Svcs .... Dr. Michael J. SMITH
66 Dean College of Nursing .... Dr. Judy DIDION
50 Dean College Business & Leadership .... Dr. Dean LUDWIG
58 Dean of Graduate School .... Dr. Deborah SCHWARTZ
35 Dean of Students & Retention .... Dr. Kim GRIEVE
37 Director Financial Aid .... Ms. Denise MCCLUSKEY
26 Director of University Relations .... Ms. Helene SHEETS
08 Director of Library Services .... Sr. Sandra RUTKOWSKI
06 Registrar .... Ms. Michelle A. RABLE
13 Director of Information Technology .... Dr. LeRoy BUTLER
07 Director of Admissions .... Ms. Amy MERGEN
15 Director of Human Resources .... Mr. Scott SIMON
85 Director Foreign Students .... Vacant
36 Director of Career Counseling .... Ms. Janet DICKSON
11 Director of Administrative Systems .... Ms. Laurie ORZECHOWSKI
21 Director of Finance .... Ms. Brigette SADOWSKI
88 Director of Advising Center .... Ms. Mary DOUGLAS
44 Dir Development/Annual Fund Officer .... Mr. Michael GEORGE
18 Director of Facilities & Grounds .... Vacant
09 Director of Institutional Research .... Ms. Pam CURAVO
40 Manager of Bookstore .... Ms. Ann MORRIS

Malone University (F)

2600 Cleveland Avenue NW, Canton OH 44709-3897
County: Stark　FICE Identification: 003072
Unit ID: 203775
Telephone: (330) 471-8100　Carnegie Class: Master's M
FAX Number: (330) 471-8478　Calendar System: Semester
URL: www.malone.edu
Established: 1892　Annual Undergrad Tuition & Fees: $24,536
Enrollment: 2,428　Coed
Affiliation or Control: Friends　IRS Status: 501(c)3
Highest Offering: Master's
Program: Liberal Arts And General; Teacher Preparatory; Professional
Accreditation: NH, ACBSP, CACREP, NURSE, SW, TED

01 President .... Dr. David A. KING
10 Vice President for Finance/CFO .... Mrs. Joy E. BRATHWAITE
05 Provost .... Dr. Donald L. TUCKER
30 Vice Pres for Univ Advancement .... Mr. Howard E. TAYLOR
84 Vice Pres for Enrollment Management .... Vacant
32 Vice Pres for Student Development ... Dr. Christopher T. ABRAMS
49 Dean Col of Theol/Arts & Sciences .... Dr. D. Nathan PHINNEY
51 Dean Sch of Business & Leadership .... Dr. Marjorie F. CARLSON HURST
53 Dean Sch of Education & Human Devel .... Dr. Rhoda C. SOMMERS
66 Dean Sch of Nursing & Health Sci .... Dr. Debra A. LEE
35 Assoc Dean Student Development .... Mr. Joshua L. PERKINS
21 Controller .... Mr. Ronald B. MESSNER
06 Registrar .... Mr. Gary L. PHELPS
07 Director of Admissions .... Vacant
29 Dir of Alumni & Parent Relations .... Mrs. Deborah M. ROBINSON
44 Director of The Malone Fund .... Mr. F. Allen FRALEY
36 Director of Alumni Career Services .... Mr. Douglas C. REICHENBERGER
27 Director of University Relations .... Mrs. Suzanne W. THOMAS
30 Senior Dev Officer for Intercol Ath .... Mr. John C. FEHLMAN
88 Director of Church Relations .... Mr. Timothy G. PITZER
105 Web Administrator .... Mr. Michael R. MILLER
37 Director of Financial Aid .... Mrs. Pamela S. PUSTAY
15 Director of Human Resources .... Mr. Michael J. FAIRLESS
13 Director of Info Technologies .... Mr. Clark D. HOOPES
41 Athletic Director .... Mr. Charles R. GRIMES
08 Acting Director of Library Services .... Ms. Rebecca L. FORT
93 Director of Multicultural Services .... Mrs. Brenda D. STEVENS
18 Director of Physical Plant .... Mr. James E. PALONE
88 Director of Student Retention .... Mrs. Patricia L. LITTLE
108 Director of Assessment .... Dr. Charles R. LARTEY
91 Asst Dir of Info Technologies .... Mr. John D. RIVERS
90 Senior Systems Engineer .... Mr. Alexander YU
42 University Chaplain .... Rev. L. Randall HECKERT
40 Bookstore Manager .... Ms. Rebecca E. ABEL
09 Assistant to the Provost .... Ms. Karen R. WARNER
92 Director of Honors Programs .... Dr. Diane M. CHAMBERS
89 Dir of the College Experience Pgm .... Dr. Marcia K. EVERETT
38 Director of Counseling Center .... Mr. Timothy T. MORBER
23 Health Center Nurse .... Mrs. Janet A. PERKO
24 Technology Services Coordinator .... Mr. M. Adam KLEMANN

Marietta College (G)

215 Fifth Street, Marietta OH 45750-4033
County: Washington　FICE Identification: 003073
Unit ID: 203845
Telephone: (740) 376-4000　Carnegie Class: Bac/Diverse
FAX Number: (740) 376-4896　Calendar System: Semester
URL: www.marietta.edu
Established: 1835　Annual Undergrad Tuition & Fees: $40,510
Enrollment: 1,615　Coed
Affiliation or Control: Independent Non-Profit　IRS Status: 501(c)3
Highest Offering: Master's
Program: Liberal Arts And General; Teacher Preparatory; Professional
Accreditation: NH, ARCPA, ENG, TED

01 President .... Dr. Joseph W. BRUNO
05 Interim Provost/Dean of Faculty ..... Dr. Gamaliel (Gama) PERRUCI
10 Vice President for Admin & Finance .... Mr. Daniel C. BRYANT
30 Interim VP for College Advancement .... Mr. Crompton B. BURTON
28 VP for Diversity & Inclusion .... Dr. Richard DANFORD
84 Vice President for Enrollment .... Mr. David J. RHODES
32 Vice President for Student Life .... Dr. Robert A. PASTOOR
29 Assoc VP Alumni/College Relations .... Mr. Crompton (Hub) B. BURTON
44 Asst VP Advancement/Planned Giving .... Mr. Evan BOHNEN
88 Dean McDonough Ctr for Leadership .... Dr. Gamaliel (Gama) PERRUCI
101 Secretary Board of Trustees .... Mr. William H. DONNELLY
08 Director of Library .... Dr. N. Douglas ANDERSON
21 Controller .... Mr. Dan HUNGERFORD
37 Director Student Financial Services .... Mr. Kevin D. LAMB
18 Director of Physical Plant .... Mr. Fred R. SMITH
38 Director of Counseling Services .... Dr. Eric LIMEGROVER
06 Registrar .... Ms. Tina K. PERDUE
15 Director of Human Resources .... Ms. Victoria A. FORD
19 Chief of Campus Police .... Mr. Thomas M. SACCENTI
26 Director of College Relations .... Mr. Thomas D. PERRY
07 Director of Admissions .... Mr. Jason J. TURLEY
09 Director of Institutional Research ... Dr. Gregory J. DELEMEESTER
36 Career Center Director .... Ms. B. Hilles HUGHES
41 Director of Athletics .... Mr. Larry R. HISER
27 Chief Information Officer .... Mr. John R. DAVIS
63 Dir Physician Assistant Programs .... Dr. Gloria STEWART
85 Dir International Student Programs .... Ms. Christy BURKE
105 Webmaster .... Mr. Chris J. CRAIG
25 Grants Officer .... Ms. Elizabeth B. MCNALLY
51 Continuing Education .... Ms. Tina K. PERDUE
35 Dean of Students .... Mr. Bruce E. PETERSON
20 Assoc Provost for Academic Admin .... Dr. Mark A. MILLER

Marion Technical College (H)

1467 Mount Vernon Avenue, Marion OH 43302-5694
County: Marion　FICE Identification: 010736
Unit ID: 203881
Telephone: (740) 389-4636　Carnegie Class: Assoc/Pub-R-M
FAX Number: (740) 389-6136　Calendar System: Semester
URL: www.mtc.edu
Established: 1971　Annual Undergrad Tuition & Fees (In-State): $3,984
Enrollment: 2,791　Coed
Affiliation or Control: State　IRS Status: 501(c)3
Highest Offering: Associate Degree
Program: Occupational; 2-Year Principally Bachelor's Creditable
Accreditation: NH, ADNUR, MAC, MLTAD, OTA, PTAA, RAD

01 President .... Dr. J. Richard BRYSON
05 Vice Pres Instructional Services .... Mr. Dennis BUDKOWSKI
32 VP of Student Svcs & Inst Advance .... Vacant
84 Dean of Enrollment Services .... Mr. Joel O. LILES
06 Registrar .... Mr. Jim LAVERY
13 Director Mgmt Information Systems .... Ms. Joy A. MOORE
26 Director of Public Relations .... Ms. Nikki WORKMAN
66 Dean of Nursing Technology .... Ms. Mary MCWILLIAMS
103 Director Ctr Workforce Development .... Vacant
15 Director Human Resources .... Ms. Brenda MCKINNON
88 Dir Physical Therapist Asst Pgm .... Ms. Susan COTTERMAN
88 Dir Occupational Therapy .... Mr. Chad SCHNEIDER
04 Assistant to Pres for Research/Plng .... Ms. Teresa PARKER
18 Coord Facil Improvements/Operations .... Ms. Leeann GRAU
37 Coordinator Student Financial Aid .... Ms. Deb LANGDON
54 Dean of Engineering Technology .... Mr. Dave WAGNER
50 Dean of Business/Information Tech .... Ms. Vicky WOOD
49 Dean of Arts and Sciences .... Mr. Scott POTTER
76 Dean of Allied Health .... Ms. Deborah BATES

Mercy College of Ohio (I)

2221 Madison Avenue, Toledo OH 43604
County: Lucas　FICE Identification: 030970
Unit ID: 203960
Telephone: (419) 251-1313　Carnegie Class: Spec/Health
FAX Number: (419) 251-1570　Calendar System: Semester
URL: www.mercycollege.edu
Established: 1993　Annual Undergrad Tuition & Fees: $8,736
Enrollment: 1,210　Coed
Affiliation or Control: Roman Catholic　IRS Status: 501(c)3
Highest Offering: Baccalaureate
Program: 2-Year Principally Bachelor's Creditable; Nursing Emphasis
Accreditation: NH, ADNUR, CVT, NUR, NURSE, POLYT, RAD

01 President .... Mr. John HAYWARD
05 VP Acad Affs/Dean of Faculty .... Dr. Anne LOOCHTAN

11 Vice Pres Administrative Services .... Mr. James L. HARTER
66 Associate Dean Nursing .... Dr. Maria NOWICKI
81 Associate Dean Scimatics Division .... Dr. Barbara STOOS
97 Assoc Dean Humanities/Social Scis .... Dr. Regan BROCK
76 Assoc Dean Allied Health/Dist Ed .... Dr. Kimberly WATSON
10 Director College Finances/Res Plng ..Ms. Joan M. RUTHERFORD
30 Director College Advancement .... Mr. Michael WHALEN
84 Dir Enroll Svcs/Chief Admiss Ofcr .Dr. Shelly MCCOY GRISSOM
08 Director Library/Resource Services ....Ms. Deborah JOHNSON
91 Manager College Admin Info Systems ....Mr. Gary BROCK
06 Registrar ....Ms. Heather HOPPE
37 Financial Aid Director .... Ms. Julie LESLIE
26 Director of Communications ....Ms. Denise HUDGIN
42 Dir Campus Ministry/Coord Ser Learn ....Sr. Sally BOHNETT
21 Business Officer ....Ms. Diane RAHN
103 Director Short Term Educ Programs .... Ms. Cheryl NUTTER
09 Director of Institutional Research ....Ms. Heather HOPPE
15 Director Personnel Services ....Ms. Joan BUNCH
18 Chief Facilities/Physical Plant ....Mr. James HARTER
29 Director Alumni Relations .... Sr. Barbara DAVIS
32 Chief Student Life Officer .... Ms. Megan GRAY
35 Assoc Dean Student Affs/Placement ....Ms. Jennifer PIZIO
38 Director Student Counseling .... Ms. Wendy NATHAN
108 Director Institutional Assessment ....Ms. Lori EDGEWORTH
07 Director of Admissions ....Ms. Aimee BISHOP STUART
36 Director of Career & Prof Develop .... Ms. Megan GRAY

Methodist Theological School in Ohio (A)

3081 Columbus Pike, Delaware OH 43015-3211

County: Delaware — FICE Identification: 003075
Unit ID: 203997
Telephone: (740) 363-1146 — Carnegie Class: Spec/Faith
FAX Number: (740) 362-3135 — Calendar System: 4/1/4
URL: www.mtso.edu
Established: 1958 — Annual Graduate Tuition & Fees: $15,660
Enrollment: 224 — Coed
Affiliation or Control: United Methodist — IRS Status: 501(c)3
Highest Offering: Doctorate; No Undergraduates
Program: Professional; Religious Emphasis
Accreditation: NH, THEOL

01 President ....Rev. Jay A. RUNDELL
05 Academic Dean ....Dr. Randy I. LITCHFIELD
11 VP for Administrative Services ....Mr. Jonathan D. JUMP
04 Executive Asst to the President ....Ms. Linda J. OGDEN
27 Director of Communications ....Mr. Danny RUSSELL
07 Director of Admissions ....Ms. April CASPERSON
06 Registrar ....Ms. Sue LAMPHERE
08 Librarian ....Mr. Paul BURNAM
10 Controller .... Mrs. Carolyn ROTHERMEL
18 Director Buildings/Grounds .... Mr. James ROHLER
32 Director of Student Services .... Rev. Leslie TAYLOR
13 Director of Information Services ....Mr. Matthew REHM

Miami-Jacobs Career College (B)

150 E Gay Street, 1st Floor, Columbus OH 43215-3227

County: Franklin — Identification: 666465
Unit ID: 369862
Telephone: (614) 221-7770 — Carnegie Class: Assoc/PrivFP
FAX Number: N/A — Calendar System: Quarter
URL: www.miamijacobs.edu.com
Established: 1980 — Annual Undergrad Tuition & Fees: $16,032
Enrollment: 303 — Coed
Affiliation or Control: Proprietary — IRS Status: Proprietary
Highest Offering: Associate Degree
Program: Occupational
Accreditation: ACICS

01 President/Director ....Ms. Joanie KREIN
05 Director Education/Academic Affairs .... Ms. Erin DORMAN
37 Director Financial Aid ....Ms. Lori BEARD
36 Director of Career Plng/Placement .... Mr. Joseph BARKER
06 Registrar .... Ms. Linsday ROBERTS
07 Senior Admissions Rep .... Ms. Natalie MCDANIEL
88 Director of Employer Relations ....Ms. Jessica PARSONS

Miami-Jacobs Career College (C)

110 N Patterson Boulevard, Dayton OH 45402-1771

County: Montgomery — FICE Identification: 003076
Unit ID: 204060
Telephone: (937) 222-7337 — Carnegie Class: Assoc/PrivFP
FAX Number: (937) 461-3384 — Calendar System: Quarter
URL: www.miamijacobs.edu
Established: 1860 — Annual Undergrad Tuition & Fees: $13,750
Enrollment: 235 — Coed
Affiliation or Control: Proprietary — IRS Status: Proprietary
Highest Offering: Associate Degree
Program: Occupational; 2-Year Principally Bachelor's Creditable
Accreditation: ACICS, MAC, SURGT

01 Regional Vice President .... Mr. Ned SYNDER
12 Campus Director ....Ms. Angela MARTIN
05 Academic Dean .... Ms. Jennifer FRIEND
37 Director Student Financial Aid .... Ms. Marcia BYRD

Miami-Jacobs Career College (D)

6400 Rockside Road, Independence OH 44131

County: Cuyahoga — FICE Identification: 021521
Unit ID: 200633
Telephone: (216) 834-1400 — Carnegie Class: Assoc/PrivFP
FAX Number: (216) 861-4517 — Calendar System: Quarter
URL: www.miamijacobs.edu
Established: 1970 — Annual Undergrad Tuition & Fees: $22,765
Enrollment: 266 — Coed
Affiliation or Control: Proprietary — IRS Status: Proprietary
Highest Offering: Associate Degree
Program: Occupational
Accreditation: ACICS

01 School Director ....Mrs. Lynn M. MIZANIN

Miami University (E)

501 E High Street, Oxford OH 45056-1846

County: Butler — FICE Identification: 003077
Unit ID: 204024
Telephone: (513) 529-1809 — Carnegie Class: RU/H
FAX Number: (513) 529-3841 — Calendar System: Semester
URL: www.muohio.edu
Established: 1809 — Annual Undergrad Tuition & Fees (In-State): $13,067
Enrollment: 23,240 — Coed
Affiliation or Control: State — IRS Status: 501(c)3
Highest Offering: Doctorate
Program: Liberal Arts And General; Teacher Preparatory; Professional
Accreditation: NH, ART, BUS, BUSA, CIDA, CLPSY, CS, DIETD, ENG, ENGT, IPSY, MUS, NUR, NURSE, SP, SW, TED, THEA

01 President ....Dr. David HODGE
05 Exec Vice Pres Academic Affs/Prov ....Dr. Bobby GEMPESAW
10 VP Finance & Bus Svcs/Treasurer .... Dr. David CREAMER
32 Vice President Student Affairs .... Dr. Barbara JONES
30 Int VP University Advancement .... Mr. Bradley M. BUNDY
13 VP Information Technology .... Ms. Debra A. ALLISON
15 Ast Prov Personnel/Dir Acad Per Svc .... Dr. Janet L. COX
21 Assoc VP Finance/Business Svcs ....Dr. David A. ELLIS
20 Int Assoc Provost for Ugrad Studies ....Dr. Carolyn A. HAYNES
35 Assoc VP Student Affs/Dean Students ....Dr. Gerri S. MOSLEY-HOWARD
27 Assoc VP Comm/Marketing ....Ms. Deedie Kay DOWDLE
18 Assoc VP Facilities Planning & Op ....Mr. Robert G. KELLER
84 Assoc VP Enrollment Mgmt ....Mr. Michael S. KABBAZ
28 Assoc VP Inst Diversity ....Dr. Ronald B. SCOTT
29 Asst Vice Pres Alumni Relations ....Mr. Raymond F. MOCK
26 Director Institutional Relations ....Mr. Randi Malcolm THOMAS
100 Secy Board/Exec Asst to President ....Mr. Ted O. PICKERILL
49 Dean College Arts & Science .... Dr. Phyllis CALLAHAN
76 Dean Education/Health & Society .... Dr. Carine FEYTEN
50 Dean School of Business ....Dr. Roger L. JENKINS
57 Dean School of Fine Arts .... Dr. James P. LENTINI
72 Dean Sch Engineering/Applied Sci .... Dr. Marek DOLLAR
08 Dean & University Librarian ....Ms. Judith A. SESSIONS
58 Dean Graduate School .... Dr. James T. ORIS
12 Dean Regional Campus ....Dr. G. Michael PRATT
88 Assoc Provost/Assoc Vice Pres ....Dr. Raymond F. GORMAN
07 Interim Director of Admission ....Ms. Ann LARSON
51 Director of Lifelong Learning ....Ms. Cheryl D. YOUNG
88 Univ Dir/Teach Effectiveness Pgm .... Dr. Cecilia M. SHORE
88 Univ Dir Liberal Educ/Assessment ....Dr. John P. TASSONI
92 Univ Dir Honors & Scholars Program .... Dr. Carolyn HAYNES
15 Sr Director Human Resources .... Ms. Carol HAUSER
88 Dir Center American/World Cultures ....Dr. Mary Jane BERMAN
23 Medical Director Student Health Svc ....Dr. Gregory CALKINS
104 Director Intl Education Services ....Dr. David KEITGES
06 University Registrar .... Mr. David M. SAUTER
36 Director Career Services ....Vacant
38 Director Student Counseling Service .... Dr. Kip C. ALISHIO
09 Director Institutional Research ....Ms. Denise A. KRALLMAN
27 Assoc Dir Univ Communications ....Ms. Claire M. WAGNER
19 Chief of Police/Dir Public Safety .... Mr. John MCCANDLESS
96 Sr Director Purchasing/Central Svcs .... Mr. William G. SHAWVER
43 University General Counsel ....Ms. Robin L. PARKER
22 Director Equity & Equal Opportunity .... Mr. Matthew L. BOAZ
41 Director Intercollegiate Athletics ....Mr. Brad J. BATES
23 Asst VP for Student Health & Svcs ....Ms. Gail A. WALENGA
04 Assistant to the President ....Ms. Deborah P. MASON

Miami University Hamilton Campus (F)

1601 University Boulevard, Hamilton OH 45011-3399

County: Butler — FICE Identification: 003079
Unit ID: 204006
Telephone: (513) 785-3000 — Carnegie Class: Assoc/Pub4
FAX Number: (513) 785-3145 — Calendar System: Semester
URL: www.ham.muohio.edu
Established: 1968 — Annual Undergrad Tuition & Fees (In-State): $4,958
Enrollment: 3,673 — Coed
Affiliation or Control: State — IRS Status: 501(c)3
Highest Offering: Baccalaureate
Program: Occupational; 2-Year Principally Bachelor's Creditable; Liberal Arts And General
Accreditation: &NH, ADNUR

01 Asc Provost/Dn of Regional Campuses .... Dr. G. Michael PRATT
05 Assoc Dean for Academic Affairs .... Dr. Rob SCHORMAN
32 Regional Assoc Dean of Students ....Dr. Robert H. RUSBOSIN
11 Assoc Dean Administrative Affairs ....Dr. Lee K. SANDERS
10 Senior Budget Director .... Mr. Gary STEELMAN
06 Regional Dir Registration Records ....Ms. Joanna SHOFIELD
30 Sr Regional Director of Advancement .... Mrs. Ellen PAXTON
27 Campus Communications Officer .... Mr. Perry RICHARDSON
11 Sr Director of Administration ....Mr. Christopher CONNELL
08 Director Regional Campus Library ....Ms. Krista MCDONALD
22 Director of Multicultural Services ....Mr. Jimmie L. JONES
26 Director of Marketing ....Ms. Michele DIENNO
18 Director of Physical Facilities ....Mr. Scott BROWN
88 Director of Conference Services ....Mr. Brett COUCH
85 Regnl Dir International Initiatives ....Ms. Chen FERGUSON
31 Director of Civic Engagement ....Ms. Sarah WOITESHER
07 Assoc Dir Admission/Financial Aid ....Ms. Jane LEE

† Regional accreditation is carried under the parent institution in Oxford, OH.

Miami University Middletown (G)

4200 E University Boulevard, Middletown OH 45042-3497

County: Butler — FICE Identification: 003080
Unit ID: 204015
Telephone: (513) 727-3200 — Carnegie Class: Assoc/Pub4
FAX Number: (513) 727-3223 — Calendar System: Semester
URL: www.mid.muohio.edu
Established: 1963 — Annual Undergrad Tuition & Fees (In-State): $3,758
Enrollment: 2,233 — Coed
Affiliation or Control: State — IRS Status: 501(c)3
Highest Offering: Baccalaureate
Program: Occupational; 2-Year Principally Bachelor's Creditable; Liberal Arts And General
Accreditation: &NH, ADNUR

01 Regional Assoc Dean for Admin .... Dr. Lee SANDERS
07 Assoc Dir of Admiss/Finanical Aid ....Mrs. Megan SPANEL
05 Regional Assoc Dean Academic Affs .... Dr. Rob SCHORMAN
32 Regional Sr Assoc Dean of Students ....Dr. Robert RUSBOSIN
08 Director of Regional Campus Library ....Mr. John BURKE
06 Regional Dir Records & Registration ....Ms. Joanna SHOFIELD
31 Dir Corporate Community Institute ....Ms. Pat MCNAB
10 Director Business Services ....Vacant
26 Director Public Affairs .... Mrs. Jan TOENNISSON
30 Regional Director of Development ....Ellen PAXTON
18 Chief Facilities/Physical Plant ....Mr. Chuck MACK
35 Assistant Dean for Student Affairs ....Vacant
37 Director Student Financial Aid .... Ms. Stacey ADAMS
38 Coord Counseling/Disability Svcs .... Ms. Nancy FERGUSON

† Regional accreditation is carried under the parent institution in Oxford, OH.

Mount Carmel College of Nursing (H)

127 S Davis Avenue, Columbus OH 43222-1504

County: Franklin — FICE Identification: 030719
Unit ID: 204176
Telephone: (614) 234-5800 — Carnegie Class: Spec/Health
FAX Number: (614) 234-2875 — Calendar System: Semester
URL: www.mccn.edu
Established: 1990 — Annual Undergrad Tuition & Fees: $17,197
Enrollment: 914 — Coed
Affiliation or Control: Roman Catholic — IRS Status: 501(c)3
Highest Offering: Master's
Program: Professional; Nursing Emphasis
Accreditation: NH, NURSE

01 President ....Dr. Ann E. SCHIELE
05 Associate Dean Undergrad Nsg Pgm .... Dr. Barbara BARTA
05 Associate Dean Graduate Nursing Pgm .... Dr. Angela PHILLIPS-LOWE
106 Assistant Dean Online Learning Pgm .... Ms. Tara SPALLA
06 Director of Records & Registration ....Ms. Karen L. GREENE
10 Director Business Affairs ....Ms. Kathy SMITH
07 Director Recruitment & Admissions .... Ms. Kim CAMPBELL
13 Systems Administrator ....Mr. Tim TABOL
37 Director Financial Aid ....Dr. Alyncia BOWEN
32 Director Student Life ....Ms. Colleen CIPRIANI
28 Director Diversity/Comm Initiative .... Ms. Kathlynne D. ESPY
04 Coord Administrative/Support Svcs ....Ms. Robin L. SHOCKLEY
29 Coordinator Alumni Affairs ....Ms. Phylis CROOK
26 Director College Relations ....Ms. Robin HUTCHINSON BELL
08 Director Library Services ....Mr. Stevo ROKSANDIC

Mount Vernon Nazarene University (I)

800 Martinsburg Road, Mount Vernon OH 43050-9500

County: Knox — FICE Identification: 007085
Unit ID: 204194
Telephone: (740) 392-6868 — Carnegie Class: Master's M
FAX Number: (740) 397-2769 — Calendar System: 4/1/4
URL: www.mvnu.edu
Established: 1968 — Annual Undergrad Tuition & Fees: $22,890
Enrollment: 2,521 — Coed
Affiliation or Control: Church Of The Nazarene — IRS Status: 501(c)3
Highest Offering: Master's
Program: Liberal Arts And General; Teacher Preparatory
Accreditation: NH, ACBSP, MUS, NURSE, SW, TED

01 Interim President ....Dr. Henry W. SPAULDING, II
10 Vice President Finance/Treasurer ....Mr. Jeffrey B. SPEAR
05 Provost and CAO ....Dr. Henry W. SPAULDING, II

84 Vice President for Enrollment Dev ... Mr. Doug BANBURY
32 Vice President Student Life ... Dr. Lanette SESSINK
42 University Chaplain ... Rev. Scott PETERSON
20 Assoc VP for Academic Affairs ... Dr. Robert P. HAMILL
20 Associate VP for Academic Programs ... Dr. Brock SCHROEDER
30 Mgr Development Operations ... Mr. Ben BLAKE
21 Director of Business Services ... Mr. Alan D. SHAFFER
06 University Registrar ... Mr. Mel SEVERNS
24 Educational Resource Ctr Specialist ... Mrs. Vicki SNYDER
15 Director of Human Resources ... Mrs. Tricia POKOSH
38 Director Counseling and Wellness ... Mr. Eric BROWNING
91 Director of Information Technology ... Mr. Chris MILLER
19 Director of Campus Safety ... Mr. Patrick RHOTON
29 Director of Alumni Relations ... Mr. Thomas H. WEST
40 Director of the Bookstore ... Mrs. Gina A. BLANCHARD
41 Athletic Director ... Mr. Paul P. SWANSON
27 Director Communications ... Mr. Jeffrey SCOTT
53 Dir Teacher Education/ Certification ... Dr. Debbie SHEPHERD-GREGG
37 Dir of Student Financial Services ... Mrs. Mary CANNON
18 Director of Facilities Management ... Mr. Dennis D. TAYLOR
21 Controller ... Mr. Steven JENKINS
35 Director of Student Involvement ... Mr. Travis KELLER
39 Director of Residence Life ... Vacant
28 Director Multicultural Affairs ... Mr. James M. SINGLETARY
09 Director Inst Research & Compliance ... Mrs. Kathy GRIFFITH

Muskingum University (A)

163 Stormont Street, New Concord OH 43762-1199
County: Muskingum FICE Identification: 003084
Unit ID: 204264
Telephone: (740) 826-8211 Carnegie Class: Master's M
FAX Number: (740) 826-8404 Calendar System: Semester
URL: www.muskingum.edu
Established: 1837 Annual Undergrad Tuition & Fees: $22,628
Enrollment: 2,292 Coed
Affiliation or Control: Presbyterian Church (U.S.A.) IRS Status: 501(c)3
Highest Offering: Master's
Program: Liberal Arts And General; Teacher Preparatory
Accreditation: NH, MUS, NURSE, TED

01 President ... Dr. Anne C. STEELE
05 Vice President Academic Affairs ... Dr. James CALLAGHAN
10 Vice President Business & Finance ... Mr. James R. WILSON
30 Vice President of Inst Advancement ... Vacant
32 Dean of Student Life ... Mrs. Janet A. HEETER-BASS
84 Dean Enrollment/Dir Financial Aid ... Mr. Jeff W. ZELLERS
20 Associate Academic Dean ... Vacant
08 Director of Library ... Dr. Sheila J. ELLENBERGER
06 Registrar ... Mr. Daniel B. WILSON
36 Assistant Director Career Services ... Mrs. Jacquelyn L. VASCURA
13 Director of Computing Services ... Mr. Lewis M. DREBLOW
26 Director Public Relations ... Ms. Janice TUCKER-MCCLOUD
29 Director Alumni Relations ... Ms. Jennifer BRONNER
07 Director of Admissions ... Mrs. Beth DALONZO
19 Director of Public Safety ... Mr. Danny VINCENT
42 College Minister ... Rev. William MULLINS
18 Supt of Building & Grounds ... Mr. Kevin J. WAGNER
41 Director of Athletics ... Mr. Larry SHANK
21 Associate Business Officer ... Mr. Philip LAUBE
35 Director of Student Affairs ... Ms. Susan HOGLUND
37 Director of Student Financial Aid ... Mrs. Janet VEJSICKY
38 Director of Student Counseling ... Mrs. Tracy BUGGLIN
40 Manager of Bookstore ... Mr. Lee MILLER
15 Coordinator of Human Resources ... Ms. Kathy J. MOORE

National Institute of Massotherapy (B)

3681 Manchester Road, Suite 304, Akron OH 44319
County: Summit FICE Identification: 034684
Unit ID: 412003
Telephone: (330) 867-1996 Carnegie Class: Assoc/PrivFP
FAX Number: (330) 867-6422 Calendar System: Other
URL: www.nim.edu
Established: N/A Annual Undergrad Tuition & Fees: $15,540
Enrollment: 64 Coed
Affiliation or Control: Proprietary IRS Status: Proprietary
Highest Offering: Associate Degree
Program: Occupational
Accreditation: CNCE

01 President ... Mr. Stephen PERKINSON

North Central State College (C)

2441 Kenwood Circle, Mansfield OH 44906
County: Richland FICE Identification: 005313
Unit ID: 204422
Telephone: (419) 755-4800 Carnegie Class: Assoc/Pub-R-M
FAX Number: (419) 755-4750 Calendar System: Semester
URL: www.ncstatecollege.edu
Established: 1961 Annual Undergrad Tuition & Fees (In-State): $4,290
Enrollment: 3,382 Coed
Affiliation or Control: State IRS Status: 501(c)3
Highest Offering: Associate Degree
Program: Occupational; 2-Year Principally Bachelor's Creditable
Accreditation: NH, ACBSP, ADNUR, OTA, PTAA, RAD

01 President ... Mr. Donald L. PLOTTS
04 Exec Assistant to the President ... Mr. Stephen R. WILLIAMS
10 VP Business Svcs ... Mr. Koffi AKAKPO
05 Vice President Academic Services ... Dr. Karen A. REED
26 Chief Public Affairs Officer ... Ms. Betty E. PRESTON
32 Vice President Student Services ... Ms. Margaret (Peg) A. MOIR
15 Director of Human Resources ... Mr. R. Douglas HANUSCIN
37 Director of Financial Aid ... Mr. James PHINNEY
08 Director Library ... Ms. Beth BURNS
22 Counselor/Coord Disability Services ... Ms. Sandra LUCKIE
50 Dean of Business/Lib Arts/Public Sv ... Mr. Gregory BUSCH
103 Dean of Tech/Workforce Develop ... Dr. Gregory TIMBERLAKE
76 Dean Health & Public Services ... Mr. James L. HULL
13 Director Information Technology ... Mr. Jim TURNER
06 Registrar ... Mr. Mark J. MONNES
18 Chief Facilities/Physical Plant ... Mr. Dean SCHAAD
96 Director of Purchasing ... Ms. Renee NUSSBAUM
102 Foundation Director ... Ms. Chriss HARRIS
09 Director of Institutional Research ... Mr. Thomas M. PRENDERGAST
88 Director of Retention Services ... Ms. Bev WALKER
88 Phi Theta Kappa Advisor ... Ms. Barb KEENER
66 Director of Nursing Programs ... Ms. Kelly GRAY
40 Campus Bookstore Manager ... Ms. Carla BUTDORFF
21 Controller ... Ms. Lori MCKEE
26 Director Marketing/Creative Design ... Mr. Keith STONER
105 Web Master ... Mr. Mark HUPP
88 Director of Tech Prep ... Mr. Tom KLUDING
51 Continuing Education Director ... Ms. Gina KAMWITHI
32 Coord Student Life Activities ... Ms. Elise RIGGLE
41 Int Coord Recreation/Intra Sports ... Ms. Jennifer RACER
29 Coord of Alumni/Employer Relations ... Ms. Mary J. RODRIGUEZ
36 Coordinator of Career Development ... Mr. Troy SHUTLER
103 Exec Dir Workforce Partnerships ... Ms. Marybeth BUSCH

Northeast Ohio Medical University (D)

PO Box 95, State Route 44, Rootstown OH 44272-0095
County: Portage FICE Identification: 024544
Unit ID: 204477
Telephone: (330) 325-2511 Carnegie Class: Spec/Med
FAX Number: (330) 325-7943 Calendar System: Other
URL: www.neomed.edu
Established: 1973 Annual Graduate Tuition & Fees: $34,455
Enrollment: 778 Coed
Affiliation or Control: State IRS Status: 501(c)3
Highest Offering: First Professional Degree; No Undergraduates
Program: Professional
Accreditation: NH, IPSY, MED, PH, PHAR

01 President ... Dr. Jay A. GERSHEN
100 Special Assistant to the President ... Ms. Kathleen C. RUFF
10 VP Administration/Finance ... Mr. John WRAY
30 VP External Affairs ... Vacant
46 VP Research ... Dr. Walter E. HORTON, JR.
67 Dean College of Pharmacy ... Dr. Charles TAYLOR
63 Dean College of Medicine ... Dr. Jeffrey L. SUSMAN
58 Dean College of Graduate Studies ... Dr. Walter E. HORTON, JR.
43 General Counsel ... Mrs. Maria R. SCHIMER
32 Chief Student Affairs Officer ... Ms. Sandra EMERICK
88 Executive Director Wasson Center ... Ms. Holly GERZINA
88 Executive Director Research ... Ms. Elizabeth CLINE
88 Executive Director Ind Relations ... Dr. Walter HORNE
88 Executive Director Faculty ... Dr. Robert EAGLEN
09 Executive Director Inst Research ... Dr. Margarita D. KOKINOVA
26 Director Public Relations ... Ms. Cristine BOYD
13 Director Information Technology ... Mr. Ronald L. MCGRADY
24 Dir Academic Technology Svcs ... Mr. Rey T. NOTARESCHI
86 Dir Government Relations/Sec BOT ... Mr. Richard LEWIS
21 Director Budget and Business Svcs ... Ms. Carrie BAST
18 Director Physical Plant ... Mr. Blaine M. WYCKOFF
35 Dir Career Development & Advising ... Ms. Anita R. POKORNY
36 Director Academic Support ... Ms. Amanda YOCUM
40 Supervisor Bookstore ... Ms. Christine KOVACICH
19 Supervisor Public Safety ... Ms. Kali MEONSKE
15 Senior HR Business Partner ... Ms. Barbara TOBIAS
04 Assistant to the President ... Ms. Michelle MULHERN

Northwest State Community College (E)

22-600 State Route 34, Archbold OH 43502-9542
County: Henry FICE Identification: 008677
Unit ID: 204440
Telephone: (419) 267-5511 Carnegie Class: Assoc/Pub-R-M
FAX Number: (419) 267-3688 Calendar System: Semester
URL: www.northweststate.edu
Established: 1968 Annual Undergrad Tuition & Fees (In-State): $4,300
Enrollment: 3,017 Coed
Affiliation or Control: State IRS Status: 501(c)3
Highest Offering: Associate Degree
Program: Occupational; 2-Year Principally Bachelor's Creditable
Accreditation: NH, ACBSP, ADNUR, MAC

01 President ... Dr. Thomas L. STUCKEY
05 VP for Academics ... Ms. Cindy KRUEGER
30 VP for Institutional Advancement ... Ms. Mari YODER
103 VP Workforce Development ... Mr. Thomas WYLIE
50 Dean of Business Technologies ... Dr. Von R. PLESSNER
69 Dean of Allied Health & Public Svcs ... Mrs. Lori ROBISON
49 Dean of Arts & Science ... Ms. Lana EVANS
66 Dean of Nursing ... Mrs. Lori BIRD
06 Registrar ... Ms. Connie KLINGSHIRN
40 Bookstore Manager ... Mr. Kemp STAPLETON
08 Director of Student Resources ... Ms. Kristi ROTROFF
18 Director of Plant Operations ... Mr. Timothy NELSON
90 Exec Director of Info Tech ... Mr. Matthew OSBORN
15 Director of Human Resources ... Mr. Denis CIACIUCH
21 Director of Business Services ... Ms. Lynn SPEISER
07 Director of Admissions ... Mr. Dennis GIACOMINO
10 Chief Fiscal Officer ... Ms. Kathy SOARDS
44 Chief Development ... Ms. Robbin WILCOX
37 Director Student Financial Aid ... Ms. Charlotte SORG
88 Dir Facil/Construction/Renovations ... Mrs. Lise' KONECNY
32 Coordinator Student Activities ... Mr. Keith F. VAN HORN

Notre Dame College (F)

4545 College Road, South Euclid OH 44121-4293
County: Cuyahoga FICE Identification: 003085
Unit ID: 204468
Telephone: (216) 381-1680 Carnegie Class: Bac/Diverse
FAX Number: (216) 381-3802 Calendar System: Semester
URL: www.notredamecollege.edu
Established: 1922 Annual Undergrad Tuition & Fees: $25,514
Enrollment: 2,147 Coed
Affiliation or Control: Roman Catholic IRS Status: 501(c)3
Highest Offering: Master's
Program: Liberal Arts And General; Teacher Preparatory
Accreditation: NH, NURSE, TED

01 President ... Dr. Andrew P. ROTH
05 Vice Pres Academic Affairs ... Dr. Nick SANTILLI
10 Sr Vice Pres Finance/Administration ... Mr. John C. PHILLIPS
45 Vice Pres for Assessment Planning ... Vacant
30 Vice Pres for Development ... Mr. David A. ARMSTRONG
31 Vice Pres for Board/Community Rels ... Ms. Karen L. POELKING
20 Assoc Dean of Academic Affairs ... Vacant
66 Nursing Division Chair ... Ms. Beth KASKEL
53 Education Division Chair ... Dr. John GALOVIC
81 Math & Science Division Chair ... Mr. David OROSZ
50 Business Division Chair ... Ms. Karen PENLER
57 Fine Arts Division Chair ... Ms. Rachel MORRIS
26 Director of Public Relations ... Vacant
07 Director of Traditional Admissions ... Ms. Beth FORD
88 Director of the Finn Center (Adult) ... Vacant
32 Dean for Student Affairs ... Mr. Brian EMERSON
06 Registrar ... Ms. Jameka WINDHAM
37 Dir Student Financial Assistance ... Ms. Mary MCCRYSTAL
88 Director of Student Accounts ... Mr. Jason LAPINSKI
19 Director Security/Safety ... Mr. Michael DUGAN
18 Director Physical Plant ... Mr. Tom MEEKS
13 Director Information Technology ... Mr. Michael KIEC
15 Director Personnel Services ... Ms. Susan ANDERSON
08 Director of Library ... Ms. Karen ZOLLER
42 Director Ctr Campus Theol/Ministry ... Mr. Anthony CAMINO
78 Director Coop Educ & Career Devel ... Ms. Kimberly LANE
38 Director of Counseling Center ... Ms. Susan LIPIEC
39 Director of Residence Life ... Mr. Ronald WIAFE
29 Dir Alumni Rels/Asc Dir Development ... Mrs. Mary Elizabeth COTLEUR
04 Admin Assistant to the President ... Ms. April KENNEDY
27 Chief Information Officer ... Ms. Deborah SHEREN
26 Chief Communications Officer ... Mr. Brian JOHNSTON
106 Online Education/E-learning ... Vacant

Oberlin College (G)

173 West Lorain Street, Oberlin OH 44074-1057
County: Lorain FICE Identification: 003086
Unit ID: 204501
Telephone: (440) 775-8121 Carnegie Class: Bac/A&S
FAX Number: (440) 775-8886 Calendar System: 4/1/4
URL: www.oberlin.edu
Established: 1833 Annual Undergrad Tuition & Fees: $44,905
Enrollment: 2,948 Coed
Affiliation or Control: Independent Non-Profit IRS Status: 501(c)3
Highest Offering: Master's
Program: Liberal Arts And General; Teacher Preparatory; Professional
Accreditation: NH, MUS

01 President ... Mr. Marvin KRISLOV
10 Vice President for Finance ... Mr. Ronald R. WATTS
30 VP Development/Alumni Affair ... Mr. William BARLOW
26 Vice President College Relations ... Mr. Ben JONES
49 Dean College Arts & Sciences ... Dr. Sean DECATUR
64 Dean Conservatory Music ... Dr. David H. STULL
32 Dean of Student Life ... Dr. Eric ESTES
35 Dean of Studies/VP Strategic Init ... Dr. Kathryn STUART
07 Dean Admissions/Financial Aid ... Ms. Debra J. CHERMONTE
43 VP General Counsel and Secretary ... Ms. Sandhya SUBRAMANIAN
86 Spec Asst Community/Govt Relations ... Vacant
21 Assoc Vice Pres Finance/Controller ... Mr. Mark R. BATES
29 Exec Director Alumni Assoc ... Ms. Danielle YOUNG
20 Assoc Dean of College Arts & Sci ... Ms. Joyce BABYAK
20 Assoc Dean of College Arts & Sci ... Dr. Heather HOGAN
14 Chief Tech Ofcr/Dir Computing Ctr ... Dr. John E. BUCHER
08 Director of Libraries ... Dr. Raymond A. ENGLISH
07 Director Admissions Conservatory ... Mr. Michael C. MANDEREN
38 Director of Counseling Center ... Vacant
57 Director of Allen Art Museums ... Dr. Andria DERSTINE
06 Registrar ... Ms. Elizabeth CLERKIN
37 Director of Financial Aid ... Mr. Robert A. REDDY, JR.
09 Director of Institutional Research ... Mr. Ross PEACOCK
18 Asst VP for Facilities ... Mr. Tom PICCORELLI
36 Director Career Devel/Placement ... Vacant

42 Director Religious Life ... Mr. Gregory MCGONIGLE
39 Dir Residential/Dining Services ... Mr. Adrian BATISTA
41 Director of Physical Educ/Athletics ... Vacant
19 Director of Safety & Security ... Ms. Marjorie BURTON
28 Director Multicultural Affairs ... Vacant
96 Director of Purchasing ... Mr. Gary W. KOEPP
15 Manager of Employee Relations ... Vacant

Ohio Business College (A)

1880 E Dublin-Granville Road, Columbus OH 43229
County: Franklin FICE Identification: 030658
Unit ID: 453747
Telephone: (614) 891-5030 Carnegie Class: Assoc/PrivFP
FAX Number: (614) 891-5130 Calendar System: Other
URL: www.ohiobusinesscollege.edu
Established: 1903 Annual Undergrad Tuition & Fees: $8,140
Enrollment: 194 Coed
Affiliation or Control: Proprietary IRS Status: Proprietary
Highest Offering: Associate Degree
Program: Occupational; 2-Year Principally Bachelor's Creditable
Accreditation: ACICS, MAC

01 President ... Mr. Dave GLEASON
12 Director ... Mr. Dennis HIRSH

Ohio Business College (B)

5202 Timber Commons Drive, Sandusky OH 44870-5894
County: Erie Identification: 666467
Unit ID: 203739
Telephone: (419) 627-8345 Carnegie Class: Assoc/PrivFP
FAX Number: (419) 627-1958 Calendar System: Quarter
URL: www.OhioBusinessCollege.Edu
Established: 1982 Annual Undergrad Tuition & Fees: $10,800
Enrollment: 460 Coed
Affiliation or Control: Proprietary IRS Status: Proprietary
Highest Offering: Associate Degree
Program: Occupational; 2-Year Principally Bachelor's Creditable; Business Emphasis
Accreditation: ACICS

01 School Director ... Theresa M. FISHER
37 Lead Financial Aid Administrator ... Geri WILSON
36 Director of Career Services ... Tarina OGLESBY
06 Registrar ... Emily COLWELL
07 Director of Admissions ... Cecilia BLEVINS
05 Director of Education ... Greg SCHULTZ
32 Student Success Liaison ... Erin CREMEAN

† Branch campus of Ohio Business College, Sheffield Village, OH.

Ohio Business College, Lorain Branch (C)

5095 Waterford Drive, Sheffield Village OH 44035-0701
County: Lorain FICE Identification: 021585
Unit ID: 203720
Telephone: (440) 934-3101 Carnegie Class: Assoc/PrivFP
FAX Number: (440) 934-3105 Calendar System: Quarter
URL: www.ohiobusinesscollege.edu
Established: 1903 Annual Undergrad Tuition & Fees: $12,000
Enrollment: 360 Coed
Affiliation or Control: Proprietary IRS Status: Proprietary
Highest Offering: Associate Degree
Program: Occupational; 2-Year Principally Bachelor's Creditable
Accreditation: ACICS, MAC

01 Executive Director ... Mrs. Rosanne CATELLA
07 Admissions Director ... Mrs. Rosemerry NICKELS
37 Financial Manager ... Mrs. Christine TODD
36 Career Services ... Ms. Cheryl JANKOWSKI

Ohio Christian University (D)

1476 Lancaster Pike, Circleville OH 43113-0458
County: Pickaway FICE Identification: 003030
Unit ID: 201964
Telephone: (740) 474-8896 Carnegie Class: Bac/Diverse
FAX Number: (740) 477-7755 Calendar System: Semester
URL: www.ohiochristian.edu
Established: 1948 Annual Undergrad Tuition & Fees: $17,350
Enrollment: 2,382 Coed
Affiliation or Control: Other Protestant IRS Status: 501(c)3
Highest Offering: Master's
Program: 2-Year Principally Bachelor's Creditable; Teacher Preparatory; Professional; Religious Emphasis
Accreditation: NH, BI, TEAC

01 President ... Dr. Mark A. SMITH
03 Provost ... Dr. Hank KELLY
05 Vice President of Academics ... Vacant
10 Vice President of Finance ... Mr. Robert HARTMAN
30 Vice President for Advancement ... Mr. Mark TAYLOR
32 Vice President Student Development ... Rev. Rick CHRISTMAN
11 Vice President of Operations ... Mr. Curtis CHRISTOPHER
13 Assistant VP for IT ... Mr. Ryan WHISLER
09 Director of Institutional Research ... Mr. David PENNINGTON
06 Registrar ... Dr. Rodney SONES
84 Associate Vice Pres Enrollment ... Mr. Michael EGENREIDER
55 VP College of Adult & Graduate Stds ... Mr. Tim EADES
08 Director of Library Services ... Mrs. Barbara MEISTER
37 Director Student Financial Services ... Mr. Wes BROTHERS
41 Athletic Director ... Mr. Ben BELLMAN
29 Director Alumni Relations ... Ms. Julie SORLEY

Ohio College of Massotherapy (E)

225 Heritage Woods Drive, Akron OH 44321-1363
County: Summit FICE Identification: 031163
Unit ID: 204592
Telephone: (330) 665-1084 Carnegie Class: Assoc/PrivNFP
FAX Number: (330) 665-5021 Calendar System: Semester
URL: www.ocm.edu
Established: 1973 Annual Undergrad Tuition & Fees: $20,545
Enrollment: 150 Coed
Affiliation or Control: Proprietary IRS Status: Proprietary
Highest Offering: Associate Degree
Program: 2-Year Principally Bachelor's Creditable; Technical Emphasis
Accreditation: ACCSC

01 President ... Mr. Jeffrey S. MORROW
11 Director of Administration ... Mrs. Debra M. SMITH

Ohio Dominican University (F)

1216 Sunbury Road, Columbus OH 43219-2099
County: Franklin FICE Identification: 003035
Unit ID: 204617
Telephone: (614) 251-4500 Carnegie Class: Master's L
FAX Number: (614) 251-4634 Calendar System: Semester
URL: www.ohiodominican.edu
Established: 1911 Annual Undergrad Tuition & Fees: $28,104
Enrollment: 2,913 Coed
Affiliation or Control: Roman Catholic IRS Status: 501(c)3
Highest Offering: Master's
Program: Liberal Arts And General; Teacher Preparatory; Professional
Accreditation: NH, ACBSP, #ARCPA, SW, TED

01 President ... Dr. Peter CIMBOLIC
05 Vice President Academic Affairs ... Dr. Alison BENDERS
32 Vice President Student Development ... Dr. James A. CARIDI
10 Vice President Finance & Admin ... Mr. David KOSANOVIC
04 Executive Asst to the President ... Ms. Candie LESTER
35 Asst Vice Pres Student Development ... Ms. Sharon REED
20 Assoc Vice Pres Academic Affairs ... Dr. Linda SCHOEN
58 Dean Graduate/Professional Studies ... Dr. Jay YOUNG
06 Registrar ... Ms. Shirley MCBRAYER
07 Director of Admissions ... Ms. Nicole EVANS
08 Director of the Library ... Mr. James E. LAYDEN
37 Director of Financial Aid ... Ms. Laura MEEK
36 Director Career Services ... Mr. Gary SWISHER
38 Director of Counseling Services ... Mr. Michael LEWIS
85 Director of Intercultural Office ... Ms. Melissa OCHAL
26 Director of PR & Communications ... Ms. Beth KOWALSKI
42 Director of Campus Ministry ... Rev. Richard GROSS
27 Chief Information Officer ... Mr. Fred LASSITER
15 Director of Human Resources ... Ms. Michelle GEIMAN
18 Director of Physical Facilities ... Ms. Jackie HENSON
29 Director of Alumni/AE Relations ... Ms. Ann SNIDER
39 Director of Resident Life ... Ms. Kerry SOLLER
41 Athletic Director ... Mr. Jeff BLAIR
24 Dir Center for Instruct Technology ... Vacant
96 Director of Purchasing ... Sr. Margaret WALSH
19 Director of Safety & Security ... Mr. John RACE
92 Director of Honors Program ... Mr. Matthew PONESSE
88 Dean Learning Enhanced Adult Degree ... Dr. Deborah SERLING
09 Director of Institutional Research ... Vacant

Ohio Mid-Western College (Formerly Temple Baptist College) (G)

19 Triangle Park Drive, Sharonville OH 45246
County: Hamilton FICE Identification: 037263
Unit ID: 206002
Telephone: (513) 772-9888 Carnegie Class: Spec/Faith
FAX Number: (513) 771-0702 Calendar System: Quarter
URL: www.omw.edu
Established: 1972 Annual Undergrad Tuition & Fees: $10,944
Enrollment: 134 Coed
Affiliation or Control: Baptist IRS Status: 501(c)3
Highest Offering: Baccalaureate
Program: Religious Emphasis
Accreditation: TRACS

01 President ... Dr. Scott REESE
10 Chief Financial Officer ... Mr. Tyler CLEM
05 VP/Dean of Academic Affairs ... Dr. Bill G. DYKES
37 Director of Financial Aid ... Mrs. Gail GOODE
08 Director of Library Services ... Ms. Wren SHAVER
06 Registrar ... Mr. Stephen KLEINER
32 Director of Student Success ... Mrs. Susan SICKLES
41 Athletics Director ... Mr. David POOL
07 Director of Recruiting ... Mr. Ricardo HILL

Ohio Northern University (H)

525 S Main Street, Ada OH 45810-1599
County: Hardin FICE Identification: 003089
Unit ID: 204635
Telephone: (419) 772-2000 Carnegie Class: Bac/Diverse
FAX Number: (419) 772-1932 Calendar System: Quarter
URL: www.onu.edu
Established: 1871 Annual Undergrad Tuition & Fees: $35,824
Enrollment: 3,611 Coed
Affiliation or Control: United Methodist IRS Status: 501(c)3
Highest Offering: First Professional Degree
Program: Liberal Arts And General; Teacher Preparatory; Professional; Business Emphasis
Accreditation: NH, BUS, CS, ENG, EXSC, LAW, MT, MUS, NAIT, NURSE, PHAR, TED

01 President ... Dr. Daniel A. DIBIASIO
05 Provost/Vice Pres Academic Affairs ... Dr. David C. CRAGO
10 Vice President Financial Affairs ... Mr. William H. BALLARD
30 Acting VP of University Advancement ... Mr. Ken W. BLOCK
84 Vice Pres Enrollment Management ... Dr. Lawrence T. LESICK
32 VP Student Affairs/Dean of Students ... Dean Adriane THOMPSON-BRADSHAW
49 Dean of Arts & Sciences ... Dr. Catherine ALBRECHT
54 Dean of Engineering ... Dr. Eric T. BAUMGARTNER
67 Dean of Pharmacy ... Dr. Jon E. SPRAGUE
50 Dean Business Administration ... Dr. James W. FENTON
61 Interim Dean of Law ... Dr. Stephen C. VELTRI
35 Dean of Students ... Vacant
30 Senior Director of Development ... Mr. Scott D. WILLS
06 Assistant Registrar ... Mrs. Andrea RICHARDSON
08 Librarian ... Mr. Paul M. LOGSDON
14 Director of Computer Center ... Mr. C. Lawrence BUSCH
36 Interim Director Career Services ... Mr. Justin COURTNEY
61 Dir Law Ext Affs/Career Strategies ... Mrs. Cheryl KITCHEN
38 Director of Counseling ... Dr. Michael SCHAFER
29 Director of Alumni Relations ... Ms. Ann DONNELLY HAMILTON
08 Law Librarian ... Dr. Nancy A. ARMSTRONG
42 University Chaplain ... Rev. David MACDONALD
18 Director of Physical Plant ... Mr. Marc STALEY
13 Interim Director of Technology ... Mr. Scott N. WALTHOUR
09 Director of Institutional Research ... Dr. Omer MINHAS
15 Director of Human Resources ... Ms. Tonya PAUL
20 Associate Academic Officer ... Dr. Juliet K. HURTIG
37 Director of Student Financial Aid ... Mrs. Melanie WEAVER
92 Director of Honors Program ... Dr. Patrick T. CROSKERY
21 Bursar ... Mrs. Amber L. CARPENTER
26 Dir of Communications & Marketing ... Ms. Carol FLAX
07 Director of Admissions ... Ms. Deborah MILLER
06 Registrar ... Ms. Tamela S. BASH
28 Director Multicultural Development ... Mr. Clyde W. PICKETT
41 Athletic Director ... Mr. Thomas SIMMONS
27 Assoc Director Public Information ... Ms. Mary WILKIN
44 Director of Annual Giving ... Ms. Kelly BRANT
96 Manager of Purchasing ... Ms. Vicki J. NIESE

The Ohio State University Main Campus (I)

154 W. 12th Avenue, Columbus OH 43210-1358
County: Franklin FICE Identification: 003090
Unit ID: 204796
Telephone: (614) 292-6446 Carnegie Class: RU/VH
FAX Number: (614) 292-9180 Calendar System: Semester
URL: www.osu.edu
Established: 1870 Annual Undergrad Tuition & Fees (In-State): $10,036
Enrollment: 56,867 Coed
Affiliation or Control: State IRS Status: 501(c)3
Highest Offering: Doctorate
Program: Liberal Arts And General; Teacher Preparatory; Professional
Accreditation: NH, ART, AUD, BUS, BUSA, CIDA, CLPSY, CS, DANCE, DENT, DH, DIETC, DIETD, DIETI, ENG, FOR, HSA, IPSY, LAW, LSAR, MED, MFCD, MIDWF, MT, MUS, NMT, NURSE, OPT, OPTR, OT, PH, PHAR, PLNG, PTA, RTT, SP, SPAA, SW, TED, THEA, VET

01 President ... Dr. E. Gordon GEE
100 Spc Asst to Pres for Op & Strgc Com ... Ms. Melinda CHURCH
05 Executive Vice Pres/Provost ... Dr. Joseph A. ALUTTO
32 Vice President for Student Life ... Dr. Javaune ADAMS-GASTON
10 Senior VP Business & Finance & CFO ... Mr. Geoffrey CHATAS
20 Vice Provost for Academic Planning ... Mr. Michael J. BOEHM
43 Sr VP & General Counsel ... Mr. Christopher M. CULLEY
15 VP for Human Resources ... Ms. Kathleen MCCUTCHEON
46 Vice Pres for Research ... Dr. Caroline WHITACRE
86 Sr Vice Pres of Govt Relations ... Mr. Herb ASHER
23 Sr Vice Pres Health Sci ... Dr. Steve G. GABBE
47 Vice Pres & Exec Dean FAES ... Dr. Bobby D. MOSER
30 Sr Vice President for Advancement ... Mr. Michael EICHER
28 Vice Prov Div & Incl & VP O & E ... Dr. Valerie LEE
58 Vice Provost/Dean Grad School ... Dr. Patrick S. OSMER
18 Assoc VP Facilities Op/Dev ... Ms. Mary L. READEY
07 Assoc VP UG Admissions/First-Yr Exp ... Mr. Vern GRANGER
21 Asst Vice Pres Business/Finance ... Vacant
13 Chief Information Officer ... Ms. Kathleen STARKOFF
08 Director of Libraries ... Ms. Carol P. DIEDRCHS
101 Secretary Board of Trustees ... Dr. David G. HORN
17 VP Health Svcs ... Dr. Peter E. GEIER
85 Vice Prov Global Strat/Intl Affs ... Dr. William I. BRUSTEIN
90 Int Exec Dir Ohio Supercomputr Ctr ... Mr. Steve GORDON
29 Sr VP for Alumni Relations ... Mr. Archie GRIFFIN
41 Director Athletics ... Mr. Gene SMITH
12 Executive Dean of Reg Campuses ... Vacant
49 Exec Dean Arts & Sciences ... Dr. Joseph E. STEINMETZ
88 Int Dean Colleges of Bio Sci & MPS ... Vacant
50 Dean Fisher Col of Business ... Dr. Christine A. POON
52 Dean College of Dentistry ... Dr. Patrick M. LLOYD
53 Dean College of Educ & Hum Ecology ... Dr. Cheryl L. ACHTERBERG

54 Dean College of Engineering ... Dr. David B. WILLIAMS
57 Dean Colleges of the Arts & Hum ... Vacant
79 Dean College of Humanities ... Vacant
61 Dean College of Law ... Dr. Alan C. MICHAELS
63 Dean College of Medicine ... Dr. Charles J. LOCKWOOD
81 Dean College Math/Physical Science ... Vacant
88 Dean College of Optometry ... Dr. Melvin D. SHIPP
67 Dean College of Pharmacy ... Dr. Robert W. BRUEGGEMEIER
69 Dean College of Public Health ... Dr. Stanley A. LEMESHOW
83 Dean College of Soc & Behav Sci ... Vacant
70 Dean College of Social Work ... Dr. Tom GREGOIRE
74 Dean Col Veterinary Medicine ... Dr. Lonnie KING
66 Dean College of Nursing ... Dr. Bernadette MELNYK
84 VP Strategic Enrollment Planning ... Mr. Dolan EVANOVICH
09 Asst VP Inst Research/Planning ... Ms. Julie CARPENTER-HUBIN
37 Director Student Financial Aid ... Ms. Diane L. STEMPER
88 Director of OES Analysis & Reportng ... Ms. Gail C. STEPHENOFF
39 Asst VP Student Life/Housing ... Mr. Fred FOTIS
06 University Registrar ... Mr. Bradley A. MYERS
38 Asst VP & Dir Younkin Success Ctr ... Ms. Louise A. DOUCE
96 Assoc Director of Purchasing ... Ms. Cris PENN
11 Sr Vice Pres Admin & Planning ... Mr. Jay D. KASEY
40 General Manager OSU Bookstores ... Ms. Kathy SMITH

The Ohio State University Agricultural Technical Institute (A)

1328 Dover Road, Wooster OH 44691-4000
County: Wayne FICE Identification: 010687
Unit ID: 204662
Telephone: (330) 264-3911 Carnegie Class: Assoc/Pub2in4
FAX Number: (330) 287-1333 Calendar System: Semester
URL: ati.osu.edu/
Established: 1971 Annual Undergrad Tuition & Fees (In-State): $6,327
Enrollment: 666 Coed
Affiliation or Control: State IRS Status: 501(c)3
Highest Offering: Associate Degree
Program: Occupational; 2-Year Principally Bachelor's Creditable
Accreditation: NH

01 Director ... Dr. Stephen P. NAMETH
20 Associate Director ... Dr. Steven M. NEAL
26 Public Relations Coordinator ... Ms. Frances P. WHITED
03 Assistant Director ... Dr. Rhonda BILLMAN
37 Coordinator Student Financial Aid ... Ms. Barbara LAMOREAUX
07 Manager of Enrollment ... Mr. David DIETRICH
21 Business Manager 2 ... Ms. Rita M. SMOLKO
32 Coordinator Student Programs ... Ms. Kathy E. MAKSYMICZ
40 Bookstore Manager ... Ms. Patricia A. PAXTON
08 Library Director ... Ms. Sharon HOLDERMAN
19 Assistant Chief Campus Police ... Mr. Gregory K. FERRELL
13 Systems Manager ... Mr. Rick L. MITCHELL
23 Staff Nurse ... Ms. Karen S. MYERS
50 Director Business Trng & Educ Svcs ... Ms. Kimberly J. SAYERS
39 Housing Coordinator ... Ms. Ashley E. BRIGHTBILL
88 Coordinator Disability Services ... Ms. Silvia H. HENRISS
88 Program Director Program EXCEL ... Ms. Dee Dee SNYDER
06 Academic Records Manager ... Ms. Peggy E. LAMBERT
29 Assistant to Director ... Ms. Helen THOMPSON
38 SOAR Coordinator Stdnt Success Svcs ... Ms. Nancy BROOKER

The Ohio State University at Lima Campus (B)

4240 Campus Drive, Lima OH 45804-3597
County: Allen FICE Identification: 003092
Unit ID: 204671
Telephone: (419) 995-8600 Carnegie Class: Bac/Diverse
FAX Number: (419) 995-8483 Calendar System: Semester
URL: lima.osu.edu/
Established: 1959 Annual Undergrad Tuition & Fees (In-State): $6,327
Enrollment: 1,306 Coed
Affiliation or Control: State IRS Status: 501(c)3
Highest Offering: Baccalaureate
Program: Liberal Arts And General
Accreditation: &NH

01 Dean & Director ... Dr. John R. SNYDER
05 Associate Dean ... Dr. Michael A. CUNNINGHAM
10 Assoc Director ... Mr. Devon N. PHELPS
101 Exec Asistant to Dean & Director ... Ms. Jeanne M. MOORMAN
20 Assistant Dean ... Dr. Roger L. NIMPS
37 Assistant Director Financial Aid ... Mr. Josh LUKE
08 Head Librarian ... Dr. Tina SCHNEIDER
27 Director of Communications ... Ms. Pamela K. JOSEPH
15 Human Resources Generalist ... Ms. Whitney CLARK
13 Director of Technology Services ... Mr. James M. KERR
24 Director Educational Technology ... Ms. Lynn A. TRINKO
88 Dir Academic Advising & Fin Aid ... Mr. Bryan ALBRIGHT
36 Coordinator of Career Services ... Vacant
30 Director of Development ... Ms. Amanda L. MILLER
06 Coordinator Student Records ... Mr. Kevin SMITH
32 Director of Student Life ... Mr. John UPSHAW
07 Sr Assistant Director of Admissions ... Ms. Sara AMBROZA
21 Business Services Officer ... Ms. Cheri L. WISE
35 Coordinator Student Programs ... Vacant
28 Coordinator Minority Affairs ... Ms. Temple PATTON

† Regional accreditation is carried under the parent institution in Columbus, OH.

The Ohio State University Mansfield Campus (C)

1760 University Drive, Mansfield OH 44906-1599
County: Richland FICE Identification: 003093
Unit ID: 204680
Telephone: (419) 755-4011 Carnegie Class: Bac/Assoc
FAX Number: (419) 755-4241 Calendar System: Semester
URL: mansfield.osu.edu/
Established: 1958 Annual Undergrad Tuition & Fees (In-State): $6,327
Enrollment: 1,388 Coed
Affiliation or Control: State IRS Status: 501(c)3
Highest Offering: Baccalaureate
Program: Liberal Arts And General; Teacher Preparatory
Accreditation: &NH

01 Dean & Director ... Dr. Stephen M. GAVAZZI
05 Associate Dean ... Dr. David TOVEY
08 Int Director Broomfield Library ... Vacant
07 Director Admissions & Financial Aid ... Mr. Kenneth SIGLER
15 Human Resources Officer ... Ms. Cathy STIMPERT
18 Supt Phys Fac Security & Custodial ... Mr. Brian WHITE
32 Chief Student Life & Retention Ofcr ... Dr. Donna HIGHT
10 Fiscal Officer ... Ms. Carol FREYTAG
26 Asst Director University Relations ... Mr. Rodger C. SMITH
13 Senior Systems Manager ... Mr. Major PRICE
06 Registrar ... Vacant
21 Office Assistant Business Office ... Ms. Heather ARMSTRONG
30 Director of Development ... Mr. Andronic OROSAN
88 Coord Min Affairs & Student Success ... Mr. Dametraus JAGGERS
88 Coordinator of Student Engagement ... Ms. Elise RIGGLE

† Regional accreditation is carried under the parent institution in Columbus, OH.

The Ohio State University at Marion (D)

1465 Mount Vernon Avenue, Marion OH 43302-5628
County: Marion FICE Identification: 003094
Unit ID: 204699
Telephone: (740) 389-6786 Carnegie Class: Bac/Assoc
FAX Number: (614) 292-5817 Calendar System: Semester
URL: osumarion.osu.edu
Established: 1957 Annual Undergrad Tuition & Fees (In-State): $6,327
Enrollment: 1,525 Coed
Affiliation or Control: State IRS Status: 501(c)3
Highest Offering: Master's
Program: Liberal Arts And General
Accreditation: &NH

01 Dean & Director ... Dr. Gregory S. ROSE
05 Associate Dean ... Dr. Bishun PANDEY
20 Assistant Dean ... Dr. Leslie BEYER-HERMSEN
08 Head Librarian ... Ms. Betsy BLANKENSHIP
88 Director Alber Enteprise Center ... Ms. Myra WILSON
06 Records Mgmt Officer/Registrar ... Ms. Karin LANIUS
15 Human Resource Manager ... Ms. Maryjo MUNDEY
07 Asst Dir Enrollment Management ... Mr. Matt MOREAU
32 Director Student Activities ... Mr. Dave BECKEL
30 Dir Community Rels & Development ... Mr. Dave CLABORN
18 Supt/Facility Maint & Security ... Mr. Ron TURNER
10 Senior Fiscal Officer ... Ms. Karen CARROLL
26 Manager Communications/Marketing ... Mr. Wayne ROWE
38 Asst Dir Academic Advising ... Ms. Chris TRAPP
36 Coordinator Career Services ... Mr. Will SMITH
28 Coordinator Diversity Initiatives ... Mr. Shawn JACKSON
41 Director Athletics ... Mr. Mark SISLER

† Regional accreditation is carried under the parent institution in Columbus, OH.

The Ohio State University Newark Campus (E)

1179 University Drive, Newark OH 43055-9990
County: Licking FICE Identification: 003095
Unit ID: 204705
Telephone: (740) 366-3321 Carnegie Class: Bac/Assoc
FAX Number: (740) 366-5047 Calendar System: Semester
URL: www.newark.osu.edu
Established: 1957 Annual Undergrad Tuition & Fees (In-State): $6,327
Enrollment: 2,627 Coed
Affiliation or Control: State IRS Status: 501(c)3
Highest Offering: Baccalaureate
Program: Liberal Arts And General
Accreditation: &NH

01 Dean/Director ... Dr. William L. MACDONALD
32 Director of Student Life ... Mr. John BERRY
10 Dir Business & Finance ... Mr. David BRILLHART
16 Dir HR/Camp Rel & Planning Support ... Ms. Jacqueline PARRILL
08 Directory of Library ... Ms. Susan SCOTT
05 Associate Dean ... Dr. Paul SANDERS
07 Director of Enrollment ... Ms. Ann DONAHUE
37 Director of Financial Aid ... Ms. Faith PHILLIPS
96 Purchasing/Auxiliary Services Mgr ... Vacant
18 Supt Facilities Operations ... Vacant
06 Registrar ... Vacant
21 Director of Business Affairs ... Mr. Douglas WARTHEN
28 Pgm Manager Multi-Cultural Affairs ... Ms. Vorley TAYLOR

38 Personal Counselor ... Ms. Susan ADAMS
41 Pgm Coord Athletics/Phys Ed & Rec ... Mr. Bret WHITAKER
30 Director of Development ... Ms. Jennifer ROBERTS
26 Marketing & Public Relations Dir ... Ms. Alice HUTZEL-BATESON

† Regional accreditation is carried under the parent institution in Columbus, OH.

Ohio Technical College (F)

1374 E 51st Street, Cleveland OH 44103-1269
County: Cuyahoga FICE Identification: 011745
Unit ID: 204608
Telephone: (216) 881-1700 Carnegie Class: Assoc/PrivFP
FAX Number: (216) 881-9145 Calendar System: Quarter
URL: www.ohiotechnicalcollege.com
Established: 1969 Annual Undergrad Tuition & Fees: $26,280
Enrollment: 1,107 Coed
Affiliation or Control: Proprietary IRS Status: Proprietary
Highest Offering: Associate Degree
Program: Occupational
Accreditation: ACCSC

01 Director ... Mr. Tom KING

Ohio University Main Campus (G)

Athens OH 45701-2979
County: Athens FICE Identification: 003100
Unit ID: 204857
Telephone: (740) 593-1000 Carnegie Class: RU/H
FAX Number: N/A Calendar System: Quarter
URL: www.ohiou.edu
Established: 1804 Annual Undergrad Tuition & Fees (In-State): $10,216
Enrollment: 36,126 Coed
Affiliation or Control: State IRS Status: 501(c)3
Highest Offering: Doctorate
Program: Liberal Arts And General; Teacher Preparatory; Professional
Accreditation: NH, AAFCS, ADNUR, ART, AUD, BUS, BUSA, CACREP, CIDA, CLPSY, CORE, CS, DANCE, DIETD, ENG, ENGR, JOUR, MUS, NAIT, NRPA, NURSE, OSTEO, PH, PTA, SP, SW, TED, THEA

01 President ... Dr. Roderick J. MCDAVIS
100 Chief of Staff ... Ms. Jennifer KIRKSEY
05 Executive Vice President & Provost ... Dr. Pam BENOIT
10 VP for Finance & Administration ... Mr. Stephen T. GOLDING
32 Interim VP for Student Affairs ... Mr. Ryan LOMBARDI
30 VP Univ Advance/Pres/CEO OU Fdn ... Mr. Bryan BENCHOFF
27 Chief Information Officer ... Mr. J. Brice BIBLE
46 VP Research & Dean Grad College ... Dr. Joseph SHIELDS
84 Vice Provost Enrollment Management ... Mr. Craig CORNELL
43 General Counsel ... Mr. John J. BIANCAMANO
26 Exec Dir Comm/Marketing ... Ms. Renea MORRIS
80 Director of Government Relations ... Mr. Eric BURCHARD
88 Exec V Provost /Dean Univ Col ... Dr. David N. DESCUTNER
49 Dean College of Arts & Sciences ... Dr. Robert FRANK
50 Dean College of Business ... Dr. Hugh SHERMAN
60 Int Dean Scripps Col Communication ... Dr. Scott TITSWORTH
53 Dean Patton College of Education ... Dr. Renee A. MIDDLETON
54 Dean Russ Col Engineering/Tech ... Dr. Dennis IRWIN
57 Int Dean College of Fine Arts ... Ms. Madeleine SCOTT
69 Dean Col Health/Human Services ... Dr. Randy LEITE
92 Dean Honors Tutorial College ... Dr. Jeremy WEBSTER
63 Dean Heritage Col Osteopathic Med ... Dr. Kenneth JOHNSON
62 Dean University Libraries ... Mr. Scott H. SEAMAN
35 Int Dean of Students ... Dr. Jenny HALL-JONES
12 Int Exec Dean Regional Campuses ... Dr. James W. FONSECA
12 Dean Eastern Campus ... Dr. Richard GREENLEE
12 Dean Southern Campus ... Dr. William WILLAN
12 Int Dean Chillicothe Campus ... Dr. Martin TUCK
12 Dean Lancaster Campus ... Dr. James SMITH
12 Dean Zanesville Campus ... Dr. James W. FONSECA
20 Associate Provost Academic Affairs ... Vacant
58 Director Graduate Student Services ... Dr. Katherine TADLOCK
88 Int Exec Dir Ctr for Intl Studies ... Dr. Ming LI
28 Int Vice Prov Diversity & Inclusion ... Dr. David DESCUTNER
09 Assoc Prov Inst Rsrch/Assessment ... Dr. A. Michael WILLIFORD
41 Director of Athletics ... Mr. Jim SCHAUS
06 University Registrar ... Mrs. Debra M. BENTON
18 Assoc VP Finance/Admin/Facilities ... Mr. Harry WYATT
15 Assoc VP for Human Resources ... Ms. Linda LONSINGER
22 Director Institutional Equity ... Dr. Laura MYERS
29 Int Exec Director Alumni Relations ... Ms. Connie ROMINE
36 Asst Dean for Career Services ... Mr. Imants JAUNARAJS
07 Asst Vice Provost/Dir Ungrad Admiss ... Ms. Candice BOEHNINGER
38 Director Counseling Services ... Vacant
44 Exec Dir of Develop Planned Giving ... Ms. Kelli BELL
37 Director Student Financial Aid ... Ms. Valerie MILLER
23 Medical Dir of Campus Care ... Dr. John J. KEMERER
87 Director Summer Sessions ... Dr. Pamela J. BROWN
96 Director of Procurement Services ... Ms. Laura NOWICKI
19 Chief of Police/Dir Campus Safety ... Mr. Andrew POWERS
85 Assoc Dir Intl Students/Fac Svcs ... Ms. Krista M. BEATTY
39 Asst Vice Pres Auxiliary Services ... Ms. Christine SHEETS
88 Asst VP for Economic & Tech Devel ... Vacant
25 Asst VP Res & Sponsored Programs ... Mr. Shane L. GILKEY
24 Media Library Manager ... Ms. Robin KRIVESTI

Ohio University Chillicothe Campus (A)

PO Box 629, 101 University Drive, Chillicothe OH 45601-0629

County: Ross FICE Identification: 003102
Unit ID: 204820
Telephone: (740) 774-7200 Carnegie Class: Assoc/Pub4
FAX Number: (740) 774-7295 Calendar System: Semester
URL: www.chillicothe.ohiou.edu
Established: 1946 Annual Undergrad Tuition & Fees (In-State): $5,034
Enrollment: 2,400 Coed
Affiliation or Control: State IRS Status: 501(c)3
Highest Offering: Baccalaureate
Program: Occupational; 2-Year Principally Bachelor's Creditable
Accreditation: &NH

01 Dean .... Dr. Martin TUCK
05 Associate Dean .... Dr. James MCKEAN
08 Head Librarian .... Mr. Allan POLLCHIK
13 Dir Information/Technology Services .... Vacant
18 Director Facilities Management .... Mr. David SCOTT
15 Director Personnel Services .... Ms. Jonna DEPUGH
26 Chief Public Relations Officer .... Mr. Jack JEFFERY
30 Chief Development .... Ms. Joyce ATWOOD
41 Athletic Director .... Ms. Kim MCKIMMY
36 Coordinator of Student Support .... Mrs. Martha TANEDO
32 Coord of Student Affs/Stdnt Fin Aid ... Mrs. Ashlee RAUCKHORST
07 Coordinator of Student Recruitment .... Mrs. Neeley CLARY

† Regional accreditation is carried under the parent institution in Athens, OH.

Ohio University Eastern Campus (B)

45425 National Road, Saint Clairsville OH 43950-9724

County: Belmont FICE Identification: 003101
Unit ID: 204802
Telephone: (740) 695-1720 Carnegie Class: Assoc/Pub4
FAX Number: (740) 695-7077 Calendar System: Quarter
URL: www.eastern.ohiou.edu
Established: 1957 Annual Undergrad Tuition & Fees (In-State): $4,527
Enrollment: 1,017 Coed
Affiliation or Control: State IRS Status: 501(c)3
Highest Offering: Master's
Program: 2-Year Principally Bachelor's Creditable; Liberal Arts And General; Teacher Preparatory; Professional
Accreditation: &NH

01 Campus Dean .... Dr. Richard W. GREENLEE
05 Associate Dean .... Mr. Michael MCTEAGUE
30 Assistant Dean for Development .... Vacant
20 Faculty Chairperson .... Dr. David CASTLE
10 Chief Business Officer .... Ms. Rosanna LEMASTERS
08 Director of Library .... Ms. Donna CAPEZZUTO
24 Director of Media .... Mr. Jay MORRIS
26 Director of Marketing .... Mr. E.J SCHODZINSKI
18 Director of Physical Plant .... Mr. Steven MCGUFFIN
17 Director Health/Phys Educ Center .... Mr. E.J SCHODZINSKI
40 Director Bookstore .... Mrs. Tammy WARD
32 Director Student Services .... Mr. Kevin CHENOWETH
13 Computer Resources Coordinator .... Mr. Trent DUFFY
14 Computer/Technology Specialist .... Mr. Peter LIM

† Regional accreditation is carried under the parent institution in Athens, OH.

Ohio University Lancaster Campus (C)

1570 Granville Pike, Lancaster OH 43130-1097

County: Fairfield FICE Identification: 003104
Unit ID: 204848
Telephone: (740) 654-6711 Carnegie Class: Assoc/Pub4
FAX Number: (740) 687-9497 Calendar System: Semester
URL: www.ohiou.edu/lancaster
Established: 1968 Annual Undergrad Tuition & Fees (In-State): $4,956
Enrollment: 2,514 Coed
Affiliation or Control: State IRS Status: 501(c)3
Highest Offering: Master's
Program: Occupational; 2-Year Principally Bachelor's Creditable; Liberal Arts And General
Accreditation: &NH, MAC

01 Dean .... Dr. James SMITH
05 Associate Dean .... Dr. Paul ABRAHAM
30 Director of Development .... Ms. Mandi CUSTER
18 Interim Director of Physical Plant .... Mr. Mark BATESON
41 Athletic Director .... Mr. Jeff WHITEHEAD
08 Librarian .... Ms. Judy CAREY NEVIN
84 Student Services Enrollment Manager .... Ms. Patricia FOX
51 Interim Dir of Community & Corp .... Mr. Ron CULLUMS
49 Coord Arts/Communicatns/ Humanities .... Dr. Candice THOMAS-MADDOX
72 Coord Science & Technology Division ..... Dr. Franco GUERRIERO
83 Coord Social Sciences/Applied Stds .... Ms. Janet BECKER
90 Director Computer Svcs/Instr Tech .... Mr. Paul ALLEN
26 Mgr of Communications & Mktg .... Ms. Cheri RUSSO
10 Budget Manager .... Ms. Gwen WHITEHEAD

† Regional accreditation is carried under the parent institution in Athens, OH.

Ohio University Southern Campus (D)

1804 Liberty Avenue, Ironton OH 45638-2279

County: Lawrence Identification: 666000
Unit ID: 204839
Telephone: (740) 533-4600 Carnegie Class: Assoc/Pub4
FAX Number: (740) 533-4632 Calendar System: Quarter
URL: www.southern.ohiou.edu
Established: 1953 Annual Undergrad Tuition & Fees (In-State): $4,527
Enrollment: 1,983 Coed
Affiliation or Control: State IRS Status: 501(c)3
Highest Offering: Associate Degree
Program: Occupational; 2-Year Principally Bachelor's Creditable
Accreditation: &NH

01 President .... Dr. Roderick J. MCDAVIS
05 Dean .... Dr. William WILLAN
84 Dir Enrollment/Student Services .... Mr. Robert PLEASANT

† Regional accreditation is carried under the parent institution in Athens, OH.

Ohio University Zanesville Branch (E)

1425 Newark Road, Zanesville OH 43701-2695

County: Muskingum FICE Identification: 003108
Unit ID: 204866
Telephone: (740) 453-0762 Carnegie Class: Assoc/Pub4
FAX Number: (740) 453-6161 Calendar System: Quarter
URL: www.zanesville.ohiou.edu
Established: 1946 Annual Undergrad Tuition & Fees (In-State): $5,038
Enrollment: 2,106 Coed
Affiliation or Control: State IRS Status: 501(c)3
Highest Offering: Master's
Program: Occupational; 2-Year Principally Bachelor's Creditable; Liberal Arts And General
Accreditation: &NH

01 Interim Dean .... Dr. Richard GREENLEE
05 Associate Dean .... Dr. Alan PUNCHES
30 Assistant Dean for Development .... Mrs. Cindy LINN
32 Director of Student Services .... Ms. Susan MONTGOMERY
08 Library Director .... Mr. Tony HOPKINS
66 Associate Director of Nursing .... Mrs. Pamela SEALOVER
18 Director of Operations .... Mr. Joe KEATING
35 Associate Director Student Services .... Mr. Jason HOWARD
37 Financial Aid Coordinator .... Mrs. Vicki DELUCAS

† Regional accreditation is carried under the parent institution in Athens, OH.

Ohio Valley College of Technology (F)

15258 State Route 170, East Liverpool OH 43920

County: Columbiana FICE Identification: 023014
Unit ID: 204884
Telephone: (330) 385-1070 Carnegie Class: Assoc/PrivFP
FAX Number: (330) 385-4606 Calendar System: Semester
URL: www.ovct.edu
Established: 1886 Annual Undergrad Tuition & Fees: $10,580
Enrollment: 206 Coed
Affiliation or Control: Proprietary IRS Status: Proprietary
Highest Offering: Associate Degree
Program: Occupational; 2-Year Principally Bachelor's Creditable; Technical Emphasis
Accreditation: ACICS, MAC

01 President/Executive Director .... Mr. Scott S. ROGERS

Ohio Wesleyan University (G)

61 S Sandusky Street, Delaware OH 43015-2398

County: Delaware FICE Identification: 003109
Unit ID: 204909
Telephone: (740) 368-2000 Carnegie Class: Bac/A&S
FAX Number: (740) 368-3299 Calendar System: Semester
URL: www.owu.edu
Established: 1842 Annual Undergrad Tuition & Fees: $38,890
Enrollment: 1,850 Coed
Affiliation or Control: United Methodist IRS Status: 501(c)3
Highest Offering: Baccalaureate
Program: Liberal Arts And General
Accreditation: NH, MUS, TED

01 President .... Dr. Rockwell F. JONES
05 Interim Provost .... Dr. Charles L. STINEMETZ
10 VP for Finance/Administration .... Mr. Eric S. ALGOE
26 Vice Pres for University Relations .... Ms. Colleen GARLAND
84 Vice Pres for Enrollment .... Ms. Rebecca R. ECKSTEIN
32 Vice President for Student Affairs .... Dr. Craig E. ULLOM
07 Asst VP Admissions/Financial Aid .... Mr. Lee HARRELL
30 Asst Vice Pres University Relations .... Mr. Christopher J. DELISIO
20 Interim Dean of Academic Affairs .... Dr. Barbara S. ANDERECK
09 Assoc Dean Inst Research .... Dr. Dale E. SWARTZENTRUBER
88 Assoc Dean Assessment/Accreditation . Dr. Barbara S. ANDERECK
36 Director of Career Services .... Ms. Leslie DELERME
06 Registrar .... Ms. Shelly A. MCMAHON
08 Chief Info Officer/Dir of Libraries .... Ms. Cathi CARDWELL
14 Director of Computer Center .... Mr. Harold D. WIEBE
13 Exec Director Information Tech .... Mr. Brian A. RELLINGER
19 Director of Public Safety .... Mr. Robert A. WOOD
29 Director Alumni Relations .... Ms. Brenda E. DEWITT
26 Director Marketing/Communications .... Mr. Mark E. COOPER
85 Director International Student Svcs .... Mr. Darrell J. ALBON
18 Director Physical Plant .... Mr. Peter K. SCHANTZ
15 Director Human Resources .... Ms. Debra A. GUILBERT
31 Director Community Svc Learning .... Ms. Sally LEBER
11 Director of Administrative Services .... Ms. Susan COOPERIDER
04 Asst to President/Board Secy .... Ms. Lisa D. JACKSON
23 Director Wellness Center .... Ms. Marsha A. TILDEN
35 Dean of Students .... Dr. Kimberlie L. GOLDSBERRY
39 Director Residential Life .... Ms. Wendy L. PIPER
41 Director of Athletics .... Mr. Roger D. INGLES
42 Chaplain .... Rev. Jon R. POWERS
89 Dean First Year Students .... Vacant
92 Honors Program Codirector .... Dr. Edward H. BURTT
92 Honors Program Codirector .... Dr. Amy MCCLURE
93 Dir Multicultural Student Affairs .... Ms. Terree L. STEVENSON
102 Dir Foundation/Corp/Govt Relations .... Ms. Karen CROSMAN
07 Associate Director of Admissions .... Ms. Alisha M. COUCH
88 Special Assistant to the President .... Mr. Mark H. SHIPPS
40 Bookstore Manager .... Mr. Kevin U. STITH
38 Coord Counseling/Career/Health Svcs .... Dr. Colleen M. COOK

Otterbein University (H)

1 South Grove Street, Westerville OH 43081-2006

County: Franklin FICE Identification: 003110
Unit ID: 204936
Telephone: (614) 890-3000 Carnegie Class: Master's M
FAX Number: (614) 823-3114 Calendar System: Semester
URL: www.otterbein.edu
Established: 1847 Annual Undergrad Tuition & Fees: $30,658
Enrollment: 2,997 Coed
Affiliation or Control: United Methodist IRS Status: 501(c)3
Highest Offering: Doctorate
Program: Liberal Arts And General; Teacher Preparatory; Professional
Accreditation: NH, ANEST, MUS, NUR, NURSE, TED, THEA

01 President .... Dr. Kathy A. KRENDL
100 Chief of Staff .... Ms. Kristi ROBBINS
05 Vice President Academic Affairs .... Dr. Victoria MCGILLIN
32 Vice President Student Affairs .... Mr. Robert M. GATTI
10 Vice President for Business Affairs .... Mrs. Rebecca D. VAZQUEZ-SKILLINGS
30 VP Institutional Advancement .... Ms. Heidi L. TRACY
84 Vice President for Enrollment .... Mr. Jefferson BLACKBURN-SMITH
20 Assoc VP AA/Dean Academic Services .... Dr. Susan R. FAGAN
91 Exec Director of Information Tech .... Mr. Jeff KASSON
08 Director of the Library .... Mrs. Lois F. SZUDY
06 Registrar .... Mr. Donald W. FOSTER
26 Exec Dir Marketing/Communications .... Mrs. Jennifer PEARCE
36 Director Career Planning/Placement .... Mr. Ryan BRECHBILL
37 Director of Financial Aid .... Mr. Thomas V. YARNELL
41 Athletic Director .... Ms. Dawn STEWART
42 Chaplain .... Rev. Monty E. BRADLEY
51 Assoc Dean Grad & Cont Studies .... Ms. Kate CAREY
107 Dean School of Prof Studies .... Dr. Barbara H. SCHAFFNER
49 Dean School of Arts/Sciences .... Dr. Paul EISENSTEIN
85 Exec Director Intl Programs .... Mr. Chris MUSICK
07 Director of Admissions .... Mr. Ben SHOEMAKER
15 Director Human Resources .... Vacant
18 Director/Physical Plant .... Mr. David D. BELL
29 Director Alumni Relations .... Ms. Rebecca F. SMITH
28 Director of Diversity .... Dr. Lisa PATTERSON
96 Director of Purchasing .... Mr. Steven H. ROSENBERGER
21 Inst Rsrch Spec/Financial Analyst .... Mr. Christopher A. HAYTER
09 Asst VP for Institutional Planning .... Dr. Barbara I. WHARTON
19 Director of Security .... Mr. Larry BANASZAK
04 Executive Assistant to President .... Vacant

Owens Community College (I)

30335 Oregon, PO Box 10000, Toledo OH 43699-1947

County: Wood FICE Identification: 005753
Unit ID: 204945
Telephone: (567) 661-7000 Carnegie Class: Assoc/Pub-U-MC
FAX Number: N/A Calendar System: Semester
URL: www.owens.edu
Established: 1965 Annual Undergrad Tuition & Fees (In-State): $3,674
Enrollment: 16,669 Coed
Affiliation or Control: State IRS Status: 501(c)3
Highest Offering: Associate Degree
Program: Occupational; 2-Year Principally Bachelor's Creditable
Accreditation: NH, ACBSP, DH, DIETT, DMS, EMT, MAC, NAIT, OTA, PTAA, RAD, SURGT

01 President .... Dr. Mike BOWER
101 Secretary to the Board of Trustees .... Ms. Patricia JEZAK
04 Executive Assistant to President .... Ms. Vicki HENERY
05 Vice President/Provost .... Dr. Renay SCOTT
10 Vice Pres Finance Admin/CFO .... Mr. John SATKOWSKI
16 VP Human Resources .... Mr. Jack WITT
108 Assoc VP Assessment/Accreditation .... Mr. Thomas PERIN
20 Associate Vice Provost .... Ms. Tamara WILLIAMS
30 Exec Director College Development .... Ms. Ann SAVAGE
103 Associate VP Workforce/Cmty Service .... Dr. Michael BANKEY
12 Associate VP Findlay Campus .... Dr. Melissa GREEN
32 Assoc Vice Provost Student Svcs .... Dr. Cynthia SPIERS
21 Assoc VP Business Affs/Controller .... Ms. Pam BECK
13 Chief Information Officer .... Ms. Connie SCHAFFER
19 Chief of Police .... Mr. John BETORI

37 Associate Director Financial Aid ... Ms. Susanne SCHWARCK
18 Assoc Vice President Operations ... Mr. Michael MCDONALD
09 Director Organizational Research ... Ms. Debra RATHKE
72 Dean School of Technology ... Mr. Randy WHARTON
84 Dean Student Enrollment ... Dr. Betsy JOHNSON
76 Dean School of Health Sciences ... Dr. Doug MEAD
66 Dean School of Nursing ... Ms. Dawn WETMORE
50 Interim Dean School of Business ... Dr. Gretchen CARROLL
49 Dean School of Arts & Sciences ... Dr. Laurie FATHE
62 Dean Library ... Mr. Tom SINK
106 Director eLearning ... Mr. Mark KARAMOL
43 In-House Legal Counsel ... Dr. Natalie JACKSON
22 Equal Opp/Inclusiveness Officer ... Ms. Lisa DUBOSE
06 Registrar ... Vacant
26 Director Marketing/Communications ... Dr. Gary CORRIGAN
29 Director Alumni Affairs ... Ms. Laura MOORE
35 Director Student Life ... Mr. Chris GIORDANO
07 Director Admissions/Career Service ... Mr. Joseph CARONE
36 Specialist Admiss/Career Services ... Ms. Gentry DIXON
40 Director Bookstore/Food Services ... Mr. David WAHR
85 Director International Programs ... Ms. Deborah GAVLIK
41 Athletics Director ... Vacant

Payne Theological Seminary (A)

PO Box 474, Wilberforce OH 45384-0474
County: Greene FICE Identification: 010017
Unit ID: 204990
Telephone: (937) 376-2946 Carnegie Class: Spec/Faith
FAX Number: (937) 376-3330 Calendar System: 4/1/4
URL: www.payne.edu
Established: 1844 Annual Graduate Tuition & Fees: $7,240
Enrollment: 151 Coed
Affiliation or Control: African Methodist Episcopal IRS Status: 501(c)3
Highest Offering: Master's; No Undergraduates
Program: Professional
Accreditation: THEOL

01 President ... Rev Dr. Leah GASKIN-FITCHUE
05 Interim Academic Dean ... Dr. William J. AUGMAN, JR.
30 Director of Development ... Rev. Jules HOWIE
36 Director of Planning & Placement ... Vacant
08 Head Librarian ... Mr. George JOHNSON

Pontifical College Josephinum (B)

7625 N High Street, Columbus OH 43235-1498
County: Franklin FICE Identification: 003113
Unit ID: 205027
Telephone: (614) 885-5585 Carnegie Class: Spec/Faith
FAX Number: (614) 885-2307 Calendar System: Semester
URL: www.pcj.edu
Established: 1888 Annual Undergrad Tuition & Fees: $19,239
Enrollment: 175 Male
Affiliation or Control: Roman Catholic IRS Status: 501(c)3
Highest Offering: Master's
Program: Liberal Arts And General; Professional; Religious Emphasis
Accreditation: NH, THEOL

01 Rector/President ... R.Msgr. Christopher J. SCHRECK
03 Vice President ... Vacant
03 Vice Rector School of Theology ... Rev. Walter R. OXLEY
30 Vice President Advancement ... R.Msgr. Christopher J. SCHRECK
49 Vice Rector College Liberal Arts ... Rev. John F. HEISLER
05 Academic Dean ... Dr. Michael D. ROSS
20 Assistant Academic Dean ... Dr. David J. DE LEONARDIS
10 Treasurer ... Mr. John ERWIN
06 Registrar ... Ms. Danielle ANDREWS
08 Librarian ... Mr. Peter G. VERACKA
33 Dean of Men In Theology ... R.Msgr. Micahel A. OSBORN
33 Dean of Men In College ... Rev. John ROZEMBAJGIER
07 Director of Admissions College ... Rev. John F. HEISLER
37 Financial Aid Director ... Mrs. Marky LEICHTNAM

Professional Skills Institute (C)

1505 Holland Road, Maumee OH 43537
County: Lucas FICE Identification: 023377
Unit ID: 205054
Telephone: (419) 720-6670 Carnegie Class: Assoc/PrivFP
FAX Number: (419) 720-6674 Calendar System: Quarter
URL: www.proskills.edu
Established: 1984 Annual Undergrad Tuition & Fees: $11,550
Enrollment: 490 Coed
Affiliation or Control: Proprietary IRS Status: Proprietary
Highest Offering: Associate Degree
Program: Occupational; 2-Year Principally Bachelor's Creditable; Nursing Emphasis
Accreditation: ABHES, PTAA

01 CEO ... Mr. Daniel FINCH
07 Admissions Coordinator ... Mr. Tony DICKENS

Rabbinical College of Telshe (D)

28400 Euclid Avenue, Wickliffe OH 44092-2584
County: Lake FICE Identification: 003115
Unit ID: 205124
Telephone: (440) 943-5300 Carnegie Class: Spec/Faith
FAX Number: (440) 943-5303 Calendar System: Quarter
Established: 1941 Annual Undergrad Tuition & Fees: $8,000
Enrollment: 74 Male
Affiliation or Control: Independent Non-Profit IRS Status: 501(c)3
Highest Offering: Doctorate
Program: Teacher Preparatory; Professional
Accreditation: RABN

01 President ... Rabbi Shlomo EISENBERGER
06 Registrar ... Rabbi Abraham MATITIA

Remington College Cleveland Campus (E)

14445 Broadway Avenue, Cleveland OH 44125-1900
County: Cuyahoga FICE Identification: 007777
Unit ID: 375416
Telephone: (216) 475-7520 Carnegie Class: Assoc/PrivFP
FAX Number: (216) 475-6055 Calendar System: Other
URL: www.remingtoncollege.edu
Established: 1990 Annual Undergrad Tuition & Fees: $16,686
Enrollment: 592 Coed
Affiliation or Control: Proprietary IRS Status: Proprietary
Highest Offering: Associate Degree
Program: Occupational
Accreditation: ACCSC

01 President ... Mr. Patrick RESETAR

Rosedale Bible College (F)

2270 Rosedale Road, Irwin OH 43029-9517
County: Madison FICE Identification: 034253
Unit ID: 439899
Telephone: (740) 857-1311 Carnegie Class: Assoc/PrivNFP
FAX Number: (877) 857-1312 Calendar System: Semester
URL: www.rosedale.edu
Established: 1952 Annual Undergrad Tuition & Fees: $8,401
Enrollment: 80 Coed
Affiliation or Control: Mennonite Church IRS Status: 501(c)3
Highest Offering: Associate Degree
Program: 2-Year Principally Bachelor's Creditable; Religious Emphasis
Accreditation: BI

01 President ... Mr. Daniel ZIEGLER
05 Academic Dean ... Mr. Phil WEBER
32 Dean of Students ... Mr. Chris JONES
10 Business Manager ... Mr. Alfred YODER
84 Director of Enrollment Services ... Ms. Elizabeth DILLER
08 Director of Library Services ... Mr. Reuben SAIRS
06 Registrar ... Ms. Bethany GEIB
21 Associate Business Officer ... Mr. Lynford SCHROCK
26 Chief Public Relations Officer ... Mr. Kenneth MILLER

Saint Mary Seminary and Graduate School of Theology (G)

28700 Euclid Avenue, Wickliffe OH 44092-2585
County: Lake FICE Identification: 004061
Unit ID: 205319
Telephone: (440) 943-7600 Carnegie Class: Not Classified
FAX Number: (440) 943-7577 Calendar System: Semester
URL: www.stmarysem.edu
Established: 1848 Annual Graduate Tuition & Fees: $9,825
Enrollment: 130 Coed
Affiliation or Control: Roman Catholic IRS Status: 501(c)3
Highest Offering: Doctorate; No Undergraduates
Program: Professional; Religious Emphasis
Accreditation: NH, THEOL

01 President/Rector ... V.Rev. Mark A. LATCOVICH
05 Academic Dean/Dean of Students ... V.Rev. Mark A. LATCOVICH
06 Registrar ... Sr. Brendon ZAJAC, SND
08 Librarian ... Mr. Alan K. ROME
42 Spiritual Director ... Rev. Mark HOLLIS
10 Treasurer ... Mr. Philip GUBAN

School of Advertising Art (H)

1725 E David Road, Dayton OH 45440-1612
County: Montgomery FICE Identification: 025530
Unit ID: 205391
Telephone: (877) 300-9866 Carnegie Class: Assoc/PrivFP
FAX Number: (937) 294-5869 Calendar System: Quarter
URL: www.saa.edu
Established: 1983 Annual Undergrad Tuition & Fees: $267,230
Enrollment: 110 Coed
Affiliation or Control: Proprietary IRS Status: Proprietary
Highest Offering: Associate Degree
Program: Occupational; 2-Year Principally Bachelor's Creditable; Technical Emphasis
Accreditation: ACCSC

00 Owner ... Ms. Linda POTTER
01 President/Creative Director ... Ms. Jessica GRAVES
03 Vice President ... Mr. Matt FLICK
06 Vice President/HR/Registrar ... Mr. Nathan SUMMERS
05 Director of Education ... Ms. Jennifer LORENZETTI
36 Director of Career Services & PR ... Ms. Roxann PATRICK
37 Director of Financial Aid ... Ms. Tracy GARDNER

Shawnee State University (I)

940 Second Street, Portsmouth OH 45662-4344
County: Scioto FICE Identification: 009942
Unit ID: 205443
Telephone: (740) 351-3205 Carnegie Class: Bac/A&S
FAX Number: (740) 351-3470 Calendar System: Semester
URL: www.shawnee.edu
Established: 1975 Annual Undergrad Tuition & Fees (In-State): $6,988
Enrollment: 4,684 Coed
Affiliation or Control: State IRS Status: 501(c)3
Highest Offering: Master's
Program: Occupational; Liberal Arts And General; Teacher Preparatory
Accreditation: NH, ADNUR, DH, MLTAD, NUR, OT, OTA, PTAA, RAD, TED

01 President ... Dr. Rita R. MORRIS
05 Provost/VP Academic Affairs ... Dr. David TODT
10 Vice President for Finance & Admin ... Ms. Elinda C. BOYLES
32 Vice President for Student Affairs ... Dr. Mary OLING-SISAY
43 General Counsel/Asst to the Pres ... Ms. Cheryl HACKER
84 Assoc Vice Pres Enrollment Mgmt ... Mr. Robert J. TRUSZ
20 Associate Provost ... Dr. Paul MADDEN
26 Director Communications ... Ms. Elizabeth BLEVINS
107 Dean Professional Studies ... Dr. Jim KADEL
49 Dean College Arts & Sciences ... Dr. Timothy E. SCHEURER
08 Director Library ... Vacant
13 Director Univ Information Systems ... Mr. Charles WARNER
30 Director of Development ... Mr. Eric BRAUN
07 Director of Admission & Retention ... Mr. Robert J. TRUSZ
06 Registrar ... Mr. Mark MOORE
15 Director of Human Resources/Payroll ... Vacant
41 Athletic Director ... Mr. Jeff HAMILTON
37 Director of Financial Aid ... Dr. Nicole NEAL
36 Director Career Services ... Mr. Stephen GREGORY
38 Director of Counseling & Psych Svcs ... Dr. Michael J. HUGHES
21 Assoc VP for Finance & Admin ... Ms. Joanne CHARLES
88 Dean University College ... Dr. Brenda HAAS
86 Director of Government Relations ... Mr. John CAREY
85 Director for International Pgms ... Ms. Rita HAIDER
24 Director Instructional Technology ... Mr. Pete DUNCAN
96 Dir of Purchasing & Mail Services ... Ms. Pat CARSON
29 Coordinator Alumni & Retirees ... Ms. Denise GREGORY
18 Director of Facilities ... Mr. Butch KOTCAMP
97 Director General Education Program ... Dr. Phil BLAU
09 Dir of Institutional Effectiveness ... Mr. Christopher SHAFFER
21 Controller ... Mr. Greg A. BALLENGEE
35 Dean of Students ... Dr. Jessie GRANT
19 Chief of Police ... Mr. David THOROUGHMAN

Sinclair Community College (J)

444 W Third Street, Dayton OH 45402-1460
County: Montgomery FICE Identification: 003119
Unit ID: 205470
Telephone: (937) 512-2500 Carnegie Class: Assoc/Pub-U-SC
FAX Number: (937) 512-5192 Calendar System: Quarter
URL: www.sinclair.edu
Established: 1887 Annual Undergrad Tuition & Fees (In-District): $2,481
Enrollment: 21,106 Coed
Affiliation or Control: State/Local IRS Status: 501(c)3
Highest Offering: Associate Degree
Program: Occupational; 2-Year Principally Bachelor's Creditable
Accreditation: NH, ACBSP, ACFEI, ADNUR, ART, DH, DIETT, ENGT, MAC, MUS, OTA, PTAA, RAD, SURGT, THEA

00 President Emeritus ... Dr. Ned J. SIFFERLEN
01 President ... Dr. Steven L. JOHNSON
05 Senior Vice President/Provost ... Dr. Helen GROVE
10 Vice Pres Business Operations ... Dr. Ty STONE
32 Sr Vice Pres Student Services ... Mr. Michael CARTER
13 Sr Vice Pres for Info Technology ... Mr. Kenneth MOORE
103 VP Workforce Develop/Corporate Svcs ... Ms. Deb NORRIS
45 Vice Pres Organizational Dev ... Dr. Mary GAIER
30 Vice President Advancement ... Ms. Madeline ISELI
20 Associate Provost ... Dr. Gloria GOLDMAN
106 Dean Distance Learning/Inst Support ... Ms. Nancy THIBEAULT
81 Dean of Science/Math/Engineering ... Dr. Roger ABERNATHY
50 Dean Business & Public Services ... Dr. Sue MERRELL
83 Int Dean Liberal Arts/Comm/Soc Sci ... Dr. Lori ZAKEL
76 Dean Life & Health Sciences ... Dr. David L. COLLINS
26 Director of Media Relations ... Ms. Natasha BAKER
07 Int Director Outreach Services ... Ms. Rebecca BUTLER
84 Int Sr Dir Enrollment Management ... Ms. Melissa TOLLE
38 Director Counseling Services ... Dr. Bobby J. BEAVERS
37 Director Financial Aid/Scholarships ... Ms. Carlyn BOZEMAN
08 Int Dir Learning Resources Center ... Ms. Rebecca BUTLER
09 Dir Research/Analytics/Reporting ... Ms. Laura MERCER
15 Director Human Resources ... Ms. Janet JONES
13 Director Info Technology Services ... Mr. Scott MCCOLLUM
25 Director Grants Devel/Govt Info ... Mr. Neil HERBKERSMAN
18 Director Facilities Management ... Mr. Thomas MESSINGER
88 Senior Director of Marketing ... Ms. Rebecca BUTLER
19 Director of Public Safety ... Mr. Charles GIFT
28 Diversity Officer ... Ms. Gwen JONES
86 Director Government Relations ... Ms. Madeline ISELI
43 Legal Counsel/Legal Affairs ... Ms. Lauren ROSS
45 Director Curriculum & Assessment ... Mr. Jared CUTLER
90 Manager Info Processing/Tech Svcs ... Ms. Donna BLANKENSHIP
72 Mgr Adv Integrated Manufacture Ctr ... Mr. Mike DONOVAN
36 Manager Career Services ... Mr. Matt MASSIE
96 Manager of Purchasing ... Mr. Mark SCHMID
24 Manager Media Services ... Ms. Susanne SMITH

35 Manager Student Activities .... Ms. Gwendolyn JONES
84 Manager Enrollment Services .... Mr. Peter BOLMIDA
40 Manager Tartan Campus Store .... Mr. Ron BULTEMA
29 Coordinator Alumni Affairs .... Ms. Karen USREY

Southern State Community College (A)

100 Hobart Drive, Hillsboro OH 45133-9488
County: Highland FICE Identification: 012870
Unit ID: 205966
Telephone: (937) 393-3431 Carnegie Class: Assoc/Pub-R-M
FAX Number: (937) 393-9370 Calendar System: Quarter
URL: www.sscc.edu
Established: 1975 Annual Undergrad Tuition & Fees (In-State): $4,032
Enrollment: 3,350 Coed
Affiliation or Control: State IRS Status: 501(c)3
Highest Offering: Associate Degree
Program: Occupational; 2-Year Principally Bachelor's Creditable
Accreditation: NH, ADNUR, MAC

01 President .... Dr. Kevin S. BOYS
05 Vice President Academic Affairs .... Dr. Ryan MCCALL
10 Vice President Business & Finance .... Mr. James E. BUCK
32 Vice Pres Student Svcs/Enroll Mgmt .... Mr. James BLAND
30 Vice Pres Instl Advancement .... Ms. Nicole ROADES
12 Director of Fayette Campus .... Ms. Jessica WISE
12 Director of South Campus .... Dr. Peggy CHALKER
12 Director of North Campus .... Ms. Therese LIMBERT
20 Dean Instruction .... Ms. Karen S. DAVIS
103 Dean Workforce Dev/Community Svcs .... Mr. John JOY
15 Director of Human Resources .... Ms. Mindy MARKEY-GRABILL
88 Dean of Adult Opportunity Center .... Ms. Karyn EVANS
88 Dean of Course Studies .... Mr. JR ROUSH
102 Executive Director Foundation .... Vacant
91 Computer System/Communication Mgr .... Ms. Shirley A. CORNWELL
26 Director of Public Relations .... Ms. Kris CROSS
06 Registrar .... Ms. Sharon PURVIS
66 Director of Nursing .... Dr. Julianne KREBS
08 Librarian .... Mr. Louis E. MAYS
37 Director Financial Aid .... Ms. Janeen S. DEATLEY
07 Dir Admission/Student Activities .... Ms. Wendy JOHNSON
41 Athletic Director .... Mr. Adam HOLBROOK
40 Bookstore Manager .... Ms. Jessica STEADMAN
13 Director Information Tech .... Mr. Dennis R. GRIFFITH
36 Director of Recruitment .... Mr. Tom PAYTON
84 Coordinator Enrollment Management .... Ms. Lisa COPAS

Stark State College (B)

6200 Frank Avenue, NW, North Canton OH 44720-7299
County: Stark FICE Identification: 010881
Unit ID: 205841
Telephone: (330) 494-6170 Carnegie Class: Assoc/Pub-R-L
FAX Number: (330) 497-6313 Calendar System: Semester
URL: www.starkstate.edu
Established: 1960 Annual Undergrad Tuition & Fees (In-District): $4,410
Enrollment: 15,551 Coed
Affiliation or Control: State/Local IRS Status: 501(c)3
Highest Offering: Associate Degree
Program: 2-Year Principally Bachelor's Creditable; Technical Emphasis
Accreditation: NH, ACBSP, ADNUR, DH, ENGT, MAC, MLTAD, OTA, PTAA

01 President .... Dr. Para M. JONES
05 Provost .... Dr. Dorey DIAB
10 Chief Operating Officer and Treas .... Mr. Thomas A. CHIAPPINI
27 Chief Information Officer .... Mr. Michael DRONEY
84 VP Student Services/Enrollment Mgmt .... Mrs. Cheryl RICE
16 VP for Human Resources .... Ms. Celeste JONES
15 Director of Human Resources .... Ms. Melissa A. GLANZ
49 Dean Liberal Arts .... Dr. Lada GIBSON-SHREVE
81 Dean Sciences .... Mr. James TREACLE
81 Dean Mathematics .... Mr. Andrew STEPHAN
50 Dean Business and Entrep Studies .... Dr. Glenda ZINK
76 Dean Health Technologies .... Mr. John THORNTON
07 Dean Admissions/Student Services .... Mr. Wallace C. HOFFER
51 Dean Corp Svcs and Cont Educ .... Mrs. Barbara MILLIKEN
21 Controller .... Mr. David A. JOHNSON
14 Director Computer Services .... Mr. Greg LANKA
88 Sr Dir Emerg Tech and Strat Grant .... Ms. Rebecca PRIEST
36 Director of Career Development .... Ms. Kristin HANNON
37 Dean Financial Aid and Registration .... Ms. Amy SMUCKER
51 Director Continuing Education .... Mr. Russ O'NEILL
18 Director of Physical Plant and Cons .... Mr. Steve SPRADLING
90 Director Academic Computing .... Mr. Jeff LASH
40 Bookstore Manager .... Ms. Kathryn FEICHTER
06 Registrar .... Ms. Lisa KASUNIC
26 Director Marketing & Communications .... Ms. Irene LEWIS-MOTTS
21 Director of Budget .... Mr. Bruce WYDER
09 Director of Institutional Research .... Mr. Peter TRUMPOWER
88 Dean Teaching and Learning .... Ms. Wendy FORD
54 Dean Eng/Indus and Emerg Tech .... Mr. Don BALL
72 Dean Information Technology Div .... Ms. Cindy CLOSE
38 Dean Advising & Student Engagement .... Ms. Renee LILLY
106 Director eStarkState .... Ms. Linda MOROSKO
53 Dean Education and Human Services .... Ms. Carrilyn LONG

Stautzenberger College (C)

1796 Indian Wood Circle, Maumee OH 43537-4007
County: Lucas FICE Identification: 004866
Unit ID: 205887
Telephone: (419) 866-0261 Carnegie Class: Assoc/PrivFP
FAX Number: (419) 867-9821 Calendar System: Quarter
URL: www.sctoday.edu
Established: 1926 Annual Undergrad Tuition & Fees: $10,939
Enrollment: 952 Coed
Affiliation or Control: Proprietary IRS Status: Proprietary
Highest Offering: Associate Degree
Program: Occupational; 2-Year Principally Bachelor's Creditable; Technical Emphasis
Accreditation: ACICS, MAC

01 President/Director .... Mr. George A. SIMON
03 Executive Vice President .... Mr. Brian E. NIEDZWIECKI
07 Dir of Admissions and Marketing .... Ms. Karen L. FITZGERALD
05 Dean of Academics .... Ms. Susan M. LIPPENS
37 Financial Aid Director .... Mrs. Mari L. HUFFMAN
36 Career Services Director .... Mr. Robert A. GARVER

Terra State Community College (D)

2830 Napoleon Road, Fremont OH 43420-9670
County: Sandusky FICE Identification: 008278
Unit ID: 206011
Telephone: (419) 334-8400 Carnegie Class: Assoc/Pub-R-M
FAX Number: (419) 334-3719 Calendar System: Semester
URL: www.terra.edu
Established: 1968 Annual Undergrad Tuition & Fees (In-State): $3,395
Enrollment: 3,566 Coed
Affiliation or Control: State IRS Status: 501(c)3
Highest Offering: Associate Degree
Program: Occupational; 2-Year Principally Bachelor's Creditable; Technical Emphasis
Accreditation: NH, @PTAA

01 President .... Dr. Jerome WEBSTER
32 Senior VP Academic & Student Affs .... Ms. Lisa WILLIAMS
05 Assistant VP for Instruction .... Mr. John FATICA
10 VP for Financial Affairs .... Mr. Randy MCCULLOUGH
54 Dean Engineering Technology/Math .... Mr. Andrew G. CARROLL
49 Dean Liberal Arts and Public Svcs .... Ms. Lynette SULLIVAN
37 Director Financial Aid .... Mr. Joseph SPENCER
102 Exec Dir of Foundation .... Mr. Ed MAYER
09 Registrar .... Vacant
13 Director Information Technology .... Mr. Tim KINCAID
21 Director of Finance .... Ms. Renee D. BROWN
18 Director Plant Operations .... Vacant
08 Librarian .... Ms. Mary K. BROESTL
26 Dir Mktg Public Rels/Enroll Svcs .... Ms. Mary E. MCCUE
36 Coordinator Career Services .... Ms. Joan GAMBLE
19 Coord Campus Safety/Evening Svcs .... Mr. Jeffery HUFFMAN

Tiffin University (E)

155 Miami Street, Tiffin OH 44883-2161
County: Seneca FICE Identification: 003121
Unit ID: 206048
Telephone: (419) 447-6442 Carnegie Class: Master's L
FAX Number: (419) 443-5022 Calendar System: Semester
URL: www.tiffin.edu
Established: 1888 Annual Undergrad Tuition & Fees: $19,890
Enrollment: 6,816 Coed
Affiliation or Control: Independent Non-Profit IRS Status: 501(c)3
Highest Offering: Master's
Program: 2-Year Principally Bachelor's Creditable; Liberal Arts And General
Accreditation: NH, ACBSP

01 President .... Dr. Paul MARION
05 Vice President for Academic Affairs .... Dr. Charles CHRISTENSEN
30 Vice Pres Development/Pub Affairs .... Mr. Ron SCHUMACHER
10 Vice Pres Finance/Administration .... Mr. Leon WYDEN
16 VP Human Resources/Campus Services .... Ms. Lori HALL
07 Dean of Admissions/Financial Aid .... Mr. Jeremy MARINIS
106 Dean Online/Off-Campus Programs .... Dr. Jason SLONE
88 Dean of Academic Support Programs .... Ms. Annette STAUNTON
04 Assistant to the President .... Ms. Nancy GILBERT
32 Dean of Students .... Mr. Mike HERDLICK
13 Exec Dir Information/Tech Services .... Mr. Leonard REAVES
07 Director Undergrad Admissions .... Mr. Joe BORICH
26 Exec Dir Media Rels/Publications .... Ms. Lisa WILLIAMS
38 Director of Academic Advising .... Ms. Judith GARDNER
06 Registrar .... Ms. Alice NICHOLS
41 Director Athletics .... Mr. Lonny ALLEN
21 Controller .... Mr. Robert WATSON
08 Head Librarian .... Ms. Frances FLEET
09 Director of Institutional Research .... Mr. Michael HERDLICK
29 Director Alumni Relations .... Ms. Celinda SCHERGER
36 Director of Career Development .... Ms. Carol MCDANNELL
18 Director of Facilities .... Mr. Harold KINN
22 Equal Opportunity Officer .... Ms. Lori HALL
39 Director of Residence Life .... Mr. Tom NELLSON
44 Director of Annual Fund .... Mr. Donnie JOHNSON
28 Director of Institutional Diversity .... Dr. Sharon PERRY-NAUSE
37 Director Student Financial Aid .... Ms. Andrea FABER
40 Bookstore Manager .... Mr. Charles LUTZ
49 Dean of Arts & Sciences .... Dr. Gene CRUTSINGER
50 Dean of Business .... Dr. Lillian SCHUMACHER
88 Int Dean Criminal Justice/Soc Sci .... Dr. Jaimie ORR
92 Chair of Freshman Honors Program .... Prof. Pat MCLEOD

Tri-State Bible College (F)

506 Margaret Street, PO Box 445, South Point OH 45680-8402
County: Lawrence FICE Identification: 034754
Unit ID: 206154
Telephone: (740) 377-2520 Carnegie Class: Spec/Faith
FAX Number: (740) 377-0001 Calendar System: Semester
URL: www.tsbc.edu
Established: 1970 Annual Undergrad Tuition & Fees: $7,700
Enrollment: 75 Coed
Affiliation or Control: Independent Non-Profit IRS Status: 501(c)3
Highest Offering: Master's
Program: 2-Year Principally Bachelor's Creditable; Professional; Religious Emphasis
Accreditation: BI

00 Chancellor .... Dr. Clifford L. MARQUARDT
01 President .... Dr. Jack R. FINCH
05 Chief Academic Administrator .... Mr. Phillip KINNEY
10 Chief Financial Administrator .... Ms. Clyda HESTER
11 Chief Administrative Administrator .... Ms. Bobby MERCER

Trinity Lutheran Seminary (G)

2199 E Main Street, Columbus OH 43209-2334
County: Franklin FICE Identification: 003044
Unit ID: 206215
Telephone: (614) 235-4136 Carnegie Class: Spec/Faith
FAX Number: (614) 238-0263 Calendar System: Semester
URL: www.TLSohio.edu
Established: 1830 Annual Graduate Tuition & Fees: $14,330
Enrollment: 136 Coed
Affiliation or Control: Evangelical Lutheran Church In America
IRS Status: 501(c)3
Highest Offering: Doctorate; No Undergraduates
Program: Professional; Religious Emphasis
Accreditation: NH, THEOL

01 President .... Dr. Mark R. RAMSETH
05 Academic Dean .... Dr. Brad A. BINAU
20 Associate Academic Dean .... Dr. Diane J. HYMANS
88 Dean of Leadership Formation .... Rev. Emlyn A. OTT
84 Director Vocation and Enrollment .... Rev. Shari L. AYERS
06 Registrar .... Mrs. Carol M. DIXON
08 Director Hamma Library .... Mr. Ray A. OLSON
26 Director Communications/Marketing .... Ms. Margaret L. FARNHAM
37 Director Financial Aid .... Mrs. Melissa CURTIS POWELL
88 Director Contextual Education .... Rev. Jane E. JENKINS
88 Director MA in Church Music Program .... Ms. May L. SCHWARZ
58 Director Graduate Studies .... Dr. Walter F. TAYLOR, JR.
88 Director MACE/MAYFM/MTS Programs .... Dr. Mary E. HUGHES
21 Controller .... Mrs. Patricia A. FORK
42 Director Church Relations .... Rev. Gary A. SANDBERG
18 Director Facilities Management .... Ms. Laura K. PETERSON

Trumbull Business College (H)

3200 Ridge Road, Warren OH 44484-3272
County: Trumbull FICE Identification: 020543
Unit ID: 206224
Telephone: (330) 369-3200 Carnegie Class: Assoc/PrivFP
FAX Number: (330) 369-6792 Calendar System: Quarter
URL: www.tbc-trumbullbusiness.com
Established: 1972 Annual Undergrad Tuition & Fees: $11,671
Enrollment: 318 Coed
Affiliation or Control: Proprietary IRS Status: Proprietary
Highest Offering: Associate Degree
Program: Occupational
Accreditation: ACICS

01 President .... Mr. Dennis J. GRIFFITH
37 Director of Financial Aid .... Ms. Florence HENNING
36 Director of Student Placement .... Ms. Kimberly STRANIAK
12 Director of Branch Campus .... Mr. Kimberly STRANIAK
06 Registrar .... Ms. Teresa SHAMBACH

Union Institute & University (I)

440 E McMillan Street, Cincinnati OH 45206-1947
County: Hamilton FICE Identification: 010923
Unit ID: 206279
Telephone: (513) 861-6400 Carnegie Class: DRU
FAX Number: (513) 861-0779 Calendar System: Semester
URL: www.myunion.edu
Established: 1964 Annual Undergrad Tuition & Fees: $11,664
Enrollment: 1,822 Coed
Affiliation or Control: Independent Non-Profit IRS Status: 501(c)3
Highest Offering: Doctorate
Program: Liberal Arts And General; Teacher Preparatory
Accreditation: NH, @SW

01 President .... Dr. Roger H. SUBLETT
05 Provost .... Dr. Richard HANSEN
04 Executive Assistant to President .... Ms. Carolyn KRAUSE
10 Chief Fiscal Officer .... Mr. Edward WALTON
15 Vice President Human Resources .... Ms. Deborah EAMOE
84 VP Enrollment Management .... Mr. Jon MAYS
20 Assoc Provost Academic Programs .... Dr. Patricia BREWER
46 Assoc Provost Inst Effectiveness .... Dr. Elizabeth PRUDEN

88	Assoc VP Special Projects	Dr. James ROCHELEAU
58	Interim Dean PhD Pgm	Dr. Karsten PIEP
58	Dean Graduate Studies in Education	Dr. Arlene SACKS
58	Dean Graduate Studies in Psychology	Dr. William LAX
21	Controller	Mr. Anthony DENNIS
06	Registrar	Ms. Lew Rita MOORE
09	Director Institutional Research	Ms. Linda C. VAN VOLKENBURGH
13	Asst VP Information Technology	Mr. Greg THOMPSON
18	Director Building Management	Ms. Janet DAY
26	Assoc VP Communications	Ms. Carolyn KRAUSE
96	Director of Purchasing	Mrs. Ruth A. RIDGE
12	Dean Undergrad Studies Miami Center	Dr. Beryl WATNICK
12	Dean Undergrad Studies LA Center	Dr. Elizabeth PASTORRES-PALFFY
12	Dean Undergrad Studies Cincinnati	Dr. Carolyn TURNER
12	Dean Undergrad Studies Sacramento	Dr. Frederick ROCCO
12	Dean Vermont Centers	Dr. Dan LERNER
08	Director Gary Library	Mr. Matthew PAPPATHAN
37	Director Financial Aid	Ms. Lisa PERDOMO
29	Director Alumni Relations & Vet Aff	Dr. Neal MEIER
30	Director of Development	Mr. Jeffrey SELLERS
51	Director Lifelong Learning	Ms. Dayle DEARDURFF

United Theological Seminary (A)

4501 Denlinger Road, Dayton OH 45426-2308

County: Montgomery — FICE Identification: 003122 — Unit ID: 206288
Telephone: (937) 529-2201 — Carnegie Class: Spec/Faith
FAX Number: (866) 433-8235 — Calendar System: Semester
URL: www.united.edu
Established: 1871 — Annual Graduate Tuition & Fees: $16,016
Enrollment: 398 — Coed
Affiliation or Control: United Methodist — IRS Status: 501(c)3
Highest Offering: Doctorate; No Undergraduates
Program: Professional; Religious Emphasis
Accreditation: **NH**, THEOL

01	President & CEO	Dr. Wendy J. DEICHMANN
05	Vice Pres Academic Affairs & Dean	Dr. David WATSON
10	Vice Pres Finance/Treasurer	Mr. Ronald KUKER
30	Vice Pres Development	Rev. Timothy FORBESS
84	VP Enrollment/Dir Doctoral Studies	Dr. Harold HUDSON
06	Registrar	Ms. Martha M. ANDERSON
13	Director of Information Technology	Mr. Rick MOHR
106	Dir Distance Learning/Educ Tech	Ms. Phyllis ENNIST
08	Librarian	Ms. Sarah D. BROOKS BLAIR
88	Director of Contextual Ministries	Rev. Gary EUBANK
26	Director of Communications	Ms. JoAnn WAGNER
29	Assoc Dir Alumni/ae Services	Rev. Brice THOMAS
18	Facility Manager	Mr. Roger BOWYER

The University of Akron, Main Campus (B)

302 Buchtel Common, Akron OH 44325

County: Summit — FICE Identification: 003123 — Unit ID: 200800
Telephone: (330) 972-7111 — Carnegie Class: RU/H
FAX Number: (330) 972-6990 — Calendar System: Semester
URL: www.uakron.edu
Established: 1870 — Annual Undergrad Tuition & Fees (In-State): $9,552
Enrollment: 29,699 — Coed
Affiliation or Control: State — IRS Status: 501(c)3
Highest Offering: Doctorate
Program: 2-Year Principally Bachelor's Creditable; Liberal Arts And General; Teacher Preparatory; Professional
Accreditation: **NH**, AAFCS, ACBSP, ANEST, ART, AUD, BUS, BUSA, CACREP, CIDA, COPSY, DANCE, DIETC, DIETD, ENG, ENGR, ENGT, IFSAC, IPSY, LAW, MAC, MFCD, MUS, NURSE, PH, SP, SPAA, SURGT, SW, TED

01	President	Dr. Luis M. PROENZA
05	Senior Vice President & Provost	Dr. Mike SHERMAN
46	Vice Pres Research/Dean of Grad Sch	Dr. George R. NEWKOME
32	Vice President for Student Affairs	Dr. Charles J. FEY
10	VP Finance & Administration/CFO	Mr. David J. CUMMINS
43	Vice President & General Counsel	Mr. Ted A. MALLO
44	Vice Pres Public Affs/Development	Mr. John A. LAGUARDIA
13	VP Information Technology/CIO	Mr. James L. SAGE
18	Vice Pres Capital Plng/Facil Mgmt	Mr. Ted CURTIS
88	VP of Strategic Engagement	Mr. James P. TRESSEL
88	Assistant Secretary of the BOT	Mr. Paul A. HEROLD
100	Vice President/Chief of Staff	Mrs. Candace CAMPBELL JACKSON
101	Secretary Board of Trustees	Mr. Ted A. MALLO
32	Assoc VP & Dean of Student Life	Ms. Denine M. ROCCO
30	Assoc Vice Pres Development	Mr. Timothy R. DUFORE
44	Special Assistant to the President	Mr. Paul A. HEROLD
31	Assoc VP Community Relations	Mr. David NYPAVER
21	Assc VP Treasury/Financial Planning	Mr. Brian E. DAVIS
46	Assoc Vice President for Research	Mr. Kenneth G. PRESTON
46	Assoc Vice President for Research	Mr. Wayne H. WATKINS
21	Assoc Vice President & Controller	Mr. John E. KOVATCH
84	Assoc VP Strategic Enrollment	Mr. William KRAUS
38	Associate Vice Pres for Campus Life	Mrs. Oletha THOMPSON
88	Assoc VP Strategic Init & Engage	Mrs. Holly HARRIS BANE
88	Assoc VP Inclusion & Equity	Mr. Lee A. GILL
27	Assoc Vice Pres/Chief Comm Officer	Ms. Eileen KOREY
26	Assoc VP/Chief Marketing Officer	Mr. Wayne R. HILL
19	Ast VP Camp Safety/Chf Univ Police	Mr. Paul J. CALLAHAN
43	Asst VP & Assoc General Counsel	Mr. Sidney C. FOSTER, JR.
29	Asst VP Alumni/College Cen Programs	Mrs. Kimberly M. KARSON
15	VP Talent Dev & Human Resources	Dr. Becky J. HOOVER
38	Director Academic Advising Center	Mrs. Nancy L. ROADRUCK
06	Registrar	Mrs. Debra L. HAYES
07	Director of Admissions	Ms. Diane R. RAYBUCK
09	Director Institutional Research	Ms. Sabrina L. ANDREWS
13	Director Technology Transfer	Mr. Kenneth G. PRESTON
08	Dean of University Libraries	Ms. Cheryl KERN-SIMIRENKO
49	Dean Buchtel College of Arts & Sci	Dr. Chand MIDHA
54	Dean College of Engineering	Dr. George K. HARITOS
53	Dean College of Education	Dr. Mark D. SHERMIS
50	Dean College of Business Admin	Dr. Ravi KROVI
76	Int Dean College Health Professions	Dr. Roberta A. DEPOMPEI
72	Dean Summit College	Mr. Stanley B. SILVERMAN
61	Interim Dean School of Law	Ms. Elizabeth H. REILLY
20	Dean University College	Mr. Stanley B. SILVERMAN
54	Dean of Polymer Science/Engineering	Dr. Stephen Z D. CHENG
12	Interim Dean Wayne College	Dr. Neil B. SAPIENZA
37	Director Student Financial Aid	Mrs. Michelle ELLIS
96	Director of Purchasing	Mr. Andrew W. ROTH
88	Director of Internal Communications	Mr. Robert KROPFF
105	University Webmaster	Mr. Eric W. KRIEDER
92	Dean Honors College	Dr. Dale H. MUGLER
88	Director UA Adult Focus	Mrs. Laura H. CONLEY
41	Director Athletics	Mr. Tom WISTRCILL
36	Director Counseling/Test/Career Ctr	Dr. Juanita K. MARTIN
39	Asst VP & Chief Housing Officer	Mr. John A. MESSINA
25	Director Rsrch Svcs/Sponsored Pgms	Ms. Katie WATKINS-WENDELL
85	Director International Programs	Mr. Peter B. LI
23	Director Health Services	Ms. Diane J. FASHINPAUR
14	Dir Hardware Opers/Oper Sys Svcs	Mr. Thomas R. BEITL
21	Spec Asst to VP/IT & Spec Proj Mgr	Mr. David G. WASIK
28	Dir Multicultural Development	Ms. Fedearia A. NICHOLSON
88	Exec Dir University Park Alliance	Mr. Eric A. JOHNSON
88	Information Security Officer	Mrs. Deborah WHITE
88	Mgr Editorial Svcs/Inst Marketing	Ms. Joette DIGNAN WEIR

The University of Akron-Wayne College (C)

1901 Smucker Road, Orrville OH 44667-9758

County: Wayne — FICE Identification: 010818 — Unit ID: 200846
Telephone: (330) 683-2010 — Carnegie Class: Assoc/Pub2in4
FAX Number: (330) 684-8989 — Calendar System: Semester
URL: www.wayne.uakron.edu
Established: 1972 — Annual Undergrad Tuition & Fees (In-State): $6,093
Enrollment: 2,509 — Coed
Affiliation or Control: State — IRS Status: 501(c)3
Highest Offering: Associate Degree
Program: Occupational; 2-Year Principally Bachelor's Creditable
Accreditation: **NH**

01	Interim Dean	Mr. Neil SAPIENZA
04	Senior Administrative Assistant	Ms. Lindsie B. WEBB
05	Associate Dean of Instruction	Vacant
10	Sr Dir Business Operations/Finance	Mrs. Tamara A. LOWE
32	Sr Dir Student Life/Enroll Mgmt	Mr. Gordon K. HOLLY
18	Chief Facilities/Physical Plant	Mr. W. Russ PUGH
26	Chief Public Relations Officer	Mrs. Regina L. SCHWARTZ
08	Manager Library Services	Mrs. Maureen T. LERCH
06	Registrar	Mrs. Charlene LANCE
07	Director of Admissions	Mrs. Alicia BROADUS
09	Director of Institutional Research	Mr. William CLARK
15	Director Personnel Services	Ms. Kathy BATCHELDER
20	Associate Academic Officer	Mr. Garth D. SCHOFFMAN
88	Assistant to the Dean	Mr. Kevin E. ENGLE
35	Student Activities Coordinator	Ms. Jackie E. ASHBAUGH
36	Coord Career and Assessment Svcs	Ms. Carol J. PLEUSS
37	Manager Student Svcs/Financial Aid	Ms. Barb CAILLET
38	Coordinator of Academic Advising	Vacant
96	Accounting Clerk Sr	Ms. Amy M. HAYNES
13	Manager Technical Support Services	Ms. Cher DEEDS
19	University Police	Lt. Tom WYKOFF
40	Director Bookstore	Ms. Pat PAXTON
41	Athletic Director	Mr. Patrick S. RUFENER
103	Dir Cont Ed & Workforce Development	Ms. Amy H. MAST

University of Cincinnati Main Campus (D)

2624 Clifton Avenue, Cincinnati OH 45221-0001

County: Hamilton — FICE Identification: 003125 — Unit ID: 201885
Telephone: (513) 556-6000 — Carnegie Class: RU/VH
FAX Number: (513) 556-3237 — Calendar System: Quarter
URL: www.uc.edu
Established: 1819 — Annual Undergrad Tuition & Fees (In-State): $10,784
Enrollment: 42,421 — Coed
Affiliation or Control: State — IRS Status: 501(c)3
Highest Offering: Doctorate
Program: 2-Year Principally Bachelor's Creditable; Liberal Arts And General; Teacher Preparatory; Professional
Accreditation: **NH**, ANEST, ART, AUD, BBT, BUS, CACREP, CIDA, CLPSY, CONST, CS, DANCE, DENT, DIETC, DIETD, ENG, ENGR, ENGT, LAW, MED, MIDWF, MT, MUS, NMT, NURSE, PHAR, PLNG, PTA, PTAA, SP, SURGA, SW, TED, THEA

01	Interim President	Dr. Santa J. ONO
05	Sr VP/Provost Academic Affairs	Dr. Lawrence J. JOHNSON
11	Sr VP for Administration & Finance	Mr. Robert AMBACH
03	Executive VP	Ms. Karen K. FAABORG
46	Interim Vice President for Research	Dr. William S. BALL
63	Dean Medicine/VP for Health Affairs	Dr. Thomas F. BOAT
30	Interim VP Development/Alumni Rels	Mr. Steve WILSON
86	Vice Pres Govt Rels/University Comm	Mr. Gregory J. VEHR
32	Vice Pres Student Affairs & Svcs	Dr. Mitchel D. LIVINGSTON
10	Vice President for Finance	Mr. James D. PLUMMER
13	VP & CIO for Information Technology	Dr. Michael LIEBERMAN
43	General Counsel	Mr. Mitchell D. MCCRATE
15	Acting Sr Assoc VP Human Resources	Ms. Theresa MURPHY
84	Sr Assoc Vice President Enrollment	Dr. Caroline B. MILLER
21	Assoc VP Community Development	Mr. Gerald A. SIEGERT
27	Assoc VP PR/Univ Spokesperson	Mr. Greg HAND
07	Assoc Vice Pres for Admissions	Dr. Thomas CANEPA
76	Dean Allied Health Sciences	Dr. Elizabeth C. KING
49	Dean Arts & Sciences	Dr. Ronald JACKSON
50	Dean Business Administration	Dr. David M. SZYMANSKI
64	Dean College Conservatory of Music	Peter LANDGREN
48	Dean Design/Architecture/Art & Plng	Dr. Robert PROBST
53	Dean Education	Dr. Lawrence J. JOHNSON
54	Dean Engineering & Applied Science	Dr. Carlo D. MONTEMAGNO
61	Dean Law	Mr. Louis D. BILIONIS
66	Dean Nursing	Dr. Greer L. GLAZER
67	Interim Dean Pharmacy	Dr. William K. FANT
70	Director School Social Work	Dr. Gerald J. BOSTWICK
08	Dean Library	Mr. Xuemao WANG
29	Executive Director Alumni Affairs	Mr. Myron HUGHES
41	Director Athletics	Mr. Whit BABCOCK
40	Director Bookstore	Ms. Linda K. GINDELE
36	Director Career Development	Dr. Katrina JORDAN
38	Director Counseling Center	Dr. Tow Y. YAU
22	Interim Director Equal Opportunity	Ms. Theresa MURPHY
39	Director Housing/Food Service	Mr. Todd DUNCAN
37	Director Student Financial Aid	Ms. Connie WILLIAMS
09	Director Institutional Research	Mr. Lee E. MORTIMER
19	Director Public Safety	Mr. Michael CURETON
06	Registrar	Dr. Douglas BURGESS
96	Director of Purchasing	Mr. Thomas B. GUERIN
45	CoDir Institute for Policy Research	Dr. Eric RADEMACHER
45	CoDir Institute for Policy Research	Dr. Kimberly DOWNING

University of Cincinnati-Clermont College (E)

4200 Clermont College Drive, Batavia OH 45103-1785

County: Clermont — FICE Identification: 010805 — Unit ID: 201946
Telephone: (513) 732-5200 — Carnegie Class: Assoc/Pub2in4
FAX Number: (513) 732-5275 — Calendar System: Quarter
URL: www.ucclermont.edu
Established: 1972 — Annual Undergrad Tuition & Fees (In-State): $5,210
Enrollment: 3,871 — Coed
Affiliation or Control: State — IRS Status: 501(c)3
Highest Offering: Baccalaureate
Program: Occupational; 2-Year Principally Bachelor's Creditable; Technical Emphasis
Accreditation: **NH**, MAC, SURGT

01	Dean	Dr. Gregory S. SOJKA
05	Assoc Dean Academic Affairs	Dr. Rajiv S. SOMAN
20	Sr Assistant Dean Academic Affairs	Ms. Mary F. STEARNS
08	Senior Librarian	Ms. Rosemary YOUNG
24	Dir Learning Center	Ms. Pam MAVI
76	Director Allied Health	Ms. Sharman WILLMORE
09	Director of Institutional Research	Ms. Susan RILEY
10	Asst Dean Administrative Services	Mr. John R. NELSON
32	Asst Dean Enroll & Student Svcs	Ms. Ann APPLETON
84	Director Advising & Registration	Mr. Ryan HALL
84	Director of Enrollment Services	Ms. Martha GEIGER
06	Asst Dir Registration & Scheduling	Ms. Kristine LOUGHRAN
88	Director Disability Services	Ms. Jennifer RADT
35	Director of Student Life	Ms. Kimberly ELLISON
41	Program Coord/Athletic Director	Mr. Brian SULLIVAN
18	Asst Dean Facilities & Tech Svcs	Mr. Stephen W. YOUNG
30	Director of Development	Ms. Meredith DELANEY
26	Asst Dean Communications & Mktg	Ms. Mae HANNA

University of Cincinnati-Raymond Walters College (F)

9555 Plainfield Road, Blue Ash OH 45236-1096

County: Hamilton — FICE Identification: 004868 — Unit ID: 201955
Telephone: (513) 745-5600 — Carnegie Class: Assoc/Pub2in4
FAX Number: (513) 745-5780 — Calendar System: Quarter
URL: www.rwc.uc.edu
Established: 1967 — Annual Undergrad Tuition & Fees (In-State): $5,691
Enrollment: 5,221 — Coed
Affiliation or Control: State — IRS Status: 501(c)3
Highest Offering: Baccalaureate
Program: Occupational; 2-Year Principally Bachelor's Creditable
Accreditation: **NH**, ADNUR, ART, DH, EMT, MAC, RAD, RTT

01	Dean	Dr. Cady SHORT-THOMPSON
05	Assoc Dean Academic Affairs	Dr. Marlene R. MINER
10	Asst Dean Administrative Svcs	Mr. Eugene KRAMER
32	Asst Dean Student Services	Ms. Pamela LINEBACK
26	Int Director College Relations	Mr. Tom CRUSE

90 Int Director Network Resources ... Mr. Dale HOFSTETTER
84 Director Enrollment Services ... Mr. Christopher POWER
09 Director Institutional Research ... Ms. Sandra PARKER
06 Registration Officer ... Ms. Deborah L. SMITH
08 Library Director ... Ms. Stephena HARMONY
24 Director Media Services ... Mr. H. Michael SANDERS
36 Career Development Specialist ... Ms. Tresha LEWIS
35 Student Life Coordinator ... Ms. Shelia YATES-MATTINGLY

University of Dayton (A)

300 College Park, Dayton OH 45469-0001
County: Montgomery FICE Identification: 003127
Unit ID: 202480
Telephone: (937) 229-1000 Carnegie Class: RU/H
FAX Number: (937) 229-4000 Calendar System: Semester
URL: www.udayton.edu
Established: 1850 Annual Undergrad Tuition & Fees: $33,400
Enrollment: 11,063 Coed
Affiliation or Control: Roman Catholic IRS Status: 501(c)3
Highest Offering: Doctorate
Program: Liberal Arts And General; Teacher Preparatory; Professional
Accreditation: NH, ART, BUS, BUSA, CACREP, DIETD, ENG, ENGT, LAW, MUS, PTA, SPAA, TED

01 President ... Dr. Daniel J. CURRAN
05 Provost ... Dr. Joseph E. SALIBA
32 VP Student Development ... Mr. William M. FISCHER
10 VP Finance & Admin Services ... Mr. Thomas E. BURKHARDT
30 Int VP Univ Advancement ... Mr. David HARPER
41 VP/Director of Athletics ... Mr. Timothy J. WABLER
15 VP Human Resources ... Ms. Joyce M. CARTER
84 VP for Enrollment Mgmt ... Mr. Sundar KUMARASAMY
46 VP of Research/Exec Dir UDRI ... Dr. Michael V. MCCABE
26 Assoc VP University Communications ... Ms. Teresa J. RIZVI
44 Assoc VP Development ... Mr. James F. BROTHERS
42 Director Campus Ministry ... Ms. Crystal C. SULLIVAN
88 VP for Mission and Rector ... Rev. James F. FITZ, SM
88 Univ Prof Faith/Culture ... Vacant
31 Dir Ctr for Leadership in Community .. Mr. Richard T. FERGUSON
20 Assoc Provost Faculty & Admin Affs ... Dr. Patrick G. DONNELLY
88 Asc Prov Lrng Spprt/Dir Rch Tch Ctr .. Dr. Deborah J. BICKFORD
90 Assoc Prov/Chief Information Ofcr ... Dr. Thomas D. SKILL
06 Registrar ... Mr. Thomas J. WESTENDORF
07 Asst VP/ Dean of Admission ... Mr. Robert F. DURKLE
19 Director Public Safety ... Mr. Bruce E. BURT
09 Director Institutional Studies ... Ms. Susan K. SEXTON
21 Comptroller ... Ms. Angela K. BUECHELE
88 Assoc VP/Dean of Students ... Ms. Christine M. SCHRAMM
36 Director Career Services ... Mr. Jason C. ECKERT
38 Asst VP Student Dev/Dir Counseling ... Dr. Steven D. MUELLER
18 VP for Facilities Management ... Ms. Beth H. KEYES
23 Medical Director Univ Health Ctr ... Dr. Mary P. BUCHWALDER
62 Dean University Libraries ... Ms. Kathleen M. WEBB
49 Dean College Arts & Sciences ... Dr. Paul H. BENSON
61 Dean School of Law ... Mr. Paul E. MCGREAL
50 Dean Sch of Business Admin ... Dr. Paul BOBROWSKI
58 Assoc Provost and Dean Grad Studies ... Dr. Paul M. VANDERBURGH
53 Dean School of Educ & Allied Prof ... Dr. Kevin R. KELLY
54 Dean School of Engineering ... Dr. Tony E. SALIBA
29 Asst VP Principal Gifts ... Mr. Todd W. IMWALLE
35 Dir Student Life & Kennedy Union ... Ms. Amy L. LOPEZ-MATTHEWS
37 Dean of Admission/Dir of Fin Aid ... Ms. Kathy M. HARMON
39 Asst Dean Students & Dir Res Life ... Mr. Steven T. HERNDON
40 Manager UD Bookstore ... Ms. Julie M. BANKS
43 Director Legal Affairs/Univ Counsel ... Vacant
96 Director of Purchasing ... Mr. Ken R. SOUCY
92 Dir University Honors/Scholars Pgm ... Dr. David W. DARROW
94 Director of Women's Studies ... Dr. Rebecca S. WHISNANT
22 Dir Affirmative Action & Compliance ... Ms. Patricia BERNAL-OLSON
86 Government/Regional Relations Dir ... Mr. S. Ted BUCARO
28 Exe Dir Inst Diversity & Inclusion ... Dr. Jack T. LING

The University of Findlay (B)

1000 North Main Street, Findlay OH 45840-3653
County: Hancock FICE Identification: 003045
Unit ID: 202763
Telephone: (419) 422-8313 Carnegie Class: Master's L
FAX Number: (419) 434-4822 Calendar System: Semester
URL: www.findlay.edu
Established: 1882 Annual Undergrad Tuition & Fees: $29,189
Enrollment: 4,982 Coed
Affiliation or Control: Church Of God IRS Status: 501(c)3
Highest Offering: Doctorate
Program: Occupational; Liberal Arts And General; Teacher Preparatory; Professional
Accreditation: NH, ARCPA, ENGR, NMT, OT, PHAR, PTA, SW, TED

01 President ... Dr. Katherine R. FELL
05 Vice President for Academic Affairs ... Dr. Daniel J. MAY
10 Vice President for Business Affairs ... Mr. Martin L. TERRY
30 Vice Pres University Advancement ... Dr. John W. MOSSER
32 Vice President for Student Affairs ... Mr. David W. EMSWELLER
04 Assistant to the President ... Ms. Meg FLEMION
46 Dean Undergraduate Education ... Dr. Marie A. LOUDEN-HANES
81 Interim Dean College of Sciences ... Dr. Jeffrey FRYE
50 Dean College of Business ... Dr. Paul SEARS
49 Interim Dean College of Liberal Art ... Dr. Nicole DIEDERICH
76 Dean College of Health Sciences ... Dr. Andrea KOEPKE
67 Dean College of Pharmacy ... Dr. Donald STANSLOSKI
53 Dean College of Education ... Dr. Julie MCINTOSH
58 Dean of Graduate/Professional Stds ... Dr. Thomas DILLON
18 Director of Physical Plant ... Mr. Myreon K. COBB
09 Director of Institutional Research ... Mr. Tony G. GOEDDE
06 Registrar ... Mr. Tony G. GOEDDE
07 Director of Admissions ... Ms. Donna GRUBER
41 Athletic Director ... Mr. Steven P. RACKLEY
08 Director of Shafer Library ... Mr. Andrew WHITIS
37 Director of Financial Aid ... Mr. Edward R. RECLER
13 Director of Computer Services ... Dr. Raymond MCCANDLESS
29 Director of Alumni Affairs ... Ms. Deanna SPRAW
26 Dir Public Relations/Media Rels ... Ms. Suzanne ENGLISH
44 Assoc VP Univ Advancement ... Mr. Charles SHEPARD, II
36 Director of Career Services ... Ms. Janet M. TAYLOR
15 Director of Human Resources ... Mr. Robert LINK
23 Director of Health Services ... Ms. Julie R. YINGLING
38 Director Counseling Services ... Ms. Karyn J. WESTRICK
40 Manager of Bookstore ... Mr. Jay CANTERBURY
42 Director Christian Ministries ... Rev. William D. MILLER
19 Director of Security/Safety ... Mr. Kenneth WALERIUS
93 Dir Intercultural Student Services ... Mr. Almar WALTER
21 Business Manager ... Mr. Robert LINK
28 Director of Diversity ... Mr. Almar WALTER
35 Chief Student Life Officer ... Mr. David W. EMSWELLER
85 Dir Intl Student Admissions & Svcs ... Ms. Penny GERDEMAN
101 Secretary to the Board of Trustees ... Ms. C. Sue PIRSCHEL
25 Dir of Grants and Contract Admin ... Ms. Jill GEAR

University of Mount Union (C)

1972 Clark Avenue, Alliance OH 44601-3993
County: Stark FICE Identification: 003083
Unit ID: 204185
Telephone: (330) 821-5320 Carnegie Class: Bac/Diverse
FAX Number: (330) 823-3457 Calendar System: Semester
URL: www.mountunion.edu
Established: 1846 Annual Undergrad Tuition & Fees: $26,650
Enrollment: 2,231 Coed
Affiliation or Control: United Methodist IRS Status: 501(c)3
Highest Offering: Master's
Program: Liberal Arts And General; Teacher Preparatory
Accreditation: NH, ARCPA, MUS, TED

01 President ... Dr. Richard F. GIESE
05 Vice Pres Acad Affs/Dean of Univ ... Dr. Patricia H. DRAVES
10 Vice Pres Business Affs/Treasurer ... Mr. Patrick D. HEDDLESTON
30 Vice President Univ Advancement ... Mr. Gregory KING
32 Vice Pres Student Affs/Dean Stdnts ... Mr. John FRAZIER
84 Vice President for Enrollment Mgmt ... Ms. Amy A. TOMKO
26 Vice President for Marketing ... Ms. Melissa GARDNER
08 Librarian ... Mr. Robert R. GARLAND
06 Registrar ... Ms. Karen MORIARTY
07 Director of Admissions ... Ms. Grace CHALKER
44 Director Annual Fund ... Ms. Kim RODSTROM
44 Director of Planned Giving ... Mr. David WOLPERT
14 Director Computer Information Sys ... Ms. Tina STUCHELL
88 Director of Advance for Major Gifts ... Mr. Matt STINSON
09 Director Assesment/Program Develop ... Dr. Fang DU
29 Director Alumni/College Activities ... Ms. Anne GRAFFICE
85 Director Center for Global Educ ... Dr. Jennifer HALL
18 Director of Physical Plant ... Mr. Blaine D. LEWIS
16 Director of Human Resources ... Ms. Pamela NEWBOLD
39 Director of Housing ... Ms. Michelle GAFFNEY
42 Chaplain ... Rev. Martha D. CASHBURLESS
36 Director of Career Services ... Ms. Rebecca DOAK
37 Director of Student Financial Svcs ... Ms. Emily SWAIN
40 Manager of College Bookstore ... Mr. Rod PETERSON
41 Athletic Director ... Mr. Larry T. KEHRES
04 Exec Assistant to the President ... Ms. Laura E. GOOD
21 Assoc VP for Business Affairs ... Mr. Ronald CROWL
28 Director of Diversity ... Dr. Ivory LYONS
20 Associate Academic Officer ... Dr. James THOMA
35 Associate Dean of Students ... Ms. Karen PETKO
96 Director of Purchasing ... Mr. John GREGORY

University of Northwestern Ohio (D)

1441 N Cable Road, Lima OH 45805-1498
County: Allen FICE Identification: 004861
Unit ID: 204486
Telephone: (419) 227-3141 Carnegie Class: Assoc/PrivNFP4
FAX Number: (419) 229-6926 Calendar System: Quarter
URL: www.unoh.edu
Established: 1920 Annual Undergrad Tuition & Fees: $13,430
Enrollment: 4,167 Coed
Affiliation or Control: Independent Non-Profit IRS Status: 501(c)3
Highest Offering: Master's
Program: Occupational
Accreditation: NH, ACBSP, MAC

01 President ... Dr. Jeffrey A. JARVIS
05 Vice Pres Academic Affairs/Provost ... Dr. Cheryl MUELLER
10 Vice President Finance ... Mrs. Marcia EICKHOLT
84 Vice Pres Enrollment Management ... Mr. Ricky MORRISON
18 Vice Pres of Property Management ... Mr. Don RICKER
26 Vice Pres Public Relations/Mktg ... Mrs. Cheryl STEINWEDEL
30 Vice President Development ... Mr. Steve FARMER
32 Vice President Campus Life ... Mr. Bob FRICKE
39 Director of Housing ... Mr. Pat FINNERTY
15 Exec Director of Human Resources ... Ms. Geri MORRIS
10 Controller/Chief Financial Officer ... Mr. James S. BRONDER
06 Director of Registration & Advising ... Mr. Loren KORZAN
37 Director of Financial Aid ... Mr. Wendell SCHICK
88 Director MBA Program ... Mr. Michael CALLAHAN
20 Assoc Vice Pres Academic Affairs ... Mrs. Jenell BRAMLAGE
36 Co-Director Career Services ... Mr. Justin FLANAGAN
36 Co-Director Career Services ... Mrs. Nicole NEIMEYER
25 Coordinator of Grant Writing ... Ms. Jessica SPIERS
04 Executive Assistant to President ... Mrs. Jennifer BENDELE
50 Dean College of Business ... Mr. Dean HOBLER
72 Dean College of Technologies ... Mr. Tom GROTHOUS

University of Rio Grande (E)

218 N College Avenue, PO BOX 500,
Rio Grande OH 45674-3100
County: Gallia FICE Identification: 003116
Unit ID: 205203
Telephone: (740) 245-5353 Carnegie Class: Master's M
FAX Number: (740) 245-5266 Calendar System: Semester
URL: www.rio.edu
Established: 1876 Annual Undergrad Tuition & Fees: $20,300
Enrollment: 1,928 Coed
Affiliation or Control: Independent Non-Profit IRS Status: 501(c)3
Highest Offering: Master's
Program: 2-Year Principally Bachelor's Creditable; Liberal Arts And General; Teacher Preparatory; Professional
Accreditation: NH, ADNUR, DMS, IACBE, NUR, RAD, SW, TED

01 President ... Dr. Barbara GELLMAN-DANLEY
05 Provost/VP of Academic Affairs ... Dr. Kenneth PORADA
30 Executive VP & VP for Inst Advance ... Mr. Paul D. HARRISON
10 Vice President for Finance/CFO ... Mr. Tim PRUETT
15 VP Human Resources ... Ms. Phyllis MASON
88 Chief Compliance Officer ... Ms. Sophia CHIOU
49 Dean Col of Arts & Sciences ... Dr. David LAWRENCE
76 Dean Col of Health & Behav Science ... Dr. Donna MITCHELL
107 Dean Col of Professional Studies ... Dr. Zaki SHARIF
84 Dean of Enrollment Management ... Mr. Mark ABELL
07 Director Admissions ... Mr. Thomas MANSPERGER
11 RGCC Chief Admin Officer ... Mrs. Rebecca LONG
25 Exec to Provost & Dir of Grants ... Dr. Yasmin SHARIF
32 Dean of Students ... Mr. Aaron QUINN
41 Athletics Director ... Mr. Jeff LANHAM
08 Director of the Library ... Mr. J. David MAUER
14 Dir Campus Computing & Networking ... Mr. Kingsley MEYER
13 MIS Director ... Dr. Steve COX
06 Registrar ... Mrs. Debbie BROWNING
29 Director of Alumni Relations ... Mrs. Annette P. WARD
04 Exec Assistant to the President ... Mrs. Lori TAYLOR

University of Toledo (F)

2801 W Bancroft, Toledo OH 43606-3390
County: Lucas FICE Identification: 003131
Unit ID: 206084
Telephone: (419) 530-4636 Carnegie Class: RU/H
FAX Number: (419) 530-4984 Calendar System: Semester
URL: www.utoledo.edu
Established: 1872 Annual Undergrad Tuition & Fees (In-State): $9,192
Enrollment: 22,610 Coed
Affiliation or Control: State IRS Status: 501(c)3
Highest Offering: Doctorate
Program: Liberal Arts And General; Teacher Preparatory; Professional
Accreditation: NH, ARCPA, ART, BUS, CACREP, CLPSY, CS, DENT, ENG, ENGR, ENGT, LAW, MED, MUS, NRPA, NURSE, OT, PH, PHAR, PTA, SP, SPAA, SW, TED

01 President ... Dr. Lloyd A. JACOBS
17 Exec VP/Chancellor Health Affairs ... Dr. Jeffrey P. GOLD
05 Exec VP/Provost Academic Affairs ... Dr. William MCMILLEN
17 Sr VP and Exec Director of UTMC .. Dr. Scott L. SCARBOROUGH
10 CFO and VP for Finance ... Mr. David O. DABNEY
43 Vice President General Counsel ... Mr. Peter J. PAPADIMOS
32 Vice President for Student Affairs .... Dr. Kaye PATTEN WALLACE
30 Vice Pres Institutional Advancement ... Mr. C. Vernon SNYDER
26 VP Ext Affairs/Equity & Diversity ... Mr. Lawrence J. BURNS
86 VP Government Relations ... Dr. Frank J. CALZONETTI
46 Vice President Research ... Dr. James P. TREMPE
11 Vice President Administration ... Mr. Charles LEHNERT
13 VP for Info Tech/CIO ... Dr. Godfrey ORWIGHO
41 Vice Pres and Director of Athletics ... Mr. Michael E. O'BRIEN
58 Dean College of Graduate Studies ... Dr. Patricia R. KOMUNIECKI
50 Dean Business & Innovation ... Dr. Thomas GUTTERIDGE
53 Dean Educ/Hlth Science/Human Serv ... Dr. Beverly J. SCHMOLL
54 Dean Engineering ... Dr. Nagi NAGANATHAN
83 Dean Languages/Lit & Soc Sciences ... Dr. Jamie BARLOWE
61 Dean Law ... Mr. Daniel STEINBOCK
63 Dean Medicine & Life Sciences ... Dr. Jeffrey GOLD
81 Dean Natural Sciences & Mathematics ... Dr. Karen BJORKMAN
66 Dean Nursing ... Dr. Timothy GASPAR
67 Dean Pharmacy ... Dr. Johnnie EARLY
88 Dean Visual & Performing Arts ... Ms. Debra DAVIS
88 Dean Adult & Lifelong Learning ... Dr. Dennis LETTMAN
92 Dean Honors College ... Dr. Thomas BARDEN
09 Vice Provost Institutional Research ... Dr. Geoffrey MARTIN
35 Dean of Students ... Ms. Michele C. MARTINEZ
39 Assoc Director Residence Life ... Ms. Virginia SPEIGHT
37 Director Student Financial Aid ... Ms. Carolyn G. BAUMGARTNER
15 Sr Human Resources Officer ... Mr. Kevin WEST
102 President Foundation ... Ms. Brenda LEE
29 Assoc Vice Pres Alumni Relations ... Mr. Daniel J. SAEVIG

06 University Registrar ... Ms. Sherri ARMSTRONG
36 Director Career Development ... Ms. Beth E. NICHOLSON
85 Director Immigration Services ... Mr. Peter I. THOMAS
21 Director Internal Audit ... Mr. David CUTRI
19 Chief of Police ... Mr. Jeff NEWTON
101 Secretary to Brd of Trustees ... Ms. Joan STASA
25 Contract Compliance Specialist HSC ... Ms. Colleen MILLER
40 General Manager Bookstore SU ... Ms. Colleen STRAYER

Urbana University (A)

579 College Way, Urbana OH 43078-2091
County: Champaign FICE Identification: 003133
Unit ID: 206330
Telephone: (937) 484-1400 Carnegie Class: Bac/Diverse
FAX Number: (937) 484-1322 Calendar System: Semester
URL: www.urbana.edu
Established: 1850 Annual Undergrad Tuition & Fees: $20,984
Enrollment: 1,509 Coed
Affiliation or Control: Independent Non-Profit IRS Status: 501(c)3
Highest Offering: Master's
Program: Liberal Arts And General; Teacher Preparatory
Accreditation: NH, IACBE, NURSE

01 President ... Dr. Stephen JONES
05 VP Academic Affairs/Dean of Faculty ... Dr. Kirk PETERSON
30 Vice Pres Institutional Advancement ... Mr. James THORNTON
32 VP Student & Enrollment Services ... Dr. James (Chip) WEISGERBER
06 Registrar ... Dr. Hedwig (Hedy) FRICK
37 Director of Financial Aid ... Mr. Larry BRICKMAN
09 Dean of Institutional Research ... Dr. Denise BOLDMAN
08 University Librarian ... Ms. Julie MCDANIEL
39 Director of Residence Life ... Mr. Mitch JOSEPH
14 Director Computer Center ... Vacant
26 Director of University Relations ... Mrs. Christina BRUUN-HORRIGAN
29 Director of Alumni Relations ... Ms. Kat STEINER
15 Director of Human Resources/Payroll ... Mrs. Audrey STEVENS
19 Director of Security/Safety ... Mr. Larry GLEESON
10 Vice Pres Admin Svcs/CFO ... Ms. Barbara STEWART
41 Athletic Director ... Mr. Doug YOUNG
40 Bookstore Manager ... Mr. Eric LATHAM

Ursuline College (B)

2550 Lander Road, Cleveland OH 44124-4398
County: Cuyahoga FICE Identification: 003134
Unit ID: 206349
Telephone: (440) 449-4200 Carnegie Class: Master's S
FAX Number: (440) 646-8318 Calendar System: Semester
URL: www.ursuline.edu
Established: 1871 Annual Undergrad Tuition & Fees: $25,530
Enrollment: 1,488 Female
Affiliation or Control: Roman Catholic IRS Status: 501(c)3
Highest Offering: Doctorate
Program: Liberal Arts And General; Teacher Preparatory; Professional; Technical Emphasis
Accreditation: NH, IACBE, NURSE, SW, TED

01 President ... Sr. Diana STANO
05 Vice President Academic Affairs ... Dr. JoAnne PODIS
10 Vice Pres & Chief Financial Officer ... Mr. David STEINER
30 Vice Pres Institutional Advancement ... Mr. Kevin GLADSTONE
18 Vice Pres of Facility Management ... Ms. June GRACYK
32 Vice President of Student Affairs ... Ms. Deanne HURLEY
84 Vice Pres of Enrollment Management ... Vacant
58 Dean of Graduate Studies ... Vacant
49 Dean of Arts & Sciences ... Dr. Elizabeth KAVRAN
66 Dean Division of Nursing ... Dr. Christine WYND
88 Exec Director Accelerated Program ... Vacant
08 Director of Library ... Ms. Betsey BELKIN
06 Registrar ... Ms. Leah SULLIVAN
21 Accounting Manager ... Mr. Timothy REARDON
44 Director of Development ... Dr. Patrick RILEY
07 Director of Admissions ... Mr. Matthew MCCAFFREY
37 Director of Financial Aid ... Ms. Mary Lynn PERRI
29 Director Alumnae ... Ms. Tiffany MUSHRUSH
26 Dir of Marketing/Communications ... Ms. Angela DELPRETE
38 Director Counseling & Career Svcs .. Ms. Geraldine M. SULLIVAN
15 Director of Personnel ... Ms. Kelli KNAUS
13 Dir of Computer Information Svcs ... Mr. Tim FARRIS
09 Director of Institutional Research ... Ms. Diane PETRUCCIO
102 Dir of Corp & Foundation Relations ... Vacant
39 Director of Residence Life ... Ms. Amy LECHKO
42 Director Campus Ministry ... Ms. Joann PIOTRKOWSKI
28 Director of Multicultural Affairs ... Ms. Tina ROAN
93 Director of Wellness Program ... Vacant
24 Media Coordinator ... Vacant
40 Manager Bookstore ... Ms. Jennifer BRAZALOVICS
41 Athletic Director ... Ms. Cynthia MCKNIGHT

Valor Christian College (C)

PO Box 800, Columbus OH 43216
County: Franklin Identification: 667093
Telephone: (614) 837-4088 Carnegie Class: Not Classified
FAX Number: (614) 837-6904 Calendar System: Semester
URL: www.valorcollege.com
Established: 1990 Annual Undergrad Tuition & Fees: $3,754
Enrollment: N/A Coed
Affiliation or Control: Independent Non-Profit IRS Status: 501(c)3
Highest Offering: Associate Degree
Program: Religious Emphasis
Accreditation: @BI

01 President ... Charles ESTRIDGE
05 Chief Academic Officer ... Ronald JEWETT
10 CFO ... Andrew STURDON
30 Chief Development Officer ... Ben BUCKNER
07 Director of Enrollment ... Aziza DEGROAT
06 Registrar ... Horace SIMONS

Vatterott College-Cleveland (D)

5025 E Royalton Road,
Broadview Heights OH 44147-3502
County: Cuyahoga Identification: 666156
Unit ID: 442408
Telephone: (440) 526-1660 Carnegie Class: Assoc/PrivFP
FAX Number: (440) 526-1933 Calendar System: Other
URL: www.vatterott-college.edu
Established: 2002 Annual Undergrad Tuition & Fees: $11,650
Enrollment: 321 Coed
Affiliation or Control: Proprietary IRS Status: Proprietary
Highest Offering: Associate Degree
Program: Occupational
Accreditation: ACCSC

01 CEO & President ... Ms. Pam BELL
10 Chief Financial Officer ... Mr. Dennis BEAVERS
05 Vice President Academic Affairs ... Dr. Brandon SHEDRON
45 VP Regulatory Affs/Strategic Devel ... Mr. Aaron LACEY
43 General Counsel/Chief Administrator ... Mr. Scott CASANOVER
12 Campus Director ... Ms. Nicole FOCARETO

† Branch campus of Vatterott College-North Park, Berkeley, MO.

Virginia Marti College of Art & Design (E)

11724 Detroit Avenue, Lakewood OH 44107-3002
County: Cuyahoga FICE Identification: 012896
Unit ID: 206394
Telephone: (216) 221-8584 Carnegie Class: Assoc/PrivFP
FAX Number: (216) 221-2311 Calendar System: Quarter
URL: www.vmcad.edu
Established: 1966 Annual Undergrad Tuition & Fees: $16,560
Enrollment: 221 Coed
Affiliation or Control: Proprietary IRS Status: Proprietary
Highest Offering: Associate Degree
Program: Occupational
Accreditation: ACCSC

01 Director ... Mrs. Virginia MARTI-VEITH
03 Assistant Director ... Mr. Dennis N. MARTI
37 Financial Aid Administrator ... Mrs. Jennifer V. MINKIEWICZ
06 Registrar ... Mrs. Lisa ALESSANDRO
07 Director of Admissions ... Mr. Quinn E. MARTI
36 Director of Career Services ... Ms. Diane NAHRA

Walsh University (F)

2020 East Maple Street, North Canton OH 44720
County: Stark FICE Identification: 003135
Unit ID: 206437
Telephone: (330) 490-7090 Carnegie Class: Master's M
FAX Number: (330) 499-7165 Calendar System: Semester
URL: www.walsh.edu
Established: 1958 Annual Undergrad Tuition & Fees: $23,765
Enrollment: 2,913 Coed
Affiliation or Control: Roman Catholic IRS Status: 501(c)3
Highest Offering: Doctorate
Program: Liberal Arts And General; Teacher Preparatory; Professional
Accreditation: NH, CACREP, NUR, PTA, TED

01 President ... Mr. Richard JUSSEAUME
05 Provost/VP Academic Affairs ... Dr. Laurence BOVE
10 Vice Pres Finance/Business Affairs ... Ms. Shelley BROWN
32 VP Student Affairs/Dean of Students ... Ms. Amy MALASKA
30 Vice Pres of Advancement/Univ Rels ... Mr. Eric BELDEN
84 Vice Pres of Enrollment Management ... Mr. Brett FRESHOUR
41 Vice Pres for Athletics ... Mr. Dale S. HOWARD
26 Asst Vice Pres University Relations ... Ms. Teresa GRIFFIN
20 Dean for Academic Affairs ... Dr. Andrew GRANT
35 Dean of Students ... Ms. Amy K. MALASKA
18 Director of Facilities & Grounds ... Mr. John SCHISSLER
09 Dean Inst Effectiveness/Lib Svcs ... Mr. Daniel S. SUVAK
13 Director of Information Systems ... Mr. Timothy OBERSCHLAKE
91 Director Administrative Computing ... Ms. Hope STANCIU
22 Director of Compliance ... Mrs. Ellen M. KUTZ
36 Director of Career Services ... Mrs. Shaanette FOWLER
38 Director Counseling Services ... Ms. Frances MORROW
42 Director of Campus Ministry ... Mr. Miguel CHAVEZ
06 University Registrar ... Mrs. Edna MCCULLOH
31 Dir Campus & Community Programs ... Ms. Jacqueline M. MANSER
37 Director Financial Aid ... Mrs. Holly VAN GILDER
15 Director of Human Resources ... Mr. Frank MCKNIGHT
29 Director of Alumni Relations ... Mr. Daniel GRAVO
43 Assoc Dean Stdt Life/Judicial Affs ... Ms. Amy MALASKA

Washington State Community College (G)

710 Colegate Drive, Marietta OH 45750-9225
County: Washington FICE Identification: 010453
Unit ID: 206446
Telephone: (740) 374-8716 Carnegie Class: Assoc/Pub-R-M
FAX Number: (740) 374-9562 Calendar System: Semester
URL: www.wscc.edu
Established: 1971 Annual Undergrad Tuition & Fees (In-State): $4,140
Enrollment: 2,211 Coed
Affiliation or Control: State IRS Status: 501(c)3
Highest Offering: Associate Degree
Program: Occupational; 2-Year Principally Bachelor's Creditable; Technical Emphasis
Accreditation: NH, MLTAD, PTAA

01 President ... Dr. Bradley J. EBERSOLE
10 Chief Financial Officer & Treasurer ... Mr. Jess N. RAINES
84 Chief Enrollment Management Officer ... Ms. Amanda K. HERB
27 Chief Information Officer ... Mr. John BILLERMAN
05 Vice President for Academic Affairs ... Dr. John W. TIGUE
103 Exec Dir of Workforce Development ... Ms. Laurene K. HUFFMAN
76 Dean of Health Sciences ... Dr. Dixie L. VAUGHAN
49 Dean of Arts and Sciences ... Vacant
50 Dean of Bus/Engr/Industrial Tech ... Ms. Brenda L. KORNMILLER
30 Director of Development ... Ms. Gail REYNOLDS
36 Director of Advising & Transfer ... Ms. Deb GOINS
06 Registrar ... Mr. Michael D. WHITNABLE
07 Senior Director of Admissions ... Mr. Paul S. WELLS
15 Director Human Resources ... Ms. Susan MURDOCK
26 Dir of Marketing & Communications ... Ms. Claudia OWENS
37 Director of Financial Aid ... Ms. Emily G. SCHUCK
18 Director Plant Opers & Maintenance ... Mr. Eric LANKFORD
38 Director of Student Development ... Vacant
08 Head Librarian ... Ms. Georgene T. JOHNSON
40 Bookstore Operations Director ... Ms. Jennifer L. DAVIS
91 Dir Management Information Systems ... Vacant
37 Assistant Director of Financial Aid ... Ms. Kathy PATTERSON
88 Business Intelligence Specialist ... Mr. Michael P. HOWERTON
25 Exec Dir of Inst Advan/Grant Writer ... Ms. Robyn HOFFMAN
88 Director of Outreach ... Mr. Gary WILLIAMS

Wilberforce University (H)

PO Box 1001, Wilberforce OH 45384-1001
County: Greene FICE Identification: 003141
Unit ID: 206491
Telephone: (937) 376-2911 Carnegie Class: Bac/Diverse
FAX Number: (937) 376-2627 Calendar System: Semester
URL: www.wilberforce.edu
Established: 1856 Annual Undergrad Tuition & Fees: $19,350
Enrollment: 608 Coed
Affiliation or Control: African Methodist Episcopal IRS Status: 501(c)3
Highest Offering: Master's
Program: Liberal Arts And General
Accreditation: NH, CORE

01 President ... Dr. Patricia L. HARDAWAY
05 Vice President Academic Affairs ... Vacant
10 Vice Pres Financial/Admin Affairs ... Ms. Mary MORALE
30 Vice President Devel/Univ Relations ... Mr. Eppechal T. SMALLS
51 Vice Pres Adult/Continuing Educ ... Dr. Emeka O. MORAH
84 VP Student Devel/Enrollment Mgmt ... Dr. Jo-Ann ROBINSON
04 Executive Assistant to President ... Vacant
32 Dean of Students ... Mr. Parris CARTER
07 Director of Admissions ... Mrs. Junell MCCALL
26 Director of Public Relations ... Vacant
06 Registrar ... Mrs. Gail D. LASH
08 Chief Librarian ... Ms. Willette STINSON
29 Dir Alumni Relations/Development ... Mr. Milton WIGGINS
36 Director Coop Education/Career Svcs ... Mrs. Hila WILLIAMS
14 Director Computer Services ... Mr. Jeff CHOI
19 Campus Police Chief ... Chief David FOX
37 Director of Financial Services ... Mr. Lloyd DIXON
38 Director Counseling Services ... Vacant
41 Athletic Director ... Mr. Parris CARTER
18 Chief Facilities/Physical Plant ... Mr. William CANADAY
15 Human Resources Manager ... Mr. Lyman MONTGOMERY
40 Bookstore Manager ... Vacant

Wilmington College (I)

1870 Quaker Way, Wilmington OH 45177-2499
County: Clinton FICE Identification: 003142
Unit ID: 206507
Telephone: (937) 382-6661 Carnegie Class: Bac/Diverse
FAX Number: (937) 383-8583 Calendar System: Semester
URL: www.wilmington.edu
Established: 1870 Annual Undergrad Tuition & Fees: $27,970
Enrollment: 1,432 Coed
Affiliation or Control: Friends IRS Status: 501(c)3
Highest Offering: Master's
Program: Liberal Arts And General; Teacher Preparatory
Accreditation: NH, TEAC

01 President ... Dr. James M. REYNOLDS
04 Assistant to the President ... Ms. Leslie A. NICHOLS
05 Interim Vice Pres Academic Affairs ... Dr. Erika A. GOODWIN
10 Vice Pres Business/Finance ... Mr. Bradley J. MITCHELL
30 Vice President College Advancement ... Mr. Robert C. HARROD

84 Vice Pres Enrollment Management .... Mr. Mark DENNISTON
12 Vice President External Programs .... Ms. Iris KELSEN
32 Vice President for Student Affairs .... Ms. Sigrid B. SOLOMON
41 Vice President Athletic Admin .... Dr. Terry A. RUPERT
20 Interim Assoc VP Academic Affairs ..... Dr. Martha S. HENDRICKS
35 Assoc Vice Pres Student Affairs .... Mr. Kenneth A. LYDY
26 Director of Public Relations .... Mr. Randall F. SARVIS
06 Registrar/Asst Dean Acad Affairs .... Ms. Karen M. GARMAN
58 Director of Graduate Studies .... Dr. Terry MILLER
08 Director of Watson Library .... Dr. Jean K. MULHERN
15 Director of Human Resources .... Mr. Scott M. FARKAS
36 Director of Career Services .... Ms. Barbara E. KAPLAN
18 Director of Physical Plant .... Mr. Terry L. JOHNSON
29 Dir Alumni and Parent Relations .... Ms. Kathy L. MILAM
37 Director Student One Stop Center .... Ms. Cheryl LOUALLEN
07 Director of Admission .... Ms. Tina M. GARLAND
09 Director of Institutional Research .... Vacant
28 Director of Multicultural Affairs .... Vacant
96 Purchasing Manager .... Ms. Laura BAESSLER

Winebrenner Theological Seminary (A)

950 N Main Street, Findlay OH 45840-3652

County: Hancock FICE Identification: 004060
Unit ID: 206516
Telephone: (419) 434-4200 Carnegie Class: Spec/Faith
FAX Number: (419) 434-4267 Calendar System: Trimester
URL: www.winebrenner.edu
Established: 1942 Annual Graduate Tuition & Fees: $13,125
Enrollment: 131 Coed
Affiliation or Control: Independent Non-Profit IRS Status: 501(c)3
Highest Offering: Doctorate; No Undergraduates
Program: Professional; Religious Emphasis
Accreditation: NH, THEOL

01 President/CEO .... Dr. David E. DRAPER
30 VP of Institutional Advancement .... Mr. Jim SMARKEL
05 VP of Academic Advancement .... Rev. Joel COCKLIN
07 Regional Coordinator Admiss/Devel .... Mr. Jim WILDER
08 Director of Library Services .... Mrs. Margaret HIRSCHY
06 Registrar .... Mrs. Shari BRANDEBERRY
04 Assistant to the President .... Ms. Marilynn C. DUNN

Wittenberg University (B)

PO Box 720, Springfield OH 45501-0720

County: Clark FICE Identification: 003143
Unit ID: 206525
Telephone: (937) 327-6231 Carnegie Class: Bac/A&S
FAX Number: (937) 327-6340 Calendar System: Semester
URL: www.wittenberg.edu
Established: 1845 Annual Undergrad Tuition & Fees: $47,766
Enrollment: 1,827 Coed
Affiliation or Control: Evangelical Lutheran Church In America
IRS Status: 501(c)3
Highest Offering: Master's
Program: Liberal Arts And General; Teacher Preparatory
Accreditation: NH, MUS, TED

01 President .... Dr. Laurie M. JOYNER
05 Provost .... Dr. Chris DUNCAN
10 Vice President Business & Finance .... Mr. Darrell B. KITCHEN
32 Vice Pres Stdnt Devel/Dean Students .... Dr. Sarah M. KELLLY
30 Vice Pres University Advancement .... Mr. Jim GEIGER
20 Assistant Provost Academic Svcs .... Ms. Van RUTHERFORD
89 Associate Provost/Undergraduate Aff .... Dr. Ty BUCKMAN
31 Dean of Community Education .... Dr. Thomas T. TAYLOR
85 Director International Education .... Ms. JoAnn BENNETT
42 Director of Church Relations .... Mr. Robert L. WHITE
42 Co-Pastor to the University .... Rev. Rachel SANDUM TUNE
42 Co-Pastor to the University .... Rev. Anders S. TUNE
08 Director of the Library .... Mr. Douglas K. LEHMAN
14 Chief Information Officer .... Mr. Richard MICKOOL
26 Chief Marketing & Communications Of .... Mr. Mark SULLIVAN
31 Director Community Service .... Ms. Kristen L. COLLIER
06 Registrar .... Mr. Jack M. CAMPBELL
24 Director Audio-Visual Services .... Mr. Lyndon C. MCCURDY
41 Director Athletics/Recreation .... Mr. Garnett H. PURNELL
58 Director Graduate Studies in Educ .... Dr. Regina POST
92 Director of Honors Program .... Dr. J. Fitz SMITH
94 Director of Women's Studies .... Dr. Lori J. ASKELAND
09 Director Institutional Research .... Dr. Jeff A. ANKROM
44 Exec Dir Major & Planned Giving ...... Mr. Richard W. STENBERG
102 Dir Govt/Corporate & Found Rels .... Vacant
29 Director of Alumni Relations .... Ms. Linda M. BEALS
26 Director of Univ Communications .... Ms. Karen L. GERBOTH
27 Dir of News Services/Sports Info .... Mr. Ryan S. MAURER
105 Webmaster .... Vacant
35 Senior Dean of Students .... Ms. Dawn H. WHITE
39 Associate Dean for Residence Life .... Mr. Mark B. DEVILBISS
38 Director Student Counseling ...... Ms. Linda M. LAUFFENBURGER
88 Director of Greek Life .... Ms. Kasey STEVENS
88 Director Student Activities .... Mr. Jonathan DURAJ
28 Director Multicultural Stdnt Pgms .... Mr. John YOUNG
23 Physician/Dir Health Services .... Dr. Kathrine MCKEE
07 Director of Admission .... Ms. Karen HUNT
37 Director of Financial Aid .... Mr. Jonathan RANDY GREEN
21 Director Budget .... Ms. Deborah S. DEWITT
18 Director Plant/Safety & Environment .... Mr. John E. PAULSEN
96 Director of Business Services .... Mrs. Donna M. PICKLESIMER

15 Assoc VP Human Resources .... Mrs. Maureen SHEEHAN MASSARO
19 Chief of Police .... Mr. Carl E. LONEY
40 Manager of Bookstore .... Mr. Tim GOGNAT

Wright State University Main Campus (C)

3640 Colonel Glenn Highway, Dayton OH 45435-0001

County: Greene FICE Identification: 003078
Unit ID: 206604
Telephone: (937) 775-3333 Carnegie Class: RU/H
FAX Number: (937) 775-3301 Calendar System: Quarter
URL: www.wright.edu
Established: 1964 Annual Undergrad Tuition & Fees (In-State): $8,424
Enrollment: 19,600 Coed
Affiliation or Control: State IRS Status: 501(c)3
Highest Offering: Doctorate
Program: Liberal Arts And General; Teacher Preparatory; Professional
Accreditation: NH, BUS, BUSA, CACREP, CLPSY, CORE, CS, ENG, IPSY, MED, MT, MUS, NURSE, PH, SPAA, SW, TED

01 President .... Dr. David R. HOPKINS
03 Senior Vice President .... Dr. Steven R. ANGLE
05 Provost .... Dr. Thomas A. SUDKAMP
10 Vice Pres Business/Fiscal Affairs .... Dr. Mark M. POLATAJKO
32 Vice President Student Affairs .... Dr. Dan ABRAHAMOWICZ
46 Vice Pres Research/Graduate Studies .... Dr. Robert FYFFE
30 Vice President Univ Advancement .... Ms. Rebecca S. COLE
84 Vice Pres Enrollment Management ...... Dr. Jacqueline MCMILLAN
20 Assoc Provost Undergrad Studies .... Dr. Thomas A. SUDKAMP
58 Dean Sch Graduate Studies .... Dr. Andrew T. HSU
04 Exec Vice President for Planning .... Dr. Robert J. SWEENEY
08 University Librarian .... Dr. Stephen P. FOSTER
26 Assoc VP Mktg/Communications .... Mr. George HEDDLESTON
15 Asst Vice Pres for Human Resources .... Mr. Allan BOGGS
18 Assc VP Facilities Plng/Development ...... Ms. Vicky L. DAVIDSON
32 Associate Vice Pres Student Affairs ..... Ms. Katherine W. MORRIS
50 Dean Raj Soin College of Business .... Dr. Joanne LI
53 Dean Education/Human Services .... Dr. Charlotte HARRIS
54 Dean Engineering/Computer Science .... Dr. S. NARAYANAN
12 Dean WSU Lake Campus .... Dr. Bonnie MATHIES
49 Interim Dean Liberal Arts .... Dr. Linda CARON
66 Dean College of Nursing & Health .... Dr. Rosalie O'DELL MAINOUS
63 Dean Boonshaft School of Medicine .... Dr. Marjorie BOWMAN
83 Dean Sch of Professional Psychology .... Dr. Larry C. JAMES
81 Dean Science/Mathematics .... Dr. Yi LI
06 Registrar .... Ms. Marian J. BRAINERD
07 Director Undergraduate Admissions .... Ms. Cathleen M. DAVIS
13 Director Computing/Telecomm Svcs ..... Mr. Paul R. HERNANDEZ
46 Asst VP Research/Sponsored Pgms ..Ms. Ellen REINSCH FRIESE
36 Director Career Services .... Ms. Cheryl KRUEGER
37 Director of Financial Aid .... Ms. Amy BARNHART
38 Director Counsel/Wellness Svcs .... Dr. Robert A. RANDO
29 Exec Dir Alumni Relations .... Mr. Gregory SCHARER
22 Director Affirmative Action Program .... Dr. Juanita L. WEHRLE-EINHORN
31 Assoc Director Event Svcs .... Ms. Jane SHELB
88 Director Disability Services .... Mr. Jeffrey A. VERNOOY
27 Assoc VP Public Affairs .... Mr. Robert E. HICKEY, JR.
41 Director of Athletics .... Mr. Bob GRANT
43 General Counsel .... Ms. Gwen M. MATTISON
24 Director CTR Teaching/Learning .... Dr. Sarah TWILL
40 Store Manager .... Ms. Jennifer L. GEBHART
85 Director Intl Student/Scholar Svcs .... Mr. Steven J. LYONS
39 Director Residence Services .... Mr. Daniel BERTSOS
19 Chief Police Department .... Mr. Michael MARTINSEN
96 Director of Purchasing .... Mr. Jerry D. BLACK
92 Director Honors Program .... Dr. Susan CARRAFIELLO
94 Director Womens Studies Program .... Dr. Kelli ZAYTOUN
09 Director of Institutional Research .... Mrs. Barbara J. BULLOCK

Wright State University Lake Campus (D)

7600 Lake Campus Drive, Celina OH 45822-2952

County: Mercer FICE Identification: 009169
Unit ID: 206613
Telephone: (419) 586-0300 Carnegie Class: Assoc/Pub2in4
FAX Number: (419) 586-0358 Calendar System: Quarter
URL: www.wright.edu/lake
Established: 1969 Annual Undergrad Tuition & Fees (In-State): $5,614
Enrollment: 1,417 Coed
Affiliation or Control: State IRS Status: 501(c)3
Highest Offering: Master's
Program: Liberal Arts And General
Accreditation: &NH

01 Dean .... Dr. Bonnie MATHIES
05 Associate Dean .... Dr. Robert M. HISKEY
32 Dir Student Svcs/Public Relations .... Ms. Sandi HOLDHEIDE
06 Registrar .... Ms. Billie J. HOBLER
30 Development Officer .... Ms. Julie MILLER
08 Librarian .... Mr. Alexander PITTMAN
13 Director Computing & Telecommun .... Mr. Ronald E. DORSTEN
38 Chief Academic Advising & Testing ..... Ms. Evelyn LAUTERBACK
53 Director of Teacher Education .... Ms. Paula K. BRYAN
20 Dir Tech/Acad/Instruct Pgms & Svcs .... Dr. John R. WOLFE
07 Dir of Admissions/Pub Rels Speclst .... Ms. Jill PUTHOFF
18 Supervisor Buildings & Grounds .... Ms. Elizabeth J. STAUGLER
40 Manager of the Bookstore .... Ms. Katie DABBELT
10 Business Manager .... Ms. Cassandra L. DORSTEN
37 Student Financial Aid Coordinator .... Ms. Gretchen RENTZ

† Regional accreditation is carried under the parent institution in Dayton, OH.

Xavier University (E)

3800 Victory Parkway, Cincinnati OH 45207-1096

County: Hamilton FICE Identification: 003144
Unit ID: 206622
Telephone: (513) 745-3000 Carnegie Class: Master's L
FAX Number: (513) 745-4223 Calendar System: Semester
URL: www.xavier.edu
Established: 1831 Annual Undergrad Tuition & Fees: $32,070
Enrollment: 6,945 Coed
Affiliation or Control: Roman Catholic IRS Status: 501(c)3
Highest Offering: Doctorate
Program: Liberal Arts And General; Teacher Preparatory; Professional
Accreditation: NH, BUS, CACREP, CEA, CLPSY, HSA, MACTE, MUS, NURSE, OT, RAD, SW, TEAC

01 President .... Rev. Michael J. GRAHAM, SJ
11 Administrative Vice President .... Dr. John F. KUCIA
05 Provost & Chief Academic Officer .... Dr. Scott CHADWICK
10 Sr VP Financial Administration/CFO .... Ms. Maribeth AMYOT
26 Vice Pres for University Relations .... Mr. Gary R. MASSA
88 Asst to Pres for Mission & Identity .... Dr. Debra MOONEY
13 Assoc Provost Information Resources .... Ms. Annette MARKSBERRY
84 Vice Pres for Student Enrollment .... Mr. Terry RICHARDS
28 Asst to Pres Diversity/Inclusion .... Ms. Cheryl L. NUNEZ
26 Director for Public Relations .... Ms. Deb DEL VALLE
30 Assoc VP for University Relations .... Ms. Susan ABEL
32 Assoc Provost for Student Affairs .... Mr. David J. JOHNSON
18 Asc VP Facility Mgt/Capital Project .... Mr. Robert M. SHEERAN
41 Assoc Vice Pres/Director Athletics .... Mr. Michael A. BOBINSKI
15 Assoc Vice Pres for Human Resources .... Mrs. Shari MICKEY-BOGGS
07 Dean Undergraduate Admission .... Mr. Aaron MEIS
12 Director Cintas Center .... Mr. Michael DUNN
44 Exec Dir Gifts & Estate Planning .... Mr. Mark MCLAUGHLIN
42 Dir Center for Mission/Identity .... Mr. Joseph SHADLE
06 Registrar .... Ms. Mary Alyce ORAHOOD
88 Director of Scholarships .... Mr. Paul H. CALME
85 Director for Internatl Student Svcs .... Ms. Lea MINNITI
105 Exec Dir Ofc University Commun .... Mr. Doug RUSCHMAN
39 Director of Residence Life .... Ms. Lori A. LAMBERT
40 Director of Bookstore .... Ms. Susan GRIFFIN
86 Dir of Comm & Government Relations ... Dr. Eugene L. BEAUPRE'
83 Dean College Social Sci/Health/Educ .... Dr. Mark MEYERS
36 Dir Student Involvement/Leadership .... Ms. Leah BUSAM
23 Director for Health Services .... Ms. Mary ROSENFELDT
49 Dean College Arts & Sciences .... Dr. Janice B. WALKER
19 Director of Campus Police/Security .... Mr. Michael COUCH
37 Director of Financial Aid .... Mr. Todd EVERETT
43 General Counsel .... Mr. Joseph H. FELDHAUS
29 Dir Alumni Rels/Ex Dir Athletic Dev .... Mr. Brian MALEY
09 Sr Policy/Plng Analyst/Ofc of SIR .... Dr. Tammy KAHRIG
50 Dean Williams College of Business .... Dr. Brian TILL
51 Actg Dean Center Adults/PT Students .... Ms. Sheila DORAN

Youngstown State University (F)

One University Plaza, Youngstown OH 44555-0001

County: Mahoning FICE Identification: 003145
Unit ID: 206695
Telephone: (330) 941-3000 Carnegie Class: Master's L
FAX Number: (330) 941-7169 Calendar System: Semester
URL: www.ysu.edu
Established: 1908 Annual Undergrad Tuition & Fees (In-State): $7,451
Enrollment: 14,483 Coed
Affiliation or Control: State IRS Status: 501(c)3
Highest Offering: Doctorate
Program: Occupational; Liberal Arts And General; Teacher Preparatory; Professional; Technical Emphasis
Accreditation: NH, AAFCS, ANEST, ART, BUS, CACREP, DH, DIETC, DIETD, DIETT, EMT, ENG, ENGT, HT, MAC, MLTAD, MUS, NUR, PH, PTA, SW, TED, THEA

01 President .... Dr. Cynthia E. ANDERSON
05 Provost .... Dr. Ikram KHAWAJA
11 Vice President for Finance/Admin .... Mr. Eugene P. GRILLI
04 Executive Assoc to the President .... Ms. Shannon TIRONE
32 VP for Student Affairs .... Mr. Jack FAHEY
30 VP for University Advancement .... Mr. R. Scott EVANS
43 Univ General Counsel/Asst to Pres .... Ms. Holly A. JACOBS
49 Dean of Liberal Arts/Social Science .... Dr. Shearle FURNISH
50 Dean of Business Administration .... Dr. Betty Jo LICATA
53 Dean of Education .... Dr. Charles HOWELL
54 Dean of Science/Tech/Eng/Math .... Dr. Martin A. ABRAHAM
57 Dean Fine & Performing Arts .... Mr. Byran DEPOY
76 Dean Health & Human Services .... Dr. Joseph L. MOSCA
58 Dean of Graduate Studies/Research .... Dr. Peter J. KASVINSKY
45 Assoc Provost Acad Pgms/Planning .... Dr. Kevin BALL
20 Int Assoc Prov Acad Admin/Info Svcs .... Dr. Teri RILEY
15 Chief Human Resources Officer .... Mr. Kevin W. REYNOLDS
13 Interim Chief Technology Officer .... Mr. Richard J. MARSICO
10 Exec Director Financial Services .... Ms. Eileen GREAF
41 Exec Director of Athletics .... Mr. Ronald A. STROLLO
26 Exec Dir of Mktg/Communications ..... Mr. Mark W. VANTILBURG

35 Vice President for Student Affairs ... Mr. John P. FAHEY
35 Exec Director of Student Life ... Mr. Matthew NOVOTNY
84 Exec Dir Enrollment Mgmt ... Vacant
08 Executive Director Library ... Mr. Paul J. KOBULNICKY
29 Int Exec Dir of Alumni Relations ... Ms. Jacquelyn LEVISEUR
28 Director Equal Oppty/Diversity .. Ms. Yulanda MCCARTY-HARRIS
07 Director Undergrad Recruit/Admiss ... Ms. Sue E. DAVIS
06 Registrar ... Ms. Jeanne HERMAN
19 Chief of University Police ... Mr. John BESHARA
18 Director of University Facilities ... Mr. John P. HYDEN
21 Director-Student Accts/Receivables ... Ms. Beth A. YEATTS
23 Dir Environ/Occup Health & Safety ... Mr. Daniel SAHLI
37 Director Financial/Scholarships ... Ms. Elaine RUSE
21 Director General Accounting ... Ms. Katrena J. DAVIDSON
88 Director Budget Planning ... Mr. Neal P. MCNALLY
21 Cash Management Officer ... Ms. Akhande KHAN
25 Director Grants & Sponsored Pgms ... Mr. Edward ORONA
09 Exec Dir Institutional Research ... Vacant
39 Director Housing Services ... Ms. Danielle MEYER
85 Administrator International Studies ... Mr. Jef C. DAVIS
14 Director Computer Center ... Mr. Richard J. MARSICO
30 Interim Chief Development Officer ... Ms. Catherine CALA
28 Director Student Diversity Programs ... Mr. William J. BLAKE
88 Dir Assoc Degree/Tech Prep Pgms ... Ms. Arlene FLOYD
40 Director of Bookstore ... Mr. Charles A. SABATINO
88 Director Support Services ... Mr. Danny J. O'CONNELL
88 Dir Electronic Maintenance Svcs ... Mr. Michael REPETSKI
90 Director Media/Acad Computing ... Mr. Michael S. HRISHENKO
92 Director Univ Scholars/Honors Pgm ... Dr. Ronald SHAKLEE
36 Director of Career Services ... Ms. Marijean BENEDICK
96 Director Procurement Services ... Mr. William WHEELOCK
88 Director Degree Audit ... Ms. Marie D. CULLEN
91 Director Network Services ... Mr. Jason T. RAKERS
35 Director for Student Progress ... Ms. Jonelle BEATRICE
35 Dir Campus Rec/Intramural Sports ... Mr. Jack RIGNEY
88 Director WYSU-FM ... Mr. Gary SEXTON

Zane State College (A)

1555 Newark Road, Zanesville OH 43701-2626
County: Muskingum — FICE Identification: 008133
Unit ID: 204255
Telephone: (740) 454-2501 — Carnegie Class: Assoc/Pub-R-M
FAX Number: (740) 454-0035 — Calendar System: Quarter
URL: www.zanestate.edu
Established: 1969 — Annual Undergrad Tuition & Fees (In-State): $4,672
Enrollment: 2,943 — Coed
Affiliation or Control: State — IRS Status: 501(c)3
Highest Offering: Associate Degree
Program: 2-Year Principally Bachelor's Creditable; Technical Emphasis
Accreditation: NH, ACFEI, ENGT, MAC, MLTAD, OTA, PTAA, RAD

01 President ... Dr. Paul R. BROWN
102 Exec Dir Inst Advancemnt/Foundation ... Ms. Pamela A. JIRA
05 Provost/Executive Vice President ... Dr. Chad BROWN
10 Vice Pres for Business Services ... Mr. Albert F. BROWN
32 Vice Pres for Student Svcs/Registra ... Dr. Dotty WELCH
54 Acad Dean Business & Engineering ... Mr. George HICKS
12 Dean Cambridge Campus ... Mr. Mike WITSON
15 Director of Human Resources ... Dr. James KEMPER
13 Exec Dir of Info Tech Svcs ... Mr. Jeffrey DEVLIN
08 Library Director ... Mr. Tony HOPKINS
09 Director of Institutional Research ... Dr. Beth FISCHER
25 Director of Grants & Contracts ... Mrs. Larisa HARPER
07 Director of Admissions ... Mr. Paul J. YOUNG
37 Director Student Financial Aid ... Ms. Amanda B. REISINGER
36 Director Career/Employment Services ... Ms. Jamie K. CLARK
26 Director Marketing & Communications ... Ms. Tamra PACE
20 Assoc Dean of Dev Ed & First Year ... Ms. Rebecca R. AMENT
38 Director of Student Success Center ... Ms. Stacie J. MAHAFFEY
21 Director of Accounting Services ... Ms. Tammy S. HUFFMAN
40 Director of Bookstore Operations ... Ms. Linda D. METZ
19 Int Director of Safety and Security ... Mr. Joe KEATING
49 Dean of Arts and Sciences ... Mrs. Susan HOLDREN
76 Dean of Educ Health & Human Svcs ... Dr. Barbara SHELBY

OKLAHOMA

Bacone College (B)

2299 Old Bacone Road, Muskogee OK 74403-1568
County: Muskogee — FICE Identification: 003147
Unit ID: 206817
Telephone: (918) 683-4581 — Carnegie Class: Bac/Assoc
FAX Number: (918) 781-7422 — Calendar System: Semester
URL: www.bacone.edu
Established: 1880 — Annual Undergrad Tuition & Fees: $13,510
Enrollment: 1,111 — Coed
Affiliation or Control: American Baptist — IRS Status: 501(c)3
Highest Offering: Baccalaureate
Program: 2-Year Principally Bachelor's Creditable; Liberal Arts And General; Teacher Preparatory
Accreditation: NH, IACBE, NUR, RAD

01 President ... Rev Dr. Robert J. DUNCAN, JR.
03 Exec Vice Pres & Dean of Faculty ... Dr. Robert K. BROWN
88 VP Center for American Indians ... Dr. Pete COSER
30 Asst VP Institutional Advancement ... Mr. Eugene BLANKENSHIP
84 VP of Enrollment Management ... Vacant
42 VP Christian Ministry ... Rev Dr. Leroy THOMPSON
10 VP Finance ... Mr. Mustafa YUNDEM
88 Asst VP Ctr for Christian Ministry ... Rev Dr. Stephen WILEY
32 Asst VP Student Life ... Ms. Shelli HOPKINS
06 Registrar ... Mrs. Virginia THOMPSON
40 Bookstore Manager ... Ms. Christin SWAGERS
41 Asst VP Athletics ... Mr. Alan FOSTER
39 Dir Residential Life & Hospitality ... Ms. Denise WILCOX
37 Director Financial Aid ... Ms. Kathye WATSON
15 Director Human Resources ... Ms. Tammy MCDANIELS
18 Chief Facilities/Physical Plant ... Vacant
35 Director of Student Services ... Mr. Dustin HOPKINS
29 Asst Director Alumni Relations ... Vacant
09 Coord Institutional Assessment Data ... Ms. Linda MILAM
26 Director of External Relations ... Ms. Susie CAGLE
21 Controller ... Mr. Joe SNOW
36 Director of Career Services ... Ms. Jo COLLIER
105 Dir Web/Video Design Studio ... Mr. Dwayne PARTON
08 Dir Betts Library/Head Librarian ... Ms. Faye DAVIS
13 Director of Network Systems ... Mr. Chris EHLERS

Brown Mackie College-Tulsa (C)

4608 South Garnett Road, Ste. 110, Tulsa OK 74146
County: Tulsa — Identification: 666783
Unit ID: 455619
Telephone: (918) 628-3700 — Carnegie Class: Assoc/PrivFP4
FAX Number: (918) 828-9083 — Calendar System: Other
URL: www.brownmackie.edu
Established: N/A — Annual Undergrad Tuition & Fees: $11,124
Enrollment: 463 — Coed
Affiliation or Control: Proprietary — IRS Status: Proprietary
Highest Offering: Baccalaureate
Program: Occupational; 2-Year Principally Bachelor's Creditable; Business Emphasis
Accreditation: ACICS, OTA, SURGT, SURTEC

01 President ... John PAPPAS
07 Senior Director of Admissions ... Jim LILLARD
05 Dean of Academic Affairs ... James FOUNTAIN

† Branch campus of Brown Mackie College, South Bend, IN.

Cameron University (D)

2800 W Gore Boulevard, Lawton OK 73505-6377
County: Comanche — FICE Identification: 003150
Unit ID: 206914
Telephone: (580) 581-2200 — Carnegie Class: Master's S
FAX Number: (580) 581-2867 — Calendar System: Semester
URL: www.cameron.edu
Established: 1908 — Annual Undergrad Tuition & Fees (In-State): $4,770
Enrollment: 6,463 — Coed
Affiliation or Control: State — IRS Status: 501(c)3
Highest Offering: Master's
Program: Liberal Arts And General; Teacher Preparatory
Accreditation: NH, ACBSP, MUS, TED

01 President ... Dr. Cynthia S. ROSS
05 Provost ... Dr. John M. MCARTHUR
10 Vice Pres for Business & Finance ... Mr. Glen P. PINKSTON
30 Vice Pres University Advancement ... Mr. Albert D. JOHNSON, JR.
32 Vice President for Student Services ... Ms. Jennifer L. HOLLAND
84 Assoc Vice Pres Enrollment Mgmt ... Mrs. Jamie L. GLOVER
50 Dean School of Business ... Dr. Oris ODOM, II
79 Dean School of Liberal Arts ... Dr. Von E. UNDERWOOD
53 Dean Sch of Educ/Behav Science ... Dr. Ronna J. VANDERSLICE
81 Dean School Science/Tech ... Dr. Terry CONLEY
31 Director of Public Affairs ... Mr. Josh LEHMAN
08 Librarian ... Dr. Sheridan YOUNG
29 Director Alumni Relations ... Ms. Jennifer MCGRAIL
41 Director Athletic Administration ... Mr. Jim C. JACKSON
07 Director of Admissions ... Ms. Zoe W. DURANT
06 Registrar ... Mrs. Linda PHILLIPS
45 Dir Inst Rsrch/Assess/Accountablty ... Dr. Karla OTY
37 Director of Financial Assistance ... Mr. Donald HALL
13 Director Information Tech Services ... Ms. Debbie GOODE
15 Director of Human Resources ... Mr. Chase MASSIE
38 Director Student Development ... Dr. Jennifer PRUCHNICKI
35 Director Student Activities ... Mr. Zeak NAIFEH
19 Director Public Safety ... Mr. John DEBOARD
18 Int Director Physical Facilities ... Mr. Robert HANEFIELD
96 Director of Purchasing ... Mr. Richard MCCOMAS

Carl Albert State College (E)

1507 S McKenna, Poteau OK 74953-5208
County: Le Flore — FICE Identification: 003176
Unit ID: 206923
Telephone: (918) 647-1200 — Carnegie Class: Assoc/Pub-R-M
FAX Number: (918) 647-1201 — Calendar System: Semester
URL: www.carlalbert.edu
Established: 1933 — Annual Undergrad Tuition & Fees (In-State): $2,490
Enrollment: 2,622 — Coed
Affiliation or Control: State — IRS Status: 501(c)3
Highest Offering: Associate Degree
Program: Occupational; 2-Year Principally Bachelor's Creditable
Accreditation: NH, ACBSP, ADNUR, PTAA, RAD

01 President ... Dr. Brandon R. WEBB
32 Vice President for Student Affairs ... Ms. Leah MCLAUGHLIN
05 Vice President of Academic Affairs ... Dr. James YATES
10 Vice Pres for Business Operations ... Ms. Ramona BUCKNER
13 Information Technology Director ... Mr. Michael MARTIN
04 Assistant to the President ... Mr. Garry IVEY
26 Public Relations Director ... Ms. Judi WHITE
06 Registrar/Director Admissions ... Ms. Dee Ann DICKERSON
37 Director of Financial Aid ... Ms. Robin BENSON
86 Director Federal Programs ... Ms. Michelle WHITE
18 Chief Facilities/Physical Plant ... Mr. Garry IVEY
15 Director Personnel Services ... Ms. Vicki HILL
21 Assistant Finance Officer ... Ms. Melinda PIERCE

Clary Sage College (F)

3131 South Sheridan Road, Tulsa OK 74145-1102
County: Tulsa — Identification: 666368
Unit ID: 450401
Telephone: (918) 298-8200 — Carnegie Class: Assoc/PrivFP
FAX Number: (918) 298-0099 — Calendar System: Other
URL: www.clarysagecollege.com
Established: 2005 — Annual Undergrad Tuition & Fees: $17,807
Enrollment: 340 — Coed
Affiliation or Control: Proprietary — IRS Status: Proprietary
Highest Offering: Associate Degree
Program: Occupational; 2-Year Principally Bachelor's Creditable; Technical Emphasis
Accreditation: ACICS

00 CEO ... Ms. Teresa KNOX
01 President ... Dr. Kevin KIRK
05 Campus Director ... Dr. Raye MAHLBERG

† Branch campus of Community Care College, Tulsa, OK.

Community Care College (G)

4242 S Sheridan Road, Tulsa OK 74145-1119
County: Tulsa — FICE Identification: 033674
Unit ID: 439570
Telephone: (918) 610-0027 — Carnegie Class: Assoc/PrivFP
FAX Number: (918) 610-0029 — Calendar System: Other
URL: www.communitycarecollege.edu
Established: 1995 — Annual Undergrad Tuition & Fees: $21,071
Enrollment: 618 — Coed
Affiliation or Control: Proprietary — IRS Status: Proprietary
Highest Offering: Associate Degree
Program: Occupational; 2-Year Principally Bachelor's Creditable
Accreditation: ACICS, MAAB, SURGT

00 CEO ... Ms. Teresa L. KNOX
01 President ... Mr. Kevin L. KIRK

Connors State College (H)

Route 1, Box 1000, Warner OK 74469-9700
County: Muskogee — FICE Identification: 003153
Unit ID: 206996
Telephone: (918) 463-2931 — Carnegie Class: Assoc/Pub-R-M
FAX Number: (918) 463-2233 — Calendar System: Semester
URL: www.connorsstate.edu
Established: 1908 — Annual Undergrad Tuition & Fees (In-State): $2,997
Enrollment: 2,563 — Coed
Affiliation or Control: State — IRS Status: 501(c)3
Highest Offering: Associate Degree
Program: Occupational; 2-Year Principally Bachelor's Creditable
Accreditation: NH, ADNUR

01 President ... Dr. Timothy W. FALTYN
05 Vice Pres Academic Svcs/Stdnt Affs ... Dr. Ron RAMMING
10 Vice President of Fiscal Services ... Mrs. Shirley TWILLEY
37 Director of Financial Aid ... Ms. Jennifer WATKINS
08 Director of Learning Center ... Mrs. Margaret RIGNEY
13 Director Information Technology ... Mr. Heath HODGES
06 Registrar ... Ms. Kwanna KING
07 Director of Recruitment ... Ms. Logan KNAPPER
26 Director of Public Information ... Mr. Lyndsey SULLIVAN
15 Director Human Resources ... Ms. Gwendolyn DERRICK
09 Int Dir of Institutional Research ... Mr. Eric SYNAR
30 Dir of Development Foundation ... Mr. Ryan BLANTON

DeVry University - Oklahoma City (I)

4013 NW Expressway Street, Ste 100,
Oklahoma City OK 73116-1695
County: Oklahoma — Identification: 666566
Unit ID: 447485
Telephone: (405) 767-9516 — Carnegie Class: Spec/Bus
FAX Number: (405) 842-4573 — Calendar System: Semester
URL: www.devry.edu
Established: 1931 — Annual Undergrad Tuition & Fees: $16,156
Enrollment: 252 — Coed
Affiliation or Control: Proprietary — IRS Status: Proprietary
Highest Offering: Master's
Program: Professional; Business Emphasis
Accreditation: &NH

01 Campus Director ... Anthony SPANO

† Regional accreditation is carried under the parent institution in Downers Grove, IL.

East Central University (J)

1100 E 14th Street, Ada OK 74820-6899
County: Pontotoc — FICE Identification: 003154
Unit ID: 207041

Telephone: (580) 332-8000 Carnegie Class: Master's L
FAX Number: (580) 332-1623 Calendar System: Semester
URL: www.ecok.edu
Established: 1909 Annual Undergrad Tuition & Fees (In-State): $4,838
Enrollment: 4,816 Coed
Affiliation or Control: State IRS Status: 501(c)3
Highest Offering: Master's
Program: Liberal Arts And General; Teacher Preparatory; Professional
Accreditation: NH, ACBSP, CORE, MUS, NUR, SW, TED

01 President .... Dr. John R. HARGRAVE
05 Provost/Vice Pres Academic Affairs .... Dr. Duane C. ANDERSON
32 Vice President Student Development .... Dr. Gerald FORBES
10 Vice Pres Administration/Finance .... Ms. Jessica BOLES
20 Asst VP Academic Affairs .... Dr. Katricia PIERSON
53 Dean of Education .... Dr. Brenda WALLING
50 Dean of Business .... Mr. Wendell GODWIN
51 Director Continuing Education .... Dr. G. Richard WETHERILL
35 Dean of Students .... Vacant
37 Director of Financial Aid .... Ms. Becky ISAACS
09 Director of Institutional Research .... Dr. Sheilynda STEWART
08 Librarian .... Dr. Adrianna LANCASTER
06 Registrar .... Ms. Pamla ARMSTRONG
14 Director Computer Center .... Mr. Frank WILLIAMS
41 Athletic Director .... Mr. Brian DEANGELIS
15 Director of Human Resources .... Mr. Lynn LOFTIN
19 Chief of Police .... Mr. Henry MILLER
18 Director Physical Plant .... Mr. Robert CASTLEBERRY
26 Dir of Marketing & Communication .... Ms. Amy FORD
29 Director Alumni Relations .... Ms. Buffy LOVELIS
84 Director Enrollment Management .... Mr. B. J ECHARD
96 Director of Purchasing .... Ms. Jo Ann JOHNSON

Eastern Oklahoma State College (A)

1301 W Main Street, Wilburton OK 74578-4999
County: Latimer FICE Identification: 003155
Unit ID: 207050
Telephone: (918) 465-2361 Carnegie Class: Assoc/Pub-R-S
FAX Number: (918) 465-2431 Calendar System: Semester
URL: www.eosc.edu
Established: 1909 Annual Undergrad Tuition & Fees (In-State): $3,200
Enrollment: 1,946 Coed
Affiliation or Control: State IRS Status: 501(c)3
Highest Offering: Associate Degree
Program: Occupational; 2-Year Principally Bachelor's Creditable
Accreditation: NH, ADNUR, MLTAD

01 President .... Dr. Stephen E. SMITH
05 Vice President of Academic Affairs .... Dr. Karen D. HARRISON
10 Vice Pres of Business Affairs .... Ms. La Donna HOWELL
32 Vice Pres for Student Affairs .... Mr. Victor WOODS
12 Director of McAlester Campus .... Dr. Janet WANSICK
35 Dean of Students .... Mr. Greg WARREN
30 Exec Dir Development/Alumni Rels .... Mrs. Ann OWENS
27 Director Public Information .... Mr. Hank MOONEY
84 Dir Enrollment Mgmt/Financial Aid .... Mrs. Victor WOODS
13 Chief Technical Officer .... Mr. Jeff WEEMS
08 Director Library & Media Services .... Ms. Maria MARTINEZ
15 Director Personnel Services .... Mrs. Joyce BILLS
06 Registrar .... Ms. Karen CLARK
18 Chief Facilities/Physical Plant .... Mr. Rudy O'DONLEY
44 Dir of Institutional Advancement .... Ms. Treva KENNEDY
37 Financial Aid Officer .... Ms. Patricia RECTOR

Family of Faith College (B)

PO Box 1805, Shawnee OK 74802-1805
County: Pottawatomie FICE Identification: 036763
Unit ID: 443058
Telephone: (405) 273-5331 Carnegie Class: Spec/Faith
FAX Number: (405) 273-8535 Calendar System: Semester
URL: www.familyoffaithcollege.edu
Established: 1992 Annual Undergrad Tuition & Fees: $5,410
Enrollment: 25 Coed
Affiliation or Control: Independent Non-Profit IRS Status: 501(c)3
Highest Offering: Baccalaureate
Program: Professional; Religious Emphasis
Accreditation: BI

01 President .... Dr. Samuel W. MATTHEWS
05 Vice President Academic Affairs .... Mrs. Elaine W. PHILLIPS
10 Vice President Operations/Finance .... Mr. Vaughn NEWMAN
32 Vice Pres Student Affs/Dir Fin Aid .... Mrs. Rhonda GAINES
46 Director of Resource Development .... Vacant
42 Director of Spiritual Life .... Mr. Daniel J. MATTHEWS
108 Dir of Accreditation/Assessment .... Mrs. Elaine W. PHILLIPS

Heritage College (C)

7100 I-35 Services Road, Suite 7118,
Oklahoma City OK 73149-2740
County: Oklahoma FICE Identification: 031151
Unit ID: 410070
Telephone: (405) 631-3399 Carnegie Class: Assoc/PrivFP
FAX Number: (405) 631-6711 Calendar System: Quarter
URL: www.heritage-education.com
Established: 2002 Annual Undergrad Tuition & Fees: $23,220
Enrollment: 1,001 Coed
Affiliation or Control: Proprietary IRS Status: Proprietary
Highest Offering: Associate Degree
Program: Occupational
Accreditation: ABHES, SURTEC

01 Director .... Ms. Cheryl MORRIS

Hillsdale Free Will Baptist College (D)

PO Box 7208, Moore OK 73153-1208
County: Cleveland FICE Identification: 010266
Unit ID: 207157
Telephone: (405) 912-9000 Carnegie Class: Spec/Faith
FAX Number: (405) 912-9050 Calendar System: Semester
URL: www.hc.edu
Established: 1959 Annual Undergrad Tuition & Fees: $13,600
Enrollment: 263 Coed
Affiliation or Control: Free Will Baptist Church IRS Status: 501(c)3
Highest Offering: Master's
Program: Liberal Arts And General; Religious Emphasis
Accreditation: TRACS

01 President .... Dr. Timothy W. EATON
05 Chief Academic Officer .... Dr. Thomas L. MARBERRY
03 Executive Vice President .... Dr. Mark H. BRAISHER
30 Director Institutional Advancement .... Mr. Bob THOMPSON
07 Dir of Admissions/Dean of Students .... Vacant
37 Financial Aid Coordinator .... Ms. Denise CONKLIN
08 LRC Director .... Ms. Nancy J. DRAPER
13 Director of MIS .... Mr. Quentin C. LOOP
06 Registrar .... Ms. Patti ASHBY
58 Dean of Graduate Studies .... Dr. Mark H. BRAISHER
33 Men's Resident Life Coordinator .... Mr. Sam CRILLY
34 Women's Resident Life Coordinator .... Ms. Sammi MCCRARY
41 Athletic Director .... Ms. Autumn DRAKE
42 Chaplain/Director Campus Ministries .... Rev. Jeff SLOAN
40 Bookstore Manager .... Ms. Taylor PAULK
51 Coordinator of Adult Studies .... Ms. Patti ASHBY

ITT Technical Institute (E)

50 Penn Place Ofc Tower, Ste 305R,
Oklahoma City OK 73118
County: Oklahoma Identification: 666159
Unit ID: 448503
Telephone: (405) 810-4100 Carnegie Class: Assoc/PrivFP4
FAX Number: N/A Calendar System: Quarter
URL: www.itt-tech.edu
Established: 2006 Annual Undergrad Tuition & Fees: N/A
Enrollment: 450 Coed
Affiliation or Control: Proprietary IRS Status: Proprietary
Highest Offering: Baccalaureate
Program: Technical Emphasis
Accreditation: ACICS

† Branch campus of ITT Technical Institute, Indianapolis, IN.

ITT Technical Institute (F)

4500 S. 129th East Avenue, Ste. 152, Tulsa OK 74134
County: Tulsa Identification: 666147
Unit ID: 448512
Telephone: (918) 615-3900 Carnegie Class: Assoc/PrivFP4
FAX Number: N/A Calendar System: Quarter
URL: www.itt-tech.edu
Established: 2006 Annual Undergrad Tuition & Fees: N/A
Enrollment: 593 Coed
Affiliation or Control: Proprietary IRS Status: Proprietary
Highest Offering: Baccalaureate
Program: Technical Emphasis
Accreditation: ACICS

† Branch campus of ITT Technical Institute, Indianapolis, IN.

Langston University (G)

PO Box 1500, Langston OK 73050
County: Logan FICE Identification: 003157
Unit ID: 207209
Telephone: (405) 466-2231 Carnegie Class: Master's S
FAX Number: (405) 466-3461 Calendar System: Semester
URL: www.langston.edu
Established: 1897 Annual Undergrad Tuition & Fees (In-State): $4,112
Enrollment: 2,840 Coed
Affiliation or Control: State IRS Status: 501(c)3
Highest Offering: Doctorate
Program: Liberal Arts And General; Teacher Preparatory; Professional
Accreditation: NH, ACBSP, CORE, DIETD, NUR, PTA, TED

01 President .... Dr. Kent J. SMITH, JR.
05 Vice President Academic Affairs .... Dr. Clyde MONTGOMERY
10 Vice President Fiscal/Admin Affairs .... Mrs. Angela R. WATSON
32 VP Student Affairs/Enrollment Mgmt .... Dr. Rafael MOFFETT
30 Vice Pres Inst Development/Advance .... Vacant
100 Chief of Staff .... Mrs. Cynthia S. BUCKLEY
13 Chief Information Officer .... Mr. Pritchard MONCRIFFE
20 Assoc VP Academic Affairs LU/OKC .... Dr. Blayne E. HINDS
20 COO/Assoc VP Academic Affs LU/Tulsa .... Dr. Bruce W. MCGOWAN
21 Asst VP of Fiscal Affairs .... Ms. Debra G. MASTERS
44 Asst VP Inst Advanc/Campaign Dir .... Mr. James R. DUNAVANT
35 Assistant VP of Student Affairs .... Vacant
29 Director Alumni Affairs .... Mrs. Vonnie W. ROBERTS
36 Dir Assessment/Career Placement .... Mr. James A. WALLACE
26 Director Public Relations .... Ms. Vickie G. JACKSON
07 Director of Admissions .... Ms. Josita L. BAKER
37 Director Financial Aid .... Ms. Shelia MCGILL
15 Director of Human Resources .... Mrs. Beverly H. SMITH
22 Dir LCDC Affirm Action/EEO Ofc .... Vacant
18 Director Facilities/Physical Plant .... Mr. Ruben D. OLIVER
38 Dir Professional Counseling Center .... Dr. William PRICE CURTIS
09 Director Inst Research & Planning .... Ms. Hala KHOURY
08 Director of Libraries .... Ms. Bettye R. BLACK
06 Registrar .... Mrs. Kathy SIMMONS
41 Athletic Director .... Mr. Mike GARRETT
21 Comptroller .... Mr. J.I JOHNSON
58 Director of Graduate Programs .... Dr. Alex O. LEWIS
19 Chief of Police .... Mr. Frank ATKINSON
96 Director of Purchasing .... Mrs. Deirdra M. STEVENSON
49 Dean School of Arts & Sciences .... Dr. Clarence A. HEDGE
50 Dean School of Business .... Dr. Solomon S. SMITH
46 Dean School Agric/Applied Science .... Dr. Marvin BURNS
66 Dean Sch Nursing/Health Professions .... Dr. Carolyn T. KORNEGAY
53 Acting Dean Sch Educ/Behav Sci .... Dr. Joe N. HORNBEAK
92 Dean Honors Program .... Dr. Joanne CLARK
88 Dean Physical Therapy Program .... Dr. Milagros JORGE
88 Dean Entrepreneurial Studies .... Dr. Surya P. SINGH

Mid-America Christian University (H)

3500 SW 119th Street, Oklahoma City OK 73170-4500
County: Cleveland FICE Identification: 006942
Unit ID: 245953
Telephone: (405) 691-3800 Carnegie Class: Bac/Diverse
FAX Number: (405) 692-3165 Calendar System: Semester
URL: www.macu.edu
Established: 1953 Annual Undergrad Tuition & Fees: $15,092
Enrollment: 2,255 Coed
Affiliation or Control: Church Of God IRS Status: 501(c)3
Highest Offering: Master's
Program: Liberal Arts And General; Teacher Preparatory; Religious Emphasis
Accreditation: NH

01 President .... Dr. John D. FOZARD
05 Provost .... Dr. Kathaleen REID-MARTINEZ
30 Vice Pres for Univ Advancement .... Mr. Steven SEATON
84 Assoc VP Student Affairs/Enrollment .... Mrs. Jessica RIMMER
88 Dean Academic Scholarships .... Dr. Shirley RODDY
10 Chief Financial Officer .... Ms. Mici SARTIN
15 Chief Administration Officer (HR) .... Mr. Owen SEVIER
20 Chief Academic Assessment Officer .... Mrs. Julia CARPENTER
88 Exec Dir of Church Relations .... Rev. Morgan ALSIP
06 Registrar .... Vacant
37 Director Student Financial Services .... Vacant
07 Director of Admissions .... Mr. Dustin ROWTON
18 Director Facilities/Physical Plant .... Mr. Clark BAREFOOT
29 Director Alumni Relations .... Vacant

Murray State College (I)

One Murray Campus, Tishomingo OK 73460-3130
County: Johnston FICE Identification: 003158
Unit ID: 207236
Telephone: (580) 371-2371 Carnegie Class: Assoc/Pub-R-M
FAX Number: (580) 371-9844 Calendar System: Semester
URL: www.mscok.edu
Established: 1908 Annual Undergrad Tuition & Fees (In-State): $3,200
Enrollment: 2,674 Coed
Affiliation or Control: State IRS Status: 501(c)3
Highest Offering: Associate Degree
Program: Occupational; 2-Year Principally Bachelor's Creditable
Accreditation: NH, ADNUR, OTA, PTAA

01 President .... Ms. Joy MCDANIEL
04 Exec Assistant to President/Board .... Mr. Michael BURRELL
10 VP for Administration and Finance .... Vacant
05 VP for Academic Affairs .... Dr. Roger STACY
32 VP of Student Affairs .... Ms. Michaelle GRAY
37 Assoc Financial Aid Director .... Ms. Machelle ELLIS
08 Director of Library .... Ms. Mary RIXEN
74 Veterinary Tech Program Director .... Dr. Carey FLOYD
66 Director of Nursing .... Ms. Joni JETER
30 Dir of Development/External Rels .... Vacant
20 Director of Academic Advisement .... Ms. Amanda BALDRIDGE
07 Registrar/Director of Admissions .... Ms. Genna MARTEN
15 Director of Human Resources .... Mr. Joe Pat HUGHES
35 Director of Student Life .... Ms. Linda ROBINS
18 Assistant VP of Facilities .... Mr. Gary COOK
26 Public Information Officer .... Ms. Erin KNIGHT
21 Comptroller .... Ms. Sherry GRAY-DEVINE

Northeastern Oklahoma Agricultural and Mechanical College (J)

200 I Street, NE, Miami OK 74354-6434
County: Ottawa FICE Identification: 003160
Unit ID: 207290
Telephone: (918) 542-8441 Carnegie Class: Assoc/Pub-R-M
FAX Number: (918) 542-9759 Calendar System: Semester
URL: www.neo.edu
Established: 1919 Annual Undergrad Tuition & Fees (In-State): $3,195
Enrollment: 2,501 Coed
Affiliation or Control: State IRS Status: 501(c)3
Highest Offering: Associate Degree

Program: Occupational; 2-Year Principally Bachelor's Creditable
Accreditation: NH, ADNUR, MLTAD, PTAA

01	President	Dr. Jeffery L. HALE
05	Vice President Academic Affairs	Dr. Bethene FAHNESTOCK
10	Vice President for Fiscal Affairs	Mr. Mark RASOR
32	VP Student Affairs/Enrollment Svcs	Mrs. Amy ISHMAEL
20	Asst VP for Academic Affairs	Vacant
37	Director of Financial Aid	Mr. David FISHER
26	Chief Public Relations Officer	Ms. Katie SWEETEN
15	Director Human Resources	Vacant
18	Director Facilities/Physical Plant	Mr. Steve GRIMES
27	Dir Public Information/Relations	Ms. Katie SWEETEN
14	Asst Director Technology Services	Mr. Brian SPARKS
30	Dir Devel/Alumni Rels/Foundation	Ms. Jennifer HESSEE
38	Director Academic Advising Center	Mrs. Rachel LLOYD
41	Athletic Director	Mr. Dale PATTERSON
88	Economic Development Coordinator	Vacant
105	Webmaster	Mr. Jeremiah FRENCH
06	Registrar	Mrs. Michelle SHACKELFORD
21	Asst Vice Pres for Fiscal Affairs	Vacant
40	Bookstore Manager	Mrs. Kathryn VANOVER
36	Dir Ctr for Academic Success & Adv	Ms. Rachel LLOYD
08	Coordinator Library Services	Ms. Sloane BROWN
47	Department Chair Agriculture	Mrs. Shannon CUNNINGHAM
83	Department Chair Social Science	Dr. Jeff BIRDSONG
57	Dept Chair Commun/Performing Arts	Mr. Steve MCCURLEY
81	Dept Chair Mathematics/Science	Dr. Mark GRIGSBY
66	Dept Chr Nursing/Allied Hlth/Phy Ed	Mrs. Deborah MORGAN
50	Dept Chair Business and Technology	Mrs. Pat CREECH

Northeastern State University (A)

601 N Grand Avenue, Tahlequah OK 74464-2399
County: Cherokee — FICE Identification: 003161 — Unit ID: 207263
Telephone: (918) 456-5511 — Carnegie Class: Master's L
FAX Number: (918) 458-2193 — Calendar System: Semester
URL: www.nsuok.edu
Established: 1851 — Annual Undergrad Tuition & Fees (In-State): $4,857
Enrollment: 9,361 — Coed
Affiliation or Control: State — IRS Status: 501(c)3
Highest Offering: First Professional Degree
Program: Liberal Arts And General; Teacher Preparatory; Professional; Business Emphasis
Accreditation: NH, ACBSP, DIETD, MT, MUS, NUR, OPT, OPTR, SP, SW, TED

01	President	Dr. Steve TURNER
05	Provost & Vice Pres Academic Affs	Vacant
11	Vice President for Administration	Mr. David KOEHN
26	Int Exec Dir University Relations	Mr. Jerry COOK
21	Vice Pres for Operations	Mr. Tim FOUTCH
32	Vice President Student Affairs	Ms. Laura BOREN
20	Assoc Vice Pres Academic Affairs	Dr. Janet BAHR
58	Asst VP Acad Affs/Dean Grad College	Dr. Tom JACKSON
88	Int Asst VP Ctr Teaching/Learning	Dr. Chuck ZIEHR
12	Dean Broken Arrow Campus	Dr. Christee JENLINK
12	Dean Muskogee Campus	Dr. Tim MCELROY
49	Dean College of Liberal Arts	Dr. Phillip BRIDGMON
50	Dean College of Business/Technology	Dr. Roger COLLIER
53	Dean College of Education	Dr. Debbie LANDRY
81	Dean Science & Health Professions	Dr. Martin VENNEMAN
88	Dean Optometry	Dr. Douglas PENISTEN
13	Chief Information Officer	Mr. Chuck MIZE
10	Director Business Affairs	Ms. Sue CATRON
08	Interim Dean of NSU Libraries	Ms. Paula SETTOON
21	Director of Budget	Ms. Christy LANDSAW
30	Director of Development	Ms. Peggy GLENN-SUMMITT
44	Director of Annual Giving	Vacant
15	Director of Human Resources	Dr. Martha ALBIN
37	Director Student Financial Services	Dr. Teri COCHRAN
06	Associate Registrar	Ms. Paula PAGE
26	Director High School & College Rels	Mr. Jason JESSIE
84	Int Exec Dir Enrollment Management	Mr. Jerrett PHILLIPS
18	Interim Director of Physical Plant	Mr. Jonathan ASBILL
41	Director of Athletics	Mr. Tony DUCKWORTH
27	Director of Communications	Mr. Thomas SMITH
19	Director of Campus Police	Ms. Patti BUHL
29	Director Alumni Services	Mr. Daniel JOHNSON
07	Director of Admission	Dr. Dawn CAIN
06	Registrar	Dr. Julie SAWYER
88	Int Director of Auxiliary Services	Mr. Todd ENLOW
39	Director of Housing	Mr. E. Thayne KING
38	Director Student Counseling	Ms. Sheila SELF
96	Director of Purchasing	Mr. Jerry COZBY
09	Coordinator Institutional Research	Vacant

Northern Oklahoma College (B)

1220 E Grand Avenue, PO Box 310,
Tonkawa OK 74653-0310
County: Kay — FICE Identification: 003162 — Unit ID: 207281
Telephone: (580) 628-6200 — Carnegie Class: Assoc/Pub-R-M
FAX Number: (580) 628-6209 — Calendar System: Semester
URL: www.north-ok.edu
Established: 1901 — Annual Undergrad Tuition & Fees (In-State): $2,845
Enrollment: 5,427 — Coed
Affiliation or Control: State — IRS Status: 501(c)3
Highest Offering: Associate Degree
Program: Occupational; 2-Year Principally Bachelor's Creditable
Accreditation: NH, ACBSP, ADNUR

01	President	Dr. Cheryl EVANS
05	Vice President for Academic Affairs	Dr. Judy COLWELL
10	Vice President Financial Affairs	Mrs. Anita SIMPSON
12	Vice President for Enid Campus	Dr. Ed VINEYARD
32	Vice President for Student Affairs	Dr. Mark EDWARDS
26	Vice Pres for Devel/Cmty Rels	Mrs. Sheri SNYDER
14	Director Information Technology	Mr. Michael MACHIA
15	Director Human Resources	Ms. Shannon CRANFORD
20	Dean of Instruction	Dr. Pamela STINSON
35	Dean of Students-Enid	Mr. Boomer APPLEMAN
35	Dean of Students-Tonkawa	Mr. Jason JOHNSON
12	Assoc Vice Pres Stillwater Campus	Ms. Debbie QUIREY
06	Assoc Vice Pres Enroll Mgt/Registr	Dr. Rick EDGINGTON
08	Director of Library Services	Mr. Benjamin HAINLINE
18	Assoc Vice Pres of Physical Plant	Mr. Larry DYE
41	Athletic Director	Mr. Greg KRAUSE
29	Director Alumni Relations	Ms. Kirby HILL
37	Director Student Financial Aid	Ms. Linda BROWN
40	Manager Student Bookstore	Mrs. Jimilea JANSSON
96	Purchasing Agent	Ms. Anita BARTLETT

Northwestern Oklahoma State University (C)

709 Oklahoma Boulevard, Alva OK 73717-2799
County: Woods — FICE Identification: 003163 — Unit ID: 207306
Telephone: (580) 327-1700 — Carnegie Class: Master's S
FAX Number: (580) 327-1881 — Calendar System: Semester
URL: www.nwosu.edu
Established: 1897 — Annual Undergrad Tuition & Fees (In-State): $5,175
Enrollment: 2,273 — Coed
Affiliation or Control: State — IRS Status: 501(c)3
Highest Offering: Master's
Program: Liberal Arts And General; Teacher Preparatory; Professional
Accreditation: NH, ACBSP, NUR, SW, TED

01	President	Dr. Janet L. CUNNINGHAM
05	Exec Vice Pres/Chief Acad Affairs	Dr. Steven L. LOHMANN
11	Vice President for Administration	Mr. David M. PECHA
35	VP Student Affairs/Enrollment Mgmt	Mr. Brad M. FRANZ
26	Assoc VP for University Relations	Mr. Steven J. VALENCIA
58	Assoc Dean of Graduate Studies	Dr. Shawn P. HOLLIDAY
08	Director of Libraries	Mrs. Susan K. JEFFRIES
06	Registrar	Mrs. Sheri K. LAHR
39	Director of Students/Housing	Mr. Marcus L. WALLACE
41	Athletic Director	Mr. Andrew V. CARTER
18	Chief Facilities/Physical Plant	Mr. Jim DETGEN
29	Director Alumni Relations	Mrs. Lizabeth R. RICHEY
37	Director Student Financial Aid	Mr. Calleb N. MOSBURG
38	Director of Student Life/Counselor	Mrs. Kaylyn L. HANSEN
07	Director of Recruitment	Mr. Matt ADAIR
15	Human Resource Director	Mrs. Tami L. COOPER
09	Institutional Research Specialist	Ms. Tara D. HALL

Oklahoma Baptist University (D)

500 W University, Shawnee OK 74804-2590
County: Pottawatomie — FICE Identification: 003164 — Unit ID: 207403
Telephone: (405) 585-4000 — Carnegie Class: Bac/Diverse
FAX Number: N/A — Calendar System: Semester
URL: www.okbu.edu
Established: 1910 — Annual Undergrad Tuition & Fees: $26,996
Enrollment: 1,871 — Coed
Affiliation or Control: Southern Baptist — IRS Status: 501(c)3
Highest Offering: Master's
Program: Liberal Arts And General; Teacher Preparatory; Professional
Accreditation: NH, ACBSP, MUS, NUR, NURSE, TED

01	President	Dr. David W. WHITLOCK
05	Provost/Exec Vice Pres Campus Life	Dr. Robert S. NORMAN
10	Exec VP Business Affs/Admin Svcs	Mr. Randy L. SMITH
30	Vice Pres University Advancement	Mr. Will SMALLWOOD
81	Dean College of Math and Science	Mrs. Debbie BLUE
42	Campus Minister	Mr. Dale M. GRIFFIN
44	Assoc VP University Advancement	Mrs. Paula GOWER
79	Assc Provost/Dn Humanities/Soc Sci	Dr. Pam ROBINSON
13	Asst Vice Pres Info Sys/Services	Mr. Gary NICKERSON
08	Dean Library Services	Vacant
32	Dean of Students	Mr. Brandon SKAGGS
29	Exec Director OBU Alumni Assn	Mrs. Lori R. HAGANS
11	Director of Executive Offices	Mrs. Tonia KELLOGG
37	Director Student Financial Services	Mrs. Jonna G. RANEY
12	Director Geiger Center	Ms. Cynthia K. GATES
06	Director Academic Records	Mrs. Marcia MCQUERRY
20	Academic Director/Asst Registrar	Mrs. Teri F. WALKER
21	Controller	Mrs. Lauri A. FLUKE
15	Director of Human Resources	Mr. Mike JOHNSON
35	Director of Campus Services	Mr. Larry A. WALKER
19	Chief of University Police	Mr. David SHANNON
41	Athletic Director	Mr. Robert DAVENPORT
18	Dir Facilities Mgt & Services	Mr. Robert CASH
96	Director of Purchasing	Mr. Larry WALKER
07	Director of Admissions	Mr. Bruce PERKINS
58	Director OBU Graduate School	Dr. Scott HARRIS
36	Career Planning Counselor	Ms. Stephanie MILLER
38	Counselor	Mrs. Rilda SMITH
57	Dean of Fine Arts	Dr. Ken GABRIELSE
73	Dean School Christian Service	Dr. Mack MCCLELLAN
50	Dean School of Business	Dr. David C. HOUGHTON
66	Dean School of Nursing	Dr. Lana BOLHOUSE

Oklahoma Christian University (E)

PO Box 11000, Oklahoma City OK 73136-1100
County: Oklahoma — FICE Identification: 003165 — Unit ID: 207324
Telephone: (405) 425-5000 — Carnegie Class: Master's M
FAX Number: (405) 425-5090 — Calendar System: Semester
URL: www.oc.edu
Established: 1950 — Annual Undergrad Tuition & Fees: $18,800
Enrollment: 2,194 — Coed
Affiliation or Control: Independent Non-Profit — IRS Status: 501(c)3
Highest Offering: Master's
Program: Liberal Arts And General; Teacher Preparatory; Professional
Accreditation: NH, ACBSP, CIDA, ENG, MUS, NURSE, TED

01	President	Mr. John DESTEIGUER
03	Executive Vice President	Dr. William GOAD
05	Sr Vice Pres for Academic Affairs	Dr. Allison GARRETT
11	Exec Dir of University Services	Mr. Kinney BRYANT
10	Vice President for Finance	Mr. Jeff BINGHAM
27	VP for Marketing	Mrs. Risa FORRESTER
29	Exec Dir for Alumni Relations	Mr. Bob LASHLEY
44	Vice Presiden Estate/Planned Giving	Mr. Stephen ECK
32	Vice Pres and Dean of Student Life	Mr. Neil ARTER
84	Vice President for Admissions	Mrs. Risa FORRESTER
14	Vice President for Information Tech	Mr. John HERMES
43	Vice President & General Counsel	Mr. Stephen ECK
30	Vice President for Advancement	Mr. Kent ALLEN
58	Dean of Graduate Programs	Dr. Don DREW
107	Dean Col of Professional Studies	Dr. Phil LEWIS
73	Dean College of Biblical Studies	Dr. Alan MARTIN
49	Dean College Arts & Sciences	Dr. David LOWRY
06	Registrar	Dr. Mickey D. BANISTER
08	Library Director	Mrs. Tamie L. WILLIS
19	Chief of Police Dept	Mr. John MATLOCK
41	Athletic Director	Mr. Curtis JANZ
18	Director of Building Maintenance	Mr. Cary FALLING
26	Assoc Director Marketing Services	Mr. Wes MCKINZIE
37	Dir Student Financial Services	Mr. Clint LARUE
104	Director of International Programs	Mr. John OSBORNE
15	Human Resources Director	Mr. Lynn HOOPER
31	Director of Church Relations	Mr. Bob ROWLEY
42	Assoc Dean for Spiritual Life	Mr. Chance VANOVER
89	Dir of Freshman Programs & ADA	Mrs. Amy JANZEN
102	Dir Foundation & Corporate Rels	Ms. Jo GRIFFIN
88	Director of Creative Services	Mr. Judson COPELAND
40	Manager of Bookstore	Mr. James MENCER
09	Director of Institutional Research	Mr. Gary LYONS
21	Controller	Mr. Chris BOWMAN
07	Director of Admissions	Mrs. Darci THOMPSON
36	Director of Career Services	Mr. Mark CHAN
85	International Student Adviser	Mrs. Tamara J. NEWELL
23	Director of Health Services	Vacant
38	Director of Counseling Services	Dr. Sheldon ADKINS
88	Director of Retention	Mrs. Katy ROYBAL

Oklahoma City Community College (F)

7777 S May Avenue, Oklahoma City OK 73159-4444
County: Oklahoma — FICE Identification: 010391 — Unit ID: 207449
Telephone: (405) 682-1611 — Carnegie Class: Assoc/Pub-U-SC
FAX Number: (405) 682-7585 — Calendar System: Other
URL: www.occc.edu
Established: 1972 — Annual Undergrad Tuition & Fees (In-District): $2,970
Enrollment: 14,972 — Coed
Affiliation or Control: State/Local — IRS Status: 501(c)3
Highest Offering: Associate Degree
Program: Occupational; 2-Year Principally Bachelor's Creditable
Accreditation: NH, ACBSP, ADNUR, EMT, ENGT, OTA, PTAA

01	President	Dr. Paul W. SECHRIST
03	Executive Vice President	Dr. Jerry STEWARD
43	Legal Counsel	Dr. Nancy GERRITY
05	Vice President Academic Affairs	Dr. Felix J. AQUINO
32	VP Enrollment/Student Services	Dr. Marion PADEN
15	Vice Pres Human Resources	Mr. Gary A. LOMBARD
10	Vice President Business & Finance	Dr. John BOYD
31	Vice Pres Community Development	Mr. Steven BLOOMBERG
20	Associate VP Academic Affairs	Mr. Greg GARDNER
37	Dean Student Financial Support Svcs	Mr. Harold CASE
38	Dean of Student Development	Dr. Liz LARGENT
06	Registrar	Mr. Alan STRINGFELLOW
30	Exec Director Inst Advancement	Mr. Lealon TAYLOR
45	Executive Director of Planning	Mr. Stu HARVEY
13	Dir Info Tech Infrastructure	Mr. David ANDERSON
88	Director Recreation and Fitness	Ms. Roxanna BUTLER
44	Director of Development	Ms. Jennifer HARRISON
88	Director Students Support Svcs	Ms. Patricia STOWE
07	Dir of Recruitment & Admissions	Mr. Jon HORINEK
35	Director of Student Life	Vacant
18	Director of Facilities Management	Mr. J. B. MESSER
40	Director of Student Store	Ms. Brenda REINKE
88	Director Corporate Learning	Ms. Delores JACKSON
26	Dir of Marketing & Public Relations	Ms. Paula GOWER
35	Director Student Relations	Ms. Erin LOGAN
25	Director of Grants & Contracts	Mr. Joe SWALWELL
12	Director OKC Downtown College	Dr. Gus PEKARA
36	Director Career Transitions Program	Ms. Nora PUGH-SEEMSTER
88	Dir Child Development/Lab School	Dr. Mary MCCOY
21	Bursar	Ms. Brandi HENSON

08 Director of Library Services ... Ms. Barbara KING
09 Dir Institutional Effectiveness ... Dr. Janet PERRY
88 Director Cooperative Alliances ... Ms. Alexa MASHLAN
22 EEO/AA Compliance Officer ... Vacant
31 Dir Community Outreach & Education ... Ms. Jessica MARTINEZ-BROOKS
88 Coord OCCC Capitol Hill Center ... Mr. Sergio GALLEGOS
96 Purchasing Manager ... Ms. Lori WALKER
19 Dir Emergency Planning/Risk Mgmt ... Ms. Lisa TEEL

Oklahoma City University (A)

2501 N Blackwelder, Oklahoma City OK 73106-1493
County: Oklahoma FICE Identification: 003166
Unit ID: 207458
Telephone: (405) 208-5000 Carnegie Class: Master's L
FAX Number: (405) 208-5916 Calendar System: Semester
URL: www.okcu.edu
Established: 1904 Annual Undergrad Tuition & Fees: $28,190
Enrollment: 3,546 Coed
Affiliation or Control: United Methodist IRS Status: 501(c)3
Highest Offering: First Professional Degree
Program: Liberal Arts And General; Teacher Preparatory; Professional
Accreditation: NH, ACBSP, LAW, MACTE, MUS, NUR

01 President ... Mr. Robert H. HENRY
05 Provost/Vice Pres Academic Affairs ... Dr. Susan C. BARBER
30 Vice Pres University Advancement ... Vacant
26 Vice Pres Univ/Church Relations ... Rev. Margaret A. BALL
10 Chief Financial Officer ... Ms. Donna S. NANCE
32 Vice President for Student Affairs ... Dr. Richard HALL
84 Asst VP/Dean Enrollment Services ... Mr. Kevin WINDHOLZ
35 Dean of Students ... Dr. Liz DONNELLY
06 Registrar ... Mr. Charles MONNOT
09 Director of Institutional Research ... Mr. Michael JACKSON
08 Director Dulaney-Browne Library ... Dr. Victoria SWINNEY
37 Director of Financial Aid ... Ms. Denise FLIS
27 Director of Communications ... Vacant
15 Chief Human Resources Officer ... Ms. Joey CROSLIN
92 Director of Honors Program ... Dr. James BUSS
07 Director of Undergrad Admissions ... Ms. Michelle COOK
18 Chief Facilities/Physical Plant ... Mr. Jeff CASTLEBERRY
29 Director Alumni Relations ... Mr. Cary PIRRONG
36 Director Career Planning/Placement ... Mr. Josh WADDELL
49 Dean College of Arts & Sciences ... Dr. Mark Y. DAVIES
50 Dean School of Business ... Dr. Steve AGEE
61 Dean School of Law ... Dr. Valerie COUCH
64 Dean School of Music ... Mr. Mark PARKER
66 Dean of School of Nursing ... Dr. Marvel WILLIAMSON
73 Dean School of Religion ... Dr. Mark DAVIES
88 Dean School of Amer Dance/Arts Mgt ... Mr. John BEDFORD
100 Chief of Staff ... Mr. Craig KNUTSON

Oklahoma Panhandle State University (B)

Box 430, Goodwell OK 73939-0430
County: Texas FICE Identification: 003174
Unit ID: 207351
Telephone: (580) 349-2611 Carnegie Class: Bac/Diverse
FAX Number: (580) 349-2302 Calendar System: Semester
URL: www.opsu.edu
Established: 1909 Annual Undergrad Tuition & Fees (In-State): $6,737
Enrollment: 1,463 Coed
Affiliation or Control: State IRS Status: 501(c)3
Highest Offering: Baccalaureate
Program: Liberal Arts And General
Accreditation: NH, NUR, TED

01 President ... Dr. David A. BRYANT
05 Vice Pres Academic Affairs/Outreach ... Dr. Wayne MANNING
10 Vice Pres Business & Fiscal Affairs ... Mr. Larry PETERS
47 Dean Agriculture ... Dr. Peter CAMFIELD
50 Dean Business & Technology ... Ms. Diane MURPHEY
53 Dean Education ... Dr. R. Wayne STEWART
57 Dean Liberal Arts ... Dr. Sara RICHTER
66 Dean Science/Mathematics/Nursing ... Dr. Justin COLLINS
32 Dean of Student Affairs ... Ms. Jessica LOFLAND
06 Registrar/Director of Admissions ... Mr. Bobby JENKINS
37 Director Student Financial Aid ... Ms. Lori FERGUSON
09 Director Institutional Research ... Mr. Nick TUTTLE
13 Director of Technology ... Mr. Howard HENDERSON
15 Director Personnel Services ... Ms. Cheryl ASHPAUGH
08 Director of Library ... Ms. Alton (Tony) HARDMAN
21 Comptroller ... Mr. Benny DAIN
38 Director Counseling/Career Services ... Ms. Christi HALE
26 Campus Communications Director ... Ms. Laura HAYS
41 Athletic Officer ... Dr. R. Wayne STEWART
40 Bookstore Manager ... Ms. Mandy BATENHORST
18 Director Physical Plant ... Mr. Bob SCOTT
29 Director Alumni Relations ... Mr. Nick TUTTLE
96 Director of Purchasing ... Ms. Jena MARR

Oklahoma State University (C)

Stillwater OK 74078
County: Payne FICE Identification: 003170
Unit ID: 207388
Telephone: (405) 744-5000 Carnegie Class: RU/H
FAX Number: N/A Calendar System: Semester
URL: osu.okstate.edu/
Established: 1890 Annual Undergrad Tuition & Fees (In-State): $7,442
Enrollment: 24,231 Coed
Affiliation or Control: State IRS Status: 501(c)3
Highest Offering: Doctorate
Program: Liberal Arts And General; Teacher Preparatory; Professional
Accreditation: NH, AAB, BUS, BUSA, CACREP, CIDA, CLPSY, COPSY, DIETD, DIETI, ENG, ENGT, FOR, JOUR, LSAR, MFCD, MUS, NRPA, SCPSY, SP, TED, THEA, VET

01 President ... Dr. V. Burns HARGIS
04 Exec Assistant to the President ... Ms. Deborah LANE
05 Provost & Senior Vice President ... Dr. Robert STERNBERG
10 Vice Pres Administration & Finance . Mr. Joseph B. WEAVER, JR.
03 Vice President for Univ Relations ... Mr. Gary C. CLARK
32 Vice President Student Affairs ... Dr. Lee E. BIRD
46 Vice Pres Research/Tech Transfer ... Dr. Stephen W. MCKEEVER
28 Assoc VP Institutional Diversity ... Dr. Jason KIRKSEY
47 VP Agri Programs & Dean CASNR ... Dr. Robert E. WHITSON
41 Vice President Athletic Programs ... Mr. Mike HOLDER
20 Assoc Provost ... Dr. Pamela FRY
21 Assoc Vice President & Controller ... Ms. Kathy ELLIOTT
15 Asst Vice Pres Human Resources ... Ms. Jamie A. PAYNE
102 President & CEO OSU Foundation ... Mr. Kirk A. JEWELL
29 President & CEO/Alumni Association ... Mr. Larry SHELL
88 Pres Ctr for Innovation & Econ Dev .. Dr. Joseph W. ALEXANDER
54 Dean Engineering ... Dr. Paul J. TIKALSKY
49 Dean Arts & Sciences ... Dr. Bret S. DANILOWICZ
50 Dean Spears School of Business ... Dr. Lawrence CROSBY
53 Dean Education ... Dr. Pamela CARROLL
59 Dean College of Human Sciences ... Dr. Stephan M. WILSON
74 Dean Veterinary Medicine ... Dr. Jean E. SANDER
58 Dean Graduate College ... Dr. Sheryl TUCKER
08 Dean Library ... Ms. Sheila G. JOHNSON
23 Director University Health Services ... Mr. Stephen K. ROGERS
27 Director Communication Services ... Mr. Gary SHUTT
26 Vice Pres Enroll Mgmt/Univ Mktg ... Mr. Kyle WRAY
07 Director Undergraduate Admissions ... Ms. Christine CRENSHAW
13 Chief Information Officer ... Ms. Darlene HIGHTOWER
43 Board of Regents Legal Counsel ... Mr. Charles E. DRAKE
06 Registrar ... Dr. K. Celeste CAMPBELL
39 Director University Housing ... Dr. Matthew S. BROWN
38 Director University Counseling Svcs ... Dr. Suzanne M. BURKS
37 Director Financial Aid ... Dr. Charles W. BRUCE
92 Director Honors College ... Dr. Robert L. SPURRIER
36 Director Career Services ... Ms. Pam EHLERS
19 Director & Chief of Public Safety ... Mr. Michael ROBINSON
25 Dir Grants/Contracts/Financial Admn ... Dr. Robert DIXON
22 Director Affirmative Action ... Ms. Mackenzie WILFONG
24 Asst Prov/Dir Inst Tch/Lrng Excel ... Ms. Christine ORMSBEE
09 Director Inst Research/Info Mgmt ... Dr. Christie HAWKINS
96 Director of Purchasing ... Ms. Sharon S. TOY
18 Chief Facilities Officer ... Mr. Richard KRYSIAK
88 Asst VP/Director Student Union ... Mr. Mitch KILCREASE
40 Asst Dir Student Union Bookstore ... Mr. Lance HINKLE
85 Manager Intl Students & Scholars ... Mr. Tim T. HUFF

Oklahoma State University Center for Health Sciences College of Osteopathic Medicine (D)

1111 W 17th Street, Tulsa OK 74107-1898
County: Tulsa FICE Identification: 011282
Unit ID: 207315
Telephone: (918) 582-1972 Carnegie Class: Spec/Med
FAX Number: (918) 561-8412 Calendar System: Semester
URL: www.healthsciences.okstate.edu
Established: 1972 Annual Undergrad Tuition & Fees (In-State): $23,150
Enrollment: 427 Coed
Affiliation or Control: State IRS Status: 501(c)3
Highest Offering: First Professional Degree
Program: Professional
Accreditation: &NH, OSTEO

01 President ... Dr. Howard BARNETT
05 Provost and Dean ... Dr. Kayse SHRUM
10 COO/Vice Pres for Healthcare Admin ... Dr. James D. HESS
46 Vice Pres Research/Inst Advancement ... Dr. Leigh GOODSON
30 Assoc Vice President of Development ... Mr. Stephen MASON
20 Int Vice Provost/Asoc Dn Biomed Sci ... Dr. Bruce A. BENJAMIN
84 Assoc Dean for Enrollment Mgmt ... Dr. Vivian M. STEVENS
20 Assoc Dean for Clinical Services ... Dr. Jenny ALEXOPULOS
20 Assoc Dean for Clinical Education ... Dr. Joan E. STEWART
13 Dir Info Technology/Lrng Tech Svcs ... Mr. Randall POPP
29 Director Alumni Affairs ... Mr. Ryan MILLER
88 Director Health Information Tech ... Ms. Heidi HOLMES
26 Director of Mktg/Communication Svcs ... Dr. Mary Bea DRUMMOND
06 Registrar ... Ms. Amanda SUMNER
07 Asst Dir of Admissions & Recruitmnt ... Ms. Lindsey KIRKPATRICK

† Regional accreditation is carried under the parent institution in Stillwater, OK.

Oklahoma State University Institute of Technology-Okmulgee (E)

1801 E Fourth Street, Okmulgee OK 74447-3901
County: Okmulgee FICE Identification: 003172
Unit ID: 207564
Telephone: (918) 293-4678 Carnegie Class: Assoc/Pub4
FAX Number: (918) 293-4644 Calendar System: Trimester
URL: www.osuit.edu
Established: 1946 Annual Undergrad Tuition & Fees (In-State): $141
Enrollment: 2,654 Coed
Affiliation or Control: State IRS Status: 501(c)3
Highest Offering: Baccalaureate
Program: Occupational; 2-Year Principally Bachelor's Creditable; Technical Emphasis
Accreditation: NH, ADNUR, CS

01 President ... Dr. Bill PATH
03 Executive VP ... Dr. Linda AVANT
10 VP Fiscal Services ... Mr. Jim SMITH
05 VP Academic Affairs ... Dr. Greg MOSIER
84 VP Enrollment Management ... Ms. Ina AGNEW
26 VP University & External Relations .. Ms. Anita GORDY-WATKINS
76 Allied Health Sciences ... Ms. Jana MARTIN
49 Arts & Sciences ... Dr. Mark ALLEN
72 Automotive Technologies ... Mr. Bill VOORHEES
72 Construction Technologies ... Mr. Steve OLMSTEAD
88 Culinary Arts ... Mr. Rene JUNGO
54 Engineering Technologies ... Mr. Dolph HAYDEN
88 Heavy Equipment & Vehicle Institute ... Mr. Roy ACHEMIRE
77 Information Technologies ... Dr. Scott NEWMAN
88 Visual Communications ... Mr. James MCCULLOUGH
37 Dir Student Financial Services ... Ms. Diana SANDERS
45 Dir Inst Assessment & Research ... Vacant
13 Dir Computer Information Systems ... Mr. Kevin HULETT
07 Dir Admissions & Records ... Ms. Genie TRAMMELL
15 Dir Human Resources ... Ms. Paula NORTH
18 Dir Physical Plant Services ... Mr. Mark PITCHER
88 Dir Student Union & Auxiliary Svcs ... Mr. James BYRD
32 Director Student Life ... Mr. Bruce FORCE
39 Director Residential Life ... Mr. Devin DEBOCK
08 Dir Learning Resource Center ... Ms. Jenny DUNCAN
96 Director Purchasing ... Mrs. Chandra MILLER
12 Dir MAIP-Pryor Campus ... Mr. Scott FRY
06 Registrar ... Ms. Crystal BOWLES
38 Counselor ... Ms. Kathy AVERY
40 Manager Bookstore ... Ms. Barbara WRIGHT
27 Public Relations Officer ... Mr. Rex DAUGHERTY
19 Campus Police Chief ... Mr. Steve RODRIQUEZ
04 Admin Asst to President ... Ms. Claudette BUTCHER
103 Dir Econ Dev & Training Ctr ... Mr. Mark HAYS
26 Director of Marketing ... Ms. Shari ERWIN
106 Director of Distance Learning ... Ms. Kari CHANCEY
88 Dir Tutorial Ctr/Acad Accommodation ... Mr. Chad SPURLOCK

Oklahoma State University - Oklahoma City (F)

900 N Portland Ave, Oklahoma City OK 73107-6195
County: Oklahoma FICE Identification: 009647
Unit ID: 207397
Telephone: (405) 947-4421 Carnegie Class: Assoc/Pub4
FAX Number: (405) 945-3289 Calendar System: Semester
URL: www.osuokc.edu
Established: 1961 Annual Undergrad Tuition & Fees (In-State): $3,926
Enrollment: 7,721 Coed
Affiliation or Control: State IRS Status: 501(c)3
Highest Offering: Baccalaureate
Program: Occupational; 2-Year Principally Bachelor's Creditable; Technical Emphasis
Accreditation: NH, ADNUR, @DIETT, DMS

01 President ... Ms. Natalie SHIRLEY
05 Vice President Academic Affairs ... Dr. Bill PINK
10 Vice President Finance & Operations ... Ms. Ronda REECE
32 Vice President Student Services ... Mr. Brad WILLIAMS
50 VP for Business and Industry ... Ms. Robin ROBERTS KRIEGER
20 Associate VP Academic Affairs ... Ms. Kim PEARSALL
84 Director Enrollment Mgmt/Admissions ... Mr. Kyle WILLIAMS
30 Associate VP Development OKC Region ... Ms. Sue REEL
13 Senior Director Information Svcs ... Mr. Jonathan FOZARD
08 Librarian ... Mr. David ROBINSON
37 Director Financial Aid ... Ms. Bessie CARTER
15 Director Personnel Services ... Ms. Melissa HERREN
18 Chief Facilities/Physical Plant ... Mr. Wade REED
26 Chief Public Relations Officer ... Ms. Evelyn BOLLENBACH
07 Assistant Director of Admissions ... Ms. Melissa GARNER
72 Dir of Technology Education Center ... Ms. Adrianne COVINGTON-GRAHAM
29 Director Alumni Relations ... Dr. JoElla FLINTON
96 Director of Purchasing ... Ms. Sharon FITZPATRICK
06 Registrar ... Ms. Keila WHITAKER
09 Director Inst Grants & Research ... Ms. Anna ROYER

Oklahoma State University - Tulsa (G)

700 N Greenwood Avenue, Tulsa OK 74106-0702
County: Tulsa Identification: 666053
Telephone: (918) 594-8000 Carnegie Class: Not Classified
FAX Number: (918) 594-8009 Calendar System: Semester
URL: www.osu-tulsa.okstate.edu
Established: 1999 Annual Undergrad Tuition & Fees (In-State): $6,748
Enrollment: 3,118 Coed
Affiliation or Control: State IRS Status: 501(c)3
Highest Offering: Doctorate
Program: Liberal Arts And General; Professional; Business Emphasis
Accreditation: &NH

01 President ... Dr. Howard G. BARNETT, JR.
11 Vice Pres Administration/Finance ... Dr. Ronald BUSSERT
05 VP Academic Affs/Chief Acad Ofcr ... Dr. Raj BASU

† Regional accreditation is carried under the parent institution in Stillwater, OK.

Oklahoma Technical College (A)

4444 South Sheridan, Tulsa OK 74145-1122

County: Tulsa — Identification: 666718
Telephone: (918) 895-7500 — Carnegie Class: Not Classified
FAX Number: (918) 665-7335 — Calendar System: Other
URL: www.oklahomatechnicalcollege.com
Established: 2009 — Annual Undergrad Tuition & Fees: $27,677
Enrollment: 164 — Coed
Affiliation or Control: Proprietary — IRS Status: Proprietary
Highest Offering: Associate Degree
Program: Occupational; 2-Year Principally Bachelor's Creditable; Technical Emphasis
Accreditation: ACICS

00 CEO .... Ms. Teresa L. KNOX
01 President .... Dr. Kevin L. KIRK
05 Campus Director .... Ms. Jamie KIDDER

Oklahoma Wesleyan University (B)

2201 Silver Lake Road, Bartlesville OK 74006-6299

County: Washington — FICE Identification: 003151
Unit ID: 206835
Telephone: (918) 333-6151 — Carnegie Class: Bac/Diverse
FAX Number: (918) 335-6228 — Calendar System: Semester
URL: www.okwu.edu
Established: 1910 — Annual Undergrad Tuition & Fees: $21,140
Enrollment: 1,150 — Coed
Affiliation or Control: Wesleyan Church — IRS Status: 501(c)3
Highest Offering: Master's
Program: 2-Year Principally Bachelor's Creditable; Liberal Arts And General; Teacher Preparatory; Professional
Accreditation: NH, IACBE, NURSE, TED

01 President .... Dr. Everett G. PIPER
05 Exec Vice Pres for Academic Affairs .... Vacant
10 Vice President for Business Affairs .... Mrs. Andrea ZEPEDA
30 Vice President for Development .... Vacant
32 Vice President for Student Life .... Mr. Kyle WHITE
88 VP for Academic Program Development .... Dr. Brett ANDREWS
07 Vice President Admissions .... Mr. John MEANS
20 Assoc VP for Academic Affairs .... Dr. Mark WEETER
42 Assoc VP for Student Dev .... Rev. Ben ROTZ
53 Dean of School of Education .... Dr. Sheldon BUXTON
73 Dean of School of Religion & Phil .... Dr. Mark WEETER
49 Dean of School of Arts & Sciences .... Mrs. Gail RICHARDSON
50 Dean of School of Business .... Dr. Brett ANDREWS
66 Dean School of Nursing .... Mrs. Rebecca LE
07 Director Adult/Grad Admissions .... Mrs. Samantha PETERSON
106 Director of Online Learning .... Dr. Devon SMITH
108 Director of Assessment .... Mrs. Julia CROUCH
21 Director of Accounting .... Mrs. Margaret FRIEND
14 Director of Computer Services .... Mr. Eric GOINGS
37 Director of Financial Aid .... Mrs. Kandi MOLDER
41 Athletic Director .... Mr. Mark MOLDER
29 Director of Alumni .... Mrs. Janet ODDEN
06 Registrar .... Mrs. Cindy RIFFE
04 Executive Assistant to President .... Mrs. Kathy LINDQUIST
15 Human Resources Administrator .... Mrs. Jessica MORROW
33 Men's Resident Director .... Mr. Chris BREILAND
34 Women's Resident Director .... Ms. Sheresa GRATE
23 Director Student Health .... Mrs. Debra COOK
18 Director of Buildings and Grounds .... Mr. Mark SPENCER
40 Bookstore Manager .... Mrs. Jessica JARRETT

Oral Roberts University (C)

7777 S Lewis, Tulsa OK 74171-0003

County: Tulsa — FICE Identification: 003985
Unit ID: 207582
Telephone: (918) 495-6161 — Carnegie Class: Master's S
FAX Number: (918) 495-6033 — Calendar System: Semester
URL: www.oru.edu
Established: 1965 — Annual Undergrad Tuition & Fees: $20,862
Enrollment: 3,259 — Coed
Affiliation or Control: Independent Non-Profit — IRS Status: 501(c)3
Highest Offering: Doctorate
Program: Liberal Arts And General; Teacher Preparatory; Professional
Accreditation: NH, ACBSP, ENG, MUS, NURSE, SW, TED, THEOL

01 President .... Dr. Mark RUTLAND
03 Provost .... Dr. Ralph FAGIN
10 EVP and Chief Financial Officer .... Ms. Michelle FINLEY
11 EVP and Chief Operations Officer .... Mr. Tim PHILLEY
26 Vice Pres for University Relations .... Mr. Ossie MILLS
05 VP Academic Affairs .... Dr. Debra SOWELL
84 VP for Enrollment Management .... Dr. Nancy BRAINARD
88 VP of Sponsored Pgm & Admn Affairs .... Vacant
32 Vice President Student Development .... Dr. Dan GUAJARDO
13 Chief Information Officer .... Mr. Tannie OLSEN
21 Controller .... Ms. Ann Marie ELFRINK
42 Dean of Spiritual Formation .... Dr. Clarence BOYD
08 Dean Learning Resources .... Dr. William JERNIGAN
50 Dean Col of Science & Engineering .... Dr. Dominic HALSMER
49 Dean Col of Arts & Cultural Studies .... Dr. Wendy SHIRK
73 Dean College Theology/Ministry .... Dr. Thomson MATHEW
50 Dean College of Business .... Dr. Steve GREENE
66 Dean & Chairman College of Nursing .... Dr. Kenda JEZEK
53 Dean College of Education .... Dr. Kim BOYD
33 Dean of Men .... Mr. Matthew OLSEN
34 Dean of Women .... Ms. Lori SYLVESTER
09 Director of Institutional Research .... Dr. Cal EASTERLING
41 Director for Athletics .... Mr. Mike CARTER
25 Director of Sponsored Programs .... Ms. Kim FALCON
38 Director of Student Counseling .... Ms. Michelle TAYLOR
89 Director of Freshmen Studies .... Mr. Tom BELLATTI
92 Director of Honors Program .... Dr. John KORSTAD
21 Director Student Accounts .... Mr. Steve THANNICKAL
96 Director of Purchasing .... Ms. Jeanine HORTON
06 Registrar .... Mr. David FULMER
07 Director of Admissions .... Mr. Chris BELCHER
37 Director of Financial Aid .... Mr. William WOMACK
29 Director of Alumni Relations .... Mr. Jesse PISORS
19 Director of Security/Safety .... Mr. Jerry ISAACS
15 Director of Human Resources .... Mr. Bill WEBB
36 Director of Student Placement .... Ms. Allison JONES

Phillips Theological Seminary (D)

901 N Mingo Road, Tulsa OK 74116-5612

County: Tulsa — FICE Identification: 025602
Unit ID: 414966
Telephone: (918) 610-8303 — Carnegie Class: Spec/Faith
FAX Number: (918) 610-8404 — Calendar System: Semester
URL: www.ptstulsa.edu
Established: 1907 — Annual Graduate Tuition & Fees: $10,080
Enrollment: 152 — Coed
Affiliation or Control: Christian Church (Disciples Of Christ)
IRS Status: 501(c)3
Highest Offering: Doctorate; No Undergraduates
Program: Professional; Religious Emphasis
Accreditation: NH, THEOL

01 President .... Gary PELUSO-VERDEND
51 Special Assistant to the President .... John M. IMBLER
05 Vice Pres Academic Affairs & Dean .... Don A. PITTMAN
108 Assoc Dean Assessment and Faculty .... Joseph BESSLER
07 Assoc Dean Admissions/Student Svcs .... Belva Brown JORDAN
20 Assoc Dn/Dir Supervised Ministries .... John THOMAS
10 Chief Financial Officer .... Lora CONGER
88 Director Doctor of Ministry Program .... Nancy PITTMAN
07 Director of Recruitment .... Linda FORD
37 Director Student Financial Aid .... Ann JORDAN
08 Director of Library .... Sandy SHAPOVAL
44 Director of Planned Giving .... Virginia WALKER
29 Director of Alumni Relations .... Geoffrey BREWSTER
44 Director of Annual Fund .... Malisa PIERCE
60 Director of Communications .... Sara E. SMITH
06 Registrar .... Toni IMBLER
04 Executive Assistant to President .... Melanie K. TIPTON

Platt College (E)

3801 S Sheridan, Tulsa OK 74145-1132

County: Tulsa — FICE Identification: 023068
Unit ID: 245962
Telephone: (918) 663-9000 — Carnegie Class: Assoc/PrivFP
FAX Number: (918) 622-1240 — Calendar System: Other
URL: www.plattcollege.org
Established: 1979 — Annual Undergrad Tuition & Fees: $29,000
Enrollment: 536 — Coed
Affiliation or Control: Proprietary — IRS Status: Proprietary
Highest Offering: Baccalaureate
Program: Occupational
Accreditation: ACCSC, ACFEI

01 President .... Mr. Mike A. PUGLIESE
05 Director of Campus .... Ms. Stephanie THRASHER
66 Director of Nursing LPN Program .... Ms. Ella ABELA
07 Director of Admission & Marketing .... Mr. Richard DIXON

Platt College-OKC Central (F)

309 South Ann Arbor Avenue,
Oklahoma City OK 73128-1112

County: Oklahoma — Identification: 666341
Unit ID: 445258
Telephone: (405) 946-7799 — Carnegie Class: Assoc/PrivFP4
FAX Number: (405) 943-2150 — Calendar System: Other
URL: www.plattcollege.org
Established: 1979 — Annual Undergrad Tuition & Fees: $28,900
Enrollment: 209 — Coed
Affiliation or Control: Proprietary — IRS Status: Proprietary
Highest Offering: Associate Degree
Program: Occupational; Nursing Emphasis
Accreditation: ACCSC, ACFEI, SURGT

01 Director .... Mr. Joey KEEFER

† Branch campus of Platt College, Tulsa, OK.

Redlands Community College (G)

1300 S Country Club Road, El Reno OK 73036-5304

County: Canadian — FICE Identification: 003156
Unit ID: 207069
Telephone: (405) 262-2552 — Carnegie Class: Assoc/Pub-S-SC
FAX Number: (405) 422-1200 — Calendar System: Semester
URL: www.redlandscc.edu
Established: 1938 — Annual Undergrad Tuition & Fees (In-District): $3,330
Enrollment: 2,574 — Coed
Affiliation or Control: State/Local — IRS Status: 501(c)3
Highest Offering: Associate Degree
Program: Occupational; 2-Year Principally Bachelor's Creditable
Accreditation: NH, ADNUR

01 President .... Dr. Larry F. DEVANE
05 Vice President Instruction .... Mr. Bill BAKER
103 VP Workforce/Economic Development .... Mr. Jack BRYANT
10 Vice Pres Finance/Campus Services .... Mrs. Karen BOUCHER
30 VP Inst Advancement/Student Svcs .... Mr. Joel DRURY
46 Vice Pres Undergraduate Research .... Dr. Amanda EVERT
18 Director Physical Plant .... Mr. Richard BUCHHOLZ
66 Director Nursing/Allied Health .... Mrs. Deborah BUTTTRUM
72 Dir Liberal Studies/Mgmt Science .... Dr. Laura GRUNTMEIR
81 Dir Math/Science/Developmental Stds .... Ms. Barbara KNOP-COX
08 Director Learning Resource Center .... Mrs. Christine DETTLAFF
06 Registrar/Director Student Records .... Mr. Dennis HARRIS
37 Director Financial Aid .... Ms. Paris PRZEKURAT
41 Athletic Director .... Mr. Matt NEWGENT
14 Director Administrative Computing .... Mr. Troy MILLIGAN
22 Director of Upward Bound .... Mrs. Linda MCDOWN
09 Director of Institutional Research .... Mr. Troy MILLIGAN
84 Director Enrollment Management .... Mrs. Tricia HOBSON
21 Associate Business Officer .... Mrs. Maxine CALVERT
56 Coordinator Alternative Education .... Ms. Arlie SCHRODER
36 Coordinator Career Services .... Mrs. Terri BARGER
15 Coordinator Personnel/Payroll .... Mrs. Kim ANDRADE
26 Coordinator Public Information .... Ms. Deirdre STEINER
29 Coordinator Alumni Relations .... Mrs. Jill WORTHINGTON
39 Coordinator of Resident Life .... Ms. Margie MOORE

Rogers State University (H)

1701 W Will Rogers Boulevard,
Claremore OK 74017-2099

County: Rogers — FICE Identification: 003168
Unit ID: 207661
Telephone: (918) 343-7777 — Carnegie Class: Bac/Assoc
FAX Number: (918) 343-7898 — Calendar System: Semester
URL: www.rsu.edu
Established: 1909 — Annual Undergrad Tuition & Fees (In-State): $4,777
Enrollment: 4,632 — Coed
Affiliation or Control: State — IRS Status: 501(c)3
Highest Offering: Baccalaureate
Program: 2-Year Principally Bachelor's Creditable; Liberal Arts And General; Business Emphasis
Accreditation: NH, ADNUR, EMT, NUR

01 President .... Dr. Larry D. RICE
05 Vice President for Academic Affairs .... Dr. Richard BECK
03 Exec VP for Admin & Finance .... Mr. Tom VOLTURO
30 Vice President for Development .... Vacant
32 Vice Pres for Student Affairs .... Dr. Tobie TITSWORTH
31 Vice Pres Community/Economic Devel .... Vacant
09 Asst VP Accountability & Academics .... Dr. Mary MILLIKIN
12 Director Pryor Campus .... Ms. Sherry ALEXANDER
12 Provost Bartlesville Campus .... Mr. Bill BEIERSCHMITT
50 Dean School of Business & Tech .... Dr. Bruce GARRISON
83 Dean School of Liberal Arts .... Dr. Frank ELWELL
81 Dean Sch of Math/Sci/Hlth Sci .... Dr. Keith MARTIN
04 Assistant to the President .... Vacant
35 Director of Student Development .... Ms. Misty SMITH
08 Director of the Library .... Mr. J. Alan LAWLESS
07 Director of Admissions .... Ms. Joy Lin HUSTED
06 Registrar .... Mr. David BARRON
29 Director Alumni & Special Events .... Ms. Marisa LITTLEFIELD
21 Comptroller/Asst Vice Pres Bus Affs .... Mr. Mark MEADORS
04 Exec Assistant to the President .... Ms. Rhonda SPURLOCK
18 Director Physical Plant .... Mr. Leonard SZOPINSKI
19 Director Campus Public Safety .... Mr. Gary BOERGERMANN
27 Director Public Relations .... Mr. David HAMBY
37 Director of Financial Aid .... Ms. Kelly HICKS
91 Director Administrative Computing .... Ms. Cathy BURNS
90 Director Information Technology .... Mr. Brian REEVES
15 Employment & Benefits Coordinator .... Ms. Kristi MALLETT
41 Director of Athletics .... Mr. Ryan BRADLEY
39 Director Residential Life .... Ms. Kyla SHORT
23 Director Student Health Clinic .... Ms. Lisa MARTIN

Rose State College (I)

6420 SE 15th, Midwest City OK 73110-2799

County: Oklahoma — FICE Identification: 009185
Unit ID: 207670
Telephone: (405) 733-7311 — Carnegie Class: Assoc/Pub-S-SC
FAX Number: (405) 733-7399 — Calendar System: Semester
URL: www.rose.edu
Established: 1970 — Annual Undergrad Tuition & Fees (In-District): $2,968
Enrollment: 8,150 — Coed
Affiliation or Control: State/Local — IRS Status: 501(c)3
Highest Offering: Associate Degree
Program: Occupational; 2-Year Principally Bachelor's Creditable
Accreditation: NH, ADNUR, DA, DH, MLTAD, RAD

01 President .... Dr. Terry BRITTON
05 Vice President for Academic Affairs .... Dr. Frances HENDRIX
10 Vice President for Business Affairs .... Mr. Keith OGANS
32 Vice President for Student Affairs .... Dr. Jeanie WEBB
14 Vice President for Info Technology .... Mr. John PRIMO
103 Vice President for Workforce Devel .... Mr. Stan GREIL
84 Asoc Vice Pres Enrollment Mgmt .... Mr. Dean FISHER
20 Associate VP Academic Affairs .... Dr. Jeff CALDWELL
35 Assoc Vice Pres for Student Life .... Dr. Kent LASHLEY
30 Exec Dir Institutional Advancement .... Ms. Lisa PITSIRI

16	Exec Dir Human Res/Affirm Act Ofcr	Ms. Kim DELK
06	Registrar/Dir Admissions & Records	Ms. Mechelle AITSON-ROESSLER
37	Director Financial Aid	Mr. Steve DAFFER
26	Director Marketing/Public Relations	Mr. John CAIN
31	Director Community Learning Center	Mr. Joey DAVAULT
18	Director Operations	Mr. Ardie RODGERS
41	Dir Health & Wellness Activities	Mr. Chris LELAND
09	Dir Information Sys/Inst Research	Ms. Isabelle BILLEN
21	Director of Finance	Mr. Raymond BLANKE
36	Director Spec Svcs/Student Outreach	Dr. Joanne STAFFORD
25	Dir Grants and Contracts	Dr. Alan NEITZEL
29	Director Alumni Relations	Ms. Lindsay LANCASTER
08	Dean Learning Resources Center	Vacant
50	Dean Business & Info Tech Division	Mr. Art ZENNER
54	Dean Engineering & Science Division	Mr. Dawcett MIDDLETON
79	Dean Humanities Division	Dr. Betty EDWARDS
76	Dean Health Sciences Division	Mr. Dan POINTS
83	Dean Social Sciences Division	Dr. Bret WOOD

St. Gregory's University (A)

1900 W MacArthur, Shawnee OK 74804-2499

County: Pottawatomie | FICE Identification: 003183 | Unit ID: 207689

Telephone: (405) 878-5100 | Carnegie Class: Bac/Diverse

FAX Number: (405) 878-5198 | Calendar System: Semester

URL: www.stgregorys.edu

Established: 1875 | Annual Undergrad Tuition & Fees: $19,725

Enrollment: 739 | Coed

Affiliation or Control: Roman Catholic | IRS Status: 501(c)3

Highest Offering: Master's

Program: Liberal Arts And General; Technical Emphasis

Accreditation: NH

01	President	Mr. Gregory MAIN
03	Executive Vice President	Mr. Harley W. LINGERFELT
05	Provost	Vacant
26	Vice Pres Marketing & Development	Ms. Becky BEAUCHAMP
10	Chief Financial Officer	Ms. Catherine MANINGER
88	VP for Mission & Identity	Rev. Nicholas AST
84	Vice Pres for Enrollment Management	Mr. William KUEHL
55	Dean College for Working Adults	Dr. Jean THORNBRUGH
49	Dean College of Arts & Sciences	Dr. Ron H. FAULK
32	Dean of Student Life	Mr. Joshua CLARY
06	Registrar	Mrs. Kay K. STITH
08	Library Director	Mrs. Anita SEMTNER
26	Director of Public Relations	Mr. Brad M. COLLINS
38	Director Student Counseling	Mrs. Melody HARRINGTON
37	Director Student Financial Aid	Ms. Debra GAMBILL
41	Athletic Director	Dr. Jeff POTTER
85	Director of International Office	Mr. Spencer RYAN
15	Director of Human Resources	Mrs. Marria L. BRYDON
18	Director Facilities/Physical Plant	Mr. Mark SAUNDERS
13	Int Director of Information Systems	Mr. Max A. JENKINS

Seminole State College (B)

PO Box 351, Seminole OK 74818-0351

County: Seminole | FICE Identification: 003178 | Unit ID: 207740

Telephone: (405) 382-9950 | Carnegie Class: Assoc/Pub-R-M

FAX Number: (405) 382-3122 | Calendar System: Semester

URL: www.sscok.edu

Established: 1931 | Annual Undergrad Tuition & Fees (In-District): $3,231

Enrollment: 2,241 | Coed

Affiliation or Control: State/Local | IRS Status: 501(c)3

Highest Offering: Associate Degree

Program: Occupational; 2-Year Principally Bachelor's Creditable

Accreditation: NH, ADNUR, MLTAD

01	President	Dr. Jim W. UTTERBACK
05	Vice President Academic Affairs	Dr. Melanie CROY
32	Vice President for Student Affairs	Dr. Brad WALCK
10	Vice President Fiscal Affairs	Mrs. Katherine BENTON
30	Vice Pres Institutional Advancement	Ms. Lana REYNOLDS
84	Director of Enrollment Management	Dr. Mark AMES
13	Director Mgmt Information Systems	Mr. Jack WHISENNAND
08	Librarian/Director Education Media	Mrs. Marguerite HEAROD
66	Director of Nursing	Mrs. Donna CHAMBERS
06	Registrar	Mrs. Debbie ROBERTSON
15	Director Personnel Services	Mrs. Courtney JONES
18	Chief Facilities/Physical Plant	Mr. Braden BROWN
20	Associate Academic Officer	Ms. Pam KOENIG
26	Coordinator of Media Relations	Ms. Dustie BUTNER

Southeastern Oklahoma State University (C)

1405 N 4th Avenue, Durant OK 74701-3330

County: Bryan | FICE Identification: 003179 | Unit ID: 207847

Telephone: (580) 745-2000 | Carnegie Class: Master's M

FAX Number: (580) 745-2515 | Calendar System: Semester

URL: www.se.edu

Established: 1909 | Annual Undergrad Tuition & Fees (In-State): $4,127

Enrollment: 4,127 | Coed

Affiliation or Control: State | IRS Status: 501(c)3

Highest Offering: Master's

Program: Liberal Arts And General; Teacher Preparatory; Professional

Accreditation: NH, AAB, ACBSP, BUS, MUS, TED

01	President	Dr. Larry MINKS
05	Vice Pres Acad Affairs	Dr. Douglas MCMILLAN
10	Vice President Business Affairs	Mr. Ross WALKUP
32	Vice President Student Affairs	Ms. Sharon ROBINSON
20	AVP Acad Aff/Supprt/Dn Grad Studies	Dr. William Jerry POLSON
20	Asst VP Academic Affs/Instruction	Dr. Bryon CLARK
04	Exec Asst to President	Ms. Michele CAMPBELL
35	Dean of Students	Dr. Camille PHELPS
49	Dean of Instruction	Dr. Lucretia SCOUFOS
07	Assoc Dean Admissions/Registrar	Ms. Kristie LUKE
88	Assoc Dean Academic Services	Mr. Tim BOATMUN
13	Exec Dir of Information Technology	Mr. Dan MOORE
30	Exec Director of Univ Advancement	Mr. Kyle STAFFORD
37	Director Student Financial Aid	Mr. Tony LEHRLING
36	Director of Career Management Ctr	Mr. Scott HENSLEY
08	Library Director	Ms. Sharon MORRISON
51	Director Continuing Education	Mr. Scott HENSLEY
41	Director of Athletics	Mr. Keith BAXTER
26	Director University Communications	Mr. Alan BURTON
15	Director Human Resources	Mrs. Cathy CONWAY
21	Director Finance/Controller	Ms. Kay Lynn ROBERTS
38	Director Student Counseling	Ms. Jane MCMILLAN
18	Director Facilities/Physical Plant	Mr. Eddie HARBIN
28	Special Asst to the Pres/Diversity	Dr. Claire STUBBLEFIELD
96	Purchasing Agent	Mrs. Carol COATS
40	Book Store Manager	Ms. Jackie CODNER
29	Director Alumni Relations	Ms. Stephanie SHADE-DAVISON

Southern Nazarene University (D)

6729 NW 39 Expressway, Bethany OK 73008-2694

County: Oklahoma | FICE Identification: 003149 | Unit ID: 206862

Telephone: (405) 789-6400 | Carnegie Class: Master's L

FAX Number: (405) 491-6381 | Calendar System: Semester

URL: www.snu.edu

Established: 1899 | Annual Undergrad Tuition & Fees: $21,174

Enrollment: 2,042 | Coed

Affiliation or Control: Church Of The Nazarene | IRS Status: 501(c)3

Highest Offering: Master's

Program: Liberal Arts And General; Teacher Preparatory; Professional; Business Emphasis

Accreditation: NH, ACBSP, MUS, NURSE, TED

01	President	Dr. Loren P. GRESHAM
03	Provost	Dr. Mary JONES
05	Acting Vice Pres Academic Affairs	Dr. Mary JONES
10	Vice President Financial Affairs	Dr. Scott STRAWN
30	VP of Univ Advance & Church Rels	Dr. Terry TOLER
32	Vice President Student Development	Dr. Mike REDWINE
42	University Pastor	Dr. Blair SPINDLE
84	Vice Pres of Enrollment Management	Dr. Linda CANTWELL
20	Dean College of Humanities	Dr. Melany KYZER
81	Dean College of Sci & Health	Dr. Mark WINSLOW
06	Registrar	Mr. Charles CHITWOOD
07	Director Admissions	Dr. Linda CANTWELL
37	Director Student Financial Aid	Mrs. Diana LEE
35	Director Student Affairs	Mrs. Marian REDWINE
38	Director Student Counseling	Mrs. Kimberly CAMPBELL
36	Director Career Planning/Placement	Vacant
08	Director Learning Resources Center	Prof. Katie KING
29	Director Alumni Relations	Ms. Kendra THOMSON
14	Director Information Technology	Mrs. Laureen SPRINGER
88	Director Academic Services	Mr. Wes LEE
09	Director Institutional Research	Dr. Randy ZABEL
58	Dean Col of Grad & Prof Study	Dr. Davis BERRYMAN
66	Director of Nursing	Dr. Katie SIGLER
15	Director Human Resources	Mr. Chris PETERSON
18	Director of Physical Plant	Mr. Ron LESTER
24	Director Network	Mrs. Chichi FREELANDER
26	Director Communications & Marketing	Mrs. Sarah ROBERTS
40	Bookstore Manager	Mr. Reggie COLEMAN
41	Athletic Director	Mr. Bobby MARTIN
88	Dean College of Teach & Learn	Dr. Dennis WILLIAMS
50	Dean Col of Bus/Educ & KSM	Dr. Sylvia GOODMAN

Southwestern Christian University (E)

PO Box 340, 7210 NW 39th Expressway, Bethany OK 73008-0340

County: Oklahoma | FICE Identification: 003180 | Unit ID: 207856

Telephone: (405) 789-7661 | Carnegie Class: Bac/Diverse

FAX Number: (405) 495-0078 | Calendar System: Semester

URL: www.swcu.edu

Established: 1946 | Annual Undergrad Tuition & Fees: $13,500

Enrollment: 644 | Coed

Affiliation or Control: Pentecostal Holiness Church | IRS Status: 501(c)3

Highest Offering: Master's

Program: Liberal Arts And General; Religious Emphasis

Accreditation: NH

01	President	Dr. Ed HUCKEBY
05	Provost & VP Academic Affairs	Dr. Reggies WENYIKA
10	Vice President for Fiscal Affairs	Mr. Wallace O. HAMILTON
30	Vice President for Advance/Develop	Mr. Kevin RICHARDSON
32	Vice President for Student Affairs	Mr. David H. CHISSOE
41	Athletic Director	Mr. Mark ARTHUR
37	Director of Financial Aid	Mrs. Kellye JOHNSON
07	Director of Admissions & Enrollment	Mr. Chad PUGH
08	Director of Library Services	Mrs. Marilyn HUDSON
06	Registrar	Mrs. Sherri HENDRIX
58	Dean of Adult & Graduate Studies	Vacant
107	Dean of Professional Studies	Mrs. Adrian HINKLE
49	Dean of Arts & Sciences	Dr. Donna MCCOY
18	Director of Plant/Property Mgmt	Vacant
26	Director of Sports Information/PR	Ms. Kasey GARDNER
13	Director of Information Technology	Mr. David WIGGINS
12	Director of Tulsa Campus Branch	Mrs. Lorena RAY
42	Director of Campus Spiritual Life	Dr. Mark CULHAM
106	Director of Online Education	Mr. Julian COWART
108	Director of Institution Assessment	Dr. James BOWEN

Southwestern Oklahoma State University (F)

100 Campus Drive, Weatherford OK 73096-3098

County: Custer | FICE Identification: 003181 | Unit ID: 207865

Telephone: (580) 772-6611 | Carnegie Class: Master's M

FAX Number: (580) 774-3795 | Calendar System: Semester

URL: www.swosu.edu

Established: 1901 | Annual Undergrad Tuition & Fees (In-State): $4,905

Enrollment: 5,340 | Coed

Affiliation or Control: State | IRS Status: 501(c)3

Highest Offering: First Professional Degree

Program: Liberal Arts And General; Teacher Preparatory; Professional

Accreditation: NH, ENGT, IACBE, MLTAB, MUS, NAIT, NUR, OTA, PHAR, PTAA, RAD, SW, TED

01	President	Dr. Randy L. BEUTLER
05	Senior Vice President & Provost	Dr. Blake I. SONOBE
10	Vice Pres Administration & Finance	Mr. Thomas W. FAGAN
30	Asst to Pres for Inst Advancement	Ms. Lynne F. THURMAN
32	VP Student Affairs/Assoc Provost	Dr. Cynthia R. FOUST
26	Assoc VP Marketing/Public Relations	Mr. Brian D. ADLER
96	Dir Business Affairs/Comptroller	Ms. Brenda K. BURGESS
35	Dean of Students/Dir Student Act	Ms. Cynthia R. DOUGHERTY
13	Dir Information Technology Services	Mr. Mark D. ENGELMAN
06	Registrar	Mr. Daniel R. ARCHER
08	Library Director	Dr. Jonathan D. SPARKS
37	Director Student Financial Services	Mr. Jerome L. WICHERT
15	Dir Human Resources/Affirm Action	Mr. M. David MISAK
84	Dir Enrollment Mgmt/Career Svcs	Mr. Todd T. BOYD
57	Director Fine Arts Center	Mr. Kyle J. BARTEL
41	Athletic Director	Mr. Todd A. THURMAN
09	Director Institutional Research	Ms. Denisa A. ENGELMAN
06	Registrar Sayre Campus	Ms. G. Kim SEYMOUR
37	Dir Financial Svcs/Sayre Campus	Mr. Ron KISTLER
38	Director Counseling Services	Ms. Kim K. LIEBSCHER
18	Director Physical Plant	Mr. Rick SKINNER
36	Career Services Coordinator	Ms. Jonna MYERS
58	Dean College of Prof/Grad Studies	Dr. Ken G. ROSE
49	Dean College of Arts & Sciences	Dr. James D. SOUTH
67	Dean College of Pharmacy	Dr. Dennis F. THOMPSON
12	Dean College of Assoc/Applied Prog	Ms. Sherron K. MANNING
76	Associate Dean Sch of Allied Health	Ms. Marion L. PRICHARD
53	Assoc Dean Sch of Behavioral Sci	Dr. L. Chad KINDER
50	Assoc Dean School of Business/Tech	Dr. Leslie D. CRALL
66	Associate Dean School of Nursing	Dr. Barbara A. PATTERSON

† Campus at Sayre offers a two-year degree and is regionally accredited (NH) under parent institution. Other specialized accreditation: RAD, MLTAB.

Spartan College of Aeronautics and Technology (G)

8820 E Pine Street, Tulsa OK 74115

County: Tulsa | FICE Identification: 007678 | Unit ID: 207254

Telephone: (918) 836-6886 | Carnegie Class: Spec/Tech

FAX Number: (918) 831-5287 | Calendar System: Other

URL: www.spartan.edu

Established: 1928 | Annual Undergrad Tuition & Fees: $15,450

Enrollment: 1,051 | Coed

Affiliation or Control: Proprietary | IRS Status: Proprietary

Highest Offering: Baccalaureate

Program: Occupational; 2-Year Principally Bachelor's Creditable; Technical Emphasis

Accreditation: ACCSC

01	CEO/President	Mr. Jeremy GIBSON
10	CFO/Vice President Finance	Mr. Blaine WALKER
05	Vice Pres Educ/Lic/Accreditation	Mr. Ryan GOERTZEN
11	Vice President Administration	Mr. Dean RILING

Tulsa Community College (H)

6111 E Skelly Drive, Tulsa OK 74135-6198

County: Tulsa | FICE Identification: 009763 | Unit ID: 207935

Telephone: (918) 595-7000 | Carnegie Class: Assoc/Pub-U-MC

FAX Number: (918) 595-7910 | Calendar System: Semester

URL: www.tulsacc.edu

Established: 1968 | Annual Undergrad Tuition & Fees (In-State): $3,180

Enrollment: 27,704 | Coed

Affiliation or Control: State | IRS Status: 501(c)3

Highest Offering: Associate Degree

Program: Occupational; 2-Year Principally Bachelor's Creditable

Accreditation: NH, ADNUR, DH, MAC, MLTAD, OTA, PTAA, RAD

01	President	Dr. Thomas K. MCKEON
04	Assistant to the President	Ms. Norma L. RODGERS

10 Controller & CFO ... Mr. Shane NETHERTON
05 Vice President for Academic Affairs ... Dr. Ric N. BASER
13 VP Administration/Chief Tech Ofcr ... Mr. Sean A. WEINS
32 Assoc Vice Pres Student Affairs ... Dr. Jan L. CLAYTON
20 Assoc Vice Pres Academic Affairs ... Dr. Donna G. WOOD
15 Asst Vice Pres for Human Resources ... Ms. Patricia L. FISCHER
12 Provost Southeast Campus ... Dr. Brett S. CAMPBELL
12 Provost Northeast Campus ... Dr. John GIBSON
12 Provost Metro Campus ... Dr. Flo E. POTTS
12 Provost West Campus ... Dr. Peggy D. DYER
26 Vice President External Affairs ... Ms. Lauren F. BROOKEY
08 Dean Learning Res Ctr/Librarian ... Ms. Paula SETTOON
28 Dean of Diversity/Civic Engagement ... Mr. Tony J. ALONSO
51 Dean Corporate & Continuing Educ ... Ms. Lisa PALMER
07 Dean Admissions/College Registrar ... Ms. Traci HECK
18 Director Physical Facilities ... Ms. Jemina C. LOTTI
37 Director Financial Aid ... Ms. Karen JEFFERS
96 Dir Purch & Inventory Control ... Mr. Bill CREECH
09 Dir Planning/Institutional Research ... Dr. Kevin DAVID
19 Director Campus Police ... Vacant
40 Director Campus Store Operations ... Mr. Ken A. JONES
27 Director Marketing Communications ... Ms. Sue A. BROWN
21 Director Administrative Services ... Dr. Frederick D. ARTIS
92 Director of Honors Program ... Ms. Susan ONEAL

Tulsa Welding School (A)

2545 E 11th Street, Tulsa OK 74104-3909

County: Tulsa | FICE Identification: 009618 | Unit ID: 207962
Telephone: (918) 587-6789 | Carnegie Class: Assoc/PrivFP
FAX Number: (918) 587-8170 | Calendar System: Other
URL: www.weldingschool.com
Established: 1949 | Annual Undergrad Tuition & Fees: $16,195
Enrollment: 1,033 | Coed
Affiliation or Control: Proprietary | IRS Status: Proprietary
Highest Offering: Associate Degree
Program: Occupational
Accreditation: ACCSC

01 President ... Ms. Aleco BABIKI
03 Vice Pres/Executive Director ... Mrs. Debbie BURKE
05 Director of Training ... Mr. Jamie PEARSON
07 Director of Admissions ... Mr. Stephen STIERWALT
37 Director of Financial Aid ... Mrs. Teresa FRANKLIN
36 Director of Employment ... Ms. Tiffany JORDAN

University of Central Oklahoma (B)

100 N University Drive, Edmond OK 73034-5209

County: Oklahoma | FICE Identification: 003152 | Unit ID: 206941
Telephone: (405) 974-2000 | Carnegie Class: Master's L
FAX Number: (405) 341-4964 | Calendar System: Semester
URL: www.uco.edu
Established: 1890 | Annual Undergrad Tuition & Fees (In-State): $5,408
Enrollment: 17,262 | Coed
Affiliation or Control: State | IRS Status: 501(c)3
Highest Offering: Master's
Program: Liberal Arts And General; Teacher Preparatory; Professional
Accreditation: NH, ACBSP, CIDA, CS, DIETD, DIETI, ENG, EXSC, FUSER, MUS, NUR, SP, TED

01 President ... Dr. Don BETZ
03 Executive Vice President ... Mr. Steve KREIDLER
05 Provost/Vice Pres Academic Affairs ... Dr. William RADKE
32 Vice President Student Affairs ... Dr. Kathryn GAGE
13 Vice President Information Tech ... Dr. Cynthia ROLFE
84 Vice Pres Enrollment Management ... Dr. Myron POPE
26 Vice Pres University Relations ... Mr. Charlie JOHNSON
86 Vice Pres Government Relations ... Mr. Mark KINDERS
11 Assoc VP Administration ... Mr. Mark MOORE
20 Vice Prov/Assoc VP Academic Affairs ... Dr. Patricia LAGROW
20 Asst Vice Pres Academic Affairs ... Dr. Lori BEASLEY
10 Asst VP Admin Financial Services ... Ms. Lisa HARPER
18 Asst Vice Pres Admin/Facilities Mgt ... Mr. Mark RODOLF
35 Asst Vice Pres Student Affairs ... Mr. Cole STANLEY
04 Special Assistant to Vice President ... Ms. Amy ROGALSKY
102 President UCO Foundation ... Mrs. Anne HOLZBERLEIN
41 Athletic Director ... Mr. Joe MULLER
04 Executive in Residence ... Dr. Douglas FOX
09 Director Institutional Research ... Ms. Cindy BOLING
31 Exec Director Auxiliary Enterprises ... Mr. Robert LINDLEY
08 Exec Director University Libraries ... Dr. Bonnie MCNEELY
37 Director Student Financial Aid ... Ms. Susan PRATER
29 Director Alumni Relations ... Mr. Al JONES
38 Dir Counsel/Test/Disabl Support Svc ... Dr. Bruce LOCHNER
85 Director International Student Svcs ... Dr. Dennis DUNHAM
39 Director Residential Life ... Mr. Josh OVEROCKER
19 Director Public Safety ... Mr. Jeff HARP
23 Director Wellness Center ... Mr. Mark HERRIN
14 Director Project Management ... Ms. Sandra THOMAS
15 Director Employee Services ... Ms. Jeanette PATTON
88 Exec Dir Leadership Central ... Mr. Jarrett JOBE
36 Career Counselor ... Ms. Carrol MCALLISTER
22 Equity/Affirmative Action Officer ... Dr. Brad MORELLI
50 Dean of Business Administration ... Dr. Mickey HEPNER
53 Dean College Education ... Dr. James MACHELL
49 Dean College of Liberal Arts ... Dr. Pamela WASHINGTON
81 Dean College Math/Science ... Dr. John BARTHELL
58 Dean Graduate Studies ... Dr. Richard BERNARD
57 Dean College Fine Arts & Design ... Dr. John CLINTON

University of Oklahoma Norman Campus (C)

660 Parrington Oval, Norman OK 73019-3070

County: Cleveland | FICE Identification: 003184 | Unit ID: 207500
Telephone: (405) 325-0311 | Carnegie Class: RU/VH
FAX Number: (405) 325-7605 | Calendar System: Semester
URL: www.ou.edu
Established: 1890 | Annual Undergrad Tuition & Fees (In-State): $7,340
Enrollment: 27,138 | Coed
Affiliation or Control: State | IRS Status: 501(c)3
Highest Offering: Doctorate
Program: Liberal Arts And General; Teacher Preparatory; Professional
Accreditation: NH, AAB, BUS, BUSA, CIDA, CONST, COPSY, CS, ENG, JOUR, LAW, LIB, LSAR, MUS, PLNG, SW, TED, THEA

01 President ... Mr. David L. BOREN
10 VP Administration & Finance ... Mr. Nick HATHAWAY
101 VP Univ Gov/Exec Secy Bd of Regents ... Dr. Chris PURCELL
05 Senior Vice President/Provost ... Dr. Nancy L. MERGLER
43 VP of Univ/General Counsel ... Mr. Anil GOLLAHALLI
32 Vice President for Student Affairs ... Mr. Clarke STROUD
30 Vice Pres for University Devel ... Mr. Jim HALL, III
51 VP Univ Outreach/Dn Col Lib Std ... Dr. James P. PAPPAS
58 Dean Grad College ... Dr. T. H. Lee WILLIAMS
46 Vice President for Research ... Dr. Kelvin DROEGEMEIER
26 Vice President for Public Affairs ... Ms. Catherine BISHOP
13 Assoc VP/Chief Information Ofcr ... Ms. Loretta EARLY
86 Vice Pres for Governmental Relation ... Mr. Danny C. HILLIARD
20 Associate Provost/Dir of Acad Integ ... Dr. Gregory M. HEISER
20 Assoc Provost for Academic Advising ... Dr. Joyce L. ALLMAN
09 Assoc Provost/Dir Inst Research ... Ms. Cheryl K. JORGENSON
06 Registrar/VP Enroll/Stdnt Fin Svcs ... Mr. Matt HAMILTON
35 Director Student Life ... Ms. Kristen PARTRIDGE
21 Assoc VP Administration & Finance ... Mr. Byron MILLSAP
21 Assoc VP Admin & Finance ... Mr. Chris KUWITZKY
29 Assoc VP Alum&Dev/Ex Dir Alum Assoc ... Mr. Jean Paul AUDAS
18 Director Facilities Management ... Mr. Brian ELLIS
39 Director of Housing & Food Services ... Mr. David L. ANNIS
41 Director of Athletics ... Mr. Joe CASTIGLIONE
21 Controller ... Ms. Terri B. PINKSTON
23 AVP/Director Goddard Health Center ... Dr. William WAYNE
36 Director Career Services ... Ms. Bette J. SCOTT
19 Chief of Police ... Ms. Liz WOOLLEN
15 AVP/Director of Human Resources ... Mr. Julius HILBURN
22 Equal Opportunity Officer ... Dr. Shad B. SATTERTHWAITE
22 Inst Eq Ofcr & Title IX Coordinator ... Ms. Laura PALK
07 Director of Admissions ... Mr. Mark MCMASTERS
25 Assoc VP for Research Services ... Ms. Andrea D. DEATON
85 Director Internatl Student Services ... Ms. Monica A. SHARP
104 Director Education Abroad ... Ms. Alice KLOKER
37 Director of Financial Aid ... Ms. Caryn L. PACHECO
48 Dean College of Architecture ... Dr. Charles W. GRAHAM
49 VP/Dean College Arts & Sciences ... Dr. Paul BELL
53 Dn Jeannine Rainbolt Col of Educ ... Dr. Gregg GARN
54 Dean College of Engineering ... Dr. Thomas L. LANDERS
57 Dn Weitzenhoffer Col of Fine Arts ... Mr. Rich TAYLOR
61 VP/Dean College of Law ... Mr. Joseph HARROZ, JR.
62 Dean University Libraries ... Mr. Richard E. LUCE
65 VP/Dn Col Atmospheric/Geographic Sc ... Dr. Berrien MOORE, III
50 Dn Michael F. Price Col of Business ... Dr. Kenneth R. EVANS
92 Dean McClendon Honors College ... Dr. David H. RAY
60 Dn Gaylord Col Journ/Mass Comm ... Dr. Joe S. FOOTE
89 Interim Dean University College ... Dr. Nicole J. CAMPBELL
88 Dean Mewborne Col of Earth & Energy ... Dr. Larry R. GRILLOT
82 Interim Dean Col Intl Studies ... Dr. Suzette R. GRILLOT

† Tuition is now based on 30 credit hour year rather than 24 as in the past.

University of Oklahoma Health Sciences Center (D)

1000 Stanton L. Young Boulevard, Oklahoma City OK 73117

County: Oklahoma | FICE Identification: 005889 | Unit ID: 207342
Telephone: (405) 271-4000 | Carnegie Class: Spec/Med
FAX Number: N/A | Calendar System: Semester
URL: www.ouhsc.edu
Established: 1910 | Annual Undergrad Tuition & Fees (In-State): $6,052
Enrollment: 3,624 | Coed
Affiliation or Control: State | IRS Status: 501(c)3
Highest Offering: Doctorate
Program: Occupational; Professional
Accreditation: &NH, ARCPA, AUD, DENT, DH, DIETC, DIETD, DIETI, DMS, ENGR, HSA, IPSY, MED, NMT, NUR, OT, PDPSY, PH, PHAR, PTA, RAD, RADDOS, RTT, SP

01 Senior Vice President & Provost ... Dr. M. Dewayne ANDREWS
05 Vice Provost Academic Affairs ... Dr. Valerie WILLIAMS
23 Vice Provost for Health Sciences ... Dr. Marcia M. BENNETT
10 Vice Pres Administrative & Finance ... Mr. Kenneth D. ROWE
32 Vice President Student Affairs ... Mr. Clarke STROUD
46 Vice President for Research ... Dr. John J. IANDOLO
27 Vice President for Public Affairs ... Ms. Catherine F. BISHOP
13 Int Vice Pres Info Technology/CIO ... Ms. Loretta M. EARLY
28 Asst Provost Diversity/Cmty Prtnshp ... Mr. Brian K. CORPENING
35 Exec Director HSC Student Affairs ... Ms. Kate STANTON
102 Dir Oklahoma Health Ctr Foundation ... Mr. Hershel LAMIRAND
30 Director Development ... Ms. Stacey MAXON
06 Registrar ... Ms. Lori KLIMKOWSKI
07 Director of Admissions ... Mr. Scott BOEH
29 Director Alumni & Annual Programs ... Ms. Carol MODISETTE
18 Director of Operations ... Mr. Don P. CAIL
43 Legal Counsel ... Ms. Peggy CLAY
22 Univ Equal Opportunity Officer ... Dr. Shad SATTERTHWAITE
37 Director Student Financial Aid ... Ms. Pamela JORDAN
08 Director Robert M Bird Library ... Mr. C. Marty THOMPSON
15 Director of Human Resources ... Mr. Julius HILBURN
96 Director of Purchasing ... Ms. Jean WILSON
63 Exec Dean College of Medicine ... Dr. Dewayne ANDREWS
76 Dean College Allied Health ... Dr. P. Kevin RUDEEN
52 Dean College of Dentistry ... Dr. Stephen K. YOUNG
66 Dean College of Nursing ... Dr. Lazelle BENEFIELD
67 Dean College of Pharmacy ... Dr. JoLaine DRAUGALIS
69 Dean College Public Health ... Dr. Gary E. RASKOB
63 Dean College of Medicine-Tulsa ... Dr. Daniel DUFFY
58 Dean Graduate College ... Dr. James J. TOMASEK

† Regional accreditation is carried under the parent institution in Norman, OK.

University of Science and Arts of Oklahoma (E)

1727 W Alabama, Chickasha OK 73018-5322

County: Grady | FICE Identification: 003167 | Unit ID: 207722
Telephone: (405) 224-3140 | Carnegie Class: Bac/A&S
FAX Number: (405) 574-1220 | Calendar System: Trimester
URL: www.usao.edu
Established: 1908 | Annual Undergrad Tuition & Fees (In-State): $5,400
Enrollment: 1,033 | Coed
Affiliation or Control: State | IRS Status: 501(c)3
Highest Offering: Baccalaureate
Program: Liberal Arts And General; Teacher Preparatory
Accreditation: NH, MUS, TED

01 President ... Dr. John H. FEAVER
05 VP for Academic Affairs ... Dr. Dexter MARBLE
10 Vice Pres for Business & Finance ... Mr. Mike D. COPONITI
84 Vice Pres for Enrollment Management ... Ms. Monica TREVINO
30 Vice Pres University Advancement ... Dr. Michael NEALEIGH
13 VP for Information Services & Tech ... Ms. Lynn BOYCE
06 Registrar/Dir of Enrollment/Records ... Mr. Joe W. EVANS
08 Director of Nash Library ... Ms. Kelly BROWN
37 Director of Financial Aid ... Ms. Nancy I. MOATS
32 Dean of Students/Dir Student Svcs ... Ms. Nancy HUGHES
26 Director Media/Community Relations ... Mr. Randy TALLEY
29 Director of Alumni Development ... Mr. Eric FEUERBORN
18 Director of Physical Plant ... Mr. Tim A. STIGER
14 Director of Data Processing ... Mr. Jim HOPKINS
09 Director of Institutional Research ... Ms. Lynn BOYCE
15 Director Personnel Services ... Mr. Mike COPONITI
49 Chair Div of Arts & Humanities ... Dr. Stephen WEBER
50 Chair Div of Business & Social Sci ... Dr. Christopher WALKER
53 Chair Division of Education ... Dr. Vicki FERGUSON
81 Chair Div of Science/Physical Educ ... Dr. Darryel REIGH
88 Chair Interdisciplinary Studies ... Dr. Jennifer LONG

University of Tulsa (F)

800 S Tucker, Tulsa OK 74104

County: Tulsa | FICE Identification: 003185 | Unit ID: 207971
Telephone: (918) 631-2000 | Carnegie Class: DRU
FAX Number: (918) 631-2033 | Calendar System: Semester
URL: www.utulsa.edu
Established: 1894 | Annual Undergrad Tuition & Fees: $43,079
Enrollment: 4,092 | Coed
Affiliation or Control: Independent Non-Profit | IRS Status: 501(c)3
Highest Offering: Doctorate
Program: Liberal Arts And General; Teacher Preparatory; Professional
Accreditation: NH, BUS, CLPSY, CS, ENG, LAW, MUS, NUR, SP, TEAC

01 President ... Dr. Geoffrey ORSAK
03 Exec Vice President & Treasurer ... Mr. Kevan C. BUCK
05 Provost/Vice Pres Academic Affairs ... Dr. Roger N. BLAIS
30 Sr Vice Pres Planning & Outreach ... Dr. Janis I. ZINK
20 Sr Vice Provost & Assoc VP ... Ms. Winona M. TANAKA
84 VP Enrollment & Student Svcs ... Dr. Roger W. SOROCHTY
13 VP Info Services & CIO ... Dr. Dale A. SCHOENEFELD
26 VP Public Relations ... Dr. Kayla K. ACEBO
88 VP Museum Affs/Exec Dir Gilcrease ... Dr. Duane KING
46 Vice Prov Research/Dean Grad School ... Dr. Janet A. HAGGERTY
100 Chief of Staff ... Ms. Jacqueline H. CALDWELL
86 Assoc VP Pub Affairs/Econ Devel ... Ms. Susan NEAL
09 Director Inst Research & Records ... Dr. Michael W. BARNES
41 Athletic Director ... Mr. Ross PARMLEY
42 University Chaplain ... Dr. Jeffrey FRANCIS
49 Dean Arts & Sciences ... Dr. Dale T. BENEDIKTSON
50 Dean Business Administration ... Dr. A. Gale SULLENBERGER
54 Interim Dean Engineering ... Dr. James SOREM
61 Dean Law ... Ms. Janet LEVIT
08 RM & Ida McFarlin Dean of Library ... Mr. Adrian W. ALEXANDER
104 Vice Provost Intl Studies ... Dr. Cheryl MATHERLY
06 Registrar ... Ms. Ginna V. LANGSTON
15 Associate VP Human Resources ... Mr. Wayne PAULISON
18 Assoc VP Operations/Physical Plant ... Mr. Robert SHIPLEY
21 Assoc VP & Controller ... Mr. Michael D. THESENVITZ
07 Assoc VP Enrollment Dean Admission ... Mr. Earl JOHNSON
32 Assoc VP Enrollment Dean Students ... Ms. Yolanda D. TAYLOR

39 Assoc VP Director Housing ..... Ms. Melissa H. FRANCE
85 Dean International Students ..... Ms. Pamela A. SMITH
51 Dean Lifelong Learning ..... Dr. J. Phillip APPLEGATE
62 Assoc Dean McFarlin Library ..... Ms. Francine J. FISK
23 Director Health Center ..... Ms. Stephanie FELL
38 Director Student Counseling ..... Dr. Thomas J. BRIAN
19 Director Campus Security ..... Mr. Joseph F. TIMMONS
29 Director Alumni Relations ..... Ms. Amy M. FREIBERGER
36 Director Career Services ..... Ms. Shelly HOLLY
37 Director Student Financial Svcs ..... Ms. Vicki A. HENDRICKSON
96 Director Purchasing ..... Mr. Jerry R. HOLLOWAY
90 Dir Academic Tech Services ..... Ms. Janet CAIRNS
91 Dir Admin Computing ..... Mr. Martin PAGE
31 Assoc Dean Community Relations ..... Mr. Michael MILLS
27 Assoc Dir News & Public Rels ..... Ms. Mona CHAMBERLIN
88 Sr Director Creative Svcs ..... Ms. Leslie CAIRNS
105 Director Web Communications ..... Mr. Matt CASTEEL
101 Secretary Board of Trustees ..... Ms. June E. BROWN
04 Sr Admin Associate to President ..... Ms. Tia CREAMER

Vatterott College-Oklahoma City (A)

4621 NW 23rd Street, Oklahoma City OK 73127-2103
County: Oklahoma — Identification: 666061
Unit ID: 437060
Telephone: (405) 945-0088 — Carnegie Class: Assoc/PrivFP
FAX Number: (405) 945-0788 — Calendar System: Other
URL: www.vatterott-college.edu
Established: 1997 — Annual Undergrad Tuition & Fees: $10,213
Enrollment: 371 — Coed
Affiliation or Control: Proprietary — IRS Status: Proprietary
Highest Offering: Associate Degree
Program: Occupational; Technical Emphasis
Accreditation: **ACCSC**

01 CEO & President ..... Ms. Pam BELL
10 Chief Financial Officer ..... Mr. Dennis BEAVERS
05 Chief Academic Officer ..... Mr. Brandon SHEDRON
11 Chief Administrative Officer ..... Mr. Scott CASANOVER
12 Campus Director ..... Mr. Christopher PIATT

† Branch campus of Vatterott College, Quincy, IL.

Vatterott College-Tulsa (B)

4343 S 118th E Avenue, Ste A, Tulsa OK 74146-4406
County: Tulsa — Identification: 666102
Unit ID: 440882
Telephone: (918) 835-8288 — Carnegie Class: Assoc/PrivFP
FAX Number: (918) 836-9698 — Calendar System: Other
URL: www.vatterott-college.edu
Established: 1997 — Annual Undergrad Tuition & Fees: $10,899
Enrollment: 259 — Coed
Affiliation or Control: Proprietary — IRS Status: Proprietary
Highest Offering: Associate Degree
Program: Occupational; Technical Emphasis
Accreditation: **ACCSC**

01 CEO & President ..... Ms. Pam BELL
10 Chief Financial Officer ..... Mr. Dennis BEAVERS
05 Vice President Academic Affairs ..... Dr. Brandon SHEDRON
30 VP Regulatory Affs/Strategic Devel ..... Mr. Aaron LACEY
43 General Counsel/Chief Administrator ..... Mr. Scott CASANOVER
12 Campus Director ..... Ms. Heather ANSON

† Branch campus of Vatterott College-NorthPark, Berkeley, MO.

Western Oklahoma State College (C)

2801 N Main Street, Altus OK 73521-1397
County: Jackson — FICE Identification: 003146
Unit ID: 208035
Telephone: (580) 477-2000 — Carnegie Class: Assoc/Pub-R-M
FAX Number: (580) 477-7777 — Calendar System: Semester
URL: www.wosc.edu
Established: 1926 — Annual Undergrad Tuition & Fees (In-State): $3,003
Enrollment: 5,035 — Coed
Affiliation or Control: State — IRS Status: 501(c)3
Highest Offering: Associate Degree
Program: Occupational; 2-Year Principally Bachelor's Creditable
Accreditation: **NH**, ADNUR, RAD

01 President ..... Dr. Phil BIRDINE
04 Admin Secretary to the President ..... Ms. Briar JENKINS
05 VP for Academic & Student Supp Svcs ..... Ms. Lisa GREENLEE
10 Vice President for Business Affairs ..... Ms. Tricia LATHAM
30 Vice Pres Development & Alumni Rels ..... Mr. Larry K. DUFFY
49 Dean Arts & Sciences ..... Dr. Jason MORRISON
20 Dean of Student Support Services ..... Mr. Chad WIGINTON
72 Dean of Technical Programs ..... Ms. Chrystal OVERTON
13 Dir of Information Technology ..... Mr. Steve PRATER
27 Director Public Information ..... Ms. Judith NORTON
07 Director of Admissions & Registrar ..... Ms. Lana SCOTT
37 Director of Student Financial Aid ..... Ms. Myrna J. CROSS
29 Dir Development/Alumni Relations ..... Ms. Haley THOMPSON
40 Bookstore Manager ..... Ms. Kass DEWEESE
68 Dir Physical Educ/Athletic Devel ..... Mr. Bob PEARSON
62 Director of Learning Resources ..... Ms. Suzanne ROOKER
15 Director Personnel Services ..... Ms. April NELSON
18 Director Physical Plant & Safety ..... Mr. Doyle JENCKS
38 Counselor ..... Ms. April DILL
96 Asst Director of Purchasing ..... Ms. Vicki ELKINS
81 Science Instructor ..... Dr. Toni COAKLEY
79 Art Instructor ..... Mr. Jerry BRYAN
88 History Instructor ..... Mr. Mickey GRAHAM

OREGON

American College of Healthcare Sciences (D)

5940 SW Hood Avenue, Portland OR 97239-3719
County: Multnomah — Identification: 666365
Telephone: (503) 244-0726 — Carnegie Class: Not Classified
FAX Number: (503) 244-0727 — Calendar System: Semester
URL: www.achs.edu
Established: 1978 — Annual Undergrad Tuition & Fees: $13,500
Enrollment: 500 — Coed
Affiliation or Control: Proprietary — IRS Status: Proprietary
Highest Offering: Master's
Program: Occupational; 2-Year Principally Bachelor's Creditable; Professional
Accreditation: **DETC**

01 President ..... Dorene PETERSEN
11 Director of Operations ..... Tracey ABELL
03 Chief Institutional Officer ..... Erika YIGZAW
06 Assistant Registrar ..... Brooke PILLSBURY-GUYOT
26 Director of Marketing ..... Kate HARMON

The Art Institute of Portland (E)

1122 NW Davis Street, Portland OR 97209-2911
County: Multnomah — FICE Identification: 007819
Unit ID: 208239
Telephone: (503) 228-6528 — Carnegie Class: Spec/Arts
FAX Number: (503) 228-4227 — Calendar System: Quarter
URL: www.artinstitutes.edu/portland
Established: 1963 — Annual Undergrad Tuition & Fees: $17,616
Enrollment: 1,676 — Coed
Affiliation or Control: Proprietary — IRS Status: Proprietary
Highest Offering: Baccalaureate
Program: Occupational; Liberal Arts And General
Accreditation: **NW**, CIDA

01 President ..... Dr. Timothy MOSCATO
05 Dean of Academic Affairs ..... Dr. Cassandra KELLY
06 Registrar ..... Ms. Kristin MCGILLIVRAY
07 Director of Admission ..... Mr. Hector VERDUGO
08 Head Librarian ..... Ms. Jennifer COX
37 Financial Aid Director ..... Ms. Kathy MARTIN

† Granted candidacy at the Master's level.

Birthingway College of Midwifery (F)

12113 SE Foster Road, Portland OR 97266-4042
County: Multnomah — FICE Identification: 036683
Unit ID: 442949
Telephone: (503) 760-3131 — Carnegie Class: Spec/Health
FAX Number: (503) 760-3332 — Calendar System: Quarter
URL: www.birthingway.edu
Established: 1993 — Annual Undergrad Tuition & Fees: $17,277
Enrollment: 91 — Coed
Affiliation or Control: Independent Non-Profit — IRS Status: 501(c)3
Highest Offering: Baccalaureate
Program: Professional
Accreditation: **MEAC**

01 President ..... Ms. Holly SCHOLLES
03 Faculty Coordinator ..... Ms. Nancy LONGATAN
05 Academic Coordinator ..... Ms. Nichole REDING
10 Finance Coordinator ..... Ms. Nina THOMPSON
37 Financial Aid Coordinator ..... Ms. Julia REID
06 Registrar ..... Ms. Dawn BAKER
88 Midwifery Program Coordinator ..... Ms. Rhonda RAY
88 Lactation Program Coordinator ..... Ms. Stacey MARSHALL

Blue Mountain Community College (G)

PO Box 100, Pendleton OR 97801-0100
County: Umatilla/Morrow/Baker — FICE Identification: 003186
Unit ID: 208275
Telephone: (541) 276-1260 — Carnegie Class: Assoc/Pub-R-M
FAX Number: (541) 278-5886 — Calendar System: Quarter
URL: www.bluecc.edu
Established: 1962 — Annual Undergrad Tuition & Fees (In-District): $4,290
Enrollment: 2,923 — Coed
Affiliation or Control: State/Local — IRS Status: 501(c)3
Highest Offering: Associate Degree
Program: Occupational; 2-Year Principally Bachelor's Creditable; Business Emphasis
Accreditation: **NW**, DA

01 President ..... Mr. John H. TURNER
05 Vice President of Instruction ..... Mr. Dan LANGE
10 Vice President of Operations ..... Mr. Clark WILLIAMS
20 Vice Pres of Economic Development ..... Mr. Art HILL
15 Director for Human Resources ..... Mr. Arthur DOHERTY
08 Director of Library & Media Svcs ..... Ms. Shannon VAN KIRK
07 Registrar/Dir of Admiss & Records ..... Ms. Theresa BOSWORTH
18 Supervisor Facilities/Phy Plant ..... Mr. Steve PLATT
102 Director Foundation ..... Ms. Margaret GIANOTTI
29 Director Alumni Relations ..... Ms. Stacey SIMPSON
25 Director of Grants ..... Mr. Casey BEARD
37 Director of Student Financial Aid ..... Ms. Cristina SWEEK

Carrington College - Portland (H)

2004 Lloyd Center, 3rd Floor, Portland OR 97232-1309
County: Multnomah — FICE Identification: 030425
Unit ID: 246035
Telephone: (503) 761-6100 — Carnegie Class: Assoc/PrivFP
FAX Number: (503) 761-3351 — Calendar System: Other
URL: www.carrington.edu
Established: 1991 — Annual Undergrad Tuition & Fees: $14,200
Enrollment: 627 — Coed
Affiliation or Control: Proprietary — IRS Status: Proprietary
Highest Offering: Associate Degree
Program: Occupational; 2-Year Principally Bachelor's Creditable
Accreditation: **ACICS**, DH, MAAB, PNUR

01 Executive Campus Director ..... Ms. Leslie GONZALES

Central Oregon Community College (I)

2600 NW College Way, Bend OR 97701-5998
County: Deschutes — FICE Identification: 003188
Unit ID: 208318
Telephone: (541) 383-7700 — Carnegie Class: Assoc/Pub-R-M
FAX Number: (541) 383-7506 — Calendar System: Quarter
URL: www.cocc.edu
Established: 1949 — Annual Undergrad Tuition & Fees (In-District): $3,195
Enrollment: 7,286 — Coed
Affiliation or Control: Local — IRS Status: 501(c)3
Highest Offering: Associate Degree
Program: Occupational; 2-Year Principally Bachelor's Creditable
Accreditation: **NW**, DA, MAC

01 President ..... Dr. James E. MIDDLETON
05 Vice President for Instruction ..... Dr. Karin M. HILGERSOM
11 Vice Pres for Administration ..... Mr. Matthew J. MCCOY
10 Chief Financial Officer ..... Mr. Kevin KIMBALL
51 Dean of Extended Learning ..... Dr. Shirley METCALF
20 Instructional Dean ..... Dr. Leslie MINOR
20 Instructional Dean ..... Dr. Michael FISHER
20 Instructional Dean ..... Ms. Jennifer NEWBY
84 Dean of Student/Enrollment Svcs ..... Ms. Alicia MOORE
07 Director of Admissions & Records ..... Vacant
08 Director Library Services ..... Mr. David D. BILYEU
26 Director College Relations ..... Mr. Ronald S. PARADIS
14 Director Information Technology ..... Mr. Dan CECCHINI
18 Director Campus Services ..... Mr. Joe VIOLA
15 Director Human Resources ..... Mr. Eric BUCKLES
22 Affirmative Action Officer ..... Mrs. Sharla ANDRESEN
37 Director Financial Aid ..... Mr. Kevin MULTOP
28 Dir of Multicultural Activities ..... Ms. Karen ROTH
32 Director of Student Life ..... Mr. Gordon PRICE
09 Dir Institutional Effectiveness ..... Ms. Brynn PIERCE
21 Associate Business Officer ..... Mr. David DONA
38 Director Student Counseling ..... Ms. Vickery VILES
96 Director of Purchasing ..... Ms. Julie MOSIER
40 Bookstore Manager ..... Ms. Lori A. WILLIS
36 Coordinator of Career Services ..... Ms. Vickery VILES

Chemeketa Community College (J)

PO Box 14007, Salem OR 97309-7070
County: Marion — FICE Identification: 003218
Unit ID: 208390
Telephone: (503) 399-5000 — Carnegie Class: Assoc/Pub-R-L
FAX Number: (503) 399-5214 — Calendar System: Quarter
URL: www.chemek.cc.or.us
Established: 1962 — Annual Undergrad Tuition & Fees (In-District): $3,240
Enrollment: 4,021 — Coed
Affiliation or Control: Local — IRS Status: 501(c)3
Highest Offering: Associate Degree
Program: Occupational; 2-Year Principally Bachelor's Creditable
Accreditation: **NW**, ADNUR, DA, EMT, IFSAC

01 President/Chief Executive Officer ..... Dr. Cheryl ROBERTS
05 Chief Academic Officer ..... Dr. Patrick LANNING
10 Chief Financial Officer ..... Ms. Julie A. HUCKESTEIN
12 Campus President Yamhill Valley ..... Dr. Patrick LANNING
20 Dean General Education/Trans Stds ..... Dr. David HALLETT
16 Executive Dean ..... Mr. Andrew BONE
32 Ex Dean Student Devel/Learning Res ..... Mr. Jim EUSTROM
88 Exec Dean Academic Advancement ..... Vacant
68 Dean Life Sci/Health/PE/Athletics ..... Mr. Johnny MACK
79 Dean Humanities & Communications ..... Mr. Don BRASE
66 Dean Dental Asst/Med Asst/Nursing ..... Ms. Kay CARNEGIE
37 Dean Financial Aid/Enrollment Svcs ..... Ms. Kathy CAMPBELL
38 Dean Counseling/Career Services ..... Ms. Jill WARD
72 Dean Applied Technologies ..... Mr. Glen MILLER
81 Dean Math/Science/Technologies ..... Mr. Michael MILHAUSEN
83 Dean Early Chld/Hum Svc/Soc Sci/Ed ..... Vacant
84 Dean Marketing/Student Recruitment ..... Mr. Greg HARRIS
45 Dean Curriculum Resource Center ..... Vacant
65 Dean Natural Resources ..... Dr. Greg SANDOR
102 Executive Director Foundation ..... Mr. Andrew BONE
08 Director Learning Resource Center ..... Ms. Natalie BEACH

88 Director Enterprise Services ....Mr. Brian RADER
21 Director Business Services ....Ms. Miriam ROZIN
18 Director Facilities & Operations ....Mr. Phil WRIGHT
15 Director Human Resources ....Ms. Peggy BORJESSON
19 Director Public Safety ....Mr. Bill KOHLMEYER
40 Manager Auxiliary Services ....Vacant
06 Registrar ....Ms. Minna GELDER
41 Athletic Director ....Ms. Cassie BELMODIS
50 Dir Chemeketa Ctr for Bus/Industry ....Ms. Diane MCLARAN
88 Director Reg Prof Tech Educ ....Ms. Trish CONLON
28 Director of Diversity & Equity ....Ms. Linda HERRERA
35 Director Student Life/Retention ....Mr. Manuel GUERRA
07 Director of Admissions ....Ms. Melissa FREY
96 Director of Purchasing ....Ms. Eileen MILLER
30 Development ....Ms. Nancy DUNCAN
25 Grants Coordinator ....Ms. Diane SCHMITZ

Clackamas Community College (A)

19600 Molalla Avenue, Oregon City OR 97045-7998
County: Clackamas FICE Identification: 004878
Unit ID: 208406
Telephone: (503) 594-6000 Carnegie Class: Assoc/Pub-S-MC
FAX Number: N/A Calendar System: Quarter
URL: www.clackamas.edu
Established: 1966 Annual Undergrad Tuition & Fees (In-District): $3,138
Enrollment: 3,598 Coed
Affiliation or Control: Local IRS Status: 501(c)3
Highest Offering: Associate Degree
Program: Occupational; 2-Year Principally Bachelor's Creditable
Accreditation: NW, MAC

01 President ....Dr. Joanne TRUESDELL
05 VP Instruct & Stdnt Svcs/Provost ....Ms. Elizabeth LUNDY
11 Vice President of College Services ....Mr. Courtney WILTON
04 Executive Asst to the President ....Ms. Debbie JENKINS
30 Dn Col Advanc/Chf Govt/Cmty Rel Dir ....Ms. Shelly PARINI
102 Executive Director Foundation ....Mr. Greg FITZGERALD
27 Public Information Officer ....Ms. Janet PAULSON
88 Dean Acad Found/Connections Div ....Mr. Phillip KING
06 Registrar ....Ms. Tara SPREHE
32 Assoc Dean Acad Found/Connect Div ....Mr. Jim MARTINEAU
13 Dean/CIO Information Technology ....Ms. Kim CAREY
49 Dean Arts & Sciences ....Mr. Bill BRIARE
46 Dean Curriculum/Planning/Research ....Mr. Steffen MOLLER
88 Director Educational Partnerships ....Ms. Cyndi ANDREWS
72 Dean Tech/Hlth Occup/Workforce Div ....Mr. Scott GILTZ
12 Dean Regional Educational Services ....Ms. Theresa TUFFLI
15 Dean Human Resources ....Ms. Marsha EDWARDS
21 Director Business Services ....Ms. Chris ROBUCK
11 Dean Campus Services ....Mr. Bob COCHRAN
18 Director Plant Operations ....Mr. Kirk PEARSON
35 Director Student Activities ....Ms. Mindy BROWN
37 Director Student Financial Svcs ....Ms. Chippi BELLO
41 Director Athletics/Health/PE ....Mr. Jim MARTINEAU

Clatsop Community College (B)

1651 Lexington Avenue, Astoria OR 97103
County: Clatsop FICE Identification: 003189
Unit ID: 208415
Telephone: (503) 325-0910 Carnegie Class: Assoc/Pub-R-M
FAX Number: (503) 325-5738 Calendar System: Quarter
URL: www.clatsopcc.edu
Established: 1958 Annual Undergrad Tuition & Fees (In-District): $4,104
Enrollment: 1,307 Coed
Affiliation or Control: State/Local IRS Status: 501(c)3
Highest Offering: Associate Degree
Program: Occupational; 2-Year Principally Bachelor's Creditable
Accreditation: NW

01 President ....Dr. Larry GALIZIO
05 VP Academic & Student Affairs ....Dr. Donna LARSON
10 Vice President Finance & Operations ....Ms. JoAnn ZAHN
06 Registrar ....Dr. Chris OUSLEY
26 Chief Public Rels Officer/Marketing ....Ms. Patricia WARREN
78 Dir Co-op Educ & Special Project ....Ms. Joanie WEATHERLY
51 Director Distance Education ....Mrs. Kirsten HORNING
15 Director Personnel Services ....Ms. Leslie LIPE
37 Director Student Financial Aid ....Mr. Lloyd MUELLER
09 Director of Institutional Research ....Mr. Tom GILL
18 Chief Facilities/Physical Plant ....Mr. Greg DORCHEUS
21 Associate Business Officer ....Ms. Margaret ANTILLA
29 Director of Alumni Relations/Devel ....Ms. Patricia WARREN
84 Assoc Dean Enrollment Management ....Mr. Chris OUSLEY

Columbia Gorge Community College (C)

400 East Scenic Drive, The Dalles OR 97058
County: Wasco FICE Identification: 041519
Unit ID: 420556
Telephone: (541) 506-6000 Carnegie Class: Assoc/Pub-R-S
FAX Number: N/A Calendar System: Quarter
URL: www.cgcc.cc.or.us/
Established: 1977 Annual Undergrad Tuition & Fees (In-District): $4,545
Enrollment: 1,290 Coed
Affiliation or Control: State/Local IRS Status: 501(c)3
Highest Offering: Associate Degree
Program: 2-Year Principally Bachelor's Creditable
Accreditation: @NW, MAC

01 President ....Dr. Frank TODA
05 Chief Academic Officer ....Vacant
10 Chief Financial Officer ....Saundra BUCHANAN
88 Chief Talent and Operations Officer ....Robb VAN CLEAVE
32 Chief Student Services Officer ....Karen CARTER
30 Chief Inst Advancement Officer ....Dan SPATZ
13 Chief Technology Officer ....Bill BOHN

Concorde Career College (D)

1425 NE Irving Street, Suite 300, Portland OR 97232
County: Multnomah FICE Identification: 008887
Unit ID: 208479
Telephone: (503) 281-4181 Carnegie Class: Assoc/PrivFP
FAX Number: (503) 281-6739 Calendar System: Other
URL: www.concorde.edu/campus/portland
Established: N/A Annual Undergrad Tuition & Fees: N/A
Enrollment: 983 Coed
Affiliation or Control: Proprietary IRS Status: Proprietary
Highest Offering: Associate Degree
Program: Occupational
Accreditation: ACCSC, MAC, SURGT

01 Campus President ....Kim IERIEN

Concordia University (E)

2811 NE Holman, Portland OR 97211-6099
County: Multnomah FICE Identification: 003191
Unit ID: 208488
Telephone: (503) 288-9371 Carnegie Class: Master's L
FAX Number: (503) 280-8518 Calendar System: Quarter
URL: www.cu-portland.edu
Established: 1905 Annual Undergrad Tuition & Fees: $26,420
Enrollment: 2,509 Coed
Affiliation or Control: Lutheran Church - Missouri Synod
IRS Status: 501(c)3
Highest Offering: Master's
Program: Liberal Arts And General; Teacher Preparatory
Accreditation: NW, SW

01 President ....Dr. Charles E. SCHLIMPERT
26 Exec Vice Pres External Affairs ....Dr. Gary WITHERS
102 Exec Vice Pres Strategic Planning ....Mr. Johnnie DRIESSNER
05 Provost/Chief Academic Officer ....Dr. Mark E. WAHLERS
10 Chief Financial Officer ....Mr. Dennis J. STOECKLIN
32 VP Student Svcs/Enrollment Mgmt ....Dr. Glenn C. SMITH
04 Assistant to the President ....Ms. Linda JAMES
30 Chief Development Officer ....Mr. Kevin MATHENY
06 Registrar ....Mr. Jim CULLEN
07 Director Admissions & Enroll Mgmt ....Ms. Bobi SWAN
09 Director of Institutional Research ....Mr. Ron FONGER
15 Director of Human Resources ....Ms. Andrea STEN
18 Chief Facilities/Physical Plant ....Mr. Doug MEYER
20 Associate Academic Officer ....Vacant
88 Chief Public Relations Officer ....Ms. Madeline TURNOCK
29 Director Alumni Relations ....Ms. Brooke KRYSTOSEK
35 Dean of Students ....Mr. Steve DEKLOTZ
08 Librarian ....Mr. Brent MAI
37 Director Student Financial Aid ....Ms. Rhoda RESEBURG
41 Athletic Director ....Dr. Matthew ENGLISH
38 Director Student Counseling ....Ms. Jaklin PEAKE
85 Director of International Studies ....Ms. Linda ROUNTREE
42 Campus Pastor ....Rev. Greg FAIROW
13 Chief Information Officer ....Vacant
50 Dean School of Management ....Dr. Steve BRAUN
53 Dean College of Education ....Dr. Joe MANNION
49 Dean Theol Studies/Arts/Sciences .... Dr. Charles KUNERT
88 Dean Col of Health/Human Service ....Dr. Mark JAGER
61 Dean School of Law ....Ms. Cathy SILAK

Corban University (F)

5000 Deer Park Drive, SE, Salem OR 97317
County: Marion FICE Identification: 001339
Unit ID: 210331
Telephone: (503) 581-8600 Carnegie Class: Bac/Diverse
FAX Number: (503) 585-4316 Calendar System: Semester
URL: www.corban.edu
Established: 1935 Annual Undergrad Tuition & Fees: $25,974
Enrollment: 1,275 Coed
Affiliation or Control: Independent Non-Profit IRS Status: 501(c)3
Highest Offering: Master's
Program: Liberal Arts And General; Teacher Preparatory; Professional
Accreditation: NW

01 President ....Dr. Reno R. HOFF
88 President Elect ....Dr. Sheldon NORD
05 Provost/Executive Vice President ....Dr. Matthew LUCAS
10 Vice President For Business ....Mr. Kevin BRUBAKER
32 Vice President For Student Life ....Dr. Nancy HEDBERG
26 Vice President for Marketing ....Mr. J. Steven HUNT
30 Vice President for Advancement ....Mr. Mike BATES
84 Vice Pres for Enrollment Management ....Mr. Marty ZIESEMER
35 Dean of Students ....Miss Brenda ROTH
11 Campus Administrator ....Dr. Leroy GOERTZEN
23 Dean of Education ....Dr. Janine ALLEN
51 Dean of Adult Services ....Miss Nancy MARTYN
50 Dean of Business ....Mr. P. Griffith LINDELL
91 Chief Information Systems Officer ....Mr. Brian SCHMIDT
18 Director of Campus Care ....Mr. Tom SAMEK

06 Registrar ....Dr. Chris VETTER
08 Librarian ....Mr. Floyd VOTAW
39 Director of Residential Life ....Mr. Nathan GEER
42 Director of Campus Ministries ....Dr. Dan HUBER
41 Athletic Director ....Mr. Dave JOHNSON
36 Director Academic & Career Services ....Mr. Daren MILIONIS
37 Director Student Financial Aid ....Mr. Nathan WARTHAN
29 Director Alumni Relations ....Mrs. Deleen WILLS
38 Director Student Counseling ....Mrs. Stephanie HUSK
21 Associate Business Officer ....Mr. Brian ELLIOTT
40 Bookstore Manager ....Ms. Heather ULBRIGHT

DeVry University - Portland (G)

9755 SW Barnes Road, Suite 150,
Portland OR 97225-6651
County: Washington Identification: 666567
Unit ID: 444033
Telephone: (503) 296-7468 Carnegie Class: Spec/Bus
FAX Number: (503) 296-6114 Calendar System: Semester
URL: www.devry.edu
Established: 1931 Annual Undergrad Tuition & Fees: $16,156
Enrollment: 352 Coed
Affiliation or Control: Proprietary IRS Status: Proprietary
Highest Offering: Master's
Program: Professional; Business Emphasis
Accreditation: &NH

01 Campus Director ....Matt HANUSA

† Regional accreditation is carried under the parent institution in Downers Grove, IL.

Everest College (H)

425 Southwest Washington, Portland OR 97204-2296
County: Multnomah FICE Identification: 009079
Unit ID: 210359
Telephone: (503) 222-3225 Carnegie Class: Assoc/PrivFP
FAX Number: (503) 228-6926 Calendar System: Quarter
URL: www.everest-college.com
Established: 1955 Annual Undergrad Tuition & Fees: $14,212
Enrollment: 559 Coed
Affiliation or Control: Proprietary IRS Status: Proprietary
Highest Offering: Associate Degree
Program: Occupational; 2-Year Principally Bachelor's Creditable
Accreditation: ACICS, MAC

01 President ....Ms. Siri DIXON
05 Chief Academic Officer ....Ms. Elaine SEYMAN
07 Director of Admissions ....Ms. Cindy SLUSHER
06 Registrar ....Mrs. Renee HATFIELD
37 Director Student Financial Aid ....Mrs. Nicole TONE
36 Director of Student Placement ....Ms. Michelle MESMAN MICHAELIS

George Fox University (I)

414 N Meridian, Newberg OR 97132-2697
County: Yamhill FICE Identification: 003194
Unit ID: 208822
Telephone: (503) 538-8383 Carnegie Class: Master's L
FAX Number: (503) 554-3834 Calendar System: Semester
URL: www.georgefox.edu
Established: 1891 Annual Undergrad Tuition & Fees: $30,230
Enrollment: 3,519 Coed
Affiliation or Control: Friends IRS Status: 501(c)3
Highest Offering: Doctorate
Program: Liberal Arts And General; Teacher Preparatory; Business Emphasis
Accreditation: NW, ACBSP, CACREP, CLPSY, ENG, MUS, NURSE, @PTA, SW, TED, THEOL

01 President ....Dr. Robin E. BAKER
03 Vice President/Dean of Seminary .....Dr. Charles J. CONNIRY, JR.
05 Provost ....Dr. Patrick ALLEN
10 Exec VP Finance/Business Operations ....Mr. Ted ALLEN
30 Vice President Advancement ....Dr. Brian GARDNER
32 Vice President Student Life ....Dr. Bradley A. LAU
26 Vice Pres Marketing/ Communications ....Mr. Robert K. WESTERVELT
04 Executive Assistant to President ....Ms. Missy D. TERRY
21 Asst VP Financial Affairs ....Ms. Cris BANTON
08 University Librarian ....Mr. Merrill L. JOHNSON
06 Registrar ....Ms. Melissa THOMAS
26 Asst Dir of University Engagement ....Vacant
36 Director of Career Services ....Ms. Bonnie J. JERKE
18 Director of Plant Services ....Mr. Clyde G. THOMAS
37 Interim Dir Student Financial Svcs ....Mr. James OSHIRO
96 Director Purchasing/Admin Services ....Mr. Andy DUNN
41 Director of Athletics ....Mr. Craig B. TAYLOR
105 Director of Web Development ....Mr. Peter CRACKENBERG
15 Director Human Resources ....Ms. Peggy L. KILBURG
42 University Pastor ....Ms. Sarah BALDWIN
27 Director Public Information ....Mr. Rob FELTON
13 Chief Information Officer ....Mr. Greg SMITH
19 Director Security Services ....Mr. Ed GIEROK
38 Dir Health and Counseling Services ....Dr. William C. BUHROW
49 Dean School of Arts & Sciences ....Mr. Hank HELSABECK
83 Dean Sch Behavioral/Health Sci ....Dr. James E. FOSTER
53 Dean School of Education ....Dr. Linda SAMEK

50 Dean School of Business ... Dr. Dirk BARRAM
88 Dean of Transitions & Inclusion ... Mr. Joel PEREZ

Gutenberg College (A)

1883 University Street, Eugene OR 97403-1368
County: Lane FICE Identification: 039324
Unit ID: 420510
Telephone: (541) 683-5141 Carnegie Class: Not Classified
FAX Number: (541) 683-6997 Calendar System: Quarter
URL: www.gutenberg.edu
Established: 1994 Annual Undergrad Tuition & Fees: $24,650
Enrollment: 27 Coed
Affiliation or Control: Independent Non-Profit IRS Status: 501(c)3
Highest Offering: Baccalaureate
Program: Liberal Arts And General; Religious Emphasis
Accreditation: TRACS

01 President ... David CRABTREE
03 Vice President ... Richard BOOSTER
05 Dean ... Thomas DEWBERRY
07 Admissions Director ... Tim MCINTOSH
06 Registrar ... Chris SWANSON

Heald College, Portland (B)

6035 NE 78th Court, Portland OR 97218
County: Multnomah FICE Identification: 037454
Unit ID: 430148
Telephone: (503) 229-0492 Carnegie Class: Assoc/PrivFP
FAX Number: (503) 229-0498 Calendar System: Quarter
URL: www.heald.edu
Established: 1863 Annual Undergrad Tuition & Fees: N/A
Enrollment: 1,073 Coed
Affiliation or Control: Independent Non-Profit IRS Status: 501(c)3
Highest Offering: Associate Degree
Program: Occupational
Accreditation: &WJ, MAC

01 Campus President ... Mr. Jason FERGUSON
36 Director of Career Services ... Ms. Taunji FALKENBERG
37 Director of Financial Aid ... Ms. Elizabeth VONAU

† Regional accreditation is carried under the parent institution Heald College, Central Office in San Francisco, CA.

ITT Technical Institute (C)

9500 NE Cascades Parkway, Portland OR 97220
County: Multnomah FICE Identification: 011852
Unit ID: 208965
Telephone: (503) 255-6500 Carnegie Class: Spec/Tech
FAX Number: (503) 255-8381 Calendar System: Quarter
URL: www.itt-tech.edu
Established: 1971 Annual Undergrad Tuition & Fees: N/A
Enrollment: 856 Coed
Affiliation or Control: Proprietary IRS Status: Proprietary
Highest Offering: Baccalaureate
Program: Technical Emphasis
Accreditation: ACICS

† Branch campus of ITT Technical Institute, Indianapolis, IN.

Klamath Community College (D)

7390 S 6th Street, Klamath Falls OR 97603-7121
County: Klamath FICE Identification: 034283
Unit ID: 428392
Telephone: (541) 882-3521 Carnegie Class: Assoc/Pub-R-S
FAX Number: (541) 885-7758 Calendar System: Quarter
URL: www.klamathcc.edu
Established: 1996 Annual Undergrad Tuition & Fees (In-District): $3,073
Enrollment: 1,448 Coed
Affiliation or Control: State/Local IRS Status: 501(c)3
Highest Offering: Associate Degree
Program: Occupational; 2-Year Principally Bachelor's Creditable
Accreditation: NW

01 President ... Dr. Roberto GUTIERREZ
11 Exec Vice Pres Administrative Svcs ... Ms. Renee FERGUSON
05 Vice Pres for Learning Services ... Ms. Terri ARMSTRONG
32 Vice Pres for Student Services ... Ms. Julie MURRAY-JENSEN
10 Chief Business Officer ... Mr. Jack NOWAK
13 Director Information Services ... Mr. Paul BREEDLOVE
15 Exec Director Human Resources ... Ms. Karren ANDREWS
18 Chief Facilities/Physical Plant ... Mr. Mike GRIFFITH
37 Financial Aid Specialist ... Ms. Donna FULTON

Lane Community College (E)

4000 E 30th Avenue, Eugene OR 97405-0640
County: Lane FICE Identification: 003196
Unit ID: 209038
Telephone: (541) 463-3000 Carnegie Class: Assoc/Pub-R-L
FAX Number: (541) 463-5201 Calendar System: Quarter
URL: www.lanecc.edu
Established: 1964 Annual Undergrad Tuition & Fees (In-District): $4,537
Enrollment: 20,632 Coed
Affiliation or Control: Local IRS Status: 501(c)3
Highest Offering: Associate Degree
Program: Occupational; 2-Year Principally Bachelor's Creditable
Accreditation: NW, ACFEI, DA, DH, EMT, MAC, PTAA

01 President ... Dr. Mary SPILDE
05 Vice Pres Instruction/Student Svcs ... Dr. Sonya CHRISTIAN
11 Vice President College Operations ... Vacant
32 Exec Dean/Student Svc/Career Tech ... Ms. Andrea NEWTON
20 Executive Dean/Transfer ... Mr. Don MCNAIR
35 Div Dean Student Life/Leadership ... Dr. Barbara DELANSKY
68 Div Dean Health/Physical Education ... Mr. Chris HAWKIN
28 Interim Chief Diversity Officer ... Dr. Donna KOECHIG
13 Chief Information Officer ... Mr. Bill SCHUETZ
10 Chief Financial Officer ... Mr. Greg MORGAN
35 Executive Dean/Student Affairs ... Ms. Helen GARRETT
15 Director Human Resources ... Mr. Dennis CARR
09 Dir Inst Research/Assess/Planning ... Dr. Craig TAYLOR
84 Director Enrollment Services ... Vacant
18 Director Facilities Mgmt/Planning ... Mr. Dave WILLIS
19 Director Public Safety ... Mr. Jace SMITH
08 Interim Library Director ... Ms. Marika PINEDA
38 Dir Counseling/Student Placement ... Mr. Jerry DELEON
37 Director of Financial Aid ... Ms. Helen FAITH
96 Director of Finance/Purchasing ... Mr. Stan BARKER
26 Chief Public Relations Officer ... Ms. Tracy SIMMS
102 Foundation Director ... Ms. Janet ANDERSON

Le Cordon Bleu College of Culinary Arts in Portland (F)

600 SW 10th Avenue, Suite 500, Portland OR 97205-2793
County: Multnomah FICE Identification: 030226
Unit ID: 375841
Telephone: (503) 223-2245 Carnegie Class: Assoc/PrivFP
FAX Number: (503) 223-0126 Calendar System: Other
URL: www.chefs.edu/portland
Established: 1983 Annual Undergrad Tuition & Fees: $17,550
Enrollment: 750 Coed
Affiliation or Control: Proprietary IRS Status: Proprietary
Highest Offering: Associate Degree
Program: Occupational
Accreditation: ACICS, ACFEI

01 Campus President ... Julia BROOKS
05 Vice President Academic Affairs ... Matt KUERBIS
07 Vice Pres of Admissions & Marketing ... Tom BARKER
10 Vice Pres of Finance/Accounting ... Katie STONE
32 Vice President Student Services ... Marsha PARMER
13 Director of IT & Facilities ... Bryan LEVINE
06 Registrar ... Linda M. SCHOEN
37 Director Student Finances ... Katie STONE
21 Controller ... David COFFMAN

Lewis and Clark College (G)

0615 SW Palatine Hill, Portland OR 97219-7899
County: Multnomah FICE Identification: 003197
Unit ID: 209056
Telephone: (503) 768-7000 Carnegie Class: Bac/A&S
FAX Number: (503) 768-7055 Calendar System: Semester
URL: www.lclark.edu
Established: 1867 Annual Undergrad Tuition & Fees: $39,970
Enrollment: 3,712 Coed
Affiliation or Control: Independent Non-Profit IRS Status: 501(c)3
Highest Offering: Doctorate
Program: Liberal Arts And General; Teacher Preparatory; Professional
Accreditation: NW, CACREP, LAW, MFCD, TED

01 President ... Dr. Barry GLASSNER
03 Vice President & Provost ... Dr. Jane M. ATKINSON
05 Dean of College of Arts & Sciences ... Dr. Tuajuanda C. JORDAN
10 Vice Pres Business/Finance/Treas ... Mr. Carl VANCE
30 Vice Pres Institutional Advancement ... Mr. Gregory A. VOLK
43 VP General Counsel/Secy of College ... Mr. David ELLIS
88 Assoc Vice President Campus Life ... Dr. Michael B. FORD
44 Director of Annual Giving & Develop ... Mr. Aaron WHITEFORD
18 Assoc Vice Pres Facilities ... Mr. Michel GEORGE
26 Assoc VP Public Affs/Communications ... Mr. Tom KRATTENMAKER
15 Assoc VP/Director Human Resources ... Mr. Isaac DIXON
29 Director Alumni/Parent Pgms ... Mr. Andrew MCPHEETERS
21 Associate Vice Pres for Finance/Con ... Mr. George BATTISTEL
53 Dean Grad Sch Education/Counseling ... Dr. Scott FLETCHER
61 Dean of the Law School ... Mr. Robert KLONOFF
49 Assoc Dean College of Arts/Science ... Dr. Jane HUNTER
32 Dean of Students ... Dr. Anna GONZALEZ
28 Asc Dn Stdnts/Dir Multicultural Aff ... Ms. Latricia BRAND
85 Assoc Dean Intl Stdnts & Scholars ... Mr. Brian WHITE
08 Director of Library ... Mr. Mark DAHL
13 Assoc Vice Pres & Chief Info Ofcr ... Mr. Adam BUCHWALD
06 Registrar College of Arts/Sciences ... Ms. Judy FINCH
06 Registrar Law School ... Ms. Susan GALYEN
06 Registrar Graduate School ... Mr. Curt LUTTRELL
07 Dean of Admissions & Financial Aid ... Ms. Lisa MEYER
37 Interim Director of Financial Aid ... Ms. Anastacia DILLON
27 Senior Communications Officer ... Vacant
19 Director of Campus Safety ... Mr. Timothy O'DWYER
42 Dean of the Chapel ... Dr. Mark DUNTLEY
41 Director of Phys Educ & Athletics ... Mr. Clark YEAGER
39 Director of Residential Services ... Ms. Sandi BOTTEMILLER
24 Dir of Instructional Media Svcs ... Mr. Patrick RYALL
39 Assoc Dean of Students ... Mr. Jeffrey FELD-GORE
17 Asc Dean Stdnts/Wellness Svcs/Psych ... Dr. John HANCOCK
09 Director of Institutional Research ... Dr. Mark FIGUEROA

Linfield College (H)

900 SE Baker Street, McMinnville OR 97128-6894
County: Yamhill FICE Identification: 003198
Unit ID: 209065
Telephone: (503) 883-2200 Carnegie Class: Bac/A&S
FAX Number: (503) 883-2472 Calendar System: 4/1/4
URL: www.linfield.edu
Established: 1858 Annual Undergrad Tuition & Fees: $34,328
Enrollment: 2,664 Coed
Affiliation or Control: American Baptist IRS Status: 501(c)3
Highest Offering: Baccalaureate
Program: Liberal Arts And General; Teacher Preparatory; Professional
Accreditation: NW, MUS, NURSE

01 President ... Dr. Thomas HELLIE
05 Vice Pres Acad Affs/Dean of Faculty ... Ms. Susan AGRE-KIPPENHAN
10 Vice Pres Finance/Administration ... Mr. W. Glenn FORD
26 Vice Pres for College Relations ... Mr. Bruce WYATT
84 Vice Pres for Enrollment Management ... Mr. Daniel PRESTON
32 VP Student Svcs/Dean of Students ... Ms. Susan HOPP
43 Advisor to the Pres & General Couns ... Mr. John MCKEEGAN
66 Interim Dean of Nursing ... Dr. Pamela WHEELER
20 Associate Dean of Faculty ... Dr. Nancy DRICKEY
20 Associate Dean of Faculty ... Dr. Martha VAN CLEAVE
35 Associate Dean of Students ... Mr. Jeff MACKAY
15 Senior Director of Human Resources ... Ms. Linda POWELL
18 Director Facilities & Auxiliary Svc ... Ms. Allison HORN
28 Director Multicultural Programs ... Mr. Jason RODRIQUEZ
06 Registrar ... Dr. Eileen BOURASSA
07 Director of Admission ... Ms. Lisa KNODLE-BRAGIEL
08 Library Director ... Ms. Susan BARNES WHYTE
09 Director of Institutional Research ... Ms. Jennifer BALLARD
37 Director of Financial Aid ... Ms. Keri BURKE
13 Chief Technology Officer ... Mr. Irv WISWALL
91 Assoc Director Integrated Tech Svcs ... Mr. Phil SETH
105 Webmaster ... Mr. Jonathan PIERCE
85 Director of International Programs ... Dr. Shaik ISMAIL
51 Int Dean of Continuing Education ... Dr. Martha VAN CLEAVE
19 Director of Security ... Ms. Rebecca WALE
38 Director of Counseling Services ... Dr. John F. KERRIGAN, JR.
26 Director of Public Relations ... Ms. Mardi MILEHAM
44 Director of Annual Giving ... Ms. Christina DISS
44 Director of Planned Giving ... Mr. Craig HAISCH
102 Dir Corp & Foundation Relations ... Ms. Catherine JARMIN MILLER
29 Director of Alumni Relations ... Ms. Debbie HARMON
36 Director Career & Community Svcs ... Mr. Michael HAMPTON
42 Chaplain ... Dr. David MASSEY
41 Athletic Director ... Mr. Scott CARNAHAN
40 Bookstore Manager ... Mr. Chad COTTRILL

Linn-Benton Community College (I)

6500 SW Pacific Boulevard, Albany OR 97321-3774
County: Linn FICE Identification: 006938
Unit ID: 209074
Telephone: (541) 917-4999 Carnegie Class: Assoc/Pub-R-L
FAX Number: (541) 917-4445 Calendar System: Quarter
URL: www.linnbenton.edu
Established: 1966 Annual Undergrad Tuition & Fees (In-District): $4,500
Enrollment: 8,000 Coed
Affiliation or Control: State/Local IRS Status: 501(c)3
Highest Offering: Associate Degree
Program: Occupational; 2-Year Principally Bachelor's Creditable
Accreditation: NW, DA, MAC, OTA, POLYT

01 President ... Dr. Gregory J. HAMANN
05 Vice President Academic Affairs ... Ms. Beth HOGELAND
10 Vice Pres Finance & Operations ... Mr. Jim HUCKESTEIN
32 Vice President Student Services ... Dr. Bruce CLEMETSEN
15 Director Human Resources ... Mr. Scott ROLEN
37 Director of Student Financial Aid ... Ms. Bev GERIG
12 Director Albany Community Education ... Mr. Joel WHITE
12 Director East Linn Centers ... Mr. Gary PRICE
12 Director Benton Center ... Mr. Jeff DAVIS
84 Director Enrollment Services ... Mr. Danny AYNES
88 Dean Instructional Facilities Plng ... Vacant
68 Dean Athletics and Emergency Plng ... Vacant
81 Dean Science/Engr & Tech ... Mr. Dan LARA
49 Dean Liberal Arts/Soc Sys & HP ... Ms. Katie WINDER
20 Dean Instruction ... Mr. Jonathan PAVER
30 Director Institutional Advancement ... Ms. B.J NICOLETTI
21 Budget Officer ... Ms. Betty NIELSEN
35 Director Student Life & Leadership ... Vacant
36 Dir Career Svcs/Stdnt Counseling ... Mr. Mark WEISS
13 Director Information Services ... Ms. Ann ADAMS
26 Director College Advancement ... Ms. Marlene PROPST
20 Dean of Instruction ... Vacant
50 Dean Business/Health Care & Work ... Ms. Ann MALOSH
06 Registrar ... Vacant
18 Chief Facilities/Physical Plant ... Mr. Scott KRAMBUHL
44 Chief Development Officer ... Mr. John MCARDLE
08 Dean Academic Devel/Library Svcs ... Vacant
88 Assoc Dean Student Development ... Ms. Lynne COX

Marylhurst University (J)

PO Box 261, 17600 Pacific Highway, Marylhurst OR 97036-0261
County: Clackamas FICE Identification: 003199
Unit ID: 209108
Telephone: (503) 636-8141 Carnegie Class: Master's L

FAX Number: (503) 636-9526 Calendar System: Quarter
URL: www.marylhurst.edu
Established: 1893 Annual Undergrad Tuition & Fees: $18,945
Enrollment: 1,835 Coed
Affiliation or Control: Independent Non-Profit IRS Status: 501(c)3
Highest Offering: Master's
Program: Liberal Arts And General
Accreditation: NW, CIDA, IACBE, MUS

01 President Dr. Judith JOHANSEN
05 Provost/VP Academic Affairs Dr. David PLOTKIN
10 CFO/Exec VP Finance & Admin Mr. Michael LAMMERS
30 Vice Pres Institutional Advancement Ms. Lynn MAWE
15 Vice President for Human Resources Ms. Celina RATLIFFE
27 Vice President Info Tech/CIO Dr. Ethan BENATAN
84 VP Enrollment Mgmt Ms. Beth WOODWARD
04 Assistant to the President Ms. Judy MILLENBACH
32 Dean of Students Mr. Bill ZUELKE
07 Director of Admissions Mr. Chris SWEET
88 Dean of Assessment Dr. Melanie BOOTH
06 Registrar Ms. Gwen HYATT
08 University Librarian Ms. Nancy HOOVER
26 Director Marketing & Communications Ms. Shirley SKIDMORE
44 Manager Annual Giving Vacant
25 Director of University Events Ms. Cheryl HANSEN
37 Director of Financial Aid Ms. Tracy REISINGER
88 Director Art Therapy Graduate Pgm Ms. Christine TURNER
72 Director Center for Learning Tech Dr. Vicki SUTER
13 Director of Information Systems Mr. Rick CAMPBELL
18 Director of Facilities Mr. Mark STRULOEFF
50 Dean School of Business Ms. Mary BRADBURY JONES
58 Dean School of Graduate Studies Dr. Debrah BOKOWSKI
49 Dean College of Arts & Sciences Dr. Jan DABROWSKI
88 Director Music Therapy Ms. Christine KORB
64 Chairperson Music Department Dr. John PAUL
57 Co-Chairperson & Dir Art Department Mr. Paul SUTINEN
57 Co-Chrpn Art Dpt/Dir Int Design Dpt Ms. Nancy HISS
73 Chrpsn Religious Studies & Phil Dr. Jeroid ROUSSELL
88 Chrpsn Grad Interdisciplinary Stds Dr. Susan CARTER
88 Chrpsn Interdisciplinary Studies Mr. Simeon DREYFUSS
79 Chrpsn Culture & Media Dr. David DENNY
81 Chair Science&Math Mr. Greg DARDIS
83 Chairperson Human Sciences Dr. Jennifer SASSER
88 Chairperson Real Estate Studies Vacant
88 Chrpsn English Literature/Writing Dr. Meg ROLAND
60 Chairperson Communication Studies Mr. Jeff SWEENEY
88 Chair Sustainable Business Mr. Paul VENTURA

Mount Angel Seminary (A)

1 Abbey Drive, Saint Benedict OR 97373-0505
County: Marion FICE Identification: 003203
Unit ID: 209241
Telephone: (503) 845-3951 Carnegie Class: Spec/Faith
FAX Number: (503) 845-3128 Calendar System: Semester
URL: www.mountangelabbey.org
Established: 1887 Annual Undergrad Tuition & Fees: $31,817
Enrollment: 183 Coed
Affiliation or Control: Roman Catholic IRS Status: 501(c)3
Highest Offering: Master's
Program: Liberal Arts And General; Professional
Accreditation: NW, THEOL

01 President/Rector Rev. Joseph V. BETSCHART
05 Vice President/Academic Dean Dr. Owen CUMMINGS
08 Librarian Ms. Victoria ERTELT
10 Business Manager Fr. Martin GRASSEL, OSB
06 Registrar & Student Financial Aid Ms. Marina KEYS
32 Dean of Students College Rev. Paschal CHELINE, OSB
32 Dean of Students Theology Abbot Peter EBERLE, OSB
20 Academic Dean College Dr. Creighton LINDSAY
85 Director of Foreign Students Ms. Tamara SWANSON-ORR
07 Director of Admissions Fr. Ralph RECKER, OSB
04 Admin Assistant to the President Ms. Graciela CORTES
13 Director of Information Technology Mr. Francisco MORA
40 Director of Bookstore Mrs. Beth WELLS
20 Academic Dean Theology Dr. Seymour HOUSE

Mt. Hood Community College (B)

26000 SE Stark, Gresham OR 97030-3300
County: Multnomah FICE Identification: 003204
Unit ID: 209250
Telephone: (503) 491-6422 Carnegie Class: Assoc/Pub-S-SC
FAX Number: (503) 491-7389 Calendar System: Quarter
URL: www.mhcc.edu
Established: 1965 Annual Undergrad Tuition & Fees (In-District): $4,056
Enrollment: 9,905 Coed
Affiliation or Control: Local IRS Status: 501(c)3
Highest Offering: Associate Degree
Program: Occupational; 2-Year Principally Bachelor's Creditable
Accreditation: NW, DH, FUSER, MAC, PTAA, SURGT

01 President Dr. Michael D. HAY
11 Int VP of Administrative Services Mr. Bill FARVER
05 Vice President of Instruction Ms. Christie PLINSKI
32 Vice Pres Student Svcs & Enrollment Dr. David MINGER
20 Assoc Vice President of Instruction Dr. Ursula IRWIN
38 Dean Student Success Services Mr. Robert COX
15 Director Human Resources Ms. Mara KERSHAW
26 Chief Public Relations Officer Ms. Maggie HUFFMAN
88 Dir Child Dev/Family Support Pgms Ms. Jean WAGNER
18 Director Facilities Management Mr. Richard BYERS
31 Dir Board Relations & Comm Devel Ms. Michelle GREGORY
21 Director Auxiliary Services Ms. Sue ASCHIM
10 Director of Finance Ms. Jennifer DEMENT
06 Registrar Vacant
37 Director Student Financial Aid Ms. Christi HART
13 Chief Information Officer Ms. Linda VIGESAA
08 Dean Information Resources Vacant
76 Dean Health Professions & Nursing Ms. Janie GRIFFIN
81 Dean Social Science Ms. Janet MCINTYRE
79 Dean Humanities Mr. Eric TSCHUY
72 Dean Science & Technology Vacant
50 Dean Business Mr. Rod BARKER
88 Dean Adult Basic Skills/Econ WF Dev Mr. Marc GOLDBERG
08 Dean Learning Commons Mr. Jeff RING

Multnomah University (C)

8435 NE Glisan Street, Portland OR 97220-5898
County: Multnomah FICE Identification: 003206
Unit ID: 209287
Telephone: (503) 255-0332 Carnegie Class: Spec/Faith
FAX Number: (503) 254-1268 Calendar System: Semester
URL: www.multnomah.edu
Established: 1936 Annual Undergrad Tuition & Fees: $21,240
Enrollment: 939 Coed
Affiliation or Control: Independent Non-Profit IRS Status: 501(c)3
Highest Offering: First Professional Degree
Program: Liberal Arts And General; Teacher Preparatory; Professional; Religious Emphasis
Accreditation: NW, BI, THEOL

01 President Dr. Daniel R. LOCKWOOD
05 Chief Academic Officer/Provost Dr. Wayne G. STRICKLAND
11 Chief Administrative Officer Ms. Gina BERQUIST
10 Chief Financial Officer Mr. Russell LACY
20 Academic Dean for College and Grad Dr. Rex KOIVISTO
73 VP/Academic Dean Biblical Seminary Dr. Robert R. REDMAN
32 Director/Dean of Students Mr. Jon MATHIS
30 Executive Director of Advancement Mr. John ZAREVA
39 Dean of Resident & Commuter Life Mr. David GROOM
35 Dean of Seminary Students Dr. Karen J. FANCHER
108 Dir of Institutional Effectiveness Dr. David FUNK
20 Associate Academic Dean Mr. David W. JONGEWARD
06 Registrar Miss Amy M. STEPHENS
21 Controller Mr. Brian YAW
18 Executive Director of Facilities Mr. Lloyd L. HELM
08 Librarian Dr. Philip M. JOHNSON
37 Director Student Financial Aid Mrs. Mary MCGLOTHLAN
36 Seminary Director of Placement Dr. Roger TRAUTMANN
13 Director Information Technology Mrs. Brenda GIBSON
15 Director of Human Resources Miss Tracy L. MORESCHI
23 Director Health Services Mrs. Jana POLING
41 Athletic Director Miss Lois VOS
26 Dir of Promotions & Communication Mr. Robert LEARY
07 Director of Admissions Mr. Palmer MUNTZ
29 Director Alumni Relations Miss Michelle PEEL
04 Assistant to the President Mrs. Denise STONE

National College of Natural Medicine (D)

049 SW Porter Street, Portland OR 97201-4878
County: Multnomah FICE Identification: 025340
Unit ID: 209296
Telephone: (503) 552-1555 Carnegie Class: Spec/Health
FAX Number: (503) 499-0022 Calendar System: Quarter
URL: www.ncnm.edu
Established: 1956 Annual Graduate Tuition & Fees: $13,500
Enrollment: 551 Coed
Affiliation or Control: Independent Non-Profit IRS Status: 501(c)3
Highest Offering: Doctorate; No Undergraduates
Program: Professional
Accreditation: NW, ACUP, NATUR

01 President Dr. David J. SCHLEICH
05 Provost/VP Academic Dr. Andrea SMITH
10 Chief Financial Officer/VP Finances Mr. Gerald BORES
30 VP of Advancement Ms. Susan HUNTER
26 VP Marketing Ms. Sandra SNYDER
09 Dir of Inst Research & Compliance Ms. Laurie MCGRATH
17 Dean of Naturopathic Medicine Dr. Margot LONGENECKER
88 Dean Classical Chinese Medicine Dr. Laurie REGAN
32 Dean of Student Affairs Ms. Cheryl MILLER
46 Dean Helfgott Research Inst Dr. Heather ZWICKEY
23 Dean of Clinical Operations Dr. Jill SANDERS
88 Assoc Dean Naturopathic Medicine Dr. Melanie HENRIKSEN
20 Associate Dean Academic Progress Ms. Catherine DOWNEY
15 Director of Human Resources Mr. Steve JOHNSON
07 Director of Admissions Mr. Rigo NUNEZ
37 Director of Financial Aid Ms. Laurie RADFORD
06 Registrar Ms. Kelly GAREY
04 Executive Asst to the President Ms. Colleen CORDER
40 Dir Retail Operations Ms. Nora SANDE
88 Director of Professional Formation Dr. Marnie LOOMIS
08 Director of Library Dr. Rick SEVERSON

New Hope Christian College (E)

2155 Bailey Hill Road, Eugene OR 97405-1194
County: Lane FICE Identification: 021597
Unit ID: 208725
Telephone: (541) 485-1780 Carnegie Class: Spec/Faith
FAX Number: (541) 343-5801 Calendar System: Semester
URL: www.newhope.edu
Established: 1925 Annual Undergrad Tuition & Fees: $13,190
Enrollment: 146 Coed
Affiliation or Control: Other IRS Status: 501(c)3
Highest Offering: Baccalaureate
Program: Religious Emphasis
Accreditation: BI

00 Chancellor Mr. Wayne CORDEIRO
01 President/Dir College Advancement Dr. Guy HIGASHI
03 Executive Director Mr. Gary MATSDORF
04 Executive Assistant to President Mrs. Lori HIGASHI
05 Academic Dean Dr. Larry R. BURKE
29 Director of Alumni Relations Mrs. Jan HORNSHUH KENT
32 Director of Student Life Mr. Steven POETZL
10 Business Administrator Mr. Paul SHERIDON
06 Registrar Ms. Sarah SLATER
07 Enrollment Management Mr. Sean MCCARTIN
37 Director of Financial Aid Mr. Nathan ICENHOWER
08 Head Librarian Ms. Jan KELLEY
38 Director of Christian Counseling Mr. David F. ORTEGA

Northwest Christian University (F)

828 E 11th Avenue, Eugene OR 97401-3745
County: Lane FICE Identification: 003208
Unit ID: 209409
Telephone: (541) 343-1641 Carnegie Class: Bac/Diverse
FAX Number: (541) 343-9159 Calendar System: Semester
URL: www.nwcu.edu
Established: 1895 Annual Undergrad Tuition & Fees: $24,780
Enrollment: 610 Coed
Affiliation or Control: Christian Church (Disciples Of Christ)
IRS Status: 501(c)3
Highest Offering: Master's
Program: Liberal Arts And General; Teacher Preparatory
Accreditation: NW, IACBE

01 President Dr. Joe WOMACK
05 VP Academic Affairs/Dean of Faculty Dr. Dennis LINDSAY
10 Vice Pres Finance/Administration Ms. Lisa CASTLEBURY
30 Vice President Advancement Dr. Greg STRAUSBAUGH
32 VP Student Development/Enrollment Mr. Michael FULLER
49 Dean Arts & Sciences Vacant
50 Dean Business & Management Vacant
53 Dean School Education & Counseling Dr. Jim HOWARD
26 Director University Relations Ms. Jeannine JONES
39 Dir Residence Life/Asst Dean Stdnts Ms. Jocelyn HUBBS
08 Director Kellenberger Library Mr. Steve SILVER
06 Registrar Mr. Aaron PRUITT
42 Campus Pastor Mr. Troy DEAN
37 Director Financial Aid Mr. Scott PALMER
07 Director Admissions Ms. Kacie GERDRUM
35 Director Student Activities Ms. Sarah HALSTEAD
18 Plant Manager Mr. Oskar BUCHER
40 Bookstore Manager Vacant
41 Athletic Director Mr. Corey R. ANDERSON
36 Dir Career Dev & Disability Service Ms. Angela DOTY
24 Media/Computer Lab Supervisor Mr. Doug VERMILYEA
04 Administrative Assistant Ms. Carla AYDELOTT
29 Director Alumni & Church Relations Ms. Shannon BALMER
44 Director Annual Fund Ms. Glenda GORDON

Oregon College of Art and Craft (G)

8245 SW Barnes Road, Portland OR 97225-6349
County: Washington FICE Identification: 030073
Unit ID: 209533
Telephone: (503) 297-5554 Carnegie Class: Spec/Arts
FAX Number: (503) 297-3155 Calendar System: Semester
URL: www.ocac.edu
Established: 1907 Annual Undergrad Tuition & Fees: $24,200
Enrollment: 151 Coed
Affiliation or Control: Independent Non-Profit IRS Status: 501(c)3
Highest Offering: Baccalaureate
Program: Fine Arts Emphasis
Accreditation: NW, ART

01 President Ms. Denise MULLEN
10 Chief Financial Officer Mr. Lee MILLIGAN
05 Academic Dean Vacant
30 Chief Advanc/Marketing & CP Officer Ms. Roma PEYSER
07 Chief Enroll Officer/Dir of Admiss Ms. Anne BOERNER
06 Registrar Vacant
08 Head of Library Services Ms. Lori JOHNSON
32 Coordinator of Student Services Ms. Meaghen PORTE
31 Coordinator of Community Programs Mr. Jeffrey BAKER
37 Director of Financial Aid Ms. Linda ANDERSON
29 Dir of Exhibitions/Alumni Affairs Mr. Arthur DEBOW
04 Exec Assistant to the President Ms. Kris KEBISEK

Oregon College of Oriental Medicine (H)

10525 SE Cherry Blossom Drive, Portland OR 97216-2859
County: Multnomah FICE Identification: 026037
Unit ID: 369659
Telephone: (503) 253-3443 Carnegie Class: Spec/Health
FAX Number: (503) 253-2701 Calendar System: Quarter
URL: www.ocom.edu
Established: 1983 Annual Graduate Tuition & Fees: $24,495
Enrollment: 315 Coed

Affiliation or Control: Independent Non-Profit IRS Status: 501(c)3
Highest Offering: Doctorate; No Undergraduates
Program: Professional
Accreditation: @NW, ACUP

01 President Dr. Michael GAETA
05 Vice President for Academic Affairs Dr. Tim CHAPMAN
10 Vice President for Finance Susan SLOAN
32 Dean of Academic & Student Affairs Carol TAUB
09 Planning & Inst Assessment Officer Shelley STUMP
88 Dean of Doctoral Studies Dr. Beth BURCH
46 Associate Dean of Research Dr. Deborah ACKERMAN
30 Development Officer Glenn FEE
15 Director of Human Resources Michelle VALINTIS
26 Director of Community Relations Gretchen HORTON
23 Assoc Dean of Clinical Education Dr. Debra MULROONEY
06 Registrar Carol ACHESON
13 Director of Operations & Technology Chris CHIACCHIERINI

Oregon Culinary Institute (A)

1701 SW Jefferson Street, Portland OR 97201-2571
County: Multnomah Identification: 666177
Telephone: (503) 961-6200 Carnegie Class: Not Classified
FAX Number: (503) 961-6240 Calendar System: Other
URL: www.oregonculinaryinstitute.com
Established: 2006 Annual Undergrad Tuition & Fees: $16,735
Enrollment: 235 Coed
Affiliation or Control: Proprietary IRS Status: Proprietary
Highest Offering: Associate Degree
Program: Occupational; Fine Arts Emphasis
Accreditation: ACICS

01 President Mr. Eric STROMQUIST
05 Director of Education Mr. Brian WILKE
07 Location Director/Admissions Mr. Ray COLVIN
36 Career Services Director Ms. Nina TUTHILL-RANGER
37 Financial Aid Director Ms. Sarah PETERS
31 Community Relations Director Mr. Kevin RICHARDS
06 Education Coordinator Mr. Ryan GAGE

† Branch campus of Pioneer Pacific College, Wilsonville, OR.

*Oregon University System (B)

PO Box 3175, Eugene OR 97403-0175
County: Lane FICE Identification: 009190
Unit ID: 209445
Telephone: (541) 346-5794 Carnegie Class: N/A
FAX Number: (541) 346-5764
URL: www.ous.edu

01 Chancellor Mr. George P. PERNSTEINER
10 VC Finance & Administration Dr. Jay KENTON
05 Vice Chanc for Academic Strategies Vacant
21 Asst VC Budget/Operations Ms. Jan LEWIS
15 Director Labor & Employee Relations Vacant
43 Director Legal Services Dr. Ryan HAGEMANN
86 Director Government Relations Vacant
09 Director Institutional Research Mr. Robert KIERAN

*Eastern Oregon University (C)

One University Boulevard, La Grande OR 97850-2807
County: Union FICE Identification: 003193
Unit ID: 208646
Telephone: (541) 962-3672 Carnegie Class: Master's S
FAX Number: (541) 962-3493 Calendar System: Quarter
URL: www.eou.edu
Established: 1929 Annual Undergrad Tuition & Fees (In-State): $7,238
Enrollment: 4,298 Coed
Affiliation or Control: State IRS Status: 501(c)3
Highest Offering: Master's
Program: Liberal Arts And General; Teacher Preparatory; Professional
Accreditation: NW, IACBE

02 President Dr. Robert DAVIES
05 Provost/Senior VP Academic Affairs Dr. Stephen ADKISON
32 Vice President for Student Affairs Dr. Camille CONSOLVO
10 Vice President for Finance & Admin Mr. Lon WHITAKER
30 Vice Pres UA & Admissions Mr. Tim SEYDEL
20 Associate VP for Academic Affairs Dr. Sarah WITTE
49 Dean College Arts & Science Dr. Steven GAMMON
50 Interim Dean College of Bus & Educ Dr. Dan MIELKE
37 Director of Financial Aid Ms. Lara MOORE
08 Director of Pierce Library Ms. Karen CLAY
07 Director of Admissions Mr. Arlyn LOVE
06 Registrar Ms. Carolyn BLOYED
15 Director of Human Resources Mr. Michael LAMBRECHT
29 Dir of Annual Giving and Alumni Rel Mr. Jon LARKIN
41 Interim Director of Athletics Ms. Anji WEISSENFLUH
39 Director of Residence Life Mr. Stephen JENKINS
18 Director of Facilities & Planning Mr. David LAGESON
38 Director Counseling Center Vacant
04 Exec Assistant to the President Ms. Kristen KRUSE
21 Director of Business Affairs Ms. Lara MOORE
36 Director of Acad & Career Advising Ms. Liz BURTON
88 Director of Learning Center Ms. Anna Maria DILL
35 Director of Student Relations Ms. Colleen DUNNE-CASCIO
19 Campus Security/Public Safety Ofcr Mr. Bill BENSON

*Oregon Health & Science University (D)

3181 SW Sam Jackson, Portland OR 97201-3098
County: Multnomah FICE Identification: 004882
Unit ID: 209490
Telephone: (503) 494-8311 Carnegie Class: Spec/Med
FAX Number: (503) 494-5738 Calendar System: Quarter
URL: www.ohsu.edu
Established: 1974 Annual Undergrad Tuition & Fees (In-State): $16,192
Enrollment: 2,802 Coed
Affiliation or Control: State IRS Status: 501(c)3
Highest Offering: Doctorate
Program: Professional
Accreditation: NW, ANEST, ARCPA, DENT, DIETI, EMT, IPSY, MED, MIDWF, MT, NURSE, PH, RTT

02 President Dr. Joseph E. ROBERTSON
03 Executive Vice Provost Dr. David W. ROBINSON
05 Provost Education & Research Dr. Jeanette MLADENOVIC
18 Assoc VP Facilities/Physical Plant Mr. Scott PAGE
32 Vice Provost for Student Affairs Dr. Robert VIEIRA
63 Dean School of Medicine Dr. Mark RICHARDSON
52 Interim Dean School of Dentistry Dr. Gary CHIODO
66 Interim Dean School of Nursing Dr. Chris A. TANNER
06 Registrar/Director of Financial Aid Ms. Cherie HONNELL
17 Director University Hospital Mr. Peter RAPP
88 Director Vollum Inst Adv Biomed Res Dr. Richard H. GOODMAN
15 Director of Human Resources Vacant
08 Director Health Sciences Libraries Mr. Chris SHAFFER
46 Director of Research Services Dr. Daniel DORSA
27 Director Corporate Communications Ms. Lora L. CUYKENDALL
88 Director Child Devel/Rehab Center Dr. Brian ROGERS
37 Director Student Financial Aid Ms. Cherie HONNELL
28 Director of Diversity Ms. Leslie GARCIA

*Oregon Institute of Technology (E)

3201 Campus Drive, Klamath Falls OR 97601-8801
County: Klamath FICE Identification: 003211
Unit ID: 209506
Telephone: (541) 885-1000 Carnegie Class: Bac/Diverse
FAX Number: (541) 885-1101 Calendar System: Quarter
URL: www.oit.edu
Established: 1947 Annual Undergrad Tuition & Fees (In-State): $8,308
Enrollment: 3,911 Coed
Affiliation or Control: State IRS Status: 501(c)3
Highest Offering: Master's
Program: Liberal Arts And General; Technical Emphasis
Accreditation: NW, DH, ENG, ENGR, ENGT, IACBE, MT, POLYT

02 President Dr. Christopher MAPLES
05 Provost/Vice Pres Academic Affairs Mr. Bradley BURDA
10 Int VP Finance/Administration Ms. Mary Ann ZEMKE
32 VP Student Affairs/Enrollment Mgmt Dr. Erin FOLEY
30 Int Vice Pres of Development Mrs. Robin THOMPSON
35 Dean of Students Dr. Erin FOLEY
37 Director of Financial Aid Ms. Tracey A. LEHMAN
15 Director of Human Resources Mr. Ron MCCUTCHEON
07 Director of Admissions Mr. Carl THOMAS
06 Registrar Ms. Wendy PEDERSEN
38 Director of Counseling Vacant
21 Int Director of Business Affairs Ms. Sara REUTER
13 Chief Information Officer Mr. Andy ABBOTT
23 Director Student Health Services Mr. James PITTMAN
18 Director Facilities Services Mr. David W. EBSEN
41 Athletic Director Mr. Michael J. SCHELL
35 Director Campus Life Vacant
36 Director of Career Services Vacant
09 Director of Institutional Research Mr. David WAITE
29 Director Alumni Relations Mrs. Robin THOMPSON

*Oregon State University (F)

Corvallis OR 97331-8507
County: Benton FICE Identification: 003210
Unit ID: 209542
Telephone: (541) 737-0123 Carnegie Class: RU/VH
FAX Number: (541) 737-3033 Calendar System: Quarter
URL: www.oregonstate.edu
Established: 1868 Annual Undergrad Tuition & Fees (In-State): $8,139
Enrollment: 24,977 Coed
Affiliation or Control: State IRS Status: 501(c)3
Highest Offering: Doctorate
Program: Liberal Arts And General; Teacher Preparatory; Professional
Accreditation: NW, BUS, BUSA, CACREP, CONST, CS, DIETD, DIETI, ENG, ENGR, FOR, IPSY, PH, PHAR, TED, VET

02 President Dr. Edward J. RAY
05 Provost/Executive Vice President Dr. Sabah U. RANDHAWA
10 Vice Pres Finance/Administration Mr. Mark E. MCCAMBRIDGE
30 Vice Pres University Advancement Mr. Steve CLARK
46 Vice President for Research Mr. Rick SPINRAD
20 Vice Prov Academic Affs/Intl Pgms Dr. Rebecca WARNER
13 Vice Prov for Information Svcs/CIO Ms. Lois BROOKS
32 Vice Prov for Student Affairs Dr. Larry D. ROPER
56 Vice Prov Univ Outreach/Engagement Dr. Scott REED
12 V Prov/Campus Ex Ofcr OSU-Cascades Dr. Rebecca JOHNSON
84 Asst Provost Enrollment Management Ms. Kate M. PETERSON
102 President & CEO OSU Foundation Mr. Mike GOODWIN
47 Dean of Agricultural Sciences Dr. Dan ARP
50 Dean of Business Dr. Ilene K. KLEINSORGE
54 Dean of Engineering Vacant
65 Dean of Forestry Vacant
68 Dean of Health & Human Sciences Dr. Tammy BRAY
49 Interim Dean of Liberal Arts Dr. Larry RODGERS
88 Dean of Oceanic & Atmos Science Dr. Mark R. ABBOTT
67 Dean of Pharmacy Dr. Mark ZABRISKIE
81 Dean of Science Dr. Vince REMCHO
74 Dean of Veterinary Medicine Dr. Cyril CLARKE
51 Assoc Provost Extended Campus Dr. David A. KING
58 Dean of Graduate School Dr. Brenda MCCOMB
35 Dean of Student Life Dr. Mamta ACCAPADI
92 Dean University Honors College Vacant
53 Dean of Education Dr. Larry FLICK
08 University Librarian Ms. Faye CHADWELL
22 Dir Affirmative Action/Equal Oppty Mr. Angelo GOMEZ
43 General Counsel Ms. Meg REEVES
41 Director Intercollegiate Athletics Mr. Robert J. DE CAROLIS
88 Director Intl Education & Outreach Dr. Sunil KHANNA
36 Director of Career Services Mr. Douglas COCHRAN
37 Dir of Financial Aid/Scholarship Mr. Doug SEVERS
31 Director Memorial Union Mr. Michael HENTHORNE
23 Director Student Health Services Dr. Phillip C. HISTAND
38 Dir Univ Counseling/Psych Svcs Dr. Mariette BROUWERS
39 Director Univ Housing/Dining Svcs Mr. Thomas A. SCHEUERMANN
06 Registrar Mr. Thomas K. KUO
07 Director of Admissions Mr. Noah BUCKLEY
24 Director Media & Outreach Services Mr. John GREYDANUS
14 Dir of Enterprise Computing Service Ms. Catherine M. WILLIAMS
21 Director of Business Affairs Mr. Aaron D. HOWELL
88 Director Business Services Mr. Brian K. THORSNESS
15 Director of Human Resources Vacant
18 Director Facility Services Mr. Vincent MARTORELLO
19 Director Public Safety Mr. Jack T. ROGERS
29 Exec Dir of Alumni Association Mr. Scott GREENWOOD
86 Director Government Relations Mr. Jock S. MILLS
44 Director of Annual Giving Ms. Lacie LA RUE
27 Dir News/Comm Svcs/Asst Vice Pres Mr. Mark FLOYD
26 Director of University Marketing Ms. Melody K. OLDFIELD
105 Asst Director Web Communications Mr. David A. BAKER
20 Dir Academic Planning/Assessment Mr. Gary BEACH
28 Director of Community & Diversity Dr. Terryl J. ROSS
09 Director of Institutional Research Mr. Salvador CASTILLO
40 General Mgr & CEO OSU Bookstores Mr. Steve E. ECKRICH
96 Manager Procurement/Contract Svcs Ms. Kelly L. KOZISEK

*Portland State University (G)

PO Box 751, Portland OR 97207-0751
County: Multnomah FICE Identification: 003216
Unit ID: 209807
Telephone: (503) 725-3000 Carnegie Class: RU/H
FAX Number: (503) 725-4882 Calendar System: Quarter
URL: www.pdx.edu
Established: 1946 Annual Undergrad Tuition & Fees (In-State): $6,729
Enrollment: 25,883 Coed
Affiliation or Control: State IRS Status: 501(c)3
Highest Offering: Doctorate
Program: Liberal Arts And General; Teacher Preparatory; Professional
Accreditation: NW, BUS, BUSA, CACREP, CORE, CS, ENG, MUS, PH, PLNG, SP, SPAA, SW, TED, THEA

02 President Dr. Wim WIEWEL
43 General Counsel Mr. David REESE
05 Provost Dr. Sona ANDREWS
10 Vice President Finance/Admin Dr. Monica RIMAI
30 VP for University Advancement Ms. Francoise AYLMER
100 Chief of Staff Ms. Lois DAVIS
84 VP Enroll Mgmt & Student Affairs Dr. Jackie BALZER
46 VP Rsrch & Strategic Partnerships Dr. Jonathan FINK
51 Interim Vice Provost of Ext Studies Mr. Kevin REYNOLDS
20 Vice Prov Acad Personnel Dr. Carol MACK
88 Vice Provost International Affairs Dr. Gil LATZ
21 Assoc VP Finance & Planning Mr. Alan FINN
15 Assc VP HR & Univ Policy/Practice Ms. Shana SECHRIST
20 Assoc Vice Prov Academic Services Mr. Dan FORTMILLER
39 Director Housing & Transportation Mr. John ECKMAN
32 Asoc V Prov Stdnt Affs/Enroll Mgmt Mrs. Agnes HOFFMAN
88 Assistant VP Enrollment Management Ms. Cindy SKARUPPA
22 Chief Diversity Officer Dr. Jilma MENESES
26 Asst Vice Pres Communications Mr. Christopher BRODERICK
09 Director Inst Research/Planning Dr. Kathi A. KETCHESON
19 Chief of Campus Safety & Security Mr. Phil ZERZAN
96 Purchasing Mgr/Contractor Admin Ms. Karen PRESTON
13 AVP Strategic Plng/Prtnrshps/Tech Mr. Mark GREGORY
91 Director of Information Services Ms. Ann HARRIS
90 Director User Support Services Mr. Jahed SUKHUN
88 Dir Ctr for Academic Excellence Dr. Gary BROWN
08 University Librarian Dr. Marilyn MOODY
36 Assoc Vice Provost Career Services Mr. Dan FORTMILLER
85 Director International Affairs Ms. Judy VAN DYCK
18 Director Facilities & Planning Ms. Robyn PIERCE
41 Athletics Director Mr. Michael T. CHISHOLM
07 Associate Director of Admissions Ms. Cindy BACCAR
89 AVP Undergraduate Success Mr. Sukhwant S. JHAJ
92 Director University Honors Program Dr. Ann Marie FALLON
38 Dir Student Health & Counseling Dr. Dana TASSON
44 Director for Annual Giving Ms. Melinda PETERSEN
49 Dean Col of Liberal Arts/Sciences Dr. Susan BEATTY
50 Dean School Business Administration Dr. Scott DAWSON
53 Dean Graduate Sch of Education Dr. Randy HITZ

54 Dean Col Engr/Computer Science ... Dr. Renjeng SU
57 Dean School Fine/Performing Arts ... Ms. Barbara SESTAK
70 Dean Graduate School Social Work ... Dr. David SPRINGER
80 Dean College Urban/Public Affairs ... Dr. Lawrence WALLACK
37 Director Student Financial Aid ... Mr. Phillip RODGERS
21 Vice Provost Fiscal Strategies ... Mr. Kevin REYNOLDS
35 Assoc Vice Provost Student Affairs ... Ms. Michele TOPPE
88 Associate Director of Career Center ... Mr. Greg FLORES
27 Chief Information Officer ... Ms. Sharon BLANTON

*Southern Oregon University (A)

1250 Siskiyou Boulevard, Ashland OR 97520-5001
County: Jackson FICE Identification: 003219
Unit ID: 210146
Telephone: (541) 552-7672 Carnegie Class: Master's L
FAX Number: (541) 552-6329 Calendar System: Quarter
URL: www.sou.edu
Established: 1872 Annual Undergrad Tuition & Fees (In-State): $7,230
Enrollment: 6,745 Coed
Affiliation or Control: State IRS Status: 501(c)3
Highest Offering: Master's
Program: Liberal Arts And General; Professional
Accreditation: NW, ACBSP, CACREP, MUS

02 President ... Dr. Mary CULLINAN
05 Provost and VP for Academic Affairs ... Dr. James KLEIN
11 VP for Administration & Finance ... Mr. Craig MORRIS
32 Vice President for Student Affairs ... Mr. Jon ELDRIDGE
30 Vice President Development ... Ms. Sylvia KELLEY
15 Director for Human Resource Svcs ... Mr. Jay STEPHENS
100 Chief of Staff/Dir Governmt Rels ... Ms. Liz SHELBY
84 Asst VP of Enrollment ... Mr. Rick WEEMS
26 Dir Interactive Mktg & Media Rels ... Mr. James BEAVER
18 Dir for Facilities Mgmt & Planning ... Mr. Drew GILLELAND
58 Assoc Provost/Dean Graduate Stds ... Dr. Susan WALSH
21 Director of Business Services ... Mr. Steve LARVICK
08 Dean of Library ... Mr. Paul ADALIAN
35 Executive Director for Student Life ... Vacant
51 Exec Dir Division of Continuing Edu ... Ms. Jeanne STALLMAN
35 Dean of Students ... Dr. Laura O'BRYON
49 Dean College of Arts & Sciences ... Dr. Alissa ARP
19 Co-Director of Campus Public Safety ... Mr. Stephen ROSS
19 Co-Director of Campus Public Safety ... Mr. Richard WALSH
14 Director of Information Technology ... Mr. Brad CHRIST
29 Director of Alumni Affairs ... Ms. Doreen O'SKEA
21 Assoc Director of Business Services ... Vacant
106 Director of Distance Education ... Dr. Jennifer MCVAY-DYCHE
88 Exec Dir of Schneider Museum of Art ... Vacant
88 Dir of Accelerated Baccalureate Pgm ... Mr. Curt BACON
28 Director of Diversity ... Mr. Jonathan ELDRIDGE
44 Annual Fund Coordinator ... Ms. Chava FLORENDO
88 Donor Relations Coordinator ... Ms. Sarah KASSEL
88 Director of Performing Arts ... Mr. Noel KORAN

*University of Oregon (B)

Eugene OR 97403-1226
County: Lane FICE Identification: 003223
Unit ID: 209551
Telephone: (541) 346-1000 Carnegie Class: RU/VH
FAX Number: (541) 346-3017 Calendar System: Quarter
URL: www.uoregon.edu
Established: 1876 Annual Undergrad Tuition & Fees (In-State): $9,310
Enrollment: 24,396 Coed
Affiliation or Control: State IRS Status: 501(c)3
Highest Offering: Doctorate
Program: Liberal Arts And General; Professional
Accreditation: NW, ART, BUS, BUSA, CEA, CIDA, CLPSY, COPSY, IPSY, JOUR, LAW, LSAR, MFCD, MUS, PLNG, SCPSY, SP, SPAA

02 President ... Dr. Michael R. GOTTFREDSON
04 Senior Assistant to the President ... Dr. David R. HUBIN
04 Assistant Vice President ... Mr. Timothy R. BLACK
05 Senior Vice President & Provost ... Dr. James C. BEAN
10 VP Finance & Admin & CFO ... Ms. Jamie H. MOFFITT
32 Vice President for Student Affairs ... Dr. Robin H. HOLMES
30 Vice Pres University Relations ... Dr. Michael W. REDDING
46 VP Research/Dean Graduate School ... Dr. Kimberly A. ESPY
20 Vice Provost Undergraduate Studies ... Dr. Karen U. SPRAGUE
28 Vice Pres Inst Equity/Diversity ... Dr. Yvette ALEX-ASSENSOH
13 Vice Prov Information Services/CIO ... Vacant
85 Vice Provost International Affairs ... Dr. Dennis GALVAN
30 Asst VP Campaign Initiatives ... Vacant
21 Assoc Vice Pres Budget & Finance ... Vacant
86 Assoc Vice Pres Public/Govt Affairs ... Ms. Betsy A. BOYD
29 AVP Alumni Affairs/Exec Dir UOAA .. Mr. Timothy R. CLEVENGER
43 General Counsel to the University ... Mr. L. Randy GELLER
102 Chief Investment Officer Foundation ... Mr. Jay NAMYET
06 University Registrar ... Ms. Susan M. EVELAND
07 Director of Admissions ... Mr. Brian L. HENLEY
08 Philip H Knight Dean of Libraries ... Ms. Deborah A. CARVER
21 Dir Business Affairs and Controller ... Mr. Kelly B. WOLF
37 Director Student Financial Aid ... Mr. James J. BROOKS
36 Director of Career Center ... Ms. Deborah T. CHERECK
15 Assoc VP Human Resources ... Ms. Linda L. KING
18 Assoc VP Campus Operations ... Mr. George E. HECHT
22 Director Affirmative Action ... Ms. Penny J. DAUGHERTY
41 Director Intercollegiate Athletics ... Mr. Rob A. MULLENS
56 Senior Dir UO Academic Extension ... Mr. Curt D. LIND
49 Dean College Arts & Sciences ... Dr. Scott L. COLTRANE
48 Dean Architecture & Allied Arts ... Ms. Frances BRONET
50 Dean College of Business ... Dr. Cornelis A. DE KLUYVER
53 Dean College of Education ... Dr. Michael D. BULLIS
60 Dean School of Journalism & Comm ... Dr. Timothy W. GLEASON
58 Vice Prov Grad Studies & Assoc Dean ... Dr. Sandra MORGEN
61 Dean School of Law ... Ms. Margaret L. PARIS
64 Dean School of Music & Dance ... Dr. C. Brad FOLEY
92 Dean Clark Honors College ... Dr. David FRANK
09 Director of Institutional Research ... Dr. J.P MONROE
35 Associate VP for Student Affairs ... Mr. Michael E. EYSTER
38 Dir Counseling & Testing Center ... Dr. Shelly K. KERR
84 Vice Provost Enrollment Management ... Mr. Roger J. THOMPSON
96 Dir Purchasing & Contracting Svcs ... Ms. Catherine D. SUSMAN

*Western Oregon University (C)

345 N Monmouth Avenue, Monmouth OR 97361-1394
County: Polk FICE Identification: 003209
Unit ID: 210429
Telephone: (503) 838-8000 Carnegie Class: Master's M
FAX Number: (503) 838-8474 Calendar System: Quarter
URL: www.wou.edu
Established: 1856 Annual Undergrad Tuition & Fees (In-State): $7,818
Enrollment: 6,217 Coed
Affiliation or Control: State IRS Status: 501(c)3
Highest Offering: Beyond Master's But Less Than Doctorate
Program: Liberal Arts And General; Teacher Preparatory
Accreditation: NW, CORE, MUS, TED

02 President ... Mr. Mark D. WEISS
05 Provost/VP Academic Affairs ... Dr. Monty K. NEELY
32 Vice President Student Affairs ... Dr. Gary DUKES
10 Vice President Business & Finance ... Vacant
35 Dean of Students ... Ms. Tina M. FUCHS
49 Dean Col Liberal Arts & Sciences ... Dr. Stephen SCHECK
53 Dean College of Education ... Dr. Hilda ROSSELLI
07 Asc Prov Admiss Retent/Enroll Mgmt ... Mr. David MCDONALD
56 Exec Dir Division Extended Pgms ... Ms. JoNan LEROY
06 Registrar ... Ms. Nancy FRANCE
30 Director of Development ... Mr. Tommy LOVE
08 Director Hamersly Library ... Dr. Allen MCKIEL
13 Director University Computing Svcs ... Mr. William KERNAN
15 Director Human Resources ... Ms. Judy J. VANDERBURG
18 Director Physical Plant ... Mr. Tom NEAL
19 Director University Public Safety ... Mr. Jay CAREY
23 Dir Student Health/Counseling Ctr ... Ms. Michele J. COX
26 Dir Public Relations/Communications ... Ms. Denise VISUANO
32 Director Student Life ... Mr. Jon TUCKER
37 Director Financial Aid ... Ms. Donna KIRK
41 Athletic Director ... Mr. Daniel HARE
46 Dir of Teaching Research Institute ... Dr. Ella TAYLOR
85 Dir Intl Students/Scholars Affairs ... Mr. Neng YANG
88 Dir Multicultural Student Svcs/ Pgms ... Ms. Anna HERNANDEZ-HUNTER
22 Director AAEO ... Ms. Judy J. VANDERBURG
29 Dir Leadership Giving/Athletic Dev ... Mr. Michael FEULING
25 Project & Contract Officer ... Mr. Stan HAGEN

Pacific Northwest College of Art (D)

1241 NW Johnson Street, Portland OR 97209-3023
County: Multnomah FICE Identification: 003207
Unit ID: 209603
Telephone: (503) 226-4391 Carnegie Class: Spec/Arts
FAX Number: (503) 226-3587 Calendar System: Semester
URL: www.pnca.edu
Established: 1909 Annual Undergrad Tuition & Fees: $30,730
Enrollment: 596 Coed
Affiliation or Control: Independent Non-Profit IRS Status: 501(c)3
Highest Offering: Master's
Program: Fine Arts Emphasis
Accreditation: NW, ART

01 President ... Dr. Thomas MANLEY
05 Dean of Academic Affairs ... Mr. Mark TAKIGUCHI
10 Chief Financial Officer/HR Dir ... Mr. Larry HUDSPETH
84 Vice Pres Enrollment Services ... Mr. Kavin BUCK
04 Interim Assistant to the President ... Ms. Elizabeth CAMPBELL
51 Director of Continuing Education ... Mr. Patrick FORSTER
37 Director Financial Aid ... Ms. Heidi LOCKE
26 Director of Communications ... Mrs. Becca BIGGS
06 Registrar ... Ms. Jenifer DE KALB
08 Director of Library Services ... Mr. Dan MCCLURE
07 Director of Admissions ... Ms. D. Jean HESTER

Pacific University (E)

2043 College Way, Forest Grove OR 97116-1797
County: Washington FICE Identification: 003212
Unit ID: 209612
Telephone: (503) 357-6151 Carnegie Class: Master's L
FAX Number: (503) 352-2242 Calendar System: Semester
URL: www.pacificu.edu
Established: 1849 Annual Undergrad Tuition & Fees: $35,260
Enrollment: 3,302 Coed
Affiliation or Control: Independent Non-Profit IRS Status: 501(c)3
Highest Offering: Doctorate
Program: Liberal Arts And General; Teacher Preparatory; Professional
Accreditation: NW, ARCPA, @AUD, CLPSY, DH, IPSY, MUS, OPT, OPTR, OT, PHAR, PTA, @SP, SW, TED

01 President ... Dr. Lesley M. HALLICK
05 Vice Pres Academic Affairs/Provost ... Dr. John MILLER
10 Vice Pres Finance & Administration ... Mr. Mike MALLERY
30 Vice Pres University Advancement ... Ms. Cassie MCVEETY
32 Interim VP of Student Affairs ... Mr. Will PERKINS
46 Vice Provost for Research ... Dr. Chris WILKES
21 Assistant Vice Pres for Finance ... Mr. William RAY
26 Assoc VP for University Relations ... Ms. Jan STRICKLIN
18 Dir of Facilities/Safety Management ... Mr. Harold ROARK
07 Executive Director of Admissions ... Ms. Karen DUNSTON
84 Registrar ... Ms. Anne HERMAN
37 Director Financial Aid ... Mr. Mike JOHNSON
27 Chief Information Officer ... Mr. James FLEMING
88 Director of Conference Services ... Ms. Lois HORNBERGER
88 Director University Events ... Ms. Paula THATCHER
76 Exec Dean Col of Health Professions ... Dr. Ann BARR
49 Dean of Arts & Sciences ... Dr. Lisa CARSTENS
63 Dean of Optometry ... Dr. Jennifer SMYTHE
67 Dean of Pharmacy ... Dr. Sue STEIN
53 Dean College of Education ... Dr. Mark ANKENY
83 Dean Sch Professional Psychology ... Dr. Christiane BREMS
41 Athletic Director ... Mr. Kenneth SCHUMANN
76 Director School Physical Therapy ... Dr. Richard RUTT
76 Dir School Occupational Therapy ... Dr. John WHITE
15 Director of Human Resources ... Mr. Troy STRASS
23 Director of Health Services ... Ms. Kathryn L. EISENBARTH
88 Acad Coord/English Language Inst ... Ms. Monique GRINDELL
44 Director of Annual Giving ... Ms. Kristin STORFA
07 Exec Director of Grad/Prof Admiss ... Mr. Jon-Erik LARSEN
76 Director Physician Asst Studies ... Ms. Judy ORTIZ
29 Director Alumni Relations ... Ms. Martha CALUS-MCLAIN
88 Dir External Relations Optometry ... Ms. Jeanne OLIVER
08 Library Director ... Ms. Marita KUNKEL
88 Senior Editor/Writer ... Ms. Jenni LUCKETT
32 Dir Univ Center/Student Activities ... Mr. Steve KLEIN
36 Director Career Development ... Mr. Brian O'DRISCOLL
52 Program Director-Dental ... Ms. Lisa ROWLEY
40 Manager Bookstore ... Ms. Stacie BLANKENHORN
38 Director Counseling Center ... Ms. Robin KEILLOR
09 Director of Institutional Research ... Mr. William O'SHEA

Pioneer Pacific College (F)

27501 SW Parkway Avenue, Wilsonville OR 97070-9296
County: Clackamas FICE Identification: 023301
Unit ID: 210076
Telephone: (503) 682-3903 Carnegie Class: Assoc/PrivFP4
FAX Number: (503) 682-1514 Calendar System: Other
URL: www.pioneerpacific.edu
Established: 1981 Annual Undergrad Tuition & Fees: $12,237
Enrollment: 1,688 Coed
Affiliation or Control: Proprietary IRS Status: Proprietary
Highest Offering: Baccalaureate
Program: Occupational
Accreditation: ACICS

01 President ... Mr. Don MOUTOS
00 Board Chairman ... Mr. Raymond C. GAUTHIER
12 Portland Metro Campus President ... Mr. Don MOUTOS
12 OCI Campus President ... Mr. Eric STROMQUIST
12 Springfield Campus President ... Mr. Eric ARMSTRONG
10 Chief Financial Officer ... Mr. Mark MORELAND
05 Vice President of Academic Affairs ... Ms. Sandra WIGGINS
07 Vice President of Admissions ... Ms. Vicki CHURCH
37 Executive Director of Financial Aid ... Mr. Michael HARGRAVE
22 Compliance Officer ... Mr. Andrew BERNHARD
21 Controller ... Mr. Don ECK
26 Director of Marketing ... Ms. Basia PETRI
06 Lead Registrar ... Ms. Etta SCHWAB
50 Program Director Business-WLS ... Ms. Carin DYKZEUL
50 Program Director Business-CLK ... Mr. David WILHOYTE
50 Program Director Business-SPR ... Ms. Linda FARMER
61 Program Director Legal-WLS ... Ms. Vanesa PANCIC-MEIER
61 Program Director Legal-CLK ... Mr. Warren MOE
76 Program Director Medical-HCI ... Ms. Jennifer SCHILLING
76 Program Director Health-WLS & HCI ... Ms. Roxanne STEVENS
76 Program Director Massage-HCI ... Dr. Kim SCHMALTZ
76 Program Director Limited Xray ... Ms. Monica QUINTERO-DEVLAEMINCK
76 Program Director Limited X-Ray-SPR ... Ms. Katheryn MADISON
76 Program Director Medical-SPR ... Ms. Jody WEARIN
77 Program Director IT-WLS ... Mr. Rob MORRISON
77 Program Director IT-SPR ... Mr. Ed MCLAUGHLIN
66 Program Director Nursing ... Ms. Kim VOGEL
80 Program Director Criminal Just-WLS ... Mr. James FORD
80 Program Director Criminal Just-SPR ... Ms. Pamela MOORE
67 Program Director Pharmacy-HCI ... Dr. Kim SCHMALTZ
67 Program Director Pharmacy- SPR ... Ms. Lisa RUSSELL
08 Librarian ... Ms. Jill SLED

Portland Community College (G)

PO Box 19000, Portland OR 97280-0990
County: Multnomah FICE Identification: 003213
Unit ID: 209746
Telephone: (971) 722-6111 Carnegie Class: Assoc/Pub-U-MC
FAX Number: (503) 977-4960 Calendar System: Quarter
URL: www.pcc.edu
Established: 1961 Annual Undergrad Tuition & Fees (In-District): $2,990
Enrollment: 27,000 Coed
Affiliation or Control: Local IRS Status: 501(c)3
Highest Offering: Associate Degree
Program: Occupational; 2-Year Principally Bachelor's Creditable
Accreditation: NW, ADNUR, DA, DH, DT, EMT, MAC, MLTAD, RAD

01 District President Dr. Preston PULLIAMS
03 District Vice President Mr. Randy MCEWEN
05 VP Academic & Student Affairs Dr. Christine CHAIRSELL
11 Vice Pres Administrative Services Mr. Wing-Kit CHUNG
10 Assoc VP Financial Services Mr. Jim Langstraat CHEVALIER
91 Assoc VP Information Tech Svcs Ms. Leslie RIESTER
26 Assoc VP Institutional Advancement Ms. Kristin WATKINS
12 Campus President Sylvania Dr. Linda GERBER
12 Campus President Cascade Dr. Algie GATEWOOD
12 Campus President Rock Creek Dr. David RULE
12 Campus President Extended Lrng Dr. Jessica HOWARD
20 Dean Instruction Sylvania Campus Mr. Jeff TRIPLET
20 Dean Instruction Cascade Campus Mr. Scott HUFF
20 Dean Instr Rock Creek Campus Ms. Birgitte RYSLINGE
20 Dean Instr/Stdnt Dev/Ext Lrng Camp Dr. Craig KOLINS
32 Dean Student Dev Sylvania Campus Ms. Heather LANG
32 Dean Stdnt Dev Rock Creek Campus Ms. Narce RODRIGUEZ
32 Dean Student Dev Cascade Campus Dr. Linda REISSER
32 Dean Student Affairs Ms. Veronica GARCIA
15 Interim Director Human Resources Ms. Lisa BLEDSOE
18 Director Facilities Management Mr. Tim DONAHUE
08 Director Libraries Dr. Donna REED
09 Dir Institutional Effectiveness Ms. Laura MASSEY
19 Director Public Safety Mr. Ken GOODWIN
37 Director Financial Aid Mr. Bert LOGAN
22 Interim Dir Affirmative Action Ms. Claire OLIVEROS
30 Director of Development Ms. Kim KONO

Reed College (A)

3203 SE Woodstock Boulevard, Portland OR 97202-8199
County: Multnomah FICE Identification: 003217
Unit ID: 209922
Telephone: (503) 771-1112 Carnegie Class: Bac/A&S
FAX Number: (503) 777-7769 Calendar System: Semester
URL: www.reed.edu
Established: 1908 Annual Undergrad Tuition & Fees: $44,460
Enrollment: 1,474 Coed
Affiliation or Control: Independent Non-Profit IRS Status: 501(c)3
Highest Offering: Master's
Program: Liberal Arts And General
Accreditation: NW

01 President Mr. John KROGER
05 Dean of the Faculty Dr. Patrick G. MCDOUGAL
26 Vice President College Relations Dr. Hugh PORTER
10 Vice President & Treasurer Mr. Edwin O. MCFARLANE
32 Vice Pres/Dean Student Services Dr. Michael BRODY
04 Exec Asst to the President Ms. Dawn THOMPSON
28 Dean Institutional Diversity Ms. Crystal WILLIAMS
35 Assoc Dean of Stdnts for Acad Supp Ms. Lily COPENAGLE
39 Assoc Dean Student & Campus Life Mr. Bruce SMITH
23 Director Health & Counseling Ms. Kathryn SMITH
07 Dean of Admission Mr. Keith TODD
06 Registrar Ms. Nora MCLAUGHLIN
08 College Librarian Ms. Victoria L. HANAWALT
30 Director of Development Ms. Jan KURTZ
37 Director of Financial Aid Ms. Leslie LIMPER
09 Director of Institutional Research Mr. Mike TAMADA
26 Director of Public Affairs Ms. Jennifer BATES
29 Director of Alumni Relations Mr. Michael TESKEY
13 Chief Technology Officer Dr. Martin D. RINGLE
90 Director of Academic Computing Mr. Gary G. SCHLICKEISER
91 Director Administrative Computing Mr. Gary D. NORBRATEN
21 Controller Ms. Tracy L. FRANTEL
15 Director of Human Resources Ms. Connie HELLESON
44 Dir Annual Funds/Special Gifts Ms. Mary ASKELSON
102 Dir Corporate/Foundation Support Ms. Diane GUMZ
104 Director International Programs Dr. Paul DEYOUNG
36 Director of Career Services Mr. Ron ALBERTSON
88 Director of Special Programs Ms. Barbara A. AMEN
18 Director Facilities Operations Mr. Townsend ANGELL
19 Director Community Safety Mr. Gary GRANGER
68 Director of Physical Education Mr. Michael LOMBARDO
40 Manager of the Bookstore Mr. Ueli STADLER

Rogue Community College (B)

3345 Redwood Highway, Grants Pass OR 97527-9298
County: Josephine FICE Identification: 010182
Unit ID: 209940
Telephone: (541) 956-7500 Carnegie Class: Assoc/Pub-R-L
FAX Number: (541) 471-3591 Calendar System: Quarter
URL: www.roguecc.edu
Established: 1970 Annual Undergrad Tuition & Fees (In-District): $3,681
Enrollment: 8,188 Coed
Affiliation or Control: Local IRS Status: 501(c)3
Highest Offering: Associate Degree
Program: Occupational; 2-Year Principally Bachelor's Creditable
Accreditation: NW

01 President Dr. Peter ANGSTADT
05 VP of Instrution/CAO Mr. Kirk GIBSON
10 VP of College Services/CFO/AA Mr. Curtis SOMMERFELD
103 Dean School of Workforce/Col Prep Ms. Linda RENFRO
72 Dean School of Arts and Technology Ms. Rena B. DENHAM
76 Dean School of Health/Public Svcs Mr. John OSBOURN
88 Director SBDC Mr. Rick LEIBOWITZ
81 Dean School of Science and Tech Mr. Jacob JACKSON
13 Chief Infomation Office/CIO Mr. Curtis SOMMERFELD
08 Head Librarian Mr. Thomas MILLER
18 Facilities and Project Manager Mr. Pat HUEBSCH
32 VP of Student Services/CSSO Ms. Kori BIEBER
102 Executive Director Foundation Ms. Jennifer WHEATLEY
15 Director HR & Risk Management Ms. Jenny ROSSKNECHT
84 Director Enrollment Services Ms. Claudia SULLIVAN
24 Director Instructional Media Mr. Rich KIRK
21 Dir Budget & Financial Services/CFO Ms. Lisa STANTON
40 Director Auxiliary Services Ms. Pat GUNTER
26 Dir Marketing & Recruitment Ms. Margaret BRADFORD
37 Director Student Financial Aid Ms. Anna MANLEY
13 Director I/T Network & User Support Mr. Mike MCCLURE
105 Director Internet & Telecommunic Ms. Susie ASHBRIDGE
71 Director TRiO-EOC Mr. Jason FIANO
71 Director TRiO-SSS Ms. Colletta YOUNG
51 Apprenticeship Coordinator Ms. Cathy PIERSON
96 Contract and Procurment Manager Ms. Jodie FULTON
25 Grants and Planning Coordinator Ms. Mary O'KIEF
91 Coordinator of IT Programming Svcs Mr. Jeff MILLER
91 Applications Programmer/Analyst II Mr. Grant HUBLER

Southwestern Oregon Community College (C)

1988 Newmark Avenue, Coos Bay OR 97420-2911
County: Coos FICE Identification: 003220
Unit ID: 210155
Telephone: (541) 888-2525 Carnegie Class: Assoc/Pub-R-M
FAX Number: (541) 888-7285 Calendar System: Quarter
URL: www.socc.edu
Established: 1961 Annual Undergrad Tuition & Fees (In-District): $5,082
Enrollment: 4,092 Coed
Affiliation or Control: Local IRS Status: 501(c)3
Highest Offering: Associate Degree
Program: Occupational; 2-Year Principally Bachelor's Creditable
Accreditation: NW, ACFEI

01 President Dr. Patty SCOTT
11 VP Administrative Services Ms. Linda KRIDELBAUGH
05 VP Instructional Services Mr. Phill ANDERSON
12 Dean Curry County Ms. Janet PRETTI
32 Dean Student Services Mr. Tim DAILEY
84 Exec Director Enrollment Management Mr. Tom NICHOLLS
102 Exec Director Foundation Ms. Karen PRINGLE
13 Exec Director Integrated Technology Ms. Kat FLORES
88 Exec Director OCCI (Culinary) Mr. Shawn HANLIN
20 Associate Dean Learning Vacant
20 Associate Dean Learning Ms. Diana SCHAB
41 Director Athletics Mr. Mike HERBERT
07 Director of Admissions Mr. Tom NICHOLLS
19 Director Campus Safety Mr. Joe THOMAS
30 Director College Advancement Vacant
103 Director Community & Workforce Dev Ms. Karen HELLAND
18 Director Facilities Services Mr. David MCKINEY
29 Director of Alumni Relations Ms. Karen PRINGLE
06 Registrar Ms. Shawn LIGGETT
37 Director Financial Aid Ms. Avena SINGH
15 Exec Director Human Resources Ms. Rachele SUMMERVILLE
08 Director Learning Resources Vacant
66 Director Nursing Ms. Susan WALKER
39 Director Residence Life Mr. Jeff WHITEY
88 Director SOCC Business Dev Center Ms. Arlene SOTO
38 Director Student Support Srvcs Mr. Tim DAILEY
40 Manager Bookstore Ms. Dede CLEMENTS
09 Institutional Researcher Ms. Robin BUNNELL
35 Coordinator Student Life and Events Ms. Karina SMITH
04 Exec Asst to the Pres/Board of Educ Ms. Deb NICHOLLS

Tillamook Bay Community College (D)

4301 3rd Street, Tillamook OR 97141
County: Tillamook Identification: 666647
Unit ID: 420723
Telephone: (503) 842-8222 Carnegie Class: Assoc/Pub-R-S
FAX Number: (503) 842-8336 Calendar System: Semester
URL: www.tillamookbay.cc
Established: 1981 Annual Undergrad Tuition & Fees (In-District): $4,750
Enrollment: 550 Coed
Affiliation or Control: State/Local IRS Status: 501(c)3
Highest Offering: Associate Degree
Program: 2-Year Principally Bachelor's Creditable
Accreditation: @NW

01 President Dr. Constance C. GREEN
05 Chief Academic Officer Dr. Lori GATES
11 Dean of Administrative Services Mr. Ron ELLISON

Treasure Valley Community College (E)

650 College Boulevard, Ontario OR 97914-3423
County: Malheur FICE Identification: 003221
Unit ID: 210234
Telephone: (541) 881-8822 Carnegie Class: Assoc/Pub-R-M
FAX Number: (541) 881-2717 Calendar System: Quarter
URL: www.tvcc.cc
Established: 1961 Annual Undergrad Tuition & Fees (In-District): $4,725
Enrollment: 2,418 Coed
Affiliation or Control: Local IRS Status: 501(c)3
Highest Offering: Associate Degree
Program: Occupational; 2-Year Principally Bachelor's Creditable
Accreditation: NW

01 President Ms. Dana YOUNG
05 Interim Dean of Instruction Mr. John MICHAELSON
11 Dean of Administrative Services Mr. Randy R. GRIFFIN
08 Librarian Mr. Dennis GILL
32 Dean Student Services Dr. Paul KRAFT
37 Financial Aid Advisor Mr. Jonathan GILLEN
14 Director Data Processing Mr. Scott CARPENTER
07 Director of Admissions Ms. Stephanie OESTER
15 Director of Human Resources Vacant
51 Director of Continuing Education Ms. Andrea TESTI
18 Dir of Housing/Building & Grounds Mr. Bernie BABCOCK
10 Comptroller Mr. Jonathan GILLEN
35 Director of Student Activities Mr. Justin CORE
41 Athletic Director Mr. Ed ARONSON
88 Corrections Education Director Ms. Carol FITZGERALD
06 Registrar Ms. Debbie KRIEGH
09 Director of Institutional Research Vacant
28 Director of Diversity Dr. Paul KRAFT
30 Chief Development Ms. Cathy YASUDA
40 Bookstore Manager Mr. Kjetil ROM
38 Vocational Counselor Ms. Lori EYLER

Umpqua Community College (F)

PO Box 967, Roseburg OR 97470-0226
County: Douglas FICE Identification: 003222
Unit ID: 210270
Telephone: (541) 440-4600 Carnegie Class: Assoc/Pub-R-M
FAX Number: (541) 440-4637 Calendar System: Quarter
URL: www.umpqua.edu
Established: 1964 Annual Undergrad Tuition & Fees (In-District): $4,796
Enrollment: 4,234 Coed
Affiliation or Control: Local IRS Status: 501(c)3
Highest Offering: Associate Degree
Program: Occupational; 2-Year Principally Bachelor's Creditable
Accreditation: NW, ADNUR

01 President Dr. Joe OLSON
05 Vice President Instruction Services Dr. Roxanne KELLY
11 Vice President Administrative Svcs Dr. Lynn MOORE
32 Vice President Student Development Dr. Lynn MOORE
84 Director Enrollment Management Mr. David FARRINGTON
38 Director Counseling Services Ms. Mandie PRITCHARD
37 Director of Financial Aid Ms. Michelle BERGMANN
14 Director Instructional Technology Vacant
08 Director of Library Services Mr. David HUTCHISON
18 Director of Facilities Mr. Jess MILLER
31 Director of Community Education Ms. Robynne VAN WINKLE
09 Director Inst Research/Assess/Plng Mr. Dan YODER
15 Director Personnel Services Ms. Joanne HAYES
26 Chief Public Rel/Dir Community Rel Mr. Bentley GILBERT
96 Director of Purchasing Ms. Cathy VAUGHN

University of Portland (G)

5000 N Willamette Boulevard, Portland OR 97203-5798
County: Multnomah FICE Identification: 003224
Unit ID: 209825
Telephone: (503) 943-8000 Carnegie Class: Master's L
FAX Number: (503) 943-7491 Calendar System: Semester
URL: www.up.edu
Established: 1901 Annual Undergrad Tuition & Fees: $35,120
Enrollment: 3,973 Coed
Affiliation or Control: Independent Non-Profit IRS Status: 501(c)3
Highest Offering: Master's
Program: Liberal Arts And General; Teacher Preparatory; Professional
Accreditation: NW, BUS, CS, ENG, MUS, NURSE, SW, TED, THEA

01 President Rev. E. William BEAUCHAMP, CSC
05 Interim Provost Dr. Thomas G. GREENE
03 Executive Vice President Rev. Mark L. POORMAN, CSC
26 Vice Pres for University Relations Mr. James LYONS
11 Vice Pres for Univeristy Operations Mr. James B. RAVELLI
10 Vice Pres for Financial Affairs Mr. Alan P. TIMMINS
32 Vice President for Student Affairs Rev. Gerard J. OLINGER, CSC
100 Executive Asst to the Pres Ms. Danielle E. HERMANNY
35 Assoc VP for Student Development Rev. John J. DONATO, CSC
07 Dean of Admissions Mr. Jason MCDONALD
21 Controller Mr. Eric BARGER
06 Registrar Ms. Roberta LINDAHL
30 Assoc Vice President Development Mr. Bryce STRANG
36 Director Career Services Ms. Amy CAVANAUGH
15 Director for Human Resources Ms. Bryn SOPKO
37 Director Student Financial Aid Ms. Janet TURNER
27 Assoc VP of Univ Relations/CMO Ms. Laurie C. KELLEY
49 Interim Dean of Arts & Sciences Dr. Michael F. ANDREWS
50 Dean of the Business School Dr. Robin ANDERSON
66 Dean of Nursing Dr. Joanne WARNER
54 Dean of Engineering Dr. Sharon JONES
53 Dean of Education Dr. John WATZKE
23 Director University Health Services Dr. Paul MYERS
19 Director of Public Safety Mr. Gerald A. GREGG
29 Director Alumni Relations Ms. Carmen GASTON
39 Director Residence Life Mr. Michael WALSH
41 Athletic Director Mr. Scott LEYKAM
42 Director Campus Ministry Rev. Gary S. CHAMBERLAND, CSC
102 Director Foundation Development Ms. Kathy A. KENDALL-JOHNSTON
18 Director Facilities Planning Constr Mr. Paul J. LUTY
18 Director Physical Plant Mr. Andre HUTCHINSON
40 Director Bookstore Ms. Erin SCHUMACHER-BRIGHT
88 Director University Events Mr. William O. REED

09 Director of Institutional Research .... Ms. Karen NELSON
35 Director Student Activities .... Mr. Jeromy KOFFLER

† Granted candidacy at the Doctorate level.

University of Western States (A)

2900 NE 132nd Avenue, Portland OR 97230-3099
County: Multnomah FICE Identification: 012309
Unit ID: 210438
Telephone: (503) 256-3180 Carnegie Class: Spec/Health
FAX Number: (503) 251-5723 Calendar System: Quarter
URL: www.uws.edu
Established: 1904 Annual Undergrad Tuition & Fees: $8,935
Enrollment: 531 Coed
Affiliation or Control: Independent Non-Profit IRS Status: 501(c)3
Highest Offering: Doctorate
Program: Professional
Accreditation: NW, CHIRO

01 President .... Dr. Joseph BRIMHALL
10 Vice Pres Finance & Administration .... Mr. Eric BLUMENTHAL
05 Vice President Academic Affairs .... Dr. Gary SCHULTZ
84 VP Enrollment & Student Affairs .... Dr. Patrick BROWNE
23 Vice President of Clinics .... Dr. Joseph PFEIFER
46 Assoc Vice President of Research .... Dr. Mitch HAAS
13 Chief Information Officer .... Mr. Kris ROSENBERG
04 Assistant to the President .... Ms. Bonnie FLATT
27 Director of Communications .... Mr. Todd LOGGAN
15 Director Human Resources .... Ms. Carrie LOEWEN
37 Director Financial Aid .... Mr. Peter GROSS
06 Registrar .... Ms. Michelle DODGE
07 Assoc Director of Admissions .... Ms. Mary STAFFORD
08 University Librarian .... Ms. Janet TAPPER
18 Director Campus Facilities .... Mr. Todd BENSON

Warner Pacific College (B)

2219 SE 68th Avenue, Portland OR 97215
County: Multnomah FICE Identification: 003225
Unit ID: 210304
Telephone: (503) 517-1000 Carnegie Class: Bac/Diverse
FAX Number: (503) 517-1350 Calendar System: Semester
URL: www.warnerpacific.edu
Established: 1937 Annual Undergrad Tuition & Fees: $19,030
Enrollment: 1,679 Coed
Affiliation or Control: Church Of God IRS Status: 501(c)3
Highest Offering: Master's
Program: Liberal Arts And General; Teacher Preparatory
Accreditation: NW

01 President .... Dr. Andrea P. COOK
03 Executive Vice President .... Vacant
05 Vice Pres Acad Affs/Dean of Faculty .... Dr. Cole DAWSON
10 Vice Pres of Operations .... Mr. Steve STENBERG
30 Vice President for Inst Advancement .... Mr. Kevin BRYANT
32 Vice President for Community Life .... Dr. Daymond GLENN
20 Assoc VP for Acad Affairs/Dean ADP .... Vacant
84 VP for Enrollment and Marketing .... Mr. Dale SEIPP
37 Dir of Student Financial Services .... Mrs. Katrina SARTIN MANTANO
41 Director of Athletics .... Vacant
08 Director of Library Services .... Ms. Sue KOPP
06 Registrar .... Ms. Victoria CUMINGS
13 Director of Information Technology .... Ms. Linda RUDAWITZ
29 Dir of Alumni/Church Relations .... Mrs. Cindy POLLARD
27 Director of College Communications .... Vacant
42 Dir of Contextualized Ministries .... Mr. Jess BIELMAN
39 Dir of Res Life & Judicial Affairs .... Mr. Jared VALENTINE
18 Director of Plant Services .... Vacant
15 Dir of Human Resources/Prof Devel .... Mrs. Bev FITTS
09 Dir of Institutional Effectiveness .... Dr. Warren J. BEAMAN
40 Director Bookstore .... Mrs. Mimi FONSECA
26 Marketing/College Relations .... Ms. Shirell HENNESSY
38 Director Student Counseling .... Dr. Denise LOPEZ HAUGEN
21 Associate Business Officer .... Mr. Nathan DUNBAR
35 Dir Leadership Dev and Stdnt Pgm .... Vacant
36 Director of Academic Success .... Mr. Rod JOHANSON
28 Urban Recruitment Coordinator .... Mr. James BROADOUS

Western Seminary (C)

5511 SE Hawthorne Boulevard, Portland OR 97215-3399
County: Multnomah FICE Identification: 007178
Unit ID: 210368
Telephone: (503) 517-1800 Carnegie Class: Spec/Faith
FAX Number: (503) 517-1801 Calendar System: Semester
URL: www.westernseminary.edu
Established: 1927 Annual Graduate Tuition & Fees: $11,280
Enrollment: 732 Coed
Affiliation or Control: Independent Non-Profit IRS Status: 501(c)3
Highest Offering: Doctorate; No Undergraduates
Program: Professional; Religious Emphasis
Accreditation: NW, THEOL

01 President .... Dr. Randal R. ROBERTS
05 Academic Dean .... Dr. Marc CORTEZ
30 Vice President for Advancement .... Mr. Greg MOON
20 Associate Academic Dean .... Vacant
06 Dean Student Devel/Registrar .... Dr. Robert W. WIGGINS
10 Controller/Business/Finance .... Ms. Patricia A. PRICHARD
32 Dean of Students .... Dr. Ken EPP
36 Director of Student Placement .... Dr. Larry MCCRACKEN
13 Director of Information Services .... Mrs. Valerie MAINRIDGE
37 Financial Aid Director .... Ms. Shelle RIEHL
56 Asst Director of Distance Education .... Mr. Jon RAIBLEY
21 Associate Business Officer .... Mrs. Christina BOTTIGLIA
15 Human Resources Dir/Dir Communic .... Miss Julia SEAL
08 Library Director .... Dr. Robert A. KRUPP
84 Director Enrollment Services/Mktg .... Mr. P.J OSWALD
29 Director Alumni Relations .... Dr. Larry MCCRACKEN
18 Chief Facilities/Physical Plant .... Mr. Cliff STEIN
106 Director of Distance Education .... Mr. James STEWART

Willamette University (D)

900 State Street, Salem OR 97301-3930
County: Marion FICE Identification: 003227
Unit ID: 210401
Telephone: (503) 370-6300 Carnegie Class: Bac/A&S
FAX Number: (503) 370-6148 Calendar System: Semester
URL: www.willamette.edu
Established: 1842 Annual Undergrad Tuition & Fees: $40,560
Enrollment: 2,815 Coed
Affiliation or Control: Independent Non-Profit IRS Status: 501(c)3
Highest Offering: Doctorate
Program: Liberal Arts And General; Teacher Preparatory; Professional
Accreditation: NW, BUS, LAW, MUS, SPAA, TED

01 President .... Dr. Stephen THORSETT
10 Vice President Financial Affs .... Mr. W. Arnold YASINSKI
30 Interim Vice President Development .... Ms. Denise CALLAHAN
07 Vice President Enrollment .... Mr. James SUMNER
13 Vice President Integrated Tech .... Dr. John D. BALLING
11 Vice President Administrative Svcs .... Mr. James R. BAUER
04 Exec/Admin Assistant to President .... Ms. Kristen GRAINGER
32 Dean of Campus Life .... Dr. David A. DOUGLASS
49 Dean of Liberal Arts .... Dr. Marlene MOORE
61 Dean of Law .... Mr. Peter LETSOU
50 Dean Graduate School Management .... Ms. Debra RINGOLD
42 Chaplain .... Dr. Charles I. WALLACE, JR.
23 Director of Bishop Wellness Center .... Ms. Margaret TROUT
88 Director Center Dispute Resolution .... Dr. Richard BIRKE
91 Director Administrative Computing .. Mr. Harvey J. PRUDHOMME
37 Director Student Financial Aid .... Ms. Patricia K. HOBAN
09 Director of Institutional Research .... Dr. Michael J. MOON
06 University Registrar .... Ms. Patricia K. HOBAN
08 University Librarian .... Ms. Deborah B. DANCIK
21 Controller .... Mr. Robert N. OLSON
40 Bookstore Director .... Mr. Donald C. BECKMAN
104 Director of International Education .... Mr. Kris LOU
41 Interim Athletic Director .... Mr. Dave RIGSBY
29 Senior Director Alumni Relations .... Vacant
44 Director of Planned Giving .... Mr. Stephen F. BRIER
15 Director of Human Resources .... Mr. Keith GRIMM
35 Director of Student Activities .... Ms. Lisa C. HOLLIDAY
36 Director Career Services .... Dr. Gerald B. HOUSER
28 Director of Multicultural Affairs .... Mr. Gordon K. TOYAMA
18 Manager Operations/Energy .... Mr. Gary GRIMM
96 Purchasing Coordinator .... Mr. Micheal K. SERAPHIN
26 Int Director Marketing Communic .... Mr. Adam TORGERSON

PENNSYLVANIA

Albright College (E)

13th & Bern Streets, PO Box 15234,
Reading PA 19612-5234
County: Berks FICE Identification: 003229
Unit ID: 210571
Telephone: (610) 921-2381 Carnegie Class: Bac/A&S
FAX Number: (610) 921-7530 Calendar System: 4/1/4
URL: www.albright.edu
Established: 1856 Annual Undergrad Tuition & Fees: $35,320
Enrollment: 2,391 Coed
Affiliation or Control: United Methodist IRS Status: 501(c)3
Highest Offering: Master's
Program: Liberal Arts And General; Teacher Preparatory; Professional
Accreditation: M

01 President .... Dr. Lex O. MCMILLAN, III
05 Provost/Vice Pres Academic Affairs . Dr. Andrea E. CHAPDELAINE
10 Vice President Finance & Admin .... Mr. William W. WOOD
30 Vice President Advancement .... Dr. Timothy A. MCELWEE
84 VP Enrollment Mgt/Dean Admission ... Mr. Gregory E. EICHHORN
32 VP Student Affairs/Dean of Students .... Dr. Gina-Lyn CRANCE
26 Assoc VP College Relations/Mktg .... Mr. Thomas W. DURSO
13 Chief Technology Officer .... Ms. Dana B. GERMAN
04 Executive Assistant to President .... Mrs. Kathy L. CAFONCELLI
20 Dean of Undergraduate Studies .... Dr. Joseph M. THOMAS
08 Library Director .... Ms. Rosemary L. DEEGAN
44 Assoc VP for Development .... Mr. John SHORT
14 Director of Core Technologies .... Mr. Hoerr U. JASON
91 Dir of Enterprise Applications .... Ms. Gena HOWARD
21 Controller .... Mr. Rick W. MELCHER
37 Director of Financial Aid .... Mr. Christopher HANLON
58 Dean of Graduate & Professional Div ...... Dr. Joseph YARWORTH
35 Assistant Dean of Students .... Ms. Amanda HANINCIK
06 Registrar .... Mr. David C. BALLABAN
36 Director Career Development Center .... Ms. Karen V. EVANS
39 Int Director of Residential Life .... Ms. Rebecca PEAL MORROW
38 Director of Counseling Center .... Dr. Brenda J. INGRAM-WALLACE
29 Dir of Alumni Relations .... Mrs. Megan BERMUDEZ
18 Director Facilities/Operations/Svcs .... Mr. Kevin GAFFNEY
41 Co-Athletic Director .... Mr. Richard E. FERRY
41 Co-Athletic Director .... Ms. Janice J. LUCK
19 Director of Safety & Security .... Mr. Thomas MCDANIEL
40 Book Store Manager .... Ms. Coreen MCCAFFERTY
23 Director of Gable Health Center .... Ms. Samantha WESNER
42 Chaplain .... Rev. Paul E. CLARK
22 Affirmative Action Coord/Dir HR .... Mr. Timothy J. STEINROCK
85 Asst Dir Multi-Ethnic Student Affs .... Ms. Tiffany CLAYTON
88 Int Dir of Accelerated Degree Pgm .... Mr. Kevin EZZELL
09 Director of Institutional Research .... Mr. Jack LAFAYETTE
35 Director of Student Activities .... Mr. Bradley A. SMITH
25 Director of Grants .... Ms. Darlene ROTH
92 Director Honors Program .... Dr. Julia F. HEBERLE
07 Director of Admission .... Mr. Christopher H. BOEHM
107 Dean of Adult & Prof Studies .... Dr. Andra M. BASU
88 Director of Conferences .... Ms. Lois A. KUBINAK

Allegheny College (F)

520 N Main, Meadville PA 16335-3902
County: Crawford FICE Identification: 003230
Unit ID: 210669
Telephone: (814) 332-3100 Carnegie Class: Bac/A&S
FAX Number: (814) 724-6032 Calendar System: Semester
URL: www.allegheny.edu
Established: 1815 Annual Undergrad Tuition & Fees: $37,260
Enrollment: 2,123 Coed
Affiliation or Control: Independent Non-Profit IRS Status: 501(c)3
Highest Offering: Baccalaureate
Program: Liberal Arts And General
Accreditation: M

01 President .... Dr. James H. MULLEN
03 Exec Vice President & Treasurer .... Dr. David W. MCINALLY
30 Vice Pres Devel & Alumni Affairs .... Ms. Marjorie S. KLEIN
84 Vice Pres Enrollment/Communication .... Dr. Brian F. DALTON
04 Assistant to the President .... Ms. Pamela S. HIGHAM
28 Chief Diversity Ofce/Asc Dn of Col .... Vacant
21 Senior Associate Vice President .... Mr. Larry K. LEE
45 Assoc Vice Pres for Advancement .... Mr. Bruce WHITEHAIR
05 Provost & Dean of the College .... Dr. Linda C. DEMERITT
32 Dean of Students .... Mr. Joseph J. DICHRISTINA
20 Associate Dean of the College .... Dr. Terry BENSEL
37 Assoc Dean Enrollment/Financial Aid .... Ms. Sheryle A. PROPER
88 Ex Dir Learning Info/Tech Svcs .... Dr. Richard A. HOLMGREN
06 Registrar .... Dr. Ann D. SHEFFIELD
08 Library Director .... Ms. Linda G. BILLS
15 Director of Human Resources .... Ms. Patricia A. FERREY
19 Director Campus Safety & Security ...... Dr. Jeffrey A. SCHNEIDER
44 Director of Annual Giving .... Ms. Melena MEARS
18 Director Physical Plant .... Mr. Cliff K. WILLIS
91 Director Administrative Computing .... Mr. Richard A. METZGER
29 AVP Development & Alumni Affairs .... Mr. Philip R. FOXMAN
41 Director of Athletics .... Ms. Portia HOEG
31 Director Community Service .... Dr. David RONCOLATO
14 Dir Tech Computer & Networking Svcs .... Mr. Tim W. HUNTER
100 Chief of Staff .... Ms. Gillian F. FORD
38 Director of Counseling Center ...... Ms. Yvonne M. EATON-STULL
102 Director of Found/Corporate Rels .... Dr. Ann H. ARESON
28 Director of Diversity Affairs .... Vacant
09 Director of Institutional Research .... Ms. Marian D. SHERWOOD
36 Director Career Services .... Ms. Michaeline M. SHUMAN
35 Director Student Involvement .... Ms. Gretchen A. SYMONS
21 Associate Vice President of Finance .... Ms. Linda S. WETSELL
42 Chaplain .... Dr. Jane Ellen NICKELL
88 Dir Center Political Participation .... Dr. Brian HARWARD
88 Assoc Director Learning Commons .... Mr. John J. MAGINNIE
84 Assoc Dir Enrollment/Communication .... Ms. Penny M. FRANK
40 Manager of Bookstore .... Mr. Peter M. LEBAR
96 Purchasing Coordinator .... Ms. Kathleen M. CONAWAY

Alvernia University (G)

400 Saint Bernardine Street, Reading PA 19607-1799
County: Berks FICE Identification: 003233
Unit ID: 210775
Telephone: (610) 796-8200 Carnegie Class: Master's M
FAX Number: (610) 777-6632 Calendar System: Semester
URL: www.alvernia.edu
Established: 1958 Annual Undergrad Tuition & Fees: $26,830
Enrollment: 3,011 Coed
Affiliation or Control: Roman Catholic IRS Status: 501(c)3
Highest Offering: Doctorate
Program: Liberal Arts And General; Teacher Preparatory; Professional
Accreditation: M, ACBSP, NURSE, OT, SW

01 President .... Dr. Thomas F. FLYNN
05 Provost .... Dr. Shirley J. WILLIAMS
10 VP for Finance & Administration .... Mr. Douglas F. SMITH
30 Vice Pres for Advancement .... Mr. J. Michael PRESSIMONE
32 Vice Pres Univ Life/Dean of Stdnts .. Dr. Joseph J. CICALA, RSM
84 Vice Pres for Enrollment Management .... Mr. John R. MCCLOSKEY, JR.
42 Asst to the President For Mission .... Sr. Roberta MCKELVIE, OSF
26 VP Mktg & Comms/Chief PR Ofcr .... Mr. Brad DREXLER
35 Dean of Students .... Vacant
35 Director of Student Activities .... Ms. Abby SWATCHICK
39 Director Residence Life .... Ms. Karolina DREHER
06 Registrar .... Ms. Beki STEIN
21 Controller .... Ms. Jada D. CAMPBELL

29 Director Alumni Donor Relations ... Thomas MINICK
08 Grad Program Librarian/Archivist ... Vacant
92 Director Honors Program ... Vacant
41 Director Athletics & Recreation ... Bill STILES
07 Director of Admissions ... Ms. Stacy ADAMSPERRY
09 Director of Institutional Research ... Dr. Evelina PANAYOTOVA
15 Director Human Resources ... Ms. Laurel CLINE
18 Chief Facilities/Physical Plant ... Mr. David REPPERT
26 Chief Public Relations Officer ... Mr. Brad DREXLER
36 Director of Career Services ... Ms. Jennifer GITTINGS-DALTON
37 Int Dir Student Financial Planning ... Ms. Christine SAADL
96 Director of Purchasing ... Ms. Cynthia URICK
28 Director of Diversity ... Ms. Mary LOZADA
21 Associate Business Officer ... Ms. Gwynne KOLODZIEJSKI
31 Dir Ctr for Community Engagement ... Mr. Jay WORRALL
58 Dean of Graduate & Cont Studies ... Ms. Daria LATORRE
49 Dean of Arts & Sciences ... Dr. Beth ARACENA
76 Dean Professional Programs ... Ms. Karen S. THACKER

The American College (A)

270 S Bryn Mawr Avenue, Bryn Mawr PA 19010-2196
County: Delaware FICE Identification: 033173
Unit ID: 210809
Telephone: (610) 526-1000 Carnegie Class: Spec/Bus
FAX Number: (610) 526-1310 Calendar System: Quarter
URL: www.theamericancollege.edu
Established: 1927 Annual Graduate Tuition & Fees: $5,040
Enrollment: 533 Coed
Affiliation or Control: Independent Non-Profit IRS Status: 501(c)3
Highest Offering: Doctorate; No Undergraduates
Program: Professional
Accreditation: M

01 President & CEO ... Dr. Laurence BARTON
03 Senior Vice President ... Mr. Steven TARR
05 Vice Pres Academic Affairs & Dean ... Dr. Walter J. WOERHEIDE
30 Sr Vice President Advancement ... Mr. Charles CRONIN
11 Chief Operating Officer ... Mr. Neal R. FEGELY
26 Chief Marketing Officer ... Mr. Jack HONDROS
13 Chief Technology Officer ... Mr. Ed M. MCEVOY
107 Vice Pres Professional Education ... Mr. Russell J. FIGUEIRA
15 Vice Pres Human Resources ... Ms. Amy DEWEY
04 Admin Assistant to the President ... Ms. Mary C. VARNER
06 Registrar ... Ms. Antoinette CHRISTALDI
08 Librarian/Mgr Knowledge Center ... Ms. Virginia E. WEBB
88 Managing Director Exam Systems ... Ms. Diane M. HAMMONDS

Antonelli Institute of Art and Photography (B)

300 Montgomery Avenue, Erdenheim PA 19038-8242
County: Montgomery FICE Identification: 007430
Unit ID: 210890
Telephone: (215) 836-2222 Carnegie Class: Assoc/PrivFP
FAX Number: (215) 836-2794 Calendar System: Semester
URL: www.antonelli.edu
Established: 1938 Annual Undergrad Tuition & Fees: $19,730
Enrollment: 183 Coed
Affiliation or Control: Proprietary IRS Status: Proprietary
Highest Offering: Associate Degree
Program: Occupational
Accreditation: ACCSC

01 President ... Dr. John D. HAYDEN
05 Director of Education/Student Svcs ... Ms. Trish FLEMING
37 Financial Aid Officer ... Ms. Stephanie SHOWALTER

Arcadia University (C)

450 S Easton Road, Glenside PA 19038-3295
County: Montgomery FICE Identification: 003235
Unit ID: 211088
Telephone: (215) 572-2900 Carnegie Class: Master's L
FAX Number: (215) 572-0240 Calendar System: Semester
URL: www.arcadia.edu
Established: 1853 Annual Undergrad Tuition & Fees: $35,620
Enrollment: 3,932 Coed
Affiliation or Control: Independent Non-Profit IRS Status: 501(c)3
Highest Offering: Doctorate
Program: Liberal Arts And General; Teacher Preparatory; Professional
Accreditation: M, ACBSP, ARCPA, ART, PTA

01 President ... Mr. Carl OXHOLM, III
05 Provost & VP Academic Affairs ... Dr. Steve O. MICHAEL
104 VP The College of Global Studies ... Dr. Nicolette D. CHRISTENSEN
30 VP Development ... Dr. Janet E. WALBERT
84 VP Enrollment Management ... Mr. Mark LAPREZIOSA
10 VP Finance & Treasurer ... Mr. Michael J. COVENEY
27 VP Global Info Svcs & CIO ... Mr. Steven ALTER
43 VP Legal Affairs & Univ Counsel ... Ms. Valerie HARRISON
30 VP University Advancement ... Vacant
32 Assoc VP Student Affairs/Dean ... Mr. Joshua STERN
07 Assoc VP Enrollment Management ... Vacant
18 Assoc VP Facilities/Capital Plng ... Mr. Thomas J. MACCHI
21 Assoc VP Finance & COO TCGS ... Ms. Colleen BURKE
88 Assoc VP & Dir Strategic Dev TCGS ... Ms. Lorna STERN LANIAK
26 Chief Mktg & Communications Officer ... Ms. Lori BAUER
15 Asst VP Human Resources/AAO ... Ms. Lynette ALLEN-PERRY
44 Asst VP University Advancement ... Ms. Diana FRAZIER
21 Controller ... Ms. Julie A. ROSNER-LENGELE
06 Registrar ... Mr. William ELNICK
06 Associate Registrar ... Mrs. Nicole M. ZUCKER
49 Dean College of Arts and Sciences ... Dr. Barbara F. NODINE
88 Academic Dean TCGS ... Dr. Dennis DUTSCHKE
76 Dean College of Health Sciences ... Dr. Archie J. VOMACHKA
51 Dean School of Continuing Studies ... Dr. Erik NELSON
50 Dean School of Global Business ... Dr. N.J DELENER
58 Dean Graduate & Undergraduate Pgms ... Ms. Nancy ROSOFF
88 Dean International Affairs ... Dr. Warren HAFFAR
108 Asst Provost Planning Assessment ... Dr. Mark P. CURCHACK
28 Assoc Dean Institutional Diversity ... Ms. Judith DALTON
35 Assoc Dean of Students ... Ms. Dian TAYLOR-ALLEYNE
20 Assoc Dean Undergraduate Studies ... Mr. Bruce KELLER
88 Asst Dean Graduate Studies ... Ms. Mary Kate MCNULTY
37 Exec Dir Financial Aid Systems ... Ms. Elizabeth RIHL-LEWINSKY
08 Exec Dir Program Excellence ... Mr. Eric MCCLOY
88 Director Administrative Services ... Ms. Mimi BASSETTI
29 Director Alumni Relations ... Mr. Kevin BROWN
44 Director Annual Fund ... Ms. Judith MCNAMARA
88 Director Art Gallery ... Mr. Richard TORCHIA
41 Director Athletics & Recreation ... Mr. Brian GRANATA
88 Director Campus Visits and EM ... Ms. Kathleen BEARDSLEY
36 Interim Director Career Education ... Ms. Stephenie F. WILSON
38 Director Counseling Services ... Ms. Cynthia RUTHERFORD
88 Director EM & Financial Aid ... Ms. Holly R. KIRKPATRICK
91 Director Enterprise Applications ... Mr. Scott GRABUS
25 Director Grant Writing ... Ms. Maryanne D. BOWERS
09 Director Institutional Research ... Mr. Will PADDOCK
88 Director Lib Svcs & Instr Tech ... Ms. Jeanne BUCKLEY
88 Dir Network & Info Security Systems ... Mr. Marc ROCQUE
96 Payroll and Purchasing Manager ... Ms. Sharon ANTHONY
19 Director of Public Safety ... Mr. James BONNER
39 Director Residence & Commuter Life . Ms. Catherine MATTINGLY
25 Director Sponsored Research Pgms ... Vacant
60 Director Communications ... Dr. Shekhar DESHPANDE
79 Director MA in English/Humanities ... Dr. Richard A. WERTIME
69 Director Public Health/Health Educ ... Dr. Andrea COVELLI-KOVACH
88 Director EdD in Special Educ ... Dr. Christina AGER
88 Director Theater Arts ... Mr. Mark WADE

Art Institute of Philadelphia (D)

1622 Chestnut Street, Philadelphia PA 19103-5198
County: Philadelphia FICE Identification: 008350
Unit ID: 210942
Telephone: (215) 567-7080 Carnegie Class: Spec/Arts
FAX Number: (215) 405-6398 Calendar System: Quarter
URL: www.aiph.aii.edu
Established: 1966 Annual Undergrad Tuition & Fees: $22,275
Enrollment: 3,556 Coed
Affiliation or Control: Proprietary IRS Status: Proprietary
Highest Offering: Baccalaureate
Program: Occupational
Accreditation: M, ACICS, ACFEI, CIDA

01 President ... Mr. Michael DEPRISCO
05 Dean of Academic Affairs ... Dr. Raymond BECKER
10 Director Admin & Financial Services ... Mr. James MORETTI
07 Director of Admissions ... Mr. Steven COHEN
36 Director of Career Services ... Ms. Emily AMBROSE
04 Exec Assistant to the President ... Vacant
09 Dir of Institutional Effectiveness ... Ms. Heather RAMSEY
20 Assoc Dean of Academic Affairs ... Mr. Harry COSTIGAN
32 Dean of Students ... Ms. Ashley FORSYTH
37 Director Student Financial Services ... Ms. Fatisha STRICKLAND
06 Registrar ... Ms. Adriane MEDFORD
08 Library Director ... Ms. Ruth SCHACHTER
38 Counselor ... Ms. Eileen MCMULLEN
40 Manager-Supply Store ... Ms. Sharon MASULLO
85 Regional Internatl Student Advisor ... Vacant

Art Institute of Pittsburgh (E)

420 Boulevard of the Allies, Pittsburgh PA 15219-1301
County: Allegheny FICE Identification: 007470
Unit ID: 210960
Telephone: (412) 263-6600 Carnegie Class: Spec/Arts
FAX Number: (412) 263-3715 Calendar System: Quarter
URL: www.artinstitutes.edu/pittsburgh
Established: 1921 Annual Undergrad Tuition & Fees: $21,915
Enrollment: 14,725 Coed
Affiliation or Control: Proprietary IRS Status: Proprietary
Highest Offering: Baccalaureate
Program: Occupational
Accreditation: M, ACFEI, CIDA

01 President ... Mr. George W. SEBOLT
10 Vice Pres/Dir Admin/Financial Svcs ... Vacant
05 VP/Dean Academic Affairs ... Mr. Daniel GARLAND
32 Vice Pres/Director Student Affairs ... Ms. Nadine W. JOSEPHS
36 VP/Director Career Services ... Vacant
07 Director of Admissions ... Mr. Lee COLKER
37 Director Student Financial Aid ... Ms. Gayle J. KNIGHT
15 Director Human Resources ... Ms. Jacquie DEMIANCZYK
97 Director General Education ... Ms. Maria BOADA
88 Dir Graphic/Dig Design/Web Design ... Ms. Tamara PAVLOCK
72 Director of Technology ... Mr. George ALBERT
88 Dir Indust Dsgn Tech/Entertnmt Dsgn ... Mr. Greg L. BUTLER
88 Dir Media Animation/Game Design ... Mr. Hans WESTMAN
88 Director of Photography ... Mr. Andrew ENGLISH
88 Dir Interior Design/Residential Pln ... Ms. Kelly J K. SPEWOCK
06 Registrar ... Ms. Diane E. CARNEY
84 Enrollment Management Supervisor ... Ms. Lara SEBOLT
88 Director Culinary ... Mr. Michael ZAPPONE
88 Dir Fashion/Retail Mktng/Fashn Dsgn ... Ms. Stephanie TAYLOR
88 Dir Video Production/Visual Effects ... Mr. Andres TAPIA URZUA
88 College Affiliate/HS Articulation ... Ms. Karen SOLTIS

The Art Institute of York - Pennsylvania (F)

1409 Williams Road, York PA 17402-9012
County: York FICE Identification: 025578
Unit ID: 210906
Telephone: (717) 755-2300 Carnegie Class: Assoc/PrivFP
FAX Number: (717) 757-5552 Calendar System: Other
URL: www.artinstitutes.edu/york
Established: 1952 Annual Undergrad Tuition & Fees: $24,862
Enrollment: 582 Coed
Affiliation or Control: Proprietary IRS Status: Proprietary
Highest Offering: Baccalaureate
Program: Liberal Arts And General; Professional
Accreditation: ACICS

01 President ... Mr. Tim HOWARD
05 Dean of Academic Affairs ... Ms. Marla PRICE
07 Senior Director of Admissions ... Mr. Scott VUKODER
32 Director of Student Affairs ... Ms. Laura RYDER

Baptist Bible College and Seminary (G)

538 Venard Road, Clarks Summit PA 18411-1297
County: Lackawanna FICE Identification: 002670
Unit ID: 211024
Telephone: (570) 586-2400 Carnegie Class: Spec/Faith
FAX Number: (570) 586-1753 Calendar System: Semester
URL: www.bbc.edu
Established: 1932 Annual Undergrad Tuition & Fees: $19,030
Enrollment: 1,053 Coed
Affiliation or Control: Baptist IRS Status: 501(c)3
Highest Offering: Doctorate
Program: Teacher Preparatory; Religious Emphasis
Accreditation: M, BI

01 President ... Mr. James E. JEFFERY
05 Vice President & Provost ... Dr. James R. LYTLE
10 Vice President Business/Finance ... Mr. Hal G. CROSS
30 Vice Pres Inst Advancement ... Mr. Don PATTEN
84 Vice Pres Enrollment/External Rels ... Mr. Mel WALKER
20 Seminary Dean ... Dr. Michael STALLARD
32 Dean of Students ... Mr. Matthew POLLOCK
33 Associate Dean of Men ... Mr. Ted BOYKIN
34 Assoc Dean/Dir Women Ministries ... Mrs. Carol S. KING
04 President's Assistant ... Mrs. Kathy M. COMPTON
06 Registrar ... Mr. Allen R. DREYER
08 Librarian ... Mr. Joshua B. MICHAEL
09 Director of Institutional Research ... Dr. Barry C. SMITH
37 Director of Financial Aid ... Mr. Steve BROWN
26 Exec Dir Communications/Marketing ... Mr. Ken KNELLY
19 Director Safety/Security ... Mr. Tom MORRIS
84 Director of Enrollment ... Mr. Sean MCPHERSON
18 Chief Facilities/Physical Plant ... Mr. Wayne STEVENS
13 Manager of Information/Technology ... Mr. Timothy COREY
73 Dean School of Bible and Theology ... Dr. David A. LACKEY
53 Dean of School of Education ... Dr. Ritch KELLEY
49 Dean of School of Arts & Sciences ... Dr. Steve A. SHUMAKER
88 Dean of School of Global Ministries ... Dr. Dennis WILHITE
15 Director Personnel Services ... Mr. Manning BROWN
29 Coordinator Alumni Relations ... Ms. Michelle HAMMAKER
36 Director Student Placement ... Mr. Roddy HANNAH

Berks Technical Institute (H)

2205 Ridgewood Road, Wyomissing PA 19610-1168
County: Berks FICE Identification: 022539
Unit ID: 213534
Telephone: (610) 372-1722 Carnegie Class: Assoc/PrivFP
FAX Number: (610) 376-4684 Calendar System: Other
URL: www.berks.edu
Established: 1974 Annual Undergrad Tuition & Fees: $14,400
Enrollment: 997 Coed
Affiliation or Control: Proprietary IRS Status: Proprietary
Highest Offering: Associate Degree
Program: Occupational; Technical Emphasis
Accreditation: ACCSC, MAC

01 President ... Mr. Joseph F. REICHARD
05 Dean ... Ms. Cheryl GARMAN

Biblical Theological Seminary (I)

200 N Main Street, Hatfield PA 19440-2499
County: Montgomery FICE Identification: 023230
Unit ID: 211130
Telephone: (215) 368-5000 Carnegie Class: Spec/Faith
FAX Number: (215) 368-2301 Calendar System: Semester
URL: www.biblical.edu
Established: 1971 Annual Graduate Tuition & Fees: $13,700
Enrollment: 319 Coed
Affiliation or Control: Independent Non-Profit IRS Status: 501(c)3
Highest Offering: Doctorate; No Undergraduates

Program: Professional; Religious Emphasis
Accreditation: M, THEOL

01 President ....Dr. David G. DUNBAR
32 VP for Student Advancement ....Mrs. Pamela J. SMITH
05 Academic Dean ....Dr. R. Todd MANGUM
10 Controller ....Mr. Wayne A. DAVIDSON
20 Director of Academic Services ....Mr. Eric T. HOUSEKNECHT
08 Director of Library Services ....Mr. Daniel N. LAVALLA
13 Director of Information Technology ....Mr. Kelly PFLEIGER
18 Director of Physical Plant ....Mr. Anthony W. PLETSCHER
88 Associate Director of DMin Program ....Dr. Larry ANDERSON
88 Associate Director of DMin Program ....Dr. Derek COOPER
30 Director of Development ....Mr. William G. MEINEL

Bidwell Training Center (A)

1815 Metropolitan Street, Pittsburgh PA 15233-2200
County: Allegheny FICE Identification: 031015
Unit ID: 211149
Telephone: (412) 323-4000 Carnegie Class: Assoc/PrivNFP
FAX Number: (412) 325-7378 Calendar System: Semester
URL: www.bidwell-training.org
Established: 1968 Annual Undergrad Tuition & Fees: $8,200
Enrollment: 181 Coed
Affiliation or Control: Independent Non-Profit IRS Status: 501(c)3
Highest Offering: Associate Degree
Program: Occupational
Accreditation: ACCSC

01 Exec Director/Sr Vice President ....Ms. Valerie NJIE
07 Director of Admissions ....Mr. Ken HUSELTON

Bradford School (B)

125 W Station Square Dr, Ste 129,
Pittsburgh PA 15219-2602
County: Allegheny FICE Identification: 009721
Unit ID: 211200
Telephone: (412) 391-6710 Carnegie Class: Assoc/PrivFP
FAX Number: (412) 471-6714 Calendar System: Semester
URL: www.bradfordpittsburgh.edu
Established: 1968 Annual Undergrad Tuition & Fees: $14,820
Enrollment: 441 Coed
Affiliation or Control: Proprietary IRS Status: Proprietary
Highest Offering: Associate Degree
Program: Occupational
Accreditation: ACICS, DA, MAC, @PTAA

01 President ....Mr. Vincent S. GRAZIANO

Bryn Athyn College of the New Church (C)

PO Box 717, Bryn Athyn PA 19009-0717
County: Montgomery FICE Identification: 003228
Unit ID: 210492
Telephone: (267) 502-2400 Carnegie Class: Bac/A&S
FAX Number: (215) 938-2658 Calendar System: Trimester
URL: www.brynathyn.edu
Established: 1876 Annual Undergrad Tuition & Fees: $16,878
Enrollment: 230 Coed
Affiliation or Control: Church of New Jerusalem IRS Status: 501(c)3
Highest Offering: Master's
Program: Liberal Arts And General; Teacher Preparatory; Professional
Accreditation: M

01 President ....Dr. Kristin KING
10 Chief Finance Officer ....Mr. Daniel T. ALLEN
03 Dean ....Dr. Charles W. LINDSAY
73 Dean of Theological School ....Rev. Andrew M T. DIBB
05 Dean of Academic Affairs ....Dr. Allen BEDFORD
32 Dean of Student Affairs ....Ms. Kiri ROGERS
84 Dir Admission/Enrollment Management ....Mr. Allen LINNELL
08 Director of Swedenborg Library ....Mrs. Carroll C. ODHNER
41 Director of Athletics ....Mr. Matthew KENNEDY
13 Director of Information Technology ....Ms. Lelia HOWARD
15 Director of Human Resources ....Ms. T. Muriel ALLEN
19 Director of Security & Safety ....Mr. R. Scott COOPER
42 Chaplain ....Rev. Thane GLENN

Bryn Mawr College (D)

101 N Merion Avenue, Bryn Mawr PA 19010-2899
County: Montgomery FICE Identification: 003237
Unit ID: 211273
Telephone: (610) 526-5000 Carnegie Class: Bac/A&S
FAX Number: (610) 526-7450 Calendar System: Semester
URL: www.brynmawr.edu
Established: 1885 Annual Undergrad Tuition & Fees: $41,956
Enrollment: 1,785 Female
Affiliation or Control: Independent Non-Profit IRS Status: 501(c)3
Highest Offering: Doctorate
Program: Liberal Arts And General
Accreditation: M, SW

01 President ....Jane D. MCAULIFFE
05 Provost ....Kimberly E. CASSIDY
49 Dean of Undergraduate College ....Michele A. RASMUSSEN
11 Chief Administrative Officer ....Jerry A. BERENSON
10 Chief Financial Officer & Treasurer ....John GRIFFITH
30 Chief Development Officer ....Ms. Donna FRITHSEN
07 Chief Enrollmnt/Communications Ofcr ....Jennifer J. RICKARD
08 Director Libraries/Chief Info Ofcr ....Elliott SHORE
58 Dean of Graduate Studies ....Mary OSIRIM
28 Asst Dean/Dir Intercultural Affairs ....Vanessa CHRISTMAN
06 Registrar ....Kirsten O'BEIRNE
37 Director of Financial Aid ....Ethel M. DESMARAIS
19 Director of Public Safety ....Tom KING
29 Exec Director Alumnae Association ....Wendy M. GREENFIELD
68 Director of Athletics & Physical Ed ....Kathleen TIERNEY
21 Controller ....Ms. Betsy STEWART
09 Director of Institutional Research ....Mark A. FREEMAN
18 Chief Facilities/Physical Plant ....Glenn R. SMITH

Bucknell University (E)

701 Moore Avenue, Lewisburg PA 17837
County: Union FICE Identification: 003238
Unit ID: 211291
Telephone: (570) 577-2000 Carnegie Class: Bac/A&S
FAX Number: (570) 577-3760 Calendar System: Semester
URL: www.bucknell.edu
Established: 1846 Annual Undergrad Tuition & Fees: $45,378
Enrollment: 3,635 Coed
Affiliation or Control: Independent Non-Profit IRS Status: 501(c)3
Highest Offering: Master's
Program: Liberal Arts And General; Teacher Preparatory; Professional
Accreditation: M, CS, ENG, MUS

01 President ....Dr. John C. BRAVMAN
05 Provost ....Dr. Michael A. SMYER
10 VP for Finance & Administration ....Mr. David J. SURGALA
30 VP Development & Alumni Rels ....Dr. Scott G. ROSEVEAR
43 General Counsel ....Mr. Wayne A. BROMFIELD
27 VP Communications & Cmty Rels ....Dr. Peter F. MACKEY
13 VP Library & Information Technology ....Mr. Param S. BEDI
84 VP for Enrollment Management ....Mr. William T. CONLEY
88 Chief Investment Officer ....Mr. Christopher D. BROWN
49 Dean of Arts & Sciences ....Dr. George C. SHIELDS
54 Dean of Engineering ....Dr. Keith W. BUFFINTON
32 Dean of Students ....Ms. Susan LANTZ
20 Assoc Provost/Dean of Grad Studies ....Dr. James P. RICE
20 Assoc Prov/Dean Summer Sch/ Registr ....Dr. Robert M. MIDKIFF, JR.
50 Director School of Management ....Dr. Michael E. JOHNSON-CRAMER
21 Associate VP for Finance ....Mr. Dennis W. SWANK
29 Assoc VP Development & Alumni Rels ....Ms. Kathleen GRAHAM
41 Director of Athletics & Recreation ....Mr. John P. HARDT
88 Treasurer and Controller ....Mr. Michael S. COVER
28 Assoc Provost for Diversity ....Vacant
46 Assistant Provost for Research ....Vacant
18 Associate VP for Facilities ....Mr. Dennis W. HAWLEY
16 Executive Director Human Resources ....Ms. Marcia K. HOFFMAN
88 Exec Dir of Alumni Relations ....Mr. Joshua L. GRILL
09 Director of Institutional Research ....Mr. Kevork T. HORISSIAN
88 Director of Internal Audit ....Mr. Robert L. HOSTER
45 Director of Strategy Implementation ....Mr. Edward J. LOFTUS
08 Dir Library Services & Inst Tech ....Ms. Carrie E. RAMPP
14 Dir Tech Infrastructure & User Svcs ....Mr. J. Christopher WEBER
91 Dir of Enterprise Systems ....Mr. Mark YERGER
07 Dean of Admissions ....Mr. Robert G. SPRINGALL
19 Chief of Public Safety ....Vacant
88 Director of Business Services ....Ms. Lori J. WILSON
36 Exec Director of Career Services ....Ms. Pamela G. KEISER
88 Executive Dir Leadership Gifts ....Mr. Robert D. RATHBUN
88 Dir Dev Research & Prospect Mgmt ....Ms. Cynthia D. JANESCH
102 Dir Corporate & Foundation Rels ....Mr. David M. FOREMAN
88 Dir Parents Fund & Family Programs ....Ms. Ann L. DISTEFANO
44 Director of Gift Planning ....Ms. Melissa M. DIEHL
44 Director of the Annual Fund ....Ms. Loni N. KLINE
88 Director of Principal Gifts ....Mr. Kenneth C. HALL
88 Dir Donor & Volunteer Recognition ....Ms. Cynthia J. GARRETT
88 Director of Facility Services ....Mr. Michael J. PATTERSON
88 Director of Construction & Design ....Mr. James HOSTETLER
88 Dir Business Operations for Provost ....Ms. Pamela A. BENFER
15 Dir Compensation & Employment Svcs ....Ms. Gene L. CRAWFORD
15 Director of Benefits & HRIS ....Ms. Cindy L. BILGER
88 Director Office of the President ....Ms. Carol M. KENNEDY
07 Asst VP for Enrollment Management ....Mr. Mark D. DAVIES
88 Exec Director of Events Mgmt Office ....Ms. Judith L. MICKANIS
37 Director of Financial Aid ....Ms. Andrea C. LEITHNER STAUFFER
23 Director Student Health Services ....Dr. Donald W. STECHSCHULTE
38 Director of Psychological Services ....Dr. Linda L. LOCHER
88 Sr Assoc Director for Maintenance ....Mr. Jeffrey W. LOSS
88 Sr Assoc Dir Energy & Utilities ....Mr. James C. KNIGHT
06 Associate Registrar ....Ms. Melissa A. WEBER
06 Associate Registrar ....Mr. Dennis M. HOPPLE
35 Associate Dean of Students ....Ms. Kari M. CONRAD
88 Associate Dean Student Diversity ....Mr. Thomas L. ALEXANDER
35 Associate Dean of Students ....Ms. Amy A. BADAL
35 Associate Dean of Students ....Mr. Daniel C. REMLEY
42 University Chaplain ....Mr. John P. KOLATCH
104 Director of International Education ....Mr. Stephen K. APPIAH-PADI
88 Director of Media Communications ....Mr. Andrew H. HIRSCH
88 Dir of Publications/Print & Mail ....Ms. Lisa D. HOOVER
105 Dir Digital Communications ....Ms. Roberta L. SIMS
88 Exec Dir Weis Center Perform Arts ....Ms. Kathryn L. MAGUET
88 Dir of Samek Art Gallery ....Mr. Richard J. RINEHART
88 Associate Controller ....Mr. William D. GEORGE
88 Associate Director Budgets ....Ms. Judy STABOLEPSZY
88 Assoc Controller Financial Services ....Mr. Ronald E. STAUFFER, II
88 Director of Financial Services ....Ms. Kathy M. GUYER
96 Director of Procurement Services ....Mr. Donald A. KRECH
22 Affirmative Action Officer ....Ms. Linda L. BENNETT
88 Director Events Technology Services ....Mr. George A. LINCOLN, III
88 Dir Card Services & Student Transit ....Mr. Glenn R. FISHER
88 Dir Financial Information Systems ....Ms. Pamela K. NOONE
88 Dir Civic Engagement & Service Lrng ....Ms. Janice R. BUTLER
88 Director of Events ....Ms. Patricia M. RINGKAMP
88 Dir International Student Services ....Ms. Jennifer E. FIGUEROA
93 Director Multicultural Student Svcs ....Mr. Vincent L. STEPHENS
88 Director of Women's Resource Center ....Ms. Tracy E. SHAYNAK
88 Director Office of LGBT Awareness ....Mr. William K. MCCOY
92 Honors Council Chair ....Dr. Erin L. JABLONSKI
88 Director of Writing Center ....Ms. Deirdre M. O'CONNOR
94 Dir Women's & Gender Studies Pgm ....Dr. Coralynn V. DAVIS

Bucks County Community College (F)

275 Swamp Road, Newtown PA 18940-4106
County: Bucks FICE Identification: 003239
Unit ID: 211307
Telephone: (215) 968-8000 Carnegie Class: Assoc/Pub-S-MC
FAX Number: (215) 968-8129 Calendar System: Semester
URL: www.bucks.edu
Established: 1964 Annual Undergrad Tuition & Fees (In-District): $3,698
Enrollment: 10,300 Coed
Affiliation or Control: Local IRS Status: 501(c)3
Highest Offering: Associate Degree
Program: Occupational; 2-Year Principally Bachelor's Creditable
Accreditation: M, ACBSP, ADNUR, ART, MUS, RAD

05 Provost/Dean of Academic Affairs ....Dr. Annette L. CONN
10 VP for Administrative Affairs & CFO ....Mr. Dennis W. MATTHEWS
32 VP Student Affairs/Dean of Students ....Ms. Barbara H. YETMAN
51 Vice Pres Cont Educ/Workforce Devel ....Ms. Barbara A. MILLER
27 Vice Pres/Chief Info Tech Officer ....Vacant
21 Exec Dir Budget & Internal Audit ....Ms. Nancy PRUSKOWSKI
20 Dean Academic & Curricular Svcs ....Ms. Catherine C. MCELROY
88 Dean Learning Resources ....Dr. Maureen MCCREADIE
84 Asst Dean for Enrollment Services ....Ms. Liz M. KULICK
38 Asst Dean Advising & Stdnt Planning ....Ms. Christine HAGEDORN
102 Exec Director of the Foundation ....Mr. Tobias BRUHN
18 Exec Director Physical Plant ....Mr. Mark P. GRISI
26 Exec Dir Marketing/Public Relations ....Ms. Marta KAUFMANN
12 Exec Director Upper County Campus ....Dr. Rodney E. ALTEMOSE
04 Exec Assistant to President ....Ms. Kathleen C. FEDORKO
15 Exec Director Human Resources ....Ms. Tracey DONALDSON
96 Director of Purchasing ....Mr. James F. LOUGHERY
106 Director Online Learning ....Ms. Georglyn L. DAVIDSON
37 Director Financial Aid ....Ms. Donna M. WILKOSKI
36 Director Career Services ....Ms. Sharon STEPHENS
35 Director of Student Life Programs ....Mr. Matt J. CIPRIANO
09 Exec Dir Inst Research & Assessment ....Dr. Christine BOYLE
103 Asst VP Cont Educ/Workforce Devel ....Ms. Christine GILLESPIE
19 Director of Security/Safety ....Mr. Dennis MCCAULEY
08 Director Library Services ....Ms. Linda MCCANN
41 Athletic Director ....Dr. Priscilla RICE
20 Executive Assistant to Provost ....Dr. William FORD
07 Director of Admissions ....Ms. Marlene T. BARLOW
12 Exec Dir Lower Bucks Campus ....Mr. James H. SELL
88 Exec Dir Public Safety Training ....Mr. Fred HUNSINGER
06 Registrar ....Mr. Robert MALEY
29 Director Alumni Relations ....Ms. Adrienne CLARKE

Butler County Community College (G)

107 College Drive, Butler PA 16002
County: Butler FICE Identification: 003240
Unit ID: 211343
Telephone: (724) 287-8711 Carnegie Class: Assoc/Pub-S-SC
FAX Number: (724) 285-6047 Calendar System: Semester
URL: www.bc3.edu
Established: 1965 Annual Undergrad Tuition & Fees (In-District): $3,264
Enrollment: 4,211 Coed
Affiliation or Control: Local IRS Status: 501(c)3
Highest Offering: Associate Degree
Program: Occupational; 2-Year Principally Bachelor's Creditable
Accreditation: M, ACBSP, ADNUR, MAC, PTAA

01 President ....Dr. Nicholas C. NEUPAUER
05 Vice President for Academic Affairs ....Dr. Francie P. SPIGELMYER
11 VP for Administration & Finance ....Mr. James A. HRABOSKY
32 Vice President for Student Services ....Dr. Gordon C. WILLOUGHBY
51 VP Continuing Ed Off-Campus Centers ....Mr. William T. O'BRIEN
10 Chief Business Officer ....Mr. Wm. Jake FRIEL
50 Dean of Business ....Ms. Rosemary C. KEASEY
83 Dean of Social Science/Humanities ....Mr. William L. MILLER
66 Dean of Nursing/Allied Health ....Dr. Patricia MIHALCIN
72 Interim Dean of Nat Science/Tech ....Mr. Matt KOVAC
106 Dean of Education Technology ....Ms. Ann MCCANDLESS
08 Dean of Library Services ....Mr. Stephen M. JOSEPH
35 Interim Dean of Students ....Mr. Joshua NOVAK
103 Exec Dir Workforce Dev Training ....Dr. Stephen R. CATT
16 Director Human Resources ....Ms. Linda M. DODD
26 Director of Public Relations ....Ms. Susan J. CHANGNON
51 Director Adult/Continuing Education ....Mr. Paul M. LUCAS
06 Director of Records & Registration ....Ms. Ruth A. SCOTT
13 Director Telecommunications & MIS ....Mr. Rick H. MICHELINI
32 Director of Student Life ....Mr. Rob A. SNYDER

09 Dir Instl Research/Strategic Plng ....Ms. Sharla M. ANKE
18 Director of Facilities ....Mr. Brian R. OPITZ
07 Director of Admissions ....Ms. Pattie A. BAJUSZIK
12 Director of Lawrence County Center ....Ms. Diane M. DECARBO
12 Director Cranberry Center ....Mr. Alex J. GLADIS
12 Director of Linden Pointe-Mercer Co ....Mr. John P. SUESSER
12 Director of Upper Allegheny Region ....Ms. Jill MARTIN-REND
37 Financial Aid Director ....Ms. Julianne E. LOUTTIT
41 Athletic Director ....Mr. Rob A. SNYDER
21 Director of College Services ....Vacant
50 Director of Business/Industry Trng ....Ms. Lisa M. CAMPBELL
38 Director Student Counseling ....Vacant
29 Director Alumni Relations ....Ms. Michelle E. JAMIESON
45 Director of Advancement ....Ms. Ruth PURCELL
19 Director of Campus Police/Security ...... Mr. Patrick W. MASSARO
88 Director of Cultural Center ....Mr. Lawrence E. STOCK
88 Director of Children's Center ....Ms. Judith A. ZUZACK
88 Associate Director Admissions ....Mr. Sean M. CARROLL
40 Bookstore Manager ....Ms. Donna L. PALLONE

Byzantine Catholic Seminary of SS. Cyril and Methodius (A)

3605 Perrysville Avenue, Pittsburgh PA 15214-2229

County: Allegheny FICE Identification: 041180
Unit ID: 444103
Telephone: (412) 321-8383 Carnegie Class: Spec/Faith
FAX Number: (412) 321-9936 Calendar System: Semester
URL: www.byzcathsem.edu
Established: 1950 Annual Graduate Tuition & Fees: $19,200
Enrollment: 15 Coed
Affiliation or Control: Other IRS Status: 501(c)3
Highest Offering: Master's; No Undergraduates
Program: Liberal Arts And General; Religious Emphasis
Accreditation: THEOL

01 Rector ....Rev. John G. PETRO
04 Administrative Assistant ....Sr. Margaret A. ANDRAKO
05 Academic Dean ....Rev. Joseph RAPTOSH

Cabrini College (B)

610 King of Prussia Road, Radnor PA 19087-3698

County: Delaware FICE Identification: 003241
Unit ID: 211352
Telephone: (610) 902-8100 Carnegie Class: Master's L
FAX Number: (610) 902-8309 Calendar System: Semester
URL: www.cabrini.edu
Established: 1957 Annual Undergrad Tuition & Fees: $29,000
Enrollment: 3,291 Coed
Affiliation or Control: Roman Catholic IRS Status: 501(c)3
Highest Offering: Master's
Program: Liberal Arts And General
Accreditation: M, SW

01 President ....Dr. Marie A. GEORGE
05 Provost/Vice Pres Academic Affairs .... Dr. Anne SKLEDER
10 Vice Pres Finance/Admin & Treasurer ....Dr. Steven FELD
30 VP Advancement/External Relations .... Mr. Gene CASTELLANO
32 Vice Pres for Student Development ....Dr. Christine LYSIONEK
84 Vice Pres of Enrollment Management ....Mr. Dennis M. KELLY
26 Vice Pres Marketing/Communications ..... Mr. Gene CASTELLANO
20 Dean for Academic Affairs .... Dr. Jeffrey GINGERICH
35 Dean of Students ....Mr. George STROUD
58 Dean of Grad Studies ....Dr. Martha COMBS
04 Exec Assistant to the President ....Ms. Betsy STILES
06 Registrar ....Ms. Phyllis BEAN
08 Library Director ....Dr. Roberta JACQUET
14 Director of Info Tech & Resources ....Ms. Marlayne DUNOVICH
19 Director of Public Safety ....Vacant
18 Dir Construction/Plng/Facilities .... Mr. Howard HOLDEN
29 Dir of Alumni Programs and Giving ....Ms. Rachel MCCARTER
37 Director of Financial Aid ....Ms. Michelle TAYLOR
36 Dir of Cooperative Educ/Career Svcs ...... Ms. Nancy HUTCHISON
41 Director of Athletics ....Vacant
15 Director of Human Resources ....Ms. Susan ROHANNA
21 Controller ....Ms. Diane SCUTTI
24 Coord of Education Resources Center ... Ms. Mary BUDZILOWICZ
40 Bookstore Manager ....Ms. Michele CONROY
105 Web Master ....Mr. Matt HOLMES
09 Director of Institutional Research .... Ms. Lisa PLUMMER
35 Director of Student Activities ....Mrs. Anne FILIPPONE
11 Dir of Admin Services/Purchasing .... Ms. Heather CARDAMONE
92 Co-Director of the Honors Program .... Dr. Paul WRIGHT
92 Co-Director of the Honors Program ....Dr. Leonard PRIMIANO
28 Dir Student Diversity Initiatives ....Ms. Stephanie REED
38 Director Student Counseling ....Ms. Sara MAGGITTI
39 Director of Residence Life ....Ms. Sue KRAMER

Calvary Baptist Theological Seminary (C)

1380 S Valley Forge Road, Lansdale PA 19446-4797

County: Montgomery FICE Identification: 038993
Unit ID: 211370
Telephone: (215) 368-7538 Carnegie Class: Spec/Faith
FAX Number: (215) 368-1003 Calendar System: Semester
URL: www.cbs.edu
Established: 1976 Annual Graduate Tuition & Fees: $13,050
Enrollment: 69 Coed
Affiliation or Control: Independent Non-Profit IRS Status: 501(c)3
Highest Offering: Doctorate; No Undergraduates
Program: Professional; Religious Emphasis
Accreditation: M

01 President ....Dr. Samuel L. HARBIN
05 Seminary Dean ....Dr. Charles MCLAIN
06 Registrar ....Mr. Clint J. BANZ
08 Director of Library Services ....Mr. Clint J. BANZ
10 Business Manager ....Mr. Nicholas Y. YZZI

Cambria-Rowe Business College (D)

422 S 13th Street, Indiana PA 15701-2804

County: Indiana Identification: 666476
Unit ID: 428329
Telephone: (724) 463-0222 Carnegie Class: Assoc/PrivFP
FAX Number: (724) 463-7246 Calendar System: Quarter
URL: www.crbc.net
Established: 1891 Annual Undergrad Tuition & Fees: $12,980
Enrollment: 106 Coed
Affiliation or Control: Proprietary IRS Status: Proprietary
Highest Offering: Associate Degree
Program: Occupational; 2-Year Principally Bachelor's Creditable; Business Emphasis
Accreditation: ACICS

01 President ....Mr. William COWARD
03 Executive Director ....Mr. Michael ARTIM
12 Director ....Mr. Jeffrey ALLEN
05 Director of Education ....Mrs. Angela SEIDEL
20 Assistant Director of Education ....Mrs. Amy BEITEL
37 Director of Financial Aid Services ....Mrs. Linda WESS
36 Director of Career Services ....Mrs. Missy HILL
07 Director of Admissions ....Mrs. Amanda ARTIM

† Branch campus of Cambria-Rowe Business College, Johnstown, PA.

Cambria-Rowe Business College (E)

221 Central Avenue, Johnstown PA 15902-2494

County: Cambria FICE Identification: 004889
Unit ID: 211398
Telephone: (814) 536-5168 Carnegie Class: Assoc/PrivFP
FAX Number: (814) 536-5160 Calendar System: Quarter
URL: www.crbc.net
Established: 1891 Annual Undergrad Tuition & Fees: $12,980
Enrollment: 148 Coed
Affiliation or Control: Proprietary IRS Status: Proprietary
Highest Offering: Associate Degree
Program: Occupational; 2-Year Principally Bachelor's Creditable; Business Emphasis
Accreditation: ACICS

01 President ....Mr. William COWARD
03 Executive Director ....Mr. Michael ARTIM
88 Director ....Mr. Jeffrey ALLEN
05 Director of Education ....Mrs. Angela SEIDEL
36 Director of Career Services ....Mrs. Amy HORWATH
37 Director of Financial Aid Services ....Mrs. Linda WESS
07 Director of Admission ....Mrs. Amanda ARTIM
10 Business Manager ....Mrs. LeAnna BRKOVICH
07 Admissions Representative ....Mrs. Katherine BAYS

Career Training Academy (F)

4314 Old William Penn Hwy, Ste 103, Monroeville PA 15146-1455

County: Allegheny Identification: 666051
Unit ID: 408312
Telephone: (412) 372-3900 Carnegie Class: Assoc/PrivFP
FAX Number: (412) 373-4262 Calendar System: Other
URL: www.careerta.edu
Established: 1992 Annual Undergrad Tuition & Fees: $8,516
Enrollment: 74 Coed
Affiliation or Control: Proprietary IRS Status: Proprietary
Highest Offering: Associate Degree
Program: Occupational; 2-Year Principally Bachelor's Creditable; Technical Emphasis
Accreditation: ACCSC

01 Director ....Ms. Donna BROWN

† Branch campus of Career Training Academy, New Kensington, PA.

Career Training Academy (G)

950 Fifth Avenue, New Kensington PA 15068-6308

County: Westmoreland FICE Identification: 026095
Unit ID: 210951
Telephone: (724) 337-1000 Carnegie Class: Assoc/PrivFP
FAX Number: (724) 335-7140 Calendar System: Other
URL: www.careerta.edu
Established: 1986 Annual Undergrad Tuition & Fees: $8,965
Enrollment: 87 Coed
Affiliation or Control: Proprietary IRS Status: Proprietary
Highest Offering: Associate Degree
Program: Occupational; 2-Year Principally Bachelor's Creditable; Technical Emphasis
Accreditation: ACCSC

01 President ....Mr. John M. REDDY

Career Training Academy (H)

1500 Shoppes at Northway, Pittsburgh PA 15237-3015

County: Allegheny Identification: 666100
Unit ID: 440174
Telephone: (412) 367-4000 Carnegie Class: Assoc/PrivFP
FAX Number: (412) 369-7223 Calendar System: Other
URL: www.careerta.edu
Established: 1986 Annual Undergrad Tuition & Fees: $19,529
Enrollment: 59 Coed
Affiliation or Control: Proprietary IRS Status: Proprietary
Highest Offering: Associate Degree
Program: Occupational; 2-Year Principally Bachelor's Creditable; Technical Emphasis
Accreditation: ACCSC

01 Director ....Carla RYBA

† Branch campus of Career Training Academy, New Kensington, PA.

Carlow University (I)

3333 Fifth Avenue, Pittsburgh PA 15213-3165

County: Allegheny FICE Identification: 003303
Unit ID: 211431
Telephone: (412) 578-6000 Carnegie Class: Master's M
FAX Number: (412) 578-6668 Calendar System: Semester
URL: www.carlow.edu
Established: 1929 Annual Undergrad Tuition & Fees: $24,438
Enrollment: 2,346 Coed
Affiliation or Control: Roman Catholic IRS Status: 501(c)3
Highest Offering: Doctorate
Program: Liberal Arts And General; Teacher Preparatory; Professional
Accreditation: M, COPSY, NURSE, SW

01 President ....Dr. Mary E. HINES
05 Provost/VP Academic Affairs ....Dr. Margaret K. MCLAUGHLIN
10 CFO/VP Finance and Operations ....Vacant
30 VP Advancement ....Ms. Karen E. GALENTINE
26 VP Communications & External Rels ....Ms. Louise C. SCIANNAMEO
88 Special Asst to Pres/Mercy Heritage .... Sr. Sheila A. CARNEY
32 Dean Student Affairs ....Ms. Jennifer CARLO
04 Asst to the President ....Ms. Barbara L. GILLES
15 Director Human Resources ....Ms. Andra M. TOKARSKY
42 Campus Minister ....Ms. Siobhan K. DEWITT
58 Interim Dean Graduate School ....Dr. Robert A. REED
49 Dean Arts and Sciences ....Dr. Karyn Z. SPROLES
06 Registrar ....Mr. Jason KRALL
20 Assoc Provost Enrollment Management ....Ms. Judith A. BOLSINGER
88 Exec Dir & Principal Campus School ....Ms. Michelle A. PEDUTO
58 Sr Dir Adult & Graduate Admissions ....Ms. Susan S. SHUTTER
07 Director Admissions ....Ms. Susan M. WINSTEL
12 Dir Cranberry Education Center ....Mr. James V. SHANKEL
12 Dir Greensburg Education Center ....Ms. Wendy S. PHILLIPS
36 Director Career Center ....Vacant
08 Director Library Services ....Ms. Elaine J. MISKO
85 Coordinator Center for Global Lrng ... Mr. Garrett D. MARGLIOTTI
09 Sr Dir Inst Research & Effective .... Ms. Anne M. CANDREVA
35 Director Campus Life ....Mr. Christopher M. MEANER
39 Asst Director Campus Life ....Ms. Carrie R. BENSON
23 Director Health Services ....Ms. Mary Frances REIDELL
41 Director Athletics ....Mr. George S. SLIMAN
88 Director Wellness & Fitness Svcs ....Ms. Julie M. GAUL
28 Director Diversity Initiative ....Ms. Barbara G. JOHNSON
21 Controller ....Ms. Dorothy M. ANTONUCCI
13 Interim Chief Technology Operation ....Dr. Howard A. STERN
26 Interim Chief Technology Strategy .... Ms. Anne M. CANDREVA
18 Director Facilities ....Mr. Taylor G. BLICE
19 Chief of Police ....Ms. Tami L. ALLIAS
37 Director Financial Aid ....Ms. Natalie L. WILSON
88 Director Student Accounts ....Ms. Linda C. ROOT
40 Manager Bookstore ....Ms. Tracy HILL
44 Exec Director Advancement ....Ms. Anita S. DACAL
29 Director Alumnae/i Relations ....Ms. Rose M. WOOLLEY
44 Senior Director of Major Gifts .... Ms. Marcia M. WALLANDER
102 Director of Corp & Found Relations .... Ms. Marjorie P. BERNARD
27 Asst Dir Media & Public Rels ....Mr. Andrew G. WILSON
105 Manager Web Communications ....Ms. Kristin A. RAUP

Carnegie Mellon University (J)

5000 Forbes Avenue, Pittsburgh PA 15213-3890

County: Allegheny FICE Identification: 003242
Unit ID: 211440
Telephone: (412) 268-2000 Carnegie Class: RU/VH
FAX Number: (412) 268-2330 Calendar System: Semester
URL: www.cmu.edu
Established: 1900 Annual Undergrad Tuition & Fees: $45,554
Enrollment: 12,058 Coed
Affiliation or Control: Independent Non-Profit IRS Status: 501(c)3
Highest Offering: Doctorate
Program: Liberal Arts And General; Teacher Preparatory; Professional
Accreditation: M, BUS, ENG, MUS, SPAA

01 President ....Dr. Jared L. COHON
05 Provost/Executive Vice President ....Dr. Mark S. KAMLET
10 Vice President and CFO ....Ms. Deborah J. MOON
30 Vice President for Univ Advancement ....Mrs. Robbee KOSAK
46 Vice President for Research ....Dr. Richard D. MCCULLOUGH
43 Vice President/General Counsel ....Ms. Mary Jo DIVELY

101 Secretary Board of Trustees .... Ms. Cheryl M. HAYS
04 Exec Asst to Pres & Office Mgr .... Ms. Cathy A. LIGHT
20 Vice Provost for Education .... Dr. Amy L. BURKERT
11 Vice President for Campus Services .... Dr. Michael C. MURPHY
13 Vice Provost for Comp Svcs/CIO .... Mr. Steven K. HUTH
15 Assoc VP Chief Human Resources Ofcr .... Ms. Dianne KENNEY
29 Assoc Vice Pres Alumni Relations .... Mr. Andrew SHAINDLIN
18 Asc VP Campus Design/Facility Devel .... Mr. Ralph R. HORGAN
22 Asst Vice Pres for Diversity & EOS .... Mr. Everett L. TADEMY
26 Asst Vice Pres For Media Relations .... Ms. Teresa THOMAS
28 Asst Vice Pres for Diversity & EOS .... Mr. Everett L. TADAMY
102 Exec Director Foundation Relations .... Dr. Peter F. COHEN
45 Director University Planning .... Mr. Russell D. O'LARE
41 Director Athletics & Physical Educ .... Ms. Susan BASSETT
19 Director Security/Chief Univ Police .... Mr. Thomas A. OGDEN
84 Co-Director of Enrollment Services .... Mr. John R. PAPINCHAK
84 Co-Director of Enrollment Services .... Mrs. Linda M. ANDERSON
14 Director Software Engr Inst .... Dr. Paul D. NIELSEN
07 Director of Admission .... Mr. Michael STEIDEL
08 Dean of University Libraries .... Dr. Gloriana ST. CLAIR
96 Director of Procurement .... Mr. Shawn G. FRONZAGLIA
06 Registrar .... Mr. John R. PAPINCHAK
09 Director of Institutional Research .... Ms. Janel SUTKUS
36 Director of Career Center .... Mr. Farouk DEY
38 Dir Counseling & Psychological Svcs .... Dr. Cynthia K. VALLEY
32 Dean Student Affairs .... Ms. Gina CASALEGNO
54 Dean Carnegie Inst of Technology .... Vacant
57 Interim Dean College Fine Arts .... Dr. Dan J. MARTIN
49 Dean Human & Social Science .... Dr. John P. LEHOCZKY
50 Dean Tepper School of Business .... Dr. Robert DAMMON
81 Dean Mellon College of Science .... Dr. Frederick J. GILMAN
80 Dean Heinz Sch Publ Policy/Mgmt .... Dr. Ramayya KRISHNAN
77 Dean School of Computer Science .... Dr. Randal E. BRYANT
35 Asst Dean of Student Affairs .... Ms. Anne WITCHNER

Cedar Crest College (A)

100 College Drive, Allentown PA 18104-6196

County: Lehigh — FICE Identification: 003243 — Unit ID: 211468
Telephone: (610) 437-4471 — Carnegie Class: Bac/Diverse
FAX Number: (610) 437-5955 — Calendar System: Semester
URL: www.cedarcrest.edu
Established: 1867 — Annual Undergrad Tuition & Fees: $31,196
Enrollment: 1,620 — Female
Affiliation or Control: United Church Of Christ — IRS Status: 501(c)3
Highest Offering: Master's
Program: Liberal Arts And General; Teacher Preparatory; Professional
Accreditation: M, ACBSP, DIETD, @DIETI, NMT, NUR, SW

01 President .... Ms. Carmen T. AMBAR
05 Acting Provost .... Dr. Elizabeth MEADE
10 Chief Financial Officer .... Ms. Audra KAHR
84 Interim VP for Enrollment Mgmt .... Ms. Mariea NOBLITT
30 Vice Pres Institutional Advancement .... Ms. Patricia MORAN
32 Vice President of Student Affairs .... Dr. Kimberly OWENS
06 Registrar .... Ms. Janet BAKER
29 Exec Director for Alumnae Affairs .... Mrs. Susan S. COX
19 Chief of Campus Safety and Security .... Mr. Mark VITALOS
18 Director of Facilities .... Mr. Joseph HARTNER
08 Library Director .... Ms. Mary Beth FREEH
91 Director Administrative Technology .... Mrs. Kathleen CUNNINGHAM
09 Dir of Institutional Research .... Ms. Lyn WILLIAMS
04 Exec Assistant to the President .... Ms. Cheryl WENNER
26 Director Marketing/Cmty Outreach .... Ms. Kerri PUSKAR
15 Director Personnel Services .... Ms. Margie GRANDINETTI
37 Dir Student Financial Services .... Ms. Valerie KREISER
22 Director Health/Counseling Services .... Ms. Nancy ROBERTS
27 Media Relations Associate .... Mr. David JWANIER
96 Purchasing Coordinator .... Ms. Karen KHATTARI
40 Manager Bookstore .... Ms. Maureen YOACHIM

Central Penn College (B)

College Hill Road, Summerdale PA 17093-0309

County: Cumberland — FICE Identification: 004890 — Unit ID: 211477
Telephone: (800) 759-2727 — Carnegie Class: Bac/Diverse
FAX Number: (717) 732-5254 — Calendar System: Quarter
URL: www.centralpenn.edu
Established: 1881 — Annual Undergrad Tuition & Fees: $20,580
Enrollment: 1,462 — Coed
Affiliation or Control: Proprietary — IRS Status: Proprietary
Highest Offering: Baccalaureate
Program: Occupational; 2-Year Principally Bachelor's Creditable; Professional; Business Emphasis
Accreditation: M, MAC, PTAA

01 President .... Mr. Todd A. MILANO
05 Vice Pres/Chief Academic Officer .... Dr. Melissa M. VAYDA
06 Director Records & Registration .... Mr. Jen CORRELL
03 Provost .... Ms. Janice MOORE
20 Academic Dean .... Ms. Kathy ANDERSEN
26 Marketing Services Manager .... Mrs. Mary E. WETZEL
07 Enrollment Director .... Ms. Kristin HORN
51 Dir Continuing Education Admissions .... Ms. Michelle MEISER
18 Facilities Director .... Mr. Rodney GROFF
37 Financial Aid Director .... Ms. Kathy J. SHEPARD
32 Asst Dean Student Services .... Mr. Ed LIESCH
09 Institutional Research Director .... Col. Wilbur E. GRAY
36 Career Services Coordinator .... Mr. Steven HASSINGER

Chatham University (C)

Woodland Road, Pittsburgh PA 15232-2826

County: Allegheny — FICE Identification: 003244 — Unit ID: 211556
Telephone: (412) 365-1100 — Carnegie Class: Master's L
FAX Number: (412) 365-1505 — Calendar System: Other
URL: www.chatham.edu
Established: 1869 — Annual Undergrad Tuition & Fees: $31,532
Enrollment: 2,220 — Female
Affiliation or Control: Independent Non-Profit — IRS Status: 501(c)3
Highest Offering: Doctorate
Program: Liberal Arts And General; Teacher Preparatory; Professional
Accreditation: M, #ARCPA, CIDA, LSAR, NURSE, OT, PTA, SW

01 President .... Dr. Esther L. BARAZZONE
94 Dean College for Women .... Dr. Karol DEAN
10 Vice Pres Finance/Administration .... Mr. Walter B. FOWLER
05 Vice President Academic Affairs .... Dr. Wenying XU
84 Vice Pres Enrollment Management .... Vacant
32 Vice President Student Affairs .... Dr. Zauyah WAITE
27 Vice Pres for Mktg & Communications .... Mr. Bill CAMPBELL
30 Vice Pres University Advancement .... Ms. Ann BOYD-STEWART
51 Dean Continuing/Prof Studies .... Vacant
88 Dean Sch Sustainability/Environment .... Dr. David HASSENZAHL
21 Asst Vice Pres Finance .... Ms. Jennifer LUNDY
04 Executive Assistant to President .... Mr. Sean COLEMAN
20 Asst VP of Academic Affairs .... Vacant
58 Dean College of Graduate Studies .... Vacant
09 Director of Institutional Research .... Dr. Robert ZHANG
06 Registrar .... Ms. Jennifer BRONSON
37 Director of Financial Aid .... Ms. Jennifer A. BURNS
08 Director of Library .... Ms. Jill AUSEL
29 Director Alumnae Affairs .... Vacant
44 Director of Annual Giving .... Ms. Donna HOLMES
102 Director of Foundation/Corp Support .... Ms. Kate FREED
15 Director of Human Resources .... Mr. Frank M. GRECO
18 Director of Facilities Management .... Mr. Robert R. DUBRAY
19 Director of Safety & Security .... Mr. Bernard D. MERRICK
41 Director of Athletics .... Mr. Scott KOSKOSKI
36 Director Career Development .... Ms. Monica RITTER
38 Director of Student Counseling .... Ms. Elsa M. ARCE
35 Director Student Activities .... Ms. Heather BLACK

Chestnut Hill College (D)

9601 Germantown Avenue, Philadelphia PA 19118-2693

County: Philadelphia — FICE Identification: 003245 — Unit ID: 211583
Telephone: (215) 248-7000 — Carnegie Class: Master's L
FAX Number: (215) 248-7155 — Calendar System: Semester
URL: www.chc.edu
Established: 1924 — Annual Undergrad Tuition & Fees: $30,620
Enrollment: 2,323 — Coed
Affiliation or Control: Roman Catholic — IRS Status: 501(c)3
Highest Offering: Doctorate
Program: Liberal Arts And General; Teacher Preparatory
Accreditation: M, CLPSY, MACTE

01 President .... Sr. Carol Jean VALE, SSJ
05 Vice Pres for Academic Affairs .... Dr. Steven GUERRIERO
09 Vice Pres Admin Instl Svcs & Events .... Vacant
10 Sr Vice Pres for Financial Affairs .... Ms. Lauri STRIMKOVSKY
30 Vice President for Inst Advancement .... Mr. Kenneth HICKS
32 Vice President for Student Life .... Dr. Lynn ORTALE
90 VP for Information Technology & CIO .... Vacant
11 Asst to Pres for Administration .... Sr. Kathryn MILLER, SSJ
42 Asst to Pres for Mission & Ministry .... Sr. Mary DARRAH, SSJ
58 Dean School of Graduate Studies .... Dr. Steven GUERRIERO
34 Dean School of Undergrad Studies .... Sr. Cecelia J. CAVANAUGH, SSJ
51 Dean of Continuing Studies .... Dr. Elaine GREEN
08 Dean Library/Information Resources .... Sr. Mary Josephine LARKIN, SSJ
07 Vice President for Admissions .... Ms. Jodie KING
20 Assoc Dir Acad Adv Student Svcs .... Ms. Clare DOYLE
20 Assoc Dir Acad Adv Tech Support .... Mr. Michael PETERSON
06 Registrar .... Ms. Deborah EBBERT
35 Director of Student Activities .... Ms. Emily SCHADEMAN
38 Director Counseling Center .... Sr. Sheila KENNEDY, SSJ
85 Foreign Student Advisor .... Ms. Trachanda BROWN
28 Dir Cultural Diversity Initiatives .... Vacant
92 Director of Honors Programs .... Vacant
23 Director Health Services .... Ms. Shannon ROBERTS
36 Director of Career Services .... Ms. Nancy DACHILLE
07 Dir Admission/Sch Graduate Studies .... Ms. Jayne MASHETT
07 Director Accelerated Admissions .... Sr. Mary Esther LEE, SSJ
21 Controller .... Mr. Michael GAVANUS
37 Director Financial Aid .... Mr. Michael COLAHAN
44 Director of Development .... Ms. Catherine QUINN
09 Director of Institutional Research .... Sr. Patricia O'DONNELL, SSJ
102 Dir Corporate/Found/Govt Relations .... Vacant
29 Director of Alumnae/i Affairs .... Ms. Patricia CANNING
41 Director of Athletics .... Ms. Lynn TUBMAN
15 Director Human Resources .... Ms. Michelle MOCARSKY
19 Dir Security/Safety/Bldgs/Grounds .... Mr. Raymond HALLMAN
18 Director of Physical Plant .... Mr. Mark MCGRATH
91 Administrative Software Manager .... Ms. Darlene BROWN
24 Audio Visual Manager .... Vacant
26 Public Relations Director .... Ms. Kathleen SPIGELMYER
40 Manager of Campus Store .... Vacant

CHI Institute/Broomall Campus (E)

1991 Sproul Road, Suite 42, Broomall PA 19008-3516

County: Delaware — FICE Identification: 007781 — Unit ID: 215646
Telephone: (610) 353-7630 — Carnegie Class: Assoc/PrivFP
FAX Number: (610) 359-1370 — Calendar System: Quarter
URL: www.chitraining.com
Established: 1958 — Annual Undergrad Tuition & Fees: $21,000
Enrollment: 783 — Coed
Affiliation or Control: Proprietary — IRS Status: Proprietary
Highest Offering: Associate Degree
Program: Occupational; 2-Year Principally Bachelor's Creditable; Technical Emphasis
Accreditation: ACCSC

01 President .... Mrs. Adrienne SCOTT
05 Director of Education .... Mr. Warren HOWELL
36 Placement Director .... Mr. James LINCKE
07 Director of Admissions .... Mr. Bill SCHNELL

The Commonwealth Medical College (F)

525 Pine Street, Scranton PA 18509

County: Lackawanna — FICE Identification: 041672 — Unit ID: 456542
Telephone: (570) 504-7000 — Carnegie Class: Assoc/PrivNFP4
FAX Number: (570) 504-7289 — Calendar System: Semester
URL: www.thecommonwealthmedical.com
Established: 2009 — Annual Graduate Tuition & Fees: $37,650
Enrollment: 235 — Coed
Affiliation or Control: Independent Non-Profit — IRS Status: 501(c)3
Highest Offering: Doctorate; No Undergraduates
Program: Professional
Accreditation: @M, #MED

00 President Emeritus & Founding Dean .... Dr. Robert D'ALESSANDRI
01 Interim President and Dean .... Dr. Robert E. WRIGHT
45 Vice Pres & Assoc Dean for Planning .... Ms. Virginia HUNT
28 Vice Pres Cmty Engagement/Diversity .... Ms. Ida L. CASTRO
05 Senior Assoc Dean Academic Affairs .... Dr. Maurice CLIFTON
32 Associate Dean for Student Affairs .... Dr. David AXLER
30 Chief Development Officer .... Mr. Brian CAMPBELL
13 Dir of Technology Infrastructure .... Mr. Douglas CARROLL, JR.
15 Director of Human Resources .... Mr. Joseph CORTESE
10 Interim Chief Financial Officer .... Mr. Richard CRATER
21 Dir Budgeting & Financial Services .... Mr. Sam DIAZ
58 Dir Fac Affairs/Grad Medical Educ .... Ms. Andrea DIMATTIA
105 Director of Web Services .... Mr. Jay FORTIN
35 Director of Student Affairs .... Ms. Julia KOLCHARNO
06 Registrar .... Mr. Edward LAHART
37 Director of Financial Aid .... Ms. Ellen MCGUIRE
91 Director of Administrative Systems .... Mr. John KEARNEY
08 Director of Library .... Ms. Joanne MUELLENBACH
18 Director Facility/Public Safety .... Mr. Joe ROSS
07 Director of Admissions .... Ms. Debra STALK
27 CIO/Assoc Dean for Technology .... Mr. Wayne THOMPSON
09 Dir Alumni Relations/Annual Giving .... Ms. Nina Cecelia DEI TOS

Commonwealth Technical Institute at the Hiram G. Andrews Center (G)

727 Goucher Street, Johnstown PA 15905-3092

County: Cambria — FICE Identification: 025366 — Unit ID: 212975
Telephone: (814) 255-8200 — Carnegie Class: Assoc/PrivNFP
FAX Number: (814) 255-5709 — Calendar System: Semester
URL: www.hgac.org
Established: 1959 — Annual Undergrad Tuition & Fees: $15,128
Enrollment: 262 — Coed
Affiliation or Control: Proprietary — IRS Status: Proprietary
Highest Offering: Associate Degree
Program: Occupational
Accreditation: ACCSC

01 President .... Carol MACKEL
03 Executive Vice President .... Jill MORICONI
05 Chief Academic Officer .... Barbara PETERSEN
07 Director of Admissions .... Jason GIES
32 Chief Student Life Officer .... Vacant
37 Director Student Financial Aid .... Sylvia SABO
38 Director Student Counseling .... Keith RAGER

Community College of Allegheny County (H)

800 Allegheny Avenue, Pittsburgh PA 15233-1895

County: Allegheny — FICE Identification: 003231 — Unit ID: 210605
Telephone: (412) 323-2323 — Carnegie Class: Assoc/Pub-U-MC
FAX Number: (412) 237-3037 — Calendar System: Semester
URL: www.ccac.edu
Established: 1966 — Annual Undergrad Tuition & Fees (In-District): $3,312
Enrollment: 20,430 — Coed
Affiliation or Control: State/Local — IRS Status: 501(c)3
Highest Offering: Associate Degree
Program: Occupational; 2-Year Principally Bachelor's Creditable
Accreditation: M, ADNUR, DIETT, DMS, MAC, MLTAD, NMT, OTA, PTAA, RAD, RTT, SURGT

01 President ... Dr. Alex JOHNSON
05 VP Learning & Student Development ... Dr. Mary Frances ARCHEY
10 VP Business & Admin/CFO ... Ms. Joyce BRECKENRIDGE
12 Campus President Allegheny ... Vacant
12 Campus President Boyce ... Hon. Charles MARTONI
12 Campus President North ... Dr. Donna IMHOFF
12 Campus President South ... Dr. Charlene NEWKIRK
30 VP Inst Advance/External Relations ... Ms. Nancilee BURZACHECHI
103 VP Workforce Development ... Vacant
16 VP Human Resources ... Vacant
102 Exec Director of Foundation ... Ms. Rose Ann DICOLA
13 Exec Dir Information Tech Svcs ... Mr. Ibrahim GARBIOGLU
20 Assistant Dean Academic Management ... Ms. Frances DICE
06 Registrar ... Ms. Frances DICE
51 Exec Dir Center Professional Dev ... Mr. Reginald OVERTON
09 Exec Dir of Strategic Planning ... Mr. Kevin SMAY
18 Director of Facilities Management ... Mr. Bob HAMILTON
21 Controller ... Mr. Paul SWEARENGIN
25 Director Contracts & Grants ... Dr. Carol YOANNONE
96 Director Purchasing/Contracts Admin ... Mr. James CAIRNS
28 Special Asst to the Pres for Diversity ... Vacant
100 Assistant to the President ... Ms. Bonita L. RICHARDSON
22 Human Resources Generalist ... Mr. Paul SCHWARZMILLER
86 Exec Dir Gov Relations ... Dr. Charles BLOCKSIDGE
29 Dir Alumni Affairs ... Ms. Susan GALL
04 Exec Assistant to the President ... Mr. David HOOVLER

Community College of Beaver County (A)

1 Campus Drive, Monaca PA 15061-2588
County: Beaver FICE Identification: 006807
Unit ID: 211079
Telephone: (724) 480-2222 Carnegie Class: Assoc/Pub-S-SC
FAX Number: (724) 480-3573 Calendar System: Semester
URL: www.ccbc.edu
Established: 1966 Annual Undergrad Tuition & Fees (In-District): $3,780
Enrollment: 2,714 Coed
Affiliation or Control: State/Local IRS Status: 501(c)3
Highest Offering: Associate Degree
Program: Occupational; 2-Year Principally Bachelor's Creditable
Accreditation: M, ADNUR

01 President ... Dr. Joe D. FORRESTER
05 Provost/VP Learning/Student Success ... Mrs. Melissa D. DENARDO
10 Vice President Finance & Operations ... Mr. Stephen R. DANIK
16 Vice Pres Human Resource Dev ... Mr. Jeff A. FARLEY
26 VP Community Relations/Development ... Ms. Nancy DICKSON
13 Vice Pres Information Technology ... Mr. Walter LUKHAUP
38 Dean Academic Support Services ... Ms. Janice M. KAMINSKI
06 Dean of Enrollment Services ... Mr. Scott F. ENSWORTH
103 Assoc VP Career & Workforce Dev ... Ms. Karen DEICHERT
09 Director Institutional Research ... Mr. Brian HAYDEN
18 Director Physical Plant Ops ... Mr. Robert MOLLENKOPF
37 Director Student Financial Svcs ... Ms. Janet DAVIDSON
04 Assistant to President ... Ms. Jo Ann COATES
76 Division Dir Health Sciences ... Mrs. Linda A. GALLAGHER
50 Division Dir Business/Technologies ... Ms. Deborah MICHEALS
49 Division Dir Liberal Arts & Science ... Dr. John GALL
88 Division Dir Aviation ... Vacant

Community College of Philadelphia (B)

1700 Spring Garden Street, Philadelphia PA 19130-3991
County: Philadelphia FICE Identification: 003249
Unit ID: 215239
Telephone: (215) 751-8000 Carnegie Class: Assoc/Pub-U-SC
FAX Number: (215) 751-8762 Calendar System: Semester
URL: www.ccp.edu
Established: 1965 Annual Undergrad Tuition & Fees (In-District): $4,320
Enrollment: 19,751 Coed
Affiliation or Control: State/Local IRS Status: 501(c)3
Highest Offering: Associate Degree
Program: Occupational; 2-Year Principally Bachelor's Creditable
Accreditation: M, ADNUR, DH, MAC, MLTAD, RAD

01 President ... Dr. Stephen M. CURTIS
10 Vice President Finance/Planning ... Dr. Thomas R. HAWK
05 Vice President Academic Affairs ... Dr. Judith R. GAY
30 Vice Pres Institutional Advancement ... Ms. Marsha M. RAY
32 Vice President Student Affairs ... Dr. Samuel HIRSCH
86 Vice Pres Marketing/Government Rels ... Ms. Lynette BROWN-SOW
43 General Counsel/VP Human Resources ... Ms. Jill GARFINKLE-WEITZ
13 Chief Information Officer ... Ms. Jody BAUER
35 Dean of Students ... Mr. Ronald C. JACKSON
88 Dean of Student Systems ... Dr. Beatrice JONES
49 Dean Liberal Studies ... Dr. Sharon THOMPSON
51 Dean Div Adult/Community Education ... Dr. David E. THOMAS
72 Div Dean of Business/Technology ... Dr. Wayne WORMLEY
09 Director Institutional Research ... Dr. Jane M. GROSSET
06 Director Stdnt Records/Registration ... Ms. Bonnie HARRINGTON
18 Chief Facilities/Physical Plant ... Mr. Harry MOORE
28 Affirmative Action Director ... Mr. Simon BROWN
07 Director of Recruitment/Admissions ... Ms. Jeri DRAPER
37 Director Financial Aid ... Mr. Gim LIM
96 Director of Purchasing ... Ms. Marsia HENLEY
38 Dept Head Student Counseling ... Mr. Todd JONES
36 Coord Career Info/Placement Svcs ... Ms. Tarsha SCOVENS
29 Coord Alumni Rels/Annual Giving ... Ms. Lyvette BROOKS
25 Coord Grants/Prospect Research ... Ms. Anne GRECO

Consolidated School of Business (C)

2124 Ambassador Circle, Lancaster PA 17603-2389
County: Lancaster FICE Identification: 030299
Unit ID: 260354
Telephone: (717) 394-6211 Carnegie Class: Assoc/PrivFP
FAX Number: (717) 394-6213 Calendar System: Other
URL: www.csb.edu
Established: 1981 Annual Undergrad Tuition & Fees: $24,900
Enrollment: 122 Coed
Affiliation or Control: Proprietary IRS Status: Proprietary
Highest Offering: Associate Degree
Program: Occupational
Accreditation: ACICS

01 CEO/President ... Mr. Robert L. SAFRAN
03 Vice President ... Mr. William HOYT
10 Controller ... Mr. Craig D. ELLIS
37 Financial Aid Director ... Ms. Gail DOUGHERTY
36 Placement Director ... Ms. Derena CEDENO
13 Data Systems Director ... Mr. Gholamereza SALARI
32 Student Services Director ... Ms. Linda CLYMAR
21 Bursar ... Mrs. Diane GRANT
23 Medical Coordinator ... Ms. Joan COPP

Consolidated School of Business (D)

1605 Clugston Road, York PA 17404-1798
County: York FICE Identification: 022896
Unit ID: 211820
Telephone: (717) 764-9550 Carnegie Class: Assoc/PrivFP
FAX Number: (717) 764-9469 Calendar System: Other
URL: www.csb.edu
Established: 1981 Annual Undergrad Tuition & Fees: $24,900
Enrollment: 128 Coed
Affiliation or Control: Proprietary IRS Status: Proprietary
Highest Offering: Associate Degree
Program: Occupational
Accreditation: ACICS

01 CEO/President ... Mr. Robert L. SAFRAN
10 Vice President/Controller ... Mr. Craig D. ELLIS
36 Placement Director ... Mr. Paul CULBERTSON
07 Director of Admissions ... Ms. Derena CEDENO
21 Bursar ... Mrs. Gail E. DOUGHERTY
13 Data Systems Director ... Ms. Linda L. HOFFMASTER
32 Director Student Services ... Ms. Jennifer HATCH
37 Financial Aid Director ... Mr. Bill HOYT
23 Medical Coordinator ... Mrs. Cynthia L. DESTAFANO

Curtis Institute of Music (E)

1726 Locust Street, Philadelphia PA 19103-6187
County: Philadelphia FICE Identification: 003251
Unit ID: 211893
Telephone: (215) 893-5252 Carnegie Class: Spec/Arts
FAX Number: (215) 893-9065 Calendar System: Semester
URL: www.curtis.edu
Established: 1924 Annual Undergrad Tuition & Fees: $2,300
Enrollment: 165 Coed
Affiliation or Control: Independent Non-Profit IRS Status: 501(c)3
Highest Offering: Master's
Program: Professional; Music Emphasis
Accreditation: M, MUS

01 President & Director ... Mr. Roberto DIAZ
03 Executive Vice President ... Ms. Elizabeth WARSHAWER
05 Dean ... Mr. John MANGAN
06 Registrar ... Mr. Paul BRYAN
07 Admissions Officer ... Mr. Christopher HODGES
08 Librarian ... Ms. Elizabeth WALKER
29 Director Alumni/Parent Relations ... Ms. Anne O'DONNELL

Dean Institute of Technology (F)

1501 W Liberty Avenue, Pittsburgh PA 15226-1197
County: Allegheny FICE Identification: 009186
Unit ID: 211909
Telephone: (412) 531-4433 Carnegie Class: Assoc/PrivFP
FAX Number: (412) 531-4435 Calendar System: Quarter
URL: www.deantech.edu
Established: 1947 Annual Undergrad Tuition & Fees: $12,800
Enrollment: 205 Coed
Affiliation or Control: Proprietary IRS Status: Proprietary
Highest Offering: Associate Degree
Program: Occupational; Technical Emphasis
Accreditation: ACCSC

01 President ... Mr. James S. DEAN
05 Director of Education ... Mr. Richard D. ALI
07 Director of Admissions ... Mr. Nicholas D. ALI
37 Director Student Financial Aid ... Ms. Valerie L. VELTRI
36 Placement Director ... Ms. Valerie A. HAGEDORN
27 Director Information Office ... Mr. Nicholas D. ALI

Delaware County Community College (G)

901 S Media Line Road, Media PA 19063-1094
County: Delaware FICE Identification: 007110
Unit ID: 211927
Telephone: (610) 359-5000 Carnegie Class: Assoc/Pub-S-SC
FAX Number: (610) 359-5343 Calendar System: Semester
URL: www.dccc.edu
Established: 1967 Annual Undergrad Tuition & Fees (In-District): $6,024
Enrollment: 13,248 Coed
Affiliation or Control: State/Local IRS Status: 501(c)3
Highest Offering: Associate Degree
Program: Occupational; 2-Year Principally Bachelor's Creditable
Accreditation: M, ADNUR, MAC, SURGT

01 President ... Dr. Jerome S. PARKER
10 Vice Pres Administration/Treasurer ... Mr. John A. GLAVIN, JR.
05 Provost ... Dr. Virginia M. CARTER
30 Vice President for Advancement ... Ms. Kathleen A. BRESLIN
12 Vice Provost & Vice Pres Chester Co ... Dr. Mary Jo BOYER
15 Vice President of Human Resources ... Ms. Connie L. MCCALLA
84 Vice President of Enrollment Mgmt ... Ms. Frances M. CUBBERLEY
13 VP & CIO Information Technology ... Mr. George J. SULLIVAN
32 Vice Provost Student/Instr Support ... Dr. Grant S. SNYDER
96 Assoc VP Admin & Facilities Plng ... Mr. Jeffrey S. BAUN
88 Director Learning Centers ... Ms. Dawn M. MOSCARIELLO
88 Director Municipal Police Academy ... Mr. William DAVIS
106 Director Distance Learning Services ... Mr. Alexander PLUCHUTA
37 Director of Financial Aid ... Mr. Raymond L. TOOLE
08 Director of Library Services ... Dr. Karen M. REGE
07 Dir Admissions/Enrollment Services ... Ms. Hope L. DIEHL
36 Director Career/Counseling Center ... Ms. Christine M. DOYLE
06 Registrar ... Mr. Thomas W. LUGG
09 Assoc Vice Prov Inst Effectiveness ... Dr. Christopher TOKPAH
21 Associate VP Finance ... Mr. William J. MARKLE
103 Director Workforce Entry Center ... Ms. Susan E. BOND
85 Director International Student Svs ... Ms. Lydia J. DELL'OSA
15 Director Human Resources ... Mr. Christopher M. DICKERMAN
14 Director OIT/Technical Services ... Ms. Bianca VALENTE
91 Director Admin Computing ... Mr. Bob HARDCASTLE
29 Director Alumni Programs ... Mr. Douglas J. FERGUSON
25 Director Grants Management ... Ms. Susan M. SHISLER-RAPP
31 Director Community Education ... Ms. Nan L. SMITH
35 Director Campus Life ... Ms. Amy WILLIAMS-GAUDIOSO
19 Director Safety & Security ... Mr. Raymond VISCUSI
12 Director Pennocks Bridge Campus ... Ms. Jane SCHURMAN
88 Director Southeast & UD Centers ... Ms. Shantelle K. JENKINS
89 Director First Year Experiences ... Dr. Kendrick MICKENS
88 Director Assessment Center ... Ms. Carol MULLIN
96 Director Purchasing ... Ms. Jenny M. RARIG
18 Dir Plant Oper/Construction Svcs ... Mr. Tony DELUCA
103 Dean Workforce Dev & Cmty Educ ... Ms. Karen KOZACHYN
80 Acting Dean Public Svcs & Soc Svcs ... Dr. Clayton RAILEY, III
72 Dean Tech/Engineering & Math ... Dr. John R. AGAR
88 Acting Dean Learning Support Svcs ... Ms. Dolores E. MARTINO
50 Dean Business & Computer Info Sys ... Dr. Eric R. WELLINGTON
12 Acting Dean Branch Campuses ... Mr. John CRAIG
79 Dean Comm/Arts & Humanities ... Dr. Clayton A. RAILEY III
40 Manager Bookstore ... Mr. Kris STACHOWIAK

Delaware Valley College (H)

700 E Butler Avenue, Doylestown PA 18901-2697
County: Bucks FICE Identification: 003252
Unit ID: 211981
Telephone: (215) 345-1500 Carnegie Class: Bac/Diverse
FAX Number: (215) 345-5277 Calendar System: Semester
URL: www.delval.edu
Established: 1896 Annual Undergrad Tuition & Fees: $33,746
Enrollment: 1,712 Coed
Affiliation or Control: Independent Non-Profit IRS Status: 501(c)3
Highest Offering: Master's
Program: Liberal Arts And General
Accreditation: M

01 President ... Dr. Joseph S. BROSNAN
04 Exec Assistant to the President ... Ms. Angela T. RECKNER
05 VP Acad Affairs/Dean of the Faculty ... Dr. Bashar W. HANNA
32 VP Student Affairs/Dean of Students ... Mr. John BROWN
10 VP for Finance & Administration ... Mr. Arthur GLASS
30 Vice President for Inst Advancement ... Mr. Joseph ERCKERT
84 Vice Pres for Enrollment Management ... Mr. Norman JONES
49 Dean Bus/Educ/Arts & Sciences ... Dr. Benjamin RUSILOSKI
47 Interim Dean Agriculture/Environ ... Mr. Russell REDDING
06 Registrar ... Ms. Lucy DRENTH
41 Athletic Director ... Mr. Frank F. WOLFGANG
26 Chief Marketing Officer ... Ms. Laurie WARD
07 Director of Admissions ... Mr. Dwayne WALKER
36 Director Career Services ... Ms. Tracy DEPEDRO
08 Librarian ... Mr. Peter A. KUPERSMITH
37 Director Student Financial Aid ... Mrs. Joan HOCK
51 Director Continuing Education ... Vacant
38 Director Counseling/Learn Support ... Mrs. Karen KRZYZKOWSKI
23 Director Health Services ... Ms. Miriam TORRES
14 Director of Client Services ... Mr. James LINDEN
39 Director of Residence Life ... Mr. Derek SMITH
19 Director Security/Public Safety ... Mr. Steven JOHNSON
09 Director Institutional Research ... Ms. Elisabeth ERVIN-BLANKENHEIM
15 Director Human Resources ... Ms. Elaine SPIRO
18 Director Physical Plant ... Mr. Theodore STANIEWICZ

44 Director Annual Fund .... Ms. Jennifer ROCK
96 Director of Purchasing .... Mr. William LYLE
04 Special Assistant to President .... Mr. Donald FELDSCHER

DeSales University (A)

2755 Station Avenue, Center Valley PA 18034-9568
County: Lehigh FICE Identification: 003986
Unit ID: 210739
Telephone: (610) 282-1100 Carnegie Class: Master's L
FAX Number: (610) 282-2254 Calendar System: Semester
URL: www.desales.edu
Established: 1965 Annual Undergrad Tuition & Fees: $30,150
Enrollment: 3,171 Coed
Affiliation or Control: Roman Catholic IRS Status: 501(c)3
Highest Offering: Master's
Program: Liberal Arts And General; Teacher Preparatory; Professional
Accreditation: M, ACBSP, ARCPA, NUR

01 President .... Dr. Bernard F. O'CONNOR, OSFS
04 Admin Assistant to the President .... Ms. Mary A. GOTZON
05 Provost/Vice Pres Academic Affairs .... Dr. Karen WALTON
06 Registrar .... Mr. Thomas MANTONI
08 Librarian .... Ms. Deborah MALONE
51 Dean of Lifelong Learning .... Ms. Deborah BOOROS
88 Dean of Undergraduate Education .... Dr. Robert BLUMENSTEIN
36 Director Career Svcs & Internships .... Ms. Kristin EICHOLTZ
30 Vice Pres Institutional Advancement .... Mr. Thomas L. CAMPBELL
86 Director of Government Relations .... Dr. Bernard F. O'CONNOR, OSFS
102 Director Corp/Foundation Relations .... Mrs. Judith BARBERICH
26 Executive Director of Communication .... Mr. Thomas MCNAMARA
44 Executive Dir of Annual Giving .... Ms. Lina BARBIERI
29 Director of Alumni Relations .... Mr. Dug SALLEY
10 VP for Admin/Finance & Campus Env .... Mr. Robert J. SNYDER
45 Assoc VP for Admin & Planning .... Mr. Peter RAUTZHAN
21 Director of Finance/Treasurer .... Mr. Michael SWEETANA
19 Director of Security .... Chief Stuart BEDICS
09 Director of Institutional Research .... Deacon George KELLY
88 Assoc VP of Campus Environment .... Mr. Marc ALBANESE
18 Director of Facilities .... Mr. Jim MOLCHANY
40 Campus Store Manager .... Mr. Robert BREEN
16 Director of Human Resources .... Mr. Joseph TRELLA
15 Employment Benefits Coordinator .... Ms. Elizabeth GARCIA
13 Director of Information Technology .... Mr. Jim MAHACHEK
32 Vice President Student Life .... Dr. Gerard JOYCE
84 Dean of Enrollment Mgmt .... Mrs. Mary BIRKHEAD
35 Dean of Students .... Mrs. Linda ZERBE
39 Director of Residence Life .... Ms. Leah BREISCH
07 Director of Admissions .... Mr. Derrick WETZEL
37 Director of Student Financial Aid .... Mrs. Joyce FARMER
42 Chaplain .... Vacant
38 Director of Counseling Center .... Ms. Wendy KRISAK
41 Athletic Director .... Mr. Scott COVAL
28 Director Multicultural/Intl Affairs .... Vacant
58 Dean of Graduate Education .... Dr. Peter LEONARD, OSFS

DeVry University - Fort Washington Campus (B)

1140 Virginia Drive, Fort Washington PA 19034-3204
County: Montgomery Identification: 666218
Unit ID: 442824
Telephone: (215) 591-5700 Carnegie Class: Master's S
FAX Number: (215) 591-5863 Calendar System: Semester
URL: www.devry.edu
Established: 1931 Annual Undergrad Tuition & Fees: $16,156
Enrollment: 1,055 Coed
Affiliation or Control: Proprietary IRS Status: Proprietary
Highest Offering: Master's
Program: Occupational; Professional; Business Emphasis
Accreditation: &NH, ENGT

01 Metro President .... Joyce WHEATLEY
03 Group Vice President .... Darryl FIELD
05 Manager Academic Operations .... Lynn COPPOLA
32 Student Services Manager .... Abby GODFREY
06 Registrar .... Olivia MARTINEZ
07 Director of Admissions .... Harry LINENBERG
37 Manager Student Finance .... Robert FRYER
08 Director Library Services .... Pam JOHNSON
15 HR Business Partner .... Vacant
36 Assoc Dean of Career Services .... Jeffrey GREENBERG
31 Director of Community Outreach .... Emily MCGILL

† Regional accreditation is carried under the parent institution in Downers Grove, IL.

DeVry University - King of Prussia (C)

150 Allendale Road, Suite 3201,
King of Prussia PA 19406-2926
County: Montgomery Identification: 666570
Telephone: (610) 205-3130 Carnegie Class: Not Classified
FAX Number: (610) 205-3170 Calendar System: Semester
URL: www.devry.edu
Established: 1931 Annual Undergrad Tuition & Fees: $16,156
Enrollment: 224 Coed
Affiliation or Control: Proprietary IRS Status: Proprietary
Highest Offering: Master's
Program: Professional; Business Emphasis
Accreditation: &NH

01 Center Dean .... Deidre SHAFFER

† Regional accreditation is carried under the parent institution in Downers Grove, IL.

DeVry University - Philadelphia (D)

1800 JFK Boulevard, Suite 200,
Philadelphia PA 19103-7410
County: Philadelphia Identification: 666568
Telephone: (215) 568-2911 Carnegie Class: Not Classified
FAX Number: (215) 568-1255 Calendar System: Semester
URL: www.devry.edu
Established: 1931 Annual Undergrad Tuition & Fees: $16,176
Enrollment: 971 Coed
Affiliation or Control: Proprietary IRS Status: Proprietary
Highest Offering: Master's
Program: Professional; Business Emphasis
Accreditation: &NH

01 Campus President .... Jerry WARGO

† Regional accreditation is carried under the parent institution in Downers Grove, IL.

DeVry University - Pittsburgh (E)

210 Sixth Avenue, Suite 200, Pittsburgh PA 15222-2606
County: Allegheny Identification: 666569
Telephone: (412) 642-9072 Carnegie Class: Not Classified
FAX Number: (412) 642-9201 Calendar System: Semester
URL: www.devry.edu
Established: 1931 Annual Undergrad Tuition & Fees: $16,156
Enrollment: 447 Coed
Affiliation or Control: Proprietary IRS Status: Proprietary
Highest Offering: Master's
Program: Professional; Business Emphasis
Accreditation: &NH

01 Campus Director .... Al MCLAUGHLIN

† Regional accreditation is carried under the parent institution in Downers Grove, IL.

Dickinson College (F)

Box 1773, College & Louther Street,
Carlisle PA 17013-2896
County: Cumberland FICE Identification: 003253
Unit ID: 212009
Telephone: (717) 243-5121 Carnegie Class: Bac/A&S
FAX Number: N/A Calendar System: Semester
URL: www.dickinson.edu
Established: 1783 Annual Undergrad Tuition & Fees: $44,551
Enrollment: 2,397 Coed
Affiliation or Control: Independent Non-Profit IRS Status: 501(c)3
Highest Offering: Baccalaureate
Program: Liberal Arts And General; Teacher Preparatory
Accreditation: M

01 President .... Dr. William G. DURDEN
05 Provost and Dean of the College .... Dr. Neil B. WEISSMAN
84 VP Enroll/Comm & Dean Admissions .... Ms. Stephanie BALMER
32 VP Student Development .... Dr. April L. VARI
10 VP Finance & Administration .... Mr. Thomas A K. QUEENAN
30 Int VP College Advancement .... Ms. Carolyn YEAGER
27 VP & Chief Information Officer .... Mr. Robert E. RENAUD
15 VP Human Resource Services .... Mr. John A. WEIS
43 General Counsel .... Ms. Dana E. SCADUTO
100 Chief of Staff/Secretary of College .... Ms. Karen N. FARYNIAK
18 Assoc VP Campus Operations .... Mr. Kenneth E. SHULTES
20 Associate Provost .... Dr. Robert P. WINSTON
30 Assoc VP Advancement/Assoc Provost .... Ms. Christina P. VAN BUSKIRK
88 Associate Provost for Curriculum .... Dr. Brenda K. BRETZ
28 Spcl Asst Pres Inst & Divrsty Init .... Ms. Joyce A. BYLANDER
21 Assoc VP Financial Op & Aux Svcs .... Mr. Stephen C. HIETSCH
26 Associate VP Enroll/Communications .... Vacant
06 Registrar/Summer School .... Ms. Karen A. WEIKEL
09 Director Institutional Research .... Dr. Michael J. JOHNSON
37 Director of Financial Aid .... Mr. Richard A. HECKMAN
104 Exec Dir of Global Ed/Assoc Provost .... Mr. Stephen C. DEPAUL
94 Professor American Studies .... Dr. Amy E. FARRELL
38 Dir Wellness-Counseling Center .... Dr. Alecia D. SUNDSMO
36 Dean Career Dev/Asst VP Stdnt Dev .... Mr. Philip JONES
35 Dean of Students/Assoc VP .... Mr. Leonard E. BROWN, JR.
24 Director Instruct & Media Services .... Ms. Patricia A. PEHLMAN
27 Director of Media Relations .... Ms. Christine M. DUGAN
44 Exec Dir Annual Fund/Alum & Prnt .... Ms. Kathleen A. MARCELLO
41 Dir Physical Education & Athletics .... Dr. Leslie J. POOLMAN
23 Director Wellness-Health Center .... Ms. Mary E. POLSON
40 Dir College Bookstore/Central Svcs .... Mr. David A. NELSON
19 Director of Public Safety .... Ms. Dolores A. DANSER
91 Assoc VP Enterprise Systems .... Ms. Jill M. FORRESTER
29 Director Alumni & Parent Relations .... Vacant
42 Director Religious Life/Cmty Svcs .... Vacant
28 Director of Diversity Initiatives .... Ms. Paula M. LIMA-JONES

Douglas Education Center (G)

130 Seventh Street, Monessen PA 15062-1097
County: Westmoreland FICE Identification: 020683
Unit ID: 212045
Telephone: (724) 684-3684 Carnegie Class: Assoc/PrivFP
FAX Number: (724) 684-7463 Calendar System: Semester
URL: www.dec.edu
Established: 1904 Annual Undergrad Tuition & Fees: $20,630
Enrollment: 268 Coed
Affiliation or Control: Proprietary IRS Status: Proprietary
Highest Offering: Associate Degree
Program: Occupational; 2-Year Principally Bachelor's Creditable; Fine Arts Emphasis
Accreditation: ACICS

01 President .... Mr. Jeffrey D. IMBRESCIA
05 Vice President of Academic Affairs .... Ms. Patricia A. DECONCILIS
10 Chief Financial Officer .... Mr. Jay B. CLAYTON
20 Director of Academic Progress .... Ms. Susan F. WEAVER
20 Academic Affairs Coordinator .... Ms. N. Renee MCDOWELL
07 Director of Admissions .... Mr. Tony BAEZ MILAN
37 Director of Financial Aid .... Ms. Amanda PHILLIPS
26 Director of Marketing .... Mr. Kevin G. FEAR
88 Director of Cosmetology .... Ms. Karen S. NELSON
36 Manager of Career Services .... Mrs. Donna STAIRS
27 Public Relations Coordinator .... Ms. Katharine E. KELLAR
13 Information Technology Coordinator .... Mr. Wayne NAGLE

Drexel University (H)

3141 Chestnut Street, Philadelphia PA 19104-2875
County: Philadelphia FICE Identification: 003256
Unit ID: 212054
Telephone: (215) 895-2000 Carnegie Class: RU/H
FAX Number: (215) 895-1414 Calendar System: Quarter
URL: www.drexel.edu
Established: 1891 Annual Undergrad Tuition & Fees: $34,505
Enrollment: 24,860 Coed
Affiliation or Control: Independent Non-Profit IRS Status: 501(c)3
Highest Offering: Doctorate
Program: Liberal Arts And General; Professional
Accreditation: M, ANEST, ARCPA, ART, BUS, CEA, CIDA, CLPSY, CONST, CS, DENT, DIETD, ENG, ENGT, HT, LAW, LIB, MED, MFCD, NURSE, PA, PH, PTA, RAD

01 President .... Mr. John A. FRY
05 Provost/Sr Vice Pres Acad Affairs .... Dr. Mark L. GREENBERG
17 Dean/Senior VP Health Sciences .... Dr. Richard V. HOMAN
30 Sr VP Institutional Advancement .... Dr. Elizabeth DALE
10 Sr Vice Pres Finance/Treasurer/CFO .... Mrs. Helen Y. BOWMAN
32 Sr VP Admin Services/Student Life .... Mr. James R. TUCKER
84 Senior VP Enrollment Management .... Ms. Joan T. MCDONALD
26 Sr VP University Communications .... Ms. Lori DOYLE
11 Sr Vice Provost Budget Plan, Admin .... Dr. Janice BIROS
43 Sr VP & General Counsel .... Mr. Michael J. EXLER
03 Sr VP & Executive Director .... Mr. Brian KEECH
20 Sr Vice Provost Academic Affairs .... Dr. N. John DINARDO
13 Vice Pres Info Resources/Technology .... Dr. John BIELEC
88 Vice President Internal Audit .... Mr. James SEAMAN
21 Vice Pres & Assoc Treasurer .... Mr. Eric OLSON
86 VP Gov't & Community Relations .... Mr. David E. WILSON
88 VP of Institutional Advancement .... Mr. Peter FRISKO
46 Vice Provost of Research .... Dr. Deborah CRAWFORD
09 Vice Provost Institutional Research .... Dr. Craig BACH
88 Vice Provost Partnerships .... Dr. Lucy E. KERMAN
18 Vice Pres Univ Facilities .... Dr. Robert FRANCIS
16 Vice President Human Resources .... Ms. Deborah GLENN
88 Vice President & Comptroller .... Ms. Susan WILMER
49 Dean College Arts & Sciences .... Dr. Donna MURASKO
50 Dean LeBow College of Business .... Dr. George TSETSEKOS
54 Dean College of Engineering .... Dr. Joseph B. HUGHES
107 Dean Goodwin Col Professional Stds .... Dr. William F. LYNCH
72 Dean Col Info Science & Technology .... Dr. David E. FENSKE
92 Dean of Pennoni Honors College .... Dr. D.B JONES
62 Dean of Libraries .... Dr. Danuta NITECKI
58 Exec Dir Center for Grad Studies .... Dr. Sandra G. KIRSCHENMANN
61 Dean Earle Mack School of Law .... Mr. Roger J. DENNIS
60 Dean Coll of Media Arts & Design .... Mr. Allen SABINSON
63 Sr VP & Dean College of Medicine .... Dr. Daniel SCHIDLOW
66 Dean College of Nursing/Health Prof .... Dr. Gloria DONNELLY
69 Dean School of Public Health .... Dr. Marla J. GOLD
88 Pres & CEO Acad of Natural Sciences .... Mr. George W. GEPHART, JR.
88 Dir Sch Biomed Eng, Sci, Hlth Sys .... Dr. Banu ONARAL
19 Sr Assoc VP Public Safety .... Mr. Domenic CECCANECCHIO
88 Senior Assoc Vice President .... Ms. Rita LARUE
25 Sr Assoc Vice Provost for Research .... Mr. Michael EDWARDS
41 Athletic Director .... Dr. Eric A. ZILLMER
45 VP Fin Planning & Student Srvcs .... Ms. Amy BOSIO
14 Assoc VP Info Resources & Tech .... Mr. Kenneth BLACKNEY
90 Assoc VP Info Resources & Tech .... Dr. Michael SCHEUERMANN
29 Associate VP Alumni Relations .... Ms. Cristina A. GESO
102 Assoc Vice Pres Corp & Found Rels .... Ms. Patricia DAVIS AUSTIN
32 Assoc Vice Pres/Dean of Students .... Mr. David A. RUTH
96 Sr Assoc VP Stu Life, Admin Srvcs .... Dr. Joseph A. CAMPBELL
44 Assoc VP Planned Giving .... Mr. David J. TOLL
78 Sr Assoc Vice Prov Career Dev Cent .... Mr. Peter FRANKS
93 Assoc Vice Provost AARD .... Ms. Antoinette TORRES
22 Asst Vice Pres Equality & Diversity .... Ms. Michele ROVINSKY
88 Asst Vice Pres Recruitment .... Dr. Lois "Casey" TURNER
07 Asst Vice Pres Admissions .... Ms. Erin FINN
35 Assoc Dean of Students .... Dr. Rebecca L. WEIDENSAUL
23 Asst Dean Counseling & Health Svc .... Dr. Annette MOLYNEUX
85 Asst Dean Intl Stdnts Scholars Svc .... Ms. Adrienne GIGANTINO
06 Registrar .... Mr. Joseph J. SALOMONE
24 Director Instructional Media Svcs .... Mr. Christopher GIBSON

37 Asst VP EM Planning/Financial Aid .... Ms. Melissa M. ENGLUND
38 Assoc Director of Counseling .... Dr. Amy HENNING
39 Director University Housing .... Mr. Joseph RUSSO
104 Asst Vice Provost Study Abroad .... Ms. Daniela ASCARELLI
105 Director of Web Development .... Mr. James MERGENTHAL
04 Executive Asst President's Office .... Ms. Anita MCEVOY
36 Sr Asst Director Career Services .... Mr. Andrew DUFFY
40 Manager Bookstore .... Mr. John RORER
106 President Drexel e-Learning .... Dr. Kenneth HARTMAN
88 Ombuds .... Dr. David FLOOD
88 Vice Provost Strategic Dev & Init .... Dr. Janet FLEETWOOD
88 Coll of Med VP Instit Advancement .... Mr. John J. ZABINSKI
88 Vice Provost Intl Programs .... Dr. Julie MOSTOV

DuBois Business College (A)

One Beaver Drive, DuBois PA 15801-2401

County: Clearfield FICE Identification: 004893
Unit ID: 212072
Telephone: (814) 371-6920 Carnegie Class: Assoc/PrivFP
FAX Number: (814) 371-3974 Calendar System: Quarter
URL: www.dbcollege.com
Established: 1885 Annual Undergrad Tuition & Fees: $12,250
Enrollment: 255 Coed
Affiliation or Control: Proprietary IRS Status: Proprietary
Highest Offering: Associate Degree
Program: Occupational
Accreditation: ACICS

01 President and Director .... Ms. Jackie D. SYKTICH
05 Academic Dean .... Ms. Mary O. JONES
37 Financial Aid Director .... Ms. Karen S. ALDERTON
07 Director of Admissions .... Ms. Terry KHOURY
36 Career Services .... Ms. Barbara M. MARTINI
12 Director Huntingdon Campus .... Mr. Howard DIVINS
12 Director Oil City Campus .... Mrs. Kathie BROWN

DuBois Business College (B)

1001 Moore Street, Huntingdon PA 16652-1800

County: Huntingdon Identification: 666479
Unit ID: 439303
Telephone: (814) 641-0440 Carnegie Class: Assoc/PrivFP
FAX Number: (814) 641-0205 Calendar System: Quarter
URL: www.dbcollege.com
Established: 1885 Annual Undergrad Tuition & Fees: $9,390
Enrollment: 61 Coed
Affiliation or Control: Proprietary IRS Status: Proprietary
Highest Offering: Associate Degree
Program: Occupational
Accreditation: ACICS

01 Director .... Ms. Susan RAMEY

† Branch campus of DuBois Business College, DuBois, PA.

DuBois Business College (C)

701 E Third Street, Oil City PA 16301-2407

County: Venango Identification: 666480
Unit ID: 439312
Telephone: (814) 677-1322 Carnegie Class: Assoc/PrivFP
FAX Number: (814) 677-8237 Calendar System: Quarter
URL: www.dbcollege.com
Established: 1996 Annual Undergrad Tuition & Fees: $14,050
Enrollment: 60 Coed
Affiliation or Control: Proprietary IRS Status: Proprietary
Highest Offering: Associate Degree
Program: Occupational
Accreditation: ACICS

01 Director .... Ms. Kathryn A. BROWN

† Branch campus of DuBois Business College, DuBois, PA.

Duquesne University (D)

600 Forbes Avenue, Pittsburgh PA 15282-0001

County: Allegheny FICE Identification: 003258
Unit ID: 212106
Telephone: (412) 396-6000 Carnegie Class: RU/H
FAX Number: (412) 396-4186 Calendar System: Semester
URL: www.duq.edu
Established: 1878 Annual Undergrad Tuition & Fees: $30,034
Enrollment: 10,011 Coed
Affiliation or Control: Roman Catholic IRS Status: 501(c)3
Highest Offering: Doctorate
Program: Liberal Arts And General; Teacher Preparatory; Professional
Accreditation: M, ARCPA, BUS, CACREP, CEA, CLPSY, LAW, MUS, NURSE, OT, PHAR, PTA, SCPSY, SP, TED

01 President .... Dr. Charles J. DOUGHERTY
04 Assistant to President .... Ms. Mary F. MCINTYRE
05 Provost/Academic Vice President .... Dr. Ralph L. PEARSON
10 Vice President Management Business .... Mr. Stephen A. SCHILLO
32 Exec Vice Pres for Student Life .... Rev. Sean HOGAN, CSSP
30 VP for University Advancement .... Mr. John J. PLANTE
88 Vice President Mission & Identity .... Rev. James MCCLOSKEY
43 VP Legal Affairs & General Counsel .... Ms. Linda S. DRAGO
20 Assoc Academic Vice Pres Research .... Dr. Alan W. SEADLER
20 Assoc Academic Vice President .... Dr. Jeffrey A. MILLER
21 Assoc Vice Pres Financial Affairs .... Mr. David P. GROUSOSKY
13 Executive Director CTS .... Dr. John H. ZIEGLER
31 Exec Director Auxiliary Services .... Mr. David DIPETRO
85 Exec Director Intl Programs .... Dr. Roberta C. ARONSON
84 Assoc Vice Pres Enrollment Mgmt .... Mr. Paul-James CUKANNA
06 Registrar .... Ms. Kim HOERITZ
08 Librarian .... Dr. Laverna M. SAUNDERS
29 Director Alumni Relations .... Ms. Sarah SPERRY
35 Director Student Affairs .... Rev. Sean HOGAN, CSSP
09 Director of Institutional Research .... Mr. Matthew NORTH
37 Director Financial Aid .... Mr. Richard C. ESPOSITO
15 Director of Human Resource Mgmt .... Ms. Mary Ellen BANEY
19 Director of Security .... Mr. Thomas HART
88 Dir Environmental Health/Safety .... Mr. George BENDER
18 Director of Facilities Management .... Mr. Rodney W. DOBISH
36 Director of Career Services .... Ms. Nicole FELDHUES
41 Director of Athletics .... Mr. Greg J. AMODIO
26 Assoc Vice Pres of Public Affairs .... Ms. Bridget M. FARE
22 Director Affirmative Action .... Dr. Judith R. GRIGGS
23 Director Health Service .... Ms. Dessa MRVOS
38 Director Univ Counseling Center .... Dr. Ian C. EDWARDS
39 Director Residence Life .... Mrs. Sharon G. OELSCHLAGER
42 Director Campus Ministry .... Rev. Raymond FRENCH, CSSP
28 Director of Multicultural Affairs .... Dr. Rahmon HART
96 Director of Purchasing/Support Svcs .... Ms. Cynthia A. VINARSKI
50 Dean Business & Administration .... Dr. Alan R. MICIAK
66 Dean of Nursing .... Dr. Mary Ellen S. GLASGOW
67 Dean of Pharmacy .... Dr. J. Douglas BRICKER
64 Dean of Music .... Dr. Edward W. KOCHER
53 Dean of Education .... Dr. Olga M. WELCH
76 Dean of Health Sciences .... Dr. Gregory H. FRAZER
61 Dean of Law .... Mr. Ken GORMLEY
49 Dean of Liberal Arts/Graduate .... Dr. James SWINDAL
65 Dean of Natural/Environment Sci .... Dr. David W. SEYBERT
88 Dean Leadership & Profess Advanc .... Dr. Dorothy E. BASSETT
40 Bookstore Manager .... Mr. John KACHUR
88 Internal Auditor .... Mr. Aaron MITCHAM

Eastern University (E)

1300 Eagle Road, Saint Davids PA 19087-3696

County: Delaware FICE Identification: 003259
Unit ID: 212133
Telephone: (610) 341-5800 Carnegie Class: Master's L
FAX Number: (610) 341-1377 Calendar System: Semester
URL: www.eastern.edu
Established: 1925 Annual Undergrad Tuition & Fees: $26,934
Enrollment: 4,464 Coed
Affiliation or Control: American Baptist IRS Status: 501(c)3
Highest Offering: Doctorate
Program: 2-Year Principally Bachelor's Creditable; Liberal Arts And General; Teacher Preparatory; Professional
Accreditation: M, EXSC, NURSE, SW

01 President .... Dr. David R. BLACK
73 Chancellor/Dean of the Seminary .... Dr. Christopher A. HALL
10 Vice Pres for Finance/Operations .... Mr. J. Pernell JONES
03 Senior Vice President/Chief Mkt Ofc . Dr. M. Thomas RIDINGTON
05 Interim Provost .... Dr. Kenton SPARKS
32 Vice Pres for Student Development .... Dr. Bettie Ann BRIGHAM
30 Vice President Development .... Mr. Derek RITCHIE
84 Exec Director Enrollment (CAS) .... Mr. Michael DZIEDZIAK
84 Interim Exec Dir of Enroll(CCGPS) .... Mr. Peter J. BEROL
84 Dir of Seminary Admissions .... Rev. Alexander HOUSTON
15 Director of Human Resources .... Mrs. Kacey BERNARD
06 Registrar/VP Administration .... Mrs. Diana S. BACCI
04 Exec Asst to the President .... Mrs. Heather NORCINI
35 Dean of Students .... Mr. Daryl HAWKINS
12 Dean Esperanza College .... Dr. Elizabeth CONDE-FRAZIER
49 Dean Arts and Sciences .... Dr. Beth M. DORIANI
58 Dean Grad/Professional Studies ... Dr. Debra HEATH-THORNTON
53 Assoc Dean Education .... Dr. Harry GUTELIUS
66 Chair Department of Nursing .... Dr. MaryAnne PETERS
18 Exec Director Campus Services .... Mr. Carl ALTOMARE
91 Exec Director Admin Computing .... Mr. Dwight FOWLER
105 Webmaster .... Mr. Valdimir GORDYNSKIY
09 Director Institutional Research .... Mr. Thomas A. DAHLSTROM
09 Assoc Provost Inst Effectiveness .... Dr. Christine P. MAHAN
27 Exec Director of Communications .... Mrs. Linda OLSON
88 Director Student Accounts .... Ms. Lisa WELLER
08 Library Director .... Mr. James L. SAUER
42 University Chaplain .... Rev Dr. Joseph B. MODICA
42 Seminary Chaplain .... Rev. Willette BURGIE-BRYANT
37 Director of Financial Aid .... Ms. Christal JENNINGS
90 Director of Academic Computing .... Mr. Philip MUGRIDGE
36 Director of Careers and Calling .... Ms. Tess BRADLEY
29 Director Alumni Relations .... Mrs. Mary GARDNER
41 Director of Athletics .... Mr. Brad FIELDS
19 Director of Campus Security .... Mr. Jim MAGEE
88 Director of Conferences .... Ms. Meggin CAPERS
38 Dir Counseling/Academic Support .... Dr. Lisa M. HEMLICK
23 Director College Health Center .... Mrs. Janet TOPPER
96 Manager of Purchasing .... Ms. Patricia G. ROOT
85 Dir Intl Student & Scholar Services .... Rev. Kathy KAUTZ DE ARANGO
39 Coordinator of Housing .... Mr. Anthony HARRIS
40 Bookstore Manager .... Mr. Frank MARTINEZ, JR.
88 Chair Urban Studies .... Dr. K-Lee JOHNSON
28 Dir Multicultural Stdnt Initiatives .... Ms. Jacqueline IRVING
89 Director Advising/1st Yr Programs .... Mrs. Julie ELLIOTT
92 Dean Honors College .... Dr. Jonathan YONAN

† Parent institution of Palmer Theological Seminary.

Elizabethtown College (F)

1 Alpha Drive, Elizabethtown PA 17022-2298

County: Lancaster FICE Identification: 003262
Unit ID: 212197
Telephone: (717) 361-1000 Carnegie Class: Bac/Diverse
FAX Number: (717) 361-1207 Calendar System: Semester
URL: www.etown.edu
Established: 1899 Annual Undergrad Tuition & Fees: $45,600
Enrollment: 1,848 Coed
Affiliation or Control: Church Of The Brethren IRS Status: 501(c)3
Highest Offering: Master's
Program: Liberal Arts And General; Teacher Preparatory; Professional
Accreditation: M, ACBSP, ENG, MUS, OT, SW

01 President .... Dr. Carl J. STRIKWERDA
05 Provost & Sr Vice President .... Dr. Susan TRAVERSO
10 Vice President for Finance .... Mr. Richard L. BAILEY
30 Vice President for Advancement .... Mr. David C. BEIDLEMAN
11 Vice President for Administration .... Mr. David B. DENTLER
84 VP Admissions/Enrollment Mgmt .... Mr. Paul CRAMER
15 Associate VP for Human Resources .... Ms. Nancy E. FLOREY
32 Dean of Students .... Ms. Marianne CALENDA
20 Dean of Faculty .... Dr. Fletcher MCCLELLAN
51 Dean Ctr Continuing Educ/Dist Lrng .... Mr. John KOKOLUS
06 Associate Academic Dean/Registrar .... Dr. Elizabeth A. RIDER
07 Assoc Dean Admissions/Enroll Mgmt .... Ms. Debra H. MURRAY
35 Asst Dean of Students & Dir of CSS .... Ms. Stephanie A. RANKIN
26 Exec Dir Marketing/ Communications .... Ms. Elizabeth A. BRAUNGARD
13 Exec Director Information/Tech Svcs .... Mr. Ronald P. HEASLEY
102 Exec Dir Foundation/Govt Relations .... Ms. Lesley M. FINNEY
46 Exec Dir Ofc Sponsored Rsrch/Pgms .... Dr. Richard BASOM
27 Director of Communications .... Ms. Amy MOUNTAIN
37 Director of Financial Aid .... Ms. Elizabeth K. MCCLOUD
08 College Librarian & Dir of Library .... Ms. BethAnn ZAMBELLA
29 Director Alumni Devel & Programs .... Mr. Mark A. CLAPPER
19 Director of Campus Security .... Mr. Jack R. LONGENECKER
41 Director of Athletics .... Ms. Nancy J. LATIMORE
23 Dir Health Promotion/Campus Health .... Ms. Alexandra SPAYD
40 Director of Business Services .... Vacant
88 Director of Food Services .... Mr. Eric C. TURZAI
42 Chaplain of the College .... Dr. Tracy SADD
92 Director Honor Program .... Dr. Dana G. MEAD
18 Dir of Facilities Mgmt/Construction .... Mr. Joseph METRO
28 Director of Diversity .... Ms. Diane ELLIOTT
21 Business Office Support .... Vacant

Erie Business Center, Main (G)

246 W Ninth Street, Erie PA 16501-1392

County: Erie FICE Identification: 004894
Unit ID: 212425
Telephone: (814) 456-7504 Carnegie Class: Assoc/PrivFP
FAX Number: (814) 456-6015 Calendar System: Trimester
URL: www.eriebc.edu
Established: 1884 Annual Undergrad Tuition & Fees: $11,800
Enrollment: 300 Coed
Affiliation or Control: Proprietary IRS Status: Proprietary
Highest Offering: Associate Degree
Program: Occupational
Accreditation: ACICS

01 President .... Mr. Charles P. MCGEARY
03 Chief Executive Officer .... Mr. Samuel L. MCCAUGHTRY
12 Executive Director .... Ms. Donna B. PERINO

Erie Business Center South (H)

170 Cascade Galleria, New Castle PA 16101-3900

County: Lawrence FICE Identification: 003305
Unit ID: 213686
Telephone: (724) 658-9066 Carnegie Class: Assoc/PrivFP
FAX Number: (724) 658-3083 Calendar System: Trimester
URL: www.eriebc.edu/newcastle
Established: 1884 Annual Undergrad Tuition & Fees: $7,164
Enrollment: 65 Coed
Affiliation or Control: Proprietary IRS Status: Proprietary
Highest Offering: Associate Degree
Program: Occupational; 2-Year Principally Bachelor's Creditable; Business Emphasis
Accreditation: ACICS

01 Director .... Mr. Steven R. OROURKE

† Branch campus of Erie Business Center Main, Erie, PA.

Erie Institute of Technology (I)

940 Millcreek Mall, Erie PA 16565-1002

County: Erie FICE Identification: 022039
Unit ID: 212434
Telephone: (814) 868-9900 Carnegie Class: Assoc/PrivFP
FAX Number: (814) 868-9977 Calendar System: Semester
URL: www.erieit.edu
Established: 1958 Annual Undergrad Tuition & Fees: $18,000
Enrollment: 243 Coed
Affiliation or Control: Proprietary IRS Status: Proprietary
Highest Offering: Associate Degree
Program: Occupational; Technical Emphasis
Accreditation: ACCSC

01 Director .... Mr. Paul FITZGERALD
05 Director of Education .... Ms. Kate HUSHON
37 Financial Aid Officer .... Ms. Kim CLARK
07 Admissions Director .... Ms. Barb BOLT
36 Placement Director .... Mr. Bill BURCHFIELD

Evangelical Theological Seminary (A)

121 S College Street, Myerstown PA 17067-1222
County: Lebanon FICE Identification: 003263
Unit ID: 212443
Telephone: (717) 866-5775 Carnegie Class: Spec/Faith
FAX Number: (717) 866-4667 Calendar System: 4/1/4
URL: www.evangelical.edu
Established: 1953 Annual Graduate Tuition & Fees: $11,500
Enrollment: 125 Coed
Affiliation or Control: Evangelical Congregational Church
IRS Status: 501(c)3
Highest Offering: Master's; No Undergraduates
Program: Professional; Religious Emphasis
Accreditation: M, THEOL

01 President .... Dr. Anthony L. BLAIR
30 Vice Pres Institutional Advancement .... Rev. Ann E. STEEL
10 Vice President Finance & Operations .... Mr. Kevin C. HENRY
05 Dean of Academic Programs .... Dr. Laurie A. MELLINGER
07 Dean of Admissions .... Mr. Thomas M. MAIELLO
08 Head Librarian .... Dr. Terry M. HEISEY
18 Director of Buildings & Grounds .... Mr. William J. ROBERTSON
88 Database Manager .... Mrs. Marsha A. CONLEY
06 Registrar/Financial Aid Admin .... Mr. Ellis I. KIRK

Everest Institute (B)

100 Forbes Avenue, Suite 1200,
Pittsburgh PA 15222-3618
County: Allegheny FICE Identification: 007091
Unit ID: 212090
Telephone: (412) 261-4520 Carnegie Class: Assoc/PrivFP
FAX Number: (412) 261-4546 Calendar System: Quarter
URL: www.everest.edu
Established: 1840 Annual Undergrad Tuition & Fees: $12,996
Enrollment: 636 Coed
Affiliation or Control: Proprietary IRS Status: Proprietary
Highest Offering: Associate Degree
Program: Occupational; 2-Year Principally Bachelor's Creditable; Business Emphasis
Accreditation: ACICS, MAC

01 President/Director .... Vacant
05 Dean .... Mrs. Michele ZOLLNER
07 Director of Admissions .... Ms. Lynn FISCHER
36 Director of Career Services .... Ms. Dana MELVIN
37 Director of Student Finance .... Mrs. Annette VOSE

Fortis Institute (C)

5757 West Ridge Road, Erie PA 16506-1013
County: Erie FICE Identification: 030108
Unit ID: 216418
Telephone: (814) 838-7673 Carnegie Class: Assoc/PrivFP
FAX Number: (814) 838-8642 Calendar System: Quarter
URL: www.fortis.edu
Established: 1984 Annual Undergrad Tuition & Fees: $12,538
Enrollment: 1,215 Coed
Affiliation or Control: Proprietary IRS Status: Proprietary
Highest Offering: Associate Degree
Program: Occupational; 2-Year Principally Bachelor's Creditable
Accreditation: ACICS, DH, MAAB, MAC, MLTAD, RAD

01 President .... Mr. Guy EULIANO
05 Academic Dean .... Mr. Jerry KNIGHT
10 Business Officer .... Ms. Shelley FAYTAK
07 Admissions .... Ms. Karen LAPAGLIA
37 Financial Aid .... Ms. Renee WRIGHT
36 Placement .... Ms. Wendy FUGATE

Fortis Institute (D)

166 Slocum Street, Forty Fort PA 18704-2347
County: Luzerne FICE Identification: 030115
Unit ID: 249609
Telephone: (570) 288-8400 Carnegie Class: Assoc/PrivFP
FAX Number: (570) 287-7936 Calendar System: Other
URL: www.fortis.edu
Established: 1984 Annual Undergrad Tuition & Fees: $13,575
Enrollment: 521 Coed
Affiliation or Control: Proprietary IRS Status: Proprietary
Highest Offering: Associate Degree
Program: Occupational
Accreditation: ACCSC

01 Campus President .... Ruth BRUMAGIN
05 Director of Education .... Joanne GIOVANNINI
07 Director of Admissions .... Heather CONTARDI

Fortis Institute (E)

517 Ash Street, Scranton PA 18509
County: Lackawanna FICE Identification: 030116
Unit ID: 385503
Telephone: (570) 558-1818 Carnegie Class: Assoc/PrivFP
FAX Number: (570) 342-4537 Calendar System: Other
URL: www.fortis.edu/scranton-pennsylvania.php
Established: 1922 Annual Undergrad Tuition & Fees: N/A
Enrollment: 230 Coed
Affiliation or Control: Proprietary IRS Status: Proprietary
Highest Offering: Associate Degree
Program: Occupational
Accreditation: ACCSC, DH

01 Campus President .... Ms. Madeline LEVY CRUZ

† Tuition varies by degree program.

Franklin & Marshall College (F)

PO Box 3003, Lancaster PA 17604-3003
County: Lancaster FICE Identification: 003265
Unit ID: 212577
Telephone: (717) 291-3911 Carnegie Class: Bac/A&S
FAX Number: (717) 291-4183 Calendar System: Semester
URL: www.fandm.edu
Established: 1787 Annual Undergrad Tuition & Fees: $44,260
Enrollment: 2,324 Coed
Affiliation or Control: Independent Non-Profit IRS Status: 501(c)3
Highest Offering: Baccalaureate
Program: Liberal Arts And General
Accreditation: M

01 President .... Dr. Daniel R. PORTERFIELD
10 Vice Pres for Finance and Treasurer .... Mr. David R. PROULX
30 Vice Pres for College Advancement .... Vacant
84 VP Enroll Mgmt & Dean of Admission .... Mr. Daniel G. LUGO
27 Vice Pres for College Communication .... Ms. Cass CLIATT
05 Provost/Dean of Faculty .... Dr. Ann STEINER
20 Dean of the College .... Dr. Kent C. TRACHTE
88 Assoc Dean of Col & Dir Klehr Ctr .... Dr. Ralph TABER
21 Assoc Vice President for Finance .... Mr. Gregory L. FULMER
11 Associate VP for Administration .... Mr. Barry BOSLEY
88 Associate VP of Development .... Ms. Mary D. WOOLSON
45 Sr Asc Dean Fac/VP Plng & Inst Res .... Dr. Alan S. CANIGLIA
20 Associate Dean of Faculty .... Dr. Carol DEWET
100 Chief of Staff .... Dr. Samuel HOUSER
08 College Librarian .... Ms. Pamela SNELSON
44 Major Gifts Officer .... Ms. Catherine T. FERRY
85 Assoc Dean International Programs .... Ms. Sue MENNICKE
36 Associate Dean/House Prefect .... Dr. Roger A. GODIN
46 Associate Dean of Faculty .... Dr. Michael BILLIG
46 Associate Dean of Faculty .... Dr. Carmen TISNADO
32 Associate Dean of Students .... Dr. Marion A. COLEMAN
88 Associate Dean/House Prefect .... Ms. Katharine J. SNIDER
88 Associate Dean/House Prefect .... Dr. Suzanna L. RICHTER
88 Senior Assoc Dean of the College .... Dr. Steven P. O'DAY
88 Associate Dean/House Prefect .... Dr. David M. STAMESHKIN
88 Associate Dean/House Prefect .... Dr. Amy R. MORENO
88 Associate Dean/Senior Prefect .... Dr. Todd DEKAY
21 Assistant Controller .... Ms. Kathryn ELLIEHAUSEN-SLOBOZIEN
15 Director Human Resources .... Ms. Nancy ESHLEMAN
18 Director Facilities & Operations .... Vacant
19 Director Public Safety .... Vacant
23 Director Health Services .... Dr. Amy A. MYERS
13 Assoc Provost & Chief Info Officer .... Dr. Jonathan C. ENOS
37 Director Financial Aid .... Mr. Clarke C. PAINE
38 Clinical Dir Counseling Services .... Dr. Christine G. CONWAY
90 Dir Instructional & Emerg Technol .... Dr. Oscar RETTERER
09 Director of Institutional Research .... Dr. Alan CANIGLIA
06 Registrar & Assoc Director Inst Res .... Ms. Christine D. ALEXANDER
29 Director of Alumni Programs .... Ms. Cathy ROMAN
07 Director of Admission .... MS. Julie A. KERICH

Gannon University (G)

University Square, Erie PA 16541-0001
County: Erie FICE Identification: 003266
Unit ID: 212601
Telephone: (814) 871-7000 Carnegie Class: Master's L
FAX Number: (814) 871-7338 Calendar System: Other
URL: www.gannon.edu
Established: 1925 Annual Undergrad Tuition & Fees: $26,526
Enrollment: 4,076 Coed
Affiliation or Control: Roman Catholic IRS Status: 501(c)3
Highest Offering: Doctorate
Program: Liberal Arts And General; Teacher Preparatory; Professional
Accreditation: M, ACBSP, ANEST, ARCPA, CACREP, CS, ENG, NURSE, OT, PTA, RAD, SW

01 President .... Dr. Keith TAYLOR
05 Provost/VP Academic Affairs .... Dr. Andrew NOVOBILSKI
10 Vice President Finance/Admin .... Mrs. Linda L. WAGNER
30 Vice Pres University Advancement .... Mr. Jack SIMS
88 Assoc Vice President for Mission .... Rev. Michael KESICKI
84 Vice President for Enrollment .... Mr. William EDMONDSON
32 VP Student Development & Engagement .... Vacant
04 Assistant to the President .... Mrs. Darlene A. THEISEN
50 Dean Col Humanities/Business/Educ .... Dr. Linda FLEMING
76 Dean Norosky Col Health Profess/Sci ... Dr. Carolyn B. MASTERS
49 Director of Liberal Studies .... Dr. Penny L. SMITH
08 Director Nash Library .... Mr. Ken BRUNDAGE
37 Director of Financial Aid .... Ms. Sharon A. KRAHE
06 Registrar .... Ms. Marilyn A. MOORE
36 Dir Career Develop/Employment Svcs .... Mr. James M. FINEGAN
35 Director of Student Living .... Mr. Doug R. ZIMMERMAN
23 Head Nurse .... Ms. Ali SCHNEIDER
88 Dir Student Organiz/Leadership Dev .... Ms. Beth Ann SCHICK
29 Director Development & Alumni Rels .... Ms. Cathy FRESCH
27 Dir Pub Rels & Communications .... Mrs. Karla M. WLUDYGA
44 Dir of Research/Foundation Rels .... Ms. Anita L. MILLER
21 Controller .... Mr. Jeffrey S. TAYLOR
45 Director of Budgeting .... Ms. Mary Kathleen DRAGHI
16 Director of Human Resources .... Mr. Robert J. CLINE
41 Director of Athletics .... Mr. Mark RICHARD
19 Director Campus Police & Safety .... Mr. Ted MARNEN
14 Director of Computing/Telecomm .... Mr. Mark JORDANO
42 University Chaplain .... Rev. George STROHMEYER
07 Director of Admissions .... Mr. Terrence R. KIZINA
09 Director of Institutional Research .... Ms. Margaret JAMES
15 Director Human Resources .... Mr. Robert J. CLINE
18 Chief Facilities/Physical Plant .... Mr. Gary G. GARNIC
26 Chief Media Relations Officer .... Mr. Nick G. PRONKO
38 Director Student Counseling .... Mr. James M. FINEGAN
86 Dir Community/Government Relations .... Ms. Erika A. RAMALHO
96 Director of Purchasing .... Mr. Andrew TEETS
40 Bookstore Manager .... Ms. Amber COOK

Geneva College (H)

3200 College Avenue, Beaver Falls PA 15010-3599
County: Beaver FICE Identification: 003267
Unit ID: 212656
Telephone: (724) 846-5100 Carnegie Class: Bac/Diverse
FAX Number: (724) 847-6687 Calendar System: Semester
URL: www.geneva.edu
Established: 1848 Annual Undergrad Tuition & Fees: $24,480
Enrollment: 1,990 Coed
Affiliation or Control: Reformed Presbyterian Church IRS Status: 501(c)3
Highest Offering: Master's
Program: Liberal Arts And General; Teacher Preparatory; Professional
Accreditation: M, ACBSP, CACREP, CVT, ENG

01 President .... Dr. Kenneth A. SMITH
03 Executive Vice President .... Mr. Larry K. GRIFFITH
05 Provost .... Dr. Kenneth P. CARSON
30 Vice Pres of Advancement .... Dr. Jeffrey A. JONES
10 Assoc Vice Pres & Controller .... Mr. Stephen C. ROSS
15 Assoc Vice Pres & Director of HR .... Mr. Timothy R. BAIRD
32 Dean of Students .... Dr. Michael J. LOOMIS
20 Dean of Faculty and Administration .... Dr. Terri B. WILLIAMS
07 Assoc VP for Enrollment .... Mr. David B. LAYTON
35 Associate Dean of Students .... Vacant
51 Director of Adult Education .... Dr. Ralph N. PHILLIPS
06 Registrar .... Mrs. Andrea L. KORCAN-BUZZA
37 Director of Financial Aid .... Mr. Steven K. BELL
08 Librarian .... Dr. John G. DONCEVIC
26 Director Public Relations .... Mrs. Cheryl L. JOHNSTON
29 Director of Alumni Relations .... Mr. Thomas J. STEIN
88 Assoc Dir Parent & Church Relations .... Mrs. Rebecca J. PHILLIPS
14 Director of Computer Services .... Mr. Larry R. WINGARD
41 Director of Athletics .... Dr. Kimerly R. GALL
18 Director of Physical Plant .... Mr. Jeffrey LYDIC
36 Director of Career Development .... Mr. Robert L. ROSTONI
85 International Admissions Counselor .... Mr. Joel A. BRUBAKER
88 Director International Student Svcs .... Ms. Ann E. BURKHEAD
40 Campus Store Manager .... Ms. Rachael E. VAN DERVEER
19 Director of Security .... Mr. Dennis E. DAMAZO
44 Director of Planned Giving .... Mrs. Wendy B. SMITH
93 Dir Multiethnic Student Services .... Miss Kathy Y. KINZER
92 Director Honors Program .... Dr. David S. GUTHRIE
39 Director of Residence Life .... Mr. Neil A. BEST
23 Health Services Director .... Mrs. Connie I. ERWIN
96 Director of Purchasing .... Mrs. Nancy D. GRAHAM
21 Accounting and Payroll Manager .... Mrs. Ruth Ann HARTZEL
38 ACCESS Director .... Miss Christy M. COULTER

Gettysburg College (I)

300 N Washington Street, Gettysburg PA 17325-1486
County: Adams FICE Identification: 003268
Unit ID: 212674
Telephone: (717) 337-6000 Carnegie Class: Bac/A&S
FAX Number: (717) 337-6008 Calendar System: Semester
URL: www.gettysburg.edu
Established: 1832 Annual Undergrad Tuition & Fees: $44,210
Enrollment: 2,714 Coed
Affiliation or Control: Evangelical Lutheran Church In America
IRS Status: 501(c)3
Highest Offering: Baccalaureate
Program: Liberal Arts And General
Accreditation: M

01 President .... Dr. Janet MORGAN RIGGS
03 Executive Vice President .... Ms. Jane D. NORTH
05 Provost .... Dr. Christopher ZAPPE
30 Vice Pres Dev & Alumni/Parent Rels .... Mr. Robert KALLIN
10 Vice President Finance/Treasurer .... Mr. Daniel T. KONSTALID
32 Vice President for College Life .... Dr. Julie L. RAMSEY
84 Vice Pres Enrollment/Education Svcs .... Ms. Barbara B. FRITZE
13 Vice President Information Tech .... Dr. Rod TOSTEN
45 Assoc Provost for Planning .... Mrs. Rhonda GOOD
20 Assoc Provost for Faculty .... Ms. Elizabeth VITI
21 Associate Vice President/Treasurer .... Mr. Christopher DELANEY
26 Exec Dir of Comm & Marketing .... Mr. Paul W. REDFERN
35 Associate Dean of College Life .... Mr. Thomas J. MOTTOLA
44 Assistant Vice Pres for Development .... Ms. Susan PYRON
93 Dean Intercultural Advancement .... Mr. H. Pete CURRY, JR.

06 Registrar .... Mr. James DUFFY
37 Director of Financial Aid .... Ms. Christina L. GORMLEY
07 Director Admissions .... Ms. Gail M. SWEEZEY
42 Chaplain .... Rev. Joseph A. DONNELLA, II
09 Director for Institutional Analysis .... Ms. Suhua DONG
38 Exec Dir of Health & Counseling .... Ms. Kathy BRADLEY
36 Director of Career Services .... Ms. Kathleen L. WILLIAMS
08 Head Librarian .... Ms. Robin WAGNER
44 Director of Annual Giving .... Mr. Christopher HARMON
29 Director of Alumni Relations .... Mr. Joe LYNCH
41 Athletic Director .... Mr. David W. WRIGHT
19 Director of Campus Safety/Security .... Mr. William J. LAFFERTY
18 Director Facilities Planning & Mgmt .... Mr. James BIESECKER
21 Controller .... Ms. Christine M. HARTMAN
80 Director Center for Public Service .... Ms. Gretchen NATTER
39 Director Residence Life .... Mr. Victor ARCELUS
20 Director of Academic Advising .... Ms. Gail Ann RICKERT
23 Director Health Services .... Mr. Frederick W. KINSELLA
35 Director Student Activities .... Ms. Morgan A. STOCKER
40 Director of College Bookstore .... Mr. Michael J. KOTLINSKI
94 Coord Women/Gender/Sexuality Stds .... Ms. Nathalie LEBON
96 Director of Procurement .... Ms. Patricia K. VERDEROSA
15 Co-Director Human Resources .... Ms. Jennifer R. LUCAS
15 Co-Director Human Resources .... Ms. Regina Z. CAMPO
25 Director of Found/Govt Grant .... Mr. Richard M. ROSENBERG
31 Assoc VP for Govt & Comm Relatio .... Ms. Patricia A. LAWSON
104 Director of Off-Campus Studies .... Ms. Rebecca A. BERGREN

Gratz College (A)

7605 Old York Road, Melrose Park PA 19027-3010
County: Montgomery FICE Identification: 004058
Unit ID: 212771
Telephone: (215) 635-7300 Carnegie Class: Master's L
FAX Number: (215) 635-1046 Calendar System: Semester
URL: www.gratz.edu
Established: 1895 Annual Undergrad Tuition & Fees: $13,200
Enrollment: 1,023 Coed
Affiliation or Control: Independent Non-Profit IRS Status: 501(c)3
Highest Offering: Doctorate
Program: Liberal Arts And General; Teacher Preparatory; Professional
Accreditation: M

01 President .... Ms. Joy W. GOLDSTEIN
05 Dean Academic Affairs/Dir Cont Educ .... Dr. Jerry M. KUTNICK
04 Executive Asst to President .... Ms. Dodi KLIMOFF
26 Chief Public Relations Officer .... Ms. Dodi KLIMOFF
08 Director of Tuttleman Library .... Mr. Eliezer WISE
10 Director of Finance .... Mr. Joseph WEHR
07 Director of Student Life/Admissions .... Ms. Shira WEISSBACH
06 Director of Student Records .... Ms. Lovisa WOODSON
15 Director Personnel Services .... Ms. Yaffa HOWARD
30 Dir of Institutional Advancement .... Ms. Beth SCHONBERGER
88 Actg Dir Jewish Community High Sch .... Ms. Ruth SCHAPIRA
37 Student Financial Services Advisor .... Ms. Dana MOORE

Grove City College (B)

100 Campus Drive, Grove City PA 16127-2104
County: Mercer FICE Identification: 003269
Unit ID: 212805
Telephone: (724) 458-2000 Carnegie Class: Bac/A&S
FAX Number: (724) 458-2190 Calendar System: Semester
URL: www.gcc.edu
Established: 1876 Annual Undergrad Tuition & Fees: $14,212
Enrollment: 2,461 Coed
Affiliation or Control: Presbyterian Church (U.S.A.) IRS Status: 501(c)3
Highest Offering: Baccalaureate
Program: Liberal Arts And General; Teacher Preparatory; Professional
Accreditation: M, ENG

01 President .... Dr. Richard G. JEWELL
05 Provost & VP for Academic Affairs .... Dr. William P. ANDERSON, JR.
10 Vice Pres for Financial Affairs .... Mr. Roger K. TOWLE
32 Vice Pres For Student Life/Learning .... Mr. Larry E. HARDESTY
30 Vice President for Inst Advancement .. Mr. Jeffrey D. PROKOVICH
11 Vice President for Operations .... Mr. Thomas W. GREGG
13 Vice Pres/Chief Information Officer .... Dr. Vincent F. DISTASI
04 Assistant to the President .... Ms. Betty L. TALLERICO
49 Dean of School of Arts/Letters .... Dr. John A. SPARKS
81 Dean School of Engr/Science .... Dr. Stacy G. BIRMINGHAM
84 Dean Enrollment Svcs/Registrar .... Dr. John G. INMAN
35 Assistant Dean of Students .... Mr. John M. COYNE
15 Dir of HR & Business Operations .... Mrs. Marci K. WAGNER
07 Director of Admissions .... Ms. Sarah E. ZWINGER
88 Admn Dir For Ctr For Vision/Values .... Mr. Lee S. WISHING, III
36 Director of Career Services .... Mr. James T. THRASHER
08 Librarian .... Ms. Diane H. GRUNDY
37 Director of Financial Aid .... Mr. Thomas G. BALL
88 Dir Std Rec/Club Sports/Frat Life .... Mr. Andrew A. TONCIC, JR.
35 Director Stdnt Activities/Programs .... Mr. T. Scott GORDON
19 Director of Campus Safety .... Mr. Seth J. VAN TIL
23 Director of Health & Wellness Ctr .... Mrs. Amy E. PAGANO
40 Bookstore Manager .... Mrs. Carrie J. GAULT
41 Athletic Director .... Dr. Donald L. LYLE
42 Dean of the Chapel .... Rev. F. Stanley KEEHLWETTER
29 Sr Dir Alumni & College Relations .... Ms. Melissa A. MACLEOD
38 Director of College Counseling .... Dr. Suzanne N. HOUK
39 Director of Residence Life .... Ms. Jamie R. SWANK

Gwynedd-Mercy College (C)

1325 Sumneytown Pike, PO Box 901,
Gwynedd Valley PA 19437-0901
County: Montgomery FICE Identification: 003270
Unit ID: 212832
Telephone: (215) 646-7300 Carnegie Class: Master's M
FAX Number: (215) 641-5596 Calendar System: Semester
URL: www.gmc.edu
Established: 1948 Annual Undergrad Tuition & Fees: $28,340
Enrollment: 2,710 Coed
Affiliation or Control: Roman Catholic IRS Status: 501(c)3
Highest Offering: Master's
Program: Occupational; Liberal Arts And General; Teacher Preparatory; Nursing Emphasis
Accreditation: M, ADNUR, CVT, IACBE, NUR, RTT

01 President .... Dr. Kathleen C. OWENS
05 VP Academic Affairs .... Dr. Frank E. SCULLY, JR.
10 Vice President Finance .... Mr. Kevin O'FLAHERTY
30 Vice Pres Institutional Advancement .... Mr. Gerald (Jerry) MCLAUGHLIN
84 Vice Pres for Enrollment & SS .... Dr. Cheryl HORSEY
101 Secretary of the Institution/Board .... Ms. Barbara MCHALE
108 AVP for Assessment & Compliance .... Dr. Dawn HAYWARD
20 AVP Off-Campus/On-line Programs .... Dr. Raymond CAMPBELL
88 AVP for Enrollment & Marketing .... Mr. Jamison KRAVCAK
06 Registrar .... Ms. Therese ANDERSON
08 Director of Library .... Mr. Daniel SCHABERT
37 Director of Student Financial Aid .... Vacant
13 Chief Information Officer .... Dr. Karl HORVATH
88 Dean of Students .... Dr. Carol GRUBER
29 Director Alumni Relations .... Ms. Gianna QUINN
35 Director Student Activities .... Vacant
09 Director of Institutional Research .... Vacant
15 Director Human Resources .... Ms. Donna HAWKINS
18 Chief Facilities/Physical Plant .... Vacant
21 Controller .... Ms. Mary GILBERT
38 Director Counseling .... Ms. Jeanne MCGOWAN
07 Director of Undergrad Admissions .... Ms. Michele DIEHL
07 Dir Undergrad Adult Accel Admission .... Ms. Christine GEIB
07 Director of Graduate Admissions .... Ms. Michele VITELLI
96 Manager of Purchasing .... Ms. Joyce SCHARLE

Harcum College (D)

750 Montgomery Avenue, Bryn Mawr PA 19010-3476
County: Montgomery FICE Identification: 003272
Unit ID: 212869
Telephone: (610) 525-4100 Carnegie Class: Assoc/PrivNFP
FAX Number: (610) 526-6009 Calendar System: Semester
URL: www.harcum.edu
Established: 1915 Annual Undergrad Tuition & Fees: $19,900
Enrollment: 1,523 Coed
Affiliation or Control: Independent Non-Profit IRS Status: 501(c)3
Highest Offering: Associate Degree
Program: Occupational; 2-Year Principally Bachelor's Creditable; Technical Emphasis
Accreditation: M, ADNUR, DA, DH, HT, MLTAD, NDT, OTA, PTAA, RAD

01 President .... Dr. Jon Jay DETEMPLE
05 VP of Academic & Legal Affairs .... Ms. Julia INGERSOLL
10 Vice Pres of Finance & Operations .... Ms. Patricia BENSON
32 Dean of Student Affairs .... Dr. George THORNTON
07 Director of Admissions .... Ms. Rachel BOWEN
30 VP of College Advancement .... Ms. Sachi MALLACH
51 Exec Director of Contining Studies .... Dr. Denise BEAUCHAMP
18 Facilities Director .... Mr. Nikolay KARPALO
15 Director of Human Resources .... Ms. Claudine VITA
06 Registrar .... Ms. Madeleine V. WRIGHTSON
08 Director of Library Services .... Ms. Ann E. RANIERI
85 Director International Student Pgms .... Ms. Debra L. YOUNG-YASSINE
26 Chief Public Relations Officer .... Mr. Andy BACK
29 Director of Alumni Relations .... Ms. Melissa SAMANGO
38 Director of Student Counseling .... Ms. Kathy ANTHONY
36 Dir of Career & Transfer Services .... Ms. Danyele DOVE
37 Director of Student Financial Aid .... Mr. Eli MOINESTER
39 Director of Residence Life .... Mr. Urick LEWIS
35 Director of Campus Activities .... Ms. Laurie PLAZA
09 Coordinator Institutional Research .... Ms. Donna PARKER
106 Asst VP for Distance Learning .... Mr. Tim ELY

Harrisburg Area Community College (E)

1 HACC Drive, Harrisburg PA 17110-2999
County: Dauphin FICE Identification: 003273
Unit ID: 212878
Telephone: (717) 780-2300 Carnegie Class: Assoc/Pub-U-MC
FAX Number: (717) 780-2551 Calendar System: Semester
URL: www.hacc.edu
Established: 1964 Annual Undergrad Tuition & Fees (In-District): $4,044
Enrollment: 22,500 Coed
Affiliation or Control: State/Local IRS Status: 501(c)3
Highest Offering: Associate Degree
Program: Occupational; 2-Year Principally Bachelor's Creditable
Accreditation: M, ACBSP, ACFEI, ADNUR, CVT, DA, DH, DMS, EMT, MAC, MLTAD, PNUR, RAD, SURGT

01 President/CEO .... Dr. John J. SYGIELSKI
05 Provost/VP Academic Affairs .... Mr. James E. BAXTER
32 VP Student Affairs/Enrollment Mgmt .... Dr. Rob R. STEINMETZ
10 Interim VP Finance/College .... Mr. John M. EBERLY
30 VP College Advancement .... Dr. Linnie S. CARTER
16 Executive Director Human Resources .... Ms. Lisa A. SANFORD
12 Campus VP Lancaster .... Dr. L. Marshall WASHINGTON
12 Campus VP Lebanon .... Dr. Kathleen R. KRAMER
12 Interim Campus VP Gettysburg .... Ms. Shannon S. HARVEY
12 Campus VP York .... Ms. Jean M. TREUTHART
106 Director Virtual Campus Operations .... Ms. Amy S. WITHROW
08 Executive Director HACC Libraries .... Ms. Beth A. EVITTS
20 Dean Acad Affs Admn/Retention Svcs .... Vacant
84 Dean Enrollment Services/Registrar .... Vacant
91 Int Director Information Tech Sys .... Ms. Tammy T. WITKOWSKI
102 Exec Director HACC Foundation .... Dr. Linnie S. CARTER
96 Exec Director Business/Aux Svcs .... Mr. Thomas J. FOGARTY
88 Director Performing Artist Series .... Ms. Theresa L. GUERRISI
19 Director Public Safety .... Mr. Todd C. CRAWLEY
29 Director Alumni Affairs .... Ms. Maureen G. HOEPFER
40 Director College Bookstores .... Mr. Kyle J. DIBRITO
21 Controller .... Ms. Barbara L. HUTCHINSON
18 Director Construction & Real Estate .... Mr. Robert R. DERCK
88 Director Center for Global Educ .... Mr. Michael B. SANDY
09 Director Institutional Research .... Vacant
37 Director Financial Aid .... Mr. James J. CARIDEO
07 Dir Enrollment Services .... Ms. Tisa R. RILEY
102 Board Manager HACC Foundation .... Ms. Bonny R. ELLIS

Harrisburg University of Science and Technology (F)

326 Market Street, Harrisburg PA 17101-2116
County: Dauphin FICE Identification: 039483
Unit ID: 446640
Telephone: (717) 901-5100 Carnegie Class: Bac/A&S
FAX Number: (717) 901-3152 Calendar System: Trimester
URL: www.harrisburgu.edu
Established: 2001 Annual Undergrad Tuition & Fees: $22,500
Enrollment: 322 Coed
Affiliation or Control: Independent Non-Profit IRS Status: 501(c)3
Highest Offering: Master's
Program: Professional; Technical Emphasis
Accreditation: M

01 Interim President .... Dr. Eric D. DARR
05 Interim Provost/Chief Academic Ofcr .... Ms. Bili MATTES
10 Vice Pres Finance & Chief Fin Ofcr .... Mr. Duane F. MAUN
30 Assoc VP Devel & Alumni Relations .... Vacant
26 Associate VP Comm & Marketing .... Mr. Steven M. INFANTI
15 Associate VP Human Resources .... Ms. Linda WRIGHT
88 Assoc VP for University Centers .... Mr. Dale HAMBY
32 Director of Student Services .... Ms. Laura DIMINO
13 Director of Technology Services .... Mr. Alex C. PITZNER
09 Director Compliance & Research .... Mr. Keith A. GREEN
37 Director Financial Aid Services .... Mr. Vincent P. FRANK
06 Director Records & Registration .... Ms. Jeanne A. WAGNER
84 Director Enrollment Mgmt/Admissions .... Mr. Timothy DAWSON

Haverford College (G)

370 Lancaster Avenue, Haverford PA 19041-1392
County: Delaware & Montgomery FICE Identification: 003274
Unit ID: 212911
Telephone: (610) 896-1000 Carnegie Class: Bac/A&S
FAX Number: (610) 896-4202 Calendar System: Semester
URL: www.haverford.edu
Established: 1833 Annual Undergrad Tuition & Fees: $42,208
Enrollment: 1,198 Coed
Affiliation or Control: Independent Non-Profit IRS Status: 501(c)3
Highest Offering: Master's
Program: Liberal Arts And General
Accreditation: M

01 Interim President .... Joanne V. CREIGHTON
05 Interim Provost .... Kimberly BENSTON
10 Vice Pres Finance & Administration .... G. Richard WYNN
30 VP of Advancement .... Michael KIEFER
20 Dean of the College .... Martha DENNEY
07 Dean of Admission .... Jess LORD
85 Dean of Intl Academic Programs .... Donna MANCINI
89 Dean of Freshmen Students .... Raisa WILLIAMS
21 Asst VP for Budgeting and Finance .... Michael CASEL
88 Assistant VP of Inst Advancement .... Diane WILDER
11 Senior Executive Administrator .... Violet BROWN
41 Director of Athletics .... Wendall SMITH
26 Exec Dir Marketing & Communication .... Chris MILLS
09 Director of Institutional Research .... Catherine FENNELL
08 Librarian .... Terry SNYDER
15 Director of Human Resources .... Christopher CHANDLER
21 Controller & Assistant Treasurer .... Kathi RUFFIN
96 Director of Purchasing .... Samuel WILLIAMS
18 Director of Physical Plant .... Ron TOLA
19 Director of Safety & Security .... Thomas KING
88 Director Conferences/Dir Campus Ctr .... Dorothy LABE
88 Director of Dining Services .... Bernie CHUNG
40 Bookstore Manager .... Lydia WHITELAW
39 Director of Student Housing .... Marianne SMITH
34 Director of Women's Center .... Mary Louise ALLEN
23 Director of Health Services .... Catherine SHARBAUGH
38 Director Counseling/Disability Svcs .... Richard E. WEBB
36 Director of Career Development .... Liza BERNARD
06 Registrar .... Lee WATKINS

37 Director of Financial Aid ... David HOY
88 Director Leadership Gifts ... Ann WEST FIGUEREDO
44 Director of Annual Giving ... Deborah STRECKER
88 Director of Gift Planning ... Steven KAVANAUGH
102 Dir Foundation/Corporate Relations ... John MOSTELLER
28 Director of Diversity/Assoc Dean ... Vacant
29 Director of Alumni Relations ... Deborah STRECKER
32 Coordinator of Student Activities ... Jason MCGRAW
27 Chief Information Officer ... Joseph SPADARO

Holy Family University (A)

9801 Frankford Avenue, Philadelphia PA 19114-2009
County: Philadelphia FICE Identification: 003275
Unit ID: 212984
Telephone: (215) 637-7700 Carnegie Class: Master's L
FAX Number: (215) 637-3787 Calendar System: Semester
URL: www.holyfamily.edu
Established: 1954 Annual Undergrad Tuition & Fees: $25,590
Enrollment: 3,184 Coed
Affiliation or Control: Roman Catholic IRS Status: 501(c)3
Highest Offering: Doctorate
Program: Liberal Arts And General; Teacher Preparatory; Professional
Accreditation: M, ACBSP, IFSAC, NURSE, RAD, @TEAC

01 President ... Sr. Francesca ONLEY
05 Provost ... Sr. Maureen MCGARRITY
10 Vice Pres Finance & Administration ... Mr. John JASZCZAK
30 Vice Pres Mission ... Ms. Margaret S. KELLY
13 Vice Pres Information Technology ... Mr. Robert LAFOND
32 Vice President for Student Life ... Sr. Marcella BINKOWSKI
30 Interim Vice Pres for Development ... Mr. Robert WETZEL
21 AVP Finance/Budget/Inst Rsrch ... Mr. Michael E. VAN THUYNE
84 Assoc VP for Enrollment Services ... Mr. Robert REESE
06 Assoc VP Academic Svcs/Registrar ... Ms. Ann Marie VICKERY
12 Exec Director of Newtown Campus ... Ms. Karen GALARDI
37 Director of Student Financial Aid ... Mrs. Janice HETRICK
21 Treasurer ... Sr. M. Paul ROZANSKA
15 Asst Vice Pres Human Resources ... Ms. Renee ROSENFELD
08 Director of Library Services ... Ms. Lori SCHWABENBAUER
36 Director of the Career Center ... Mr. Donald BROM
26 Senior Dir Marketing-Communications ... Vacant
38 Director Counseling Center ... Dr. Diana PIPERATA
42 Chaplain/Campus Minister ... Rev. James MACNEW
07 Director of Undergraduate Admission ... Ms. Lauren CAMPBELL
41 Athletic Director ... Mrs. Sandra MICHAEL
58 Dean of the School of Education ... Dr. Leonard G. SOROKA
66 Dean Sch Nursing/Allied Hlth Profns ... Dr. Christine ROSNER
49 Dean of School of Arts & Sciences ... Dr. Michael MARKOWITZ
50 Dean of School of Business Admin ... Dr. Jack V. KIRNAN
51 Assoc Vice Pres Extended Learning ... Mrs. Honour MOORE
58 Assoc Dean School of Education ... Dr. Antoinette SCHIAVO
29 Director Alumni & Parent Giving ... Ms. Marie ZECCA
09 Dir of Inst Research & Assessment ... Mr. Chad L. MAY
18 Chief Facilities/Physical Plant ... Mr. John JASZCZAK
96 Director of Purchasing ... Mrs. Marie MELNICK
28 Coordinator Diversity ... Dr. Gloria KERSEY-MATUSIAK
39 Director of Residence Life ... Mr. Brett BUCKRIDGE

Hussian School of Art (B)

111 S Independence Mall East, #300,
Philadelphia PA 19106-2521
County: Philadelphia FICE Identification: 007469
Unit ID: 212993
Telephone: (215) 574-9600 Carnegie Class: Assoc/PrivFP
FAX Number: (215) 574-9800 Calendar System: Semester
URL: www.hussianart.edu
Established: 1946 Annual Undergrad Tuition & Fees: $14,550
Enrollment: 133 Coed
Affiliation or Control: Proprietary IRS Status: Proprietary
Highest Offering: Associate Degree
Program: Occupational; Technical Emphasis
Accreditation: ACCSC

03 Vice President ... Mr. Wilbur O. CRAWFORD
05 Dean of Academic Affairs ... Ms. Melissa MORGAN
06 Dir of Student Services/ Registrar ... Ms. Maureen P. FLANAGAN
37 Director Financial Aid ... Ms. Susan J. COHEN
07 Admissions Representative ... Ms. Siobhan CUSUMANO
10 Director of Finance ... Mr. Eric STRUBEL
11 Administrative Coordinator ... Ms. Jodi BRABAZON

Immaculata University (C)

1145 King Road, Immaculata PA 19345-0654
County: Chester FICE Identification: 003276
Unit ID: 213011
Telephone: (610) 647-4400 Carnegie Class: DRU
FAX Number: (610) 251-1668 Calendar System: Semester
URL: www.immaculata.edu
Established: 1920 Annual Undergrad Tuition & Fees: $29,000
Enrollment: 4,306 Coed
Affiliation or Control: Roman Catholic IRS Status: 501(c)3
Highest Offering: Doctorate
Program: 2-Year Principally Bachelor's Creditable; Liberal Arts And General; Teacher Preparatory; Professional
Accreditation: M, ACBSP, CLPSY, DIETD, DIETI, MUS, NURSE

01 President ... Sr. R. Patricia FADDEN
05 Vice President Academic Affairs ... Sr. Ann HEATH
10 Vice Pres Finance/Administration ... Ms. Jenni SAUER
30 Vice Pres University Advancement ... Vacant
32 Vice President Student Development ... Dr. Stephen PUGLIESE
27 VP of University Communications ... Mr. Robert COLE
20 Associate VP of Academic Affairs ... Mr. Phillip HUBBARD
06 Registrar ... Ms. Janice BATES
09 Director Inst Research/Assessment ... Ms. Erin R. EBERSOLE
08 Director of Library ... Dr. Jeffrey D. ROLLISON
37 Director Student Financial Aid ... Mr. Robert FOREST
44 Senior Director of Gift Planning ... Sr. Rita O'LEARY
91 Director Administrative Computing ... Dr. Thomas EGAN
26 Director Public Relations ... Ms. Marie MOUGHAN
29 Alumni Director ... Ms. Karen MATWEYCHUK
36 Director Career Advisement ... Ms. Diane MASSEY
41 Athletic Director ... Ms. Patricia CANTERINO
85 International Student Advisor ... Sr. Catarin CONJAR
90 Director Academic Technology ... Ms. Sharon AINSLEY
42 Chaplain ... Fr. Christopher ROGERS
58 Dean Graduate Division ... Dr. Janet KANE
34 Dean College of Undergrad Studies ... Sr. Jo CARTER
51 Dean College of Lifelong Learning ... Dr. Sam WRIGHTSON
19 Director Campus Safety ... Mr. Eugene BIAGIOTTI
15 Director of Personnel Services ... Mrs. Cathey PASSIN
18 Director of Physical Plant ... Mr. Dennis SHORES
44 Director of the Annual Fund ... Vacant
42 Director of Campus Ministry ... Sr. Cathy NALLY
07 Director of Admissions ... Dr. Nicola DIFRONZO-HEITZER
20 Associate Dean of Academic Affairs ... Ms. Mary Kate BOLAND

International Institute for Restorative Practices (D)

P.O. Box 229, Bethlehem PA 18016-0229
County: Northampton Identification: 666688
Unit ID: 448691
Telephone: (610) 807-9221 Carnegie Class: Assoc/PrivNFP4
FAX Number: (610) 807-0423 Calendar System: Semester
URL: www.iirp.org
Established: N/A Annual Graduate Tuition & Fees: $19,800
Enrollment: 60 Coed
Affiliation or Control: Independent Non-Profit IRS Status: 501(c)3
Highest Offering: Master's; No Undergraduates
Program: Professional
Accreditation: M

01 President ... Mr. Theodore WACHTEL
05 Vice President for Academic Affairs ... Dr. Patrick MCDONOUGH

ITT Technical Institute (E)

3330 Tillman Drive, Bensalem PA 19020-2030
County: Bucks Identification: 666320
Unit ID: 440642
Telephone: (215) 244-8871 Carnegie Class: Assoc/PrivFP
FAX Number: (215) 244-8872 Calendar System: Quarter
URL: www.itt-tech.edu
Established: 2003 Annual Undergrad Tuition & Fees: N/A
Enrollment: 651 Coed
Affiliation or Control: Proprietary IRS Status: Proprietary
Highest Offering: Associate Degree
Program: Technical Emphasis
Accreditation: ACICS

† Branch campus of ITT Technical Institute, Indianapolis, IN.

ITT Technical Institute (F)

1000 Meade Street, Dunmore PA 18512-3195
County: Lackawanna Identification: 666150
Unit ID: 448460
Telephone: (570) 330-0600 Carnegie Class: Assoc/PrivFP
FAX Number: N/A Calendar System: Quarter
URL: www.itt-tech.edu
Established: 2006 Annual Undergrad Tuition & Fees: N/A
Enrollment: 273 Coed
Affiliation or Control: Proprietary IRS Status: Proprietary
Highest Offering: Associate Degree
Program: Technical Emphasis
Accreditation: ACICS

† Branch campus of ITT Technical Institute, Indianapolis, IN.

ITT Technical Institute (G)

449 Eisenhower Blvd., Suite 100,
Harrisburg PA 17111-2302
County: Cumberland Identification: 666548
Unit ID: 430351
Telephone: (717) 565-1700 Carnegie Class: Assoc/PrivFP
FAX Number: (717) 691-9273 Calendar System: Quarter
URL: www.itt-tech.edu
Established: 1994 Annual Undergrad Tuition & Fees: N/A
Enrollment: 352 Coed
Affiliation or Control: Proprietary IRS Status: Proprietary
Highest Offering: Associate Degree
Program: Technical Emphasis
Accreditation: ACICS

† Branch campus of ITT Technical Institute, Indianapolis, IN.

ITT Technical Institute (H)

760 Moore Road, King of Prussia PA 19406-1212
County: Montgomery Identification: 666322
Unit ID: 442347
Telephone: (610) 491-8004 Carnegie Class: Assoc/PrivFP
FAX Number: (610) 491-9047 Calendar System: Quarter
URL: www.itt-tech.edu
Established: 2002 Annual Undergrad Tuition & Fees: N/A
Enrollment: 480 Coed
Affiliation or Control: Proprietary IRS Status: Proprietary
Highest Offering: Associate Degree
Program: Technical Emphasis
Accreditation: ACICS

† Branch campus of ITT Technical Institute, Indianapolis, IN.

ITT Technical Institute (I)

10 Parkway Center, Pittsburgh PA 15220-3801
County: Allegheny Identification: 666483
Unit ID: 414841
Telephone: (412) 937-9150 Carnegie Class: Assoc/PrivFP
FAX Number: (412) 937-9425 Calendar System: Quarter
URL: www.itt-tech.edu
Established: 1992 Annual Undergrad Tuition & Fees: N/A
Enrollment: 350 Coed
Affiliation or Control: Proprietary IRS Status: Proprietary
Highest Offering: Associate Degree
Program: Technical Emphasis
Accreditation: ACICS

† Branch campus of ITT Technical Institute, Indianapolis, IN.

ITT Technical Institute (J)

100 Pittsburgh Mills Cir, Ste 100, Tarentum PA 15084
County: Allegheny Identification: 666482
Unit ID: 430360
Telephone: (724) 274-1400 Carnegie Class: Assoc/PrivFP
FAX Number: (412) 856-4501 Calendar System: Quarter
URL: www.itt-tech.edu
Established: 1996 Annual Undergrad Tuition & Fees: N/A
Enrollment: 282 Coed
Affiliation or Control: Proprietary IRS Status: Proprietary
Highest Offering: Associate Degree
Program: Technical Emphasis
Accreditation: ACICS

† Branch campus of ITT Technical Institute, Indianapolis, IN.

JNA Institute of Culinary Arts (K)

1212 S Broad Street, Philadelphia PA 19146-3119
County: Philadelphia FICE Identification: 031033
Unit ID: 419341
Telephone: (215) 468-8800 Carnegie Class: Assoc/PrivFP
FAX Number: (215) 468-8838 Calendar System: Quarter
URL: www.culinaryarts.edu
Established: 1988 Annual Undergrad Tuition & Fees: $22,075
Enrollment: 99 Coed
Affiliation or Control: Proprietary IRS Status: Proprietary
Highest Offering: Associate Degree
Program: Occupational; 2-Year Principally Bachelor's Creditable; Technical Emphasis
Accreditation: ACCSC

01 Director ... Mr. Joseph DIGIRONIMO
07 Director of Admission ... Mr. Robert FOX

Johnson College (L)

3427 N Main Avenue, Scranton PA 18508-1495
County: Lackawanna FICE Identification: 021142
Unit ID: 213233
Telephone: (570) 342-6404 Carnegie Class: Assoc/PrivNFP
FAX Number: (570) 348-2181 Calendar System: Semester
URL: www.johnson.edu
Established: 1916 Annual Undergrad Tuition & Fees: $16,530
Enrollment: 438 Coed
Affiliation or Control: Independent Non-Profit IRS Status: 501(c)3
Highest Offering: Associate Degree
Program: 2-Year Principally Bachelor's Creditable; Technical Emphasis
Accreditation: ACCSC, RAD

01 President & CEO ... Dr. Ann L. PIPINSKI
05 Vice President Academic Affairs ... Mr. Dominick A. CARACHILO
13 Director of Information Services ... Ms. Sue PHILLIPS
37 Financial Aid Director ... Mr. Matthew PETERS
84 Vice Pres of Enrollment Services ... Ms. Melissa IDE
88 Student Support Coordinator ... Ms. Lynn KRUSHINSKI
10 Chief Financial Officer ... Mr. Jeffrey NOVAK
08 Head Librarian ... Mrs. Michele M. SREBRO
04 Assistant to the President ... Ms. Lisa TOOLE
06 Associate Registrar ... Mrs. Cathy BECKAGE
38 Asst Dir Student Support Services ... Ms. Linda LEARN
51 Director of Continuing Education ... Vacant
39 Residence/Student Life Coordinator ... Ms. Tara RHODES
30 VP of Institutional Advancement ... Ms. Katie LEONARD
15 Human Resources Assistant ... Ms. Diane DOLINSKY

36 Assoc Dir of Career Services .... Ms. Roseann MARTINETTI
32 Director of Student Life .... Ms. Sara WILLIAMS
07 Assoc Director of Admissions .... Vacant
18 Facilities Manager .... Mr. Bill KELLY
09 Dir of Program & Research .... Mrs. Shirley HELBING

Juniata College (A)

1700 Moore Street, Huntingdon PA 16652-2119
County: Huntingdon FICE Identification: 003279
Unit ID: 213251
Telephone: (814) 641-3000 Carnegie Class: Bac/A&S
FAX Number: (814) 641-3199 Calendar System: Semester
URL: www.juniata.edu
Established: 1876 Annual Undergrad Tuition & Fees: $35,780
Enrollment: 1,619 Coed
Affiliation or Control: Independent Non-Profit IRS Status: 501(c)3
Highest Offering: Baccalaureate
Program: Liberal Arts And General; Teacher Preparatory
Accreditation: M, SW

01 President .... Dr. Thomas R. KEPPLE, JR.
05 Provost/Exec Vice Pres Student Dev .... Dr. James J. LAKSO
84 Exec VP Enrollment and Retention .... Mr. John S. HILLE
10 Vice President Finance/Operations .... Mr. Robert E. YELNOSKY
26 Vice President Advancement/Mkt .... Mr. Gabriel WELSCH
27 Assoc Vice President & CIO .... Mr. David J. FUSCO
30 Exec Director of Development .... Ms. Kimberly KITCHEN
26 Exec Director of Marketing .... Ms. Rosann BROWN
07 Dean of Enrollment .... Ms. Michelle M. BARTOL
85 Dean International Programs .... Ms. Jenifer S. CUSHMAN
06 Registrar .... Ms. Athena D. FREDERICK
36 Director Career Services .... Dr. Darwin V. KYSOR
37 Enrollment Mgr/Dir Student Fin Plng ...... Ms. Valerie D. RENNELL
08 Library Director .... Mr. John W. MUMFORD
91 Director Admin Information Svcs .... Ms. Barbara J. HUGHES
15 Director of Human Resources .... Ms. Gail L. ULRICH
32 Dean of Students .... Mr. Kris R. CLARKSON
09 Dir Institutional Planning/Research .... Ms. Carlee K. RANALLI
18 Director of Facilities Services .... Mr. Tristan S. DEL GIUDICE
19 Director Public Safety .... Mr. Jesse W. LEONARD
41 Athletic Director .... Mr. Greg M. CURLEY
90 Dir Technology Solutions Center .... Mr. Joel C. PHEASANT
21 Budget Director & Bursar .... Ms. Susan F. SHONTZ
21 Controller .... Mr. Jeffrey L. SAVINO
44 Exec Dir Constituent Relations .... Mrs. Linda M. CARPENTER
35 Assistant Dean of Students .... Mr. Daniel J. COOK-HUFFMAN
42 College Chaplain .... Mr. Lowell D. WITKOVSKY
20 Director of Academic Support Svcs ...... Ms. Sarah M. CLARKSON
88 Director of Student Activities .... Ms. Jessica JACKSON
88 Assoc Dir Conferences & Events .... Ms. Lorri P. SHIDELER
07 Director of Enrollment
Operations .... Ms. Terri L. BOLLMAN-DALANSKY
38 College Counselor .... Ms. Mary B. WILLIAMS
28 Asst to Pres Diversity & Inclusion ... Ms. Rosalie M. RODRIGUEZ
29 Director Alumni Relations .... Mr. David D. MEADOWS
39 Director of Residential Life .... Ms. Lauren O'DONNELL

Kaplan Career Institute (B)

5650 Derry Street, Harrisburg PA 17111-4112
County: Dauphin FICE Identification: 004910
Unit ID: 251075
Telephone: (717) 564-4112 Carnegie Class: Assoc/PrivFP
FAX Number: (717) 564-3779 Calendar System: Quarter
URL: www.kci-harrisburg.com
Established: 1918 Annual Undergrad Tuition & Fees: N/A
Enrollment: 439 Coed
Affiliation or Control: Proprietary IRS Status: Proprietary
Highest Offering: Associate Degree
Program: Occupational
Accreditation: ACICS, MAC

01 Executive Director .... Adrian SCOTT
07 Director Admissions .... Mark HALE
36 Director Student Placement .... Jennifer RIORDAN
05 Acting Director of Education .... Adrian SCOTT
37 Director Student Financial Aid .... Sarah BROOKER

Kaplan Career Institute (C)

177 Franklin Mills Boulevard, Philadelphia PA 19154-3140
County: Bucks FICE Identification: 022898
Unit ID: 211617
Telephone: (215) 612-6600 Carnegie Class: Assoc/PrivFP
FAX Number: (215) 612-6695 Calendar System: Quarter
URL: www.chitraining.com
Established: 1982 Annual Undergrad Tuition & Fees: $14,916
Enrollment: 780 Coed
Affiliation or Control: Proprietary IRS Status: Proprietary
Highest Offering: Associate Degree
Program: Occupational
Accreditation: ACCSC

01 President .... Ms. Jamie PEAK
07 Director of Admissions .... Mr. Dan WATKINS
05 Education Department Head .... Mrs. Dorothy MCCADEN
36 Director of Placement .... Ms. Cheryl BRAIDES
37 Director Financial Aid .... Ms. Nina BALAGOUR

Kaplan Career Institute - ICM Campus (D)

10-14 Wood Street, Pittsburgh PA 15222
County: Allegheny FICE Identification: 007436
Unit ID: 213002
Telephone: (412) 261-2647 Carnegie Class: Assoc/PrivFP
FAX Number: (412) 261-6491 Calendar System: Quarter
URL: www.kcipittsburgh.com
Established: 1963 Annual Undergrad Tuition & Fees: $17,310
Enrollment: 719 Coed
Affiliation or Control: Proprietary IRS Status: Proprietary
Highest Offering: Associate Degree
Program: Occupational; 2-Year Principally Bachelor's Creditable; Technical Emphasis
Accreditation: ACICS, MAC, OTA

01 President .... Mr. Hunter H. HOPKINS
05 Director of Education .... Mr. Thomas E. ROCKS, JR.
37 Director of Financial Aid .... Mr. Chris FOX
89 Director of New Students .... Ms. Rebekah SABO
07 Director of Admissions .... Ms. Lori MILLER
10 Director of Finance .... Ms. Denise RINGER-FISHER
36 Director of Career Services .... Ms. Jennifer KELLY

Keystone College (E)

One College Green, P.O. Box 50,
La Plume PA 18440-0200
County: Lackawanna FICE Identification: 003280
Unit ID: 213303
Telephone: (570) 945-8000 Carnegie Class: Bac/Diverse
FAX Number: (570) 945-8962 Calendar System: Semester
URL: www.keystone.edu
Established: 1868 Annual Undergrad Tuition & Fees: $20,400
Enrollment: 1,799 Coed
Affiliation or Control: Independent Non-Profit IRS Status: 501(c)3
Highest Offering: Baccalaureate
Program: Liberal Arts And General
Accreditation: M

01 President .... Dr. Edward G. BOEHM, JR.
05 VP Academic Affairs/Dean of College .... Dr. Thea HARRINGTON
32 VP Student Affairs/Dean Students .... Dr. Robert J. PERKINS
84 Vice Pres Enrollment .... Ms. Sarah KEATING
10 Vice Pres Finance & Administration .... Mr. Kevin WILSON
30 Exec Dir Institutional Advancement .... Ms. Sharon BURKE
91 Director Information Technology .... Mr. Charles L. PROTHERO
06 Registrar .... Ms. Kate OWENS
26 Senior Director College Relations .... Mr. Fran CALPIN
37 Dir Financial Assistance & Planning .... Mr. Brian WEBER
29 Director of Alumni Outreach .... Ms. Christina FENTON-MACE
36 Director Career Development .... Ms. Rhea V. ELLIS DUKE
08 Director Miller Library .... Ms. Mari FLYNN
15 Director of Human Resources .... Ms. Alberta GRUSHINSKI
35 Director Student Activities .... Ms. Lucilia MCCONKEY
09 Institutional Researcher .... Ms. Linda WOZNIAK

Keystone Technical Institute (F)

2301 Academy Drive, Harrisburg PA 17112-1012
County: Dauphin FICE Identification: 022342
Unit ID: 210483
Telephone: (717) 545-4747 Carnegie Class: Assoc/PrivFP
FAX Number: (717) 901-9090 Calendar System: Semester
URL: www.kti.edu
Established: 1980 Annual Undergrad Tuition & Fees: $15,000
Enrollment: 679 Coed
Affiliation or Control: Proprietary IRS Status: Proprietary
Highest Offering: Associate Degree
Program: Occupational; 2-Year Principally Bachelor's Creditable; Technical Emphasis
Accreditation: ACCSC

01 President .... Mr. David W. SNYDER
03 Vice President .... Mrs. Andrea SNYDER
05 Dean of Education .... Mrs. Nancy NAVETTA
06 Registrar/Dir Stdnt Financial Aid .... Ms. Tracy STEWART
10 Chief Business Officer .... Mr. Dennis FIELDS
07 Admissions Officer .... Mr. Mark DYKEMA

King's College (G)

133 N River Street, Wilkes-Barre PA 18711-0801
County: Luzerne FICE Identification: 003282
Unit ID: 213321
Telephone: (570) 208-5900 Carnegie Class: Master's S
FAX Number: (570) 825-9049 Calendar System: Semester
URL: www.kings.edu
Established: 1946 Annual Undergrad Tuition & Fees: $29,174
Enrollment: 2,621 Coed
Affiliation or Control: Roman Catholic IRS Status: 501(c)3
Highest Offering: Master's
Program: Liberal Arts And General; Teacher Preparatory; Professional; Business Emphasis
Accreditation: M, ARCPA, BUS, TED

01 President .... Rev. John RYAN, CSC
05 Vice President for Academic Affairs ..... Dr. Nicholas A. HOLODICK
10 Interim VP Business Affs/Treasurer .... Mr. Frederick PETTIT
30 Vice President for Inst Advancement .... Mr. Frederick PETTIT
32 Vice President for Student Affairs .. Ms. Janet E. MERCINCAVAGE
04 Assistant to the President .... Vacant
20 Assoc VP for Academic Affairs .... Dr. Joseph EVAN
13 Exec Dir Info & Tech Svc Div .... Mr. Paul J. MORAN
08 Director of Library .... Dr. Terrence F. MECH
84 Assoc VP Enroll/Academic Svcs .... Ms. Teresa M. PECK
35 Assoc Vice Pres Student Affairs .... Mr. Robert B. MCGONIGLE
07 Director of Admissions .... Mr. James ANDERSON
50 Dean Wm G McGowan Sch Business .... Dr. Barry WILLIAMS
06 Registrar .... Mr. Daniel T. CEBRICK
37 Director of Financial Aid .... Ms. Donna CERZA
42 Chaplain/Director Campus Ministry ... Rev. Thomas LOONEY, CSC
36 Director Career Planning & Placemnt ..... Mr. Christopher SUTZKO
14 Computer Operations Manager .... Ms. Patricia L. KELLAR
16 Interim Director of Human Resources .... Ms. Lita PIEKARA
26 Director of Public Relations .... Mr. John MCANDREW
29 Director of Alumni Relations .... Ms. Laura HADEN
18 Director Facilities & Grounds .... Mr. Patrick MULLARKEY
19 Director of Security/Safety .... Mr. Francis HACKEN
41 Dir of Intercollegiate Athletics .... Ms. Cheryl J. ISH
21 Comptroller .... Mr. Thomas GRABER
39 Director of Residence Life .... Ms. Megan SELLICK
44 Director of Annual Giving Programs .... Ms. Kimberly K. CARDONE
58 Dean of Graduate Programs .... Dr. Elizabeth S. LOTT
55 Director Evening/Weekend Programs .. Ms. Maureen E. SHERIDAN
09 Director of Institutional Research .... Ms. Marian K. PALMERI
28 Director of College Diversity .... Mr. Nathan WARD
96 Director of Purchasing .... Mr. Herbert G. GODFREY
92 Director of the Honors Program .... Dr. William IRWIN
90 Managing Dir of User Services .... Mr. Raymond G. PRYOR
91 Managing Director for MIS .... Mr. William M. CORCORAN

La Roche College (H)

9000 Babcock Boulevard, Pittsburgh PA 15237-5898
County: Allegheny FICE Identification: 003987
Unit ID: 213358
Telephone: (412) 367-9300 Carnegie Class: Bac/Diverse
FAX Number: (412) 536-1062 Calendar System: Semester
URL: www.laroche.edu
Established: 1963 Annual Undergrad Tuition & Fees: $24,058
Enrollment: 1,419 Coed
Affiliation or Control: Roman Catholic IRS Status: 501(c)3
Highest Offering: Master's
Program: Liberal Arts And General; Professional
Accreditation: M, ACBSP, ADNUR, ANEST, ART, CIDA, NUR

01 President .... Sr. Candace INTROCASO, CDP
04 Admin Asst to the President .... Ms. Karen P. WILLOUGHBY
05 Vice President Academic Affairs .... Dr. Howard J. ISHIYAMA
84 VP for Enrollment Mgmt & Mktg ..... Mr. William H. FIRMAN, JR.
10 Vice President for Finance .... Mr. Robert VOGEL
32 Vice Pres Student Life/Dean Stdnts .... Ms. Colleen RUEFLE
11 Vice Pres Administrative Services .... Mr. George T. ZAFFUTO
30 VP for Institutional Advancement .... Mr. Michael ANDREOLA
43 General Counsel .... Ms. Mary Beth FETCHKO
20 Assoc VP Academic Affairs .... Dr. Rosemary MCCARTHY
20 Assoc Vice Pres Academic Affairs .... Dr. Thomas G. SCHAEFER
36 Assoc Dean Academic/Student Support .... Ms. Marie DEEM
35 Director of Student Development .... Mr. David DAY
83 Div Chair Natural & Behavioral Sci .... Ms. Jane ARNOLD
79 Div Chair Humanities .... Sr. Michele BISBEY, CDP
50 Div Chair Business .... Vacant
57 Div Chair Design .... Ms. Maria RIPEPI
53 Div Chair Education & Nursing .... Dr. Kathleen A. SULLIVAN
06 Registrar .... Ms. Joan CUTONE
08 Director Library/Learning Center .... Ms. Laverne COLLINS
07 Director of Admissions .... Mr. Stephen STEPPE
26 Director of Mktg & Media Relations ... Ms. Mary Gray DELBUONO
37 Director of Financial Aid .... Ms. Sharon PLATT
41 Director of Athletics .... Mr. Jim TINKEY
42 Director of Campus Ministry .... Fr. Peter HORTON
07 Director Grad Studies/Adult Ed .... Ms. Hope SCHIFFGENS
39 Director Residence Life .... Mr. Christopher WILLIS
14 Director Information Technology .... Ms. Terri BALLARD
85 Director International Student Svcs .... Dr. Natasha GARRETT
29 Director Alumni Relations .... Ms. Gina MILLER
88 Director of Special Events .... Ms. Bobbi LAPLACE
21 Director Budget & Finance .... Mr. John PETRUS
09 Director of Institutional Research .... Ms. Patricia A. CONNOLLY
18 Director of Facilities Management .... Mr. J.R YOUNG
38 Director Counseling Services .... Ms. Lori AREND
19 Director Public Safety .... Mr. David HILKE
15 Director Human Resources .... Ms. Melissa KIM
40 Bookstore Manager .... Mr. Tim JONES
88 Director of Student Accounts .... Ms. Danya TINKEY

La Salle University (I)

1900 W Olney Avenue, Philadelphia PA 19141-1199
County: Philadelphia FICE Identification: 003287
Unit ID: 213367
Telephone: (215) 951-1000 Carnegie Class: Master's L
FAX Number: (215) 951-1488 Calendar System: Semester
URL: www.lasalle.edu
Established: 1863 Annual Undergrad Tuition & Fees: $37,450
Enrollment: 6,685 Coed
Affiliation or Control: Roman Catholic IRS Status: 501(c)3
Highest Offering: Doctorate
Program: 2-Year Principally Bachelor's Creditable; Liberal Arts And General; Professional
Accreditation: M, ANEST, BUS, CLPSY, DIETC, DIETD, MFCD, NURSE, SP, SW

01 President .... Bro. Michael J. MCGINNISS
05 Vice Pres Academic Affairs/Provost .... Dr. Joseph R. MARBACH
04 Exec Assistant to the President .... Dr. Alice L. HOERSCH
04 Exec Assistant to the President .... Bro. Joseph WILLARD
30 Vice Pres University Advancement .... Mr. R. Brian ELDERTON
84 Interim VP Enrollment Services .... Mr. Michael J. PAYNE
10 VP Finance and Admin and Treasurer .... Mr. Matthew MCMANNESS
32 VP Student Affairs/Dean of Students .... Dr. James E. MOORE
20 Assistant Provost .... Bro. John MCGOLDRICK
49 Dean School of Arts & Sciences .... Dr. Thomas A. KEAGY
50 Dean Sch of Business Administration .... Mr. Paul R. BRAZINA
51 Dean Col of Professional/Cont Stds .... Dr. Joseph Y. UGRAS
66 Dean Sch of Nursing/Health Sciences .... Dr. Brian GOLDSTEIN
22 Asst VP Admin/Plng/Affirm Action .... Ms. Rose Lee PAULINE
26 Asst VP Mktg & Communications .... Mr. Joseph W. DONOVAN
29 Asst Vice Pres of Alumni Relations .... Mr. Trey P. ULRICH
86 Asst Vice Pres Government Affairs .... Mr. Edward A. TURZANSKI
44 Asst Vice President Development .... Ms. Terry K. TRAVIS
21 Asst VP Finance & Asst Treasurer .... Ms. Rebecca L. HORVATH
88 Asst Vice Pres Enrollment Services .... Ms. Kathryn E. PAYNE
88 Asst Vice Pres Enrollment Services .... Mr. Paul J. REILLY
88 Director Advancement Services .... Ms. Elizabeth LOCHNER
88 Director Economic Development .... Mr. William J. DEVITO
88 Director Graduate Bilingual Studies .... Dr. Carmen LAMAS
82 Director Grad Ctr/East Europe Stds .... Dr. Bernard G. BLUMENTHAL
77 Director Grad Computer Info Science .... Ms. Margaret MCCOEY
53 Interim Dir Graduate Education Pgm .... Dr. Greer RICHARDSON
83 Director Grad Clinic-Counsel Psych .... Dr. Donna A. TONREY
73 Director Grad Theol & Ministry .... Fr. Francis J. BERNA
60 Director Grad Prof Communication .... Dr. Pamela LANNUTTI
66 Director Undergraduate Nursing .... Dr. Barbara HOERST
66 Director Graduate Nursing .... Dr. Kathleen CZEKANSKI
102 Director Corporate Relations .... Ms. Gloria PUGLIESE
25 Director Grants/Research .... Dr. Fred J. FOLEY
35 Senior Assoc Dean of Students .... Mr. Alan B. WENDALL
35 Associate Dean of Students .... Dr. Lane B. NEUBAUER
35 Associate Dean of Students .... Ms. Anna M. ALLEN
51 Asst Dean Prof/Continuing Studies .... Ms. Elizabeth A. HEENAN
42 Director Univ Ministry & Service .... Bro. Robert J. KINZLER
92 Director University Honors Program .... Dr. Richard A. NIGRO
13 Chief Information Officer .... Mr. Edward NICKERSON
08 Director of the Library .... Mr. John S. BAKY
18 Asst VP Facilities Mgmt/Capital Dev .... Mr. Robert C. KROH, JR.
19 Asst VP for Safety & Security .... Mr. Arthur GROVER
16 Director Human Resources .... Dr. Margurete WALSH
41 Athletic Director .... Dr. Thomas BRENNAN
88 Director of Major Gifts .... Bro. Charles E. GRESH
30 Director of Development .... Bro. John MCDONNELL
44 Director of The La Salle Fund .... Ms. Helene HOLMES
30 Director of Prospect Development .... Ms. Sarah PARNUM CADBURY
36 Director of Career Services .... Mr. Louis A. LAMORTE, JR.
36 Exec Dir Career & Employ Svcs .... Mr. Steve MCGONIGLE
07 Executive Director of Admission .... Mr. James C. PLUNKETT
37 Director Student Financial Services .... Mr. Michael WISNIEWSKI
06 Registrar .... Mr. Dominic J. GALANTE
09 Director Institutional Research .... Dr. Michael J. ROSZKOWSKI
88 Dir Doctoral Clinical Psychology .... Dr. Kelly MCCLURE
88 Director Graduate English Studies .... Dr. Stephen P. SMITH
88 Grad Director Instr Technology Mgt .... Dr. Bobbe G. BAGGIO
88 Director Part-time MBA Program .... Ms. Denise SAURENNANN
88 Director Full-time MBA Program .... Ms. Elizabeth A. SCOFIELD
40 Manager Campus Store .... Mr. Mark ALLAN
28 Multicultural Education Coordinator .... Ms. Cherlyn L. RUSH

Lackawanna College (A)

501 Vine Street, Scranton PA 18509-3206
County: Lackawanna FICE Identification: 003283
Unit ID: 213376
Telephone: (570) 961-7810 Carnegie Class: Assoc/PrivNFP
FAX Number: (570) 961-7858 Calendar System: 4/1/4
URL: www.lackawanna.edu
Established: 1894 Annual Undergrad Tuition & Fees: $12,210
Enrollment: 1,515 Coed
Affiliation or Control: Independent Non-Profit IRS Status: 501(c)3
Highest Offering: Associate Degree
Program: Occupational; 2-Year Principally Bachelor's Creditable; Business Emphasis
Accreditation: M, DMS, @PTAA, SURGT

01 President .... Mr. Mark VOLK
03 Executive Vice President .... Dr. Jill MURRAY
10 Vice President Financial Affairs .... Ms. Alycia SCHWARTZ
11 Vice President Administration .... Dr. Gail SCARAMUZZO
05 Associate VP Academic Affairs .... Dr. Erica PRICCI
30 Assoc VP for Inst Advancement .... Mrs. Bridget FITZPATRICK
32 Dean of Student Affairs .... Mrs. Suellen MUSEWICZ
35 Dean of Students .... Mr. Mark DUDA
84 Dean of Enrollment Management .... Mr. Brian COSTANZO
20 Associate Dean of Faculty .... Vacant
26 Exec Dir Communications & Marketing .... Mr. Chris KUCHARSKI
29 Director Alumni Relations .... Ms. Ashley FETTERMAN
09 Director Institutional Research .... Mrs. Laura DUDA
88 Dir Programming & Special Events .... Mr. Jim CULLEN
88 Director Community Concerts .... Ms. Wendy EVANS
51 Director of Adult Education .... Mrs. Anita COLA
41 Director of Athletics .... Mrs. Kim MECCA
88 Director of Advising & Transfer Svc .... Mrs. Barbara NOWOGORSKI
88 Director Community Outreach & Pgms .... Ms. Jo-Ann ORCUTT
06 Registrar .... Mrs. Theresa SCOPELLITI
19 Direcrtor of Public Safety .... Mr. Gary SHOENER
12 Director of Hazleton Center .... Vacant
12 Director of Lake Region Center .... Ms. Kim VANGARELLI
12 Director New Milford Center .... Ms. Katherine TUTTLE
91 Director Admin Computing Svcs .... Mr. Edward WARGO
08 Library Director .... Mrs. Mary Beth ROCHE
102 Director of Grant Support Services .... Ms. Michelle WILLIAMS
39 Director Housing & Residence Life .... Mr. Stephen DUDA
15 Director of Human Resources .... Mrs. Sharon EBERT
18 Director of Facilities .... Mr. Joseph ERRICO
37 Director of Financial Aid .... Mrs. Barbara HAPEMAN
12 Director Towanda Center .... Vacant
13 Director of MIS .... Mrs. Melanie KOWALSKI
35 Director of Student Activities .... Ms. Karen LEGGE
88 Director of Health Club Facilities .... Mr. Joseph LUCIANO
07 Asst Director of Admissions .... Ms. Stacey MUCHAL

Lafayette College (B)

Easton PA 18042-1798
County: Northampton FICE Identification: 003284
Unit ID: 213385
Telephone: (610) 330-5000 Carnegie Class: Bac/A&S
FAX Number: (610) 330-5127 Calendar System: Semester
URL: www.lafayette.edu
Established: 1826 Annual Undergrad Tuition & Fees: $41,920
Enrollment: 2,442 Coed
Affiliation or Control: Independent Non-Profit IRS Status: 501(c)3
Highest Offering: Baccalaureate
Program: Liberal Arts And General; Professional
Accreditation: M, CS, ENG

01 President .... Mr. Daniel H. WEISS
05 Provost .... Dr. Wendy L. HILL
30 Vice Pres Devel/College Relations .... Mr. James W. DICKER
10 Vice Pres Business Affairs/Treas .... Mr. Mitchell L. WEIN
32 VP Campus Life/Sr Diversity Officer .... Dr. Celestino Jose LIMAS
16 Vice President Human Resources .... Ms. Leslie F. MUHLFELDER
27 Vice President for Communications .... Mr. Robert J. MASSA
21 Assoc VP Bus Affairs/Controller .... Mr. Paul H. ZIMMERMAN
54 Director of Engineering .... Vacant
04 Executive Assistant .... Dr. James F. KRIVOSKI
84 Dean Admissions & Financial Aid .... Mr. Gregory MACDONALD
20 Dean of the College .... Dr. Hannah W. STEWART-GAMBINO
08 Dean of Libraries/Info Tech Svcs .... Mr. Neil J. MCELROY
35 Dean of Students .... Dr. Paul J. MCLOUGHLIN
07 Director of Admissions .... Mr. Matthew HYDE
37 Director Student Financial Aid .... Ms. Arlina B. DENARDO
09 Director of Institutional Research .... Dr. James P. SCHAFFER
06 Registrar .... Mr. Francis A. BENGINIA
41 Director of Athletics .... Dr. Bruce E. MCCUTCHEON
36 Director Career Services .... Ms. Linda N. ARRA
23 Director Health Services .... Dr. Jeffrey E. GOLDSTEIN
38 Director Counseling Center .... Dr. Karen J. FORBES
19 Director of Public Safety .... Mr. Hugh W. HARRIS
18 Dir Physical Planning & Plant Oper .... Mr. Bruce S. FERRETTI
29 Executive Director Alumni Relations .... Ms. Rachel NELSON MOELLER
15 Director Employment .... Ms. Lisa Youngkin REX
96 Manager of Procurement .... Ms. Linda L. JROSKI

Lake Erie College of Osteopathic Medicine (C)

1858 W Grandview Boulevard, Erie PA 16509-1025
County: Erie FICE Identification: 030908
Unit ID: 407629
Telephone: (814) 866-6641 Carnegie Class: Spec/Med
FAX Number: (814) 866-8123 Calendar System: Semester
URL: www.lecom.edu
Established: 1993 Annual Graduate Tuition & Fees: $29,820
Enrollment: 3,044 Coed
Affiliation or Control: Independent Non-Profit IRS Status: 501(c)3
Highest Offering: First Professional Degree; No Undergraduates
Program: Professional
Accreditation: M, DENT, OSTEO, PHAR

01 President/CEO .... Dr. John M. FERRETTI
05 Provost/Sr Vice Pres/Dean Acad Affs .... Dr. Silvia M. FERRETTI
10 Vice Pres of Fiscal Affairs/CFO .... Mr. Richard P. OLINGER
67 VP Acad Affs/Dn LECOM Sch Pharmacy .... Dr. Hershey BELL
12 Vice Pres for LECOM at Seton Hill .... Dr. Irving FREEMAN
52 Dean School of Dental Medicine .... Dr. Robert HIRSCH
05 Assoc Dean Acad Affairs Bradenton .... Dr. Robert GEORGE
12 Assc Dn Ops/Dist Ed Pharm Bradenton .... Dr. Sunil JAMBHEKAR
88 Asst Dean of Clinical Education .... Dr. Regan SHABLOSKI
88 Assoc Dean of Preclinical Educ .... Dr. Christine KELL
88 Asst Dean Clinical Educ Bradenton .... Dr. Anthony J. FERRETTI
88 Asst Dean Preclinical Ed Bradenton .... Dr. Mark COTY
20 Asst Dean Acad Affairs Bradenton .... Dr. Ronald BEREZNIAK
63 VP Med Educ & Program Development .... Dr. Chet EVANS
20 Assoc Dean of Faculty .... Dr. Rachel OGDEN
20 Assoc Dean of Curriculum .... Dr. Julie WILKINSON
108 Assistant Dean for Assessment .... Dr. Theresa SCHWEIGER
09 Director of Institutional Research .... Mr. Matt CETIN
32 Dir Stdnt Affs/Fin Aid/Enrol Mgmt .... Ms. Susan LAZZARO
30 Vice President of Institutional Dev .... Dr. James K. MOORE
26 Director Communications/Marketing .... Mr. Pierre A. BELLICINI
08 Dir of Learning Resources/Educ Tech .... Mr. Robert M. SCHNICK
72 Director of Information Technology .... Mr. Michael E. LEE
46 Director of Research .... Dr. Bertalan DUDAS
15 Director of Human Resources .... Ms. JoAnn I. JEWELL
38 Director Behavioral Health .... Vacant
20 Director of Faculty Development .... Dr. Mark TERRELL
27 Asst Dir Communications/Marketing .... Mr. Michael POLIN
18 Building Operations Supervisor .... Mr. Carl F. MULLINAX
37 Associate Director of Financial Aid .... Ms. Bonnie CRILLEY
06 Registrar .... Mr. Jeremy SIVILLO
07 Admissions Coordinator .... Ms. Amy W. ROWE
40 Bookstore Manager .... Ms. Alice PUZAROWSKI

Lancaster Bible College (D)

901 Eden Road, Lancaster PA 17601-5036
County: Lancaster FICE Identification: 003285
Unit ID: 213400
Telephone: (717) 569-7071 Carnegie Class: Spec/Faith
FAX Number: (717) 560-8260 Calendar System: Semester
URL: www.lbc.edu
Established: 1933 Annual Undergrad Tuition & Fees: $17,740
Enrollment: 1,018 Coed
Affiliation or Control: Independent Non-Profit IRS Status: 501(c)3
Highest Offering: Doctorate
Program: Religious Emphasis
Accreditation: M, BI

01 President .... Dr. Peter W. TEAGUE
04 Assistant to the President .... Mrs. Judith M. HECKAMAN
05 Vice President for Academic Affairs .... Dr. Philip E. DEARBORN
84 VP for Enrollment Management .... Mr. Josh BEERS
30 VP of Advancement .... Mr. Tim HEITZ
10 Director of Finance .... Mr. Matthew MASON
09 AVP of Institutional Effectiveness .... Dr. Dale MORT
20 Dean of iLEAD Center .... Dr. Gary BREDFELDT
06 Associate VP & Registrar .... Mr. Jeffrey HOOVER
32 Associate VP for Student Services .... Mr. Robert MCMICHAEL
26 Director of Marketing .... Mr. Peter CASTOR
07 Director of Admissions .... Mr. Scott BOYER
38 Dean of Student Development .... Ms. Annette HERNANDEZ
08 Interm Director of Library Services .... Dr. Philip E. DEARBORN
37 Director of Financial Aid .... Mrs. Karen L. FOX
21 Controller .... Mr. Lonnie MARTIN
18 Director of Plant Operations .... Mr. Steve MUSSER
23 Director of Health Services .... Mrs. Mary Lou JOLINE
29 Dir of Alumni & Career Services .... Mr. Cameron MARTIN
41 Athletic Director .... Mr. Peter BEERS
15 Director of People Development & HR .... Mrs. Paula POOLE

Lancaster General College of Nursing and Health Sciences (E)

410 N Lime Street, Lancaster PA 17602-2337
County: Lancaster FICE Identification: 009863
Unit ID: 442356
Telephone: (717) 544-4912 Carnegie Class: Assoc/PrivNFP
FAX Number: (717) 544-5970 Calendar System: Semester
URL: www.lancastergeneralcollege.edu
Established: 1903 Annual Undergrad Tuition & Fees: $19,000
Enrollment: 1,165 Coed
Affiliation or Control: Independent Non-Profit IRS Status: 501(c)3
Highest Offering: Baccalaureate
Program: 2-Year Principally Bachelor's Creditable; Nursing Emphasis
Accreditation: M, ADNUR, CVT, DMS, MT, NMT, NURSE, RAD, SURGT

01 President .... Dr. Mary Grace SIMCOX
05 Vice President of Academic Affairs .... Ms. Penni LONGENECKER
10 Vice President of Finance & Admin .... Mr. Thomas HULSTINE
20 Vice President Learning Development .... Ms. Donna WILLIAMSON
06 Registrar .... Mr. James DONOHUE
07 Director of Admissions .... Mr. Lyn LONGENECKER
84 Int Dean of Enrollment Management .... Ms. JoAnn HENDRICKS

Lancaster Theological Seminary (F)

555 W James Street, Lancaster PA 17603-2812
County: Lancaster FICE Identification: 003286
Unit ID: 213446
Telephone: (717) 393-0654 Carnegie Class: Spec/Faith
FAX Number: (717) 393-4254 Calendar System: Semester
URL: www.lancasterseminary.edu
Established: 1825 Annual Graduate Tuition & Fees: $14,600
Enrollment: 130 Coed
Affiliation or Control: United Church Of Christ IRS Status: 501(c)3
Highest Offering: Doctorate; No Undergraduates
Program: Professional; Religious Emphasis
Accreditation: M, THEOL

01 President .... Dr. Carol E. LYTCH
10 Vice President Business & Finance .... Ms. Valerie A. CALHOUN
05 Vice Pres Academic Affairs & Dean .... Dr. David M. MELLOTT
07 Director of Admissions .... Rev. Kendal N. BROWN
08 Director Library Services .... Rev. Richard R. BERG
06 Registrar .... Mrs. Judith G. HUMMER
29 Director Alumni Relations .... Rev. Paul EYER
13 Director Computing/Information Mgmt .... Rev. Chris BELDAN
30 Exec Director of Advancement .... Ms. Crystal MILLS
04 Assistant to the President .... Vacant

Lansdale School of Business (G)

290 Wissahickon Ave, North Wales PA 19454-4114
County: Montgomery FICE Identification: 007779
Unit ID: 213473
Telephone: (215) 699-5700 Carnegie Class: Assoc/PrivFP
FAX Number: (215) 699-8770 Calendar System: Semester

URL: www.LSB.edu
Established: 1918 Annual Undergrad Tuition & Fees: $10,395
Enrollment: 535 Coed
Affiliation or Control: Proprietary IRS Status: Proprietary
Highest Offering: Associate Degree
Program: Occupational; 2-Year Principally Bachelor's Creditable; Business Emphasis
Accreditation: ACICS

01 President ... Mr. Marlon D. KELLER
03 Executive Director ... Mrs. Marianne H. JOHNSON
05 Academic Dean ... Mr. David P. HEFFLEY
32 Student Services Coordinator ... Ms. Debora GAHMAN
08 Librarian ... Mrs. Marie B. WALCROFT
10 Director of Student Finance ... Mr. Robert RUSSO
36 Career Services Coordinator ... Ms. Jodi L. TASHMAN

Laurel Business Institute (A)

11 East Penn Street, Uniontown PA 15401-3453
County: Fayette FICE Identification: 025462
Unit ID: 250027
Telephone: (724) 439-4900 Carnegie Class: Assoc/PrivFP
FAX Number: (724) 439-3607 Calendar System: Semester
URL: www.laurel.edu
Established: 1985 Annual Undergrad Tuition & Fees: $12,285
Enrollment: 223 Coed
Affiliation or Control: Proprietary IRS Status: Proprietary
Highest Offering: Associate Degree
Program: Occupational; Technical Emphasis
Accreditation: ACICS, MLTAD

01 President ... Mrs. Nancy M. DECKER
05 Vice President of Education ... Mrs. Valerie S. BACHARACH
12 Campus Director ... Mrs. Bonnie Jean MARSH
13 Network Administrator ... Mrs. JoAnna MEESE
15 Vice President of Human Resources ... Mr. Chuck SANTORE, JR.
37 Director of Financial Aid ... Ms. Stephanie M. MIGYANKO
10 Vice President of Finance ... Ms. Vicki M. JOLLIFFE
07 Director of Admission/Marketing ... Mr. Douglas S. DECKER

Laurel Technical Institute (B)

200 Sterling Avenue, Sharon PA 16146
County: Mercer FICE Identification: 020925
Unit ID: 215992
Telephone: (724) 983-0700 Carnegie Class: Assoc/PrivFP
FAX Number: (724) 983-8355 Calendar System: Quarter
URL: www.laurel.edu
Established: 1925 Annual Undergrad Tuition & Fees: $9,079
Enrollment: 275 Coed
Affiliation or Control: Proprietary IRS Status: Proprietary
Highest Offering: Associate Degree
Program: Occupational; 2-Year Principally Bachelor's Creditable
Accreditation: ACICS

01 President ... Ms. Nancy DECKER
05 Director ... Mr. Douglas DECKER

Lebanon Valley College (C)

101 N College Avenue, Annville PA 17003-1400
County: Lebanon FICE Identification: 003288
Unit ID: 213507
Telephone: (717) 867-6161 Carnegie Class: Bac/Diverse
FAX Number: (717) 867-6124 Calendar System: Semester
URL: www.lvc.edu
Established: 1866 Annual Undergrad Tuition & Fees: $34,470
Enrollment: 2,102 Coed
Affiliation or Control: United Methodist IRS Status: 501(c)3
Highest Offering: Doctorate
Program: Liberal Arts And General; Teacher Preparatory; Professional
Accreditation: M, ACBSP, MUS, PTA

01 President ... Dr. Lewis E. THAYNE
05 Vice Pres Acad Affs/Dean of Faculty ... Dr. Michael R. GREEN
30 Vice President of Advancement ... Vacant
11 Vice President Administration/IT ... Mr. Robert A. RILEY
10 Vice President of Finance ... Mrs. Deborah R. FULLAM
84 Vice President of Enrollment ... Mr. William J. BROWN
32 VP Student Affairs/Dean of Students . Mr. Gregory H. KRIKORIAN
04 Exec Assistant to the President ... Ms. Beth ESLER
20 Associate Dean of the Faculty ... Dr. Ann E. DAMIANO
06 Registrar ... Mr. Jeremy A. MAISTO
08 Librarian ... Mr. Frank MOLS
42 Chaplain ... Rev. Paul FULLMER
51 Dir Cont Educ/Professional Devel ... Ms. Mary M. HERSTER
35 Associate Dean Student Services ... Mr. Robert L. MIKUS
37 Director of Financial Aid ... Mrs. Kendra M. FEIGERT
36 Director of Career Services ... Ms. Sharon M. GIVLER
41 Director of Athletics ... Mr. Richard L. BEARD
29 Director of Alumni Programs ... Ms. Jayanne HAYWARD
44 Director of Development ... Mrs. Jamie N. CECIL
26 Exec Dir Marketing/Communications ... Mr. Martin J. PARKES
27 Director Marketing & Communications ... Dr. Thomas M. HANRAHAN
21 Controller ... Ms. Eleanor LEWIS
18 Sr Director of Facilities Services ... Mr. Donald SANTOSTEFANO
19 Director of Public Safety ... Mr. Brent OBERHOLTZER
15 Director of Human Resources ... Mrs. Ann C. HAYES
28 Director of Multicultural Affairs ... Ms. Venus RICKS
35 Director of Student Activities ... Mrs. Jennifer M. EVANS
104 Director of Study Abroad ... Ms. Jill T. RUSSELL
90 Director of Client Services ... Mr. Michael C. ZEIGLER
91 Director of Info Mgt Services ... Mr. Robert J. DILLANE
39 Director of Residential Life ... Mr. Jason A. KUNTZ
38 Director of Counseling ... Dr. Stephanie A. FALK
38 Director of Disability Services ... Ms. Yvonne FOSTER
09 Director of Institutional Research ... Mr. Lynold K. MCGHEE
50 Director of the MBA Program ... Ms. Jennifer K. EASTER
96 Director of Business Services ... Mr. Todd M. LATSHAW

Lehigh Carbon Community College (D)

4525 Education Park Drive, Schnecksville PA 18078-2598
County: Lehigh FICE Identification: 006810
Unit ID: 213525
Telephone: (610) 799-2121 Carnegie Class: Assoc/Pub-S-SC
FAX Number: (610) 799-1527 Calendar System: Semester
URL: www.lccc.edu
Established: 1966 Annual Undergrad Tuition & Fees (In-District): $3,390
Enrollment: 7,710 Coed
Affiliation or Control: Local IRS Status: 501(c)3
Highest Offering: Associate Degree
Program: Occupational; 2-Year Principally Bachelor's Creditable
Accreditation: M, ACBSP, ADNUR, MAC, OTA, PNUR, PTAA

01 President ... Dr. Donald W. SNYDER
05 VP Academic/Student Dev ... Dr. Thomas C. LEAMER
11 Sr VP Administrative Services ... Dr. Ann D. BIEBER
10 VP Finance & Facilities ... Mr. Larry W. ROSS
04 Admin Secy to President and Board ... Mrs. Cindy L. BROOKS
32 Dean of Students ... Ms. Peggy M. HEIM
62 Dean Library and Info Tech ... Mr. David S. VOROS
88 Dean of Academic Services ... Dr. Barry L. SPRIGGS
13 Exec Dir Information Technology ... Mr. Ervin J. MEASE
106 Assoc Dean Distance Education ... Mr. Dominic CHRISTISON
20 Associate Academic Dean ... Dr. Richard W. WILT
20 Associate Academic Dean ... Ms. Larissa M. VERTA
103 Ex Dir Workforce/Community Ed ... Ms. Terri K. KEEFE
88 Assoc Dean Educational Support Svcs . Dr. Michael L. TORRENCE
30 Assoc Dean Inst Advancement ... Ms. Heather L. KUHNS
09 Assoc Dean Inst Research/Planning ... Dr. Glynis A. DANIELS
45 Assoc Dean Planning & Assessment ... Dr. Cecelia A. CONNELLY-WEIDA
21 Assistant Controller-Accounting ... Ms. Shannon HELMER
102 Executive Director of Foundation ... Mr. Timothy J. HERRLINGER
38 Director Advising and Counseling ... Ms. Susan J. FREAD
07 Director of Recruitment/Admissions ... Mr. Louis L. HEGYES
88 Dir of Application Support Services ... Ms. Shirley DELONG
36 Director Career Development ... Ms. Christina L. MOYER
88 Assoc Dean Prof Accred/Curriculum ... Mr. Scott W. AQUILA
88 Director of High School Connections ... Ms. Jennifer K. NEEB
15 Director of Human Resources ... Ms. Donna M. WILLIAMS
88 Dir Infrastructure Svcs/Client Sol ... Mr. Frank D. MROZ
88 Dir Fac Dev/Student Retention ... Ms. Cheryl A. DOLL
103 Director Workforce Training ... Ms. Lois M. YEAKEL
66 Director Nursing/Healthcare Science ... Ms. Barbara H. LUPOLE
35 Director of Student Life ... Ms. Gene F. EDEN
14 Director IT Support Services ... Mr. George C. HEGEDUS
18 Director of Facilities Management ... Mr. Carl S. PECKITT, JR.
37 Director of Financial Aid ... Ms. Marian L. SNYDER
25 Director of Academic Grants ... Ms. Linda L. MESICS
106 Dir of Distance Lrng/Instruct Tech ... Ms. Beverly J. BENFER
41 Director of Athletics ... Ms. Jocelyn M. BECK
88 Director of Early Learning Center ... Vacant
96 Purchasing Manager ... Ms. Susan E. LINDENMUTH
12 Dir Carbon/Schuylkill Cty Ed Svcs ... Ms. Jeanne Y. MILLER
88 Dir of Literacy and Job Training ... Ms. Suzy L. WELLIVER
31 Director of Community Education ... Vacant
88 Controller ... Ms. Connie BURNS
88 ESC Lab Supervisor ... Ms. Debra A. CONDON
25 Dir Institutional Advancement Grant .. Mr. Thomas J. MULDERICK
74 Dir Veterinary Tech Program ... Ms. Samantha FRIEDENBERG
27 Director Marketing and Publications ... Ms. Paula A. HANNAM
06 Registrar ... Ms. Sandra L. MOSSER
19 Supervisor of Security & Safety ... Mr. Kevin J. MILES
40 Bookstore Manager ... Ms. Jennifer ERB
88 Assoc Dean Student Success ... Mr. Brian C. DELONG
19 Director of Public Safety ... Vacant

Lehigh University (E)

27 Memorial Drive W, Bethlehem PA 18015-3094
County: Northampton FICE Identification: 003289
Unit ID: 213543
Telephone: (610) 758-3000 Carnegie Class: RU/H
FAX Number: (610) 691-5420 Calendar System: Semester
URL: www.lehigh.edu
Established: 1865 Annual Undergrad Tuition & Fees: $53,450
Enrollment: 7,036 Coed
Affiliation or Control: Independent Non-Profit IRS Status: 501(c)3
Highest Offering: Doctorate
Program: Liberal Arts And General; Teacher Preparatory; Professional
Accreditation: M, BUS, BUSA, COPSY, CS, ENG, SCPSY, THEA

01 President ... Dr. Alice P. GAST
05 Provost & VP for Academic Affairs ... Dr. Patrick V. FARRELL
10 Vice Pres Finance & Administration . Ms. Margaret F. PLYMPTON
88 VP for International Affairs ... Dr. Mohamed S. EL-AASSER
30 Vice President Advancement ... Mr. Joseph P. KENDER, JR.
46 VP & Assoc Prov Research/Graduate ... Dr. Alan J. SNYDER
26 VP Communications & Public Affairs ... Mr. Frederick J. MCGRAIL
88 Chief Investment Officer ... Mr. Peter M. GILBERT
09 Vice Provost Institutional Research ... Dr. J. Gary LUTZ
32 Vice Provost Student Affairs ... Dr. John W. SMEATON
13 Vice Provost Library & Tech Svcs ... Dr. Bruce M. TAGGART
86 Assoc VP for Govt Relations ... Mr. William D. MICHALERYA
21 Assoc VP Finance/Asst Secy Board ... Ms. Denise M. BLEW
15 Assoc Vice Pres for Human Resources ... Ms. Jacqueline MATTHEWS
18 Assoc Vice Pres Facilities Services .. Mr. Henry (Van) V. DOBSON
20 Deputy Provost Academic Affairs ... Mr. Gerald P. LENNON
35 Assoc Vice Provost Dean of Students ... Ms. Sharon K. BASSO
29 Asst Vice Pres of Alumni Relations ... Mr. Robert W. WOLFENDEN
31 Asst VP Community & Regional Affs ... Mr. Dale A. KOCHARD
54 Dean Engineering & Applied Science ... Dr. S. David WU
49 Dean Arts & Sciences ... Dr. Donald E. HALL
50 Dean of Business & Economics ... Dr. Paul R. BROWN
53 Dean of Education ... Dr. Gary M. SASSO
07 Dean of Admissions/Financial Aid ... Mr. J. Leon WASHINGTON
41 Murray H Goodman Dean of Athletics ... Mr. Joseph D. STERRETT
06 Registrar ... Mr. Emil A. GNASSO
37 Director Financial Aid ... Ms. Jennifer L. MERTZ
106 Director Distance Education ... Ms. Margaret A. PORTZ
36 Director Career Services ... Ms. Donna L. GOLDFEDER
23 Director Health Center ... Dr. Susan C. KITEI
39 Director Residential Services ... Mr. Ozzie BREINER
40 Director Bookstore ... Mr. Steve A. SCHATTEN
19 Chief University Police ... Mr. Edward K. SHUPP
38 Director of Counseling Services ... Dr. Ian T. BIRKY
42 Chaplain ... Rev. Lloyd H. STEFFEN
43 General Counsel ... Mr. Frank A. ROTH
21 Director of Budget ... Mr. Stephen J. GUTTMAN
28 Director of Diversity ... Mr. Henry U. ODI
96 Manager Strategic Sourcing ... Ms. Jane ALTEMOSE
84 Director Enrollment Management ... Ms. Jennifer E. O'BRIEN

Lincoln Technical Institute (F)

5151 Tilghman Street, Allentown PA 18104-3298
County: Lehigh FICE Identification: 007759
Unit ID: 213570
Telephone: (610) 398-5300 Carnegie Class: Assoc/PrivFP
FAX Number: (610) 395-2706 Calendar System: Semester
URL: www.lincolntech.com
Established: 1946 Annual Undergrad Tuition & Fees: N/A
Enrollment: 627 Coed
Affiliation or Control: Proprietary IRS Status: Proprietary
Highest Offering: Associate Degree
Program: Occupational
Accreditation: ACCSC

01 Executive Director ... Mrs. Lisa M. KUNTZ
05 Director of Education ... Ms. Anne CONNELY
11 Director of Administrative Services ... Mrs. Jennie I. HUNSICKER
37 Director of Financial Aid ... Ms. Erica BETZ
07 Director of Admissions ... Mr. Mark GARNER
36 Director of Career Services ... Mrs. Charmain BRODY

Lincoln Technical Institute (G)

9191 Torresdale Avenue, Philadelphia PA 19136-1595
County: Philadelphia FICE Identification: 007832
Unit ID: 213589
Telephone: (215) 335-0800 Carnegie Class: Assoc/PrivFP
FAX Number: (215) 335-1443 Calendar System: Other
URL: www.lincolntech.com
Established: 1946 Annual Undergrad Tuition & Fees: $29,731
Enrollment: 545 Coed
Affiliation or Control: Proprietary IRS Status: Proprietary
Highest Offering: Associate Degree
Program: Occupational
Accreditation: ACCSC

01 Executive Director ... Mr. John WILLI
07 Dir Admiss High School/Adult Educ ... Mr. Pat FITTIPALDI
32 Director of Student Services ... Ms. Kristin DRUST
05 Director of Education ... Mr. Norman NORBILLE
11 Director Administrative Services ... Ms. Gina ALTSHULER
36 Int Director of Career Services ... Ms. Merle MOYER

Lincoln University (H)

PO Box 179, 1570 Baltimore Pike,
Lincoln University PA 19352-0999
County: Chester FICE Identification: 003290
Unit ID: 213598
Telephone: (484) 365-8000 Carnegie Class: Master's L
FAX Number: (484) 365-7316 Calendar System: Semester
URL: www.lincoln.edu
Established: 1854 Annual Undergrad Tuition & Fees (In-State): $9,984
Enrollment: 2,240 Coed
Affiliation or Control: State Related IRS Status: 501(c)3
Highest Offering: Master's
Program: Liberal Arts And General
Accreditation: M

01 President ... Dr. Robert R. JENNINGS
03 Executive Vice President ... Mr. Michael B. HILL
100 Asst to Pres/Mgr Board of Trustees ... Ms. Diane M. BROWN
05 Sr VP Academic & Student Affairs ... Vacant
10 Vice Pres Fiscal Affairs/Treasurer ... Mr. Charles GRADOWSKI

32 Vice Pres for Student Affairs .... Dr. F. Carl WALTON
20 Int Asst VP Academic Affs/Info Tech .... Mr. Harry WASHINGTON
09 Asst VP Institutional Effectiveness ...... Dr. Renford A B. BREVETT
07 Director Admissions .... Ms. Germel EATON-CLARKE
08 Director of Library .... Mr. Tracey HUNTER HAYES
26 Director of Communications .... Vacant
29 Director of Alumni Relations .... Ms. Theresa BRASWELL
06 Registrar .... Ms. Catherine RUTLEDGE
30 Director Development & Major Gifts .... Vacant
15 Chief Human Resources Officer .... Dr. Debbie BULLOCK
19 Director of Public Safety/Security .... Mr. Larry WOODS
102 Dir Foundation/Corporate Relations .... Mr. Andre DIXON
36 Director Counseling/Career Svcs Ctr .... Mr. Ralph SIMPSON
41 Director of Athletics .... Ms. Dianthia FORD-KEE
42 Chaplain .... Mr. Frederick FAISON
21 Controller .... Ms. Danielle JONES
18 Chief Facilities/Physical Plant .... Mr. John THOMPSON
39 Int Dean Students and Campus Life .... Ms. Thelma ROSS
85 Director International Services .... Ms. Constance L. LUNDY
23 Director Health Services .... Ms. Velva GREENE-RAINEY
58 Dir Graduate Student Svcs/Admission .... Ms. Jernice LEA
37 Director Financial Aid .... Ms. Thelma L. ROSS
96 Director of Purchasing .... Ms. Lynnette F. SCOTT
81 Dean Sch of Natural Sciences & Math ....Dr. John O. CHIKWEM
83 Int Dean Sch Soc Sci/Behavioral Std ....Dr. Patricia A. JOSEPH
79 Dean School of Humanities/Grad Stds ...Dr. Cheryl Renee GOOCH

Lutheran Theological Seminary at Gettysburg (A)

61 Seminary Ridge, Gettysburg PA 17325-1795
County: Adams — FICE Identification: 003291
Unit ID: 213631
Telephone: (717) 334-6286 — Carnegie Class: Spec/Faith
FAX Number: (717) 334-3469 — Calendar System: 4/1/4
URL: www.ltsg.edu
Established: 1826 — Annual Graduate Tuition & Fees: $13,650
Enrollment: 128 — Coed
Affiliation or Control: Evangelical Lutheran Church In America
IRS Status: 501(c)3
Highest Offering: Doctorate; No Undergraduates
Program: Professional; Religious Emphasis
Accreditation: M, THEOL

01 President .... Rev. Michael L. COOPER-WHITE
30 Chief Advancement Officer .... Rev. Kathleen O. REED
10 Chief Financial Officer .... Dr. Marty STEVENS
05 Dean of the Seminary .... Dr. Robin J. STEINKE
08 Library Director and Archivist .... Dr. Briant BOHLEKE
06 Registrar .... Dr. Marty STEVENS
26 Exec Asst to Pres for Comm/Plng .... Rev. John R. SPANGLER
91 Director of Info Systems/Ed Tech .... Mr. Donald L. REDMAN
15 Asst to the Pres/Personnel Officer .... Mrs. Carol A. TROYER
07 Director of Admissions .... Rev. Virginia PRICE
21 Financial Services Manager .... Ms. Debra ECK

Lutheran Theological Seminary at Philadelphia (B)

7301 Germantown Avenue, Philadelphia PA 19119-1794
County: Philadelphia — FICE Identification: 003292
Unit ID: 213640
Telephone: (215) 248-4616 — Carnegie Class: Spec/Faith
FAX Number: (215) 248-4577 — Calendar System: Other
URL: www.ltsp.edu
Established: 1864 — Annual Graduate Tuition & Fees: $15,300
Enrollment: 330 — Coed
Affiliation or Control: Evangelical Lutheran Church In America
IRS Status: 501(c)3
Highest Offering: Doctorate; No Undergraduates
Program: Professional; Religious Emphasis
Accreditation: M, THEOL

01 President .... Dr. Philip D. KREY
05 Dean .... Dr. J. Jayakiran SEBASTIAN
10 Vice President Finance & Operation .... Vacant
30 Vice President LTSP Foundation .... Rev. John V. PUOTINEN
58 Director of Graduate Studies .... Dr. David GRAFTON
08 Director of the Library .... Dr. Karl KRUEGER
07 Director of Admissions .... Rev. Louise N. JOHNSON
21 Business Office Manager .... Mr. Martin SCHWAB
15 Human Resources Manager .... Ms. Lisa HUTCHINSON
32 Director of Student Services .... Rev. Heidi RODRICK-SCHNAATH
06 Registrar .... Ms. Rene DIEMER
37 Director of Financial Aid .... Ms. Elizabeth BRUNTON
39 Coordinator of Housing .... Ms. Sara CALDERON
19 Director of Security/Safety .... Mr. Vincent FERGUSON
13 Director Information Technology .... Mr. Kyle BARGER
27 Director of Communications .... Ms. Merri BROWN
42 Chaplain .... Dr. Nelson RIVERA

Luzerne County Community College (C)

1333 S Prospect Street, Nanticoke PA 18634-3899
County: Luzerne — FICE Identification: 006811
Unit ID: 213659
Telephone: (570) 740-0200 — Carnegie Class: Assoc/Pub-S-SC
FAX Number: (570) 740-0386 — Calendar System: Semester
URL: www.luzerne.edu
Established: 1966 — Annual Undergrad Tuition & Fees (In-District): $3,150
Enrollment: 6,779 — Coed
Affiliation or Control: Local — IRS Status: 501(c)3
Highest Offering: Associate Degree
Program: Occupational; 2-Year Principally Bachelor's Creditable
Accreditation: M, ADNUR, DA, DH, SURGT

01 President .... Mr. Thomas P. LEARY
04 Spec Ast to Pres Policy/Staff Devel .... Ms. Laura KATRENICZ
05 Vice Pres Academic Affairs/Provost .... Dr. Dana CLARK
32 Dean Enrollment Mgmt/Student Dev .... Ms. Rosana REYES
103 VP Workforce/Community Development .... Ms. Susan SPRY
16 Dean Human Resources .... Mr. John SEDLAK
66 Dean of Nursing/Health Sciences ... Ms. Deborah VILEGI-PETERS
50 Dean of Business/Technologies .... Mr. Gary MROZINSKI
49 Dean of Arts & Sciences .... Vacant
10 Dean Finance .... Mr. Joseph GASPER
13 Chief Technology Office .... Mr. Don NELSON
07 Director Admissions & Recruiting .... Mr. James DOMZALSKI
37 Director of Student Financial Aid .... Ms. Mary KOSIN
08 Director of Library Services .... Mrs. Mia W. BASSHAM
38 Dir Counseling/Stdnt Support Svcs .... Mrs. Linda WALTERS
35 Dir Student Activities/Athletics .... Ms. Mary SULLIVAN
09 Director Inst Research/Planning .... Ms. Graceann PLATUKUS
36 Director Career Services .... Ms. Mary GHILANI
18 Director of Physical Plant .... Mr. Keith GRAHAM
30 Exec Dir of Institutional Advance .... Ms. Sandra NICHOLAS
84 Director Enrollment Management .... Mr. Jim DOMZALSKI
26 Chief Public Relations Officer .... Mrs. Lisa NELSON
29 Director Alumni Relations .... Ms. Bonnie LAUER
96 Director of Purchasing .... Mr. Len OLZINSKI

Lycoming College (D)

700 College Place, Williamsport PA 17701-5192
County: Lycoming — FICE Identification: 003293
Unit ID: 213668
Telephone: (570) 321-4000 — Carnegie Class: Bac/A&S
FAX Number: (570) 321-4337 — Calendar System: Semester
URL: www.lycoming.edu
Established: 1812 — Annual Undergrad Tuition & Fees: $31,818
Enrollment: 1,366 — Coed
Affiliation or Control: United Methodist — IRS Status: 501(c)3
Highest Offering: Baccalaureate
Program: Liberal Arts And General; Fine Arts Emphasis
Accreditation: M

01 President .... Dr. James E. DOUTHAT
05 Provost and Dean of the College .... Dr. Philip W. SPRUNGER
10 Vice Pres Administration/Planning .... Dr. Sue S. GAYLOR
30 Vice President for Advancement .... Mr. Charles W. EDMONDS
07 Vice Pres Admissions/Financial Aid .... Mr. James D. SPENCER
21 Controller/Chf Financial Ofcr/Treas .... Ms. Michelle M. JONES
32 Dean Student Affairs .... Dr. Daniel P. MILLER
89 Assistant Dean for Freshmen .... Mr. Andrew W. KILPATRICK
08 Director of Snowden Library .... Ms. Janet M. HURLBERT
06 Registrar .... Ms. Whitney A. MERINAR
26 Director of College Relations .... Mr. Jerry T. RASHID
37 Director of Financial Aid .... Mr. James LAKIS
14 Assoc Dean/Chief Information Ofcr .... Mr. David B. HEFFNER
36 Director of Career Services .... Ms. MaryJo CAMPANA
29 Director Alumni Relations .... Ms. Amy S. DOWLING
44 Planned Giving Officer .... Ms. Karen M. SHEAFFER
19 Director of Safety & Security .... Mr. Donald TROUTMAN
35 Director of Student Programs ... Mr. Lawrence P. MANNOLINI, III
39 Director Residence Life .... Mr. Andrew W. KILPATRICK
41 Director of Athletics .... Mr. Michael CLARK
30 Senior Major Gift Officer .... Mr. Gregory J. BELL
44 Director of Annual Giving .... Ms. Meghan E. HEPLER
42 Campus Minister .... Rev. Jeffrey L. LECRONE
16 Director of Human Resources .... Ms. Jackie BILGER
18 Chief Facilities/Physical Plant .... Mr. F. Douglas KUNTZ
23 Director of Health Services .... Ms. Sondra L. STIPCAK
38 Director Student Counseling .... Mr. Townsend VELKOFF
40 Campus Store Manager .... Ms. Patricia E. BAUSINGER
92 Lycoming Scholars .... Dr. Michelle A. BRIGGS
94 Women's Studies .... Dr. N. J. STANLEY
15 Human Resources Coordinator .... Mrs. Cathleen A. LUTZ

Manor College (E)

700 Fox Chase Road, Jenkintown PA 19046-3399
County: Montgomery — FICE Identification: 003294
Unit ID: 213774
Telephone: (215) 885-2360 — Carnegie Class: Assoc/PrivNFP
FAX Number: (215) 576-6564 — Calendar System: Semester
URL: www.manor.edu
Established: 1947 — Annual Undergrad Tuition & Fees: $14,620
Enrollment: 938 — Coed
Affiliation or Control: Independent Non-Profit — IRS Status: 501(c)3
Highest Offering: Associate Degree
Program: Occupational; 2-Year Principally Bachelor's Creditable; Business Emphasis
Accreditation: M, ACBSP, DA, DH

01 President .... Sr. M. Cecilia JURASINSKI, OSBM
05 Dean Academic Affs/Exec Vice Pres .... Mrs. Sally P. MYDLOWEC
10 Director Finance & Physical Plant .... Mr. John WINICKI
08 Library Director .... Ms. Beth LANDER
32 Dean of Students .... Sr. Marie Francis WALCHONSKY, OSBM
30 Director of Development .... Ms. Marialice STANZESKI
38 Director Counseling Office .... Ms. Linda PETERSON
07 Director of Admissions .... Mr. Jeffrey P. LEVINE
26 Director Marketing Communications .... Mr. Steve GREENBAUM
06 Registrar .... Mr. Edwin EIGENBROT
29 Director Alumni Relations .... Ms. Marialice STANZESKI
41 Director of Athletics .... Mr. Robert REEVES
37 Director of Financial Aid .... Mr. Peter LYSIONEK
18 Maintenance Supervisor .... Mr. Petro DOLINAY
09 Director of Institutional Research ..... Sr. Monica LESNICK, OSBM
15 Human Resources Generalist .... Ms. Brittney RICHARDSON
40 Bookstore Manager .... Ms. Mary ZAKRZEWSKI
20 Assistant Dean Academic Affairs ...... Ms. Jane R. ZEGESTOWSKY

Marywood University (F)

2300 Adams Avenue, Scranton PA 18509-1598
County: Lackawanna — FICE Identification: 003296
Unit ID: 213826
Telephone: (570) 348-6211 — Carnegie Class: Master's L
FAX Number: (570) 961-4769 — Calendar System: Semester
URL: www.marywood.edu
Established: 1915 — Annual Undergrad Tuition & Fees: $29,380
Enrollment: 3,398 — Coed
Affiliation or Control: Roman Catholic — IRS Status: 501(c)3
Highest Offering: Doctorate
Program: Liberal Arts And General; Teacher Preparatory; Professional
Accreditation: M, ACBSP, ARCPA, ART, CACREP, CLPSY, DIETC, DIETD, DIETI, MUS, NUR, SP, SW, TED

01 President .... Sr. Anne MUNLEY
05 Vice Pres Academic Affairs .... Dr. Alan LEVINE
10 VP Business Affairs/Treasurer .... Mr. Joseph X. GARVEY, JR.
30 Vice Pres University Advancement .... Dr. Clayton N. PHEASANT
32 Vice President Student Life .... Dr. Raymond P. HEATH
84 Vice Pres Enrollment Management .... Ms. Ann BOLAND-CHASE
101 Secretary Univ & General Counsel .... Ms. Mary T. GARDIER PATERSON
15 Asst Vice Pres for Human Resources ... Dr. Patricia E. DUNLEAVY
26 Asst VP for Marketing and Comm .... Mr. Peter KILCULLEN
18 Asst VP for Buildings & Grounds .... Mrs. Wendy YANKELITIS
44 Asst Vice Pres for Development .... Vacant
35 Dean of Students .... Dr. Amy PACIEJ-WOODRUFF
49 Dean College Liberal Arts/Sciences .... Dr. Michael FOLEY
53 Dean Reap College Educ/Human Dev ...... Dr. Mary Anne FEDRICK
76 Dean Col of Health/Human Svcs .... Dr. Mark E. RODGERS
88 Dn Col of Creative Performing Arts .... Mr. Collier B. PARKER
48 Dean School of Architecture .... Mr. Gregory K. HUNT
90 Director User Support Services .... Dr. Michael MIRABITO
70 Director School of Social Work .... Dr. Lloyd L. LYTER
08 Director of Library Services .... Vacant
06 Registrar .... Ms. Rosemary BURGER
07 Dir of University Admissions .... Mr. Christian DIGREGORIO
21 Controller/Asst Treasurer .... Vacant
21 Senior Accountant .... Ms. Melissa A. SADDLEMIRE
13 Dir of ERP Migration .... Mr. Michael P. GIBBONS
88 Asst Director Buildings & Grounds .... Mr. Myron MARCINEK
37 Director of Financial Aid .... Mr. Stanley F. SKRUTSKI
102 Dir Corp/Found/Govt Relations .... Ms. Renee GREGORI ZEHEL
44 Director of Planned Giving .... Ms. Elizabeth A. CONNERY
26 Communications Director .... Ms. Juneann GRECO
44 Director of Capital Resources .... Mr. Paul J. STRUNK
29 Director of Alumni Development .... Mr. Leon JOHN, JR.
42 Chaplain/Asst Dir Campus Ministry ... Rev. Brian F. VAN FOSSEN
39 Director Housing/Residence Life .... Vacant
41 Director Athletics/Recreation .... Dr. Mary Jo GUNNING
36 Director of Career Services .... Dr. Carole R. GUSTITUS
42 Director of Campus Ministry .... Sr. Catherine LUXNER
88 Director of Dining Services .... Mr. Thomas K. NOTCHICK
27 Chief Information Officer .... Mr. Anthony SPINILLO
27 Telecommunications Manager .... Mr. Martin O'CONNOR
19 Sr Dir Sec/Safety/Environ Complnce .... Mr. David R. ELLIOTT
23 Director of Student Health Services .... Ms. Linda MCDADE
38 Director Counseling & Student Devel .... Dr. Robert S. SHAW
40 Bookstore Manager .... Ms. Joan DIEHL
104 Assoc Dir International Affairs .... Mr. David A. CRISCI
14 Director of Operations .... Mr. John B. PORTER
30 Director Advancement Services .... Ms. Gretchen FRITZ
30 Dir Constituent Rels/Marywood Fund .... Ms. Michele ZABRISKI
35 Dir of Student Act/Leadership Devel .... Mr. Carl OLIVERI
28 Director of Diversity Services .... Dr. Lia Richards PALMITER
88 Director Human Physiology Lab .... Dr. Gerald S. ZAVORSKY
09 Director Inst Rsrch/Assessment .... Dr. Ellen BOYLAN
45 Chief Planning Officer .... Vacant
90 Asst Director of User Support .... Ms. Katherine P. LEWIS

McCann School of Business & Technology (G)

370 Maplewood Drive, Humbolt Ind Pk, Hazleton PA 18202-9790
County: Luzerne — Identification: 666484
Unit ID: 213871
Telephone: (570) 454-6172 — Carnegie Class: Not Classified
FAX Number: (570) 454-6286 — Calendar System: Quarter
URL: www.mccann.edu
Established: 1897 — Annual Undergrad Tuition & Fees: $11,520
Enrollment: 550 — Coed
Affiliation or Control: Proprietary — IRS Status: Proprietary
Highest Offering: Associate Degree
Program: Occupational
Accreditation: ACICS, MAC, SURGT

01 Director .... Ms. Barbara J. REESE
05 Director of Education .... Mr. Frank BERLETH
36 Career Services Director .... Mr. William BURKE

07 Director of Admissions .... Mr. Jason BLOZOWSKY

† Branch campus of McCann School of Business & Technology, Pottsville, PA.

McCann School of Business & Technology (A)

2650 Woodglen Road, Pottsville PA 17901-1335
County: Schuylkill FICE Identification: 004898
Unit ID: 438212
Telephone: (570) 622-7622 Carnegie Class: Assoc/PrivFP
FAX Number: (570) 622-7770 Calendar System: Quarter
URL: www.mccann.edu
Established: 1897 Annual Undergrad Tuition & Fees: $25,000
Enrollment: 539 Coed
Affiliation or Control: Proprietary IRS Status: Proprietary
Highest Offering: Associate Degree
Program: Occupational
Accreditation: ACICS, MAC

01 Director Pottsville Campus .... Ms. Shannon BRENNAN
05 Director of Education .... Ms. MaryLou ORAM
36 Director of Career Services .... Ms. Michelle SCRIBBICK

McCann School of Business & Technology (B)

1147 N Fourth Street, Sunbury PA 17801-3413
County: Northumberland Identification: 666485
Unit ID: 438221
Telephone: (570) 286-3058 Carnegie Class: Not Classified
FAX Number: (570) 286-4723 Calendar System: Quarter
URL: www.mccannschool.com
Established: 1897 Annual Undergrad Tuition & Fees: $12,400
Enrollment: 1,230 Coed
Affiliation or Control: Proprietary IRS Status: Proprietary
Highest Offering: Associate Degree
Program: Occupational
Accreditation: ACICS, MAC, SURGT

01 Campus Director .... Ms. Susan M. LYNCH
07 Admissions Representative .... Ms. Angela BRICKER
36 Career Services Representative .... Ms. Carol SHAFER

† Branch campus of McCann School of Business & Technology, Pottsville, PA.

Mercyhurst University (C)

501 E 38th Street, Erie PA 16546-0001
County: Erie FICE Identification: 003297
Unit ID: 213987
Telephone: (814) 824-2000 Carnegie Class: Master's S
FAX Number: (814) 824-2438 Calendar System: Trimester
URL: www.mercyhurst.edu
Established: 1926 Annual Undergrad Tuition & Fees: $29,037
Enrollment: 4,298 Coed
Affiliation or Control: Roman Catholic IRS Status: 501(c)3
Highest Offering: Master's
Program: Occupational; 2-Year Principally Bachelor's Creditable; Liberal Arts And General; Teacher Preparatory; Professional
Accreditation: M, ADNUR, DANCE, IACBE, MLTAD, MUS, OTA, PTAA, SW

01 President .... Dr. Thomas J. GAMBLE
03 Provost/Sr Counselor to President .... Dr. James M. ADOVASIO
05 Vice Pres Acad Affs/Dean of College .... Dr. Phil J. BELFIORE
10 Exec Vice Pres and CFO .... Dr. Gary BROWN
84 VP Enrollment & Adult/Grad Pgm .... Dr. Michael P. LYDEN
10 Vice Pres of Finance & Treasurer .... Ms. Jane M. KELSEY
12 Exec VP Mercyhurst - NE/West .... Dr. Kenneth ZIRKLE
30 Vice Pres Development/Alumni Rels .... Dr. David J. LIVINGSTON
32 Vice Pres of Student Development .... Dr. Gerry A. TOBIN
21 Associate Business Officer .... Mr. James F. LIEB
14 Director Computing Services .... Ms. Jeanette BRITT
18 Director Facilities/Physical Plant .... Mr. Kenneth STEPHERSON
38 Director Student Counseling Service .... Ms. Judy SMITH
07 Director of Undergrad Admissions .... Mr. Christopher COONS
06 Registrar .... Sr. Patricia WHALEN
08 Director of Libraries .... Ms. Darcy JONES
39 Dir Residential Life/Stdnt Conduct .... Ms. Alice AGNEW
19 Director of Public Safety Programs .... Mr. Robert KUHN
29 Director of Alumni Services .... Mr. Ryan PALM
42 Director of Campus Ministry .... Fr. James PISZKER
37 Director of Student Financial Svcs .... Ms. Carrie NEWMAN
41 Director of Athletics .... Mr. Joseph KIMBALL
09 Director of Institutional Research .... Mrs. Sheila W. RICHTER
15 Director Human Resources .... Mr. Jim TOMETSKO
28 Director Multicultural Affairs .... Ms. Petrina WILLIAMS

Messiah College (D)

One College Avenue, Mechanicsburg PA 17055
County: Cumberland FICE Identification: 003298
Unit ID: 213996
Telephone: (717) 766-2511 Carnegie Class: Bac/Diverse
FAX Number: (717) 691-6025 Calendar System: Semester
URL: www.messiah.edu
Established: 1909 Annual Undergrad Tuition & Fees: $29,460
Enrollment: 2,805 Coed
Affiliation or Control: Interdenominational IRS Status: 501(c)3
Highest Offering: Master's
Program: Liberal Arts And General; Teacher Preparatory; Professional
Accreditation: M, THEA, ACBSP, ART, CACREP, DIETD, ENG, MUS, NURSE, SW

01 President .... Dr. Kim S. PHIPPS
05 Provost .... Dr. Randall G. BASINGER
10 Vice Pres for Finance & Planning .... Mr. David S. WALKER
30 Vice President for Advancement .... Mr. Barry G. GOODLING
11 Vice President for Operations .... Mrs. Kathrynne G. SHAFER
84 Vice Pres for Enrollment Management .... Mr. John A. CHOPKA
32 Vice Provost & Dean of Students .... Dr. Kristin M. HANSEN-KIEFFER
27 Assoc Provost/Chief Info Officer .. Dr. William G. STRAUSBAUGH
28 Spec Asst Prov & Pres Div Affairs .... Dr. Bernardo A. MICHAEL
42 College Pastor .... Rev. Eldon E. FRY
57 Dean School of the Arts .... Dr. Richard E. ROBERSON
53 Int Dean Sch Bus/Educ/Soc Sci .... Dr. John ADDLEMAN
79 Dean School of Humanities .... Dr. Peter K. POWERS
81 Dean School of Sci/Engr/Health .... Dr. W. Ray NORMAN
104 Director Intl Programs & EpiCenter .... Mrs. Wendy S. LIPPERT
93 Director of Multicultural Programs .... Ms. Tatiana A. DIAZ
85 Director Intl Student Programs .... Mr. Kevin J. VILLEGAS
35 Associate Dean of Students .... Mr. Douglas M. WOOD
07 Director of Admissions .... Mrs. Dana J. BRITTON
37 Director of Financial Aid .... Mr. Gregory L. GEARHART
39 Director of Housing .... Ms. Rhonda L. GOOD
15 VP for Human Res & Compliance .... Ms. Amanda A. COFFEY
21 Dir Financial Operations/Controller .... Mrs. Wendy S. STARNER
96 Director of Procurement .... Mrs. Danelle L. WATSON
06 Registrar .... Mr. James J. SOTHERDEN
08 Director of the Murray Library .... Mr. Jonathan D. LAUER
91 Director Information Services .... Mr. John P. LUFT
90 Dir Learning Technology Services .... Mrs. Susan K. SHANNON
09 Assoc Dir Institutional Research .... Ms. Laura M. MILLER
30 Director of Development .... Dr. Jon C. STUCKEY
26 Dir of Marketing & Public Relations .... Mrs. Carla E. GROSS
29 Director Alumni & Parent Relations .... Mr. Jay W. MCCLYMONT
44 Director of Annual Giving .... Vacant
38 Director Counseling/Health Services .... Dr. Philip J. LAWLIS
12 Program Dir Philadelphia Campus .... Mr. Ryan R. GLADWIN
41 Director of Athletics .... Mr. Jack T. COLE
92 Dir of the College Honors Program .... Dr. Dean C. CURRY
18 Director of Facility Services .... Mr. Bradley A. MARKLEY
36 Director of Career Development .... Mrs. Christina R. HANSON
40 Director of Campus Store .... Ms. Mindy W. LANGE
19 Director Safety/Dispatch Services .... Ms. Cindy L. BURGER
23 Coordinator of Health Services .... Mrs. Judith M. GROOP

Metropolitan Career Center Computer Technology Institute (E)

100 S Broad Street, Suite 830,
Philadelphia PA 19110-1018
County: Philadelphia FICE Identification: 031091
Unit ID: 214023
Telephone: (215) 568-9215 Carnegie Class: Assoc/PrivNFP
FAX Number: (215) 568-3511 Calendar System: Semester
URL: www.CareersInIT.org
Established: 1974 Annual Undergrad Tuition & Fees: $23,994
Enrollment: 170 Coed
Affiliation or Control: Independent Non-Profit IRS Status: 501(c)3
Highest Offering: Associate Degree
Program: Occupational; Technical Emphasis
Accreditation: ACCSC

01 President .... Dr. Richard COHEN
03 Executive Director .... Ms. Amy MILLER
10 Controller .... Mr. Timothy DONOHOE
88 School Director .... Ms. Amy MILLER
05 Director of Education .... Ms. Josanne FORD
37 Financial Aid Director .... Ms. Madeline SARGENT
07 Admissions Representative .... Mr. Samuel JOHNSON
36 Relationship Manager .... Ms. Christina HARRIS

Misericordia University (F)

301 Lake Street, Dallas PA 18612-1098
County: Luzerne FICE Identification: 003247
Unit ID: 214069
Telephone: (570) 674-6400 Carnegie Class: Master's M
FAX Number: (570) 675-2441 Calendar System: Semester
URL: www.misericordia.edu
Established: 1924 Annual Undergrad Tuition & Fees: $13,615
Enrollment: 2,089 Coed
Affiliation or Control: Roman Catholic IRS Status: 501(c)3
Highest Offering: Doctorate
Program: Liberal Arts And General; Teacher Preparatory; Professional
Accreditation: M, #ARCPA, DMS, IACBE, NMT, NURSE, OT, PTA, RAD, SP, SW

01 President .... Dr. Michael A. MACDOWELL
10 Vice Pres Finance & Administration .... Mr. Eric NELSON
05 Vice President Academic Affairs .... Dr. Mari P. KING
30 VP of Institutional Advancement .... Ms. Susan M. HELWIG
32 Vice President of Student Affairs .... Sr. Jean MESSAROS
45 VP of Planning/Assessment & Rsrch .... Dr. Barbara SAMUEL LOFTUS
45 Chief Information/Planning Officer .... Vacant
21 Controller .... Mr. Ronald S. HROMISIN
06 Registrar .... Mr. Joseph REDINGTON
84 Director Enrollment Management .... Ms. Jane F. DESSOYE
29 Director Alumni Relations .... Ms. Denise MISCAVAGE
08 Librarian .... Ms. Martha STEVENSON
04 Admin Assistant to the President .... Ms. Carol FAHNESTOCK
96 Director of Purchasing .... Mr. Thomas F. KANE
38 Exec Dir Learning Resource Ctr .... Ms. Amy LAHART
42 Co-Director Campus Ministry .... Ms. Christine SOMERS
42 Chaplain/Co-Dir Campus Ministry .... Fr. Donald WILLIAMS
41 Director of Athletics .... Mr. David MARTIN
39 Director of Residents .... Ms. Donna ELLIS
13 Director of Management Info Systems .... Mr. Joseph J. MACK
14 Director of Information Technology .... Mr. Val APANOVICH
35 Director of Student Activities .... Ms. Darcy BRODMERKEL
36 Dir Insalaco Ctr Career Development .... Ms. Bernadette RUSHMER
102 Dir Foundation/Government Relations .... Mr. Larry PELLEGRINI
51 Director of Adult Education .... Mrs. Barbara LEGGAT
16 Director of Human Resources .... Ms. Pamela PARSNIK
07 Director of Admissions .... Mr. Glenn BOZINSKI
26 Dir of Public Relations/Marketing .... Mr. James ROBERTS
37 Director of Financial Aid .... Ms. Susan FRONZONI
28 Director of Multicultural Initiativ .... Dr. Scott RICHARDSON
19 Assoc Director Security/Safety .... Mr. Robert ZAVADA
18 Director of Facilities .... Mr. Paul MURPHY
09 Asst Dir of Institutional Research .... Ms. Sharon HUDAK
90 Manager of User Services .... Mr. David A. JOHNDROW

Montgomery County Community College (G)

340 Dekalb Pike, Blue Bell PA 19422-1400
County: Montgomery FICE Identification: 004452
Unit ID: 214111
Telephone: (215) 641-6300 Carnegie Class: Assoc/Pub-S-MC
FAX Number: (215) 641-6647 Calendar System: Semester
URL: www.mc3.edu
Established: 1964 Annual Undergrad Tuition & Fees (In-District): $3,240
Enrollment: 13,985 Coed
Affiliation or Control: State/Local IRS Status: 501(c)3
Highest Offering: Associate Degree
Program: Occupational; 2-Year Principally Bachelor's Creditable
Accreditation: M, ADNUR, DH, IFSAC, MAC, MLTAD, RAD, SURGT

01 President .... Dr. Karen A. STOUT
04 Exec Assistant to the President .... Mr. Joshua SCHWARTZ
101 Exec Asst to the Board of Trustees .... Ms. Deborah ROGERS
12 VP of the West Campus .... Dr. Steady MOONO
27 VP for Information Technology .... Ms. Celeste M. SCHWARTZ
10 VP for Finance & Administration .... Mr. Thomas FREITAG
26 Vice Pres of Devel & External Rels .... Ms. Sharon BEALES
84 VP for Student Affairs & Enrol Mgt .... Dr. Kathrine SWANSON
05 VP for Academic Affairs & Provost .... Dr. Victoria BASTECKI-PEREZ
06 Registrar .... Ms. Cynthia MCCABE
30 Exec Director of Foundation .... Vacant
15 Executive Director Human Resources .... Ms. Diane O'CONNOR
21 Assoc VP for Finance & Admin .... Mr. Brent PARKER
21 Controller .... Ms. Kathleen MCGIRR
44 Dir of Annual Giving & Adv Services .... Ms. Megan SNEERINGER
19 Director of Campus Safety .... Mr. Joseph MCGURIMAN
07 Director of Admissions .... Ms. Penelope SAWYER
08 Director of Library Services .... Ms. Diane LOVELACE
37 Director of Financial Aid .... Ms. Tracey RICHARDS
09 Director of Institutional Research .... Mr. Leon HILL
28 Dir Equity & Diversity Initiatives .... Ms. Rose MAKOFSKE
29 Director of Major Gifts and Alumni .... Ms. Leslie BLUESTONE
27 Director Media/Public Relations .... Ms. Alana MAUGER
103 Dean Workforce Development & CE .... Ms. Suzanne HOLLOMAN
86 Exec Dir of Govt Relations .... Ms. Margaret LEE-CLARK
41 Dir of Athletics & Campus Rec .... Mr. Bruce BACH

Moore College of Art and Design (H)

20th and The Parkway, Philadelphia PA 19103-1179
County: Philadelphia FICE Identification: 003300
Unit ID: 214148
Telephone: (215) 568-4515 Carnegie Class: Spec/Arts
FAX Number: (215) 568-8017 Calendar System: Semester
URL: www.moore.edu
Established: 1848 Annual Undergrad Tuition & Fees: $31,478
Enrollment: 526 Female
Affiliation or Control: Independent Non-Profit IRS Status: 501(c)3
Highest Offering: Master's
Program: Fine Arts Emphasis
Accreditation: M, ART, CIDA

01 President .... Dr. Cecelia FITZGIBBON
10 Vice Pres Finance & Administration .... Mr. William L. HILL, II
05 Academic Dean .... Ms. Dona LANTZ
32 Dean of Students .... Ms. Ruth ROBBINS
20 Assoc Dean Educational Support Svcs .... Mrs. Claudine R. THOMAS
39 Asst Dean Res Life/Events Mkt Mgr .... Ms. Carienne MYSLINSKI
88 Executive Director of Galleries .... Ms. Kaytie JOHNSON
51 Co-Director of Continuing Education .... Ms. Judith WOODWORTH
51 Co-Director of Continuing Education .... Mrs. Natalie PAYNE
26 Director of Communications .... Ms. Amanda MOTT
30 Director of Development .... Ms. Linda PORCH
29 Director Alumnae Affairs .... Ms. Doris CHORNEY
08 Library Director .... Ms. Sharon WATSON-MAURO
07 Director of Admissions/Enrollment .... Ms. Hesseung LEE
37 Director of Financial Aid .... Ms. Melissa WALSH
06 Registrar .... Ms. Dianne SARIDAKIS
18 Director Facilities/Physical Plant .... Mr. Kenneth FERRETTI
15 Director Human Resources .... Ms. Rachel PHILLIPS
36 Director Career Services .... Ms. Belena CHAPP

58 Director of Graduate Programs ... Mr. Ian VERSTEGEN
38 Director Student Counseling ... Ms. Ruth R. GAYLE
90 Academic Computing Manager ... Mr. Dennis DAWTON

Moravian College (A)

1200 Main Street, Bethlehem PA 18018-6650
County: Northampton FICE Identification: 003301
Unit ID: 214157
Telephone: (610) 861-1300 Carnegie Class: Bac/A&S
FAX Number: (610) 625-7918 Calendar System: Semester
URL: www.moravian.edu
Established: 1742 Annual Undergrad Tuition & Fees: $34,484
Enrollment: 2,003 Coed
Affiliation or Control: Moravian Church IRS Status: 501(c)3
Highest Offering: Master's
Program: Liberal Arts And General; Teacher Preparatory; Professional; Nursing Emphasis
Accreditation: M, MUS, NURSE, THEOL

01 President ... Dr. Christopher M. THOMFORDE
04 Assistant to the President ... Ms. Julie DEL GIORNO
05 Vice President Academic Affairs ... Dr. Gordon WEIL
10 Vice President Finance & Admin ... Mr. Mark F. REED
21 Treasurer ... Ms. Anne M. REID
30 Vice Pres Institutional Advancement ... Mr. Gary CARNEY
32 Vice President Student Affairs ... Dr. Nicole L. LOYD
73 Vice Pres/Dean of the Seminary ... Dr. Frank CROUCH
84 Vice President for Enrollment ... Mr. Kenneth T. HUUS
35 Dean of Students ... Mr. Thomas DUBREUIL
88 Director of Leadership Development ... Ms. Catherine DANTSIN
20 Assoc Dean for Academic Affairs ... Dr. Carol TRAUPMAN-CARR
24 Director of Learning Services ... Ms. Laurie ROTH
88 Director of Event Management ... Mrs. Ann E. CLAUSSEN
21 Dir Business/Financial Operations ... Ms. Amy JOHNSON
21 Bursar ... Ms. Susan O'HARE
96 Assoc Director of Business Affairs ... Mr. Brian G. BLENIS
15 Chief Human Resources Officer ... Mr. Jon B. CONRAD
44 Director of Leadership Giving ... Ms. Bertie KNISELY
18 Dir Facilities Mgt Plng/Construct ... Mr. Douglas J. PLOTTS
19 Director of Campus Safety ... Mr. George BOKSAN
26 Director of Public Relations ... Mr. Michael P. WILSON
08 Library Director ... Mr. David SCHAPPERT
06 Registrar ... Mrs. Mary Margaret GROSS
88 Director of Sports Information ... Mr. Mark J. FLEMING
27 Director of Publications ... Mrs. Susan O. WOOLLEY
29 Director of Alumni Relations ... Ms. Marsha STILES
37 Director of Financial Aid ... Ms. Colby MCCARTHY
36 Director Career Development Svcs ... Ms. Amy SAUL
38 Director of Counseling ... Dr. Ronald J. KLINE
58 Dean Continuing/Graduate Studies ... Dr. Donna SMITH
13 Director Information Technology ... Mr. Stephen MCKINNEY
40 Director of Bookstore ... Mrs. Sandra M. GIORDANO
41 Director of Athletics ... Mr. Paul R. MOYER
42 College Chaplain ... Rev. Hopeton C. CLENNON
88 Director of the Payne Gallery ... Dr. Diane C. RADYCKI
88 Director of Constituent Relations ... Ms. Deborah L. EVANS
23 Health Services Coordinator ... Mrs. Mary S. SEK
88 Director of International Studies ... Mr. Kerry SETHI
28 Dir Instl Diversity/Multicul Affs ... Ms. Sharon A. BROWN
24 Media Center Manager ... Mr. Craig UNDERWOOD
09 Director Institutional Research ... Ms. Carole A. REESE

Mount Aloysius College (B)

7373 Admiral Peary Highway, Cresson PA 16630-1999
County: Cambria FICE Identification: 003302
Unit ID: 214166
Telephone: (814) 886-4131 Carnegie Class: Bac/Assoc
FAX Number: (814) 886-2978 Calendar System: Semester
URL: www.mtaloy.edu
Established: 1853 Annual Undergrad Tuition & Fees: $18,640
Enrollment: 1,692 Coed
Affiliation or Control: Independent Non-Profit IRS Status: 501(c)3
Highest Offering: Master's
Program: Occupational; 2-Year Principally Bachelor's Creditable; Liberal Arts And General
Accreditation: M, ADNUR, DMS, MAC, MLTAD, NUR, PTAA, SURGT

01 President ... Dr. Thomas P. FOLEY
05 Sr VP Academic Affs/Dean of Faculty ... Dr. Timothy FULOP
11 Sr VP Administrative Services ... Ms. Suzanne P. CAMPBELL
32 VP Student Affs/Dean Students ... Dr. Jane M. GRASSADONIA
84 VP Enrollment Mgmt/Dean Admissions ... Mr. Francis C. CROUSE, JR.
07 Director of Freshmen Admissions ... Mr. Andrew D. CLOUSE
07 Director of Transfer Admissions ... Mr. Richard MISHLER
30 VP Institutional Advancement ... Mr. John H. ANDERSON
10 Controller/CFO ... Ms. Donna K. YODER
06 Registrar ... Mr. Christopher M. LOVETT
08 Director of Library Services ... Vacant
37 Director of Financial Aid ... Ms. Stacy L. SCHENK
15 Director of Human Resources ... Ms. Tonia J. GORDON
26 Director of Communications ... Mr. John COYLE
44 Major Gifts Officer ... Mr. Michael A. GREER
13 Director of Information Technology ... Mr. Rich J. SHEA
23 Director of Health Services ... Ms. Shannon D. GROVE
40 Director of Bookstore ... Ms. Christine M. CLINTON
41 Director of Athletics ... Mr. Ryan M. SMITH
19 Director of Safety & Security ... Mr. William H. TREXLER
18 Director of Physical Plant ... Mr. Gerald RUBRITZ
09 Institutional Researcher ... Mr. Bryan J. PEARSON

36 Director Career Services ... Mr. Larry W. BRUGH
38 Dir Student Counseling/Disabilities ... Ms. Marisa L. EVANS
39 Director of Residence Life ... Ms. Christina KOREN
42 Director Campus Ministry ... Sr. Nancy E. DONOVAN, RSM
44 Director Annual Giving ... Ms. Sally GORDON

Muhlenberg College (C)

2400 West Chew Street, Allentown PA 18104-5586
County: Lehigh FICE Identification: 003304
Unit ID: 214175
Telephone: (484) 664-3100 Carnegie Class: Bac/A&S
FAX Number: (484) 664-3234 Calendar System: Semester
URL: www.muhlenberg.edu
Established: 1848 Annual Undergrad Tuition & Fees: $41,540
Enrollment: 2,298 Coed
Affiliation or Control: Evangelical Lutheran Church In America
IRS Status: 501(c)3
Highest Offering: Baccalaureate
Program: Liberal Arts And General; Teacher Preparatory
Accreditation: M

01 President ... Dr. Peyton R. HELM
05 Provost ... Dr. John G. RAMSAY
10 Treasurer & Vice Pres for Finance ... Mr. Kent DYER
26 Vice President of Public Relations ... Mr. Michael S. BRUCKNER
30 VP Development & Alumni Relations ... Ms. Rebekkah L. BROWN
15 Vice President of Human Resources ... Ms. Anne SPECK
04 Exec Assistant to the President ... Mr. Ken BUTLER
102 Asst VP Corporate/Found & Govt Rels ... Ms. Deborah J. KIPP
32 Dean of Students ... Ms. Karen GREEN
88 Dean of College for Academic Life ... Dr. Michael HUBER
20 Assoc Dean Institutional Assessment ... Dr. Kathleen E. HARRING
86 Assoc Dean International Programs ... Dr. Donna M. KISH-GOODLING
37 Associate Dean Financial Aid ... Mr. Gregory S. MITTON
88 Assistant Dean of Academic Life ... Ms. Wendy P. COLE
29 Alumni Relations Director ... Ms. Jenny MCLARIN
55 Dean Wescoe Sch Muhlenberg College ... Ms. Jane E. HUDAK
07 Dean Admissions/Financial Aid ... Mr. Christopher HOOKER-HARING
08 Director of Trexler Library ... Ms. Tina L. HERTEL
06 Registrar ... Ms. Deborah TAMTE-HORAN
13 Director Information Technology ... Mr. Harry E. MILLER
19 Director of Campus Safety/Security ... Mr. Robert GERKEN
39 Director of Residence Life ... Ms. Janette SCHUMACHER
36 Director of the Career Center ... Ms. Cailin M. PACHTER
21 Assistant Treasurer ... Mr. Jason FEIERTAG
23 Director of Student Health Services ... Ms. Brynnmarie DORSEY
38 Director Counseling Services ... Ms. Anita KELLY
42 Chaplain ... Rev. Callista S. ISABELLE
09 Director of Institutional Research ... Ms. Nicole HAMMEL
18 Chief Facilities/Physical Plant ... Mr. Michael H. BREWER
96 Director of Purchasing ... Ms. Elizabeth M. LEES
40 Bookstore Manager ... Ms. Karen R. DELARCO

Neumann University (D)

One Neumann Drive, Aston PA 19014-1298
County: Delaware FICE Identification: 003988
Unit ID: 214272
Telephone: (610) 459-0905 Carnegie Class: Master's M
FAX Number: (610) 459-1370 Calendar System: Semester
URL: www.neumann.edu
Established: 1965 Annual Undergrad Tuition & Fees: $24,232
Enrollment: 3,087 Coed
Affiliation or Control: Roman Catholic IRS Status: 501(c)3
Highest Offering: Doctorate
Program: Liberal Arts And General; Teacher Preparatory; Professional
Accreditation: M, ACBSP, CACREP, MT, NUR, PTA

01 President ... Dr. Rosalie M. MIRENDA
05 Vice President Academic Affairs ... Dr. Gerard P. O'SULLIVAN
43 Vice President and General Counsel ... Mr. Jonathan PERI
10 Vice Pres Finance/Administration ... Mr. Joseph GORMAN
42 Vice President Mission/Ministry ... Sr. Marguerite O'BEIRNE, OSF
30 Vice Pres Inst Advance/Univ Rels ... Mr. Henry A. SUMNER
84 Vice Pres Enrollment/Student Affs ... Mr. Dennis J. MURPHY
15 Vice President HR & Risk Management ... Mr. David W. BROWNLEE
49 Dean Division of Arts & Science ... Dr. Mac GIVEN
50 Dean Div of Business & Info Mgmt ... Ms. Janet MASSEY
53 Dean Div of Education/Human Svcs ... Dr. Joseph E. GILLESPIE
51 Dean Div Cont Adult/Prof Studies ... Dr. Patricia SZYMURSKI
66 Dean Div Nursing/Health Sciences ... Dr. Kathleen HOOVER
04 Assistant to President ... Ms. Danielle WAGNER
06 Registrar ... Mr. Larry S. FRIEDMAN
18 Facilities Director ... Mr. Earl WORSHAM
19 Director Safety & Security ... Mr. Leon FRANCIS
08 Director Library ... Ms. Tiffany MCGREGOR
26 Exec Director Mktg/Communications ... Mr. Stephen BELL
09 Director Institutional Research ... Ms. Melissa THORPE
42 Chaplain ... Rev. Philip J. LOWE, OFM
44 Director Annual Giving/Prospect Mgt ... Ms. Christina FARRELL
29 Dir Alumni Rels/Special Programs ... Ms. Judi STANAITIS
88 Director Inst Gifts/Donor Rels ... Ms. Josephina E. BANNER
38 Director Counseling ... Mr. Fritz HAAS
39 Director Residence Life ... Mr. Michael WEBSTER
13 Exec Director University Computing ... Mr. David O'LEARY
24 Director Academic Resource Center ... Ms. Theresa HUKE
41 Director Athletics ... Mr. Chuck SACK
36 Director Career Services ... Mrs. Carol A. DOUGHERTY

88 Director of Academic Advising ... Mr. Michael MULLEN
88 Director Child Development Center ... Ms. Mary Ann MELISI
21 Controller ... Mr. John YOUHOUSE
37 Director Financial Assistance ... Ms. Deborah CRAWLEY
23 Director Health Services ... Ms. Janet GEDDIS
96 Director of Purchasing ... Ms. Elena BARRAR
88 Director Physical Therapy Program ... Dr. Robert POST
07 Director of Admissions ... Ms. Kidesti TEKLEGIORGIS
88 Dir Cntr for Sport/Spir/Char Devel ... Dr. Edward T. HASTINGS
90 Director Instructional Technology ... Mr. Scott BEADENKOPF
88 Director Conference&Scheduling Serv ... Ms. Alexis SINKOW
40 Director University Bookstore ... Ms. Natalie VAN WYK
108 Assistant VP for Assessmen/Learning ... Dr. Janet THIEL, OFM
88 Director Development Education ... Ms. Lori PELLESCKI
104 Coord International Studies Educ ... Mr. Scott KELLER
88 Director Student Retention ... Dr. Erin WALSH-KANE

New Castle School of Trades (E)

4117 Pulaski Road, New Castle PA 16101
County: Lawrence FICE Identification: 007780
Unit ID: 214290
Telephone: (724) 964-8811 Carnegie Class: Assoc/PrivFP
FAX Number: (724) 202-6147 Calendar System: Other
URL: www.ncstrades.edu
Established: 1945 Annual Undergrad Tuition & Fees: $16,650
Enrollment: 543 Coed
Affiliation or Control: Proprietary IRS Status: Proprietary
Highest Offering: Associate Degree
Program: Occupational; 2-Year Principally Bachelor's Creditable; Technical Emphasis
Accreditation: ACCSC

01 Director ... Mr. Jim BUTTERMORE
05 Director of Education ... Mr. Tony GIOVANNELLI
07 Director Admiss/Veterans Affs Ofcr ... Mr. Jim CATHELINE
10 Fiscal Director ... Mrs. JoAnn MELNIK
36 Director Student Placement ... Ms. Carrie KRAYNAK
37 Director Student Financial Aid ... Miss Trudy SOTTER

Newport Business Institute (F)

945 Greensburg Road, Lower Burrell PA 15068-3929
County: Westmoreland FICE Identification: 004901
Unit ID: 214315
Telephone: (724) 339-7542 Carnegie Class: Assoc/PrivFP
FAX Number: (724) 339-2950 Calendar System: Quarter
URL: www.nbi.edu
Established: 1895 Annual Undergrad Tuition & Fees: $10,600
Enrollment: 70 Coed
Affiliation or Control: Proprietary IRS Status: Proprietary
Highest Offering: Associate Degree
Program: Occupational
Accreditation: ACICS

01 Director ... Mr. Ray WROBLEWSKI
05 Dean of Academic Affairs ... Mr. Michael CHOMA
58 Director of Graduate Services ... Mrs. Nancy DONATUCCI
37 Director of Financial Aid ... Mrs. Rosemary LEIPERTZ
07 Admissions Coordinator ... Mr. Don ACKER

Newport Business Institute (G)

941 W Third Street, Williamsport PA 17701-5855
County: Lycoming FICE Identification: 004914
Unit ID: 216986
Telephone: (570) 326-2869 Carnegie Class: Assoc/PrivFP
FAX Number: (570) 326-2136 Calendar System: Quarter
URL: www.nbi.edu
Established: 1955 Annual Undergrad Tuition & Fees: $12,075
Enrollment: 78 Coed
Affiliation or Control: Proprietary IRS Status: Proprietary
Highest Offering: Associate Degree
Program: Occupational
Accreditation: ACICS

01 Director ... Mr. John M. KIERNAN

Northampton Community College (H)

3835 Green Pond Road, Bethlehem PA 18020-7599
County: Northampton FICE Identification: 007191
Unit ID: 214379
Telephone: (610) 861-5300 Carnegie Class: Assoc/Pub-S-MC
FAX Number: (610) 861-5070 Calendar System: Semester
URL: www.northampton.edu
Established: 1966 Annual Undergrad Tuition & Fees (In-District): $3,570
Enrollment: 11,350 Coed
Affiliation or Control: State/Local IRS Status: 170(c)1
Highest Offering: Associate Degree
Program: Occupational; 2-Year Principally Bachelor's Creditable
Accreditation: M, ACBSP, ADNUR, DH, DMS, FUSER, PNUR, RAD, SURGT

01 President ... Dr. Mark H. ERICKSON
05 Vice President Academic Affairs ... Dr. Jeffrey W. FOCHT
11 Vice Pres Administrative Affairs ... Ms. Helene M. WHITAKER
10 Vice President Finance & Operations ... Mr. James F. DUNLEAVY
30 Vice Pres Institutional Advancement ... Ms. Sheri JONES
32 Vice President Student Affairs ... Ms. Margaret MCGUIRE-CLOSSON

31 Vice President Community Education ....Dr. Paul E. PIERPOINT
12 Dean Monroe Campus ....Dr. Matthew J. CONNELL
79 Dean Humanities & Social Sciences ....Dr. Christine PENSE
53 Dean Education/Academic Success ....Dr. Elizabeth BUGAIGHIS
50 Interim Dean Business & Technology ....Ms. Denise FRANCOIS-SEENY
76 Dean Allied Health & Sciences ....Ms. Carolyn BORTZ
13 Dean & Chief Information Officer ....Dr. Deborah BURAK
27 Director Public Info/Community Rels ....Ms. Heidi BUTLER
06 Registrar ....Ms. Carolyn H. MOYER
07 Director Admissions ....Mr. James MCCARTHY
37 Director Financial Aid ....Ms. Cynthia L. KING
45 Dir Plng/Assessment/Instl Effective ....Dr. E. Jill HIRT
15 Director of Human Resources ....Ms. Kathy SIEGFRIED
09 Director of Institutional Research ....Ms. Kathy KAPCSOS
18 Director Buildings & Grounds ....Mr. Mark K. CULP
29 Director Alumni Relations ....Ms. Melissa STARACE
36 Director Career Services ....Ms. Karen VERES
38 Director Counseling & Support Svcs ....Ms. Carolyn M. BRADY
96 Director of Purchasing ....Vacant

Oakbridge Academy of Arts (A)

1250 Greensburg Road, Lower Burrell PA 15068-3843
County: Westmoreland FICE Identification: 021535
Unit ID: 376039
Telephone: (724) 335-5336 Carnegie Class: Assoc/PrivFP
FAX Number: (724) 335-3367 Calendar System: Quarter
URL: www.oaa.edu
Established: 1972 Annual Undergrad Tuition & Fees: $15,300
Enrollment: 55 Coed
Affiliation or Control: Proprietary IRS Status: Proprietary
Highest Offering: Associate Degree
Program: 2-Year Principally Bachelor's Creditable; Fine Arts Emphasis
Accreditation: ACCSC

01 Director ....Ms. Janie GATTY
07 Admissions Coordinator ....Ms. Sharon PANAIA
06 Registrar ....Ms. Debra WELLS

Orleans Technical Institute (B)

2770 Red Lion Road, Philadelphia PA 19114-1014
County: Philadelphia FICE Identification: 021830
Unit ID: 214528
Telephone: (215) 728-4700 Carnegie Class: Assoc/PrivNFP
FAX Number: (215) 745-1689 Calendar System: Semester
URL: www.orleanstech.edu
Established: 1986 Annual Undergrad Tuition & Fees: $11,815
Enrollment: 787 Coed
Affiliation or Control: Independent Non-Profit IRS Status: Exempt
Highest Offering: Associate Degree
Program: Occupational; 2-Year Principally Bachelor's Creditable; Technical Emphasis
Accreditation: ACCSC

01 Campus Director ....Ms. Jayne SINIARI
88 Director Court Reporting Program ....Ms. Carol CRAWFORD

Pace Institute (C)

606 Court Street, Reading PA 19601-3542
County: Berks FICE Identification: 022895
Unit ID: 214838
Telephone: (610) 375-1212 Carnegie Class: Assoc/PrivFP
FAX Number: (610) 375-1924 Calendar System: Semester
URL: www.paceinstitute.com
Established: 1980 Annual Undergrad Tuition & Fees: $7,464
Enrollment: 256 Coed
Affiliation or Control: Proprietary IRS Status: Proprietary
Highest Offering: Associate Degree
Program: Occupational
Accreditation: ACICS

01 President ....Ms. Rhoda E. DERSH
05 School Director ....Ms. Christine WULLERT

Palmer Theological Seminary of Eastern University (D)

6 E. Lancaster Avenue, Wynnewood PA 19096-3430
County: Montgomery FICE Identification: 003260
Unit ID: 212124
Telephone: (610) 896-5000 Carnegie Class: Not Classified
FAX Number: (610) 649-3834 Calendar System: 4/1/4
URL: www.palmerseminary.edu
Established: 1925 Annual Graduate Tuition & Fees: $24,015
Enrollment: 438 Coed
Affiliation or Control: American Baptist IRS Status: 501(c)3
Highest Offering: Doctorate; No Undergraduates
Program: Professional
Accreditation: THEOL

01 University President ....Dr. David R. BLACK
05 Dean ....Dr. Chris HALL
10 Chief Operating Officer ....Mr. Anup KAPUR
04 President's Assistant ....Ms. Ruth E. MCFARLAND
20 Associate Dean ....Dr. Colleen DIRADDO
15 Director of Human Resources ....Ms. Kacey BERNARD
29 Director Alumni & Church Relations ....Ms. Mary GARDNER
42 Dir Stdnt Form/Seminary Chaplain ....Rev. Willette A. BURGIE-BRYANT
88 Director D Min Marriage & Family ....Dr. Peter SCHRECK
08 Director University Libraries ....Mr. James SAUER
09 Director of Institutional Research ....Dr. Thomas DAHLSTROM
06 Associate Registrar ....Mr. Craig MILLER
07 Director Admissions ....Dr. Alexander G. HOUSTON
26 Exec Dir Marketing & Communications ......Mr. Randall L. FRAME
18 Manager Plant Operations ....Mr. Carmen ANUZZI
24 Educational Technologist ....Ms. Masego KEBAETSE

† Affiliated with Eastern University, Saint Davids, PA.

Peirce College (E)

1420 Pine Street, Philadelphia PA 19102-4699
County: Philadelphia FICE Identification: 003309
Unit ID: 214883
Telephone: (215) 545-6400 Carnegie Class: Bac/Diverse
FAX Number: (215) 670-9366 Calendar System: Semester
URL: www.peirce.edu
Established: 1865 Annual Undergrad Tuition & Fees: $16,500
Enrollment: 2,276 Coed
Affiliation or Control: Independent Non-Profit IRS Status: 501(c)3
Highest Offering: Baccalaureate
Program: Occupational; Business Emphasis
Accreditation: M, ACBSP

01 President & CEO ....Mr. James J. MERGIOTTI
05 Senior VP Acad Advancement/Provost ......Dr. Patricia A. RUCKER
10 Senior VP Finance & Administration ....Mr. James M. VITALE
13 Chief Information Officer ....Mr. Christopher L. DUFFY
32 Dean of Students ....Dr. Rita J. TOLIVER-ROBERTS
26 Asst VP Marketing/Communication ....Ms. Lisa PARIS
18 Chief Auxiliary Services Officer ....Mr. Vito R. CHIMENTI
16 Asst VP Human Resources ....Ms. Harriet S. GOLEN
20 Associate Dean Academic Operations ....Mr. Jon LENROW
84 Dean Enrollment Management ....Ms. Nadine M. MAHER
37 Chief Business & Financial Svc Ofcr ....Mr. Brad K. HODGE
09 Dean Academic Programs & Research ....Ms. Debra S. SCHRAMMEL
21 Controller ....Ms. Karen M. BRIGGS
88 Program Manager Inst Support ....Ms. Amy A. CALIENDO

Penn Commercial Business/ Technical School (F)

242 Oak Spring Road, Washington PA 15301-6822
County: Washington FICE Identification: 004902
Unit ID: 214892
Telephone: (724) 222-5330 Carnegie Class: Assoc/PrivFP
FAX Number: (724) 222-4722 Calendar System: Quarter
URL: www.penncommercial.edu
Established: 1929 Annual Undergrad Tuition & Fees: $19,000
Enrollment: 392 Coed
Affiliation or Control: Proprietary IRS Status: Proprietary
Highest Offering: Associate Degree
Program: Occupational; Technical Emphasis
Accreditation: ACICS, MAC

01 Director ....Mr. Robert S. BAZANT
11 Vice President of Operations ....Ms. Marianne ALBERT
04 Assistant to the President ....Ms. Jennifer POLAND
07 Director of Admissions ....Ms. Jayme TUITE
32 Director of Student Affairs ....Ms. Betty SHINGLE
37 Director of Financial Aid ....Ms. Jenny SLESH
88 Director of Education ....Ms. Nicole LANE
05 Director of Academic Affairs ....Ms. Sandy PHILLIPS
09 Dir of Reports & Statistics ....Mrs. Melissa PAPSON
88 Dir of Student Support Services ....Mr. Larry BEVAN
36 Director of Career Services ....Mrs. Kristin WISSINGER

Penn State University Park (G)

201 Old Main, University Park PA 16802-1503
County: Centre FICE Identification: 003329
Unit ID: 214777
Telephone: (814) 865-4700 Carnegie Class: RU/VH
FAX Number: N/A Calendar System: Semester
URL: www.psu.edu
Established: 1855 Annual Undergrad Tuition & Fees (In-State): $16,444
Enrollment: 44,485 Coed
Affiliation or Control: State Related IRS Status: 501(c)3
Highest Offering: Doctorate
Program: 2-Year Principally Bachelor's Creditable; Liberal Arts And General; Teacher Preparatory; Professional
Accreditation: M, ADNUR, ART, BUS, CACREP, CEA, CLPSY, COPSY, CORE, DIETD, DIETI, ENG, FOR, HSA, IPSY, JOUR, LSAR, MUS, NUR, NURSE, SCPSY, SP, TED, THEA

01 President ....Dr. Rodney A. ERICKSON
46 Vice Pres Research/Dean Grad School ....Dr. Henry FOLEY
32 Vice President Student Affairs ....Dr. Damon SIMS
26 Vice President University Relations .....Mr. William M. MAHON, III
30 Sr Vice Pres Devel/Alumni Relations ....Mr. Rodney P. KIRSCH
10 Sr Vice Pres Finance & Business ....Mr. David J. GRAY
31 Vice President Outreach ....Dr. Craig D. WEIDEMANN
11 VP for Administration ....Dr. Thomas G. POOLE
104 Vice Provost for Global Programs ....Dr. Michael A. ADEWUMI
43 Vice President & General Counsel ....Mr. Stephen S. DUNHAM
05 Int Exec Vice Pres & Provost ....Dr. Robert N. PANGBORN
49 Vice Pres & Dean Undergrad Educ ......Dr. Robert N. PANGBORN
20 Vice Provost Academic Affairs ....Dr. Blannie E. BOWEN
28 Vice Provost Educational Equity ....Dr. W. Terrell JONES
12 Vice Pres Commonwealth Campuses ....Dr. Madlyn HANES
13 Vice Provost Information Tech ....Mr. Kevin M. MOROONEY
108 Exec Dir Ofc Plng/Inst Assessment ....Mr. Michael J. DOORIS
22 Vice Provost for Affirmative Action . Dr. Kenneth F. LEHRMAN, III
45 University Budget Officer ....Ms. Rachel E. SMITH
21 Corporate Controller ....Mr. Joseph J. DONCSECZ
21 Assoc VP Finance/Business Comm Oper ....Mr. Daniel W. SIEMINSKI
16 Assoc Vice Pres Human Resources ....Dr. Susan BASSO
18 Assoc Vice Pres Physical Plant ....Mr. H. Ford STRYKER
21 Assoc Vice Pres Aux & Business Svcs ....Ms. Gail A. HURLEY
51 Associate Vice President Outreach ....Mr. Wayne D. SMUTZ
27 Director of Public Information ....Ms. Lisa M. POWERS
39 Asst Vice President HFS & Res Life ....Dr. Stanley LATTA
37 Exec Director for Student Aid ....Ms. Anna M. GRISWOLD
29 Exec Director Alumni Association ....Mr. Roger L. WILLIAMS
21 Exec Director Investment Management ....Mr. David BRANIGAN
07 Exec Dir of Undergrad Admissions ....Ms. Anne L. ROHRBACH
38 Sr Director Counseling/Psych Svcs .....Dr. Dennis E. HEITZMANN
41 Acting Athletic Director ....Mr. David M. JOYNER
86 Special Asst for Government Affairs ....Dr. Richard D. DIEUGENIO
06 University Registrar ....Ms. Karen L. SCHULTZ
36 Sr Director Career Services ....Dr. Jack R. RAYMAN
17 Sr VP for Health Affairs & Dean ....Dr. Harold L. PAZ
08 Dean of Univ Libraries/Scholar Comm ....Ms. Barbara I. DEWEY
47 Dean of Agricultural Sciences ....Dr. Bruce A. MCPHERON
48 Dean Arts & Architecture ....Dr. Barbara O. KORNER
50 Dean of Business ....Dr. Charles H. WHITEMAN
60 Dean of Communications ....Dr. Douglas A. ANDERSON
65 Dean Earth & Mineral Sciences .. Dr. William E. EASTERLING, III
53 Dean of Education ....Dr. David H. MONK
54 Dean of Engineering ....Dr. David N. WORMLEY
58 Dean of the Graduate School ....Dr. Henry FOLEY
76 Dean Health & Human Development ....Dr. Ann C. CROUTER
66 Director School of Nursing ....Dr. Paula F. MILONE-NUZZO
56 Assoc Dean Cooperative Extension ....Dr. Dennis D. CALVIN
83 Dean of Liberal Arts ....Dr. Susan WELCH
81 Dean of Science ....Dr. Daniel J. LARSON
72 Dean Info Sciences/Technology ....Dr. David L. HALL
92 Dean of Honors College ....Dr. Christian BRADY
61 Dean School of Law ....Mr. Philip MCCONNAUGHAY
63 Dean College of Medicine ....Dr. Harold L. PAZ
75 Chief College of Technology ....Dr. Davie J. GILMOUR
44 Director of Annual Giving ....Ms. Ann LEHMAN
25 Sr Assoc Dir Sponsored Programs ....Dr. John W. HANOLD
19 Director University Police ....Mr. Stephen G. SHELOW
23 Dir University Health Services ....Dr. Margaret E. SPEAR
96 Director of Procurement Services ....Ms. Joyce A. HANEY
31 Director Campus & Comm Affairs ....Ms. Barbara ETTARO
102 Interim Dir Corp/Foundation Rels ....Mr. John DIETZ
04 Exec Admin Asst to President ....Mrs. Carmella MULROY-DEGENHART
40 General Manager Bookstore ....Mr. Steve J. FALKE
25 Contract Coordinator ....Mr. Richel PERRETTI
15 Director Human Resources ....Mr. Robert L. MANEY
21 Director of Internal Audit ....Mr. Daniel P. HEIST

† The legal name of Penn State and all its campuses is The Pennsylvania State University. For communication purposes, the name is shortened to Penn State followed by the name of the campus.

Penn State Abington (H)

1600 Woodland Road, Abington PA 19001-3900
County: Montgomery FICE Identification: 003342
Unit ID: 214801
Telephone: (215) 881-7300 Carnegie Class: Bac/A&S
FAX Number: (215) 881-7412 Calendar System: Semester
URL: www.abington.psu.edu
Established: 1950 Annual Undergrad Tuition & Fees (In-State): $13,356
Enrollment: 3,425 Coed
Affiliation or Control: State Related IRS Status: 501(c)3
Highest Offering: Baccalaureate
Program: Occupational; 2-Year Principally Bachelor's Creditable; Liberal Arts And General; Teacher Preparatory
Accreditation: &M

01 Chancellor ....Dr. Karen WILEY SANDLER
05 Academic Affairs ....Dr. Samir OUZOMGI
32 Student Affairs ....Ms. Gale J. SIEGEL
06 Registrar ....Ms. Joan M. RAUDENBUSH
30 Development/Alumni Relations ....Ms. Lydia D. KOKOLSKYJ

† Regional accreditation is carried under the parent institution in University Park, PA.

Penn State Altoona (I)

3000 Ivyside Park, Altoona PA 16601-3777
County: Blair FICE Identification: 003331
Unit ID: 214689
Telephone: (814) 949-5000 Carnegie Class: Bac/Diverse
FAX Number: (814) 949-5011 Calendar System: Semester
URL: www.aa.psu.edu
Established: 1929 Annual Undergrad Tuition & Fees (In-State): $13,900
Enrollment: 4,105 Coed
Affiliation or Control: State Related IRS Status: 501(c)3
Highest Offering: Baccalaureate
Program: Occupational; 2-Year Principally Bachelor's Creditable; Liberal Arts And General; Teacher Preparatory
Accreditation: &M, ENGT

01 Chancellor .... Dr. Lori J. BECHTEL-WHERRY
05 Academic Affairs .... Dr. Kenneth A. WOMACK
32 Student Affairs .... Mr. Sean C. KELLY
06 Registrar .... Ms. Margaret B. MC NULTY
30 Development/Alumni Relations .... Ms. N. Susan WOODRING

† Regional accreditation is carried under the parent institution in University Park, PA.

Penn State Beaver (A)

100 University Drive, Monaca PA 15061-2799
County: Beaver FICE Identification: 003332
Unit ID: 214698
Telephone: (724) 773-3800 Carnegie Class: Bac/A&S
FAX Number: (724) 773-3557 Calendar System: Semester
URL: www.br.psu.edu
Established: 1964 Annual Undergrad Tuition & Fees (In-State): $13,350
Enrollment: 870 Coed
Affiliation or Control: State Related IRS Status: 501(c)3
Highest Offering: Master's
Program: Occupational; 2-Year Principally Bachelor's Creditable; Liberal Arts And General
Accreditation: &M

01 Chancellor .... Dr. Gary B. KEEFER
05 Academic Affairs .... Dr. Donna J. KUGA
32 Student Affairs .... Dr. Christopher RIZZO
06 Registrar .... Ms. Gloria S. DESCHLER
30 Development/Allumni Relations .... Ms. Diana L. PATTERSON

† Regional accreditation is carried under the parent institution in University Park, PA.

Penn State Berks (B)

Tulpehocken Road, PO Box 7009, Reading PA 19610-6009
County: Berks FICE Identification: 003334
Unit ID: 214704
Telephone: (610) 396-6000 Carnegie Class: Bac/Diverse
FAX Number: (610) 396-6024 Calendar System: Semester
URL: www.bk.psu.edu
Established: 1924 Annual Undergrad Tuition & Fees (In-State): $13,900
Enrollment: 2,873 Coed
Affiliation or Control: State Related IRS Status: 501(c)3
Highest Offering: Baccalaureate
Program: Occupational; 2-Year Principally Bachelor's Creditable; Liberal Arts And General; Teacher Preparatory
Accreditation: &M, ENGT, OTA

01 Chancellor .... Dr. Susan P. SPEECE
05 Academic Affairs .... Dr. Paul ESQUEDA
32 Student Affairs .... Dr. Blaine E. STEENSLAND
06 Registrar .... Dr. David BENDER
30 Director of Development/Alumni .... Mr. David DELOZIER

† Regional accreditation is carried under the parent institution in University Park, PA.

Penn State Brandywine (C)

25 Yearsley Mill Road, Media PA 19063-5596
County: Delaware FICE Identification: 006922
Unit ID: 214731
Telephone: (610) 892-1350 Carnegie Class: Bac/Diverse
FAX Number: (610) 892-1357 Calendar System: Semester
URL: www.de.psu.edu
Established: 1966 Annual Undergrad Tuition & Fees (In-State): $13,356
Enrollment: 1,630 Coed
Affiliation or Control: State Related IRS Status: 501(c)3
Highest Offering: Baccalaureate
Program: Occupational; 2-Year Principally Bachelor's Creditable; Liberal Arts And General; Teacher Preparatory
Accreditation: &M

01 Chancellor .... Dr. Sophia T. WISNIEWSKA
05 Academic Affairs .... Dr. Paul J. DEGATEGNO
32 Student Affairs .... Mr. Matthew R. SHUPP
06 Registrar .... Ms. Joanna MCGOWAN
30 Development/Alumni Relations .... Ms. Michelle C. JOHNSON

† Regional accreditation is carried under the parent institution in University Park, PA.

The Penn State Dickinson School of Law (D)

150 S College Street, Carlisle PA 17013-2861
County: Cumberland FICE Identification: 003254
Unit ID: 212018
Telephone: (717) 240-5000 Carnegie Class: Spec/Law
FAX Number: (717) 243-4443 Calendar System: Semester
URL: www.dsl.psu.edu
Established: 1834 Annual Graduate Tuition & Fees: $40,532
Enrollment: 629 Coed
Affiliation or Control: State Related IRS Status: 501(c)3
Highest Offering: First Professional Degree; No Undergraduates
Program: Professional
Accreditation: &M, LAW

01 Dean .... Mr. Philip J. MCCONNAUGHAY
05 Academic Affairs .... Ms. Marie T. REILLY
06 Registrar .... Ms. Shari L. WELCH
32 Student Affairs .... Ms. Holly A. PARRISH
30 Development/Alumni Relations .... Ms. Kelly R. RIMMER

† Regional accreditation is carried under the parent institution in University Park, PA.

Penn State DuBois (E)

One College Place, DuBois PA 15801-3199
County: Clearfield FICE Identification: 003335
Unit ID: 214740
Telephone: (814) 375-4700 Carnegie Class: Bac/Assoc
FAX Number: (814) 375-4784 Calendar System: Semester
URL: www.ds.psu.edu
Established: 1935 Annual Undergrad Tuition & Fees (In-State): $13,244
Enrollment: 795 Coed
Affiliation or Control: State Related IRS Status: 501(c)3
Highest Offering: Master's
Program: Occupational; 2-Year Principally Bachelor's Creditable; Liberal Arts And General
Accreditation: &M, ENGT, OTA, #PTAA

01 Chancellor .... Dr. Anita D. MCDONALD
05 Academic Affairs .... Ms. Maureen T. HORAN
32 Student Affairs .... Ms. Rebecca A. PENNINGTON
06 Registrar .... Ms. Jeanne HUNTER
30 Development/Alumni Relations .... Ms. Jean A. WOLF

† Regional accreditation is carried under the parent institution in University Park, PA.

Penn State Erie, The Behrend College (F)

5091 Station Road, Erie PA 16563-0001
County: Erie FICE Identification: 003333
Unit ID: 214591
Telephone: (814) 898-6000 Carnegie Class: Master's S
FAX Number: (814) 898-6461 Calendar System: Semester
URL: www.pserie.psu.edu
Established: 1926 Annual Undergrad Tuition & Fees (In-State): $13,900
Enrollment: 4,226 Coed
Affiliation or Control: State Related IRS Status: 501(c)3
Highest Offering: Master's
Program: Occupational; 2-Year Principally Bachelor's Creditable; Liberal Arts And General
Accreditation: &M, BUS, ENG, ENGT

01 Chancellor .... Dr. Donald L. BIRX
05 Academic Affairs .... Dr. David J. CHRISTIANSEN
32 Student Affairs .... Dr. Kenneth P. MILLER
06 Registrar .... Dr. Mary Ellen BAYUK
30 Development/Alumni Relations .... Ms. Margaret TAYLOR

† Regional accreditation is carried under the parent institution in University Park, PA.

Penn State Fayette, The Eberly Campus (G)

PO BOX 519, Rt 119 N, One Univ Dr, Uniontown PA 15401-0519
County: Fayette FICE Identification: 003336
Unit ID: 214759
Telephone: (724) 430-4100 Carnegie Class: Bac/Assoc
FAX Number: (724) 430-4184 Calendar System: Semester
URL: www.fe.psu.edu
Established: 1934 Annual Undergrad Tuition & Fees (In-State): $13,300
Enrollment: 957 Coed
Affiliation or Control: State Related IRS Status: 501(c)3
Highest Offering: Baccalaureate
Program: Occupational; 2-Year Principally Bachelor's Creditable; Liberal Arts And General
Accreditation: &M, ENGT, @PTAA

01 Chancellor .... Dr. Francis K. ACHAMPONG
05 Academic Affairs .... Dr. Delia B. CONTI
32 Student Affairs .... Mr. Jason M. BROADWATER
06 Registrar .... Ms. Maria E. MCDONALD
30 Development/Alumni Relations .... Ms. Lori A. OMATICK

† Regional accreditation is carried under the parent institution in University Park, PA.

Penn State Great Valley School of Graduate Professional Studies (H)

30 E Swedesford Road, Malvern PA 19355-1488
County: Chester FICE Identification: 003348
Unit ID: 214607
Telephone: (610) 648-3200 Carnegie Class: Master's L
FAX Number: (610) 889-1334 Calendar System: Semester
URL: www.gv.psu.edu
Established: 1963 Annual Graduate Tuition & Fees: $21,934
Enrollment: 691 Coed
Affiliation or Control: State Related IRS Status: 501(c)3
Highest Offering: Master's; No Undergraduates
Program: Professional
Accreditation: &M, BUS

01 Chancellor .... Dr. Craig S. EDELBROCK
05 Interim Director Academic Affairs .... Dr. James NEMES
32 Student Affairs .... Ms. Carla A. HOLWAY
29 Development/Alumni Relations .... Ms. Suzanne CRUIT
06 Registrar .... Vacant

† Regional accreditation is carried under the parent institution in University Park, PA.

Penn State Greater Allegheny (I)

4000 University Drive, McKeesport PA 15132-7698
County: Allegheny FICE Identification: 003339
Unit ID: 214786
Telephone: (412) 675-9000 Carnegie Class: Bac/A&S
FAX Number: (412) 675-9043 Calendar System: Semester
URL: www.mk.psu.edu
Established: 1947 Annual Undergrad Tuition & Fees (In-State): $13,356
Enrollment: 701 Coed
Affiliation or Control: State Related IRS Status: 501(c)3
Highest Offering: Master's
Program: Occupational; 2-Year Principally Bachelor's Creditable; Liberal Arts And General
Accreditation: &M

01 Chancellor .... Dr. Curtiss E. PORTER
05 Academic Affairs .... Dr. Kurt C. TORELL
06 Registrar .... Ms. Victoria GARWOOD
30 Development/Alumni Relations .... Mr. Joseph R. EDMISTON
32 Student Affairs .... Mr. Glenn J. BEECH

† Regional accreditation is carried under the parent institution in University Park, PA.

Penn State Harrisburg (J)

777 W Harrisburg Pike, Middletown PA 17057-4898
County: Dauphin FICE Identification: 006814
Unit ID: 214713
Telephone: (717) 948-6452 Carnegie Class: Master's L
FAX Number: (717) 948-6008 Calendar System: Semester
URL: www.hbg.psu.edu
Established: 1966 Annual Undergrad Tuition & Fees (In-State): $13,900
Enrollment: 4,269 Coed
Affiliation or Control: State Related IRS Status: 501(c)3
Highest Offering: Doctorate
Program: Occupational; 2-Year Principally Bachelor's Creditable; Liberal Arts And General; Teacher Preparatory
Accreditation: &M, BUS, ENG, ENGT, SPAA, TED

01 Chancellor .... Dr. Mukund S. KULKARNI
05 Academic Affairs .... Dr. Omid ANSARY
32 Student Affairs .... Ms. Felicia L. BROWN-HAYWOOD
30 Development/Alumni Relations .... Ms. Marissa HOOVER
06 Registrar .... Dr. Margaret BOMAN

† Regional accreditation is carried under the parent institution in University Park, PA.

Penn State Hazleton (K)

76 University Drive, Hazleton PA 18202-1291
County: Luzerne FICE Identification: 003338
Unit ID: 214768
Telephone: (570) 450-3000 Carnegie Class: Bac/A&S
FAX Number: (570) 450-3182 Calendar System: Semester
URL: www.hn.psu.edu
Established: 1934 Annual Undergrad Tuition & Fees (In-State): $13,300
Enrollment: 1,172 Coed
Affiliation or Control: State Related IRS Status: 501(c)3
Highest Offering: Baccalaureate
Program: Occupational; 2-Year Principally Bachelor's Creditable; Liberal Arts And General
Accreditation: &M, ENGT, MLTAD, PTAA

01 Chancellor .... Dr. Gary M. LAWLER
05 Academic Affairs .... Dr. Elizabeth J. WRIGHT
32 Student Affairs .... Mr. Marquis L. BENNETT
30 Development/Alumni Relations .... Mr. Kevin J. SALAWAY
06 Registrar .... Ms. Michele JAIS

† Regional accreditation is carried under the parent institution in University Park, PA.

Penn State Lehigh Valley (L)

8380 Mohr Lane, Fogelsville PA 18051-9999
County: Lehigh FICE Identification: 003330
Unit ID: 214670
Telephone: (610) 285-5000 Carnegie Class: Bac/Diverse
FAX Number: (610) 285-5220 Calendar System: Semester
URL: www.lv.psu.edu
Established: 1912 Annual Undergrad Tuition & Fees (In-State): $13,350
Enrollment: 942 Coed
Affiliation or Control: State Related IRS Status: 501(c)3
Highest Offering: Baccalaureate
Program: Occupational; 2-Year Principally Bachelor's Creditable; Liberal Arts And General; Teacher Preparatory
Accreditation: &M

01 Chancellor .... Dr. Ann M. WILLIAMS
05 Academic Affairs .... Dr. Kenneth A. THIGPEN
06 Registrar .... Ms. Katherine D. ECK
30 Development/Alumni Relations .... Ms. Maureen S. JOLY
32 Student Affairs .... Ms. Tiffany CRESSWELL-YEAGER

† Regional accreditation is carried under the parent institution in University Park, PA.

Penn State Milton S. Hershey Medical Center College of Medicine (A)

500 University Drive, Box 850, Hershey PA 17033-2360
County: Dauphin FICE Identification: 006813
Unit ID: 214616
Telephone: (717) 531-8521 Carnegie Class: Spec/Med
FAX Number: N/A Calendar System: Semester
URL: www.hmc.psu.edu
Established: 1964 Annual Graduate Tuition & Fees: $42,392
Enrollment: 787 Coed
Affiliation or Control: State Related IRS Status: 501(c)3
Highest Offering: Doctorate; No Undergraduates
Program: Professional
Accreditation: &M, MED

01 Chancellor .... Dr. Harold L. PAZ
05 Academic Affairs .... Dr. Richard J. SIMONS
30 Development/Alumni Relations .... Ms. Kristen B. ROZANSKY
32 Student Affairs .... Ms. Susan KELLEY
06 Registrar .... Ms. Diane E. GILL

† Regional accreditation is carried under the parent institution in University Park, PA.

Penn State Mont Alto (B)

One Campus Drive, Mont Alto PA 17237-9703
County: Franklin FICE Identification: 003340
Unit ID: 214795
Telephone: (717) 749-6000 Carnegie Class: Bac/Assoc
FAX Number: (717) 749-6069 Calendar System: Semester
URL: www.ma.psu.edu
Established: 1929 Annual Undergrad Tuition & Fees (In-State): $13,356
Enrollment: 1,217 Coed
Affiliation or Control: State Related IRS Status: 501(c)3
Highest Offering: Baccalaureate
Program: Occupational; 2-Year Principally Bachelor's Creditable; Liberal Arts And General
Accreditation: &M, OTA, PTAA

01 Chancellor .... Dr. David C. GNAGE
05 Academic Affairs .... Dr. Michael DONCHESKI
32 Student Affairs .... Ms. Andrea D. CHRISTOPHER
06 Registrar .... Ms. Linda S. MONN
30 Development/Alumni Relations .... Mr. Randall R. ACKERMAN

† Regional accreditation is carried under the parent institution in University Park, PA.

Penn State New Kensington (C)

3550 Seventh Street Road, Route 780,
Upper Burrell PA 15068-1798
County: Westmoreland FICE Identification: 003341
Unit ID: 214625
Telephone: (724) 334-5466 Carnegie Class: Bac/Diverse
FAX Number: (724) 334-6052 Calendar System: Semester
URL: www.nk.psu.edu
Established: 1958 Annual Undergrad Tuition & Fees (In-State): $13,300
Enrollment: 801 Coed
Affiliation or Control: State Related IRS Status: 501(c)3
Highest Offering: Master's
Program: Occupational; 2-Year Principally Bachelor's Creditable; Liberal Arts And General
Accreditation: &M, ENGT, RAD

01 Chancellor .... Dr. Kevin J. SNIDER
05 Academic Affairs .... Dr. Arlene E. HALL
32 Student Affairs .... Ms. Theresa A. BONK
06 Registrar .... Ms. Mary T. DUBBINK
30 Development/Alumni Relations .... Ms. Donna M. SPEER

† Regional accreditation is carried under the parent institution in University Park, PA.

Penn State Schuylkill (D)

200 University Drive, Schuylkill Haven PA 17972-2208
County: Schuylkill FICE Identification: 003343
Unit ID: 214810
Telephone: (570) 385-6000 Carnegie Class: Bac/Diverse
FAX Number: (570) 385-3672 Calendar System: Semester
URL: www.sl.psu.edu
Established: 1934 Annual Undergrad Tuition & Fees (In-State): $13,238
Enrollment: 1,012 Coed
Affiliation or Control: State Related IRS Status: 501(c)3
Highest Offering: Baccalaureate
Program: Occupational; 2-Year Principally Bachelor's Creditable; Liberal Arts And General
Accreditation: &M, RAD

01 Chancellor .... Dr. Kelly M. AUSTIN
05 Academic Affairs .... Dr. Stephen R. COUCH
32 Student Affairs .... Mr. Matthew J. SWATCHICK
06 Registrar .... Ms. Elyce M. LYKINS
30 Development/Alumni Relations .... Ms. Jane ZINTAK

† Regional accreditation is carried under the parent institution in University Park, PA.

Penn State Shenango (E)

147 Shenango Avenue, Sharon PA 16146-1597
County: Mercer FICE Identification: 003345
Unit ID: 214634
Telephone: (724) 983-2803 Carnegie Class: Bac/Diverse
FAX Number: (724) 983-2820 Calendar System: Semester
URL: www.shenango.psu.edu
Established: 1965 Annual Undergrad Tuition & Fees (In-State): $13,244
Enrollment: 651 Coed
Affiliation or Control: State Related IRS Status: 501(c)3
Highest Offering: Baccalaureate
Program: Occupational; 2-Year Principally Bachelor's Creditable; Liberal Arts And General
Accreditation: &M, ENGT, PTAA

01 Chancellor .... Dr. Fredric M. LEEDS
05 Academic Affairs .... Dr. Ira S. SALTZ
32 Interim Student Affairs .... Ms. Stephanie M. CHASTAIN
30 Development/Alumni Relations .... Mr. Steven L. HESSMANN
06 Registrar .... Mr. Matthew E. GORAL

† Regional accreditation is carried under the parent institution in University Park, PA.

Penn State Wilkes-Barre (F)

PO Box PSU, Old Route 115, Lehman PA 18627-0217
County: Luzerne FICE Identification: 003346
Unit ID: 214643
Telephone: (570) 675-2171 Carnegie Class: Bac/Diverse
FAX Number: (570) 675-8308 Calendar System: Semester
URL: www.wb.psu.edu
Established: 1916 Annual Undergrad Tuition & Fees (In-State): $13,238
Enrollment: 683 Coed
Affiliation or Control: State Related IRS Status: 501(c)3
Highest Offering: Baccalaureate
Program: Occupational; 2-Year Principally Bachelor's Creditable; Liberal Arts And General
Accreditation: &M, ENG, ENGT

01 Chancellor .... Dr. Charles H. DAVIS
05 Academic Affairs .... Dr. Albert LOZANO-NIETO
32 Student Affairs .... Ms. Katherine M. FLANAGAN-HERSTEK
06 Registrar .... Ms. Margaret B. ESOPI
30 Development/Alumni Relations .... Mr. Anthony J. SHIPULA

† Regional accreditation is carried under the parent institution in University Park, PA.

Penn State Worthington-Scranton (G)

120 Ridge View Drive, Dunmore PA 18512-1602
County: Lackawanna FICE Identification: 003344
Unit ID: 214652
Telephone: (570) 963-2500 Carnegie Class: Bac/Diverse
FAX Number: (570) 963-2543 Calendar System: Semester
URL: www.sn.psu.edu
Established: 1923 Annual Undergrad Tuition & Fees (In-State): $13,230
Enrollment: 1,270 Coed
Affiliation or Control: State Related IRS Status: 501(c)3
Highest Offering: Baccalaureate
Program: Occupational; 2-Year Principally Bachelor's Creditable; Liberal Arts And General
Accreditation: &M, ENGT

01 Chancellor .... Dr. Mary-Beth KROGH-JESPERSEN
05 Academic Affairs .... Dr. Molly WERTHEIMER
06 Registrar .... Ms. Allison L. BURNS
30 Development/Alumni Relations .... Ms. Maria J. RUSSONIELLO
35 Director Student Affairs .... Ms. Michelle K. SCHUTT

† Regional accreditation is carried under the parent institution in University Park, PA.

Penn State York (H)

1031 Edgecomb Avenue, York PA 17403-3398
County: York FICE Identification: 003347
Unit ID: 214829
Telephone: (717) 771-4000 Carnegie Class: Bac/Diverse
FAX Number: (717) 771-4062 Calendar System: Other
URL: www.yk.psu.edu
Established: 1926 Annual Undergrad Tuition & Fees (In-State): $13,238
Enrollment: 1,329 Coed
Affiliation or Control: State Related IRS Status: 501(c)3
Highest Offering: Master's
Program: Occupational; 2-Year Principally Bachelor's Creditable; Liberal Arts And General
Accreditation: &M, ENGT

01 Chancellor .... Dr. Lisa Ann PLOWFIELD
05 Academic Affairs .... Dr. Joseph P. MCCORMICK
32 Student Affairs .... Dr. Sharon CHRIST
06 Registrar .... Mr. Frank P. MILLER, JR.
30 Development/Alumni Relations .... Ms. Diane K. HERSHEY

† Regional accreditation is carried under the parent institution in University Park, PA.

Pennco Tech (I)

3815 Otter Street, Bristol PA 19007-3696
County: Bucks FICE Identification: 009449
Unit ID: 214944
Telephone: (215) 785-0111 Carnegie Class: Assoc/PrivFP
FAX Number: (215) 785-1945 Calendar System: Other
URL: www.penncotech.edu
Established: 1973 Annual Undergrad Tuition & Fees: $18,500
Enrollment: 410 Coed
Affiliation or Control: Proprietary IRS Status: Proprietary
Highest Offering: Associate Degree
Program: Occupational; Technical Emphasis
Accreditation: ACCSC

01 CEO .... Michael S. HOBYAK
03 School Director .... Fred PARCELLS
05 Director of Education .... Vern LUCAS
07 Director of Admissions .... Glenn SLATER
06 Registrar .... Sondra KOOB
35 Director Student Services .... Todd JANZER
37 Admin Mgr/Dir Student Financial Aid .... Fran GRANDVILLE
36 Director Student Placement .... Teresa SCHEERER

Pennsylvania Academy of the Fine Arts (J)

128 N Broad Street, Philadelphia PA 19102-1424
County: Philadelphia FICE Identification: 021073
Unit ID: 214971
Telephone: (215) 972-7600 Carnegie Class: Spec/Arts
FAX Number: (215) 569-0153 Calendar System: Semester
URL: www.pafa.edu
Established: 1805 Annual Undergrad Tuition & Fees: $29,020
Enrollment: 348 Coed
Affiliation or Control: Independent Non-Profit IRS Status: 501(c)3
Highest Offering: Master's
Program: Liberal Arts And General; Professional; Fine Arts Emphasis
Accreditation: @M, ART

01 President & CEO .... Dr. David R. BRIGHAM
30 Exec Vice President Development .... Ms. Melissa DERUITER
26 Exec Vice President of Marketing .... Ms. Heike RASS
05 Dean School of Fine Arts .... Mr. Jeffrey CARR
10 Exec Vice Pres of Finance/Operation .... Mr. John BERG
07 Dean of Enrollment .... Mr. André S.F. VAN DE PUTTE
32 Dean of Students .... Ms. Anne K. STASSEN
18 Director of Operations and Safety .... Mr. Ed POLETTI
19 Director of Security .... Mr. Jimmie GREENO
37 Director of Financial Aid .... Vacant
06 Registrar .... Mr. Peter MEDWICK
08 Head Librarian .... Mr. Brian DUFFY

Pennsylvania College of Art & Design (K)

204 N Prince Street, Box 59, Lancaster PA 17608-0059
County: Lancaster FICE Identification: 022699
Unit ID: 215053
Telephone: (717) 396-7833 Carnegie Class: Spec/Arts
FAX Number: (717) 396-1339 Calendar System: Semester
URL: www.pcad.edu
Established: 1982 Annual Undergrad Tuition & Fees: $19,680
Enrollment: 257 Coed
Affiliation or Control: Independent Non-Profit IRS Status: 501(c)3
Highest Offering: Baccalaureate
Program: Professional; Fine Arts Emphasis
Accreditation: M, ART

01 President .... Ms. Mary Colleen HEIL
05 Academic Dean .... Mr. Marc TORICK
32 Dean of Students .... Ms. Pamela RICHARDSON
26 Director of Public Relations .... Mrs. Mary STADDEN
10 Director of Finance .... Mrs. Patricia ERNST
84 Dir of Admiss/Mktg & Recruitment .... Ms. Natalie LASCEK-SPEAKMAN
37 Director Financial Aid .... Mr. J. David HERSHEY
08 Library Director .... Ms. Karen HUTCHISON
30 Director of Development .... Ms. Angela SPICKLER
51 Director of Continuing Education .... Mrs. Tracy BEYL
18 Director of Physical Plant .... Mr. Dan FREILER
06 Registrar .... Ms. Faith GADDIE

Pennsylvania College of Technology (L)

One College Avenue, Williamsport PA 17701-5799
County: Lycoming FICE Identification: 003395
Unit ID: 366252
Telephone: (570) 326-3761 Carnegie Class: Bac/Assoc
FAX Number: (570) 327-4503 Calendar System: Semester
URL: www.pct.edu
Established: 1941 Annual Undergrad Tuition & Fees (In-State): $14,370
Enrollment: 5,976 Coed
Affiliation or Control: State IRS Status: 501(c)3

Highest Offering: Baccalaureate
Program: Occupational; 2-Year Principally Bachelor's Creditable; Technical Emphasis
Accreditation: M, ACBSP, ACFEI, ADNUR, ARCPA, CONST, DH, EMT, ENGT, IACBE, NAIT, NUR, OTA, PNUR, RAD, SURGT

01 President .... Dr. Davie Jane GILMOUR
05 VP for Academic Affairs/Provost .... Dr. Paul L. STARKEY
108 VP Assessment/Research/Planning .... Vacant
10 VP for Finance/CFO .... Ms. Suzanne T. STOPPER
30 Vice Pres Institutional Advancement .... Mr. Barry R. STIGER
13 VP for Info Tech and Business .... Mr. Michael M. CUNNINGHAM
20 Assistant VP for Academic Services .... Mrs. Carolyn R. STRICKLAND
20 Associate VP for Instruction .... Mr. Tom F. GREGORY
04 Administrative Asst to President .... Mrs. Valerie A. BAIER
88 Spec Asst to the President ITS .... Mr. James E. CUNNINGHAM
32 Special Asst to Pres Student Affs .... Vacant
103 Asst VP for Workforce Develop .... Mr. Larry L. MICHAEL
50 Dean Business & Computer Technology .... Dr. Edward A. HENNINGER
88 Dean Construction & Design Tech .... Mr. Marc E. BRIDGENS
76 Dean Health Sciences .... Mrs. Sharon WATERS
54 Dean Indust & Engineer Tech .... Mr. Donald O. PRASTER
49 Dean Integrated Studies .... Dr. Clifford P. COPPERSMITH
65 Dean Natural Resource Management .... Dr. Mary A. SULLIVAN
88 Dean Transportation Technology .... Mr. Colin W. WILLIAMSON
88 Dean for Hospitality .... Mr. Frederick W. BECKER
102 Exec Dir of Penn College Foundation ..... Mr. Robert C. DIETRICH
08 Director of the Madigan Library .... Vacant
56 Director Instruc Tech/Distance Lrng .... Mr. Walter J. SHULTZ
37 Assoc Dean of Admissions & Fin Aid ..... Mr. Dennis L. CORRELL
18 Director of General Services .... Mr. Walter D. NYMAN
09 Director Institutional Research .... Mr. Brian CYGAN
22 VP Human Resources/Employees/EEO ..... Mrs. Linda M. MORRIS
15 VP for College Services .... Mr. R. David KAY
06 Registrar .... Mr. Dennis L. DUNKLEBERGER
38 Director of Advisement Center .... Mr. Stephen R. HAEFNER
36 Dir Counsel/Career & Disability Svc .... Dr. Jennifer MCLEAN
39 Director Residence Life .... Mr. Brian M. JOHNSON
19 Chief of Police .... Mr. Chris E. MILLER
27 Director College Info/Cmty Rels .... Mrs. Elaine J. LAMBERT
88 Director Academic Support Services .... Dr. Kimberly L. BOLIG
35 Director Student Activities .... Mrs. Kimberly R. CASSEL
29 Director Alumni Relations .... Ms. Valerie L. FESSLER
26 Director of Corporate Relations .... Ms. Debra M. MILLER
88 Director Children Learning Center .... Ms. Karen W. PAYNE
40 Director of College Store .... Mr. Matthew P. BRANCA
41 Director of Athletics .... Mr. Scott E. KENNELL
90 Manager Academic Computing .... Ms. Constance M. VITOLINS
91 Director Administrative Info Sys .... Mr. Randall L. MONROE
23 Student Health Center Director .... Mr. Carl L. SHANER
88 Coordinator of Disability Services ... Ms. Kay E. DUNKLEBERGER
85 International Programs Specialist .... Ms. Shanin L. DOUGHERTY
25 Director of Grants & Contracts .... Ms. Alice M. SCHUSTER
96 Director/Procurement Services .... Ms. Karen P. FESSLER

† Affiliate of Pennsylvania State University.

Pennsylvania Highlands Community College (A)

101 Community College Way, Johnstown PA 15904-2949
County: Cambria FICE Identification: 031804
Unit ID: 414911
Telephone: (814) 262-6400 Carnegie Class: Assoc/Pub-R-M
FAX Number: (814) 269-9700 Calendar System: Semester
URL: www.pennhighlands.edu
Established: 1994 Annual Undergrad Tuition & Fees (In-District): $4,420
Enrollment: 1,436 Coed
Affiliation or Control: State/Local IRS Status: 501(c)3
Highest Offering: Associate Degree
Program: Occupational; 2-Year Principally Bachelor's Creditable
Accreditation: M

01 President .... Dr. Walter J. ASONEVICH
05 Vice Pres/Dean Academic Affairs .... Dr. Edward NICHOLS
10 Vice Pres Finance & Admin Services .... Lorraine DONAHUE
32 Vice Pres Student Svcs .... Dr. David VOLPE
26 AVP for External Relations .... Trish CORLE
51 AVP for Continuing Education .... Grace MARKUM
08 Assoc Dean for Learning Resources .... Dr. Barbara ZABOROWSKI
20 Assoc Dean of Instruction .... Erica REIGHARD
20 Assoc Dean of Instruction .... Michele RICE
06 Registrar .... Michelle STUMPF
07 Director of Admissions .... Jeffrey MAUL
15 AVP of Human Resources .... Ginny ALTEMUS
21 Director of Finance/Admin Services .... Christopher PRIBULSKY
37 Director Student Financial Aid .... Brenda COUGHENOUR
26 Director of Marketing .... Raymond WEIBLE, JR.
35 Director of Student Activities .... Suzanne BRUGH
18 Director of Facilities Operation .... Reb BROWNLEE
13 Director of IT .... Danielle GERKO

Pennsylvania Institute of Health and Technology (B)

PO Box 278, Mount Braddock PA 15465-0278
County: Fayette Identification: 666035
Unit ID: 261861
Telephone: (724) 437-4600 Carnegie Class: Assoc/PrivFP
FAX Number: (724) 437-6053 Calendar System: Quarter
URL: www.piht.edu
Established: 1987 Annual Undergrad Tuition & Fees: $12,585
Enrollment: 150 Coed
Affiliation or Control: Proprietary IRS Status: Proprietary
Highest Offering: Associate Degree
Program: Occupational
Accreditation: ACICS

01 Director .... Ms. Robin ADDIS
03 Executive Director .... Ms. Patricia A. CALLEN
32 Director of Student Services .... Mrs. Mary Jo BARNHART
36 Career Services Director .... Ms. Sue Ann PRIEMER
37 Financial Aid Office .... Ms. Lisa JANESKO

† Branch campus of West Virginia Junior College, Morgantown, WV.

Pennsylvania Institute of Technology (C)

800 Manchester Avenue, Media PA 19063-4098
County: Delaware FICE Identification: 010998
Unit ID: 214582
Telephone: (610) 892-1500 Carnegie Class: Assoc/PrivNFP
FAX Number: (610) 892-1510 Calendar System: Semester
URL: www.pit.edu
Established: 1953 Annual Undergrad Tuition & Fees: $11,400
Enrollment: 870 Coed
Affiliation or Control: Independent Non-Profit IRS Status: 501(c)3
Highest Offering: Associate Degree
Program: Occupational; 2-Year Principally Bachelor's Creditable; Technical Emphasis
Accreditation: M

01 President .... Mr. Walter GARRISON
05 Dean of Academic Affairs .... Dr. Robert E. HANCOX
32 Dean Student Services .... Dr. Dona M. FABRIZIO
20 Asst Dean of Academic Affairs .... Ms. Susanne LEHMAN
13 Chief Information Officer .... Mr. Jack BACON
10 Chief Financial Officer .... Ms. Annamarie CASSIDY
06 Registrar .... Mr. Craig M. JACOBS
08 Director of the Library .... Ms. Lynea ANDERMAN
18 Director of Facilities .... Mr. Frederick FIVECOAT
36 Director Career Placement/Transfer .... Ms. Adina TAYAR
36 Dir Career Plct/Extrn Sch Prof Pgms .... Ms. Kamira EVANS
37 Financial Aid Director .... Ms. Kristina FRIPPS
07 Director of Admissions .... Mr. John DETURRIS

Pennsylvania School of Business (D)

406 W Hamilton Street, Allentown PA 18101-1604
County: Lehigh FICE Identification: 022552
Unit ID: 213057
Telephone: (610) 841-3333 Carnegie Class: Assoc/PrivFP
FAX Number: (610) 841-3334 Calendar System: Semester
URL: www.psb.edu
Established: 1980 Annual Undergrad Tuition & Fees: $11,115
Enrollment: 279 Coed
Affiliation or Control: Proprietary IRS Status: Proprietary
Highest Offering: Associate Degree
Program: Occupational
Accreditation: ACCSC

01 President .... Mr. Michael J. O'BRIEN
10 Controller .... Ms. Michele TAYLOR
05 Dean of Education .... Ms. Dani J. PHELPS
07 Director of Admissions .... Mr. Sam JARVIS
37 Director of Financial Aid .... Ms. Stephanie A. AZUR
36 Director of Career Services .... Ms. Cynthia PHILLIPS

*Pennsylvania State System of Higher Education, Office of the Chancellor (E)

Dixon University Ctr, 2986 N 2nd St,
Harrisburg PA 17110-1201
County: Dauphin FICE Identification: 029371
Unit ID: 214661
Telephone: (717) 720-4010 Carnegie Class: N/A
FAX Number: (717) 720-4011
URL: www.passhe.edu

01 Chancellor .... Dr. John C. CAVANAUGH
03 Executive Vice Chancellor .... Dr. Peter H. GARLAND
10 Vice Chancellor Admin/Finance .... Mr. James S. DILLON
21 Assoc Vice Chancellor Admin/Finance ...... Ms. Lois M. JOHNSON
18 Asst Vice Chancellor Facilities .... Mr. Steven DUPES
05 Vice Chanc Academic/Student Affairs .... Dr. James D. MORAN, III
20 Sr Assoc Vice Chanc A/S Affairs .... Dr. Kathleen HOWLEY
16 Vice Chancellor HR/LR .... Mr. Gary K. DENT
15 Asst Vice Chancellor LR .... Mr. Michael A. MOTTOLA
86 Vice Chancellor External Relations .... Ms. Karen BALL
43 Chief Legal Counsel .... Mr. Leo PANDELADIS

*Bloomsburg University of Pennsylvania (F)

400 E Second Street, Bloomsburg PA 17815-1399
County: Columbia FICE Identification: 003315
Unit ID: 211158
Telephone: (570) 389-4000 Carnegie Class: Master's L
FAX Number: (570) 389-3700 Calendar System: Semester
URL: www.bloomu.edu
Established: 1839 Annual Undergrad Tuition & Fees (In-State): N/A
Enrollment: 10,159 Coed
Affiliation or Control: State IRS Status: 501(c)3
Highest Offering: Doctorate
Program: Liberal Arts And General; Teacher Preparatory; Professional
Accreditation: M, ANEST, ART, AUD, BUS, CS, ENGR, ENGT, EXSC, MUS, NURSE, SP, SW, TED, THEA

02 President .... Dr. David L. SOLTZ
05 Sr VP/Provost Academic Affairs .... Dr. Ira BLAKE
10 Vice Pres Finance/Administration .... Dr. Richard RUGEN
32 Vice Pres Student Affairs .... Dr. Dionne D. SOMERVILLE
30 Vice Pres University Advancement .... Mr. Erik EVANS
22 Deputy to Pres for Equity .... Dr. Robert WISLOCK
04 Exec Asst to the President .... Ms. Brenda CROMLEY
20 Vice Provost/Dean Undergraduate Ed .... Dr. Jonathan LINCOLN
58 Interim Assoc VP/Dean Grad Studies .... Dr. Robert GATES
13 Assoc VP Technology & Library Serv .... Mr. Wayne C. MOHR
51 Assoc VP/Dean Extended Programs .... Mr. Thomas FLETCHER
18 Asst VP for Facilities Management .... Mr. Eric NESS
21 Asst VP Finance/Budget & Bus Svcs .... Ms. Claudia THRUSH
35 Asst VP Student Affairs/Comm Act .... Dr. Jeff C. LONG
39 Asst VP Student Affairs/Campus Life .... Mr. Thomas KRESCH
26 Asst VP External Relations .... Mr. Jim HOLLISTER
49 Dean College of Liberal Arts .... Dr. James BROWN
50 Dean College of Business .... Vacant
81 Dean College of Science/Technology ...... Dr. Robert P. MARANDE
53 Dean College of Education .... Dr. Elizabeth MAUCH
88 Acting Assoc Dean Acad Achievement .... Dr. Irvin WRIGHT
15 Director Human Resources/Labor Rel .... Mr. Jerry REED
46 Director of Research/Sponsored Pgms .... Dr. Jerrold R. HARRIS
06 Registrar .... Mr. Joseph KISSELL
07 Director of Admissions .... Mr. Christopher J. KELLER
36 Interim Director Career Development . Ms. Jeanne R. FITZGERALD
38 Director of Counsel & Human Devel .... Dr. William R. HARRAR
37 Director Financial Aid .... Mr. John BIERYLA
90 Manager Technology Support Services .... Mr. David S. CELLI
29 Director of Alumni Affairs .... Ms. Lynda MICHAELS
40 Manager University Store .... Ms. Beth CHRISTIAN
41 Director of Athletics .... Mr. Michael S. MCFARLAND
85 Director International Education .... Dr. Madhav P. SHARMA
42 Director Protestant Campus Ministry .... Rev. Maggie GILLESPIE
42 Director Catholic Campus Ministry .... Rev. Timothy MARCOE
19 Dir Univ Safety & Police .... Mr. Tom PHILLIPS
92 Director University Honors Program .... Dr. Stephen KOKOSKA
96 Director of Purchasing & Operations .... Mr. Jeffrey MANDEL
08 Director Library Services .... Ms. Charlotte DROLL
91 Dir Applications Develop/Operations .... Mr. James C. GESSNER
09 Director of Institutional Research .... Ms. Karen L. SLUSSER
27 Director of Communications .... Ms. Rosalee RUSH
108 Director of Planning & Assessment .... Dr. Sheila JONES
104 Director Global & Multicultural Ed .... Dr. Doreen JOWI
102 Exec Dir BU Foundation .... Mr. Jerome DVORAK

*California University of Pennsylvania (G)

250 University Avenue, California PA 15419-1394
County: Washington FICE Identification: 003316
Unit ID: 211361
Telephone: (724) 938-4000 Carnegie Class: Master's L
FAX Number: (724) 938-4138 Calendar System: Semester
URL: www.calu.edu
Established: 1852 Annual Undergrad Tuition & Fees (In-State): $9,034
Enrollment: 9,483 Coed
Affiliation or Control: State IRS Status: 501(c)3
Highest Offering: Master's
Program: 2-Year Principally Bachelor's Creditable; Liberal Arts And General; Teacher Preparatory; Professional
Accreditation: M, ART, CACREP, CS, ENGT, NAIT, NRPA, NURSE, PTAA, SP, SW, TED, THEA

02 Acting President .... Ms. Geraldine JONES
05 Provost/Vice Pres Academic Affairs .... Ms. Geraldine JONES
10 Interim VP Administration & Finance .... Mr. Robert THORN
32 VP Student Development & Services .... Dr. Lenora ANGELONE
30 VP for University Development .... Mr. Ron HUIATT
13 VP Information Technology .... Dr. Charles MANCE
04 Special Assistant to the President ... Mr. Norman G. HASBROUCK
09 Director Institutional Research .... Mr. Richard L. KLINE
88 Executive Dir Special Initiatives .... Mr. Timothy M. BUCHANAN
58 Interim Dean of Graduate Studies .... Dr. John CENCICH
20 Associate Provost .... Dr. Bruce BARNHART
20 Interim Associate Provost .... Dr. Stanley KOMACEK
20 Assoc Provost/Student Retent Ofcr .... Dr. Harry M. LANGLEY
30 Assoc Vice Pres for Development .... Mr. Howard GOLDSTEIN
30 Assoc Vice Pres for Development .... Mr. Mitch KOZIKOWSKI
56 Exec Director Southpointe Center .... Ms. Ellen NESSER
72 Dean of Science/Technology .... Dr. Leonard A. COLELLI
49 Interim Dean of Liberal Arts .... Dr. Mohamed YAMBA
53 Act Dean Col Education/Human Svcs .... Dr. Kevin A. KOURY
62 Dean of Library Services .... Mr. Douglas HOOVER
07 Dean of Admissions .... Dr. William A. EDMONDS
37 Director of Financial Aid .... Mrs. Jill FERNANDES
37 Sr Assoc Director of Financial Aid .... Mr. Jeff DERUBBO
06 Registrar .... Ms. Heidi WILLIAMS
36 Director of Career Services .... Ms. Rhonda GIFFORD
92 Director Honors Program .... Dr. Donald S. LAWSON
29 Director of Alumni Relations .... Ms. Amy LOMBARD
88 Director of University Exhibitions .... Mr. Walter P. CZEKAJ
44 Director of Planned Giving .... Mr. Gordon CORE
38 Assoc VP Student Development & Svcs .... Dr. Timothy SUSICK
14 Computer Systems Manager .... Ms. Rebecca NICHOLS

39 Director of Housing ... Mr. Shawn URBINE
94 Director Women's Studies ... Dr. Marta MCCLINTOCK
85 International Student Advisor ... Mr. John WATKINS
41 Athletic Director ... Dr. Tom PUCCI
88 Assoc VP of Athletic Development ... Mr. Frank BAUER
15 Interim Director of Personnel ... Ms. Pamela MURPHY
22 Special Assistant to President EEEO ... Dr. Lisa MCBRIDE
19 Chief of Police ... Mr. Robert F. DOWNEY
18 Director of Physical Plant ... Mr. Michael PEPLINSKI
26 Director of Communications & PR ... Mrs. Christine KINDL
27 Director of Publications ... Mr. Greg SOFRANKO
40 Book Store Manager ... Mr. David ALBERTS
96 Director of Purchasing ... Ms. Judith LAUGHLIN
26 Interim Vice Pres Marketing ... Mr. Craig S. BUTZINE

*Cheyney University of Pennsylvania (A)

Cheyney and Creek Roads, Cheyney PA 19319-0200
County: Delaware FICE Identification: 003317
Unit ID: 211608
Telephone: (610) 399-2000 Carnegie Class: Master's S
FAX Number: (610) 399-2415 Calendar System: Semester
URL: www.cheyney.edu
Established: 1837 Annual Undergrad Tuition & Fees (In-State): $8,404
Enrollment: 1,200 Coed
Affiliation or Control: State IRS Status: 501(c)3
Highest Offering: Master's
Program: Liberal Arts And General; Teacher Preparatory
Accreditation: M

02 President ... Dr. Michelle R. HOWARD-VITAL
03 Chief of Staff/Deputy to President ... Ms. Sheilah VANCE, ESQ.
05 Provost/VP Academic Affairs ... Dr. Ivan BANKS
10 Vice Pres Finance & Administration ... Vacant
30 Vice President Inst Advancement ... Ms. Nancy JONES
32 VP Student Affairs/Student Life ... Dr. Susanne D. PHILLIPS
08 Dean Library Services ... Dr. Lut NERO
49 Dean of Faculty & Academic Schools ... Dr. Donna PARKER
38 Chairperson,Guidance&Counseling ... Ms. Jolly RAMAKRISHNAN
06 Registrar ... Ms. Brenda SHIELDS
37 Director Financial Aid ... Vacant
13 Director of Information Technology ... Mr. Sheng YAO
07 Director of Enrollment Management ... Dr. Eric HILTON
09 Director Institutional Research ... Mr. Sesime ADANU, JR.
15 Director Human Resources ... Ms. Jo-Anne HARRIS
18 Deputy Dir Facilities Management ... Mr. Carl M. WILLIAMS
19 Director Public Safety ... Mr. Lawrence RICHARDS
36 Director Career Services ... Ms. Ruth BRICE
41 Athletic Director ... Mr. Ruffin BELL
17 College Physician ... Dr. Pamela HADLEY
43 University Legal Counsel ... Ms. Jacqualine BARNETT
35 Director Student Affairs ... Ms. Sharon THORN
21 Dir Business Support Service ... Ms. Monique BAYLOR
25 Contract Compliance Officer ... Mr. Michael FLANAGAN
22 Social Equity ... Vacant
29 Director Alumni Relations ... Mr. Gregory BENJAMIN
39 Mg HousingOp&Auxiliary Services ... Ms. Elizabeth BURTON
103 Dir Economic/Workforce Devel ... Ms. Sharon CANNON
24 Director Telecommunications ... Mr. Phil PAGLIARO

*Clarion University of Pennsylvania (B)

840 Wood Street, Clarion PA 16214-1232
County: Clarion FICE Identification: 003318
Unit ID: 211644
Telephone: (814) 393-2000 Carnegie Class: Master's L
FAX Number: (814) 393-1826 Calendar System: Semester
URL: www.clarion.edu
Established: 1867 Annual Undergrad Tuition & Fees (In-State): $9,269
Enrollment: 6,991 Coed
Affiliation or Control: State IRS Status: 501(c)3
Highest Offering: Master's
Program: 2-Year Principally Bachelor's Creditable; Liberal Arts And General; Teacher Preparatory; Professional
Accreditation: M, ART, BUS, LIB, MUS, NUR, SP, TED

02 President ... Dr. Karen M. WHITNEY
05 Provost/Academic Vice President ... Dr. Ronald NOWACZYK
32 Vice Pres Student & University Affs ... Mr. Harry E. TRIPP
10 Vice Pres Finance/Administration ... Mr. Paul BYLASKA
20 Associate Provost ... Dr. Susan C. TURELL
102 Chief Exec Officer Foundation ... Mr. Michael R. KEEFER
30 Director of Development ... Mr. John CATONE
21 Assoc VP for Finance/Administration ... Mr. Timothy P. FOGARTY
22 Asst to President for Social Equity ... Dr. Jocelind E. GANT
12 Executive Dean Venango College ... Dr. Christopher M. REBER
84 Dean of Enrollment Management ... Mr. William D. BAILEY
08 Dean of Libraries ... Dr. Terry S. LATOUR
49 Dean of Arts & Sciences ... Dr. Rachelle P. PRIOLEAU
50 Dean of Business Administration ... Dr. James G. PESEK
66 Director Nursing & Allied Health ... Dr. Sharon FALKENSTERN
58 Associate VP for Graduate Studies ... Dr. Arthur J. ACTON
09 Int Director Institutional Research ... Ms. Rose M. LOGUE
06 Registrar ... Ms. Lisa L. HEPLER
21 Director of Budgets ... Vacant
14 Assoc VP for Information Technology ... Mr. Samuel T. PULEIO
46 Director Faculty Research ... Dr. Brenda S. DEDE
26 Dir of Marketing & Communications ... Mr. David LOVE
37 Director of Financial Aid ... Mr. Kenneth E. GRUGEL
18 Director of Facilities Mgmt & Plng ... Mr. Richard TAYLOR
88 Exec Dir Programming & Devel Ctr ... Ms. Carol A. ROTH
29 Director of Alumni Relations ... Ms. Laura C. KING
36 Int Director Career Services ... Ms. Diana BRUSH
39 Director of Residence Life ... Ms. Michelle L. KEALEY
19 Director of Public Safety ... Ms. Glen L. REID
41 Athletic Director ... Mr. David J. KATIS
96 Director of Purchasing ... Mr. Rein A. POLD

*Clarion University-Venango Campus (C)

1801 W First Street, Oil City PA 16301-3297
County: Venango FICE Identification: 003319
Unit ID: 211662
Telephone: (814) 676-6591 Carnegie Class: Not Classified
FAX Number: (814) 676-1348 Calendar System: Semester
URL: www.clarion.edu/venango
Established: 1961 Annual Undergrad Tuition & Fees (In-State): $8,820
Enrollment: 1,036 Coed
Affiliation or Control: State IRS Status: 501(c)3
Highest Offering: Master's
Program: Liberal Arts And General
Accreditation: &M, ADNUR, NAIT, NUR

02 Executive Dean ... Dr. Christopher M. REBER
32 Director of Student Affairs ... Ms. Emily AUBELE
26 Dir of Marketing & Univ Relations ... Ms. Hope LINEMAN
10 Director of Finance/Administration ... Ms. Debra SOBINA
07 Coord Admissions/Financial Aid ... Mr. LaTrobe BARNITZ
04 Assistant to the Executive Dean ... Ms. Kay E. ENSLE

*East Stroudsburg University of Pennsylvania (D)

200 Prospect Street, East Stroudsburg PA 18301-2999
County: Monroe FICE Identification: 003320
Unit ID: 212115
Telephone: (570) 422-3211 Carnegie Class: Master's L
FAX Number: (570) 422-3777 Calendar System: Semester
URL: www.esu.edu
Established: 1893 Annual Undergrad Tuition & Fees (In-State): $8,699
Enrollment: 7,353 Coed
Affiliation or Control: State IRS Status: 501(c)3
Highest Offering: Master's
Program: Liberal Arts And General; Teacher Preparatory; Professional
Accreditation: M, CS, EXSC, NRPA, NUR, PH, SP, TED

02 President ... Dr. Marcia G. WELSH
05 Provost ... Dr. Van A. REIDHEAD
32 Vice President Student Affairs ... Dr. Doreen TOBIN
10 Vice Pres Finance & Administration ... Mr. Richard A. STANESKI
46 Vice Pres Econ Dev & Research Supp ... Ms. Mary Frances POSTUPACK
102 President & CEO ESU Foundation ... Mr. Frank FALSO
84 Vice Pres Enrollment Management ... Dr. Victoria SANDERS
58 Vice Provost & Graduate Dean ... Dr. Marilyn WELLS
49 Dean of Arts & Sciences ... Dr. Peter HAWKES
68 Dean of Health Sciences ... Dr. Mark KILKER
53 Dean of Education ... Dr. Pamela KRAMER-ERTEL
50 Dean of Business and Management ... Dr. Alla WILSON
08 Dean of Library & Univ Collections ... Dr. Edward OWUSU-ANSAH
20 Associate Provost ... Dr. Yun KIM
35 Asst Vice President Student Affairs ... Mr. Warren ANDERSON
100 Interim Chief of Staff ... Mr. Miguel BARBOSA
88 Asst Vice Pres Instruct Supp & Outr ... Mr. Michael SOUTHWELL
07 Director of Admissions ... Mr. Jeffrey JONES
06 Registrar/Dir Enrollment Services ... Ms. Kizzy MORRIS
37 Assoc Dir Enroll Svcs/Financial Aid ... Ms. Phyllis SWINSON
36 Director of Career Services ... Vacant
38 Director Counseling Center ... Dr. John A. ABBRUZZESE
41 Director Intercollegiate Athletics ... Dr. Thomas GIOGLIO
39 Director of Residence Life ... Mr. Robert M. MOSES
88 Dir of Student Activity Association ... Mr. Fredric A. MOSES
21 Controller ... Ms. Donna R. BULZONI
14 Director of Computing Services ... Mr. Robert D'AVERSA
15 Director of Human Resources ... Ms. Teresa FRITSCHE
18 Director Facilities Management ... Mr. Syed S. ZAIDI
96 Director of Procurement/Contracting ... Mr. Michael CRAPP
29 Director of Alumni Relations ... Mr. Mike SARAKA
26 Int Director University Relations ... Dr. Brenda FRIDAY
108 Dir Institutional/Academic Effect ... Ms. Joann STRYKER

*Edinboro University of Pennsylvania (E)

219 Meadville Street, Edinboro PA 16444-0001
County: Erie FICE Identification: 003321
Unit ID: 212160
Telephone: (814) 732-2000 Carnegie Class: Master's L
FAX Number: (814) 732-2880 Calendar System: Semester
URL: www.edinboro.edu
Established: 1857 Annual Undergrad Tuition & Fees (In-State): $8,577
Enrollment: 8,262 Coed
Affiliation or Control: State IRS Status: 501(c)3
Highest Offering: Beyond Master's But Less Than Doctorate
Program: Occupational; 2-Year Principally Bachelor's Creditable; Liberal Arts And General; Teacher Preparatory; Professional
Accreditation: M, ART, ACBSP, CACREP, CORE, CS, MUS, NUR, NURSE, SP, SW, TED

02 President ... Dr. Julie E. WOLLMAN
05 Provost/VP Academic Affairs ... Dr. Philip E. GINNETTI
10 Vice Pres Finance & Administration ... Mr. Gordon J. HERBST
32 Vice President for Student Affairs ... Dr. Kahan SABLO
30 Vice Pres University Advancement ... Ms. Tina MENGINE
04 Special Assistant to the President ... Mr. Sean BLILEY
20 Sr Exec Associate to the Provost ... Ms. Judy KUBEJA
14 Assoc VP Tech & Communications ... Dr. Andrew C. LAWLOR
15 Assoc VP Human Res/Fac Rels ... Mr. Sid BOOKER
08 Assoc Vice President Univ Libraries ... Dr. Donald H. DILMORE
18 Director of Facilities Management ... Mr. James MILLER
27 Director of Comm and Marketing ... Mr. Matthew CUMMINGS
37 Asst VP Student Financial Aid ... Ms. Dorothy H. BODY
07 Director of Undergrad Admissions ... Mr. Craig GROOMS
92 Director Honors Program ... Dr. Jean JONES
22 Dir of Social Equity/Ombudsperson ... Ms. Valerie O. HAYES
49 Dean College of Arts and Sciences ... Dr. Terry L. SMITH
58 Dean of Graduate Studies/Research ... Dr. Alan BIEL
53 Dean School of Education ... Dr. Nomsa GELETA
50 Dean School of Business ... Dr. Michael HANNAN
06 Registrar ... Mr. Tim W. PILEWSKI
36 Dir Ctr for Career Develop ... Dr. Jody GALLAGHER
29 Director Alumni Relations ... Mr. Jon PULICE
41 Athletic Director ... Mr. Bruce BAUMGARTNER
38 Dir Counseling/Psychological Svcs ... Dr. Michael BUCELL
19 Chief University Police ... Mr. Clark PETERS
39 Dir Residence Life & Orientation ... Ms. Kim KENNEDY
12 Dir & Outreach Coord EUP in Erie ... Ms. Janet L. BOWKER
23 Medical Dir Student Health Services ... Dr. Ronald C. MARTIN
106 Manager of Online Programs ... Dr. James BOULDER
40 Director Auxiliary Operations ... Mr. Paul B. KIGHTLINGER
85 Director Intl Student Svcs ... Ms. Linda KIGHTLINGER
25 Director Sponsored Programs ... Ms. Rene HEARNS
88 Dir Networks & Telecommunications ... Ms. Karen MURDZAK
90 Dir Desktop Systems/Learning Tech ... Mr. Dennis J. BRADLEY
13 Director Enterprise Systems ... Ms. Sallie A. TERPACK
96 Director Purchasing & Contract ... Ms. Darla SPAID
102 Director of Major Gifts ... Ms. Julie A. CHACONA
44 Dir of Annual Fund & Stewardship ... Ms. Marilyn GOELLNER
88 Director of Budget and Payroll ... Ms. Theresa VILLELLA
21 Controller ... Mr. Wayne T. OCHS
35 Director of Campus Life ... Ms. Michelle BARBICH
17 Nurse Supervisor ... Ms. Darla ELDER
24 Learning Technology Svcs Manager ... Mr. Randall MCCASLIN
88 Coordinator Non-Credit Programs ... Ms. Beth ZEWE

*Indiana University of Pennsylvania (F)

Indiana PA 15705-0001
County: Indiana FICE Identification: 003277
Unit ID: 213020
Telephone: (724) 357-2100 Carnegie Class: DRU
FAX Number: (724) 357-6213 Calendar System: Semester
URL: www.iup.edu
Established: 1875 Annual Undergrad Tuition & Fees (In-State): $8,672
Enrollment: 15,132 Coed
Affiliation or Control: State IRS Status: 501(c)3
Highest Offering: Doctorate
Program: Liberal Arts And General; Teacher Preparatory; Professional
Accreditation: M, ACFEI, ART, BUS, CACREP, CLPSY, CS, DIETD, DIETI, ENGR, EXSC, MUS, NURSE, PLNG, SP, TED, THEA

02 President ... Dr. Michael DRISCOLL
05 Provost & VP Academic Affairs ... Dr. Gerald W. INTEMANN
11 Vice Pres Administration/Finance ... Dr. Cornelius WOOTEN
32 Vice President Student Affairs ... Dr. Rhonda H. LUCKEY
30 Vice Pres University Advancement ... Mr. William SPEIDEL
20 Assoc VP Academic Administration ... Dr. John N. KILMARX
58 Dean Grad School and Research ... Dr. Timothy P. MACK
16 Associate VP Human Resources ... Vacant
79 Dean College Human Social Science ... Dr. Yaw A. ASAMOAH
50 Dean Eberly Col Bus/Inform Tech ... Dr. Robert C. CAMP
20 Assoc Provost for Acad Pgms & Plng ... Dr. Inno ONWUEME
53 Interim Dean College Educ/Educ Tech ... Dr. Edward NARDI
81 Dean Col Natural Science & Math ... Dr. Deanne SNAVELY
57 Dean College of Fine Arts ... Mr. Michael J. HOOD
66 Int Dean Col Health & Human Svcs ... Dr. Mary SWINKLER
84 Assoc VP Enrollment Management ... Mr. James BEGANY
08 Dean of Libraries ... Dr. Luis GONZALEZ
35 Dean of Students ... Vacant
06 Registrar ... Mr. Robert SIMON
38 Counseling Center ... Dr. Patti SHAFFER
27 Chief Information Officer ... Mr. Bill BALINT
04 Inst Research Planning & Assessment ... Mrs. Barbe MOORE
14 Exec Dir of Technology Services Ctr ... Mr. Todd CUNNINGHAM
37 Asst VP Enrollment/Dir of Fin Aid ... Ms. Patricia MCCARTHY
28 Dir Social Equity/Civic Engagement ... Vacant
19 Director University Safety/Police ... Mr. Sam CLUTTER
36 Director of Career Services ... Mr. Mark E. ANTHONY
29 Exec Director Alumni Association ... Mrs. Mary Jo LYTTLE
44 Director Annual Giving ... Ms. Emily SMELTZ
85 Director International Affairs ... Ms. Michele PETRUCCI
46 Assistant Dean for Research ... Dr. Hilliary CREELY
39 Director Housing/Residence Life ... Mr. Michael LEMASTERS
40 Bookstore Director ... Mr. Tim SHARBAUGH
41 Director Athletics ... Dr. Francis CONDINO
23 Director Health Services ... Mr. Scott GIBSON
12 Dean Northpointe Campus ... Mr. Richard MUTH
12 Dean Punxsutawney Campus ... Dr. Terry APPOLONIA
43 Staff Attorney ... Ms. Jacqueline R. MORROW
26 Director of Public Relations ... Ms. Michelle SHAFFER FRYLING
96 Director of Purchasing ... Mr. Robert BOWSER
10 Assoc Vice President for Finance ... Mrs. Susanna C. SINK
04 Exec Assistant to the President ... Ms. Robin GORMAN

*Kutztown University of Pennsylvania (A)

15200 Kutztown Road, Kutztown PA 19530-0730
County: Berks FICE Identification: 003322
Unit ID: 213349
Telephone: (610) 683-4000 Carnegie Class: Master's L
FAX Number: (610) 683-4693 Calendar System: Semester
URL: www.kutztown.edu
Established: 1866 Annual Undergrad Tuition & Fees (In-State): $8,596
Enrollment: 9,877 Coed
Affiliation or Control: State IRS Status: 501(c)3
Highest Offering: Master's
Program: Liberal Arts And General; Teacher Preparatory; Professional
Accreditation: M, ART, MUS, NUR, SW, TED

02 President .... Dr. F. Javier CEVALLOS
05 Vice Pres Academic & Stdnt Affairs .... Dr. Carlos VARGAS-ABURTO
10 VP Administration & Finance .... Mr. Gerald L. SILBERMAN
100 Chief of Staff to the President .... Ms. Elsa G. COLLINS
102 Executive Director KU Foundation .... Mr. Jason KETTER
30 Assoc Vice Pres Univ Advancement .... Mr. John C. GREEN
22 Assoc Vice Pres Equity & Compliance .... Mr. Jesus PENA
20 Vice Provost Academic Affairs .... Dr. Carole WELLS
21 Asst Vice Pres Admin & Finance .... Mr. Kenneth LONG
32 Assoc Vice Provost & Dean Students .... Mr. Robert WATROUS
27 Asst Vice Provost/Info Technology .... Mr. Mitchell FREED
15 Executive Director Human Resources .... Ms. Sharon M. PICUS
18 Asst Vice President for Facilities .... Mr. Robert J. GRIMM
84 Assistant Provost Enrollment Svcs .... Vacant
88 Dean College Visual/Performing Arts .... Dr. William J. MOWDER
49 Dean College Liberal Arts/Sci .... Dr. Anne E. ZAYAITZ
50 Dean College of Business .... Dr. William DEMPSEY
53 Dean College Education .... Dr. Darrell GARBER
62 Dean Library Services .... Dr. Barbara DARDEN
88 Dean for Students/Campus Life .... Mr. Robert T. WATROUS
26 Director of University Relations .... Mr. Matthew SANTOS
09 Institutional Research Manager .... Ms. Natalie SNOW
06 Registrar .... Ms. Michelle HUGHES
37 Director of Financial Aid .... Mr. Bernard L. MCCREE
39 Director Housing/Residential Svcs .... Mr. Kent R. DAHLQUIST
41 Director of Athletics .... Mr. Gregory BAMBERGER
38 Director Counseling & Psych Svcs .... Dr. Bruce SHARKIN
96 Director of Purchasing .... Mr. Joseph COCO
07 Director of Admissions .... Ms. Nancy WUNDERLY
19 Acting Chief of Police .... Mr. John DILLON
36 Director Career/Community Services .... Ms. Kerri GARDI
29 Director Alumni Engagement .... Mr. Alex OGEKA

*Lock Haven University (B)

401 N Fairview Street, Lock Haven PA 17745-2390
County: Clinton FICE Identification: 003323
Unit ID: 213613
Telephone: (570) 484-2001 Carnegie Class: Master's S
FAX Number: (570) 484-2432 Calendar System: Semester
URL: www.lhup.edu
Established: 1870 Annual Undergrad Tuition & Fees (In-State): $8,238
Enrollment: 5,366 Coed
Affiliation or Control: State IRS Status: 170(c)1
Highest Offering: Master's
Program: Liberal Arts And General; Teacher Preparatory
Accreditation: M, ADNUR, ARCPA, NRPA, SW, TED

02 President .... Dr. Michael FIORENTINO, JR.
05 Provost/Vice Pres Academic Affs .... Dr. Donna WILSON
10 Vice Pres Finance/Admin/Technology .... Mr. William HANELLY
32 Vice President for Student Affairs .... Dr. Linda D. KOCH
45 Asst to Pres for Planning Assess .... Vacant
49 Int Dean Arts & Sciences .... Dr. Zakir HOSSAIN
53 Int Dean Education & Human Services .... Dr. Jane PENMAN
12 Int Dean Clearfield Branch Campus .... Dr. Marianne HAZEL
85 Dean of International Studies .... Vacant
09 Director Institutional Research .... Mr. Mike ABPLANALP
15 Director of Human Resources .... Ms. Deana HILL
07 Director of Admissions .... Ms. Robin ROCKEY
06 Registrar .... Mrs. Jill MITCHLEY
28 Director of Diversity .... Mr. Albert W. JONES
37 Director of Financial Aid .... Ms. Heidi HUNTER-GOLDSWORTHY
36 Director of Career Services .... Ms. Joan C. WELKER
26 Director Marketing & Communications .... Vacant
19 Director of Public Safety .... Mr. Paul ALTIERI
18 Director of Facilities .... Mr. Keith ROUSH
41 Int Director of Athletics .... Mr. Peter CAMPBELL
66 Director of Nursing Program .... Ms. Kimberly OWENS
38 Director of Counseling .... Dr. Dan E. TESS
90 Dir Computing/Instructional Tech .... Mr. Donald W. PATTERSON
17 Director of Physician Asst Program .... Mr. Walt EISENHAUER
92 Director Honors Program .... Dr. Jacqueline WHITLING
94 Director Women's Studies .... Dr. Kimberly ALEXANDER
93 Director Minority Students .... Mr. Kenneth L. HALL
40 Manager University Bookstore .... Mr. James KOWNACKI
29 Director Alumni Relations .... Ms. Tammy RICH

*Mansfield University of Pennsylvania (C)

Academy Street, Mansfield PA 16933-1697
County: Tioga FICE Identification: 003324
Unit ID: 213783
Telephone: (570) 662-4000 Carnegie Class: Master's M
FAX Number: (570) 662-4995 Calendar System: Semester
URL: www.mansfield.edu
Established: 1857 Annual Undergrad Tuition & Fees (In-State): $8,926
Enrollment: 3,300 Coed
Affiliation or Control: State IRS Status: 501(c)3
Highest Offering: Master's
Program: Liberal Arts And General; Teacher Preparatory
Accreditation: M, DIETD, MUS, NUR, RAD, SW, TED

02 Interim President .... Dr. Alan J. GOLDEN
05 Provost/Vice Pres Academic Affairs .... Dr. Peter KELLER
10 Vice Pres Finance/Administration .... Mr. Daniel DOBELL
30 Vice Pres for Univ Advancement .... Vacant
32 Vice President of Student Affairs .... Dr. James PARKER
39 Assoc Vice Pres Residence Life .... Mr. Chuck COLBY
49 Dean of Arts & Sciences .... Mr. James BROWN
53 Dean of Education .... Ms. Joy BURKE
15 Exec Dir Org Dev & Employee Rels .... Ms. Dia CARLETON
08 Director Library/Info Resource Svcs .... Dr. Scott L. DIMARCO
13 Director of Information Technology .... Ms. Connie L. BECKMAN
84 Exec Director Enrollment Management .... Mr. Brian D. BARDEN
26 Director Public Rels/Publications .... Mr. Dennis R. MILLER
37 Director of Financial Aid .... Ms. Barbara SCHMITT
88 Dir Center for Lifelong Learning .... Ms. Susan W. SWEET
19 Director University Police & Safety .... Ms. Christine SHEGAN
41 Director of Athletics .... Mr. Roger N. MAISNER
85 Director of Multicultural Affairs .... Ms. Annie L. COOPER
25 Director of Grants Development .... Ms. Anne LOUDENSLAGER
09 Dir Institutional Rsrch/Assess Data .... Dr. John COSGROVE
29 Director of Alumni Relations .... Ms. Denise BERG
96 Director of Purchasing .... Mr. Tekeste B. ABRAHAM
18 Director of Facilities .... Mr. Benjamin JONES
06 Registrar .... Ms. Lori CASS
38 Director of Counseling Center .... Mr. William S. CHABALA
90 Coord Academic Computing Support .... Ms. Tamela BASTION

*Millersville University of Pennsylvania (D)

PO Box 1002, Millersville PA 17551-0302
County: Lancaster FICE Identification: 003325
Unit ID: 214041
Telephone: (717) 872-3024 Carnegie Class: Master's L
FAX Number: (717) 872-3968 Calendar System: 4/1/4
URL: www.millersville.edu
Established: 1855 Annual Undergrad Tuition & Fees (In-State): $8,600
Enrollment: 8,725 Coed
Affiliation or Control: State IRS Status: 501(c)3
Highest Offering: Master's
Program: Liberal Arts And General; Teacher Preparatory; Professional
Accreditation: M, ACBSP, ART, CS, ENGR, MUS, NAIT, NUR, SW, TED

02 President .... Dr. Francine G. MCNAIRY
05 Vice Pres Academic Affs/Provost .... Dr. Vilas A. PRABHU
10 Vice Pres Finance & Administration .... Mr. Roger BRUSZEWSKI
32 Vice President for Student Affairs .... Dr. Aminta H. BREAUX
30 Vice Pres University Advancement .... Mr. Gerald C. ECKERT
13 Vice Pres Information Resources .... Mr. Robert (Chip) GERMAN, JR.
22 Asst to Pres Soc Equity/Div .... Mr. Hiram G. MARTINEZ
20 Associate Provost Academic Admin .... Dr. Jeffrey R. ADAMS
20 Asst Vice President Academic Svc .... Dr. Minor (Will) REDMOND
45 Asst VP Plng Assessment/Analysis .... Dr. Lisa R. SHIBLEY
21 Assoc Vice Pres Finance/ Admin .... Mr. Kenneth E. DEARSTYNE, JR.
35 Assoc VP Student Affairs .... Ms. Michelle PEREZ
15 Associate Vice Pres Human Resources .... Mr. Louis P. DESOL
26 Asst Vice Pres for Advancement .... Ms. Amy H. DMITZAK
37 Asst VP Stdnt Affs/Dir Fin Aid .... Mr. Dwight G. HORSEY
39 Asst VP Stdnt Affs/Dir Housing .... Mr. Thomas J. RICHARDSON
25 Asst Vice President Development .... Vacant
18 Asst VP Facilities .... Mr. Thomas A. WALTZ, JR.
53 Dean of Education .... Dr. Jane S. BRAY
79 Int Dean Humanities/Social Sciences .... Dr. Diane UMBLE
81 Dean of Science & Mathematics .... Dr. Robert T. SMITH
58 Dean Graduate Studies .... Dr. Victor DESANTIS
84 Assoc Provost Enrollment Management .... Dr. Douglas ZANDER
06 Registrar .... Ms. Candace DEEN
36 Director Career Services .... Ms. Margo J. SASSAMAN
18 Dir Capital Const/Contract/Design .... Vacant
38 Director Counseling/Human Devel .... Dr. Kelsey K. BACKELS
19 Chief of University Police .... Mr. Peter J. ANDERS
23 Director of Univ Health Service .... Dr. Susan F. NORTHWALL
41 Dir of Intercollegiate Athletics .... Ms. Peg KAUFFMAN
40 Manager University Bookstore .... Ms. Audrey HERR
42 Minister-Campus .... Rev. Darrell WOOMER
42 Minister-Catholic .... Fr. Pang TCHEOU
44 Director of Planned Giving .... Mr. Francis SCHODOWSKI
29 Exec Dir for Alumni/Cmty Rels .... Mr. Steven A. DIGUISEPPE
44 Asst Director Major Gifts .... Ms. Alice MCMURRY
44 Asst Dir Advancement Services .... Mr. Derek M. HOFFMAN
09 Director Institutional Research .... Mr. Joseph E. REVELT
30 Director of Development .... Ms. Martha P. MACADAM
30 Dir of Major Gifts .... Ms. Linda ROUSH
102 Dir of Foundation & Govt Support .... Mr. Rene MUNOZ
96 Director of Purchasing .... Mr. David C. ERRICKSON
18 Interim Dir of Maint Operations .... Mr. Frederick G. EDDINGER
100 Executive Deputy/Chief of Staff .... Dr. James MCCOLLUM
12 Dir The Ware Center .... Mr. Harvey OWEN
12 Director The Winter Center .... Ms. Laura KENDALL
04 Assistant to the President .... Vacant

*Shippensburg University of Pennsylvania (E)

1871 Old Main Drive, Shippensburg PA 17257-2200
County: Cumberland FICE Identification: 003326
Unit ID: 216010
Telephone: (717) 477-7447 Carnegie Class: Master's L
FAX Number: (717) 477-1273 Calendar System: Semester
URL: www.ship.edu
Established: 1871 Annual Undergrad Tuition & Fees (In-State): $8,856
Enrollment: 8,183 Coed
Affiliation or Control: State IRS Status: 501(c)3
Highest Offering: Master's
Program: Liberal Arts And General; Teacher Preparatory; Professional; Fine Arts Emphasis
Accreditation: M, BUS, CACREP, CS, SW, TED

02 President .... Dr. William N. RUUD
03 Exec VP Ext & University Relations .... Dr. G. F. (Jody) HARPSTER
05 Provost & Sr VP Academic Affairs .... Dr. Barbara G. LYMAN
10 Vice Pres Administration/Finance .... Dr. Jan (Denny) TERRELL
102 Pres Shippensburg Univ Foundation .... Mr. John CLINTON
32 Vice Pres for Student Affairs .... Dr. Roger L. SERR
13 Vice Pres Information Tech/Services .... Dr. Rick RUTH
20 Associate Provost .... Dr. Tracy A. SCHOOLCRAFT
20 Assoc Provost/Dean of Acad Outreach .... Dr. Christine SAX
84 Dean of Admiss/Dir of Enroll Mgmt .... Dr. Thomas SPEAKMAN
35 Dean of Students .... Dr. David L. LOVETT
06 Registrar .... Ms. Cathy J. SPRENGER
36 Director Career Development .... Vacant
37 Director Financial Aid .... Dr. Sandra TARBOX
29 Exec Dir University/AlumniRelations .... Dr. Tim EBERSOLE
27 Director Publications & Advertising .... Ms. Laura LUDLAM
88 Exec Dir Univ Communications/Mrktg .... Dr. Peter GIGLIOTTI
08 Dean Library & Multi-Media Services .... Vacant
22 Director Social Equity .... Dr. Melodye WEHRUNG
88 Director Womens Center .... Ms. Stephanie ERDICE
09 Director Inst Research & Planning .... Mr. Mark PILGRIM
25 Dir Spons Pgm/Inst Public Svc .... Mr. Christopher WONDERS
15 Director Human Resources .... Dr. David TOPPER
38 Director Counseling Services .... Dr. Philip W. HENRY
88 Director of Conferences .... Mr. Randy HAMMOND
53 Dean College Education & Human Svcs .... Dr. James R. JOHNSON
49 Dean College Arts & Science .... Dr. James MIKE
50 Dean College of Business .... Dr. John KOOTI
88 Dean Academic Engagement & Student .... Dr. Sarah STOKELY
18 Chief Facilities/Physical Plant .... Mr. Lance BRYSON
96 Director of Purchasing/Contracting .... Ms. Deborah MARTIN
19 Director Public Safety .... Ms. Cytha D. GRISSOM
41 Athletic Director .... Mr. Jeff A. MICHAELS
04 Exec Asst to the President .... Ms. Robin MAUN

*Slippery Rock University of Pennsylvania (F)

1 Morrow Way, Slippery Rock PA 16057-1326
County: Butler FICE Identification: 003327
Unit ID: 216038
Telephone: (724) 738-9000 Carnegie Class: Master's L
FAX Number: (724) 738-2169 Calendar System: Semester
URL: www.sru.edu
Established: 1889 Annual Undergrad Tuition & Fees (In-State): $8,777
Enrollment: 8,712 Coed
Affiliation or Control: State IRS Status: 501(c)3
Highest Offering: Doctorate
Program: Liberal Arts And General; Teacher Preparatory; Professional
Accreditation: M, ART, ACBSP, CACREP, CS, DANCE, EXSC, MUS, NRPA, NUR, PTA, SW, TED, THEA

02 President .... Dr. Cheryl NORTON
05 Provost/Vice Pres Academic Affairs .... Dr. William F. WILLIAMS
10 Vice Pres Finance/Administration .... Dr. Charles T. CURRY
32 Vice President Student Life .... Dr. Constance L. FOLEY
30 Vice President for Univ Advancement .... Ms. Barbara A. ENDER
21 Asst Vice Pres for Finance .... Ms. Molly MERCER
18 Asst Vice Pres for Facilities .... Mr. Herbert F. CARLSON
35 Asst Vice Pres for Student Services .... Dr. John S. BONANDO
38 Asst Vice Pres for Student Devel .... Dr. Paula OLIVERO
15 Asst Vice Pres Human Resources .... Ms. Lynne M. MOTYL
28 Asst VP Diversity & Equal Oppty .... Ms. Holly M. MCCOY
04 Assistant to the President .... Ms. Tina L. MOSER
13 Assoc Provost Info & Admin Tech .... Mr. Simeon ANANOU
84 Assoc Provost Enrollment Services .... Dr. Amanda A. YALE
30 Exec Director Univ Advancement .... Dr. Edward R. BUCHA
26 Exec Director Public Relations .... Ms. Rita E. ABENT
37 Director Student Financial Aid .... Ms. Patricia A. HLADIO
19 Director Public Safety .... Mr. William J. RUDLOFF
19 Director University Police .... Mr. Michael SIMMONS
09 Assoc Prov Inst Rsrch/Acad Fin Mgmt .... Ms. Carrie J. BIRCKBICHLER
08 Director of Library Services .... Mr. Philip J. TRAMDACK
14 Director Computer Services .... Vacant
06 Director Acad Records/Summer School .... Mr. Eliott G. BAKER
07 Director Undergraduate Admissions .... Mr. Michael MAY
23 Director Health Services .... Ms. Kristina B. CHIPREAN
36 Associate Director Career Services .... Mr. John F. SNYDER
29 Director Alumni Affairs .... Ms. Kelly BAILEY
76 Dean Col Health Environment/Sci .... Dr. Susan E. HANNAM
07 Int Director Graduate Admissions .... Ms. Rebecca TRINCHESE
41 Athletic Director .... Mr. Paul A. LUEKEN
39 Director Housing/Residence Life .... Mr. Kevin D. CURRIE

85 Director International Services .... Ms. Pamela J. FRIGOT
25 Director Grants & Sponsored Rsrch . Ms. Nancy L. CRUIKSHANK
38 Director of Student Counseling .... Dr. Carol L. HOLLAND
93 Director of Minority Students .... Ms. Corinne J. GIBSON
96 Director of Purchasing .... Mr. Mark S. COMBINE
92 Director of Honors Program .... Dr. Bradley WILSON
57 Dean Col of Hum/Fine/Perf Arts .... Dr. Eva TSUQUIASHI-DADDESIO
50 Dean Col Business/Info/Social Scs .... Dr. Kurt SHIMMEL
53 Dean College of Education .... Dr. Keith DILS

*West Chester University of Pennsylvania (A)

University & High Street, West Chester PA 19383-0001
County: Chester — FICE Identification: 003328
Unit ID: 216764
Telephone: (610) 436-1000 — Carnegie Class: Master's L
FAX Number: (610) 436-3115 — Calendar System: Semester
URL: www.wcupa.edu
Established: 1871 — Annual Undergrad Tuition & Fees (In-State): $6,786
Enrollment: 15,100 — Coed
Affiliation or Control: State — IRS Status: 501(c)3
Highest Offering: Master's
Program: Liberal Arts And General; Teacher Preparatory; Professional
Accreditation: M, ART, BUS, CACREP, CS, DIETD, EXSC, MUS, NURSE, PH, SP, SW, TED, THEA

02 President .... Dr. Greg R. WEISENSTEIN
86 Executive Deputy/Govt Relations Ofc .... Mr. Lawrence A. DOWDY
04 Sr Assoc to the President .... Ms. Rebecca HOOK
22 Director Social Equity .... Ms. Barbara SCHNELLER
05 Vice Pres Academic Affairs/Provost .... Dr. Linda L. LAMWERS
11 Vice President Admin/Finance .... Mr. Mark P. MIXNER
13 Vice Pres Information Services .... Mr. Adel BARIMANI
30 Vice President Advancement .... Dr. Mark G. PAVLOVICH
32 VP Student Affs/Dean of Students .... Dr. Matthew M. BRICKETTO
88 AVP Planning/Academic Admin .... Mr. Vernon HARPER
64 Dean College Visual/Performing Arts .... Dr. Timothy V. BLAIR
76 Interim Dean College Health Science .... Dr. Raymond ZETTS
53 Dean College Education .... Dr. Kenneth D. WITMER
50 Assoc Provost/Dean College of BPA .... Dr. Christopher M. FIORENTINO
49 Dean College Arts/Sciences .... Dr. Lori A. VERMEULEN
20 Dean Undergrad Stds/Stdt Suppt Svcs .... Dr. Idna M. CORBETT
23 Asst Dean Stdnts/Dir Health Center .... Ms. Mary Ann HAMMOND
88 Assoc VP Sponsored Research .... Dr. Michael AYEWOH
58 Interim AVP AA/Dean Grad Studies .... Dr. Lorraine BERNOTSKY
15 Assoc Vice Pres Human Resources .... Mr. Michael T. MALOY
35 Asst Vice Pres Student Affairs .... Ms. Diane DEVESTERN
35 Asst Vice Pres Student Affairs .... Dr. Thomas J. PURCE
10 Asst VP Finance/Business Svcs .... Ms. Bernadette HINKLE
06 Asst VP Enrollment Mgmt/Registrar .... Mr. Joeseph SANTIVASCI
85 Asst VP International Programs .... Dr. David A. WRIGHT
102 Exec Director WCU Foundation .... Mr. Richard T. PRZYWARA
18 Exec Director Facilities Management .... Mr. Greg CUPRAK
18 Exec Direct Facilities Design/Const .... Ms. Dolores GIARDINA
106 Exec Director Distance Education .... Dr. Rui LI
21 Dir Accounting/Financial Reporting .... Mr. Kevin MCCADDEN
07 Director Admissions .... Ms. Marsha L. HAUG
88 Director Graduate Enrollment .... Dr. Lawrence WALSH
09 Director Institutional Research .... Ms. Lisa YANNICK
21 Bursar/Director Student Finan Svcs .... Mr. Daniel PAULETTI
88 Director Budget/Financial Planning .... Ms. Colleen BRADLEY
26 Director Public Relations/Marketing .... Ms. Pamela SHERIDAN
88 Director Publications/Printing Svcs .... Ms. Cynthia BEDNAR
31 Director Cultural/Community Affairs .... Mr. John RHEIN
08 Director Library Services .... Mr. Richard SWAIN
88 Director Teacher Education Center .... Dr. James B. PRICE
36 Director Career Devel Center .... Ms. Rebecca ROSS
88 Int Dir Academic Development Pgm .... Dr. Allan HILL
88 Dir Learning Asst/Resource .... Ms. Gerardina MARTIN
37 Director Financial Aid .... Mr. Dana C. PARKER
38 Director Counseling Center .... Dr. Julie PERONE
29 Interim Director Alumni Relations .... Ms. Nichole MORAN
41 Director Athletics .... Dr. Edward M. MATEJKOVIC
88 Director Sports Information .... Mr. James ZUHLKE
28 Director Multicultural Affairs .... Mr. Jerome HUTSON
94 Director Women's Center .... Dr. Adale SHOLOCK
19 Director Public Safety .... Mr. Michael D. BICKING
96 Director Purchasing/Contract Svcs .... Ms. Marianne PEFFALL
91 Dir Administrative Computing Systms .... Mr. Patrick LENZI
88 Dir Admin Computing Application Dev .... Ms. Chaw-ye CHANG
90 Spec Asst to VP Information Svcs .... Dr. James FABREY
88 Director Comm/Infrastructure Svcs .... Mr. Joseph SINCAVAGE
39 Director Housing Services .... Mr. Peter GALLOWAY
39 Director Residence Life .... Ms. Marion MCKINNEY
88 Dir Judicial Affairs/Student Assist .... Ms. Lynn KLINGENSMITH
88 Director Sykes Student Union .... Mr. David TIMMANN
88 Dir Pre-major Academic Advising .... Dr. Joanne CONLON
92 Director Honors College .... Dr. Kevin DEAN
40 Student Svcs Inc Bookstore Manager .... Mr. Stephen MANNELLA

Philadelphia Biblical University (B)

200 Manor Avenue, Langhorne Manor PA 19047-2990
County: Bucks — FICE Identification: 003351
Unit ID: 215114
Telephone: (215) 752-5800 — Carnegie Class: Master's S
FAX Number: (215) 702-4341 — Calendar System: Semester
URL: www.pbu.edu
Established: 1913 — Annual Undergrad Tuition & Fees: $21,705
Enrollment: 1,227 — Coed
Affiliation or Control: Independent Non-Profit — IRS Status: 501(c)3
Highest Offering: First Professional Degree
Program: Liberal Arts And General; Teacher Preparatory; Professional; Religious Emphasis
Accreditation: M, BI, IACBE, MUS, SW

01 President .... Dr. Todd J. WILLIAMS
05 Provost .... Dr. Brian G. TOEWS
11 Sr Vice Pres Finance & Admin .... Mr. Jan M. HAAS
30 Sr Vice Pres Univ Advancement .... Mr. Scott A. KEATING
15 Vice Pres Human Resources .... Ms. Mary BOYER
20 Vice Pres Educational Resources .... Dr. Timothy K. HUI
32 Vice Pres Student Life .... Mr. J. Scott CAWOOD
26 Vice Pres Marketing/Communications .... Vacant
06 Registrar .... Dr. Steven SCHLENKER
09 Associate Dir, UG Admissions .... Mr. Eric RIVERA
10 Controller .... Mr. Jeff EUBANK
18 Director Campus Services .... Mr. Robert WATSON
12 Director Wisconsin Campus .... Mr. Mark A. JALOVICK
04 Assistant to President .... Ms. Jodi L. TODD
13 Director Information Technology .... Mr. Curt D. WINTERS
37 Director Financial Aid .... Mr. Stephen CASSEL
09 Director Institutional Research .... Dr. Lynn H. WALLACE
42 Director University Ministries .... Ms. Michele MCALACK
39 Director Resident Life .... Mr. Stephen HAUSER
29 Director Alumni Relations .... Mr. Jamie GLEASON
19 Chief of Security .... Mr. Chris LLOYD
23 Director Health Services .... Ms. Alison KIKENDALL
40 Manager of Bookstore .... Mr. Charles GLOVER
38 Director Student Counseling .... Mr. Baron KING
36 Director Career Center .... Ms. Teri T. CANTANIO
21 Asst Director Business Services .... Dr. Andrew HUI
96 Purchasing Agent .... Vacant
09 Director Graduate Admissions .... Mr. Binu ABRAHAM

Philadelphia College of Osteopathic Medicine (C)

4170 City Avenue, Philadelphia PA 19131-1694
County: Philadelphia — FICE Identification: 003352
Unit ID: 215123
Telephone: (215) 871-6100 — Carnegie Class: Spec/Med
FAX Number: (215) 871-6719 — Calendar System: Semester
URL: www.pcom.edu
Established: 1899 — Annual Graduate Tuition & Fees: $42,965
Enrollment: 2,418 — Coed
Affiliation or Control: Independent Non-Profit — IRS Status: 501(c)3
Highest Offering: Doctorate; No Undergraduates
Program: Professional
Accreditation: M, ARCPA, CLPSY, OSTEO

01 President & CEO .... Dr. Matthew SCHURE
05 Provost/Senior VP Acad Affairs/Dean .... Dr. Kenneth J. VEIT
10 Vice Pres Finance/Treasurer/CFO .... Mr. Peter DOULIS
30 Vice Pres Alumni Rels/Development .... Ms. Florence D. ZELLER
58 Vice Pres Grad Pgms/Academic Plng .... Dr. Robert G. CUZZOLINO
84 Assoc Vice Pres Enrollment Mgmt .... Vacant
88 Vice Dean Clinical Education .... Dr. Richard A. PASCUCCI
76 Sr Assoc Dean Preclinical Ed/Rsrch .... Dr. Richard M. KRIEBEL
51 Assoc Dean Primary Care/Cont Educ .... Dr. Eugene MOCHAN
32 Assistant Dean of Student Affairs .... Dr. Tina WOODRUFF
88 Dir of Ungraduate Educ Clinical .... Dr. Allan MCLEOD
26 Director Marketing/Communications .... Ms. Wendy ROMANO
37 Director Student Financial Aid .... Mr. Samuel MATHENY
15 Director Human Resources .... Mr. Edward POTTS
08 Chair of Library/Exec Director .... Ms. Etheldra TEMPLETON
06 Registrar .... Ms. Deborah CASTELLANO
20 Chief Academic Officer .... Ms. Deborah A. BENVENGER
18 Chief Facilities/Plant Operations .... Mr. Frank H. WINDLE
29 Dir Alumni Relations/Development .... Ms. Pamela J. RUOFF
96 Director of Purchasing .... Ms. Natalie COOPER

Philadelphia University (D)

School House Ln & Henry Avenue, Philadelphia PA 19144-5497
County: Philadelphia — FICE Identification: 003354
Unit ID: 215099
Telephone: (215) 951-2700 — Carnegie Class: Master's L
FAX Number: (215) 951-2615 — Calendar System: Semester
URL: www.philau.edu
Established: 1884 — Annual Undergrad Tuition & Fees: $31,874
Enrollment: 3,600 — Coed
Affiliation or Control: Independent Non-Profit — IRS Status: 501(c)3
Highest Offering: Doctorate
Program: Professional
Accreditation: M, ARCPA, ART, CIDA, ENG, LSAR, MIDWF, OT, OTA

01 President .... Dr. Stephen SPINELLI, JR.
11 VP for Administration/COO .... Dr. Geoffrey CROMARTY
10 Chief Financial Officer .... Mr. James P. HARTMAN
05 Provost .... Dr. Randy SWEARER
30 VP Development & Alumni Relations .... Mr. Jesse SHAFER
26 Vice Pres Marketing/Public Rels .... Ms. Patricia M. BALDRIDGE
13 Vice President Campus Info Res .... Mr. Jeff CEPULL
84 Dean of Enrollment Management .... Ms. Christine GREB
32 Dean of Students .... Dr. Mark GOVONI
18 Asst Vice Pres for Operations .... Mr. J. Thomas BECKER
15 Asst Vice Pres Human Resources .... Ms. Katherine FLANNERY
48 Dean College of Architecture .... Vacant
81 Dean Col of Science & Health .... Dr. Matt BAKER
88 Dean College of Design Engineering .... Dr. Ron KANDER
50 Dean School of Business Admin .... Dr. Sue LEHRMAN
58 Director Sch Grad Continuing Stds .... Mr. Frank CONGDON
08 Director of Library Services .... Ms. Karen ALBERT
38 Director Advising/Counseling .... Dr. Patricia THATCHER
41 Athletic Director .... Mr. Thomas R. SHIRLEY, JR.
29 Director Alumni Relations .... Ms. Elona LAKURIQI
36 Director of Career Placement .... Ms. Patricia SHAFER
40 Director College Store .... Ms. Shirley A. LANDIS
37 Director Financial Aid .... Ms. Lisa J. COOPER
23 Director Health Services .... Vacant
06 Registrar .... Ms. Julia AGGREH
39 Director of Residence Life Educ .... Vacant
19 Director Safety & Security .... Mr. Jeffrey BAIRD
35 Director Student Activities .... Mr. Timothy J. BUTLER
09 Director of Institutional Research .... Mr. Mark PALLADINO

Pittsburgh Institute of Aeronautics (E)

5 Allegheny County Airport, West Mifflin PA 15122-2674
County: Allegheny — FICE Identification: 005310
Unit ID: 215381
Telephone: (412) 346-2100 — Carnegie Class: Assoc/PrivNFP
FAX Number: (412) 466-0513 — Calendar System: Quarter
URL: www.pia.edu
Established: 1929 — Annual Undergrad Tuition & Fees: $19,770
Enrollment: 297 — Coed
Affiliation or Control: Independent Non-Profit — IRS Status: 501(c)3
Highest Offering: Associate Degree
Program: Occupational
Accreditation: ACCSC

01 President/CFO .... Mr. John GRAHAM, III
03 Executive Vice President .... Ms. Sue MARKLE
05 Director .... Dr. James MADER
29 Director of Alumni Services .... Mr. Greg NULL
07 Supervisor of Admissions .... Mr. Steven SABOLD

Pittsburgh Institute of Mortuary Science (F)

5808 Baum Boulevard, Pittsburgh PA 15206-3706
County: Allegheny — FICE Identification: 010814
Unit ID: 215390
Telephone: (412) 362-8500 — Carnegie Class: Assoc/PrivNFP
FAX Number: (412) 362-1684 — Calendar System: Trimester
URL: www.pims.edu
Established: 1939 — Annual Undergrad Tuition & Fees: $15,600
Enrollment: 230 — Coed
Affiliation or Control: Independent Non-Profit — IRS Status: 501(c)3
Highest Offering: Associate Degree
Program: Occupational; 2-Year Principally Bachelor's Creditable
Accreditation: FUSER

01 President & CEO .... Eugene C. OGRODNIK
06 Registrar .... Karen S. ROCCO

Pittsburgh Technical Institute (G)

1111 McKee Road, Oakdale PA 15071-3205
County: Allegheny — FICE Identification: 007437
Unit ID: 215415
Telephone: (412) 809-5100 — Carnegie Class: Assoc/PrivFP
FAX Number: (412) 809-5320 — Calendar System: Quarter
URL: www.pti.edu
Established: 1946 — Annual Undergrad Tuition & Fees: $15,250
Enrollment: 1,939 — Coed
Affiliation or Control: Proprietary — IRS Status: Proprietary
Highest Offering: Associate Degree
Program: Occupational; 2-Year Principally Bachelor's Creditable; Technical Emphasis
Accreditation: M, MAC, SURGT

01 President .... Mr. Gregory DEFEO
03 Executive Vice President .... Mr. George PRY
05 Sr Vice Pres Academic Affairs .... Mr. Mark SCOTT
10 Sr Vice Pres Financial Affairs .... Mr. Terry FARRELL
07 Vice Pres Admissions .... Mr. Eric STONEKING
26 Vice President of Marketing .... Mr. Bart LEVITT
10 Vice President of Business Affairs .... Mr. Chuck CUBELIC
21 Vice President Financial Services .... Mrs. Connie FRIEDBERG
32 Vice President Student Services .... Mr. Keith MERLINO
20 Vice President Education .... Ms. Eileen RILEY
30 Vice President of Inst Advancement .... Mrs. Ruth DELACH
09 Vice Pres of Strategic Initiatives .... Mr. Jeff BELSKY
43 General Counsel .... Mr. Jack MCGINTY
06 Registrar .... Mrs. Patricia TARVIN
08 Library Director .... Mrs. Ruth WALTER
36 Director of Graduate Services .... Mrs. Josephine SMITH
26 Director of Public Relations .... Mrs. Linda ALLAN
16 Director of Human Resources .... Ms. Nancy SHEPPARD
13 IT Department Director .... Mr. John KOVAC
19 Director of Public Safety .... Dr. James LAURIA
39 Director of Resident Life .... Ms. Gloria RITCHIE
86 Manager of Compliance .... Ms. Melissa BROWN
40 Campus Store Manager .... Mrs. Cynthia KLEIN
29 Alumni Coordinator .... Mrs. Christine IOLI

Pittsburgh Theological Seminary (H)

616 N. Highland Avenue, Pittsburgh PA 15206-2596
County: Allegheny — FICE Identification: 003356
Unit ID: 215424
Telephone: (412) 362-5610 — Carnegie Class: Spec/Faith

FAX Number: (412) 363-3260 Calendar System: Quarter
URL: www.pts.edu
Established: 1794 Annual Graduate Tuition & Fees: $10,956
Enrollment: 307 Coed
Affiliation or Control: Presbyterian Church (U.S.A.) IRS Status: 501(c)3
Highest Offering: Doctorate; No Undergraduates
Program: Professional; Religious Emphasis
Accreditation: M, THEOL

01 President .... Dr. William J. CARL, III
05 VP Academic Affs/Dean of Faculty .... Dr. Byron H. JACKSON
30 VP Strategic Advance/Mktg .... Mr. Thomas J. PAPPALARDO
32 VP Student Svcs/Dean of Students .... Mr. John WELCH
45 VP Planning/Inst Effectiveness .... Dr. James DOWNEY
07 Associate Dean Admissions/Vocations .... Ms. Sherry SPARKS
06 Registrar .... Ms. Anne B. MALONE
08 Director of the Library .... Dr. Sharon TAYLOR
88 Director of Field Education .... Dr. Carolyn J. JONES
29 Director of Alumni/ae Services .... Ms. Carolyn CRANSTON
88 Director Doctor of Ministry Program .... Dr. Susan KENDALL
51 Director Cont Educ/Special Events .... Dr. James DAVISON
37 Dir Financial Aid/Admissions Ofcr .... Ms. Cheryl DEPAOLIS

Point Park University (A)

201 Wood Street, Pittsburgh PA 15222-1984
County: Allegheny FICE Identification: 003357
Unit ID: 215442
Telephone: (412) 391-4100 Carnegie Class: Master's L
FAX Number: (412) 392-3998 Calendar System: Semester
URL: www.pointpark.edu
Established: 1960 Annual Undergrad Tuition & Fees: $25,190
Enrollment: 3,920 Coed
Affiliation or Control: Independent Non-Profit IRS Status: 501(c)3
Highest Offering: Master's
Program: Liberal Arts And General; Teacher Preparatory; Professional
Accreditation: M, DANCE, ENGT, IACBE

01 President .... Dr. Paul HENNIGAN
05 Sr VP Academic and Student Affairs .... Dr. Karen MCINTYRE
10 Sr VP Finance and Operations .... Ms. Bridget MANCOSH
26 VP of External Affairs .... Ms. Mariann GEYER
18 Vice Pres for Operations .... Mr. William D. CAMERON
30 Vice Pres Development/AlumniAffairs .... Mr. Richard HASKINS
84 Asst VP Strategic Plng/Enrollment .... Ms. Trudy WILLIAMS
96 Asst VP Procurement/Business Svcs .... Ms. Ruth RAULUK
32 Dean of Student Affairs .... Mr. Keith PAYLO
53 Chair Education .... Dr. Darlene MARNICH
79 Actg Chair Humanities/Human Science .... Mr. William PURCELL
88 Chair of Faculty .... Dr. Heather STARR FIEDLER
54 Act Chair Natural Science/Engr Tech .... Dr. Mark FARRELL
88 Chair Criminal Justice/Intell Stds .... Mr. Greg ROGERS
88 Chair Management .... Ms. Margaret GILFILLAN
88 Chair Theatre .... Ms. Sheila MCKENNA
88 Chair Dance .... Ms. Susan STOWE
88 Chair Cinema .... Mr. Nelson CHIPMAN
57 Dean Conservatory of Perform Arts .... Mr. Frederick JOHNSON
49 Actg Dean School Arts and Sciences .... Dr. Robert FESSLER
60 Acting Dean School of Communication .... Mr. Ronald ALLAN-LINDBLOM
50 Acting Dean School of Business . Mr. Ronald ALLAN-LINDBLOM
04 Exec Assistant to the President .... Ms. Nina CAMPBELL
06 Registrar .... Ms. Jennifer FEDELE
15 Director Human Resources .... Mr. Guy CATANIA
21 Director of Finance/Controller .... Mr. Jim HARDT
29 Assoc VP Development/Alumni Affairs .... Mr. Scott GLUCK
08 Director/Librarian/Academic Svcs .... Ms. Liz EVANS
37 Director of Financial Aid .... Ms. Sheila NELSON-HENSLEY
26 Sr Dir Marketing & Communications .. Ms. Mary Ellen SOLOMON
39 Director of Campus Life .... Ms. Janet D. EVANS
07 Director of Admissions .... Ms. Joell MINFORD
36 Director of Career Services .... Mr. Jan-Mitchell SHERRILL
41 Director of Athletics .... Mr. Dan SWALGA
09 Director Institutional Research .... Mr. Christopher CHONCEK
54 Dir of Sciences/Engineering Mgmt .... Dr. John KUDLAC
88 Dir Conference & Event Services .... Ms. Terri SNOE
38 Student Counseling .... Ms. Patti SCHWARTZ

Prism Career Institute-Upper Darby Campus (B)

6800 Market Street, Upper Darby PA 19082-1926
County: Delaware FICE Identification: 023013
Unit ID: 215433
Telephone: (610) 789-6700 Carnegie Class: Assoc/PrivFP
FAX Number: (610) 789-5208 Calendar System: Semester
URL: www.prismcareerinstitute.edu
Established: 1981 Annual Undergrad Tuition & Fees: $10,897
Enrollment: 426 Coed
Affiliation or Control: Proprietary IRS Status: Proprietary
Highest Offering: Associate Degree
Program: Occupational
Accreditation: ACCSC

01 Campus Director .... Ms. Carole HEININGER
05 Director of Education .... Vacant
07 Director of Admissions .... Ms. Dina M. GENTILE

Reading Area Community College (C)

PO Box 1706, Reading PA 19603-1706
County: Berks FICE Identification: 010388
Unit ID: 215585
Telephone: (610) 372-4721 Carnegie Class: Assoc/Pub-R-M
FAX Number: (610) 372-4264 Calendar System: Semester
URL: www.racc.edu
Established: 1971 Annual Undergrad Tuition & Fees (In-District): $4,350
Enrollment: 5,175 Coed
Affiliation or Control: State/Local IRS Status: 501(c)3
Highest Offering: Associate Degree
Program: Occupational; 2-Year Principally Bachelor's Creditable
Accreditation: M, ADNUR, MLTAD, PNUR

01 President .... Dr. Anna D. WEITZ
05 Sr VP of Academic Affairs/Provost .... Dr. A. Wade DAVENPORT
10 Sr VP Business Svcs/Treasurer .... Mr. Theodore BASSANO
103 VP Workforce Dev/Community Educ .... Dr. Robert VAUGHN
30 VP of Institutional Advancement .... Mr. Michael NAGEL
84 VP Enrollment Management .... Ms. Maria MITCHELL
21 Assoc VP for Business/Controller .... Ms. Dolores PETERSON
08 Asst Dean Library Svcs/Learning Res ... Ms. Mary Ellen HECKMAN
37 Director Financial Aid/Registrar .... Mr. Benjamin ROSENBERGER
15 Director Human Resources .... Mr. Scott HEFFELFINGER
26 Director of Public Relations .... Ms. Melissa KUSHNER
13 Director Information Technology .... Mr. Chet WINTERS
09 Dir of Asessment/Research/Planning .... Ms. Mary FLAGG
88 Dir of Miller Center for the Arts .... Ms. Cathleen STEPHEN
84 Director of Enrollment Services .... Ms. Calley STEVENS-TAYLOR
96 Purchasing Manager .... Mr. Michael HODOWANEC
35 Coordinator of Student Activities .... Ms. Sue GELSINGER

Reconstructionist Rabbinical College (D)

1299 Church Road, Wyncote PA 19095-1898
County: Montgomery FICE Identification: 022734
Unit ID: 215619
Telephone: (215) 576-0800 Carnegie Class: Spec/Faith
FAX Number: (215) 576-6143 Calendar System: Semester
URL: www.rrc.edu
Established: 1968 Annual Graduate Tuition & Fees: $20,000
Enrollment: 59 Coed
Affiliation or Control: Jewish IRS Status: 501(c)3
Highest Offering: Doctorate; No Undergraduates
Program: Professional
Accreditation: M

01 President .... Rabbi Dan EHRENKRANTZ
05 Chief Academic Officer/Dean .... Dr. Tamar KAMIONKOWSKI
11 Vice President Administration .... Mrs. Jennifer S. ABRAHAM
10 Controller .... Ms. Lisa COHEN
20 Dean Academic Administration .... Ms. Barbara HIRSH
07 Asst VP Rabbinic Formation/Admiss .... Rabbi Amber POWERS
08 Director of the Library .... Ms. Deborah STERN

Reformed Episcopal Seminary (E)

826 Second Avenue, Blue Bell PA 19422-1257
County: Montgomery Identification: 667050
Telephone: (610) 292-9852 Carnegie Class: Not Classified
FAX Number: (610) 292-9853 Calendar System: Quarter
URL: www.reseminary.edu
Established: 1887 Annual Graduate Tuition & Fees: $6,190
Enrollment: 23 Coed
Affiliation or Control: Reformed Episcopal Church IRS Status: 501(c)3
Highest Offering: Master's; No Undergraduates
Program: Professional; Religious Emphasis
Accreditation: @THEOL

01 Chancellor and President .... Rt Rev. David L. HICKS
05 Dean .... Rev Dr. Jonathan S. RICHES
10 Provost .... Ven Dr. Jon W. ABBOUD
90 Director Information & Technology .... Mr. Gregory R. WRIGHT

Reformed Presbyterian Theological Seminary (F)

7418 Penn Avenue, Pittsburgh PA 15208-2594
County: Allegheny FICE Identification: 003358
Unit ID: 215628
Telephone: (412) 731-8690 Carnegie Class: Spec/Faith
FAX Number: (412) 731-4834 Calendar System: Quarter
URL: www.rpts.edu
Established: 1810 Annual Graduate Tuition & Fees: $10,296
Enrollment: 111 Coed
Affiliation or Control: Reformed Presbyterian Church IRS Status: 501(c)3
Highest Offering: Master's; No Undergraduates
Program: Professional; Religious Emphasis
Accreditation: THEOL

01 President .... Dr. Jerry F. O'NEILL
05 Dean of the Faculty .... Dr. Dennis J. PRUTOW
06 Registrar/Head Librarian .... Mr. Thomas G. REID, JR.
40 Bookstore Manager .... Ms. Sharon SAMPSON
10 Treasurer .... Mr. James MCFARLAND
07 Director of Admissions .... Mr. John MCCOMBS
37 Director of Financial Aid .... Ms. Yasuko KANAMORI

The Restaurant School at Walnut Hill College (G)

4207 Walnut Street, Philadelphia PA 19104-3518
County: Philadelphia FICE Identification: 021928
Unit ID: 215637
Telephone: (215) 222-4200 Carnegie Class: Spec/Other
FAX Number: (215) 222-4219 Calendar System: Other
URL: www.walnuthillcollege.edu
Established: 1974 Annual Undergrad Tuition & Fees: $22,575
Enrollment: 450 Coed
Affiliation or Control: Proprietary IRS Status: Proprietary
Highest Offering: Baccalaureate
Program: 2-Year Principally Bachelor's Creditable
Accreditation: ACCSC

01 President .... Mr. Daniel LIBERATOSCIOLI
30 Vice President College Advancement .... Mr. Karl D. BECKER
11 Vice President Administrative Svcs .. Ms. Peggy LIBERATOSCIOLI
07 Director of Admissions .... Vacant
05 Dean of Academic Affairs .... Ms. Lenore BOCCIA
10 Chief Business Officer .... Mr. Chris MOLZ
32 Chf Student Life Ofcr/Stdnt Plcmnt .... Ms. Sabrina JORDAN
51 Director Continuing Education .... Ms. Jocelyn WOOD
88 Director of Culinary Arts .... Chef Tom DELCAMP
88 Director School of Management .... Mr. David MORROW

Robert Morris University (H)

6001 University Boulevard,
Moon Township PA 15108-1189
County: Allegheny FICE Identification: 003359
Unit ID: 215655
Telephone: (412) 397-3000 Carnegie Class: Master's L
FAX Number: (412) 397-5958 Calendar System: Semester
URL: www.rmu.edu
Established: 1921 Annual Undergrad Tuition & Fees: $24,064
Enrollment: 4,984 Coed
Affiliation or Control: Independent Non-Profit IRS Status: 501(c)3
Highest Offering: Doctorate
Program: Teacher Preparatory; Professional
Accreditation: M, BUS, CS, ENG, NMT, NURSE, TEAC

01 President .... Dr. Gregory G. DELL'OMO
10 Sr Vice Pres for Business Affairs .... Mr. Dan W. KIENER
05 Provost/Sr VP Academic Affairs .... Mr. David L. JAMISON
30 Sr VP Institutional Advancement .... Mr. Jay T. CARSON
43 Vice President & General Counsel .... Mr. Sidney ZONN
21 Vice President Financial Operations .... Mr. Jeffrey A. LISTWAK
15 Vice President of Human Resources .... Mr. Peter K. FAIX
106 VP Online and Off-Campus Programs .... Dr. Darcy B. TANNEHILL
84 VP Enrollment Management .... Ms. Wendy C. BECKEMEYER
32 Vice President for Student Life .... Mr. John MICHALENKO
30 Vice President for Development .... Ms. Kimberley HAMMER
13 Vice Pres Information Technology ...... Ms. Ellen G. WIECKOWSKI
18 Vice Pres for Facilities .... Mr. Perry F. ROOFNER
26 Vice Pres Public Rels/Marketing .... Ms. Kyle FISHER
20 Vice Provost for Academic Affairs .... Dr. Lawrence A. TOMEI
46 Vice Provost Research/Grad Study .... Dr. Derya JACOBS
88 Exec Dir Bayer Ctr Nonprofit Mgmt .... Ms. Peggy M. OUTON
60 Dean School Comm/Info Systems .... Dr. Barbara J. LEVINE
50 Interim Dean School of Business .... Dr. Patrick J. LITZINGER
54 Dean School of Engr/Math/Science .... Dr. Maria V. KALEVITCH
53 Dean Sch Education/Social Sciences .... Dr. Mary Ann RAFOTH
66 Dean School Nursing/Health Sciences .... Dr. Lynda J. DAVIDSON
88 Assoc VP/Director of Sponsorships .... Vacant
07 Dean of Admissions .... Ms. Kellie L. LAURENZI
41 Director of Athletics .... Dr. Craig S. COLEMAN
08 Dean University Libraries .... Dr. Frances J. CAPLAN
21 Controller .... Ms. Melissa A. MICCO
06 Registrar .... Mr. Frank E. PERRY
19 Director Public Safety .... Mr. Randy L. MINK
36 Director Career Center .... Ms. Kishma DECASTRO-SALLIS
39 Director Residence Life .... Vacant
38 Director Center for Student Success .... Ms. Cassandra L. ODEN
27 Senior Director Public Relations .... Mr. Jonathan POTTS
09 Director Institutional Research .... Dr. David R. MAJKA
96 Senior Director Business Operations .... Mr. Neal F. BINSTOCK
37 Director Student Financial Aid ... Ms. Stephanie N. HENDERSHOT
29 Dir Development/Alumni Relations .... Mr. Warner O. JOHNSON
88 Dean Engaged Learning .... Dr. Shari L. PAYNE

Rosedale Technical Institute (I)

215 Beecham Drive, Suite 2, Pittsburgh PA 15205-9791
County: Allegheny FICE Identification: 012050
Unit ID: 215682
Telephone: (412) 521-6200 Carnegie Class: Assoc/PrivNFP
FAX Number: (412) 521-2520 Calendar System: Semester
URL: www.rosedaletech.org
Established: 1949 Annual Undergrad Tuition & Fees: $12,230
Enrollment: 328 Coed
Affiliation or Control: Independent Non-Profit IRS Status: 501(c)3
Highest Offering: Associate Degree
Program: Occupational; 2-Year Principally Bachelor's Creditable; Technical Emphasis
Accreditation: ACCSC

01 President .... Dennis F. WILKE
05 Director of Education .... Jim SHORE
07 Director of Admissions .... Debbie BIER

Rosemont College (J)

1400 Montgomery Avenue, Rosemont PA 19010-1699
County: Montgomery FICE Identification: 003360
Unit ID: 215691
Telephone: (610) 527-0200 Carnegie Class: Master's M
FAX Number: (610) 527-0341 Calendar System: Semester

URL: www.rosemont.edu
Established: 1921 Annual Undergrad Tuition & Fees: $30,450
Enrollment: 883 Coed
Affiliation or Control: Roman Catholic IRS Status: 501(c)3
Highest Offering: Master's
Program: Liberal Arts And General; Teacher Preparatory
Accreditation: M

01 President ....Dr. Sharon LATCHAW HIRSH
05 Provost/VP Academic/Student Affairs ....Dr. B. Christopher DOUGHERTY
10 VP for Finance & Administration ....Mr. Randy ELDRIDGE
37 Director of Financial Aid ....Ms. Sarah FEVIG
30 Vice Pres College Relations ....Ms. Christyn MORAN
32 Dean of Students ....Mr. David A. SURRATT
84 Vice President for Enrollment Mgmt ....Mr. Kevin M. MCINTYRE
88 Vice President for Mission ....Sr. Jeanne Marie HATCH, SHCJ
08 Exec Director of Library Services ....Mrs. Catherine FENNELL
58 Dean School Graduate/Prof Studies ....Dr. Dennis R. DOUGHERTY
20 Academic Dean Undergrad College ....Mrs. Paulette HUTCHINSON
29 Director of Alumni Relations ....Vacant
26 Director of Public Relations ....Ms. Roberta PERRY
06 Registrar/Dir of Inst Research ....Mr. Joseph T. ROGERS
41 Director of Athletics ....Ms. Lynn S. ROTHENHOEFER
15 Director of Human Resources ....Ms. Jane FEDEROWICZ
42 Director of Campus Ministry ....Vacant
40 Store Manager Campus Bookstore ....Ms. Isel A. PIZARRO
18 Chief Facil/Phys Plant/Pub Safety ....Mr. Raymond A. BROWN
38 Director Student Counseling ....Vacant
39 Director of Res Life/Asst Dean ....Ms. Dianne VILLAR
19 Director of Public Safety ....Mr. Chuck LORENZ
21 Controller ....Mr. Ronald LAHER

Saint Charles Borromeo Seminary (A)

100 E Wynnewood Road, Wynnewood PA 19096-3099
County: Montgomery FICE Identification: 003364
Unit ID: 216047
Telephone: (610) 667-3394 Carnegie Class: Spec/Faith
FAX Number: (610) 667-7635 Calendar System: Semester
URL: www.scs.edu
Established: 1832 Annual Undergrad Tuition & Fees: $19,150
Enrollment: 195 Male
Affiliation or Control: Roman Catholic IRS Status: 501(c)3
Highest Offering: Master's
Program: Liberal Arts And General; Professional
Accreditation: M, THEOL

01 Rector & President ....M.Rev. Timothy C. SENIOR
03 Vice Rector ....Rev. Joseph W. BONGARD
10 Vice Pres of Finance & Operations ....Mrs. Elaine K. RICE
73 Academic Dean Theology Division ....Rev. Robert A. PESARCHICK
49 Academic Dean College Division ....Mr. James F. GROWDON
73 Acad Dean Religious Studies Div ....Dr. Kelly BOWRING
33 Dean of Men College ....Rev. Robert B. MCDERMOTT
33 Dean of Men Theol/Dir of Liturgy ....Rev. Patrick J. WELSH
06 Registrar ....Mr. Lawrence A. HEYMAN
08 Director of Library Services ....Mrs. Cait KOKOLUS
42 Director Spiritual Formation Col ....Rev. Paul J. ODONNELL
42 Director Spiritual Formation Theol ....Rev. Joseph F. GLEASON
88 Director Pastoral/Apostolic Form ....Rev. Joseph T. SHENOSKY
64 Director of Music ....Dr. Theodore E. KIEFER
21 Director of Financial Services ....Ms. Mary D. D'URSO
37 Director Student Financial Aid ....Ms. Nora DOWNEY
19 Director of Safety and Security ....Mr. Nicholas MANCINI

Saint Francis University (B)

PO Box 600, Loretto PA 15940-0600
County: Cambria FICE Identification: 003366
Unit ID: 215743
Telephone: (814) 472-3000 Carnegie Class: Master's L
FAX Number: (814) 472-3003 Calendar System: Semester
URL: www.francis.edu
Established: 1847 Annual Undergrad Tuition & Fees: $28,878
Enrollment: 2,398 Coed
Affiliation or Control: Roman Catholic IRS Status: 501(c)3
Highest Offering: Doctorate
Program: Liberal Arts And General; Teacher Preparatory; Professional
Accreditation: M, ARCPA, IACBE, NURSE, OT, PTA, SW, @TEAC

01 President ....Rev. Gabriel ZEIS, TOR
05 Provost ....Dr. Wayne POWEL
10 Vice President for Finance ....Mr. Robert G. DATSKO
32 Vice Pres for Student Development ....Dr. Frank MONTECALVO
42 VP Mission Effective & Integration ....Rev. Daniel F. SINISI
45 Vice Pres for Strategic Initiatives ....Ms. Patricia SEROTKIN
30 Vice President for Advancement ....Mr. Robert CRUSCIEL
84 Vice Pres for Enrollment Management ....Ms. Erin E. MCCLOSKEY
08 Dean of Library Services ....Ms. Sandra A. BALOUGH
97 Assoc Dean of General Education ....Vacant
06 Registrar ....Dr. Stephen R. ROMBOUTS
09 Director of Institutional Research ....Mr. Daniel KOSHUTE
37 Financial Aid Director ....Mr. Jamie KOSH
26 Director Marketing & Public Affairs ....Ms. Marie YOUNG
44 Director of Development ....Ms. Marie B. MELUSKY
38 Director of Counseling Center ....Mr. David P. WILSON
14 Director Computer Services ....Mr. George F. PYO
29 Director of Alumni Relations ....Ms. Anita M. BAUMANN
51 Director Continuing Education ....Ms. Julie BARRIS
18 Director of Physical Plant ....Mr. Doug EPPLEY
21 Controller ....Mr. Thomas R. FRITZ
41 Director of Athletics ....Mr. Bob S. KRIMMEL
88 Dir Small Business Devel Center ....Mr. Edward R. HUTTENHOWER
19 Director Security & Safety ....Mr. Donald MILES
39 Director of Residence Life ....Mr. T. J BRECCIAROLI
42 Director of Campus Ministry ....Rev. John Mark KLAUS
24 Dir Academic Center for Enrichment ....Vacant
35 Assoc Dean of Student Life ....Mr. Dominick F. PERUSO
15 Director of Human Resources ....Ms. Heather J. MECK
28 Director of Multicultural Affairs ....Ms. Lynne BANKS
96 Director of Purchasing ....Mr. William AGOSTA
20 Associate Provost ....Dr. Peter R. SKONER
40 Manager of Bookstore ....Ms. Barbara SHINGLE

Saint Joseph's University (C)

5600 City Avenue, Philadelphia PA 19131-1376
County: Philadelphia FICE Identification: 003367
Unit ID: 215770
Telephone: (610) 660-1000 Carnegie Class: Master's L
FAX Number: (610) 660-3300 Calendar System: Semester
URL: www.sju.edu
Established: 1851 Annual Undergrad Tuition & Fees: $37,830
Enrollment: 9,011 Coed
Affiliation or Control: Roman Catholic IRS Status: 501(c)3
Highest Offering: Doctorate
Program: Liberal Arts And General; Teacher Preparatory; Professional
Accreditation: M, ANEST, BUS, BUSA

01 President ....Rev. C. Kevin GILLESPIE, SJ
05 Provost ....Dr. Brice R. WACHTERHAUSER
03 Senior Vice President ....Mr. John W. SMITHSON
88 Vice President Mission & Identity ....Dr. E. Springs STEELE
32 VP Student Life/Assoc Provost ....Dr. Cary M. ANDERSON
11 Vice Pres Administrative Services ....Mr. Kevin W. ROBINSON
30 VP Dev/Alumni Relations ....Mr. Martin F. FARRELL
26 Vice President External Affairs ....Ms. Joan F. CHRESTAY
10 Vice President Financial Affairs ....Dr. Louis J. MAYER
45 Vice President Planning ....Dr. Kathleen D. GAVAL
43 General Counsel ....Ms. Marianne SCHIMELFINIG
04 Assistant Vice President ....Ms. Sarah F. QUINN
20 Vice Provost ....Dr. Paul L. DEVITO
49 Dean College Arts & Sciences ....Dr. William MADGES
50 Dean Haub School of Business ....Dr. Joseph A. DIANGELO, JR.
41 Assoc VP/Director Athletics ....Mr. Dominick J. DIJULIA
107 Assoc Dean Col Prof & Liberal Stds ....Ms. Patricia GRIFFIN
58 Assoc Dean & Exec Dir Grad A&S ....Dr. Sabrina DETURK
84 Assoc Provost Enrollment Mgmt ....Mr. John G. HALLER
06 Registrar ....Mr. Gerard J. DONAHUE
08 University Librarian Drexel Library ....Ms. Evelyn MINICK
21 Asst VP Financial Affs & Treasury ....Mr. James B. QUERY
21 Asst VP & Controller ....Mr. Joseph CASSIDY
86 Asst VP Govt & Community Rels ....Mr. Wadell RIDLEY, JR.
15 Assistant VP Human Resources ....Ms. Sharon O'GRADY EISENMANN
13 Asst VP Information Technology ....Mr. Joseph F. PETRAGNANI
13 Chief Information Officer ....Mr. Francis J. DISANTI
27 Asst VP Marketing Communications ....Mr. Joseph M. LUNARDI
108 Asst VP Planning & Assessment ....Ms. Dawn M. BURDSALL
88 Asst VP Student Development ....Dr. Mary Elaine PERRY
88 Asst VP Student Ed Support Services ....Ms. Jacqueline M. STARKS
26 Asst VP Univ Communications ....Ms. Harriet K. GOODHEART
29 Exec Dir Saint Joseph's Fund ....Mr. Douglas KLEINTOP
24 Exec Dir Acad Tech/Dist Learning ....Dr. David LEES
07 Exec Director UG Admissions ....Ms. Maureen MATHIS
105 Exec Dir Web & Support Services ....Mr. Jeffery J. BACHOVCHIN
22 Director Benefits and Wellness ....Mr. James MOLNAR
42 Director Campus Ministry ....Mr. Thomas J. SHEIBLEY
36 Director Career Development Center ....Mr. Brett WOODARD
38 Director Counseling/Pers Dev Ctr ....Dr. Gregory NICHOLLS
18 Director Facilities Management ....Mr. Kevin M. KANE
37 Director Financial Assistance ....Ms. Eileen TUCKER
92 Director Honors Program ....Dr. Maria S. MARSILIO
28 Director Institutional Diversity ....Dr. Valerie DUDLEY
88 Director Multicultural Life ....Dr. Shoshanna EDWARDS-ALEXANDER
19 Director Public Safety & Security ....Mr. John M. HENFEY
96 Director Purchasing ....Mr. William O. ANDERSON
39 Director Residence Life ....Mr. John A. JEFFERY
23 Director Student Health Center ....Ms. Laura HURST
35 Dir Student Leadership/Activities ....Dr. Beth HAGOVSKY
09 Assoc Dir Institutional Research ....Ms. Annemarie M. BARTLETT

St. Tikhon's Orthodox Theological Seminary (D)

PO Box 130, South Canaan PA 18459-0130
County: Wayne FICE Identification: 039193
Unit ID: 216180
Telephone: (570) 561-1818 Carnegie Class: Not Classified
FAX Number: (570) 937-3100 Calendar System: Semester
URL: www.stots.edu
Established: 1938 Annual Undergrad Tuition & Fees: $5,250
Enrollment: 96 Male
Affiliation or Control: Other IRS Status: 501(c)3
Highest Offering: First Professional Degree
Program: Religious Emphasis
Accreditation: THEOL

01 Acting President ....ABP. Nathaniel POPP
03 Rector ....Rt Rev. Mchael DAHULICH
05 Dean/COO ....V.Rev. Alexander ATTY

Saint Vincent College (E)

300 Fraser Purchase Road, Latrobe PA 15650-2690
County: Westmoreland FICE Identification: 003368
Unit ID: 215798
Telephone: (724) 805-2500 Carnegie Class: Bac/A&S
FAX Number: (724) 805-2019 Calendar System: Semester
URL: www.stvincent.edu
Established: 1846 Annual Undergrad Tuition & Fees: $39,723
Enrollment: 1,929 Coed
Affiliation or Control: Roman Catholic IRS Status: 501(c)3
Highest Offering: Doctorate
Program: Liberal Arts And General; Professional
Accreditation: M, ACBSP, ANEST

01 President ....Br. Norman W. HIPPS, OSB
03 Executive Vice President ....Rev. Paul TAYLOR, OSB
05 VP Academic Affairs ....Dr. John SMETANKA
10 VP/Chief Finance/Admin Officer ....Mr. Dennis THIMONS
32 VP Student Affairs ....Ms. Mary COLLINS
26 VP Marketing and Communication ....Ms. Suzanne ENGLISH
07 Asst Vice Pres Admission ....Mr. David A. COLLINS
13 Chief Information Officer ....Mr. Peter E. MAHONEY
20 Dean of Studies ....Ms. Alice J. KAYLOR
50 Dean McKenna Sch Bus/Econ/Govt ....Dr. Gary QUINLIVAN
60 Dean Sch Soc Sci/Communication/Educ ....Dr. MaryBeth SPORE
79 Dean Humanities & Fine Arts ....Rev. Rene KOLLAR, OSB
81 Dean Science/Math & Computing ....Dr. Stephen M. JODIS
06 Registrar ....Ms. Celine R. BRUDNOK
08 Librarian ....Bro. David KELLY, OSB
29 Director of Alumni Affairs ....Mr. Michael GERDICH
26 Director of Public Relations ....Mr. Donald A. ORLANDO
36 Director Career Services ....Ms. Courtney BAUM
15 Director of Human Resources ....Ms. Judith MAHER
42 Director of Campus Ministry ....Rev. Killian LOCH, OSB
23 Director Wellness Center ....Ms. Mary Alice ARMOUR
19 Director Public Safety ....Mr. Steve BROWN
41 Athletic Director ....Rev. Myron KIRSCH, OSB
39 Director Resident Life ....Mr. Robert BAUM
96 Dir of Purchasing/Chief Fire Dept ....Mr. Terry NOEL
09 Director of Institutional Research ....Ms. Maren HESS
18 Director of Facility Management ....Mr. Larry HENDRICK
40 Manager Book Center ....Rev. Anthony GROSSI, OSB
88 Exec Dir Fred Rogers Center ....Ms. Rita CATALANO
88 Coord of Grad Admission & Cont Educ ....Ms. Lisa GLESSNER

Saint Vincent Seminary (F)

300 Fraser Purchase Road, Latrobe PA 15650-2690
County: Westmoreland Identification: 666018
Unit ID: 215813
Telephone: (724) 805-2592 Carnegie Class: Spec/Faith
FAX Number: (724) 532-5052 Calendar System: Semester
URL: www.saintvincentseminary.edu
Established: 1846 Annual Undergrad Tuition & Fees: $33,886
Enrollment: 62 Coed
Affiliation or Control: Roman Catholic IRS Status: 501(c)3
Highest Offering: Master's
Program: Religious Emphasis
Accreditation: THEOL

01 Rector ....V.Rev. Timothy F. WHALEN
88 Director of Spiritual Formation ....Rev. Aaron N. BUZZELLI, OSB
05 Academic Dean ....Dr. Michel THERRIEN
03 Vice-Rector ....Rev. John-Mary TOMPKINS, OSB

Salus University (G)

8360 Old York Road, Elkins Park PA 19027-1516
County: Philadelphia FICE Identification: 003311
Unit ID: 214564
Telephone: (215) 780-1400 Carnegie Class: Spec/Health
FAX Number: (215) 780-1325 Calendar System: Quarter
URL: www.salus.edu
Established: 1919 Annual Undergrad Tuition & Fees: $32,810
Enrollment: 1,007 Coed
Affiliation or Control: Independent Non-Profit IRS Status: 501(c)3
Highest Offering: Doctorate
Program: Professional
Accreditation: M, ARCPA, AUD, OPT, OPTR

01 President ....Dr. Michael H. MITTLEMAN
05 Vice President Faculty Affairs ....Dr. Anthony F. DISTEFANO
10 Vice Pres Finance/Business Affairs ....Mr. Donald KATES
17 VP/Exec Director The Eye Institute ....Dr. Susan OLESZEWSKI
32 Vice President Student Affairs ....Mr. Robert HORNE
45 Vice President for Inst Planning ....Ms. Lynne CORBOY
35 Dean Student Affairs ....Dr. James CALDWELL
20 Exec Assistant to the Dean ....Ms. Karen BOYKIN
09 Asst Dir Research Admin ....Ms. Lydia PARKE
06 Registrar ....Ms. Shannon BOSS
07 Director of Admissions ....Dr. James CALDWELL
13 Director Management Info Services ....Mr. Alex ANDERSON
38 Director Personal/Prof Development ....Ms. Natalie LECKERMAN
37 Assoc Dean Student Financial Affs ....Dr. H. Lawrence MCCLURE
18 Director Physical Plant ....Mr. Richard ECHEVARRI
30 Director of Development ....Ms. Lynne CORBOY
26 Chief Public Relations Officer ....Ms. Peggy SHELLY
27 Director Publications/Communication ....Ms. Peggy SHELLY
29 Director Alumni Relations/Giving ....Ms. Heather GIAMPAPA
51 Coord Continuing/Post-Graduate Educ ....Mrs. Melissa PADILLA
58 Chairperson Graduate Studies ....Dr. Kathleen HUEBNER

40 Bookstore Manager .... Mr. Joe NOCE
12 Director Bennett Center .... Ms. Janice MIGNOGNA
24 Director Instructional Media .... Mr. Glenn ROEDEL
36 Director Student Placement .... Ms. Janice MIGNOGNA
84 Director Enrollment Management .... Dr. Larry MCCLURE
88 Exec Dir Inst Visually Impaired .... Dr. Audrey SMITH
08 Head Librarian .... Mr. Keith LAMMERS
19 Director of Security .... Mr. Joe KELLENBENZ
15 Dir Human Resources/Affirm Action .... Ms. Maura ALEXANDER
96 Director of Purchasing .... Mr. Steve SCHEPS

Sanford-Brown Institute-Pittsburgh (A)

421 Seventh Avenue, Pittsburgh PA 15219-1907
County: Allegheny FICE Identification: 022023
Unit ID: 216782
Telephone: (412) 281-2600 Carnegie Class: Assoc/PrivFP
FAX Number: (412) 281-0319 Calendar System: Other
URL: www.sanfordbrown.edu/Pittsburgh
Established: 1979 Annual Undergrad Tuition & Fees: N/A
Enrollment: 1,043 Coed
Affiliation or Control: Proprietary IRS Status: Proprietary
Highest Offering: Associate Degree
Program: Occupational
Accreditation: ACCSC, ACICS, DMS, MAAB, RAD

01 President-Pittsburgh .... Patti L. YAKSHE
12 President-Monroeville .... R. Thomas CONTRELLA
05 Director of Education .... Charles LONG
07 Director of Admissions .... Clinton ALEXANDER
06 Registrar .... Amy ROBERTS
13 Director of Information Technology .... Mark MARCI
36 Director of Career Services .... George MORE
10 Business Manager .... George SANTUCCI

Sanford-Brown Institute-Wilkins Township (B)

777 Penn Center Boulevard, Bldg 7, Pittsburgh PA 15235
County: Allegheny Identification: 666526
Unit ID: 376136
Telephone: (412) 373-6400 Carnegie Class: Assoc/PrivFP
FAX Number: (412) 373-2544 Calendar System: Semester
URL: www.sanfordbrown.edu/Wilkins-Township
Established: 1987 Annual Undergrad Tuition & Fees: $12,319
Enrollment: 602 Coed
Affiliation or Control: Proprietary IRS Status: Proprietary
Highest Offering: Associate Degree
Program: Occupational; 2-Year Principally Bachelor's Creditable
Accreditation: ACCSC, ACICS, MAAB, SURGT

01 President .... Mr. R. Thomas CONTRELLA

† Branch campus of Sanford-Brown Institute-Pittsburgh, Pittsburgh, PA.

Seton Hill University (C)

Seton Hill Drive, Greensburg PA 15601-1599
County: Westmoreland FICE Identification: 003362
Unit ID: 215947
Telephone: (724) 834-2200 Carnegie Class: Bac/Diverse
FAX Number: (724) 830-4611 Calendar System: Semester
URL: www.setonhill.edu
Established: 1883 Annual Undergrad Tuition & Fees: $29,054
Enrollment: 2,137 Coed
Affiliation or Control: Roman Catholic IRS Status: 501(c)3
Highest Offering: Master's
Program: Liberal Arts And General; Teacher Preparatory; Professional
Accreditation: M, ARCPA, DENT, DIETC, IACBE, MFCD, MUS, SW

01 President .... Dr. JoAnne W. BOYLE
32 Vice President Mission/Student Life .... Dr. Lois SCULCO, SC
05 Provost & Dean of the Faculty .... Dr. Mary Ann GAWELEK
10 Vice Pres Finance & Business .... Mr. Paul ROMAN
11 Vice Pres Administration .... Mrs. Barbara C. HINKLE
44 Vice Pres Institutional Advancement .... Ms. Christine MUESELER
13 Vice Pres Computers & Technology .... Mr. Phil KOMARNY
84 Vice Pres Enrollment Management .... Mr. Michael POLL
21 Controller .... Mr. Paul EDSALL
35 Dean of Student Services .... Dr. Charmaine R. STRONG
07 Director Admissions .... Ms. Ashley JOSAY
08 Director of Library .... Mr. David STANLEY
30 Director Development .... Ms. Molly ROBB SHIMKO
29 Director of Alumni Relations .... Ms. Mary COX
37 Director of Financial Aid .... Ms. Maryann DUDAS
36 Director of Career Development .... Ms. Renee STAREK
15 Director Personnel Services .... Mrs. Darlene SAUERS
18 Director Facilities .... Mr. Bill VOKES
41 Executive Athletic Director .... Mr. Chris SNYDER
42 Director Campus Ministry .... Sr. Maureen O'BRIEN
88 Dir Natl Educ Ctr Women in Business .... Mrs. Jayne HUSTON
04 Assistant to the President .... Mrs. Carol ZOLA
06 Registrar .... Ms. Barbara HINKLE
38 Director Student Counseling .... Ms. Teresa BASSI-COOK

South Hills School of Business and Technology (D)

480 Waupelani Drive, State College PA 16801-4516
County: Centre FICE Identification: 013263
Unit ID: 216083
Telephone: (814) 234-7755 Carnegie Class: Assoc/PrivFP
FAX Number: (814) 234-0926 Calendar System: Quarter
URL: www.southhills.edu
Established: 1970 Annual Undergrad Tuition & Fees: $14,961
Enrollment: 706 Coed
Affiliation or Control: Proprietary IRS Status: Proprietary
Highest Offering: Associate Degree
Program: Occupational
Accreditation: ACICS, DMS, MAAB

01 President & Owner .... Mr. S. Paul MAZZA
05 Director .... Mr. Mark MAGGS

Susquehanna University (E)

514 University Avenue, Selinsgrove PA 17870-1025
County: Snyder FICE Identification: 003369
Unit ID: 216278
Telephone: (570) 372-4395 Carnegie Class: Bac/A&S
FAX Number: (570) 372-4040 Calendar System: Semester
URL: www.susqu.edu
Established: 1858 Annual Undergrad Tuition & Fees: $37,280
Enrollment: 2,261 Coed
Affiliation or Control: Evangelical Lutheran Church In America
IRS Status: 501(c)3
Highest Offering: Baccalaureate
Program: Liberal Arts And General; Teacher Preparatory
Accreditation: M, BUS, MUS

01 President .... Dr. L. Jay LEMONS
03 Senior Vice President .... Ms. Sara G. KIRKLAND
05 Provost .... Dr. Carl O. MOSES
10 Vice Pres for Finance .... Mr. Michael COYNE
26 Vice President for Univ Relations .... Mr. Ronald A. COHEN
84 Vice Pres Enrollment Management .... Ms. Deborah STIEFFEL
32 Vice Pres of Student Life & Dean .... Dr. Philip E. WINGER
27 Chief Communications Officer .... Ms. Angie BURROWS
30 Asst Vice President Gift Planning .... Mr. Doug SEABERG
28 Chief Diversity Officer .... Ms. Lisa M. SCOTT
04 Assistant to the President .... Ms. Joann B. ANTES
04 Senior Admin Asst to the President .... Ms. Sharon POPE
57 Dean Sch Arts/Humanities/Comm .... Dr. Valerie G. MARTIN
50 Dean Weis School of Business .... Dr. Alicia JACKSON
38 Assoc Dean & Director of Counseling .... Ms. Anna Beth PAYNE
89 Asst Dean/First Year Programs .... Ms. Caroline MERCADO
28 Dir Center for Diversity & Soc Just .... Ms. Dena SALERNO
07 Director of Admissions .... Mr. Chris A. MARKLE
08 Director of the Library .... Ms. Kathleen GUNNING
37 Director of Financial Aid .... Ms. Helen S. NUNN
06 Registrar .... Mr. Alex G H. SMITH
42 University Chaplain .... Rev. Mark Wm RADECKE
13 Chief Information Officer .... Mr. Mark D. HUBER
41 Director of Athletics .... Ms. Pamela SAMUELSON
18 Director of Facilities Management .... Mr. Chris C. BAILEY
36 Director of Career Services .... Ms. Brenda FABIAN
88 Director of Event Management .... Ms. Brenda MULL
29 Director of Alumni Relations .... Ms. Becky DEITRICK
09 Dir of Institutional Research .... Dr. Colleen FLEWELLING
102 Dir of Corp/Foundation Support .... Mr. Ed CLARKE
104 Dir Cross Cultural Off-Campus Pgm .... Dr. Scott MANNING
15 Director Human Resources/Risk Mgmt .... Ms. Maureen N. PUGH
19 Director of Public Safety .... Mr. Tom RAMBO
44 Director of the Annual Fund .... Mr. Jason MCCAHAN
92 Director of Honors Program .... Dr. James POMYKALSKI
20 Dir of Inst Research & Asst Provost .... Dr. Colleen FLEWELLING

Swarthmore College (F)

500 College Avenue, Swarthmore PA 19081-1390
County: Delaware FICE Identification: 003370
Unit ID: 216287
Telephone: (610) 328-8000 Carnegie Class: Bac/A&S
FAX Number: (610) 328-8673 Calendar System: Semester
URL: www.swarthmore.edu
Established: 1864 Annual Undergrad Tuition & Fees: $43,080
Enrollment: 1,545 Coed
Affiliation or Control: Independent Non-Profit IRS Status: 501(c)3
Highest Offering: Baccalaureate
Program: Liberal Arts And General
Accreditation: M, ENG

01 President .... Rebecca S. CHOPP
05 Provost .... Thomas STEPHENSON
10 Vice President Finance/Treasurer .... Suzanne P. WELSH
30 Vice President Alumni/Development .... Karl CLAUSS
04 VP Col/Cmty Rels/Exec Asst to Pres .... Maurice G. ELDRIDGE
18 Vice Pres Facilities & Services .... C. Stuart HAIN
16 Vice Pres for Human Resources .... Pamela PRESCOD-CAESAR
26 Vice President for Communications .... Nancy NICELY
07 Vice Pres & Dean of Admissions .... Jim BOCK
21 Asst Vice Pres Finance & Controller .... Eileen E. PETULA
32 Dean of Students .... Elizabeth BRAUN
28 Assoc Dean Multicultural Affairs .... Vacant
06 Registrar .... Martin O. WARNER
08 College Librarian .... Peggy SEIDEN
09 Director Institutional Research .... Robin H. SHORES
29 Director of Alumni Relations .... Lisa LEE
37 Director of Financial Aid .... Laura TALBOT
36 Director Career Services .... Nancy BURKETT
19 Director Security/Safety Services .... Michael HILL
22 Director Equal Opportunity Office .... Sharmaine LAMAR
23 Director Worth Health Center .... Beth KOTARSKI

38 Director Psychological Services .... David RAMIREZ
41 Director Physical Educ/Athletics .... Adam HERTZ
44 Director Annual and Parent Giving .... Danielle SHEPHERD
13 Actg Chief Info Technology Officer .... Glen STAUFFER
35 Student Activities Coordinator .... Paury FLOWERS

Talmudical Yeshiva of Philadelphia (G)

6063 Drexel Road, Philadelphia PA 19131-1296
County: Philadelphia FICE Identification: 012523
Unit ID: 216311
Telephone: (215) 473-1212 Carnegie Class: Spec/Faith
FAX Number: (215) 477-5065 Calendar System: Semester
Established: 1953 Annual Undergrad Tuition & Fees: $8,100
Enrollment: 230 Male
Affiliation or Control: Independent Non-Profit IRS Status: 501(c)3
Highest Offering: Second Talmudic Degree
Program: Teacher Preparatory; Professional; Religious Emphasis
Accreditation: RABN

01 President .... Mr. Erwin WEINBERG
05 Dean .... Rabbi Shmuel KAMENETSKY
05 Dean .... Rabbi Yehuda SVEI
05 Dean .... Rabbi Sholom KAMENETSKY

Temple University (H)

1801 N. Broad Street, Philadelphia PA 19122-6072
County: Philadelphia FICE Identification: 003371
Unit ID: 216339
Telephone: (215) 204-7000 Carnegie Class: RU/H
FAX Number: (215) 204-5694 Calendar System: Semester
URL: www.temple.edu
Established: 1884 Annual Undergrad Tuition & Fees (In-State): $13,006
Enrollment: 36,855 Coed
Affiliation or Control: State Related IRS Status: 501(c)3
Highest Offering: Doctorate
Program: 2-Year Principally Bachelor's Creditable; Liberal Arts And General; Teacher Preparatory; Professional
Accreditation: M, ART, BUS, CLPSY, DANCE, DENT, ENG, ENGT, HSA, IPSY, JOUR, LAW, LSAR, MED, MUS, NRPA, NURSE, OT, PH, PHAR, PLNG, POD, PTA, SCPSY, SP, SW, TEAC, THEA

01 Acting President .... Dr. Richard ENGLERT
03 Vice President .... Mr. William T. BERGMAN, JR.
05 Int Provost/Sr VP Academic Affairs .... Dr. Hai-Lung DAI
43 Univ Counsel/Univ Secretary/Sr VP .... Mr. George E. MOORE
32 VP for Student Affairs .... Dr. Theresa A. POWELL
27 VP Computer/Financial Svcs/CIO .... Mr. Timothy C. O'ROURKE
17 Sr EVP Health Sci/CEO Health System .... Dr. Larry R. KAISER
03 Sr Vice Provost Strategic Init/ Comm .... Dr. Elizabeth LEEBRON TUTELMAN
10 Sr VP/CFO & Treasurer .... Mr. Anthony E. WAGNER
26 Sr VP Govt/Community & Public Affs .... Mr. Kenneth LAWERENCE, JR.
35 Assoc VP/Dean of Students .... Dr. Stephanie IVES
30 Sr VP Institutional Advancement .... Mr. David UNRUH
46 Sr VP Research/Graduate Education .... Mr. Kenneth J. BLANK
18 Sr VP Construction & Facilities .... Mr. James CREEDON
16 Sr Assoc VP Finance/HR .... Mr. Kenneth H. KAISER
21 Assoc VP Finance .... Mr. William J. WILKINSON
39 Assoc VP Student Affairs/Housing .... Mr. Michael SCALES
15 Assoc VP HR .... Mr. Harry A. YOUNG
21 Assoc VP/ Controller .... Mr. Frank ANNUNZIATO
88 Assoc VP Business Services .... Mr. Richard RUMER
22 Assoc VP Multicultural Affairs .... Ms. Rhonda L. BROWN
11 Asst VP Administration/Planning .... Ms. Kathryn P. D'ANGELO
29 Asst Vice Pres Alumni Relations .... Ms. Audrey SCHNEIDER
88 Sr Vice Provost Faculty Dev/Affairs .... Dr. Diane C. MAELSON
84 Senior Vice Provost Enrollment .... Mr. William N. BLACK
20 Vice Provost Undergraduate Programs .... Dr. Peter JONES
20 Vice Prov Acad Affairs/ Assessment .... Dr. Jodi LEVINE LAUFGRABEN
88 Assoc Vice Provost Faculty Affairs .... Ms. Nelia VIVEIROS
08 Int Dean for University Libraries .... Ms. Carol LANG
06 Registrar .... Ms. Wendy KUTCHNER
41 Director Intercollegiate Athletics .... Mr. William BRADSHAW
38 Director Tuttleman Counseling Svcs .... Dr. John L. DIMINO
36 Sr Dir Student Svcs/Career Services .... Ms. Rachel BROWN
09 Sr Director Measurement/Research .... Dr. James W. DEGNAN
85 Sr Vice Provost Intl Affairs .... Dr. Hai-Lung DAI
88 Sr Dir International Student Svcs .... Dr. Martyn J. MILLER
88 Asst VP International Affairs .... Ms. Denise A. CONNERTY
23 Assoc Director Health Services .... Dr. Mark DENYS
37 Director Student Financial Services .... Mr. Craig FENNELL
88 Vice Provost University College .... Dr. Vicki Lewis MCGARVEY
96 Director of Purchasing .... Ms. Theresa E. BURT
88 Bursar .... Mr. David R. GLEZERMAN
97 Director General Education .... Mr. Istvan L. VARKONYI
12 Exec Dir Ambler/Ctr City Campuses .... Mr. William PARSHALL
40 Bookstore Manager .... Mr. Jim HANLEY
49 Dean Liberal Arts .... Dr. Teresa SCOTT SOUFAS
53 Interim Dean of Education .... Dr. James Earl DAVIS
61 Dean Law School .... Dr. Joanne A. EPPS
64 Dean Center for the Arts .... Dr. Robert STROKER
50 Dean Business/Management .... Dr. Moshe PORAT
52 Dean of Dentistry .... Dr. Amid ISMAIL
63 Dean of Medicine .... Dr. Larry KAISER
67 Dean of Pharmacy .... Dr. Peter H. DOUKAS
54 Dean Engineering .... Dr. Keya SADEGHIPOUR
88 Dean Podiatric Medicine .... Dr. John A. MATTIACCI

72 Dean Science & Technology ... Dr. Hai-Lung DAI
60 Int Dean Media & Communications ... Dr. Thomas JACOBSON
76 Dean Health Professions & Social Wk ... Dr. Michael SITLER
88 Dean of Tourism/Hospitality Mgmt ... Dr. Moshe PORAT
88 Dean Environmental Design ... Dr. Teresa SCOTT SOUFAS
88 Dean Temple Japan ... Dr. Bruce STRONACH
88 Dean Temple Rome ... Mr. Kim STROMMEN

Thaddeus Stevens College of Technology (A)

750 E King Street, Lancaster PA 17602-3198
County: Lancaster FICE Identification: 007912
Unit ID: 216296
Telephone: (717) 299-7730 Carnegie Class: Assoc/Pub-R-S
FAX Number: (717) 299-7748 Calendar System: Semester
URL: www.stevenscollege.edu
Established: 1905 Annual Undergrad Tuition & Fees (In-State): $6,900
Enrollment: 838 Coed
Affiliation or Control: State IRS Status: 501(c)3
Highest Offering: Associate Degree
Program: Occupational; 2-Year Principally Bachelor's Creditable
Accreditation: M

01 President ... Dr. William E. GRISCOM
32 Vice President for Student Services ... Mr. Christopher METZLER
10 Vice President Finance and Admin ... Mrs. Betty TOMPOS
05 Vice President Academic Affairs ... Dr. William R. THOMPSON
84 Dir Enrollment Services/Admissions ... Dr. Erin NELSEN
08 Learning Resources Center Director ... Ms. Diane AMBRUSO
09 Director of Research & Planning ... Vacant
15 Director of Personnel Services ... Ms. Sue EMSWILER
26 Dir of Marketing/Public Information ... Mr. Chad BAKER
38 Director of Student Counseling ... Ms. Debra SCHUCH
28 Director Multicultural Affairs ... Mr. Paul CULBRETH
29 Alumni Foundation Exec Director ... Mr. Alex MUNRO
37 Director Financial Aid/Registrar ... Mr. Michael DEGROFT
41 Athletic Director ... Mr. Christopher METZLER
30 Director of Development ... Mr. Allen TATE
36 Career Services Director ... Ms. Laurie GROVE
18 Facilities Maintenance Manager ... Mr. Gene DUNCAN, JR.

† Qualified individuals are eligible for full scholarships based on family/financial status.

Thiel College (B)

75 College Avenue, Greenville PA 16125-2181
County: Mercer FICE Identification: 003376
Unit ID: 216357
Telephone: (724) 589-2000 Carnegie Class: Bac/Diverse
FAX Number: (724) 589-2850 Calendar System: Semester
URL: www.thiel.edu
Established: 1866 Annual Undergrad Tuition & Fees: $26,288
Enrollment: 1,083 Coed
Affiliation or Control: Evangelical Lutheran Church In America
IRS Status: 501(c)3
Highest Offering: Baccalaureate
Program: Liberal Arts And General; Teacher Preparatory
Accreditation: M

01 President ... Dr. Troy D. VAN AKEN
05 Vice Pres Academic Affairs ... Dr. Lynn FRANKEN
30 Vice President College Advancement ... Mr. Samuel D. SIPLE
10 Vice President for Finance & CFO ... Vacant
13 Chief Information Officer ... Mr. Kurt ASHLEY
04 Special Assistant to the President ... Ms. Nancy HOLCOMB
32 Dean of Students ... Mr. Michael MCKINNEY
84 Dean of Enrollment ... Ms. Amy BECHER
44 Dir of Special & Planned Giving ... Mr. Mario MARINI
08 Library Director ... Mr. Allen MORRILL
27 Director Information Office ... Ms. Joyce DEFRANCESCO
15 Director Human Resources ... Mrs. Susan SWARTZBECK
36 Career Service Director ... Mrs. Heather BALAS
19 Chief of Public Safety ... Mr. Donald AUBRECHT
41 Director of Athletics ... Mr. John LEIPHEIMER
06 Registrar ... Ms. Denise UREY
29 Director of Alumni Services ... Ms. Darlene MCCLINTOCK
42 Campus Pastor ... Rev. Bill BIXBY
37 Financial Aid Director ... Ms. Cynthia H. FARRELL
44 Dir Annual Giving/Parent Relations ... Ms. Lauren OMAN
23 Coordinator Health Services ... Mrs. Pamela M. DESPO

Thomas Jefferson University (C)

11th and Walnut Streets, Philadelphia PA 19107-5083
County: Philadelphia FICE Identification: 012393
Unit ID: 216366
Telephone: (215) 955-6000 Carnegie Class: Spec/Med
FAX Number: (215) 955-5587 Calendar System: Quarter
URL: www.jefferson.edu
Established: 1824 Annual Undergrad Tuition & Fees: $33,931
Enrollment: 3,730 Coed
Affiliation or Control: Independent Non-Profit IRS Status: 501(c)3
Highest Offering: Doctorate
Program: Liberal Arts And General; Professional
Accreditation: M, ANEST, CYTO, DENT, DMS, MED, MT, NMT, NURSE, OT, PH, PHAR, PTA, RAD, RADDOS, RADMAG, RTT

01 President ... Mr. Richard C. GOZON
63 Dean Jefferson Medicial College ... Dr. Mark L. TYKOCINSKI
05 Sr VP Academic Affairs ... Dr. Michael J. VERGARE
26 Senior VP Univ Marketing/Relations ... Ms. Carmhiel J. BROWN
10 Sr Vice President for Finance ... Mr. Alfred SALVATO
30 Sr VP for Development ... Mr. Frederick E. RUCCIUS
43 Sr VP & University Counsel ... Ms. Cristina G. CAVALIERI
46 Vice President for Research ... Dr. Steven E. MCKENZIE
18 Vice Pres for Facilities Mgmt ... Mr. Ronald E. BOWLAN
15 Interim VP Human Resources ... Mr. Alfred C. SALVATO
100 Chief of Staff ... Ms. Janice K. MARINI
58 Dean Jeff Col Grad Studies ... Dr. Gerald GRUNWALD
20 Assoc Sr VP Academic Affairs ... Dr. James ERDMANN
66 Dean Jefferson School of Nursing ... Dr. Beth Ann SWAN
67 Dean Jefferson School of Pharmacy ... Dr. Rebecca FINLEY
76 Dean Jefferson Sch Hlth Professions ... Dr. Janice P. BURKE
69 Dean Jefferson Sch of Pop Health ... Dr. David NASH
32 Dean of Student & Admissions JMC ... Dr. Clara A. CALLAHAN
07 Asst Dean of Admissions ... Dr. Karen JACOBS ASTLE
06 University Registrar ... Dr. Raelynn COOTER
29 Exec Director of Alumni Assoc JMC ... Dr. Phillip J. MARONE
08 University Librarian ... Mr. Anthony FRISBY
22 Univ Affirmative Action Officer ... Dr. Karen GLASER
23 Medical Director Univ Health Svcs ... Dr. Ellen M. O'CONNOR
24 Director Medical Media Services ... Mr. Pejman MAKARECHI
35 Assoc VP Student Affairs ... Dr. James ERDMANN
39 Manager Housing/Residence Life ... Ms. Patricia CRISTIANO KELLY
37 Univ Director Student Financial Aid ... Ms. Susan BATCHELOR
40 Director Bookstore ... Ms. Patricia HAAS
91 Chief Information Officer ... Mr. P. Douglas HERRICK
19 Director of Security ... Mr. Robert B. HENDRICK
85 Dir International Exchange Services ... Ms. Janice M. BOGEN
07 Dir Admission/Recruitment/Grad Stds ... Mr. Marc STEARNS
28 Asst Dean Diversity/Minority Affs ... Ms. Luz M. ORTIZ
96 Director of Purchasing ... Mr. Robert C. BURKHOLDER
35 Associate Dean Student Affairs ... Dr. Charles A. POHL

Triangle Tech, Dubois (D)

PO Box 551, Dubois PA 15801-0551
County: Clearfield FICE Identification: 021744
Unit ID: 216454
Telephone: (814) 371-2090 Carnegie Class: Assoc/PrivFP
FAX Number: (814) 371-9227 Calendar System: Semester
URL: www.triangle-tech.edu
Established: 1982 Annual Undergrad Tuition & Fees: $15,286
Enrollment: 212 Coed
Affiliation or Control: Proprietary IRS Status: Proprietary
Highest Offering: Associate Degree
Program: Occupational; 2-Year Principally Bachelor's Creditable; Technical Emphasis
Accreditation: ACCSC

01 Director ... Mrs. Stephanie A. CRAIG
03 Assistant Director ... Mr. Steve CURLL
05 Academic Affairs Advisor ... Mrs. Joan HOCKMAN
07 Admiss/Recruiting/Training Coord ... Mrs. Peggy SHILK
07 Admiss/Recruiting/Training Coord ... Ms. Janie A. DEJESUS
36 Career Advisor ... Mrs. Dori FORDOSKI
37 Financial Aid Administrator ... Ms. Michelle L. JASHINSKI

Triangle Tech, Erie (E)

2000 Liberty Street, Erie PA 16502-2594
County: Erie FICE Identification: 020902
Unit ID: 216427
Telephone: (814) 453-6016 Carnegie Class: Assoc/PrivFP
FAX Number: (814) 454-2818 Calendar System: Semester
URL: www.triangle-tech.edu
Established: 1976 Annual Undergrad Tuition & Fees: $15,604
Enrollment: 104 Coed
Affiliation or Control: Proprietary IRS Status: Proprietary
Highest Offering: Associate Degree
Program: Occupational
Accreditation: ACCSC

00 CEO ... Mr. James R. AGRAS
01 Campus Director ... Mr. Ken ADAMS
03 Executive Vice President ... Mr. Rudy K. AGRAS
07 Vice President of Admissions ... Vacant

Triangle Tech, Greensburg (F)

222 E Pittsburgh Street, Suite A, Greensburg PA 15601-3304
County: Westmoreland FICE Identification: 021290
Unit ID: 216445
Telephone: (724) 832-1050 Carnegie Class: Assoc/PrivFP
FAX Number: (724) 834-0325 Calendar System: Semester
URL: www.triangle-tech.edu
Established: 1944 Annual Undergrad Tuition & Fees: $15,594
Enrollment: 191 Coed
Affiliation or Control: Proprietary IRS Status: Proprietary
Highest Offering: Associate Degree
Program: Occupational; 2-Year Principally Bachelor's Creditable; Technical Emphasis
Accreditation: ACCSC

00 Chairman/CEO ... James R. AGRAS
01 President ... Timothy J. MCMAHON
07 Director of Admissions ... John A. MAZZARESE
05 Senior Director ... Deborah G. HEPBURN
12 Director of Branch Campus/CEO ... Paul BEADLE

Triangle Tech, Pittsburgh (G)

1940 Perrysville Avenue, Pittsburgh PA 15214-3897
County: Allegheny FICE Identification: 007839
Unit ID: 216436
Telephone: (412) 359-1000 Carnegie Class: Assoc/PrivFP
FAX Number: (412) 359-1012 Calendar System: Semester
URL: www.triangle-tech.edu
Established: 1944 Annual Undergrad Tuition & Fees: $15,651
Enrollment: 280 Coed
Affiliation or Control: Proprietary IRS Status: Proprietary
Highest Offering: Associate Degree
Program: Occupational; 2-Year Principally Bachelor's Creditable; Technical Emphasis
Accreditation: ACCSC

00 Chairman/CEO ... James R. AGRAS
01 President ... Timothy J. MCMAHON
07 Director of Admissions ... Jason VALLOZZI
05 Senior Director ... Deborah G. HEPBURN
12 School Director ... Anthony VARGO

Trinity Episcopal School for Ministry (H)

311 11th Street, Ambridge PA 15003-2397
County: Beaver FICE Identification: 022993
Unit ID: 216463
Telephone: (724) 266-3838 Carnegie Class: Spec/Faith
FAX Number: (724) 266-4617 Calendar System: Semester
URL: www.tsm.edu
Established: 1976 Annual Graduate Tuition & Fees: $10,860
Enrollment: 135 Coed
Affiliation or Control: Protestant Episcopal IRS Status: 501(c)3
Highest Offering: Doctorate; No Undergraduates
Program: Professional; Religious Emphasis
Accreditation: THEOL

01 Dean/President ... V.Rev. Justyn TERRY
05 Academic Dean ... Rev Dr. Mark STEVENSON
11 Dean Administration/Dir DMin Degree ... Rev Dr. H. Lawrence THOMPSON, III
32 Dean of Students ... Rev. Tina LOCKETT
37 Financial Aid Director ... Ms. Stacey WILLIARD
06 Dir Academic Support Tech/Registrar ... Rev. William STARKE
07 Director of Admissions ... Rev. Tina LOCKETT
08 Library Director ... Ms. Susanah HANSON
21 Director of Accounting ... Mrs. Karen GETZ
30 Director of Development ... Mr. Jack WALSH

The University of the Arts (I)

320 S Broad Street, Philadelphia PA 19102-4944
County: Philadelphia FICE Identification: 003350
Unit ID: 215105
Telephone: (215) 717-6000 Carnegie Class: Spec/Arts
FAX Number: (215) 717-6045 Calendar System: Semester
URL: www.uarts.edu
Established: 1876 Annual Undergrad Tuition & Fees: $34,840
Enrollment: 2,246 Coed
Affiliation or Control: Independent Non-Profit IRS Status: 501(c)3
Highest Offering: Master's
Program: Liberal Arts And General; Teacher Preparatory; Professional; Fine Arts Emphasis
Accreditation: M, ART, MUS

01 President ... Mr. Sean T. BUFFINGTON
05 Provost ... Dr. Kirk E. PILLOW
26 Director University Communications ... Mr. Paul F. HEALY
32 VP Student Affs & Dean of Students ... Dr. Gregory NAYOR
20 Assistant Provost ... Mr. James SAVOIE
30 Vice Pres Advancement ... Ms. Lucille HUGHES
04 Exec Assistant to the President ... Ms. Pamela SHROPSHIRE
10 Vice Pres Finance/Administration ... Mr. Stephen LIGHTCAP
15 Director of Personnel Services ... Ms. Jennifer EDWARDS
08 Assoc Provost/Director of Libraries ... Ms. Carol GRANEY
19 Director of Public Safety ... Mr. Randolph MERCED
27 Vice Pres Technology & Info Svcs ... Mr. Thomas CARNWATH
90 Director Academic Computing ... Vacant
91 Director of Information Systems ... Mr. Jack POST
91 Director Network Services ... Mr. Kevin BRENNAN
07 VP Enroll Mgmt/Dean of Admissions ... Vacant
06 Registrar ... Ms. Margaret KIP
37 VP Enroll Mgmt/Dean of Fin Aid ... Ms. Chris PESOTSKI
57 Dean College Art/Media & Design ... Mr. Christopher SHARROCK
79 Dean of Liberal Arts ... Dr. Catherine KODAT
51 Dean of Continuing Studies ... Ms. Erin ELMAN
35 Director of Student Life ... Ms. Kathleen EMBLETON
36 Director of Career Services ... Ms. Elisa SEEHERMAN
38 Director Student Counseling ... Mr. Brian HAINSTOCK
09 Director of Institutional Research ... Ms. Beth E. FREDERICK
85 Dir International Student Services ... Ms. Mara FLAMM
29 Director Alumni & Parent Relations ... Ms. Lauren VILLANUEVE

University of Pennsylvania (J)

34th & Spruce Streets, Philadelphia PA 19104
County: Philadelphia FICE Identification: 003378
Unit ID: 215062
Telephone: (215) 898-5000 Carnegie Class: RU/VH
FAX Number: (215) 898-5756 Calendar System: Semester
URL: www.upenn.edu

Established: 1740 Annual Undergrad Tuition & Fees: $43,738
Enrollment: 24,832 Coed
Affiliation or Control: Independent Non-Profit IRS Status: 501(c)3
Highest Offering: Doctorate
Program: Liberal Arts And General; Teacher Preparatory; Professional
Accreditation: M, ANEST, BUS, CEA, CS, DENT, ENG, IPSY, LAW, LSAR, MED, MIDWF, NURSE, PH, SW, VET

01 President .... Dr. Amy GUTMANN
03 Executive Vice President .... Mr. Craig CARNAROLI
05 Provost .... Dr. Vincent PRICE
06 Registrar .... Vacant
07 Dean of Admissions .... Mr. Eric J. FURDA
32 Vice Provost University Life .... Dr. Valarie S. MCCOULLUM
10 Vice Pres Finance & Treasurer .... Mr. Stephen D. GOLDING
18 Vice Pres Facil/Real Est Svcs .... Ms. Anne PAPAGEORGE
17 CEO Univ of PA Health System .... Dr. Ralph W. MULLER
08 Vice Provost/Dir of Libraries .... Mr. Harry C. ROGERS
13 Vice Pres Info Systems/Computing .... Ms. Robin H. BECK
100 Vice Pres & Chief of Staff .... Mr. Gregory S. ROST
88 Vice Pres Institutional Affairs .... Ms. Joann MITCHELL
30 Vice Pres Dev/Alumni Relations .... Mr. John H. ZELLER
16 Vice Pres Human Resources .... Dr. John J. HEUER
86 Vice Pres Govt & Community Affairs .... Mr. Jeffrey COOPER
19 Vice President Public Safety .... Ms. Maureen RUSH
26 Vice Pres for Univ Communications .... Mr. Stephen J. MACCARTHY
88 Vice Pres Business Services .... Ms. Marie D. WITT
45 Vice Pres Budget Mgmt Analysis .... Ms. Bonnie C. GIBSON
43 Senior Vice Pres/General Counsel .... Ms. Wendy S. WHITE
101 Secretary of the University .... Ms. Leslie L. KRUHLY
20 Vice Provost for Education .... Dr. Andrew N. BINNS
20 Vice Provost Faculty Affairs .... Dr. Lynn H. LEES
29 Asst Vice Pres Alumni Relations .... Mr. Fredrick H. WAMPLER
88 Vice Provost for Research .... Dr. Steven J. FLUHARTY
88 Assoc Vice Provost Rsrch Svcs .... Ms. Pamela S. CAUDILL
14 Assoc Vice Pres Networking/ Telecom .... Mr. Michael A. PALLADINO
88 Assoc VP Audit Compl & Privacy .... Ms. Mary Lee BROWN
31 Assoc VP/Dir Ctr Cmty Partnerships .... Dr. Ira HARKAVY
28 Associate Vice Prov Equity & Access .... Rev. William GIPSON
21 Comptroller .... Mr. John F. HORN
63 Exec Vice Pres/Dean Sch of Medicine .... Dr. J. L. JAMESON
49 Dean School Arts & Sciences .... Dr. Rebecca W. BUSHNELL
54 Dean School of Engr/Applied Science .... Dr. Eduardo D. GLANDT
66 Dean School of Nursing .... Dr. Afaf I. MELEIS
50 Dean Wharton School .... Dr. Thomas S. ROBERTSON
60 Dean Annenberg Sch Communications .... Dr. Michael X. DELLI CARPINI
52 Dean School of Dental Medicine .... Dr. Denis F. KINANE
57 Dean PennDesign .... Ms. Marilyn J. TAYLOR
53 Dean Graduate School Education .... Dr. Andrew C. PORTER
61 Dean School of Law .... Mr. Michael A. FITTS
70 Dean School Social Policy/Practice .... Dr. Richard J. GELLES
74 Dean School of Veterinary Medicine .... Dr. Joan C. HENDRICKS
51 Vice Dean Cont & Profession Studies .... Ms. Nora E. LEWIS
35 Assoc VP Student Services .... Ms. Michelle H. BROWN-NEVERS
09 Asst VP Inst Research & Analysis .... Ms. Stacey J. LOPEZ
85 Dir Intl Student & Scholar Svcs .... Dr. Rodolfo R. ALTAMIRANO
36 Dir of Career Services .... Ms. Patricia L. ROSE
37 Dir Student Financial Aid .... Vacant
35 Executive Director Student Affairs .... Mr. Hikaru KOZUMA
38 Int Dir Counseling/Psych Services .... Dr. William B. ALEXANDER
102 Exec Dir Corp Rels/Int Dir Fnd Rels .... Dr. Don BONE
22 Exec Dir Affirm Action & Equal Op .... Mr. Sam B. STARKS
23 Dir Student Health Services .... Dr. Evelyn WIENER
88 Mgng Dir Annenberg Cr/Penn Presents .... Dr. Michael J. ROSE
88 Dir Morris Arboretum .... Mr. Paul W. MEYER
88 Dir Institute of Contempory Art .... Ms. Amy SADAO
88 Dir Museum of Archlgy/Anthrplgy .... Dr. Richard A. HODGES
88 Director Research Services .... Ms. Deborah M. FISHER
41 Dir Intercollegiate Athletics .... Mr. Steven BILSKY
24 IT Director .... Mr. James F. JOHNSON
91 IT Exec Dir Admin Info Tech .... Ms. Jeanne F. CURTIS
39 Dir College Houses & Academic Svcs .... Dr. Leslie J. DELAUTER
96 Chief Procurement Officer .... Vacant
42 Associate University Chaplain .... Rev. Charles L. HOWARD
104 Dir Study Abroad .... Ms. Barbara C. GORKA
106 Online Learning Manager .... Ms. Jacqueline P. CANDIDO

University of Pittsburgh (A)

4200 Fifth Avenue, Pittsburgh PA 15260-3583
County: Allegheny FICE Identification: 003379
Unit ID: 215293
Telephone: (412) 624-4141 Carnegie Class: RU/VH
FAX Number: N/A Calendar System: Semester
URL: www.pitt.edu
Established: 1787 Annual Undergrad Tuition & Fees (In-State): $15,730
Enrollment: 28,766 Coed
Affiliation or Control: State Related IRS Status: 501(c)3
Highest Offering: Doctorate
Program: Liberal Arts And General; Teacher Preparatory; Professional
Accreditation: M, ANEST, ARCPA, AUD, BUS, CEA, CLPSY, CORE, DENT, DH, DIETC, DIETD, ENG, HSA, HT, IPSY, LAW, LIB, MED, NURSE, OPE, OT, PERF, PH, PHAR, PTA, SP, SPAA, SW, @TEAC, THEA

01 Chancellor and Chief Exec Officer .... Mr. Mark A. NORDENBERG
05 Sr Vice Chancellor & Provost .... Dr. Patricia E. BEESON
63 Sr VC Health Sci/Dean Sch of Med .... Dr. Arthur S. LEVINE
03 Exec Vice Chanc/General Counsel .... Mr. Jerome COCHRAN
101 Secy of Brd of Trustees/Asst Chanc .... Dr. B. Jean FERKETISH
88 Associate Chancellor .... Dr. Vijai P. SINGH
10 Chief Financial Officer .... Mr. Arthur G. RAMICONE
30 Vice Chancellor Inst Advancement .... Mr. Albert J. NOVAK, JR.
43 Exec Vice Chanc & General Counsel .... Mr. Jerome COCHRAN
22 Dir Aff Action/Diversity & Inclus .... Ms. Carol W. MOHAMED
26 Vice Chancellor Public Affairs .... Mr. Robert HILL
100 Vice Chanc Cmty Init/Chief of Staff .... Mr. G. Reynolds CLARK
86 Vice Chanc Governmental Relations .... Mr. Paul A. SUPOWITZ
18 Assoc Vice Chanc Facilities Mgmt .... Mr. Joseph W. FINK
15 Assoc Vice Chanc Human Resources .... Mr. Ronald W. FRISCH
88 Assoc Vice Chanc Mgmt Info & Analy .... Ms. Jane W. THOMPSON
27 Sr Assoc Vice Chanc Univ News/Mag .... Mr. John HARVITH
20 Vice Provost Undergraduate Studies .... Dr. Juan J. MAFREDI
58 Vice Provost Graduate Studies .... Dr. Alberta M. SBRAGIA
88 Asst Provost Strategic/Program Dev .... Ms. Sheila W. RATHKE
45 Vice Prov Acad Plng/Resource Mgmt .... Dr. David N. DEJONG
46 Vice Provost for Research .... Dr. George E. KLINZING
20 Vice Provost for Faculty Affairs .... Dr. Andrew R. BLAIR
29 Assoc Vice Chanc Alumni Relations .... Mr. Jeffery T. GLEIM
39 Associate Vice Chancellor Business .... Mr. James V. EARLE
06 Interim University Registrar .... Mr. Ralph E. HERTEL
41 Athletic Director .... Mr. Steve C. PEDERSON
07 Chief Enrollment Officer .... Mr. Marc L. HARDING
32 Vice Provost and Dean of Students .... Dr. Kathy W. HUMPHREY
49 Dean Deitrich Sch Arts & Sci/CGS .... Dr. N. John COOPER
92 Dean University Honors College .... Dr. Edward M. STRICKER
50 Dean Jos M Katz Gr Sch Bus .... Dr. John T. DELANEY
53 Dean of School of Education .... Dr. Alan M. LESGOLD
54 Dean Swanson School of Engineering .... Dr. Gerald D. HOLDER
61 Dean of School of Law .... Mr. William M. CARTER
80 Dean Grad Sch Public/Intl Affs .... Dr. John T. KEELER
70 Dean School of Social Work .... Dr. Larry E. DAVIS
62 Dean School Information Sciences .... Dr. Ronald L. LARSEN
52 Dean School of Dental Medicine .... Dr. Thomas W. BRAUN
66 Dean of School of Nursing .... Dr. Jaqueline DUNBAR-JACOB
67 Dean School of Pharmacy .... Dr. Patricia D. KROBOTH
69 Dean Grad School Public Health .... Dr. Donald S. BURKE
76 Dean School Health & Rehab Science .... Dr. Clifford E. BRUBAKER
40 Interim Director Book Centers .... Ms. Debra R. FYOCK
24 Dir Ctr Instruct Dev/Distance Educ .... Ms. Cynthia GOLDEN
13 Dir Computer Svcs/Systems Devel .... Ms. Jinx P. WALTON
104 Dir International Services .... Dr. Charles L. NIEMAN
09 Director Institutional Research .... Ms. Cynthia A. ROBERTS
21 Director Internal Audit .... Mr. John P. ELLIOTT
36 Dir Career Dev/St Empl/Place Asst .... Ms. Cheryl S. FINLAY
25 Director Research .... Mr. Allen A. DIPALMA
38 Director of Counseling Center .... Dr. Tevya ZUKOR
08 Director Univ Library System .... Mr. Rush G. MILLER
19 Chief University Police .... Mr. Timothy R. DELANEY
23 Director Student Health Svcs .... Dr. Elizabeth WETTICK
96 Manager Purchasing Services .... Mr. Thomas E. YOUNGS, JR.
44 Sr Exec Director Planned Giving .... Mr. Walter E. BROWN
102 Exec Dir Corp & Found Relations .... Mr. Andrew B. KOVALCIK
04 Exec Asst to the Chancellor .... Ms. Mary Jo RACE

University of Pittsburgh at Bradford (B)

300 Campus Drive, Bradford PA 16701-2812
County: McKean FICE Identification: 003380
Unit ID: 215266
Telephone: (814) 362-7500 Carnegie Class: Bac/Diverse
FAX Number: (814) 362-7578 Calendar System: Semester
URL: www.upb.pitt.edu
Established: 1963 Annual Undergrad Tuition & Fees (In-State): $12,810
Enrollment: 1,564 Coed
Affiliation or Control: State Related IRS Status: 501(c)3
Highest Offering: Baccalaureate
Program: Liberal Arts And General; Teacher Preparatory; Professional
Accreditation: &M, ADNUR, NUR

01 President .... Dr. Livingston ALEXANDER
05 Vice President Academic Affairs .... Dr. Steven E. HARDIN
32 Vice Pres/Dean Student Affairs .... Dr. K. James EVANS
10 Vice President for Business Affairs .... Mr. Richard T. ESCH
20 Associate Dean of Academic Affairs .... Dr. Stephen F. ROBAR
35 Assoc Dn Stdnt Affs/Dir Career Svcs .... Dr. Holly J. SPITTLER
39 Assc Dn Stdnt Affs/Dir Judicial Aff .... Dr. Ronald S. BINDER
30 Exec Dir Institutional Advancement .... Mrs. Jill M. BALLARD
26 Director Communications & Marketing .... Mrs. Patricia FRANTZ CERCONE
07 Director of Admissions .... Mr. Alex P. NAZEMETZ
06 Registrar/Asst Dean Academic Affs .... Mr. James L. BALDWIN
37 Director Financial Aid .... Ms. Melissa IBANEZ
88 Director Academic Sucess Center .... Vacant
66 Director of Nursing .... Dr. Lisa FIORENTINO
08 Director of Library Services .... Vacant
51 Director Adult Continuing Education .... Mr. Raymond R. GEARY, JR.
41 Director Athletics/Recreat Sports .... Ms. Lorraine R. MAZZA
21 Director Budget & Fiscal Reporting .... Mr. Steve WILLIAMS
18 Director Facilities Management .... Mr. Peter J. BUCHHEIT
19 Director of Campus Police & Safety .... Mr. Dan SONGER
13 Dir Computing/Telecom/Media Svcs .... Mr. Donald C. LEWICKI
88 Coordinator of Community Engagement .... Mrs. Tonya J. ACKLEY
29 Director Alumni Relations .... Ms. Lindsay RETCHLESS
88 Director Student Activities .... Ms. Christina L. GRAHAM
23 Director of Student Health Services .... Ms. Bonnie K. MCMILLEN
38 Director Counseling Services .... Dr. Leslie L. RHINEHART
31 Director of Auxiliary Services .... Mr. Rhett KENNEDY
88 Director of Arts Programming .... Vacant
15 Manager Human Resources .... Ms. Laurel E. PHILLIPS
40 Manager Book Center .... Ms. Leasa A. MALEY
96 Manager of Purchasing .... Ms. Heidi A. ANDERSON
83 Chair Div Behavioral/Social Sci .... Vacant
76 Chair Div Biological/Health Sci .... Dr. Mary MULCAHY
79 Chair Div Communications/Arts .... Mr. Jeff GUTERMAN
50 Chair Div of Management/Education .... Dr. Betsy MATZ
81 Chair Div Phys/Computational Sci .... Dr. Yong-Zhuo CHEN
09 Director of Institutional Research .... Vacant
28 Director of Diversity .... Mrs. Liza J. GREVILLE
36 Director Student Placement .... Dr. Holly J. SPITTLER

† Regional accreditation is carried under the parent institution in Pittsburgh, PA.

University of Pittsburgh at Greensburg (C)

150 Finoli Drive, Greensburg PA 15601-5898
County: Westmoreland FICE Identification: 003381
Unit ID: 215275
Telephone: (724) 837-7040 Carnegie Class: Bac/A&S
FAX Number: (724) 836-9901 Calendar System: Semester
URL: www.upg.pitt.edu
Established: 1963 Annual Undergrad Tuition & Fees (In-State): $12,890
Enrollment: 1,846 Coed
Affiliation or Control: State Related IRS Status: 501(c)3
Highest Offering: Baccalaureate
Program: Liberal Arts And General; Business Emphasis
Accreditation: &M

01 President .... Dr. Sharon P. SMITH
05 Vice Pres of Academic Affairs .... Dr. J. Wesley JAMISON
11 Vice President Administration .... Mr. Carl A. ROSSMAN
32 Dean of Student Services .... Mr. Rick A. FOGLE
07 Director of Admissions .... Ms. Heather KABALA
08 Director Millstein Library .... Dr. Patricia M. DUCK
14 Interim Dir Comp Svcs & Info Sys .... Mr. Robert W. SMITH
06 Registrar .... Ms. Linda SMITH
15 Director Human Resources .... Ms. Karen M. ANTONIAK
37 Director of Financial Aid .... Ms. Brandi DARR
41 Director of Athletics/Recreation .... Mr. Anthony BERICH
18 Director Plant Maintenance .... Mr. Robert KAUFMAN
21 Director Business Affairs .... Mrs. Ronna COLLAND
30 Dir Univ Rels/Instl Advancement .... Ms. Jodi KRAISINGER
36 Director Career Services .... Ms. Elizabeth TIEDEMANN
38 Director of Counseling .... Ms. Gayle PAMERLEAU
26 Director Media Relations .... Ms. Susan ISOLA
96 Purchasing Administrator .... Mr. Allen TEDROW
29 Coordinator Alumni Affairs .... Mr. Joshua GMYS

† Regional accreditation is carried under the parent institution in Pittsburgh, PA.

University of Pittsburgh at Johnstown (D)

450 Schoolhouse Road, Johnstown PA 15904-2990
County: Cambria FICE Identification: 003382
Unit ID: 215284
Telephone: (814) 269-7000 Carnegie Class: Bac/Diverse
FAX Number: (814) 269-2096 Calendar System: Semester
URL: www.pitt-johnstown.pitt.edu
Established: 1927 Annual Undergrad Tuition & Fees (In-State): $12,966
Enrollment: 2,881 Coed
Affiliation or Control: State Related IRS Status: 501(c)3
Highest Offering: Baccalaureate
Program: Liberal Arts And General; Teacher Preparatory
Accreditation: &M, ENGT

01 President .... Dr. Jem SPECTAR
11 Assoc VP Admin Services & Planning .... Mr. Christian J. STUMPF
10 Vice Pres Finance & Administration .... Ms. Amy BUXBAUM
05 Vice Pres for Academic Affairs .... Dr. Janet L. GRADY
32 Vice Pres for Student Affairs .... Mr. Jon WESCOTT
04 Secretary to the President .... Mrs. Susan K. PALOV
29 Assoc VP Inst Advance & Comm Rels .... Mr. Robert W. KNIPPLE
30 Exec Dir Institutional Advancement .... Mrs. Lynn I. BARGER
08 Director Library .... Ms. Deborah RINDERKNECHT
13 Associate Vice Pres for Info Tech .... Mr. J. Jeffrey SERNELL
06 Registrar .... Vacant
22 Sr Officer for Equity & Inclusion .... Ms. Laura PERRY-THOMPSON
26 Director Marketing .... Vacant
15 Campus Director Of Human Resources .... Mrs. Pamela J. SABOL
18 Director of Facilities Operations .... Mr. Andrew M. CSIKOS
35 Director of Student Life .... Ms. Sherri RAE
38 Director Wellness Center .... Ms. Katrin A. WOLFE
37 Director Financial Aid .... Mrs. Jeanine M. LAWN
19 Director of Campus Police .... Mr. Eric ZANGAGLIA
23 Exec Dir of Health & Wellness Svcs .... Mrs. Theresa M. HORNER
39 Director Housing & Residence Life .... Mr. Mark A. DOUGHERTY
40 Dir Bookstore/Convenience Store .... Mr. John ZIATS
41 Athletics Director .... Mr. Patrick PECORA
96 Exec Dir of Budget & Purchasing .... Ms. Dolores BERKEY
21 Director of Business Office Opers .... Ms. Amanda E. REED
85 Director of International Services .... Mrs. Jennifer S. KIST
88 Exec Dir of Auxiliary Services .... Mrs. Joyce A. RADOVANIC
07 Dir of Admissions & Recruitment .... Ms. Therese GRIMES
51 Dir of Advanced & Continuing Educ .... Mrs. Stephanie KORBER
88 Director of Academic Success Center .... Mrs. Katherine KINSINGER
36 Director Career Services .... Mr. Bernard J. SARNESO

† Regional accreditation is carried under the parent institution in Pittsburgh, PA.

University of Pittsburgh at Titusville (A)

504 E Main, Titusville PA 16354-2097
County: Crawford FICE Identification: 003383
Unit ID: 215309
Telephone: (814) 827-4400 Carnegie Class: Assoc/Pub2in4
FAX Number: (814) 827-4448 Calendar System: Semester
URL: www.upt.pitt.edu
Established: 1963 Annual Undergrad Tuition & Fees (In-State): $11,118
Enrollment: 448 Coed
Affiliation or Control: State Related IRS Status: 501(c)3
Highest Offering: Associate Degree
Program: 2-Year Principally Bachelor's Creditable
Accreditation: &M, ADNUR, PTAA

01 President .... Dr. Livingston ALEXANDER
05 Int Vice Pres for Academic Affairs .... Dr. David FITZ
10 Vice President for Business Affairs .... Vacant
32 Vice Pres for Student Affairs .... Dr. Checka LEINWALL
84 Exec Director Enrollment Management .... Vacant
13 Director of Computing and Telecomm .... Vacant
08 Library Director .... Mr. Patrick HALL
06 Registrar .... Mr. Christopher COAT
07 Director of Admissions .... Mr. Robert WYANT
21 Director Student Accounts .... Ms. Nicole NEELY
15 Director Human Resources .... Ms. Debra BIGGERSTAFF
18 Director of Facilities Management .... Mr. Jon N. EDWARDS
26 Director Public Relations .... Ms. Tammy KNAPP
40 Director of Bookstore .... Ms. Margaret WAGNER
29 Director Alumni Relations .... Ms. Tammy KNAPP
37 Director Student Financial Aid .... Ms. Sue Ann BLOOM
96 Director of Purchasing .... Ms. Pamela KREPPS
41 Int Athletic Director .... Mr. Harry MILLER

† Regional accreditation is carried under the parent institution in Pittsburgh, PA.

University of the Sciences in Philadelphia (B)

600 S 43rd Street, Philadelphia PA 19104-4495
County: Philadelphia FICE Identification: 003353
Unit ID: 215132
Telephone: (215) 596-8800 Carnegie Class: Spec/Health
FAX Number: (215) 895-1100 Calendar System: Semester
URL: www.usciences.edu
Established: 1821 Annual Undergrad Tuition & Fees: $31,774
Enrollment: 2,807 Coed
Affiliation or Control: Independent Non-Profit IRS Status: 501(c)3
Highest Offering: Doctorate
Program: Professional
Accreditation: M, OT, PHAR, PTA

01 President .... Dr. Helen GILES-GEE
05 Provost .... Vacant
10 Senior VP for Finance & CFO .... Mr. Joseph G. TRAINOR
88 Senior VP for Div External Affairs .... Mr. William ASHTON
30 VP for Institutional Advancement .... Ms. Carrie COLLINS
31 Vice Pres Community Partnerships .... Ms. Elizabeth BRESSI-STOPPE
26 Vice President of Marketing .... Ms. Maria BUEHLER
102 VP Corporate Relatons .... Dr. Susan BARRETT
100 Chief of Staff/VP Inst Effect .... Dr. Peter MILLER
13 Exec Dir Information Technology .... Mr. John MASCIANTONIO
84 Assoc Provost for Enrollment Mgmt .... Ms. Barbara ELLIOTT
27 Associate Provost/CIO .... Dr. Mark NESTOR
37 Director of Financial Aid .... Ms. Paula LEHRBERGER
06 Registrar .... Mr. Alan SIMS
07 Executive Director of Admissions .... Ms. Diana COLLINS
29 Director of Alumni Relations .... Ms. Nancy SHILS
08 Director of Library Services .... Mr. Charles MYERS
58 Dean Graduate Studies .... Dr. Rodney WIGENT
32 Dean of Students .... Dr. William J. CUNNINGHAM
67 Dean of Pharmacy .... Dr. Lisa LAWSON
49 Dean Misher College Arts & Sci .... Dr. Suzanne K. MURPHY
76 Dean Samson College of Health Sci .... Dr. Laurie SHERWEN
88 Dean of Mayes College .... Dr. Andrew PETERSON
15 Exec Director Human Resources .... Ms. Rosalie I. JONES
19 Executive Director Public Safety .... Mr. Michael ROSSANO
41 Athletic Director .... Mr. Paul KLIMITAS
88 Director of Student Engagement .... Mr. Ross RADISH
35 Director of Student Life .... Ms. Susanne E. FERRIN
39 Residence Life Administrator .... Mr. Ryan CROCETTO
85 Director of Multicultural Affairs .... Mr. Walter PERRY
09 Director of Institutional Research .... Ms. Anne B. HOROWITZ
21 Controller/Asst VP Finance .... Ms. Brigid K. ISACKMAN
36 Director Career Services .... Ms. Kimberly BRYANT
38 Director Student Counseling .... Dr. Paul FURTAW
96 Manager University Purchasing .... Mr. Thomas MOIANI
88 Assistant Provost Spec Projects .... Dr. John CONNORS
88 Director Academic Advising .... Mr. Joseph CANADAY
18 Director of Facilities .... Mr. Dan SEVERINO

The University of Scranton (C)

800 Linden St, Scranton PA 18510-4622
County: Lackawanna FICE Identification: 003384
Unit ID: 215929
Telephone: (570) 941-7400 Carnegie Class: Master's L
FAX Number: (570) 941-6369 Calendar System: Semester
URL: www.scranton.edu
Established: 1888 Annual Undergrad Tuition & Fees: $37,281
Enrollment: 6,034 Coed
Affiliation or Control: Roman Catholic IRS Status: 501(c)3
Highest Offering: Doctorate
Program: Liberal Arts And General; Teacher Preparatory; Professional
Accreditation: M, ANEST, BUS, CACREP, CORE, CS, HSA, NURSE, OT, PTA, @TEAC, TED

01 President .... Rev. Kevin P. QUINN, SJ
05 Sr VP Academic Affairs & Provost .... Dr. Harold BAILLIE
10 Sr VP Finance & Administration .... Mr. Edward J. STEINMETZ
32 Vice President Student Affairs .... Dr. Vincent CARILLI
45 Vice President Planning/CIO .... Dr. Jerome P. DESANTO
26 Vice President for External Affairs .... Mr. Gerald ZABOSKI
16 Vice President Human Resources .... Ms. Patricia A. DAY
42 VP for University Ministries .... Rev. Richard G. MALLOY, SJ
43 General Counsel .... Mr. Robert B. FARRELL
49 Dean Arts & Sciences .... Dr. Brian P. CONNIFF
50 Dean Kania School Management .... Dr. Michael O. MENSAH
58 Dean Grad School/Continuing Educ .... Dr. William J. WELSH
88 Dean Panuska Col of Prof Studies .... Dr. Debra A. PELLEGRINO
35 Asst VP Stdnt Affs/Dean of Students .... Ms. Anitra M. MCSHEA
08 Dean of the Library/Info Fluency .... Mr. Charles E. KRATZ, JR.
51 Asst Dean of OL/Off Campus Program .... Mrs. Lisa M. LOBASSO
21 Assistant Vice President Finance .... Mr. Robert J. THOMAS
20 Assoc Provost for Academic Affairs .... Dr. Joseph H. DREISBACH
07 Assoc VP Admiss & Undergrad Enroll .... Mr. Joseph M. ROBACK
84 Asst VP Admissions & Enrollment .... Ms. Mary Kay ASTON
21 Assistant Provost for Operations .... Ms. Anne Marie STAMFORD
06 Registrar .... Ms. Helen H. STAGER
37 Director of Financial Aid .... Mr. William R. BURKE
36 Director of Career Services .... Mrs. Constance F. MCDONNELL
29 Director of Alumni Relations .... Ms. Maryjane S. ROONEY
28 Director of Equity/Diversity Office .... Ms. Rosette B. ADERA
09 Dir Inst Research/Assessment .... Ms. Valerie A. TAYLOR
38 Director of Counseling Center .... Mr. Thomas P. SMITH
96 Director of Purchasing .... Mr. Gary S. ZAMPANO
100 Chf of Staff/Int VP Dev & Alum Rel .... Mr. Robert W. DAVIS, JR.
18 Asst VP Facilities Operations .... Mr. James DEVERS
30 Assistant VP Development .... Ms. Marise GAROFALO

Ursinus College (D)

PO Box 1000, 601 E Main Street, Collegeville PA 19426-1000
County: Montgomery FICE Identification: 003385
Unit ID: 216524
Telephone: (610) 409-3000 Carnegie Class: Bac/A&S
FAX Number: (610) 489-0627 Calendar System: Semester
URL: www.ursinus.edu
Established: 1869 Annual Undergrad Tuition & Fees: $43,100
Enrollment: 1,750 Coed
Affiliation or Control: Independent Non-Profit IRS Status: 501(c)3
Highest Offering: Baccalaureate
Program: Liberal Arts And General; Teacher Preparatory
Accreditation: M

01 President .... Dr. Bobby FONG
05 Vice Pres Acad Affs/Dean of College .... Dr. Lucien T. WINEGAR
10 Vice Pres Finance & Administration .... Mr. Winfield L. GUILMETTE
30 Senior Vice Pres for Advancement .... Ms. Jill A. MARSTELLER
84 Vice President for Enrollment .... Mr. Richard G. DIFELICIANTONIO
32 Vice Pres of Student Affairs/Dean .... Ms. Deborah O. NOLAN
21 Associate Vice Pres/Controller .... Mr. James COOPER
07 Dean of Admissions .... Mr. Richard FLOYD
44 Exec Director of Planned Giving .... Mr. Mark P. GADSON
08 Library Director .... Mr. Charles JAMISON
36 Director of Career Services .... Mrs. Carla M. RINDE
18 Director of Physical Facilities .... Mr. Andrew FEICK
41 Director of Athletics .... Mrs. Laura MOLIKEN
27 Director College Communications .... Ms. Wendy GREENBERG
37 Director Student Financial Services .... Mrs. Suzanne SPARROW
06 Registrar .... Ms. Barbara A. BORIS
29 Director of Alumni Relations .... Vacant
20 Associate Dean of the College .... Dr. Annette V. LUCAS
15 Director Human Resources .... Ms. Kelly WILLIAMS

Valley Forge Christian College (E)

1401 Charlestown Road, Phoenixville PA 19460-2399
County: Chester FICE Identification: 003306
Unit ID: 216542
Telephone: (610) 935-0450 Carnegie Class: Bac/Diverse
FAX Number: (610) 935-9353 Calendar System: Semester
URL: www.vfcc.edu
Established: 1939 Annual Undergrad Tuition & Fees: $18,292
Enrollment: 1,128 Coed
Affiliation or Control: Assemblies Of God Church IRS Status: 501(c)3
Highest Offering: Master's
Program: Liberal Arts And General; Teacher Preparatory; Professional; Religious Emphasis
Accreditation: M, SW

01 President .... Dr. Donald G. MEYER
05 VP of Academic Affairs .... Dr. Kevin E. BEERY
10 VP of Finance .... Mr. Richard A. DUNHAM
32 VP of Student Life .... Rev. Jennifer D. GALE
30 Executive Director of Development .... Mr. Samuel J. LUFI
108 Dean Inst Assessment/Online Educ .... Dr. Judy DUNHAM
21 Comptroller .... Mr. Jonathan CAPECI
84 Exec Director Enrollment Management .... Mrs. Evie MEYER
49 Arts & Sciences Dept Chair .... Dr. Michael DI GIACOMO
83 Behavioral Sciences Dept Chair .... Dr. David SCOLFORO
50 Business Dept Chair .... Dr. William CLARKSON
73 Church Ministry Dept Chair .... Dr. Ronald HALL
73 Deaf Pastoral Minstries Dept Chair .... Dr. JoAnn SMITH
72 Digital Media/Commun Dept Chair .... Mr. Leone BILOTTA
53 Education Dept Chair .... Dr. A. Glann MCCLURE
88 Intercultural Studies Dept Chair .... Rev. Jennifer DUNCAN
64 Music Dept Chair .... Dr. William DESANTLO
88 Director of Accounting .... Mrs. Betty SMITH
07 Director of Admissions .... Rev. William CHENCO
29 Director Alumni Relations .... Mrs. Kristie OVERLY
41 Director of Athletics .... Mr. Jon MACK
36 Director Career Services .... Mrs. Amy THURSTON
37 Director of Financial Aid .... Mrs. Linda STEIN
15 Director Human Resources .... Mrs. Veronica BIRD
14 Director of Information Technology .... Mr. Brian SWOMLEY
08 Librarian/Dir Storms Research Ctr .... Mrs. Deborah HIRNEISEN
26 Director of Marketing .... Mrs. Michelle MALONEY
06 Registrar .... Mr. Russell CAMBRIA
35 Campus Director .... Mrs. Wendy BEERY
35 Campus Director .... Mr. Anthony ROSS
39 Residence Director .... Ms. Trinidad ANDINO
39 Residence Director .... Mr. Yung Won PARK

Valley Forge Military College (F)

1001 Eagle Road, Wayne PA 19087-3695
County: Delaware FICE Identification: 003386
Unit ID: 216551
Telephone: (610) 989-1450 Carnegie Class: Not Classified
FAX Number: (610) 975-9642 Calendar System: Semester
URL: www.vfmac.edu
Established: 1935 Annual Undergrad Tuition & Fees: $30,395
Enrollment: 268 Coed
Affiliation or Control: Independent Non-Profit IRS Status: 501(c)3
Highest Offering: Associate Degree
Program: 2-Year Principally Bachelor's Creditable
Accreditation: M

00 President Military Academy/ College .... Col. David R. GRAY
01 President of the College .... Dr. Kathleen M. ANDERSON
32 Commandant of Cadets .... WO2. Rik THORNTON
30 Vice President for Development .... Mr. Dennis SPIZUOCO
05 Dean Academic Services .... Col. Nan S. HOOD
10 Chief Financial Officer/COO .... Mr. Vincent VUONO
18 Director of Facilities .... Mr. Bryan K. GEILING
07 Director of College Admissions .... Ms. Kristen ROSE
08 Director of Library Services .... LTC. Jean L. SMITH
37 Director of Financial Aid .... Ms. Heather SHALLEY
102 Director Corporate/Foundation Rels .... Mrs. Ann SINATRA
15 Director of Human Resources .... Ms. Marianne MEADE
13 Director Information Technology .... Mr. Michael BROCK
41 Director of Athletics .... Col. Dominick P. LORUSSO
35 Dean Student Services .... Maj. Robert WOOD
09 Institutional Rsrch/Online Learning .... Ms. Gloria OIKELOME
06 Assistant Dean/Registrar .... Ms. Maureen MALONE
88 Transfer Advisor .... Ms. Joann MCCRACKEN

Vet Tech Institute (G)

125 Seventh Street, Pittsburgh PA 15222-3400
County: Allegheny FICE Identification: 008568
Unit ID: 213914
Telephone: (412) 391-7021 Carnegie Class: Assoc/PrivFP
FAX Number: (412) 232-4348 Calendar System: Semester
URL: www.vettechinstitute.edu
Established: 1958 Annual Undergrad Tuition & Fees: $14,116
Enrollment: 340 Coed
Affiliation or Control: Proprietary IRS Status: Proprietary
Highest Offering: Associate Degree
Program: Occupational; Technical Emphasis
Accreditation: ACCSC

01 Director .... Jackie FLYNN

Villanova University (H)

800 Lancaster Avenue, Villanova PA 19085-1699
County: Delaware FICE Identification: 003388
Unit ID: 216597
Telephone: (610) 519-4500 Carnegie Class: Master's L
FAX Number: (610) 519-5000 Calendar System: Semester
URL: www.villanova.edu
Established: 1842 Annual Undergrad Tuition & Fees: $42,740
Enrollment: 10,467 Coed
Affiliation or Control: Roman Catholic IRS Status: 501(c)3
Highest Offering: Doctorate
Program: Liberal Arts And General; Teacher Preparatory; Professional
Accreditation: M, ANEST, BUS, BUSA, CS, ENG, LAW, NURSE, SPAA

01 President .... Rev. Peter M. DONOHUE, OSA
43 Vice President & General Counsel .... Ms. Dorothy A. MALLOY
05 Vice President for Academic Affairs .... Rev. Kail C. ELLIS, OSA
30 Vice Pres University Advancement .... Mr. Michael O'NEILL
11 Vice Pres Administration/Finance .... Mr. Kenneth G. VALOSKY
13 Vice Pres/Chief Information Officer .... Mr. Stephen FUGALE
32 Vice President for Student Life .... Rev. John P. STACK, OSA
27 Vice Pres University Communication .... Ms. Ann DIEBOLD
20 Assoc Vice Pres Academic Affairs .... Dr. Craig WHEELAND
15 AVP Human Res/Affirm Action Ofcr .... Ms. Ellen KRUTZ
45 Assoc Vice Pres for Auxiliary Svcs .... Mr. Frederick C. SIEBER

42 Assoc Vice Pres Mission & Ministry .... Rev. Joseph L. FARRELL, OSA
29 Asst Vice Pres for Alumni Affairs .... Mr. Gary R. OLSEN
46 Asst Vice Pres for Research .... Dr. Milton T. COLE
51 Asst Vice Pres for Academic Affairs .... Dr. Robert D. STOKES
28 Asst VP Multicultural Affairs .... Dr. Teresa A. NANCE
84 Dean Enrollment Management .... Mr. Stephen R. MERRITT
09 Exec Dir Planning/Inst Research .... Dr. James F. TRAINER
18 Exec Director Facilities Management .... Mr. Robert MORRO
88 Asoc Dean Enrol Mgt For Stdnt Info ... Ms. Catherine H. CONNOR
88 Asc Dn Enr Mgt Univ Admiss/Fin Asst .... Mr. George J. WALTER
07 Director University Admission .... Mr. Michael GAYNOR
08 Librarian/Dir of Falvey Library .... Mr. Joseph LUCIA
35 Dean of Students .... Mr. Paul F. PUGH
49 Dean Liberal Arts & Sciences .... Dr. Jean A. LINNEY
50 Dean Villanova School of Business .... Dr. Patrick G. MAGGITTI
58 Dean Graduate Studies LA&S .... Dr. Adele LINDENMEYR
61 Dean School of Law .... Mr. John GOTANDA
66 Dean of Nursing .... Dr. M. Louise FITZPATRICK
54 Dean of Engineering .... Dr. Gary A. GABRIELE
55 Director Part Time Studies .... Mr. James R. JOHNSON
85 Director Intl/Human Services .... Mr. Stephen T. MCWILLIAMS
37 Director Financial Assistance .... Ms. Bonnie Lee BEHM
19 Director of Public Safety .... Mr. David TEDJESKE
36 Director Career Services .... Ms. Nancy J. DUDAK
92 Director of the Honors Program .... Dr. Thomas W. SMITH
38 Director of Univ Counseling Center .... Dr. Joan G. WHITNEY
94 Dir Women's Studies Programming .... Dr. Lisa SEWELL
94 Dir Women's Studies Academics .... Dr. Jean LUTES
39 Director Office of Residence Life .... Mr. Thomas DE MARCO
96 Director of Procurement .... Mr. John R. DURHAM
26 Director of Media Relations .... Mr. Jonathan GUST
40 Director of University Shop .... Mr. Frank L. HENNINGER
41 Director of Athletics .... Mr. Vincent P. NICASTRO
23 Medical Director Student Health Ctr .... Dr. Brian BULLOCK
23 Director Student Health Center .... Dr. Mary MCGONIGLE
06 Associate Registrar .... Ms. Melissa D. GERDING
24 Assoc Director Media Technologies .... Mr. Michael C. HOFFBERG
22 Asc Dir Center Multicultural Affs .... Ms. Linda COLEMAN
04 Special Asst to President/Ext Rels .... Rev. George F. RILEY

Washington & Jefferson College (A)

60 S Lincoln Street, Washington PA 15301-4801

County: Washington FICE Identification: 003389
Unit ID: 216667

Telephone: (724) 222-4400 Carnegie Class: Bac/A&S
FAX Number: (724) 223-6534 Calendar System: 4/1/4
URL: www.washjeff.edu
Established: 1781 Annual Undergrad Tuition & Fees: $37,850
Enrollment: 1,457 Coed
Affiliation or Control: Independent Non-Profit IRS Status: 501(c)3
Highest Offering: Baccalaureate
Program: Liberal Arts And General; Teacher Preparatory
Accreditation: M

01 President .... Dr. Tori HARING-SMITH
04 Special Assistant to the President .... Vacant
05 VP Academic Affairs/Dean of Faculty ... Dr. John E. ZIMMERMAN
10 CFO/VP Business/Finance .... Mr. Dennis MCMASTER
30 VP Development/Alumni Relations .... Mr. Michael P. GRZESIAK
84 Vice President for Enrollment .... Mr. Alton E. NEWELL
21 Assoc VP for Business & Finance .... Mr. Thomas SZEJKO
32 VP and Dean of Student Life .... Mr. Byron MCCRAE
44 Exec Dir Campaigns/Advancement Oper ... Ms. Karen CRENSHAW
20 Associate Dean of the Faculty .... Dr. Charles HANNON
28 Asst Dean Stdnt Life/Dir Diver Pgm .... Ms. Teanca SHEPHERD
18 Director of Facilities and Planning .... Mr. Troy BONTE
26 Dir Comm/Special Asst to President .... Ms. Karen OOSTERHOUS
06 Registrar .... Ms. Leslie MAXIN
29 Exec Dir Alumni Relations & Dev .... Ms. Michele HUFNAGEL
07 Director of Admission .... Mr. Robert ADKINS
37 Director Financial Aid .... Ms. Michelle ANDERSON
13 Dir of Information/Technology Svcs .... Mr. Daniel FAULK
15 Director Human Resources .... Ms. Susan MEHALIK
19 Director Protection Services .... Mr. Edward E. COCHRAN
36 Director Career Services .... Ms. Roberta CROSS
40 Bookstore Manager .... Ms. Cynthia BRICELAND
41 Director of Athletics .... Mr. William DUKETT
08 Director of Library Services .... Ms. Alexis RITTENBERGER
102 Foundation & Corp Relations Officer .... Ms. Julie THROCKMORTON
35 Associate Dean Student Life .... Mr. Steven ANDERSON
91 Assoc Director for Admin Computing .... Mr. Michael A. TIMKO
104 Dir of Global Education .... Ms. Tracie SEBASTIAN-FRUEHAUF
88 Associate Dean for Assessment .... Vacant
88 Asst Dean for Academic Advising .... Ms. Catherine SHERMAN
88 Director Conferences and Events .... Ms. Maureen VALENTINE
38 Director of Counseling Services .... Ms. Lisa HAMILTON

Waynesburg University (B)

51 W College Street, Waynesburg PA 15370-1222

County: Greene FICE Identification: 003391
Unit ID: 216694

Telephone: (724) 627-8191 Carnegie Class: Master's L
FAX Number: (724) 627-6416 Calendar System: Semester
URL: www.waynesburg.edu
Established: 1849 Annual Undergrad Tuition & Fees: $19,810
Enrollment: 2,458 Coed
Affiliation or Control: Presbyterian Church (U.S.A.) IRS Status: 501(c)3
Highest Offering: Doctorate
Program: Liberal Arts And General; Teacher Preparatory; Professional
Accreditation: M, CACREP, NURSE

01 President .... Dr. Timothy R. THYREEN
05 Provost .... Dr. Robert J. GRAHAM
30 Exec VP Institutional Advancement .... Mr. Doug LEE
10 Sr VP Business & Finance .... Mr. Roy R. BARNHART
07 Sr VP Enrollment & Univ Relations .... Ms. Robin L. KING
32 VP of Student Services .... Mrs. Mary CUMMINGS
06 Registrar .... Mrs. Vicki WILSON
41 Athletic Director .... Mr. Larry MARSHALL
13 Exec Dir Information Technology .... Mrs. Donna POSIVAK
08 Int Library Director .... Ms. Rea REDD
18 Director of Facilites Management .... Mr. John BURKE
26 Director of News and Publications .... Mrs. Pam CUNNINGHAM
36 Director of Placement .... Mrs. Marie E. COFFMAN
38 Student Counselor .... Mrs. Jane S. OWEN
21 Business Ofc Supervisor/Controller .... Mr. Dave MARTIN
23 Director of Health Services .... Vacant
42 Chaplain .... Mr. Tom RIBAR
15 Director Human Resources .... Mr. Tom HELMICK
37 Director Student Financial Aid .... Mr. Matthew STOKAN

Westminster College (C)

319 South Market Street, New Wilmington PA 16172-0001

County: Lawrence FICE Identification: 003392
Unit ID: 216807

Telephone: (724) 946-8761 Carnegie Class: Bac/A&S
FAX Number: (724) 946-7132 Calendar System: Semester
URL: www.westminster.edu
Established: 1852 Annual Undergrad Tuition & Fees: $31,510
Enrollment: 1,522 Coed
Affiliation or Control: Presbyterian Church (U.S.A.) IRS Status: 501(c)3
Highest Offering: Master's
Program: Liberal Arts And General; Teacher Preparatory
Accreditation: M, MUS

01 President .... Dr. Richard H. DORMAN
05 Vice Pres Academic Affs/Dean of Col .... Dr. Jesse T. MANN
30 VP Inst Advancement/Chief Dev Ofcr .... Ms. Gloria C. CAGIGAS
10 Vice Pres Finance/Mgmt Services .... Mr. Kenneth J. ROMIG
06 Registrar .... Ms. June PIERCE
07 Vice President for Enrollment .... Mr. Bradley P. TOKAR
42 Dean of the Chapel .... Rev. James R. MOHR
32 VP Student Affairs/Dean of Students .... Dr. Neal A. EDMAN
35 Assoc Dean of Student Affairs .... Ms. Camille HAWTHORNE
37 Director Student Financial Aid .... Ms. Cheryl GERBER
08 Head Librarian .... Ms. Erin T. SMITH
36 Director of Career Center .... Ms. Linda B. MEADE
29 Director of Alumni Relations .... Ms. Mary C. JAMES
27 Sr Dir Marketing/Communications .... Mr. Mark A. MEIGHEN
13 Director of Information Systems .... Mr. Paul N. WALLACE
51 Dir Cont Educ/Lifelong Learning .... Ms. Elizabeth E. HINES
58 Director Graduate Programs .... Ms. Elizabeth E. HINES
41 Athletic Director .... Mr. James E. DAFLER
18 Director of Physical Plant .... Mr. Owen W. WAGNER
21 Business Manager .... Ms. Janet M. SMITH
24 Director of Audio-Visual Aids .... Mr. Gary L. SWANSON
19 Director of Public Safety .... Mr. William A. BRANDT
09 Director of Institutional Research .... Dr. Gary D. LILLY
23 Director Health Services .... Ms. Melissa M. BARON
40 Bookstore Manager .... Ms. Kay A. GALANSKI
21 Controller .... Ms. Christine A. MILLER
15 Director of Human Resources .... Ms. Kimberlee K. CHRISTOFFERSON
38 Counselor .... Ms. Barbara I. QUINCY
28 Director of Diversity Services .... Ms. Jeannette HUBBARD

Westminster Theological Seminary (D)

Chestnut Hill, PO Box 27009, Philadelphia PA 19118-0009

County: Montgomery FICE Identification: 003393
Unit ID: 216816

Telephone: (215) 887-5511 Carnegie Class: Spec/Faith
FAX Number: (215) 887-5404 Calendar System: 4/1/4
URL: www.wts.edu
Established: 1929 Annual Graduate Tuition & Fees: $13,330
Enrollment: 613 Coed
Affiliation or Control: Independent Non-Profit IRS Status: 501(c)3
Highest Offering: Doctorate; No Undergraduates
Program: Liberal Arts And General; Professional; Religious Emphasis
Accreditation: M, THEOL

01 President .... Dr. Peter A. LILLBACK
30 Vice Pres Development .... Mr. William B. VINCENT
05 Vice President Academic Affairs .... Dr. Jeffrey K. JUE
45 Vice Pres Institutional Projects .... Dr. David GARNER
10 Chief Financial Officer .... Mr. Mark WILSON
11 Chief Administartive Officer .... Mr. Steven CARTER
88 Dean Student/Ministerial Formation .... Rev. Greg HOBAUGH
06 Registrar .... Ms. Melinda E. DUGAN
07 Director of Admissions .... Mr. Jonathan M. BRACK
08 Director of Library Services ... Mr. Alexander (Sandy) FINLAYSON
73 Director D.Min/Supervised Ministry .... Mr. Timothy Z. WITMER
40 Director Bookstore .... Mr. Chun LAI
37 Financial Aid Officer .... Ms. Fiona E. DAVENPORT
15 Director Human Resources .... Ms. Karin DEUSSING
13 Director Information Technology .... Mr. Matt HOGG
18 Physical Plant Manager .... Mr. Robert M. SEXTON
29 Dir Student Develop/Alumni Support .... Mr. John CURRIE
09 Dir Institutional Assess/Accred .... Ms. Rebecca M. LIPPERT

Westmoreland County Community College (E)

145 Pavilion Lane, Youngwood PA 15697-1895

County: Westmoreland FICE Identification: 010176
Unit ID: 216825

Telephone: (724) 925-4000 Carnegie Class: Assoc/Pub-S-SC
FAX Number: (724) 925-1150 Calendar System: Semester
URL: www.wccc.edu
Established: 1970 Annual Undergrad Tuition & Fees (In-District): $2,910
Enrollment: 6,943 Coed
Affiliation or Control: Local IRS Status: 501(c)3
Highest Offering: Associate Degree
Program: Occupational; 2-Year Principally Bachelor's Creditable
Accreditation: M, ACFEI, ADNUR, DA, DH, MAC

01 President .... Dr. Daniel J. OBARA
05 Vice Pres Academic Affs/Stdnt Svcs .... Dr. Nicole REAVES
11 Vice Pres Administrative Services .... Mr. Ronald E. EBERHARDT
51 VP Cont Educ/Workforce & Cmty Devel .... Dr. Patrick E. GERITY
20 Assoc VP Academic Affairs .... Dr. Nicole REAVES
10 Chief Business Officer .... Mr. Ronald E. EBERHARDT
25 Director of Grants .... Ms. Debra J. WILLIAMS
15 Director Human Resources .... Ms. Lauren M. FARRELL
08 Director Learning Res & Sp Projects .... Ms. Kathleen A. KEEFE
77 Dean Computer Tech/Business .... Mr. Edwin C. NELSON
76 Dean Health Profess/Biology .... Dr. Kathleen A. MALLOY
81 Dean Mathematics/Sciences .... Vacant
79 Dean Public Svc/Human/Soc Science .... Dr. Andrew BARNETTE
32 Dean of Students .... Ms. Diane D. HIGHTOWER
103 Dean Workforce Development .... Mr. Douglas J. JENSEN
84 Director Enrollment Management .... Vacant
102 Exec Director Education Foundation .... Ms. Debra D. WOODS
37 Director Financial Aid .... Mr. Gary A. MEANS
18 Director Facilities .... Mr. John C. DETISCH
21 Controller .... Mr. Timothy W. STAHL
14 Director Information Technology .... Mr. Patrick R. MCKULA
88 Director College Services .... Mr. Ronald A. KRIVDA
26 Director Public Relations .... Ms. Anna Marie PALATELLA
07 Director Admissions .... Ms. Janice T. GRABOWSKI
41 Director Student Life/Athletics .... Mr. Richard G. HOLLER
09 Dir Institutional Research/Data Svc .... Mr. Randal M. FINFROCK
96 Coordinator of Purchasing .... Ms. Kim A. HIMLER
36 Coord Student Placement/Coop Ed .... Ms. Cheryl A. NOEL

Widener University (F)

One University Place, Chester PA 19013-5792

County: Delaware FICE Identification: 003313
Unit ID: 216852

Telephone: (610) 499-4000 Carnegie Class: DRU
FAX Number: (610) 876-9751 Calendar System: Semester
URL: www.widener.edu
Established: 1821 Annual Undergrad Tuition & Fees: $36,382
Enrollment: 6,464 Coed
Affiliation or Control: Independent Non-Profit IRS Status: 501(c)3
Highest Offering: Doctorate
Program: Liberal Arts And General; Teacher Preparatory; Professional
Accreditation: M, BUS, CLPSY, ENG, HSA, IPSY, LAW, NURSE, PTA, SW, TED

01 President .... Dr. James T. HARRIS, III
05 Provost/Sr Vice Pres Academic Affs .... Dr. Stephen C. WILHITE
10 Sr Vice Pres Administration/Finance .... Mr. Joseph J. BAKER
30 Vice Pres University Advancement .... Ms. Linda S. DURANT
13 Chief Information Officer .... Mr. Peter D. SHOUDY
21 Associate VP & Controller .... Ms. Catherine MCGEEHAN
11 Associate VP of Administration .... Mr. George E. HASSEL
26 Asst Vice Pres University Relations .... Ms. Lou Anne BULIK
18 Director of Operations .... Mr. Carl G. PIERCE
58 Assoc Provost Grad Studies .... Dr. Michael W. LEDOUX
20 Associate Provost Undergraduate .... Dr. Geraldine A. BLOEMKER
32 Assoc Provost/Dean of Students .... Dr. Denise D. GIFFORD
54 Dean School of Engineering .... Dr. Fred A. AKL
49 Dean College Arts & Sciences .... Dr. Matthew POSLUSNY
50 Dean School of Business Admin .... Dr. Savas OZATALAY
66 Dean School of Nursing .... Dr. Deborah R. GARRISON
51 Dean Sch of Educ/Innov/Cont Studies .... Dr. Michael W. LEDOUX
88 Dean Sch of Hospitality Management .... Mr. Nicholas J. HADGIS
88 Dean Sch Human Svc Professions .... Dr. Paula SILVER
21 Bursar .... Ms. Diana BARRACLOUGH
08 Librarian .... Dr. Robert E. DANFORD
37 Exec Dir Student Financial Services .... Mr. Thomas K. MALLOY
06 Director of Records/Registration .... Ms. Kristen CHANDO
29 Director of Alumni Engagement .... Ms. Tina A. PHILLIPS
09 Dir of Inst Res & Effectiveness .... Dr. Stephen W. THORPE
36 Placement Director .... Ms. Jan MOPPERT
41 Director of Athletics .... Mr. Jack L. SHAFER
85 Director International Student Svcs .... Ms. Lois J. FULLER
19 Director of Campus Safety .... Mr. Patrick SULLIVAN
23 Director of Health Services .... Ms. Lynn A. NELSON-RUSSOM
24 Head of Multimedia/Classroom Spprt .... Mr. Eric WOEBKENBERG
40 Manager Campus Bookstore .... Mr. Chester HENSEL
91 Director Information Systems .... Mrs. Linda TAYLOR
88 Director Technical Resources .... Mr. Perry M. DRAYFAHL
15 Director of Human Resources .... Ms. Christine M. LLOYD
96 Director of Purchasing .... Vacant
07 Exec Director of Admissions .... Mr. Edwin R. WRIGHT
89 Dir Student Success/Retention .... Mr. Timothy J. CAIRY
97 Dir Honors Program in General Educ .... Dr. Ilene LIEBERMAN
94 Director of Women's Studies .... Dr. Annalisa CASTALDO

† See Delaware listing of Widener University School of Law - Delaware Campus.

Wilkes University (A)

84 W South Street, Wilkes-Barre PA 18766-0001
County: Luzerne FICE Identification: 003394
Unit ID: 216931
Telephone: (570) 408-5000 Carnegie Class: Master's L
FAX Number: (570) 408-2934 Calendar System: Semester
URL: www.wilkes.edu
Established: 1933 Annual Undergrad Tuition & Fees: $29,326
Enrollment: 5,163 Coed
Affiliation or Control: Independent Non-Profit IRS Status: 501(c)3
Highest Offering: Doctorate
Program: Liberal Arts And General; Teacher Preparatory; Professional
Accreditation: M, ACBSP, CEA, ENG, NURSE, PHAR

01 President .... Dr. Patrick F. LEAHY
05 Provost .... Vacant
30 Vice Pres University Advancement .... Mr. Michael WOOD
10 Vice President & General Counsel .... Mr. Loren D. PRESCOTT
21 Controller .... Ms. Janet KOBYLSKI
84 Vice President Enrollment Services .... Ms. Melanie WADE
32 Vice President Student Affairs .... Dr. Paul S. ADAMS
16 Vice President Human Resources Dev .... Vacant
20 Associate Provost .... Vacant
35 Dean of Students .... Mr. Mark R. ALLEN
35 Associate Dean Student Affairs .... Ms. Barbara E. KING
54 Dean Col of Science & Engineering .... Vacant
49 Dean College of Arts & Humanities .... Dr. Linda WINKLER
67 Dean Nesbitt Col Pharm/Nursing .... Dr. Bernard GRAHAM
58 Dean Grad/Prof Studies/Sch of Educ .... Dr. Michael SPEZIALE
50 Int Dean Sidh School of Business .... Dr. Jeffrey ALVES
62 Dean Library .... Mr. John STACHACZ
09 Exec Director Info/Analysis/Plng .... Mr. Brian BOGERT
29 Director Alumni Relations .... Mr. Mirko WIDENHORN
41 Director of Athletics .... Ms. Addy MALATESTA
23 Director Health Services .... Ms. Diane E. O'BRIEN
36 Director Career Services .... Mrs. Carol A. BOSACK-KOSEK
39 Director Residence Life .... Ms. Elizabeth ROVEDA
58 Director Graduate Teach Education .... Ms. Kristine PRUETT
06 Registrar .... Mrs. Susan A. HRITZAK
37 Dir of Financial Aid/Stdnt Services .... Mr. Joseph ALAIMO
26 Dir Mktg/Com/Sp Ast to Pres Gov Rel .... Mr. Jack A. CHIELLI
18 Director Facilities Services .... Mr. John PESTA
14 Chief Information Officer .... Ms. Gloria BARLOW
07 Assoc Director of Admissions .... Ms. Amy PATTON
07 Assoc Director of Admissions .... Mr. Alex SPERAZZA
28 Spec Asst to Pres for Multicul Affs .... Vacant
96 Director Procurement & Finan Svcs .... Mr. Justin KRAYNACK
15 Director Human Resource Services .... Mr. Joseph HOUSENICK
38 Campus Counselor .... Ms. Melissa GAUDIO
38 Campus Counselor .... Ms. Susan BISKUP
102 Director of Corp/Found/Govt Rels .... Mrs. Anne PELAK
35 Dir Student Svc Ctr/Student Svcs .... Ms. Janine BECKER
04 Admin Asst to the President .... Ms. Susan DIBONIFAZIO

Williamson Free School of Mechanical Trades (B)

106 S New Middletown Road, Media PA 19063-5299
County: Delaware FICE Identification: 041238
Unit ID: 216940
Telephone: (610) 566-1776 Carnegie Class: Not Classified
FAX Number: (610) 566-6502 Calendar System: Semester
URL: www.williamson.edu
Established: 1888 Annual Undergrad Tuition & Fees: N/A
Enrollment: 270 Male
Affiliation or Control: Independent Non-Profit IRS Status: 501(c)3
Highest Offering: Associate Degree
Program: Occupational
Accreditation: ACCSC

01 President .... Mr. Guy S. GARDNER
05 Vice President of Education & CAO .... Mr. Thomas E. WISNESKI
10 Vice President of Finance & CFO .... Mr. Gregory L. LINDEMUTH
30 Vice President of Inst Advancement .... Mr. Peter D'ORAZIO
11 Vice Pres of Plans & Operations .... Mr. Jim HANNIGAN
32 Dean of Students .... Mr. Thomas J. MOFFITT
84 Director of Enrollments .... Mr. Jason C. MERILLAT
41 Director of Athletics .... Mr. Dale H. PLUMMER
42 Chaplain/Counselor .... Rev. Mark A. SPECHT
06 Registrar .... Ms. Anne M. HAYES
36 Director of Placement .... Ms. Margaret T. KINGHAM
26 Director of Public Relations .... Mr. Carl A. VAIRO

Wilson College (C)

1015 Philadelphia Avenue, Chambersburg PA 17201-1285
County: Franklin FICE Identification: 003396
Unit ID: 217013
Telephone: (717) 262-4141 Carnegie Class: Bac/Diverse
FAX Number: (717) 264-1578 Calendar System: 4/1/4
URL: www.wilson.edu
Established: 1869 Annual Undergrad Tuition & Fees: $29,340
Enrollment: 746 Female
Affiliation or Control: Presbyterian Church (U.S.A.) IRS Status: 501(c)3
Highest Offering: Master's
Program: Liberal Arts And General; Teacher Preparatory
Accreditation: M

01 President .... Dr. Barbara K. MISTICK
05 VP for Academic Affairs/Dean of Fac .... Dr. Mary HENDRICKSON
30 Vice President College Advancement .... Vacant
10 Vice Pres Finance & Administration .... Mr. Brian ECKER
84 Vice President/Dean of Enrollment .... Ms. Mary Ann NASO
32 Vice President for Student Dev/Dean .... Ms. Carolyn PERKINS
06 Registrar .... Ms. Jean B. HOOVER
37 Dean of Financial Aid .... Ms. Linda D. BRITTAIN
09 Asst Dean IR and Assesment .... Dr. Elizabeth ANDERSON
08 Director of Library .... Ms. Kathleen MURPHY
18 Director of Physical Plant .... Mr. Jack KELLY
27 Communications Associate .... Ms. Cathy MENTZER
40 Director of Bookstore .... Ms. Deborah GAYNOR
41 Athletic Director .... Ms. Lori FREY
51 Director of Conferences .... Mr. Joel PAGLIARO
29 Director of Alumnae Programs .... Vacant
44 Director of Annual Fund .... Ms. Denise MCDOWELL
15 Director Human Resources .... Vacant
20 Assoc Dean of Academic Advising .... Dr. Deborah AUSTIN
21 Assoc VP for Finance/Admin .... Ms. Lori TOSTEN
26 Chief Public Relations Officer .... Ms. Debra COLLINS
36 Director of Career Development .... Mr. Jay PFEIFFER
38 Director of Student Counseling .... Ms. Cindy SHOEMAKER
88 Director of Women With Children Pgm .... Ms. Katherine KOUGH
37 Coordinator of Financial Aid .... Ms. Christine KNOUSE
28 Coordinator of Diversity .... Vacant
42 Chaplain .... Rev. Rosie MAGEE
39 Director of Residence Life .... Ms. Sherri SADOWSKI

Won Institute of Graduate Studies (D)

137 S Easton Road, Glenside PA 19038
County: Montgomery FICE Identification: 039493
Unit ID: 442064
Telephone: (215) 884-8942 Carnegie Class: Spec/Health
FAX Number: (215) 884-9002 Calendar System: Trimester
URL: www.woninstitute.edu
Established: 2002 Annual Graduate Tuition & Fees: $16,900
Enrollment: 71 Coed
Affiliation or Control: Independent Non-Profit IRS Status: 501(c)3
Highest Offering: Master's; No Undergraduates
Program: Professional; Religious Emphasis
Accreditation: M, ACUP

01 President .... Dr. Bokin KIM
11 Chief Administrative Officer .... Ms. Colleen O'CONNELL
10 Chief Financial Officer .... Ms. Maria PERRY
05 Chief Academic Officer .... Ms. Lynn MITCHELL
06 Registrar .... Rev. Sangwon HWANG
08 Librarian .... Mrs. Pat KING
07 Admissions Officer .... Rev. Hojin PARK

WyoTech-Blairsville (E)

500 Innovation Drive, Blairsville PA 15717-8060
County: Indiana Identification: 666305
Unit ID: 441089
Telephone: (724) 459-9500 Carnegie Class: Assoc/PrivFP
FAX Number: (724) 459-6499 Calendar System: Quarter
URL: www.wyotech.edu
Established: 1966 Annual Undergrad Tuition & Fees: $29,250
Enrollment: 1,300 Coed
Affiliation or Control: Proprietary IRS Status: Proprietary
Highest Offering: Associate Degree
Program: Occupational; Technical Emphasis
Accreditation: ACCSC

01 President .... Mr. Arthur HERMAN

† Branch campus of Wyoming Technical Institute, Laramie, WY.

Yeshiva Beth Moshe (F)

930 Hickory Street, Scranton PA 18505-2196
County: Lackawanna FICE Identification: 013134
Unit ID: 217040
Telephone: (570) 346-1747 Carnegie Class: Spec/Faith
FAX Number: (570) 346-2251 Calendar System: Semester
Established: 1965 Annual Undergrad Tuition & Fees: $7,800
Enrollment: 65 Male
Affiliation or Control: Independent Non-Profit IRS Status: 501(c)3
Highest Offering: Second Talmudic Degree
Program: Teacher Preparatory; Professional; Religious Emphasis
Accreditation: RABN

01 Chief Executive Officer .... Rabbi Yaakov SCHNAIDMAN
03 Executive Director .... Rabbi Avraham PRESSMAN

York College of Pennsylvania (G)

Country Club Road, York PA 17405-7199
County: York FICE Identification: 003399
Unit ID: 217059
Telephone: (717) 846-7788 Carnegie Class: Master's S
FAX Number: (717) 849-1607 Calendar System: Semester
URL: www.ycp.edu
Established: 1787 Annual Undergrad Tuition & Fees: $16,520
Enrollment: 4,669 Coed
Affiliation or Control: Independent Non-Profit IRS Status: 501(c)3
Highest Offering: Doctorate
Program: Liberal Arts And General; Teacher Preparatory; Professional
Accreditation: M, ACBSP, ANEST, CS, ENG, MUS, NRPA, NURSE

01 President .... Dr. George W. WALDNER
05 Dean of Academic Affairs .... Dr. Dominic DELLICARPINI
11 Dean of Administrative Service .... Dr. Frank P. MUSSANO
10 Chief Financial Officer .... Mr. Matthew SMITH
20 Dean of Academic Services .... Dr. Deborah D. RICKER
32 Dean of Student Affairs .... Mr. Joseph F. MERKLE
18 Dean of Campus Operations .... Dr. Kenneth M. MARTIN
44 Dean of College Advancement .... Mr. Daniel S. HELWIG
41 Asst Dean Athletics & Recreation .... Mr. Paul SAIKIA
84 Asst Dean Enrollment Management .... Mr. Stephen NEITZ
26 Asst Dean Institutional Advancement .... Ms. Mary E. DOLHEIMER
30 Director Development .... Ms. Camilla B. RAWLEIGH
07 Director of Admissions .... Mrs. Nancy C. SPATARO
06 Registrar .... Ms. Rebecca C. LINK
08 Librarian .... Ms. Susan M. CAMPBELL
37 Director of Financial Aid .... Mr. Calvin H. WILLIAMS
13 Director of Information Technology .... Mr. Robert L. ROBINSON
29 Director Alumni Relations .... Mr. Bruce WALL
36 Director of Career Services .... Ms. Beverly A. EVANS
06 Director of Records .... Mrs. Debra L. SHIMMEL
19 Director of Public Safety .... Mr. Edward C. BRUDER
39 Director of Residence Life .... Mr. Kevin D. FEIL
31 Director Community Education .... Mr. Leroy M. KEENEY
15 Director Human Resources .... Mrs. Vicki L. STEWART
38 Director Counseling Services .... Mrs. Karen JONES
91 Dir Administrative Computer Center .... Mr. Brian K. SMELTZER
23 Director Health Services .... Mrs. Rita CLAYTON
40 Director Bookstore .... Mrs. Lynn P. FERRO
88 Director College & Special Events .... Ms. Sherry HEFLIN
102 Dir Corporate/Foundation/Govt Rels .... Mr. Chad LINDER
27 College Editor .... Mrs. Alicia BRUMBACH
42 Director of Religious Activities .... Mrs. Louise WORLEY
31 Dir Center for Community Engagement .... Vacant
09 Director of Institutional Research .... Ms. Elizabeth CARROLL
28 Director of Multicultural Affairs .... Mr. Darrien DAVENPORT
24 Learning Center Coordinator .... Mrs. Cindy CRIMMINS
44 Sr Dir Principal & Planned Gifts .... Mr. Mark RANK

Yorktowne Business Institute (H)

West Seventh Avenue, York PA 17404-9946
County: York FICE Identification: 021208
Unit ID: 217086
Telephone: (717) 846-5000 Carnegie Class: Assoc/PrivFP
FAX Number: (717) 848-4584 Calendar System: Other
URL: www.ybi.edu
Established: 1977 Annual Undergrad Tuition & Fees: $8,955
Enrollment: 835 Coed
Affiliation or Control: Proprietary IRS Status: Proprietary
Highest Offering: Associate Degree
Program: Occupational
Accreditation: ACICS

01 President .... Dr. James P. MURPHY
03 Executive Director .... Ms. Elizabeth M. DREIBELBIS
50 Business Department Chair .... Ms. Lynda R. MEYERS
06 Registrar .... Ms. Lisa MCGOWAN
37 Director Student Financial Aid .... Ms. Deborah BOSTIC
08 Director Library Services .... Ms. Lynda MEYERS
36 Director Student Placement .... Mrs. Nan JOURDAN
18 Chief Facilities/Physical Plant .... Mr. Frederick WEIBLE
88 Acting Director Culinary Arts .... Mr. Robert GENET
10 Business Officer .... Vacant
55 Evening Administrator .... Mr. Dean FRIEND
26 Marketing Director .... Mr. John A. DREIBELBIS
88 Teaching Kitchen Manager .... Ms. Kim CRIM

YTI Career Institute (I)

2900 Fairway Drive, Altoona PA 16602
County: Blair FICE Identification: 030819
Unit ID: 375939
Telephone: (814) 944-5643 Carnegie Class: Not Classified
FAX Number: (814) 944-5309 Calendar System: Quarter
URL: www.yti.edu
Established: 2006 Annual Undergrad Tuition & Fees: $23,296
Enrollment: 382 Coed
Affiliation or Control: Proprietary IRS Status: Proprietary
Highest Offering: Associate Degree
Program: Occupational
Accreditation: ACCSC

01 Director of Education .... Mr. Ken LOENDOWSKI

YTI Career Institute (J)

1405 Williams Road, York PA 17402-9017
County: York FICE Identification: 021274
Unit ID: 217077
Telephone: (717) 757-1100 Carnegie Class: Assoc/PrivFP
FAX Number: (717) 757-4964 Calendar System: Quarter
URL: www.yti.edu
Established: 1967 Annual Undergrad Tuition & Fees: $22,250
Enrollment: 1,754 Coed
Affiliation or Control: Proprietary IRS Status: Proprietary
Highest Offering: Associate Degree
Program: Occupational
Accreditation: ACCSC, ACFEI, DA, MAC

01 Chairman and CEO .... Mr. Timothy FOSTER
12 President - York .... Ms. Carla HORN

12	President - Capital Region	Mr. Erin CARLIN
12	President - Lancaster	Mr. Michael MARINO
12	President - Altoona	Mr. Kenneth LEWANDOWSKI
12	President - MTC	Mr. Michael MARINO
03	Executive Vice President	Mr. Mike WRIGHT
05	Sr VP Education & Regulatory	Mrs. Sherry BOMBERGER
10	CFO	Mr. Andrew EMMERLING
13	Director of Technology	Mr. Andrew HIPPLE

YTI Career Institute-Capital Region (A)

401 East Winding Hill Rd, Mechanicsburg PA 17055

County: Cumberland — FICE Identification: 023044 — Unit ID: 211750
Telephone: (717) 761-1481 — Carnegie Class: Not Classified
FAX Number: (717) 761-0558 — Calendar System: Quarter
URL: www.yti.edu
Established: N/A — Annual Undergrad Tuition & Fees: $23,296
Enrollment: 285 — Coed
Affiliation or Control: Proprietary — IRS Status: Proprietary
Highest Offering: Associate Degree
Program: Occupational
Accreditation: ACCSC

RHODE ISLAND

Brown University (B)

Providence RI 02912

County: Providence — FICE Identification: 003401 — Unit ID: 217156
Telephone: (401) 863-1000 — Carnegie Class: RU/VH
FAX Number: (401) 863-3700 — Calendar System: Semester
URL: www.brown.edu
Established: 1764 — Annual Undergrad Tuition & Fees: $43,758
Enrollment: 8,768 — Coed
Affiliation or Control: Independent Non-Profit — IRS Status: 501(c)3
Highest Offering: Doctorate
Program: Liberal Arts And General; Professional
Accreditation: EH, ENG, IPSY, MED, PDPSY, PH

01	President	Christina H. PAXSON
05	Provost	Mark S. SCHLISSEL
30	Sr Vice Pres for Advancement	Steven A. KING
102	Exec Vice Pres Planning & Policy	Russell C. CAREY
10	Exec VP Finance/Administration	Elizabeth HUIDEKOPER
26	VP Public Affairs/Univ Relations	Marisa A. QUINN
43	Vice President/General Counsel	Beverly E. LEDBETTER
13	Vice Pres Computing/Info Services	Michael P. PICKETT
44	VP of Development/Campaign Director	Vacant
29	Vice President Alumni Affairs	Todd G. ANDREWS
18	Vice Pres for Facilities Management	Stephen M. MAIORISI
46	Vice President for Research	Clyde L. BRIANT
15	Vice Pres for Human Resources	Karen DAVIS
35	Vice Pres Campus Life/Student Svcs	Margaret M. KLAWUNN
20	Deputy Provost	Joseph S. MEISEL
28	Assoc Provost Acad Devel/Diversity	Liza CARIAGA-LO
63	Dean Medicine & Biological Sciences	Edward WING
58	Dean of Graduate School	Peter M. WEBER
20	Dean of the Faculty	Kevin MCLAUGHLIN
20	Dean of the College	Katherine BERGERON
07	Dean of Admission	James S. MILLER
31	Director State/Community Relations	Albert A. DAHLBERG
08	University Librarian	Harriette HEMMASI
21	University Controller/Assistant VP	Donald S. SCHANCK
11	Sr Business Analyst/Project Manager	Vacant
41	Director of Athletics	Jack HAYES
06	Registrar	Robert F. FITZGERALD
37	Director of Financial Aid	James TILTON
19	Dir Public Safety/Chief of Police	Mark J. PORTER
38	Director Psychological Services	Belinda JOHNSON
09	Director of Institutional Research	Katharine T. BARNES
96	Assistant Director Purchasing	Raymond STEWART

Bryant University (C)

1150 Douglas Pike, Smithfield RI 02917-1291

County: Providence — FICE Identification: 003402 — Unit ID: 217165
Telephone: (401) 232-6000 — Carnegie Class: Master's M
FAX Number: (401) 232-6319 — Calendar System: Semester
URL: www.bryant.edu
Established: 1863 — Annual Undergrad Tuition & Fees: $35,940
Enrollment: 3,180 — Coed
Affiliation or Control: Independent Non-Profit — IRS Status: 501(c)3
Highest Offering: Beyond Master's But Less Than Doctorate
Program: Liberal Arts And General; Business Emphasis
Accreditation: EH, BUS

00	Chairman Board of Trustees	Mr. Michael FISHER
01	President	Mr. Ronald K. MACHTLEY
04	Exec Asst & Corp Secretary	Dr. Roger L. ANDERSON
05	VP Academic Affairs	Dr. Jose-Marie GRIFFITHS
32	VP & Dean Student Affairs	Dr. J. Thomas EAKIN
84	VP Enrollment Management	Vacant
10	VP Business Affairs	Mr. Barry F. MORRISON
30	VP University Advancement	Mr. James DAMRON
13	VP Information Services	Mr. Chuck LOCURTO
16	Assoc VP Human Resources	Ms. Linda S. LULLI
18	Asst VP Campus Management	Mr. Brian J. BRITTON
21	Asst VP Business & Controller	Mr. Farokh BHADA
49	Dean College of Arts & Sciences	Dr. David LUX
50	Dean College of Business	Dr. Michael COOPER
58	Asst Dean Graduate School	Mr. Kristopher T. SULLIVAN
51	Dir Exec Development Center	Ms. Annette CERILLI
88	Exec Dir Inst for Family Enterprise	Dr. William T. O'HARA
88	Dir RI Export Assistance Center	Mr. Raymond FOGARTY
89	Dir Academic Center for Excellence	Dr. Laurie L. HAZARD
20	Asst to VP Academic & Dir Advising	Vacant
06	Registrar	Ms. Susan MCLACKEN
20	Asst to VP Academic Affairs	Ms. Elizabeth A. POWERS
35	Assoc Dean of Students	Mr. Robert E. SLOSS
39	Assoc Dean Residence Life	Mr. John DENIO
35	Assoc Dean Student Life	Ms. Judy KAWAMOTO
88	Dir Bryant Center Operations	Mr. Richard DANKEL
36	Dir Career Services	Ms. Judith CLARE
42	Chaplain Campus Ministry	Rev. Philip DEVENS
38	Dir Counseling Services	Mr. William PHILLIPS
23	Dir Health Services	Ms. Susan CURRAN
28	Dir Intercultural Center	Ms. Shontay DELALUE-KING
19	Dir Public Safety	Mr. Stephen BANNON
31	Dir Student Involvement Center	Mr. John LINDSAY
88	Dir Women's Center	Ms. Toby SIMON
07	Dir Admission	Ms. Michelle BEAUREGARD
07	Dir Transfer Admission	Ms. Brenda DORAN
07	Sr Assoc Dir Mulitcult Admission	Ms. Priscilla ALICEA
07	Assoc Dir International Admission	Mr. John ERIKSEN
37	Dir Financial Aid	Mr. John B. CANNING
88	Dir Conferences & Special Events	Ms. Sheila GUAY
96	Dir Purchasing & Support Services	Ms. Paulette RATTIGAN
44	Exec Dir Development	Ms. Robin MAREK
29	Dir Alumni Relations	Ms. Robin T. WARDE
90	Dir Acad Computing & Media Svcs	Mr. Phillip LOMBARDI
91	Dir Admin Systems	Ms. Janice FAGAN
14	Dir Computer & Telecomm Svcs	Mr. Richard SIEDZIK
08	Dir Library Services	Ms. Mary F. MORONEY
15	Assoc Dir Human Resources	Ms. Catherine CURRIE
41	Dir Athletics	Mr. Bill SMITH
09	Dir Planning & Inst Research	Mr. Robert JONES
82	Exec Dir US-China Institute	Dr. Hong YANG
40	Manager Bookstore	Mr. Stanley STOWIK

Community College of Rhode Island (D)

400 East Avenue, Warwick RI 02886-1807

County: Kent — FICE Identification: 003408 — Unit ID: 217475
Telephone: (401) 825-1000 — Carnegie Class: Assoc/Pub-U-MC
FAX Number: (401) 825-2365 — Calendar System: Semester
URL: www.ccri.edu
Established: 1964 — Annual Undergrad Tuition & Fees (In-State): $3,676
Enrollment: 17,893 — Coed
Affiliation or Control: State — IRS Status: 501(c)3
Highest Offering: Associate Degree
Program: Occupational; 2-Year Principally Bachelor's Creditable
Accreditation: EH, ACBSP, ADNUR, COMTA, DA, DH, DMS, HT, MLTAD, MUS, OTA, PNUR, PTAA, RAD

01	President	Mr. Ray DI PASQUALE
05	Vice President for Academic Affairs	Ms. Lela M. MORGAN
10	Vice President for Business Affairs	Mr. Robert SHEA, JR.
32	Assoc VP for Student Services	Dr. Ronald L. SCHERTZ
84	Int Dean of Enrollment Services	Ms. Deborah J. AIKEN
11	Director of Administration	Mr. William R. FERLAND
49	Dean Arts/Humanities/Soc Sciences	Dr. Lois A. WIMS
66	Dean of Nursing/Allied Health	Dr. Maureen MCGARRY
50	Dean Business/Science/Technology	Dr. Peter N. WOODBERRY
51	Dean of CWCE	Ms. Robin Ann SMITH
08	Dean Library	Ms. Ruth D. SULLIVAN
07	Asst Dean of Enrollment Services	Mr. John PANZICA
21	Controller	Mr. Carl TOFT
35	Associate Dean of Students	Dr. Rebecca H. YOUNT
15	Director of Human Resources	Ms. Sheri L. NORTON
12	Dir Ctr Advanced Tech & Careers	Mr. Vincent BALASCO
13	Chief Information Officer	Mr. Stephen A. VIEIRA
19	Director of Safety & Security	Mr. Dale R. WETHERELL
26	Director Marketing & Communications	Mr. Richard H. COREN
30	VP for Institutional Advancement	Mr. Joseph APRIL
41	Director of Athletics	Mr. Joseph PAVONE
09	Director Inst Research/Planning	Dr. William LEBLANC
21	Bursar	Mr. Dennis J. GRASSINI
88	Director Access to Opportunity	Ms. Tracy KARASINSKI
40	Director Bookstore Operations	Mr. Donald B. BAKER
29	Director of Alumni Affairs	Ms. Marisa ALBINI
18	Chief Facilities/Physical Plant	Mr. Kenneth MCCABE
96	Director of Purchasing	Mr. Raymond DEANGELIS
21	Business Manager	Ms. Ruth A. BARRINGTON
36	Coordinator Career Services	Ms. Camille NUMRICH
37	Director of Financial Aid	Mr. Joel FRIEDMAN

Johnson & Wales University (E)

8 Abbott Park Place, Providence RI 02903-3703

County: Providence — FICE Identification: 003404 — Unit ID: 217235
Telephone: (401) 598-1000 — Carnegie Class: Master's L
FAX Number: (401) 598-2880 — Calendar System: Quarter
URL: www.jwu.edu
Established: 1914 — Annual Undergrad Tuition & Fees: $26,112
Enrollment: 10,848 — Coed
Affiliation or Control: Independent Non-Profit — IRS Status: 501(c)3
Highest Offering: Doctorate
Program: Occupational; 2-Year Principally Bachelor's Creditable; Teacher Preparatory; Professional
Accreditation: EH, DIETD

00	Chairman of the Board	Mr. John A. YENA
01	Chancellor	Mr. John J. BOWEN
12	Providence Campus President/COO	Ms. Mim L. RUNEY
32	Vice President of Student Affairs	Mr. Ronald MARTEL
05	University Provost	Ms. Veera GAUL
30	Exec Dir of University Advancement	Ms. Page C. SCIOTTO
85	Senior VP of Special Projects	Mr. Kenneth R. LEVY
10	Treasurer and CFO	Mr. William F. MCARDLE
18	Sr Vice Pres Facilities Management	Mr. Merlin A. DECONTI
43	Sr VP and General Counsel	Mr. Wayne M. KEZIRIAN
20	Associate Provost	Mr. James GRIFFIN
10	Vice Chancellor & Executive VP	Mr. Thomas L. DWYER, JR.
36	VP of Experiential Ed & Career Svc	Ms. Maureen DUMAS
11	Sr VP of Compliance/Int Audit/Risk	Ms. Robin KRAKOWSKY
84	Sr VP of Enrollment Management	Mr. Kenneth F. DISAIA
20	Vice President of Academic Affairs	Mr. Jeffrey SENESE
15	Vice President of Human Resources	Ms. Diane D'AMBRA
21	Asst Treasurer & VP of Finance	Mr. Joseph J. GREENE
58	Dean of Graduate School	Mr. Frank SARGENT
88	Dean of The Hospitality College	Mr. Richard BRUSH
50	Int Dean of the College of Business	Mr. Frank SARGENT
49	Dean of A&S	Ms. Angela RENAUD
72	Dean of the School of Technology	Mr. Frank TWEEDIE
88	Vice President of Auxiliary Service	Mr. Michael DOWNING
18	Vice President of Facilities Mgmt	Mr. Christopher PLACCO
13	VP of IT and CIO	Mr. John A. SMITHERS
32	Sr VP of Student Services	Ms. Marie BERNARDO-SOUSA
43	Sr VP of Law & Policy & Corp Secret	Ms. Barbara L. BENNETT
96	Director of Procurement	Mr. Michael GILLARDI
36	Director of Ext Educ & Career Svcs	Ms. Sheri ISPIR
09	Director of Institutional Research	Vacant
19	Exec Dir of Campus Safety/Security	Major Michael P. QUINN
21	University Budget Director	Ms. Eileen T. HASKINS
88	University Dean of Culinary Educ	Mr. Karl J. GUGGENMOS
88	Director of Student Communications	Ms. Kristine E. MCNAMARA
88	Dean of Culinary Academics	Mr. Paul J. MCVETY
88	Dir of Acad Accountability & Init	Ms. Cynthia L. PARKER
51	Director of Continuing Education	Mr. Ian CANNING

Mater Ecclesiae College (F)

60 Austin Avenue, Greenville RI 02828-1440

County: Providence — FICE Identification: 041449
Telephone: (401) 949-2820 — Carnegie Class: Not Classified
FAX Number: (401) 949-0291 — Calendar System: Semester
URL: www.mecollege.org
Established: 1991 — Annual Undergrad Tuition & Fees: N/A
Enrollment: 70 — Female
Affiliation or Control: Independent Non-Profit — IRS Status: 501(c)3
Highest Offering: Baccalaureate
Program: Liberal Arts And General; Religious Emphasis
Accreditation: EH

01	President	Ms. Deb BAUER
32	Vice Pres/Dir Student Affairs	Ms. Cecilia AZCUNAGA
05	Dean of Academic Affairs	Dr. Patricia CAMARERO
06	Registrar	Ms. Jennifer RISTINE
10	Director of Financial/Admin Affairs	Vacant
21	Business Manager	Ms. Maritza SILVA

New England Institute of Technology (G)

One New England Tech Blvd., East Greenwich RI 02818

County: Kent — FICE Identification: 007845 — Unit ID: 217305
Telephone: (401) 467-7744 — Carnegie Class: Bac/Assoc
FAX Number: (401) 886-0859 — Calendar System: Quarter
URL: www.neit.edu
Established: 1940 — Annual Undergrad Tuition & Fees: $19,980
Enrollment: 2,933 — Coed
Affiliation or Control: Independent Non-Profit — IRS Status: 501(c)3
Highest Offering: Master's
Program: Occupational; 2-Year Principally Bachelor's Creditable; Liberal Arts And General; Technical Emphasis
Accreditation: EH, ADNUR, ENGT, OT, OTA, PTAA, SURGT

01	President	Dr. Richard I. GOUSE
03	Executive Vice President	Mr. Seth A. KURN
05	Senior Vice President and Provost	Dr. Thomas F. WYLIE
10	Sr VP Financial Affs & Endowment	Ms. Cheryl C. CONNORS
32	Vice Pres Student Support Services	Ms. Catherine B. KENNEDY
21	VP of Finance & Business Admin	Mr. Robert R. THEROUX
20	Associate Provost	Vacant
07	Director of Admissions	Mr. Mark BLONDIN
37	Director Financial Aid	Ms. Anna KELLY
04	Assoc Provost & Spec Asst to Pres	Mr. Douglas SHERMAN, JR.
08	Director Library	Ms. Susan WARTHMAN
36	Director of Career Services	Ms. Patricia BLAKEMORE
31	Director Auxiliary Services	Mr. Patrick TRACEY
06	Registrar	Ms. Doreen LASIEWSKI
35	Director Student Affairs	Ms. Lee PEEBLES
29	Dir Institutional Dev & Alumni Rels	Ms. Lynne DONAHUE

Providence College (H)

1 Cunningham Square, Providence RI 02918-0001

County: Providence — FICE Identification: 003406 — Unit ID: 217402
Telephone: (401) 865-1000 — Carnegie Class: Master's L
FAX Number: (401) 865-2057 — Calendar System: Semester

URL: www.providence.edu
Established: 1917 Annual Undergrad Tuition & Fees: $42,080
Enrollment: 4,863 Coed
Affiliation or Control: Roman Catholic IRS Status: 501(c)3
Highest Offering: Master's
Program: Liberal Arts And General; Teacher Preparatory
Accreditation: EH, BUS, MT, MUS, SW

Code	Title	Name
01	President	Rev. Brian J. SHANLEY, OP
03	Asst to Pres & Exec Vice President	Ms. Ann MANCHESTER-MOLAK
03	Executive Vice President	Rev. Kenneth R. SICARD, OP
05	Sr Vice President Academic Affairs	Dr. Hugh F. LENA
10	Sr VP for Finance & Business/CFO	Mr. John M. SWEENEY
30	Sr VP for Institutional Advancement	Mr. David C. WEGRZYN
32	Vice Pres Student Affairs Admin	Ms. Kristine C. GOODWIN
43	Vice President/General Counsel	Ms. Marifrances MCGINN
42	Vice Pres for Mission & Ministry	Rev. Joseph J. GUIDO, OP
04	Special Asst to Pres for Devel Proj	Mr. Joseph P. BRUM
21	Assoc VP for Finance/Asst Treasurer	Ms. Jacqueline M. WHITE
35	Assoc VP for Student Affairs Admin	Dr. Steven A. SEARS
20	Associate VP for Academic Affairs	Dr. Brian J. BARTOLINI
44	Assoc VP Institutional Advancement	Ms. Lisa M. BOUSQUET
41	Assoc Vice Pres for Athletics	Mr. Robert G. DRISCOLL, JR.
15	Assoc Vice Pres for Human Resources	Ms. Kathleen M. ALVINO
43	Assoc VP/Assoc General Counsel	Ms. Gail A. DYER
28	Assoc VP/Chief Diversity Officer	Mr. Rafael A. ZAPATA
26	Ast VP for Public Affairs/Cmty Rels	Mr. Steven J. MAURANO
20	Asst Vice Pres for Academic Affairs	Mr. Charles J. HABERLE
21	Asst Vice Pres for Business Svcs	Mr. Warren S. GRAY
29	Asst Vice Pres for Alumni Relations	Mr. Robert FERREIRA, JR.
13	Asst VP for Information Technology	Ms. Rebecca RAMOS
46	Asst VP Capital Projects & Fac Plng	Mr. Mark F. RAPOZA
58	Dean of Undergrad & Grad Studies	Rev. Mark D. NOWEL, OP
49	Dean School of Arts & Sciences	Dr. Sheila M. ADAMUS LIOTTA
107	Dean School of Professional Studies	Dr. Brian M. MCCADDEN
07	Dean of Admissions/Financial Aid	Mr. Raul A. FONTS
50	Interim Dean School of Business	Dr. Mary Jane LENON
51	Dean School of Continuing Education	Dr. Janet L. CASTLEMAN
39	Dean of Residence Life	Ms. Tiffany D. GAFFNEY
84	Dean of Enrollment Services	Ms. Yvonne D. ARRUDA
104	Dean of International Studies	Mr. Adrian G. BEAULIEU
88	Dean of Student Programming	Ms. Sharon L. HAY
51	Assoc Dean Sch of Continuing Educ	Ms. Madeleine A. METZLER
37	Exec Director of Financial Aid	Ms. Sandra J. OLIVEIRA
19	Exec Director Safety & Security	Mr. John J. LEYDEN
36	Director for Career Services	Ms. Patricia A. GOFF
18	Exec Director of Physical Plant	Mr. William J. HARTIGAN
08	Director Library	Dr. Donald Russell BAILEY
21	Treasurer	Rev. Kenneth R. SICARD, OP
09	Director of Institutional Research	Mr. Thomas E. FRANK
88	Director of Advancement Services	Vacant
88	Director of Telecommunications	Mr. Carmine R. PISCOPO
92	Program Dir Liberal Arts Honors	Dr. Stephen J. LYNCH
96	Director Cntrl Purchasing/Receiving	Mr. Mark S. MCGOVERN
88	Director of Academic Services	Mr. Bryan D. MARINELLI
38	Exec Director Personal Counseling	Dr. John T. HOGAN

Rhode Island College (A)

600 Mount Pleasant Avenue, Providence RI 02908-1991
County: Providence FICE Identification: 003407
Unit ID: 217420
Telephone: (401) 456-8000 Carnegie Class: Master's L
FAX Number: (401) 456-8379 Calendar System: Semester
URL: www.ric.edu
Established: 1854 Annual Undergrad Tuition & Fees (In-State): $7,558
Enrollment: 9,044 Coed
Affiliation or Control: State IRS Status: 501(c)3
Highest Offering: Doctorate
Program: Liberal Arts And General; Teacher Preparatory; Professional
Accreditation: EH, ART, MUS, NURSE, SW, TED

Code	Title	Name
01	President	Dr. Nancy CARRIUOLO
05	Vice President Academic Affairs	Dr. Ronald E. PITT
10	Vice Pres Administration & Finance	Mr. William H. GEARHART
32	Vice President Student Affairs	Dr. Gary M. PENFIELD
30	Vice President College Advancement	Mr. James G. SALMO
107	Assoc VP Prof Studies & Cont Ed	Vacant
20	Int Asst Vice Pres Academic Affairs	Dr. Holly L. SHADOIAN
21	Asst Vice Pres Finance/Controller	Mr. Paul D. FORTE
14	Asst Vice Pres Information Services	Dr. Richard W. PRULL
15	Asst Vice President Human Resources	Mr. Robert G. TETREAULT
49	Dean Faculty Arts & Sciences	Dr. Earl L. SIMSON
53	Dean School Education & Human Dev	Dr. Alexander SIDORKIN
66	Dean School of Nursing	Dr. Jane WILLIAMS
50	Dean School of Management	Dr. David M. BLANCHETTE
70	Dean School of Social Work	Dr. Roberta S. PEARLMUTTER
58	Int Dean of Graduate Studies	Dr. Leslie SCHUSTER
08	Director of the Library	Mr. Hedi BENAICHA
35	Dean of Students	Dr. Scott D. KANE
100	Assistant to the President	Vacant
26	Director of News & Public Relations	Vacant
105	Director Web Services	Ms. Karen M. RUBINO
07	Director of Admissions	Mr. John MCLAUGHLIN
06	Director of Records	Mr. James C. DORIAN
37	Director Student Financial Aid	Mr. James T. HANBURY
25	Director of Research & Grants	Ms. Lisa SMOLSKI
18	Director Facilities & Operations	Vacant
90	Director User Support Services	Ms. Pamela CHRISTMAN
91	Director MIS	Dr. Bin YU
13	Director Network/Telecommunications	Mr. Henk E. SONDER
19	Director of Security	Mr. Frederick W. GHIO
09	Asst Dir Inst Research/Planning	Mrs. Jennifer A. ELLIS
96	Director of Purchasing	Ms. Jessica L. SILVA
41	Director of Athletics	Mr. Donald E. TENCHER
39	Director Residential Life/Housing	Ms. Teresa L. BROWN
36	Director Career Development Center	Ms. Linda S. KENT-DAVIS
23	Director College Health Services	Ms. Lynn A. WACHTEL
38	Director Counseling Center	Dr. Thomas J. LAVIN
29	Director Alumni Affairs	Ms. Kate BREZINA
04	Admin Assistant to the President	Ms. Donna NARODOWY

Rhode Island School of Design (B)

2 College Street, Providence RI 02903-2784
County: Providence FICE Identification: 003409
Unit ID: 217493
Telephone: (401) 454-6100 Carnegie Class: Spec/Arts
FAX Number: (401) 454-6320 Calendar System: 4/1/4
URL: www.risd.edu
Established: 1877 Annual Undergrad Tuition & Fees: $41,022
Enrollment: 2,396 Coed
Affiliation or Control: Independent Non-Profit IRS Status: 501(c)3
Highest Offering: Master's
Program: Liberal Arts And General; Professional; Fine Arts Emphasis
Accreditation: EH, ART, LSAR

Code	Title	Name
01	President	Dr. John MAEDA
100	Chief of Staff/Trustee Relations	Ms. Molly GARRISON
88	Special Assistant to President	Ms. Mara HERMANO
04	Executive Assistant to President	Ms. Marina MIHALAKIS
05	Provost	Ms. Rosanne SOMERSON
10	Exec Vice Pres Admin/Finance	Mr. William DECATUR
32	Senior VP for Students & Enrollment	Ms. Jean EDDY
30	Vice Pres Institutional Engagement	Mr. Eric GRAAGE
26	VP Media	Ms. Becky BERMONT
16	Vice Pres Human Resource	Ms. Candace BAER
88	Director RISD Museum of Art	Mr. John W. SMITH
20	Interim Assoc Provost Acad Affairs	Ms. Patricia PHILLIPS
48	Dean Architecture & Design	Vacant
57	Interim Dean of Fine Arts	Ms. Anais MISSAKIAN
58	Interim Dean of Graduate Studies	Mr. Brian GOLDBERG
89	Dean of Foundation Studies	Ms. Joanne STRYKER
49	Dean of Liberal Arts	Dr. Barbara VON ECKARDT
51	Dean Continuing Education	Dr. Brian K. SMITH
08	Director Library Services	Ms. Carol S. TERRY
21	Assoc VP Finance & Business Svcs	Mr. Richard RUMMEL
13	Interim Assoc VP Info Technology	Mr. Joseph BERNIER
18	Assoc VP Facilities & EHS	Mr. Jack SILVA
07	Director of Admissions	Mr. Edward NEWHALL, JR.
35	Dean of Students	Ms. Jerri DRUMMOND
105	Assistant VP Communications	Mr. Brian CLARK
43	General Counsel	Mr. Steven MCDONALD
31	Director of Media Relations	Ms. Jaime MARLAND
19	Director Public Safety	Mr. Ken BILODEAU
09	Director Institutional Research	Ms. Jennifer DUNSEATH
45	Director Budget	Ms. Linda MURPHY CHURCH
86	Director Government Relations	Ms. Babette ALLINA
29	Director of Alumni Relations	Ms. Christina HARTLEY
102	Dir Corp & Foundation Relations	Ms. Pamela HARRINGTON
44	Director of Leadership Giving	Ms. Louise OLSON
44	Director Annual Fund	Vacant
06	Registrar	Mr. Steven BERENBACK
25	Director Grants & Contracts	Ms. Stacy RISEMAN
96	Director Procurement Services	Mr. James NEWMAN
14	Director Network Services	Mr. Steven BOUDREAU
27	Director Editorial Services/Media	Ms. Liisa SILANDER
23	Director Health Services	Ms. Catherine VOLTAS
39	Director of Residence Life	Mr. Brian JANES
38	Dir Student Development/Counseling	Mr. Wayne ASSING
37	Director Financial Aid	Mr. Anthony GALLONIO
36	Director of Career Center	Mr. Gregory J. VICTORY
40	Dir of Dining & Retail Operations	Ms. Virginia DUNLEAVY
85	Director International Programs	Vacant

Roger Williams University (C)

One Old Ferry Road, Bristol RI 02809-2921
County: Bristol FICE Identification: 003410
Unit ID: 217518
Telephone: (401) 253-1040 Carnegie Class: Master's S
FAX Number: N/A Calendar System: Semester
URL: www.rwu.edu
Established: 1956 Annual Undergrad Tuition & Fees: $29,976
Enrollment: 4,844 Coed
Affiliation or Control: Independent Non-Profit IRS Status: 501(c)3
Highest Offering: Doctorate
Program: Liberal Arts And General; Teacher Preparatory; Professional
Accreditation: EH, BUS, CONST, ENG, LAW

Code	Title	Name
01	President	Dr. Donald J. FARISH
05	Provost/Sr VP Academic Affairs	Dr. Andrew WORKMAN
11	EVP Finance/Administration	Mr. Jerome WILLIAMS
43	Sr VP Legal Affs/General Counsel	Mr. Robert H. AVERY
84	Sr VP Enrollment Mgmt/ Retention	Ms. Lynn M. FAWTHROP
04	Executive Assistant to President	Ms. Brenda L. LITTLEFIELD
10	VP for Accounting/Treasury Mgmt	Mr. David GILMORE
32	Vice President for Student Affairs	Mr. John J. KING
30	Vice Pres University Advancement	Mr. Robert WEST
08	Int Dn Univ Lib Svcs/Dir Honors Pgm	Ms. Betsy P. LEARNED
32	Dean of Students	Dr. Kathleen N. MCMAHON
88	Asst VP Enrollment Mgmt/Retenton	Ms. Tracy M. DACOSTA
28	Assoc Dean/Dir Intercultural Center	Ms. Andrea DIAZ
61	Dean School of Law	Mr. David A. LOGAN
48	Dean Sch Arch/Art & Hist Preserv	Mr. Stephen E. WHITE
50	Dean Gabelli School of Business	Dr. Jerry DAUTERIVE
54	Dean Sch Engrng/Comput/Constr Mgmt	Dr. Robert A. POTTER
61	Dean School of Justice Studies	Dr. Stephanie PICOLO MANZI
53	Dean School of Education	Dr. Robert A. COLE
51	Dir Cont Studies/Grad Admiss	Ms. Jamie GRENON
49	Dean Feinstein Col Arts & Sciences	Dr. Robert COLE
55	Dean Instruct Sys Dev/Spec Projects	Mr. Kenneth T. OSBORNE
96	Director of Purchasing	Mr. Thomas KANE
29	Assoc Dean/Dir of Conferences	Ms. Allison CHASE PADULA
06	Registrar	Ms. Ann RUSSELL
45	Assoc VP Community/Govt Relations	Mr. Peter WILBUR
19	Director of Public Safety	Mr. Steven MELARAGNO
41	Director of Athletics	Mr. Dave KEMMY
18	Director of Facilities Management	Mr. John TAMEO
36	Director of Career Center	Ms. Robin L. BEAUCHAMP
38	Director Counseling & Student Devel	Dr. James A. AZAR
23	Director Health Services	Ms. Anne M. ANDRADE
39	Director of Housing	Mr. Anthony MONTEFUSCO
46	Director of Prospect Research	Ms. Nancy L. RAMOS
39	Director Residence Life/Women's Ctr	Ms. Jennifer STANLEY
09	Int Director Institutional Research	Mr. Eric SPONSELLER
37	Int Director Student Financial Aid	Ms. Tracy M. DACOSTA
40	Manager Bookstore	Vacant

Salve Regina University (D)

100 Ochre Point Avenue, Newport RI 02840-4192
County: Newport FICE Identification: 003411
Unit ID: 217536
Telephone: (401) 847-6650 Carnegie Class: Master's M
FAX Number: (401) 341-2925 Calendar System: Semester
URL: www.salve.edu
Established: 1947 Annual Undergrad Tuition & Fees: $33,950
Enrollment: 2,604 Coed
Affiliation or Control: Roman Catholic IRS Status: 501(c)3
Highest Offering: Doctorate
Program: Liberal Arts And General; Teacher Preparatory; Professional
Accreditation: EH, ART, CORE, IACBE, NUR, SW

Code	Title	Name
01	President	Dr. Jane GERETY, RSM
05	Vice President Academic Affairs	Dr. Dean DE LA MOTTE
32	Vice President Student Affairs	Dr. Margaret HIGGINS
30	VP University Rels/Advancement	Mr. Michael L. SEMENZA
10	Vice President Administration & CFO	Mr. William B. HALL
84	Vice President Enrollment Services	Dr. Laura E. MCPHIE-OLIVEIRA
88	Vice Pres Mission Integration	Sr. Leona MISTO, RSM
27	Assoc Vice Pres Univ Rels/CCO	Ms. Kristine HENDRICKSON
21	Assoc Vice Pres Finance/ Controller	Mr. Michael N. GRANDCHAMP
13	Assoc Vice Pres Info Technology/CIO	Mr. Thomas H. BRENNAN
15	Assoc Vice Pres Human Resources/ AAO	Mrs. Diane F. BLANCHETTE
20	Asst Vice Pres Academic Affairs	Dr. Donna M. COOK
07	Dean of Undergraduate Admissions	Ms. Colleen EMERSON
35	Dean of Students	Mr. John F. QUINN, JR.
49	Dean of Art & Sciences	Dr. Laura L. O'TOOLE
20	Dean of Professional Studies	Dr. Traci WARRINGTON
06	Registrar	Ms. Louise MONAST
37	Director of Financial Aid	Ms. Aida MIRANTE
29	Assoc Director Alumni & Parent Pgms	Mr. John RISTAINO
41	Athletic Director	Mr. Colin SULLIVAN
09	Director Institutional Research	Dr. Frederick C. PROMADES
08	Director of Library Services	Ms. Kathleen BOYD
39	Interim Director Campus Life	Dr. Gerry WILLIS
90	Director Academic Computing	Mr. Brian A. MCDONNELL
18	Director of Facilities	Mr. Eric MILNER
19	Director of Security/Safety	Mr. John MIXTER
40	Director of Bookstore	Mr. Michael LEDDY
44	Assoc Director of Annual Giving	Ms. Victoria DUCLOS-BARRETT
23	Director of Health Services	Mrs. Mary Kay CONNELL
35	Director of Student Activities	Ms. Heather BARBOUR
36	Director of Career Development	Mr. Michael WISNEWSKI
96	Director of Purchasing	Ms. Francine MONFETTE
104	Director of International Programs	Ms. Erin FITZGERALD
38	Dir of Student Counseling Services	Vacant

University of Rhode Island (E)

Kingston RI 02881-0806
County: Washington FICE Identification: 003414
Unit ID: 217484
Telephone: (401) 874-1000 Carnegie Class: RU/H
FAX Number: (401) 874-7149 Calendar System: Semester
URL: www.uri.edu
Established: 1892 Annual Undergrad Tuition & Fees (In-State): $12,450
Enrollment: 16,317 Coed
Affiliation or Control: State IRS Status: 501(c)3
Highest Offering: Doctorate
Program: Liberal Arts And General; Teacher Preparatory; Professional
Accreditation: EH, BUS, BUSA, CLPSY, CYTO, DIETD, DIETI, ENG, LIB, LSAR, MFCD, MUS, NURSE, PHAR, PTA, SCPSY, SP, TED

Code	Title	Name
01	President	Dr. David M. DOOLEY
100	Exec Asst to Pres & Dir PSPD	Mr. Abu BAKR
04	Sr Assistant to the President	Ms. Michelle S. CURRERI
05	Provost/Vice Pres Academic Affairs	Dr. Donald H. DEHAYES

88 Spec Asst to the Prov for Acad Plng ....Ms. Ann M. MORRISSEY
45 Vice Prov Acad Finance/Personnel ....Dr. Clifford H. KATZ
84 Vice Provost Enrollment Management ....Mr. Dean LIBUTTI
20 Int Vice Provost Faculty Affairs ....Dr. Laura BEAUVAIS
32 Vice President Student Affairs ....Dr. Thomas R. DOUGAN
10 Vice President for Administration ....Mr. Robert A. WEYGAND
46 Vice Pres Research/Economic Devel ....Dr. Peter ALFONSO
51 V Prov Urban Pgms/Dn Col Cont Educ ....Dr. John H. MCCRAY, JR.
28 Int Dir Community/Equity/Diversity ....Mr. Abu BAKR
49 Dean of Arts & Sciences ....Dr. Winifred E. BROWNELL
50 Dean Business Administration ....Dr. Mark M. HIGGINS
54 Dean of Engineering ....Dr. Raymond M. WRIGHT
88 Int Dean Grad School Oceanography ....Dr. Steven L. D'HONDT
69 Int Dean Human Sciences & Services ..Dr. Lori CICCOMOSCOLO
66 Dean of Nursing ....Dr. Dayle F. JOSEPH
67 Dean of Pharmacy ....Mr. Ronald P. JORDAN
07 Dean of Admissions ....Ms. Cynthia L. BONN
08 Dean University Libraries ....Mr. Dave MASLYN
88 Dean Univ Col & Spec Acad Pgms ....Dr. Jayne E. RICHMOND
58 Dean of Graduate School ....Dr. Nasser H. ZAWIA
53 Director School of Education ....Dr. David BYRD
92 Director Honors Program ....Dr. Richard MCINTYRE
43 General Counsel ....Mr. Louis J. SACCOCCIO
16 Asst Vice Pres Human Resource Admin ....Ms. Anne Marie COLEMAN
88 Asst VP Intell Property Mgmt/Comm ....Mr. David SADOWSKI
35 Asst VP Stdnt Affs & Dean of Stdnts ....Dr. Jason B. PINA
18 Asst Vice Pres Business Services ....Mr. J. Vernon WYMAN
39 Asst VP Student Affairs & Dir HRL ....Mr. Lester K. YENSAN
21 Dir Budget & Financial Planning ....Ms. Linda BARRETT
21 Controller ....Ms. Sharon B. BELL
27 Chief Information Officer ....Mr. Garrett A. BOZYLINSKY
37 Sr Assoc Dir Enrol Svcs/Fin Aid ....Ms. Bonnie A. SACCUCCI
22 Director Affirm Act/Equal Oppty/Div ....Ms. Roxanne GOMES
27 Director of Communications ....Ms. Linda A. ACCIARDO
23 Director Health Services ....Mr. Charles M. HENDERSON, III
38 Director Counseling Center ....Dr. Robert SAMUELS
41 Director of Athletics ....Mr. Thorr D. BJORN
15 Director Personnel Services ....Ms. Laura KENERSON
90 Dir Media & Technology Services ....Mr. David S. PORTER
91 Dir University Computing Systems ....Mr. Charlie SCHIFINO
104 Dir Intl Educ & Natl Student Exchg ....Dr. Dania C. BRANDFORD-CALVO
19 Int Director Public Safety ....Mr. Stephen N. BAKER
96 Director Purchasing & Univ Stores ....Ms. Elizabeth A. GIL
36 Director Career Services ....Dr. Roberta K. KOPPEL
40 Administrator Bookstore ....Mr. Paul WHITNEY
31 Dir Public Programming/Events ....Ms. Diane M. BLANDA
26 Int Dir Public Affairs ....Ms. Kerrie BENNETT
102 President RIU Foundation ....Mr. Michael J. SMITH
30 Interim Dir University Advancement ....Ms. Michele NOTA
29 Exec Dir Alumni Relations/Secy Assn ....Ms. Michele NOTA

SOUTH CAROLINA

Aiken Technical College (A)

PO Drawer 696, Aiken SC 29802-0696
County: Aiken FICE Identification: 010056
Unit ID: 217615
Telephone: (803) 593-9231 Carnegie Class: Assoc/Pub-R-M
FAX Number: (803) 593-6641 Calendar System: Semester
URL: www.atc.edu
Established: 1972 Annual Undergrad Tuition & Fees (In-District): $3,706
Enrollment: 3,071 Coed
Affiliation or Control: State/Local IRS Status: 501(c)3
Highest Offering: Associate Degree
Program: Occupational; 2-Year Principally Bachelor's Creditable; Technical Emphasis
Accreditation: SC, ACBSP, ADNUR, DA, MAC, RAD, SURGT

01 President ....Dr. Susan A. WINSOR
05 Vice President Academic Affairs ....Dr. Gemma FROCK
11 Vice Pres Administrative Services ....Mr. Andy JORDAN
103 VP Workforce & Business Devel ....Vacant
84 Dean of Enrollment Management ....Mr. Bryan NEWTON
09 Director Inst Planning/Research ....Vacant
102 Int Director Foundation & Grants ....Ms. Mary COMMONS
38 Director Counseling/Stdnt Placement ....Mr. Rich WELDON
37 Director of Financial Aid ....Vacant
27 Director of Information Services ....Vacant
13 Director of Computer Center/MIS ....Mr. Ray TIMMONS
16 Personnel Officer ....Ms. Sylvia BYRD
18 Chief of Maintenance ....Mr. Mike DUNCAN
10 Chief Business Officer ....Mr. Don TRUE
96 Director of Purchasing ....Ms. Toni MARSHALL

Allen University (B)

1530 Harden Street, Columbia SC 29204-1085
County: Richland FICE Identification: 003417
Unit ID: 217624
Telephone: (803) 376-5700 Carnegie Class: Bac/A&S
FAX Number: N/A Calendar System: Semester
URL: www.allenuniversity.edu
Established: 1870 Annual Undergrad Tuition & Fees: $11,940
Enrollment: 644 Coed
Affiliation or Control: African Methodist Episcopal IRS Status: 501(c)3
Highest Offering: Baccalaureate
Program: Liberal Arts And General; Teacher Preparatory
Accreditation: SC

01 President ....Dr. Pamela M. WILSON
03 Executive Vice President ....Vacant
51 Sr Vice Pres College Prof Adults ....Vacant
05 Vice President Academic Affairs . Dr. Lady June HUBBARD-COLE
10 Assoc Vice Pres Fiscal Affairs ....Mrs. Lavinia TEJADA
13 Vice Pres Information Technology ....Vacant
30 Vice Pres Institutional Advancement ....Vacant
32 Vice Pres Student Life ....Dr. Orlando LEWIS
45 VP Planning/Research/Sponsored Pgms ....Mr. Marcus V. BELL
43 General Counsel ....Mr. Renardo L. HICKS
06 Registrar ....Ms. Marilyn YOUNG
07 Director of Admissions ....Mr. Nathaniel CANTALL
15 Director of Human Resources ....Mrs. Paige MOORE
18 Facilities/Physical Plant Director ....Mr. Timothy TAYLOR
23 Director Health Services ....Mrs. Stephanie BRANTLEY
26 Director of Public Relations ....Vacant
09 Director of Institutional Research ....Ms. Marilyn C. YOUNG
29 Director of Alumni Relations ....Vacant
37 Director of Student Financial Aid ....Mrs. Shelline WARRENS
36 Director Student Placement ....Vacant
38 Director Counseling Services ....Vacant

Anderson University (C)

316 Boulevard, Anderson SC 29621-4035
County: Anderson FICE Identification: 003418
Unit ID: 217633
Telephone: (864) 231-2000 Carnegie Class: Bac/Diverse
FAX Number: (864) 231-2004 Calendar System: Semester
URL: www.andersonuniversity.edu
Established: 1911 Annual Undergrad Tuition & Fees: $21,730
Enrollment: 2,705 Coed
Affiliation or Control: Other IRS Status: 501(c)3
Highest Offering: Doctorate
Program: Liberal Arts And General; Teacher Preparatory
Accreditation: SC, ACBSP, ART, MUS, TED

01 President ....Dr. Evans P. WHITAKER
05 Provost ....Dr. Danny M. PARKER
10 VP for Finance and Operations ....Mr. James A. WRIGHT, JR.
30 VP for Institutional Advancement ....Mr. R. Dean WOODS
84 VP for Enrollment Management ....Mr. D. Omar RASHED
42 Vice President for Christian Life ....Dr. J. Robert CLINE
32 Vice Pres of Student Development ....Dr. Bob L. HANLEY
14 Chief Information Officer ....Mr. Peter B. HARVIN
41 Director of Athletics ....Mrs. Nancy P. SIMPSON
09 Dir of Enrollment Mgt Sys & Ext Rpt ....Mr. Daryl A. IVERSON
20 Associate Provost ....Mrs. Susan B. WOOTEN
28 Assoc VP for Student Development . Dr. Beverly RICE MCADAMS
06 University Registrar ....Mrs. Kendra B. WOODSON
08 Director of Library Services ....Mr. Kent A. MILLWOOD
26 Director Marketing & Communications ....Mr. Barry D. RAY
07 Director of Admissions ....Ms. Pam ROSS
37 Dir Financial Aid Planning ....Mrs. Rebekah BURDICK
15 Director of Human Resources ....Mrs. Darlene M. FISHER
18 Dir of Facilities and Procurement ....Mr. Dane S. SLAUGHTER
38 Director of Counseling Services ....Ms. Erin C. MAURER
29 Director of Alumni Relations ....Mr. Chad NELMS
36 Director Career Services ....Ms. Kelly A. BELL
39 Assoc Director of Residence Life ....Mr. Tim JARED
23 Director Health Services ....Mrs. Deb A. TAYLOR
21 Controller ....Ms. Kristie C. COLE
32 Dean of Student Life ....Mr. Jonathan GROPP
88 Director for Student Success ....Ms. L. Dianne KING
35 Director of Student Activities ....Ms. Sara MUDD

Benedict College (D)

Harden and Bland Streets, Columbia SC 29204-1086
County: Richland FICE Identification: 003420
Unit ID: 217721
Telephone: (803) 253-5000 Carnegie Class: Bac/Diverse
FAX Number: (803) 253-5059 Calendar System: Semester
URL: www.benedict.edu
Established: 1870 Annual Undergrad Tuition & Fees: $18,286
Enrollment: 3,224 Coed
Affiliation or Control: Independent Non-Profit IRS Status: 501(c)3
Highest Offering: Baccalaureate
Program: Liberal Arts And General; Teacher Preparatory
Accreditation: SC, ACBSP, ART, NRPA, SW, TED

01 President ....Dr. David H. SWINTON
05 Senior Vice Pres Academic Affairs ....Dr. Janeen WITTY
03 Executive Vice President ....Dr. Ruby W. WATTS
10 Vice President Business/Finance ....Ms. Brenda S. WALKER
32 Vice President Student Affairs ....Mr. Gary E. KNIGHT
44 Vice Pres Institutional Advancement ....Mrs. Barbara C. MOORE
35 Dean of Students ....Mr. Rufus C. WATTS
20 Assoc Vice Pres Academic Affairs ....Dr. George A. DEVLIN
21 Asst VP for Business & Finance ....Ms. Kathryn JONES
26 Asst VP for Comm & Marketing ....Ms. Kymm HUNTER
07 Director of Admissions/Student Mktg ....Mrs. Phyllis THOMPSON
29 Assistant VP for Alumni Relations ....Mrs. Ada A. BELTON
13 Dir Management Information Systems ....Mr. Robert SQUIREWELL
15 Director of Human Resources ....Mrs. Betty A. JENKINS
06 Registrar/Director Student Records ....Mrs. Wanda A. SCOTT-KINNEY
41 Athletics Director ....Mr. Willie WASHINGTON
38 Director Service Learning & Leaders ....Ms. Tondaleya JACKSON
39 Director Community Life ....Mr. Michael REBIMBUS
42 Dir Campus Ministry/Dean of Chapel ....Mr. Thomas DAVIS
19 Director Campus Safety ....Mr. Haywood M. BAZEMORE

36 Director Career Services ....Ms. Karen W. RUTHERFORD
37 Director Financial Aid ....Ms. Sul BLACK
19 Director Physical Plant ....Mr. Abu AHMED
08 Director of Library ....Mrs. Darlene ZINNERMAN-BETHEA
25 Coordinator Title III ....Mrs. Doris W. JOHNSON
49 Dean Sch Human/Arts/Soc Sci ....Dr. Charles AUSTIN
50 Dean School of Business/Econ ....Mr. Gerald SMALLS
53 Dean School of Education ....Dr. Allen COLES
72 Dean Sch Science/Tech/Engrng/ Math ....Dr. Samir S. RAYCHOUDHURY
92 Dean School of Honors ....Dr. Warren ROBINSON
57 Chair Fine Arts ....Mr. Charles BROOKS
50 Int Chair Business Admin/Mgmt/Mktg ....Dr. Ebuta EKURE
57 Int Chair Education and Family Stds ....Dr. Mona THORNTON
70 Chair Social Work ....Dr. Dorothy OSGOOD
88 Chair English/Foreign Language Dept ... Dr. Carolyn DRAKEFORD
88 Chair Bio/Chem/Enviroment Hlth Sci ....Dr. Helene TAMBOUE
81 Chair Math/Computer Science ....Ms. Fereshtah ZAHED
54 Int Chair Physics/Engineering ....Dr. Fouzi H. ARAMMASH
88 Int Chair Economics/Finance/Acctg ....Dr. Syed MAHDI

Bob Jones University (E)

1700 Wade Hampton Boulevard, Greenville SC 29614-0001
County: Greenville FICE Identification: 003421
Unit ID: 217749
Telephone: (864) 242-5100 Carnegie Class: Spec/Faith
FAX Number: (864) 235-6661 Calendar System: Semester
URL: www.bju.edu
Established: 1927 Annual Undergrad Tuition & Fees: $13,090
Enrollment: 3,631 Coed
Affiliation or Control: Proprietary IRS Status: Proprietary
Highest Offering: Doctorate
Program: Liberal Arts And General; Religious Emphasis
Accreditation: TRACS

00 Chancellor ....Dr. Bob JONES, III
01 President ....Dr. Stephen JONES
05 Exec Vice Pres for Academic Affairs ....Dr. Gary M. WEIER
11 Executive Vice Pres for Operations ....Mr. Marshall E. FRANKLIN
10 Vice President for Finance ....Mr. John D. MATTHEWS
05 Provost ....Dr. David A. FISHER
32 Dean of Students ....Dr. Eric D. NEWTON
20 Director of Educational Services ....Dr. N. Daniel SMITH
18 Chief Facilities Management Officer ....Mr. Mark W. KOPP
26 Chief Publications Officer ....Mr. Bill APELIAN
27 Chief Communication Officer ....Ms. Carol A. KEIRSTEAD
13 Chief Information Officer ....Mr. Marvin P. REEM
84 Director of Enrollment Planning ....Dr. Jeffrey D. HEATH
09 Dir of Institutional Effectiveness ....Rev. Phillip R. GERARD
06 Registrar ....Dr. N. Daniel SMITH
07 Director of Admissions ....Mr. Gary A. DEEDRICK
08 Director of Libraries ....Mr. Joseph L. ALLEN
88 Director of Ministerial Training ....Dr. M. Bruce MCALLISTER
30 Director of Advancement ....Mr. Thomas H. HALL
37 Director of Financial Aid ....Mr. Kevin DELP
41 Athletic Director ....Mr. Neal RING
33 Dean of Men ....Mr. Jonathan G. DAULTON
34 Dean of Women ....Ms. Deneen LAWSON
49 Dean College of Arts and Science ....Dr. Renae WENTWORTH
50 Dean School of Business ....Mr. Mike BUITER
53 Dean School of Education ....Dr. Brian A. CARRUTHERS
57 Dean Sch Fine Arts & Communication ....Dr. Darren P. LAWSON
73 Dean School of Religion ....Dr. Royce B. SHORT
73 Dean Seminary/Grad Sch of Religion ....Dr. Stephen J. HANKINS

Brown Mackie College-Greenville (F)

75 Beattie Place, Ste. 100, Greenville SC 29601-2155
County: Greenville Identification: 666781
Unit ID: 456791
Telephone: (864) 239-5301 Carnegie Class: Assoc/PrivFP
FAX Number: (864) 232-4094 Calendar System: Other
URL: www.brownmackie.edu
Established: 2009 Annual Undergrad Tuition & Fees: $11,124
Enrollment: 832 Coed
Affiliation or Control: Proprietary IRS Status: Proprietary
Highest Offering: Baccalaureate
Program: Occupational; 2-Year Principally Bachelor's Creditable; Business Emphasis
Accreditation: ACICS, OTA, SURTEC

01 President ....Karen BURGESS
07 Senior Director of Admissions ....Laura WALKER
05 Dean of Academic Affairs ....Brian WYSKO

† Branch campus of Brown Mackie College, Tucson, AZ.

Central Carolina Technical College (G)

506 N Guignard Drive, Sumter SC 29150-2499
County: Sumter FICE Identification: 003995
Unit ID: 218858
Telephone: (803) 778-1961 Carnegie Class: Assoc/Pub-R-M
FAX Number: (803) 778-7880 Calendar System: Semester
URL: www.cctech.edu
Established: 1962 Annual Undergrad Tuition & Fees (In-State): $3,584
Enrollment: 4,456 Coed
Affiliation or Control: State IRS Status: 501(c)3
Highest Offering: Associate Degree
Program: Occupational; 2-Year Principally Bachelor's Creditable; Technical Emphasis

Accreditation: SC, ADNUR, MAC, PNUR, SURGT

01 President ....Dr. Tim HARDEE
05 Interim Vice Pres Academics ....Mr. David WATSON
11 VP for Administration & Planning ....Mrs. Ann A. COOPER
10 Vice President for Business Affairs ....Ms. Terry L. BOOTH
32 Vice President for Student Affairs ....Ms. Lisa BRACKEN
04 Assistant to the President ....Ms. Emma Lee RICKARD
51 Director Cont Educ/Workforce Devel ....Ms. Elizabeth WILLIAMS
08 Dean of Learning Resources ....Ms. Nancy BISHOP
102 Director Foundation ....Ms. Meree MCALISTER
26 Director Public Relations ....Mr. Neal CROTTS
15 Director of Personnel ....Mrs. Ronalda S. STOVER
13 Director Information Systems ....Dr. Vicky G. MALONEY
06 Registrar ....Ms. Henrietta SCOTT
37 Director Student Financial Aid ....Ms. Sarah DOWD
09 Dir Research/Institutional Effect ....Mr. Bryan MAY
07 Director of Admissions & Counseling ....Mrs. Barbara WRIGHT
54 Dean of Industrial and Engineering ....Mr. Brent RUSSELL
76 Dean of Health Sciences ....Ms. Miriam LANEY
50 Dean of Business/Public Service ....Mr. David WATSON
53 Dean of General Education ....Mr. Myles WILLIAMS

Charleston School of Law (A)

81 Mary Street, PO Box 535, Charleston SC 29402
County: Charleston FICE Identification: 040963
Unit ID: 451510
Telephone: (843) 329-1000 Carnegie Class: Spec/Law
FAX Number: N/A Calendar System: Semester
URL: www.charlestonlaw.edu
Established: 2003 Annual Graduate Tuition & Fees: $37,874
Enrollment: 708 Coed
Affiliation or Control: Proprietary IRS Status: Proprietary
Highest Offering: First Professional Degree; No Undergraduates
Program: Professional
Accreditation: LAW

01 Dean ....Mr. Andrew L. ABRAMS
05 Associate Dean Academic Affairs ....Ms. Margaret M. LAWTON
07 Associate Dean Admissions ....Mr. John S. BENFIELD
32 Associate Dean of Students ....Ms. Abby EDWARDS SAUNDERS
08 Assoc Dean of Library/Tech Svcs ....Ms. Lisa SMITH-BUTLER
10 Chief Financial Officer ....Ms. Wende WOOD

Charleston Southern University (B)

PO Box 118087, Charleston SC 29423-8087
County: Charleston FICE Identification: 003419
Unit ID: 217688
Telephone: (843) 863-7000 Carnegie Class: Master's M
FAX Number: (843) 863-8074 Calendar System: Semester
URL: www.csuniv.edu
Established: 1964 Annual Undergrad Tuition & Fees: $21,400
Enrollment: 3,300 Coed
Affiliation or Control: Southern Baptist IRS Status: 501(c)3
Highest Offering: Master's
Program: Liberal Arts And General; Teacher Preparatory; Professional
Accreditation: SC, IACBE, MUS, NUR, TED

01 President ....Dr. Jairy C. HUNTER, JR.
05 Vice President Academic Affairs ....Dr. Jacqueline FISH
10 Vice President for Business Affairs ....Mr. Luke BLACKMON
04 Exec Assistant to the President ....Mrs. Faye WOOD
84 Vice Pres Enrollment Management ....Mrs. Debbie WILLIAMSON
45 Vice Pres Planning/Athletics ....Dr. Rick BREWER
26 Vice Pres Advancement & Marketing ....Mr. David BAGGS
30 Executive Director of Development ....Mr. Bill WARD
32 Dean of Students ....Mr. Clark CARTER
91 Director of Administrative Services ....Mr. Shannon PHILLIPS
08 Director of the Library ....Mrs. Sandra HUGHES
06 Registrar ....Mrs. Amanda SISSION
29 Director of BUC Club ....Ms. Cathryn BRODERHAUSEN
88 Asst to the VP for Retention ....Dr. Scott YARBROUGH
21 Associate Business Officer ....Mrs. Janet MIMS
26 Director of Integrated Marketing ....Mr. John STRUBEL
09 Dir of Institutional Effectiveness ....Mr. Jeffrey BABETZ
50 Dean of Business ....Dr. John B. DUNCAN
58 Director MBA Program ....Dr. Darin GERDES
58 Dean Education ....Dr. Kari SIKO
83 Dean Humanities/Social Sciences ....Dr. Keith CALLIS
81 Dean Science & Mathematics ....Dr. Jeryl JOHNSON
66 Dean of Nursing ....Dr. Tara HULSEY
51 College of Adult Professional Stds ....Dr. James JONES
41 Athletic Director ....Mr. Hank SMALL
42 Director Campus Ministry ....Mr. Jon DAVIS
19 Director Security ....Mr. Guy VAN HORN
90 Director Computing & Info Science ....Mr. James ROBERTS
18 Director Physical & Auxiliary Svcs ....Mr. Nick CIMORELLI
29 Director of Alumni Relations ....Mrs. Beth MYERS
07 Director of Admission ....Mr. James M. RHOTON
15 Director of Personnel Services ....Mrs. Lindsey WALKE
36 Director Career Planning ....Mrs. Hester YOUNG
38 Director Student Counseling ....Mr. Rufus WOFFORD
96 Director of Purchasing ....Mrs. Linda PARKER
37 Director Student Financial Aid ....Mrs. Teri KARGES
39 Director Residence Life ....Mr. Tyler DAVIS

The Citadel, The Military College of South Carolina (C)

171 Moultrie Street, Charleston SC 29409-0001
County: Charleston FICE Identification: 003423
Unit ID: 217864
Telephone: (843) 225-3294 Carnegie Class: Master's L
FAX Number: (843) 953-5287 Calendar System: Semester
URL: www.citadel.edu
Established: 1842 Annual Undergrad Tuition & Fees (In-State): $10,523
Enrollment: 3,390 Coed
Affiliation or Control: State IRS Status: 501(c)3
Highest Offering: Beyond Master's But Less Than Doctorate
Program: Liberal Arts And General; Teacher Preparatory; Professional
Accreditation: SC, BUS, CACREP, CS, ENG, TED

01 President ....LtGen. John W. ROSA
05 Provost/Dean of College ....BGen. Samuel M. HINES, JR.
10 Exec VP Finance Admin & Operations ....BGen. Thomas J. ELZEY
18 Vice Pres Facilities/Engineering ....Col. George D. YEATTS
26 Vice President for External Affairs ....Col. L. Jeffrey PEREZ
30 VP Inst Advanc/Citadel Fndtn Ex Dir ....Vacant
11 Associate Vice Pres for Operations ....Col. Thomas G. PHILIPKOSKY
04 Executive Assistant to President ....Vacant
32 Commandant of Cadets ....Col. Leo A. MERCADO
43 General Counsel ....Mr. Mark C. BRANDENBURG
20 Assoc Provost Academic Affairs ....Col. Mark A. BEBENSEE
20 Assoc Prov Plng/Assess/Evaluation ....LtCol. Tara F. MCNEALY
58 Assoc Provost/Citadel Graduate Col ....Vacant
07 Director of Admissions ....LtCol. John W. POWELL, JR.
06 Registrar ....LtCol. Sylvia L. NESMITH
41 Director Intercollegiate Athletics ....Mr. Larry W. LECKONBY
35 Director of Cadet Activities ....LtCol. Robert A. SBERNA
29 Director Alumni Affairs/Placement ....Mr. Michael F. ROGERS
08 Director of Library ....LtCol. David S. GOBLE
13 Director Info Technology Services ....Mr. Richard NELSON
37 Director Financial Aid/ Scholarships ....LtCol. Henry M. FULLER, JR.
15 Director of Human Resources ....Col. Dennis D. CARPENTER
36 Director of Student Placement ....Mr. Brent A. STEWART
38 Director of Student Counseling ....Dr. Suzanne BUFANO
09 Institutional Research Coordinator ....Mrs. Lisa L. PACE
19 Director Security/Safety ....Maj. William A. FLETCHER
23 College Physician ....Dr. Carey M. CAPELL
40 Director of the Cadet Store ....Mr. Kenneth A. WOODRUFF
42 Chaplain/Dir Religious Activities ....LtCol. Joel C. HARRIS
92 Director Honors Program ....Col. Jack W. RHODES
86 Director Govt & Community Affairs ....Col. Cardon B. CRAWFORD
96 Director of Purchasing ....Mr. James P. DE LUCA
28 Chief Diversity Officer ....Ms. Emma BENNETT-WILLIAMS
50 Dean of the School of Bus Admin ....Col. Ronald F. GREEN
53 Dean of the School of Education ....Col. Tony W. JOHNSON
54 Dean of the School of Engineering ....Col. Ronald W. WELCH
81 Dean of the School of Science/ Math ....Col. Lok C. LEW YAN VOON
79 Dean Sch Humanities/Social Sciences ....Col. Winifred B. MOORE

Claflin University (D)

400 Magnolia Street, Orangeburg SC 29115-4477
County: Orangeburg FICE Identification: 003424
Unit ID: 217873
Telephone: (803) 535-5000 Carnegie Class: Bac/A&S
FAX Number: (803) 531-2860 Calendar System: Semester
URL: www.claflin.edu
Established: 1869 Annual Undergrad Tuition & Fees: $14,308
Enrollment: 1,961 Coed
Affiliation or Control: United Methodist IRS Status: 501(c)3
Highest Offering: Master's
Program: Liberal Arts And General
Accreditation: SC, MUS, ACBSP, TED

01 President ....Dr. Henry N. TISDALE
03 Executive Vice President ....Mr. Drexel B. BALL
05 Int Vice Pres for Academic Affairs ....Dr. Vermelle J. JOHNSON
10 Vice President for Fiscal Affairs ....Vacant
30 Vice Pres Institutional Advancement ....Rev. Whittaker V. MIDDLETON
32 Vice Pres Student Devel & Services ....Dr. Leroy A. DURANT
45 VP Plng/Assessment/Information Svcs ....Dr. Zia HASAN
20 Associate VP for Academic Affairs ....Dr. Rebecca BULLARD-DILLARD
21 Associate VP for Fiscal Affairs ....Mrs. Tijuana R. HUDSON
26 Asst VP Communications & Marketing ....Ms. Sonja BENNETT
35 Asst VP Student Devel & Services ....Vacant
07 Director of Admissions ....Mr. Michael ZEIGLER
79 Dean Sch Humanities & Soc Science ....Dr. Peggy STEVENSON-RATLIFF
50 Dean School of Business ....Dr. Harpal S. GREWAL
53 Interim Dean School of Education ....Dr. Valerie E. HARRISON
81 Dean Sch Natural Sciences & Math ....Dr. Verlie A. TISDALE
13 Asst VP Information Tech Svcs ....Mr. James E. BRENN
51 Interim Dir of Prof & Cont Studies ....Dr. Gloria SEABROOK
88 Director of Special Events ....Ms. Franette BOYD
08 Library Director ....Ms. Marilyn Y. GIBBS
37 Director of Financial Aid ....Ms. Terria C. WILLIAMS
36 Director of Career Development ....Mrs. Carolyn R. SNELL
18 Director Plant Operations ....Mr. Adrian PARKS
41 Athletic Director ....Dr. Timothy J. AUTRY
15 Director of Human Resources ....Ms. Shirley A. BIGGS
06 Registrar ....Mrs. Roe B. HUNT
29 Director Alumni Relations ....Vacant
19 Chief of Campus Public Safety ....Mr. Steven A. PEARSON
96 Director of Auxiliary Services ....Mr. Rodeny B. HUDSON
88 Director of Sponsored Programs ....Ms. Veronica GOODMAN
09 Dir of Institutional Effectiveness ....Mrs. Bridget DEWEES
04 Executive Admin Asst to President ....Ms. Melvenia WILLIAMS

Clemson University (E)

201 Sikes Hall, Clemson SC 29634-0001
County: Pickens FICE Identification: 003425
Unit ID: 217882
Telephone: (864) 656-3311 Carnegie Class: RU/H
FAX Number: (864) 656-4040 Calendar System: Semester
URL: www.clemson.edu
Established: 1889 Annual Undergrad Tuition & Fees (In-State): $12,674
Enrollment: 19,914 Coed
Affiliation or Control: State IRS Status: 501(c)3
Highest Offering: Doctorate
Program: Liberal Arts And General; Teacher Preparatory; Professional
Accreditation: SC, ART, BUS, BUSA, CACREP, CONST, CS, DIETD, ENG, ENGR, FOR, IPSY, LSAR, NRPA, NURSE, PLNG, TED

01 President ....Mr. James F. BARKER
43 General Counsel ....Mr. W.C. (Chip) HOOD
05 Vice President Acad Affairs/Provost ....Dr. Doris R. HELMS
10 Chief Financial Officer ....Mr. Brett A. DALTON
32 Vice President Student Affairs ....Ms. Gail DISABATINO
101 Executive Secretary to the Board ....Ms. Angie LEIDINGER
30 Vice President for Advancement ....Mr. A. Neill CAMERON, JR.
88 Vice Pres Public Svc/Agriculture ....Dr. John W. KELLY, JR.
46 Vice President for Research ....Dr. Gerald SONNENFELD
27 Vice Prov Computer/Info Technology ....Mr. James R. BOTTUM
20 Vice Prov/Dean Undergrad Studies ....Dr. Janice W. MURDOCH
29 Chief Alumni Officer ....Mr. Brian J. O'ROURKE
18 Chief Facilities Officer ....Mr. Robert J. WELLS, JR.
35 Associate VP/Dean of Students ....Dr. Joy S. SMITH
26 Chief Public Affairs Officer ....Ms. Catherine T. SAMS
08 Dean of Libraries ....Ms. Kay WALL
07 Director of Admissions ....Mr. Robert S. BARKLEY
06 Registrar ....Mr. Stanley B. SMITH
37 Director of Financial Aid ....Mr. Chuck KNEPFLE
36 Director of Career Center ....Vacant
38 Director Counseling/Psych Services ....Dr. Raquel J. CONTRERAS
47 Dean Col Agric/Forestry/Life Sci ....Dr. Thomas R. SCOTT
58 Dean Grad School/Assoc Vice Provost ....Vacant
48 Dean Col Arch/Arts/Humanities ....Dr. Richard E. GOODSTEIN
54 Interim Dean Col Engr/Sciences ....Dr. Larry DOOLEY
50 Int Dn Col Business/Behavioral Sci ....Dr. Charles K. WATT
53 Dean Col Health/Educ/Human Dev ....Dr. Lawrence R. ALLEN
09 Director Institutional Research ....Dr. S. Wickes WESTCOTT, III
39 Executive Director of Housing ....Ms. Verna G. HOWELL
41 Director of Athletics ....Dr. Terry Don PHILLIPS
44 Director of Estate & Planned Giving ....Ms. Jovanna J. KING
22 Director Access & Equity ....Mr. Byron A. WILEY
23 Director Student Health Services ....Mr. George W. CLAY
15 Chief Human Resources ....Vacant
91 Executive Director Enterprise Appl ....Ms. Deborah WHITTEN
25 Director Sponsored Programs ....Dr. Vincent S. GALLICCHIO
19 Director Law Enforcement & Safety ....Chief Johnson LINK
96 Director of Purchasing ....Mr. Michael NEBESKY

Clinton Junior College (F)

1029 Crawford Road, Rock Hill SC 29730-5152
County: York FICE Identification: 004923
Unit ID: 217891
Telephone: (803) 327-7402 Carnegie Class: Assoc/PrivNFP
FAX Number: (803) 327-3261 Calendar System: Semester
URL: www.clintonjuniorcollege.edu
Established: 1894 Annual Undergrad Tuition & Fees: $12,237
Enrollment: 174 Coed
Affiliation or Control: African Methodist Episcopal Zion Church
IRS Status: 501(c)3
Highest Offering: Associate Degree
Program: Liberal Arts And General
Accreditation: TRACS

01 President ....Dr. Elaine J. COPELAND
04 Assistant to the President ....Ms. Cheryl A. WEBB
05 VP for Academic Affairs/Dean ....Ms. Janis S. PENDLETON
30 VP for Development ....Mr. William TABOR
32 VP for Student Affairs ....Dr. Robert M. COPELAND, JR.
10 VP of Business & Finance ....Ms. Archinya INGRAM
09 VP for Institutional Effectiveness ....Ms. Judith COWAN
06 Registrar ....Mrs. Altavese HUNT
37 Financial Aid ....Ms. Sadie PYE-JUMPER
08 Librarian ....Ms. Minora HICKS
41 Athletic Dir/Womens Basketbl Coach ....Mr. Roderick WOODS
18 Director Facilities/Bldgs/Grounds ....Rev. Lloyd SNIPES
07 Admissions Director ....Dr. Robert COPELAND
35 Coord Student Support Services ....Ms. Omega HONEYWOOD

Coastal Carolina University (G)

PO Box 261954, Conway SC 29528-6054
County: Horry FICE Identification: 003451
Unit ID: 218724
Telephone: (843) 347-3161 Carnegie Class: Master's S
FAX Number: (843) 349-2990 Calendar System: Semester
URL: www.coastal.edu
Established: 1954 Annual Undergrad Tuition & Fees (In-State): $9,760
Enrollment: 9,084 Coed
Affiliation or Control: State IRS Status: 501(c)3
Highest Offering: Master's
Program: Liberal Arts And General
Accreditation: SC, ART, BUS, CS, MUS, NUR, TED, THEA

01 President ... Dr. David A. DECENZO
05 Provost/Sr VP Acad & Student Affs ... Dr. Robert J. SHEEHAN
03 Executive Vice President ... Dr. Edgar L. DYER
10 Vice Pres Finance/Administration ... Ms. Staci A. BOWIE
84 Vice Pres for Enrollment Services ... Dr. Judy W. VOGT
30 Interim Vice Pres Philanthropy ... Mr. Lawson HOLLAND
27 Vice Pres University Communications ... Vacant
50 Dean Business Administration ... Dr. J. Ralph BYINGTON
53 Dean of Education ... Dr. Edward JADALLAH
79 Int Dean of Humanities & Fine Arts ... Dr. Daniel ENNIS
81 Dean of Science ... Dr. Michael H. ROBERTS
08 Dean Library Services ... Dr. Barbara BURD
32 Vice President Student Affairs ... Dr. Deborah CONNER
16 Exec Dir HR & Organizational Dev ... Ms. Pat WEST
13 Exec Director Info Technology Svcs ... Mr. Abdallah HADDAD
20 Assoc Provost Admin/Academic ... Ms. Sallie CLARKSON
20 Assoc Prov Assessment/Accreditation ... Dr. John P. BEARD
58 Assoc Provost/Dir Graduate Studies ... Dr. James O. LUKEN
20 Assoc Provost/QEP ... Dr. Michael RUSE
09 Director of Inst Rsrch/Assessment ... Ms. Christine L. MEE
06 University Registrar ... Mr. Daniel M. LAWLESS
19 Director Public Safety ... Mr. David ROPER
21 Controller ... Ms. Lori CHURCH
28 Dir Multicultural Student Services ... Ms. Patricia SINGLETON-YOUNG
41 Director of Athletics ... Mr. Hunter R. YURACHEK
38 Director of Counseling Services ... Dr. Jennie M. CASSIDY
85 Director of International Programs ... Mr. Geoffrey J. PARSONS
39 Director of Housing/Residence Life ... Mr. Steve HARRISON
37 Director of Financial Aid ... Mr. Greg THORNBURG
92 Director Honors Program ... Dr. Philip E. WHALEN
36 Director Career Services ... Dr. Tom WOODLE
96 Dir Procurement/Business Services ... Mr. Dean P. HUDSON
18 Dir University Projects & Planning ... Mr. T. Rein MUNGO
26 Chief Public Relations Officer ... Ms. Martha S. HUNN
29 Director Alumni Relations ... Ms. Jean Ann BRAKEFIELD
104 Exec Dir Global Initiatives ... Dr. Darla J. DOMKE-DAMONTE
07 Dir Enrollment/Assoc Dir Admissions ... Vacant

Coker College (A)

300 E College Avenue, Hartsville SC 29550-3797
County: Darlington
FICE Identification: 003427
Unit ID: 217907
Telephone: (843) 383-8000
Carnegie Class: Bac/Diverse
FAX Number: (843) 383-8048
Calendar System: Semester
URL: www.coker.edu
Established: 1908
Annual Undergrad Tuition & Fees: $23,640
Enrollment: 1,141
Coed
Affiliation or Control: Independent Non-Profit
IRS Status: 501(c)3
Highest Offering: Master's
Program: Liberal Arts And General; Teacher Preparatory
Accreditation: SC, MUS, SW

01 President ... Dr. Robert L. WYATT
04 Exec Assistant to the President ... Ms. Bonnie WILCOX
05 Provost & Dean of the Faculty ... Dr. Tracy PARKINSON
30 VP Institutional Advancement ... Mr. Charles SULLIVAN
10 Vice President Business Operations ... Vacant
84 VP Enrollment/Student Services ... Dr. Stephen B. TERRY
32 Dean of Students ... Dr. Jason UMFRESS
55 Assoc Dean Adult Learner Pgm ... Dr. Barbara JACKOWSKI
78 Asst Dean/Dir CTR Engaged Learning ... Ms. Darlene SMALL
26 Exec Dir Marketing/Communication ... Mr. R. Kyle SAVERANCE
39 Director of Residence Life ... Ms. April A. PALMER
41 Director of Athletics ... Dr. Lynn GRIFFIN
07 Director of Admissions ... Mr. Adam CONNOLLY
06 Registrar ... Ms. Stacy R. ATKINSON
18 Director of Plant Operations ... Mr. Russell CROFT
21 Controller ... Mrs. Robin A. PERDUE
37 Director of Financial Aid ... Mrs. Betty B. WILLIAMS
44 Director of Major Gifts ... Mr. Wesley J. DANIELS
29 Dir of Alumni & Advancement Svcs ... Ms. Pat DAMPIER
38 Director Counseling Services ... Vacant
35 Dir Student Activities/Leadership ... Ms. Lisa POTOKA
15 Director of Human Resources ... Ms. Brianna DOUGLAS
38 Director of Career Services ... Ms. Deanne FRYE
08 Director of Library ... Ms. Alexa BARTEL
13 Director of Information Technology ... Mr. Wally BOATWRIGHT
19 Director of Campus Safety ... Mr. Michael WILLIAMSON

College of Charleston (B)

66 George Street, Charleston SC 29424-0100
County: Charleston
FICE Identification: 003428
Unit ID: 217819
Telephone: (843) 953-5507
Carnegie Class: Master's M
FAX Number: (843) 953-5811
Calendar System: Semester
URL: www.cofc.edu
Established: 1770
Annual Undergrad Tuition & Fees (In-State): $9,918
Enrollment: 11,649
Coed
Affiliation or Control: State
IRS Status: 501(c)3
Highest Offering: Master's
Program: Liberal Arts And General
Accreditation: SC, BUS, BUSA, CS, MUS, SPAA, TED, THEA

01 President ... Dr. George BENSON
05 VP Acad Affairs/Provost ... Mr. George W. HYND
10 Exec VP Business Affairs ... Mr. Steven C. OSBORNE
32 Exec VP Student Affairs ... Dr. Victor K. WILSON
30 Exec VP Institutional Advancement ... Mr. George P. WATT, JR.
84 Assoc Vice Pres Enrollment Planning ... Mr. Donald C. BURKARD
26 Exec VP External Relations ... Mr. Mike HASKINS
31 Assoc Dean Community Relations ... Ms. Evelyn H. NADEL
43 Senior VP Legal Affairs ... Mr. Thomas A. TRIMBOLI
100 Chief of Staff ... Dr. Brian MCGEE
12 Int Director Lowcountry Grad Ctr ... Dr. Sue SOMMER-KRESSE
20 Assoc VP Academic Experience ... Dr. Kay SMITH
22 Director Human Rels/Minority Affs ... Ms. Jo Ann DIAZ
08 Dean Libraries/Acad Info Svcs ... Dr. David J. COHEN
58 Dean Grad School/Asc Prov Research ... Dr. Amy T. MCCANDLESS
20 Senior Vice Provost Academic Affair ... Dr. Beverly E. DIAMOND
20 Assoc Provost for Faculty Affairs ... Dr. Deanna M. CAVENY
35 Dean of Students ... Dr. Jeri O. CABOT
57 Dean School of the Arts ... Ms. Valerie B. MORRIS
50 Dean School of Business ... Dr. Alan T. SHAO
53 Dean School of Education ... Dr. Frances C. WELCH
79 Dean Humanities/Social Science ... Dr. Cynthia J. LOWENTHAL
81 Dean School of Science & Math ... Dr. Michael AUERBACH
79 Dean Languages/Culture & World Affs ... Dr. David J. COHEN
92 Dean Honors College ... Dr. John H. NEWELL, JR.
36 Director of Career Services ... Mr. Denny D. CIGANOVIC
06 Registrar ... Ms. Catherine C. BOYD
15 Director of Human Resources ... Mr. Tom R. CASEY
21 Director of Budgets ... Mr. Samuel B. JONES
51 Director Adult Student Services ... Ms. Dorinda Q. HARMON
29 Dir Institutional Advancement Comm ... Ms. Karen B. JONES
37 Director Financial Asst/Veteran Aff ... Mr. Donald R. GRIGGS
91 Director IT Network & Program Svcs ... Ms. Marcia K. MOORE
27 Chief Information Officer ... Dr. Robert E. CAPE
19 Chief Public Safety ... Chief Paul VERRECCHIA
41 Athletic Director ... Mr. Joe HULL, JR.
23 Director Health Services ... Ms. Jane RENO-MUNRO
39 Dean Residence Life & Housing ... Mr. John T. CAMPBELL
38 Dir Counseling/Substance Abuse Svcs ... Dr. Frank C. BUDD
09 Director of Institutional Research ... Vacant
25 Director of Research/Grants Admin ... Ms. Susan A. RIVALEAU
40 Bookstore Manager ... Ms. Rebecca GRAY
18 Director of Physical Plant ... Mr. John A. CORDRAY, JR.
12 Interim Dir Col of Charleston North ... Dr. Sue SOMMER-KRESSE
104 Director Intl Education & Programs ... Dr. Andrew SOBIESUO
26 Dir College Publications ... Mr. Mark E. BERRY
87 Director Summer Programs ... Mr. Michael C. PHILLIPS
96 Director of Procurement ... Ms. Wendy E. WILLIAMS

Columbia College (C)

1301 Columbia College Drive, Columbia SC 29203-5998
County: Richland
FICE Identification: 003430
Unit ID: 217934
Telephone: (803) 786-3012
Carnegie Class: Master's M
FAX Number: (803) 754-3178
Calendar System: Semester
URL: www.columbiasc.edu
Established: 1854
Annual Undergrad Tuition & Fees: $26,030
Enrollment: 1,145
Female
Affiliation or Control: United Methodist
IRS Status: 501(c)3
Highest Offering: Master's
Program: Liberal Arts And General; Teacher Preparatory
Accreditation: SC, ART, DANCE, MUS, SW, TED

01 President ... Ms. Elizabeth A. DINNDORF
05 Provost/VP for Academic Affairs ... Dr. Laurie B. HOPKINS
10 Vice President for Finance ... Mr. John D. JONES
84 Vice Pres for Enrollment Management ... Dr. Ronald G. WHITE
46 Exec Director Leadership Institute ... Dr. Linda B. SALANE
30 Interim VP for Advancement ... Ms. Amy S. LANIER
32 Dean Student Affairs ... Ms. LaNae R. BRIGGS
29 Exec Director of Alumnae Relations ... Ms. Sara S. JOHNSON
11 Director of Administrative Services ... Ms. Virginia A. RICKER
06 Registrar/Dir Institutional Rsrch ... Dr. Scott A. SMITH
08 Dir of Library & Info Tech Services ... Mr. Dan MURPHY
19 Chief of Police ... Chief Howard M. COOK
25 Director of Grants ... Vacant
37 Director of Financial Aid ... Ms. Donna QUICK
36 Director of the Career Center ... Ms. Kim FRANKLIN
14 Director of Info Technology ... Mr. Dave MEDEIROS
18 Director of Facilities Management ... Mr. Lowell CUPPS
23 Director of Student Health Services ... Vacant
26 Executive Director Public Relations ... Ms. Rebecca B. MUNNERLYN
41 Director of Athletics ... Ms. Kelly COX
40 Director Bookstore ... Mr. Chris FREEMAN
38 Director Counseling Services ... Ms. Birma GAINOR
04 Executive Assistant to President ... Ms. Joye G. HIPP
07 Director of Admissions ... Ms. Julie A. KING
92 Director Honors Program/Faculty Dev ... Dr. John ZUBIZARRETA

Columbia International University (D)

PO Box 3122, Columbia SC 29230-3122
County: Richland
FICE Identification: 003429
Unit ID: 217925
Telephone: (803) 754-4100
Carnegie Class: Master's S
FAX Number: (803) 786-4209
Calendar System: Semester
URL: www.ciu.edu
Established: 1923
Annual Undergrad Tuition & Fees: $18,065
Enrollment: 1,177
Coed
Affiliation or Control: Independent Non-Profit
IRS Status: 501(c)3
Highest Offering: Doctorate
Program: Liberal Arts And General; Professional
Accreditation: SC, BI, THEOL

01 President ... Dr. William H. JONES
00 Chancellor ... Dr. George W. MURRAY
05 Senior Vice President/Provost ... Dr. Jim LANPHER
30 Sr Vice Pres Development/Operations ... Mr. D. Keith MARION
84 VP Enrollment Mgmt/Communications ... Mr. Michael BLACKWELL
73 Dean Columbia Biblical Seminary ... Dr. John HARVEY
49 Dean College of Arts and Sciences ... Dr. Bryan BEYER
53 Dean College of Education ... Dr. Milton V. UECKER
38 Dean College of Counselling ... Dr. Harvey PAYNE
104 Dean College Intercultural Studies ... Dr. Michael BARNETT
09 Dir Institutional Research/Assess ... Mr. Jeff MILLER
56 Director of Distance Education ... Mr. Rob MCDOLE
08 Director of Library ... Mrs. Jo Ann RHODES
06 University Registrar ... Mrs. Tammy TURKETT
15 Director Human Resources ... Mr. Donald E. JONES
29 Director of Alumni ... Dr. Roy KING
32 Dean of Students ... Mr. Rick SWIFT
07 Director University Admissions ... Ms. Sandra RHYNE
14 Director Computer Services ... Mrs. Michele BRANCH-FRAPPIER
18 Director Physical Plant ... Mr. Robert REGISTER
40 Director of Business Services ... Mr. Roger L. TILTON
21 Controller ... Mr. Larry F. HUSS
30 Director Development ... Mr. Frank BEDELL
37 Director Financial Aid ... Ms. Sandra RHYNE
26 Chief Public Relations Officer ... Mrs. Polly SHOEMAKER
88 General Mgr WMHK/WRCM Radio ... Mr. Joseph PAULO
36 Director Student Placement ... Mrs. Stephanie BRYANT

Converse College (E)

580 E Main, Spartanburg SC 29302-0006
County: Spartanburg
FICE Identification: 003431
Unit ID: 217961
Telephone: (864) 596-9000
Carnegie Class: Master's M
FAX Number: (864) 596-9158
Calendar System: 4/1/4
URL: www.converse.edu
Established: 1889
Annual Undergrad Tuition & Fees: $27,320
Enrollment: 1,296
Female
Affiliation or Control: Independent Non-Profit
IRS Status: 501(c)3
Highest Offering: Beyond Master's But Less Than Doctorate
Program: Liberal Arts And General; Teacher Preparatory; Professional; Business Emphasis
Accreditation: SC, ART, CIDA, MFCD, MUS, TED

01 President ... Dr. Elizabeth A. FLEMING
03 Senior Vice President ... Dr. Thomas MCDANIEL
05 VP Academic Affs/Dean Sch Human/Sci ... Dr. Jeffrey H. BARKER
10 Vice Pres Finance/Administration ... Mrs. Susan A. STEVENSON
84 Vice Pres Enrollment Management ... Ms. Sally J. HAMMOND
30 Vice President Inst Advancement ... Dr. Robert STEWART
32 Vice Pres Student life/Dn Students ... Dr. Molly DUESTERHAUS
58 Dean Graduate Educ/Special Programs ... Dr. Kathy GOOD
64 Dean School of the Arts ... Mr. Richard HIGGS
35 Asst Dean Students for Engage/Lrng ... Ms. Rhonda MINGO
08 Librarian ... Mr. Wade WOODWARD
37 Director of Financial Assistance ... Mrs. Peggy P. COLLINS
06 Registrar ... Mrs. Mary L. BROWN
15 Human Resources Director ... Mrs. Sandy GORDIN
29 Director of Alumnae/Donor Rels ... Ms. Carrie COLEMAN
13 Chief Technology Officer ... Mr. John JAMES
36 Director of Career Services ... Ms. Witney FISHER
26 Director of Media/Communications ... Mrs. Beth LANCASTER
04 Admin Assistant to the President ... Mrs. Stacey BREWER
38 Director Student Counseling ... Dr. Carol EPPS
09 Director Institutional Research ... Mrs. Ann M. PLETCHER
07 Director of Admissions ... Ms. April LEWIS
18 Chief Facilities/Physical Plant ... Mr. Hayden HUTCHINGS
18 Facilities Planner ... Mr. Mark L. OSINGA

Denmark Technical College (F)

PO Box 327, Denmark SC 29042-0327
County: Bamberg
FICE Identification: 005363
Unit ID: 217989
Telephone: (803) 793-5176
Carnegie Class: Assoc/Pub-R-S
FAX Number: (803) 793-5942
Calendar System: Semester
URL: www.denmarktech.edu
Established: 1948
Annual Undergrad Tuition & Fees (In-State): $2,662
Enrollment: 1,606
Coed
Affiliation or Control: State
IRS Status: 501(c)3
Highest Offering: Associate Degree
Program: Occupational; 2-Year Principally Bachelor's Creditable
Accreditation: SC, ACBSP, ENGT

01 President ... Dr. Joann BOYD-SCOTLAND
05 VP Academic Affairs ... Mrs. Carolyn FENNELL-MCGAY
09 Vice Pres Inst Research/Plng/Dev ... Dr. Ashok KABISATPATHY
10 VP Fiscal Affairs ... Mr. Clarence BONNETTE
16 Human Resources Director ... Ms. Tonya OTTS
32 Dean of Student Services ... Mrs. Avis GATHERS
08 Dean of Learning Resources Center ... Vacant
13 Information Technology Director ... Mr. Derrick STEWARD
19 Chief of Public Safety ... Mrs. Judy HALMON
84 Director of Enrollment Management ... Vacant
25 Director of Grants & Contracts ... Mrs. Teresa MACK
36 Director Career Plng/Placement ... Mr. Jay FIELDS
37 Financial Aid Director ... Mrs. Connie WILLIAMS
40 Dean of Public Service ... Ms. Bijayalaxmi KABISATPATHY
49 Dean of Arts & Sciences ... Vacant
54 Dean Industrial/Related Technology ... Dr. Ambrish LAVANIA
50 Dean Business/Computer/Related Tech ... Ms. Antonia ROBERTS
60 Dean of Transitional Studies ... Ms. Colleen WHETSTONE
07 Director of Recruitment ... Ms. Margaree BONNETTE
103 AVP Economic/Workforce Develpoment ... Mr. Stephen MASON

Erskine College (A)

PO Box 338, 2 Washington Street,
Due West SC 29639-0338

County: Abbeville FICE Identification: 003432
Unit ID: 217998
Telephone: (864) 379-2131 Carnegie Class: Bac/A&S
FAX Number: (864) 379-2167 Calendar System: 4/1/4
URL: www.erskine.edu
Established: 1837 Annual Undergrad Tuition & Fees: $29,790
Enrollment: 773 Coed
Affiliation or Control: Other IRS Status: 501(c)3
Highest Offering: Doctorate
Program: Liberal Arts And General; Professional
Accreditation: SC, TED, THEOL

01 President .... Dr. David A. NORMAN
05 Interim Vice President & Dean .... Dr. N. Bradley CHRISTIE
10 Vice President Finance & Operations . Mr. Gregory W. HASELDEN
32 Vice President Student Services .... Dr. Robyn R. AGNEW
73 Interim VP Theological Seminary .... Dr. Steve D. LOWE
06 Registrar .... Mrs. Tracy M. SPIRES
37 Director of Student Financial Aid .... Mrs. Becky PRESSLEY
08 Librarian .... Mr. John F. KENNERLY
13 Director of Information Technology .... Mr. Robert S. CLARKE, III
09 Director of Institutional Research .... Mr. Buck F. BROWN, JR.
41 Athletic Director .... Mr. Mark L. PEELER
42 Chaplain .... Mr. Paul G. PATRICK
21 Controller .... Mr. Christian M. HABEGER
15 Director Human Resources .... Ms. Hope S. HARRISON
19 Director of Public Safety .... Mr. Charles R. ESTEP
40 Interim Manager of Bookstore .... Mr. Christian M. HABEGER
35 Dean of Students .... Dr. S. Bryan RUSH
36 Director Career Services .... Vacant
26 Vice President for Communications .... Mr. Cliff L. SMITH
29 Director of Alumni Affairs .... Mr. William L. FERGUSON
44 Interim Director of Sem Development .... Ms. Jane D. GREENE
73 Dean Theological Seminary .... Dr. Robert W. BELL

Florence - Darlington Technical College (B)

PO Box 100548, Florence SC 29501-0548

County: Florence FICE Identification: 003990
Unit ID: 218025
Telephone: (843) 661-8324 Carnegie Class: Assoc/Pub-R-M
FAX Number: (843) 661-8011 Calendar System: Semester
URL: www.fdtc.edu
Established: 1964 Annual Undergrad Tuition & Fees (In-District): $3,766
Enrollment: 6,011 Coed
Affiliation or Control: State/Local IRS Status: 501(c)3
Highest Offering: Associate Degree
Program: Occupational; 2-Year Principally Bachelor's Creditable
Accreditation: SC, ACBSP, ADNUR, DA, DH, MLTAD, RAD, SURGT

01 President .... Dr. Charles W. GOULD
05 Vice President Academic Affairs .... Dr. Dale DOTY
10 Vice President Business & Finance .... Mr. Tim O'DELL
32 Vice President Student Services .... Dr. Shelley FORTIN
30 Vice Pres Institutional Advancement .... Ms. Jill HEIDEN
72 Assoc VP Technical & General Educ .... Ms. Suzanne JENNINGS
76 Assoc VP Health & Sciences .... Dr. Lynn BROWN-BULLOCH
13 Assoc Vice Pres Information Tech .... Mr. Bill GRIFFENBERG
15 Director Internal Relations .... Ms. Terry DINGLE
09 Director Institutional Research .... Ms. Melissa MILLER
26 Director Public Relations .... Mr. Edward BETHEA
72 Director Manufacturing/Technology .... Mr. Jack ROACH
06 Registrar .... Ms. Abby VILLAR
37 Director Financial Aid .... Mr. Joseph DURANT
18 Chief Facilities/Physical Plant .... Mr. Harrison FORD, III
40 Director Bookstore .... Mr. Bob GARAND
96 Director of Purchasing .... Ms. Angela JORDAN
07 Director of Admissions .... Ms. Elaine HODGES

Forrest College (C)

601 E River Street, Anderson SC 29624-2498

County: Anderson FICE Identification: 004924
Unit ID: 218043
Telephone: (864) 225-7653 Carnegie Class: Assoc/PrivFP
FAX Number: (864) 261-7471 Calendar System: 4/1/4
URL: www.forrestcollege.edu
Established: 1946 Annual Undergrad Tuition & Fees: $9,420
Enrollment: 97 Coed
Affiliation or Control: Proprietary IRS Status: Proprietary
Highest Offering: Associate Degree
Program: Occupational; 2-Year Principally Bachelor's Creditable
Accreditation: ACICS, MAC

00 Chairman Board of Directors .... Dr. John RE
01 Interim President .... Laura LEE
05 Academic Dean .... Linda REEVES
101 Secy/Treasurer Board of Directors .... Charles PALMER
06 Fin Records Coordinator/Registrar .... Elizabeth FLOYD
08 Information Resource Coordinator .... Vacant
76 Allied Health Programs Coordinator .... Sandra CARTER
07 Admissions Rep .... Janie TURMON
07 Admissions Rep .... Linda PERRYMAN
07 Admissions Rep .... Jamey BOWEN

Francis Marion University (D)

PO Box 100547, Florence SC 29501-0547

County: Florence FICE Identification: 009226
Unit ID: 218061
Telephone: (843) 661-1362 Carnegie Class: Master's S
FAX Number: (843) 661-1202 Calendar System: Semester
URL: www.fmarion.edu
Established: 1970 Annual Undergrad Tuition & Fees (In-State): $8,802
Enrollment: 4,187 Coed
Affiliation or Control: State IRS Status: 501(c)3
Highest Offering: Master's
Program: Liberal Arts And General; Teacher Preparatory; Professional
Accreditation: SC, ART, BUS, NUR, TED, THEA

01 President .... Dr. Luther F. CARTER
05 Provost/Dean Col of Liberal Arts .... Dr. Richard N. CHAPMAN
10 Vice President Business Affairs .... Mr. John J. KISPERT
11 Vice President Administration .... Dr. Charlene WAGES
30 Vice President Devel/Exec Dir .... Mr. John P. DOWD
26 VP Public & Community Affairs .... Mr. Darryl L. BRIDGES
32 Vice President for Student Affairs .... Mrs. Teresa RAMEY
84 Assoc Provost For Academic Affiars .... Dr. Peter KING
21 Asst Vice Pres for Accounting .... Mr. M. Augustus MCDILL
88 Asst Vice Pres Financial Services .... Mrs. Brinda A. JONES
08 Dean of the Library .... Mrs. Joyce M. DURANT
20 Asst Provost/Dir Graduate Programs .... Dr. Jeannette MYERS
37 Financial Assistance Director .... Ms. Kimberly M. ELLISOR
41 Athletic Director .... Mr. Murray G. HARTZLER
06 Registrar .... Ms. Dollie NEWHOUSE
38 Director Counseling and Testing .... Dr. Rebecca L. LAWSON
18 Director of Facilities Management .... Mr. Ralph U. DAVIS
36 Director Career Development .... Vacant
07 Director of Admissions .... Mrs. Perry T. WILSON
35 Asst Dean of Students .... Ms. R. Daphne CARTER
29 Director of Alumni Affairs .... Mr. Julian M. YOUNG
96 Director of Purchasing .... Mr. Eric L. GARRIS
92 Director of Honors Program .... Dr. Pamela A. ROOKS
27 Chief Information Officer .... Mr. John DIXON

Furman University (E)

3300 Poinsett Highway, Greenville SC 29613-0001

County: Greenville FICE Identification: 003434
Unit ID: 218070
Telephone: (864) 294-2000 Carnegie Class: Bac/A&S
FAX Number: (864) 294-3001 Calendar System: Semester
URL: www.furman.edu
Established: 1826 Annual Undergrad Tuition & Fees: $41,532
Enrollment: 3,028 Coed
Affiliation or Control: Independent Non-Profit IRS Status: 501(c)3
Highest Offering: Master's
Program: Liberal Arts And General; Teacher Preparatory; Professional
Accreditation: SC, MUS, TED

01 President .... Mr. Rodney A. SMOLLA
03 VP Academic Affairs & Dean .... Dr. John S. BECKFORD
10 VP for Finance & Administration .... Ms. Mary Lou MERKT
32 Vice President for Student Life .... Ms. Connie L. CARSON
30 Vice President for Development .... Mr. Michael D. GATCHELL
26 VP Marketing/Public Relations .... Mr. Mark L. KELLY
20 Associate Academic Dean .... Dr. Paula S. GABBERT
06 University Registrar .... Mr. Brad E. BARRON
87 Director Graduate Studies .... Dr. Troy M. TERRY
08 Director Libraries .... Dr. Janis M. BANDELIN
19 Director of Public Safety .... Mr. Robert M. MILLER
45 Director Planning & Inst Research .... Mr. Donald E. PIERCE
37 Assoc Vice Pres of Financial Aid .... Mr. Forrest M. STUART
29 Director of Alumni Association .... Mr. Tom A. TRIPLITT
07 Assoc Vice President of Admissions .... Mr. Brad POCHARD
44 Director of Annual Giving .... Mr. John KEMP
44 Director of Planned Giving .... Mr. Steve PERRY
25 Grants Administrator .... Ms. Judith J. ROMANO
28 Director of Multicultural Affairs .... Ms. Idella G. GLENN
94 Director of Women's Studies .... Dr. Nicholas F. RADEL
15 Asst VP Human Resources/AAO .... Ms. Pamela BARKETT
27 Chief Information Officer .... Mr. Fred MILLER
85 Asst Dean Intl Educ/Study Away .... Dr. Kailash KHANDKE
36 Director Career Services .... Mr. John D. BARKER
88 Aux Services Director .... Ms. Rebecca VUKSTA
18 Asst VP for Facilities Services .... Mr. Jeff P. REDDERSON
51 Director Continuing Education .... Dr. Brad BECHTOLD
41 VP & Director of Athletics .... Dr. Gary E. CLARK
88 Director UG Research & Internships .... Dr. Tim G. FEHLER
88 Director CTEL .... Dr. Jane LOVE
17 Director Student Health Services .... Dr. Paul V. CATALANA
38 Director Counseling Center .... Dr. Stephen DAWES
39 Director University Housing .... Mr. Ronald C. THOMPSON
88 Director Disability Services .... Ms. Gina PARRIS
42 Chaplain .... Dr. Vaughn CROWETIPTON
40 Director Bookstore .... Ms. Jessica ELLIS
04 Assistant to President .... Ms. Cindy ALEXANDER
21 Budget Director .... Ms. Amy BLACKWELL
96 Director of Purchasing .... Ms. Lishan YAU
35 Director Student Activities .... Mr. Scott DERRICK

Golf Academy of America (F)

3268 Waccamaw Boulevard, Myrtle Beach SC 29579-9451

County: Horry Identification: 666490
Unit ID: 434690
Telephone: (800) 342-7342 Carnegie Class: Assoc/PrivFP
FAX Number: (843) 236-4448 Calendar System: Semester
URL: www.golfacademy.edu
Established: 1998 Annual Undergrad Tuition & Fees: $33,390
Enrollment: 331 Coed
Affiliation or Control: Proprietary IRS Status: Proprietary
Highest Offering: Associate Degree
Program: Occupational; Business Emphasis
Accreditation: ACICS

01 President .... Mr. Michael LARGENT
12 Campus Director .... Mr. James HART, JR.

† Branch campus of Virginia College, Birmingham, AL.

Greenville Technical College (G)

PO Box 5616, Greenville SC 29606-5616

County: Greenville FICE Identification: 003991
Unit ID: 218113
Telephone: (864) 250-8000 Carnegie Class: Assoc/Pub-U-MC
FAX Number: (864) 250-8507 Calendar System: Semester
URL: www.gvltec.edu
Established: 1962 Annual Undergrad Tuition & Fees (In-State): $1,933
Enrollment: 14,453 Coed
Affiliation or Control: State IRS Status: 501(c)3
Highest Offering: Associate Degree
Program: Occupational; 2-Year Principally Bachelor's Creditable; Technical Emphasis
Accreditation: SC, ACBSP, ACFEI, ADNUR, DA, DH, DMS, EMT, ENGT, MAC, MLTAD, OTA, PNUR, PTAA, RAD, SURGT

01 President .... Dr. Keith MILLER
05 Vice President for Education .... Mr. Steven B. VALAND
10 Vice President for Finance .... Mrs. Jacqueline R. DIMAGGIO
32 VP Student Diversity & Student Affs .... Vacant
36 Vice Pres Corp & Career Development .... Mrs. Cynthia G. EASON
45 VP Institutional Effectiveness .... Mrs. Lauren SIMER

Horry-Georgetown Technical College (H)

2050 Highway 501 E, Conway SC 29526-9521

County: Horry FICE Identification: 004925
Unit ID: 218140
Telephone: (843) 347-3186 Carnegie Class: Assoc/Pub-R-M
FAX Number: (843) 347-4207 Calendar System: Semester
URL: www.hgtc.edu
Established: 1966 Annual Undergrad Tuition & Fees (In-District): $1,775
Enrollment: 7,492 Coed
Affiliation or Control: State/Local IRS Status: 501(c)3
Highest Offering: Associate Degree
Program: Occupational; 2-Year Principally Bachelor's Creditable
Accreditation: SC, ACBSP, ACFEI, ADNUR, DA, DH, DMS, EMT, ENGT, PNUR, PTAA, RAD, SURGT

01 President .... Mr. Neyle WILSON
05 Senior VP .... Dr. Marilyn FORE
10 Vice President for Business Affairs .... Mr. Harold HAWLEY
13 VP for Tech/Institutional Planning .... Mr. Ralph SELANDER
103 VP Workforce Devel & Continuing Ed .... Mr. Gregory MITCHELL
84 AVP Enrollment Dev/Registration .... Mr. George SWINDOLL
32 Asc VP Student Affs/Campus Life .... Mr. Greg THOMPSON
20 AVP Acad Affs/Dean Academic Support .... Ms. Rene SMITH
20 AVP Acad Affs/Dn Univ Paral/Bus/Leg .... Dr. Shirley BUTLER
15 AVP Human Res/Employee Rel .... Ms. Judy HARDEE
08 AVP/Dn Library/Stdnt Succ/Tech Ctr .... Ms. Peggy SMITH
20 AVP Acad Affs/Dn Allied Hlth/Agri .... Dr. Philip RENDER
21 AVP/Controller .... Ms. Ellen BLACK
38 AVP Student Success .... Ms. Melissa BATTEN
12 Provost Georgetown Campus .... Mr. Murray VERNON
26 Chief Public Relations Officer .... Ms. Mary EADDY
18 Superintendent Bulidings & Grounds .... Mr. Kevin BROWN
37 Dir of Financial Aid/Veterans Affs .... Ms. Susan THOMPSON
07 Dir Stdnt Recruitment/Admissions .... Ms. Thyssene FREDERICK
36 Career Resource Ctr Coordinator .... Ms. April GARNER
09 Dir Institutional Rsrch/Assessment .... Ms. Lori HEAFNER
96 Procurement Manager .... Ms. Diana CECALA

ITT Technical Institute (I)

1628 Browning Road, Suite 180, Columbia SC 29210

County: Greenville Identification: 666162
Unit ID: 450225
Telephone: (803) 216-6000 Carnegie Class: Assoc/PrivFP4
FAX Number: N/A Calendar System: Quarter
URL: www.itt-tech.edu
Established: 2006 Annual Undergrad Tuition & Fees: N/A
Enrollment: 536 Coed
Affiliation or Control: Proprietary IRS Status: Proprietary
Highest Offering: Baccalaureate
Program: Technical Emphasis
Accreditation: ACICS

† Branch campus of ITT Technical Institute, Indianapolis, IN.

ITT Technical Institute (J)

6 Independence Pointe, Greenville SC 29615-4506

County: Greenville Identification: 666549
Unit ID: 413866
Telephone: (864) 288-0777 Carnegie Class: Spec/Tech
FAX Number: (864) 297-0930 Calendar System: Quarter
URL: www.itt-tech.edu
Established: 1992 Annual Undergrad Tuition & Fees: N/A

Enrollment: 517 Coed
Affiliation or Control: Proprietary IRS Status: Proprietary
Highest Offering: Baccalaureate
Program: Technical Emphasis
Accreditation: ACICS

† Branch campus of ITT Technical Institute, Indianapolis, IN.

Lander University (A)

320 Stanley Avenue, Greenwood SC 29649-2099
County: Greenwood FICE Identification: 003435
Unit ID: 218229
Telephone: (864) 388-8000 Carnegie Class: Bac/Diverse
FAX Number: (864) 388-8890 Calendar System: Semester
URL: www.lander.edu
Established: 1872 Annual Undergrad Tuition & Fees (In-State): $9,720
Enrollment: 3,045 Coed
Affiliation or Control: State IRS Status: 501(c)3
Highest Offering: Master's
Program: Liberal Arts And General; Teacher Preparatory; Professional; Business Emphasis
Accreditation: SC, ART, BUS, MACTE, MUS, NURSE, TED

01 President .... Dr. Daniel W. BALL
05 Provost/Vice Pres Academic Affairs .... Dr. David MASH
10 Vice Pres Business/Administration .... Mrs. Glenda RIDGELY
32 Vice President for Student Affairs .... Mr. H. Randall BOUKNIGHT
30 Vice President for Univ Advancement .... Mr. Ralph PATTERSON
84 Dean of Enrollment Services .... Vacant
07 Director of Admissions .... Mrs. Jennifer M. MATHIS
08 Librarian .... Ms. Lisa WIECKI
38 Director Counseling .... Ms. Debra J. FRANKS
41 Athletic Director .... Mr. Jefferson J. MAY
15 Director Human Resources .... Ms. Jeannie MCCALLUM
19 Director University Police .... Mr. Ray O. MANLEY
26 Director of Public Information .... Mrs. Megan PRICE
37 Director of Financial Aid .... Mr. Fred HARDIN
36 Director of Career Services .... Vacant
21 Controller .... Mr. Tom COVAR
40 Dir Bookstore/Procurement/Print Svc .... Mrs. Mary W. MCDANIEL
13 Dir Office Inform Tech Services .... Ms. Robin P. LAWRENCE
18 Director Physical Plant/Engr Svcs .... Mr. Jeff S. BEAVER
09 Dir Institutional Rsrch/Registrar .... Mr. Mac KIRKPATRICK
29 Director Alumni Relations .... Ms. Myra SHAFFER

Limestone College (B)

1115 College Drive, Gaffney SC 29340-3799
County: Cherokee FICE Identification: 003436
Unit ID: 218238
Telephone: (864) 489-7151 Carnegie Class: Bac/Diverse
FAX Number: (864) 487-8706 Calendar System: Semester
URL: www.limestone.edu
Established: 1845 Annual Undergrad Tuition & Fees: $21,000
Enrollment: 3,411 Coed
Affiliation or Control: Independent Non-Profit IRS Status: 501(c)3
Highest Offering: Master's
Program: Liberal Arts And General; Teacher Preparatory; Professional
Accreditation: SC, MUS, SW, TED

01 President .... Dr. Walt R. GRIFFIN
03 Exec Vice Pres/VP Academic Affairs .... Dr. Karen W. GAINEY
10 Vice President Financial Affairs .... Mr. David S. RILLING
30 Vice Pres Institutional Advancement .... Dr. William H. BAKER
84 Vice President Enrollment Services .... Mr. Christopher N. PHENICIE
32 Vice President Student Services .... Mr. Robert A. OVERTON
13 Vice Pres Information Technology .... Mr. C. R. HORTON
41 Vice Pres Intercollegiate Athletics .... Mr. Michael H. CERINO
30 Assoc Vice Pres for Development .... Ms. Kelly T. CURTIS
14 Assoc VP Information Technology .... Mr. C. Adam LONG
20 Assoc Vice Pres Academic Affairs .... Dr. Mark A. REGER
45 Assoc Vice Pres Planning/Assessment .... Dr. Bonnie M. WRIGHT
88 Dean of Retention Services .... Dr. Charles J. CUNNING
04 Administrative Asst to President .... Mrs. Nani Lou S. COOPER
106 Dir Extended Campus Internet Pgm .... Mr. C. R. HORTON
56 Dir Extended Campus Classroom Pgm .... Mrs. Patricia L. SOKOLS
06 Registrar .... Ms. Brenda F. WATKINS
37 Director Financial Aid .... Mr. Bobby T. GREER
44 Director of Development .... Ms. Tisha L. THOMPSON
08 Director Library .... Mrs. Lori J. HETRICK
26 Director Communications .... Mr. Eric LAWSON
35 Director Student Services .... Ms. Jessica D. GOINS
36 Director Career Services .... Ms. Ileka L. LEAKS
90 Director Network Services .... Dr. Scott D. BERRY
18 Director Physical Plant .... Mr. R. Lynn LAWHON
09 Dir Institutional Rsrch/Effective .... Mr. Franklin L. MITCHELL
92 Director Academic Honors Program .... Dr. Thomas J. THOMSON
83 Assoc Dean/Director Social Work .... Mr. Jackie A. PUCKETT
19 Chief of Public Safety .... Mr. Richard E. SIMMONS
21 Controller .... Mr. L. Wayde DAWSON
23 Campus Nurse .... Mrs. Sandy B. GREEN
44 Director Advancement Services .... Mrs. Brandi P. HARTMAN
20 Director of Academic Advising .... Mrs. Brenda F. WATKINS
29 Director Alumni/Parent Programs .... Mr. Kristopher C. BARNHILL
88 Dir Christian Ed/Leadership Program .... Rev. J. Ron SINGLETON
88 Director of Food Services .... Mr. Geoffrey W. ELKINS
88 Director of Sports Information .... Mr. Joshua J. DARLING
88 Assoc Business Manager .... Mr. Franklin L. MITCHELL
42 College Chaplain .... Rev. J. Ron SINGLETON
88 Dir Accessibility Services/PALS .... Ms. Tina E. VIRES
15 Dir Human Resources/AAEEO Officer .... Ms. Sharon D. HAMMONDS
50 Director of MBA Program .... Mr. Brandon J. GIBSON
88 Sr Assoc Athletics Dir Compliance .... Mr. Dennis L. BLOOMER
88 Assoc Athletics Dir for Media Rels .... Mr. Ernest G. MEYERS
88 Assoc Dir Extended Internet Pgm .... Ms. Diana L. BEDENBAUGH
40 Campus Store Manager .... Mrs. Patti H. MCCRAW
38 College Counselor .... Mrs. Mary B. CAMPBELL
107 Chair Div of Professional Studies .... Dr. Paul R. LEFRANCOIS
88 Chair Div of Natural Sciences .... Mr. Brian F. AMELING
49 Chair Div of Arts & Letters .... Dr. Gena E. POOVEY
83 Chair Div Social & Behav Sciences .... Dr. Betsy A. WITT
53 Chair Div Educ/Phys Ed/Teacher Educ .... Dr. Shelly MEYERS

Lutheran Theological Southern Seminary of Lenoir-Rhyne University (C)

4201 N Main Street, Columbia SC 29203-5898
County: Richland FICE Identification: 003437
Unit ID: 218265
Telephone: (803) 786-5150 Carnegie Class: Spec/Faith
FAX Number: (803) 786-6499 Calendar System: Semester
URL: ltss.lr.edu
Established: 1830 Annual Graduate Tuition & Fees: $14,900
Enrollment: 140 Coed
Affiliation or Control: Evangelical Lutheran Church In America
IRS Status: 501(c)3
Highest Offering: Master's; No Undergraduates
Program: Professional; Religious Emphasis
Accreditation: THEOL

01 Provost .... Rev Dr. Clayton J. SCHMIT
05 Associate Dean .... Rev Dr. Virginia C. BARFIELD
10 Dir of Administration and Finance .... Mr. Andrew D. SMITH
30 Director of Development .... Mr. Ron WALRATH
84 Director Enrollment/Communications .... Mr. Andrew BOOZER
88 Asst Director Enrollment Services .... Ms. Jenn CASEY

Medical University of South Carolina (D)

179 Ashley Avenue, Charleston SC 29425
County: Charleston FICE Identification: 003438
Unit ID: 218335
Telephone: (843) 792-2300 Carnegie Class: Spec/Med
FAX Number: N/A Calendar System: Semester
URL: www.musc.edu
Established: 1824 Annual Undergrad Tuition & Fees (In-State): $14,500
Enrollment: 2,678 Coed
Affiliation or Control: State IRS Status: Exempt
Highest Offering: Doctorate
Program: Professional
Accreditation: SC, ANEST, ARCPA, DENT, DIETI, HSA, HT, IPSY, MED, NURSE, OT, PERF, PTA

01 President .... Dr. Raymond S. GREENBERG
100 Chief of Staff .... Dr. Sabra C. SLAUGHTER
05 VP Acad Affairs & Provost .... Dr. Mark S. SOTHMANN
17 VP Med Affairs & Dean Col of Med .... Dr. Etta D. PISANO
10 Vice President Finance & Admin .... Ms. Lisa P. MONTGOMERY
30 Vice President Development .... Mr. William J. FISHER
17 VP Clinical Opers/CEO Medical Ctr .... Mr. W. Stuart SMITH
13 VP Information Technology/CIO .... Dr. Frank C. CLARK
20 Assoc Prov Education/Student Life .... Dr. Darlene L. SHAW
46 Associate Provost Research .... Dr. Stephen M. LANIER
52 Dean of Dental Medicine .... Dr. John J. SANDERS
76 Interim Dean of Health Professions .... Dr. Lisa SALADIN
58 Dean of Graduate Studies .... Dr. Perry V. HALUSHKA
66 Dean of Nursing .... Dr. Gail W. STUART
67 Exec Dean SC College of Pharmacy .... Dr. Joseph T. DIPIRO
67 Int Campus Dean SC Col of Pharmacy .... Dr. Philip D. HALL
88 Exec Dir SC Area Hlth Ed Consortium .... Dr. David R. GARR
08 Director of Libraries .... Dr. Thomas G. BASLER
84 Director Enrollment Management .... Mr. George W. OHLANDT
28 Exec Director Student Programs .... Dr. Willette S. BURNHAM
43 General Counsel .... Mr. Joseph C. GOOD
26 Director Public Relations .... Dr. Sarah KING
22 Dir Affirm Act/Equal Opportunity .... Mr. Wallace T. BONAPARTE
07 Director of Admissions .... Ms. Lyla HUDSON
18 Chief Facilities/Physical Plant .... Mr. John MALMROSE
06 Registrar .... Ms. Sandra L. MORRIS
15 Director Personnel Services .... Ms. Susan H. CARULLO
38 Director Student Counseling .... Dr. Alice Q. LIBET
29 Director Alumni Affairs .... Ms. Jean M. GROOMS
37 Director Student Financial Aid .... Dr. Cecile E. KAMATH
96 Director of Purchasing .... Ms. Betty SANDIFER

Midlands Technical College (E)

PO Box 2408, Columbia SC 29202-2408
County: Richland FICE Identification: 003993
Unit ID: 218353
Telephone: (803) 738-8324 Carnegie Class: Assoc/Pub-U-MC
FAX Number: (803) 738-7784 Calendar System: Semester
URL: www.midlandstech.edu
Established: 1974 Annual Undergrad Tuition & Fees (In-District): $4,366
Enrollment: 12,078 Coed
Affiliation or Control: State/Local IRS Status: 501(c)3
Highest Offering: Associate Degree
Program: Occupational; 2-Year Principally Bachelor's Creditable
Accreditation: SC, ACBSP, ADNUR, DA, DH, ENGT, MAC, MLTAD, NMT, PNUR, PTAA, RAD, SURGT

01 President .... Dr. Marshall Sonny WHITE, JR.
04 Exec Assistant to the President .... Ms. Nancy PEDERSEN
05 Vice President Academic Affairs .... Dr. Ronald DRAYTON
10 Sr Vice Pres of Business Affairs .... Dr. Ronald RHAMES
49 Assoc Vice Pres Arts & Sciences .... Dr. Diane CARR
32 Vice Pres Student Development Svcs .... Ms. Sandi OLIVER
30 Vice President for Advancement .... Ms. Starnell BATES
51 VP Economic Devel & Continuing Educ .... Dr. Barrie KIRK
21 Assoc Vice Pres for Business Affs .... Ms. Debbie WALKER
88 AVP SDS: Trio Cmty Support Pgms .... Ms. Mary HOLLOWAY
15 Director of Human Resources .... Ms. Crystal ROOKARD
06 Registrar .... Ms. Susan HOUCK
13 Director Information Resource Mgmt .... Mr. Tony HOUGH
25 Director of Resource Development .... Ms. Alice APPLEBY
37 Director of Student Financial Aid .... Mrs. Angela WILLIAMS
08 Interim Director of Library .... Ms. Florence MAYES
09 Dir Assessment/Research/Planning .... Ms. Dorcas A. KITCHINGS
18 Director of Operations .... Mr. Craig E. HESS
35 Director of Campus Life .... Mr. Hart HAYDEN
31 Director of Auxiliary Services .... Mr. Stanley BOLTON
38 Director of Counseling .... Mr. Phil MORRIS
50 Dept Chair of Business Department .... Mr. Melvin HAWKINS, JR.
54 Dept Chair of Engineering Tech .... Dr. Clint CHANDLER
76 Director of Health Science Dept .... Ms. Martha HANKS
84 Director of Enrollment Services .... Ms. Sylvia LITTLEJOHN
27 Director of Public Affairs .... Mr. Todd GAVIN
44 Director of Development .... Mr. Tom SCHLICTMAN
36 Director Student Employment Service .... Ms. Sarah TRICE
96 Procurement Manager .... Ms. Rochelle DANIELS
14 Manager Tech Support .... Mr. Carl CARRAWAY

Miller-Motte Technical College (F)

8085 Rivers Avenue, Suite E, North Charleston SC 29406
County: Charleston Identification: 666256
Unit ID: 441025
Telephone: (843) 574-0101 Carnegie Class: Assoc/PrivFP
FAX Number: (843) 266-3424 Calendar System: Semester
URL: www.miller-motte.edu
Established: 1916 Annual Undergrad Tuition & Fees: $9,900
Enrollment: 701 Coed
Affiliation or Control: Proprietary IRS Status: Proprietary
Highest Offering: Associate Degree
Program: Occupational
Accreditation: ACICS, MAC, SURGT

01 Director of Branch Campus .... Ms. Sara EICHELMAN

† Branch campus of Miller-Motte Technical College, Clarksville, TN.

Morris College (G)

100 W College Street, Sumter SC 29150-3599
County: Sumter FICE Identification: 003439
Unit ID: 218399
Telephone: (803) 934-3200 Carnegie Class: Bac/Diverse
FAX Number: (803) 773-3687 Calendar System: Semester
URL: www.morris.edu
Established: 1908 Annual Undergrad Tuition & Fees: $10,840
Enrollment: 979 Coed
Affiliation or Control: Baptist IRS Status: 501(c)3
Highest Offering: Baccalaureate
Program: Liberal Arts And General; Teacher Preparatory
Accreditation: SC, ACBSP, TED

01 President .... Dr. Luns C. RICHARDSON
05 Academic Dean .... Dr. Leroy STAGGERS
10 Director of Business Affairs .... Mr. Robert EAVES
86 Director Planning/Govt Relations .... Mrs. Dorothy S. CHEAGLE
32 Interim Dean Student Affairs .... Rev. Eliza E. BLACK
15 Personnel Officer .... Mr. Roy GRAHAM
42 College Minister .... Dr. Charles M. PEE
07 Director Admissions & Records .... Ms. Deborah C. CALHOUN
08 Director Learning Resources Ctr .... Mrs. Janet S. CLAYTON
37 Director of Financial Aid .... Mrs. Sandra S. GIBSON
13 Director MIS/Computer Center .... Mr. Rodney JOHNSON
36 Director Career Services Center .... Ms. Margaret A. BAILEY
09 Director of Assessment .... Vacant
29 Alumni Affairs Officer .... Mrs. Altoya A. FELDER-DEAS
38 Director Counseling & Testing Ctr .... Dr. Lula J. GARY
39 Director Residential Life .... Mr. Permon MITCHELL
23 Director of Health Services .... Mrs. Johnell ROGERS
41 Director of Athletics .... Mr. Clarence M. HOUCK
26 Director Public Relations .... Ms. Vicky L. SUTTON-JACKSON
30 Director Inst Advanc/Church Rels .... Rev. Melvin MACK
96 Director of Purchasing .... Mr. Robert EAVES
97 Director of Freshmen Studies .... Dr. Reginald A. BESS
92 Director of Honors Program .... Dr. Joseph K. POPOOLA
06 Registrar .... Ms. Deborah C. CALHOUN
18 Chief Facilities/Physical Plant .... Mr. Roy GRAHAM
20 Associate Academic Officer .... Ms. Kay M. RHOADS
21 Associate Business Officer .... Vacant
40 Bookstore Manager .... Ms. Jeanette MOSES-HOLMES
35 Coordinator Student Activities .... Mr. Alston FREEMAN
19 Coordinator Security Services .... Ms. Lucille W. WILLIAMS

Newberry College (H)

2100 College, Newberry SC 29108-2126
County: Newberry FICE Identification: 003440
Unit ID: 218414
Telephone: (800) 845-4955 Carnegie Class: Bac/Diverse

FAX Number: (803) 321-5627 Calendar System: Semester
URL: www.newberry.edu
Established: 1856 Annual Undergrad Tuition & Fees: $23,575
Enrollment: 1,095 Coed
Affiliation or Control: Evangelical Lutheran Church In America
IRS Status: 501(c)3
Highest Offering: Baccalaureate
Program: Liberal Arts And General; Teacher Preparatory
Accreditation: SC, MUS, NURSE, TED

01 President ... Dr. Maurice W. SCHERRENS
05 Interim VP for Academic Affairs ... Dr. Timothy G. ELSTON
10 Int CFO & Exec VP for Admin Affs ... Dr. Ronald MATTHIAS
84 Acting Dir of Enroll Management ... Ms. Sheila WENDELN
32 Dean of Students ... Dr. Kay BANKS
41 Director of Athletics ... Mr. Brad EDWARDS
15 Director of Human Resources ... Mrs. Peggy SHULER
09 Exec Dir of Inst Effectiveness ... Dr. Don W. JOHNSON-TAYLOR
06 Registrar ... Mrs. Carol A. BICKLEY
29 Director of Alumni Relations ... Rev. John D. DERRICK
08 Librarian ... Ms. Nancy ROSENWALD
18 Director of Facilities ... Mr. Fred ERRIGO
26 Director of Public Relations ... Ms. Sharon LACKEY
42 Chaplain ... Rev. Ernie WORMAN
21 Director of Accounting ... Mrs. Landee BUZHARDT
38 Director of Wellness Services ... Mrs. Martha DORRELL
37 Director Student Financial Aid ... Mrs. Danielle BELL

North Greenville University (A)

PO Box 1892, Tigerville SC 29688-1892
County: Greenville FICE Identification: 003441
Unit ID: 218441
Telephone: (864) 977-7000 Carnegie Class: Bac/Diverse
FAX Number: (864) 977-7021 Calendar System: Semester
URL: www.ngu.edu
Established: 1892 Annual Undergrad Tuition & Fees: $13,936
Enrollment: 2,438 Coed
Affiliation or Control: Southern Baptist IRS Status: 501(c)3
Highest Offering: Doctorate
Program: Liberal Arts And General; Religious Emphasis
Accreditation: SC, MUS, TED

01 President/CEO ... Dr. James B. EPTING
04 Admin Assistant for President ... Ms. Elise STYLES
05 Vice President Academics ... Dr. Randall PANNELL
32 Vice President Student Services ... Dr. Tony BEAM
58 Vice Pres/Dean Graduate Studies ... Dr. J. Samuel ISGETT
10 Vice President Business Affairs ... Ms. Michelle L. SABOU
07 VP Admissions/Financial Planning ... Ms. Keli SEWELL
30 Vice President Advancement ... Mr. Alex MILLER
88 Vice Pres Denominational Relations ... Rev. Mayson EASTERLING
42 Vice President Campus Ministries ... Dr. Steve CROUSE
44 VP Crusader Club/Corp Found Giving ... Mr. J. Wayne LANDRITH
45 Director Academic Plng & Assessment ... Mr. Paul GARRETT
35 Director Student Services ... Mr. Billy WATSON
09 Director of Institutional Research ... Dr. George A. HOPSON
06 Registrar ... Ms. Pam FARMER
18 Director of College Properties ... Mr. Larry BARNWELL
41 Athletic Director ... Ms. Jan MCDONALD
34 Director Residential Living Women ... Ms. Lorry GREEN
33 Director Residential Living Men ... Mr. Donald LILLY
08 Director Learning Center ... Ms. Carla MCMAHAN
19 Director Public Safety ... Mr. Rick MORRIS
88 Dean of Graduate Enrollment ... Mrs. Tawana SCOTT
26 Director Public Rels/Stewardship ... Mr. LaVerne B. HOWELL
29 Director Alumni Affairs/Annual Fund ... Mr. Jason ROSS
15 Human Resource Manager ... Mrs. Lindi FOWLER
40 Bookstore Manager ... Mrs. Cindy COWAN
38 Personal Counselor ... Dr. Bill MCMANUS
36 Career Services Coordinator ... Ms. Lisa SNYDER
23 Director Health Services ... Ms. Kathy BAILEY
30 Executive Director Development ... Rev. Joe F. HAYES
14 Director Computer Services ... Mr. Paul GARRETT
37 Financial Aid Director ... Mr. Michael JORDAN
53 Dean Education ... Dr. Constance WRIGHT
79 Dean Humanities ... Dr. Cathy SEPKO
57 Dean Fine Arts ... Dr. Jacquelyn H. GRIFFIN
81 Dean Sciences ... Dr. Tom ALLEN
73 Dean Christian Studies ... Dr. Walter JOHNSON
50 Dean Business ... Dr. Ralph JOHNSON

Northeastern Technical College (B)

1201 Chesterfield Hwy, Cheraw SC 29520
County: Chesterfield FICE Identification: 007602
Unit ID: 217837
Telephone: (843) 921-6900 Carnegie Class: Assoc/Pub-R-S
FAX Number: (843) 537-6148 Calendar System: Semester
URL: www.netc.edu
Established: 1969 Annual Undergrad Tuition & Fees (In-State): $6,390
Enrollment: 1,222 Coed
Affiliation or Control: State IRS Status: 501(c)3
Highest Offering: Associate Degree
Program: Occupational; 2-Year Principally Bachelor's Creditable
Accreditation: SC

01 President ... Dr. Ron BARTLEY
05 Vice Pres Instruction/Student Svcs ... Dr. Forest MAHAN
10 Vice Pres Administration & Finance ... Mrs. Debbie Q. CHEEK
30 Director for Inst Advancement ... Vacant
15 Director for Human Resources ... Mrs. Donna CHAVIS

Orangeburg-Calhoun Technical College (C)

3250 Saint Matthews Road, Orangeburg SC 29118-8299
County: Orangeburg FICE Identification: 006815
Unit ID: 218487
Telephone: (803) 536-0311 Carnegie Class: Assoc/Pub-R-M
FAX Number: (803) 535-1388 Calendar System: Semester
URL: www.octech.edu
Established: 1966 Annual Undergrad Tuition & Fees (In-State): $3,650
Enrollment: 3,005 Coed
Affiliation or Control: State IRS Status: 501(c)3
Highest Offering: Associate Degree
Program: Occupational; 2-Year Principally Bachelor's Creditable
Accreditation: SC, ACBSP, ADNUR, ENGT, MAC, PNUR, RAD

01 President ... Dr. Walt TOBIN, JR.
05 Vice Pres Academic Affairs ... Mrs. Donna ELMORE
10 Vice President Business Affairs ... Mrs. Henrietta C. GUTHRIE
32 Vice President of Student Services ... Mrs. Barbara M. FELDER
11 Assoc VP of Administration ... Mr. Mike HAMMOND
36 Assoc VP Corp Trng/Econ Develop ... Mrs. Rebecca BATTLE-BRYANT
21 Assoc Vice Pres of Business Affairs ... Mr. Kim R. HUFF
46 Dean Planning/Research/Development ... Ms. Faith MCCURRY
13 Director Information Technology ... Mr. Gary A. FOLEY
62 Dean Learning Resource Center ... Mrs. Harris MURRAY
18 Chief Facilities/Physical Plant ... Mr. James S. BRYANT, III
37 Director Student Financial Aid ... Mr. Chris DOOLEY
08 Director Library Services ... Mrs. Harris MURRAY
07 Director of Recruiting ... Ms. Semetta QUICK
19 Chief of Safety/Security ... Mr. Douglas STOKES
09 Dir Acad Spprt/Institutional Effect ... Mr. Cleveland WILSON
15 Human Resource Director ... Ms. Marie HOWELL
96 Procurement Manager ... Mrs. Scarlet GEDDINGS

Piedmont Technical College (D)

620 N. Emerald Road, PO Box 1467,
Greenwood SC 29648-1467
County: Greenwood FICE Identification: 003992
Unit ID: 218520
Telephone: (864) 941-8324 Carnegie Class: Assoc/Pub-R-M
FAX Number: (864) 941-8555 Calendar System: Semester
URL: www.ptc.edu
Established: 1966 Annual Undergrad Tuition & Fees (In-District): $3,523
Enrollment: 6,213 Coed
Affiliation or Control: State/Local IRS Status: 501(c)3
Highest Offering: Associate Degree
Program: Occupational; 2-Year Principally Bachelor's Creditable
Accreditation: SC, ADNUR, ENGT, FUSER, MAC, RAD, SURGT

01 President ... Dr. L. Rayburn BROOKS
10 Vice Pres Business & Finance ... Ms. Paige CHILDS
05 Vice President Educational Affairs ... Dr. Susan TIMMONS
32 Vice Pres Student Devel/Mrktng Div ... Ms. Becky R. MCINTOSH
51 Assoc Vice Pres Cont Educ/Econ Dev ... Mr. Rusty DENNING
24 Assoc VP Instructional Technology ... Dr. Joel GRIFFIN
108 Assoc VP Institutional Assessment ... Ms. Donna FOSTER
12 Dean County Centers ... Dr. Jennifer WILBANKS
76 Dean Health Sciences ... Mr. Jerry ALEWINE
54 Dean Engr/Industrial Technologies ... Mr. Keith LASURE
66 Dean Nursing Education ... Ms. Rosalie STEVENSON
35 Dean Student Services ... Mr. J. Andrew OMUNDSON
09 Director of Inst Effectiveness ... Ms. Zeolean F. KINARD
26 Director Marketing/Public Relations ... Mr. Joshua BLACK
88 Director College Outreach ... Mr. Steve B. COLEMAN
18 Director Facilities/Management ... Mr. S. Dale WILSON
102 Foundation Exec Dir/Alumni Affairs ... Ms. Fran K. WILEY
08 Librarian ... Mr. Daniel MEREDITH
19 Director Public Safety ... Mr. Terry LEDFORD
36 Assoc Dean Student Services ... Mr. David R. ROSENBAUM
37 Director of Financial Aid ... Ms. Deborah H. WILLIAMS
06 Registrar ... Ms. Tanisha LATIMER
21 Controller ... Ms. Paige CHILDS
15 Human Resource Manager ... Ms. Debbie THARPE
21 Manager Business Office ... Ms. Crystal PITTMAN

Presbyterian College (E)

503 S Broad Street, Clinton SC 29325-2865
County: Laurens FICE Identification: 003445
Unit ID: 218539
Telephone: (864) 833-2820 Carnegie Class: Bac/A&S
FAX Number: (864) 833-8481 Calendar System: Semester
URL: www.presby.edu
Established: 1880 Annual Undergrad Tuition & Fees: $32,680
Enrollment: 1,359 Coed
Affiliation or Control: Presbyterian Church (U.S.A.) IRS Status: 501(c)3
Highest Offering: Doctorate
Program: Liberal Arts And General; Teacher Preparatory
Accreditation: SC, MUS, @PHAR, TED

01 President ... Dr. Claude C. LILLY
04 Assistant to the President ... Ms. Rosanne R. BRASWELL
05 Provost ... Dr. Anita O. GUSTAFSON
10 Exec VP Finance/Administration ... Mr. Morris M. GALLOWAY, JR.
30 Vice President for Advancement ... Mr. Raymond CARNLEY
84 VP of Enrollment/Communications ... Ms. Deborah THOMPSON
67 Dean School of Pharmacy ... Dr. Richard E. STULL
13 Int Dir Information Technology ... Mr. David WALKER
35 Dean of Student Life ... Vacant
20 Dean Academic Programs ... Dr. Donald R. RABER, II
42 Dean of Religious Life ... Dr. Jeri Parris PERKINS
32 Interim Dean of Campus Life ... Ms. Linda C. JAMEISON
30 Exec Dir Foundation/Corporate Dev ... Ms. M. Genevra KELLY
27 Exec Director of Communications ... Vacant
41 Exec Director of Athletics ... Mr. Brian P. REESE
29 Director Alumni Relations ... Ms. Justine R. SCHWINDEL
08 Librarian ... Mr. David W. CHATHAM
38 Director Counseling Services ... Mrs. Susan C. GENTRY-WRIGHT
37 Director of Financial Aid ... Vacant
21 Controller ... Mr. Michael D. CHASTEEN
19 Director of Campus Police ... Mr. Lawrence P. MULHALL
06 Registrar ... Mr. W. Keith KARRIKER
15 Director Human Resources ... Ms. Barbara H. FAYAD
09 Director of Institutional Research ... Dr. Norman B. BRYAN, JR.
18 Exec Director Business Operations ... Mr. L. David WALKER

Sherman College of Chiropractic (F)

PO Box 1452, Spartanburg SC 29304-1452
County: Spartanburg FICE Identification: 020637
Unit ID: 218751
Telephone: (864) 578-8770 Carnegie Class: Spec/Health
FAX Number: (864) 599-7145 Calendar System: Quarter
URL: www.sherman.edu
Established: 1973 Annual Graduate Tuition & Fees: $26,812
Enrollment: 189 Coed
Affiliation or Control: Independent Non-Profit IRS Status: 501(c)3
Highest Offering: Doctorate; No Undergraduates
Program: Professional
Accreditation: SC, CHIRO

01 President ... Dr. Jon C. SCHWARTZBAUER
05 Vice Pres for Academic Affairs ... Dr. Robert IRWIN
84 Vice Pres for Enrollment Services ... Mrs. Kelley ASHCRAFT
10 Vice Pres for Business & Finance ... Mr. Tim D. REVELS
32 Dean of Student Services ... Mrs. LaShanda HUTTO-HARRIS
29 Dir Alumni Rels/Instl Advancement ... Ms. Marggi ROLDAN
06 Registrar ... Ms. Melody SABIN
08 Librarian ... Mrs. Crissy LEWIS
37 Financial Aid Director ... Mrs. Kathy WILSON
45 Director of Planning Assessment ... Vacant

South Carolina State University (G)

300 College Street, NE, Orangeburg SC 29117-0001
County: Orangeburg FICE Identification: 003446
Unit ID: 218733
Telephone: (803) 536-7000 Carnegie Class: DRU
FAX Number: (803) 533-3622 Calendar System: Semester
URL: www.scsu.edu
Established: 1896 Annual Undergrad Tuition & Fees (In-State): $9,258
Enrollment: 4,326 Coed
Affiliation or Control: State IRS Status: 501(c)3
Highest Offering: Doctorate
Program: Liberal Arts And General; Teacher Preparatory; Professional; Business Emphasis
Accreditation: SC, AAFCS, ART, BUS, CACREP, CORE, CS, DIETD, ENG, ENGT, MUS, NURSE, SP, SW, TED

01 Interim President ... Dr. Cynthia WARRICK
04 Exec Asst to the President ... Mrs. Shondra N. ABRAHAM
05 Vice President Academic Affairs ... Dr. W. Franklin EVANS
10 Vice Pres Fiscal Affs/Mgt Info Sys ... Vacant
32 Int Vice President Student Affairs ... Dr. Valerie FIELDS
30 Vice Pres Inst Advancement ... Vacant
46 VP Research/EconDevel/Pub Svc ... Mr. John ROSENTHALL
100 Chief of Staff & Gen Counsel ... Vacant
20 Assoc Vice Pres Academic Affs ... Dr. M. Evelyn FIELDS
20 Int Assoc Vice Pres Academic Affs ... Dr. Christine R. BOONE
44 Asst Vice President Development ... Vacant
21 Asst Vice Pres Fiscal Affs/Mgt Info ... Mr. Eric EATON
35 Int Asst Vice Pres Student Affairs ... Dr. Tamera J. HUGHES
84 Asst VP Enrollment Management ... Mr. Antonio BOYLE
29 Asst Vice Pres Alumni Relations ... Vacant
46 Int Asst VP Sponsored Programs ... Mr. Elbert R. MALONE
72 Dean Col Sci/Math/Engineering Tech ... Dr. Kenneth D. LEWIS
53 Dean Col Educ/Humanities/Soc Sci ... Dr. Leonard A. MCINTYRE
58 Dean School of Graduate Studies ... Dr. Thomas E. THOMPSON
50 Dean Col Business/Applied Prof Sci ... Dr. Robert T. BARRETT
08 Dean Library & Information Services ... Ms. Mary L. SMALLS
09 Exec Dir Institutional Effectivenes ... Dr. Rita J. TEAL
45 Exec Director of Planning ... Ms. Joyce GREEN
88 Asst Exec Dir Stdnt Success Retent ... Mr. Terrence M. CUMMINGS
06 Registrar ... Mrs. Annie R. BELTON
07 Director Admissions/Recruitment ... Mr. Antonio BOYLE
13 Dir Univ Computing/Info Tech Svcs ... Dr. James L. MYERS
37 Director Financial Aid to Students ... Mrs. Sandra DAVIS
38 Director Counsel/Hlth/Psycmtrc Svcs ... Dr. Cherilyn Y. TAYLOR
21 Controller ... Mr. Ernie M. TORRES
09 Director Institutional Research ... Ms. Betty R. BOATWRIGHT
26 Director Univ Relations & Mktg ... Ms. Erica PRIOLEAU-TAYLOR
36 Int Director of Career Placement ... Mr. Joseph THOMAS
15 Director Human Resource Mgmt ... Ms. Anna D. HAIGLER
41 Director Athletics ... Mrs. Charlene M. JOHNSON
18 Director of Facilities Mgmt ... Mr. Charles ALEXANDER
96 Director Procurement Services ... Mrs. Mary L. SIMS
39 Asst Director of Residential Life ... Ms. Jennifer TOWNSEND-GAMBLE
19 Chief of Campus Police ... Mr. Gregory HARRIS

92 Dir Honors Exchange/intl Program ....Dr. Harriet A. ROLAND
88 Director Sports Information ....Mr. William P. HAMILTON
35 Director of Student Life ....Mr. Terrance ALDRIDGE
88 Int Director of Internal Audit ....Mr. Kelvin WASHINGTON
25 Dir Grants & Contract Accounting ....Ms. Mildred L. DANIELS
88 Director of Title III ....Ms. Gloria D. PYLES
88 Director of Staff Development ...... Ms. Patricia GIBSON-HAIGLER
28 Director of Multicultural Affairs ....Ms. Carolyn G. FREE
88 Asst Dir Educational Technology Svc ....Dr. Frederick M. EVANS
88 Station Manager WSSB-FM ....Mr. Milton E. MCKISSICK
88 Athletics Compliance Coordinator ....Mr. Robert CHATMAN

South University Columbia Campus (A)

9 Science Court, Columbia SC 29203-6400
County: Richland　FICE Identification: 004922
Unit ID: 251312
Telephone: (803) 799-9082　Carnegie Class: Master's S
FAX Number: (803) 935-4382　Calendar System: Quarter
URL: www.southuniversity.edu
Established: 1899　Annual Undergrad Tuition & Fees: $15,910
Enrollment: 1,568　Coed
Affiliation or Control: Proprietary　IRS Status: Proprietary
Highest Offering: Master's
Program: Professional; Business Emphasis
Accreditation: &SC, MAC, NURSE

01 President ....Mr. Gregory J. SHIELDS
04 Exec Assistant to the President ....Ms. Missy WHITE
05 Dean of Academic Affairs ....Mr. David SHOOP
32 Dean of Student Affairs ....Ms. Aimee CARTER
10 Business Officer .... Mr. John BALLENTINE
06 Registrar .... Ms. Melinda WILLIAMS
07 Director of Admissions .... Ms. Shannon JONES
08 Librarian ....Mrs. Amanda DIFETERICI
37 Director Student Financial Aid ....Mr. Walt HAVERSAT
40 Director Bookstore .... Mr. Todd POWELL

† Regional accreditation is carried under the parent institution in Savannah, GA.

Southern Wesleyan University (B)

907 Wesleyan Drive, PO Box 1020,
Central SC 29630-1020
County: Pickens　FICE Identification: 003422
Unit ID: 217776
Telephone: (864) 644-5000　Carnegie Class: Master's L
FAX Number: (864) 644-5900　Calendar System: Semester
URL: www.swu.edu
Established: 1906　Annual Undergrad Tuition & Fees: $20,850
Enrollment: 1,858　Coed
Affiliation or Control: Wesleyan Church　IRS Status: 501(c)3
Highest Offering: Master's
Program: Liberal Arts And General; Teacher Preparatory; Professional
Accreditation: SC, MUS, TED

01 President ....Dr. Todd S. VOSS
04 Admin Assistant to the President ....Mrs. Andrea PILGRIM
10 Sr VP for Finance & Treasurer ....Mr. Marshall L. ATCHESON
37 Assoc VP of Student Financial Svcs .... Mr. Jeff DENNIS
13 Director Information Technology ....Mr. Mike PREUSZ
37 Director of Financial Aid ....Mrs. Melanie GILLESPIE
18 Director of Physical Plant ....Mr. Jonathan CATRON
40 Bookstore Manager ....Mrs. Darlene STANCIL
05 Provost ....Dr. Keith IDDINGS
09 Assoc VP for Planning & Assessment .... Dr. Daryl D. COUCH
20 AVP for Curriculum & Instruction ....Dr. Laurie HILLSTOCK
06 Registrar .... Mr. Rock MCCASKILL
08 Director of Library Services ....Mr. Robert E. SEARS
84 VP for Enrollment Management ....Mr. Chad PETERS
07 Dir of Admissions & Enrollment Mgmt ....Mrs. Amanda YOUNG
26 Director of Communications ....Mr. Greg WILSON
32 Vice President for Student Life ....Dr. W. Joseph BROCKINTON
42 AVP Spiritual Life/Univ Chaplain ....Rev. Ken DILL
35 Assoc Vice Pres for Student Life ....Dr. Justin CARTER
41 Athletic Director ....Mr. Chris WILLIAMS
38 Director of Counseling & Health Svc ....Mrs. Carol SINNAMON
30 Asst to President-Church/Donor Rels ....Dr. Gary CARR
29 Exec Dir of Alumni/Constituent Rels ....Mrs. Joy L. BRYANT
49 Dean College of Arts & Sciences ....Dr. Walt SINNAMON
57 Chair Fine Arts ....Mrs. Jane P. DILL
73 Acting Chair Religion ....Dr. Walt SINNAMON
79 Chair Humanities ....Dr. Ken MYERS
83 Chair Social Sciences ....Dr. Chris ACCORNERO
50 Dean School of Business ....Dr. Jeannie TRUDEL
53 Dean of School of Education ....Dr. Paul SHOTSBERGER
16 Director of Human Resources ....Mrs. Dana L. FROST

Spartanburg Community College (C)

I-85 Business, PO Box 4386, Spartanburg SC 29305-4386
County: Spartanburg　FICE Identification: 003994
Unit ID: 218830
Telephone: (864) 592-4600　Carnegie Class: Assoc/Pub-U-SC
FAX Number: (864) 592-4642　Calendar System: Semester
URL: www.sccsc.edu
Established: 1963　Annual Undergrad Tuition & Fees (In-State): $3,820
Enrollment: 6,008　Coed
Affiliation or Control: State　IRS Status: 501(c)3
Highest Offering: Associate Degree
Program: Occupational; 2-Year Principally Bachelor's Creditable
Accreditation: SC, ACBSP, ACFEI, ADNUR, DA, ENGT, MAC, MLTAD, RAD, SURGT

01 Interim President ....Mr. Henry C. GILES, JR.
03 Executive Vice President ....Mr. Henry C. GILES, JR.
05 Vice President Academic Affairs ....Dr. Cheryl COX
45 Vice President for Planning & Info ....Dr. Patricia P. ABELL
32 Vice President for Student Affairs .... Mr. Ron JACKSON
51 Int Dir Corporate/Community Educ ....Mr. Michael P. FORRESTER
12 Exec Director Tyger River Campus ....Mrs. Lynn F. DALE
12 Executive Director Cherokee Campus .... Mr. Daryl SMITH
102 Exec Director SCC Foundation ....Mr. Sam HOOK
20 Dean of Instruction ....Dr. Keith POMAKOY
08 Dean of Learning Resources .... Mr. Mark ROSEVEARE
46 Dean of Assessment/Cont Improvement ....Vacant
76 Dean Health & Human Services ....Dr. Rita A. MELTON
15 Director of Human Resources ....Mr. Rick TEAL
13 Director Information Technologies ....Mr. Peter C. GALLEN
18 Director of Physical Plant ....Mr. Ray SWITZER
84 Director Enrollment Services ....Mrs. Kathy F. MCKINZIE
09 Director of Institutional Research ....Mr. Jack R. BOURGEOIS
26 Chief Public Relations Officer ....Mrs. Cheri A. HUCKS
29 Director Alumni Relations ....Vacant
38 Director Student Counseling ....Mrs. Phyllis ROGERS
14 Director Computer Center ....Mrs. Tina S. REID
19 Director Security/Safety ....Mr. Andre KERR
96 Director of Procurement ....Vacant
06 Registrar ....Ms. Celia N. BAUSS
21 Business Manager ....Mr. Cecil L. HUTCHERSON
37 Director of Financial Aid ....Mrs. Nancy T. GARMROTH

Spartanburg Methodist College (D)

1000 Powell Mill Road, Spartanburg SC 29301-5899
County: Spartanburg　FICE Identification: 003447
Unit ID: 218821
Telephone: (864) 587-4000　Carnegie Class: Assoc/PrivNFP
FAX Number: (864) 587-4355　Calendar System: Semester
URL: www.smcsc.edu
Established: 1911　Annual Undergrad Tuition & Fees: $15,293
Enrollment: 803　Coed
Affiliation or Control: United Methodist　IRS Status: 501(c)3
Highest Offering: Associate Degree
Program: 2-Year Principally Bachelor's Creditable
Accreditation: SC

01 President ....Dr. Colleen P. KEITH
05 Vice President for Academic Affairs ....Dr. Anita K. BOWLES
10 Vice President for Business Affairs .... Mr. Eric MCDONALD
84 Vice Pres for Enrollment Management .... Mr. Daniel L. PHILBECK
30 Vice President for Inst Advancement .... Mr. Bob FUZY
32 Dean of Students ....Mr. Ron LAFFITTE
06 Registrar ....Ms. Jill R. JOHNSON
08 Librarian ....Mr. James P. HALLER
04 Admin Assistant to the President ....Ms. Vicki D. KENNEDY
20 Exec Dir of Academic Services ....Vacant
14 Exec Dir Info Tech/Campus Svcs ....Mr. Bill ROACH
27 Dir Public Information/Webmaster ....Vacant
44 Director of Development ....Mr. Don TATE
37 Director of Financial Aid ....Mrs. Emily STAGGS
38 Director of Student Counseling ....Mr. Pete AYLOR
42 Chaplain/Director of Church Rels ....Rev. Candice Y. SLOAN
41 Athletic Director ....Mr. Tim WALLACE
18 Director Facilities Mgmt/Purchasing ....Mr. Rick JOLLEY
29 Director Alumni Relations ....Mrs. Leah L. PRUITT
15 Dir of Human Resources/College Acct ....Mrs. Jeanette R. DUNN
35 Director of Student Support Svcs ....Ms. Sharon PORTER
44 Director Gift Planning ....Rev. Michael E. BOWERS
19 Chief of Campus Safety ....Ms. Teresa D. FERGUSON
07 Director of Admissions ....Mr. Michael QUEEN
09 Director of Assessment Activities ....Mr. Robert W. ISENHOWER

Technical College of the Lowcountry (E)

921 S Ribaut Road, PO Box 1288,
Beaufort SC 29901-1288
County: Beaufort　FICE Identification: 009910
Unit ID: 217712
Telephone: (843) 525-8211　Carnegie Class: Assoc/Pub-R-M
FAX Number: (843) 525-8330　Calendar System: Semester
URL: www.tcl.edu
Established: 1972　Annual Undergrad Tuition & Fees (In-State): $3,772
Enrollment: 2,632　Coed
Affiliation or Control: State　IRS Status: 501(c)3
Highest Offering: Associate Degree
Program: Occupational; 2-Year Principally Bachelor's Creditable
Accreditation: SC, ACBSP, ADNUR, COMTA, PNUR, PTAA, RAD, SURGT

01 President ....Dr. Thomas C. LEITZEL
10 Vice President for Finance ....Mr. Hayes WISER
05 Vice President for Academic Affairs .... Dr. Gina MOUNFIELD
26 VP Marketing/Enrollment Management .... Ms. Nancy WEBER
32 Vice President for Student Affairs ....Dr. Matteel JONES
09 Director for Research ....Ms. Camille MYERS
15 Director of Personnel .... Ms. Sonya LYTTLE
20 Director for Learning Resources ....Ms. Cindy HALSEY
50 Div Dean Business Technologies ....Dr. Kenneth FLICK
49 Div Dean Arts & Sciences ....Dr. Wesla FLETCHER
76 Division Dean Health Sciences .... Ms. Marge SAPP
86 Dir Retention & Federal Programs .... Mr. Rodney ADAMS
14 Director of Computer Center ....Mr. Floyd HENDERSON

37 Director Financial Aid ....Ms. Cleo MARTIN
45 Director of Inst Effectiveness ....Vacant
26 Public Relations Director ....Ms. Leigh COPELAND
21 Associate Business Officer ....Ms. Irina GREER
40 Bookstore Director ....Ms. Louise RENNIX
18 Director of Facility Management ....Mr. Larry BECKLER
38 Campus Life Manager .... Ms. Mackenzie MCGREW
96 Director of Purchasing ....Ms. Carol MACK
06 Registrar ....Dr. Debralee MCCLELLAN
36 Career & Transfer Services Manager .... Ms. Melanie GALLION

Tri-County Technical College (F)

PO Box 587, Pendleton SC 29670-0587
County: Anderson　FICE Identification: 004926
Unit ID: 218885
Telephone: (864) 646-8361　Carnegie Class: Assoc/Pub-S-SC
FAX Number: (864) 646-1895　Calendar System: Semester
URL: www.tctc.edu
Established: 1962　Annual Undergrad Tuition & Fees (In-District): $3,648
Enrollment: 6,800　Coed
Affiliation or Control: State/Local　IRS Status: 501(c)3
Highest Offering: Associate Degree
Program: Occupational; 2-Year Principally Bachelor's Creditable
Accreditation: SC, ACBSP, ADNUR, DA, MAC, MLTAD, PNUR, SURGT

01 President ....Dr. Ronnie L. BOOTH
05 Vice President Academic Affairs ....Vacant
10 Vice Pres Administration & Finance .... Mr. Gregg STAPLETON
30 VP Economic & Institutional Advance ....Mr. John LUMMUS
51 Dean of Continuing Education ....Mr. Rick COTHRAN
84 Dean of Enrollment Management ....Mrs. Amanda BLANTON
88 Dean of Student Development ....Mr. Dan HOLLAND
49 Dean Arts & Sciences Division ....Vacant
72 Dean Engineering Technology Div ....Vacant
50 Dean Business/Human Services Div ....Mrs. Jackie BLAKLEY
76 Dean Health Education Division ....Dr. Lynn LEWIS
08 Head Librarian ....Ms. Marla ROBERSON
37 Student Financial Aid Director ....Vacant
13 Director Computer Operations ....Mr. Lee TENNENT
26 Dir Public Relations/Communication ..... Mrs. Rebecca W. EIDSON
44 Director of Development ....Mrs. Elisabeth GADD
29 Manager of Donor Relations & Alumni ....Mrs. Courtney WHITE
15 Director of Personnel Services ....Mrs. Sharon COLCOLOUGH
07 Director of Admissions ....Ms. Renae FRAZIER
06 Registrar ....Mr. Scott HARVEY
09 Director of Institutional Research ....Mr. Chris MARINO
18 Chief Facilities/Physical Plant ....Mr. Ken KOPERA
21 Associate Business Officer ....Mrs. Faye ALLEN
96 Director of Purchasing .... Ms. Kristal DOHERTY
41 Athletic Director ....Vacant
38 Director of Student Life/Counseling .... Ms. Croslena JOHNSON

Trident Technical College (G)

PO Box 118067, Charleston SC 29423-8067
County: Charleston　FICE Identification: 004920
Unit ID: 218894
Telephone: (843) 574-6111　Carnegie Class: Assoc/Pub-U-MC
FAX Number: (843) 574-6541　Calendar System: Semester
URL: www.tridenttech.edu
Established: 1964　Annual Undergrad Tuition & Fees (In-District): $3,683
Enrollment: 16,781　Coed
Affiliation or Control: State/Local　IRS Status: 501(c)3
Highest Offering: Associate Degree
Program: Occupational; 2-Year Principally Bachelor's Creditable
Accreditation: SC, ACBSP, ACFEI, ADNUR, DA, DH, EMT, MAC, MLTAD, #OTA, PNUR, PTAA, RAD

01 President .... Dr. Mary THORNLEY
10 Vice Pres Finance & Administration ....Mr. Scott POELKER
05 Vice President Academic Affairs ....Dr. Patricia ROBERTSON
32 Vice President Student Services ....Dr. Elise DAVIS-MCFARLAND
30 Vice President Advancement ....Ms. Meg HOWLE
51 Vice Pres Continuing Educ/Econ Dev ....Mr. Robert WALKER
13 Vice Pres Information Technology ....Mr. Bernie STRAUB
45 Assoc VP Planning/Accreditation ....Ms. Suzy BARR
20 Asst Vice Pres Academic Programs ....Ms. Susan NORTON
51 Asst Vice Pres Continuing Education .... Ms. Yvonne NOISETTE
72 Asst Vice Pres Info Technology ....Mr. Henry COPE
35 Asst Vice Pres for Student Svcs ....Ms. Lynne ANKERSEN
20 Asst Vice President Instruction ....Mr. Eddie SIMMONS
16 Director Human Resources ....Ms. DeVetta HUGHES
96 Dir Procurement/Risk Management ....Ms. Carol BELCHER
40 Dir Auxiliary Enterprises/Bookstore ....Ms. Jloundia PINCKNEY
18 Director Facilities ....Mr. Eric HAMILTON
21 Director Finance .... Ms. Doris BRUMGARDT
26 Director Marketing .... Ms. Tina AHLEMANN
27 Director Public Info ....Mr. David HANSEN
88 Director High School Programs .... Ms. Melissa STOWASSER
30 Associate VP Development ....Ms. Kimberley STURGEON
14 Dir Information Technology Training .... Mr. Joseph GIBSON
36 Director Career Employment Services ....Mr. Brian ALMQUIST
81 Dean Science & Mathematics ....Mr. Bill LANDRY
79 Dean Humanities & Social Sciences .... Dr. Tim BROWN
88 Dean The Learning Center ....Ms. Pamela LEONARD-RAY
50 Dean Business Technology ....Ms. Connie JOLLY
76 Dean Allied Health Sciences ....Dr. Richard HERNANDEZ
57 Dean Fil/ Media and Visual Arts ....Ms. Pat FOX
54 Dean Industrial/Engineering Tech ....Ms. Christine LANG
88 Dean Culinary Inst of Charleston ....Mr. Mike SABOE
61 Dean Law-Related Studies ....Mr. John UNGARO

66 Dean Nursing ... Ms. Muriel HORTON
38 Dean Student Development ... Ms. Pamela BROWN
88 Dean Comm/Family/Child Studies ... Ms. Stephany HEWITT
84 Dean Enrollment Management ... Mr. John JAMROGOWICZ
75 Dean Aeronautical Studies ... Dr. Barry FRANCO
12 Dean Berkeley Campus ... Ms. Karen WRIGHTEN
12 Dean Mount Pleasant Campus ... Mr. Michael PATTERSON
12 Dean Palmer Campus ... Dr. Louester ROBINSON
19 Director Public Safety ... Mr. Lawrence SAVIDGE

University of South Carolina Columbia (A)

Columbia SC 29208-0001

County: Richland — FICE Identification: 003448
Unit ID: 218663
Telephone: (803) 777-7000 — Carnegie Class: RU/VH
FAX Number: (803) 777-0101 — Calendar System: Semester
URL: www.sc.edu
Established: 1801 — Annual Undergrad Tuition & Fees (In-State): $4,884
Enrollment: 30,721 — Coed
Affiliation or Control: State — IRS Status: 501(c)3
Highest Offering: Doctorate
Program: Liberal Arts And General; Teacher Preparatory; Professional
Accreditation: SC, ANEST, ART, BUS, BUSA, CACREP, CEA, CLPSY, CORE, CS, ENG, HSA, IPSY, JOUR, LAW, LIB, MED, MUS, NURSE, PH, PTA, SCPSY, SP, SPAA, SW, TED, THEA

01 President ... Dr. Harris PASTIDES
03 Vice President & CIO ... Dr. William F. HOGUE
05 Exec VP Academic Affs/Provost ... Dr. Michael AMIRIDIS
45 Sr Vice Prov/Dir Strategic Planning ... Dr. Christine W. CURTIS
10 Vice President Finance & Planning ... Mr. Edward I. WALTON
32 VP Student Affairs/VProv Acad Suppt ... Dr. Dennis A. PRUITT
16 Vice President Human Resources ... Mr. Christopher D. BYRD
30 VP Development & Alumni Relations ... Mrs. Michelle DODENHOFF
12 VP/Exec Dean Regional Campuses ... Dr. Chris P. PLYLER
46 VP Research & Grad Education ... Dr. Prakash NAGARKATTI
26 Vice President Communications ... Ms. Luanne M. LAWRENCE
101 Secretary to Board of Trustees ... Ms. Amy E. STONE
20 Vice Provost & Dean Undergrad Stds ... Dr. Helen I. DOERPINGHAUS
58 Vice Provost & Dean Graduate School ... Dr. Lacy K. FORD
84 Asst Vice Provost Enrollment Mgmt ... Mr. Scott VERZYL
08 Dean of Libraries ... Dr. Tom MCNALLY
43 General Counsel ... Mr. Walter H. PARHAM
09 Dir Inst Assessment & Compliance ... Dr. Philip S. MOORE
18 Assoc VP for Facilities ... Mr. Thomas D. QUASNEY
27 Director University Creative Servic ... Mr. Laurence W. PEARCE
19 Director Law Enforcement & Safety ... Mr. Christopher L. WUCHENICH
37 Dir Stdnt Financial Aid/Scholarshp ... Dr. Edgar MILLER
36 Director Career Center ... Mr. Thomas HALASZ
06 University Registrar ... Mr. Aaron C. MARTERER
22 Exec Asst to Pres Equal Oppty Pgm ... Mr. Bobby D. GIST
21 Budget Director ... Mrs. Leslie G. BRUNELLI
07 Director of Admissions ... Dr. Mary WAGNER
39 Director Housing & Residential Svcs ... Dr. Gene LUNA
38 Dir Counseling/Human Devel Center ... Dr. Deborah C. BECK
41 Director of Athletics ... Mr. Eric C. HYMAN
35 Assoc VP for Student Life ... Mr. Jerry T. BREWER
23 Director of Student Health Services ... Ms. Deborah BECK
27 Director News & Internal Relations ... Mr. Wesley T. HICKMAN
96 Director of Purchasing ... Mrs. Venis MANIGO
29 Int Exec Dir Alumni Association ... Ms. Amy E. STONE
49 Dean College Arts & Sciences ... Dr. Mary Anne FITZPATRICK
88 Dean Hospitality/Retail/Sport Mgt ... Mr. Brian MIHALIK
50 Dean Moore School of Business ... Dr. Hildy TEEGEN
53 Dean College of Education ... Dr. Lemuel WATSON
54 Dean Col Engineering & Computing ... Dr. Anthony P. AMBLER
69 Dean Arnold School of Public Health ... Dr. G. Thomas CHANDLER
60 Dn College of Mass Comm/Infor Stdys ... Mr. Charles BIERBAUER
61 Dean School of Law ... Dr. Robert M. WILCOX
63 Dean School of Medicine ... Dr. Richard A. HOPPMANN
63 Dean Greenville School of Medicine ... Dr. Jerry R. YOUKEY
64 Dean School of Music ... Dr. Tayloe HARDING
66 Dean College of Nursing ... Dr. Peggy HEWLETT
67 Exec Dean College of Pharmacy ... Dr. Joseph T. DIPIRO
67 Dean College of Pharmacy ... Dr. Randall C. ROWEN
70 Dean College of Social Work ... Dr. Anna M. SCHEYETTE
92 Dir Fellowships & Scholar Programs ... Ms. Novella BESKID
88 Director of Academic Programs ... Dr. Kristia H. FINNIGAN
88 Executive Director USC Connect ... Dr. Irma J. VANSCOY

University of South Carolina Aiken (B)

471 University Parkway, Aiken SC 29801-6399

County: Aiken — FICE Identification: 003449
Unit ID: 218645
Telephone: (803) 648-6851 — Carnegie Class: Bac/Diverse
FAX Number: (803) 641-3362 — Calendar System: Semester
URL: www.usca.edu
Established: 1961 — Annual Undergrad Tuition & Fees (In-State): $8,460
Enrollment: 3,277 — Coed
Affiliation or Control: State — IRS Status: 501(c)3
Highest Offering: Master's
Program: Liberal Arts And General; Teacher Preparatory
Accreditation: SC, BUS, MUS, NUR, NURSE, TED

01 Chancellor ... Dr. Sandra JORDAN
05 Exec Vice Chanc Academic Affairs ... Dr. Jeffrey M. PRIEST
30 Vice Chancellor Advancement ... Dr. Deidre MARTIN
32 Vice Chancellor Student Life & Svcs ... Dr. Deborah KLADIVKO
27 Vice Chancellor Information Tech ... Mr. Ernest PRINGLE
84 Vice Chancellor Enrollment Services ... Mr. Randy R. DUCKETT
18 Asst Chanc Facilities Management ... Mr. Mike JARA
79 College Coordinator Hum & Soc Sci ... Dr. Tom MACK
83 College Coordinator Sciences ... Vacant
50 Dean of the School of Business ... Dr. Clifton JONES
53 Dean of the School of Education ... Dr. Wendy SCHWEDER
66 Dean of the School of Nursing ... Dr. Sara CAMPBELL
88 Dir Academic Success Center ... Dr. Stacie WILLIAMS
09 Dir Institutional Effectiveness ... Dr. Lloyd A. DAWE
08 Dir of Library ... Ms. Jane TUTEN
88 Dir Ruth Patrick Sci Ed Center ... Dr. Gary SENN
25 Dir Sponsored Research ... Dr. Bill PIRKLE
24 Dir Center for Teaching Excellence ... Mr. Chad LEVERETTE
10 Vice Chanc Business & Finance ... Ms. Virginia S. HUDOCK
40 Dir Bookstore ... Ms. Heidi DIFRANCO
88 Dir Campus Support Services ... Mr. Jeff JENIK
88 Dir Children's Center ... Ms. Lynn WILLIAMS
88 Dir Convocation Center ... Mr. Matt HERPICH
88 Dir Dining Services ... Mr. Brent WUSTMAN
12 Dir of Etherredge Center ... Ms. Jane SCHUMACHER
21 Dir of Business Services ... Ms. Gwen ASHLEY
15 Dir Human Resources & Affirm Action ... Ms. Maria CHANDLER
17 Dir Wellness Center ... Ms. Mila PADGETT
07 Dir of Admissions ... Mr. Andrew HENDRIX
58 Coord Citizenshp Residenc Grad Stds ... Ms. Karen MORRIS
36 Dir of Career Services ... Mr. Corey FERALDI
37 Dir Financial Aid ... Mr. Glenn SHUMPERT
06 Registrar ... Ms. Vivian D. GRICE
14 Director of Client Services ... Mr. Chris SPIRES
90 Dir Communications & Hardware ... Mr. Bob WIESNER
105 Dir Network Sys/Infrastructure/Arch ... Ms. Joann WILLIAMSON
41 Dir of Athletics ... Mr. Douglas R. WARRICK, JR.
38 Dir Counseling & Disablilities ... Ms. Cynthia B. GELINAS
23 Interim Dir Student Health Center ... Ms. Cynthia B. GELINAS
39 Dir Housing & Univ Police ... Mr. Deri WILLS
28 Dir International Programs ... Dr. Maria ANASTASIOU
35 Dir of Student Involvement ... Mr. Ahmed SAMAHA
19 Chief of Police ... Mr. Kevin LILES
29 Dir of Alumni Relations/Annual Fund ... Ms. Ashley HOWELL
51 Dir Conferences & Continuing Ed ... Ms. Mary Anne CAVANAUGH
44 Dir Major Gifts ... Ms. Linda EVANS
26 Dir Marketing & Community Relations ... Mr. Preston SPARKS
105 Dir Visual Comm & Web Development ... Mr. Jeff MASTROMONICO

University of South Carolina Beaufort (C)

1 University Boulevard, Bluffton SC 29909-6085

County: Beaufort — FICE Identification: 003450
Unit ID: 218654
Telephone: (843) 208-8000 — Carnegie Class: Bac/Diverse
FAX Number: (843) 208-8299 — Calendar System: Semester
URL: www.uscb.edu
Established: 1959 — Annual Undergrad Tuition & Fees (In-State): $7,722
Enrollment: 1,874 — Coed
Affiliation or Control: State — IRS Status: 501(c)3
Highest Offering: Baccalaureate
Program: Liberal Arts And General; Teacher Preparatory; Professional
Accreditation: SC, NURSE, TED

01 Chancellor ... Dr. Jane UPSHAW
05 Exec Vice Chanc Academic Affairs ... Dr. Harvey VARNET
32 Vice Chanc for Student Development ... Dr. Douglas OBLANDER
10 Vice Chancellor Finance/Operations ... Mr. Earle HOLLEY
26 Vice Chanc University Advancement ... Dr. Lynn MCGEE
18 Director of Facilities ... Mr. Mike PARROTT
20 Assoc Vice Chanc Acad Affairs ... Dr. Harvey VARNET
13 Chief Information Officer ... Mr. Eddie KING
08 Director of Library ... Dr. Harvey VARNET
06 Registrar ... Dr. James TISDALE
07 Director of Admissions ... Mrs. Joffery GAYMON
37 Director of Financial Aid ... Ms. Patricia GREENE
30 Director of Development ... Ms. Colleen CALLAHAN
09 Dir Inst Effectiveness/Research ... Ms. Jodi HERRIN
19 Director of Security ... Dr. Henry GARBADE
35 Director of Student Life ... Ms. Kate VERMILYEA
15 Manager of Human Resources ... Dr. Sue GOLABEK

University of South Carolina Lancaster (D)

PO Box 889, Lancaster SC 29721-0889

County: Lancaster — FICE Identification: 003453
Unit ID: 218672
Telephone: (803) 313-7000 — Carnegie Class: Assoc/Pub2in4
FAX Number: (803) 313-7106 — Calendar System: Semester
URL: usclancaster.sc.edu
Established: 1959 — Annual Undergrad Tuition & Fees (In-State): $5,700
Enrollment: 1,744 — Coed
Affiliation or Control: State — IRS Status: 501(c)3
Highest Offering: Associate Degree
Program: Occupational; 2-Year Principally Bachelor's Creditable
Accreditation: &SC, ACBSP, ADNUR, PNUR

01 Dean ... Dr. John CATALANO
05 Assoc Dean for Acad & Student Affs ... Dr. M. Ron COX
84 Director of Enrollment Management ... Mrs. Karen FAILE
08 Director of the Library ... Ms. Lorene B. HARRIS
10 Business Manager/Dir of Planning ... Mr. Paul C. JOHNSON, III
37 Director Financial Aid ... Mr. Kenneth COLE
32 Director of Student Life ... Ms. Laura HUMPHREY
16 Human Resources Specialist ... Ms. Tracey A. MOBLEY
51 Director Trio Programs ... Ms. Thelathia B. BAILEY
30 Director of Development ... Vacant
26 Director of Public Information ... Ms. Shana DRY
14 Director of Computer Services ... Mr. Blake FAULKENBERRY
41 Athletics Director ... Mr. Rick WALTERS
18 Dir Custodial Svcs Groundskeeping ... Mr. Butch LUCAS
23 Director of Health Services ... Dr. William F. RINER
19 Dir Law Enforcement & Safety ... Dr. John E. RUTLEDGE
88 Dir Academic Success Center ... Dr. Dana LAWRENCE
88 Director of Archives ... Mr. Brent BURGIN

† Regional accreditation is carried under University of South Carolina - Columbia.

University of South Carolina Salkehatchie (E)

PO Box 617, Allendale SC 29810-0617

County: Allendale — FICE Identification: 003454
Unit ID: 218681
Telephone: (803) 584-3446 — Carnegie Class: Assoc/Pub2in4
FAX Number: (803) 584-5038 — Calendar System: Semester
URL: uscsalkehatchie.sc.edu
Established: 1965 — Annual Undergrad Tuition & Fees (In-State): $5,700
Enrollment: 1,155 — Coed
Affiliation or Control: State — IRS Status: 501(c)3
Highest Offering: Associate Degree
Program: 2-Year Principally Bachelor's Creditable
Accreditation: &SC

01 Dean ... Dr. Ann C. CARMICHAEL
05 Assoc Dean Academic Affairs ... Dr. Roberto REFINETTI
32 Asc Dean Student Svcs/Dir Athletics ... Ms. Jane T. BREWER
08 Head Librarian ... Mr. Daniel JOHNSON
37 Director Financial Aid ... Ms. Julie HADWIN
18 Director Facilities/Safety ... Dr. William A. SANDIFER
40 Bookstore Manager ... Mr. Lamar HEWETT
15 Director of Human Resources ... Dr. William A. SANDIFER
07 Director of Admissions ... Ms. Carmen BROWN
30 Chief Development ... Dr. Ann C. CARMICHAEL
84 Director Enrollment Mgmt Svcs ... Mr. Mike SMITH
88 Director Leadership Center ... Ms. Ann RICE
88 Dir Opportunity Scholars Program ... Ms. Carolyn BANNER
88 Dir Ctr Leadership Development ... Mr. Warren CHAVOUS
88 Sports Information Director ... Mr. Trent KINARD
96 Director of Purchasing ... Mr. Caleb MORRISON
45 Dir Planning/Business Manager ... Mr. Paul C. JOHNSON, III
17 Dir Gregory Health Wellness Ctr ... Dr. Sarah HUNT-SELLHORST

† Regional accreditation is carried under University of South Carolina - Columbia.

University of South Carolina School of Medicine-Greenville (F)

607 Grove Road, Greenville SC 29605

County: Greenville — Identification: 667114
Telephone: (864) 455-7992 — Carnegie Class: Not Classified
FAX Number: (864) 455-8404 — Calendar System: Semester
URL: greenvillemed.sc.edu
Established: 2010 — Annual Graduate Tuition & Fees: $33,808
Enrollment: 53 — Coed
Affiliation or Control: State — IRS Status: 501(c)3
Highest Offering: Doctorate; No Undergraduates
Program: Professional
Accreditation: #MED

01 Dean ... Dr. Jerry R. YOUKEY
05 Sr Assc Dean Academic Affs/Diverity ... Dr. Spence TAYLOR
20 Assoc Dean for Faculty Affairs ... Dr. Robert BEST
32 Assoc Dean Student Affairs/Admiss ... Dr. James BUGGY
53 Assoc Dean for Education ... Dr. Lynn CRESPO
07 Assoc Dean for Admissions ... Dr. Paul CATALANA

University of South Carolina Sumter (G)

200 Miller Road, Sumter SC 29150-2498

County: Sumter — FICE Identification: 003426
Unit ID: 218690
Telephone: (803) 775-8727 — Carnegie Class: Assoc/Pub2in4
FAX Number: (803) 775-2180 — Calendar System: Semester
URL: www.uscsumter.edu
Established: 1966 — Annual Undergrad Tuition & Fees (In-State): $5,700
Enrollment: 1,018 — Coed
Affiliation or Control: State — IRS Status: 501(c)3
Highest Offering: Associate Degree
Program: 2-Year Principally Bachelor's Creditable
Accreditation: &SC

01 Interim Dean of the University ... Mr. Lynwood WATTS
05 Assoc Dean Academic Affairs ... Dr. Anthony M. COYNE
30 Asst Dean University Advancement ... Mr. Carl R. MCINTOSH
32 Assoc Dean for Student Affairs ... Vacant
10 Assoc Dean for Admin/Financial Svcs ... Mr. Bruce K. BLUMBERG
79 Chr Div of Hum/Social Science/Educ ... Dr. Richard S. BELL
49 Chair Division of Arts & Letters ... Dr. Hayes D. HAMPTON

81 Chr Div of Science/Math & Engr ... Dr. James E. PRIVETT
50 Chr Div of Business/Admin/ Economics ... Dr. Kay OLDHOUSER DAVIS
09 Director of Institutional Research ... Mr. Charles W. WRIGHT
08 Head Librarian ... Ms. Sharon H. CHAPMAN
07 Director of Admissions ... Mr. Keith E. BRITTON
38 Director Advisement/Counseling ... Ms. C. Gail PACK
56 Director of Distance Education ... Ms. Jean B. CARRANO
51 Director of Continuing Education ... Ms. Susan S. BRABHAM
35 Director Student Life ... Vacant
14 Director of Computer Services ... Mr. George R. THOMPSON, III
26 Dir of Public Relations/Marketing ... Ms. Becky BEAN
40 Bookstore Manager ... Ms. Julie MCCOY
15 Human Resources Officer ... Ms. Marchetta L. WILLIAMS
21 Budget/Planning/Grants Director ... Ms. Joann V. GROOVER
29 Director of Alumni Relations ... Ms. Erica G. CHRISTMAS
37 Coord Fin Aid/Scholarships/Vet Affs ... Ms. Sue A. SIMS
06 Records & Registration Coordinator ... Ms. Alicia CURTIS
36 Career Planning & Placement Coord ... Ms. Toni J. WILLIAMS
88 Director Opportunity Scholars ... Ms. Lisa ROSDAIL
88 Director Upstate Education Programs ... Ms. Marilyn IZZARD
18 Superintendent Buildings & Grounds ... Mr. Jeff LINGEFELT

† Regional accreditation is carried under University of South Carolina - Columbia.

University of South Carolina Union (A)

PO Drawer 729, Union SC 29379-0729

County: Union   FICE Identification: 004927
Unit ID: 218706
Telephone: (864) 429-8728   Carnegie Class: Assoc/Pub2in4
FAX Number: (864) 427-3682   Calendar System: Semester
URL: uscunion.sc.edu
Established: 1965   Annual Undergrad Tuition & Fees (In-State): N/A
Enrollment: 492   Coed
Affiliation or Control: State   IRS Status: 501(c)3
Highest Offering: Associate Degree
Program: Occupational; 2-Year Principally Bachelor's Creditable
Accreditation: &SC

01 Interim Dean ... Dr. Stephen H. LOWE
84 Director Enrollment Services ... Mr. M. Bradley GREER
37 Director Financial Aid ... Mr. Robert HOLCOMBE
15 Human Resources ... Ms. Susan P. JETT
10 Business Manager ... Ms. Michele S. LEE
40 Bookstore Manager ... Ms. Tanja BLACK
14 Director of Information Technology ... Mr. Wesley C. BELK
108 Inst Effectiveness Officer ... Mr. Thomas W. SIMPSON
08 Library Manager ... Ms. Sharon L. RUPP

† Regional accreditation is carried under University of South Carolina - Columbia.

University of South Carolina Upstate (B)

800 University Way, Spartanburg SC 29303-4996

County: Spartanburg   FICE Identification: 006951
Unit ID: 218742
Telephone: (864) 503-5000   Carnegie Class: Bac/Diverse
FAX Number: (864) 503-5375   Calendar System: Semester
URL: www.uscupstate.edu
Established: 1967   Annual Undergrad Tuition & Fees (In-State): $9,146
Enrollment: 5,493   Coed
Affiliation or Control: State   IRS Status: 501(c)3
Highest Offering: Master's
Program: Liberal Arts And General; Teacher Preparatory
Accreditation: SC, ART, BUS, CS, ENGT, NURSE, TED

01 Chancellor ... Dr. Thomas MOORE
05 Sr Vice Chanc for Acad Affair ... Dr. Marsha DOWELL
13 Vice Chanc Information Technology ... Ms. Jeanne SKUL
11 Vice Chanc Admin & Business Affs ... Ms. Sheryl TURNER-WATTS
30 Vice Chanc University Advancement ... Mr. Michael E. IRVIN
12 Vice Chanc Greenville Campus ... Dr. Judith PRINCE
88 Asst Vice Chanc Student Success ... Dr. Mary THEOKAS
32 Dean of Students ... Mrs. Laura PUCKETT-BOLER
06 Registrar ... Ms. Mary David FOX
84 Asst Vice Chanc Enrollment Services ... Ms. Donette STEWART
38 Director of Counseling Services ... Ms. Frances L. JARRETT-HORTIS
27 Telecommunications Manager ... Mr. Robbie COTHRAN
08 Dean of the Library ... Ms. Frieda M. DAVISON
37 Director Financial Aid ... Ms. Allison SULLIVAN
49 Dean of Arts & Sciences ... Dr. Dirk SCHLINGMANN
50 Dean Johnson Col Business & Econ ... Dr. Darrell F. PARKER
53 Dean of Education ... Dr. Charles LOVE
66 Interim Dean of Nursing ... Dr. Katharine GIBB
58 Director of Graduate Education ... Dr. Tina HERZBERG
102 Director Dev & Found Scholarships ... Mrs. Bea W. SMITH
40 Director of the Bookstore ... Mr. Jerry CARROLL
41 Director of Athletics ... Mr. H. Michael HALL
18 Director of Facilities Management ... Mr. Frederick D. PUNCKE
108 Dir of Inst Assessment & Planning ... Mr. C. Sam BINGHAM
96 Director of Purchasing ... Ms. Janice DELLINGER
26 Director University Communications ... Ms. Tammey E. WHALEY
19 Chief of Police ... Mr. Klay PETERSON
35 Director of Student Life ... Ms. Khrystal SMITH
39 Director of Housing ... Vacant
23 Director of Health Services ... Ms. Lou Anne WEBER
88 Exec Dir Univ Boards & Public Affs ... Mr. John F. PERRY
09 Dir Inst Effectiveness & Compliance ... Mr. Brian MALLORY
88 Dir Campus Fitness & Recreation ... Mr. Mark RITTER
88 Dir Disability Services ... Ms. Margaret CAMP

Voorhees College (C)

PO Box 678, Denmark SC 29042-0678

County: Bamberg   FICE Identification: 003455
Unit ID: 218919
Telephone: (803) 780-1010   Carnegie Class: Bac/Diverse
FAX Number: (803) 780-1015   Calendar System: Semester
URL: www.voorhees.edu
Established: 1897   Annual Undergrad Tuition & Fees: $18,126
Enrollment: 642   Coed
Affiliation or Control: Protestant Episcopal   IRS Status: 501(c)3
Highest Offering: Baccalaureate
Program: Liberal Arts And General
Accreditation: SC, ACBSP

01 President ... Dr. Cleveland L. SELLERS, JR.
05 Exec Vice Pres Academic Affairs ... Dr. Paul K. BAKER
32 Vice President Student Affairs ... Mr. Willie JEFFERSON
10 VP Fiscal/Admin Affairs/CFO ... Mrs. V. Diane O'BERRY
30 Vice Pres Institutional Advancement ... Vacant
09 VP Planning & Information Mgmt ... Mr. Samuel BLACKWELL
35 Director of Student Life/Counseling ... Mrs. Sarah SIMPSON
08 Administrative Librarian ... Dr. Marie MARTIN
37 Director of Financial Aid ... Mr. Augusta KITCHEN
18 Director of Physical Plant ... Mr. Eddie PATTERSON
29 Director Alumni Affairs ... Ms. Dorothy PATTERSON
36 Director Career Planning & Outreach ... Mr. Gerald DEVAUGHN
42 Chaplain ... Rev. James YARSIAH
41 Director of Athletics ... Mr. Willie JEFFERSON
19 Director of Security ... Mr. James WELDON
23 Director of Health Services ... Ms. Sheila CUNNINGHAM
06 Registrar ... Ms. Melika JACKSON
07 Director of Admissions ... Mr. Benjamin O. WATSON
15 Director of Human Resources ... Ms. Andraea HERRIN
13 Chief Technology Officer ... Mr. Timothy KENTOPP
21 Internal Auditor ... Vacant
40 Bookstore Manager ... Mrs. Shanda RUFFIN
26 Coordinator Media Rels/Marketing ... Mrs. Teesa BRUNSON
04 Exec Assistant to the President ... Ms. Sandra GLOSTER
50 Chrpn Business & Professional Stds ... Dr. Bernard MOSES
49 Chairperson of Arts & Sciences ... Dr. Doris WARD

Williamsburg Technical College (D)

601 Martin Luther King, Jr. Avenue, Kingstree SC 29556-4103

County: Williamsburg   FICE Identification: 009322
Unit ID: 218955
Telephone: (843) 355-4110   Carnegie Class: Assoc/Pub-R-S
FAX Number: (843) 355-4296   Calendar System: Semester
URL: www.wiltech.edu
Established: 1969   Annual Undergrad Tuition & Fees (In-District): $5,310
Enrollment: 694   Coed
Affiliation or Control: State/Local   IRS Status: 501(c)3
Highest Offering: Associate Degree
Program: Occupational; 2-Year Principally Bachelor's Creditable
Accreditation: SC, ACBSP

01 President ... Dr. Patricia A. LEE
05 Vice Pres for Academic Affairs ... Mr. Clifton R. ELLIOTT
10 Vice Pres Business Affairs ... Ms. Melissa A. COKER
32 Vice Pres Student Affairs ... Dr. Eric A. BROWN
46 Dir Planning/Research/Grants ... Mr. Andrew MULLER
08 Library Director ... Ms. Demetra WALKER
07 Admissions Counselor ... Ms. Cheryl DUBOSE
30 Chief Devel Officer/Grants Coord/PR ... Mrs. Mona B. DUKES
37 Financial Aid Officer ... Mrs. Jean BOOS
09 Research/Systems Analyst ... Mr. T. Kent COKER
06 Director Enrollment and Record Svcs ... Dr. Alexis WRIGHT-DUBOSE
18 Director of Physical Plant ... Mr. Tyrone THOMAS
15 Director Human Resources ... Vacant
26 Dir Development/Public Relations ... Mrs. Mona B. DUKES

Winthrop University (E)

Oakland Avenue, Rock Hill SC 29733-0001

County: York   FICE Identification: 003456
Unit ID: 218964
Telephone: (803) 323-2211   Carnegie Class: Master's L
FAX Number: (803) 323-3001   Calendar System: Semester
URL: www.winthrop.edu
Established: 1886   Annual Undergrad Tuition & Fees (In-State): $12,698
Enrollment: 5,913   Coed
Affiliation or Control: State   IRS Status: 501(c)3
Highest Offering: Beyond Master's But Less Than Doctorate
Program: Liberal Arts And General; Teacher Preparatory; Professional
Accreditation: SC, ART, BUS, CACREP, CIDA, CS, DANCE, DIETD, DIETI, JOUR, MUS, SW, TED, THEA

01 President ... Dr. Anthony J. DIGIORGIO
05 Vice Pres Academic Affairs ... Dr. Debra BOYD
10 Vice President Finance & Business ... Mr. J. P. MCKEE
30 Vice Pres University Advancement ... Dr. Kathryn HOLTEN
32 Vice President of Student Life ... Dr. Frank P. ARDAIOLO
29 Vice Pres Development and Alumni ... Ms. Kimberly KEEL
21 Associate VP Finance/Business ... Ms. Amanda F. MAGHSOUD
18 Assoc VP Facilities Management ... Mr. Walter A. HARDIN
15 Associate VP Human Resource ... Ms. Lisa COWART
29 Assoc Vice Pres Alumni Relations ... Ms. Debbie GARRICK
13 Assoc VP Information Technology ... Mr. James HAMMOND
26 Assoc VP/Exec Dir University Rels ... Ms. Ellen M. WILDER-BYRD
100 Exec Assistant to President ... Dr. Kimberly A. FAUST
26 Asst to President Public Affairs ... Ms. Rebecca MASTERS
04 Asst to Pres University Events ... Ms. DeeAnna BROOKS
20 Asst Vice Pres Academic Affairs ... Mr. Tim DRUEKE
58 Dean of Graduate School ... Dr. Jack DEROCHI
49 Interim Dean College Arts & Science ... Dr. Peter JUDGE
50 Dean Col of Business Administration ... Dr. Roger D. WEIKLE
53 Dean College of Education ... Dr. Jennie RAKESTRAW
64 Dean College of Visual/Perf ... Dr. David WOHL
08 Dean Library Services ... Dr. Mark Y. HERRING
88 Dean University College ... Dr. Gloria JONES
35 Dean of Students ... Ms. Bethany MARLOWE
41 Athletic Director ... Mr. Thomas N. HICKMAN
25 Director Sponsored Pgms/Research ... Ms. Teresa R. JUSTICE
90 Director Academic Computing ... Mr. Patrice BRUNEAU
91 Director Admin System/Programming ... Mr. Larry W. FERGUSON
06 Registrar ... Ms. Gina JONES
07 Director of Admissions ... Ms. Deborah G. BARBER
37 Director of Financial Aid ... Ms. Leah STURGIS
19 Chief of Campus Police ... Chief Frank J. ZEBEDIS
38 Interim Director Health/Counseling ... Ms. Mary Jo BARRETO
39 Director of Residence Life ... Ms. Cynthia A. CASSENS
36 Director Career Development /Svcs ... Ms. Amy SULLIVAN
96 Director Procurement/Risk Mgmt ... Mr. Bob REID
53 Director Teaching/Learning Ctr ... Dr. John BRYD

W.L. Bonner College (F)

4430 Argent Court, Columbia SC 29203-5901

County: Richland   FICE Identification: 038564
Unit ID: 446613
Telephone: (803) 754-3950   Carnegie Class: Spec/Faith
FAX Number: (803) 754-9700   Calendar System: Semester
URL: www.wlbc.edu
Established: 1995   Annual Undergrad Tuition & Fees: $7,152
Enrollment: 43   Coed
Affiliation or Control: Independent Non-Profit   IRS Status: 501(c)3
Highest Offering: Baccalaureate
Program: Liberal Arts And General; Religious Emphasis
Accreditation: #BI

01 President and Founder ... Bishop William L. BONNER
05 College Dean - CEO ... Ms. Elaine MCQUEEN
10 Chief Fiscal Officer ... Vacant

Wofford College (G)

429 N Church Street, Spartanburg SC 29303-3663

County: Spartanburg   FICE Identification: 003457
Unit ID: 218973
Telephone: (864) 597-4000   Carnegie Class: Bac/A&S
FAX Number: (864) 597-4018   Calendar System: 4/1/4
URL: www.wofford.edu
Established: 1854   Annual Undergrad Tuition & Fees: $34,555
Enrollment: 1,536   Coed
Affiliation or Control: United Methodist   IRS Status: 501(c)3
Highest Offering: Baccalaureate
Program: Liberal Arts And General; Teacher Preparatory
Accreditation: SC

01 President ... Dr. Benjamin B. DUNLAP
10 Chief Financial Officer ... Ms. Barbie F. JEFFERSON
05 Sr VP Academic Affs/Dean of College ... Dr. David S. WOOD
30 Sr VP Development/College Relations ... Mr. Marion B. PEAVEY
11 Sr Vice Pres for Administration ... Mr. David M. BEACHAM
32 Vice President Student Affairs ... Ms. Roberta H. BIGGER
46 Vice Pres Education Technology ... Dr. David M. WHISNANT
84 Vice President for Enrollment ... Mr. Brand R. STILLE
09 Vice Pres Academic Admin & Planning ... Dr. Boyce M. LAWTON, III
27 Assoc VP Communications/Marketing ... Dr. Doyle W. BOGGS
18 Assoc VP Facilities/Cap Projects ... Mr. Jason H. BURR
36 Dean Ctr for Professional Excellnce ... Mr. Scott COCHRAN
08 Dean of Library/Dir Cultural Events ... Mr. Oakley H. COBURN
82 Dean of International Programs ... Dr. Ana Maria WISEMAN
23 Assoc Dean Students/Dir Health Svcs ... Ms. Beth D. WALLACE
04 Exec Assistant to the President ... Ms. Mary A. GILMAN
41 Director of Athletics ... Mr. Richard A. JOHNSON
06 College Registrar ... Ms. Jennifer R. ALLISON
42 Chaplain ... Dr. Ronald R. ROBINSON
29 Dir of Alumni Affairs/Parent Assn ... Mrs. Debbi N. THOMPSON
19 Campus Safety Director ... Mr. Randy HALL
15 Human Resources Director ... Ms. Carole B. LISTER

York Technical College (H)

452 S Anderson Road, Rock Hill SC 29730-3395

County: York   FICE Identification: 003996
Unit ID: 218991
Telephone: (803) 327-8000   Carnegie Class: Assoc/Pub-S-SC
FAX Number: (803) 327-8059   Calendar System: Semester
URL: www.yorktech.edu
Established: 1964   Annual Undergrad Tuition & Fees (In-State): $3,712
Enrollment: 5,621   Coed
Affiliation or Control: State   IRS Status: 501(c)3
Highest Offering: Associate Degree
Program: Occupational; 2-Year Principally Bachelor's Creditable

Accreditation: SC, ACBSP, ADNUR, DA, DH, ENGT, MLTAD, PNUR, RAD, SURGT

01	President	Dr. Greg F. RUTHERFORD
05	Exec Vice Pres Acad/Student Affs	Dr. Carolyn G. STEWART
10	VP Business & Support Svcs	Dr. Marc TARPLEE
32	Assoc VP Academic/Student Affairs	Ms. Bridgett GOLMAN
30	Vice President for Advancement	Ms. Melanie E. JONES
50	Assoc VP Business/Computer/AA/AS	Mr. Jack BAGWELL
76	Assoc VP Health & Human Services	Ms. Linda WEAVER-GRIGGS
54	Assoc VP Industry/Engineering Tech	Mr. Sidney VALENTINE
103	Assoc VP Economic/Workforce Devel	Dr. Joanne ZUKOWSKI
08	Librarian	Vacant
35	Dean of Students	Ms. Kelly T. DAWKINS
88	Dean Center for Teaching/Learning	Ms. Kathy L. HOELLEN
71	ReadySC Program Manager	Ms. Marianne BORDERS
09	Director of Institutional Research	Ms. Mary Beth SCHWARTZ
15	Director of Human Resources	Ms. Edwina ROSEBORO-BARNES
37	Director Student Financial Aid	Mrs. Angela FOWLER
13	Information Services Director	Mr. Ronald G. SCOTT
18	Facilities Management Director	Mr. Robert L. BROWN
45	Director of Planning	Mrs. Jacquelyn H. NESBITT
06	Registrar	Mrs. Brandy PINER
07	Director of Admissions	Mr. Kenny ALDRIDGE

SOUTH DAKOTA

Augustana College (A)

2001 S Summit, Sioux Falls SD 57197-0001

County: Minnehaha — FICE Identification: 003458 — Unit ID: 219000

Telephone: (605) 274-0770 — Carnegie Class: Bac/Diverse

FAX Number: (605) 274-5299 — Calendar System: 4/1/4

URL: www.augie.edu

Established: 1860 — Annual Undergrad Tuition & Fees: $27,780

Enrollment: 1,870 — Coed

Affiliation or Control: Evangelical Lutheran Church In America — IRS Status: 501(c)3

Highest Offering: Master's

Program: Liberal Arts And General; Teacher Preparatory; Professional

Accreditation: NH, MUS, NURSE, TED

01	President	Mr. Robert C. OLIVER
05	Sr Vice Pres Academic Affairs	Dr. Susan HASSELER
32	Vice President Student Services	Dr. James B. BIES
10	Vice Pres Finance/Administration	Mr. Thomas MEYER
30	Vice President for Advancement	Vacant
07	Vice President for Admission	Ms. Nancy DAVIDSON
15	Vice President of Human Resources	Ms. Jane T. KUPER
11	Assoc VP Admin/Chief Info Officer	Mr. Daniel D. DRENKOW
21	Assoc Vice President for Finance	Ms. Carol SPILLUM
20	Associate Academic Dean	Dr. Mike WANOUS
32	Associate Dean of Students	Vacant
37	Director of Financial Aid	Ms. Brenda MURTHA
08	Director of Library	Ms. Ronelle THOMPSON
36	Director Career Center	Ms. Sandi VIETOR
13	Director Mgmt Information Systems	Ms. Debra FREDERICK
18	Chief Facilities/Physical Plant	Mr. Frank HUGHES
29	Director of Alumni Relations	Ms. Mary TOSO
41	Athletic Director	Mr. Bill GROSS
06	Registrar	Ms. Joni KRUEGER

Colorado Technical University (B)

3901 W 59th Street, Sioux Falls SD 57108-2272

County: Lincoln — Identification: 666731 — Unit ID: 402615

Telephone: (605) 361-0200 — Carnegie Class: Master's S

FAX Number: (605) 361-5954 — Calendar System: Quarter

URL: www.coloradotech.edu

Established: 1965 — Annual Undergrad Tuition & Fees: $12,700

Enrollment: 899 — Coed

Affiliation or Control: Proprietary — IRS Status: Proprietary

Highest Offering: Master's

Program: 2-Year Principally Bachelor's Creditable; Professional

Accreditation: &NH, MAC

01	President	Dr. David HEFLIN
10	Controller	Ms. Amy WARWICK
07	Vice President of Admissions	Ms. Catherine ALLEN
05	Director of Education	Dr. Michelle LAUGHLIN
32	Director of Student Services	Ms. Christie DECKER
37	Assistant Director of Financial Aid	Vacant

† Regional accreditation is carried under the parent institution in Colorado Springs, CO.

Dakota Wesleyan University (C)

1200 W University, Mitchell SD 57301-4398

County: Davison — FICE Identification: 003461 — Unit ID: 219091

Telephone: (605) 995-2600 — Carnegie Class: Bac/Diverse

FAX Number: (605) 995-2699 — Calendar System: Semester

URL: www.dwu.edu

Established: 1885 — Annual Undergrad Tuition & Fees: $21,750

Enrollment: 757 — Coed

Affiliation or Control: United Methodist — IRS Status: 501(c)3

Highest Offering: Master's

Program: Liberal Arts And General; Teacher Preparatory

Accreditation: NH, ADNUR

01	President	Dr. Robert G. DUFFETT
03	Provost & Executive Vice President	Ms. Amy NOVAK
10	Vice Pres Business & Advancement	Ms. Theresa KRIESE
26	Vice Pres of University Relations	Ms. Lori ESSIG
06	Registrar	Ms. Karen KNOELL
08	Chief Info Ofcr/Dir Lrng Resources	Mr. Kevin KENKEL
88	Dir Kelley Ctr for Entrepreneurship	Ms. Rhonda POLE
88	Dn Col Ldrshp/Pub Svc/Dir McGov Ctr	Dr. Donald SIMMONS
81	Dean Col Health/Fitness & Science	Dr. Rochelle VON EYE
79	Dean College Arts & Humanities	Dr. Vince REDDER
30	Development Officer	Ms. Kitty ALLEN
29	Director of Alumni Relations	Ms. Jackie WENTWORTH
37	Director of Financial Aid	Ms. Kristy O'KIEF
13	Director of Information Technology	Mr. Matt MOORE
15	Director of Human Resources	Mr. Corey MELLEGAARD
42	Campus Pastor	Rev. Brandon VETTER
66	Administrative Chair Nursing Dept	Dr. Adele JACOBSON
41	Athletic Director	Mr. Curt HART
18	Director of Physical Plant	Mr. Louis SCHOENFELDER
32	Director of Student Life	Ms. Diana GOLDAMMER
35	Director Student Support Services	Ms. Kate MILLER
07	Director of Recruitment	Ms. Melissa HERR-VALBURG
38	Student Support Services Counselor	Ms. Sara THOMPSON
40	Director of University Services	Ms. Lori SOLBERG
88	Day Care Director/Teacher	Ms. Linda HOFER

Kilian Community College (D)

300 E 6th Street, Sioux Falls SD 57103-7020

County: Minnehaha — FICE Identification: 021446 — Unit ID: 219055

Telephone: (605) 221-3100 — Carnegie Class: Assoc/PrivNFP

FAX Number: (605) 336-2606 — Calendar System: Semester

URL: www.kilian.edu

Established: 1976 — Annual Undergrad Tuition & Fees: $8,580

Enrollment: 335 — Coed

Affiliation or Control: Independent Non-Profit — IRS Status: 501(c)3

Highest Offering: Associate Degree

Program: Occupational; 2-Year Principally Bachelor's Creditable

Accreditation: NH

01	President	Mr. Mark MILLAGE
11	Dean of Institutional Services	Mr. Craig JUCHT
37	Financial Aid Director	Ms. Carolyn HELGERSON
06	Registrar/Dir of Inst Research	Ms. Janet K. GARCIA
26	Director of Marketing	Vacant
88	Director Student Success Center	Ms. Rose TOERING
07	Director of Admissions	Ms. Mary KLOCKMAN
30	Director of Development	Ms. Wendy MCDONNEL
04	Assistant to the President	Ms. Joyce HUBREGTSE
08	Librarian	Vacant
10	Manager Business Office	Vacant
18	Chief Facilities/Physical Plant	Mr. Herb ROE
49	Instruction Liberal Arts Division	Ms. Cheryl J. HARTMAN
50	Instruction Business Division	Ms. Wendy JANSEN

Lake Area Technical Institute (E)

1201 Arrow Avenue, PO Box 730, Watertown SD 57201-2869

County: Codington — FICE Identification: 005309 — Unit ID: 219143

Telephone: (605) 882-5284 — Carnegie Class: Assoc/Pub-R-S

FAX Number: (605) 882-6299 — Calendar System: Semester

URL: www.lakeareatech.edu

Established: 1965 — Annual Undergrad Tuition & Fees (In-District): $5,904

Enrollment: 1,468 — Coed

Affiliation or Control: Local — IRS Status: 501(c)3

Highest Offering: Associate Degree

Program: Occupational; 2-Year Principally Bachelor's Creditable; Technical Emphasis

Accreditation: NH, DA, EMT, MAC, MLTAD, OTA, PNUR, PTAA

01	President	Ms. Debra SHEPHARD
03	Executive Vice President	Mr. Michael CARTNEY
84	Director of Enrollment	Mr. Lee QUALE
05	Dean of Instruction	Ms. Kim BELLUM
26	Chief Public Relations Officer	Ms. LuAnn STRAIT
31	Business/Industry Coordinator	Mr. Steven HAUCK
32	Student Services Coordinator	Mr. Shane ORTMEIER
37	Financial Aid Coordinator	Ms. Marlene SEEKLANDER
38	Academic Counselor	Ms. Jeanette TRUE

Mitchell Technical Institute (F)

1800 E Spruce, Mitchell SD 57301-2002

County: Davison — FICE Identification: 008284 — Unit ID: 219189

Telephone: (605) 995-3025 — Carnegie Class: Assoc/Pub-R-S

FAX Number: (605) 995-3083 — Calendar System: Semester

URL: www.mitchelltech.edu

Established: 1968 — Annual Undergrad Tuition & Fees (In-District): $6,000

Enrollment: 1,055 — Coed

Affiliation or Control: Local — IRS Status: 501(c)3

Highest Offering: Associate Degree

Program: Occupational; 2-Year Principally Bachelor's Creditable; Technical Emphasis

Accreditation: NH, MAC, MLTAD, RAD

01	President	Mr. Greg VON WALD
05	Vice President for Academic Affairs	Ms. Vicki WIESE
11	Vice Pres for Admin Svcs/CFO	Mr. Michael HOFFMAN
13	Vice President for Technology	Mr. Dan MUCK
88	Vice Pres for Industrial Relations	Mr. Mark GERHARDT
84	Dean of Enrollment	Mr. Scott FOSSUM
06	Registrar	Ms. Janet GREENWAY
37	Director Student Financial Aid	Mr. Grant UECKER
07	Admissions Coordinator	Mr. Clayton DEUTER
38	Learning Services Coordinator	Ms. Julie HART-SCHUTTE
09	Director of Institutional Research	Ms. Marla SMITH
20	Associate Academic Officer	Ms. Carol GRODE-HANKS
26	Director of Marketing	Ms. Julie BROOKBANK
30	Foundation Director	Ms. Heather LENTZ

Mount Marty College (G)

1105 W 8th, Yankton SD 57078-3724

County: Yankton — FICE Identification: 003465 — Unit ID: 219198

Telephone: (605) 668-1011 — Carnegie Class: Bac/Diverse

FAX Number: (605) 668-1607 — Calendar System: Semester

URL: www.mtmc.edu

Established: 1936 — Annual Undergrad Tuition & Fees: $22,130

Enrollment: 1,242 — Coed

Affiliation or Control: Roman Catholic — IRS Status: 501(c)3

Highest Offering: Master's

Program: Liberal Arts And General; Teacher Preparatory; Professional; Nursing Emphasis

Accreditation: NH, ANEST, NURSE

01	President	Dr. Joseph N. BENOIT
04	Asst to the Pres/Asst Sec to Board	Ms. Carla ENG
05	VP for Academic Affairs	Mr. Robert TERESHINSKI
10	VP for Finance/Administration	Ms. Daisy HALVORSON
32	VP of Student Affairs	Ms. Sarah CARDA
84	VP for Marketing & Admissions	Ms. Paula TACKE
42	Director of Campus Ministry	Vacant
30	Chief Advancement Officer	Ms. Barb REZAC
27	Chief Information Officer	Mr. Ed KOSTER
09	Director of Institutional Research	Ms. Kristen WELKER
58	Director of Nurse Anesthesia	Dr. Alfred LUPIEN
88	Director of Pastoral Ministries	Vacant
12	Director of Watertown Campus	Dr. Linda SCHURMANN
37	Director Student Financial Aid	Mr. Ken KOCER
06	Registrar	Ms. Jonna SUPURGECI
13	Director Information Support Servic	Mr. Paul LAMMERS
08	Director of Library	Ms. Sandra BROWN
40	Dir Bookstore/Central Scheduling	Ms. Mary ABBOTT
38	Dir Student Counseling	Vacant
41	Athletic Director	Mr. Chuck IVERSON
36	Director Student Placement	Ms. Estelle JOHNSON
18	Chief Facilities/Physical Plant	Mr. Steve HERMANSON
15	Human Resources Specialist	Ms. Julie DATHER

National American University (H)

5301 S Highway 16, Suite 200, Rapid City SD 57701-8932

County: Pennington — FICE Identification: 004057 — Unit ID: 219204

Telephone: (605) 721-5200 — Carnegie Class: Master's S

FAX Number: (605) 721-5241 — Calendar System: Quarter

URL: www.national.edu

Established: 1941 — Annual Undergrad Tuition & Fees: $27,684

Enrollment: 10,898 — Coed

Affiliation or Control: Proprietary — IRS Status: Proprietary

Highest Offering: Master's

Program: Occupational; Liberal Arts And General; Professional

Accreditation: NH, IACBE, MAC

01	University President	Dr. Jerry L. GALLENTINE
05	Provost/General Counsel	Dr. Samuel KERR
58	System VP Grad Stds/Dean Grad Sch	Dr. Samuel KERR
12	President of Campus Operations	Ms. Michaelle HOLLAND
20	Assoc Provost/Sys VP Curricul/Instr	Ms. Marilyn HOLMGREN
10	Chief Executive Officer	Dr. Ronald SHAPE
06	Registrar	Mr. Tom MAHON
37	Director of Financial Aid	Ms. Cheryl BULLINGER
29	Director Alumni Relations	Mr. Guy TILLETT
21	Director of Student Accounts	Ms. Linda POTTORFF
08	System Librarian	Ms. Pat HAMILTON
12	Campus Exec Ofcr-Ellsworth AFB	Mr. John TERRY
12	Campus Exec Ofcr-Rapid City	Dr. John QUINN
12	Campus Exec Ofcr-Albuquerque	Ms. Jessica CARR
12	Campus Exec Ofcr-Bloomington	Mr. Roger SAGE
12	Campus Exec Ofcr-Brooklyn Center	Mr. Travis JENSEN
12	Campus Exec Ofcr-Colorado Springs	Ms. Audrey DERUBIS
12	Campus Exec Ofcr-Overland Park KS	Mr. Ken MARCH
12	Campus Exec Ofcr-Roseville	Mr. Michael KNAPP
12	Campus Exec Ofcr-Sioux Falls	Ms. Lisa HOUTSMA
12	Campus Exec Ofcr-Independence	Mr. Tyre SMITH
12	Campus Exec Ofcr-Zona Rosa	Mr. Tim DZUBAY
12	Campus Exec Ofcr-Austin	Mr. Brooke JOECKEL
12	Campus Exec Ofcr-Denver	Mr. Grant NUSTAD
12	Director-Watertown Education Center	Ms. Traci MAAG
12	Campus Exec Ofcr-Wichita West	Mr. Eric DENNIS
12	Campus Exec Ofcr-Burnsville MN	Ms. Kristin MARTHALER
12	Campus Exec Ofcr-Minnetonka MN	Mr. Aaron ZELLMER
12	Campus Exec Ofcr-Rochester MN	Ms. Samantha THOMPSON
12	Campus Exec Ofcr-Bellevue NE	Mr. Trevor MISCHKE
12	Campus Exec Ofcr-Wichita (East) KS	Ms. Colleen SCHNEIDER
12	Campus Exec Ofcr-Lee's Summit MO	Ms. Tunya CARR

12 Campus Exec Ofcr-Weldon Spring MO .... Vacant
12 Campus Exec Ofcr-Tulsa OK .... Ms. Amanda OPPEL
12 Campus Exec Ofcr-Centennial CO .... Mr. Brian DEBOSKEY
12 Camp Ex Ofcr-Col Springs (South) CO .... Ms. Courtney HANSEN
12 Camp Ex Ofcr-Albuquerque (West) NM .... Mr. Steve RIGNEY
12 Campus Exec Ofcr-Austin (South) TX .... Dr. Mark WINKLEMAN
12 Campus Exec Ofcr-Lewinsville TX .... Mr. David IRVIN
12 Campus Exec Ofcr-Mesquite TX .... Mr. Mark PULLMAN
12 Campus Exec Ofcr-Richardson TX .... Mr. Rodney BROWN
12 Campus Exec Ofcr-Georgetown TX .... Mr. Joel LEE

Oglala Lakota College (A)

Box 490, Kyle SD 57752-0490

County: Shannon FICE Identification: 014659
Unit ID: 219277
Telephone: (605) 455-6000 Carnegie Class: Tribal
FAX Number: (605) 455-2787 Calendar System: Semester
URL: www.olc.edu
Established: 1971 Annual Undergrad Tuition & Fees: $2,825
Enrollment: 1,688 Coed
Affiliation or Control: Tribal Control IRS Status: 501(c)3
Highest Offering: Master's
Program: Liberal Arts And General
Accreditation: NH, SW

01 President .... Mr. Thomas H. SHORTBULL
05 Vice President for Instruction .... Ms. Ursula GAERTNER
10 Vice President for Business .... Ms. Arlene QUIST
06 Registrar .... Ms. Leslie MESTETH
08 Director Learning Resources .... Ms. Michelle MAY
15 Personnel Director .... Ms. Faith RICHARDS
37 Financial Aid Director .... Ms. Billi HORNBECK
84 Director Enrollment Management .... Ms. Leslie MESTETH
07 Director of Admissions .... Ms. Leslie MESTETH
09 Director of Institutional Research .... Ms. Lori BROBERG
21 Assoc Business Ofcr/Dir Purchasing .... Ms. Mia ALBERS
29 Director Alumni Relations .... Ms. Marilyn POURIER
89 Director of Freshman Studies .... Mr. Gerry LESSERT
13 MIS Director .... Mr. Cliff DELONG
30 Inst Development Coordinator .... Ms. Marilyn POURIER
51 Community/Cont Education Coord .... Ms. Susan KOLB
88 Applied Science Department Chair .... Mr. Doug NOYES
81 Math & Science Department Chair .... Mr. Jason TINANT
49 Art & History Department Chair .... Mr. Anthony FRESQUEZ
53 Education Department Chair .... Mr. Thomas RAYMOND
66 Nursing Department Chair .... Ms. Joan NELSON
83 Human Services Department Chair .... Dr. Jeffrey OLSON
88 LAKOTA Studies Department Chair .... Ms. Karen LONE HILL

Presentation College (B)

1500 N Main Street, Aberdeen SD 57401-1280

County: Brown FICE Identification: 003467
Unit ID: 219295
Telephone: (605) 225-1634 Carnegie Class: Bac/Diverse
FAX Number: (605) 229-8330 Calendar System: Semester
URL: www.presentation.edu
Established: 1951 Annual Undergrad Tuition & Fees: $16,514
Enrollment: 731 Coed
Affiliation or Control: Roman Catholic IRS Status: 501(c)3
Highest Offering: Baccalaureate
Program: Liberal Arts And General
Accreditation: NH, ADNUR, IACBE, MAC, NUR, RAD, SURGT, SW

01 President .... Dr. Margaret HUBER
05 Vice Pres for Academics .... Dr. Michelle METZINGER
10 Vice Pres for Finance .... Ms. Cathy HALL
84 Vice Pres for Enrollment .... Ms. JoEllen LINDNER
32 Vice Pres for Student Services .... Mr. Bob SCHUCHARDT
30 Vice President for Advancement .... Ms. Lori HARMEL
06 Registrar .... Ms. Maureen SCHUCHARDT
08 Librarian .... Ms. Fran RICE
37 Director Student Financial Aid .... Ms. Janel WAGNER
09 Assessment Coordinator .... Ms. Nancy VANDER HOEK
15 Director of Human Resources .... Mr. Jason PETTIGREW
26 Coord Marketing/Graphic Design .... Mr. Mark ZOELLNER

Sinte Gleska University (C)

Antelope Lake Circle, PO Box 105,
Mission SD 57555-0105

County: Todd FICE Identification: 021437
Unit ID: 219374
Telephone: (605) 856-5880 Carnegie Class: Tribal
FAX Number: (605) 856-5401 Calendar System: Semester
URL: www.sintegleska.edu
Established: 1970 Annual Undergrad Tuition & Fees: $3,154
Enrollment: 835 Coed
Affiliation or Control: Independent Non-Profit IRS Status: 501(c)3
Highest Offering: Master's
Program: Liberal Arts And General; Teacher Preparatory; Professional
Accreditation: NH

01 President .... Mr. Lionel BORDEAUX
11 Vice Pres Admin/Dean Student Svcs .... Ms. Cheryl MEDEARIS
06 Registrar .... Mr. Harvey HERMAN
08 Librarian .... Ms. Diana DILLION
10 Fiscal Officer .... Ms. Alisa BARLETT
37 Director Financial Aid .... Mr. William HAY
55 Director Adult Education .... Mr. James SHERMAN, III
15 Director Personnel Dept .... Ms. Lynette BORDEAUX

Sioux Falls Seminary (D)

2100 S Summit Ave, Sioux Falls SD 57105-2729

County: Minnehaha FICE Identification: 004056
Unit ID: 219240
Telephone: (605) 336-6588 Carnegie Class: Spec/Faith
FAX Number: (605) 335-9090 Calendar System: 4/1/4
URL: www.sfseminary.edu
Established: 1858 Annual Graduate Tuition & Fees: $15,848
Enrollment: 164 Coed
Affiliation or Control: North American Baptist IRS Status: 501(c)3
Highest Offering: Doctorate; No Undergraduates
Program: Professional; Religious Emphasis
Accreditation: NH, THEOL

01 President .... Dr. G. Michael HAGAN
05 Academic Vice President & Dean .... Dr. Ronald D. SISK
10 Chief Financial Officer .... Mr. Jason D. KLEIN
30 Executive Dir/Leadership Foundation .... Mr. Benjamin G. LEE
58 Director of Doctoral Studies .... Dr. Gary E. STRICKLAND
06 Registrar .... Ms. Brenda L. MEDALEN
26 Director Public Relations/Marketing .... Ms. Shanda L. STRICHERZ
84 Director of Enrollment & Fin Aid .... Mr. Nathan M. HELLING

Sisseton-Wahpeton College (E)

PO Box 689, Sisseton SD 57262-0689

County: Roberts FICE Identification: 022773
Unit ID: 219408
Telephone: (605) 698-3966 Carnegie Class: Tribal
FAX Number: (605) 698-3132 Calendar System: Semester
URL: www.swc.tc
Established: 1979 Annual Undergrad Tuition & Fees (In-District): $3,960
Enrollment: 164 Coed
Affiliation or Control: Local IRS Status: 501(c)3
Highest Offering: Associate Degree
Program: Occupational; 2-Year Principally Bachelor's Creditable
Accreditation: NH

01 President .... Dr. Rafe E. TRICKEY, JR.
05 Vice President of Academic Affairs .... Dr. Jeanette GRAVDAHL
10 Chief Financial Officer .... Mr. Dennis STUGELMEYER
37 Financial Aid Officer .... Ms. Janel MANY LIGHTNINGS
07 Director of Admissions .... Mrs. Darlene REDDAY
45 Planner/Developer .... Ms. Pam WYNIA
66 Director Nursing .... Ms. Nola RAGAN

*South Dakota State Board of Regents System Office (F)

306 E Capitol Avenue, Suite 200, Pierre SD 57501-2545

County: Hughes FICE Identification: 033438
Telephone: (605) 773-3455 Carnegie Class: N/A
FAX Number: (605) 773-5320
URL: www.sdbor.edu

01 Executive Director .... Dr. Jack R. WARNER
11 System VP Administrative Services .... Dr. Monte KRAMER
05 System Vice Pres Academic Affairs .... Dr. Samuel GINGERICH
46 System VP Research and Economic Dev .... Dr. Paul TURMAN
43 General Counsel .... Dr. James F. SHEKLETON
21 Internal Auditor .... Ms. Shelly ANDERSON
15 Director of Human Resources .... Dr. Barbara BASEL
09 Director of Communications .... Dr. Janelle TOMAN
45 Director of Policy & Planning .... Dr. Paul GOUGH
09 Director of Institutional Research .... Mr. Daniel PALMER
13 Int Director Information Systems .... Mr. David HANSEN
46 Information Research Analyst .... Ms. Tracy MERCER

*The University of South Dakota (G)

414 E Clark, Vermillion SD 57069-2390

County: Clay FICE Identification: 003474
Unit ID: 219471
Telephone: (605) 677-5011 Carnegie Class: RU/H
FAX Number: (605) 677-5073 Calendar System: Semester
URL: www.usd.edu
Established: 1862 Annual Undergrad Tuition & Fees (In-State): $7,704
Enrollment: 9,970 Coed
Affiliation or Control: State IRS Status: 501(c)3
Highest Offering: Doctorate
Program: Liberal Arts And General; Teacher Preparatory; Professional
Accreditation: NH, ADNUR, ARCPA, ART, AUD, BUS, CACREP, CLPSY, DH, DIETI, JOUR, LAW, MED, MUS, OT, PTA, SP, SPAA, SW, TED, THEA

02 President .... Mr. James W. ABBOTT
05 Provost/Vice Pres Academic Affairs .... Dr. Charles A. STABEN
17 Vice President Health Affairs .... Dr. Mary DEKKER NETTLEMAN
10 Vice Pres Finance - CFO .... Ms. Sheila GESTRING
46 Vice President for Research .... Dr. Laura J. JENSKI
26 VP of Marketing/Enrollment Svcs .... Mr. Jeffrey S. BAYLOR
11 Vice Pres Administration & ITS .... Ms. Roberta S. AMBUR
20 Assoc Vice Pres Academic Affairs .... Ms. Lynn B. ROGNSTAD
28 Associate VP of Diversity .... Dr. Jesus TREVINIO
08 Interim Dean of Libraries .... Mr. Daniel R. DAILY
32 Dean of Students .... Dr. Kimberly GRIEVE
29 Exec Dir Alumni Association .... Ms. Kersten JOHNSON
96 Director of Purchasing .... Mr. Darby GANSCHOW
15 Director Human Resources .... Ms. Diane S. ZAK
22 Affirmative Action Officer .... Ms. Roberta H. HAKL
18 Acting Dir Facilities Management .... Mr. John DAVIS
37 Director of Financial Aid .... Ms. Julie H. PIER
09 Director of Institutional Research .... Dr. Biao ZHANG
36 Dir Ctr for Academic & Career Plng .... Mr. Steve WARD
06 Acting Registrar .... Dr. Kurt HACKEMER
41 Athletic Director .... Mr. David SAYLER
38 Director Student Counseling .... Vacant
19 Director Public Safety .... Mr. Peter E. JENSEN
84 Dean of Enrollment .... Mr. Scott POHLSON
49 Dean College Arts & Sciences .... Dr. Matthew C. MOEN
50 Dean School of Business .... Mr. Michael J. KELLER
51 Dean Continuing Education .... Dr. Laurie J. BECVAR
53 Dean School of Education .... Dr. Rick MELMER
57 Dean College Fine Arts .... Dr. Larry SCHOU
58 Dean of Graduate Education .... Dr. Laurie J. BECVAR
63 Dean Sanford School of Medicine .... Dr. Mary DEKKER NETTLEMAN
61 Interim Dean School of Law .... Mr. Thomas GEU

*Black Hills State University (H)

1200 University Street, Spearfish SD 57799-9500

County: Lawrence FICE Identification: 003459
Unit ID: 219046
Telephone: (605) 642-6011 Carnegie Class: Master's S
FAX Number: (605) 642-6214 Calendar System: Semester
URL: www.bhsu.edu
Established: 1883 Annual Undergrad Tuition & Fees (In-State): $7,808
Enrollment: 4,415 Coed
Affiliation or Control: State IRS Status: 501(c)3
Highest Offering: Master's
Program: 2-Year Principally Bachelor's Creditable; Liberal Arts And General; Teacher Preparatory
Accreditation: NH, MUS, TED

02 President .... Dr. Kay SCHALLENKAMP
05 Provost/Vice Pres Academic Affairs .... Dr. Rodney CUSTER
10 Vice President Finance/Admin .... Ms. Kathy J. JOHNSON
30 Vice Pres University Advancement .... Mr. Steve L. MEEKER
32 Vice President for Student Life .... Dr. Lois FLAGSTAD
20 Assoc Vice Pres Academic Affairs .... Dr. Curtis CARD
26 Director Marketing & Communications .... Ms. Corinne HANSEN
27 Chief Information Officer .... Dr. Warren WILSON
37 Director Student Financial Aid .... Ms. Deb HENRIKSEN
38 Director Counseling Center .... Dr. James FLEMING
39 Director Residence Life .... Dr. Michael L. ISAACSON
35 Director Student Services .... Dr. Jane KLUG
15 Director of Human Resources .... Ms. Nancy GRASSEL
06 Registrar .... Ms. April M. MEEKER
07 Director of Admissions .... Ms. Beth OAKS
21 Director of Business Services .... Mr. Rob HOUDEK
18 Director Facilities/Physical Plant .... Mr. Art JONES
29 Director Alumni Relations .... Mr. Tom WHEATON
09 Director of Institutional Research .... Dr. Erin HOLMES
08 Director Library Operations .... Mr. Scott AHOLA
36 Director of Career Center .... Vacant
104 Director International Studies .... Dr. James FLEMING
30 Director of Development .... Mr. Dwight HANSEN
19 Director Security/Safety .... Mr. Myron SULLIVAN
40 Director University Bookstore .... Mr. Michael JASTORFF
41 Director of Athletics .... Mr. Jhett ALBERS
13 Director Network & Computer Svcs .... Mr. Fred NELSON
49 Dean College of Liberal Arts .... Dr. David WOLFF
50 Dean Col of Business & Natural Sci .... Dr. Priscilla ROMKEMA
53 Dean Col of Educ & Behavioral Sci .... Dr. Patricia SIMPSON
106 Dean Educational Outreach .... Vacant
92 Director of Honors Program .... Dr. Amy FUQUA

*Dakota State University (I)

820 N Washington Avenue, Madison SD 57042-1799

County: Lake FICE Identification: 003463
Unit ID: 219082
Telephone: (605) 256-5111 Carnegie Class: Master's S
FAX Number: (605) 256-5316 Calendar System: Semester
URL: www.dsu.edu
Established: 1881 Annual Undergrad Tuition & Fees (In-State): $7,212
Enrollment: 3,102 Coed
Affiliation or Control: State IRS Status: 501(c)3
Highest Offering: Doctorate
Program: 2-Year Principally Bachelor's Creditable; Liberal Arts And General; Teacher Preparatory; Technical Emphasis
Accreditation: NH, ACBSP, TED

02 Interim President .... Dr. David BOROFSKY
05 Vice President for Academic Affairs .... Dr. Cecelia M. WITTMAYER
10 Vice Pres for Business & Admin Svcs .... Mr. Stacy L. KRUSEMARK
32 Vice Pres/Dean Student Affairs .... Mr. Jesse KANE
30 Vice Pres for Univ Advancement .... Ms. Judith PAYNE
50 Dean College Business/Info Systems .... Dr. Tom L. HALVERSON
53 Dean College of Education .... Dr. Judith L. DITTMAN
49 Dean College of Arts and Sciences .... Dr. Kari L. FORBES-BOYTE
58 Dean of Graduate Studies/Research .... Dr. Omar F. EL-GAYAR
41 Director of Athletics .... Mr. Jeff DITTMAN
36 Asst VP Stdnt Affs/Dir Career Svcs .... Dr. Marie A. LOHSANDT
08 Director of Library .... Ms. Ethelle S. BEAN
13 Director of Computing Services .... Mr. W. David ZOLNOWSKY
29 Director of Alumni .... Ms. Jona M. SCHMIDT
18 Director of Physical Plant .... Mr. Patrick C. KEATING
06 Registrar .... Ms. Sandra E. ANDERSON
37 Director Financial Aid .... Ms. Denise R. GRAYSON
38 Asst Dean for Student Development .... Mr. O. Keith BUNDY

39 Dir of Student Union/Residence Life .... Mr. Steven J. BARTEL
35 Director of Student Activities .... Ms. Amanda L. PARPART
04 Admin Assistant to the President .... Ms. Linda J. BROZIK
16 Director Human Resources .... Ms. Maria D. HARDER
88 Director Extended Programs .... Dr. Margaret A. O'BRIEN
84 Assoc VP of Enr Mgmt & Marketing .... Ms. Amy S. CRISSINGER
92 Dir Ctr Excell Computer Info Sys .... Dr. Wayne E. PAULI
09 Director of Assessment .... Ms. Carrie A. AHERN
21 Comptroller .... Ms. Amy L. DOCKENDORF
25 Dir of Ctr for Adv of HIT .... Mr. Dan FRIEDRICH
85 International Programs Coordinator .... Ms. Jacy FRY
40 Director of Bookstore .... Mr. Dale P. DAVIS
88 Director Center of Info Assurance .... Dr. Kevin F. STREFF
25 Director of Budget & Grants Admin .... Ms. Sara HARE
25 Director of Sponsored Programs .... Dr. Mickie L. KREIDLER
28 Diversity Coordinator .... Ms. Jennifer ARANDA

*Northern State University (A)

1200 S Jay Street, Aberdeen SD 57401-7198
County: Brown FICE Identification: 003466
Unit ID: 219259
Telephone: (605) 626-3011 Carnegie Class: Bac/Diverse
FAX Number: (605) 626-3022 Calendar System: Semester
URL: www.northern.edu
Established: 1901 Annual Undergrad Tuition & Fees (In-State): $7,269
Enrollment: 3,580 Coed
Affiliation or Control: State IRS Status: 501(c)3
Highest Offering: Master's
Program: Liberal Arts And General; Teacher Preparatory; Business Emphasis
Accreditation: NH, MUS, TED

02 President .... Dr. James M. SMITH
05 Vice Pres Academic Affs/Provost .... Dr. Thomas HAWLEY
10 Vice Pres Finance/Administration .... Ms. Veronica PAULSON
32 Vice President for Student Affairs .... Vacant
29 Vice Pres Alumni Relations .... Mr. Mike BIRGEN
102 President/CEO of Foundation .... Mr. Todd JORDRE
06 Registrar .... Ms. Peggy HALLSTROM
07 Director of Admissions .... Mr. Allan VOGEL
08 Director of Library .... Mr. Robert RUSSELL
36 Director Counsel/Service Learning .... Ms. Deb THORSTENSON
09 Institutional Research Officer .... Mr. Ross NORMAN
25 Director Grants Sponsored Research .... Ms. Karen MARCHANT
13 Director of Computer Services .... Ms. Joann POMPLUN
37 Dir Student Financial Assistance .... Ms. Sharon KIENOW
39 Director Student Devel/Residence .... Mr. Todd TUCKER
21 Controller .... Ms. Kay FREDRICK
15 Director of Human Resources .... Ms. Susan BOSTIAN
26 Director of University Relations .... Ms. Brenda DREYER
43 General Counsel .... Mr. John MEYER
18 Director of Facilities Management .... Mr. Monte MEHLHOFF
49 Dean College of Arts & Science .... Dr. Celestino MENDEZ
50 Dean School of Business .... Dr. Willard BROUCEK
53 Dean School of Education .... Dr. Connie GEIER
57 Dean School of Fine Arts .... Dr. Alan LAFAVE
56 Director of Extended Studies .... Mr. Ronald BROWNIE
41 Director of Athletics .... Mr. Joshua MOON
40 Director of Bookstore .... Ms. Beth RASMUSSON
38 Director Student Counseling .... Ms. Deb THORSTENSON
96 Director of Purchasing .... Mr. Earl WEISENBURGER
92 Director Honors Program .... Dr. Erin FOUBERG
28 Multicultural Advisor .... Mr. Peni MOUNGA
35 Director Student Activities .... Mr. Bart CARITHERS

*South Dakota School of Mines and Technology (B)

501 E Saint Joseph, Rapid City SD 57701-3995
County: Pennington FICE Identification: 003470
Unit ID: 219347
Telephone: (605) 394-2511 Carnegie Class: Spec/Engg
FAX Number: (605) 394-6131 Calendar System: Semester
URL: www.sdsmt.edu
Established: 1885 Annual Undergrad Tuition & Fees (In-State): $9,370
Enrollment: 2,311 Coed
Affiliation or Control: State IRS Status: 501(c)3
Highest Offering: Doctorate
Program: Professional; Technical Emphasis
Accreditation: NH, CS, ENG

02 President .... Dr. Robert A. WHARTON
05 Provost/Vice Pres Academic Affs .... Dr. Duane HRNCIR
10 Vice Pres Business/Administration .. Mr. Timothy G. HENDERSON
46 Vice President of Research .... Dr. Ronald J. WHITE
32 VP Student Affs/Dean of Students .... Dr. Patricia G. MAHON
30 VP University Relations .... Ms. Christy A. HORN
20 Associate Provost Academic Affairs .... Dr. Kathryn E. ALLEY
84 Assoc Provost for Enrollment Mgmt .... Dr. Michael C. GUNN
96 Purchasing Manager .... Ms. Barbara MUSTARD
07 Director of Admissions .... Ms. Molly E. FRANKL
29 Director of Alumni Association .... Mr. Timothy J. VOTTERO
90 Director Information Tech Svcs .... Mr. Bryan J. SCHUMACHER
08 Director Devereaux Library .... Ms. Patricia M. ANDERSEN
36 Director Career Services .... Dr. Darrell R. SAWYER
37 Director of Financial Aid .... Mr. David W. MARTIN
88 Dir Inst Atmospheric Sciences .... Dr. Andrew G. DETWILER
41 Director of Athletics .... Dr. Dick KAISER
102 President SDSM&T Foundation .... Mr. Michael M. SELZER
15 Director Human Resources .... Ms. Kelli R. SHUMAN
18 Director of Facilities Services .... Mr. Thomas BLUME
11 Director of Administrative Services .... Ms. Terry H. GRANT
39 Dir Residence Life/Student Conduct .... Dr. Dan SEPION
85 Director Ivanhoe International Ctr .... Ms. Susan R. AADLAND
58 Dean of Graduate Education .... Dr. Douglas WELLS
38 Director Student Counseling Svcs .... Ms. Jolie A. MCCOY
84 Registrar and Dir Academic Services .... Ms. Barbara DOLAN
09 Director of Retention & Testing .... Dr. Pat BEU
06 Registration Officer .... Mrs. Kathryn CRAWFORD
40 Manager College Bookstore .... Mr. Marlin L. KINZER
35 Student Activities Coordinator .... Mr. Michael KEEGAN

*South Dakota State University (C)

Brookings SD 57007-2298
County: Brookings FICE Identification: 003471
Unit ID: 219356
Telephone: (605) 688-4151 Carnegie Class: RU/H
FAX Number: (605) 688-5822 Calendar System: Semester
URL: www.sdstate.edu
Established: 1881 Annual Undergrad Tuition & Fees (In-State): $7,404
Enrollment: 12,725 Coed
Affiliation or Control: State IRS Status: 501(c)3
Highest Offering: Doctorate
Program: Liberal Arts And General; Teacher Preparatory; Professional
Accreditation: NH, AAFCS, CACREP, CIDA, CONST, @CORE, CS, DIETD, ENG, ENGT, EXSC, JOUR, MT, MUS, NURSE, PHAR, TED

02 President .... Dr. David L. CHICOINE
05 Provost/Vice Pres Academic Affairs .... Dr. Laurie NICHOLS
32 Vice President Student Affairs .... Dr. Marysz RAMES
45 Vice President of Research .... Dr. Kevin KEPHART
13 VP for Information Technology .... Dr. Michael ADELAINE
10 Vice Pres Finance & Budget .... Mr. Wesley G. TSCHETTER
20 Assoc Vice Pres for Academic Affs .... Dr. Mary Kay HELLING
18 Asst Vice Pres Facilities Services .... Mr. Dean KATTELMANN
88 Asst VP AA Intl Affairs/Outreach .... Dr. Kathleen FAIRFAX
04 Executive Asst to the President .... Mr. Robert OTTERSON
08 Dean of the Library .... Dr. Kristi TORNQUIST
97 Dean of General Studies .... Dr. Keith CORBETT
51 Dean Continuing & Extended Educ .... Vacant
07 Director of Admissions .... Ms. Tracy WELSH
06 Registrar .... Dr. Aaron AURE
38 Director Wellness .... Mr. Jeffrey HUSKEY
37 Financial Aid Officer .... Mr. Jay A. LARSEN
15 Interim Director Human Resources .... Mr. Wesley TSCHETTER
102 President & CEO of Foundation .... Mr. Steve ERPENBACH
29 President & CEO Alumni Affairs .... Mr. Matt FUKS
14 Director Admin & Information Svcs .... Mr. William (Joe) MOORE
19 Chief Security/Safety .... Mr. Tim HEATON
39 Director of Residential Life .... Ms. Connie CRANDALL
40 Director of Bookstore .... Mr. Derek PETERSON
41 Director of Athletics .... Mr. Justin SELL
28 Dir of Diversity/Equal Opportunity .... Dr. Jennifer (Jaime) NOLAN
56 Interim Director of Extension .... Dr. Barry DUNN
26 Dir Marketing/Image/Communications .... Mr. Michael LOCKREM
24 Mgr Instructional Design Services .... Dr. Shouhong ZHANG
85 International Students Advisor .... Ms. Stephanie DESOUSA
47 Dean Agriculture/Biological Sci .... Dr. Barry DUNN
49 Dean of Arts & Sciences .... Dr. Dennis PAPINI
54 Dean of Engineering .... Dr. Lewis BROWN
53 Dean Education & Human Science .... Dr. Jill THORNGREN
66 Dean of Nursing .... Dr. Roberta K. OLSON
67 Dean of Pharmacy .... Dr. Dennis HEDGE
58 Dean of Graduate School .... Dr. Kinchel DOERNER
92 Dean Honors College .... Dr. Timothy NICHOLS

Southeast Technical Institute (D)

2320 N Career Avenue, Sioux Falls SD 57107-1302
County: Minnehaha FICE Identification: 007764
Unit ID: 219426
Telephone: (605) 367-7624 Carnegie Class: Assoc/Pub-R-M
FAX Number: (605) 367-8305 Calendar System: Semester
URL: www.southeasttech.edu
Established: 1968 Annual Undergrad Tuition & Fees (In-District): $3,864
Enrollment: 2,507 Coed
Affiliation or Control: Local IRS Status: 501(c)3
Highest Offering: Associate Degree
Program: Occupational
Accreditation: NH, CVT, DMS, NDT, NMT, SURGT

01 President .... Mr. Jeffrey R. HOLCOMB
05 Vice President of Academics .... Mr. Jim JACOBSEN
10 Vice President Finance & Operations .... Mr. Rich KLUIN
32 Vice Pres Student Affs/Inst Rsrch .... Mr. Tracy NOLDNER
35 Director of Students .... Mr. Jim ROKUSEK
50 Training Solutions Institute .... Mr. Lon HIRD
06 Registrar .... Ms. Kristie VORTHERMS
15 Human Resources Specialist .... Ms. Kathy STRUCK
20 Director of Academic Support .... Dr. Craig PETERS
26 Marketing Coordinator .... Ms. Margaret PENNOCK
102 Foundation Director .... Ms. Nancee STURDEVANT
37 Financial Aid Officer .... Ms. Lynette GRABOWSKA
21 Business Manager .... Mr. James WESTCOTT
38 Personal Counselor .... Ms. Nicole MCMILLIN

University of Sioux Falls (E)

1101 W 22nd Street, Sioux Falls SD 57105-1699
County: Minnehaha FICE Identification: 003469
Unit ID: 219383
Telephone: (605) 331-5000 Carnegie Class: Bac/Diverse
FAX Number: (605) 331-6615 Calendar System: 4/1/4
URL: www.usiouxfalls.edu
Established: 1883 Annual Undergrad Tuition & Fees: $23,740
Enrollment: 1,213 Coed
Affiliation or Control: American Baptist IRS Status: 501(c)3
Highest Offering: Master's
Program: Liberal Arts And General; Teacher Preparatory; Professional
Accreditation: NH, IACBE, NURSE, SW, TED

01 President .... Dr. Mark BENEDETTO
04 Exec Assistant to the President .... Ms. Karen BANGASSER
10 VP for Business and Finance .... Ms. Marsha DENNISTON
05 Provost/Vice Pres Academic Affairs .... Dr. Brett BRADFIELD
30 VP Institutional Advancement .... Mr. Jon HIATT
15 VP of Human Resources .... Ms. Julie GEDNALSKE
32 VP of Student Development .... Mr. Gene BROOKS
13 AVP Information Tech .... Mr. William BARTELL
42 Dean of the Chapel .... Rev. Dennis L. THUM
06 Registrar .... Ms. Anna HECKENLAIBLE
21 Controller .... Ms. Susan THIE
37 Director of Financial Aid .... Ms. Laura A. OLSON
07 Director of Admissions .... Ms. Aimee VANDER FEEN
08 Director of Library Services .... Ms. Rachel CROWLEY
84 Director of Academic Success Center .... Ms. Billie STREUFERT
18 Director Buildings/Grounds .... Mr. Ralph SMITH
41 Athletic Director .... Mr. William SANCHEZ
88 Dir of Degree Completion Program .... Ms. LuAnn GROSSMAN
40 Bookstore Manager .... Ms. Lesley GORBY
58 Chair Business/Dir of MBA/Asst Prof ...... Ms. Rebecca MURDOCK
53 Chair Fredrikson School Education .... Ms. Julie MCAREAVEY
57 Chair Fine Arts/Associate Professor .... Ms. Nancy OLIVE
81 Chair Natural Sciences/Assoc Prof .... Dr. William SOEFFING
79 Chair Humanities/Asst Professor .... Ms. Nicholle SCHUELKE
66 Founding Director School of Nursing .... Dr. Barbara VELLENGA
83 Chair Social Sciences .... Dr. Sharon COOL

Western Dakota Technical Institute (F)

800 Mickelson Drive, Rapid City SD 57703-4018
County: Pennington FICE Identification: 010170
Unit ID: 219480
Telephone: (605) 394-4034 Carnegie Class: Assoc/Pub-R-S
FAX Number: (605) 394-1789 Calendar System: Semester
URL: www.wdt.edu
Established: 1968 Annual Undergrad Tuition & Fees (In-District): $6,400
Enrollment: 1,045 Coed
Affiliation or Control: Local IRS Status: 501(c)3
Highest Offering: Associate Degree
Program: Occupational; 2-Year Principally Bachelor's Creditable
Accreditation: NH, SURGT

01 President .... Mr. Mark WILSON
03 Vice President .... Dr. Cathy ANDERSON
32 Dean Student Services .... Ms. Janell OBERLANDER
26 Director of Marketing/Admissions .... Mr. Stephen BUCHHOLZ
37 Financial Aid Coordinator .... Ms. Starla RUSSELL
36 Student Placement Coordinator .... Mr. Curt LAUINGER

TENNESSEE

All Saints Bible College (G)

930 Mason Street, Memphis TN 38126
County: Shelby Identification: 667014
Telephone: (901) 322-0120 Carnegie Class: Not Classified
FAX Number: (901) 947-3504 Calendar System: Semester
URL: www.allsaintsonline.info
Established: 2002 Annual Undergrad Tuition & Fees: N/A
Enrollment: 70 Coed
Affiliation or Control: Church of God in Christ IRS Status: 501(c)3
Highest Offering: Baccalaureate
Program: Religious Emphasis
Accreditation: @BI

01 Chancellor .... Bishop Charles E. BLAKE
11 Administrator .... Dr. Granville SCRUGGS

American Baptist College (H)

1800 Baptist World Center Drive, Nashville TN 37207
County: Davidson FICE Identification: 010460
Unit ID: 219505
Telephone: (615) 256-1463 Carnegie Class: Spec/Faith
FAX Number: (615) 226-7855 Calendar System: Semester
URL: www.abcnash.edu
Established: 1924 Annual Undergrad Tuition & Fees: $8,594
Enrollment: 103 Coed
Affiliation or Control: Baptist IRS Status: 501(c)3
Highest Offering: Baccalaureate
Program: Liberal Arts And General
Accreditation: BI

01 President .... Dr. Forrest E. HARRIS, SR.
05 Vice President Academic Affairs .... Dr. Renita WEEMS
84 Director of Enrollment Management .. Ms. Marcella F. LOCKHART
10 Chief Financial Officer .... Ms. Clara A. WILLIAMS
11 Chief of Campus Operations .... Ms. Joyce ACKLEN
08 Interim Director Library Services .... Ms. Cherisna JEAN-MARIE
04 Asst to Pres for Faculty Support .... Mr. Marcus TUBBS
32 Dir Student Svcs/Extention Pgms .... Mr. James SANFORD
09 Director of Institutional Research .... Dr. Joanne FLOWERS
07 Admissions/Registrar Admin .... Ms. Pam TABOR

Aquinas College (A)

4210 Harding Road, Nashville TN 37205-2005
County: Davidson FICE Identification: 003477
Unit ID: 219578
Telephone: (615) 297-7545 Carnegie Class: Bac/Assoc
FAX Number: (615) 279-3892 Calendar System: Semester
URL: www.aquinascollege.edu
Established: 1961 Annual Undergrad Tuition & Fees: $19,800
Enrollment: 646 Coed
Affiliation or Control: Roman Catholic IRS Status: 501(c)3
Highest Offering: Master's
Program: 2-Year Principally Bachelor's Creditable; Liberal Arts And General; Teacher Preparatory; Nursing Emphasis
Accreditation: SC, ADNUR, NUR

01 President ... Sr. Mary Sarah GALBRAITH, OP
11 Vice Pres Administrative Affairs . Sr. Mary Cecilia GOODRUM, OP
05 Vice President for Academic Affairs ... Sr. Elizabeth Anne ALLEN, OP
30 Vice Pres Institutional Advancement ... Mr. Timothy STRANSKY
27 Director of Communications ... Mr. Ron KERMAN
07 Director of Admissions ... Mrs. Connie HANSOM
06 Registrar ... Ms. Etta MASON
08 Librarian ... Mr. Mark HALL
30 Director of Development ... Ms. Jeanne SCHULLER
40 Bookstore Manager ... Mr. Alan BRADLEY
66 Dean School of Nursing ... Bro. Ignatius PERKINS, OP
66 Director of ASN Nursing Program ... Mrs. Margaret DANIEL
53 Dean School of Education ... Sr. Mary Anne ZUBERBUELER, OP
37 Director of Financial Aid ... Ms. Martha MARTINEZ
10 Business Manager ... Mr. Roger MUEHE
32 Director of Student Affairs ... Mrs. Suzette TELLI
09 Director of Institutional Research ... Sr. Mary BENDYNA, OP
29 Director of Alumni Relations ... Ms. Rachel LEACH
18 Chief of Facilities/Physical Plant ... Mr. John WALL
15 Director Personnel Services ... Mrs. Loretta CLARK
88 Director of Student Learning Svcs ... Ms. Nancy ARNOLD
88 Director of Catechetics ... Sr. Mary Michael FOX, OP
49 Dean School of Arts and Sciences ... Dr. William SMART
50 Dean School of Business ... Dr. Daniel DONNELLY

Argosy University, Nashville (B)

100 Centerview Drive, Suite 225,
Nashville TN 37214-3438
County: Davidson Identification: 666668
Unit ID: 450535
Telephone: (615) 525-2800 Carnegie Class: Spec/Health
FAX Number: (615) 525-2900 Calendar System: Semester
URL: www.argosy.edu
Established: 2001 Annual Undergrad Tuition & Fees: $13,224
Enrollment: 562 Coed
Affiliation or Control: Proprietary IRS Status: Proprietary
Highest Offering: Doctorate
Program: Professional
Accreditation: &WC

01 Campus President ... Dr. Roger H. WIDNER
07 Senior Director of Admissions ... Ms. Erica BLIGEN
32 Director of Student Services ... Ms. Stacy A. WADDELL
06 Registrar ... Ms. Christine DYBATA
37 Director of Student Finance ... Mr. Josh YARBOROUGH
15 Human Resources ... Mr. Thomas A. TUCKER
11 Dir of Admin and Financial Svcs ... Mr. Brian GARDNER

† Regional accreditation is carried under the parent institution in Orange, CA.

Baptist Memorial College of Health Sciences (C)

1003 Monroe Avenue, Memphis TN 38104-3199
County: Shelby FICE Identification: 034403
Unit ID: 219639
Telephone: (901) 575-2247 Carnegie Class: Spec/Health
FAX Number: (901) 572-2461 Calendar System: Trimester
URL: www.bchs.edu
Established: 1994 Annual Undergrad Tuition & Fees: $10,680
Enrollment: 975 Coed
Affiliation or Control: Independent Non-Profit IRS Status: 501(c)3
Highest Offering: Baccalaureate
Program: Occupational; Professional
Accreditation: SC, DMS, NMT, NURSE, RAD, RTT

01 President ... Dr. Betty S. MCGARVEY
10 Vice President Business/Admin Svcs ... Ms. Leanne SMITH
05 Chief Academic Officer/Provost ... Dr. William J. SOBOTOR
97 Dean General Studies ... Dr. Barry SCHULTZ
66 Dean Nursing ... Dr. Anne M. PLUMB
76 Dean Allied Health ... Dr. Linda REED
32 Dean Student Services ... Ms. Nancy REED
16 Exec Director Admin Support Svcs ... Ms. Adonna CALDWELL
06 Registrar ... Ms. Jana D. TURNER
07 Director of Admissions ... Ms. Lissa MORGAN
09 Dir of Institutional Effectiveness ... Ms. Pam MOSS
29 Director Alumni Relations ... Mrs. Bamby COUNCE
35 Manager Student Affairs ... Mr. Jeremy WILKES
37 Supervisor Student Financial Aid ... Ms. Janet BONNEY-BAKER

Belmont University (D)

1900 Belmont Boulevard, Nashville TN 37212-3757
County: Davidson FICE Identification: 003479
Unit ID: 219709
Telephone: (615) 460-6000 Carnegie Class: Master's L
FAX Number: (615) 460-6446 Calendar System: Semester
URL: www.belmont.edu
Established: 1890 Annual Undergrad Tuition & Fees: $24,960
Enrollment: 6,395 Coed
Affiliation or Control: Non-denominational IRS Status: 501(c)3
Highest Offering: Doctorate
Program: Liberal Arts And General; Teacher Preparatory; Professional
Accreditation: SC, ART, BUS, BUSA, ENGT, MACTE, MUS, NURSE, OT, PHAR, PTA, SW, TED

01 President ... Dr. Robert C. FISHER
05 Provost ... Dr. Thomas D. BURNS
11 Vice Pres for Admin & Univ Counsel ... Dr. Jason ROGERS
30 Vice Pres University Advancement ... Dr. Bethel THOMAS
10 Vice President Finance & Operations ... Mr. Steven T. LASLEY
100 Vice President/Chief of Staff ... Dr. Susan H. WEST
42 Vice Pres Spiritual Development ... Dr. Todd LAKE
32 Assoc Provost/Dean of Students ... Mr. Andrew J. JOHNSTON
84 Assoc Provost/Dean Enrollment Svcs ... Dr. David MEE
09 Asst Provost/Assess/Instl Research ... Dr. Tracy ROKAS
50 Dean College of Business ... Dr. Patrick RAINES
88 Dean College Visual/Performing Arts ... Dr. Cynthia A. CURTIS
49 Dean College Arts & Sciences ... Dr. Bryce SULLIVAN
76 Dean Col Health Sciences/Nursing ... Dr. Cathy TAYLOR
73 Dean School of Religion ... Dr. Darrell GWALTNEY
61 Dean College of Law ... Mr. Jeffrey S. KINSLER
81 Assoc Dean School of Science ... Dr. Robert GRAMMER
85 Director of International Education ... Ms. Katherine SKINNER
15 Director of Human Resources ... Mrs. Sally MCKAY
37 Director of Financial Aid ... Mrs. Patricia SMEDLEY
29 Director of Alumni Relations ... Ms. Debbie COPPINGER
18 Director of Facilities Management ... Mr. Fred THOMPSON
19 Director of Safety & Security ... Mr. Terry A. WHITE
90 Director Technology Services ... Mr. Randall REYNOLDS
06 University Registrar ... Mr. Steven REED
08 Director of Library Services ... Dr. Ernest W. HEARD, JR.
41 Athletic Director ... Mr. Michael D. STRICKLAND
40 Manager Bookstore ... Mrs. Catherine MURPHY
36 Dir Career Svcs/Cooperative Educ ... Mrs. Patricia JACOBS
27 Director of Communications ... Mr. Greg S. PILLON
20 Assistant Provost ... Vacant

Bethel University (E)

325 Cherry Avenue, McKenzie TN 38201-1705
County: Carroll FICE Identification: 003480
Unit ID: 219718
Telephone: (731) 352-4000 Carnegie Class: Master's M
FAX Number: (731) 352-4069 Calendar System: Semester
URL: www.bethelu.edu
Established: 1842 Annual Undergrad Tuition & Fees: $13,870
Enrollment: 5,225 Coed
Affiliation or Control: Cumberland Presbyterian IRS Status: 501(c)3
Highest Offering: Master's
Program: Liberal Arts And General; Teacher Preparatory; Professional; Business Emphasis
Accreditation: SC, #ARCPA, NURSE

01 President ... Dr. Robert D. PROSSER
05 Chief Academic Officer ... Dr. Phyllis CAMPBELL
49 VP College of Liberal Arts ... Dr. Ronald DEMING
107 VP College of Prof Studies ... Ms. Kelly SANDERS-KELLEY
06 University Registrar ... Ms. Becky HAMES
10 Asst to Pres of Financial Affairs ... Mr. Keith PRIESTLEY
07 Dean of Enrollment CLA ... Mrs. Tina HODGES
30 Director of Development ... Mr. Mike PARKER
32 Dean of Student Development ... Mr. James STEWART
37 Director of Financial Aid ... Ms. Janie BURNS
26 Director of Public Relations ... Ms. Jennifer GLASS
38 Director Student Counseling ... Mrs. Sandy LOUDEN
18 Director of Physical Facilities ... Mr. Steve PROSSER
42 Chaplain ... Rev. Anne HAMES
08 Library Director ... Ms. Jill WHITFILL
15 Human Resource Director ... Ms. Carolyn FLOOD
41 Athletic Director ... Vacant
09 Director of Institutional Research ... Dr. Mary Jane HAWTHORNE
29 Director Alumni Relations ... Mrs. Myra CARLOCK
88 Dir College of Criminal Justice ... Mr. Jimmy Ray FARRIS
53 Dir College of Education ... Dr. J. Randolph CROMWELL
58 Dean College of Graduate Studies ... Dr. Dorothy BLACK
76 Director of Col of Health Sciences ... Mr. Steve PROSSER
88 Director Sch of Global Studies ... Mr. John HALL
88 Dir Sch of Conflict Resolution ... Mr. Clay PHILLIPS

Bryan College (F)

PO Box 7000, Dayton TN 37321-7000
County: Rhea FICE Identification: 003536
Unit ID: 219790
Telephone: (423) 775-2041 Carnegie Class: Bac/Diverse
FAX Number: (423) 775-7330 Calendar System: Semester
URL: www.bryan.edu
Established: 1930 Annual Undergrad Tuition & Fees: $20,150
Enrollment: 1,270 Coed
Affiliation or Control: Independent Non-Profit IRS Status: 501(c)3
Highest Offering: Master's
Program: Liberal Arts And General; Teacher Preparatory
Accreditation: SC, IACBE

01 President ... Dr. Stephen D. LIVESAY
04 Exec Assistant to the President ... Ms. Margaret A. LEGG
05 Academic Vice President ... Dr. Bradford W. SAMPLE
10 Vice President for Finance ... Mr. Vance J. BERGER
30 Vice Pres for College Advancement ... Mr. Blake W. HUDSON
11 Vice President of Operations ... Mr. Timothy J. HOSTETLER
84 Vice Pres for Enrollment Management .. Dr. Michael C. SAPIENZA
42 Vice Pres for Spiritual Formation ... Dr. Matt A. BENSON
58 Dean Sch of Adult & Graduate Stds ... Dr. Michael K. CHASE
32 Dean of Students ... Mr. Bruce MORGAN
37 Director of Financial Aid ... Mr. David L. HAGGARD
13 Director of Information Systems ... Mr. Stephen M. PAULSON
06 Registrar ... Ms. Janet M. PIATT
08 Director of Library Sciences ... Dr. Gary N. FITSIMMONS
26 Director of Public Information ... Mr. Thomas A. DAVIS
15 Director Personnel Services ... Mrs. Barbara J. FAVORITE
41 Athletic Director ... Dr. Sanford ZENSEN
18 Director of Physical Plant ... Mr. Doug W. SCHOTT
29 Director of Alumni Affairs ... Mr. David C. TROMANHAUSER
07 Director of Admissions ... Mr. Aaron K. PORTER
88 Accreditation Liaison ... Dr. Kenneth M. FROEMKE

Carson-Newman College (G)

1646 Russell Avenue, PO Box 557,
Jefferson City TN 37760-2204
County: Jefferson FICE Identification: 003481
Unit ID: 219806
Telephone: (865) 471-2000 Carnegie Class: Bac/Diverse
FAX Number: (865) 471-3502 Calendar System: Semester
URL: www.cn.edu
Established: 1851 Annual Undergrad Tuition & Fees: $23,276
Enrollment: 2,100 Coed
Affiliation or Control: Southern Baptist IRS Status: 501(c)3
Highest Offering: Master's
Program: Liberal Arts And General; Teacher Preparatory; Professional
Accreditation: SC, AAFCS, ART, DIETD, MUS, NURSE, TED

01 President ... Dr. J. Randall O'BRIEN
05 Provost ... Dr. Kina S. MALLARD
30 Vice President for Advancement ... Dr. Danny NICHOLSON
32 Vice President Student Affairs ... Dr. Ross BRUMMETT
35 Dean of Student Affairs ... Ms. Shelley BALL
08 Dean of Library Services ... Mr. Bruce KOCOUR
27 Senior Director for Communications ... Mr. Parker LEAKE
36 Director of Life Directions Center ... Mrs. Amy HUMPHREY
37 Director Financial Aid ... Mrs. Danette SEALE
38 Director Counseling Services ... Mrs. Jennifer CATLETT
07 Director of Admissions ... Mrs. Melanie REDDING
44 Dir Charitable Gift Plan/Annual Fnd ... Mr. Chris CATES
13 Chief Information Officer/IT ... Mrs. Valerie STEPHENS
09 Director of Institutional Research ... Ms. Gail GREENE
18 Chief Facilities/Physical Plant ... Mr. Ondes WEBSTER
84 Director of Enrollment Services ... Mrs. Sheryl GRAY
92 Director of Honors Program ... Dr. Brian AUSTIN
20 Associate Provost ... Dr. Naomi LARSEN
15 Director Personnel Services ... Mr. Jimmy WYATT
41 Athletic Director ... Mr. Allen MORGAN
10 Chief Financial/Business Officer ... Mrs. Martha CHAMBERS
51 Dir Adult/Professional Studies ... Dr. Mel HAWKINS
85 Dean of Global Education ... Dr. Danny HINSON

Chattanooga College (H)

3805 Brainerd Road, Chattanooga TN 37411-3798
County: Hamilton FICE Identification: 022042
Unit ID: 220118
Telephone: (423) 624-0077 Carnegie Class: Assoc/PrivFP
FAX Number: (423) 624-1575 Calendar System: Quarter
URL: www.chattanoogacollege.edu
Established: 1968 Annual Undergrad Tuition & Fees: $9,825
Enrollment: 326 Coed
Affiliation or Control: Proprietary IRS Status: Proprietary
Highest Offering: Associate Degree
Program: Occupational
Accreditation: ACCSC

01 President ... Mr. William G. FAOUR
03 Vice President ... Mr. Toney C. MCFADDEN
37 Director Financial Aid ... Mrs. Evelyn DAVIS

Christian Brothers University (I)

650 East Parkway S, Memphis TN 38104-5581
County: Shelby FICE Identification: 003482
Unit ID: 219833
Telephone: (901) 321-3000 Carnegie Class: Master's M
FAX Number: (901) 321-3494 Calendar System: Semester
URL: www.cbu.edu
Established: 1871 Annual Undergrad Tuition & Fees: $26,700
Enrollment: 1,641 Coed
Affiliation or Control: Roman Catholic IRS Status: 501(c)3
Highest Offering: Master's
Program: Liberal Arts And General; Teacher Preparatory; Professional
Accreditation: SC, #ARCPA, ENG, TED

01 President ... Dr. John SMARRELLI, JR.
05 Vice President Academic Affairs ... Dr. Frank BUSCHER
11 Vice Pres Administration & Finance ... Mr. Dan WORTHAM
30 Vice Pres Institutional Advancement ... Mr. Andrew PRISLOVSKY

84 VP for Enrollment Management .... Mr. Jim SCHLIMMER
32 Vice Pres Mission and Identity .... Dr. Evelyn MCDONALD
35 Dean of Students .... Ms. Karen CONWAY
13 Dean Information Technology .... Mr. David PALMER
26 Vice Pres Communications/Marketing .... Ms. Elisa MARUS
06 Registrar .... Mrs. Melody L. NABORS
36 Director Career Center .... Vacant
08 Director of Plough Library .... Ms. Kay CUNNINGHAM
07 Director of Admissions .... Dr. Anne H. KENWORTHY
38 Director of Counseling .... Mrs. Sadie LISENBY
37 Director Financial Resources .... Mr. Jim SHANNON
09 Dir Inst Research/Effectiveness .... Ms. Melissa S. HANSON
39 Director Residence Life .... Vacant
35 Director Student Life .... Vacant
42 Director of Ministry and Mission ..... Br. Dominic EHRMANTRAUT
92 Director Honors Program .... Dr. Tracie L. BURKE
41 Athletic Director .... Mr. Joseph P. NADICKSBERND
44 Director Development .... Mr. Stephen KIRKPATRICK
29 Director Alumni .... Ms. Karen VIOTTI
21 Controller .... Mr. Thomas COCHRAN
15 Director of Personnel .... Mr. Greg ELLER
18 Chief Facility/Physical Plant .... Mr. Philip R. YELVINGTON
19 Director of Security .... Mr. John D. LOTRIONTE
40 Director Bookstore .... Ms. Diane DUDENHEFER
50 Dean School of Business .... Dr. Jack HARGETT
54 Dean School of Engineering .... Dr. Eric WELCH
49 Dean School of Arts .... Dr. Paul A. HAUGHT
81 Dean School of Science .... Dr. Johnny B. HOLMES
107 Dir Graduate/Professional Stds Pgms .... Ms. Julie YANCEY
58 Director Graduate Education Program .... Dr. Samantha ALPERIN
58 Director MBA Program .... Dr. Scott LAWYER
58 Director Engineering Management Pgm .. Dr. Gregory A. SEDRICK
66 Director Nursing Program .... Dr. Margaret I. VEESER
88 Director Physician Assistant Stds .... Mr. Mark J. SCOTT

Concorde Career College (A)

5100 Poplar Avenue, Suite 132, Memphis TN 38137-0132

County: Shelby FICE Identification: 021571
Unit ID: 219903
Telephone: (901) 761-9494 Carnegie Class: Assoc/PrivFP
FAX Number: (901) 761-3293 Calendar System: Semester
URL: www.concorde.edu
Established: 1967 Annual Undergrad Tuition & Fees: $8,045
Enrollment: 804 Coed
Affiliation or Control: Proprietary IRS Status: Proprietary
Highest Offering: Associate Degree
Program: Occupational
Accreditation: **COE**, DA, DH, PTAA, RAD, SURGT

01 Executive Campus Director .... Mr. Tommy STEWART

Cumberland University (B)

1 Cumberland Square, Lebanon TN 37087-3554

County: Wilson FICE Identification: 003485
Unit ID: 219949
Telephone: (615) 444-2562 Carnegie Class: Master's M
FAX Number: (615) 444-2569 Calendar System: Semester
URL: www.cumberland.edu
Established: 1842 Annual Undergrad Tuition & Fees: $20,200
Enrollment: 1,941 Coed
Affiliation or Control: Independent Non-Profit IRS Status: 501(c)3
Highest Offering: Master's
Program: Liberal Arts And General; Teacher Preparatory; Professional
Accreditation: **SC**, ACBSP, NUR, TED

01 President .... Dr. Harvill C. EATON
03 Executive Vice President .... Mr. Eddie PAWLAWSKI
05 Vice President for Academic Affairs . Dr. Wilbur (Pete) PETERSON
11 Vice President for Administration .... Dr. Joe GRAY
10 Vice President of Finance .... Ms. Judy G. JORDAN
106 Vice President Online Professional .... Ms. Stacey A. GARRETT
30 Vice President of Advancement .... Mr. Rusty RICHARDSON
20 Associate VP for Academic Affairs .... Dr. Lisa COBB
45 Associate VP for Strategic Affairs .... Ms. Stephanie WALKER
32 Dean of Students .... Mrs. Lisa MACKE
53 Dean Education .... Dr. Eric CUMMINGS
49 Dean Liberal Arts & Sciences .... Dr. Laurie DISHMAN
50 Dean Labry School/Technology .... Dr. Paul STUMB
66 Dean Nursing .... Dr. Carol Anne BACH
57 Dean Music & the Arts .... Dr. Ted ROSE
101 Sec to President/Board of Trustees .... Ms. Leslie STEELE
29 Exec Dir Development/Alumni Rels .... Mr. Jonathan HAWKINS
08 Director Library Services .... Ms. Eloise HITCHCOCK
07 Exec Director Enrollment Services .... Ms. Beatrice LACHANCE
41 Athletic Director .... Mr. Ron PAVAN
06 Registrar .... Ms. Tammi PAVAN
15 Human Resources Director .... Ms. Vickie RICKARD
38 Director Student Counseling .... Vacant
13 Chief Information Officer .... Mr. Tony DEDMAN
09 Director of Institutional Research .... Mr. Larry F. VAUGHAN
26 Chief Public Relations Officer .... Mr. Phillip CARTER
40 Manager Bookstore .... Ms. Stephani DE ROUEN
36 Dir of Career Services/Internships .... Mrs. Ronie MCPEAK
39 Director of Residence Life .... Mr. Eddie LOVIN

Daymar Institute (C)

1860 Wilma Rudolph Boulevard,
Clarksville TN 37040-6718

County: Montgomery Identification: 666492
Unit ID: 368443
Telephone: (931) 552-7600 Carnegie Class: Assoc/PrivFP
FAX Number: (931) 552-3624 Calendar System: Quarter
URL: www.daymarinstitute.edu
Established: 1954 Annual Undergrad Tuition & Fees: $16,610
Enrollment: 623 Coed
Affiliation or Control: Proprietary IRS Status: Proprietary
Highest Offering: Baccalaureate
Program: Technical Emphasis
Accreditation: **ACICS**, PTAA

01 President .... Mr. Mark GABIS
12 Campus President .... Ms. Katharine PURNELL
05 Director of Education .... Ms. Elizabeth ASHY
07 Director of Admissions .... Mr. Alphonse PRATHER

† Branch campus of Daymart Institute, Nashville, TN.

Daymar Institute (D)

415 Golden Bear Court, Murfreesboro TN 37128-5508

County: Rutherford Identification: 666392
Unit ID: 444255
Telephone: (615) 217-9347 Carnegie Class: Assoc/PrivFP
FAX Number: (615) 217-9348 Calendar System: Quarter
URL: www.daymarinstitute.edu
Established: 2003 Annual Undergrad Tuition & Fees: $16,610
Enrollment: 464 Coed
Affiliation or Control: Proprietary IRS Status: Proprietary
Highest Offering: Baccalaureate
Program: Technical Emphasis
Accreditation: **ACICS**

01 President .... Mark A. GABIS
12 Campus President .... Deborah BROWN
05 Director of Education .... Jackie RODDY
07 Director of Admissions .... Jennifer VIOLA
32 Director of Student Services .... Kandy BRASHEAR
37 Director of Financial Services .... Julia FRIEDNER
06 Senior Registrar .... Julie ROHALY

† Branch campus of Daymar Institute, Nashville, TN.

Daymar Institute (E)

340 Plus Park Boulevard, Nashville TN 37217-1056

County: Davidson FICE Identification: 004934
Unit ID: 220002
Telephone: (615) 361-7555 Carnegie Class: Assoc/PrivFP
FAX Number: (615) 367-2736 Calendar System: Quarter
URL: www.daymarinstitute.edu
Established: 1884 Annual Undergrad Tuition & Fees: $16,610
Enrollment: 400 Coed
Affiliation or Control: Proprietary IRS Status: Proprietary
Highest Offering: Baccalaureate
Program: Technical Emphasis
Accreditation: **ACICS**

01 President .... Mr. Mark A. GABIS
12 Campus Director .... Mr. Kevin SUHR
07 Director of Admissions .... Ms. Elizabeth COLLIER
10 Director of Financial Services .... Ms. Janie RAGER
36 Director of Career Services .... Mr. Barry HOWARD
06 Registrar .... Mr. Michael GILLIAM
36 Director of Career Services .... Ms. Sara COLLIVER

DeVry University - Memphis (F)

6401 Poplar Avenue, Suite 600, Memphis TN 38119-4808

County: Shelby Identification: 666571
Unit ID: 450517
Telephone: (901) 537-2560 Carnegie Class: Spec/Bus
FAX Number: (901) 682-1326 Calendar System: Semester
URL: www.devry.edu
Established: 1931 Annual Undergrad Tuition & Fees: $16,156
Enrollment: 270 Coed
Affiliation or Control: Proprietary IRS Status: Proprietary
Highest Offering: Master's
Program: Professional; Business Emphasis
Accreditation: **&NH**

01 Campus Director .... Mr. William WEST

† Regional accreditation is carried under the parent institution in Downers Grove, IL.

DeVry University - Nashville (G)

3343 Perimeter Hill Drive, Ste 200,
Nashville TN 37211-4147

County: Davidson Identification: 666589
Telephone: (615) 445-3456 Carnegie Class: Not Classified
FAX Number: (615) 331-1635 Calendar System: Semester
URL: www.devry.edu
Established: 1931 Annual Undergrad Tuition & Fees: $16,156
Enrollment: 304 Coed
Affiliation or Control: Proprietary IRS Status: Proprietary
Highest Offering: Master's
Program: Professional; Business Emphasis
Accreditation: **&NH**

01 Campus Director .... Peter POWELL

† Regional accreditation is carried under the parent institution in Downers Grove, IL.

Emmanuel Christian Seminary (H)

1 Walker Drive, Johnson City TN 37601-9989

County: Carter FICE Identification: 012547
Unit ID: 220136
Telephone: (423) 926-1186 Carnegie Class: Spec/Faith
FAX Number: (423) 926-6198 Calendar System: Semester
URL: www.ecs.edu
Established: 1961 Annual Graduate Tuition & Fees: $11,040
Enrollment: 135 Coed
Affiliation or Control: Christian Churches And Churches of Christ
IRS Status: 501(c)3
Highest Offering: Doctorate; No Undergraduates
Program: Professional
Accreditation: **SC**, THEOL

01 President .... Dr. Michael L. SWEENEY
05 Dean .... Dr. Jack HOLLAND
10 Director of Finance .... Mr. David B. MARSHALL
30 Executive Director of Development .... Mr. Dan R. LAWSON
08 Librarian .... Mr. John M. WADE
07 Director of Admissions & Recruitmen .... Ms. Erin C. LAYTON
42 Chaplain .... Mrs. Heather E. HOLLAND

Fisk University (I)

1000 17th Avenue N, Nashville TN 37208-3051

County: Davidson FICE Identification: 003490
Unit ID: 220181
Telephone: (615) 329-8500 Carnegie Class: Bac/A&S
FAX Number: N/A Calendar System: Semester
URL: www.fisk.edu
Established: 1866 Annual Undergrad Tuition & Fees: $20,001
Enrollment: 533 Coed
Affiliation or Control: Independent Non-Profit IRS Status: 501(c)3
Highest Offering: Master's
Program: Liberal Arts And General; Teacher Preparatory
Accreditation: **#SC**, MUS

01 President .... Dr. Hazel R. O'LEARY
05 Executive Vice President & Provost .... Dr. Princilla E. MORRIS
10 Vice President for Finance and CFO .... Mr. Gary MOORE
04 Exec Assistant to the President .... Mrs. Sherri B. RUCKER
30 Vice President of Inst Advancement .... Mrs. Edwina H. HAMBY
26 Public Relations Specialist .... Vacant
09 VP of Inst Assessment & Research .... Dr. Michael SELF
32 VP of Student Engagement & Enroll ..... Mr. Jason MERIWETHER
13 Acting Dir Info Technology Svcs .... Mr. Joseph CURTIS
29 Exec Director of Alumni Affairs .... Mrs. Adrienne LATHAM
20 Vice Provost for Acad Initiatives .... Dr. Arnold BURGER
07 Dean of Admission .... Mr. Anthony JONES
37 Director of Financial Aid .... Mrs. Mary CHAMBLISS
06 Registrar .... Ms. Stephanie CAGE
08 University Librarian .... Dr. Jessie C. SMITH
58 Interim Dean of Graduate Studies .... Dr. Lee LIMBIRD
41 Dir of Athletics & Intramural Pgms .... Mr. Anthony OWENS
42 Dean of the Chapel .... Dr. Jason CURRY
25 Director of Sponsored Programs .... Ms. Beverly ROBINSON
44 Director of Annual Giving .... Vacant
18 Director of Facilities .... Mr. Norman RAPP
19 Director of Public Safety .... Mr. Mickey WEST
96 Director of Purchasing .... Vacant
36 Director Career Development .... Ms. Natara GARVIN
38 Coordinator of Student Counseling .... Dr. Sheila PETERS
15 Director of Human Resources .... Dr. JaCenda DAVIDSON
21 Comptroller .... Vacant
35 Dean of Student Engagement .... Ms. LaMetrius DANIELS

Fortis Institute (J)

1025 Highway 111, Cookeville TN 38501-4305

County: Putnam FICE Identification: 023263
Unit ID: 418870
Telephone: (931) 526-3660 Carnegie Class: Assoc/PrivFP
FAX Number: (931) 372-2603 Calendar System: Quarter
URL: www.fortis.edu/cookeville-tennessee.php
Established: 1970 Annual Undergrad Tuition & Fees: $13,600
Enrollment: 365 Coed
Affiliation or Control: Proprietary IRS Status: Proprietary
Highest Offering: Associate Degree
Program: Occupational
Accreditation: **COE**, MLTAD, RAD, SURGT

01 Campus Director .... Mr. Bill STRADLEY
05 Dean of Education .... Ms. Rebecca BLALOCK

Fountainhead College of Technology (K)

3203 Tazewell Pike, Knoxville TN 37918-2530

County: Knox FICE Identification: 007439
Unit ID: 221795
Telephone: (865) 688-9422 Carnegie Class: Spec/Tech
FAX Number: (865) 688-2419 Calendar System: Semester
URL: www.fountainheadcollege.edu
Established: 1947 Annual Undergrad Tuition & Fees: $14,550
Enrollment: 250 Coed
Affiliation or Control: Proprietary IRS Status: Proprietary
Highest Offering: Baccalaureate
Program: Occupational; 2-Year Principally Bachelor's Creditable; Technical Emphasis

Accreditation: ACCSC

01 President .... Mr. Richard W. RACKLEY

Free Will Baptist Bible College (A)

3606 West End Avenue, Nashville TN 37205-2498
County: Davidson FICE Identification: 030018
Unit ID: 220206
Telephone: (615) 383-1340 Carnegie Class: Bac/Diverse
FAX Number: (615) 269-6028 Calendar System: Semester
URL: www.fwbbc.edu
Established: 1942 Annual Undergrad Tuition & Fees: $21,584
Enrollment: 300 Coed
Affiliation or Control: Free Will Baptist Church IRS Status: 501(c)3
Highest Offering: Baccalaureate
Program: Liberal Arts And General; Teacher Preparatory; Religious Emphasis
Accreditation: SC, BI

01 President .... Dr. J. Matthew PINSON
05 Provost .... Dr. Paul G. KETTEMAN
10 Vice President Financial Affairs .... Mr. Craig MAHLER
45 Dir Institutional Planning/Assess .... Dr. Kevin HESTER
30 Vice Pres Institutional Advancement .... Mr. David WILLIFORD
32 VP Student Svcs/Dean of Students .... Dr. Jon FORLINES
34 Dean of Women .... Mrs. Susan FORLINES
21 Comptroller .... Mr. Jeff BENNETT
08 Librarian .... Mrs. Carol REID
18 Director of Plant Operations .... Mr. Sandy GOODFELLOW
26 Director of Public Relations .... Dr. Jack WILLIAMS
84 Dir of Enrollment Svcs/Fin Aid .... Mr. Rusty CAMPBELL
106 Dir of Online and Adult Studies .... Mr. Allan CROWSON
09 Director of Institutional Research .... Mr. Wayne SPRUILL
41 Athletic Director .... Mr. Gary TURNER

Freed-Hardeman University (B)

158 E Main, Henderson TN 38340-2398
County: Chester FICE Identification: 003492
Unit ID: 220215
Telephone: (731) 989-6000 Carnegie Class: Master's M
FAX Number: (731) 989-6065 Calendar System: Semester
URL: www.fhu.edu
Established: 1869 Annual Undergrad Tuition & Fees: $20,468
Enrollment: 1,972 Coed
Affiliation or Control: Churches Of Christ IRS Status: 501(c)3
Highest Offering: Beyond Master's But Less Than Doctorate
Program: Liberal Arts And General; Teacher Preparatory
Accreditation: SC, ACBSP, SW, TED

01 President .... Dr. Joe A. WILEY
04 Executive Assistant to President .... Mrs. Donna M. STEELE
10 Exec VP and CFO .... Dr. Dwayne H. WILSON
30 Vice President for Univ Advancement .... Mr. Dave CLOUSE
05 Vice Pres Academics/Enrollment Mgmt .... Dr. Charles VIRES
88 VP for Spiritual Development .... Dr. Samuel T. JONES
32 Vice Pres Student Services .... Dr. Wayne SCOTT
13 VP for Innovation and Technology .... Mr. Mark SCOTT
20 Associate Vice President Academics .... Dr. Vicki M. JOHNSON
41 Director of Athletics .... Mr. Michael F. MCCUTCHEN
29 Asst VP for Alumni Relations .... Mrs. Betsy HESSELRODE
07 Director of Admissions .... Mr. Joseph ASKEW
35 Dean of Students .... Dr. Wayne SCOTT
35 Dean of Student Life .... Mr. Tony M. ALLEN
06 Registrar .... Mr. Larry R. OLDHAM
37 Director Student Financial Services .... Mrs. Summer JUDD
40 University Book Store Manager .... Mr. Dan LUSSIER
08 Head Librarian .... Mrs. A. Hope SHULL
70 Director of Social Work Program .... Mrs. Nadine G. MCNEAL
24 A-V Supervisor .... Mrs. Gail B. NASH
21 Controller/Purchasing Coordinator .... Mr. Barry V. SMITH
45 Asst VP for Instnl Effectiveness .... Dr. James Q. EDMONDS
09 Director of Institutional Research .... Mr. Micah SMITH
15 Human Resources Coordinator .... Mr. Jay SATTERFIELD
18 Director Facilities .... Mr. Jeff BARKMAN
26 Director Marketing & Univ Relations .... Mr. Judson B. DAVIS
73 Dean of School Biblical Studies .... Dr. Billy R. SMITH
50 Dean School of Business .... Dr. Keith SMITH
53 Dean School of Education .... Dr. Sharen CYPRESS
49 Dean School of Arts & Humanities .... Dr. W. Stephen JOHNSON
81 Dean School of Science & Math .... Dr. LeAnn SELF-DAVIS
92 Dean of Honors College .... Dr. Jenny JOHNSON
23 Campus Physician .... Dr. Kenneth R. CARGILE
104 Dir of International Studies .... Dr. Jenny JOHNSON
38 Director of Counseling .... Mrs. Nicole YOUNG

Harding School of Theology (C)

1000 Cherry Road, Memphis TN 38117-5499
County: Shelby FICE Identification: 004081
Unit ID: 107035
Telephone: (901) 761-1350 Carnegie Class: Not Classified
FAX Number: (901) 761-1358 Calendar System: Semester
URL: www.hst.edu
Established: 1958 Annual Graduate Tuition & Fees: $14,592
Enrollment: 198 Coed
Affiliation or Control: Churches Of Christ IRS Status: 501(c)3
Highest Offering: Doctorate; No Undergraduates
Program: Professional; Religious Emphasis
Accreditation: &NH, THEOL

01 President .... Dr. David B. BURKS
05 Vice President/Dean .... Dr. Evertt W. HUFFARD
07 Director of Admissions .... Mr. Matt R. CARTER
08 Librarian .... Mr. Don L. MEREDITH
10 Business Office Manager .... Ms. Brenda M. DAVID
30 Director of Advancement .... Mr. Larry J. ARICK
20 Associate Dean .... Dr. Steve MCLEOD

† Regional accreditation is carried under Harding University, Searcy, AR.

Hiwassee College (D)

225 Hiwassee College Drive, Madisonville TN 37354
County: Monroe FICE Identification: 003494
Unit ID: 220312
Telephone: (423) 442-2001 Carnegie Class: Assoc/PrivNFP
FAX Number: (423) 420-1929 Calendar System: Semester
URL: www.hiwassee.edu
Established: 1850 Annual Undergrad Tuition & Fees: $17,040
Enrollment: 350 Coed
Affiliation or Control: United Methodist IRS Status: 501(c)3
Highest Offering: Baccalaureate
Program: Liberal Arts And General
Accreditation: @TRACS, DH

01 President .... Dr. Robin J. TRICOLI
05 Vice President/Academic Dean .... Dr. Beth R. SCRUGGS
10 VP Business Affairs & Treasurer .... D. D THOMPSON
37 Director of Financial Aid .... Ronda EVERETT

Huntington College of Health Sciences (E)

1204 Kenesaw Avenue, Suite D, Knoxville TN 37919-7700
County: Knox Identification: 666971
Unit ID: 371274
Telephone: (800) 290-4226 Carnegie Class: Not Classified
FAX Number: (865) 524-8339 Calendar System: Semester
URL: www.hchs.edu
Established: 1985 Annual Undergrad Tuition & Fees: $4,950
Enrollment: 430 Coed
Affiliation or Control: Proprietary IRS Status: Proprietary
Highest Offering: Master's
Program: Occupational
Accreditation: DETC

01 Chief Executive Officer .... Dr. Art PRESSER
05 Dean of Academics .... Mr. Gene BRUNO
10 Director of Finance .... Mr. Robert SCHMAEF
07 Director of Admissions .... Ms. Kim GALYON

International Academy of Design and Technology (F)

1 Bridgestone Park, Nashville TN 37214-2428
County: Davidson Identification: 666347
Unit ID: 446817
Telephone: (615) 232-7384 Carnegie Class: Spec/Arts
FAX Number: (615) 883-5285 Calendar System: Other
URL: www.iadtnashville.com
Established: 2004 Annual Undergrad Tuition & Fees: $18,687
Enrollment: 550 Coed
Affiliation or Control: Proprietary IRS Status: Proprietary
Highest Offering: Baccalaureate
Program: Occupational; Liberal Arts And General
Accreditation: ACICS

01 Interim Campus Director .... Ms. Julie O'GUIN
37 Director of Financial Aid .... Mr. Jason ERICKSON

† Branch campus of International Academy of Design and Technology, Chicago, IL.

ITT Technical Institute (G)

5600 Brainerd Road, Suite G-1, Chattanooga TN 37411
County: Hamilton Identification: 666708
Unit ID: 450261
Telephone: (423) 510-6800 Carnegie Class: Assoc/PrivFP4
FAX Number: (423) 510-6850 Calendar System: Quarter
URL: www.itt-tech.edu
Established: N/A Annual Undergrad Tuition & Fees: N/A
Enrollment: 274 Coed
Affiliation or Control: Proprietary IRS Status: Proprietary
Highest Offering: Baccalaureate
Program: Technical Emphasis
Accreditation: ACICS

† Branch campus of ITT Technical Institute, Indianapolis, IN.

ITT Technical Institute (H)

7260 Goodlett Farms Parkway, Cordova TN 38016-4908
County: Shelby Identification: 666550
Unit ID: 413884
Telephone: (901) 381-0200 Carnegie Class: Spec/Tech
FAX Number: (901) 381-0299 Calendar System: Quarter
URL: www.itt-tech.edu
Established: 1994 Annual Undergrad Tuition & Fees: N/A
Enrollment: 719 Coed
Affiliation or Control: Proprietary IRS Status: Proprietary
Highest Offering: Baccalaureate
Program: Technical Emphasis
Accreditation: ACICS

† Branch campus of ITT Technical Institute, Indianapolis, IN.

ITT Technical Institute (I)

10208 Technology Drive, Knoxville TN 37932-3343
County: Knox FICE Identification: 030734
Unit ID: 366650
Telephone: (865) 671-2800 Carnegie Class: Spec/Tech
FAX Number: (865) 671-2811 Calendar System: Quarter
URL: www.itt-tech.edu
Established: 1988 Annual Undergrad Tuition & Fees: N/A
Enrollment: 727 Coed
Affiliation or Control: Proprietary IRS Status: Proprietary
Highest Offering: Baccalaureate
Program: Technical Emphasis
Accreditation: ACICS

† Branch campus of ITT Technical Institute, Indianapolis, IN.

ITT Technical Institute (J)

2845 Elm Hill Pike, Nashville TN 37214-3717
County: Davidson FICE Identification: 023598
Unit ID: 151494
Telephone: (615) 889-8700 Carnegie Class: Spec/Tech
FAX Number: (615) 872-7209 Calendar System: Quarter
URL: www.itt-tech.edu
Established: 1984 Annual Undergrad Tuition & Fees: N/A
Enrollment: 753 Coed
Affiliation or Control: Proprietary IRS Status: Proprietary
Highest Offering: Baccalaureate
Program: Technical Emphasis
Accreditation: ACICS

† Branch campus of ITT Technical Institute, Indianapolis, IN.

John A. Gupton College (K)

1616 Church Street, Nashville TN 37203-2920
County: Davidson FICE Identification: 008859
Unit ID: 220464
Telephone: (615) 327-3927 Carnegie Class: Assoc/PrivNFP
FAX Number: (615) 321-4518 Calendar System: Semester
URL: www.guptoncollege.com
Established: 1946 Annual Undergrad Tuition & Fees: $9,280
Enrollment: 146 Coed
Affiliation or Control: Independent Non-Profit IRS Status: 501(c)3
Highest Offering: Associate Degree
Program: Occupational; 2-Year Principally Bachelor's Creditable
Accreditation: SC, FUSER

01 President .... Mr. B. Steven SPANN
08 Library Director .... Mr. William P. BRUCE
06 Registrar .... Ms. Lisa MOFFITT

Johnson University (L)

7900 Johnson Drive, Knoxville TN 37998-0001
County: Knox FICE Identification: 003495
Unit ID: 220473
Telephone: (865) 573-4517 Carnegie Class: Spec/Faith
FAX Number: (865) 251-2337 Calendar System: Semester
URL: www.johnsonu.edu
Established: 1893 Annual Undergrad Tuition & Fees: $10,250
Enrollment: 845 Coed
Affiliation or Control: Christian Churches And Churches of Christ
IRS Status: 501(c)3
Highest Offering: Doctorate
Program: Liberal Arts And General; Teacher Preparatory
Accreditation: SC, BI

01 President .... Dr. Gary E. WEEDMAN
00 President Emeritus .... Dr. David L. EUBANKS
05 Vice President for Academics .... Dr. Christopher DAVIS
10 Vice Pres for Business and Finance .... Mr. Chris ROLPH
32 Vice President for Student Services .... Mr. David LEGG
30 Vice President for Advancement .... Mr. Philip A. EUBANKS
08 Librarian .... Miss Carrie B. LOWE
06 Registrar .... Mrs. Sandra J. BLEVINS
07 Deanof Enrollment Services .... Dr. Tim WINGFIELD
37 Financial Aid Director .... Mr. Larry RECTOR
45 Dir Institutional Effectiveness .... Dr. Mark PIERCE
41 Athletic Director .... Mr. Ken UNDERWOOD
18 Director of Plant Services .... Mr. John LINSENBIGLER
92 Director of Honors Program .... Dr. Gerald L. MATTINGLY
15 Director Human Resources .... Mrs. Ruthanne BEAM
26 Director of Public Relations .... Mr. Kevin O'BRIEN
38 Director Student Counseling .... Dr. Sean RIDGE

Kaplan Career Institute (M)

750 Envious Lane, Nashville TN 37217-1342
County: Davidson FICE Identification: 023262
Unit ID: 246202
Telephone: (615) 279-8300 Carnegie Class: Assoc/PrivFP
FAX Number: (615) 297-6678 Calendar System: Other
URL: www.kci-nashville.com
Established: 1981 Annual Undergrad Tuition & Fees: $14,844

Enrollment: 475 Coed
Affiliation or Control: Proprietary IRS Status: Proprietary
Highest Offering: Associate Degree
Program: Occupational
Accreditation: **COE**, DA

01 Executive Director ... Mr. Adam BUTLER

King College (A)

1350 King College Road, Bristol TN 37620-2699
County: Sullivan FICE Identification: 003496
Unit ID: 220516
Telephone: (423) 968-1187 Carnegie Class: Master's M
FAX Number: (423) 968-4456 Calendar System: Other
URL: www.king.edu
Established: 1867 Annual Undergrad Tuition & Fees: $24,052
Enrollment: 2,126 Coed
Affiliation or Control: Presbyterian Church (U.S.A.) IRS Status: 501(c)3
Highest Offering: Master's
Program: Liberal Arts And General; Teacher Preparatory; Professional; Nursing Emphasis
Accreditation: **SC**, NURSE

01 President ... Dr. Gregory D. JORDAN
05 Provost/Dean of Faculty ... Dr. Paul M. PERCY
10 Vice President Finance/Operations ... Mr. James P. DONAHUE
32 Vice President for Student Affairs ... Dr. Robert A. LITTLETON
84 Vice President of Enrollment Mgmt ... Mr. Micah R. CREWS
26 Assoc Vice Pres Marketing & Devel ... Mrs. A. LeAnn HUGHES
08 Dean of Library Services ... Ms. Erika BRAMMER
35 Assoc Dean Student Development ... Mr. Matthew S. PELTIER
06 Registrar/Dir Regist & Records ... Mrs. Sarah L. DILLOW
30 Chief Development Officer ... Mr. John W. KING
09 Director of Institutional Research ... Dr. J. Kevin DEFORD
29 Director of Alumni Relations ... Mrs. Finley L. GREEN
42 Chaplain ... Dr. Fred F. STRANG
21 Director of Business Operations ... Mr. Thomas R. LARSON
36 Director of Career Development ... Ms. Donna H. FELTY
41 Athletic Director ... Mr. J. David HICKS
38 Director of Counseling ... Mr. Charles S. THOMPSON
88 Sports Information Director ... Mr. Glen G. RENFRO
40 Bookstore Manager ... Ms. Susan D. MARSHALL
37 Director Student Financial Aid ... Ms. Nancy M. BEVERLY
84 Director of Recruitment ... Mr. Charles G. KING
18 Chief Facilities/Physical Plant ... Mr. Todd THOMAS
92 Director of Honors Program ... Dr. Mark E. DOLLAR
26 Director Marketing & Communications .. Ms. Sarah CLEVENTURE
27 Assoc Director of Communication ... Mrs. Laura K. BOGGAN

Lane College (B)

545 Lane Avenue, Jackson TN 38301-4598
County: Madison FICE Identification: 003499
Unit ID: 220598
Telephone: (731) 426-7500 Carnegie Class: Bac/A&S
FAX Number: (731) 427-3987 Calendar System: Semester
URL: www.lanecollege.edu
Established: 1882 Annual Undergrad Tuition & Fees: $8,560
Enrollment: 2,003 Coed
Affiliation or Control: Christian Methodist Episcopal IRS Status: 501(c)3
Highest Offering: Baccalaureate
Program: Liberal Arts And General; Teacher Preparatory
Accreditation: **SC**, @TEAC

01 President ... Dr. Wesley C. MCCLURE
03 Executive Vice President ... Ms. Sharron T. BURNETT
05 Vice President Academic Affairs ... Dr. Deborah B. BUCHANAN
10 Vice President Business & Finance ... Mr. Melvin R. HAMLETT
32 Vice President Student Affairs ... Ms. Sherrill B. SCOTT
30 Vice Pres Inst Advance/Dir Alum Aff ... Mr. Richard H. DONNELL
04 Exec Assistant to the President ... Ms. Darlette C. SAMUELS
18 Chief Facilities/Physical Plant ... Mr. Michael BATES
26 Chief Public Relations Officer ... Ms. Darlette C. SAMUELS
09 Director Institutional Research ... Dr. Fred OKANDA
08 Librarian ... Ms. Lan WANG
07 Director of Admissions ... Ms. Evelyn BROWN
06 Registrar ... Mr. Terry W. BLACKMON
37 Director of Financial Aid ... Mr. Tony CALHOUN
20 Director Academic Assessment ... Dr. Juanita MORRIS
84 Director Enrollment Management ... Ms. Kelly R. BOYD
89 Director of Freshman Studies ... Dr. David POINTS
96 Director of Purchasing ... Ms. Tammy MCDOUGAL
36 Director Placement Services ... Ms. Virginia S. CRUMP
13 Director Information Technology ... Mr. Earnest L. MITCHELL, III
15 Director of Personnel ... Ms. Juanita MARSHALL
19 Director Security ... Mr. Ernest BOYD
40 Director Bookstore ... Mr. Carter B. MCCLURE
19 Director of Safety ... Ms. Aleshia COX
20 Associate Academic Officer ... Dr. Virginia S. CRUMP
21 Associate Business Officer ... Mr. Duan ROBINSON
41 Director of Athletics ... Ms. Penny MINTER
29 Director Alumni Relations ... Ms. Monica CLAYBORNE SCOTT
35 Director Student Affairs ... Mr. Reginald CLEVELAND
27 Chief Information Officer ... Ms. Tori L. HALIBURTON

Lee University (C)

1120 N Ocoee Street, Cleveland TN 37320-3450
County: Bradley FICE Identification: 003500
Unit ID: 220613
Telephone: (423) 614-8100 Carnegie Class: Master's M
FAX Number: (423) 614-8083 Calendar System: Semester
URL: www.leeuniversity.edu
Established: 1918 Annual Undergrad Tuition & Fees: $13,370
Enrollment: 4,411 Coed
Affiliation or Control: Church Of God IRS Status: 501(c)3
Highest Offering: Beyond Master's But Less Than Doctorate
Program: Liberal Arts And General; Teacher Preparatory
Accreditation: **SC**, ACBSP, MUS, TED

01 President ... Dr. C. Paul CONN
04 Executive Assistant to President ... Mrs. Stephanie TAYLOR
10 Vice President Business & Finance ... Mr. Chris CONINE
05 Vice President for Academic Affairs ... Dr. Carolyn DIRKSEN
11 Vice President for Administration ... Dr. Walter MAULDIN
84 Vice President for Enrollment ... Mr. Phil COOK
26 VP for University Relations ... Dr. Jerome HAMMOND
32 VP for Student Development ... Mr. Mike HAYES
27 VP for Information Services ... Dr. Jayson VAN HOOK
21 Comptroller ... Mr. Duane PACE
37 Director of Student Aid ... Mr. Mike ELLIS
35 Dean of Students ... Mr. Alan MCCLUNG
15 Director of Human Resources ... Mrs. Ann MCELRATH
14 Director of IT Operations ... Mr. Chris GOLDEN
13 Director of IT Systems ... Mr. Nate TUCKER
29 Director of Alumni Relations ... Mrs. Mitzi MEW
39 Director of Residential Life ... Ms. Tracey CARLSON
06 Registrar ... Mrs. Cathy THOMPSOM
21 Bursar ... Ms. Kristy HARNER
08 Librarian ... Ms. Barbara MCCULLOUGH
42 Director of Campus Ministries ... Rev. Jimmy HARPER
25 Director of Grants ... Mrs. Vanessa HAMMOND
19 Director of Campus Safety ... Mr. Ashley MEW
23 Director of Health Services ... Mr. Mickey MOORE
27 Director of Public Information ... Mr. Brian CONN
73 Dean School of Religion ... Dr. Terry CROSS
49 Dean College of Arts & Sciences ... Dr. Matthew MELTON
53 Dean College of Education ... Dr. Deborah MURRAY
64 Dean School of Music ... Dr. William GREEN
51 Exec Dir of Div of Adult Learning ... Mr. Joshua BLACK
07 Director of Graduate Enrollment ... Ms. Vicki GLASSCOCK
38 Director Counseling & Testing ... Ms. Christin LOGUE
18 Director of Physical Plant ... Mr. Larry BERRY
41 Athletic Director ... Mr. Larry CARPENTER
104 Director of Global Perspectives ... Mrs. Angeline MCMULLIN
36 Director of Calling and Career ... Ms. Stacy BALLINGER

LeMoyne-Owen College (D)

807 Walker Avenue, Memphis TN 38126-6595
County: Shelby FICE Identification: 003501
Unit ID: 220604
Telephone: (901) 435-1000 Carnegie Class: Bac/Diverse
FAX Number: (901) 435-1699 Calendar System: Semester
URL: www.loc.edu
Established: 1862 Annual Undergrad Tuition & Fees: $10,460
Enrollment: 1,051 Coed
Affiliation or Control: Multiple Protestant Denominations
IRS Status: 501(c)3
Highest Offering: Baccalaureate
Program: Liberal Arts And General; Teacher Preparatory; Business Emphasis
Accreditation: **SC**, TED

01 President ... Mr. Johnnie B. WATSON
05 VP/Chief Academic Officer ... Dr. Barbara FRANKLE
10 Chief Financial Officer ... Mr. Jim DUGGER
88 Director Title III Administration ... Ms. Shirley HILL
32 Dean of Students ... Ms. Edythe COBB
30 Exec Dir Institutional Advancement ... Mr. Roger BROWN
84 Exec Dir Enrollment Management ... Ms. June CHINN-JOINTER
16 Director of Human Resources ... Mr. Michael WASHINGTON
08 Librarian ... Ms. Annette BERHE
37 Director Student Financial Services ... Ms. Phyllis TORRY
06 Registrar ... Mr. Addie HARVEY
36 Director Career Services/Placement ... Dr. Denita HEDGEMAN
29 Director of Alumni Relations ... Ms. Frankie JEFFRIES
14 Director Information Technology ... Mr. Angus SMALL
21 Controller ... Ms. Colleen GIBSON
09 Director Institutional Research ... Mr. Reoungeneria MCFARLAND
92 Director Dubois Honors Program ... Dr. Elton WEAVER, III
35 Director Student Activities ... Ms. Felecia FOSTER
50 Chair Div Business & Econ Devel ... Dr. Katherine CAUSEY
53 Chair Education Division ... Dr. Ralph CALHOUN
57 Chair Div Fine Arts & Humanities ... Dr. Linda WHITE
65 Chair Div Natural & Math Science ... Dr. Delphia HARRIS
83 Chair Div Social & Behavioral Sci ... Dr. Cheryl GOLDEN
38 Director Student Counseling ... Mr. Tony WHITSON
26 Dir Public Relations & Marketing ... Ms. Daphne J. THOMAS
41 Director of Athletics ... Mr. William ANDERSON
11 Director Administrative Services ... Mr. Jesse CHATMAN

Lincoln Memorial University (E)

6965 Cumberland Gap Parkway,
Harrogate TN 37752-1901
County: Claiborne FICE Identification: 003502
Unit ID: 220631
Telephone: (423) 869-3611 Carnegie Class: Master's L
FAX Number: (423) 869-6250 Calendar System: Semester
URL: www.lmunet.edu
Established: 1897 Annual Undergrad Tuition & Fees: $18,240
Enrollment: 4,550 Coed
Affiliation or Control: Independent Non-Profit IRS Status: 501(c)3
Highest Offering: Doctorate
Program: Liberal Arts And General; Teacher Preparatory; Professional
Accreditation: **SC**, ACBSP, ADNUR, ANEST, ARCPA, MT, NUR, OSTEO, SW

01 President ... Dr. B. James DAWSON
11 Dean for Administration ... Ms. Lisa COX
30 Vice Pres University Advancement ... Ms. Cynthia L. WHITT
05 Vice President for Academic Affairs ... Dr. Clayton HESS
10 Vice President of Finance ... Ms. Kimberlee BONTRAGER
61 VP/Dean School of Law ... Mr. Sydney BECKMAN
84 Dean of Enrollment ... Mr. Bryan ERSLAN
53 Dean of School of Education ... Dr. Michael CLYBURN
49 Dean of Arts and Sciences ... Dr. Amiel JARSTFER
66 Dean School of Nursing ... Dr. Mary Anne MODRCIN
50 Dean School of Business ... Dr. Jack MCCANN
32 Dean of Students ... Mr. Frank E. SMITH
04 Exec Assistant to the President ... Mrs. Janet SMITH
37 Executive Director of Financial Aid ... Mr. Bryan ERSLAN
09 Director of Institutional Research ... Vacant
41 Athletic Director ... Mr. Roger VANNOY
18 Director Properties/Physical Plant ... Mr. Rodney COCHRAN
15 Director of Human Resources ... Ms. Libby KING
96 Director Purchasing/Accts Payable ... Ms. Pat TENNYSON
06 Registrar ... Ms. Helen BAILEY
90 Director of Acad Computing Support ... Vacant
42 University Chaplain ... Dr. Ray PENN
43 Legal Counsel ... Mr. J. Thomas BAUGH
13 Chief Information Officer ... Mr. Jason MCCONNELL
26 Senior Director of Marketing ... Mrs. Kate M. REAGAN
29 Director Alumni Services ... Mr. Donnie LIPSCOMB
40 Bookstore Manager ... Mr. Rick CROWDER

Lipscomb University (F)

One University Park Dr., Nashville TN 37204-3951
County: Davidson FICE Identification: 003486
Unit ID: 219976
Telephone: (615) 966-1000 Carnegie Class: Master's L
FAX Number: (615) 966-1798 Calendar System: Semester
URL: www.lipscomb.edu
Established: 1891 Annual Undergrad Tuition & Fees: $24,654
Enrollment: 4,010 Coed
Affiliation or Control: Churches Of Christ IRS Status: 501(c)3
Highest Offering: Doctorate
Program: Liberal Arts And General; Teacher Preparatory; Professional
Accreditation: **SC**, ACBSP, DIETD, DIETI, ENG, MUS, NUR, PHAR, SW, TED, THEOL

01 President ... Dr. L. Randolph LOWRY, III
05 Provost ... Dr. W. Craig BLEDSOE
45 Senior VP Strategic Initiatives ... Dr. Nancy MAGNUSSON DURHAM
10 Senior VP Finance & Administration ... Mr. Danny TAYLOR
30 Senior VP Advancement ... Vacant
26 VP University Relations ... Mr. Walt LEAVER
29 VP Development & Alumni Relations ... Dr. Bennie L. HARRIS
32 VP Student Develop/Dean Campus Life ... Dr. Scott MCDOWELL
26 VP Communications & Marketing ... Ms. Deby K. SAMUELS
42 Vice President for Church Services ... Dr. Scott SAGER
13 Vice President Info Technology/CIO ... Mr. Mike GREEN
20 Assoc Prov Acad Admin & Strat Init ... Dr. Susan C. GALBREATH
43 General Counsel ... Dr. Phillip ELLENBURG
41 Director of Athletics ... Mr. Philip HUTCHESON
20 Associate Provost Academic Support ... Mr. Steve PREWITT
20 Assoc Provost for Grad Studies ... Dr. Randy BOULDIN
88 Assoc Prov for Inst Effectiveness ... Dr. Elaine GRIFFIN
79 Dean College of Arts & Sciences ... Dr. Norma BURGESS
73 Dean College of Bible & Ministry ... Dr. Terry BRILEY
50 Dean College of Business ... Mr. Turney STEVENS
53 Dean College of Education ... Dr. Candice MCQUEEN
81 Dean College of Engineering ... Vacant
67 Dean College of Pharmacy ... Dr. Roger DAVIS
107 Dean College of Prof Studies ... Dr. Charla LONG
55 Dir School of Computing/Informatics ... Dr. Fortune MHLANGA
39 Associate Dean & Dir Residence Life ... Dr. Sam SMITH
35 Associate Dean of Campus Life ... Ms. Sarah GAMBLE
21 Associate VP Finance ... Mr. Darrell DUNCAN
102 Associate VP Advancement ... Mr. David ENGLAND
88 Asst VP Develop & Alumni Relations ... Mrs. Carrie THOMPSON
44 Senior Director of Development ... Mr. Mark MEADOR
07 Senior Director of Admissions ... Mr. Rick HOLAWAY
06 Registrar ... Mrs. Janet CATES
37 Director of Financial Aid ... Ms. Tiffany SUMMERS
08 Director of Library Services ... Mrs. Carolyn WILSON
19 Director of Campus Safety ... Mr. Brad WYATT
36 Director of Career Development Ctr ... Mrs. Monica WENTWORTH
88 Director of Student Advocacy ... Ms. Teresa WILLIAMS
55 Director Adult Degree Program ... Dr. Teresa CLARK
73 Dir of Hazelip School of Theology ... Dr. Mark BLACK
88 Dir of Grad Exercise & Nutrition ... Dr. Karen ROBICHAUD
58 Director of Graduate Education ... Dr. Deborah BOYD
83 Dir of Grad Studies in Psychology ... Dr. Jake MORRIS
58 Associate Dean of Graduate Business ... Dr. Mike KENDRICK
88 Asst Dean of Executive Education ... Dr. John LOWRY
88 Dir Inst for Conflict Management ... Dr. Steve JOINER
88 Dir Inst for Chistian Spirituality ... Dr. Earl LAVENDER
88 Dir Inst for Law Justice & Society ... Dr. Randy SPIVEY
88 Exec Dir Inst for Civic Leadership ... Dr. Linda SCHACHT
88 Exec Dir Inst for Sustain Practice ... Mr. Dodd GALBREATH
38 Director Counseling Center ... Dr. Paul CATES
23 Director of Health Services ... Mrs. Bethany MASSEY
88 Director of Spiritual Outreach ... Mr. Steve DAVIDSON
28 Asst Dean Intercultural Development ... Mrs. Tenielle BUCHANAN
28 Asst Dean Intercultural Engagement ... Mrs. Jessica GARCIA VAN DE GRIEK

09 Director of Institutional Research ....Mr. Matt REHBEIN
15 Director Human Resources ....Mr. Matt TILLER
88 Director of Campus Enhancement ....Mr. Tom WOOD
18 Director of Campus & Retail Ops ....Mr. Jeff WILSON
91 Director of Admin Computing ....Mr. Joe TRIMBLE
105 Director of Information Security ....Mr. Dave WAGNER

Martin Methodist College (A)

433 W Madison Street, Pulaski TN 38478-2799
County: Giles FICE Identification: 003504
Unit ID: 220701
Telephone: (931) 363-9804 Carnegie Class: Bac/Diverse
FAX Number: (931) 363-9818 Calendar System: Semester
URL: www.martinmethodist.edu
Established: 1870 Annual Undergrad Tuition & Fees: $20,998
Enrollment: 1,107 Coed
Affiliation or Control: United Methodist IRS Status: 501(c)3
Highest Offering: Baccalaureate
Program: Liberal Arts And General
Accreditation: SC, NURSE

01 President ....Dr. Ted R. BROWN
05 Vice President of Academic Affairs ....Dr. James T. MURRELL
10 VP for Finance & Administration ....Mr. David J. STEPHENS
32 VP Campus Life/Enrollment Mgmt ....Mr. Robby C. SHELTON
30 Vice Pres for College Advancement ....Dr. Jack L. GREGORY
06 Registrar/Dir Institutional Rsrch ....Dr. Dennis E. HASKINS
41 Athletic Director ....Mr. Jeff N. BAIN
42 Chaplain ....Rev. Laura KIRKPATRICK
08 Librarian ....Mr. Richard MADDEN
40 Director of Bookstore ....Mrs. Margaret W. JACKSON
29 Alumni Affairs Director ....Mrs. Edna LUNA
04 Assistant to the President ....Mrs. Kim W. HARRISON
07 Director of Admissions ....Mrs. Lisa SMITH
15 Director Personnel Services ....Mr. James R. HLUBB
21 Controller ....Ms. Rhonda CLINARD
37 Director Student Financial Aid ....Mrs. Emma HLUBB
18 Chief Facilities/Physical Plant ....Mr. Fred HYDE
26 Director of Public Relations ....Mr. Grant VOSBURGH
38 Dir Student Counseling/Career/Svcs ....Ms. Doris F. WOSSUM
85 Director Foreign Students ....Ms. Georgia UDE
13 Director of Technology ....Mr. Edward MARTIN

Maryville College (B)

502 E Lamar Alexander Parkway,
Maryville TN 37804-5907
County: Blount FICE Identification: 003505
Unit ID: 220710
Telephone: (865) 981-8000 Carnegie Class: Bac/A&S
FAX Number: (865) 981-8010 Calendar System: Semester
URL: www.maryvillecollege.edu
Established: 1819 Annual Undergrad Tuition & Fees: $30,522
Enrollment: 1,078 Coed
Affiliation or Control: Presbyterian Church (U.S.A.) IRS Status: 501(c)3
Highest Offering: Baccalaureate
Program: Liberal Arts And General; Teacher Preparatory; Professional
Accreditation: SC, MUS

01 President ....Dr. William T. BOGART
05 Vice President & Dean of College ....Dr. Barbara WELLS
10 Vice President & Treasurer ....Mr. Dana SMITH
32 Vice President & Dean of Students ....Ms. Vandy KEMP
84 Vice President for Enrollment ....Dr. Dolph HENRY
30 VP of Advancement & Cmty Rels ....Ms. Holly SULLIVAN
09 Associate Dean & Dir of IR ....Dr. Martha P. CRAIG
35 Associate Dean of Students ....Dr. Andy LEWTER
21 Asst Vice Pres for Finance ....Ms. Nancy PYANOE
26 Director of Marketing ....Ms. Mary LEIDIG
27 Director of Communications ....Ms. Karen ELDRIDGE
06 Registrar ....Ms. Kathy WILSON
13 Director of Information Technology ....Mr. Mark FUGATE
90 Dir of Instructional Technology ....Dr. Steven JAMES
24 Director of Learning Center ....Ms. Lori HUNTER
36 Director of Career Resources ....Ms. Thema MCCOWAN
37 Director of Financial Aid ....Mr. Richard BRAND
41 Athletic Director ....Ms. Kandis SCHRAM
08 Director of the Library ....Ms. Angela QUICK
18 Director of Physical Plant ....Mr. Andy K. MCCALL
42 Campus Minister ....Rev. Anne MCKEE
04 Assistant to President ....Ms. Laura M. CASE
15 Director of Human Resources ....Ms. Keni LANAGAN
38 Director of Counseling ....Mr. Bruce HOLT
44 Director of Annual Giving ....Mr. Eric BELLAH
22 Director of Minority Services ....Mr. Larry ERVIN
29 Dir of Stewardship & Alumni Bd Rels ....Ms. Diana CANACARIS

Meharry Medical College (C)

1005 Dr. D. B. Todd Jr. Boulevard,
Nashville TN 37208-3501
County: Davidson FICE Identification: 003506
Unit ID: 220792
Telephone: (615) 327-6111 Carnegie Class: Spec/Med
FAX Number: (615) 327-6540 Calendar System: Semester
URL: www.mmc.edu
Established: 1876 Annual Graduate Tuition & Fees: $47,736
Enrollment: 772 Coed
Affiliation or Control: Independent Non-Profit IRS Status: 501(c)3
Highest Offering: Doctorate; No Undergraduates
Program: Professional
Accreditation: SC, DENT, MED, PH

01 President & Chief Executive Officer ....Dr. Wayne J. RILEY
05 Executive Vice President & Provost ....Vacant
32 Int Assoc Dean Student/Academic Aff .....Dr. Mildred D. COLLINS
17 Sr Vice President Health Affairs ....Dr. Charles P. MOUTON
30 Sr VP Institutional Advancement ....Mr. Robert S. POOLE
10 Senior Vice President & CFO ....Mrs. LaMel BANDY-NEAL
45 Vice President for Research ....Dr. Russell POLAND
35 Assoc VP Student Svcs/Enroll Mgmt ....Mrs. Karen LEWIS
13 Assoc VP Information Technology ....Mr. Andrew JACKSON
31 Sr Assoc Vice Pres External Affairs ....Mr. Osei MEVS
11 Assoc Vice President Administration ....Dr. Bernard RAY
16 Assoc Vice Pres Human Resources ....Ms. Leslie CARROLL
26 Assoc VP Marketing/Communications ....Ms. Janet CALDWELL
21 Assoc Vice Pres Financial Systems ....Mr. Larry HOLDEN
43 General Counsel/Corporate Sec/Sr VP .... Mr. Benjamin RAWLINS
58 Dean Graduate Studies .... Dr. Maria DE FATIMA LIMA
51 Director Lifelong Learning .... Dr. Allyson FLEMING
63 Dean School of Medicine .... Dr. Charles P. MOUTON
76 Dean Allied Health Professions ....Vacant
52 Dean School of Dentistry .... Dr. Janet H. SOUTHERLAND
29 Executive Director Alumni Affairs ....Dr. Henry MOSES
07 Director Admissions & Recruitment ....Mr. Angelo C. LEE
08 Director of Library ....Ms. Fatima MNCUBE-BARNES
19 Director Campus Safety & Security .... Ms. Theresa MCKINNON
25 Director Grants & Contracts .... Mr. George WILLIAMS
46 Assoc VP for Research-Grants Mgmt ....Vacant
37 Director Student Financial Aid .... Ms. Barbara THARPE
09 Director Institutional Research ....Dr. Chau-Kuang CHEN
100 Special Assistant & Chief of Staff ....Mrs. Lisa JOHNSON
18 Director Facilities ....Mr. George N. KELLY
38 Director Counseling Center .... Ms. Sharda D. MISHRA
06 Registrar .... Ms. Shanita BROWN

Memphis College of Art (D)

1930 Poplar Avenue, Overton Park,
Memphis TN 38104-2764
County: Shelby FICE Identification: 003507
Unit ID: 220808
Telephone: (901) 272-5100 Carnegie Class: Spec/Arts
FAX Number: (901) 272-5104 Calendar System: Semester
URL: www.mca.edu
Established: 1936 Annual Undergrad Tuition & Fees: $25,600
Enrollment: 433 Coed
Affiliation or Control: Independent Non-Profit IRS Status: 501(c)3
Highest Offering: Master's
Program: Professional; Fine Arts Emphasis
Accreditation: SC, ART

01 President ....Dr. Ronald L. JONES
05 Dean of Faculty ....Mr. Remy MILLER
10 Vice Pres Finance & Administration ...... Ms. Sherry YELVINGTON
30 Vice President College Advancement ....Ms. Shawna ENGEL
84 Vice Pres Enrollment/Student Svcs ....Ms. Susan S. MILLER
08 Librarian .... Ms. Leslie HOLLAND
04 Assistant to President ....Ms. Becky RUPE
07 Director Admissions .... Ms. Annette JAMES-MOORE
32 Director Student Life ....Ms. Carla RUFFER
37 Director Financial Aid ....Mr. Aaron WHITE
06 Registrar ....Mr. Sean SCOTT
13 Director Computing Services .... Mr. Gordon DOVER
19 Director Safety & Security .... Mr. Donald KELLY
26 Director College Communications .... Ms. Cara SIEVERS
29 Director Alumni & Donor Relations ....Ms. LeeAnn WARNER
31 Coordinator Community Education .... Ms. Cecelia PALAZOLA
21 Assoc Business Officer/Staff Acct .... Ms. Heather RAGLAND
36 Director Career Services .... Ms. Gadsby CRESON

Memphis Theological Seminary (E)

168 East Parkway S at Union, Memphis TN 38104-4395
County: Shelby FICE Identification: 010529
Unit ID: 220871
Telephone: (901) 458-8232 Carnegie Class: Spec/Faith
FAX Number: (901) 452-4051 Calendar System: Semester
URL: www.memphisseminary.edu
Established: 1852 Annual Graduate Tuition & Fees: $13,080
Enrollment: 325 Coed
Affiliation or Control: Cumberland Presbyterian IRS Status: 501(c)3
Highest Offering: Doctorate; No Undergraduates
Program: Professional; Religious Emphasis
Accreditation: SC, THEOL

01 President .... Dr. Daniel J. EARHEART-BROWN
05 Vice President Academic Affs & Dean ....Dr. Robert S. WOOD
30 Vice President of Advancement ....Mrs. Cathi JOHNSON
08 Librarian ....Mr. Steven R. EDSCORN
51 Assoc Dean Continuing Education ....Mr. Pete GATHJE
10 Vice President of Operations/
CFO ....Mrs. Cassandra F. PRICE-PERRY
32 Director of Student Services ....Dr. Barry L. ANDERSON
06 Dir Acad Rec/Regist & Accreditation ....Dr. Gail D. ROBINSON

Mid-America Baptist Theological Seminary (F)

2095 Appling Road, Cordova TN 38016-4911
County: Shelby FICE Identification: 029172
Unit ID: 220914
Telephone: (901) 751-8453 Carnegie Class: Not Classified
FAX Number: (901) 751-8454 Calendar System: Semester
URL: www.mabts.edu
Established: 1972 Annual Undergrad Tuition & Fees: $4,825
Enrollment: 415 Coed
Affiliation or Control: Independent Non-Profit IRS Status: 501(c)3
Highest Offering: Doctorate
Program: 2-Year Principally Bachelor's Creditable; Teacher Preparatory; Professional
Accreditation: SC

01 President .... Dr. Michael R. SPRADLIN
03 Executive Vice President .... Dr. Bradley THOMPSON
05 Academic Vice President ....Dr. Timothy SEAL
30 Vice Pres Institutional Advancement ....Mr. Duffy GUYTON
10 Chief Financial Officer ....Mr. Randy REDD
20 Director of Masters & Associate Pgm .... Dr. Kirk KILPATRICK
12 Director NE Branch ....Dr. Shawn BUICE
06 Registrar ....Mrs. Rose MINK
08 Director of Library Services .... Mr. Terrence BROWN
42 Director of Practical Missions ....Dr. Jeff BRAWNER
07 Director of Admissions ....Dr. Andy HYNES
04 Admin Assistant to the President ....Mrs. Maria WOOTEN
18 Supt of Buildings & Grounds .... Mr. Gene APPLEBURY
40 Manager Bookstore ....Mr. Brad JOHNSON

Mid-South Christian College (G)

PO Box 181056, Memphis TN 38181
County: Shelby Identification: 667046
Telephone: (901) 375-4400 Carnegie Class: Not Classified
FAX Number: (901) 375-4085 Calendar System: Semester
URL: www.midsouthcc.org
Established: 1959 Annual Undergrad Tuition & Fees: $5,900
Enrollment: 22 Coed
Affiliation or Control: Independent Non-Profit IRS Status: 501(c)3
Highest Offering: Baccalaureate
Program: Religious Emphasis
Accreditation: @BI

01 President .... Mr. Larry GRIFFIN
05 Academic Dean .... Mr. Wray GRAHAM
32 Director of Student Services ....Mr. Brent LINN
30 Chief Development Officer .... Mr. John BLIFFEN
88 Director Institutional Improvement ....Mr. Greg WADDELL

Middle Tennessee School of Anesthesia (H)

PO Box 417, 315 Hospital Drive, Madison TN 37116-6414
County: Davidson FICE Identification: 007783
Unit ID: 220996
Telephone: (615) 868-6503 Carnegie Class: Spec/Health
FAX Number: (615) 868-9885 Calendar System: Quarter
URL: www.mtsa.edu
Established: 1950 Annual Graduate Tuition & Fees: $30,966
Enrollment: 216 Coed
Affiliation or Control: Independent Non-Profit IRS Status: 501(c)3
Highest Offering: Doctorate; No Undergraduates
Program: Professional
Accreditation: SC, ANEST

01 President ....Dr. Kenneth L. SCHWAB
05 Dean/Program Administrator ....Dr. Christopher P. HULIN

Miller-Motte Technical College (I)

1820 Business Park Drive, Clarksville TN 37040-6023
County: Montgomery FICE Identification: 026142
Unit ID: 382771
Telephone: (931) 553-0071 Carnegie Class: Assoc/PrivFP
FAX Number: (931) 552-2916 Calendar System: Quarter
URL: www.miller-motte.com
Established: 1916 Annual Undergrad Tuition & Fees: $10,900
Enrollment: 573 Coed
Affiliation or Control: Proprietary IRS Status: Proprietary
Highest Offering: Associate Degree
Program: Occupational
Accreditation: ACICS, MAC, POLYT, SURGT

01 Director .... Ms. Gina CASTLEBERRY
05 Director of Education ....Ms. Kala MATHIS
37 Financial Aid Director .... Ms. Debbie STRATMAN
06 Registrar ....Ms. Patricia CLINE
36 Director of Career Development .... Mr. John MCCASLIN
07 Director of Admissions .... Ms. Gayle KILGORE
72 CIS/Technology Division .... Mr. Bruce LIVESAY

Milligan College (J)

1 Milligan College, Milligan College TN 37682-4000
County: Carter FICE Identification: 003511
Unit ID: 221014
Telephone: (423) 461-8700 Carnegie Class: Bac/Diverse
FAX Number: (423) 461-8755 Calendar System: Semester
URL: www.milligan.edu
Established: 1866 Annual Undergrad Tuition & Fees: $26,760
Enrollment: 1,208 Coed
Affiliation or Control: Independent Non-Profit IRS Status: 501(c)3
Highest Offering: Master's
Program: Liberal Arts And General; Teacher Preparatory; Professional
Accreditation: SC, NURSE, OT, TED

01 President ..... Dr. William B. GREER
05 Vice Pres Academic Affairs/Dean ..... Dr. Garland YOUNG
32 Vice President Student Affairs ..... Mr. Mark FOX
30 Vice Pres Institutional Advancement ..... Mr. Jack SIMPSON
84 Vice Pres Enrollment Management ..... Dr. Lee FIERBAUGH
21 Vice Pres Business & Finance ..... Mrs. Jacqui STEADMAN
06 Registrar/Institutional Research ..... Mrs. Sue SKIDMORE
07 Director of Admissions ..... Ms. Tracy BRINN
08 Director of Library Services ..... Mr. Gary DAUGHT
35 Director of Student Activities ..... Mrs. Katy MOSBY
29 Director of Alumni Relations ..... Ms. Theresa GARBE
15 Director Personnel Services ..... Ms. Linda LAWSON
37 Coordinator of Financial Aid ..... Ms. Diane KEASLING
26 Director of Church Relations ..... Mrs. Phyllis FOX
36 Director Student Placement ..... Ms. Beth ANDERSON
18 Service Manager Facilities ..... Mr. Ken BROYLES
28 Director of Diversity ..... Mr. Ernesto VILLARREAL

Nashville Auto-Diesel College (A)

1524 Gallatin Road, Nashville TN 37206-3298
County: Davidson FICE Identification: 007440
Unit ID: 221148
Telephone: (615) 226-3990 Carnegie Class: Assoc/PrivFP
FAX Number: (615) 262-8466 Calendar System: Other
URL: www.nadcedu.com
Established: 1919 Annual Undergrad Tuition & Fees: $25,800
Enrollment: 2,200 Coed
Affiliation or Control: Proprietary IRS Status: Proprietary
Highest Offering: Associate Degree
Program: Occupational
Accreditation: ACCSC

01 President ..... Mr. Jim COAKLEY
03 Vice President ..... Mr. Doug FOX
05 Vice President Education ..... Mr. Scott REYNOLDS
26 Vice President Marketing ..... Mr. Cary OLIVER
37 Director of Financial Aid ..... Mr. Chris BIDDLE
06 Registrar ..... Mr. Gary WHITE

National College of Business and Technology (B)

1328 Highway 11 W, Bristol TN 37620-8530
County: Sullivan Identification: 666500
Telephone: (423) 878-4440 Carnegie Class: Not Classified
FAX Number: (923) 793-1060 Calendar System: Quarter
URL: www.ncbt.edu
Established: 1886 Annual Undergrad Tuition & Fees: $9,500
Enrollment: 492 Coed
Affiliation or Control: Proprietary IRS Status: Proprietary
Highest Offering: Baccalaureate
Program: Occupational; Technical Emphasis
Accreditation: ACICS, MAC

01 Director ..... Mr. Michael STOUT

National College of Business and Technology (C)

1638 Bell Road, Nashville TN 37211
County: Davidson FICE Identification: 004617
Unit ID: 388043
Telephone: (615) 333-3344 Carnegie Class: Assoc/PrivFP
FAX Number: (615) 333-3429 Calendar System: Quarter
URL: www.ncbt.edu
Established: 1991 Annual Undergrad Tuition & Fees: $11,101
Enrollment: 1,225 Coed
Affiliation or Control: Proprietary IRS Status: Proprietary
Highest Offering: Baccalaureate
Program: Occupational
Accreditation: ACICS, MAC

01 Director ..... Mr. Patrick PATTERSON

North Central Institute (D)

168 Jack Miller Boulevard Suite A,
Clarksville TN 37042-4810
County: Montgomery FICE Identification: 030791
Unit ID: 418889
Telephone: (931) 431-9700 Carnegie Class: Assoc/PrivFP
FAX Number: (931) 431-9771 Calendar System: Semester
URL: www.nci.edu
Established: 1988 Annual Undergrad Tuition & Fees: $13,770
Enrollment: 380 Coed
Affiliation or Control: Proprietary IRS Status: Proprietary
Highest Offering: Associate Degree
Program: Occupational; 2-Year Principally Bachelor's Creditable; Technical Emphasis
Accreditation: COE

01 President ..... Ms. Tamela K. TALIENTO

Nossi College of Art (E)

590 Cheron Road, Nashville TN 37115
County: Davidson FICE Identification: 025782
Unit ID: 368452
Telephone: (615) 514-2787 Carnegie Class: Spec/Arts
FAX Number: (615) 514-2788 Calendar System: Trimester
URL: www.nossi.edu
Established: 1973 Annual Undergrad Tuition & Fees: $14,100
Enrollment: 408 Coed
Affiliation or Control: Proprietary IRS Status: Proprietary
Highest Offering: Baccalaureate
Program: Occupational; 2-Year Principally Bachelor's Creditable
Accreditation: ACCSC

01 President ..... Ms. Nossi VATANDOOST
07 Admissions Director ..... Ms. Mary ALEXANDER
37 Financial Aid Director ..... Ms. Mary KIDD

O'More College of Design (F)

423 S Margin Street, Franklin TN 37064
County: Williamson FICE Identification: 021064
Unit ID: 221254
Telephone: (615) 794-4254 Carnegie Class: Spec/Arts
FAX Number: (615) 790-1662 Calendar System: Semester
URL: www.omorecollege.edu
Established: 1970 Annual Undergrad Tuition & Fees: $25,000
Enrollment: 205 Coed
Affiliation or Control: Independent Non-Profit IRS Status: 501(c)3
Highest Offering: Baccalaureate
Program: Occupational; Liberal Arts And General; Fine Arts Emphasis
Accreditation: ACCSC, CIDA

01 President and CEO ..... Dr. Mark HILLIARD
05 VP of Academics/Chair Liberal Arts ..... Ms. Shari FOX
06 Registrar ..... Ms. Amy SHELTON
10 Director of Business Affairs ..... Ms. Teresa CORLEY
19 Director of Security ..... Mr. DeWayne PULLIAM
07 Director of Admissions ..... Ms. Melinda DABBS
08 Librarian and Bookstore Manager ..... Ms. Allison CRAWFORD
88 Chair Visual Communications ..... Mr. Josh LOMELINO
88 Chair Fashion Design/Merch ..... Ms. Jamie ATLAS
88 Chair Interior Design ..... Mr. David KOELLEIN
57 Chair Fine Arts ..... Ms. Janet CRUZ

Oxford Graduate School (G)

500 Oxford Drive, Dayton TN 37321-6736
County: Rhea FICE Identification: 038403
Telephone: (423) 775-6596 Carnegie Class: Not Classified
FAX Number: (423) 775-6599 Calendar System: Trimester
URL: www.ogs.edu
Established: 1981 Annual Graduate Tuition & Fees: $31,500
Enrollment: 92 Coed
Affiliation or Control: Independent Non-Profit IRS Status: 501(c)3
Highest Offering: Doctorate; No Undergraduates
Program: Professional
Accreditation: TRACS

01 President ..... Dr. Donald PRICE
00 Chancellor ..... Dr. Rollin VAN BROEKHOVEN
05 Vice President Acadmic Affairs ..... Dr. Richard P. WALTERS
07 Vice President of Recruitment ..... Vacant
08 Head Librarian ..... Dr. Sara LAMBERT
09 Director Institutional Research ..... Mr. Richard NTI
10 Chief Business Officer ..... Ms. Sharlene DANIEL
29 Director Alumni Relations ..... Dr. Jimmilea BERRYHILL
37 Director Financial Aid/Admissions ..... Mr. Michael FARRAND
42 Chaplain ..... Dr. Richard HUMPHREY
06 Registrar ..... Mrs. Joanne PHILLIPS

Pentecostal Theological Seminary (H)

900 Walker Street, NE, Cleveland TN 37311
County: Bradley FICE Identification: 021883
Unit ID: 219842
Telephone: (423) 478-1131 Carnegie Class: Spec/Faith
FAX Number: (423) 478-7711 Calendar System: 4/1/4
URL: www.ptseminary.edu
Established: 1975 Annual Graduate Tuition & Fees: $14,328
Enrollment: 171 Coed
Affiliation or Control: Church Of God IRS Status: 501(c)3
Highest Offering: Doctorate; No Undergraduates
Program: Professional
Accreditation: SC, THEOL

01 President ..... Dr. Steven J. LAND
05 VP for Academics ..... Dr. Sang-Ehil HAN
42 VP for Ministry Formation ..... Dr. Oliver L. MCMAHAN
10 VP for Finance ..... Mr. Robert E. BUXTON
30 VP for Institutional Advancement ..... Rev. Ken R. DAVIS
04 Exec Assistant to the President ..... Mrs. Teresa GILBERT
27 Director Recruitment/Communications ..... Dr. J. Anthony LOMBARD
07 Director of Admissions/Registrar ..... Ms. Anita F. BLEVINS
15 Director of Administrative Services ..... Mrs. Alanna L. HENRY
18 Dir of Facilities/Support Services ..... Dr. Welton WRISTON
29 Dir Donor and Alumni Relations ..... Mrs. Joylita TERPSTRA
32 Director of Student Services ..... Dr. Jimmy DUPREE
37 Director of Financial Aid ..... Mrs. Robin SLUDER
38 Director of Counseling/Testing ..... Dr. Douglas SLOCUMB

Remington College (I)

2710 Nonconnah Boulevard, Memphis TN 38132-2110
County: Shelby Identification: 666062
Unit ID: 412599
Telephone: (901) 345-1000 Carnegie Class: Assoc/PrivFP4
FAX Number: (901) 396-8310 Calendar System: Quarter
URL: www.remingtoncollege.edu
Established: 1987 Annual Undergrad Tuition & Fees: $15,495
Enrollment: 1,000 Coed
Affiliation or Control: Proprietary IRS Status: Proprietary
Highest Offering: Baccalaureate
Program: Occupational; 2-Year Principally Bachelor's Creditable
Accreditation: ACCSC

01 President ..... Dr. Lori K. MAY

† Branch campus of Remington College, Mobile, AL.

Remington College (J)

441 Donelson Pike, Suite 150, Nashville TN 37214-3558
County: Davidson Identification: 666307
Unit ID: 445249
Telephone: (615) 889-5520 Carnegie Class: Assoc/PrivFP
FAX Number: (615) 493-9385 Calendar System: Other
URL: www.remingtoncollege.edu
Established: 2003 Annual Undergrad Tuition & Fees: $15,495
Enrollment: 373 Coed
Affiliation or Control: Proprietary IRS Status: Proprietary
Highest Offering: Associate Degree
Program: Occupational
Accreditation: ACCSC, DH

01 Campus President ..... Mr. Larry COLLINS

† Branch campus of Remington College, Mobile, AL.

Rhodes College (K)

2000 North Parkway, Memphis TN 38112-1690
County: Shelby FICE Identification: 003519
Unit ID: 221351
Telephone: (901) 843-3000 Carnegie Class: Bac/A&S
FAX Number: N/A Calendar System: Semester
URL: www.rhodes.edu
Established: 1848 Annual Undergrad Tuition & Fees: $37,782
Enrollment: 1,712 Coed
Affiliation or Control: Presbyterian Church (U.S.A.) IRS Status: 501(c)3
Highest Offering: Master's
Program: Liberal Arts And General
Accreditation: SC, MUS

01 President ..... Dr. William E. TROUTT
05 Provost ..... Dr. Michael R. DROMPP
10 VP for Finance & Business Affairs ..... Mr. J. Allen BOONE
13 Vice Pres for Information Services . Dr. Robert M. JOHNSON, JR.
30 Vice President for Development ..... Ms. Jennifer G. WADE
84 Vice Pres Enrollment/Communications ..... Mr. Carey THOMPSON
32 Dean of Students ..... Ms. Carol E. CASEY
35 Associate Dean of Students ..... Ms. Kathleen LAAKSO
20 Assoc Dean of Academic Affairs ..... Dr. Brian W. SHAFFER
20 Assoc Dean of Academic Affairs ..... Dr. John S. OLSEN
20 Assoc Dean of Academic Affairs ..... Dr. Anita A. DAVIS
06 Registrar ..... Ms. DeAnna ADAMS
37 Director of Financial Aid ..... Ms. Ashley BIANCHI
08 Librarian ..... Ms. Darlene D. BROOKS
21 Comptroller ..... Mr. Kyle WEBB
29 Director of Alumni Relations ..... Mr. Warren A. RICHEY
15 Director of Human Resources ..... Ms. Claire R. SHAPIRO
14 Director of Info Tech Services ..... Dr. Charles LEMOND
19 Director of Campus Safety ..... Mr. Ike SLOAS
41 Director of Athletics ..... Mr. Michael T. CLARY
36 Director of Career Services ..... Ms. Sandra G. TRACY
38 Director of Counseling Services ..... Mr. Robert B. DOVE
18 Director of Physical Plant ..... Mr. Brian E. FOSHEE
44 Director of Planned Giving ..... Mr. Jim DUNCAN
27 Director of Communications ..... Mr. Ken WOODMANSEE
09 Director of Institutional Research ..... Vacant
04 Exec Assistant to the President ..... Ms. Melody H. RICHEY
96 Physical Plant Business Manager ..... Ms. Amy J. RADFORD

Sewanee: The University of the South (L)

735 University Avenue, Sewanee TN 37383-1000
County: Franklin FICE Identification: 003534
Unit ID: 221519
Telephone: (931) 598-1000 Carnegie Class: Bac/A&S
FAX Number: (931) 598-1145 Calendar System: Semester
URL: www.sewanee.edu
Established: 1857 Annual Undergrad Tuition & Fees: $34,714
Enrollment: 1,557 Coed
Affiliation or Control: Protestant Episcopal IRS Status: 501(c)3
Highest Offering: Doctorate
Program: Liberal Arts And General; Professional
Accreditation: SC, THEOL

01 Vice Chancellor & President ..... Dr. John M. MCCARDELL, JR.
05 Provost ..... Dr. John R. SWALLOW
30 Vice President for Advancement ..... Mr. Jay FISHER
13 Assoc Provost Info Tech/Librarian ..... Dr. Vicki G. SELLS
20 Associate Provost Academic Affairs ..... Dr. Nancy BERNER
49 Dean College of Arts & Sciences ..... Dr. John J. GATTA
73 Dean School of Theology ..... Rev Dr. William S. STAFFORD
32 Dean of Students ..... Mr. Eric G. HARTMAN
20 Assoc Dean Arts & Sciences ..... Dr. Larry H. JONES
20 Assoc Dean Arts and Sciences ..... Dr. Richard G. SUMMERS
10 Vice President for Finance & Admin ..... Dr. Jerry FORSTER
09 Director of Institutional Research ..... Dr. Robert A. LESTER, III

06 Registrar .... Mr. Paul G. WILEY
07 Dean of Admission & Financial Aid .... Ms. Lee Ann M. AFTON
26 Exec Dir Marketing/Communications .... Mr. Parker OLIVER
15 Director of Human Resources .... Ms. Mary WILSON
41 Director of Athletics .... Mr. Mark F. WEBB
29 Director of Alumni Relations .... Ms. Susan S. ASKEW
36 Director of Career Services .... Ms. Kim D. HEITZENRATER
38 Director of University Counseling .... Dr. David L. SPAULDING
93 Director of Minority Affairs .... Mr. Eric V. BENJAMIN
18 Director of Physical Plant Services .... Mr. John P. VINEYARD
43 University Legal Counsel .... Ms. Donna L. PIERCE
35 Associate Dean of Students .... Dr. Alex M. BRUCE
19 Chief of Police .... Mr. Robert W. WHITE
21 Assistant Treasurer .... Ms. Sarah R. SUTHERLAND
23 Director of Univ Health Services .... Ms. Karen THARP
24 Director of Media Services .... Mr. Larry E. WOOD
42 University Chaplain .... V.Rev. Thomas E. MACFIE
11 Assoc Vice President for Admin .... Mr. Frank GLADU

South College (A)

3904 Lonas Drive, Knoxville TN 37909-3323
County: Knox FICE Identification: 004938
Unit ID: 220552
Telephone: (865) 251-1800 Carnegie Class: Bac/Assoc
FAX Number: (865) 584-7335 Calendar System: Quarter
URL: www.southcollegetn.edu
Established: 1882 Annual Undergrad Tuition & Fees: $17,550
Enrollment: 1,049 Coed
Affiliation or Control: Proprietary IRS Status: Proprietary
Highest Offering: Doctorate
Program: Occupational; Teacher Preparatory; Professional
Accreditation: SC, ARCPA, MAC, NMT, NUR, @PHAR, PTAA, RAD

01 President .... Mr. Stephen A. SOUTH
05 Executive Vice President .... Dr. Kim B. HALL
11 Vice Pres Administrative Services .... Mr. Steve WOODFORD
13 VP Information Tech/Facilities .... Mr. Ron HALL
09 VP Inst Effective/Student Svcs .... Ms. Barbara BRIMI
84 VP Enrollment Management .... Mr. Walter HOSEA
10 Chief Financial Officer .... Mr. Mark HAUB
21 Controller .... Mr. Kevin SPARKS
26 Public Relations Coordinator .... Mr. Norman HAMMITT
36 Job Placement Coordinator .... Mr. Gary TAYLOR
06 Registrar .... Ms. Kim WOOD
37 Director of Financial Aid .... Mr. Larry BROADWATER
08 Librarian .... Ms. Mary MCHUGH
72 Director Instructional Technology .... Dr. Jennifer GRAMLING

Southern Adventist University (B)

Box 370, 5010 University Drive,
Collegedale TN 37315-0370
County: Hamilton FICE Identification: 003518
Unit ID: 221661
Telephone: (423) 236-2000 Carnegie Class: Bac/Diverse
FAX Number: (423) 236-1000 Calendar System: Semester
URL: www.southern.edu
Established: 1892 Annual Undergrad Tuition & Fees: $18,324
Enrollment: 3,200 Coed
Affiliation or Control: Seventh-day Adventist IRS Status: 501(c)3
Highest Offering: Doctorate
Program: Liberal Arts And General; Teacher Preparatory
Accreditation: SC, ADNUR, CS, IACBE, MUS, NUR, SW, TED

01 President .... Dr. Gordon BIETZ
05 Vice Pres Academic Administration .... Dr. Robert YOUNG
10 Vice President Finance .... Mr. Tom VERRILL
32 Vice President Student Services .... Dr. William R. WOHLERS
45 Vice Pres Strategic Initiatives .... Mrs. Vinita R. SAUDER
30 Vice President Advancement .... Mr. Chris CAREY
84 Vice Pres Enrollment Services .... Mr. Marc A. GRUNDY
20 Associate VP Academic Admin .... Dr. Volker HENNING
21 Associate VP Financial Admin .... Mr. Marty HAMILTON
13 Assoc VP Information Systems .... Mr. Gary SEWELL
09 Director Inst Research/Planning .... Dr. Hollis JAMES
08 Director of Libraries .... Vacant
06 Director Records & Advisement .... Mrs. Joni I. ZIER
15 Director Personnel Services .... Mrs. Pat COVERDALE
26 Chief Public Relations Officer .... Ms. Ingrid SKANTZ
29 Director Alumni Relations .... Ms. Evonne CROOK
38 Director Student Counseling .... Dr. Jim WAMPLER
33 Dean of Men .... Mr. Dwight E. MAGERS
34 Dean of Women .... Ms. Kassy KRAUSE
50 Dean School of Business/Mgmt .... Dr. Donald C. VAN ORNAM
53 Dean School of Education/Psych .... Dr. John MCCOY
57 Dean School of Visual Art/Design .... Mr. Randy CRAVEN
60 Dean School of Journalism/Comm .... Dr. Greg RUMSEY
64 Dean School of Music .... Dr. Scott BALL
66 Dean School of Nursing .... Dr. Barbara JAMES
68 Dean Sch of Phys Ed/Health/Wellness .... Dr. Phil GARVER
73 Dean School of Religion .... Dr. Greg KING
77 Dean School of Computing .... Dr. Rick HALTERMAN
70 Chair Social Work/Family Studies .... Dr. Rene' DRUMM
72 Chair Technology .... Mr. Dale WALTERS
81 Chair Mathematics .... Dr. Kevin BROWN
76 Chair Biology/Allied Health .... Dr. Keith SNYDER
88 Chair Chemistry .... Dr. Rhonda J. SCOTT
88 Chair English .... Dr. Jan HALUSKA
88 Chair History .... Dr. Lisa C. DILLER
88 Chair Modern Languages .... Dr. Carlos P. PARRA
88 Chair Physics .... Dr. Chris HANSEN

18 Chief Facilities/Physical Plant .... Mr. Clair KITSON
35 Director Student Affairs .... Ms. Kari SHULTZ
37 Director Student Financial Aid .... Mr. Jason MERRYMAN
96 Director of Purchasing .... Mr. Russell ORRISON

Southern College of Optometry (C)

1245 Madison Avenue, Memphis TN 38104-2222
County: Shelby FICE Identification: 003517
Unit ID: 221670
Telephone: (901) 722-3200 Carnegie Class: Spec/Health
FAX Number: (901) 722-3279 Calendar System: Trimester
URL: www.sco.edu
Established: 1932 Annual Graduate Tuition & Fees: $27,882
Enrollment: 494 Coed
Affiliation or Control: Independent Non-Profit IRS Status: 501(c)3
Highest Offering: Doctorate; No Undergraduates
Program: Professional
Accreditation: SC, OPT, OPTR

01 President .... Dr. Richard W. PHILLIPS
04 Executive Admin Assistant to Pres .... Ms. Sandra S. STEPHENS
05 Vice President for Academic Affairs .... Dr. Lewis REICH
30 Vice President for Inst Advancement .... Dr. Kristin K. ANDERSON
102 Dir of Corp & Foundation Relations .... Ms. Christine M. WEINREICH
10 Vice President for Finance & Admin .... Mr. David L. WEST
13 Director of Information Services .... Mr. Dean SWICK
18 Director of Physical Plant .... Mr. Danny ANDERSON
17 Vice Pres for Clinical Programs .... Dr. James E. VENABLE
23 Director of Clinic Operations .... Mr. Gary SNUFFIN
06 Vice President for Student Services .... Mr. Joseph H. HAUSER
07 Dir of Admissions/Enrollment Svcs .... Mr. Michael N. ROBERTSON
07 Director of Student Recruitment .... Ms. Sunnie EWING
08 Director of Library .... Dr. Sharon E. TABACHNICK
27 Dir of Communications/Media Svcs .... Mr. Jim HOLLIFIELD
16 Vice President for Human Resources .... Ms. Ann Z. FIELDS
37 Director of Financial Aid .... Ms. Cindy GARNER

*Tennessee Board of Regents Office (D)

1415 Murfreesboro Road, Nashville TN 37217-2833
County: Davidson FICE Identification: 029031
Unit ID: 409379
Telephone: (615) 366-4400 Carnegie Class: N/A
FAX Number: (615) 366-3922
URL: www.tbr.edu

01 Chancellor .... Mr. John G. MORGAN
05 Int Vice Chanc Academic Affairs .... Dr. Kay CLARK
10 Vice Chanc Business & Finance .... Mr. Dale SIMS
11 Vice Chanc Admin & Fac Mgmt .... Mr. David B. GREGORY
12 Vice Chanc TN Technology Centers .... Mr. James KING
13 Vice Chanc Information Systems .... Mr. Tom DANFORD
88 Vice Chanc for Community Colleges .... Dr. Warren NICHOLS
43 General Counsel .... Ms. Christine A. MODISHER
09 Asst Vice Chanc Research/Assess .... Mr. Greg SCHUTZ
20 Assoc Vice Chanc Academic Affairs .... Dr. Treva G. BERRYMAN
20 Assoc Vice Chanc Academic Affairs .... Dr. S. Kay CLARK
20 Assoc Vice Chance Academic Affairs .... Dr. Pamela KNOX
21 Assistant Vice Chancellor Business .... Vacant
15 Asst Vice Chanc for Human Resources .... Ms. April PRESTON
21 Assistant Vice Chancellor Business .... Ms. Renee STEWART
88 Exec Dir of Operations for ROCC .... Dr. Raylean HENRY
26 Director of Communications .... Ms. Monica GREPPIN

*Austin Peay State University (E)

601 College Street, Clarksville TN 37044-0002
County: Montgomery FICE Identification: 003478
Unit ID: 219602
Telephone: (931) 221-7011 Carnegie Class: Master's L
FAX Number: (931) 221-7475 Calendar System: Semester
URL: www.apsu.edu
Established: 1927 Annual Undergrad Tuition & Fees (In-State): $6,648
Enrollment: 10,873 Coed
Affiliation or Control: State IRS Status: 501(c)3
Highest Offering: Beyond Master's But Less Than Doctorate
Program: Liberal Arts And General; Teacher Preparatory; Professional; Fine Arts Emphasis
Accreditation: SC, ART, ENGT, MT, MUS, NUR, RAD, SW, TED

02 President .... Mr. Timothy L. HALL
04 Exec Asst to the President .... Ms. Carol D. CLARK
05 Provost/VP Acad Affairs .... Dr. Tristan M. JOSEPH DENLEY
10 Vice President for Finance & Admin .... Mr. Mitch ROBINSON
43 University Attorney .... Ms. Stephanie REEVERS
20 Assistant VP Academic Affairs .... Mr. Brian JOHNSON
32 VP for Student Affairs .... Dr. Sherryl BYRD
21 Asst Vice Pres for Finance .... Mr. Timothy HURST
84 Assoc Provost for Enrollment Mgmt .... Dr. Beverly BOGGS
30 Exec Director Univ Advancement .... Mr. J. Roy GREGORY
31 Dir Community/Business Rels .... Ms. Carol CLARK
26 Exec Dir Marketing/Public Rels .... Mr. Bill PERSINGER
12 Exec Dir APSU Fort Campbell .... Dr. William COX
29 Dir Alumni and Annual Giving .... Ms. Nicole PETERSON
21 Director Budgets .... Ms. Sonja STEWART
08 Director Library .... Mr. Joe WEBER
13 Director of Information Technology .... Mr. Charles B. WALL
09 Dir Inst Research & Effectiveness .... Ms. Melissa HUNTER
07 Director of Admissions .... Ms. Amy DEATON

06 Registrar .... Ms. Telaina WRIGLEY
18 Director of Plant Administration .... Mr. Thomas HUTCHINS
45 Dir Facilities Planning & Projects .... Mr. Al WESTERMAN
41 Athletics Director .... Mr. David H. LOOS
27 Director of Athletic Information .... Mr. Brad J. KIRTLEY
37 Director of Student Financial Aid .... Ms. Donna PRICE
36 Director Academic Advisement .... Ms. Barbara BLACKSTON
38 Dir of Student Counseling Services .... Dr. Lowell RODDY
35 Dean of Students .... Mr. Gregory SINGLETON
88 Dir African Amer Cultural Ctr .... Mr. Henderson HILL
15 Director Human Resources .... Mr. Michael HAMLET
19 Director Public Safety .... Mr. Terence CALLOWAY
39 Director Housing/Resident Life .... Mr. F. Joe MILLS
21 Director Internal Audit .... Ms. Jacqueline STRUCKMEYER
25 Director of Grants .... Mr. Andrew SHEPARD-SMITH
96 Director of Purchasing .... Ms. Judy BLAIN
22 Dir Affirmative Action .... Ms. Sheila M. BRYANT
49 Dean College Arts & Letters .... Dr. Dixie WEBB
81 Dean Col Science & Math .... Dr. Jaime TAYLOR
53 Dean Col Behav Health Science .... Dr. David DENTON
58 Dean College Graduate Studies .... Dr. Dixie DENNIS
51 Exec Dir Extended & Distance Educ .... Mr. Dana WILLETT

*East Tennessee State University (F)

807 University Parkway, Johnson City TN 37614-6500
County: Washington FICE Identification: 003487
Unit ID: 220075
Telephone: (423) 439-1000 Carnegie Class: DRU
FAX Number: (423) 439-5770 Calendar System: Semester
URL: www.etsu.edu
Established: 1911 Annual Undergrad Tuition & Fees (In-State): $6,715
Enrollment: 14,662 Coed
Affiliation or Control: State IRS Status: 501(c)3
Highest Offering: Doctorate
Program: Occupational; Liberal Arts And General; Teacher Preparatory; Professional; Business Emphasis
Accreditation: SC, ART, AUD, BUS, BUSA, CACREP, CS, DH, DIETD, DIETI, ENGR, ENGT, JOUR, MED, MUS, NURSE, PH, PHAR, POLYT, PTA, RAD, SP, SW, TED

02 President .... Dr. Brian E. NOLAN
100 Chief of Staff/Assoc VP .... Dr. Jane M. JONES
05 Provost/Vice Pres Academic Affairs .... Dr. Bert C. BACH
10 Vice Pres Finance & Administration .... Dr. David D. COLLINS
17 Vice President Health Affairs/COO .... Dr. Wilsie S. BISHOP
30 Vice Pres University Advancement .... Dr. Richard A. MANAHAN
41 Athletic Director .... Mr. C. David MULLINS, JR.
28 Special Asst to Pres Cultural Div .... Ms. Mary V. JORDAN
88 Director of Internal Audit .... Ms. Rebecca B. LEWIS
43 University Counsel .... Mr. Edward J. KELLY
26 Exec Director of Univ Relations .... Mr. Fred W. SAUCEMAN
84 Vice Provost Enrollment Services .... Dr. Ramona A. WILLIAMS
51 Dean Cont Studies & Acad Outreach .... Dr. Richard E. OSBORN
46 Vice Prov Research/Sponsored Pgms .... Dr. William R. DUNCAN
32 VProv Student Aff/Dean of Students .... Dr. Joe H. SHERLIN
20 Vice Provost Academic Affairs .... Dr. M. Marshall GRUBE
20 VProv Ugrad Ed/Dir Plan & Analysis .... Dr. William G. KIRKWOOD
18 Assoc VP for Facilities Management .... Mr. William B. RASNICK, JR.
35 Associate Vice Pres Student Affairs .... Dr. Sally LEE
13 Assoc VP/Chief Information Officer .... Mr. Mark S. BRAGG
96 Assoc VP Procurement/Contract Svcs .... Dr. Katherine M. KELLEY
21 Assoc VP Financial Services .... Dr. B. J. KING
44 Assoc VP Univ Adv/Planned Giving .... Mr. Jeffrey W. ANDERSON
29 Assoc VP Univ Adv/Exec Dir Alumni .... Mr. Robert M. PLUMMER
106 AVP/Ex Dir E-Learning & Online Ed .... Dr. Karen D. KING
09 Asst VP Institutional Research .... Dr. Jack A. SANDERS
86 Asst VP for Governmental Relations .... Dr. Robert V. ACUFF
49 Dean College Arts & Science .... Dr. Gordon K. ANDERSON
50 Dean College of Business/Technology .... Dr. Linda R. GARCEAU
76 Dean College of Clin & Rehab Sci .... Dr. Nancy J. SCHERER
53 Dean College of Education .... Dr. W. Hal KNIGHT
92 Dean Honors College .... Dr. Rebecca A. PYLES
63 Dean College of Medicine .... Dr. Philip C. BAGNELL
67 Dean College of Pharmacy .... Dr. Larry D. CALHOUN
66 Dean College of Nursing .... Dr. Wendy M. NEHRING
69 Dean College of Public Health .... Dr. Randolph F. WYKOFF
58 Dean School of Graduate Studies .... Dr. Cecilia A. MCINTOSH
08 Dean of Libraries .... Ms. Patricia R. VAN ZANDT
06 University Registrar .... Ms. Sheryl L. BURNETTE
07 Interim Director of Admissions .... Mr. Paul S. HAYES
36 Dir Career & Internship Services .... Dr. David E. MAGEE, JR.
38 Director Counseling Center .... Dr. Steve D. BROWN
12 Director of ETSU at Kingsport .... Ms. Patricia L. STAFFORD
37 Director of Financial Aid .... Ms. Margaret L. MILLER
92 Director University Honors Program .... Dr. Michael A. CODY
39 Director Student Housing .... Dr. Bonnie L. BURCHETT
85 Dir International Programs/Services .... Ms. Maria D. COSTA
93 Multicultural Director .... Ms. Laura C. TERRY
19 Director Public Safety .... Chief Jack R. COTREL
25 Director of Sponsored Programs .... Dr. Louise C. NUTTLE
87 Director of Summer School .... Ms. Sarah E. BRADFORD
94 Director of Women's Studies .... Dr. Phyllis THOMPSON
105 Web Manager .... Ms. Michaele D. LAWS
15 Dir Empl Relations/Compensation/Dev .... Ms. Diana D. MCCLAY
15 Director Benefits/Retirement/HRIS .... Ms. Tammy S. HAMM

*Middle Tennessee State University (G)

1301 E Main Street, Murfreesboro TN 37132-0001
County: Rutherford FICE Identification: 003510
Unit ID: 220978
Telephone: (615) 898-2300 Carnegie Class: DRU
FAX Number: (615) 898-5538 Calendar System: Semester

URL: www.mtsu.edu
Established: 1911 Annual Undergrad Tuition & Fees (In-State): $6,753
Enrollment: 26,442 Coed
Affiliation or Control: State IRS Status: 501(c)3
Highest Offering: Doctorate
Program: Liberal Arts And General; Teacher Preparatory
Accreditation: SC, AAB, AAFCS, ART, BUS, BUSA, CACREP, CIDA, CS, DIETD, ENGT, JOUR, MUS, NAIT, NRPA, NURSE, SW, TED

02 President ..... Dr. Sidney A. MCPHEE
03 University Provost ..... Dr. Brad BARTEL
10 Senior Vice Pres Business & Finance ..... Dr. John W. COTHERN
30 Vice President Devel/Univ Relations ..... Mr. William J. BALES
32 VP Stdnt Affs/V Prov Enroll Mgmt ..... Dr. Debra K. SELLS
14 VP Info Tech/Chief Info Officer ..... Mr. Bruce PETRYSHAK
05 Vice Prov for Academic Affairs ..... Dr. John OMACHONU
58 Vice Provost Rsrch/Dean Grad Stds ..... Dr. Michael ALLEN
43 Univ Counsel & Asst to the Pres ..... Ms. Heidi ZIMMERMAN
04 Exec Assistant to the President ..... Ms. Kimberly S. EDGAR
22 Exec Dir Institutional Equity/Com ..... Ms. Barbara L. PATTON
31 Community Engagement/Asst to Pres ..... Dr. Gloria L. BONNER
07 Assoc Vice Prov Admis & Enroll Svcs ..... Vacant
13 Assoc Vice Pres Info Technology ..... Mr. Tom WALLACE
21 Assoc Vice Pres Business Office ..... Mr. Michael E. GOWER
35 Assoc Vice Pres/Dean Student Life ..... Ms. Sarah SUDAK
27 Assoc Vice Pres Mktg/Communications ..... Mr. Andrew OPPMANN
15 Asst Vice Pres Human Resource Svcs ..... Ms. Kathy I. MUSSELMAN
18 Asst Vice Pres Facilities Services ..... Mr. David W. GRAY
11 Asst Vice Pres Admin/Business Svcs ..... Ms. Kathryn CRISP
45 Asst Vice Pres Entrprse Rsrce Plng ..... Mrs. Lisa C. ROGERS
90 Asst Vice Pres Acad & Instruct Tech ..... Ms. Barbara J. DRAUDE
81 Dean Col Basic/Applied Science ..... Dr. Robert W. FISCHER, JR.
83 Dean College Behavioral & Hlth Sci ..... Dr. Harold WHITESIDE
60 Dean College Mass Communication ..... Dr. Roy MOORE
50 Dean College of Business ..... Dr. E. James BURTON
53 Dean College of Education ..... Dr. Lana SEIVERS
49 Dean College of Liberal Arts ..... Dr. Mark BYRNES
51 Dean University College ..... Dr. Mike A. BOYLE
92 Dean University Honors College ..... Dr. John R. VILE
08 Dean University Library ..... Bonnie ALLEN
09 Exec Dir Inst Effect/Plng/Research ..... Vacant
36 Dir Career & Employment Center ..... Mr. Bill FLETCHER
93 Dir Intercultural/Diversity Affairs ..... Mr. Vincent WINDROW
37 Dir of Financial Aid & Scholarship ..... Mr. Stephen WHITE
25 Dir Research & Sponsored Programs ..... Dr. Myra K. NORMAN
29 Director Alumni Relations ..... Ms. Ginger C. FREEMAN
40 Director Bookstore ..... Mr. Jeff WHITWELL
24 Director Center for Educational Med ..... Vacant
38 Director Counseling Services ..... Dr. Jane TIPPS
44 Director Development Office ..... Mr. Nick PERLICK
06 Director Enrollment Technical Sys ..... Ms. Teresa THOMAS
26 Director News & Media Relations ..... Mr. Jimmy HART
41 Director of Athletics ..... Mr. Chris John MASSARO
23 Director of Health Services ..... Mr. Richard L. CHAPMAN
94 Director Women's and Gender Studies ..... Dr. Tina JOHNSON
06 Registrar ..... Ms. Cathy KIRCHNER
19 Chief of Police/Dir Public Safety ..... Mr. Carl S. PEASTER

*Tennessee State University (A)

3500 John A Merritt Boulevard, Nashville TN 37209-1561
County: Davidson FICE Identification: 003522
Unit ID: 221838
Telephone: (615) 963-5000 Carnegie Class: DRU
FAX Number: (615) 963-7412 Calendar System: Semester
URL: www.tnstate.edu
Established: 1912 Annual Undergrad Tuition & Fees (In-State): $6,700
Enrollment: 9,165 Coed
Affiliation or Control: State IRS Status: 501(c)3
Highest Offering: Doctorate
Program: Occupational; Liberal Arts And General; Teacher Preparatory; Professional
Accreditation: SC, AAFCS, ADNUR, ART, BUS, COPSY, CS, DH, DIETD, ENG, MUS, NAIT, NUR, OT, PTA, SP, SPAA, SW, TED

02 President ..... Dr. Portia H. SHIELDS
05 Interim Provost ..... Dr. Millicent LOWNES JACKSON
04 Exec Ast to Pres/Chf Diversity Ofcr ..... Dr. Jewell WINN
10 VP Business & Finance ..... Mrs. Cynthia BROOKS
32 VP Student Affairs ..... Dr. A. Dexter SAMUELS
30 VP Univ Relations & Development ..... Vacant
41 Athletic Director ..... Mrs. Teresa LAWRENCE-PHILLIPS
43 University Legal Counsel ..... Mr. Laurence PENDLETON
84 Assoc Provost Enrollment Mgmt ..... Dr. John CADE
20 Assoc VP Academic Affairs ..... Dr. Patricia CROOK
20 Assoc VP Academic Affairs Ext Ed ..... Dr. Evelyn NETTLES
20 Assoc VP Academic Affairs ..... Dr. Ken LOONEY
20 Assoc VP Academic Aff Planning ..... Dr. Peter NWOSU
15 Assoc VP/Dir Human Resources ..... Ms. Linda C. SPEARS
46 Assoc VP Research & Sponsored Pgm ..... Dr. Michael BUSBY
21 Assoc VP Finance/Accounting ..... Mr. Robert HUGHES
18 Assoc VP Facilities/Physical Plant ..... Mr. Ronnie BROOKS
35 Asst VP Student Affairs ..... Ms. Michelle VIERA
88 Asst VP Budget/Travel ..... Mr. Bradley WHITE
09 Dir Inst Effectiveness & Research ..... Dr. G. Pamela BURCH-SIMS
28 Dir Equity Diversity & Compliance ..... Ms. Tiffa COX
37 Director Financial Aid ..... Ms. Amy B. WOOD
06 Registrar ..... Mrs. Thelria HARDAWAY
27 Director Media Relations ..... Mr. Richard DELAHAYA
19 Chief TSU Police Department ..... Mr. Richard BRIGGANCE
08 Dean Libraries & Media Centers ..... Dr. Yildiz B. BINKLEY
49 Int Dean College of Liberal Arts ..... Dr. Gloria JOHNSON
50 Int Dean College of Business ..... Dr. James ELLZY
53 Interim Dean College of Education ..... Dr. Heraldo RICHARDS
54 Dean College of Engr/Tech/Comp Sci ..... Dr. S. Keith HARGROVE
47 Dean Agriculture/Human & Nat Sci ..... Dr. Chandra REDDY
58 Dean School of Graduate Studies ..... Dr. Michael OROK
88 Int Dean Coll Public Svcs/Urban Aff ..... Dr. Stephanie BAILEY
76 Dean College of Health Sciences ..... Dr. Kathleen MCENERNEY
66 Assoc Dean/Dir of Nursing ..... Dr. Kathy MARTIN

*Tennessee Technological University (B)

1000 N Dixie Avenue, Cookeville TN 38505-0001
County: Putnam FICE Identification: 003523
Unit ID: 221847
Telephone: (931) 372-3101 Carnegie Class: Master's L
FAX Number: (931) 372-3898 Calendar System: Semester
URL: www.tntech.edu
Established: 1915 Annual Undergrad Tuition & Fees (In-State): $6,724
Enrollment: 11,768 Coed
Affiliation or Control: State IRS Status: 501(c)3
Highest Offering: Doctorate
Program: Liberal Arts And General; Teacher Preparatory; Professional
Accreditation: SC, AAFCS, ART, BUS, BUSA, CS, DIETD, EMT, ENG, MUS, NAIT, NURSE, TED

02 President ..... Dr. Philip B. OLDHAM
05 Provost/Vice President Acad Affairs ..... Dr. Mark STEPHENS
10 Vice Pres Planning & Finance ..... Dr. Claire STINSON
32 Vice President Student Affairs ..... Mr. Marc BURNETT
56 VP Extended Pgms/Regional Devel ..... Dr. Susan ELKINS
30 Vice President Univ Advancement ..... Mr. Mark HUTCHINS
20 Assoc Provost/Vice Pres Acad Affs ..... Dr. Xiaoming (Sharon) HUO
58 Assoc VP for Research/Grad Studies ..... Dr. Francis O. OTUONYE
13 Assoc VP for Info Tech Svcs ..... Mr. Danny R. REESE
32 Dean of Students ..... Mr. Ed BOUCHER
37 Director Financial Aid ..... Mr. Lester MCKENZIE
08 Director Library & Learning Assist ..... Dr. Doug BATES
09 Director Institutional Research ..... Dr. Glenn W. JAMES
45 Director of Institutional Planning ..... Vacant
15 Director of Human Resources ..... Mr. Michael COWAN
19 Director of University Police ..... Ms. Gay SHEPHERD
39 Director of Housing ..... Mr. Charles MACKE
41 Director of Athletics ..... Mr. Mark WILSON
18 Director of Physical Plant ..... Mr. Jack BUTLER
38 Director Counseling Center ..... Ms. Patricia SMITH
36 Director Career Services ..... Ms. Alice CAMUTI
27 Assoc VP Communications & Mkting ..... Ms. Karen LYKINS
85 Director Intl Student Affairs ..... Mr. Charles WILKERSON
06 Director Records & Registrar ..... Ms. Elizabeth ROGERS
92 Director Honors Program ..... Dr. Rita BARNES
93 Director Minority Affairs ..... Dr. Robert OWENS
96 Director of Purchasing ..... Ms. Judy M. HULL
21 Associate Business Officer ..... Mr. Jeff YOUNG
26 Chief Public Relations Officer ..... Ms. Karen LYKINS
29 Director Alumni Relations ..... Ms. Tracey DUNCAN
28 Director of Diversity/Legal Affairs ..... Ms. Rachel RADER
07 Director of Admissions ..... Mr. Alexis POPE
19 Dir Campus Safety & Environment ..... Mr. James COBB
84 Assoc VP Enr Mgmt & Student Success ..... Dr. Robert HODUM
49 Dean of Arts & Sciences ..... Dr. Paul SEMMES
54 Dean of Engineering ..... Dr. Joseph RENCIS
47 Dean of Agricultural/Human Sciences ..... Dr. Pat BAGLEY
50 Dean of Business Administration ..... Dr. James JORDAN WAGNER
53 Dean College of Education ..... Dr. Matt SMITH

*The University of Memphis (C)

Memphis TN 38152
County: Shelby FICE Identification: 003509
Unit ID: 220862
Telephone: (901) 678-2000 Carnegie Class: RU/H
FAX Number: N/A Calendar System: Semester
URL: www.memphis.edu
Established: 1912 Annual Undergrad Tuition & Fees (In-State): $7,390
Enrollment: 22,864 Coed
Affiliation or Control: State IRS Status: 501(c)3
Highest Offering: Doctorate
Program: Liberal Arts And General; Teacher Preparatory; Professional
Accreditation: SC, ART, AUD, BUS, BUSA, CACREP, CIDA, CLPSY, COPSY, CORE, CS, DIETD, DIETI, ENG, ENGT, HSA, IPSY, JOUR, LAW, MUS, NURSE, PLNG, SP, SPAA, SW, TED, THEA

02 President ..... Dr. Shirley C. RAINES
05 Provost ..... Dr. Ralph J. FAUDREE
04 Exec Assistant to the President ..... Dr. David N. COX
10 Vice President Business & Finance ..... Mr. David G. ZETTERGREN
13 Int Vice Pres Information Sys/CIO ..... Dr. Ellen WATSON
86 Exec Asst Pres Govt Relations ..... Mr. Kevin F. ROPER
30 Vice President Advancement ..... Mrs. Julie A. JOHNSON
32 Vice President Student Affairs ..... Dr. Rosie P. BINGHAM
26 Int VP Marketing/Communication ..... Ms. Linda BONNIN
41 Director of Athletics ..... Mr. Tom BOWEN
43 University Counsel ..... Ms. Sheryl H. LIPMAN
46 Vice Provost for Research ..... Dr. Andrew W. MEYERS
45 VP Assessment/Inst Rsrch/Reporting ..... Dr. Thomas J. NENON
84 Asst Vice Provost Enrollment Svcs ..... Ms. Betty HUFF
58 Vice Prov Graduate Studies ..... Dr. Karen D. WEDDLE-WEST
88 VP Undergrad Programs ..... Dr. Shannon BLANTON
35 Asst VP Student Affs/Stdnt Dev ..... Dr. Stephen H. PETERSEN
18 Asst Vice Pres Physical Plant ..... Mr. Michael L. ALLEN
21 Assistant Vice President Finance ..... Ms. Jeannie SMITH
15 Asst Vice Pres Human Resources ..... Ms. Maria ALAM
44 Assoc Vice Pres Development ..... Mr. Bobby A. PRINCE
102 Director Donor Relations ..... Dr. Dan S. BEASLEY
27 Assoc Vice Pres Marketing/Comm ..... Ms. Linda H. BONNIN
08 Dean U of M Libraries ..... Dr. Sylverna V. FORD
09 Director Institutional Research ..... Dr. Gary L. DONHARDT
36 Director Career & Employment Svcs ..... Ms. Alisha D. ROSE
06 Registrar ..... Ms. Donna S. VAN CANNEYT
37 Director of Student Aid ..... Mr. Richard RITZMAN
96 Director of Purchasing ..... Ms. Canty ROBBINS
29 Dir Alumni Programs Special Events ..... Ms. Tammy L. HEDGES
92 Director University Honors Program ..... Dr. Melinda L. JONES
07 Sr Assoc Director of Admissions ..... Ms. Kate HOWARD
22 Equal Oppty/Affirm Action Comp Ofcr ..... Ms. Michelle R. BANKS
88 Dn Sch Audio/Speech-Lang Pathology ..... Dr. Maurice I. MENDEL
49 Dean of Arts & Science ..... Dr. Henry A. KURTZ
50 Dean Business & Economics ..... Dr. Rajiv GROVER
53 Dean of Education ..... Dr. Donald I. WAGNER
54 Dean of Engineering ..... Vacant
55 Vice Provost Extended Programs ..... Dr. Dan L. LATTIMORE
57 Dean Communication & Fine Arts ..... Dr. Richard R. RANTA
61 Interim Dean School of Law ..... Mr. William P. KRATZKE
66 Dean School of Nursing ..... Dr. Lin ZHAN
69 Dean School of Public Health ..... Dr. Lisa M. KLESGES
94 Director Women's Studies ..... Dr. Wanda RUSHING

*Chattanooga State Community College (D)

4501 Amnicola Highway, Chattanooga TN 37406-1097
County: Hamilton FICE Identification: 003998
Unit ID: 219824
Telephone: (423) 697-4400 Carnegie Class: Assoc/Pub-R-L
FAX Number: N/A Calendar System: Semester
URL: www.chattanoogastate.edu
Established: 1963 Annual Undergrad Tuition & Fees (In-State): $3,717
Enrollment: 11,840 Coed
Affiliation or Control: State IRS Status: 501(c)3
Highest Offering: Associate Degree
Program: Occupational; 2-Year Principally Bachelor's Creditable
Accreditation: SC, ACBSP, ADNUR, DA, DH, DMS, EMT, ENGT, MAC, NMT, PTAA, RAD, RTT, SURGT

02 President ..... Dr. James L. CATANZARO
04 Special Assistant to the President ..... Mr. Joe HELSETH
09 Asc VP Institutional Effectiveness ..... Ms. Eva LEWIS
05 Provost/Vice Pres Academic Affairs ..... Dr. Fannie HEWLETT
10 Exec Vice Pres Business & Finance ..... Ms. Tammy SWENSON
32 Vice President Student Services ..... Vacant
31 Vice President Economic & Comm Dev ..... Vacant
72 Vice President for Technology ..... Dr. Jim BARROTT
44 Assoc Vice Pres Fund Development ..... Ms. Holly REEVE
20 Assoc Vice Pres Academic Affairs ..... Ms. Kimberly MCCORMICK
21 Assistant VP Business & Finance ..... Ms. Susan JOSEPH
35 Asst Vice Pres Student Affairs ..... Ms. Debbie ADAMS
18 Asst VP Plant Operations/Facil Plng ..... Mr. Steve HUSKINS
56 Asst VP Distributed Education ..... Ms. Judy LOWE
25 Asst VP Grants/Contracts/Stdnt Acct ..... Ms. Debbie MAILEN
51 Director Continuing Education ..... Ms. Ju-Hsin LUSK
09 Director of Institutional Research ..... Ms. Bonnie RIGGS
26 Director of Marketing ..... Ms. Patty BROWN
15 Director Human Resources ..... Mr. Tom CRUM
06 Registrar ..... Ms. Norma LEE
36 Director Student Placement ..... Ms. Sheila ALBRITTON
37 Director Student Financial Aid ..... Ms. Jeanne HINCHEE
28 Director of Diversity ..... Ms. Mary KNAFF
41 Athletic Director ..... Mr. Steve JAECKS
08 Dean Library Services ..... Vacant
76 Dean Allied Health & Nursing ..... Dr. Howard YARBROUGH
79 Dean Humanities & Fine Arts ..... Dr. Don ANDREWS
83 Dean Social/Behavioral Sciences ..... Ms. Anne CARROLL
81 Dean Math & Sciences ..... Dr. Mosunmola GEORGE-TAYLOR
50 Dean Business/Info Tech ..... Mr. Barry JENNISON
32 Dean Student Life/Judicial Affairs ..... Ms. Sandy KLUTTZ
75 Dean Tennessee Technology Center ..... Dr. Mike RICKETTS
54 Dean Engineering Technology ..... Mr. Tim MCGHEE

*Cleveland State Community College (E)

PO Box 3570, Cleveland TN 37320-3570
County: Bradley FICE Identification: 003999
Unit ID: 219879
Telephone: (423) 472-7141 Carnegie Class: Assoc/Pub-R-M
FAX Number: (423) 478-6255 Calendar System: Semester
URL: www.clevelandstatecc.edu
Established: 1967 Annual Undergrad Tuition & Fees (In-State): $3,671
Enrollment: 3,814 Coed
Affiliation or Control: State IRS Status: 501(c)3
Highest Offering: Associate Degree
Program: Occupational; 2-Year Principally Bachelor's Creditable
Accreditation: SC, ADNUR, MAC, NAIT

02 President ..... Dr. Carl HITE
05 Vice President for Academic Affairs ..... Dr. Denise KING
32 Vice President for Student Services ..... Dr. Michael STOKES
11 Vice President Admin & Finance ..... Dr. Thomas WRIGHT
09 Director of Institutional Research ..... Mrs. Marcia O'CONNOR
37 Director of Financial Aid ..... Mrs. Brenda DISORBO
30 Director of Inst Advancement ..... Mr. Adam LOWE
26 Director Marketing & Promotions ..... Mr. Tony BARTOLO

06 Asst Dir Enrollment Svcs/Registrar .... Mrs. Gail GREENWOOD
15 Director of Human Resources .... Mrs. Joan BATES
08 Director of the Library .... Ms. Sarah COPELAND
14 Director of College Computing .... Mr. Rick CUMBY
19 Coordinator Campus Security .... Vacant
50 Dean of Business & Technology .... Ms. Sherra WITT
66 Dean of Health & Wellness .... Mrs. Nancy LABINE
79 Int Dean Humanities/Social Sciences .... Mr. Fred WOOD
81 Dean of Math/Science .... Dr. Mitchell RHEA
38 Dir Student Development/ACCESS Ctr .... Mr. Mark WILSON
31 Dir Training & Continuing Education .... Vacant
18 Director of Plant Operations .... Vacant
21 Director of Budget & Accounting .... Mrs. Shirley ELDREDGE
84 Director of Enrollment Services .... Mr. Jason SEWELL
07 Asst Dir Enrollment Services Admiss .... Mrs. Suzanne BAYNE
10 Business Manager .... Mrs. Shirley ELDREDGE
41 Athletic Director .... Mr. Mike POLICASTRO

*Columbia State Community College (A)

1665 Hampshire Pike, Columbia TN 38401-5653
County: Maury FICE Identification: 003483
Unit ID: 219888
Telephone: (931) 540-2722 Carnegie Class: Assoc/Pub-R-M
FAX Number: (931) 540-2535 Calendar System: Semester
URL: www.columbiastate.edu
Established: 1966 Annual Undergrad Tuition & Fees (In-State): $3,367
Enrollment: 5,460 Coed
Affiliation or Control: State IRS Status: 501(c)3
Highest Offering: Associate Degree
Program: Occupational; 2-Year Principally Bachelor's Creditable
Accreditation: SC, ACBSP, ADNUR, EMT, RAD

02 President .... Dr. Janet F. SMITH
03 Executive Vice President/Provost .... Dr. Margaret D. SMITH
10 Vice Pres Financial/Admin Services .... Mr. Kenneth R. HORNER
30 Executive for Advancement .... Ms. Bethany LAY
20 Assoc VP Faculty/Curric & Programs .... Ms. Joni L. LENIG
32 Assoc VP Student Services .... Ms. Cecelia JOHNSON
13 Assoc VP Info Technology .... Ms. Emily SICIENSKY
21 Assoc VP Business Services .... Ms. Elaine CURTIS
27 Director Marketing & Public Rels .... Ms. Amy GREEN
28 Asst to Pres for Access & Diversity .... Ms. Christa S. MARTIN
07 Director Recruitment & Admissions .... Mr. David OGDEN
06 Director Records .... Ms. Sharon G. BOWEN
15 Director Human Resources .... Mr. Randy L. ELSTON
08 Director Library .... Ms. Kathy BREEDEN
38 Coord Counseling & Student Succ Svc .... Dr. Paula J. PETTY-WARD
09 Director Inst Effect and Planning .... Ms. Nancy RAMSEY
37 Director Financial Aid .... Mrs. Brenda D. BURNEY
41 Director Athletics .... Mr. Louis M. CONNER
18 Director Facility Services .... Mr. David HALL
56 Dean Extended Svcs & Will Campus .... Dr. Shanna JACKSON
35 Director Student Success .... Vacant
96 Coordinator Purchasing .... Ms. Jerri H. GROOMS

*Dyersburg State Community College (B)

1510 Lake Road, Dyersburg TN 38024-2450
County: Dyer FICE Identification: 006835
Unit ID: 220057
Telephone: (731) 286-3200 Carnegie Class: Assoc/Pub-R-M
FAX Number: (731) 286-3333 Calendar System: Semester
URL: www.dscc.edu
Established: 1967 Annual Undergrad Tuition & Fees (In-State): $3,521
Enrollment: 3,751 Coed
Affiliation or Control: State IRS Status: 501(c)3
Highest Offering: Associate Degree
Program: Occupational; 2-Year Principally Bachelor's Creditable
Accreditation: SC, ACBSP, ADNUR

02 President .... Dr. Karen A. BOWYER
05 Vice President for the College .... Dr. Mary Ann SELLARS
10 Vice President Finance/Admin Svcs .... Mr. Lowell HOFFMANN
30 Vice Pres Institutional Advancement .... Ms. Youlanda JONES-WILCOX
13 Vice President Technology .... Ms. Diane CAMPER
32 Asst VP for Acad & Student Affairs .... Mr. J. Dan GULLETT
20 Assistant VP for Learning .... Dr. Kay PATTERSON
35 Dean of Student Services .... Ms. Larenda FULTZ
08 Dean Learning Resources Center .... Ms. Teresa JOHNSON
37 Director of Financial Aid .... Mrs. Sandra ROCKETT
09 Director of Institutional Research .... Ms. Youlanda JONES-WILCOX
15 Director Personnel Services .... Ms. Sheilah GILLAHAN
103 Director of Workforce Development .... Ms. Margaret PRATER
29 Dir Alumni Relations/Public Info .... Ms. Jane PATE
38 Director Student Counseling .... Vacant
41 Director of Athletics .... Mr. Alan BARNETT
18 Director of Physical Plant .... Mr. Kent JETTON
07 Director of Admissions .... Mr. J. Dan GULLETT
96 Director of Purchasing .... Ms. Amy WATTS
45 Manager of Assessment .... Mr. Doug HODGE
21 Business & Student Fin Svcs Manager .... Ms. Donna MEALER
72 Coord Business/Technology Div .... Mr. James BARHAM
66 Dean of Nursing & Allied Health Div .... Dr. Evelyn MILLER
51 Dean of Continuing Education .... Ms. Youlanda JONES-WILCOX

*Jackson State Community College (C)

2046 North Parkway, Jackson TN 38301-3797
County: Madison FICE Identification: 004937
Unit ID: 220400
Telephone: (731) 424-3520 Carnegie Class: Assoc/Pub-R-M
FAX Number: (731) 425-2647 Calendar System: Semester
URL: www.jscc.edu
Established: 1965 Annual Undergrad Tuition & Fees (In-State): $3,679
Enrollment: 4,928 Coed
Affiliation or Control: State IRS Status: 501(c)3
Highest Offering: Associate Degree
Program: Occupational; 2-Year Principally Bachelor's Creditable
Accreditation: SC, ACBSP, ADNUR, EMT, MLTAD, NAIT, PTAA, RAD

02 President .... Dr. Bruce BLANDING
05 Interim VP of Academic Affairs .... Mr. Bobby SMITH
10 Vice Pres of Finance & Admin Affs .... Mr. Horace W. CHASE
30 Exec Dir Institutional Advancement .... Ms. Dee HENDERSON
32 Interim VP of Student Services .... Dr. Bill SEYMOUR
88 Internal Auditor .... Mrs. Angela P. BROWN
15 Dir Human Resources/Affirm Action .... Mrs. Amy WEST
09 Dir Inst Research & Accountability .... Mr. Scott WOODS
51 Dean of Continuing Education .... Ms. Leah GRAY
13 Director of Information Technology .... Ms. Dana NAILS
21 Director of Business Services .... Mr. Tim DELLINGER
18 Director of Physical Plant .... Mr. Gerald BATCHELOR
96 Director of Purchasing .... Mr. Robert D. HEMRICK
12 Director Lexington Campus .... Ms. Sandy STANFILL
12 Director Savannah Campus .... Mrs. Meda FALLS
12 Director Humboldt Campus .... Ms. Lisa BARKER
07 Director Admissions .... Mrs. Andrea WINCHESTER
26 Director Public Relations .... Vacant
37 Director Student Financial Aid .... Ms. Dewana LATIMER
06 Registrar .... Ms. Frances EDMONSON

*Motlow State Community College (D)

PO Box 8500, Lynchburg TN 37352-8500
County: Moore FICE Identification: 006836
Unit ID: 221096
Telephone: (931) 393-1500 Carnegie Class: Assoc/Pub-R-M
FAX Number: (931) 393-1681 Calendar System: Semester
URL: www.mscc.edu
Established: 1969 Annual Undergrad Tuition & Fees (In-State): $3,372
Enrollment: 4,988 Coed
Affiliation or Control: State IRS Status: 501(c)3
Highest Offering: Associate Degree
Program: Occupational; 2-Year Principally Bachelor's Creditable
Accreditation: SC, ACBSP, ADNUR

02 President .... Dr. MaryLou APPLE
05 Provost .... Dr. Bonny COPENHAVER
10 Vice Pres for Business Affairs .... Ms. Hilda TUNSTILL
13 VP for Technology & Admin Services .... Dr. Eddie STONE
13 VP for Student Affairs .... Mr. Jerry TUNSTILL
20 Asst Vice Pres for Academic Affair .... Ms. Dawn COPELAND
18 Director of Facilities .... Mr. Billy GARNER
14 Director of Technical Operations .... Mr. Ron GAULT
31 Director Student & Campus Relations .... Ms. Brenda CANNON
32 Asst Vice President Student Affairs .... Ms. Regina BURDEN
08 Director of Libraries .... Mr. Stuart GAETJENS
37 Executive Director of Financial Aid .... Mr. Joe MYERS
38 Director of Disability & Testing .... Ms. Sonya HOOD
07 Director of Admissions & Records .... Ms. Greer ALSUP
66 Director of Nursing .... Ms. Amy HUFF
41 Director of Athletics .... Mr. Jerry NICHOLS
09 Dir of Research/Planning & Comm .... Ms. Sylvia COLLINS
90 Director Center for Academic Tech .... Dr. Shelly MCCOY
12 Director McMinnville Center .... Ms. Melody EDMONDS
12 Director Fayetteville Center .... Ms. Laura MONKS
12 Director Smyrna Site .... Ms. Cheryl HYLAND
36 Dir of Career Placement & Extended .... Mr. Tom DILLINGHAM
04 Admin Assistant to the President .... Ms. Christy GLENN
15 Director of Human Resources .... Ms. Laura JENT
96 Director of Purchasing .... Ms. Sandy SCHAFFER

*Nashville State Community College (E)

120 White Bridge Road, Nashville TN 37209-4515
County: Davidson FICE Identification: 008145
Unit ID: 221184
Telephone: (615) 353-3333 Carnegie Class: Assoc/Pub-U-MC
FAX Number: (615) 353-3713 Calendar System: Semester
URL: www.nscc.edu
Established: 1969 Annual Undergrad Tuition & Fees (In-State): $3,627
Enrollment: 9,876 Coed
Affiliation or Control: State IRS Status: 501(c)3
Highest Offering: Associate Degree
Program: Occupational; 2-Year Principally Bachelor's Creditable; Business Emphasis
Accreditation: SC, ACBSP, ACFEI, NAIT, OTA, SURGT

02 President .... Dr. George H. VAN ALLEN
05 Vice President of Academic Affairs .... Dr. Kimberly K. ESTEP
10 Vice Pres Finance & Administration .... Mrs. Mary M. CROSS
88 Exec Assistant to the President .... Vacant
45 Assoc VP Planning/Assessment .... Mr. Ted M. WASHINGTON
09 Assoc VP Institutional Research .... Mr. Ted M. WASHINGTON
30 Exec Dir of Devel/Dir Public Affs .... Mr. Keith D. FERGUSON
32 Dean of Students .... Dr. Carol J. MARTIN-OSORIO
21 Internal Auditor .... Mr. Robert HANKINS
06 Registrar .... Mr. Lance L. WOODARD
07 Director of Admissions .... Ms. Laura L. POTTER
14 Director of Computer Services .... Mr. Carl G. DURY
19 Director of Safety and Security .... Mr. Derrek G. SHEUCRAFT
37 Director of Financial Aid .... Mr. James J. MORAN
15 Dir Human Res/Affirm Act/Diversity .... Ms. Lori B. MADDOX
18 Director of Operations/Maintenance .... Mr. Jim T. DAWSON
103 Dir Workforce and Community Dev .... Ms. Gail G. PHILLIPS
27 Manager of Publications .... Ms. Ellen L. ZINK
106 Director of Online Learning .... Ms. Kathy S. EMERY
51 Coord Special Interest/CEUs .... Ms. Betty P. BROZ
83 Dean of Social and Life Sciences .... Mr. Charles B. DEWITT
72 Dean of Info/Eng Technologies .... Ms. Karen L. STEVENSON
81 Dean Math & Natural Sciences .... Dr. Jennifer A. KNAPP
79 Dean English/Humanities & Arts .... Ms. Valerie S. BELEW
62 Dean Lrng Resources & Distance Educ .... Dr. Faye JONES
50 Dean Bus Technology & Applied Arts .... Ms. Karen L. STEVENSON
96 Director of Purchasing .... Ms. Jo SMITH
29 Director Alumni Relations .... Mr. Keith D. FERGUSON
66 Director of Nursing .... Dr. Cynthia G. WALLER

*Northeast State Community College (F)

PO Box 246, 2425 Highway 75, Blountville TN 37617-0246
County: Sullivan FICE Identification: 005378
Unit ID: 221908
Telephone: (423) 323-3191 Carnegie Class: Assoc/Pub-R-M
FAX Number: (423) 279-7636 Calendar System: Semester
URL: www.northeaststate.edu
Established: 1965 Annual Undergrad Tuition & Fees (In-State): $3,522
Enrollment: 6,478 Coed
Affiliation or Control: State IRS Status: 501(c)3
Highest Offering: Associate Degree
Program: Occupational; 2-Year Principally Bachelor's Creditable
Accreditation: SC, ACBSP, ADNUR, CVT, DA, EMT, MLTAD, NAIT, SURGT

02 President .... Dr. Janice H. GILLIAM
04 Exec Assistant to the President .... Ms. Megan JONES
05 Vice Pres Academic Affairs .... Dr. Allana R. HAMILTON
10 Vice President Business Affairs .... Dr. Steven CAMPBELL
32 Vice President for Student Affairs .... Dr. Jon P. HARR
13 Vice Pres Info Tech/Computer Svcs .... Mr. Fred LEWIS
09 VP of Institutional Effectiveness .... Dr. Susan E. GRAYBEAL
12 VP for Northeast State at Kingsport .... Mr. Jeff D. MCCORD
56 Asst VP Evening/Distance Educ .... Dr. James C. LEFLER
15 Director Human Resources .... Ms. Gerri S. BROCKWELL
31 Director Community Relations .... Mr. Robert CARPENTER
08 Dean Library .... Mr. Duncan A. PARSONS
79 Dean Humanities .... Mr. William WILSON
81 Dean Math .... Ms. Nancy FORRESTER
76 Dean Health Related Profession .... Mr. Don COLEMAN
72 Dean Advance Technologies .... Mr. Sam S. ROWELL
83 Dean Behavior/Social Sciences .... Dr. Xiaoping WANG
81 Dean Science .... Dr. Carolyn MCCRACKEN
50 Dean Business Technologies .... Mr. Danny L. LAWSON
66 Dean Nursing .... Dr. Melessia D. WEBB

*Pellissippi State Community College (G)

PO Box 22990, Knoxville TN 37933-0990
County: Knox FICE Identification: 012693
Unit ID: 221643
Telephone: (865) 694-6400 Carnegie Class: Assoc/Pub-U-MC
FAX Number: (865) 694-6435 Calendar System: Semester
URL: www.pstcc.edu
Established: 1974 Annual Undergrad Tuition & Fees (In-State): $3,558
Enrollment: 11,259 Coed
Affiliation or Control: State IRS Status: 501(c)3
Highest Offering: Associate Degree
Program: Occupational; 2-Year Principally Bachelor's Creditable
Accreditation: SC, ACBSP

02 President .... Dr. L. Anthony WISE
05 Vice President of Academic Affairs .... Dr. Ted A. LEWIS
13 Vice President Information Services .... Mr. Robert G. BRYAN
10 Vice President Business & Finance .... Mr. Ronald L. KESTERSON
30 VP College Advancement/Exec Dir Fdn .... Ms. Peggy M. WILSON
32 Vice President of Student Affairs .... Dr. Rebecca L. ASHFORD
103 Exec Dir Business/Workforce Dev .... Ms. Teri T. BRAHAMS
20 Dean Instructional Programs .... Dr. Dennis R. ADAMS
12 Asst Dean Blount County Programs .... Ms. Holly L. BURKETT
12 Asst Dean Strawberry Plains Program .... Dr. Mike NORTH
12 Asst Dean Magnolia Ave Programs .... Ms. Rosalyn P. TILLMAN
12 Asst Dean Division Street Programs .... Ms. Esther L. DYER
35 Asst Vice President Dean of Student .... Ms. Mary C. BLEDSOE
20 Asst VP of Academic Affairs .... Ms. Lois G. REYNOLDS
84 Asst VP Enrollment Services .... Ms. Leigh A. TOUZEAU
36 Director of Placement .... Ms. Carolyn N. CARSON
88 Dir Svc for Students w/Disabilities .... Ms. Ann E. SATKOWIAK
38 Director Counseling Department .... Dr. Elizabeth E. FIRESTONE
26 Director Marketing & Communications .... Ms. Julia H. WOOD
06 Registrar .... Ms. Melanie PARADISE
08 Director of Library Services .... Mr. J. Peter NERZAK
24 Dir Educ Technology Svcs .... Ms. Audrey WILLIAMS
37 Director of Financial Aid .... Mr. Dick SMELSER
09 Dir Inst Effectiveness/Res/Plan .... Vacant
18 Interim Director of Facilities .... Ms. Regina MCNEW

19 Director Safety/Security .... Mr. Fred BREINER
21 Director/Budget & Payroll .... Ms. Nancy DONAHUE
96 Director of Purchasing .... Mr. John S. CLARK
15 Exe Dir HR/Affirm Action .... Ms. Karen D. QUEENER
21 Asst VP Business Services .... Ms. Renee R. MOORE
44 Director Major Gift Development .... Mr. Leslie G. FOUT
29 Dir Alum Relations & Annual Giving .... Ms. Patricia T. MYERS
91 Dir Applications Programming Sup .... Mr. James "Dean" COPPLE
90 Dir Network & Technical Services .... Ms. Linda C. PETERSON
07 Director of Admissions & Com Ctr .... Ms. Heather HATFIELD
28 Director of Access & Diversity .... Ms. Gayle E. WOOD

*Roane State Community College (A)

276 Patton Lane, Harriman TN 37748-5011
County: Roane FICE Identification: 009914
Unit ID: 221397
Telephone: (865) 354-3000 Carnegie Class: Assoc/Pub-R-M
FAX Number: (865) 882-4585 Calendar System: Semester
URL: www.roanestate.edu
Established: 1971 Annual Undergrad Tuition & Fees (In-State): $3,387
Enrollment: 6,801 Coed
Affiliation or Control: State IRS Status: 501(c)3
Highest Offering: Associate Degree
Program: Occupational; 2-Year Principally Bachelor's Creditable
Accreditation: SC, ACBSP, ADNUR, COMTA, DH, EMT, OPD, OTA, POLYT, PTAA, RAD

02 President .... Dr. Gary GOFF
05 Vice Pres for Student Learning .... Dr. Chris WHALEY
10 Vice Pres for Business & Finance .... Mr. Danny C. GIBBS
32 VP Student Services/Enrollment Mgmt .... Ms. Teresa S. DUNCAN
12 VP ORBC & Ctrs/Exec Dir RSCC Found .... Ms. Melinda HILLMAN
21 Asst VP Fiscal/Auxiliary Services .... Ms. Jamie WILMOTH
35 Asst VP Student Services .... Ms. Beverly J. BONNER
84 Asst Vice President Enrollment Svcs .... Ms. Joy GOLDBERG
72 Asst Vice Pres of Info Technology .... Mr. Timothy D. CARROLL
09 Asst VP Institutional Research .... Ms. Karen L. BRUNNER
15 Director of Human Resources .... Mr. Odell FEARN
08 Director of Library Services .... Mr. Robert M. BENSON
11 Director of Administrative Systems .... Mr. Chris PANKRATZ
06 Director of Records & Registration .... Ms. Brenda RECTOR
07 Director of Admissions/Recruitment .... Ms. Maria GONZALES
18 Director Physical Plant & Expo Ctr .... Mr. Stan R. STARKEY
29 Director Alumni Relations .... Ms. Tamsin MILLER
96 Director of Purchasing .... Mr. Jack WALKER
36 Placement Coordinator .... Ms. Kim HARRIS

*Southwest Tennessee Community College (B)

PO Box 780, Memphis TN 38101-0780
County: Shelby FICE Identification: 010439
Unit ID: 221485
Telephone: (901) 333-5020 Carnegie Class: Assoc/Pub-U-MC
FAX Number: (901) 333-5024 Calendar System: Semester
URL: www.southwest.tn.edu
Established: 2000 Annual Undergrad Tuition & Fees (In-State): $3,381
Enrollment: 12,958 Coed
Affiliation or Control: State IRS Status: 501(c)3
Highest Offering: Associate Degree
Program: Occupational; 2-Year Principally Bachelor's Creditable
Accreditation: SC, ACBSP, ADNUR, DIETT, EMT, ENGT, MLTAD, PTAA, RAD

02 President .... Dr. Nathan L. ESSEX
04 Assistant to the President .... Ms. Carol BROWN
05 Provost/Executive Vice President .... Dr. Joanne BASSETT
41 Athletic Director .... Mr. Verties SAILS, JR.
30 Vice Pres Institutional Advancement .... Ms. Karen F. NIPPERT
10 Vice Pres Finance & Admin Services .... Mr. Ronald G. PARR
32 Vice Pres Student Svcs/Enroll Mgmt .... Dr. Carol TOSH
84 Exec Director Enrollment Management .... Ms. Kathryn JOHNSON
26 Exec Director of Comm & Marketing .... Mr. Robert G. MILLER
15 Exec Director Hum Res/Affirm Action .... Mr. Paul THOMAS
06 Registrar .... Ms. Barbara WELLS
18 Director Physical Plant .... Vacant
96 Director of Purchasing .... Ms. Michelle NEWMAN
37 Dir Student Financial Aid-Macon .... Ms. Chateeka FARRIS
37 Dir Student Financial Aid-Union .... Ms. Tina STUDAWAY
09 Institutional Research Analyst .... Mr. Donald C. MYERS

*Volunteer State Community College (C)

1480 Nashville Pike, Gallatin TN 37066-3188
County: Sumner FICE Identification: 009912
Unit ID: 222053
Telephone: (615) 452-8600 Carnegie Class: Assoc/Pub-S-SC
FAX Number: (615) 230-3577 Calendar System: Semester
URL: www.volstate.edu
Established: 1970 Annual Undergrad Tuition & Fees (In-State): $3,505
Enrollment: 8,653 Coed
Affiliation or Control: State IRS Status: 501(c)3
Highest Offering: Associate Degree
Program: Occupational; 2-Year Principally Bachelor's Creditable
Accreditation: SC, ACBSP, DA, DMS, EMT, MLTAD, POLYT, PTAA, RAD

02 President .... Dr. Jerry FAULKNER
04 Exec Assistant to the President .... Vacant
05 Vice President Academic Affairs .... Dr. Bruce SCISM
10 Vice President Business & Finance .... Ms. Beth COOKSEY
32 Vice President Student Services .... Ms. Patty T. POWELL
30 Vice Pres for Resource Development .... Ms. Karen MITCHELL
45 Vice Pres Inst Planning/Research .... Ms. Jane MCGUIRE
20 Asst VP of Academic Affairs .... Mr. Jim HIETT
21 Asst Vice Pres Business & Finance .... Ms. Kathy Y. JOHNSON
35 Asst VP Student Svcs/Enrollment Mgt .... Ms. Emily SHORT
51 Asst VP/Dean Continuing Education .... Mrs. Hilary B. MARABETI
76 Assoc Vice Pres/Dean Allied Health .... Mr. Elvis BRANDON
79 Dean Humanities .... Dr. Alycia EHLERT
53 Dean Social Science/Education .... Ms. Phyllis FOLEY
81 Dean Math & Science .... Ms. Nancy MORRIS
50 Dean Business .... Dr. John ESPEY
88 Director of Development Studies Pgm .... Ms. Kay DAYTON
15 Dir Personnel/Affirm Act/Human Res .... Ms. Lori CUTRELL
08 Director Library Services .... Ms. Louise KELLY
07 Director Admissions & Records .... Mr. Tim AMYX
13 Director Information Technology .... Mr. Brian KRAUS
37 Director Student Financial Aid .... Mrs. Sue H. PEDIGO
26 Director Public Relations .... Mrs. Tami WALLACE
18 Senior Director Physical Plant .... Mr. Gary HUME
19 Chief Security & Safety .... Mr. William D. ROGAN
41 Director of Athletics .... Mr. Bobby HUDSON
56 Director Distance Learning .... Vacant
88 Special Adult Programs/ADA Director .... Ms. Kathy SOWELL
55 Director of Evening Services .... Ms. Brenda BUFFINGTON
09 Director of Institutional Research .... Mrs. Ann Marie CALDERON
96 Director Purchasing .... Mr. Terry MCGOVERN
24 Director Media Services .... Mr. Terry HEINEN
88 Director Retention Support Services .... Ms. Heather HARPER
36 Director of Career Placement .... Dr. Rick PARRENT
38 Director Counseling & Testing .... Mrs. Teresa BROWN
28 Director Student Life & Diversity .... Mr. Kenny YARBROUGH
45 Specialist Resource Development .... Ms. Lori JOHNSON
88 Director Center of Emphasis .... Vacant
06 Registrar .... Mr. Tim AMYX
29 Director Alumni Relations .... Ms. Lori JOHNSON

*Walters State Community College (D)

500 S Davy Crockett Parkway, Morristown TN 37813-6899
County: Hamblen FICE Identification: 008863
Unit ID: 222062
Telephone: (423) 585-2600 Carnegie Class: Assoc/Pub-R-L
FAX Number: (423) 585-6853 Calendar System: Semester
URL: www.ws.edu
Established: 1969 Annual Undergrad Tuition & Fees (In-State): $3,534
Enrollment: 6,738 Coed
Affiliation or Control: State IRS Status: 501(c)3
Highest Offering: Associate Degree
Program: Occupational; 2-Year Principally Bachelor's Creditable
Accreditation: SC, ACBSP, ACFEI, ADNUR, EMT, NAIT, PTAA

02 President .... Dr. Wade B. MCCAMEY
04 Exec Director to the President .... Ms. Brenda L. SMALL
05 Vice President Academic Affairs .... Dr. Lori CAMPBELL
10 Vice President Business Affairs .... Dr. Rosemary JACKSON
32 Vice President Student Affairs .... Dr. Foster CHASON
30 Vice Pres for College Advancement .... Dr. Mark HURST
45 VP for Planning/Research/Assessment . Dr. Debbie L. MCCARTER
20 Asst Vice Pres for Academic Affairs .... Vacant
35 Asst Vice Pres Student Affairs .... Mr. Michael A. CAMPBELL
18 Ast Vice Pres Facilities Management .... Mr. Max E. WILLIAMS
21 Asst Vice Pres Business Affairs .... Mr. Roger D. BEVERLY
28 Spec Asst to Pres for Diversity .... Ms. W. Ann BOWEN
08 Dean of Library .... Dr. Douglas D. CROSS
31 Dean/Dir Cmty & Economic Devel .... Mr. Joseph L. COMBS
19 Dean of Public Safety Division .... Mr. Thomas STRANGE
17 Dean Health Programs .... Ms. Marty K. RUCKER
12 Dean Greenville/Greene Co Center .... Ms. Drucilla W. MILLER
12 Dean Sevier County Campus .... Ms. Sue FRAZIER
83 Dean of Behavioral/Social Sciences .... Dr. Marilyn R. BOWERS
50 Dean of Business .... Dr. Evelyn J. HONAKER
79 Dean of Humanities .... Dr. James E. CRAWFORD, JR.
81 Dean of Mathematics .... Dr. John P. LAPRISE
49 Dean of Natural Science .... Dr. Jeffrey T. HORNER
75 Dean of Technical Education .... Mr. Thomas R. SEWELL
06 Dean Student Info System/Records .... Ms. Linda MASON
103 Dean Ctr for Workforce Development .... Dr. Nancy B. BROWN
37 Dean of Financial Aid .... Ms. Terri STANSBERRY
38 Exec Director Counseling/Testing .... Mr. Andy HALL
15 Exec Dir of Human Resources .... Ms. Tammy GOODE
26 Exec Director of Public Information .... Mr. James B. PECTOL
13 Exec Director for Information .... Mr. Joe E. SARGENT
41 Director of Athletics .... Dr. Foster CHASON
07 Director of Admissions .... Ms. Mary A. RUSH
19 Chief of Campus Police .... Ms. Sarah ROSE
89 Director Freshmen Studies .... Dr. Marilyn R. BOWERS
36 Director Student Placement .... Mr. Andy HALL
92 Director Honors Program .... Ms. Janice M. DONAHUE
96 Director of Purchasing .... Mr. Shawn A. WILLIAMS
27 Int Dir of Communication Services .... Mr. Bill R. MOREFIELD
29 Coordinator of Alumni Relations .... Ms. Wanda HARRELL
84 Coordinator Enrollment Development .... Mr. Marlin R. CURNUTT
93 Coord Minority Student Recruit .... Ms. Roxanne BOWEN

Tennessee Temple University (E)

1815 Union Avenue, Chattanooga TN 37404-3587
County: Hamilton FICE Identification: 003524
Unit ID: 221856
Telephone: (423) 493-4100 Carnegie Class: Spec/Faith
FAX Number: (423) 493-4497 Calendar System: Semester
URL: www.tntemple.edu
Established: 1946 Annual Undergrad Tuition & Fees: $17,640
Enrollment: 556 Coed
Affiliation or Control: Baptist IRS Status: 501(c)3
Highest Offering: Doctorate
Program: Liberal Arts And General; Teacher Preparatory; Professional; Business Emphasis
Accreditation: TRACS

00 Chancellor .... Dr. David E. BOULER
01 President .... Dr. Steve ECHOLS
03 Dean of Seminary .... Dr. Jim O'NEILL
05 Vice President of Academic Services .... Dr. Francis KIMMITT
11 Chief Operations Officer .... Dr. Jeff RECTOR
106 Director of Online Learning .... Mr. Byron EDENS
06 Registrar .... Mr. Richard D. VAUPEL
08 Librarian .... Mr. Kevin WOODRUFF
32 Director of Student Services .... Mrs. Pam FREJOSKY
41 Interim Athletic Director .... Mr. Joe FREJOSKY
19 Director of Security .... Mr. Donny BEAM
13 Director of Information Technology .... Mr. Darwin BLANDON
20 Director of Academic Support .... Vacant
35 Director Student Development .... Mr. Joe FREJOSKY
37 Director Student Financial Aid .... Mr. Jeff DAVIS
26 Dir of Mktg/Strategic Initiatives .... Vacant

Tennessee Wesleyan College (F)

204 East College St., Athens TN 37303
County: McMinn FICE Identification: 003525
Unit ID: 221731
Telephone: (423) 745-7504 Carnegie Class: Bac/Diverse
FAX Number: (423) 744-9968 Calendar System: Semester
URL: www.twcnet.edu
Established: 1857 Annual Undergrad Tuition & Fees: $20,500
Enrollment: 1,116 Coed
Affiliation or Control: United Methodist IRS Status: 501(c)3
Highest Offering: Master's
Program: Liberal Arts And General; Teacher Preparatory; Professional
Accreditation: SC, NURSE

01 President .... Dr. Harley KNOWLES
05 Vice President for Academic Affairs .... Dr. Suzanne A. HINE
11 Vice Pres Administration .... Mr. Larry WALLACE
10 Vice Pres Financial/Business Affs .... Mrs. Gail HARRIS
32 Vice President for Student Life .... Dr. Scott MASHBURN
84 Vice President for Enrollment .... Mr. Stan HARRISON
09 Asst VP Inst Research & Retention .... Mrs. Traci N. WILLIAMS
04 Admin Assistant to President .... Mrs. Gail ROGERS
08 Assoc Dean of Library Svcs .... Mrs. Sandra CLARIDAY
06 Registrar .... Mrs. Julie MCCASLIN
37 Director of Financial Aid .... Mr. Robert K. PERRY
29 Director of Alumni Relations .... Ms. Jessica EDWARDS
41 Athletic Director .... Mr. Donny MAYFIELD
15 Human Resources Director .... Mrs. Pam DAVIS
18 Chief of Facilities/Physical Plant .... Mr. Mike INGRAM
26 Director Public Relations .... Mr. Blake MCCASLIN
35 Director of Student Activities .... Ms. Kerrie LYNN
13 Director of Information Technoloy .... Mr. Joe PASSMORE

Trevecca Nazarene University (G)

333 Murfreesboro Road, Nashville TN 37210-2877
County: Davidson FICE Identification: 003526
Unit ID: 221892
Telephone: (615) 248-1200 Carnegie Class: DRU
FAX Number: (615) 248-7728 Calendar System: Semester
URL: www.trevecca.edu
Established: 1901 Annual Undergrad Tuition & Fees: $19,990
Enrollment: 2,478 Coed
Affiliation or Control: Church Of The Nazarene IRS Status: 501(c)3
Highest Offering: Doctorate
Program: Liberal Arts And General; Teacher Preparatory; Professional
Accreditation: SC, ARCPA, MUS, NURSE, @SW, TED

01 President .... Dr. Dan BOONE
05 University Provost .... Dr. Stephen M. PUSEY
10 Exec Vice Pres Finance & Admin .... Mr. David CALDWELL
26 Vice President External Relations .... Mrs. Peggy J. COONING
20 Assoc Provost/Dean Academic Affairs .... Dr. Carol MAXSON
32 Assoc Provost/Dean of Student Dev .... Mr. Stephen A. HARRIS
84 Assoc Provost/Dean of Enroll Mgmt .... Dr. Kathy BAUGHER
73 Dean of School of Religion .... Dr. Timothy M. GREEN
50 Dean of Business and Technology .... Dr. Jim HIATT
51 Dean of College Lifelong Learning .... Dr. Dave PHILLIPS
35 Assoc Dean Student Community Life .... Mr. Matt SPRAKER
39 Asc Dean Students Residential Life .... Mrs. Ronda LILIENTHAL
53 Dean of the School of Education .... Dr. Suzann HARRIS
49 Dean of School of Arts & Science .... Dr. Lena WELCH
13 Chief Information Officer/ITS .... Mr. Scott CREEL
08 Director Library Services .... Mrs. Ruth KINNERSLEY
09 Director Institutional Research .... Ms. Donna K. TUDOR
06 Registrar .... Mrs. Becky NIECE
19 Director of Security .... Mr. Norm ROBINSON
07 Director of Admissions .... Ms. Holly WHITBY
41 Athletic Director .... Vacant
36 Director Counseling Services .... Dr. Sara HOPKINS
88 Coordinator of Sophomore Year Pgm .... Ms. Jennifer NEELY
88 Coordinator of Senior Year Programs .... Ms. Nicole RABALAIS
106 Director Online Learning .... Ms. Angela WETMORE
21 Director of Financial Services .... Mr. Chuck SEAMAN
15 Director Human Resources .... Mr. Steve SEXTON
37 Financial Aid Director .... Mr. Eddie WHITE
76 Director Physician Asst Pgm .... Dr. Gerald M. MOREDOCK

Code	Title	Name
18	Director Plant Operations	Mr. Glen LINTHICUM
44	Sr Stewardship Ofcr/Dir Plan Giving	Mr. Richard UNDERWOOD
29	Director of Alumni Services	Mrs. Nancy DUNLAP
26	Director of Public Relations	Mrs. Jan GREATHOUSE

Tusculum College (A)

60 Shiloh Road, Greeneville TN 37743-9997
County: Greene FICE Identification: 003527
Unit ID: 221953
Telephone: (423) 636-7300 Carnegie Class: Master's S
FAX Number: (423) 638-7166 Calendar System: Other
URL: www.tusculum.edu
Established: 1794 Annual Undergrad Tuition & Fees: $21,620
Enrollment: 2,128 Coed
Affiliation or Control: Presbyterian Church (U.S.A.) IRS Status: 501(c)3
Highest Offering: Master's
Program: Liberal Arts And General; Teacher Preparatory
Accreditation: SC

Code	Title	Name
01	President	Dr. Nancy B. MOODY
05	VP Academic Affairs	Dr. Melinda DUKES
30	VP Institutional Advancement	Ms. Heather PATCHETT
10	Vice Pres/Chief Financial Officer	Mr. Steve GEHRET
84	VP for Enrollment Management	Dr. Tom STEIN
20	Int Assoc VP for Academic Affairs	Dr. Lisa JOHNSON
32	Dean of Students	Dr. David MCMAHAN
35	Associate Dean of Students	Ms. Jonita ASHLEY-PAULEY
29	Assoc VP Institutional Advancement	Ms. Susan VANCE
06	Registrar	Ms. Bobbie CLARKSON
21	Controller	Ms. Tracey JULIAN
07	Director of Operations/Admissions	Ms. Melissa RIPLEY
45	Asst to Pres Inst Plng/Effectivenes	Dr. Keith LARSON
15	Director Human Resources	Ms. Mary SONNER
36	Director Career Counseling	Ms. Amanda WADDELL
08	Librarian	Mr. Myron J. SMITH, JR.
42	College Minister	Mr. Mark STOKES
37	Director of Financial Aid	Ms. Melena VERITY
41	Athletic Director	Mr. Frankie DEBUSK
27	Director of Communications	Ms. Suzanne RICHEY
13	Director of Information Systems	Dr. Blair HENLEY
18	Director Facilities Management	Mr. David MARTIN
92	Director of Honors Program	Dr. Angela KEATON
40	Bookstore Manager	Mr. Cliff HOY

Union University (B)

1050 Union University Drive, Jackson TN 38305-3697
County: Madison FICE Identification: 003528
Unit ID: 221971
Telephone: (731) 668-1818 Carnegie Class: Master's L
FAX Number: (731) 661-5175 Calendar System: 4/1/4
URL: www.uu.edu
Established: 1823 Annual Undergrad Tuition & Fees: $25,650
Enrollment: 4,007 Coed
Affiliation or Control: Southern Baptist IRS Status: 501(c)3
Highest Offering: Doctorate
Program: Liberal Arts And General
Accreditation: SC, ANEST, ART, ENG, MUS, NURSE, PHAR, SW, TED

Code	Title	Name
01	President	Dr. David S. DOCKERY
05	Exec Vice Pres Acad Administration	Dr. Gene FANT
10	Sr Vice Pres Business Services	Mr. Gary L. CARTER
30	Sr Vice Pres University Relations	Dr. Jerry TIDWELL
84	Sr Vice Pres Enrollment Services	Mr. Rich GRIMM
32	Sr VP Student Svcs/Dean of Students	Dr. Kimberly THORNBURY
26	Vice Pres for Church Relations	Dr. Todd BRADY
108	Vice Pres Institutional Assessment	Dr. Jimmy H. DAVIS
42	Vice President for Spiritual Life	Dr. Gregory THORNBURY
04	Exec Assistant to the President	Mrs. Cynthia L. MEREDITH
21	Assoc Vice Pres Business Svcs	Mr. Robert SIMPSON
08	Assoc VP Academic Res/Dir Library	Ms. Anna B. MORGAN
27	Assoc VP University Communications	Mr. Mark KAHLER
90	Assoc VP Information Technology	Mr. James AVERY
15	Assoc VP Business Svcs/Human Res	Mr. John CARBONELL
07	Asst VP for Undergraduate Admiss	Mr. Robbie GRAVES
37	Assistant VP for Financial Planning	Mr. John BRANDT
49	Acting Dean College Arts & Sciences	Dr. Hunter BAKER
46	Exec Vice Pres Strategic Initiative	Dr. Carla D. SANDERSON
50	Dean School of Business	Dr. Keith ABSHER
66	Dean School of Nursing	Dr. Timothy SMITH
53	Exec Dean Col Educ/Human Studies	Dr. Tom ROSEBROUGH
88	Dean School of Theology Missions	Dr. Gregory THORNBURY
67	Dean School of Pharmacy	Dr. Sheila MITCHELL
91	Assoc Dir Information Technology	Miss Karen MCWHERTER
36	Asst Dean Students/Dir Career Svcs	Mrs. Jackie TAYLOR
29	Director of Alumni Relations	Mr. Josh CLARKE
13	Director of Data Management	Mr. David PORTER
46	Director of Development Services	Mrs. Katrina BRADFIELD
06	Registrar	Vacant
19	Director of Security/Safety	Mr. Carson HAWKINS
41	Director of Athletics	Mr. Tommy SADLER
18	Chief Facilities/Physical Plant	Mr. David MCBRIDE

*University of Tennessee System Office (C)

800 Andy Holt Tower, Knoxville TN 37996-0180
County: Knox FICE Identification: 008051
Unit ID: 221722
Telephone: (865) 974-1000 Carnegie Class: N/A
FAX Number: (865) 974-3753
URL: www.tennessee.edu

Code	Title	Name
01	President	Dr. Joe DIPIETRO
03	Executive Vice President	Dr. David E. MILLHORN
05	Interim VP Acad Affs/Stdnt Success	Dr. Katherine N. HIGH
30	CEO UT Found/VP Develop & Alumni	Mr. Johnnie RAY
26	VP for Public & Govt Relations	Mr. Hank C. DYE
45	Vice President for Research	Dr. David E. MILLHORN
10	Treasurer & CIO/Acting CFO	Mr. Charles (Butch) M. PECCOLO, JR.
43	VP/General Counsel/Secretary	Ms. Catherine S. MIZELL
16	Chief Human Resources Officer	Ms. Linda HENDRICKS
86	Vice President of Public Service	Dr. Mary JINKS
28	VP for Equity and Diversity	Mr. Theotis ROBINSON
04	Exec Assistant to the President	Mr. Keith CARVER
21	Exec Dir Auditing/Consulting Svcs	Ms. Sandy JANSEN
29	Exec Dir UT Natl Alumni Assn	Mr. Lofton K. STUART

*University of Tennessee, Knoxville (D)

1331 Circle Park, Andy Holt Tower,
Knoxville TN 37996-0184
County: Knox FICE Identification: 003530
Unit ID: 221759
Telephone: (865) 974-1000 Carnegie Class: RU/VH
FAX Number: (865) 974-1182 Calendar System: Semester
URL: www.utk.edu
Established: 1794 Annual Undergrad Tuition & Fees (In-State): $9,092
Enrollment: 30,194 Coed
Affiliation or Control: State IRS Status: 501(c)3
Highest Offering: Doctorate
Program: Liberal Arts And General; Teacher Preparatory; Professional
Accreditation: SC, ANEST, ART, AUD, BUS, BUSA, CACREP, CIDA, CLPSY, COPSY, CORE, DENT, DIETD, DIETI, ENG, FOR, IPSY, JOUR, LAW, LIB, MT, MUS, NRPA, NURSE, PH, RAD, SCPSY, SP, SW, TED, VET

Code	Title	Name
02	Chancellor	Dr. Jimmy G. CHEEK
100	Chancellor's Chief of Staff	Vacant
05	Provost/Senior VC for Acad Affairs	Dr. Susan D. MARTIN
32	Vice Chancellor for Student Affairs	Mr. W. Timothy ROGERS
46	Int Vice Chanc Research/Engagement	Dr. Lee RIEDINGER
10	Vice Chanc Finance & Administration	Mr. Chris CIMINO
27	Vice Chanc for Communications	Ms. Margie NICHOLS
30	Vice Chanc Development/Alumni Affs	Mr. Scott RABENOLD
20	Vice Provost for Faculty Affairs	Vacant
20	Vice Provost Academic Operations	Vacant
58	Vice Provost/Dean Graduate School	Dr. Carolyn R. HODGES
39	Asst VC/Exec Dir Univ Housing	Mr. Ken STONER
51	Asst Provost Univ Outrch/Cont Educ	Dr. Norvel BURKETT
07	Asst Provost Enrollment Svcs	Mr. Richard L. BAYER
18	Exec Director Facilities Services	Mr. J. Michael SHERRELL
41	Men's Athletic Director	Mr. Michael E. HAMILTON
41	Women's Athletic Director	Ms. Joan CRONAN
28	Director Equity/Diversity Office	Dr. Marva RUDOLPH
37	Director of Financial Aid	Mr. Jeffrey G. GERKIN
09	Dir Inst Research/Assessmt	Ms. Denise GARDNER
38	Director of Student Counseling	Dr. Victor BARR
06	Registrar	Ms. Monique W. ANDERSON
47	Dean Ag Sciences/Natural Resources	Dr. Caula BEYL
48	Dean of Architecture and Design	Dr. Scott POOLE
50	Dean Business Administration	Dr. Jan R. WILLIAMS
60	Dean Communication/Information	Dr. Michael WIRTH
53	Dean Educ/Health/Human Sciences	Dr. Robert RIDER
54	Dean of Engineering	Dr. Wayne DAVIS
61	Dean of Law	Prof. Douglas BLAZE
49	Dean of Arts & Sciences	Dr. Theresa LEE
66	Dean of Nursing	Dr. Joan L. CREASIA
70	Dean of Social Work	Dr. Karen SOWERS
74	Dean of Veterinary Medicine	Dr. James P. THOMPSON
47	Dean of Agricultural Extension Svc	Dr. Tim L. CROSS
08	Dean of Libraries	Dr. Steve SMITH

*University of Tennessee Health Science Center (E)

800 Madison Avenue, Memphis TN 38163-0002
County: Shelby FICE Identification: 006725
Unit ID: 221704
Telephone: (901) 448-5500 Carnegie Class: Not Classified
FAX Number: (901) 448-7750 Calendar System: Semester
URL: www.uthsc.edu
Established: 1911 Annual Undergrad Tuition & Fees (In-State): $9,092
Enrollment: 2,815 Coed
Affiliation or Control: State IRS Status: 501(c)3
Highest Offering: Doctorate
Program: Professional
Accreditation: &SC, ANEST, CYTO, DENT, DH, HT, IPSY, MED, MT, NURSE, OT, PHAR, PTA

Code	Title	Name
02	Chancellor	Dr. Steve J. SCHWAB
100	Executive Vice Chancellor	Dr. Kennard D. BROWN
76	Dean of Allied Health Sci	Dr. Noma B. ANDERSON
52	Dean of Dentistry	Dr. Timothy L. HOTTEL
58	Dean of Graduate Health Sciences	Dr. Don THOMASON
63	Dean of Medicine	Dr. David STERN
63	Dean Medicine Chattanooga	Dr. David C. SEABERG
63	Dean Medicine Knoxville	Dr. James J. NEUTENS
66	Dean of Nursing	Dr. Laura TALBOT
67	Dean of Pharmacy	Dr. Marie CHISHOLM- BURNS
05	VC Academic/Faculty/Student Affs	Dr. Cheryl R. SCHEID
13	Chief Information Officer	Dr. Kennard D. BROWN
30	Int VC Development/Alumni Affairs	Ms. Bethany GOOLSBY
10	Vice Chancellor Finance/Operations	Mr. Anthony A. FERRARA
09	Asst VC of Inst Research/Educ Tech	Dr. Chanchai MCDONALD
32	Asst VC for Student Affairs	Ms. Sonya SMITH
07	Director of Admissions	Mr. Ron K. PATTERSON
19	Director of Campus Police	Chief L. Ida WALLS-UPCHURCH
35	Dir of Campus Rec/Student Life	Mr. Frank HARRISON
27	Director of Communications/Mktg	Ms. Sheila CHAMPLIN
31	Dir of Community Affairs	Ms. Pam HOUSTON
28	Director of Equity & Diversity	Dr. Michael L. ALSTON
18	Director of Facilities	Mr. J. Bruce STILES
37	Director of Financial Aid	Mr. John H. LEWIS
15	Director of Human Resources	Mr. Jerry S. HALL
62	Director of Lib/Biocomm Ctr	Dr. Thomas A. SINGARELLA
96	Director of Purchasing Svcs	Mr. Victor CRUTCHFIELD
38	Dir of Student Acad Support Svcs	Ms. Kathy L. GIBBS
06	Registrar	Dr. Glenda K. ALEXANDER
40	Director of Bookstore	Ms. Bobbie BALDWIN
48	Director of Architecture and Plng	Mr. Kenny BRADSHAW
88	VC Clinical Affairs	Dr. David STERN
88	Asst VC Faculty Administration	Dr. Cynthia RUSSELL

*University of Tennessee at Chattanooga (F)

615 McCallie Avenue, Chattanooga TN 37403-2504
County: Hamilton FICE Identification: 003529
Unit ID: 221740
Telephone: (423) 425-4111 Carnegie Class: Master's L
FAX Number: (423) 425-2200 Calendar System: Semester
URL: www.utc.edu
Established: 1886 Annual Undergrad Tuition & Fees (In-State): $9,092
Enrollment: 11,438 Coed
Affiliation or Control: State IRS Status: 501(c)3
Highest Offering: Doctorate
Program: Liberal Arts And General; Teacher Preparatory; Professional
Accreditation: SC, ANEST, ART, BUS, BUSA, CACREP, CIDA, CS, DIETD, ENG, JOUR, MUS, NURSE, PTA, SPAA, SW, TED, THEA

Code	Title	Name
02	Chancellor	Dr. Roger G. BROWN
05	Interim Provost	Dr. Mary TANNER
30	Vice Chanc University Advancement	Mr. Bob LYON
10	Sr Vice Chanc Fin/Operations & IT	Dr. Richard BROWN
32	Vice Chanc Student Development	Dr. John DELANEY
20	Assoc Provost for Academic Affairs	Dr. Jocelyn SANDERS
21	Assoc Vice Chanc Business/Fin Affs	Ms. Vanasia Conley PARKS
26	Assoc VC University Relations	Mr. Chuck CANTRELL
18	Asst VC Operations/Fac Plng & Mgt	Mr. Tom M. ELLIS
91	Assoc VC & CIO	Mr. Tom HOOVER
35	Asst VC Student Development	Dr. Dee Dee ANDERSON
100	Chief of Staff	Ms. Terry DENNISTON
08	Dean of Lupton Library	Ms. Theresa LIEDTKA
88	Assoc Dean of Student Life	Mr. Jim HICKS
07	Asst VC Enrollment Services	Mr. Yancy FREEMAN
06	Director of Records and Registrar	Ms. Linda ORTH
13	Director of Information Systems	Mr. Richard GAMBRELL
09	Dir of Planning/Eval/Inst Research	Dr. Richard R. GRUETZEMACHER
36	Dir of Placement/Student Employment	Mrs. Jean DAKE
15	Director of Human Resources	Mr. Dan WEBB
38	Director of Counseling	Dr. Nancy BADGER
37	Director of Financial Aid	Ms. Dianne COX
41	Director of Athletics	Mr. Rick HART
49	Dean of Arts & Sciences	Dr. Herbert BURHENN
50	Dean of Business Administration	Dr. Robert DOOLEY
53	Dean of Health/Educ/Prof Studies	Dr. Mary TANNER
54	Dean of Engineering/Comp Science	Dr. William SUTTON
58	Dean of Graduate School	Dr. Jerald AINSWORTH
66	Director of Nursing	Dr. Katherine S. LINDGREN
22	Director of Equity & Diversity	Dr. Bryan SAMUEL
78	Director of Cooperative Education	Mr. Hugh L. PREVOST, JR.
46	Director of Grants/Research	Ms. Meredith PERRY
29	Director of Alumni Affairs	Ms. Jayne HOLDER
14	Director of Admin Computing	Ms. Glenda F. SULLIVAN
96	Mgr of Business Svcs (Purchasing)	Mr. Charles SCOTT

*University of Tennessee at Martin (G)

544 University Street, Martin TN 38238-0001
County: Weakley FICE Identification: 003531
Unit ID: 221768
Telephone: (731) 881-7000 Carnegie Class: Master's M
FAX Number: (731) 881-7019 Calendar System: Semester
URL: www.utm.edu
Established: 1900 Annual Undergrad Tuition & Fees (In-State): $9,092
Enrollment: 7,910 Coed
Affiliation or Control: State IRS Status: 501(c)3
Highest Offering: Master's
Program: Liberal Arts And General; Teacher Preparatory; Professional
Accreditation: SC, AAFCS, BUS, #DIETD, #DIETI, ENG, JOUR, MUS, NUR, SW, TED

Code	Title	Name
02	Chancellor	Dr. Thomas A. RAKES
05	Provost & Vice Chanc for Acad Affs	Dr. E. Jerald OGG
10	Int Vice Chanc for Finance & Admin	Ms. Nancy J. YARBROUGH
32	Vice Chancellor for Student Affairs	Dr. Margaret Y. TOSTON
30	Vice Chancellor for Univ Advancemnt	Vacant
20	Assoc Vice Chanc for Academic Affr	Dr. Victoria S. SENG
27	CIO	Mr. Terry W. LEWIS
21	Int Dir of Budget & Mgmt Reporting	Ms. Petra R. MCPHEARSON
35	Asst Vice Chanc for Student Affairs	Mr. David J. BELOTE
44	Asst VChanc Devel & Planned Giving	Ms. Jeanna C. SWAFFORD

04 Exec Assistant to the Chancellor ... Ms. Edie B. GIBSON
29 Asst Vice Chanc for Alumni Rels ... Mr. Charley T. DEAL
06 Dir of Acad Records & Registrar ... Ms. Brandy D. CARTMELL
07 Director of Admissions ... Ms. Judy M. RAYBURN
28 Equity and Diversity Officer ... Vacant
15 Director of Human Resources ... Mr. James (Phillip) BRIGHT
09 Int Dir Institutional Research ... Dr. Desiree A. MCCULLOUGH
41 Director Intercollegiate Athletics ... Mr. Phil W. DANE
08 Director of Library ... Ms. Mary V. CARPENTER
18 Director of Physical Plant Opers ... Mr. Tim J. NIPP
19 Director of Public Safety ... Mr. Scott D. ROBBINS
96 Purchasing Agent ... Ms. Lori A. DONAVANT
37 Int Dir Financial Aid & Scholarship ... Ms. Sheryl FRAZIER
38 Dir Student Health & Counseling Svc ... Ms. Shannon DEAL
39 Director of Student Housing ... Mr. Earl WRIGHT
26 Director of University Relations ... Mr. Robert (Bud) D. GRIMES
85 Int Dir Tenn Intensive English Pgm ... Mr. Charles (Gary) WILSON
47 Int Dean Col Agri & App Sciences ... Dr. Jerry GRESHAM
50 Dean Col Business & Global Affairs ... Dr. Ernest R. MOSER
53 Dean Col Educ/Health & Behav Sci ... Dr. Mary Lee HALL
79 Dean Col Humanities/Fine Arts ... Dr. Lynn M. ALEXANDER
54 Interim Dean Col Engr & Natural Sci ... Dr. Richard J. HELGESON

Vanderbilt University (A)

2201 West End Avenue, Nashville TN 37240-0002
County: Davidson FICE Identification: 003535
Unit ID: 221999
Telephone: (615) 322-7311 Carnegie Class: RU/VH
FAX Number: (615) 343-5555 Calendar System: Semester
URL: www.vanderbilt.edu
Established: 1873 Annual Undergrad Tuition & Fees: $42,118
Enrollment: 12,836 Coed
Affiliation or Control: Independent Non-Profit IRS Status: 501(c)3
Highest Offering: Doctorate
Program: Liberal Arts And General; Teacher Preparatory; Professional
Accreditation: SC, AUD, BUS, CACREP, CLPSY, DENT, DIETI, DMS, ENG, IPSY, LAW, MED, MIDWF, MT, MUS, NMT, NUR, PERF, PH, RTT, SP, TED, THEOL

01 Chancellor ... Dr. Nicholas ZEPPOS
05 Provost/Vice Chancellor ... Dr. Richard C. MCCARTY
17 Vice Chancellor Health Affairs ... Dr. Jeffrey BALSER
10 Vice Chanc/Chief Financial Officer ... Mr. Brett SWEET
11 Vice Chanc Administration ... Mr. Jerry FIFE
30 Vice Chanc Dev & Alumni Relations ... Ms. Susie STALCUP
15 Chief Human Resouce Ofcr ... Ms. Traci NORDBERG
26 VC Univ Affs/Gen Counsel/Univ Secy ... Dr. David WILLIAMS
29 Exec Asc VC Development/Alumni Rels ... Mr. Robert EARLY
20 Assoc Vice Chanc Academic Affairs ... Mr. John MCDANIEL
18 Deputy VC Facilities & Environment ... Mr. Judson NEWBERN
27 Vice Chancellor for Public Affairs ... Ms. Beth FORTUNE
09 Director Institutional Research ... Dr. Roberta BELL
21 Vice Chancellor for Investments ... Mr. Matthew WRIGHT
20 Assoc Provost Undergrad Education ... Ms. Cynthia CYRUS
58 Vice Prov Research/Dean Grad Sch ... Dr. Dennis G. HALL
84 Vice Provost Enrollment ... Dr. Douglas CHRISTIANSEN
13 Dean Student Info Tech Support ... Mr. F. Clark WILLIAMS
21 Assistant VC Finance/Controller ... Mr. Kevin WALKER
06 Registrar ... Mr. Cheng KHOO
07 Dean of Admissions ... Dr. Douglas CHRISTIANSEN
07 Dir Undergraduate Admissions ... Mr. John GAINES
37 Exec Director of Financial Aid ... Dr. David D. MOHNING
38 Director Counseling Center ... Dr. Rhonda VENABLE
36 Director of Career Center ... Ms. Cynthia FUNK
46 Director Contract & Research Adm ... Dr. John CHILDRESS
14 Assoc Vice Chancellor ITS ... Vacant
32 Dean of Students/Assoc Provost ... Dr. Mark BANDAS
49 Dean College Arts & Science ... Dr. Carolyn DEVER
63 Dean School of Medicine ... Dr. Jeffrey R. BALSER
54 Dean School of Engineering ... Dr. Philippe FAUCHET
66 Dean School of Nursing ... Dr. Colleen CONWAY-WELCH
53 Dean of Peabody College ... Dr. Camilla P. BENBOW
64 Dean Blair School of Music ... Dr. Mark WAIT
73 Dean of the Divinity School ... Dr. James HUDNUT-BEUMLER
61 Dean of the School of Law ... Dr. Chris GUTHRIE
50 Dean Owen Grad School of Mgmt ... Dr. James BRADFORD
88 Dean of the Commons ... Dr. Frank WCISLO
42 University Chaplain ... Rev. Gretchen PERSON
19 Chief of Police/Asst Vice Chanc ... Mr. August WASHINGTON
22 Dir EO/AA & Disability Svcs ... Ms. Anita JENIOUS
23 Assoc Dean Health & Wellness ... Dr. John W. GREENE
41 Director of Sport Operations ... Mr. Brockton WILLIAMS

Vatterott College-Memphis (B)

2655 Dividend Drive, Memphis TN 38132-1713
County: Shelby Identification: 666308
Unit ID: 440873
Telephone: (901) 761-5730 Carnegie Class: Assoc/PrivFP
FAX Number: (901) 763-2897 Calendar System: Other
URL: www.vatterott-college.edu
Established: 1969 Annual Undergrad Tuition & Fees: $10,930
Enrollment: 1,014 Coed
Affiliation or Control: Proprietary IRS Status: Proprietary
Highest Offering: Associate Degree
Program: Occupational
Accreditation: ACCSC

01 CEO & President ... Ms. Pam BELL
10 Chief Financial Officer ... Mr. Dennis BEAVERS
05 Chief Academic Officer ... Mr. Brandon SHEBRON
11 Chief Administrative Officer ... Mr. Scott CASANOVER
12 Campus Director ... Mr. Christopher COLEMAN

† Branch campus of Vatterott College-NorthPark, Berkeley, MO.

Victory University (formerly Crichton College) (C)

255 N Highland Street, Memphis TN 38111-1375
County: Shelby FICE Identification: 009982
Unit ID: 220941
Telephone: (901) 320-9700 Carnegie Class: Bac/Diverse
FAX Number: (901) 320-9709 Calendar System: Semester
URL: www.victory.edu
Established: 1941 Annual Undergrad Tuition & Fees: $10,050
Enrollment: 994 Coed
Affiliation or Control: Proprietary IRS Status: Proprietary
Highest Offering: Master's
Program: Occupational; 2-Year Principally Bachelor's Creditable; Liberal Arts And General; Teacher Preparatory; Professional; Business Emphasis
Accreditation: SC

01 President ... Dr. Shirley ROBINSON PIPPINS
03 Provost ... Dr. Jim JEREMIAH
11 Dir Operations & Public Safety ... Mr. Troy GRAHAM
13 Director IT & Telecommunications ... Mr. Todd WILLIAMS
09 Dir Inst Effectiveness & Research ... Dr. Suzan SMITH
84 Exec Dir Enrollment Management ... Mrs. Carolyn CATES
07 Director of Admissions ... Ms. Shelley DUNN
05 Vice President Academic Affairs ... Dr. William CHANEY
06 Registrar ... Ms. Erica TAYLOR
73 Chair Bible & Theology ... Dr. Troy MILLER
83 Chair Behavioral Studies ... Dr. William CHANEY
50 Chair Business ... Dr. Brodie I. JOHNSON
53 Interim Chair Education ... Dr. William CHANEY
79 Chair Arts and Science ... Dr. Yolanda HARPER
08 Director Library ... Ms. Pamela B. WALKER
37 Director Student Finance Center ... Mr. Todd WILLIAMS
32 Director Student Development ... Mr. Brian DUFFY
10 Chief Financial Officer ... Mr. Troy GRAHAM
15 Director Human Resources ... Mrs. Julie TYLER
41 Athletic Director ... Mr. Scott ROBINSON

Virginia College School of Business and Health (D)

721 Eastgate Loop, Chattanooga TN 37411-5600
County: Hamilton Identification: 666136
Unit ID: 450289
Telephone: (423) 893-2000 Carnegie Class: Assoc/PrivFP4
FAX Number: (423) 893-2010 Calendar System: Quarter
URL: www.vc.edu
Established: 2006 Annual Undergrad Tuition & Fees: $15,616
Enrollment: 501 Coed
Affiliation or Control: Proprietary IRS Status: Proprietary
Highest Offering: Baccalaureate
Program: 2-Year Principally Bachelor's Creditable; Liberal Arts And General
Accreditation: ACICS

01 Campus President ... Mr. Dominick DELORENZO
05 Academic Dean ... Mr. James RAY
06 Registrar ... Ms. Sandra MCMANUS
03 Director of Admissions ... Mr. William KILGORE

Visible Music College (E)

200 Madison Avenue, Memphis TN 38103
County: Shelby FICE Identification: 039823
Unit ID: 449764
Telephone: (901) 381-3939 Carnegie Class: Spec/Arts
FAX Number: (901) 377-0544 Calendar System: Semester
URL: www.visible.edu
Established: 2000 Annual Undergrad Tuition & Fees: $22,700
Enrollment: 126 Coed
Affiliation or Control: Independent Non-Profit IRS Status: 501(c)3
Highest Offering: Baccalaureate
Program: Professional; Music Emphasis
Accreditation: TRACS

01 President ... Ken STEORTS
05 Interim Academic Dean ... Robert MURPHY
32 Vice President Student Development ... Peet STRYDOM
07 Director of Admissions ... Emily SPONSLER
10 Vice President Business ... Christy MCFARLAND
08 Librarian ... Vacant
26 Communications Coordinator ... Sue STRYDOM
37 Director of Financial Aid ... LaKeisha MURRY
06 Registrar ... Mary Ann GARDNER

Watkins College of Art, Design & Film (F)

2298 Rosa L. Parks Boulevard, Nashville TN 37228-1306
County: Davidson FICE Identification: 030888
Unit ID: 392840
Telephone: (615) 383-4848 Carnegie Class: Spec/Arts
FAX Number: (615) 383-4849 Calendar System: Semester
URL: www.watkins.edu
Established: 1885 Annual Undergrad Tuition & Fees: $21,300
Enrollment: 394 Coed
Affiliation or Control: Independent Non-Profit IRS Status: 501(c)3
Highest Offering: Baccalaureate
Program: Fine Arts Emphasis
Accreditation: SC, ART, CIDA

01 President ... Ms. Ellen MEYER
30 Vice Pres Institutional Advancement ... Ms. Hilrie BROWN
05 Interim Dean ... Ms. Joy MCKENZIE
10 Vice Pres Finance and Operations ... Ms. Mary Ellen LOTHAMER
07 Dir Admissions ... Ms. Linda SCHWAB
26 Dir External Relations ... Ms. Caroline DAVIS
06 Registrar ... Ms. Tracie JOHNSON
37 Dir Financial Aid ... Ms. Regina GILBERT
08 Library Dir ... Ms. Lisa WILLIAMS
13 Dir Information Technology ... Mr. Chris MCQUISTION
18 Dir of Facilities ... Mr. Martin DILLINGHAM
88 Chair Film School ... Mr. Van FLESHER
57 Chair Fine Art Department ... Ms. Kristi HARGROVE
88 Chair Graphic Design Department ... Mr. Dan BRAWNER
88 Chair Interior Design Department ... Ms. Cheryl GULLEY
88 Chair Photography Department ... Ms. Robin PARIS
97 Dir General Education ... Ms. Cary Beth MILLER
51 Dir Community Education ... Ms. Meredith EASTBURN
32 Dir Student Life ... Ms. Samantha BRZOZOWSKI

West Tennessee Business College (G)

1186 Highway 45 Bypass, Jackson TN 38301
County: Madison FICE Identification: 004947
Unit ID: 222099
Telephone: (731) 668-7240 Carnegie Class: Assoc/PrivFP
FAX Number: (731) 668-3824 Calendar System: Other
URL: www.wtbc.edu
Established: 1888 Annual Undergrad Tuition & Fees: $14,800
Enrollment: 279 Coed
Affiliation or Control: Proprietary IRS Status: Proprietary
Highest Offering: Associate Degree
Program: Occupational
Accreditation: ACICS

01 Executive Director ... C. Vicki BURCH
05 Academic Dean ... LaVerne ADAMS
10 Chief Fiscal Officer ... Kim JONES
06 Registrar ... Sheila JOHNSON
07 Admissions Director ... Ann RECORD

† Tuition for each program includes books.

Williamson Christian College (H)

200 Seaboard Lane, Franklin TN 37067-8237
County: Williamson FICE Identification: 035135
Unit ID: 443340
Telephone: (615) 771-7821 Carnegie Class: Spec/Faith
FAX Number: (615) 771-7810 Calendar System: Semester
URL: www.williamsoncc.edu
Established: 1996 Annual Undergrad Tuition & Fees: $9,450
Enrollment: 118 Coed
Affiliation or Control: Non-denominational IRS Status: 501(c)3
Highest Offering: Baccalaureate
Program: Professional; Religious Emphasis
Accreditation: BI

01 President ... Dr. Ed SMITH
05 Exec Vice Pres Academic Affairs ... Dr. Sharon LANDERS
30 Int Vice President Advancement ... Dr. Ed SMITH
11 Vice President for Operations ... Vacant
06 Registrar ... Ms. Karen HUDSON
09 Dir Institutional Effectiveness ... Dr. Tony BUCHANAN
08 Librarian ... Ms. Elizabeth HUTCHISON
07 Dir of Admissions/Enrollment Mgmt ... Ms. Susan MAYS
37 Manager of Financial Aid ... Ms. Becky WILLENBERG

TEXAS

Abilene Christian University (I)

ACU Box 29100, Abilene TX 79699-9100
County: Taylor FICE Identification: 003537
Unit ID: 222178
Telephone: (325) 674-2000 Carnegie Class: Master's L
FAX Number: (325) 674-2202 Calendar System: Semester
URL: www.acu.edu
Established: 1906 Annual Undergrad Tuition & Fees: $26,770
Enrollment: 4,558 Coed
Affiliation or Control: Churches Of Christ IRS Status: 501(c)3
Highest Offering: Doctorate
Program: Liberal Arts And General; Teacher Preparatory; Professional
Accreditation: SC, BUS, CIDA, DIETD, JOUR, MFCD, MUS, NURSE, SP, SW, TEAC, THEOL

01 President ... Dr. Phil SCHUBERT
100 Senior Advisor to the President ... Ms. Suzanne ALLMON
05 Provost ... Dr. Robert RHODES
03 Vice President of the University ... Dr. Gary D. MCCALEB
30 Vice President for Advancement ... Mr. Phil BOONE
32 VP for Student Life/Dean Students ... Dr. Jean-Noel THOMPSON
88 Chief Investment Ofcr/Pres ACIMCO ... Mr. Jack W. RICH
43 General Counsel ... Mr. Slade SULLIVAN
00 Chancellor ... Dr. Royce MONEY
88 Exec Assistant to the Chancellor ... Mr. Jim HOLMANS
102 Vice Chancellor/Pres ACU Foundation ... Mr. Dan T. GARRETT
88 Senior Vice President Emeritus ... Dr. Robert D. HUNTER

20 Interim Vice Provost ....Dr. Susan LEWIS
97 Asst Provost for General Educ ....Dr. Nancy SHANKLE
49 Int Dean College of Arts & Sciences ....Dr. Greg STRAUGHN
73 Int Dean CBS/GST ....Dr. Ken R. CUKROWSKI
50 Dean College of Business Admin ....Dr. Rick S. LYTLE
53 Int Dean College of Educ/Human Svcs ....Dr. Donnie SNIDER
92 Dean Honors College ....Dr. Stephen JOHNSON
58 Dean Graduate School ....Dr. Carley DODD
66 Dean School of Nursing ....Dr. Becky HAMMACK
89 Director of First-Year Program ....Dr. Eric GUMM
08 Dean Library/Information Resources ....Dr. John WEAVER
104 Int Director of the Ctr Intl Educ ....Dr. Stephen SHEWMAKER
106 Managing Director Online Programs ....Mr. Corey PATTERSON
42 Assistant Dean for Spiritual Life ....Mr. Mark LEWIS
36 Director Career Center ....Ms. MaryEllen OLSON
06 Registrar ....Mr. Bart HERRIDGE
37 Director Student Financial Services ....Mr. Ed KERESTLY
84 Chief Enrollment Officer ....Mr. Kevin CAMPBELL
26 Chief Marketing Officer ....Mr. Jason GROVES
35 Associate VP for Student Life ....Dr. Jeff ARRINGTON
23 Director of Medical Clinic ....Dr. Ellen B. LITTLE
39 Director Residence Life ....Mr. John DELONY
38 Director Univ Counseling Center ....Mr. Steve ROWLANDS
31 Director Ministery & Service ....Mr. Bob A. STRADER
45 Chief Info & Planning Officer ....Mr. Kevin J. ROBERTS
18 Exec Dir Facilities/Campus Develop ....Mr. Corey RUFF
10 Chief Financial Officer ....Mr. Craig FISHER
13 Exec Dir of Information Technology ....Mrs. Kay REEVES
24 Exec Dir Adams Ctr Teaching/Lrng ....Dr. Lesa BREEDING
105 Director Web Integration/Prgmng ....Dr. James D. LANGFORD
29 Dir of Alumni Rels & Annual Project ....Mr. Craig FISHER
19 Chief of ACU Police ....Mr. Jimmy ELLISON
44 Director of Major Gifts ....Mr. Don GARRETT
41 Director of Athletics ....Mr. Jared MOSLEY
15 Director of Human Resources ....Mrs. Wendy JONES
88 Director Instruction/Faculty Devel ....Dr. Dwayne HARAPNUIK
09 Asst Prov Dir Inst Research/Assess ....Dr. Tom A. MILHOLLAND
96 University Purchasing Manager ....Ms. Sandy HALL
40 Chief Business Services Officer ....Mr. Anthony T. WILLIAMS
101 Secretary to the Board of Trustees ....Mr. Slade SULLIVAN
04 Exec Assistant Office of President ....Mrs. Stephanie A. WOODLEE

*Alamo Community College District Central Office (A)

201 W Sheridan, San Antonio TX 78204-1429
County: Bexar FICE Identification: 003607
Unit ID: 222497
Telephone: (210) 485-0020 Carnegie Class: N/A
FAX Number: (210) 486-9166
URL: www.alamo.edu

01 Chancellor ....Dr. Bruce LESLIE
05 Vice Chanc for Academic Success ....Vacant
11 Vice Chanc for Finance & Admin ....Ms. Diane E. SNYDER
32 Vice Chancellor for Student Success ....Dr. Adelina SILVA
103 Vice Chanc Economic/Workforce Devel ....Dr. Federico ZARAGOZA
44 VC Plng/Performance/Inform/Systems ....Dr. Thomas CLEARY
15 Assoc Vice Chanc Human Resources ....Ms. Linda BOYER-OWENS
27 Assoc Vice Chanc Communications ....Mr. Leo ZUNIGA
18 Assoc Vice Chanc Facilities ....Mr. John STRYBOS
20 Assoc VC Acad Partnershp/Initatives ....Dr. Jo-Carol FABIANKE
10 Assoc VC Finance & Fiscal Services ....Ms. Pamela ANSBOURY
04 Deputy to the Chancellor/Dist Dir ....Dr. Adriana CONTRERAS
30 Exec Director Inst Advancement ....Mr. Jim ESKIN
21 Director of Internal Audit ....Ms. Patricia MAJOR
96 Director Acquisitions & Admin Svcs ....Mr. Gary O'BAR
41 Athletic Director ....Vacant
19 Chief Department of Public Safety ....Mr. Don ADAMS
21 Comptroller ....Ms. Angelia DEBARROS
12 President Northwest Vista College ....Dr. Jacqueline CLAUNCH
12 President San Antonio College ....Dr. Robert ZEIGLER
12 President St Philip's College ....Dr. Adena WILLIAMS LOSTON
12 President Palo Alto College ....Dr. Ana (Cha) GUZMAN
12 President Northeast College ....Dr. Eric RENO

*Northwest Vista College (B)

3535 N Ellison Drive, San Antonio TX 78251-4217
County: Bexar FICE Identification: 033723
Unit ID: 420398
Telephone: (210) 486-4000 Carnegie Class: Assoc/Pub-U-MC
FAX Number: (210) 486-9105 Calendar System: Semester
URL: www.alamo.edu/nvc
Established: 1995 Annual Undergrad Tuition & Fees (In-District): $1,662
Enrollment: 16,067 Coed
Affiliation or Control: Local IRS Status: 501(c)3
Highest Offering: Associate Degree
Program: 2-Year Principally Bachelor's Creditable
Accreditation: SC

02 President ....Dr. Jacqueline CLAUNCH
03 Vice President for College Services ....Mrs. Julie PACE
05 Vice President of Academics ....Dr. Jimmie BRUCE
32 Vice President of Student Success ....Mrs. Deborah GAITAN
30 Director Institutional Advancement ....Mrs. Lynne DEAN
08 Learning Resources Chair ....Ms. Judy MCMILLAN
36 Dean of Student Success ....Mrs. Jennifer COMEDY-HOLMES
26 Dir of Public Relations & Marketing ....Mrs. Renata SERAFIN
27 Director Info/Communications Tech ....Mr. Felix SALINAS
37 Director of Financial Aid ....Mr. Noe ORTIZ
21 Assistant Bursar ....Ms. Jennifer ORTIZ
39 Assoc Director of Residency/Reports ....Ms. Cynthia ZAMUDIO
15 Sr Human Resources Generalist ....Mr. Manuel CERDA
45 Director of Resources & College Dev ....Mr. Carlos AGUIRRE
18 Superintendent NVC ....Mr. Bernie ZERTUCHE
103 Dean of Workforce Development ....Mr. Patrick FONTENOT
88 Dean of Interdisciplinary Programs ....Dr. Mary DIXSON
09 Director of Institutional Research ....Dr. Eliza HERNANDEZ
88 Coordinator Scholarship ....Mrs. Lucy GAUNA
84 Director of Enrollment Management ....Mrs. Robin CARRILLO

*Palo Alto College (C)

1400 W Villaret, San Antonio TX 78224-2499
County: Bexar FICE Identification: 023413
Unit ID: 246354
Telephone: (210) 486-3000 Carnegie Class: Assoc/Pub-U-MC
FAX Number: (210) 921-5005 Calendar System: Semester
URL: www.alamo.edu
Established: 1985 Annual Undergrad Tuition & Fees (In-District): $1,952
Enrollment: 9,163 Coed
Affiliation or Control: Local IRS Status: 501(c)3
Highest Offering: Associate Degree
Program: Occupational; 2-Year Principally Bachelor's Creditable
Accreditation: SC

02 President ....Dr. Michael FLORES
05 Vice President Academic Affairs ....Vacant
10 Vice Pres College Services ....Dr. Beatriz JOSEPH
32 Vice President of Student Affairs ....Dr. Robert GARZA
49 Dean Arts & Sciences ....Ms. Elizabeth TANNER
49 Dean Science/Advanced/Applied Tech ....Mr. Gary SHELMAN
08 Dean of Learning Resources ....Ms. Tina MESA
26 Int Director of Public Relations ....Ms. Ginger HALL CARNES
21 Bursar ....Mr. Daniel ROCHA
84 Director of Enrollment Management ....Ms. Elizabeth VILLARUAL
37 Director Student Financial Services ....Mr. Lamar DUARTE
41 Athletic Director ....Mr. Adrian MONTOYA
32 Dean of Student Affairs ....Vacant
18 Chief Facilities/Physical Plant ....Mr. Sergio RIVERA
38 Director Student Counseling ....Ms. Yolanda REYNA
29 Director Alumni Relations ....Ms. Danielle ESPINOZA
09 Dir Inst Rsrch/Plng/Effectiveness ....Ms. Lanette GARZA
30 Chief Development ....Ms. Christina ALDRETE

*St. Philip's College (D)

1801 Martin Luther King, San Antonio TX 78203-2098
County: Bexar FICE Identification: 003608
Unit ID: 227854
Telephone: (210) 486-2000 Carnegie Class: Assoc/Pub-U-MC
FAX Number: N/A Calendar System: Semester
URL: www.alamo.edu/spc/
Established: 1898 Annual Undergrad Tuition & Fees (In-District): $1,952
Enrollment: 10,710 Coed
Affiliation or Control: Local IRS Status: 501(c)3
Highest Offering: Associate Degree
Program: Occupational; 2-Year Principally Bachelor's Creditable
Accreditation: SC, ACFEI, HT, MLTAD, OTA, PTAA, RAD, SURGT

02 President ....Dr. Adena WILLIAMS LOSTON
05 Vice Pres for Academic Affairs ....Ms. Ruth DALRYMPLE
32 Vice Pres of Student Success ....Dr. Sherrie LANG
11 Vice President for College Svcs ....Ms. Lacy HAMPTON
12 Vice Pres Admin Southwest Campus ....Vacant
35 Dean Student Success ....Mr. Paul MACHEN
08 Dean Interdisciplinary Programs ....Dr. Karen SIDES
75 Dean Applied Science & Tech ....Ms. Maureen CARTLEDGE
49 Dean Arts & Science ....Ms. Mary COTTIER
76 Dean of Health Sciences ....Ms. Rose SPRUILL
51 Director Continuing Ed/Extend Svcs ....Mr. Erick AKINS
37 Director of Financial Aid ....Mr. Diego BERNAL
45 Director Planning & Research ....Ms. Mecca SALAHUDDIN
10 Bursar ....Ms. Sophia GONZALEZ
26 Dir Community & Public Relations ....Vacant
30 Director Institutional Advancement ....Dr. Sharon CROCKETT-BELL
72 Director Instructional Technology ....Vacant
18 Chief Facilities/Physical Plant ....Ms. Sherry TOLIVER
29 Director Alumni Relations ....Dr. Sharon CROCKETT-BELL
96 Chief Budget Manager ....Mr. Paul BORREGO
84 Director Enrollment Management ....Ms. Beautrice BUTLER

*San Antonio College (E)

1300 San Pedro Avenue, San Antonio TX 78212-4299
County: Bexar FICE Identification: 009163
Unit ID: 227924
Telephone: (210) 486-0000 Carnegie Class: Assoc/Pub-U-MC
FAX Number: N/A Calendar System: Semester
URL: www.alamo.edu/sac
Established: 1925 Annual Undergrad Tuition & Fees (In-District): $2,568
Enrollment: 27,074 Coed
Affiliation or Control: Local IRS Status: 501(c)3
Highest Offering: Associate Degree
Program: Occupational; 2-Year Principally Bachelor's Creditable
Accreditation: SC, ADNUR, DA, DT, EMT, FUSER, MAC

02 President ....Dr. Robert E. ZEIGLER
05 Vice President of Academic Affairs ....Vacant
32 Vice President of Student Affairs ....Dr. Robert H. VELA
11 Vice President of College Services ....Mr. David E. MRIZEK
72 Dean Professional & Tech Educ ....Ms. Vernell E. WALKER
49 Dean of Arts & Sciences ....Dr. Conrad KRUEGER
51 Dean Cont Educ/Training Network ....Mr. Tim ROCKEY
08 Dean of Learning Resources ....Dr. Alice JOHNSON
84 Director of Enrollment Services ....Mr. J. Martin ORTEGA
37 Coordinator of Financial Aid ....Mr. Tom CAMPOS
35 Director of Student Activities ....Mr. Jorge POSADAS
85 Coordinator International Students ....Vacant
26 Director Public Relations ....Ms. Vanessa TORRES
45 Director Resource & College Devel ....Ms. Susan B. ESPINOZA
23 Director Health Services ....Ms. Paula DAGGETT
29 Coordinator of Alumni and Friends ....Vacant
18 Chief Facilities/Physical Plant ....Mr. David ORTEGA
38 Dean of Student Affairs ....Ms. Emma MENDIOLA

Alvin Community College (F)

3110 Mustang Road, Alvin TX 77511-4898
County: Brazoria FICE Identification: 003539
Unit ID: 222567
Telephone: (281) 756-3500 Carnegie Class: Assoc/Pub-R-L
FAX Number: (281) 756-3854 Calendar System: Semester
URL: www.alvincollege.edu
Established: 1948 Annual Undergrad Tuition & Fees (In-District): $1,432
Enrollment: 5,242 Coed
Affiliation or Control: Local IRS Status: 501(c)3
Highest Offering: Associate Degree
Program: Occupational; 2-Year Principally Bachelor's Creditable
Accreditation: SC, ADNUR, DMS, NDT, POLYT

01 President ....Dr. A. Rodney ALLBRIGHT
05 Dean Instruction/Provost ....Dr. John BETHSCHEIDER
11 Dean Financial/Admin Services ....Dr. Darryl STEVENS
06 Registrar ....Ms. Irene M. ROBINSON
08 Director Library Services ....Mr. Tom BATES
10 Director Fiscal Affairs/Controller ....Mr. Karl STAGER
13 Int Director Info Technology ....Mr. Jeff CERNOCH
37 Dir Student Financial Aid Placement ....Ms. Dora SIMS
45 Dir Institutional Effectiveness ....Mr. Patrick SANGER
15 Director Human Resources ....Ms. Lang WINDSOR
18 Director Physical Plant ....Vacant
29 Director Alumni Relations ....Ms. Wendy DEL BELLO
07 Director Admissions/Acad Advising ....Ms. Stephanie STOCKSTILL
09 Director of Inst Effective/Research ....Mr. Patrick SANGER
51 Dean Cont Educ/Pearland Center ....Dr. Patricia HERTENBERGER
32 Dean of Students ....Ms. JoAn ANDERSON
75 Dean Technical Programs ....Dr. John BETHSCHEIDER
26 Chief Public Relations Officer ....Ms. Wendy DEL BELLO

Amarillo College (G)

PO Box 447, Amarillo TX 79178-0001
County: Potter FICE Identification: 003540
Unit ID: 222576
Telephone: (806) 371-5000 Carnegie Class: Assoc/Pub-R-L
FAX Number: (806) 371-5370 Calendar System: Semester
URL: www.actx.edu
Established: 1929 Annual Undergrad Tuition & Fees (In-District): $2,176
Enrollment: 11,598 Coed
Affiliation or Control: State/Local IRS Status: 501(c)3
Highest Offering: Associate Degree
Program: Occupational; 2-Year Principally Bachelor's Creditable
Accreditation: SC, ADNUR, DH, FUSER, MLTAD, MUS, NMT, OTA, PTAA, RAD, RTT, SURGT

01 President ....Dr. Paul MATNEY
05 VP of Academic Affairs ....Dr. Russell LOWERY-HART
10 VP of Business Affairs ....Mr. Terry BERG
51 Dean of Continuing Education ....Mrs. Kim D. DAVIS
32 VP of Student Affairs ....Mr. Robert C. AUSTIN
13 Chief Information Officer ....Mr. Lee M. COLAW
46 Chief of Planning/Advancement ....Ms. Danita L. MCANALLY
102 Dir AC Foundation/Development ....Mrs. Kathleen B. DOWDY
76 Director Ctr Cont Health Care Educ ....Mrs. Kimberly A. CROWLEY
18 Director Physical Plant ....Mr. Bruce COTGREAVE
37 Director Financial Aid ....Mrs. Mary K. MOONEY
08 Director AC Library Network ....Mr. Mark HANNA
06 Registrar ....Mrs. Diane BRICE
27 Chief of Communication/Mktg ....Mrs. Ellen R. GREEN
15 Director of Admin Svcs/Human Res ....Mr. Lynn L. THORNTON
19 Director of Police ....Mr. Michael W. DUVAL
26 Director Found Mktg/Special Events ....Mrs. Tracy D. DOUGHERTY
35 Assoc VP of Student Affairs ....Mrs. April L. SESSLER
38 Director Advising & Counseling ....Mr. Jason A. NORMAN
88 Director Amarillo Museum of Art ....Vacant
88 Director Criminal Justice Program ....Ms. Toni GRAY
96 Director of Purchasing ....Mrs. Vickie SHELTON
88 Dean of Academic Transfer Pgms ....Mr. Jerry E. MOLLER
76 Dean of Health Sciences ....Mr. Bill E. CRAWFORD
75 Dean of Career/Tech Education ....Dr. Shawn M. FOUTS
88 Dean of Academic Success ....Dr. Tamara T. CLUNIS

Amberton University (H)

1700 Eastgate Drive, Garland TX 75041
County: Dallas FICE Identification: 022594
Unit ID: 222628
Telephone: (972) 279-6511 Carnegie Class: Master's L
FAX Number: (972) 279-9773 Calendar System: Quarter
URL: www.amberton.edu
Established: 1971 Annual Undergrad Tuition & Fees: $5,600
Enrollment: 1,380 Coed
Affiliation or Control: Independent Non-Profit IRS Status: 501(c)3
Highest Offering: Master's
Program: Professional; Business Emphasis

Accreditation: SC

01 President ... Dr. Melinda REAGAN
05 Academic Dean ... Dr. Don HEBBARD
30 Dean Univ Advance/VP Strategic Svcs ... Dr. Jo Lynn LOYD
10 Chief Business Officer ... Mr. Brent BRADSHAW
06 Registrar ... Ms. Marge MASSEY
32 Director Student Services ... Mr. Bill GILBREATH
84 Director for Recruiting ... Mr. Glenn SORRELLS
08 Head Librarian ... Ms. Judy GIBSON
29 Dir Alumni Relations & Inst Rsch ... Dr. Jo Lynn LOYD
07 Director of Admissions ... Dr. Don HEBBARD

American College of Acupuncture and Oriental Medicine (A)

9100 Park West Drive, Houston TX 77063-4104
County: Harris FICE Identification: 031533
Unit ID: 429085
Telephone: (713) 780-9777 Carnegie Class: Spec/Health
FAX Number: (713) 781-5781 Calendar System: Trimester
URL: www.acaom.edu
Established: 1991 Annual Graduate Tuition & Fees: $13,000
Enrollment: 129 Coed
Affiliation or Control: Proprietary IRS Status: Proprietary
Highest Offering: Master's; No Undergraduates
Program: Professional
Accreditation: SC, ACUP

01 President ... Dr. John Paul LIANG
11 Vice President of Operations ... Ms. Angel GUINARA
05 Dean of Academic Affairs ... Dr. Wen HUANG
20 Dean of Clinical Training ... Dr. Baisong ZHONG

American InterContinental University-Houston Campus (B)

9999 Richmond Avenue, Houston TX 77042-4516
County: Harris Identification: 666335
Unit ID: 445133
Telephone: (832) 201-3600 Carnegie Class: Spec/Bus
FAX Number: (832) 201-3633 Calendar System: Quarter
URL: www.houston.aiuniv.edu
Established: 2003 Annual Undergrad Tuition & Fees: N/A
Enrollment: 557 Coed
Affiliation or Control: Proprietary IRS Status: Proprietary
Highest Offering: Master's
Program: Professional; Business Emphasis
Accreditation: &NH, ACBSP

01 Campus President ... Mr. Stephen MALUTICH

† Regional accreditation is carried under the parent institution in Hoffman Estates, IL.

Anamarc College (C)

3210 Dyer, El Paso TX 79930
County: El Paso FICE Identification: 037563
Unit ID: 444389
Telephone: (915) 351-8100 Carnegie Class: Assoc/PrivFP
FAX Number: (915) 351-8300 Calendar System: Other
URL: www.anamarc.edu
Established: N/A Annual Undergrad Tuition & Fees: $11,813
Enrollment: 710 Coed
Affiliation or Control: Proprietary IRS Status: Proprietary
Highest Offering: Associate Degree
Program: Occupational
Accreditation: ACICS, OTA

01 President ... Mr. Pablo FUENTES
03 Chief Executive Officer ... Dr. Ana Maria PINA HOUDE
10 Vice President of Finance ... Mr. Jaime LOWENBERG
15 Vice President of Human Resources ... Ms. Elena LIGGINGS
46 VP of Educ Research & Technology ... Mr. Sergio ZAPATA
06 Registrar ... Ms. Elsa PINA
37 Financial Aid Director ... Mr. Rick AMBRIZ

Angelina College (D)

PO Box 1768, Lufkin TX 75902-1768
County: Angelina Identification: 006661
Unit ID: 222822
Telephone: (936) 639-1301 Carnegie Class: Assoc/Pub-R-M
FAX Number: (936) 639-4299 Calendar System: Semester
URL: www.angelina.edu
Established: 1966 Annual Undergrad Tuition & Fees (In-District): $1,770
Enrollment: 5,850 Coed
Affiliation or Control: State/Local IRS Status: 501(c)3
Highest Offering: Associate Degree
Program: Occupational; 2-Year Principally Bachelor's Creditable
Accreditation: SC, DMS, RAD, SURGT

01 President ... Dr. Larry M. PHILLIPS
05 Vice President/Dean of Instruction ... Dr. Patricia M. MCKENZIE
10 Vice President Business Services ... Mr. Joe MADDEN
31 Vice Pres of Community Services ... Dr. Frederick W. KANKE
32 Dean of Student Services ... Mr. James TWOHIG
13 Dir Management Information Systems ... Mr. Kenneth STREET
37 Director Student Financial Aid ... Mrs. Sue JONES
18 Chief Facilities/Physical Plant ... Mr. Steve CAPPS
84 Director Enrollment Services ... Mr. Jeremy THOMAS
09 Coord Instnl Effectiveness & Q.E.P. ... Dr. Monica PETERS
26 Coordinator Marketing/Development ... Mr. Gary STALLARD
15 Coord of Human Resources ... Mrs. Tifini WHIDDON
06 Registrar & Records Coordinator ... Mrs. Sandra COX

Angelo State University (E)

2601 West Avenue N, San Angelo TX 76909-0001
County: Tom Green FICE Identification: 003541
Unit ID: 222831
Telephone: (325) 942-2555 Carnegie Class: Master's M
FAX Number: (325) 942-2038 Calendar System: Semester
URL: www.angelo.edu
Established: 1928 Annual Undergrad Tuition & Fees (In-State): $6,326
Enrollment: 7,084 Coed
Affiliation or Control: State IRS Status: 501(c)3
Highest Offering: Doctorate
Program: Liberal Arts And General; Teacher Preparatory; Professional; Business Emphasis
Accreditation: SC, ACBSP, ADNUR, MUS, NUR, PTA, @SW, TED

01 President ... Dr. Joseph C. RALLO
05 Provost/Vice Pres Academic Affairs ... Dr. Brian J. MAY
30 Vice President for Dev & Alumni Rel ... Dr. Jason C. PENRY
10 VP for Finance and Administration ... Mr. Michael REID
32 VP for Student Affs & Enroll Mgmt ... Dr. Javier FLORES
20 Vice Provost ... Dr. Nancy ALLEN
58 Dean College of Graduate Studies ... Dr. Brian MAY
49 Dean of College of Arts & Sciences ... Dr. Paul SWETS
50 Dean College Business ... Dr. Corbett F. GAULDEN, JR.
53 Dean College of Education ... Dr. John MIAZGA
66 Dean College Health & Human Service ... Dr. Leslie MAYRAND
84 Assoc VP for Enrollment Mgmt ... Vacant
06 Director of Registrar Services ... Ms. Cindy WEEAKS
09 Asst VP Inst Res & Effectiveness ... Dr. Sarah LOGAN
08 Exec Director of Library ... Dr. Maurice G. FORTIN
36 Director Career Development ... Ms. Julie J. RUTHENBECK
15 Director of Human Resources ... Mr. Kurtis R. NEAL
14 Director Process/Integ Tech Archite ... Mr. Jeff SEFCIK
37 Director Student Financial Aid ... Ms. Michelle BENNETT
27 Director Communications & Mktg ... Mr. Preston LEWIS
29 Executive Director Alumni Assoc ... Ms. Erin WHITFORD
35 Exec Dir Student Life & Services ... Mr. Philip N. MEARS
18 Director of Facilities Management ... Mr. Jay HALBERT
39 Director of Residential Programs ... Ms. Connie H. FRAZIER
40 Manager Bookstore ... Ms. Margaret BOX
41 Athletic Director ... Vacant
19 Chief of University Police ... Mr. James E. ADAMS
13 Assoc VP Information Technology/CIO ... Mr. Douglas FOX
21 Exec Director of Business Services ... Mr. Greg PECINA
96 Director Purchasing and Operations ... Ms. Margaret MATA
92 Director of Honors Program ... Dr. Shirley EOFF
04 Executive Asst to the President ... Ms. Adelina C. MORALES
104 Director Center International Stds ... Dr. Sharynn TOMLIN

† Affiliated with Texas Tech University in Lubbock, TX

AOMA Graduate School of Integrative Medicine (F)

4701 West Gate Boulevard, Austin TX 78745
County: Travis FICE Identification: 031564
Unit ID: 429094
Telephone: (512) 454-1188 Carnegie Class: Spec/Health
FAX Number: (512) 454-7001 Calendar System: Quarter
URL: www.aoma.edu
Established: 1993 Annual Graduate Tuition & Fees: $11,900
Enrollment: 202 Coed
Affiliation or Control: Proprietary IRS Status: Proprietary
Highest Offering: Doctorate; No Undergraduates
Program: Professional
Accreditation: SC, ACUP

01 President ... Dr. William R. MORRIS
11 VP Student Svcs/Operations ... Ms. Anne PROVINCE
05 Vice President of Faculty ... Dr. Qianzhi WU
32 Dean of Students ... Mr. Robert LAGUNA
20 Program Director ... Ms. Lesley HAMILTON
08 Head Librarian ... Mr. David YORK
07 Dir Admissions & Student Services ... Ms. Hannah THORNTON
06 Registrar ... Ms. Kristen BORTHWICK
58 Dean of Academics ... Dr. Yuxin HE
88 Director of Herbal Studies ... Dr. Dongxin MA
88 Director of Biomedical Sciences ... Dr. Raja MANDYAM
45 Director of Research ... Dr. Yuxing LIU
88 Director Acupuncture ... Dr. Zheng ZENG
23 Clinic Business Director ... Ms. Laura COFFEY
18 Facilities Manager ... Mr. Stuart A. BAILEY
20 Academic Advisor ... Mr. Robert LAGUNA
31 Community Services Coordinator ... Ms. Sarah BENTLEY

Argosy University, Dallas (G)

5001 Lyndon B. Johnson Freeway,
Farmers Branch TX 75244
County: Dallas Identification: 666181
Unit ID: 442222
Telephone: (214) 890-9900 Carnegie Class: Spec/Health
FAX Number: (214) 696-3900 Calendar System: Semester
URL: www.argosy.edu/dallas
Established: 2002 Annual Undergrad Tuition & Fees: $13,224
Enrollment: 586 Coed
Affiliation or Control: Proprietary IRS Status: Proprietary
Highest Offering: Doctorate
Program: Professional
Accreditation: &WC

01 Campus President ... Dr. Ronald HYSON
05 Vice President of Academic Affairs ... Dr. Nannette GLENN
07 Senior Director of Admissions ... Michael C. MCMULLEN
32 Director of Student Services ... Brigit MATTIX
06 Registrar ... Vacant
15 Human Resources ... Ruby CHAVEZ
11 Dir of Admin and Financial Svcs ... Rich BINDER

† Regional accreditation is carried under the parent institution in Orange, CA.

Arlington Baptist College (H)

3001 W Division, Arlington TX 76012-3497
County: Tarrant FICE Identification: 020814
Unit ID: 222877
Telephone: (817) 461-8741 Carnegie Class: Spec/Faith
FAX Number: (817) 274-1138 Calendar System: Semester
URL: www.abconline.edu
Established: 1939 Annual Undergrad Tuition & Fees: $7,000
Enrollment: 248 Coed
Affiliation or Control: Baptist IRS Status: 501(c)3
Highest Offering: Master's
Program: Teacher Preparatory; Professional; Religious Emphasis
Accreditation: BI

01 President ... Dr. D. L MOODY
05 Academic Dean ... Dr. Ergun CANER
32 Dean of Students ... Rev. Emil BALLIET
10 Business Manager/Dir Financial Aid ... Mr. Gerald SMITH
06 Registrar/Director Admissions ... Ms. Janie TAYLOR
08 Head Librarian ... Ms. Jill BOTTICELLI
18 Director Physical Plant ... Mr. Stan SPENCE
21 Office Manager ... Mrs. Kim MARVIN
40 Director Bookstore ... Mrs. Vickie BRYANT
30 Director Institutional Advancement ... Rev. Michael EVANS
41 Athletic Director ... Mr. Cliff MCDANIEL

Art Institute of Dallas (I)

8080 Park Lane, Suite 100, Dallas TX 75231-5900
County: Dallas FICE Identification: 025396
Unit ID: 224776
Telephone: (214) 692-8080 Carnegie Class: Spec/Arts
FAX Number: (214) 696-4898 Calendar System: Quarter
URL: www.aid.edu
Established: 1964 Annual Undergrad Tuition & Fees: $23,424
Enrollment: 1,893 Coed
Affiliation or Control: Proprietary IRS Status: Proprietary
Highest Offering: Baccalaureate
Program: Occupational; Fine Arts Emphasis
Accreditation: &SC, ACFEI, CIDA

01 President ... Dr. Thomas W. NEWSOM
05 Vice President of Academic Affairs ... Dr. Leslie C. BAUGHMAN
07 Sr Director of Admissions ... Mrs. Dawn POLK-BRIDGES
11 Director Admin & Financial Svcs ... Mrs. Cecilia COLBERT
32 Dean of Student Affairs ... Mrs. April CHATHAM
36 Director Career Services ... Ms. Miriam K. JOHNSTON
15 Director Human Resources ... Ms. Shannon FULMER

† Regional accreditation is carried under the parent institution, South University, Savannah, GA.

The Art Institute of Houston (J)

4140 Southwest Freeway, Houston TX 77027
County: Harris FICE Identification: 021171
Unit ID: 222938
Telephone: (713) 623-2040 Carnegie Class: Spec/Arts
FAX Number: (713) 966-2700 Calendar System: Quarter
URL: www.aih.aii.edu
Established: 1978 Annual Undergrad Tuition & Fees: $29,280
Enrollment: 2,347 Coed
Affiliation or Control: Proprietary IRS Status: Proprietary
Highest Offering: Baccalaureate
Program: Occupational
Accreditation: SC, ACFEI, CIDA

01 President ... Larry HORN
05 Dean of Academic Affairs ... Dr. Kenneth C. PASCAL
32 Dean of Student Affairs ... Michael MCKENNA
11 Dir Administrative/Financial Svcs ... Tom KUPER
07 Senior Director of Admissions ... Jane CHASTANT
15 Director of Human Resources ... Vacant
36 Director of Career Services ... Mary Kate ROBINSON

ATI Career Training Center (K)

10003 Technology Boulevard W, Dallas TX 75220-4316
County: Dallas FICE Identification: 025966
Unit ID: 249247
Telephone: (214) 902-8191 Carnegie Class: Assoc/PrivFP
FAX Number: (214) 358-7500 Calendar System: Semester
URL: www.aticareertraining.edu
Established: 1986 Annual Undergrad Tuition & Fees: $19,875
Enrollment: 455 Coed

Affiliation or Control: Proprietary — IRS Status: Proprietary
Highest Offering: Associate Degree
Program: Occupational
Accreditation: #ACCSC

01 Executive Director of the School ....Mr. Anthony GOSS
37 Director Student Financial Aid ....Ms. Lyn CROSS
06 Registrar ....Ms. Christe MILLER

Austin College (A)

900 N Grand Avenue, Sherman TX 75090-4400
County: Grayson — FICE Identification: 003543
Unit ID: 222983
Telephone: (903) 813-2000 — Carnegie Class: Bac/A&S
FAX Number: (903) 813-3199 — Calendar System: 4/1/4
URL: www.austincollege.edu
Established: 1849 — Annual Undergrad Tuition & Fees: $31,270
Enrollment: 1,353 — Coed
Affiliation or Control: Presbyterian Church (U.S.A.) — IRS Status: 501(c)3
Highest Offering: Master's
Program: Liberal Arts And General; Teacher Preparatory
Accreditation: SC

01 President ....Dr. Marjorie HASS
05 Vice President Academic Affairs ....Dr. Michael A. IMHOFF
32 Vice Pres Student Affairs/Athletics ......Mr. Timothy P. MILLERICK
30 Vice Pres Institutional Advancement ....Mr. Brooks A. HULL
10 Vice President for Business Affairs ....Ms. Heidi B. ELLIS
84 Vice President for Inst Enrollment ....Ms. Nan M. DAVIS
45 Associate VP for Inst Effectiveness ....Vacant
07 Asst VP Institutional Enrollment ....Ms. Laurie COULTER
44 Assistant VP for Inst Advancement ....Ms. Cary E. WACKER
29 AVP Inst Adv/Exec Dir Alumni Rels ....Ms. Paula JONSE
09 Director Inst Planning/Research ....Vacant
88 Exec Dir Transfer/Intrntl Admission ....Mr. David DILLMAN
42 Chaplain/Dir of Church Relations ....Dr. John D. WILLIAMS
35 Director of Student Life ....Mr. Michael DEEN
06 Registrar ....Mr. Texas RUEGG
08 College Librarian/Library Director ....Mr. John R. WEST
21 Director of Finance ....Ms. Sheryl BRADSHAW
79 Dean of Humanities ....Dr. Patrick DUFFEY
81 Dean of Sciences ....Dr. Steve GOLDSMITH
83 Dean of Social Sciences ....Dr. Jerry B. JOHNSON
15 Director of Human Resources ....Mr. Keith L. LAREY
88 Dean of Student Services ....Dr. Rosemarie ROTHMEIER
36 Director Career Services ....Ms. Margie A. NORMAN
13 Exec Director Information Tech ....Mr. Bill EDGETTE
58 Director of Graduate Program ....Dr. Barbara N. SYLVESTER
104 Director Study Abroad ....Dr. Truett CATES
26 Director of Public Affairs ....Dr. Lynn Z. WOMBLE
25 Director of Stewardship ....Ms. Dara MCCOY
19 Chief of Police ....Mr. James PERRY
40 Manager of Campus Store ....Ms. Linda FRANZEO
27 Sr Dir Editorial Communications ....Ms. Vickie S. KIRBY
18 Director of Physical Plant ....Mr. John L. JENNINGS
51 Coordinator of Continuing Education ..... Ms. Carolyn CRANFORD
96 Purchasing Representative ....Ms. Jeannean SMITH

Austin Community College District (B)

5930 Middle Fiskville Road, Austin TX 78752-4390
County: Travis — FICE Identification: 012015
Unit ID: 222992
Telephone: (512) 223-7000 — Carnegie Class: Assoc/Pub-U-MC
FAX Number: (512) 223-7185 — Calendar System: Semester
URL: www.austincc.edu
Established: 1972 — Annual Undergrad Tuition & Fees (In-District): $2,340
Enrollment: 45,100 — Coed
Affiliation or Control: State/Local — IRS Status: 501(c)3
Highest Offering: Associate Degree
Program: Occupational; 2-Year Principally Bachelor's Creditable
Accreditation: SC, ACBSP, ACFEI, ADNUR, DH, DMS, EMT, MLTAD, OTA, PNUR, PTAA, RAD, SURGT

01 President/CEO ....Dr. Richard M. RHODES
05 Provost/Exec Vice President ....Dr. Enrique SOLIS
03 Exec Vice Pres College Operations ....Dr. Mary HENSLEY
10 Exec VP Finance & Administration ....Mr. Ben B. FERRELL
05 VP Instruction ....Mr. Michael T. MIDGLEY
32 VP Student Support/Success Systems ....Dr. Kathleen E. CHRISTENSEN
16 VP Human Resources ....Dr. Geraldine TUCKER
09 VP Effectiveness & Accountability ....Ms. Soon O. MERZ
20 AVP College Access Programs ....Dr. Stephanie HAWLEY
24 AVP Instructional Resources/Tech ....Dr. Richard L. SMITH
13 AVP Information Technology ....Mr. Stanley T. GUNN
21 AVP Finance & Budget ....Mr. Neil W. VICKERS
88 AVP Student Success ....Dr. Richard R. ARMENTA
17 Executive Dean Health Sciences ....Dr. Eileen KLEIN
51 Executive Dean Continuing Education ....Dr. Hector AGUILAR
88 Dean Appl Tech/Multimedia/Pub Svc ....Dr. Gary W. HAMPTON
50 Dean Business Studies ....Mr. Charles C. QUINN
72 Dean Computer Studies/Adv Tech ....Ms. Linda S. SMARZIK
57 Dean Arts & Humanities ....Mr. Lyman W. GRANT
60 Dean Communications ....Dr. Hazel WARD
81 Dean Math & Science ....Dr. David FONKEN
83 Dean Social & Behavioral Sciences ....Ms. Gaye Lynn SCOTT
62 Dean Library Services ....Dr. Julie B. TODARO
35 Dean Student Services-South Austin ....Ms. Yolanda M. CHAPA
35 Dean Student Services-Riverside ....Dr. Virginia M. FRAIRE
35 Dean Student Services-Cypress Creek ....Ms. Amber L. KELLEY
35 Dean Student Services-Eastview ....Mr. Dorado M. KINNEY
35 Dean Student Services-Northridge ....Mr. Clint R. RODENFELS
35 Dean Student Services-Pinnacle ....Mr. George R. REYES
35 Dean Student Services-Round Rock ....Dr. Louella H. TATE
35 Dean Student Services-Rio Grande ....Dr. Voncille T. WRIGHT
88 Executive Director Adult Education ....Mr. David S. BORDEN
88 Exec Dir Customized Trng/Bus Assmt ....Dr. Kathy M. WALTON
88 Exec Director School Relations ....Mr. Patrick W. ABBOTT
88 Exec Dir Early College HS ....Dr. Sharon H. FREDERICK
25 Exec Dir Grant Development ....Ms. Mary E. HARRIS
88 Exec Dir College & Career Prep Pgm ...Ms. Annette K. GREGORY
18 Exec Dir Facilities & Construction ....Mr. William S. MULLANE
27 Exec Dir Public Info & College Mktg ....Ms. Brette E. LEA
102 Executive Director ACC Foundation ....Ms. Stephanie C. DIINA-DEMPSEY
88 Executive Director ....Ms. Susan P. DAWSON
88 Exec Dir EHS & Insurance ....Ms. Rebecca S. COLE
07 Director Admissions/Records ....Ms. Linda A. KLUCK
80 Dir Ctr for Pub Policy & Pol Stds ....Mr. William R. YOUNG
88 Director Internal Audit ....Mr. Imad A. MOUCHAYLEH
37 Director Student Asst/Veterans ....Ms. Teresita BAZAN
88 Director P-16 Initiatives ....Mr. Gary L. MADSEN
88 Director Analysis & Policy ....Mr. Jim VANOVERSCHELDE
04 Spec Asst to Pres External Affairs ....Ms. Linda K. YOUNG
04 Special Asst to VP Instruction ....Mr. Joe M. LOSTRACCO
19 Chief District Police ....Mr. Chester L. DIXON

Austin Graduate School of Theology (C)

7640 Guadalupe Street, Austin TX 78752
County: Travis — FICE Identification: 023628
Unit ID: 247825
Telephone: (512) 476-2772 — Carnegie Class: Spec/Faith
FAX Number: (512) 476-3919 — Calendar System: Semester
URL: www.austingrad.edu
Established: 1976 — Annual Undergrad Tuition & Fees: $9,300
Enrollment: 59 — Coed
Affiliation or Control: Independent Non-Profit — IRS Status: 501(c)3
Highest Offering: Master's
Program: Liberal Arts And General; Professional; Religious Emphasis
Accreditation: SC

01 President ....Dr. Stanley G. REID
37 Vice President/Dir Financial Aid .... Mr. Dave ARTHUR
07 Director Recruiting & Admissions ..Mrs. Celeste SCARBAROUGH
30 Director of Development ....Mr. Neil HANEY

Austin Presbyterian Theological Seminary (D)

100 E 27th Street, Austin TX 78705-5797
County: Travis — FICE Identification: 003544
Unit ID: 223001
Telephone: (512) 472-6736 — Carnegie Class: Spec/Faith
FAX Number: (512) 479-0738 — Calendar System: Semester
URL: www.austinseminary.edu
Established: 1902 — Annual Graduate Tuition & Fees: $10,780
Enrollment: 126 — Coed
Affiliation or Control: Presbyterian Church (U.S.A.) — IRS Status: 501(c)3
Highest Offering: Doctorate; No Undergraduates
Program: Professional
Accreditation: SC, THEOL

01 President ....Rev. Theodore J. WARDLAW
05 Academic Dean ....Dr. Michael JINKINS
10 Vice President for Business Affairs ....Mr. Kurt A. GABBARD
26 Vice Pres Institutional Advancement ....Ms. Donna SCOTT
32 Vice Pres Student Affairs/Vocation ....Rev. Jackie SAXON
07 Vice President for Admissions ....Rev. John H. BARDEN
51 VP Education Beyond the Walls ....Ms. Melissa WIGINTON
29 Director Alumni & Church Relations ....Rev. Lemuel GARCIA-ANOYO
30 Sr Dir of Development/Instl Advance ....Ms. Lisa HOLLERAN
08 Director of the Stitt Library ....Rev. Timothy LINCOLN
06 Registrar ....Ms. Jacqueline D. HEFLEY
37 Director of Financial Aid ....Ms. Glenna BALCH

Baptist Health System School of Health Professions (E)

8400 Datapoint Drive, San Antonio TX 78229
County: Bexar — Identification: 006606
Unit ID: 223083
Telephone: (210) 297-9630 — Carnegie Class: Assoc/PrivFP
FAX Number: (210) 297-0075 — Calendar System: Semester
URL: www.bshp.edu
Established: 1903 — Annual Undergrad Tuition & Fees: N/A
Enrollment: 514 — Coed
Affiliation or Control: Proprietary — IRS Status: Proprietary
Highest Offering: Associate Degree
Program: Occupational
Accreditation: ABHES, ADNUR, RAD, SURGT, SURTEC

01 Interim Dean ....Dr. Marion JEWEL

† Tuition varies by degree program.

Baptist Missionary Association Theological Seminary (F)

P.O. Box 670/1530 E Pine Street, Jacksonville TX 75766-5407
County: Cherokee — FICE Identification: 023312
Unit ID: 223117
Telephone: (903) 586-2501 — Carnegie Class: Spec/Faith
FAX Number: (903) 586-0378 — Calendar System: Semester
URL: www.bmats.edu
Established: 1957 — Annual Undergrad Tuition & Fees: $5,340
Enrollment: 120 — Coed
Affiliation or Control: Baptist — IRS Status: 501(c)3
Highest Offering: Master's
Program: Professional
Accreditation: SC, THEOL

01 President ....Dr. Charley HOLMES
06 Registrar ....Dr. Philip ATTEBERY

Baptist University of the Americas (G)

8019 S Pan Am Expressway, San Antonio TX 78224-1336
County: Bexar — FICE Identification: 037333
Unit ID: 444398
Telephone: (210) 924-4338 — Carnegie Class: Spec/Faith
FAX Number: (210) 924-2701 — Calendar System: Semester
URL: www.bua.edu
Established: 1947 — Annual Undergrad Tuition & Fees: $6,600
Enrollment: 259 — Coed
Affiliation or Control: Baptist — IRS Status: 501(c)3
Highest Offering: Baccalaureate
Program: 2-Year Principally Bachelor's Creditable; Liberal Arts And General; Religious Emphasis
Accreditation: BI

01 President ....Mr. Rene MACIEL
10 Chief Financial Officer ....Vacant
30 Vice President for Development ....Rev. Teo CISNEROS
03 Executive Vice President & Provost ....Vacant
05 Dean of Curriculum & Faculty Devel ...Dr. F. Marconi MONTEIRO
04 Special Assistant to the President ....Mr. Craig BIRD
84 Director of Enrollment Management ....Ms. Mary RANJEL
37 Financial Aid Administrator ....Mrs. Araceli ACOSTA
88 Dean of the Bible Baptist Institute ....Dr. Moises RODRIGUEZ

Baylor College of Medicine (H)

One Baylor Plaza, Houston TX 77030-3411
County: Harris — FICE Identification: 004949
Unit ID: 223223
Telephone: (713) 798-4951 — Carnegie Class: Spec/Med
FAX Number: (713) 798-3692 — Calendar System: Quarter
URL: www.bcm.edu
Established: 1900 — Annual Graduate Tuition & Fees: $19,868
Enrollment: 1,486 — Coed
Affiliation or Control: Independent Non-Profit — IRS Status: 501(c)3
Highest Offering: Doctorate; No Undergraduates
Program: Professional
Accreditation: SC, ANEST, ARCPA, DIETI, IPSY, MED

00 Chancellor ....Dr. Bobby R. ALFORD
01 President and CEO ....Dr. Paul KLOTMAN
88 Dean Natl Sch Tropical Medicine ....Dr. Peter HOTEZ
17 Vice Pres/Chief Medical Officer ....Dr. Steve SIGWORTH
10 Sr VP Finance & Admin/CFO ....Mrs. Kim DAVID
30 Vice Pres Development ....Ms. Kristi SHERWOOD COOPER
43 Vice Pres/General Counsel/Corp Sec ....Mr. Robert F. CORRIGAN, JR.
27 VP Communications & Marketing ....Ms. Claire M. BASSETT
15 Vice President Human Resources ....Mr. Dane FRIEND
46 Vice President for Research ....Dr. Adam KUSPA
13 VP/Chief Technology Ofcr/Info Tech ......Dr. Alexander IZAGUIRRE
86 Vice Pres Government Relations ....Mr. Tom KLEINWORTH
63 Dean of Medical Education ....Dr. Stephen B. GREENBERG
58 Dean Grad School of Biomed Sciences ....Dr. Hiram (Gil) F. GILBERT
76 Dean School Allied Health Programs ....Dr. J. David HOLCOMB
88 Senior Associate Dean ....Dr. James L. PHILLIPS
07 Senior Associate Dean Admissions ....Dr. Lloyd H. MICHAEL
51 Sr Assoc Dean Continuing Education ....Dr. C. Michael FORDIS, JR.
32 Sr Associate Dean Student Affairs .... Dr. Donald T. DONOVAN
88 Associate Dean Graduate School ....Dr. Scott F. BASINGER
63 Sr Assoc Dean Grad Medical Educ ....Dr. Linda ANDREWS
88 Associate Dean Res Assurances ....Dr. Stacey L. BERG
88 Associate Dean Medical Education ....Dr. Elizabeth A. NELSON
88 Asst Dean Graduate Education ....Dr. Gayle R. SLAUGHTER
88 Asst Dean Graduate Medical Educ ....Dr. Jacqueline LEVESQUE
88 Associate Dean for Admissions ....Dr. Graciela B. VILLARREAL
35 Assoc Dean Student Affairs & Admin ....Dr. Florence F. EDDINS-FOLENSBEE
09 Associate Dean for Research ....Dr. Placido GRINO
88 Associate Dean Clinical Affairs ....Dr. John W. BURRUSS
88 Assoc Dean Undergrad Med Education .....Dr. Jerry C. GOODMAN
21 Controller ....Mr. Douglas R. SPADE
88 Chief Performance Improvement Ofcr .... Mr. Navneet KATHURIA
37 Director Student Financial Planning ....Ms. Hilda DELEON
06 Registrar/Dir of Student Affairs ....Mr. John RAPP
88 Director Environmental Safety ....Mr. Paul MURACA
23 Director Occupational Medicine ....Dr. James E. KELAHER

29 Sr Director Alumni Affairs ... Ms. Barbara WALKER
19 Director of Security ... Vacant
85 Director Center for Globalization ... Dr. Bobby KAPUR
22 Sr Director Employee Relations ... Mr. Dane K. FRIEND
96 Director Supply Chain Management ... Mr. Bud BOCCHINO
28 Co-Chair Diversity Council ... Dr. Gayle R. SLAUGHTER

Baylor University (A)

One Bear Place #97096, Waco TX 76798-7096
County: McLennan FICE Identification: 003545
Unit ID: 223232
Telephone: (254) 710-1011 Carnegie Class: RU/H
FAX Number: (254) 710-3557 Calendar System: Semester
URL: www.baylor.edu
Established: 1845 Annual Undergrad Tuition & Fees: $33,716
Enrollment: 15,029 Coed
Affiliation or Control: Baptist IRS Status: 501(c)3
Highest Offering: Doctorate
Program: Liberal Arts And General; Teacher Preparatory; Professional
Accreditation: **SC**, AAFCS, BUS, BUSA, CIDA, CLPSY, CS, DIETD, ENG, HSA, JOUR, LAW, MIDWF, MUS, NMT, NURSE, PTA, RAD, SP, SW, TED, THEA, THEOL

01 President & CEO ... Judge Kenneth W. STARR
05 Executive Vice President & Provost ... Dr. Elizabeth DAVIS
100 Chief of Staff ... Dr. Karla LEEPER
10 Senior VP for Operations & CFO ... Dr. Reagan RAMSOWER
30 Vice President Univ Development ... Vacant
32 Vice President Student Life ... Dr. Kevin JACKSON
29 Exec Vice President of Alumni Assoc ... Mr. Jeffrey L. KILGORE
26 Vice President Marketing & Comm ... Mr. John BARRY
13 VP for IT & Dean of Libraries ... Ms. Pattie ORR
31 Vice Pres Constituent Engagement ... Ms. Tommye Lou DAVIS
43 General Counsel ... Mr. Charles D. BECKENHAUER
41 Director of Athletics ... Mr. Ian J. MCCAW
88 Dir Internal Audit & Mgmt Anlys ... Mr. Juan ALEJANDRO
09 Director Inst Research/Testing ... Dr. Kathleen MORLEY
84 Assoc Vice Pres Enrollment Mgmt ... Mrs. Diana M. RAMEY
21 Assoc VP Financial Svcs & Treasurer ... Mr. Bob C. SPENCE
21 Assoc VP Oper Plng & Budget Dir ... Mr. Wilson E. MCGREGOR
88 Assoc VP Planning & Construction ... Mr. Brian W. NICHOLSON
15 Associate Vice Pres Human Resources ... Mr. John WHELAN
91 Associate VP Information Sys/Svcs ... Mrs. Becky L. KING
08 Assoc Dean & Director of Libraries ... Mr. Jeffrey STEELY
35 Associate Vice Pres Student Life ... Dr. Martha Lou SCOTT
06 Registrar ... Mr. Jonathan C. HELM
88 Assoc Vice Pres Campus Svcs ... Mr. Chris KRAUSE
90 Assoc Vice Pres Electronic Library ... Mr. Timothy M. LOGAN
88 Vice Prov Strategic Edu Initiatives ... Dr. Edward BURGER
108 Vice Provost Inst Effectiveness ... Dr. Michael MATIER
97 Vice Provost Undergrad Education ... Dr. Wesley NULL
20 Vice Provost of Academic Affairs ... Dr. James BENNIGHOFF
46 Vice Provost for Research ... Dr. Truell HYDE
07 Asst Vice Pres Admissions Svcs ... Ms. Jennifer CARRON
88 Asst Vice President & Controller ... Ms. Susan ANZ
37 Asst VP Student Financial Svcs ... Mrs. Jackie DIAZ
88 Chief Investment Officer ... Mr. R. Brian WEBB
19 Chief of Police ... Mr. James W. DOAK
93 Director Multiculture Affairs ... Mrs. Pearlie BEVERLY
20 Director Academic Support Programs ... Ms. Sally E. FIRMIN
23 Medical Director Health Center ... Dr. Sharon STERN
36 Director Career Services Center ... Vacant
18 Director Facilities Management ... Mr. Don BAGBY
25 Director Sponsored Programs ... Ms. Lisa H. MCKETHAN
38 Director Counseling Svcs ... Dr. James G. MARSH
40 Director Baylor Bookstore ... Mr. Billy NORS
86 Director Governmental Relations ... Ms. Rochonda FARMER-NEAL
96 Director Procurement Services ... Mr. Tom HOFFMEYER
31 Director Community Relations ... Ms. Jana HIXSON
49 Dean College of Arts/Sciences ... Dr. Lee C. NORDT
50 Dean School of Business ... Dr. Terry S. MANESS
53 Dean School of Education ... Dr. Jon ENGELHARDT
61 Dean School of Law ... Mr. Bradley J B. TOBEN
64 Dean School of Music ... Dr. William V. MAY
66 Dean School of Nursing ... Dr. Shelley F. CONROY
58 Dean Graduate School ... Dr. Larry LYON
73 Dean Truett Theological Sem ... Dr. David GARLAND
54 Dean Engineering & Computer Science ... Dr. Dennis O'NEAL
92 Dean Honors College ... Dr. Thomas S. HIBBS
85 Interim Dir Ctr International Educ ... Mr. Naymond KEATHLEY
35 Dean Student Development ... Dr. Elizabeth PALACIOS
39 Dean Student Learning & Engagement ... Dr. Jeff DOYLE
42 University Chaplain ... Dr. Burt BURLESON
88 Assoc Dean Student Conduct Admin ... Ms. Bethany J. MCCRAW

B.H. Carroll Theological Institute (B)

301 S. Center St, Ste 100, Arlington TX 76010-7140
County: Tarrant Identification: 667089
Telephone: (817) 274-4284 Carnegie Class: Not Classified
FAX Number: (817) 274-2226 Calendar System: Semester
URL: www.bhcarroll.edu
Established: 2004 Annual Graduate Tuition & Fees: N/A
Enrollment: N/A Coed
Affiliation or Control: Southern Baptist IRS Status: 501(c)3
Highest Offering: Doctorate; No Undergraduates
Program: Religious Emphasis
Accreditation: **BI**

01 President ... Dr. Bruce CORLEY
10 CFO ... Dr. Bruce MUSKRAT

06 Registrar ... Dr. Stan MOORE
07 Director of Enrollment ... Mrs. Fran WILSON
08 Chief Librarian ... Mr. Don DAY

Blinn College (C)

902 College Avenue, Brenham TX 77833-4098
County: Washington FICE Identification: 003549
Unit ID: 223427
Telephone: (979) 830-4000 Carnegie Class: Assoc/Pub-R-L
FAX Number: (979) 830-4030 Calendar System: Semester
URL: www.blinn.edu
Established: 1883 Annual Undergrad Tuition & Fees (In-District): $1,824
Enrollment: 18,156 Coed
Affiliation or Control: State/Local IRS Status: 501(c)3
Highest Offering: Associate Degree
Program: Occupational; 2-Year Principally Bachelor's Creditable
Accreditation: **SC**, ADNUR, DH, EMT, IFSAC, PTAA, RAD

01 President/CEO ... Dr. Harold NOLTE
05 Vice President Academic Affairs ... Dr. Debra R. LACOUR
32 Vice Pres Student Services ... Dr. Dennis CROWSON
10 Vice Pres Administrative Services ... Vacant
103 VP Applied Science/Workforce Educ ... Dr. Robert BRICK
12 President Brazos County Campuses ... Dr. Ted RASPILLER
32 Dean of Students ... Dr. John D. HARRIS
20 Dean Academic Affairs ... Dr. John BEAVER
09 Dean Inst Effectiveness/Accred ... Vacant
35 Judicial Officer ... Mr. Keith THOMAS
35 Associate Dean Student Affairs ... Mrs. Ann E. WEIR
27 Exec Admin of External Affairs ... Ms. Cathy BOEKER
11 Exec Dir Operations Brazos County ... Mr. Ted HAJOVSKY
102 Executive Director Foundation ... Mr. Joe Al PICONE
18 Exec Dir Facilities/Planning/Constr ... Mr. Richard O'MALLEY
12 Director Schulenburg Campus ... Ms. Rebecca GARLICK
12 Director Sealy Campus ... Ms. Jeri DULANEY
06 Registrar ... Ms. Julie MAASS
21 Director Accounting ... Mr. Thomas BRAZZEL
08 Director Library Services ... Ms. Linda FLYNN
38 Director of Counseling ... Mr. Robert LOVELIDGE
13 Dir Administrative Computing Svcs ... Ms. Christine WIED
37 Director Financial Aid ... Ms. Melanie MORGAN
15 Director Human Resources ... Ms. Karla ROPER
41 Athletic Director ... Vacant
18 Dir Facilities Maint/Transportation ... Mr. Dennis KOCICH
19 Chief College Police Department ... Mr. Claude FREE
96 Director Purchasing ... Mr. Ross SCHROEDER
07 Director Admissions & Records ... Ms. Sonia WINNEY
27 Dir Prospective Student Relations ... Ms. Jennifer BYNUM
26 Dir Marketing/Media Relations ... Mr. Jeff TILLEY
35 Dir Student Leadership/Activities ... Mr. Mordecai BROWNLEE
27 Asst Dir Marketing/Media Relations ... Mr. Brandon WEBB
29 Coord Campus Events/Alumni Affairs ... Mr. Glen VIERUS

Brazosport College (D)

500 College Drive, Lake Jackson TX 77566-3199
County: Brazoria FICE Identification: 007287
Unit ID: 223506
Telephone: (979) 230-3000 Carnegie Class: Assoc/Pub4
FAX Number: (979) 230-3443 Calendar System: Semester
URL: www.brazosport.edu
Established: 1948 Annual Undergrad Tuition & Fees (In-District): $1,912
Enrollment: 5,000 Coed
Affiliation or Control: Local IRS Status: 501(c)3
Highest Offering: Baccalaureate
Program: Occupational; 2-Year Principally Bachelor's Creditable
Accreditation: **SC**, EMT

01 President ... Dr. Millicent M. VALEK
05 Provost/Dean Academic & Stdnt Affs ... Dr. Ken TASA
31 Dean Industry & Community Res ... Dr. John C. RAY
32 Associate Dean of Students ... Mr. David SHAW
10 Dean Administrative Services & CFO ... Mr. Fred SCOTT
15 Dean Human Resources ... Dr. Herb E. MILES
08 Director Library Services ... Ms. Tami WISOFSKY
09 Director Institutional Research ... Dr. David PRESTON
07 Director Admissions/Registrar ... Ms. Carrie STREETER
31 Director Community Education ... Ms. Catherine HANSON
21 Internal Auditor ... Mr. Christopher BAHR
27 Director Marketing & Communications ... Ms. Patty SAYES
13 Director/Information Technology ... Mr. Ron PARKER
37 Director of Financial Aid ... Ms. Kay WRIGHT

Brite Divinity School (E)

2925 Princeton Street, Fort Worth TX 76129-0001
County: Tarrant Identification: 666228
Unit ID: 450304
Telephone: (817) 257-7575 Carnegie Class: Spec/Faith
FAX Number: (817) 257-6932 Calendar System: Semester
URL: www.brite.tcu.edu
Established: 1873 Annual Graduate Tuition & Fees: $18,000
Enrollment: 229 Coed
Affiliation or Control: Independent Non-Profit IRS Status: 501(c)3
Highest Offering: Doctorate; No Undergraduates
Program: Professional; Religious Emphasis
Accreditation: **SC**, THEOL

01 President & Chief Executive Officer ... Dr. D. Newell WILLIAMS
10 Vice President Business/Finance ... Beverly COTTON
07 Director of Admission ... Dr. Valerie FROSTMAN

Career Point College (F)

355-1 Spencer Lane, San Antonio TX 78201
County: Bexar FICE Identification: 025911
Unit ID: 224439
Telephone: (210) 732-3000 Carnegie Class: Assoc/PrivFP
FAX Number: (210) 734-9225 Calendar System: Other
URL: www.careerpointcollege.edu
Established: 1921 Annual Undergrad Tuition & Fees: $16,930
Enrollment: 1,820 Coed
Affiliation or Control: Proprietary IRS Status: Proprietary
Highest Offering: Baccalaureate
Program: Occupational; 2-Year Principally Bachelor's Creditable
Accreditation: **ACICS**

01 Director ... Ms. Kim MURGUIA

Center for Advanced Legal Studies (G)

3910 Kirby Drive, Suite 200, Houston TX 77098-4151
County: Harris FICE Identification: 026047
Unit ID: 379782
Telephone: (713) 529-2778 Carnegie Class: Assoc/PrivFP4
FAX Number: (713) 523-2715 Calendar System: Other
URL: www.paralegal.edu
Established: 1987 Annual Undergrad Tuition & Fees: $11,550
Enrollment: 220 Coed
Affiliation or Control: Proprietary IRS Status: Proprietary
Highest Offering: Associate Degree
Program: Occupational; Technical Emphasis
Accreditation: **COE**

01 President/CEO ... Mr. Doyle HAPPE

Central Texas College (H)

PO Box 1800, Killeen TX 76540-9990
County: Bell FICE Identification: 004003
Unit ID: 223816
Telephone: (254) 526-7161 Carnegie Class: Assoc/Pub-Spec
FAX Number: (254) 526-0817 Calendar System: Semester
URL: www.ctcd.edu
Established: 1965 Annual Undergrad Tuition & Fees (In-District): $1,512
Enrollment: 31,194 Coed
Affiliation or Control: Local IRS Status: 501(c)3
Highest Offering: Associate Degree
Program: Occupational; 2-Year Principally Bachelor's Creditable
Accreditation: **SC**, ADNUR, EMT, MLTAD

01 Chancellor ... Dr. Thomas D. KLINCAR
03 Deputy Chanc Resource Management ... Mr. Al ERDMAN
03 Deputy Chanc International/Navy Op ... Mr. Jim YEONOPOLUS
03 Deputy Chanc DL/TX Campus Op ... Mr. John HUNT
05 Deputy Chanc Educ Pgm/Supp Svcs ... Dr. Dana WATSON
12 Dean Ft Hood/Service Area Campus ... Dr. Tina ADY
12 Dean Central Campus ... Ms. Janice ANDERSON
32 Dean Student Services ... Dr. Johnelle WELSH
08 Dean Library Services ... Ms. Deba SWAN
38 Associate Dean Guidance/Counseling ... Mr. David MCCLURE
06 Systems Registrar ... Ms. Lillian KROEGER
10 Comptroller ... Mr. Bob LIBERTY
15 Director Human Resource Mgmt ... Ms. Holly JORDAN
88 Director Risk Management ... Ms. Deborah SHIBLEY
106 Director Distance Education/Ed Tech ... Ms. Sharon DAVIS
18 Director Facilities Management ... Mr. Mark HARMSEN
21 Director Business Services ... Ms. Michele CARTER
30 Director College Development ... Ms. Judy HEARTFIELD
09 Director Institutional Effectivenes ... Ms. Amy BAWCOM
13 Director Information Technology ... Mr. Bruce KENDALL
07 Director Admissions/Recruitment ... Mr. Stephen O'DONOVAN
88 Director Testing ... Mr. George ERSKINE
85 Director International Student Svcs ... Ms. Marta GRANT
88 Director Student Support Services ... Ms. Denise PERGL
88 Director Substance Abuse Resource . Dr. Gerald MAHONE-LEIWS
36 Director Career Planning/Placement ... Ms. Elaine RILEY
27 Dir Community Relations/Marketing ... Ms. Barbara MERLO
88 Liaison Military Programs ... Ms. Diana CASTILLO
19 Chief Police/Security Services ... Ms. Mary WHEELER
40 Manager Bookstore ... Mr. Gary FUDA

Cisco College (I)

101 College Heights, Cisco TX 76437-1900
County: Eastland FICE Identification: 003553
Unit ID: 223898
Telephone: (254) 442-5000 Carnegie Class: Assoc/Pub-R-M
FAX Number: (254) 442-5100 Calendar System: Semester
URL: www.cisco.edu
Established: 1940 Annual Undergrad Tuition & Fees (In-State): $2,400
Enrollment: 4,375 Coed
Affiliation or Control: State IRS Status: 501(c)3
Highest Offering: Associate Degree
Program: Occupational; 2-Year Principally Bachelor's Creditable
Accreditation: **SC**, MAC, PNUR, SURGT

01 President ... Mr. Bobby SMITH
03 Executive Vice President ... Vacant
05 Vice Pres of Learning Services ... Vacant
32 Vice President for Student Services ... Dr. Jerry DODSON

13 Vice President of IT .... Mr. Joe BUTLER
12 Provost Abilene Education Center .... Dr. Carol DUPREE
84 Dean of Enrollment Management .... Mr. Olin O. ODOM, III
38 Dean of Counseling .... Mr. Randy LEATH
30 Director of Development .... Ms. Martha MONTGOMERY
37 Director of Financial Aid .... Ms. Dianne PHARR
15 Director Human Resources .... Ms. Pamela PAGE
35 Director New Student Services .... Ms. Shae WHITE
08 Director of Libraries .... Ms. Heather WILLIAMSON

Clarendon College (A)

PO Box 968, Clarendon TX 79226-0968
County: Donley FICE Identification: 003554
Unit ID: 223922
Telephone: (806) 874-3571 Carnegie Class: Assoc/Pub-R-S
FAX Number: (806) 874-3201 Calendar System: Semester
URL: www.clarendoncollege.edu
Established: 1898 Annual Undergrad Tuition & Fees (In-District): $2,730
Enrollment: 1,341 Coed
Affiliation or Control: State/Local IRS Status: 501(c)3
Highest Offering: Associate Degree
Program: Occupational; 2-Year Principally Bachelor's Creditable
Accreditation: SC

01 President .... Dr. Phil E. SHIRLEY
05 Acting Dean of Instruction .... Mr. Tex BUCKHAULTS
11 Vice Pres of Campus Affairs .... Mr. Ray JARAMILLO
32 Dean of Student Services .... Mr. Tex BUCKHAULTS
08 Librarian .... Ms. Pamela REED
07 Dean of Admission Services .... Ms. Annette FERGUSON
37 Director of Financial Aid .... Ms. Michele COPELIN
06 Registrar .... Ms. Brandi HAVENS
81 Div Chr Science/Health/Liberal Arts .... Mrs. Scarlet ESTLACK

Coastal Bend College (B)

3800 Charco Road, Beeville TX 78102-2197
County: Bee FICE Identification: 003546
Unit ID: 223320
Telephone: (361) 358-2838 Carnegie Class: Assoc/Pub-R-M
FAX Number: (361) 358-3971 Calendar System: Semester
URL: www.coastalbend.edu
Established: 1965 Annual Undergrad Tuition & Fees (In-District): $2,696
Enrollment: 3,931 Coed
Affiliation or Control: State/Local IRS Status: 501(c)3
Highest Offering: Associate Degree
Program: Occupational; 2-Year Principally Bachelor's Creditable
Accreditation: SC, DH, RAD

01 President .... Dr. Beatriz T. ESPINOZA
32 Dean of Student Services .... Ms. Velma ELIZALDE
11 Dean of Administrative Services .... Ms. Ruth CUDE
07 Director of Admissions/Registrar .... Ms. Alicia ULLOA
30 Dir Institutional Advancement/PR .... Ms. Susan SMEDLEY
05 Director of Academic Programs .... Dr. Bruce EXSTROM
25 Director of Grants/Special Projects .... Mrs. Velma ELIZALDE
37 Director of Financial Aid .... Ms. Nora MORALES
12 Director of Alice Campus .... Dr. Patricia CANDIA
12 Director of Kingsville Campus .... Vacant
12 Coordinator Pleasanton Campus .... Ms. Teresa VILLANUEVA
09 Institutional Research Director .... Mr. Randy LINDEMAN
08 Director Library Services .... Ms. Sarah MILNARICH
15 Personnel Director .... Ms. Kathlyn PATTON
18 Chief Facilities/Physical Plant .... Mr. Michael SLAUGHTER
26 Chief Public Relations Officer .... Ms. Monica CRUZ

College of Biblical Studies-Houston (C)

7000 Regency Square, Houston TX 77036-3211
County: Harris FICE Identification: 034224
Unit ID: 388520
Telephone: (713) 785-5995 Carnegie Class: Spec/Faith
FAX Number: (713) 785-5998 Calendar System: Trimester
URL: www.cbshouston.edu
Established: 1976 Annual Undergrad Tuition & Fees: $9,036
Enrollment: 501 Coed
Affiliation or Control: Independent Non-Profit IRS Status: 501(c)3
Highest Offering: Baccalaureate
Program: Religious Emphasis
Accreditation: @SC, BI

01 President .... Dr. Bill BLOCKER
04 Exec Administrative Assistant .... Mrs. Vicki PATTERSON
05 VP Academic Affairs/Acad Dean .... Mr. Joseph D. PARLE
10 VP Finance & Business Affairs .... Vacant
30 Vice President Development .... Vacant
32 VP Enrollment Services .... Mr. Paul D. KEITH
08 Director of Library Services .... Mr. Artis LOVELADY, III
09 Assoc VP Institutionl Effectiveness .... Dr. Beverly R. LUCAS
13 Director Information Technology .... Mr. M. Shane BOOTHE
06 Registrar .... Ms. Laura Y. HAMILTON
88 Dir Christian Service Program .... Dr. Andre MORGAN
21 Controller .... Mrs. Betty-Ann W. MCNAIR
15 Director Human Resources .... Mrs. Patricia ARBUCKLE
37 Director Student Financial Aid .... Ms. Roshanna HARDISON
40 Director Bookstore .... Mr. Terry BRYAN
84 Director of Marketing and PR .... Ms. Meliinda MERILAT

The College of Health Care Professions (D)

6505 Airport Blvd, Suite 102, Austin TX 78752
County: Travis FICE Identification: 034263
Unit ID: 437635
Telephone: (512) 892-2835 Carnegie Class: Not Classified
FAX Number: (512) 892-6643 Calendar System: Other
URL: www.chcp.edu
Established: N/A Annual Undergrad Tuition & Fees: N/A
Enrollment: 244 Coed
Affiliation or Control: Proprietary IRS Status: Proprietary
Highest Offering: Associate Degree
Program: Occupational
Accreditation: ABHES

01 Director .... Ms. Lori BJORGO

The College of Health Care Professions (E)

240 Northwest Mall, Houston TX 77092
County: Harris FICE Identification: 031281
Unit ID: 392257
Telephone: (713) 425-3100 Carnegie Class: Assoc/PrivFP
FAX Number: (713) 425-3192 Calendar System: Other
URL: www.ahcp.edu
Established: 1988 Annual Undergrad Tuition & Fees: N/A
Enrollment: 378 Coed
Affiliation or Control: Proprietary IRS Status: Proprietary
Highest Offering: Associate Degree
Program: Occupational; 2-Year Principally Bachelor's Creditable
Accreditation: ABHES, SURGT, SURTEC

College of the Mainland (F)

1200 Amburn Road, Texas City TX 77591-2499
County: Galveston FICE Identification: 007096
Unit ID: 226408
Telephone: (409) 933-8271 Carnegie Class: Assoc/Pub-R-M
FAX Number: (409) 933-8010 Calendar System: Semester
URL: www.com.edu
Established: 1966 Annual Undergrad Tuition & Fees (In-District): $1,773
Enrollment: 4,168 Coed
Affiliation or Control: Local IRS Status: 501(c)3
Highest Offering: Associate Degree
Program: Occupational; 2-Year Principally Bachelor's Creditable
Accreditation: SC, ADNUR, EMT, MAC

01 Interim President .... Dr. J. Larry DURRENCE
05 Vice President Instruction .... Dr. Amy LOCKLEAR
10 VP College & Financial Services .... Ms. Lisa TEMPLER
20 Interim Dean Gen Education Programs .... Dr. Amy LOCKLEAR
35 Assoc VP Student Success & Conduct .... Ms. Kris KIMBARK
06 Assoc VP for Enrollment/Registrar .... Mrs. Kelly MUSICK
18 Assoc VP Facility Services .... Mr. Peter EARLY
08 Director Library Services .... Ms. Kathryn PARK
27 Chief Information Officer .... Mr. David DIVINE
37 Director of Student Financial Svcs .... Mr. Carl GORDON
28 Director of Diversity & Equity .... Ms. Lonica BUSH
96 Director of Purchasing .... Ms. Sonja BLINKA
09 Director of Inst Research & Effec .... Dr. Katherine FRIEDRICH
21 Controller .... Ms. Helen DUVALL

The College of Saints John Fisher & Thomas More (G)

3020 Lubbock Avenue, Fort Worth TX 76109-2323
County: Tarrant FICE Identification: 031894
Unit ID: 420352
Telephone: (817) 923-8459 Carnegie Class: Bac/A&S
FAX Number: (817) 924-3206 Calendar System: Semester
URL: www.fishermorecollege.edu
Established: 1981 Annual Undergrad Tuition & Fees: $12,800
Enrollment: 16 Coed
Affiliation or Control: Roman Catholic IRS Status: 501(c)3
Highest Offering: Baccalaureate
Program: Liberal Arts And General
Accreditation: SC

00 Chancellor Emeritus .... Dr. James A. PATRICK
01 President .... Mr. Michael KING
05 Dean .... Dr. Taylor MARSHALL
09 Dir Institutional Effectiveness .... Mr. Raymond PFANG
84 Dir Enrollment Management .... Mr. Peter CAPANI
32 Director Student Life .... Ms. Lindsay JENNINGS
26 Director Communications .... Mr. Shanti GUY
08 Head Librarian .... Ms. Marilyn ANKENBAUER
10 Bursar .... Mr. Joe MARSHALL
88 Office Manager .... Ms. Marilyn ANKENBAUER

Collin County Community College District (H)

3452 Spur 399, McKinney TX 75069
County: Collin FICE Identification: 023614
Unit ID: 247834
Telephone: (972) 758-3800 Carnegie Class: Assoc/Pub-S-MC
FAX Number: (972) 758-5468 Calendar System: Semester
URL: www.collin.edu
Established: 1985 Annual Undergrad Tuition & Fees (In-District): $1,024
Enrollment: 27,593 Coed
Affiliation or Control: State/Local IRS Status: 501(c)3
Highest Offering: Associate Degree
Program: Occupational; 2-Year Principally Bachelor's Creditable
Accreditation: SC, ADNUR, DH, EMT, SURGT

01 President .... Dr. Cary A. ISRAEL
05 Sr VP Acad Affairs/Student Dev .... Dr. Colleen SMITH
12 VP/Provost Spring Creek Campus .... Dr. Mary MCRAE
12 VP/Provost Preston Ridge Campus .... Dr. Brenda K. KIHL
12 VP/Provost Central Park Campus .... Dr. Sherry SCHUMANN
32 Vice President Student Development .... Dr. Barbara MONEY
10 Vice President Admin Svcs & CFO .... Mr. Ralph G. HALL
16 Vice Pres Org Effectiveness & HR .... Ms. Kim K. DAVISON
26 Executive Director College & PR .... Ms. Lisa R. VASQUEZ
09 Assoc VP Rsrch & Inst Effectiveness .... Dr. Thomas K. MARTIN
20 Assoc VP Teaching & Learning .... Ms. Dani DAY
20 Dean Acad Affs-STEM Preston Ridge .... Mr. Jon HARDESTY
20 Dean Acad Aff Preston Ridge Campus .... Dr. Michael MCCONACHIE
20 Dean Acad Affs Central Park Campus .... Ms. Brenda C. CARTER
57 Dean Fine Arts .... Ms. Gaye M. COOKSEY
50 Dean Business/Computer Systems .... Mr. William J. BLITT
79 Dean Communications/Humanities .... Ms. Marianne LAYER
83 Dean Social/Behavioral Sciences .... Mr. Gary B. HODGE
81 Dean Mathematics/Natural Science .... Dr. L. Cameron NEAL, JR.
76 Dean Health Sciences/Emergency Svcs .... Mr. Abe JOHNSON
88 Dean Developmental Education .... Dr. Donald WEASENFORTH
51 Assoc VP Cont Educ/Workforce Dev .... Mr. Stephen R. HARDY
102 Executive Director of Foundation .... Vacant
35 Dean Student Dev Spring Creek .... Mr. Terrence BRENNAN
35 Dean Student Dev Preston Ridge .... Ms. Stephanie MEINHARDT
35 Dean Student Dev Central Park .... Mr. Douglas WILLIS
06 Registrar/Director Admissions .... Mr. Todd E. FIELDS
84 Dean Enroll/Acad Success Momentum .... Dr. Alicia L. HUPPE
38 Assoc Dean Counseling/Career Svcs .... Dr. Linda R. QUALIA
37 Director Financial Aid/Vets Affairs .... Ms. Debra WILKISON
85 International Student Coordinator .... Ms. Rebecca C. CROWELL
13 Chief Information Systems Officer .... Mr. David R. HOYT
21 Assoc VP/Controller .... Ms. Julie BRADLEY
21 Assoc VP Financial Svcs & Reporting .... Ms. Barbara JINDRA
19 Dist Dir Safety/Sec/Fac/Construct .... Mr. Ed C. LEATHERS
96 Director Purchasing .... Ms. Cynthia L. WHITE
40 Director Auxiliary Services .... Mr. David S. HUSTED
15 AVP Human Resources/Org Dev .... Ms. Norma SMITH
08 Exec Dir Library Preston Ridge Cam .... Mr. John MULLIN
08 Exec Dir Library Central Park Cam .... Ms. Bobbie LONG
08 Exec Dir Library Spring Creek Cam .... Ms. Linda KYPRIOS

Commonwealth Institute of Funeral Service (I)

415 Barren Springs, Houston TX 77090-5913
County: Harris FICE Identification: 003556
Unit ID: 366261
Telephone: (281) 873-0262 Carnegie Class: Assoc/PrivNFP
FAX Number: (281) 873-5232 Calendar System: Quarter
URL: www.commonwealth.edu
Established: 1936 Annual Undergrad Tuition & Fees: $14,456
Enrollment: 211 Coed
Affiliation or Control: Independent Non-Profit IRS Status: 501(c)3
Highest Offering: Associate Degree
Program: Occupational
Accreditation: FUSER

01 President .... Mr. Jason C. ALTIERI
05 Chief Academic Officer .... Mr. Stuart MOEN
20 Associate Academic Officer .... Mr. Christopher LAYTON
37 Director Student Financial Aid .... Ms. Jessika JENKINS
06 Registrar .... Ms. Patricia MORENO
08 Head Librarian .... Ms. Therisa MASSEY

Computer Career Center (J)

6101 Montana Avenue, El Paso TX 79925-2021
County: El Paso FICE Identification: 025720
Unit ID: 365204
Telephone: (915) 779-8031 Carnegie Class: Assoc/PrivFP
FAX Number: (915) 779-8097 Calendar System: Semester
URL: www.computercareercenter.com
Established: 1987 Annual Undergrad Tuition & Fees: $17,762
Enrollment: 1,498 Coed
Affiliation or Control: Proprietary IRS Status: Proprietary
Highest Offering: Associate Degree
Program: Occupational
Accreditation: COE, MAAB, MAC

01 Campus Director .... Mr. Antonio RICO
01 Campus Director .... Ms. Rebecca CANCHOLA
06 Registrar .... Ms. Valerie PARKS
07 Director of Admissions .... Ms. Andre ROYOS
36 Director Career Services .... Vacant
37 Director Student Financial Aid .... Ms. Jennifer PHILLIPS
63 Director Medical .... Ms. Juana CERVANTES

Concordia University Texas (K)

11400 Concordia University Drive, Austin TX 78726
County: Travis FICE Identification: 003557
Unit ID: 224004
Telephone: (512) 313-3000 Carnegie Class: Master's L
FAX Number: (512) 313-3339 Calendar System: Semester

URL: www.concordia.edu
Established: 1926 Annual Undergrad Tuition & Fees: $23,600
Enrollment: 2,632 Coed
Affiliation or Control: Lutheran Church - Missouri Synod
IRS Status: 501(c)3
Highest Offering: Master's
Program: Liberal Arts And General; Teacher Preparatory; Professional
Accreditation: SC, IACBE

01 President & CEO ... Dr. Thomas CEDEL
05 Provost ... Dr. Alan RUNGE
10 Vice President Business Services ... Ms. Pamela LEE
11 Vice President University Services ... Mr. C. Gary BELCHER
03 Vice President External Relations ... Mr. Don ADAM
20 Asst Provost Quality Enhancement ... Dr. Trey BUCHANAN
84 Vice Prov Enrollmnt/Student Support ... Ms. Kristi KIRK
55 Vice Provost for Remote Operations ... Ms. Tammy STEWART
42 Campus Pastor ... Rev. Bruce PEFFER
50 Dean College of Business ... Dr. Donald CHRISTIAN
53 Dean College of Education ... Dr. James MCCONNELL
49 Int Dean College of Liberal Arts ... Dr. Carl TROVALL
81 Dean College of Science ... Dr. Janet WHITSON
12 Center Dean Austin ... Dr. DeEadra ALBERT-GREEN
106 Center Online Dean ... Ms. Alex FITTERER
12 Center Dean Ft Worth ... Dr. Mary MAY
12 Center Dean Houston ... Ms. Renae LISTER
12 Center Dean San Antonio ... Dr. Mary DARDEN
06 Registrar ... Ms. Connie BERAN
41 Athletic Director ... Mr. Stan BONEWITZ
32 Director of Student Services ... Mr. Richard POWERS
08 Director of Library Services ... Ms. Mikail MCINTOSH-DOTY
66 Director Nursing Program ... Dr. Joy PENTICUFF
58 Director MED Graduate Program ... Dr. Chris WINKLER
58 Director MBA Graduate Program ... Dr. Elise BRAZIER
37 Director Student Financial Services ... Mr. Russell JEFFREY
07 Director of Admissions ... Ms. Kristin COULTER
13 Director of Information Systems ... Mr. DeWayne MANGAN
19 Chief of Police ... Mr. H.E JENKINS
15 Human Resources Manager ... Ms. Holly JUNG
40 Bookstore Manager ... Ms. Jessica BRIGHT
09 Director of Institutional Research ... Vacant
29 Director Alumni Relations ... Ms. Amy HUTH
18 Director Facilities Management ... Mr. Eric BOOTH
38 Director Student Success Center ... Ms. Ruth COOPER
36 Director Career Center ... Ms. Joyce SINCLAIR
26 Associate VP Communications ... Ms. Melinda BRASHER
35 Assistant Director Student Services ... Mr. John ADAMS
39 Director of Residential Life ... Ms. Sarah EBERLE
27 Chief Information Officer ... Ms. Linda Beth BRADY

Court Reporting Institute of Dallas (A)

1341 W Mockingbird Lane, Suite 200E,
Dallas TX 75247-4968
County: Dallas FICE Identification: 021192
Unit ID: 224183
Telephone: (214) 350-9722 Carnegie Class: Assoc/PrivFP
FAX Number: (214) 631-0143 Calendar System: Quarter
URL: www.cri.edu
Established: 1978 Annual Undergrad Tuition & Fees: $13,800
Enrollment: 472 Coed
Affiliation or Control: Proprietary IRS Status: Proprietary
Highest Offering: Associate Degree
Program: Occupational; 2-Year Principally Bachelor's Creditable; Technical Emphasis
Accreditation: ACICS

01 Campus Director ... Mr. Larry P. PAIZ

Criswell College (B)

4010 Gaston Avenue, Dallas TX 75246-1537
County: Dallas FICE Identification: 041218
Unit ID: 224208
Telephone: (214) 821-5433 Carnegie Class: Not Classified
FAX Number: (214) 370-0497 Calendar System: Semester
URL: www.criswell.edu
Established: 1970 Annual Undergrad Tuition & Fees: $9,700
Enrollment: 327 Coed
Affiliation or Control: Independent Non-Profit IRS Status: 501(c)3
Highest Offering: Master's
Program: Religious Emphasis
Accreditation: SC

01 President ... Jerry JOHNSON
05 Vice President Academic Affairs ... Barry CREAMER
30 Vice President for Development ... Jay GRAHAM
10 Vice President Business & Finance ... Mike RODGERS
84 Assoc Vice Pres Enrollment Services ... Russell MARRIOTT

Culinary Institute LeNotre (C)

7070 Allensby, Houston TX 77022-4322
County: Harris FICE Identification: 037233
Unit ID: 444565
Telephone: (713) 692-0077 Carnegie Class: Assoc/PrivFP
FAX Number: (713) 692-7399 Calendar System: Other
URL: www.culinaryinstitute.edu
Established: 1998 Annual Undergrad Tuition & Fees: N/A
Enrollment: 536 Coed
Affiliation or Control: Proprietary IRS Status: Proprietary
Highest Offering: Associate Degree
Program: Occupational
Accreditation: ACCSC, ACFEI

01 School Director ... Mark STROEH

Dallas Baptist University (D)

3000 Mountain Creek Parkway, Dallas TX 75211-9299
County: Dallas FICE Identification: 003560
Unit ID: 224226
Telephone: (214) 333-7100 Carnegie Class: Master's L
FAX Number: (214) 333-6863 Calendar System: 4/1/4
URL: www.dbu.edu
Established: 1898 Annual Undergrad Tuition & Fees: $20,910
Enrollment: 5,545 Coed
Affiliation or Control: Baptist IRS Status: 501(c)3
Highest Offering: Doctorate
Program: Liberal Arts And General; Teacher Preparatory; Professional
Accreditation: SC, ACBSP, MUS

01 President ... Dr. Gary R. COOK
04 Assistant to the President ... Mr. Mitchell BENNETT
03 Executive Vice President ... Dr. J. Blair BLACKBURN
05 Provost ... Dr. Gail G. LINAM
10 Vice President Financial Affairs ... Mr. Eric BRUNTMYER
20 VP Graduate/Corp Affs/Sr Asc Prov ... Dr. Dennis C. DOWD
31 Vice Pres External Affairs ... Dr. Cory HINES
30 Vice Pres University Advancement ... Dr. Adam WRIGHT
32 Dean of Students and Spiritual Life ... Mr. Jay HARLEY
13 Vice Pres for Technology ... Mr. Matt MURRAH
27 Vice Pres for Communications ... Dr. Blake KILLINGSWORTH
11 Assoc Vice Pres for Admin Affairs ... Dr. Ozzie INGRAM
20 Associate Provost ... Mrs. Deemie J. NAUGLE
50 Dean College of Business ... Dr. Charlene CONNER
81 Acting Dean Col Natural Sci & Math ... Dr. Dionisio FLEITAS
53 Dean College of Education ... Dr. Charles CARONA
57 Dean College of Fine Arts ... Mr. Ronald BOWLES
73 Dean College Christian Faith ... Dr. Steven K. MULLEN
79 Dean Col Humanities/Social Sciences ... Dr. Jack GOODYEAR
107 Dean College Professional Studies ... Dr. Donovan FREDRICKSEN
06 Registrar ... Mrs. Linda M. RONEY
07 Director Undergrad Admissions ... Mr. Bobby SOTO
08 Director of Library ... Ms. Debra COLLINS
37 Director of Financial Aid ... Mr. Lee FERGUSON
15 Director of Human Resources ... Ms. Tamy ROGERS
56 Director Weekend College ... Ms. Joyce WALLACE
41 Director of Athletics ... Mr. Ryan ERWIN
19 Director of Security ... Mr. Donald KABETZKE
85 Director of International Students ... Mrs. Rebecca BROWN
38 Director Student Counseling Center ... Mrs. Joan DAVIS
18 Asst Vice Pres for Admin Affairs ... Mr. Jonathan TEAT
36 Director of Career Services ... Ms. Marion A. HILL
35 Associate Dean of Students ... Dr. Heather HADLOCK
42 Dir Intercessory Prayer Ministry ... Ms. Cyndi PETTIT
88 Academic Projects Administrator ... Ms. Lou ESPARZA
58 Director of Graduate Programs ... Mrs. Kit P. MONTGOMERY
43 General Counsel ... Mr. Dan MALONE
21 Controller ... Mrs. Mendi M. MCMAHAN
96 Accounts Payable Administrator ... Mrs. Becky BUTLER
40 Manager Bookstore ... Mr. Jason SMITH
09 Coordinator Institutional Reporting ... Mrs. Valerie FERGUSON
24 Coordinator Media Services ... Mr. Jonathan HOOVER

Dallas Christian College (E)

2700 Christian Parkway, Dallas TX 75234-7299
County: Dallas FICE Identification: 006941
Unit ID: 224244
Telephone: (972) 241-3371 Carnegie Class: Spec/Faith
FAX Number: (972) 241-8021 Calendar System: 4/1/4
URL: www.dallas.edu
Established: 1950 Annual Undergrad Tuition & Fees: $13,148
Enrollment: 327 Coed
Affiliation or Control: Christian Churches And Churches of Christ
IRS Status: 501(c)3
Highest Offering: Baccalaureate
Program: Teacher Preparatory; Professional; Religious Emphasis
Accreditation: BI

01 President ... Mr. Dustin D. RUBECK
05 Vice President of Academic Affairs ... Dr. Paul KISSLING
30 Vice Pres Institutional Advancement ... Dr. Ron RIFE
31 Vice President of Community ... Mr. Mark WORLEY
10 Controller ... Dr. Tom DODGEN
06 Registrar ... Mrs. Crystal LAIDACKER
37 Director Financial Aid ... Ms. Pamela JONES
07 Director Admissions ... Mr. Matthew MEEKS
18 Director of Facilities ... Mr. Gary ADAMS

*Dallas County Community College District Office (F)

1601 South Lamar, Dallas TX 75215
County: Dallas FICE Identification: 009331
Unit ID: 224253
Telephone: (214) 378-1601 Carnegie Class: N/A
FAX Number: (214) 378-1810
URL: www.dcccd.edu

01 Chancellor ... Dr. Wright L. LASSITER, JR.
05 Provost Educational Affairs ... Dr. Sharon L. BLACKMAN
10 Exec Vice Chanc Business Affairs ... Mr. Ed DESPLAS
20 Exec Dist Dir WF Educ & Compliance ... Mr. Don PERRY
18 Asc Vice Chanc Facil Mgmt/Architect ... Mr. Clyde PORTER
43 District Legal Counsel ... Mr. Robert J. YOUNG
26 Vice Chanc Public & Govt Affairs ... Mr. Justin H. LONON
102 Assoc Vice Chanc Foundation ... Mrs. Betheny REID
101 Executive Director Board Relations ... Mrs. Susan HALL
30 Assoc Vice Chanc Resource Develop ... Mrs. Betheny REID
96 Director of Purchasing ... Mr. Steve PARK
62 Director of Technical Services ... Mr. John CRISWELL

*Brookhaven College (G)

3939 Valley View, Dallas TX 75244-4997
County: Dallas FICE Identification: 021002
Unit ID: 223524
Telephone: (972) 860-4700 Carnegie Class: Assoc/Pub-U-MC
FAX Number: (972) 860-4897 Calendar System: Semester
URL: www.brookhavencollege.edu
Established: 1978 Annual Undergrad Tuition & Fees (In-District): $1,350
Enrollment: 13,571 Coed
Affiliation or Control: State/Local IRS Status: 501(c)3
Highest Offering: Associate Degree
Program: Occupational; 2-Year Principally Bachelor's Creditable
Accreditation: SC, ADNUR, EMT, RAD

02 President ... Dr. Thom D. CHESNEY
05 Vice President of Academic Affairs ... Mr. Rodger BENNETT
10 Vice President of Business Services ... Mr. George HERRING
32 Vice Pres of Student Services ... Mr. Oscar LOPEZ
50 Exec Dean Business Studies ... Mr. Sandy WYCHE
36 Assoc VP Career & Program Resources ... Ms. Marilyn K. KOLESAR-LYNCH
103 Assoc VP Workforce/Continuing Educ ... Mr. Vernon L. HAWKINS
45 Exec Dean Educational Resources ... Ms. Sarah FERGUSON
57 Exec Dean Fine Arts/Phys Ed ... Mr. Rick MAXWELL
81 Executive Dean Science/Math ... Ms. Doris ROUSEY
23 Exec Dean of Health/Human Svcs ... Dr. Juanita FLINT
09 AVP Plng/Rsrch/Inst Effectiveness ... Dr. Michael DENNEHY
90 Director of Info Tech ... Mr. Michael DEASON
83 Exec Dean Social Sci/Distance Lrng ... Mr. Sam GOVEA
27 Executive Dean Communications ... Ms. Kendra VAGLIENTI
88 Dean of Student Success ... Ms. Brenda DALTON
26 Asst Dir Marketing & Public Info ... Ms. Meridith DANFORTH
07 Director of Admissions/Registrar ... Ms. Thoa Hoang VO
41 Director of Athletics ... Ms. Lynne LEVESQUE
21 Director of Business Operations ... Vacant
36 Director Career Development Center ... Ms. Annette WILSON
88 Dir Ellison Miles Geotech Institute ... Vacant
18 Director of Facilities Services ... Mr. Tommy GALLEGOS
15 Exec Dir of Human Resources ... Ms. Terri EDRICH
85 Director of Multicultural Center ... Vacant
35 Dir Office of Student Life ... Mr. Brian BORSKI
19 Captain of College Police ... Mr. John KLINGENSMITH
23 Nurse Health Services ... Ms. Mildred KELLEY
04 Assistant to President ... Ms. Carrie SCHWEITZER

*Cedar Valley College (H)

3030 N Dallas Avenue, Lancaster TX 75134-3799
County: Dallas FICE Identification: 003561
Unit ID: 223773
Telephone: (972) 860-8201 Carnegie Class: Assoc/Pub-U-MC
FAX Number: (972) 682-7075 Calendar System: Semester
URL: www.cedarvalleycollege.edu
Established: 1974 Annual Undergrad Tuition & Fees (In-District): $1,350
Enrollment: 6,802 Coed
Affiliation or Control: State/Local IRS Status: 501(c)3
Highest Offering: Associate Degree
Program: Occupational; 2-Year Principally Bachelor's Creditable
Accreditation: SC

02 President ... Dr. Jennifer L. WIMBISH
05 Vice President for Instruction ... Dr. Nancy CURE
32 Vice Pres Student Svcs/Enroll Mgmt ... Ms. Anna MAYS
10 Vice President Business Services ... Mr. Huan LUONG
81 Director Dean Math/Science/Health ... Dr. Jennie POLLARD
09 Dir Inst Research/Effectiveness ... Mr. Marlon MOTE
49 Division Dean Liberal Arts ... Dr. Mickey BEST
50 Div Dean Bus/Science/Technology ... Dr. Ruben JOHNSON
20 Dean Instructional SupportDist Ed ... Mrs. Lisa NIGHTINGALE
51 Executive Dean Cmty & Resource Dev ... Mrs. Patricia DAVIS
08 Assoc Dean Educ Resource/Librarian ... Ms. Dana M. CORBIN
26 Assoc Dean External Relations ... Vacant
07 Director of Admissions/Registrar ... Ms. Lucia JOHNSON
18 Director Facilities Management ... Mrs. Cindy A. ROGERS
26 Dir Marketing & Public Relations ... Mrs. Megan PALSA
15 Director Human Resources ... Mr. Willie NEAL
37 Director of Financial Aid ... Ms. Cathryn ADAMS
88 Director of Upward Bound ... Ms. Olivia GUERRA
88 Director of Independent Study ... Vacant
35 Coordinator Office Student Life ... Ms. Myioshi U. HOLMES
36 Senior Placement Coordinator ... Mr. Mike J. ALFORD

*Eastfield College (I)

3737 Motley Drive, Mesquite TX 75150-2099
County: Dallas FICE Identification: 008510
Unit ID: 224572
Telephone: (972) 860-7100 Carnegie Class: Assoc/Pub-U-MC
FAX Number: (972) 860-8373 Calendar System: Semester
URL: www.eastfieldcollege.edu
Established: 1970 Annual Undergrad Tuition & Fees (In-District): $1,350
Enrollment: 14,016 Coed
Affiliation or Control: State/Local IRS Status: 170(c)1

Highest Offering: Associate Degree
Program: Occupational; 2-Year Principally Bachelor's Creditable
Accreditation: SC

02 President .... Dr. Jean L. CONWAY
05 Exec VP Academic Affairs .... Mr. Michael J. GUTIERREZ
45 VP Organizational Development .... Dr. Thomas J. GRACA
10 VP Business Services .... Dr. Adrian H. DOUGLAS
32 Executive Dean Student Services .... Ms. Linda C. RICHARDSON
35 Dean Outreach & Student Development .... Ms. Dina M. SOSA-HEGARTY
26 Assistant to the President .... Ms. Sharon L. COOK
15 Executive Director Human Resources .... Mr. Larry L. WILSON
12 Exec Dir Pleasant Grove Campus .... Mr. Javier E. OLGUIN
45 Associate Vice President .... Mr. Donald BAYNHAM
04 Admin Assistant to the President .... Ms. Gloria JOHNSON
20 Dean Academic Enrichment .... Ms. Elizabeth M. NICHOLS
57 Executive Dean Arts & Literature .... Ms. Rachel B. WOLF
72 Executive Dean Career Technologies ... Mr. Gerald F. KOZLOWSKI
81 Executive Dean College Readiness .... Mr. Ricardo S. RODRIGUEZ
81 Executive Dean Science .... Dr. Gretchen K. RIEHL
83 Executive Dean Social Sciences .... Dr. Richard J. CINCLAIR
103 Executive Dean Workforce Devel .... Dr. Lindle D. GRIGSBY
51 Dean Continuing Education .... Mr. Roy L. BOND
08 Dean Educational Resources .... Ms. Karla J. GREER
88 Director Advising .... Ms. Kimberly M. MOORE
37 Director Financial Aid .... Ms. Susan M. GROVE
35 Interim Director Student Life .... Ms. Judy A. SCHWARTZ
41 Director Intercollegiate Athletics .... Mr. Anthony S. FLETCHER
23 Director Health Center .... Ms. Cynthia S. TAYLOR
38 Professional Counselor .... Mr. Jeff QUAN
88 Director Disability Services .... Ms. Barbara L. WHITE
21 Financial Manager .... Ms. Heidi M. BASSETT
21 Director Business Operations .... Ms. Linda S. ZABOJNIK
18 Director Facilities Management .... Mr. Arthur SYKES
90 Interim Dean Information Tech .... Mr. Jack O. THIEHOFF
91 Manager Administrative Computing .... Ms. Dana R. HASKINS
46 Dean Resource Development .... Ms. Whitney C. HOUSTON
19 Acting Director College Police .... Capt. Michael D. HORAK
88 Director Decision Support .... Dr. Richard K. PLOTT

*El Centro College (A)

801 Main Street, Dallas TX 75202-3604
County: Dallas FICE Identification: 004453
Unit ID: 224615
Telephone: (214) 860-2037 Carnegie Class: Assoc/Pub-U-MC
FAX Number: (214) 860-2335 Calendar System: Semester
URL: www.elcentrocollege.edu
Established: 1966 Annual Undergrad Tuition & Fees (In-District): $1,620
Enrollment: 12,028 Coed
Affiliation or Control: State/Local IRS Status: 501(c)3
Highest Offering: Associate Degree
Program: Occupational; 2-Year Principally Bachelor's Creditable
Accreditation: SC, ACFEI, ADNUR, CVT, DMS, MAC, MLTAD, PNUR, RAD, SURGT

02 President .... Dr. Paul J. MCCARTHY
05 Exec VP Acad Affairs/Stdnt Success .... Dr. Micheal B. JACKSON
17 VP Health/Economic Development .... Ms. Sondra G. FLEMMING
10 VP Business Services .... Mr. David A. BROWNING
50 Exec Dean Bus/Pub Svc/Info Tech .... Mr. Howard H. FINNEY
60 Exec Dean Communications/Math .... Ms. Lisa M. THERIOT
49 Interim Exec Dean Arts & Sciences .... Mr. Eddy RAWLINSON
76 Exec Dean Health Occupations .... Dr. Mary L. MCPHERSON
84 Exec Dean Student/Enrollment Svcs .... Ms. Fela ALFARO
32 Exec Dean Student Dev/Support Svcs .... Mr. James L. HANDY
12 Executive Dean BJP Campus .... Ms. Pyeper L. WILKINS
12 Executive Director West Campus .... Ms. Ana-Maria RAMOS
88 Ombudsman .... Dr. Bettie L. TULLY
09 Dean Institutional Effectiveness .... Ms. Teresa S. ISBELL
08 Asst Dean Educational Resources .... Dr. Norman HOWDEN
06 Director Admissions/Registrar .... Ms. Rebecca J. GARZA
37 Dir Student Financial Support/Svcs .... Ms. Pam A. LUCAS
88 Dist Dir Health Career Res Ctr .... Vacant
19 College Director College Police .... Mr. Calvin R. RICHARDS
26 Director Marketing/Communications .... Ms. Priscilla A. STALEY
15 Exec Director Human Resources .... Mr. Robert P. GARCIA
38 Director Testing Center .... Mr. Monty E. FRANCIS
18 Director Facilities Services .... Mr. William E. BUTLER
21 College Director Business Operation .... Ms. Susan G. PIERCE
85 Coordinator International Center .... Mr. Robert G. REYES
35 Director Ofc of Student Life .... Ms. Shanee' S. MOORE
23 College Nurse .... Mr. Ken L. JOHNSON
91 Director Information Technology .... Mr. Michael C. JOHNSON
40 Manager Bookstore .... Mr. Bobby WATSON

*Mountain View College (B)

4849 W Illinois, Dallas TX 75211-6599
County: Dallas FICE Identification: 008503
Unit ID: 226930
Telephone: (214) 860-8680 Carnegie Class: Assoc/Pub-U-MC
FAX Number: (214) 860-8521 Calendar System: Semester
URL: www.mountainviewcollege.edu
Established: 1970 Annual Undergrad Tuition & Fees (In-District): $540
Enrollment: 9,462 Coed
Affiliation or Control: State/Local IRS Status: 501(c)3
Highest Offering: Associate Degree
Program: Occupational; 2-Year Principally Bachelor's Creditable
Accreditation: SC

02 President .... Mr. Felix A. ZAMORA
05 VP Academic Affairs & Student Succ .... Dr. John DELEON
32 VP Student Svcs/Enrollment Mgmt .... Dr. Leonard GARRETT
10 Vice President of Business Services .... Ms. Sharon DAVIS
84 Exec Dean Student Support Svcs .... Dr. John PRUIT
90 Exec Dean Curriculum & Instruction .... Dr. Karen VALENCIA
45 Dean Education Center/Dir Title V .... Mr. Moises ALMENDARIZ
06 Assoc Dean Student Support Svcs .... Ms. Glenda GARRETT
18 Director Facilities Services .... Mr. Allan KNOTT
09 Dir of Planning/Research & IE .... Mr. Jerry SCHEERER
37 Director Financial Aid .... Mr. James HUBENER
35 Director of Student Life .... Ms. Cathy EDWARDS
103 Associate Dean of Workforce Develop .... Ms. Vonice CHAMP
26 Director Public Info/Marketing .... Ms. Marci GARROTT
21 Director of Business Operations .... Mr. Tim SOYARS
07 Asst Director of Admissions .... Ms. Linda OSAGIE
38 Director of Advising .... Vacant
15 Director Human Resources .... Mr. Willie NEAL
36 Director Career Development .... Ms. Regina GARNER
45 Dean Resource Development .... Ms. Heather A. MARSH

*North Lake College (C)

5001 N MacArthur Boulevard, Irving TX 75038-3899
County: Dallas FICE Identification: 020774
Unit ID: 227191
Telephone: (972) 273-3000 Carnegie Class: Assoc/Pub-U-MC
FAX Number: (972) 273-3014 Calendar System: Semester
URL: www.dcccd.edu
Established: 1977 Annual Undergrad Tuition & Fees (In-District): $1,080
Enrollment: 12,107 Coed
Affiliation or Control: State/Local IRS Status: 501(c)3
Highest Offering: Associate Degree
Program: Occupational; 2-Year Principally Bachelor's Creditable; Technical Emphasis
Accreditation: SC, CONST

02 Interim President .... Ms. Christa SLEJKO
05 Vice President Academic Affairs .... Dr. Martha HUGHES
31 VP Community and Economic Develop .... Dr. Paul KELEMEN
10 Interim Vice Pres Business Services .... Ms. Shannon WEAVER
45 Vice Pres Planning & Development .... Ms. Candace CASTILLO
84 VP Stdnt Svcs/Enrollment Mgmt .... Ms. Mary CIMINELLI
88 Director of Learning Resources .... Mr. Kent SEAVER
07 Director Admissions & Registration .... Ms. Francyenne MAYNARD
26 Director Marketing & Public Info .... Ms. Gina FEDERER
12 Ex Director North and South Campus .... Mr. Arthur JAMES
08 Head Librarian .... Dr. Enrique CHAMBERLAIN
18 Director Facilities Services .... Mr. John WATSON
19 Director Campus Police .... Mr. Chris DRAKE
09 Director of Institutional Research .... Dr. Karen LALJIANI
15 Director Human Resources .... Ms. Ella BARBER
21 Interim Associate Business Officer .... Ms. Pamela MAYS
32 Dir Stdnt Prog/Resources/Hlth Svcs .... Ms. Virginia JONES
103 Interim Director Workforce Dev/CE .... Ms. Lynn SMITH-BRUSH
38 Dir Acad Advising Career Edu Pl .... Ms. DeAira HOLLOWAY
83 Executive Dean Liberal Arts .... Dr. Zena JACKSON
81 Exec Dean Math/Science .... Dr. Marilyn MAYS
50 Exe Dean Arts/Bus/Sports Sci Tech .... Dr. David EVANS
12 Exec Dean West Campus .... Mr. Mike COOLEY

*Richland College (D)

12800 Abrams Road, Dallas TX 75243-2199
County: Dallas FICE Identification: 008504
Unit ID: 227766
Telephone: (972) 238-6194 Carnegie Class: Assoc/Pub-U-MC
FAX Number: (972) 238-6978 Calendar System: Semester
URL: www.rlc.dcccd.edu
Established: 1972 Annual Undergrad Tuition & Fees (In-District): $1,080
Enrollment: 20,000 Coed
Affiliation or Control: State/Local IRS Status: 501(c)3
Highest Offering: Associate Degree
Program: Occupational; 2-Year Principally Bachelor's Creditable
Accreditation: SC, MAC

02 President .... Dr. Kathryn K. EGGLESTON
04 Dean/Exec Assistant to President .... Ms. Janet C. JAMES
05 Interim VP Teaching & Learning .... Dr. Zarina BLANKENBAKER
32 VP for Student Development .... Mr. Tony E. SUMMERS
10 VP for Business Services .... Mr. Ron M. CLARK
50 Exec Dean Sch of Engr/Business/Tech .... Ms. Martha A. HOGAN
79 Exec Dean Human/Fine & Perf Arts .... Dr. Sherry L. DEAN
81 Exec Dean of Math/Science/Hlth Prof .... Dr. Raymond P. CANHAM
09 Exec Dean Plng/Rsrch/Inst Effect .... Ms. Fonda L. VERA
60 Exec Dean World Lang/Cultures/Comm ... Ms. Susan E. BARKLEY
88 Exec Dean Lrng Enrich & Acad Dev .... Ms. Mary K. DARIN
41 Director Athletic Programs .... Mr. Tony E. SUMMERS
76 Assoc Dean of Health Professions .... Ms. Shannon YDOYAGA
35 Director of Student Life .... Ms. Bobbie J. HARRISON
08 Director of Library Services .... Ms. Lennijo HENDERSON
26 Dir College Comm and Marketing .... Ms. Whitney ROSENBALM
18 Director of Facilities Services .... Mr. Eddie C. HUESTON
15 Executive Director Human Resources .... Mr. Daniel GUTIERREZ
19 Chief of College Police .... Mr. Robert D. BAKER
12 Principal Richland Collegiate HS .... Dr. Kristyn EDNEY
84 Assoc VP Enrollment/Supt RCHS .... Ms. Donna WALKER

Dallas Institute of Funeral Service (E)

3909 S Buckner Boulevard, Dallas TX 75227-4314
County: Dallas FICE Identification: 010761
Unit ID: 224271
Telephone: (214) 388-5466 Carnegie Class: Assoc/PrivNFP
FAX Number: (214) 388-0316 Calendar System: Quarter
URL: www.dallasinstitute.edu
Established: 1945 Annual Undergrad Tuition & Fees: $15,000
Enrollment: 156 Coed
Affiliation or Control: Independent Non-Profit IRS Status: 501(c)3
Highest Offering: Associate Degree
Program: Occupational; 2-Year Principally Bachelor's Creditable; Technical Emphasis
Accreditation: FUSER

01 President .... Mr. James M. SHOEMAKE

Dallas Theological Seminary (F)

3909 Swiss Avenue, Dallas TX 75204-6493
County: Dallas FICE Identification: 003562
Unit ID: 224305
Telephone: (214) 824-3094 Carnegie Class: Spec/Faith
FAX Number: (214) 841-3625 Calendar System: Semester
URL: www.dts.edu
Established: 1924 Annual Graduate Tuition & Fees: $13,430
Enrollment: 1,978 Coordinate
Affiliation or Control: Independent Non-Profit IRS Status: 501(c)3
Highest Offering: Doctorate; No Undergraduates
Program: Professional; Religious Emphasis
Accreditation: SC, THEOL

01 President .... Dr. Mark L. BAILEY
05 Vice Pres Academic Affs/Acad Dean .... Dr. Mark M. YARBROUGH
32 VP Dean Stdnt Svcs/Dir Stdnt Affs .... Dr. Robert J. GARIPPA
10 Vice President Business & Finance .... Mr. Dale C. LARSON
30 Vice President for Advancement .... Ms. Kimberly B. TILL
11 Vice President Campus Operations .... Mr. Robert F. RIGGS
100 Exec Assistant to the President .... Mr. Robert F. RIGGS
26 Exec Director of Communications .... Mr. John C. DYER
102 President Dallas Sem Foundation .... Mr. Stephen M. GOLDING
108 Dean of Assessment .... Dr. Eugene W. POND
20 Dean of Academic Administration .... Dr. James H. THAMES
12 Dean of DTS Houston .... Dr. Bruce W. FONG
37 Director of Financial Aid & HR .... Ms. Karen G. HOLDER
58 Director of Ph.D. Studies .... Dr. Richard A. TAYLOR
58 Director of D.Min. Studies .... Dr. D. Scott BARFOOT
09 Director of Inst Research/Effective .... Dr. Eugene W. POND
06 Registrar .... Mr. Billy R. TODD, JR.
88 Exec Dir of Leadership Center .... Dr. Andrew B. SEIDEL
07 Director of Admissions .... Mr. Joshua J. BLEEKER
08 Library Director .... Mr. Marvin T. HUNN, II
29 Director of Alumni .... Mr. Gregory A. HATTEBERG
36 Director of Placement .... Dr. Paul E. PETTIT
24 Director of Media Support .... Mr. James W. HOOVER
105 Director of Web Development .... Mr. John C. DYER
42 Chaplain .... Rev. G. William BRYAN
34 Adviser to Women Students .... Ms. Lynn Etta G. MANNING
93 Adviser to African-American Studnts ... Dr. Terrance S. WOODSON
18 Dir Facilities & Plant Operations .... Mr. B. Kevin FOLSOM
13 Director of Information Technology .... Mr. Richard D. BLAKE
19 Director of Campus Police .... Mr. John S. BLOOM
39 Director of Housing & Food Services ...... Mr. Drew H. WILLIAMS
106 Dir Online and External Studies .... Mr. Robert M. ABEGG
88 Director of Online Chinese Studies .... Dr. Samuel CHIA
38 Director of Counseling Services .... Dr. J. Lee JAGERS
15 Director Personnel Services .... Ms. Karen G. HOLDER
21 Associate Business Officer .... Ms. Patricia MAYABB
40 Bookstore Manager .... Mr. Kevin D. STERN
85 International Student Adviser .... Ms. Jenny MCGILL

Del Mar College (G)

101 Baldwin, Corpus Christi TX 78404-3897
County: Nueces FICE Identification: 003563
Unit ID: 224350
Telephone: (361) 698-1200 Carnegie Class: Assoc/Pub-R-L
FAX Number: (361) 698-1559 Calendar System: Semester
URL: www.delmar.edu
Established: 1935 Annual Undergrad Tuition & Fees (In-District): $2,700
Enrollment: 12,139 Coed
Affiliation or Control: Local IRS Status: 501(c)3
Highest Offering: Associate Degree
Program: Occupational; 2-Year Principally Bachelor's Creditable
Accreditation: SC, ACFEI, ADNUR, ART, DA, DH, DMS, MLTAD, MUS, NMT, OTA, PTAA, RAD, SURGT, THEA

01 President .... Dr. Mark ESCAMILLA
05 VP of Instruction & Provost .... Dr. Fernando FIGUEROA
10 VP Administration/Finance .... Dr. Lee SLOAN
45 Exec Dir Strategic Planning .... Ms. Lenora KEAS
26 Exec Director Comm and Legis Affs .... Ms. Claudia JACKSON
30 Director Development .... Ms. Mary MCQUEEN
07 Dean Student Outreach/Enrol .... Mr. Gilbert BECERRA
35 Dean Student Eng & Retention .... Ms. Cheryl GARNER
49 Dean Division Arts & Sciences .... Dr. Jonda HALCOMB
50 Dean Div Business/Prof/Tech Ed .... Dr. Larry LEE
15 Director of Human Resources/EO .... Ms. Tammy MCDONALD
21 Comptroller .... Mr. John J. JOHNSON
96 Director of Purchasing/Business Svc .... Mr. James ROBERTSON
13 Chief Information/Technology Ofcr .... Mr. August ALFONSO
19 Director Risk Mgmt/Safety .... Mr. Kelly L. WHITE
37 Director Financial Aid .... Mr. Enrique GARCIA, JR.
06 Registrar .... Ms. Angalynn BISHOP
32 Dir Stdnt Leadership/Campus Life .... Ms. Beverly CAGE
88 Director Cash Management .... Ms. Cathy WEST
08 Director of Learning Resources .... Ms. Chris M. TETZLAFF-BELHASEN

DeVry University - Austin (A)

11044 Research Boulevard, Ste B100,
Austin TX 78759-5292

County: Travis — Identification: 666573
Telephone: (512) 231-2500 — Carnegie Class: Not Classified
FAX Number: (512) 342-1716 — Calendar System: Semester
URL: www.devry.edu
Established: 1931 — Annual Undergrad Tuition & Fees: $16,156
Enrollment: 350 — Coed
Affiliation or Control: Proprietary — IRS Status: Proprietary
Highest Offering: Master's
Program: Professional; Business Emphasis
Accreditation: &NH

01 Campus Director .... Lorraine BEACH

† Regional accreditation is carried under the parent institution in Downers Grove, IL.

DeVry University - Fort Worth (B)

301 Commerce Street, Suite 2000,
Fort Worth TX 76102-4120

County: Tarrant — Identification: 666574
Telephone: (817) 810-9114 — Carnegie Class: Not Classified
FAX Number: (817) 810-9112 — Calendar System: Semester
URL: www.devry.edu
Established: 1931 — Annual Undergrad Tuition & Fees: $16,156
Enrollment: 306 — Coed
Affiliation or Control: Proprietary — IRS Status: Proprietary
Highest Offering: Master's
Program: Professional; Business Emphasis
Accreditation: &NH

01 Center Dean .... Vacant

† Regional accreditation is carried under the parent institution in Downers Grove, IL.

DeVry University - Houston Campus (C)

11125 Equity Drive, Houston TX 77041-8217

County: Harris — Identification: 666219
Telephone: (713) 973-3100 — Carnegie Class: Not Classified
FAX Number: (713) 896-0293 — Calendar System: Semester
URL: www.devry.edu
Established: 1931 — Annual Undergrad Tuition & Fees: $16,156
Enrollment: 1,840 — Coed
Affiliation or Control: Proprietary — IRS Status: Proprietary
Highest Offering: Master's
Program: Occupational; Professional; Business Emphasis
Accreditation: &NH, ENGT

01 Metro President .... Kim NUGENT
37 Director of Student Finance .... Dong SUH
36 Director Career Services .... Janet CAMINOS-GORERT
15 HR Business Partner .... Sandra NEWMAN
08 Director of Library Services .... Lloyd WEDES
07 Vice President of Admissions .... David WOOD
05 Dean Academic Affairs .... Adrian SHAPIRO
06 Registrar .... Amynah MITHANI

† Regional accreditation is carried under the parent institution in Downers Grove, IL.

DeVry University - Irving Campus (D)

4800 Regent Boulevard, Irving TX 75063-2439

County: Dallas — FICE Identification: 010139
Unit ID: 224402
Telephone: (972) 929-6777 — Carnegie Class: Master's M
FAX Number: (972) 929-2802 — Calendar System: Semester
URL: www.devry.edu
Established: 1931 — Annual Undergrad Tuition & Fees: $16,156
Enrollment: 1,740 — Coed
Affiliation or Control: Proprietary — IRS Status: Proprietary
Highest Offering: Master's
Program: Occupational; Professional; Business Emphasis
Accreditation: &NH, ENGT

01 Metro President .... Mr. John STUART
06 Registrar .... Ms. Sandhya PATEL
07 Director of Admissions .... Ms. Pierre-Carly LAFAILLE
36 Director Career Services .... Ms. Joan LONG
05 Dean of Academic Affairs .... Ms. Emily SMITH
15 HR Business Partner .... Ms. Shingai CHIGWEDERE
54 Dean of Electronics .... Mr. Christian PENCIU
50 Dean of Business & Technology .... Mr. Craig LASSEIGNE
77 Dean of CIS .... Mr. William MCCLURE

† Regional accreditation is carried under the parent institution in Downers Grove, IL.

DeVry University - Richardson (E)

2201 North Central Expressway,
Richardson TX 75080-2754

County: Dallas — Identification: 666575
Telephone: (972) 792-7450 — Carnegie Class: Not Classified
FAX Number: (972) 437-6892 — Calendar System: Semester
URL: www.devry.edu
Established: 1931 — Annual Undergrad Tuition & Fees: $16,156
Enrollment: 379 — Coed
Affiliation or Control: Proprietary — IRS Status: Proprietary
Highest Offering: Master's
Program: Professional; Business Emphasis
Accreditation: &NH

01 Center Dean .... Renee DOYAL

† Regional accreditation is carried under the parent institution in Downers Grove, IL.

East Texas Baptist University (F)

One Tiger Drive, Marshall TX 75670-1498

County: Harrison — FICE Identification: 003564
Unit ID: 224527
Telephone: (903) 935-7963 — Carnegie Class: Bac/Diverse
FAX Number: (903) 938-1705 — Calendar System: Semester
URL: www.etbu.edu
Established: 1912 — Annual Undergrad Tuition & Fees: $21,530
Enrollment: 1,214 — Coed
Affiliation or Control: Southern Baptist — IRS Status: 501(c)3
Highest Offering: Master's
Program: Liberal Arts And General
Accreditation: SC, MUS, NURSE

01 President .... Dr. Samuel W. "Dub" OLIVER
05 Provost/Vice Pres Academic Affairs .... Dr. Sherilyn EMBERTON
20 Assistant Provost .... Dr. Marila D. PALMER
30 Vice Pres University Advancement .... Mrs. Catherine CRAWFORD
42 Vice Pres Spiritual Development .... Dr. Scott BRYANT
10 Vice Pres Administration & Finance .... Mr. Ned CALVERT
32 Vice President for Student Affairs .... Vacant
84 Vice Pres for Enrollment Mgmt/Mktg .... Mr. Vince BLANKENSHIP
35 Dean of Students .... Ms. Magen BUNYARD
09 Dir Inst Research/Effectiveness .... Mrs. Karen WILEY
07 Director of Admissions .... Mr. Jason SOLES
13 Director of Inst Technology .... Mr. Barry HALE
06 University Registrar .... Mr. Chris WOOD
29 Director of Alumni Relations .... Ms. Lindsay CULBERTSON
66 Dean School of Nursing .... Dr. Ellen FINEOUT-OVERHOLT
08 Director of Library .... Ms. Cynthia PETERSON
26 Director of Public Relations .... Mr. Mike MIDKIFF
37 Director of Financial Aid .... Mr. Tommy YOUNG
41 Director of Athletics .... Mr. Kent REEVES
88 Director Baptist Student Ministry .... Mr. Mark YATES
40 Director of Bookstore .... Mr. Bill WARDEN
44 Director of Alumni Development .... Mr. Paul TAPP
18 Director of Physical Facilities .... Mr. Eric WILBURN
88 Director Rec & Athletic Facilities .... Mr. Randy PRINGLE
35 Director of Student Activities .... Mr. Blair PREVOST
88 Director Great Commission Center .... Vacant
53 Dean School of Education .... Dr. Donna LUBCKER
53 Associate Dean of Education .... Dr. Joseph D. BROWN
88 Dean School of Christian Studies .... Dr. John HARRIS
83 Dean School of Nat/Soc Sciences .... Dr. Lynn NEW
50 Dean School of Business .... Dr. Scott RAY
79 Dean School of Humanities .... Dr. Jerry SUMMERS
85 Director of International Education .... Mr. Alan HUESING
21 Director of Financial Services .... Mr. Richard HUTSELL
88 Director of Student Success .... Mrs. Bonnie JONES
57 Dean School of Fine Arts .... Dr. Tom WEBSTER
102 Director of Major Gifts .... Dr. Dane FOWLKES

El Paso Community College (G)

PO Box 20500, El Paso TX 79998-0500

County: El Paso — FICE Identification: 010387
Unit ID: 224642
Telephone: (915) 831-2000 — Carnegie Class: Assoc/Pub-U-MC
FAX Number: (915) 831-6507 — Calendar System: Semester
URL: www.epcc.edu
Established: 1969 — Annual Undergrad Tuition & Fees (In-District): $2,430
Enrollment: 30,812 — Coed
Affiliation or Control: Local — IRS Status: 501(c)3
Highest Offering: Associate Degree
Program: Occupational; 2-Year Principally Bachelor's Creditable
Accreditation: SC, ADNUR, DA, DH, DMS, MAC, MLTAD, PTAA, RAD, SURGT

01 President .... Dr. William SERRATA
05 Interim Vice President Instruction .... Mr. Steve SMITH
10 Vice Pres Admin & Fin Operations .... Dr. Ernst E. ROBERTS
13 Vice Pres Information Tech/CIO .... Dr. Jenny GIRON
103 Vice Pres Wrkfc/Economic Dev & CE .... Ms. Yolanda AHNER
32 Vice President Student Services .... Ms. Linda GONZALEZ
46 Vice Pres Research & Accountability .... Mr. Saul C. CANDELAS
10 Assoc VP Budget & Financial Svcs .... Ms. Josette SHAUGHNESSY
15 Assoc VP Employee Relations .... Ms. Nancy N. NELSON
26 Dir Marketing & Community Rels .... Ms. Joyce CORDELL
88 Dean Instruct Programs-MDP Campus .... Dr. Julie PENLEY
76 Dean Health Occupations/Math/Sci .... Dr. Paula MITCHELL
50 Dean Arts/Bask/Comp/Oc Educ/Soc Sci .... Dr. Eileen CONKLIN
57 Dean Arts/Bask/Comm & Soc Sci .... Vacant
79 Dean ESL Reading Social Science .... Ms. Susana RODARTE
81 Dean Arch/Arts/Math/Science .... Ms. Toni BADILLO
88 Dean American Lang/BS/Comm/PA .... Mr. Claude MATHIS
53 Dean Education & Occ Programs .... Dr. Jaime D. FARIAS
66 Dean Nursing .... Ms. Paula G. MEAGHER
12 Dean Instructional Pgms-NW Campus .... Dr. Lydia TENA
45 Director Inst Effectiveness .... Dr. Ron STROUD
08 Director Library Technical Services .... Mr. Luis CHAPARRO
21 Comptroller .... Mr. Fernando FLORES
36 Director Career Services .... Ms. Carla CARDOZA
18 Director Physical Plant .... Mr. Richard L. LOBATO
19 Chief of Police .... Chief Jose L. RAMIREZ
24 Director Center Instr Telecommunic .... Vacant
15 Exec Director Personnel Services .... Ms. Elizabeth OLGUIN-RYAN
07 Exec Director Admissions/Registrar .... Mr. Daryle HENDRY
96 Dir Purchasing & Contract Mgmt .... Mr. Ruben C. GALLARDO
09 Director Institutional Research .... Dr. Carol KAY
16 Director Human Resources Devel .... Mr. Alex HERNANDEZ
31 Director Inst & Community Planning .... Ms. Dolores GROSS
21 Director Budget .... Vacant
88 Manager Literacy Programs .... Mrs. Sara MARTINEZ
85 Director International Education .... Dr. Miguel A. MARTINEZ-LASSO
102 Exec Dir Foundation/Development .... Dr. Christy PONCE
88 Dir Ctr for Students w/Disabilities .... Ms. Janet M. LOCKHART
88 Director Recruitment/School Rels .... Ms. Nita CORRAL-NAVA
88 Director Testing Service .... Ms. Marisa PIERCE
25 Director Grants Management .... Mr. Alfred C. LAWRENCE
103 Director Workforce Development .... Ms. Luz E. TABOADA
56 Director Distance Learning .... Mr. Robert P. JONES
88 Director Student Success .... Ms. Irma G. CAMACHO
88 Dir Law Enforcement Trng Academy .... Mr. Barry J. BOGLE
28 Director of Diversity Programs .... Mrs. Olga CHAVEZ

Everest College (H)

6080 N Central Expressway, Dallas TX 75206-5202

County: Dallas — Identification: 666254
Unit ID: 442790
Telephone: (214) 234-4850 — Carnegie Class: Assoc/PrivFP
FAX Number: (214) 696-6208 — Calendar System: Quarter
URL: www.everest-college.com
Established: 2003 — Annual Undergrad Tuition & Fees: $14,976
Enrollment: 1,252 — Coed
Affiliation or Control: Proprietary — IRS Status: Proprietary
Highest Offering: Associate Degree
Program: Occupational; Business Emphasis
Accreditation: ACICS, MAAB

01 President .... Vacant
05 Academic Dean .... Glenn THAXTON
07 Acting Director of Admissions .... Chris EIFLER
37 Director of Financial Aid .... Kevin HODGE

† Branch campus of Everest College, Portland, OR.

Frank Phillips College (I)

PO Box 5118, Borger TX 79008-5118

County: Hutchinson — FICE Identification: 003568
Unit ID: 224891
Telephone: (806) 457-4200 — Carnegie Class: Assoc/Pub-R-S
FAX Number: (806) 457-4224 — Calendar System: Semester
URL: www.fpctx.edu
Established: 1948 — Annual Undergrad Tuition & Fees (In-District): $1,023
Enrollment: 1,227 — Coed
Affiliation or Control: Local — IRS Status: 501(c)3
Highest Offering: Associate Degree
Program: Occupational; 2-Year Principally Bachelor's Creditable
Accreditation: SC

01 President .... Dr. Jud HICKS
11 Vice Pres Administrative Services .... Dr. Jud HICKS
05 Vice President of Academic Affairs .... Ms. Shannon CARROLL
12 Dean of FPC Allen Campus .... Dr. Lew HUNNICUTT
08 Director of the Library .... Mr. Jason PRICE
06 Registrar .... Vacant
09 Director of Institutional Research .... Vacant
18 Chief Facilities/Physical Plant .... Ms. Regina HANEY
26 Col Advancement/Community Rels Ofcr .... Ms. Jerri AYLOR
103 Dean of Career & Technical Educ .... Mr. Jack STANLEY
37 Co-Dir Student Financial Services .... Ms. Beverly FIELDS
37 Co-Dir Student Financial Services .... Ms. Dianne ENSEY
38 Director Student Counseling .... Ms. Marilee COOPER
84 Director Enrollment Management .... Ms. Michele STEVENS
56 Coordinator of Extended Education .... Ms. Kim PIEDRA
10 Director of Accounting .... Ms. Bridey MCCORMACK

Franklin College (J)

5700 Cromo Drive, El Paso TX 79912

County: El Paso — FICE Identification: 009082
Unit ID: 225779
Telephone: (915) 842-0422 — Carnegie Class: Assoc/PrivFP
FAX Number: (915) 584-5325 — Calendar System: Other
URL: www.franklin-college.edu
Established: N/A — Annual Undergrad Tuition & Fees: $12,762
Enrollment: 323 — Coed
Affiliation or Control: Proprietary — IRS Status: Proprietary
Highest Offering: Associate Degree
Program: Occupational
Accreditation: ACICS

01 President .... Margie AGUILAR

Galveston College (K)

4015 Avenue Q, Galveston TX 77550-7496

County: Galveston — FICE Identification: 004972
Unit ID: 224961
Telephone: (409) 944-4242 — Carnegie Class: Assoc/Pub-R-M
FAX Number: (409) 944-1500 — Calendar System: Semester

URL: www.gc.edu
Established: 1966 Annual Undergrad Tuition & Fees (In-District): $1,558
Enrollment: 2,222 Coed
Affiliation or Control: State/Local IRS Status: 501(c)3
Highest Offering: Associate Degree
Program: Occupational; 2-Year Principally Bachelor's Creditable; Business Emphasis
Accreditation: SC, ADNUR, EMT, NMT, RAD, RTT, SURGT

01 President Dr. Myles SHELTON
05 Vice President of Instruction Dr. Cissy MATTHEWS
11 Vice President for Administration Dr. Gaynelle H. HAYES
32 Vice President of Student Services Dr. Phyllis A. PEPIN
75 Dean of Tech & Prof Education Ms. Vera LEWIS-JASPER
10 Director of Business Services Mr. M. Jeff ENGBROCK
14 Dir of Information Technology Mr. George CROSSLAND
30 Dir of Inst Advancement/Foundation Mr. Joseph E. HUFF, III
15 Dir Human Resources/Risk Management Ms. Mary Jan LANTZ
41 Athletic Director/Head Coach Mr. Ken DELCAMBRE
07 Director Admissions/Registrar Dr. Kimberly ELLIS
66 Director of Nursing Ms. Elaine RENOLA
09 Director Inst Effectiveness/Rsrch Dr. Deeanna L. ANTOSH
18 Director of Facilities/Security Mr. Tim W. SETZER
37 Director of Financial Aid Mr. Ron C. CRUMEDY
62 Dir of Library/Learning Resources Dr. Alan M. UYEHARA
04 Executive Assistant Ms. Carla D. BIGGERS

Grace School of Theology (A)

PO Box 7477, The Woodlands TX 77387
County: Montgomery Identification: 667100
Telephone: (877) 476-8674 Carnegie Class: Not Classified
FAX Number: N/A Calendar System: Semester
URL: www.gsot.org
Established: 2002 Annual Graduate Tuition & Fees: N/A
Enrollment: N/A Coed
Affiliation or Control: Independent Non-Profit IRS Status: 501(c)3
Highest Offering: Master's; No Undergraduates
Program: Religious Emphasis
Accreditation: @TRACS

01 President Dr. Dave ANDERSON

Graduate Institute of Applied Linguistics (B)

7500 W Camp Wisdom Road, Dallas TX 75236-5629
County: Dallas FICE Identification: 038513
Telephone: (972) 708-7340 Carnegie Class: Not Classified
FAX Number: (972) 708-7396 Calendar System: Other
URL: www.gial.edu
Established: 1999 Annual Graduate Tuition & Fees: $13,560
Enrollment: 113 Coed
Affiliation or Control: Independent Non-Profit IRS Status: 501(c)3
Highest Offering: Master's; No Undergraduates
Program: Professional; Religious Emphasis
Accreditation: SC

01 President Dr. David A. ROSS
05 Chief Academic Officer Dr. Doug TIFFIN
10 Chief Financial Officer Mr. Rod JENKINS
30 Vice President for Advancement Mr. James W. WALTON
32 Dean of Students Ms. Ruth E. SCHILBERG
06 Registrar Mrs. Lynne LAMIMAN
07 Director of Admissions Mrs. Maggie JOHNSON
08 Librarian Ms. Ferne L. WEIMER
44 Director of Development Ms. Rebecca BRIDGES
09 Director of Inst Research/Svcs Mr. Richard E. LYNCH
13 Director of Computing Services Mr. Chuck WALEK
26 Chief Public Relations Officer Mr. Richard M. SMITH
21 Business Manager Mr. Paul W. SETTER

Grayson County College (C)

6101 Grayson Drive, Denison TX 75020-8299
County: Grayson FICE Identification: 003570
Unit ID: 225070
Telephone: (903) 465-6030 Carnegie Class: Assoc/Pub-R-M
FAX Number: (903) 463-5284 Calendar System: Semester
URL: www.grayson.edu
Established: 1963 Annual Undergrad Tuition & Fees (In-District): $1,850
Enrollment: 4,909 Coed
Affiliation or Control: State/Local IRS Status: 501(c)3
Highest Offering: Associate Degree
Program: Occupational; 2-Year Principally Bachelor's Creditable
Accreditation: SC, ADNUR, DA, EMT, MLTAD

01 President Dr. Jeremy P. MCMILLEN
05 Vice President of Instruction Dr. Jeanie HARDIN
10 Vice President of Business Services Mr. Giles BROWN
13 Vice Pres of Information Technology Mr. Gary PAIKOWSKI
32 Vice President Student Services Mr. Marc PAYNE
31 Vice Pres Resource/Community Devel Dr. Roy E. RENFRO
07 Director of Admissions/Records Mr. Gary HENSLER
37 Director of Financial Aid Ms. Donna KING
14 Director of Computer Center Mr. Mike BROWN
19 Director Campus Police Mr. Andy MACPHERSON
26 Dir of Public Information/Marketing Mrs. Shelle R. CASSELL
21 Director of Fiscal Services Mr. Danny HYATT
40 Bookstore Manager Ms. Brenda FOX
41 Athletic Director Ms. Theresa BARNETT

Hallmark College of Aeronautics (D)

10401 W IH 10, San Antonio TX 78230
County: Bexar Identification: 666623
Unit ID: 225201
Telephone: (210) 690-9000 Carnegie Class: Assoc/PrivFP
FAX Number: (210) 690-8225 Calendar System: Other
URL: www.hallmarkcollege.edu
Established: 1969 Annual Undergrad Tuition & Fees: $29,872
Enrollment: 900 Coed
Affiliation or Control: Proprietary IRS Status: Proprietary
Highest Offering: Associate Degree
Program: Occupational
Accreditation: ACCSC

01 Campus President Mr. Bret JOHNSON
07 Vice Pres of Marketing/Admissions Ms. Sonia ROSS

Hallmark College of Technology (E)

10401 IH-10 W, San Antonio TX 78230-1737
County: Bexar FICE Identification: 010509
Unit ID: 225201
Telephone: (210) 690-9000 Carnegie Class: Assoc/PrivFP
FAX Number: (210) 697-8225 Calendar System: Other
URL: www.hallmarkcollege.edu
Established: 1969 Annual Undergrad Tuition & Fees: $23,925
Enrollment: 798 Coed
Affiliation or Control: Proprietary IRS Status: Proprietary
Highest Offering: Baccalaureate
Program: Occupational; 2-Year Principally Bachelor's Creditable; Technical Emphasis
Accreditation: ACCSC, MAC

00 College Systems President Mr. Joseph B. FISHER
01 Campus President Mr. Brent FESSLER
05 Vice Pres of Academics Mr. Sal ROSS
26 Vice President of Marketing Ms. Sonia ROSS
07 Director of Admissions Mr. Joe LONG

Hardin-Simmons University (F)

2200 Hickory, Abilene TX 79698-0001
County: Taylor FICE Identification: 003571
Unit ID: 225247
Telephone: (325) 670-1000 Carnegie Class: Master's M
FAX Number: (325) 670-1267 Calendar System: Semester
URL: www.hsutx.edu
Established: 1891 Annual Undergrad Tuition & Fees: $22,560
Enrollment: 2,358 Coed
Affiliation or Control: Baptist IRS Status: 501(c)3
Highest Offering: Doctorate
Program: Liberal Arts And General; Teacher Preparatory; Professional
Accreditation: SC, ACBSP, MUS, NURSE, PTA, SW, THEOL

01 President Dr. Lanny HALL
05 Provost & Chief Academic Officer Dr. Thomas V. BRISCO
10 Sr VP Finance & Chief Oper Ofcr Mr. Harold R. PRESTON
30 VP for Advancement Mr. Mike HAMMACK
32 Sr Vice Pres Student Development Dr. Michael A. WHITEHORN
84 Vice Pres for Enrollment Management Dr. J. Shane DAVIDSON
07 Assoc VP for Enrollment Svcs Mr. Jim JONES
04 Exec Assistant to the President Ms. Vicki D. HOUSE
53 Dean Irvin School of Education Dr. Pamela K. WILLIFORD
49 Dean College of Liberal Arts Dr. Alan STAFFORD
50 Dean School of Business Mr. Michael MONHOLLON
64 Dean School of Music/Fine Arts Mr. Bob BROOKS
73 Dean Logsdon School of Theology Dr. Don WILLIFORD
58 Dean of Graduate School Dr. Nancy KUCINSKI
66 Dean School of Nursing Dr. Nina OUIMETTE
81 Dean School Sciences/Mathematics Dr. Christopher L. MCNAIR
14 Assoc Vice Pres Technical Services Mr. Travis P. SEEKINS
21 Assoc VP/Controller for Finance/Mgt Mr. Don P. ASHMORE
38 Assoc VP Academic Advising/Retent Mrs. Gracie CARROLL
08 Dean/Dir of University Libraries Mrs. Alice W. SPECHT
09 Director of Institutional Research Mrs. Lori BLAKE
06 Registrar Mrs. Kacey HIGGINS
35 Dean of Students Mr. Forrest MCMILLAN
29 Director of Alumni Relations Mrs. Britt E. JONES
19 Chief of Police Mr. Frank LOZA
23 University Nurse Mrs. Sue A. BIGGS
42 Chaplain Dr. Kelly PIGOTT
39 Associate Dean of Students Mr. Ben JOHNSON
36 Director of Career Services Mrs. Kelley WOOD
15 Director of Human Resources Mr. John SNAPP
27 Dir of University Communications Mrs. Brenda HARRIS
37 Dir Student Fin Aid & Scholarships Mrs. Bridget MOORE
18 Facilities Services Director Mr. Tim MCCARRY
41 Athletic Director Mr. John M. NEESE
85 Director of International Studies Dr. Allan J. LANDWER
26 Public Relations Director Mrs. Janlyn THAXTON
93 Coordinator of Minority Programs Dr. Joe H. ALCORTA
28 Coord of Student Diversity Dr. Kelvin J. KELLEY

Hill College (G)

112 Lamar Drive, Hillsboro TX 76645-2711
County: Hill FICE Identification: 003573
Unit ID: 225371
Telephone: (254) 659-7500 Carnegie Class: Assoc/Pub-R-M
FAX Number: (254) 582-7591 Calendar System: Semester
URL: www.hillcollege.edu
Established: 1923 Annual Undergrad Tuition & Fees (In-District): $1,480
Enrollment: 4,307 Coed
Affiliation or Control: Local IRS Status: 501(c)3
Highest Offering: Associate Degree
Program: Occupational; 2-Year Principally Bachelor's Creditable
Accreditation: SC

01 President Dr. Sheryl S. KAPPUS
04 Executive Asst to the President Ms. Sharon MIDDLEBROOK
05 Vice President Instruction Mr. Rex PARCELLS
11 Vice Pres Administrative Services Mr. Billy D. CURBO
32 Vice President Student Services Dr. Robert RIZA
13 Vice Pres Information Technology Mrs. Jessie WHITE
84 Exec Dean of Enrollment Services Ms. Lizza TRENKLE
88 Exec Dean President's Office Ms. Leslie CANNON
09 Dean Institutional Plng & Research Mrs. Jessyca BROWN
21 Dean Financial Services Mrs. Debbie GERIK
08 Librarian Mr. Joseph SHAUGHNESSY
08 Librarian - Cleburne Campus Mr. Kevin HENARD
16 Human Resources Executive Director Dr. Heather KISSACK
12 Exec Dir JCC/Dean of Students Mr. Bill GILKER
41 Athletic Director Mr. Paul BROWN
26 Director of Marketing & Public Rels Ms. Nikki WILMOTH
06 Dir Stdnt Records & Registration Ms. Sherry DAVIS
37 Director of Financial Aid Ms. Susan RUSSELL
07 Dir School Relations & Recruiting Mr. Scott WARREN
18 Facilities Coordinator Ms. Wendie HERNANDEZ

Houston Baptist University (H)

7502 Fondren Road, Houston TX 77074-3298
County: Harris FICE Identification: 003576
Unit ID: 225399
Telephone: (281) 649-3000 Carnegie Class: Master's M
FAX Number: (281) 649-3012 Calendar System: Semester
URL: www.hbu.edu
Established: 1960 Annual Undergrad Tuition & Fees: $26,795
Enrollment: 2,432 Coed
Affiliation or Control: Southern Baptist IRS Status: 501(c)3
Highest Offering: Master's
Program: Liberal Arts And General; Teacher Preparatory; Professional
Accreditation: SC, ACBSP, ADNUR, NUR

01 President Dr. Robert B. SLOAN
05 Provost Dr. John Mark REYNOLDS
10 Vice President Financial Operations Ms. Sandra N. MOONEY
26 Vice Pres University Communication Mr. Kimberly GAYNOR
30 Vice President for Advancement Mr. Charles BACARISSE
26 Vice Pres University Relations Mrs. Sharon E. SAUNDERS
84 Vice Pres Enrollment Management Mr. James STEEN
20 Associate Provost Ms. Ritamarie TAUER
20 Associate Provost Dr. Robert D. STACEY
21 Asst VP for Treasury Operations Mr. Hugh MCCLUNG
79 Int Dean College Arts & Humanities Dr. Chris HAMMONS
50 Dean School of Business Dr. Mohan KURUVILLA
81 Dean College of Science & Math Dr. Doris C. WARREN
92 Dean Honors College Dr. Robert STACEY
53 Dean School of Education Dr. Cynthia SIMPSON
66 Int Dean Sch Nursing & Allied Hlth Ms. Carol LAVENDER
41 Athletic Director Mr. Steve C. MONIACI
06 University Registrar Ms. Erinn HUGHES
40 Director of University Store Mr. Anthony MARTIN
07 Director of Admissions Mr. Eduardo BORGES
08 Director of Libraries Ms. Ann NOBLE
42 University Minister Mr. Tom MOSLEY
21 Sr Director Financial Services Ms. Jene GABBARD
88 Assoc Director Scholarships Ms. Janet FENG
29 Director of Alumni Relations Vacant
39 Director Housing Operations Mr. Mark ENDRASKE
13 Int Dir of Information Technology Mr. Trent CARROLL
19 Director Police Mr. Charles MILLER
09 Sr Director Institutional Research Dr. Phil RHODES
32 Chief Student Life Officer Mr. Whittington GOODWIN
88 SACS Liaison Ms. Ritamarie TAUER
04 Sr Admin Asst to the President Ms. Judy FERGUSON
04 Admin Asst to the President Ms. Karen FRANCIES

Houston Community College (I)

3100 Main Street, Houston TX 77002
County: Harris FICE Identification: 010633
Unit ID: 225423
Telephone: (713) 718-2000 Carnegie Class: Assoc/Pub-U-MC
FAX Number: N/A Calendar System: Semester
URL: www.hccs.edu
Established: 1971 Annual Undergrad Tuition & Fees (In-State): $813
Enrollment: 64,333 Coed
Affiliation or Control: State IRS Status: 501(c)3
Highest Offering: Associate Degree
Program: Occupational; 2-Year Principally Bachelor's Creditable
Accreditation: SC, DA, DH, DMS, EMT, ENGT, HT, MAC, MLTAD, NMT, OTA, PTAA, RAD, SURGT

01 Chancellor Dr. Mary S. SPANGLER
04 Executive Officer to the Chancellor Ms. Shantay GRAYS
03 COO/Deputy Chancellor Dr. Arthur Q. TYLER
43 General Counsel Ms. Renee BYAS
05 Vice Chancellor Instruction Dr. Charles M. COOK
32 Vice Chancellor Student Success Dr. Diana PINO
14 Vice Chancellor Information Tech Mr. William E. CARTER
45 VC Planning and Inst Effectiveness Vacant
11 Chief Administration Officer Mr. Winston DAHSE
15 Chief Human Resource Officer Mr. Willie WILLIAMS

22 Director EEO/Compliance .... Mr. David CROSS
10 Controller/Chief Financial Officer .... Mr. Ron E. DEFALCO
26 Chief Communications Officer .... Mr. Daniel ARGUIJO, JR.
76 Dean Health Science Programs .... Dr. Michael EDWARDS
66 Department Chair Vocational Nursing .... Ms. Deborah SIMMONS-JOHNSON
07 Director of Admissions & Registrar .... Ms. Mary LEMBURG
09 Exec Dir of Inst Research & Innov .... Dr. Martha OBURN
46 Director Resource Development .... Ms. Georgia CARMICHAEL
102 Executive Director Foundation .... Dr. Kelly ZUNIGA
19 Environmental Safety Manager .... Mr. Oscar GONZALES
12 President-Northeast College .... Dr. Margaret FORD FISHER
12 President-Southwest College .... Dr. Fena GARZA
12 President-Central College .... Dr. William HARMON
12 President-Southeast College .... Dr. Irene PORCARELLO
12 President-Northwest College .... Dr. Zachary HODGES
12 President-Coleman College .... Dr. Betty K. YOUNG
85 Ex Dir International Initiatives .... Ms. Gigi Diemuyen DO-NGUYEN
18 Dir Bldg Operations/Property Mgmt .... Ms. Jackquline SWINDLE
29 Alumni Relations Officer .... Ms. Lauren STROMAN
96 Ex Dir Purchasing/Procurement Oper .... Mr. Rogelio ANASAGASTI
35 Director Student/Financial Services .... Mr. Hernando BALDONADO
37 Director Student Financial Aid .... Vacant
20 Assoc VC of Academic Instruction .... Dr. Steve LEVEY
21 Ex Dir Financial & Budget Control .... Ms. Karla BENDER

Houston Graduate School of Theology (A)

2501 Central Parkway, Suite A19,
Houston TX 77092-7726

County: Harris FICE Identification: 023202
Unit ID: 246345
Telephone: (713) 942-9505 Carnegie Class: Spec/Faith
FAX Number: (713) 942-9506 Calendar System: Semester
URL: www.hgst.edu
Established: 1983 Annual Graduate Tuition & Fees: $10,600
Enrollment: 186 Coed
Affiliation or Control: Independent Non-Profit IRS Status: 501(c)3
Highest Offering: Doctorate; No Undergraduates
Program: Professional; Religious Emphasis
Accreditation: **THEOL**

01 President .... Dr. James FERR
05 Assoc Dean-Curriculum & Instruction .... Dr. Chuck PITTS
73 Dir of D.Min Program .... Dr. Becky L. TOWNE
10 Chief Financial Officer .... Ms. Janell RAY
06 Registrar .... Ms. Kristin DOMERACKI
08 Director of Library Services .... Ms. Janet KENNARD

Howard College (B)

1001 Birdwell Lane, Big Spring TX 79720-3799

County: Howard FICE Identification: 003574
Unit ID: 225520
Telephone: (432) 264-5000 Carnegie Class: Assoc/Pub-R-M
FAX Number: (432) 264-5082 Calendar System: Semester
URL: www.howardcollege.edu
Established: 1945 Annual Undergrad Tuition & Fees (In-District): $2,222
Enrollment: 4,695 Coed
Affiliation or Control: State/Local IRS Status: 501(c)3
Highest Offering: Associate Degree
Program: Occupational; 2-Year Principally Bachelor's Creditable
Accreditation: **SC**, ADNUR, DH, RAD, SURGT

01 President .... Dr. Cheryl T. SPARKS
03 Executive Vice President .... Mr. Terry HANSEN
05 Vice President Academic Affairs .... Dr. Amy BURCHETT
12 Int Prov SW Col Inst for the Deaf .... Mr. Dominick BONURA
12 Provost San Angelo .... Ms. LeAnne BYRD
12 Executive Dean Big Spring .... Mr. Terry L. HANSON
103 Campus Dean for Workforce Devel .... Ms. Kinsey HANSEN
04 Executive Asst to the President .... Ms. Julie BAILEY
06 Registrar .... Mr. Scott RAINES
08 Dean of Libararies .... Mr. Luis KINCADE
14 Director of Computer Services .... Mr. Ed ROBERTS
56 Distance Learning Coordinator .... Ms. Kym CLARK
18 Director of Physical Plant .... Mr. Robert WILLIAMS
27 Director Information/Marketing .... Ms. Cindy SMITH
41 Athletic Director .... Mr. Britt SMITH
10 Controller .... Ms. Brenda CLAXTON
15 Director Human Resources/Payroll .... Ms. Rhonda KERNICK
96 Director of Purchasing .... Mr. Jason MIMS
37 Director of Financial Aid .... Ms. Liz ADAMSON
35 Director Student Affairs .... Ms. Lorinda HERROD
21 Assistant Controller-Student Acct .... Ms. Margaret CERVANTES
21 Assistant Controller-Fiscal Acct .... Mrs. Cherry FURQUERON
30 Director Institutional Advancement .... Mrs. Jan FORESYTH

Howard Payne University (C)

1000 Fisk Street, Brownwood TX 76801-2794

County: Brown FICE Identification: 003575
Unit ID: 225548
Telephone: (325) 646-2502 Carnegie Class: Bac/Diverse
FAX Number: (325) 649-8975 Calendar System: Semester
URL: www.hputx.edu
Established: 1889 Annual Undergrad Tuition & Fees: $22,560
Enrollment: 1,209 Coed
Affiliation or Control: Baptist IRS Status: 501(c)3
Highest Offering: Master's
Program: Liberal Arts And General; Teacher Preparatory
Accreditation: **SC**, IACBE, MUS, SW

01 President .... Dr. William N. ELLIS
05 Provost/Chief Academic Officer .... Dr. Mark TEW
10 Sr Vice Pres Finance/Administration .... Mrs. Brenda ALEXANDER
30 Sr VP Institutional Advancement .... Dr. Brad JOHNSON
32 Vice Pres Stdnt Life/Dean Stdnts .... Dr. Brent A. MARSH
26 Assoc VP Mktg/Comm/Sp Asst to Pres .... Ms. Louise SHARP
44 Vice President Development .... Mr. Paul A. DUNNE
15 Asst VP for Bus & Hum Resources .... Mr. Bill FISHBACK
06 Registrar .... Mrs. Lana WAGNER
37 Director Financial Aid .... Mrs. Glenda HUFF
07 Director of Admission .... Mrs. P.J GRAMLING
36 Dir Academic Testing/Career Svcs .... Ms. Wendy MCNEELEY
40 Director Bookstore .... Ms. Teresa BAIRD
29 Coordinator of Alumni Relations .... Ms. Nancy HEADY
27 Director of Publications .... Mr. Kyle C. MIZE
88 Alumni and Media Relations Asst .... Ms. Kathy JAMES
41 Athletic Director .... Mr. Mike JONES
91 Database Administrator .... Mr. Randy GINTHER
18 Facilities Coordinator .... Ms. Debbie CHILDS
90 Computer Network Administrator .... Mr. Russell EZZELL
09 Director Institutional Research .... Ms. Shannon PITTMAN
04 Executive Assistant to President .... Ms. Susan HAYNES
38 University Counselor .... Dr. Athena BEAN
56 Dean Extended Education .... Dr. Robert TUCKER
08 Dean of Libraries .... Mrs. Nancy K. ANDERSON
81 Dean School of Science & Math .... Dr. Lynn LITTLE
50 Dean School of Business .... Dr. Leslie F. PLAGENS
53 Dean School of Ecucation .... Dr. Mike ROSATO
64 Dean Sch Music/Fine Arts/Extend Ed .... Dr. Robert TUCKER
73 Dean School of Christian Studies .... Dr. Donnie AUVENSHINE
79 Dean School of Humanities .... Dr. Justin MURPHY

Huston-Tillotson University (D)

900 Chicon Street, Austin TX 78702-2795

County: Travis FICE Identification: 003577
Unit ID: 225575
Telephone: (512) 505-3000 Carnegie Class: Bac/A&S
FAX Number: (512) 505-3190 Calendar System: Semester
URL: www.htu.edu
Established: 1875 Annual Undergrad Tuition & Fees: $13,054
Enrollment: 904 Coed
Affiliation or Control: Multiple Protestant Denominations
IRS Status: 501(c)3
Highest Offering: Baccalaureate
Program: Liberal Arts And General
Accreditation: **SC**

01 President & CEO .... Dr. Larry L. EARVIN
04 Executive Assistant to President .... Dr. Terry S. SMITH
05 Provost/VP Academic & Student Affs .... Dr. Vicki V. LOTT
32 Dean of Student Affairs .... Dr. LaTanya LOWERY
30 VP for Institutional Advancement .... Dr. Roderick L. SMOTHERA
10 VP for Administration & Finance .... Mrs. Valerie D. HILL
20 Associate Provost .... Dr. Archibald W. VANDERPUYE
08 Director Library & Media Services .... Ms. Patricia A. WILKINS
36 Director Career & Grad Development .... Mr. Paul LEVERINGTON
41 Director of Athletics .... Vacant
84 Dean Enrollment Management .... Mr. B. Sherrance RUSSELL
06 Registrar .... Mrs. Earnestine J. STRICKLAND
25 Dir Sponsored PRGs/Title III Coord .... Ms. Janice B. SMITH
09 Director Inst Research & Assessment .... Vacant
13 Director Information Technology .... Vacant
26 Dir Communication & Marketing .... Mrs. Linda Y. JACKSON
18 Director of Facilities .... Mr. William S. GRIMES
30 Director of Development/Major Gifts .... Vacant
29 Director of Alumni Affairs .... Ms. LaJuana R. NAPIER
35 Interim Dir Campus Life & FYE .... Ms. Destiny S. THOMPSON
88 Dir of Ctr for Academic Excellence .... Ms. Ericka D. JONES
15 Director of Human Resources .... Ms. Joy S. KING
37 Director Student Financial Aid .... Mr. Antonio HOLLOWAY
38 Dir Counseling & Consultation Ctr .... Dr. Erika GONZALEZ-LIMA
42 University Chaplain .... Rev. Donald E. BREWINGTON
07 Director of Admissions .... Mrs. Shakitha STINSON
49 Interim Dean of Arts & Sciences .... Dr. Michael L. HIRSCH
50 Dean of Business & Technology .... Dr. Steven EDMOND
88 Director of Disability Services .... Mr. James E. TYSON
23 University Nurse .... Vacant

International Academy of Design and Technology (E)

4511 Horizon Hill Boulevard, San Antonio TX 78229

Identification: 666733
Unit ID: 450465
Telephone: (210) 530-9449 Carnegie Class: Assoc/PrivFP
FAX Number: (210) 530-9463 Calendar System: Semester
URL: www.iadtsanantonio.com
Established: N/A Annual Undergrad Tuition & Fees: $11,900
Enrollment: 637 Coed
Affiliation or Control: Proprietary IRS Status: Proprietary
Highest Offering: Baccalaureate
Program: 2-Year Principally Bachelor's Creditable; Fine Arts Emphasis
Accreditation: **ACICS**

01 Campus Director .... Mr. Gilbert DELEON

† Branch campus of International Academy of Design and Technology, Tampa, FL.

ITT Technical Institute (F)

551 Ryan Plaza Drive, Arlington TX 76011-3919

County: Tarrant FICE Identification: 023286
Unit ID: 225849
Telephone: (817) 794-5100 Carnegie Class: Assoc/PrivFP
FAX Number: (817) 275-8446 Calendar System: Quarter
URL: www.itt-tech.edu
Established: 1982 Annual Undergrad Tuition & Fees: N/A
Enrollment: 756 Coed
Affiliation or Control: Proprietary IRS Status: Proprietary
Highest Offering: Baccalaureate
Program: Technical Emphasis
Accreditation: **ACICS**

† Branch campus of ITT Technical Institute, Indianapolis, IN.

ITT Technical Institute (G)

6330 Highway 290 E, Suite 150, Austin TX 78723-1035

County: Travis Identification: 666551
Unit ID: 366678
Telephone: (512) 467-6800 Carnegie Class: Assoc/PrivFP
FAX Number: (512) 467-6677 Calendar System: Quarter
URL: www.itt-tech.edu
Established: 1985 Annual Undergrad Tuition & Fees: N/A
Enrollment: 632 Coed
Affiliation or Control: Proprietary IRS Status: Proprietary
Highest Offering: Baccalaureate
Program: Technical Emphasis
Accreditation: **ACICS**

† Branch campus of ITT Technical Institute, Indianapolis, IN.

ITT Technical Institute (H)

2950 South Gessner, Houston TX 77063-3751

County: Harris FICE Identification: 023287
Unit ID: 225858
Telephone: (713) 952-2294 Carnegie Class: Assoc/PrivFP
FAX Number: (713) 952-2393 Calendar System: Quarter
URL: www.itt-tech.edu
Established: 1983 Annual Undergrad Tuition & Fees: N/A
Enrollment: 630 Coed
Affiliation or Control: Proprietary IRS Status: Proprietary
Highest Offering: Baccalaureate
Program: Technical Emphasis
Accreditation: **ACICS**

† Branch campus of ITT Technical Institute, Indianapolis, IN.

ITT Technical Institute (I)

15651 North Freeway, Houston TX 77090-5903

County: Harris Identification: 666554
Unit ID: 366696
Telephone: (281) 873-0512 Carnegie Class: Assoc/PrivFP
FAX Number: (281) 873-0518 Calendar System: Quarter
URL: www.itt-tech.edu
Established: 1985 Annual Undergrad Tuition & Fees: N/A
Enrollment: 837 Coed
Affiliation or Control: Proprietary IRS Status: Proprietary
Highest Offering: Baccalaureate
Program: Technical Emphasis
Accreditation: **ACICS**

† Branch campus of ITT Technical Institute, Indianapolis, IN.

ITT Technical Institute (J)

2101 Waterview Parkway, Richardson TX 75080-2208

County: Dallas Identification: 666327
Unit ID: 434052
Telephone: (972) 690-9100 Carnegie Class: Assoc/PrivFP
FAX Number: (972) 690-0853 Calendar System: Quarter
URL: www.itt-tech.edu
Established: 2003 Annual Undergrad Tuition & Fees: N/A
Enrollment: 730 Coed
Affiliation or Control: Proprietary IRS Status: Proprietary
Highest Offering: Baccalaureate
Program: Technical Emphasis
Accreditation: **ACICS**

† Branch campus of ITT Technical Institute, Indianapolis, IN.

ITT Technical Institute (K)

5700 Northwest Parkway, San Antonio TX 78249-3303

County: Bexar FICE Identification: 030714
Unit ID: 377069
Telephone: (210) 694-4612 Carnegie Class: Assoc/PrivFP
FAX Number: (210) 694-4651 Calendar System: Quarter
URL: www.itt-tech.edu
Established: 1988 Annual Undergrad Tuition & Fees: N/A
Enrollment: 814 Coed
Affiliation or Control: Proprietary IRS Status: Proprietary
Highest Offering: Baccalaureate
Program: Technical Emphasis
Accreditation: **ACICS**

† Branch campus of ITT Technical Institute, Indianapolis, IN.

ITT Technical Institute (A)

1001 Magnolia Avenue, Webster TX 77598-5418
County: Harris Identification: 666552
Unit ID: 427663
Telephone: (281) 316-4700 Carnegie Class: Assoc/PrivFP
FAX Number: N/A Calendar System: Quarter
URL: www.itt-tech.edu
Established: 1995 Annual Undergrad Tuition & Fees: N/A
Enrollment: 443 Coed
Affiliation or Control: Proprietary IRS Status: Proprietary
Highest Offering: Baccalaureate
Program: Technical Emphasis
Accreditation: **ACICS**

† Branch campus of ITT Technical Institute, Indianapolis, IN.

Jacksonville College (B)

105 B. J. Albritton Drive, Jacksonville TX 75766-4759
County: Cherokee FICE Identification: 003579
Unit ID: 225876
Telephone: (903) 586-2518 Carnegie Class: Assoc/PrivNFP
FAX Number: (903) 586-0743 Calendar System: Semester
URL: www.jacksonville-college.edu
Established: 1899 Annual Undergrad Tuition & Fees: $7,640
Enrollment: 457 Coed
Affiliation or Control: Baptist IRS Status: 501(c)3
Highest Offering: Associate Degree
Program: 2-Year Principally Bachelor's Creditable
Accreditation: **SC**

01 President .... Dr. Mike SMITH
05 Academic Dean/Registrar .... Dr. Tampa J. CLARK
32 Dean of Students .... Mr. Ken RAWSON
10 Business Officer .... Mr. David PITTMAN
41 Athletic Director .... Mr. Lynn NABI

Jarvis Christian College (C)

Highway 80 E, PR 7631, Hawkins TX 75765-1470
County: Wood FICE Identification: 003637
Unit ID: 225885
Telephone: (903) 730-4890 Carnegie Class: Bac/Diverse
FAX Number: (903) 769-4852 Calendar System: Semester
URL: www.jarvis.edu
Established: 1912 Annual Undergrad Tuition & Fees: $11,369
Enrollment: 511 Coed
Affiliation or Control: Christian Church (Disciples Of Christ)
IRS Status: 501(c)3
Highest Offering: Baccalaureate
Program: Liberal Arts And General; Teacher Preparatory
Accreditation: **SC**, ACBSP

01 President .... Dr. Lester C. NEWMAN
05 Provost/Vice Pres Academic Affairs .... Vacant
11 Vice Pres Administration & Finance .... Mr. Reginald DICKENS
32 Vice President Student Affairs .... Vacant
30 Vice Pres Institutional Advancement .... Dr. William SMIALEK
45 Vice Pres for Inst Effectiveness .... Vacant
13 Director Information Technology .... Vacant
06 Registrar .... Mr. Autry ACREY
35 Dean of Students/Dir of Housing .... Mr. William HAMPTON
29 Director of Alumni Affairs .... Mr. Chris WOOTEN
07 Dir Admissions & Enrollment Svcs .... Vacant
26 Director Public Relations/Publicity .... Vacant
19 Chief of Security .... Mr. Reginald DICKENS
04 Exec Asst to the President .... Mrs. Cynthia HOLLMAN-STANCIL
88 Dir TItle III and Sponsored Program .... Vacant
08 Head Librarian .... Mr. Rodney ATKINS
38 Dir Student Dev &Career Services .... Vacant
37 Director of Financial Aid .... Ms. Alice COPELAND
41 Athletic Director .... Mrs. Elissia BURWELL
42 College Pastor .... Mr. Olin FREGIA
18 Physical Plant Director .... Mr. Reginald DICKENS
15 Dir HR/Prof Dev & Compliance .... Mrs. Dorothy LANGLEY
09 Dir Institutional Research .... Vacant
108 Dir Assessment .... Vacant

Kaplan College (D)

12005 Ford Road, Suite 100, Dallas TX 75234
County: Dallas FICE Identification: 032723
Unit ID: 382896
Telephone: (972) 385-1446 Carnegie Class: Assoc/PrivFP
FAX Number: (972) 385-0641 Calendar System: Other
URL: dallas.kaplancollege.com
Established: N/A Annual Undergrad Tuition & Fees: $14,104
Enrollment: 290 Coed
Affiliation or Control: Proprietary IRS Status: Proprietary
Highest Offering: Associate Degree
Program: Occupational; Technical Emphasis
Accreditation: **COE**, @PTAA

01 Campus Director .... Vacant

Kaplan College (E)

8360 Burnham Road, Ste 100, El Paso TX 79907
County: El Paso FICE Identification: 025919
Telephone: (915) 595-1935 Carnegie Class: Not Classified
FAX Number: N/A Calendar System: Other
URL: www.kaplan.edu
Established: N/A Annual Undergrad Tuition & Fees: $15,200
Enrollment: 836 Coed
Affiliation or Control: Proprietary IRS Status: Proprietary
Highest Offering: Associate Degree
Program: Occupational
Accreditation: **ACCSC**, MAC

01 Director of Education .... Ms. Nova PENA

Kaplan College (F)

7142 San Pedro Avenue, Suite 100,
San Antonio TX 78216
County: Bexar FICE Identification: 009466
Unit ID: 364955
Telephone: (210) 733-0777 Carnegie Class: Assoc/PrivFP
FAX Number: (210) 340-6603 Calendar System: Other
URL: nsan-antonio.kaplancollege.com
Established: N/A Annual Undergrad Tuition & Fees: $15,451
Enrollment: 881 Coed
Affiliation or Control: Proprietary IRS Status: Proprietary
Highest Offering: Associate Degree
Program: Occupational; 2-Year Principally Bachelor's Creditable; Technical Emphasis
Accreditation: **ACCSC**, MAC

01 Executive Director .... Rene CANDELARIA

Kaplan College (G)

6441 NW Loop 410, San Antonio TX 78238
County: Bexar FICE Identification: 031158
Telephone: (210) 308-8584 Carnegie Class: Not Classified
FAX Number: (210) 308-8985 Calendar System: Other
URL: www.kaplancollege.com
Established: N/A Annual Undergrad Tuition & Fees: $15,005
Enrollment: 710 Coed
Affiliation or Control: Proprietary IRS Status: Proprietary
Highest Offering: Associate Degree
Program: Occupational
Accreditation: **COE**

01 President .... Ms. Liza RINCONES

KD Studio-Actors Conservatory (H)

2600 N Stemmons Fwy, Suite 117, Dallas TX 75207-2111
County: Dallas FICE Identification: 023182
Unit ID: 225991
Telephone: (214) 638-0484 Carnegie Class: Assoc/PrivFP
FAX Number: (214) 630-5140 Calendar System: Semester
URL: www.kdstudio.com
Established: 1979 Annual Undergrad Tuition & Fees: $13,350
Enrollment: 163 Coed
Affiliation or Control: Proprietary IRS Status: Proprietary
Highest Offering: Associate Degree
Program: Occupational
Accreditation: **THEA**

00 Chief Executive Officer .... Ms. Kathy TYNER
01 President .... Mr. Gary TYNER, JR.
05 Director/CAO .... Mr. T. A TAYLOR

Kilgore College (I)

1100 Broadway, Kilgore TX 75662-3299
County: Gregg FICE Identification: 003580
Unit ID: 226019
Telephone: (903) 984-8531 Carnegie Class: Assoc/Pub-R-M
FAX Number: (903) 983-8600 Calendar System: Semester
URL: www.kilgore.edu
Established: 1935 Annual Undergrad Tuition & Fees (In-District): $1,368
Enrollment: 6,391 Coed
Affiliation or Control: Local IRS Status: 501(c)3
Highest Offering: Associate Degree
Program: Occupational; 2-Year Principally Bachelor's Creditable
Accreditation: **SC**, ADNUR, PTAA, SURGT

01 President .... Dr. William M. HOLDA
05 Vice President of Instruction .... Dr. Gerald M. STANGLIN
11 Vice Pres Administrative Services .... Mr. Duane MCNANEY
32 Vice President Student Development .... Dr. Mike JENKINS
57 Div Dean Liberal & Fine Arts .... Dr. Richard HARRISON
81 Div Dean Science/Math/Health Sci .... Mrs. Louise WILEY
50 Div Dean Business/Tech/Lang Devel/ .... Mr. Randy LEWELLEN
88 Div Dean of Public Services .... Mr. Randy LEWELLEN
72 Dir of Adult Voc Educ .... Ms. Martha WOODRUFF
12 Div Dean of Longview Center .... Dr. Julie H. FOWLER
06 Registrar .... Mrs. Staci MARTIN
15 Director of Human Resources .... Mr. Tony JOHNSON
13 Director of Information Technology .... Mr. John COLVILLE
08 Director Library .... Ms. Kathy FAIR
40 Manager of Bookstore .... Ms. Carolyn WILLIAMS
18 Director Physical Plant .... Mr. Dalton SMITH
19 Chief of Police .... Chief Martin PESSINK
84 Dir of Marketing & Enrollment Mgmt .... Mr. Trey HATTAWAY
04 Assistant to the President .... Mrs. Nancy LAW
30 Director of Development .... Mrs. Leah GORMAN
37 Financial Aid Officer .... Mrs. Annette MORGAN
85 International Student Advisor .... Mrs. Brenda THORNHILL
27 Coordinator of Public & Sports Info .... Mr. Chris CRADDOCK
09 Coord of Institutional Research .... Ms. Robin HUSKEY
36 Coordinator of Career Services .... Ms. Patty BELL
29 Coordinator of Alumni Relations .... Mrs. Paula JAMERSON
38 Coordinator of Counseling .... Mrs. Pam GATTON
96 Purchasing Agent .... Ms. Tammie PASCOE

Laredo Community College (J)

West End Washington Street, Laredo TX 78040-4395
County: Webb FICE Identification: 003582
Unit ID: 226134
Telephone: (956) 722-0521 Carnegie Class: Assoc/Pub-R-L
FAX Number: (956) 721-5381 Calendar System: Semester
URL: www.laredo.edu
Established: 1946 Annual Undergrad Tuition & Fees (In-District): $3,948
Enrollment: 10,076 Coed
Affiliation or Control: Local IRS Status: 501(c)3
Highest Offering: Associate Degree
Program: Occupational; 2-Year Principally Bachelor's Creditable; Technical Emphasis
Accreditation: **#SC**, ADNUR, MLTAD, OTA, PTAA, RAD

01 President .... Dr. Juan L. MALDONADO
05 Vice President for Instruction .... Dr. Dianna L. MILLER
32 Vice President for Student Services .... Dr. Vincent R. SOLIS
25 Vice President for Resource Develop .... Dr. Nora R. GARZA
10 Chief Admin & Financial Officer .... Mr. Eleazar GONZALEZ
88 Institutional Effectiveness Officer .... Dr. Federico SOLIS, JR.
26 Communications & Outreach Officer .... Ms. Deirdre REYNA
49 Dean Arts & Humanities .... Mr. Phil W. WORLEY
12 Dean - LCC South .... Mr. Luciano RAMON
103 Dean of Workforce Education .... Ms. Roxanne VEDIA
81 Dean of Sciences .... Mr. J. Alfredo INIGUEZ-JIMENEZ
35 Dean of Student Affairs .... Mr. Robert L. OCHOA
84 Dean of Enrollment & Reg Services .... Dr. Alberto SALINAS
09 Dir Institutional Research & Plng .... Mrs. Maria Luisa RAMIREZ
08 Director of Library .... Vacant
13 Director Information Technology .... Mr. Jose A. PENA, JR.
21 Comptroller .... Mr. Cesar E. VELA, JR.
18 Director Physical Plant .... Mr. Jacob C. FLORES
26 Dir Marketing/Public Relations .... Mr. Esteban TREVINO, JR.
88 Internal Auditor .... Vacant
37 Director of Financial Aid .... Mr. Steven AGUILAR
07 Director Enrollment & Registration .... Vacant
51 Director of Continuing Education .... Ms. Sandra L. CORTEZ
41 Athletic Director .... Mr. Troy G. VAN BRUNT
06 Registrar .... Ms. Olga D. RUBIO
15 Director of Human Resources .... Mr. Lee SPAIN
102 Dir Donor Relations & Spec Proj .... Ms. Millicent SLAUGHTER
38 Director of Student Success Ctr .... Mr. Carmelino CASTILLO, JR.
96 Director of Purchasing .... Mr. Ramiro V. MARTINEZ
19 Chief of Campus Police .... Mr. Ray CORTEZ
23 Director of Health Services .... Ms. Melissa GARCIA
24 Associate Director of Media Center .... Mr. Ceferino IZAGUIRRE

Le Cordon Bleu College of Culinary Arts in Austin (K)

3110 Esperanza Crossing Suite 100, Austin TX 78758
County: Travis FICE Identification: 025693
Unit ID: 364973
Telephone: (512) 837-2665 Carnegie Class: Assoc/PrivFP
FAX Number: (512) 977-9753 Calendar System: Other
URL: www.chefs.edu/austin
Established: 1981 Annual Undergrad Tuition & Fees: $12,150
Enrollment: 1,037 Coed
Affiliation or Control: Proprietary IRS Status: Proprietary
Highest Offering: Associate Degree
Program: Occupational; Technical Emphasis
Accreditation: **ACICS**, ACFEI

01 President .... Steve SMITH

Le Cordon Bleu College of Culinary Arts in Dallas (L)

11830 Webb Chapel Road, Suite 1200, Dallas TX 75234
Identification: 666728
Unit ID: 452063
Telephone: (214) 647-8505 Carnegie Class: Assoc/PrivFP
FAX Number: (972) 406-9935 Calendar System: Semester
URL: www.chefs.edu/dallas
Established: N/A Annual Undergrad Tuition & Fees: $12,822
Enrollment: 1,256 Coed
Affiliation or Control: Proprietary IRS Status: Proprietary
Highest Offering: Associate Degree
Program: Occupational; 2-Year Principally Bachelor's Creditable
Accreditation: **ACICS**

01 President .... Ms. Maureen K. CLEMENTS

† Branch campus of Le Cordon Bleu College of Culinary Arts, Austin, TX.

Lee College (M)

511 S Whiting, PO Box 818, Baytown TX 77522-0818
County: Harris FICE Identification: 003583
Unit ID: 226204
Telephone: (281) 427-5611 Carnegie Class: Assoc/Pub-S-MC
FAX Number: (281) 425-6555 Calendar System: Semester

URL: www.lee.edu
Established: 1934 Annual Undergrad Tuition & Fees (In-District): $1,470
Enrollment: 6,554 Coed
Affiliation or Control: State/Local IRS Status: 501(c)3
Highest Offering: Associate Degree
Program: Occupational; 2-Year Principally Bachelor's Creditable
Accreditation: SC, ADNUR

01 President .... Dr. Dennis BROWN
101 Admin Asst Pres/Secy to Board .... Vacant
05 VP Instruction .... Dr. Cathy KEMPER
32 VP Student Affairs .... Dr. Donnetta SUCHON
38 Assoc Dean/Dir Counseling Services .... Dr. Rosemary COFFMAN
10 VP Finance & Administration .... Mr. Steve EVANS
21 Executive Dir Accounting .... Mr. Keith SCHEFFLER
12 Dean of Huntsville Center at TDCJ .... Ms. Donna P. ZUNIGA
30 Exec Dir Institutional Advancement .... Ms. Mary Ann AMELANG
14 Exec Dir Tech/Research/Planning .... Dr. Carolyn A. LIGHTFOOT
18 Executive Director Physical Plant .... Mr. Alvin SCHNEIDER
06 Registrar .... Ms. Becki S. GRIFFITH
07 Director College Relations .... Mr. Steve LESTARJETTE
96 Director Purchasing .... Mr. Mike SPARKES
103 Director Continuing Education .... Ms. Jonna CAGLE-PAGE
15 Director Human Resources .... Mrs. Amanda SUMMERS
37 Director Financial Aid .... Mrs. Sharon MULLINS
40 Director Auxiliary Services .... Ms. Suzanne MACHALA
41 Director Athletics .... Mr. Roy CHAMPAGNE
08 Dir Library/Instructional Support .... Mr. Paul ARRIGO
25 Grants Development Officer .... Ms. Pam WARFORD
26 Public Relations Manager .... Mrs. Anikka AYALA-ROGERS
36 Stdnt Career/Employment Specialist .... Mrs. Cindy FLETCHER
29 Director of Alumni Relations .... Mrs. Virgina "Ginni" WHITTEN

LeTourneau University (A)

PO Box 7001, 2100 S Mobberly Ave,
Longview TX 75607-7001
County: Gregg FICE Identification: 003584
Unit ID: 226231
Telephone: (903) 233-3000 Carnegie Class: Master's M
FAX Number: (903) 233-3101 Calendar System: Semester
URL: www.letu.edu
Established: 1946 Annual Undergrad Tuition & Fees: $24,120
Enrollment: 2,950 Coed
Affiliation or Control: Independent Non-Profit IRS Status: 501(c)3
Highest Offering: Master's
Program: Liberal Arts And General; Teacher Preparatory; Professional
Accreditation: SC, ENG, ENGT, IACBE

01 President .... Dr. Dale A. LUNSFORD
05 Provost & Executive Vice President .... Dr. Philip COYLE
30 VP University Development .... Mr. Ben MARCH
10 VP Finance/Administration .... Mr. Mike HOOD
32 Dean of Students .... Mr. Corey ROSS
84 VP Enrollment Services .... Dr. Steve CONDON
58 VP Grad/Professional Studies .... Dr. Carol GREEN
20 Assoc VP Provost Office .... Dr. Steven D. MASON
26 Asst VP Enroll Mgmt/Mkt Research .... Mr. Christopher W. FONTAINE
18 Asst VP of Facilities Services .... Mr. Daniel FIEDLER
53 Dean School of Education .... Dr. Wayne JACOBS
50 Dean School of Business .... Dr. Bob WHARTON
54 Dean Sch Engineering & Engr Tech .... Dr. Ronald DELAP
49 Dean School of Arts & Sciences .... Dr. Larry FRAZIER
88 Dean School of Aeronautical Science .... Mr. Fred L. RITCHEY
35 Assoc Dean Student Life .... Mr. Chad MELTON
44 Assoc VP University Development .... Vacant
08 Director Learning Resource Center .... Vacant
41 Director of Athletics .... Ms. Terri DEIKE
46 Director Office of Sponsored Pgms .... Mr. Paul R. BOGGS
56 Director Distance Lrng .... Vacant
13 Chief Information Officer .... Mr. Matthew HENRY
15 Director of Human Resources .... Mr. Sam PALOMARIA
23 Director Health Services .... Ms. Shela B. DAWSON
42 University Chaplain .... Dr. Harold F. CARL
19 Chief of Police .... Mr. Terrance A. TURNER
36 Director of Career Development .... Mr. Steven J. GATTON
06 University Registrar .... Vacant
07 Director of Admissions .... Vacant
29 Director of Alumni & Parent Rels .... Mrs. Martha STEED
26 Director of Univ Relations .... Ms. Janet RAGLAND
102 Dir of Corp/Foundation Relations .... Mr. Randall YEAKLEY
44 Dir of Gift Planning and Endowed .... Mr. Bryan E. BENSON
12 Director Austin Educational Ctr .... Dr. R. Murlene WATWOOD
12 Director Dallas Educational Center .... Dr. Bonita VINSON
12 Director Houston Education Center .... Dr. R. Murlene WATWOOD
71 Dir Curriculum/Academic Resources .... Vacant
21 Controller .... Ms. Vikki KEILERS
09 Sr Dir Inst Effective/Retention .... Dr. Pamela JOHNSON
88 Asst to the President for Outreach .... Dr. Tim WATSON
96 Purchasing Agent .... Mrs. Jana CAMPBELL
88 Executive Dir Ctr for Faith & Work .... Mr. Bill PEEL

Lighthouse College (B)

9400 North Central Expwy., Ste. 200, Dallas TX 75231
County: Dallas Identification: 667106
Telephone: (214) 368-3680 Carnegie Class: Not Classified
FAX Number: (214) 368-3682 Calendar System: Other
URL: www.lhc.edu
Established: N/A Annual Undergrad Tuition & Fees: $13,450
Enrollment: N/A Coed
Affiliation or Control: Proprietary IRS Status: Proprietary
Highest Offering: Associate Degree
Program: Occupational
Accreditation: ACICS

Lincoln College of Technology (C)

2915 Alouette Drive, Grand Praire TX 75052
County: Tarrant FICE Identification: 008353
Unit ID: 226277
Telephone: (972) 660-5701 Carnegie Class: Assoc/PrivFP
FAX Number: (972) 660-6148 Calendar System: Other
URL: www.lincolntech.com
Established: N/A Annual Undergrad Tuition & Fees: $23,189
Enrollment: 1,033 Coed
Affiliation or Control: Proprietary IRS Status: Proprietary
Highest Offering: Associate Degree
Program: Occupational
Accreditation: ACCSC

01 Executive Director .... Mr. Paul MCGURIK

Lon Morris College (D)

800 College Avenue, Jacksonville TX 75766-2900
County: Cherokee FICE Identification: 003585
Unit ID: 226329
Telephone: (903) 589-4000 Carnegie Class: Assoc/PrivNFP
FAX Number: (903) 586-8562 Calendar System: Semester
URL: www.lonmorris.edu
Established: 1873 Annual Undergrad Tuition & Fees: $14,790
Enrollment: 609 Coed
Affiliation or Control: United Methodist IRS Status: 501(c)3
Highest Offering: Associate Degree
Program: 2-Year Principally Bachelor's Creditable; Business Emphasis
Accreditation: SC

01 President .... Dr. Miles L. MCCALL
10 Vice Pres Business Admin Affairs .... Mr. Tommy FERGUSON
05 Provost .... Dr. Loretta GALLEGOS
06 Academic Dean/Registrar .... Dr. John ROSS
32 Dean of Students .... Mr. David HUBBARD
37 Director Financial Aid .... Ms. Kayla CHRISTIANSEN
07 Director Admissions .... Mr. Lance LEISSNER
08 Librarian .... Ms. Linda GRAY
35 Director of Campus Life .... Mr. David GEHRELS
09 Director of Institutional Research .... Dr. Danny POTTER
15 Director Human Resources .... Ms. Carolyn NANNI
41 Athletic Director .... Mr. Dale DOTSON
42 Chaplain .... Rev. Rhett ANSLEY

† Fall 2012 semester suspended. Southern Association Colleges and Schools will review accreditation December 2012.

Lone Star College System (E)

5000 Research Forest Drive,
The Woodlands TX 77381-4356
County: Harris FICE Identification: 011145
Unit ID: 227182
Telephone: (832) 813-6500 Carnegie Class: Assoc/Pub-S-MC
FAX Number: N/A Calendar System: Semester
URL: www.lonestar.edu
Established: 1972 Annual Undergrad Tuition & Fees (In-District): $1,600
Enrollment: 75,680 Coed
Affiliation or Control: State/Local IRS Status: 501(c)3
Highest Offering: Associate Degree
Program: Occupational; 2-Year Principally Bachelor's Creditable
Accreditation: SC, ADNUR, CEA, DH, DMS, EMT, MAC, OTA, PTAA, RAD, SURGT

01 Chancellor .... Dr. Richard CARPENTER
03 Senior Executive Vice Chancellor .... Dr. Rand KEY
05 Interim Vice Chanc Acad Affairs .... Dr. Keri ROGERS
32 Interim Vice Chanc Student Success .... Ms. Juanita CHRYSANTHOU
10 Vice Chanc for Admin & Finance .... Ms. Cynthia GILLIAM
27 Interim Vice Chanc Info Technology .... Mr. Link ALANDER
26 Vice Chancellor External Affairs .... Mr. Ray LAUGHTER
43 General Counsel .... Mr. Brian NELSON
101 Special Asst to Chancellor/Board .... Ms. Helen CLOUGHERTY
12 President of LSC-Kingwood .... Dr. Katherine PERSSON
12 President of LSC-Tomball .... Dr. Susan KARR
12 President of LSC-North Harris .... Dr. Steve HEAD
12 President of LSC-Montgomery .... Dr. Austin LANE
12 President of LSC-CyFair .... Dr. Audre LEVY
12 Chief Exec Officer LSC-Univ Park .... Mr. Shah ARDALAN
27 AVC Marketing & Comm .... Ms. Laura MORRIS
18 AVC Construction/Facilities .... Mr. Jimmy MARTIN
28 Exec Dir Employmnt Svcs & Diversity .... Vacant
15 Sys Dir Compensatn/Records/Benefits .... Ms. Lisa COWART
105 Exec Director Portal Services .... Ms. Jennifer MURILLO
21 AVC Admin & Finance .... Ms. Tammy CORTES
21 AVC Business Services .... Ms. Carin HUTCHINS
21 AVC Accounting .... Ms. Diane NOVAK
16 Assoc Gen Counsel Human Resources .... Ms. Anne ZEMEK
106 Exec Director/LSC-Online .... Mr. Marwin BRITTO
103 AVC Workforce & Econ Dev .... Ms. Linda HEAD
86 AVC Govt Affairs & Stdnt Completion .... Mr. Jonathan DURFIELD
09 AVC Ofc Research/Inst Effectiveness .... Dr. Siobhan FLEMING
13 Assoc VC Office Tech Services .... Vacant
08 Director Library/LSC-Kingwood .... Vacant
08 Director Library/LSC-Tomball .... Ms. Pamela SHAFER
08 Director Library/LSC-North Harris .... Ms. Pradeep LELE
08 Director Library/LSC-Cy Fair .... Mr. Michael STAFFORD
08 Director Library/LSC-Montgomery .... Dr. Janice PEYTON
08 Director Library/LSC-Univ Park .... Vacant
37 System Exec Dir Financial Aid .... Ms. Carolyn WADE
21 Director Internal Audit .... Ms. Donna HYPOLITE
19 Chief of Police/Dir Pub Safety .... Mr. Richard GREGORY
96 Director of Purchasing .... Ms. Laura RIVERA

Lubbock Christian University (F)

5601 19th Street, Lubbock TX 79407-2099
County: Lubbock FICE Identification: 003586
Unit ID: 226383
Telephone: (806) 796-8800 Carnegie Class: Master's S
FAX Number: (806) 720-7255 Calendar System: Semester
URL: www.lcu.edu
Established: 1957 Annual Undergrad Tuition & Fees: $17,760
Enrollment: 2,038 Coed
Affiliation or Control: Churches Of Christ IRS Status: 501(c)3
Highest Offering: Master's
Program: Liberal Arts And General; Teacher Preparatory; Professional
Accreditation: SC, NUR, SW

01 President .... Mr. L. Timothy PERRIN
03 Executive Vice President .... Dr. Brian STARR
05 Provost & Chief Academic Officer .... Dr. Rodney B. BLACKWOOD
43 General Counsel .... Mrs. Monica BARNARD
26 Vice President University Relations .... Mr. John C. KING
10 Vice Pres for Financial Services .... Mrs. Tia CLARY
13 Vice President for Technology .... Dr. Karl MAHAN
107 Dean Col of Professional Studies .... Dr. Gary ESTEP
49 Dean College Liberal Arts/Education .... Dr. Susan BLASSINGAME
73 Dean Col Biblical Stds/Behavior Sci .... Dr. Jesse LONG
09 Asst VP for Instl Effectiveness .... Mr. Randy SELLERS
41 Athletic Director .... Mr. Paul HISE
06 Registrar .... Mrs. Janice STONE
37 Director of Financial Assistance .... Mrs. Amy HARDESTY
35 Dean of Students .... Mr. Josh STEPHENS
08 Director of Library Services .... Ms. Rebecca J. VICKERS
18 Director of Campus Facilities .... Mr. Mike SELLECK
38 Director Student Counseling .... Ms. Janelle M. BUCHANAN
92 Director of Honors Program .... Dr. Stacy PATTY
23 Director of Medical Clinic .... Dr. Jeff SMITH
13 Director of Technology Services .... Mr. Robert SMITH
88 Director of Disability Services .... Mrs. Elizabeth JACKSON
39 Director of Residental Life .... Mrs. Sunny PARK
07 Director of Admissions .... Mr. Charlie WEBB
15 Human Resources Director .... Mrs. Brenda LOWE
29 Director Alumni Relations .... Dr. Matt PADEN
19 Director of Security .... Mr. Michael SMITH
40 Bookstore Manager .... Mrs. Denise MCNEILL

McLennan Community College (G)

1400 College Drive, Waco TX 76708-1498
County: McLennan FICE Identification: 003590
Unit ID: 226578
Telephone: (254) 299-8000 Carnegie Class: Assoc/Pub-R-L
FAX Number: (254) 299-8654 Calendar System: Semester
URL: www.mclennan.edu
Established: 1965 Annual Undergrad Tuition & Fees (In-District): $2,568
Enrollment: 10,185 Coed
Affiliation or Control: State/Local IRS Status: 501(c)3
Highest Offering: Associate Degree
Program: Occupational; 2-Year Principally Bachelor's Creditable; Nursing Emphasis
Accreditation: SC, ADNUR, MLTAD, NDT, PTAA, RAD, SURGT

01 President .... Dr. Johnette MCKOWN
10 Vice Pres Finance & Administration .... Mr. Gene GOOCH
05 Vice President Instruction .... Dr. Donald BALMOS
46 Vice President Program Development .... Mr. Al POLLARD
32 Vice President Student Services .... Dr. Drew CANHAM
09 Vice Pres Research/Plng & Info Tech .... Dr. Paul ILLICH
102 Exec Director McLennan CC Found .... Mr. Harry HARELIK
11 Director of Administrative Services .... Ms. Lori SOUTHERN
37 Director of Financial Aid .... Mr. James KUBACAK
26 Director Community Relations .... Ms. Lisa WILHELMI
41 Director Athletics .... Mrs. Shawn TROCHIM
06 Director Records & Registration .... Mr. Herman V. TUCKER
07 Director Admissions & Recruitment .... Mrs. Karen CLARK
08 Director Library Services .... Mr. Daniel MARTINSEN
15 Director Human Resources .... Mrs. Phyllis BLACKWOOD
18 Director Physical Plant .... Mrs. Dianne E. FEYERHERM
21 Director Financial Services .... Mrs. Terry LECHLER
103 Dean of Workforce Education .... Dr. Ronald EPPS
49 Dean of Arts & Sciences .... Dr. Fred HILLS
51 Dean of Continuing Education .... Mr. Frank GRAVES

McMurry University (H)

1400 Sayles Boulevard, Abilene TX 79697-0002
County: Taylor FICE Identification: 003591
Unit ID: 226587
Telephone: (325) 793-3800 Carnegie Class: Bac/Diverse
FAX Number: (325) 793-6800 Calendar System: Semester
URL: www.mcm.edu
Established: 1923 Annual Undergrad Tuition & Fees: $23,305
Enrollment: 1,469 Coed
Affiliation or Control: United Methodist IRS Status: 501(c)3
Highest Offering: Master's
Program: Liberal Arts And General; Teacher Preparatory

Accreditation: **SC**, NURSE

01 President .... Dr. John H. RUSSELL
05 Vice President for Academic Affairs .... Dr. Paul FABRIZIO
10 Vice Pres for Financial Affairs .... Mrs. Lisa L. WILLIAMS
30 Vice Pres for Development .... Ms. Debra HULSE
26 Vice President Marketing Services .... Mr. Steve CRISMAN
11 Vice Pres for Info & Support Svcs .... Mr. Brad POORMAN
105 Webmaster .... Mr. Jim QUINNETT
14 Customer Service Director .... Mr. Freddie FAMBLE, JR.
13 Director of Administrative Systems .... Ms. Kathy DENSLOW
06 Registrar .... Mrs. Carolyn A. CALVERT
08 Director Jay-Rollins Library .... Ms. Terry YOUNG
24 Director of Media Center .... Mr. David WILLIAMS
32 Dean of Students .... Ms. Vanessa ROBERTS
81 Dean Sch Natural/Computational Sci .... Dr. Alicia WYATT
83 Dean Sch Social Sciences/Religion .... Dr. Phil LEMASTERS
57 Dean School of Arts & Letters .... Dr. Christina WILSON
50 Dean School of Business .... Dr. K. O. LONG
53 Dean School of Education .... Dr. Perry Kay HALEY-BROWN
66 Dean School of Nursing .... Dr. Nina OUIMETTE
07 Director of Admission .... Mr. Jon CROOK
35 Dir Student Activities/Orientation .... Ms. Megan BALDREE
37 Director of Financial Aid .... Mrs. Rachel ATKINS
18 Director Physical Plant .... Mr. John HARVEY
21 Controller .... Mrs. Carole RICKETTS
15 Director of Human Resources .... Ms. Lecia HUGHES
108 Dir of Institutional Effectiveness .... Dr. Thomas BENOIT
09 Director of Institutional Research .... Ms. Terry NIXON
29 Director Alumni/Church Relations .... Mr. Joshua POORMAN
36 Director of Counseling/Career Svcs .... Mr. James GREER
38 Director Counseling & Career Svcs .... Mr. James GREER
41 Athletic Director .... Mr. Ron HOLMES
42 University Chaplain .... Rev. Tim KENNEDY
19 Director of Security/Safety .... Mr. Mark R. ODOM
23 Dir of Health Services & Univ Nurse .... Ms. Ronda HOELSCHER
39 Director of Residence Life .... Mr. Jason FELTZ
102 Exec Dir Alumni Dev & Major Gifts .... Mr. Clark WILLIAMS
92 Director Honors Program .... Dr. Philip LE MASTERS
106 Online Ed Design Support Specialist .... Ms. Vicki DUNNAM

Midland College (A)

3600 N Garfield, Midland TX 79705-6397
County: Midland FICE Identification: 009797
Unit ID: 226806
Telephone: (432) 685-4500 Carnegie Class: Assoc/Pub4
FAX Number: (432) 685-4714 Calendar System: Semester
URL: www.midland.edu
Established: 1969 Annual Undergrad Tuition & Fees (In-District): $2,490
Enrollment: 6,067 Coed
Affiliation or Control: Local IRS Status: 501(c)3
Highest Offering: Baccalaureate
Program: Occupational; 2-Year Principally Bachelor's Creditable
Accreditation: **SC**, ADNUR, DMS

01 President .... Dr. Steve THOMAS
03 Executive Vice President .... Dr. Richard C. JOLLY
05 Vice President of Instruction .... Dr. Rex PEEBLES
10 Vice Pres Administrative Services .... Mr. Rick BENDER
32 Vice President Student Services .... Ms. Rita Nell DIFFIE
13 Vice Pres Information Techonology .... Mr. Dennis SEVER
20 Assoc Vice Pres of Instruction .... Dr. Deana M. SAVAGE
20 Assoc Vice Pres of Instruction .... Dr. Stan G. JACOBS
101 Asst to President/Sec to Board .... Mrs. Bahola EDWARDS
106 Dean of Distance Learning .... Mr. Dale BEIKIRCH
50 Dean of Business Studies .... Mr. Gavin FRANTZ
57 Dean of Fine Arts/Communication .... Mr. Billy FEELER
72 Dean of Applied Technology .... Mr. Curt PERVIER
76 Dean of Health Sciences .... Dr. Becky HAMMACK
81 Dean of Natural Sciences .... Dr. Margaret WADE
83 Dean Social & Behavioral Sciences .... Dr. William MORRIS
06 Registrar .... Mrs. Angela BALCH
08 Head Librarian .... Mr. John DEATS
30 Exec Dir Inst Advancement/Col Fndn .... Ms. Erin C. TRESNER
15 Director of Human Services .... Ms. Zaira VALERIANO
18 Director Physical Plant .... Mr. Ken RILEY
19 Director Security .... Vacant
27 Dean of Public Information .... Ms. Rebecca BELL
35 Director Student Affairs .... Vacant
40 Director Bookstore .... Vacant
41 Athletic Director .... Mr. Forrest ALLEN
09 Dir Institutional Effect/Planning .... Mr. Thomas CORLL
36 Director Student Placement .... Vacant
37 Director Student Financial Aid .... Ms. Yolanda RAMOS
96 Purchasing Agent .... Ms. Barbara FENNELL
84 Dean of Enrollment Management .... Dr. Michael CHAVEZ
07 Director of Admissions/Recruitment .... Mr. Jeremy MARTINEZ

Midwestern State University (B)

3410 Taft Boulevard, Wichita Falls TX 76308-2095
County: Wichita FICE Identification: 003592
Unit ID: 226833
Telephone: (940) 397-4000 Carnegie Class: Master's M
FAX Number: (940) 397-4042 Calendar System: Semester
URL: www.mwsu.edu
Established: 1922 Annual Undergrad Tuition & Fees (In-State): $6,910
Enrollment: 6,181 Coed
Affiliation or Control: State IRS Status: 501(c)3
Highest Offering: Master's
Program: Liberal Arts And General; Teacher Preparatory; Professional
Accreditation: **SC**, ART, BUS, DH, ENG, ENGT, MUS, NURSE, RAD, SW, TED

01 President .... Dr. Jesse W. ROGERS
05 Provost .... Dr. Betty STEWART
46 VP Inst Effectiveness .... Dr. Robert E. CLARK
10 VP Business Affairs & Finance .... Dr. Marilyn FOWLE
30 VP Univ Advncmnt & Stdnt Affairs .... Dr. Howard M. FARRELL
32 VP Student Affairs/Enrollment Mgmt .... Dr. Keith LAMB
18 Assoc VP Facilities Services .... Mr. Kyle OWEN
35 Dean of Students .... Mr. Dail NEELY
14 Director Information Systems .... Mr. Michael DYE
06 Registrar .... Ms. Darla INGLISH
08 University Librarian .... Dr. Clara LATHAM
37 Director of Student Financial Aid .... Ms. Kathy PENNARTZ
38 Director of Counseling Center .... Dr. Pam MIDGETT
51 Director of Extended Education .... Dr. Pamela MORGAN
07 Director of Admissions .... Ms. Barbara MERKLE
19 Chief of Police .... Mr. Dan WILLIAMS
27 Director Public Info/Marketing .... Ms. Julie GAYNOR
30 Dir Donor Services and Scholarships .... Ms. Laura PETERSON
36 Director Career Management Center .... Mr. Dirk WELCH
41 Director of Athletics .... Mr. Charles CARR
15 Director of Human Resources .... Ms. Dianne WEAKLEY
09 Director Inst Research & Planning .... Mr. Mark MCCLENDON
21 Controller .... Ms. Gail FERGUSON
23 Director Vinson Health Center .... Vacant
58 Int Dean of Graduate School .... Dr. Jane OWEN
50 Dean College Business Admin .... Dr. Terry PATTON
53 Dean College of Education .... Dr. Matthew CAPPS
57 Dean College of Fine Arts .... Dr. Ron FISCHLI
76 Int Dean Col Health Sci/Human Svcs .... Dr. James JOHNSTON
79 Dean College Humanities/Social Sci .... Dr. Samuel E. WATSON, III
81 Dean College of Science & Math .... Dr. Lynn LITTLE
86 Director Board & Govt Relations .... Ms. Deborah L. BARROW
29 Director of Alumni Relations .... Ms. Leslee PONDER
88 Director of Academic Success Center .... Ms. Naoma CLARK
105 Webmaster .... Mr. Robert STEFLIK
96 Director of Purchasing .... Mr. Stephen SHELLEY
88 Dir Disability Support Services .... Ms. Debra HIGGINBOTHAM
88 Dir Student Development/Orientation .... Mr. Matthew PARK
39 Director Housing & Residence Life .... Mr. Michael MILLS
30 Director University Development .... Mr. Steve SHIPP
85 Director of International Education .... Vacant
88 Director Testing Center .... Ms. Lynn DUCIOAME
88 Director International Services .... Dr. Randy GLEAN
88 Director Budget & Management .... Ms. Valarie MAXWELL
88 Director Museum .... Mrs. Frances CARRARO
88 Director Student Support Services .... Ms. Lisa ESTRADA-HAMBY
88 Campus Postal Supervisor .... Ms. Cindy LOVELESS
92 Coordinator Honors Program .... Mrs. Juliana LEHMAN-FELTS

Navarro College (C)

3200 W Seventh Avenue, Corsicana TX 75110-4899
County: Navarro FICE Identification: 003593
Unit ID: 227146
Telephone: (903) 874-6501 Carnegie Class: Assoc/Pub-R-L
FAX Number: (903) 874-4636 Calendar System: Semester
URL: www.navarrocollege.edu
Established: 1946 Annual Undergrad Tuition & Fees (In-District): $1,386
Enrollment: 10,433 Coed
Affiliation or Control: Local IRS Status: 501(c)3
Highest Offering: Associate Degree
Program: Occupational; 2-Year Principally Bachelor's Creditable
Accreditation: **SC**, ADNUR, MLTAD, OTA

01 District President .... Dr. Richard M. SANCHEZ
12 President Ellis Co Campuses .... Dr. Kenneth MARTIN
05 Vice President Academic Affairs .... Dr. Harold HOUSLEY
10 Vice President Finance & Admin .... Ms. Gertrud MORENO
30 Vice Pres Institutional Advancement .... Dr. Tommy STRINGER
32 Vice President Student Services .... Ms. Maryann HAILEY
84 VP Enroll Mgmt/Stdnt Succ/Inst Stds .... Mr. T. Dewayne GRAGG
15 Director Human Resources .... Ms. Marcy BALLEW
26 Director Marketing Relations .... Mr. Matthew CATES
41 Athletic Director .... Mr. Roark MONTGOMERY
49 Dean of Arts/Sciences/Humanities .... Dr. Larry WEAVER
50 Dean of Business/Prof & Tech Educ .... Ms. Judy CUTTING
12 Dean of Midlothian Campus .... Mr. Guy FEATHERSTON
12 Dean of Mexia Campus .... Ms. Linda DAVIS
21 Comptroller .... Mr. Aaron YORK
51 Director Continuing Education .... Ms. Kristin WALKER
08 Director of Libraries .... Mr. Tim KEVIL
06 Registrar .... Mr. David EDWARDS
18 Chief Facilities/Physical Plant .... Mr. Karl HUMPHRIES
14 Director of Computer Center .... Ms. Dana HOLLAND
37 Director Student Financial Aid .... Ms. Kristal NICHOLSON
35 Director Student Affairs .... Mr. Phil W. SIMS
40 College Store Coordinator .... Ms. Nancy JOHNSON

North American College (D)

3203 North Sam Houston Pkwy West, Houston TX 77038
County: Harris FICE Identification: 041795
Unit ID: 461795
Telephone: (832) 230-5555 Carnegie Class: Not Classified
FAX Number: (832) 230-5546 Calendar System: Semester
URL: www.northamerican.edu
Established: N/A Annual Undergrad Tuition & Fees: $10,950
Enrollment: 169 Coed
Affiliation or Control: Independent Non-Profit IRS Status: 501(c)3
Highest Offering: Baccalaureate
Program: Occupational
Accreditation: **ACICS**

01 President .... Dr. Yuksel A. ASLANDOGON
11 Vice Pres Administrative Affairs .... Dr. John C. TOPUZ
05 Vice Pres Academic Affairs .... Dr. Coskun CETINKAYA

North Central Texas College (E)

1525 W California Street, Gainesville TX 76240-4699
County: Cooke FICE Identification: 003558
Unit ID: 224110
Telephone: (940) 668-7731 Carnegie Class: Assoc/Pub-R-L
FAX Number: (940) 668-6049 Calendar System: Semester
URL: www.nctc.edu
Established: 1924 Annual Undergrad Tuition & Fees (In-District): $1,530
Enrollment: 9,945 Coed
Affiliation or Control: State/Local IRS Status: 501(c)3
Highest Offering: Associate Degree
Program: Occupational; 2-Year Principally Bachelor's Creditable
Accreditation: **SC**, ADNUR, SURGT

01 President .... Dr. Eddie L. HADLOCK
05 Vice President of Instruction .... Dr. Brent WALLACE
32 Vice President of Student Services .... Dr. Billy ROESSLER
11 Dean of Administrative Services .... Dr. Stephen BROYLES
10 Vice President Financial Services .... Dr. Janie NEIGHBORS
30 Vice Pres Institutional Advancement .... Ms. Debbie SHARP
12 Dean of Denton County Campuses .... Mr. Roy CULBERSON
18 Sr Dir of Campus Operations .... Mr. Robbie BAUGH
12 Dean of Bowie & Graham Campuses .... Dr. Emily KLEMENT
09 Dir Inst Research & Effectiveness .... Mr. David BROWN
06 Registrar/Director of Admission .... Ms. Kari FORD
08 Librarian .... Ms. Diane ROETHER
37 Financial Aid Director .... Ms. Ashley TATUM
38 Director of Advisement .... Mrs. Tracey FLENIKEN
26 Dir Marketing and Public Relations .... Mrs. Dianne WALTERSCHEID
41 Athletic Director .... Mr. Van HEDRICK
66 Dean of Nursing Program .... Mrs. Gie ARCHER
32 Director of Student Life .... Ms. Kim BROWN
72 Dean of Instruction Gainesville .... Mrs. Debbie HUFFMAN
49 Dean of Instruction Corinth .... Dr. Larry GILBERT
49 Dean of Instruction Flower Mound .... Mrs. Sara ALFORD

Northeast Texas Community College (F)

PO Box 1307, Mount Pleasant TX 75456-1307
County: Titus FICE Identification: 023154
Unit ID: 227225
Telephone: (903) 434-8100 Carnegie Class: Assoc/Pub-R-M
FAX Number: (903) 572-6712 Calendar System: Semester
URL: www.ntcc.edu
Established: 1984 Annual Undergrad Tuition & Fees (In-District): $1,740
Enrollment: 3,324 Coed
Affiliation or Control: Local IRS Status: 501(c)3
Highest Offering: Associate Degree
Program: Occupational; 2-Year Principally Bachelor's Creditable; Teacher Preparatory
Accreditation: **SC**, DH, MAC, MLTAD, PTAA

01 President .... Dr. Brad W. JOHNSON
04 Executive Asst to the President .... Ms. Pat L. TALLANT
05 Executive Vice Pres for Instruction .... Dr. Ron CLINTON
11 Vice Pres Administrative Services .... Ms. Beth THOMPSON
30 Vice Pres Institutional Advancement .... Dr. Jonathan W. MCCULLOUGH
32 VP for Student & Outreach Services .... Dr. Judy G. TRAYLOR
103 Assoc VP for Workforce Development .... Mr. Kevin ROSE
37 Dean Enroll/Dir Student Fin Assist .... Ms. Kim LAWRENCE
76 Dean of Allied Health Professions .... Dr. Jena HAMRA
84 Associate Dean of Outreach Services .... Ms. Melody HENRY
18 Director of Plant Services .... Mr. Tim JOHNSTON
51 Director of Continuing Education .... Ms. Teresa WOOTEN
08 Director Learning Resource Center .... Mr. Ron BOWDEN
91 Director of Computer Services .... Mr. Kenneth GOODSON
26 Director Marketing/Public Relations .... Ms. Jodi WEBER
06 Registrar .... Ms. Betsy GOODING
15 Director Human Resources .... Ms. Diana HALL
10 Controller .... Ms. Jaci M. MERRITT
09 Dir Institutional Effectiveness .... Ms. Toni LABEFF
88 Advisor/Retention Specialist .... Mr. Miles YOUNG
36 Career Development/Advisor .... Ms. Lynda WATSON

Oblate School of Theology (G)

285 Oblate Drive, San Antonio TX 78216-6693
County: Bexar FICE Identification: 003595
Unit ID: 227289
Telephone: (210) 341-1366 Carnegie Class: Spec/Faith
FAX Number: (210) 341-4519 Calendar System: Semester
URL: www.ost.edu
Established: 1903 Annual Graduate Tuition & Fees: $13,385
Enrollment: 127 Coed
Affiliation or Control: Roman Catholic IRS Status: 501(c)3
Highest Offering: Doctorate; No Undergraduates
Program: Professional; Religious Emphasis
Accreditation: **SC**, THEOL

01 President .... Rev. Ronald ROLHEISER
05 Vice Pres Academic Affairs/Dean .... Dr. Scott WOODWARD
10 Vice Pres Finance/Human Resources .... Mr. Rene ESPINOSA
11 Vice Pres Administrative Affairs .... Rev. David KALERT

30 Vice Pres Institutional Advancement .... Mrs. Lea KOCHANEK
20 Associate Dean .... Sr. Linda GIBLER
88 Director Oblate Renewal Center .... Mr. Brian WALLACE
18 Director of Physical Plant .... Mr. Morris LIM
08 Director of the Library .... Ms. Maria GARCÍA
06 Registrar & Director of Admissions .... Mr. Mario PORTER
51 Assoc Dean of Continuing Educ .... Mrs. Rose MARDEN
88 Director Lay Ministry Institute .... Mrs. Bonnie ABADIE
88 Director Ministry to Ministers Pgm .... Rev. Vincent LOUWAGIE
09 Dir Instl Research/Plng/Assessment .... Rev. David KALERT
88 Director DMin Program .... Rev. John MARKEY

Odessa College (A)

201 W University Boulevard, Odessa TX 79764-7127
County: Ector FICE Identification: 003596
Unit ID: 227304
Telephone: (432) 335-6400 Carnegie Class: Assoc/Pub-R-M
FAX Number: (432) 335-6860 Calendar System: Semester
URL: www.odessa.edu
Established: 1946 Annual Undergrad Tuition & Fees (In-District): $2,400
Enrollment: 5,112 Coed
Affiliation or Control: Local IRS Status: 501(c)3
Highest Offering: Associate Degree
Program: Occupational; 2-Year Principally Bachelor's Creditable
Accreditation: SC, ADNUR, MUS, PTAA, RAD

01 President .... Dr. Gregory D. WILLIAMS
05 Vice President for Instruction .... Dr. Ken TUNSTALL
10 Vice President Business Affairs .... Ms. Virginia E. CHISUM
32 Interim VP for Student Services .... Dr. Tanya G. HUGHES
100 Chief of Staff .... Dr. Tanya G. HUGHES
09 VP for Institutional Effectiveness .... Dr. Donald WOOD
30 Exec Dir of Resource Development .... Vacant
11 Exec Dir of Administration & HR .... Mr. Ken ZARTERN
75 Dean of Career/Tech & Wrkforce Educ .... Mr. Ian ROARK
49 Dean of Arts & Sciences .... Ms. Kathryn KEEN
84 Exec Director of Enrollment Mgmt .... Mr. Trey WETENDORF
06 Registrar .... Ms. Rebecca BEARD
41 Director Intercollegiate Athletics .... Mr. Wayne BAKER
37 Director Student Financial Svcs .... Ms. Dee NESMITH
18 Director Facilities & Construction .... Mr. Bryan HEIFNER
26 Dir Media Relations/Publications .... Ms. Cheri DALTON
38 Director Counseling/Recruiting .... Mr. Trey WETENDORF
96 Dir of Purchasing/Business Services .... Ms. Cindy CURNUTT

Our Lady of the Lake University (B)

411 SW 24th Street, San Antonio TX 78207-4689
County: Bexar FICE Identification: 003598
Unit ID: 227331
Telephone: (210) 434-6711 Carnegie Class: DRU
FAX Number: (210) 431-3928 Calendar System: Semester
URL: www.ollusa.edu
Established: 1895 Annual Undergrad Tuition & Fees: $23,588
Enrollment: 2,614 Coed
Affiliation or Control: Roman Catholic IRS Status: 501(c)3
Highest Offering: Doctorate
Program: Liberal Arts And General; Teacher Preparatory
Accreditation: SC, ACBSP, COPSY, SP, SW

01 President .... Dr. Tessa M. POLLACK
03 Executive Vice President .... Dr. David C. ESTES
05 Vice President for Academic Affairs .... Dr. Helen J. STREUBERT
32 Vice President of Student Life .... Mr. Jack L. HANK
10 Vice President Finance & Facilities .... Mr. Allen R. KLAUS
30 Vice Pres Institutional Advancement .... Mr. Daniel YOXALL
84 Vice Pres of Enrollment Management .... Mr. Michael E. ACOSTA
26 Vice Pres Communications/Marketing .... Mr. Daniel YOXALL
42 Vice President of Mission/Ministry .... Ms. Gloria URRABAZO
13 Chief Technology Officer .... Mr. Joseph G. DECK
35 Asst Vice Pres Student Life .... Ms. Mary F. SCOTKA
100 Chief of Staff to the President .... Ms. Susan SCHLEICHER
04 Exec Asst to President/Govt Rels .... Mrs. Susan A. SCHLEICHER
44 Exec Director Inst Advancement .... Ms. Paula PARISH
18 Director Physical Plant .... Mr. Darrell R. GLASSCOCK
15 Director Human Resources .... Mr. Phillip VARGAS
06 Registrar .... Mrs. Norma J. ANDERSON
14 Director Network & Telecomm .... Mr. David LYTLE
45 Dir Institutional/Effectiveness .... Dr. Lei WANG
19 Chief of Police/Dir Campus Safety .... Mr. David JUAREZ
39 Director Residence Life .... Mr. Mark R. CENTER
36 Director Career Counsel/Placement .... Ms. Rhonda J. BOYLES
38 Director of Counseling Services .... Dr. Rosa ESPINOSA
23 Director Student Health Services .... Ms. Julie STUCKEY
40 Director Bookstore .... Mr. Edward CROCE
102 Corporate Relations Officer .... Ms. Roxanne SANCHEZ
46 Director of Advancement Services .... Mr. John SANCHEZ
30 Dir of Stewardship/Constituent Rels .... Ms. Asia CIARAVINO
37 Director of Financial Aid .... Ms. Karla VARGAS
29 Asst Dir Stewrdshp/Constituent Rels .... Ms. Alexandra GARCIA
88 Asst Dir of Advancement Services .... Ms. Cyndi CAVAZOS

Panola College (C)

1109 West Panola Street, Carthage TX 75633-2397
County: Panola FICE Identification: 003600
Unit ID: 227386
Telephone: (903) 693-2000 Carnegie Class: Assoc/Pub-R-M
FAX Number: (903) 693-5588 Calendar System: Semester
URL: www.panola.edu
Established: 1947 Annual Undergrad Tuition & Fees (In-District): $2,010
Enrollment: 2,561 Coed
Affiliation or Control: Local IRS Status: 501(c)3
Highest Offering: Associate Degree
Program: Occupational; 2-Year Principally Bachelor's Creditable
Accreditation: SC, ADNUR, OTA

01 President .... Dr. Gregory S. POWELL
05 Vice President of Instruction .... Dr. Joe SHANNON
32 Vice President of Student Services .... Mr. Don CLINTON
10 Vice President of Fiscal Services .... Mr. Steve WILLIAMS
08 Director of Library .... Mrs. Cristie FERGUSON
07 Director of Admissions/Registrar .... Mr. Jeremy DORMAN
26 Director Recruiting/College Rels .... Dr. Van PATTERSON
103 Dir of Workforce & Economic Devel .... Mrs. Linda BARLOW
30 VP of Institutional Advancement .... Dr. Van PATTERSON
09 Director of Institutional Research .... Mrs. Christine BLAIR
106 Dean Distance Education/Webmaster .... Mrs. Ann MORRIS
12 Director of Shelby County Operation .... Mrs. Natalie OSWALT
12 Director of Marshall Operations .... Mrs. Laura WOOD
76 Dean of Health Sciences .... Dr. Barbara CORDELL
14 Computer Services Director .... Mr. Allen WEST
11 Director of Administrative Services .... Mr. Mike EDENS
19 Campus Police Chief .... Mr. Ernie DAVIS
37 Director Student Financial Aid .... Mrs. Denise WELCH

Paris Junior College (D)

2400 Clarksville Street, Paris TX 75460-6298
County: Lamar FICE Identification: 003601
Unit ID: 227401
Telephone: (903) 785-7661 Carnegie Class: Assoc/Pub-R-M
FAX Number: (903) 782-0370 Calendar System: Semester
URL: www.parisjc.edu
Established: 1924 Annual Undergrad Tuition & Fees (In-District): $1,650
Enrollment: 5,957 Coed
Affiliation or Control: State/Local IRS Status: 501(c)3
Highest Offering: Associate Degree
Program: Occupational; 2-Year Principally Bachelor's Creditable
Accreditation: SC, ADNUR, EMT, RAD, SURGT

01 President .... Dr. Pamela D. ANGLIN
10 VP Business Services .... Mr. John EASTMAN
05 VP/Dean Academic Studies .... Mr. L. D. CHANEY
81 Associate Dean Math/Social Sciences .... Mr. Ed MCCRAW
60 Associate Dean Communications/Arts .... Mrs. Beth SHELTON
106 Associate Dean Distance Education .... Dr. Ken HALEY
103 VP/Dean Workforce Education .... Mr. John SPRADLING
51 Associate Dean Workforce Training .... Dr. Charles GEORGE
32 Assoc Dean Student Access/Success .... Mrs. Sheila REECE
07 Director of Admissions .... Mrs. Amie CATO
06 Registrar .... Mrs. Rita TAPP
37 Director Student Financial Aid .... Mrs. Linda SLAWSON
08 Director Library Services .... Mr. Carl COVERT
38 Director Counseling .... Mrs. Barbara THOMAS
09 Director Institutional Research .... Mrs. Beverly MATTHEWS
30 Director Institutional Advancement .... Mr. Derald BULLS
35 Director Student Affairs .... Mr. Kenneth WEBB
14 Director Computer Center .... Mrs. Mary HOLBROOK MIMS
26 Chief Public Relations Officer .... Ms. Margaret RUFF
18 Manager Plant Operations .... Mr. Randall COX

Parker University (E)

2540 Walnut Hill Lane, Dallas TX 75229-5609
County: Dallas FICE Identification: 023053
Unit ID: 243823
Telephone: (972) 438-6932 Carnegie Class: Spec/Health
FAX Number: (214) 902-2496 Calendar System: Trimester
URL: www.parker.edu
Established: 1982 Annual Undergrad Tuition & Fees: $29,319
Enrollment: 847 Coed
Affiliation or Control: Independent Non-Profit IRS Status: 501(c)3
Highest Offering: Doctorate
Program: Professional
Accreditation: SC, CHIRO, COMTA

01 President .... Dr. Fabrizio MANCINI
05 Provost .... Dr. Gery HOCHANADEL
20 Vice President of Academics .... Dr. Kenneth THOMAS
10 Chief Financial Officer .... Mr. David GARAFOLA
20 Academic Dean .... Dr. Gene GIGGLEMAN
46 Dean of Research .... Dr. Ronald RUPPERT
84 Dean of Enrollment .... Ms. Valory HEMPHILL
32 Dean of Students .... Mr. Victor BALLESTEROS
51 Director Continuing Education .... Ms. Michelle YUNGBLUT
06 Registrar .... Ms. Paula BROWN
37 Director Financial Aid .... Vacant
08 Head Librarian .... Mrs. Becky SULLIVAN
38 Student Counseling Director .... Dr. Jacqueline ELBEL
16 Chief Human Resources Officer .... Ms. Sandra MCLEAN
19 Director Safety/Security .... Mr. Scott CHRISTENSEN
41 Athletic Director .... Mr. Steve WELLER
29 Director Alumni Relations .... Mr. Tim GUNN
26 Chief Marketing Officer .... Mr. Matt EISERLOH
91 Director of Information Services .... Mr. Tom PHAM
18 Dir of Facilities/Procurement .... Mr. Philip CERVANTES
35 Director Student Activities .... Mrs. Wendy NULPH
17 Asst Dean of Clinic .... Vacant

Paul Quinn College (F)

3837 Simpson Stuart Road, Dallas TX 75241-4398
County: Dallas FICE Identification: 003602
Unit ID: 227429
Telephone: (214) 376-1000 Carnegie Class: Bac/Diverse
FAX Number: (214) 379-5559 Calendar System: Semester
URL: www.pqc.edu
Established: 1872 Annual Undergrad Tuition & Fees: $15,640
Enrollment: 201 Coed
Affiliation or Control: African Methodist Episcopal IRS Status: 501(c)3
Highest Offering: Baccalaureate
Program: Liberal Arts And General; Teacher Preparatory
Accreditation: TRACS

01 President .... Mr. Michael J. SORRELL
05 Vice Pres Academic Affairs .... Dr. Kizuwanda GRANT
10 COO & Vice President Fiscal .... Mr. Antwane OWENS
84 Int Dir of Enrollment Management .... Ms. Eddie FRANCIS
32 Dean of Students .... Ms. Kelsel THOMPSON
06 Registrar .... Ms. Beverly SMITH
08 Librarian/Director LRC .... Ms. Clarice MEDLEY-WEEKS
13 Director Technology .... Mr. Justin WIRPEL
41 Dir Athletics/Intramural Sports .... Mr. James SUMMERS
37 Director of Financial Aid .... Vacant
35 Director Student Support Svcs .... Dr. Marguerite MCCLINTON
18 Director of Facilities .... Mrs. Marieta OGLESBY
09 Director of Institutional Research .... Vacant
29 Director of Alumni Relations .... Vacant
23 Nurse .... Ms. Glenda DAVIS
107 Div Chair Professional Studies .... Mr. Reginald GRAY
53 Division Chair Education .... Dr. Kizuwanda GRANT
100 Chief of Staff .... Ms. Lori PRICE
88 Director of Service Learning .... Ms. Elizabeth WATTLEY

Ranger College (G)

1100 College Circle, Ranger TX 76470-3298
County: Eastland FICE Identification: 003603
Unit ID: 227687
Telephone: (254) 647-3234 Carnegie Class: Assoc/Pub-R-S
FAX Number: (254) 647-1656 Calendar System: Semester
URL: www.rangercollege.edu
Established: 1926 Annual Undergrad Tuition & Fees (In-District): $2,160
Enrollment: 1,741 Coed
Affiliation or Control: Local IRS Status: 501(c)3
Highest Offering: Associate Degree
Program: Occupational; 2-Year Principally Bachelor's Creditable; Technical Emphasis
Accreditation: #SC

01 President .... Dr. William J. CAMPION
12 Executive VP Brownwood .... Dr. Don BOSTIC
12 Vice President Erath County .... Dr. Kerry SCHINDLER
10 Chief Financial Officer .... Mrs. Tammy ADAMS
84 Dean of Enrollment Management .... Mr. John SLAUGHTER
32 Dean of Students .... Mr. Johnny GANN
05 Dean of Student Learning .... Mr. Billy ADAMS
11 Dean of Administration .... Dr. Dava WASHBURN
08 Director of Learning Resources .... Mrs. Cherie BELTRAN
18 Director of Maintenance & Grounds .... Mr. Charles LEMASTER
37 Director of Financial Aid .... Mr. Don HILTON
41 Athletic Director .... Mr. Jack ALLEN
15 Director of Personnel .... Miss Laura YECK
36 Director Student Placement .... Ms. Vicki LOWRANCE
38 Dir Academic Counseling & Testing .... Ms. Vicki LOWRANCE
21 Bursar .... Ms. Evonne CHERRY
40 Director Bookstore .... Miss Cindy STRINGER

Redeemer Theological Seminary (H)

6060 N Central Expressway, Ste. 700, Dallas TX 75206
County: Dallas Identification: 667055
Telephone: (214) 528-8600 Carnegie Class: Not Classified
FAX Number: N/A Calendar System: Semester
URL: www.redeemerseminary.org
Established: 1999 Annual Graduate Tuition & Fees: $12,000
Enrollment: 136 Coed
Affiliation or Control: Independent Non-Profit IRS Status: 501(c)3
Highest Offering: Master's; No Undergraduates
Program: Professional; Religious Emphasis
Accreditation: @THEOL

01 President .... Dr. Steven T. VANDERHILL
05 Academic Dean .... Dr. Douglas M. GROPP

Remington College (I)

3110 Hayes Road, Suite 380, Houston TX 77082-2782
County: Harris FICE Identification: 030265
Unit ID: 380094
Telephone: (281) 899-1240 Carnegie Class: Assoc/PrivFP
FAX Number: (281) 597-8466 Calendar System: Quarter
URL: www.remingtoncollege.edu
Established: 1981 Annual Undergrad Tuition & Fees: $14,995
Enrollment: 382 Coed
Affiliation or Control: Proprietary IRS Status: Proprietary
Highest Offering: Baccalaureate
Program: Occupational
Accreditation: ACCSC

01 President .... Ms. Lori BANKY
05 Director of Education .... Vacant
07 Director of Admissions .... Mr. Michael HOLMES
37 Director of Financial Aid .... Mrs. Rhoda HAMILTON

Remington College-Dallas Campus (A)

1800 Eastgate Drive, Garland TX 75041-5513

County: Dallas | Identification: 666037
Unit ID: 223463
Telephone: (972) 686-7878 | Carnegie Class: Assoc/PrivFP
FAX Number: (972) 686-5116 | Calendar System: Quarter
URL: www.remingtoncollege.edu
Established: 1987 | Annual Undergrad Tuition & Fees: $14,995
Enrollment: 1,212 | Coed
Affiliation or Control: Proprietary | IRS Status: Proprietary
Highest Offering: Baccalaureate
Program: 2-Year Principally Bachelor's Creditable
Accreditation: ACCSC

01 Campus President .... Mr. Skip WALLS
05 Academic Dean .... Mr. Billy FERRELL

† Branch campus of Remington College, Houston, TX.

Remington College-Fort Worth Campus (B)

300 E Loop 820, Fort Worth TX 76112-1225

County: Tarrant | Identification: 666063
Unit ID: 377111
Telephone: (817) 451-0017 | Carnegie Class: Assoc/PrivFP
FAX Number: (817) 496-1257 | Calendar System: Quarter
URL: www.remingtoncollege.edu
Established: 1988 | Annual Undergrad Tuition & Fees: N/A
Enrollment: 574 | Coed
Affiliation or Control: Proprietary | IRS Status: Proprietary
Highest Offering: Baccalaureate
Program: Occupational
Accreditation: ACCSC

01 President .... Mr. Greg FALCON

† Branch campus of Remington College, Houston, TX.

Rice University (C)

PO Box 1892, Houston TX 77251-1892

County: Harris | FICE Identification: 003604
Unit ID: 227757
Telephone: (713) 348-0000 | Carnegie Class: RU/VH
FAX Number: N/A | Calendar System: Semester
URL: www.rice.edu
Established: 1891 | Annual Undergrad Tuition & Fees: $37,292
Enrollment: 6,224 | Coed
Affiliation or Control: Independent Non-Profit | IRS Status: 501(c)3
Highest Offering: Doctorate
Program: Liberal Arts And General; Professional
Accreditation: SC, BUS, ENG, @TEAC

01 President .... Mr. David W. LEEBRON
101 Deputy Sec to Board of Trustees .... Ms. Cynthia L. WILSON
05 Provost .... Dr. George L. MCLENDON
11 Vice President Administration .... Dr. Kevin KIRBY
10 Vice President Finance .... Ms. Kathy COLLINS
30 Vice President Resource Development .. Mr. Darrow ZEIDENSTEIN
88 Vice Pres Investments/Treasurer .... Ms. Allison THACKER
84 Vice President for Enrollment .... Mr. Chris MUNOZ
26 Vice President for Public Affairs .... Ms. Linda THRANE
13 Vice Provost Information Technology .... Dr. Kamran KHAN
46 Vice Provost Research .... Dr. Vicki L. COLVIN
20 Vice Provost for Academic Affairs .... Dr. Paula SANDERS
15 Associate Vice Pres Human Resources .... Ms. Mary A. CRONIN
91 Assoc Vice Pres for Admin Systems ...... Mr. Randy CASTIGLIONI
18 Assoc VP Facil Engr & Planning .... Ms. Barbara BRYSON
04 Sr Asst to the President .... Dr. David K. VASSAR
43 General Counsel .... Mr. Richard A. ZANSITIS
06 Registrar .... Mr. David TENNEY
07 Dean for Undergraduate Enrollment .... Ms. Julie BROWNING
29 Director Alumni Affairs/Univ Events .... Ms. Carrie BROWN
88 Director International Opportunity .... Ms. Erika P. ZANETTI
37 Director Student Financial Services .... Ms. Anne E. WALKER
13 Director Enterprise Application .... Ms. Andrea MARTIN
25 Director of Sponsored Research .... Ms. Melinda COTTEN
41 Director of Athletics .... Mr. Richard GREENSPAN
85 Director Intl Students/Scholars .... Dr. Adria BAKER
31 Dir of Community Involvement Ctr .... Mr. Mac GRISWOLD
39 Director of Housing & Dining .... Mr. Mark DITMAN
23 Director Student Health Services .... Dr. Mark JENKINS
09 Director of Institutional Research .... Dr. Ratna SARKAR
21 University Controller .... Ms. Evelyn STEWART
21 Director of Internal Audit .... Ms. Janet COVINGTON
19 Chief of Campus Police .... Mr. Johnny WHITEHEAD
22 Director of Affirmative Action .... Mr. Russell BARNES
27 Director of News & Media Relations .... Mr. B.J ALMOND
21 Director Administrative Services .... Mr. Eugen RADULESCU
28 Director of Diversity .... Dr. Roland B. SMITH
36 Dir Center for Career Development .... Ms. Nicole VAN DEN HEUVEL
96 Director of Purchasing .... Mr. Brian SOIKA
40 Manager Bookstore .... Mr. Tim JACKSON
79 Dean of School of Humanities .... Dr. Nicolas SHUMWAY
58 Dean Graduate/Postdoctoral Stds .... Dr. Paula SANDERS
20 Dean of Undergraduate Education .... Dr. John S. HUTCHINSON
48 Dean of Architecture .... Dr. Sarah M. WHITING
64 Dean of Shepherd School of Music .... Dr. Robert YEKOVICH
54 Dean GR Brown School Engineering .... Dr. Ned THOMAS
50 Dean JH Jones Graduate Sch Business .... Dr. William H. GLICK
83 Dean of Social Sciences .... Dr. Lyn RAGSDALE
81 Dean of Wiess Sch Natural Science .... Dr. Daniel CARSON
51 Dean Glasscock Sch Continuing Stds .... Dr. Mary MCINTIRE
88 Asst Dean Student Judicial Pgms .... Dr. Donald OSTDIEK
38 Asst Dean Student Counseling .... Dr. Donald OSTDIEK

Rio Grande Bible Institute (D)

4300 South Business 281, Edinburg TX 78539-9650

County: Hidalgo | Identification: 666395
Telephone: (956) 380-8100 | Carnegie Class: Not Classified
FAX Number: (956) 380-8256 | Calendar System: Semester
URL: www.riogrande.edu
Established: 1946 | Annual Undergrad Tuition & Fees: $1,954
Enrollment: 136 | Coed
Affiliation or Control: Independent Non-Profit | IRS Status: 501(c)3
Highest Offering: Baccalaureate
Program: Professional; Religious Emphasis
Accreditation: BI

01 President .... Dr. Lawrence B. WINDLE
04 Administrative Assistant to Pres ... Ms. Lidia PLACENCIO-ABREU
05 Vice President of Education .... Mr. David LOYOLA
32 Dean of Students .... Mr. David LOYOLA
10 Vice President of Administration .... Mr. Larry DICK
21 Comptroller .... Mr. Keith HEPPNER
08 Chief Librarian .... Ms. Mary CANO
06 Registrar .... Mr. Keith SWARTZBAUGH
15 Personnel Director .... Mr. Larry DICK
18 Vice President of Campus Services .... Mr. Gary WILLIAMS
26 Director of Ministerial Advancement .... Dr. Robert CRANE

† 2011-2012 Tuition should have been $1724/2010 Fall Enrollment should be 121.

St. Edward's University (E)

3001 S Congress Avenue, Austin TX 78704-6489

County: Travis | FICE Identification: 003621
Unit ID: 227845
Telephone: (512) 448-8400 | Carnegie Class: Master's L
FAX Number: (512) 448-8492 | Calendar System: Semester
URL: www.stedwards.edu
Established: 1885 | Annual Undergrad Tuition & Fees: $30,710
Enrollment: 5,330 | Coed
Affiliation or Control: Independent Non-Profit | IRS Status: 501(c)3
Highest Offering: Master's
Program: Liberal Arts And General; Teacher Preparatory; Professional; Business Emphasis
Accreditation: SC, SW

01 President .... Dr. George E. MARTIN
03 Executive Vice President/Provost .... Sr. Donna M. JURICK
10 Vice President Financial Affairs ..... Ms. Rhonda D. CARTWRIGHT
30 Vice President for Advancement .... Mr. Michael F. LARKIN
26 Vice Pres Marketing/Enrollment Mgmt .... Ms. Paige BOOTH
32 Vice President for Student Affairs .... Dr. Sandra L. PACHECO
13 Vice President Information Tech .... Mr. David E. WALDRON
42 Director of Campus Ministry .... Fr. Richard S. WILKINSON
05 Interim VP for Academic Affairs .... Dr. Brenda J. VALLANCE
09 Assoc VP Inst Effectiveness/Rsrch .... Mr. Bhuban R. PANDEY
21 Assoc Vice Pres Financial Affairs .... Mr. Barton G. GLASER
107 AVP for Global Initiatives .... Mr. William CLABBY
20 Assoc VP for Academic Affairs .... Dr. Molly E. MINUS
07 Assoc VP/Dean Undergrad Admission .... Ms. Tracy L. MANIER
37 Assoc VP Student Financial Services .... Ms. Doris F. CONSTANTINE
32 Assoc VP/Dean of Students .... Ms. Lisa L. KIRKPATRICK
29 Assoc VP Alumni/Parent Programs .... Ms. Kippi R. GRIFFITH
101 Asst to Pres Institutional Rels .... Ms. Cristina L. BORDIN
04 Executive Assistant to President .... Ms. Lorraine M. PAGAN
83 Interim Dean Behavior/Social Sci .... Dr. Russell FROHARDT
50 Dean Management & Business .... Ms. Marsha C. KELLIHER
53 Dean School of Education .... Dr. Grant W. SIMPSON, JR.
79 Dean School of Humanities .... Dr. Sharon NELL
81 Dean School of Natural Sciences .... Dr. Thomas M. MITZEL
88 Dean of New College .... Dr. Helene L. CAUDILL
88 Dean University Programs .... Dr. Marianne F. HOPPER
08 Director of Library .... Mr. Pongracz SENNYEY
06 Registrar .... Dr. Lance R. HAYES
36 Director Career Planning .... Ms. Barbara J. HENDERSON
108 Dir of Institutional Assessment .... Mr. David A. BLAIR
44 Associate VP Development .... Mr. Joe DEMEDEIROS
104 Director Ofc of International Educ .... Vacant
90 Director Instructional Technology .... Ms. Mary T. HOWERTON
18 Assoc VP Facilities .... Mr. Michael W. PETERSON
91 Director Administrative Computing ... Mr. Raymond J. SPINHIRNE
88 Director Digital Infrastructure .... Mr. Benjamin R. HOCKENHULL
88 Dir of Enterprise Info Systems .... Ms. Angela M. SVOBODA
88 Director Info Technology Resources .... Vacant
19 Chief of Police .... Mr. Rudolph L. RENDON
27 Director of Communications .... Ms. Mischelle R. DIAZ
15 Director Human Resources .... Ms. Rosemary RUDNICKI
38 Director Health & Counseling Center .... Dr. Claudia C. CAROL
41 Athletic Director .... Ms. Debora W. TAYLOR
35 Director of Student Life .... Mr. Thomas B. SULLIVAN
39 Director Residence Life .... Mr. Dave ROZEBOOM
31 Director Auxiliary Services .... Mr. Michael C. STONE
88 Risk Manager .... Ms. Rebekah M. NAGY
21 Controller .... Mr. Paul R. SINTEF
102 Director Foundation Relations .... Ms. Carol A. JANUSZESKI
89 Director Freshman Studies .... Ms. Alexandra L. BARRON
92 Director Honors Program .... Dr. Barbara FILIPPIDIS
88 Director Capstone Course .... Ms. Cory LOCK
40 Bookstore Director .... Ms. Melanie FOSTER

St. Mary's University (F)

One Camino Santa Maria, San Antonio TX 78228-8572

County: Bexar | FICE Identification: 003623
Unit ID: 228149
Telephone: (210) 436-3011 | Carnegie Class: Master's L
FAX Number: (210) 436-3500 | Calendar System: Semester
URL: www.stmarytx.edu
Established: 1852 | Annual Undergrad Tuition & Fees: $24,226
Enrollment: 4,188 | Coed
Affiliation or Control: Roman Catholic | IRS Status: 501(c)3
Highest Offering: Doctorate
Program: Liberal Arts And General; Teacher Preparatory; Professional
Accreditation: SC, BUS, CACREP, ENG, LAW, MFCD, MUS

01 President .... Mr. Thomas M. MENGLER
05 Provost/Vice Pres Academic Affairs .... Mr. Andre HAMPTON
10 Vice Pres Administration & Finance .... Ms. Rebeckah J. DAY
84 Vice Pres Enrollment Management ... Ms. Suzanne M. PETRUSCH
32 Vice President Student Development .... Ms. Katherine SISOIAN
30 Vice Pres University Advancement ...... Mr. Rocky KETTERING, III
88 Vice President Mission & Identity .... Rev. Rudy VELA, SM
50 Dean/Prof Bill Greehey Sch Business .... Dr. Tanuja SINGH
79 Dean/Assoc Prof Hum & Social Sci .... Dr. Janet B. DIZINNO
54 Dean/Prof Science/Engrng/Technology ... Dr. Winston EREVELLES
58 Dean & Professor Graduate School .... Dr. Henry FLORES
61 Dean of Law .... Mr. Charles CANTU
39 Director Residence Life .... Mr. James VILLARREAL
09 Director of Institutional Research ...... Mr. Christopher M. ANTONS
100 Chief of Staff/Office of President .... Ms. Dianne L. PIPES
06 Registrar .... Ms. Christina VILLANUEVA
07 Director of Admissions .... Vacant
08 Director Louis J Blume Library .... Dr. Palmer H. HALL
37 Director Financial Assistance .... Mr. David R. KRAUSE
38 Director Student Counseling .... Dr. Barbara HARDIN
36 Director of Career Services .... Ms. Amy DIEPENBROCK
90 Exec Director Academic Technology ... Mr. Daxing (Michael) CHEN
15 Director Human Resources .... Ms. Elsa YBANEZ
72 Exec Dir Tech Operations/Info Tech .... Vacant
91 Ex Dir Resource Mgt/Plng/Info/Tech .... Ms. Louisa A. MARTIN
13 Dir Network Tech Services/Info Tech .. Mr. Robert STOOKSBERRY
88 Director Tech User Support .... Vacant
42 Director University Ministry .... Mr. Wayne ROMO
30 Director University Advancement .... Mr. Peter HANSEN
21 Director of Finance .... Ms. Mei-Lin LEE
21 Director of Accounting Operations .... Ms. Sheila NIX
26 Dir Media Relations/Communications .... Mrs. Gina FARRELL
18 Facilities Administrator .... Mr. William M. TAM

*San Jacinto College District (G)

4624 Fairmont Parkway, Pasadena TX 77504-3323

County: Harris | FICE Identification: 029137
Unit ID: 227988
Telephone: (281) 998-6150 | Carnegie Class: N/A
FAX Number: (281) 479-8127
URL: www.sanjac.edu

01 Chancellor .... Dr. Brenda HELLYER
05 VC Learning & Student Success .... Dr. Laurel WILLIAMSON
10 Vice Chancellor Fiscal Affairs .... Mr. Ken LYNN
16 Vice Chanc Human Resources .... Mr. Stephen TRNCAK
27 Interim CIO .... Mr. Rob STANICIC
26 Associate Vice Chanc Marketing .... Ms. Teri FOWLE
84 Vice Pres Enrollment Services .... Dr. William RAFFETTO
32 Vice Pres Student Development .... Ms. Amy AMMERMAN
51 Vice President CPD .... Ms. Sarah JANES
88 Vice Pres Educational Technology .... Ms. Niki WHITESIDE
88 Vice Pres Org Development .... Ms. Susan TEMPLE
88 Asst Vice Chanc Educ Partnerships .... Ms. Pamela CAMPBELL
30 Exec Dir Advance of SJC Foundation .... Ms. Ruth KEENAN
06 Dean Enroll Mgmt/Col Registrar .... Dr. Wanda MUNSON
20 Associate Vice Chanc Learning .... Dr. Catherine O'BRIEN
88 Assoc Vice Chancellor Col Prep .... Dr. Rebecca GOOSEN
09 Dir Research/Institutional Effectiv .... Mr. George GONZALEZ
21 Dir Accting and Financial Svcs .... Mr. Bill DICKERSON
96 Dir Contracts & Purchasing Svcs .... Ms. Ann KOKX-TEMPLET
37 Director Financial Aid Services .... Mr. Robert MERINO
88 Dir Small Business Development .... Mr. Richard PRETS

*San Jacinto College Central (H)

8060 Spencer Highway, Pasadena TX 77505-5903

County: Harris | FICE Identification: 003609
Unit ID: 227979
Telephone: (281) 476-1501 | Carnegie Class: Assoc/Pub-S-MC
FAX Number: (281) 476-1892 | Calendar System: Semester
URL: www.sanjac.edu
Established: 1960 | Annual Undergrad Tuition & Fees (In-District): $1,943
Enrollment: 15,255 | Coed
Affiliation or Control: Local | IRS Status: 501(c)3
Highest Offering: Associate Degree
Program: Occupational; 2-Year Principally Bachelor's Creditable
Accreditation: &SC, ADNUR, EMT, MLTAD, RAD, SURGT

02 President .... Dr. Laurel WILLIAMSON
05 Vice President of Learning .... Dr. Barbara HANSON
56 Dean Evening Div/Weekend College .... Ms. Denise EVANS

49 Dean of Liberal Arts .... Dr. Van WIGGINTON
75 Dean of Industrial and Applied Tech .... Mr. Jeffrey PARKS
76 Dean of Allied Health .... Ms. Veronica JAMMER
50 Dean of Business/Ag and Prof Svcs .... Mr. Michael KANE
11 Dean of Administration .... Dr. James BRASWELL
84 Dean of Enrollment Services .... Mr. Kevin MCKISSON
32 Dean of Student Development .... Dr. Deborah MYLES
62 Director of Library .... Ms. Karen BLANKENSHIP
41 Director of Athletics .... Mr. Scott HORSTMAN
88 Dir of Educ Planning and Counseling .... Mr. Daniel NEULS
88 Director of Dual Credit .... Ms. Jaynie MITCHELL
06 Associate College Registrar .... Ms. Joan RONDOT
35 Coordinator Student Life .... Ms. Amanda ROSE
37 Coordinator of Financial Aid .... Ms. Vicki KANE
88 Coordinator of Testing .... Ms. Carita WEBSTER
36 Coordinator Career/Employment Ctr .... Ms. Shannon HINTON

† Regional accreditation is carried under the parent institution (district office) in Pasadena, TX.

*San Jacinto College North (A)

5800 Uvalde Road, Houston TX 77049-4599
County: Harris — Identification: 666747
Unit ID: 227997
Telephone: (281) 458-4050 — Carnegie Class: Not Classified
FAX Number: (281) 459-7125 — Calendar System: Semester
URL: www.sanjac.edu
Established: 1974 — Annual Undergrad Tuition & Fees (In-District): $1,943
Enrollment: 7,043 — Coed
Affiliation or Control: Local — IRS Status: 501(c)3
Highest Offering: Associate Degree
Program: Occupational; 2-Year Principally Bachelor's Creditable
Accreditation: &SC, ACFEI, EMT, MAC

02 President .... Dr. Allatia HARRIS
05 Vice President of Learning .... Dr. Richard BAILEY
76 Dean of Allied Health .... Ms. Serita DICKEY
90 Dean Educational Technology .... Dr. Gary FRIERY
55 Dean Evening/Weekend College .... Mr. James HALL
84 Interim Dean of Enrollment Services .... Ms. Tami KELLY
32 Dean of Student Development .... Ms. Clare IANNELLI
62 Director of Library .... Dr. Jan CRENSHAW
88 Dir Educ Planning Counsel .... Ms. Christine TORRES
88 Director of Dual Credit .... Ms. Jennifer MOWDY
49 Dean of Liberal Arts .... Mr. Shawn SILMAN
07 Coordinator Enrollment Services .... Ms. Faye ALLEN
35 Coordinator of Student Life .... Mr. Lamar MCWAINE
37 Coordinator of Financial Aid .... Mr. Art ESCOBAR
88 Coordinator of Testing .... Mr. Ronald HOPKINS
36 Coordinator Career/Employment Ctr .... Ms. Natiesha WALKER
88 Coordinator Wellness Program .... Mr. Kory KOEHLER

† Regional accreditation is carried under the parent institution (district office) in Pasadena, TX.

*San Jacinto College South (B)

13735 Beamer Road, Houston TX 77089-6099
County: Harris — Identification: 666748
Unit ID: 228006
Telephone: (281) 484-1900 — Carnegie Class: Not Classified
FAX Number: (281) 922-3401 — Calendar System: Semester
URL: www.sanjac.edu
Established: 1979 — Annual Undergrad Tuition & Fees (In-District): $1,943
Enrollment: 11,159 — Coed
Affiliation or Control: Local — IRS Status: 501(c)3
Highest Offering: Associate Degree
Program: Occupational; 2-Year Principally Bachelor's Creditable
Accreditation: &SC, ADNUR, PTAA

02 President .... Dr. Laurel WILLIAMSON
05 Vice President of Learning .... Dr. Brenda JONES
49 Dean of Liberal Arts .... Ms. Kathryn ROOSA
50 Dean Business & Technology .... Mr. Kevin MORRIS
11 Dean of Administration .... Mr. Joseph HEBERT
84 Dean of Enrollment Mgmt .... Dr. Kerry MIX
32 Dean of Student Development .... Ms. Joanna ZIMMERMANN
55 Director of Evening Division .... Mr. John BOGGS
62 Director of Library .... Mr. Richard MCKAY
88 Dir of Educ Planning and Counseling .... Ms. Shelley RINEHART
88 Director of Dual Credit .... Ms. Quiana BROWN
92 Dean Honors Program .... Mr. Scott FURTWENGLER
07 Coordinator Enrollment Services .... Ms. Renee HUMAN
35 Coordinator of Student Life .... Ms. Ellie MEYER
37 Coordinator of Financial Aid .... Ms. Sonia TOWNSEND
88 Coordinator of Testing .... Mr. Jeff WYLIN
36 Coordinator Career/Employment Ctr .... Ms. Deborah SMITH

† Regional accreditation is carried under the parent institution (district office) in Pasadena, TX.

Sanford-Brown College (C)

1250 W. Mockingbird Lane, Ste 150, Dallas TX 75247
County: Dallas — FICE Identification: 026150
Unit ID: 404514
Telephone: (214) 459-8490 — Carnegie Class: Assoc/PrivFP
FAX Number: (214) 638-6401 — Calendar System: Other
URL: www.sanfordbrown.edu
Established: N/A — Annual Undergrad Tuition & Fees: $14,300
Enrollment: 1,009 — Coed
Affiliation or Control: Proprietary — IRS Status: Proprietary
Highest Offering: Associate Degree
Program: Occupational
Accreditation: ACICS, DA, DH, MAAB, SURTEC

01 Campus President .... David B. BOWMAN

Sanford-Brown College-Houston (D)

9999 Richmond Avenue, Houston TX 77042
County: Harris — Identification: 666382
Unit ID: 404499
Telephone: (713) 779-1110 — Carnegie Class: Assoc/PrivFP
FAX Number: (713) 779-2408 — Calendar System: Other
URL: www.sanfordbrown.edu/Houston
Established: 1992 — Annual Undergrad Tuition & Fees: $15,400
Enrollment: 2,400 — Coed
Affiliation or Control: Proprietary — IRS Status: Proprietary
Highest Offering: Associate Degree
Program: Occupational; 2-Year Principally Bachelor's Creditable; Nursing Emphasis
Accreditation: ACICS, DMS, MAAB, MLTAD, SURGT, SURTEC

01 President .... Mr. Jeffrey D. FOWLER
07 Director of Admissions .... Mr. William HARRIS
05 Director of Education .... Dr. Khawar AIZAZ

† Branch campus of Sanford-Brown College, Atlanta, GA.

Schreiner University (E)

2100 Memorial Boulevard, Kerrville TX 78028-5697
County: Kerr — FICE Identification: 003610
Unit ID: 228042
Telephone: (830) 896-5411 — Carnegie Class: Bac/Diverse
FAX Number: (830) 896-3232 — Calendar System: Semester
URL: www.schreiner.edu
Established: 1923 — Annual Undergrad Tuition & Fees: $20,940
Enrollment: 1,078 — Coed
Affiliation or Control: Presbyterian Church (U.S.A.) — IRS Status: 501(c)3
Highest Offering: Master's
Program: Liberal Arts And General; Teacher Preparatory; Professional
Accreditation: SC

01 President .... Dr. Timothy SUMMERLIN
05 Provost/Vice Pres Acad Affairs .... Dr. Charlie T. MCCORMICK
10 Vice Pres Administration & Finance .... Mr. Bill MUSE
30 Vice Pres Advancement/Public Rels .... Mr. Mark TUSCHAK
84 Vice Pres Enrollment/Student Svcs .... Ms. Peg A. LAYTON
20 Assistant Provost .... Ms. Darlene BANNISTER
13 Chief Information Ofcr/Library/IT .... Dr. Candice SCOTT
27 Assistant Vice President Marketing .... Ms. Lane H. TAIT
21 Asst Vice Pres Finance/Controller .... Ms. Barbara SIEMERS
07 Dean Admission/Financial Aid .... Vacant
42 Campus Minister .... Rev. Virginia NORRIS-LANE
37 Director Student Financial Aid .... Ms. Toni BRYANT
06 Registrar .... Ms. Darlene A. BANNISTER
26 Director of University Relations .... Ms. Amy ARMSTRONG
41 Athletic Director .... Mr. Ron MACOSKO
16 Director of Human Resources .... Ms. Mary WOODS
88 Director Environment Management .... Mr. Dale MYERS
29 Director Alumni Relations .... Mr. Paul CAMFIELD
38 Director Student Counseling .... Ms. Carolyn S. OSBORN
36 Director Career Development .... Ms. Cristina MARTINEZ
09 Director of Institutional Research .... Dr. Gloria STEWART

Seminary of the Southwest (F)

Box 2247, Austin TX 78768-2247
County: Travis — FICE Identification: 003566
Unit ID: 224712
Telephone: (512) 472-4133 — Carnegie Class: Spec/Faith
FAX Number: (512) 472-3098 — Calendar System: 4/1/4
URL: www.ssw.edu
Established: 1952 — Annual Graduate Tuition & Fees: $13,227
Enrollment: 139 — Coed
Affiliation or Control: Protestant Episcopal — IRS Status: 501(c)3
Highest Offering: Master's; No Undergraduates
Program: Professional
Accreditation: SC, THEOL

01 Dean & President .... V.Rev. Douglas B. TRAVIS
05 Academic Dean .... Rev Dr. Cynthia BRIGGS KITTREDGE
11 Exec VP Administration & Finance .... Mr. John B. WATERS
27 Exec VP of Communications .... Ms. Nancy SPRINGER-BALDWIN
84 Vice Pres Enrollment Management .... Ms. Jennielle STROTHER
21 Accounting Director .... Ms. Kathy LEBRUN
06 Registrar .... Mrs. Madelyn SNODGRASS
08 Director of the Booher Library .... Dr. Donald KEENEY
18 Director of Facilities Management .... Mr. Marty ROBBINS
13 Director Instructional Technology .... Mr. Fito KAHN
44 Dir Annual Giving/Alumni Relations .... Mr. Andrew WEST

South Plains College (G)

1401 College Avenue, Levelland TX 79336-6595
County: Hockley — FICE Identification: 003611
Unit ID: 228158
Telephone: (806) 894-9611 — Carnegie Class: Assoc/Pub-R-L
FAX Number: (806) 894-5274 — Calendar System: Semester
URL: www.southplainscollege.edu
Established: 1957 — Annual Undergrad Tuition & Fees (In-State): $2,654
Enrollment: 10,482 — Coed
Affiliation or Control: State — IRS Status: 501(c)3
Highest Offering: Associate Degree
Program: Occupational; 2-Year Principally Bachelor's Creditable
Accreditation: SC, ADNUR, EMT, @PTAA, SURGT

01 President .... Dr. Kelvin W. SHARP
05 Vice President Academic Affairs .... Mr. Jim WALKER
10 Vice Pres Finance & Administration .... Mr. Anthony G. RILEY
32 Vice President of Student Affairs .... Mrs. Cathy MITCHELL
30 Vice Pres Institutional Advancement .... Mr. Stephen S. JOHN
76 Dean of Health Occupations .... Ms. Sue Ann LOPEZ
49 Dean of Arts & Sciences .... Mr. Yancy NUNEZ
75 Dean of Technical Education .... Mr. Rob M. BLAIR
51 Dean Continuing & Distance Educ .... Mr. Ronald SPEARS
07 Dean of Admissions & Records .... Mrs. Andrea RANGEL
35 Dean of Students .... Mr. David CONNER
12 Dean of Reese Center .... Ms. Kara MARTINEZ
09 Assoc Dean of Research & Reports .... Mr. Jack WARDLOW
26 Assoc Dean of College Relations .... Mr. Dane DEWBRE
13 Assoc Dean Information Technology .... Mr. Tim WINDERS
88 Assoc Dean Dual Credit .... Mr. Ron SPEARS
103 Assoc Dean Workforce Development .... Mr. Rafael AGUILERA
38 Director of Counseling & Guidance .... Mrs. Christi ANDERSON
37 Director of Financial Aid .... Ms. Jim Ann BATENHORST
08 Director of Libraries .... Ms. Fran COTTON
44 Director of Development .... Mr. Russell HALL
15 Director of Human Resources .... Mrs. Jeri Ann DEWBRE
41 Director of Athletics .... Mr. Joe TUBB
06 Registrar .... Mr. Andrew RUIZ
18 Director of Physical Plant .... Mr. Cary MARROW
84 Director of Enrollment Management .... Mrs. Kimbra QUINN
96 Director of Purchasing .... Mr. Dennis CHURCHWELL
40 Bookstore Manager .... Mr. Roger SHULL
28 Diversity Coord/Career Counselor .... Ms. Maria LOPEZ-STRONG

South Texas College (H)

3201 W Pecan, McAllen TX 78501-6699
County: Hidalgo — FICE Identification: 031034
Unit ID: 409315
Telephone: (956) 872-5051 — Carnegie Class: Assoc/Pub4
FAX Number: (956) 971-3739 — Calendar System: Semester
URL: www.southtexascollege.edu
Established: 1993 — Annual Undergrad Tuition & Fees (In-District): $2,460
Enrollment: 30,558 — Coed
Affiliation or Control: State/Local — IRS Status: 501(c)3
Highest Offering: Baccalaureate
Program: 2-Year Principally Bachelor's Creditable
Accreditation: SC, ACBSP, OTA, PTAA

01 President .... Dr. Shirley A. REED
05 Vice Pres Academic Affairs .... Mr. Juan E. MEJIA
10 Vice Pres Financial Services .... Ms. Diana A. PENA
32 Vice Pres Stdnt Affairs/Enroll Mgmt .... Vacant
13 Vice Pres Info Services/Planning .... Mr. Jose CRUZ
30 Vice Pres Institutional Advancement .... Vacant
88 Exec Officer for NAAMRIE .... Ms. Wanda GARZA
83 Dean Liberal Arts/Soc Sci .... Dr. Margaretha BISCHOFF
50 Dean Business/Technology .... Mr. Mario REYNA
76 Int Dean Nursing/Allied Health .... Ms. Melba TREVINO
81 Interim Dean Math/Science .... Dr. Ali ESMAEILI
88 Dean Bach Deg Prog/Univ Rels .... Dr. Ali ESMAEILI
84 Interim Dean Enrollment Svcs .... Ms. Kimberly MCKAY
24 Dir Instructional Technologies .... Mr. Cody GREGG
37 Assoc Dean Student Financial Svcs .... Mr. Mike CARRANZA
21 Comptroller .... Ms. Maria ELIZONDO
16 Director Human Resources .... Ms. Shirley M. INGRAM
51 Dir Continuing/Prof & Workforce Ed .... Mr. Juan Carlos AGUIRRE
96 Director Purchasing .... Ms. Rebecca CAVAZOS
09 Dir Research/Analytical Svcs .... Mr. Serkan CELTEK
38 Dean Student Support Svcs .... Mr. Paul HERNANDEZ, JR.
18 Director Operations .... Mr. George MCCALEB
18 Director Facilities Plan/Construct .... Mr. Gerardo RODRIGUEZ, JR.
25 Dir Gr Dev/Accountability/Mgmt Svcs .... Vacant
12 Campus Administrator Starr Cty .... Mr. Ruben SAENZ
12 Campus Administrator Mid-Valley .... Mr. Monte CHURCHILL
88 Employee Relations Officer .... Vacant
106 Interim Director Distance Education .... Dr. Brett MILLAN
26 Director Public Rels/Marketing .... Mr. Daniel RAMIREZ
88 Dir Outreach/Orient/Wel Centers .... Ms. Kimberly MCKAY
07 Director Admissions/Registrar .... Mr. Matthew HEBBARD
88 Dir of Professional Development .... Ms. Lee GRIMES
20 Asst to VP Instructional Svcs .... Dr. Anahid PETROSIAN
19 Director Security .... Mr. Paul VARVILLE
09 Dir Inst Effectiv/Assessment .... Dr. Jinhao WANG
62 Interim Dean Lib Svcs/Instr Tech .... Mr. Cody GREGG
103 Int Assc Dean Cmty Engage/Wkfrc Dev .... Vacant
14 Director for IT Services .... Mr. Daniel DE LEON
08 Director Library Technical Services .... Mr. Jesus CAMPOS
08 Director Library Public Services .... Ms. Noemi GARZA
88 Dir Student Lrg Outcomes/Achievemnt .... Mr. Oscar HERNANDEZ
88 Int Dir Centers for Lrg Excellence .... Ms. Jennifer KNECHT
88 Director High School Programs .... Mr. Guadalupe CHAVEZ
90 Dir Info Commons Open Labs .... Dr. Lelia SALINAS
35 Int Assoc Dean Stdnt Life/Wellness .... Mr. Mike SHANNON
27 Chief Information Officer .... Vacant
88 Asst Chief Information Officer .... Ms. Alicia GOMEZ
88 Chief Information Security Officer .... Mr. Steve BOURDON
88 Curriculum/Accreditation Officer .... Ms. Laura TALBOT

South Texas College of Law (I)

1303 San Jacinto Street, Houston TX 77002-7000
County: Harris — FICE Identification: 004977
Unit ID: 228194
Telephone: (713) 659-8040 — Carnegie Class: Spec/Law
FAX Number: (713) 646-2909 — Calendar System: Semester

URL: www.stcl.edu
Established: 1923 Annual Graduate Tuition & Fees: $27,000
Enrollment: 1,354 Coed
Affiliation or Control: Independent Non-Profit IRS Status: 501(c)3
Highest Offering: First Professional Degree; No Undergraduates
Program: Professional
Accreditation: **LAW**

01 President & Dean ... Mr. Donald J. GUTER
03 Executive Vice President ... Ms. Helen JENKINS
101 Sr Exec Assistant to President/Dean ... Ms. Jennifer M. HUDSON
10 Senior Vice President & CFO ... Mr. Gregory A. BROTHERS
09 Vice Pres Strategic Plng/Inst Rsrch .. Mr. Jeffrey L. RENSBERGER
30 VP Development/Alumni Relations ... Ms. Kim PARKER
08 Vice Pres & Director Library Svcs ... Mr. David G. COWAN
20 Vice President & Associate Dean ... Mr. Bruce MCGOVERN
20 Vice President & Associate Dean ... Mr. T. Gerald TREECE
20 Vice President & Associate Dean ... Ms. Catherine G. BURNETT
13 Vice President Technology ... Mr. Randy MARAK
15 Vice President Human Resources ... Mr. Steve ALDERMAN
38 Asst Dean for Academic Assistance ... Ms. Gena L. SINGLETON
06 Registrar ... Ms. Mandi GIBSON
51 Assoc Director of Cont Legal Educ ... Vacant
36 Director of Career Resources ... Ms. Ginna GALBRAITH
07 Assistant Dean for Admissions ... Ms. Alicia CRAMER
21 Controller ... Ms. Nancy N. JOHNSON
37 Director of Financial Aid ... Ms. Pat HOLLENBECK
26 Dir Marketing/Communications ... Ms. Cheryl MCENTIRE
32 Assistant Dean ... Ms. Wanda MORROW
19 Director Security & Office Services ... Ms. Debbie GIBBINS
51 Director of Cont Legal Education ... Ms. Lisa DAHM
09 Exec Dir of Institutional Research ... Ms. Julie SAUNDERS
24 Dir Instructional Technology Svcs ... Mr. Terry SMITH
27 Director Information Services ... Mr. George MILZ
43 General Counsel ... Mr. Harry REED
30 Dir Development/Alumni Relations ... Ms. Jackie LAMINACK
26 Manager of Public Relations ... Ms. Sheila HANSEL
44 Asst Director of Development ... Ms. Alice H. MORRIS
44 Manager of Gift Administration ... Mr. Anthony DAVIS

Southern Methodist University (A)

6425 Boaz Lane, Dallas TX 75205-0100
County: Dallas FICE Identification: 003613
Unit ID: 228246
Telephone: (214) 768-2000 Carnegie Class: RU/H
FAX Number: (214) 768-1001 Calendar System: Semester
URL: www.smu.edu
Established: 1911 Annual Undergrad Tuition & Fees: $41,750
Enrollment: 10,982 Coed
Affiliation or Control: United Methodist IRS Status: 501(c)3
Highest Offering: Doctorate
Program: Liberal Arts And General; Professional
Accreditation: **SC**, ART, BUS, CLPSY, CS, DANCE, ENG, LAW, MUS, THEA, THEOL

01 President ... Dr. R. Gerald TURNER
05 Provost/Vice Pres Academic Affairs ... Dr. Paul W. LUDDEN
10 Vice President Business & Finance ... Ms. Chris C. REGIS
32 Vice President for Student Affairs ... Dr. Lori S. WHITE
30 Vice Pres Devel & External Affairs ... Mr. Brad E. CHEVES
43 Gen Counsel/VP Leg Affs/Govt Rels ... Mr. Paul J. WARD
11 Vice President Executive Affairs ... Dr. Thomas E. BARRY
49 Dean Dedman College ... Dr. William M. TSUTSUI
35 Assoc VP/Dean Student Life ... Dr. Lisa WEBB
21 Associate Vice President/Controller ... Mr. John O'CONNOR
45 Associate Vice President/Budgets ... Mr. Ernie BARRY
26 Assoc Vice President/Public Affairs ... Ms. Patti LASALLE
44 Asst Vice Pres Univ Development ... Ms. Pam CONLIN
15 Assoc VP Human Res & Business Svcs ... Dr. William DETWILER
84 Assoc Vice Pres Enrollment Mgmt ... Dr. Stephanie DUPAUL
88 Exec Dir of Program Services ... Ms. Dana AYRES
57 Dean Meadows School of the Arts ... Dr. Jose A. BOWEN
61 Dean Dedman School of Law ... Mr. John B. ATTANASIO
54 Interim Dean Lyle School of Engr ... Dr. Marc CHRISTENSEN
73 Dean Perkins School of Theology ... Dr. William B. LAWRENCE
50 Dean Cox School of Business ... Dr. Albert W. NIEMI, JR.
58 Assoc VP Research & Grad Studies ... Dr. James E. QUICK
53 Dean Sch of Educ/Human Devel ... Dr. David J. CHARD
08 Dean/Dir Central Univ Libraries ... Ms. Gillian M. MCCOMBS
20 Assoc Provost ... Dr. Harold W. STANLEY
20 Assoc Provost ... Ms. Linda S. EADS
25 Asst VP for Research Administration ... Ms. Alicia BROSSETTE
41 Interim Director of Athletics ... Mr. Tim LEONARD
06 Registrar ... Mr. John A. HALL
07 Dean Admiss/Exec Dir Enroll Mgmt ... Mr. Wes K. WAGGONER
37 Director Financial Aid ... Mr. Marc PETERSON
36 Asst VP/ Exec Dir Career Center ... Dr. Troy T. BEHRENS
27 Chief Information Officer ... Mr. Joe GARGIULO
38 Director Counseling & Testing ... Dr. Karen SETTLE
23 Exec Director Health Services ... Mr. Patrick HITE
39 Dir Residence Life/Student Housing ... Mr. Steve LOGAN
04 Ex Ast to Pres/Dir Inst Access/Eqty ... Ms. Beth WILSON
09 Director of Institutional Research ... Dr. John M. KALB
21 Treasurer/Chief Investment Officer ... Mr. Michael A. CONDON
96 Director of Procurement ... Mr. Terrence CONNOR
42 University Chaplain ... Mr. Stephen RANKIN
24 Dir Ctr for Media/Instr Technology ... Dr. Bill DWORACZYK
29 Interim Exec Dir Alumni Relations ... Ms. Marianne B. PIEPENBURG

Southwest Career College (B)

1414 Geronimo Drive, El Paso TX 79925
County: El Paso FICE Identification: 041317
Unit ID: 451556
Telephone: (915) 778-4001 Carnegie Class: Assoc/PrivFP
FAX Number: (915) 778-1575 Calendar System: Other
URL: www.swci-ep.com
Established: 2001 Annual Undergrad Tuition & Fees: N/A
Enrollment: 813 Coed
Affiliation or Control: Proprietary IRS Status: Proprietary
Highest Offering: Associate Degree
Program: Occupational
Accreditation: **ABHES**

01 School Director ... Mr. Benjamin ARRIOLA

Southwest Institute of Technology (C)

5424 Highway 290 W, Suite 200, Austin TX 78735-8890
County: Travis FICE Identification: 020936
Unit ID: 228291
Telephone: (512) 892-2640 Carnegie Class: Assoc/PrivFP
FAX Number: (512) 892-1045 Calendar System: Quarter
URL: www.swse.net
Established: 1958 Annual Undergrad Tuition & Fees: $40,200
Enrollment: 28 Coed
Affiliation or Control: Proprietary IRS Status: Proprietary
Highest Offering: Associate Degree
Program: Occupational; Technical Emphasis
Accreditation: **ACCSC**

01 Director ... Ms. Frances DAVIS
32 Director of Student Services ... Ms. Lori GARZA

Southwest Texas Junior College (D)

2401 Garner Field Road, Uvalde TX 78801-6221
County: Uvalde FICE Identification: 003614
Unit ID: 228316
Telephone: (830) 278-4401 Carnegie Class: Assoc/Pub-R-M
FAX Number: (830) 591-7354 Calendar System: Semester
URL: www.swtjc.net
Established: 1946 Annual Undergrad Tuition & Fees (In-District): $2,468
Enrollment: 5,664 Coed
Affiliation or Control: Local IRS Status: 501(c)3
Highest Offering: Associate Degree
Program: Occupational; 2-Year Principally Bachelor's Creditable; Teacher Preparatory
Accreditation: **SC**

01 President ... Dr. Ismael SOSA
05 Dean Instructional Services/CFO ... Dr. Hector GONZALES
30 Dean of Inst Advancement/Technology ... Dr. Blaine BENNETT
06 Registrar ... Mr. Luis FERNANDEZ
07 Dean of Admissions & Student Svc ... Mr. Joe BARKER
09 Coordinator Institutional Research ... Dr. Julie THOMAS
15 Director Human Resources ... Mr. Oscar S. GARCIA
18 Chief Facilities/Physical Plant ... Mr. Jesus MARTINEZ
26 Chief Public Relations Officer ... Mr. Willie EDWARDS
32 Chief Student Life Officer ... Mr. Joe BARKER
35 Director Student Affairs ... Ms. Jessica NUNEZ
37 Director Student Financial Aid ... Ms. Yvette HERNANDEZ
38 Director Student Counseling ... Ms. Lorena LOPEZ
84 Director Enrollment Management ... Mr. Joe BARKER
96 Director of Purchasing ... Mr. Jesse MARTINEZ

Southwestern Adventist University (E)

PO Box 567, 100 W Hillcrest St, Keene TX 76059-0567
County: Johnson FICE Identification: 003619
Unit ID: 228468
Telephone: (817) 645-3921 Carnegie Class: Bac/Diverse
FAX Number: (817) 202-6744 Calendar System: Semester
URL: www.swau.edu
Established: 1893 Annual Undergrad Tuition & Fees: $17,800
Enrollment: 635 Coed
Affiliation or Control: Seventh-day Adventist IRS Status: 501(c)3
Highest Offering: Master's
Program: Liberal Arts And General; Teacher Preparatory; Professional
Accreditation: **SC**, IACBE, NURSE

01 President ... Dr. Eric D. ANDERSON
05 VP for Academic Administration ... Dr. Amy ROSENTHAL
10 VP for Financial Administration ... Mr. Larry W. GARRETT
30 VP for University Advancement ... Mr. Gary M. TEMPLE
84 VP for Enrollment ... Ms. Enga ALMEIDA
32 VP for Student Services ... Mr. James THE
42 VP for Spiritual Development ... Mr. Russ LAUGHLIN
45 Director of Planning ... Dr. Thomas G. BUNCH
37 Asst VP for Student Finance ... Ms. Patricia A. NORWOOD
21 Asst VP Financial Administration ... Mr. Greg A. WICKLUND
06 Registrar ... Dr. Robert GARDNER
08 Librarian ... Ms. Cristina M. THOMSEN
34 Dean of Women ... Mrs. Janelle D. WILLIAMS
33 Dean of Men ... Mr. William IVERSON
13 Dir Information Technology Svcs ... Mr. E. Charles LEWIS
18 Plant Engineer ... Mr. Dale E. HAINEY
26 Director of Marketing ... Ms. Darcy FORCE
29 Director of Alumni Relations ... Ms. Beverly A. MENDENHALL
38 Director of Counseling & Testing ... Dr. R. Mark ALDRIDGE

Southwestern Assemblies of God University (F)

1200 Sycamore, Waxahachie TX 75165-2397
County: Ellis FICE Identification: 003616
Unit ID: 228325
Telephone: (972) 937-4010 Carnegie Class: Master's S
FAX Number: (972) 923-0488 Calendar System: Semester
URL: www.sagu.edu
Established: 1927 Annual Undergrad Tuition & Fees: $16,630
Enrollment: 2,023 Coed
Affiliation or Control: Assemblies Of God Church IRS Status: 501(c)3
Highest Offering: Master's
Program: Liberal Arts And General; Teacher Preparatory; Religious Emphasis
Accreditation: **SC**

01 President ... Dr. Kermit S. BRIDGES
05 Vice President for Academics ... Dr. Paul BROOKS
32 Vice President for Student Services ... Rev. Terry PHIPPS
10 Vice Pres for Business & Finance ... Rev. Jay TREWERN
30 Vice President for Univ Advancement ... Rev. Irby MCKNIGHT
84 Vice Pres Enrollment & Retention ... Rev. Eddie DAVIS
20 Dean of Academic Services ... Rev. Donny LUTRICK
58 Dean of Graduate Studies ... Dr. Robert HARDEN
73 Dean Col Bible & Church Ministries ... Dr. LeRoy BARTEL
79 Dean College of Arts & Professions ... Dr. Larry GOODRICH
09 Assoc Dean of Inst Effectiveness ... Dr. Kim BERNECKER
106 Asst Dean for Distance Education ... Rev. Joseph HARTMAN
06 Registrar ... Ms. Heather FRANCIS
35 Dean of Students ... Rev. Lance MECHE
89 Asst Dean for Student Success ... Rev. Rob BLAKNEY
88 Director of Achievement Center ... Mr. Nolan JONES
14 Sr Dir Information Technology ... Rev. David BUSH
29 Director of Alumni Relations ... Mr. Devin FERGUSON
08 Director of Learning Resources ... Mr. Eugene HOLDER
13 Director of Campus Software ... Mr. Mark WALKER
21 Sr Dir of Business Services ... Mr. Jimmie LAMB
88 Senior Director of Accounting ... Ms. Candee LUTRICK
37 Sr Director of Financial Aid ... Mr. Jeff FRANCIS
19 Director of Security ... Mr. Ron CRANE
07 Assistant Dean of Admissions ... Rev. Bryan BROOKS
24 Director of Media Services ... Mr. John COOKMAN
88 Director of Accounts Receivable ... Ms. Joan BUTLER
44 Sr Dir of Dev & Planned Giving ... Mr. Craig RINAS
36 Director of Career Services ... Ms. Beverly ROBINSON
41 Athletic Director ... Mr. Jesse GODDING
26 Director of University Marketing ... Mr. Ryan MCELHANY
15 Director of Human Resources ... Mrs. Ruth ROBERTS
88 Director of Educator Cert ... Ms. Janice WHITAKER
18 Projects Manager ... Mr. James DAVIS
38 Counselor ... Dr. Tim MYERS
88 Admissions Counselor ... Ms. Pat THOMPSON
88 Director of On Campus Admissions ... Ms. Sara ESCAMILLA
88 Director of Online Admissions ... Ms. Valerie FITZWATER

Southwestern Baptist Theological Seminary (G)

PO Box 22607, Fort Worth TX 76122-0150
County: Tarrant FICE Identification: 003617
Unit ID: 228477
Telephone: (817) 923-1921 Carnegie Class: Spec/Faith
FAX Number: (817) 921-8766 Calendar System: Semester
URL: www.swbts.edu
Established: 1908 Annual Undergrad Tuition & Fees: $6,536
Enrollment: 2,808 Coed
Affiliation or Control: Southern Baptist IRS Status: 501(c)3
Highest Offering: Doctorate
Program: Professional; Religious Emphasis
Accreditation: **SC**, MUS, THEOL

01 President ... Dr. Paige PATTERSON
05 Executive Vice President/Provost ... Dr. Craig A. BLAISING
10 Vice Pres Business Administration ... Mr. Kevin ENSLEY
30 Vice Pres Institutional Advancement ... Mr. Mike C. HUGHES
32 Vice Pres for Student Services/Comm ... Dr. Thomas WHITE
88 Vice Pres of Strategic Initiatives ... Dr. Jason G. DUESING
20 Vice Provost for Academic Programs ... Dr. Edward PAULEY
06 Registrar & Assoc VP Inst Assessmnt ... Dr. Mark LEEDS
08 Dean of Libraries ... Dr. C. Berry DRIVER
73 Dean of the School of Theology ... Dr. David ALLEN
88 Dean Marshall Center for Theol Stds ... Dr. Rudy GONZALEZ
53 Dean Sch of Church & Fam Ministries ... Dr. Waylan OWENS
64 Dean School of Church Music ... Dr. Stephen JOHNSON
12 Dean Havard Sch for Theol Studies ... Dr. Denny AUTREY
73 Dean Sch of Evangelism & Missions ... Dr. Keith EITEL
49 Dean College at Southwestern ... Dr. Steven SMITH
94 Dean of Women's Programs ... Dr. Terri STOVALL
56 Dean Center for Extension Education ... Dr. Deron BILES
07 Director of Admissions ... Mr. Kyle WALKER

Southwestern Christian College (H)

Box 10, Terrell TX 75160-9002
County: Kaufman FICE Identification: 003618
Unit ID: 228486
Telephone: (972) 524-3341 Carnegie Class: Bac/Assoc
FAX Number: (972) 563-7133 Calendar System: Semester
URL: www.swcc.edu
Established: 1949 Annual Undergrad Tuition & Fees: $6,910
Enrollment: 216 Coed
Affiliation or Control: Churches Of Christ IRS Status: 501(c)3

Highest Offering: Baccalaureate
Program: Liberal Arts And General
Accreditation: SC

01 President .... Dr. Jack EVANS, SR.
30 Vice President for Instl Expansion .... Dr. James MAXWELL
05 Vice President Academic Affairs .... Mrs. Zoa Ann TURNER
10 Vice President Fiscal Affairs .... Mr. Douglas HOWIE
32 Vice President Student Affairs .... Mr. Ben FOSTER
08 Librarian .... Mrs. Doris JOHNSON
07 Director of Admissions .... Mr. Walter PRICE
37 Director of Financial Aid .... Ms. Tanya DEAN
44 Director of Development .... Mr. Jack EVANS, JR.

Southwestern University (A)

1001 E University Avenue, Georgetown TX 78626-6144
County: Williamson FICE Identification: 003620
Unit ID: 228343
Telephone: (512) 863-6511 Carnegie Class: Bac/A&S
FAX Number: (512) 863-5788 Calendar System: Semester
URL: www.southwestern.edu
Established: 1840 Annual Undergrad Tuition & Fees: $34,410
Enrollment: 1,347 Coed
Affiliation or Control: United Methodist IRS Status: 501(c)3
Highest Offering: Baccalaureate
Program: Liberal Arts And General; Teacher Preparatory
Accreditation: SC, MUS

01 President .... Dr. Jake B. SCHRUM
42 University Chaplain .... Ms. Beverly JONES
04 Executive Asst to the President .... Ms. Francie SCHROEDER
04 Sr Advisor Strategic Plng/Assess .... Dr. Ronald L. SWAIN
05 Provost/Dean of Faculty .... Dr. James W. HUNT
84 Vice Pres for Enrollment Services .... Mr. Dave VOSKUIL
30 Vice Pres Institutional Advancement .... Mr. C. Richard MCKELVEY
10 Vice President for Fiscal Affairs .... Mr. Richard L. ANDERSON
32 Vice President for Student Life .... Mr. Gerald D. BRODY
27 VP for Information Services and CIO .... Dr. Pam MCQUESTEN
57 Dean of Sarofim School of Fine Arts .... Dr. Paul J. GAFFNEY
08 Dean of Library Services .... Ms. Lynne BRODY
20 Assoc VP Academic Administration .... Ms. Julie A. COWLEY
26 Assoc VP for University Relations .... Ms. Cindy LOCKE
21 Assoc Vice President for Finance .... Vacant
88 Assoc VP for Facility/Campus Svcs .... Mr. Bob D. MATHIS
13 Assoc VP for Information Tech Svcs .... Vacant
15 Assoc VP for Human Resources .... Ms. Elma F. BENAVIDES
39 Assoc VP and Dean of Students .... Ms. Jaime WOODY
07 Assoc VP for Enrollment Services .... Vacant
29 Assoc VP for Alumni Relations .... Vacant
44 Associate Vice Pres for Development .... Mr. Kent HUNTSMAN
41 Assoc VP/Dir Intercollegiate Athl .... Dr. Glada C. MUNT
35 Associate Dean for Student Life .... Vacant
88 Asst Dean Faculty Dev & Spons Pgms .... Dr. John MCCANN
06 Registrar .... Mr. David H. STONES
21 Controller .... Ms. Brenda THOMPSON
19 Chief of Police .... Ms. Deborah BROWN
37 Director of Financial Aid .... Mr. James GAETA
36 Director Career Services .... Mr. Roger YOUNG
20 Dir Academic Success .... Ms. Kimberly MURPHY
20 Dir Paideia Program/Assoc Professor .... Dr. David J. GAINES
85 Director Intercultural Learning .... Ms. Tisha TEMPLE
27 Director of Communications .... Ms. Ellen DAVIS
38 Director Counseling/Health Services .... Dr. Judith SONNENBERG
18 Director Physical Plant .... Mr. Joe LEPAGE
09 Director Institutional Research .... Dr. Michelle ACHACOSO
28 Asst Director of Diversity Educ .... Vacant
31 Coordinator of Civic Engagement .... Vacant

Stephen F. Austin State University (B)

2008 Alumni Drive, Rusk 206,
Nacogdoches TX 75961-3940
County: Nacogdoches FICE Identification: 003624
Unit ID: 228431
Telephone: (936) 468-2011 Carnegie Class: Master's L
FAX Number: (936) 468-2202 Calendar System: Semester
URL: www.sfasu.edu
Established: 1921 Annual Undergrad Tuition & Fees (In-State): $7,929
Enrollment: 12,903 Coed
Affiliation or Control: State IRS Status: 501(c)3
Highest Offering: Doctorate
Program: Liberal Arts And General; Teacher Preparatory; Professional
Accreditation: SC, AAFCS, ART, BUS, CACREP, CIDA, CORE, CS, DIETD, DIETI, FOR, MUS, NUR, SP, SW, TED, THEA

01 President .... Dr. Baker PATTILLO
05 Provost/Vice Pres Academic Affairs .... Dr. Richard A. BERRY
10 Vice Pres Finance/Administration .... Mr. Danny R. GALLANT
32 Vice Pres for University Affairs .... Dr. Steve WESTBROOK
30 Vice Pres University Advancement .... Mrs. Jill STILL
29 Exec Director SFA Alumni Affairs .... Mr. Jeff DAVIS
20 Assoc Provost/VP Academic Affairs .... Dr. Mary Nelle BRUNSON
84 Exec Dir of Enrollment Management .... Ms. Monique COSSICH
26 Inr Exec Dir Public Affs/Marketing .... Mrs. Shirley LUNA
43 General Counsel .... Mr. Damon DERRICK
06 Registrar .... Ms. Lynda LANGHAM
09 Director Institutional Research .... Ms. Karyn HALL
08 Library Director .... Ms. Shirley DICKERSON
39 Director of Residence Life .... Mr. Winston BAKER
18 Director of Physical Plant .... Mr. Lee BRITTAIN
37 Director of Financial Aid .... Mr. Michael C. O'REAR
22 Director Affirmative Action .... Ms. Glenda HERRINGTON
13 Dir Computer/Communication Svcs .... Mr. Paul DAVIS
15 Personnel Director .... Ms. Glenda HERRINGTON
19 Chief of University Police .... Mr. Marc COSSICH
23 Director Health Services .... Dr. Penny JEFFERY
41 Director of Intercol Athletics .... Mr. Robert W. HILL
35 Dean Student Affairs .... Dr. Adam PECK
36 Director Counsel/Career Services .... Mrs. Jill MILEM
96 Director of Procurement .... Ms. Diana BOUBEL
45 Dir Research/Sponsored Programs .... Dr. Carrie BROWN
28 Director Multicultural Affairs .... Dr. Terrence FRAZIER
58 Dean Graduate School .... Dr. Mary Nelle BRUNSON
49 Dean College Liberal/Applied Arts .... Dr. Brian MURPHY
47 Dean College Forestry/Agriculture .... Dr. Steven BULLARD
53 Dean of College of Education .... Dr. Judy A. ABBOTT
57 Dean College Fine Arts .... Dr. A.C. (Buddy) HIMES
50 Int Dean College of Business .... Dr. Geralyn FRANKLIN
81 Dean College Sciences & Math .... Dr. Kimberly M. CHILDS

Tarrant County College District (C)

1500 Houston Street, Fort Worth TX 76102-6599
County: Tarrant FICE Identification: 003626
Unit ID: 228547
Telephone: (817) 515-5100 Carnegie Class: Assoc/Pub-U-MC
FAX Number: (817) 515-5350 Calendar System: Semester
URL: www.tccd.edu
Established: 1965 Annual Undergrad Tuition & Fees (In-District): $1,248
Enrollment: 50,062 Coed
Affiliation or Control: State/Local IRS Status: 501(c)3
Highest Offering: Associate Degree
Program: Occupational; 2-Year Principally Bachelor's Creditable
Accreditation: SC, ADNUR, DH, DIETT, EMT, PTAA, RAD, SURGT

01 Chancellor .... Mrs. Erma C. JOHNSON HADLEY
05 Vice Chancellor Academic Affairs .... Dr. David A. WELLS
11 Vice Chanc Admin and Gen Counsel .... Mrs. Angela ROBINSON
10 Vice Chancellor for Finance .... Mr. Mark MCCLENDON
13 Vice Chanc Info/Technical Services .... Mr. Timothy (Tim) MARSHALL
88 Vice Chancellor for Student Success .... Dr. Joy GATES BLACK
18 Vice Chanc Real Estate/Facilities .... Ms. Nina PETTY
27 VC Communications/External Affairs .... Mr. Reginald GATES
20 VP Academic Affairs/SO Campus .... Dr. Jo K. BAGLEY
20 VP Academic Affairs/NE Campus .... Mr. Gary SMITH
20 VP Academic Affairs/NW Campus .... Dr. Leann ELLIS
20 VP Academic Affairs/SE .... Ms. Barbara COAN
20 VP Academic Affairs/TR .... Dr. Bryan STEWART
32 VP Student Dev Services/NE Campus . Dr. Magdalena DELA TEJA
32 VP Student Dev Services/SE Campus .... Mr. Rusty FOX
32 VP Student Dev Services/So Campus .... Dr. Nicole BRADFORD
32 VP Student Dev Services/TR Campus .... Mr. Adrian RODRIGUEZ
32 VP Student Dev Services/NW .... Dr. Joe RODE
12 President South Campus .... Dr. Peter JORDAN
12 President Northwest Campus .... Dr. Elva C. LEBLANC
12 President Northeast Campus .... Dr. Larry J. DARLAGE
12 President Southeast Campus .... Dr. William COPPOLA
12 President Trinity River Campus .... Dr. Tahita M. FULKERSON
84 Assoc Vice Chanc Enrollment Svcs .... Mr. David XIMENEZ
88 Assoc Vice Chanc Student Success .... Dr. Kimberly A. BEATTY
15 Assoc Vice Chanc Human Resources .... Dr. Ricardo CORONADO
25 Assoc Vice Chanc Grants Dev/Compl .... Ms. Jackie MAKI
21 Assoc Vice Chancellor Finance .... Mrs. Nancy H. CHANG
20 Assoc Vice Chanc Academic Affairs .... Dr. Jane HARPER
51 Assoc Vice Chanc Cont Ed Svcs .... Mr. Troy VAUGHN
88 AVC Col Readiness Educ Foundations .... Mr. Rick GARCIA
30 Executive Director of Development .... Dr. Joe MCINTOSH
09 Exec Dir Inst Rsrch/Plng/Effect .... Dr. Terri L. DAY
09 Dir Inst Rsrch/Plng/Effect .... Dr. Steven W. HAGSTROM
26 Director Public Rels/Marketing .... Mr. Frank GRIFFIS
18 Dir of Physical Plant Operations .... Mr. Gary PREATHER
19 Chief of Police .... Mr. Shaun WILLIAMS
56 Director Distance Learning .... Dr. Kevin EASON
08 Dir Library Svcs Northeast Campus .... Mr. Mark DOLIVE
08 Director Library Svcs South Campus .... Ms. Linda JENSON
08 Dir Library Svcs Northwest Campus .... Ms. Sandra MCGORDY
08 Dir Library Svcs Southeast Campus .... Mr. Mark DOLIVE
06 Registrar South Campus .... Mr. John D. SPENCER
06 Registrar Northeast Campus .... Mr. Brian D. BARRETT
06 Registrar Northwest Campus .... Dr. Aubra J. GANTT
06 Registrar Southeast Campus .... Mr. Juan C. TORRES
06 Registrar Trinity Campus .... Mr. Gerald RACIOPPI
38 Director Counseling South Campus .. Ms. Marisa GARCIA-LUNA
38 Dir Counseling Northeast Campus .... Dr. Condoa PARRENT
38 Dir Counseling Southeast Campus .... Mr. Steve RAKOFF
37 Director Financial Aid South Campus .... Ms. JoLynn F. SPROLE
37 Dir Financial Aid Northeast Campus .... Vacant
37 Dir Financial Aid Northwest Campus .... Ms. Trina SMITH-PATTERSON
37 Dir Financial Aid Southeast Campus .... Ms. Erika T. WILLIAMS
37 Dir Financial Aid Trinity Campus .... Mr. William MCMULLEN
23 Dir Student Devel Svcs NE Campus .... Dr. Paula VASTINE-NORMAN
24 Dir Instruction Media South Campus .... Ms. Sue E. SANDERS
24 Dir Instruction Media NE Campus .... Mr. David B. MEAD
24 Dir Learning Resources NW Campus .... Dr. John R. MARTIN, JR.
35 Dir Student Activities So Campus ... Mr. Bobby (BJ) A. SULLIVAN
35 Dir Student Activities NW Campus .... Ms. Vesta M. MARTINEZ
35 Dir Student Devel Svcs SE Campus .... Mr. Douglas C. PEAK
96 Director of Business Svcs .... Mrs. Kathy CRUSTO-WAY
38 Dir Counseling Northwest Campus .... Dr. Ricks EDMONDSON
96 Director of Procurement .... Mr. Michael (Mike) HERNDON
36 Coord Student Career/Employmnt Svcs .... Ms. Sandra L. WALKER

Temple College (D)

2600 S First Street, Temple TX 76504-7435
County: Bell FICE Identification: 003627
Unit ID: 228608
Telephone: (254) 298-8282 Carnegie Class: Assoc/Pub-R-M
FAX Number: (254) 298-8277 Calendar System: Semester
URL: www.templejc.edu
Established: 1926 Annual Undergrad Tuition & Fees (In-District): $2,112
Enrollment: 5,807 Coed
Affiliation or Control: Local IRS Status: 501(c)3
Highest Offering: Associate Degree
Program: Occupational; 2-Year Principally Bachelor's Creditable
Accreditation: SC, ADNUR, DH, DMS, EMT, SURGT

01 President .... Dr. Glenda O. BARRON
11 AVP Finance/Info Tech Svcs .... Dr. Van MILLER
05 Vice Pres of Educational Services .... Dr. Mark A. SMITH
31 AVP Acad Outreach & Ext Programs .... Dr. Dan SPENCER
13 Senior Dir IT Services .... Mr. Donnie CARPENTER
15 Director Div of Resource Management .... Dr. Randy BACA
84 Div Dir Stdnt & Enroll Srvcs .... Mrs. Carey ROSE
08 Div Director of Learning Resources .... Mrs. Kathy FULTON
102 Exec Dir Temple College Foundation .... Mrs. Jennifer GRAHAM
09 AVP Comm Init & Spec Programs .... Dr. Jimmy ROBERTS
38 Director Student Advising .... Ms. Amy FLINN
04 Assistant to the President & Board .... Mrs. Judith DOHNALIK
37 Director of Financial Aid .... Mr. Fred PENA
27 Director College Communications .... Ms. Erin SPENCER
18 Dir Facilities/Physical Plant .... Mr. Skeet POWELL
96 Director of Purchasing .... Mrs. Deborah SVAJDA
32 Chief Student Life Officer .... Mrs. Ruth BRIDGES
07 Assoc Dir Admission & Records .... Mrs. Toni CUELLAR
41 Athletic Director .... Mr. Danny SCOTT
19 Chief of Police .... Mr. David BLANKEMEIER

Texarkana College (E)

2500 N Robison Road, Texarkana TX 75501-3099
County: Bowie FICE Identification: 003628
Unit ID: 228699
Telephone: (903) 823-3456 Carnegie Class: Assoc/Pub-R-M
FAX Number: (903) 823-5030 Calendar System: Semester
URL: www.texarkanacollege.edu
Established: 1927 Annual Undergrad Tuition & Fees (In-District): $1,808
Enrollment: 4,663 Coed
Affiliation or Control: Local IRS Status: 501(c)3
Highest Offering: Associate Degree
Program: Occupational; 2-Year Principally Bachelor's Creditable
Accreditation: SC, ADNUR

01 President .... Mr. James H. RUSSELL
10 Chief Finance Officer .... Ms. Kim JONES
27 Int Chief Information Officer .... Dr. Vernon WILDER
45 Dir of Institutional Effectiveness .... Mrs. Jamie ASHBY
07 Director of Admissions .... Mr. Tom ELDER
51 Assoc Dean Evening & Cont Education .... Mr. Bill MOSS
18 Chief Facilities/Physical Plant .... Mr. Rick BOYETTE
30 Inst Advancement & Public Rels .... Mrs. Suzy IRWIN
84 Recruitment Coordinator .... Ms. Jennifer GOODWIN

*The Texas A & M University System Office (F)

301 Tarrow Street, 7th Floor, College Station TX 77840
County: Brazos FICE Identification: 003629
Unit ID: 228732
Telephone: (979) 458-6000 Carnegie Class: N/A
FAX Number: (979) 458-6044
URL: www.tamus.edu

01 Chancellor .... Mr. John SHARP
05 Vice Chanc Academic Affairs .... Dr. James HALLMARK
86 Vice Chanc for Federal & State Rels .... Dr. Gui DIEDRICH
09 Vice Chanc for Strategic Initiative .... Dr. Brett GIROIR
07 Vice Chanc Recruitment/Diversity .... Dr. Frank ASHLEY
26 Vice Chanc Marketing/Communications .... Mr. Steve B. MOORE
10 Chief Financial Officer/Treasurer .... Mr. Greg ANDERSON
21 Chief Auditor .... Ms. Cathy SMOCK
43 General Counsel .... Mr. Ray BONILLA
46 Chief Research Officer .... Dr. Jeffrey R. SEEMANN
19 Chief Safety Officer .... Mr. Chris MEYER
13 Chief Information Officer .... Mr. Pierce CANTRELL

*Prairie View A & M University (G)

L. W. Minor Street, Prairie View TX 77446-0519
County: Waller FICE Identification: 003630
Unit ID: 227526
Telephone: (936) 261-3311 Carnegie Class: Master's L
FAX Number: (936) 261-2115 Calendar System: Semester
URL: www.pvamu.edu
Established: 1876 Annual Undergrad Tuition & Fees (In-State): $6,485
Enrollment: 8,425 Coed
Affiliation or Control: State IRS Status: 501(c)3
Highest Offering: Doctorate
Program: Liberal Arts And General; Teacher Preparatory; Professional
Accreditation: SC, BUS, CS, DIETD, DIETI, ENG, ENGT, MUS, NUR, NURSE, SW, TED

02 President .... Dr. George C. WRIGHT

05 Provost/SR VP Academic Affairs .... Dr. E. Joahanne THOMAS-SMITH
20 Assoc Prov & Assoc VP Acad Afairs .. Dr. James J. WILSON, JR.
20 Assoc Prov & Assoc VP Acad Affairs .... Dr. Felicia M. NAVE
92 Director of Honors Program .... Dr. James J. WILSON, JR.
10 Sr Vice President Business Affairs .... Dr. Corey S. BRADFORD, SR.
32 VP for Student Affs/Inst Relations .... Dr. Lauretta F. BYARS
46 Vice President Research/Development .... Dr. Willie F. TROTTY
35 Vice Pres Student/Enrollment Svcs .... Mr. Don BYARS
10 Vice Pres Administration/Aux Svcs ...... Mr. Fred E. WASHINGTON
20 Vice Provost & Dean of NWHC .... Dr. Michael L. MCFRAZIER
84 Assoc Provost Enrollment Mgmt .... Mr. Don BYARS
21 Asst VP for Financial Accounting .... Mr. Rod MIRELES
21 Asst VP for Financial Services .... Ms. Patricia BAUGHMAN
30 Director of Development .... Mr. Nelson E. BOWMAN
09 Director Institutional Research .... Mr. Dean WILLIAMSON
07 Dir of Undergraduate Admissions .... Ms. Mary E. GOOCH
18 Assistant VP of Physical Plant .... Mr. Larry J. WATSON
08 Director of Library .... Dr. Rosie L. ALBRITTON
15 Asst VP for Human Resources .... Mr. Albert R. GEE
37 Director of Financial Aid .... Mr. K. Michael FRANCOIS
36 Program Coord Residence Life .... Mr. Charles E. CROCKETT
63 Director Undergrad Med Acad .... Dr. Dennis E. DANIELS
41 Director of Athletics .... Mr. Fred E. WASHINGTON
14 Chief Information Officer .... Mr. Luis-Pablo GRIJALVA
58 Dean of the Graduate School .... Dr. Willie F. TROTTY
50 Dean College of Business .... Dr. Munir QUDDUS
53 Dean College of Education .... Dr. Lucian YATES
54 Dean College of Engineering .... Dr. Kendall T. HARRIS
47 Dean Col Agriculture/Human Sci .... Dr. Freddie L. RICHARDS
66 Dean College of Nursing .... Dr. Betty ADAMS
49 Dean College of Arts & Sciences .... Dr. Danny R. KELLEY
48 Dean School of Architecture .... Dr. Ikhlas SABOUNI
88 Int Dean Col of Juv Just/Psychology .... Dr. Dennis E. DANIELS
21 Manager of Treasury Services .... Ms. Equilla JACKSON
23 Director Health Center .... Ms. Thelma J. PIERRE
56 Administrator Coop Extension .... Dr. Freddie L. RICHARDS
19 Director Security/Safety .... Mr. Algray L. PETTUS
31 Asst VP Auxiliary Enterprises .... Ms. Tressey D. WILSON
29 Executive Dir for Comm/Alumni Affs .... Mrs. Sheleah D. REED
06 Registrar/Records .... Ms. Deborah J. DUNGEY
12 Exec Dir University College .... Ms. Lettie M. RAAB
28 Director of Diversity .... Ms. Elma D. GONZALEZ
85 Immigration Services Coord .... Mrs. Evelyn J. MCGINTY
26 Executive Dir for Communications .... Mrs. Sheleah D. REED
96 Procurement Sup/HUB Coordinator .... Mr. Jim A. NELMS
88 Director Budget & Reconciliation .... Mrs. Diane T. EVANS

*Tarleton State University (A)

1333 W Washington, Box T-0001,
Stephenville TX 76402-0001

County: Erath | FICE Identification: 003631 | Unit ID: 228529
Telephone: (254) 968-9000 | Carnegie Class: Master's L
FAX Number: (254) 968-9920 | Calendar System: Semester
URL: www.tarleton.edu
Established: 1899 | Annual Undergrad Tuition & Fees (In-State): $6,450
Enrollment: 11,693 | Coed
Affiliation or Control: State | IRS Status: 501(c)3
Highest Offering: Doctorate
Program: Liberal Arts And General; Teacher Preparatory
Accreditation: SC, ACBSP, ENG, HT, MLTAD, MT, MUS, NURSE, SW

02 President .... Dr. F. Dominic DOTTAVIO
04 Executive Asst to the President .... Ms. Vickie E. SWAM
05 Provost/Exec VPAA .... Dr. Karen MURRAY
30 Vice Pres Inst Advancement .... Dr. Rick RICHARDSON
10 Vice Pres Finance/Administration .... Mr. Tye MINCKLER
32 VP Student Life/Dean Students .... Mr. Rusty JERGINS
84 Assoc VP Enrollment/Inform Mgmt . Dr. David WEISSENBURGER
20 Assoc VP for Academic Affairs .... Dr. Dwayne SNIDER
38 Asst VP Wellness/Career Devel .... Vacant
46 Assoc VP Academic Research/Grants .... Dr. Bert LITTLE
18 Assoc Vice Pres Physical Facilities .... Mr. Joe STANDRIDGE
21 Asst VP Finance/Administration .... Ms. Cynthia CARTER
35 AVP Student Success/Multicul Init .... Dr. Jennifer T. EDWARDS
26 Assoc VP Marketing/Communications .... Ms. Janice HORAK
35 Asst VP Student Life Studies .... Dr. Ashley TULL
21 Asst VP Business Svcs/Controller .... Mr. Mike TATE
49 Dean College Science & Technology .... Dr. James PIERCE
50 Dean Col of Business Administration .... Dr. Adolfo BENAVIDES
47 Dean Col Agricul & Environ Sciences .... Dr. Donald L. CAWTHON
53 Dean College of Education .... Dr. Jill BURK
57 Int Dean College Liberal/Fine Arts .... Ms. Kelli STYRON
58 Dean College of Graduate Studies .... Dr. Linda M. JONES
07 Director Undergraduate Admissions .... Ms. Cynthia HESS
28 Dir Student Disability Services .... Ms. Trina GEYE
08 University Librarian .... Mrs. Donna SAVAGE
31 Director of External Relations .... Ms. Janice HORAK
37 Director Student Financial Aid .... Ms. Betty MURRAY
09 Director Institutional Research .... Dr. Wayne ATCHLEY
13 CIO/Exec Dir Information Tech Svcs .... Ms. Rebecca GRAY
15 Director Human Resources .... Ms. Angela C. BROWN
36 Director Career Services .... Ms. Darla DOTY
41 Athletic Director .... Mr. Lonn REISMAN
23 Director Student Health Center .... Ms. Bridgette BEDNARZ
19 Director University Police .... Mr. Justin WILLIAMS
39 Director Housing & Residence Life .... Ms. Elizabeth WALLACE
28 Int Dir Ofc Diversity/Inclusion .... Dr. Moumin QUAZI
24 Dir Instruct Tech/Distribut Educ .... Dr. Credence BAKER
44 Director of Development .... Ms. Sabra GUERRA

104 Dir International Academic Programs .... Dr. Marilyn ROBITAILLE
06 Registrar .... Ms. Denise GROVES
96 Director of Purchasing/HUB .... Ms. Beth CHANDLER
25 Grants/Contracts Administrator .... Ms. DeAnna POWELL
40 Manager Campus Store .... Ms. Christina STRADLEY
105 Web Administrator .... Ms. Daphne HUNT

*Texas A & M University System Health Science Center (B)

8441 State HWY 47, CB1 Suite 3100, Bryan TX 77807

County: Brazos | FICE Identification: 004948 | Unit ID: 223214
Telephone: (979) 436-9100 | Carnegie Class: Spec/Med
FAX Number: (979) 436-0072 | Calendar System: Semester
URL: www.tamhsc.edu
Established: 1999 | Annual Undergrad Tuition & Fees (In-State): $10,010
Enrollment: 2,122 | Coed
Affiliation or Control: State | IRS Status: 501(c)3
Highest Offering: Doctorate
Program: Professional
Accreditation: SC

02 President .... Dr. Nancy W. DICKEY
05 Vice President for Academic Affairs . Dr. Roderick W. MCCALLUM
10 Vice Pres Finance & Administration .... Dr. Barry C. NELSON
86 Vice President Governmental Affairs .... Ms. Jenny E. JONES
46 Vice Pres Research/Graduate Studies .... Dr. David S. CARLSON
30 VP for Institutional Advancement .... Dr. Russell A. GIBBS
13 Assistant Vice President/CIO .... Mr. Scott HONEA
52 Dean Baylor College of Dentistry .... Dr. Lawrence E. WOLINSKY
63 Dean Col of Medicine/VP Clin Affs .... Dr. Thomas S. SHOMAKER
66 Dean College of Nursing .... Dr. Sharon A. WILKERSON
67 Dean College of Pharmacy .... Dr. Indra K. REDDY
69 Dean School of Rural Public Health .... Dr. Craig H. BLAKELY
88 Dir Inst for Biosciences & Tech .... Dr. Cheryl WALKER
100 Chief of Staff .... Dr. Lee Ann RAY

† Tuition varies by program.

*Texas A & M Health Science Center Baylor College of Dentistry (C)

3302 Gaston Avenue, Dallas TX 75246-2098

County: Dallas | Identification: 666240
Telephone: (214) 828-8100 | Carnegie Class: Not Classified
FAX Number: (214) 874-4536 | Calendar System: Semester
URL: www.bcd.tamhsc.edu
Established: 1905 | Annual Undergrad Tuition & Fees (In-State): $6,894
Enrollment: 573 | Coed
Affiliation or Control: State | IRS Status: 501(c)3
Highest Offering: Doctorate
Program: Professional
Accreditation: &SC, DENT, DH

02 Dean .... Dr. Lawrence E. WOLINSKY
10 Special Assistant to the Dean .... Ms. Juanna S. MOORE
05 Assoc Dean Academic Affairs .... Dr. Charles W. BERRY
46 Assoc Dean Research/Grad Studies .... Dr. Larry L. BELLINGER
88 Associate Dean Clinical Affairs .... Dr. Dean A. HUDSON
26 Exec Dir of Comm/Devel & Alumni Aff .... Ms. Susan MITCHELL JACKSON
07 Exec Dir of Recruitment/Admissions .... Dr. Barbara H. MILLER
51 Exec Dir Continuing Education .... Dr. Amerian SONES
09 Exec Dir of Institutional Research .... Dr. Eric S. SOLOMON
18 Exec Dir of Facilities Services .... Mr. Dale A. CHRISTENSEN
32 Associate Dean Student Affairs .... Dr. Jack L. LONG
76 Director Dental Hygiene .... Dr. Janice P. DEWALD
90 Director of Academic Computing .... Ms. Regina L. COURTNEY
15 Regional Director Human Resources .... Ms. Pat LOPEZ
37 Director Student Financial Aid .... Ms. Kay EGBERT
08 Director Library .... Ms. Rosanna RATLIFF
17 Director of Hospital Affairs .... Dr. R. Gilbert TRIPLETT
83 Director of Social Services .... Mrs. Leeanna BARTLETT
96 Assistant Manager Purchasing .... Ms. Debbie RUFF
35 Director Student Affairs .... Ms. Moira ALLEN

*Texas A & M International University (D)

5201 University Boulevard, Laredo TX 78041-1900

County: Webb | FICE Identification: 009651 | Unit ID: 226152
Telephone: (956) 326-2001 | Carnegie Class: Master's L
FAX Number: (956) 326-2348 | Calendar System: Semester
URL: www.tamiu.edu
Established: 1969 | Annual Undergrad Tuition & Fees (In-State): $6,558
Enrollment: 7,037 | Coed
Affiliation or Control: State | IRS Status: 501(c)3
Highest Offering: Doctorate
Program: Liberal Arts And General; Teacher Preparatory
Accreditation: SC, BUS, NUR

02 President .... Dr. Ray M. KECK, III
05 Provost/Vice Pres Academic Affs .... Dr. Pablo ARENAZ
10 Vice Pres Finance & Administration ... Mr. Juan J. CASTILLO, JR.
30 Vice Pres Institutional Advancement .... Mrs. Candy HEIN
32 Vice Pres for Student Success .... Ms. Minita RAMIREZ
20 Assoc Vice Pres Academic Affairs .... Mrs. Mary T. TREVINO
11 Assoc Vice Pres for Administration .. Mrs. Elizabeth N. MARTINEZ

13 Assoc VP Information Technology/CIO .. Mr. Leebrian E. GASKINS
88 Regents Professor/Associate Provost .... Dr. Juan R. LIRA
49 Dean College Arts & Sciences .... Dr. Thomas R. MITCHELL
50 Dean AR Sanchez Jr Sch of Business .... Dr. Steve R. SEARS
66 Dean Canseco School of Nursing .... Dr. Regina C. AUNE
08 Dir Sue & Radcliffe Killam Library .... Mr. Douglas M. FERRIER
07 Director Admissions .... Mrs. Rosie A. DICKINSON
06 University Registrar .... Mr. Oscar E. REYNA
15 Director of Human Resources .... Mrs. Sandra V. PENA
26 Director Public Rels Mktg/Info Svcs .... Mr. Steve K. HARMON
37 Director Financial Aid .... Mrs. Laura M. ELIZONDO
41 Athletic Director .... Dr. Leonard J. NARDONE
18 Director Physical Plant .... Mr. Richard E. GENTRY
29 Director Alumni Relations .... Mrs. Yelitza Marie HOWARD
36 Director Career Services .... Mrs. Cassandra L. WHEELER
23 Assoc Director Student Health .... Ms. Elizabeth DODIER
39 Director of Residence Life/Housing .... Mr. Trevor C. LIDDLE
38 Dir of Student Couns/Hlth Svcs .... Mr. Gilberto SALINAS
96 Dir Purchasing & Support Services .... Mr. Hector G. CAVAZOS
92 Dir D.D. Hachar Honor Scholars Pgm .... Mr. Sergio D. GARZA
21 Comptroller .... Ms. Elena M. MARTINEZ
32 Director Student Affairs .... Mr. Gerardo ALVA
35 Assoc Director Student Affairs .... Mr. Miguel A. TREVINO
09 Director of Institutional Research .... Ms. Elizabeth MARTINEZ

*Texas A & M University (E)

1246 TAMU, College Station TX 77843-1246

County: Brazos | FICE Identification: 003632 | Unit ID: 228723
Telephone: (979) 845-2217 | Carnegie Class: RU/VH
FAX Number: (979) 845-5027 | Calendar System: Semester
URL: www.tamu.edu
Established: 1876 | Annual Undergrad Tuition & Fees (In-State): $8,480
Enrollment: 49,861 | Coed
Affiliation or Control: State | IRS Status: 501(c)3
Highest Offering: Doctorate
Program: Liberal Arts And General; Teacher Preparatory; Professional
Accreditation: SC, BUS, BUSA, CEA, CLPSY, CONST, COPSY, CS, DIETD, DIETI, ENG, ENGT, FOR, HSA, IPSY, LSAR, MED, NRPA, NURSE, PH, PLNG, SCPSY, SPAA, VET

02 President .... Dr. R. Bowen LOFTIN
05 Provost/Exec VP Academic Affairs .... Dr. Karan L. WATSON
11 Vice Pres Administration .... Dr. Rodney P. MCCLENDON
10 Vice President Finance/CFO .... Mr. B. J. CRAIN
32 Vice Pres Student Affairs .... LtGen. Joseph F. WEBER
46 Vice Pres Research .... Dr. Jeffrey R. SEEMANN
27 Vice Pres Marketing/Communications .... Mr. Jason D. COOK
86 Vice Pres Governmental Relations .... Mr. Michael O'QUINN
12 Vice Pres/CEO Texas A&M Galveston .... RAdm. Robert SMITH, III
13 Vice Pres/Assoc Prov IT .... Dr. Pierce E. CANTRELL, JR.
28 Vice Pres/Assoc Prov Diversity .... Dr. Christine STANLEY
20 Vice Provost for Academic Affairs .... Dr. Pamela R. MATTHEWS
43 Deputy General Counsel .... Mr. Scott A. KELLY
47 Dean Agriculture & Life Science .... Dr. Mark A. HUSSEY
48 Dean Architecture .... Dr. Jorge VANEGAS
50 Dean Business .... Dr. Jerry STRAWSER
53 Dean Educ & Human Dev .... Dr. Douglas J. PALMER
54 Dean Engineering .... Dr. M. Katherine BANKS
65 Dean Geosciences .... Dr. Kate C. MILLER
80 Acting Dean Govt & Public Policy .... Mr. Andrew H. CARD, JR.
49 Dean Liberal Arts .... Dr. Jose Luis BERMUDEZ
81 Dean Science .... Dr. H. Joseph NEWTON
74 Dean Vet Med & Biomed Sciences .... Dr. Eleanor M. GREEN
08 Int Dean/Director Libraries .... Mr. David H. CARLSON
12 Dean & CEO Texas A&M at Qatar .... Dr. Mark H. WEICHOLD
20 Dean of Faculties/Associate Provost .... Dr. Antonio CEPEDA-BENITO
20 Int Assoc Prov Undergrad Studies .... Dr. Christine A. STANLEY
20 Assoc Prov Graduate Studies .... Dr. Karen L. BUTLER-PURRY
07 Asst VP Acad Services/Admissions .... Mr. Scott MCDONALD
37 Exec Dir Student Financial Aid .... Ms. Delisa F. FALKS
06 Registrar .... Ms. Venesa A. HEIDICK
41 Interim Athletic Director .... Dr. John H. THORNTON
26 Assoc VP Mktg & Comm/News .... Ms. Sherylon CARROLL
15 Chief Human Resources Officer .... Ms. Kathryn B. SYMANK
14 Exec Dir Computing & Info Svcs .... Mr. Pete MARCHBANKS
19 Chief University Police .... Mr. Elmer E. SCHNEIDER, JR.
18 Exec Dir Facilities .... Mr. Rodney E. WEIS
36 Exec Dir Career Center .... Dr. J. Leigh TURNER
23 Director Student Health Center .... Dr. Martha C. DANNENBAUM
38 Exec Dir Student Counseling Svcs .... Dr. Maggie GARTNER
39 Director Residence Life/Housing .... Ms. Chareny L. RYDL
92 Exec Dir Honors Programs .... Dr. Sumana DATTA
104 Dir Study Abroad .... Dr. Jane FLAHERTY
96 Exec Dir Strategic Sourcing .... Mr. Rex JANNE
09 Exec Dir for Data & Research Svcs .... Dr. David J. MARTIN
30 Sr Executive Development .... Dr. Robert L. WALKER
102 Pres Texas A&M Foundation .... Dr. Eddie J. DAVIS
29 Pres Assoc of Former Students .... Mr. Porter GARNER
100 Chief of Staff to President .... Mr. Matt FRY

*Texas A & M University at Galveston (F)

PO Box 1675, Galveston TX 77553-1675

County: Galveston | FICE Identification: 010298 | Unit ID: 228714
Telephone: (409) 740-4400 | Carnegie Class: Bac/Diverse
FAX Number: (409) 740-4407 | Calendar System: Semester
URL: www.tamug.edu
Established: 1962 | Annual Undergrad Tuition & Fees (In-State): $7,834
Enrollment: 2,035 | Coed

Affiliation or Control: State IRS Status: 501(c)3
Highest Offering: Master's
Program: Professional
Accreditation: &SC, ENG, ENGT

02 President & CEO RADM. Robert SMITH, III
05 Vice Pres Academic Affairs Dr. Donna LANG
20 Sr Vice Pres/Assoc Provost Dr. William SEITZ
12 Supt Texas State Maritime Acad RADM. William W. PICKAVANCE, JR.
10 Vice President Finance Ms. Susan HERNANDEZ LEE
11 Assoc Vice Pres for Administration Vacant
32 Assoc VP Stdnt Affs/Auxiliary Svcs Mr. Grant W. SHALLENBERGER
09 Assoc VP Research/Graduate Studies Dr. Tammy L. HOLLIDAY
46 Assoc VP Research/Development Dr. Antonietta QUIDGG
30 Director Development Mr. Shaun MILLIGAN
15 Director Personnel Services Mr. Jeff BOYER
35 Director Student Affairs Mr. Todd SUTHERLAND
37 Director Student Financial Aid Mr. Truman GLENN
07 Exec Dir Admissions/Enrollment Mgmt Ms. Cheryl GREFFENSTEET-MOON
18 Chief Facilities/Physical Plant Ms. Wie HEIDEL
26 Dir Media Relations/Communications Ms. Cathy CASHIO
36 Dir Student Placement/Counseling Mr. Ken BAILEY
14 Dir Computing/Information Svcs Mr. Steven CONWAY
88 Head Dept of Marine Biology Dr. John SCHWARZ
97 Head Dept of General Academics Dr. Joseph SZUCS
88 Int Head Dept Maritime Sys Engineer Dr. Martin MILLER
88 Hd Dept Marine Sci/Ocean/Coast Rec Dr. Patrick LOUCHOUARN
88 Int Hd Marine Transp/Maritime Admn Dr. Augusta ROTH

† Regional accreditation is carried under the parent institution Texas A & M University, College Station, TX.

*Texas A & M University - Central Texas (A)

1901 South Clear Creek Rd, Killeen TX 76549
County: Bell Identification: 667086
Telephone: (245) 519-5400 Carnegie Class: Not Classified
FAX Number: (245) 519-5482 Calendar System: Semester
URL: www.ct.tamus.edu
Established: 1999 Annual Undergrad Tuition & Fees (In-State): $6,420
Enrollment: N/A Coed
Affiliation or Control: State IRS Status: 501(c)3
Highest Offering: Master's
Program: Liberal Arts And General
Accreditation: &SC, ACBSP

02 President Dr. Marc A. NIGLIAZZO

† Regional accreditation is carried under the parent institution, Tarleton State University, Stephenville, TX.

*Texas A & M University - Commerce (B)

PO Box 3011, Commerce TX 75429-3011
County: Hunt FICE Identification: 003565
Unit ID: 224554
Telephone: (903) 886-5102 Carnegie Class: DRU
FAX Number: (903) 886-5888 Calendar System: Semester
URL: www.tamu-commerce.edu
Established: 1889 Annual Undergrad Tuition & Fees (In-State): $5,470
Enrollment: 10,726 Coed
Affiliation or Control: State IRS Status: 501(c)3
Highest Offering: Doctorate
Program: Liberal Arts And General; Teacher Preparatory; Professional
Accreditation: SC, ART, BUS, CACREP, ENG, MUS, SW

02 President Dr. Dan JONES
05 Provost/VP Academic Affairs Dr. Larry LEMANSKI
10 Vice Pres Business & Administration Mr. Bob BROWN
30 Vice Pres Institutional Advancement Mr. Randy VAN DEVEN
26 Assoc VP for Mktg Communications Mr. Randy JOLLY
20 Int Assoc Provost for Academic Affs Dr. Dan EDLEMAN
20 Assoc VP Student Access & Success Dr. Sharon JOHNSON
09 Assoc Prov of Inst Effectiveness Dr. Roseann HOGAN
84 Dean of Enrollment Management Mrs. Stephanie HOLLEY
21 Assoc VP & Dir of Financial Svcs Ms. Alicia CURRIN
18 Exec Dir Facil Mgmt & Support Svcs Mr. David MCKENNA
06 Registrar Ms. Paige BUSSELL
21 Asst VP Business & Dir Employee Svc Mr. Rex GIDDENS
88 Comptroller/Director of Accounting Ms. Kim LAIRD
08 Library Director Dr. Gregory MITCHELL
27 Chief Information Officer Mr. Anwar KARIM
37 Director of Financial Aid Ms. Maria RAMOS
36 Director of Career Development Mrs. Tina BOITNOTT
58 Dean Graduate Studies/Research Vacant
53 Dean Education & Human Services Dr. Brent MANGUS
79 Dean of Humanities/Soc Sci & Art Dr. Salvatore ATTARDO
92 Dean of the Honors College Dr. Ray GREEN
81 Dean Science/Engr & Agric Dr. Grady PRICE BLOUNT
50 Dean of Business & Entrepreneurship Dr. Harold (Hal) P. LANGFORD
88 Dean of University College Dr. Ricky DOBBS
07 Director of Undergraduate Admiss Mr. Jody TODHUNTER
108 Director of Student Assessment Ms. Wendy GRUVER
32 Dean of Campus Life & Student Dev Mr. Brian NICHOLS
29 Director of Alumni Relations Mr. Derryle PEACE
19 University Police Chief Mrs. Donna SPINATO
12 Director Metroplex Center Mrs. SuzAnne KEIFER
38 Director Counseling Center Dr. Linda T. CLINTON
39 Residential Living & Learning Mr. Dennis KOCH
41 Athletic Director Mr. Carlton COOPER
88 Dir of Risk Management Mr. Jeffrey MCMURRAY
23 Director Student Health Services Ms. Maxine MENDOZA-WELCH
15 Asst VP for Business/Dir Empl Svcs Mr. Rex GIDDENS
85 Dir International Student Services Mr. John MARK JONES
96 Director of Purchasing/HUB Coord Mr. Travis BALL
28 Dir of Diversity & Cultural Affair Mr. Robert DOTSON
88 Safety Manager Mr. Derek PREAS

*Texas A & M University - Corpus Christi (C)

6300 Ocean Drive, Unit 5756,
Corpus Christi TX 78412-5756
County: Nueces FICE Identification: 011161
Unit ID: 224147
Telephone: (361) 825-5700 Carnegie Class: DRU
FAX Number: (361) 825-5887 Calendar System: Semester
URL: www.tamucc.edu
Established: 1947 Annual Undergrad Tuition & Fees (In-State): $7,669
Enrollment: 10,162 Coed
Affiliation or Control: State IRS Status: 501(c)3
Highest Offering: Doctorate
Program: Liberal Arts And General; Teacher Preparatory; Professional
Accreditation: SC, BUS, BUSA, CACREP, CS, ENGR, ENGT, MT, MUS, NURSE

02 President Dr. Flavius C. KILLEBREW
05 Provost/VP for Academic Affairs Dr. Christopher L. MARKWOOD
10 Exec VP for Finance/Administration Ms. Kathryn FUNK-BAXTER
30 Vice Pres Institutional Advancement Dr. S. Trent HILL
32 VP Student Engagement & Success Dr. Don ALBRECHT
46 VP Rsrch/Commercialization/Outreach Dr. Luis CIFUENTES
20 Vice Provost Academic Affairs Dr. Paul MEYER
100 Chief of Staff Dr. Mary SHERWOOD
13 Assoc Vice Pres Info Technology/CIO Mr. Terry TATUM
20 Assoc VP for Academic Affairs Dr. David BILLEAUX
84 Assoc VP Enrollment Management Ms. Margaret DECHANT
35 Assoc Vice Pres/Dean of Students Ms. Ann DEGAISH
08 Asst VP & Director of Bell Library Ms. Christine SHUPALA
09 Dir Planning & Instl Research Dr. Colby STOEVER
26 Dir Communications/Public Affairs Ms. Gloria GALLARDO
44 Director of Development Ms. Kimberly MCNIERNEY
06 University Registrar Mr. Michael RENDON
07 Director of Admissions Dr. J. Christopher FLEMING
37 Director of Financial Assistance Ms. Jeannie GAGE
31 Director Community Outreach Dr. James NEEDHAM
15 Director Human Resources Ms. Debra CORTINAS
18 Director Facilities Services Mr. Mark NASH
29 Director Alumni Relations Ms. Evon ENGLISH
36 Director Career Services Ms. Joanna BENAVIDES-FRANKE
38 Dir Student Counseling/Development Dr. Carla BERKICH
28 Dir Equal Opportunity/Employee Rels Mr. Sam RAMIREZ
11 Exec Dir Administrative Services Ms. Judy HARRAL
96 Dir Procurement & Disbursements Mr. David DAVILA
21 Bursar Ms. Christina HOLZHEUSER
58 Int Dean College of Grad Studies Ms. Jo Ann CANALES
49 Dean College Liberal Arts Dr. Kelly QUINTANILLA
50 Dean College of Business Dr. Moustafa H. ABDELSAMAD
53 Dean College of Education Dr. Arthur HERNANDEZ
54 Dean of Col Science & Engrng Dr. Frank PEZOLD
66 Dean College Nursing & Health Sci Dr. Mary Jane HAMILTON

*Texas A & M University - Kingsville (D)

700 University Boulevard, Kingsville TX 78363-8202
County: Kleberg FICE Identification: 003639
Unit ID: 228705
Telephone: (361) 593-2111 Carnegie Class: DRU
FAX Number: (361) 593-3107 Calendar System: Semester
URL: www.tamuk.edu
Established: 1925 Annual Undergrad Tuition & Fees (In-State): $6,940
Enrollment: 6,737 Coed
Affiliation or Control: State IRS Status: 501(c)3
Highest Offering: Doctorate
Program: Liberal Arts And General; Teacher Preparatory
Accreditation: SC, ACBSP, DIETD, DIETI, ENG, MUS, NAIT, PHAR, SP, SW

02 President Dr. Steven H. TALLANT
100 Chief of Staff Mr. Randy HUGHES
88 Dir of Compliance Dr. John BURNETT
05 Provost & Vice Pres Acad Affs Dr. Rex F. GANDY
10 Interim Sr VP Fiscal Affairs Dr. Terisa RILEY
88 Interim Dir of Budgets Ms. Jennifer ALEXANDER
88 Comptroller Ms. Paula HANSON
88 Risk Management Dr. Shane CREEL
30 Vice Pres Institutional Advancement Mr. Scott GINES
36 Director of Career Services Mr. Christian FERRIS
32 Vice President Student Affairs Dr. Terisa C. RILEY
35 Dir Student Affairs Auxiliary Svcs Mr. Crispin TREVINO
88 Dir of Campus Rec & Fitness Mr. Charles ESPINOSA
84 VP Enrollment Management Mr. Manuel LUJAN
27 Assoc VP Information Technology/CIO Mr. Robert PAULSON
88 Assoc CIO Mr. Lonnie NAGEL
88 Dir Enterprise Information Systems Mr. Lee MOORE
88 Dir Compliance & Client Support Mr. Val RAMIREZ
32 Dean of Students Ms. Kristin COMPARY
20 Associate VP Academic Affairs Dr. Duane GARDINER
85 Director International Studies Ms. Marilu SALAZAR
88 Dir Center Teaching Effectiveness Dr. Jaya GOSWAMI
88 Asst Dir Cntr Teaching Effectiven Ms. Brenda MELENDY
58 Assoc VP Research & Grad Studies Dr. Mohamed ABDELRAHMAN
88 Asst VP Student Access Dr. Mary GONZALEZ
47 Dean Agriculture/Nat Res/Human Sci Dr. George A. RASMUSSEN
88 Dir Center for Young Childrean Ms. Lisa TURCOTTE
49 Dean Arts & Sciences Dr. Abbey ZINK
50 Dean Business Administration Vacant
53 Dean Education & Human Performance Dr. Alberto RUIZ
54 Dean Engineering Dr. Stephan NIX
92 Dean Honors College Dr. Dolores GUERRERO
89 Assoc VP for Student Success Dr. Nancy KING SANDERS
26 Exec Dir Mktg & Comm Ms. Cheryl CAIN
08 Librarian Mr. Bruce R. SCHUENAMAN
09 Interim Dir Planning & Assessment Mr. Lee MOORE
88 Director Citrus Center Dr. John DA GRACA
88 Director King Ranch Mgmt Institute Dr. Clay P. MATHIS
88 Director Wildlife Research Inst Dr. Fred BRYANT
88 Interim Dir Nat Toxins Res Ctr Dr. Elda E. SANCHEZ
88 Director Inst Sust Energy & Env Dr. Kim JONES
06 Registrar Mr. George WEIR
07 Director of Admission Mr. Ramon BLAKLEY
29 Director Development and Alumni Rel Ms. Yvonne TRACHTA
41 Director Athletics Mr. Brian DEANGELIS
40 Director Bookstore Ms. Mary GUTIERREZ
106 Director Distance Learning Ms. Michelle DURAN
44 Exec Dir Development & Alumni Ms. Lori RUSSEK
88 Interim Dir Health and Wellness Ms. Jo Elda CASTILLO-ALANIZ
09 Director Institutional Research Ms. Miao ZHUANG
88 Director John E. Conner Museum Mr. Jonathan PLANT
16 Exec Dir HR & Payroll Mr. Leon BAZAR
18 Director Physical Plant Mr. Roberto RAMIREZ
26 Coordinator Public Relations Mr. Jason MARTON
88 Coordinator Publications Mr. Robert PENA
96 Assoc VP Support Services Mr. Ralph STEPHENS
25 Contract Administrator Ms. Rachel L. BUENTELLO
39 Director Residence Life Mr. Tom MARTIN
46 Interim Director Sponsored Research Dr. Rebecca DAVIS
35 Director Student Activities Ms. Erin MCCLURE
19 Director of University Police Mr. Felipe GARZA
37 Director Student Financial Aid Mr. Ralph PERRI
38 Director Student Counseling Vacant
21 Supervisor Business Services Ms. Janet L. POLLARD
88 Advisor Pre-profession Programs Ms. Amanda MUNIZ
88 Bible Chair Baptist Mr. Mike CERVANTES
88 Bible Chair Catholic Mr. Victor RODRIGUEZ

*Texas A & M University-San Antonio (E)

One University Way, San Antonio TX 78224
County: Bexar Identification: 666689
Telephone: (210) 784-1000 Carnegie Class: Not Classified
FAX Number: (210) 784-6219 Calendar System: Semester
URL: www.tamusa.tamus.edu
Established: 2009 Annual Undergrad Tuition & Fees (In-District): $3,072
Enrollment: 3,057 Coed
Affiliation or Control: State/Local IRS Status: 501(c)3
Highest Offering: Master's
Program: Liberal Arts And General
Accreditation: &SC

02 President Dr. Maria Hernandez FERRIER
05 Chief Academic Officer/Provost Dr. Brent SNOW
10 Vice Pres Finance/Administration Kenneth MITTS
30 VP Strategic Init/Inst Advance Dr. Charles RODRIGUEZ
32 Assoc VP for Student Affairs Dr. Mary Ann GRAMS
26 Assc VP Univ Communications Ms. Marilu A. REYNA
09 Director of Institutional Research Dr. Raymond S. BOTELLO
50 Head School of Business Dr. Tracy HURLEY
53 Int Head Sch Education/Kinesiology Mr. Joe GARCIA

† Regional accreditation is carried under the parent institution, Texas A&M University-Kingsville in Kingsville, TX.

*Texas A & M University - Texarkana (F)

7101 University Avenue, Texarkana TX 75503
County: Bowie FICE Identification: 031703
Unit ID: 224545
Telephone: (903) 223-3000 Carnegie Class: Master's L
FAX Number: (903) 832-8890 Calendar System: Semester
URL: www.tamut.edu
Established: 1971 Annual Undergrad Tuition & Fees (In-State): $5,568
Enrollment: 1,952 Coed
Affiliation or Control: State IRS Status: 501(c)3
Highest Offering: Doctorate
Program: Liberal Arts And General; Professional
Accreditation: SC, NURSE

02 President Dr. Carlisle B. RATHBURN, III
05 Provost/Vice Pres Academic Affairs Dr. Rosanne STRIPLING
10 Vice Pres Finance & Administration Mr. Randy RIKEL
32 VP Student Engagement & Success Dr. Kent KELSO
88 Dean College of STEM Dr. Arthur LINKINS
53 Dean College Education/Liberal Art Dr. Glenda BALLARD
50 Dean College of Business Dr. Larry DAVIS

21 Controller ... Mr. James SCOGIN
07 Exec Dir Enrollment Services ... Mr. Richard BOLLINGER
37 Director Fin Aid & Veteran Svcs ... Ms. Alyssa MCCLURE
15 Director Human Resources & EEO ... Mr. Jerry HENRY
30 Director Institutional Advancement ... Mrs. LeAnne WRIGHT
09 AVP Institutional Effectiveness ... Vacant
08 Director Library ... Mrs. Teri STOVER
18 Director Physical Plant ... Mr. John MILLS
18 Director of Security ... Mr. John GANN
96 Director Purchasing ... Mrs. Cynthia HENDERSON
13 Int AVP of Information Technology ... Mr. Scott LENT
88 Director Payroll ... Mrs. Ramona GREEN
35 Director Student & Career Services ... Mr. Carl GREIG
84 Director Enrollment Management ... Mr. Toney FAVORS
27 Mgr Communications/Alumni Relation ... Mr. Bob BRUGGEMAN

*West Texas A & M University (A)

2403 Russell C. Long Blvd., Canyon TX 79015
County: Randall FICE Identification: 003665
Unit ID: 229814
Telephone: (806) 651-0000 Carnegie Class: Master's L
FAX Number: (806) 651-2126 Calendar System: Semester
URL: www.wtamu.edu
Established: 1910 Annual Undergrad Tuition & Fees (In-State): $6,728
Enrollment: 7,902 Coed
Affiliation or Control: State IRS Status: 501(c)3
Highest Offering: Doctorate
Program: Liberal Arts And General; Teacher Preparatory; Professional
Accreditation: SC, BUS, ENG, MUS, NURSE, SP, SW

02 President ... Dr. J. Patrick O'BRIEN
05 Int Provost/Vice Pres Acad Affairs ... Dr. Wade SHAFFER
10 Vice Pres for Business & Finance ... Mr. Gary W. BARNES
32 Int Vice Pres for Student Affairs ... Ms. Denese SKINNER
26 Vice Pres Institutional Advancement ... Dr. Neal WEAVER
84 Vice Pres of Enrollment Management ... Mr. Dan D. GARCIA
30 Executive Director of Development ... Dr. Neal WEAVER
06 Registrar ... Ms. Tana J. MILLER
07 Director of Admissions ... Mr. Kyle MOORE
08 Dir Information/Library Resources ... Ms. Shawna J. KENNEDY-WITTHAR
36 Int Dir Career Planning & Placement ... Ms. Kim MULLER
37 Director Student Financial Aid ... Mr. James D. REED
51 Interim Dir Continuing Education ... Ms. Roxie PRANGLIN
23 Director Medical Service ... Dr. Jim GIBBS
18 Director Physical Plant ... Mr. Dan K. SMITH
19 Police Chief ... Chief Shawn G. BURNS
27 Director Communication Services ... Ms. Ann UNDERWOOD
29 Director of Alumni Relations ... Ms. Becky STOGNER
38 Int Director Counseling Services ... Mr. Orvie NIX
41 Director of Athletics ... Mr. Michael MCBROOM
09 Director Institutional Research ... Dr. Gary D. KELLEY
13 Chief Information Officer ... Mr. James D. WEBB
96 Director of Purchasing ... Mr. Brian GLENN
40 Manager Bookstore ... Mr. Terry S. NEPPER
15 Director Personnel Services ... Mr. Harvey L. HUDSPETH
47 Dean Col Agr/Science/Engineering ... Dr. Don TOPLIFF
50 Dean College of Business ... Dr. Neil W. TERRY
53 Dean Col Education & Social Science ... Dr. Eddie W. HENDERSON
57 Dean College Fine Arts/Humanities ... Dr. Jessica MALLARD
58 Dean Graduate School & Research ... Dr. Angela SPAULDING
66 Dean College of Nursing/Health Sci ... Dr. Dirk NELSON
21 Controller ... Mr. Rick JOHNSON

Texas Chiropractic College (B)

5912 Spencer Highway, Pasadena TX 77505-1699
County: Harris FICE Identification: 003635
Unit ID: 228866
Telephone: (281) 487-1170 Carnegie Class: Spec/Health
FAX Number: (281) 487-2009 Calendar System: Trimester
URL: www.txchiro.edu
Established: 1908 Annual Undergrad Tuition & Fees: N/A
Enrollment: 279 Coed
Affiliation or Control: Independent Non-Profit IRS Status: 501(c)3
Highest Offering: Doctorate
Program: Professional
Accreditation: SC, CHIRO

01 President/CEO ... Dr. Richard G. BRASSARD
05 Vice President/Provost ... Dr. Clay MCDONALD
10 Chief Financial Officer ... Mr. Bill QUINN
20 VP Academics & Program Development ... Dr. Al ADAMS
32 Vice President Student Affairs ... Dr. Steve HASLUND
20 Dean of Academic Affairs ... Dr. John MROZEK
84 Dean of Enrollment Management ... Dr. Fred ZUKER
23 Dean of Clinics ... Dr. Barry WIESE
06 Registrar ... Dr. Karlene DENBY
46 Director Research ... Vacant
15 Director of Human Resources ... Mrs. Sue ARNOLD
26 Director of Communications ... Ms. Patty BARNES
09 Director Institutional Research ... Vacant
51 Director of Postgraduate ... Dr. Jason FLANAGAN
08 Director of Library Services ... Ms. Carol WEBB
37 Director Financial Aid ... Mr. Arthur GOUDEAU
96 Director of Purchasing ... Ms. Joanna LITTLE
29 Director of Alumni Relations ... Ms. Gabrielle GREENWADE
35 Director of Student Services ... Ms. Mary SUTTLE
07 Associate Director of Admissions ... Ms. Kristina HANSON
04 Admin Asst to President ... Ms. Glenda RAMIREZ
18 Physical Plant Supervisor ... Mr. Perry LATIOLAIS

Texas Christian University (C)

2800 S University Drive, Fort Worth TX 76129-2800
County: Tarrant FICE Identification: 003636
Unit ID: 228875
Telephone: (817) 257-7000 Carnegie Class: DRU
FAX Number: (817) 257-7333 Calendar System: Semester
URL: www.tcu.edu
Established: 1873 Annual Undergrad Tuition & Fees: $34,590
Enrollment: 9,518 Coed
Affiliation or Control: Christian Church (Disciples Of Christ)
IRS Status: 501(c)3
Highest Offering: Doctorate
Program: Liberal Arts And General; Teacher Preparatory; Professional
Accreditation: SC, ANEST, ART, BUS, BUSA, CIDA, CS, DANCE, DIETC, DIETD, ENG, JOUR, MUS, NURSE, SP, SW

01 Chancellor ... Dr. Victor J. BOSCHINI, JR.
05 Provost/Vice Chanc Academic Affairs ... Dr. R. Nowell DONOVAN
10 Vice Chanc Finance & Administration ... Mr. Brian G. GUTIERREZ
30 Vice Chanc University Advancement . Mr. Donald J. WHELAN, JR.
32 Vice Chancellor Student Affairs ... Dr. Kathryn CAVINS-TULL
26 Vice Chanc Mktg & Communication ... Ms. Tracy SYLER-JONES
86 Vice Chanc Government Affairs ... Mr. Larry D. LAUER
35 Assoc Vice Chanc Student Affairs ... Dr. Barbara B. HERMAN
35 Assoc Vice Chanc/Dean Campus Life ... Ms. Susan W. ADAMS
88 Assoc Vice Chanc Advancement Ops ... Dr. Roby V. KEY
29 Assoc Vice Chanc Alumni Relations ... Ms. Kristi M. HOBAN
16 Assoc Vice Chanc HR/Risk Mgmt ... Ms. Jill L. LASTER
21 Assoc Vice Chanc & Controller ... Ms. Cheryl L. WILSON
18 Assoc Vice Chanc for Facilities ... Vacant
44 Asst Vice Chanc College & Reg Devel ... Mr. Adam BAGGS
28 Asst VC of Student Services ... Mr. Darron TURNER
88 Chief Investment Officer ... Mr. Jim HILLE
41 Director Athletics ... Mr. Christopher DEL CONTE
100 Chief of Staff ... Ms. Karen M. BAKER
20 Assoc Provost Academic Affairs ... Dr. Bonnie MELHART
20 Assoc Provost Academic Support ... Dr. Leo W. MUNSON
20 Assoc Provost Academic Plan/Budget ... Dr. Ann C. SEWELL
20 Assoc Provost Technology Support ... Mr. Ruben D. CHANLATTE
20 Asst Provost Inst Effectiveness ... Dr. Catherine WEHLBURG
49 Dean Addran College of Liberal Arts ... Dr. Andrew SCHOOLMASTER
50 Dean Neeley School of Business ... Dr. Homer EREKSON
60 Dean College of Communication ... Dr. David WHILLOCK
53 Dean College of Education ... Dr. Mary PATTON
57 Dean College of Fine Arts ... Dr. Scott SULLIVAN
66 Dean Harris Col Nurs/Hlth Science ... Dr. Paulette BURNS
54 Dean Col of Science & Engineering ... Dr. Demitris KOURIS
92 Dean John V Roach Honors College ... Dr. Peggy WATSON
08 Dean of the Library ... Dr. June KOELKER
07 Dean of Admission ... Mr. Raymond A. BROWN
13 Director Information Technology ... Mr. Bryan LUCAS
88 Exec Dir Acad Resource Mgmt & Compl ... Ms. Susan G. CAMPBELL
22 Affirmative Action Officer ... Mr. Darron TURNER
06 Registrar/Dir Enrollment Management ... Mr. Patrick MILLER
19 Chief TCU Police ... Mr. Steve G. MCGEE
42 Minister to the University ... Rev. Angela KAUFMAN
21 Dir Budget & Financial Planning ... Mr. Kenneth JANAK
85 Director Center for Intl Studies ... Dr. Jane KUCKO
15 Director Compensation ... Ms. Dindy ROBINSON
25 Director Contract Administration ... Mr. Matthew WALLIS
15 Director Employee Relations ... Ms. Sharon E. BARNES
51 Director Extended Education ... Mr. David A. GREBEL
88 Director Freshman Admission ... Mr. Heath EINSTEIN
23 Director Health Center ... Dr. Jane TORGERSON
09 Director Institutional Research ... Dr. Cathy COGHLAN
24 Director Instructional Services ... Mr. Larry E. KITCHENS
85 Director International Student Svcs ... Mr. John L. SINGLETON
38 Director Mental Health Services ... Dr. Linda WOLSZON
96 Director Purchasing ... Mr. Roger D. FULLER
39 Director Residential Services ... Mr. Craig ALLEN
37 Director Student Aid ... Mr. Michael H. SCOTT
88 Assoc Dean Student Development Svc ... Ms. Cynthia WALSH
25 Coord Research & Sponsored Projects ... Vacant
36 Exec Director Univ Career Svcs ... Dr. John THOMPSON

Texas College (D)

2404 N Grand Avenue, Tyler TX 75702-1962
County: Smith FICE Identification: 003638
Unit ID: 228884
Telephone: (903) 593-8311 Carnegie Class: Bac/Diverse
FAX Number: (903) 593-0588 Calendar System: Semester
URL: www.texascollege.edu
Established: 1894 Annual Undergrad Tuition & Fees: $9,682
Enrollment: 883 Coed
Affiliation or Control: Christian Methodist Episcopal IRS Status: 501(c)3
Highest Offering: Baccalaureate
Program: 2-Year Principally Bachelor's Creditable; Liberal Arts And General; Teacher Preparatory
Accreditation: SC

01 President ... Dr. Dwight FENNELL
05 Vice President Academic Affairs ... Dr. Rhonda SALDIVOR
10 Vice Pres Business & Finance ... Mr. James HARRIS
32 Vice Pres Student Affairs ... Dr. Willie CHAMPION
30 Director of Development ... Mr. Anthony MEYERS
07 Dean of Enrollment Services ... Mr. John ROBERTS
35 Dean of Students ... Ms. Vickie KENNEDY
06 Registrar ... Mr. John ROBERTS

09 Dir Inst Research/Effectiveness ... Mrs. Cynthia MARSHALL-BIGGINS
08 Director of Library Services ... Ms. Joyce ARPS
13 Director of Information Technology ... Mr. Dave PICKINS
15 Director Human Resources ... Ms. Lois BOWIE
21 Comptroller ... Mr. Walter MOSLEY
36 Coord Counseling & Career Services ... Mr. Anthony MEYERS
41 Athletic Director ... Mr. Randy BUTLER
37 Director Financial Aid ... Ms. Cecelia K. JONES
18 Director Physical Plant ... Mr. James HARGRAVE
26 Coordinator Public Relations ... Ms. Christie HOWARD
29 Coordinator Alumni Affairs ... Ms. Orenthia MASON
88 Asst to VP for AA/Dean Lower Col ... Dr. Robert HARPER
88 Coordinator of Special Projects ... Mrs. Angelia FENNELL

Texas College of Traditional Chinese Medicine (E)

4005 Manchaca Road, Austin TX 78704-6737
County: Travis FICE Identification: 031795
Unit ID: 430704
Telephone: (512) 444-8082 Carnegie Class: Spec/Health
FAX Number: (512) 444-6345 Calendar System: Trimester
URL: www.texastcm.edu
Established: 1990 Annual Undergrad Tuition & Fees: $14,000
Enrollment: 144 Coordinate
Affiliation or Control: Proprietary IRS Status: Proprietary
Highest Offering: Master's; No Lower Division
Program: Professional
Accreditation: ACUP

01 President ... Ms. Lisa LIN
05 Academic Dean ... Dr. Maoyi CAI
20 Vice Pres of Academics/Assessment ... Dr. Joseph MCMILLAN
11 Administrator ... Ms. Wai-Lan KUO
37 Financial Aid Officer ... Mr. Moe GONZALEZ
07 Director of Admission ... Dr. Steve RENAUD
17 Clinic Director ... Mr. Dragon CHU
88 Director Herbal Department ... Dr. Guili ZHENG
88 Director of Acupuncture Department ... Dr. Shao LI
88 Director Bio-Med Dept/Dean Students ... Dr. Maoyi CAI
08 Director of Library ... Ms. Teresa BOGAR
46 Director of Research Department ... Dr. Lin-Ying TAN
10 Opers Dir Budget/Human Resources ... Mr. Paul LIN
06 Registrar ... Ms. Laura KRAUS

Texas Lutheran University (F)

1000 W Court Street, Seguin TX 78155-5999
County: Guadalupe FICE Identification: 003641
Unit ID: 228981
Telephone: (830) 372-8000 Carnegie Class: Bac/Diverse
FAX Number: (830) 372-8096 Calendar System: Semester
URL: www.tlu.edu
Established: 1891 Annual Undergrad Tuition & Fees: $24,860
Enrollment: 1,415 Coed
Affiliation or Control: Evangelical Lutheran Church In America
IRS Status: 501(c)3
Highest Offering: Master's
Program: Liberal Arts And General; Teacher Preparatory
Accreditation: SC, ACBSP, MUS, TEAC

01 President ... Dr. Stuart B. DORSEY
05 Vice Pres for Academic Affairs ... Dr. Debbie COTTRELL
11 Asst to Pres Admin/Public Affairs ... Mr. Stephen P. ANDERSON
10 Vice President Finance ... Mr. Andrew NELSON
84 Vice President Enrollment Services ... Mr. Thomas OLIVER
30 VP for Development/Alumni Relations ... Vacant
44 Vice President for Principal Gifts ... Vacant
32 VP/Dean of Student Life & Learning ... Ms. Kristi QUIROS
06 Director of Records & Registration ... Mr. Glenn YOCKEY
08 Library Director ... Ms. Martha RINN
37 Director of Financial Aid ... Ms. Cathleen WRIGHT
42 Campus Pastor ... Rev. Greg RONNING
36 Director Career Services ... Ms. Kimberly WATTS
38 Director Counseling Services ... Ms. Terry WEERS
07 Director of Admissions ... Mr. Adam NAVARRO-JUSINO
15 Director Personnel Services ... Mr. Andrew VASQUEZ
41 Director of Athletics ... Mr. Bill MILLER
09 Director of Institutional Research ... Ms. Jean CONSTABLE
04 Exec Assistant to the President ... Ms. Sharon CRAIG

Texas School of Business (G)

711 Airtex Drive, Houston TX 77073
County: Harris FICE Identification: 023122
Unit ID: 229036
Telephone: (281) 443-8900 Carnegie Class: Assoc/PrivFP
FAX Number: (281) 443-0777 Calendar System: Other
URL: www.tsb.edu
Established: 1983 Annual Undergrad Tuition & Fees: $15,506
Enrollment: 501 Coed
Affiliation or Control: Proprietary IRS Status: Proprietary
Highest Offering: Associate Degree
Program: Occupational
Accreditation: ACICS

01 Campus Director ... Mr. Greg GARRETT

Texas School of Business-Friendswood (A)

3208 FM 528, Friendswood TX 77546

County: Harris — Identification: 667051
Unit ID: 439127
Telephone: (281) 648-0880 — Carnegie Class: Assoc/PrivFP
FAX Number: (281) 648-0821 — Calendar System: Other
URL: www.tsb.edu
Established: N/A — Annual Undergrad Tuition & Fees: $15,506
Enrollment: 293 — Coed
Affiliation or Control: Proprietary — IRS Status: Proprietary
Highest Offering: Associate Degree
Program: Occupational
Accreditation: ACICS, MAC

01 Executive Director .... Ms. Kimberly ITO

† Branch campus of Texas School of Business, Houston, TX.

Texas Southern University (B)

3100 Cleburne Street, Houston TX 77004-4584

County: Harris — FICE Identification: 003642
Unit ID: 229063
Telephone: (713) 313-7011 — Carnegie Class: DRU
FAX Number: (713) 313-1092 — Calendar System: Semester
URL: www.tsu.edu
Established: 1947 — Annual Undergrad Tuition & Fees (In-State): $7,462
Enrollment: 9,730 — Coed
Affiliation or Control: State — IRS Status: 170(c)1
Highest Offering: Doctorate
Program: Liberal Arts And General; Teacher Preparatory; Professional
Accreditation: SC, BUS, #DIETD, ENGT, LAW, MT, NAIT, PHAR, PLNG, SPAA, SW

01 President .... Dr. John M. RUDLEY
05 Provost/VP Academic Affs & Research .... Dr. Sunny E. OHIA
86 VP Govt Relations & Community Affs .... Dr. James M. DOUGLAS
10 Vice President for Admin & Finance .... Mr. Jim C. MCSHAN
30 Vice Pres University Advancement .... Ms. Wendy H. ADAIR
100 Chief of Staff .... Ms. Janis J. NEWMAN
43 General Counsel .... Mr. Andrew C. HUGHEY
41 Athletic Director .... Dr. Charles F. MCCLELLAND
32 VP Student Svcs/Dean of Students .... Dr. William T. SAUNDERS
09 Int Assoc Provost/Assoc VP Research .... Dr. Adebayo O. OYEKAN
88 Dir Title III & Ofc of Sponsored Pr .... Ms. Demetria JOHNSON-WEEKS
15 Exec Director of Human Resources .... Mr. Brian K. DICKENS
26 Exec Director of Communications .... Ms. Eva K. PICKENS
84 Executive Director Enrollment Svc .... Mr. Hasan JAMIL
06 University Registrar .... Ms. Marilyn C. SQUARE
08 Int Exec Dir Libraries/Museums .... Ms. Norma P. BEAN
50 Dean School of Business .... Dr. Ronald A. JOHNSON
51 Dean Col of Cont Educ/Asst Provost .... Dr. Kingston NYAMAPFENE
53 Dean College of Education .... Dr. Lillian B. POATS
80 Dean School of Public Affairs .... Dr. Robert D. BULLARD
61 Dean School of Law .... Dr. Dannye HOLLEY
67 Int Dean Col Pharmacy & Health Sci .... Dr. Shirlette G. MILTON
88 Int Assoc Prov/VP Stdt Acad Enh Svc .... Dr. Betty B. COX
72 Dean College of Science/Technology .... Dr. Lei YU
60 Dean School of Communications .... Dr. James W. WARD
19 Chief of Police .... Chief Roger D. BYARS
35 Associate Dean of Students .... Dr. William A. THOMAS
21 Exec Dir of Business Affairs .... Ms. Beverly W. RUFFIN
92 Dean Freeman Honors College .... Dr. Humphrey A. REGIS
96 Exec Dir Procurement Services .... Mr. Gregory G. WILLIAMS
102 Executive Director of Development .... Ms. Carolyne B. OLIVER
18 Exec Director Facilities & Maint .... Mr. Tim RYCHLEC
13 CIO/Information Technology .... Mr. Billy C. RECTOR
20 Assoc Provost/Assoc VP Acad Affairs .... Dr. Elizabeth BROWN-GUILLORY
58 Dean Graduate School .... Dr. Gregory H. MADDOX
21 Exec Dir Provost of Business Svcs .... Mr. Charles E. HENRY
88 Dir Acad Ret Svcs Spec Asst/Provost .... Ms. Lori A. LABRIE
35 Associate Dean of Students .... Ms. Najla F. NAJIEB
88 Exec Director Budget .... Mr. Elias HAILU
88 Treasurer .... Mr. Louis W. EDWARDS
45 Director of Marketing .... Mr. Gregory K. HOLLAND
09 Int Ex Dir Inst Assess Plng & Effec .... Dr. Chander S. MEHTA
29 Dir Alumni Relations/Special Event .... Ms. Connie L. COCHRAN
88 Coordinator Academic Services .... Ms. Michara N. MAYES
88 Director of Scholarships .... Ms. Jeanette J. OLIVER
88 Int Dir Teaching & Learning Center .... Dr. Kimberly R. MCLEOD
88 Program Director Urban Academic Vil .... Dr. Isiah D. BROWN
88 Associate Director of QEP Office .... Dr. Arbolina L. JENNINGS

*Texas State Technical College System (C)

3801 Campus Drive, Waco TX 76705-1607

County: McLennan — FICE Identification: 009642
Unit ID: 228671
Telephone: (254) 867-4891 — Carnegie Class: N/A
FAX Number: (254) 867-3973
URL: www.tstc.edu

01 Chancellor .... Mr. Michael L. REESER
100 Vice Chancellor & Chief of Staff .... Mr. Jonathan HOEKSTRA
10 VC Financial Svcs & CFO .... Dr. J. Gary HENDRICKS
09 VC of IR & Commercialization .... Dr. Cesar MALDONADO
26 VC of Business Development .... Mr. Randall WOOTEN
05 VC of Instructional Services .... Dr. Elton E. STUCKLY, JR.
16 VC of Human Organizational Dev .... Mrs. Gail LAWRENCE
13 VC & Chief Technology Officer .... Mr. Rick HERRERA
102 Executive Director Foundation .... Mr. Mike HARDER
101 Board of Regents Secretary/Ofc Mgr .... Ms. Lillian MACIK
04 Admin Asst Office of Chancellor .... Ms. Beverly E. CLARK

*Texas State Technical College Harlingen (D)

1902 North Loop 499, Harlingen TX 78550-3697

County: Cameron — FICE Identification: 009225
Unit ID: 229319
Telephone: (956) 364-4000 — Carnegie Class: Assoc/Pub-R-M
FAX Number: (965) 364-5100 — Calendar System: Trimester
URL: www.harlingen.tstc.edu
Established: 1969 — Annual Undergrad Tuition & Fees (In-State): $6,096
Enrollment: 5,807 — Coed
Affiliation or Control: State — IRS Status: 501(c)3
Highest Offering: Associate Degree
Program: Occupational; 2-Year Principally Bachelor's Creditable; Technical Emphasis
Accreditation: SC, DA, DH, MAC, SURGT

02 President .... Dr. Cesar MALDONADO
100 Chief of Staff .... Ms. Stella GARCIA
32 Vice President for Student Devel .... Mrs. Cathy MAPLES
05 Associate VP of Academic Affairs .... Mrs. Barbara BENNETT
10 Vice Pres Financial/Admin Services .... Ms. Teri ZAMORA
20 Vice President for Student Learning .... Vacant
88 Assoc VP Col Readiness & Advancmnt .... Mr. Javier DELEON
13 Chief Technology Officer .... Mr. Rick HERRERA
31 Assoc VP External Relations .... Vacant
26 Executive Director of Marketing .... Ms. Lynda LOPEZ
09 Exec Dir for Institutional Complian .... Ms. Lisa CAVAZOS
15 Director Human/Organizational Dev .... Mrs. Mary PREPEJCHAL
19 Chief of Public Safety .... Mr. Aurelio TORRES
18 Director of Physical Plant .... Mr. Juan LOPEZ
55 Director of Evening School & ACE .... Mr. Juan LEAL
38 Director Student Counseling .... Ms. Liz SILVA
37 Director of Financial Aid .... Mr. Fred PENA
35 Director of Student Life .... Mrs. Adele CLINTON
41 Supervisor of Intramurals .... Mr. Joe DOMINGUEZ
08 Director of the Library .... Ms. Nancy HENDRICKS
96 Director of Purchasing .... Ms. Linda RODRIGUEZ-GUILLEN
36 Director of Placement/Coop Service .... Ms. Susan HOLMES
40 Supervisor Bookstore .... Ms. Susan FLORES
39 Supervisor Housing/Dormitories .... Mr. Carlos PEREZ
18 Assoc VP for Administrative Svcs .... Mr. Chuck SMITH
88 Director Staff Professional Dev .... Mrs. Cindy MATA
106 Director Distance Learning Educ .... Vacant
27 Director College Information .... Ms. Dora COLVIN
22 Director Support Services .... Ms. Edda URREA
88 Director Instructional Support Svcs .... Mr. Steve SZYMONIAK
88 Director of Curriculum .... Mr. Juan GARCIA

*Texas State Technical College Marshall (E)

2650 East End Boulevard S, Marshall TX 75672-7402

County: Harrison — FICE Identification: 033965
Unit ID: 408394
Telephone: (903) 935-1010 — Carnegie Class: Assoc/Pub-R-S
FAX Number: (903) 935-9554 — Calendar System: Semester
URL: www.marshall.tstc.edu
Established: 1993 — Annual Undergrad Tuition & Fees (In-District): $2,886
Enrollment: 831 — Coed
Affiliation or Control: State/Local — IRS Status: 501(c)3
Highest Offering: Associate Degree
Program: Occupational; 2-Year Principally Bachelor's Creditable; Technical Emphasis
Accreditation: SC

02 President .... Mr. Randall E. WOOTEN
05 Vice Pres of Student Learning .... Dr. Irene CRAVEY
10 Vice Pres of Financial Services .... Mrs. Deborah L. SANDERS
84 Dean of Enrollment Management .... Vacant
32 Vice Pres of Student Services .... Mr. Brett O. BRIGHT
102 Assoc Vice Pres Corporate College .... Vacant
20 Associate Dean Learning Community .... Ms. Annette M. ELLIS
04 Exec Assistant to the President .... Mr. Marshal V. JOSLIN
06 Registrar .... Ms. Patricia A. ROBBINS
09 Dir of Inst Effect/Rsrch & Planning .... Mrs. Mittie D. HUTCHINS
15 Human & Organ Develop Executive .... Mr. Jeff W. BELL
36 Coordinator of Placement .... Mr. Benjamin CANTU
37 Financial Aid Specialist .... Mrs. Susan F. WINGATE
103 Director Workforce & Economic Dev .... Mr. Bryan MAERTINS
13 Dir Network/Telecommunications Svcs .... Mr. Dennis J. BURRER
26 Chief Public Relations Officer .... Mr. Baily BRIGGS
96 Director of Purchasing .... Mrs. Eloise REED

*Texas State Technical College Waco (F)

3801 Campus Drive, Waco TX 76705-1695

County: McLennan — FICE Identification: 003634
Unit ID: 228680
Telephone: (254) 799-3611 — Carnegie Class: Assoc/Pub-R-M
FAX Number: (254) 867-2006 — Calendar System: Semester
URL: www.tstc.edu
Established: 1965 — Annual Undergrad Tuition & Fees (In-State): $3,324
Enrollment: 4,730 — Coed
Affiliation or Control: State — IRS Status: 501(c)3
Highest Offering: Associate Degree
Program: Occupational; 2-Year Principally Bachelor's Creditable; Technical Emphasis
Accreditation: SC, DA

00 Chancellor .... Dr. Bill SEGURA
02 President .... Mr. Elton E. STUCKLY, JR.
05 Provost .... Dr. Becky MUSIL
03 Executive Vice President .... Mr. Rob WOLAVER
10 VP Admin & Financial Svcs .... Mr. Paul WOODFIN
05 VP Student Learning .... Mr. Ron SANDERS
45 VP Institutional Advancement .... Ms. Carliss HYDE
09 Exec Dir Inst Effect Rsrch/Plng .... Dr. Ben COX
13 Exec Dir Support Operations .... Ms. Shelli SCHERWITZ
20 Assoc VP Student Learning .... Dr. Terry CONROY
20 Assoc VP Student Development .... Ms. Sarah PATTERSON
20 Assoc VP Student Development .... Mr. Marcus BALCH
06 Registrar/Dir of Adm & Records .... Ms. Mary DANIEL
37 Director of Financial Aid .... Ms. Jackie ADLER

*Texas State Technical College West Texas (G)

300 Homer K. Taylor Drive, Sweetwater TX 79556-4108

County: Nolan — FICE Identification: 009932
Unit ID: 229328
Telephone: (325) 235-7300 — Carnegie Class: Assoc/Pub-R-S
FAX Number: (325) 235-7320 — Calendar System: Semester
URL: www.tstc.edu
Established: 1970 — Annual Undergrad Tuition & Fees (In-State): $7,722
Enrollment: 1,036 — Coed
Affiliation or Control: State — IRS Status: 501(c)3
Highest Offering: Associate Degree
Program: Occupational; 2-Year Principally Bachelor's Creditable; Technical Emphasis
Accreditation: SC, EMT

02 President/Vice Chancellor .... Ms. Gail LAWRENCE
05 Vice President Student Learning .... Mr. Kyle SMITH
32 Vice President Student Development .... Mrs. Kathleen P. BUTLER
88 Vice Pres Corporate College .... Mr. Dixon BAILEY
10 Vice President Financial Services .... Ms. Karen WALLER
11 Vice President Admin Svcs .... Mr. Ray FRIED
35 Assoc VP Student Development .... Mr. Jeff HOWARD
20 Associate VP Student Learning .... Mrs. Debbie KARL
84 Associate VP Enrollment Management .... Mrs. Janyth USSERY
84 Associate VP Enrollment Management .... Mrs. Maria AGUIRRE-ACUNA
84 Associate VP Enrollment Management .... Mr. Brian KIGHT
84 Associate VP Enrollment Management .... Mrs. Sherry STRICKLAND
21 Assistant CFO .... Mr. Kevin SHIPP
19 Chief of Police .... Mr. Mike KELLER
15 Director Human Resources .... Ms. Hannah LOVE
37 Director of Financial Aid .... Mrs. Connie CHANCE
08 Director Library .... Mr. Steven PERRY
96 Director of Purchasing .... Ms. Jessica CHAVIRA
45 Staff Development Officer .... Vacant
46 Manager Inst Planning & Research .... Mr. John ARNOLD
38 Coordinator Counseling & Testing .... Mr. Donald J. ARMSTRONG, JR.
36 Coord Career Planning & Placement .... Mr. Nick ALVARADO
35 Coordinator Student Activities .... Mr. Tod RYDEN
07 Director of Retention .... Mr. Giles MONTGOMERY
26 Chief Public Relations Officer .... Mrs. Julie CROMEENS
39 Housing Supervisor .... Mr. Lupe NAVARRETTE
40 Bookstore Manager .... Mrs. Sherrie PARKS
13 Dir Network & Telecommunications .... Mrs. Shelli SCHERWITZ
46 Exec Director Strategic Initiatives .... Ms. Hannah LOVE

*The Texas State University System (H)

208 E 10th Street, Suite 600, Austin TX 78701-2407

County: Travis — FICE Identification: 033442
Telephone: (512) 463-1808 — Carnegie Class: N/A
FAX Number: (512) 463-1816
URL: www.tsus.edu

01 Chancellor .... Brian MCCALL
43 Vice Chanc & General Counsel .... Fernando C. GOMEZ
10 Vice Chancellor for Finance .... Roland K. SMITH
86 VC Governmental Rels/Educ Policy .... Sean CUNNINGHAM
25 Vice Chanc Contract Administration .... Peter E. GRAVES
88 Associate General Counsel .... Diane CORLEY
18 Assoc Vice Chanc Facilities .... Rob Roy PARNELL
27 Assoc VC Govt Rels/Dir of Communic .... Mike WINTEMUTE
21 Director of Audits & Analysis .... Carole M. FOX
11 Director of Administration .... Kelly WYLIE

*Lamar Institute of Technology (I)

PO Box 10043, Beaumont TX 77710-0043

County: Jefferson — FICE Identification: 036273
Unit ID: 441760
Telephone: (409) 880-8321 — Carnegie Class: Assoc/Pub-S-SC
FAX Number: (409) 880-1711 — Calendar System: Semester
URL: www.lit.edu
Established: 1995 — Annual Undergrad Tuition & Fees (In-State): $3,916
Enrollment: 3,025 — Coed
Affiliation or Control: State — IRS Status: 501(c)3

Highest Offering: Associate Degree
Program: Occupational; 2-Year Principally Bachelor's Creditable; Technical Emphasis
Accreditation: SC, DH, DMS, RAD

02 President .... Dr. Paul SZUCH
05 Vice President for Academic Affairs .... Dr. Betty REYNARD
103 Vice Pres for Workforce Development .... Mr. Sam WILLIAMS
10 Vice President Finance & Operations .... Mr. Jonathan WOLFE
32 Vice President of Student Services .... Dr. Vivian JEFFERSON
15 Vice President for Human Resources .... Ms. Bertha FREGIA
37 Director of Student Financial Aid .... Ms. Lisa SCHROEDER
13 Director of Technology Services .... Mr. Isaac BARBOSA
30 Dir of Development/Alumni Relations .... Ms. Joanne BROWN
26 Director of Marketing/Public Info .... Ms. Beth MILLER
18 Facilities Coordinator .... Mr. Jack WIGGINS
36 Job Plcmnt/Student Activities Coord .... Vacant
09 Coord Inst Effectiveness and Grants .... Mr. David MOSLEY

*Lamar University (A)

PO Box 10009, Beaumont TX 77710-0009
County: Jefferson FICE Identification: 003581
Unit ID: 226091
Telephone: (409) 880-7011 Carnegie Class: DRU
FAX Number: (409) 880-8404 Calendar System: Semester
URL: www.lamar.edu
Established: 1923 Annual Undergrad Tuition & Fees (In-State): $8,544
Enrollment: 14,021 Coed
Affiliation or Control: State IRS Status: 501(c)3
Highest Offering: Doctorate
Program: Liberal Arts And General; Teacher Preparatory; Professional
Accreditation: SC, ACFEI, ADNUR, AUD, BUS, CS, DIETD, DIETI, ENG, MUS, NUR, SP, SW, TED

02 President .... Dr. James M. SIMMONS
05 Provost/Vice Pres Academic Affairs .... Dr. Stephen A. DOBLIN
10 Vice President Finance/Operations .... Dr. Gregg LASSEN
30 Vice President for Inst Advancement .... Ms. Camille MOUTON
58 Interim Dean of Graduate Studies .... Dr. Victor ZALOOM
20 Sr Assoc Provost for Academic Affs .... Dr. Kevin B. SMITH
16 Assoc Vice Pres Human Resources .... Ms. Bertha FREGIA
18 Int Assoc VP Facilities/Maint .... Mr. Gerald MCCAIG
21 Associate Vice President Finance/Co .... Ms. Vicki WARD
13 Assoc Vice Pres for Information Sys .... Ms. Priscilla PARSONS
84 Assoc VP Strategic Enrollment Mgmt .... Ms. Sherry WELLS
49 Dean College Arts & Sciences .... Dr. Brenda NICHOLS
50 Dean College of Business .... Dr. Henry VENTA
53 Dean College of Education .... Dr. Hollis LOWERY-MOORE
54 Dean College of Engineering .... Dr. Jack HOPPER
57 Dean Col Fine Arts & Communication .... Dr. Russ SCHULTZ
08 Director Library Services .... Mr. David J. CARROLL
06 Registrar .... Mr. David SHORT, JR.
106 Dir Division of Distance Learning .... Dr. Paula NICHOLS
35 Director of Academic Services .... Mr. James C. RUSH
44 Director of Development .... Ms. Janice TRAMMELL
09 Director Institutional Research .... Dr. Gregory MARSH
36 Dir Career Development/Placement .... Ms. Teresa SIMPSON
23 Director Health Services .... Ms. Janet WARNER
19 Chief University Police .... Mr. Curtis Jason GOODRICH
26 Public Relations Director .... Mr. Brian SATTLER
29 Director Alumni Relations .... Mr. Juan ZABALA
37 Director Student Financial Aid .... Ms. Jill ROWLEY
96 Director of Purchasing .... Mr. Jack D. TENNER

*Lamar State College-Orange (B)

410 Front Street, Orange TX 77630-5802
County: Orange FICE Identification: 023582
Unit ID: 226107
Telephone: (409) 883-7750 Carnegie Class: Assoc/Pub-R-M
FAX Number: (409) 882-3374 Calendar System: Semester
URL: www.lsco.edu
Established: 1969 Annual Undergrad Tuition & Fees (In-State): $3,880
Enrollment: 2,760 Coed
Affiliation or Control: State IRS Status: 501(c)3
Highest Offering: Associate Degree
Program: Occupational; 2-Year Principally Bachelor's Creditable
Accreditation: SC

02 President .... Dr. J. Michael SHAHAN
05 Vice President Academic Affairs .... Dr. Joseph KIRKLAND
10 Vice President Finance & Operations .... Mrs. Dana ROGERS
32 Vice Pres Student Svcs & Aux Ent .... Mrs. Barbara BURGESS
08 Director of Library Services .... Ms. Mary MCCOY
06 Registrar .... Mrs. Rebecca J. CAMPBELL
37 Director Student Financial Aid .... Mr. Kerry J. OLSON
15 Human Resources Director .... Mrs. Alicia GRAY
18 Director of Physical Plant .... Mr. David GOINS
26 Dir Marketing & Public Information .... Ms. Amanda ROWELL
13 Coord Information Resources .... Ms. Linda G. BURNETT
09 Coordinator Institutional Research .... Mr. Bishar M. SETHNA
25 Contracts/Grants Administrator .... Mrs. Dana N. ROGERS
76 Director of Allied Health .... Ms. Gina A. SIMAR
72 Director of Business/Technology .... Ms. Jacqueline A. SPEARS
49 Division Chair Arts & Science .... Mr. Mike MCNAIR
96 Director of Purchasing .... Ms. Tabitha EVANS

*Lamar State College-Port Arthur (C)

1500 Procter Street, Port Arthur TX 77640-6604
County: Jefferson FICE Identification: 023485
Unit ID: 226116
Telephone: (409) 983-4921 Carnegie Class: Assoc/Pub-R-M
FAX Number: (409) 984-6032 Calendar System: Semester
URL: www.lamarpa.edu
Established: 1909 Annual Undergrad Tuition & Fees (In-State): $5,052
Enrollment: 2,169 Coed
Affiliation or Control: State IRS Status: 501(c)3
Highest Offering: Associate Degree
Program: Occupational; 2-Year Principally Bachelor's Creditable
Accreditation: SC, SURGT

02 President .... Dr. W. Sam MONROE
05 Vice President Academic Affairs .... Dr. Gary D. STRETCHER
10 Vice President for Finance .... Ms. Mary WICKLAND
32 Vice President Student Services .... Mr. Thomas G. NEAL
04 Admin Assistant to the President .... Mrs. Donna SCHION
08 Dean Library Services .... Mr. Peter B. KAATRUDE
06 Registrar .... Ms. Connie NICHOLAS
37 Director Financial Aid .... Mr. Pedro SALDANA
45 Director Inst Effectiveness .... Dr. Ben STAFFORD
18 Director of Physical Plant .... Mr. Stephen ARNOLD
27 Public Information Officer .... Mr. Gerry DICKERT
36 Career Placement Counselor .... Vacant
56 Dir Inmate Instructional Program .... Dr. Barbara HUVAL
13 Dir Information Technology Services .... Mr. Samir GHORAYEB
15 Director Human Resources .... Ms. Linda MCGEE
07 Director of Admissions .... Ms. Connie NICHOLAS
09 Director of Institutional Research .... Mrs. Petra UZORUO
51 Dean Academic/Continuing Educ Pgms .... Dr. Charles GONGRE
72 Dean Technical Programs .... Dr. Nancy CAMMACK
81 Department Head Science & Math .... Dr. Percy JORDAN
50 Dept Head Business/CIS Technology .... Mr. Michael TRAHAN
83 Department Head Liberal Arts .... Dr. Barbara HUVAL
76 Department Head Allied Health .... Ms. Janet HAMILTON

*Sam Houston State University (D)

1806 Avenue J, Suite 303, Huntsville TX 77341-0001
County: Walker FICE Identification: 003606
Unit ID: 227881
Telephone: (936) 294-1111 Carnegie Class: DRU
FAX Number: (936) 294-1465 Calendar System: Semester
URL: www.shsu.edu
Established: 1879 Annual Undergrad Tuition & Fees (In-State): $8,120
Enrollment: 17,539 Coed
Affiliation or Control: State IRS Status: 501(c)3
Highest Offering: Doctorate
Program: Liberal Arts And General; Teacher Preparatory; Professional
Accreditation: SC, BUS, CACREP, CIDA, CLPSY, CS, DIETD, DIETI, MUS, TED

02 President .... Dr. Dana L. GIBSON
05 Provost/Vice Pres Academic Affairs .... Dr. Jaimie HEBERT
10 Vice President Finance & Operations .... Mr. Al HOOTEN
84 Vice Pres Enrollment Management .... Dr. Heather THIELEMANN
32 Vice Pres Student Services .... Mr. Frank PARKER
30 Vice President of Univ Advancement .... Mr. Frank R. HOLMES
13 VP for Information Technology .... Mr. Mark ADAMS
41 Athletic Director .... Mr. Bobby WILLIAMS
20 Assoc Provost Academic Affairs .... Dr. Richard EGLSAER
20 Assoc VP Academic Affairs .... Dr. Kandi TAYEBI
21 Assoc VP Financial Services .... Ms. Paige SMITH
18 Assoc VP Facilities Management .... Mr. Doug J. GREENING
16 Assoc VP for HR & Risk Mgmt .... Mr. Dave HAMMONDS
96 Assoc VP Business Svcs .... Mr. John HITZEMAN
44 Assoc VP for Development .... Ms. Thelma MOONEY
26 Assoc VP Marketing & Comm .... Ms. Kris RUIZ
100 Chief of Staff .... Ms. Kathy J. GILCREASE
06 Registrar .... Ms. Teresa T. RINGO
07 Director of Undergrad Admissions .... Mr. Trevor THORN
08 Director of Library Services .... Ms. Ann H. HOLDER
29 Director of Alumni Relations .... Mr. Charlie VIENNE
09 Exec Dir Inst Effectiveness .... Ms. Donna ARTHO
37 Director Student Financial Aid .... Ms. Lisa TATOM
26 Director Marketing & Communications .... Mr. Bruce O'NEAL
38 Director Counseling Services .... Dr. Drew MILLER
39 Director Residence Life .... Ms. Joellen N. TIPTON
19 Director Public Safety Services .... Mr. Kevin MORRIS
92 Director of Honors College .... Dr. Gene YOUNG
21 Controller .... Mr. Aaron LEMAY
50 Dean of Business Administration .... Dr. Mitchell MUEHSAM
81 Dean of Sciences .... Dr. John PASCARELLA
57 Interim Dean of Fine Arts/Mass Comm .... Dr. Mary ROBBINS
61 Dean of Criminal Justice .... Dr. Vincent WEBB
53 Dean Education .... Dr. Genevieve BROWN
58 Dean of Graduate Studies .... Dr. Kandi TAYEBI
83 Dean Humanities/Social Sciences .... Dr. John DECASTRO

*Sul Ross State University (E)

PO Box C-114, Alpine TX 79832-0001
County: Brewster FICE Identification: 003625
Unit ID: 228501
Telephone: (432) 837-8032 Carnegie Class: Master's L
FAX Number: (432) 837-8334 Calendar System: Semester
URL: www.sulross.edu
Established: 1917 Annual Undergrad Tuition & Fees (In-State): $4,764
Enrollment: 2,940 Coed
Affiliation or Control: State IRS Status: 501(c)3
Highest Offering: Master's
Program: Occupational; Liberal Arts And General; Teacher Preparatory; Professional
Accreditation: SC

02 President .... Dr. Ricardo MAESTAS
05 Int Provst/VP Acad & Student Affs .... Dr. Jim CASE
10 Vice Pres for Finance & Operations .... Mr. Cesario E. VALENZUELA
12 Vice President Rio Grande College .... Vacant
84 Vice Pres Enrollment Management .... Ms. Denise GROVES
11 Assoc VP Fac/Plng/Construct/Ops .... Mr. Jim W. CLOUSE
30 Assoc Vice President Advancement .... Mr. Leo G. DOMINGUEZ
12 Associate Provost & Dean RGC .... Dr. Paul SORRELS
04 Special Assistant to President .... Vacant
04 Assistant to the President .... Ms. Yvonne REALIVASQUEZ
06 Registrar .... Vacant
08 Dean Library & Info Technology .... Mr. Don DOWDEY
32 Dean of Student Life .... Mr. Leo DOMINGUEZ
92 Dir Honors Prog/Acad Ctr Excellence .... Dr. Kathy STEIN
27 Director News & Publications .... Mr. Stephen W. LANG
37 Dir Financial Assistance .... Mr. Mickey CORBETT
49 Dean Arts & Science .... Dr. Jimmy CASE
107 Dean Professional Studies .... Dr. Melanie CROY
47 Dean Agricult/Natural Resource Sci .... Dr. Robert J. KINUCAN
15 Director of Human Resources .... Mrs. Judy A. PERRY
18 Asst Director of Physical Plant .... Mr. Edmundo NATERA
19 Director Dept of Public Safety .... Mr. Johnnie L. HOLBROOKS
21 Controller .... Mr. Oscar JIMENEZ
39 Director Residential Living .... Mr. Mark CHASZAR
41 Athletic Director .... Ms. Kay E. WHITLEY
38 Director Counseling Ctr .... Ms. Helen CRANE
13 Chief Information Officer .... Mr. Chandragupta GUDENA
96 Director of Purchasing .... Mr. Noe HERNANDEZ
88 Dir Center for Big Bend Studies .... Mr. Andy CLOUD
29 Intrm Director Alumni Affairs .... Ms. Karen BROWN
66 Director of Vocational Nursing .... Ms. Donna KUENSTLER
88 Director Museum of the Big Bend .... Ms. Elizabeth JACKSON
88 Director of Upward Bound .... Ms. Barbara VEGA
88 Director of University Archives .... Ms. Melleta BELL
88 Director Small Business Devel Ctr .... Mr. David WILSON
88 Director Law Enforcement Academy .... Mr. Lloyd DRAGOO
88 Dir Publication Services Coord .... Ms. Lauren MENDIAS
07 Director Admissions & Records .... Ms. Claudia WRIGHT
88 Mail Service Supervisor .... Ms. Angela BERMUDEZ
88 Internal Auditor .... Mrs. Stephanie NELSON
36 Coord Career Services & Testing .... Ms. Susan FOX-FORRESTER

*Texas State University-San Marcos (F)

601 University Drive, San Marcos TX 78666-4615
County: Hays FICE Identification: 003615
Unit ID: 228459
Telephone: (512) 245-2111 Carnegie Class: Master's L
FAX Number: (512) 245-3040 Calendar System: Semester
URL: www.txstate.edu
Established: 1899 Annual Undergrad Tuition & Fees (In-State): $8,772
Enrollment: 34,087 Coed
Affiliation or Control: State IRS Status: 501(c)3
Highest Offering: Doctorate
Program: Liberal Arts And General; Teacher Preparatory; Professional
Accreditation: SC, BUS, CACREP, CIDA, CS, DIETD, DIETI, ENG, HSA, IPSY, JOUR, MT, MUS, NRPA, NURSE, PTA, RTT, SP, SPAA, SW, TEAC

02 President .... Dr. Denise M. TRAUTH
05 Provost/Vice Pres Academic Affairs .... Dr. Gene BOURGEOIS
100 Special Assistant to the President .... Dr. Robert D. GRATZ
32 Vice President Student Affairs .... Dr. Joanne H. SMITH
10 Vice Pres Finance/Support Services .... Mr. William A. NANCE
30 Vice President Univ Advancement .... Dr. Barbara BREIER
13 Vice Pres Information Technology .... Dr. Carl V. WYATT
41 Director of Athletics .... Dr. Lawrence B. TEIS
83 Dean College of Applied Arts .... Dr. T. Jaime CHAHIN
50 Dean McCoy Col of Business Admin .... Dr. Denise T. SMART
57 Dean Col Fine Arts & Communication .... Dr. Timothy MOTTET
53 Dean College of Education .... Dr. Stan CARPENTER
76 Dean College Health Professions .... Dr. Ruth B. WELBORN
83 Dean College Liberal Arts .... Dr. Michael HENNESSY
81 Dean Col of Science & Engineering .... Dr. Stephen B. SEIDMAN
58 Dean The Graduate College .... Dr. J. Michael WILLOUGHBY
97 Dean Univ Col & Dir PACE Center .... Dr. Daniel BROWN
92 Dean Honors College .... Dr. Heather GALLOWAY
20 Assoc Vice Pres Academic Affairs .... Dr. Debbie M. THORNE
20 Associate Provost .... Dr. Cynthia L. OPHEIM
18 Associate VP of Facilities .... Mr. Juan M. GUERRA
86 Assoc VP Research & Dir of Fed Rels .... Dr. Bill C. COVINGTON
35 Assoc VP Stdnt Affs/Dean of Stdnt .... Dr. Margarita M. ARELLANO
20 Assoc Vice Pres for Inst Effective .... Dr. Cathy A. FLEURIET
21 Assoc VP Financial Services .... Mr. Terry ONDREYKA
84 Assoc VP Enrollment Mgmt/Marketing .... Dr. Michael R. HEINTZE
08 Associate VP University Library .... Ms. Joan L. HEATH
20 Assistant VP for Academic Services .... Dr. Ronald C. BROWN
38 Asst VP/Director Counseling Center .... Dr. Gregory SNODGRASS
88 Assoc VP Finance/Support Svcs Plng .... Ms. Nancy NUSBAUM
14 Assoc VP for Technology Resources .... Mr. Mark HUGHES
90 Assoc VP Instructional Tech Support .... Dr. Milton C. NIELSEN
106 Interim Dir Disatnce/Extended Lrng .... Dr. Debbie M. THORNE
06 Registrar .... Ms. Lloydean M. ECKLEY
07 Asst VP Enroll Mgmt/Dir Ug Admiss .... Ms. Stephanie ANDERSON
91 Director Enterprise Systems .... Mr. Bill RAMPY
37 Director of Fin Aid & Scholarships .... Dr. Christopher MURR
36 Director Career Services .... Mr. Curtis P. SCHAFER
29 Director of Alumni Affairs .... Ms. Kim GANNON
27 Director News Services .... Mr. Mark S. HENDRICKS
31 Chief Community Relations .... Ms. Kim PORTERFIELD
15 Director of Human Resources .... Mr. John E. MCBRIDE
12 Director Round Rock Higher Educ Ctr .... Dr. Edna REHBEIN
25 Director of Sponsored Programs .... Mr. W. Scott ERWIN
19 Director University Police .... Mr. Ralph MEYER

23 Director Student Health Center .... Dr. Emilio CARRANCO
39 Director Housing & Residential Life .... Dr. Rosanne PROITE
85 Director International Office .... Dr. Robert M. SEESE
40 Manager University Bookstore .... Ms. Jacqueline SLAUGHTER
24 Director Education Technology Ctr .... Mr. Michael W. FARRIS
09 Director of Institutional Research .... Mr. Joseph M. MEYER
22 Chief Divsty Offc/Dir Equity & Acce .... Mr. Herman HORN
93 Dir Center for Multicul/Gender Stds .... Dr. Sandra MAYO
96 Director Purchasing .... Ms. Jacque ALLBRIGHT
26 Director of University Marketing .... Ms. Diana HARRELL
88 Director of Audit & Compliance .... Mr. Steve R. MCGEE
89 Asst Dean of University College .... Dr. Pam J. WUESTENBERG
88 Asst VP/Dir of Multicul Stdnt Affs .... Dr. Sherri BENN
88 Asst VP for Development .... Mr. Ted M. MCKINNON
88 Asst VP University Advancement .... Mr. Matt FLORES
88 Director Campus Recreation .... Dr. Glenn HANLEY
88 Interim Director LBJ Student Center .... Dr. Margarita ARELLANO
88 Director Retention Mgmt & Planning .... Dr. Jen BECK
88 Interim Directr Disability Services .... Dr. Sherri BENN

Texas Tech University (A)

Lubbock TX 79409-2005

County: Lubbock FICE Identification: 003644
Unit ID: 229115
Telephone: (806) 742-2121 Carnegie Class: RU/H
FAX Number: (806) 742-2138 Calendar System: Semester
URL: www.ttu.edu
Established: 1923 Annual Undergrad Tuition & Fees (In-State): $4,621
Enrollment: 32,327 Coed
Affiliation or Control: State IRS Status: 170(c)1
Highest Offering: Doctorate
Program: Liberal Arts And General; Teacher Preparatory; Professional
Accreditation: SC, AAFCS, ARCPA, ART, BUS, BUSA, CACREP, CIDA, CLPSY, COPSY, DIETD, DIETI, ENG, ENGT, HSA, IPSY, LAW, LSAR, MED, MFCD, @MIDWF, MUS, SPAA, SW, TED, THEA

00 Chancellor .... Mr. Kent HANCE
01 President .... Dr. Guy BAILEY
101 Sec Board Regents/Ex Asst to Chanc .... Mr. Ben W. LOCK
03 Provost and Sr VP .... Dr. Bob SMITH
05 Vice Chancellor for Academic Affair .... Dr. Joseph RALLO
10 Chief Operating Ofcr/SVP Admin/Fin .... Mr. Kyle CLARK
30 Vice Chancellor Inst Advancement .... Dr. Kelly OVERLEY
86 Vice Chancellor Govt Relations .... Mr. J. Michael SANDERS
43 Vice Chanc & General Counsel .... Mr. John HUFFAKER
18 VC Facilities Planning Construction .... Mr. Michael MOLINA
20 Vice Provost & SVP Academic Affairs .... Dr. Valerie PATON
100 President's Chief of Staff .... Ms. Grace HERNANDEZ
29 EVP & CEO Texas Tech Alumni Assoc .... Dr. Bill DEAN
46 Vice President for Research .... Dr. Taylor EIGHMY
28 VP Inst Diversity & Vice Provost .... Dr. Juan S. MUNOZ
84 Sr Assoc VP Enrollment Management .... Dr. James BURKHALTER
20 Assoc Vice Provost Academic Affairs .... Dr. Gary ELBOW
20 Sr Vice Provost .... Dr. Rob STEWART
88 Assoc VP External Relations & Strat .... Ms. Mary LARSON DIAZ
21 Interim Asst Vice Pres & Controller .... Ms. Sharon WILLIAMSON
16 AVP Human Resources .... Mr. Doug BUCHANAN
106 VC Distance & Online Learning .... Vacant
82 Assoc Vice Prov International Affs .... Mr. Tibor P. NAGY
13 Assoc VP Information Technology .... Mr. Sam SEGRAN
88 Asst VP & Dir Hospitality Services .... Dr. Samuel BENNETT
08 Dean of Libraries .... Dr. Donald DYAL
60 Dean Mass Communications .... Dr. Jerry HUDSON
35 Int Dean Stdnts/Dir Campus Life .... Ms. Amy L. MURPHY
37 Managing Dir Financial Aid .... Ms. Becky WILSON
27 Chief Information Officer .... Ms. Kay RHODES
06 Registrar .... Ms. Bobbie BROWN
07 Managing Director of Admissions .... Dr. Ethan LOGAN
26 Managing Dir Comms & Marketing .... Mr. Chris COOK
104 Director Study Abroad .... Ms. Sandy CROSIER
04 Administrative Asst to President .... Ms. Jessica CARRILLO
31 Assoc Dir Community Engagment .... Dr. Heather MARTINEZ
44 Senior Dir Annual Giving Programs .... Ms. Deborah FINLAYSON
23 Director Student Health Services .... Ms. Evelyn MCPHERSON
39 Managing Dir Student Housing .... Mr. Sean DUGGAN
36 Managing Director Career Center .... Mr. Jay KILLOUGH
15 Managing Director of HR Management .... Mr. Justin CLARK
22 Asst Vice Chanc Admin/Dir EEO .... Ms. Charlotte BINGHAM
38 Managing Dir Student Counseling .... Dr. Eileen NATHAN
41 Director of Athletics .... Mr. Kirby HOCUTT
47 Dean Agricult Sci/Nat Res .... Dr. Michael GALYEAN
49 Dean of Arts & Sciences .... Dr. Lawrence SCHOVANEC
48 Dean of Architecture .... Mr. Andrew VERNOOY
50 Dean Business Administration .... Dr. Lance NAIL
53 Dean of Education .... Dr. Scott RIDLEY
54 Dean of Engineering .... Dr. Albert SACCO
88 Dean of Human Sciences .... Dr. Linda HOOVER
61 Dean School of Law .... Ms. Darby DICKERSON
58 Interim Dean of Graduate School .... Dr. Peggy MILLER
92 Interim Dean Honors College .... Dr. Stephen FRITZ
57 Dean Visual & Performing Arts .... Dr. Carol EDWARDS
19 Chief of Police .... Mr. Ronald SEACRIST
09 Managing Dir Institutional Research .... Ms. Vicki WEST
96 Dir Purchasing & Contracting .... Ms. Jennifer ADLING

Texas Tech University Health Sciences Center (B)

3601 4th Street, Lubbock TX 79430-0001

County: Lubbock FICE Identification: 010674
Unit ID: 229337
Telephone: (806) 743-1000 Carnegie Class: Spec/Med
FAX Number: (806) 743-2118 Calendar System: Semester
URL: www.ttuhsc.edu
Established: 1969 Annual Undergrad Tuition & Fees (In-State): $7,533
Enrollment: 4,094 Coed
Affiliation or Control: State IRS Status: 501(c)3
Highest Offering: Doctorate
Program: Professional
Accreditation: SC, AUD, CORE, DMOLS, MED, MT, NURSE, OT, PHAR, PTA, SP

01 President .... Dr. Tedd MITCHELL
10 Exec Vice Pres for Finance Admin .... Mr. Elmo M. CAVIN, JR.
05 Sr Vice Pres Academic Affairs .... Dr. Rial D. ROLFE
26 Dir Communications & Marketing .... Ms. Mary CROYLE
17 Vice Pres Rural/Community Hlth .... Dr. Billy U. PHILIPS, JR.
13 Vice Pres Info Tech/Chief Info Ofcr .... Dr. Chip SHAW
100 Chief of Staff .... Ms. Didit MARTINEZ
43 Senior Assoc General Counsel .... Ms. Glenda HELFRICH
21 Assoc Vice Pres Business Affairs .... Mr. Mike CROWDER
46 Exec Vice President for Research .... Dr. Douglas M. STOCCO
19 Information Security Officer .... Mr. Andrew HOWARD
15 Asst Vice Pres of Human Resources .... Dr. Gena JONES
18 Asst Vice Pres of Physical Plant .... Mr. George MORALES
63 Dean of Medical School .... Dr. Steven L. BERK
58 Dean Grad Sch Biomed Sciences .... Dr. Douglas M. STOCCO
66 Dean of Nursing School .... Dr. Michael L. EVANS
76 Dean of Allied Health Sciences Sch .... Dr. Robin SATTERWHITE
67 Dean of Pharmacy School .... Dr. Arthur NELSON, JR.
12 Reg Dean Medicine Amarillo Campus .... Dr. Richard JORDAN
12 Found Dean Medicine El Paso Campus .... Dr. J. Manuel DE LA ROSA
12 Reg Dean Medicine Odessa Campus .... Dr. Gary VENTOLINI
66 Reg Dean Nursing Odessa Campus .... Dr. Sharon CANNON
76 Reg Dean Allied Health Amarillo .... Dr. Michael HOOTEN
76 Reg Dean Allied Health Odessa .... Dr. Manuel DOMENECH
06 Registrar .... Ms. Tamara LANE
08 Exec Director of HSC Libraries .... Mr. Richard C. WOOD
21 Director of Accounting Services .... Mr. Todd BASH
22 Director of Equal Employment .... Ms. Charlotte BINGHAM
25 Director of Sponsored Programs .... Ms. Victoria RIVERA
37 Director of Financial Aid .... Mr. Marcus WILSON
25 Sr Director of Contracting .... Mr. Jim LEWIS
96 Sr Director of Purchasing .... Mr. John G. HAYNES
09 Lead Analyst Inst Research .... Mr. Kevin MCINTYRE
35 Managing Director Student Services .... Ms. Margret DURAN
29 Director of Alumni Relations .... Mr. Nathan RICE
21 Asst Vice Pres of Budget .... Ms. Penny HARKEY
30 Asst VC Development .... Ms. Kendra BURRIS

Texas Wesleyan University (C)

1201 Wesleyan, Fort Worth TX 76105-1536

County: Tarrant FICE Identification: 003645
Unit ID: 229160
Telephone: (817) 531-4444 Carnegie Class: Master's L
FAX Number: (817) 531-4425 Calendar System: Semester
URL: www.txwes.edu
Established: 1890 Annual Undergrad Tuition & Fees: $20,840
Enrollment: 3,181 Coed
Affiliation or Control: United Methodist IRS Status: 501(c)3
Highest Offering: Doctorate
Program: Liberal Arts And General; Teacher Preparatory; Professional
Accreditation: SC, ACBSP, ANEST, LAW, MUS

01 President .... Mr. Frederick G. SLABACH
05 Provost .... Dr. Allen HENDERSON
10 Sr VP Finance & Administration .... Ms. Karen L. MONTGOMERY
30 VP University Advancement .... Ms. Joan CANTY
84 VP for Enrollment & Student Svcs .... Ms. Pati ALEXANDER
26 Vice Pres Marketing/Communications .... Mr. John VEILLEUX
11 Assoc VP Admin Svcs/Human Resources .... Mr. Steve ROBERTS
26 Assistant Vice President for Mktg .... Mr. Chuck BURTON
20 Associate Provost .... Dr. Helena BUSSELL
41 Athletic Director .... Mr. Steven TRACHIER
53 Dean School of Education .... Dr. Carlos MARTINEZ
50 Dean of School of Business .... Dr. Hector QUINTANILLA
49 Dean School Arts & Letters .... Dr. Steven DANIELL
61 Dean School of Law .... Mr. Fred WHITE
83 Dean School of Natural & Social Sci .... Dr. Trevor MORRIS
35 Dean of Students .... Mr. Cary POOLE
39 Director of Residence Life .... Ms. Sharon MANSON
06 Registrar .... Ms. Kay VANTOORN
08 Library Science Assoc Professor .... Ms. Cindy POTTER
21 Controller .... Ms. Lori LOGAN
27 Communications Director .... Ms. Laura HANNA
07 Director of Admissions .... Ms. Holly KISER
37 Director Financial Aid .... Ms. Shanna HOLLIS
42 Chaplain .... Dr. Robert FLOWERS
38 Director of Counseling .... Dr. Michael ELLISON
29 Director Alumni Relations .... Ms. Gina PHILLIPS
15 Human Resources Director .... Ms. Kristi TAYLOR
96 Director of Purchasing .... Ms. Deborah CAVITT
36 Director of Career Services .... Ms. Sherri MATA
18 Director of Facilities/Security .... Mr. Ken DUNSON
45 Director Institutional Research .... Ms. Sherri CARABALLO
25 Director of Grants & Research .... Ms. Deborah ROARK
13 CIO/Info & Communications Tech .... Mr. Marcus KERR

Texas Woman's University (D)

Box 425589, Denton TX 76204-5587

County: Denton FICE Identification: 003646
Unit ID: 229179
Telephone: (940) 898-2000 Carnegie Class: DRU
FAX Number: (940) 898-3198 Calendar System: Semester
URL: www.twu.edu
Established: 1901 Annual Undergrad Tuition & Fees (In-State): $5,156
Enrollment: 14,700 Coed
Affiliation or Control: State IRS Status: 501(c)3
Highest Offering: Doctorate
Program: Liberal Arts And General; Teacher Preparatory; Professional
Accreditation: SC, ACBSP, CACREP, COPSY, DANCE, DH, DIETD, DIETI, HSA, IPSY, LIB, MUS, NURSE, OT, PTA, SCPSY, SP, SW

01 President .... Dr. Ann STUART
05 Provost & VP Academic Affairs .... Dr. Robert NEELY
10 Vice Pres Finance/Administration .... Dr. Brenda L. FLOYD
32 Vice President Student Life .... Dr. Richard A. NICHOLAS
13 Chief Information Officer .... Mr. Rob PLACIDO
20 Assoc Provost .... Dr. Michael STANKEY
58 Sr Assoc Provost/Dean Graduate Sch .... Dr. Jennifer MARTIN
26 Assoc Vice Pres Mktg/Communication .... Ms. Carolyn BARNES
84 Assoc Vice Pres Enrollment Services .... Mr. Gary RAY
21 Associate Vice President Finance .... Mr. Robert L. TUGGLE
18 Assoc Vice Pres Facilities .... Mr. Harold JOHNSON
15 Assoc Vice Pres Human Resources .... Mr. Lewis BENAVIDES
49 Dean College Arts & Sciences .... Dr. Ann STATON
69 Dean College Health Sciences .... Dr. Jimmy ISHEE
62 Dean College Professional Education .... Dr. Nan RESTINE
66 Dean College of Nursing .... Dr. Patricia HOLDEN-HUCHTON
07 Director of Admissions .... Ms. Erma M. NIETO
58 Assoc Dean for Graduate Studies .... Dr. JoAnn ENGLEBRECHT
09 Director of Institutional Research .... Dr. Mark HAMNER
43 General Counsel .... Mr. John LAWHON
08 Director of Libraries .... Ms. Sherilyn BYRD
37 Director Student Financial Aid .... Mr. Governor E. JACKSON
36 Director Career & Employment Svcs .... Ms. Deidre Lynn LESLIE
38 Director Counseling Center .... Dr. Denise LUCERO-MILLER
27 Director News & Information .... Ms. Amanda SIMPSON
19 Director of Public Safety .... Mr. John W. ERWIN
06 Registrar .... Mr. Bobby LOTHRINGER
41 Athletic Director .... Ms. Chalese CONNORS
23 Director Student Health Services .... Dr. Connie MENARD
39 Director University Housing .... Dr. Joe BERTHIAUME
28 Director of Diversity .... Mr. Lewis BENAVIDES
29 Director Alumni Relations .... Ms. Anne SCOTT
30 Director Development .... Mr. Phil TRAMMELL
40 Bookstore Manager .... Ms. Jennifer MADISON
96 Procurement Services .... Ms. Vanna PARR

Trinity University (E)

One Trinity Place, San Antonio TX 78212-7200

County: Bexar FICE Identification: 003647
Unit ID: 229267
Telephone: (210) 999-7011 Carnegie Class: Master's M
FAX Number: (210) 999-7696 Calendar System: Semester
URL: www.trinity.edu
Established: 1869 Annual Undergrad Tuition & Fees: $33,678
Enrollment: 2,635 Coed
Affiliation or Control: Independent Non-Profit IRS Status: 501(c)3
Highest Offering: Master's
Program: Liberal Arts And General; Teacher Preparatory; Professional
Accreditation: SC, BUS, ENG, HSA, TED

01 President .... Dr. Dennis A. AHLBURG
05 VP Faculty and Student Affairs .... Dr. Michael R. FISCHER
10 VP Finance and Administration .... Mr. Gary LOGAN
30 Interim VP External Affairs .... Mr. Rick ROBERTS
27 VP Information Resources .... Dr. Charles B. WHITE
20 AVP Faculty and Student Affairs .... Dr. Sheryl R. TYNES
20 AVP Faculty and Student Affairs .... Dr. Duane COLTHARP
20 AVP Faculty and Student Affairs .... Dr. Mark BRODL
21 AVP Finance and Administration .... Ms. Ana M. WINDHAM
07 AVP Enrollment & Student Retention .... Mr. Christopher J. ELLERTSON
08 University Librarian .... Ms. Diane J. GRAVES
06 Registrar .... Mr. Alfred RODRIGUEZ
37 Director of Financial Aid .... Ms. Glendi GADDIS
38 Director Counseling/Health Svcs .... Dr. Gary W. NEAL
32 AVP Student Affairs & Dean of Stdnt .... Mr. David M. TUTTLE
31 Dir Campus/Community Involvement .... Dr. Raphael MOFFETT
36 Director of Career Services .... Mr. Brian HIRSCH
15 Assistant VP Human Resources .... Ms. Pamela JOHNSTON
13 Director of Information Technology .... Mr. Fred ZAPATA
26 AVP University Communications .... Ms. Sharon JONES SCHWEITZER
30 Director of Development .... Ms. Kathy MCNEILL
44 Director of Planned Giving .... Ms. Kristine HOWLAND
29 Director of Alumni Relations .... Dr. MaryKay COOPER
51 Director Conferences/Special Pgms .... Ms. Ann G. KNOEBEL
04 Assistant to the President .... Ms. Claire SMITH
19 Chief of Police .... Mr. Paul CHAPA
18 Acting Director Buildings & Grounds .... Mr. Mike SCHWEITZER
40 Director of Bookstore .... Ms. Dora AMADOR
42 Chaplain .... Rev. Stephen R. NICKLE
09 Director Institutional Research .... Dr. Diane G. SAPHIRE
96 Director of Purchasing .... Ms. Cynthia LARA

Trinity Valley Community College (F)

100 Cardinal Drive, Athens TX 75751-2734

County: Henderson FICE Identification: 003572
Unit ID: 225308
Telephone: (903) 677-8822 Carnegie Class: Assoc/Pub-S-MC
FAX Number: (903) 675-6316 Calendar System: Semester
URL: www.tvcc.edu
Established: 1946 Annual Undergrad Tuition & Fees (In-District): $2,100
Enrollment: 7,677 Coed
Affiliation or Control: State/Local IRS Status: 501(c)3

Highest Offering: Associate Degree
Program: Occupational; 2-Year Principally Bachelor's Creditable
Accreditation: SC, ADNUR, SURGT

01 President ... Dr. Glendon S. FORGEY
05 Vice President for Instruction ... Dr. Jerry KING
30 VP of Institutional Advancement ... Ms. Mary NICHOLSON
32 Vice President Student Services ... Dr. Jay KINZER
13 VP of Information Technology ... Mr. Mike ABBOTT
10 Vice Pres Administrative Services ... Mrs. Jean MCSPADDEN
20 Assoc VP Instruction Academic Educ ... Dr. Jeremy MCMILLEN
103 Associate VP of Workforce Education ... Mr. David MCANALLY
91 Assoc VP of Information Technology ... Mr. Brett DANIEL
12 Assoc VP of TDCJ Programs ... Dr. Sam HURLEY
46 Asst VP of Institutional Research ... Ms. Kay PULLEY
18 Asst VP of Facilities Management ... Mr. David GRAEM
76 Provost Health Occupations ... Dr. Helen REID
12 Provost Kaufman County Campus ... Dr. Algia ALLEN
12 Provost Anderson County Campus ... Dr. Jeff WATSON
06 Registrar/Dean Enrollment Mgmt ... Dr. Colette HILLIARD
09 Director of Institutional Research ... Ms. Tina RUMMEL
08 Director Learning Resource Center ... Ms. Janice SUTTON
38 Director Guidance Center ... Ms. Linda DANIEL
27 Public Information Officer ... Mrs. Jennifer HANNIGAN
07 Director School Relations ... Ms. Audrey HAWKINS
37 Dir Student Finan Aid/Veteran's Svc ... Ms. Julie LIVELY
41 Athletic Director ... Mr. Brad SMILEY
19 Director of Campus Police ... Mr. Heath CARIKER
36 Placement Officer ... Mr. Dennis NOLLEY
40 Bookstore Manager ... Mr. James QUATTLEBAUM
35 Director Student Activities ... Mr. Harold JONES
31 Director Community Services ... Ms. Gayla ROBERTS
15 Director of Human Resources ... Ms. Jennifer ROBERTSON

Tyler Junior College (A)

PO Box 9020, Tyler TX 75711-9020
County: Smith FICE Identification: 003648
Unit ID: 229355
Telephone: (903) 510-2200 Carnegie Class: Assoc/Pub-R-L
FAX Number: (903) 510-2632 Calendar System: Semester
URL: www.tjc.edu
Established: 1926 Annual Undergrad Tuition & Fees (In-District): $1,856
Enrollment: 11,540 Coed
Affiliation or Control: State/Local IRS Status: 501(c)3
Highest Offering: Associate Degree
Program: Occupational; 2-Year Principally Bachelor's Creditable; Business Emphasis
Accreditation: SC, DH, DMS, MLTAD, OPD, RAD, SURGT

01 President ... Dr. L. Michael METKE
10 Vice President Business Affairs ... Ms. Sarah E. VAN CLEEF
30 VP Advancement/External Affairs ... Dr. Kimberly A. RUSSELL
32 Int Vice President Student Affairs ... Dr. Charles B. FLORIO
05 Provost ... Dr. Homer M. HAYES
81 Dean Engineering/Math and Sciences ... Dr. Kenneth R. MURPHY
79 Dean Humanities/Comm/Fine Arts ... Dr. Rosemary REYNOLDS-SUNDET
76 Dean Nursing & Health Professions ... Mr. Paul R. MONAGAN
72 Dean Prof & Tech Programs ... Dr. W. Clayton ALLEN
84 Exec Dir Enrollment Mgmt Svcs ... Mrs. Janna L. CHANCEY
09 Exec Dir Inst Effect/Plng & Rsrch ... Dr. Cheryl L. ROGERS
62 Director Library Services ... Ms. Marian D. JACKSON
51 Dean Continuing Studies ... Dr. Aubrey D. SHARPE
21 Controller ... Ms. Carol A. HUTSON
06 Registrar ... Mrs. Andrea H. LINER
37 Director Financial Aid ... Ms. Devon WIGGINS
26 Dir Public Affairs and Grant Dev ... Mr. Fred M. PETERS
35 Director Student Success ... Mr. Vincent NGUYEN
29 Director Alumni Relations ... Ms. Betty S. BRIGGS
36 Coordinator Career Services ... Mrs. Felecia NEELY-MORRIS
07 Director Admissions ... Mrs. Nidia HASSAN
16 Exec Dir Human Resources ... Mr. S. Kevin FOWLER
41 Director Intercol Athletics ... Dr. Timothy S. DRAIN
09 Dir Institutional Research ... Ms. Jacquelyn MESSINGER
18 Exec Dir Facilities & Construction ... Mr. William L. KING
96 Director Purchasing & Contracts ... Mr. Michael CARUSO
19 Exec Director Campus Safety ... Dr. Thomas A. JOHNSON
13 Chief Information Officer ... Mr. Larry MENDEZ
39 Director Auxiliary Svcs ... Ms. Diana KAROL
44 Director Principal Gifts ... Mr. Mitch ANDREWS
36 Director Testing/Career Services ... Mr. Paul GOERTEMILLER
88 Director Academic Advising ... Mrs. Jan ADAMS
88 Dean Academic Foundations ... Ms. Lisa M. HARPER
88 Director SBDC ... Mr. Donald W. PROUDFOOT

University of Dallas (B)

1845 E Northgate Drive, Irving TX 75062-4736
County: Dallas FICE Identification: 003651
Unit ID: 224323
Telephone: (972) 721-5000 Carnegie Class: Master's L
FAX Number: (972) 721-5017 Calendar System: Semester
URL: www.udallas.edu
Established: 1956 Annual Undergrad Tuition & Fees: $31,070
Enrollment: 2,725 Coed
Affiliation or Control: Roman Catholic IRS Status: 501(c)3
Highest Offering: Doctorate
Program: Liberal Arts And General; Teacher Preparatory
Accreditation: SC, ACBSP

01 President ... Mr. Thomas W. KEEFE
04 Exec Admin Asst to the President ... Ms. Cathy MCCALEB
05 Executive VP & Provost ... Dr. J. William BERRY
20 Associate Provost ... Dr. Brian MURRAY
10 Executive VP for Fince/Admin ... Mr. Robert M. GALECKE
11 Assoc VP for Administration ... Mr. Patrick DALY
50 Dean College of Business ... Dr. Robert SCHERER
20 Dean of Undergraduate College ... Dr. C. W. EAKER
58 Dean Grad School of Liberal Arts ... Dr. David SWEET
73 Dean School of Ministry ... Dr. Mark GOODWIN
84 VP of Enroll Mgmt & Student Affairs ... Dr. John PLOTTS
38 Assoc Dean for Constantin College ... Dr. Margaret BROWN MARSDEN
06 Registrar ... Mrs. Jan BURK
19 Campus Safety Supervisor ... Mr. Charles STEADMAN
90 Director of Academic Computing ... Mr. Malik DULANEY
91 Director Administrative Computing ... Mr. Richard HAYTER
44 Director of Annual Giving ... Mr. Jim LIVERNOIS
41 Director of Athletics ... Mr. Richard STROCKBINE
42 Director of Campus Ministry ... Mrs. Denise PHILLIPS
18 Director of Facilities ... Mr. Jerry HABA
21 Director of Finance ... Mr. Leonard A. ROBERTSON
15 Director of Human Resources ... Mrs. Janis TOWNSEND
09 Director of Institutional Research ... Dr. Leslie R. ODOM
08 Director of Library ... Dr. Robert S. DUPREE
27 Director of Marketing & Comm ... Mr. William HARTLEY
96 Director of Purchasing ... Mr. Alan STERLING
104 Director for Rome/Summer Programs ... Mrs. Becky DAVIES
23 Director of Student Health ... Dr. Laurie KUGELMANN DEKAT
36 Director of Career Services ... Ms. Julie JANIK

*University of Houston System (C)

212 Ezekiel Cullen Building, Houston TX 77204-2018
County: Harris FICE Identification: 011721
Unit ID: 229407
Telephone: (713) 743-1000 Carnegie Class: N/A
FAX Number: (713) 743-8837
URL: www.uhsa.uh.edu

01 Chancellor ... Dr. Renu KHATOR
05 Sr VC for Academic Affairs/Provost ... Dr. John J. ANTEL
43 Vice Chancellor/General Counsel ... Ms. Dona G. CORNELL
10 Exec VC Administration/Finance ... Dr. Carl P. CARLUCCI
32 Vice Chancellor Student Affairs ... Dr. Richard WALKER
46 Vice Chancellor Research IPM ... Dr. Rathindra N. BOSE
30 VC University Advancement ... Ms. Eloise D. STUHR
26 AVC University Relations ... Ms. Karen CLARKE
13 Assoc VC CIO/Information Technology ... Dr. Dennis FOUTY
20 Assoc VC Academic Affairs ... Dr. Elaine M. CHARLSON
21 Associate Vice Chancellor Finance ... Mr. Thomas EHARDT
11 Assoc VC Administration ... Ms. Emily MESSA
45 Associate Vice Chancellor Planning ... Mr. Edward T. HUGETZ
44 Assoc VC University Advancement ... Mr. Eli CIPRIANO
88 Assoc VC Planning & Administration ... Dr. Marshall SCHOTT
86 Asst Vice Chanc Govt Relations ... Ms. Laura CALFEE
88 Asst VC for Planning & Policy ... Mr. Chris STANICH
15 Exec Director Human Resources ... Ms. Joan M. NELSON
21 Director Internal Auditing ... Mr. Don GUYTON
88 Treasurer ... Mr. Raymond BARTLETT
86 Exec Director for Govt Relations ... Mr. Darrin HALL

*University of Houston (D)

4800 Calhoun Road, Houston TX 77204
County: Harris FICE Identification: 003652
Unit ID: 225511
Telephone: (713) 743-1000 Carnegie Class: RU/VH
FAX Number: (713) 743-8837 Calendar System: Semester
URL: www.uh.edu
Established: 1927 Annual Undergrad Tuition & Fees (In-State): $9,311
Enrollment: 39,820 Coed
Affiliation or Control: State IRS Status: Exempt
Highest Offering: Doctorate
Program: Liberal Arts And General; Teacher Preparatory; Professional
Accreditation: SC, AAFCS, BUS, BUSA, CEA, CLPSY, CONST, COPSY, CS, DIETD, DIETI, ENG, ENGT, IPSY, LAW, MUS, OPT, OPTR, PHAR, SCPSY, SP, SW, TED

02 President ... Dr. Renu KHATOR
05 Sr Vice Chanc/VP Acad Affs/Prov ... Dr. John ANTEL
10 Exec VP Administration/Finance ... Dr. Carl CARLUCCI
30 Vice Pres University Advancement ... Dr. Eloise D. STUHR
32 Vice President Student Affairs ... Dr. Richard WALKER
86 Exec Dir Governmental Relations ... Mr. Darrin HALL
43 VP Legal Affairs & General Counsel ... Ms. Dona G. CORNELL
46 VP for Research & Tech Transfer ... Dr. Rathindra N. BOSE
31 VP for Community Rels & Inst Access ... Dr. Elwyn C. LEE
29 President/CEO Alumni Association ... Mr. Mike PEDE
13 Assoc VP Information Tech/CIO ... Dr. Dennis FOUTY
26 Assoc VP University Relations ... Ms. Karen B. CLARKE
30 Assoc Vice Pres for Development ... Mr. Cliff REDD
20 Exec Asc VP Academic & Faculty Affs ... Dr. Elaine M. CHARLSON
84 Assoc VP for Enrollment Management ... Mr. Stephen C. SOUTULLO
35 Assoc VP for Student Affairs ... Mr. Daniel MAXWELL
88 Assoc VP Stdnt Affs/Dean of Stdnts ... Dr. William MUNSON
91 Assoc VP Enterprise Sys Adm ... Dr. Arun JAIN
45 Assoc VP Planning/Univ Outreach ... Mr. Edward HUGETZ
21 Associate Vice President Finance ... Mr. Tom EHARDT
88 Asst VP Undergraduate Studies ... Dr. Agnes L. DEFRANCO
22 Asst VP Equal Opportunity Services ... Dr. Richard A. BAKER
09 Asst VP Academic Affairs ... Dr. Elizabeth A. BARLOW
41 VP Intercollegiate Athletics ... Mr. Mack B. RHOADES, IV
37 Exec Dir Scholarships & Fin Aid ... Mr. Sal LORIA
16 Exec Director Human Resources ... Ms. Joan NELSON
18 Exec Dir Facilities Management ... Ms. Melissa ROCKWELL-HOPKINS
51 Director Continuing Education ... Ms. Mercedes SURATY-CLARKE
06 Registrar ... Ms. Debbie HENRY
07 Executive Director of Admissions ... Ms. Djuana YOUNG
19 Asst VP for Univ Safety & Security ... Mr. Malcolm DAVIS
96 Director of Purchasing & Stores ... Mr. Christopher E. BURTON
79 Dean Col Liberal Arts/Soc Sci ... Dr. John ROBERTS
81 Dean Col Natural Sciences & Math ... Dr. Mark A. SMITH
88 Dean College of Optometry ... Dr. Earl SMITH, III
72 Dean College of Technology ... Dr. William FITZGIBBON
54 Dean Cullen College of Engineering ... Dr. Joseph W. TEDESCO
48 Dean College of Architecture ... Ms. Patricia Belton OLIVER
70 Dean Graduate Coll of Social Work ... Dr. Ira COLBY
67 Dean College of Pharmacy ... Dr. Lamar PRITCHARD
53 Dean College of Education ... Dr. Robert MCPHERSON
50 Dean Bauer Col Business Admin ... Dr. Latha RAMCHAND
88 Dean Hilton Col Htl/Restaurant Mgt ... Dr. John BOWEN
92 Dean Honors College ... Dr. William MONROE
61 Dean UH Law Center ... Dr. Raymond NIMMER
08 Dean University Libraries ... Ms. Dana C. ROOKS
88 Assoc VP for Administration ... Ms. Emily MESSA
44 Assoc VP for Univ Advancement ... Mr. Eli D. CIPRIANO
88 Assoc VP Univ Outreach/Pgm ... Mr. Marshall SCHOTT

*University of Houston - Clear Lake (E)

Houston TX 77058-1098
County: Harris FICE Identification: 011711
Unit ID: 225414
Telephone: (281) 283-7600 Carnegie Class: Master's L
FAX Number: (281) 283-2219 Calendar System: Semester
URL: www.uhcl.edu
Established: 1971 Annual Undergrad Tuition & Fees (In-State): $5,304
Enrollment: 8,185 Coed
Affiliation or Control: State IRS Status: 501(c)3
Highest Offering: Doctorate
Program: Liberal Arts And General; Teacher Preparatory; Professional
Accreditation: SC, BUS, BUSA, CS, ENG, ENGR, HSA, #MFCD, SW, TED

02 President ... Dr. William A. STAPLES
05 Sr Vice Pres for Academic Affairs ... Dr. Carl A. STOCKTON
10 Vice Pres Administration & Finance ... Ms. Michelle DOTTER
04 Executive Assoc to the President ... Ms. Mary Ann H. SHALLBERG
13 Assoc VP Information Resources ... Dr. A. Glen HOUSTON
20 Assoc Vice Pres Academic Affairs ... Dr. Mrinal MUGDH
30 Assoc VP University Advancement ... Mr. Dion MCINNIS
32 Assoc Vice Pres Student Services ... Dr. Darlene BIGGERS
21 Associate Vice President Finance ... Mr. John CORDARY
84 Assoc Vice Pres Enrollment Mgmt ... Dr. Yvette BENDECK
18 Assoc VP Facilities Mgmt/Construct ... Mr. Ward MARTAINDALE
50 Dean School Business ... Dr. Wm. Theodore CUMMINGS
81 Dean School Science/Computer Engr ... Dr. Zbigniew CZAJKIEWICZ
79 Dean Sch Human Sci/Humanities ... Dr. Rick SHORT
53 Dean School Education ... Dr. Dennis W. SPUCK
35 Interim Dean of Students ... Mr. David A. RACHITA
28 Asst Dean Student Diversity ... Ms. Linda C. BULLOCK
08 Exec Director Neumann Library ... Ms. Karen WIELHORSKI
85 Exec Director Intl Initiatives ... Dr. Sameer PANDE
45 Exec Director Planning & Assessment ... Mr. Kevin BARLOW
15 Executive Director Human Resources ... Ms. Katherine JUSTICE
14 Exec Director University Computing ... Mr. Rodger CARR
21 Exec Dir of Procurement & Payables ... Ms. Debra CARPENTER
25 Exec Dir Sponsored Programs ... Mr. Paul MEYERS
37 Executive Director Financial Aid ... Mr. Billy SATTERFIELD
88 Exec Dir Environment Inst Houston ... Dr. George GUILLEN
06 Registrar/Director Academic Records ... Vacant
56 Director Distance/Off-Campus Educ ... Ms. Lisa GABRIEL
27 Director Communications ... Ms. Theresa PRESSWOOD
29 Director Alumni & Cmty Relations ... Ms. Charity ELLIS
19 Director Police ... Mr. Paul WILLINGHAM
36 Director Career/Counseling Services ... Dr. Alfred KAHN
09 Assoc Dir Institutional Research ... Ms. Peggy JOHNSON
12 Dir Camp Operat/UHCL Pearland Camp ... Ms. Kathy DUPREE
23 Dir Health & Disability Services ... Ms. Susan L. PRIHODA
07 Exec Director of Admissions ... Ms. Rauchelle JONES
40 Manager Bookstore ... Mr. Brent WELLS

*University of Houston - Downtown (F)

One Main Street, Houston TX 77002-1014
County: Harris FICE Identification: 003612
Unit ID: 225432
Telephone: (713) 221-8001 Carnegie Class: Bac/Diverse
FAX Number: (713) 221-8075 Calendar System: Semester
URL: www.uhd.edu
Established: 1974 Annual Undergrad Tuition & Fees (In-State): $5,022
Enrollment: 12,918 Coed
Affiliation or Control: State IRS Status: Exempt
Highest Offering: Master's
Program: Liberal Arts And General
Accreditation: SC, BUS, ENGT, SW

02 President ... Dr. William V. FLORES
04 Director Presidential Affairs ... Ms. Gilda PARKER
05 Provost/Sr Vice Pres Acad Affairs ... Dr. Brian R. CHAPMAN
20 Assoc VPAA/Vice Prov/Dean Grad Std ... Dr. Michael R. DRESSMAN
20 Asst VP Acad Affairs/Dean Ungrad ... Dr. Gary L. STADING

108 Assoc VP Inst Effectiveness .... Dr. Patrick S. WILLIAMS
50 Dean College of Business .... Vacant
79 Int Dean Col Humanities/Social Sci .... Dr. Robert JARRETT
88 Dean College of Public Service .... Dr. Beth PELZ
81 Interim Dean Col Sciences & Tech .... Dr. Akif UZMAN
97 Dean University College .... Dr. Chris BIRCHAK
08 Executive Director WI Dykes Library .... Ms. Pat ENSOR
106 Exec Dir Distance Education .... Mr. Louis D. EVANS, III
09 Director of Institutional Research .... Ms. Carol M. TUCKER
88 Asst VP Research & Spon Programs .... Ms. Sandra GARCIA
88 Director Sponsored Programs .... Ms. Carolyn IVEY
88 Director of Academic Assessment .... Dr. Lea CAMPBELL
88 Director Creative Services .... Mr. Joe WYNNE
88 Executive Dir Global Citizenship .... Dr. Jean DEWITT
88 Director International Programs .... Mr. Spencer LIGHTSY
92 Director of Scholars Academy .... Dr. Mary Jo PARKER
88 Director Advising .... Ms. Jemma CAESAR
88 Director Advising Services .... Ms. Reyna ROMERO
88 Director Academic Support Center .... Dr. Isidro GRAU
88 Director Academic Services .... Mr. David MORALES
72 Dir Applied Business/Technology Ctr .... Mr. G. V. KRISHNAN
88 Director English Language Institute .... Dr. Gail KELLERSBERGER
88 Director Criminal Justice Center .... Mr. Rex WHITE
88 Dir Inst for Financial Literacy .... Dr. James KANE
10 VP Administration & Finance .... Mr. David M. BRADLEY
13 Assoc VP Information Technology .... Mr. Hossein SHAHROKHI
88 Executive Director IT .... Ms. Erin MAYER
91 Director Enterprise Systems .... Mr. Kong YIN
88 Dir Technology Learning Services .... Dr. Deborah CARRUTHERS
88 Dir User Support Services .... Mr. Said FATTOUH
88 Director Technical Services .... Ms. Grace DAVILA
88 Dir Comp/Telecom & Video Networks .... Vacant
21 Asst VP Business Affairs .... Mr. George W. ANDERSON
21 Dic Budget & Procurement .... Ms. Theresa MENELEY
21 Dir Accounting & Fin Reporting .... Ms. Jacqueline SUPENSKY
21 Director Accounts Payable .... Ms. Cynthia CONNER
21 Dir Student Accounting & Collection .... Ms. Trisha JACOBSON
25 Director Risk Mgmt & Compliance .... Ms. Mary COOK
96 Coordinator Purchasing .... Mr. Cory ODSTRCIL
18 Asst VP Facilities Management .... Mr. Chris MCCALL
19 Chief of Police .... Mr. Richard BOYLE
16 VP Employment Svcs & Operations .... Ms. Ivonne MONTALBANO
15 Asst VP Employee Svcs/Records Mgmt .... Ms. Betty POWELL
22 Asst VP Empl Trng/Camp Rels/AA Ofcr .... Dr. Doug TEDUITS
84 VP Student Success & Enrollment Mgt .. Dr. Lisa MONTGOMERY
35 Asst VP Student Success/Dean .... Mr. Tommy N. THOMASON
35 Assistant Dean of Students .... Ms. Liza ALONZO
06 Registrar .... Ms. Cynthia SANTOS
07 Director Admissions & Recruitment .... Vacant
37 Director of Scholarships & Fin Aid .... Ms. LaTasha GOUDEAU
41 Director Sports & Fitness .... Mr. Richard SEBASTIANI
36 Director Career Services .... Mr. Stephen MARKERT
88 Director Testing Services .... Ms. Po-Chu A. LEUNG
88 Director Disability Services .... Dr. Christopher KAIO
88 Exec Director Talent Search .... Ms. Jennifer HIGHTOWER
88 Director Upward Bound .... Ms. Dawanna LEWIS
88 Assoc Director Learning Success .... Ms. Michelle FALCON
31 Director Community Relations .... Ms. Janet HEITMILLER
30 VP Advancement & External Rels .... Ms. Johanna WOLFE
26 Executive Dir University Relations .... Ms. Diane SUMMERS
88 Dir Advancement Svc & Operations .... Ms. Karen P. ALFARO

*University of Houston - Victoria (A)

3007 N Ben Wilson, Victoria TX 77901-4450
County: Victoria FICE Identification: 013231
Unit ID: 225502
Telephone: (361) 570-4848 Carnegie Class: Master's L
FAX Number: (361) 580-5534 Calendar System: Semester
URL: www.uhv.edu
Established: 1973 Annual Undergrad Tuition & Fees (In-State): $4,963
Enrollment: 4,330 Coed
Affiliation or Control: State IRS Status: 501(c)3
Highest Offering: Master's
Program: Liberal Arts And General; Teacher Preparatory; Professional
Accreditation: SC, BUS, CACREP, NURSE, @TEAC

02 President .... Dr. Philip D. CASTILLE
11 Vice Pres Administration & Finance .... Mr. Wayne B. BERAN
05 Provost/Vice Pres Academic Affairs .... Dr. Jeffrey CASS
100 Chief of Staff .... Dr. Margaret H. RICE
32 Associate Vice Pres Student Affairs .... Ms. Chari NORGARD
49 Dean Arts & Sciences .... Dr. Jeffrey DILEO
50 Dean Business Administration .... Dr. Farhang NIROOMAND
53 Dean Education & Human Development .... Dr. Freddie LITTON
66 Dean Nursing .... Dr. Kathryn TART
30 VP University Advancement .... Vacant
08 Senior Director of Library .... Dr. Joe F. DAHLSTROM
14 Sr Director Information Technology .... Mr. Joseph S. FERGUSON
15 Dir Human Resource/Affirmative Act .... Ms. Laura L. SMITH
84 Sr Director of Enrollment Mgmt .... Dr. Denee THOMAS
88 Dir Small Business Development Ctr .... Mr. Joe HUMPHREYS
06 Registrar .... Ms. Trudy WORTHAM
37 Director Financial Aid .... Ms. Carolyn R. MALLORY
18 Director Facilities .... Mr. Kevin MYERS
10 Director Business Services .... Mr. Tim MICHALSKI
21 Comptroller .... Ms. Valerie WALDEN
41 Director Athletics .... Mr. Ashley WALYUCHOW
44 Director Stewardship/Planned Giving .... Vacant
102 Dir Corp & Foundation Relations .... Ms. Amy MUNDY
26 Interim Director Marketing .... Ms. Paula COBLER
38 Director of Counseling Center .... Dr. Jesse AROS
35 Director of Student Life & Services .... Ms. Lindsey KOCH

09 Director Institutional Research .... Dr. Tong-Ai ZHANG
88 Director Retention & Student Succ .... Ms. Sandra HEINOLD
88 Director of Budget .... Ms. Darlene PULLIN

University of the Incarnate Word (B)

4301 Broadway, San Antonio TX 78209-6397
County: Bexar FICE Identification: 003578
Unit ID: 225627
Telephone: (210) 829-6000 Carnegie Class: Master's L
FAX Number: (210) 829-1220 Calendar System: Semester
URL: www.uiw.edu
Established: 1881 Annual Undergrad Tuition & Fees: $22,800
Enrollment: 8,455 Coed
Affiliation or Control: Roman Catholic IRS Status: 501(c)3
Highest Offering: Doctorate
Program: Liberal Arts And General; Teacher Preparatory; Professional
Accreditation: SC, ACBSP, CIDA, DIETD, DIETI, NMT, NURSE, @OPT, PHAR, @PTA, THEA

01 President .... Dr. Louis J. AGNESE, JR.
00 Chancellor .... Dr. Denise DOYLE
88 Mission Effectiveness .... Sr. Walter MAHER
04 Executive Assistant to President .... Ms. Yvonne BURNS
26 Asst to the President/Communication .... Mr. Vincent RODRIQUEZ
43 General Counsel .... Ms. Cindy ESCAMILLA
05 Provost .... Dr. Kathleen LIGHT
84 Vice Pres Enrollment Mgt/Stdnt Svcs .Dr. David M. JURENOVICH
30 Vice Pres Institutional Advancement .... Sr. Kathleen COUGHLIN
10 Vice Pres for Business & Finance .... Mr. Douglas ENDSLEY
104 Vice Pres International Programs .... Mr. Marcos FRAGOSO
56 Vice Pres of Ext Academic Programs .... Dr. Cyndi WILSON-PORTER
13 Vice Pres Information Resources .... Mr. Marshall EIDSON
21 Comptroller .... Ms. Edith COGDELL
50 Dean H-E-B Sch Business & Admin .... Vacant
57 Dean Humanities Arts & Social Sci .... Dr. John HEALY
66 Dean Nursing & Health Professions .... Dr. Mary HOKE
53 Dean Dreeben School of Education .... Dr. Denise STAUDT
54 Dean Math Science Engineering .... Dr. Carlos GARCIA
08 Dean Interactve Media & Design .... Dr. Sharon WELKEY
67 Dean Feik School of Pharmacy .... Dr. Arcelia JOHNSON-FANNIN
88 Acting Dean School of Optometry .... Dr. Andrew BUZZELLI
58 Dean of Grad Studies/Research .... Dr. Kevin VICHCALES
62 Dean of Library Services .... Dr. Cheryl ANDERSON
108 Assoc Provost/Dir of Assessment .... Dr. Glenn JAMES
55 Dean Sch of Extended Studies .... Mr. Vincent PORTER
106 Dean of Virtual University .... Vacant
88 Dean Univ Preparatory Programs .... Mr. Daniel OCHOA
29 Director of Alumni Relations .... Ms. Lisa SCHULTZ
26 Director of Public Relations .... Ms. Debra DEL TORO
84 Dean of Enrollment .... Ms. Andrea CYTERSKI-ACOSTA
32 Dean of Student Success .... Ms. Sandy MCMAKIN
38 Director of Counseling .... Dr. Keith TUCKER
20 Director of Academic Advising .... Mr. Moises TORRESCANO
88 Director Learning Assistance Center .... Ms. Cristina ARIZA
06 Registrar .... Dr. Bobbye G. FRY
37 Director of Financial Aid .... Ms. Amy CARCANAGUES
32 Dean of Campus Life .... Dr. Renee MOORE
39 Director of Residence Life .... Ms. Diane SANCHEZ
35 Dir University Events/Student Pgms .... Mr. Paul AYALA
23 Director of Health Services .... Ms. Marveen MAHON
42 Chaplain .... Fr. Tom DYMOWSKI
42 Director of Campus Ministry .... Ms. Elisabeth VILLARREAL
15 Director of Human Resources .... Ms. Annette THOMPSON
96 Director of Purchasing .... Mr. Sam WAGES
18 Director Facilities Mgmt & Services .... Mr. Steve HEYING
41 Director of Athletics .... Mr. Mark PAPICH
88 Director of Infrastructure Support .... Mr. Carl HAYWOOD
88 Director of Enterprise Systems .... Ms. Sandy GIVENS
88 Director Instructional Technology .... Ms. Ana GONZALES
72 Director of Technology Support .... Mr. Anthony RAMOS
09 Director of Institutional Research .... Ms. Robin LOGAN
07 Director of Admissions .... Ms. Heather RODRIGUEZ
36 Coordinator of Career Services .... Mr. Juan ALMENDAREZ

University of Mary Hardin-Baylor (C)

900 College Street, Belton TX 76513-2578
County: Bell FICE Identification: 003588
Unit ID: 226471
Telephone: (254) 295-8642 Carnegie Class: Master's S
FAX Number: (254) 295-4535 Calendar System: Semester
URL: www.umhb.edu
Established: 1845 Annual Undergrad Tuition & Fees: $22,640
Enrollment: 3,137 Coed
Affiliation or Control: Southern Baptist IRS Status: 501(c)3
Highest Offering: Doctorate
Program: Liberal Arts And General; Teacher Preparatory; Professional
Accreditation: SC, CACREP, MUS, NURSE, SW

01 President/CEO .... Dr. Randy G. O'REAR
03 Sr Vice Pres Admin/COO .... Dr. Steve THEODORE
05 Provost/Sr Vice Pres Academics .... Dr. Steve OLDHAM
45 Sr Vice Pres Campus Planning .... Mr. Edd MARTIN
00 President Emeritus .... Dr. Jerry G. BAWCOM
30 Vice Pres for Development .... Mr. Brent DAVISON
102 Vice Pres Communication/Spec Proj .... Dr. Paula TANNER
32 Vice Pres for Student Life .... Dr. Byron WEATHERSBEE
41 Vice Pres Athletics .... Mr. Randy MANN
10 Vice Pres Business/Finance/CFO .... Mrs. Jennifer RAMM
15 Assoc Vice Pres Human Resources .... Mrs. Susan OWENS

13 Assoc Vice Pres Information Tech .... Mr. Brent HARRIS
84 Assoc Vice Pres Enrollment Mgmt .... Mr. Gary LAMM
18 Assoc Vice Pres for Facilities .... Mr. Bob PATTEE
20 Asst Provost .... Dr. Tammi COOPER
21 Controller .... Ms. Charla KAHLIG
49 Dean of Sciences .... Mr. Carl GILBERT
66 Dean of Nursing .... Dr. Sharon SOUTER
53 Dean of Education .... Dr. Marlene ZIPPERLEN
50 Dean Global Engagmnt/Dir Global Ctr .... Dr. Jim KING
58 Dean Graduate School .... Dr. Colin WILBORN
88 Dean of Christian Studies .... Dr. Tim CRAWFORD
57 Dean Visual/Performing Arts .... Mr. Ted BARNES
35 Dean of Students .... Mr. Ray MARTIN
39 Assoc Dean Students/Dir Residence .... Ms. Donna PLANK
04 Executive Assistant to President .... Mrs. Phyllis ROGERS
06 Registrar .... Mrs. Amy MCGILVRAY
07 Director of Admissions & Recruiting .... Mr. Brent BURKS
08 Director Learning Resources .... Ms. Denise KARIMKHANI
26 Director Marketing/Public Relations .... Mr. James STAFFORD
09 Director Institutional Research .... Ms. Bethany CHAPMAN
37 Director Financial Aid .... Mr. Ron BROWN
92 Director Honors Program .... Dr. David HOLCOMB
19 Director Campus Police .... Mr. Gary SARGENT
96 Director of Purchasing .... Mr. Mike FRAZIER
29 Director Alumni Relations .... Ms. Rebecca O'BANION
42 University Chaplain .... Dr. George LOUTHERBACK
36 Director Career Services .... Mr. Don OWENS
38 Director Couns Testing & Health .... Mr. Nate WILLIAMS
85 Dir International Student Services .... Mrs. Elizabeth TANAKA
44 Director Planned Giving .... Dr. Gene KIMES
40 Bookstore Manager .... Mrs. Debbie COTTRELL

University of North Texas (D)

1155 Union Circle #311277, Denton TX 76203-5013
County: Denton FICE Identification: 003594
Unit ID: 227216
Telephone: (940) 565-2000 Carnegie Class: RU/H
FAX Number: (940) 565-7600 Calendar System: Semester
URL: www.unt.edu
Established: 1890 Annual Undergrad Tuition & Fees (In-State): $8,357
Enrollment: 35,694 Coed
Affiliation or Control: State IRS Status: 501(c)3
Highest Offering: Doctorate
Program: Liberal Arts And General; Teacher Preparatory; Professional
Accreditation: SC, ART, AUD, BUS, BUSA, CACREP, CEA, CIDA, CLPSY, COPSY, CORE, CS, ENG, ENGT, JOUR, LIB, MUS, NRPA, SP, SPAA, SW, TED

00 Chancellor .... Mr. Lee F. JACKSON
01 President .... Dr. V. Lane RAWLINS
05 Provost/Vice Pres Academic Affairs .... Dr. Warrewn BURGGREN
10 Vice Pres Finance/Administration .... Mr. Andrew M. HARRIS
46 VP Research/Economic Development .... Dr. Geoff GAMBLE
32 Vice President Student Affairs .... Dr. Elizabeth WITH
43 Vice Chancellor/General Counsel .... Ms. Nancy FOOTER
26 Vice President University Relations .... Ms. Deborah S. LELIAERT
30 VP for Advancement/Dir of Develop .... Ms. Lisa Birley BARONIO
20 Vice Provost for Academic Resources .... Dr. Allen CLARK
20 Vice Provost for Faculty Success .... Dr. Christy CRUTSINGER
41 Athletic Director .... Mr. Rick VILLARREAL
35 Dean Students .... Dr. Maureen MCGUINNESS
13 Vice President for Information Tech .... Mr. John HOOPER
21 Senior Assoc VP for Finance .... Ms. Jean BUSH
21 Assoc VP Finance & Cont .... Dr. Carlos HERNANDEZ
28 VP Institutional Equity & Diversity .... Dr. Gilda GARCIA
20 Vice Provost for Educ Innovation .... Dr. Celia WILLIAMSON
18 Asst Vice President for Facilities .... Mr. Charles JACKSON
84 Vice Provost for Enrollment .... Dr. Troy JOHNSON
08 Dean of Libraries .... Dr. Martin HALBERT
37 Director Financial Aid .... Ms. Zelma DELEON
49 Dean College of Arts/Sciences .... Dr. Michael MONTICINO
50 Dean College Business .... Dr. Finley GRAVES
53 Dean College of Education .... Dr. Jerry R. THOMAS
57 Dean Col Visual Arts & Design .... Dr. Robert W. MILNES
88 Dean Col Public Affs/Community Svc .... Dr. Thomas L. EVENSON
64 Dean College of Music .... Dr. James C. SCOTT
59 Dean Col of Merch/Hosp & Tourism .... Dr. Judith FORNEY
62 Dean College of Information .... Dr. Herman L. TOTTEN
58 Dean Toulouse Grad School .... Dr. Jean MILLER
92 Dean Honors College .... Dr. Gloria COX
60 Actg Dean Mayborn Sch of Journalism .... Dr. Roy BUSBY
54 Dean College of Engineering .... Dr. Costas TSATSOULIS
90 Director Acad Computing/User Svcs .... Dr. Philip C. BACZEWSKI
09 Director Institutional Research .... Dr. Mary BARTON
07 Director of Admissions .... Dr. Rebecca LOTHRINGER
51 Dir Ctr for Achvmnt & Lifelng Lrng .... Ms. Marilyn D. WAGNER
06 Registrar .... Ms. Lynn MCCREARY
15 Asst Vice Pres Human Resources .... Ms. Donna L. KEENER
36 Dir Career & Counseling Svcs .... Mr. Dan NAEGELI
38 Director of Counseling & Testing .... Dr. Judy A. MCCONNELL
19 Director/Chief of Police .... Mr. Richard S. DETER
39 Director Housing .... Dr. Elisabeth B. WARREN
85 Vice Provost International Affairs .... Dr. Richard NADER
40 Director UNT Bookstore .... Mr. Rodney DAVISON
23 Dir Stdnt Health Ctr/Wellness Svcs .... Dr. Herschel VOORHEES
29 Exec Dir Alum Rels/N Texas Exes .... Mr. Derrick MORGAN

University of North Texas Health Science Center at Fort Worth (E)

3500 Camp Bowie Boulevard, Fort Worth TX 76107-2699
County: Tarrant FICE Identification: 009768
Unit ID: 228909
Telephone: (817) 735-2000 Carnegie Class: Spec/Med

FAX Number: (817) 735-2486 Calendar System: Semester
URL: www.hsc.unt.edu
Established: 1966 Annual Graduate Tuition & Fees: $16,330
Enrollment: 1,760 Coed
Affiliation or Control: State IRS Status: 501(c)3
Highest Offering: Doctorate; No Undergraduates
Program: Professional
Accreditation: SC, ARCPA, OSTEO, PH, @PTA

01 President ... Dr. Scott B. RANSOM
10 VP for Finance and CFO ... Mr. Michael R. MUELLER
86 Vice President Governmental Affairs ... Mr. Dan JENSEN
63 Dean Texas Col of Osteopathic Med ... Dr. Don PESKA
32 Vice Pres Student Affairs ... Dr. Thomas D. MOORMAN
08 VP Information Resources & Technolo ... Dr. Renee DRABIER
15 Vice Pres Human Resource Svcs ... Vacant
81 VP Research & Biotechnology ... Vacant
51 Assoc VP for Professional/Cont Edu ... Ms. Pam MCFADDEN
58 Dean Grad Sch Biomedical Sciences ... Dr. Jamboor K. VISHWANATHA
76 Dean School of Health Professions ... Vacant
69 Dean of School of Public Health ... Dr. Richard KURZ
37 Director Student Financial Aid ... Mr. Joseph SANCHEZ
84 Executive Director Enrollment Svcs ... Mr. A.J RANDOLPH
19 Chief of Police ... Mr. Gary GAILLIARD
30 VP Institutional Advancement ... Mr. Gary GRANT
09 VP Strategy & Measurement ... Dr. Thomas FAIRCHILD
21 Controller & Chief Budget Officer ... Mr. Geoff SCARPELLI
07 Asst Dean of Admissions & Outreach ... Mr. Joel DABOUB
18 Vice President for Operations ... Mr. Stephen BARRETT
26 VP Marketing & Communications ... Ms. Jean TIPS
96 Dir Of Contract Administration ... Mrs. Lane NESTMAN

University of St. Thomas (A)

3800 Montrose Boulevard, Houston TX 77006-4696
County: Harris FICE Identification: 003654
Unit ID: 227863
Telephone: (713) 522-7911 Carnegie Class: Master's L
FAX Number: (713) 525-2125 Calendar System: Semester
URL: www.stthom.edu
Established: 1947 Annual Undergrad Tuition & Fees: $26,550
Enrollment: 3,726 Coed
Affiliation or Control: Roman Catholic IRS Status: 501(c)3
Highest Offering: Doctorate
Program: Liberal Arts And General; Teacher Preparatory; Professional
Accreditation: SC, ACBSP, BUS, TEAC, THEOL

01 President ... Dr. Robert IVANY
04 Exec Assistant to the President ... Ms. Sandra CACKOWSKI
04 Admin Assistant to the President ... Ms. Cindy VIAUD
10 Vice President for Finance ... Mr. James M. BOOTH
05 Vice President Academic Affairs ... Dr. Dominic AQUILA
11 Assoc VP of Administrative Svcs ... Mr. John MEUSER
20 Associate VP Academic Affairs ... Dr. John PALASOTA
49 Dean Arts & Sciences ... Fr. Joseph PILSNER
73 Dean School of Theology ... Dr. Sandra C. MAGIE, CM
50 Int Dean Cameron School of Business ... Dr. Barry WILBRATTE
53 Dean School of Education ... Dr. Robert LEBLANC
08 Dean of Libraries ... Mr. James PICCININNI
58 Dir Center for Thomistic Studies ... Dr. Mary C. SOMMERS
88 Director Center for Business Ethics ... Dr. Michele SIMMS
82 Director Center for Intl Studies ... Dr. Hans STOCKTON
88 Director Center for Irish Studies ... Ms. Lori GALLAGHER
13 Vice Pres Information Technology ... Mr. Gary MCCORMACK
30 Vice President for Inst Advancement ... Ms. Cynthia COLBERT RILEY
84 Vice Pres Marketing & Enroll Mgmt ... Ms. Vickie ALLEMAN
88 Director Center for Faith & Culture ... Fr. Donald NESTI, CSSP
06 Registrar ... Ms. Kimberly SANDERS
90 Dir of Network & Campus Computing ... Mr. Tony REYNA
90 Director Technology Support Svcs ... Mr. Mark HENDERSON
91 Dir Administrative Computing Svcs ... Ms. Joanna E. PALASOTA
88 Director Central Computing Services ... Ms. Christine BARRY
32 Vice Pres Student Affairs ... Ms. Patricia MCKINLEY
35 Dean of Students ... Ms. Lindsey MCPHERSON
38 Exec Dir Counseling & Disability ... Dr. Rose SIGNORELLO
35 Assistant VP of Campus Life ... Mr. Matthew PRASIFKA
42 Dir of Campus Ministry/Chaplain ... Fr. Michael BUENTELLO
39 Director Residence Life ... Ms. Yolanda NORMAN
88 Director of Student Activities ... Ms. Angie MONTELONGO
88 Director of Recreational Sports ... Ms. Jessica DOMANN
18 Asst VP Facilities Operations ... Mr. Howard A. ROSE
21 Controller ... Ms. Karen S. BURNS
88 Treasurer ... Ms. Susan ROSE
44 Exec Dir Institutional Advancement ... Ms. Susan E. BRADFORD
44 Director of Development/Major Gifts ... Ms. Deborah CROFOOT-MORLEY
29 Director of Major Constitutents ... Ms. Kia WISSMILLER
07 Director Admissions ... Mr. Phil BUTCHER
37 Dean of Scholarships/Financial Aid ... Ms. Lynda MCKENDREE
26 Dir of Marketing Communications ... Ms. Sandra SOLIZ
27 Director Publications ... Ms. Marionette MITCHELL

*University of Texas System Administration (B)

601 Colorado Street, Austin TX 78701-2982
County: Travis FICE Identification: 003655
Unit ID: 229090
Telephone: (512) 499-4201 Carnegie Class: N/A
FAX Number: (512) 499-4215
URL: www.utsystem.edu

01 Chancellor ... Dr. Francisco G. CIGARROA
05 Int Exec VC Academic Affairs ... Dr. Pedro REYES
17 Exec Vice Chanc Health Affairs ... Dr. Kenneth I. SHINE
10 Exec Vice Chanc Business Affairs ... Dr. Scott C. KELLEY
43 Vice Chanc & General Counsel ... Mr. Barry D. BURGDORF
86 Vice Chanc for Govt Relations ... Mr. Barry MCBEE
26 Vice Chanc for External Relations ... Dr. Randa S. SAFADY
86 Vice Chanc Federal Relations ... Mr. William SHUTE
45 Vice Chanc Strategic Initiatives ... Ms. Sandra K. WOODLEY
18 Assoc VC Facil Plng/Construction ... Mr. Michael O'DONNELL
13 Assoc VC & Chief Info Officer ... Mrs. Marg KNOX
21 Asst VC/Controller/Chief Budget Ofc ... Mr. Randy WALLACE
15 Assist Vice Chanc Employee Services ... Mr. Dan STEWART
27 Director Public Affairs ... Mr. Anthony P. DE BRUYN
88 Executive Director Real Estate ... Ms. Florence P. MAYNE
30 Dir Development/Gift Planning Svcs ... Ms. Julie LYNCH
19 Director of Police ... Mr. Michael J. HEIDINGSFIELD

*The University of Texas at Arlington (C)

701 S Nedderman Drive, Arlington TX 76013
County: Tarrant FICE Identification: 003656
Unit ID: 228769
Telephone: (817) 272-2101 Carnegie Class: RU/H
FAX Number: (817) 272-5656 Calendar System: Semester
URL: www.uta.edu
Established: 1895 Annual Undergrad Tuition & Fees (In-State): $8,878
Enrollment: 33,439 Coed
Affiliation or Control: State IRS Status: 170(c)1
Highest Offering: Doctorate
Program: Liberal Arts And General; Teacher Preparatory; Business Emphasis
Accreditation: SC, ART, BUS, BUSA, CIDA, CS, ENG, LSAR, MUS, NURSE, PLNG, SPAA, SW, TED

02 President ... Mr. James D. SPANIOLO
05 Provost & Vice Pres Acad Affairs ... Dr. Ronald L. ELSENBAUMER
10 Vice Pres Business Affs/Controller ... Ms. Kelly DAVIS
32 Vice President Student Affairs ... Dr. Frank LAMAS
30 Vice President Development ... Mr. Jim LEWIS
46 Int Vice President Research ... Dr. Carolyn CASON
13 Vice Pres Information Technology ... Dr. Maurice LEATHERBURY
11 Vice Pres Admin & Campus Operations ... Mr. John D. HALL
27 Vice President of Communications ... Mr. Jerry LEWIS
16 Vice President for Human Resources ... Ms. Jean HOOD
84 Sr Assoc VP Student Enrollment Svcs ... Dr. Dale WASSON
45 Assoc VP & Dir Inst Research/Plng ... Dr. Pamela M. HAWS
15 Asst Vice Pres Human Resources ... Ms. Eunice M. CURRIE
26 Asst Vice President Media Services ... Ms. Kristin SULLIVAN
18 Asst VP Campus Operation/Facilities ... Mr. Bill POOLE
88 Executive Dir University College ... Dr. Dawn REMMERS
04 Exec Associate to the President ... Ms. Marcy SANDERS
58 Dean of Graduate Studies ... Dr. Phil COHEN
48 Dean of Architecture ... Mr. Donald GATZKE
50 Dean Business Administration ... Dr. Daniel HIMARIOS
54 Dean of Engineering ... Dr. Jean-Pierre BARDET
49 Dean of Liberal Arts ... Dr. Beth WRIGHT
66 Dean of Nursing ... Dr. Elizabeth C. POSTER
81 Dean of Science ... Dr. Pamela JANSMA
70 Dean School of Social Work ... Dr. Scott RYAN
71 Dean Urban & Public Affairs ... Dr. Barbara BECKER
53 Dean College of Education ... Dr. Jeanne M. GERLACH
92 Dean Honors College ... Dr. Karl PETRUSO
08 Dean of Libraries ... Dr. Rebecca BICHEL
07 Exec Director Admissions & Records ... Dr. Hans GATTERDAM
29 Exec Director Alumni Association ... Ms. Lora MALONE
12 Exec Dir of UTA Ft Worth Center ... Mr. Mike WEST
37 Director of Financial Aid ... Dr. Karen KRAUSE
23 Director Student Health Center ... Mr. Robert BLUM
22 Director Equal Opportunity Services ... Mr. Eddie FREEMAN
24 Director of Art Services ... Mr. Joel QUINTANS
41 Athletic Director ... Mr. Jim BAKER
19 Dir Environmental Health Safety ... Ms. Leah HOY
85 Interim Exec Dir Intl Education ... Mr. Jay HORN
88 Director Multicultural Outreach ... Mr. Casey GONZALES
88 Director Multicultural Affairs ... Ms. Leticia MARTINEZ

*University of Texas at Austin (D)

Austin TX 78712-1026
County: Travis FICE Identification: 003658
Unit ID: 228778
Telephone: (512) 471-3434 Carnegie Class: RU/VH
FAX Number: (512) 471-8102 Calendar System: Semester
URL: www.utexas.edu
Established: 1883 Annual Undergrad Tuition & Fees (In-State): $9,792
Enrollment: 51,112 Coed
Affiliation or Control: State IRS Status: 170(c)1
Highest Offering: Doctorate
Program: Liberal Arts And General; Teacher Preparatory; Professional
Accreditation: SC, ART, AUD, BUS, BUSA, CIDA, CLPSY, COPSY, CORE, DANCE, DIETC, DIETD, ENG, IPSY, JOUR, LAW, LIB, LSAR, MUS, NURSE, PHAR, PLNG, SCPSY, SP, SPAA, SW

02 President ... Dr. William C. POWERS, JR.
05 Executive Vice Pres & Provost ... Dr. Steven W. LESLIE
10 Vice Pres & Chief Financial Officer ... Mr. Kevin P. HEGARTY
28 VP Diversity & Community Engagement ... Dr. Gregory J. VINCENT
11 Vice Pres for University Operations ... Dr. Patricia L. CLUBB
43 Vice President Legal Affairs ... Dr. Patricia A. OHLENDORF
26 Director University Media Relations ... Mr. Gary J. SUSSWEIN
46 Vice President Research ... Dr. Juan M. SANCHEZ
32 Vice President Student Affairs ... Dr. Gage PAINE
04 Deputy to the President ... Dr. Charles A. ROECKLE
04 Deputy to the President ... Ms. Nancy A. BRAZZIL
04 Executive Assistant to President ... Ms. Kathy R. BARTSCH
88 Vice Prov for Resource Management ... Dr. Daniel A. SLESNICK
07 Vice Prov & Dir Admissions ... Dr. Kedra B. ISHOP
20 Vice Provost for Faculty Affairs ... Dr. Neal E. ARMSTRONG
20 Vice Provost ... Dr. Victoria RODRIGUEZ
88 Vice Provost for Health Affairs ... Dr. William M. SAGE
08 Vice Provost/Dir General Libraries ... Dr. Fred M. HEATH
45 V Prov Forecasting/Inst Res/Modelng ... Dr. John D. DOLLARD
104 Vice Provost International Programs ... Dr. Janet L. ELLZEY
58 Vice Provost/Interim Dean Grad Stds ... Dr. Judith H. LANGLOIS
20 V Prov UG Educ & Faculty Governance ... Dr. Gretchen RITTER
88 Vice Provost for Special Projects ... Dr. N. Bruce WALKER
88 Vice Provost for Higher Ed Policy ... Dr. Harrison KELLER
21 Associate Vice President ... Ms. Mary E. KNIGHT
21 Budget Director ... Ms. Elvia H. ROSALES
09 Assoc V Prov/Dir Info Mgmt/Analysis ... Ms. Kristi D. FISHER
88 Associate Vice Provost ... Dr. R. Michael KERKER
88 Associate Vice President ... Ms. Renee L. WALLACE
30 Associate Vice Pres Development ... Mr. John H. MCCALL
30 Sr Associate Vice Pres Development ... Mr. David S. ONION
19 Assoc VP Campus Safety/Security ... Mr. Gerald R. HARKINS
18 Sr Assoc VP Facilities Management ... Dr. Steven A. KRAAL
15 Associate Vice Pres Human Resources ... Dr. Debra G. KRESS
22 Assoc VP/ADA Coordinator ... Ms. Linda H. MILLSTONE
38 Director University Health Services ... Ms. Jamie L. SHUTTER
46 Assoc VP Rsrch/Dir Spnsrd Projects ... Dr. Susan W. SEDWICK
06 Assoc VP Registrar ... Mr. Vincent (Shelby) STANFIELD
29 Assoc VP Off Rel Mgmt/Univ Events ... Vacant
37 Director Student Financial Svcs ... Dr. Thomas G. MELECKI
35 Sr Assoc Vice Pres/Dean of Students ... Dr. Soncia R. REAGINS-LILLY
39 Director Housing & Food Service ... Dr. Floyd B. HOELTING
41 Men's Athletics Director ... Mr. DeLoss DODDS
41 Women's Athletics Director ... Ms. Christine A. PLONSKY
29 CEO/Exec Director Ex-Students Assn ... Ms. Leslie CEDAR
19 Chief University Police ... Mr. Robert E. DAHLSTROM
48 Dean of Architecture ... Dr. Frederick R. STEINER
50 Dean McCombs School of Business ... Dr. Thomas W. GILLIGAN
60 Dean of Communication ... Dr. Roderick P. HART
53 Dean of Education ... Dr. Manuel J. JUSTIZ
54 Dean of Engineering ... Dr. Gregory L. FENVES
57 Dean of Fine Arts ... Dr. Douglas J. DEMPSTER
62 Dean School of Information ... Dr. Andrew P. DILLON
65 Dean Jackson School of Geosciences ... Dr. Sharon MOSHER
61 Dean School of Law ... Mr. Ward FARNSWORTH
49 Dean of Liberal Arts ... Dr. Randy L. DIEHL
81 Interim Dean of Natural Sciences ... Dr. David A. LAUDE
66 Dean of Nursing ... Dr. Alexa M. STUIFBERGEN
67 Dean of Pharmacy ... Dr. M. Lynn CRISMON
80 Dean LBJ School Public Affs ... Mr. Robert L. HUTCHINGS
70 Dean Social Work ... Dr. Luis H. ZAYAS
97 Dean of Undergraduate Studies ... Dr. Paul B. WOODRUFF
51 Ex Dir Continuing/Innovat Education ... Dr. Linda L. GLESSNER
88 Director Internal Audits ... Mr. Michael W. VANDERVORT
18 Director Facilities Services ... Mr. Michael A. MILLER
88 Executive Director Univ Union ... Mr. W. Andrew (Andy) SMITH
27 Dir Univ of Texas Press ... Mr. David S. HAMRICK
88 Assoc Athl Dir/Dir Spec Events Ctr ... Mr. John M. GRAHAM
96 Assistant VP/Dir of Procurement ... Mr. Jerry A. FULLER

*The University of Texas at Brownsville and Texas Southmost College (E)

80 Fort Brown, Brownsville TX 78520-4993
County: Cameron FICE Identification: 030646
Unit ID: 227377
Telephone: (956) 882-8200 Carnegie Class: Master's M
FAX Number: (956) 548-0020 Calendar System: Semester
URL: www.utb.edu
Established: 1973 Annual Undergrad Tuition & Fees (In-State): $5,116
Enrollment: 15,320 Coed
Affiliation or Control: State IRS Status: 501(c)3
Highest Offering: Doctorate
Program: Liberal Arts And General
Accreditation: SC, ADNUR, BUS, CACREP, CS, DMS, EMT, ENG, MLTAD, MUS, NUR

02 President ... Dr. Juliet V. GARCIA
05 Provost/VP for Academic Affairs ... Dr. Alan ARTIBISE
10 Vice President of Business Affairs ... Ms. Rosemary MARTINEZ
32 Vice President Student Affairs ... Dr. Hilda SILVA
13 Vice Pres Information Tech/CIO ... Dr. Clair GOLDSMITH
26 Vice Pres Economic Dev/Cmty Svcs ... Dr. Irvine DOWNING
20 Associate Provost ... Dr. Ruth A. RAGLAND
04 Special Assistant to the Provost ... Dr. Wayne MOORE
84 Assoc Vice Pres Enrollment Mgmt ... Mr. Rene VILLARREAL
100 Chief of Staff ... Dr. Marilyn J. WOODS
35 Dean of Students ... Dr. Mari FUENTES-MARTIN
58 Dean Graduate Studies ... Dr. Charles LACKEY
50 Dean School of Business ... Dr. Mark KROLL
76 Int Dean Biomed Scis/Health Profess ... Dr. Eldon NELSON
81 Dean College Science/Math/Tech ... Dr. Mikhail BOUNIAEV
53 Dean School of Education ... Dr. Miguel ESCOTET
49 Dean College Liberal Arts ... Dr. Javier MARTINEZ
103 Dean Workforce Trng/Cont Education ... Mr. Jim HOLT
06 Registrar ... Mr. Albert BARREDA

07 Director of Admissions .... Ms. Rene VILLARREAL
09 Director of Institutional Research .... Ms. Blanca TREVINO BAUER
18 Director Physical Plant .... Mr. Abraham HERNANDEZ
37 Director Student Financial Aid .... Ms. Mari F. CHAPA
38 Director of Student Success .... Ms. Beatriz BECERRA-BARCKHOLTZ
15 Director Human Resources .... Vacant
21 Director Business Office .... Ms. Yolanda DE LA RIVA
96 Director of Purchasing .... Mr. William M. DODD
89 Dir New Student Relations/Admission .... Mr. Carlo TAMAYO
29 Coordinator of Alumni Relations .... Ms. Veronica GARCIA

*The University of Texas at Dallas (A)

800 West Campbell Road, Richardson TX 75080

County: Collin FICE Identification: 009741
Unit ID: 228787
Telephone: (972) 883-2111 Carnegie Class: RU/H
FAX Number: (972) 883-2237 Calendar System: Semester
URL: www.utdallas.edu
Established: 1969 Annual Undergrad Tuition & Fees (In-State): $11,592
Enrollment: 18,864 Coed
Affiliation or Control: State IRS Status: 501(c)3
Highest Offering: Doctorate
Program: Liberal Arts And General; Professional
Accreditation: SC, AUD, BUS, BUSA, CS, ENG, SP, SPAA

02 President .... Dr. David E. DANIEL
03 Provost/Exec VP Academic Affairs .... Dr. B. Hobson WILDENTHAL
10 Vice President for Business Affairs .... Dr. Calvin D. JAMISON
32 Vice President Student Affairs .... Dr. Darrelene RACHAVONG
30 VP Development/Alumni Relations .... Dr. Aaron CONLEY
46 VP Research/Economic Development .... Dr. Bruce GNADE
20 Vice Provost .... Dr. John WIORKOWSKI
26 Vice President for Communications .... Ms. Susan ROGERS
13 Interim VP/Chief Info Officer .... Dr. Andrew BLANCHARD
28 Vice President of Diversity .... Dr. Magaly SPECTOR
21 Asst Dir Budget/Resource Plng .... Mr. David K. GAARDER
84 Vice Provost Enrollment Mgmt .... Mr. Curt ELEY
21 Assoc VP Finance & Controller .... Ms. Wanda MIZUTOWICZ
09 Exec Director Strategic Planning .... Dr. Lawrence J. REDLINGER
35 Dean of Students .... Dr. Gene FITCH
58 Dean Graduate Studies .... Dr. Austin J. CUNNINGHAM
53 Dean Undergraduate Education .... Dr. Sheila AMIN GUTIERREZ DE PINERES
79 Dean School Arts & Humanities .... Dr. Dennis KRATZ
50 Dean School of Management .... Dr. Hasan PIRKUL
81 Dean Sch of Natural Science/Math .... Dr. Bruce NOVAK
83 Dean School of Econ/Pol/Policy Sci .... Dr. James W. MARQUART
76 Dean Sch Behavioral/Brain Science .... Dr. Bert S. MOORE
97 Dean School General Studies .... Dr. George W. FAIR
54 Dean EJ Sch of Engr/Computer Sci .... Dr. Mark W. SPONG
08 Director of Libraries .... Dr. Ellen SAFLEY
37 Asst Provost/Acad Records .... Vacant
12 Exec Director of Callier Center .... Dr. Thomas F. CAMPBELL
25 Assoc VP Research Administration .... Mr. Rafael MARTIN
18 Assoc VP Facilities Management .... Mr. Richard DEMPSEY
16 Asst VP Human Resource Management .... Ms. Colleen DUTTON
96 Asst VP Procurement Management .... Mr. Peter BOND
91 Asst VP Information Resources .... Dr. Sue TAYLOR
19 Chief of Police .... Mr. Larry ZACHARIAS
36 Director Career Services .... Vacant
38 Director Student Counseling .... Mr. James P. CANNICI
88 Director of Audit and Compliance .... Ms. Toni MESSER
88 Director Teacher Education .... Dr. Scherry F. JOHNSON
41 Athletics Director .... Mr. Chris GAGE
78 Director Co-operative Education .... Mr. Michael J. CHOATE
90 Director Tech Customer Services .... Mr. Donald L. DAVIS
29 Director of Alumni Relations .... Ms. Erin DOUGHERTY

*University of Texas at El Paso (B)

500 W University Avenue, El Paso TX 79968-8900

County: El Paso FICE Identification: 003661
Unit ID: 228796
Telephone: (915) 747-5000 Carnegie Class: RU/H
FAX Number: (915) 747-5111 Calendar System: Semester
URL: www.utep.edu
Established: 1914 Annual Undergrad Tuition & Fees (In-State): $7,123
Enrollment: 22,640 Coed
Affiliation or Control: State IRS Status: 501(c)3
Highest Offering: Doctorate
Program: Liberal Arts And General; Teacher Preparatory; Professional
Accreditation: SC, BUS, BUSA, CORE, CS, ENG, MT, MUS, NURSE, OT, PTA, SP, SPAA, SW

02 President .... Dr. Diana S. NATALICIO
03 Sr Executive Vice President .... Dr. Howard DAUDISTEL
03 Executive Vice President .... Mr. Ricardo ADAUTO, III
04 Assistant to the President .... Ms. Estrella ESCOBAR
05 Provost/Vice Pres Academic Affairs .... Dr. Junius GONZALES
10 Vice President for Business Affairs .... Ms. Cindy VILLA
46 Vice President for Research .... Dr. Roberto OSEGUEDA
09 Vice Pres Info Resources & Planning .... Dr. Steve RITER
58 Acting Dean of Graduate School .... Dr. Ben FLORES
50 Dean of Business Administration .... Dr. Robert NACHTMANN
53 Dean of Education .... Dr. Josefina V. TINAJERO
54 Dean of Engineering .... Dr. Richard T. SCHOEPHOERSTER
49 Dean of Liberal Arts .... Dr. Patricia WITHERSPOON
66 Dean of Health Sciences .... Dr. Kathleen A. CURTIS
81 Dean of Science .... Dr. Anny MORROBEL-SOSA
66 Dean of School of Nursing .... Dr. Elias PROVENCIO-VASQUEZ

32 Interim VP Student Affairs .... Dr. Gary EDENS
18 Assoc VP Business Affs/Facilities .... Mr. Greg L. MCNICOL
08 Assoc Vice President/Library .... Mr. Robert L. STAKES
26 Asst Vice Pres University Relations .... Mr. Beto LOPEZ
27 Assoc VP University Communications .... Mr. Chris LOPEZ
22 Asst Vice Pres EO/AA Dept .... Ms. Sandy VASQUEZ
29 Asst VP Development/Alumni Rels .... Dr. Richard DANIEL
46 Assoc Provost for Resource Mgmt .... Ms. Elizabeth FLORES
84 Assoc Vice Provost Enrollment Mgmt .... Dr. Craig E. WESTMAN
06 Registrar .... Mr. Miguel SIFUENTES
15 Director of Human Resources Svcs .... Mr. Andrew PENA
19 Chief Campus Police .... Mr. Clifton WALSH
37 Interim Dir of Student Fin Aid .... Mr. Ron WILLIAMS
23 Interim CoDir of Student Health Ctr .... Ms. Valerie FARRINGTON
36 Director of Career Services .... Mr. George BARTON
35 Associate VP/Dean of Students .... Ms. Catherine M. MCCORRY-ANDALIS
46 Assoc VP Inst Eval/Rsrch & Planning .... Dr. Roy MATHEW
39 Director of Housing Services .... Mr. Charlie E. GIBBENS
40 Director of University Bookstore .... Mr. Fernando PADULA
41 Athletics Director .... Mr. Robert W. STULL
38 Director Counseling Services .... Ms. Sherri I. TERRELL
96 Dir Purchasing/General Services .... Ms. Diane N. DEHOYOS
07 Exec Dir Admissions/Recruitment .... Dr. Luisa M. HAVENS

*University of Texas - Pan American (C)

1201 W University Drive, Edinburg TX 78539-2970

County: Hidalgo FICE Identification: 003599
Unit ID: 227368
Telephone: (956) 665-2011 Carnegie Class: Master's L
FAX Number: (956) 665-2150 Calendar System: Semester
URL: www.utpa.edu
Established: 1927 Annual Undergrad Tuition & Fees (In-State): $6,124
Enrollment: 19,034 Coed
Affiliation or Control: State IRS Status: 501(c)3
Highest Offering: Doctorate
Program: Liberal Arts And General; Teacher Preparatory; Professional
Accreditation: SC, ARCPA, BUS, CORE, CS, DIETC, ENG, MT, MUS, NURSE, OT, SP, SW, THEA

02 President .... Dr. Robert S. NELSEN
100 Chief of Staff .... Ms. Lisa PRIETO
05 Provost/VP Academic Affairs .... Dr. Havidan RODRIGUEZ
20 Associate Provost .... Dr. Kenneth BUCKMAN
88 Vice Provost for Faculty Affairs .... Dr. Ala QUBBAJ
10 Vice President for Business Affairs .... Mr. Martin BAYLOR
30 VP for University Advancement .... Ms. Veronica GONZALES
32 Vice President for Student Affairs .... Dr. Martha CANTU
13 CIO for Information Technology .... Dr. Jeffrey GRAHAM
20 Vice Prov for Undergraduate Stds .... Dr. Kristin CROYLE
21 Assoc Vice Pres BA & Comptroller .... Mr. Esequiel GRANADO
07 Sr Assoc VP for Enrollment Services .... Dr. Maggie HINOJOSA
31 Exec Dir Ofc Ctr Oper/Community Svc .... Ms. Jessica SALINAS
08 Dean of the University Library .... Dr. Farzaneh RAZZAGHI
06 University Registrar .... Dr. Jeff RHODES
14 Executive Director for IT Services .... Mr. Frank ZECCA
15 Director of Human Resources .... Ms. Francisca RIOS
19 Chief University Police .... Mr. Roger STEARNS
26 Director University Relations .... Ms. Sandra Q. GUZMAN
36 Director Career Placement Services .... Ms. Lourdes SERVANTES
37 Director Student Financial Services .... Mrs. Elaine RIVERA
29 Director Alumni Rels/Special Events .... Mrs. Debby GRANT
41 Director Intercollegiate Athletics .... Mr. Christopher KING
09 Exec Dir Inst Rsrch Effectiveness .... Dr. S.J SETHI
53 Dean College of Education .... Dr. Salvador H. OCHOA
35 Dean of Students .... Vacant
50 Dean Col Business Admin .... Dr. Teofilo OZUNA
38 Director of Couseling/Advisement .... Ms. Lise BLANKENSHIP
81 Dean College of Science and Math .... Dr. John M. TRANT
54 Dean College Engr/Computer Science .... Dr. David ALLEN
84 Director of Recruitment .... Ms. Debbie GILCHRIST
76 Dean Col Health Sci/Human Svcs .... Dr. Bruce REED
49 Dean College Arts & Humanities .... Dr. Dahlia GUERRA
83 Dean Social/Behavioral Sciences .... Dr. Walter DIAZ
18 Dir for Facilities & Physical Plant .... Mr. Oscar VILLARREAL
96 Director Materials Management .... Ms. Norma DRYER
25 Supervisor for Grants & Contracts .... Vacant
22 EEO ADA Coordinator .... Ms. Esmeralda GUERRA

*University of Texas at San Antonio (D)

One UTSA Circle, San Antonio TX 78249-0169

County: Bexar FICE Identification: 010115
Unit ID: 229027
Telephone: (210) 458-4011 Carnegie Class: RU/H
FAX Number: (210) 458-4187 Calendar System: Semester
URL: www.utsa.edu
Established: 1969 Annual Undergrad Tuition & Fees (In-State): $9,003
Enrollment: 30,968 Coed
Affiliation or Control: State IRS Status: 501(c)3
Highest Offering: Doctorate
Program: Liberal Arts And General; Teacher Preparatory; Professional
Accreditation: SC, ART, BUS, BUSA, CACREP, CIDA, ENG, MUS, SPAA, SW

02 President .... Dr. Ricardo ROMO
05 Provost/Vice Pres Academic Affairs .... Dr. John FREDERICK
10 Vice President for Business Affairs .... Mr. Kerry L. KENNEDY
32 Vice President Student Affairs .... Vacant
31 Vice President Community Services .... Dr. Jude VALDEZ
30 Vice Pres Univ Advancement .... Ms. Marjie M. FRENCH

11 Assoc Vice Pres for Administration .... Ms. Pamela BACON
20 Executive Vice Provost .... Mr. Julius M. GRIBOU
09 V Prov Acad Compliance/Inst Effect .... Dr. Sandra T. WELCH
12 Vice Provost for Downtown Campus .... Dr. Jesse T. ZAPATA
14 Vice Provost Information Officer .... Mr. Kenneth PIERCE
20 V Prov Acad Supt/Dean UGrad Studies .... Dr. Lawrence R. WILLIAMS
21 Assoc Vice Pres Financial Affairs .... Vacant
15 Assoc VP Human Resources/Developmt .... Ms. Barbara CENTENO
35 Asst VP Student Svcs/Admin/Plng .... Mr. Samuel M. GONZALES
08 Dean of Libraries .... Ms. Krisellen MALONEY
92 Dean Honors College .... Dr. Richard A. DIEM
58 Dean Graduate School .... Dr. Dorothy A. FLANNAGAN
50 Dean College of Business .... Dr. Lynda Y. DE LA VINA
57 Dean College of Liberal & Fine Arts .... Dr. Daniel J. GELO
54 Dean College of Engineering .... Dr. C. Mauli AGRAWAL
83 Dean College of Sciences .... Dr. George PERRY
48 Dean School of Architecture .... Prof. John MURPHY
53 Dean College Educ/Human Development .... Dr. Betty MERCHANT
80 Dean College of Public Policy .... Dr. Rogelio SAENZ
19 Chief of Police .... Mr. Steve V. BARRERA
41 Director Intercol Athletics .... Ms. Lynn HICKEY
29 ASCT VP Alumni Program Mkt .... Mr. James C. MICKEY
43 Chief Legal Officer .... Ms. Gail JENSEN
26 Chief Communications Officer .... Mr. Joe IZBRAND
86 Director External Affairs .... Mr. Albert A. CARRISALEZ

*University of Texas at Tyler (E)

3900 University Boulevard, Tyler TX 75799-6699

County: Smith FICE Identification: 011163
Unit ID: 228802
Telephone: (903) 566-7000 Carnegie Class: Master's L
FAX Number: (903) 566-7068 Calendar System: Semester
URL: www.uttyler.edu
Established: 1971 Annual Undergrad Tuition & Fees (In-State): $6,740
Enrollment: 6,696 Coed
Affiliation or Control: State IRS Status: 501(c)3
Highest Offering: Doctorate
Program: Liberal Arts And General; Teacher Preparatory; Professional
Accreditation: SC, BUS, ENG, NAIT, NURSE, TEAC

02 President .... Dr. Rodney H. MABRY
05 Provost/Sr VP Academic Affairs .... Dr. Alisa WHITE
10 Vice President for Business Affairs .... Mr. Randall POWELL
30 Vice President Univ Advancement .... Mr. Jerre IVERSEN
41 Vice Pres Auxilary Svcs & Athletics .... Dr. Howard PATTERSON
13 Vice President & CIO IT .... Dr. Sherri WHATLEY
20 Vice Provost AA/Grad Studies .... Dr. Donna DICKERSON
20 Associate Provost UG Programs .... Vacant
46 Assoc Vice President for Research .... Vacant
21 Associate VP for Business Affairs .... Ms. Sheryl DENNIS
11 Associate VP for Adminstration .... Mr. Jesse ACOSTA
15 Assoc VP/Director Human Resources .... Mr. Joe VORSAS
84 Asst VP Enroll Mgmt & Mktg .... Ms. Candice LINDSEY
88 Asst Vice Pres for Assessment/IE .... Dr. Lou Ann BERMAN
32 Asst VP Student Affs/Dean Students .... Ms. Ona TOLLIVER
49 Dean College of Arts & Sciences .... Dr. Martin SLANN
50 Dean College Business & Technology .... Dr. Harold DOTY
53 Dean College Education & Psychology .... Dr. William GEIGER
54 Dean College Engineering & Comp Sci .... Dr. James NELSON
66 Dean College Nursing & Health Sci .... Dr. Linda KLOTZ
08 Director of the Library .... Ms. Jeanne PYLE
21 Director of Financial Services .... Ms. Carrie CLAYTON
18 Dir Facility/Plng/Construct/Oper .... Mr. Chip CLARK
29 Coordinator of Alumni Relations .... Ms. Derrith BONDURANT
100 Chief of Staff .... Vacant
27 Director Mktg & Communiation .... Ms. Beverley GOLDEN
38 Dir Stdnt Svc/Stdnt Couns/Test Ctr .... Ms. Ida MACDONALD
39 Director of Residence Life .... Mr. David R. HILL
96 Asst Dir Financial Services .... Mrs. Cindy TROYER
06 Registrar .... Ms. Sonja MORALE
09 Director of Institutional Analysis .... Dr. Sherri WHATLEY
19 Chief University Police .... Mr. Mike W. MEDDERS

*The University of Texas Health Science Center at Houston (UTHealth) (F)

PO Box 20036, Houston TX 77225-0036

County: Harris FICE Identification: 004951
Unit ID: 229300
Telephone: (713) 500-4472 Carnegie Class: Spec/Med
FAX Number: (713) 500-3026 Calendar System: Semester
URL: www.uthouston.edu
Established: 1972 Annual Undergrad Tuition & Fees (In-State): $9,000
Enrollment: 3,994 Coed
Affiliation or Control: State IRS Status: 501(c)3
Highest Offering: Doctorate
Program: Professional
Accreditation: SC, ANEST, DENT, DH, DIETI, ENGR, MED, NURSE, PH

02 Interim President .... Dr. Giuseppe N. COLASURDO
03 CFO/COO & Exec VP for Admin .... Mr. T. Kevin DILLON
45 Senior VP for Strategic Planning .... Dr. Osama I. MIKHAIL
05 Exec VP Acad & Res Affs .... Dr. George M. STANCEL
46 Vice Dn Rsrch/Int Molecular Med .... Dr. John HANCOCK
26 Vice Pres Institutional Advancement .... Vacant
15 VP/Chief Human Resources Officer .... Mr. Eric FERNETTE
43 VP/Chief Legal & Compliance Officer .... Ms. Arlene D. STALLER
86 VP/Chief Govt Relations Officer .... Ms. Sabrina MIDKIFF

104 VP Global Health Initiatives .... Dr. Bruce D. BUTLER
31 VP Auxiliary Enterprises .... Mr. Charles A. FIGARI
13 VP/Chief Information Officer .... Mr. Richard L. MILLER
18 VP Facilities Planning & Engr .... Mr. Richard L. MCDERMOTT
10 Sr VP Finance & Budget .... Mr. Michael TRAMONTE
30 Asst VP Fundraising & Advancemnt .... Ms. Betsy C. FRANTZ
90 Asst VP Academic Technology .... Dr. William A. WEEMS
91 Director Administrative Technology .... Vacant
21 Director Internal Audit .... Ms. Lois K. PIERSON
06 Registrar .... Mr. Robert JENKINS
19 Chief of Police .... Mr. William ADCOX
41 Director Recreation/Intramural Pgms .... Ms. Pauline M. HABETZ
85 Director International Affairs .... Ms. Maria C. AREVALO-SANCHEZ
39 Director University Housing .... Mr. Billy C. HINTON
27 Dir Univ Communications/Pubs .... Ms. Karen K. KAPLAN
88 Director of Media Relations .... Ms. Meredith RAINE
37 Director Student Financial Svcs .... Ms. Wanda K. WILLIAMS
28 Chief Academic Diversity Officer .... Dr. Ronald JOHNSON
52 Dean School of Dentistry .... Dr. John A. VALENZA
63 Dean Medical School .... Dr. Giuseppe N. COLASURDO
17 Exec Vice Dean Clinical Affairs .... Dr. Brent KING
66 Dean School of Nursing .... Dr. Patricia L. STARCK
69 Dean School of Public Health .... Dr. Roberta B. NESS
88 Interim Dean Sch of Biomed Info .... Dr. Jiajie W. ZHANG
58 Dean Grad Sch Biomed Science .... Vacant
25 Exec Direc Sponsored Projects Admin .... Ms. Jodi OGDEN
23 Executive Director Clinical-MS .... Dr. Thomas A. MACKEY
14 Director Data Center Operations .... Mr. Kevin B. GRANHOLD
22 EEO Advisor .... Mr. John RAYBURN
24 Director Educational & Tech-DB .... Dr. David TAYLOR
24 Director Ctr Education & Info-SON .... Ms. Linda L. CRAYS
72 Director Biomedical Info Tech-MS .... Dr. Stephen J. FATH
07 Associate Dean Admissions-MS .... Dr. Margaret MCNEESE
29 Assoc Dean Student & Alumni-SOD .... Dr. Hugh P. PIERPONT
07 Asst Dean Admissions-GSBS .... Vacant
07 Asst Dir of Admissions-SHIS .... Ms. Carolyn ELLIOTT
35 Director Student Affairs-SON .... Ms. Laurie G. RUTHERFORD
35 Director of Student Affairs-SPH .... Dr. Mary A. SMITH

*University of Texas Health Science Center at San Antonio (A)

7703 Floyd Curl Drive, San Antonio TX 78229-3900
County: Bexar — FICE Identification: 003659
Unit ID: 228644
Telephone: (210) 567-7000 — Carnegie Class: Spec/Med
FAX Number: (210) 567-2025 — Calendar System: Other
URL: www.uthscsa.edu
Established: 1959 — Annual Undergrad Tuition & Fees (In-State): $7,603
Enrollment: 3,310 — Coed
Affiliation or Control: State — IRS Status: 501(c)3
Highest Offering: Doctorate
Program: Professional
Accreditation: SC, ARCPA, BBT, DENT, DH, @DIETC, EMT, HT, IPSY, #MED, MT, NURSE, OT, PTA, RADDOS

02 President .... Dr. William L. HENRICH
03 Sr Exec Vice President & COO .... Mr. Michael E. BLACK
11 Exec VP for Facility Planning/Admin .... Mr. James D. KAZEN
10 Vice President & CFO .... Ms. Andrea M. MARKS
05 Int VP Acad/Facul & Student Affairs .... Dr. Denise WILBUR
13 Vice Pres & Chief Information Ofcr .... Vacant
46 Vice President for Research .... Dr. David WEISS
86 VP for Governmental Relations .... Mr. Armando DIAZ
30 VP for Institutional Advancement .... Ms. Deborah H. MORRILL
15 Vice Pres of Human Resources .... Mr. J. Michael TESH
100 VP Communications & Chief of Staff .... Ms. Mary G. DELAY
21 Asst Vice Pres for Business Affairs .... Mr. Gerard E. LONG
25 Asst VP Research/Sponsored Programs .... Ms. Jane A. YOUNGERS
18 Asst VP for Strategic Initiatives .... Mr. Darrell MAATSCH
63 Dean School of Medicine .... Dr. Francisco GONZALEZ-SCARANO
52 Dean Dental School .... Dr. Kenneth L. KALKWARF
58 Dean Graduate Biomed Science .... Dr. David WEISS
76 Int Dean School Health Professions .... Dr. Juanita WALLACE
66 Dean School of Nursing .... Dr. Eileen T. BRESLIN
32 Exec Dir for Student Services .... Vacant
06 Registrar .... Ms. Blanca GUERRA
08 Exec Director of Libraries .... Ms. Rajia C. TOBIA
19 Chief of Police .... Mr. Michael PARKS
22 Executive Director of EEO/AA Office .... Dr. Bonnie L. BLANKMEYER
37 Director of Financial Aid .... Vacant
38 Director of Counseling .... Dr. Kozue SHIBAZAKI
43 Senior Legal Officer .... Mr. Jack C. PARK
96 Director of Purchasing .... Ms. Vikki F. ROSS

*The University of Texas M.D. Anderson Cancer Center (B)

1515 Holcombe Boulevard, Houston TX 77030-4000
County: Harris — FICE Identification: 025554
Unit ID: 416801
Telephone: (713) 792-6161 — Carnegie Class: Spec/Health
FAX Number: N/A — Calendar System: Semester
URL: www.mdanderson.org
Established: 1941 — Annual Undergrad Tuition & Fees (In-District): N/A
Enrollment: 316 — Coed
Affiliation or Control: State/Local — IRS Status: 501(c)3
Highest Offering: Doctorate
Program: Professional
Accreditation: SC, CYTO, DENT, DMOLS, HT, MT, RAD, RADDOS, RTT

02 President .... Dr. Ronald DEPINKO
05 Provost/Executive Vice President .... Dr. Raymond DUBOIS

*The University of Texas Medical Branch (C)

301 University Boulevard, Galveston TX 77555-0100
County: Galveston — FICE Identification: 004952
Unit ID: 228653
Telephone: (409) 772-1011 — Carnegie Class: Spec/Med
FAX Number: N/A — Calendar System: Semester
URL: www.utmb.edu
Established: 1891 — Annual Undergrad Tuition & Fees (In-State): $6,712
Enrollment: 2,825 — Coed
Affiliation or Control: State — IRS Status: 170(c)1
Highest Offering: Doctorate
Program: Professional
Accreditation: SC, ARCPA, BBT, DENT, MED, MT, NURSE, OT, PH, PTA

02 President .... Dr. David L. CALLENDER
04 Exec Asst to the President .... Ms. Jandee ALARID
05 Int Exec VP/Dean Sch of Medicine .... Dr. Donald S. PROUGH
17 Exec VP & CEO Health System .... Ms. Donna K. SOLLENBERGER
10 Exec VP & Chief Business/Fin Ofcr .... Mr. William R. ELGER
86 Sr VP Health Policy & Legis Affairs .... Dr. Ben G. RAIMER
88 VP & Chief Physician .... Dr. Rex M. MCCALLUM
17 Interim Chief Medical Officer .... Dr. Steve Q. QUACH
20 VP Education & Dean Sch of Nursing .... Dr. Pamela G. WATSON
76 VP & Dean Sch of Health Professions .... Dr. Elizabeth J. PROTAS
58 VP & Dean Grad Sch of Biomed Sci .... Dr. Cary W. COOPER
16 VP HR & Employee Services .... Dr. Ronald B. MCKINLEY
13 VP Information Services & CIO .... Mr. Ralph E. FARR
18 VP Facilities & Campus Services .... Mr. Michael B. SHRINER
21 VP Finance Academic Enterprise .... Mr. Cameron W. SLOCUM
21 VP Finance Clinical Enterprise .... Mr. David M. CONNAUGHTON
45 VP for Strategic Mgmt .... Dr. Rebecca SAAVEDRA
43 VP & Chief Legal Officer .... Ms. Carolee KING
26 VP Public Affairs .... Ms. Christine F. COMER
12 Dean Austin Programs .... Dr. T. S. SHOMAKER
35 Sr Assoc Dean Grad Sch Biomed Sci .... Dr. Dorian H. COPPENHAVER
35 Assoc Dean School of Medicine .... Dr. Lauree THOMAS
07 Assoc Dean Admiss School of Nursing .... Dr. Tina CUELLAR
35 Assoc Dean Health Professions .... Mr. Henry CAVAZOS
46 Assoc Dean Research Admin .... Mr. William G. NEW
08 Assoc VP Academic Res/Dir Library .... Mr. Brett A. KIRKPATRICK
09 Assoc VP Inst Effectiveness .... Dr. John C. MCKEE
26 Assoc VP Marketing .... Vacant
21 Assoc VP Fin Plng & Perf Mgmt .... Mr. Matthew FURLONG
21 Assoc VP Finance .... Ms. Celia BAILEY-OCHOA
88 Assoc VP Audit Services .... Ms. Kimberly HAGARA
30 Assoc VP Chief Develop Officer .... Ms. Betsy B. CLARDY
32 Assoc VP for Univ Student Services .... Mr. James MARTIN
29 Asst VP Alumni Relations .... Ms. Dixie MULLINS
28 Interim Inst Compliance Officer .... Ms. Carolee KING
84 Dir Enrollment Svcs/Univ Registrar .... Mr. Shawn DEVEAU
19 Chief of University Police .... Mr. Thomas ENGELLS
22 Dir Equal Opportunity/Diversity .... Mr. Joe A. GALVAN
23 Director Student Wellness .... Ms. Cynthia A. DESANTO
96 Int ED Supply Chain/Chf Purchasing .... Mr. Kyle BARTON
39 Dir Aux Enterprises-Housing/Bkstore .... Mr. Bruno P. CRISTELLI
38 Director Student Counseling .... Ms. Cynthia DESANTOS

*University of Texas of the Permian Basin (D)

4901 E University Boulevard, Odessa TX 79762-8122
County: Ector — FICE Identification: 009930
Unit ID: 229018
Telephone: (432) 552-2020 — Carnegie Class: Master's M
FAX Number: (432) 552-2374 — Calendar System: Semester
URL: www.utpb.edu
Established: 1969 — Annual Undergrad Tuition & Fees (In-State): $6,468
Enrollment: 3,831 — Coed
Affiliation or Control: State — IRS Status: 501(c)3
Highest Offering: Master's
Program: Liberal Arts And General; Teacher Preparatory; Professional
Accreditation: SC, ART, BUS, SW, TED

02 President .... Dr. W. David WATTS
04 Assistant to the President .... Ms. Carla P. NELSON
05 Provost/Vice Pres Academic Affairs .... Dr. William R. FANNIN
32 Provost & VP Student Services .... Dr. Susan LARA
10 Vice President Business Affairs .... Mr. Dale CASSIDY
58 Asst Vice Pres Grad Stds/Research .... Dr. Juli RATHEAL
13 Asst Vice Pres/Dir Info Resources .... Mr. J. Keith YARBROUGH
49 Dean College of Arts & Science .... Dr. Mylan REDFERN
50 Dean School of Business .... Mr. Jack LADD
53 Dean School of Education .... Dr. Frank HERNANDEZ
30 Director Institutional Advancement .... Vacant
07 Director Admissions .... Mr. Scott SMILEY
06 Registrar .... Mr. Hector GOVEA
37 Director Financial Aid .... Mr. Joe SANDERS
08 Director of Library Services .... Vacant
15 Director Human Resources .... Ms. Caron PERKINS
51 Director Continuing Education .... Mr. Rey LASCANO
26 Interim Public Information Officer .... Ms. Travis WOODWARD
41 Director Athletics .... Dr. Steve AICINENA
19 Chief of Police .... Chief Tom HAIN
18 Chief Facilities/Physical Plant .... Mr. Michael RULAND
29 Director Alumni Relations .... Mr. Stacy FUQUA
35 Director Student Affairs .... Dr. Susan LARA
36 Dir Student Placement/Counseling .... Mr. Tony LOVE
96 Interim Director of Purchasing .... Ms. Ynez ALDERSON

*University of Texas Southwestern Medical Center (E)

5323 Harry Hines Boulevard, Dallas TX 75390-9002
County: Dallas — FICE Identification: 010019
Unit ID: 228635
Telephone: (214) 648-3111 — Carnegie Class: Spec/Med
FAX Number: N/A — Calendar System: Other
URL: www.utsouthwestern.edu
Established: 1943 — Annual Undergrad Tuition & Fees (In-State): $7,971
Enrollment: 2,488 — Coed
Affiliation or Control: State — IRS Status: 501(c)3
Highest Offering: Doctorate
Program: Professional
Accreditation: SC, ARCPA, BBT, CLPSY, CORE, DIETC, EMT, IPSY, MED, MIL, MT, OPE, PTA, RTT

02 President .... Dr. Daniel K. PODOLSKY
100 Vice President & Chief of Staff .... Dr. Robin M. JACOBY
05 Exec VP Acad Aff/Provost/Dean SMS .... Dr. Gregory FITZ
03 Exec VP Health System Affairs .... Dr. Bruce A. MEYER
10 Exec Vice Pres Business Affairs .... Mr. Arnim DONTES
46 Vice Provost/Dean of Basic Research .... Dr. David W. RUSSELL
88 Vice Pres Health System Fin Affairs .... Mr. Bruce M. FAIRBANKS
23 Vice President Clinical Operations .... Dr. John D. RUTHERFORD
88 Vice President University Hospitals .... Dr. John WARNER
88 Chief Quality Officer .... Dr. Gary REED
86 Vice Pres Govt Affairs & Policy .... Ms. Angelica MARIN-HILL
27 Vice Pres Comm Mktg & Public Affs .... Mr. Tim DOKE
31 Vice President External Relations .... Mrs. Cynthia B. BASSEL
16 Vice President Human Resource .... Dr. William M. BEHRENDT
43 Vice President Legal Affairs .... Ms. Leah A. HURLEY
72 Vice Pres Technology Development .... Vacant
30 Vice President Development .... Ms. Amanda BILLINGS
102 Vice Pres Community and Corp Rels .... Mr. Ruben E. ESQUIVEL
13 Vice Pres Information Resources .... Mr. Kirk A. KIRKSEY
18 Vice President Facilities Mgmt .... Mr. Kirby L. VAHLE
29 Vice Pres Stdnt/Alumni Affs/Admiss .... Mr. J. W. NORRED
88 Vice President Research Admin .... Ms. Angela WISHON
88 Assoc Vice Pres Chief Admin Ofcr .... Dr. Randall F. JONES
88 Asst Vice Pres Ambulatory Care .... Dr. Stan TAYLOR
88 Chief Med Officer University Hosp .... Dr. Steven LEACH
88 Assoc Vice Pres Chief Nursing Ofcr .... Ms. Donna RICHARDSON
96 Asst Vice Pres Materials Mgmt .... Mr. Paul D. BELEW
88 Asst Vice Pres Parkland HHS Affairs .... Dr. Christopher MADDEN
88 Asst Vice Pres Marketing .... Ms. Dorothea BONDS
21 Asst Vice President Accounting .... Mr. George S. KOKORUDA
08 Asst Vice Pres Library Services .... Mrs. Laurie L. THOMPSON
20 Sr Assoc Dean Academic Admin .... Dr. Charles M. GINSBURG
45 Sr Assoc Dean Strategic Development .... Dr. Dwain L. THIELE
28 Assoc Dean Faculty Diversity & Dev .... Dr. Byron L. CRYER
88 Assoc Dean Global Health .... Dr. Fiemu E. NWARIAKU
51 Assoc Dean Grad Medical Education .... Dr. Bradley MARPLE
63 Assoc Dean Undergrad Med Educ .... Dr. Steve CANNON
32 Assoc Dean Student Affairs .... Dr. Angela MIHALIC
32 Assoc Dean Student Affairs .... Dr. James M. WAGNER
93 Assoc Dean Minority Student Affairs .... Dr. Shawna NESBITT
88 Associate Dean .... Dr. Perrie M. ADAMS
58 Dean Grad School Biomedical Science .... Dr. Michael G. ROTH
76 Dean School of Health Professions .... Dr. Raul CAETANO
06 Registrar/Financial Aid .... Mr. Charles L. KETTLEWELL
07 Assoc Director of Admissions .... Ms. Anne P. MCLANE

Vernon College (F)

4400 College Drive, Vernon TX 76384-4092
County: Wilbarger — FICE Identification: 010060
Unit ID: 229504
Telephone: (940) 552-6291 — Carnegie Class: Assoc/Pub-R-M
FAX Number: (940) 553-3902 — Calendar System: Semester
URL: www.vernoncollege.edu
Established: 1970 — Annual Undergrad Tuition & Fees (In-District): $2,064
Enrollment: 3,252 — Coed
Affiliation or Control: State/Local — IRS Status: 501(c)3
Highest Offering: Associate Degree
Program: Occupational; 2-Year Principally Bachelor's Creditable
Accreditation: SC, SURGT

01 President .... Dr. Dusty R. JOHNSTON
04 Admin Secretary to the President .... Ms. Mary KING
05 Dean of Instructional Services .... Dr. Gary Don HARKEY
11 Dean of Administrative Services .... Mr. Garry DAVID
32 Dean of Student Svs/Athletic Dir .... Mr. John B. HARDIN, III
07 Dean Admiss/Registr/Financial Aid .... Mr. Joe HITE
103 Assoc Dean of Workforce Ed & Trng .... Mrs. Shana MUNSON
21 Assoc Dean Administrative Svcs .... Vacant
30 Director of Inst Advancement .... Ms. Michelle ALEXANDER
09 Director of Institutional Research .... Mrs. Betsy HARKEY
37 Director Financial Aid .... Mrs. Melissa J. ELLIOTT
13 Director of Information Technology .... Mr. Jim BINION
08 Director of Library Services .... Ms. Marion GRONA
18 Director Physical Plant .... Mr. John MAHONEY
15 Director of Human Resources .... Mrs. Haven DAVID
39 Director of Housing .... Mr. Tony PEREZ
35 Assoc Dean of Student Services .... Mrs. Kristin HARRIS
06 Assistant Registrar .... Mrs. Sarah DAVENPORT
66 Dir Associate Degree in Nursing .... Ms. Cathy BOLTON
66 Dir Licensed Vocational Nursing .... Mr. Lynn KALSKI

88 Director of Student Relations .... Ms. Brandi BRANNON
35 Director of Student Activities .... Mr. Sjohonton FANNER
19 Director of Campus Police .... Mr. Chris BELL
51 Coordinator Continuing Education .... Mrs. Anne PATTERSON
88 Coordinator of Testing .... Mrs. Sharron SHELTON
56 Coordinator of Distance Learning .... Vacant
24 Media Specialist .... Mr. Gene FROMMELT

Vet Tech Institute of Houston (A)

4669 Southwest Freeway, Suite 100, Houston TX 77027
County: Harris FICE Identification: 021448
Unit ID: 223472
Telephone: (713) 629-8940 Carnegie Class: Assoc/PrivFP
FAX Number: (713) 629-0059 Calendar System: Semester
URL: www.vettechinstitute.edu/houston
Established: 2007 Annual Undergrad Tuition & Fees: $13,530
Enrollment: 239 Coed
Affiliation or Control: Proprietary IRS Status: Proprietary
Highest Offering: Associate Degree
Program: Occupational
Accreditation: ACICS

01 Director/Chief Academic Officer .... Mr. Elbert HAMILTON, JR.

Victoria College (B)

2200 E Red River, Victoria TX 77901-4494
County: Victoria FICE Identification: 003662
Unit ID: 229540
Telephone: (361) 573-3291 Carnegie Class: Assoc/Pub-R-M
FAX Number: (361) 572-3850 Calendar System: Semester
URL: www.victoriacollege.edu
Established: 1925 Annual Undergrad Tuition & Fees (In-District): $1,920
Enrollment: 4,566 Coed
Affiliation or Control: Local IRS Status: 501(c)3
Highest Offering: Associate Degree
Program: Occupational; 2-Year Principally Bachelor's Creditable
Accreditation: SC, ADNUR, MLTAD, PTAA

01 President .... Dr. Thomas E. BUTLER
05 Vice President of Instruction .... Dr. Patricia A. VANDERVOORT
10 VP Administrative Svcs .... Mr. Keith BLUNDELL
32 Vice President of Student Services .... Dr. Florinda CORREA
30 VP College Advance/External Affairs .... Ms. Jennifer L. YANCEY
45 Exec Director Special Projects .... Dr. Larry GARRETT
09 Dir Inst Effect/Research/Assess .... Ms. Patricia REHAK
08 Director of Libraries .... Dr. Joe F. DAHLSTROM
06 Registrar Admissions & Records .... Ms. Michelle KLIMITCHEK
18 Director Physical Plant .... Mr. Robert DUFFIE
37 Director Financial Aid .... Ms. Kim OBSTA
15 Director Human Resources .... Ms. Terri KURTZ
26 Dir Marketing & Communications .... Mr. Darin KAZMIR
38 Director Advising/Counseling .... Vacant
96 Director of Purchasing .... Ms. Lydia HUBER
21 Director of Finance .... Ms. Tracey BERGSTROM
35 Student Center/Activities Director .... Ms. Elaine EVERETT-HENSLEY
38 Director of Testing Center .... Ms. Sharon VACLAVIK
13 Director Technology Services .... Mr. Andy FARRIOR
04 Admin Asst to President .... Ms. Debbie RAINS

Virginia College at Austin (C)

6301 E Highway 290, Austin TX 78723-1027
County: Travis Identification: 666074
Unit ID: 441928
Telephone: (512) 371-3500 Carnegie Class: Assoc/PrivFP
FAX Number: (512) 371-3502 Calendar System: Quarter
URL: www.vc.edu
Established: 2002 Annual Undergrad Tuition & Fees: $14,782
Enrollment: 900 Coed
Affiliation or Control: Proprietary IRS Status: Proprietary
Highest Offering: Associate Degree
Program: Occupational
Accreditation: ACICS, MAAB, SURGT

01 Campus President .... Mr. Harvey M. GIBLIN
05 Academic Dean .... Ms. Virginia ESCOBEDO
07 Director of Admissions .... Ms. Tyka BOOKER
06 Registrar .... Mr. Jeremy B. SAPP

† Branch campus of Virginia College, Birmingham, AL.

Wade College Infomart (D)

1950 Stemmons Fwy, Ste 4080, LB 562, Dallas TX 75207
County: Dallas FICE Identification: 010130
Unit ID: 226879
Telephone: (214) 637-3530 Carnegie Class: Assoc/PrivFP
FAX Number: (214) 637-0827 Calendar System: Trimester
URL: www.wadecollege.edu
Established: 1962 Annual Undergrad Tuition & Fees: $14,250
Enrollment: 270 Coed
Affiliation or Control: Proprietary IRS Status: Proprietary
Highest Offering: Baccalaureate
Program: Fine Arts Emphasis
Accreditation: SC

01 President .... Dr. Harry DAVROS
03 Vice President .... Mr. John CONTE

05 Director of Academic Affairs .... Mr. Rusty BELL
11 Director of Institutional Support .... Ms. Kim PARKER
08 Head Librarian .... Mrs. Bobbie BAUMGARTEN
36 Director of Career Services .... Mrs. Patti MARTINEZ
07 Director of Admissions .... Ms. Julia ANDALMAN
37 Director Student Financial Aid .... Ms. Lisa HOOVER

Wayland Baptist University (E)

1900 West Seventh, Plainview TX 79072-6998
County: Hale FICE Identification: 003663
Unit ID: 229780
Telephone: (806) 291-1000 Carnegie Class: Master's L
FAX Number: (806) 291-1960 Calendar System: Semester
URL: www.wbu.edu
Established: 1908 Annual Undergrad Tuition & Fees: $11,900
Enrollment: 6,743 Coed
Affiliation or Control: Southern Baptist IRS Status: 501(c)3
Highest Offering: Master's
Program: 2-Year Principally Bachelor's Creditable; Liberal Arts And General; Teacher Preparatory
Accreditation: SC, MUS, NUR

01 President .... Dr. Paul W. ARMES
05 Executive Vice President/Provost .... Dr. Bobby L. HALL
84 Vice Pres Enrollment Management .... Dr. D. Claude LUSK
20 Vice Pres of External Campuses .... Dr. Elane SEEBO
10 Chief Financial Officer .... Mr. Jim SMITH
20 Associate Academic Vice President .... Dr. Stan DEMERRITT
12 Exec Dir/Campus Dean Albuquerque .... Dr. Steve SMITH
12 Exec Dir/Campus Dean Altus .... Dr. Tom FISHER
12 Exec Dir/Campus Dean Amarillo .... Dr. J. B BOREN
12 Exec Dir/Campus Dean Anchorage .... Dr. Eric ASH
12 Exec Dir/Campus Dean Clovis .... Dr. Gary MITCHELL
12 Exec Dir/Campus Dean Fairbanks .... Dr. Nancy WAGNER
12 Exec Dir/Campus Dean Hawaii .... Dr. David HOWLE
12 Exec Dir/Campus Dean Lubbock .... Dr. David BISHOP
12 Exec Dir/Campus Dean Phoenix .... Dr. D. Glenn SIMMONS
12 Exec Dir/Campus Dean San Antonio .... Dr. James ANTENEN
12 Exec Dir/Campus Dean Sierra Vista .... Dr. Robert MORRIS, III
12 Exec Dir/Campus Dean Wichita Falls .... Dr. Dean DANIEL
83 Acad Dean School Behav & Soc Sci .... Dr. Estelle OWENS
50 Academic Dean School of Business .... Dr. Otto B. SCHACHT
53 Academic Dean School of Education .... Dr. Jimmie L. TODD
57 Academic Dean School of Fine Arts .... Dr. Marti R. RUNNELS
79 Academic Dean School of Lang & Lit .... Dr. Cindy M. MCCLENAGAN
81 Academic Dean School Math/Sciences .... Dr. Herbert GROVER
64 Academic Dean School of Music .... Dr. Ann B. STUTES
66 Academic Dean School of Nursing .... Dr. Diane FRAZOR
73 Academic Dean Religion & Philosophy .... Dr. Paul L. SADLER
06 Registrar .... Mrs. Julie BOWEN
32 Exec Dir Student Development .... Mr. Tom HALL
30 Executive Dir Univ Advancement .... Mr. Mike MELCHER
21 Controller .... Mrs. Lezlie HUKILL
41 Athletic Director .... Dr. Greg FERIS
07 Director Admissions .... Mrs. Debbie STENNETT
29 Director Alumni Development .... Mr. Danny ANDREWS
88 Director Church Services .... Mr. Micheal SUMMERS
44 Director of Annual Fund .... Ms. Janeen HACKNEY
44 Director Donor Relations .... Ms. Hope ENGLISH
37 Director Financial Aid .... Mrs. Karen LAQUEY
58 Director of Graduate Services .... Miss Amanda STANTON
15 Director Human Resources .... Mr. Ron APPLING
13 Director Information Technology .... Mrs. Katrina SMITH
09 Dir Inst Research/Effectiveness .... Mrs. Crhistina SPRUILL
12 Director Kenya Campus .... Dr. Richard SHAW
08 Director Library .... Dr. Polly R. LACKEY
88 Director Property Management .... Mr. Danny W. MURPHREE
26 Director Public Relations .... Mr. Jonathan PETTY
88 Director of Special Projects .... Mrs. Penny POOLE
39 Director Student Housing .... Mrs. Nancy KEITH
32 Director of Student Ldrship & Activ .... Mrs. Teresa MOORE
42 Director Student Ministries .... Mr. Donnie BROWN
40 Director University Services .... Mr. Eddie C. TURNER
106 Director Virtual Campus .... Dr. Scott FRANKLIN
105 Director Web Services .... Mrs. Charlotte SCHUMACHER
56 Co-Coordinator External Records .... Ms. Brenda GONZALEZ
56 Co-Coordinator External Records .... Mr. Daniel BROWN
38 Coord Stdnt Counseling/Career Plng .... Mr. Michael COX
19 Chief of Police/WBU .... Mr. Lonnie BURTON
18 Chief Facilities/Physical Plant .... Mr. David MURPHREE
04 Exec Admin Asst to President .... Mrs. Carolyn ANDREWS

Weatherford College (F)

225 College Park Drive, Weatherford TX 76086-5699
County: Parker FICE Identification: 003664
Unit ID: 229799
Telephone: (817) 594-5471 Carnegie Class: Assoc/Pub-S-SC
FAX Number: (817) 598-6210 Calendar System: Semester
URL: www.wc.edu
Established: 1869 Annual Undergrad Tuition & Fees (In-District): $1,704
Enrollment: 5,528 Coed
Affiliation or Control: Local IRS Status: 501(c)3
Highest Offering: Associate Degree
Program: Occupational; 2-Year Principally Bachelor's Creditable
Accreditation: SC, ADNUR, DMS, EMT, IFSAC, RAD

01 President .... Dr. Kevin EATON
04 Exec Asst to the President .... Mrs. Theresa R. HUTCHISON
32 VP of Inst & Stdnt Services .... Dr. Richard BOWERS
10 Vice Pres Financial/Admin Affairs .... Mrs. Andra R. CANTRELL
30 Vice Pres Institutional Advancement .... Mr. Brent BAKER
76 Dean of Health & Human Sciences .... Ms. Kathrine BOSWELL
05 Executive Dean of Academics .... Mr. Michael ENDY
53 Dean Educational/Instructional Sppt .... Ms. Rhonda TORRES
35 Executive Dean of Student Services .... Ms. Kathy BASSHAM
103 Dean Workforce & Economic Devel .... Ms. Kay YOUNG
27 Dir Communications/Public Relations .... Mrs. Linda BAGWELL
56 Dean of Extended Campuses .... Mr. Duane DURRETT
88 Director Truck Driving .... Mr. Bubba SWEARINGIN
09 Dir Institutional Research .... Mr. Dewayne BERRY
35 Exec Director Student Development .... Mr. Doug JEFFERSON
36 Dir of Career and Transfer Center .... Ms. Teresa BROCK
88 Director Food Services .... Ms. Erin DAVIDSON
37 Director Student Financial Aid .... Mr. Donnie PURVIS
21 Controller .... Mrs. Ruth CAMPFIELD
15 Director Human Resources .... Ms. Ralinda STONE
07 Director of Admissions .... Mr. Ralph WILLINGHAM
13 Director Technology Services .... Mr. Steven SANDIDGE
08 Director Library Services .... Mrs. Martha A. TANDY
18 Director of Facilities .... Ms. Rhonda JOHNSON
96 Director of Purchasing .... Mrs. Jeanie HOBBS
45 Director of Resource Development .... Dr. Shirley CHENAULT
19 Chief of Campus Police .... Mr. Paul STONE
38 Student Counseling .... Ms. Phyllis TIFFIN
88 Director Upward Bound .... Mr. Jeff KHALDEN
29 Director Alumni Relations .... Mr. Brent BAKER
22 Director of Workforce Education .... Ms. Janetta KRUSE
53 Director of Instructional Support .... Ms. Sue COODY
53 Director of Education .... Dr. Joyce MELTON PAGES
06 Registrar .... Mrs. Vicki TRAWEEK
88 Exec Dir of Student Engagement .... Mr. Adam FINLEY
88 Director of Testing .... Ms. Lela MORRIS
88 Dir of Outreach/Student Success .... Ms. Kay LANDRUM
88 Director Special Populations .... Ms. Bernadean CONNELL

Western Technical College (G)

9451 Diana Drive, El Paso TX 79924-6936
County: El Paso Identification: 666103
Unit ID: 224660
Telephone: (915) 566-9621 Carnegie Class: Assoc/PrivFP
FAX Number: (915) 565-9903 Calendar System: Other
URL: www.westerntech.edu
Established: 1969 Annual Undergrad Tuition & Fees: $32,600
Enrollment: 485 Coed
Affiliation or Control: Proprietary IRS Status: Proprietary
Highest Offering: Associate Degree
Program: Occupational; 2-Year Principally Bachelor's Creditable; Technical Emphasis
Accreditation: ACCSC

01 Director .... Ms. Mary CANO

Western Technical College (H)

9624 Plaza Circle, El Paso TX 79927-2105
County: El Paso FICE Identification: 020983
Unit ID: 224679
Telephone: (915) 532-3737 Carnegie Class: Assoc/PrivFP
FAX Number: (915) 532-6946 Calendar System: Other
URL: www.westerntech.edu
Established: 1969 Annual Undergrad Tuition & Fees: $31,000
Enrollment: 1,150 Coed
Affiliation or Control: Proprietary IRS Status: Proprietary
Highest Offering: Associate Degree
Program: Occupational; Technical Emphasis
Accreditation: ACCSC, PTAA

01 President .... Mr. Allan SHARPE
00 Chief Executive Officer .... Mr. Randy KUYKENDALL
11 Chief Administrative Officer .... Mr. Bill TERRELL
03 Excecutive VP/Director Branch .... Ms. Mary CANO
05 Dean of Academics .... Mr. Charles BROWN
10 Accountant .... Ms. Celi AVILA
37 Director Student Financial Services .... Ms. Danielle PICCHI
36 Director Career Services .... Ms. Helen GARCIA
07 Director Admission .... Ms. Laura PENA

Western Texas College (I)

6200 College Avenue, Snyder TX 79549-6189
County: Scurry FICE Identification: 009549
Unit ID: 229832
Telephone: (325) 573-8511 Carnegie Class: Assoc/Pub-R-M
FAX Number: (325) 573-9321 Calendar System: Semester
URL: www.wtc.edu
Established: 1969 Annual Undergrad Tuition & Fees (In-District): $1,898
Enrollment: 2,394 Coed
Affiliation or Control: State/Local IRS Status: 501(c)3
Highest Offering: Associate Degree
Program: Occupational; 2-Year Principally Bachelor's Creditable
Accreditation: SC

01 Interim President .... Mr. Mike THORNTON
05 Int Vice President of Instruction .... Dr. Jim PALMER
04 Assistant to the President .... Ms. Melanie SCHWERTNER
10 Chief Financial Officer .... Ms. Patricia CLAXTON
11 Chief Operation Officer .... Mr. Mike THORTON
09 Dean Inst Research & Effectiveness .... Mr. Britt CANADA
20 Dean of Academic Instruction .... Mr. Kyle SMITH

32 Dean of Student Services .... Mr. Ralph RAMON
72 Dean of Technology .... Mr. Roy BARTELS
30 Dean Col Advancement/Exec Dir Dev ... Mr. Jeremiah BOATRIGHT
41 Athletic Director .... Ms. Tammy DAVIS
06 Registrar .... Ms. Ann GALYEAN
37 Director Student Financial Aid .... Ms. Kathy HALL
26 Director of College Relations .... Vacant
21 Controller .... Ms. Marjann MORROW
16 Director of Human Resources .... Ms. Kelly MCGINNIS
18 Director of Physical Plant .... Mr. Tommy WATTS
85 Dir International Student Services .... Ms. Julie SENTELL
41 Coordinator of Athletic Services .... Ms. Debra BURKE

Westwood College-Dallas (A)

8390 LBJ Freeway, Ex Ctr 1, Ste 100,
Dallas TX 75243-1215
County: Dallas — Identification: 666427
Unit ID: 442505
Telephone: (214) 570-0100 — Carnegie Class: Assoc/PrivFP
FAX Number: (214) 570-8502 — Calendar System: Other
URL: www.westwood.edu
Established: 2002 — Annual Undergrad Tuition & Fees: $14,498
Enrollment: 261 — Coed
Affiliation or Control: Proprietary — IRS Status: Proprietary
Highest Offering: Baccalaureate
Program: Professional; Technical Emphasis
Accreditation: ACICS

01 Campus President .... Paul KEPIC

† Branch campus of Westwood College-O'Hare Airport, Chicago, IL.

Westwood College-Fort Worth (B)

4232 North Freeway, Fort Worth TX 76137-5021
County: Tarrant — Identification: 666434
Unit ID: 442499
Telephone: (817) 547-9600 — Carnegie Class: Assoc/PrivFP
FAX Number: (817) 547-9602 — Calendar System: Other
URL: www.westwood.edu
Established: 2002 — Annual Undergrad Tuition & Fees: $14,655
Enrollment: 166 — Coed
Affiliation or Control: Proprietary — IRS Status: Proprietary
Highest Offering: Baccalaureate
Program: Occupational
Accreditation: ACICS

01 Executive Director .... Paul KEPIC

† Branch campus of Westwood College-DuPage, Woodbridge, IL.

Westwood College-Houston South (C)

7322 Southwest Freeway, #110, Houston TX 77074-2082
County: Harris — Identification: 666309
Unit ID: 444060
Telephone: (713) 777-4433 — Carnegie Class: Assoc/PrivFP
FAX Number: (713) 219-2022 — Calendar System: Other
URL: www.westwood.edu
Established: 2003 — Annual Undergrad Tuition & Fees: N/A
Enrollment: 200 — Coed
Affiliation or Control: Proprietary — IRS Status: Proprietary
Highest Offering: Baccalaureate
Program: Occupational; 2-Year Principally Bachelor's Creditable; Technical Emphasis
Accreditation: ACICS

01 Campus President .... Mr. Rick SKINNER
05 Asst Academic Dean .... Ms. Valerie PRUITT
32 Director of Student Services .... Ms. Ashley RHODES

† Branch campus of Westwood College-Denver North, Denver, CO.

Wharton County Junior College (D)

911 Boling Highway, Wharton TX 77488-3298
County: Wharton — FICE Identification: 003668
Unit ID: 229841
Telephone: (979) 532-4560 — Carnegie Class: Assoc/Pub-R-L
FAX Number: (979) 532-6545 — Calendar System: Semester
URL: www.wcjc.edu
Established: 1946 — Annual Undergrad Tuition & Fees (In-District): $3,168
Enrollment: 6,922 — Coed
Affiliation or Control: Local — IRS Status: 501(c)3
Highest Offering: Associate Degree
Program: Occupational; 2-Year Principally Bachelor's Creditable
Accreditation: SC, DH, #EMT, PTAA, RAD, SURGT

01 President .... Ms. Betty A. MCCROHAN
05 Vice President of Instruction .... Ms. Leigh Ann COLLINS
10 Vice President Administrative Svcs .... Mr. Bryce KOCIAN
13 Vice President of Technology & IR ... Ms. Pamela YOUNGBLOOD
32 Vice President of Student Services .... Mr. David LEENHOUTS
21 Dean of Financial & Business Svcs .... Mr. Gus WESSELS
26 Director of Marketing & Comm .... Ms. Zina CARTER
07 Director Admissions & Registration .... Ms. Karen PREISLER
37 Director of Financial Aid .... Mr. Richard D. HYDE
08 Director Library Info/Tech Services .... Ms. Kwei HSU
18 Director of Facilities Management .... Mr. Mike FEYEN
15 Director of Human Resources .... Ms. Judy JONES
09 Director of Inst Effectiveness .... Dr. Danson JONES
96 Director of Purchasing .... Mr. Philip WUTHRICH

Wiley College (E)

711 Wiley Avenue, Marshall TX 75670-5199
County: Harrison — FICE Identification: 003669
Unit ID: 229887
Telephone: (903) 927-3300 — Carnegie Class: Bac/Diverse
FAX Number: (903) 938-8100 — Calendar System: Semester
URL: www.wileyc.edu
Established: 1873 — Annual Undergrad Tuition & Fees: $11,050
Enrollment: 1,356 — Coed
Affiliation or Control: United Methodist — IRS Status: 501(c)3
Highest Offering: Baccalaureate
Program: Liberal Arts And General; Teacher Preparatory
Accreditation: SC, ACBSP

01 President and CEO .... Dr. Haywood L. STRICKLAND
03 Executive Vice President & Provost .... Dr. Glenda F. CARTER
10 Vice Pres for Business & Finance .... Mrs. Willie M. HUGHEY
05 Vice President Academic Affairs .... Dr. Ernest J. PLATA
32 Vice President Student Affairs .... Dr. Joseph L. MORALE
30 Vice Pres Institutional Advancement .... Dr. Evelyn LEATHERS
13 Vice Pres Information Technology .... Mr. Nathaniel HEWITT
21 Assoc VP Business/Fiscal Affairs .... Ms. Pamela PRESSLEY
53 Dean of Education .... Dr. Henryett LOVELY-WATSON
42 College Chaplain .... Rev. Michelle HALL
04 Assistant to the President .... Mrs. Karen HELTON
50 Dean of Business & Technology .... Dr. Abdalla F. HAGAN
49 Dean of Sciences .... Dr. Walter SHUMANTE
97 Dean General Studies .... Dr. Sonya BURNETT-ANDRUS
79 Dean Social Sciences & Humanities .... Dr. Sherlynn H. BYRD
26 Director of Public Relations .... Ms. Tammy TAYLOR
08 Director of Library Services .... Mrs. Alma RAVENELL
06 Registrar .... Dr. Lalita ROGERS
07 Director of Admissions .... Ms. Ashley BENNETT
15 Director Personnel Services .... Ms. Merdis F. BUCKLEY
18 Chief Facilities/Physical Plant .... Mr. Percy MURRAY
20 Assistant VP Academic Affairs .... Dr. Sherlynn BYRD
37 Director of Financial Aid .... Mr. Alan D. JACKSON
29 Director of Alumni Relations .... Ms. Alvena JONES
09 Director of Institutional Research .... Dr. Warren H. HAWKINS
11 Director Administrative Svcs .... Mr. O. Ivan WHITE
23 College Nurse .... Ms. Shonte EPPERSON
36 Dir Student Placement/Counseling .... Ms. LaDonna GAUT
41 Director of Athletics .... Ms. Janet EATON
96 Director of Purchasing .... Mr. Darius Z. KIMBLE
35 Director of Student Development .... Ms. Karen HUNTER
84 Director Enrollment Management .... Ms. Ashley BENNETT

UTAH

Argosy University, Salt Lake City (F)

121 Election Road Suite 300, Draper UT 84020-7724
County: Salt Lake — Identification: 666655
Unit ID: 452090
Telephone: (801) 601-5000 — Carnegie Class: Assoc/PrivFP4
FAX Number: (801) 601-4990 — Calendar System: Other
URL: www.argosy.edu/saltlakecity
Established: 2006 — Annual Undergrad Tuition & Fees: $13,224
Enrollment: 334 — Coed
Affiliation or Control: Proprietary — IRS Status: Proprietary
Highest Offering: Doctorate
Program: Professional
Accreditation: &WC

01 Campus President .... David TIETJEN
05 Vice President of Academic Affairs .... Dr. Elizabeth FAWCETT
07 Senior Director of Admissions .... Todd HARRISON
32 Director of Student Services .... Steve MERRILL
37 Assoc Director of Student Finance .... Kelly JENSEN
15 Human Resources .... Jonathan BAY
11 Dir of Admin and Financial Svcs .... Jeffrey SWENSON

† Regional accreditation is carried under the parent institution in Orange, CA.

The Art Institute of Salt Lake City (G)

121 West Election Road, Draper UT 84020
County: Salt Lake — Identification: 666694
Unit ID: 450049
Telephone: (801) 601-4700 — Carnegie Class: Spec/Arts
FAX Number: (801) 601-4724 — Calendar System: Semester
URL: www.artinstitutes.edu/saltlakecity
Established: 2007 — Annual Undergrad Tuition & Fees: $18,500
Enrollment: 725 — Coed
Affiliation or Control: Proprietary — IRS Status: Proprietary
Highest Offering: Baccalaureate
Program: Liberal Arts And General; Fine Arts Emphasis
Accreditation: ACICS

01 President .... Dr. Ron MOSS

† Branch campus of The Art Institute of Phoenix, AZ.

Brigham Young University (H)

Provo UT 84602-0002
County: Utah — FICE Identification: 003670
Unit ID: 230038
Telephone: (801) 422-1211 — Carnegie Class: RU/H
FAX Number: (801) 422-0586 — Calendar System: Semester
URL: www.byu.edu
Established: 1875 — Annual Undergrad Tuition & Fees: $4,710
Enrollment: 34,101 — Coed
Affiliation or Control: Latter-day Saints — IRS Status: 501(c)3
Highest Offering: Doctorate
Program: Liberal Arts And General; Teacher Preparatory; Professional
Accreditation: NW, ART, BUS, BUSA, CLPSY, CONST, COPSY, CS, DANCE, DIETD, DIETI, ENG, ENGT, IPSY, JOUR, LAW, MFCD, MT, MUS, NRPA, NURSE, PH, SP, SPAA, SW, TEAC, THEA

01 President .... Dr. Cecil O. SAMUELSON
05 Academic Vice President .... Dr. Brent W. WEBB
11 Administrative Vice President .... Mr. Brian K. EVANS
44 Advancement Vice President .... Dr. Kevin J. WORTHEN
13 Vice Pres Info Tech/Chief Info Ofcr .... Dr. J. Kelly FLANAGAN
88 International Vice President .... Dr. Sandra ROGERS
32 Student Life Vice President .... Dr. Janet S. SCHARMAN
43 Asst to President/General Counsel .... Mr. Michael R. ORME
45 Asst to Pres Planning/Assessment ..... Mr. James D. GORDON, III
27 Asst to Pres Univ Communications .... Mrs. Carri P. JENKINS
20 Assoc Acad Vice President Faculty .... Dr. Craig H. HART
20 Assoc Acad VP Undergraduate Stds .... Dr. Jeffrey D. KEITH
46 Assoc Acad VP Research/Grad Stds .... Dr. Alan R. HARKER
32 Assoc Student Life Vice Pres .... Dr. Ronald K. CHAPMAN
10 Chief Financial Officer .... Mr. Brian K. EVANS
18 Asst Admin VP Physical Facilities .... Mr. Ole M. SMITH
15 Asst Admin VP Human Resource Svcs .... Mr. Forrest FLAKE
35 Asst Admin VP/Stdnt Auxil Svc .... Mr. David A. HUNT
26 Assoc Advance VP Univ Relations .... Mr. John C. LEWIS
30 Executive Director Development .... Dr. Tanise CHUNG-HOON
36 Exec Dir Stdnt Acad/Advisement Svcs .... Mr. Norm FINLINSON
35 Dean Student Life .... Mr. Vernon L. HEPERI
37 Director Financial Aid/Scholarships .... Mr. Steve HILL
88 Dean Undergraduate Education .... Dr. John D. BELL
08 University Librarian .... Ms. H. Julene BUTLER
58 Dean Graduate Studies .... Dr. Wynn C. STIRLING
51 Dean Continuing Education .... Dr. Wayne J. LOTT
47 Dean Life Sciences .... Dr. Rodney J. BROWN
54 Dean Engineering & Technology .... Dr. Alan R. PARKINSON
83 Dean Family Home & Social Science .... Dr. Benjamin M. OGLES
57 Dean Fine Arts & Communications .... Dr. Stephen M. JONES
79 Dean Humanities .... Dr. John ROSENBERG
61 Dean Law School .... Dr. James R. RASBAND
50 Dean Marriott School Management .... Dr. Gary C. CORNIA
53 Dean McKay School of Education .... Dr. K. Richard YOUNG
81 Dean Physical & Math Science .... Dr. Scott D. SOMMERFELDT
66 Dean Nursing .... Dr. Beth V. COLE
73 Dean Religious Education .... Dr. Terry BALL
09 Dir Institutional Assess/Analysis .... Dr. Danny R. OLSEN
06 Registrar .... Mr. Barry ALLRED
07 Director of Admissions .... Mr. Kirk STRONG
29 Managing Director Alumni Relations .... Ms. Linda PALMER
96 Director of Purchasing .... Mr. W. Timothy HILL

Broadview University (I)

1902 W 7800 S, West Jordan UT 84088-4021
County: Salt Lake — FICE Identification: 011166
Unit ID: 230056
Telephone: (801) 304-4224 — Carnegie Class: Spec/Health
FAX Number: (801) 304-4229 — Calendar System: Quarter
URL: www.broadviewuniversity.edu
Established: 1971 — Annual Undergrad Tuition & Fees: $14,400
Enrollment: 470 — Coed
Affiliation or Control: Proprietary — IRS Status: Proprietary
Highest Offering: Master's
Program: Occupational; Technical Emphasis
Accreditation: ACICS, ADNUR, MAC

01 President .... Mr. Terry MYHRE
05 Director .... Mr. Mark STAATS

DeVry University - Sandy (J)

9350 South 150 East, Suite 420, Sandy UT 84070-2704
County: Salt Lake — Identification: 666576
Unit ID: 448877
Telephone: (801) 565-5110 — Carnegie Class: Spec/Bus
FAX Number: (801) 561-1710 — Calendar System: Semester
URL: www.devry.edu
Established: 1931 — Annual Undergrad Tuition & Fees: $16,156
Enrollment: 277 — Coed
Affiliation or Control: Proprietary — IRS Status: Proprietary
Highest Offering: Master's
Program: Professional; Business Emphasis
Accreditation: &NH

01 Campus Director .... Michael TOWNSLEY

† Regional accreditation is carried under the parent institution in Downers Grove, IL.

Eagle Gate College (K)

5588 S Green Street, Murray UT 84123-6965
County: Salt Lake — FICE Identification: 021785
Unit ID: 230366
Telephone: (801) 333-8100 — Carnegie Class: Assoc/PrivFP4
FAX Number: (801) 263-6520 — Calendar System: Other
URL: www.eaglegatecollege.edu
Established: 1979 — Annual Undergrad Tuition & Fees: $13,609

Enrollment: 375 Coed
Affiliation or Control: Proprietary IRS Status: Proprietary
Highest Offering: Baccalaureate
Program: Occupational
Accreditation: **ACICS**

01 President Ms. Janet HEAD
07 Director of Admissions Mr. Raymond JOHNSON

Everest College (A)

3280 W 3500 South, West Valley City UT 84119
County: Salt Lake FICE Identification: 022985
Unit ID: 230472
Telephone: (801) 840-4800 Carnegie Class: Assoc/PrivFP4
FAX Number: (801) 969-0828 Calendar System: Quarter
URL: www.everest.edu
Established: 1982 Annual Undergrad Tuition & Fees: $13,842
Enrollment: 393 Coed
Affiliation or Control: Proprietary IRS Status: Proprietary
Highest Offering: Baccalaureate
Program: Occupational; 2-Year Principally Bachelor's Creditable; Business Emphasis
Accreditation: **ACICS**, MAC, SURGT

01 President Ms. Rebecca PEREGRINE
05 Academic Dean Ms. Daisy HERNANDEZ
10 Business Manager Ms. Amanda DUNN
07 Director of Admissions Ms. Loreen CLEVELAND
36 Director Career Services Mr. Robert PETERSON

Fortis College (B)

3949 South 700 East, Suite 150, Salt Lake City UT 84107
County: Salt Lake Identification: 666762
Unit ID: 456454
Telephone: (801) 713-0915 Carnegie Class: Assoc/PrivFP
FAX Number: (801) 281-9620 Calendar System: Quarter
URL: www.fortis.edu
Established: 2009 Annual Undergrad Tuition & Fees: $19,250
Enrollment: 325 Coed
Affiliation or Control: Proprietary IRS Status: Proprietary
Highest Offering: Baccalaureate
Program: Nursing Emphasis
Accreditation: **ACCSC**, DH

01 Campus Director Kendall DEAN

† Tuition varies by degree program.

Independence University (C)

4021 South 700 East, Suite 400,
Salt Lake City UT 84107-2453
County: Salt Lake FICE Identification: 022061
Telephone: (800) 972-5149 Carnegie Class: Not Classified
FAX Number: (801) 263-0345 Calendar System: Other
URL: www.independence.edu
Established: 1978 Annual Undergrad Tuition & Fees: $12,100
Enrollment: 104 Coed
Affiliation or Control: Proprietary IRS Status: Proprietary
Highest Offering: Master's
Program: Professional
Accreditation: **ACCSC**

01 Executive Director Mr. Carl BARNEY

ITT Technical Institute (D)

920 West LeVoy Drive, Murray UT 84123-2500
County: Salt Lake FICE Identification: 023610
Unit ID: 230384
Telephone: (801) 263-3313 Carnegie Class: Spec/Tech
FAX Number: (801) 263-3497 Calendar System: Quarter
URL: www.itt-tech.edu
Established: 1984 Annual Undergrad Tuition & Fees: N/A
Enrollment: 734 Coed
Affiliation or Control: Proprietary IRS Status: Proprietary
Highest Offering: Baccalaureate
Program: Technical Emphasis
Accreditation: **ACICS**

† Branch campus of ITT Technical Institute, Indianapolis, IN.

LDS Business College (E)

95 N 300 W, Salt Lake City UT 84101-3500
County: Salt Lake FICE Identification: 003672
Unit ID: 230418
Telephone: (801) 524-8100 Carnegie Class: Assoc/PrivNFP
FAX Number: (801) 524-1900 Calendar System: Semester
URL: www.ldsbc.edu
Established: 1886 Annual Undergrad Tuition & Fees: $3,060
Enrollment: 2,025 Coed
Affiliation or Control: Latter-day Saints IRS Status: 501(c)3
Highest Offering: Associate Degree
Program: Occupational; 2-Year Principally Bachelor's Creditable; Business Emphasis
Accreditation: **NW**

01 President Mr. Larry J. RICHARDS
04 Admin Asst to the Presidents Coun Ms. Cathy A. SMITH
05 Vice President for Academic Affairs Dr. Carolyn S. BROWN
11 Vice President Administration Mr. Jerold M. BRYAN
10 Vice President Finance/Controller Mr. Bob H. WISER
30 VP Advancement Mr. Craig V. NELSON
20 Dean of Instuctional Support Mr. Tyler S. MORGAN
26 Director of Marketing & Research Mr. Matthew D. TITTLE
13 Chief Information Officer Mr. R. Brent CHERRINGTON
88 Dir of Faculty & Staff Development Mr. Ronald E. GUYMON
84 Director of Enrollment Management Mrs. Renae L. RICHARDS
06 Registrar Ms. Tamra TAYLOR
08 Dir of Library/Inform Resources Ms. Sarah SORENSEN
88 Accounting Program Director Mr. Kitt FINLINSON
50 Business Skills Program Director Mr. Scott NEWMAN
23 Health Professions Program Director Mr. Brett MERKLEY
77 IT & Photography Program Director Ms. Lynda D. HENRIE
83 Bus Admin Support Program Director Mrs. Marjean LAKE
88 Interior Design Program Director Mr. Miles HUNSAKER
72 Business Info Systems Program Dir Mr. Kevin MCREYNOLDS
73 Institute of Religion Director Mr. Tracy WILLIAMS
21 Assistant Controller Mr. Chris REITZ
37 Director of Financial Aid Mr. J. Douglas HORNE
40 Bookstore Manager Ms. Rachel BINGHAM

Midwives College of Utah (F)

1174 E Graystone Way Suite 2,
Salt Lake City UT 84106-2671
County: Utah Identification: 666281
Telephone: (866) 680-2756 Carnegie Class: Not Classified
FAX Number: (866) 207-2024 Calendar System: Semester
URL: www.midwifery.edu
Established: 1980 Annual Undergrad Tuition & Fees: $17,650
Enrollment: 230 Coed
Affiliation or Control: Independent Non-Profit IRS Status: 501(c)3
Highest Offering: Master's
Program: Occupational
Accreditation: **MEAC**

01 President Ms. Kristi RIDD-YOUNG
05 Academic Dean Ms. Nicole CROFT
04 Administrative Assistant Ms. Cindy WINWARD

Neumont University (G)

10701 S River Front Parkway Ste 300,
South Jordan UT 84095-3524
County: Salt Lake Identification: 666125
Unit ID: 445692
Telephone: (801) 302-2800 Carnegie Class: Spec/Tech
FAX Number: (801) 302-2811 Calendar System: Quarter
URL: www.neumont.edu
Established: 2003 Annual Undergrad Tuition & Fees: $23,100
Enrollment: 346 Coed
Affiliation or Control: Proprietary IRS Status: Proprietary
Highest Offering: Master's
Program: Professional; Technical Emphasis
Accreditation: **ACICS**

01 President/Campus Dir Utah Ned LEVINE
05 Provost Sam PUICH
32 Dean of Students Erin MCCORMACK
06 Registrar/Dir Academic Programs Larry CRANDALL
07 Director of Admissions Karick HEATON

Ogden-Weber Applied Technology College (H)

200 North Washington Boulevard, Ogden UT 84404-4089
County: Weber FICE Identification: 023465
Unit ID: 230490
Telephone: (801) 627-8300 Carnegie Class: Assoc/Pub-U-MC
FAX Number: (801) 395-3727 Calendar System: Other
URL: www.owatc.edu
Established: 1971 Annual Undergrad Tuition & Fees (In-District): $2,250
Enrollment: 2,399 Coed
Affiliation or Control: State/Local IRS Status: 501(c)3
Highest Offering: Associate Degree
Program: Occupational; Technical Emphasis
Accreditation: **COE**, MAC, PNUR

01 President & Chief Executive Officer Collette R. MERCIER
05 Vice Pres Instructional Services James TAGGART
32 Vice Pres for Student Services Rhonda LAURITZEN
10 Vice Pres for Campus Svcs/CFO Tyler CALL

† Campus of Utah College of Applied Technology, Salt Lake City, UT.

Provo College (I)

1450 W 820 N, Provo UT 84601-1305
County: Utah FICE Identification: 023608
Unit ID: 380438
Telephone: (801) 818-8900 Carnegie Class: Assoc/PrivFP
FAX Number: (801) 375-9728 Calendar System: Other
URL: www.provocollege.edu
Established: 1984 Annual Undergrad Tuition & Fees: $14,346
Enrollment: 401 Coed
Affiliation or Control: Proprietary IRS Status: Proprietary
Highest Offering: Associate Degree
Program: Occupational; Nursing Emphasis
Accreditation: **ACCSC**, ACICS, ADNUR, PTAA

01 Campus President Mr. Gordon C. PETERS
05 Academic Dean Mrs. Kristy THOMPSON
10 Business Manager Mr. Mickel BLOMQUIST
07 Director of Admissions Mr. Stewart HAGBERG
37 Financial Services Assoc Director Mr. Nick JOHNSON
06 Registrar Mrs. Marrybell MONTANO
32 Director of Student Services Ms. Traci CLARIDA
36 Director of Career Services Mrs. Diann DECKER

Rocky Mountain University of Health Professions (J)

561 East 1860 South, Provo UT 84606-7312
County: Utah Identification: 666019
Telephone: (801) 375-5125 Carnegie Class: Not Classified
FAX Number: (801) 375-2125 Calendar System: Trimester
URL: www.rmuohp.edu
Established: 1998 Annual Graduate Tuition & Fees: $17,000
Enrollment: 400 Coed
Affiliation or Control: Proprietary IRS Status: Proprietary
Highest Offering: Doctorate; No Undergraduates
Program: Professional
Accreditation: **NW**, @PTA

01 President Dr. Richard P. NIELSEN
03 Executive Vice President of Admin Dr. Michael SKURJA, JR.
10 Vice President Finance Mr. Jeff BATE
30 Vice Pres of Advancement Dr. Les SMITH
05 Interim Provost/Academic Dean Dr. Sandra PENNINGTON
46 Director of Research Dr. Brent ALVAR
09 Dir of Institutional Effectiveness Ms. Jessica D. EGBERT

Stevens-Henager College (K)

PO Box 9428, Ogden UT 84409-0428
County: Weber FICE Identification: 003674
Unit ID: 230621
Telephone: (801) 394-7791 Carnegie Class: Bac/Assoc
FAX Number: (801) 621-0853 Calendar System: Quarter
URL: www.stevenshenager.edu
Established: 1891 Annual Undergrad Tuition & Fees: $18,300
Enrollment: 840 Coed
Affiliation or Control: Proprietary IRS Status: Proprietary
Highest Offering: Master's
Program: Occupational; 2-Year Principally Bachelor's Creditable
Accreditation: **ACCSC**, ADNUR, MAC, SURGT

01 Pres of Ogden Campus/Regional Dir Ms. Vicky DEWSNUP
07 Director of Admissions Mr. Brandon WRIGHT
32 Director of Student Services Mr. Doug BURCH

Stevens-Henager College (L)

1476 S Sandhill Road, Orem UT 84058-7310
County: Utah FICE Identification: 030030
Unit ID: 230630
Telephone: (801) 418-1450 Carnegie Class: Bac/Diverse
FAX Number: (801) 375-9836 Calendar System: Semester
URL: www.stevenshenager.edu
Established: 1962 Annual Undergrad Tuition & Fees: $15,858
Enrollment: 619 Coed
Affiliation or Control: Proprietary IRS Status: Proprietary
Highest Offering: Master's
Program: Business Emphasis
Accreditation: **ACCSC**, MAC

01 President Mr. Ken PLANT

Stevens-Henager College (M)

383 W Vine Street, Salt Lake City UT 84123
County: Salt Lake Identification: 666038
Unit ID: 438151
Telephone: (801) 281-7620 Carnegie Class: Bac/Diverse
FAX Number: (801) 281-7660 Calendar System: Quarter
URL: www.stevenshenager.edu
Established: 1891 Annual Undergrad Tuition & Fees: $38,500
Enrollment: 700 Coed
Affiliation or Control: Proprietary IRS Status: Proprietary
Highest Offering: Master's
Program: Occupational
Accreditation: **ACCSC**

01 Director Mr. Robert O. SALMON
06 Registrar Ms. Carrie BARNETT
07 Director of Admissions Ms. Stephanie WILLIAMSON
08 Head Librarian Mr. David LEWIS
37 Director of Financial Aid Ms. Gina SEITZ

† Branch campus of Stevens-Henager College, Ogden, UT.

Uintah Basin Applied Technology College (N)

1100 East Lagoon Street, Roosevelt UT 84066
FICE Identification: 011165
Unit ID: 230676
Telephone: (435) 722-6900 Carnegie Class: Assoc/Pub-R-S
FAX Number: (435) 722-6999 Calendar System: Semester
URL: www.ubatc.edu

Established: 1968 Annual Undergrad Tuition & Fees (In-State): $1,530
Enrollment: 1,394 Coed
Affiliation or Control: State IRS Status: 501(c)3
Highest Offering: Associate Degree
Program: Occupational; Technical Emphasis
Accreditation: COE, PNUR

01 Chief Executive Officer .... Mark D. WALKER
30 Vice Pres Economic Development .... Jean MOLD
32 Vice Pres of Student Services .... Bob NAYLOR
10 Vice Pres of Finance .... Keith SPROUSE
05 Vice Pres of Instruction .... John WAHL
04 Exec Assistant to the President .... Trenna BALLOU
06 Registrar .... Julene OLSEN
37 Financial Aid Coordinator .... Mark ANDERTON

† Campus of Utah College of Applied Technology, Salt Lake City, UT.

The Utah College of Dental Hygiene at Careers Unlimited (A)

1176 S 1480 W, Orem UT 84058-4905
County: Utah FICE Identification: 034633
Unit ID: 448239
Telephone: (801) 426-8234 Carnegie Class: Spec/Health
FAX Number: (801) 224-5437 Calendar System: Other
URL: www.ucdh.edu
Established: 2006 Annual Undergrad Tuition & Fees: $24,970
Enrollment: 120 Coed
Affiliation or Control: Proprietary IRS Status: Proprietary
Highest Offering: Baccalaureate
Program: Occupational; 2-Year Principally Bachelor's Creditable
Accreditation: ACCSC, DH

01 College President .... Mr. Brent MOLEN
05 Director of Education .... Mr. Kenneth MOLEN

*Utah System of Higher Education (B)

The Gateway, 60 S 400 W, Salt Lake City UT 84101-1284
County: Salt Lake FICE Identification: 009339
Telephone: (801) 321-7101 Carnegie Class: N/A
FAX Number: (801) 321-7199
URL: www.higheredutah.org

01 Exec Ofcr/Commissioner of Higher Ed .... Mr. David L. BUHLER
05 Assoc Commissioner Academic Affairs .... Dr. Elizabeth J. HITCH
10 Assoc Commissioner Finance/Facilit .... Dr. Gregory STAUFFER
37 Exec Director Student Financial Aid .... Mr. David A. FEITZ
45 Asc Commissioner Economic Dev/Plng .. Dr. Cameron K. MARTIN
88 UESP Executive Director .... Ms. Lynne WARD

*The University of Utah (C)

201 South 1460 East, Salt Lake City UT 84112-1107
County: Salt Lake FICE Identification: 003675
Unit ID: 230764
Telephone: (801) 581-7200 Carnegie Class: RU/VH
FAX Number: (801) 581-3007 Calendar System: Semester
URL: www.utah.edu
Established: 1850 Annual Undergrad Tuition & Fees (In-State): $7,139
Enrollment: 31,660 Coed
Affiliation or Control: State IRS Status: 501(c)3
Highest Offering: Doctorate
Program: Liberal Arts And General; Teacher Preparatory; Professional
Accreditation: NW, ARCPA, AUD, BUS, BUSA, CEA, CLPSY, COPSY, CYTO, DANCE, DENT, DIETC, EMT, ENG, ENGR, IPSY, LAW, MED, MIDWF, MT, MUS, NMT, NRPA, NURSE, OT, PH, PHAR, PLNG, PTA, SCPSY, SP, SPAA, SW, TEAC

02 President .... Dr. David W. PERSHING
05 Int Sr Vice Pres Academic Affairs .... Dr. Michael L. HARDMAN
17 Sr VP Hlth Sci/CEO Univ Ut Hlth Ctr .... Dr. Vivian S. LEE
43 Vice President & General Counsel .... Mr. John K. MORRIS
11 Vice Pres Administrative Services .... Mr. Arnold B. COMBE
32 Vice President Student Affairs .... Dr. Barbara H. SNYDER
30 Vice Pres Institutional Advancement .... Mr. Fred C. ESPLIN
86 Vice President Government Relations .... Mr. Jason PERRY
16 Vice President for Human Resources .... Dr. Loretta F. HARPER
46 Vice President Research .... Dr. Thomas N. PARKS
88 Vice Pres Technology Venture Devel .... Dr. Jack W. BRITTAIN
27 Chief Information Officer .... Dr. Eric DENNA
101 Special Ast to Pres/Sec to the Univ .... Ms. Laura SNOW
04 Exec Asst to the President .... Ms. Elizabeth W. MCCOY
20 Assoc VP AA & Dean Undergrad Stds .... Dr. Martha S. BRADLEY
84 Sr Assoc VP for Enrollment Mgmt .... Ms. Mary G. PARKER
45 Assoc VP Acad Affs/Budget/Planning .... Ms. Cathy ANDERSON
18 Assoc VP Admin Services/Facilities .... Mr. Michael G. PEREZ
10 Assoc VP Admin/Finance & Bus Svcs .... Mr. Jeffrey J. WEST
20 Assoc VP Acad Affs/Equity/Diversity .. Dr. Octavio VILLALPANDO
76 Associate Vice Pres Health Sciences .... Dr. Richard J. SPERRY
88 Associate Vice President Research .... Dr. Cynthia M. FURSE
15 Associate Vice Pres Human Resources .... Ms. Joan E. GINES
88 Assoc VP Acad Affs/Faculty .... Dr. Amy WILDERMUTH
35 Assoc VP Stdnt Affs/Bus/Auxil Svcs .... Dr. Jerry L. BASFORD
26 Chief Mktg & Commun Officer .... Mr. William J. WARREN
21 Asst Vice Pres Admin Svc/Aux Svc .... Mr. Gordon N. WILSON
58 Dean Graduate School .... Dr. Chuck WIGHT
48 Dean Architecture & Planning .... Ms. Brenda C. SCHEER
50 Dean David Eccles Sch of Business .... Dr. Taylor RANDALL
53 Interim Dean College of Education .... Dr. John MCDONNELL
54 Dean College of Engineering .... Dr. Richard B. BROWN
57 Dean Col of Fine Arts/AVP the Arts .... Dr. Raymond TYMAS-JONES
68 Dean College of Health .... Dr. James E. GRAVES
92 Dean Honors College .... Dr. Sylvia TORTI
79 Dn Col Hum/AVP Acad Affs/Indply Std .... Dr. Robert D. NEWMAN
61 Dean S J Quinney College of Law .... Mr. Hiram CHODOSH
65 Dean Coll of Mines & Earth Science .... Dr. Francis H. BROWN
63 Dean School of Medicine .... Dr. Vivian S. LEE
66 Dean College of Nursing .... Dr. Maureen R. KEEFE
67 Dean College of Pharmacy .... Dr. Chris M. IRELAND
81 Dean College of Science .... Dr. Pierre V. SOKOLSKY
83 Dean Col Social/Behavioral Science .... Dr. M. David RUDD
70 Dean College of Social Work .... Dr. Jannah H. MATHER
88 Dean of Students .... Ms. Annie NEBEKER-CHRISTENSEN
06 University Registrar .... Mr. Timothy J. EBNER
23 CEO University Hospitals & Clinics .... Mr. David E. ENTWISTLE
91 Exec Dir Proj/Apps/Univ Info Tech .... Mr. Joseph R. TAYLOR
88 Director Institutional Review Board .... Mr. John P. STILLMAN
96 Director Purchasing .... Mr. James T. PARKER
94 Director Gender Studies .... Dr. Susie PORTER
77 Department Chair Sch of Computing .... Dr. Martin BERZINS
52 Dir Dental Clinic/Gen Prac Resideny .... Dr. Craige J. OLSON
07 Director Admissions .... Vacant
29 Exec Director Alumni Association .... Mr. M. John ASHTON
44 Director Planned Giving .... Ms. Karin S. HARDY
37 Dir Financial Aid & Scholarships .... Mr. John CURL
08 Executive Director Marriott Library .... Ms. Joyce OGBURN
62 Dir Eccles Health Sciences Library .... Ms. Jean P. SHIPMAN
62 Dir S J Quinney Col of Law/Lib .... Ms. Melissa BERNSTEIN
36 Director of Career Services .... Mr. Stan D. INMAN
38 Director Counseling Center .... Dr. Lauren WEITZMAN
22 Dir Center Ethnic Student Affairs .... Ms. S. Mikiko KUMASAKA
39 Director Housing & Res Education .... Ms. Barbara REMSBURG
39 Director Univ Student Apartments .... Mr. Richard L. JAMES
88 Director UT Museum Natural History .... Dr. Sarah B. GEORGE
19 Director Public Safety .... Mr. Scott D. FOLSOM
40 Director Campus Bookstore .... Mr. Earl L. CLEGG
85 Director International Center .... Dr. Sabine KLAHR
41 Director Athletics .... Dr. Chris HILL
25 Dir Office of Sponsored Projects .... Mr. Brent K. BROWN
31 Director Univ-Neighborhood Partners .... Dr. Rosemarie HUNTER
09 Director Institutional Analysis .... Dr. Paul A. GORE

*Southern Utah University (D)

351 W Center Blvd, Cedar City UT 84720-2470
County: Iron FICE Identification: 003678
Unit ID: 230603
Telephone: (435) 586-7700 Carnegie Class: Master's L
FAX Number: (435) 586-5475 Calendar System: Semester
URL: www.suu.edu
Established: 1897 Annual Undergrad Tuition & Fees (In-State): $5,576
Enrollment: 7,750 Coed
Affiliation or Control: State IRS Status: 501(c)3
Highest Offering: Master's
Program: Occupational; Liberal Arts And General; Teacher Preparatory
Accreditation: NW, ART, ACBSP, BUS, CS, DANCE, ENG, MUS, NURSE, TEAC

02 President .... Dr. Michael T. BENSON
05 Provost .... Dr. Bradley COOK
10 Vice Pres of Finance & Govt Rels .... Mr. Dorian PAGE
32 Vice President Student Services .... Dr. Donna M. EDDLEMAN
26 Vice Pres for University Relations .... Mr. Dean O'DRISCOLL
30 Vice Pres Advancement .... Mr. Stuart JONES
58 Assoc Provost/Dean of Graduate Stds .... Mr. William J. BYRNES
13 Assoc VP for Information Tech .... Mr. Glen E. PRYOR
84 Assoc VP for Enrollment Management .... Dr. Stephen ALLEN
18 VP Facilities Management & Planning .... Mr. David F. TANNER
08 Dean/Director Library/Univ Studies .... Mr. John EYE
51 Dean of Continuing/Profess Studies .... Mr. Mark ATKINSON
21 Director Budget .... Mr. Bryant FLAKE
75 Director CTE .... Mr. David A. WARD
06 Registrar .... Mr. John ALLRED
15 Director Human Resources .... Mr. David T. MCGUIRE
88 Dean of University College .... Dr. Patrick CLARKE
27 Director of Communications .... Mrs. Jennifer A. BURT
37 Director of Financial Aid .... Ms. Jan CAREY-MCDONALD
29 Exec Director of Alumni Relations .... Ms. Mindy BENSON
41 Athletic Director .... Mr. Ken BEAZER
43 Legal Counsel .... Mr. D. Michael CARTER
79 Dean Col Humanities/Soc Sci .... Dr. James MCDONALD
50 Dean School of Business .... Dr. Carl R. TEMPLIN
53 Interim Dean College of Education .... Dr. Deborah HILL
81 Dean College of Sci and Engineering .... Dr. Robert EVES
57 Dean College Performing/Visual Arts .... Mrs. Shauna MENDINI
96 Director of Purchasing .... Mr. Peter J. HEILGEIST
09 Director of Institutional Research .... Mr. Christian REINER
38 Director Student Counseling .... Dr. Curtis HILL

*Utah State University (E)

Logan UT 84322-0001
County: Cache FICE Identification: 003677
Unit ID: 230728
Telephone: (435) 797-1000 Carnegie Class: RU/H
FAX Number: (435) 797-3880 Calendar System: Semester
URL: www.usu.edu
Established: 1888 Annual Undergrad Tuition & Fees (In-State): $5,931
Enrollment: 26,757 Coed
Affiliation or Control: State IRS Status: 501(c)3
Highest Offering: Doctorate
Program: Liberal Arts And General; Teacher Preparatory; Professional
Accreditation: NW, AUD, BUS, BUSA, CEA, CIDA, CORE, CS, DIETC, DIETD, DIETI, ENG, ENGR, FOR, IPSY, LSAR, MFCD, MUS, NRPA, PSPSY, SP, SW, TEAC

02 President .... Dr. Stan L. ALBRECHT
05 Provost .... Dr. Raymond T. COWARD
43 General Counsel .... Mr. Craig J. SIMPER
10 Vice President Business & Finance .... Mr. Dave COWLEY
32 Vice President Student Services .... Mr. James MORALES
56 Vice Pres Extension & Agriculture .... Dr. Noelle E. COCKETT
46 VP Research/Dn Sch Graduate Stds .... Dr. Mark R. MCLELLAN
30 COO/University Advancement .... Ms. Annette HERMAN
13 CIO/Assoc VP Information Technology .... Dr. Eric HAWLEY
18 Associate VP for Facilities .... Mr. Darrell E. HART
44 Associate VP University Advancement .... Ms. Joan SCHEFFKE
07 Asst VP Recruitment/Enrollment Svcs .... Mr. John MORTENSEN
20 Vice Provost .... Dr. Laurens H. SMITH
51 Vice Prov Regional Camp/Dist Educ .... Dr. Ronda R. MENLOVE
08 Dean Libraries .... Mr. Richard CLEMENT
29 Exec Director Alumni Relations .... Mrs. Patty HALAUFIA
26 Exec Dir Public Relations/Marketing .... Mr. John W. DEVILBISS
09 Dir Analysis Assess/Accreditation .... Mr. Michael TORRENS
22 Director Affirmative Action/EEO .... Mr. David OTTLEY
41 Athletic Director .... Mr. Scott BARNES
25 Director Sponsored Programs .... Mr. Jeff COLEMAN
86 Director Government Relations .... Mr. Neil N. ABERCROMBIE
15 Director of Human Resources .... Ms. BrandE FAUPELL
19 Director University Police Dept .... Mr. Steven J. MECHAM
06 Registrar .... Mr. Roland SQUIRE
36 Director Career Services/Coop Educ .... Ms. Donna E. CROW
37 Director of Financial Aid .... Mr. Steven SHARP
38 Director Counseling Center .... Dr. David BUSH
40 Director of Bookstore .... Mr. David PARKINSON
92 Director of Honors .... Dr. Christie L. FOX
96 Director of Purchasing .... Mr. Paul BOWMAN
47 Dean of Agriculture .... Dr. Noelle E. COCKETT
57 Dean of Arts .... Dr. Craig JESSOP
50 Dean of Business .... Mr. Douglas D. ANDERSON
53 Dean of Education .... Dr. Beth FOLEY
54 Dean of Engineering .... Mr. H. Scott HINTON
79 Dean Humanities/Social Science .... Dr. John C. ALLEN
65 Interim Dean of Natural Resources .... Dr. Chris LUECKE
81 Dean of Science .... Dr. James MACMAHON

*Utah Valley University (F)

800 W University Parkway, Orem UT 84058-5999
County: Utah FICE Identification: 004027
Unit ID: 230737
Telephone: (801) 863-8000 Carnegie Class: Bac/Diverse
FAX Number: (801) 226-5207 Calendar System: Semester
URL: www.uvu.edu
Established: 1941 Annual Undergrad Tuition & Fees (In-State): $2,393
Enrollment: 33,395 Coed
Affiliation or Control: State IRS Status: 501(c)3
Highest Offering: Master's
Program: Occupational; 2-Year Principally Bachelor's Creditable; Liberal Arts And General; Teacher Preparatory; Professional
Accreditation: NW, ADNUR, BUS, CEA, CS, DH, EMT, IFSAC, NUR, TEAC

02 President .... Dr. Matthew S. HOLLAND
05 Vice Pres Academic Affairs .... Dr. Ian WILSON
03 Vice Pres Finance & Administration .... Dr. Val L. PETERSON
32 Vice President Student Affairs .... Dr. Cory L. DUCKWORTH
30 Vice Pres Deveopment/Alumni .... Mr. Marc ARCHAMBAULT
26 Vice Pres University Relations .... Vacant
10 Assoc Vice Pres Finance .... Mr. Michael R. FRANCIS
20 Assoc Vice Pres Engaged Learning .... Dr. Brian BIRCH
18 Assoc Vice Pres Facilities Planning .... Mr. Jim MICHAELIS
20 Assoc VP Programs .... Dr. Maureen ANDRADE
84 Assc VP/Dean Stdnt Svcs/Enroll Mgmt .... Dr. Michelle TAYLOR
26 Assoc VP College Mktg/Communication .... Mr. Chris TAYLOR
44 Assoc Vice Pres Development .... Ms. Jane URBASKA
35 Asst VP Stdnt Life/Dean of Stdnts .... Mr. Bob RASMUSSEN
21 Asst VP/Controller Business Svcs .... Mr. Kedric BLACK
88 Asst VP Scholarship & Faculty Dev .... Vacant
07 Sr Director Admissions/One Stop .... Ms. Liz CHILDS
32 Asc Vice Pres Stdnt Adv/Sppt Svcs .... Dr. Shad SORENSON
72 Dean Computing/Technology .... Mr. Ernie CAREY
57 Dean School of the Arts .... Dr. Newell DAYLEY
81 Dean Science & Health .... Dr. Samuel RUSHFORTH
50 Dean School of Business .... Dr. Norman WRIGHT
97 Dean University College .... Dr. K.D TAYLOR
53 Dean School of Education .... Dr. Briant J. FARNSWORTH
15 Assoc VP Human Res/Equity Officer .... Mr. Ron PRICE, JR.
37 Director Financial Aid/Scholarship .... Ms. Trish HOWARD
19 Dir Public Safety/Chief of Police .... Mr. John BREWER
44 Director of Planned Giving .... Ms. Cristina PIANEZZOLA
09 Director Institutional Research .... Mr. Robert LOVERIDGE
41 Assoc VP Athletics .... Mr. Michael V. JACOBSEN
24 Director Studios & Engineering .... Mr. Will MCKINNON
40 Director Bookstore .... Ms. Louise BRIDGE
06 Registrar .... Ms. LuAnn SMITH
45 Exec Director Planning & Budgets .... Ms. Linda MAKIN
28 Director Multicultural Center .... Vacant
29 Director Alumni Relations .... Ms. Jeri L. ALLPHIN
38 Dir Career & Academic Counseling .... Mr. Adam BLACK
96 Director of Purchasing .... Mr. Ryan LINDSTROM

*Weber State University (G)

1001 University Circle, Ogden UT 84408-1001
County: Weber FICE Identification: 003680
Unit ID: 230782
Telephone: (801) 626-6000 Carnegie Class: Master's M

FAX Number: (801) 626-7922 Calendar System: Semester
URL: www.weber.edu
Established: 1889 Annual Undergrad Tuition & Fees (In-State): $4,761
Enrollment: 25,301 Coed
Affiliation or Control: State IRS Status: 501(c)3
Highest Offering: Master's
Program: Occupational; 2-Year Principally Bachelor's Creditable; Liberal Arts And General; Teacher Preparatory; Professional; Fine Arts Emphasis
Accreditation: NW, ADNUR, ART, BUS, BUSA, CIDA, CONST, DH, EMT, ENGT, MLTAD, MT, MUS, NUR, SW, @TEAC, TED

02 President ...... Dr. F. Ann MILLNER
05 Provost ...... Dr. Michael B. VAUGHAN
20 Associate Provost ...... Dr. Bruce BOWEN
20 Associate Provost ...... Dr. Ryan THOMAS
10 Vice Pres Administrative Services ...... Dr. Norm TARBOX
30 Vice Pres for Univ Advancement ...... Dr. Brad MORTENSEN
32 Vice President Student Affairs ...... Dr. Janet WINNIFORD
13 VP for Information Technology ...... Dr. Bret R. ELLIS
35 Assoc VP for Student Affairs ...... Dr. Brett PEROZZI
21 Asst VP for Financial Services ...... Mr. Steven E. NABOR
15 Asst Vice Pres for Human Resources ...... Ms. Cherrie NELSON
88 Vice Provost Innovation & Econo Dev ...... Mr. Alexander LAWRENCE
11 Asst VP for Administrative Services ...... Mr. Jerry G. GRAYBEAL
18 Assoc VP for Facilities Management ...... Mr. Kevin HANSEN
06 Registrar ...... Mr. Mark SIMPSON
19 Director Public Safety ...... Vacant
29 Exec Director Alumni Association ...... Ms. Nancy COLLINWOOD
38 Dir Counseling & Psycholog Services ...... Dr. Dianna K. ABEL
36 Director of Career Services ...... Dr. Winn STANGER
37 Director of Financial Aid ...... Mr. Jed SPENCER
51 Vice Prov & Dean Continuing Educ ...... Dr. Bruce DAVIS
76 Dean Health Professions ...... Dr. Yasmen SIMONIAN
50 Dean Business/Economics ...... Dr. Jeffrey STEAGALL
53 Dean of Education ...... Dr. Jack L. RASMUSSEN
83 Dean Social Behavioral Science ...... Dr. Frank HARROLD
79 Dean of Arts & Humanities ...... Dr. Madonne MINER
81 Dean of Science ...... Dr. David MATTY
72 Dean of Applied Science & Tech ...... Dr. David FERRO
27 Director of Media Relations ...... Mr. John L. KOWALEWSKI
35 Dean of Students ...... Dr. Jeffrey J. HURST
07 Director of Admissions ...... Mr. Scott TEICHERT
08 University Librarian ...... Ms. Joan HUBBARD
22 Dir Equal Opportunity/Affirm Action ...... Dr. Barry G. GOMBERG
41 Dir of Intercollegiate Athletics ...... Mr. Jerry BOVEE
40 Bookstore Director ...... Mr. Tim ECK
25 Director Sponsored Projects ...... Mr. James TAYLOR
85 Director Services Intl Students ...... Mr. Morteza EMAMI
23 Director Student Health Center ...... Ms. Juliana P. LARSEN
26 Director Public Relations ...... Ms. Allison B. HESS
91 Director Administrative Computing ...... Vacant
43 University Counsel ...... Dr. G. Richard HILL
39 Director Housing & Residence Life ...... Mr. Daniel KILCREASE
96 Director of Purchasing ...... Ms. Nancy E. EMENGER
28 Asst to President for Diversity ...... Dr. Forrest C. CRAWFORD
92 Director of Honors Program ...... Dr. Judy ELSLEY
88 Director Budget & Investments ...... Mr. Brian L. SHUPPY
09 Director of Institutional Research ...... Mr. Steve KERR
94 Coordinator of Women's Studies ...... Dr. Parrilla DE KOKAL

*Utah State University-College of Eastern Utah (A)

451 E 400 N, Price UT 84501-2699
County: Carbon FICE Identification: 003676
Unit ID: 230092
Telephone: (435) 637-2120 Carnegie Class: Assoc/Pub-R-M
FAX Number: (435) 613-5422 Calendar System: Semester
URL: www.ceu.edu
Established: 1937 Annual Undergrad Tuition & Fees (In-State): $3,070
Enrollment: 2,323 Coed
Affiliation or Control: State IRS Status: 501(c)3
Highest Offering: Associate Degree
Program: Occupational; 2-Year Principally Bachelor's Creditable
Accreditation: &NW, ADNUR, PNUR

02 Chancellor ...... Dr. Joe PETERSON
05 VC Academic Affairs/Student Svcs ...... Dr. Greg BENSON
30 Vice Chanc Admin/Advancement ...... Mr. Brad KING
12 Vice Chanc Blanding Campus ...... Dr. Guy DENTON
13 Assoc Vice Chanc Info Tech/CIO ...... Mr. Eric MANTZ
88 AVC Prehistoric Museum ...... Mr. Kenneth CARPENTER
32 Assoc Vice Chanc Student Services ...... Dr. Alex HERZOG
37 Director of Financial Aid ...... Mr. Kim BOOTH
06 Academic Records/Registrar ...... Ms. Jan YOUNG
07 Director of Enrollment Services ...... Mr. Greg DART
08 Director of Library ...... Ms. Lori BRASSAW
10 Director Business Information ...... Ms. Juanita MCEVOY
41 Athletic Director ...... Mr. Dave PAUR
40 Bookstore Manager ...... Ms. Susan LEONARD
19 Director of Public Safety ...... Mr. James PRETTYMAN
96 Director of Purchasing ...... Ms. Robyn SHERIFF
15 Senior HR Coordinator ...... Mrs. Tammy AUBERGER
18 Director of Facilities ...... Mrs. Sheila BURGHARDT

† Regional accreditation is carried under the parent institution in Logan, UT.

*Dixie State College of Utah (B)

225 S 700 E, Saint George UT 84770-3876
County: Washington FICE Identification: 003671
Unit ID: 230171
Telephone: (435) 652-7500 Carnegie Class: Bac/Assoc
FAX Number: (435) 656-4001 Calendar System: Semester
URL: www.dixie.edu
Established: 1911 Annual Undergrad Tuition & Fees (In-State): $4,089
Enrollment: 9,086 Coed
Affiliation or Control: State IRS Status: 501(c)3
Highest Offering: Baccalaureate
Program: Occupational; 2-Year Principally Bachelor's Creditable; Liberal Arts And General; Teacher Preparatory; Professional
Accreditation: NW, ADNUR, DH, EMT, NUR, PTAA, RAD, SURGT, TEAC

02 President ...... Dr. Stephen D. NADAULD
11 Vice Pres Administrative Services ...... Mr. Stanley J. PLEWE
05 Exec Vice Pres Academic Services ...... Dr. Donna DILLINGHAM-EVANS
32 VP Student Services/Govt Relations ...... Mr. Frank LOJKO
44 Vice Pres Development ...... Mr. George WHITEHEAD
30 Vice Pres Institutional Advancement ...... Ms. Christina SCHULTZ
49 Dean School Arts & Letters ...... Dr. Don HINTON
66 Dean School Nursing/Allied Health ...... Dr. Carole GRADY
50 Dean School Business ...... Dr. William CHRISTENSEN
81 Dean Science & Technology ...... Dr. Victor HASFURTHER
53 Dean Sch Education/Family Studies ...... Dr. Brenda SABEY
51 Dean Continuing Education ...... Mr. Steve BRINGHURST
35 Dean of Students ...... Mr. Del BEATTY
13 Dean of Information Services ...... Mr. Gary J. KOEVEN
10 Exec Director Business Services ...... Mr. A. Scott TALBOT
15 Exec Director of Human Resources ...... Ms. Pamela MONTRALLO
18 Executive Director Campus Services ...... Ms. Sherry RUESCH
08 Director Library ...... Ms. Daphne SELBERT
40 Executive Director Auxiliaries ...... Mr. T. Randy JUDD
37 Director Student Financial Aid ...... Mr. J. D ROBERTSON
84 Exec Dir Enrollment Services ...... Mr. David ROOS
06 Registrar ...... Ms. Julie STENDER
07 Director of Admissions ...... Mr. Josh SINE
38 Director Student Counseling ...... Mr. Rick PALMER
26 Director Public Relations ...... Mr. Steve JOHNSON
18 Director Facilities Operation ...... Mr. Doug WHITEHEAD
19 Director Security/Safety ...... Mr. Don C. REID
41 Athletic Director ...... Mr. Jason BOOTHE
39 Director Resident Life ...... Mr. Seth GUBLER
09 Director of Institutional Research ...... Ms. Andrea BROWN
04 Exec Assistant to the President ...... Mrs. Marilyn LAMOREAUX
35 Director of Student Involvement ...... Mr. Jordon SHARP
96 Director of Purchasing ...... Ms. Jackie FREEMAN
29 Director of Alumni Relations ...... Ms. Kalynn LARSON

*Snow College (C)

150 E College Avenue, Ephraim UT 84627-1299
County: Sanpete FICE Identification: 003679
Unit ID: 230597
Telephone: (435) 283-7000 Carnegie Class: Assoc/Pub-R-M
FAX Number: (435) 283-6879 Calendar System: Semester
URL: www.snow.edu
Established: 1888 Annual Undergrad Tuition & Fees (In-State): $3,086
Enrollment: 4,113 Coed
Affiliation or Control: State IRS Status: 501(c)3
Highest Offering: Associate Degree
Program: Occupational; 2-Year Principally Bachelor's Creditable
Accreditation: NW, ACBSP, MUS, PNUR, THEA

02 President ...... Dr. Scott L. WYATT
32 Vice President Student Success ...... Mr. Craig MATHIE
05 Vice President for Academic Affairs ...... Dr. Gary SMITH
10 VP Finance/Administrative Services ...... Mr. Marvin DODGE
35 Dean of Student Life ...... Ms. Michelle BROWN
75 Dean Business & Applied Tech ...... Mr. Mike MEDLEY
36 Director of Student Success ...... Ms. Susan LARSEN
08 Director Library/Information Svcs ...... Mr. Jon OSTLER
09 Director Institutional Research ...... Ms. Beckie HERMANSEN
15 Director Human Resource Development ...... Mr. David DYCHES
18 Director Physical Plant Operations ...... Mr. Bob OLIVER
24 Director TTC ...... Mr. Chase MITCHELL
39 Director Student Housing ...... Ms. Jessica SIEGFRIED
41 Athletic Director ...... Mr. Robert NIELSON
06 Registrar ...... Ms. Margie ANDERSON
07 Director Admissions/Communications ...... Mr. Greg DART
21 Associate Business Officer ...... Mr. John RUELL
26 Chief Public Relations Officer ...... Vacant
35 Director Student Affairs ...... Ms. Lindsey FIELD
37 Director Student Financial Aid ...... Mr. Jack DALENE
38 Director Student Counseling ...... Mr. Allen RIGGS
96 Director of Purchasing ...... Mr. Michael JORGENSEN
30 Chief Development ...... Ms. Rosie CONNOR

*Salt Lake Community College (D)

4600 S Redwood Road, Salt Lake City UT 84123-3197
County: Salt Lake FICE Identification: 005220
Unit ID: 230746
Telephone: (801) 957-4111 Carnegie Class: Assoc/Pub-U-MC
FAX Number: (801) 957-4444 Calendar System: Semester
URL: www.slcc.edu
Established: 1948 Annual Undergrad Tuition & Fees (In-State): $3,170
Enrollment: 33,420 Coed
Affiliation or Control: State IRS Status: 501(c)3
Highest Offering: Associate Degree
Program: Occupational; 2-Year Principally Bachelor's Creditable
Accreditation: NW, ACBSP, ACFEI, ADNUR, DH, MAC, OTA, PTAA, RAD, SURGT

02 President ...... Dr. Cynthia A. BIOTEAU
05 Provost ...... Dr. Chris PICARD
10 Business Services Vice Pres ...... Mr. Dennis KLAUS
32 Student Services Vice President ...... Dr. Deneece HUFTALIN
30 Vice Pres Institutional Advancement ...... Mr. Tim SHEEHAN
20 Assoc Prov Educ/Cmty Partnerships ...... Dr. Ryan CARSTENS
20 Asst VP/Dean Professnal & Econ Dev ...... Ms. Karen GUNN
09 Asst Provost Inst Effectiveness ...... Ms. Barbara GROVER
20 Asst Vice Pres of Budget Services ...... Dr. Kimberly HENRIE
15 Asst Vice Pres of Human Resources ...... Mr. Craig GARDNER
18 Assistant VP of Facilities ...... Mr. Robert ASKERLUND
35 Dean of Students/Asst Vice Pres ...... Dr. Marlin CLARK
45 Asst VP Student Planning & Support ...... Dr. Nancy SINGER
84 Asst VP Student Enrollment Services ...... Mr. Eric WEBER
26 AVP Inst Mktg/Communications ...... Ms. Alison MCFARLANE
49 Dean Arts/Communication/New Media ...... Dr. Anna SZABADOS
50 Dean School of Business ...... Mr. Dennis BROMLEY
76 Dean School of Health Sciences ...... Dr. Loredana HAEGER
79 Dean Humanities & Social Sciences ...... Dr. John MCCORMICK
81 Dean Science/Math & Engineering ...... Dr. Clifton SANDERS
75 Dean Technical Specialties ...... Mr. Rick BOUILLON
08 Dean Learning Resources ...... Vacant
41 Athletic Director ...... Ms. Norma CARR
88 Director Student Ctr/Auxiliary Svc ...... Mr. Jason BEAL
88 Executive Director Grand Theatre ...... Mr. Richard SCOTT
38 Director Academic Advising ...... Ms. Sonia PARKER
78 Director of Co-operative Education ...... Mr. Jack HESLEPH
36 Dir Student Assessment/Placement ...... Ms. Diana HARVEY
06 Registrar ...... Ms. MaryEtta CHASE
37 Director Financial Aid ...... Ms. Cristi MILLARD
19 Director Parking & Security ...... Mr. Shane CRABTREE
88 Director of Risk Management ...... Ms. Nancy SANCHEZ
27 Chief Information/Security Officer ...... Mr. Bill ZOUMADAKIS
21 Controller/Business Manager ...... Mr. Douglas HANSEN
22 EEO Director ...... Ms. Mozelle ORTON
96 Director of Purchasing ...... Ms. Lois WIESEMANN
25 Director of Grants & Contracts ...... Ms. Susan SALEM
30 Exec Director of Development ...... Mr. Benjamin KORN
09 Int Dir of Institutional Research ...... Mr. Joseph DIAZ
29 Alumni Coordinator ...... Vacant

Vista College (E)

1785 E 1450 South, Suite 300, Clearfield UT 84015
County: Davis FICE Identification: 025728
Unit ID: 377342
Telephone: (801) 774-9900 Carnegie Class: Assoc/PrivFP
FAX Number: (801) 774-0111 Calendar System: Other
URL: www.vistacollege.edu
Established: N/A Annual Undergrad Tuition & Fees: $15,695
Enrollment: 64 Coed
Affiliation or Control: Proprietary IRS Status: Proprietary
Highest Offering: Associate Degree
Program: Occupational
Accreditation: ACCSC

01 Director ...... Mr. Scott TOMLIN

Western Governors University (F)

4001 S 700 E, Suite 700, Salt Lake City UT 84107-2533
County: Salt Lake FICE Identification: 033394
Unit ID: 433387
Telephone: (801) 274-3280 Carnegie Class: Master's L
FAX Number: (801) 274-3305 Calendar System: Other
URL: www.wgu.edu
Established: 1996 Annual Undergrad Tuition & Fees: $5,780
Enrollment: 34,000 Coed
Affiliation or Control: Independent Non-Profit IRS Status: 501(c)3
Highest Offering: Master's
Program: Teacher Preparatory; Professional
Accreditation: NW, DETC, NURSE, TED

01 President ...... Dr. Robert W. MENDENHALL
10 Vice Pres Finance/Administration ...... David GROW
09 Vice Pres Quality/Inst Research ...... Jason LEVIN
88 Vice Pres of Strategic Relations ...... Ken SORBER
26 Vice President of Marketing ...... Linda Jean WESTERN
15 Vice President of Human Resources ...... Nanette BLACK
20 Associate Provost Student Mentoring ...... Chris MALLET
20 Assoc Provost Program Management ...... Dr. Larry BANKS
20 Associate Provost Academic Services ...... Dr. Stacey LUDWIG-JOHNSON
20 Assoc Provost Teachers Col/Accred ...... Dr. Phil SCHMIDT
20 Associate Provost Assessment ...... Dr. Kelli FOSTER
76 Dean College of Health Professions ...... Jan JONES-SCHENK
27 Chief Marketing Officer ...... Patrick PARTRIDGE
26 Director of Public Relations ...... Joan MITCHELL
84 Director of Enrollment ...... Eddie RIOS
37 Director of Financial Aid ...... Jenny ALLEN RYAN

Westminster College (G)

1840 S 1300 E, Salt Lake City UT 84105-3697
County: Salt Lake FICE Identification: 003681
Unit ID: 230807
Telephone: (801) 484-7651 Carnegie Class: Master's M
FAX Number: (801) 466-6916 Calendar System: Semester
URL: www.westminstercollege.edu
Established: 1875 Annual Undergrad Tuition & Fees: $28,210
Enrollment: 3,348 Coed
Affiliation or Control: Independent Non-Profit IRS Status: 501(c)3
Highest Offering: Master's

Program: Liberal Arts And General; Teacher Preparatory; Professional
Accreditation: NW, AAB, ACBSP, ANEST, NURSE, PH, TEAC

01	President	Dr. Brian L. LEVIN-STANKEVICH
05	Provost & VP Academic Affairs	Dr. James E. SEIDELMAN
30	Vice Pres Institutional Advancement	Mr. Stephen R. MORGAN
10	Vice Pres Finance & Administration	Mr. Curtis W. RYAN
84	Vice Pres Enrollment Management	Dr. Gary DAYNES
44	Asst VP Institutional Advancement	Ms. Lisa ACTOR
26	Acting Director of Communications	Mr. Jeremy PUGH
49	Dean School of Arts & Sciences	Dr. Mary Jane CHASE
66	Dean School of Nursing/Hlth Science	Dr. Sheryl STEADMAN
50	Dean School of Business	Dr. Jin WANG
53	Dean School of Education	Dr. Robert A. SHAW
106	Dean Division of New Learning	Dr. Aric KRAUSE
35	Dean of Students	Mr. Mark FERNE
86	Director of Government Relations	Dr. Gary DAYNES
29	Dir Alumni/Community & Board Rels	Ms. Annalisa A. HOLCOMBE
32	Assoc Provost Student Development	Dr. Susan D. HEATH
09	Assoc Provost Inst Research/Assess	Dr. Paul PRESSON
88	Assoc Provost Integrative Learning	Dr. Gary DAYNES
28	Assoc Provost Diversity/Global Lrng	Dr. Bridget NEWELL
13	Chief Information Officer	Mr. Robert ALLRED
88	Director of New Ventures	Mr. Rex FALKENRATH
43	General Counsel/Risk Management	Ms. Kelly D. HILL
21	Director of Accounting Services	Ms. Jennifer MEDRANO
15	Director of Human Resources	Mr. Darin JONES
06	Registrar	Ms. Mindy WENNERGREN
37	Director of Financial Aid	Mr. Sean VIEW
07	Director of Admissions	Ms. Elizabeth KEY
18	Director Plant/Facilities	Mr. Richard A. BROCKMYER
36	Director of Career Resource Center	Mr. Mike CALDWELL
08	Director of Library	Ms. Diane VANDERPOL
96	Director of Purchasing	Mr. Alfred W. JOHANSEN
35	Dir Student Involvement/Leadership	Ms. Trisha TEIG
39	Asst Director of Residential Life	Ms. Aimee FROST
88	Director Start Center	Ms. Deborah VICKERY
88	Director of Conferences	Mr. Jeff BROWN
19	Director of Campus Patrol/Safety	Mr. Saeed REZAI
41	Director of Athletics	Mr. Shay WYATT
42	Director of Spiritual Life	Ms. Jan SAAED
38	Director of Campus Counseling	Ms. Lisa JONES
92	Director of Honors Program	Dr. Richard BADENHAUSEN
91	Database Administrator	Mr. Kyle RIMA

VERMONT

Bennington College (A)

One College Drive, Bennington VT 05201-6003
County: Bennington FICE Identification: 003682
Unit ID: 230816
Telephone: (802) 442-5401 Carnegie Class: Bac/A&S
FAX Number: (802) 447-4269 Calendar System: Semester
URL: www.bennington.edu
Established: 1932 Annual Undergrad Tuition & Fees: $44,220
Enrollment: 822 Coed
Affiliation or Control: Independent Non-Profit IRS Status: 501(c)3
Highest Offering: Master's
Program: Liberal Arts And General
Accreditation: EH

01	President	Dr. Elizabeth COLEMAN
05	Dean of the College	Ms. Isabel ROCHE
10	VP and Chief Financial Officer	Ms. Laura KRAUSE
30	VP for External Relations	Ms. Paige BARTELS
45	VP for Planning & Administration	Mr. David G. REES
07	Dean of Admissions & Financial Aid	Mr. Ken HIMMELMAN
32	Dean of Students	Ms. Eva CHATTERJEE-SUTTON
26	Director of Communications	Ms. Janet L. MARSDEN
20	Associate Dean of the College	Mr. Duncan DOBBELMANN

Burlington College (B)

351 North Avenue, Burlington VT 05401-8477
County: Chittenden FICE Identification: 012183
Unit ID: 230825
Telephone: (802) 862-9616 Carnegie Class: Bac/A&S
FAX Number: (802) 660-4331 Calendar System: Semester
URL: www.burlington.edu
Established: 1972 Annual Undergrad Tuition & Fees: $22,410
Enrollment: 196 Coed
Affiliation or Control: Independent Non-Profit IRS Status: 501(c)3
Highest Offering: Master's
Program: Liberal Arts And General
Accreditation: EH

01	President	Ms. Christine A. PLUNKETT
05	Vice Pres Academic/Student Affairs	Dr. Stephen ST ONGE
10	Director of Administration/Finance	Vacant
30	Director of Development/Communicati	Vacant
32	Director of Student Life	Mr. Greg LITCHFIELD
18	Director of Physical Plant	Mr. John HAWKINS
07	Director of Admissions	Ms. Gillian HOMSTED
13	Director Information Technology	Mr. Jordan M. YOUNG
06	Registrar	Ms. Melissa LONG
08	Dir Library/Information Services	Ms. Jessica ALLARD
37	Director of Financial Aid	Ms. Lindy WALSH

Champlain College (C)

163 S Willard Street, Burlington VT 05402-0670
County: Chittenden FICE Identification: 003684
Unit ID: 230852
Telephone: (802) 860-2700 Carnegie Class: Bac/Diverse
FAX Number: (802) 860-2750 Calendar System: Semester
URL: www.champlain.edu
Established: 1956 Annual Undergrad Tuition & Fees: $29,765
Enrollment: 3,114 Coed
Affiliation or Control: Independent Non-Profit IRS Status: 501(c)3
Highest Offering: Master's
Program: Liberal Arts And General; Teacher Preparatory; Professional
Accreditation: EH, RAD, @SW

01	President	Dr. David F. FINNEY
05	Provost	Dr. Robin ABRAMSON
10	Vice President Finances	David J. PROVOST
84	Vice President Enrollment	Ian MORTIMER
30	Vice President Advancement	Michele RICHARDSON
32	Vice President Student Life	Dr. Leslie AVERILL
13	Asst Vice Pres Information Systems	Theodore LASKARIS
36	Assistant Vice Pres Career Services	Sarah POTTER
15	Assoc Vice Pres Human Resources	Mary Margaret LEE
20	Associate Provost	Dr. Michelle MILLER
104	Associate Provost-Education Abroad	Dr. James CROSS
101	Secretary of Corporation	Katie HAWLEY
53	Int Dean Education/Human Stds Div	Dr. James GAROFALO
88	Int Dean Comm/Creative Media Div	Dr. William RICHARDSON
50	Dean Business Division	Dr. David STRUBLER
77	Int Dean Information Tech/Science	Dr. Robert MARINO
51	Dean Continuing/Online Education	Vacant
09	Institutional Effectiveness Dir	Susan POWERS
07	Director of Admissions	Sarah ANDRIANO
06	Registrar	Rebecca PETERSON
37	Director of Financial Aid	Kristi JOVELL
38	Director of Counseling	Carol MORAN-BROWN
18	Director of Physical Plant	Thomas BONNETTE
19	Director of Security & Safety	Richard LONG
23	Director Health Services	Cissy MCCLELLAN
22	Director of Affirmative Action	Mary Margaret LEE
39	Director of Residential Life	Ashley MIKELL
85	Foreign Students Advisor	Kathy LYNN
21	Treasurer	Shelley NAVARI
27	Public Information & News Director	Stephen MEASE
29	Director of Alumni Relations	Erik OLIVER
08	Director Library	Janet COTTRELL
28	Dir Student Diversity/Inclusion	Ame LAMBERT
103	Director Workforce Development	Melissa HERSH
102	Dir Foundation/Corporate Relations	Susan PANKEY
04	Executive Assistant	Diana AGUSTA
40	Bookstore Manager	Susan BROWN

College of St. Joseph (D)

71 Clement Road, Rutland VT 05701-3899
County: Rutland FICE Identification: 003685
Unit ID: 231077
Telephone: (802) 773-5900 Carnegie Class: Master's S
FAX Number: (802) 776-5258 Calendar System: Semester
URL: www.csj.edu
Established: 1956 Annual Undergrad Tuition & Fees: $19,465
Enrollment: 377 Coed
Affiliation or Control: Roman Catholic IRS Status: 501(c)3
Highest Offering: Master's
Program: Liberal Arts And General; Teacher Preparatory; Professional
Accreditation: EH

01	President	Dr. Richard B. LLOYD
05	Academic Dean	Dr. Nancy J. KLINE
07	Dean of Admissions	Vacant
32	Dean of Student Services	Mr. Robert P. LUKASKIEWICZ
37	Director of Financial Aid	Mrs. Julie ROSMUS
30	Dir Development/Alumni Relations	Mr. Bates CHILDRESS
41	Director of Athletics	Mr. Phil BARTLETT
06	Registrar	Mr. Greg CHAMBERLAND
14	CIS Administrator	Mr. Raymond GIBBS
35	Director of Student Support Svcs	Ms. Linda JOHNSON
21	Controller	Mrs. Karen REYNOLDS
18	Chief Facilities/Physical Plant	Mr. Thomas BELAND
10	Business Manager	Mrs. Kristie JOHNSON
49	Chair Arts & Sciences	Dr. David BALFOUR
50	Chair Business	Dr. Robert GODDARD
53	Chair Education	Dr. Maria BOVE
15	Chair Psychology/Human Services	Dr. Michael KESLER
08	Librarian	Ms. Doreen MCCULLOUGH

Goddard College (E)

123 Pitkin Road, Plainfield VT 05667-9432
County: Washington FICE Identification: 003686
Unit ID: 230889
Telephone: (800) 468-4888 Carnegie Class: Master's M
FAX Number: (802) 454-1029 Calendar System: Semester
URL: www.goddard.edu
Established: 1863 Annual Undergrad Tuition & Fees: $14,036
Enrollment: 754 Coed
Affiliation or Control: Independent Non-Profit IRS Status: 501(c)3
Highest Offering: Master's
Program: Liberal Arts And General; Teacher Preparatory
Accreditation: EH

01	President	Dr. Barbara VACARR
05	Interim Academic Vice President	Dr. Marianne REIFF
10	Vice President Finance and Admin	Ms. Faith BROWN
88	Exec Asst to President	Ms. Karen BOUTELLE
30	Chief Advancement Officer	Ms. Lauren MOYE
32	Associate Dean of Community Life	Ms. Susan A. WILSON
06	Registrar	Mr. Josh CASTLE
15	DIrector of Human Resources	Ms. Jane BRADLEY
37	Director of Financial Aid	Ms. Beverly JENE
88	Director of Campus Services	Mr. Paul SHPER
08	Director of Information Access	Ms. Clara BRUNS
18	Director of Facilities Operations	Mr. Scott BLANCHARD
12	Director of Port Townsend Campus	Ms. Erin FRISTAD
21	Director of Business Office	Ms. Sherri MOLLEUR
04	Exec Asst to President	Ms. Caro THOMPSON
88	Manager of WGDR/WGDH Radio	Mr. Kris GRUEN

Green Mountain College (F)

1 Brennan Circle, Poultney VT 05764-1199
County: Rutland FICE Identification: 003687
Unit ID: 230898
Telephone: (802) 287-8000 Carnegie Class: Bac/A&S
FAX Number: (802) 287-8099 Calendar System: Semester
URL: www.greenmtn.edu
Established: 1834 Annual Undergrad Tuition & Fees: $30,718
Enrollment: 698 Coed
Affiliation or Control: Independent Non-Profit IRS Status: 501(c)3
Highest Offering: Master's
Program: Liberal Arts And General; Teacher Preparatory
Accreditation: EH

01	President	Dr. Paul J. FONTEYN
05	Vice President Academic Affairs	Dr. William M. THROOP
10	Vice Pres Finance/Administration	Mr. Joseph A. MANNING, III
32	Vice President Student Affairs	Dr. Joseph PETRICK
04	Executive Assistant to President	Ms. Jeanne V. ROOT
20	Dean of Faculty	Dr. Thomas J. MAUHS-PUGH
84	Dean of Enrollment Management	Mr. Robert J. GOULD
30	Director of Development	Ms. Mary Lou WILLITS
06	Registrar	Ms. Sharon L. HOFFMAN
18	Director of Facilities	Mr. Glenn LAPLANTE
19	Director of Public Safety	Mr. Steven BROWN
26	Director of Public Relations	Mr. Kevin COBURN
41	Athletic Director	Ms. Marybeth LENNOX
08	Director Library & Information Svcs	Mr. Paul MILLETTE
85	Director of International Pgms	Ms. Anne COLPITTS
13	Director Computing & Info Mgmt	Mr. Jeffrey WRIGHT
42	Chaplain	Ms. Shirley OSKAMP
29	Dir Alumni Relations/Annual Giving	Vacant
36	Director of Career Counseling	Ms. Renee BEAUPRE WHITE
92	Director of College Honors Program	Dr. Jennifer SELLERS
37	Director Student Financial Aid	Ms. Wendy ELLIS
15	Director Human Resources	Ms. Janie EVANS
38	Director Student Counseling	Ms. Heidi VAZQUEZ-GARCIA
40	Manager of Bookstore	Ms. Heather LYNG

Landmark College (G)

River Road South, Putney VT 05346
County: Windham FICE Identification: 025326
Unit ID: 247649
Telephone: (802) 387-4767 Carnegie Class: Assoc/PrivNFP
FAX Number: (802) 387-6868 Calendar System: Semester
URL: www.landmark.edu
Established: 1985 Annual Undergrad Tuition & Fees: $48,710
Enrollment: 488 Coed
Affiliation or Control: Independent Non-Profit IRS Status: 501(c)3
Highest Offering: Baccalaureate
Program: 2-Year Principally Bachelor's Creditable
Accreditation: EH

01	President	Dr. Peter A. EDEN
03	Senior Vice President	Dr. Brent BETIT
05	Academic Dean	Dr. Adrienne MAJOR
10	Vice President Administration/Finan	Mr. Alan RUSSELL
26	VP Public Relations & Marketing	Mr. Steve MULLER
84	Vice Pres Enrollment Management	Ms. Dale HEROLD
04	Assistant to the President	Vacant
88	Dean Short-Term Pgms/Transfer Svcs	Dr. John NISSEN
35	Dean of Students	Mr. Michael LUCIANI
18	Director of Physical Plant	Mr. James LOVERING
08	Head Librarian	Ms. Jennifer LANN
13	Chief of Technology	Ms. Corinne BELL
06	Registrar	Ms. Karen DAMIAN
41	Director Activities/Athletics	Mr. James AUSTIN
37	Director Student Financial Aid	Ms. Jennifer DESMARAIS
38	Director of Student Counseling	Mrs. Julie OSHERSON
23	Director of Health Services	Ms. Simone HOLTON
40	Bookstore Manager	Ms. Kimberly JUDD

Marlboro College (H)

PO Box A, Marlboro VT 05344-9999
County: Windham FICE Identification: 003690
Unit ID: 230940
Telephone: (802) 257-4333 Carnegie Class: Bac/A&S
FAX Number: (802) 257-4154 Calendar System: Semester
URL: www.marlboro.edu
Established: 1946 Annual Undergrad Tuition & Fees: $37,640
Enrollment: 326 Coed
Affiliation or Control: Independent Non-Profit IRS Status: 501(c)3
Highest Offering: Master's

Program: Liberal Arts And General
Accreditation: EH

01 President ... Ms. Ellen M. LOVELL
10 Senior Financial Mgmt Officer ... Ms. Anne PRATT
05 Dean of Faculty/Graduate Educ ... Mr. Richard GLEJZER
07 Dean of Admissions ... Ms. Nicole CURVIN
32 Dean of Students ... Mr. Ken SCHNECK
58 Associate Dean Graduate School ... Mr. Sean CONLEY
84 Dir Enrollment Stdt Svc at Grad Ctr ... Mr. Joseph HESLIN
46 Chief Planning & Budget Officer ... Mr. Bryant MORGAN
08 Librarian ... Ms. Emily ALLING
06 Registrar ... Ms. Virginia NELLIS
30 Chief Advancement Officer ... Ms. Lisa M. CHRISTENSEN
44 Annual Giving Director ... Ms. Patricia CAVANAUGH
18 Director of Plant Operations ... Mr. Dan J. COTTER
82 World Studies Director ... Ms. Cathy OSMAN
40 Bookstore Manager ... Ms. Rebecca BARTLETT

Middlebury College (A)

Old Chapel, Middlebury VT 05753-6200
County: Addison FICE Identification: 003691
Unit ID: 230959
Telephone: (802) 443-5000 Carnegie Class: Bac/A&S
FAX Number: (802) 443-2071 Calendar System: 4/1/4
URL: www.middlebury.edu
Established: 1800 Annual Undergrad Tuition & Fees: $55,950
Enrollment: 2,507 Coed
Affiliation or Control: Independent Non-Profit IRS Status: 501(c)3
Highest Offering: Doctorate
Program: Liberal Arts And General
Accreditation: EH

01 President ... Dr. Ronald D. LIEBOWITZ
05 Vice President for Academic Affairs ... Dr. Tim SPEARS
10 Vice Pres for Finance/Treasurer ... Mr. Patrick J. NORTON
88 Sr Vice Pres/Philanthropic Advisor ... Mr. Michael SCHOENFELD
58 VP Language Sch/Sch Abroad/Grad Pgm ... Dr. Michael GEISLER
30 Vice Pres College Advancement ... Mr. James R. KEYES
37 Assoc VP Student Financial Services ... Ms. Kim DOWNS
21 Assoc VP Budget/Financial Planning ... Ms. Kristen C. ANDERSON
15 Assoc VP for HR/Organiz Development ... Ms. Drew MACAN
29 Assoc VP for Alumni Relations ... Ms. Margaret STOREY GROVES
20 Dean Curriculum/Faculty Dev & Rsch ... Dr. Bob CLUSS
20 Dean of the Faculty ... Dr. Andrea LLOYD
28 Dean of College/Chf Diversity Ofcr ... Dr. Shirley COLLADO
20 Dn Plng/Assess/Dir Col Self Study ... Dr. Susan BALDRIDGE
38 Exec Dir Health & Counseling Svcs ... Dr. Augustus JORDAN
08 Dean of Library & Information Svcs ... Mr. Michael D. ROY
07 Dean of Admissions ... Mr. Gregory B. BUCKLES
06 College Registrar ... Mr. LeRoy GRAHAM
21 Asst Treasurer/Dir of Business Svcs ... Mr. Thomas CORBIN
32 Assoc Dn of the Col/Dir Pub Safety ... Ms. Elizabeth B. BURCHARD
26 Executive Director Communications ... Mr. Timothy ETCHELLS
42 Chaplain ... Ms. Laurel JORDAN
41 Director of Athletics ... Mr. Erin QUINN
26 Director of Public Affairs ... Ms. Sarah RAY
88 President MIIS ... Dr. Sunder RAMASWAMY
40 Bookstore Manager ... Ms. Georgia BEST

† Tuition figure is a comprehensive fees figure.

New England Culinary Institute (B)

56 College Street, Montpelier VT 05602-9720
County: Washington FICE Identification: 022540
Unit ID: 230977
Telephone: (802) 223-6324 Carnegie Class: Spec/Other
FAX Number: (802) 225-3280 Calendar System: Semester
URL: www.neci.edu
Established: 1980 Annual Undergrad Tuition & Fees: $30,140
Enrollment: 483 Coed
Affiliation or Control: Proprietary IRS Status: Proprietary
Highest Offering: Baccalaureate
Program: Occupational; Technical Emphasis
Accreditation: ACCSC

01 CEO/President ... Mr. Francis VOIGT
11 Chief Financial Officer ... Mr. Phillip HARKER
05 Senior Vice President Education ... Mrs. Kathleen FINCK
88 Vice President Food & Bev Ops ... Mr. Kevin O'DONNELL
88 Chair Baking & Pastry Programs ... Chef Michael RHOADS
88 Chair HRM Program ... Ms. Michelle FORD
88 Chair Culinary Arts Programs ... Mr. Lyndon VIRKLER
20 Director Academic Svcs ... Ms. Laureen GAUTHIER
106 Chair Online Programs ... Chef Peg CHECCI
32 Director of Student Services ... Dr. Eric KECK
06 Registrar ... Ms. Liz FITZGERALD
07 Director of Admissions ... Ms. Anne BLACK CONE
08 Head Librarian ... Ms. Jessica JOYAL
13 Director Information Technology ... Mr. Nik ZNAMENSKIS
15 Director Human Resources ... Ms. Jennifer ZETARSKI
18 Director of Facilities ... Mr. William COLGAN
36 Manager Career Services ... Ms. Jill LANPHER

Norwich University (C)

158 Harmon Drive, Northfield VT 05663-1000
County: Washington FICE Identification: 003692
Unit ID: 230995
Telephone: (802) 485-2000 Carnegie Class: Master's L
FAX Number: (802) 485-2032 Calendar System: Semester
URL: www.norwich.edu
Established: 1819 Annual Undergrad Tuition & Fees: $30,048
Enrollment: 2,339 Coed
Affiliation or Control: Independent Non-Profit IRS Status: 501(c)3
Highest Offering: Master's
Program: Liberal Arts And General; Teacher Preparatory; Professional
Accreditation: EH, ACBSP, ENG, NURSE

01 President ... Dr. Richard W. SCHNEIDER
05 VP Academic Affairs/Dean of Faculty ... Dr. Guiyou HUANG
107 Dean Col of Professional Studies ... Mr. Aron TEMPKIN
32 VP Student Affs/Enrollment/Tech ... Dr. Frank VANECEK
83 Dean College of Liberal Arts ... Dr. Andrea TALENTINO
81 Dean College of Science/Mathematics ... Ms. Cathy FREY
88 Dean School of National Services ... Col. Steven SMITH
30 Vice Pres Institutional Advancement ... Mr. David J. WHALEY
13 VP Strategic Partnership ... Mr. Phillip SUSMANN
29 Asst VP for Alumni and Vol Progrms ... Mr. Paul BOVA
20 Associate VP Academic Affairs ... Dr. Joseph BYRNE
04 Assistant to President ... Ms. Judith A. BAILEY
10 Chief Financial Officer ... Ms. Lauren WOBBY
11 Chief Administrative Officer ... Mr. David MAGIDA
84 Director of Retention & Enrollment ... Ms. Shelby GILE
88 Coord Office of Communications ... Mr. Mark ALBURY
35 Dean of Students ... Ms. Martha MATHIS
09 Dir Inst Research/Effectiveness ... Ms. Ellalou ZIRBLIS
15 Director of Human Resources ... Mr. Jay WISNER
08 Head Librarian ... Mr. Ravil VELI
41 Athletic Director ... Mr. Anthony A. MARIANO
18 Director Facilities/Operations ... Mr. Bizhan YAHYAZADEH
37 Director Student Financial Aid ... Ms. Tracy STEINE
38 Director Student Counseling ... Dr. Melvin MILLER
07 Director of Admissions ... Ms. Sherri GILMORE

Saint Michael's College (D)

One Winooski Park, Colchester VT 05439-0001
County: Chittenden FICE Identification: 003694
Unit ID: 231059
Telephone: (802) 654-2000 Carnegie Class: Bac/A&S
FAX Number: (802) 654-2297 Calendar System: Semester
URL: www.smcvt.edu
Established: 1904 Annual Undergrad Tuition & Fees: $37,200
Enrollment: 2,455 Coed
Affiliation or Control: Roman Catholic IRS Status: 501(c)3
Highest Offering: Master's
Program: Liberal Arts And General; Teacher Preparatory
Accreditation: EH, CEA

01 President ... Dr. John J. NEUHAUSER
04 Assistant to the President ... Ms. Tara L. ARCURY
05 Vice Pres Academic Affairs ... Dr. Karen A. TALENTINO
10 Vice President for Finance ... Mr. Neal ROBINSON
32 Vice President for Student Affairs ... Ms. Dawn M. ELLINWOOD
84 Vice President for Enrollment ... Mr. Jerry E. FLANAGAN
16 Vice President for Human Resources ... Mr. Michael J. NEW
30 VP for Institutional Advancement ... Mr. Patrick J. GALLIVAN
20 Dean of the College ... Dr. Jeffrey A. TRUMBOWER
42 Director Edmundite Campus Ministry ... Rev. Brian J. CUMMINGS, SSE
07 Director of Admission ... Ms. Jacqueline MURPHY
37 Director Student Financial Services ... Mr. Daniel R. COUTURE
06 Registrar ... Mr. John D. SHEEHEY
09 Director of Institutional Research ... Mr. John P. KULHOWVICK
29 Director of Alumni/Parent Relations ... Ms. Angela ARMOUR
35 Director Student Activities ... Ms. Grace A. KELLY
93 Dir Intercultural Student Affairs ... Mr. Moise ST. LOUIS
39 Director of Residence Life ... Mr. Louis DIMASI
88 Associate Dean of the College ... Dr. Joan R. WRY
104 Director of Study Abroad ... Ms. Peggy H. IMAI
92 Honors Program Faculty Coordinator ... Dr. Nicholas CLARY
94 Coord of Gender/Women's Studies ... Dr. Michael BOSIA
08 Dir Library & Information Services ... Mr. John K. PAYNE
13 Chief Information Officer ... Mr. William O. ANDERSON
14 Director of Information Tech ... Ms. Billie MILES
26 Dir of Marketing/Communications ... Dr. Buff L. LINDAU
86 Dir Government/Community Relations ... Ms. Marilyn E. CORMIER
19 Director of Public Safety ... Mr. Peter D. SOONS
18 Director of Facilities ... Mr. David A. CUTLER
38 Director of Personal Counseling ... Ms. Linda HOLLINGDALE
36 Director of Career Development ... Ms. Christine CLARY
23 Director of Health Services ... Ms. Mary MASSON
41 Director of Athletics ... Dr. Geraldine KNORTZ
44 Director of Advancement Services ... Ms. Linda V. DONAHUE
102 Director of Foundation Relations ... Ms. Angela IRVINE
88 Financial Accounting Manager ... Ms. Shirley J. GOODELL-LACKEY
21 Director of Finance ... Ms. Mary Jane RUSSELL
96 Director of Business Services ... Mr. Robert ROBINSON
40 Bookstore Manager ... Mr. Stephen MCMAHON
31 Community Service Coordinator ... Ms. Heidi ST. PETER
105 Dir of Web Site Development ... Mr. Brian MACDONALD
44 Director of Individual Giving ... Ms. Terri P. SELBY

SIT (E)

Kipling Road, Brattleboro VT 05302-0676
County: Windham FICE Identification: 008860
Unit ID: 231068
Telephone: (802) 257-7751 Carnegie Class: Master's L
FAX Number: (802) 258-3248 Calendar System: Other
URL: www.worldlearning.org
Established: 1964 Annual Undergrad Tuition & Fees: $20,187
Enrollment: 1,052 Coed
Affiliation or Control: Independent Non-Profit IRS Status: 501(c)3
Highest Offering: Master's
Program: Teacher Preparatory; Professional
Accreditation: EH

01 President ... Dr. Adam WEINBERG
05 Senior VP of Academic Affairs/CAO ... Dr. John LUCAS
10 CFO ... Ms. Nancy R. BROCK
16 Senior VP of Global Human Resources ... Mr. Ross GIBSON
43 General Counsel ... Ms. Lisa RAE
58 Dean SIT Graduate Institute ... Ms. Preeti SHROFF-MEHTA
84 Dean External Rels/Strtgc Enrol Mgt ... Ms. Laurie BLACK
30 Director of Advancement ... Mr. Tom NAVIN
26 Director of Communications ... Ms. Laura INGALLS
88 Director Language and Culture Dept ... Ms. Beatriz FANTINI
07 Director of Admissions ... Ms. Kim DEREGO
06 Registrar ... Ms. Ginny NELLIS
37 Director Financial Aid ... Ms. Michelle KRAJNIK
32 Director Student Services ... Vacant

Southern Vermont College (F)

982 Mansion Drive, Bennington VT 05201-6002
County: Bennington FICE Identification: 003693
Unit ID: 231086
Telephone: (802) 442-5427 Carnegie Class: Bac/Diverse
FAX Number: (802) 447-4695 Calendar System: Semester
URL: www.svc.edu
Established: 1926 Annual Undergrad Tuition & Fees: $21,273
Enrollment: 533 Coed
Affiliation or Control: Independent Non-Profit IRS Status: 501(c)3
Highest Offering: Baccalaureate
Program: Occupational; Liberal Arts And General
Accreditation: EH, ADNUR, NUR, RAD

01 Acting President ... Mr. James BECKWITH
10 Chief Financial Officer/COO ... Mr. James BECKWITH
04 Executive Assistant ... Ms. Colleen LITTLE
41 Director of Athletics ... Mr. Michael MCDONOUGH
05 Provost ... Dr. Albert C. DECICCIO
20 Associate Academic Dean ... Vacant
50 Chair Business ... Vacant
66 Chair Nursing ... Dr. Karen CLEMENT O'BRIEN
79 Chair of Humanities ... Dr. Scott O'CALLAGHAN
81 Chair of Science and Technology ... Dr. Barry FLANARY
83 Chair of Social Sciences ... Mr. Scott STEIN
08 Director Learning Resources ... Ms. Sarah SANFILIPPO
06 Registrar ... Mr. Eric PARSONS
36 Director of Career Services ... Ms. Denise SPENCER
18 Director of Facilities ... Mr. Mark J. KLAUDER
32 Dean of Students ... Ms. Anne M. HOPKINS GROSS
38 Director of Counseling ... Mr. Michael GOODWIN
39 Director of Residence Life ... Ms. Sara PATCH
19 Director of Security ... Mr. George MARSHALL
07 Director of Admissions ... Mr. Jeremy GIBBONS
37 Director of Financial Aid ... Ms. Joel PHELPS
30 Dean of Development ... Vacant
27 Director of Communications ... Ms. Susan BIGGS
29 Dir Alumni Relations/Annual Fund ... Vacant
16 Director of Human Resources ... Ms. Sue METZNER
88 Coord Learning Disabilities ... Mr. David A. LINDENBERG

Sterling College (G)

PO Box 72, Craftsbury Common VT 05827-0072
County: Orleans FICE Identification: 021435
Unit ID: 231095
Telephone: (802) 586-7711 Carnegie Class: Bac/A&S
FAX Number: (802) 586-2596 Calendar System: Semester
URL: www.sterlingcollege.edu
Established: 1958 Annual Undergrad Tuition & Fees: $29,310
Enrollment: 98 Coed
Affiliation or Control: Independent Non-Profit IRS Status: 501(c)3
Highest Offering: Baccalaureate
Program: Liberal Arts And General
Accreditation: EH

01 President ... Mr. William R. WOOTTON
03 Exec VP & Director of Financial Aid ... Mr. Ned R. HOUSTON
05 Dean of the College ... Dr. Pavel CENKL
36 Dean of Work ... Ms. Jennifer PAYNE
07 Director of Admissions ... Ms. Lynne BIRDSALL
04 Administrative Asst to President ... Ms. Michele MARTIN
10 Comptroller/Dir Student Accounts ... Ms. Deborah CLARK
08 Librarian ... Ms. Petra VOGEL
18 Director of Facilities ... Mr. Steve SMITH
38 Director Student Counseling ... Mr. Leland PETERSON
32 Dean of Students ... Ms. Jill FINEIS
30 Director Advancement ... Mr. Tim PATTERSON
06 Registrar ... Ms. Laurie LAGGNER
24 Director of Media Relations ... Mr. Tim PATTERSON

University of Vermont (H)

South Prospect Street, Burlington VT 05405-0160
County: Chittenden FICE Identification: 003696
Unit ID: 231174
Telephone: (802) 656-3131 Carnegie Class: RU/H
FAX Number: N/A Calendar System: Semester
URL: www.uvm.edu
Established: 1791 Annual Undergrad Tuition & Fees (In-State): $15,284
Enrollment: 13,478 Coed
Affiliation or Control: State IRS Status: 501(c)3
Highest Offering: Doctorate

Program: Liberal Arts And General; Teacher Preparatory; Professional
Accreditation: EH, BUS, CACREP, CLPSY, DIETC, DIETD, ENG, MED, MT, NMT, NURSE, PTA, RTT, SP, SW, TED

01 President ... Dr. E. Thomas SULLIVAN
05 Senior Vice President & Provost ... Dr. Jane E. KNODELL
10 VP for Finance & Administration ... Mr. Richard H. CATE
32 VP University Rels & Campus Life ... Dr. Thomas J. GUSTAFSON
46 VP Research & Dean Graduate Studies ... Dr. Domenico GRASSO
102 CEO & President The UVM Foundation ... Mr. O. Richard BUNDY, III
43 VP Legal Affairs & General Counsel ... Ms. Francine T. BAZLUKE
84 Vice Pres Enrollment Management ... Mr. Christopher H. LUCIER
20 Assoc Prov Faculty & International ... Dr. Gayle R. NUNLEY
20 Assoc Provost Curricular Affairs ... Dr. Brian V. REED
28 Chief Diversity Officer ... Dr. Wanda R. HEADING-GRANT
100 VP for Executive Operations ... Dr. Gary L. DERR
18 Assoc VP Admin & Facility Services ... Mr. William P. BALLARD
15 Assoc VP for Human Resources ... Ms. Barbara L. JOHNSON
35 AVP Campus Life & Dean of Students ... Dr. David A. NESTOR
29 Assoc VP for Alumni Relations ... Mr. Alan E. RYEA
63 Dean College of Medicine ... Dr. Frederick C. MORIN, III
66 Dean Nursing & Health Sciences ... Dr. Patricia A. PRELOCK
49 Dean Arts & Sciences ... Dr. Antonio CEPEDA-BENITO
47 Dean Agriculture & Life Sciences ... Dr. Thomas C. VOGELMANN
54 Int Dean Engineering & Math Sci ... Dr. Bernard F. COLE
53 Dean Education & Social Services ... Dr. Fayneese S. MILLER
50 Dean Business Administration ... Dr. Sanjay SHARMA
92 Dean Honors College ... Dr. S. Abu RIZVI
65 Dean Environment & Natural Resource ... Dr. Mary C. WATZIN
56 Dean Extension ... Dr. Douglas O. LANTAGNE
51 Dean Continuing Education ... Ms. Cynthia L. BELLIVEAU
08 Dean Libraries & Learning Resources ... Ms. Mara R. SAULE
06 Registrar ... Mr. Keith P. WILLIAMS
09 Director Institutional Research ... Dr. John F. RYAN
27 Director University Communications ... Mr. Enrique CORREDERA
13 Director Computing & Info Tech ... Dr. David TODD
25 Assoc VP Research Administration ... Ms. Ruth A. FARRELL
21 University Budget Director ... Mr. Alberto CITARELLA
19 Chief of Police Services ... Ms. Lianne M. TUOMEY
41 Director of Athletics ... Dr. Robert CORRAN
36 Director Career Services ... Ms. Pamela K. GARDNER
23 Director Ctr for Health & Wellbeing ... Dr. Jon K. PORTER
38 Counsel/Psych Services Program Dir ... Dr. Todd N. WEINMAN
39 Director Residential Life ... Ms. Stacey A. MILLER
40 Director University Bookstore ... Mr. Jay E. MENNINGER
85 Director Intl Education Services ... Ms. Kimberly A. HOWARD
30 COO & VP The UVM Foundation ... Mr. Shane M. JACOBSON
44 Assoc Director Planned Giving ... Ms. Becky P. ARNOLD
07 Director Graduate Admissions ... Mr. Ralph M. SWENSON, III
07 Director Undergraduate Admissions ... Dr. Elizabeth A. WISER
37 Director Student Financial Services ... Ms. Marie D. JOHNSON
96 Director Procurement Services ... Ms. Natalie L. GUILLETTE
94 Director Women's Center ... Ms. LuAnn K. ROLLEY
24 Access/Media Services Librarian ... Mr. Aaron F. NICHOLS
101 Board of Trustees Coordinator ... Ms. Corinne B. THOMPSON

Vermont College of Fine Arts (A)

36 College Street, Montpelier VT 05602-3145

County: Washington | FICE Identification: 003697 | Unit ID: 455992

Telephone: (802) 828-8600 | Carnegie Class: Assoc/PrivNFP4
FAX Number: (802) 828-8649 | Calendar System: Semester
URL: www.vcfa.edu
Established: 2008 | Annual Graduate Tuition & Fees: $19,619
Enrollment: 319 | Coed
Affiliation or Control: Independent Non-Profit | IRS Status: 501(c)3
Highest Offering: Master's; No Undergraduates
Program: Liberal Arts And General
Accreditation: EH

01 President ... Mr. Thomas Christopher GREENE
05 Academic Dean ... Mr. Matthew MONK
10 Chief Financial Ofcr/VP for Admin ... Ms. Erica METZGER HARE
26 Exec Dir of External Relations ... Ms. Lyn CHAMBERLIN

Vermont Law School (B)

164 Chelsea Street, PO Box 96, South Royalton VT 05068-0096

County: Windsor | FICE Identification: 011934 | Unit ID: 231147

Telephone: (802) 831-1000 | Carnegie Class: Spec/Law
FAX Number: (802) 831-1163 | Calendar System: Semester
URL: www.vermontlaw.edu
Established: 1972 | Annual Graduate Tuition & Fees: $45,207
Enrollment: 717 | Coed
Affiliation or Control: Independent Non-Profit | IRS Status: 501(c)3
Highest Offering: First Professional Degree; No Undergraduates
Program: Professional
Accreditation: EH, LAW

01 President & Dean ... Mr. Marc MIHALY
05 Vice Dean for Academic Affairs ... Mr. Gil KUJOVICH
36 VP Operations/Office Career Svcs ... Mr. Dennis STERN
10 Vice President for Finance & Admin ... Ms. Lorraine ATWOOD
20 Dep Vice Dean for Academic Affairs ... Mr. Mark LATHAM
88 Asoc Dn Env Law Pgm/Dir Env Law Ctr ... Mr. John ECHEVERRIA
32 Assoc Dean Student Affs & Diversity ... Ms. Shirley JEFFERSON
84 Assoc Dean for Enrollment Mgmt ... Ms. Magy KELLOGG
30 Exec Director Inst Advancement ... Mr. Matt RIZZO
20 Asst Dean for Academic Affairs ... Ms. Clara GIMENEZ
101 Secretary of the Institution/Board ... Ms. Kim EVANS
15 Director Human Resources ... Ms. Diane HAYES
08 Dir Cornell Library & Professor ... Mr. Carl A. YIRKA
21 Comptroller ... Mr. James OUELLETTE
06 Dir of Academic Proc & Registrar ... Ms. Magy KELLOGG
37 Associate Director of Financial Aid ... Ms. Patricia BRIGGS
18 Physical Plant Director ... Ms. Lori CAMPBELL
26 Dir of Marketing/Communications ... Ms. Carol WESTBERG
13 Director of Information Technology ... Mr. Duncan SUTHERLAND
04 Exec Asst to the President/Dean ... Ms. Rachel SAUERWEIN
40 Manager Barrister's Bookstore ... Ms. Amy MCDOWELL

*Vermont State Colleges System Office (C)

PO Box 7, Montpelier VT 05601

County: Washington | FICE Identification: 029162 | Unit ID: 231156

Telephone: (802) 241-2520 | Carnegie Class: N/A
FAX Number: N/A
URL: www.vsc.edu

01 Chancellor ... Mr. Timothy J. DONOVAN
04 Exec Assistant to the Chancellor ... Ms. Julie MASSUCCO
43 Vice President/General Counsel ... Mr. William REEDY
10 Vice Pres/Chief Financial Officer ... Mr. Thomas ROBBINS
86 Director Cmty Rels & Public Policy ... Mr. Daniel SMITH
27 Chief Information Officer ... Ms. Linda HILTON
18 Director of Facilities ... Mr. Richard ETHIER
91 Director Admin Information Systems ... Ms. Dianne POLLACK
13 Director of System Info Tech ... Mr. Rick BLOOD
15 Director of Human Resources ... Ms. Nancy SHAW
09 Director of Institutional Research ... Ms. Hope SWANSON
88 Director of Payroll/Benefits ... Ms. Tracy SWEET

*Castleton State College (D)

62 Alumni Drive, Castleton VT 05735-4454

County: Rutland | FICE Identification: 003683 | Unit ID: 230834

Telephone: (802) 468-5611 | Carnegie Class: Bac/A&S
FAX Number: (802) 468-6470 | Calendar System: Semester
URL: www.castleton.edu
Established: 1787 | Annual Undergrad Tuition & Fees (In-State): $9,668
Enrollment: 2,192 | Coed
Affiliation or Control: State | IRS Status: 501(c)3
Highest Offering: Master's
Program: Liberal Arts And General; Teacher Preparatory
Accreditation: EH, ADNUR, SW

02 President ... Mr. David S. WOLK
04 Exec Assistant to the President ... Ms. Rita B. GENO
05 Academic Dean ... Dr. Tony PEFFER
11 Dean of Administration ... Mr. Scott DIKEMAN
10 Controller ... Ms. Heidi WHITNEY
32 Dean of Students ... Mr. Dennis PROULX
20 Dean of Education ... Dr. Honoree FLEMING
84 Dean of Enrollment ... Mr. Maurice OUIMET
26 Director of Communications ... Mr. Ennis DULING
15 Director of Human Resources ... Ms. Janet HAZELTON
35 Assistant Dean for Campus Life ... Ms. Victoria ANGIS
06 Registrar ... Ms. Lori PATTEN
08 Director Calvin Coolidge Library ... Ms. Sandra DULING
37 Director Student Financial Aid ... Ms. Kathy O'MEARA
53 Director of Student Teaching ... Mr. Tim CLEARY
18 Director of Physical Plant ... Mr. Chuck LAVOIE
30 Director of Development ... Mr. George MCGURL
36 Dir of Career Planning/Placement ... Ms. Judith CARRUTHERS
23 Wellness Center Director ... Ms. Martha COULTER
38 Director Student Counseling ... Vacant

*Community College of Vermont (E)

PO Box 489, Montpelier VT 05601

County: Washington | FICE Identification: 011167 | Unit ID: 230861

Telephone: (802) 828-2800 | Carnegie Class: Assoc/Pub-R-L
FAX Number: (802) 828-2805 | Calendar System: Semester
URL: www.ccv.edu
Established: 1970 | Annual Undergrad Tuition & Fees (In-State): $6,790
Enrollment: 7,116 | Coed
Affiliation or Control: State | IRS Status: 501(c)3
Highest Offering: Associate Degree
Program: Occupational; 2-Year Principally Bachelor's Creditable
Accreditation: EH

02 President ... Ms. Joyce M. JUDY
03 Executive Dean ... Ms. Susan P. HENRY
11 Dean of Administration ... Dr. Barbara MARTIN
05 Dean of Academic Services ... Ms. Linda GABRIELSON
32 Dean of Student Services ... Ms. Deborah STEWART
84 Assoc Dean Enrollment Services ... Ms. Pam CHISHOLM
20 Associate Academic Dean ... Ms. Hester FULLER
20 Associate Academic Dean ... Ms. Darlene MURPHY
20 Associate Academic Dean ... Ms. Diane HERMANN-ARTIM
12 Exec Director of Academic Center ... Ms. Penne CIARALDI
12 Exec Director of Academic Center ... Mr. Elmer KIMBALL
12 Exec Director of Academic Center ... Ms. Dee STEFFAN
12 Exec Director of Academic Center ... Ms. Tapp BARNHILL
24 Dean of Learning Technologies ... Mr. Eric SAKAI
15 Director Personnel Services ... Mrs. Lisa YAEGER
06 Registrar ... Mr. Thomas ARNER
07 Director of Admissions ... Mr. Adam WARRINGTON
09 Dir Institutional Research/Planning ... Ms. Laura MASSELL
88 Director Student Support Services ... Ms. Heather WEINSTEIN
29 Director Alumni Relations/Develop ... Vacant
26 Chief Public Relations Officer ... Ms. Robin DUTCHER
10 Chief Business Officer ... Ms. Lorei DAWSON
18 Chief Facilities/Physical Plant ... Mr. Larry ELLIOTT
88 Director of Secondary Initiatives ... Ms. Natalie SEARLE
36 Director of Career Training Program ... Ms. Mary LOTHROP
26 Dir of Marketing/Communications ... Ms. Janette SHAFFER

*Johnson State College (F)

337 College Hill, Johnson VT 05656-9898

County: Lamoille | FICE Identification: 003688 | Unit ID: 230913

Telephone: (802) 635-2356 | Carnegie Class: Master's S
FAX Number: (802) 635-1230 | Calendar System: Semester
URL: www.jsc.edu
Established: 1828 | Annual Undergrad Tuition & Fees (In-State): $9,864
Enrollment: 1,859 | Coed
Affiliation or Control: State | IRS Status: 501(c)3
Highest Offering: Master's
Program: 2-Year Principally Bachelor's Creditable; Liberal Arts And General; Teacher Preparatory; Professional
Accreditation: EH

02 President ... Ms. Barbara E. MURPHY
05 Academic Dean ... Dr. Dan REGAN
11 Dean Administration/Chief Tech Ofcr ... Ms. Sharron R. SCOTT
32 Dean of Students ... Dr. David BERGH
84 Dean of Enrollment Services ... Ms. Penny HOWRIGAN
35 Asst Dean of Students ... Ms. Michele WHITMORE
06 Registrar ... Mr. Douglas EASTMAN
51 Co-Director External Degree Program ... Mr. David CAVANAGH
51 Co-Director of External Degree Prgm ... Ms. Valerie EDWARDS
18 Director of Physical Plant ... Mr. Woody DIONNE
41 Director of Athletics & Recreation ... Mr. Jamey VENTURA
38 Director of Counseling Services ... Ms. Cynthia HENNARD
30 Director Development/Alumni Rels ... Ms. Lauren PHILIE
36 Director Advising/Career Svcs ... Ms. Sara KINERSON
89 Director of First-Year Experience ... Ms. Margo WARDEN
19 Director Safety & Security ... Mr. Michael PALAGONIA
26 Dir College Communications ... Ms. Deborah BOUTON
37 Director Student Financial Aid ... Ms. Lisa CUMMINGS
15 Director Human Resources ... Ms. Sharon SCOTT
08 Librarian ... Mr. Joseph FARARA
79 Chair Humanities ... Dr. Frederick WISEMAN
53 Chair Education ... Dr. David MCGOUGH
65 Co-Chair Environ/Health Sciences ... Dr. Hans HAVERKAMP
65 Co-Chair Environ/Health Sciences ... Mr. Brad MOSKOWITZ
57 Co-Chair Fine & Performing Arts ... Dr. Russell LONGTIN
57 Co-Chair Fine & Performing Arts ... Mr. Ken LESLIE
50 Co-Chair Business/Economics ... Dr. James BLACK
50 Co-Chair Business/Economics ... Mr. Henrique CEZAR
60 Co-Chair Writing/Literature ... Dr. Andrea PERHAM
81 Chair Mathematics ... Dr. Julie THEORET
83 Co-Chair Behavioral Sciences ... Dr. Susan GREEN
83 Co-Chair Behavioral Sciences ... Dr. Eleanor WEBBER

*Lyndon State College (G)

1001 College Road, PO Box 919, Lyndonville VT 05851-0919

County: Caledonia | FICE Identification: 003689 | Unit ID: 230931

Telephone: (802) 626-6200 | Carnegie Class: Bac/Diverse
FAX Number: (802) 626-9770 | Calendar System: Semester
URL: www.lyndonstate.edu
Established: 1911 | Annual Undergrad Tuition & Fees (In-State): $9,864
Enrollment: 1,422 | Coed
Affiliation or Control: State | IRS Status: 501(c)3
Highest Offering: Master's
Program: Liberal Arts And General; Teacher Preparatory; Professional
Accreditation: EH, EXSC

02 President ... Dr. Joseph A. BERTOLINO
05 Dean Academic & Student Affairs ... Dr. Donna DALTON
11 Dean of Administration ... Mr. Wayne T. HAMILTON
20 Associate Academic Dean ... Dr. John R. KASCENSKA
30 Dean of Institutional Advancement ... Mr. Robert E. WHITTAKER
07 Director of Admissions ... Mr. Vincent U. MALONEY
32 Associate Dean for Student Affairs ... Mr. Jonathan M. DAVIS
18 Director of Physical Plant ... Mr. Thomas R. ARCHER
91 Chief Technology Officer ... Mr. Michael A. DENTE
29 Director of Development & Alumni ... Ms. Hannah J. MANLEY
21 Controller ... Ms. Sheilah M. LADD
08 Library Director ... Mr. Garet B. NELSON
20 Assistant Academic Dean ... Ms. Debra A. HALE
41 Director of Athletics ... Mr. Christopher T. UMMER
37 Director of Financial Aid ... Ms. Tanya W. BRADLEY
36 Director of Career Services ... Ms. Linda A. WACHOLDER
19 Director Public Safety ... Mr. George B. HACKING
88 Director Student Academic Support ... Mr. Robert G. MCCABE
88 Director of Broadcast Operations ... Ms. Darlene R. BOLDUC
88 Dir of Student Academic Development ... Ms. Debra M. BAILIN
26 Director Communications & Marketing ... Mr. Keith B. CHAMBERLIN
88 Director of Advising Resources ... Ms. Kathleen E. GOLD
89 Director of First-Year Experience ... Ms. Donna J. KEELY
15 Director Human Resources ... Ms. Sandra L. FRANZ

*Vermont Technical College (A)

PO Box 500, Randolph Center VT 05061-0500
County: Orange FICE Identification: 003698
Unit ID: 231165
Telephone: (802) 728-1000 Carnegie Class: Bac/Assoc
FAX Number: (802) 728-1390 Calendar System: Semester
URL: www.vtc.edu
Established: 1866 Annual Undergrad Tuition & Fees (In-State): $12,344
Enrollment: 1,607 Coed
Affiliation or Control: State IRS Status: 501(c)3
Highest Offering: Baccalaureate
Program: Occupational; 2-Year Principally Bachelor's Creditable; Professional; Technical Emphasis
Accreditation: EH, ADNUR, DH, ENGT, PNUR

02 President .... Dr. Philip CONROY, JR.
05 Dean Academic Affairs .... Ms. Patricia MENCHINI
11 Dean of Administration .... Mr. Geoffrey LINDEMER
32 Dean of Student Affairs .... Dr. Eric BRAUN
13 Chief Technology Officer .... Mr. Michael WOODEN
88 Exec Dir Strategic Col Operations .... Mr. Jay PATERSON
30 Assoc Dean Inst Advancement .... Ms. Martha TROMBLEY OAKES
35 Assistant Dean Student Life .... Ms. Mary Kathryn JUSKIEWICZ
06 Registrar .... Ms. Sarah LEVIN
37 Director Financial Aid .... Ms. Catherine MCCULLOUGH
29 Director Alumni Relations .... Ms. Carrie CLEMENT
23 Coordinator Health Services .... Vacant
19 Director Security/Safety .... Mr. Emile FREDETTE
18 Director Physical Plant .... Mr. Theodore MANAZIR
36 Career Counseling/Placement .... Ms. Lauri SYBEL
66 Director Nursing Education .... Ms. Anna GERAC
15 Director of Human Resources .... Ms. Pamela ANKUDA
26 Director of Marketing .... Ms. Michelle BARBER
40 Manager Bookstore .... Mr. Joe HIRAK

VIRGINIA

Advanced Technology Institute (B)

5700 Southern Boulevard, Virginia Beach VA 23462-2409
County: City of Virginia Beach FICE Identification: 031275
Unit ID: 231411
Telephone: (757) 490-1241 Carnegie Class: Assoc/PrivFP
FAX Number: (757) 499-5929 Calendar System: Semester
URL: www.auto.edu
Established: 1993 Annual Undergrad Tuition & Fees: $23,175
Enrollment: 600 Coed
Affiliation or Control: Proprietary IRS Status: Proprietary
Highest Offering: Associate Degree
Program: Occupational; Technical Emphasis
Accreditation: ACCSC

01 Campus President .... Mr. Dick DAIGLE
05 Chief Academic Officer .... Mr. Chenek PICKA
07 Director of Admissions .... Mr. Joe ARELLANO
32 Director of Student Services .... Mr. Kirk CLAYTON
37 Director Student Financial Aid .... Mr. Chad MARTS

Appalachian College of Pharmacy (C)

1060 Dragon Road, Oakwood VA 24631
County: Buchanan Identification: 667019
Unit ID: 449922
Telephone: (276) 498-4190 Carnegie Class: Spec/Health
FAX Number: (276) 498-4193 Calendar System: Semester
URL: www.acpharm.org
Established: 2003 Annual Graduate Tuition & Fees: $35,800
Enrollment: 219 Coed
Affiliation or Control: Independent Non-Profit IRS Status: 501(c)3
Highest Offering: Doctorate; No Undergraduates
Program: Professional
Accreditation: SC, PHAR

01 President .... Mr. Michael G. MCGLOTHLIN
05 Dean .... Dr. Susan L. MAYHEW

Appalachian School of Law (D)

PO Box 2825, Grundy VA 24614-2825
County: Buchanan FICE Identification: 035593
Unit ID: 432348
Telephone: (800) 895-7411 Carnegie Class: Spec/Law
FAX Number: (276) 935-8261 Calendar System: Semester
URL: www.asl.edu
Established: 1995 Annual Undergrad Tuition & Fees: $31,000
Enrollment: 327 Coed
Affiliation or Control: Independent Non-Profit IRS Status: 501(c)3
Highest Offering: First Professional Degree
Program: Professional
Accreditation: LAW

01 Dean & President .... Ms. Lucy MCGOUGH
08 Director of Library .... Mr. Charlie CONDON
36 Director of Career Services .... Ms. Janie CASTLE
13 Director of Information Services .... Mr. Brian PRESLEY
31 Director of Community Services .... Ms. Jina M. SAULS
32 Director of Student Services .... Ms. Mary RAGLAND

Argosy University, Washington DC (E)

1550 Wilson Boulevard, Suite 600,
Arlington VA 22209-2435
County: Arlington Identification: 666788
Unit ID: 419457
Telephone: (703) 526-5800 Carnegie Class: Spec/Health
FAX Number: (703) 243-8973 Calendar System: Semester
URL: www.argosy.edu/washingtondc
Established: 1994 Annual Undergrad Tuition & Fees: $13,224
Enrollment: 1,142 Coed
Affiliation or Control: Proprietary IRS Status: Proprietary
Highest Offering: Doctorate
Program: Professional
Accreditation: &WC, CACREP, CLPSY

01 Campus President .... David EREKSON
05 Vice President of Academic Affairs .... Cynthia WORTHEN
07 Sr Director of Admissions .... Frank MARRANZINI
32 Director of Student Services .... Gretchen EITT
11 Dir Admin & Financial Services .... Vacant
15 Human Resources .... Lan NGUYEN
37 Director of Student Finance .... Matthew MONSEES
06 Registrar .... Tammy COHEN

† Regional accreditation is carried under the parent institution in Orange, CA.

Atlantic University (F)

215 67th Street, Virginia Beach VA 23451-8101
County: Virginia Beach Identification: 666653
Unit ID: 231402
Telephone: (757) 631-8101 Carnegie Class: Not Classified
FAX Number: (757) 631-8096 Calendar System: Trimester
URL: www.atlanticuniv.edu
Established: 1930 Annual Graduate Tuition & Fees: $13,260
Enrollment: 13,000 Coed
Affiliation or Control: Independent Non-Profit IRS Status: 501(c)3
Highest Offering: Master's; No Undergraduates
Program: Professional
Accreditation: DETC

01 CEO .... Kevin TODESCHI
05 Director of Academic Affairs .... Dr. Nancy L. ZINGRONE
32 Dean Student Services & Admissions .... Candis COLLINS
10 Educational Business Manager .... James VAN AUKEN
06 Registrar .... Lynne MICELI
84 Enrollment Coordinator .... Nicole ARMSTRONG
51 Continuing Education Coordinator .... Rachel ALVIDREZ

Averett University (G)

420 W Main Street, Danville VA 24541-3692
County: Independent City FICE Identification: 003702
Unit ID: 231420
Telephone: (434) 791-5600 Carnegie Class: Bac/Diverse
FAX Number: (434) 791-5637 Calendar System: Semester
URL: www.averett.edu
Established: 1859 Annual Undergrad Tuition & Fees: $25,950
Enrollment: 2,568 Coed
Affiliation or Control: Independent Non-Profit IRS Status: 501(c)3
Highest Offering: Master's
Program: Liberal Arts And General; Teacher Preparatory
Accreditation: SC

01 President .... Dr. Tiffany M. FRANKS
32 Executive Vice President .... Mr. Charles S. HARRIS
05 Vice Pres for Academic Affairs .... Dr. Janet LAUGHLIN
10 Vice President Business & Finance .... Mr. Thomas DAVIS
30 Vice Pres Institutional Advancement .... Mr. Albert RAWLEY
15 Vice President for Human Resources .... Mrs. Kathie TUNE
84 Vice Pres Enrollment Management .... Dr. Stuart JONES
37 Director Student Financial Services .... Mr. Carl BRADSHER
21 Controller .... Mr. Andy FITCH
08 Director of Library .... Ms. Elaine DAY
36 Director of Career Services .... Ms. Petrina CARTER
06 Registrar .... Mrs. Janet ROBERSON
26 Dir of Marketing/Communications .... Vacant
29 Director Alumni Relations .... Mr. Dan HAYES
09 Dir Institutional Research/Effect .... Dr. Metta ALSOBROOK

Aviation Institute of Maintenance (H)

2211 S Military Highway, Chesapeake VA 23320
County: Chesapeake City FICE Identification: 031263
Unit ID: 427973
Telephone: (757) 363-2121 Carnegie Class: Assoc/PrivFP
FAX Number: (757) 363-2044 Calendar System: Other
URL: www.aviationmaintenance.edu
Established: 1993 Annual Undergrad Tuition & Fees: $13,447
Enrollment: 391 Coed
Affiliation or Control: Proprietary IRS Status: Proprietary
Highest Offering: Associate Degree
Program: Occupational
Accreditation: ACCSC

01 President .... Mr. Rondell DAVIS

Aviation Institute of Maintenance (I)

10640 Davidson Place, Manassas VA 20109
County: Prince William FICE Identification: 038834
Telephone: (703) 257-5515 Carnegie Class: Not Classified
FAX Number: (703) 257-5523 Calendar System: Quarter
URL: www.aviationmaintenance.edu
Established: N/A Annual Undergrad Tuition & Fees: $38,610
Enrollment: 219 Coed
Affiliation or Control: Proprietary IRS Status: Proprietary
Highest Offering: Associate Degree
Program: Occupational; Technical Emphasis
Accreditation: ACCSC

01 Director of Education .... Mr. Michael CAROTHERS

Baptist Theological Seminary at Richmond (J)

3400 Brook Road, Richmond VA 23227-4536
County: Independent City FICE Identification: 031169
Unit ID: 366793
Telephone: (804) 355-8135 Carnegie Class: Spec/Faith
FAX Number: (804) 355-8182 Calendar System: Semester
URL: www.btsr.edu
Established: 1991 Annual Graduate Tuition & Fees: $10,395
Enrollment: 110 Coed
Affiliation or Control: Independent Non-Profit IRS Status: 501(c)3
Highest Offering: Doctorate; No Undergraduates
Program: Professional; Religious Emphasis
Accreditation: THEOL

01 President .... Dr. Ronald W. CRAWFORD
05 Dean .... Dr. Israel GALINDO
30 VP Institutional Advancement .... Mr. Timothy Bruce HEILMAN
10 Dir Business Affairs & Facilities .... Dr. James F. PEAK, JR.
07 Director Admissions & Recruitment .... Ms. Tiffany KELLOGG PITTMAN
06 Registrar .... Ms. Erin SPENGEMAN

Bethel College (K)

1705 Todds Lane, Hampton VA 23666
County: Hampton City FICE Identification: 041538
Unit ID: 458113
Telephone: (757) 826-1883 Carnegie Class: Not Classified
FAX Number: (757) 826-0458 Calendar System: Semester
URL: www.bethel-college.com
Established: 2004 Annual Undergrad Tuition & Fees: $6,075
Enrollment: 87 Coed
Affiliation or Control: Assemblies Of God Church IRS Status: 501(c)3
Highest Offering: Baccalaureate
Program: Religious Emphasis
Accreditation: @BI

01 President .... Mr. Glenn REYNOLDS
05 Academic Dean .... Vacant
32 Dean of Students .... Dr. Jerry GOULD
06 Registrar .... Ms. Nanette BARTHOLOMEW
08 Library Director .... Ms. Janell SANFORD

Bluefield College (L)

3000 College Drive, Bluefield VA 24605-1799
County: Tazewell FICE Identification: 003703
Unit ID: 231554
Telephone: (276) 326-3682 Carnegie Class: Bac/Diverse
FAX Number: (276) 326-4288 Calendar System: Semester
URL: www.bluefield.edu
Established: 1922 Annual Undergrad Tuition & Fees: $21,060
Enrollment: 686 Coed
Affiliation or Control: Baptist IRS Status: 501(c)3
Highest Offering: Baccalaureate
Program: Liberal Arts And General; Teacher Preparatory
Accreditation: SC, TEAC

01 President .... Dr. David W. OLIVE
04 Assistant to the President .... Mrs. Diane T. SHOTT
05 VP for Academic Affairs .... Dr. Robert C. SHIPPEY, JR.
30 VP for Advancement .... Mrs. Mary R. BLANKENSHIP
10 VP for Finance & Admin .... Mrs. Sarah BEAMER
32 VP for Student Development .... Rev. David TAYLOR
84 VP for Enrollment Management .... Mr. Trent ARGO
07 Director of Trad Admissions .... Mr. Mark HIPES
07 Director of Adult Admissions .... Mrs. Cathy PAYNE
06 Registrar .... Ms. Amanda PARKS
08 Director of Library Services .... Ms. Nora LOCKETT
26 Director of Public Relations .... Mr. Chris SHOEMAKER
29 Director of Alumni Relations .... Mr. Joshua CLINE
09 Director of Institutional Research .... Mrs. Amanda JORDAN
37 Director of Financial Aid .... Mrs. Debbie CHECCHIO
42 Campus Minister .... Rev. David TAYLOR
41 Athletic Director .... Mr. Peter DRYER
40 Bookstore Manager .... Mrs. Judy VANNOY
18 Director of Maintenance .... Mr. Blair TAYLOR
19 Director of Campus Safety .... Dr. Kelly WALLS
15 Human Resources Coordinator .... Mrs. Karen THURMER

Bon Secours Memorial College of Nursing (A)

8550 Magellan Pkwy, Ste 1100, Richmond VA 23227
County: Henrico   FICE Identification: 010043
Telephone: (804) 627-5300   Carnegie Class: Not Classified
FAX Number: (804) 627-5330   Calendar System: Semester
URL: www.bsmcon.edu
Established: 1961   Annual Undergrad Tuition & Fees: $13,464
Enrollment: 340   Coed
Affiliation or Control: Independent Non-Profit   IRS Status: 501(c)3
Highest Offering: Baccalaureate
Program: Liberal Arts And General; Nursing Emphasis
Accreditation: ACICS, NURSE

05 Vice Pres Academic Affairs/Provost ....Dr. Melanie H. GREEN
66 Dean of the College ....Dr. Susan BODIN
20 Asst Dean of Curriculum/Instruction ....Vacant
11 Asst Dean of Administration ....Ms. Carol GRECO
32 Asst Dean of Student Services ....Dr. Regina WELCH

Bridgewater College (B)

402 E College Street, Bridgewater VA 22812-1599
County: Rockingham   FICE Identification: 003704
Unit ID: 231581
Telephone: (540) 828-8000   Carnegie Class: Bac/A&S
FAX Number: (540) 828-5479   Calendar System: 4/1/4
URL: www.bridgewater.edu
Established: 1880   Annual Undergrad Tuition & Fees: $28,000
Enrollment: 1,648   Coed
Affiliation or Control: Church Of The Brethren   IRS Status: 501(c)3
Highest Offering: Baccalaureate
Program: Liberal Arts And General; Teacher Preparatory
Accreditation: SC

01 Interim President ....Mr. Roy W. FERGUSON, JR.
05 Vice Pres/Dean of Academic Affairs ..... Dr. Carol A. SCHEPPARD
10 Vice Pres for Finance & Treasurer ....Ms. Anne B. KEELER
30 Vice President for Inst Advancement ....Vacant
26 Dir of Marketing & Communications .... Ms. Abbie PARKHURST
84 Vice President for Enrollment Mgmt .... Mr. Reggie WEBB
44 Director of Major Gifts ....Vacant
18 Director of Sustainability .... Mr. Teshome H. MOLALENGE
40 Bookstore Manager ....Ms. Brandi LIVESAY
20 Associate Dean of Academic Affairs ....Dr. Edward W. HUFFSTETLER
32 Dean of Students ....Dr. William D. MIRACLE
36 Director of Career Services .... Ms. Sherry TALBOTT
88 Director of Academic Support Svcs .... Dr. Raymond W. STUDWELL, II
42 Chaplain ....Rev. Robert R. MILLER
07 Director of Admissions ....Mr. Jarrett L. SMITH
37 Director of Financial Aid ....Mr. Scott D. MORRISON
21 Director of Budget & Analysis ....Mr. Jeffrey FIKE
13 Director of Info Tech Center ....Ms. Kristy K. RHEA
41 Director of Athletics ....Mr. Curtis L. KENDALL
38 Director of Counseling Services ....Mr. Randall HOOK
29 Director of Alumni Relations ....Ms. Ellen B. MILLER
09 Director of Institutional Research ....Ms. Dawn S. DALBOW
15 Director of Human Resources ....Ms. Victoria L. INGRAM
08 Library Director ....Mr. Andrew L. PEARSON
06 Registrar .... Ms. Cynthia K. HOWDYSHELL
21 Controller .... Ms. Mary S. SCHWAB
27 Editor/Dir of Media Relations ....Mr. Charles R. CULBERTSON
18 Director of Facilities ....Mr. David R. VANDEVANDER
19 Campus Police Chief ....Mr. Nicholas P. PICERNO
28 Minority Mentor ....Mr. James E. RAEFORD
23 Director of Student Health Services ....Ms. Paige FRENCH
35 Associate Dean of Students .... Ms. Crystal LYNN
28 Director of Multicultural Services ....Ms. Stephanie WILSON
88 Director of Dining Services ....Vacant

Bryant & Stratton College (C)

8141 Hull Street Road, North Chesterfield VA 23235-6411
County: Chesterfield   Identification: 666496
Unit ID: 231828
Telephone: (804) 745-2444   Carnegie Class: Bac/Assoc
FAX Number: (804) 745-6884   Calendar System: Trimester
URL: www.bryantstratton.edu
Established: 1854   Annual Undergrad Tuition & Fees: $16,570
Enrollment: 1,006   Coed
Affiliation or Control: Proprietary   IRS Status: Proprietary
Highest Offering: Baccalaureate
Program: Occupational; Business Emphasis
Accreditation: &M, MAC

01 Campus Director ....Ms. Beth M. MURPHY
05 Dean of Instruction ....Ms. Darlene M. LACHUT
32 Dean of Student Services ....Ms. Deborah J. MERRITT
36 Career Service Director ....Ms. Brenda SANDS HINES
07 Director of Admissions ....Mr. Rayford GRADY
10 Business Office Director .... Ms. Ditamichelle TERRY
06 Registrar ....Ms. Teresa TURNER

† Regional accreditation is carried under the parent institution (corporate office) in Buffalo, NY.

Bryant & Stratton College (D)

301 Centre Pointe Drive, Virginia Beach VA 23462-4417
County: Independent City   FICE Identification: 010061
Unit ID: 231785
Telephone: (757) 499-7900   Carnegie Class: Bac/Assoc
FAX Number: (757) 499-9977   Calendar System: Semester
URL: www.bryantstratton.edu
Established: 1854   Annual Undergrad Tuition & Fees: $16,050
Enrollment: 863   Coed
Affiliation or Control: Proprietary   IRS Status: Proprietary
Highest Offering: Baccalaureate
Program: 2-Year Principally Bachelor's Creditable; Business Emphasis
Accreditation: &M, MAC

01 Campus Director ....Mr. Lee H. JONES
10 Business Office Director ....Mr. Erik BLACKWELL
05 Dean of Instruction ....Ms. Vivian D. ROGERS
32 Dean of Student Services ....Ms. Anita WYCHE
07 Director of Admissions ....Ms. Deana SUTHERLAND
36 Career Services Director ....Ms. Ronda TOLL
88 Director of Military Programs .... Mr. Arch WALPOLE

† Regional accreditation is carried under the parent institution (corporate office) in Buffalo, NY.

California University of Management and Sciences Virginia (E)

400 North Washington Street, Falls Church VA 22046
County: Fairfax   Identification: 666734
Unit ID: 460075
Telephone: (703) 663-8088   Carnegie Class: Not Classified
FAX Number: (703) 663-8090   Calendar System: Quarter
URL: www.calums.edu/index_va.htm
Established: 2007   Annual Undergrad Tuition & Fees: N/A
Enrollment: N/A   Coed
Affiliation or Control: Independent Non-Profit   IRS Status: 501(c)3
Highest Offering: Master's
Program: Professional; Business Emphasis
Accreditation: ACICS

01 Branch Director ....Mr. Young KIM

† Branch campus of California University of Management and Sciences, Anaheim, CA.

Career Training Solutions (F)

10304 Spotsylvania Avenue, Ste. 400, Fredericksburg VA 22408-8605
County: Stafford   FICE Identification: 036543
Unit ID: 441858
Telephone: (540) 373-2200   Carnegie Class: Assoc/PrivFP
FAX Number: (540) 373-4465   Calendar System: Other
URL: www.careertrainingsolutions.com
Established: 2000   Annual Undergrad Tuition & Fees: N/A
Enrollment: 170   Coed
Affiliation or Control: Proprietary   IRS Status: Proprietary
Highest Offering: Associate Degree
Program: Occupational
Accreditation: COE

01 Chief Executive Officer/President ....Ms. A. Christine CARROLL

The Catholic Distance University (G)

120 E Colonial Highway, Hamilton VA 20158-9012
County: Loudoun   FICE Identification: 041242
Unit ID: 377430
Telephone: (540) 338-2700   Carnegie Class: Not Classified
FAX Number: (540) 338-4788   Calendar System: Trimester
URL: www.cdu.edu
Established: 1983   Annual Undergrad Tuition & Fees: $3,480
Enrollment: 800   Coed
Affiliation or Control: Independent Non-Profit   IRS Status: 501(c)3
Highest Offering: Master's
Program: Religious Emphasis
Accreditation: DETC

01 President ....Dr. Marianne E. MOUNT
58 Dean Graduate Programs ....Dr. Robert ROYAL
05 Undergraduate Dean ....Fr. Bevil BRAMWELL
88 Dean of Catechetical Programs .... Sr. Mary Margaret SCHLATHER
06 Graduate Registrar .... Ms. Judith WELSH
06 Undergraduate Registrar .... Mrs. Kathleen WOODDELL
08 Head Librarian ....Vacant
10 Director of Finance ....Mr. Donald FONG
30 Director of Development ....Vacant
26 Director of Communications .... Ms. Therese CASHEN
35 Director Student Affairs ....Vacant
07 Director of Admissions .... Ms. Carol CIULLO
29 Director Alumni Relations ....Vacant
37 Director Student Financial Aid ....Vacant
13 Director Computing Information Mgmt .... Mrs. Carol DALEY

Central Baptist Theological Seminary (H)

2221 Centerville Turnpike, Virginia Beach VA 23464-6847
County: Virginia Beach   FICE Identification: 039663
Telephone: (757) 479-3706   Carnegie Class: Not Classified
FAX Number: (757) 479-4232   Calendar System: Semester
URL: www.baptistseminary.edu
Established: 1995   Annual Undergrad Tuition & Fees: $4,320
Enrollment: 85   Coed
Affiliation or Control: Baptist   IRS Status: 501(c)3
Highest Offering: Master's
Program: Professional; Religious Emphasis
Accreditation: TRACS

01 Director of Operations ....Mr. Edward ESTES
05 Chief Academic Officer ....Mr. Eric LEHNER
06 Registrar/Director of Admissions .... Mr. Kyle DUNHAM
10 Chief Finance Officer ....Dr. Thomas KEISER
09 Dir Institutional Effectiveness .... Dr. Robert TOMENENDAL

Centura College (I)

7914 Midlothian Turnpike, North Chesterfield VA 23235
County: Chesterfield   FICE Identification: 031264
Unit ID: 427982
Telephone: (804) 330-0111   Carnegie Class: Assoc/PrivFP
FAX Number: (804) 330-3809   Calendar System: Other
URL: www.centuracollege.edu/college-campus/richmond-va-college.as
Established: 1992   Annual Undergrad Tuition & Fees: $14,880
Enrollment: 160   Coed
Affiliation or Control: Proprietary   IRS Status: Proprietary
Highest Offering: Associate Degree
Program: Occupational; 2-Year Principally Bachelor's Creditable
Accreditation: ACCSC

Centura College (J)

2697 Dean Drive, Suite 100, Virginia Beach VA 23452-7431
County: City of Virginia Beach   FICE Identification: 023344
Unit ID: 232016
Telephone: (757) 340-2121   Carnegie Class: Assoc/PrivFP4
FAX Number: (757) 340-9704   Calendar System: Other
URL: www.centura.edu
Established: 1969   Annual Undergrad Tuition & Fees: $13,512
Enrollment: 1,605   Coed
Affiliation or Control: Proprietary   IRS Status: Proprietary
Highest Offering: Baccalaureate
Program: Occupational
Accreditation: ACCSC

01 Director ....Ms. Beth HALL

Christendom College (K)

134 Christendom Drive, Front Royal VA 22630-6534
County: Warren   FICE Identification: 036653
Unit ID: 231703
Telephone: (540) 636-2900   Carnegie Class: Not Classified
FAX Number: (540) 636-1655   Calendar System: Semester
URL: www.christendom.edu
Established: 1977   Annual Undergrad Tuition & Fees: $21,600
Enrollment: 407   Coed
Affiliation or Control: Roman Catholic   IRS Status: 501(c)3
Highest Offering: Master's
Program: Liberal Arts And General
Accreditation: SC

01 President ....Dr. Timothy T. O'DONNELL
10 Exec Vice President Finance & Admin .... Mr. Mark C. MCSHURLEY
05 Vice President Academic Affairs ....Dr. Steven C. SNYDER
30 Vice President for Advancement ....Mr. John F. CISKANIK
18 Vice Pres Operations/Facility Plng ....Mr. Michael S. FOECKLER
32 Dean of Student Life .... Mr. Jesse DORMAN
20 Academic Dean ....Dr. Patrick KEATS
07 Director of Admissions & Marketing ...... Mr. Thomas MCFADDEN
06 Registrar ....Mr. Walter A. JANARO
08 Director of Christendom Library ......Mr. Andrew V. ARMSTRONG
37 Financial Aid Officer ....Mrs. Alisa L. POLK
29 Director Alumni & Career Devel ....Ms. Marie ANTUNES
13 Director of Computer Services ....Mr. Douglas S. BRIGGS
88 Registrar/Business Officer NDGS ....Miss Heidi KALIAN
41 Athletic Director ....Mr. Chris VANDERWOUDE
04 Assistant to the President ....Miss Melanie BAKER
58 Dean of the Graduate School .... Dr. Kristen BURNS

Christopher Newport University (L)

1 Avenue of the Arts, Newport News VA 23606-3072
County: Independent City   FICE Identification: 003706
Unit ID: 231712
Telephone: (757) 594-7000   Carnegie Class: Master's S
FAX Number: (757) 594-7713   Calendar System: Semester
URL: www.cnu.edu
Established: 1960   Annual Undergrad Tuition & Fees (In-State): $10,572
Enrollment: 4,966   Coed
Affiliation or Control: State   IRS Status: 501(c)3
Highest Offering: Master's
Program: Liberal Arts And General

Accreditation: SC, BUS, ENG, MUS, SW, THEA

01 President .... Sen. Paul S. TRIBLE
100 Chief of Staff .... Mrs. Cynthia R. PERRY
05 Provost .... Dr. Mark W. PADILLA
03 Executive Vice President .... Mr. William L. BRAUER
43 University Counsel .... Mr. William E. THRO
30 Vice Pres for Univ Advancement .... Mrs. Adelia P. THOMPSON
15 Director of Human Resources .... Mrs. Lorraine M. WESTPHAL
41 Interim Director of Athletics .... Mr. Jonathan S. WATERS
04 Exec Assistant to the President .... Mrs. Beverley D. MUELLER
10 University Comptroller .... Mrs. Diane REED
49 Dean College of Arts & Humanities .... Mr. Steven BREESE
83 Dean College of Social Sciences .... Dr. Robert E. COLVIN
88 Dean College Natural/Behav Sciences .... Dr. David C. DOUGHTY
07 Dean of Admissions .... Mr. Rob LANGE
06 Dean Enrollment Services/ Registrar .... Dr. Lisa D. DUNCAN RAINES
37 Associate Director of Financial Aid .... Ms. Clara E. JOHNSON
36 Director Center of Career Planning .... Ms. Elizabeth K. WESTLEY
35 Dean of Students .... Dr. Kevin M. HUGHES
39 Assistant Director of Housing .... Ms. Janine W. KENNELL
09 Director of Institutional Research .... Ms. Donna A. VARNER
13 Chief Information Officer .... Mr. Stephen S. CAMPBELL
08 University Librarian .... Ms. Mary SELLEN
19 Chief of University Police .... Mr. Jeffrey S. BROWN
21 Director of University Audit .... Ms. Faith D. BELOTE
18 Asst Director of Plant Operations .... Mr. Albert C. METZGAR
44 Sr Dir Advancement/Planned Giving .... Ms. Lucy L. LATCHUM
96 Director of Materiel Management .... Mr. Ryan A. FEREBEE
29 Director Alumni Rels/Univ Events .... Ms. Amie E. GRAHAM
26 Director of Public Relations .... Ms. Lori A. JACOBS
28 Director of EO/Faculty Recruitment .... Ms. Michelle L. MOODY
38 Exec Dir Counseling & HE Services .... Mr. William V. RITCHEY

College of William & Mary (A)

PO Box 8795, Williamsburg VA 23187-8795

County: Independent City FICE Identification: 003705
Unit ID: 231624
Telephone: (757) 221-4000 Carnegie Class: RU/H
FAX Number: (757) 221-1259 Calendar System: Semester
URL: www.wm.edu
Established: 1693 Annual Undergrad Tuition & Fees (In-State): $13,570
Enrollment: 8,200 Coed
Affiliation or Control: State IRS Status: 501(c)3
Highest Offering: Doctorate
Program: Liberal Arts And General; Teacher Preparatory; Professional
Accreditation: SC, BUS, BUSA, CACREP, IPSY, LAW, TED

01 President .... Mr. W. Taylor REVELEY, III
05 Provost .... Dr. Michael HALLERAN
11 Vice President for Administration .... Ms. Anna B. MARTIN
10 Vice President for Finance .... Mr. Samuel E. JONES
30 Vice President for Development .... Mr. Sean M. PIERI
45 Vice Pres for Strategic Initiatives .... Dr. James R. GOLDEN
32 Vice President for Student Affairs .... Dr. Virginia M. AMBLER
41 Director of Athletics .... Mr. Edward (Terry) C. DRISCOLL
29 Exec Vice Pres Alumni Association .... Ms. Karen R. COTTRELL
49 Dean Faculty of Arts & Sciences .... Dr. Katharine CONLEY
50 Dean School of Business Admin .... Dr. Lawrence B. PULLEY
53 Dean School of Education .... Dr. Virginia L. MCLAUGHLIN
61 Dean School of Law .... Mr. Davison M. DOUGLAS
88 Dean/Dir School of Marine Science .... Dr. John T. WELLS
08 Dean University Libraries .... Ms. Carrie COOPER
43 University Counsel .... Ms. Deborah A. LOVE
20 Vice Provost for Academic Affairs .... Dr. Kathleen F. SLEVIN
82 Vice Prov Intl Affairs/Reves Ctr .... Dr. Stephen E. HANSON
46 Vice Provost Rsch & Grad Prof Stds .... Dr. Dennis M. MANOS
13 Assoc Prov Information Technology .... Mr. Courtney M. CARPENTER
27 Chief Information Officer .... Mr. Courtney CARPENTER
108 Assoc Prov Inst Analysis /Effectiv .... Dr. Susan L. BOSWORTH
84 Associate Provost for Enrollment .... Mr. Henry R. BROADDUS
07 Dean of Admission .... Mr. Henry R. BROADDUS
06 University Registrar .... Ms. Sara L. MARCHELLO
88 Dean for Educational Policy .... Dr. Teresa LONGO
58 Dean Graduate Studies & Research .... Dr. John SWADDLE
92 Dean Honors/Interdisciplinary Stds .... Dr. Joel D. SCHWARTZ
88 Dean of Undergraduate Studies .... Dr. Kelly JOYCE
104 Director of Global Education .... Ms. Sylvia MITTERNDORFER
86 Assoc VP Government Relations .... Ms. Frances C. BRADFORD
26 Director of University Relations .... Mr. Brian WHITSON
88 Assoc VP Development/Operations .... Ms. Teresa L. MUNFORD
44 Assoc Vice Pres for Development .... Mr. Earl T. GRANGER
102 Director Corporate & Found Rels .... Ms. Suzanne ARMSTRONG
18 Assoc Vice Pres Facilities Mgmt .... Mr. Dave SHEPARD
35 Dean of Students .... Ms. Patricia M. VOLP
25 Director of Sponsored Programs .... Ms. Jane LOPEZ
22 Director of Equal Opportunity .... Ms. Tammy H. CURRIE
37 Director Student Financial Aid .... Mr. Edward P. IRISH
15 Assoc VP Human Resources .... Mr. Ron PRICE
38 Director Counseling Center .... Dr. Warrenetta C. MANN
36 Director Career Center .... Ms. Mary E. SCHILLING
19 Chief W&M Police Department .... Mr. Donald R. CHALLIS
21 Director Financial Operations .... Mr. Edmund (Bert) E. BRUMMER
23 Director Student Health Center .... Dr. Virginia D. WELLS
28 Dir of Ctr for Student Diversity .... Dr. Vernon HURTE
39 Asst VP Stdnt Affs/Dir of Res Life .... Ms. Deborah BOYKIN
96 Director of Procurement .... Mr. Gregory W. JOHNSON
40 Manager W&M Bookstore .... Ms. Kathy PACHECO
100 Asst to President/Chief of Staff .... Mr. Michael J. FOX
101 Secretary to the Board of Visitors .... Mr. Michael J. FOX
04 Executive Asst to President .... Ms. Cynthia A. BRAUER
88 Director of Creative Services .... Ms. Tina L. COLEMAN

Columbia College (B)

8300 Merrifield Avenue, Fairfax VA 22031

County: Fairfax FICE Identification: 041273
Unit ID: 455983
Telephone: (703) 206-0508 Carnegie Class: Assoc/PrivFP
FAX Number: (703) 206-0488 Calendar System: Quarter
URL: www.ccdc.edu
Established: 1999 Annual Undergrad Tuition & Fees: $6,600
Enrollment: 387 Coed
Affiliation or Control: Proprietary IRS Status: Proprietary
Highest Offering: Associate Degree
Program: Occupational; 2-Year Principally Bachelor's Creditable
Accreditation: COE

01 President .... Dr. Richard K. KIM

DeVry University - Arlington Campus (C)

2450 Crystal Drive, Arlington VA 22202-3843

County: Arlington Identification: 666220
Unit ID: 440536
Telephone: (703) 414-4000 Carnegie Class: Master's S
FAX Number: (703) 414-4023 Calendar System: Semester
URL: www.devry.edu
Established: 1931 Annual Undergrad Tuition & Fees: $16,156
Enrollment: 942 Coed
Affiliation or Control: Proprietary IRS Status: Proprietary
Highest Offering: Master's
Program: Occupational; Professional; Business Emphasis
Accreditation: &NH, ENGT

01 Metro President .... Ms. Loretta FRANKLIN
15 HR Business Partner .... Ms. Jennifer CAMDEN-CHAU
32 Dean Student Central .... Mr. Cary WHITCUP
37 Director of Student Finance .... Ms. Lisa BRANSON
07 Senior Director of Admissions .... Mr. Jeffrey PTAK
08 Director of Library Services .... Ms. Jane CARVAJAL
06 Registrar .... Ms. Cheri MAEA
05 Dean Academic Affairs .... Mr. Keith WRIGHT
36 Director of Career Services .... Mr. Jack WEBSTER

† Regional accreditation is carried under the parent institution in Downers Grove, IL.

DeVry University - Chesapeake (D)

1317 Executive Boulevard, Suite 100,
Chesapeake VA 23320-3671

County: Chesapeake City Identification: 666577
Telephone: (757) 382-5680 Carnegie Class: Not Classified
FAX Number: (757) 549-5215 Calendar System: Semester
URL: www.devry.edu
Established: 1931 Annual Undergrad Tuition & Fees: $16,156
Enrollment: 519 Coed
Affiliation or Control: Proprietary IRS Status: Proprietary
Highest Offering: Master's
Program: Professional; Business Emphasis
Accreditation: &NH

01 Campus Director .... Vacant

† Regional accreditation is carried under the parent institution in Downers Grove, IL.

DeVry University - Manassas (E)

10432 Balls Ford Rd, Suite 130,
Manassas VA 20109-3173

County: Prince William Identification: 666222
Unit ID: 430333
Telephone: (703) 396-6611 Carnegie Class: Not Classified
FAX Number: (703) 367-7242 Calendar System: Semester
URL: www.devry.edu
Established: 1931 Annual Undergrad Tuition & Fees: $16,156
Enrollment: 344 Coed
Affiliation or Control: Proprietary IRS Status: Proprietary
Highest Offering: Master's
Program: Occupational; Professional; Business Emphasis
Accreditation: &NH

01 Center Dean .... Lisa MULLALY

† Regional accreditation is carried under the parent institution in Downers Grove, IL.

Eastern Mennonite University (F)

1200 Park Road, Harrisonburg VA 22802-2462

County: Independent City FICE Identification: 003708
Unit ID: 232043
Telephone: (540) 432-4000 Carnegie Class: Bac/A&S
FAX Number: (540) 432-4444 Calendar System: Semester
URL: www.emu.edu
Established: 1917 Annual Undergrad Tuition & Fees: $27,970
Enrollment: 1,605 Coed
Affiliation or Control: Mennonite Church IRS Status: 501(c)3
Highest Offering: Master's
Program: Liberal Arts And General; Teacher Preparatory; Professional
Accreditation: SC, CACREP, NURSE, SW, TED, THEOL

01 President .... Dr. Loren E. SWARTZENDRUBER
05 Provost .... Dr. Fred L. KNISS
30 Vice President for Advancement .... Mr. Kirk L. SHISLER
10 Vice President for Finance .... Mr. Daryl W. BERT
84 Vice Pres Enrollment & Marketing .... Mr. Luke HARTMAN
32 Vice President for Student Life .... Dr. Kenneth L. NAFZIGER
20 Vice Pres & Undergrad Academic Dean .... Dr. Nancy HEISEY
73 Seminary Dean .... Dr. Michael A. KING
06 University Registrar .... Mr. David A. DETROW
27 Director of Marketing Services .... Ms. Andrea S. WENGER
07 Director Undergraduate Admissions .... Ms. Stephanie C. SHAFER
08 Director of Libraries .... Dr. Beryl H. BRUBAKER
37 Director of Financial Assistance .... Ms. Michele R. HENSLEY
36 Director Career Services/Testing .... Ms. Jennifer L. LITWILLER
29 Director of Alumni/Parent Relations .... Mr. Douglas J. NYCE
09 Director Institutional Research .... Dr. BJ MILLER
04 Assistant to the President .... Ms. Twila K. YODER
41 Athletic Director .... Mr. David A. KING
42 Campus Pastor .... Mr. Brian M. BURKHOLDER
13 Director of Information Systems .... Mr. Jack H. RUTT
18 Director of Physical Plant .... Mr. Eldon KURTZ
15 Director Human Resources .... Ms. Marcia J. ENGLE
21 Controller .... Mr. Timothy STUTZMAN
26 Chief Public Information Officer .... Mr. Michael J. ZUCCONI
35 Director Student Affairs .... Mr. Lawrence W. MILLER
38 Director Student Counseling .... Ms. Pamela D. COMER

Eastern Virginia Medical School (G)

Box 1980, Norfolk VA 23501-1980

County: Independent City FICE Identification: 010338
Unit ID: 231970
Telephone: (757) 446-5600 Carnegie Class: Spec/Med
FAX Number: (757) 446-5135 Calendar System: Other
URL: www.evms.edu
Established: 1973 Annual Graduate Tuition & Fees: $30,842
Enrollment: 1,008 Coed
Affiliation or Control: Independent Non-Profit IRS Status: 501(c)3
Highest Offering: Doctorate; No Undergraduates
Program: Professional
Accreditation: SC, ARCPA, CLPSY, IPSY, MED, PH, SURGA

01 President .... Mr. Harry T. LESTER
05 Dean & Provost .... Dr. Richard V. HOMAN
10 Vice Pres Administration/Finance .... Mr. Mark R. BABASHANIAN
100 Chief of Staff .... Ms. Claudia KEENAN
88 Vice Pres/Dean Sch of Health Prof .... Dr. Charles D. COMBS
20 Associate Dean Education .... Dr. Ronald W. FLENNER
88 Assoc Dean Clinical Affairs .... Dr. Alfred Z. ABUHAMAD
58 Assoc Dean Grad Medical Education .... Dr. Linda R. ARCHER
88 Assoc Dean Hum Sub Protection/IRB .... Dr. Robert F. WILLIAMS
09 Assoc Dean for Research .... Dr. William J. WASILENKO
50 Assoc Dean Business/Admin Affairs .... Mr. David E. HUBAND
08 Assoc Dean Library/Lrng Resource .... Ms. Judith G. ROBINSON
28 Vice President for Diversity .... Vacant
32 Asst Dean for Student Affairs .... Dr. Ann E. CAMPBELL
84 Asst Dean Admissions and Enroll .... Dr. Donald C. MEYER
43 General Counsel .... Ms. Stacy R. PURCELL
06 Registrar .... Mr. Michael J. DONLAN
07 Director of Admissions .... Ms. Susan L. CASTORA
15 Director Human Resources .... Mr. Matthew R. SCHENK
21 Director of Finance .... Ms. Helen S. HESELIUS
18 Chief Facilities/Physical Plant .... Mr. Jack D. BEASLEY
37 Director Student Financial Aid .... Ms. Margaret L. MURPHY
93 Director Minority Affairs .... Ms. Gail C. WILLIAMS
96 Director of Materials Management .... Mr. Steven LEE
21 Director for Business Management .... Ms. Tammy A. POSTON
26 Director of Mktg & Communications .... Mr. Vincent A. RHODES
29 Director Alumni Affairs .... Ms. Melissa W. LANG
30 Director of Development .... Ms. Connie L. MCKENZIE
51 Director for Continuing Med Educ .... Ms. Drucie A. PAPAFIL

† Member of Virginia Consortium for Professional Psychology.

ECPI College of Technology (H)

5555 Greenwich Road, Virginia Beach VA 23462-6554

County: Independent City FICE Identification: 010198
Unit ID: 248934
Telephone: (757) 671-7171 Carnegie Class: Assoc/PrivFP4
FAX Number: (757) 671-8661 Calendar System: Semester
URL: www.ecpi.edu
Established: 1966 Annual Undergrad Tuition & Fees: $13,700
Enrollment: 10,762 Coed
Affiliation or Control: Proprietary IRS Status: Proprietary
Highest Offering: Master's
Program: Occupational
Accreditation: SC, ACFEI, MAAB, NUR

01 President .... Mr. Mark B. DREYFUS
12 Campus President .... Mr. Kevin PAVEGLIO
03 Vice President .... Mr. Ronald J. BALLANCE
13 VP Info Systems/Financial Aid .... Mr. Jeff ARTHUR

Edward Via College of Osteopathic Medicine (I)

2265 Kraft Drive, Blacksburg VA 24060

County: Montgomery FICE Identification: 037093
Unit ID: 442806
Telephone: (540) 231-4000 Carnegie Class: Spec/Med
FAX Number: (540) 231-5252 Calendar System: Semester
URL: www.vcom.vt.edu
Established: 2002 Annual Graduate Tuition & Fees: $39,530

Enrollment: 964 Coed
Affiliation or Control: Independent Non-Profit IRS Status: 501(c)3
Highest Offering: Doctorate; No Undergraduates
Program: Professional
Accreditation: OSTEO

01 President .... Dr. James F. WOLFE
05 Executive Vice President & Dean .... Dr. Dixie TOOKE-RAWLINS
10 Associate Vice Pres Finance/CFO .... Mr. Mark HAMRIC
32 Assoc Vice Pres Student Services .... Mr. William KING
46 Assoc Vice Pres Research/Grad Stds .... Dr. Hara P. MISRA
11 Assoc Vice President Operations .... Mr. Bill PRICE
12 Vice Dean Carolinas Campus .... Dr. Timothy J. KOWALSKI
12 Vice Dean Virginia Campus .... Dr. Jan M. WILLCOX
58 Vice Dean Post-Bac/Pre-med Program .... Dr. Francine ANDERSON
63 Vice Dean Medical Education .... Dr Brian W. HILL

Emory & Henry College (A)

PO Box 947, 30461 Garnand Drive,
Emory VA 24327-0947

County: Washington FICE Identification: 003709
Unit ID: 232025
Telephone: (276) 944-4121 Carnegie Class: Bac/A&S
FAX Number: (276) 944-6934 Calendar System: Semester
URL: www.ehc.edu
Established: 1836 Annual Undergrad Tuition & Fees: $28,122
Enrollment: 982 Coed
Affiliation or Control: United Methodist IRS Status: 501(c)3
Highest Offering: Doctorate
Program: Liberal Arts And General; Teacher Preparatory
Accreditation: SC, TEAC

01 President .... Dr. Rosalind REICHARD
04 Executive Assistant to President .... Mr. Mark R. GRAHAM
05 VP Academic Affairs/Dean .... Dr. David P. HANEY
10 Vice Pres for Business and Finance .... Dr. Dirk E. WILMOTH
32 VP Student Life/Dean of Students .... Ms. Pamela L. GOURLEY
30 Int VP Institutional Advancement .... Mr. A. P. PERKINSON
84 Vice Pres for Enrollment Management .... Mr. David S. HAWSEY
09 Coordinator Institutional Research .... Ms. Elizabeth WASSUM
29 Director of Alumni Affairs .... Ms. Monica S. HOEL
37 Director of Financial Aid .... Ms. Lauren PIZZO
06 Registrar .... Ms. Lynn ELLIOTT
36 Director of Career Planning .... Ms. Amanda GARDNER
38 Director Student Counseling .... Ms. Jill M. SMELTZER
26 Director Public Relations .... Mr. Dirk S. MOORE
08 Chief Information Officer/Librarian .... Ms. Lorraine N. ABRAHAM
18 Director of Facilities Managment .... Ms. Judy YODER
40 Bookstore Manager .... Mr. Terry RICHARDSON
42 Chaplain .... Rev. Mary K. BRIGGS
15 Human Resources Manager .... Ms. Angie S. EDMONDSON
20 Associate VP Academic Affairs .... Dr. Michael J. PUGLISI
35 Assistant Dean of Students .... Mr. Todd CLARK
21 Business Affairs Manager .... Ms. Benita BARE
07 Director of Admissions .... Vacant

Everest College (B)

803 Diligence Drive, Newport News VA 23606

County: Independent City FICE Identification: 009267
Unit ID: 232502
Telephone: (757) 873-1111 Carnegie Class: Assoc/PrivFP
FAX Number: (757) 873-0728 Calendar System: Other
URL: www.everest.edu
Established: N/A Annual Undergrad Tuition & Fees: N/A
Enrollment: 420 Coed
Affiliation or Control: Proprietary IRS Status: Proprietary
Highest Offering: Associate Degree
Program: Occupational
Accreditation: ACICS

† Tuition varies by degree program.

Ferrum College (C)

PO Box 1000, 215 Ferrum Mtn Road,
Ferrum VA 24088-9001

County: Franklin FICE Identification: 003711
Unit ID: 232089
Telephone: (540) 365-2121 Carnegie Class: Bac/Diverse
FAX Number: (540) 365-4269 Calendar System: Semester
URL: www.ferrum.edu
Established: 1913 Annual Undergrad Tuition & Fees: $27,310
Enrollment: 1,512 Coed
Affiliation or Control: United Methodist IRS Status: 501(c)3
Highest Offering: Baccalaureate
Program: Liberal Arts And General
Accreditation: SC, SW

01 President .... Dr. Jennifer L. BRAATEN
11 Sr Vice Pres for Admin & Treasurer .... Mr. Bobby W. THOMPSON
05 Provost & Executive Vice President .... Dr. Leslie T. LAMBERT
10 Chief Financial Officer .... Mrs. Barb HATCHER
30 Vice Pres Institutional Advancement .... Mrs. Kimberly P. BLAIR
84 Vice Pres Enrollment Management .... Dr. Douglas E. CLARK
32 Vice President of Student Affairs .... Dr. Andrea P. ZUSCHIN
42 Dean of Chapel/Religious Life .... Rev. C. Wesley ASTIN, JR.
20 Dean Academic Pgms/Faculty Devel .... Dr. Gail SUMMER
04 Special Assistant to the President .... Mrs. Theresa M. POTTER
06 Registrar .... Mrs. Yvonne S. WALKER
84 Assoc VP for Enrollment Mgmt .... Mrs. Gilda Q. WOODS
09 Dir of Assessment & Inst Research .... Dr. Jolene D. HAMM
08 Exec Dir Stanley Library .... Ms. Brandi PORTER
37 Director of Financial Aid .... Ms. Heather HOLLANDSWORTH
29 Director Alumni & Family Programs .... Mrs. Tracy S. HOLLEY
26 Director of Public Relations .... Mr. John CARLIN
41 Director of Athletics .... Mr. J. Abraham NAFF
44 Director of Ferrum Fund .... Mr. Gene BOURNE
18 Director of Physical Plant .... Mr. Sam E. MORAN
88 Dir Student Leadership & Engagement .... Mr. David A. NEWCOMBE
13 Director of Computer Services .... Mr. Daniel K. HODGES
15 Director of Personnel Services .... Mrs. Mary Alice WHISENANT
40 Bookstore Manager .... Ms. Patty SIGMON
19 Director Ferrum College Police Dept .... Ms. Elizabeth LEGG
36 Dir Career Svcs/Student Employment .... Mr. Roland WALTERS
88 Disability Services Coordinator .... Ms. Nancy S. BEACH
91 Coord of Administrative Computing .... Mr. Tim BELCHER
28 Coordinator Multicultural Programs .... Mr. Justin MUSE
79 Dean School Arts & Humanities .... Dr. John W. BRUTON
81 Dean School Natural Science & Math .... Dr. Jason POWELL
83 Dean School Social Sciences .... Dr. Kevin REILLY

Fortis College (D)

6300 Center Drive, Suite 100, Norfolk VA 23502

County: Independent City FICE Identification: 023427
Unit ID: 233329
Telephone: (757) 499-5447 Carnegie Class: Assoc/PrivFP
FAX Number: N/A Calendar System: Quarter
Established: N/A Annual Undergrad Tuition & Fees: $22,295
Enrollment: 442 Coed
Affiliation or Control: Proprietary IRS Status: Proprietary
Highest Offering: Associate Degree
Program: Occupational
Accreditation: ACICS

01 President .... David SPLITSTONE

George Mason University (E)

4400 University Drive, Fairfax VA 22030-4444

County: Fairfax FICE Identification: 003749
Unit ID: 232186
Telephone: (703) 993-1000 Carnegie Class: RU/H
FAX Number: (703) 993-1009 Calendar System: Semester
URL: www.gmu.edu
Established: 1957 Annual Undergrad Tuition & Fees (In-State): $9,620
Enrollment: 33,320 Coed
Affiliation or Control: State IRS Status: 501(c)3
Highest Offering: Doctorate
Program: Liberal Arts And General; Teacher Preparatory; Professional
Accreditation: SC, ART, BUS, BUSA, CEA, CLPSY, CS, ENG, HSA, IPSY, LAW, MUS, NRPA, NURSE, SPAA, SW, TED

01 President .... Dr. Ángel CABRERA
100 Chief of Staff .... Mr. Frank NEVILLE
03 Vice Pres for Administration .... Vacant
05 Provost .... Dr. Peter N. STEARNS
10 Senior Vice President .... Dr. Maurice W. SCHERRENS
07 Vice President Enrollment Services .... Mr. Wayne SIGLER
18 Vice President for Facilities .... Mr. Thomas G. CALHOUN
26 Interim VP University Relations .... Mr. Paul LIBERTY
30 VP University Devel/Alumni Affairs .... Mr. Marc BRODERICK
13 VP Info Technology/Chief Info Ofcr .... Dr. Joy R. HUGHES
32 Vice President for University Life .... Dr. Sandra J. SCHERRENS
46 VP Research/Economic Development .... Dr. Roger R. STOUGH
22 Director Equity & Diversity Svcs .... Mr. Corey D. JACKSON
16 Assoc Vice Pres for HR/Payroll .... Ms. Linda HARBER
43 University Counsel .... Mr. Thomas M. MONCURE
45 Chief Budget Officer .... Mr. Guilbert L. BROWN
20 Vice Provost Academic Affairs .... Dr. Michelle MARKS
20 Assoc Prov for Undergrad Education .... Dr. Janette MUIR
84 Assoc Prov for Enroll Plng & Admin .... Ms. Renate H. GUILFORD
58 Assoc Prov for Graduate Education .... Vacant
35 Director Ofc of Student Involvement .... Ms. Lauren LONG
35 Assistant Vice Pres University Life .... Ms. Patricia J. CARRETTA
06 Registrar .... Ms. Susan H. JONES
37 Director Student Financial Aid .... Ms. Heidi GRANGER
36 Director University Career Services .... Dr. Janice SUTERA
08 University Librarian .... Mr. John G. ZENELIS
23 Exec Director Student Health Svcs .... Dr. Wagida A. ABDALLA
29 Assoc VP Alumni Affairs .... Ms. Christine CLARK-TALLEY
41 Dir of Intercollegiate Athletics .... Mr. Thomas J. O'CONNOR
19 Dir & Chief of University Police .... Mr. Michael F. LYNCH
49 Dean Col of Humanities/Social Sci .... Dr. Jack R. CENSER
61 Dean School of Law .... Dr. Daniel D. POLSBY
80 Dean School of Public Policy .... Dr. Edward RHODES
50 Dean School of Management .... Dr. Jorge HADDOCK
53 Dean College of Educ & Human Devel .... Dr. Mark R. GINSBERG
54 Dean Volgenau School of Engineering .... Dr. Kenneth BALL
66 Dean College of Health/Human Svcs .... Dr. Thomas R. PROHASKA
81 Dean College of Science .... Dr. Vikas CHANDHOKE
88 Dean Sch Conflict Analysis & Resol .... Dr. Andrea BARTOLI
88 Dean Col of Visual/Performing Arts .... Mr. William F. REEDER
38 Acting Director Counseling Center .... Dr. Adrienne M. BARNA
09 Assoc Prov Institutional Research .... Ms. Kris M. SMITH
35 Associate Dean University Life .... Dr. Todd S. ROSE
96 Director of Purchasing and AP .... Mr. William R. HARDIMAN

Global Health College (F)

25 South Quaker Lane, 1st Floor, Alexandria VA 22314

County: Independent City FICE Identification: 041400
Unit ID: 455390
Telephone: (703) 212-7410 Carnegie Class: Assoc/PrivFP
FAX Number: (703) 212-7414 Calendar System: Other
URL: www.global.edu
Established: 2004 Annual Undergrad Tuition & Fees: $15,271
Enrollment: 223 Coed
Affiliation or Control: Proprietary IRS Status: Proprietary
Highest Offering: Associate Degree
Program: Nursing Emphasis
Accreditation: ACICS

01 President .... Mariatu KARGBO
05 Vice President Academic Affairs .... Jennifer REID

Hampden-Sydney College (G)

College Road, PO Box 128,
Hampden-Sydney VA 23943-0667

County: Prince Edward FICE Identification: 003713
Unit ID: 232256
Telephone: (434) 223-6000 Carnegie Class: Bac/A&S
FAX Number: (434) 223-6350 Calendar System: Semester
URL: www.hsc.edu
Established: 1775 Annual Undergrad Tuition & Fees: $35,932
Enrollment: 1,057 Male
Affiliation or Control: Presbyterian Church (U.S.A.) IRS Status: 501(c)3
Highest Offering: Baccalaureate
Program: Liberal Arts And General
Accreditation: SC

01 President .... Dr. Christopher B. HOWARD
04 Special Asst to the President .... Mr. William P. O MOSS
05 Provost & Dean of the Faculty .... Dr. Dennis G. STEVENS
10 VP Business Affairs & Finance .... Mr. W. Glenn CULLEY, JR.
30 VP Institutional Advancement .... Dr. H. Lee KING, JR.
11 VP Strategy/Admin & Board Affs .... Dr. V. Dale JONES
07 Dean of Admissions .... Ms. Anita H. GARLAND
20 Associate Dean of the Faculty .... Dr. J. Michael UTZINGER
32 Dean of Students .... Dr. David A. KLEIN
20 Associate Dean Academic Support .... Ms. Christa D. FYE
41 Director of Athletics .... Mr. Richard P. EPPERSON, II
08 Director of the Library .... Dr. Cyrus I. DILLON, III
42 Pastor of College Church & Chaplain .... Rev Dr. David A. KECK
06 Registrar .... Ms. Dawn L. CONGLETON
37 Director of Financial Aid .... Ms. Zita M. BARREE
29 Director of Alumni Relations .... Mr. Mark G. MEITZ
18 Director of Physical Plant .... Mr. Thomas L. GREGORY
14 Director of Computing .... Mr. Robert C. MURRAY
36 Director of Career Development .... LtCol. L. Rucker SNEAD, III
23 Director of Student Health Center .... Ms. Margaret P. GRAHAM
15 Director of Human Resources .... Ms. Barbara S. ARMENTROUT
19 Director of Security & Police .... Mr. Jeffrey S. GEE
40 Bookstore Manager .... Mrs. Hazel N. BALDWIN
09 Director Inst Research/Assessment .... Dr. Christine C. ROSS
26 Director Communications & Marketing .... Mr. Thomas H. SHOMO
21 Controller .... Mr. Michael SMITH
35 Dir Student Activities & Orgs .... Mr. John RAMSAY
39 Assoc Dean Students Resident Life .... Mr. Wesley S. LAWSON
102 Dir Corporate/Foundation Relations .... Mrs. Eunice W. CARWILE
104 Dir Global Education & Study Abroad .... Mrs. Mary K. COOPER

Hampton University (H)

Hampton VA 23668-0199

County: Independent City FICE Identification: 003714
Unit ID: 232265
Telephone: (757) 727-5000 Carnegie Class: Master's M
FAX Number: (757) 727-5085 Calendar System: Semester
URL: www.hamptonu.edu
Established: 1868 Annual Undergrad Tuition & Fees: $19,738
Enrollment: 5,223 Coed
Affiliation or Control: Independent Non-Profit IRS Status: 501(c)3
Highest Offering: Doctorate
Program: Liberal Arts And General; Teacher Preparatory; Professional
Accreditation: SC, CS, ENG, IACBE, JOUR, MUS, NURSE, PHAR, PTA, SP, TED

01 President .... Dr. William R. HARVEY
03 Executive Vice President .... Dr. JoAnn HAYSBERT
05 Provost .... Dr. Pamela V. HAMMOND
10 Vice Pres Business Affs/Treasurer .... Mrs. Doretha J. SPELLS
32 Vice Pres for Student Affairs .... Dr. Barbara L. INMAN
43 Vice President/General Counsel .... Atty. Faye HARDY-LUCAS
30 Vice President for Development .... Mr. Laron J. CLARK
04 Executive Assistant to President .... Dr. Charrita D. DANLEY
46 Special Asst to President/Research .... Dr. Elnora DANIEL
31 Assoc Vice Pres External Relations .... Mrs. Joy JEFFERSON
35 Assoc Vice Pres for Student Affairs .... Vacant
21 Asst VP Business Affs/Comptroller .... Ms. Nellie CRAWFORD
25 Asst Vice Pres Grants Management .... Mrs. Lillie F. GREEN
20 Asst Provost Academic Affairs .... Dr. Pollie MURPHY
72 Assistant Provost Technology .... Mr. Keith PERKINS
33 Dean of Men .... Mr. Woodson H. HOPEWELL, JR.
34 Dean of Women .... Miss Jewel B. LONG
07 Director of Admissions .... Mrs. Angela BOYD
06 Registrar .... Mrs. Jorsene COOPER
36 Dir Career Counsel/Planning Ctr .... Mrs. Vivian DAVID
38 Interim Director the Counseling Ctr .... Dr. Linda KIRKLAND-HARRIS
08 Administrator University Libraries .... Ms. Faye WATKINS
29 Director of Alumni Affairs .... Mrs. Mildred SWANN
15 Director of Human Resources .... Ms. Rikki THOMAS
14 Interim Director Computer Center .... Mr. Christopher VERNON
37 Financial Aid Officer .... Mr. Martin MILES

26 Director of University Relations ....Mrs. Yuri Rodgers MILLIGAN
09 Director Institutional Research ....Ms. Regina GIBBONS
23 Director Student Health Services .... Dr. Hannibal E. HOWELL
42 University Chaplain ....Rev. Debra L. HAGGINS
18 Director Buildings & Grounds .... Mr. Lowell MIDDLETON
87 Director of Summer Sessions ....Dr. Pollie MURPHY
19 Chief of Campus Police ....Mr. David GLOVER
86 Director Government Relations ....Mr. Wilbert L. THOMAS
96 Director of Purchasing ....Mr. Malcolm HAINES
40 University Bookstore Manager ....Ms. Michelle R. MILLER
53 Dean School of Liberal Arts ....Dr. Mamie E. LOCKE
66 Dean School of Nursing ....Dr. Deborah JONES
81 Assistant Dean School of Science .... Dr. Michelle CLAVILLE
51 Dean Col Educ & Continuing Studies .....Dr. Cassandra HERRING
50 Dean School of Business ....Dr. Sid H. CREDLE
54 Dean Sch of Engineering/Technology ....Dr. Eric J. SHEPPARD
67 Dean School of Pharmacy ....Dr. Wayne HARRIS
58 Dean the Graduate College ....Dr. Patrena N. BENTON
60 Dean Scripps Howard Sch Journ/Comm .... Mr. Brett PULLEY

Hollins University (A)

PO Box 9688, Roanoke VA 24020-1688
County: Roanoke FICE Identification: 003715
Unit ID: 232308
Telephone: (540) 362-6000 Carnegie Class: Bac/A&S
FAX Number: (540) 362-6642 Calendar System: 4/1/4
URL: www.hollins.edu
Established: 1842 Annual Undergrad Tuition & Fees: $31,490
Enrollment: 953 Female
Affiliation or Control: Independent Non-Profit IRS Status: 501(c)3
Highest Offering: Master's
Program: Liberal Arts And General; Teacher Preparatory
Accreditation: SC, TEAC

01 President ....Ms. Nancy O. GRAY
10 Vice Pres Finance/Administration ....Ms. Kerry EDMONDS
30 Vice Pres for External Relations ....Mr. Mark W. JONES
05 Chair of the Faculty ....Mr. Joe LEEDOM
32 Dean of Students ....Ms. Patty O'TOOLE
07 Associate Dean of Admissions ...Ms. Nikki JOHNSON WILLIAMS
20 Dean Academic Services ....Dr. Patricia HAMMER
28 Associate Dean Intercultural Pgms .... Ms. Jeri L. SUAREZ
04 Executive Assistant to President ....Ms. Brook E. DICKSON
88 Exec Dir Alumnae & Donor Relations ....Ms. Brenda MCDANIEL
06 Registrar ....Ms. Anna GOODWIN
08 Acting Director of the Library ....Mr. Luke VILELLE
15 Director of Human Resources ....Ms. Alicia GODZWA
26 Director of Public Relations ....Mr. Jeff HODGES
29 Director of Alumnae Relations ....Vacant
36 Director Career Development Center .... Ms. Ashley GLENN
37 Director Financial Aid ....Ms. Mary Jean CORRISS
41 Director of Athletics ....Mr. David ZINN
09 Director of Institutional Research ....Ms. Anna GOODWIN
18 Director Plant Operations/Services .... Ms. May THOMAS

iGlobal University (B)

7700 Little River Turnpike, #600, Annandale VA 22003
County: Fairfax Identification: 667105
Telephone: (703) 941-2020 Carnegie Class: Not Classified
FAX Number: (703) 941-2025 Calendar System: Quarter
URL: www.iglobaluniversity.org
Established: 2008 Annual Undergrad Tuition & Fees: N/A
Enrollment: N/A Coed
Affiliation or Control: Proprietary IRS Status: Proprietary
Highest Offering: Master's
Program: Business Emphasis
Accreditation: ACICS

Institute for the Psychological Sciences (C)

2001 Jefferson Davis Hwy, Ste 511,
Arlington VA 22202-3609
County: Arlington FICE Identification: 038724
Unit ID: 445869
Telephone: (703) 416-1441 Carnegie Class: Spec/Health
FAX Number: (703) 416-8588 Calendar System: Semester
URL: www.ipsciences.edu
Established: 1998 Annual Graduate Tuition & Fees: $21,375
Enrollment: 82 Coed
Affiliation or Control: Independent Non-Profit IRS Status: 501(c)3
Highest Offering: Doctorate; No Undergraduates
Program: Professional
Accreditation: SC

01 President ....Rev. Charles SIKORSKY, LC
00 President Emeritus ....Rev. John HOPKINS, LC
05 Academic Dean ....Dr. William NORDLING
10 Vice President of Finance ....Mr. Roberto PARTARRIEU
84 Director Enrollment Svcs/Registrar ....Ms. Jennifer E. KARNS
30 Director Institutional Advancement .... Dr. Mary Ann LA FOEUR
07 Director of Admissions .... Ms. Anne-Marie DARDIS
08 Library Director .... Mr. Jeffrey ELLIOTT

ITT Technical Institute (D)

14420 Albemarle Point Pl, Suite 100,
Chantilly VA 20151-1750
County: Fairfax Identification: 666324
Unit ID: 441964
Telephone: (703) 263-2541 Carnegie Class: Spec/Tech
FAX Number: (703) 263-0846 Calendar System: Quarter
URL: www.itt-tech.edu
Established: 2003 Annual Undergrad Tuition & Fees: N/A
Enrollment: 697 Coed
Affiliation or Control: Proprietary IRS Status: Proprietary
Highest Offering: Baccalaureate
Program: Technical Emphasis
Accreditation: ACICS

† Branch campus of ITT Technical Institute, Indianapolis, IN.

ITT Technical Institute (E)

863 Glenrock Road, Suite 100, Norfolk VA 23502-3701
County: Norfolk City Identification: 666555
Unit ID: 368601
Telephone: (757) 466-1260 Carnegie Class: Bac/Assoc
FAX Number: (757) 466-7630 Calendar System: Quarter
URL: www.itt-tech.edu
Established: 1988 Annual Undergrad Tuition & Fees: N/A
Enrollment: 1,163 Coed
Affiliation or Control: Proprietary IRS Status: Proprietary
Highest Offering: Baccalaureate
Program: Technical Emphasis
Accreditation: ACICS

† Branch campus of ITT Technical Institute, Indianapolis, IN.

ITT Technical Institute (F)

300 Gateway Centre Parkway, Richmond VA 23235-5139
County: Chesterfield Identification: 666040
Unit ID: 437051
Telephone: (804) 330-4992 Carnegie Class: Spec/Tech
FAX Number: (804) 330-4993 Calendar System: Quarter
URL: www.itt-tech.edu
Established: 1998 Annual Undergrad Tuition & Fees: N/A
Enrollment: 713 Coed
Affiliation or Control: Proprietary IRS Status: Proprietary
Highest Offering: Baccalaureate
Program: Occupational; Technical Emphasis
Accreditation: ACICS

† Branch campus of ITT Technical Institute, Indianapolis, IN.

ITT Technical Institute (G)

7300 Boston Boulevard, Springfield VA 22153-2804
County: Fairfax Identification: 666321
Unit ID: 441955
Telephone: (703) 440-9535 Carnegie Class: Spec/Tech
FAX Number: (703) 440-9561 Calendar System: Quarter
URL: www.itt-tech.edu
Established: 2003 Annual Undergrad Tuition & Fees: N/A
Enrollment: 943 Coed
Affiliation or Control: Proprietary IRS Status: Proprietary
Highest Offering: Baccalaureate
Program: Technical Emphasis
Accreditation: ACICS

† Branch campus of ITT Technical Institute, Indianapolis, IN.

James Madison University (H)

800 S Main Street, Harrisonburg VA 22807-0001
County: Independent City FICE Identification: 003721
Unit ID: 232423
Telephone: (540) 568-6211 Carnegie Class: Master's L
FAX Number: N/A Calendar System: Semester
URL: www.jmu.edu
Established: 1908 Annual Undergrad Tuition & Fees (In-State): $8,808
Enrollment: 19,722 Coed
Affiliation or Control: State IRS Status: 501(c)3
Highest Offering: Doctorate
Program: Liberal Arts And General; Teacher Preparatory; Professional
Accreditation: SC, ARCPA, ART, AUD, BUS, BUSA, CACREP, CIDA, CS, DANCE, DIETD, ENGR, IPSY, MUS, NURSE, OT, PSPSY, SP, SW, TED, THEA

01 President ....Mr. Jonathan R. ALGER
05 Provost/Vice Pres Academic Affairs .... Dr. Jerry BENSON
11 Sr Vice Pres Administration/Finance ....Mr. Charles W. KING
32 Sr VP Student Affairs/Univ Planning ....Dr. Mark J. WARNER
30 Sr Vice Pres University Advancement ....Mr. Nick LANGRIDGE
04 Exec Assistant to the President ....Mrs. Donna L. HARPER
81 Dean College Science/Math ....Dr. David F. BRAKKE
49 Dean College Arts/Letters ....Dr. David K. JEFFREY
76 Dean Col of Health & Behav Studies ....Dr. Sharon LOVELL
50 Dean College of Business ....Dr. Irvine CLARKE, III
57 Dean College Visual Performing Arts ....Dr. George E. SPARKS
53 Dean College of Education ....Dr. Phillip M. WISHON
72 Dean College of Int Science & Engr .... Dr. Robert KOLVOORD
58 Dean Graduate School ....Dr. Reid J. LINN
97 Dean University Studies ....Dr. Linda C. HALPERN
08 Dean of Libraries/Educ Technologies ....Mr. Ralph A. ALBERICO
43 University Counsel ....Ms. Susan L. WHEELER
45 Asst Vice Pres Budget Management ....Ms. Diane L. STAMP
07 Director of Admissions ....Mr. Michael D. WALSH
37 Dir Financial Aid & Scholarships ....Ms. Lisa L. TUMER
15 Director Human Resources ....Ms. Yohna CHAMBERS
09 Director Institutional Research ....Dr. Frank J. DOHERTY
41 Director of Athletics ....Mr. Jeffrey T. BOURNE
26 Dir Public Affairs & Univ Spokesman ....Mr. Donald K. EGLE
06 University Registrar ....Ms. Michele M. WHITE
19 Chief of Police ....Mr. Lee A. SHIFFLETT

Jefferson College of Health Sciences (I)

PO Box 13186, Roanoke VA 24031-3186
County: Independent City Identification: 006622
Unit ID: 231837
Telephone: (540) 985-8483 Carnegie Class: Spec/Health
FAX Number: (540) 985-9773 Calendar System: Semester
URL: www.jchs.edu
Established: 1982 Annual Undergrad Tuition & Fees: $21,330
Enrollment: 1,063 Coed
Affiliation or Control: Independent Non-Profit IRS Status: 501(c)3
Highest Offering: Master's
Program: Nursing Emphasis
Accreditation: SC, ARCPA, EMT, MT, NURSE, OT, OTA, PTAA

01 President ....Dr. Nathaniel L. BISHOP
05 Dean Academic Affairs ....Dr. Lisa ALLISON-JONES
10 Dean Administrative Services ....Ms. Anna S. MILLIRONS
84 Director Enrollment Management ....Ms. Connie S. COOK
32 Dean Student Affairs ....Mr. Scott HILL
108 Assoc Dean for Inst Effectiveness ....Dr. Glen R. MAYHEW
17 Chair Community Health Sciences ....Dr. Sharon L. HATFIELD
88 Director Healthcare Management ....Dr. Janet E. PHILLIPS
63 Program Director Emergency Services ....Mr. John C. COOK
17 Dept Chair Arts & Sciences ....Dr. Francis C. DANE
83 Pgm Dir Humanities & Soc Sci .... Mr. Darrell K. SHOMAKER
81 Interim Director Biomed/Sci/Math ....Dr. Francis C. DANE
66 Dept Chair Nursing ....Dr. Ava G. PORTER
66 Program Director BSN ....Dr. Rebecca M. GREER
66 Program Director BSN ....Dr. Melody F. SHARP
88 Dept Chr Rehab/Wellness ....Dr. Michael S. KRACKOW
88 Director Occupation Therapy Masters ....Dr. David A. HAYNES
27 Coord Communications/Col Relations .... Mr. Mark A. LAMBERT
29 Development Resource Officer .... Ms. Catherine P. TURNER
25 Sponsored Projects Coordinator ....Ms. Amanda M. ELLINGER
07 Director of Admissions ....Ms. Judith O. MCKEON
37 Director of Financial Aid ....Ms. Debra J. JOHNSON
06 Registrar ....Ms. Linda C. WILLIAMS
08 Director Library ....Ms. Ramona H. THISS
35 Coordinator Student Affairs ....Ms. Elizabeth A. COSTA
40 Manager Bookstore ....Ms. Suzanne M. ANDERSON
21 Bursar ....Ms. Vicki R. BROWN
09 Institutional Research Manager .... Mr. Timothy R. MILLARD
18 Safety/Physical Plant Officer .... Ms. Susan L. BOOTH
38 Director Counseling and Wellness .... Dr. Jennifer J. SLUSHER
21 Director Business Services ....Mr. Glenn S. HENSLEY
04 Admin Secretary to President ....Ms. Priscilla L. DUBOIS
88 Program Director Health and Exc Sci .... Dr. Allison H. BOWERSOCK
88 Director Occupational Therapy Asst .... Ms. Ave M. MITTA
88 Program Dir Physician Asst Program .... Ms. Patricia J. AIREY
88 Program Director PTA program ....Ms. Rebecca DUFF

The John Leland Center for Theological Studies (J)

405 N. Washington Street, Suite 200,
Falls Church VA 22046
County: City of Falls Church Identification: 666340
Telephone: (703) 812-4757 Carnegie Class: Not Classified
FAX Number: (703) 812-4764 Calendar System: Other
URL: www.leland.edu
Established: 1998 Annual Graduate Tuition & Fees: $11,620
Enrollment: 75 Coed
Affiliation or Control: Baptist IRS Status: 501(c)3
Highest Offering: Master's; No Undergraduates
Program: Religious Emphasis
Accreditation: THEOL

01 President ....Dr. Mark J. OLSON
05 Academic Dean/Vice President ....Dr. Jeffrey G. WILLETTS
04 Exec Assistant to the President ....Ms. Jovan PETTY
08 Librarian ....Ms. Monica LEAK
06 Registrar .... Ms. Andrea BAKKE
07 Director Recruiting/Admissions ....Mr. Elijah HEYWARD
10 Chief Business Officer ....Mrs. Ellen TEAGUE
21 Associate Business Officer ....Mr. Jonathan RIDER
26 Chief Public Relations Officer ....Mr. Elijah HEYWARD

Liberty University (K)

1971 University Boulevard, Lynchburg VA 24502-2269
County: Independent City FICE Identification: 020530
Unit ID: 232557
Telephone: (434) 582-2000 Carnegie Class: Master's L
FAX Number: (434) 582-2304 Calendar System: Semester
URL: www.liberty.edu
Established: 1971 Annual Undergrad Tuition & Fees: $20,236
Enrollment: 65,951 Coed
Affiliation or Control: Baptist IRS Status: 501(c)3
Highest Offering: Doctorate
Program: Liberal Arts And General; Teacher Preparatory; Professional
Accreditation: SC, EXSC, LAW, NURSE, TED

01 Chancellor/President .... Mr. Jerry FALWELL, JR.
88 Vice Chancellor Spiritual Affairs .... Rev. Jonathan FALWELL
05 Vice Chancellor/Acting Provost .... Dr. Ronald S. GODWIN
10 Chief Financial Officer .... Mr. Don MOON
32 Vice President Student Affairs .... Dr. Mark L. HINE
11 Vice President Administration .... Mrs. Sharon HARTLESS
15 Vice President Human Resources .... Mrs. Laura J. WALLACE
88 Vice President for Spiritual Devel .... Vacant
26 Vice Pres Exec Projects/Media Rels .... Mr. Johnnie MOORE
20 Vice Prov Grad Sch/Online Programs ..... Dr. Ronald E. HAWKINS
20 Vice Prov Academic Administration .... Dr. Garth E. RUNION
21 Vice President Finance .... Vacant
09 Vice Pres for Admin Info Management .... Mr. Larry SHACKLETON
45 AVP for Institutional Effectiveness .... Dr. H. William WHEELER
13 Chief Information Officer .... Mr. Matthew J. ZEALAND
06 Registrar .... Mr. Larry SHACKLETON
84 Vice Pres Enrollment Management .... Mr. Chris JOHNSON
07 Director of Admissions .... Mr. Terry ELAM
29 Director of Alumni Affairs .... Mr. Tyler FALWELL
08 Dean of Library Services .... Mr. Carl MERAT
33 Dir Student Care/Conduct Offices .... Mr. Keith ANDERSON
34 Senior Student Conduct Officer .... Ms. Andrea ADAMS
42 Vice Pres & Dean of the Seminary .... Dr. Elmer TOWNS
86 Dean Helms School of Government .... Mr. Shawn D. AKERS
37 Vice President of Financial Aid .... Dr. Robert L. RITZ
41 Director of Athletics .... Mr. Jeff BARBER
49 Dean College of Arts & Sciences .... Dr. Roger D. SCHULTZ
50 Dean School of Business .... Dr. Scott M. HICKS
60 Dean School of Communication .... Dr. William G. GRIBBIN
97 Dean Ctr Acad Support/Adv Svcs .... Dr. Brian YATES
73 Dean School of Religion .... Dr. Elmer L. TOWNS
53 Dean School of Education .... Dr. Karen L. PARKER
35 Director of Campus Recreation .... Mr. Chris MISIANO
18 Vice Pres of Field Operations .... Mr. Scott STARNES
19 Chief of Police LUPD .... Col. Richard HINKLEY
72 Dean School of Engineering and CSCI .... Mr. David DONAHOO
28 Dir Ctr for Multicltrl Enrichment .... Ms. Melany PEARL
36 Director of Career Center .... Mrs. Carrie BARNHOUSE
106 Exec Director Online Programs .... Mrs. Tamela CRICKENBERGER
58 Dean Academic Admin Graduate School .... Dr. Fred MILACCI
61 Dean School of Law .... Mr. Mathew D. STAVER
88 Dean School of Aeronautics .... Mr. David L. YOUNG

Longwood University (A)

201 High Street, Farmville VA 23909-1801
County: Prince Edward FICE Identification: 003719
Unit ID: 232566
Telephone: (434) 395-2000 Carnegie Class: Master's M
FAX Number: (434) 395-2635 Calendar System: Semester
URL: www.longwood.edu
Established: 1839 Annual Undergrad Tuition & Fees (In-State): $10,890
Enrollment: 4,860 Coed
Affiliation or Control: State IRS Status: 501(c)3
Highest Offering: Master's
Program: Liberal Arts And General; Teacher Preparatory; Professional
Accreditation: SC, BUS, MUS, NRPA, SP, SW, TED, THEA

01 Interim President .... Ms. Marjorie M. CONNELLY
05 Provost/Vice Pres Academic Affairs .... Dr. Kenneth B. PERKINS
10 Vice Pres Administration & Finance .... Mrs. Kathy A. WORSTER
32 Vice President for Student Affairs .... Dr. Tim J. PIERSON
30 Vice Pres University Advancement .... Dr. Bryan K. ROWLAND
18 VP Facilities Mgmt/Real Property .... Mr. Richard W. BRATCHER
13 VP Info/Instructional Tech Svcs .... Dr. Francis X. MOORE
84 Assoc VP Enrollment Management .... Dr. Jennifer K. GREEN
26 Assoc VP Marketing/Communications .... Ms. Sabrina BROWN
07 Dean of Admissions .... Ms. Sallie D. MCMULLIN
09 Director Assessment & Inst Research .... Dr. Ling Y. WHITWORTH
06 Registrar .... Ms. Vikki LEVINE
08 Dean of Library .... Mrs. Suzy SZASZ-PALMER
29 Director Alumni Relations .... Mrs. Nancy B. SHELTON
36 Director of Acad & Career Adv Ctr .... Ms. Mary M. SAUNDERS
28 Director for Diversity & Inclusion .... Dr. Jamie R. RILEY
38 Director Student Counseling .... Dr. Wayne R. O'BRIEN
37 Director Student Financial Aid .... Ms. Karen M. SCHINABECK
96 Director of Materiel Management .... Mr. James E. SIMPSON
15 Chief Human Resources Officer .... Ms. Della H. WICKIZER
18 Director Physical Plant .... Mr. Alvin B. MYERS

Lynchburg College (B)

1501 Lakeside Drive, Lynchburg VA 24501-3199
County: Independent City FICE Identification: 003720
Unit ID: 232609
Telephone: (434) 544-8100 Carnegie Class: Master's S
FAX Number: (434) 544-8499 Calendar System: Semester
URL: www.lynchburg.edu
Established: 1903 Annual Undergrad Tuition & Fees: $30,805
Enrollment: 2,828 Coed
Affiliation or Control: Christian Church (Disciples Of Christ)
IRS Status: 501(c)3
Highest Offering: Doctorate
Program: Liberal Arts And General; Teacher Preparatory; Professional
Accreditation: SC, ACBSP, CACREP, EXSC, NURSE, @PTA

01 President .... Dr. Kenneth R. GARREN
05 Vice Pres & Dean for Academic Affs .... Dr. Julius A. SIGLER
10 Vice President Business & Finance .... Mr. Steve BRIGHT
30 Vice Pres Advancement .... Ms. Denise MCDONALD
84 Vice Pres Enrollment Management .... Mrs. Rita DETWILER
32 Vice Pres & Dean of Student Develop .... Mr. John G. ECCLES
50 Dean School Business & Economics .... Dr. Joseph TUREK
53 Dean School Education/Human Devel .... Dr. Jan STENNETTE
60 Dean Sch Communications & The Arts .... Dr. Oeida HATCHER
79 Dean Sch Humanities/Social Science .... Dr. Kim MCCABE
81 Dean School of Sciences .... Dr. Barry LOBB
76 Dean Sch Health Science/Human Perf .... Dr. Linda ANDREWS
06 Registrar/Asst Dean Acad/Stndt Info .... Mr. Jay K. WEBB
08 Director of the Library .. Mr. Christopher A. MILLSON-MARTULA
37 Director of Financial Aid .... Ms. Michelle DAVIS

Mary Baldwin College (C)

318 Prospect Street, Staunton VA 24401
County: Augusta FICE Identification: 003723
Unit ID: 232672
Telephone: (540) 887-7000 Carnegie Class: Master's S
FAX Number: (540) 886-5561 Calendar System: Other
URL: www.mbc.edu
Established: 1842 Annual Undergrad Tuition & Fees: $28,020
Enrollment: 2,250 Female
Affiliation or Control: Presbyterian Church (U.S.A.) IRS Status: 501(c)3
Highest Offering: Master's
Program: Liberal Arts And General; Teacher Preparatory
Accreditation: SC, @SW, TEAC

01 President .... Dr. Pamela FOX
05 VP Academic Affairs/Dean .... Dr. Catharine O'CONNELL
10 Sr Vice President Business/Finance .... Mr. David MOWEN
84 Sr VP Enrollment Mgmt/Dean Stdnts .... Dr. Brenda BRYANT
30 Vice Pres Institutional Advancement .... Mr. David ATCHLEY
26 Vice President for Public Relations .... Ms. Crista CABE
88 Assoc VP for Inclusive Excellence .... Rev. Andrea CORNELL-SCOTT
58 Int Dean Adult & Graduate Studies .... Ms. Lallon POND
09 Dean Inst Research/Registrar .... Dr. Lewis D. ASKEGAARD
27 Chief Information Officer .... Mr. Angus MCQUEEN
07 Executive Director Enrollment Mgmt .... Mr. Andrew MODLIN
08 Director of Library .... Ms. Carol CREAGER
58 Int Director of MAT .... Dr. James HARRINGTON
57 Director ML/MFA .... Dr. Paul MENZER
88 Director Program for Excep Gifted .... Dr. Stephanie FERGUSON
15 Director of Human Resources .... Ms. Shelly IRVINE
32 Exec Dir Stdnt Life/Asc Dean Stdnts .... Ms. Lisa WELLS
18 Chief Facilities/Physical Plant .... Mr. Brent DOUGLASS
21 Dir of Budgets/Business Operation .... Mr. Rick CZERWINSKI
29 Director of Alumni Relations .... Ms. Elizabeth SHUPE
36 Director Career Development Svcs .... Ms. Julie CHAPPELL
37 Director of Financial Aid .... Ms. Robin DIETRICH

Marymount University (D)

2807 N Glebe Road, Arlington VA 22207-4299
County: Arlington FICE Identification: 003724
Unit ID: 232706
Telephone: (703) 522-5600 Carnegie Class: Master's L
FAX Number: (703) 284-1637 Calendar System: Semester
URL: www.marymount.edu
Established: 1950 Annual Undergrad Tuition & Fees: $24,900
Enrollment: 3,633 Coed
Affiliation or Control: Roman Catholic IRS Status: 501(c)3
Highest Offering: Doctorate
Program: Liberal Arts And General; Teacher Preparatory; Professional
Accreditation: SC, ACBSP, CACREP, CIDA, HSA, NURSE, PTA, TED

01 President .... Dr. Matthew D. SHANK
05 Provost and Vice Pres Acad Affairs .... Dr. Sherri L. HUGHES
10 Vice Pres for Financial Affairs .... Dr. Ralph KIDDER
84 Vice Pres Stdnt Devel & Enrollment .... Dr. Chris E. DOMES
30 Vice President for Development .... Vacant
26 Vice Pres Communications/Marketing ...... Ms. Shelley A. DUTTON
20 Assoc Vice President Acad Affairs .... Dr. Robert OTTEN
20 Assoc Vice President Acad Affairs .... Dr. Liane SUMMERFIELD
49 Dean Arts & Sciences .... Dr. George CHEATHAM
50 Dean Business Administration .... Dr. James RYERSON
53 Dean Education & Human Services .... Vacant
76 Dean Health Professions .... Dr. Tess CAPPELLO
08 Dean Library & Learning Services .... Dr. Zary MOSTASHARI
06 University Registrar .... Mr. Scott SPENCER
13 Exec Director IT Services .... Ms. Claudia O'CONNOR
09 Exec Director Inst Effectiveness .... Mr. Michael SCHUCHERT
32 Assoc Vice President Student Dev .... Mr. Frank RIZZO
07 Director of Admissions Undergrad .... Mr. Michael CANFIELD
07 Director of Graduate Admissions .... Ms. Francesca REED
37 Director Financial Aid .... Ms. Deborah RAINES
42 Director Campus Ministry .... Rev. David SHARLAND
41 Director Athletics .... Mrs. Debbie WARREN
19 Dir of Campus Safety/Transportation .... Mr. Eric HOLS
91 Dir of Admin Information Services .... Vacant
39 Director of Residence Life .... Mr. Paul LYNCH
35 Director of Student Activities .... Mr. Vincent STOVALL
23 Director of Student Health Service .... Ms. Diane WHITE
38 Director Student Counseling .... Mr. Silvestro MENZANO
21 Asst Vice Pres and Controller .... Mr. Ronald SOMERVELL
15 Exec Dir Human Resource Svcs .... Mr. James HOBSON
18 Int Director of Physical Plant .... Mr. Robert RUSH
96 Coordinator of Purchasing .... Mrs. Amy PAPPAS
29 Exec Dir Development/Alumni Rels .... Mrs. Kathleen ZEIFANG
26 Director of Public Relations .... Ms. Laurie F. CALLAHAN

Medical Careers Institute (E)

1001 Omni Boulevard Suite 200,
Newport News VA 23606-4388
County: Newport News FICE Identification: 022472
Unit ID: 231642
Telephone: (757) 873-2423 Carnegie Class: Assoc/PrivFP
FAX Number: (757) 873-2472 Calendar System: Other
URL: www.medical.edu
Established: N/A Annual Undergrad Tuition & Fees: N/A
Enrollment: 19 Coed
Affiliation or Control: Proprietary IRS Status: Proprietary
Highest Offering: Associate Degree
Program: Occupational
Accreditation: &SC, MAAB, PTAA, RAD

01 President .... Ms. Alicia COLES
05 Vice President of Operations .... Ms. Barbara LARAR

† Regional accreditation is carried under the parent institution, ECPI College of Technology, in Virginia Beach, VA.

Medical Careers Institute (F)

2809 Emerywood Parkway, Suite 400,
Richmond VA 23294
County: Henrico Identification: 667038
Telephone: (804) 521-5999 Carnegie Class: Not Classified
FAX Number: (804) 521-5998 Calendar System: Other
URL: www.medical.edu
Established: N/A Annual Undergrad Tuition & Fees: N/A
Enrollment: N/A Coed
Affiliation or Control: Proprietary IRS Status: Proprietary
Highest Offering: Associate Degree
Program: Occupational
Accreditation: &SC, MAAB

01 Interim Campus President .... Dr. John OLSON

† Regional accreditation is carried under the parent institution ECPI College of Technology, Virginia Beach, VA.

Medtech College (G)

6565 Arlington Blvd., Suite 100, Falls Church VA 22042
County: Fairfax FICE Identification: 025889
Unit ID: 131742
Telephone: (703) 237-6200 Carnegie Class: Assoc/PrivFP
FAX Number: (703) 533-3750 Calendar System: Semester
URL: www.medtec.edu
Established: 1939 Annual Undergrad Tuition & Fees: $1,868
Enrollment: 15,500 Coed
Affiliation or Control: Proprietary IRS Status: Proprietary
Highest Offering: Associate Degree
Program: Occupational
Accreditation: COE

01 Executive Director .... Janet BARONE

Miller-Motte Technical College (H)

1011 Creekside Lane, Lynchburg VA 24502-4353
County: Lynchburg FICE Identification: 004992
Unit ID: 233091
Telephone: (434) 239-5222 Carnegie Class: Assoc/PrivFP
FAX Number: (434) 239-1069 Calendar System: Quarter
URL: www.miller-motte.com
Established: 1997 Annual Undergrad Tuition & Fees: $9,648
Enrollment: 460 Coed
Affiliation or Control: Proprietary IRS Status: Proprietary
Highest Offering: Associate Degree
Program: Occupational; Technical Emphasis
Accreditation: ACICS, MAC, SURGT

01 Director .... Ms. Suzie ROLAND

National College (I)

1819 Emmet Street, Charlottesville VA 22901-2812
County: Charlottesville City Identification: 666501
Telephone: (434) 295-0136 Carnegie Class: Not Classified
FAX Number: (434) 979-8061 Calendar System: Quarter
URL: www.ncbt.edu
Established: 1865 Annual Undergrad Tuition & Fees: N/A
Enrollment: 215 Coed
Affiliation or Control: Proprietary IRS Status: Proprietary
Highest Offering: Associate Degree
Program: Occupational; Business Emphasis
Accreditation: ACICS, MAC

01 President .... Mr. Frank LONGAKER
05 Director .... Dr. Kimberly MOORE
03 Executive Vice President .... Ms. Lenora DOWNING

† Branch campus of National College, Salem, VA.

National College (J)

336 Old Riverside Drive, Danville VA 24541-1819
County: Independent City Identification: 666502
Telephone: (434) 793-6822 Carnegie Class: Not Classified
FAX Number: (434) 793-3634 Calendar System: Quarter

URL: www.ncbt.edu
Established: N/A Annual Undergrad Tuition & Fees: $9,052
Enrollment: 365 Coed
Affiliation or Control: Proprietary IRS Status: Proprietary
Highest Offering: Baccalaureate
Program: Occupational; Business Emphasis
Accreditation: ACICS, MAC, SURGT

01 Campus Director .... Mr. Mark EVANS
03 Executive Vice President .... Ms. Lenora S. DOWNING

† Branch campus of National College, Salem, VA.

National College (A)

1515 Country Club Road, Harrisonburg VA 22801-9709
County: Rockingham Identification: 666503
Telephone: (540) 432-0943 Carnegie Class: Not Classified
FAX Number: (540) 432-1133 Calendar System: Quarter
URL: www.ncbt.edu
Established: 1986 Annual Undergrad Tuition & Fees: $12,900
Enrollment: 340 Coed
Affiliation or Control: Proprietary IRS Status: Proprietary
Highest Offering: Baccalaureate
Program: Occupational; Technical Emphasis
Accreditation: ACICS, MAC, SURGT

01 Director .... Mr. David ZIMMERMAN

† Branch campus of National College, Salem, VA.

National College (B)

104 Candlewood Court, Lynchburg VA 24502-2653
County: Lynchburg City Identification: 666504
Telephone: (434) 239-3500 Carnegie Class: Not Classified
FAX Number: (434) 239-3948 Calendar System: Quarter
URL: www.ncbt.edu
Established: 1886 Annual Undergrad Tuition & Fees: $8,900
Enrollment: 432 Coed
Affiliation or Control: Proprietary IRS Status: Proprietary
Highest Offering: Baccalaureate
Program: Occupational; Business Emphasis
Accreditation: ACICS, MAC

01 Director .... Mr. Bill BAKER

† Branch campus of National College, Salem, VA.

National College (C)

905 N. Memorial Boulevard, Martinsville VA 24112-2420
County: Martinsville City Identification: 666505
Telephone: (276) 632-5621 Carnegie Class: Not Classified
FAX Number: (276) 632-7915 Calendar System: Quarter
URL: www.ncbt.edu
Established: 1886 Annual Undergrad Tuition & Fees: $11,964
Enrollment: 475 Coed
Affiliation or Control: Proprietary IRS Status: Proprietary
Highest Offering: Associate Degree
Program: Occupational; Technical Emphasis
Accreditation: ACICS, MAC

01 Director .... Mr. John H. SCOTT

† Branch campus of National College, Salem, VA.

National College (D)

1813 E Main Street, Salem VA 24153-4598
County: Independent City FICE Identification: 003726
Unit ID: 232797
Telephone: (540) 986-1800 Carnegie Class: Assoc/PrivFP4
FAX Number: (540) 986-1344 Calendar System: Quarter
URL: www.national-college.edu
Established: 1886 Annual Undergrad Tuition & Fees: $11,412
Enrollment: 500 Coed
Affiliation or Control: Proprietary IRS Status: Proprietary
Highest Offering: Master's
Program: Business Emphasis
Accreditation: ACICS, EMT, MAC

01 President .... Mr. Frank E. LONGAKER
03 Executive Vice President .... Ms. Lenora S. DOWNING
05 Campus Director .... Mr. Lewis BISHOP
07 Regional Director of Admissions .... Mr. Larry W. STEELE

Norfolk State University (E)

700 Park Avenue, Norfolk VA 23504-8000
County: Independent City FICE Identification: 003765
Unit ID: 232937
Telephone: (757) 823-8600 Carnegie Class: Master's L
FAX Number: (757) 823-2067 Calendar System: Semester
URL: www.nsu.edu
Established: 1935 Annual Undergrad Tuition & Fees (In-State): $6,860
Enrollment: 7,091 Coed
Affiliation or Control: State IRS Status: 501(c)3
Highest Offering: Doctorate
Program: Liberal Arts And General; Teacher Preparatory; Professional
Accreditation: SC, ADNUR, BUS, CLPSY, CS, DIETD, ENG, #JOUR, KIN, MT, MUS, NAIT, NUR, SW, TED

01 President .... Dr. Tony ATWATER
03 Exec VP/Chief Operation Ofcr .... Dr. Kim LUCKES
100 Chief of Staff .... Dr. Deborah C. FONTAINE
05 Provost/Vice Pres Academic Affs .... Dr. Sandra J. DELOATCH
10 Interim Vice Pres Finance/Admin .... Mr. Gregory A. DAVIS
30 Acting Vice Pres Univ Advancement .... Mrs. Cheryl A. BATES-LEE
32 Interim Vice Pres Student Affairs .... Mr. Edward M. WILLIS
20 Vice Provost for Undergrad .... Dr. Mildred K. FULLER
20 Vice Provost .... Dr. Clarence D. COLEMAN
84 Asst Vice Pres Enrollment Mgmt .... Mrs. Terricita E. SASS
35 Asst Vice Pres Student Affairs .... Vacant
43 University Counsel .... Ms. Pamela F. BOSTON
07 Dir of Recuitment & Admissions .... Mrs. Lakeisha E. MAYES
19 Chief of Campus Police .... Mr. Anthony H. WALKER
38 Acting Director of Counseling .... Mrs. Vanessa C. JENKINS
06 Interim Registrar .... Mr. Michael CARPENTER
08 Interim Library Director .... Dr. Tommy BOGGER
37 Director of Financial Aid .... Mr. Kevin J. BURNS
36 Director of Career Services .... Mr. Nash D. MONTOGMERY
15 Human Resources Director .... Mrs. Francie H. JOHNSON
14 Director Enterprise Information Sys .Mrs. Alison D. DAVIS-TARIQ
29 Director of Alumni Relations .... Ms. Michelle D. HILL
49 Dean of Liberal Arts .... Dr. Belinda C. ANDERSON
50 Dean of Business .... Dr. Steven D. PAPMARCOS
53 Dean of Education .... Vacant
76 Acting Dean of Science & Technology .... Dr. Larry MATTIX
70 Dean of Social Work .... Dr. Dorothy C. BROWNE
58 Dean of Graduate Studies and Resear .... Vacant
86 Legislative and Community Liason .... Ms. Paula C. THOMPSON
26 Asst VP of Univ Relations .... Mrs. Cheryl A. BATES-LEE
09 Dir Institutional Research .... Dr. Alona SMOLOVA
39 Director of Residential Life .... Mrs. Faith M. FITZGERALD
40 Bookstore Manager .... Ms. Pamela WILLIAMSON
41 Athletic Director .... Mr. Marty L. MILLER
88 Univ Ombudsmen .... Vacant
18 Director of Facilities Management .... Vacant
85 Dir of Intl Student & Scholar Svcs .... Dr. William ALEXANDER
96 Director of Procurement .... Ms. Lynn MOON
21 Controller .... Mr. Barry O. HERRING

† Member of Virginia Consortium for Professional Psychology.

Old Dominion University (F)

5115 Hampton Boulevard, Norfolk VA 23529-0001
County: Independent City FICE Identification: 003728
Unit ID: 232982
Telephone: (757) 683-3000 Carnegie Class: RU/H
FAX Number: (757) 683-4505 Calendar System: Semester
URL: www.odu.edu
Established: 1930 Annual Undergrad Tuition & Fees (In-State): $8,450
Enrollment: 24,753 Coed
Affiliation or Control: State IRS Status: 501(c)3
Highest Offering: Doctorate
Program: Liberal Arts And General; Teacher Preparatory; Professional
Accreditation: SC, ANEST, ART, BUS, BUSA, CACREP, CLPSY, CYTO, DH, ENG, ENGT, EXSC, HT, MT, MUS, NMT, NRPA, NURSE, PH, PTA, SP, SPAA, TED, THEA

01 President .... Mr. John R. BRODERICK
05 Provost/VP Academic Affairs .... Dr. Carol SIMPSON
10 Vice President Admin & Finance .... Mr. Robert L. FENNING
46 Vice President for Research .... Dr. Mohammad A. KARIM
15 Act Vice Pres for Human Resources .... Ms. September C. SANDERLIN
30 Vice Pres University Advancement .... Mr. Alonzo C. BRANDON
32 VP Student Engagement & Enroll Svcs ...... Dr. Ellen J. NEUFELDT
09 Vice Prov Plng & Inst Effectiveness .... Dr. Martha S. SHARPE
88 Vice Provost for Faculty/Pgm Devel .... Dr. Chandra R. DESILVA
20 Assoc Vice Pres Academic Services .... Mr. James P. DUFFY
21 Asc VP Admn & Fin/Univ Budget Ofcr .... Ms. Deborah L. SWIECINSKI
56 Assoc VP Distance Learning .... Mr. Andrew R. CASIELLO
88 Asst Vice Pres Auxiliary Services .... Mr. Todd JOHNSON
13 Asst Vice Pres Comp & Comm Services .... Mr. James R. WATERFIELD
31 Asst Vice Pres Community Engagement .... Ms. Karen F. MEIER
84 Assoc Vice Pres Enrollment Mgmt .... Ms. Jane H. DANE
44 Assoc Vice Pres for Advancement .... Mr. Daniel J. GENARD
88 Assoc VP Student Engage/Enroll Svcs .... Mr. Johnny YOUNG
20 Asst VP Undergraduate Studies .... Ms. Judith M. BOWMAN
30 Asst Vice Pres for Development .... Dr. Anita S. FRIEDMAN
29 Asst Vice Pres of Alumni Relations .... Ms. Dana G. ALLEN
26 Asst VP Marketing & Communications .... Ms. Jennifer MULLEN
22 Asst VP Inst Equity & Diversity .... Ms. ReNee S. DUNMAN
49 Dean College Arts & Letters .... Dr. Charles E. WILSON, JR.
81 Dean College of Sciences .... Dr. Christopher PLATSOUCAS
76 Dean College Health Sciences .... Dr. Shelley C. MISHOE
50 Dean Col Business/Public Admin .... Dr. Gilbert R. YOCHUM
53 Dean College of Education .... Dr. Linda IRWIN-DEVITIS
54 Dean Col Engineering & Tech .... Dr. Oktay BAYSAL
92 Dean Honors College .... Dr. David D. METZGER
20 Int Dean Academic Enhancement .... Dr. David D. METZGER
36 Asst Dean Career Management Center .... Mr. Tom WUNDERLICH
93 Asst Dean Multicultural Stdnt Svcs .... Ms. Lesa C. CLARK
35 Dean of Students .... Mr. Donald M. STANSBURY
43 General Counsel .... Mr. Richard E. NANCE
85 Exec Dir International Programs .... Mr. Marcelo E. SILES
88 Exec Dir Cmty Development Corp .... Ms. E. Ann GRANDY
08 University Librarian .... Ms. Virginia S. O'HERRON
06 University Registrar .... Ms. Mary K. SWARTZ
07 Exec Director of Admissions .... Vacant
41 Director of Athletics .... Dr. C. Wood SELIG
37 Int Director Student Financial Aid .... Ms. Vera E. RIDDICK
31 Director Community Relations .... Ms. Cecelia T. TUCKER
88 Director Military Affairs .... Capt. F. Richard WHALEN
38 Assoc Dean Stdnts/Dir Counsel Svcs .. Dr. Lenora H. THOMPSON
23 Director Student Health Center .... Ms. Jennifer J. FOSS
85 Director Intl Students & Faculty .... Ms. Robbin S. FULMORE
91 Director Computing Information Svcs .... Mr. Michael S. LITTLE
39 Exec Director of Student Housing .... Ms. Carole S. HENRY
18 Director Facilities Management .... Mr. R. Dillard GEORGE
88 University Controller .... Vacant
19 Chief of Police .... Ms. Rhonda L. HARRIS
27 Director of Public Relations .... Mr. Stephen P. DANIEL
28 Director of Diversity and EO/AA .... Ms. Pamela E. JACKSON
96 Director of Materiel Management .... Mr. Rick BERRY
94 Director Women's Studies .... Dr. Jennifer N. FISH
16 Director of Human Resources .... Vacant
35 Dir Student Activities/Leadership .... Ms. Nicole C. KIGER
40 Manager Bookstore .... Mr. Darryl ATKINSON
04 Assistant to the President & COO .... Ms. Velvet L. GRANT
86 Asst to Pres for Govt Relations .... Ms. Elizabeth A. KERSEY

† Member of Virginia Consortium for Professional Psychology.

Patrick Henry College (G)

Ten Patrick Henry Circle, Purcellville VA 20132
County: Loudoun FICE Identification: 039513
Telephone: (540) 338-1776 Carnegie Class: Bac/A&S
FAX Number: (540) 441-8709 Calendar System: Semester
URL: www.phc.edu
Established: 2000 Annual Undergrad Tuition & Fees: $24,352
Enrollment: 461 Coed
Affiliation or Control: Independent Non-Profit IRS Status: 501(c)3
Highest Offering: Baccalaureate
Program: Liberal Arts And General
Accreditation: TRACS

01 President .... Dr. Graham WALKER
00 Chancellor .... Dr. Michael P. FARRIS
05 Provost .... Dr. Gene E. VEITH
03 Exec Vice President & Treasurer .... Mr. Carl W. SCHREIBER
84 Asst VP for Enrollment Management .... Mr. William KELLARIS
30 Vice President for Advancement .... Mr. Colin STEWART
11 Vice Pres for Campus Services .... Mr. Earl W. HALL
10 Chief Financial Officer .... Mr. Daryl WOLKING
13 Chief Information Officer .... Mr. Jeff R. BURTNER
49 Chairman Classical Liberal Arts Dep .... Dr. Stephen R. HAKE
80 Chairman Government Department .... Dr. Mark MITCHELL
06 Registrar .... Mr. Rodney J. SHOWALTER
09 Director Inst Research & Records .... Mr. Rodney SHOWALTER
56 Director of Distance Learning .... Dr. Robert G. SPINNEY
08 Director of the Library .... Ms. Charlessa E. MCCONNELL
32 Dean of Student Affairs .... Ms. Sandra K. CORBITT
07 Asst Director of Admissions .... Ms. Tia STOCKTON
26 Director of Communications .... Mr. David W. HALBROOK
15 Director of Human Resources .... Ms. Barbara A. FINLAY

Potomac College (H)

2070 Chain Bridge Road, Vienna VA 22182
County: Fairfax Identification: 666178
Unit ID: 442639
Telephone: (703) 709-5875 Carnegie Class: Bac/Diverse
FAX Number: (703) 709-8976 Calendar System: Semester
URL: www.potomac.edu
Established: 1991 Annual Undergrad Tuition & Fees: $12,760
Enrollment: 31 Coed
Affiliation or Control: Proprietary IRS Status: Proprietary
Highest Offering: Baccalaureate
Program: 2-Year Principally Bachelor's Creditable; Professional; Business Emphasis
Accreditation: &M

01 Chief Executive Officer .... Dr. Laura PALMER NOONE
05 Vice Pres Academic Affairs .... Dr. Richard RESCH
20 Academic Dean .... Mr. James MOSES
06 Registrar .... Ms. Toni NEWMAN
37 Financial Aid Director .... Ms. Phyllis CREWS
08 Librarian .... Vacant
32 Director of Student Services .... Mr. Marcus PALMORE
35 Assistant Director Student Services .... Mr. Ervan PEARSON

† Regional accreditation is carried under the parent institution in Washington, DC.

Protestant Episcopal Theological Seminary in Virginia (I)

3737 Seminary Road, Alexandria VA 22304-5201
County: Independent City FICE Identification: 003731
Unit ID: 233259
Telephone: (703) 370-6600 Carnegie Class: Not Classified
FAX Number: (703) 370-6234 Calendar System: Semester
URL: www.vts.edu
Established: 1823 Annual Graduate Tuition & Fees: $12,600
Enrollment: 181 Coed
Affiliation or Control: Protestant Episcopal IRS Status: 501(c)3
Highest Offering: Doctorate; No Undergraduates
Program: Professional; Religious Emphasis
Accreditation: THEOL

01 President/Dean .... Rev. Ian S. MARKHAM

05 Vice Pres/Assoc Dean Academic Affs .. Dr. Timothy F. SEDGWICK
11 VP for Administration/Finance .... Mrs. Heather ZDANCEWICZ
32 Assoc Dean of Students ....Dr. Amelia G. DYER
06 Registrar .... Mrs. Tamara A. SHEPHERD
08 Director of the Library ....Dr. Mitzi J. BUDDE

Radford University (A)

810 E Main Street, Radford VA 24142-0002
County: Independent City FICE Identification: 003732
Unit ID: 233277
Telephone: (540) 831-5000 Carnegie Class: Master's L
FAX Number: (540) 831-5142 Calendar System: Semester
URL: www.radford.edu
Established: 1910 Annual Undergrad Tuition & Fees (In-State): $8,590
Enrollment: 9,370 Coed
Affiliation or Control: State IRS Status: 501(c)3
Highest Offering: Doctorate
Program: Liberal Arts And General; Teacher Preparatory; Professional
Accreditation: SC, BUS, CACREP, CIDA, CS, DIETD, MUS, NRPA, NURSE, OT, @PTA, SP, SW, TED, THEA

01 President ....Ms. Penelope W. KYLE
04 Special Assistant to the President ....Ms. JoAnn KIERNAN
05 Provost & VP Academic Affairs ....Dr. Sam H. MINNER
10 Vice President for Finance & Admin ...... Mr. Richard S. ALVAREZ
32 Vice President for Student Affairs .... Dr. Mark G. SHANLEY
30 VP Univ Advancement .... Dr. Deborah ROBINSON
84 Interim Vice Prov Enroll Plng/Mgmt .... Mr. James PENNIX
20 Vice Prov for Academic Affairs ....Dr. William R. KENNAN
49 Dean Col Hum/Behav Sci ....Dr. Katherine HAWKINS
50 Dean of Business & Economics ....Dr. Faye W. GILBERT
53 Dean Education & Human Development .... Dr. Patricia B. SHOEMAKER
66 Dean Health & Human Services ....Dr. Kenneth M. COX
57 Dean Visual/Performing Arts .... Dr. Joseph P. SCARTELLI
58 Dean College of Grad & Prof Studies ....Dr. Dennis O. GRADY
72 Dean Col of Sci & Technology .... Dr. J. Orion ROGERS
35 Assoc Vice Pres & Dean of Students .... Mr. Don APPIARIUS
90 Associate VP Info Technology .... Mr. Edward OAKES
07 Dean of Admissions ....Mr. James PENNIX
06 Registrar ....Mr. Matthew S. BRUNNER
37 Director of Financial Aid .... Mrs. Barbara A. PORTER
39 Director of Residential Life .... Ms. Amber MULLEN
18 Director Facilities Operations .... Mr. Jorge W. COARTNEY
29 Assoc Dir of Alumni Relations ....Ms. Sandra BOND
41 Director Intercollegiate Athletics .... Mr. Robert LINEBURG
08 Dean of the Library ....Mr. Steve HELM
13 Vice President Info Technology/CIO ....Mr. Danny M. KEMP
15 Director of Human Resources ....Vacant
19 Director of University Police ....Chief Colleen T. ROBERTS
88 Dir Acad Engage/Career Svc/Comm ....Ms. Ellen TAYLOR
23 Director Student Health Services ....Ms. Abby UGLUM
85 Interim Dir of International Pgm ....Ms. Teresa KING
24 Director TV/Radio/Comm Svcs ....Ms. Ashlee B. CLAUD
25 Dir Sponsored Pgms/Grant Mgmt .... Mr. Thomas CRUISE
40 Manager University Bookstore .... Mr. Benjie SAUNDERS
96 Director of Material Management .... Ms. Pamela P. SIMPKINS
09 Asst Vice Provost/Dir Inst Research .....Dr. Debra R. TEMPLETON
38 Director Student Counseling .... Ms. Erin SULLIVAN
41 Director Univ Adv for Athletics .... Mr. Kelly R. UNDERWOOD
102 Exec Dir Univ Adv Corp & Foundation ....Ms. Robyn J. PORTERFIELD
88 University Controller ....Mr. William H. SHORTER
44 Director Annual Giving .... Mr. Alex SIMPSON
88 Director Planning & Construction .... Mr. Roy E. SAVILLE
88 Dir Leadership/Professional Dev ....Vacant
86 Dir Govt/Non-Profit Assistance Ctr ....Dr. Bruce W. CHASE
88 Assoc VP Student Affairs/Activities ....Mr. Kenneth J. BONK
39 Director of Housing Operations ....Mr. Jeffrey P. ORZOLEK
51 Int Dir Ctr Innovative Teach/Learn .... Mr. Charlie COSMATO
28 Dir Ctr for Diversity & Inclusion .... Ms. Crasha PERKINS
26 Asst Dir University Relations ....Ms. Christy JACKSON

Randolph College (B)

2500 Rivermont Avenue, Lynchburg VA 24503-1555
County: Independent City FICE Identification: 003734
Unit ID: 233301
Telephone: (434) 947-8000 Carnegie Class: Bac/A&S
FAX Number: (434) 947-8139 Calendar System: Semester
URL: www.randolphcollege.edu
Established: 1891 Annual Undergrad Tuition & Fees: $30,376
Enrollment: 576 Coed
Affiliation or Control: United Methodist IRS Status: 501(c)3
Highest Offering: Master's
Program: Liberal Arts And General; Teacher Preparatory
Accreditation: SC, TEAC

01 President ....Mr. John E. KLEIN
05 VP Academic Affs & Dean of College ....Dr. Carl A. GIRELLI
30 Vice Pres Institutional Advancement .... Ms. Jan MERIWETHER
10 VP Finance/Administration/ Treasurer .... Mr. Christopher L. BURNLEY
32 VP Student Affs & Dean of Students ....Dr. Martha THORNTON
26 Vice Pres College Relations ....Dr. Sandra BARTHOLOMEW
84 VP Enrollment Management .... Mr. Michael J. QUINN
101 Exec Asst to Pres/Sec Board Trust ....Mr. Wesley (Wes) FUGATE
20 Associate Dean of the College ....Ms. Paula J. WALLACE
29 Alumnae Director .... Ms. Heather A. GARNETT
09 Dir Institutional Res/Plng/Asses ....Dr. John F. KEENER
15 Director Human Resources .... Ms. Sharon SAUNDERS

18 Chief Facilities/Physical Plant ....Mr. Bobby BENNETT
21 Controller ....Mr. Jonathan TYREE
38 Director Student Counseling .... Dr. Anne HERSHBELL
08 Librarian .... Mr. Theodore J. HOSTETLER
06 Registrar .... Ms. Barbara S. THRASHER
37 Dir Student Financial Services .... Ms. Kay MATTOX
36 Director of Career Development ....Ms. Connie HAYES
13 Director of Information Technology .... Mr. Victor GOSNELL

Randolph-Macon College (C)

204 Henry Street, PO Box 5005, Ashland VA 23005-5505
County: Hanover FICE Identification: 003733
Unit ID: 233295
Telephone: (804) 752-7200 Carnegie Class: Bac/A&S
FAX Number: (804) 752-7231 Calendar System: Other
URL: www.rmc.edu
Established: 1830 Annual Undergrad Tuition & Fees: $33,525
Enrollment: 1,257 Coed
Affiliation or Control: United Methodist IRS Status: 501(c)3
Highest Offering: Baccalaureate
Program: Liberal Arts And General; Teacher Preparatory
Accreditation: SC, TEAC

01 President ....Mr. Robert R. LINDGREN
05 Provost/VP for Academic Affairs ....Dr. William T. FRANZ
10 Vice Pres of Admin & Finance .... Mr. Paul DAVIES
30 Vice Pres for College Advancement .... Ms. Diane M. LOWDER
07 Dean of Admissions/Financial Aid ....Dr. David L. LESESNE
32 Dean of Students ....Dr. Grant L. AZDELL
29 Exec Dir Col Advancement for Alumni ....Mrs. Susan H. DONAVANT
08 Director of Library ....Dr. Virginia E. YOUNG
26 Dir of Marketing & Communications .... Mrs. Anne Marie LAURANZON
07 Director of Admissions ....Mr. Anthony F. AMBROGI
37 Director of Financial Aid ....Mrs. Mary Y. NEAL
14 Director of Information & Tech Svcs ....Mr. Thomas H. COPLER
06 Registrar ....Mrs. Alana DAVIS
36 Dir Counseling/Career Services .... Dr. D. Craig ANDERSON
09 Director of Institutional Research .... Dr. Timothy W. MERRILL
18 Dir of Operations & Physical Plant ....Mr. Thomas P. DWYER
42 Chaplain .... Rev. Darrell L. HEADRICK
19 Director of Campus Safety .... Mr. Maurice J. KIELY
41 Athletic Director ....Mr. Jeffrey S. BURNS
15 Director Human Resources ....Mrs. Sharon S. JACKSON
21 Controller ....Mrs. Caroline C. BUSCH
20 Associate Dean of the College ....Dr. Lauren C. BELL
36 Director of Career Services ....Ms. Catherine A. ROLLMAN
35 Asst Dean of Students ....Mr. James D. MCGHEE, JR.
40 Bookstore Manager ....Mrs. Barclay F. DUPRIEST
88 Exec Dir Ctr Personal/Career Dev ....Mrs. Linda P. CARNE

Reformed Theological Seminary (D)

1651 Old Meadow Road, Suite 300, McLean VA 22102
County: Fairfax Identification: 666079
Telephone: (703) 448-3393 Carnegie Class: Not Classified
FAX Number: (703) 738-7389 Calendar System: 4/1/4
URL: www.rts.edu
Established: 1997 Annual Graduate Tuition & Fees: $14,940
Enrollment: 139 Coed
Affiliation or Control: Independent Non-Profit IRS Status: 501(c)3
Highest Offering: Master's; No Undergraduates
Program: Religious Emphasis
Accreditation: &SC, &THEOL

01 Campus President ....Dr. Scott REDD
05 Academic Dean ....Mr. Howard GRIFFITH
30 Vice President for Development ....Mr. Dennis FUSARO
07 Dir Admiss/Student Svcs/Registrar .... Mr. Geoffrey M. SACKETT

† Regional accreditation is carried under the parent institution in Jackson, MS.

Regent University (E)

1000 Regent University Drive,
Virginia Beach VA 23464-9800
County: Independent City FICE Identification: 030913
Unit ID: 231651
Telephone: (757) 352-4127 Carnegie Class: DRU
FAX Number: (757) 352-4381 Calendar System: Semester
URL: www.regent.edu
Established: 1977 Annual Undergrad Tuition & Fees: $15,508
Enrollment: 5,915 Coed
Affiliation or Control: Independent Non-Profit IRS Status: 501(c)3
Highest Offering: Doctorate
Program: Professional
Accreditation: SC, CACREP, CLPSY, LAW, TEAC, THEOL

01 President ....Dr. Carlos CAMPO
05 Exec Vice Pres for Academic Affairs ....Dr. Paul BONICELLI
30 Vice President for Advancement ....Mrs. Ann LEBLANC
14 Vice President for Info Technology ....Mrs. Tracy R. STEWART
10 VP of Finance .... Mr. Dean A. WOOTEN
15 Vice President for Human Resources ....Mrs. Martha J. SMITH
26 VP for Marketing & Public Relations ....Ms. Sherri STOCKS
106 Assistant VP of Online Learning ....Mrs. Ginger ZILLGES
60 Dean Communication & the Arts ....Dr. Mitch LAND
88 Dean School of Global Leadership ....Dr. Bruce E. WINSTON
38 Dean Psychology & Counseling .... Dr. William HATHAWAY

73 Dean School of Divinity ....Dr. Michael D. PALMER
53 Interim Dean School of Education ....Dr. Gail DERRICK
80 Dean School of Government .... Dr. Eric PATTERSON
61 Dean School of Law .... Mr. Jeffrey A. BRAUCH
97 Dean School of Undergrad Studies . Dr. Gerson MORENO-RIANO
08 Dean of Libraries .... Dr. Sara BARON
43 General Counsel .... Mr. Louis A. ISAKOFF
06 Registrar ....Ms. Althea KIMES
37 Director of Financial Aid .... Mr. Joseph DOBROTA
09 Director of Institutional Research .... Dr. Amanda WYNN
84 Director of Enrollment Management .... Mr. Matthew CHADWICK
18 Dir of Facilities & Engineering .... Mr. Richard JEMIOLA
29 Director of Alumni Relations ....Ms. Melissa FUQUAY
35 Director of Student Life ....Mr. Roger CHEEKS
96 Manager of Purchasing ....Mrs. Pauline CARRAWAY
42 Director of Campus Ministries ....Dr. Richard KIDD
84 Exec Dir Enrollment Marketing .... Mr. David PROFFITT
108 Director of Assessment ....Mr. Ryan MURNANE
88 Director of Military Affairs ....Mr. Dave BOISSELLE

Richard Bland College (F)

11301 Johnson Road, Petersburg VA 23805-7100
County: Independent City FICE Identification: 003707
Unit ID: 233338
Telephone: (804) 862-6100 Carnegie Class: Assoc/Pub2in4
FAX Number: (804) 862-6207 Calendar System: Semester
URL: www.rbc.edu
Established: 1960 Annual Undergrad Tuition & Fees (In-State): $3,658
Enrollment: 1,616 Coed
Affiliation or Control: State IRS Status: 501(c)3
Highest Offering: Associate Degree
Program: 2-Year Principally Bachelor's Creditable
Accreditation: SC

01 President .... Dr. Debbie L. SYDOW
05 Provost & Dean of Faculty ....Vacant
10 Vice Pres Administration & Finance .... Dr. Russell E. WHITAKER, JR.
19 Director Security/Safety ....Mr. C. Scott DAVIS
30 Director Institutional Advancement ....Dr. LeAnn M. BINGER
09 Dir of Institutional Effectiveness .... Mr. James T. HART
06 Registrar .... Ms. Lois WRAY
08 Director of Library ....Mr. Daniel L. REAM
32 Director of Student Affairs ....Mr. Randy DEAN
13 Director of Info Tech Services ....Ms. Dorothy P. EDWARDS
37 Director of Financial Aid ....Mr. James T. HART
07 Assoc Dir of Enrollment Services ..... Mrs. Whitney GERSHOWITZ
15 Director of Human Resources ....Ms. Frances SCARBROUGH
18 Facilities/Physical Plant Manager .... Mr. George JELLERSON
96 Director of Purchasing .... Ms. Nichole COLLINS
35 Assoc Dir of Student Services .... Ms. Evanda WATTS-MARTINEZ
39 Assoc Dir of Residence Life ....Mr. Casey BLANKENSHIP

Roanoke College (G)

221 College Lane, Salem VA 24153-3747
County: Independent City FICE Identification: 003736
Unit ID: 233426
Telephone: (540) 375-2500 Carnegie Class: Bac/A&S
FAX Number: (540) 375-2205 Calendar System: Semester
URL: www.roanoke.edu
Established: 1842 Annual Undergrad Tuition & Fees: $34,496
Enrollment: 2,057 Coed
Affiliation or Control: Evangelical Lutheran Church In America
IRS Status: 501(c)3
Highest Offering: Baccalaureate
Program: Liberal Arts And General; Teacher Preparatory
Accreditation: SC, ACBSP, TEAC

01 President .... Mr. Michael C. MAXEY
05 Vice President/Dean of the College ....Dr. Richard A. SMITH
84 VP of Enrollment Services ....Ms. Brenda P. POGGENDORF
32 Vice President Student Affairs ....Dr. Eugene L. ZDZIARSKI, II
10 Vice President Business Affairs .... Mr. Mark P. NOFTSINGER
30 Vice President Resource Development ...Ms. Connie K. CARMACK
13 Chief Information Officer ....Ms. Rebecca SANDLIN
09 Exec Dir Institutional Research ....Dr. Jack K. STEEHLER
20 Assoc Dean Academic Affairs/Admin ...Dr. Jennifer K. BERENSON
06 Assoc Dean Acad Affairs/Registrar .... Ms. Leah R. RUSSELL
07 Director of Admissions ....Ms. Patricia N. LEDONNE
35 Associate Dean of Student Life ....Dr. Brian T. CHISOM
39 Director of Residence Life/Housing .... Ms. Teresa P. BLETHYN
88 Director of Colket Ctr/Student Act .... Mr. Mark T. PETERSEN
92 Director of Honors Programs ....Dr. Michael A. HAKKENBERG
08 Director of the Library ....Mr. Stanley F. UMBERGER
36 Director of Career Services .... Ms. Toni D. MCLAWHORN
24 Director Instructional Tech/Res Ctr .... Mr. David H. MULFORD
31 Director Cmty Pgms/Special Events ....Ms. Stephanie P. GARST
26 Director of Public Relations .... Ms. Teresa T. GEREAUX
44 Director of Major & Planned Gifts ....Vacant
29 Director of Development/Alumni ....Mr. Jonathan E. LEE
37 Director of Financial Aid ....Mr. Thomas S. BLAIR
21 Director of Finance & Budget ....Ms. Kathryn A. VANNESS
91 Dir Appllications Systems Inf Tech .... Ms. Mitzi B. STEELE
18 Manager Planning and Projects .... Mr. Larry S. WALKER
15 Director Human Resources ....Ms. Cathy S. DICKERSON
40 Bookstore Coordinator/Buyer ....Ms. Melissa B. RUTLEDGE
19 Director Campus Safety ....Mr. Thomas H. TURNER
23 Director Student Health Services ....Ms. Sandra W. MCGHEE
41 Athletic Director ....Mr. M. Scott ALLISON
42 Chaplain .... Rev. R. Paul HENRICKSON

104 Director International Education .... Ms. Lorraine FLECK
38 Director Counseling Center .... Dr. J. P. Hap COX
28 Director of Multicultural Affairs .... Ms. Juliet J. LOWERY
04 Executive Assistant to President .... Ms. Joyce A. SINK
04 Senior Advisor to President .... Mr. McMillan H. JOHNSON

RSHT (A)

751 West Hundred Road, Chester VA 23836-2516
County: Chesterfield Identification: 666481
Telephone: (804) 751-9191 Carnegie Class: Not Classified
FAX Number: (804) 751-2599 Calendar System: Semester
URL: www.rsht.edu
Established: 1997 Annual Undergrad Tuition & Fees: N/A
Enrollment: N/A Coed
Affiliation or Control: Proprietary IRS Status: Proprietary
Highest Offering: Associate Degree
Program: Occupational
Accreditation: **COE**, #RAD

01 Campus Director .... Debbie HARRIS
05 Academic Dean .... Sandra KERRICK

Saint Paul's College (B)

115 College Drive, Lawrenceville VA 23868-1200
County: Brunswick FICE Identification: 003739
Unit ID: 233499
Telephone: (434) 848-3111 Carnegie Class: Bac/Diverse
FAX Number: (434) 848-6407 Calendar System: Semester
URL: www.saintpauls.edu
Established: 1888 Annual Undergrad Tuition & Fees: $13,210
Enrollment: 410 Coed
Affiliation or Control: Protestant Episcopal IRS Status: 501(c)3
Highest Offering: Baccalaureate
Program: Liberal Arts And General; Teacher Preparatory
Accreditation: **#SC**

01 Interim President/CEO .... Dr. Claud FLYTHE
05 Int Provost/Vice Pres Academic Affs .... Dr. Cynthia BEAMON
10 Int Vice Pres Financial Affairs .... Ms. Beverly HERNDON
32 Vice President for Student Affairs .... Dr. Willie J. HARRIS
30 Vice President for Inst Advancement .... Ms. Kimberly TETLOW
84 Director Enrollment Management .... Ms. Vivian HUNTER
06 Int Dir Registration & Records .... Ms. Helen JACKSON
08 Librarian .... Mr. Marc FINNEY
37 Director of Financial Aid .... Mrs. Antionette HOUSE
26 Director of Public Relations .... Miss Germeka AKRIE
35 Director of Student Activities .... Mrs. Kimberly JACKSON
09 Director Institutional Research .... Dr. Barbara WYCHE
36 Director Career Planning/Placement .... Ms. Denise RICE
42 Chaplain .... Rev. Harry V. NEVELS, JR.
29 Director Alumni Relations .... Dr. Dianne BARNES-RHOADES
41 Athletic Director .... Mr. Le Roy H. BACOTE
15 Director of Human Resources .... Mrs. Alta M. THOMAS
13 Dir of Information Technology .... Mr. Joe MACKLIN
88 Director of Student Support Svcs .... Ms. Audrey NELSON
18 Int Supt Facilities/Physical Plant .... Mr. LeRoy BACOTE
20 Asst Dean Academic Affairs .... Ms. Lunette ELLIS

Sanford-Brown College-Tysons Corner (C)

1761 Old Meadow Road, McLean VA 22102
County: Fairfax FICE Identification: 009420
Unit ID: 234216
Telephone: (703) 556-8888 Carnegie Class: Bac/Assoc
FAX Number: (703) 556-0953 Calendar System: Quarter
URL: www.wbscareer.com
Established: 1950 Annual Undergrad Tuition & Fees: $16,328
Enrollment: 829 Coed
Affiliation or Control: Proprietary IRS Status: Proprietary
Highest Offering: Baccalaureate
Program: Occupational; 2-Year Principally Bachelor's Creditable; Liberal Arts And General
Accreditation: **ACICS**, MAAB

01 President .... Dr. Raul GARZA

Sentara College of Health Sciences (D)

1441 Crossways Blvd, Ste 105, Chesapeake VA 23320
County: Chesapeake City FICE Identification: 031065
Telephone: (757) 388-2900 Carnegie Class: Not Classified
FAX Number: (757) 388-2905 Calendar System: Semester
URL: www.sentara.edu
Established: 1892 Annual Undergrad Tuition & Fees: $22,000
Enrollment: 330 Coed
Affiliation or Control: Independent Non-Profit IRS Status: 501(c)3
Highest Offering: Baccalaureate
Program: Professional; Nursing Emphasis
Accreditation: **ACICS**, CVT, NURSE, SURGT

01 Dean Sentara Col of Health Sciences .... Ms. Shelly COHEN
66 Dean of Nursing .... Dr. Angela TAYLOR
45 Asst Dean Institutional Effective .... Ms. Sue CARROLL
76 Asst Dean Dept of Allied Health .... Ms. Nora LEONARD
88 Asst Dean Information Technology .... Mr. Christopher NELSON
32 Asst Dean Dept of Student Svcs .... Mrs. Sandy MOORE

08 Librarian .... Ms. Suzanne DUNCAN
37 Financial Aid Representative .... Ms. Mary Ann RIVERA
07 Admissions Recruiter .... Ms. Sue LAMB

Shenandoah University (E)

1460 University Drive, Winchester VA 22601-5195
County: Independent City FICE Identification: 003737
Unit ID: 233541
Telephone: (540) 665-4500 Carnegie Class: Master's L
FAX Number: N/A Calendar System: Semester
URL: www.su.edu
Established: 1875 Annual Undergrad Tuition & Fees: $28,888
Enrollment: 4,052 Coed
Affiliation or Control: United Methodist IRS Status: 501(c)3
Highest Offering: Doctorate
Program: Liberal Arts And General; Teacher Preparatory; Professional
Accreditation: **SC**, ARCPA, BUS, MIDWF, MUS, NURSE, OT, PHAR, PTA, TEAC

01 President .... Dr. Tracy FITZSIMMONS
05 Senior VP & VP Academic Affairs .... Dr. Bryon L. GRIGSBY
10 Vice Pres Administration/Finance ... Mr. Richard C. SHICKLE, SR.
32 Vice President for Student Life ...... Dr. Rhonda VANDYKE COLBY
30 Vice Pres for Advancement .... Mr. Mitchell L. MOORE
84 VP for Enrol Mgmt & Student Success .... Dr. Clarresa MORTON
39 Dir Resident Life & Student Conduct .... Ms. Sue O'DRISCOLL
29 Assoc Vice Pres for Alumni Affairs .... Ms. Jane D. PITTMAN
44 Assoc Vice Pres for Advancement .... Ms. Vicky MEDLOCK
26 Director of Media Relations .... Ms. Emily BURNER
49 Dean of College of Arts & Sciences ...... Dr. Calvin H. ALLEN, JR.
50 Dean of Byrd School of Business .... Dr. Miles DAVIS
64 Dean of Shenandoah Conservatory .... Dr. Michael J. STEPNIAK
67 Dean of Dunn School of Pharmacy .... Dr. Alan B. MCKAY
07 Dean of Admissions .... Mr. David D. ANTHONY
35 Dir of Student Engagement .... Mr. Rick MCCLENDON
08 Director of Library Services .... Mr. Christopher A. BEAN
06 Registrar .... Vacant
21 Comptroller .... Ms. Marcene GRAVES
37 Director of Financial Aid .... Ms. Nancy S. BRAGG
36 Director of Career Services ... Ms. Jennifer A. SPATARO-WILSON
18 Director of Physical Plant .... Mr. Gene E. FISHER
23 Director of Wellness Center .... Mr. Ronald G. STICKLEY
15 Director of Human Resources .... Ms. Marie C. LANDES
41 Athletic Director .... Mr. Doug ZIPP
91 Database & System Administrator .... Mr. David HOFFMAN
13 Director of Institutional Computing .... Mr. Quaiser ABSAR
66 Director Division of Nursing .... Dr. Kathryn M. GANSKE
88 Director Div of Athletic Training .... Dr. Rose A. SCHMIEG
88 Interim Dir Div of Occupat Therapy .... Dr. Leslie DAVIDSON
88 Director Div of Physical Therapy .... Dr. Karen E. ABRAHAM
88 Sr Dir Advancement - Conservatory ..... Mr. Bradley C. SNOWDEN
19 Director of Public Safety .... Mr. Wayne SEALOCK
102 Director Foundation Relations .... Ms. Jennifer BOUSQUET
31 Director Auxiliary Services .... Mr. John V. STEVENS
88 Dir Div of Physician Asst Studies .... Mr. Anthony A. MILLER
20 Director of Learning Services .... Dr. Audrey ROBINSON
42 Dean of Spiritual Life .... Rev Dr. Justin ALLEN
88 Dir Program in Respiratory Care .... Ms. Beverly WATSON
09 Director Institutional Research .... Vacant
40 Bookstore Manager .... Ms. Mary Ellen WELCH
96 Purchasing & Accts Pay Manager .... Ms. Ginny L. NORMAN
24 Coordinator Media Services .... Ms. Val GANGWER
38 Director Student Counseling .... Ms. Nancy SCHULTE

Skyline College (F)

5234 Airport Road, Roanoke VA 24012-1603
County: Roanoke FICE Identification: 030927
Unit ID: 261931
Telephone: (540) 563-8000 Carnegie Class: Bac/Assoc
FAX Number: (540) 362-5400 Calendar System: Semester
URL: www.skyline.edu
Established: 1966 Annual Undergrad Tuition & Fees: $13,700
Enrollment: 264 Coed
Affiliation or Control: Proprietary IRS Status: Proprietary
Highest Offering: Baccalaureate
Program: Occupational; 2-Year Principally Bachelor's Creditable; Technical Emphasis
Accreditation: **ACCSC**, MAAB

01 Campus President .... Dr. Walter G. MERCHANT

Southeast Culinary and Hospitality College (G)

100 Piedmont Avenue, Bristol VA 24201-5699
County: Bristol FICE Identification: 041338
Unit ID: 451608
Telephone: (276) 591-5699 Carnegie Class: Assoc/PrivFP
FAX Number: (276) 591-5677 Calendar System: Semester
URL: www.southeastculinary.edu
Established: 2004 Annual Undergrad Tuition & Fees: $13,590
Enrollment: 71 Coed
Affiliation or Control: Proprietary IRS Status: Proprietary
Highest Offering: Associate Degree
Program: Occupational
Accreditation: **COE**

01 Chief Executive Officer .... Richard K. ERSKINE
05 Dean .... Everett HONAKER

Southern Virginia University (H)

One University Hill Drive, Buena Vista VA 24416-3097
County: Rockbridge FICE Identification: 003738
Unit ID: 233611
Telephone: (540) 261-8400 Carnegie Class: Bac/A&S
FAX Number: (540) 261-8451 Calendar System: Semester
URL: www.svu.edu
Established: 1867 Annual Undergrad Tuition & Fees: $18,900
Enrollment: 800 Coed
Affiliation or Control: Independent Non-Profit IRS Status: 501(c)3
Highest Offering: Baccalaureate
Program: Liberal Arts And General
Accreditation: **SC**

01 President .... Mr. Paul K. SYBROWSKY
05 Provost .... Dr. Madison U. SOWELL
10 Vice President Finance .... Mr. Robert E. HUCH
30 VP Institutional Advancement .... Mr. Richard G. WHITEHEAD
26 VP Communications & Marketing .... Mr. Burke OLSEN
07 VP Enrollment Services .... Mr. Brett GARCIA
13 VP Operations/Student Services .... Mr. Scott Y. DOXEY
20 Associate Provost .... Dr. Alan WHITEHURST
44 Director of Annual Giving .... Mr. Jeff ROBISON
35 Associate Dean of Students .... Mr. Joseph BOUCHELLE
10 Controller .... Mr. Jesse SEEGMILLER
08 Director of Library Services .... Dr. Christopher RICHARDSON
36 Director of Student Support .... Mr. Michael GIBBONS
41 Athletic Director .... Mr. Scott Y. DOXEY
06 Registrar .... Ms. Whitney LARSEN
37 Director of Financial Aid .... Mr. John BRANDT
29 Director of Alumni Relations .... Mr. John FEINAUER
09 Director of Institutional Research .... Dr. Alan WHITEHURST
15 Human Resources Assistant .... Ms. Kara CRAWFORD

Southside Regional Medical Center Professional Schools (I)

737 South Sycamore Street, Petersburg VA 23803-5133
County: Independent City FICE Identification: 012744
Unit ID: 233082
Telephone: (804) 765-5800 Carnegie Class: Not Classified
FAX Number: (804) 765-5937 Calendar System: Semester
URL: www.srmconline.com
Established: 1895 Annual Undergrad Tuition & Fees: $6,550
Enrollment: 140 Coed
Affiliation or Control: Proprietary IRS Status: Proprietary
Highest Offering: Associate Degree
Program: Occupational
Accreditation: **ABHES**, DMS, DNUR, RAD

03 Vice Pres for Professional Schools .... Ms. Cynthia PARSONS

Stratford University (J)

7777 Leesburg Pike, Falls Church VA 22043-2403
County: Fairfax FICE Identification: 025412
Unit ID: 438498
Telephone: (703) 821-8570 Carnegie Class: Master's L
FAX Number: (703) 734-5335 Calendar System: Quarter
URL: www.stratford.edu
Established: 1976 Annual Undergrad Tuition & Fees: $16,650
Enrollment: 1,823 Coed
Affiliation or Control: Proprietary IRS Status: Proprietary
Highest Offering: Master's
Program: Professional; Business Emphasis
Accreditation: **ACICS**, ACFEI, NURSE

01 President .... Dr. Richard R. SHURTZ, II
03 Executive Director Falls Church .... Mary Ann SHURTZ
05 Campus Dean .... Dr. Lloyd GIBSON
11 Chief Operating Officer .... Dr. James FLAGGERT
10 Chief Financial Officer .... John DOVI
50 Dean School of Business .... Dr. Lloyd GIBSON
12 Campus Director .... Christi HAYS
88 Dean School of Hospitality/Culinary .... Jordan LICHMAN
76 Dean of Allied Health .... Dr. Bennett SOLBERG
77 Dean Sch of Information Technology .... Vacant
06 Registrar .... Heather RICHARDS
07 Director of Admissions .... Carl SIEBECKER
37 Director Business/Financial Aid .... Brian FORD
36 Director Career Services .... Lenie TIONGSON
21 Assistant Business Officer A/R .... Mila SKLYAR

Sweet Briar College (K)

134 Chapel Road, Sweet Briar VA 24595-9998
County: Amherst FICE Identification: 003742
Unit ID: 233718
Telephone: (434) 381-6100 Carnegie Class: Bac/A&S
FAX Number: (434) 381-6173 Calendar System: 4/1/4
URL: www.sbc.edu
Established: 1901 Annual Undergrad Tuition & Fees: $32,325
Enrollment: 760 Female
Affiliation or Control: Independent Non-Profit IRS Status: 501(c)3
Highest Offering: Master's
Program: Liberal Arts And General
Accreditation: **SC**, ENG

01 President .... Dr. Jo Ellen PARKER

100 Vice President and Chief of Staff .... Mrs. Louise S. ZINGARO
04 Exec Asst Office of the President .... Mrs. Karen L. SUMMERS
09 Director Institutional Research .... Ms. Christy C. COLE
88 Director of the Tusculum Institute .... Dr. Lynn RAINVILLE
42 Chaplain .... Rev. Adam J. WHITE
05 Dean of the FacultyVP Acad Affs ... Dr. Amy JESSEN-MARSHALL
20 Assoc Dean Academic Affairs .... Dr. Jill GRANGER
08 Dir Integrated Information Systems .... Dr. John G. JAFFE
06 Registrar .... Ms. Deborah L. POWELL
25 Faculty Grants Officer .... Ms. Kathleen PLACIDI
85 Director International Studies .... Dr. Tiffany N. CUMMINGS
41 Director of Athletics .... Ms. Kelly S. MORRISON
104 Director Junior Year in Spain .... Ms. M. Celeste DELGADO-LIBRERO
104 Director Junior Year in France .... Dr. Margaret A. SCOUTEN
88 Director of Academic Advising .... Mrs. Kelly KRAFT-MEYER
84 Dean of Enrollment Mgmt .... Mr. Steven W. NAPE
10 Vice Pres Finance/Administration .... Mr. Scott SHANK
21 Assoc VP Finance/Administration .... Ms. Gail D. PAYNE
15 Director of Human Resources .... Ms. Caroyn BURTON
18 Director Physical Plant .... Mr. Steve BAILEY
19 Chief of Campus Police .... Mr. Willie H. NEAL
37 Director Financial Aid .... Mrs. Bobbi CARPENTER
40 Book Shop Manager .... Ms. Lynn LEWIS
96 Director Purchasing .... Ms. Cynthia L. PONTON
88 Coordinator Benefits .... Mrs. Judy SPROUSE
31 Director of Auxiliary Services .... Vacant
30 Vice Pres for Alumni/Development .... Ms. Heidi HANSEN-MCCRORY
29 Director of Alumnae Relations .... Mrs. Melissa COFFEY-GAY
44 Director of Development .... Ms. Connor FORREN
32 VP/Dean of Co-Curricular Life .... Ms. Cheryl L. STEELE
38 Mental Health Counselor/Health Svcs .... Vacant
36 Director Career Services .... Mr. Wayne F. STARK
39 Director Residence Life & Housing .... Vacant
23 Nurse Practioner/Dir Health Svcs .... Vacant
27 Director of Media/Marketing & Comm .... Mr. Zach O. KINCAID

Union Presbyterian Seminary (A)

3401 Brook Road, Richmond VA 23227-4597
County: Independent City FICE Identification: 003743
Unit ID: 233842
Telephone: (804) 355-0671 Carnegie Class: Spec/Faith
FAX Number: (804) 355-3919 Calendar System: Semester
URL: www.upsem.edu
Established: 1812 Annual Graduate Tuition & Fees: $13,000
Enrollment: 221 Coed
Affiliation or Control: Presbyterian Church (U.S.A.) IRS Status: 501(c)3
Highest Offering: Doctorate; No Undergraduates
Program: Professional; Religious Emphasis
Accreditation: SC, THEOL

01 President .... Dr. Brian K. BLOUNT
11 Vice President for Administration .... Mr. Michael B. CASHWELL
30 Vice Pres Institutional Advancement .... Mr. Richard WONG
05 Dn Union Presbyterian Sem(Richmond) ..... Dr. Stanley SKRESLET
42 Chaplain & Dean of Students .... Rev. Edna J. BANES
12 Dean Union Presby Sem (Charlotte) .... Dr. Thomas W. CURRIE
20 Associate Dean Academic Programs .... Dr. E. Carson BRISSON
10 Controller .... Ms. Sharon PAYNE
07 Director of Admissions .... Ms. Kate Fiedler BOSWELL
06 Registrar .... Mr. Stanley HARGRAVES
08 Librarian .... Dr. Milton J. COALTER
13 Director Technology Services .... Mr. John R. WILSON
36 Director Student Placement .... Dr. Susan E. FOX

University of Fairfax (B)

2070 Chain Bridge Rd, Ste G-100, Vienna VA 22182
County: Fairfax Identification: 667094
Telephone: (703) 790-3200 Carnegie Class: Not Classified
FAX Number: (703) 790-3201 Calendar System: Other
URL: www.ufairfax.net
Established: 2002 Annual Graduate Tuition & Fees: N/A
Enrollment: N/A Coed
Affiliation or Control: Independent Non-Profit IRS Status: 501(c)3
Highest Offering: Doctorate; No Undergraduates
Program: Professional
Accreditation: DETC

01 President/CEO .... Mr. David OXENHANDLER

University of Management & Technology (C)

1901 Fort Myer Drive, Suite 700, Arlington VA 22209-1609
County: Arlington FICE Identification: 041103
Unit ID: 437097
Telephone: (703) 516-0035 Carnegie Class: Not Classified
FAX Number: (703) 516-0985 Calendar System: Semester
URL: www.umtweb.edu
Established: 1998 Annual Undergrad Tuition & Fees: $11,820
Enrollment: 566 Coed
Affiliation or Control: Proprietary IRS Status: Proprietary
Highest Offering: Doctorate
Program: Professional; Business Emphasis
Accreditation: DETC

01 President .... Dr. Yanping CHEN
05 Academic Dean .... Dr. J. Davidson FRAME

University of Mary Washington (D)

1301 College Avenue, Fredericksburg VA 22401-5300
County: Independent City FICE Identification: 003746
Unit ID: 232681
Telephone: (540) 654-1000 Carnegie Class: Master's L
FAX Number: (540) 654-1073 Calendar System: Semester
URL: www.umw.edu
Established: 1908 Annual Undergrad Tuition & Fees (In-State): $9,246
Enrollment: 5,170 Coed
Affiliation or Control: State IRS Status: 501(c)3
Highest Offering: Master's
Program: Liberal Arts And General; Teacher Preparatory
Accreditation: SC, MUS

01 President .... Mr. Richard V. HURLEY
05 Interim Provost .... Dr. Ian NEWBOULD
100 Chief of Staff .... Dr. Martin A. WILDER
10 VP for Admin & Finance .... Mr. Richard R. PEARCE
32 Vice President Student Affairs .... Mr. Douglas N. SEARCY
30 Vice Pres for Advance & Univ Rels .... Mr. Salvatore M. MERINGOLO
102 CEO of UMW Foundation .... Mr. Jeffrey W. ROUNTREE
13 Actg CIO .... Mr. Justin WEBB
88 VP Econ Dev & Regional Engagement .... Dr. Meta R. BRAYMER
15 Asst Vice Pres/Human Res/AAEEO .... Ms. Sabrina C. JOHNSON
105 Director of Web Communication .... Ms. Cathy DERECKI
21 Asst Vice Pres Business Svcs/CPO .... Ms. Erma A. BAKER
20 Assocate Provost .... Dr. John T. MORELLO
18 Assoc Vice Pres Facilities Services .... Mr. John P. WILTENMUTH, III
09 Asst Prov Inst Analy & Effect .... Mr. Taiwo A. ANDE
07 Dean of Admissions .... Ms. Kimberly JOHNSTON
53 Dean of College of Education .... Dr. Mary L. GENDERNALIK-COOPER
50 Dean College of Business .... Dr. Lynne D. RICHARDSON
20 Dean College of Arts & Sciences .... Dr. Richard FINKELSTEIN
35 Dean of Student Life .... Mr. Cedric B. RUCKER
37 Director of Financial Aid .... Ms. Debra J. HARBER
09 Director of Institutional Research ...... Mr. Mathew C. WILKERSON
21 Internal Audit Director .... Ms. Tera D. KOVANES
39 Director of Residence Life .... Ms. Christine M. PORTER
06 Registrar .... Ms. Rita DUNSTON
41 Director of Athletics .... Mr. Ken D. TYLER
08 University Librarian .... Ms. Rosemary ARNESON
88 Director of Publications .... Ms. Neva S. TRENIS
24 Director of Dodd Auditorium .... Mr. Doug NOBLE
88 Assoc Dean of Advising Services .... Ms. Sallie W. BRAXTON
19 Chief of University Police .... Mr. Eddie L. PERRY
29 Director Alumni Relations .... Mr. Mark THADEN
38 Director of Counseling/Psych Svcs ...... Dr. Nicole A. SURETHING
88 Director of Disability Services .... Ms. Sally SCOTT
23 University Physician .... Dr. P. Thomas RILEY
88 Director of University Galleries .... Ms. Anne TIMPANO
27 Director News & Public Information ...... Ms. Marty G. MORRISON
28 Spec Asst Diversity & Inclusion .... Dr. Leah COX
26 Associate VP University Rels .... Ms. Anna B. BILLINGSLEY
88 Director of Design Services .... Ms. AJ NEWELL
29 Director National Alumni Engagement .... Ms. Cindy L. SNYDER
44 Assoc VP Univ Advancemnt/Alumni Rel ...... Mr. Kenneth L. STEEN

University of Richmond (E)

28 Westhampton Way, Richmond VA 23173-1903
County: Independent City FICE Identification: 003744
Unit ID: 233374
Telephone: (804) 289-8000 Carnegie Class: Bac/A&S
FAX Number: (804) 287-6540 Calendar System: Semester
URL: www.richmond.edu
Established: 1830 Annual Undergrad Tuition & Fees: $44,210
Enrollment: 4,348 Coordinate
Affiliation or Control: Independent Non-Profit IRS Status: 501(c)3
Highest Offering: Doctorate
Program: Liberal Arts And General; Professional
Accreditation: SC, BUS, BUSA, LAW, TEAC

01 President .... Dr. Edward L. AYERS
05 Provost .... Dr. Stephen ALLRED
10 Vice President Business & Finance .... Mr. Hossein SADID
32 Vice President Student Affairs .... Dr. Stephen D. BISESE
30 Vice President Advancement .... Mr. Thomas C. GUTENBERGER
13 Vice Pres for Information Services .... Ms. Kathryn J. MONDAY
84 Vice Pres Enrollment Management .... Ms. Nanci TESSIER
100 Chief of Staff .... Dr. Lori G. SCHUYLER
101 Secretary Board of Trustees .... Ms. Ann Lloyd BREEDEN
04 Executive Assistant to President .... Ms. Carolyn R. MARTIN
88 President Spider Mgmt Company .... Mr. Srinivas PULAVARTI
16 Assoc Vice Pres Human Resources .... Mr. Carl K. SORENSEN
18 Assoc Vice Pres Facilities .... Mr. Andrew S. MCBRIDE
29 Asst VP Alumni & Career Services .... Ms. Kristin J. WOODS
102 Asst VP Foundation/Corp/Govt Rels ... Ms. Michelle E. WAMSLEY
42 University Chaplain .... Rev. Craig T. KOCHER
07 Asst VP and Dean of Admissions .... Mr. Gil VILLANUEVA
08 University Librarian .... Mr. Kevin BUTTERFIELD
09 Dir Institutional Effectiveness .... Dr. Patricia B. MURPHY
06 University Registrar .... Ms. Susan D. BREEDEN
37 Director of Financial Aid .... Ms. Cynthia B. DEFFENBAUGH
36 Director Career Development Center .. Ms. Leslie W. STEVENSON
38 Director of CAPS .... Dr. Peter O. LEVINESS
96 Director of Procurement .... Ms. Jean C. HINES
35 Assoc VP Student Development .... Dr. Tinina Q. CADE
41 Director of Athletics .... Mr. James D. MILLER

104 Director Study Abroad .... Ms. Michele D. COX
105 Director Web Services .... Mr. Eric F. PALMER
33 Dean of Richmond College .... Dr. Joseph R. BOEHMAN
34 Dean Westhampton College .... Dr. Juliette L. LANDPHAIR
49 Dean School of Arts & Sciences .... Dr. Kahtleen R. SKERRETT
50 Dean School of Business .... Dr. Nancy A. BAGRANOFF
61 Dean TC Williams Law School .... Dr. Wendy C. PERDUE
51 Dean School Continuing Studies .... Dr. James L. NARDUZZI
88 Dean Jepson School Leader Stds .... Dr. Sandra J. PEART
19 Assoc VP Publc Sfty/Chief of Police .... Mr. David M. MCCOY
23 Director Health Center .... Dr. Lynne P. DEANE
26 Asst VP for Communications .... Ms. Lisa VAN RIPER
40 Manager University Bookstore .... Mr. Roger L. BROOKS

University of Virginia (F)

Charlottesville VA 22903
County: Independent City FICE Identification: 003745
Unit ID: 234076
Telephone: (434) 924-0311 Carnegie Class: RU/VH
FAX Number: (434) 924-0938 Calendar System: Semester
URL: www.virginia.edu
Established: 1819 Annual Undergrad Tuition & Fees (In-State): $12,216
Enrollment: 24,297 Coed
Affiliation or Control: State IRS Status: 501(c)3
Highest Offering: Doctorate
Program: Liberal Arts And General; Teacher Preparatory; Professional
Accreditation: SC, BUS, BUSA, CACREP, CLPSY, CS, DENT, DIETI, ENG, IPSY, LAW, LSAR, MED, NURSE, PH, PLNG, RTT, SP, TEAC

01 President .... Dr. Teresa A. SULLIVAN
03 Exec Vice Pres/Chief Operating Ofcr .... Vacant
101 Secretary Board of Visitors .... Ms. Susan G. HARRIS
05 Exec Vice President & Provost .... Dr. John D. SIMON
30 Sr Vice Pres Devel/Public Affairs .... Mr. Robert D. SWEENEY
46 Vice President for Research .... Mr. Thomas C. SKALAK
10 Vice Pres/Chief Financial Officer .... Vacant
21 Vice President Management/Budget .... Ms. Colette SHEEHY
17 Vice President & CEO Medical Center ..... Mr. R. Edward HOWELL
32 Vice Pres/Chief Student Affs Ofcr .... Ms. Patricia M. LAMPKIN
13 Vice Pres/Chief Info Officer .... Mr. James L. HILTON
63 VP & Dean School of Medicine .... Dr. Steven T. DEKOSKY
28 VP/Chief Officer Diversity/Equity .... Mr. Marcus L. MARTIN
100 Chief of Staff/Assoc VP for Admin .... Ms. Nancy A. RIVERS
44 Sr Asc VP Dev/Principal Relship Dev .... Mr. Charles B. FITZGERALD
105 Dir of Web Services & Interac Media .... Mr. Zach WHEAT
88 Vice Prov for Academic Programs .... Mr. J. Milton ADAMS
88 Vice Prov Faculty Recruitmt/Retent .... Ms. Gertrude J. FRASER
20 Asc Prov Acad Spprt/Classroom Mgmt .... Ms. Martha Wynne STUART
88 Assoc VP Business Operations .... Mr. Richard A. KOVATCH
15 VP/Chief Human Resource Officer .... Ms. Susan CARKEEK
21 Asst Vice Pres Finance/Comptroller .... Mr. Stephen A. KIMATA
88 Asst VP Research Admin .... Mr. Gerald J. KANE
26 Assoc Vice Pres for Public Affairs .... Ms. Carol S. WOOD
88 Chief Investment Officer .... Mr. Lawrence E. KOCHARD
18 Chief Facilities Officer .... Mr. Donald E. SUNDGREN
06 Registrar .... Ms. Carol A J. STANLEY
07 Dean Undergraduate Admission .... Mr. Gregory W. ROBERTS
49 Dean School of Arts & Sciences .... Ms. Meredith J. WOO
61 Dean School of Law .... Mr. Paul G. MAHONEY
66 Dean School of Nursing .... Ms. Dorrie K. FONTAINE
54 Dean Schl Engr/Applied Science .... Mr. James H. AYLOR
48 Dean School of Architecture .... Ms. Kim TANZER
50 Dean Grad School Business Admin .... Mr. Robert F. BRUNER
50 Dean School of Commerce .... Mr. Carl P. ZEITHAML
53 Dean School of Education .... Mr. Robert C. PIANTA
80 Dean Sch Leadership/Public Policy .... Mr. Harry HARDING
51 Dean Cont & Prof Studies .... Mr. Billy K. CANNADAY
35 Associate VP/Dean of Students .... Mr. Allen W. GROVES
23 Director Student Health .... Dr. James C. TURNER
41 Dir Intercollegiate Athletic Pgms .... Mr. Craig K. LITTLEPAGE
43 Gen Counsel & Corporate Secretary .... Mr. Paul J. FORCH
31 Director Community Relations .... Ms. Ida Lee WOOTTEN
22 Director Equal Opportunity Pgms ... Ms. Darlene SCOTT-SCURRY
08 University Librarian .... Ms. Karin WITTENBORG
09 Dir Institutional Assess & Studies .... Mr. George A. STOVALL
88 Exec Director The Jefferson Trust .... Mr. Wayne COZART
37 Director Student Financial Svcs .... Ms. Yvonne B. HUBBARD
36 Exec Dir Univ Career Services .... Mr. James L. MCBRIDE, JR.
87 Dir Summer & Special Academic Pgms .... Mr. Dudley J. DOANE
104 Dir International Studies Office .... Mr. Dudley J. DOANE
19 Chief of Police .... Mr. Michael A. GIBSON
39 Exec Dir Housing & Residence Life .... Ms. Gay PEREZ
40 Executive Director of UVa Bookstore .... Mr. Jonathan A. KATES
38 Director Counseling/Psych Services .... Mr. Russell FEDERMAN
93 Dean African-American Affairs .... Dr. Maurice APPREY
94 Dir Studies in Women & Gender .... Ms. Charlotte PATTERSON
96 Director of Procurement Services .... Mr. Eric N. DENBY

The University of Virginia's College at Wise (G)

One College Avenue, Wise VA 24293-4412
County: Wise FICE Identification: 003747
Unit ID: 233897
Telephone: (276) 328-0100 Carnegie Class: Bac/A&S
FAX Number: (276) 376-1012 Calendar System: Semester
URL: www.uvawise.edu
Established: 1954 Annual Undergrad Tuition & Fees (In-State): $8,107
Enrollment: 2,067 Coed
Affiliation or Control: State IRS Status: 501(c)3
Highest Offering: Baccalaureate

Program: Liberal Arts And General; Teacher Preparatory
Accreditation: SC, CS, ENG, NURSE, TEAC

01 Chancellor ... Vacant
46 Ex Asst to Chanc/Dir Strategic Plng ... Ms. Marcia K. QUESENBERRY
05 Provost/Vice Chan for Acad Affairs ... Dr. Sanders HUGUENIN
30 Vice Chanc Devel/College Relations ... Ms. Tami ELY
10 Vice Chanc Finance/ Administration ... Mr. Sim E. EWING
84 Vice Chancellor Enrollment Mgmt ... Mr. Russell D. NECESSARY
13 Vice Chanc for Info Technology ... Mr. Keith FOWLKES
41 Ast Vice Chanc Athletic Development ... Mr. Carroll W. DALE
20 Academic Dean ... Dr. Amelia J. HARRIS
32 Dean of Students ... Mrs. Jewell B. WORLEY
21 Comptroller ... Mrs. Kristy KISER
06 Registrar/Asst Academic Dean ... Ms. Narda PORTER
08 Director of the Library ... Mr. Robin P. BENKE
15 Director of Human Resources ... Ms. Stephanie D. PERRY
88 Director of College Services ... Mr. Joseph B. KISER
26 Director of News & Media Relations ... Ms. Kathy STILL
44 Director of Development ... Ms. Valerie LAWSON
29 Director of Alumni Relations ... Ms. Pamela J. COLLIE
37 Director of Financial Aid ... Ms. Rebecca HUFFMAN
35 Asst Dir of Student Activities ... Mr. Joshua JUSTICE
36 Director of Career Development ... Vacant
38 Personal Counselor/Health Services ... Ms. Rachel ROSE
19 Campus Police Chief ... Mr. Stephen L. MCCOY
12 Site Director UVA-Wise Programs ... Ms. Courtney L. CONNER
18 Director Facilities Planning/Mgmt ... Mr. Chad NODINE
09 Director of Institutional Research ... Mr. P. Scott BEVINS
24 Director of Media Services ... Mr. Randy G. GILMER
40 Bookstore Manager ... Mr. Scott LAWSON
39 Director of Residence Life ... Ms. Angela LEMKE

Virginia Baptist College (A)

4105 Plank Road, Fredericksburg VA 22407-4803
County: Spotsylvania — FICE Identification: 038626
Telephone: (540) 785-5440 — Carnegie Class: Not Classified
FAX Number: (540) 785-5441 — Calendar System: Semester
URL: www.vbc.edu
Established: 1984 — Annual Undergrad Tuition & Fees: $4,800
Enrollment: 100 — Coed
Affiliation or Control: Baptist — IRS Status: 501(c)3
Highest Offering: Master's
Program: Religious Emphasis
Accreditation: TRACS

01 President ... Dr. Don FORRESTER

Virginia Commonwealth University (B)

901 W Franklin Street, Box 842527, Richmond VA 23284-2527
County: Independent City — FICE Identification: 003735
Unit ID: 234030
Telephone: (804) 828-0100 — Carnegie Class: RU/VH
FAX Number: N/A — Calendar System: Semester
URL: www.vcu.edu
Established: 1838 — Annual Undergrad Tuition & Fees (In-State): $9,885
Enrollment: 31,899 — Coed
Affiliation or Control: State — IRS Status: 501(c)3
Highest Offering: Doctorate
Program: Liberal Arts And General; Teacher Preparatory; Professional
Accreditation: SC, ANEST, ART, BUS, BUSA, CACREP, CIDA, CLPSY, COPSY, CORE, CS, DANCE, DENT, DH, DIETI, EMT, ENG, HSA, IPSY, JOUR, MED, MT, MUS, NMT, NUR, OT, PH, PHAR, PLNG, PTA, RAD, RTT, SPAA, SW, TED, THEA

01 President VCU & VCU Health System ... Dr. Michael RAO
05 Provost & Vice Pres Academic Affs ... Dr. Beverly J. WARREN
17 Vice Pres Health Sciences ... Dr. Sheldon M. RETCHIN
10 Vice Pres Finance & Administration ... Dr. David W. HANSON
46 Vice President for Research ... Dr. Francis L. MACRINA
30 Vice Pres Development & Alumni Rel ... Mr. John I. BLOHM
86 Executive Dir For Government Rels ... Mr. Mark E. RUBIN
32 Vice Prov Student Affairs ... Dr. Henry G. RHONE
88 Vice Provost for Life Sciences ... Dr. Thomas F. HUFF
45 Vice Prov Planning & Decision Supp ... Vacant
91 Chief Information Officer Tech Svcs ... Mr. Mark D. WILLIS
18 Assoc Vice Pres Facilities Mgmt ... Mr. Brian J. OHLINGER
88 Assoc Vice Pres Gift Development ... Ms. Anne D. JACOBSON
21 Assoc Vice Pres Business Svcs/Treas ... Mr. Paul P. JEZ
21 Assoc Vice Pres Finance & Admin ... Ms. Pamela A. CURREY
84 Assoc Vice Provost Enroll Svcs ... Ms. Delores T. TAYLOR
22 Assoc Vice Prov Inst Equity ... Ms. Velma J. WILLIAMS
16 Asst Vice Pres for Human Resource ... Ms. Cynthia H. ANDREWS
08 University Librarian ... Mr. John E. ULMSCHNEIDER
43 General Counsel ... Mr. David L. ROSS
41 Dir of Intercollegiate Athletics ... Vacant
88 Director of Business Services ... Ms. Diane L. REYNOLDS
39 Interim Dir Res Life & Housing ... Dr. Reuban B. RODRIGUEZ
06 Univ Registrar & Dir Records/Regis ... Ms. Anjour B. HARRIS
07 Asst VP Student Records & Admission ... Ms. Sybil C. HALLORAN
37 Director of Financial Aid ... Ms. Brenda L. BURKE
38 Dir of Counseling Services ... Dr. Jihad N. AZIZ
36 Dir of University Career Center ... Mr. Joseph A. TESTANI
35 Assoc VProv/Dean Student Affs ... Dr. Reuban B. RODRIGUEZ
29 Asst VP University Alumni Relations ... Mr. Gordon A. MCDOUGALL
88 Exec Dir Global Eduation ... Dr. R. McKenna BROWN
88 Dir Ctr for Environmental Studies ... Dr. Gregory C. GARMAN
25 Asst Vice Pres Research Admin ... Ms. Susan E. ROBB
19 Chief of Police ... Mr. John A. VENUTI
31 VProv/Div Community Engagement ... Dr. Catherine W. HOWARD
94 Director Women's Studies ... Dr. Diana H. SCULLY
92 Dean Honors College ... Dr. Timothy L. HULSEY
67 Dean of Pharmacy ... Dr. Victor A. YANCHICK
66 Dean of Nursing ... Dr. Nancy F. LANGSTON
63 Dean of School of Medicine ... Dr. Jerome F. STRAUSS
53 Dean School of Education ... Dr. Christine S. WALTHER-THOMAS
52 Dean of Dentistry ... Dr. David C. SARRETT
50 Dean School of Business ... Mr. Ed A. GRIER
49 Dean Humanities & Sciences ... Dr. James S. COLEMAN
57 Dean School of Arts ... Mr. Joseph H. SEIPEL
70 Dean School of Social Work ... Dr. James E. HINTERLONG
76 Dean Allied Health Professions ... Dr. Cecil B. DRAIN
58 Dean Graduate School ... Dr. F. Douglas BOUDINOT
54 Interim Dean School of Engineering ... Dr. Charles JENNETT
35 Asst Vice Prov Student Affairs ... Dr. Charles J. KLINK
88 Assoc Director of GEO ... Mr. Osama ALAMI
96 Director Procurement Payment Svcs ... Mr. C. Edward GIBBS
26 Exec Dir University Relations ... Ms. Pamela D. LEPLEY

*Virginia Community College System Office (C)

101 N 14th Street, Richmond VA 23219-3658
County: Independent City — FICE Identification: 008904
Unit ID: 234146
Telephone: (804) 819-4901 — Carnegie Class: N/A
FAX Number: (804) 819-4760
URL: www.vccs.edu

01 Chancellor ... Dr. Glenn DUBOIS
11 Vice Chanc Administrative Services ... Ms. Donna VANCLEAVE
05 Vice Chancellor Academic Services ... Dr. Susan WOOD
103 Vice Chanc Workforce Development ... Dr. Craig HERNDON
13 Vice Chancellor Information Tech ... Dr. Joy A. HATCH
30 Vice Chanc Institutional Advance ... Dr. Jennifer SAGER GENTRY
15 Assoc Vice Chanc Human Resource Svc ... Dr. Christopher LEE
18 Assoc Vice Chanc/Facility Mgmt ... Mr. Bert JONES
43 General Counsel ... Ms. Rita W. BEALE
88 Director of Internal Audit ... Ms. Helen VANDERLAND
21 Controller ... Mr. Dave MAIR
04 Exec Assistant to the Chancellor ... Ms. Marlene MONDZIEL

*Blue Ridge Community College (D)

PO Box 80, Weyers Cave VA 24486-0080
County: Augusta — FICE Identification: 006819
Unit ID: 231536
Telephone: (540) 234-9261 — Carnegie Class: Assoc/Pub-R-M
FAX Number: (540) 234-8189 — Calendar System: Semester
URL: www.brcc.edu
Established: 1965 — Annual Undergrad Tuition & Fees (In-State): $4,218
Enrollment: 4,836 — Coed
Affiliation or Control: State — IRS Status: 501(c)3
Highest Offering: Associate Degree
Program: Occupational; 2-Year Principally Bachelor's Creditable
Accreditation: SC, ADNUR

02 President ... Dr. John A. DOWNEY
05 Vice Pres Instruction/Student Svcs ... Dr. Robert YOUNG
10 VP Finance/Administrative Svcs ... Dr. Robert BALDYGO
19 Security & Compliance Coordinator ... Mr. Wayne MARTIN
09 Coordinator Institutional Research ... Dr. Susan E. CROSBY
21 Associate Vice President of Finance ... Ms. Franki HAMPTON
15 Director of Human Resources ... Mr. Tim NICELY
30 Director Development ... Ms. Amy LASER KIGER
81 Dean Math/Science/Engineering ... Vacant
79 Dean Humanities/SoclSci/Workforce ... Dr. Kevin RATLIFF
76 Dean Health & Human Services ... Vacant
20 Dean Academic Support Services ... Ms. Annette WILLIAMS
08 Dean Learning Resources ... Mr. Francis J. MORAN
37 Financial Aid Officer ... Mr. Robert CLEMMER
26 Chief Public Relations Officer ... Ms. Bridget BAYLOR
36 Coord Career Services/Recruitment ... Ms. Jenny HARVEY

*Central Virginia Community College (E)

3506 Wards Road, Lynchburg VA 24502-2498
County: Independent City — FICE Identification: 004988
Unit ID: 231697
Telephone: (434) 832-7600 — Carnegie Class: Assoc/Pub-R-M
FAX Number: (434) 386-4700 — Calendar System: Semester
URL: www.cvcc.vccs.edu
Established: 1966 — Annual Undergrad Tuition & Fees (In-State): $3,906
Enrollment: 5,446 — Coed
Affiliation or Control: State — IRS Status: 501(c)3
Highest Offering: Associate Degree
Program: Occupational; 2-Year Principally Bachelor's Creditable
Accreditation: #SC, EMT, RAD

02 President ... Dr. John CAPPS
05 Vice Pres Academic Affs/Stdnt Svcs ... Dr. Geoffrey HICKS
10 Vice President Finance & Admin Svcs ... Mr. John POOLE
103 VP Ctr Workforce Dev/Cont Educ ... Dr. Ruth HENDRICK
30 Vice Pres Institutional Advancement ... Vacant
13 Vice Pres of Information Technology ... Mr. James D. LIGHTFOOT
45 Dean Instnl Effectiveness/Planning ... Dr. Joey FRONHEISER
21 Chief Business Officer ... Ms. Cathryn MOBLEY
29 Director Alumni/Public Relations ... Vacant
96 Director of Purchasing ... Dr. Kimely DAVIS
37 Financial Aid Officer ... Ms. Deborah A. MARSHALL
15 Human Resource Manager ... Ms. Leticia FORSTER
18 Capital Outlay Project Engineer ... Vacant
56 Distance Education Supervisor ... Ms. Susan S. BEASLEY
07 Coordinator of Admissions/Records ... Ms. Julie LOVING
08 Coordinator of Library Services ... Mr. Michael T. FEIN
78 Coord Apprenticeship/Coop Education ... Vacant
79 Dean Humanities/Social Science ... Dr. Muriel B. MICKLES
50 Dean of Business & Allied Health ... Dr. James LEMONS
81 Dean of Science/Math/Engineering ... Dr. Jeffrey W. LAUB

*Dabney S. Lancaster Community College (F)

PO Box 1000, Clifton Forge VA 24422-1000
County: Independent City — FICE Identification: 004996
Unit ID: 231873
Telephone: (540) 863-2800 — Carnegie Class: Assoc/Pub-R-S
FAX Number: (540) 863-2915 — Calendar System: Semester
URL: www.dslcc.edu
Established: 1967 — Annual Undergrad Tuition & Fees (In-State): $4,572
Enrollment: 1,538 — Coed
Affiliation or Control: State — IRS Status: 501(c)3
Highest Offering: Associate Degree
Program: Occupational; 2-Year Principally Bachelor's Creditable
Accreditation: SC, ACFEI, ADNUR

02 President ... Dr. Richard R. TEAFF
10 Vice President Finance/Admin Svcs ... Mrs. Angela GRAHAM
51 VP Continuing Educ/Workforce Svcs ... Mr. Gary S. KEENER
49 Dean Arts & Sciences ... Dr. Michael R. SCOTT
32 Director of Student Services ... Mr. Matt MCGRAW
35 Acting Director of Student Services ... Dr. Michael SCOTT
08 Director of Learning Resources ... Ms. Nova WRIGHT
09 Assessment Officer ... Dr. Michael SCOTT
06 Registrar ... Ms. Lorrie FERGUSON
21 Business Officer ... Ms. Melanie RICKETT
18 Buildings & Grounds Supervisor ... Mr. Ed N. KENNY
13 Coord of Computer Info Systems ... Ms. Tamra COTTRILL
37 Coord of Student Financial Aid ... Mrs. Sandra J. HAVERLACK
45 Planning & Funding Specialist ... Ms. Lynda N. THOMPSON

*Danville Community College (G)

1008 S Main Street, Danville VA 24541-4088
County: Independent City — FICE Identification: 003758
Unit ID: 231882
Telephone: (434) 797-2222 — Carnegie Class: Assoc/Pub-R-M
FAX Number: (434) 797-8514 — Calendar System: Semester
URL: www.dcc.vccs.edu
Established: 1967 — Annual Undergrad Tuition & Fees (In-State): $3,780
Enrollment: 4,390 — Coed
Affiliation or Control: State — IRS Status: 501(c)3
Highest Offering: Associate Degree
Program: Occupational; 2-Year Principally Bachelor's Creditable
Accreditation: SC

02 President ... Dr. Berkley C. RAMSEY
05 Vice Pres Academic/Student Services ... Dr. Christopher C. EZELL
10 Vice Pres Financial/Admin Services ... Mr. Scott BARNES
09 Dir of Plng/Effectiveness/Research ... Dr. Sherri H. HUFFMAN
30 Director of Development ... Mr. Shannon HAIR
26 Chief Public Relations Officer ... Ms. Andrea BURNEY

*Eastern Shore Community College (H)

29300 Lankford Highway, Melfa VA 23410-9755
County: Accomack — FICE Identification: 003748
Unit ID: 232052
Telephone: (757) 789-1789 — Carnegie Class: Assoc/Pub-R-S
FAX Number: (757) 789-1737 — Calendar System: Semester
URL: www.es.vccs.edu
Established: 1971 — Annual Undergrad Tuition & Fees (In-State): $3,795
Enrollment: 1,381 — Coed
Affiliation or Control: State — IRS Status: 501(c)3
Highest Offering: Associate Degree
Program: Occupational; 2-Year Principally Bachelor's Creditable
Accreditation: SC

02 President ... Dr. Linda THOMAS-GLOVER
05 Vice Pres Academic & Student Svcs ... Dr. James AHERN
10 Vice Pres Finance & Administration ... Miss Cynthia A. ALLEN
32 Dean of Student Services ... Mr. Bryan SMITH
08 Director Learning Resources ... Mrs. Patricia L. PHILLIPS
06 Registrar ... Mrs. Connie FENTRESS
09 Director of Institutional Research ... Ms. Judith M. GRIER
26 Chief Public Relations Officer ... Ms. Laurie SWAIN
37 Director of Student Financial Aid ... Mr. Bryan SMITH
15 Director Personnel Services ... Ms. Diane WHEATLEY
18 Chief Facilities/Physical Plant ... Mr. Bobby MEARS
29 Director Alumni Relations/Devel ... Ms. Eve BELOTE
20 Associate Academic Officer ... Mrs. Robin RICH-COATES

*Germanna Community College (I)

2130 Germanna Highway, Locust Grove VA 22508-2102
County: Orange — FICE Identification: 008660
Unit ID: 232195
Telephone: (540) 423-9030 — Carnegie Class: Assoc/Pub-R-M
FAX Number: (540) 727-3207 — Calendar System: Semester
URL: www.germanna.edu

Established: 1970 Annual Undergrad Tuition & Fees (In-State): $3,131
Enrollment: 7,778 Coed
Affiliation or Control: State IRS Status: 501(c)3
Highest Offering: Associate Degree
Program: Occupational; 2-Year Principally Bachelor's Creditable; Fine Arts Emphasis
Accreditation: SC, ADNUR, DA

02 President ....Dr. David A. SAM
04 Exec Assistant to the President ....Ms. Pamela D. SHIFFLETT
05 VP Academic & Student Services ....Dr. Ann WOOLFORD
11 VP Finance & Administrative Svcs ....Mr. Richard BREHM
103 VP Workforce & Community Educ ....Dr. Jeanne WESLEY
32 Dean of Student Services ....Ms. Pam FREDERICK
30 Exec Dir of Foundation & Alumni Rel ....Mr. Mike CATELL
09 Exec Dir of Planning & Assessement ....Dr. John DAVIS
08 Head Librarian ....Mr. George OBERLE
72 Dean Professional & Technical Study ....Ms. Denise GUEST
55 Dean Distance Educ & Lrng Resources ....Dr. Yan Yan YONG
66 Dean of Nursing & Health Technology ....Ms. Mary GILKEY
15 Exec Director of Human Resources ....Mr. Reginald RYALS
18 Building & Ground Supervisor ....Mr. Garland FENWICK
07 Dean of Enrollment Services/Registr ....Vacant
13 Manager Technology Services ....Ms. Jacque LARSEN
37 Financial Aid Officer ....Mr. Michael FARRIS
26 Director of Marketing ....Ms. Barbara TAYLOR
21 Financial Services Coordinator ....Vacant
49 Dean of Arts & Sciences ....Dr. Deborah BROCK
103 Dean of Workforce Prof Development ....Ms. Martha O'KEEFE
19 Chief of Police ....Mr. Craig BRANCH

*J. Sargeant Reynolds Community College (A)

PO Box 85622, Richmond VA 23285-5622
County: Henrico FICE Identification: 003759
Unit ID: 232414
Telephone: (804) 371-3000 Carnegie Class: Assoc/Pub-U-MC
FAX Number: (804) 371-3650 Calendar System: Semester
URL: www.reynolds.edu
Established: 1972 Annual Undergrad Tuition & Fees (In-State): $4,053
Enrollment: 13,367 Coed
Affiliation or Control: State IRS Status: 501(c)3
Highest Offering: Associate Degree
Program: Occupational; 2-Year Principally Bachelor's Creditable
Accreditation: SC, ACFEI, ADNUR, DA, DT, EMT, MLTAD, OPD, POLYT

02 President ....Dr. Gary L. RHODES
03 Executive Vice President ....Dr. Genene D. LEROSEN
05 Vice President Academic Affairs ....Dr. David R. LOOPE
30 Vice President Advancement ....Mrs. Elizabeth S. LITTLEFIELD
103 VP Comm Col Workforce Alliance ....Mr. Louis MCGINTY
10 VP Finance and Administration ....Ms. Amelia M. BRADSHAW
32 Vice President Student Affairs ....Dr. Thomas HOLLINS, JR.
45 Assoc VP Policy/Inst Effectiveness ....Mrs. Diane F. BRASINGTON
13 Assoc Vice President Technology ....Mr. John N. AMBROSE
79 Dean School of Humanities/Soc Sci ....Dr. Barbara M. GLENN
50 Dean School of Business ....Mr. David J. BARRISH
76 Dean School of Nursing/Allied Hlth ....Dr. Susan S. HUNTER
81 Dean School of Math Sci Engineering ....Mr. Raymond A. BURTON
20 Dean Educational Support Services ....Mr. Ty CORBIN
09 Director Office Inst Effectiveness ....Dr. Jackie R. BOURQUE
15 Director of Human Resources ....Ms. Corliss B. WOODSON
37 Director of Financial Aid ....Mrs. Kiesha L. POPE
07 Director of Admissions & Records ....Mrs. Karen M. PETTIS-WALDEN
88 Assistant VP Workforce Development ....Ms. Shauna N. DAVIS
88 Assistant VP Workforce Development ....Ms. Cara DILLARD
88 Director Outreach and Recruitment ....Ms. Tracy GREEN
26 Dir Communications/Public Affairs ....Mr. Malcolm T. HOLMES
26 Director of Marketing ....Ms. Kelly A. SMITH
08 Director of Info/Library Services ....Vacant
88 Director of Learning Communities ....Mr. Charles PETERSON, JR.
18 Director Facilities Mgmt/Planning ....Mr. Mark PROBST
21 Director of Financial Operations ....Ms. Shirley L. HOPKINS
30 Director of Development ....Ms. Marianne S. MCGHEE
88 Director of Middle College ....Ms. Mary Jo WASHKO
06 Registrar ....Ms. Denise S. TUNSTALL
96 Purchasing Manager ....Mr. Christopher L. COLE
19 Chief of Police & Security Services ....Mr. Paul L. RONCA

*John Tyler Community College (B)

13101 Jefferson Davis Highway, Chester VA 23831-5316
County: Chesterfield FICE Identification: 004004
Unit ID: 232450
Telephone: (804) 796-4000 Carnegie Class: Assoc/Pub-S-MC
FAX Number: (804) 796-4163 Calendar System: Semester
URL: www.jtcc.edu
Established: 1965 Annual Undergrad Tuition & Fees (In-State): $3,785
Enrollment: 10,797 Coed
Affiliation or Control: State IRS Status: 501(c)3
Highest Offering: Associate Degree
Program: Occupational; 2-Year Principally Bachelor's Creditable
Accreditation: SC, ADNUR, FUSER

02 President ....Dr. Marshall W. SMITH
04 Executive Assistant to President ....Ms. Mara M. HILLIAR
05 VP Academic Affairs ....Dr. William FIEGE
32 VP for Student Affairs ....Dr. L. Ray DRINKWATER
10 VP for Finance & Admin Services ....Mr. William F. TAYLOR
103 Vice Pres for CC Workforce Alliance ....Mr. Mac L. MCGINTY
35 Dean of Students ....Dr. Chris PFAUTZ
54 Dean Engr/Business/Public Svcs ....Dr. Melody L. MOORE
49 Dean Arts/Humanities/Soc Sciences ....Dr. Mikell BROWN
81 Dean Math/Natural & Behavorial Sci ....Dr. Johanna WEISS
102 Executive Director Foundation ....Ms. Beverley DEW
09 Dir Institutional Effectiveness ....Dr. Donna JOVANOVICH
08 Librarian Chester Campus ....Ms. Linda LUEBKE
15 Director Human Resources ....Ms. Susan GRINNAN
13 Director Information Services ....Mr. Larry RUBES
37 Director Financial Aid ....Mr. Tony JONES
07 Dir Admission/Records/Registration ....Mrs. Joy L. JAMES
21 Business Manager ....Mr. Leon R. BROWN
19 Security Manager ....Mr. Frank MEDAGLIA
35 Coordinator Student Activities ....Ms. Amanda CARPENTER
36 Director Counseling Chester Campus ....Ms. Michelle TINDALL
36 Dir Counseling Midlothian Campus ....Dr. Ruth VARNEY
18 Director Facilities Operations ....Mr. Greg A. DUNAWAY
26 Director College Relations ....Ms. Joanne M. HORTON
66 Dean of Health Sciences ....Dr. Deborah ULMER
08 Librarian Midlothian Campus ....Ms. Helen MCKANN
06 Registrar ....Ms. Joy L. JAMES
96 Director of Purchasing ....Ms. Nancy M. JIMISON

*Lord Fairfax Community College (C)

173 Skirmisher Lane, Middletown VA 22645-1745
County: Frederick FICE Identification: 008659
Unit ID: 232575
Telephone: (540) 868-7000 Carnegie Class: Assoc/Pub-R-L
FAX Number: (540) 868-7100 Calendar System: Semester
URL: www.lfcc.edu
Established: 1970 Annual Undergrad Tuition & Fees (In-State): $3,080
Enrollment: 9,719 Coed
Affiliation or Control: State IRS Status: 501(c)3
Highest Offering: Associate Degree
Program: Occupational; 2-Year Principally Bachelor's Creditable; Business Emphasis
Accreditation: SC

02 President ....Dr. Cheryl THOMPSON-STACY
05 VP of Academic and Student Affairs ....Dr. Chris COUTTS
10 VP of Financial & Admin Services ....Mr. Chris BOIES
32 Vice President of Student Success ....Vacant
103 Vice Pres Workforce Solutions ....Ms. Jeanian CLARK
20 Assoc VP of Instruction Middletown ....Ms. Kim BLOSSER
20 Assoc VP of Instruction Fauquier ....Dr. Judy BATSON
76 Assoc Dean Health Prof & Science ....Ms. Claudia J. MAZURKIEWICZ
88 Assoc Dean Bus/Tech/Dir HS Outreach ....Ms. Brenda K. BYARD
81 Assoc Dean Hum/Math/Social Sciences ....Dr. Richard L. ELAM
15 Human Resource Manager ....Ms. Karen N. FOREMAN
30 Director of Development ....Mr. David J. URSO
12 Manager Luray-Page County Center ....Ms. Judith J. SUDDITH
08 Director Learning Resources Center ....Mr. David R. GRAY
09 Dir Planning/Inst Effectiveness ....Dr. John H. MILAM
13 Coordinator Network Security ....Mr. Douglas M. SHRIER
35 Dean of Students - Middletown ....Dr. Karen H. BUCHER
84 Dir of Enrollment Mgt & Reg Service ....Vacant
38 Dir Stdnt Learning Svcs/Counseling ....Ms. Tammy LADREW
37 Coordinator Student Financial Aid ....Mr. Aaron WHITACRE
96 Procurement Officer ....Ms. Anastasia TRIPLETT
21 Budget and Finance Director ....Ms. Margaret J. BARNETT
19 Law Enforcement Manager ....Mr. Rob MARSHALL
26 Public Relations Marketing Manager ....Vacant
07 Coord Student Success ....Vacant
35 Coord Student Life & Info Services ....Ms. Brandy BOIES
36 Counselor Middle College ....Mr. Doug CUMBIA
08 Librarian ....Mr. Gregory MACDONALD
88 Coord of Dual Enrollment ....Ms. Heather BURTON
88 Coord Student Learning & TRIO SS ....Ms. Susan M. MARTIN
88 Coord/Dir LF Small Bus Dev Center ....Mr. William A. SIRBAUGH
88 Coord Business & Industry Trng ....Mr. Bill PENCE
35 Dean of Students - Fauquier ....Mr. Craig BENNETT
88 Director of Transition Programs ....Dr. Judith JAMES
27 Public Info/Grant & Sponsored Pgm ....Ms. Lyda C. KISER

*Mountain Empire Community College (D)

3441 Mountain Empire Road,
Big Stone Gap VA 24219-4634
County: Wise FICE Identification: 009629
Unit ID: 232788
Telephone: (276) 523-2400 Carnegie Class: Assoc/Pub-R-M
FAX Number: (276) 523-8297 Calendar System: Semester
URL: www.mecc.edu
Established: 1972 Annual Undergrad Tuition & Fees (In-State): $3,060
Enrollment: 3,219 Coed
Affiliation or Control: State IRS Status: 501(c)3
Highest Offering: Associate Degree
Program: Occupational; 2-Year Principally Bachelor's Creditable
Accreditation: SC

02 President ....Dr. Scott HAMILTON
05 Vice Pres Academic & Student Svcs ....Dr. Richard PHILLIPS
10 Vice Pres Finance & Admin Services ....Ms. Donna SHELTON
30 Vice Pres Institutional Advancement ....Ms. Donna G. STANLEY
32 Dean of Student Services ....Mr. Brandon DOTSON
07 Director of Enrollment Services ....Ms. Kristy HALL
08 Director of Library Services ....Mr. Michael GILLEY
51 Dir Continuing & Distance Education ....Ms. Sue Ella BOATRIGHT-WELLS
37 Director Financial Aid/Registrar ....Ms. Kristy HALL
09 Dir Inst Research/Chief PR Ofcr ....Mr. Ricky BOLLING
13 Dir Ctr Computing & Info Technology ....Mr. Rickie N. CAMPBELL
15 Director Personnel Services ....Ms. Pam GILES
18 Int Chief Facilities/Physical Plant ....Mr. Jim VICARS
49 Dean Arts & Sciences ....Ms. Carolyn H. REYNOLDS
72 Dean of Industrial Tech/Health Sci ....Mr. Tommy CLEMENTS
50 Dean of Business & Information Tech ....Ms. Vickie RATLIFF

*New River Community College (E)

PO Box 1127, Dublin VA 24084-1127
County: Pulaski FICE Identification: 005223
Unit ID: 232867
Telephone: (540) 674-3600 Carnegie Class: Assoc/Pub-R-M
FAX Number: (540) 674-3642 Calendar System: Semester
URL: www.nr.edu
Established: 1969 Annual Undergrad Tuition & Fees (In-State): $3,812
Enrollment: 5,207 Coed
Affiliation or Control: State IRS Status: 501(c)3
Highest Offering: Associate Degree
Program: Occupational; 2-Year Principally Bachelor's Creditable
Accreditation: SC

02 President ....Dr. Jack M. LEWIS
04 Assistant to the President ....Mrs. Amy J. HALL
05 VP for Instruction/Student Svcs ....Dr. Patricia B. HUBER
10 Vice Pres for Finance & Technology ....Mr. John L. VAN HEMERT
30 VP for WD and External Relations ....Dr. Mark C. ROWH
20 Assoc VP/Assessment Coordinator ....Mrs. Teri D. MOORE
49 Dean of Arts & Sciences ....Mrs. Carol P. HURST
72 Dean Business & Technologies ....Mr. Dan A. LOOKADOO
09 Dir Inst Effectiveness/Research ....Dr. Frederick M. STREFF
06 Registrar ....Ms. Margaret G. TAYLOR
15 Human Resources & Business Ofc Mgr ....Ms. Melissa P. ANDERSON
102 Executive Director of Foundation ....Mrs. Angie E. COVEY
32 Counselor/Student Life Coordinator ....Mr. Benjamin KRAMER
35 Director of Student Affairs ....Ms. Margaret G. TAYLOR
37 Director of Student Financial Aid ....Mrs. Lori A. TIBBS
38 Director of Student Counseling ....Ms. Margaret G. TAYLOR
18 Chief Facilities/Physical Plant ....Mr. Anthony J. NICOLO
21 Associate Vice President of Finance ....Ms. Bridget M. SAYLES
96 Inventory and Purchasing Technician ....Ms. Monica W. CARDEN
56 Dir Dist Educ/Offsite Campus Svcs ....Mrs. Linda C. CLAUSSEN
51 Director Transitional Programs ....Mrs. Jenny L. BOLTE
08 Coordinator of Library Services ....Mrs. Sandra B. SMITH
07 Coord Admissions/Records/Stdnt Svcs ....Ms. Margaret G. TAYLOR
88 Coordinator of WorkKeys Center ....Ms. Patricia RYAN
88 Coordinator Center Hearing Impaired ....Ms. Lucy J. HOWLETT
88 Coordinator of Learning Disabled ....Ms. Jeananne F. DIXON
84 Enrollment Manager Coordinator ....Mrs. Deborah D. KENNEDY

*Northern Virginia Community College (F)

4001 Wakefield Chapel Road, Annandale VA 22003-3796
County: Fairfax FICE Identification: 003727
Unit ID: 232946
Telephone: (703) 323-3000 Carnegie Class: Assoc/Pub-S-MC
FAX Number: (703) 323-3767 Calendar System: Semester
URL: www.nvcc.edu
Established: 1965 Annual Undergrad Tuition & Fees (In-State): $3,486
Enrollment: 50,044 Coed
Affiliation or Control: State IRS Status: 501(c)3
Highest Offering: Associate Degree
Program: Occupational; 2-Year Principally Bachelor's Creditable
Accreditation: SC, ADNUR, DH, DMS, EMT, MLTAD, PTAA

02 President ....Dr. Robert G. TEMPLIN, JR.
05 Exec VP/Chief Academic Officer ....Dr. Mel D. SCHIAVELLI
10 Vice President Finance ....Ms. Dimitrina DIMKOVA
11 Vice President Administration ....Mr. Tony A. BANSAL
13 Vice Pres of Information Technology ....Dr. Steven G. SACHS
103 Vice Pres of Workforce Development ....Mr. William H. GARY, SR.
09 VP Inst Research & Planning ....Dr. George E. GABRIEL
20 Assoc VP Academic Services ....Dr. Sharon N. ROBERTSON
104 Assoc Vice Pres Global Studies ....Dr. Paul J. MCVEIGH
84 Assoc VP Stdnt Svcs & Enroll Mgmt ....Dr. Elizabeth HARPER
12 Provost Alexandria Campus ....Dr. Peter MAPHUMULO
12 Provost Annandale Campus ....Dr. Barbara L. SAPERSTONE
12 Provost Loudoun Campus ....Dr. Julie LEIDIG
12 Interim Provost Manassas Campus ....Ms. Christine HOLT
12 Provost Medical Education Campus ....Mr. Brian P. FOLEY
12 Provost Woodbridge Campus ....Dr. Sam HILL
102 Exec Dir NVCC Education Foundation ....Mr. John J. RUFFINO
22 Dir Affirm Act/Minority/Legal Affs ....Mr. Everett V. EBERHARDT
29 Director Alumni Relations ....Ms. Bonnie L. IDLE
25 Director of Grants Development ....Ms. Deborah E. MOTTSMAN-ROSEN
15 Director of Human Resources ....Ms. Shelli W. JARVIS
96 Director of Purchasing ....Mr. Edward J. MELLON
37 Dir Stdnt Financial Aid/Support Svc ....Ms. Joan A. ZANDERS
21 Business Manager ....Mr. Frederick R. TITTMANN
18 Chief Facilities/Physical Plant ....Mr. Derek M. HODGE
27 Public Information Officer ....Ms. Jessica M. BAXTER
19 Director Security/Safety ....Mr. William FLAGLER
86 Director Government Relations ....Mr. Dana KAUFFMAN

*Patrick Henry Community College (G)

645 Patriot Avenue, Martinsville VA 24112
County: Henry FICE Identification: 003751
Unit ID: 233019

Telephone: (276) 638-8777 Carnegie Class: Assoc/Pub-R-M
FAX Number: (276) 656-0320 Calendar System: Semester
URL: www.ph.vccs.edu
Established: 1962 Annual Undergrad Tuition & Fees (In-State): $3,805
Enrollment: 2,599 Coed
Affiliation or Control: State IRS Status: 501(c)3
Highest Offering: Associate Degree
Program: Occupational; 2-Year Principally Bachelor's Creditable
Accreditation: SC, ADNUR

02 President .... Dr. Angeline D. GODWIN
05 Vice Pres Student Development Svcs .... Dr. Kristin BISHOP
10 Vice Pres Finance & Admin Services .... Dr. Ronald EPPERLY
30 Int Vice Pres Inst Advancement .... Mr. James BECKNER, JR.
56 Dean Extended Learning Services .... Mrs. Rhonda HODGES
20 Dean Institutional Support Svcs .... Mr. Greg HODGES
72 Dean Div Occupational Tech Program .... Mr. Jeff FIELDS
49 Dean Div Arts & Science Programs .... Mr. Robert CLARY
38 Dean Student Development Svcs .... Mr. Jeff PORTER
22 Affirmative Action Coordinator .... Ms. Delores EANES
37 Financial Aid/Veterans Admin .... Mrs. Cindy KELLER
09 Coord Inst Research/Plng/Evaluation .... Mr. Kevin SHROPSHIRE
07 Coord of Admissions & Records .... Mr. Travis TISDALE
06 Registrar .... Ms. Jessica CARTER
15 Director of Personnel Services .... Ms. Delores EANES
18 Chief Facilities/Physical Plant .... Mr. Wayne CARDWELL
26 Chief Public Relations/Dir Alumni .... Mrs. Kristin LANDRUM
32 Director of Student Affairs .... Mr. Jeff PORTER
96 Director of Purchasing .... Ms. Carline DEAL

*Paul D. Camp Community College (A)

100 N College Drive, Franklin VA 23851-0737
County: Independent City FICE Identification: 009159
Unit ID: 233037
Telephone: (757) 569-6700 Carnegie Class: Assoc/Pub-R-S
FAX Number: (757) 569-6795 Calendar System: Semester
URL: www.pdc.edu
Established: 1970 Annual Undergrad Tuition & Fees (In-State): $3,800
Enrollment: 1,659 Coed
Affiliation or Control: State IRS Status: 501(c)3
Highest Offering: Associate Degree
Program: Occupational; 2-Year Principally Bachelor's Creditable
Accreditation: SC

02 President .... Dr. Paul W. CONCO
05 Vice Pres Inst/Student Development .... Dr. Maxine B. SINGLETON
10 Vice President Finance/Admin Svcs .... Dr. Joe EDENFIELD
30 Vice Pres Institutional Advancement .... Ms. Felicia BLOW
20 Dean Franklin Academic Programs .... Vacant
20 Dean of Suffolk Academic Programs .... Dr. Harriette ARRINGTON
08 Director of Learning Resources .... Ms. Linza M. WEAVER
12 Academic Director-Smithfield .... Dr. Carl SWEAT
103 Director of Workforce Development .... Mr. Randy BETZ
09 Director of Institutional Research .... Dr. Jerry J. STANDAHL
18 Chief Facilities/Physical Plant .... Mr. James C. GORHAM
15 Human Resources Manager .... Vacant
21 Business Office Manager .... Vacant
88 Development Studies Program Head .... Dr. Maxine B. SINGLETON
26 Public Relations Specialist .... Ms. Wendy HARRISON
96 Buyer Specialist .... Ms. J. Lynn PHILLIPS
37 Financial Aid Coordinator .... Ms. Teresa HARRISON
04 Assistant to the President .... Ms. Diane COOKE

*Piedmont Virginia Community College (B)

501 College Drive, Charlottesville VA 22902-7589
County: Independent City FICE Identification: 009928
Unit ID: 233116
Telephone: (434) 977-3900 Carnegie Class: Assoc/Pub-R-M
FAX Number: (434) 971-8232 Calendar System: Semester
URL: www.pvcc.edu
Established: 1972 Annual Undergrad Tuition & Fees (In-State): $3,665
Enrollment: 5,684 Coed
Affiliation or Control: State IRS Status: 501(c)3
Highest Offering: Associate Degree
Program: Occupational; 2-Year Principally Bachelor's Creditable; Liberal Arts And General
Accreditation: SC, ADNUR, EMT, RAD, SURGT

02 President .... Dr. Frank FRIEDMAN
05 VP Instruction/Student Svcs .... Dr. John DONNELLY
10 Vice President Finance/Admin Svcs .... Dr. William P. JACKAMEIT
79 Dean Humanities/Fine Arts/Soc Sci .... Dr. Clifford W. HAURY
50 Dean Business/Math/Technologies .... Dr. Chuck BOHLEKE
17 Dean Health & Life Sciences .... Dr. Kathy HUDSON
103 Dean Workforce Services .... Ms. Valerie PALAMOUNTAIN
32 Director of Student Services .... Ms. Mary Lee WALSH
13 Dir Information Technology/CIO .... Mr. Shivajl SAMANTA
09 Dir Instl Research/Planning/Effect .... Dr. Tara ATKINS-BRADY
30 Dir Inst Advancement & Development .... Ms. Mary Jane KING
06 Registrar .... Ms. Lorraine CONCA
96 Director of Purchasing .... Ms. Marie C. MELTON
18 Facilities Manager .... Mr. David THOMPSON
15 Human Resources Manager .... Ms. Yvonne CAREY
26 Manager Marketing/Media Relations .... Ms. Anita SHOWERS
84 Outreach/Enrollment Services Mgr .... Ms. Heather LUTZ
08 Coordinator Library Services .... Ms. Linda CAHILL
37 Coordinator Financial Aid .... Ms. Carol LARSON
36 Coordinator Advising & Transfer .... Mr. Kemper STEELE

*Rappahannock Community College (C)

12745 College Drive, Glenns VA 23149-0287
County: Gloucester FICE Identification: 009160
Unit ID: 233310
Telephone: (804) 758-6700 Carnegie Class: Assoc/Pub-S-MC
FAX Number: (804) 758-3852 Calendar System: Semester
URL: www.rappahannock.edu
Established: 1970 Annual Undergrad Tuition & Fees (In-State): $3,089
Enrollment: 3,734 Coed
Affiliation or Control: State IRS Status: 501(c)3
Highest Offering: Associate Degree
Program: Occupational; 2-Year Principally Bachelor's Creditable
Accreditation: SC

02 President .... Dr. Elizabeth H. CROWTHER
10 Vice Pres Finance & Admin Services .... Mr. D. Kim MCMANUS
05 VP Instruction/Student Development .... Dr. A. Donna ALEXANDER
32 Dean Student Development .... Ms. Anne KORNEGAY
08 Dean of Learning Resources .... Ms. Cherie CARL
30 Dean of College Advancement .... Mr. Victor W. CLOUGH, JR.
09 Dir Institutional Effectiveness .... Dr. Glenda D. HAYNIE
06 College Registrar .... Ms. Felicia B. PACKETT
37 Financial Aid/Veteran Affairs Ofcr .... Ms. Carolyn A. WARD
15 Human Resources Manager .... Mrs. Caroline W. STELTER
18 Facilities/Physical Plant Manager .... Mr. Mark P. BEAVER

*Southside Virginia Community College (D)

109 Campus Drive, Alberta VA 23821-2930
County: Brunswick FICE Identification: 008661
Unit ID: 233639
Telephone: (434) 949-1000 Carnegie Class: Assoc/Pub-R-L
FAX Number: (434) 949-7863 Calendar System: Semester
URL: www.southside.edu
Established: 1970 Annual Undergrad Tuition & Fees (In-State): $3,048
Enrollment: 6,461 Coed
Affiliation or Control: State IRS Status: 501(c)3
Highest Offering: Associate Degree
Program: Occupational; 2-Year Principally Bachelor's Creditable
Accreditation: SC, EMT

02 President .... Dr. John J. CAVAN
12 Provost John H Daniel Campus .... Dr. Al ROBERTS
12 Provost Christanna Campus .... Dr. John D. SYKES, JR.
10 Vice Pres Finance & Administration .... Mr. Peter G. HUNT
25 VP Adult Education & Grants .... Dr. Linda SHEFFIELD
13 Dean Information Services .... Mr. Jack ANCELL
84 Dean Enrollment Mgt & Assoc Prof .... Mrs. Shannon FEINMAN
20 Dean of Instruction Daniel .... Ms. Paula M. GASTENVELD
20 Dean of Instruction Christanna .... Mr. Tom WISBEY
09 Dean Planning & Inst Effectiveness .... Mr. Chad PATTON
66 Dean of Nursing/Health Technology .... Ms. Michelle K. EDMONDS
102 Exec Director SVCC Foundation .... Mrs. Mary Jane ELKINS
08 Library Supervisor .... Ms. Earnestine LEWIS
08 College Librarian .... Ms. Libby BLANTON
26 Public Relations & Mktg Specialist .... Ms. Christie C. HALES
37 Director of Financial Aid .... Ms. Sally THARRINGTON
15 Human Resources Manager .... Ms. Bethany W. HARRIS
18 Buildings/Grounds Supt Christanna .... Mr. Roger WRAY
38 Dir Student Counseling Christanna .... Ms. Judy SHEPHERD
38 Director Student Counseling Daniel .... Mrs. Dorethea SIZEMORE
21 Business Manager .... Mrs. Diane B. DANIEL
29 Alumni Relations SVCC .... Mrs. Mary Jane ELKINS

*Southwest Virginia Community College (E)

Box SVCC, Richlands VA 24641-1101
County: Tazewell FICE Identification: 007260
Unit ID: 233648
Telephone: (276) 964-2555 Carnegie Class: Assoc/Pub-R-M
FAX Number: (276) 964-9307 Calendar System: Semester
URL: www.sw.edu
Established: 1967 Annual Undergrad Tuition & Fees (In-State): $2,988
Enrollment: 3,233 Coed
Affiliation or Control: State IRS Status: 501(c)3
Highest Offering: Associate Degree
Program: Occupational; 2-Year Principally Bachelor's Creditable
Accreditation: SC, EMT, OTA, RAD

02 President .... Dr. J. Mark ESTEPP
05 Vice President of Instruction .... Dr. Barbara J. FULLER
10 Vice Pres Finance & Admin Services .... Dr. Leonard V. KOGUT
30 Vice Pres Institutional Advancement .... Ms. Phyllis A. ROBERTS
51 Dean Continuing Education .... Ms. Sharon PEERY
24 Dean Learning Resources .... Vacant
32 Assoc Vice Pres Student Services .... Mr. Roderick B. MOORE
44 Institutional Advancement Officer .... Ms. Mary W. LAWSON
09 Institutional Research Officer .... Dr. Edmond C. SMITH
18 Physical Plant Superintendent .... Mr. Larry WHITT
19 Campus Police Chief .... Mr. Ronnie KISER
15 Human Resources Manager .... Ms. Martha L. RASNAKE
21 Financial Services Manager .... Mr. Michael BALES
26 Public Relations Coordinator .... Ms. Patsy G. BUSSARD
07 Coord Admissions/Counseling .... Mr. James E. FARRIS
11 General Admin Coordinator .... Ms. Rhonda L. VANDYKE
08 Coordinator of Library Services .... Ms. Teresa A. ALLEY
56 Coord Distributed/Distance Learning .... Vacant

*Thomas Nelson Community College (F)

99 Thomas Nelson Drive, Hampton VA 23666
County: Independent City FICE Identification: 006871
Unit ID: 233754
Telephone: (757) 825-2700 Carnegie Class: Assoc/Pub-S-SC
FAX Number: (757) 825-2763 Calendar System: Semester
URL: www.tncc.edu
Established: 1967 Annual Undergrad Tuition & Fees (In-State): $3,779
Enrollment: 9,245 Coed
Affiliation or Control: State IRS Status: 501(c)3
Highest Offering: Associate Degree
Program: Occupational; 2-Year Principally Bachelor's Creditable
Accreditation: SC, ADNUR, DH

02 President .... Dr. John T. DEVER
12 Provost Historic Triangle Campus .... Dr. William TRAVIS
05 Int Vice Pres for Academic Affairs .... Mr. Norman P. HAHN
32 Int Vice Pres for Student Affairs .... Dr. Vicki RICHMOND
11 Vice President for Admin/Finance .... Mr. Charles NURNBERGER
103 Vice Pres for Workforce Development .... Dr. Deborah G. WRIGHT
44 Vice Pres Institutional Advancement .... Ms. Cynthia CALLAWAY
35 Assoc VP for Student Affairs .... Dr. Vicki RICHMOND
13 Director of Information Tech .... Mr. Wayne DAVIS
106 Dir Distance/Distributive Learning .... Ms. Ruth SMITH
84 Director of Enrollment Management .... Ms. Kris RARIG
10 Assoc VP for Financial Services .... Ms. Teresa BAILEY
103 Assoc VP for Workforce Training/CE .... Dr. Carmen BURROWS
79 Dean Communications/Humanities .... Dr. Kimberly BRITT
81 Dean Engr/Science/Allied Health .... Ms. Patricia TAYLOR
50 Int Dean Public Services/Business .... Mr. Raymond MUZIA
38 Dean of Student Development .... Ms. Joyce JOHHSON
37 Dir Financial Aid/Veteran Affairs .... Ms. Kathryn ANDERSON
18 Physical Plant Manager .... Mr. Mark KRAMER
26 Director Public Relations/Marketing .... Ms. Cecilia RAMIREZ
08 Director of Learning Resources .... Vacant
09 Dir Inst Research and Effectiveness .... Vacant
21 Business Office Manager .... Ms. Wan HU
15 Human Resources Manager .... Ms. Lisa JOHNSON
21 Budget Office Manager .... Mr. Lisle WILKE

*Tidewater Community College (G)

121 College Place, Norfolk VA 23510
County: Independent City FICE Identification: 003712
Unit ID: 233772
Telephone: (757) 822-1122 Carnegie Class: Assoc/Pub-S-SC
FAX Number: (757) 822-1060 Calendar System: Semester
URL: www.tcc.edu
Established: 1968 Annual Undergrad Tuition & Fees (In-State): $3,645
Enrollment: 32,101 Coed
Affiliation or Control: State IRS Status: 501(c)3
Highest Offering: Associate Degree
Program: Occupational; 2-Year Principally Bachelor's Creditable
Accreditation: SC, FUSER, ACFEI, ADNUR, DMS, EMT, MAC, OTA, PTAA

02 President .... Dr. Edna BAEHRE-KOLOVANI
11 Exec Vice President Administration .... Mr. Franklin T. DUNN
05 VP Student Learning/Chief Acad Ofcr .... Dr. Daniel DEMARTE
10 Vice President Finance .... Ms. Phyllis MILLOY
13 Vice President Info Systems .... Mr. Richard ANDERSEN
103 Vice Pres Workforce Development .... Dr. Theresa BRYANT
84 VP Student Success/Enrollment Mgmt .... Dr. Alice R. MCADORY
44 Vice Pres Institutional Advancement .... Mr. James P. TOSCANO
20 Int Assoc VP Academic Effectiveness .... Dr. Kellie SOREY
20 AVP Faculty Dev/Curriculum Innovat .... Dr. Diann HOLT
106 Interim Assoc Vice Pres eLearning .... Ms. Deborah EDSON
25 Assoc Vice Pres Grants/Spons Pgms .... Ms. Valerie CHEESEMAN
20 Provost Chesapeake Campus .... Dr. Linda RICE
20 Provost Portsmouth Campus .... Dr. Michelle WOODHOUSE
20 Provost Virginia Beach Campus .... Dr. Michael SUMMERS
20 Provost Norfolk Campus .... Dr. Marvin L. BRIGHT
09 Dir Institutional Effectiveness .... Mr. Curtis K. AASEN
32 Dean of Student Svcs Chesapeake .... Dr. Judy MCMILLAN
81 Dean Lang/Math/Science Chesapeake .... Dr. Cynthia CADIEUX
50 Dean Bus/Pub Svc/Tech Chesapeake .... Mr. James PERKINSON
32 Int Dean of Student Svcs Portsmouth .... Dr. Bertha ESCOFFERY
50 Dean Bus/Pub Svcs/Tech Portsmouth .... Ms. Ann AMBROSE
81 Dean Lang/Math/Science Portsmouth .... Ms. Jenefer SNYDER
57 Director Visual Arts Center .... Ms. Christina RUPSCH
32 Dean of Student Svcs Va Beach .... Dr. Marilyn HODGE
50 Dean IT & Business Va Beach .... Ms. Carolyn MCLELLAN
54 Dean Eng & Ind Tech Va Beach .... Mr. David EKKER
76 Dean Health Professions .... Mr. Thomas CALOGRIDES, JR.
88 Dean Language & Speech Va Beach .... Ms. Marcane ANDERSON
81 Dean Math & Science Va Beach .... Mr. Greg FRANK
83 Dean Social Sci/Pub Svcs Va Beach .... Vacant
32 Dean of Student Svcs Norfolk .... Dr. Waldon HAGAN
50 Dean Bus/Pub Svcs/Tech Norfolk .... Ms. Caroline RIVERA
81 Int Dean Lang/Math/Science Norfolk .... Mr. Joseph JOYNER
30 Director of Development .... Ms. Lara OVERY
06 Registrar .... Dr. Kellie SOREY
26 Chief Communications Officer .... Vacant
96 Director of Materiel Management .... Ms. Robin MOORE
18 Director Facilities Management .... Mr. David GUGLIELMO
15 Director Human Resources .... Ms. Gretna SMITH
37 Director Student Financial Aid .... Ms. Jennifer HARPHAM

*Virginia Highlands Community College (A)

PO Box 828, Abingdon VA 24212-0828

County: Washington | FICE Identification: 007099 | Unit ID: 233903
Telephone: (276) 739-2400 | Carnegie Class: Assoc/Pub-R-M
FAX Number: (276) 739-2590 | Calendar System: Semester
URL: www.vhcc.edu
Established: 1967 | Annual Undergrad Tuition & Fees (In-State): $3,802
Enrollment: 2,824 | Coed
Affiliation or Control: State | IRS Status: 501(c)3
Highest Offering: Associate Degree
Program: Occupational; 2-Year Principally Bachelor's Creditable
Accreditation: SC, ADNUR, OTA

Code	Title	Name
02	President	Dr. Ron PROFFITT
05	VP Instruction & Student Services	Dr. Hara CHARLIER
10	VP Financial/Administrative Svcs	Ms. Christine FIELDS
30	Vice Pres Institutional Advancement	Mr. David N. MATLOCK
49	Dean Business/Human/Soc Sci	Ms. Alma Z. ROWLAND
72	Dean of Science & Engr Technologies	Mr. Robert E. MAY
66	Dean of Nursing and Allied Health	Ms. Kathy J. MITCHELL
103	Dean Workforce Training & Cont Educ	Ms. Melinda T. LELAND
08	Director Library/Instructional Svcs	Mr. Charles BOLING
37	Director of Financial Aid	Ms. Karen T. CHEERS
07	Director Admission/Records	Ms. Karen T. CHEERS
06	Registrar	Ms. Charlene EASTRIDGE
15	Director Personnel Services	Ms. Laura MCCLELLAN
32	Director Student Affs/Alumni Rels	Vacant
88	Director of Talent Search	Ms. Beth M. PAGE
88	Director Project EXCEL	Ms. Jackie T. CRAFT
38	Director Student Counseling	Vacant
21	Business Manager	Mr. Roger W. SPENCER
96	Director of Purchasing	Ms. Chelsa TAYLOR
88	Institutional Effectiveness	Ms. Jennifer D. ADDISON
90	Coord Academic Computing/Technology	Mr. Glen JOHNSON
26	Public Relations Officer	Ms. Anne M. DUNHAM
09	Institutional Research Officer	Mr. Jeff D. RUSSELL
18	Chief Facilities/Physical Plant	Mr. Ernest L. NUNLEY
19	Director of Security/Safety	Mr. David NECESSARY
36	Career Plng/Placement Spclst	Mr. Tony FULLER

*Virginia Western Community College (B)

PO Box 14007, Roanoke VA 24038-4007

County: Independent City | FICE Identification: 003760 | Unit ID: 233949
Telephone: (540) 857-8922 | Carnegie Class: Assoc/Pub-R-L
FAX Number: (540) 857-6526 | Calendar System: Semester
URL: www.virginiawestern.edu
Established: 1966 | Annual Undergrad Tuition & Fees (In-State): $4,052
Enrollment: 8,557 | Coed
Affiliation or Control: State | IRS Status: 501(c)3
Highest Offering: Associate Degree
Program: Occupational; 2-Year Principally Bachelor's Creditable
Accreditation: SC, ACBSP, DH, RAD, RTT

Code	Title	Name
02	President	Dr. Robert H. SANDEL
10	Vice Pres of Finance/Admin Services	Ms. Cheryl MILLER
05	Int Vice Pres Academic/Student Affs	Dr. Elizabeth WILMER
30	Vice Pres Institutional Advancement	Dr. Angela M. FALCONETTI
45	Dean Institutional Effectiveness	Ms. Rachelle KOUDELIK-JONES
49	Dean Liberal Arts/Social Sciences	Dr. Elizabeth WILMER
81	Dean Nat Sci/Math/Health Tech Div	Dr. Bryan SCHAUBACH
50	Dean Bus/Sciences/Engineering/WFD	Mr. James W. POYTHRESS
09	Director Institutional Research	Ms. Carol ROWLETT
32	Dean of Student Services	Ms. Lori BAKER
06	Registrar	Ms. Lorraine CONKLIN
19	Campus Police Chief	Mr. Craig HARRIS
13	Information Technology Manager	Mr. David W. HARRISON
15	Human Resources Manager	Mr. Garry M. SHELTON
21	Business Manager	Mrs. Fredona AARON
37	Financial Aid Officer	Mr. Chad SARTINI
103	Workforce Development Officer	Ms. Leah COFFMAN
35	Coordinator Advising/Retention Svc	Dr. Gloria A. LINDSAY
08	Coordinator of the Library	Ms. Lynn HURT
18	Director of Facilities Mgmt Svcs	Mr. Kevin G. WITTER
36	Counselor Career Services	Vacant
24	Coordinator Learning Tech Center	Vacant
25	Coord Grants Dev & Special Projects	Ms. Marilyn J. HERBERT-ASHTON
29	Alumni/Annual Giving Coord/Communic	Mr. Erik W. WILLIAMS

*Wytheville Community College (C)

1000 E Main Street, Wytheville VA 24382-3308

County: Wythe | FICE Identification: 003761 | Unit ID: 234377
Telephone: (276) 223-4700 | Carnegie Class: Assoc/Pub-R-M
FAX Number: (276) 223-4778 | Calendar System: Semester
URL: www.wcc.vccs.edu
Established: 1963 | Annual Undergrad Tuition & Fees (In-State): $3,810
Enrollment: 3,792 | Coed
Affiliation or Control: State | IRS Status: 501(c)3
Highest Offering: Associate Degree
Program: Occupational; 2-Year Principally Bachelor's Creditable
Accreditation: SC, ADNUR, DH, MLTAD, PTAA

Code	Title	Name
02	President	Dr. Charlie WHITE
05	Vice Pres Instruction/Student Devel	Dr. William H. HIGHTOWER, JR.
10	Vice Pres Finance & Admin Services	Ms. Crystal Y. CREGGER
09	Director of Institutional Research	Dr. Kent E. GLINDEMANN
30	Vice Pres of College Development	Dr. Rhonda K. CATRON-WOOD
75	Vice Pres Cont Ed & Tech/Occ Pgms	Ms. Angela Y. LAWSON
50	Dean of Business & Humanities	Ms. Donna FENDER
76	Dean of Health & Science	Dr. Lorri M. HUFFARD
32	Dean of Student Services	Mr. Michael L. MCHONE
13	Director Acad/Admin Computing	Mr. Shawn MCREYNOLDS
06	Registrar	Vacant
15	Human Resources Manager	Ms. Linda R. NYE
26	Public Relations Coordinator	Mr. William A. VESELIK
08	Coordinator of Library Services	Mr. George E. MATTIS, JR.
96	Procurement Officer	Ms. Vivian FANNING
106	Dir of Distance & Distrib Learning	Mr. Kenneth E. FAIRBANKS

Virginia Intermont College (D)

1013 Moore Street, Bristol VA 24201-4298

County: Independent City | FICE Identification: 003752 | Unit ID: 233912
Telephone: (276) 669-6101 | Carnegie Class: Bac/A&S
FAX Number: (276) 669-5763 | Calendar System: Semester
URL: www.vic.edu
Established: 1884 | Annual Undergrad Tuition & Fees: $24,542
Enrollment: 511 | Coed
Affiliation or Control: Baptist | IRS Status: 501(c)3
Highest Offering: Baccalaureate
Program: Liberal Arts And General; Teacher Preparatory; Business Emphasis
Accreditation: SC, SW

Code	Title	Name
01	President	Dr. E. Clorisa PHILLIPS
05	Provost	Mr. Mark ROBERTS
10	VP for Business & Finance	Ms. Linda MORGAN
32	Dean of Student Development	Ms. Ronda COLE
04	Executive Assistant to President	Mr. Robert BAIRD
07	Dean of Admissions	Mr. Richard CARROLL
37	Director of Financial Aid	Ms. Denise POSEY
08	Librarian	Mr. Jonathan TALLMAN
36	Dir Placement & Career Planning	Ms. Ronan KING
06	Registrar	Ms. Pamela HAMMOND
09	Director of Institutional Research	Ms. Charlotte INGRAM
21	Associate Business Officer	Ms. Becky COVEY
29	Director of Alumni Relations	Ms. Beth SHUMAKER
38	Director of Student Counseling	Ms. Deborah PATTERSON
92	Director of Honors Program	Dr. Robert RAINWATER
15	Director Personnel Services	Mr. Ali TRIVETT
26	Dir of Marketing/Communications	Ms. Mary Anne HOLBROOK
18	Chief Facilities/Physical Plant	Mr. Con SAULS

Virginia International University (E)

11200 Waples Mill Road, Suite 360, Fairfax VA 22030

County: Fairfax | FICE Identification: 041440
Telephone: (703) 591-7042 | Carnegie Class: Not Classified
FAX Number: (703) 591-7046 | Calendar System: Other
URL: www.viu.edu
Established: 1998 | Annual Undergrad Tuition & Fees: N/A
Enrollment: N/A | Coed
Affiliation or Control: Proprietary | IRS Status: Proprietary
Highest Offering: Master's
Program: Professional; Business Emphasis
Accreditation: ACICS

Code	Title	Name
01	President	Dr. Isa SARAC
03	Vice President University Affairs	Ms. Sue Ann MYERS

Virginia Military Institute (F)

319 Letcher Avenue, Lexington VA 24450-0304

County: Independent City | FICE Identification: 003753 | Unit ID: 234085
Telephone: (540) 464-7230 | Carnegie Class: Bac/A&S
FAX Number: (540) 464-7583 | Calendar System: Semester
URL: www.vmi.edu
Established: 1839 | Annual Undergrad Tuition & Fees (In-State): $21,568
Enrollment: 1,605 | Coed
Affiliation or Control: State | IRS Status: 501(c)3
Highest Offering: Baccalaureate
Program: Liberal Arts And General; Professional
Accreditation: SC, BUS, CS, ENG

Code	Title	Name
01	Superintendent	Gen. J. H. Benford PEAY
05	Dean of the Faculty	BGen. R. Wane SCHNEITER
10	Deputy Superintendent Finance/Admin	BGen. Robert L. GREEN
32	Commandant of Cadets	Col. Thomas H. TRUMPS
100	Chief of Staff	Col. Jeffrey H. CURTIS
04	Assistant to the Superintendent	Col. Michael M. STRICKLER
21	Assoc Business Exec/Treasurer	Col. Gary R. KNICK
07	Director of Admissions	Col. Vernon L. BEITZEL
88	Exec Director Museum Programs	Col. Keith E. GIBSON
37	Director of Financial Aid	Col. Timothy P. GOLDEN
35	Deputy Commandant Cadet Life	Col. L. E. HURLBUT
36	Director of Career Services	Col. R. Samuel RATCLIFFE
41	Director Intercollegiate Athletics	Mr. Donald T. WHITE
26	Director Communications & Marketing	Col. Stewart D. MACINNIS
29	Executive VP Alumni Association	LTC. Adam C. VOLANT
30	Exec VP VMI Foundation/Fund Raising	Mr. Brian S. CROCKETT
88	Exec VP Keydet Club/Athletic Fund	Mr. Gregory M. CAVALLARO
06	Registrar	LtCol. Janet M. BATTAGLIA
15	Director Human Resources	Col. Robert B. SPORE
18	Director Physical Plant	LTC. James L. WILLIAMS, JR.
09	Director Institutional Research	Col. Elizabeth S. SECHLER
88	Director Auxiliary Services	Col. James N. JOYNER
40	Manager Bookstore	Ms. Patricia T. RULEY
42	Institute Chaplain	Col. James S. PARK
17	Institute Physician	Dr. David L. COPELAND
88	Director of Sports Information	Mr. Wade H. BRANNER
08	Head Librarian	Col. Donald H. SAMDAHL, JR.
38	Director of Cadet Counseling	LtCol. Sarah L. JONES
14	Director Information Technology	Col. Thomas F. HOPKINS
96	Director of Purchasing	Maj. Kathy H. TOMLIN

† Tuition includes required room and board and quartermaster charges.

Virginia Polytechnic Institute and State University (G)

Blacksburg VA 24061-0202

County: Montgomery | FICE Identification: 003754 | Unit ID: 233921
Telephone: (540) 231-6000 | Carnegie Class: RU/VH
FAX Number: (540) 231-9263 | Calendar System: Semester
URL: www.vt.edu
Established: 1872 | Annual Undergrad Tuition & Fees (In-State): $10,923
Enrollment: 30,936 | Coed
Affiliation or Control: State | IRS Status: 501(c)3
Highest Offering: Doctorate
Program: Liberal Arts And General; Teacher Preparatory; Professional
Accreditation: SC, ART, BUS, BUSA, CACREP, CEA, CIDA, CLPSY, CONST, CS, DIETD, DIETI, ENG, FOR, IPSY, LSAR, MFCD, MUS, PLNG, SPAA, TED, THEA, VET

Code	Title	Name
01	President	Charles W. STEGER
05	Senior Vice President & Provost	Mark G. MCNAMEE
11	Vice President for Admin Services	Sherwood G. WILSON
13	Vice Pres for Information Tech	Scott F. MIDKIFF
32	Vice President Student Affairs	Patricia A. PERILLO
30	Vice Pres Devel & University Rels	Elizabeth A. FLANAGAN
29	Vice President Alumni Relations	Thomas C. TILLAR, JR.
28	VP Diversity and Inclusion	William T. LEWIS, SR.
46	Vice President for Research	Robert WALTERS
20	Vice President and Dean UG Educ	Daniel A. WUBAH
58	Vice President and Dean Grad Educ	Karen P. DEPAUW
56	Int VP Outreach/International Affs	Jerry NILES
10	Vice President for Finance and CFO	M. Dwight SHELTON
07	Director of Undergrad Admissions	Mildred JOHNSON
35	Dean of Students	Thomas BROWN
16	Assoc Vice Pres for Human Resources	Hal IRVIN
09	Asst Provost Institutional Research	Kristen BUSH
43	General Counsel	Kay K. HEIDBREDER
84	Asst VP Enrollment Mgmt & Registrar	Wanda H. DEAN
45	Dir for Planning & Administration	Jeb STEWART
37	Dir of Scholarships/Financial Aid	Barry W. SIMMONS
23	Director Schiffert Health Center	Kanitta CHAROENSIRI
18	Assoc Vice President for Facilities	Michael J. COLEMAN
39	Director of Dining Services	Ted FAULKNER
39	Director of Housing and Res Life	Eleanor FINGER
41	Athletic Director	James WEAVER
26	Assoc Vice Pres Univ Relations	Larry HINCKER
38	Director Student Counseling	Chris FLYNN
40	Executive Director Bookstore	Donald J. WILLIAMS
62	Dean of Libraries	Tyler WALTERS
47	Dean of Agriculture/Life Sciences	Alan GRANT
48	Dean of Architecture/Urban Studies	Jack DAVIS
49	Dean College of Science	Lay N. CHANG
50	Dean of Business	Richard E. SORENSEN
54	Dean of Engineering	Richard BENSON
79	Dean Liberal Arts & Human Sciences	Sue OTT ROWLANDS
74	Dean of Veterinary Medicine	Gerhardt SCHURIG
65	Dean of Natural Resources & Environ	Paul M. WINISTORFER
96	Director of Purchasing	W. Thomas KALOUPEK
90	Director Educational Technology	John F. MOORE
91	Assoc Vice Pres for Enterprise Sys	Deborah M. FULTON
12	Exec Dir National Capital Region	Donald J. LEO
102	COO Virginia Tech Foundation	John E. DOOLEY

Virginia State University (H)

One Hayden Street,
Virginia State University VA 23806-0001

County: Chesterfield | FICE Identification: 003764 | Unit ID: 234155
Telephone: (804) 524-5000 | Carnegie Class: Master's S
FAX Number: (804) 524-6506 | Calendar System: Semester
URL: www.vsu.edu
Established: 1882 | Annual Undergrad Tuition & Fees (In-State): $7,420
Enrollment: 5,890 | Coed
Affiliation or Control: State | IRS Status: 501(c)3
Highest Offering: Doctorate
Program: Liberal Arts And General; Teacher Preparatory
Accreditation: SC, ART, BUS, CS, DIETD, DIETI, ENG, ENGT, MUS, NAIT, @SW, TED

Code	Title	Name
01	President	Dr. Keith T. MILLER
100	Chief of Staff	Mr. Cortez K. DIAL
10	Vice Pres Finance & Administration	Mr. David J. MEADOWS
30	VP for Institutional Advancement	Mr. James B. TYSON

05 Provost/VP for Academic Affairs .... Dr. W. Weldon HILL
32 VP of Student Affairs & Enroll Mgmt .... Dr. Michael SHACKLEFORD
20 Vice Provost .... Dr. James E. HUNTER
15 Assoc VP for Human Resource .... Dr. Elliot WHEELAN
84 Asst VP/Student Enrollment Services .... Mr. Henry DEBOSE
21 Associate Business Officer .... Ms. Sheila MCNAIR
50 Dean School Business .... Dr. Mirta M. MARTIN
54 Dean Sch of Engineering Sci & Tech . Dr. Keith M. WILLIAMSON
79 Dean Sch Liberal Arts & Education .... Dr. Andrew KANU
47 Dean Sch of Agriculture .... Dr. Jewel E. HAIRSTON
58 Dean Graduate Studies/Res/Outreach .... Dr. James E. HUNTER
62 Dean Library & Media Services ... Dr. Elsie S. WEATHERINGTON
44 Director of Development .... Ms. Nancy L. JONES
06 Registrar .... Ms. Debera BONNER
09 Director Inst Planning/Assessment .... Dr. Emmett L. RIDLEY
37 Director of Financial Aid .... Mrs. Myra PHILLIPS
19 Director Police/Public Safety .... Mr. Michael WALLACE
04 Special Assistant to the President .... Mr. Jesse VAUGHAN
18 Director of Facilities .... Mr. Gilbertt HANZLIK
07 Director Admissions & Recruitment .... Ms. Irene F. LOGAN
26 Director University Relations .... Mr. Thomas REED
22 Human Resources Manager .... Ms. Gayle ONEAL
14 Assoc VP & Chief Information .... Mr. Hubert B. HARRIS
39 Director Residence Facilities .... Dr. LaVerne BRIGGS
36 Director Career Plng & Placement .... Ms. Yolanda M. CREWS
40 Bookstore Manager .... Mr. Kevin POWELL
92 Director Honors Program .... Dr. Gladys NUNNALLY
41 Athletic Director .... Mrs. Peggy DAVIS
42 Minister .... Rev. Delano DOUGLAS
44 Planned Giving Officer .... Mr. Jonathan YOUNG
29 Coordinator of Alumni Relations .... Ms. Andrea COLLINS
27 Deputy Chief Information Officer .... Ms. Stephanie A. HAYES
23 Director Student Health Services .... Mrs. Rebecca BRANCH-GRIFFIN
25 Contract Manager .... Ms. Linda SCOTT
87 Director Summer School Session .... Dr. Vykuntapathi THOTA
96 Director of Purchasing .... Mrs. Yolanda BUCK
38 Director Student Counseling .... Ms. LaKesha RONEY

Virginia Union University (A)

1500 N Lombardy Street, Richmond VA 23220-1784
County: Independent City — FICE Identification: 003766
Unit ID: 234164
Telephone: (804) 257-5600 — Carnegie Class: Bac/Diverse
FAX Number: (804) 257-5818 — Calendar System: Semester
URL: www.vuu.edu
Established: 1865 — Annual Undergrad Tuition & Fees: $14,630
Enrollment: 1,711 — Coed
Affiliation or Control: Baptist — IRS Status: 501(c)3
Highest Offering: Doctorate
Program: Liberal Arts And General; Teacher Preparatory; Professional
Accreditation: **SC**, ACBSP, SW, TED, THEOL

01 President .... Dr. Claude G. PERKINS
03 Senior Vice President .... Dr. Joseph F. JOHNSON
05 Vice President for Academic Affairs .... Dr. W. F. EVANS
32 VP Enrollmnt Mgmt & Stdnt Affs .... Vacant
10 VP Financial Affairs .... Mr. Gregory LEWIS
30 Vice Pres Institutional Advancement .... Dr. Anthony THOMPSON
09 VP Research/Planning & Spec Prog .... Dr. Joy P. GOODRICH
26 Asst to Pres/Dir Public Relations .... Vacant
53 Dean Evelyn R Syphax Sch Ed/Psy .... Dr. Marshae HORTON
81 Dean Math/Science & Technology .... Dr. Phillip W. ARCHER
50 Dean Sydney Lewis Sch of Business ..... Dr. Adelaja O. ODUTOLA
79 Dean School of Humanities & Soc Sci .... Dr. Linda G. SCHLICHTING
73 Dean School of Theology .... Dr. John W. KINNEY
25 Asst to President Title III Pgms .... Mr. Samuel T. RHOADES
15 Director Human Resources .... Ms. Hollace J. ENOCH
06 Interim Registrar .... Ms. Marilyn A. BROOKS
38 Director Counseling .... Vacant
29 Director of Alumni Affairs .... Ms. Kristie L. WHITE
08 Library Director .... Ms. Pamela FOREMAN
37 Int Director Financial Aid .... Mrs. Arcelia M. JACKSON
27 Director Information Technology .... Mr. Robert R. GRAY
88 Lan Administrator .... Mr. Bryan K. ROYAL
36 Director Career Services .... Dr. Penni SWEETENBURG-LEE
84 Director of Enrollment Management .... Ms. Renita A. JOHNSON
42 University Pastor .... Rev. Angelo V. CHATMON
41 Athletic Director .... Mr. Michael L. BAILEY
19 Chief University Police .... Col. Carlton G. EDWARDS
24 Audio Visual Coordinator .... Mr. JaPrince L. CARTER
21 Comptroller .... Ms. Stephanie M. WHITE
40 Bookstore Manager .... Ms. Terri WYATT
39 Int Director of Residence Life .... Mr. Ullin K. RIGBY
23 University Physician .... Dr. Walton M. BELLE
31 Dir of Community & Student Rels .... Ms. Claudia E. WALL
18 Director Facilities .... Mr. David E. GORDON
96 Director of Purchasing .... Mr. Michael T. ADKINS

Virginia University of Lynchburg (B)

2058 Garfield Avenue, Lynchburg VA 24501-6417
County: Independent City — FICE Identification: 003762
Unit ID: 234137
Telephone: (434) 528-5276 — Carnegie Class: Spec/Faith
FAX Number: (434) 528-4257 — Calendar System: Semester
URL: www.vul.edu
Established: 1886 — Annual Undergrad Tuition & Fees: $7,880
Enrollment: 597 — Coed
Affiliation or Control: Independent Non-Profit — IRS Status: 501(c)3
Highest Offering: Doctorate
Program: Liberal Arts And General; Business Emphasis
Accreditation: **TRACS**

01 President .... Dr. Ralph REAVIS
05 Provost/Executive Vice President .... Dr. Kathy C. FRANKLIN
10 Vice President of Finance .... Mr. Donald LESLIE
32 Vice Pres Div Student Affairs .... Dr. Terrie E. GRIFFIN
30 VP for Institutional Advancement .... Dr. Doris S. CRAWFORD

Virginia Wesleyan College (C)

1584 Wesleyan Drive, Norfolk VA 23502-5599
County: Independent City — FICE Identification: 003767
Unit ID: 234173
Telephone: (757) 455-3200 — Carnegie Class: Bac/A&S
FAX Number: (757) 461-4944 — Calendar System: 4/1/4
URL: www.vwc.edu
Established: 1961 — Annual Undergrad Tuition & Fees: $30,948
Enrollment: 1,404 — Coed
Affiliation or Control: United Methodist — IRS Status: 501(c)3
Highest Offering: Baccalaureate
Program: Liberal Arts And General; Teacher Preparatory
Accreditation: **SC**, NRPA, @SW

01 President .... Dr. William T. GREER, JR.
05 VP Academic Affs/Dean of College ..... Dr. Timothy G. O'ROURKE
10 Vice President of Finance .... Mr. Cary A. SAWYER
32 VP Student Affs/Dean of Enrollment .. Mr. David E. BUCKINGHAM
30 VP for College Advancement .... Ms. Mita K. VAIL
11 Vice President of Operations .... Mr. Bruce F. VAUGHAN
45 AVP Inst Rsrch/Effect/Strat Plng .... Mr. Bryan PRICE
26 Director of College Communications .... Mrs. Laynee H. TIMLIN
35 Dean of Students .... Dr. Keith E. MOORE
88 Assoc VP for College Advancement .... Ms. Suzanne SAVAGE
07 Dean of Admissions .... Ms. Patricia C. PATTEN
20 Assoc Dean Special Acad Projects .... Ms. Debbie L. HICKS
20 Assoc Dean of the College .... Dr. Sally SHEDD
13 Chief Technology Officer .... Mr. Jack L. DMOCH
41 Director of Athletics .... Ms. Joanne M. RENN
09 Asst Director for Instnl Research .... Mr. Donald C. STAUFFER
55 Director of Adult Studies Program .... Mr. Thomas R. FARLEY
08 Interim Library Director .... Mrs. Patricia CLARK
15 Director of Human Resources .... Ms. Karla R. RASMUSSEN
06 Registrar .... Ms. Regina BYNUM
37 Director of Financial Aid .... Ms. Teresa L. RHYNE
96 Director of Purchasing .... Ms. Midge ZIMMERMAN
31 Director of Community Service .... Ms. Diane E. HOTALING
36 Director of Career Services .... Ms. Lisa I. FENTRESS
19 Director of Security .... Mr. Jerry MANCE
39 Asst Dean Students/Dir Res Life .... Ms. McCarren CAPUTA
29 Director of Alumni Relations .... Ms. Kathleen M. JUDGE
91 Manager of Admin Computer Systems .... Mr. Greg BAPTISTE
18 Director of Physical Plant .... Mr. David R. HOPPER
42 Chaplain .... Rev. Greg WEST
38 Director of Counseling .... Mr. James W. BROWN
44 Director of Special Gifts .... Ms. Lori MCCAREL
44 Director of Annual Giving .... Ms. Megan T. SPENCER
44 Dir Leadership & Planned Giving .... Dr. Mary Kate ANDRIS
40 Bookstore Manager .... Ms. Kim S. BROWN
92 Director Honors and Scholars .... Dr. Joyce B. EASTER
28 Director of International Programs .... Ms. Lena H. JOHNSON
88 Director of Student Activities .... Ms. Jennifer E. MITCHELL
23 Director of Health Services .... Ms. Valerie L. COVINGTON

Washington and Lee University (D)

204 W Washington Street, Lexington VA 24450-2116
County: Independent City — FICE Identification: 003768
Unit ID: 234207
Telephone: (540) 458-8400 — Carnegie Class: Bac/A&S
FAX Number: (540) 458-8945 — Calendar System: Other
URL: www.wlu.edu
Established: 1749 — Annual Undergrad Tuition & Fees: $43,362
Enrollment: 2,193 — Coed
Affiliation or Control: Independent Non-Profit — IRS Status: 501(c)3
Highest Offering: Doctorate
Program: Liberal Arts And General; Professional
Accreditation: **SC**, BUS, JOUR, LAW, TEAC

01 President .... Dr. Kenneth P. RUSCIO
05 Interim Provost .... Dr. Robert A. STRONG
20 Associate Provost .... Dr. Elizabeth KNAPP
10 Vice Pres for Finance and Admin ..... Mr. Steven G. MCALLISTER
30 Vice Pres University Advancement .... Mr. Dennis W. CROSS
32 VP for Stdnt Affs & Dean of Stdnts .... Ms. Sidney S. EVANS
04 Senior Asst to the President .... Dr. Valerie J. CUSHMAN
101 Sr Asst to Pres/Sec of University .... Mr. James D. FARRAR
43 General Counsel .... Ms. Leanne M. SHANK
22 Assoc Gen Counsel Compliance Spprt .... Ms. Jennifer E. KIRKLAND
49 Interim Dean of the College .... Dr. Suzanne P. KEEN
50 Dean of Commerce/Economics/Politics ...... Dr. Larry C. PEPPERS
61 Dean of Law School .... Ms. Nora V. DEMLEITNER
26 Exec Dir of Comm/Public Affairs .... Mr. Jeffery G. HANNA
89 Assoc Dean of Students/Dn Freshmen .... Mr. David M. LEONARD
35 Assoc Dean of Students .... Ms. Tamara Y. FUTRELL
30 Exec Dir of University Development .... Mr. Tres MULLIS
41 Director of Athletics .... Ms. Janine M. HATHORN
35 Dir Univ Commons/Campus Activities .. Mr. Jason L. RODOCKER
07 Dean of Admissions/Financial Aid .... Mr. William M. HARTOG
09 Asst Dir/Inst Effectiveness .... Mr. Jamie REDWINE
06 Associate University Registrar .... Ms. Barbara L. ROWE
08 University Librarian .... Mr. Terry METZ

85 Director International Education .... Dr. Larry BOETSCH
29 Exec Director of Alumni Affairs .... Mr. Waller T. DUDLEY
15 Exec Director of Human Resources .... Ms. Amy BARNES
37 Director of Financial Aid .... Mr. James D. KASTER
18 Exec Dir Facilities/Capital Plng .... Mr. John HOOGAKKER
21 Associate Treasurer & Controller .... Mrs. Deborah Z. CAYLOR
13 Chief Technology Officer .... Mr. David SAACKE
24 Senior Academic Technologist .... Mr. Brandon R. BUCY
36 Director Undergrad Career Services .... Ms. Beverly T. LORIG
23 Director Student Health/Counseling .... Dr. Jane T. HORTON
96 Director of Auxiliary Services .... Mr. Paul F. RENZI
40 Director of Univ Bookstore .... Ms. Maureen BECKER

Washington Baptist University (E)

4300 Evergreen Lane, Annandale VA 22003
County: Fairfax — Identification: 666234
Telephone: (703) 333-5904 — Carnegie Class: Not Classified
FAX Number: (703) 333-5906 — Calendar System: Semester
URL: www.wbcs.edu
Established: N/A — Annual Undergrad Tuition & Fees: $4,590
Enrollment: N/A — Coed
Affiliation or Control: Baptist — IRS Status: 501(c)3
Highest Offering: Doctorate
Program: Religious Emphasis
Accreditation: **@BI**, @THEOL

01 President .... Dr. Peter M. CHANG
03 Executive Vice President .... Dr. Davis S. KIM
32 Dean of Students .... Mr. David Y. LEE

Westwood College-Annandale (F)

7619 Little River Turnpike 5th Fl, Annandale VA 22003
County: Fairfax — Identification: 666599
Unit ID: 448628
Telephone: (877) 305-0049 — Carnegie Class: Bac/Assoc
FAX Number: (703) 642-3772 — Calendar System: Quarter
URL: www.westwood.edu
Established: 1953 — Annual Undergrad Tuition & Fees: $15,291
Enrollment: 442 — Coed
Affiliation or Control: Proprietary — IRS Status: Proprietary
Highest Offering: Baccalaureate
Program: Occupational; Liberal Arts And General
Accreditation: **ACICS**

01 Campus President .... Mary Kay SVEDBERG

† Branch campus of Westwood College-South Bay, Torrance, CA.

Westwood College-Arlington Ballston (G)

4420 North Fairfax Drive, Arlington VA 22203
County: Arlington — Identification: 666660
Unit ID: 447069
Telephone: (703) 243-3900 — Carnegie Class: Bac/Assoc
FAX Number: (703) 243-3992 — Calendar System: Quarter
URL: www.westwood.edu
Established: N/A — Annual Undergrad Tuition & Fees: $16,500
Enrollment: 459 — Coed
Affiliation or Control: Proprietary — IRS Status: Proprietary
Highest Offering: Baccalaureate
Program: Occupational; Liberal Arts And General
Accreditation: **ACICS**

01 Campus President .... Valarie TRIMARCHI

† Branch campus of Westwood College-South Bay, Torrance, CA.

World College (H)

5193 Lake Shore Drive, Suite 105, Virginia Beach VA 23455-2500
County: Henrico — FICE Identification: 041361
Unit ID: 419448
Telephone: (757) 464-4600 — Carnegie Class: Not Classified
FAX Number: (757) 464-3687 — Calendar System: Other
URL: www.cie-wc.edu
Established: 1992 — Annual Undergrad Tuition & Fees: $4,150
Enrollment: 518 — Coed
Affiliation or Control: Proprietary — IRS Status: Proprietary
Highest Offering: Baccalaureate
Program: Technical Emphasis
Accreditation: **DETC**

01 President .... Mr. Randy DRINKO
05 Dean of Instruction .... Mr. Keith CONN
07 Admissions Counselor .... Mr. Scott KATZENMEYER

WASHINGTON

Antioch University Seattle (I)

2326 Sixth Avenue, Seattle WA 98121-1814
County: King — Identification: 666812
Unit ID: 245883
Telephone: (206) 441-5352 — Carnegie Class: Master's M
FAX Number: (206) 441-3307 — Calendar System: Quarter
URL: www.antiochseattle.edu
Established: 1975 — Annual Undergrad Tuition & Fees: $18,900

Enrollment: 931 Coed
Affiliation or Control: Independent Non-Profit IRS Status: 501(c)3
Highest Offering: Doctorate
Program: Liberal Arts And General; Teacher Preparatory; Professional; Business Emphasis
Accreditation: &NH, MFCD

01 President ... Dr. Cassandra MANUELITO-KERKVLIET
04 Exec Assistant to the President ... Ms. Wendy DAHL
05 VP Acad Affs & Dean of Faculty ... Dr. Peter M. ROJCEWICZ
30 VP Institutional Advancement ... Ms. Brigid MERCER
11 Vice Pres Administration/Finance ... Ms. Betsy RALEIGH
88 Interim Dean of Psychology ... Dr. Jane HARMON JACOBS
32 Associate Dean & Dean of Students ... Ms. Shana HORMANN
06 Registrar ... Ms. Barbara TALMADGE
84 Dean of Enrollment Svcs/Admissions ... Vacant
10 Chief Business Officer ... Ms. Betsy RALEIGH
08 Interim Library Director ... Ms. Beverly STUART
88 Administrative Services Director ... Ms. Bet DOLO
26 Director of Integrated Marketing ... Vacant
44 Director of Development ... Ms. Michelle WILKINSON
37 Financial Aid Director ... Ms. Katy STAHL
29 Director of Alumni Relations ... Mr. Eric WARN
18 Facilities Director ... Mr. Michael JOHNSON
51 Director of Continuing Education ... Ms. Debra ALDERMAN
97 Dir of BA Liberal Studies Program ... Vacant
53 Interim Dean School of Education ... Dr. Ed MIKEL
88 Interim Dir Ctr for Creative Chg ... Dr. Betsy GEIST
15 Sr HR Business Partner ... Ms. Pamela PETITT
21 Budget Manager ... Mr. Greg SCHULER

† Regional accreditation is carried under the parent institution in Yellow Springs, Ohio.

Argosy University, Seattle (A)

2601 A Elliott Avenue, Seattle WA 98121-1318
County: King Identification: 666080
Unit ID: 439057
Telephone: (206) 283-4500 Carnegie Class: Master's S
FAX Number: (206) 283-5777 Calendar System: Semester
URL: www.argosy.edu/seattle
Established: 1999 Annual Undergrad Tuition & Fees: $13,224
Enrollment: 515 Coed
Affiliation or Control: Proprietary IRS Status: Proprietary
Highest Offering: Doctorate
Program: Professional
Accreditation: &WC

01 Campus President ... Dr. Tom DYER
05 Vice President of Academic Affairs ... Dr. Russell WRIGHT
07 Senior Director of Admissions ... Tina JACOBS
32 Director of Student Services ... Deann KETCHUM
15 Human Resources ... Mark BRUNKE
37 Director of Student Finance ... Sara DEWITT
11 Dir of Admin and Financial Svcs ... Michael TOLIVER
06 Registrar ... Deann M. KETCHUM

† Regional accreditation is carried under the parent institution in Orange, CA.

The Art Institute of Seattle (B)

2323 Elliott Avenue, Seattle WA 98121-1622
County: King FICE Identification: 022913
Unit ID: 234492
Telephone: (206) 448-0900 Carnegie Class: Spec/Arts
FAX Number: (206) 448-2501 Calendar System: Quarter
URL: www.ais.edu
Established: 1946 Annual Undergrad Tuition & Fees: $23,088
Enrollment: 1,959 Coed
Affiliation or Control: Proprietary IRS Status: Proprietary
Highest Offering: Baccalaureate
Program: Occupational
Accreditation: NW, ACFEI, CIDA

01 President ... Elden R. MONDAY, JR.
05 Vice Pres/Dean of Academic Affairs ... Dr. Scott CARNZ
15 Director of Human Resources ... Natasha J. OILAR
32 Dean of Student Affairs ... Megan KIJEWSKI
07 Senior Director of Admissions ... Liane SOOHOO
11 Dir Administration/Financial Svcs ... Greg WOODARD
36 Director Career Services ... Dawn MONET

Bainbridge Graduate Institute (C)

2601 Fourth Avenue, Suite 310, Seattle WA 98121
FICE Identification: 041612
Unit ID: 458159
Telephone: (206) 855-9559 Carnegie Class: Not Classified
FAX Number: (206) 855-9045 Calendar System: Semester
URL: www.bgi.edu
Established: 2002 Annual Undergrad Tuition & Fees: $26,400
Enrollment: 164 Coed
Affiliation or Control: Independent Non-Profit IRS Status: 501(c)3
Highest Offering: Master's
Program: Professional; Business Emphasis
Accreditation: ACICS

01 President/Chief Executive Officer ... Mr. Gifford PINCHOT, III
05 Provost/Exec Vice President ... Mr. John GARDNER
06 Registrar ... Ms. Lynn BRAUN
11 Director of Operations ... Mr. Jim MCRAE

Bakke Graduate University (D)

1013 8th Avenue, Suite 401, Seattle WA 98104-1222
County: King FICE Identification: 031108
Unit ID: 420705
Telephone: (206) 264-9100 Carnegie Class: Not Classified
FAX Number: (206) 264-8828 Calendar System: Semester
URL: www.bgu.edu
Established: 1990 Annual Graduate Tuition & Fees: N/A
Enrollment: 230 Coed
Affiliation or Control: Independent Non-Profit IRS Status: 501(c)3
Highest Offering: Doctorate; No Undergraduates
Program: Professional; Religious Emphasis
Accreditation: TRACS

00 Chancellor ... Dr. Ray BAKKE
01 President ... Dr. Brad SMITH
05 Academic Dean ... Dr. Gwen DEWEY
30 Vice President Advancement ... Mr. Robert STEINHAGEN
10 Chief Operations/Financial Ofcr ... Mr. Art ZYLSTRA
06 Registrar ... Dr. Judi MELTON
07 Dir Admiss Svcs/Personnel/Facil Dir ... Ms. Julie GUSTAVSON

Bastyr University (E)

14500 Juanita Drive NE, Kenmore WA 98028-4966
County: King FICE Identification: 022425
Unit ID: 235547
Telephone: (425) 602-3000 Carnegie Class: Spec/Health
FAX Number: (425) 823-6222 Calendar System: Quarter
URL: www.bastyr.edu
Established: 1978 Annual Undergrad Tuition & Fees: $21,635
Enrollment: 1,018 Coed
Affiliation or Control: Independent Non-Profit IRS Status: 501(c)3
Highest Offering: Doctorate
Program: Professional
Accreditation: NW, ACUP, DIETD, DIETI, MEAC, NATUR

01 President ... Dr. Daniel K. CHURCH
05 Senior Vice President/Provost ... Dr. Timothy C. CALLAHAN
10 Vice President for Finance & Admin ... Mr. Sheldon R. HABER
100 Chief of Staff ... Mr. Greg J. GOODE
30 Chief Development Officer ... Ms. Sheryl STIEFEL
32 Vice President of Student Affairs ... Ms. Susan WEIDER
07 Asst Vice Pres Recruitment & Retent ... Ms. Christine MASTERSON
08 Director of Library Services ... Ms. Jane SAXTON
29 Dir Career and Alumni Svcs ... Ms. Susan FARLEY
23 Chf Medical Ofcr Ctr Natural Health ... Dr. Jamey WALLACE
15 Exec Dir of Human Resources/IT ... Mr. Keith WOODY
13 Director of Information Technology ... Ms. Marsha MCGOUGH
09 Director of Research Development ... Dr. Mark MARTZEN
26 Assoc Dir of Media/Public Rels ... Mr. Derek WING
46 Senior Research Scientist ... Dr. Leanna STANDISH
40 Bookstore Manager ... Mr. Marty PETERSEN
07 Director of Admissions ... Vacant
37 Director Financial Aid ... Ms. Danette CARTER
18 Director Facilities and Safety ... Mr. Daniel CLARK
21 Controller ... Mr. Joe PLOUF
38 Director Counseling ... Ms. Cherlyn STOVER

Bates Technical College (F)

1101 S Yakima Avenue, Tacoma WA 98405-4895
County: Pierce FICE Identification: 005306
Unit ID: 235671
Telephone: (253) 680-7000 Carnegie Class: Assoc/Pub-U-MC
FAX Number: (253) 680-7101 Calendar System: Quarter
URL: www.bates.ctc.edu
Established: 1940 Annual Undergrad Tuition & Fees (In-State): $6,864
Enrollment: 4,552 Coed
Affiliation or Control: State IRS Status: 501(c)3
Highest Offering: Associate Degree
Program: Occupational; 2-Year Principally Bachelor's Creditable; Technical Emphasis
Accreditation: NW, DA, DT, OTA

01 President ... Dr. Ron LANGRELL
04 Exec Asst to the President ... Mr. Geof KAUFMAN
05 Vice President of Instruction ... Ms. Cheri LOILAND
32 Vice President of Student Services ... Mr. Ivan GORNE
10 Vice Pres Administrative Services ... Vacant
15 Vice President of Human Resources ... Ms. Vickie LACKMAN
12 Executive Dean Mohler Campus ... Mr. David HINMAN
12 Executive Dean South Campus ... Mr. Wayne CALDWELL
88 Dean of Educational Systems ... Vacant
09 Dean of Inst Rsrch/Plng/Assessment ... Ms. Summer KENESSON
20 Dean of Academic Programs ... Mr. Mike BRANDSTETTER
30 Director of Development ... Ms. Kimberly PLEGER
21 Director of Fiscal Services ... Mr. John GINTHER
18 Director Facilities & Operations ... Mr. Marty MATTES
06 Registrar ... Mr. Patrick BROWN
96 General Services Manager ... Mr. Spiro MANTHOU
37 Financial Aid Officer ... Ms. Susan NEESE
35 Director of Student Services ... Mr. Dion TEAGUE
13 Director of Information Technology ... Mr. Tom GEORGE
28 College Diversity Coordinator ... Ms. Kathy FLORES

Bellevue College (G)

3000 Landerholm Circle, SE, Bellevue WA 98007-6484
County: King FICE Identification: 003769
Unit ID: 234669
Telephone: (425) 564-1000 Carnegie Class: Assoc/Pub4
FAX Number: (425) 564-4065 Calendar System: Quarter
URL: www.bellevuecollege.edu
Established: 1965 Annual Undergrad Tuition & Fees (In-State): $4,240
Enrollment: 14,156 Coed
Affiliation or Control: State IRS Status: 501(c)3
Highest Offering: Baccalaureate
Program: Occupational; 2-Year Principally Bachelor's Creditable; Professional
Accreditation: NW, ADNUR, CIDA, DMS, NDT, NMT, RADDOS, RTT

01 Interim President ... Mrs. Laura SAUNDERS
04 Exec Asst to the President ... Ms. Lisa CORCORAN
11 Vice Pres Administrative Services ... Mr. Ray WHITE
05 Vice President of Instruction ... Mr. Tom NIELSEN
15 Vice President Human Resources ... Mr. Cesar PORTILLO
30 Vice Pres Institutional Advancement ... Mr. Larry HERRON
32 Vice President of Student Services ... Dr. Tom PRITCHARD
103 Vice Pres of Workforce Development ... Dr. Paula BOYUM
13 Vice Pres of Information Resources ... Mr. Russell BEARD
09 Assoc VP Effect & Strat Planning ... Ms. Patricia JAMES
51 Dean Continuing Education ... Ms. Janis MACHALA
79 Dean of Arts and Humanities ... Ms. Margaret HARADA
76 Dean of HSEWI ... Mr. Kevin MCCARTHY
83 Dean of Social Science ... Ms. Virginia BRIDWELL
88 Associate Dean of Student Programs ... Mr. Faisal JASWAL
35 Associate Dean of Student Services ... Mr. Matt GROSHONG
85 Asst Dean Internatl Student Pgms ... Mr. Cris SAMIA
10 Exec Dir of Finance & Auxiliary Svc ... Ms. Jennifer STROTHER
08 Dean Library/Media ... Ms. Myra VAN VACTOR
26 Director College & Community Rels ... Mr. Bart BECKER
37 Director Financial Aid ... Ms. Sherri BALLANTYNE
19 Director of Public Safety ... Mr. Tommy VU
13 Director Computing Services ... Mr. Jason AQUI
91 Director Networking Svcs & Security ... Mr. Gary FARRIS
41 Director of Athletics ... Mr. Bill O'CONNOR
38 Student Counseling ... Mr. Harlan LEE
40 Manager Bellevue College Bookstore ... Ms. Kristen CONNELY
96 Director Proc Mgmt & Fac Plng ... Mr. Dexter JOHNSON

Bellingham Technical College (H)

3028 Lindebergh Avenue, Bellingham WA 98225-1599
County: Whatcom FICE Identification: 004999
Unit ID: 234696
Telephone: (360) 752-7000 Carnegie Class: Assoc/Pub-R-M
FAX Number: (360) 676-2798 Calendar System: Quarter
URL: www.btc.ctc.edu
Established: 1957 Annual Undergrad Tuition & Fees (In-District): $4,680
Enrollment: 3,500 Coed
Affiliation or Control: State/Local IRS Status: 501(c)3
Highest Offering: Associate Degree
Program: Occupational
Accreditation: NW, ACFEI, DA, DH, SURGT

01 President ... Dr. Patricia MCKEOWN
04 Exec Assistant to the President ... Ms. Ronda LAUGHLIN
05 Vice President of Instruction ... Ms. Carol LAGER
32 Vice President of Student Services ... Dr. Linda FOSSEN
11 VP of Administrative Services ... Ms. Debra JONES
72 Dean of Professional Technical Educ ... Mr. Dan CADWELL
30 Exec Director College Advancement ... Mr. Dean FULTON
15 Director Human Resources ... Vacant
37 Director Financial Aid ... Mr. Mike FENTRESS
06 Director Registration/Enrollment ... Ms. Joan KAMMERZELL
13 Dir Computer/Inform Support Svcs ... Mr. Curtis PERERA
08 Director Library ... Ms. Jane BLUME
18 Chief Facilities/Physical Plant ... Mr. David JUNGKUNTZ
26 Director of Communications ... Ms. Marni Saling MAYER

Big Bend Community College (I)

7662 Chanute Street NE, Moses Lake WA 98837-3299
County: Grant FICE Identification: 003770
Unit ID: 234711
Telephone: (509) 793-2222 Carnegie Class: Assoc/Pub-R-M
FAX Number: (509) 762-6329 Calendar System: Quarter
URL: www.bigbend.edu
Established: 1962 Annual Undergrad Tuition & Fees (In-State): $3,837
Enrollment: 2,398 Coed
Affiliation or Control: State IRS Status: 501(c)3
Highest Offering: Associate Degree
Program: Occupational; 2-Year Principally Bachelor's Creditable
Accreditation: NW, ADNUR

01 President ... Dr. Terry LEAS
10 Vice Pres Administrative Services ... Ms. Gail HAMBURG
05 Vice Pres Instruction/Student Svcs ... Mr. Bob MOHRBACHER
15 VP of Human Resources & Labor ... Mrs. Kim GARZA
75 Dean Prof Technical Education ... Mr. Clyde RASMUSSEN
49 Dean of Arts & Sciences ... Ms. Kara GARRETT
53 Dean Educ/Health/Language Skills ... Vacant
32 Assoc VP of Student Services ... Ms. Candis LACHER
35 Director of Student Programs ... Ms. Kim JACKSON
37 Director of Financial Aid ... Ms. Jille SHANKAR
08 Dean of Library Resources ... Mr. Tim FUHRMAN
41 Director of Athletics ... Mr. Preston WILKS
06 Registrar ... Ms. Candis LACHER
102 Dir Inst Advancement/Exec Dir Found ... Mrs. LeAnne PARTON
27 Publication & Information Director ... Mr. Doug SLY
21 Director of Business Services ... Ms. Charlene RIOS
40 Director of Bookstore ... Mrs. Caren COURTRIGHT

18 Chief Facilities/Physical Plant .... Ms. Gail HAMBURG
96 Director of Purchasing .... Ms. Kathy ARITA
39 Residence Hall Coordinator .... Mr. Hugh SCHOLTE
09 Dean of Institutional Research .... Ms. Valerie KIRKWOOD

Carrington College - Spokane (A)

10102 E Knox Ave., Suite 200, Spokane WA 99206-4187
County: Spokane Identification: 666385
Unit ID: 439118
Telephone: (509) 532-8888 Carnegie Class: Not Classified
FAX Number: (509) 533-5983 Calendar System: Other
URL: www.carrington.edu
Established: 1998 Annual Undergrad Tuition & Fees: $14,212
Enrollment: 588 Coed
Affiliation or Control: Proprietary IRS Status: Proprietary
Highest Offering: Associate Degree
Program: Occupational; 2-Year Principally Bachelor's Creditable
Accreditation: ACICS, MAAB, RAD

01 Executive Campus Director .... Mr. Peter TENNEY

Cascadia Community College (B)

18345 Campus Way, NE, Bothell WA 98011-8205
County: King FICE Identification: 034835
Unit ID: 439190
Telephone: (425) 352-8000 Carnegie Class: Assoc/Pub-S-SC
FAX Number: (425) 352-8313 Calendar System: Quarter
URL: www.cascadia.edu
Established: 2000 Annual Undergrad Tuition & Fees (In-District): $4,000
Enrollment: 3,438 Coed
Affiliation or Control: State/Local IRS Status: Exempt
Highest Offering: Associate Degree
Program: 2-Year Principally Bachelor's Creditable
Accreditation: NW

01 President .... Dr. Eric MURRAY
05 Vice Pres Student Learning/Success .... Dr. Sunny BURNS
20 Dean for Academic Affairs .... Mr. Walter HUDSICK
06 Registrar .... Ms. Bonnie ELLIS
09 Dir Institutional Research .... Ms. Susan HAMILTON
10 Chief Business Officer .... Mr. Terrence HSIAO
15 Director Personnel Services .... Ms. Gina LORENZ
18 Chief Facilities/Physical Plant .... Ms. Dee SLINEY
21 Associate Business Officer .... Vacant
27 Chief Information Officer .... Ms. Meagan WALKER
32 Interim Chief Student Life Officer .... Mr. Brian NOVAK
37 Director Student Financial Aid .... Ms. Sybil SMITH
30 Chief Development .... Ms. Rebecca HASTINGS
38 Director Student Counseling .... Ms. Ana BLACKSTAD
84 Director Enrollment Management .... Ms. Erin BLAKENEY

Central Washington University (C)

400 E University Way, Ellensburg WA 98926-7501
County: Kittitas FICE Identification: 003771
Unit ID: 234827
Telephone: (509) 963-1111 Carnegie Class: Master's M
FAX Number: (509) 963-3206 Calendar System: Quarter
URL: www.cwu.edu
Established: 1890 Annual Undergrad Tuition & Fees (In-State): $8,919
Enrollment: 10,770 Coed
Affiliation or Control: State IRS Status: 501(c)3
Highest Offering: Master's
Program: Liberal Arts And General; Teacher Preparatory; Professional
Accreditation: NW, BUS, CACREP, CONST, DIETD, DIETI, EMT, ENGT, IPSY, MUS

01 President .... Dr. James L. GAUDINO
05 Provost/VP Academic & Student Life .... Dr. Marilyn LEVINE
10 CFO/VP Business & Financial Affairs .... Mr. George CLARK
100 Chief of Staff .... Ms. Sherer HOLTER
20 Assoc Provost .... Mr. Tracy PELLETT
21 Dir Organizational Effectiveness .... Mr. Edward DAY
84 Assoc VP Enrollment Management .... Mr. John SWINEY
32 Dean of Student Success .... Dr. Sarah L. SWAGER
35 Assoc Dean Student Development .... Mr. Keith M. CHAMPAGNE
88 Assoc Dean Student Achievement .... Mr. Jesse NELSON
18 Asst VP for Facilities Management .... Mr. Bill VERTREES
15 Dir Faculty and Labor Relations .... Mr. James BUSALACCHI
14 Asst VP for Information Tech Svcs .... Mr. Carmen RAHM
58 Dean Graduate Studies and Research .... Dr. Holly CRAWFORD
49 Dean College of Arts/Humanities .... Dr. Marji MORGAN
50 Dean College of Business .... Dr. Kathryn MARTELL
53 Dean College of Educ/Prof Studies .... Dr. Connie LAMBERT
83 Dean College of the Sciences .... Dr. Kirk JOHNSON
08 Dean of Library Services .... Dr. Patricia CUTRIGHT
30 Dir University Advancement .... Mr. Scott WADE
85 Asst VP Intl Stds and Programs .... Dr. Michael LAUNIUS
06 Registrar .... Ms. Tracy TERRELL
22 Dir Employ/Student Svc/ Compliance .... Ms. Staci SLEIGH-LAYMAN
41 Director Athletics .... Mr. Jack BISHOP
51 Director Continuing Education .... Mr. Richard N. BYHAM
12 Asst VP University Centers .... Ms. Margaret BADGLEY
07 Director of Admissions .... Ms. Kathy GAER-CARLTON
37 Director of Financial Aid .... Ms. Agnes F. CANEDO
39 Assoc Dean Student Living .... Mr. Richard DESHIELDS
19 Director Public Safety .... Mr. Michael LUVERA
26 Director Public Affairs .... Ms. Linda SCHACTLER

Centralia College (D)

600 Centralia College Boulevard,
Centralia WA 98531-4035
County: Lewis FICE Identification: 003772
Unit ID: 234845
Telephone: (360) 736-9391 Carnegie Class: Assoc/Pub-R-M
FAX Number: (360) 330-7573 Calendar System: Quarter
URL: www.centralia.edu
Established: 1925 Annual Undergrad Tuition & Fees (In-State): $3,834
Enrollment: 2,643 Coed
Affiliation or Control: State IRS Status: 501(c)3
Highest Offering: Associate Degree
Program: Occupational; 2-Year Principally Bachelor's Creditable
Accreditation: NW

01 President .... Dr. James M. WALTON
05 Vice President Instruction .... Mr. John MARTENS
32 Vice President of Students .... Vacant
10 Vice Pres Finance/Administration .... Mr. Steve WARD
15 VP Human Resources/Legal Affairs .... Ms. Julie LEDFORD
103 Dean Workforce Education .... Ms. Durelle SULLIVAN
08 Dean of Library Services/E-Learning .... Ms. Sue GALLAWAY
88 Dean of Academic Transfer Programs .... T. R. GRATZ
09 Director of Institutional Research .... Vacant
103 Dir WorkFirst & Worker Retraining .... Ms. Beverley GESTRINE
84 Director of Enrollment Services .... Ms. Qy-Ana MANNING
37 Director of Financial Aid .... Ms. Tracy DAHL
13 Director Information Technology .... Mr. Patrick ALLISON
41 Director of Sports Programs .... Mr. Bob PETERS
29 Director Alumni Relations .... Ms. Julie JOHNSON
96 Director of Purchasing .... Ms. Bonnie MYER
26 Dir College Relations & Events Plng .... Mr. Don FREY
40 Bookstore Manager .... Ms. Tammy STRODEMIER
97 Program Coordinator .... Ms. Joanie ROGERSON

City University of Seattle (E)

11900 NE First Street, Bellevue WA 98005-3030
County: King FICE Identification: 013022
Unit ID: 234915
Telephone: (425) 637-1010 Carnegie Class: Master's L
FAX Number: (425) 709-7699 Calendar System: Quarter
URL: www.cityu.edu
Established: 1973 Annual Undergrad Tuition & Fees: $17,550
Enrollment: 2,302 Coed
Affiliation or Control: Independent Non-Profit IRS Status: 501(c)3
Highest Offering: Master's
Program: 2-Year Principally Bachelor's Creditable; Liberal Arts And General; Teacher Preparatory; Professional; Business Emphasis
Accreditation: NW

01 President .... Mr. E. Lee GORSUCH, II
101 Exec Asst Offfice of the President .... Ms. Ruth NICHOLS
84 Vice President Enrollment/Registrar .... Dr. Melissa E. MECHAM
05 Provost .... Dr. Steven OLSWANG
10 CFO/VP Finance & Administration .... Mr. Bruce K. BRYANT
30 Vice President for Univ Advancement .... Mr. Christopher ROSS
88 Vice President European Operations .... Dr. Jan REBRO
50 Dean School of Management .... Dr. Kurt KIRSTEIN
53 Dean School of Education .... Dr. Craig SCHIEBER
20 Dean Academic Affs-Europe .... Mr. David GRIFFIN
108 Director of Inst Effectiveness .... Ms. Sabrina CRAWFORD
21 Director of Finance .... Ms. Maria KREY
15 Director of Human Resources .... Mr. Timothy SPRAKE
08 Director Library Services .... Ms. Mary MARA
37 Director Student Financial Svcs .... Mr. Martin DANIELS
29 Alumni Relations Manager .... Mr. Alex WEBSTER
90 Director of Information Technology .... Mr. Kevin H. BROWN
88 Veterans Affairs Officer .... Ms. Ry-Yon SAO
07 Director Admissions .... Ms. Alyssa BORELLI
85 Director Intl Student Office .... Ms. Sabine SAWAY
18 Facilities Manager .... Mr. Troy CRABREE

† Granted candidacy at the Doctorate level.

Clark College (F)

1933 Fort Vancouver Way, Vancouver WA 98663-3598
County: Clark FICE Identification: 003773
Unit ID: 234933
Telephone: (360) 992-2000 Carnegie Class: Assoc/Pub-U-SC
FAX Number: (360) 992-2871 Calendar System: Quarter
URL: www.clark.edu
Established: 1933 Annual Undergrad Tuition & Fees (In-State): $3,743
Enrollment: 15,704 Coed
Affiliation or Control: State IRS Status: 501(c)3
Highest Offering: Associate Degree
Program: Occupational; 2-Year Principally Bachelor's Creditable
Accreditation: NW, ADNUR, DH, MAC

01 President .... Mr. Robert KNIGHT
05 Vice President of Instruction .... Dr. Tim COOK
32 Vice President of Student Affairs .... Mr. William BELDON
11 Vice President of Admin Services .... Mr. Bob WILLIAMSON
16 Assoc Vice Pres of Human Resources .... Ms. Darcy ROURK
45 Assoc VP Planning/Instnl Effective .... Ms. Shanda DIEHL
51 Assoc VP Corp & Continuing Educ .... Mr. Kevin KUSSMAN
84 Dean of Enrollment Services .... Ms. Diane DREBIN
50 Dean Business/Technology .... Mr. Ted KOTSAKIS
79 Dean English/Comm/Hum/Basic Educ .... Dr. Ray KORPI
76 Dean Life Sci/Health & Phys Ed .... Mr. Blake BOWERS
83 Dean Social Sciences/Fine Arts .... Mr. Miles JACKSON
66 Assoc Dean of Nursing .... Vacant
52 Director of Dental Hygiene .... Ms. Brenda WALSTEAD
04 Exec Assistant to the President .... Ms. Leigh KENT
06 Registrar .... Ms. Kimberly MARSHEL
41 Director of Athletics .... Mr. Charles GUTHRIE
15 Associate Director Human Resources .... Ms. Sue WILLIAMS
08 Dir of Library Services .... Ms. Michelle BAGLEY
13 Director of Computing Services .... Mr. Phil SHEEHAN
18 Director of Plant Services .... Mr. Jim GREEN
26 Exec Director of Communications .... Ms. Barbara KERR
36 Director Career/Employment Services .... Ms. Edie BLAKELY
37 Director of Financial Aid .... Ms. Karen DRISCOLL
07 Director of Admissions .... Vacant
10 Director of Business Services .... Ms. Karen WYNKOOP
35 Dir Stdnt Life/Multicult Stdnt Affs .... Ms. Sarah GRUHLER
38 Director Advising & Counseling .... Mr. Andrew LONG
25 Director of Grant Development .... Mr. Travis KIBOTA
28 Director of Equity & Diversity .... Ms. Sirius BONNER
19 Director of Security & Safety .... Mr. Ken PACHECO
85 International Recruitment Manager .... Ms. Jody SHULNAK
40 Bookstore Manager .... Ms. Monica KNOWLES
88 Mature Learning & Travel Stds Mgr .... Ms. Tracy REILLY-KELLY
96 Purchasing Manager .... Ms. Lisa NELSON

Clover Park Technical College (G)

4500 Steilacoom Boulevard, SW,
Lakewood WA 98499-4004
County: Pierce FICE Identification: 005752
Unit ID: 234951
Telephone: (253) 589-5800 Carnegie Class: Assoc/Pub-S-MC
FAX Number: (253) 589-5601 Calendar System: Quarter
URL: www.cptc.edu
Established: 1942 Annual Undergrad Tuition & Fees (In-State): $7,742
Enrollment: 4,738 Coed
Affiliation or Control: State IRS Status: 501(c)3
Highest Offering: Associate Degree
Program: Occupational; 2-Year Principally Bachelor's Creditable; Technical Emphasis
Accreditation: NW, DA, HT, MAC, MLTAD, SURGT

01 President .... Dr. John W. WALSTRUM
04 Executive Assistant .... Cherie STEELE
05 Vice President Instruction .... Lori BANASZAK
10 Vice President Finance .... Linda SCHOONMAKER
32 Vice President Student Services .... June STACEY-CLEMONS
26 VP Operations & College Relations .... Amy GOINGS
20 Associate Vice Pres Instruction .... Joyce LOVEDAY
16 Chief Human Res/Legal Affairs Off .... James TUTTLE
103 Dean of Workforce Development .... Mabel EDMONDS
13 Dir Information Technology .... Michael TAYLOR
37 Director Financial Aid .... Wendy JOSEPH
19 Director Plant Services & Security .... Mike ANDERSON
12 Dir Northwest Career/Technical HS .... Loren DAVIS
56 Director Extended Learning .... Vacant
84 Director of Enrollment Services .... Judy MACDOUGALL
21 Controller .... Vacant
96 Purchasing Coord/Capital Projects .... Kate PURATICH
26 Marketing/Outreach Coordinator .... Janet HOLM
36 WorkFirst Special Projects Coord .... Christeen CROUCHET
09 Institutional Researcher .... Cynthia REQUA
40 Bookstore Coordinator .... Donna KOEHLER
18 Custodial Maintenance Coordinator .... Morris MILLER
06 Registrar .... Judy MACDOUGALL

Columbia Basin College (H)

2600 N 20th Avenue, Pasco WA 99301-3397
County: Franklin FICE Identification: 003774
Unit ID: 234979
Telephone: (509) 547-0511 Carnegie Class: Assoc/Pub-R-L
FAX Number: (509) 546-0401 Calendar System: Quarter
URL: www.columbiabasin.edu
Established: 1955 Annual Undergrad Tuition & Fees (In-State): $4,508
Enrollment: 7,552 Coed
Affiliation or Control: State IRS Status: 170(c)1
Highest Offering: Baccalaureate
Program: Occupational; 2-Year Principally Bachelor's Creditable
Accreditation: NW, ADNUR, DH, EMT, MAC, SURGT

01 President .... Dr. Richard CUMMINS
05 Vice President Instruction .... Mr. Curt FREED
11 Vice President of Administration .... Mr. William SARACENO
28 Vice Pres of Diversity/Outreach .... Mr. Martin VALADEZ
32 Vice President of Student Services .... Dr. Madeline JEFFS
15 VP Human Resources/Legal Affairs .... Ms. Camilla GLATT
21 Assist VP Fiscal Operations .... Mr. Mike GRINNELL
09 Dean for Institutional Effectivenes .... Dr. Joe MONTGOMERY
49 Dean Arts & Humanities .... Mr. Bill MCKAY
62 Dean Library Services .... Vacant
102 Executive Director Foundation .... Mr. Robert ROSSELLI
36 Dean Career Development .... Mr. Derek BRANDES
84 Registrar/Assoc Dean Enroll Svcs .... Ms. Patricia CAMPBELL
13 Director of Technology Services .... Mr. Brian DEXTER
40 Bookstore Director .... Ms. Debra BRUCE
18 Director of Plant Operations .... Mr. Chuck SCHMIDT
41 Athletic Director .... Mr. Scott ROGERS
26 Director of Communications .... Mr. Frank MURRAY
35 Director of Student Programs .... Ms. Alice SCHLEGEL
37 Director Student Financial Aid .... Ms. Ceci RATLIFF
96 Director of Purchasing .... Mr. Paul PAPIESE
06 Associate Registrar .... Ms. Donna KORSTAD

*Community Colleges of Spokane District 17 (A)

501 N Riverpoint Boulevard, Ste 126,
Spokane WA 99217-6000

County: Spokane FICE Identification: 010784
Telephone: (509) 434-5107 Carnegie Class: N/A
FAX Number: (509) 434-5120
URL: www.ccs.spokane.edu

01 Chancellor .... Dr. Christine JOHNSON
12 Actg Pres Spokane Community College .... Mr. Scott MORGAN
12 Pres Spokane Falls Comm College .... Dr. Janet GULLICKSON
03 Chief Exec Ofcr Inst Extnd Lrng .... Mr. Scott MORGAN
05 Actg Vice President of Learning SCC .... Ms. Rebecca RHODES
05 Vice President of Learning SFCC .... Dr. Jim MINKLER
32 Vice Pres of Student Services SCC .... Vacant
32 VP of Student Services SFCC .... Mr. Darrin PITCHER
20 Provost/Chief Learning Officer .... Dr. Nancy FAIR-SZOFRAN
10 Chief Financial Officer .... Mr. Keith FOSTER
11 Chief Administration Officer .... Mr. Greg L. STEVENS
13 Chief Information Officer .... Mr. Dick HOL
26 Public Information Officer .... Ms. Anne M. TUCKER
41 Dist Director of Athletics PE/Rec .... Mr. Ken BURRUS
102 Executive Director CCS Foundation .... Mr. Tony D. HIGLEY
40 Director College Bookstores .... Ms. Catherine R. SCOTT
18 District Director of Facilities .... Mr. Dennis DUNHAM
96 Purchasing Manager .... Mr. Rod RAMER
07 District Outreach Coordinator .... Ms. Lori HUNT

*Spokane Community College (B)

North 1810 Greene Street, Spokane WA 99217-5499

County: Spokane FICE Identification: 003793
Unit ID: 236692
Telephone: (509) 533-7000 Carnegie Class: Assoc/Pub-R-L
FAX Number: (509) 533-8839 Calendar System: Quarter
URL: www.scc.spokane.edu
Established: 1963 Annual Undergrad Tuition & Fees (In-State): $3,945
Enrollment: 7,440 Coed
Affiliation or Control: State IRS Status: 501(c)3
Highest Offering: Associate Degree
Program: Occupational; 2-Year Principally Bachelor's Creditable; Technical Emphasis
Accreditation: NW, ACFEI, ADNUR, CVT, DA, DMS, MAC, RAD, SURGT

00 District Chancellor .... Dr. Christine JOHNSON
02 Acting President .... Mr. Scott MORGAN
05 Vice President Learning .... Ms. Carol RIESENBERG
32 VP Student/Instructional Services .... Dr. Terri MCKENZIE
84 Dean of Enrollment Services .... Mr. Michael LENKER
49 Dean Arts & Sciences .... Dr. Virginia TOMLINSON
50 Dean Business/Hospitality/Info Tech .... Ms. Kathleen SILVAS
75 Dean for Technical Education .... Mr. Dave COX
76 Dean Health & Environmental Science .... Ms. Christy DOYLE
41 Director Athletics/PE/Recreation .... Mr. Ken BURRUS
10 Chief Financial Officer .... Mr. Keith FOSTER
06 Registrar .... Ms. Robin YOUNG
37 Director Financial Aid .... Ms. Tammy ZIBELL
40 Director of College Bookstores .... Ms. Cathy SCOTT
11 Chief Administration Officer .... Mr. Greg STEVENS
26 Chief Public Information Officer .... Ms. Anne TUCKER
30 District Development Officer .... Mr. Tony HIGLEY
20 District Provost .... Dr. Nancy FAIR-SZOFRAN
28 Multicultural Director .... Ms. Kitara MCCLURE
29 Director Alumni Relations .... Ms. Janice EATHERTON
38 Student Counseling Department Chair .... Ms. Cathy SHAFFER
96 Director of Purchasing .... Mr. Rodney RAMER
09 Manager Institutional Effectiveness .... Mr. Roger REED
90 District Dir Information Technology .... Mr. Dick HOL

*Spokane Falls Community College (C)

3410 W Fort George Wright Drive,
Spokane WA 99224-5288

County: Spokane FICE Identification: 009544
Unit ID: 236708
Telephone: (509) 533-3500 Carnegie Class: Assoc/Pub-R-L
FAX Number: (509) 533-3237 Calendar System: Quarter
URL: www.spokanefalls.edu
Established: 1967 Annual Undergrad Tuition & Fees (In-State): $3,467
Enrollment: 5,735 Coed
Affiliation or Control: State IRS Status: 501(c)3
Highest Offering: Associate Degree
Program: Occupational; 2-Year Principally Bachelor's Creditable
Accreditation: NW, PTAA

02 President .... Dr. Janet GULLICKSON
04 Exec Asst to the President .... Ms. Ann KIENHOLZ JURCEVICH
05 Vice President of Learning .... Dr. James MINKLER
32 Vice President of Student Services .... Mr. Darren PITCHER
81 Dean Computing/Math & Science .... Mr. James BRADY
22 Dn Equity/Diversity/Spec Initiative .... Vacant
83 Dean Soc Science/Acad Initiatives .... Dr. Lisa AVERY
79 Dean Humanities/Acad Initiatives .... Dr. Glen COSBY
08 Dean Library/Instruct Support Svcs .... Dr. Mary Ann GOODWIN
103 Dean Bus/Prof Stds/Workforce .... Dr. Frank POWERS
68 Dean Physical Education .... Mr. Ken BURRUS
85 Dean of International Programs .... Vacant
79 Dean Visual & Performing Arts .... Vacant
84 Assoc Dean Enrollment Services .... Mr. Steven BAYS
38 Chair of Student Counseling .... Mr. Loren PEMBERTON
19 Security & Safety Supervisor .... Mr. Kenneth DEMELLO
37 Assoc Dean Fin Aid/Student Employ .... Ms. Marjorie DAVIS
36 Assoc Dn Stdnt Success/Counsel/Adv .... Ms. Chrissy JONES
07 Dir Recruit/New Stdnt Entry Center .... Ms. Chrissy JONES
30 Exec Director CCS Foundation .... Mr. Tony HIGLEY
51 Director Marketing/Outreach .... Ms. Penny BUTTERS
15 Chief Human Resources Officer .... Mr. Greg STEVENS
18 Director of Facilities .... Mr. Dennis DUNHAM
26 Public Information Officer .... Ms. Anne TUCKER
96 Director of Purchasing .... Mr. Rod RAMER
09 Mgr of Institutional Effectiveness .... Ms. Sally JACKSON

Cornish College of the Arts (D)

1000 Lenora Street, Seattle WA 98121-2707

County: King FICE Identification: 012315
Unit ID: 235024
Telephone: (206) 726-5151 Carnegie Class: Spec/Arts
FAX Number: (206) 720-1011 Calendar System: Semester
URL: www.cornish.edu
Established: 1914 Annual Undergrad Tuition & Fees: $32,180
Enrollment: 826 Coed
Affiliation or Control: Independent Non-Profit IRS Status: 501(c)3
Highest Offering: Baccalaureate
Program: Liberal Arts And General; Business Emphasis
Accreditation: NW, ART

01 President .... Dr. Nancy J. USCHER
05 Provost .... Dr. Lois A. HARRIS
30 Acting VP Institutional Advancement .... Ms. Chris STOLLERY
10 Chief Finance Officer .... Mr. Jeffrey R. RIDDELL
11 Chief Operations Officer .... Ms. Vicki CLAYTON
84 VP of Enrollment Management .... Mr. Gary CRAIG
57 Interim Art Department Chairperson .... Ms. Bonnie BIGGS
57 Dance Department Chairperson .... Ms. Kathryn DANIELS
57 Design Department Chairperson .... Mr. Grant DONESKY
64 Music Department Chairperson .... Mr. Kent DEVEREAUX
57 Performance Production Dept Chair .... Mr. Dave TOSTI-LANE
57 Theater Department Chairperson .... Mr. Richard E T. WHITE
79 Humanities & Sciences Dept Chair .... Dr. Chris KELLETT
20 Associate Provost .... Dr. Jenifer WARD
32 Dean of Student Affairs .... Mr. Jerry HEKKEL
06 Dean of Academic Services/Registrar .... Ms. Adrienne M. BOLYARD
26 Director of Communications .... Ms. Karen L. BYSTROM
38 Director of Counseling Services .... Ms. Lori KOSHORK
15 Director of Human Resources .... Ms. Beverly PAGE
13 Director of Information Technology .... Mr. Mark LEDESMA
21 Controller .... Ms. Tina CHAMBERLAIN
08 Director of Library Services .... Ms. Hollis NEAR
30 Dir of Development/Alumni Relations .... Ms. Chris STOLLERY
07 Director of Admissions .... Ms. Sharron STARLING
18 Facilities Director .... Ms. Jenny FRAZIER
88 Business & Student Accounts Manager .... Mr. Jeff WYBORNY
19 Dir of Campus Safety & Security .... Mr. Brandon BIRD
37 Director of Financial Aid .... Ms. Monique THERIAULT

DeVry University - Bellevue Center (E)

600 108th Avenue NE, Suite 230,
Bellevue WA 98004-5110

County: King Identification: 666223
Unit ID: 440703
Telephone: (425) 455-2242 Carnegie Class: Not Classified
FAX Number: (425) 455-2322 Calendar System: Semester
URL: www.devry.edu
Established: 1999 Annual Undergrad Tuition & Fees: $16,156
Enrollment: 202 Coed
Affiliation or Control: Proprietary IRS Status: Proprietary
Highest Offering: Master's
Program: Occupational; Professional; Business Emphasis
Accreditation: &NH

01 Center Dean .... Mr. Curtis SMITH

† Regional accreditation is carried under the parent institution in Downers Grove, IL.

DeVry University - Federal Way Campus (F)

3600 S 344th Way, Federal Way WA 98001-9558

County: King Identification: 666224
Unit ID: 440545
Telephone: (253) 943-2800 Carnegie Class: Master's S
FAX Number: (253) 943-3295 Calendar System: Semester
URL: www.devry.edu
Established: 1931 Annual Undergrad Tuition & Fees: $16,156
Enrollment: 794 Coed
Affiliation or Control: Proprietary IRS Status: Proprietary
Highest Offering: Master's
Program: Occupational; Professional; Business Emphasis
Accreditation: &NH, ENGT

01 Metro President .... Ms. Maria DEZENBERG
05 Dean of Academic Affairs .... Mr. Bob DANIELLE
07 Senior Director of Admissions .... Ms. Michelle VANDERBILT
32 Director Student Central .... Ms. Jill BOULANGER
06 Registrar .... Ms. Susan KURLINSKI
15 HR Business Partner .... Mr. Richard SETER
36 Director Career Services .... Ms. Chelsey KUZYK
08 Director of Library Services .... Mr. Daniel LIESTMAN
77 Dean of Technology Programs .... Mr. Richard THOMAS

† Regional accreditation is carried under the parent institution in Downers Grove, IL.

DigiPen Institute of Technology (G)

9931 Willows Road, NE, Redmond WA 98052

County: King FICE Identification: 037243
Unit ID: 443410
Telephone: (425) 558-0299 Carnegie Class: Bac/Diverse
FAX Number: (425) 558-0378 Calendar System: Semester
URL: www.digipen.edu
Established: 1988 Annual Undergrad Tuition & Fees: $25,600
Enrollment: 911 Coed
Affiliation or Control: Proprietary IRS Status: Proprietary
Highest Offering: Master's
Program: Professional; Technical Emphasis
Accreditation: ACCSC

01 President .... Mr. Claude COMAIR
03 Chief Operating Officer .... Mr. Jason Y. CHU
05 Dean of Faculty .... Mr. Xin LI
11 Sr Vice President of Administration .... Ms. Meighan SHOESMITH
10 Sr Vice President of Operations .... Mr. Raymond YAN
37 Director of Financial Aid .... Ms. Kimberly KING
32 Director of Student Services .... Mr. Gordon DUTRISAC
26 VP of External Affairs .... Ms. Angela KUGLER

Eastern Washington University (H)

526 5th Street, Cheney WA 99004-1619

County: Spokane FICE Identification: 003775
Unit ID: 235097
Telephone: (509) 359-6200 Carnegie Class: Master's L
FAX Number: (509) 359-6927 Calendar System: Quarter
URL: www.ewu.edu
Established: 1882 Annual Undergrad Tuition & Fees (In-State): $7,372
Enrollment: 12,130 Coed
Affiliation or Control: State IRS Status: 501(c)3
Highest Offering: Doctorate
Program: Liberal Arts And General; Teacher Preparatory; Professional
Accreditation: NW, BUS, CACREP, CEA, CS, DH, ENG, ENGT, MUS, NRPA, NURSE, OT, PLNG, PTA, SP, SW

01 President .... Dr. Rodolfo AREVALO
05 Vice Pres/Prov Academic Affs .... Dr. Rex FULLER
10 Vice President for Business/Finance .... Ms. Mary VOVES
32 Vice President for Student Affairs .... Ms. Stacey MORGAN FOSTER
30 Vice President of Advancement .... Mr. Michael WESTFALL
20 Vice Prov Academic Res/Admin/Plng .... Dr. Linda KIEFFER
58 Vice Prov/Dean Grad/Undergrad Std .... Dr. Ronald DALLA
08 Interim Dean of Libraries .... Dr. Theophil OTTO
84 Assoc VP Enrollment Services .... Dr. Lawrence BRIGGS
41 Director Intercollegiate Athletics .... Mr. William CHAVES
21 Assoc VP Finance/Chief Fin Officer .... Ms. Toni HABEGGER
18 Assoc Vice Pres for Facilities .... Mr. Shawn KING
04 Exec Assistant to the President/BOT .... Ms. Catherine GOFF
100 Assoc to the President .... Ms. Laurie CONNELLY
86 Director of Government Relations .... Mr. David BURI
36 Assoc Dir Career Services Center .... Ms. Virginia HINCH
92 Director of University Honors .... Dr. Dana ELDER
07 Director of Admissions .... Ms. Shannon CARR
37 Director of Fin Aid & Scholarships .... Mr. Bruce DEFRATES
40 Dir of Bookstore/Pence Union Bldg .... Mr. Robert ANDERSON
51 Dir of Continuing Education & RS .... Ms. Sara SEXTON-JOHNSON
06 Director of Registration & Records .... Ms. Debra FOCKLER
20 Interim Vice Provost .... Dr. Colin ORMSBY
15 Director of Human Resources .... Ms. Jolynn ROGERS
29 Director of Alumni Advancement .... Ms. Lisa POPLAWSKI
96 Director Purchasing .... Ms. Susan BROWN
39 Director Housing/Residential Life .... Ms. Toni TAYLOR
38 Director Counseling & Psych Svcs .... Dr. Robert QUACKENBUSH
19 Director Public Safety/Chief Police .... Chief Timothy L. WALTERS
44 Assoc Director of Annual Giving .... Ms. Pat SPANJER
27 Media Relations Specialist .... Mr. David MEANY
22 Dir Equal Opp/Affirm Action Coord .... Mrs. Gayla WRIGHT
50 Int Dean College of Business Admin .... Dr. Niel ZIMMERMAN
49 Dean College Arts/Letters/Education .... Dr. Lynn BRIGGS
83 Dean Col Social/Behav Sci/Soc Work .... Dr. Vickie SHIELDS
81 Dean Col Science Math & Technology .... Dr. Judd CASE
66 Dean Intercol Center Nursing Educ .... Dr. Patricia BUTTERFIELD
35 Dean of Student Life .... Dr. Al THOMPSON

Edmonds Community College (I)

20000 68th Avenue W, Lynnwood WA 98036-5999

County: Snohomish FICE Identification: 005001
Unit ID: 235103
Telephone: (425) 640-1459 Carnegie Class: Assoc/Pub-S-MC
FAX Number: (425) 771-3366 Calendar System: Quarter
URL: www.edcc.edu
Established: 1967 Annual Undergrad Tuition & Fees (In-State): $4,409
Enrollment: 12,734 Coed
Affiliation or Control: State IRS Status: 501(c)3
Highest Offering: Associate Degree
Program: Occupational; 2-Year Principally Bachelor's Creditable
Accreditation: NW, CONST

01 President .... Dr. Jean HERNANDEZ
05 Vice President Instruction .... Dr. Marty R. CAVALLUZZI

10 Vice Pres/Chief Financial Ofcr ... Mr. Kevin MCKAY
30 Vice Pres Col Relations/Advancement ... Ms. Carol SUMMERS
16 Vice Pres Human Resources ... Mr. Mark CASSIDY
32 Vice President Student Services ... Mr. George SMITH
103 VP Workforce Devel/Training ... Ms. Susan LOREEN
85 Vice Pres International Education ... Mr. David J. CORDELL
08 Dean Learning Resources ... Ms. Lauri KRAM
84 Sr Asc Dean Stdnt Enroll/Fin Svcs ... Ms. Rae-Ellen REAS
35 Sr Assoc Dean Student Life/Devel ... Ms. Nicola SMITH
36 Int Assoc Dean Stdnt Success/Reten ... Ms. Stephanie BARON
04 Executive Asst to the President ... Ms. Patty MICHAJLA
102 Exec Director College Foundation ... Vacant
25 Exec Dir Grants Research/Effective ... Ms. Beth NICHOLS
26 Director Communications/Marketing ... Ms. Stephanie WIEGAND
13 Int Director Information Technology ... Ms. Eva SMITH
18 Chief Facilities/Physical Plant ... Mr. Paul DOHERTY
28 Director of Equity & Diversity ... Ms. Shirley SUTTON
96 Director of Purchasing ... Ms. Marian PAANANEN
27 Public Information Officer ... Ms. Michele GRAVES
19 Director Safety & Security ... Mr. Paul DOHERTY
41 Interim Athletics Director ... Mr. Clay BLACKWOOD
85 Dir International Student Services ... Ms. Lisa THOMPSON
09 Institutional Researcher ... Ms. Pat HUFFMAN

Everest College (A)

155 Washington Ave, Ste 200, Bremerton WA 98337

County: Kitsap | FICE Identification: 023001 | Unit ID: 234739
Telephone: (360) 473-1120 | Carnegie Class: Not Classified
FAX Number: (360) 792-2404 | Calendar System: Quarter
URL: www.everest.edu
Established: 1960 | Annual Undergrad Tuition & Fees: $11,788
Enrollment: 362 | Coed
Affiliation or Control: Proprietary | IRS Status: Proprietary
Highest Offering: Associate Degree
Program: Occupational
Accreditation: ACICS, MAC

01 President ... Mr. Tim ALLEN

Everest College (B)

120 NE 136th Avenue, Suite 130, Vancouver WA 98684

County: Clark | Identification: 666737 | Unit ID: 236993
Telephone: (360) 254-3282 | Carnegie Class: Assoc/PrivFP
FAX Number: (360) 254-3035 | Calendar System: Other
URL: www.everest.edu/campus/vancouver
Established: 1976 | Annual Undergrad Tuition & Fees: $15,771
Enrollment: 402 | Coed
Affiliation or Control: Proprietary | IRS Status: Proprietary
Highest Offering: Associate Degree
Program: Occupational; 2-Year Principally Bachelor's Creditable
Accreditation: ACICS, MAC

01 President ... Mr. Brad KUCHENREUTHER

† Branch campus of Everest College, Portland, OR. Tuition varies by degree program.

Everett Community College (C)

2000 Tower Street, Everett WA 98201-1390

County: Snohomish | FICE Identification: 003776 | Unit ID: 235149
Telephone: (425) 388-9100 | Carnegie Class: Assoc/Pub-U-SC
FAX Number: (425) 388-9129 | Calendar System: Quarter
URL: www.everettcc.edu
Established: 1941 | Annual Undergrad Tuition & Fees (In-State): $3,556
Enrollment: 6,970 | Coed
Affiliation or Control: State | IRS Status: 501(c)3
Highest Offering: Associate Degree
Program: Occupational; 2-Year Principally Bachelor's Creditable
Accreditation: NW, ADNUR, MAC

01 President ... Dr. David BEYER
04 Executive Assistant to President ... Ms. Cheryl BLACKBURN
05 Vice Pres Instruction/Student Svcs ... Dr. Sandra FOWLER-HILL
30 Vice Pres of College Advancement ... Dr. John OLSON
11 Vice Pres of Administrative Svcs ... Ms. Jennifer L. HOWARD
26 Vice Pres of College Services ... Mr. Patrick SISNEROS
12 Exec Dir Univ Ctr North Puget Sound ... Vacant
60 Dean Communication/Social Sciences ... Mr. Craig LEWIS
81 Dean of Math & Science ... Mr. Al FRIEDMAN
62 Dean of Arts & Learning Resources ... Ms. Jeanne LEADER
76 Dean Health Sciences/Public Safety ... Mr. Elliott STERN
53 Dean of Basic & Adult Education ... Mr. Darrell MIHARA
28 Dean Student Dev/Diversity Advocacy ... Ms. Christina CASTORENA
51 Director Continuing Education ... Ms. Karen LANDRY
84 Dean Enrollment/Student Finan Svcs ... Ms. Laurie FRANKLIN
19 Dir of Campus Safety & Security ... Mr. Bob WRIGHT
12 Exec Director of Corporate Training ... Mr. John B. BONNER
09 Director Institutional Research ... Vacant
41 Director of Athletics ... Mr. Larry WALKER
40 Director of Bookstore ... Ms. Kerri KIRK
88 Dir Center for Disability Services ... Ms. Kathy COOK
88 Program Manager A ... Vacant

The Evergreen State College (D)

2700 Evergreen Parkway, NW, Olympia WA 98505-0005

County: Thurston | FICE Identification: 008155 | Unit ID: 235167
Telephone: (360) 867-6000 | Carnegie Class: Master's S
FAX Number: (360) 867-6577 | Calendar System: Quarter
URL: www.evergreen.edu
Established: 1967 | Annual Undergrad Tuition & Fees (In-State): $7,486
Enrollment: 4,794 | Coed
Affiliation or Control: State | IRS Status: 501(c)3
Highest Offering: Master's
Program: Liberal Arts And General
Accreditation: NW

01 President ... Dr. Thomas L. PURCE
05 Vice President/Provost ... Dr. Michael ZIMMERMAN
32 Vice President Student Affairs ... Dr. Arthur COSTANTINO
10 Vice President Finance/Admin ... Dr. John HURLEY
30 Vice President College Advancement ... Ms. D. Lee HOEMANN
84 Assoc Vice Pres for Enrollmt Mgmt ... Mr. Steve HUNTER
15 Assoc Vice Pres for Human Resources ... Ms. Laurel UZNANSKI
08 Interim Dean of Library Services ... Ms. Sarah PEDERSEN
35 Dean Student/Academic Support Svcs ... Dr. Phyllis LANE
04 Exec Assistant to the President ... Mr. John CARMICHAEL
45 Exec Dir Operational Plng/Budget ... Mr. Steve TROTTER
22 Spec Asst to Pres/Equal Opportunity ... Mr. Paul GALLEGOS
22 Civil Rights Officer ... Ms. Nicole ACK
20 Academic Dean ... Dr. Ken TABBUTT
86 Director of Government Relations ... Dr. Julie GARVER
14 Director Computing & Communications ... Mr. Aaron POWELL
26 Director of College Relations ... Mr. Todd SPRAGUE
37 Director of Financial Aid ... Ms. Tracy HALL
06 Registrar ... Ms. Andrea COKER-ANDERSON
09 Director of Institutional Research ... Ms. Laura COGHLAN
18 Director of Facilities ... Mr. Paul SMITH
21 Director of Business Services ... Mr. Collin ORR
29 Director Alumni Relations ... Ms. R.J BURT
36 Director Career Development Center ... Mr. Mychael HEUER
38 Dir Counseling & Health Services ... Ms. Elizabeth MCHUGH
96 Director of Purchasing ... Vacant
07 Director of Admissions ... Mr. Bryan GOULD
88 Sustainability Coordinator ... Mr. Scott MORGAN

Faith Evangelical College & Seminary (E)

3504 N Pearl Street, Tacoma WA 98407-2607

County: Pierce | FICE Identification: 036894 | Unit ID: 443049
Telephone: (253) 752-2020 | Carnegie Class: Spec/Faith
FAX Number: (253) 759-1790 | Calendar System: Quarter
URL: www.faithseminary.edu
Established: 1969 | Annual Undergrad Tuition & Fees: $9,100
Enrollment: 300 | Coed
Affiliation or Control: Interdenominational | IRS Status: 501(c)3
Highest Offering: Doctorate
Program: Professional; Religious Emphasis
Accreditation: TRACS

01 President ... Dr. Michael J. ADAMS
05 Executive Dean ... Dr. James D. GIBSON
09 Dir of Institutional Effectiveness ... Dr. Eric L. RICE
07 Admissions Officer ... Mrs. Lorrie WHATELY
08 Director Information/Library Svcs ... Dr. Timothy HYUN
88 Director of Korean Studies ... Dr. Kyu H. LEE
37 Financial Aid Officer ... Ms. Debi RICE
10 Chief Financial Officer ... Dr. Douglas COLLIER
06 Registrar ... Rev. Tyrone M. HARDY
35 Office Manager/Student Services ... Mrs. Alison B. HARDY

Gonzaga University (F)

502 E Boone Avenue, Spokane WA 99258-0001

County: Spokane | FICE Identification: 003778 | Unit ID: 235316
Telephone: (509) 313-4220 | Carnegie Class: Master's L
FAX Number: (509) 313-5718 | Calendar System: Semester
URL: www.gonzaga.edu
Established: 1887 | Annual Undergrad Tuition & Fees: $33,860
Enrollment: 7,764 | Coed
Affiliation or Control: Roman Catholic | IRS Status: 501(c)3
Highest Offering: Doctorate
Program: Liberal Arts And General; Teacher Preparatory; Professional; Fine Arts Emphasis
Accreditation: NW, ANEST, BUS, BUSA, CACREP, CEA, ENG, LAW, NURSE, TED

01 President ... Dr. Thayne M. MCCULLOH
05 Academic Vice President ... Dr. Patricia OCONNELL KILLEN
03 Executive Vice President ... Mr. Earl F. MARTIN
10 Vice President for Finance ... Mr. Charles J. MURPHY
88 Vice President for Mission ... Rev. Frank E. CASE, SJ
32 Vice President for Student Life ... Dr. Sue D. WEITZ
26 Acting VP University Relations ... Mr. Joe POSS
30 Sr Vice President Principal Gifts ... Ms. Margot J. STANFIELD
20 Assoc Academic Vice President ... Dr. Raymond REYES
06 Asst Academic Vice Pres/Registrar ... Ms. Jolanta A. WEBER
15 Asst Vice President Human Resources ... Mr. Dan C. BERRYMAN
88 Assistant VP for Marketing/Comm ... Mr. Dave SONNTAG
07 Dean of Admission ... Ms. Julie A. MCCULLOH
35 Dean of Students/Judicial Affairs ... Ms. Kassi KAIN
08 Dean of Libraries ... Dr. Eileen K. BELL-GARRISON
37 Dean of Student Finance Services ... Mr. James WHITE
13 Chief Information Officer ... Mr. Chris G. GILL
26 Director Cmty/Public Relations ... Ms. Mary Joan HAHN
29 Director Alumni ... Mr. Bob D. FINN
36 Director Career Center ... Dr. Mary HEITKEMPER
38 Dir Counseling/Career Assessment ... Dr. Fernando ORITZ
49 Interim Dean Arts & Sciences ... Dr. Blaine GARVIN
50 Dean School of Business ... Dr. Clarence D. BARNES
107 Dean School of Prof Studies ... Vacant
53 Dean of Education ... Dr. Jon D. SUNDERLAND
54 Dean of Engineering ... Dr. Steve SILLIMAN
61 Dean of Law ... Ms. Jane KORN
09 Director of Institutional Research ... Ms. Jolanta A. WEBER
41 Director of Athletics ... Mr. Michael L. ROTH
42 Director of University Ministry ... Fr. C. HIGHTOWER, SJ
43 Interim Corporation Counsel ... Mr. James S. CRAVEN
18 Director Plant Services ... Mr. Kenneth R. SAMMONS
86 Director Government Relations ... Vacant
92 Director Honors Program ... Rev. Tim R. CLANCY, SJ
96 Manager of Purchasing ... Mr. Steve M. LUNDEN
104 Director Study Abroad ... Vacant
25 Director Sponsored Research & Pgm ... Ms. Joann WAITE
108 Faculty Director of Assessment ... Dr. Patrick T. MCCORMICK

Grays Harbor College (G)

1620 Edward P. Smith Drive, Aberdeen WA 98520-7500

County: Grays Harbor | FICE Identification: 003779 | Unit ID: 235334
Telephone: (360) 532-9020 | Carnegie Class: Assoc/Pub-R-M
FAX Number: (360) 538-4299 | Calendar System: Quarter
URL: www.ghc.edu
Established: 1930 | Annual Undergrad Tuition & Fees (In-District): $4,000
Enrollment: 2,088 | Coed
Affiliation or Control: State/Local | IRS Status: 501(c)3
Highest Offering: Associate Degree
Program: Occupational; 2-Year Principally Bachelor's Creditable
Accreditation: NW, ADNUR

01 President ... Dr. Edward BREWSTER
05 Vice President for Instruction ... Ms. Laurie CLARY
10 Chief Financial Officer ... Ms. Barbara MCCULLOUGH
32 Vice President for Student Services ... Dr. Arlene TORGERSEN
75 Dean of Vocational Instruction ... Mr. Mike KELLY
56 Dean Transitions Pgms/Extended Lrng ... Ms. Cindy WILSON
35 Assoc Dean for Student Services ... Ms. Nancy DEVERSE
08 Assoc Dean Library/Media Services ... Mr. Stanley W. HORTON
07 Assoc Dean of Admissions ... Ms. Nancy DE VERSE
15 Chief Human Resources Officer ... Mr. David HALVERSTADT
37 Director Student Financial Aid ... Mr. Ben BEUSS
18 Dir Campus Operations/Sfty/Security ... Mr. Tony SIMONE
38 Director of Counseling ... Ms. Melissa BARNES
30 Chief Development Officer ... Ms. Jan JORGENSON
26 Director Public Relations ... Ms. Jane F. GOLDBERG
09 Director Institutional Research ... Ms. Debbie REYNVAAN

Green River Community College (H)

12401 SE 320th Street, Auburn WA 98092-3699

County: King | FICE Identification: 003780 | Unit ID: 235343
Telephone: (253) 833-9111 | Carnegie Class: Assoc/Pub-S-MC
FAX Number: (253) 288-3470 | Calendar System: Quarter
URL: www.greenriver.edu
Established: 1965 | Annual Undergrad Tuition & Fees (In-State): $3,575
Enrollment: 10,991 | Coed
Affiliation or Control: State | IRS Status: 501(c)3
Highest Offering: Associate Degree
Program: Occupational; 2-Year Principally Bachelor's Creditable
Accreditation: NW, OTA, PTAA

01 President ... Dr. Eileen E. ELY
05 Vice President of Instruction ... Mr. Derek BRANDES
13 Exec Dir of Information Technology ... Ms. Camella MORGAN
10 Vice President Business Affairs ... Mr. Rick BRUMFIELD
15 Vice President for Human Resources ... Ms. Lesley HOGAN
30 Exec Director of Development/Found ... Mr. George FRASIER
32 Vice President of Student Services ... Dr. Deborah CASEY
56 Vice Pres Extended Learning ... Ms. Edith BANNISTER
85 Assoc VP of International Programs ... Mr. Ross JENNINGS
75 Dn Prof/Tech Ed/Trades & Technology ... Mr. Josh CLEARMAN
49 Dean Instr/Math/Soc Sci/Fine Arts ... Ms. Christie GILLILAND
79 Assoc Dean Instr/English/Humanities ... Dr. Joyce HAMMER
81 Assoc Dean Instr/Science ... Ms. Cathy WELLS
76 Dean of Instr/Health/Family Studies ... Ms. Krista FOX
88 Dean of Instr/Capital Project ... Mr. Sam BALL
88 Dean Inst Lang/Acad Skill/Wellnes ... Ms. Laura DIZAZZO
06 Registrar ... Ms. Denise BENNATTS
37 Director of Financial Aid ... Ms. Mary EDINGTON
21 Director of Business Services ... Ms. Debbie KNIPSCHIELD
21 Controller ... Ms. Teresa COLLINS
18 Director of Facilities ... Mr. Michael LAMONTAGNE
27 Exec Director of College Relations ... Vacant
51 Exec Dir Cont Educ/Off-Campus Sites ... Ms. Leslie MOORE
09 Director of Research & Planning ... Ms. Fia ELIASSON-CREEK
28 Dir Multicultural & Diversity Svcs ... Mr. Michael TUNCAP
96 Purchasing Manager ... Ms. Patty SIKORA
31 Community Relations Coordinator ... Mr. Josh GERTSMAN
19 Director of Campus Safety ... Mr. Fred A. CREEK
41 Director Athletics ... Mr. Robert KICKNER

Heritage University (A)

3240 Fort Road, Toppenish WA 98948-9599
County: Yakima | FICE Identification: 003777 | Unit ID: 235422
Telephone: (509) 865-8500 | Carnegie Class: Master's M
FAX Number: (509) 865-4469 | Calendar System: Semester
URL: www.heritage.edu
Established: 1982 | Annual Undergrad Tuition & Fees: $1,200
Enrollment: 1,170 | Coed
Affiliation or Control: Independent Non-Profit | IRS Status: 501(c)3
Highest Offering: Master's
Program: 2-Year Principally Bachelor's Creditable; Liberal Arts And General; Teacher Preparatory; Professional
Accreditation: NW, MT, SW

01	President	Dr. John E. BASSETT
05	Vice President Academic Affairs	Dr. Curtis GUAGLIANONE
32	Vice Pres Student Life	Ms. Melissa FILOWSKI
100	Chief of Staff	Ms. Crystal LAME BULL
30	Vice President Advancement	Mr. Michael P. MOORE
21	Controller	Ms. Siri J. STROM
06	Registrar	Mr. Michael BUTTREY
53	Dean of Education & Psychology	Mr. Robert SMART
18	Director Physical Plant	Mr. Rob CARROLL
37	Director of Financial Aid	Vacant
08	Library Director	Mr. Bill MCCAY
13	Director Information Services	Mr. Jim BUSH
07	Dir of Admissions & Recruitment	Mr. Miguel PUENTE
26	Communications Officer	Ms. Bonnie HUGHES
04	Manager Executive Offices	Ms. Betty J. SAMPSON
09	Director of Institutional Research	Ms. Nina OMAN
10	Chief Business Officer	Mr. Rick R. GAGNIER
15	Director Personnel Services	Ms. Veronica NARANJO
49	Dean Arts & Sciences	Dr. Kazuhiro SONODA
35	Dir Stdnt Affs/Plcmnt/Counseling	Ms. Melissa HILL
29	Dir Alumni Rels/Annual Giving Ofcr	Ms. Betsy NAGLE-MCNAUGHTON
36	Director Student Placement	Ms. Irma DEPRIETO
84	Director Enrollment Management	Mr. Miguel PUENTE
96	Director of Purchasing	Ms. Geneva SAPP
38	Counselor for Student Life	Ms. Erica MACIAS

Highline Community College (B)

PO Box 98000, 2400 S 240th Street,
Des Moines WA 98198-9800
County: King | FICE Identification: 003781 | Unit ID: 235431
Telephone: (206) 878-3710 | Carnegie Class: Assoc/Pub-S-MC
FAX Number: (206) 870-3754 | Calendar System: Quarter
URL: www.highline.edu
Established: 1961 | Annual Undergrad Tuition & Fees (In-State): $4,000
Enrollment: 6,743 | Coed
Affiliation or Control: State | IRS Status: 501(c)3
Highest Offering: Associate Degree
Program: Occupational; 2-Year Principally Bachelor's Creditable
Accreditation: NW, ADNUR, MAC, POLYT

01	President	Dr. Jack BERMINGHAM
11	Vice President for Administration	Mr. Larry YOK
05	Vice Pres for Academic Affairs	Mr. Jeff WAGNITZ
30	VP Inst Advancement/Cmty Rels	Dr. Lisa SKARI
32	Vice Pres for Student Services	Ms. Toni CASTRO
20	Dean of Instruction-Vocational	Ms. Alice MADSEN
20	Dean of Instruction-Academics	Dr. Rolita EZEONU
24	Dean Instructional Resources	Ms. Monica LUCE
51	Int Dean of Extended Learning	Dr. James PEYTON
35	Assoc Dean Student Programs	Mr. Jonathan BROWN
84	Assoc Dean for Enrollment Services	Ms. Kate BLIGH
37	Director Financial Aid	Ms. Lorraine ODOM
26	Director Communications & Marketing	Mr. Jason PRENOVOST
15	Exec Director of Human Resources	Ms. Beth BROOKS
21	Director Financial Services	Ms. Shirley BEAN
13	Exec Dir Administrative Technology	Mr. Dennis COLGAN
18	Director Plant Operations	Mr. Barry HOLLDORF
19	Director Security & Safety	Mr. Rich NOYER
41	Director Athletics	Mr. John DUNN
44	Director Resources & Development	Mr. Rod STEPHENSON
09	Director Institutional Research	Ms. Tonya BENTON
38	Assoc Dean Counseling/ Judicial	Dr. Allison LAU
40	Bookstore Manager	Ms. Laura NOLE
96	Director of Purchasing	Ms. Dianna THIELE
06	Interim Registrar	Ms. Debbie FAISON
07	Director of Admissions	Ms. L. Michelle KUWASAKI
22	Dir Multicultural Svcs/Stdnt Devel	Ms. Yoshiko HARDEN-ABE

Interface College (C)

178 South Stevens Street, Spokane WA 99201
County: Spokane | FICE Identification: 023265 | Unit ID: 235495
Telephone: (509) 467-1727 | Carnegie Class: Assoc/PrivFP
FAX Number: (509) 467-3804 | Calendar System: Semester
URL: www.interface.edu
Established: 1982 | Annual Undergrad Tuition & Fees: $12,320
Enrollment: 140 | Coed
Affiliation or Control: Proprietary | IRS Status: Proprietary
Highest Offering: Associate Degree
Program: Occupational
Accreditation: CNCE

01	President	Walt LEATHERS
03	Director	Dave WILSON
37	Director of Financial Aid	Rick SINCLAIR
07	Asst Director of Admissions	Kathy HAMMONDS

International Academy of Design and Technology (D)

645 Andover Park West, Seattle WA 98188-3319
County: King | Identification: 666265 | Unit ID: 446808
Telephone: (206) 575-1865 | Carnegie Class: Spec/Arts
FAX Number: (206) 575-1724 | Calendar System: Semester
URL: www.iadtseattle.com
Established: 2004 | Annual Undergrad Tuition & Fees: N/A
Enrollment: 436 | Coed
Affiliation or Control: Proprietary | IRS Status: Proprietary
Highest Offering: Baccalaureate
Program: Fine Arts Emphasis
Accreditation: ACICS

01	President	Mr. Khaled SAKALLA

† Branch campus of International Academy of Design and Technology, Tampa, FL.

ITT Technical Institute (E)

1615 75th Street SW, Everett WA 98203-6261
County: Snohomish | Identification: 666326 | Unit ID: 414531
Telephone: (425) 583-0200 | Carnegie Class: Spec/Tech
FAX Number: (425) 485-3438 | Calendar System: Quarter
URL: www.itt-tech.edu
Established: 2003 | Annual Undergrad Tuition & Fees: N/A
Enrollment: 459 | Coed
Affiliation or Control: Proprietary | IRS Status: Proprietary
Highest Offering: Baccalaureate
Program: Technical Emphasis
Accreditation: ACICS

† Branch campus of ITT Technical Institute, Spokane Valley, WA.

ITT Technical Institute (F)

12720 Gateway Drive, Suite 100, Seattle WA 98168-3334
County: King | FICE Identification: 008443 | Unit ID: 235529
Telephone: (206) 244-3300 | Carnegie Class: Spec/Tech
FAX Number: (206) 246-7635 | Calendar System: Quarter
URL: www.itt-tech.edu
Established: 1932 | Annual Undergrad Tuition & Fees: N/A
Enrollment: 670 | Coed
Affiliation or Control: Proprietary | IRS Status: Proprietary
Highest Offering: Baccalaureate
Program: Technical Emphasis
Accreditation: ACICS

† Branch campus of ITT Technical Institute, Spokane Valley, WA.

ITT Technical Institute (G)

13518 East Indiana Avenue,
Spokane Valley WA 99216-1589
County: Spokane | FICE Identification: 030718 | Unit ID: 235510
Telephone: (509) 926-2900 | Carnegie Class: Spec/Tech
FAX Number: (509) 926-2908 | Calendar System: Quarter
URL: www.itt-tech.edu
Established: 1985 | Annual Undergrad Tuition & Fees: N/A
Enrollment: 384 | Coed
Affiliation or Control: Proprietary | IRS Status: Proprietary
Highest Offering: Baccalaureate
Program: Technical Emphasis
Accreditation: ACICS

Lake Washington Institute of Technology (H)

11605 132nd Avenue NE, Kirkland WA 98034-8506
County: King | FICE Identification: 005373 | Unit ID: 235699
Telephone: (425) 739-8100 | Carnegie Class: Assoc/Pub-S-MC
FAX Number: (425) 739-8299 | Calendar System: Quarter
URL: www.lwtech.edu
Established: 1949 | Annual Undergrad Tuition & Fees (In-State): $3,462
Enrollment: 4,151 | Coed
Affiliation or Control: State | IRS Status: 170(c)1
Highest Offering: Associate Degree
Program: Occupational; Technical Emphasis
Accreditation: NW, ACFEI, DA, DH, FUSER, MAC, OTA, PTAA

01	President	Dr. David M. WOODALL
04	Executive Asst to President	Ms. Debbie Z. ALMSTEDT
88	Accreditation Liaison Officer	Dr. Brinton SPRAGUE
05	Vice Pres Instructional Svcs	Dr. Sara BURNS
53	Dean Gen Educ/Hospitality & Svcs	Mr. Douglas J. EMORY
76	Dean Instruction Allied Health	Ms. Maria MACEDO
72	Dean Applied Design Programs	Ms. Nancy DICK
08	Assoc Dean Library/E-Learning	Mr. Ed SARGENT
76	Dir Phys Therapist Assistant Pgm	Ms. Molly VERSCHUYL
76	Director Occupational Therapy	Ms. Kay BRITTINGHAM
88	Director Funeral Services	Mr. Jack NORBELL
66	Director Nursing Programs	Ms. Colleen HEWES
27	Chief Information Officer	Mr. Mike POTTER
18	Director Facilities & Operations	Mr. Tim WHEELER
21	Controller	Ms. Debbie DEBEAUCHAMP
88	Food Service Operations Manager	Mr. Eric SAKAI
96	Purchasing Manager	Ms. Betty CONWELL
56	Associate Dean Extended Learning	Ms. Lin ZHOU
26	Director Marketing	Ms. Regine ADAMS
102	Executive Director Foundation	Ms. Laurie AUSTIN
32	Vice President Student Services	Mr. Dennis LONG
89	Principal/Dean High School Programs	Ms. Kim INFINGER
37	Director Financial Aid	Mr. Bill CHANEY
38	Dir Student Dev & Retention	Ms. Ruby HAYDEN
103	Director Workforce Development	Ms. Demetra BIROS
88	Director TRiO Student Support Svcs	Dr. Patricia HUNTER
06	Director Enroll Services/Registrar	Vacant
88	Director Title III	Ms. Christina HARTER
88	Manager Student Programs	Ms. Sheila WALTON
40	Manager Bookstore	Mr. Greg LEPAGE
85	Exec Dir Global & Extended Learning	Ms. Myung PARK
88	Associate Dean Grants	Ms. Joy HOWLAND
30	Executive Dir College Advancement	Ms. Terry BYINGTON
15	Executive Director Human Resources	Mr. Gregory W. ROBERTS

† Granted candidacy at the Baccalaureate level.

Lower Columbia College (I)

PO Box 3010, Longview WA 98632-0310
County: Cowlitz | FICE Identification: 003782 | Unit ID: 235750
Telephone: (360) 442-2000 | Carnegie Class: Assoc/Pub-R-M
FAX Number: (360) 442-2109 | Calendar System: Quarter
URL: www.lowercolumbia.edu
Established: 1934 | Annual Undergrad Tuition & Fees (In-State): $4,262
Enrollment: 4,176 | Coed
Affiliation or Control: State | IRS Status: 170(c)1
Highest Offering: Associate Degree
Program: Occupational; 2-Year Principally Bachelor's Creditable
Accreditation: NW, ADNUR, MAC

01	President	Mr. Christopher C. BAILEY
05	Vice President of Instruction	Ms. Laura BRENER
11	Vice President Administrative Svcs	Mr. Nolan WHEELER
32	Vice President for Student Success	Ms. Lisa MATYE EDWARDS
103	Dean Workforce/Continuing Educ	Mr. Brendan GLASER
20	Dean Instructional Programs	Ms. Maggie STUART
20	Dean Instructional Programs	Mr. Kyle HAMMON
76	Associate Dean Allied Health/Nurse	Ms. Karen JOINER
09	Director Institutional Research	Ms. Wendy HALL
18	Director of Campus Services	Mr. Richard HAMILTON
102	Director of Foundation	Ms. Erin BROWN
41	Athletic Director	Mr. Kirc J. ROLAND
21	Controller	Mr. Joe QUIRK
26	Director of College Relations	Ms. Sue GROTH
15	Director of Personnel Services	Ms. Kendra SPRAGUE
37	Financial Aid Officer	Ms. Marisa GREEAR
08	Director of Library Services	Mr. Jon KERR
13	Director of Information Technology	Mr. Brandon RAY
40	Director of Bookstore	Ms. Debbie CLEVELAND
07	Director of Admissions/Registrar	Ms. Lynn LAWRENCE
10	Chief Business Officer	Mr. Nolan WHEELER
84	Director Enrollment Management	Ms. Lisa MATYE EDWARDS
96	Director of Purchasing	Ms. Sherry GOHN
04	Executive Assistant	Ms. Linda J. CLARK

Northwest College of Art & Design (NCAD) (J)

16301 Creative Drive, NE, Poulsbo WA 98370-8651
County: Kitsap | FICE Identification: 026021 | Unit ID: 377546
Telephone: (360) 779-9993 | Carnegie Class: Spec/Arts
FAX Number: (360) 779-9933 | Calendar System: Semester
URL: www.ncad.edu
Established: 1982 | Annual Undergrad Tuition & Fees: $18,200
Enrollment: 99 | Coed
Affiliation or Control: Proprietary | IRS Status: Proprietary
Highest Offering: Baccalaureate
Program: Fine Arts Emphasis
Accreditation: ACCSC

01	President	Craig FREEMAN
06	Registrar/Financial Aid	Julie PERIGARD
05	Director of Education	Julius FINLEY

Northwest Indian College (K)

2522 Kwina Road, Bellingham WA 98226-9278
County: Whatcom | FICE Identification: 021800 | Unit ID: 380377
Telephone: (360) 676-2772 | Carnegie Class: Tribal
FAX Number: (360) 738-0136 | Calendar System: Quarter
URL: www.nwic.edu
Established: 1978 | Annual Undergrad Tuition & Fees: $4,960
Enrollment: 1,731 | Coed
Affiliation or Control: Tribal Control | IRS Status: 501(c)3
Highest Offering: Baccalaureate
Program: Occupational; 2-Year Principally Bachelor's Creditable

Accreditation: NW

- 01 President ... Dr. Justin GUILLORY
- 10 Vice President/Admin & Finance ... Ms. Karyl JEFFERSON
- 05 Vice Pres Instruction/Student Svcs ... Ms. Carole RAVE
- 11 Vice President Campus Development ... Mr. David OREIRO
- 45 VP for Research/Sponsored Programs ... Ms. Barbara ROBERTS
- 04 Exec Assistant to the President ... Ms. Corby DAVIS
- 106 Dean Instruction/Distant Learning ... Ms. Bernice PORTERVINT
- 20 Assoc Dean for Instruction ... Vacant
- 37 Assoc Dean of Students/Fin Aid Dir ... Ms. Crystal BAGBY
- 13 IT Director ... Mr. Michael JAMES
- 08 Librarian ... Ms. Valerie MCBETH

Northwest Institute of Literary Arts (A)

5577 Vanbarr Place Suite S1, Freeland WA 98249

County: Island FICE Identification: 041889
Unit ID: 460941
Telephone: (360) 331-0307 Carnegie Class: Not Classified
FAX Number: N/A Calendar System: Semester
URL: www.writeonwhidbey.org/mfa
Established: 2005 Annual Graduate Tuition & Fees: $11,550
Enrollment: N/A Coed
Affiliation or Control: Independent Non-Profit IRS Status: 501(c)3
Highest Offering: Master's; No Undergraduates
Program: Professional
Accreditation: DETC

- 01 Program Director ... Mr. Wayne UDE
- 32 Student Services Coordinator ... Ms. Asharaine MACHALA

Northwest School of Wooden Boatbuilding (B)

42 N Water Street, Port Hadlock WA 98339-8706

County: Jefferson FICE Identification: 041550
Unit ID: 236124
Telephone: (360) 385-4948 Carnegie Class: Not Classified
FAX Number: (360) 385-5089 Calendar System: Other
URL: www.nwboatschool.org
Established: 1981 Annual Undergrad Tuition & Fees: $13,050
Enrollment: 44 Coed
Affiliation or Control: Independent Non-Profit IRS Status: 501(c)3
Highest Offering: Associate Degree
Program: Occupational
Accreditation: ACCSC

- 01 Executive Director ... Mr. Peter LEENHOUTS
- 05 Chief Instructor ... Mr. Tim LEE

Northwest University (C)

PO Box 579, Kirkland WA 98083-0579

County: King FICE Identification: 003783
Unit ID: 236133
Telephone: (425) 822-8266 Carnegie Class: Bac/Diverse
FAX Number: (425) 827-0148 Calendar System: Semester
URL: www.northwestu.edu
Established: 1934 Annual Undergrad Tuition & Fees: $24,740
Enrollment: 1,294 Coed
Affiliation or Control: Assemblies Of God Church IRS Status: 501(c)3
Highest Offering: Master's
Program: Liberal Arts And General
Accreditation: NW, ACBSP, NURSE

- 01 President ... Dr. Joseph CASTLEBERRY
- 05 Provost ... Dr. Jim HEUGEL
- 32 Vice Pres Student Development ... Dr. Paul BANAS
- 10 Chief Financial Officer ... Mr. John JORDAN
- 102 Asst Vice Pres for Development ... Mr. Jason MILES
- 84 Asst Vice Pres Enrollment Services ... Mrs. Rose SMITH
- 42 Dean of the Chapel ... Rev. Phil RASMUSSEN
- 06 Registrar ... Mrs. Sandy HENDRICKSON
- 07 Director of Admissions ... Mrs. Jessica VELASCO
- 37 Director Student Financial Aid ... Mr. Roger WILSON
- 41 Athletic Director ... Mr. Gary MCINTOSH
- 08 College Librarian ... Mr. Adam EPP
- 38 Director of Counseling Services ... Ms. Teresa REGAN
- 29 Director of Alumni Services ... Mr. Dustin SHIRLEY
- 15 Director Human Resources ... Ms. Victoria CLARK
- 36 Director Student Success ... Mrs. Amy JONES

† Granted candidacy at the Doctorate level.

Olympic College (D)

1600 Chester Avenue, Bremerton WA 98337-1699

County: Kitsap FICE Identification: 003784
Unit ID: 236188
Telephone: (360) 792-6050 Carnegie Class: Assoc/Pub4
FAX Number: (360) 475-7151 Calendar System: Quarter
URL: www.olympic.edu
Established: 1946 Annual Undergrad Tuition & Fees (In-State): $3,999
Enrollment: 8,746 Coed
Affiliation or Control: State IRS Status: 501(c)3
Highest Offering: Baccalaureate
Program: Occupational; 2-Year Principally Bachelor's Creditable
Accreditation: NW, ACFEI, ADNUR, MAC, NURSE, PTAA

- 01 President ... Dr. David C. MITCHELL
- 05 Vice President of Instruction ... Ms. Mary GARGUILE
- 11 Vice President of Administration ... Mr. Bruce RIVELAND
- 32 Vice President of Student Services ... Dr. Ron SHADE
- 30 Exec Dir Institutional Advancement ... Dr. Joan HANTEN
- 16 Exec Director Human Resource Svcs ... Ms. Linda YERGER
- 56 Director of Extended Learning ... Vacant
- 04 Exec Assistant to the President ... Ms. Allison SMITH
- 37 Director Financial Aid ... Ms. Heidi TOWNSEND
- 27 Director of Communications ... Ms. Jennifer HAYES
- 84 Dn Enroll Svcs/Registrar/Dir Admiss ... Ms. Dianna LARSEN
- 18 Chief Facilities/Physical Plant ... Mr. William WILKIE
- 21 Director of Business Services ... Ms. Janell WHITELEY
- 96 Procurement Officer ... Ms. Diana LAKE
- 28 Multicultural Services Manager ... Mr. Daniel JOHNSON
- 40 Director of Auxiliary Services ... Vacant
- 36 Director Student Placement ... Ms. Patricia TRIGGS
- 103 Dean Workforce Development ... Ms. Amy HATFIELD
- 08 Dean Library-Media ... Ms. Ruth M. SAUCIER
- 35 Dean of Student Development ... Dr. Kimberly MCNAMARA
- 50 Dean Business & Technology ... Dr. Norma WHITACRE
- 81 Dean Math/Engineer/Sci/Health ... Dr. Judi BROWN
- 79 Dean Humanities/Social Science ... Dr. Gina HUSTON
- 09 Assoc Dean Planning/Assess/Research ... Vacant

Pacific Lutheran University (E)

Tacoma WA 98447-0003

County: Pierce FICE Identification: 003785
Unit ID: 236230
Telephone: (253) 531-6900 Carnegie Class: Master's M
FAX Number: (253) 535-8320 Calendar System: 4/1/4
URL: www.plu.edu
Established: 1890 Annual Undergrad Tuition & Fees: $32,800
Enrollment: 3,461 Coed
Affiliation or Control: Evangelical Lutheran Church In America
IRS Status: 501(c)3
Highest Offering: Master's
Program: Liberal Arts And General; Teacher Preparatory; Professional
Accreditation: NW, BUS, CS, ENG, MFCD, MUS, NURSE, SW, TED

- 01 President ... Dr. Thomas W. KRISE
- 05 Provost/Dean Graduate Studies ... Dr. Steven P. STARKOVICH
- 10 Vice President Finance & Operations ... Dr. Sheri J. TONN
- 30 Vice Pres Development/Univ Rels ... Dr. Steve J. OLSON
- 32 Vice Pres Stdnt Life/Dean of Stdnts ... Dr. Laura F. MAJOVSKI
- 07 Vice Pres Admission/Enrollment Svcs ... Mr. Karl A. STUMO
- 21 Assoc Vice Pres Finance/Controller ... Mr. Robert K. RILEY
- 20 Associate Provost ... Dr. Jan P. LEWIS
- 08 Assoc Provost for Information Tech ... Vacant
- 27 Exec Dir University Communications ... Mr. Greg W. BREWIS
- 42 University Pastor ... Rev. Dennis G. SEPPER
- 42 University Pastor ... Rev. Nancy J. CONNOR
- 57 Dean School of Arts & Communication ... Dr. Cameron D. BENNETT
- 50 Dean of School of Business ... Dr. James L. BROCK
- 53 Dean School of Educ/Movement Study ... Dr. Frank M. KLINE
- 66 Dean School of Nursing ... Dr. Terry W. MILLER
- 79 Dean of Humanities ... Dr. James M. ALBRECHT
- 88 Dean of Natural Sciences ... Dr. Matthew J. SMITH
- 83 Dean of Social Sciences ... Dr. David R. HUELSBECK
- 88 Dean of Student Academic Success ... Dr. Patricia E. ROUNDY
- 35 Dean Stdnt Dev/Dir of Stdnt Involve ... Dr. Eva R. JOHNSON
- 58 Assoc Dean Grad & Special Programs ... Dr. Laura J. POLCYN
- 88 Acting Exec Dir Wang Ctr Intl Pgm ... Dr. Tamara R. WILLIAMS
- 41 Athletic Director ... Ms. Laurie L. TURNER
- 06 Registrar ... Ms. Kristin H. PLAEHN
- 39 Asst Dean of Stdnts/Dir of Res Life ... Mr. Tom A. HUELSBECK
- 18 Director Facilities Management ... Mr. David L. KOHLER
- 29 Exec Dir Constituent Relations ... Ms. Lauralee HAGEN
- 19 Director of Campus Safety & Info ... Mr. Greg V. PREMO
- 36 Exec Dir of Career Connections ... Ms. Bobbi R. HUGHES
- 23 Director of Health & Counseling Ctr ... Dr. Matt FREEMAN
- 15 Director of Human Resource Services ... Ms. Teri P. PHILLIPS
- 90 Dir of Enterprise Systems ... Mr. David P. ALLEN
- 37 Director of Student Financial Aid ... Ms. Kay W. SOLTIS
- 40 Manager of Bookstore ... Ms. Amanda B. HAMILTON
- 09 Systems and Data Analyst ... Ms. Deirdre E. MCGOLDRICK

Pacific Northwest University of Health Sciences (F)

111 University Parkway, Suite 202, Yakima WA 98901

County: Yakima FICE Identification: 041305
Unit ID: 455406
Telephone: (509) 452-5100 Carnegie Class: Assoc/PrivNFP4
FAX Number: (509) 452-5101 Calendar System: Semester
URL: www.pnwu.edu
Established: 2005 Annual Graduate Tuition & Fees: $46,700
Enrollment: 294 Coed
Affiliation or Control: Independent Non-Profit IRS Status: 501(c)3
Highest Offering: Doctorate; No Undergraduates
Program: Professional
Accreditation: @OSTEO

- 01 President ... Dr. Keith WATSON
- 05 Chief Academic Officer ... Dr. Robert E. SUTTON
- 10 Chief Financial Officer ... Ms. Ann O'BRIEN
- 11 Interim Chief Business Officer ... Mr. Keith RIFFE
- 30 Chief Advancement Officer ... Vacant
- 88 Dean Col of Osteopathic Medicine ... Dr. Robyn PHILLIPS-MADSON

Peninsula College (G)

1502 East Lauridsen Boulevard, Port Angeles WA 98362-6698

County: Clallam FICE Identification: 003786
Unit ID: 236258
Telephone: (360) 452-9277 Carnegie Class: Assoc/Pub4
FAX Number: (360) 457-8100 Calendar System: Quarter
URL: www.pc.ctc.edu
Established: 1961 Annual Undergrad Tuition & Fees (In-District): $3,678
Enrollment: 2,733 Coed
Affiliation or Control: State/Local IRS Status: 501(c)3
Highest Offering: Baccalaureate
Program: Occupational; 2-Year Principally Bachelor's Creditable
Accreditation: NW, ADNUR

- 01 President ... Dr. Luke ROBINS
- 05 Vice President Instruction ... Dr. Mary O'NEIL-GARRETT
- 11 Vice President Administrative Svcs ... Ms. Deborah FRAZIER
- 32 Vice President Student Services ... Mr. Jack HULS
- 45 VP Institutional Effectiveness ... Dr. Paula DOHERTY
- 50 Exec Dir Cmty/Business Education ... Mr. Bob LAWRENCE-MARKARIAN
- 55 Dean Adult Basic Education ... Dr. Evelyn SHORT
- 35 Dean of Student Services ... Ms. Maria PENA
- 13 Director Information Technology ... Mr. Steven BAXTER
- 37 Director Financial Aid ... Ms. Krista FRANCIS
- 04 Executive Asst to the President ... Ms. Tina HERSCHELMAN
- 27 Public Information Officer ... Ms. Phyllis L. VAN HOLLAND
- 15 Director Human Resources ... Ms. Bonnie H. CAUFFMAN
- 85 Director of International Programs ... Ms. Nicole A. CASARES
- 102 Exec Director of the Foundation ... Ms. Mary HUNCHBERGER
- 41 Director Athletics/Student Programs ... Mr. Rick ROSS
- 09 Director of Institutional Research ... Vacant
- 18 Physical Plant Director ... Mr. Rick CROOT
- 40 Bookstore Manager ... Mrs. Patty MCCRAY-ROBERTS
- 06 Enrollment Services Manager ... Ms. Cindy LAUDERBACK

Pierce College District (H)

9401 Farwest Drive SW, Lakewood WA 98498-1999

County: Pierce FICE Identification: 005000
Unit ID: 235237
Telephone: (253) 964-6500 Carnegie Class: Assoc/Pub-S-MC
FAX Number: N/A Calendar System: Quarter
URL: www.pierce.ctc.edu
Established: 1967 Annual Undergrad Tuition & Fees (In-State): $3,826
Enrollment: 12,681 Coed
Affiliation or Control: State IRS Status: 501(c)3
Highest Offering: Associate Degree
Program: Occupational; 2-Year Principally Bachelor's Creditable
Accreditation: NW, ADNUR, DH

- 01 District Chancellor ... Dr. Michele JOHNSON
- 12 President Pierce College Puyallup ... Ms. Colette P. BURNETTE
- 12 President Fort Steilacoom ... Ms. Denise YOCHUM
- 05 Vice Pres Learning Stdnt Success-PY ... Dr. Carol GREEN
- 05 Vice Pres Learning/Stdnt Success-FS ... Ms. Debra GILCHRIST
- 10 Vice Pres Administrative Services ... Ms. Joann WISZMANN
- 30 Vice President of Advancement ... Ms. Suzy AMES
- 15 Vice President for Human Resources ... Ms. Jan BUCHOLZ
- 13 Dean of Institutional Technology ... Mr. Mike STOCKE
- 06 Registrar/Dir Enrollment Svcs-Dist ... Ms. Anne WHITE
- 08 Dean Libraries & Learning Resources ... Ms. Christie FLYNN
- 26 Dir Marketing and Communications ... Mr. Brian BENEDETTI
- 36 Dir Student Development-District ... Ms. Agnes STEWARD
- 35 Dir Student Programs-Ft Steilacoom ... Mr. Cameron COX
- 41 Director of Athletics ... Mr. Duncan STEVENSON
- 18 Director of Facilities & Const Mgt ... Mr. Jim TAYLOR
- 32 Dir of Student Life-Puyallup ... Vacant
- 85 Director of International Education ... Vacant
- 19 District Manager Campus Safety ... Mr. Chris MACKERSIE
- 21 Director of Budget and Finance ... Mr. Bill VON HASSELN
- 37 Interim Director Financial Aid ... Ms. Anne WHITE
- 84 Director Enrollment Services-Puy ... Ms. Els DEMING
- 09 Institutional Researcher ... Ms. Kris CUMMINGS
- 49 District Dean Arts & Humanities ... Dr. Holly SMITH
- 88 District Dean Transitional Ed ... Ms. Lori GRIFFIN
- 76 District Dean Tech/Allied Health ... Mr. Ronald MAY
- 88 District Dean Natural Sciences ... Mr. Thomas BROXSON
- 83 District Dean Social Sciences ... Mr. Greg BRAZELL
- 29 Alumni Relations Manager ... Ms. Paula HENSON-WILLIAMS
- 96 Procurement Officer ... Mr. Curtis LEE

Pima Medical Institute-Seattle (I)

9709 3rd Avenue NE, Suite 400, Seattle WA 98115-2052

County: King Identification: 666172
Unit ID: 368629
Telephone: (206) 322-6100 Carnegie Class: Assoc/PrivFP
FAX Number: (206) 324-1985 Calendar System: Other
URL: www.pmi.edu
Established: 1989 Annual Undergrad Tuition & Fees: N/A
Enrollment: 590 Coed
Affiliation or Control: Proprietary IRS Status: Proprietary
Highest Offering: Associate Degree
Program: Occupational; 2-Year Principally Bachelor's Creditable
Accreditation: ABHES, DH, OTA, PTAA, RAD

- 01 Director ... Mr. Carey HOCHMAN

Renton Technical College (A)

3000 NE Fourth Street, Renton WA 98056-4123

County: King　FICE Identification: 010434
Unit ID: 236382
Telephone: (425) 235-2352　Carnegie Class: Assoc/Pub-S-SC
FAX Number: (425) 235-7832　Calendar System: Quarter
URL: www.rtc.edu
Established: 1942　Annual Undergrad Tuition & Fees (In-State): $6,093
Enrollment: 5,785　Coed
Affiliation or Control: State　IRS Status: 501(c)3
Highest Offering: Associate Degree
Program: Occupational; Technical Emphasis
Accreditation: **NW**, ACFEI, DA, MAC, SURGT

01	President	Mr. Steven J. HANSON
10	VP Finance/Administration	Ms. Melinda M. MERRELL
05	Vice President Instruction	Mr. Martin R. HEILSTEDT
32	Vice President Student Services	Mr. Dave PELKEY
97	Dean Basic Studies	Ms. Jodi NOVOTNY
76	Dean Allied Health	Ms. Heather M. STEPHEN-SELBY
72	Dean Apprentice/Trade & Industry	Ms. Gay KIESLING
50	Dean Bus/Educ/Hum Svcs/Gen Educ	Ms. Peggy MOE
72	Dean Automotive/Tech/Distance Educ	Mr. Dante J. LEON
102	College Rels/Foundation Director	Ms. Susanna WILLIAMS
13	Director Technology	Ms. Mary Kay WEGNER
07	Director Admissions/Registration	Ms. Becky RIVERMAN
46	Director Research/Development	Mr. Chris JOHNSON
08	Director Library	Mr. Eric E. PALO
21	Director Financial Services	Mr. Mark JOHNSON
15	Director Human Resources Develop	Ms. Lisa HAYWARD
37	Director Financial Aid	Ms. Debbie SOLOMON
18	Director Plant Operations	Mr. Barry A. BAKER
40	Bookstore Manager	Mr. Jose A. PERDOMO
19	Safety & Security Manager	Mr. Brian GROSSMAN
103	Director Workforce Development	Ms. Maggi SUTTHOFF
88	Associate Dean Culinary Arts	Mr. Doug MEDBURY

Saint Martin's University (B)

5000 Abbey Way, SE, Lacey WA 98503-7500

County: Thurston　FICE Identification: 003794
Unit ID: 236452
Telephone: (360) 491-4700　Carnegie Class: Master's S
FAX Number: (360) 459-4124　Calendar System: Semester
URL: www.stmartin.edu
Established: 1895　Annual Undergrad Tuition & Fees: $27,897
Enrollment: 1,800　Coed
Affiliation or Control: Roman Catholic　IRS Status: 501(c)3
Highest Offering: Master's
Program: Liberal Arts And General; Teacher Preparatory; Professional
Accreditation: **NW**, ENG, TEAC

00	Chancellor	Abbot Neal G. ROTH, OSB
01	President	Dr. Roy F. HEYNDERICKX
05	Provost & Vice President	Dr. Joseph D. BESSIE
10	Vice President of Finance	Ms. Susan D. HELTSLEY
30	Vice Pres Inst Advancement	Ms. Rosanne NICHOLS
85	Vice Pres Intl Programs/Development	Ms. Josephine YUNG
26	VP of Marketing/Communications	Ms. Jennifer FELLINGER
32	Dean Student Services	Ms. Melanie RICHARDSON
84	Dean Enrollment Management	Vacant
07	Dean Admission/Stdnt Financial Svcs	Mr. Scott SCHULZ
21	Treasurer	Fr. Bede CLASSICK
37	Financial Aid Director	Ms. Shelle RIEHL
29	Director Alumni Relations	Vacant
06	Registrar	Ms. Mary Conley LAW
13	Dir Integrated Technology Systems	Dr. Michael EXTINE
18	Director Facilities Management	Mr. Alan TYLER
44	Dir of Development/Planned Giving	Ms. Katie WOJKE
36	Director of Career Placement	Ms. Ann ADAMS
41	Athletic Director	Mr. Bob GRISHAM
49	Dean Col of Arts & Sciences	Dr. Eric APFELSTADT
81	Dean of Science & Math	Dr. Katherine PORTER
83	Dean of Social Sciences	Dr. Rex CASILLAS
53	Dean of Education	Dr. Joyce WESTGARD
50	Dean of Business	Dr. Richard BEER
54	Dean of Engineering	Dr. Zella KAHN-JETTER
56	Director Extension Programs	Mr. Cruz ARROYO
08	Library Director	Mr. Scot HARRISON
42	Director Campus Ministry	Ms. Susan LEYSTER
39	Director of Housing/Residence Life	Mr. Tim MCCLAIN
38	Director Counseling Center	Ms. Jan BERNEY
09	Director Institutional Grants/Rsrch	Vacant
15	Director of Human Resources	Ms. Cynthia JOHNSON
89	Director of Freshmen Studies	Dr. Sharon TAYLOR
104	Dir International Programs/Dev	Ms. Marie BOISVERT
40	Manager Bookstore	Mr. Mark MORRIS

*Seattle Community Colleges (C)

1500 Harvard Avenue, Seattle WA 98122-3803

County: King　FICE Identification: 010106
Unit ID: 236498
Telephone: (206) 934-4100　Carnegie Class: N/A
FAX Number: (206) 934-3883
URL: www.seattlecolleges.edu

01	Chancellor	Dr. Jill WAKEFIELD
05	VC Educ/Plng/e-Lrng/Workforce Educ	Dr. Carin S. WEISS
10	Vice Chanc for Finance & Technology	Dr. Kurt BUTTLEMAN
15	Chief Human Resources Officer	Mr. Charles E. SIMS
26	Public Information Officer	Ms. Patricia PAQUETTE
30	Interim Exec Dir for Advancement	Ms. Evelyn YENSON
12	President South Seattle Cmty Col	Mr. Gary OERTLI
12	President North Seattle Cmty Col	Mr. Mark MITSUI
12	President Seattle Central Cmty Col	Dr. Paul KILLPATRICK

*North Seattle Community College (D)

9600 College Way N, Seattle WA 98103-3599

County: King　FICE Identification: 009704
Unit ID: 236072
Telephone: (206) 934-3600　Carnegie Class: Assoc/Pub-U-MC
FAX Number: (206) 934-3606　Calendar System: Quarter
URL: www.northseattle.edu
Established: 1970　Annual Undergrad Tuition & Fees (In-State): $3,984
Enrollment: 6,303　Coed
Affiliation or Control: State　IRS Status: 170(c)1
Highest Offering: Associate Degree
Program: Occupational; 2-Year Principally Bachelor's Creditable
Accreditation: **NW**, ADNUR, MAC

02	President	Mr. Mark MITSUI
05	Vice President for Instruction	Dr. Mary Ellen O'KEEFFE
32	Int Vice Pres Student Development	Ms. Marci MYER
11	Vice President Admin Services	Dr. Monty MONTERECY
36	Exec Dean Career/Workforce Educ	Mr. Steve MILLER
79	Dean Art/Humanities/Social Sciences	Dr. Alison STEVENS
81	Dean Math & Science	Mr. Peter LORTZ
17	Dean Health & Human Services	Dr. Robert FINEMAN
50	Dean Business/Eng Info Tech	Ms. Terry COX
08	Dean Library & Media Services	Ms. Sharon SIMES
35	Assoc Dean Student Develop Svcs	Ms. Alice MELLING
88	Assoc Dean Basic/Transitional Stds	Ms. Kim CHAPMAN
56	Assoc Dean e-Learning	Dr. Tom BRAZIUNAS
30	Director of Development	Ms. Anne ZACOVIC
26	Int Dir Public Relations/Marketing	Ms. Katherine MORSE
84	Assoc Dean Enrollment/Registrar	Ms. Betsy ABTS
51	Director Continuing Education	Ms. Heidi STUBER
37	Int Director Financial Aid Services	Ms. Bridget DORAN
35	Director Student Programs	Mr. Jeffrey VASQUEZ
103	Director Workforce Education	Mr. John BOWERS
09	Dir Institutional Effectiveness	Dr. Jack BAUTSCH
104	Director International Programs	Ms. Mari ACOB-NASH
15	Director Personnel Services	Mr. David BITTENBENDER
18	Mgr Facilities Planning/Operations	Mr. Bruce KIESER
38	Lead Counselor	Dr. Lydia MINATOYA
45	Director Strategic Initiatives	Mr. Gary GORLAND

*Seattle Central Community College (E)

1701 Broadway, Seattle WA 98122-2400

County: King　FICE Identification: 003787
Unit ID: 236513
Telephone: (206) 587-3800　Carnegie Class: Assoc/Pub-U-MC
FAX Number: (206) 344-4390　Calendar System: Quarter
URL: seattlecentral.edu
Established: 1966　Annual Undergrad Tuition & Fees (In-State): $3,542
Enrollment: 9,606　Coed
Affiliation or Control: State　IRS Status: 170(c)1
Highest Offering: Baccalaureate
Program: Occupational; 2-Year Principally Bachelor's Creditable
Accreditation: **NW**, ACFEI, ADNUR, DH, OPD, SURGT

02	President	Dr. Paul KILLPATRICK
05	Vice Pres of Instruction & Student	Dr. Warren BROWN
11	Vice Pres Administrative Services	Mr. Michael PHAM
103	Exec Dean Workforce Education	Mr. Al GRISWOLD
09	Exec Dir Strategic Initiatives & IR	Dr. Cherisa YARKIN
35	Dean of Student Resources & Support	Ms. Brigid MCDEVITT
37	Director of Financial Aid	Ms. Noel MCBRIDE
102	Executive Director Foundation	Mr. Adam NANCE
27	Interim Director of Communications	Ms. Janet GRIMLEY
08	Exec Dean Instructional Resources	Dr. Wai-Fong LEE
49	Dean Basic Studies	Ms. Laura DIZAZZO
50	Dean Business IT & Creative Arts	Ms. Jody LAFLEN
76	Dean of Allied Health	Mr. David GOURD
81	Dean Science & Mathematics	Dr. Wendy ROCKHILL
83	Dean Humanities/Social Sciences	Dr. Kenneth LAWSON
88	Dean International Education	Dr. Andrea INSLEY
35	Dean Student Life & Engagement	Ms. Lexie EVANS
12	Assoc Dean Seattle Culinary Academy	Ms. Linda CHAUNCEY
13	Assoc Dean Information Technology	Ms. Harriet WASSERMAN
88	Director Facilities & Capital Proj	Vacant
12	Asst Dean Seattle Maritime Academy	Dr. Carl ELLIS
51	Director Cmty Educ/Evening Pgm	Mr. Jeff WEST
06	Assoc Dean Enrollment/Registrar	Ms. Diane COLEMAN
19	Director Security/Safety	Mr. Elman MCCLAIN
18	Director Facilities	Mr. Chuck DAVIS

*South Seattle Community College (F)

6000 16th Avenue, SW, Seattle WA 98106-1499

County: King　FICE Identification: 009706
Unit ID: 236504
Telephone: (206) 934-5300　Carnegie Class: Assoc/Pub4
FAX Number: (206) 934-5393　Calendar System: Quarter
URL: www.southseattle.edu
Established: 1969　Annual Undergrad Tuition & Fees (In-State): $4,267
Enrollment: 8,108　Coed
Affiliation or Control: State　IRS Status: 501(c)3
Highest Offering: Baccalaureate
Program: Occupational; 2-Year Principally Bachelor's Creditable
Accreditation: **NW**

02	President	Mr. Gary L. OERTLI
05	Vice Pres Instruction	Ms. Donna MILLER-PARKER
11	Vice Pres Administrative Services	Dr. Frank ASHBY
32	Vice President Student Services	Dr. Rosie RIMANDO-CHAREUNSAP
45	Dean Instructional Resources	Ms. Mary Jo WHITE
75	Executive Dean Technical Education	Dr. Malcom P. GROTHE
88	Exec Dn Apprenticeshp/Special Trng	Ms. Holly MOORE
97	Int Dean Basic & Transitional Stds	Ms. Dorrienne CHINN
20	Dean of Academic Programs	Dr. Chad E. HICKOX
35	Dean Student Life	Ms. Cessa HEARD-JOHNSON
88	Dean Hosp & Service Occupations	Mr. Robert GLATT
88	Dean Transportation	Mr. Bennett C. TAVES
84	Associate Dean Enrollment Services	Mr. Greg DEMPSEY
72	Assoc Dean of Technical Education	Ms. Kim ALEXANDER
20	Assoc Dean Academic Programs	Ms. Laura KINGSTON
51	Director Continuing Education	Ms. Luisa MOTTEN
103	Dir Worksource Dev/Employment Svcs	Mr. Duncan BURGESS
37	Dir Student Financial Assistance	Ms. Patricia L. BILLINGS
27	Director Communications	Ms. Candace OEHLER
15	Director Employee Services	Ms. Kathryn A. VEDVICK
108	Dir of Planning/Research/Assessment	Ms. Marsha D. BROWN
13	Director Computer Services	Vacant
18	Dir Facilities & Plant Operations	Mr. Steve MORGAN
30	Exec Dir Foundation/College Advance	Ms. Elizabeth A. PLUHTA
28	Director of Diversity & Retention	Mr. Ricardo LEYVA-PUEBLA
19	Manager Safety/Security	Mr. James E. LEWIS
40	Manager Bookstore	Ms. Amber MERCER

Seattle Institute of Oriental Medicine (G)

444 Ravenna Boulevard, Suite 101, Seattle WA 98115

County: King　FICE Identification: 032803
Unit ID: 439914
Telephone: (206) 517-4541　Carnegie Class: Spec/Health
FAX Number: N/A　Calendar System: Trimester
URL: www.siom.edu
Established: 1994　Annual Undergrad Tuition & Fees: $19,635
Enrollment: 41　Coed
Affiliation or Control: Proprietary　IRS Status: Proprietary
Highest Offering: Master's; No Lower Division
Program: Professional
Accreditation: **ACUP**

01	President	Dr. Paul KARSTEN
05	Academic Dean	Mr. Craig MITCHELL
23	Clinic Manager	Ms. Grace MCNAMARA

Seattle Pacific University (H)

3307 Third Avenue W, Seattle WA 98119-1997

County: King　FICE Identification: 003788
Unit ID: 236577
Telephone: (206) 281-2111　Carnegie Class: Master's L
FAX Number: (206) 281-2115　Calendar System: Quarter
URL: www.spu.edu
Established: 1891　Annual Undergrad Tuition & Fees: $32,067
Enrollment: 4,167　Coed
Affiliation or Control: Free Methodist　IRS Status: 501(c)3
Highest Offering: Doctorate
Program: Liberal Arts And General; Teacher Preparatory; Professional
Accreditation: **NW**, BUS, CLPSY, DIETD, ENG, MFCD, MUS, NURSE, TED

01	President	Dr. Daniel J. MARTIN
05	Vice President for Academic Affairs	Vacant
11	VP Administration/Univ Relations	Mrs. Marjorie R. JOHNSON
10	Vice Pres for Business & Planning	Mr. Donald W. MORTENSON
30	Vice President for Univ Advancement	Mr. Thomas W. BOX
20	Asc VP Acad Affs/Curriculum Assess	Dr. Cynthia J. PRICE
13	Assoc VP Information/Data Mgmt	Ms. Janet L. WARD
32	Vice Pres for Student Life	Dr. Jeffrey C. JORDAN
21	Assoc VP for Business & Finance	Mr. Craig G. KISPERT
13	Asst VP of Technology Services	Mr. David W. TINDALL
18	Asst VP for Facility Management	Mr. David B. CHURCH
44	Assistant Vice President Endowment	Mr. Gordon A. NYGARD
50	Dean School of Business & Economics	Mr. Jeffrey B. VAN DUZER
53	Dean School of Education	Dr. Rick EIGENBROOD
66	Dean School of Health Sciences	Dr. Lorie WILD
49	Dean College of Arts & Sciences	Dr. Bruce D. CONGDON
88	Dean School of Psych/Fam & Cmty	Dr. Michael D. ROE
73	Dean School of Theology	Dr. Douglas M. STRONG
15	Director of Human Resources	Mr. Gary E. WOMELSDUFF
36	Director Career Development Center	Dr. Jacqui S. SMITH-BATES
08	University Librarian	Mr. Michael PAULUS
38	Director Student Counseling Center	Dr. Steven A. MAYBELL
07	Director Undergraduate Admissions	Mr. Jobe S. KORB-NICE
07	Dir Graduate Admissions/Marketing	Dr. John L. GLANCY
06	University Registrar	Mrs. Ruth L. ADAMS
27	Director University Communications	Mrs. Jennifer J. GILNETT
37	Director Student Financial Services	Mr. Jordan L. GRANT
27	News & Media Relations Manager	Mrs. Tracy C. NORLEN
45	Assoc Director Projects & Planning	Mr. Wayne H. ELLING
31	Director of University Services	Mr. Murray J. LAWSON
19	Director of Safety & Security	Mr. Mark REID
44	Director of Annual Giving	Mr. Dean O. CARRELL
29	Director of Alumni Relations	Mr. Kenneth E. CORNELL
41	Director of Athletics	Ms. Erin E. O'CONNELL

42 Dir Univ Ministry/Ctr for Worship ....Dr. Stephen M. NEWBY
28 Director of the John Perkins Center ....Mr. Tali HAIRSTON
35 Director Student Programs ....Mr. Dale N. ANDERSON

The Seattle School of Theology and Psychology (A)

2501 Elliot Avenue, Seattle WA 98121-1177
County: King FICE Identification: 034664
Unit ID: 441131
Telephone: (206) 876-6100 Carnegie Class: Spec/Health
FAX Number: (206) 876-6195 Calendar System: Trimester
URL: www.theseattleschool.edu
Established: 2001 Annual Graduate Tuition & Fees: $14,654
Enrollment: 264 Coed
Affiliation or Control: Independent Non-Profit IRS Status: 501(c)3
Highest Offering: Master's; No Undergraduates
Program: Religious Emphasis
Accreditation: @THEOL, TRACS

01 President ....Dr. Keith R. ANDERSON
04 Assistant to the President ....Vacant
05 Sr Vice Pres Academic Affs/CAO ....Dr. J. Derek MCNEIL
10 Chief Financial Officer ....Mr. Phil BISHOP
20 Assistant Academic Dean ....Dr. Stephanie NEIL
08 Dir Library Svcs/Inst Assessment ....Ms. Cheryl GOODWIN
06 Dir Academic Services/Registrar ....Ms. Kristen HOUSTON
07 Director of Recruitment ....Ms. Nicole GREENWALD
13 Director Computer & Info Services ....Mr. Jason BEST
15 Human Resources ....Mrs. Amy WILSON
18 Facilities Manager ....Ms. Kartha HEINZ

Seattle University (B)

901 12th Avenue, Seattle WA 98122-1090
County: King FICE Identification: 003790
Unit ID: 236595
Telephone: (206) 296-6000 Carnegie Class: Master's L
FAX Number: N/A Calendar System: Quarter
URL: www.seattleu.edu
Established: 1891 Annual Undergrad Tuition & Fees: $34,200
Enrollment: 7,755 Coed
Affiliation or Control: Roman Catholic IRS Status: 501(c)3
Highest Offering: Doctorate
Program: Liberal Arts And General; Teacher Preparatory; Professional
Accreditation: NW, BUS, CACREP, DMS, ENG, LAW, @MIDWF, NURSE, SPAA, SW, TED, THEOL

01 President ....Rev. Stephen V. SUNDBORG, SJ
05 Provost ....Dr. Isiaah CRAWFORD
03 Executive Vice President ....Dr. Tim LEARY
43 Vice Pres and University Counsel ....Ms. Mary S. PETERSEN
10 Vice President Finance ....Mr. Connie KANTER
30 Vice Pres University Advancement ....Ms. Mary Kay MCFADDEN
32 Vice President Student Development ....Dr. Jacob DIAZ
88 Vice President Mission & Ministry ....Rev. Peter ELY, SJ
45 Vice President University Planning ....Dr. Robert DULLEA
84 Vice President for Enrollment Svcs ....Ms. Marilyn CRONE
15 Vice President Human Resources ....Mr. Gerald HUFFMAN
49 Dean of Arts & Sciences ....Dr. David POWERS
50 Dean of Business & Economics ....Dr. Joseph M. PHILLIPS
53 Dean of Education ....Dr. Sue A. SCHMITT
66 Dean of Nursing ....Dr. Azita EMAMI
54 Dean of Science & Engineering ....Dr. Michael QUINN
79 Dean Matteo Ricci College ....Dr. Jodi OLSEN KELLY
61 Dean of Law ....Mr. Mark NILES
73 Dean of Theology & Ministry ....Dr. Mark MARKULY
08 University Librarian ....Mr. John P. POPKO
20 Assoc Provost Academic Affairs ....Dr. Jacquelyn MILLER
20 Assoc Provost Academic Affairs ....Dr. Charles LAWRENCE
27 Chief Information Officer/AVP ....Mr. Charles PORTER
26 Asst VP/Director Public Relations ....Vacant
21 Assoc VP Finance & Business ....Mr. James I. ADOLPHSON
18 Assoc VP Facilities Administration ....Mr. Robert SCHWARTZ
13 Chief Technology Officer ....Mr. Daniel DUFFY
29 Asst VP/Sr Dir Advance Initiatives ....Ms. Carlene BUTY
44 Asst VP/Director of Development ....Ms. Sarah FINNEY
30 Assoc VP University Advancement ....Mr. Mark BURNETT
35 Assoc Vice Pres Student Development ....Dr. Michele MURRAY
35 Asst Vice Pres Student Development ....Dr. Alvin STURDIVANT
45 Asst VP for Planning ....Dr. Robert DUNIWAY
06 Registrar ....Ms. Joyce ALLEN
07 Dean of Admissions ....Ms. Melore NIELSEN
09 Director of Institutional Research ....Dr. Robert DUNIWAY
42 Director Campus Ministry ....Fr. Mike BAYARD, SJ
37 Interim Dir Student Financial Svcs ....Ms. Lindy HALL
19 Director Public Safety ....Mr. Michael L. SLETTEN
85 Director International Student Ctr ....Mr. Ryan GREENE
41 Athletic Director ....Mr. Bill HOGAN
36 Executive Director Career Services ....Ms. Bethany KREITL
38 Director Counseling Center ....Dr. Susan HAWKINS
28 Dir Multicultural Student Affairs ....Ms. Monica NIXON
96 Director of Purchasing ....Ms. Marie PETERSON
39 Assoc Dir Housing & Resid Life ....Mr. Timothy ALBERT

Shoreline Community College (C)

16101 Greenwood Avenue N, Shoreline WA 98133-5696
County: King FICE Identification: 003791
Unit ID: 236610
Telephone: (206) 546-4101 Carnegie Class: Assoc/Pub-S-SC
FAX Number: (206) 546-4630 Calendar System: Quarter
URL: www.shoreline.edu
Established: 1964 Annual Undergrad Tuition & Fees (In-State): $4,410
Enrollment: 6,868 Coed
Affiliation or Control: State IRS Status: 170(c)1
Highest Offering: Associate Degree
Program: Occupational; 2-Year Principally Bachelor's Creditable
Accreditation: NW, ADNUR, DH, MLTAD

01 President ....Mr. Lee D. LAMBERT
05 VP Academic & Student Affairs ....Mr. James JANSEN
11 Vice Pres Administrative Svcs ....Mr. Daryl J. CAMPBELL
15 VP Human Resources/Legal Affairs ....Mr. Stephen SMITH
27 Spec Asst to Pres/Public Info/Mkt ....Mr. Jim HILLS
96 Special Asst to President Budget ....Ms. Holly M. WOODMANSEE
04 Exec Asst to the President ....Ms. Lori YONEMITSU
85 Exec Dir International Programs ....Ms. Diana SAMPSON
51 Director Cntr for Bus & Cont Educ ....Mr. Dave CUNNINGHAM
72 Director Technology Support Service ......Mr. Gary KALBFLEISCH
84 Dir Recruit & Enroll Svcs/Registrar ....Mr. Ted HAASE
18 Director Facilities ....Mr. Bob ROEHL
19 Director Safety & Security ....Ms. Robin BLACKSMITH
66 Program Director Nursing ....Ms. Lynn VON SCHLIEDER
37 Director Financial Aid ....Mr. Ted HAASE
38 Dir Advis/Counsel/High School Pgm ....Dr. Yvonne L. TERRELL-POWELL
40 Director Auxiliary Services ....Ms. Mary E. KELEMEN
88 Director Essential Skills ....Mr. William SPERLING
09 Asst Director Inst Effectiveness ....Mr. Joseph DUGGAN
08 Acting Dean Library/Media/Tech ....Mr. Robert FRANCIS
35 Dean of Students ....Dr. Tonya M. DRAKE
103 Dean Workforce Education ....Mr. Dave CUNNINGHAM
31 Dean Capital Projects/Cmty Rels ....Ms. Gillian O. LEWIS
79 Dean Humanities Division ....Dr. Norma W. GOLDSTEIN
104 Actg Dean Global Stds/Trans/Honors ....Mr. Robert FRANCIS
88 Dean Student Enroll/Environ Init ....Dr. Susan H. HOYNE

Skagit Valley College (D)

2405 College Way, Mount Vernon WA 98273-5899
County: Skagit FICE Identification: 003792
Unit ID: 236638
Telephone: (360) 416-7600 Carnegie Class: Assoc/Pub-R-L
FAX Number: (360) 416-7890 Calendar System: Quarter
URL: www.skagit.edu
Established: 1926 Annual Undergrad Tuition & Fees (In-State): $4,208
Enrollment: 5,982 Coed
Affiliation or Control: State IRS Status: 501(c)3
Highest Offering: Associate Degree
Program: Occupational; 2-Year Principally Bachelor's Creditable
Accreditation: NW, ACFEI, ADNUR, MAC

01 President ....Dr. Thomas KEEGAN
05 Vice President Educational Services ....Dr. Mick DONAHUE
10 Vice Pres Administrative Services ....Ms. Mary Alice GROBINS
12 Vice President of Whidbey Campus ....Dr. Mick DONAHUE
32 Dean of Student Services ....Dr. David PAUL
13 Dean Technology/eLearning/Library ....Mr. Tom BATES
103 Dean Workforce Education ....Ms. Laura CAILLOUX
20 Dean Academic Education ....Dr. Joan YOUNGQUIST
37 Financial Aid Officer ....Mr. Steve EPPERSON
16 Exec Director of Human Resources ....Ms. Sue WILLIAMSON
18 Director of Physical Plant ....Mr. Dave SCOTT
27 Director of Public Information ....Ms. Arden AINLEY
104 Director of International Programs ....Ms. Christa SCHULZ
40 Bookstore Manager ....Ms. Kim HALL
41 Director of Athletics ....Mr. Gary KNUTZEN
09 Director of Institutional Research ....Dr. Maureen PETTITT

South Puget Sound Community College (E)

2011 Mottman Road, SW, Olympia WA 98512-6292
County: Thurston FICE Identification: 005372
Unit ID: 236656
Telephone: (360) 754-7711 Carnegie Class: Assoc/Pub-R-L
FAX Number: (360) 664-0780 Calendar System: Quarter
URL: www.spscc.ctc.edu
Established: 1962 Annual Undergrad Tuition & Fees (In-State): $4,974
Enrollment: 6,556 Coed
Affiliation or Control: State IRS Status: 501(c)3
Highest Offering: Associate Degree
Program: Occupational; 2-Year Principally Bachelor's Creditable
Accreditation: NW, ACFEI, ADNUR, DA, MAC

01 President ....Dr. Gerald PUMPHREY
04 Exec Assistant to the President ....Ms. Diana TOLEDO
05 Vice President for Instruction ....Ms. Dorna BULLPITT
32 Vice President for Student Services ....Dr. Rhonda COATS
11 Vice Pres Administrative Services ....Ms. Nancy MCKINNEY
07 Dean of Enrollment Svcs/Registrar ....Ms. Kathy RHODES
18 Dean of Facilities Planning & Opers ....Ms. Penny KOAL
26 Dean of College Relations ....Ms. Kellie BRASETH
35 Dean of Student Life ....Dr. Dave RECTOR
37 Dean of Student Financial Services ....Ms. Carla IDOHL-CORWIN
16 Chief Human Resources Officer ....Ms. Sheila EMERY
30 Exec Director College Foundation ....Ms. Cecelia LOVELESS
28 Director of Diversity & Equity ....Ms. Eileen YOSHINA
09 Director of Institutional Research ....Ms. Jennifer TUIA
10 Chief Business Officer ....Ms. Nancy MCKINNEY
06 Registrar ....Ms. Kathy RHODES
08 Dir of Library/Media & eLearning ....Dr. Elizabeth HILL
19 Director of Security ....Mr. Lonnie HATMAN
40 Director of Auxiliary Services ....Mr. Bryce WINKELMAN
27 Chief Information Officer ....Mr. Bob BILLINGS
72 Dean of Applied Technology ....Dr. Brent CHAPMAN
45 Dean of Instruc Planning & Develop ....Ms. Lorna PATTERSON
76 Dean of Natural & Applied Sciences ....Dr. Allen MASON
79 Dean of Humanities/Communications ....Ms. Mary SOLTMAN
83 Dean of Social Sciences & Business ....Dr. Debbie TEED

Tacoma Community College (F)

6501 S 19th Street, Tacoma WA 98466-6100
County: Pierce FICE Identification: 003796
Unit ID: 236753
Telephone: (253) 566-5000 Carnegie Class: Assoc/Pub-U-MC
FAX Number: (253) 566-5169 Calendar System: Quarter
URL: www.tacomacc.edu
Established: 1965 Annual Undergrad Tuition & Fees (In-State): $3,717
Enrollment: 8,797 Coed
Affiliation or Control: State IRS Status: 501(c)3
Highest Offering: Associate Degree
Program: Occupational; 2-Year Principally Bachelor's Creditable
Accreditation: NW, ADNUR, DMS, EMT, RAD

01 President ....Dr. Pamela TRANSUE
05 Vice Pres Academic/Student Affairs ....Dr. Timothy STOKES
11 Vice Pres Administrative Services ....Ms. Silvia BARAJAS
32 Vice Pres Student Services ....Ms. Mary CHIKWINYA
20 Dean for Academic Services ....Mr. Charlie CRAWFORD
88 Director K-12 Ptnshps/Stdnt Conduct ....Ms. Dolores HAUGEN
07 Dean for Entry & Enrollment Svcs ....Mr. Steve ASHPOLE
88 Director of Advising ....Ms. Terri JONES
108 Dir Inst Effective/Instr Assessment ....Mr. Scott MARSH
18 Director Facilities/CapitalProjects ....Mr. Clint STEELE
35 Director of Student Life ....Ms. Jen MANLEY
37 Director Student Financial Aid ....Ms. Kim MATISON

Trinity Lutheran College (G)

2802 Wetmore Avenue, Everett WA 98201
County: Snohomish FICE Identification: 021067
Unit ID: 235769
Telephone: (425) 249-4800 Carnegie Class: Bac/Diverse
FAX Number: (425) 249-4801 Calendar System: 4/1/4
URL: www.tlc.edu
Established: 1944 Annual Undergrad Tuition & Fees: $23,400
Enrollment: 160 Coed
Affiliation or Control: Independent Non-Profit IRS Status: 501(c)3
Highest Offering: Baccalaureate
Program: Liberal Arts And General; Religious Emphasis
Accreditation: NW

01 President ....Mr. John REED
05 Interim Academic Dean ....Dr. Tom JOHNSON
10 Vice President Finance ....Mr. Tom RAMSEY
32 Dean of Students ....Ms. Andrea IDE
30 Associate Director of Development ....Mr. Lance GEORGESON
06 Registrar ....Sir Charles NELSON
08 Director of Educ Tech & Library ....Mr. Seong Heon LEE
37 Director of Financial Aid ....Ms. Shanna PYZER
29 Alumni Relations Coordinator ....Ms. Linda KENT
31 Campus Pastor ....Mr. Erik SAMUELSON
13 IT Administrator ....Mr. Seong Heon LEE
21 Accounting Manager ....Mrs. Miwa EASTON

University of Puget Sound (H)

1500 N Warner St., Tacoma WA 98416-0002
County: Pierce FICE Identification: 003797
Unit ID: 236328
Telephone: (253) 879-3100 Carnegie Class: Bac/A&S
FAX Number: (253) 879-3500 Calendar System: Semester
URL: www.pugetsound.edu
Established: 1888 Annual Undergrad Tuition & Fees: $40,250
Enrollment: 2,938 Coed
Affiliation or Control: Independent Non-Profit IRS Status: 501(c)3
Highest Offering: Doctorate
Program: Liberal Arts And General; Teacher Preparatory; Professional
Accreditation: NW, MUS, OT, PTA

01 President ....Dr. Ronald R. THOMAS
101 Board Secy/Dir Ofc of President ....Ms. Mary Elizabeth COLLINS
05 Academic VP/Dean of University ....Dr. Kristine M. BARTANEN
10 Vice Pres Finance & Admin ....Ms. Sherry B. MONDOU
26 Vice President University Relations ....Mr. David BEERS
84 Vice President for Enrollment ....Dr. George H. MILLS
32 VP Student Affairs/Dean of Students ....Mr. Mike SEGAWA
21 Assoc VP Accounting/Budget Svcs ....Ms. Janet S. HALLMAN
15 Assoc Vice Pres Human Resources ....Ms. Cindy MATERN
21 Assoc Vice Pres Business Services ....Mr. John M. HICKEY
18 Assoc Vice Pres Facilities Services ....Mr. Bob KIEF
37 Assoc VP for Student Financial Svcs .....Ms. Maggie A. MITTUCH
26 Executive Dir of Communications ....Ms. Gayle MCINTOSH
13 Chief Technology Officer ....Mr. William MORSE
20 Associate Academic Dean ....Dr. Martin JACKSON
20 Associate Academic Dean ....Dr. Sarah MOORE
20 Associate Academic Dean ....Dr. Lisa L. FERRARI
06 Registrar ....Mr. Brad TOMHAVE
08 Library Director ....Ms. Jane CARLIN
41 Director of Athletics ....Ms. Amy E. HACKETT
29 Director Alumni & Parent Relations ....Ms. Allison CANNADY-SMITH
85 Director International Programs ....Mr. Roy ROBINSON

53 Dean School of Education .... Dr. John WOODWARD
50 Dir School of Business/Leadership .... Dr. Alva BUTCHER
64 Director of School of Music .... Dr. Keith C. WARD
88 Director of Occupational Therapy .... Dr. George TOMLIN
88 Director of Physical Therapy .... Dr. Jennifer D. HASTINGS
09 Dir Inst Research & Retention .... Ms. C. Ellen PETERS
28 Chief Diversity Officer .... Vacant

University of Washington (A)

Seattle WA 98195-0001
County: King FICE Identification: 003798
Unit ID: 236948
Telephone: (206) 543-2100 Carnegie Class: RU/VH
FAX Number: (206) 543-9285 Calendar System: Quarter
URL: www.washington.edu
Established: 1861 Annual Undergrad Tuition & Fees (In-State): $11,305
Enrollment: 42,446 Coed
Affiliation or Control: State IRS Status: 501(c)3
Highest Offering: Doctorate
Program: Liberal Arts And General; Teacher Preparatory; Professional
Accreditation: NW, ARCPA, AUD, BUS, BUSA, CEA, CLPSY, CONST, DENT, DIETC, EMT, ENG, FOR, HSA, IPSY, JOUR, LAW, LIB, LSAR, MED, MIDWF, MT, NURSE, OPE, OT, PDPSY, PH, PHAR, PLNG, PTA, SCPSY, SP, SPAA, SW

01 President .... Mr. Michael K. YOUNG
12 Chancellor Bothell Campus .... Dr. Kenyon S. CHAN
12 Chancellor Tacoma Campus .... Dr. Patricia SPAKES
05 Provost .... Dr. Ana Mari CAUCE
20 Vice Chanc Academic Affairs Tacoma .... Dr. James W. HARRINGTON
10 Sr Vice Pres Finance/Facilities .... Ms. V'Ella WARREN
28 VP Minority Affs/V Prov Diversity .. Dr. Sheila EDWARDS LANGE
17 Exec VP Med Affs/CEO UW Med/Dean .... Dr. Paul G. RAMSEY
30 Vice Pres for Univ Advancement .... Dr. Connie KRAVAS
15 Vice President Human Resources .... Ms. Mindy KORNBERG
13 Interim VP & Vice Prov UW Info Tech .... Ms. Kelli TROSVIG
26 Vice President for External Affairs .... Mr. Randy HODGINS
46 Vice Provost Research .... Dr. Mary E. LIDSTROM
51 V Provost UW Prof & Cont Education ... Dr. David P. SZATMARY
45 Vice Prov Planning & Budgeting .... Mr. Paul JENNY
20 Executive V Provost Acad Affs .... Mr. Douglas J. WADDEN
20 Vice Prov/Dean Undergrad Acad Affs .... Dr. Ed TAYLOR
32 VP & Vice Provost Student Life .... Mr. Eric GODFREY
88 V Provost for Academic Personnel .... Dr. Cheryl A. CAMERON
88 V Prov/UW Ctr for Commercialization .... Ms. Linden RHOADS
86 Director Federal Relations .... Ms. Christy D. GULLION
43 Division Chief Attorney General .... Mr. Gary L. IKEDA
06 University Registrar .... Ms. Virjean EDWARDS
29 Exec Dir & Assoc VP Alum Assoc .... Mr. Paul RUCKER
17 Exec Dir UW Medical Ctr Admin .... Mr. Stephen P. ZIENIEWICZ
17 Exec Dir Harborview Med Ctr .... Ms. Eileen WHALEN
37 Asst Vice Pres Student Life/Dir Fin .... Ms. S. Kay LEWIS
86 Director State Relations .... Ms. Margaret A. SHEPHERD
07 Director of Admissions .... Dr. Philip BALLINGER
09 AVP Inst Research & Data Mgmt .... Mr. Todd B. MILDON
36 Director Career Center .... Ms. Susan TERRY
13 CFO UW Information Technology .... Mr. Bill FERRIS
18 Assoc Vice Pres Facilities Services .... Mr. Charles KENNEDY
92 Director Honors Program .... Dr. James J. CLAUSS
41 Director Athletics .... Mr. Scott WOODWARD
08 Dean Libraries .... Ms. Lizabeth A. WILSON
96 Assoc Director Purchasing Services .... Mr. Mark CONLEY
58 Vice Prov/Dean Graduate School .... Dr. Gerald J. BALDASTY
49 Interim Dean Arts & Sciences .... Dr. Robert STACEY
47 Dean Col of Built Environments .... Dr. Daniel FRIEDMAN
50 Dean Business School .... Dr. Jim JIAMBALVO
54 Dean Engineering .... Dr. Matthew O'DONNELL
61 Dean Law School .... Dr. Kellye Y. TESTY
70 Dean Social Work .... Dr. Edwina UEHARA
52 Dean Dentistry .... Dr. Joel H. BERG
63 Dean Medicine .... Dr. Paul G. RAMSEY
66 Dean Nursing .... Dr. Marla SALMON
67 Dean Pharmacy .... Dr. Thomas BAILLIE
69 Dean School of Public Health .... Dr. Howard FRUMKIN
53 Dean Education .... Dr. Tom STRITIKUS
80 Dean of Public Affairs .... Dr. Sandra O. ARCHIBALD
88 Dean Information School .... Dr. Harry BRUCE
88 Dean Col of the Environment .... Dr. Lisa GRAUMLICH

Walla Walla Community College (B)

500 Tausick Way, Walla Walla WA 99362-9267
County: Walla Walla FICE Identification: 005006
Unit ID: 236887
Telephone: (509) 522-2500 Carnegie Class: Assoc/Pub-R-L
FAX Number: (509) 527-4480 Calendar System: Quarter
URL: www.wwcc.edu
Established: 1967 Annual Undergrad Tuition & Fees (In-State): $4,375
Enrollment: 4,953 Coed
Affiliation or Control: State IRS Status: 170(c)1
Highest Offering: Associate Degree
Program: Occupational; 2-Year Principally Bachelor's Creditable; Technical Emphasis
Accreditation: NW, ADNUR

01 President .... Dr. Steven L. VANAUSDLE
11 VP of Administrative Services .... Mr. James R. PETERSON
05 Vice President of Academic Educ .... Dr. Marleen RAMSEY
32 Int Vice Pres of Student Services .... Mrs. Wendy SAMITORE
10 Vice Pres of Financial Services .... Mrs. Davina K. FOGG
20 Vice Pres of Instruction-Workforce .... Dr. Mindy NELSON
76 Dean of Health Sciences Education .... Ms. Kathleen ADAMSKI
30 Director of Resource Development .... Mr. Doug BAYNE
07 Director of Admissions/Registrar .... Mr. Carlos E. DELGADILLO
38 Int Dir Student Development Center .... Ms. Kim CASSETTO
37 Financial Aid Director .... Ms. Danielle HODGEN
35 Director of Student Activities .... Dr. David D. CHASE
08 Int Director of Library Services .... Mrs. Stacy PREST
12 Director of Clarkston Campus .... Dr. Janet V. DANLEY
41 Athletic Director .... Mr. Jeffrey E. REINLAND
15 Director of Human Resources .... Mrs. Sharon M. HARTFORD
18 Director of Plant Facilities .... Vacant
106 Director of eLearning .... Mrs. Sandra K. MADSEN
88 Director of Transitional Studies .... Ms. Darlene SNIDER
51 Director of Correctional Education .... Dr. Joe A. SMALL
28 Director of Multicultural Svcs .... Vacant
40 Bookstore Manager .... Ms. Alecia ANGELL
31 Coordinator of Community Education .... Vacant
09 Director of Institutional Research .... Ms. Jamie FOUTY
27 Int Dir Marketing & Communications ...... Ms. Melissa HARRISON

Walla Walla University (C)

204 S College Avenue, College Place WA 99324-1198
County: Walla Walla FICE Identification: 003799
Unit ID: 236896
Telephone: (509) 527-2615 Carnegie Class: Master's M
FAX Number: (509) 527-2397 Calendar System: Quarter
URL: www.wallawalla.edu
Established: 1892 Annual Undergrad Tuition & Fees: $27,726
Enrollment: 1,831 Coed
Affiliation or Control: Seventh-day Adventist IRS Status: 501(c)3
Highest Offering: Master's
Program: Liberal Arts And General; Teacher Preparatory; Professional
Accreditation: NW, ACBSP, ACFEI, ENG, MUS, SW

01 Interim President .... Mr. Steve ROSE
05 Vice Pres Academic Administration .... Dr. Bob CUSHMAN
10 Vice Pres Financial Administration .... Mr. Steve ROSE
32 Vice Pres Student Life and Mission .... Vacant
30 Vice Pres University Advancement .... Ms. Patsy WAGNER
84 Vice Pres Marketing and Enrollment .... Ms. Jodi WAGNER
28 Asst to President for Diversity .... Dr. Pedrito MAYNARD-REID
04 Executive Asst Office of President .... Ms. Deirdre BENWELL
20 Associate Vice Pres Academic Admin .... Dr. Scott LIGMAN
21 Associate Vice Pres Financial Admin .... Mr. Glenn CARTER
08 Director of Libraries .... Ms. Carolyn GASKELL
06 Registrar .... Ms. Carolyn DENNEY
42 Chaplain .... Mr. Paddy MCCOY
29 Director of Alumni Relations .... Vacant
14 Director Information Services .... Mr. Scott MCFADDEN
37 Director Student Financial Services ...... Ms. Cassie RAGENOVICH
15 Director Human Resources .... Vacant
18 Director of Plant Services .... Mr. Jerry MASON
26 Director of University Relations .... Ms. Rosa JIMENEZ
33 Dean of Men .... Mr. Tom BLACKWELDER
34 Dean of Women .... Ms. Misty PUYMON
58 Dean of Graduate Programs .... Dr. Joseph GALUSHA
66 Dean of School of Nursing .... Ms. Lucille KRULL
73 Dean of School of Theology .... Dr. David THOMAS
54 Dean of School of Engineering .... Mr. Larry AAMODT
07 Director of Admissions .... Mr. Dallas WEIS
09 Director of Institutional Research .... Dr. James FISHER
36 Director Career Center .... Ms. Nelle CORNELISON
38 Director Student Counseling .... Mr. Don WALLACE

Washington State University (D)

PO Box 645910, Pullman WA 99164-5910
County: Whitman FICE Identification: 003800
Unit ID: 236939
Telephone: (509) 335-3564 Carnegie Class: RU/VH
FAX Number: N/A Calendar System: Semester
URL: www.wsu.edu
Established: 1890 Annual Undergrad Tuition & Fees (In-District): $12,300
Enrollment: 27,329 Coed
Affiliation or Control: State/Local IRS Status: 501(c)3
Highest Offering: Doctorate
Program: Liberal Arts And General; Teacher Preparatory; Professional
Accreditation: NW, BUS, BUSA, CEA, CIDA, CLPSY, CONST, COPSY, CS, DIETC, ENG, FOR, HSA, IPSY, #LSAR, MUS, NURSE, PHAR, SP, VET

01 President .... Dr. Elson S. FLOYD
05 Provost/Executive Vice President .... Dr. Warwick M. BAYLY
10 VP Business and Finance .... Mr. Roger D. PATTERSON
43 Div Chief State Attorney Gen Office ..... Ms. Sharyl KAMMERZELL
03 Assoc Executive Vice President .... Dr. Larry G. JAMES
20 Vice Provost for Faculty Affairs .... Dr. Frances MCSWEENEY
106 Exec Dir Ctr for Distance/Prof Educ .... Dr. David CILLAY
84 VP Student Affairs & Enrollment .... Mr. John FRAIRE
27 VP Information Systems & CIO .... Dr. Viji MURALI
46 VP Research/Dean Grad School .... Dr. Nancy MAGNUSON
12 Chancellor WSU Spokane .... Dr. Brian PITCHER
12 Int Chancellor WSU Tri-Cities .... Mr. James PRATT
12 Chancellor WSU Vancouver .... Dr. Mel NETZHAMMER
47 Dean Agric/Human Natl Res Sci .... Dr. Daniel BERNARDO
50 Dean Business & Economics .... Dr. Eric SPANGENBERG
53 Dean Education .... Dr. A.G RUD
54 Dean Engineering & Architecture .... Dr. Candis CLAIBORN
66 Dean Nursing .... Dr. Patricia BUTTERFIELD
67 Dean Pharmacy .... Dr. Gary POLLACK
57 Dean Liberal Arts .... Dr. Doug EPPERSON
60 Dean Communication .... Dr. Lawrence E. PINTAK
81 Dean Sciences .... Dr. Daryll DEWALD
74 Dean Veterinary Medicine .... Dr. Bryan K. SLINKER
92 Dean Honors College .... Dr. Libby WALKER
45 Assoc VP & Chief Budget Office .... Ms. Joan KING
71 Dean University College .... Dr. Mary F. WACK
08 Dean Libraries .... Mr. Joseph STARRATT
06 Registrar .... Ms. Julia POMERENK
07 Director Admissions .... Ms. Wendy PETERSON
09 Director Institutional Research .... Mr. Lap-Pun LAM
18 Assoc VP Facilities Services .... Ms. Olivia YANG
37 Director Financial Aid .... Ms. Chio FLORES
41 Director Intercollegiate Athletics .... Mr. William H. MOOS
86 Assoc VP Government Relations .... Ms. Colleen KERR
88 Director Internal Audit .... Ms. Heather LOPEZ
56 Director Extension .... Dr. Daniel BERNARDO

Wenatchee Valley College (E)

1300 Fifth Street, Wenatchee WA 98801-1799
County: Chelan FICE Identification: 003801
Unit ID: 236975
Telephone: (509) 682-6800 Carnegie Class: Assoc/Pub-R-M
FAX Number: (509) 682-6541 Calendar System: Quarter
URL: www.wvc.edu
Established: 1939 Annual Undergrad Tuition & Fees (In-State): $4,105
Enrollment: 3,406 Coed
Affiliation or Control: State IRS Status: 501(c)3
Highest Offering: Associate Degree
Program: Occupational; 2-Year Principally Bachelor's Creditable
Accreditation: NW, ADNUR, MAC, MLTAD

01 President .... Mr. James RICHARDSON
05 Vice President of Instruction .... Dr. Walt TRIBLEY
11 VP of Administrative Services .... Ms. Suzie BENSON
38 Vice President Student Development .... Vacant
49 Dean Lib Arts/Sciences/Basic Skills .... Dr. Rick UNDERBAKKE
12 Dean Omak Campus .... Vacant
103 Assoc Dean Workforce Education .... Ms. Mary WATSON
23 Assoc Dean of Allied Health & Nurs .... Ms. Jenny CAPELO
15 Director Human Resources .... Ms. Reagan BELLAMY
45 Director Institution Effectiveness .... Dr. Susan MURRAY
32 Director Student Programs/Outreach .... Mr. Kelly KETCHAM
37 Director Financial Aid .... Mr. Kevin BERG
18 Facilities & Operations Manager .... Mr. Greg RANDALL
06 Registrar .... Mr. Bruce MAXWELL
13 Director of Technology .... Vacant
10 Chief Business Officer .... Mr. Gerald TOMEK
27 Communications Manager .... Ms. Libby SIEBENS
20 Coordinator of Adult Basic Skills .... Vacant

Western Washington University (F)

516 High Street, Bellingham WA 98225-5950
County: Whatcom FICE Identification: 003802
Unit ID: 237011
Telephone: (360) 650-3000 Carnegie Class: Master's L
FAX Number: (360) 650-3022 Calendar System: Quarter
URL: www.wwu.edu
Established: 1893 Annual Undergrad Tuition & Fees (In-State): $8,091
Enrollment: 14,842 Coed
Affiliation or Control: State IRS Status: 501(c)3
Highest Offering: Beyond Master's But Less Than Doctorate
Program: Liberal Arts And General; Teacher Preparatory; Professional
Accreditation: NW, ART, BUS, CACREP, CORE, CS, ENGT, MUS, NRPA, SP, TED

01 President .... Dr. Bruce SHEPARD
05 Vice Pres Academic Affairs/Provost ...... Dr. Catherine A. RIORDAN
10 Vice Pres Business/Financial Affs .. Mr. Richard D. VAN DEN HUL
84 VP Enrollment/Student Services .... Dr. Eileen V. COUGHLIN
26 Vice Pres for University Relations .... Mr. Steve SWAN
30 Vice Pres University Advancement .... Ms. Stephanie BOWERS
32 Asst VP Enrollment/Student Services .... Dr. Kunle OJIKUTU
13 Vice Prov Info/Chief Info Officer .... Dr. John D. LAWSON
58 Act Vice Prov Rsch/Act Dn Grad Sch .... Dr. Kathleen KITTO
53 Vice Prov Undergraduate Education .... Dr. Steven L. VANDERSTAAY
22 Vice Prov Equal Oppty/Employmt Div .... Dr. Sue GUENTER-SCHLESINGER
51 Vice Provost Extended Education .... Dr. Earl F. GIBBONS
35 Dean of Students .... Mr. Theodore W. PRATT, JR.
15 Director Human Resources .... Ms. Chyerl WOLFE-LEE
06 Registrar .... Mr. David BRUNNEMER
07 Exec Dir Admissions/Financial Aid .... Ms. Clara CAPRON
36 Director Career Services Center .... Ms. Tina LOUDON
37 Director Financial Aid .... Ms. Clara CAPRON
29 Executive Director Alumni Relations .... Ms. Deborah DEWEES
27 Director University Communications .... Mr. Paul COCKE
44 Dir Plan Giving/Sr Advisor to Pres .... Vacant
08 Dean of Libraries .... Mr. Christopher N. COX
39 Director University Residences .... Mr. Willy HART
04 Sr Executive Assistant to President .... Dr. Paul DUNN
09 Director of Institutional Research .... Dr. Ming ZHANG
18 Director of Facilities Management .... Mr. John A. FURMAN
19 Chief of Public Safety .... Mr. Randy STEGMEIER
41 Athletic Director .... Ms. Lynda GOODRICH
92 Director of Honors Program .... Dr. George MARIZ
96 Purchasing Manager .... Ms. Sally MCKECHNIE
79 Dean College of Humanities/Soc Sci .... Dr. Brent CARBAJAL
72 Dean College of Science/Technology .... Dr. Jeff WRIGHT
50 Dean College Business & Economics .... Dr. Brian K. BURTON
65 Dean Huxley Col of the Environment . Dr. Steven HOLLENHORST

57 Dean College Fine & Performing Arts ... Dr. Daniel G. GUYETTE
53 Dean Woodring College of Education ... Dr. Francisco RIOS
12 Dean Fairhaven College ... Dr. Roger GILMAN

Whatcom Community College (A)

237 W Kellogg Road, Bellingham WA 98226-8003

County: Whatcom FICE Identification: 010364
Unit ID: 237039
Telephone: (360) 383-3000 Carnegie Class: Assoc/Pub-R-M
FAX Number: (360) 383-4000 Calendar System: Quarter
URL: www.whatcom.ctc.edu
Established: 1970 Annual Undergrad Tuition & Fees (In-State): $4,180
Enrollment: 4,333 Coed
Affiliation or Control: State IRS Status: 501(c)3
Highest Offering: Associate Degree
Program: Occupational; 2-Year Principally Bachelor's Creditable; Technical Emphasis
Accreditation: NW, ADNUR, MAC, PTAA

01 President ... Dr. Kathi HIYANE-BROWN
05 Vice President for Instruction ... Dr. Ronald LEATHERBARROW
11 Int VP for Administrative Services ... Mr. Nate LANGSTRAAT
20 Vice Pres for Educational Services ... Ms. Patricia ONION
97 Dean for Instruction ... Mr. Ed HARRI
08 Library Director ... Ms. Linda LAMBERT
10 Director for Business & Finance ... Mr. Ken BRONSTEIN
06 Registrar ... Mr. Michael SINGLETARY
07 Coordinator of Admissions Outreach ... Ms. Laine JOHNSTON
37 Director of Financial Aid ... Mr. Jack WOLLENS
32 Director Student/Athletic Pgms ... Mr. Kris BAIER
85 Director of International Programs ... Mr. Kelly KESTER
27 Exec Director for Comm/Marketing ... Ms. Mary VERMILLION
40 Bookstore Manager ... Mr. Jon SPORES
18 Facilities Director ... Mr. Brian KEELEY
04 Exec Assistant to the President ... Ms. Keri PARRIERA
15 Director Human Resources ... Ms. Becky RAWLINGS
09 Director for Institutional Research ... Dr. Anne Marie KARLBERG
102 Executive Director for Advancement ... Ms. Anne BOWEN
27 Chief Public Information Officer ... Ms. Mary VERMILLION

Whitman College (B)

345 Boyer Avenue, Walla Walla WA 99362-2083

County: Walla Walla FICE Identification: 003803
Unit ID: 237057
Telephone: (509) 527-5411 Carnegie Class: Bac/A&S
FAX Number: (509) 527-5859 Calendar System: Semester
URL: www.whitman.edu
Established: 1882 Annual Undergrad Tuition & Fees: $41,790
Enrollment: 1,596 Coed
Affiliation or Control: Independent Non-Profit IRS Status: 501(c)3
Highest Offering: Baccalaureate
Program: Liberal Arts And General
Accreditation: NW

01 President ... Dr. George S. BRIDGES
05 Provost/Dean of Faculty ... Dr. Timothy KAUFMAN-OSBORN
30 Vice President for Development ... Mr. John W. BOGLEY
10 Treasurer/Chief Financial Officer ... Mr. Peter W. HARVEY
32 Dean of Students ... Mr. Charles E. CLEVELAND
20 Associate Dean of Faculty ... Dr. Lisa R. PERFETTI
84 Dean of Admission/Financial Aid ... Mr. Tony A. CABASCO
13 Chief Technology Officer ... Mr. Dan M. TERRIO
18 Chief Facilities/Physical Plant ... Mr. Daniel L. PARK
08 Librarian ... Mrs. Dalia L. CORKRUM
91 Director of Enterprise Technology ... Mr. Michael W. QUINER
07 Director of Admissions ... Mr. Kevin M. DYERLY
09 Director of Institutional Research ... Dr. Neal J. CHRISTOPHERSON
20 Assistant Dean of Faculty ... Dr. Michelle Y. JANNING
35 Associate Dean of Students ... Ms. Barbara A. MAXWELL
26 Director of Communications ... Ms. Ruth S. WARDWELL
38 Director Student Counseling ... Dr. Richard N. JACKS
39 Director Residence Life & Housing ... Ms. Nancy J. TAVELLI
29 Director Alumni Affairs ... Ms. Polly C. SCHMITZ
104 Director of Off-Campus Studies ... Ms. Susan H. BRICK
15 Director Human Resources ... Mr. Dennis T. HOPWOOD
06 Registrar ... Dr. Ronald F. URBAN
19 Director of Security ... Mr. Terry E. THOMPSON
23 Director Health Services ... Ms. Claudia L. NESS
36 Director of Career Center ... Ms. Susan M. BUCHANAN
37 Director of Financial Aid Services ... Ms. Marilyn K. PONTI
41 Athletic Director ... Mr. Dean C. SNIDER
42 Coordinator of Spiritual Life ... Mr. Adam M. KIRTLEY
04 Executive Assistant to President ... Ms. Jennifer A. CASPER

Whitworth University (C)

300 W Hawthorne Road, Spokane WA 99251-0001

County: Spokane FICE Identification: 003804
Unit ID: 237066
Telephone: (509) 777-1000 Carnegie Class: Master's M
FAX Number: (509) 777-4763 Calendar System: 4/1/4
URL: www.whitworth.edu
Established: 1890 Annual Undergrad Tuition & Fees: $34,346
Enrollment: 2,843 Coed
Affiliation or Control: Presbyterian Church (U.S.A.) IRS Status: 501(c)3
Highest Offering: Master's
Program: Liberal Arts And General; Teacher Preparatory; Professional
Accreditation: NW, MUS, NURSE, TED

01 President ... Dr. Beck A. TAYLOR
05 Interim Provost ... Dr. Barbara SANDERS
10 VP Finance & Administration ... Dr. Brian L. BENZEL
30 VP Institutional Advancement ... Dr. Scott A. MCQUILKIN
32 VP for Student Life ... Dr. Richard G. MANDEVILLE
84 VP Admissions & Financial Aid ... Mr. Greg ORWIG
28 Asst VP Diversity/Intercultural ... Dr. Lawrence A. BURNLEY
15 Assoc VP Human Resources ... Ms. Dolores J. HUMISTON
42 Dean of Spiritual Life ... Dr. Terry P. MCGONIGAL
53 Dean of School of Education ... Dr. Dennis W. STERNER
08 Director of Library ... Dr. Hans E. BYNAGLE
88 Assoc Provost Fac Devel/Schlrshp ... Dr. Kathleen H. STORM
06 Registrar ... Ms. Beverly S. KLEEMAN
35 Associate Dean of Students ... Dr. Jolyn DAHLVIG
20 Associate Provost of Instruction ... Dr. Randall B. MICHAELIS
91 Director of Information Systems ... Mr. Kenneth BROWN
90 Director of Instructional Resources ... Mr. Kenneth D. PECKA
21 Assoc VP Finance & Administration ... Ms. Luz I. MERKEL
29 Dir Alumni/Parent Relations ... Mr. Aaron P. MCMURRAY
51 Dean of Continuing Studies ... Dr. Terry D. RATCLIFF
07 Director of Admissions ... Ms. Marianne W. HANSEN
58 Director of Grad & Cont Studies ... Ms. Cheryl D. VAWTER
18 Director of Facilities Services ... Mr. Christopher EICHORST
23 Director of Health Center ... Ms. Kristiana L. HOLMES
41 Director of Athletics ... Mr. Aaron LEETCH
37 Director of Financial Aid ... Ms. Wendy Z. OLSON
35 Assoc Dean of Students/Dir HUB ... Ms. Dayna L. COLEMAN
39 Assoc Director of Student Housing ... Mr. Alan B. JACOB
40 Manager of Bookstore ... Ms. Nancy G. LOOMIS
26 Director of Communications ... Ms. Nancy G. HINES
38 Director of Counseling Services ... Ms. Janelle R. THAYER
09 Director of Institutional Research ... Mr. Gary D. WHISENAND
50 Dean Sch Global Commerce Mgmt ... Dr. Timothy J. WILKINSON

Yakima Valley Community College (D)

PO Box 22520, S 16th Ave & Nob Hill,
Yakima WA 98907-2520

County: Yakima FICE Identification: 003805
Unit ID: 237109
Telephone: (509) 574-4600 Carnegie Class: Assoc/Pub-R-M
FAX Number: (509) 574-6860 Calendar System: Quarter
URL: www.yvcc.edu
Established: 1928 Annual Undergrad Tuition & Fees (In-State): $4,000
Enrollment: 4,312 Coed
Affiliation or Control: State IRS Status: 170(c)1
Highest Offering: Associate Degree
Program: Occupational; 2-Year Principally Bachelor's Creditable
Accreditation: NW, ADNUR, DH, MAC, SURGT

01 President ... Dr. Linda KAMINSKI
05 Vice Pres Instruction/Student Svcs ... Mr. Tomas YBARRA
10 Vice Pres Administrative Services ... Ms. Teresa HOLLAND
12 Dean Grandview Campus ... Dr. Bryce HUMPHREYS
72 Director Tech Services ... Mr. Scott TOWSLEY
32 Dean Student Services ... Ms. Leslie BLACKABY
49 Dean Arts & Sciences ... Ms. Kerrie ABB
75 Dean Workforce Education ... Ms. Paulette LOPEZ
08 Library Director ... Ms. Joan WEBER
37 Director Student Financial Aid ... Ms. Janet CANTELON
26 Community Relations Coordinator ... Ms. Nicole HOPKINS
15 Director Human Resources ... Mr. Mark ROGSTAD
18 Director Facilities/Physical Plant ... Mr. Jeff WOOD
96 Purchasing Manager ... Ms. Claudia HOFFBAUER
35 Student Life Coordinator ... Ms. Kelly ROBBINS
97 Dean Basic Skills ... Ms. Kerrie ABB

WEST VIRGINIA

Alderson Broaddus College (E)

101 College Hill Drive, Philippi WV 26416-4600

County: Barbour FICE Identification: 003806
Unit ID: 237118
Telephone: (304) 457-1700 Carnegie Class: Bac/Diverse
FAX Number: (304) 457-6239 Calendar System: Semester
URL: www.ab.edu
Established: 1871 Annual Undergrad Tuition & Fees: $22,740
Enrollment: 624 Coed
Affiliation or Control: American Baptist IRS Status: 501(c)3
Highest Offering: Master's
Program: 2-Year Principally Bachelor's Creditable; Liberal Arts And General; Teacher Preparatory; Professional
Accreditation: NH, #ARCPA, NUR, TEAC

01 President ... Mr. Richard A. CREEHAN
05 Provost/Exec VP for Academic Affs ... Dr. Joan L. PROPST
10 Vice Pres Administration & Finance ... Mr. Bruce A. BLANKENSHIP
30 Vice Pres Institutional Advancement ... Ms. J. Nikky LUNA
84 Vice President Enrollment Mgmt ... Ms. Tanya L. SHELTON
44 Asst VP Adv/Major Gifts/Donor Rels ... Dr. Carl W. GITTINGS
20 Asst VP Institutional Accreditation ... Mr. Eric M. SHOR
108 Asst VP Institutional Assessment ... Mr. Tom J. BERLIN
32 Dean of Student Affairs ... Ms. Sarah E. WARD
13 Director of Information Technology ... Mr. Byron A. SAYRES
35 Dir of Student Engagement/Orient ... Ms. Koreen VILLERS
42 Chaplain ... Dr. James M. STINESPRING
08 Director of Library Services ... Mr. David E. HOXIE
41 Athletic Director ... Mr. Dennis W. CREEHAN
37 Director of Financial Aid ... Ms. Amy L. KING
26 Director of Mktg/Communications ... Ms. Ashley E. MITTELMEIER
29 Director of Alumni Relations ... Mr. Nathan R. PRICE
06 Registrar ... Ms. Saundra E. HOXIE
102 Dir Foundation/Corporate Giving ... Vacant
08 Director Learning Resources Center ... Vacant
18 Chief Facilities/Physical Plant ... Mr. Craig HYRE
27 Dir of Information and Research ... Ms. Julia M. MORRIS
40 Director of Campus Services ... Mr. Ed BURDA
21 Director of Accounting Services ... Ms. Jill BAKER
07 Director of Admissions ... Mr. Zachary A. WARD
38 Director of Counseling Services ... Mr. Chad HOSTETLER
36 Director of Career Services ... Ms. Teresa D. VAN ALSBURG
44 Director of Annual Giving ... Ms. Dionne T. ANDREWS
88 Director of Development ... Ms. M. Annette FETTY
105 Web Content Editor ... Mr. Aaron P. KITTLE

American Public University System (F)

111 W Congress Street, Charles Town WV 25414-1621

County: Jefferson FICE Identification: 035393
Unit ID: 449339
Telephone: (304) 724-3700 Carnegie Class: Master's L
FAX Number: (304) 724-3780 Calendar System: Other
URL: www.apus.edu
Established: 1991 Annual Undergrad Tuition & Fees: $6,400
Enrollment: 50,838 Coed
Affiliation or Control: Proprietary IRS Status: Proprietary
Highest Offering: Master's
Program: 2-Year Principally Bachelor's Creditable; Liberal Arts And General; Professional
Accreditation: NH, ACBSP

01 President/CEO ... Dr. Wallace E. BOSTON
05 Exec VP & Provost ... Dr. Karan H. POWELL
10 Exec VP & CFO ... Mr. Harry T. WILKINS
26 Exec VP Programs & Marketing ... Ms. Carol S. GILBERT
03 Exec VP/Chief Operations Officer ... Dr. Sharon VAN WYK
11 Senior VP/Chief Admin Officer ... Mr. Pete W. GIBBONS
13 Senior VP/Chief Information Officer ... Mr. W. Dale YOUNG
20 Senior VP/Academic Opers Officer ... Dr. Gwen HALL
06 VP/Registrar ... Ms. Lyn GEER
84 VP Enrollment Mgt & Student Support ... Ms. Terry GRANT
31 VP Cmty Col Relations & Outreach ... Dr. John HOUGH
46 VP Research & Development ... Dr. Phil ICE
86 VP Regulatory & Govt Relations ... Dr. Russell KITCHNER
88 VP Strategic Initiatives ... Mr. Phil MCNAIR
32 VP Student Services ... Ms. Caroline SIMPSON
09 VP Institutional Research & Assess ... Dr. Jennifer HELM
08 VP Library and Educ Materials ... Dr. Fred STIELOW
88 VP Military Relations ... Mr. Jim SWEIZER
15 VP Human Resources ... Ms. Amy PANZARELLA
37 VP Financial Aid Services ... Mr. Gary SPOALES
88 VP Institutional Accreditation ... Ms. Lynn C. WRIGHT

Appalachian Bible College (G)

161 College Drive, Mt. Hope WV 25880

County: Raleigh FICE Identification: 007544
Unit ID: 237136
Telephone: (304) 877-6428 Carnegie Class: Spec/Faith
FAX Number: (304) 877-5082 Calendar System: Semester
URL: www.abc.edu
Established: 1950 Annual Undergrad Tuition & Fees: $12,680
Enrollment: 262 Coed
Affiliation or Control: Independent Non-Profit IRS Status: 501(c)3
Highest Offering: Master's
Program: Liberal Arts And General; Teacher Preparatory; Religious Emphasis
Accreditation: NH, BI

01 President ... Dr. Daniel L. ANDERSON
05 Vice President for Academics ... Mr. Daniel S. HANSHEW
10 Vice President for Business ... Mr. Kenneth E. LILLY
30 Vice President for Development ... Rev. Jonathan A. RINKER
32 Vice President for Student Services ... Rev. David E. CHILDS
42 Vice Pres for Extension Ministries ... Mr. David J. HOLLOWAY
33 Dean of Men ... Mr. John M. SHARP
34 Dean of Women ... Mrs. Linda J. CHILDS
06 Registrar ... Dr. Charles N. BETHEL
07 Director of Admissions ... Mr. Scott T. ROSS
08 Librarian ... Mr. David W. DUNKERTON
37 Acting Director of Financial Aid ... Mrs. Deana B. STEINKE
04 Admin Assistant to the President ... Mrs. Elisabeth I. GOLDEN
26 Director of Public Relations ... Mr. Jarod K. BURRER

Bethany College (H)

Main Street, Bethany WV 26032-0417

County: Brooke FICE Identification: 003808
Unit ID: 237181
Telephone: (304) 829-7000 Carnegie Class: Bac/A&S
FAX Number: (304) 829-7700 Calendar System: 4/1/4
URL: www.bethanywv.edu
Established: 1840 Annual Undergrad Tuition & Fees: $24,780
Enrollment: 1,020 Coed
Affiliation or Control: Christian Church (Disciples Of Christ)
IRS Status: 501(c)3
Highest Offering: Master's
Program: Liberal Arts And General; Teacher Preparatory
Accreditation: NH, SW, TED

01 President of the College ....Dr. Scott D. MILLER
03 Executive VP & General Counsel ....Mr. William R. KIEFER
05 Vice President for Academic Affairs ....Dr. Darin E. FIELDS
30 Vice President for Advancement ....Mr. Sven M. DE JONG
04 Executive Asst to the President ....Ms. Deidra R. HALL-NUZUM
100 Assistant to the President ....Dr. Mort GAMBLE
32 Dean of Students ....Mr. Gerald STEBBINS
37 Director of Financial Aid ....Mr. Jason MCCLAIN
41 Director of Athletics & Recreation ....Mr. Tim WEAVER
09 Director of Institutional Research ....Vacant
88 Director of McCann Learning Center ....Dr. Christina SAMPSON
88 Director of Student Support Service ....Ms. Tracy DEPEW
89 Director of First Year Experience ....Dr. Katrina COOPER
88 Director of International Programs ....Dr. Harald MENZ
36 Director of Student Placement ....Mr. John OSBOURNE
23 Director of the Byrd Health Center ....Mrs. Carol TYLER
27 Director of Communications ....Ms. Rebecca ROSE
29 Director of Alumni/Parent Relations ....Ms. Ashley KANOTZ
88 Director of Advancement Services ....Ms. Shirley KEMP
88 Director of Sports Information ....Mr. Brian ROSE
88 Director of Church Relations ....Dr. Larry GRIMES
18 Director of Physical Plant ....Mr. Theodore D. WILLIAMS
10 Director of Financial Affairs ....Mr. Daniel T. PAJAK
21 Director of Business Services ....Ms. Saralyn DAGUE
19 Director of Safety & Security ....Mr. Robert RIBAR
15 Director of Personnel Services ....Ms. Merlinda LEES
39 Director of Residence Life ....Mr. Jonathan GEYER
35 Director of Student Activiites ....Ms. Amy COLANTONI
42 Chaplain ....Rev. Scott THAYER
08 Director of the Libraries ....Mrs. Heather MAY-RICCIUTI
88 Director of Network Operations ....Mr. Ron SHAW
88 Director of Info Tech Operations ....Mr. Thomas V. FURBEE
88 Public Services Librarian ....Mr. Trevor ONEST
06 Registrar ....Ms. Stephanie KAPPEL
38 College Counselor ....Ms. Renee STOCK
88 General Manager Conference Center ....Ms. Donna WHITE
88 Director of Dining Services ....Mrs. Necol M. DUNSON
40 Manager of the Bookstore ....Ms. Ann CRAFT
07 Director of Enrollment ....Mr. Robert ZITZELSBERGER

Davis & Elkins College (A)

100 Campus Drive, Elkins WV 26241-3996

County: Randolph　FICE Identification: 003811
Unit ID: 237358
Telephone: (304) 637-1900　Carnegie Class: Bac/Diverse
FAX Number: (304) 637-1413　Calendar System: 4/1/4
URL: www.dewv.edu
Established: 1904　Annual Undergrad Tuition & Fees: $23,500
Enrollment: 784　Coed
Affiliation or Control: Presbyterian Church (U.S.A.)　IRS Status: 501(c)3
Highest Offering: Baccalaureate
Program: 2-Year Principally Bachelor's Creditable; Liberal Arts And General; Teacher Preparatory; Business Emphasis
Accreditation: NH, ADNUR, IACBE, TEAC, THEA

01 President ....Dr. G. T. SMITH
02 Chancellor and Provost ....Dr. Michael P. MIHALYO, JR.
84 Executive Vice President/COO ....Mr. Kevin H. WILSON
10 Chief Financial Officer ....Ms. Greta J. TROASTLE
05 Vice President for Academic Affairs ....Dr. Joseph M. ROIDT
30 Vice President College Advancement . Ms. Patricia J. SCHUMANN
32 Vice President for Student Affairs ....Mr. Scott D. GODDARD
26 Assoc VP for Commun & Marketing ....Ms. Carol M. SCHULER
15 Director Human Resources ....Ms. M. J. COREY
06 Registrar ....Dr. Stephanie C. HAYNES
18 Exec Director of Physical Plant ....Mr. Ronald J. SELDERS
37 Director Financial Planning ....Mr. Matthew A. SUMMERS
08 Assistant Director Booth Library ....Ms. Kathleen DOIG
42 Chaplain ....Dr. Robert R. MCCUTCHEON
41 Director of Athletics ....Mr. Ron PALMER
19 Director of Campus Safety/Security ....Mr. Michael R. JORDAN
44 Director of Advancement Operations ....Ms. Karen L. WILMOTH
04 Executive Asst to the President ....Ms. Robin PRICE

Everest Institute (B)

5514 Big Tyler Road, Cross Lanes WV 25313-1399

County: Kanawha　FICE Identification: 010356
Unit ID: 237604
Telephone: (304) 776-6290　Carnegie Class: Assoc/PrivFP
FAX Number: (304) 776-6262　Calendar System: Other
URL: www.everest-institute.com
Established: 1968　Annual Undergrad Tuition & Fees: $18,700
Enrollment: 334　Coed
Affiliation or Control: Proprietary　IRS Status: Proprietary
Highest Offering: Associate Degree
Program: Occupational
Accreditation: ACCSC

01 President ....Ms. Aimee SWITZER
05 Director of Education ....Ms. Jennifer RICHMOND
07 Director of Admission ....Ms. Karen WILKINSON
10 Director of Finance ....Mr. Matt LANE
36 Director Career Services ....Ms. Christie CRADDOCK

Future Generations Graduate School (C)

400 Road Less Traveled, Franklin WV 26807-9201

County: Pendleton　Identification: 666714
Telephone: (304) 358-2000　Carnegie Class: Not Classified
FAX Number: (304) 358-3008　Calendar System: Other
URL: www.future.edu
Established: 2003　Annual Graduate Tuition & Fees: $17,500
Enrollment: 21　Coed
Affiliation or Control: Independent Non-Profit　IRS Status: 501(c)3
Highest Offering: Master's; No Undergraduates
Program: Liberal Arts And General
Accreditation: NH

01 President ....Dr. Daniel TAYLOR
05 Dean ....Dr. Mike RECHLIN

Huntington Junior College (D)

900 Fifth Avenue, Huntington WV 25701-2004

County: Cabell　FICE Identification: 009047
Unit ID: 237437
Telephone: (304) 697-7550　Carnegie Class: Assoc/PrivFP
FAX Number: (304) 697-7554　Calendar System: Quarter
URL: www.huntingtonjuniorcollege.edu
Established: 1936　Annual Undergrad Tuition & Fees: $7,455
Enrollment: 947　Coed
Affiliation or Control: Proprietary　IRS Status: Proprietary
Highest Offering: Associate Degree
Program: 2-Year Principally Bachelor's Creditable; Technical Emphasis
Accreditation: NH, MAC

01 President ....Carolyn A. SMITH
03 Director ....Dr. Catherine E. SNODDY
05 Academic Affairs Director ....Linda J. WEST

ITT Technical Institute (E)

5183 US Route 60, Bldg 1, Suite 40, Huntington WV 25705

County: Cabell　Identification: 666709
Unit ID: 456418
Telephone: (304) 733-8700　Carnegie Class: Assoc/PrivFP4
FAX Number: N/A　Calendar System: Other
URL: www.itt-tech.edu
Established: N/A　Annual Undergrad Tuition & Fees: N/A
Enrollment: 394　Coed
Affiliation or Control: Proprietary　IRS Status: Proprietary
Highest Offering: Associate Degree
Program: Technical Emphasis
Accreditation: ACICS

† Branch campus of ITT Technical Institute, Indianapolis, IN.

Martinsburg Institute (F)

341 Aikens Center, Martinsburg WV 25404

County: Berkeley　Identification: 667035
Telephone: (304) 263-6262　Carnegie Class: Not Classified
FAX Number: (866) 703-6611　Calendar System: Other
URL: www.martinsburginstitute.edu
Established: 1980　Annual Undergrad Tuition & Fees: $3,000
Enrollment: 775　Coed
Affiliation or Control: Proprietary　IRS Status: Proprietary
Highest Offering: Associate Degree
Program: Occupational; 2-Year Principally Bachelor's Creditable; Technical Emphasis
Accreditation: DETC

01 President ....Paul VIBOCH
05 Chief Academic Officer ....Stella GARLICK
07 Director of Admissions ....Laurie MAURO
06 Registrar ....Rita CLAYPOLE

Mountain State College (G)

1508 Spring Street, Parkersburg WV 26101

County: Wood　FICE Identification: 005008
Unit ID: 237598
Telephone: (304) 485-5487　Carnegie Class: Assoc/PrivFP
FAX Number: (304) 485-3524　Calendar System: Quarter
URL: www.msc.edu
Established: 1888　Annual Undergrad Tuition & Fees: $8,100
Enrollment: 265　Coed
Affiliation or Control: Proprietary　IRS Status: Proprietary
Highest Offering: Associate Degree
Program: Occupational; 2-Year Principally Bachelor's Creditable; Business Emphasis
Accreditation: ACICS

01 President ....Mrs. Judith SUTTON

Mountain State University (H)

410 Neville Street, Beckley WV 25801

County: Raleigh　FICE Identification: 003807
Unit ID: 237154
Telephone: (304) 253-7351　Carnegie Class: Master's L
FAX Number: (304) 253-3487　Calendar System: Semester
URL: www.mountainstate.edu
Established: 1933　Annual Undergrad Tuition & Fees: $7,680
Enrollment: 4,743　Coed
Affiliation or Control: Independent Non-Profit　IRS Status: 501(c)3
Highest Offering: Doctorate
Program: Occupational; 2-Year Principally Bachelor's Creditable; Liberal Arts And General; Teacher Preparatory; Professional; Business Emphasis
Accreditation: NH, ACFEI, ARCPA, #DMS, MAC, NUR, OTA, PTAA, RAD, SW

01 Interim President ....Dr. Richard SOURS
100 Chief Of Staff ....Ms. Rachel BRAGG
05 Provost ....Dr. Roslyn C. CLARK-ARTIS
32 Interim VP of Student Affairs ....Mr. Thomas MANN
10 Chief Financial Ofcr ....Ms. Michele SARRETT
43 General Counsel ....Mr. Dusty GWINN
84 Chief Marketing Officer ....Ms. Susan BACKOFEN
76 Dean School Health Sciences ....Ms. Karen BOWLING
49 Dean Sch of Arts & Sciences ....Vacant
58 Dean of Graduate Studies ....Dr. William WHITE
50 Dean School Business/Technology ....Dr. Marjorie SMITH
66 Dean of School of Nursing ....Dr. Sheila GARLAND
32 Dean of Students ....Ms. Mandy WRISTON
88 Dean Sch Ldrship & Prof Dev ....Dr. Ruth WYLIE
15 Director of Human Resources ....Ms. Trina LAWSON
106 Dean of Distance Learning ....Dr. James OWSTON
09 Chief Institutional Effectiveness ....Dr. Mark MILLER
66 Dean of Grad Nursing ....Dr. Jessica SHARP
12 Exec Director Orlando Campus ....Mr. Randy WHITE
12 Exec Dir Center Township Campus ....Mr. Mark CICCARELLI
12 Exec Director NC Campuses & Site ....Mr. Dallas BRAGG
13 Director of Info Technology ....Mr. Scott TERRY
26 Dir of Media & Public Relations ....Mr. Andrew WESSELS
29 Dir Alumni Relations ....Ms. Beth PERRY
40 Dir Univ Bookstores/Auxiliary Svcs ....Mr. Glenn JOHNSON
19 Dir of Security & Campus Operations ....Mr. Everette STEELE
96 Director of Purchasing ....Mr. Scott MANGUM
08 Dir Library/Technical Resources ....Ms. Judy ALTIS
88 Coordinator of Assessment ....Ms. Angela SPELOCK
88 Dir of Info Analysis/Inst Research ....Ms. Kim KEATON
06 Registrar ....Dr. Rhonda SHEPPERD
41 Athletic Director ....Mr. Robert BOLEN, III
37 Director of Financial Aid ....Ms. JoAnn ROSS
36 Dir Practicum Ctr & Career Services ....Vacant
07 Director of Admissions ....Ms. Cynthia JUSTUS
88 Director of Recruiting and Training ....Ms. Iris MCGEE
18 General Manager Facilities ....Mr. Andy BIHL
85 Director International Student Svcs ....Mr. Charles LOWRY
88 Coordinator of Accred & Licensure ....Ms. Anna-Marie ALLEN
26 Director of Marketing ....Ms. Sandy TINCHER

National College (I)

421 Hilltop Drive, Princeton WV 24740

County: Tazewell　Identification: 666499
Telephone: (304) 487-3845　Carnegie Class: Not Classified
FAX Number: (304) 487-3852　Calendar System: Quarter
URL: www.ncbt.edu
Established: 1886　Annual Undergrad Tuition & Fees: $9,790
Enrollment: 197　Coed
Affiliation or Control: Proprietary　IRS Status: Proprietary
Highest Offering: Baccalaureate
Program: Occupational; Business Emphasis
Accreditation: ACICS, MAC

01 President ....Mr. Frank LONGAKER
03 Vice President ....Ms. Lenora DOWNING
05 Campus Director ....Mr. Denver RIFFE

Ohio Valley University (J)

1 Campus View Drive, Vienna WV 26105-8000

County: Wood　FICE Identification: 003819
Unit ID: 237640
Telephone: (304) 865-6000　Carnegie Class: Bac/Diverse
FAX Number: (304) 865-6001　Calendar System: Semester
URL: www.ovu.edu
Established: 1958　Annual Undergrad Tuition & Fees: $19,050
Enrollment: 527　Coed
Affiliation or Control: Churches Of Christ　IRS Status: 501(c)3
Highest Offering: Master's
Program: Liberal Arts And General; Teacher Preparatory
Accreditation: NH, IACBE, @TEAC

01 President ....Dr. Harold SHANK
10 Executive Vice President/CFO ....Mr. Jeffrey A. DIMICK
05 Vice Pres for Academic Affairs ....Dr. Jim BULLOCK
30 Int Vice Pres for Advancement ....Dr. Keith STOTTS
29 Sr Vice Pres Alumni Services ....Mr. Jack THORN
84 Vice President for Enrollment ....Mr. Larry LYONS
37 Vice Pres Marketing/Financial Aid ....Mr. Dennis W. COX
43 General Counsel ....Dr. Becky D. MATHIS-STUMP
28 Asst to Pres for Minority Relations ....Mr. Harry OGLETREE
18 Director of Campus Operations ....Mr. David STEWART
06 Registrar ....Mrs. Sarah BARTON
36 Director of Career Services ....Mrs. Kathy MULLER
32 Student Life Officer ....Mr. Jason DOUGHERTY
08 Library Director ....Mr. Rodney WOOTEN
83 Dean Col Behav Scies/Biblical Stds ....Dr. Michael MOSS
41 Director of Athletics ....Mr. Dennis COX

Salem International University (K)

223 W Main Street, Box 500, Salem WV 26426-0500

County: Harrison　FICE Identification: 003820
Unit ID: 237783
Telephone: (304) 326-1109　Carnegie Class: Master's M
FAX Number: (304) 326-1246　Calendar System: Semester
URL: www.salemu.edu
Established: 1888　Annual Undergrad Tuition & Fees: $14,700
Enrollment: 811　Coed
Affiliation or Control: Proprietary　IRS Status: Proprietary

Highest Offering: Master's
Program: Occupational; 2-Year Principally Bachelor's Creditable; Liberal Arts And General; Teacher Preparatory; Professional; Nursing Emphasis
Accreditation: NH

00 Chancellor/CEO .... Mr. James W. BROOKS
01 President .... Mr. John A. LUOTTO
03 Executive Vice President .... Dr. Cecil E. KIRKLAND
05 Provost .... Dr. Debra HARRISON
10 CFO .... Mr. Dan NELANT
37 Director Financial Aid .... Mrs. Sri NELANT
106 Director Online Operations .... Mr. Timothy RAUSCHENBACH
27 CIO .... Mr. Pieter BRESLER
15 Director Human Resources .... Ms. Victoria HODGES
06 Registrar .... Ms. Rebecca HALL
06 Registrar Online .... Ms. Jennifer HALER
53 Dean School of Education .... Dr. Craig MCCLELLAN
66 Director Nursing Education .... Dr. Bobbie BLOCH
107 Dean Online Operations .... Dr. John M. CAVENDISH
08 Dean Library Services .... Dr. Phyllis D. FREEDMAN
32 Director Student Life .... Ms. Sarah SHEETS
19 Director Campus Security .... Mr. Joseph SHAVER
18 Director Physical Plant & Maint .... Mr. John BOWERS
41 Athletic Director .... Mr. Keith BULLION

University of Charleston (A)

2300 Maccorkle Avenue, SE, Charleston WV 25304-1099
County: Kanawha FICE Identification: 003818
Unit ID: 237312
Telephone: (304) 357-4800 Carnegie Class: Bac/Diverse
FAX Number: (304) 357-4715 Calendar System: Semester
URL: www.ucwv.edu
Established: 1888 Annual Undergrad Tuition & Fees: $19,500
Enrollment: 1,372 Coed
Affiliation or Control: Independent Non-Profit IRS Status: 501(c)3
Highest Offering: Doctorate
Program: Liberal Arts And General; Teacher Preparatory; Professional; Fine Arts Emphasis
Accreditation: NH, ADNUR, NUR, PHAR, RAD, TEAC

01 President .... Dr. Edwin H. WELCH
05 Provost & Dean of Faculty .... Dr. Letha ZOOK
10 Vice Pres Administration & Finance .... Mrs. Cleta M. HARLESS
27 Vice President for Communications .... Mrs. Jennie FERRETTI
30 Vice Pres for Development .... Mr. Ben BEAKES
06 Registrar .... Dr. Michael C. LEVY
29 Alumni Director .... Ms. Bridgette BORST
08 Director of Library .... Mr. John ADKINS
32 Dean of Students .... Ms. Bethany MEIGHEN
37 Associate Director Financial Aid .... Ms. Nina MORTON
35 Coordinator of Student Programs .... Ms. Meghan SPARROW
40 Bookstore Manager .... Ms. Sara STURGEN
18 Director Plant & Property .... Mr. Gary BOYD
19 Director Security .... Vacant
41 Athletic Director .... Dr. Bren STEVENS
88 Director of Colleague Program .... Dr. Barbara WRIGHT
85 Coord International Student Pgms .... Ms. Audrey PITONAK
13 Director of University Computing .... Mr. Tim EULER
21 Director of Operations .... Vacant
09 Director of Institutional Research .... Ms. Lisa DAWKINS
15 Director Personnel Services .... Ms. Tammy HOLSTINE
21 Associate Business Officer .... Mr. Steve DAVIS
49 Chair Division Arts & Sciences .... Dr. Barbara WRIGHT
50 Chair Division Business .... Vacant
76 Chair Division Health Sciences .... Dr. Josephine KAHLER
50 Dean Graduate School of Business .... Dr. Charles STEBBINS
67 Dean School of Pharmacy .... Dr. Michelle EASTON

Valley College - Beckley Campus (B)

713 South Oakwood Avenue, Beckley WV 25801
County: Raleigh FICE Identification: 030844
Unit ID: 377652
Telephone: (304) 252-9547 Carnegie Class: Assoc/PrivFP
FAX Number: (304) 252-1694 Calendar System: Other
URL: www.valley.edu
Established: 1983 Annual Undergrad Tuition & Fees: $9,500
Enrollment: 84 Coed
Affiliation or Control: Proprietary IRS Status: Proprietary
Highest Offering: Associate Degree
Program: Occupational; Business Emphasis
Accreditation: CNCE

01 Executive Director .... Ms. Beth GARDNER

Valley College - Martinsburg Campus (C)

287 Aikens Center, Martinsburg WV 25404-6203
County: Berkeley FICE Identification: 026094
Unit ID: 377661
Telephone: (304) 263-0979 Carnegie Class: Assoc/PrivFP
FAX Number: (304) 263-2413 Calendar System: Other
URL: www.valley.edu
Established: 1983 Annual Undergrad Tuition & Fees: $8,800
Enrollment: 60 Coed
Affiliation or Control: Proprietary IRS Status: Proprietary
Highest Offering: Associate Degree
Program: Occupational; Business Emphasis
Accreditation: ACICS

01 Executive Director .... Mr. Matt JENKINS

West Virginia Business College (D)

116 Pennsylvania Avenue, Nutter Fort WV 26301-4516
County: Harrison Identification: 666507
Unit ID: 237978
Telephone: (304) 624-7695 Carnegie Class: Assoc/PrivFP
FAX Number: (304) 622-2149 Calendar System: Quarter
URL: www.wvbc.edu
Established: 1881 Annual Undergrad Tuition & Fees: $9,500
Enrollment: 75 Coed
Affiliation or Control: Proprietary IRS Status: Proprietary
Highest Offering: Associate Degree
Program: Occupational
Accreditation: ACICS

01 Director .... Mr. Robert WRIGHT

† Branch campus of West Virginia Business College, Wheeling, WV.

West Virginia Business College (E)

1052 Main Street, Wheeling WV 26003-2702
County: Ohio FICE Identification: 010861
Unit ID: 405526
Telephone: (304) 232-0361 Carnegie Class: Assoc/PrivFP
FAX Number: (304) 232-0363 Calendar System: Quarter
URL: www.wvbc.edu
Established: 1881 Annual Undergrad Tuition & Fees: $9,150
Enrollment: 142 Coed
Affiliation or Control: Proprietary IRS Status: Proprietary
Highest Offering: Associate Degree
Program: Occupational
Accreditation: ACICS

01 Director .... Ms. Rebecca SUTER

*West Virginia Council for Community & Technical College Education (F)

1018 Kanawha Boulevard E, Suite 700, Charleston WV 25301-2800
County: Kanawha Identification: 666993
Telephone: (304) 558-0265 Carnegie Class: N/A
FAX Number: (304) 558-1646
URL: www.wvctcs.org

01 Chancellor .... James L. SKIDMORE

*Blue Ridge Community and Technical College (G)

400 W Stephen Street, Martinsburg WV 25401
County: Berkeley FICE Identification: 039573
Unit ID: 446774
Telephone: (304) 260-4380 Carnegie Class: Assoc/Pub-R-M
FAX Number: (304) 260-4376 Calendar System: Semester
URL: www.blueridgectc.edu
Established: 1974 Annual Undergrad Tuition & Fees (In-State): $3,120
Enrollment: 4,317 Coed
Affiliation or Control: State IRS Status: 501(c)3
Highest Offering: Associate Degree
Program: Occupational; 2-Year Principally Bachelor's Creditable
Accreditation: NH, ADNUR, EMT

02 President .... Dr. Peter G. CHECKOVICH
05 Vice President of Curriculum .... Dr. George PERRY
103 VP Economic and Workforce Devel .... Dr. Ann M. SHIPWAY
84 VP of Enrollment Management .... Ms. Leslie SEE
10 Chief Financial Officer .... Ms. Kimberly LINEBERG
50 Associate VP of Business and Tech .... Mr. Randall C. MILLER
06 Registrar .... Ms. Angie M. KINDER
07 Director of Access .... Ms. Brenda NEAL
15 Director Human Resources .... Dr. Justin RUBLE
14 Assoc Director of IT .... Mr. Michael BYERS
38 Director of Student Success .... Vacant
37 Director of Financial Aid .... Ms. Doris GLENN

*Bridgemont Community and Technical College (H)

619 2nd Avenue, Montgomery WV 25136
County: Fayette FICE Identification: 040473
Unit ID: 445674
Telephone: (304) 734-6600 Carnegie Class: Assoc/Pub-S-SC
FAX Number: (304) 734-6630 Calendar System: Semester
URL: www.bridgemont.edu
Established: 2004 Annual Undergrad Tuition & Fees (In-District): $3,484
Enrollment: 1,017 Coed
Affiliation or Control: State/Local IRS Status: 501(c)3
Highest Offering: Associate Degree
Program: Occupational; 2-Year Principally Bachelor's Creditable
Accreditation: NH, DH, ENGT

02 President .... Dr. Beverly Jo HARRIS
05 Vice Pres for Academic Affairs .... Dr. Kristin MALLORY
10 Chief Financial Officer .... Ms. Patricia HUNT
29 President of Alumni Relations .... Ms. Natalie PRICE
06 Registrar .... Ms. Connie KEIFFER
37 Director of Financial Aid .... Ms. Mary BLIZZARD
35 Director of Student Services .... Ms. Jeanne SMITH
26 Director of Institutional Marketing .... Mr. Jack NUCKOLS
13 Director of Computer Services .... Mr. Thomas MINNICH
09 Director of Institutional Research .... Mr. James F. FAUVER
08 Interim Director of Library .... Ms. Alena Jewel RUCKER
51 Director of Extended/Continuing Ed .... Ms. Kathy LEFTWICH
18 Director of Physical Plant .... Vacant
78 Director Career Svcs/Cooperative Ed .... Mr. Cantrell L. MILLER
22 Dir Affirm Action/Equal Opportunity .... Ms. Jennifer MCINTOSH
07 Director of Admissions .... Ms. Joyce SURBAUGH
15 Director Personnel Services .... Mr. Gene LOPEZ
21 Associate Business Officer .... Ms. Cathy AQUINO
28 Director of Diversity .... Ms. Jennifer MCINTOSH
30 Chief Development .... Mr. Jack NUCKOLS
32 Chief Student Life Officer .... Ms. Jeanne SMITH
36 Director Student Placement .... Mr. Cantrell MILLER
96 Director of Purchasing .... Mr. John POWELL
84 Director Enrollment Management .... Ms. Joyce SURBAUGH

*Eastern West Virginia Community and Technical College (I)

316 Eastern Drive, Moorefield WV 26836-1155
County: Hardy FICE Identification: 041190
Unit ID: 438708
Telephone: (304) 434-8000 Carnegie Class: Assoc/Pub-R-S
FAX Number: (304) 434-7001 Calendar System: Semester
URL: www.eastern.wvnet.edu
Established: 1999 Annual Undergrad Tuition & Fees (In-State): $2,424
Enrollment: 773 Coed
Affiliation or Control: State IRS Status: Exempt
Highest Offering: Associate Degree
Program: Occupational; 2-Year Principally Bachelor's Creditable; Technical Emphasis
Accreditation: NH

02 President .... Dr. Charles TERRELL
13 Dir Information Systems/Technology .... Mr. Tim RIGGLEMAN
10 Exec Dean for Financial & Operation .... Ms. Penny REARDON
32 Dean for Academic & Student Service .... Mr. Robert EAGLE
32 Assoc Dean Academic & Student Svcs .... Ms. Sherry BECKER-GORBY
103 Director of Workforce Education .... Ms. Sherry WATTS
75 Dean of Career/Technical/Workforce .... Mr. Ward MALCOLM

*Kanawha Valley Community & Technical College (J)

PO Box 1000; Cole Complex 102, Institute WV 25112
County: Kanawha FICE Identification: 040386
Unit ID: 445018
Telephone: (304) 766-4093 Carnegie Class: Assoc/Pub-R-S
FAX Number: (304) 766-5714 Calendar System: Semester
URL: www.kvctc.edu
Established: 1953 Annual Undergrad Tuition & Fees (In-District): $3,236
Enrollment: 1,685 Coed
Affiliation or Control: State/Local IRS Status: Exempt
Highest Offering: Associate Degree
Program: Occupational; 2-Year Principally Bachelor's Creditable
Accreditation: NH, ADNUR, NMT

02 President .... Dr. Joseph L. BADGLEY
10 Vice President Finance .... Dr. Patricia HUNT
32 Vice President of Student Services .... Dr. Susan GARDNER
04 Special Assistant to President .... Vacant
05 Vice President Academic Affairs .... Dr. Cindy KELLEY
103 Vice Pres Workforce Economic Devel .... Mrs. Laura L. MCCULLOUGH
06 Registrar .... Mr. Roy SIMMONS
07 Director of Admissions .... Ms. Michelle D. WICKS
37 Associate Director of Financial Aid .... Ms. Carla BLANKENBEUHLER
26 PR Associate and Webmaster .... Mrs. Kristin LEDFORD
16 Human Resources Representative .... Ms. Michelle BISSELL
51 Director of Continuing Education .... Mrs. Kim SOVINE
21 Business Manager .... Mrs. Kristi WILLIAMS
96 Chief Purchasing Officer .... Mr. John POWELL

*Mountwest Community and Technical College (K)

1 Mountwest Way, 2205 Fifth St Rd, Huntington WV 25701
County: Cabell FICE Identification: 040414
Unit ID: 444954
Telephone: (304) 710-3141 Carnegie Class: Assoc/Pub-R-M
FAX Number: (304) 710-3187 Calendar System: Semester
URL: www.mctc.edu
Established: 1975 Annual Undergrad Tuition & Fees (In-District): $2,952
Enrollment: 3,111 Coed
Affiliation or Control: State/Local IRS Status: 501(c)3
Highest Offering: Associate Degree
Program: Occupational; 2-Year Principally Bachelor's Creditable
Accreditation: NH, ACBSP, MAC, PTAA

02 President .... Dr. Keith J. COTRONEO
10 Vice President/CFO .... Mr. Herbert J. KARLET
05 Executive Dean .... Ms. Carol A. PERRY
32 Dean of Student Services .... Ms. Billie K. BROOKS

76 Assoc Dean Allied Health Technology ..... Ms. Jean M. CHAPPELL
103 Dean Workforce Dev/Business/Tech .... Mr. Steven L. BROWN
15 Director Employee Development/HR .... Ms. Stephanie A. NEAL
27 Chief Information Officer/COO .... Mrs. Terri L. TOMBLIN-BYRD

*New River Community and Technical College (A)

221 George Street, Suite 2, Beckley WV 25801

County: Raleigh FICE Identification: 039603
Unit ID: 447582
Telephone: (304) 929-5472 Carnegie Class: Assoc/Pub-R-M
FAX Number: (304) 929-5478 Calendar System: Semester
URL: www.newriver.edu
Established: 2003 Annual Undergrad Tuition & Fees (In-State): $3,234
Enrollment: 3,127 Coed
Affiliation or Control: State IRS Status: 501(c)3
Highest Offering: Associate Degree
Program: Occupational; 2-Year Principally Bachelor's Creditable
Accreditation: NH

02 President .... Dr. Ted D. SPRING
04 Exec Secretary to the President .... Ms. Lori A. MIDKIFF
05 Exec Vice Pres and Chief Acad Ofcr .... Dr. Harry R. FAULK
12 Campus Dean-Nicholas County .... Mr. Fred B. CULLER
12 Campus Dean-Beckley .... Dr. Carolyn G. SIZEMORE
12 Campus Dean-Greenbrier Valley .... Mr. Roger D. GRIFFITH
12 Campus Dean-Mercer County .... Mr. Steve WISE
12 Director Advanced Technology Center .... Ms. Lisa M. HATCHER
88 Director of Inst Effectiveness .... Ms. Renae R. MCGINNIS
06 Registrar .... Ms. Donna M. LEWIS
08 Staff Librarian .... Mr. Robert H. COSTON
10 Vice Pres Financial/Admin Affairs .... Mr. Stephen M. BENSON
37 Director of Financial Aid .... Ms. Patricia HARMON
96 Director of Purchasing .... Ms. Twana JACKSON
21 Controller .... Ms. Heike I. SOEFFKER-CULICERTO
18 Director of Physical Plant .... Mr. Robert RUNION
30 VP Inst Advancement/Workforce Educ .... Mr. William J. LOOPE
32 Vice Pres Student Services .... Dr. Allen B. WITHERS
07 Director of Enrollment Services .... Ms. Tracy L. EVANS
88 Vice Pres/Chief Technology Officer .... Dr. David J. AYERSMAN
24 Dir Ctr for Teaching Excellence .... Mr. Ralph C. PAYNE
16 Chief Human Resources Officer .... Ms. Leah A. TAYLOR
27 Chief Communications Officer .... Ms. Elizabeth M. BELCHER
26 Director of Public Relations .... Ms. Barbara A. ELLIOTT

*Pierpont Community & Technical College (B)

1201 Locust Avenue, Fairmont WV 26554-2470

County: Marion FICE Identification: 040385
Unit ID: 443492
Telephone: (304) 367-4692 Carnegie Class: Assoc/Pub-R-M
FAX Number: (304) 367-4881 Calendar System: Semester
URL: www.pierpont.edu
Established: 1974 Annual Undergrad Tuition & Fees (In-State): $3,860
Enrollment: 3,028 Coed
Affiliation or Control: State IRS Status: 501(c)3
Highest Offering: Associate Degree
Program: Occupational; 2-Year Principally Bachelor's Creditable
Accreditation: NH, ACFEI, MLTAD, NAIT, PTAA

02 President .... Dr. Doreen LARSON
10 VP for Finance and Administration .... Mr. Dale R. BRADLEY
05 Provost/VP for Academic Affairs .... Ms. Leslie LOVETT
86 VP for Organization and Development .... Mr. Stephen E. LEACH
103 VP Workforce & Economic Development .. Mr. Paul SCHREFFLER
26 VP for Community Engagement .... Ms. Sarah L. HENSLEY
97 Int Dean Sch of Academic Studies .... Ms. Linda KING
88 Dean Sch of Business/Aviation/Tech .... Dr. Gerald BACZA
76 Dean School of Health Careers .... Dr. Rosemarie ROMESBURG
88 Dean School of Human Services .... Dr. Beth NEWCOME

*Southern West Virginia Community and Technical College (C)

P. O. Box 2900, Mount Gay WV 25637-2900

County: Logan FICE Identification: 003816
Unit ID: 237817
Telephone: (304) 792-7098 Carnegie Class: Assoc/Pub-R-M
FAX Number: (304) 792-7046 Calendar System: Trimester
URL: www.southernwv.edu
Established: 1971 Annual Undergrad Tuition & Fees (In-State): $2,520
Enrollment: 2,457 Coed
Affiliation or Control: State IRS Status: 501(c)3
Highest Offering: Associate Degree
Program: Occupational; 2-Year Principally Bachelor's Creditable; Technical Emphasis
Accreditation: NH, ADNUR, DH, MLTAD, RAD, SURGT

02 President .... Ms. Joanne J. TOMBLIN
10 VP for Finance & Administration .... Mr. Samuel LITTERAL
05 VP Academic Affairs & Student Svcs .... Dr. Harry LANGLEY
103 VP Economic & Workforce Development ..... Ms. Allyn S. BARKER
14 Chief Information Officer .... Mr. Gary HOLEMAN
30 Vice President for Development .... Mr. Ronald E. LEMON
15 Human Resources Director .... Ms. Patricia CLAY
04 Exec Asst to President & BOG .... Ms. Emma L. BAISDEN
20 Dean Career and Techncial Programs .... Ms. Pamela L. ALDERMAN
20 Dean University Transfer Programs .... Dr. Cindy L. MCCOY
12 Director Wyoming Campus Operations .... Mr. David LORD
12 Director Wmson Campus Operations .... Ms. Rita G. ROBERSON
12 Director Logan Campus Operations .... Mr. Randy SKEENS
12 Director Boone Campus Operations .... Mr. William COOK
76 Chair Allied Health & Nursing Dept .... Ms. Alyce PATTERSON-DIAZ
50 Chair Business Department .... Dr. Gail HALL
72 Chair Technology & Engineering Dept . Ms. Carol A. HOWERTON
81 Chair Science Department .... Mr. Guy LOWES, JR.
88 Chair Transitional Studies .... Mr. Steven LACEK
83 Chair Social Sciences Department .... Vacant
81 Chair Mathematics Department .... Ms. Melinda D. SAUNDERS
79 Chair Humanities Department .... Mr. George H. MORRISON
06 Interim Registrar .... Ms. Teri WELLS
37 Director Student Financial Asst .... Ms. Cindy POWERS
08 Director of Libraries .... Ms. Kimberly L. MAYNARD
88 Director of Media .... Mr. Marcus GIBBS
96 Director of Purchasing .... Ms. Melissa CREAKMAN
84 Dean Enrollment Mgmt & Student Dev .... Mr. Darrell TAYLOR

*West Virginia Northern Community College (D)

1704 Market Street, Wheeling WV 26003-3643

County: Ohio FICE Identification: 009054
Unit ID: 238014
Telephone: (304) 233-5900 Carnegie Class: Assoc/Pub-R-M
FAX Number: (304) 232-4651 Calendar System: Semester
URL: www.wvncc.edu
Established: 1972 Annual Undergrad Tuition & Fees (In-State): $2,646
Enrollment: 2,994 Coed
Affiliation or Control: State IRS Status: 501(c)3
Highest Offering: Associate Degree
Program: Occupational; 2-Year Principally Bachelor's Creditable
Accreditation: NH, ACFEI, ADNUR, MAC, RAD, SURGT

02 President .... Dr. Martin OLSHINSKY
05 Vice President Academic Affairs .... Dr. Vicki RILEY
10 CFO & VP Administrative Services .... Mr. Stephen LIPPIELLO
103 Vice Pres Workforce Dev .... Mr. J. Michael KOON
32 Vice President Student Services .... Mrs. Janet FIKE
31 Dean Community Relations .... Mr. Robert DEFRANCIS
13 Director Information Technology .... Mr. David HANES
09 Dir Inst Research .... Mrs. Pamela WOODS
18 Director of Facilities .... Mr. Jim BALLER
06 Dir of Records/Registrar .... Ms. Nancy ALBERT
15 Chief Human Resource Officer .... Mrs. Peggy CARMICHAEL
30 Exec to the Pres for Development .... Mrs. Emily FISHER
36 Counselor I Career Plng/Placement .... Vacant
12 Campus Dean Weirton .... Vacant
12 Campus Dean Wheeling .... Vacant
12 Campus Dean New Martinsville .... Mr. Larry TACKETT
32 Director Student Union Activities .... Mrs. Shannon PAYTON
07 Associate Director Admissions .... Mr. Richard MCCRAY

*West Virginia Higher Education Policy Commission (E)

1018 Kanawha Boulevard E, Ste 700,
Charleston WV 25301-2887

County: Kanawha FICE Identification: 033440
Unit ID: 237941
Telephone: (304) 558-2101 Carnegie Class: N/A
FAX Number: (304) 558-5719
URL: www.hepc.wvnet.edu

01 Chancellor .... Dr. Paul L. HILL
05 Chancellor Comm/Tech College Educ ... Mr. James L. SKIDMORE
88 Interim Program Director .... Dr. Jan TAYLOR
100 Sr Director Board Public Relation ..... Ms. Ashley L. SCHUMAKER
20 Vice Chancellor for Academic Affs .... Dr. Kathy BUTLER
10 Vice Chancellor for Finance .... Dr. Edward MAGEE
45 Vice Chancellor Policy and Planning .... Dr. Angela BELL
43 General Counsel .... Mr. Bruce R. WALKER
11 Exec Vice Chancellor Administration .... Mr. Robert E. ANDERSON
32 Dir Student/Educational Services .... Mr. Daniel E. CROCKETT
37 Senior Director of Financial Aid .... Mr. Brian WEINGART
88 Director Administrative Services .... Ms. Cindy L. ANDERSON

*Bluefield State College (F)

219 Rock Street, Bluefield WV 24701-2198

County: Mercer FICE Identification: 003809
Unit ID: 237215
Telephone: (304) 327-4000 Carnegie Class: Bac/Diverse
FAX Number: (304) 325-7747 Calendar System: Semester
URL: www.bluefieldstate.edu
Established: 1895 Annual Undergrad Tuition & Fees (In-State): $5,180
Enrollment: 1,929 Coed
Affiliation or Control: State IRS Status: 501(c)3
Highest Offering: Baccalaureate
Program: Liberal Arts And General; Teacher Preparatory
Accreditation: NH, ACBSP, ADNUR, ENGT, NURSE, RAD, TED

02 President .... Dr. Martha V. KROTSENG
05 Vice Pres Academic Affs/Provost .... Dr. Lewis JONES
10 Vice Pres Financial/Admin Affairs .... Ms. Shelia JOHNSON
32 Vice President Student Affairs .... Mr. John C. CARDWELL
04 Dir Inst/Media Rels/Asst to Pres .... Mr. James A. NELSON
88 Executive Director Title III .... Dr. Felica WILLIAMS
06 Registrar .... Mr. Ray MULL
08 Director Library Services .... Ms. Joanna THOMPSON
24 Interim Chief Technology Officer .... Mr. Tom G. COOK
14 Director of Computer Services .... Mr. Tom G. COOK
36 Director of Placement .... Mr. Thomas HARRISON
07 Director of Admissions .... Mr. Kenneth MANDEVILLE
37 Director of Financial Aid .... Mr. Thomas ILSE
15 Director of Human Resources .... Ms. Christina BROGDON
18 Admin Asst Senior of Physical Plant .... Ms. Diana GIBSON
19 Director Public Safety .... Mr. Richard AKERS
09 Director of Institutional Research .... Dr. Tracey ANDERSON
38 Director of Counseling .... Dr. Cravor JONES
29 Director Alumni Affairs .... Ms. Deirdre GUYTON
40 Manager Bookstore .... Ms. Virginia RICHARDSON
41 Athletic Director .... Mr. Terry BROWN
50 Dean School of Business .... Dr. Steve BOURNE
49 Dean School of Arts and Sciences .... Dr. David HAUS
54 Dean School of Eng Tech/Comp Sci .... Vacant
53 Interim Dean School of Education .... Dr. Betsy STEENKEN
66 Dean School Nursing/Allied Health .... Ms. Angela LAMBERT
66 ADN Program Director .... Ms. Sandra WYNN
66 BSN Program Director .... Ms. Beth PRITCHETT
88 Program Dir of Radiologic Tech .... Ms. Melissa HAYE
61 Program Dir Criminal Justice .... Mr. Michael LILLY
28 Director of Multicultural Affs .... Dr. Sapphire CUREG
96 Director of Purchasing .... Mr. Paul RUTHERFORD
30 Director of Advancement/Planning .... Vacant

*Concord University (G)

PO Box 1000, Athens WV 24712-1000

County: Mercer FICE Identification: 003810
Unit ID: 237330
Telephone: (304) 384-3115 Carnegie Class: Bac/Diverse
FAX Number: (304) 384-9044 Calendar System: Semester
URL: www.concord.edu
Established: 1872 Annual Undergrad Tuition & Fees (In-State): $5,716
Enrollment: 2,797 Coed
Affiliation or Control: State IRS Status: 501(c)3
Highest Offering: Master's
Program: Liberal Arts And General; Teacher Preparatory; Professional
Accreditation: NH, SW, TED

02 President .... Dr. Gregory F. ALOIA
05 Interim VP & Academic Dean .... Dr. Kendra BOGGESS
30 Interim VP for Advancement .... Mrs. Alicia BESENYEI
20 Associate Dean .... Dr. George TOWERS
32 VP Student Aff/Dir of Retention .... Dr. Marjie FLANIGAN
10 VP for Business & Finance .... Dr. Charles P. BECKER
07 VP for Admissions & Financial Aid .... Vacant
11 VP of Administration .... Mr. Rick DILLON
06 Registrar .... Mrs. Carolyn COX
08 Director of Libraries .... Dr. Stephen ROWE
37 Director of Student Financial Aid .... Mrs. Debra TURNER
84 Director of Enrollment Management .... Mr. Kent GAMBLE
29 Director of Alumni Relations .... Ms. Sarah TURNER
88 Director Bonner Scholars Program .... Mrs. Kathy BALL
14 Chief Technology Officer .... Mr. Charles ELLIOTT
16 Human Resources Director .... Mr. Marshall CAMPBELL
18 Director Physical Plant .... Mr. Gerry VONVILLE
19 Director of Public Safety .... Chief Mark STELLA
36 Director of Career Services .... Ms. Tammy MONK
38 Director of Counseling .... Ms. Sandy GRIM
40 Bookstore Manager .... Mr. Carl SLATE
41 Athletic Director .... Mr. Kevin GARRETT
21 Financial Reporting Officer .... Ms. Elizabeth J. CAHILL
96 Interim Purchasing Agent .... Mr. Gary HYLTON
09 Director of Institutional Research .... Mr. George TOWERS
24 Ctr for Academic Technologies .... Mr. Steve MEADOWS
26 Public Relations/Mktg Specialist .... Mr. Lance MCDANIEL
25 Director of Grants and Contracts .... Mr. Scott INGHRAM
12 Director of the Beckley Center .... Dr. Jennifer ROBINETTE

*Fairmont State University (H)

1201 Locust Avenue, Fairmont WV 26554-2470

County: Marion FICE Identification: 003812
Unit ID: 237367
Telephone: (304) 367-4000 Carnegie Class: Master's S
FAX Number: (304) 367-4789 Calendar System: Semester
URL: www.fairmontstate.edu
Established: 1865 Annual Undergrad Tuition & Fees (In-State): $5,326
Enrollment: 4,617 Coed
Affiliation or Control: State IRS Status: 501(c)3
Highest Offering: Master's
Program: Liberal Arts And General; Teacher Preparatory; Business Emphasis
Accreditation: NH, ACBSP, ADNUR, ENGR, ENGT, NURSE, TED

02 President FSU .... Dr. Maria C. ROSE
05 Interim Provost/VP Academic Affairs .Dr. Christina M. LAVORATA
10 Vice Pres Admin & Fiscal Affairs .... Mr. Enrico A. PORTO
30 Interim VP for Inst Advancement .... Dr. Fred FIDURA
27 VP/Chief Information Officer .... Mr. David A. TAMM
32 Senior VP Enrollment/Student Svcs .... Vacant
04 Assistant to the President .... Miss Alicia NIEMAN
20 Assoc Provost for Academic Affs .... Vacant
26 Director of Communications .... Mrs. Ann BOOTH
18 Asst Vice Pres for Facilities .... Mr. Raymond T. TUCKER
16 Asst VP HR/Campus Community .... Mrs. Cynthia S. CURRY
06 Registrar .... Ms. Evie BRANTMAYER

49 Dean College of Liberal Arts ... Dr. Deanna J. SHIELDS
72 Dean College of Science and Tech ... Dr. Anthony F. GILBERTI
50 Dean School of Business ... Dr. Richard C. HARVEY
53 Dean School of Education ... Dr. Van O. DEMPSEY
57 Dean School of Fine Arts ... Mr. Peter LACH
66 Dean School of Nursing ... Dr. M. Sharon BONI
07 Director of Admissions & Recruiting ... Mrs. Lori A. SCHOONMAKER
29 Director Alumni Relations ... Mrs. Emily L. SWAIN
91 Dir of Applications Develop Svcs ... Mr. Andy RAISOVICH
41 Director of Athletics ... Mr. James ELLIOTT
19 Director of Emergency Mgmt/Police ... Mr. Jack A. CLAYTON
38 Director of Counseling ... Ms. Kat STEVENS
37 Director Financial Aid/Scholarships ... Ms. Cynthia K. HUDOK
39 Director of Housing ... Mr. Daniel L. GOCKLEY
09 Director of Institutional Research ... Mr. William D. FINLEY
08 Director of Library Services ... Ms. Thelma J. HUTCHINS
96 Director of Procurement ... Ms. Monica J. COCHRAN
26 Director of Public Relations ... Ms. Amy E. PELLEGRIN
36 Director of Student Development ... Ms. Sally V. FRY
90 Director of Solutions Center ... Ms. Joanie RAISOVICH
23 Director of Student Health Services ... Ms. Yolanda S. KIRCHARTZ

*Glenville State College (A)

200 High Street, Glenville WV 26351-1292

County: Gilmer | FICE Identification: 003813 | Unit ID: 237385
Telephone: (304) 462-7361 | Carnegie Class: Bac/Diverse
FAX Number: (304) 462-7610 | Calendar System: Semester
URL: www.glenville.edu
Established: 1872 | Annual Undergrad Tuition & Fees (In-State): $2,676
Enrollment: 1,857 | Coed
Affiliation or Control: State | IRS Status: 501(c)3
Highest Offering: Baccalaureate
Program: Liberal Arts And General; Teacher Preparatory
Accreditation: NH, TED

02 President ... Dr. Peter B. BARR
05 Provost & Senior Vice President ... Dr. John PEEK
32 Dean of Student Affairs ... Mr. Jerry L. BURKHAMMER
10 Exec Vice Pres Business & Finance . Mr. Robert O. HARDMAN, II
26 Sr Vice Pres for External Relations ... Mr. James SPEARS
30 VP Advancement/Exec Dir GSC Found ... Mr. Dennis J. POUNDS
84 Vice Pres for Enrollment Management ... Mr. D. Duane CHAPMAN
04 Executive Assistant to President ... Ms. Teresa G. STERNS
53 Dean of Teacher Education ... Dr. Kevin G. CAIN
15 Director of Human Resources ... Ms. Krystal SMITH
37 Director of Financial Aid ... Ms. Karen D. LAY
14 Director of Data Management ... Mr. Neal L. BENSON
18 Director of Physical Plant ... Mr. Thomas R. RATLIFF
19 Director of Public Safety ... Mr. Daniel R. BELL
41 Director of Athletics ... Ms. Janet BAILEY
23 Director for Campus Health ... Ms. Julia R. BARR
08 Director of Library ... Ms. Gail L. WESTBROOK
06 Associate Registrar ... Ms. Ann REED
27 Director of Public Relations ... Ms. Annette BARNETTE
21 Controller ... Mr. Richard D. ACCORD
36 Director Academic Support Center ... Vacant
96 Director of Purchasing ... Ms. Joyce E. RIDDLE
29 Director of Alumni Affairs ... Ms. Debra A. NAGY
35 Director of Student Activities ... Ms. Jodi OCHELTREE

*Marshall University (B)

1 John Marshall Drive, Huntington WV 25755-0001

County: Cabell | FICE Identification: 003815 | Unit ID: 237525
Telephone: (304) 696-3170 | Carnegie Class: Master's L
FAX Number: (304) 696-6565 | Calendar System: Semester
URL: www.marshall.edu
Established: 1837 | Annual Undergrad Tuition & Fees (In-State): $5,930
Enrollment: 13,971 | Coed
Affiliation or Control: State | IRS Status: 501(c)3
Highest Offering: Doctorate
Program: Occupational; 2-Year Principally Bachelor's Creditable; Liberal Arts And General; Teacher Preparatory; Professional
Accreditation: NH, ADNUR, ANEST, BUS, BUSA, CLPSY, CYTO, DIETD, DIETI, ENG, ENGR, JOUR, MED, MLTAD, MT, MUS, NUR, @PHAR, @PTA, SP, SW, TED

02 President ... Dr. Stephen J. KOPP
05 Provost/Sr VP Academic Affairs ... Dr. Gayle L. ORMISTON
43 Sr VP/Exec Affairs & Gen Counsel ... Mr. F. Layton COTTRILL
63 Dean of Medicine ... Dr. Joseph I. SHAPIRO
102 CEO MU Foundation Inc ... Dr. Ron AREA
11 Interim Sr VP for Finance/Admin ... Ms. Karen KIRTLEY
46 VP Research ... Mr. John MAHER
86 VP Federal Programs/Dir CEO RCBI ... Ms. Charlotte WEBER
12 VP South Charleston/VP Regional Op ... Mr. Kemp W. WINFREE
53 Dean GSEPD ... Dr. Teresa EAGLE
26 Sr VP Communication/Chief of Staff ... Mr. Matt TURNER
29 Vice President Alumni Relations ... Ms. Tish LITTLEHALES
13 VP Information Technology/CIO ... Dr. Jan I. FOX
44 Vice President Major Gifts ... Mr. Lance WEST
28 VP Multicultural Affairs ... Dr. Shari CLARKE
20 Assoc Vice Pres Academic Affairs ... Dr. Frances S. HENSLEY
14 Asst VP Information Technology ... Dr. Arnold R. MILLER
10 Chief Financial Officer ... Ms. Mary Ellen HEUTON
07 Dir Admission Undergrad/Grad Pgms ... Ms. Tammy JOHNSON
32 Dean Student Affairs ... Mr. Stephen W. HENSLEY
27 Deputy CIO ... Ms. Monica BROOKS
58 Dean Graduate College ... Dr. Donna SPINDEL
49 Dean College Liberal Arts ... Dr. David PITTENGER
50 Interim Dean College of Business ... Dr. Deanna MADER
57 Dean College of Fine Arts ... Mr. Donald L. VAN HORN
67 Dean School of Pharmacy ... Dr. Kevin W. YINGLING
66 Dean College of Health Prof ... Dr. Michael PREWITT
53 Dean College of Education ... Dr. Robert BOOKWALTER
54 Interim Dean Col of Info Tech/Engr ... Dr. Wael ZATAR
60 Dean Sch Journalism/Mass Comm ... Dr. Corley F. DENNISON
81 Dean College of Science ... Dr. Charles SOMERVILLE
41 Director of Athletics ... Mr. Mike HAMRICK
06 Registrar ... Ms. Roberta FERGUSON
37 Director Student Financial Aid ... Ms. Kathy BIALK
36 Director Career Services ... Ms. Denise HOGSETT
15 Director Human Resource Services ... Ms. Michelle DOUGLAS
19 Director of Public Safety ... Mr. James E. TERRY
96 Director of Purchasing ... Mr. Dennis MEADOWS
18 Director of Physical Plant ... Mr. Mark CUTLIP
39 Director Residence Services ... Mr. John YAUN
09 Asst to the Pres/Dir Inst Rsch/Plng ... Mr. Michael J. MCGUFFEY
85 Exec Dir Ctr for Intl Programs ... Dr. Clark EGNOR
40 Manager of Bookstore ... Mr. Mike CAMPBELL
22 Director Equity Programs ... Ms. Debra HART
88 Director Recruitment ... Ms. Elizabeth WOLFE

*Shepherd University (C)

PO Box 5000, Shepherdstown WV 25443-5000

County: Jefferson | FICE Identification: 003822 | Unit ID: 237792
Telephone: (304) 876-5000 | Carnegie Class: Master's S
FAX Number: (304) 876-3101 | Calendar System: Semester
URL: www.shepherd.edu
Established: 1871 | Annual Undergrad Tuition & Fees (In-State): $5,834
Enrollment: 4,393 | Coed
Affiliation or Control: State | IRS Status: 501(c)3
Highest Offering: Master's
Program: Liberal Arts And General; Teacher Preparatory
Accreditation: NH, IACBE, MUS, NURSE, SW, TED

02 President ... Dr. Suzanne SHIPLEY
05 Acting Vice Pres Academic Affairs ... Dr. Diane MELBY
10 Vice Pres Finance & Administration ... Ms. Deborah JUDD
32 Vice President Student Affairs ... Dr. Thomas SEGAR
30 Acting Vice President Advancement ... Mr. Aaron RYAN
84 Vice Pres Enrollment Management ... Ms. Kimberly SCRANAGE
43 General Counsel ... Mr. K. Alan PERDUE
100 Chief of Staff ... Ms. Shelli DRONSFIELD
88 Assoc VP/Business Decision Support ... Mr. James VIGIL
35 Asst VP Stdnt Aff/Student Success ... Ms. Christana JOHNSON
81 Dean Sch of Natural Sciences/Math ... Dr. Colleen NOLAN
79 Dean School of Arts & Humanities ... Mr. Dow BENEDICT
50 Dean Sch of Bus/Social Sciences ... Dr. Ann M. LEGREID
53 Dean Sch Educ/Profess Studies ... Dr. Virginia HICKS
58 Dean Grad Studies/Cont Education ... Dr. Scott BEARD
88 Dean Teaching & Learning ... Dr. Laura RENNINGER
26 Exec Director Univ Communications ... Ms. Valerie OWENS
09 Director Institutional Research ... Ms. Sara MAENE
39 Director Residence Life ... Ms. Elizabeth SECHLER
21 Comptroller ... Ms. Rebecca STOTTLEMEYER
35 Asst VP Student Aff/Student Engage ... Ms. Holly FRYE
15 Director Human Resources ... Dr. Marie DEWALT
13 Director Info Technology Services ... Mr. Joey DAGG
06 Registrar ... Ms. Tracy SEFFERS
07 Director of Admissions ... Vacant
37 Director Student Financial Aid ... Ms. Sandra OERLY-BENNETT
19 Act Dir Pub Safety/Univ Police Chf ... Mr. Ed BOOBER
53 Director Teacher Education ... Dr. Douglas KENNARD
18 Director Physical Plant ... Mr. Dan YANNA
41 Athletics Director ... Mr. B.J PUMROY
96 Director of Purchasing ... Ms. Debra LANGFORD
38 Director Student Counseling ... Ms. Barbara BYERS
29 Director Alumni Relations ... Ms. Alexis REED
92 Director Honors Program ... Dr. Sally BRASHER
44 Director Annual Giving ... Ms. Julia KRALL

*West Liberty University (D)

PO Box 295, West Liberty WV 26074-0295

County: Ohio | FICE Identification: 003823 | Unit ID: 237932
Telephone: (304) 336-5000 | Carnegie Class: Bac/Diverse
FAX Number: (304) 336-8403 | Calendar System: Semester
URL: www.westliberty.edu
Established: 1837 | Annual Undergrad Tuition & Fees (In-State): $5,530
Enrollment: 2,789 | Coed
Affiliation or Control: State | IRS Status: 501(c)3
Highest Offering: Master's
Program: Liberal Arts And General; Teacher Preparatory; Professional; Business Emphasis
Accreditation: NH, #ARCPA, DH, IACBE, MT, MUS, NURSE, TED

02 President ... Mr. Robin C. CAPEHART
05 Vice Provost ... Dr. Melinda KREISBERG
43 Vice President & General Counsel ... Mr. John L. DAVIS
32 Vice President of Student Affairs ... Vacant
10 Executive VP & CFO ... Mr. John E. WRIGHT
11 Provost ... Dr. Anthony KOYZIS
88 VP for Community Engagement ... Mr. Jeff KNIERIM
81 Dean College of Sciences ... Dr. Robert KREISBERG
49 Dean College Liberal Arts ... Dr. Brian CRAWFORD
57 Dean College Arts & Comm ... Dr. William M. BARONAK
53 Dean College of Education ... Dr. Keely O. CAMDEN
66 Dir of Nursing Programs ... Dr. Donna J. LUKICH
50 Dean College of Business ... Dr. Loren A. WENZEL
35 Assoc Dean Student Services ... Ms. Marcella SNYDER
06 Ex Dir Enr Svc/Regr/Dean Std ... Mr. Scott A. COOK
15 Vice President of Human Resources ... Mr. James L. STULTZ
13 Chief Technology Officer ... Mr. James T. CLARK
09 Dir of Inst Research & Assessment ... Ms. Paula J. TOMASIK
41 Director of Athletics ... Mr. James W. WATSON
07 Director of Admissions ... Ms. Brenda M. KING
51 Director of Cont Educ/Special Pgm ... Vacant
08 Director of Library ... Ms. Cheryl R. HARSHMAN
26 Director of University Engagement ... Ms. Tammi SECRIST
29 Director of Alumni Association ... Mr. Shane STACK
37 Director Student Financial Aid ... Mrs. Katie COOPER
30 VP of Institutional Advancement ... Mr. Jason W. KOEGLER
31 Director of Auxiliary Services ... Mr. John L. DAVIS
18 Chief of Operations ... Mr. Patrick J. HENRY
38 Director of Counseling ... Ms. Bridgette DAWSON
92 Director of the Honors Program ... Dr. Peter L. STAFFEL
93 Minority Student Coordinator ... Vacant
88 Director Dental Hygiene Programs ... Ms. Margaret J. SIX
88 Dir Clinical Lab Science Program ... Dr. William C. WAGENER
20 Associate Academic Officer ... Vacant
21 Associate Business Officer ... Ms. Cindy R. MCGEE
84 Assoc Dean Enrollment Services ... Ms. Brenda M. KING
23 Director of Health Services ... Ms. Cheryl BENNINGTON
88 Vice President of Broadcasting ... Mr. Reid AMOS
88 Director Physican Assistant Program ... Dr. Allan M. BEDASHI
21 Controller ... Ms. Stephanie L. HOOPER
04 Executive Asst to the President ... Dr. John P. MCCULLOUGH
85 Coord International Student Rec ... Ms. Mihaela A. SZABO
88 Marketing Director ... Ms. Stefanie K. TROUTEN
44 Director of Major Gifts ... Ms. Angela R. ZAMBITO

*West Virginia School of Osteopathic Medicine (E)

400 N Lee Street, Lewisburg WV 24901-1196

County: Greenbrier | FICE Identification: 011245 | Unit ID: 237880
Telephone: (304) 645-6270 | Carnegie Class: Spec/Med
FAX Number: (304) 645-4859 | Calendar System: Semester
URL: www.wvsom.edu
Established: 1972 | Annual Graduate Tuition & Fees: $21,150
Enrollment: 813 | Coed
Affiliation or Control: State | IRS Status: 501(c)3
Highest Offering: First Professional Degree; No Undergraduates
Program: Professional
Accreditation: OSTEO

02 President ... Dr. Michael D. ADELMAN
05 Vice Pres Academic Affairs & Dean ... Dr. Lorence L. PENCE
10 Vice Pres Finance & Administration ... Mr. Larry WARE
11 Vice Pres for Administration ... Dr. James W. NEMITZ
17 Assoc Dean Graduate Med Education ... Dr. Victoria SHUMAN
20 Asst Dean Graduate Med Educ ... Dr. David LEECH
20 Assoc Dean Predoctoral Clinical Ed ... Dr. Robert W. FOSTER
20 Asst Dean Predoctoral Clinical Educ ... Ms. Stephanie SCHULER
20 Assoc Dean Preclinical Education ... Dr. John SCHRIEFER
20 Assoc Dean Osteopathic Med Educ ... Vacant
20 Assoc Dean Affiliated/Spons Pgms ... Dr. Malcolm MODRZAKOWSKI
108 Assoc Dean Assessment/Educ Devel ... Dr. Elaine SOPER
37 Director Financial Aid ... Ms. Sharon L. HOWARD
26 Director of Marketing and PR ... Ms. Denise GETSOM
15 Associate VP of Human Resources ... Ms. Leslie BICKSLER
08 Director of Library ... Vacant
25 Director of Contracts ... Ms. Pam OCHALA
06 Registrar ... Ms. Jennifer SEAMS
07 Director of Admissions ... Ms. Donna VARNEY
29 Director Alumni Relations ... Ms. Shannon WARREN
18 Director of Physical Plant II ... Mr. William ALDER

*West Virginia State University (F)

PO Box 1000, Institute WV 25112-1000

County: Kanawha | FICE Identification: 003826 | Unit ID: 237899
Telephone: (304) 766-3000 | Carnegie Class: Bac/A&S
FAX Number: (304) 768-9842 | Calendar System: Semester
URL: www.wvstateu.edu
Established: 1891 | Annual Undergrad Tuition & Fees (In-State): $5,442
Enrollment: 2,827 | Coed
Affiliation or Control: State | IRS Status: 501(c)3
Highest Offering: Master's
Program: Liberal Arts And General; Teacher Preparatory
Accreditation: NH, ACBSP, SW, TED

02 President ... Dr. Brian O. HEMPHILL
10 Interim Vice President for Finance ... Mr. Melvin JONES
05 Provost and VP for Academic Affairs ... Dr. R. Charles BYERS
32 Vice President Student Affairs ... Vacant
45 Vice President Planning/Advancement ... Vacant
20 Asst Vice Pres Academic Affairs ... Dr. John TEEUWISSEN
35 Asst Vice Pres Student Affairs ... Mr. Joseph ODEN, JR.
45 Asst Vice Pres Planning/Advancement ... Vacant
11 Spec Asst to Pres/Strategic Plng ... Vacant
86 Spec Asst to Pres Rsch/Pub Svc ... Dr. Orlando F. MCMEANS
100 Exec Asst to Pres & Chief of Staff ... Vacant
79 Dean College of Arts & Humanities ... Dr. Barbara LADNER
81 Dean College of Natural Sci/Math ... Dr. Katherine HARPER
107 Dean Col of Professional Studies ... Dr. Robert L. HARRISON, JR.

50 Dean Col of Business Admin/Soc Sci .... Dr. Abainesh MITIKU
53 Chrmn Department of Education .... Dr. Sandra ORR
70 Chairman Department Sociology .... Dr. Gail MOSBY
64 Chairman Music Department .... Ms. Brenda VANDERFORD
68 Chrmn Health & Human Performance .... Mrs. Debra ANDERSON-CONLIFFE
26 Chief Public Relations Officer .... Ms. Patricia DICKINSON
14 Director Computer Services .... Mr. Robert H. HUSTON
09 Dir Inst Effective/Rsrch/Assessmt .... Dr. Barry PELPHREY
18 Director Physical Facilities .... Vacant
06 Director Records & Registration .... Ms. Donna L. HUNTER
19 Director of Public Safety .... Chief Joseph SAUNDERS
10 Director of Fiscal Affairs .... Mr. Lawrence J. SMITH
08 Director of the Library .... Mr. David CLENDINNING
37 Interim Director Financial Aid .... Ms. Sally MARCUS BURGER
29 Director Alumni Relations .... Mr. Phillip BRIGHT
15 Director of Human Resources .... Miss Barbara ROWELL
36 Dir Career Services & Coop Educ .... Ms. Sandhya (Sandy) G. MAHARAJ
07 Interim Director of Admissions .... Ms. Trina D. SWEENEY
38 Director New Student Programs .... Mrs. Sharon S. BANKS
96 Director of Purchasing .... Mrs. Janis A. BENNETT
88 Interim Director of Recruiting .... Mr. Christopher D. JACKSON
09 Coord of Institutional Research .... Dr. Danny R. CANTRELL

*West Virginia University (A)

1500 University Avenue, Morgantown WV 26506-0002
County: Monongalia FICE Identification: 003827
Unit ID: 238032
Telephone: (304) 293-0111 Carnegie Class: RU/H
FAX Number: (304) 293-5883 Calendar System: Semester
URL: www.wvu.edu
Established: 1867 Annual Undergrad Tuition & Fees (In-State): $5,800
Enrollment: 29,617 Coed
Affiliation or Control: State IRS Status: 501(c)3
Highest Offering: Doctorate
Program: Liberal Arts And General; Teacher Preparatory; Professional
Accreditation: NH, ART, AUD, BUS, BUSA, CACREP, CIDA, CLPSY, COPSY, CORE, CS, DENT, DH, DIETD, DIETI, DMS, ENG, ENGR, FOR, IPSY, JOUR, LAW, LSAR, MED, MT, MUS, NMT, NURSE, OT, PA, PH, PHAR, PTA, RAD, RADMAG, RTT, SP, SPAA, SW, TED, THEA

02 President .... Dr. James P. CLEMENTS
05 Provost & VP Acad Affairs .... Dr. Michele G. WHEATLY
10 Vice President for Admin & Finance .... Mr. Narvel G. WEESE, JR.
26 Vice Pres University Relations .... Ms. Christine M. MARTIN
17 Chancellor of Health Sciences .... Dr. Christopher C. COLENDA
32 Vice President Student Affairs .... Mr. Kenneth D. GRAY
46 Interim VP Research & Econ Develop .... Dr. Fred L. KING
15 Vice President for Human Resources .... Ms. Margaret R. PHILLIPS
58 Vice Pres Health Sci Rsrch/Grad Ed .... Dr. Glen DILLON
76 Interim Sr Assoc VP/Health Sciences .... Mr. Fred R. BUTCHER
20 Sr Assoc Provost Academic Affairs .... Dr. Russell K. DEAN
20 Assoc Provost Academic Personnel .... Dr. Cecil B. WILSON
88 Director Research & Rural Health .... Ms. Jodie JACKSON
100 Chief of Staff .... Mr. John J. COLE
88 Exec Officer for Policy Development .... Dr. Jennifer L. FISHER
88 Exec Officer for Social Justice .... Ms. Jennifer A. MCINTOSH
43 VP Legal Affairs/General Counsel . Mr. William H. HUTCHENS, III
88 Chief Financial Officer .... Ms. Wendy L. KING
21 Sr Assoc Vice Pres for Finance .... Mr. Daniel A. DURBIN
56 Int Assoc Prov Exten/Public Svcs .... Dr. Steve BONANNO
102 President WVU Foundation .... Mr. R. Wayne KING
20 Assoc Provost Academic Programs .... Dr. Elizabeth A. DOOLEY
13 Interim Assoc Provost IT/CIO .... Mr. Mark SIX
18 Interim Assoc VP Facilities & Svcs .... Mr. Randy HUDAK
35 Assoc Vice Pres Student Affairs .... Mr. Michael A. ELLINGTON
88 Asst VP Hlth Sci & Tech Academy .... Ms. Ann M. CHESTER
88 Associate Vice President Marketing .... Ms. Tricia L. PETTY
84 Associate VP Enroll Mgmt Svcs .... Ms. Brenda S. THOMPSON
45 Assoc Vice Pres Planning & Treasury .... Ms. Elizabeth P. REYNOLDS
25 Asst VP Office of Sponsored Pgms .... Mr. Alan B. MARTIN
09 Director of Institutional Research .... Ms. Roberta A. DEAN
39 Director Housing & Residence Life .... Mr. G. Corey FARRIS
41 Director Intercollegiate Athletics .... Mr. Oliver F. LUCK
23 Director of Health Services .... Dr. Jan E. PALMER
24 Director of Radio & TV Services .... Mr. John E. DUWALL
27 Asst VP News/Information Services .... Ms. Rebecca B. LOFSTEAD
29 Exec Director Alumni Association .... Mr. Stephen L. DOUGLAS
37 Director Financial Aid .... Ms. Kaye C. WIDNEY
07 Exec Director Admissions & Records .... Dr. Stephen E. LEE
06 Registrar .... Dr. Steve E. ROBINSON
08 Interim Dean of Library Services .... Ms. Myra LOWE
38 Asst VP Student Wellness .... Dr. Catherine A. YURA
21 Director Financial Services .... Ms. Lisa A. LIVELY
19 Chief of Police/Univ Police Dept .... Capt. Bob E. ROBERTS
96 Dir Purchasing/Cont & Pay .... Ms. Brenda K. MOWEN
88 Assoc VP Intl & Global Outreach .... Dr. David C. STEWART
50 Dean Business and Economics .... Dr. Jose V. SARTARELLI
49 Dean of Arts & Sciences .... Dr. Robert H. JONES
57 Dean College Creative Arts .... Dr. Paul K. KREIDER
53 Int Dean Human Resources/Educ .... Dr. Elizabeth DOOLEY
61 Dean of Law .... Dr. Joyce E. MCCONNELL
63 Dean of Medicine .... Dr. Arthur J. ROSS
52 Dean of Dentistry .... Dr. David A. FELTON
54 Dean of Engr/Mineral Resources .... Dr. Eugene V. CILENTO
47 Dean of Agriculture & Forestry .... Dr. Daniel J. ROBISON
67 Dean of Pharmacy .... Dr. Patricia A. CHASE
60 Dean of Journalism .... Dr. Maryanne REED
68 Dean Physical Education .... Dr. Dana D. BROOKS
66 Dean of Nursing .... Dr. Georgia L. NARSAVAGE
56 Dean Extended Learning .... Dr. Susan D. DAY-PERROOTS
36 Director Career Services .... Mr. David L. DURHAM
88 Assoc Provost Intl Acad Affairs .... Dr. Michael LASTINGER
88 Assoc VP Acad Strategic Plng .... Dr. Nigel N. CLARK
88 Assoc Provost Graduate Acad Affairs .... Dr. Jonathan CUMMINGS
35 Interim Dean Students & Dir Housing .... Mr. G. Corey FARRIS
88 Director of Internal Audit .... Mr. William R. QUIGLEY

*Potomac State College of West Virginia University (B)

Keyser WV 26726-2698
County: Mineral FICE Identification: 003829
Unit ID: 237701
Telephone: (304) 788-6800 Carnegie Class: Assoc/Pub2in4
FAX Number: (304) 788-6940 Calendar System: Semester
URL: www.potomacstatecollege.edu
Established: 1901 Annual Undergrad Tuition & Fees (In-State): $3,178
Enrollment: 1,800 Coed
Affiliation or Control: State IRS Status: 501(c)3
Highest Offering: Associate Degree
Program: Occupational; 2-Year Principally Bachelor's Creditable
Accreditation: &NH

02 Campus Provost .... Dr. Leonard A. COLELLI
10 Senior Business Planning Officer .... Mr. Harlan N. SHREVE
05 Dean for Curriculum & Instruction .... Dr. Douglas R. WILMES
32 Dean of Student Affairs .... Mr. William M. LETRENT
84 Director of Enrollment Services .... Mrs. Beth E. LITTLE
08 Librarian .... Mrs. Jill M. GARDNER
27 Public Information Officer .... Mrs. Rene M. TREZISE
41 Athletic Director .... Mr. Shawn A. WHITE
18 Dir of Facilities/Physical Plant .... Mr. Michael A. SIMPSON
37 Financial Aid/Veterans Coordinator .... Mrs. Beth E. LITTLE
13 Information Technology Coordinator .... Mr. Geoffrey L. CHENGER
29 Coordinator of Alumni Affairs .... Mrs. Libby M. NICHOLS

*West Virginia University at Parkersburg (C)

300 Campus Drive, Parkersburg WV 26104-8647
County: Wood FICE Identification: 003828
Unit ID: 237686
Telephone: (304) 424-8000 Carnegie Class: Bac/Assoc
FAX Number: (304) 424-8315 Calendar System: Semester
URL: www.wvup.edu
Established: 1961 Annual Undergrad Tuition & Fees (In-State): $2,276
Enrollment: 4,210 Coed
Affiliation or Control: State IRS Status: 501(c)3
Highest Offering: Baccalaureate
Program: Occupational; 2-Year Principally Bachelor's Creditable; Liberal Arts And General; Teacher Preparatory; Technical Emphasis
Accreditation: NH, ADNUR, SURGT, TED

02 President .... Dr. Marie FOSTER GNAGE
05 Sr Vice President Academic Affairs .... Dr. Rhonda TRACY
32 Vice President for Student Services .... Mr. Anthony UNDERWOOD
103 Vice Pres Workforce/Community Educ .... Mrs. Mary Beth BUSCH
10 Chief Financial Officer .... Dr. Vincent MENSAH
26 Director Marketing/Communications .... Mrs. Katie WOOTTON
13 Director Information Technology .... Vacant
22 Special Asst to President .... Mrs. Debra L. RICHARDS
12 Director Jackson County Center .... Mr. John GORRELL
102 Director of Development .... Mrs. Geni ASTORG
18 Director Facilities & Services .... Mr. David WHITE
15 Director Human Resources .... Mrs. Cynthia ASHBY
09 Dir Inst Rsrch/Outcomes Assessment .... Mr. Jeremy STARKEY
06 Registrar .... Mrs. Leslie SIMS
07 Asst Dean of Enrollment .... Mrs. Christine POST
37 Director of Financial Aid .... Mr. August KAFER
96 Director of Purchasing .... Vacant
20 Associate Dean Academic Affairs .... Vacant
04 Executive Assistant to President .... Mrs. Patsy BEE
35 Director Student Activities .... Mr. Tom YENCHA
08 Director of Library .... Mr. Stephen HUPP
50 Chair Business/Economics/Math Div .... Mr. Steven MORGAN
53 Chair Education/Humanities Division .... Dr. Cindy GISSY
76 Chair Health Sciences Division .... Mrs. Rose BEEBE
83 Chair Social Science/Languages Div .... Mrs. Denise MCCLUNG
72 Chair Science/Technology Division .... Mr. David THOMPSON

*West Virginia University Institute of Technology (D)

405 Fayette Pike, Montgomery WV 25136-2436
County: Fayette FICE Identification: 003825
Unit ID: 237950
Telephone: (304) 442-1000 Carnegie Class: Bac/Diverse
FAX Number: (304) 442-3067 Calendar System: Semester
URL: www.wvutech.edu
Established: 1895 Annual Undergrad Tuition & Fees (In-State): $5,344
Enrollment: 1,316 Coed
Affiliation or Control: State IRS Status: 501(c)3
Highest Offering: Baccalaureate
Program: Liberal Arts And General; Business Emphasis
Accreditation: &NH, ENG, ENGT

02 Chief Executive Officer .... Ms. Carolyn LONG
05 Associate Provost .... Mr. Garth E. THOMAS, JR.
10 Chief Business Officer .... Mr. George LASNIER
84 Dir Enrollment Mgmt .... Vacant
32 Dean of Students .... Mr. Richard CARPINELLI
07 Dir Admissions .... Ms. Reeta PIIRALA-SKOGLUND
50 Dean Bus/Humanities & Social Sci .... Dr. Stephen W. BROWN
54 Dean LCN College of Engr & Science .... Dr. Zeljko TORBICA
26 Marketing Communications Specialist .... Ms. Adrienne KING
41 Athletic Director .... Mr. Frank PERGOLIZZI
15 Director Human Resources .... Mr. Kevin A. LAWHON
18 Director Facilities Mgmt/Planning .... Mr. Rick LINIO
39 Assistant Dean .... Ms. Amy COTNET-KLINGLER
19 Director of Public Safety .... Mr. Tim MCKINNEY
37 Director of Financial Aid .... Mr. Michael WHITE
36 Director of Career Services .... Mr. Cantrell L. MILLER
08 Director of the Library .... Ms. Jewel RUCKER
85 International Student Advisor .... Vacant
40 Bookstore Manager .... Ms. Sarah J. SIMMONS
06 Registrar .... Vacant

West Virginia Junior College (E)

1000 Virginia Street East, Charleston WV 25301-2817
County: Kanawha FICE Identification: 010573
Unit ID: 237987
Telephone: (304) 345-2820 Carnegie Class: Assoc/PrivFP
FAX Number: (304) 345-1425 Calendar System: Quarter
URL: www.wvjc.edu
Established: 1892 Annual Undergrad Tuition & Fees: $11,725
Enrollment: 232 Coed
Affiliation or Control: Proprietary IRS Status: Proprietary
Highest Offering: Associate Degree
Program: 2-Year Principally Bachelor's Creditable
Accreditation: ACICS

01 Executive Director .... Mr. Thomas A. CROUSE

West Virginia Junior College (F)

148 Willey Street, Morgantown WV 26505-5596
County: Monongalia FICE Identification: 005007
Unit ID: 237996
Telephone: (304) 296-8282 Carnegie Class: Assoc/PrivFP
FAX Number: (304) 581-6990 Calendar System: Quarter
URL: www.wvjcmorgantown.edu
Established: 1922 Annual Undergrad Tuition & Fees: $12,650
Enrollment: 205 Coed
Affiliation or Control: Proprietary IRS Status: Proprietary
Highest Offering: Associate Degree
Program: 2-Year Principally Bachelor's Creditable; Business Emphasis
Accreditation: ACICS

01 President & CEO .... Ms. Patricia A. CALLEN
05 Academic Director .... Ms. Leanne CARDOSA
36 Career Services .... Ms. Carissa COLLINS
37 Financial Aid Director .... Ms. Savannah MCCONNELL

West Virginia Wesleyan College (G)

59 College Avenue, Buckhannon WV 26201-2699
County: Upshur FICE Identification: 003830
Unit ID: 237969
Telephone: (304) 473-8000 Carnegie Class: Bac/Diverse
FAX Number: (304) 472-2571 Calendar System: Semester
URL: www.wvwc.edu
Established: 1890 Annual Undergrad Tuition & Fees: $25,804
Enrollment: 1,452 Coed
Affiliation or Control: United Methodist IRS Status: 501(c)3
Highest Offering: Master's
Program: Liberal Arts And General; Teacher Preparatory; Professional
Accreditation: NH, MUS, NUR, TED

01 President .... Dr. Pamela M. BALCH
05 VP Academic Affs/Dean Faculty .... Dr. Larry R. PARSONS
10 Vice Pres Administration & Finance .... Dr. Barry R. PRITTS
30 Vice Pres Institutional Advancement .... Mr. Robert SKINNER
32 VP Student Devel/Enrollment Mgmt .... Ms. Julia A. KEEHNER
27 Vice Pres/Chief Information Officer .... Mr. R. Duwane SQUIRES
42 Dean of the Chapel .... Rev. Angela Gay KINKEAD
58 Dean of Graduate Stds/Extended Lrng .... Dr. Kathleen M. LONG
102 Director Foundation/Government Rels .... Ms. Nicki BENTLEY-COLTHART
07 Director of Admission .... Mr. John WALTZ
11 Director of Administrative Services .... Mr. Keith NICHOLS
37 Director Financial Planning .... Ms. Susan GEORGE
29 Director of Alumni Affairs .... Mrs. Kristi WILKERSON
08 Director of Library Services .... Ms. Paula L. MCGREW
06 Dir Acad & Career Svcs/Registrar .... Ms. Alice J. CREASMAN
39 Director Campus Life .... Mrs. Alisa LIVELY
09 Director of Institutional Research .... Ms. Tammy J. CRITES
15 Director of Personnel .... Ms. Vickie J. CROWDER
18 Director of the Physical Plant .... Vacant
30 Director Development Operations .... Ms. Rose Ellen LOUDIN
08 Director of the Learning Center .... Dr. Shawn M. KUBA
41 Director of Athletics .... Mr. Randall TENNEY
21 Comptroller .... Mr. Randall W. CRITES
40 Director of Bookstore .... Ms. Jennifer DALTON
92 Director Honors Program .... Mr. Doug VAN GUNDY
93 Director Intercultural Relations .... Vacant
44 Director of Planned & Major Gifts .... Rev. David R. PETERS
38 Dir of Counseling & Wellness Center .... Mr. Michael KUBA
31 Dir of Leadership Development .... Ms. LeeAnn BROWN

Wheeling Jesuit University (A)

316 Washington Avenue, Wheeling WV 26003-6295
County: Ohio FICE Identification: 003831
Unit ID: 238078
Telephone: (304) 243-2000 Carnegie Class: Bac/Diverse
FAX Number: (304) 243-2243 Calendar System: Semester
URL: www.wju.edu
Established: 1954 Annual Undergrad Tuition & Fees: $25,875
Enrollment: 1,429 Coed
Affiliation or Control: Roman Catholic IRS Status: 501(c)3
Highest Offering: Doctorate
Program: Liberal Arts And General; Professional
Accreditation: NH, ACBSP, NMT, NURSE, PTA, TEAC

01 President ... Mr. Richard Allen BEYER
03 University Vice President ... Rev. James J. FLEMING
05 Vice President for Academic Affairs ... Dr. Stephen D. STAHL
10 Chief Financial Officer ... Mr. Kevin LUSK
30 VP for Institutional Advancement ... Vacant
84 Vice President for Enrollment Mgmt ... Mr. Larry VALLAR
32 Dean for Student Development ... Ms. Christine OHL-GIGLIOTTI
90 Assoc VP for Info Tech Services ... Mr. Daniel T. FEELEY
37 Director Financial Aid ... Ms. Christie L. TOMCZYK
21 Controller ... Mr. Stephen CRINITI
21 Senior Accountant ... Mr. Donald YAQUINTA
06 Registrar ... Ms. Joy CRONIN
08 Librarian ... Ms. Kelly MUMMERT
91 Systems Administrator ... Mr. Richard M. KLEMPA
42 Director of Campus Ministry ... Mr. Jamey BROGAN
41 Athletic Director ... Mr. Danny SANCOMB
18 Director of Physical Plant ... Mr. Frank P. CONNELLY
85 International Student Advisor ... Mrs. Eileen P. VIGLIETTA
15 Director of Human Resources ... Mr. Donald KAMINSKI
44 Dir Planned Giving/Major Gifts ... Vacant
45 Director of Research ... Ms. Lauri STAHL

WISCONSIN

Alverno College (B)

3400 S 43rd Street, Box 343922,
Milwaukee WI 53234-3922
County: Milwaukee FICE Identification: 003832
Unit ID: 238193
Telephone: (414) 382-6000 Carnegie Class: Master's S
FAX Number: (414) 382-6354 Calendar System: Semester
URL: www.alverno.edu
Established: 1887 Annual Undergrad Tuition & Fees: $22,126
Enrollment: 2,605 Female
Affiliation or Control: Independent Non-Profit IRS Status: 501(c)3
Highest Offering: Master's
Program: Liberal Arts And General; Teacher Preparatory; Professional
Accreditation: NH, MUS, NURSE, TED

01 President ... Dr. Mary J. MEEHAN
10 Sr Vice Pres Finance & Mgmt Svcs ... Mr. James OPPERMANN
05 Sr Vice Pres Academic Affairs ... Dr. Kathleen O'BRIEN
30 Vice President College Advancement ... Ms. Julie QUINLAN BRAME
20 Exec Director Academic Services ... Sr. Marlene NEISES
84 VP Marketing & Enrollment Mgmt ... Ms. Susan SMITH
32 Assoc Vice Pres/Dean of Students ... Ms. Virginia WAGNER
07 Dir Communications for Admissions ... Ms. Cecelia CASPRAM
20 Associate Vice President Academic ... Dr. Kathy LAKE
20 Associate Vice President Academic ... Dr. Jeanna ABROMEIT
06 Registrar ... Ms. Patricia HARTMANN
08 Director Library ... Ms. Carol BRILL
36 Director Career Development ... Ms. Joanna PATTERSON
13 Exec Dir Information Technology ... Ms. Anita EIKENS
37 Director Student Financial Plng ... Mr. Dan GOYETTE
29 Director Alumnae Relations ... Ms. Mary FRIESEKE
38 Director Advising ... Ms. Katherine BUNDALO
51 Dir Institute Educational Outreach .. Ms. Judith REISETTER-HART
15 Director Human Resources ... Ms. Sharon WILCOX
41 Director of Athletics ... Mr. Brad DUCKWORTH
42 Campus Minister ... Ms. Connie POPP
96 Purchasing Agent ... Ms. Anne MCCARRON
09 Director of Institutional Research ... Dr. Glen ROGERS
27 Chief Information Officer ... Mr. Jim HILBY
50 Dean School of Business ... Mr. Dan HORTON
66 Dean School of Nursing ... Ms. Patricia SCHROEDER
53 Dean of School of Education ... Dr. Mary DIEZ
49 Dean School of Arts & Sciences ... Dr. Sandra GRAHAM
50 Director Master of Business Admin ... Dr. Patricia JENSEN
79 Assoc Dean Humanities Division ... Dr. Mimi CZARNIK
81 Asc Dean Natl Science/Math/Tech Div ... Dr. Angela FREY
83 Assoc Dean Behavioral Sciences Div ... Dr. Julia ULLMAN
60 Assoc Dean Arts/Comm/Tech Div ... Dr. Patricia GEENEN
28 Sp Asst to VP Acad Affs/Multclt Iss ... Dr. Celia JACKSON
04 Assistant to the President ... Ms. Jill DESMOND
101 Executive Assistant ... Ms. Joan WALTER-SCHUMACHER

Anthem College-Milwaukee (C)

440 South Executive Drive, Ste 200,
Brookfield WI 53005-4283
County: Waukesha Identification: 666613
Unit ID: 450155
Telephone: (262) 641-9944 Carnegie Class: Assoc/PrivFP
FAX Number: (262) 641-9955 Calendar System: Other
URL: www.hightechinstitute.edu
Established: 2006 Annual Undergrad Tuition & Fees: N/A
Enrollment: 291 Coed
Affiliation or Control: Proprietary IRS Status: Proprietary
Highest Offering: Associate Degree
Program: Occupational
Accreditation: ABHES, SURTEC

01 Campus President ... Ms. Jennifer PAUGH

† Branch campus of Anthem College, Maryland Heights, MO.

Bellin College, Inc. (D)

3201 Eaton Road, Green Bay WI 54311
County: Brown Identification: 006639
Unit ID: 238324
Telephone: (920) 433-6699 Carnegie Class: Spec/Health
FAX Number: (920) 433-1923 Calendar System: Semester
URL: www.bellincollege.edu
Established: 1909 Annual Undergrad Tuition & Fees: $19,800
Enrollment: 310 Coed
Affiliation or Control: Independent Non-Profit IRS Status: 501(c)3
Highest Offering: Master's
Program: Professional; Nursing Emphasis
Accreditation: NH, NURSE, RAD

01 President & CEO of the College ... Dr. Connie BOERST
32 Vice President Student Services ... Ms. Joann M. WOELFEL
10 Vice President Business & Finance ... Mr. Joseph E. KEEBAUGH
05 Vice President Academic Affairs ... Dr. Emily A. LITT
30 Vice President Development & PR ... Mr. Matt G. RENTMEESTER
13 Vice Pres Technology & Facilities ... Mr. Colin J. POMEROY
06 Registrar ... Ms. Aubrey A. SCHRAMM
37 Director Financial Aid ... Ms. Lena C. GOODMAN
07 Director of Admissions ... Ms. Katie KLAUS

Beloit College (E)

700 College Street, Beloit WI 53511-5595
County: Rock FICE Identification: 003835
Unit ID: 238333
Telephone: (608) 363-2000 Carnegie Class: Bac/A&S
FAX Number: (608) 363-2718 Calendar System: Semester
URL: www.beloit.edu
Established: 1846 Annual Undergrad Tuition & Fees: $38,474
Enrollment: 1,293 Coed
Affiliation or Control: Independent Non-Profit IRS Status: 501(c)3
Highest Offering: Baccalaureate
Program: Liberal Arts And General; Teacher Preparatory
Accreditation: NH

01 President ... Dr. Scott BIERMAN
05 Provost ... Dr. Ann DAVIES
11 Vice President Administration ... Mr. John M. NICHOLAS
84 Vice President Enrollment Services ... Ms. Nancy BENEDICT
30 Vice President External Affairs ... Mr. Jeff PUCKETT
32 Dean of Students ... Dr. Christina KLAWITTER
06 Registrar ... Ms. Mary BOROS-KAZAI
07 Director of Admissions ... Mr. James S. ZIELINSKI
09 Director of Institutional Research ... Dr. Cynthia B. GRAY
08 Chief Information Officer ... Ms. Megan E. FITCH
15 Director of Human Resources ... Ms. Lori RHEAD
29 Sr Dir Annual Supp & Alumni/Parent ... Mr. Mark C. WOLD
26 Director of Communications ... Mr. Jason HUGHES
39 Director Resident Life/Conferences ... Mr. John F. WINKELMANN
18 Director of Physical Plant ... Mr. Michael BRADY
36 Director of Career Development ... Vacant
38 College Counselor ... Vacant
40 Bookstore Director ... Mr. Peter FRONK
37 Dir of Student Financial Services ... Mr. Jonathan E. URISH
41 Athletic Director ... Ms. Peggy CARL
28 Dir Intercult Pgm/Asst Dean Stdnts ... Mr. Cecil YOUNGBLOOD

Bryant & Stratton College (F)

310 W Wisconsin Avenue, Suite 500 E,
Milwaukee WI 53203
County: Milwaukee FICE Identification: 005009
Unit ID: 239929
Telephone: (414) 276-5200 Carnegie Class: Assoc/PrivFP4
FAX Number: (414) 276-3930 Calendar System: Semester
URL: www.bryantstratton.edu
Established: 1863 Annual Undergrad Tuition & Fees: $15,605
Enrollment: 1,089 Coed
Affiliation or Control: Proprietary IRS Status: Proprietary
Highest Offering: Baccalaureate
Program: Occupational; Professional; Business Emphasis
Accreditation: &M, MAC

01 Director/Business Office Director ... Mr. Peter J. PAVONE
07 Admissions Director ... Ms. Kathryn M. COTEY
05 Dean of Academic Affairs ... Ms. Catherine R. REBHOLZ
20 Dean of Academic Administration ... Mr. Brian R. SPORLEDER
36 Director of Career Services ... Ms. Betty A. ERBY
37 Financial Aid Manager ... Mr. Kevin MCSHANE

† Regional accreditation is carried under the parent institution (corporate office) in Buffalo, NY.

Cardinal Stritch University (G)

6801 N Yates Road, Milwaukee WI 53217-3985
County: Milwaukee FICE Identification: 003837
Unit ID: 238430
Telephone: (414) 410-4000 Carnegie Class: DRU
FAX Number: (414) 410-4239 Calendar System: Semester
URL: www.stritch.edu
Established: 1937 Annual Undergrad Tuition & Fees: $24,330
Enrollment: 5,358 Coed
Affiliation or Control: Roman Catholic IRS Status: 501(c)3
Highest Offering: Doctorate
Program: 2-Year Principally Bachelor's Creditable; Liberal Arts And General; Teacher Preparatory; Professional
Accreditation: NH, ACBSP, ADNUR, NUR, NURSE, TED

01 President ... Dr. James P. LOFTUS
00 Chancellor ... Sr. Camille KLIEBHAN
04 Assistant to the President ... Ms. Kathryn HOWELL
03 Executive Vice President/CFO .. Mr. Thomas W. VANHIMBERGEN
05 Executive VP Academic Affairs ... Dr. Anthea L. BOJAR
42 Vice President Mission & Identity ... Fr. James G. GANNON
84 Vice President Enrollment Services ... Mr. John P. MUELLER
10 Vice President Finance & Controller ... Ms. Tammy M. HOWARD
13 Vice President Info Services/CIO ... Mr. TJ RAINS
26 Vice President of Public Relations ... Vacant
30 Vice President for Advancement ... Dr. Robert J. BUCKLA
30 Assoc VP for University Advancement . Ms. Judy M. HAUGSLAND
32 Vice Pres for Student Development .. Ms. Christine M. ROBINSON
21 Dir Treasury & Risk Management ... Mr. Brian B. BLANK
21 Asst VP for Business & Finance ... Vacant
15 Director of Human Resources ... Ms. Deborah R. JOHNSON
49 Dean College of Arts & Sciences ... Dr. Daniel J. SCHOLZ
50 Dean College of Business & Mgmt ... Dr. Peter J. HOLBROOK
53 Dean College of Education & Ldrship ... Dr. Freda R. RUSSELL
66 Dean College of Nursing ... Ms. Kelly J. DRIES
06 Registrar ... Ms. Christine L. GLYNN
21 Bursar ... Ms. Lisa M. LEWIN
20 Director of Academic Affairs ... Ms. Nancy A. DAWKINS
85 Director of International Programs ... Ms. Laine M. PHILIPPA
39 Director of Residence Life ... Mr. Joseph R. NISWONGER
41 Director of Athletics ... Mr. Patrick J. CLEMENS
07 Sr Dir of Student Recruitment ... Mr. Kirk D. MESSER
08 Director of University Library .. Mr. David W. WEINBERG-KINSEY
37 Director of Financial Aid ... Mr. Ben J. BAERBOCK
36 Director of Career Services ... Mr. Tom E. KIPP
09 Dir of Quality Data & Inst Research ... Ms. Lynsey A. SCHWABROW
18 Director of Facilities ... Mr. John B. GLYNN
91 Director of Enterprise Systems ... Ms. Susan L. INGLES
19 Director of Security ... Mr. Andrew DE RUBERTIS
44 Director Major Gifts/Planned Giving ... Mr. Chris J. LANGE
29 Dir Alumni Relations/Annual Giving ... Mr. Joel F. CENCIUS
38 Dir for Counseling/Mental Wellness ... Ms. Laura J. HEMPE

Carroll University (H)

100 N East Avenue, Waukesha WI 53186-5593
County: Waukesha FICE Identification: 003838
Unit ID: 238458
Telephone: (262) 547-1211 Carnegie Class: Master's S
FAX Number: (262) 524-7646 Calendar System: Semester
URL: www.carrollu.edu
Established: 1846 Annual Undergrad Tuition & Fees: $26,476
Enrollment: 3,523 Coed
Affiliation or Control: Presbyterian Church (U.S.A.) IRS Status: 501(c)3
Highest Offering: Doctorate
Program: Liberal Arts And General; Teacher Preparatory; Professional
Accreditation: NH, #ARCPA, NURSE, PTA

01 President ... Dr. Doug N. HASTAD
05 Provost ... Dr. Joanne PASSARO
10 Vice President for Finance ... Mr. Ron LOSTETTER
84 Vice President for Enrollment ... Mr. James V. WISEMAN
30 Vice President for Advancement ... Mr. Stephen KUHN
09 Vice Provost ... Vacant
32 Dean of Students ... Dr. Theresa BARRY
13 Chief Information Officer ... Ms. Debra JENKINS
06 Registrar ... Ms. Ann HANDFORD
44 Sr Advancement Ofcr for Development ... Ms. Cherie SWENSON
26 Director of Public Relations ... Ms. Claire M. BEGLINGER
15 Director of Human Resources ... Ms. Lorraine FORCINITO
08 Director of Library Services ... Vacant
37 Director of Student Financial Svcs ... Ms. Dawn M. SCOTT
41 Athletic Director ... Mr. Joe BAKER
88 Director of Part-Time Studies ... Vacant
28 Director of Cultural Diversity ... Mr. Carl ERVIN
29 Director Alumni Relations ... Ms. Dolores M. BROWN
96 Director of Purchasing ... Ms. Char RICHARDS
07 Director of Admissions ... Ms. Kelly J. HEIMAN
18 Chief Facilities/Physical Plant ... Mr. Dan LAPAZ
38 Director Student Counseling ... Ms. Angie R. BRANNAN
04 Exec Assistant to the President ... Ms. Gina M. EHLER

Carthage College (I)

2001 Alford Park Drive, Kenosha WI 53140-1994
County: Kenosha FICE Identification: 003839
Unit ID: 238476
Telephone: (262) 551-8500 Carnegie Class: Bac/A&S
FAX Number: (262) 551-6208 Calendar System: 4/1/4
URL: www.carthage.edu
Established: 1847 Annual Undergrad Tuition & Fees: $33,000
Enrollment: 3,376 Coed
Affiliation or Control: Evangelical Lutheran Church In America
IRS Status: 501(c)3
Highest Offering: Master's
Program: Liberal Arts And General; Teacher Preparatory

Accreditation: NH, MUS, SW

01 President .... Dr. Gregory S. WOODWARD
11 Sr VP Administration/Business .... Mr. William R. ABT
05 Provost .... Dr. Julio C. RIVERA
51 Assoc Vice Pres Adult Education .... Mr. Michael WEST
20 Sr Vice Pres Academic Resources .... Mr. Brad J. ANDREWS
90 Vice Pres Academic Information Svcs .... Mr. Todd KELLEY
26 Assoc Vice Pres for College Rels .... Ms. Elaine L. WALTON
27 Assoc Vice Pres for Communications .... Mr. Robert J. ROSEN
21 Associate Vice President Business .... Mr. William D. HOARE
07 Assoc Vice Pres for Admissions .... Mr. Dean CLARK
04 Special Assistant to President .... Mr. Paul R. HEGLAND
32 Dean of Students .... Ms. Louise PASKEY
42 Dean of Siebert Chapel .... Rev. Ross LARSON
20 Associate Dean of the College .... Dr. David STEEGE
06 Registrar .... Ms. Abby HEINRICHS
36 Director Career Center .... Ms. Jean FREDERICK
91 Director Administrative Computing .... Mr. Richard HUENINK
88 Director of Conferences .... Mr. Kevin SLONAC
19 Director of Campus Security .... Mr. John KLABECHEK, IV
37 Director Student Financial Aid .... Mr. Vatistas VATISTAS
44 Asst Dir Alumni Rels/Annual Giving .... Ms. Lauren HANSEN
14 Director of Computer Center .... Mrs. Carol SABBAR
41 Athletic Director .... Dr. Robert R. BONN
58 Director of Graduate Program .... Dr. Paul ZAVADA
10 Chief Business Officer .... Mr. David MISSURELLI
18 Chief Facilities/Physical Plant .... Mr. William D. HOARE
35 Director Student Affairs .... Ms. Nina FLEMING
38 Director Student Counseling .... Ms. Deborah BETSWORTH
92 Director of Honors Program .... Dr. Paul ULRICH
07 Director of Admissions .... Ms. Michelle HAMILTON
40 Bookstore Manager .... Mrs. Pam ROBERS
29 Asst Director of Alumni Relations .... Mrs. Mardell FISHER
31 Counselor for Community Partnership .... Mr. John M. ANTARAMIAN

College of Menominee Nation (A)

PO Box 1179, Keshena WI 54135-1179
County: Menominee FICE Identification: 031251
Unit ID: 413617
Telephone: (800) 567-2344 Carnegie Class: Tribal
FAX Number: (715) 799-1336 Calendar System: Semester
URL: www.menominee.edu
Established: 1992 Annual Undergrad Tuition & Fees: $7,670
Enrollment: 699 Coed
Affiliation or Control: Tribal Control IRS Status: 501(c)3
Highest Offering: Baccalaureate
Program: Occupational; 2-Year Principally Bachelor's Creditable; Teacher Preparatory; Business Emphasis
Accreditation: NH, ADNUR

01 President .... Dr. Verna M. FOWLER
05 Chief Academic Officer .... Dr. Diana MORRIS
10 Chief Financial Officer .... Ms. Laurie REITER
12 Vice Pres of CMN Green Bay Campus .... Mr. Chad WAUKECHON
26 Dean External Relations .... Dr. Holly YOUNGBEAR-TIBBETS
32 Dean of Student Services .... Mr. Gary BESAW
49 Dean of Letters & Science .... Mrs. Stephanie ERDMANN
66 Dean of Nursing .... Ms. Linda TAYLOR
75 Dean of Technical Education .... Mrs. Deanna BISLEY
59 Dean of Continuing Education .... Mr. Brian BOWALKOWSKI
04 Assistant to the President .... Ms. Melinda COOK
09 Director Institutional Research .... Mr. Ronald JURGENS
30 Advancement Director .... Mrs. Irene KIEFER
25 Director of Sponsored Programs .... Mrs. Jill MARTIN
13 IT Director .... Ms. Renita WILBER
18 Director of Operations .... Mr. Richard WARRINGTON
21 Business Manager .... Mr. Victor ESCALANTE
15 Human Resources Director .... Ms. Gail SWANKE
37 Director Financial Aid .... Ms. Nicole FISH
06 Registrar .... Mrs. Juanita WAUKAU-WILBER
07 Admissions Director .... Ms. Tessa JAMES
88 Voc Rehab Director .... Mr. Norman SHAWANOKASIC
08 Library Director .... Ms. Maria ESCALANTE
88 Campus Planner .... Mr. Joel KROENKE
40 Director of Bookstore .... Ms. Verna DELEON

Columbia College of Nursing (B)

4425 N Port Washington Rd, Milwaukee WI 53212-1099
County: Milwaukee Identification: 006640
Unit ID: 238573
Telephone: (414) 326-2330 Carnegie Class: Not Classified
FAX Number: (414) 236-2331 Calendar System: Semester
URL: www.ccon.edu
Established: 1901 Annual Undergrad Tuition & Fees: $24,150
Enrollment: 158 Coed
Affiliation or Control: Independent Non-Profit IRS Status: 501(c)3
Highest Offering: Baccalaureate
Program: Professional; Nursing Emphasis
Accreditation: NH, NURSE

01 Dean & CEO .... Dr. Jill M. WINTERS
10 Chief Financial/Business Officer .... Ms. Christina ITALIANO
05 Associate Academic Officer .... Ms. Haley GEIGER
37 Director Student Financial Aid .... Ms. Wendy HILVO
06 Registrar .... Ms. Joua XIONG
24 Director Educational Media .... Mr. Keith JACKSON
04 Admin Assistant to the President .... Ms. Gail PETERSON

Concordia University Wisconsin (C)

12800 N Lake Shore Drive, Mequon WI 53097-2402
County: Ozaukee FICE Identification: 003842
Unit ID: 238616
Telephone: (262) 243-5700 Carnegie Class: Master's L
FAX Number: (262) 243-4351 Calendar System: 4/1/4
URL: www.cuw.edu
Established: 1881 Annual Undergrad Tuition & Fees: $24,200
Enrollment: 7,618 Coed
Affiliation or Control: Lutheran Church - Missouri Synod
IRS Status: 501(c)3
Highest Offering: Doctorate
Program: Liberal Arts And General; Teacher Preparatory; Professional
Accreditation: NH, IACBE, MAC, NURSE, OT, @PHAR, PTA, SW

01 President .... Rev Dr. Patrick T. FERRY
11 Executive VP & Chief Oper Ofcr .... Mr. Allen J. PROCHNOW
05 Senior Vice President of Academics .... Dr. William R. CARIO
32 Vice President of Student Life .... Dr. Andrew J. LUPTAK
07 Vice Pres of Enrollment Services .... Mr. Kenneth K. GASCHK
30 Sr Vice Pres of Advancement .... Mr. Duane H. HILGENDORF
13 Vice Pres of Information Technology .... Mr. Thomas G. PHILLIP
26 Vice President of Marketing .... Ms. Anita CLARK
10 VP Finance & CFO .... Ms. Joan M. SCHOLZ
20 Assistant Vice Pres of Academics ....Rev Dr. Randy L. FERGUSON
44 Assistant Vice Pres of Advancement .... Rev Dr. Roy PETERSON
42 Campus Pastor .... Rev. Steven N. SMITH
36 Director Counseling .... Mr. David T. ENTERS
37 Financial Aid Officer .... Mr. Steve P. TAYLOR
06 Registrar .... Dr. Steven MONTREAL
50 Dean School of Business .... Dr. David BORST
88 Dean School Human Services .... Dr. Terri S. KAUL
49 Dean School Arts/Sciences .... Dr. Gaylund K. STONE
53 Dean School of Education .... Dr. Michael UDEN
35 Dean Student Affairs .... Mr. Steve W. CROOK
08 Library Director .... Mr. Christian HIMSEL
09 Institutional Research .... Dr. Tamara R. FERRY
29 Director of Alumni Relations .... Ms. Lisa LILJEGREN
39 Director Student Housing .... Ms. Barbara A. WILSON
41 Athletic Director .... Dr. Rob M. BARNHILL
88 Chair Faculty Senate .... Dr. Brad CONDIE
36 Director Career Services .... Ms. Kim DUNISCH
40 Director Bookstore .... Ms. Laurie COHEN
19 Director Campus Safety .... Mr. Mario VALDES
18 Superintendent Buildings & Grounds .... Mr. Steve V. HIBBARD
15 Director Human Resources .... Ms. Kim MASENTHIN
24 Director Instructional Technology .... Mr. Sean B. YOUNG
26 Public Relations Officer .... Mr. Jeff J. BANDURSKI
28 Minority Student Group Advisor .... Mr. Adam WALKER
86 Asst to President for Govern & Plng .... Dr. Ross STUEBER

DeVry University - Milwaukee Center (D)

411 E Wisconsin Avenue, Ste 300,
Milwaukee WI 53202-4400
County: Milwaukee Identification: 666225
Unit ID: 238935
Telephone: (414) 278-7677 Carnegie Class: Spec/Bus
FAX Number: (414) 278-0137 Calendar System: Semester
URL: www.devry.edu
Established: 1931 Annual Undergrad Tuition & Fees: $16,156
Enrollment: 294 Coed
Affiliation or Control: Proprietary IRS Status: Proprietary
Highest Offering: Master's
Program: Occupational; Professional; Business Emphasis
Accreditation: &NH

01 Campus Director .... Jeunet DAVENPORT

† Regional accreditation is carried under the parent institution in Downers Grove, IL.

DeVry University - Waukesha Center (E)

N 14 W23833 Stone Ridge Dr, Ste 450,
Waukesha WI 53188-1157
County: Waukesha Identification: 666226
Unit ID: 439260
Telephone: (262) 347-2911 Carnegie Class: Not Classified
FAX Number: (262) 798-9912 Calendar System: Semester
URL: www.devry.edu
Established: 1931 Annual Undergrad Tuition & Fees: $16,156
Enrollment: 173 Coed
Affiliation or Control: Proprietary IRS Status: Proprietary
Highest Offering: Master's
Program: Professional; Business Emphasis
Accreditation: &NH

01 Center Dean .... Kate PELCHAT

† Regional accreditation is carried under the parent institution in Downers Grove, IL.

Edgewood College (F)

1000 Edgewood College Drive, Madison WI 53711-1997
County: Dane FICE Identification: 003848
Unit ID: 238661
Telephone: (608) 663-4861 Carnegie Class: DRU
FAX Number: (608) 663-3291 Calendar System: Semester
URL: www.edgewood.edu
Established: 1927 Annual Undergrad Tuition & Fees: $23,740
Enrollment: 1,711 Coed
Affiliation or Control: Roman Catholic IRS Status: 501(c)3
Highest Offering: Doctorate
Program: Liberal Arts And General; Teacher Preparatory; Professional
Accreditation: NH, ACBSP, MFCD, NURSE, TED

01 President .... Dr. Daniel J. CAREY
03 Executive Vice President .... Dr. Scott FLANAGAN
05 VP Academic Affs/Academic Dean .... Dr. Dean PRIBBENOW
32 VP Student Devel/Dean of Students .... Dr. Margaret R. BALISTRERI-CLARKE
10 Vice President Business & Finance .... Mr. Michael GUNS
30 Vice Pres Inst Advancement/Dir Dev .... Mr. John USELMAN
13 Director of Information Technology .... Mr. Deron KLING
20 Associate Academic Dean .... Dr. Kelly GRORUD
58 Dean Grad Adult/Profess Studies .... Dr. Scott CAMPBELL
06 Registrar .... Ms. Michelle KELLY
08 Library Director .... Dr. Sylvia CONTRERAS
36 Director for Career Counseling Svcs .... Ms. Shawn JOHNSON-WILLIAMS
29 Alumni Director .... Ms. Kathleen O'CONNOR
26 Director Public Relations .... Mr. Edward TAYLOR
15 Director of Human Resources .... Ms. Annie STROUD
18 Director Facilities & Operations .... Ms. Susan SERRAULT
35 Director Student Activities .... Dr. Beth JOHN
38 Director Student Counseling .... Ms. Stephanie GRAHAM
07 Director of Admissions .... Ms. Christine BENEDICT
21 Controller .... Ms. Jane WILHELM
28 Director of Diversity .... Ms. Pearl LEONARD-ROCK
37 Director Student Financial Aid .... Ms. Kari GRIBBLE
09 Director of Institutional Research .... Dr. Yang ZHANG

Herzing University (G)

5218 E Terrace Drive, Madison WI 53718-8340
County: Dane FICE Identification: 009621
Unit ID: 240392
Telephone: (608) 249-6611 Carnegie Class: Bac/Assoc
FAX Number: (608) 249-8593 Calendar System: Semester
URL: www.herzing.edu
Established: 1948 Annual Undergrad Tuition & Fees: $17,100
Enrollment: 874 Coed
Affiliation or Control: Proprietary IRS Status: Proprietary
Highest Offering: Master's
Program: Technical Emphasis
Accreditation: NH, ADNUR, MAAB

01 President .... Ms. Renee HERZING
02 Campus President .... Mrs. Chris MONTAGNINO
10 CFO & Vice President of Finance .... Mr. Ryan O'DESKY
05 Academic Dean .... Mr. Brian WILLISON
37 Director of Educational Funding .... Mr. Donald FINCH
06 Director of Registration .... Ms. Ginger SCHMELZER
07 Director of Admissions .... Mr. Matthew SCHNEIDER
36 Director of Career Development .... Mr. Jeff WESTRA

ITT Technical Institute (H)

470 Security Boulevard, Green Bay WI 54313-9705
County: Brown Identification: 666317
Unit ID: 440165
Telephone: (920) 662-9000 Carnegie Class: Spec/Tech
FAX Number: (920) 662-9384 Calendar System: Quarter
URL: www.itt-tech.edu
Established: 2003 Annual Undergrad Tuition & Fees: N/A
Enrollment: 600 Coed
Affiliation or Control: Proprietary IRS Status: Proprietary
Highest Offering: Baccalaureate
Program: Technical Emphasis
Accreditation: ACICS

† Branch campus of ITT Technical Institute, Indianapolis, IN.

ITT Technical Institute (I)

6300 West Layton Avenue, Greenfield WI 53220-4612
County: Milwaukee FICE Identification: 030875
Unit ID: 238892
Telephone: (414) 282-9494 Carnegie Class: Spec/Tech
FAX Number: (414) 282-9698 Calendar System: Quarter
URL: www.itt-tech.edu
Established: 1989 Annual Undergrad Tuition & Fees: N/A
Enrollment: 885 Coed
Affiliation or Control: Proprietary IRS Status: Proprietary
Highest Offering: Baccalaureate
Program: Technical Emphasis
Accreditation: ACICS

† Branch campus of ITT Technical Institute, Indianapolis, IN.

Lac Courte Oreilles Ojibwa Community College (J)

13466 W Trepania Road, Hayward WI 54843-2181
County: Sawyer FICE Identification: 025322
Unit ID: 260372
Telephone: (715) 634-4790 Carnegie Class: Tribal
FAX Number: (715) 634-5049 Calendar System: Semester
URL: www.lco.edu

Established: 1982 Annual Undergrad Tuition & Fees: $3,870
Enrollment: 433 Coed
Affiliation or Control: Tribal Control IRS Status: 501(c)3
Highest Offering: Associate Degree
Program: Occupational; 2-Year Principally Bachelor's Creditable
Accreditation: **NH**, MAC

01 Interim President ....Dr. Raymond BURNS
05 Interim Academic Dean ....Dr. Beth PAAP
32 Dean Student Services/Enroll Mgmt ....Mr. Raymond BURNS
10 Controller ....Ms. Anne ADAMS
06 Registrar ....Mrs. Annette WIGGINS
37 Int Financial Aid Director ....Ms. Jill MATCHETT
46 Bus Affairs Dir/Ofc Sponsored Pgms ....Mr. Dan GETZ
15 Human Resource Director ....Mr. Peter WHITENECK

Lakeland College (A)

PO Box 359, Sheboygan WI 53082-0359
County: Sheboygan FICE Identification: 003854
Unit ID: 238980
Telephone: (920) 565-1000 Carnegie Class: Master's L
FAX Number: (920) 565-1206 Calendar System: Semester
URL: www.lakeland.edu
Established: 1862 Annual Undergrad Tuition & Fees: $21,242
Enrollment: 3,881 Coed
Affiliation or Control: United Church Of Christ IRS Status: 501(c)3
Highest Offering: Master's
Program: Liberal Arts And General
Accreditation: **NH**, TEAC

01 President ....Dr. Michael A. GRANDILLO
04 Assistant to the President ....Ms. Ann M. FLAD-JESION
05 Vice Pres Academic Affairs ....Dr. Margaret L. ALBRINCK
11 Senior Vice Pres Administration ....Mr. Daniel W. ECK
30 Vice President for Advancement ....Dr. Kenneth D. STRMISKA
10 Vice President Finance/CFO ....Mr. Joseph D. BOTANA, II
32 Vice President Student Development ....Mr. Nathan D. DEHNE
56 Vice Pres Kellett Adult Education ....Mr. Zach r. VOELZ
35 Dean of Students ....Ms. Sandra L. GIBBONS-VOLLBRECHT
43 VP Intl Programs/General Counsel ....Mr. Anthony E. FESSLER
06 Registrar ....Ms. Erin K. KOHL
09 Director of Institutional Research ....Vacant
08 Director of Library Services ....Ms. Ann K. PENKE
07 Director of Admissions ....Mr. Nick A. SPAETH
37 Director of Financial Aid ....Ms. Patty L. TAYLOR
85 International Student Advisor ....Mr. Pei Patrick LIU
27 Director of Communications ....Mr. David D. GALLIANETTI
41 Athletic Director ....Ms. Jane A. BOUCHE
21 Controller ....Ms. Sharon L. ROOB
29 Director of Alumni Relations ....Ms. Lisa B. VIHOS
36 Director of Career Development ....Ms. Lisa M. STEPHAN

Lawrence University (B)

711 E. Boldt Way, Appleton WI 54911
County: Outagamie FICE Identification: 003856
Unit ID: 239017
Telephone: (920) 832-7000 Carnegie Class: Bac/A&S
FAX Number: (920) 832-6606 Calendar System: Other
URL: www.lawrence.edu
Established: 1847 Annual Undergrad Tuition & Fees: $38,481
Enrollment: 1,487 Coed
Affiliation or Control: Independent Non-Profit IRS Status: 501(c)3
Highest Offering: Baccalaureate
Program: Liberal Arts And General
Accreditation: **NH**, MUS

01 President ....Dr. Jill BECK
04 Executive Asst to the President ....Ms. Laurie PETRICK
05 Provost and Dean of the Faculty ....Dr. David BURROWS
10 VP Business & Operations ....Mr. Brian RISTE
30 VP Development/Alumni Rels ....Mr. Calvin D. HUSMANN
32 VP Student Affairs & Dean ....Ms. Nancy D. TRUESDELL
29 VP Alumni/Constituency Engagement ....Mr. Mark D. BRESEMAN
27 Assoc Vice Pres Communications ....Mr. Craig L. GAGNON
44 Assoc VP Major & Planned Giving ....Ms. Barbara J. STACK
21 Assoc VP of Business & Operations ....Ms. Dawn ROST
64 Dean Conservatory of Music ....Mr. Brian G. PERTL
36 Dean of Career Services ....Ms. Mary T. MEANY
35 Dean Student Academic Services ....Mr. Geoff GAJEWSKI
09 Director of Research Administration ....Dr. William F. SKINNER
07 Director of Admissions ....Mr. Kenneth L. ANSELMENT
37 Director of Financial Aid ....Ms. Sara C. HOLMAN
20 Associate Dean of the Faculty ....Ms. Ruth M. LANOUETTE
28 Asst Dean Students Multicul Affs ....Ms. Pa Lee MOUA
06 Registrar ....Ms. Anne S. NORMAN
08 Librarian ....Mr. Peter J. GILBERT
30 Director of Development ....Ms. Stacy J. MARA
41 Athletic Director ....Mr. Michael W. SZKODZINSKI
36 Director of the Career Center ....Ms. Kathleen M. HEINZEN
13 Director Information Tech Svcs ....Mr. Steven M. ARMSTRONG
15 Director of Human Resources ....Ms. Sandy ISSELMANN
18 Director of Facility Services ....Mr. Daniel R. MEYER
38 Director Counseling Services ....Ms. Kathleen F. FUCHS

Madison Media Institute-College of Media Arts (C)

2702 Agriculture Drive, Madison WI 53718-6787
County: Dane FICE Identification: 010913
Unit ID: 364168
Telephone: (608) 663-2000 Carnegie Class: Assoc/PrivFP
FAX Number: (608) 442-0141 Calendar System: Semester
URL: www.mediainstitute.edu
Established: 1969 Annual Undergrad Tuition & Fees: $16,500
Enrollment: 582 Coed
Affiliation or Control: Proprietary IRS Status: Proprietary
Highest Offering: Baccalaureate
Program: 2-Year Principally Bachelor's Creditable; Technical Emphasis
Accreditation: **ACCSC**

01 President ....Mr. Donald G. MADELUNG
10 Chief Financial/Business Officer ....Ms. Laura KLOCKE
07 Admissions Director ....Mr. Francisco TORRES
53 Dean of Education ....Mr. Rich DENHART
36 Director Student Placement ....Ms. Laura MAEL

Maranatha Baptist Bible College & Seminary (D)

745 W Main Street, Watertown WI 53094-7600
County: Jefferson FICE Identification: 023172
Unit ID: 239071
Telephone: (920) 261-9300 Carnegie Class: Bac/Diverse
FAX Number: (920) 261-9109 Calendar System: Semester
URL: www.mbbc.edu
Established: 1968 Annual Undergrad Tuition & Fees: $12,860
Enrollment: 804 Coed
Affiliation or Control: Independent Non-Profit IRS Status: 501(c)3
Highest Offering: Master's
Program: Liberal Arts And General; Teacher Preparatory; Professional; Religious Emphasis
Accreditation: **NH**

01 President ....Dr. Martin MARRIOTT
03 Executive Vice President ....Dr. Matthew DAVIS
05 Vice President for Academic Affairs ....Dr. John R. BROCK
30 Vice President for Inst Advancement ....Dr. Jim H. HARRISON
10 Vice President for Business Affairs ....Mr. Mark W. STEVENS
32 Dean of Students ....Mr. John DAVIS
06 Registrar ....Dr. Steve CARLSON
07 Director of Admissions ....Dr. James H. HARRISON
30 Director of Development ....Mr. Steve BOARD
09 Director of Institutional Research ....Dr. Matthew DAVIS
15 Director Personnel Services ....Mr. Kevin MONTNEY
18 Chief Facilities/Physical Plant ....Dr. Werner LUMM
26 Chief Public Relations Officer ....Mr. Peter WRIGHT
41 Athletic Director ....Mr. Robert THOMPSON
08 Librarian ....Miss Lois OETKEN
29 Director Alumni Relations ....Mr. John DAVIS
37 Director Student Financial Aid ....Mr. Randy HIBBS

Marian University (E)

45 S National Avenue, Fond Du Lac WI 54935-4699
County: Fond Du Lac FICE Identification: 003861
Unit ID: 239080
Telephone: (920) 923-7600 Carnegie Class: Master's L
FAX Number: (920) 923-7154 Calendar System: Semester
URL: www.marianuniversity.edu
Established: 1936 Annual Undergrad Tuition & Fees: $23,440
Enrollment: 2,615 Coed
Affiliation or Control: Roman Catholic IRS Status: 501(c)3
Highest Offering: Doctorate
Program: Liberal Arts And General; Teacher Preparatory; Professional
Accreditation: **NH**, IACBE, NURSE, RAD, SW, TED

01 President ....Dr. Steven R. DISALVO
05 Exec VP Academic & Student Affairs ....Dr. Edward H. OGLE
84 VP Enrollment Management ....Ms. Stacey L. AKEY
88 VP for Mission & Retention ....Ms. Kate CANDEE
30 Vice President for Advancement ....Mr. Paul M. NEUBERGER
10 Dir Business & Finance/Controller ....Ms. Mary K. KOSMER
04 Executive Assistant to President ....Ms. Carey C. GARDIN
53 Dean School of Education ....Dr. Sue A. STODDART
66 Dean Nursing/Health Professions ....Dr. Julie A. LUETSCHWAGER
49 Dean Arts/Sciences ....Dr. James VAN DYKE
50 Dean Business/Public Safety ....Dr. Jeffrey G. REED
32 Dean of Students ....Ms. Kerry STRUPP
08 Director of Libraries ....Ms. Mary Ellen GORMICAN
55 Director Adult/Graduate Studies ....Vacant
18 General Manager/Facilities ....Mr. Layne D. SESSIONS
06 Registrar ....Ms. Cheryl A. TEICHMILLER
09 Director of Institutional Research ....Dr. Sylvia K. REED
37 Director of Financial Aid ....Ms. Pamela WARREN
42 Director of Campus Ministry ....Sr. Marie SCOTT, CSA
26 Director University Relations ....Ms. Lisa L. KIDD
29 Director Alumni Relations ....Ms. Mary SCHWINER
07 Senior Director of Admission ....Ms. Shannon S. LALUZERNE
16 Director of Human Resources ....Ms. Cathy T. FLOOD
41 Director of Athletics ....Mr. Jason J. MURPHY
88 Dean Advising/Academic Services ....Ms. Cathy M. MATHWEG
23 Director of Health Services ....Ms. Connie DIENER
36 Director Career & Grad School Svcs ....Ms. Ashly G. GARNER
88 Director of Campus Dining Services ....Ms. Nikki A. KRAMER
13 Director of Information Technology ....Mr. Keith L. FALK
40 Director of Bookstore ....Ms. Mary MANGAN-FLOOD
38 Director of Counseling ....Ms. Ellen MERCER
92 Director Honors Program ....Dr. Abbey E. ROSEN
108 Director of Inst Assessment ....Mr. Gregory M. CANARD
35 Dir Student Activities/Greek Life ....Ms. Julie A. GNIEWEK
39 Director of Student Services ....Ms. Dee HARMSEN
104 Coordinator of Study Abroad ....Vacant
25 Director Research & Sponsored Grnts ....Mr. Marc D. HEIMERL

Marquette University (F)

PO Box 1881, Milwaukee WI 53201-1881
County: Milwaukee FICE Identification: 003863
Unit ID: 239105
Telephone: (414) 288-7700 Carnegie Class: DRU
FAX Number: (414) 288-3300 Calendar System: Semester
URL: www.mu.edu
Established: 1881 Annual Undergrad Tuition & Fees: $33,244
Enrollment: 10,740 Coed
Affiliation or Control: Roman Catholic IRS Status: 501(c)3
Highest Offering: Doctorate
Program: Liberal Arts And General; Teacher Preparatory; Professional
Accreditation: **NH**, ARCPA, BUS, BUSA, CLPSY, COPSY, DENT, ENG, JOUR, LAW, MIDWF, MT, NURSE, PTA, SP, TED, THEA

01 President ....Rev. Scott R. PILARZ, SJ
03 Executive Vice President ....Dr. Mary DISTANISLAO
05 Provost ....Dr. John J. PAULY
10 Vice President Finance ....Mr. John C. LAMB
11 Vice President Administration ....Mr. Arthur F. SCHEUBER
32 Vice President for Student Affairs ....Dr. L. Christopher MILLER
30 Interim VP University Advancement ....Mr. Thomas S. MACKINNON
27 Vice President Public Affairs ....Ms. Rana H. ALTENBURG
43 Vice President/General Counsel ....Ms. Cynthia M. BAUER
26 Vice Pres Marketing/Communication ....Ms. Patricia L. GERAGHTY
35 Assoc Vice Pres Student Affairs ....Dr. Linda J. LEE
15 Asst Vice Pres/Dir Human Resources ....Mr. Octavio CASTRO
39 Asst Vice Pres/Dean Residence Life ....Dr. James P. MCMAHON
88 Sr Assoc VP Development ....Mr. Timothy RIPPINGER
20 Vice Prov Undergrad Pgms/Teaching ....Dr. Gary MEYER
58 V Prov Research/Dean Graduate Sch ....Dr. Jeanne HOSSENLOPP
90 Assoc Vice Prov Educational Tech ....Mr. G. Jon PRAY
88 Assoc Vice Prov Acad Support Pgm ....Ms. Anne D. DEAHL
28 Sr Advisor Prov Diversity Init ....Dr. William WELBURN
06 Registrar ....Ms. Georgia D. MCRAE
49 Interim Dean of Arts & Sciences ....Rev. Philip J. ROSSI, SJ
50 Dean of Business Administration ....Dr. Linda M. SALCHENBERGER
52 Dean of Dentistry ....Dr. William K. LOBB
54 Dean of Engineering ....Dr. Robert BISHOP
60 Dean of Communication ....Dr. Lori BERGEN
76 Dean of Health Sciences ....Dr. William CULLINAN
61 Dean of the Law School ....Mr. Joseph D. KEARNEY
66 Dean of Nursing ....Dr. Margaret CALLAHAN
53 Dean College of Education ....Dr. William A. HENK
107 Dean Col of Professional Studies ....Dr. Robert J. DEAHL
08 Dean of Libraries ....Ms. Janice WELBURN
07 Dean of Admissions ....Mr. Robert BLUST
35 Dean of Students ....Dr. Stephanie QUADE
25 Exec Director of Research Support ....Ms. Katherine DURBEN
104 Dir Office International Education ....Mr. Terence MILLER
37 Director of Financial Aid ....Ms. Susan M. TEERINK
36 Director Career Services Center ....Ms. Laura F. KESTNER
41 VP and Director of Athletics ....Mr. Lawrence WILLIAMS
23 Exec Dir Student Health Services ....Dr. Carolyn S. SMITH
38 Director of Counseling Center ....Dr. Michael J. ZEBROWSKI
42 Vice Pres of Univ Mission/Ministry ....Dr. Stephanie J. RUSSELL
13 Chief Information Officer ....Ms. Kathy J. LANG
18 Director Facilities Services ....Mr. Ronald L. RIPLEY
19 Director Public Safety ....Mr. Lawrence R. RICKARD
40 Director Marquette Spirit Shop ....Mr. James K. GRAEBERT
96 Director of Purchasing ....Ms. Jenny ALEXANDER
29 Exec Director of Alumni Association ....Mr. Timothy J. SIMMONS

Medical College of Wisconsin (G)

PO Box 26509, Milwaukee WI 53226-0509
County: Milwaukee FICE Identification: 024535
Unit ID: 239169
Telephone: (414) 955-8296 Carnegie Class: Spec/Med
FAX Number: (414) 955-6560 Calendar System: Other
URL: www.mcw.edu
Established: 1893 Annual Graduate Tuition & Fees: $46,851
Enrollment: 1,257 Coed
Affiliation or Control: Independent Non-Profit IRS Status: 501(c)3
Highest Offering: Doctorate; No Undergraduates
Program: Professional
Accreditation: **NH**, DENT, MED, PDPSY, PH

01 President & CEO ....Dr. John R. RAYMOND, SR.
05 Dean/Executive Vice President ....Dr. Joseph E. KERSCHNER
10 Sr Vice Pres Finance/ Administration ....Mr. Glenn Allen BOLTON, JR.
88 Dean Grad Sch Biomedical Science ....Dr. Ravi P. MISRA
30 Vice Pres Institutional Advancement ....Mr. James W. HEALD
15 Vice President Human Resources ....Ms. Sherri DUCHARME-WHITE
86 Vice Pres Government/Community Affs ....Ms. Kathryn A. KUHN
28 VP Corporate Compliance Risk Mgmt ....Mr. Daniel WICKEHAM
100 Chief of Staff ....Ms. Mara LORD
44 Assoc Vice President Development ....Ms. Pamela J. GARVEY
26 Assoc Vice Pres Public Affairs ....Mr. Richard N. KATSCHKE
20 Senior Assoc Dean Education ....Dr. Karen MARCDANTE
22 Sr Asc Dean Faculty Affs/Diversity ....Dr. Alonzo P. WALKER
32 Assoc Dean for Student Affairs ....Dr. Richard L. HOLLOWAY
63 Assoc Dean Graduate Med Educ ....Dr. Kenneth B. SIMONS
46 Senior Associate Dean Research ....Dr. David D. GUTTERMAN
20 Associate Dean Curriculum ....Dr. Philip N. REDLICH
45 Assoc Dean Educ Support/Evaluation ....Dr. Deborah E. SIMPSON
21 Director Budget Administration ....Ms. Deidre ERWIN
13 Director Application Development ....Ms. Rebecca L. MORRISON

08 Director Medical Libraries .... Ms. Mary B. BLACKWELDER
07 Director Admissions .... Ms. Jennifer L. HALUZAK
06 Registrar .... Ms. Lesley A. MACK
18 Dir Facil Engineering/Maintenance .... Mr. Jeffrey BORNEMANN
37 Director Student Financial Services .... Ms. Linda L. PASCHAL
25 Director Grants & Contracts .... Ms. April HAVERTY
29 Exec Director Alumni Relations .... Mr. William A. SCHULTZ
21 Director Business Services .... Ms. Paulette PECARD
88 Medical Dir Clinical Informatics .... Dr. Rick D. GILLIS
40 Manager of Bookstore .... Ms. Cathy GRANFIELD

Midwest College of Oriental Medicine (A)

6232 Bankers Road, Racine WI 53403-9747

County: Racine FICE Identification: 030612
Unit ID: 383020
Telephone: (800) 593-2320 Carnegie Class: Spec/Health
FAX Number: (262) 554-7475 Calendar System: Quarter
URL: www.acupuncture.edu
Established: 1979 Annual Undergrad Tuition & Fees: $15,751
Enrollment: 226 Coed
Affiliation or Control: Proprietary IRS Status: Proprietary
Highest Offering: Master's; No Lower Division
Program: Professional
Accreditation: ACUP

01 President .... Dr. William J. DUNBAR
05 Academic Director .... Dr. Robert CHELNICK
20 Academic Dean/Research Director .... Dr. Alan URETZ
88 Projects Director .... Dr. Kristine L. LA POINT
37 Director of Financial Aid .... Ms. Elizabeth M. HOJAN-FIGGE
07 Admissions Coord/Transfer Credit ..... Ms. Kelly A. WESTERLUND
06 Records Officer/Registrar .... Ms. Amy L. BENISH
08 Dean of Students/Librarian .... Mr. John BALLARINI
32 Dean of Students .... Ms. Olga GAJDOSIK
09 Research Director .... Mr. Jin Hua XIE
63 Dean of Biomedicine Science .... Dr. Peter NIKAS
85 Dean of Foreign Students .... Dr. Duckin SUH
17 Internship Director .... Dr. Helen WU
09 Clinic Tracking/Inst Evaluation .... Ms. Deirdre M. DUNBAR
86 Compliance Officer .... Mr. Harry S. HEIFETZ
91 Information Systems .... Mr. William H. LEHMAN
26 Marketing/Student Affairs .... Mr. Chris A. KRAJNIAK
88 Office Manager .... Ms. Stephanie M. PITTMAN

Milwaukee Institute of Art & Design (B)

273 E Erie Street, Milwaukee WI 53202-6003

County: Milwaukee FICE Identification: 020771
Unit ID: 239309
Telephone: (414) 847-3200 Carnegie Class: Spec/Arts
FAX Number: (414) 291-8077 Calendar System: Semester
URL: www.miad.edu
Established: 1974 Annual Undergrad Tuition & Fees: $29,942
Enrollment: 724 Coed
Affiliation or Control: Independent Non-Profit IRS Status: 501(c)3
Highest Offering: Baccalaureate
Program: Liberal Arts And General; Fine Arts Emphasis
Accreditation: NH, ART

01 President .... Mr. Neil J. HOFFMAN
05 VP of Academic Affairs .... Mr. David MARTIN
84 VP for Enrollment Management .... Ms. Mary C. SCHOPP
04 Executive Assistant to President .... Ms. Dagmar L. CARNDUFF
09 Assoc VP Academic Plng/Assessment .... Ms. Cynthia LYNCH
10 Chief Financial Officer .... Ms. Brenda JONES
32 Dean of Students .... Mr. Tony J. NOWAK
30 Director of Development .... Mr. Ryan DANIELS
37 Executive Director of Financial Aid .... Ms. Carol MASSE
07 Executive Director of Admissions .... Ms. Stacey STEINBERG
26 Director of Communications .... Ms. Vivian M. ROTHSCHILD
08 Director of Library Services .... Ms. Cynthia D. LYNCH
36 Director of Career Services .... Mr. Duane P. SEIDENSTICKER
51 Dir Pre-College & Adult Learning .... Ms. Jill F. KUNSMANN
19 Director Security/Safety .... Mr. Keith A. KOTOWICZ
06 Director of Registration Services .... Ms. Jean WEIMER
38 Director of College Advising .... Ms. Rebecca BALISTRERI
18 Building Maintenance Manager .... Mr. Michael A. GOETZ
29 Dir Cultural & Alumni Relations .... Ms. Melissa RICHARDS
15 Director of Human Resources .... Ms. Edie MCCLELLAN
20 Director of Academic Operations .... Ms. Marie KAMINSKI

Milwaukee School of Engineering (C)

1025 N Broadway, Milwaukee WI 53202-3109

County: Milwaukee FICE Identification: 003868
Unit ID: 239318
Telephone: (414) 277-7300 Carnegie Class: Master's S
FAX Number: (414) 277-7454 Calendar System: Quarter
URL: www.msoe.edu
Established: 1903 Annual Undergrad Tuition & Fees: $31,920
Enrollment: 2,486 Coed
Affiliation or Control: Independent Non-Profit IRS Status: 501(c)3
Highest Offering: Master's
Program: Professional; Technical Emphasis
Accreditation: NH, CONST, ENG, ENGT, NURSE, PERF

01 President .... Dr. Hermann VIETS
05 Vice President Academics .... Dr. Fred BERRY
10 Vice President of Finance and CFO .... Mr. Armund M. JANTO
30 Vice President of Development .... Mr. A. Frank HABIB
18 Facility Manager .... Vacant
32 Vice President Student Life .... Mr. Patrick J. COFFEY
84 Vice Pres of Enrollment Management .... Mr. Timothy VALLEY
09 Dean of Institutional Research .... Mr. Leonard A. VANDEN BOOM
25 Dean Grants & Projects .... Mr. Thomas E. BRAY
48 Chair Architectural Engr Dept .... Dr. Deborah JACKMAN
50 Chair School of Business .... Mr. Steve BIALEK
54 Chair Electrical Engr/CPU Sci Dept .... Dr. Stephen WILLIAMS
97 Chair General Studies Department .... Dr. David KENT
81 Chair Mathematics Department .... Dr. Karl H. DAVID
54 Chair Mechanical Engineering Dept ...... Dr. Matthew A. PANHANS
81 Chair Physics/Chemistry Dept .... Dr. Matey KALTCHEV
66 Chair Nursing Department .... Dr. Debra JENKS
21 Controller .... Ms. Janda VAVRICKA
06 Registrar .... Ms. Mary F. NIELSEN
26 Director Marketing Public Affairs .... Ms. Sandra L. EVERTS
27 Director Public & Media Relations .... Ms. JoEllen BURDUE
15 Director of Human Resources .... Mr. Kevin A. MORIN
37 Director of Financial Aid .... Mr. Steve MIDTHUN
21 Director of Student Accounts .... Ms. Debra A. DANNECKER
44 Director of Development .... Mr. Jonathan V. KOWALSKI, JR.
38 Director of Counseling .... Mr. Joseph P. MELOY
88 Director Learning Resource Center .... Mr. Brian E. BURKE
35 Director Student Activities .... Mr. Richard GAGLIANO
39 Director Residence Halls .... Dr. William E. BREESE
41 Director Athletics .... Mr. Dan I. HARRIS
08 Director of Library & Info Services .... Mr. Gary S. SHIMEK
105 Director of Services/Webmaster .... Mr. Kent A. PETERSON
19 Director of Public Safety .... Mr. William P. FADROWSKI
88 Director Fluid Power Institute .... Mr. Tom S. WANKE
13 Dir Computer/Communications Svcs .... Vacant
29 Director Alumni Affairs .... Ms. Cathy VAREBROOK
07 Director of Admissions .... Ms. Dana GRENNIER
36 Director Student Placement .... Ms. Mary SPENCER
88 Asst Director of Student Life .... Mr. Nick SEIDLER
40 Bookstore Manager .... Mr. David P. ABRAHAMSON

Mount Mary College (D)

2900 N Menomonee River Parkway, Milwaukee WI 53222-4597

County: Milwaukee FICE Identification: 003869
Unit ID: 239390
Telephone: (414) 258-4810 Carnegie Class: Master's S
FAX Number: (414) 256-1224 Calendar System: Semester
URL: www.mtmary.edu
Established: 1913 Annual Undergrad Tuition & Fees: $23,600
Enrollment: 1,856 Female
Affiliation or Control: Roman Catholic IRS Status: 501(c)3
Highest Offering: Master's
Program: Liberal Arts And General; Teacher Preparatory; Professional
Accreditation: NH, CIDA, DIETC, DIETI, OT, SW

01 President .... Dr. Eileen SCHWALBACH
05 Acting VP Academic/Student Affairs .... Dr. Karen FRIEDLEN
10 Vice Pres Finance & Administration .... Mr. Reyes GONZALEZ
30 Vice Pres External Relations .... Ms. Donna GASTEVICH
26 VP Communications/Comm Engage .... Ms. Lynn SPRANGERS
84 Vice Pres Enrollment Services .... Mr. David WEGENER
88 Vice President Mission/ Identity .... Sr. Joan PENZENSTADLER, SSND
20 Assoc Dean Academic Affairs .... Dr. Wendy MCCREDIE
32 Assoc Dean for Student Affairs .... Ms. Martha NELSON
58 Assoc Dean Graduate Education .... Dr. Doug MICKELSON
66 Dean Nursing Program .... Dr. Jill WINTERS
88 Exec Dir Women's Leadership Inst .... Ms. Beth WNUK
21 Controller .... Ms. Janet MCKNIGHT
06 Registrar .... Dr. Mary KARR
102 Senior Director of Development .... Ms. Cynthia ECHOLS
44 Annual Giving Officer .... Ms. Sophia KINTIS MENENDEZ
27 Senior Dir of Public Relations/Mktg .... Ms. Susan SEILER
29 Senior Dir of Alumnae Relations .... Ms. Susan NIEBERLE
07 Director of Graduate Admissions .... Ms. Judy BORAWSKI
07 Director of Undergraduate Admission ..... Ms. Rachel GONNERING
09 Director of Inst Research .... Vacant
08 Director of Library .... Ms. Julie KAMIKAWA
13 Director of Information Technology .... Mr. Praveen KRISHNAMURTI
37 Director Financial Aid .... Ms. Debra DUFF
35 Director of Student Engagement .... Ms. Amy DANIELSON
39 Residence Life Director .... Ms. Beth SCHOENWETTER
36 Dir of Advising/Career Development .... Ms. Michelle SMALLEY
104 Director of International Studies .... Ms. Nan METZGER
15 Director of Human Resources .... Ms. Teri COX
41 Athletic Director .... Ms. Janae MAGNUSON
42 Director of Campus Ministry .... Ms. Lea ROSENBERG
18 Director of Buildings & Grounds .... Sr. Georgeann KRZYZANOWSKI, SSND
19 Director of Security .... Mr. Paul LESHOK
40 Mgr Barnes & Noble Bookstore .... Ms. Whitney BAUMGARTEN
105 Website and Photo Manager .... Ms. Eichelle THOMPSON
04 Executive Assistant to President .... Ms. Pamela SALOUN

Nashotah House (E)

2777 Mission Road, Nashotah WI 53058-9793

County: Waukesha FICE Identification: 003874
Unit ID: 239424
Telephone: (262) 646-6500 Carnegie Class: Spec/Faith
FAX Number: (262) 646-6504 Calendar System: Semester
URL: www.nashotah.edu
Established: 1842 Annual Graduate Tuition & Fees: $11,850
Enrollment: 119 Coed
Affiliation or Control: Protestant Episcopal IRS Status: 501(c)3
Highest Offering: Doctorate; No Undergraduates
Program: Professional; Religious Emphasis
Accreditation: THEOL

01 President & Dean .... Rt Rev. Edward L. SALMON
03 Provost .... Mr. Richard LONGABAUGH
11 Assoc Dean of Admin & Development .... Vacant
05 Associate Dean for Academic Affairs .... Rev. Steven A. PEAY
32 Assoc Dean Student Affs/Dir Admiss .... Dr. Carol K. KLUKAS
08 Library Director .... Mr. David G. SHERWOOD
26 Director of Communications .... Vacant
30 Dir Development & Alumni Relations .. Mr. Charleston D. WILSON
18 Chief Facilities/Physical Plant .... Mr. Charlie RICHARDS
40 Bookstore Director .... Ms. Charlotte BOOTH
04 Secretary to the Dean .... Mrs. Sandy MILLS

Northland College (F)

1411 Ellis Avenue, Ashland WI 54806-3999

County: Ashland FICE Identification: 003875
Unit ID: 239512
Telephone: (715) 682-1699 Carnegie Class: Bac/A&S
FAX Number: (715) 682-1308 Calendar System: Other
URL: www.northland.edu
Established: 1892 Annual Undergrad Tuition & Fees: $28,568
Enrollment: 519 Coed
Affiliation or Control: United Church Of Christ IRS Status: 501(c)3
Highest Offering: Baccalaureate
Program: Liberal Arts And General; Teacher Preparatory
Accreditation: NH

01 President .... Dr. Michael MILLER
05 Vice President of Academic Affairs .... Ms. Cheryl CONTANT
30 Int VP of Institutional Advancement .... Ms. Kristin LIPHART
10 VP Finance & Administration .... Mr. Robert JACKSON
84 VP of Inst Marketing & Enroll Mgmt .... Mr. Rick SMITH
32 VP of Stdnt Affairs & Inst Sustain .... Ms. Michele MEYER
20 Associate Academic Dean .... Mr. Alan BREW
07 Associate Director of Admissions .... Mr. Max METZ
06 Registrar .... Ms. Kathy TRAYNOR
08 Library Director .... Ms. Julia WAGGONER
29 Sr Advanc Officer Alumni Relations .... Ms. Michelle CHASE
13 Director of IT .... Mr. Ray GREGOR
41 Athletic Director .... Mr. William WILSON
15 Director Human Resources .... Mr. Paul SKORACZEWSKI
35 Dir Career Educ & Retention .... Ms. Patti FENNER-LEINO
18 Director of Facilities .... Mr. Thomas HMIELEWSKI
37 Director of Student Financial Aid .... Ms. Heather SHELLY
21 Controller .... Ms. Lori BENNETTS
44 Director of Gift Planning .... Ms. Lois ALBRECHT
09 Institutional Research Specialist .... Ms. Petra HOFSTEDT
04 Exec Assistant to the President .... Ms. Lisa MCGINLEY
39 Director of Residential Life .... Mr. Jared FRIESEN
42 Campus Minister .... Mr. David SAETRE

Northland International University (G)

W10085 Pike Plains Road, Dunbar WI 54119-9285

County: Marinette FICE Identification: 038725
Unit ID: 239503
Telephone: (715) 324-6900 Carnegie Class: Bac/Diverse
FAX Number: (715) 324-6214 Calendar System: Semester
URL: www.ni.edu
Established: 1976 Annual Undergrad Tuition & Fees: $13,080
Enrollment: 571 Coed
Affiliation or Control: Baptist IRS Status: 501(c)3
Highest Offering: Doctorate
Program: 2-Year Principally Bachelor's Creditable; Teacher Preparatory; Professional; Religious Emphasis
Accreditation: TRACS

00 Chancellor .... Dr. Les OLLILA
01 President .... Dr. Matthew OLSON
05 Vice President Academic Affairs/CAO .... Dr. Antone GOYAK
10 Vice Pres Financial Affairs/CFO .... Mr. Cary SMITH
11 Vice Pres Operational Affairs/COO .... Mr. Hugh MCCOY
32 Vice President Student Affairs .... Mr. Hugh MCCOY
30 Vice Pres for Business Development .... Mr. Peter SULLIVAN
06 Registrar .... Dr. Kevin PRIEST
07 Admissions Director .... Mr. Trevor GEARHART
09 Dir Institutional Effectiveness .... Mr. Brent GRIFFIN
37 Director Student Financial Aid .... Mrs. Mandy MCLAIN
08 Head Librarian .... Mr. Van CARPENTER
41 Athletic Director .... Mr. Peter WEHRY

Ottawa University Wisconsin (H)

245 South Executive Drive, Brookfield WI 53005-4204

County: Waukesha Identification: 666084
Unit ID: 428259
Telephone: (262) 879-0200 Carnegie Class: Bac/Diverse
FAX Number: (262) 879-0096 Calendar System: Other
URL: www.ottawa.edu/wi
Established: 1992 Annual Undergrad Tuition & Fees: $10,920
Enrollment: 438 Coed
Affiliation or Control: American Baptist IRS Status: 501(c)3
Highest Offering: Master's
Program: Liberal Arts And General
Accreditation: &NH

01 President .... Mr. Kevin EICHNER
12 Campus Executive .... Dr. Wade MAULAND
05 Univ Provost/Chief Academic Officer .... Dr. Terry HAINES
10 Vice Pres Administration/CFO .... Mr. J. Clark RIBORDY
26 Mgr Public Relations & Publications .... Ms. Paula PAINE
30 Vice Pres University Advancement .... Mr. Paul BEAN
86 VP Regulatory/Governmental Affairs .... Dr. Donna LEVENE
88 Vice President Enterprise Division .... Dr. Brian SANDUSKY
21 Director Finance/Controller .... Ms. Noelle TESTA
21 Director Business Operations .... Mr. Tom CORLEY
15 Director Human Resources .... Ms. Joanna WALTERS
37 Director Financial Aid .... Mr. Howard FISCHER
06 University Registrar .... Ms. Karen ADAMS
21 Business Administrator .... Mr. Brian PATTERSON
07 Executive Enrollment Advisor .... Ms. Leigh-Anne IVERSON-SOMMERS
106 Vice President for Online .... Mr. Brian MESSER
88 VP and COO APOS .... Mr. Shane SMEED
20 Dean of Instruction .... Dr. Joyce CALDWELL

† Regional accreditation is carried under the parent institution in Ottawa, KS.

Rasmussen College - Appleton (A)

3500 E. Destination Drive, Appleton WI 54915
County: Calumet Identification: 667059
Unit ID: 45057101
Telephone: (920) 750-5900 Carnegie Class: Not Classified
FAX Number: (920) 750-5901 Calendar System: Quarter
URL: www.rasmussen.edu
Established: 1900 Annual Undergrad Tuition & Fees: $16,340
Enrollment: 44 Coed
Affiliation or Control: Proprietary IRS Status: Proprietary
Highest Offering: Baccalaureate
Program: Occupational; 2-Year Principally Bachelor's Creditable
Accreditation: &NH, MAAB

01 Campus Director .... Bill PANELLA

† Regional accreditation is carried under the parent institution in Lake Elmo, MN.

Rasmussen College - Green Bay (B)

904 South Taylor Street, Suite 100, Green Bay WI 54303
County: Brown Identification: 667063
Unit ID: 450571
Telephone: (920) 593-8400 Carnegie Class: Assoc/PrivFP
FAX Number: (920) 593-8401 Calendar System: Quarter
URL: www.rasmussen.edu
Established: 1900 Annual Undergrad Tuition & Fees: $16,340
Enrollment: 914 Coed
Affiliation or Control: Proprietary IRS Status: Proprietary
Highest Offering: Baccalaureate
Program: Occupational; 2-Year Principally Bachelor's Creditable
Accreditation: &NH, MAC, MLTAD

01 Campus Director .... Jon OTTERBACHER

† Regional accreditation is carried under the parent institution in Lake Elmo, MN.

Rasmussen College - Wausau (C)

1101 Westwood Drive, Wausau WI 54401
County: Marathon Identification: 667068
Unit ID: 45057102
Telephone: (715) 841-8000 Carnegie Class: Not Classified
FAX Number: (715) 841-8001 Calendar System: Quarter
URL: www.rasmussen.edu
Established: 1900 Annual Undergrad Tuition & Fees: $16,340
Enrollment: 444 Coed
Affiliation or Control: Proprietary IRS Status: Proprietary
Highest Offering: Baccalaureate
Program: Occupational; 2-Year Principally Bachelor's Creditable
Accreditation: &NH, MAAB

01 Campus Director .... Sue WILLIAMS

† Regional accreditation is carried under the parent institution in Lake Elmo, MN.

Ripon College (D)

300 Seward Street, PO Box 248, Ripon WI 54971-0248
County: Fond du Lac FICE Identification: 003884
Unit ID: 239628
Telephone: (920) 748-8115 Carnegie Class: Bac/A&S
FAX Number: (920) 748-7243 Calendar System: Semester
URL: www.ripon.edu
Established: 1851 Annual Undergrad Tuition & Fees: $30,110
Enrollment: 968 Coed
Affiliation or Control: Independent Non-Profit IRS Status: 501(c)3
Highest Offering: Baccalaureate
Program: Liberal Arts And General; Teacher Preparatory
Accreditation: NH

01 President .... Zachariah MESSITTE
04 Interim Admin Asst to President .... Danielle FICEK
05 Vice President & Dean of Faculty .... Gerald E. SEAMAN
30 Vice President for Advancement .... Wayne P. WEBSTER
10 Vice President for Finance .... Mary M. DEREGNIER
32 Vice President Dean of Students .... Christophor M. OGLE
07 Interim VP/Dean Admission/Fin Aid .... Ruth A. VEDVIK
06 Assoc Dean of Faculty/Registrar .... Michele A. WITTLER
36 Assoc Dean Students/Dir Career Dev .... Thomas M. VAUBEL
88 Exec Dir Ethical Leadership Program .... Lindsay BLUMER
07 Director of Admissions .... Leigh D. MLODZIK
21 Controller .... Lori A. SCHULZE
08 User Services Librarian .... Andrew PRELLWITZ
35 Dir Student Activities/Orientation .... Melissa L. BEMUS
88 Director Student Support Svcs .... Daniel J. KRHIN
39 Interim Director of Residence Life .... Jessica L. JOANIS
26 Dir Publication/Institutional Image .... Richard T. DAMM
26 Dir Media & Public Relations .... Vacant
44 Director of Development-Major Gifts .... Larry P. MALCHOW
14 Dir Information Technology Services .... Ronald I. HAEFNER
88 General Manager Food Service .... Sarjit SINGH
18 Director Physical Plant .... Brian SKAMRA
41 Director of Athletics .... Julie H. JOHNSON
102 Dir Foundation & Gov Relations .... Terri HOLZMAN
29 Dir Annual Fund/Alumni Relations .... Nancy HINTZ
15 Human Resource Administrator .... Jennifer FRANZ
38 Director of Counseling Services .... Cynthia S. VIERTEL
40 Bookstore Manager .... Rose BALSER

Sacred Heart School of Theology (E)

7335 S Highway 100, Box 429, Hales Corners WI 53130-0429
County: Milwaukee FICE Identification: 020780
Unit ID: 239637
Telephone: (414) 425-8300 Carnegie Class: Spec/Faith
FAX Number: (414) 529-6999 Calendar System: Semester
URL: www.shst.edu
Established: 1933 Annual Graduate Tuition & Fees: $14,850
Enrollment: 14,550 Coed
Affiliation or Control: Roman Catholic IRS Status: 501(c)3
Highest Offering: Master's; No Undergraduates
Program: Professional; Religious Emphasis
Accreditation: NH, THEOL

01 President-Rector .... Msgr. Ross A. SHECTERLE
10 VP Finance .... Ms. Sally A. SMITS
03 Vice Rector/VP External Affairs .... Rev. Thomas L. KNOEBEL
05 VP Academic Affairs .... Dr. Patrick J. RUSSELL
42 VP Human and Spiritual Formation .... Rev. Stephen MALKIEWICZ, OFM
20 VP Pastoral Formation .... Rev. Robert W. SCHIAVONE
08 Director Acad Information Services .... Ms. Susanna PATHAK
07 Director of Recruitment/Admissions .... Rev. Thomas L. KNOEBEL
06 Registrar .... Ms. Rose M. KOPENEC
26 Director Communications .... Mr. Jonathan DRAYNA
18 Director Plant Operations .... Mr. Michael J. ERATO
04 Admin Asst to President-Rector .. Ms. Josephine A. CALCAGNINO
13 Information Systems Coordinator .... Mr. Thomas WEIS

Saint Norbert College (F)

100 Grant Street, De Pere WI 54115-2099
County: Brown FICE Identification: 003892
Unit ID: 239716
Telephone: (920) 403-3181 Carnegie Class: Bac/A&S
FAX Number: (920) 403-4008 Calendar System: Semester
URL: www.snc.edu
Established: 1898 Annual Undergrad Tuition & Fees: $30,675
Enrollment: 2,225 Coed
Affiliation or Control: Roman Catholic IRS Status: 501(c)3
Highest Offering: Master's
Program: Liberal Arts And General; Teacher Preparatory; Professional
Accreditation: NH

01 President .... Mr. Thomas KUNKEL
05 Vice Pres Acad Affs/Dean of Col .... Dr. Jeffrey FRICK
10 Vice President Business & Finance .... Ms. Eileen JAHNKE
30 Vice Pres Institutional Advancement .... Mr. Phil OSWALD
32 Vice Pres Mission & Student Affairs .... Rev. Jay J. FOSTNER
84 Vice Pres Enrollment Mgmt/ Comm .... Ms. Bridget KRAGE O'CONNER
44 Assoc Vice Pres Inst Advancement .... Mr. Patrick WAGNER
09 Assoc VP Institutional Effective .... Dr. Robert RUTTER
20 Associate Academic Dean .... Dr. Kevin QUINN
36 Director Career Services .... Ms. Mandy NYCZ
35 Associate Dean Student Life .... Ms. Cynthia BARNETT
07 Exec Director of Admissions .... Mr. Edward LAMM
29 Director Alumni & Parent Relations .... Mr. Todd DANEN
21 Director of Finance .... Mr. Curt KOWALESKI
37 Director of Financial Aid .... Mr. Jeffrey A. ZAHN
26 Director Communications/Marketing .... Mr. Drew VAN FOSSEN
08 Director of Library .... Dr. Kristin D. VOGEL
15 Director Human Resources .... Mr. Gary A. UMHOEFER
41 Director Physical Educ/Athletics .... Mr. Tim BALD
38 Director Student Counseling Center .... Vacant
06 Registrar .... Mr. Richard L. GUILD
14 Dir Technology Support Services .... Ms. Raechelle CLEMMONS
104 Director of VIE & Study Abroad .... Mr. Joseph D. TULLBANE
28 Dir Multicultural Student Services .... Ms. Bridgit MARTIN
18 Director Facilities/Physical Plant .... Mr. John J. BARNES
40 Manager Bookstore Operations .... Ms. Monica WITTROCK

Sanford-Brown College-Milwaukee (G)

6737 W. Washington Street, Ste 2355, West Allis WI 53214
Identification: 666306
Unit ID: 448789
Telephone: (414) 771-2200 Carnegie Class: Assoc/PrivFP
FAX Number: (414) 771-9860 Calendar System: Semester
URL: www.sanfordbrown.edu/Milwaukee
Established: 2005 Annual Undergrad Tuition & Fees: N/A
Enrollment: 919 Coed
Affiliation or Control: Proprietary IRS Status: Proprietary
Highest Offering: Associate Degree
Program: Occupational
Accreditation: ACICS, DMS, MAAB, RAD

01 Campus President .... Mr. Winn SANDERSON

† Branch campus of Sanford-Brown Institute, Jacksonville, FL.

Silver Lake College of the Holy Family (H)

2406 S Alverno Road, Manitowoc WI 54220-9319
County: Manitowoc FICE Identification: 003850
Unit ID: 239743
Telephone: (920) 684-6691 Carnegie Class: Bac/Diverse
FAX Number: (920) 684-7082 Calendar System: Semester
URL: www.sl.edu
Established: 1935 Annual Undergrad Tuition & Fees: $22,250
Enrollment: 635 Coed
Affiliation or Control: Roman Catholic IRS Status: 501(c)3
Highest Offering: Master's
Program: Liberal Arts And General; Teacher Preparatory; Professional
Accreditation: NH, MUS, NURSE

01 President .... Dr. George F. ARNOLD
05 Int VP Academic Affs/Dean Faculty .... Ms. Vicki ANSORGE
10 VP of Finance & Business .... Ms. Debra WIGAND
32 VP Admissions/Stdnt Life/Dean Stdts .... Dr. Julie MAYROSE
30 VP Advancement/External Relations .... Mr. Jake CZARNIK-NEIMEYER
42 Director of Campus Ministry .... Mr. Tommy NELSON
06 Registrar .... Vacant
08 Head Librarian .... Sr. Ritarose STAHL
37 Director Student Financial Aid .... Ms. Jodi POPP
29 Director Alumni/Parent Relations .... Mr. Dan CONNOLLY
18 Director of Facilities .... Mr. Dale FETTERER
13 Director Technology Services .... Mr. Joe KRUSE
15 Director Human Resources .... Ms. Jan GRAUNKE
36 Dir Career Res/Experiential Lrng .... Ms. Jan L. ALGOZINE
21 Associate Business Officer .... Ms. Melissa DIENER
26 Director Marketing/Communications .... Ms. Carrie KOST
20 Associate Academic Officer .... Vacant
09 Director of Institutional Research .... Vacant
28 Director of Diversity .... Sr. Carmen Marie DIAZ
19 Director of Campus Security .... Mr. Randy AMMERMAN
44 Director of Annual Fund/Major Gifts .... Ms. Roxanna STRAWN
07 Director of Admissions/Adult Market .... Ms. Cynthia ST. JOHN
41 Athletic Director .... Mr. Mike FLENTJE

*University of Wisconsin System (I)

1220 Linden Dr, 1720 Van Hise Hall, Madison WI 53706-1559
County: Dane FICE Identification: 003894
Unit ID: 240435
Telephone: (608) 262-2321 Carnegie Class: N/A
FAX Number: (608) 262-3985
URL: www.wisconsin.edu

01 President .... Kevin P. REILLY
05 Sr Vice Pres Academic Affairs .... Mark NOOK
11 Sr VP Administration/Fiscal Affairs .... Michael L. MORGAN
10 Vice President Finance .... Deborah A. DURCAN
16 Associate Vice Pres Human Resources .... Alan N. CRIST
09 Assoc VP Policy Analysis/Research .... Heather H. KIM
91 Int Assoc VP Learning/Inform Tech .... Lori DOCKEN
45 Assoc VP Budget & Planning .... Freda J. HARRIS
43 General Counsel .... Tomas L. STAFFORD

*University of Wisconsin-Madison (J)

500 Lincoln Drive, Madison WI 53706-1380
County: Dane FICE Identification: 003895
Unit ID: 240444
Telephone: (608) 262-1234 Carnegie Class: RU/VH
FAX Number: (608) 262-0123 Calendar System: Semester
URL: www.wisc.edu
Established: 1848 Annual Undergrad Tuition & Fees (In-State): $10,384
Enrollment: 42,441 Coed
Affiliation or Control: State IRS Status: 501(c)3
Highest Offering: Doctorate
Program: Liberal Arts And General; Teacher Preparatory; Professional
Accreditation: NH, ARCPA, ART, AUD, BUS, BUSA, CIDA, CLPSY, COPSY, CORE, CYTO, DIETD, DIETI, DMS, ENG, FOR, IPSY, LAW, LIB, LSAR, MED, MT, MUS, NURSE, OT, PH, PHAR, PLNG, PTA, RAD, SCPSY, SP, SW, THEA, VET

02 Interim Chancellor .... Dr. David WARD
05 Provost Academic Affairs .... Dr. Paul M. DELUCA
11 Vice Chancellor Administration .... Mr. Darrell BAZZELL

13 CIO/Vice Provost Info Technology .... Mr. Bruce MAAS
43 Director of Admin Legal Services .... Ms. Lisa H. RUTHERFORD
100 Chancellor's Chief of Staff .... Ms. Becci MENGHINI
58 VC Research/Dean Graduate School .... Dr. Martin T. CADWALLADER
30 Vice Chanc University Relations .... Mr. Vince SWEENEY
49 Dean College Letters & Science .... Dr. Gary SANDEFUR
63 Dean Medicine and Public Health .... Dr. Robert N. GOLDEN
53 Dean School of Education .... Dr. Julie K. UNDERWOOD
50 Dean School of Business .... Dr. Francois ORTALO-MAGNE'
67 Dean School of Pharmacy .... Dr. Jeanette C. ROBERTS
54 Dean of College of Engineering .... Dr. Paul S. PEERCY
32 Dean of Students .... Ms. Lori BERQUAM
47 Dean of Agricultural/Life Sciences .... Dr. Kathryn VANDENBOSCH
66 Dean of School of Nursing .... Dr. Katharyn A. MAY
59 Dean of Human Ecology .... Dr. Robin A. DOUTHITT
74 Dean of Veterinary Medicine .... Dr. Daryl D. BUSS
61 Dean of the Law School .... Dr. Margaret RAYMOND
18 Assoc Vice Chanc Facil Plng/Mgmt .... Vacant
82 Int Dean International Studies .... Dr. Guido PODESTÁ
88 Int Director Environmental Studies .... Dr. Gregg MITMAN
41 Director Intercollegiate Athletics .... Mr. Barry L. ALVAREZ
88 Director of Physical Plant .... Mr. John HARROD
84 Assoc Vice Chanc Enrollment Mgmt .... Ms. Joanne E. BERG
88 Director of Arboretum .... Mr. Kevin D. MCSWEENEY
88 Director State Lab of Hygiene .... Dr. Charles BROKOPP
88 Director of Wisconsin Union .... Mr. Mark C. GUTHIER
07 Director of Admissions .... Ms. Adele BRUMFIELD
08 Int Director of Libraries .... Mr. Edward VANGEMERT
26 Director University Communications .... Ms. Amy TOBUREN
102 President UW Foundation .... Dr. Michael M. KNETTER
29 Director of Alumni Association .... Ms. Paula E. BONNER
37 Director Student Financial Services .... Ms. Susan FISCHER
38 Director of Counseling Services .... Dr. Danielle OAKLEY
16 Director Human Resources .... Mr. Robert LAVIGNA
39 Director of University Housing .... Mr. Paul N. EVANS
51 Int Dean Continuing Studies .... Dr. James CAMPBELL
19 Director of University Police .... Ms. Susan RISELING
88 Director of Archives .... Mr. David NULL
28 Vice Provost Diversity and Climate .... Dr. Damon WILLIAMS
20 Assoc Vice Chanc Faculty/Staff Pgms .... Dr. Steve STERN
23 Director University Health Service .... Dr. Sarah A. VAN ORMAN
88 Assoc Vice Chanc Teaching/Learning .... Dr. Aaron BROWER
88 Director of Space Management .... Mr. Douglas N. ROSE
17 President Hospital & Clinics .... Ms. Donna KATEN-BAHENSKY
21 Dir Auxiliary Operations Analysis .... Ms. Donna HALLERAN
10 Asst Vice Chanc Business Services .... Ms. Martha KERNER
88 Asst Vice Chanc Extended Pgms .... Mr. Peyton SMITH
25 Assoc Dean/Graduate/Research Svcs .Mr. James F. KNICKMEYER
06 Registrar .... Mr. Scott OWCZAREK
88 Secretary of the Faculty .... Mr. David E. MUSOLF
88 Secretary of Academic Staff .... Ms. Donna L. SILVER
88 Director of Recreational Sports .... Mr. Dale CARRUTHERS
15 Director of Academic Personnel .... Mr. Stephen R. LUND
15 Director Classified Personnel .... Mr. Mark WALTERS
85 Director Intl Student Services .... Ms. Laurie COX
22 Dir Office of Equity & Diversity .... Mr. Luis A. PINERO
96 Director of Purchasing .... Mr. Michael R. HARDIMAN
09 Dir Instl Rsrch/Acad Plng/Analysis .... Dr. Jocelyn L. MILNER
88 Special Asst to Provost .... Dr. Eden INOWAY-RONNIE
86 Sr Special Asst to Chanc Fed Rels .. Ms. Rhonda D. NORSETTER

*University of Wisconsin-Eau Claire (A)

105 Garfield Avenue, PO Box 4004,
Eau Claire WI 54702-4004

County: Eau Claire — FICE Identification: 003917
Unit ID: 240268
Telephone: (715) 836-2637 — Carnegie Class: Master's M
FAX Number: (715) 836-2902 — Calendar System: Semester
URL: www.uwec.edu
Established: 1916 — Annual Undergrad Tuition & Fees (In-State): $8,700
Enrollment: 11,233 — Coed
Affiliation or Control: State — IRS Status: 501(c)3
Highest Offering: Doctorate
Program: Liberal Arts And General; Teacher Preparatory; Professional
Accreditation: NH, BUS, CS, JOUR, MUS, NURSE, SP, SW

02 Interim Chancellor .... Dr. Giles BOUSQUET
05 Prov/Vice Chanc Academic Affairs .... Dr. Patricia A. KLEINE
10 Asst Chanc Budget & Finance .... Mr. David GESSNER
32 Vice Chanc Student Affairs .... Dr. Beth A. HELLWIG
46 Asst VC Research/Sponsored Pgm .... Dr. Karen G. HAVHOLM
18 Asst Chanc Facil/Univ Relations .... Mr. Michael J. RINDO
20 Assoc Vice Chanc Academic Affairs .... Dr. Michael R. WICK
97 Asc Vice Chanc Undergraduate Stds .... Dr. Robert KNIGHT
45 Dir Marketing/Comm/Strategic Plng ... Ms. Mary Jane BRUKARDT
22 Affirmative Action Officer .... Ms. Teresa O'HALLORAN
102 Executive Director Foundation .... Ms. Kimera WAY
32 Dean of Students .... Dr. Brian A. CARLISLE
07 Exec Dir Enrol Svcs/Admin/ Admission .... Ms. Kristina C. ANDERSON
28 Director of Multicultural Affairs .... Mr. Jesse L. DIXON
08 Director of Libraries .... Mr. John H. POLLITZ
13 Dir Learning & Technology Services .... Mr. Craig A. MEY
27 Chief Information Officer .... Mr. Chip ECKARDT
15 Director of Human Resources .... Ms. Donna J. WEBER
37 Director of Financial Aid .... Ms. Kathleen A. SAHLHOFF
38 Director of Counseling .... Ms. Lynn WILSON
06 Registrar .... Mr. James BARRETT
36 Assoc Director Career Services .... Ms. Staci L. HEIDTKE
18 Director of Facilities Mgmt .... Mr. Terry L. CLASSEN
19 Director of University Police .... Mr. David W. SPRICK

23 Director of Student Health Services .... Ms. Laura G. CHELLMAN
39 Director of Housing/Residence Life .... Mr. Charles H. MAJOR
41 Director of Athletics .... Mr. J. Scott KILGALLON
51 Director Continuing Education .... Mr. Durwin LONG
85 Director International Education .... Dr. Karl F. MARKGRAF
29 Director Alumni Relations .... Mr. John BACHMEIER
92 Director of Honors Program .... Dr. Jefford B. VAHLBUSCH
21 Director of Budget & Finance .... Mr. Mark REEVES
26 Chief Public Relations Officer .... Mr. Michael J. RINDO
09 Institutional Planner .... Mr. Andrew J. NELSON
49 Interim Dean of Arts & Sciences .... Dr. David BAKER
66 Dean Nursing/Health Sciences .... Dr. Linda K. YOUNG
53 Dean of Education/Human Sciences .... Dr. Gail SCUKANEC
50 Dean of Business .... Ms. Diane HOADLEY

*University of Wisconsin-Green Bay (B)

2420 Nicolet Drive, Green Bay WI 54311-7001

County: Brown — FICE Identification: 003899
Unit ID: 240277
Telephone: (920) 465-2000 — Carnegie Class: Master's S
FAX Number: (920) 465-2032 — Calendar System: Semester
URL: www.uwgb.edu
Established: 1965 — Annual Undergrad Tuition & Fees (In-State): $7,648
Enrollment: 6,671 — Coed
Affiliation or Control: State — IRS Status: 501(c)3
Highest Offering: Master's
Program: Liberal Arts And General; Teacher Preparatory; Professional
Accreditation: NH, DIETD, DIETI, MUS, NURSE, SW

02 Chancellor .... Dr. Thomas K. HARDEN
05 Provost/Vice Chancellor .... Dr. Julia E. WALLACE
10 Vice Chanc Business & Finance .... Mr. Kelly FRANZ
30 Asst Chanc University Advancement .... Dr. Beverly CARMICHAEL
32 Dean of Students .... Dr. Brenda AMENSON-HILL
14 Assoc Provost Information Services .... Ms. Kathy PLETCHER
20 Assoc Provost for Academic Affairs .... Dr. Timothy SEWALL
31 Assoc Provost Outreach/Adult Access . Dr. Steve VANDENAVOND
58 Dean Professional/Graduate Studies .... Dr. Sue JOSEPH MATTISON
49 Dean Liberal Arts & Sciences .... Dr. Scott FURLONG
43 Legal Counsel .... Vacant
07 Director of Admissions .... Ms. Pam HARVEY-JACOBS
15 Director of Human Resources .... Ms. Sheryl VAN GRUENSVEN
18 Dir Facilities Management/Planning .... Mr. Paul PINKSTON
19 Director Public Safety .... Mr. Thomas KUJAWA
41 Director Athletics .... Mr. Ken BOTHOF
21 Interim Controller .... Ms. SuAnn DETAMPEL
09 Director Institutional Research .... Dr. Deborah FURLONG
84 Dean Enrollment & Acad Svcs .... Mr. Michael STEARNEY
88 Asst Dean Professional Stds & Rsch .... Mr. Mike MARINETTI
49 Assoc Dean Lib Arts & Sciences .... Dr. Donna RITCH
82 Director of International Education .... Mr. Brent BLAHNIK
46 Director of Institute for Research .... Ms. Lidia NONN
37 Director Financial Aid .... Mr. James P. ROHAN
39 Director of Residence Life .... Mr. Glenn GRAY
40 Manager Bookstore .... Mr. Patrick SORELLE
24 Director Media Svcs/Telecomm .... Mr. William HUBBARD
23 Director Health Services .... Ms. Amy HENNIGES
96 Director of Institutional Support .... Vacant
38 Director Counseling Services .... Mr. Gregory L. SMITH
100 Special Asst to Chancellor .... Mr. Dan SPIELMANN
27 Director University Communications .. Mr. Christopher SAMPSON
36 Director Career Services .... Ms. Linda G. PEACOCK-LANDRUM
29 Director Alumni Relations .... Vacant
35 Director Student Life .... Ms. Lisa TETZLOFF
06 Registrar .... Ms. Amanda HRUSKA

*University of Wisconsin-La Crosse (C)

1725 State Street, La Crosse WI 54601-3788

County: La Crosse — FICE Identification: 003919
Unit ID: 240329
Telephone: (608) 785-8000 — Carnegie Class: Master's L
FAX Number: (608) 785-8492 — Calendar System: Semester
URL: www.uwlax.edu
Established: 1909 — Annual Undergrad Tuition & Fees (In-State): $8,725
Enrollment: 10,074 — Coed
Affiliation or Control: State — IRS Status: 501(c)3
Highest Offering: Doctorate
Program: Liberal Arts And General; Teacher Preparatory; Professional
Accreditation: NH, ANEST, ARCPA, BUS, MUS, NRPA, OT, PH, PTA, RADDOS, RTT

02 Chancellor .... Dr. Joe GOW
05 Provost/Vice Chanc Acad Affairs .... Ms. Heidi MACPHERSON
30 Asst Chancellor Advancement .... Mr. Greg REICHERT
10 Vice Chancellor Admin & Finance .... Dr. Bob HETZEL
50 Dean of Business Administration .... Dr. Bruce MAY
53 Director School of Education .... Dr. Marcie WYCOFF-HORN
79 Dean of Liberal Studies .... Dr. Ruthann E. BENSON
76 Dean Science Health .... Dr. Bruce RILEY
58 Assoc V Chan Acad/Dir Univ Grad Std .... Dr. Robert HOAR
32 Asst Chancellor & Dean of Students .... Dr. Paula M. KNUDSON
27 Chief Information Officer .... Dr. Mohamed ELHINDI
15 Director of Human Resources .... Ms. Madeline HOLZEM
51 Director Continuing Educ/Exten .... Ms. Penny TIEDT
08 Interim Director of Library .... Mr. John JAX
85 Director International Education .... Mr. Jay M. LOKKEN
07 Director ES/Admissions .... Mr. Corey SJOQUIST
06 Registrar .... Dr. Christine S. BAKKUM

37 Director ES/Financial Aid .... Ms. Louise L. JANKE
38 Exec Director Counseling/Testing .... Dr. Bridgette C. HENSLEY
36 Director of Career Services .... Ms. Karla E. STANEK
41 Athletic Director .... Mr. Joshua WHITMAN
26 Director News and Marketing .... Mr. Brad R. QUARBERG
29 Director Alumni Relations .... Ms. Janie M. SPENCER
23 Director Student Health Center .... Dr. Brian K. ALLEN
09 Director Institutional Research .... Ms. Natalie SOLVERSON
19 Chief of University Police .... Mr. Scott W. ROHDE
18 Director Physical Plant .... Mr. Hank M. KLOS
28 Assoc Dean Campus Climate/Diversity .Ms. Barbara E. STEWART
22 Director Affirmative Action .... Mr. Nizam ARAIN

*University of Wisconsin-Milwaukee (D)

PO Box 413, Milwaukee WI 53201-0413

County: Milwaukee — FICE Identification: 003896
Unit ID: 240453
Telephone: (414) 229-1122 — Carnegie Class: RU/H
FAX Number: (414) 229-6329 — Calendar System: Semester
URL: www.uwm.edu
Established: 1885 — Annual Undergrad Tuition & Fees (In-State): $9,380
Enrollment: 29,768 — Coed
Affiliation or Control: State — IRS Status: 501(c)3
Highest Offering: Doctorate
Program: Liberal Arts And General; Teacher Preparatory; Professional
Accreditation: NH, BUS, CEA, CLPSY, COPSY, CS, CYTO, DANCE, ENG, LIB, MT, MUS, NURSE, OT, PLNG, PTA, SCPSY, SP, SW

02 Chancellor .... Dr. Michael R. LOVELL
05 Provost/Vice Chanc Academic Affairs .... Dr. Johannes BRITZ
10 Vice Chanc Finance & Admin Affs .... Ms. Christy L. BROWN
26 Vice Chanc Univ Rels/Communications .... Mr. Thomas L. LULJAK
46 Vice Chanc Research/Dean Grad Sch .... Vacant
32 Vice Chancellor Student Affairs .... Dr. Michael R. LALIBERTE
30 Vice Chancellor Development .... Dr. Patricia A. BORGER
20 Assoc Vice Chanc Academic Affairs .... Dr. Devarajan VENUGOPALAN
20 Actg Assoc Vice Chanc Academic Affs .... Dr. Phyllis KING
28 Act Assoc Vice Chancellor Diversity .... Ms. Cheryl AJIROTUTU
88 Assoc Vice Chancellor .... Dr. Patricia ARREDONDO
13 Interim Chief Information Officer .... Mr. David M. STACK
18 Assoc VC Facilities Planning/Mgmt .... Mr. Geoffrey HURTADO
04 Senior Advisor to the Chancellor .... Mr. David H. GILBERT
76 Dean College Health Sciences .... Dr. Chukuka S. ENWEMEKA
48 Dean Architecture & Urban Planning .... Dr. Robert C. GREENSTREET
50 Dean School Business Administration .... Dr. Timothy L. SMUNT
53 Dean of School of Education .... Dr. Carol COLBECK
54 Dean Col Engr & Applied Science .... Dr. Brett PETERS
57 Int Dean Peck School of the Arts .... Dr. Scott EMMONS
88 Dean of Freshwater Science .... Dr. David GARMAN
69 Dean School of Public Health .... Dr. Magda PECK
58 Interim Dean Graduate School .... Dr. David YU
49 Dean College Letters & Science .... Dr. Rodney SWAIN
62 Int Dean School Information Studies .... Dr. Wooseob JEONG
66 Dean of College of Nursing .... Dr. Sally LUNDEEN
70 Dean Helen Bader Sch Social Welfare .... Dr. Stan STOJKOVIC
51 Int Dean School of Continuing Educ .... Dr. Patricia ARREDONDO
35 Dean of Students .... Mr. Thomas G. MCGINNITY
22 Act Dir Equity/Diversity Services .... Ms. Patricia VILLARREAL
08 Director of the Library .... Ms. Ewa BARCZYK
43 Director Legal Affairs .... Ms. Robin VAN HARPEN
06 Registrar .... Ms. Beth WARNER
15 Director of Human Resources .... Ms. Suzanne WESLOW
19 Director University Police .... Mr. Michael J. MARZION
25 Director Office Sponsored Research .... Mr. Thomas MARCUSSEN
23 Director Health Center .... Dr. Julia BONNER
09 Dir Assessment/Institutional Rsrch .... Dr. Gesele DURHAM
85 Director Center for Intl Education .... Dr. Patrice S. PETRO
37 Director Student Financial Aid .... Ms. Jane HOJAN-CLARK
39 Director of Residence Life .... Mr. Scott S. PEAK
41 Athletic Director .... Mr. Andy GEIGER
40 Director Bookstore .... Mr. Erik G C. HEMMING
36 Int Dir Career Development Center .... Ms. Cindy PETRIETES
27 Dir Univ Communications & Media Rel .... Ms. Laura GLAWE
21 Int Dir Business & Financial Svcs .... Mr. Jerry TARRER
29 Director Alumni Relations .... Vacant
96 Director of Purchasing .... Vacant
09 Coordinator Resource Analysis .... Mr. Donald A. WEILL

*University of Wisconsin-Oshkosh (E)

800 Algoma Boulevard, Oshkosh WI 54901-3551

County: Winnebago — FICE Identification: 003920
Unit ID: 240365
Telephone: (920) 424-1234 — Carnegie Class: Master's L
FAX Number: (920) 424-7317 — Calendar System: Semester
URL: www.uwosh.edu
Established: 1871 — Annual Undergrad Tuition & Fees (In-State): $7,360
Enrollment: 13,513 — Coed
Affiliation or Control: State — IRS Status: 501(c)3
Highest Offering: Doctorate
Program: Liberal Arts And General; Teacher Preparatory; Professional
Accreditation: NH, BUS, CACREP, CS, JOUR, MUS, NURSE, SW

02 Chancellor .... Dr. Richard H. WELLS
05 Provost & Vice Chancellor .... Dr. Lane R. EARNS
20 Associate Vice Chancellor .... Dr. Perry R. RETTIG
20 Asst Vice Chanc Curricular Affairs .... Dr. Carleen VANDE ZANDE
20 Int Asst Vice Chanc Acad Support .... Ms. Irma BURGOS

Code	Title	Name
51	Asst Vice Chanc Lifelong Learning	Dr. Karen HEIKEL
32	Vice Chancellor Student Affairs	Dr. Petra ROTER
10	Vice Chancellor Administrative Svcs	Mr. Thomas G. SONNLEITNER
21	Associate Vice Chanc Admin Svcs	Ms. Lori M. WORM
06	Registrar	Ms. Lisa M. DANIELSON
22	Affirmative Action Officer	Ms. Pamela LASSITER
09	Director of Institutional Research	Mr. Michael W. WATSON
38	Director of Counseling Center	Dr. Joseph J. ABHOLD
14	Int CIO Director Info Technology	Mr. Nick DVORACEK
50	Dean Business	Dr. William TALLON
66	Dean Nursing	Dr. Rosemary SMITH
53	Dean Education & Human Services	Dr. Frederick L. YEO
49	Dean Letters & Sciences	Dr. John J. KOKER
102	Pres Univ of Wisc Oshkosh Foundatn	Mr. Arthur H. RATHJEN
29	Director of Alumni Association	Ms. Christine M. GANTNER
37	Director of Financial Aid	Ms. Beatriz D. CONTRERAS
26	Exec Director Integrated Marketing	Ms. Jamie CEMAN
25	Director Grants/Faculty Development	Ms. Linda S. FREED
35	Dean of Students	Dr. Sharon KIPETZ
58	Director Graduate Studies	Mr. Gregory WYPISZYNSKI
07	Director of Admissions	Ms. Jill M. ENDRIES
15	Director of Human Resources	Mr. Timothy DANIELSON
18	Facilities/Physical Plant Director	Mr. Steven A. ARNDT
36	Director of Career Services	Ms. Jaime PAGE-STADLER
96	Purchasing/Printing Manager	Mr. Brian KLINGER
92	Director University Honors Program	Dr. Laurence CARLIN
08	Director Library	Mr. Patrick J. WILKINSON

*University of Wisconsin-Parkside (A)

900 Wood Road, Box 2000, Kenosha WI 53141-2000

County: Kenosha — FICE Identification: 005015 — Unit ID: 240374

Telephone: (262) 595-2345 — Carnegie Class: Bac/A&S

FAX Number: (262) 595-2202 — Calendar System: Semester

URL: www.uwp.edu

Established: 1968 — Annual Undergrad Tuition & Fees (In-State): $7,258

Enrollment: 4,887 — Coed

Affiliation or Control: State — IRS Status: 501(c)3

Highest Offering: Master's

Program: Liberal Arts And General; Teacher Preparatory; Professional

Accreditation: NH, BUS

Code	Title	Name
02	Chancellor	Deborah L. FORD
05	Provost/Vice Chancellor	Terry BROWN
10	Vice Chanc Admin/Fiscal Affairs	Melvin KLINKNER
32	Dean of Students	Tammy MCGUCKIN
84	Assoc Vice Chanc Enrollment Mgmt	DeAnn L. POSSEHL
30	Asst Chanc Univ Rels/Advancement	John JARACZEWSKI
20	Associate Provost	Dennis ROME
88	Asst VC Ofc of Inst Effectiveness	Kimberly KELLEY
28	Senior Diversity Officer	Edward TWYMAN
50	Dean College of Bus Econs & Tech	Fred EBEID
49	Dean College of Arts/Humanities	Dean YOHNK
51	Dean College of Nat & Hlth Sciences	Emmanual OTU
31	Exec Dir Ctr for Comty Partnerships	Jane SCHAEFER
08	Director of the Library	Jo CATES
13	Chief Information Officer	Ilya YAKOVLEV
92	Director of Honors Program	Gary M. WOOD
93	Director Minority Student Services	Damian EVANS
21	Dir Business Services/Controller	Scott MENKE
15	Interim Director Human Resources	Barbara FARRAR
19	Dir Campus Police/Public Safety	James HELLER
51	Manager Continuing Education	Kelly BOKHARI
37	Director Financial Aid	Randall MCCREADY
26	Director of Public Information	Dave BUCHANAN
29	Interim Alumni Relations Manager	Priscilla O'NEILL
06	Registrar	Rhonda KIMMEL
36	Director of Advising/Career Center	Vacant
18	Director Facilities Management	Donald A. KOLBE
94	Director of Women's Studies	Mary LENARD
96	Director of Purchasing	Robert FINK
35	Interim Director of Student Life	Steve WALLNER
38	Director Student Health/Counseling	Sandra LEICHT
40	Manager Bookstore	Daryl COHEN

*University of Wisconsin-Platteville (B)

1 University Plaza, Platteville WI 53818-3099

County: Grant — FICE Identification: 003921 — Unit ID: 240462

Telephone: (608) 342-1491 — Carnegie Class: Master's L

FAX Number: (608) 342-1232 — Calendar System: Semester

URL: www.uwplatt.edu

Established: 1866 — Annual Undergrad Tuition & Fees (In-State): $8,880

Enrollment: 8,214 — Coed

Affiliation or Control: State — IRS Status: 501(c)3

Highest Offering: Master's

Program: Liberal Arts And General; Teacher Preparatory; Professional

Accreditation: NH, ENG, MUS, NAIT, TED

Code	Title	Name
02	Chancellor	Mr. Dennis J. SHIELDS
05	Provost & Vice Chancellor	Dr. Mittie NIMOCKS DEN HERDER
103	Spec Asst to Chanc/Chief of Staff	Vacant
11	Vice Chanc Administrative Services	Mr. Robert G. CRAMER
32	Int Asst Chancellor Student Affairs	Ms. Joanne WILSON
58	Assoc Vice Chanc/Grad School Dean	Dr. David P. VAN BUREN
30	Asst Chanc Univ Advance/Foundation	Mr. Dennis R. COOLEY
06	Registrar	Mr. David S. KIECKHAFER
07	Dir Admissions and Enrollment Svcs	Ms. Angela M. UDELHOFEN
37	Director of Financial Aid	Ms. Sheila R. TROTTER
09	Director of Institutional Research	Mr. Mark R. MAILLOUX
38	Director Student Counseling	Ms. Deirdre L. DALSING
26	Dir Univ Info/Comm/Public Rels	Mr. Paul J. ERICKSON
41	Director Intercollegiate Athletics	Mr. Mark D. MOLESWORTH
39	Interim Director of Student Housing	Ms. Linda A. MULROY-BOWDEN
15	Director Personnel Services	Ms. Elaine Jeanne DURR
19	Director Security/Safety	Mr. Scott E. MARQUARDT
92	Director of Honors Program	Dr. Nancy L. TURNER
93	Dir Multicultural Educ Resource Ctr	Ms. Angela M. MILLER
96	Director of Purchasing	Mr. Lewis BETTINGER
08	Director of Library	Ms. Zora J. SAMPSON
18	Director of Physical Plant	Mr. Pete D. DAVIS
36	Director of Placement Services	Ms. Diana J. TRENDT
51	Director Continuing Education	Ms. Marian G. MACIEJ-HINER
29	Coordinator Alumni Relations	Ms. Kimberly G. SCHMELZ
49	Dean Col Liberal Arts/Education	Dr. Elizabeth A. THROOP
54	Dean Col of Engr/Math/Science	Dr. William B. HUDSON
47	Dean Business Life Sci/Agric	Dr. Wayne C. WEBER

*University of Wisconsin-River Falls (C)

410 S Third Street, River Falls WI 54022-5013

County: Pierce — FICE Identification: 003923 — Unit ID: 240471

Telephone: (715) 425-3911 — Carnegie Class: Master's M

FAX Number: (715) 425-4487 — Calendar System: Semester

URL: www.uwrf.edu

Established: 1874 — Annual Undergrad Tuition & Fees (In-State): $7,276

Enrollment: 6,803 — Coed

Affiliation or Control: State — IRS Status: 501(c)3

Highest Offering: Beyond Master's But Less Than Doctorate

Program: Liberal Arts And General; Teacher Preparatory; Professional

Accreditation: NH, BUS, MUS, SP, SW

Code	Title	Name
02	Chancellor	Dr. Dean A. VAN GALEN
05	Vice Chancellor & Provost	Dr. Fernando P. DELGADO
10	Vice Chancellor Admin/Finance	Vacant
20	Associate VC Academic Affairs	Dr. Michael MILLER
47	Dean Agricult/Food/Environ Sci	Dr. Dale GALLENBERG
53	Dean Education/Profess Studies	Dr. Larry SOLBERG
49	Dean of Arts & Sciences	Dr. Bradley J. CASKEY
50	Dean Business & Economics	Dr. Glenn T. POTTS
58	Director Graduate Studies	Dr. Michael MILLER
04	Special Assistant to Chancellor	Dr. Blake W. FRY
30	Exec Director for Advancement	Mr. Chris MUELLER
07	Director of Admissions	Mr. Mark R. MEYDAM
06	Registrar	Mr. Dan VANDE YACHT
08	Director of Library	Ms. Valerie I. MALZACHER
46	Int Director Grants & Research	Ms. Molly VAN WAGNER
21	Budget Director	Ms. Elizabeth FRUEH
13	Chief Information Officer	Mr. Stephen REED
22	Director Affirmative Action	Ms. Andriel DEES
32	Chief Student Life Officer	Mr. Paul SHEPHERD
41	Athletic Director	Mr. Roger TERNES
40	Manager Bookstore	Ms. Sherry REHNELT
37	Director Financial Assistance	Ms. Barbara J. STINSON
39	Director Residential Services	Ms. Sandra SCOTT-DUEX
15	Director of Human Resources	Ms. Donna ROBOLE
18	Director Facilities Management	Mr. Michael J. STIFTER
45	Director Campus Planning	Mr. Dale K. BRAUN
19	Director of Public Safety	Mr. Richard TRENDE
21	Controller	Mr. Terry N. HALVORSON
26	Chief Public Relations Officer	Mr. Blake FRY
96	Director Purchasing Services	Mr. Terry HALVORSON
88	Int Dir Academic Success Center	Dr. Jennifer WILLIS-RIVERA
35	Dir Student Services & Programs	Mr. Gregg M. HEINSELMAN
85	Director International Programs	Mr. Brent D. GREENE
29	Director Alumni Relations	Mr. Daniel E. MCGINTY
09	Director of Institutional Research	Vacant
92	Director Honors Program	Ms. Nanette J. JORDAHL
28	Director of Diversity	Ms. Andriel DEES
38	Director Student Counseling	Ms. Alice REILLY-MYKLEBUST
84	Director Enrollment Management	Vacant
56	Director Outreach Programs	Ms. Katrina LARSEN

*University of Wisconsin-Stevens Point (D)

2100 Main Street, Stevens Point WI 54481-3871

County: Portage — FICE Identification: 003924 — Unit ID: 240480

Telephone: (715) 346-0123 — Carnegie Class: Master's M

FAX Number: (715) 346-4841 — Calendar System: Semester

URL: www.uwsp.edu

Established: 1894 — Annual Undergrad Tuition & Fees (In-State): $7,504

Enrollment: 9,600 — Coed

Affiliation or Control: State — IRS Status: 501(c)3

Highest Offering: Doctorate

Program: Liberal Arts And General; Teacher Preparatory; Professional

Accreditation: NH, ART, AUD, CIDA, DANCE, DIETD, ENG, FOR, MT, MUS, SP, @SW, THEA

Code	Title	Name
02	Chancellor	Dr. Bernie PATTERSON
05	Interim Provost & Vice Chancellor	Dr. Greg SUMMERS
10	Vice Chancellor Business Affairs	Mr. Gregory M. DIEMER
32	Vice Chancellor Student Affairs	Dr. Al THOMPSON
20	Interim AVC for Tech/Lrng/Acad Pgms	Dr. James SAGE
04	Exec Assistant to Chancellor	Mr. Rob MANZKE
15	AVC Person/Bdgt/Grants/Summer Pgms	Dr. Katie JORE
51	Exec Dir UWSP Continuing Ed	Mr. Tom GOSPODARCZYK
07	Director Admissions	Ms. Terri CRUMLEY
37	Interim Director of Financial Aid	Mr. Paul WATSON
19	Director Safety & Loss Control	Mr. Jeff KARCHER
30	Int Vice Chanc Univ Advancement	Ms. Kathy BUENGER
29	Director of Alumni Affairs	Ms. Laura GEHRMAN-ROTTIER
26	Director University Relations/Comm	Ms. Kate WORSTER
16	Director of Personnel	Mr. Robert TABOR
38	Director Counseling Center	Dr. Stacey GERKEN
13	Dir of Information Technology	Mr. David DUMKE
22	Director Equity & Affirm Act	Ms. Mai VANG
08	Director University Library	Dr. Kathy DAVIS
06	Registrar	Mr. Dan KELLOGG
18	Int Chief Facilities/Physical Plant	Mr. Paul HASLER
36	Director Student Placement	Dr. Angie KELLOGG
96	Director of Purchasing	Ms. Katie SCHROTH
57	Dean Col of Fine Arts & Communic	Mr. Jeff MORIN
49	Dean College of Letters & Science	Dr. Christopher CIRMO
65	Dean Coll of Natural Resources	Dr. Christine L. THOMAS
107	Dean Col of Professional Studies	Dr. Marty LOY
09	Director of Institutional Research	Dr. Shari ELLERTSON
28	Director of Multicultural Affairs	Mr. Ron STREGE
35	Director Student Affairs	Dr. Al THOMPSON

*University of Wisconsin-Stout (E)

712 Broadway Street South, Menomonie WI 54751-2458

County: Dunn — FICE Identification: 003915 — Unit ID: 240417

Telephone: (715) 232-1122 — Carnegie Class: Master's L

FAX Number: (715) 232-1416 — Calendar System: 4/1/4

URL: www.uwstout.edu

Established: 1891 — Annual Undergrad Tuition & Fees (In-State): $9,400

Enrollment: 9,356 — Coed

Affiliation or Control: State — IRS Status: 501(c)3

Highest Offering: Beyond Master's But Less Than Doctorate

Program: Liberal Arts And General; Teacher Preparatory; Professional

Accreditation: NH, ACBSP, ART, CACREP, CIDA, CONST, CORE, DIETD, DIETI, ENG, MFCD, TED

Code	Title	Name
02	Chancellor	Dr. Charles W. SORENSEN
05	Interim Provost & Vice Chancellor	Dr. Mary HOPKINS-BEST
11	Vice Chanc for Admin/Student Life	Mr. Phil LYONS
20	Associate Vice Chancellor	Dr. Janice M. COKER
30	Vice Chanc Univ Advance/Mktg	Mr. Mark PARSON
35	Interim Asst VC Student Life Svcs	Mr. Joe KRIER
28	Asst Vice Chanc for Diversity	Vacant
10	Director Budget/Plng/Analysis	Dr. Meridith WENTZ
50	Dean College of Management	Dr. Abel ADEKOLA
49	Dean Col Arts/Humanities/Social Sci	Dr. Maria ALM
53	Int Dean Col of Ed/Hlth/Hum Sci	Dr. Robert PETERS
81	Dean Col of Science/Tech/Engr/Math	Dr. Jeff ANDERSON
32	Dean of Students	Ms. Joan THOMAS
06	Registrar	Mr. Scott CORRELL
84	Director Enrollment Management	Dr. Pamela HOLSINGER-FUCHS
36	Director Career Services	Ms. Amy LANE
08	Interim Director University Library	Mr. William JOHNSTON
04	Special Assistant to the Chancellor	Ms. Kristi KRIMPELBEIN
37	Director Student Financial Aid	Ms. Beth BOISEN
26	Director University Communications	Mr. Doug MELL
21	Director Business/Financial Svcs	Ms. Kim SCHULTE-SHOBERG
13	Chief Information Officer	Mr. Doug J. WAHL
76	Exec Director Health & Safety	Mr. James UHLIR
15	Director Human Resources	Ms. Deb GEHRKE
38	Director Counseling Center	Dr. John ACHTER
88	Director Online Services	Mr. Doug STEVENS
23	Director Student Health Services	Ms. Janice LAWRENCE-RAMAEKER
40	Director Bookstore	Ms. Cathy CLOSE
44	Director of the Annual Fund	Ms. Jennifer RUDIGER
85	Director International Education	Mr. Hong ROST
18	Director Physical Plant	Ms. Shirley KLEBESADEL
96	Director Procurement/Materials Mgmt	Mr. Brent TILTON
39	Director University Housing	Mr. Scott GRIESBACH
41	Director Athletics	Mr. Duey NAATZ
29	Director Alumni Relations	Ms. Sue PITTMAN
19	Dir of Safety & Risk Management	Mr. Dean A. SANKEY
19	Coordinator University Police	Ms. Lisa A. WALTER

*University of Wisconsin-Superior (F)

Belknap and Catlin, PO Box 2000, Superior WI 54880-4500

County: Douglas — FICE Identification: 003925 — Unit ID: 240426

Telephone: (715) 394-8101 — Carnegie Class: Master's S

FAX Number: (715) 394-8454 — Calendar System: Semester

URL: www.uwsuper.edu

Established: 1893 — Annual Undergrad Tuition & Fees (In-State): $7,542

Enrollment: 2,825 — Coed

Affiliation or Control: State — IRS Status: 501(c)3

Highest Offering: Beyond Master's But Less Than Doctorate

Program: Liberal Arts And General; Teacher Preparatory; Professional

Accreditation: NH, MUS, SW

Code	Title	Name
02	Chancellor	Dr. Renee WACHTER
05	Provost/Vice Chanc Academic Affairs	Dr. Faith HENSRUD
11	Vice Chanc Administration & Finance	Ms. Janet K. HANSON
30	Vice Chanc University Advancement	Ms. Jeanne E. THOMPSON
32	Dean of Students	Ms. Vicki HAJEWSKI

10 Controller .... Mr. Robert B. WAKSDAHL
15 Director Human Resources .... Ms. Peggy A. FECKER
18 Director Facilities Management .... Mr. Tom FENNESSEY
26 Director Marketing & Communications . Ms. Lynne M. WILLIAMS
06 Registrar .... Dr. Diane J. DOUGLAS
08 Librarian .... Ms. Debra L. NORDGREN
07 Director of Admissions .... Ms. Tonya ROTH
41 Athletic Director .... Mr. Steve NELSON
37 Director Student Financial Aid .... Ms. Donna R. DAHLVANG
14 Director Administrative Info Svcs .... Ms. Mary SCHOELER
51 Dir Center Cont Educ/Online Svcs .... Ms. Faith C. HENSRUD
88 Dir Distance Learning & Cont Educ .... Mr. Peter D. NORDGREN
40 Director Bookstore .... Mr. Vaughn N. RUSSOM
29 Director Alumni Relations .... Mr. Thomas K. BERGH
38 Director Advisement .... Dr. Christopher R. CHERRY
28 Director of Diversity .... Mr. Alvin (Chip) BEAL
84 Director Enrollment Management .... Vacant
09 Policy & Planning Analyst .... Vacant

*University of Wisconsin-Whitewater (A)

800 W Main, Whitewater WI 53190-1790

County: Walworth FICE Identification: 003926
Unit ID: 240189
Telephone: (262) 472-1234 Carnegie Class: Master's L
FAX Number: (262) 472-1518 Calendar System: Semester
URL: www.uww.edu
Established: 1868 Annual Undergrad Tuition & Fees (In-State): $7,528
Enrollment: 11,629 Coed
Affiliation or Control: State IRS Status: 501(c)3
Highest Offering: Beyond Master's But Less Than Doctorate
Program: Liberal Arts And General; Teacher Preparatory; Professional
Accreditation: NH, ART, BUS, CACREP, MUS, SP, SW, TED, THEA

02 Chancellor .... Dr. Richard J. TELFER
05 Prov/Vice Chanc Academic Affs .... Dr. Beverly KOPPER
32 Vice Chancellor Student Affairs .... Dr. Thomas R. RIOS
30 VC Univ Advance/Foundation Pres .... Mr. Jonathan ENSLIN
11 Vice Chanc Administrative Affs .... Mr. Jeff (Dean) ARNOLD
20 Assoc Vice Chanc Academic Affairs .... Dr. Greg COOK
13 Asst Vice Chanc Tech/Info Resource .... Dr. Elena POKOT
84 Asst Vice Chanc Enroll/Retention .... Mr. Matt ASCHENBRENER
09 Director of Institutional Research .... Dr. Chunju CHEN
20 AVC Multicult Affs/Stdnt Success .... Dr. Richard MCGREGORY
37 Director of Financial Aid .... Ms. Carol A. MILLER
10 Chief Business Officer .... Mr. Jeff (Dean) ARNOLD
26 Chief Public Relations Officer .... Ms. Sara KUHL
21 Director of Budget .... Ms. Aimee C. MCCANN
07 Director of Admissions .... Mr. Jeff BLAHNIK
06 Registrar .... Ms. Jodi M. HARE-PAYNTER
36 Director of Career Services .... Mr. Ron BUCHHOLZ
15 Director Human Resources/Diversity .... Ms. Judith M. TRAMPF
85 Dir Center for Global Education .... Ms. Candace A. CHENOWETH
44 Exec Dir University Development .... Ms. Kate LOFTUS
18 Director Facility Planning/Mgmt .... Mr. Greg SWANSON
38 Exec Dir Univ Health/Counseling Svc .... Dr. Richard L. JAZDZEWSKI
96 Director of Purchasing .... Mr. Michael T. HIRSCHFIELD
28 Director of Diversity .... Dr. Elizabeth OGUNSOLA
92 Director of Honors Program .... Dr. Marjorie RHINE
88 Int Dir Acad Advising/Explor Ctr .... Ms. Pamela TANNER
35 Dean Student Life .... Ms. Mary Beth MACKIN
57 Dean Arts/Communication .... Dr. Mark MCPHAIL
50 Dean of Business & Economics .... Dr. Christine CLEMENTS
53 Dean Education/Professional Studies .... Dr. Katharina E. HEYNING
49 Dean Letters & Sciences .... Dr. Mary PINKERTON
58 Dean Grad Stds/Continuing Educ .... Dr. John STONE

*University of Wisconsin Colleges (B)

780 Regent Street, Suite 130, Madison WI 53715-2635

County: Dane FICE Identification: 003897
Unit ID: 240055
Telephone: (608) 262-3786 Carnegie Class: Assoc/Pub2in4
FAX Number: (608) 262-7872 Calendar System: Semester
URL: www.uwc.edu
Established: 1964 Annual Undergrad Tuition & Fees (In-State): $4,882
Enrollment: 14,429 Coed
Affiliation or Control: State IRS Status: 501(c)3
Highest Offering: Associate Degree
Program: 2-Year Principally Bachelor's Creditable
Accreditation: NH

02 Chancellor .... Dr. Raymond CROSS
05 Provost/Vice Chancellor .... Dr. Gregory P. LAMPE
11 Vice Chancellor Admin & Fin Svcs .... Mr. Steven C. WILDECK
32 Assoc VC Stdt Svcs & Enroll Mgmt .... Dr. Richard BARNHOUSE
12 Int Vice Chanc/Provost UW-Extension .... Dr. Greg HUTCHINS
20 Associate Vice Chancellor .... Dr. Lisa SEALE
13 Chief Information Officer .... Ms. Marsha HENFER
15 Director Human Resources .... Ms. Pam DOLLARD
06 Registrar .... Mr. Larry GRAVES
37 Director Student Financial Aid .... Mr. William TRIPPETT
26 Exec Director University Relations .... Ms. Teri H. VENKER
28 Director of Diversity .... Dr. Stephan GILCHRIST
51 Dir Continuing Ed/Extended Svcs .... Mr. Tim URBONYA
12 Dean UW Baraboo/Sauk County .... Dr. Tom PLEGER
12 Int Dean UW Barron Cty (Rice Lake) .... Dr. Tracy WHITE
12 Dean UW Fond Du Lac .... Dr. John SHORT
12 Dean UW Fox Valley (Menasha) .... Dr. Martin RUDD
12 Dean UW Manitowoc .... Dr. Charles E. CLARK
12 Dean UW Marathon County .... Dr. Keith MONTGOMERY
12 Dean UW Marinette .... Ms. Paula LANGTEAU
12 Dean UW Marshfield/Wood Co. .... Dr. Patricia L. STUHR
12 Dean UW Richland .... Dr. Patrick HAGEN
12 Dean UW Rock County .... Dr. Carmen WILSON
12 Dean UW Sheboygan .... Dr. Al HARDERSEN
12 Dean UW Washington County .... Dr. Alan Paul PRICE
12 Dean UW Waukesha .... Dr. Harry P. MUIR, JR.

Viterbo University (C)

900 Viterbo Drive, La Crosse WI 54601-8802

County: La Crosse FICE Identification: 003911
Unit ID: 240107
Telephone: (608) 796-3000 Carnegie Class: Master's L
FAX Number: (608) 796-3050 Calendar System: Semester
URL: www.viterbo.edu
Established: 1890 Annual Undergrad Tuition & Fees: $21,870
Enrollment: 3,092 Coed
Affiliation or Control: Roman Catholic IRS Status: 501(c)3
Highest Offering: Master's
Program: Liberal Arts And General; Teacher Preparatory; Professional
Accreditation: NH, ACBSP, DIETC, DIETI, MUS, NURSE, SW, TED

01 President .... Dr. Richard B. ARTMAN
05 Vice President for Academic Affairs .... Dr. Barbara M. GAYLE
32 Vice President Student Development .... Dr. Diane L. BRIMMER
10 Vice Pres Administration/Finance .... Mr. Todd M. ERICSON
30 Vice Pres Institutional Advancement .... Mr. Gary L. KLEIN
26 Vice Pres Communications Marketing .... Mr. Patrick G. KERRIGAN
21 Assistant Vice President Finance .... Mr. Eugene R. ALBERTS
07 Dean of Admission .... Mr. Robert L. FORGET
42 Chaplain .... Fr. Conrad A. TARGONSKI
66 Dean School of Nursing .... Dr. Silvana F. RICHARDSON
53 Dean School of Education .... Dr. Sue S. BATELL
49 Dean School Letters & Sciences .... Dr. Glena G. TEMPLE
57 Dean School of Fine Arts .... Dr. Timothy B. SCHORR
50 Dean School of Business .... Dr. Thomas E. KNOTHE
58 Dean Graduate/Prof/Adult Education .... Vacant
88 Director of Ethics in Leadership .... Dr. Richard L. KYTE
06 Registrar .... Ms. Amy S. GLEASON
08 Director of Library .... Ms. Gretel L. STOCK KUPPERMAN
14 Director of Computer Services .... Mr. Tom L. HAUSMANN
41 Athletic Director .... Mr. Barry J. FRIED
37 Director of Financial Aid .... Ms. Terry W. NORMAN
29 Director Alumni/Parent Relations .... Ms. Kathleen A. DUERWACHTER
36 Director Career Planning/Placement . Ms. Beth D. DOLDER-ZIEKE
15 Director of Human Resources .... Ms. Sonya GANTHER
09 Director Institutional Research .... Ms. Naomi R. STENNES-SPIDAHL
18 Director Facilities/Physical Plant .... Mr. Eugene M. MCCURDY
38 Director of Counseling .... Ms. Lesley A. STUGELMAYER
39 Director of Residence Life .... Ms. Vickie L. UNFERTH
53 Director Grad Studies in Education .... Ms. Rhonda M. RABBITT
88 Dir Faculty Dev/Internship Coord .... Dr. Theresa MOORE
88 Director of Global Education .... Mr. Shaojie JIANG
19 Campus Safety & Security Director .... Mr. David J. PLEASANTS
07 Assoc Dir of Freshman Admissions .... Ms. Jessica K. MILLER
07 Associate Director of Admissions .... Mr. Eric R. SCHMIDT
04 Executive Administrative Assistant .... Ms. Diane M. HAUGEN

Wisconsin Lutheran College (D)

8800 W Bluemound Road, Milwaukee WI 53226-4699

County: Milwaukee FICE Identification: 021366
Unit ID: 240338
Telephone: (414) 443-8800 Carnegie Class: Bac/A&S
FAX Number: (414) 443-8514 Calendar System: Semester
URL: www.wlc.edu
Established: 1973 Annual Undergrad Tuition & Fees: $23,470
Enrollment: 1,022 Coed
Affiliation or Control: Independent Non-Profit IRS Status: 501(c)3
Highest Offering: Master's
Program: Liberal Arts And General
Accreditation: NH, NURSE

01 President .... Dr. Daniel W. JOHNSON
05 Provost & VP of Academic Affairs .... Dr. John D. KOLANDER
32 Vice President Student Affairs .... Dr. Dennis L. MILLER
10 Vice Pres Finance & Administration .... Mr. Gary SCHMID
26 Exec DIrector of Pulbic Affairs .... Mr. Jason VANACKER
30 Vice Pres Development .... Mr. Craig RUSSOW
21 Asst VP Finance .... Mrs. Diane HOEHNKE
84 Dean of Student Retention .... Mr. Joel P. MISCHKE
06 Registrar .... Mr. Brett VALERIO
08 Director of Library Services .... Mrs. Starla C. SIEGMANN
37 Director Student Financial Aid .... Mrs. Linda L. LOEFFEL
42 Campus Pastor .... Rev. Nathan STROBEL
53 Director Teacher Education .... Prof. James HOLMAN
39 Director Residential Life/Housing .... Mrs. Judy K. EGGERS
07 Executive Director of Admissions .... Mr. Jeff WEBER
41 Athletic Director .... Mr. Edward NOON
35 Director of Student Life .... Vacant
88 Director of Arts Programming .... Mr. Daniel SCHMAL
27 Director of Information Technology .... Mr. John MEYER
29 Director of Alumni Relations .... Mrs. Lisa LEFFEL
24 Director of Media Services .... Vacant
44 Director of Planned Giving .... Mrs. Kris METZGER
09 Information Systems Analyst .... Mrs. Olya FINNEGAN
44 Director Corp Foundation Relations .... Ms. Sharon PATTERSON
15 VP of Human Resources .... Mr. Steven SCHROEDER
18 Chief Facilities/Physical Plant .... Mr. Gary SCHMID

Wisconsin School of Professional Psychology (E)

9120 W Hampton Avenue, Suite 212,
Milwaukee WI 53225-4960

County: Milwaukee FICE Identification: 022713
Unit ID: 240213
Telephone: (414) 464-9777 Carnegie Class: Spec/Health
FAX Number: (414) 358-5590 Calendar System: Semester
URL: www.wspp.edu
Established: 1979 Annual Graduate Tuition & Fees: $24,850
Enrollment: 88 Coed
Affiliation or Control: Independent Non-Profit IRS Status: 501(c)3
Highest Offering: Doctorate; No Undergraduates
Program: Professional
Accreditation: NH, CLPSY

01 President .... Dr. Kathleen M. RUSCH
05 Dean .... Dr. Dale A. BESPALEC
04 Assistant to the President .... Ms. Sheri LINDGREN
17 Director Clinical Training .... Dr. Susan DVORAK

*Wisconsin Technical College System (F)

PO Box 7874, Madison WI 53707-7874

County: Dane Identification: 666185
Telephone: (608) 266-1207 Carnegie Class: N/A
FAX Number: (608) 266-1285
URL: www.wtcsystem.edu

01 President .... Mr. Daniel CLANCY
05 Vice President Academic Programs .... Ms. Kathleen CULLEN
10 Vice President Finance .... Mr. James ZYLSTRA
86 Vice President Policy/Govt Rels .... Ms. Morna FOY

*Blackhawk Technical College (G)

PO Box 5009, Janesville WI 53547-5009

County: Rock FICE Identification: 005390
Unit ID: 238397
Telephone: (608) 758-6900 Carnegie Class: Assoc/Pub-R-M
FAX Number: (608) 757-7740 Calendar System: Semester
URL: www.blackhawk.edu
Established: 1912 Annual Undergrad Tuition & Fees (In-District): $3,803
Enrollment: 3,263 Coed
Affiliation or Control: State/Local IRS Status: 501(c)3
Highest Offering: Associate Degree
Program: Occupational
Accreditation: NH, ACFEI, ADNUR, DA, DMS, MAC, MLTAD, #PTAA, RAD

02 President .... Dr. Thomas C. ECKERT
05 Vice President Learning .... Dr. Sharon A. KENNEDY
11 Vice President Finance/College Oper .... Ms. Renea L. RANGUETTE
16 Vice President Human Resources .... Mr. Brian B. GOHLKE
32 Vice President Student Services .... Mr. Edward G. ROBINSON
09 Dir Institutional Effectiveness .... Mr. Michael J. GAGNER
04 Asst to President/Board Liaison .... Ms. Jacqueline J. PINS
14 Chief Information Officer .... Vacant
26 Director Marketing & Communications .... Mr. Len E. WALKER
20 Dean Academic Support Division .... Ms. Mona L. ANTONELLI
97 Dean General Education .... Dr. Gabrielle BANICK
76 Dean Health Sciences .... Ms. Nancy R. LIGHTFIELD
88 Dean Public Safety .... Mr. Mark I. BROWN
66 Associate Degree Nursing Coord .... Ms. Ruth L. WHEATON-COX
72 Dean Mfg/Trades/Transportation .... Mr. Kirke E. PLANK
50 Dean Business and Econ Dev .... Mr. Donald S. SMITH
12 Dean Monroe Campus .... Dr. Jennifer THAYER
21 Controller .... Mr. David MCDONALD
25 Manager Grants Administration .... Mr. Andrew S. MCGRATH
37 Financial Aid Coordinator .... Ms. Sue ULLRICK
06 Director Student Development .... Ms. Kerry K. FROEHLICH-MUELLER
18 Facilities Manager .... Mr. Jeffrey R. AMUNDSON
96 Manager Purchasing/Fac Design .... Ms. Kelly J. DEMPSEY
51 Continuing Education Coord .... Mr. Mark V. TRILLER
08 Librarian .... Ms. Janet C. WHITE
102 Director of Foundation & Alumni .... Ms. Kelli CAMERON

*Chippewa Valley Technical College (H)

620 W Clairemont Avenue, Eau Claire WI 54701-6162

County: Eau Claire FICE Identification: 005304
Unit ID: 240116
Telephone: (715) 833-6200 Carnegie Class: Assoc/Pub-R-M
FAX Number: (715) 833-6470 Calendar System: Semester
URL: www.cvtc.edu
Established: 1912 Annual Undergrad Tuition & Fees (In-District): $4,056
Enrollment: 6,058 Coed
Affiliation or Control: Local IRS Status: 501(c)3
Highest Offering: Associate Degree
Program: Occupational; 2-Year Principally Bachelor's Creditable; Technical Emphasis
Accreditation: NH, ADNUR, DH, DMS, MAC, MLTAD, PNUR, PTAA, RAD, SURGT

02 President .... Bruce A. BARKER
05 Vice President Education .... Vacant
11 Vice President Operations .... Tom G. HUFFCUTT
32 Vice President Student Services .... Margo A. KEYS

12 River Falls Campus Manager .... John R. KLEVEN
12 Chippewa Falls Campus Manager ...... Timothy M. SHEPARDSON
12 Menomonie Campus Manager .... Roxann S. VANDERWYST
12 Nanorite Innovation Center Manager .... Pam D. OWEN
88 Dean Manufacturing/Nano Programs .... Mark R. HENDRICKSON
46 Dir of Research/Special Projects .... Margaret A. DICKENS
88 Dean Energy/Transp/Ag & Constructn .... Aliesha R. CROWE
06 Registrar .... Tessa A. PERCHINSKY
07 Director of Enrollment Services .... Paige WEGNER
37 Financial Aid Officer .... Mary E. GORUD
26 Public Communications Manager .... Carla S. LEUCK
31 Director of Community Relations .... Doug A. OLSON
10 Director of Budget & Finance .... Kirk L. MOIST
88 Director of Staff Development .... Roger J. STANFORD
13 Director of Info Technology .... Tom J. LANGE
88 Customer Service Center Spec/Mgr .... Karen L. CALLAWAY
35 Student Life Specialist .... Alisa S. SCHLEY
96 Purchasing Agent .... Doug D. DEKAN
21 Budget Manager .... Tracy M. DRIER
19 Safety/Security and Risk Manager .... Carrie L. HALLQUIST
28 Diversity/Equal Opportunity Spec .... Michael A. OJIBWAY
50 Dean Business .... Beth A. HEIN
35 Student Services Grants/Operations .... Natalyn M. MARLAIRE
35 Student Services Learning Support .... Kristen A. RANEY
102 Dir of CVTC Foundation/Alumni Assoc .... Heidi L. FISHER
25 Grants Specialist .... Shana SCHMIDT
108 Manager of Assessment .... Philip V. PALSER
88 Coord of Curriculum & Assessment .... Julia E. RAEHPOUR
18 Facilities Manager .... Rod BAGLEY
15 Human Resources Director .... Vacant
21 Business Office Manager .... Sara J. NICK
76 Dean Health & Public Safety .... Shelly Y. OLSON
97 Dean General Studies .... Cherrie BERGANDI

*Fox Valley Technical College (A)

1825 N Bluemound Drive, Appleton WI 54914-1643

County: Outagamie FICE Identification: 009744
Unit ID: 238722
Telephone: (920) 735-5600 Carnegie Class: Assoc/Pub-R-L
FAX Number: (920) 735-2582 Calendar System: Semester
URL: www.fvtc.edu
Established: 1967 Annual Undergrad Tuition & Fees (In-District): $4,178
Enrollment: 10,580 Coed
Affiliation or Control: State/Local IRS Status: 501(c)3
Highest Offering: Associate Degree
Program: Occupational; 2-Year Principally Bachelor's Creditable
Accreditation: NH, ACFEI, ADNUR, DA, DH, MAC, OTA

02 President .... Dr. Susan A. MAY
11 VP Administrative Services .... Ms. Jill MCEWEN
32 VP Student/Community Development .... Ms. Patti JORGENSEN
04 Assistant to the President .... Ms. Vicky VAN HOUT
05 VP Instructional Services .... Mr. Christopher MATHENY
76 Exec Dean Business/Health/Service .... Ms. Donna ELLIOTT
72 Ex Dn Mnfctng/Transp/Info/Agri Tech .... Mr. Steve STRAUB
97 Dean General Studies .... Ms. Carol MAY
19 Executive Dean Public Safety .... Dr. Patricia ROBINSON
102 Exec Dir FVTC Foundation/Cmty Rels .... Ms. Alyce DUMKE
12 Oshkosh Campus Director .... Ms. Melissa KOHN
10 Chief Financial Officer .... Ms. Amy VAN STRATEN
13 Chief Information Officer .... Mr. Troy KOHL
37 Director Student Financial Svcs .... Ms. Stacy DORAN
35 Director Student Affairs .... Ms. Denise MARTINEZ
06 Registrar .... Mr. Brian BUSS
26 Director of College Marketing .... Ms. Barb DREGER
88 Director Compensation & Benefits .... Ms. Barb KIEFFER
88 Director Venture Center .... Ms. Amy PIETSCH
15 Director Employee Rels/Staff Dev .... Ms. Deb GORMAN
88 NCJTC Technology Director .... Ms. Karen ALESCH
88 Director Articulated Programs .... Ms. Marge RUBIN
46 Director College Effectiveness .... Dr. Patti FROHRIB
36 Specialist Student Employment Svcs .... Mr. Bruce WEILAND
35 Director Student Life .... Ms. Vicky BARKE

*Gateway Technical College (B)

3520 30th Avenue, Kenosha WI 53144-1690

County: Kenosha FICE Identification: 005389
Unit ID: 238759
Telephone: (262) 564-2200 Carnegie Class: Assoc/Pub-R-L
FAX Number: (262) 564-2201 Calendar System: Semester
URL: www.gtc.edu
Established: 1912 Annual Undergrad Tuition & Fees (In-District): $3,072
Enrollment: 6,400 Coed
Affiliation or Control: State/Local IRS Status: 501(c)3
Highest Offering: Associate Degree
Program: Occupational
Accreditation: NH, ADNUR, DA, MAC, PTAA, SURGT

02 President .... Mr. Bryan D. ALBRECHT
05 Exec VP/Prov/Chief Academic Officer .... Ms. Zina HAYWOOD
12 Dean Racine Campus .... Mr. Ray KOUKARI
12 Dean Elkhorn Campus .... Mr. Michael O'DONNELL
12 Dean Kenosha Campus .... Mr. Dennis SHERWOOD
10 Vice President/Provost Finance .... Mr. Mark ZLEVOR
86 VP Government/Community Affairs .... Ms. Stephanie SKLBA
103 VP Workforce/Economic Develop Div .... Ms. Debbie DAVIDSON
20 Associate VP Academic Affairs .... Mr. John THIBODEAU
84 Dean of Student Enrollment .... Ms. Stacy RILEY
32 Dean Student Development .... Mr. Steve WILKES
06 Registrar .... Ms. Chrystal MOEZ
09 Assoc VP Institutional Research .... Ms. Anne WHYNOTT
15 Director Personnel Services .... Mr. William WHYTE
26 Marketing Director .... Ms. Jayne HERRING
36 Director Student Placement .... Ms. Sheri EISCH
07 Director of Admissions .... Ms. Susan ROBERTS
18 Chief Facilities/Physical Plant .... Mr. Mark ZLEVOR
21 Associate Business Officer .... Ms. Beverly HANSEN
37 Director Student Financial Aid .... Ms. Janice RIUTTA
28 Director of Diversity .... Ms. Debbie MILLER
102 Foundation Executive Director .... Ms. Jennifer CHARPENTIER

*Lakeshore Technical College (C)

1290 North Avenue, Cleveland WI 53015-1414

County: Manitowoc FICE Identification: 009194
Unit ID: 239008
Telephone: (920) 693-1000 Carnegie Class: Assoc/Pub-R-M
FAX Number: (920) 693-1363 Calendar System: Semester
URL: www.gotoltc.edu
Established: 1913 Annual Undergrad Tuition & Fees (In-District): $3,540
Enrollment: 2,471 Coed
Affiliation or Control: State/Local IRS Status: 501(c)3
Highest Offering: Associate Degree
Program: Occupational; 2-Year Principally Bachelor's Creditable
Accreditation: NH, ADNUR, EMT, RAD

02 President .... Dr. Michael LANSER
04 Executive Assistant .... Ms. Allison WEBER
05 Vice President of Instruction .... Dr. Deryl DAVIS-FULMER
32 Vice President of Student Services .... Dr. Douglas GOSSEN
103 Vice President Workforce Solutions .... Mr. Peter THILLMAN
15 Director Human Resources .... Ms. Kathy KOTAJARVI
10 Director Financial Services .... Ms. Cindy DROSS
09 Dir Institutional Effectiveness .... Ms. Nikki KISS
26 Dir Marketing & College Relations .... Ms. Julie MIRECKI
28 Diversity Coordinator .... Ms. Nicole YANG
47 Dean Agric/Trade & Industry/Appr .... Mr. Michael THOMPSON
50 Dean Business & Technology .... Dr. Allyn FRENCH
97 Dean General Education/Basic Skills .... Ms. Lynn RETZAK
76 Dean Health & Human Services .... Dr. Barbara DODGE
19 Dean Public Safety & Agriculture .... Mr. Richard HOERTH
07 Student Services Manager .... Mr. Don GEIGER
37 Financial Aid Manager .... Ms. Corey GIVENS
32 Student Success Manager .... Ms. Foua HANG
18 Physical Plant Manager .... Mr. Bryan KOESER
08 Library Services Manager .... Ms. Karla ZAHN
22 Affirm Action Officer .... Ms. Kathy KOTAJARVI
40 Bookstore Manager .... Ms. Kelly WOLFERT
13 Chief Information Officer .... Vacant
30 Director of Advancement .... Ms. Katie WILLINGER
29 Director Alumni Relations .... Ms. Katie WILLINGER

*Madison Area Technical College (D)

3550 Anderson Street, Madison WI 53704-2599

County: Dane FICE Identification: 004007
Unit ID: 238263
Telephone: (608) 246-6100 Carnegie Class: Assoc/Pub-R-L
FAX Number: (608) 246-6880 Calendar System: Semester
URL: www.madisoncollege.org
Established: 1912 Annual Undergrad Tuition & Fees (In-District): $3,836
Enrollment: 18,434 Coed
Affiliation or Control: State/Local IRS Status: 501(c)3
Highest Offering: Associate Degree
Program: Occupational; 2-Year Principally Bachelor's Creditable
Accreditation: NH, ACFEI, ADNUR, DH, MAC, MLTAD, OPTT, OTA, @PTAA, RAD, SURGT

02 President .... Dr. Bettsey L. BARHORST
05 Provost .... Mr. Terrance S. WEBB
11 Sr Vice Pres Administration .... Mr. Roger W. PRICE
20 Vice Pres Student Development .... Dr. Keith T. CORNILLE
20 Assoc Vice Pres Learner Success .... Ms. Turina R. BAKKEN
28 Assoc VP Diversity/Comm Rel .... Ms. Maria G. BANUELOS
10 Chief Finance Officer/Controller .... Mr. Edwin R. NOEHRE
13 Chief Information Officer .... Mr. Igor R. STEINBERG
15 Vice Pres Human Resources .... Mr. Charles E. MCDOWELL
84 Vice Pres Enrollment Management .... Ms. Diane K. WALLESER
25 Director Grants/Special Projects .... Vacant
41 Athletic Director .... Mr. Stephen C. HAUSER
09 Dir Inst Research & Effectiveness .... Mr. Ali R. ZARRINNAM
32 Director Student Life .... Ms. Renee M. ALFANO
38 Director Testing and Assessment .... Mr. James A. MERRITT
26 Manager Public Relations .... Mr. Cary R. HEYER
21 Assistant Controller .... Mr. Jeffrey J. KUHN
18 Facilities Director .... Mr. Michael M. STARK
08 Director Library Services .... Ms. Julie C. GORES
07 Director Enrollment Services .... Ms. Jennifer L. HOEGE
40 Bookstore Manager .... Mr. Scott R. HEIMAN
37 Associate Manager Financial Aid .... Ms. Marcia E. FORBES
86 Public Affs/Govt Relations Mgr .... Mr. Timothy L. CASPER
22 Diversity Recruitment/Employ Coord .... Ms. Malika S. MONGER
102 Exec Dir Foundation & Alumni Rel .... Mr. Robert J. DINNDORF
38 Assoc Dean Student Development .... Dr. Geraldo G. VILA CRUZ
88 Dean Applied Technology .... Mr. Kenneth J. STARKMAN
47 Dean Agriscience & Technologies .... Mr. David L. SHONKWILER
50 Dean Business/Applied Arts .... Mr. Bryan M. WOODHOUSE
49 Dean Arts & Sciences .... Dr. Todd H. STEBBINS
76 Dean Health Education .... Dr. Mark C. LAUSCH
51 Dean Community & Corporate Learning .... Ms. Kathleen A. RADIONOFF
19 Dean Human/Protective Services .... Mr. Richard F. RAEMISCH
88 Chief of Public Safety .... Mr. James A. BOTTONI
88 Assoc Dean Retention/Student Devt .... Ms. Carlotta V. CALMESE
88 Assoc Dean Arts & Sciences .... Ms. Sarah B. FRITZ
106 Assoc Dean Online/Accelerated Learn .... Ms. Shawna M. CARTER
88 Assoc Dean Academic Advancement .... Ms. Janice L. METTAUER
88 Director Operations .... Ms. Lori A. SEBRANEK
88 Assoc Dean Academic Advancement .... Mr. Christopher P. VANDALL
88 Assoc Dean Business/Applied Arts .... Ms. Denise M. REIMER

*Mid-State Technical College (E)

500 32nd Street N, Wisconsin Rapids WI 54494-5599

County: Wood FICE Identification: 005380
Unit ID: 239220
Telephone: (715) 422-5300 Carnegie Class: Assoc/Pub-R-M
FAX Number: (715) 422-5345 Calendar System: Semester
URL: www.mstc.edu
Established: 1967 Annual Undergrad Tuition & Fees (In-District): $3,675
Enrollment: 3,206 Coed
Affiliation or Control: State/Local IRS Status: 501(c)3
Highest Offering: Associate Degree
Program: 2-Year Principally Bachelor's Creditable; Technical Emphasis
Accreditation: NH, ADNUR, MAC, SURGT

02 President .... Dr. Susan BUDJAC
05 Vice President Academic Affairs .... Dr. Ann Marie KRAUSE
32 VP Student Affairs/Information Tech .... Ms. Connie WILLFAHRT
10 Vice President Finance .... Mr. Nelson D. DAHL
15 Vice President Human Resources .... Mr. Richard O'SULLIVAN
50 Dean General Education & Business .... Dr. John HIGGS
75 Dean Technical/Industrial Division .... Mr. Alan JAVOROSKI
76 Dean Service & Health Careers .... Ms. Janet NEWMAN
12 Dean Stevens Point Campus .... Mr. Steven SMITH
12 Dean Marshfield Campus .... Ms. Brenda DILLENBURG
26 Director of Communications .... Mr. Karl EASTTORP
30 Director College Advancement .... Ms. Patty FAIRCHILD
102 Foundation and Alumni Director .... Ms. Chris MAGUIRE
18 Director of Facilities/Procurement .... Mr. Larry CIHLAR
84 Director of Enrollment Management .... Ms. Mandy LANG
35 Director Student Support .... Ms. Nancy SCHAPERKOTTER
96 Director of Purchasing .... Vacant
06 Student Records Manager .... Ms. Denise KINNEY
08 Library Services Manager .... Ms. Maria HERNANDEZ
37 Financial Aid Supervisor .... Mrs. Mary Jo GREEN

*Milwaukee Area Technical College (F)

700 W State Street, Milwaukee WI 53233-1443

County: Milwaukee FICE Identification: 003866
Unit ID: 239248
Telephone: (414) 297-6600 Carnegie Class: Assoc/Pub-U-MC
FAX Number: (414) 297-7990 Calendar System: Semester
URL: www.matc.edu
Established: 1912 Annual Undergrad Tuition & Fees (In-District): $3,153
Enrollment: 26,448 Coed
Affiliation or Control: Local IRS Status: 501(c)3
Highest Offering: Associate Degree
Program: Occupational; 2-Year Principally Bachelor's Creditable
Accreditation: NH, ACFEI, ADNUR, CVT, DH, DIETT, FUSER, MAC, MLTAD, OTA, PNUR, PTAA, RAD, SURGT

02 President .... Dr. Michael L. BURKE
05 Provost .... Dr. Vicki J. MARTIN
32 Int Vice Pres Student Services .... Mr. Al PINCKNEY
10 Vice President of Finance .... Dr. James WILLIAMS
43 Vice President & Legal Counsel .... Ms. Janice FALKENBERG
15 Assoc Vice Pres Human Resource .... Dr. Pablo CARDONA
13 Assoc VP Information Technology .... Mr. Michael WALSH
23 Dean Health Occupation .... Dr. Dessie LEVY
49 Int Dean Liberal Arts & Sciences .... Dr. Wilma BONAPARTE
50 Int Dean Business & Graphic Arts .... Dr. Mohammad DAKWAR
24 General Manager Public Television .... Mr. Ellis BROMBERG
11 Director Operations .... Mr. Richard DRIES
35 Director Student Life .... Mr. Archie GRAHAM
08 Director of Library .... Vacant
37 Interim Director Student Finances .... Mr. Jerry MANZ
90 Director Technical Services .... Mr. Michael GAVIN
21 Controller .... Ms. Terri GAYHART
19 Director Public Safety .... Mr. Bradford HINES
06 Registrar .... Ms. Sarah ADAMS
09 Director Institutional Research .... Dr. Thomas PILARZYK
84 Director Recruitment .... Ms. Brunetta SOWARD
29 Director Alumni Relations .... Ms. Christine MCGEE
38 Int Director Student Counseling .... Dr. Daniel BURRELL
26 Chief Public Relations Officer .... Ms. Kathleen HOHL
96 Procurement Manager .... Mr. Edward BUSHMAN
41 Coordinator Athletics .... Mr. Randy CASEY

*Moraine Park Technical College (G)

235 N National Avenue, Fond Du Lac WI 54935-2897

County: Fond Du Lac FICE Identification: 009256
Unit ID: 239372
Telephone: (920) 922-8611 Carnegie Class: Assoc/Pub-R-L
FAX Number: (920) 929-2471 Calendar System: Semester
URL: www.morainepark.edu
Established: 1967 Annual Undergrad Tuition & Fees (In-District): $3,691
Enrollment: 6,734 Coed
Affiliation or Control: State/Local IRS Status: 501(c)3
Highest Offering: Associate Degree
Program: Occupational; 2-Year Principally Bachelor's Creditable; Technical Emphasis

Accreditation: NH, ADNUR, MAC, MLTAD, RAD, SURGT

02 President .... Sheila RUHLAND
05 Vice Pres Academic Affairs .... James R. EDEN
15 Vice President Human Resources .... Kathleen M. BROSKE
30 VP Marketing/College Advancement .... Sharon N. HOLMES
32 Vice President Student Affairs .... Stanley CRAM
13 CIO/Vice Pres Inform Technology .... Jim BLAKESLEE
10 Vice Pres Finance & Facilities .... Bonnie BAERWALD
84 Vice Pres of Enrollment Management .... Bethany M. RAFFAELLI
88 VP Strategic Advancement .... Josh B. BULLOCK
12 WB & Online Campus/Cmty Partner .... Peter J. RETTLER
12 Beaver Dam Campus/Cmty Prtnr .... Karen COLEY
20 Executive Dean of Instruction .... James V. EDEN
24 Exec Dean Instructional Support .... Gerald R. EDGREN, III
76 Exec Dean Hlth Sciences/Public Svcs .... Kathy S. VANEERDEN
88 Dean of Health Sciences/Public Svcs .... Kristin M. FINNEL
06 Registrar .... Amanda HRUSKA
07 Recruitment & Retention Associate .... Sally A. RUBACK
08 Learning Resource Center Associate .... Charlene M. PETTIT
40 Auxiliary Services Associate .... Jon A. SHAPIRO
18 Facilities Associate .... Timothy J. FLOOD
22 Employment/Affirmative Action Assoc .... Beth A. MENDOZA
96 Purchasing Associate .... Charles E. BIRRINGER
37 Student Financials Partner .... Karen A. ZUEHLKE

*Nicolet Area Technical College (A)

Box 518, Rhinelander WI 54501-0518

County: Oneida — FICE Identification: 005384
Unit ID: 239442
Telephone: (715) 365-4410 — Carnegie Class: Assoc/Pub-R-S
FAX Number: (715) 365-4445 — Calendar System: Semester
URL: www.nicoletcollege.edu
Established: 1967 — Annual Undergrad Tuition & Fees (In-State): $3,507
Enrollment: 1,344 — Coed
Affiliation or Control: State — IRS Status: 501(c)3
Highest Offering: Associate Degree
Program: Occupational; 2-Year Principally Bachelor's Creditable
Accreditation: NH, ADNUR, MAC

02 President .... Ms. Elizabeth BURMASTER
10 Vice Pres Finance/Coll Operations .... Ms. Roxanne M. LUTGEN
05 Vice Pres Teaching/Learning .... Dr. Kenneth E. URBAN
88 Dean of Trade & Industry .... Ms. Brigitte PARSONS
49 Dn Instr Lib Arts/Early Chldhd Educ .... Ms. Rose PRUNTY
50 Dean Instr Bus/Institutional Effect .... Mr. Chuck KOMP
76 Dean Instr Health Occupations .... Ms. Lenore MANGLES
103 Dean Workforce/Econ Devel/Security .... Mr. Ron SKALLERUD
102 Executive Director Foundation .... Ms. Heather SCHALLOCK
16 Director of Human Resources .... Dr. Dan GROLEAU
21 Dir of Accounting/Business Services .... Mr. John VAN DE LOO
18 Director of Facilities .... Mr. Pete VANNEY
26 Dir Communications/Col Cmty Init .... Ms. Sandy KINNEY
37 Director Financial Aid .... Ms. Jill PRICE
93 Director Multicultural Services .... Ms. Rachelle ASHLEY
88 Disability Support Case Manager .... Ms. Janelle CARY
19 Director Protective Services .... Mr. Jason GOELDNER
06 Registrar/Dir Enrollment Services .... Ms. Kyle GRUENING
08 Director Library Services .... Mr. Todd MOUNTJOY
13 Director Information Technology .... Mr. Greg MILJEVICH
103 Director Workforce Tr/Econ Develop .... Ms. Sandy BISHOP
88 Director Academic Success .... Ms. Rose PRUNTY
07 PK-16/Admissions Coordinator .... Ms. Teri PHALIN

*Northcentral Technical College (B)

1000 W Campus Drive, Wausau WI 54401-1880

County: Marathon — FICE Identification: 005387
Unit ID: 239460
Telephone: (715) 675-3331 — Carnegie Class: Assoc/Pub-R-M
FAX Number: (715) 675-9776 — Calendar System: Semester
URL: www.ntc.edu
Established: 1912 — Annual Undergrad Tuition & Fees (In-District): $3,852
Enrollment: 5,053 — Coed
Affiliation or Control: Local — IRS Status: 501(c)3
Highest Offering: Associate Degree
Program: Occupational; 2-Year Principally Bachelor's Creditable
Accreditation: NH, ADNUR, DH, EMT, MAC, MLTAD, RAD, SURGT

02 President .... Dr. Lori A. WEYERS
05 Vice President for Learning .... Mrs. Shelly MONDEIK
15 Vice President of Human Resources .... Mrs. Jeannie M. WORDEN
32 Vice President of Student Services .... Mrs. Laurie BOROWICZ
10 Vice President of Finance & CFO .... Ms. Jane KITTEL
13 Chief Information Officer .... Mr. Chet A. STREBE
18 Director of Facilities .... Mr. Rob ELLIOTT
26 Director of Marketing & PR .... Mrs. Katrina FELCH
19 Dean Public Safety .... Mr. Bryce KOLPACK
97 Dean General Studies .... Mrs. Rachelle PHAKITTHONG
75 Dean Tech/Trades/Agric/Cmty Svcs .... Ms. Vicky PIETZ
50 Dean Business/International Educ .... Mr. Russ ROTHAMER
103 Dean Workforce Learning Solutions .... Mr. Mark BOROWICZ
12 Director East & Southeast Campuses .... Mr. Larry KIND
12 Dir North/West & Southwest Campuses .... Ms. Bobbi DAMROW
88 Director of Continuous Improvement .... Mr. Nick BLANCHETTE
22 Employment Coord/Affirm Action Ofcr .... Ms. Cindy THELEN
88 Director Organizational Development .... Mr. Dan DOUGHERTY
35 Director of Student Relations .... Mr. Shawn P. SULLIVAN
85 Assoc Dean International Education .... Ms. Bonita S. BISSONETTE
06 Lead Registrar .... Mr. James D. BLIESE
88 Dean K-16 Relations/Student Success .... Mrs. Laurie SAGER BOROWICZ
84 Director Enrollment Management .... Ms. Sarah DILLON

*Northeast Wisconsin Technical College (C)

PO Box 19042, 2740 W Mason Street, Green Bay WI 54307-9042

County: Brown — FICE Identification: 005301
Unit ID: 239488
Telephone: (920) 498-5500 — Carnegie Class: Assoc/Pub-R-L
FAX Number: (920) 498-6260 — Calendar System: Semester
URL: www.nwtc.edu
Established: 1913 — Annual Undergrad Tuition & Fees (In-District): $3,807
Enrollment: 9,549 — Coed
Affiliation or Control: State/Local — IRS Status: 501(c)3
Highest Offering: Associate Degree
Program: Occupational; 2-Year Principally Bachelor's Creditable; Technical Emphasis
Accreditation: NH, ADNUR, DA, DH, DMS, ENGT, MAC, MLTAD, PTAA, RAD, SURGT

02 President .... Dr. H. Jeffrey RAFN
05 Vice President of Learning .... Ms. Lori SUDDICK
32 Vice President of Student Services .... Dr. Pamela PHILLIPS
30 Vice Pres of College Advancement .... Ms. Karen SMITS
15 Vice President of Human Resources .... Ms. Sandy RYCZKOWSKI
13 Chief Information Officer .... Ms. Linda HARTFORD
10 Chief Financial Officer .... Mr. Jim BLUMREICH
12 Dean Marinette Campus .... Mr. Patrick O'HARA
12 Dean Sturgeon Bay Campus .... Vacant
50 Dn Business/Information Technology .... Mr. Randy SMITH
76 Dean Health Science .... Ms. Kay TUPALA
72 Dean Trades & Engr Technologies .... Mr. Mark WEBER
97 Dean General Education .... Ms. Michele SCHMIT
31 Dean Community/Regional Lrning Svcs .... Mrs. Sally L. MARTIN
20 Dean Learning Solutions .... Ms. Anne KAMPS
103 Dean Corp Training & Economic Devel .... Mr. Dean STEWART
38 Dean of Student Success .... Vacant
28 Director of College Diversity .... Dr. Alem ASRES
06 Registrar & Dean Enrollment Svcs .... Mr. Mark FRANKS
84 Dir Assessment/Enrollment/Retention .... Ms. Sally LANGAN
37 Financial Aid Director .... Ms. Emily YSEBAERT
09 Director Planning and Development .... Ms. Karen J. SMITS
96 Director of Purchasing .... Mr. Mark CICHON
102 Director Educational Foundation .... Ms. Crystal HARRISON
40 Director Bookstore .... Ms. Bonita ZIMA
26 Chief Public Relations Officer .... Vacant
18 Director of Facilities .... Mr. Daniel J. SEIDL
24 Media & Telecom Services Manager .... Mr. John SIEMERING
08 Manager Library Services .... Ms. Kim LAPLANTE
104 Manager Center for Global Cultures .... Ms. Kelly HOLTMEIER
21 Director of Financial Operations .... Mr. Clark WAGNER

*Southwest Wisconsin Technical College (D)

1800 Bronson Boulevard, Fennimore WI 53809-9778

County: Grant — FICE Identification: 007669
Unit ID: 239910
Telephone: (608) 822-3262 — Carnegie Class: Assoc/Pub-R-M
FAX Number: (608) 822-6019 — Calendar System: Semester
URL: www.swtc.edu
Established: 1967 — Annual Undergrad Tuition & Fees (In-District): $4,010
Enrollment: 3,431 — Coed
Affiliation or Control: State/Local — IRS Status: 501(c)3
Highest Offering: Associate Degree
Program: Occupational; 2-Year Principally Bachelor's Creditable
Accreditation: NH, ADNUR, MAC, @PTAA

02 President .... Dr. Duane M. FORD
10 VP for Administrative Services .... Mr. Caleb WHITE
05 VP for Student & Academic Services .... Dr. Phil THOMAS
50 Dean Business/Agric/General Educ .... Dr. Joyce CZAJKOWSKI
76 Dean Health & Service Occupations .... Ms. Kathleen E. GARRITY
13 Director of Information Technology .... Vacant
15 Director of Human Resources .... Ms. Laura BODENBENDER
26 Director of External Relations .... Mr. Derek DACHELET
30 Director Institutional Advancement .... Ms. Barbara TUCKER
32 Director of Student Services .... Ms. Laura NYBERG-COMINS
37 Student Financial Assistance Mgr .... Ms. Joy A. KITE
18 Director of Facilities .... Mr. Doug PEARSON
102 Foundation Manager .... Ms. Heather FIFRICK
88 Human Resources Assistant .... Ms. Connie HABERKORN
88 Administrative Asst Admin Services .... Ms. Helen LAUFENBERG
88 Fire EMS & Early Childhood Coord .... Ms. Rita LUNA
88 Criminal Justice & Drivers Ed Coord .... Ms. Kris WUBBEN
04 Executive Asst to Board/President .... Ms. Karen M. CAMPBELL
21 Finance Accountant/Payroll Suprvsr .... Ms. Mary UREN
88 Teaching/Learning/Outreach Coord .... Ms. Julie PLUEMER

*Waukesha County Technical College (E)

800 Main Street, Pewaukee WI 53072-4696

County: Waukesha — FICE Identification: 005294
Unit ID: 240125
Telephone: (262) 691-5566 — Carnegie Class: Assoc/Pub-S-MC
FAX Number: (262) 691-5593 — Calendar System: Semester
URL: www.wctc.edu
Established: 1923 — Annual Undergrad Tuition & Fees (In-District): $3,717
Enrollment: 9,483 — Coed
Affiliation or Control: State/Local — IRS Status: 501(c)3
Highest Offering: Associate Degree
Program: Occupational; 2-Year Principally Bachelor's Creditable; Technical Emphasis
Accreditation: NH, ACFEI, ADNUR, DH, EMT, ENGT, MAC, SURGT

02 President .... Dr. Barbara A. PRINDIVILLE
03 Executive VP .... Ms. Kaylen BETZIG
45 VP Strategic Effectiveness & Advanc .... Dr. Margaret A. ELLIBEE
05 VP Learning .... Ms. Denine ROOD
10 Chief Financial Officer .... Ms. Cary A. TESSMANN
32 Associate VP Student Services .... Ms. Deborah WALLENDAL
75 Dean Industrial & Engineering Tech .... Mr. Michael SHIELS
76 Dean Service .... Mr. Greg WEST
76 Dean Health .... Ms. Sandra STEARNS
50 Dean Business .... Mr. Bradley PIAZZA
103 Dean Center/Business Performance .... Dr. Joseph WEITZER
97 Dean Academic Foundations/Gen Ed .... Ms. Susan MINNICK
15 Assoc VP Human Resource Svcs .... Mr. David BROWN
06 Registrar .... Ms. Jacki VANDYKE
38 Director Counsel/Retent/Spec Svcs .... Ms. Deborah JILBERT
14 Chief Information Officer .... Mr. Rodney NOBLES
40 Bookstore Manager .... Mr. Rick MILLER
18 Director Facilities Services .... Mr. Jeffrey LEVERENZ
35 Director Student Development .... Ms. Susanne FENSKE
90 Director Academic Technologies .... Mr. Randall COOROUGH
08 Director of Library Services .... Dr. Margaret A. ELLIBEE
88 Mgr Executive Operations Pres Ofc .... Mr. James F. REHAGEN
26 Dir Marketing & Public Relations .... Ms. Susan STERN
07 Manager Admissions & Assessment .... Ms. Kathleen KAZDA
37 Manager Financial Aid .... Mr. Timothy K. JACOBSON
35 Student Life Coordinator .... Mr. Jonathan N. PEDRAZA
28 Recruitment Supervisor .... Ms. Trisha L. HORNBURG
25 Manager of Grants & Contracts .... Ms. Linda J. MILLER
23 Safety/Enviro & Health Coord .... Mr. Jayson R. SCHERER
24 Media Services Coordinator .... Mr. Donald DUGAN
96 Purchasing Specialist .... Ms. Victoria NASH
36 Career Development Services .... Ms. Barbara SUYAMA
09 Inst Research & Effectiveness .... Dr. Margaret ELLIBEE
85 International Educ Coordinator .... Mr. K.Austin BAADE
28 Diversity Coordinator .... Mr. Rolando DELEON

*Western Technical College (F)

400 N Seventh Street, La Crosse WI 54601-3368

County: La Crosse — FICE Identification: 003840
Unit ID: 240170
Telephone: (608) 785-9200 — Carnegie Class: Assoc/Pub-R-M
FAX Number: (608) 785-9205 — Calendar System: Semester
URL: www.westerntc.edu
Established: 1912 — Annual Undergrad Tuition & Fees (In-District): $3,927
Enrollment: 3,810 — Coed
Affiliation or Control: State/Local — IRS Status: 501(c)3
Highest Offering: Associate Degree
Program: Occupational; 2-Year Principally Bachelor's Creditable; Technical Emphasis
Accreditation: NH, ADNUR, DA, MAC, MLTAD, OTA, PTAA, RAD, SURGT

02 President .... Dr. J. Lee RASCH
10 Vice President Finance/Operations .... Mr. Michael C. PIEPER
05 Vice President for Instruction .... Dr. Peg BOUDREAU
32 VP Student Support Svc/Col Rels .... Dr. Denise T. VUJNOVICH
45 Vice Pres Strategic Effectiveness .... Ms. Connie HOVELAND-BELDEN
12 Admin Regional Learning Centers .... Ms. Mary Ann HERLITZKE
102 Executive Director Foundation .... Ms. Lynn RUDIG
14 Director Computer/Telecomm Svcs .... Mr. Bruce E. MATHEW
37 Financial Aid Manager .... Ms. Jerolyn R. GRANDALL
21 Business Services Director .... Ms. Amy SCHMIDT
26 Director Marketing & Communications .... Ms. Amy L. THORNTON
56 Director Economic Development .... Ms. Patti BALACEK
38 Director Counseling Support Svcs .... Ms. Ann BRANDAU-HYNEK
29 Director Alumni Relations .... Ms. Sally EMERSON
07 Manager Admissions/Registration .... Ms. Jayne E. WELLS
35 Manager of Campus Activities .... Ms. Shelley MCNEELY
08 Manager Library Services .... Mr. Ron EDWARDS
24 Manager Instructional Media Center .... Ms. Joan PIERCE
40 Bookstore Manager .... Mr. David R. WIGNES
72 Dean Industrial Technologies .... Mr. William BRENDEL
76 Dean Health & Public Safety .... Ms. Diane NEEFE
97 Dean General Education .... Dr. Douglas STRAUSS
50 Dean Business Education .... Mr. Gary BROWN

*Wisconsin Indianhead Technical College (G)

505 Pine Ridge Drive, Shell Lake WI 54871-9300

County: Washburn — FICE Identification: 011824
Unit ID: 240198
Telephone: (715) 468-2815 — Carnegie Class: Assoc/Pub-R-M
FAX Number: (715) 468-2819 — Calendar System: Semester
URL: www.witc.edu
Established: 1968 — Annual Undergrad Tuition & Fees (In-State): $3,808
Enrollment: 4,447 — Coed
Affiliation or Control: State — IRS Status: Exempt
Highest Offering: Associate Degree
Program: Occupational; 2-Year Principally Bachelor's Creditable; Technical Emphasis
Accreditation: NH, ADNUR, MAC, OTA

02 President .... Dr. Robert M. MEYER
10 Assc Vice Pres Finance/Bus Svcs/CFO .... Mr. Steven DECKER
05 Vice President Academic Affairs .... Dr. Diane VERTIN
32 Vice President Student Affairs .... Mr. Steve BITZER
20 Vice President Instruct Technology .... Mr. Joe HUFTEL
51 Vice President Cont Educ/Foundation .... Mr. Craig FOWLER

09 Assoc VP Inst Effectiveness Ms. Ellen RILEY HAUSER
15 Assc VP Hum Res/Employee Rels Ms. Cher VINK
14 Sr Director Information Technology Mr. James DAHLBERG
37 Director Financial Aid Mr. Terry KLEIN
06 Registrar Mr. Shane EVENSON
08 Director Learning Resources Mr. Matthew ROSENDAHL
84 Director Enrollment Ms. Laura SULLIVAN
26 Director Marketing & Recruitment Ms. Kathy MAAS

WYOMING

Casper College (A)

125 College Drive, Casper WY 82601-2458
County: Natrona FICE Identification: 003928
Unit ID: 240505
Telephone: (307) 268-2110 Carnegie Class: Assoc/Pub-R-M
FAX Number: (307) 268-2682 Calendar System: Semester
URL: www.caspercollege.edu
Established: 1945 Annual Undergrad Tuition & Fees (In-District): $2,232
Enrollment: 4,426 Coed
Affiliation or Control: Local IRS Status: 501(c)3
Highest Offering: Associate Degree
Program: Occupational; 2-Year Principally Bachelor's Creditable
Accreditation: NH, ACBSP, ADNUR, ART, EMT, MLTAD, MUS, OTA, RAD, THEA

01 President Dr. Walter H. NOLTE
05 Vice President Academic Affairs Dr. Tim WRIGHT
32 Vice President Student Services Dr. Joanna ANDERSON
11 Vice Pres Administrative Services Ms. Lynnde COLLING
51 Dean of Continuing Education Dr. Laura DRISCOLL
15 Director Human Resources Mr. Chauncy JOHNSON
07 Director Admissions/Student Records Mrs. Linda NICHOLS
26 Director College Relations Mr. Rich FUJITA
18 Director Physical Plant Mr. Michael SAWYER
38 Director Student Counseling Mrs. Teresa WALLACE
08 Director of the Library Mr. Brad MATTHIES
13 Director Information Technology Mr. Kent BROOKS
36 Director Placement Ms. Janet DEVRIES
39 Director of Housing Ms. Barb MERYHEW
41 Athletic Director Mr. William LANDEN
24 Director of Media Services Mr. Todd WYKERT
19 Director Campus Security Mr. Lance JONES
102 Exec Director Foundation Ms. Paulann T. DOANE
09 Institutional Researcher Mrs. Lynn FLETCHER
37 Director of Student Financial Aid Mr. Darry VOIGT
21 Dir Financial Services/Controller Mrs. Robyn LANDEN
96 Purchasing Coordinator Mr. Paul CHRISTMAN

Central Wyoming College (B)

2660 Peck Avenue, Riverton WY 82501-1520
County: Fremont FICE Identification: 007289
Unit ID: 240514
Telephone: (307) 855-2000 Carnegie Class: Assoc/Pub-R-M
FAX Number: (307) 855-2095 Calendar System: Semester
URL: www.cwc.edu
Established: 1966 Annual Undergrad Tuition & Fees (In-District): $2,472
Enrollment: 2,316 Coed
Affiliation or Control: Local IRS Status: 501(c)3
Highest Offering: Associate Degree
Program: Occupational; 2-Year Principally Bachelor's Creditable
Accreditation: NH, ADNUR

01 President Dr. JoAnne Y. MCFARLAND
03 Exec Vice Pres Student/Acad Svcs Mr. Jason WOOD
10 Vice Pres Admin Svcs/CFO Mr. Ron GRANGER
13 Chief Information Officer Mr. John WOOD
18 Chief Facilities/Physical Plant Mr. Wayne ROBINSON
08 Director of Library Services Vacant
27 Director of Public Information Ms. Carolyn AANESTAD
15 Exec Dir for Human Resources Ms. Jennifer REY
21 Finance Officer Ms. Lindy PASKETT
19 Director of Campus Safety/Security Mr. Steve BARLOW
96 Director of Purchasing Ms. Suzie KOEHN
84 Asst Dean for Enrollment Services Ms. Jacquelyn BURNS
103 Dean for Workforce & Cmty Educ Ms. Lynne MCAULIFFE
41 Director of Athletics Mr. Serol STAUFFENBERG
06 Assistant Registrar Ms. Connie NYBERG
49 Dean for Arts/English/Math Dr. Mark NORDEEN
50 Dean for Commerce/Allied Health Ms. Charlotte DONELSON
32 Assoc VP Student Services Ms. Cory DALY
35 Asst Dean Student Services Mr. Steve BARLOW
05 Assoc VP Academic Services Ms. Martha DAVEY

Eastern Wyoming College (C)

3200 W C Street, Torrington WY 82240-1699
County: Goshen FICE Identification: 003929
Unit ID: 240596
Telephone: (307) 532-8200 Carnegie Class: Assoc/Pub-R-S
FAX Number: (307) 532-8229 Calendar System: Semester
URL: ewc.wy.edu/
Established: 1948 Annual Undergrad Tuition & Fees (In-District): $2,376
Enrollment: 1,965 Coed
Affiliation or Control: State/Local IRS Status: 501(c)3
Highest Offering: Associate Degree
Program: Occupational; 2-Year Principally Bachelor's Creditable
Accreditation: NH

01 President Dr. Thomas J. ARMSTRONG
04 Exec Asst to President/Board Ms. Holly L. BRANHAM
05 Vice President for Learning Dr. Dee LUDWIG
10 VP for Finance and Admin Services Mr. Robert COX
32 VP for Student Services Dr. Rex COGDILL
20 Assoc VP for Outreach & Learning Mr. Mike DURFEE
30 Dir of Institutional Development Mr. Oliver SUNDBY
08 Director of Library Services Mrs. Casey DEBUS
41 Director of College Athletics Mr. Verl E. PETSCH
26 Director of College Relations Ms. Tami AFDAHL
09 Director of Institutional Research Ms. Kimberly RUSSELL
18 Director of Physical Plant Mr. Keith JARVIS
39 Director of Residence Life Ms. Kellee GOODER
37 Director of Financial Aid Ms. Molly WILLIAMS
38 Director Counseling & Testing Mrs. Debbie OCHSNER
15 Director Human Resources Mr. Tom MCDOWELL
21 Business Office Director Ms. Karen PARRIOTT

Institute of Business and Medical Careers (D)

1854 Dell Range Boulevard, Cheyenne WY 82009
County: Laramie Identification: 666738
Telephone: (307) 433-8363 Carnegie Class: Not Classified
FAX Number: (307) 638-2348 Calendar System: Semester
URL: www.ibmc.edu
Established: 1987 Annual Undergrad Tuition & Fees: N/A
Enrollment: N/A Coed
Affiliation or Control: Proprietary IRS Status: Proprietary
Highest Offering: Associate Degree
Program: Occupational
Accreditation: ACICS

01 Director Mr. Archie RANDALL

† Branch campus of Institute of Business and Medical Careers, Fort Collins, CO.

Laramie County Community College (E)

1400 E College Drive, Cheyenne WY 82007-3299
County: Laramie FICE Identification: 009259
Unit ID: 240620
Telephone: (307) 778-5222 Carnegie Class: Assoc/Pub-R-M
FAX Number: (307) 778-1399 Calendar System: Semester
URL: www.lccc.wy.edu
Established: 1968 Annual Undergrad Tuition & Fees (In-District): $2,640
Enrollment: 5,302 Coed
Affiliation or Control: State/Local IRS Status: 501(c)3
Highest Offering: Associate Degree
Program: Occupational; 2-Year Principally Bachelor's Creditable
Accreditation: NH, ADNUR, DH, DMS, EMT, PTAA, RAD, SURGT

01 President Dr. Joe SCHAFFER
05 Int Vice Pres of Academic Affairs Dr. Jim JOHNS
10 Vice Pres of Administration/Finance Ms. Carol HOGLUND
32 Vice President of Student Services Vacant
13 Chief Technology Officer Mr. Chad MARLEY
103 Vice Pres of Workforce & Cmty Devel Mr. Stan TORVIK
16 Executive Director Human Resources Ms. Peggie KRESL-HOTZ
30 Int Assoc VP Inst Advancement Ms. Lisa MURPHY
12 Assoc VP of Albany County Campus Dr. Lynn STALNAKER
08 Librarian Ms. Karen LANGE
37 Director of Financial Aid Ms. Jennifer ALMLI
84 Dean of Enrollment Services Ms. Jenny HARGETT
26 Int Director of Public Relations Mr. Ty STOCKTON
18 Director of Physical Plant Mr. Timothy MACNAMARA
21 Director of Accounting Services Mr. Herry ANDREWS
44 Dir Scholarships & Annual Giving Ms. Brenda LAIRD
29 Director of Alumni Affairs Ms. Lisa TRIMBLE
09 Manager of Institutional Research Ms. Ann MURRAY
96 Director of Contracting/Procurement Mr. Jerry HARRIS
07 Director of Admissions Ms. Holly BRUEGMAN
06 Registrar Ms. Stacy MAESTAS
35 Dean of Campus Living & Learning Ms. Jenny RIGG
36 Dir Advising & Career Services Ms. Chrissy RENFRO
38 Dir Counseling & Camp Wellness Vacant
49 Dean of Arts & Humanities Ms. Kathleen URBAN
50 Dean of Business/Agric/ComputerTech Dr. Dean BARTOW
69 Int Dean of Health Sci & Wellness Mr. Stan TORVIK
83 Dean of Ed Natural & Social Science Vacant

Northern Wyoming Community College District (F)

PO Box 1500, 3059 Coffeen Avenue,
Sheridan WY 82801-1500
County: Sheridan FICE Identification: 003930
Unit ID: 240666
Telephone: (307) 674-6446 Carnegie Class: Assoc/Pub-R-M
FAX Number: (307) 674-4293 Calendar System: Semester
URL: www.sheridan.edu
Established: 1948 Annual Undergrad Tuition & Fees (In-District): $2,398
Enrollment: 4,296 Coed
Affiliation or Control: Local IRS Status: 501(c)3
Highest Offering: Associate Degree
Program: Occupational; 2-Year Principally Bachelor's Creditable
Accreditation: NH, ADNUR, DH

01 President Dr. Paul R. YOUNG
05 VP Academic Affairs Dr. Jon H. CONNOLLY
10 VP Admin & Finance/CFO Ms. Cheryl A. HEATH
12 VP Gillette College Dr. Mark G. ENGLERT
30 VP Development Dr. Susan BIGELOW
20 Asst VP Academic Affairs Dr. James BAKER
06 Dean Enrollment Services Ms. Sharon K. ELWOOD
32 Dean of Students Ms. Carol GARCIA
49 Dean Arts & Sciences Dr. Mercedes AGUIRRE BATTY
76 Dean Health Sciences Ms. Trudy R. MUNSICK
75 Dean Ag & Technical Careers Dr. Ami N. ERICKSON
15 Director Human Resources Ms. Jennifer MCARTHUR
26 Dir Marketing/College Information Ms. Wendy M. SMITH
37 Director Financial Aid Services Ms. Amanda STEINMETZ
13 Dir Information Technology Services Mr. Brady R. FACKRELL
21 Controller Ms. Karen B. BURTIS
39 Director Housing & Residential Ed Ms. Larissa B. BONNET
07 Director of Admissions - SC Mr. Zane S. GARSTAD
07 Director of Admissions - GC Ms. Jeri L. RUSSELL
88 Director Veteran Services Mr. Brett K. BURTIS
18 Director Facilities/Physical Plant Mr. Kent A. ANDERSEN
18 Director Gillette Facilities Mr. Mark N. ANDERSEN
106 Dir Distance & Distributive Learn Mr. Stoney GADDY
103 Dir Workforce Development & CE Ms. Karen ST. CLAIR
08 Librarian Ms. Katrina M. BROWN

Northwest College (G)

231 W 6th Street, Powell WY 82435
County: Park FICE Identification: 003931
Unit ID: 240657
Telephone: (307) 754-6000 Carnegie Class: Assoc/Pub-R-S
FAX Number: (307) 754-6245 Calendar System: Semester
URL: www.northwestcollege.edu
Established: 1946 Annual Undergrad Tuition & Fees (In-District): $2,437
Enrollment: 2,145 Coed
Affiliation or Control: State/Local IRS Status: 501(c)3
Highest Offering: Associate Degree
Program: Occupational; 2-Year Principally Bachelor's Creditable
Accreditation: NH, ADNUR, MUS

01 President Dr. Paul PRESTWICH
05 Vice Pres Academic Affairs Dr. Gerald GIRAUD
32 Vice Pres Student Affairs Dr. Sean FOX
11 Vice Pres Administrative Services Mr. Kim MILLS
26 Vice Pres College Relations Mr. Mark KITCHEN
102 Executive Director NWC Foundation Ms. Shelby WETZEL
20 Dean Student Learning/Acad Support Dr. Matthew EWERS
103 Dean Extended Campus/Workforce Ms. Ronda PEER
08 Library Director Dr. Susan RICHARDS
10 Finance Director Mr. Sheldon FLOM
15 Human Resources Director Ms. Jill ANDERSON
14 Computing Services Director Mr. Casey DEARCORN
18 Facilities Director Mr. David PLUTE
06 Registrar/Admissions Director Mr. Brad HAMMOND
37 Financial Aid/Scholarships Director Mr. Shaman QUINN
39 Residence/Campus Life Director Mr. Dee HAVIG

University of Wyoming (H)

Dept 3434, 1000 E University Avenue,
Laramie WY 82071-3434
County: Albany FICE Identification: 003932
Unit ID: 240727
Telephone: (307) 766-1121 Carnegie Class: RU/H
FAX Number: (307) 766-2271 Calendar System: Semester
URL: www.uwyo.edu
Established: 1886 Annual Undergrad Tuition & Fees (In-State): $4,278
Enrollment: 13,922 Coed
Affiliation or Control: State IRS Status: 501(c)3
Highest Offering: Doctorate
Program: Liberal Arts And General; Teacher Preparatory; Professional
Accreditation: NH, BUS, CACREP, CLPSY, CS, DIETD, ENG, LAW, MUS, NURSE, PHAR, SP, SW, TED

01 President Dr. Thomas BUCHANAN
05 Provost Dr. Myron B. ALLEN
10 Vice President Administration Vacant
86 Vice Pres Govt & Community Affairs Mr. Chris BOSWELL
46 Vice President Research & Econ Dev Dr. William A. GERN
32 Vice President Student Affairs Dr. Sara L. AXELSON
13 Vice President Information Tech Mr. Robert R. AYLWARD
30 Vice Pres Institutional Advancement Mr. W. Ben BLALOCK, III
88 Vice President Special Projects Dr. Carol FROST
43 University Counsel Ms. Susan WEIDEL
41 Director Intercollegiate Athletics Mr. Tom BURMAN
20 Associate VP Academic Affairs Dr. Nicole BALLENGER
20 Associate VP Academic Affairs Dr. Andrew C. HANSEN
56 Assoc VP Acad Affs/Dean Outreach Dr. Margaret MURDOCK
11 Assoc Vice Pres Operations Mr. Mark A. COLLINS
21 Assoc VP Fiscal Administration Ms. Janet S. LOWE
15 Assoc Vice Pres Human Resources Ms. Laura ALEXANDER
21 Asst Vice Pres Budget/Inst Analysis Ms. Arley WILLIAMS
88 Assoc Vice President Research Ms. Dorothy C. YATES
35 AVP Student Affairs/Dn of Students Dr. David COZZENS
88 Assoc VP Institutional Advancement Mr. John D. STARK
47 Dean of Agriculture Dr. Frank D. GALEY
49 Dean of Arts & Sciences Dr. B. Oliver WALTER
50 Dean of Business Dr. Brent HATHAWAY
53 Dean of Education Dr. Kay A. PERSICHITTE
54 Dean of Engineering Dr. Robert ETTEMA
76 Dean of Health Sciences Dr. Joseph F. STEINER
61 Dean of Law Mr. Stephen D. EASTON

08 Dean of Libraries .... Ms. Maggie FARRELL
12 Dean UW/Casper College Center .... Dr. Brent PICKETT
88 Director School of Energy Resources .... Dr. Mark NORTHAM
65 Director Haub Sch Env/Nat Resources .... Dr. Ingrid BURKE
07 Director of Admissions .... Ms. Shelley DODD
36 Director Advising/Career Services .... Ms. Evelyn J. CHYTKA
28 Director Affirmative Action/EEO .... Vacant
29 Director Alumni Relations .... Mr. Keener FRYE
88 Director American Heritage Center .... Mr. Mark GREENE
88 Director Art Museum .... Ms. Susan MOLDENHAUER
88 Director Auxiliary Services .... Ms. Carolyn SMITH
88 Director Campus Recreation .... Mr. Patrick MORAN
45 Director Facilities Planning .... Mr. Roger BAALMAN
92 Director Honors Program .... Dr. Duncan HARRIS
18 Director Physical Plant .... Mr. James SCOTT
26 Director Inst Communications .... Mr. Chad BALDWIN
06 Interim Registrar .... Ms. Evelyn J. CHYTKA
39 Exec Dir Res Life/Dining/Stdnt Un .... Mr. Patrick N. CALL
37 Director Student Financial Aid .... Ms. Joanna CARTER
23 Director Student Health Services .... Dr. Joanne E. STEANE
38 Director Univ Counseling Ctr .... Dr. Keith EVASHEVSKI
19 Chief University Police Dept .... Mr. Mike SAMP

Western Wyoming Community College (A)

PO Box 428, Rock Springs WY 82902-0428

County: Sweetwater FICE Identification: 003933
Unit ID: 240693
Telephone: (307) 382-1600 Carnegie Class: Assoc/Pub-R-M
FAX Number: (307) 382-1636 Calendar System: Semester
URL: www.wwcc.wy.edu
Established: 1959 Annual Undergrad Tuition & Fees (In-District): $1,145
Enrollment: 4,013 Coed
Affiliation or Control: State/Local IRS Status: 501(c)3
Highest Offering: Associate Degree
Program: Occupational; 2-Year Principally Bachelor's Creditable
Accreditation: NH

01 President .... Dr. Karla N. LEACH
05 VP of Student Learning .... Mr. Lou FLAIM
32 VP of Student Success Services .... Dr. Jackie FREEZE
11 VP for Administrative Services .... Mr. Marty KELSEY
88 Assoc VP for Administrative Svcs .... Ms. Carla BUDD
21 Controller .... Ms. Debbie BAKER
07 Director of Admissions .... Mr. Joseph MUELLER
06 Registrar .... Ms. Kay LEUM
37 Director of Financial Aid .... Mr. Javier FLORES
08 Director of Library Services .... Ms. Janice GROVER-ROOSA
18 Director of Physical Resources .... Mr. Paul ROSS
39 Director Housing/Student Activities .... Mr. Dustin CONOVER
40 Bookstore Manager .... Ms. Natalie LANE
35 Director Student Development Center .... Ms. Kim DRANE
41 Athletic Director .... Dr. Lu SWEET
92 Director of Honors Program .... Mr. Richard KEMPA
09 Director of Institutional Research .... Dr. Sandra CALDWELL
15 Director Personnel Services .... Ms. Carla BUDD
26 Coord of Marketing/Public Info .... Ms. Allyson CROSS
30 Director Community College Relation .... Mr. David TATE
36 Director Student Placement .... Mr. Mark REMBACZ
10 Chief Business Officer .... Ms. Debbie BAKER
20 Associate VP of Student Learning .... Dr. Sandy CALDWELL
88 Associate VP for Student Success .... Ms. Laurie WATKINS
38 Director Student Counseling .... Ms. Kim DRANE
96 Director of Purchasing .... Ms. Tammy REGISTER

WyoTech (B)

4373 N 3rd Street, Laramie WY 82072-9519

County: Albany FICE Identification: 009157
Unit ID: 240718
Telephone: (307) 742-3776 Carnegie Class: Assoc/PrivFP
FAX Number: (307) 721-4854 Calendar System: Other
URL: www.wyotech.edu
Established: 1966 Annual Undergrad Tuition & Fees: $29,250
Enrollment: 1,600 Coed
Affiliation or Control: Proprietary IRS Status: Proprietary
Highest Offering: Associate Degree
Program: Occupational
Accreditation: ACCSC

01 President .... Mr. Wm. Guy WARPNESS
05 Director of Education .... Mr. Caleb PERRITON
07 Director of Admissions .... Mr. Glenn HALSEY
37 Director of Financial Aid .... Ms. Thecla WOOLCOTT
32 Director of Student Services .... Mr. Kyle MORRIS
36 Director of Career Services .... Mr. Martin AXLUND
06 Registrar .... Ms. Revalee WEERHEIM
84 Admissions Manager .... Mr. Greg TAYLOR
39 Housing Manager .... Mr. Gabe LUCERO
04 Admin Assistant to the President .... Ms. Courtney SCHELL

US SERVICE SCHOOLS

Air Force Institute of Technology (C)

2950 Hobson Way, Wright Patterson AFB OH 45433-7765

County: Greene FICE Identification: 003009
Unit ID: 200697
Telephone: (937) 255-2321 Carnegie Class: DRU
FAX Number: (937) 656-7600 Calendar System: Quarter
URL: www.afit.edu
Established: 1919 Annual Graduate Tuition & Fees: $16,512
Enrollment: 798 Coed
Affiliation or Control: Federal IRS Status: Exempt
Highest Offering: Doctorate; No Undergraduates
Program: Professional; Technical Emphasis
Accreditation: NH, ENG

01 Chancellor .... Dr. Todd I. STEWART
05 Actg Director of Academic Affairs .... Dr. Marlin U. THOMAS
54 Dean Graduate School of Engr & Mgt .... Dr. Marlin U. THOMAS
20 Associate Dean for Academic Affairs .... Dr. Paul J. WOLF
46 Dean for Research .... Dr. Heidi R. RIES
10 Chief Financial Officer .... Ms. Ann M. MARBURGER
09 Director Institutional Research .... Dr. William F. ADAMS
06 Director Admissions/Registrar .... Mr. Robert J. LAVERRIERE
32 Associate Dean of Students .... Col. Christopher R. MANN
13 Dir Communications & Information .... LtCol. Lance CARMACK
08 Director D'Azzo Research Library .... Dr. Laurene E. ZAPROROZHETZ
15 Director Personnel Services .... Ms. Leanne HEAGLE
18 Chief Facilities/Physical Plant .... Mr. Daniel W. ROHRBACH
29 Manager Alumni Affairs .... Ms. Kathleen E. SCOTT
35 Director Student Services .... Mr. Richard GAMMON
85 Director of Intl Student Affairs .... Ms. Annette D. ROBB
40 Bookstore Supervisor .... Ms. Evelyn HALL

Air University (D)

55 LeMay Plaza South, Maxwell AFB AL 36112-6335

County: Montgomery FICE Identification: 001001
Telephone: (334) 953-5613 Carnegie Class: Not Classified
FAX Number: (334) 953-2749 Calendar System: Other
URL: www.au.af.mil
Established: 1946 Annual Undergrad Tuition & Fees: N/A
Enrollment: 53,887 Coed
Affiliation or Control: Federal IRS Status: Exempt
Highest Offering: Doctorate
Program: Professional
Accreditation: SC

01 Commander and President .... Lt Gen. David S. FADOK
03 Vice Commander .... MajGen. Thomas K. ANDERSEN
05 Vice President for Academic Affairs .... Dr. Bruce T. MURPHY
06 Registrar .... Mr. Lloyd L. WILSON

† Parent institution of Community College of the Air Force, School of Advanced Air and Space Studies, and the Air Force Institute of Technology

Community College of the Air Force (E)

100 South Turner Blvd,
Maxwell AFB, Gunter Annex AL 36114-3011

County: Montgomery FICE Identification: 012308
Unit ID: 100636
Telephone: (334) 649-5000 Carnegie Class: Assoc/Pub-Spec
FAX Number: (334) 649-5100 Calendar System: Other
URL: www.maxwell.af.mil
Established: 1972 Annual Undergrad Tuition & Fees: N/A
Enrollment: 315,254 Coed
Affiliation or Control: Federal IRS Status: Exempt
Highest Offering: Associate Degree
Program: Occupational; 2-Year Principally Bachelor's Creditable
Accreditation: &SC, PTAA

01 Commandant .... LtCol. Jonathan T. HAMILL
03 Vice Commandant .... CMSgt. James PEPIN
05 Dean Academic Affairs .... Mr. Lloyd WILSON
20 Superintendent Academic Operations .... MSgt. Brian NELSON
20 Assoc Dean Academic Programs .... Mr. Donald HOUSE
09 Assoc Dean Campus Relations .... Mr. William NICHOLAS
84 Director Enrollment Management .... Mrs. Teresa AMATUZZI
88 Superintendent Campus Relations .... MSgt. Joydette GALLOWAY

† Regional accreditation is carried under the parent institution, Air University, Maxwell AFB, AL.

Defense Language Institute (F)

Presido of Monterey CA 93944-3229

County: Monterey FICE Identification: 001195
Unit ID: 428222
Telephone: (831) 242-5291 Carnegie Class: Not Classified
FAX Number: (831) 242-6495 Calendar System: Other
URL: www.dliflc.edu
Established: 1941 Annual Undergrad Tuition & Fees: N/A
Enrollment: 3,800 Coed
Affiliation or Control: Federal IRS Status: Exempt
Highest Offering: Associate Degree
Program: Occupational; 2-Year Principally Bachelor's Creditable
Accreditation: WJ, CEA

01 Commandant .... Col. Danial PICK
05 Provost .... Dr. Donald FISCHER
20 Associate Provost .... Dr. Jielu ZHAO
46 Dean Program Eval Research Testing .... Dr. Deniz BILGIN

† Associate Arts in Foreign Language authorized by US Congress in December 2001 and approved by ACCJC/WASC in June 2002.

The Judge Advocate General's Legal Center & School (G)

600 Massie Road, Charlottesville VA 22903-1781

County: Albemarle Identification: 666974
Telephone: (434) 971-3300 Carnegie Class: Not Classified
FAX Number: (434) 971-3338 Calendar System: Quarter
URL: www.jagcnet.army.mil/tjaglcs
Established: 1951 Annual Graduate Tuition & Fees: N/A
Enrollment: 115 Coed
Affiliation or Control: Federal IRS Status: Exempt
Highest Offering: Master's; No Undergraduates
Program: Professional
Accreditation: LAW

01 Commander/Commandant .... BGen. Thomas E. AYRES
05 Dean .... Col. David DINER
20 Associate Dean of Academics .... Mr. Maurice A. LESCAULT, JR.

Marine Corps University (H)

2076 South Street, Quantico VA 22134-5068

County: Prince William Identification: 666745
Unit ID: 438513
Telephone: (703) 784-2105 Carnegie Class: Not Classified
FAX Number: (703) 784-1271 Calendar System: Semester
URL: www.mcu.usmc.mil
Established: 1989 Annual Graduate Tuition & Fees: N/A
Enrollment: 535 Coed
Affiliation or Control: Federal IRS Status: Exempt
Highest Offering: Master's; No Undergraduates
Program: Professional; Technical Emphasis
Accreditation: SC

01 President .... Col. William F. MULLEN, III
05 Vice President for Academic Affairs .... Dr. Jerre W. WILSON
20 Director Academic Support Division .... Mr. Joel S. WESTA
09 Director Institutional Research .... Dr. Susan JOHNSTON

National Defense University (I)

Fort Lesley J. McNair, Washington DC 20319-5066

FICE Identification: 031893
Unit ID: 423494
Telephone: (202) 685-0080 Carnegie Class: Not Classified
FAX Number: (202) 685-3920 Calendar System: Semester
URL: www.ndu.edu
Established: 1976 Annual Graduate Tuition & Fees: N/A
Enrollment: 1,275 Coed
Affiliation or Control: Federal IRS Status: Exempt
Highest Offering: Master's; No Undergraduates
Program: Professional
Accreditation: M

01 President .... MajGen. Gregg F. MARTIN
03 Senior VP Intl Programs & Outreach .... Amb. Nancy MCELDOWNEY
05 Vice Pres Academic Affairs .... Dr. John W. YAEGER
26 Director Public Affairs .... Mr. David THOMAS
20 Deputy Vice Pres Academic Affairs .... Dr. Brenda F. ROTH
27 Chief Information Officer .... Vacant
08 Head Librarian .... Ms. Helen (Meg) TULLOCH
45 Director Resource Management .... Mr. Jay HELMING
23 Director Health Fitness .... Mr. Tony SPINOSA
25 Director Contracting .... Ms. Jenifer CUOZZO
43 General Counsel .... Ms. Mollie MURPHY
06 Registrar .... Mr. Larry JOHNSON
15 Director Personnel .... Ms. Marcia MILLER
102 Acting President/CEO NDU Foundation .... Mr. Albert C. ZIMMERMAN
85 Director International Fellows .... Mr. John CHARLTON
18 Chief Facilities/Physical Plant .... Mr. Charles FANSHAW
11 Events Director .... Mr. Jerry FABER
100 Chief of Staff & Administration .... Mr. Michael CANNON
88 Deputy Chief of Staff & Admin .... Col. Bradley W. BOOTH
28 Director of Diversity .... Vacant
86 Director University Outreach .... Vacant
09 Director of Institutional Research .... Dr. R. Joel FARRELL

National Intelligence University (J)

200 MacDill Boulevard, Washington DC 20340-5100

Identification: 666393
Unit ID: 131380
Telephone: (202) 231-3344 Carnegie Class: Not Classified
FAX Number: (202) 231-3294 Calendar System: Quarter
URL: www.dia.mil
Established: 1962 Annual Undergrad Tuition & Fees: N/A
Enrollment: 730 Coed
Affiliation or Control: Federal IRS Status: Exempt
Highest Offering: Master's
Program: Professional
Accreditation: M

01 President .... Dr. David R. ELLISON
100 Chief of Staff .... Col. James C. LAUGHREY
04 Executive Assistant to President .... Ms. Jessica M. STEINRUCK
05 Provost .... Dr. Susan M. STUDDS
88 Dir Ctr for International Pgms .... Mr. Lorenzo S. HIPONIA
46 Dir Ctr for Strategic Intel Rsrch .... Dr. Cathryn Q. THURSTON

09 Dir Inst Effectiveness .... Dr. Felicia BRADSHAW
10 VP Finance & Administration .... Mr. Caleb TEMPLE
10 Chief Operating Officer .... Mr. Kevin C. TALIAFERRO
11 Director of Operations .... Mr. Stephen J. KERDA
18 Facilities .... Dr. Richard MESTAS
19 Security Officer .... Ms. Thelma FLAMER
06 Registrar .... Mr. Eric H. STUPAR
07 Director of Admissions .... Ms. Alteia L. ROBINSON
90 Director Eductional Technology .... Ms. Elvia E. CORTES
08 Director Library Services .... Ms. Denise CAMPBELL
58 Dean College of Strategic Intel .... Dr. Vance R. SKARSTEDT
88 Associate Dean College Strat Intel .... Col. Douglas KIELY
12 Director NSA Campus .... Vacant
12 Director NGA Campus .... Mr. Timothy J. CHRISTENSON
58 Dean School of Science & Tech Intel .... Dr. Brian R. SHAW
88 Associate Dean School of S&T Intel .... Dr. Duncan MCGILL
29 Dir Outreach & Alumni Affairs .... Mr. Thomas VAN WAGNER

Naval Postgraduate School (A)

1 University Circle, Room M10, Monterey CA 93943-5100

County: Monterey FICE Identification: 001310
Unit ID: 119678
Telephone: (831) 656-2441 Carnegie Class: Master's L
FAX Number: (831) 656-2921 Calendar System: Quarter
URL: www.nps.edu
Established: 1909 Annual Undergrad Tuition & Fees: N/A
Enrollment: 2,989 Coed
Affiliation or Control: Federal IRS Status: Exempt
Highest Offering: Doctorate
Program: Professional
Accreditation: WC, BUS, ENG, SPAA

01 President .... ADM. Daniel T. OLIVER
100 Chief of Staff .... Col. Zoe M. HALE
05 Executive Vice President & Provost .... Dr. Leonard A. FERRARI
10 Vice Pres Finance/Administration .... Ms. Colleen A. NICKLES
46 Vice President/Dean of Research .... Dr. Jeffrey D. PADUAN
13 Vice Pres Information Resources/CIO .... Dr. Christine M. HASKA
20 Vice Provost for Academic Affairs .... Dr. Orrin Douglas MOSES
54 Dean Grad Sch Engr/Applied Sci .... Dr. Phillip A. DURKEE
58 Dean Sch of Intl Graduate Studies .... Dr. James J. WIRTZ
50 Dean Grad Sch Bus/Public Policy .... Dr. William R. GATES
72 Dean Grad Sch Oper & Info Sciences .... Dr. Peter P. PURDUE
32 Dean of Students .... CDR. Matthew VANDERSLUIS
10 Comptroller .... Mr. Kevin K. LITTLE
18 Director Facilities/Support Svcs .... Mr. Peter G. DAUSEN
08 University Librarian .... Ms. Eleanor S. UHLINGER
06 Registrar .... Mr. Mike ANDERSEN
15 Director Human Resources .... Ms. Julie CARPENTER
29 Director of Alumni Relations .... Mr. Kari L. MIGLAW
19 Sr Lecturer NPS/Chief Security Ofcr .... CAPT. Robert SIMERAL, RET.
88 Senior Intelligence Officer .... Capt. Jennith E. HOYT
09 Exec Dir Inst Plng/Communications .... Dr. Fran HORVATH
28 EEO Director .... Ms. Deborah A. BAITY
56 Dir Office of Continuous Learning .... Mr. Tom M. MASTRE
07 Director of Admissions .... Ms. Sue DOOLEY
88 Deputy Comptroller .... Mr. Jack L. SHISIDO
88 Director of Programs .... CDR. Mary J. SIMS

Naval War College (B)

686 Cushing Road, Newport RI 02841-1207

County: Newport FICE Identification: 003413
Unit ID: 432320
Telephone: (401) 841-3089 Carnegie Class: Not Classified
FAX Number: (401) 841-1297 Calendar System: Trimester
URL: www.usnwc.edu
Established: 1884 Annual Graduate Tuition & Fees: N/A
Enrollment: N/A Coed
Affiliation or Control: Federal IRS Status: Exempt
Highest Offering: Master's; No Undergraduates
Program: Professional
Accreditation: EH

01 President .... RADM. John N. CHRISTENSON
04 Exec Assistant to the President .... LT. Robert J. DAFOE
05 Provost .... Amb. MaryAnn PETERS, RET.
88 Chief of Staff to the Provost .... Mr. Richard R. MENARD
20 Associate Provost .... Prof. William R. SPAIN
100 Chief of Staff .... CAPT. William J. NAULT
20 Dean of Academic Affairs .... Prof. John GAROFANO
09 Dean Center for Warfare Studies .... Prof. Robert J. RUBEL
32 Dean of Students .... CAPT. Raymond F. KELEDEI
08 Director Library Services .... Vacant
56 Dir College of Distance Education .... Dr. Jay HICKEY
06 Registrar .... CAPT. Raymond F. KELEDEI
46 Chairman Strategy & Policy .... Dr. John MAURER
88 Chairman National Security Affairs .... Dr. David COOPER
88 Chairman Joint Military Operations .... CAPT. Alan ABRAMSON
10 Chief Business Officer .... Mr. Robert SAMPSON
15 Director Personnel Services .... CDR. Mary E. SMITH
18 Chief Facilities/Physical Plant .... Ms. Beth LEINBERRY
26 Chief Public Relations Officer .... CDR. Carla M. MCCARTHY
27 Chief Information Officer .... Mr. Joseph PANGBORN
19 Director of Security .... Vacant
29 Director Alumni Affairs .... Prof. Julia A. GAGE
88 Director Writing Center .... Dr. Donna CONNOLLY
88 Director International Programs .... Vacant
88 Dean Col Operatnl/Strategic Ldrshp ... RADM. James KELLY, RET.

School of Advanced Air and Space Studies (C)

600 Chennault Circle, Maxwell AFB AL 36112-6424

County: Montgomery Identification: 666746
Telephone: (334) 953-5155 Carnegie Class: Not Classified
FAX Number: (334) 953-3015 Calendar System: Other
URL: www.au.af.mil/au/saass
Established: 1991 Annual Graduate Tuition & Fees: N/A
Enrollment: 45 Coed
Affiliation or Control: Federal IRS Status: Exempt
Highest Offering: Master's; No Undergraduates
Program: Professional
Accreditation: &SC

01 Commandant .... Col. Jeffrey SMITH
03 Vice Commandant .... Dr. Stephen D. CHIABOTTI

† Regional accreditation is carried under the parent institution, Air University, Maxwell AFB, AL.

Uniformed Services University of the Health Sciences (D)

4301 Jones Bridge Road, Bethesda MD 20814-4799

County: Montgomery FICE Identification: 021610
Unit ID: 164137
Telephone: (301) 295-3013 Carnegie Class: Not Classified
FAX Number: (301) 295-3431 Calendar System: Quarter
URL: www.usuhs.mil
Established: 1972 Annual Graduate Tuition & Fees: N/A
Enrollment: 999 Coed
Affiliation or Control: Federal IRS Status: Exempt
Highest Offering: Doctorate; No Undergraduates
Program: Professional
Accreditation: M, ANEST, CLPSY, ENGR, MED, NURSE, PH

01 President .... Dr. Charles L. RICE
03 Senior Vice President .... Dr. Dale C. SMITH
05 Sr Vice Pres University Programs .... Dr. Patrick SCULLEY
10 Vice Pres Finance & Administration .... Mr. Stephen C. RICE
26 Acting Vice Pres External Affairs .... Dr. Jeffrey LONGACRE
46 Acting Vice President for Research .... Dr. Richard LEVINE
88 VP Affiliation/International Affs .... Dr. Jeffrey LONGACRE
04 Exec Assistant to the President .... Ms. Mary L. SCHWARTZ
100 Chief of Staff .... Mr. Robert J. THOMPSON
63 Dean School of Medicine .... Dr. Larry W. LAUGHLIN
63 Vice Dean School of Medicine .... Dr. John MCMANIGLE
58 Assoc Dean Graduate Education .... Dr. Eleanor S. METCALF
07 Assoc Dean Admiss & Recruiting SOM .... CAPT. Margaret CALLOWAY
88 Assoc Dean Graduate Medical Educ .... CAPT. Jerri CURTIS
32 Assoc Dean Student Affairs .... Dr. Richard M. MACDONALD
88 Assistant Dean Academic Support .... Dr. William WITTMAN
88 Assistant Dean Clinical Sciences .... COL. Lisa MOORES
66 Dean Graduate School of Nursing .... Dr. Ada Sue HINSHAW
20 Associate Dean Acad Affairs GSN .... Dr. Carol A. ROMANO
46 Director AFRRI .... Col. Lester HUFF
27 Chief Information Officer .... Mr. Timothy RAPP
43 General Counsel .... Mr. John E. BAKER
06 Registrar .... Ms. Gail HEWITT-CLARKE
15 Director Civilian Human Res .... Mr. Darryl BROWN
08 Acting University Librarian .... Ms. Linda SPITZER
18 Director of Facilities .... Ms. Cheryl KING
96 Director of Contracting .... Mr. Anthony REVENIS
21 Associate Business Officer .... Mr. Walter TINLING
29 Director Alumni Relations .... Ms. Sharon WILLIS

United States Air Force Academy (E)

2304 Cadet Drive, Suite 2400,
USAF Academy CO 80840-5025

County: El Paso FICE Identification: 001369
Unit ID: 128328
Telephone: (719) 333-3070 Carnegie Class: Bac/A&S
FAX Number: (719) 333-3647 Calendar System: Semester
URL: www.academyadmissions.com
Established: 1954 Annual Undergrad Tuition & Fees: N/A
Enrollment: 4,413 Coed
Affiliation or Control: Federal IRS Status: Exempt
Highest Offering: Baccalaureate
Program: Liberal Arts And General; Professional
Accreditation: NH, BUS, CS, DENT, ENG

United States Army Command and General Staff College (F)

1 Reynolds Avenue, Building 111,
Fort Leavenworth KS 66027-1352

County: Leavenworth FICE Identification: 001947
Unit ID: 156055
Telephone: (913) 684-3097 Carnegie Class: Not Classified
FAX Number: (913) 684-2906 Calendar System: Trimester
URL: www.cgsc.army.mil
Established: 1881 Annual Undergrad Tuition & Fees: N/A
Enrollment: 1,002 Coed
Affiliation or Control: Federal IRS Status: Exempt
Highest Offering: Master's
Program: Professional
Accreditation: NH

01 Commandant .... LtGen. David G. PERKINS
03 Deputy Commandant .... BGen. Gordon DAVIS, JR.
04 Assistant Deputy Commandant .... Col. Michael J. JOHNSON
05 Dean of Academics .... Dr. Wendell KING
100 Chief of Staff .... Col. Jeff P. LAMOE
58 Director Graduate Degree Programs .... Dr. Robert BAUMANN
08 Director of Library .... Mr. Ed BURGESS
32 Director CGSS School .... Col. Drew MEYEROWICH
06 Registrar .... Mr. Kenneth A. NORRIS
26 Chief Public Relations Officer .... Mr. Harry SARLES

United States Army War College (G)

122 Forbes Avenue, Carlisle PA 17013-5050

County: Cumberland Identification: 666235
Telephone: (717) 245-4711 Carnegie Class: Not Classified
FAX Number: (717) 245-4721 Calendar System: Other
URL: www.carlisle.army.mil
Established: N/A Annual Graduate Tuition & Fees: N/A
Enrollment: N/A Coed
Affiliation or Control: Federal IRS Status: Exempt
Highest Offering: Master's; No Undergraduates
Program: Professional
Accreditation: M

01 Commandant .... MajGen. Anthony CUCOLO
05 Dean Academics .... Dr. Lance BETROLS

United States Coast Guard Academy (H)

15 Mohegan Avenue, New London CT 06320-8100

County: New London FICE Identification: 001415
Unit ID: 130624
Telephone: (860) 444-8444 Carnegie Class: Bac/Diverse
FAX Number: (860) 444-8288 Calendar System: Semester
URL: www.cga.edu
Established: 1876 Annual Undergrad Tuition & Fees: N/A
Enrollment: 1,045 Coed
Affiliation or Control: Federal IRS Status: Exempt
Highest Offering: Baccalaureate
Program: Occupational; Technical Emphasis
Accreditation: EH, BUS, ENG

01 Superintendent .... RADM. Sandra L. STOSZ
03 Assistant Superintendent .... CAPT. Eric C. JONES
45 Planning Officer .... CDR. Alan G. LAPENNA
05 Dean of Academics .... Dr. Kurt J. COLELLA
20 Associate Dean .... CDR. David C. CLIPPINGER
45 Assoc Dean Acad Support Services .... Vacant
07 Director of Admissions .... CAPT. Stephan FINTON
32 Commandant of Cadets .... CAPT. James L. MCCAULEY
06 Registrar .... Mr. Donald E. DYKES
08 Librarian .... Ms. Patricia A. DARAGAN
10 Comptroller .... CDR. Richard G. BOSTON
26 Public Affairs Officer .... CWO Kimberly SMITH
09 Institutional Research .... Dr. Leonard M. GIAMBRA
46 Director of Research .... Vacant
13 Head of Information Services .... CDR. Robert R. OATMAN
15 Personnel Management Specialist .... Mrs. Sunnie ROBINSON
16 Chief Personnel/Administration .... CAPT. Sean P. GILL
18 Chief Facilities Engineer .... CDR. Michael A. CLYBURN
19 Security Chief .... CGPO. Timothy M. NUGENT
22 Civil Rights Officer .... Mr. Bradley S. SHAFF
23 Chief Health Services .... CDR. Joseph L. PEREZ
29 President Alumni Association .... CDR. James SYLVESTER
38 Chief Cadet Counselor .... Dr. Robert MURRAY
40 Bookstore Manager .... Ms. Lauri KERP
41 Director of Athletics .... Mr. Timothy M. FITZPATRICK
42 Command Chaplain .... Capt. Brian K. FINCH
43 Staff Legal Officer .... CDR. Stephen J. ADLER
85 International Cadet Advisor .... Dr. Alina M. ZAPALSKA
28 Director of Diversity .... Mr. Antonio FARIAS
88 Director Leadership Development Ctr .... Capt. Andrea M. MARCILLE

† There is a one-time entrance fee of $3,000 to cover uniform, laptop, and supplies.

United States Merchant Marine Academy (I)

300 Steamboat Road, Kings Point NY 11024-1634

County: Nassau FICE Identification: 002892
Unit ID: 197027
Telephone: (516) 773-5000 Carnegie Class: Bac/Diverse
FAX Number: (516) 773-5509 Calendar System: Trimester
URL: www.usmma.edu
Established: 1943 Annual Undergrad Tuition & Fees: $2,530
Enrollment: 1,086 Coed
Affiliation or Control: Federal IRS Status: Exempt
Highest Offering: Master's
Program: Liberal Arts And General; Professional
Accreditation: M, ENG

01 Superintendent & Dean .... RADM. James HELIS
03 Deputy Superintendent .... Vacant
05 Academic Dean/Asst Supt Acad Affs .... Dr. Shashi KUMAR
18 Asst Supt for Facilities .... Capt. Theodore DOGONNIUCK
20 Assistant Academic Dean .... Ms. Dianne TAHA
32 Commandant Midshipmen .... Capt. John KENNEDY

30 Director Office of External Affairs .... Capt. Marcie KATCHER
07 Director of Admissions .... Capt. Robert JOHNSON
06 Registrar .... Ms. Lisa JERRY
08 Chief Librarian .... Dr. George J. BILLY
13 Director Computer/Information Mgmt .... Mr. Kevin CLARKE
15 Director Human Resources .... Mr. Andrew GREEN
21 Asst Chief Financial Officer .... Ms. Jennifer FALLIS
29 Director Alumni Relations .... Mr. Peter RACKETT
35 Director Student Affairs .... Ms. Mary CUNNINGHAM
36 Dir of Prof Develop/Career Services .... Capt. Gene ALBERT
37 Director Student Financial Aid .... Vacant
96 Director of Purchasing .... Mr. Max DIAH

United States Military Academy (A)

West Point NY 10996-5000

County: Orange FICE Identification: 002893
Unit ID: 197036
Telephone: (845) 938-4041 Carnegie Class: Bac/A&S
FAX Number: (845) 938-3021 Calendar System: Semester
URL: www.westpoint.edu
Established: 1802 Annual Undergrad Tuition & Fees: N/A
Enrollment: 4,624 Coed
Affiliation or Control: Federal IRS Status: Exempt
Highest Offering: Baccalaureate
Program: Liberal Arts And General; Professional
Accreditation: M, CS, ENG

01 Superintendent/President .... LTG. David H. HUNTOON, JR.
05 Dean of Academic Board .... BG. Timothy TRAINOR
20 Vice Dean .... Dr. Jean BLAIR
32 Commandant of Cadets .... BG. Theodore D. MARTIN
100 Chief of Staff .... COL. Charles A. STAFFORD
88 Garrison Commander .... COL. Dane RIDEOUT
07 Director of Admissions .... COL. Deborah MCDONALD
06 Assoc Dean Operations/Registrar .... Dr. James DALTON
45 Associate Dean for Research .... LTC. John GRAHAM
09 Institutional Research .... Dr. John PICCIUTO
13 Chief Information Officer .... COL. Ron DODGE
10 Director of Resource Management .... Mrs. Deborah A. POOL
26 Public Affairs Officer .... LTC. Shari REED
08 USMA Library .... Mr. Christopher BARTH
29 President Association of Graduates .... COLRet. Robert MCCLURE
38 Dir Center for Personal Development .... LTC. Brian CRANDALL
20 Assoc Dean Academic Affairs .... Vacant
41 Director Intercollegiate Athletics .... Mr. Boo CORRIGAN
18 Chief Facilities/Physical Plant .... Mr. Matthew TALABER
15 Dir Center for Faculty Excellence .... Dr. Mark EVANS
35 Dir Ctr for Enchanced Performance .... COL. Carl J. OHLSON
88 Director of Cadet Activities .... LTC. Todd MESSITT

United States Naval Academy (B)

121 Blake Road, Annapolis MD 21402-5000

County: Anne Arundel FICE Identification: 030430
Unit ID: 164155
Telephone: (410) 293-1000 Carnegie Class: Bac/A&S
FAX Number: (410) 293-3734 Calendar System: Semester
URL: www.usna.edu
Established: 1845 Annual Undergrad Tuition & Fees: N/A
Enrollment: 4,595 Coed
Affiliation or Control: Federal IRS Status: Exempt
Highest Offering: Baccalaureate
Program: Liberal Arts And General; Professional; Technical Emphasis
Accreditation: M, CS, ENG

01 Superintendent .... VADM. Michael H. MILLER
32 Commandant of Midshipmen .... Capt. Robert E. CLARK, II
05 Academic Dean & Provost .... Dr. Andrew T. PHILLIPS
20 Vice Academic Dean .... Dr. Boyd A. WAITE
07 Dean of Admissions .... Capt. Bruce J. LATTA
10 Associate Dean for Finances .... Capt. Peter A. NARDI
20 Assoc Dean for Academic Affairs .... Dr. Frederic I. DAVIS
08 Assoc Dean Information Svcs/Library .... Mr. James RETTIG
21 Deputy for Finance .... Mr. Joseph RUBINO
100 Chief of Staff .... Capt. Steven S. VAHSEN
11 CO Naval Support Activity Annapolis .... Capt. Thomas L. REESE
06 Registrar .... Dr. Christopher A. DAVIS
26 Public Affairs Officer .... CDR. William MARKS
29 Exec Director Alumni Association .... Mr. William OCONNER
21 Comptroller .... CDR. Todd W. HAUGE
14 Chief Information Officer .... CDR. Louis J. GIANNOTTI
88 Director Academic Center .... Dr. Bruce J. BUKOWSKI
09 Director Institutional Research .... Capt. Glenn F. GOTTSCHALK
18 Public Works Officer .... Capt. Donald B. CAMPBELL
41 Athletic Director .... Mr. Chet GLADCHUK
42 Command Chaplain .... Capt. Michael PARISI
30 Director Officer Development .... Capt. Mike MICHEL
15 Director Human Resources .... Mr. William COFFIN
28 Director of Diversity .... Capt. Roger ISOM

AMERICAN SAMOA

American Samoa Community College (C)

PO Box 2609, Pago Pago AS 96799-2609

County: American Samoa FICE Identification: 010010
Unit ID: 240736
Telephone: (684) 699-9155 Carnegie Class: Assoc/Pub-S-SC
FAX Number: (684) 699-6259 Calendar System: Semester
URL: www.amsamoa.edu
Established: 1970 Annual Undergrad Tuition & Fees (In-State): $3,400
Enrollment: 2,042 Coed
Affiliation or Control: State IRS Status: 501(c)3
Highest Offering: Baccalaureate
Program: Occupational; 2-Year Principally Bachelor's Creditable
Accreditation: @WC, WJ

01 President .... Dr. Seth P. GALEA'I
05 Vice Pres Academic/Student Affairs .... Dr. Kathleen KOLHOFF
11 Vice Pres Administrative Services .... Mr. Mikaele ETUALE
32 Dean of Student Services .... Dr. Emilia LE'I
51 Dir of Adult Educ/Lit Ext Learning .... Mr. Tauvela FALE
20 Dean of Academic Affairs .... Dr. Irene HELSHAM
08 Director of Library Services .... Mrs. Emma FUNG CHEN PENN
25 Dir Land Grant/Cmty & Natural Res .... Dr. Daniel F. AGA
45 Dir Institutional Effectiveness .... Mrs. Rosevonne PATO
37 Financial Aid Manager .... Mr. Peteru LAM YUEN
88 Dir Teacher Education Program .... Dr. Lina GALEA'I-SCANLAN
10 Chief Financial Officer .... Ms. Emey SILAFAU
88 Director of SAMPAC .... Mrs. Okenaisa FAUOLO-MANILA
88 Director of Upward Bound Program .... Mrs. Elizabeth LEUMA
102 Dir of ASCC Research Foundation .... Mr. John AH SUE
88 Director of Small Business Devel .... Mr. Herbert THWEATT
06 Dir of Admissions Records Finan Aid .... Mrs. Sifagatogo TUITASI
15 Director Human Resources .... Mrs. Komiti EMMSLEY
26 Press Officer .... Mr. James KNEUBUHL
72 Acting Dean Trades & Technology .... Mr. Michael LEAU
27 Chief Information Officer .... Ms. Grace TULAFONO
38 Director of Student Support Svcs .... Mrs. Repeka ALAIMOANA-NUUSA
18 Dir Physical Facilities-Maintenance .... Mr. Loligi SEUMANUTAFA

FEDERATED STATES OF MICRONESIA

College of Micronesia-FSM (D)

PO Box 159 Kolonia, Pohnpei FM 96941-0159

FICE Identification: 010343
Unit ID: 243638
Telephone: (691) 320-2480 Carnegie Class: Assoc/Pub-R-M
FAX Number: (691) 320-2479 Calendar System: Semester
URL: www.comfsm.fm
Established: 1963 Annual Undergrad Tuition & Fees (In-State): $3,891
Enrollment: 2,915 Coed
Affiliation or Control: State IRS Status: 501(c)3
Highest Offering: Associate Degree
Program: Occupational; 2-Year Principally Bachelor's Creditable
Accreditation: #WJ

01 President .... Mr. Joseph DAISY
05 Vice Pres Instructional Affairs .... Vacant
32 Vice Pres Support/Student Affairs .... Mr. Ringlen P. RINGLEN
56 VP Coop Research/Ext (Land Grant) .... Mr. Walter James CURRIE
11 Vice Pres Dept of Admin Services .... Mr. Joesph HABUCHMAI
10 Comptroller .... Mr. Danilo DUMANTAY
12 Director Chuuk Campus .... Mr. Joakim PETER
12 Director Pohnpei Campus .... Ms. Penny WEILBACHER
12 Director Kosrae Campus .... Mr. Kalwin KEPHAS
12 Director Yap Campus .... Ms. Lourdes ROBOMAN
12 Director FSM-FMI Campus .... Mr. Matthias EWARMAI
45 Director Research & Planning .... Mr. Jimmy HICKS
15 Director Human Resources .... Ms. Rencelly NELSON
20 Director Academic Programs .... Mrs. Karen SIMION
07 Director Admissions & Records .... Vacant
08 Director Learning Res Center .... Vacant
75 Director Vocational Programs .... Vacant
18 Director Physical Plant/Maintenance .... Mr. Francisco MENDIOLA
06 Registrar .... Mr. Joey ODUCADO
09 Director of Institutional Research .... Vacant
21 Business Officer Manager .... Ms. Pelma PALIK
37 Director Student Financial Aid .... Mr. Eddie HALEYALIG
38 Counselor .... Ms. Penselyn ETSE
26 Director Devel/Public Relations .... Mr. Joseph SAIMON
13 Director Information Technology .... Mr. Gordon SEGAL
35 Director Residential/Campus Life .... Mr. Reedson ABRAHAM

GUAM

Guam Community College (E)

PO Box 23069, Barrigada GU 96921-3069

County: Guam FICE Identification: 015361
Unit ID: 240745
Telephone: (671) 735-5531 Carnegie Class: Assoc/Pub-R-S
FAX Number: (671) 734-5238 Calendar System: Semester
URL: www.guamcc.edu
Established: 1977 Annual Undergrad Tuition & Fees (In-District): $4,446
Enrollment: 2,536 Coed
Affiliation or Control: State/Local IRS Status: 501(c)3
Highest Offering: Associate Degree
Program: Occupational; 2-Year Principally Bachelor's Creditable; Technical Emphasis
Accreditation: WJ, MAC

01 President .... Dr. Mary Y. OKADA
05 Vice President Academic Affairs .... Dr. R. Ray D. SOMERA
10 Vice President Finance & Admin .... Ms. Carmen K. SANTOS
10 Controller .... Mr. Edwin E. LIMTUATCO
75 Dean Trades & Professional Services .... Mr. Reilly A. RIDGELL
72 Dean Technology & Student Services .... Dr. Virginia C. TUDELA
26 Asst Dir Communications & Promo .... Ms. Jayne T. FLORES
29 Asst Dir Dev & Alumni Relations .... Ms. Lolita C. REYES
04 Private Secretary .... Ms. Esther A. MUNA
101 Admin Secretary II BOT-Pres Ofc .... Ms. Bertha M. GUERRERO
06 Coordinator Admissions/Registration .... Mr. Patrick L. CLYMER
45 Asst Dir Planning & Development .... Ms. Doris U. PEREZ
103 Asst Dir Cont Ed & Workforce Dev .... Mr. Victor RODGERS
88 Assoc Dean Trades & Prof Svcs .... Dr. Michael L. CHAN
32 Assoc Dean Student Support Svcs .... Ms. Joanne A. IGE
15 Administrator Human Resources .... Ms. Joann W. MUNA
18 Coordinator Facilities Maintenance .... Vacant
08 Librarian .... Ms. Christine B. MATSON
20 Admin Ofcr VP's Ofc-Academic Affs .... Ms. Ava M. GARCIA
09 Institutional Researcher .... Ms. Marlena O. MONTAGUE
88 Pgm Specialist AIER .... Ms. Priscilla C. JOHNS
46 Asst Director AIER .... Vacant
88 Pgm Specialist Project Aim TRIO .... Ms. Christine B. SISON
35 Pgm Spc Ctr Student Involvement .... Ms. Barbara B. LEON GUERRERO
26 Program Specialist .... Mr. Wesley T. GIMA
23 School Health Counselor .... Ms. Maria Cecilia H. DELOS SANTOS
37 Coordinator Student Financial Aid .... Ms. Micki L. LONSDALE
88 Pgm Specialist Adult Educ/GED .... Mr. Huan F. HOSEI
29 Pgm Specialist Dev & Alumni Rels .... Ms. Bonnie Mae M. DATUIN
96 Supply Management Administrator .... Ms. Joleen M. EVANGELISTA
14 Data Processing Administrator .... Mr. Francisco C. CAMACHO
51 Pgm Specialist Continuing Educ .... Ms. Terry L. BARNHART
51 Pgm Specialist Continuing Educ .... Ms. Rowena Ellen PEREZ
40 Bookstore Manager .... Mr. Daniel T. OKADA
55 Pgm Specialist Night Administrator .... Mr. John F. PAYNE
19 Safety Admin Envir Safety Ofc .... Mr. Gregorio T. MANGLONA
88 Adjunct Assoc Dean TSS .... Mr. Barry L. MEAD
88 Pgm Specialist Accomodative Svcs .... Ms. Kasinda C. LUDWIG

Pacific Islands University (F)

172 Kinneys Road, Mangilao GU 96913

County: Guam FICE Identification: 034383
Unit ID: 439862
Telephone: (671) 734-1812 Carnegie Class: Spec/Faith
FAX Number: (671) 734-1813 Calendar System: Semester
URL: piu.edu
Established: 1976 Annual Undergrad Tuition & Fees: $12,130
Enrollment: 84 Coed
Affiliation or Control: Independent Non-Profit IRS Status: 501(c)3
Highest Offering: Master's
Program: Liberal Arts And General; Religious Emphasis
Accreditation: TRACS

01 President/CEO .... Dr. David L. OWEN
05 Academic Vice President .... Dr. Cristel WOOD
10 Vice President of Administration .... Mr. Nino PATE
20 Dean of the Seminary .... Vacant
44 Interim Advancement Director .... Ms. Samantha OWEN
32 Director of Student Life .... Mr. Robert WATT
08 Librarian .... Ms. Lisa COLLINS
06 Registrar .... Ms. Urte SCHERER
21 Operations Director .... Ms. Celia ATOIGE

University of Guam (G)

UOG Station, Mangilao GU 96923-1800

County: Guam FICE Identification: 003935
Unit ID: 240754
Telephone: (671) 735-2990 Carnegie Class: Master's S
FAX Number: (671) 734-2296 Calendar System: Semester
URL: www.uog.edu
Established: 1952 Annual Undergrad Tuition & Fees (In-State): $5,098
Enrollment: 3,721 Coed
Affiliation or Control: State IRS Status: 501(c)3
Highest Offering: Master's
Program: Occupational; Liberal Arts And General; Teacher Preparatory; Professional
Accreditation: WC, IACBE, NUR, SW, TED

01 President .... Dr. Robert A. UNDERWOOD
05 Sr VP Academic & Student Affairs .... Dr. Helen J D. WHIPPY
10 Vice Pres Administration & Finance .... Mr. David M. O'BRIEN
58 AVP Graduate Studies/Research & SP .... Dr. John A. PETERSON
43 University Legal Counsel .... Ms. Victorina M Y. RENACIA
88 Institutional Compliance Officer .... Ms. Elaine FACULO-GOGUE
04 Executive Assistant to President .... Ms. Louise M. TOVES
26 Director Integrated Mktg Comm .... Mr. Jonas D. MACAPINLAC
45 Chief Planning Officer .... Mr. David S. OKADA
29 Director Dev & Alumni Affairs .... Mr. Norman ANALISTA
102 Exec Director Endowment Foundation .... Mr. Mark B. MENDIOLA
108 Dir Academic Assess/Inst Research .... Ms. Deborah D. LEON GUERRERO
49 Dean Col of Lib Arts & Social Sci .... Dr. James D. SELLMANN
47 Dean Col of Natural & Applied Sci .... Dr. Lee S. YUDIN
50 Dean Sch Bus & Pub Admin .... Dr. Anita B. ENRIQUEZ
53 Dean School of Education .... Dr. Frankie S. LAANAN
66 Actg Dir Sch of Nursing & Hlth Sci .... Ms. Kathryn WOOD
84 Dean Enroll Mgmt & Student Services .... Dr. Julie ULLOA-HEATH
06 Registrar .... Ms. Remy B. CRISTOBAL
37 Director Financial Aid .... Mr. Mark A. DUARTE
32 Student Life Officer .... Ms. Sallie MCDONALD
88 Director Guam CEDDERS .... Dr. Heidi E. SAN NICOLAS
08 Director Learning Resources .... Ms. Christine K. SCOTT-SMITH
14 Dir Info Tech Resource/Computer Ctr .... Dr. Luan P. NGUYEN

88 Actg Dir Micronesia Area Res Center .... Ms. Monique C. STORIE
88 Director Marine Laboratory .... Dr. Laurie RAYMUNDO
88 Dir Watr Env Rsrch Inst Wstrn Pac .... Dr. Gary R W. DENTON
88 Dir Ctr for Island Sustainability .... Dr. John A. PETERSON
51 Director Prof/International Pgm .... Ms. Cathleen MOORE-LINN
88 Director TRIO Programs .... Mr. Yoichi K. RENGIIL
15 Chief Human Resources Officer .... Mr. Larry GAMBOA
18 Chief Plant Fac Ofcr Fac & Util .... Mr. Sonny P. PEREZ
41 Field House/Athletics Director .... Mr. Bob O. PELKEY
19 Chief of Safety .... Mr. William PALOMO
40 Director Bookstore & Auxillary Svcs .... Ms. Ann S A. S.A. LEON GUERRERO
21 Comptroller .... Ms. Zeny ASUNCION-NACE

MARSHALL ISLANDS

College of the Marshall Islands (A)

PO Box 1258, Majuro MH 96960-1258

County: Marshalls | FICE Identification: 030224 | Unit ID: 376695
Telephone: (692) 625-3394 | Carnegie Class: Assoc/Pub-R-S
FAX Number: (692) 625-7203 | Calendar System: Semester
URL: www.cmi.edu
Established: 1989 | Annual Undergrad Tuition & Fees (In-State): $4,415
Enrollment: 989 | Coed
Affiliation or Control: State | IRS Status: 501(c)3
Highest Offering: Associate Degree
Program: 2-Year Principally Bachelor's Creditable
Accreditation: WJ

01 Interim President .... Dr. Carl HACKER
05 VP Academic & Student Affairs .... Mr. Donald HESS
11 Vice Pres Administration .... Ms. Diane C. MYAZOE-DEBRUM
10 VP Finance//Chief Financial Officer .... Mr. Stevenson KOTTON
45 VP for Research & Planning .... Dr. Rafe Edward TRICKEY, JR.
20 Dean of Academic Affairs .... Ms. Ruth ABBOTT
32 Dean of Students .... Ms. Rachel SALOMON
46 Dean of Voc & Continuing Education .... Ms. Diane C. MYAZOE-DEBRUM
06 Registrar .... Ms. Monica GORDON
07 Director of Admissions & Records .... Ms. Rosita V. CAPELLE
08 Director of Library Services .... Vacant
15 Human Resources Director .... Mr. Robert W. WILLSON
51 Director Continuing/Adult Education .... Vacant
18 Director Physical Plant .... Mr. William REIHER
88 Dir Stdnt Support Svcs/Upward Bound .... Ms. Aluka RAKIN
13 Director Information & Technology .... Mr. Bonifacio SANCHEZ
88 Director Nuclear Institute .... Ms. Mary L. SILK
53 Chair Education/Marshallese Stds .... Mr. Max VOELZKE
37 Financial Aid Director .... Ms. Jacinta SAMUEL
49 Chair Liberal Arts .... Ms. Janet HESS
50 Chair Business & IT .... Vacant
66 Chair Nursing .... Ms. Florence L. PETER
81 Chair Mathematics/Science .... Mr. Donald HESS
04 Special Assistant to the President .... Vacant
19 Director Security/Safety .... Mr. David DEBRUM
38 Director of Student Counseling .... Dr. Donna SEPPY
09 Dean Rsrch/Planning/Effectiveness .... Vacant

NORTHERN MARIANAS

Northern Marianas College (B)

PO Box 501250, Saipan MP 96950-1250

FICE Identification: 030330 | Unit ID: 240790
Telephone: (670) 234-5498 | Carnegie Class: Bac/Assoc
FAX Number: (670) 234-0759 | Calendar System: Semester
URL: www.nmcnet.edu
Established: 1976 | Annual Undergrad Tuition & Fees (In-District): $3,820
Enrollment: 1,046 | Coed
Affiliation or Control: State/Local | IRS Status: 501(c)3
Highest Offering: Baccalaureate
Program: 2-Year Principally Bachelor's Creditable; Liberal Arts And General; Teacher Preparatory
Accreditation: WC, #WJ

01 President .... Dr. Sharon Y. HART
05 Dean of Academic Programs & Svcs .... Ms. Barbara K. MERFALEN
32 Dean of Student Services .... Mr. Leo PANGELINAN
10 Dean of Finance & Administration .... Mr. David J. ATTAO
31 Dean Community Programs & Services .... Mr. Ross MANGLONA
04 Executive Secretary to President .... Ms. Becky SABLAN
13 Acg Dir of Information Technology .... Mr. Eric ABRAGAN
09 Dir Institutional Effectiveness .... Mr. Galvin S. DELEON GUERRERO
30 Director Institutional Advancement .... Mr. Frankie M. ELIPTICO
08 Director Library Services .... Mr. Matthew PASTULA
51 Director of Adult Basic Education .... Ms. Lorraine T. CABRERA
07 Director Admissions & Records .... Vacant
38 Director of Counseling Services .... Dr. Timothy BAKER
26 Director External Relations .... Mr. Frankie ELIPTICO
06 Registrar/Acting Dir Admissions .... Ms. Rosaline CEPEDA
37 Director of Financial Aid .... Ms. Daisy MANGLONA-PROPST
96 Procurement Manager .... Ms. Anita C. CAMACHO
15 Acting Human Resources Manager .... Ms. Barbara (Bobbie) HUNTER
21 Chief Accountant .... Ms. Solita K. BARNES
36 Career Planning/Placement Coord .... Ms. Neda C. DELEON GUERRERA
18 Facilities Manager .... Mr. John GUERRERO
18 Maintenance Manager .... Mr. George DAVID
29 President NMC Alumni Association .... Mr. Jack O. KIYOSHI

PALAU

Palau Community College (C)

PO Box 9, Koror PW 96940-0009

County: Koror | FICE Identification: 011009 | Unit ID: 243647
Telephone: (680) 488-2470 | Carnegie Class: Assoc/Pub-R-S
FAX Number: (680) 488-2447 | Calendar System: Semester
URL: www.palau.edu
Established: 1969 | Annual Undergrad Tuition & Fees: $4,215
Enrollment: 742 | Coed
Affiliation or Control: Federal | IRS Status: Exempt
Highest Offering: Associate Degree
Program: Occupational; 2-Year Principally Bachelor's Creditable
Accreditation: WJ

01 President .... Dr. Patrick U. TELLEI
05 Vice President Education & Training .... Vacant
11 Vice Pres Administration & Finance .... Mr. Jay OLEGERIIL
46 Vice Pres Cooperative Rsrch/Exten .... Mr. Thomas TARO
04 Exec Assistant to the President .... Mr. Todd NGIRAMENGIOR
32 Dean of Students .... Mr. Sherman DANIEL
20 Dean of Academic Affairs .... Mr. Tutii CHILTON
51 Dean of Continuing Education .... Mr. William WALLY
30 Director of Development .... Ms. Alvina O. MARCIL
07 Director Admissions & Financial Aid .... Mrs. Dahlia M. KATOSANG
06 Registrar .... Ms. Lesley B. ADACHI
15 Director of Human Resources .... Mr. Omdasu T. UEKI
18 Director of Physical Plant .... Mr. Clement KAZUMA
13 Director of Computer Systems .... Mr. Bruce RIMIRCH
08 Librarian .... Ms. Jessica P. BROOKS
35 Director of Student Life .... Ms. Hilda NGIRALMAU
10 Director of Finance .... Ms. Uroi N. SALII
09 Institutional Researcher .... Ms. Ligaya SARA
38 Counselor .... Ms. Maurine ALEXANDER
38 Counselor .... Mr. Winfred RECHEIUNGEL
38 Counselor .... Ms. Glendalynn NGIRMERIIL
91 System Analyst .... Ms. Grace ALEXANDER
26 Public Relations Manager .... Ms. Adora NOBUO
40 Bookstore/Supply Supervisor .... Mr. Gibson TOWAI

PUERTO RICO

American University of Puerto Rico (D)

Box 2037, Bayamon PR 00960-2037

County: Bayamon | FICE Identification: 011941 | Unit ID: 241100
Telephone: (787) 620-2040 | Carnegie Class: Bac/Diverse
FAX Number: (787) 785-7377 | Calendar System: Other
URL: www.aupr.edu
Established: 1963 | Annual Undergrad Tuition & Fees: $4,872
Enrollment: 3,500 | Coed
Affiliation or Control: Independent Non-Profit | IRS Status: 501(c)3
Highest Offering: Master's
Program: Liberal Arts And General; Teacher Preparatory; Business Emphasis
Accreditation: M

01 President .... Lcdo. Juan C. NAZARIO-TORRES
05 Vice President Acad Student Affairs .... Dr. Consuelo CASTRO-MELENDEZ
10 Vice Pres Finance & Admin Affairs .... Mrs. Magda A. CANCEL-PEREZ
32 Dean Student Affairs .... Prof. Tamara FELIX-RODRIGUEZ
06 Registrar .... Prof. Maria RODRIGUEZ-PAZ
07 Admissions Officer .... Ms. Keren LLANOS
08 Learning Resources Center Director .... Mrs. Wanda HERNANDEZ-SANCHEZ
35 Dir Student Affairs/Public Rels .... Mrs. Nereida CRISTOBAL
37 Director Financial Aid .... Mrs. Yahaira MELENDEZ
21 Director Accounting .... Mrs. Jeanette AVILES-FERRAN
38 Director Guidance Counseling .... Mrs. Luz S. HERNANDEZ
24 Director Educational Media .... Ms. Carol SANTIAGO
41 Athletic Director .... Mr. Manfredo VEGA
14 Director Computer Center .... Mr. Juan L. RIVERA
15 Director Personnel Services .... Mrs. Lillian BELEN-NAZARIO
12 Director Bayamon Campus .... Dr. Josephine RESTO-OLIVO
12 Director Manati Campus .... Prof. Rosa RODRIGUEZ
09 Dir Research/Institutional Planning .... Vacant
18 Chief Facilities/Physical Plant .... Mr. Efrain LUGO
36 Director of Student Placement .... Vacant
84 Director Enrollment Management .... Mrs. Mariela CRUZ
96 Director of Purchasing .... Mrs. Celeste TRAVERSO
92 Director of Honors Program .... Prof. Claribel RODRIGUEZ
30 Chief Development .... Mr. Jaime GONZALEZ
20 Associate Academic Officer .... Prof. Milagros RIVERA
14 Director Acad Computer Center .... Vacant
53 Dept Chair School of Education .... Dr. Jose RAMIREZ
50 Dept Chair Business Admin/Sec Sci .... Prof. Norma ORTIZ
49 Department Chair Arts & Sciences .... Prof. Carmen T. LANDRON

Atenas College (E)

101 Paseo de las Atenas, Manati PR 00674

FICE Identification: 035443 | Unit ID: 440651
Telephone: (787) 884-3838 | Carnegie Class: Assoc/PrivNFP4
FAX Number: (787) 884-6754 | Calendar System: Semester
URL: www.atenascollege.edu
Established: 1996 | Annual Undergrad Tuition & Fees: $5,117
Enrollment: 1,455 | Coed
Affiliation or Control: Independent Non-Profit | IRS Status: 501(c)3
Highest Offering: Baccalaureate
Program: Liberal Arts And General
Accreditation: ACCSC

01 President .... Ms. Maria L. HERNANDEZ NUNEZ

Atlantic University College (F)

PO Box 3918, Guaynabo PR 00970

County: Guaynabo | FICE Identification: 025054 | Unit ID: 241216
Telephone: (787) 720-1022 | Carnegie Class: Bac/Diverse
FAX Number: (787) 720-1092 | Calendar System: Quarter
URL: www.atlanticu.edu
Established: 1983 | Annual Undergrad Tuition & Fees: $6,255
Enrollment: 1,433 | Coed
Affiliation or Control: Independent Non-Profit | IRS Status: 501(c)3
Highest Offering: Baccalaureate
Program: 2-Year Principally Bachelor's Creditable; Liberal Arts And General; Professional
Accreditation: ACICS

01 President .... Dr. Teresa DE DIOS UNANUE
05 Dean of Academics .... Prof. Ivette CARBONELL
11 Dean of Administration .... Prof. Heriberto MARTINEZ-ABREU
26 Dean of Technology & Marketing .... Prof. Heriberto MARTINEZ-DE DIOS
81 Dean of Science and Digital Arts .... Prof. Frances GRAU
06 Registrar .... Mrs. Edna I. GUTIERREZ
38 Dir Student Counseling/ Placement .... Mrs. Maria C. LOPEZ-CEPERO
37 Director Financial Aid .... Mrs. Janice RIVERA
08 Head Librarian .... Mrs. Tania DÍAZ
07 Officer of Admissions .... Mrs. Margarita FIGUEROA
21 Bursar's Officer .... Mrs. María del C MONTESINO
15 Officer of Human Services .... Mrs. Urania GONZALEZ

Bayamon Central University (G)

PO Box 1725, Bayamon PR 00960-1725

County: Bayamon | FICE Identification: 005022 | Unit ID: 241225
Telephone: (787) 786-3030 | Carnegie Class: Master's M
FAX Number: (787) 740-2200 | Calendar System: Semester
URL: www.ucb.edu.pr
Established: 1961 | Annual Undergrad Tuition & Fees: $5,600
Enrollment: 2,185 | Coed
Affiliation or Control: Roman Catholic | IRS Status: 501(c)3
Highest Offering: Master's
Program: Liberal Arts And General; Teacher Preparatory; Professional
Accreditation: M, CORE, @TEAC

01 President .... Dr. Lillian NEGRON
05 Academic Dean .... Dr. Pura ECHANDI
11 Administrative Dean .... Mrs. Rosimar FERRER
32 Dean of Students .... Mrs. Niza ZAYAS
49 Dir College Liberal Arts/Humanities .... Dr. Oscar CRUZ
53 Dir Col of Education and Behaviora .... Dr. Caroline GONZALEZ
50 Dir Business Development & Tech .... Prof. Nidia COLON
08 Director Learning Resources .... Mrs. Annette VALENTIN
15 Director of Human Resources .... Mrs. Virna RIVERA
30 Director Institutional Development .... Mr. Pedro BERMUDEZ
07 Director of Admissions .... Mrs. Christine HERNANDEZ
37 Director Student Financial Aid .... Mrs. Edna ORTIZ
38 Director Guidance Center .... Mrs. Milagros M. RIVERA
06 Registrar .... Mr. Victor COLON
35 Director Transition Services (STAE) .... Mrs. Myrna PEREZ
90 Dir Center for Faculty Development .... Mr. Jorge DIAZ
68 Director of Sports Facilities .... Mr. Edwin MORALES
13 Director of Information System .... Vacant
18 Director Physical Facilities .... Eng. Eliezer GARCIA
26 Public Relations Officer .... Mrs. Niza ZAYAS
96 Purchase Officer .... Mrs. Jessica OJEDA
09 Specialist Institutional Research .... Mrs. Luz M. PALACIOS
66 Nursing Program Coordinator .... Prof. Floridalia VIDAL
20 Associate Academic Dean .... Dr. Luz C. VALENTIN
29 Alumni Relations .... Prof. Josean FELICIANO
84 Director Enrollment Management .... Mrs. Christine HERNANDEZ
58 Graduate Studies Director .... Dr. Nitza MARQUEZ
88 Dir Collegue Sciences/Health Profes .... Dr. Pedro ROBLES

Caribbean University (H)

Box 493, Bayamon PR 00960-0493

County: Bayamon | FICE Identification: 012525 | Unit ID: 241377
Telephone: (787) 780-0070 | Carnegie Class: Master's M
FAX Number: (787) 785-0101 | Calendar System: Semester
URL: www.caribbean.edu
Established: 1969 | Annual Undergrad Tuition & Fees: $5,550
Enrollment: 1,576 | Coed
Affiliation or Control: Independent Non-Profit | IRS Status: 501(c)3

Highest Offering: Master's
Program: Liberal Arts And General; Teacher Preparatory
Accreditation: M, @TEAC

01 President/CEO ... Dr. Ana E. CUCURELLA-ADORNO
03 Executive Director ... Mr. Victor T. ADORNO
05 Vice President of Academic Affairs ... Prof. Ann M. COPPIN
45 Vice President of Planning and Info ... Mr. Jorge RIEFKOHL
11 Dean Administration Affairs ... Mr. Israel RODRIGUEZ
32 Dean of Student Affairs ... Mr. Luis J. DELGADO
13 IT Interim Director ... Mr. Luis N. PRATTS
15 Human Resources Director ... Mrs. Lourdes LUACES
37 Director Student Financial Aid ... Mr. Hector GRACIA
06 Registrar ... Mrs. Kendra ORTIZ
08 Librarian/Director Audio-Visual ... Mrs. Carmen L. APONTE
07 Director of Admissions ... Dr. Ida ALVARADO
12 Director of Carolina Campus ... Dr. Jaime CRUZ
12 Director of Ponce Campus ... Dr. Ramon VAZQUEZ
12 Director Vega Baja Campus ... Ms. Lilliam MATOS
20 Provost ... Dr. Luis GOMEZ
71 Director Special Service Program ... Mrs. Maryliz AUBRET
26 Public Relations Director ... Mr. Enrique ROSARIO
49 Director Department Arts/Science ... Prof. William PEREZ
50 Director Dept Business Admin/Sec Sc ... Mr. Jose M. CUETO
76 Health Services ... Ms. Mara MEDINA
54 Director Department of Engineering ... Dr. Hermes CALDERON
66 Director Department of Nursing ... Dr. Mildred FLORES
53 Director Department Education ... Vacant
77 Director of Computer Science ... Dr. Augusto CARVAJAL
18 Chief Facilities/Physical Plant ... Mr. Henry SEVILLA
43 Legal Advisor ... Mr. Rafael SANTIAGO
38 Director Student Counseling ... Dr. Ida Y. ALVARADO
41 Athletic Director ... Mr. Jaime VAZQUEZ
22 Director of Compliance ... Mrs. Elena GARCIA
84 Director Enrollment Management ... Mrs. Janette TORRES

Carlos Albizu University (A)

Box 9023711, San Juan PR 00902-3711
County: San Juan — FICE Identification: 010724
Unit ID: 241331
Telephone: (787) 725-6500 — Carnegie Class: Spec/Health
FAX Number: (787) 721-7187 — Calendar System: Semester
URL: www.albizu.edu
Established: 1966 — Annual Undergrad Tuition & Fees: $4,790
Enrollment: 924 — Coed
Affiliation or Control: Independent Non-Profit — IRS Status: 501(c)3
Highest Offering: Doctorate
Program: Professional
Accreditation: M, CLPSY, SP

00 Chair Board of Trustees ... Mr. Jaime L. ALBORS BIGAS
01 President ... Dr. Ileana RODRIGUEZ-GARCIA
12 Chancellor of San Juan Campus . Dr. Jose J. CABIYA-MORALES
12 Chancellor of Miami Campus ... Dr. Carmen ROCA
11 Spec Asst to Chanc for Admin Affs ... Mr. Luis ECHEGARAY
05 Spec Asst to Chanc for Acad Affs ... Dr. Jaime VERAY
88 Special Assistant to Vice President ... Ms. Sylvia LOPEZ
10 Director of Finance ... Mrs. Maria FIGUEROA
07 Dir Student Services & Admissions ... Mr. Carlos RODRIGUEZ-IRIZARRY
46 Director Research Training ... Dr. Lymaries PADILLA-COTTO
88 Director General Psychology Program ... Dr. Jaime VERAY
51 Director Continuing Education Ofc ... Mrs. Constancia RAMOS-ROMAN
88 Director Internship ... Dr. Aida GARCIA
37 Director Student Financial Aid ... Mrs. Doris QUERO-MENDEZ
08 Librarian ... Ms. Yolanda ROSARIO-ROSARIO
06 Registrar ... Mr. Victor BONILLA-RODRIGUEZ
88 Dir Industrial/Org Psych Program ... Dr. Miguel MARTINEZ-LUGO
13 Information Technology Director ... Mr. Hugo SOLANO
88 Administrator Community Svcs Clinic ... Mr. Rafael ORTIZ
31 Director Community Services Clinic ... Dr. Jose RODRIGUEZ-QUINONES
88 Director PhD Clinical Psych Program ... Dr. Aida JIMENEZ-TORRES
88 Dir PsyD Clinical Psychology Pgm ... Dr. Gladys ALTIERI-RAMIREZ
15 Director of Human Resources ... Mrs. Carmen ACEVEDO-RIOS
30 Director Development ... Ms. Angeles PEREZ-TORO
88 Director Clinical Training ... Dr. Noel QUINTERO-JIMENEZ
88 Director Bachelor's Program ... Dr. Jaime VERAY
38 President Student Counseling ... Mr. Ricardo DEL RIO-MORALES
11 Director Administration ... Mr. John FERNANDEZ
26 Public Relations Officer ... Rochely ESCALANTE
29 Director Alumni Relations ... Ms. Angeles PEREZ

Center for Advanced Studies On Puerto Rico and the Caribbean (B)

PO Box 902-3970, Old San Juan PR 00902-3970
County: San Juan — FICE Identification: 021660
Unit ID: 241793
Telephone: (787) 723-4481 — Carnegie Class: Spec/Other
FAX Number: (787) 723-4810 — Calendar System: Semester
URL: www.ceaprc.edu
Established: 1976 — Annual Graduate Tuition & Fees: $4,300
Enrollment: 649 — Coed
Affiliation or Control: Independent Non-Profit — IRS Status: 501(c)3
Highest Offering: Doctorate; No Undergraduates
Program: Professional; Fine Arts Emphasis
Accreditation: M

01 Chancellor ... Mr. Miguel A. RODRIGUEZ-LOPEZ
05 Academic Dean ... Dr. Jaime L. RODRIGUEZ-CANCEL
06 Registrar ... Mrs. Mayra I. RAMIREZ
08 Head Librarian ... Mr. Francis J. MOJICA
10 Administration Dean ... Mrs. Lizzette CARRILLO
04 Chancellor's Assistant ... Ms. Clarissa SANTIAGO-TORO
07 Admissions and Marketing Officer ... Mrs. Monica D. GONZALEZ
37 Financial Aid Officer ... Mrs. Lillian M. OLIVER

Centro de Estudios Multidisciplinarios (C)

Calle 13 #1206, Ext San Agustin, Rio Piedras PR 00926
County: San Juan — FICE Identification: 021891
Unit ID: 241517
Telephone: (787) 765-4210 — Carnegie Class: Assoc/PrivNFP
FAX Number: (787) 765-4277 — Calendar System: Semester
URL: www.cempr.edu
Established: 1980 — Annual Undergrad Tuition & Fees: $10,000
Enrollment: 1,224 — Coed
Affiliation or Control: Independent Non-Profit — IRS Status: 501(c)3
Highest Offering: Baccalaureate
Program: Occupational; 2-Year Principally Bachelor's Creditable; Nursing Emphasis
Accreditation: ACCSC

01 President ... Mr. Juan C. PAGANI-SOTO
05 Academic Dean ... Dr. Nereida NALES
07 Director of Admissions ... Mr. Juan RESTO TORRES
06 Registrar ... Mrs. Margarita RIVERA
10 Finance Director ... Mr. Carlos RODRIGUEZ
12 Branch Director ... Mrs. Laura M. DELGADO
15 Human Resources Director ... Mrs. Lilliana M. LOPEZ-MEDERO

Colegio de las Ciencias Artes y Television (D)

51 Dr. Veve St, Degutau St Corner, Bayamon PR 00960
County: Bayamon — FICE Identification: 031576
Unit ID: 430935
Telephone: (787) 779-2500 — Carnegie Class: Assoc/PrivFP
FAX Number: (787) 995-2525 — Calendar System: Semester
URL: ccat.edu
Established: 1993 — Annual Undergrad Tuition & Fees: $5,995
Enrollment: 488 — Coed
Affiliation or Control: Proprietary — IRS Status: Proprietary
Highest Offering: Associate Degree
Program: Occupational
Accreditation: ACCSC

01 President ... Mr. Jorge GARCIA

Colegio Universitario de San Juan (E)

180 Jose R. Oliver Street, San Juan PR 00918
County: San Juan — FICE Identification: 010567
Unit ID: 241720
Telephone: (787) 480-2379 — Carnegie Class: Bac/Assoc
FAX Number: (787) 250-7395 — Calendar System: Semester
URL: www.cunisanjuan.edu
Established: 1972 — Annual Undergrad Tuition & Fees (In-District): $2,950
Enrollment: 1,608 — Coed
Affiliation or Control: Local — IRS Status: 501(c)3
Highest Offering: Baccalaureate
Program: Occupational; 2-Year Principally Bachelor's Creditable
Accreditation: M, ADNUR

01 Acting Chancellor ... Ms. Deborah DRAHUS-CAPO
45 Dir Planning/Inst Research/Ext Rels ... Dr. Haydee ZAYAS
04 Administrative Asst to the Chanc ... Prof. Annelis RIVERA
10 Acting Dean Administrative Affairs ... Mr. Cruz CORRALIZA-TORRES
05 Dean Academic Affairs ... Prof. Mercy FALERO
32 Dean Student Affairs ... Prof. Virgen PAGAN
06 Registrar ... Mrs. Kennia SANTOS
08 Head Librarian ... Mrs. Sheila VERA
84 Director of Enrollment Management ... Mr. Victor RIVERA
07 Director of Admissions ... Mrs. Sandra RIVERA
38 Counselor ... Mrs. Mara MALAVE
37 Director Student Financial Aid ... Ms. Gloria MIRABAL
13 Director Info Systems/Telecomm ... Mr. Zacarias POURIET
50 Director Business Administration ... Prof. Marie A. OLIVER TORRES
51 Dir Continuing Educ/Extension Pgm ... Vacant
55 Director of Evening Division ... Mr. Jose Luis ROMAN
76 Director Health Related Science ... Prof. Luz D. ORTEGA
72 Manager Science & Technology ... Prof. Ramon RIVERA
97 Manager General Education ... Prof. Carmen J. RODRIGUEZ
09 Coordinator Institutional Research ... Prof. Ailin MARTINEZ
15 Analyst Human Resources ... Ms. Isabel LOZADA
36 Student Placement Officer ... Vacant
66 Nursing Program Coordinator ... Prof. Brunilda ROMAN

Columbia Centro Universitario (F)

PO Box 8517, Caguas PR 00726-8517
County: Caguas — FICE Identification: 008902
Unit ID: 241304
Telephone: (787) 743-4041 — Carnegie Class: Master's S
FAX Number: (787) 746-5616 — Calendar System: Semester
URL: www.columbiaco.edu
Established: 1966 — Annual Undergrad Tuition & Fees: $9,435
Enrollment: 1,595 — Coed
Affiliation or Control: Proprietary — IRS Status: Proprietary
Highest Offering: Master's
Program: Business Emphasis
Accreditation: M

01 President ... Mr. Alex A. DEJORGE
05 VP Academic Affairs ... Mrs. Carmen J. LOPEZ
03 Senior VP of Operations ... Mrs. Carmen M. RIVERA
10 VP Finance and Administration ... Mrs. Daritza MULERO
32 VP Student Affairs ... Mrs. Brendaliz ZAYAS
26 VP Marketing and Communication ... Ms. Ana R. BURGOS
12 Chancellor of Caguas Campus ... Mr. Alex R. DEJORGE
12 Chancellor of Yauco Branch ... Ms. Rosario PADILLA
35 Dean Student Affairs ... Mr. Luis LOPEZ
20 Dean Academic Affairs ... Mrs. Myrna TORRES
08 Institutional Librarian ... Ms. Luz NEGRON
11 Administrative Support Director ... Ms. Carmen I. ROJAS
37 Financial Aid Director ... Mrs. Virginia GUANG
07 Director of Admissions ... Mrs. Xiomara SANCHEZ
06 Registrar ... Ms. Wilmarie TORRES
38 Student Counselor ... Ms. Ingrid CARRION
15 Director Human Resources ... Ms. Elsie M. TORRES
36 Director Student Placement ... Ms. Iris TIZOL
18 Facilities & Development Director ... Mr. Jesus M. RIVERA

Columbia Centro Universitario (G)

Box 3062, Yauco PR 00698-3062
County: Yauco — Identification: 666036
Unit ID: 404806
Telephone: (787) 856-0845 — Carnegie Class: Spec/Health
FAX Number: (787) 267-2335 — Calendar System: Semester
URL: www.columbiaco.edu
Established: 1986 — Annual Undergrad Tuition & Fees: $6,390
Enrollment: 430 — Coed
Affiliation or Control: Proprietary — IRS Status: Proprietary
Highest Offering: Baccalaureate
Program: Occupational; Nursing Emphasis
Accreditation: &M

01 Director ... Mrs. Rosario PADILLA

† Regional accreditation is carried under the parent institution in Caguas, PR.

Conservatory of Music of Puerto Rico (H)

951 Ponce de Leon Ave. Miramar, Santurce PR 00907
County: San Juan — FICE Identification: 010819
Unit ID: 241766
Telephone: (787) 751-0160 — Carnegie Class: Spec/Arts
FAX Number: (787) 766-1216 — Calendar System: Semester
URL: www.cmpr.edu
Established: 1959 — Annual Undergrad Tuition & Fees (In-State): $4,200
Enrollment: 463 — Coed
Affiliation or Control: State — IRS Status: 501(c)3
Highest Offering: Master's
Program: Music Emphasis
Accreditation: M

01 Chancellor ... Prof. Maria DEL CARMEN GIL
05 Dean of Academic Affairs ... Ms. Melanie SANTANA
11 Dean of Administration ... Mr. Juan Carlos HERNANDEZ
32 Dean Student Affairs/Financial Aid ... Mr. Michael RAJABALLEY
88 Dean of Preparatory School ... Mr. Germán CESPEDES
07 Director of Admissions ... Mrs. Ilsamar HERNANDEZ
08 Librarian ... Mrs. Damaris CORDERO
20 Associate Dean of Studies ... Vacant
30 Development & Public Relations Dir ... Ms. Lissette GONZÁLEZ
15 Human Resources Director ... Ms. Alba DÁNILA
38 Counselor ... Mrs. Pilar RUIBAL

Dominican Study Center of the Caribbean (I)

PO Box 1968, Bayamon PR 00960-1968
County: Bayamon — Identification: 666337
Telephone: (787) 786-4508 — Carnegie Class: Not Classified
FAX Number: (787) 798-2712 — Calendar System: Semester
URL: www.cedoc.edu
Established: 1980 — Annual Undergrad Tuition & Fees: $5,100
Enrollment: 70 — Coed
Affiliation or Control: Independent Non-Profit — IRS Status: 501(c)3
Highest Offering: Master's
Program: Religious Emphasis
Accreditation: THEOL

01 Dean ... Rev Dr. Yamil A. SAMALOT-RIVERA, OP
05 Associate Dean ... Dr. Oscar CRUZ-CUEVAS

EDIC College (J)

PO Box 9120, Caguas PR 00726-9120
County: Caguas — FICE Identification: 030219
Unit ID: 376321
Telephone: (787) 744-8519 — Carnegie Class: Assoc/PrivFP
FAX Number: (787) 743-0855 — Calendar System: Semester
URL: www.ediccollege.com
Established: 1987 — Annual Undergrad Tuition & Fees: $6,350
Enrollment: 988 — Coed

Affiliation or Control: Proprietary IRS Status: Proprietary
Highest Offering: Associate Degree
Program: Occupational
Accreditation: ACICS

01 President Mr. Jose A. CARTAGENA
05 Academic Dean Mrs. Loida R. RAMIREZ
11 Administrator Mrs. Milagros CARTAGENA

EDP College of Puerto Rico (A)

PO Box 192303, San Juan PR 00919-2303
County: San Juan FICE Identification: 021651
Unit ID: 243832
Telephone: (787) 765-3560 Carnegie Class: Bac/Diverse
FAX Number: (787) 777-0025 Calendar System: Semester
URL: www.edpcollege.edu
Established: 1968 Annual Undergrad Tuition & Fees: $5,400
Enrollment: 1,193 Coed
Affiliation or Control: Proprietary IRS Status: Proprietary
Highest Offering: Master's
Program: Occupational; Business Emphasis
Accreditation: M

01 President Mrs. Gladys T. NIEVES
00 Chancellor Dr. Elsa RODRIGUEZ
10 Vice President Finance Mr. Luis RIVERA
26 VP Institutional/International Rels Dr. Marilyn PASTRANA
05 VP Academic Planning and Inst Dev Dr. Rosa H. ALICEA
13 VP Technology/Distance Education Prof. Mayra RIVERA
14 Inst Information Systems Dir Mr. Angel RIVERA
06 Registrar Mrs. Glenda RODRIGUEZ
08 Librarian Mrs. Igrí ENRIQUEZ
21 Finance Dean Mrs. Marie Luz PASTRANA
32 Student Services Dean Dr. Leila M. ANDINO
18 Director Facilities/Physical Plant Mr. Jorge RAMOS
88 Director of CaSa Mrs. Maria COLON
07 Director of Admissions Mrs. Enid CARTAGENA

EDP College of Puerto Rico (B)

PO Box 1674, 49 Betances Street,
San Sebastian PR 00685-1674
County: San Sebastian Identification: 666488
Unit ID: 241836
Telephone: (787) 896-2137 Carnegie Class: Bac/Diverse
FAX Number: (787) 896-0066 Calendar System: Semester
URL: www.edpcollege.edu
Established: 1978 Annual Undergrad Tuition & Fees: $5,520
Enrollment: 1,077 Coed
Affiliation or Control: Proprietary IRS Status: Proprietary
Highest Offering: Baccalaureate
Program: Occupational; Nursing Emphasis
Accreditation: &M

01 President Ing. Gladys NIEVES VAZQUEZ
03 Vice Pres for International Affs Dra. Marilyn PASTRANA MURIEL
12 Chancellor Dra. Melba RIVERA DELGADO
13 Technology Director Prof. Angel F. RIVERA BAEZ
09 Data Base Administrator Prof. Veronica RIVERA MOLINA
88 Assc Dir Stdnt & Acad Affair Virtua Mrs. Carmen QUINTANA HERNANDEZ
14 Computer Center Director Prof. Jose A. ARCE COLON
05 Academic Affairs Dean Prof. Juan AVILES FONT
50 Acad Area Director - Administration Prof. Noelia JIMENEZ
97 Acad Area Director - Art & Gen Educ Prof. Aracelia SOTO MENDEZ
66 Acad Area Director - Nursing Prof. Carmen ROSA ARCE
76 Acad Area Director - Health Prof. Lilliam ALERS SOTO
32 Student Affairs Dean Mrs. Pilar CORDERO DE VIDAL
46 Assoc Dean Institutional Develop Prof. Nydia N. RIVERA-VERA
38 Counselor Prof. Maria E. DELGADO ALTIERI
08 Librarian Prof. Marisol GIRAUD MEJIAS
26 Marketing & Promotion Director Mrs. Rosa E. GONZALEZ NIEVES
06 Registar Prof. Nydia T. MENDEZ VARGAS
37 Financial Aid Director Mrs. Luz E. RIVERA CRESPO
07 Assoc Director of CASA Mrs. Zenaida OLAVARRIA RODRIGUEZ
106 Assc Dir Tech Devel & Dist Learning Mrs. Ileana ORTIZ FLORES
88 Practice's Students Coordinator Prof. Edith RAMIREZ HERNANDEZ
18 General Affairs Coordinator Mr. Reinaldo MARIN CRESPO
88 Bursars Office Coordinator Prof. Julio MENDEZ FERREIRA
15 Human Resources Officer Mrs. Aurea TORRES SEGARRA

† Regional accreditation is carried under the parent institution in San Juan, PR.

Escuela de Artes Plasticas de Puerto Rico (C)

PO Box 9021112, San Juan PR 00902-1112
County: San Juan FICE Identification: 025694
Unit ID: 241951
Telephone: (787) 725-8120 Carnegie Class: Spec/Arts
FAX Number: (787) 725-8111 Calendar System: Semester
URL: www.eap.edu
Established: 1966 Annual Undergrad Tuition & Fees (In-State): $3,248
Enrollment: 527 Coed
Affiliation or Control: State IRS Status: 501(c)3
Highest Offering: Baccalaureate
Program: Liberal Arts And General; Teacher Preparatory; Fine Arts Emphasis
Accreditation: M, ART

01 Acting Chancellor Arch. Ivonne M. MARCIAL VEGA
11 Dean of Administration Mr. Ismael GARCIA ORTEGA
05 Acting Dean Acad/Student Affairs Prof. Teresa LOPEZ
06 Registrar Ms. Ileana MALDONADO
07 Officer of Admissions Ms. Nitza MELENDEZ
13 Director Information Technology Ms. Limaris SOTO
37 Director Student Financial Aid Mr. Alfred DIAZ
36 Counselor Stdnt Affairs/Placement Ms. Ivette MUNOZ
45 Director of Planning Office Mr. Carlos E. RIVERA
09 Assistant Institutional Research Dr. Shirley A. TAVARES
10 Chief Financial Officer Ms. Evelyn Camille OTERO PABON
18 Coord Facilities/Physical Plant Mr. Edwin ALICEA
56 Coordinator Extension Program Ms. Liliam NIEVES
38 Counselor Stdnt Life/Counseling Dr. Yadira ORTIZ COLON
88 Coordinator Cultural Activities Mr. Adrian O. RIVERA NEGRON
105 Director Web Services Mr. Celso E. PORTELA IRIGOYEN
96 Officer of Purchasing Ms. Delia N. SANCHEZ BAEZ
20 Asst Dean Acad/Student Affairs Vacant
15 Director Personnel Services Ms. Carmen D. ROSARIO-MORALES
28 Director of Projects Dr. Shirley A. TAVARES
53 Director Education Prof. Grisselle SOTO
97 Director General Studies Dr. Maria VAZQUEZ
88 Director Fashion/Apparel Design Prof. Ana COLORADO
88 Director Industrial/Product Design Prof. Alfredo MONTALVO
88 Dir Design/Visual Communications Prof. Mayela CARDENAS
88 Director Painting Prof. Ivelisse JIMENEZ
88 Director Sculpture Prof. Adelino GONZALEZ VELEZ

Evangelical Seminary of Puerto Rico (D)

Ponce De Leon Avenue 776, San Juan PR 00925-2207
County: San Juan FICE Identification: 006823
Unit ID: 243498
Telephone: (787) 763-6700 Carnegie Class: Spec/Faith
FAX Number: (787) 751-0847 Calendar System: Semester
URL: www.se-pr.edu
Established: 1919 Annual Undergrad Tuition & Fees: $4,984
Enrollment: 268 Coed
Affiliation or Control: Interdenominational IRS Status: 501(c)3
Highest Offering: Doctorate
Program: Professional
Accreditation: M, THEOL

01 President Dr. Sergio OJEDA-CARCAMO
05 Academic Dean/Chaplain Dr. Jose R. IRIZARRY MERCADO
10 Director Administration & Finances Ms. Myrna E. PEREZ-LOPEZ
06 Registrar Miss Mari Lillian RIVERA
08 Head Librarian Mrs. Sonia ARRILLAGA MONTALVO
30 Director of Development/Planning Ms. Ruth M. DIAZ
37 Student Financial Aid Ms. Lourdes JESUS CESAREO

Huertas Junior College (E)

PO Box 8429, Caguas PR 00726-8429
County: Caguas FICE Identification: 022608
Unit ID: 242112
Telephone: (787) 746-1400 Carnegie Class: Assoc/PrivFP
FAX Number: (787) 747-0170 Calendar System: Semester
URL: www.huertas.edu
Established: 1945 Annual Undergrad Tuition & Fees: $9,600
Enrollment: 1,676 Coed
Affiliation or Control: Proprietary IRS Status: Proprietary
Highest Offering: Associate Degree
Program: Occupational; 2-Year Principally Bachelor's Creditable; Technical Emphasis
Accreditation: M, @PTAA

01 President Maria del Mar LOPEZ-AVILES
03 Exec Vice President and Compliance Raul HERNANDEZ
05 Vice Pres of Students & Academics Amarillys GARCIA
06 Registrar Krishna MARQUEZ
08 Head Librarian Glenda PEREZ
10 Vice Pres of Administrative/Finance Jose BAEZ
32 Associate VP of Student Services Eva VEGA
38 Director Student Counseling Evelyn COTTO
88 Counselor Vacant
30 VP Planning and Development Barbara FLORES
22 Compliance Officer Vacant
21 Director of Finance & Federal Funds Celestino CRUZ
15 VP of Human Resources Sarai GONZALEZ

Humacao Community College (F)

PO Box 9139, Humacao PR 00792-9139
County: Humacao FICE Identification: 023406
Unit ID: 242121
Telephone: (787) 852-1430 Carnegie Class: Assoc/PrivNFP
FAX Number: (787) 850-1577 Calendar System: Trimester
Established: 1978 Annual Undergrad Tuition & Fees: $5,640
Enrollment: 696 Coed
Affiliation or Control: Independent Non-Profit IRS Status: 501(c)3
Highest Offering: Baccalaureate
Program: Occupational; 2-Year Principally Bachelor's Creditable; Business Emphasis
Accreditation: ACICS

01 President Lic. Jorge E. MOJICA
03 Executive Vice President Prof. Aida E. RODRIGUEZ
05 Exec Director/Chief Academic Ofcr Mrs. Gladys E. FLECHA
55 Director of Evening Session Prof. Ada BAEZ
37 Director Student Financial Aid Mrs. Cheryle PEREZ
36 Student Placement Officer Mr. Luis GARCIA
07 Director Admissions Vacant
06 Registrar Mrs. Nildalee MELENDEZ
08 Head Librarian Mrs. Lourdes ELIZA
10 Treasury Officer (Finance) Mrs. Diana RODRIGUEZ
38 Student Counselor Mr. Angel MORALES
11 Chief College Administrator Mrs. Marianne BERRIOS
04 Adm Asst to Pres/Dir Personnel Mrs. Nilda E. RODRIGUEZ

ICPR Junior College (G)

558 Munoz Rivera Avenue, Hato Rey PR 00919-0304
County: San Juan FICE Identification: 011940
Unit ID: 243841
Telephone: (787) 753-6000 Carnegie Class: Assoc/PrivFP
FAX Number: (787) 622-3416 Calendar System: Semester
URL: www.icprjc.edu
Established: 1946 Annual Undergrad Tuition & Fees: $6,330
Enrollment: 604 Coed
Affiliation or Control: Proprietary IRS Status: Proprietary
Highest Offering: Associate Degree
Program: Occupational; 2-Year Principally Bachelor's Creditable; Business Emphasis
Accreditation: M

01 President/Chief Executive Officer Dr. Olga RIVERA
02 Hato Rey Campus Director Mrs. Maria de los M. RIVERA
20 Academic Affairs Dean Mrs. Maribel BAYONA
07 Admissions Director Hato Rey Mr. Axel CALDERON
07 Admissions Director Mayaguez Mrs. Aracelis GASTON
07 Admissions Director Arecibo Mrs. Vimarie ASENCIO
07 Admissions Director Manati Mrs. Viviana TORRES
10 Finance and Accounting Director Mr. Noel ORTIZ
37 Financial Aid Director Mrs. Velma APONTE
12 Mayaguez Campus Director Dr. Luz M. ORTIZ
12 Arecibo Campus Director Mrs. Ivette CHARRIEZ
12 Manati Campus Director Mr. Fernando GONZALEZ
06 Registrar Hato Rey Mrs. María C. VELEZ
06 Registrar Mayaguez Mrs. Olga NEGRON
06 Registrar Arecibo Mrs. Glenda PADIN
06 Registrar Manati Mrs. Vanessa TRINIDAD
06 Registrar Bayamon Extension Mrs. Diana FREYTES
26 Institutional Admissions/Mrktng Dir Mr. Isander VELAZQUEZ
13 Information Systems Director Mr. Nelson MEJIAS
08 Learning Res Librarian Hato Rey Mrs. Sulynet TORRES
08 Lrng Resources Librarian Mayaguez Mrs. Jessica CARO
08 Lrng Resources Librarian Arecibo Mrs. Irma JIMENEZ
08 Learning Resources Librarian Mr. Martin ROSADO
38 Professional Counselor Mayaguez Mrs. Barbarita CUMPIANO
38 Professional Counselor Arecibo Mrs. Milagros AGUILAR
38 Professional Counselor Manati Mrs. Edith RAMOS
38 Professional Counselor Hato Rey Mrs. Lourdes RIOS
38 Professional Counselor Hato Rey Mrs. Yarelis COLON
15 Human Resources Director Mrs. Daisy CASTRO
88 Institutional Compliance Director Mrs. Lizzette VARGAS
56 Bayamon Extension Director Mr. Manuel MELO
20 Academic Coordinator Mayaguez Dr. Mayra RUIZ
20 Academic Coordinator Arecibo Mrs. Edith RAMOS
20 Academic Coordinator Manati Mrs. Maribel TORRES
20 Academic Coordinator Hato Rey Mr. Josue CINTRON

Instituto de Banca y Comercio (H)

61 Ponce de Leon Ave, San Juan PR 00917
Identification: 667107
Telephone: (787) 754-7120 Carnegie Class: Not Classified
FAX Number: (787) 754-7143 Calendar System: Other
URL: www.ibanca.net
Established: N/A Annual Undergrad Tuition & Fees: N/A
Enrollment: N/A Coed
Affiliation or Control: Proprietary IRS Status: Proprietary
Highest Offering: Associate Degree
Program: Occupational
Accreditation: ACICS

01 President Sr. Guillermo NIGAGLIONI

*Inter American University of Puerto Rico Central Office (I)

GPO Box 363255, San Juan PR 00936-3255
County: San Juan FICE Identification: 008242
Unit ID: 242671
Telephone: (787) 766-1912 Carnegie Class: N/A
FAX Number: (787) 751-3375
URL: www.inter.edu

01 President Mr. Manuel J. FERNOS
03 Exec Director President's Office Mr. Tomas M. JIMENEZ
05 Vice Pres Academic & Student Affrs Mr. Agustin ECHEVARRIA
10 VP Financial Affairs/Services Mr. Luis ESQUILIN
42 Vice President Religious Affairs Rudo. Norberto DOMINGUEZ
20 Associate VP Academic Affairs Dr. Rafael CABRERA
21 Assoc VP Financial Affairs/Services Ms. Olga LUNA
32 Associate Vice Pres Student Affairs Dr. Elba ENCARNACION
04 Exec Assistant to the President Mrs. Sonnybel ZENO
26 Exec Dir Public Rels & Marketing Ms. Rosa MELENDEZ
30 Executive Director Development Mr. Eduardo LAMADRID

09 Exec Director Inst Research ....Dr. Elizabeth SCALLEY
13 Dir Information/Telecommunications ....Mrs. Jossie SALGUERO
43 Director Legal Services .... Mrs. Lorraine JUARBE
43 Director Federal Legal Services .... Mr. Vladimir ROMAN
15 Exec Director Human Resources ....Ms. Maggie COLON

*Inter American University of Puerto Rico Aguadilla Campus (A)

Box 20000, Aguadilla PR 00605-9001
County: Aguadilla　FICE Identification: 003939
Unit ID: 242626
Telephone: (787) 891-0925　Carnegie Class: Master's S
FAX Number: (787) 882-3020　Calendar System: Other
URL: www.aguadilla.inter.edu
Established: 1957　Annual Undergrad Tuition & Fees: $5,582
Enrollment: 5,033　Coed
Affiliation or Control: Independent Non-Profit　IRS Status: 501(c)3
Highest Offering: Master's
Program: Occupational; Liberal Arts And General; Teacher Preparatory; Professional
Accreditation: M, NUR, @TEAC

02 Chancellor .... Dr. Elie AGESILAS
05 Dean of Studies ....Prof. Nilsa M. ROMAN
32 Dean of Student Affairs ....Mrs. Ana C. LAUSELL
13 Director Information and Technology ....Mr. Asdrubal JIMENEZ
90 Information Systems Administrator .... Mr. Jossue MORALES
11 Dean of Administrative Affairs .... Mr. Israel AYALA
20 Associate Dean of Studies .... Mrs. Lymari NEGRON
30 Development Director ....Miss Sacha M. RUIZ
08 Library Director .... Mrs. Monserrate YULFO
07 Admissions Director ....Mrs. Doris PEREZ
06 Registrar ....Mrs. Maria PEREZ
37 Financial Aid Director ....Mrs. Gloria CORTES
21 Bursar .... Mrs. Yanira GONZALEZ
16 Human Resources Director .... Mr. Jose R. AREIZAGA
96 Purchasing Officer .... Ms. Wanda VARGAS
35 Student Support Services Director .... Mrs. Ivonne ACEVEDO
81 Director of Science and Technology .... Prof. Rosa GONZALEZ
79 Director of Education & Hum Studies .... Mrs. Ramonita ROSA
50 Director Economic Science & Admin ......Prof. Elidine GONZALEZ
53 Dir of Social & Behavioral Sciences ....Prof. Ricardo BADILLO
42 Chaplain .... Mr. Francisco GONZALEZ
88 Director of Upward Bound Program .... Ms. Mayra ROZADA
92 Dir Campus Learning Center Title V ....Ms. Yamilette PROSPER
18 Dir Building Maintenance/Univ Guard ....Mr. Jose CABAN
38 Director of Counseling Office .... Ms. Gladys ACEVEDO
41 Sports Director ....Ms. Yolanda PAGAN
84 Enrollment Manager ....Prof. Myriam MARCIAL

*Inter American University of Puerto Rico Arecibo Campus (B)

PO Box 4050, Arecibo PR 00614-4050
County: Arecibo　FICE Identification: 005026
Unit ID: 242635
Telephone: (787) 878-5475　Carnegie Class: Master's S
FAX Number: (787) 880-1624　Calendar System: Semester
URL: www.arecibo.inter.edu
Established: 1957　Annual Undergrad Tuition & Fees: $4,600
Enrollment: 5,493　Coed
Affiliation or Control: Independent Non-Profit　IRS Status: 501(c)3
Highest Offering: Master's
Program: Occupational; Liberal Arts And General; Teacher Preparatory
Accreditation: M, ANEST, NUR, SW, @TEAC

02 Chancellor ....Dr. Rafael RAMIREZ- RIVERA
05 Dean of Academic Affairs .... Dr. Annette VEGA
11 Dean of Administrative Affairs ....Ms. Wanda PEREZ
32 Dean of Student Affairs ....Prof. Ilvis AGUIRRE
20 Assoc Dean of Academic Affairs .... Prof. Wanda BALSEIRO
08 Educational Resources Center Dir .... Mrs. Sara ABREU
10 Bursar .... Mr. Victor MALDONADO
37 Student Financial Aid Director ....Mr. Ramon DE JESUS
06 Registrar ....Mrs. Carmen RODRIGUEZ
07 Director of Admissions ....Mrs. Provi MONTALVO
04 Executive Assistant to Chancellor .... Mrs. Enid ARBELO
56 Distance Learning Director .... Prof. Aida ALVAREZ
45 Planning Director .... Mrs. Enid ARBELO
42 Religious Life Director ....Mr. Amilcar SOTO
15 Personnel Director .... Mrs. Maritza SANTOS
41 Athletic Department ....Ms. Ileana MORALES
50 Director Econ & Adms Sciences Dept ....Prof. Elba TORO
51 Continuing Education Director .... Mrs. Mariel LLERANDI
53 Director of Education Department ....Prof. Magda VAZQUEZ
66 Director of Nursing Department .... Dr. Frances CORTES
79 Dir of Humanities Department ....Prof. Maria L. DELGADO
81 Director of Sciences & Tech Dept ....Prof. Hector PAGAN
83 Director of Social Sciences Dept ....Prof. Lourdes CARRION
30 Development Director ....Vacant
38 Director Student Counseling .... Ms. Nydia DELGADO
14 Director of Computing Center ....Mr. Jose SEGARRA
58 Director Graduate Program in Educ .... Dra. Ramonita DIAZ
18 Chief Facilities/Physical Plant .... Mr. Jose SANCHEZ
84 Director Enrollment Management ....Mrs. Carmen MONTALVO
88 Dir Graduate Program Anesthesia ....Prof. Josue RAMOS
96 Purchasing Officer ....Mrs. Sonia VILLAIZAN
92 Coordinator Honor Program .... Ms. Vilmaris VAZQUEZ

*Inter American University of Puerto Rico Barranquitas Campus (C)

PO Box 517, Barranquitas PR 00794-0517
County: Barranquitas　FICE Identification: 005027
Unit ID: 242644
Telephone: (787) 857-3600　Carnegie Class: Bac/Diverse
FAX Number: (787) 857-2244　Calendar System: Semester
URL: www.br.inter.edu
Established: 1957　Annual Undergrad Tuition & Fees: $5,500
Enrollment: 2,394　Coed
Affiliation or Control: Independent Non-Profit　IRS Status: 501(c)3
Highest Offering: Master's
Program: 2-Year Principally Bachelor's Creditable; Liberal Arts And General
Accreditation: M, @TEAC

02 Chancellor ....Dr. Irene FERNANDEZ
05 Dean Academic Affairs .... Dr. Patricia ALVAREZ
09 Director of Institutional Research .... Mr. Joseph E. ORTIZ
10 Bursar Director .... Mr. Antonio J. ROSARIO
06 Registrar .... Mrs. Sandra MORALES
32 Dean Student Affairs .... Mrs. Aramilda CARTAGENA
11 Dean Administrative Affairs .... Mr. Jose E. ORTIZ-ZAYAS
08 Librarian .... Mrs. Clanbette RODRIGUEZ
38 Director Upward Bound Program .... Mrs. Saraliz GONZALEZ
84 Director Recruitment/Promotion ....Mrs. Ana Isabel COLON
37 Financial Aid Director .... Mr. Eduardo FONTANEZ
71 Adult Program Director ....Mrs. Lydia ARCE
07 Director of Admissions .... Mr. Edgardo CINTRON
53 Dir Education/Social Sci/Humanities .... Dr. Sifilonena CINTRON
81 Dir Natural Sciences/Technology ....Prof. Wilson LOZANO
88 Director Admin & Economics Sciences ....Prof. Carmen I. GONZALEZ
51 Director Continuing Education .... Mrs. Aixa SERRANO
29 Director Alumni Relations .... Mrs. Aramilda CARTAGENA
15 Director Human Resources .... Mr. Victor SANTIAGO
30 Chief Development .... Dr. Patricia ALVAREZ
18 Chief Facilities/Physical Plant .... Mr. Jose E. ORTIZ-ZAYAS

*Inter American University of Puerto Rico Bayamon Campus (D)

500 Road 830, Bayamon PR 00957
County: Bayamon　FICE Identification: 005028
Unit ID: 242705
Telephone: (787) 279-1912　Carnegie Class: Bac/Diverse
FAX Number: (787) 279-2205　Calendar System: Semester
URL: bayamon.inter.edu
Established: 1912　Annual Undergrad Tuition & Fees: $4,596
Enrollment: 5,239　Coed
Affiliation or Control: Independent Non-Profit　IRS Status: 501(c)3
Highest Offering: Master's
Program: Technical Emphasis
Accreditation: M, ENG, OPTR

02 Chancellor ....Prof. Juan F. MARTINEZ
04 Assistant to Chancellor .... Mr. Antonio L. PANTOJA
30 Chief Development ....Mr. Jaime COLON
05 Chief Academic Officer .... Dr. Carlos OLIVARES
20 Associate Academic Officer .... Dra. Irma ALVARADO
55 Assoc Dean Studies II-Evening Pgm ....Vacant
88 Director Student Support Services .... Mrs. Zoraida CRUZ
08 Head Librarian .... Mrs. Sandra ROSA
36 Student Placement and Coop Educ .... Mrs. Maritza ZAMBRANA
88 Dean School of Aeronautics ....Prof. Jorge CALAF
54 Dean School of Engineering .... Dr. Javier QUINTANA
54 Director Electrical Engr Dept .... Prof. Ruben FLORES
54 Director Industrial Engr Dept .... Dr. Heriberto BARRIERA
54 Director Mechanical Engr Dept .... Prof. Eduardo LAY
81 Director Mathematics/Sciences .... Dr. Omar CUETO
50 Dir Business Administration Dept .... Prof. Esther MOURE
60 Director Communications Dept .... Prof. Ruth E. HERNANDEZ
77 Director Computer Sciences Dept .... Prof. Jose RODRIGUEZ
76 Director of Health Science ....Dra. Evelyn CROUCH
79 Director Humanities/Language Dept .... Prof. Laura RIOS
75 Director Tech Institute ....Mrs. Liza FREYTES
32 Chief Students Life Officer .... Mrs. Gema C. TORRES
35 Student Affairs Assistant ....Mrs. Grace GOMEZ
38 Director Student Counseling ....Mrs. Magali PALMER
35 Student Activities Director .... Mrs. Cybel BETANCOURT
41 Athletic Director .... Mr. Reynaldo ROLON
23 Infirmary .... Mrs. Maria ROSADO
10 Chief Financial/Business Officer .... Mr. Luis M. CRUZ
96 Director of Purchasing .... Mrs. Gladys ARROYO
21 Associate Business Officer ....Mr. Serafin RIVERA
18 Chief Facilities/Physical Plant ....Eng. Jose A. FUENTES
15 Human Resources Director .... Mrs. Migdalia ORTIZ
46 Chief Research and Development .... Dr. Armando RODRIGUEZ
84 Director Enrollment Services .... Miss Ivette NIEVES
07 Director of Admissions .... Mr. Carlos ALICEA
06 Registrar .... Mr. Eddie AYALA
13 Directo Information Technology ....Mr. Edwin RIVERA
45 Planning Inst Research Officer .... Dr. Francisco N. MONTALVO
42 Director of Chaplaincy Office .... Rvda. Carmen I. PEREZ

*Inter American University of Puerto Rico Fajardo Campus (E)

Call Box 70003, Fajardo PR 00738-7003
County: Fajardo　FICE Identification: 022828
Unit ID: 242680
Telephone: (787) 863-2390　Carnegie Class: Bac/Diverse
FAX Number: (787) 860-3470　Calendar System: Semester
URL: fajardo.inter.edu
Established: 1960　Annual Undergrad Tuition & Fees: $6,300
Enrollment: 2,296　Coed
Affiliation or Control: Independent Non-Profit　IRS Status: 501(c)3
Highest Offering: Master's
Program: Liberal Arts And General; Fine Arts Emphasis
Accreditation: M, SW, TEAC

02 Chancellor ....Dr. Ismael SUAREZ-HERRERO
05 Dean Academic Affairs .... Dr. Paula SAGARDIA OLIVERAS
11 Dean Administrative Affairs .....Ms. Lydia E. SANTIAGO ROSADO
32 Dean for Student Affairs .... Ms. Hilda VELAZQUEZ
06 Registrar .... Mrs. Abigail RIVERA
07 Director of Admissions ....Mrs. Ada CARABALLO
37 Director Student Financial Aid ....Mrs. Marilyn MARTINEZ
08 Librarian ....Ms. Angie COLON
15 Director of Personnel Office ....Mrs. Maria A. RAMOS
09 Planning Director ....Ms. Hilda L. ORTIZ
41 Athletic Director .... Mr. Jose RUIZ
18 Physical Plant Supervisor ....Mrs. Milagros RONDÓN
42 Chaplain/Director Campus Ministry .... Rev. Rafael HIRALDO
50 Chairperson Business Department .... Prof. Wilfredo DEL VALLE
53 Chairperson Educ & Social Sci Dept .... Dr. Porfirio MONTES
79 Chairperson Humanities Dept .... Mr. Javier MARTINEZ
81 Chairperson Math/Science Dept .... Prof. Irma MORALES
84 Director Enrollment Management ....Ms. Veronica VELAZQUEZ

*Inter American University of Puerto Rico Guayama Campus (F)

Call Box 10004, Guayama PR 00785
County: Guayama　FICE Identification: 022827
Unit ID: 242699
Telephone: (787) 864-2222　Carnegie Class: Bac/Diverse
FAX Number: (787) 866-5006　Calendar System: Semester
URL: www.guayama.inter.edu
Established: 1956　Annual Undergrad Tuition & Fees: $4,080
Enrollment: 2,431　Coed
Affiliation or Control: Independent Non-Profit　IRS Status: 501(c)3
Highest Offering: Master's
Program: 2-Year Principally Bachelor's Creditable; Liberal Arts And General; Nursing Emphasis
Accreditation: M, @TEAC

02 Chancellor ....Prof. Carlos E. COLON-RAMOS
06 Registrar .... Mr. Luis A. SOTO
08 Librarian .... Mrs. Edny SANTIAGO
10 Bursar .... Ms. Teresa MANAUTOU
05 Dean of Studies ....Dr. Angela DE JESUS
11 Dean of Administration .... Mr. Nestor A. LEBRON
32 Dean of Students .... Dr. Rosa J. MARTINEZ
07 Director Admissions ....Mrs. Laura FERRER
37 Director Financial Aid ....Mr. Jose A. VECHINI
29 Director Alumni Relations .... Dr. Rosa J. MARTINEZ
51 Director Continuing Education .... Mrs. Dianne RIVERA
15 Human Resources Officer ....Mrs. Maria MARES
18 Chief Facilities/Physical Plant .... Mr. Benjamin AYALA
45 Chief Plng Officer/Research & Devel .... Mrs. Nitza J. TORRES
30 Chief Devel/Dir Annual Plan Giv ....Vacant
42 Chaplain Director .... Rvda. Estebania BAEZ
84 Director Enrollment Management ....Mrs. Eileen RIVERA
96 Director of Purchasing .... Mrs. Maria VAZQUEZ
31 Dir of Community & New Student Rels ....Mrs. Luz ORTIZ
23 Director Health Services .... Mrs. Arcilia RIVERA
66 Director Nursing Program ....Dr. Minerva MULERO
88 Dir Adult Higher Education Program ....Mrs. Carmen G. RIVERA
50 Dir Dept Business Admin/Econ Sci ....Dr. Rosalia MORALES
53 Dir Dept Education/Soc Sci/Hum Std ....Dr. Ray ROBLES
81 Dir Dept Natural & Applied Science .... Prof. Carmen TORRES

*Inter American University of Puerto Rico Metropolitan Campus (G)

PO Box 191293, San Juan PR 00919-1293
County: San Juan　FICE Identification: 003940
Unit ID: 242653
Telephone: (787) 250-1912　Carnegie Class: DRU
FAX Number: (787) 250-0742　Calendar System: Trimester
URL: metro.inter.edu
Established: 1962　Annual Undergrad Tuition & Fees: $6,663
Enrollment: 6,663　Coed
Affiliation or Control: Independent Non-Profit　IRS Status: 501(c)3
Highest Offering: Doctorate
Program: 2-Year Principally Bachelor's Creditable; Liberal Arts And General; Teacher Preparatory; Professional
Accreditation: M, ADNUR, MT, NUR, SW, TEAC

02 Chancellor ....Prof. Marilina L. WAYLAND
05 Dean of Studies ....Prof. Migdalia TEXIDOR
32 Dean of Students ....Dr. Carmen OQUENDO
10 Dean of Administration .... Mr. Jimmy CANCEL
11 Dean of Faculty Cs Economics & Adm .... Prof. Fredrick VEGA
53 Dean of Education & Behavioral Sci .... Dr. Carmen COLLAZO
83 Director School of Psychology .... Dr. Jaime SANTIAGO
79 Dean Faculty of Humanities ....Dr. Olga VILLAMIL
66 Director of Nursing .... Dr. Aurea AYALA
72 Director of Medical Technology .... Dr. Ida A. MEJIAS
81 Dean Faculty of Science & Technolog .... Dr. Izander ROSADO
06 Registrar .... Ms. Lisette RIVERA
84 Enrollment Management ....Mr. Luis E. RUIZ
20 Associate Dean of Studies ....Ms. Blanca M. GONZALEZ

08 Director of Ctr for Access to Info .... Mrs. Rosa PIMENTEL
15 Human Resources Officer .... Mrs. Darlin TORRES
37 Director of Financial Aid ....Mrs. Glenda DIAZ
18 Dir Conservation & General Services ...Ms. Kelyma O. MARRERO
38 Dir Student Placement/Guidanc/Couns ....Ms. Beatriz RIVERA
83 Director School of Social Work ....Dr. Elizabeth MIRANDA
58 Director School of Education ....Dr. Maria D. RUBERO
88 Director International Rel Office ....Prof. Ramon AYALA
73 Dir School of Theology ....Dr. Angel VELEZ
88 Dir School of Criminal Justice ....Prof. Luis ACEVEDO
26 Public Relations Officer .... Mr. Pedro-Rabel PEREZ
14 Director Informatic/Telecomm Center ....Mr. Eduardo ORTIZ
36 Director Student Placement ....Mrs. Adabel-Vanessa COLON
07 Director of Admissions .... Ms. Janies OLIVIERI
09 Dean Inst Research/External Rsrch ....Vacant
21 Associate Dean of Administration .... Mr. Jose L. DEJESUS
30 Development & Fund Raising ....Prof. Armando CARDONA
96 Purchasing Officer ....Mrs. Patricia GONZALEZ
92 Coordinator of Honors Program ....Prof. Mariusz JACKO
88 Bursar .... Ms. Carmen RIVERA

*Inter American University of Puerto Rico Ponce Campus (A)

104 Turpo Industrial Park Road, #1,
Mercedita PR 00715-1602

County: Ponce FICE Identification: 005029
Unit ID: 242662
Telephone: (787) 284-1912 Carnegie Class: Bac/Diverse
FAX Number: (787) 841-0103 Calendar System: Semester
URL: ponce.inter.edu
Established: 1962 Annual Undergrad Tuition & Fees: $4,600
Enrollment: 6,404 Coed
Affiliation or Control: Independent Non-Profit IRS Status: 501(c)3
Highest Offering: Master's
Program: 2-Year Principally Bachelor's Creditable; Liberal Arts And General; Teacher Preparatory
Accreditation: M, @PTAA, @TEAC

02 Chancellor .... Dr. Vilma E. COLON
05 Dean of Studies ....Dr. Jacqueline ALVAREZ
32 Dean of Students .... Mrs. Edda COSTAS
11 Dean of Administrative Affairs ....Eng. Victor A. FELIBERTY
08 Director Education Resource Center ....Mrs. Maria SILVESTRINI
35 Director Student Services .... Mrs. Miriam MARTINEZ
10 Bursar ....Mrs. Nilda RODRIGUEZ
06 Registrar ....Mrs. Maria del C PEREZ
84 Director Enrollment Management .... Mrs. Miriam MARTINEZ
30 Director of Development ....Mrs. Eunice CORDERO
07 Director of Admissions ....Mr. Franco L. DIAZ
88 Ctr Academic Retention/Integration ....Vacant
15 Human Resource Officer .... Mrs. Ivonne COLLAZO
19 Supervisor of University Guard .... Mr. Reinaldo ROSADO
37 Director Student Financial Aid .... Mrs. Debra MARTINEZ
41 Athletic Director .... Mr. Raul HERNANDEZ
58 Director of Graduate Programs .... Dr. Lilliam LABOY
50 Director Business & Administration ....Prof. Maria P. GALARZA
51 Director Continuing Education .... Mrs. Maria MUNOZ
79 Act Dir Humanistics/Pedagogical Std ....Mrs. Santy CORREA
81 Director Mathematics/Sciences ....Prof. Lourdes DIAZ
83 Dir Social/Behavioral Science ....Dr. Manuel E. BAHAMONDE
76 Director Health Science ....Prof. Gerardo RIVERA
38 Dir Univ Integration Services Ofc .... Mr. Hector MARTINEZ
14 Director Computer Center ....Mr. Antonio RAMOS
26 Public Relations Officer ....Mr. Rolando J. MENDEZ
04 Chief Executive Assistant .... Mrs. Diana RIVERA
88 Dir Marketing & Student Promotion ....Mrs. Yinaira SANTIAGO
106 Director Distance Education Program .....Dr. Omayra CARABALLO
88 Accreditation/Certification Officer ....Mrs. Evelyn CASTILLO
45 Director of Evaluation & Planning .... Mr. Anselmo ALVAREZ

*Inter American University of Puerto Rico San German Campus (B)

PO Box 5100, San German PR 00683-9801

County: San German FICE Identification: 003938
Unit ID: 242617
Telephone: (787) 264-1912 Carnegie Class: Master's M
FAX Number: (787) 892-6350 Calendar System: Semester
URL: www.sg.inter.edu
Established: 1912 Annual Undergrad Tuition & Fees: $5,620
Enrollment: 5,916 Coed
Affiliation or Control: Independent Non-Profit IRS Status: 501(c)3
Highest Offering: Doctorate
Program: Occupational; 2-Year Principally Bachelor's Creditable; Liberal Arts And General; Teacher Preparatory; Professional
Accreditation: M, MT, RAD, TEAC

02 Chancellor ....Prof. Agnes MOJICA
05 Dean of Studies .... Dr. Nyvia ALVARADO
11 Dean of Administration .... Mrs. Frances CARABALLO
32 Dean of Students ....Vacant
20 Associate Dean of Studies .... Prof. Carmen TORRES
21 Auxiliary Dean of Administration .... Mrs. Marisol GONZALEZ
15 Director of Human Resources ....Mrs. Evelyn TORES
18 Chief Facilities/Physical Plant ....Mr. Jose A. RIVERA
37 Director Financial Aid ....Mrs. Maria Ines LUGO
06 Registrar .... Mrs. Arleen SANTANA
07 Director of Admissions ....Mrs. Mildred CAMACHO
08 Director of Library ....Mrs. Doris ASENCIO
38 Acting Director Student Counseling .... Mrs. Daisy PEREZ

09 Dir Plng Evaluation/Inst Studies .... Miss Maria MORALES-MARTINEZ
19 Director of Security .... Mr. Victor BONILLA
14 Director of Computer Center .... Mr. Rogelio TORO-ZAPATA
41 Athletic Director ....Prof. Francisco ACEVEDO
39 Acting Manager of Student Housing .... Mrs. Erlinda VEGA
40 Bookstore Manager ....Vacant
42 Dir Chaplaincy/Spiritual Well-being .... Rev. Sara SALIVA
04 Special Assistant of the Chancellor .... Mrs. Tary GARCIA
35 Manager of Student Services ....Mrs. Maria Gil MARTINEZ
51 Director of Continuing Education .... Mrs. Eva GARCIA
58 Director Graduate Programs ....Dr. Elba T. IRIZARRY
88 Manager of Food Services ....Vacant
17 Director of Medical Services ....Vacant
88 Auxiliary Dean of Students ....Mrs. Janet RIVERA
30 Chief Development Officer ....Miss Leticia MARTINEZ
96 Director of Purchasing .... Mr. Israel CRUZ
10 Acting Director Bursar's Office ....Mr. Carlos SEGARRA

*Inter American University of Puerto Rico School of Law (C)

PO Box 70351, San Juan PR 00936-8351

County: San Juan Identification: 666813
Unit ID: 242723
Telephone: (787) 751-1912 Carnegie Class: Spec/Law
FAX Number: (787) 751-2975 Calendar System: Semester
URL: www.derecho.inter.edu
Established: 1961 Annual Graduate Tuition & Fees: $14,403
Enrollment: 893 Coed
Affiliation or Control: Independent Non-Profit IRS Status: 501(c)3
Highest Offering: First Professional Degree; No Undergraduates
Program: Professional
Accreditation: M, LAW

02 Dean ....Dr. Luis M. NEGRON-PORTILLO
05 Dean of Academic Affairs ....Prof. Evelyn BENVENUTTI-TORO
32 Dean of Students ....Mrs. Marilucy GONZALEZ-BAEZ
11 Dean of Administration .... Mr. Heriberto SOTO
06 Registrar ....Mrs. Maria de Lourdes RIVERA
08 Head Librarian ....Mr. Hector Ruben SANCHEZ
61 Director of Legal Aid Clinic .... Mrs. Rosabelle PADIN
37 Director of Financial Aid ....Mr. Ricardo CRESPO
07 Director of Admissions .... Mrs. Angela TORRES
18 Chief Facilities/Physical Plant .... Mr. Jose A. RIVERA
96 Director of Purchasing ....Mrs. Yajahira VIDAL
88 Director of Bursar Office ....Mr. Samuel SANCHEZ

*Inter American University of Puerto Rico School of Optometry (D)

500 John Will Harris Road, Bayamon PR 00957-6257

County: San Juan Identification: 666601
Unit ID: 404222
Telephone: (787) 765-1915 Carnegie Class: Spec/Health
FAX Number: (787) 767-3920 Calendar System: Semester
URL: www.optonet.inter.edu
Established: 1981 Annual Graduate Tuition & Fees: $25,500
Enrollment: 224 Coed
Affiliation or Control: Independent Non-Profit IRS Status: 501(c)3
Highest Offering: First Professional Degree; No Undergraduates
Program: Professional
Accreditation: M, OPT

02 Dean ....Dr. Andres PAGAN
05 Dean for Academic Affairs .... Dr. Jose M. DE JESUS
11 Dean of Administration ....Mr. Francisco RIVERA
32 Dean of Student Affair .... Dra. Iris CABELLO
42 Director Religious Life .... Dra. Ileana VARGAS
07 Director Admissions .... Mr. Jose A. COLON
30 Director Development .... Mrs. Maria J. AULET
88 Director Basic Sciences .... Dr. John MORDI
20 Director Academic Affairs ....Dr. Angel F. ROMERO
88 Dean of Clinical Affairs ....Dra. Damaris PAGAN
08 Library Director .... Mrs. Wilma MARRERO
90 Director of Computing ....Mr. Elias SANTIAGO
21 Bursar's Officer ....Mr. Eduardo SALICHS
15 Director Human Resources .... Ms. Milagros RODRIGUEZ
37 Director Financial Aid .... Mrs. Lourdes M. NIEVES

John Dewey College (E)

PO Box 19538, San Juan PR 00910-1538

County: San Juan FICE Identification: 031121
Unit ID: 431309
Telephone: (787) 753-0039 Carnegie Class: Assoc/PrivNFP
FAX Number: (787) 764-6303 Calendar System: Other
URL: www.jdc.edu
Established: N/A Annual Undergrad Tuition & Fees: $8,553
Enrollment: 332 Coed
Affiliation or Control: Independent Non-Profit IRS Status: 501(c)3
Highest Offering: Baccalaureate
Program: Occupational
Accreditation: ACICS

01 President/CEO .... Mr. Carlos A. QUINONES
10 Director of Finance ....Ms. Mirna BAEZ

Mech-Tech College (F)

PO Box 6118, Caguas PR 00726

County: Caguas FICE Identification: 030255
Unit ID: 414461
Telephone: (787) 744-1060 Carnegie Class: Assoc/PrivFP
FAX Number: (787) 744-1035 Calendar System: Quarter
URL: www.mechtech.edu
Established: 1984 Annual Undergrad Tuition & Fees: $8,754
Enrollment: 4,518 Coed
Affiliation or Control: Proprietary IRS Status: Proprietary
Highest Offering: Associate Degree
Program: Occupational; 2-Year Principally Bachelor's Creditable; Technical Emphasis
Accreditation: CNCE

01 President .... Mr. Edwin J. COLON COSME
03 Chief Operating Officer .... Miss Yadexy SIERRA CONCEPCION
32 Vice President of Student Affairs .... Mrs. Lydia ROJAS
05 Vice President for Academic Affairs ....Vacant
45 Vice President Planning & Develop ....Mr. Jose ALGORRI NAVARRO
11 Vice President for Administration ....Mrs. Aguilda GOMEZ
13 Vice President Information Tech .... Mr. Luis CAMACHO
10 Comptroller .... Mr. Edwin RODRIGUEZ
06 Registrar .... Mrs. Blanca RIVERA SANTIAGO
37 Financial Aid Director ....Mrs. Jessica CRUZ BONILLA
07 Admissions Director .... Miss Rocio ROSARIO
36 Placement Director ....Mrs. Maria RAMON
20 Dean of Academic Affairs .... Dr. Delma SANTIAGO
35 Dean of Student Affairs .... Mrs. Aurea ROQUE
08 Library Director ....Mrs. Carmen AVILES
12 Bayamón Branch Campus Coordinator ....Mrs. Rosa PENA
12 Ponce Branch Campus Coordinator ... Mr. Carlos CRUZ GORRITZ
12 Vega Baja Branch Campus Coordinator ....Mr. David COLLAZO
12 Mayaguez Branch Campus Coordinator ....Mr. James RODRIGUEZ

National University College (G)

MSC 452, PO Box 144035, Arecibo PR 00614

County: Arecibo Identification: 666489
Unit ID: 242981
Telephone: (787) 879-5044 Carnegie Class: Bac/Assoc
FAX Number: (787) 879-5047 Calendar System: Trimester
URL: www.nuc.edu
Established: 1984 Annual Undergrad Tuition & Fees: $6,915
Enrollment: 1,683 Coed
Affiliation or Control: Proprietary IRS Status: Proprietary
Highest Offering: Baccalaureate
Program: Occupational
Accreditation: ACICS

01 President ....Dr. Francisco NUNEZ
05 Exec & Academic Affairs Director ....Ms. Lydia COLLAZO
37 Vice Pres Financial Aid/Compliance ....Mr. Desi LOPEZ

National University College (H)

State Road#2 Km.11.2 #1660, Bayamon PR 00960-2036

County: Bayamon FICE Identification: 022606
Unit ID: 242972
Telephone: (787) 780-5134 Carnegie Class: Bac/Assoc
FAX Number: (787) 779-4906 Calendar System: Trimester
URL: www.nuc.edu
Established: 1982 Annual Undergrad Tuition & Fees: $6,590
Enrollment: 2,300 Coed
Affiliation or Control: Proprietary IRS Status: Proprietary
Highest Offering: Master's
Program: 2-Year Principally Bachelor's Creditable; Nursing Emphasis
Accreditation: @M, ACICS, @TEAC

01 President ....Dr. Gloria E. BAQUERO
88 VP of Compliance .... Mr. Desi LOPEZ
05 VP Academic Affairs .... Dr. Maria ESTRADA
32 VP of Student Affairs ....Ms. Ana M. LUCUMI
02 Chancellor ....Ms. Daliana RIVERA
46 Director Research & Development ....Mr. Angel AVILES
37 Institutional Dir Financial Aid .... Ms. Damaris RODRIGUEZ
07 Enrollment & Admissions Coord .... Ms. Blanca GONZALEZ
06 Registrar .... Ms. Glorimar RODRIGUEZ

Ponce Paramedical College (I)

1213 Acacia Street Villa Flores Urb,
Ponce PR 00716-2901

County: Ponce FICE Identification: 025349
Unit ID: 243072
Telephone: (787) 848-1589 Carnegie Class: Assoc/PrivFP
FAX Number: (787) 259-0169 Calendar System: Other
URL: www.popac.edu
Established: 1983 Annual Undergrad Tuition & Fees: $13,300
Enrollment: 4,583 Coed
Affiliation or Control: Proprietary IRS Status: Proprietary
Highest Offering: Associate Degree
Program: Occupational; 2-Year Principally Bachelor's Creditable
Accreditation: ACCSC

01 President .... Mrs. María PAGÁN
04 Executive Assistant ....Vacant
05 Academic Dean ....Mrs. Rosa E. CRUZ

06 Registrar ..... Mrs. Ivette OLIVERAS
37 Director Student Financial Aid ..... Mrs. Amarilis ROCHE

Ponce School of Medicine & Health Sciences (A)

PO Box 7004, Ponce PR 00732-7004
County: Ponce FICE Identification: 024824
Unit ID: 243081
Telephone: (787) 840-2575 Carnegie Class: Assoc/PrivNFP4
FAX Number: (787) 840-9756 Calendar System: Semester
URL: www.psm.edu
Established: 1977 Annual Graduate Tuition & Fees: $24,359
Enrollment: 625 Coed
Affiliation or Control: Independent Non-Profit IRS Status: 501(c)3
Highest Offering: Doctorate; No Undergraduates
Program: Professional
Accreditation: M, CLPSY, MED

01 Interim President/Dean ..... Dr. Olga RODRIGUEZ DE ARZOLA
05 Assoc Dean Faculty/Clinical Affairs ..... Dr. Raul ARMSTRONG
58 Director of Graduate Studies ..... Dr. Jose A. TORRES
11 Asst Dean Administration & Finance ... Ms. Bethzaida CRUZ SOTO

The Pontifical Catholic University of Puerto Rico (B)

2250 Las Americas Avenue, Suite 564,
Ponce PR 00717-9997
County: Ponce FICE Identification: 003936
Unit ID: 241410
Telephone: (787) 841-2000 Carnegie Class: DRU
FAX Number: (787) 651-2034 Calendar System: Semester
URL: www.pucpr.edu
Established: 1948 Annual Undergrad Tuition & Fees: $5,418
Enrollment: 11,210 Coed
Affiliation or Control: Roman Catholic IRS Status: 501(c)3
Highest Offering: Doctorate
Program: Liberal Arts And General; Teacher Preparatory; Professional
Accreditation: M, CORE, LAW, MT, NUR, SW, @TEAC

00 Chancellor ..... M.Rev. Felix LAZARO
01 President ..... Dr. Jorge I. VELEZ AROCHO
04 Executive Assistant to President ..... Lcdo. Jose A. FRONTERA
05 Vice President Academic Affairs ..... Dr. Leandro COLON
10 Vice President of Finance ..... Prof. Irma I. RODRIGUEZ
32 Vice President for Student Affairs ..... Prof. Freddie MARTINEZ
20 Assoc Vice Pres Academic Affairs ..... Dr. Herminio IRIZARY
35 Asst to Vice Pres Student Affairs ..... Prof. Myriam D. LOPEZ
09 Vice President Inst Rsrch/Dev Plng ..... Dr. Felix CORTES
12 Rector Arecibo Branch ..... Dr. Edwin HERNANDEZ
12 Rector Mayaguez Branch ..... Dr. Mei-Ling VELAZQUEZ
06 Registrar ..... Prof. Ivan E. DAVILA
07 Director of Admissions ..... Dr. Ana O. BONILLA
08 Director of the Library ..... Prof. Magda VARGAS
37 Director of Student Aid ..... Mrs. Rosalia MARTINEZ
36 Director of Placement Services ..... Mr. Enrique ARROYO
14 Director Computer Center ..... Mr. Moises CABRERA
89 Director of Freshmen ..... Dr. Maria D. FERRER
55 Director of Evening Studies ..... Dra. Adalecia HASSELL
24 Director Educational Technology ..... Dr. Edgar RODRIGUEZ
79 Dean of Arts & Humanities ..... Prof. Alfonso SANTIAGO
81 Dean of Sciences ..... Dra. Alma L. SANTIAGO
61 Dean of the School of Law ..... Lic. Angel GONZALEZ
50 Dean Business Administration ..... Dr. Jaime L. SANTIAGO-CANET
53 Dean of Education ..... Dr. Myriam ZAYAS
58 Dean Institute of Graduate Studies ..... Dr. Hernan VERA
48 Organizing Dean School of Arquit ..... Mr. Javier DEJESUS
51 Coord Continuing Education Inst ..... Mrs. Karen G. MORALES
27 Communications ..... Mrs. Jalibeth RODRIGUEZ
29 Alumni Relations Officer ..... Mrs. Maria S. MASCARO
15 Director Human Resources ..... Mr. Wilfredo CORNIER
40 Director Bookstore ..... Mrs. Ashley VELEZ
41 Athletic Director ..... Prof. Louis ARCHEVAL
42 Chaplain ..... Rev. Juan INIGO
31 Director Auxiliary Enterprises ..... Mr. Julio FELIU
26 Director Public Relations ..... Mrs. Irem POVENTUD
38 Director Student Counseling ..... Prof. Carmen GONZALEZ
18 Physical Plant/Safety & Security ..... Mr. Julio PALMER
21 Treasurer Bursar's Office ..... Mr. Juan E. ROMAN
28 Director of Diversity ..... Vacant
96 Director of Purchasing ..... Mrs. Zoraida VELAZQUEZ
88 Exec Dir International Relations ..... Dra. Enid MIRANDA
88 Director of Biotechnology ..... Dra. Cariluz SANTIAGO
88 Acreditation Liaison Officer ..... Dr. Carmen J. ACOSTA-FUMERO
30 Infrastructure Director ..... Ing. Armando RODRIGUEZ
84 Coord Institutional Recruitment ..... Mrs. Linnette MILETTI
88 Coordinator of Outcomes Assessment ..... Prof. Maria MUÑIZ

Pontifical Catholic University of Puerto Rico-Arecibo Campus (C)

Box 144045, Arecibo PR 00614-4045
County: Arecibo Identification: 666603
Unit ID: 241395
Telephone: (787) 881-1212 Carnegie Class: Master's S
FAX Number: (787) 881-0777 Calendar System: Semester
URL: www.arecibo.pucpr.edu
Established: 1960 Annual Undergrad Tuition & Fees: $6,750
Enrollment: 879 Coed
Affiliation or Control: Roman Catholic IRS Status: 501(c)3
Highest Offering: Master's
Program: Occupational; 2-Year Principally Bachelor's Creditable; Liberal Arts And General; Teacher Preparatory; Business Emphasis
Accreditation: &M, @TEAC

01 Campus Rector/President ..... Dr. Edwin HERNANDEZ VERA
00 Chancellor ..... Dr. Jose Arnaldo TORRES
05 Dean/Chief Academic Officer ..... Dr. Wiefredo LOPEZ MARA
10 Director Business Office ..... Ms. Yazdel MARTINEZ
07 Admissions ..... Mrs. Rosa SANTIAGO MENDEZ

† Regional accreditation is carried under the parent institution in Ponce, PR.

Pontifical Catholic University of Puerto Rico-Mayaguez Campus (D)

Box 1326, Mayaguez PR 00681-1326
County: Mayaguez Identification: 666605
Unit ID: 243586
Telephone: (787) 834-5151 Carnegie Class: Bac/Diverse
FAX Number: (787) 833-8478 Calendar System: Semester
URL: www.pucpr.edu
Established: 1960 Annual Undergrad Tuition & Fees: $6,150
Enrollment: 1,549 Coed
Affiliation or Control: Roman Catholic IRS Status: 501(c)3
Highest Offering: Master's
Program: 2-Year Principally Bachelor's Creditable; Liberal Arts And General; Professional
Accreditation: &M, @TEAC

01 Chancellor ..... Prof. Mei-Ling VELAZQUEZ-SEPULVEDA
05 Dean of Academic Affairs ..... Dr. Frank Jimmy SIERRA-CORTES
11 Assoc Dean of Administration ..... Prof. Nilsa SOTO-CRUZ
32 Assoc Dean of Student Affairs ..... Prof. Astrid J. RODRIGUEZ-MONTALVO
06 Registrar ..... Mrs. Iris CRUZ-JIMENEZ
07 Admissions Officer ..... Ms. Jenniffer BIGAS-GONZALEZ
37 Student Financial Aid Officer ..... Mrs. Marilyn MARTI

† Branch campus of The Pontifical Catholic University of Puerto Rico, Ponce, PR.

San Juan Bautista School of Medicine (E)

PO Box 4968, Carretera 172, Caguas PR 00726-4968
County: San Juan FICE Identification: 031773
Unit ID: 430670
Telephone: (787) 743-3038 Carnegie Class: Spec/Med
FAX Number: (787) 746-3093 Calendar System: Semester
URL: www.sanjuanbautista.edu
Established: 1978 Annual Graduate Tuition & Fees: $22,800
Enrollment: 314 Coed
Affiliation or Control: Proprietary IRS Status: Proprietary
Highest Offering: First Professional Degree; No Undergraduates
Program: Professional
Accreditation: M, #MED

01 President/Dean ..... Dr. Yocasta BRUGAL-MENA
10 Chief Financial Officer ..... Mr. Jose A. COLON

*Sistema Universitario Ana G. Mendez (F)

Apartado 21345, Rio Piedras PR 00928-1341
County: San Juan FICE Identification: 029078
Unit ID: 242060
Telephone: (787) 751-0178 Carnegie Class: N/A
FAX Number: (787) 766-1706
URL: www.suagm.edu

01 President ..... Mr. Jose F. MENDEZ
03 Executive Vice President ..... Mr. Jose F. MENDEZ, JR.
05 Vice President for Academic Affairs ..... Mr. Jorge L. CRESPO
10 Vice Pres Financial Affairs ..... Mr. Alfonso L. DAVILA
26 Vice Pres Student/Marketing Affairs . Mr. Francisco BARTOLOMEI
45 Vice President Planning & Research ..... Mr. Jorge CRESPO
11 Vice Pres Administrative Affairs ..... Mr. Jesus A. DIAZ
15 Vice President Human Resources ..... Dr. Victoria DE JESUS
13 Chief Information Officer ..... Sr. Kenneth MALDONADO
26 Director Public Relations ..... Ms. Maria MARTINEZ
04 Exec Assistant to President ..... Ms. Lydia I. MASSARI

*Universidad del Este (G)

PO Box 2010, Carolina PR 00984-2010
County: San Juan FICE Identification: 003941
Unit ID: 243346
Telephone: (787) 257-7373 Carnegie Class: Master's L
FAX Number: (787) 776-1220 Calendar System: Semester
URL: www.suagm.edu/une
Established: 1949 Annual Undergrad Tuition & Fees: $5,484
Enrollment: 13,720 Coed
Affiliation or Control: Independent Non-Profit IRS Status: 501(c)3
Highest Offering: Master's
Program: Occupational; 2-Year Principally Bachelor's Creditable; Liberal Arts And General; Teacher Preparatory
Accreditation: M, ACBSP, ACFEI, @SW, @TEAC

02 Chancellor ..... Mr. Alberto MALDONADO-RUIZ
05 Vice Chancellor Academic Affairs ..... Dr. Mildred HUERTAS
11 Vice Chanc Admin Affs/Ofce of Chanc ..... Mrs. Maria S. DIAZ
32 Vice Chancellor Student Affairs ..... Mrs. Nahomy CURET
24 Vice Chanc Information Resources ..... Mrs. Carmen ORTEGA
46 Vice Chanc External Resources ..... Mrs. Mayra M. FERRAN
20 Assoc VC Licensing/Accreditation ..... Ms. Nilda I. ROSADO
88 Assoc Vice Chanc Admin Affairs ..... Mrs. Magalie ALVARADO
35 Assoc Vice Chanc Student Affairs ..... Dr. Nahomy CURET
84 Assoc VC Enrollment Management ..... Mrs. Magda A. OSTOLAZA
38 Assoc VC for Multidisciplinary Svcs ..... Vacant
23 AVC Stdnt Quality of Life/Wellness . Mrs. Carmen G. VELAZQUEZ
07 Asst Vice Chan Admiss/Financial Aid ..... Mr. Ramon FUENTES
09 Asst Vice Chanc Academic Effective .... Dr. Claribette RODRIGUEZ
36 Director Employment Placement ..... Mrs. Diana M. COLON
30 Asst VC for University Advancement ... Mrs. Maria I. DE GUZMAN
15 Asst Vice Pres Human Resources ..... Mr. Jorge RODRIGUEZ
10 Assistant Vice President of Budget ..... Mr. Jorge A. TORRES
18 Physical Plant/Operations Manager ..... Mr. Edgar D. RODRIGUEZ
06 Registrar ..... Mrs. Elisa QUILES
37 Director of Financial Aid ..... Mr. Norberto PAGAN
08 Director of Library ..... Mrs. Elsa MARIANI
26 Director Public Relations ..... Mrs. Ivonne D. ARROYO
29 Director Alumni & Fund Raising ..... Ms. Gisela NEGRON
88 Dean Intl Sch Hosp/Culinary Arts ..... Mr. Ivan O. PUIG
107 Assoc Dean Professional Studies ..... Mr. Emmanuel HERNANDEZ
13 Information/Telecommunications Dir ..... Mr. Nestor MAS
41 Athletic Director ..... Mr. Julio FIGUEROA
19 Safety & Security Director ..... Mr. Nazario LUGO

*Universidad Del Turabo (H)

Estacion Universidad, Box 3030, Gurabo PR 00778-3030
County: Gurabo FICE Identification: 011719
Unit ID: 243601
Telephone: (787) 743-7979 Carnegie Class: DRU
FAX Number: (787) 744-5394 Calendar System: Semester
URL: www.suagm.edu
Established: 1972 Annual Undergrad Tuition & Fees: $5,216
Enrollment: 5,050 Coed
Affiliation or Control: Independent Non-Profit IRS Status: 501(c)3
Highest Offering: Doctorate
Program: Liberal Arts And General; Teacher Preparatory; Professional
Accreditation: M, BUS, DIETC, ENG, NURSE, SP, TEAC

02 Chancellor ..... Dr. Dennis ALICEA
11 Vice Chancellor of Admin Affairs ..... Dr. Gladys BETANCOURT
05 Vice Chancellor Academic Affairs ..... Dr. Roberto LORAN
32 Vice Chancellor of Student Affairs ..... Mrs. Ana M. ORTEGA
08 Vice Chancellor Information Res ..... Dr. Sarai LASTRA
92 Vice Chancellor Honors Program ..... Ms. Maricarmen SANTOS
88 Asst Vice Chanc Eval & Development .. Dra. Maria del C. SANTOS
21 Asst Vice Chanc Admin Affairs ..... Mrs. Edna ORTA
53 Dean Education ..... Dra. Angela CANDELARIO
50 Dean Business Administration ..... Dr. Marcelino RIVERA
54 Dean Engineering ..... Dr. Jack T. ALLISON
72 Dean Science & Technology ..... Dr. Teresa LIPSETT
83 Dean Social Sciences & Humanities ..... Mr. Marco A. GIL DE LA MADRID
58 Dean of Graduate Studies ..... Dr. Sharon CANTRELL
06 Registrar ..... Mrs. Zoraida ORTIZ
27 Director of Marketing ..... Ms. Rosa Enid TOLEDO
37 Director Office of Financial Aid ..... Mrs. Carmen J. RIVERA
26 Director Public Relations ..... Ms. Iris SERRANO
18 Chief Facilities/Physical Plant ..... Eng. Mayra RODRIGUEZ
29 Coordinator Alumni Relations ..... Ms. Maricruz ROLON
30 Chief Development Officer ..... Ms. Alba RIVERA
96 Director of Purchasing ..... Mr. Jose BERRIOS
07 Director of Admissions ..... Mrs. Virginia GONZALEZ
09 Director of Institutional Research ..... Ms. Mari G. GONZALEZ
15 Director Personnel Services ..... Mrs. Iris BERRIOS
36 Assoc Vice Chanc Student Placement ..... Ms. Betsy VIDAL
84 Director Enrollment Management ..... Ms. Maria V. FIGUEROA
10 Chief Business Officer ..... Ms. Jessica M. PERRY
38 Assoc Vice Chanc Student Counseling ..... Ms. Betsy VIDAL

*Universidad Metropolitana (I)

PO Box 21150, Rio Piedras PR 00928-1150
County: San Juan FICE Identification: 025875
Unit ID: 241739
Telephone: (787) 766-1717 Carnegie Class: Master's L
FAX Number: (787) 759-7663 Calendar System: Quarter
URL: www.suagm.edu/umet
Established: 1980 Annual Undergrad Tuition & Fees: $6,547
Enrollment: 13,529 Coed
Affiliation or Control: Independent Non-Profit IRS Status: 501(c)3
Highest Offering: Doctorate
Program: Liberal Arts And General; Teacher Preparatory; Professional; Business Emphasis
Accreditation: M, ADNUR, NUR, @TEAC

02 SUAGM President ..... Dr. José F. MENDEZ
00 Chancellor ..... Dr. Federico M. MATHEU
05 Vice Chancellor Academic Affairs ..... Dr. Omar PONCE
11 Assoc Vice Chanc Admin Affairs ..... Mrs. Maria del Pilar CHARNECO
08 Head Librarian ..... Mrs. Maria de los A. LUGO
88 Asst Vice Chanc for Eval/Devel ..... Prof. Adanid PRIETO
108 Vice Chanc Institutional Assessment ..... Dr. Nellie PAGAN
11 Asst Vice Chanc for Admin Affairs ..... Dr. Mildred ARBONA
15 Asst Vice Pres for Human Resources ..... Mrs. Marisol MUNOZ
18 Chief Facilities/Physical Plant ..... Vacant

13 Asst Vice Chanc Info Resources ... Mr. Carlos FUENTES
29 Vice Chanc Alumni Relations ... Ms. Belissa AQUINO
32 Vice Chanc for Student Affairs ... Mrs. Carmen ROSADO
102 Vice Chanc of International Affairs ... Dr. Zaida VEGA
20 Assoc Vice Chanc Eval and Develop ... Mr. Eric BARRIOS
32 Assoc Vice Chanc Retention/Devep ... Mrs. Awilda PEREZ
88 Assoc Vice Chanc External Resources ... Mrs. Gladys CORA
10 Asst Vice Pres Analysis & Budget ... Mrs. Aixa ALDARONDO
45 Asst Vice President of Planning ... Mrs. Mariela COLLAZO
49 Dean of Liberal Arts, Huma & Commun ... Dr. Eloisa GORDON
50 Dean of Business Administration ... Dr. Juan OTERO
53 Dean of Education ... Dr. Judith GONZALEZ
76 Dean of Health Science ... Dr. Lourdes MALDONADO
81 Dean of Science & Technology ... Dr. Karen GONZALEZ
32 Asst Vice Chanc Retention/Develop ... Mr. Ariel MENDEZ
65 Dean of Environmental Affairs ... Dr. Carlos PADIN
83 Assoc Dean of Social Sciences ... Dr. Mariveliz CABAN
107 Assoc Dean of Professional Studies ... Ms. Melissa GUILLIANI
60 Assoc Dean of Communications ... Mr. Alfredo NIEVES
79 Assoc Dean of Humanities ... Dr. Martin CRUZ
75 Assoc Dean of Technical Studies ... Prof. Felipe ROSA
51 Assoc Dean of Continuing Education ... Ms. Lorna MARTINEZ
53 Assoc Dean of Education ... Dr. Daisy RODRIGUEZ
53 Assoc Dean of Education ... Dr. Angel CANALES
72 Director Educational Production ... Mr. Luis MARTINEZ
76 Director of Respiratory Therapy ... Mrs. Linette CLAUDIO
66 Director of Nursing ... Mrs. Yolanda TORRES
26 Director Public Relations Officer ... Ms. Yvonne GUADALUPE
06 Registrar ... Mrs. Beatriz NIEVES
12 Additional Location Dir Bayamón ... Mrs. Ibis RODRÍGUEZ
12 Addtional Location Dir Aguadilla ... Mr. Luis A. RUIZ
12 Additional Location Dir Jayuya ... Mrs. Irma del Pilar CRUZ
12 Additional Location Dir Comerío ... Mr. José I. CARMONA
07 Director of Admissions ... Mr. Julio RODRIGUEZ
41 Athletic Director ... Mr. Ariel ORTIZ

Universal Technology College of Puerto Rico (A)

Apartado 1955, Victoria Station, Aguadilla PR 00605-1955
County: Aguadilla FICE Identification: 030297
Unit ID: 376385
Telephone: (787) 882-2065 Carnegie Class: Assoc/PrivNFP
FAX Number: (787) 891-2370 Calendar System: Semester
URL: www.unitecpr.edu
Established: 1987 Annual Undergrad Tuition & Fees: $7,814
Enrollment: 1,395 Coed
Affiliation or Control: Independent Non-Profit IRS Status: 501(c)3
Highest Offering: Baccalaureate
Program: Occupational; 2-Year Principally Bachelor's Creditable; Technical Emphasis
Accreditation: ACCSC

01 Chief Executive Officer ... Mrs. Keila LOPEZ
11 Administrative Manager ... Mr. Ivan F. ROMAN
04 Executive Secretary ... Mrs. Marilyn GONZALEZ
05 Chief Academic Officer ... Vacant
06 Registrar ... Ms. Maria ALVAREZ
08 Director of Library ... Ms. Airlyn VAZQUEZ
10 Controller ... Mr. Alexis ROSADO
12 Director of Branch Campus ... Ms. Nelida CARDONA
14 Director Computer Center ... Mr. Zain CORDERO
15 Director Human Resources ... Ms. Jemilis GONZALEZ
18 Chief Facilities/Physical Plant ... Mr. Danily NIEVES
32 Director Student Affairs ... Vacant
36 Director Student Placement ... Mrs. Ada MORALES
45 Director Planning & Development ... Mrs. Evelyn TORRES
37 Director Student Financial Aid ... Mr. Samuel HERNANDEZ
38 Director Student Counsel ... Mrs. Dalia SANTIAGO
96 Purchasing Officer ... Mrs. Dolores MITJANS
23 Healthcare Services ... Mr. Silverio JIMENEZ
07 Coordinator of Admissions ... Mrs. Teresita RIVERA
50 Director of Business Administration ... Mrs. Sandra GONZALEZ
72 Director of Industrial Technology ... Mr. Eduardo FIGUEROA

Universidad Adventista de las Antillas (B)

Box 118, Mayaguez PR 00681-0118
County: Mayaguez FICE Identification: 005019
Unit ID: 241191
Telephone: (787) 834-9595 Carnegie Class: Bac/Diverse
FAX Number: (787) 834-9597 Calendar System: Semester
URL: www.uaa.edu
Established: 1961 Annual Undergrad Tuition & Fees: $11,140
Enrollment: 1,234 Coed
Affiliation or Control: Seventh-day Adventist IRS Status: 501(c)3
Highest Offering: Master's
Program: 2-Year Principally Bachelor's Creditable; Liberal Arts And General; Teacher Preparatory; Professional
Accreditation: M, NUR, @TEAC

01 President ... Dr. Obed JIMENEZ
05 Vice President for Academic Affairs ... Dr. Jose D. GOMEZ
10 Vice President Financial Affairs ... Mr. Misael JIMENEZ
32 Vice President for Students Affairs ... Dr. Javier DIAZ
26 VP Institutional Advancement ... Dr. Aurea ARAUJO
06 Registrar ... Mrs. Ana D. TORRES
07 Director of Admissions ... Mrs. Yolanda FERRER
08 Librarian ... Mrs. Aixa VEGA
33 Dean of Men ... Mr. Angel RODRIGUEZ
34 Dean of Women ... Mrs. Felicita CRUZ
38 Counselor ... Mrs. Ivelisse PEREZ
09 Official Institutional Research ... Mrs. Magda HERNANDEZ
88 Director of Special Projects ... Vacant
37 Director of Student Financial Aid ... Mrs. Awilda MATOS
29 Director of Recruitment and Alumni ... Miss Lorell VARELA
30 Chief Development ... Vacant
96 Director of Purchasing ... Mr. Obed RODRIGUEZ
18 Chief Facilities/Physical Plant ... Mr. Abel RODRIGUEZ

Universidad Central Del Caribe (C)

PO Box 60-327, Bayamon PR 00960-6032
County: Bayamon FICE Identification: 021633
Unit ID: 243568
Telephone: (787) 798-3001 Carnegie Class: Spec/Med
FAX Number: (787) 798-6836 Calendar System: Semester
URL: www.uccaribe.edu
Established: 1976 Annual Undergrad Tuition & Fees: $6,604
Enrollment: 494 Coed
Affiliation or Control: Independent Non-Profit IRS Status: 501(c)3
Highest Offering: Doctorate
Program: Professional
Accreditation: M, MED, RAD

01 President ... Dr. Jose Ginel RODRIGUEZ
05 Dean for Academic Affairs ... Dr. Nereida DIAZ-RODRIGUEZ
11 Dean Administrative Affairs ... Ms. Emilia SOTO
32 Dean Student Affairs ... Dr. Omar PEREZ
17 Dean of Medicine ... Dr. Jose Ginel RODRIGUEZ
63 Associate Dean of Medicine ... Mrs. Zilka RIOS
53 Asst Dean Professional Services ... Ms. Emilia SOTO
06 Registrar ... Ms. Nilda MONTANEZ-LOPEZ
07 Director of Admissions ... Ms. Irma L. CORDERO
37 Director Student Financial Aid ... Ms. Lisandra VIERA
10 Director of Finances ... Mrs. Iris J. FONT
08 Librarian ... Ms. Mildred RIVERA
51 Director of Continuing Education ... Dr. Frances GARCIA
38 Counselor ... Ms. Yari M. MARRERO
46 Dean of Research and Graduate Pgms ... Dr. Luis A. CUBANO
20 Dean for Clinical & Faculty Affairs ... Dr. Harry MERCADO

Universidad Pentecostal Mizpa (D)

PO Box 20966, San Juan PR 00928-0966
County: San Juan FICE Identification: 031983
Unit ID: 441690
Telephone: (787) 720-4476 Carnegie Class: Spec/Faith
FAX Number: (787) 720-2012 Calendar System: Semester
URL: www.colmizpa.edu
Established: 1937 Annual Undergrad Tuition & Fees: $3,400
Enrollment: 1,302 Coed
Affiliation or Control: Pentecostal Church of God IRS Status: 501(c)3
Highest Offering: Baccalaureate
Program: Religious Emphasis
Accreditation: BI

01 President ... Mr. Angel A. RIVERA
05 Dean of Academic Affairs ... Mr. Leonardo MELENDEZ
11 Dean Administration/Finance ... Mr. Elisamuel RODRIGUEZ
32 Dean of Student Affairs ... Mr. Jorge BURGOS
42 Director Christian Service ... Ms. Aida DIAZ
18 Director of Physical & Facilities ... Vacant
06 Registrar ... Ms. Sara MARTINEZ
08 Librarian ... Mr. Julio RAMOS
37 Student Financial Aid Officer ... Mrs. Myriam JUARBE
26 Chief Public Relations Officer ... Mr. Rafael LABOY

Universidad Politecnica De Puerto Rico (E)

Ponce de Leon 377, Box 192017, San Juan PR 00919
County: San Juan FICE Identification: 021000
Unit ID: 243577
Telephone: (787) 622-8000 Carnegie Class: Spec/Engg
FAX Number: (787) 763-8919 Calendar System: Trimester
URL: www.pupr.edu
Established: 1966 Annual Undergrad Tuition & Fees: $7,548
Enrollment: 7,548 Coed
Affiliation or Control: Independent Non-Profit IRS Status: 501(c)3
Highest Offering: Master's
Program: Liberal Arts And General
Accreditation: M, ENG, ENGR, IACBE, LSAR

01 President ... Prof. Ernesto VAZQUEZ-BARQUET
84 Vice Pres/Enrollment Management ... Mr. Carlos PEREZ
05 Chief Academic Officer ... Dr. Miguel A. RIESTRA
06 Registrar ... Mrs. Mayra I. LOPEZ
07 Director Admissions ... Mrs. Teresa CARDONA
08 Head Librarian ... Mrs. Mirta COLON
37 Director Financial Aid ... Mr. Sergio VILLOLDO
09 Director of Institutional Research ... Dr. Miguel A. RIESTRA
10 Chief Business Officer ... Mr. Ernesto VÁZQUEZ-MARTÍNEZ
15 Director Personnel Services ... Ms. Ana CASTELLANO
18 Chief Facilities/Physical Plant ... Mr. Herminio ROMERO
29 Alumni Relations ... Vacant
35 Director Student Affairs ... Mr. Carlos PEREZ
36 Director Student Placement ... Mrs. Angie ESCALANTE
38 Director Student Counseling ... Ms. Sidnia VÉLEZ
21 Associate Business Officer ... Mrs. Olga CANCEL

Universidad Teologica Del Caribe (F)

PO Box 901, Saint Just PR 00978-0901
County: Trujillo Alto FICE Identification: 023355
Unit ID: 241614
Telephone: (787) 761-0808 Carnegie Class: Spec/Faith
FAX Number: (787) 748-9220 Calendar System: Semester
URL: www.utcpr.edu
Established: 1956 Annual Undergrad Tuition & Fees: $3,784
Enrollment: 205 Coed
Affiliation or Control: Church Of God IRS Status: 501(c)3
Highest Offering: Baccalaureate
Program: Religious Emphasis
Accreditation: BI

01 President ... Francisco ORTIZ
05 Academic Dean ... Carmen AYALA
06 Registrar ... Caroline FIGUEROA
10 Administration Dean ... Frankie NEGRON
32 Dean of Students ... Marcos VELEZ
37 Financial Aid Director ... Sandra BARRETO
08 Librarian ... Leticia SOSA

*University of Puerto Rico-Central Administration (G)

1187 Flamboyan Street, San Juan PR 00926-1117
County: San Juan FICE Identification: 003942
Unit ID: 243160
Telephone: (787) 250-0000 Carnegie Class: N/A
FAX Number: (787) 759-6917
URL: www.upr.edu

01 President ... Dr. Miguel A. MUÑOZ-MUÑOZ
03 Executive Director ... Mrs. Desirée M. APONTE
05 Vice President for Academic Affairs ... Prof. Ibis L. APONTE-AVELLANET
09 Vice President for Research ... Dr. José A. LASALDE-DOMINICCI
32 Vice Pres Student Affairs ... Vacant
12 Chancellor Rio Piedras Campus ... Dr. Ana R. GUADALUPE
12 Acting Chancellor Mayaguez Campus ... Dr. Jorge RIVERA-SANTOS
12 Chanc Medical Sciences Campus ... Dr. Rafael RODRÍGUEZ-MERCADO
12 Chanc University College at Cayey ... Dr. Juan N. VARONA-ECHEANDÍA
12 Chanc University Col Humacao ... Dr. Carmen HERNÁNDEZ-CRUZ
12 Chanc Univ College at Bayamon ... Dr. Arturo AVILÉS-GONZÁLEZ
12 Chanc Univ College at Ponce ... Dr. Fernando RODRÍGUEZ-RODRÍGUEZ
12 Chanc Univ College at Carolina ... Prof. Trinidad FERNÁNDEZ-MIRANDA
12 Chanc Univ College at Utuado ... Dr. Iris M. MERCADO-OCASIO
12 Chanc Univ College Aguadilla ... Prof. Ivelice CARDONA-CORTÉS
12 Chanc Univ College at Arecibo ... Prof. Juan RAMÍREZ-SILVA
30 Dir Devel & Alumni Affairs Office ... Ms. Sandra M. TORRES-CLEMENTE
18 Dir Ctrl Designer Construction Ofc ... Mr. Adrián LÓPEZ-NUNCI
10 Director Finance Office ... Mr. Edwin REYES GONZÁLEZ
15 Director Human Resources Office ... Mrs. Sheyla MENDEZ
11 Director Administrative Service ... Ms. Miriam D. MARTÍNEZ
13 Director Information Systems Office ... Mrs. Alina DÍAZ
37 Director Student Financial Aid ... Mr. Hernán VAZQUEZTELL
43 Director Legal Affairs Office ... Ms. Martha L. VÉLEZ
88 Administrator Botanical Garden ... Dr. Rafael F. DÁVILA-LÓPEZ
27 University Press & Communications ... Mrs. Azyadeth N. VÉLEZ
101 Exec Secretary University Board ... Dr. Myrna MAYOL
21 Director Budget Office ... Mr. Willie ROSARIO

*University of Puerto Rico-Aguadilla (H)

PO Box 6150, Aguadilla PR 00604-6150
County: Aguadilla FICE Identification: 012123
Unit ID: 243106
Telephone: (787) 890-2681 Carnegie Class: Bac/Diverse
FAX Number: (787) 891-3455 Calendar System: Semester
URL: www.uprag.edu
Established: 1972 Annual Undergrad Tuition & Fees (In-State): $2,751
Enrollment: 2,948 Coed
Affiliation or Control: State IRS Status: 501(c)3
Highest Offering: Baccalaureate
Program: Occupational; 2-Year Principally Bachelor's Creditable; Liberal Arts And General
Accreditation: M, ACBSP, TED

02 Chancellor ... Dr. Ivelice CARDONA CORTES
05 Dean Academic Affairs ... Dr. Sonia RIVERA GONZALEZ
11 Dean Administrative Affairs ... Mr. Hector VELEZ
32 Dean Student Affairs ... Prof. Pablo A. RAMIREZ-MENDEZ
06 Registrar ... Mrs. Zaida SERRANO
07 Admissions Officer ... Mrs. Melba SERRANO
08 Head Librarian ... Prof. Cande GOMEZ
14 Director of Computer Center ... Mr. Carlos JIMENEZ
16 Interim Head of Personnel ... Mr. Miguel AROCHO
19 Director of Security/Safety ... Vacant
37 Director Student Financial Aid ... Mrs. Carmen E. SANTIAGO SOTO
51 Director Continuing Education ... Prof. U. Birilo SANTIAGO VELAZQUEZ
38 Director Student Counseling ... Prof. Elba I. ROMAN
45 Dir Planning/Inst Research Office ... Mr. Gerardo JAVARIZ

18 Chief Facilities/Physical Plant ... Vacant
29 Director Alumni Relations ... Mrs. Jeannette AQUINO
96 Purchasing Supervisor ... Mrs. Widylia MEDINA

*University of Puerto Rico at Arecibo (A)

Call Box 4010, Arecibo PR 00614-4010
County: Arecibo FICE Identification: 007228
Unit ID: 243115
Telephone: (787) 815-0000 Carnegie Class: Bac/Diverse
FAX Number: (787) 880-2245 Calendar System: Semester
URL: www.upra.edu
Established: 1967 Annual Undergrad Tuition & Fees (In-State): $2,944
Enrollment: 3,577 Coed
Affiliation or Control: State IRS Status: 501(c)3
Highest Offering: Baccalaureate
Program: Occupational; Liberal Arts And General
Accreditation: M, ACBSP, ADNUR, CS, NUR, TED

02 Chancellor ... Dr. Juan RAMIREZ SILVA
05 Dean of Academic Affairs ... Dr. Manuel SAPONARA
11 Dean of Administrative Affairs ... Prof. Juan PEREZ
32 Dean of Student Affairs ... Prof. Diomedes PAGAN
09 Dir Planning/Institutional Research ... Prof. Soriel SANTIAGO
06 Registrar ... Mrs. Milagros PITRE
07 Director of Admissions ... Mrs. Magaly MENDEZ
08 Head Librarian ... Prof. Robert ROSADO
15 Director Human Resources ... Ms. Sandra DE JESUS
38 Director Student Counseling ... Prof. Celia MEDINA
04 Assistant to the Chancellor ... Dr. Cynthia CARDONA
51 Dir Continuing Education/Prof Stds ... Mr. Sixto BERMUDEZ VARGAS
37 Director Student Financial Aid ... Ms. Myrta ORTIZ
41 Athletic Director ... Prof. Jose COLON
13 Computing & Information Management ... Prof. Carlos VALLE
20 Assoc Dean of Academic Affairs ... Prof. Melquiades ADAMES
29 Director Alumni Relations ... Mrs. Hilda ANTOMMARCHI
92 Director Honors Program ... Dra. Olga CRUZ
96 Director of Purchasing ... Mrs. Rosaura QUINTANA
18 Chief Facilities/Physical Plant ... Mr. Flor SERRANO

*University of Puerto Rico at Bayamon (B)

Carr. 174 #170 Industrial Minillas, Bayamon PR 00959-1911
County: Bayamon FICE Identification: 010975
Unit ID: 243133
Telephone: (787) 993-0000 Carnegie Class: Bac/Diverse
FAX Number: (787) 993-8900 Calendar System: Semester
URL: www.uprb.edu
Established: 1971 Annual Undergrad Tuition & Fees (In-State): $3,012
Enrollment: 4,948 Coed
Affiliation or Control: State IRS Status: 501(c)3
Highest Offering: Baccalaureate
Program: Liberal Arts And General
Accreditation: M, ACBSP, ENGT, TED

02 Chancellor ... Dr. Arturo AVILÉS-GONZÁLEZ
05 Dean Academic Affairs ... Dr. Edna MIRANDA-RODRÍGUEZ
32 Dean Student Affairs ... Mr. Nelson VÁZQUEZ-ESPEJO
06 Registrar ... Ms. Carmen CINTRON-OTERO
07 Director Admissions ... Mrs. Carmen MONTES-BURGOS
08 Director Learning Resources ... Prof. Maria de los Angeles ZAVALA-COLÓN
11 Dean Administrative Affairs ... Mr. Abdiel MARTÍNEZ-BARRIOS
15 Director Human Resources ... Mrs. Idalia MORELL-MARRERO
35 Director Student Activities ... Mrs. Maribelle PERGOLA-RIVERA
36 Director Student Placement ... Prof. Judith DIAZ-DIAZ
37 Director Student Financial Aid ... Mr. Héctor CUADRADO-GARCÍA
38 Director Student Counseling ... Mr. Angel RUCABADO
81 Director Biology/Coord Chemistry ... Dr. Orlando GONZÁLEZ-GONZÁLEZ
50 Director Business Administration ... Prof. Lydia UBARRI-DE LEÓN
51 Director Continuing Education ... Ms. Verónica FUENTES-RUÍZ
09 Director Planning & Inst Research ... Mr. Javier ZAVALA-QUIÑONES
53 Director of Education ... Dr. Carmen A. RIVERA-TORRES
54 Director of Engineering ... Prof. Jesús ORTIZ-CINTRÓN
68 Director Physical Education ... Prof. Carlos MARICHAL-LUGO
79 Director Humanities ... Dr. Luis H. PABÓN-BATLLE
83 Director Social Sciences ... Dr. Elizabeth CRESPO-KEBLER
77 Director Computer Science ... Prof. Antonio HUERTAS-BERMÚDEZ
75 Director Secretarial Sciences ... Prof. Nancy JIMÉNEZ-PÉREZ
72 Director Electronics ... Prof. Jesús ORTIZ-CINTRÓN
23 Director Health Services ... Dr. Jorge L. TORRES-SÁNCHEZ
96 Director of Purchasing ... Mr. Agustin GRATEROLE-ROSARIO
88 Director Special Services ... Ms. Shelciy COLLAZO
81 Director of Physics ... Dr. Javier AVALOS-SÁNCHEZ
88 Director English ... Dr. Luis PABÓN-BATLLE
88 Director Spanish ... Dr. Luis H. PABÓN-BATLE
81 Director Mathematics ... Prof. Angel MORERA-GONZÁLEZ
18 Coord Facilities/Physical Plant ... Mr. Samuel SÁEZ-HERNÁNDEZ

*University of Puerto Rico-Carolina University College (C)

PO Box 4800, Carolina PR 00984-4800
County: San Juan FICE Identification: 030160
Unit ID: 243142
Telephone: (787) 257-0000 Carnegie Class: Bac/Diverse
FAX Number: (787) 750-7940 Calendar System: Quarter
URL: www.uprc.edu
Established: 1974 Annual Undergrad Tuition & Fees (In-State): $4,350
Enrollment: 3,530 Coed
Affiliation or Control: State IRS Status: 501(c)3
Highest Offering: Baccalaureate
Program: Occupational; 2-Year Principally Bachelor's Creditable; Liberal Arts And General
Accreditation: M, ACBSP

02 Chancellor ... Prof. Trinidad FERNANDEZ-MIRANDA
05 Dean of Academic Affairs ... Dra. Ana E. FALCON
11 Dean Administrative Affairs ... Mr. Rafael GEIRBOLINI
32 Dean Student Affairs ... Dr. Gerardo PERFECTO
06 Registrar ... Mr. Abelardo MARTINEZ
16 Human Resources Director ... Mrs. Elizabeth NEGRON
09 Director of Planning/Inst Research ... Prof. Carmen L. CRUZ
08 Director Learning Resources Center ... Prof. Stanley PORTELA
51 Director Continuing Education ... Prof. Roberto VIZCARRONDO
07 Admissions Officer ... Mrs. Celia MENDEZ
14 Coord/Dir Computer Sys Center ... Mr. Christian TOLEDO
37 Financial Aid Director ... Mr. Rafael RUIZ
22 Affirmative Action Officer ... Mrs. Rosa QUINONES
88 Director Graphic Arts/Advertising ... Prof. Orlando TORRES
50 Director Banking/Finance/Insurance ... Prof. Mario MAURA
81 Director Natural Sciences ... Prof. Marisol RODRIGUEZ
88 Director Secretarial Sciences ... Prof. Josifina RODRIGUEZ
83 Director Social Sciences ... Dra. Carmen A. BALSA
68 Director Physical Education ... Prof. Felipe ROSA
88 Director Auto Tech/Mech Engineering ... Prof. Walbert MARCANO
79 Director Humanities ... Prof. Jose QUINONES
88 Director Spanish ... Vacant
88 Director English ... Prof. Wanda RODRIGUEZ
88 Dean Hotel Administration School ... Prof. Miguel E. PEREZ
23 Director Health Care ... Dr. Jesus M. AYUSO
18 Supt Operations & Maintenance ... Ing. Herman MUNIZ
41 Athletic Director ... Mr. Arcadio OCASIO
96 Director of Purchasing ... Mrs. Lourdes Z. ORTIZ
10 Chief Business Officer ... Mrs. Sarahi GUADALUPE

*University of Puerto Rico at Cayey (D)

205 Antonio R Barcelo Avenue, Cayey PR 00736
County: Cayey FICE Identification: 007206
Unit ID: 243151
Telephone: (787) 738-2161 Carnegie Class: Bac/Diverse
FAX Number: (787) 738-8039 Calendar System: Semester
URL: web1.oss.cayey.upr.edu/main/
Established: 1967 Annual Undergrad Tuition & Fees (In-State): $2,944
Enrollment: 3,550 Coed
Affiliation or Control: State IRS Status: 501(c)3
Highest Offering: Baccalaureate
Program: Liberal Arts And General; Teacher Preparatory; Professional
Accreditation: #M, ACBSP, TED

02 Chancellor ... Dr. Juan N. VARONA
05 Dean of Academic Affairs ... Dr. Jose A. MOLINA
11 Dean of Administration Affairs ... Prof. Angel RIVERA
32 Dean of Student Affairs ... Dr. Ivonne BAYRON
08 Director Library ... Prof. Aixa LEON
06 Interim Registrar ... Mrs. Daisy RAMOS
15 Director Human Resources ... Mr. Jose R. POLO
56 Head Extension Division ... Dr. Enid CARABALLO
37 Director Student Financial Aid ... Mrs. Sonia PLACERES
38 Director Student Counseling ... Dr. Lino HERNANDEZ
36 Interim Director Student Placement ... Mrs. Rosa ORTIZ
14 Director Computer Center ... Mr. Ramon MARTINEZ
45 Director Planning & Development ... Prof. Irmannette TORRES-LUGO
07 Director Admissions ... Mrs. Jesus MARTINEZ
18 Director Facilities/Physical Plant ... Mr. Edwin MELENDEZ
23 Director Health Services ... Dr. Sandra LISBOA
19 Director Security/Safety ... Mr. Carlos GUTIERREZ
92 Director Honor Program ... Prof. Samuel FIGUEROA
88 Director External Resources ... Prof. Gladys RAMOS
20 Associate Academic Officer ... Dr. Glorivee ROSARIO
20 Associate Academic Officer ... Prof. Ricardo COLON
04 Assistant to the Chancellor ... Prof. Gladys RAMOS
04 Assistant to the Chancellor ... Prof. Ismael QUILES
41 Director Athletic ... Prof. Efrain COLON
26 Chief Public Relations Officer ... Mr. Angel R. ROSA
29 Director Alumni Relations ... Mrs. Gema C. FIGUEROA
44 Director Annual or Planned Giving ... Mrs. Lourdes VEGA
96 Director Purchasing ... Mrs. Candida COLON
43 Director Legal Services ... Mr. Pedro CRUZ
88 Student Ombudsman ... Prof. Evelyn COLLAZO
53 Education ... Dr. William RIOS
79 Humanities ... Prof. Harry HERNANDEZ
83 Social Sciences ... Dr. Luis GALANES
88 Hispanic Studies ... Prof. Jose PEREZ
88 English ... Dr. Maria RODRIGUEZ
81 Chemistry ... Vacant
65 Natural Science ... Vacant
88 Biology ... Dr. Vivian MESTEY
94 Women's Studies ... Dr. Sarah MALAVE
09 Director Assess & Inst Research ... Prof. Irmannette TORRES-LUGO
10 Chief Business Officer ... Mr. Jose COLON
88 Director Budgeting ... Mr. Gonzalo COLON
81 Mathematics-Physics ... Prof. Rolando CID
50 Business Administration ... Prof. Edfel RIVERA
72 Technology & Office Administration ... Dr. Elizabeth MIRANDA
68 Physical Education ... Prof. Pedro FERRER

*University of Puerto Rico-Humacao (E)

Bo. Tejas Estacion Postal CUH, Humacao PR 00791
County: Humacao FICE Identification: 003943
Unit ID: 243179
Telephone: (787) 850-0000 Carnegie Class: Bac/Diverse
FAX Number: (787) 852-4638 Calendar System: Semester
URL: www.uprh.edu
Established: 1962 Annual Undergrad Tuition & Fees (In-State): $3,012
Enrollment: 3,774 Coed
Affiliation or Control: State IRS Status: 501(c)3
Highest Offering: Baccalaureate
Program: Occupational; 2-Year Principally Bachelor's Creditable; Liberal Arts And General; Teacher Preparatory
Accreditation: M, ACBSP, ADNUR, ENGT, NUR, #OTA, PTAA, SW, TED

02 Chancellor ... Dra. Carmen H. HERNANDEZ
05 Dean of Academic Affairs ... Prof. Ruth VARGAS
11 Dean of Administrative Affairs ... Mr. Luis LIZARDI
04 Assistant to the Chancellor ... Vacant
32 Dean of Student Affairs ... Dr. Nereida CRUZ
20 Assistant Dean of Academic Affairs ... Dr. Moises CARTAGENA
09 Dir Planning/IR and Accreditation ... Vacant
06 Registrar ... Mr. Jorge ACEVEDO
07 Director of Admissions ... Mrs. Elizabeth GERENA
08 Director of the Library ... Mr. Luis RODRÍGUEZ
13 Dir Computer/Commun & Info Mgmt ... Mr. Hiram ORTIZ
15 Acting Director Human Resources ... Mrs. Maria ROSA
10 Director of Finance ... Mrs. Ines SANCHEZ
37 Asst Financial Aid Officer ... Mr. Larry CRUZ
88 Director Interdis/Intreg Dev Std ... Vacant
51 Dir Continuing Education/Extension ... Prof. José LÓPEZ
23 Director Health Services ... Vacant
18 Chief Facilities/Physical Plant ... Mr. Larry CRUZ
19 Director Security/Safety ... Mr. Julio VELÁZQUEZ
96 Director of Purchasing ... Mr. Javier A. MUYET
88 Student Ombuds Person ... Dr. Cástula SANTIAGO
41 Athletic Coordinator ... Prof. María CORDOVEZ
92 Academic Honor Coordinator ... Dr. Maritza REYES
21 Director of Budget Office ... Mrs. Iris N. CARRASQUILLO
108 Office of Institutional Assessment ... Prof. Luis NEGRÓN
88 Director Svcs Population Disabil ... Prof. Carmen SEPÚLVEDA
88 Director of Cultural Activities ... Vacant
88 Envir Health & Occupational Safety ... Mrs. Angélica TORRES

*University of Puerto Rico-Mayaguez Campus (F)

PO Box 9000, Mayaguez PR 00681-9000
County: Mayaguez FICE Identification: 003944
Unit ID: 243197
Telephone: (787) 832-4040 Carnegie Class: DRU
FAX Number: (787) 834-3031 Calendar System: Semester
URL: www.uprm.edu
Established: 1911 Annual Undergrad Tuition & Fees (In-State): $3,012
Enrollment: 12,474 Coed
Affiliation or Control: State IRS Status: 501(c)3
Highest Offering: Doctorate
Program: Occupational; Liberal Arts And General; Teacher Preparatory; Professional
Accreditation: M, ENG, NUR, TED

02 Chancellor ... Dr. Jorge RIVERA SANTOS
05 Dean of Academic Affairs ... Dr. Darnyd W. ORTIZ
11 Dean Administration ... Lcdo. Angel L. MATOS FLORES
32 Acting Dean of Students ... Arq. Wilma SANTIAGO GABRIELINI
49 Acting Dean of Arts & Sciences ... Dr. Juan LÓPEZ GARRIGA
54 Dean of Engineering ... Dr. Jaime SEGUEL
47 Dean of Agricultural Sciences ... Dr. Héctor SANTIAGO
50 Dean Business Administration ... Prof. Héctor BRAVO VICK
58 Director of Graduate Studies ... Dr. Anand D. SHARMA
14 Director of Computer Center ... Mr. José CUEVAS
06 Registrar ... Mrs. Briseida MELENDEZ
08 Acting Director of the Library ... Prof. Norma I. SOJO
07 Director of Admissions ... Ms. Norma TORRES
37 Director Student Financial Aid ... Mrs. Lynette FELICIANO RIOS
36 Director Student Placement ... Mrs. Nancy NIEVES
26 Press Office Director ... Mrs. Mariam L. ROSA VELEZ
45 Director Inst Research/Planning ... Dr. Noel ARTILES LEON
29 Director Alumni Association ... Miss Yomarachaliff LUCIANO-FIGUEROA
15 Director of Personnel Services ... Mrs. Cynthia THOMAS FRATICELLI
18 Director of Physical Resources ... Eng. Roberto AYALA
38 Director Student Counseling ... Mr. Edwin MORALES
21 Acting Director Financial Services ... Mr. José E. AVILES
51 Director Continuing Education ... Prof. Silvestre COLÓN
19 Director Security/Safety ... Mr. Roberto TORRES
23 Director Health Services ... Mrs. Rosie TORRES
41 Athletic Director ... Prof. Fernando GAZTAMBIDE
43 Director Legal Services ... Lcda. Lizbeth J. RIVERA MORALES

*University of Puerto Rico-Medical Sciences Campus (G)

PO Box 365067, San Juan PR 00936-5067
County: San Juan FICE Identification: 024600
Unit ID: 243203
Telephone: (787) 758-2525 Carnegie Class: Spec/Med
FAX Number: (787) 767-0755 Calendar System: Semester
URL: www.rcm.upr.edu

Established: 1950 Annual Undergrad Tuition & Fees (In-State): $4,460
Enrollment: 2,517 Coed
Affiliation or Control: State IRS Status: 501(c)3
Highest Offering: Doctorate
Program: Professional
Accreditation: M, AUD, CYTO, DA, DENT, DIETI, HSA, MED, MIDWF, MT, NMT, NURSE, OT, PH, PHAR, PTA, RAD, SP

Code	Title	Name
02	Chancellor	Dr. Rafael RODRIGUEZ-MERCADO
05	Dean of Academic Affairs	Dr. Ilka C. RIOS
32	Dean of Students	Dr. Maria HERNANDEZ
11	Dean of Administration	Mr. Eleuterio POMALES
63	Dean of School of Medicine	Dr. Pedro J. SANTIAGO-BORRERO
52	Dean of School of Dental Medicine	Dr. Humberto VILLA
69	Dean of Grad School Public Health	Dr. Jose CORDERO
67	Dean of School of Pharmacy	Dr. Wanda MALDONADO
76	Dean School of Health Professions	Dr. Estela ESTAPE
66	Dean of School of Nursing	Dr. Maria CASTRO
100	Chief of Staff	Dr. Lyvia ALVAREZ
20	Associate Academic Officer	Dr. Juanita VILLAMIL
13	Director Information Technology	Prof. Sandra SANTOS
43	Director Legal Services	Mr. Raul BANDAS
27	Chief Information Officer	Ms. Milady GOMEZ
06	Registrar	Mr. Reinaldo POMALES
08	Library Director	Dr. Irma QUINONES
09	Director Inst & Academic Research	Dr. Wanda BARRETO
24	Director Educational Media	Prof. Efrain FLORES
35	Director Student Affairs	Mrs. Rosa VELEZ
07	Director of Admissions	Mrs. Yolanda RIVERA
38	Director of Student Counseling	Prof. Blanca AMOROS
37	Director of Student Financial Aid	Mr. Rafael SOLIS
10	Chief Financial Officer	Mrs. Maribel HERNANDEZ
15	Director Personnel Services	Mr. Nelson RIVERA
18	Chief Facilities/Physical Plant	Mr. Julio A. COLLAZO
96	Director of Purchasing	Mr. Jose CARDONA
19	Director Security Office	Mr. William FIGUEROA

*University of Puerto Rico at Ponce (A)

PO Box 7186, Ponce PR 00732-7186
County: Ponce FICE Identification: 009652
Unit ID: 243212
Telephone: (787) 844-8181 Carnegie Class: Bac/Diverse
FAX Number: (787) 844-8679 Calendar System: Semester
URL: www.uprp.edu
Established: 1970 Annual Undergrad Tuition & Fees (In-State): $12,057
Enrollment: 2,909 Coed
Affiliation or Control: State IRS Status: 501(c)3
Highest Offering: Baccalaureate
Program: Occupational; Liberal Arts And General
Accreditation: M, ACBSP, PTAA, TED

Code	Title	Name
02	Chancellor	Dr. Fernando A. RODRIGUEZ
04	Assistant to the Chancellor	Mrs. Reina M. GONZALEZ
05	Dean Academic Affairs	Prof. Lizzette A. ROIG
11	Dean Administrative Affairs	Mr. Harry BENGOCHEA
32	Dean Student Affairs	Prof. Felix A. CUEVAS
20	Associate Academic Dean	Prof. Pier LECOMPTE
45	Dir Inst Research/Planning Officer	Prof. Ivonne VILARINO
08	Director Library	Prof. Saulo COTTO
06	Registrar	Mr. Francisco TORO
38	Director of Student Counseling	Dr. Margarita VILLAMIL
07	Director of Admissions	Mrs. Acmin VELAZQUEZ
37	Director of Financial Aid	Mrs. Ada HERENCIA
15	Director of Personnel Services	Mr. Juan C. LEON
88	Director of Cultural Activities	Mr. Jose L. PONS
14	Director of Computer Center	Prof. Juan VEGA
18	Chief Facilities/Physical Plant	Mr. Alberto GARCIA
40	Director Bookstore	Mr. Juan VEGA
41	Athletic Director	Mrs. Lesbia COLON
23	Director Health Services	Dr. Claudio SANTOS
29	Director Alumni Relations	Prof. Felix A. CUEVAS
30	Chief Development	Vacant
19	Director of Security/Traffic	Mr. German PIMENTEL
88	Coordinator Security/Safety	Mr. Francisco HERNANDEZ
22	Coordinator Affirmative Action	Mrs. Ginny VELEZ

*University of Puerto Rico-Rio Piedras Campus (B)

PO Box 23300, Rio Piedras PR 00931-3300
County: San Juan FICE Identification: 007108
Unit ID: 243221
Telephone: (787) 763-3877 Carnegie Class: RU/H
FAX Number: (787) 764-8799 Calendar System: Semester
URL: www.uprrp.edu
Established: 1903 Annual Undergrad Tuition & Fees (In-State): $2,462
Enrollment: 15,402 Coed
Affiliation or Control: State IRS Status: 501(c)3
Highest Offering: Doctorate
Program: Liberal Arts And General; Teacher Preparatory; Professional
Accreditation: #M, ACBSP, CORE, CS, DIETD, JOUR, LAW, LIB, PLNG, SPAA, SW, TED

Code	Title	Name
02	Chancellor	Dr. Ana R. GUADALUPE
05	Dean Academic Affairs	Dr. Beatriz RIVERA
11	Dean of Administration	Mr. Alberto FELICIANO
32	Dean of Students	Dr. Mayra CHARRIEZ
38	Director of Student Counseling	Mrs. Maritza PÉREZ
20	Associate Dean Academic Affairs	Prof. Leticia M. FERNANDEZ
30	Int Dir Devel & Alumni Relations	Mrs. Rosita A. RIVERA
06	Registrar	Mr. Juan M. APONTE
08	Director of Library System	Dr. Snejanka PENKOVA
15	Acting Director of Personnel	Mrs. Aida ROSARIO
07	Director of Admissions	Mrs. Cruz Belinda VALENTIN
14	Director of Computer Center	Mr. Rafael LLANOS
50	Dean Business Administration	Dr. Paul LATORTUE
48	Dean of Architecture	Prof. Francisco RODRIGUEZ
81	Dean of Natural Sciences	Dr. Brad WEINER
83	Dean of Social Sciences	Dr. Blanca ORTIZ
61	Dean of Law	Ms. Vivian NEPTUNE
97	Dean of General Studies	Dr. Luis FERRAO
79	Dean of Humanities	Dr. Luis A. ORTIZ
58	Dean Graduate Studies/Research	Dr. Haydee SEIJO
53	Dean of Education	Dr. Juanita RODRIGUEZ
35	Associate Dean Student Affairs	Prof. Gloria DIAZ
62	Director Grad Sch Library/Info Sci	Dr. Luisa VIGO
60	Director School of Communication	Dr. Eliseo COLON
58	Dir Graduate Sch of Planning	Dr. Elias R. GUTIERREZ
51	Dir Continuing Educ/Extension	Mrs. Melba MARTINEZ
09	Director of Institutional Research	Prof. Zulyn RODRIGUEZ
18	Chief Planning/Physical Devel Ofc	Ing. Raul CINTRON
26	Chief Public Relations Officer	Mrs. Lorna CASTRO
37	Director of Student Financial Aid	Mrs. Ana HERNANDEZ
96	Director of Purchasing	Mrs. Ivonne MATIENZO-CARRERO

*University of Puerto Rico at Utuado (C)

PO Box 2500, Utuado PR 00641-2500
County: Utuado FICE Identification: 029384
Unit ID: 243188
Telephone: (939) 292-8924 Carnegie Class: Bac/Diverse
FAX Number: (787) 894-6918 Calendar System: Semester
URL: www.uprutuado.edu/cormo.htm
Established: 1979 Annual Undergrad Tuition & Fees (In-State): $2,944
Enrollment: 1,145 Coed
Affiliation or Control: State IRS Status: 501(c)3
Highest Offering: Baccalaureate
Program: Occupational; 2-Year Principally Bachelor's Creditable; Liberal Arts And General
Accreditation: #M, ACBSP, TED

Code	Title	Name
02	Chancellor	Dra. Yanaira VAZQUEZ
05	Chief Academic Officer	Prof. Debra GONZALEZ
10	Chief Business Officer	Mr. Edgar DEL TORO
32	Chief Student Life Officer	Prof. Magda MALDONADO
08	Head Librarian	Dr. Miguel SANTIAGO
09	Director Institutional Research	Dr. Javier LUGO
06	Registrar	Mrs. Marilia SANTIAGO
07	Director of Admission	Mrs. Livette REYES
15	Director Personnel Services	Mrs. Idalia NIEVES
38	Director Student Counseling	Mr. Amilcar GONZALEZ
37	Director Student Financial Aid	Mrs. Edymariel CORTES
14	Director Computer Center	Mr. Juan MOLINA
18	Chief Facilities/Physical Plant	Mr. Josue LUGO
19	Director Security/Safety	Mr. Miguel TORRES
41	Director of Athletics	Mr. Miguel RODRIGUEZ
47	Director of Agriculture	Prof. Eladio GONZALEZ
50	Dir Office Systems/Business Admin	Prof. Vivian VELEZ
96	Director of Purchasing	Mrs. Luz MARTINEZ
51	Director Continuing Education	Prof. Miralys PEREZ
53	Director Education	Prof. Vilmaris CESTERO
88	Director Natural Sciences	Mr. Jorge TORRES
79	Director Humanities/Spanish/English	Dra. Ivette APONTE

University of the Sacred Heart (D)

Box 12383 Loiza Station, Santurce PR 00914-0383
County: San Juan FICE Identification: 003937
Unit ID: 243443
Telephone: (787) 728-1515 Carnegie Class: Master's M
FAX Number: (787) 728-1692 Calendar System: Semester
URL: www.sagrado.edu
Established: 1935 Annual Undergrad Tuition & Fees: $6,500
Enrollment: 5,521 Coed
Affiliation or Control: Roman Catholic IRS Status: 501(c)3
Highest Offering: Master's
Program: Occupational; Liberal Arts And General; Teacher Preparatory; Professional
Accreditation: M, NUR, SW

Code	Title	Name
01	President	Dr. Jose J. RIVERA
84	Dir Inst Plng/Assessmt/Enroll Mgmt	Prof. Lilia PLANELL
05	Dean Academic/Student Affairs	Dr. Lydia ESPINET
11	Dean of Administration	Mr. Jose L. RICCI
30	Dean of Development	Prof. Adlin RIOS
20	Associate Academic Dean	Prof. Yezmin HERNANDEZ
32	Associate Students Dean	Prof. Pedro FRAILE
09	Director of Inst Research Office	Dr. Carmen PADIAL
07	Director of Admissions	Prof. Lilia PLANELL
06	Registrar	Ms. Mildred PINEIRO
26	Chief Public Relations Officer	Mrs. Maria E. MADRID
21	Director of Budgeting	Mrs. Lourdes BERTRAN
91	Director Admin Computer Center	Ms. Carmen CINTRON
18	Chief Facilities/Physical Plant	Mr. Jose L. RICCI
15	Director Personnel Services	Ms. Sol A. GOMILA
29	Director Alumni Relations	Mrs. Elizabeth VARGAS
08	Head Librarian	Mrs. Sonia DIAZ
37	Director of Financial Aid	Mrs. June ANDRADE
39	Director Student Housing	Ms. Livia D. PASTRANA
41	Athletic Director	Mr. Jose L. BURGOS
42	Chaplain	Vacant
10	Director Finance Office	Vacant
50	Director Business Administration	Prof. Marta ALMEYDA
53	Director Education Department	Dr. Migdalia OQUENDO
60	Director Communication Department	Prof. Elmer GONZALEZ
83	Director Social Science Department	Vacant
81	Director Natural Sciences	Prof. Zaida GRACIA
79	Dir Fac Intdspln Human/Social Stds	Prof. Isabel YAMIN
21	Internal Auditor	Mr. Ricardo AGUIRRE
24	Dir Center for FAC/Rchmnt/Educ Tech	Mrs. Sylvia ALVAREZ
51	Assoc Director Continuing Education	Mrs. Elvia AGOSTO
19	Coordinator Security/Safety	Mr. Jose LOZADA
21	Coord Inst Devel Center for CFRET	Mr. Wally ALVARANZA
88	Coord Edu Tech CFRET/FAC/Rchmnt	Ms. Sylvia ALVAREZ
24	Coord Multimedia Product of CFRET	Mr. Benigno ROSA

VIRGIN ISLANDS

University of the Virgin Islands (E)

2 John Brewers Bay, Saint Thomas VI 00802-9990
FICE Identification: 003946
Unit ID: 243665
Telephone: (340) 776-9200 Carnegie Class: Bac/Diverse
FAX Number: (340) 693-1005 Calendar System: Semester
URL: www.uvi.edu
Established: 1962 Annual Undergrad Tuition & Fees (In-State): $4,594
Enrollment: 2,635 Coed
Affiliation or Control: State IRS Status: 501(c)3
Highest Offering: Master's
Program: Liberal Arts And General; Teacher Preparatory; Professional
Accreditation: M, ADNUR, NUR

Code	Title	Name
01	President	Dr. David HALL
100	Chief of Staff	Dr. Noreen M. MICHAEL
88	Special Asst to the President	Dr. Haldene DAVIES
05	Interim Provost	Dr. Camille MCKAYLE-STOLZ
20	Director of Academic Affairs	Ms. Maria FLEMING
53	Interim Dean School of Education	Dr. Linda THOMAS
81	Int Dean Col Science & Mathematics	Dr. Sandra ROMANO
50	Interim Dean School of Business	Prof. Aubrey WASHINGTON
79	Interim Dean Col Lib Arts/Soc Sci	Dr. Simon B. JONES-HENDRICKSON
66	Dean School of Nursing	Dr. Cheryl P. FRANKLIN
46	VP Research/Public Service	Dr. Henry H. SMITH
84	Vice Provost Access/Enroll Services	Dr. Judith EDWIN
07	Dir Admissions/Recruitment	Dr. Xuri M. ALLEN
06	Registrar	Ms. Heather HOGARTH-SMITH
37	Director of Financial Aid	Ms. Cheryl A. ROBERTS
41	Director of Athletics	Mr. Peter SAUER
88	Director Comm/Personal Development	Ms. ILene HEYWARD
09	Dir Institutional Research/Planning	Vacant
30	VP Institutional Advancement	Ms. Dionne V. JACKSON
29	Director of Alumni Affairs	Ms. Linda SMITH
30	Director of Development Services	Ms. Ardrina SCOTT-ELIOTT
44	Director of Major Gifts	Mr. Mitchell NEAVES
26	Director Public Relations	Ms. Patrice JOHNSON
88	Director of Special Events	Ms. Liza MARGOLIS
96	Purchasing Supervisor	Mr. Eric CHRISTIAN
10	VP Administration & Finance	Ms. Shirley LAKE-KING
21	Controller	Ms. Peggy SMITH
15	Director of HR/Org Development	Ms. Bettina MILLER
88	Assoc Dir HR/Org Development	Ms. Yvonne D. LAWRENCE
88	Director of Capital Projects	Mr. Gerard BUGGY
40	Bookstore Manager-St Thomas	Mr. Mervin V. TAYLOR
40	Bookstore Manager-St Croix	Ms. Laurel A. HECKER
19	Chief of Security	Mr. Roderick C. PULLEN
18	Plant Maintenance Manager	Mr. Charles MARTIN
27	Chief Information Officer	Ms. Tina M. KOOPMANS
14	Mgr Enterprise Data/User Services	Ms. Sharlene J. HARRIS
08	Manager of Library/Fac Tech Svcs	Ms. Judith ROGERS
35	Assoc Campus Exec Dir Stdnt Aff-STT	Dr. Doris BATTISTE
36	Counseling Supervisor-St Thomas	Ms. Verna RIVERS
35	Assoc Campus Exec Dir Stdnt Aff-STC	Ms. Miriam OSBORNE-ELLIOTT
36	Counseling Supervisor-St Croix	Ms. Patricia TOWAL

Index of Key Administrators

A

ABU-GHAZALEH, Nabil, S 310-287-4325 55 F abughans@wlac.edu
ABUD, Jorge, J 202-885-2731 97 D jorge@american.edu
ABUHAMAD, Alfred, Z 757-446-7979 518 G abuhamaz@evms.edu
ABUKHALAF, Ronnie 561-912-2166 107 B rabukhalaf@evergladesuniversity.edu
ABUSOUD, Zeina 630-829-6607 145 G zabusoud@ben.edu
ABUTIN, Albert 714-992-7076 59 E aabutin@fullcoll.edu
ABUZNEID, Abdelshakour, A 203-576-4113 94 F abuzneid@bridgeport.edu
ACCAPADI, Mamta 541-737-8748 418 F mamta.accapadi@oregonstate.edu
ACCARDI, Michael 978-837-5062 242 A accardim@merrimack.edu
ACCIARDO, Linda, A 401-874-2116 454 E lindaa@advance.uri.edu
ACCOMANDO, Annette 504-278-6422 211 E aaccomando@nunez.edu
ACCORD, Richard, D 304-462-4107 544 A richard.accord@glenville.edu
ACCORNERO, Chris 864-644-5294 461 B caccornero@swu.edu
ACEBO, Kayla, K 918-631-3288 413 F kayla-acebo@utulsa.edu
ACEVEDO, Beatriz 212-924-5900 357 B bursar@swedishinstitute.edu
ACEVEDO, Francisco 787-264-1912 564 B facevedo@sg.inter.edu
ACEVEDO, Gladys 787-891-0925 563 A gacevedo@aguadilla.inter.edu
ACEVEDO, Ivonne 787-891-0925 563 A iaecheva@ns.inter.edu
ACEVEDO, Jorge 787-850-9380 567 E jorge.acevedo4@upr.edu
ACEVEDO, Luis 787-250-1912 563 G laacevedo@metro.inter.edu
ACEVEDO-RIOS, Carmen 787-725-6500 561 A cacevedo@albizu.edu
ACEVES, William, C 619-239-0391 37 F waceves@cwsl.edu
ACHACOSO, Michelle 512-863-1939 496 A achacosm@southwestern.edu
ACHAMPONG, Francis, K 724-430-4200 439 G fka3@psu.edu
ACHARYA, Suresh 269-749-7666 257 A sacharya@olivetcollege.edu
ACHEMIRE, Roy 918-293-4724 410 E roy.achemire@okstate.edu
ACHENBACH, USMS, Gerard 231-995-1203 256 D gachenbach@nmc.edu
ACHENBACH, Laurie 618-453-7984 165 B laurie@micro.siu.edu
ACHESON, Carol 503-253-3443 417 H cacheson@ocom.edu
ACHING, Gerard 607-255-4625 331 B gla23@cornell.edu
ACHS, Carol 480-461-7742 15 I carol.achs@mcmail.maricopa.edu
ACHTER, John 715-232-2468 552 E achterj@uwstout.edu
ACHTERBERG, Cheryl, L 614-292-2461 398 I achterberg.1@osu.edu
ACHTERMAN, Douglas 408-848-4809 48 C dachterman@gavilan.edu
ACIERNO, Kevin, K 440-964-4245 393 E kacierno@kent.edu
ACIERNO, Lou 212-752-1530 338 C lou.acierno@limcollege.edu
ACK, Nicole 360-867-5371 534 D ackn@evergreen.edu
ACKER, Don 724-339-7542 437 F dacker@nbi.edu
ACKERKNECHT, Steven, M 518-255-5214 354 E ackerksm@cobleskill.edu
ACKERLEY, Roseanne 513-487-3234 335 B rackerley@huc.edu
ACKERMAN, Ben 812-330-6087 175 J backerma@ivytech.edu
ACKERMAN, Debbie 217-732-3155 156 I dackerman@lincolncollege.edu
ACKERMAN, Deborah 503-253-3443 417 H dackerman@ocom.edu
ACKERMAN, Denise 845-758-7625 323 D ackerman@bard.edu
ACKERMAN, Eric 954-262-2063 114 B esa@nova.edu
ACKERMAN, Judy 240-567-5010 224 D judy.ackerman@montgomerycollege.edu
ACKERMAN, Kate 617-217-9225 231 A kackerman@baystate.edu
ACKERMAN, Kathy 828-395-1522 371 D kackerman@isothermal.edu
ACKERMAN, Mary 320-762-4673 265 F marya@alextech.edu
ACKERMAN, Randall, R 717-749-6116 440 B rra14@psu.edu
ACKERMAN, Robert, M 313-577-3933 260 A ackerman@wayne.edu
ACKERMAN, Traci 954-492-5353 103 F ackerman@citycollege.edu
ACKERMANN, Arthur, J 314-935-5582 292 I ackermann@wustl.edu
ACKLAND, Terri 520-494-5227 13 D terri.ackland@centralaz.edu
ACKLEN, Joyce 615-687-6905 466 H jacklen@abcnash.edu
ACKLEY, Brian 607-844-8222 357 I ackleyb@tc3.edu
ACKLEY, Lavon 229-430-0415 124 B lackley@albanytech.edu
ACKLEY, Tonya, J 814-362-7592 449 B tja7@pitt.edu
ACKLIN, Anthony, E 515-574-1368 185 I acklin@iowacentral.edu
ACLAND, Francis 641-784-5302 185 B acland@graceland.edu
ACOB-NASH, Mari 206-934-7804 537 D mari.acob-nash@seattlecolleges.edu
ACORACE, Joan 603-206-8012 304 D jacorace@ccsnh.edu
ACOSTA, Araceli 210-924-4338 481 G araceli.acosta@bua.edu
ACOSTA, Jesse 903-566-7044 506 E jacosta@uttyler.edu
ACOSTA, Lydia, M 954-262-4640 114 B lacosta@nsu.nova.edu
ACOSTA, Michael, E 210-434-6711 492 B meacosta@lake.ollusa.edu
ACOSTA, Pilar 407-708-2432 117 H acostap@seminolestate.edu
ACOSTA, R. Alexander 305-348-1118 119 C
ACOSTA, Reynold 407-303-8016 100 G reynold.acosta@adu.edu
ACOSTA-FUMERO, Carmen, J 787-841-2000 565 B cacosta@pucpr.edu
ACQUAAH, George 301-860-3610 228 A gacquaah@bowiestae.edu
ACREE, Elizabeth, A 520-621-3432 18 L acree@email.arizona.edu
ACREE, Jenny 785-243-1435 192 A jacree@cloud.edu
ACREY, Autry 903-730-4890 489 C autry.acrey@jarvis.edu
ACTON, Anne 617-422-7282 243 B aacton@nesl.edu
ACTON, Arthur, J 814-393-2337 442 B aacton@clarion.edu
ACTON, James 561-297-3057 119 A jacton2@fau.edu
ACTON, James 312-567-5000 153 C jacton@iit.edu
ACTOR, Lisa 801-832-2731 512 G lactor@westminstercollege.edu
ACUESTA, Sylvia 718-636-3750 346 D sacuesta@pratt.edu
ACUFF, Robert, V 423-439-8174 473 F acuffr@etsu.edu
ADACHI, Lesley, B 680-488-2471 560 C lbadachi@gmail.com
ADACHI, Themy 510-430-3285 57 D themy@mills.edu
ADADE, Anthony, K 252-335-3203 377 F akadade@mail.ecsu.edu
ADADEVOH, Vidal 205-453-6300 99 G
ADAIR, Adam 870-512-7801 20 F adam_adair@asun.edu
ADAIR, Matt 580-327-8545 409 C wmadair@nwosu.edu
ADAIR, Troy 973-278-5400 307 F
ADAIR, Troy 212-986-4343 323 H taa@berkeleycollege.edu
ADAIR, Wendy, H 713-313-7455 500 B adairw@tsu.edu
ADAKI, Rose 505-863-7505 321 D radaki@gallup.unm.edu
ADALIAN, Paul 541-552-6833 419 A adalianp@sou.edu
ADAM, Audrey 508-286-5839 246 B adam_audrey@wheatonma.edu
ADAM, Baba 530-895-2987 31 H adamba@butte.edu
ADAM, Charles, A 563-333-6151 188 F adamcharlesa@sau.edu
ADAM, Cynthia 315-312-5555 354 A cynthia.adam@oswego.edu
ADAM, Don 512-313-3000 483 K don.adam@concordia.edu
ADAM, Johnna 309-794-7578 145 E johnnaadam@augustana.edu
ADAMCIK, Barbara 208-282-2171 143 H adambarb@isu.edu
ADAMES, Jose, A 201-447-7237 307 E jadames@bergen.edu
ADAMES, Melquiades 787-815-0000 567 A melquiades.adames@upr.edu
ADAMKIEWICZ, Marsha 586-791-6610 248 B marsha.adamkiewicz@baker.edu
ADAMO, Clare 860-632-3009 93 B library@holyapostles.edu
ADAMO, Paul, J 607-436-2535 353 E adamopj@oneonta.edu
ADAMONIS, Roberta 305-892-7594 112 A roberta.adamonis@jwu.edu
ADAMS, Al 281-487-1170 499 B aadams@txchiro.edu
ADAMS, Amy 614-236-6242 386 E adams@capital.edu
ADAMS, Andrea 434-582-2681 520 K ahepburn@liberty.edu
ADAMS, Ann 541-917-4353 416 I adamsa@linnbenton.edu
ADAMS, Ann 312-503-0054 160 E a-adams@northwestern.edu
ADAMS, Ann 360-438-4382 537 B aadams@stmartin.edu
ADAMS, Ann Clay 404-687-4524 127 F adamsa@ctsnet.edu
ADAMS, Anne 715-634-4790 547 J aadams@lco.edu
ADAMS, Barbara, B 847-866-3939 151 D barbara.adams@garrett.edu
ADAMS, Beth 678-839-5567 139 A badams@westga.edu
ADAMS, Beth 218-855-8186 265 J badams@clcmn.edu
ADAMS, Betty 713-797-7000 496 G bnadams@pvamu.edu
ADAMS, Billy 254-647-3234 492 G badams@rangercollege.edu
ADAMS, Bobby 252-335-0821 369 G badams@albemarle.edu
ADAMS, Brett, C 443-352-4250 226 E bcadams@stevenson.edu
ADAMS, Bridgett 229-217-4148 134 F badams@moultrietech.edu
ADAMS, Brittany 909-599-5433 54 A badams@lifepacific.edu
ADAMS, Carey 912-344-2589 124 G carey.adams@armstrong.edu
ADAMS, Carol, J 314-968-6907 292 J caroladams05@webster.edu
ADAMS, Cathryn 972-860-8269 484 H cadams@dcccd.edu
ADAMS, Chadd 205-665-6155 9 B cadams3@montevallo.edu
ADAMS, Christine, M 240-895-4446 226 A cmadams@smcm.edu
ADAMS, Christopher, J 631-451-4118 356 D adamsc@sunysuffolk.edu
ADAMS, Clinton 909-469-5423 78 I cadams@westernu.edu
ADAMS, Colin, B 919-516-4078 376 D cbadams@st-aug.edu
ADAMS, Cynthia 620-365-5116 190 D adams@allencc.edu
ADAMS, Danette, D 404-880-8783 127 C dadams@cau.edu
ADAMS, David 301-696-3400 223 C adamsd@hood.edu
ADAMS, David 219-866-6258 179 D davida@saintjoe.edu
ADAMS, David, R 626-584-5462 48 B dadams@fuller.edu
ADAMS, Dean 270-384-8036 204 D adamsd@lindsey.edu
ADAMS, DeAnna 901-843-3885 472 K registrar@rhodes.edu
ADAMS, Debbie 423-697-3300 474 D
ADAMS, Denise 530-895-2329 31 H adamsde@butte.edu
ADAMS, Dennis, R 865-694-6448 475 G dadams@pstcc.edu
ADAMS, Diane 407-569-1336 107 I diane.adams@fcc.edu
ADAMS, Don 210-485-0088 479 A dadams@alamo.edu
ADAMS, Dorenda 334-229-4324 1 C dadams@alasu.edu
ADAMS, Dreidre 859-622-2977 200 J dreidre.adams@eku.edu
ADAMS, Edward 704-337-2543 376 A adamse@queens.edu
ADAMS, Eileen 407-569-1315 107 I eileen.adams@fcc.edu
ADAMS, Elisa 617-578-7100 244 D eadams@sbboston.com
ADAMS, Elizabeth, T 818-677-2969 35 F elizabeth.t.adams@csun.edu
ADAMS, Ellen 718-631-6269 328 F eadams@qcc.cuny.edu
ADAMS, Gary 218-733-2005 266 H g.adams@lsc.edu
ADAMS, Gary 972-241-3371 484 E gadams@dallas.edu
ADAMS, Grantley 860-738-6333 92 B gadams@nwcc.commnet.edu
ADAMS, Guy 916-789-8600 50 B guy_adams@heald.edu
ADAMS, Gwen 603-880-8308 306 A gadams@thomasmorecollege.edu
ADAMS, Hiuko 404-627-2681 126 D hiukongari.adams@beulah.org
ADAMS, J. Milton 434-924-3728 525 F jma@virginia.edu
ADAMS, Jacob 909-607-3318 40 F jacob.adams@cgu.edu
ADAMS, Jamele 781-736-3600 232 F jadams@brandeis.edu
ADAMS, James, E 325-942-2071 480 E james.adams@angelo.edu
ADAMS, JR., James, P 859-257-6654 207 D james.adams@uky.edu
ADAMS, Jan 903-510-3287 503 A jada@tjc.edu
ADAMS, Jane, A 352-392-4574 120 C jane-adams@ufl.edu
ADAMS, Jason 303-762-6936 84 D jason.adams@denverseminary.edu
ADAMS, Jeff 479-788-7221 24 D jeff.adams@uafs.edu
ADAMS, Jeffrey, M 336-841-4581 365 C jeadams@highpoint.ed
ADAMS, Jeffrey, R 717-872-3703 443 D jeffrey.adams@millersville.edu
ADAMS, Jennifer 925-424-1002 39 D jradams@laspositascollege.edu
ADAMS, Jennifer 315-792-7810 356 B jennifer.adams@sunyit.edu
ADAMS, Jennifer 614-236-6170 386 E jadams@capital.edu
ADAMS, John 512-313-3000 483 K john.adams@concordia.edu
ADAMS, Josh 707-527-4492 68 E jadams@santarosa.edu
ADAMS, Julie 317-955-6213 177 I jadams@marian.edu
ADAMS, Julie 973-655-7067 311 F adamsju@mail.montclair.edu
ADAMS, Karen 785-242-5200 178 I
ADAMS, Karen 785-242-5200 195 I karen.adams@ottawa.edu
ADAMS, Karen 785-242-5200 196 A
ADAMS, Karen 785-242-5200 17 B
ADAMS, Karen 785-242-5200 549 H
ADAMS, Karen, H 812-856-5596 173 D kadams@indiana.edu
ADAMS, Katherine 601-974-1124 275 B adamska@millsaps.edu
ADAMS, Keith 318-345-9266 210 H kadams@ladelta.edu
ADAMS, Kelly, L 315-792-3047 359 E kadams@utica.edu
ADAMS, Ken 814-453-6016 448 E
ADAMS, Kent 620-672-5641 196 D kenta@prattcc.edu
ADAMS, Kevin 718-270-6050 328 C kadams@mec.cuny.edu
ADAMS, Kim 815-394-4376 163 A kadams@rockford.edu
ADAMS, LaVerne 731-668-7240 478 G laverne.adams@wtbc.edu
ADAMS, Lesley 315-781-3671 335 F ladams@hws.edu
ADAMS, Linda 706-379-3111 140 A leadams@yhc.edu
ADAMS, Lisa 678-839-6428 139 A ladams@westga.edu
ADAMS, Lisa 413-565-1000 230 G ladams@baypath.edu
ADAMS, Lita 413-748-3695 244 H ladams@springfieldcollege.edu
ADAMS, Mack 575-527-7550 319 G madams@nmsu.edu
ADAMS, Mark 936-294-1158 501 D ucs_mca@shsu.edu
ADAMS, Mary, A 303-991-1575 81 B mary.adams@americansentinel.edu
ADAMS, Mary Beth 205-934-3254 8 F marybeth@uab.edu
ADAMS, Melvin 614-236-6901 386 E madams@capital.edu
ADAMS, Merrill 505-566-3371 320 D adamsm@sanjuancollege.edu
ADAMS, Michael, B 415-476-4753 75 A madams@aaeod.ucsf.edu
ADAMS, Michael, F 706-542-1214 138 G presuga@uga.edu
ADAMS, Michael, J 888-777-7675 534 E mjadams@faithseminary.edu
ADAMS, Michelle 773-291-6359 147 G madams@ccc.edu
ADAMS, N. Scott 828-669-8012 367 E nadams@montreat.edu
ADAMS, Natasha, A 302-857-6009 96 C nadams@desu.edu
ADAMS, Neale, J 515-574-1284 185 I adams_n@iowacentral.edu
ADAMS, Patricia, A 504-280-7477 213 E paadams@uno.edu
ADAMS, Patrick 516-876-3194 353 D adamsp@oldwestbury.edu
ADAMS, Paul, S 570-408-4114 452 A paul.adams@wilkes.edu
ADAMS, Perrie, M 214-648-2258 507 E perrie.adams@utsouthwestern.edu
ADAMS, Philip 309-438-5677 153 D pmadams@ilstu.edu

AHERN, Michael ... 620-227-9359 ... 192 E
mfahern@dc3.edu
AHERN, Susan ... 603-513-5123 ... 306 E
susan.ahern@law.unh.edu
AHERN, Tim ... 319-208-5247 ... 189 D
tahern@scciowa.edu
AHERNE, John ... 845-341-4710 ... 345 E
john.aherne@sunyorange.edu
AHLBURG, Dennis, A ... 210-999-8401 ... 502 E
dennis.ahlburg@trinity.edu
AHLEMANN, Tina ... 843-574-6142 ... 461 G
tina.ahlemann@tridenttech.edu
AHLQUIST, Michelle ... 320-762-4918 ... 265 F
michellea@alextech.edu
AHMADI, Goodarz ... 315-268-6446 ... 329 B
ahmadi@clarkson.edu
AHMED, Abu ... 803-210-9798 ... 455 D
ahmeda@benedict.edu
AHMED, Andrea ... 520-383-8401 ... 18 I
aahmed@tocc.cc.az.us
AHMED, Haseeb ... 419-448-2284 ... 391 F
hahmed@heidelberg.edu
AHMED, Ismael ... 313-593-5030 ... 259 B
inahmed@umd.umich.edu
AHMED, Juzar ... 812-465-7160 ... 181 B
juzar@usi.edu
AHMED, Mirza, F ... 313-496-2674 ... 259 G
fahmed1@wcccd.edu
AHMED, Mustaq ... 419-358-3237 ... 385 D
ahmedm@bluffton.edu
AHMED, Tanveer ... 904-398-4141 ... 121 E
AHMED, Zahir ... 573-986-6863 ... 289 K
zahmed@semo.edu
AHN, Young Jin ... 714-533-1495 ... 70 B
admission@southbaylo.edu
AHNER, Yolanda ... 915-831-7724 ... 486 G
yahner@epcc.edu
AHO, Duane ... 906-487-7349 ... 251 A
duane.aho@finlandia.edu
AHO, Marie, M ... 906-227-2981 ... 256 C
mariaho@nmu.edu
AHOLA, Scott ... 605-642-6359 ... 465 H
scott.ahola@bhsu.edu
AHORRIO, Beatriz ... 212-694-1000 ... 324 C
bahorrio@boricuacollege.edu
AHOUSE, Michele, L ... 781-309-6768 ... 236 C
mahouse@mariancourt.edu
AHRENS, Jennifer ... 478-240-5143 ... 135 B
jahrens@oftc.edu
AHUJA, Sunil ... 440-365-5222 ... 395 D
AICHELE, Christina, M ... 815-740-3363 ... 167 E
caichele@stfrancis.edu
AICINENA, Steve ... 432-552-2675 ... 507 D
aicinena_s@utpb.edu
AIKEN, Deborah, J ... 401-825-2100 ... 453 D
daiken@ccri.edu
AIKEN, George ... 415-433-9200 ... 68 F
gaiken@saybrook.edu
AIKEN, Katherine, G ... 208-885-6426 ... 144 G
kaiken@uidaho.edu
AIKEN, Ryan ... 413-775-1309 ... 239 E
aikenr@gcc.mass.edu
AIKEN, Wallace ... 330-382-7428 ... 393 F
waiken@kent.edu
AILSTOCK, M. Stephen ... 410-777-2230 ... 221 C
smailstock@aacc.edu
AIMONE, Chris ... 812-877-8498 ... 179 B
aimone@rose-hulman.edu
AINA, Saga ... 907-852-3333 ... 10 F
saga.aina@ilisagvik.edu
AINLAY, Stephen, C ... 518-388-6101 ... 358 G
ainlays@union.edu
AINLEY, Arden ... 360-416-7716 ... 538 D
arden.ainley@skagit.edu
AINSLEY, Sharon ... 610-647-4400 ... 431 C
sainsley@immaculata.edu
AINSLIE, Carolyn, N ... 609-258-1447 ... 312 G
ainslie@princeton.edu
AINSWORTH, Emma, L ... 662-685-4771 ... 273 E
eainsworth@bmc.edu
AINSWORTH, Jerald ... 423-425-4666 ... 477 F
jerald-ainsworth@utc.edu
AINSWORTH, Jerry ... 618-634-3396 ... 164 E
jerrya@shawneecc.edu
AINSWORTH, Patricia ... 978-542-6446 ... 238 E
painsworth@salemstate.edu
AIREN, Osaro ... 403-375-7112 ... 299 G
osairen1@wsc.edu
AIREY, Patricia, J ... 540-985-8376 ... 520 I
pjairey@jchs.edu
AITCHISON, Bridget ... 765-677-2389 ... 175 B
bridget.aitchison@indwes.edu
AITKEN-JULIN, Molly ... 218-755-2876 ... 265 I
maitken@bemidjistate.edu
AITSON-ROESSLER,
Mechelle ... 405-733-7308 ... 411 I
maitson-roessler@rose.edu
AIZAZ, Khawar ... 713-779-1110 ... 494 D
kaizaz@sbhouston.com
AIZENSTAT, Stephen ... 805-969-3626 ... 60 J
saizenstat@pacifica.edu
AJI, Aron, R ... 563-333-6053 ... 188 F
ajiaronr@sau.edu

AJIROTUTU, Cheryl ... 414-229-1122 ... 551 D
yinka@uwm.edu
AJMAL, Mohammad ... 225-292-5464 ... 208 B
ajmal@brc.edu
AJOHDA, Sadia ... 912-583-3216 ... 126 F
sajohda@bpc.edu
AKAJUOBI, Cajetan ... 334-229-4316 ... 1 C
cakajuobi@alasu.edu
AKAKPO, Koffi ... 419-755-4702 ... 397 C
kakakpo@ncstatecollege.edu
AKANDE, Benjamin, O ... 314-968-5951 ... 292 J
akandeb@webster.edu
AKCHIN, Lisa, G ... 410-455-2889 ... 227 D
akchin@umbc.edu
AKE, David ... 775-682-8803 ... 303 A
dake@unr.edu
AKEKE, Peter ... 508-588-9100 ... 240 A
AKENS, Cathy ... 305-919-5943 ... 119 C
akens@fiu.edu
AKENS, Jeff ... 916-388-2800 ... 38 B
jakens@carrington.edu
AKERMAN, Kate ... 617-217-9006 ... 231 A
kakerman@baystate.edu
AKERMAN, Patricia ... 320-308-5966 ... 269 B
pakerman@sctcc.edu
AKERS, Elaine ... 909-384-8273 ... 65 C
eakers@sbccd.cc.ca.us
AKERS, Lex, A ... 309-677-2721 ... 146 C
lakers@bradley.edu
AKERS, Mary Anne ... 443-885-3225 ... 224 E
maryanne.akers@morgan.edu
AKERS, Richard ... 304-327-4181 ... 543 F
rakers@bluefieldstate.edu
AKERS, Shawn, D ... 434-592-5451 ... 520 K
sdakers@liberty.edu
AKERSON, Joni ... 320-308-6158 ... 269 B
jakerson@sctcc.edu
AKEY, Stacey, L ... 920-923-7652 ... 548 E
sakey@marianuniversity.edu
AKIN, Daniel, L ... 919-761-2222 ... 377 A
dakin@sebts.edu
AKIN, Hudson ... 765-285-1633 ... 169 G
hakin@bsu.edu
AKIN, Joeleen ... 404-471-6133 ... 123 I
jakin@agnesscott.edu
AKIN, Renea ... 270-534-3461 ... 203 E
renea.akin@kctcs.edu
AKINC, Mufit ... 515-294-9988 ... 182 E
makinc@iastate.edu
AKINLEYE, Johnson, O ... 910-962-3876 ... 379 D
akinleyej@uncw.edu
AKINS, Erick ... 210-486-2778 ... 479 D
eakins@alamo.edu
AKINS, Richie ... 912-478-5393 ... 131 E
rakins@georgiasouthern.edu
AKKAWI, Kayed ... 312-935-6025 ... 162 G
kakkawi@robertmorris.edu
AKL, Fred, A ... 610-499-4036 ... 451 F
faakl@widener.edu
AKMAL, Hassan ... 212-312-4440 ... 332 A
hakmal@devry.edu
AKMAN, Jeffrey, S ... 202-741-2880 ... 98 C
akman@gwu.edu
AKOJIE, Patricia, A ... 270-686-4200 ... 199 B
patricia.akojie@brescia.edu
AKRIDGE, Jay, T ... 765-494-8391 ... 178 J
akridge@purdue.edu
AKRIE, Germeka ... 434-848-1864 ... 524 B
gakrie@saintpauls.edu
AKST JONES, Ellen ... 641-472-7000 ... 187 E
eajones@mum.edu
AKSU, Mert ... 313-994-6620 ... 258 G
aksumn@udmercy.edu
AL-AMIN, John ... 925-229-6942 ... 43 D
jalamin@4cd.edu
AL-HASSAN, Marilyn ... 909-472-0675 ... 29 D
malhassan@argosy.edu
AL-HAZZAM DAWASARI,
Elizabeth ... 480-860-2700 ... 14 F
edawsari@taliesin.edu
ALADE, Ayodele, J ... 410-651-6327 ... 227 E
ajalade@umes.edu
ALAIMO, Joseph ... 570-408-4512 ... 452 A
joseph.alaimo@wilkes.edu
ALAIMO, Kathleen ... 773-298-3090 ... 163 I
alaimo@sxu.edu
ALAIMOANA-NUUSA,
Repeka ... 684-699-9155 ... 559 C
r.nuusa@amsamoa.edu
ALAM, Maria ... 901-678-2867 ... 474 C
malam@memphis.edu
ALAM, Nadia ... 617-236-5422 ... 234 G
nalam@fisher.edu
ALAMI, Osama ... 804-827-7474 ... 526 B
oalami@vcu.edu
ALAMPI, Janet ... 860-512-2813 ... 91 F
jalampi@mcc.commnet.edu
ALAN, Patricia ... 772-462-5604 ... 111 B
palan@irsc.edu
ALANDER, Link ... 832-813-6842 ... 490 E
link.s.alander@lonestar.edu
ALANGAR, Sadhana ... 734-929-9089 ... 249 D
sadhana@cleary.edu
ALARCIO, Rebecca ... 805-922-6966 ... 26 L
ralarcio@hancockcollege.edu

ALARID, Jandee ... 409-772-9868 ... 507 C
jalarid@utmb.edu
ALASIO, Claire ... 732-571-3463 ... 311 E
calasio@monmouth.edu
ALAWIYE, Osman ... 320-308-3023 ... 269 A
oalawiye@stcloudstate.edu
ALBANESE, Linda ... 516-678-5000 ... 341 F
lalbanese@molloy.edu
ALBANESE, Marc ... 610-282-1100 ... 427 A
marc.albanese@desales.edu
ALBANESE, Robert, C ... 815-753-2755 ... 160 B
rca@niu.edu
ALBANO, John ... 209-386-6777 ... 57 C
albano.j@mccd.edu
ALBANO, Mark, A ... 212-821-0737 ... 360 C
maa2034@med.cornell.edu
ALBANO, Ralph ... 202-319-5218 ... 97 E
albano@cua.edu
ALBARRAN, Agustin ... 619-644-7600 ... 49 C
agustin.albarran@gcccd.edu
ALBARRON, Charo ... 707-864-7122 ... 70 A
charo.albarron@solano.edu
ALBAYYARI, J ... 260-481-6391 ... 174 C
albayyaj@ipfw.edu
ALBEE, David ... 415-257-1308 ... 45 C
david.albee@dominican.edu
ALBER, Antone, F ... 716-888-2160 ... 325 F
albera@canisius.edu
ALBERICO, Ralph, A ... 540-568-3828 ... 520 H
alberira@jmu.edu
ALBERLE-CANNATA,
Denise ... 800-806-1917 ... 93 C
dalberle-cannata@lincolncollegene.edu
ALBERS, Jhett ... 605-642-6885 ... 465 H
jhett.albers@bhsu.edu
ALBERS, Mia ... 605-455-6016 ... 465 A
malbers@olc.edu
ALBERS, Sarah ... 785-442-6008 ... 193 F
salbers@highlandcc.edu
ALBERT, David ... 860-768-4482 ... 95 B
dalbert@hartford.edu
ALBERT, Eric ... 847-566-6401 ... 167 F
ealbert@usml.edu
ALBERT, Gene ... 516-773-5517 ... 558 I
ALBERT, George ... 412-291-6313 ... 422 E
galbert@aii.edu
ALBERT, J, L ... 404-413-4519 ... 131 G
jalbert@gsu.edu
ALBERT, Juline ... 712-274-6400 ... 190 B
juline.albert@witcc.edu
ALBERT, Karen ... 215-951-2847 ... 444 D
albertk@philau.edu
ALBERT, Katrice, A ... 225-578-5736 ... 212 H
kalber2@lsu.edu
ALBERT, Laurie ... 919-508-2025 ... 380 E
lalbert@peace.edu
ALBERT, Louis ... 520-206-6752 ... 17 H
lalbert@pima.edu
ALBERT, Marianne ... 724-222-5330 ... 438 F
malbert@penncommercial.edu
ALBERT, Nancy ... 304-214-8852 ... 543 D
nalbert@wvncc.edu
ALBERT, OP, Peg ... 517-264-7000 ... 258 B
palbert@sienaheights.edu
ALBERT, Rachel, E ... 207-834-7510 ... 220 D
realbert@maine.edu
ALBERT, Rita ... 561-237-7231 ... 113 D
ralbert@lynn.edu
ALBERT, Robert ... 606-783-5158 ... 204 I
r.albert@moreheadstate.edu
ALBERT, Timothy ... 206-296-6305 ... 538 B
albertt@seattleu.edu
ALBERT-GREEN, DeEadra ... 512-313-3000 ... 483 K
deeadra.green@concordia.edu
ALBERT LINK, Cindy ... 617-266-1400 ... 231 E
ALBERTA, Richard ... 415-282-7600 ... 28 B
richardalberta@actcm.edu
ALBERTELLI, Denise ... 718-409-4946 ... 356 C
dalbertelli@sunymaritime.edu
ALBERTO, Paul, A ... 404-413-8100 ... 131 G
palberto@gsu.edu
ALBERTS, David ... 724-938-4324 ... 441 G
alberts@calu.edu
ALBERTS, Eugene, R ... 608-796-3849 ... 553 C
eralberts@viterbo.edu
ALBERTS, Kristin, R ... 904-256-7180 ... 111 L
kalbert@ju.edu
ALBERTS, Trev ... 402-554-2305 ... 301 A
talberts@unomaha.edu
ALBERTSON, Eugene ... 336-887-3000 ... 366 C
ealbertson@laureluniversity.edu
ALBERTSON, Kay, H ... 919-735-5151 ... 375 A
kha@waynecc.edu
ALBERTSON, Mark, R ... 336-278-6572 ... 364 D
albertso@elon.edu
ALBERTSON, Ron ... 503-517-7421 ... 420 A
ron.albertson@reed.edu
ALBES, Beth ... 314-529-9380 ... 284 C
balbes@maryville.edu
ALBIN, John ... 212-650-3811 ... 327 E
jalbi@hunter.cuny.edu
ALBIN, Martha ... 918-456-5511 ... 409 A
albinml@nsuok.edu

ALBIN-HILL, Jill ... 708-524-6980 ... 150 C
jalbin@dom.edu
ALBINA, Adam, R ... 603-641-7266 ... 305 G
aalbina@anselm.edu
ALBINI, Marisa ... 401-333-7150 ... 453 D
malbini@ccri.edu
ALBINSON, Erik ... 319-399-8741 ... 183 F
ealbinso@coe.edu
ALBISTON, Steve, K ... 208-524-3000 ... 143 G
steven.albiston@my.eitc.edu
ALBON, Darrell, J ... 740-368-3070 ... 400 G
djalbon@owu.edu
ALBORS BIGAS, Jaime, L ... 787-725-6500 ... 561 A
jalbors@pfizer.com
ALBRECHT, Bryan, D ... 262-564-3000 ... 554 B
albrechtb@gtc.edu
ALBRECHT, Catherine ... 419-772-2130 ... 398 H
c-albrecht@onu.edu
ALBRECHT, Christal, M ... 904-632-5094 ... 109 F
christal.albrecht@fscj.edu
ALBRECHT, Don ... 361-825-2612 ... 498 C
don.albrecht@tamucc.edu
ALBRECHT, James, M ... 253-535-7317 ... 536 E
albrecjm@plu.edu
ALBRECHT, Jana ... 309-438-2231 ... 153 D
jalbre2@ilstu.edu
ALBRECHT, Jon ... 813-257-3375 ... 123 A
jalbrecht@ut.edu
ALBRECHT, Lois ... 715-682-1394 ... 549 F
lalbrecht@northland.edu
ALBRECHT, Shauna ... 406-265-3711 ... 295 E
albrecht@msun.edu
ALBRECHT, Stan, L ... 435-797-7172 ... 511 E
stan.albrecht@usu.edu
ALBRECHT, William, G ... 337-475-5816 ... 215 G
walbrecht@mcneese.edu
ALBRIGHT, Bryan ... 419-995-8264 ... 399 B
albright.34@osu.edu
ALBRIGHT, Geri ... 205-929-6315 ... 5 E
galbright@lawsonstate.edu
ALBRIGHT, Janet ... 530-242-7555 ... 69 D
jalbright@shastacollege.edu
ALBRIGHT, Ken ... 530-895-2298 ... 31 H
albrightke@butte.edu
ALBRIGHT, Mike ... 845-341-4728 ... 345 E
mike.albright@sunyorange.edu
ALBRIGHT, Thomas ... 601-979-2580 ... 274 G
thomas.e.albright@jsums.edu
ALBRINCK, Jill ... 630-515-4526 ... 149 B
jalbrinck@devry.edu
ALBRINCK, Margaret, L ... 920-565-1290 ... 548 A
albrinckm@lakeland.ede
ALBRITTEN, Arna, T ... 229-430-4638 ... 124 A
arna.albritten@asurams.edu
ALBRITTON, Rosie, L ... 936-261-1510 ... 496 G
rlalbritton@pvamu.edu
ALBRITTON, Sheila ... 423-697-4710 ... 474 D
ALBURCHER, Ronald ... 650-723-2300 ... 71 G
ALBURY, Mark ... 802-485-2305 ... 514 C
malbury@norwich.edu
ALCAINO, Ricardo ... 805-893-4504 ... 75 B
ricardo.alcaino@oeo.ucsb.edu
ALCALA, Celena ... 310-287-4290 ... 55 F
alcalac@wlac.edu
ALCALA, Juana, J ... 406-243-2049 ... 294 I
juana.alcala@umontana.edu
ALCARAZ, Arturo ... 951-328-3871 ... 64 A
arturo.alcaraz@rcc.edu
ALCOCK, Sherry, B ... 563-387-1862 ... 187 D
alcock@luther.edu
ALCORN, Gena ... 309-341-5327 ... 146 D
galcorn@sandburg.edu
ALCORTA, Joe, H ... 325-670-1594 ... 487 F
jalcorta@hsutx.edu
ALDAMA, Ben ... 479-986-6939 ... 22 H
baldama@nwacc.edu
ALDARONDO, Aixa ... 787-766-1717 ... 565 I
aialdarondo@suagm.edu
ALDAY, Katherine, E ... 770-423-6290 ... 133 A
kalday@kennesaw.edu
ALDEN, Alison ... 617-253-6512 ... 241 D
ALDEN, Michael, F ... 573-882-2055 ... 291 B
aldenm@missouri.edu
ALDEN, III, Raymond, W ... 815-753-0493 ... 160 B
ralden@niu.edu
ALDEN, Robin ... 575-461-4413 ... 318 G
robina@mesalands.edu
ALDENDERFER, Mark, S ... 209-228-7742 ... 74 D
maldenderfer@ucmerced.edu
ALDER, William ... 304-647-6203 ... 544 E
walder@osteo.wvsom.edu
ALDERMAN, Charles, W ... 334-844-6406 ... 1 F
aldercw@auburn.edu
ALDERMAN, Debra ... 206-268-4100 ... 530 I
dalderman@antioch.edu
ALDERMAN, Norman, M ... 863-667-5129 ... 118 F
nmalderman@seu.edu
ALDERMAN, Pamela, L ... 304-896-7302 ... 543 C
pamela.alderman@southernwv.edu
ALDERMAN, Steve ... 713-646-1812 ... 494 I
salderman@stcl.edu
ALDERSON, Philip, O ... 314-977-9801 ... 289 C
palderso@slu.edu

ALLARD, Jessica .... 802-862-9616.... 513 B
jallard@burlington.edu
ALLARD, Lee .... 518-782-6737.... 350 I
lallard@siena.edu
ALLARD, Michael .... 518-828-4181.... 330 E
allard@sunycgcc.edu
ALLARD, Nicholas, W .... 718-780-7902.... 324 F
nicholas.allard@brooklaw.edu
ALLBEE, Bob .... 563-288-6002.... 184 G
ballbee@eicc.edu
ALLBRIGHT, A. Rodney ..... 281-756-3598.... 479 F
ara@alvincollege.edu
ALLBRIGHT, Jacque .... 512-245-2521.... 501 F
ja14@txstate.edu
ALLBRITTEN, Jeffery .... 239-489-9211.... 105 F
president@edison.edu
ALLCORN, Terry .... 407-569-1162.... 107 I
terry.allcorn@fcc.edu
ALLCORN, Terry, A .... 417-268-6062.... 278 J
tallcorn@gobbc.edu
ALLEE, Kelly .... 217-234-5215.... 156 B
kallee@lakeland.cc.il.us
ALLEMAN, Vickie .... 713-942-3466.... 505 A
alleman@stthom.edu
ALLEN, Al .... 386-822-8808.... 121 F
aallen@stetson.edu
ALLEN, Algia .... 972-563-9573.... 502 F
aallen@tvcc.edu
ALLEN, Andrea .... 305-899-3310.... 101 M
aallen@mail.barry.edu
ALLEN, Andrew, T .... 619-260-4553...... 76 D
andrewt@sandiego.edu
ALLEN, Ann .... 217-854-5506.... 146 A
aalle@blackburn.edu
ALLEN, Ann, M .... 217-854-5506.... 146 A
aalle@blackburn.edu
ALLEN, Anna, M .... 215-951-1374.... 432 I
aallen@lasalle.edu
ALLEN, Anna-Marie .... 304-929-1419.... 541 H
annamarie@mountainstate.edu
ALLEN, Anthony .... 718-933-6700.... 341 G
aallen@monroecollege.edu
ALLEN, Anthony, W .... 573-629-3252.... 282 E
anthony.allen@hlg.edu
ALLEN, B. Connie .... 919-516-4001.... 376 D
bcallen@st-aug.edu
ALLEN, Benjamin, J .... 319-273-2566.... 182 G
ben.allen@uni.edu
ALLEN, Bill .... 252-985-5111.... 375 E
ballen@ncwc.edu
ALLEN, Bob .... 260-484-4400.... 170 A
roallen@brownmackie.edu
ALLEN, Bonita .... 251-405-7053........ 2 C
ballen@bishop.edu
ALLEN, Bonnie .... 615-898-2772.... 473 G
bonnie.allen@mtsu.edu
ALLEN, Brenda .... 336-750-2200.... 380 B
allenba@wssu.edu
ALLEN, Brian .... 815-939-5258.... 161 A
ballen@olivet.edu
ALLEN, Brian, K .... 608-785-8558.... 551 C
ballen@uwlax.edu
ALLEN, JR., Calvin, H .... 540-665-4587.... 524 E
callen@su.edu
ALLEN, Carl .... 212-799-5000.... 337 H
ALLEN, Carol, M .... 443-412-2144.... 223 B
caallen@harford.edu
ALLEN, Carolyn, H .... 479-575-6702...... 24 C
challen@uark.edu
ALLEN, Catherine .... 605-361-0200.... 464 B
callen@sf.coloradotech.edu
ALLEN, Charles .... 650-949-6150...... 47 F
allencharles@fhda.edu
ALLEN, SJ, Charles, H ...... 203-254-4000...... 92 H
executive@fairfield.edu
ALLEN, Chaunda .... 225-578-4339.... 212 H
calle18@lsu.edu
ALLEN, Cindy .... 517-787-0800.... 252 J
allencynthiaa@jccmi.edu
ALLEN, Craig .... 817-257-7865.... 499 C
c.allen2@tcu.edu
ALLEN, Cynthia, A .... 757-789-1768.... 526 H
callen@es.vccs.edu
ALLEN, Dale .... 508-854-4337.... 240 F
dallen@qcc.mass.edu
ALLEN, Dana, G .... 757-683-3097.... 522 F
dallen@odu.edu
ALLEN, Daniel, T .... 267-502-2636.... 423 C
daniel.allen@brynathyn.edu
ALLEN, Darren .... 205-929-6361........ 5 E
dallen@lawsonstate.edu
ALLEN, David .... 817-923-1921.... 495 G
dallen@swbts.edu
ALLEN, David .... 508-678-2811.... 239 B
david.allen@bristolcc.edu
ALLEN, David .... 956-665-3510.... 506 C
allendh@utpa.edu
ALLEN, David, D .... 662-915-7265.... 277 D
allen@olemiss.edu
ALLEN, David, P .... 253-535-7524.... 536 E
david.allen@plu.edu
ALLEN, David, W .... 916-339-1500...... 58 D
dallen@mticollege.edu
ALLEN, Dee Dee .... 501-450-1228...... 22 A
allendd@hendrix.edu
ALLEN, Derick, A .... 573-840-9649.... 290 F
dallen@trcc.edu
ALLEN, Diane, D .... 410-548-3374.... 228 D
ddallen@salisbury.edu
ALLEN, Donna, Y .... 870-235-4012...... 23 I
dyallen@saumag.edu
ALLEN, Douglas, W .... 320-222-5202.... 268 G
douglas.allen@ridgewater.edu
ALLEN, OP,
Elizabeth Anne .... 615-297-7545.... 467 A
sreanne@aquinascollege.edu
ALLEN, Erin .... 704-991-0261.... 374 D
eallen4640@stanly.edu
ALLEN, Faye .... 864-646-1797.... 461 F
fallen@tctc.edu
ALLEN, Faye .... 281-998-6150.... 494 A
faye.allen@sjcd.edu
ALLEN, Forrest .... 432-685-4580.... 491 A
fallen@midland.edu
ALLEN, Gary, K .... 573-882-9200.... 291 A
allengk@umsystem.edu
ALLEN, Gary, K .... 573-882-9200.... 291 B
allengk@missouri.edu
ALLEN, Greg .... 402-557-7581.... 296 H
greg.allen@bellevue.edu
ALLEN, Gregg, N .... 207-780-5097.... 220 G
gregg@usm.maine.edu
ALLEN, Helen .... 205-348-7949........ 8 E
helen.allen@ua.edu
ALLEN, Hengameh, G .... 919-516-4488.... 376 D
hgallen@st-aug.edu
ALLEN, Hilary .... 919-760-8548.... 367 A
allenh@meredith.edu
ALLEN, Hilary .... 601-484-8699.... 275 A
hallen@meridiancc.edu
ALLEN, Ivan .... 478-757-3501.... 127 A
mmoye@centralgatech.edu
ALLEN, Jack .... 254-647-3234.... 492 G
jallen@rangercollege.edu
ALLEN, JR., James .... 301-387-3059.... 222 H
james.allen@garrettcollege.edu
ALLEN, JR., James .... 301-387-3006.... 222 H
james.allen@garrettcollege.edu
ALLEN, James, S .... 618-453-7653.... 165 B
jsallen@siu.ed
ALLEN, Janel, S .... 812-464-1756.... 181 B
jallen@usi.edu
ALLEN, Janine .... 503-581-8166.... 415 F
jallen@corban.edu
ALLEN, Jason .... 502-897-4142.... 206 C
jallen@sbts.edu
ALLEN, Jay .... 601-928-6250.... 275 E
jay.allen@mgccc.edu
ALLEN, Jeff .... 816-604-3063.... 285 D
jeff.allen@mcckc.edu
ALLEN, Jeffrey .... 612-332-3361.... 261 A
jallen@aii.edu
ALLEN, Jeffrey .... 814-536-5168.... 424 E
jallen@crbc.net
ALLEN, Jeffrey .... 724-463-0222.... 424 D
jallen@crbc.net
ALLEN, Jen .... 706-419-1119.... 128 B
jennifer.allen@covenant.edu
ALLEN, Jennie .... 909-447-2502...... 40 H
jallen@cst.edu
ALLEN, Jerry .... 510-594-3641...... 32 C
jallen@cca.edu
ALLEN, Jo .... 919-760-8511.... 367 A
jallen@meredith.edu
ALLEN, Joanne .... 559-438-4222...... 49 I
joanne_allen@heald.edu
ALLEN, Jodi .... 270-789-6229.... 199 F
jmallen@campbellsville.edu
ALLEN, Joel .... 704-991-0294.... 374 D
jallen7581@stanly.edu
ALLEN, John .... 217-824-4004.... 156 B
john.d.allen@doc.illinois.gov
ALLEN, John, C .... 435-797-1195.... 511 E
john.allen@usu.edu
ALLEN, John, M .... 718-270-2680.... 352 D
jallen@downstate.edu
ALLEN, Johnny, L .... 662-720-7226.... 276 C
jlallen@nemcc.edu
ALLEN, Joseph, L .... 864-242-5100.... 455 E
ALLEN, Joyce .... 206-296-2000.... 538 B
jallen@seattleu.edu
ALLEN, Judy .... 207-288-5015.... 217 H
jallen@coa.edu
ALLEN, Julian, O .... 404-413-4723.... 131 G
joallen@gsu.edu
ALLEN, Justin .... 540-535-3561.... 524 E
jallen3@su.edu
ALLEN, Kanya .... 270-707-3827.... 202 E
kanya.allen@kctcs.edu
ALLEN, Karen, H .... 919-742-2715.... 369 C
kallen@cccc.edu
ALLEN, Katherine .... 313-593-5300.... 259 B
kmaallen@umd.umich.edu
ALLEN, Kellie, L .... 606-326-2044.... 201 F
kellie.allen@kctcs.edu
ALLEN, Kent .... 405-425-5194.... 409 E
kent.allen@oc.edu
ALLEN, Kirsten .... 316-322-3192.... 191 G
kallen@butlercc.edu
ALLEN, Kitty .... 605-995-2612.... 464 C
kiallen1@dwu.edu
ALLEN, Lana .... 662-329-7409.... 276 A
thebookend@bkstr.com
ALLEN, Lawrence, R .... 864-656-7640.... 456 E
lalln@clemson.edu
ALLEN, Linda, A .... 319-296-4201.... 185 F
linda.allen@hawkeyecollege.edu
ALLEN, Linda, D .... 617-373-2307.... 243 F
ALLEN, Lonny .... 419-448-3359.... 402 E
lallen@tiffin.edu
ALLEN, Lori .... 575-527-7727.... 319 G
allen@nmsu.edu
ALLEN, Lori .... 312-942-8708.... 163 D
lori_j_allen@rush.edu
ALLEN, Mark .... 719-384-6830...... 87 A
mark.allen@ojc.edu
ALLEN, Mark .... 918-293-4830.... 410 E
mark.allen@okstate.edu
ALLEN, Mark, R .... 570-408-4103.... 452 A
mark.allen@wilkes.edu
ALLEN, Mary, E .... 302-477-2175...... 97 B
mallen@widener.edu
ALLEN, Mary Louise .... 610-896-1183.... 430 G
mlallen@haverford.edu
ALLEN, Max .... 910-962-3030.... 379 D
allenm@uncw.edu
ALLEN, Melissa .... 607-431-4130.... 335 A
allenm2@hartwick.edu
ALLEN, Michael .... 615-898-2840.... 473 G
michael.allen@mtsu.edu
ALLEN, Michael, L .... 901-678-2077.... 474 C
mlallen@memphis.edu
ALLEN, Michael, S .... 202-319-5286...... 97 E
allen@cua.edu
ALLEN, Michele .... 816-604-4023.... 285 E
michele.allen@mcckc.edu
ALLEN, Moira .... 214-828-8210.... 497 C
mallen@bcd.tamhsc.edu
ALLEN, Myrna, L .... 386-312-4249.... 116 F
myrnaallen@sjrstate.edu
ALLEN, Myron, B .... 307-766-4286.... 556 H
allen@uwyo.edu
ALLEN, Nancy .... 919-684-2965.... 364 C
nancy.allen@duke.edu
ALLEN, Nancy .... 325-942-2165.... 480 E
nancy.allen@angelo.edu
ALLEN, Nancy, T .... 303-871-2007...... 89 A
nallen@du.edu
ALLEN, Owen .... 336-887-3000.... 366 C
oallen@laureluniversity.edu
ALLEN, Patricia .... 718-951-5074.... 326 F
pallen@brooklyn.cuny.edu
ALLEN, Patrick .... 518-631-9875.... 358 H
allenp@uniongraduatecollege.edu
ALLEN, Patrick .... 503-554-2142.... 415 I
pallen@georgefox.edu
ALLEN, Paul .... 740-654-6711.... 400 C
allenp1@ohio.edu
ALLEN, Preston, C .... 805-756-1521...... 33 I
pallen@calpoly.edu
ALLEN, Preston, C .... 805-756-1226...... 33 I
pallen@calpoly.edu
ALLEN, Ray .... 410-225-2289.... 224 B
rallen@mica.edu
ALLEN, Rebecca, A .... 812-314-8533.... 176 A
rallen@ivytech.edu
ALLEN, Rosemary .... 502-863-8146.... 201 A
rosemary_allen@georgetowncollege.edu
ALLEN, Rusty .... 620-947-3121.... 197 A
rustya@tabor.edu
ALLEN, Samira .... 845-848-7407.... 332 B
samira.allen@dc.edu
ALLEN, JR., Samuel .... 603-641-7492.... 305 G
sallen@anselm.edu
ALLEN, Scott, T .... 203-596-4590...... 93 G
scallen@post.edu
ALLEN, Seth .... 909-621-8134...... 63 A
seth.allen@pomona.edu
ALLEN, Sharon .... 928-428-8342...... 14 B
sharon.allen@eac.edu
ALLEN, Sheila, W .... 706-542-3461.... 138 G
sallen01@uga.edu
ALLEN, Shelli .... 816-604-3175.... 285 D
shelli.allen@mcckc.edu
ALLEN, Stacey .... 505-566-3515.... 320 D
allens@sanjuancollege.edu
ALLEN, Stanley, T .... 609-258-3737.... 312 G
stallen@princeton.edu
ALLEN, Stephen .... 435-865-8499.... 511 D
allen@suu.edu
ALLEN, Steve .... 317-845-0100.... 178 D
ALLEN, Steve .... 606-539-4219.... 207 C
steve.allen@ucumberlands.edu
ALLEN, Susan .... 478-445-5650.... 130 B
susan.allen@gcsu.edu
ALLEN, Susan, K .... 603-862-3600.... 306 C
suzy.allen@unh.edu
ALLEN, T. Muriel .... 267-502-2632.... 423 C
muriel.allen@brynathyn.edu
ALLEN, Ted .... 503-554-2161.... 415 I
tallen@georgefox.edu
ALLEN, Teresa .... 912-287-5809.... 135 F
tallen@okefenokeetech.edu
ALLEN, Terry, D .... 859-257-8927.... 207 D
tallen@uky.edu
ALLEN, Thomas .... 845-437-7267.... 359 F
thallen@vassar.edu
ALLEN, Tim .... 360-473-1120.... 534 A
ALLEN, Tom .... 443-334-2955.... 226 E
tallen@stevenson.edu
ALLEN, Tom .... 864-977-7135.... 460 A
tom.allen@ngu.edu
ALLEN, Tony, M .... 731-989-6055.... 469 B
tallen@fhu.edu
ALLEN, W. Clayton .... 903-510-2507.... 503 A
call2@tjc.edu
ALLEN, William, R .... 530-898-5623...... 34 C
ballen@csuchico.edu
ALLEN, Xuri, M .... 340-693-1224.... 568 E
xallen@live.uvi.edu
ALLEN, Zachery .... 701-224-2524.... 382 D
zachery.allen@bismarckstate.edu
ALLEN-COVINO, Carol ...... 973-278-5400.... 307 F
cja@berkeleycollege.edu
ALLEN-DIAZ, Barbara, H ... 510-987-9359...... 73 G
barbara.allen-diaz@ucop.edu
ALLEN GRANT, Tameiko ... 904-731-4949.... 106 D
taallen@cci.edu
ALLEN-JONES, Vara .... 907-786-6471...... 10 H
afvda@uaa.alaska.edu
ALLEN-MEARES, Paula ...... 312-413-3350.... 167 A
pameares@uic.edu
ALLEN-MEARES, Paula ...... 312-413-3350.... 167 B
pameares@uic.edu
ALLEN-PERRY, Lynette ...... 215-572-2173.... 422 C
collins@arcadia.edu
ALLEN RYAN, Jenny .... 801-274-3280.... 512 F
jallenryan@wgu.edu
ALLEN-SHARPE,
Regina, C .... 302-356-6790...... 97 C
regina.a.sharpe@wilmu.edu
ALLENBY, Daniel .... 617-353-1068.... 232 E
dallenby@bu.edu
ALLER, Gary .... 202-448-6968...... 98 B
gary.aller@gallaudet.edu
ALLETTO, Philip .... 912-525-5000.... 136 F
palletto@scad.edu
ALLEVA, Joe .... 225-578-3600.... 212 H
athletics@lsu.edu
ALLEY, Ashlee, E .... 620-229-6362.... 196 G
ashlee.alley@sckans.edu
ALLEY, Brien .... 402-363-5624.... 301 E
balley@york.edu
ALLEY, Carolyn .... 828-694-1730.... 368 E
carolyna@blueridge.edu
ALLEY, Jerome .... 303-867-1155...... 90 A
alley@taftu.edu
ALLEY, Kathryn, E .... 605-394-6952.... 466 B
kate.jansak@sdsmt.edu
ALLEY, Kristen .... 660-359-3948.... 287 A
kalley@mail.ncmissouri.edu
ALLEY, Teresa, A .... 276-964-7266.... 528 E
teresa.alley@sw.edu
ALLGOOD, John .... 225-214-6975.... 214 C
john.allgood@ololcollege.edu
ALLIAS, Tami, L .... 412-578-8898.... 424 I
tlallias@carlow.edu
ALLIGOOD, Bennye, J .... 352-395-5182.... 117 F
bennye.alligood@sfcollege.edu
ALLIGOOD, Phillip, N .... 252-334-2014.... 367 C
phillip.alligood@macuniversity.edu
ALLINA, Babette .... 401-454-6317.... 454 B
ballina@risd.edu
ALLING, David, C .... 860-628-4751...... 93 C
dalling@lincolncollegene.edu
ALLING, Emily .... 802-258-9221.... 513 H
ealling@marlboro.edu
ALLIS, Celeste, H .... 336-342-4261.... 373 E
allisc@rockinghamcc.edu
ALLISON, Angela .... 559-934-2152...... 78 B
angelaallison@whccd.edu
ALLISON, Dale .... 808-236-5811.... 140 G
dallison@hpu.edu
ALLISON, Debra, A .... 313-529-5322.... 396 E
allisodh@muohio.edu
ALLISON, Jack, T .... 787-743-7979.... 565 H
jaallison@suagm.edu
ALLISON, JR., James, M .. 410-810-7490.... 229 D
jallison2@washcoll.edu
ALLISON, Jennifer, R .... 864-597-4030.... 463 G
allisonjr@wofford.edu
ALLISON, Jim .... 502-863-7922.... 201 A
jim_allison@georgetowncollege.edu
ALLISON, Lon, J .... 630-752-5918.... 168 H
lon.allison@wheaton.edu
ALLISON, Lorri .... 336-506-4133.... 368 A
lorri.allison@alamancecc.edu
ALLISON, M. Scott .... 540-375-2337.... 523 G
allison@roanoke.edu
ALLISON, Maria, T .... 480-965-7279...... 11 J
icmta@asu.edu
ALLISON, Mark .... 980-598-1430.... 365 I
mark.allison@jwu.edu
ALLISON, Patrick .... 360-736-9391.... 532 D
pallison@centralia.edu

AMELING, Brian, F ... 864-488-8200 ... 459 B
bameling@limestone.edu
AMELSBERG, James ... 641-585-8164 ... 189 I
amelsbergj@waldorf.edu
AMEN, Barbara, A ... 503-777-7259 ... 420 A
barbara.amen@reed.edu
AMEND, John ... 402-554-2242 ... 301 A
jamend@unomaha.edu
AMENDOLA, Shawnya ... 513-241-4338 ... 384 C
shawnya.amendola@antonellicollege.edu
AMENSON-HILL, Brenda ... 920-465-2159 ... 551 B
hillb@uwgb.edu
AMENT, Rebecca, R ... 740-588-1322 ... 407 A
bament@zanestate.edu
AMENTA, Paula ... 847-214-7717 ... 150 F
pamenta@elgin.edu
AMENTA, Peter, S ... 732-235-6300 ... 316 G
amenta@umdnj.edu
AMERIO, Barbara ... 661-763-7881 ... 72 E
bamerio@taftcollege.edu
AMERMAN, Jordan ... 928-350-4109 ... 17 K
jamerman@prescott.edu
AMERO, Carolina ... 678-466-4217 ... 127 D
carolinaamero@clayton.edu
AMERSHEK, Tom ... 620-235-4775 ... 196 C
tamershe@pittstate.edu
AMERSON, Philip, A ... 847-866-3901 ... 151 D
philip.amerson@garrett.edu
AMES, Christopher ... 410-778-7202 ... 229 D
cames2@washcoll.edu
AMES, Kim ... 330-869-3600 ... 385 H
kames@brownmackie.edu
AMES, Lynda, J ... 518-564-3310 ... 354 B
ameslj@plattsburgh.edu
AMES, Mark ... 405-382-9950 ... 412 B
m.ames@sscok.edu
AMES, Orrin ... 334-983-6556 ... 8 A
oames@troy.edu
AMES, Pam ... 714-997-6712 ... 39 F
ames@chapman.edu
AMES, Susan, E ... 315-445-4277 ... 338 B
amesse@lemoyne.edu
AMES, Suzy ... 253-864-3262 ... 536 H
sames@pierce.ctc.edu
AMES, Trevor, R ... 612-624-6244 ... 272 A
amesx001@umn.edu
AMES, W. Edward ... 407-582-5528 ... 123 B
eames@valenciacollege.edu
AMEY, Carol, J ... 859-858-3511 ... 198 E
camey@asbury.edu
AMICK, Michael ... 218-855-8268 ... 265 J
mamick@clcmn.edu
AMICK, Patricia, A ... 816-604-1130 ... 284 H
patricia.amick@mcckc.edu
AMICO, Theresa ... 727-725-2688 ... 106 F
tamico@cci.edu
AMIDON, Howard ... 978-921-4242 ... 242 C
howard.amidon@montserrat.edu
AMIDON, Jacob, E ... 585-785-1418 ... 334 A
amidonje@flcc.edu
AMIDON, James, L ... 765-361-6364 ... 181 E
amidonj@wabash.edu
AMIN, Sejal ... 630-652-8450 ... 149 C
samin@devry.edu
AMIN GUTIERREZ DE PINERES,
Sheila ... 972-883-6706 ... 506 A
pineres@utdallas.edu
AMIRIDIS, Michael ... 803-777-2808 ... 462 A
provost@sc.edu
AMIRTHARAJ, Merlin ... 704-991-0207 ... 374 D
mamirtharaj5283@stanly.edu
AMKRAUT, Brian, D ... 216-464-4050 ... 394 H
bamkraut@siegalcollege.edu
AMLANER, Charles, J ... 770-423-6738 ... 133 A
camlaner@kennesaw.edu
AMLER, Robert, W ... 914-594-4531 ... 343 F
robert_amler@nymc.edu
AMMAR, Mohamed ... 310-314-6030 ... 30 A
AMMAR, Salwa ... 718-862-7440 ... 339 H
salwa.ammar@manhattan.edu
AMMERMAN, Amy ... 281-998-6150 ... 493 G
amy.ammerman@sjcd.edu
AMMERMAN, Randy ... 920-686-6179 ... 550 H
randy.ammerman@sl.edu
AMMERMAN, Richard ... 973-655-5460 ... 311 F
ammermanr@mail.montclair.edu
AMMERMAN, Rocky ... 218-683-8540 ... 268 C
rocky.ammerman@northlandcollege.edu
AMMIDOWN, Darla ... 603-577-6533 ... 304 I
dammidown@dwc.edu
AMMIRATI, Theresa, P ... 860-439-2050 ... 92 G
tpamm@conncoll.edu
AMMON, Janice, S ... 609-497-7890 ... 312 F
chapel@ptsem.edu
AMMONS, Brian ... 828-298-3325 ... 380 D
bammons@warren-wilson.edu
AMMONS, Don ... 704-922-6240 ... 370 G
ammons.don@gaston.edu
AMMONS, James, H ... 850-599-3225 ... 118 L
james.ammons@famu.edu
AMMONS, Linda, L ... 302-477-2278 ... 97 B
llammons@widener.edu
AMOA, Kwesi ... 718-270-6450 ... 328 C
kamoa@mec.cuny.edu
AMODIO, Francis ... 845-569-3154 ... 342 A
francis.amodio@msmc.edu
AMODIO, Greg, J ... 412-396-5589 ... 428 D
amodiog@duq.edu
AMOKE, William ... 619-298-1829 ... 71 C
AMOO, Judith, L ... 308-635-6702 ... 301 D
amooj@wncc.edu
AMORE, Elizabeth ... 305-284-6266 ... 122 I
eamore@miami.edu
AMOROS, Blanca ... 787-758-2525 ... 567 G
blanca.amoros@upr.edu
AMORY, Deborah ... 518-587-2100 ... 355 G
deb.amory@esc.edu
AMOS, Anthea ... 850-484-4436 ... 115 B
aamos@pensacolastate.edu
AMOS, Kristy ... 909-868-4153 ... 44 K
kamos@devry.edu
AMOS, Maureen, T ... 773-442-5000 ... 160 A
m-amos@neiu.edu
AMOS, Ralph ... 310-206-8962 ... 74 C
ralphamos@support.ucla.edu
AMOS, Reid ... 304-336-5500 ... 544 D
ramos@westliberty.edu
AMOS, Stephanie, S ... 812-374-5113 ... 176 A
samos4@ivytech.edu
AMOS PALMER,
Susan, M ... 651-793-1823 ... 267 A
sueamos.palmer@metrostate.edu
AMOTT, Teresa, L ... 309-341-7210 ... 155 F
tamott@knox.edu
AMOUZEGAR, Mahyar ... 909-869-2472 ... 33 J
mahyar@csupomona.edu
AMPARO, Frank ... 623-935-8872 ... 15 F
frank.amparo@estrellamountain.edu
AMPERSAND, Stephen ... 410-287-1003 ... 222 A
sampersand@cecil.edu
AMPUERO, Rosemary ... 212-774-0739 ... 340 C
rampuero@mmm.edu
AMREIN, Mark ... 865-288-6810 ... 19 A
mark.amrein@phoenix.edu
AMRIKHAS, Violet ... 818-947-2533 ... 55 E
amrikhv@lavc.edu
AMRIR, Dacuia ... 310-577-3000 ... 80 E
admissions@yosan.edu
AMROZOWICZ, Barbara ... 716-896-0700 ... 359 H
amrozowicz@villa.edu
AMSELMI, Michael, A ... 410-704-4008 ... 228 E
manselmi@towson.edu
AMSPAUGH, Melissa, A ... 440-525-7357 ... 394 F
mamspaugh@lakelandcc.edu
AMSTER, Yosef ... 516-295-5700 ... 361 N
AMSTUTZ, Margaret, A ... 706-542-0054 ... 138 G
mamstutz@uga.edu
AMSTUTZ, Marilyn ... 402-449-2849 ... 297 H
mamstutz@graceu.edu
AMUNDSEN, Scott ... 714-816-0366 ... 73 B
scott.amundsen@trident.edu
AMUNDSON, Elizabeth, A ... 202-994-4900 ... 98 C
amundson@gwu.edu
AMUNDSON, Jeffrey, R ... 608-757-7766 ... 553 G
jamundson@blackhawk.edu
AMYOT, Maribeth ... 513-745-3445 ... 406 E
amyotm@xavier.edu
AMYX, Tim ... 615-230-3614 ... 476 C
tim.amyx@volstate.edu
AN, Nana ... 202-885-2729 ... 97 D
nanaan@american.edu
ANAHITA, Sine ... 907-474-6515 ... 10 I
sine.anahita@alaska.edu
ANALISTA, Norman ... 671-735-2586 ... 559 G
nanalista@uguam.uog.edu
ANAND, Brij, B ... 718-990-6350 ... 348 G
anandb@stjohns.edu
ANANDALINGAM,
G. Anand ... 301-405-2308 ... 227 B
ganand@rhsmith.umd.edu
ANANOU, Simeon ... 724-738-2522 ... 443 F
simeon.ananou@sru.edu
ANASAGASTI, Rogelio ... 713-718-5001 ... 487 I
rogelio.anasagasti@hccs.edu
ANASTASIO, Denise ... 847-543-2444 ... 148 B
danastasio@clcillinois.edu
ANASTASIOU, Maria ... 803-641-3671 ... 462 B
maria@usca.edu
ANASTASSIOU, Pamela, L ... 928-523-2109 ... 16 I
pamela.anastassiou@nau.edu
ANAWALT, Deborah ... 410-626-2504 ... 225 G
debbie.anawalt@sjca.edu
ANAYA, Angela ... 505-888-8898 ... 320 G
financialaid@acupuncturecollege.edu
ANAYA, Jose ... 310-660-6464 ... 45 E
janaya@elcamino.edu
ANCELL, Jack ... 434-949-1066 ... 528 D
jack.ancell@southside.edu
ANCH, Vincent, M ... 816-604-1411 ... 284 H
vincent.anch@mcckc.edu
ANCHOR, Rebecca, E ... 585-245-5100 ... 353 C
anchor@geneseo.edu
ANCI, Diane ... 413-538-2515 ... 242 D
danci@mtholyoke.edu
ANCONA, Jorge ... 949-824-9741 ... 74 B
jancona@uci.edu
ANCTIL, Robin ... 641-844-5571 ... 186 B
robin.anctil@iavalley.edu
ANCTIL, Robin ... 641-844-5571 ... 186 D
robin.anctil@iavalley.edu
ANDALMAN, Julia ... 214-658-8800 ... 508 D
jandalman@wadecollege.edu
ANDE, Taiwo, A ... 540-654-1282 ... 525 D
tande@umw.edu
ANDERECK, Barbara, S ... 740-368-3773 ... 400 G
bsandere@owu.edu
ANDERLEY, Gerald, M ... 651-962-6531 ... 272 B
gmanderley@stthomas.edu
ANDERMAN, Lynea ... 610-892-1524 ... 441 C
landerman@pit.edu
ANDERS, Lee ... 620-862-5252 ... 190 G
andle@barclaycollege.edu
ANDERS, Peter, J ... 717-872-3433 ... 443 D
peter.anders@millersville.edu
ANDERS, Steven ... 641-784-5178 ... 185 B
anders@graceland.edu
ANDERSEN, Belinda ... 212-982-3456 ... 345 G
ANDERSEN, Charles, N ... 208-496-1124 ... 143 A
andersenc@byui.edu
ANDERSEN, Jim ... 209-384-6396 ... 57 C
andersen.j@mccd.edu
ANDERSEN, Kathy ... 717-728-2503 ... 425 B
kathyandersens@centralpenn.edu
ANDERSEN, Kent ... 205-226-4679 ... 2 B
kanderse@bsc.edu
ANDERSEN, Kent, A ... 307-674-6446 ... 556 F
kandersen@sheridan.edu
ANDERSEN, Laura, A ... 269-337-7248 ... 252 K
laura.andersen@kzoo.edu
ANDERSEN, Margaret ... 302-831-2101 ... 96 I
mla@udel.edu
ANDERSEN, Mark, N ... 307-686-0254 ... 556 F
mandersen@sheridan.edu
ANDERSEN, Mary ... 719-775-8873 ... 86 G
mary.andersen@morgancc.edu
ANDERSEN, Mike ... 831-656-2845 ... 558 A
manderse@nps.edu
ANDERSEN, Patricia, M ... 605-394-1261 ... 466 B
patricia.andersen@sdsmt.edu
ANDERSEN, Richard ... 757-822-1970 ... 528 G
randersen@tcc.edu
ANDERSEN, Robert ... 309-298-2446 ... 168 C
r-andersen@wiu.edu
ANDERSEN, Russ ... 402-557-7069 ... 296 H
russ.andersen@bellevue.edu
ANDERSEN, Sherry ... 508-362-2131 ... 239 D
sanderse@capecod.edu
ANDERSEN, Thomas, K ... 334-953-7442 ... 557 D
ANDERSEN, Thomas Ove ... 828-884-8320 ... 362 H
ove.andersen@brevard.edu
ANDERSON, Aime ... 662-562-3305 ... 276 D
aanderson@northwestms.edu
ANDERSON, Al ... 406-275-4833 ... 296 D
al_anderson@skc.edu
ANDERSON, Alex ... 215-780-1270 ... 446 G
alex@salus.edu
ANDERSON, Alice ... 219-989-2335 ... 178 K
andersag@purduecal.edu
ANDERSON, Amy ... 813-253-7264 ... 110 M
aanderson@hccfl.edu
ANDERSON, Amy ... 269-782-1367 ... 258 C
aanderson@swmich.edu
ANDERSON, Amy, A ... 212-749-2802 ... 339 I
admission@msmnyc.edu
ANDERSON, Andrew ... 207-780-5585 ... 220 G
aanders@usm.maine.edu
ANDERSON, Angela ... 970-521-6659 ... 86 K
angela.anderson@njc.edu
ANDERSON, Angela, D ... 301-322-0699 ... 225 F
andersad@pgcc.edu
ANDERSON, Angela, R ... 252-328-6747 ... 377 E
andersona@ecu.edu
ANDERSON, Antje ... 402-461-7351 ... 298 A
aanderson@hastings.edu
ANDERSON, Art ... 406-496-4399 ... 296 B
aanderson@mtech.edu
ANDERSON, Arthur ... 406-496-4399 ... 296 A
aanderson@mtech.edu
ANDERSON, Barbara ... 660-248-6320 ... 279 G
banderso@centralmethodist.edu
ANDERSON, Barbara ... 206-708-4995 ... 200 K
barbara.anderson@frontier.edu
ANDERSON, Barry, L ... 901-334-5806 ... 471 E
banderson@memphisseminary.edu
ANDERSON, Belinda, C ... 757-823-8118 ... 522 E
bcanderson@nsu.edu
ANDERSON, Ben ... 859-572-5282 ... 205 H
andersonb5@nku.edu
ANDERSON, Benjamin, J ... 828-298-3325 ... 380 D
benjand@warren-wilson.edu
ANDERSON, Beth ... 937-376-6588 ... 387 A
banderson@centralstate.edu
ANDERSON, Beth ... 423-461-8316 ... 471 J
banderson@milligan.edu
ANDERSON, Beth ... 218-322-2451 ... 266 G
beth.anderson@itascacc.edu
ANDERSON, Betty, H ... 337-475-5127 ... 215 G
anderson@mcneese.edu
ANDERSON, Betty, L ... 573-629-3055 ... 282 E
banderson@hlg.edu
ANDERSON, Bobby ... 209-386-6730 ... 57 C
robert.anderson@mccd.edu
ANDERSON, Brett, B ... 970-491-7530 ... 83 F
brett.anderson@colostate.edu
ANDERSON, Bridges ... 334-222-6591 ... 5 F
banderson@lbwcc.edu
ANDERSON, Bridgette ... 845-431-8655 ... 332 D
banderso@sunydutchess.edu
ANDERSON, Bruce, W ... 651-635-8051 ... 261 D
bw-anderson@bethel.edu
ANDERSON, C. Colt ... 718-817-4802 ... 334 C
coltanderson@fordham.edu
ANDERSON, Carl, A ... 202-526-3799 ... 99 D
ANDERSON, Carsbia ... 831-646-4191 ... 57 G
canderson@mpc.edu
ANDERSON, Cary, M ... 610-660-1045 ... 446 C
cander01@sju.edu
ANDERSON, Cathleen, R ... 315-445-4300 ... 338 B
anderscr@lemoyne.edu
ANDERSON, Cathy ... 302-736-2410 ... 97 A
andersca@wesley.edu
ANDERSON, Cathy ... 605-394-4034 ... 466 F
cathy.anderson@wdt.edu
ANDERSON, Cathy ... 801-581-6940 ... 511 C
cathy.anderson@hsc.utah.edu
ANDERSON, JR., Charles ... 606-436-5721 ... 202 C
chuck.anderson@kctcs.edu
ANDERSON, Charlotte ... 785-227-3380 ... 191 B
andersonc@bethanylb.edu
ANDERSON, Cheryl ... 210-829-3837 ... 504 B
cheryla@uiwtx.edu
ANDERSON, Cheryl, A ... 315-255-1743 ... 325 G
cheryl.anderson@cayuga-cc.edu
ANDERSON, Chris, S ... 906-487-3539 ... 255 B
csanders@mtu.edu
ANDERSON, Christi ... 806-894-9611 ... 494 G
canderson@southplainscollege.edu
ANDERSON, Christina ... 815-394-4388 ... 163 A
canderson@rockford.edu
ANDERSON, Cindy, L ... 304-558-4016 ... 543 E
canderson@hepc.wvnet.edu
ANDERSON, Corey, R ... 541-684-7354 ... 417 F
canderson@nwcu.edu
ANDERSON, Cynthia, E ... 330-941-3101 ... 406 F
ceanderson@ysu.edu
ANDERSON, D. Craig ... 804-752-7270 ... 523 C
canderson@rmc.edu
ANDERSON, Dale, N ... 206-281-2483 ... 537 H
dale@spu.edu
ANDERSON, Dale, O ... 301-405-5648 ... 227 B
danderso@umd.edu
ANDERSON, Dan, J ... 515-574-2813 ... 185 I
anderson_dan@iowacentral.edu
ANDERSON, Daniel, J ... 336-278-7410 ... 364 D
andersd@elon.edu
ANDERSON, Daniel, L ... 304-877-6428 ... 540 G
president@abc.edu
ANDERSON, Danny ... 901-722-3204 ... 473 C
danderson@sco.edu
ANDERSON, Danny, J ... 785-864-3661 ... 197 B
djand@ku.edu
ANDERSON, Daryl ... 718-779-1430 ... 346 B
danderson1@mail.plazacollege.edu
ANDERSON, Dave ... 609-984-1164 ... 316 A
danderson@tesc.edu
ANDERSON, Dave ... 877-476-8674 ... 487 A
ANDERSON, David ... 949-582-4835 ... 70 F
danderson@saddleback.edu
ANDERSON, David ... 405-682-1611 ... 409 F
danderson@occc.edu
ANDERSON, David, R ... 507-786-3000 ... 271 C
anderson@stolaf.edu
ANDERSON, Dawn, L ... 619-260-7733 ... 76 D
dawn@sandiego.edu
ANDERSON, Deborah ... 812-429-1387 ... 177 C
danderson128@ivytech.edu
ANDERSON, Deborah ... 575-769-4081 ... 318 A
deborah.anderson@clovis.edu
ANDERSON, Deborah ... 906-786-5802 ... 248 I
andersod@baycollege.edu
ANDERSON, Dee Dee ... 423-425-4761 ... 477 F
deedee-anderson@utc.edu
ANDERSON, Delia, C ... 617-732-2910 ... 241 C
delia.anderson@mcphs.edu
ANDERSON, Demetria, B ... 330-569-5182 ... 391 G
andersondb@hiram.edu
ANDERSON, Diane, K ... 269-387-2152 ... 260 C
diane.anderson@wmich.edu
ANDERSON, Dianna ... 704-886-6500 ... 99 G
ANDERSON, Dianne ... 505-277-1807 ... 321 C
ANDERSON, Don, K ... 515-964-0601 ... 185 A
andersond@faith.edu
ANDERSON, Donna ... 607-431-4827 ... 335 A
andersond@hartwick.edu
ANDERSON, Donna, M ... 941-359-6116 ... 116 B
danderso@ringling.edu
ANDERSON, Dorothy ... 575-646-1694 ... 319 D
dtanders@nmsu.edu
ANDERSON, Doug ... 701-845-7227 ... 382 C
doug.anderson@vcsu.edu
ANDERSON, Douglas, A ... 814-863-1484 ... 438 G
daa7@psu.edu
ANDERSON, Douglas, D ... 435-797-2376 ... 511 E
douglas.anderson@usu.edu
ANDERSON, Douglas, P ... 651-523-2203 ... 264 A
danderson@hamline.edu

ANDRESS, Reinhard 773-508-3505 157 C
randress@luc.edu
ANDRESS-MARTIN, Holly . 583-288-6421 280 I
ANDREU, Angel, E 585-292-3031 341 H
aandreu@monroecc.edu
ANDREU, Frank 305-821-3333 109 B
fandreu@mm.fnc.edu
ANDREU, Frank 305-821-3333 109 D
fandreu@mm.fnc.edu
ANDREU, Frank 305-821-3333 109 C
fandreu@mm.fnc.edu
ANDREW, Aletha 919-735-5151 375 A
raandrew@waynecc.edu
ANDREW, Damon 334-670-3712 8 A
dandrew@troy.edu
ANDREW, Matt 314-968-6955 292 J
matthewandrew91@webster.edu
ANDREW, Sylvia, R 505-863-7501 321 D
sandrew@gallup.unm.edu
ANDREWS, Aaron 870-759-4105 26 B
aandrews@wbcoll.edu
ANDREWS, Adrienne 530-642-5644 56 C
ANDREWS, Arthur, W 919-866-5688 374 H
awandrews@waketech.edu
ANDREWS, Bev 269-467-9945 251 B
bandrews@glenoaks.edu
ANDREWS, Beverly 269-467-9945 251 B
bandrews@glenoaks.edu
ANDREWS, Brad, J 262-551-5850 546 I
bandrews@carthage.edu
ANDREWS, Brett 918-335-6250 411 B
bandrews@okwu.edu
ANDREWS, Carolyn 806-291-3400 508 E
andrewsc@wbu.edu
ANDREWS, Chip, L 770-534-6759 126 E
candrews@brenau.edu
ANDREWS, Cyndi 503-594-3025 415 A
cyndia@clackamas.edu
ANDREWS, Cynthia, H 804-828-0177 526 B
candrews@vcu.edu
ANDREWS, Danielle 614-885-5585 401 B
dandrews@pcj.edu
ANDREWS, Danny 806-291-3600 508 E
andrewsd@wbu.edu
ANDREWS, David, W 410-516-7820 223 F
davidandrews@jhu.edu
ANDREWS, Dewayne 405-271-3223 413 D
dewayne-andrews@ouhsc.edu
ANDREWS, Dianna, L 904-264-2172 116 C
dianna.andrews@iws.edu
ANDREWS, Dionne, T 304-457-6324 540 E
andrewsdt@ab.edu
ANDREWS, Don 423-697-4747 474 D
ANDREWS, Donald, R 225-771-5640 214 I
jazandrews@yahoo.com
ANDREWS, Douglas, M 863-784-7177 117 J
doug.andrews@southflorida.edu
ANDREWS, Evelyn 707-654-1794 33 C
eandrews@csum.edu
ANDREWS, George 305-237-3316 113 H
gandrews@mdc.edu
ANDREWS, Gregg, L 330-339-3391 394 A
gandrews@kent.edu
ANDREWS, Herry 307-778-1231 556 E
handrews@lccc.wy.edu
ANDREWS, Jacqueline 845-257-3227 352 B
andrewsj@newpaltz.edu
ANDREWS, Jeff 601-318-6741 278 C
jeff.andrews@wmcarey.edu
ANDREWS, John, L 562-624-9530 80 B
jandrews@cci.edu
ANDREWS, Karen, B 770-423-6555 133 A
kandrews@kennesaw.edu
ANDREWS, Karren 541-880-2203 416 D
andrews@klamathcc.edu
ANDREWS, Laura, B 603-283-2128 303 F
landrews@antioch.edu
ANDREWS, Lenora 716-286-8708 344 D
laa@niagara.edu
ANDREWS, Leslie, A 859-858-2206 198 D
ANDREWS, Linda 713-798-4606 481 H
landrews@bcm.edu
ANDREWS, Linda 434-544-8324 521 B
andrews@lynchburg.edu
ANDREWS, Loretta 406-447-4508 293 G
landrews@carroll.edu
ANDREWS, M. Dewayne 405-271-2332 413 D
dewayne-andrews@ouhsc.edu
ANDREWS, Margaret 810-762-3420 259 C
mmandrew@umflint.edu
ANDREWS, Mark 770-228-7367 137 F
mandrews@sctech.edu
ANDREWS, Michael, F 503-943-8628 420 G
andrews@up.edu
ANDREWS, Mitch 903-510-2034 503 A
mand@tjc.edu
ANDREWS, Nancy 919-684-2455 364 C
nancy.andrews@mc.duke.edu
ANDREWS, Nikki 508-373-9701 231 B
nikki.andrews@becker.edu
ANDREWS, Penny 518-445-2321 322 C
pandr@albanylaw.edu
ANDREWS, Richard 916-691-7423 56 B
andrewr@crc.losrios.edu
ANDREWS, Robert 510-885-4297 34 E
robert.andrews@csueastbay.edu
ANDREWS, Sabrina, L 330-972-6959 403 B
sabrin7@uakron.edu
ANDREWS, Sarah 415-257-1333 45 C
sarah.andrews@dominican.edu
ANDREWS, Sona 503-725-5257 418 G
asona@pdx.edu
ANDREWS, Susan 309-677-3296 146 C
susancan@bradley.edu
ANDREWS, Tim 913-360-7367 191 A
tandrews@benedictine.edu
ANDREWS, Todd, G 401-863-6331 453 B
todd_andrews@brown.edu
ANDREWS, Todd, J 860-727-6937 92 I
tandrews@goodwin.edu
ANDREWS, Trisha 847-543-2007 148 B
tandrews@clcillinois.edu
ANDREWS, Wayne, D 606-783-2022 204 I
w.andrews@moreheadstate.edu
ANDRIANO, Sarah 802-865-5740 513 C
sandriano@champlain.edu
ANDRIATCH, Michael 585-395-5809 352 F
mandriat@brockport.edu
ANDRIEN, Susan 415-485-9552 42 B
susan.andrien@marin.edu
ANDRIOTIS-BAITINGER,
Katerina 908-737-7030 311 A
andriotk@kean.edu
ANDRIS, Mary Kate 757-455-2136 530 C
mandris@vwc.edu
ANDRITZ, Mary, H 317-940-9735 170 F
mandritz@butler.edu
ANDROUIN, George 904-620-4222 120 D
gandroui@unf.edu
ANDRUS, Michael 704-334-6882 367 H
mandrus@nlts.edu
ANDRUSKI, Mike 619-321-3052 29 G
mandruski@argosy.edu
ANDRUSKI, Mike 909-472-0639 29 D
mandruski@argosy.edu
ANDRUSKI, Mike 909-472-0639 29 E
mandruski@argosy.edu
ANDRZEJEWSKI, Margaret 716-827-2564 358 D
andrzejewskim@trocaire.edu
ANDRZJEWSKI, Linda, M . 302-356-6754 97 C
linda.m.andrzjewski@wilmu.edu
ANDUJAR-WENDLAND,
Sandra 212-686-9040 360 F
s.andujar@woodtobecoburn.edu
ANEMA, Laurie 708-974-5343 159 B
anema@morainevalley.edu
ANER, Max 954-965-7272 107 H
maner@careercollege.edu
ANG, Helen, C 773-442-5110 160 A
h-ang@neiu.edu
ANGE, Crystal 252-940-6216 368 C
crystala@beaufortccc.edu
ANGEL, Daniel, D 415-442-6570 48 F
dangel@ggu.edu
ANGEL, David, P 508-793-7320 233 B
dangel@clarku.edu
ANGELES, Rocio 805-893-6189 75 B
rangeles@ltsc.ucsb.edu
ANGELIS, Peter 310-825-4941 74 C
pangelis@ha.ucla.edu
ANGELL, Alecia 509-527-3683 539 B
alecia.angell@wwcc.edu
ANGELL, Lance, R 270-707-3709 202 E
lance.angell@kctcs.edu
ANGELL, Mary 505-473-6322 320 F
mary.angell@santafeuniversity.edu
ANGELL, Townsend 503-777-7283 420 A
townsend.angell@reed.edu
ANGELO, Caroline 706-355-5013 125 C
cangelo@athenstech.edu
ANGELO, Dan 909-384-4400 65 C
dangelo@sbccd.cc.ca.us
ANGELONE, Lenora 724-938-4439 441 G
angelone@calu.edu
ANGELONI, Lisa 609-771-3080 308 F
angeloni@tcnj.edu
ANGELOTTI, Linda 408-855-5123 78 F
linda.angelotti@wvm.edu
ANGEMI, Karen 909-621-8384 49 F
karen_angemi@hmc.edu
ANGER, Donna 907-474-6131 10 I
dmanger@alaska.edu
ANGER, Paul 928-428-6260 14 B
paul.anger@eac.edu
ANGERINE, Roger, L 606-878-4801 203 C
rogerl.angerine@kctcs.edu
ANGIER, Kendra 714-338-1710 19 A
kendra.angier@phoenix.edu
ANGIOLLIO, Elise 561-297-0202 119 A
elise@fau.edu
ANGIS, Victoria 802-468-1231 515 D
victoria.angis@castleton.edu
ANGLE, J. Scott 706-542-3924 138 G
caesdean@uga.edu
ANGLE, Nick 517-629-0305 247 A
nangle@albion.edu
ANGLE, Ray 919-962-4481 378 E
rayangle@email.unc.edu
ANGLE, Steven, R 937-775-3035 406 C
steven.angle@wright.edu
ANGLIM, Sean 315-568-3092 342 H
sanglim@nycc.edu
ANGLIN, Marcus 213-763-7227 55 D
anglimj@lattc.edu
ANGLIN, Mark 209-575-2000 80 H
anglinm@mjc.edu
ANGLIN, Pamela, D 903-785-7661 492 D
panglin@parisjc.edu
ANGRISANI, Vincent 718-997-5600 328 E
vincent.angrisani@qc.cuny.edu
ANGST, JR., Arthur, H 516-876-3094 353 D
angsta@oldwestbury.edu
ANGSTADT, Peter 541-956-7000 420 B
pangstadt@roguecc.edu
ANGSTER, Sherrie 626-966-4576 28 F
studentservices@agu.edu
ANGULO, Susan, B 305-628-6566 117 A
sangulo@stu.edu
ANID, Nada 516-686-7931 343 D
nanid@nyit.edu
ANKE, Sharla, M 724-287-8711 423 G
sharla.anke@bc3.edu
ANKENBAUER, Marilyn 817-923-8459 483 G
marilyn.ankenbauer@fishermore.edu
ANKENY, Mark 503-352-1431 419 E
anke9541@pacificu.edu
ANKER, Laura, M 516-876-3460 353 D
ankerl@oldwestbury.edu
ANKER, Perryne 310-824-1586 26 D
ANKER, Steve 661-255-1050 32 F
sanker@calarts.edu
ANKERSEN, Lynne 843-574-6137 461 G
lynne.ankersen@tridenttech.edu
ANKROM, Jeff, A 937-327-6231 406 B
jankrom@wittenberg.edu
ANKTON, Darlene, S 760-747-3990 41 G
dankton@coleman.edu
ANKUDA, Pamela 802-728-1530 516 A
pankuda@vtc.vsc.edu
ANNA, Gary, M 309-677-3150 146 C
gma@bradley.edu
ANNAN, Jack 970-521-6690 86 K
jack.annan@njc.edu
ANNARELLI, James, J 727-864-8421 105 E
annarejj@eckerd.edu
ANNETT, JR., Bruce, J 248-204-2200 254 B
bannett@ltu.edu
ANNETTE, Harold 218-322-2353 266 G
harold.annette@itascacc.edu
ANNING, Peter 408-855-5125 78 F
peter.anning@wvm.edu
ANNINO, Louis 203-932-7153 95 C
lannino@newhaven.edu
ANNIS, David, L 405-325-2300 413 C
dannis@ou.edu
ANNIS, Dominique, A 815-740-3398 167 E
dannis@stfrancis.edu
ANNIS, Patricia, O 207-942-6781 217 B
pannis@bts.edu
ANNIS, Robert, L 609-921-7100 313 F
annis@rider.edu
ANNUNZIATO, Frank 215-204-7366 447 H
frank.annunziato@temple.edu
ANOUBI, Amjad 504-865-5107 215 C
aamjad@tulane.edu
ANSARI, Parviz 856-256-4850 314 A
ansari@rowan.edu
ANSARI, Shahid 781-239-4277 230 E
sansari@babson.edu
ANSARY, Omid 717-948-6103 439 J
axa8@psu.edu
ANSBOURY, Pamela 210-485-0307 479 A
pansboury@alamo.edo
ANSEL, Stuart 718-252-7800 358 B
sansel@touro.edu
ANSELMENT, Kenneth, L 920-832-6992 548 B
ken.anselment@lawrence.edu
ANSLEY, Rhett 903-589-4003 490 D
ransley@lonmorris.edu
ANSLEY, Sharon, L 228-896-9727 273 D
ANSON, Heather 918-835-8288 414 B
heather.anson@vatterott-college.edu
ANSON, Regan 402-872-2429 299 F
ranson@peru.edu
ANSORGE, Vicki 920-686-6203 550 H
vicki.ansorge@sl.edu
ANSTROM, Deborah 828-298-3325 380 D
purchasing@warren-wilson.edu
ANSTROM, Deborah 828-298-3325 380 D
danstrom@warren-wilson.edu
ANTARAMIAN, John, M 262-551-5955 546 I
jantaramian@carthage.edu
ANTCZAK, Frederick 616-331-2495 251 F
antczakf@gvsu.edu
ANTEL, John 832-842-0550 503 D
jantel@uh.edu
ANTEL, John, J 713-743-9101 503 C
antel@uh.edu
ANTEL, Lisa 203-596-4585 93 G
lantel@post.edu
ANTENEN, James 210-826-7595 508 E
antenenj@wbu.edu
ANTENORCRUC, Connie 714-953-6500 46 B
ANTENUCCI, Lindsay 818-785-2726 38 K
ANTER, Dave 310-314-6076 30 A
ANTES, Joann, B 570-372-4049 447 E
antes@susqu.edu
ANTHONY, Booker, T 910-672-1347 377 G
banthony@uncfsu.edu
ANTHONY, Cromartie 973-877-1873 309 H
cromartie@essex.edu
ANTHONY, Cynthia 205-929-3510 5 E
canthony@lawsonstate.edu
ANTHONY, David, D 540-665-4581 524 E
danthony@su.edu
ANTHONY, Jonetta, C 219-981-4404 176 G
janthony@ivytech.edu
ANTHONY, Kathy 610-526-6045 430 D
kanthony@harcum.edu
ANTHONY, Lewis 301-736-3631 224 A
lewis.anthony@msbbcs.edu
ANTHONY, Linda 410-843-8217 272 C
linda.anthony@laureate.net
ANTHONY, Lorraine 518-587-2100 355 G
lorraine.anthony@esc.edu
ANTHONY, Mark, E 724-357-2235 442 F
anthony@iup.edu
ANTHONY, Neil 465-289-2291 176 B
nanthony@ivytech.edu
ANTHONY, Pamela 515-294-1022 182 E
ANTHONY, Patrick 404-385-7344 130 F
patrick.anthony@dopp.gatech.edu
ANTHONY, Richard, M 202-408-2400 99 G
ANTHONY, Sharon 215-572-2850 422 C
anthony@arcadia.edu
ANTHWAL, Sunny 845-398-4061 349 H
sunny@stac.edu
ANTILLA, Margaret 503-338-2428 415 B
mantilla@clatsopcc.edu
ANTILLON, Susan 386-506-3656 104 F
antills@daytonastate.edu
ANTKOWIAK, Alex 410-337-6060 222 I
alex.antkowiak@goucher.edu
ANTMAN, Karen, H 617-638-5300 232 E
kha4@bu.edu
ANTOINE, Kevin 718-270-1738 352 D
kevin.antoine@downstate.edu
ANTOINE, Linda, B 225-771-4580 214 I
linda_antoine@subr.edu
ANTOKHIN, Kathleen 510-649-2463 48 J
kantokhin@gtu.edu
ANTOKHIN, Kathleen 510-649-2469 40 A
kantokhin@gtu.edu
ANTOMMARCHI, Hilda 787-815-0000 567 A
hilda.antommarchi@upr.edu
ANTON, Janis, K 312-777-8508 153 B
janton@aii.edu
ANTONACCI, Heather 407-215-9705 110 L
heathera@orl.herzing.edu
ANTONELLI, Mona, L 608-757-7655 553 G
mantonelli@blackhawk.edu
ANTONIA, Keith 706-867-2712 134 G
kantonia@northgeorgia.edu
ANTONIAK, Karen, M 724-836-7116 449 C
kma4@pitt.edu
ANTONICH, Cheryl 708-456-0300 166 F
cantonic@triton.edu
ANTONIO, Andrew 765-269-5241 176 D
aantonio@ivytech.edu
ANTONIO, Edward 303-765-3163 85 D
eantonio@iliff.edu
ANTONS, Christopher, M 210-431-6718 493 F
cantons@stmarytx.edu
ANTONUCCI, Carl 860-832-2099 90 G
antonucci@ccsu.edu
ANTONUCCI, Dorothy, M 412-578-8770 424 I
dmantonucci@carlow.edu
ANTONUCCI, Frank 716-896-0700 359 H
antonucci@villa.edu
ANTONUCCI, Robert, V 978-665-3101 237 E
rantonucci@fitchburgstate.edu
ANTONUCCI, Toni, C 734-763-5846 259 A
tca@umich.edu
ANTOSH, Deeanna, L 409-944-1208 486 K
dantosh@gc.edu
ANTROBUS, Barbara 859-858-2285 198 D
ANTUN, AJ 213-251-3636 29 J
ajantun@aii.edu
ANTUN, AJ 310-314-6049 30 A
ANTUNES, Marie 540-636-2900 517 K
alumni@christendom.edu
ANTURKAR, Anjali, N 734-764-5132 259 A
anturkar@umich.edu
ANUZZI, Carmen 484-384-2976 438 D
canuzzi@eastern.edu
ANYANWU, Fitzpatrick, U 337-491-2648 212 E
fitzpatrick.anyanwu@sowela.edu
ANZ, Susan 254-710-8641 482 A
susan_anz@baylor.edu
ANZALDVA, Ricardo 212-237-8316 327 F
ANZALONE, Roseann 518-743-2242 355 D
anzalonr@sunyacc.edu
ANZELONE, Paulette, A 716-839-8214 331 F
panzelon@daemen.edu
AOUN, Joseph, E 617-373-2101 243 F

ARMOUR, Angela ... 802-654-2527 ... 514 D aarmour@smcvt.edu
ARMOUR, Catherine ... 202-639-1803 ... 98 A carmour@corcoran.org
ARMOUR, Janet, Y ... 662-842-5192 ... 274 E jyamour@iccms.edu
ARMOUR, Lisa ... 352-381-3642 ... 117 F lisa.armour@sfcollege.edu
ARMOUR, Mary Alice ... 724-805-2209 ... 446 E maryalice.armour@email.stvincent.edu
ARMOUR, Robert ... 606-546-1799 ... 207 B rarmour@unionky.edu
ARMOUR, Robin ... 925-439-2181 ... 43 G rarmour@losmedanos.edu
ARMOZA, Marcela ... 718-260-4999 ... 328 D marmoza@citytech.cuny.edu
ARMS, Gina ... 719-389-6323 ... 82 D garms@coloradocollege.edu
ARMSTEAD, Beth ... 505-287-6628 ... 319 H barmstea@nmsu.edu
ARMSTRONG, Amy ... 830-792-7405 ... 494 E anarmstrong@schreiner.edu
ARMSTRONG, Andrew, V ... 540-636-2900 ... 517 K armstrong@christendom.edu
ARMSTRONG, Booker, S ... 816-604-6732 ... 285 A booker.armstrong@mcckc.edu
ARMSTRONG, Colleen ... 719-549-3005 ... 87 F colleen.armstrong@pueblocc.edu
ARMSTRONG, Cynthia, P ... 318-797-5005 ... 213 D cindy.armstrong@lsus.edu
ARMSTRONG, Daniel ... 719-389-6248 ... 82 D daniel.armstrong@coloradocollege.edu
ARMSTRONG, Dave ... 719-389-6870 ... 82 D david.armstrong@coloradocollege.edu
ARMSTRONG, David ... 706-865-2134 ... 138 E darmstrong@truett.edu
ARMSTRONG, David, A ... 216-373-5214 ... 397 F darmstrong@ndc.edu
ARMSTRONG, David, M ... 816-501-2423 ... 278 I david.armstrong@avila.edu
ARMSTRONG, Donald ... 716-614-5950 ... 344 C armstrong@niagaracc.suny.edu
ARMSTRONG, Donald ... 716-614-5950 ... 344 C hr@niagaracc.suny.edu
ARMSTRONG, JR., Donald, J ... 325-235-7414 ... 500 G donnie.armstrong@tstc.edu
ARMSTRONG, Doreen ... 520-206-4622 ... 17 H darmstrong@pima.edu
ARMSTRONG, Eric ... 541-684-4644 ... 419 F earmstrong@pioneerpacific.edu
ARMSTRONG, Franca ... 315-792-5321 ... 341 E farmstrong@mvcc.edu
ARMSTRONG, Heather ... 419-755-4386 ... 399 C armstrong.286@osu.edu
ARMSTRONG, J. David ... 954-201-7401 ... 102 E darmstro@broward.edu
ARMSTRONG, Jacquelyn, B ... 404-627-2681 ... 126 D jacquelyn.armstrong@beulah.org
ARMSTRONG, Jane ... 973-328-5181 ... 309 A jarmstrong@ccm.edu
ARMSTRONG, Jeff ... 563-336-3460 ... 184 E jarmstrong@eicc.edu
ARMSTRONG, Jeffrey, D ... 805-756-1111 ... 33 I presidentsoffice@calpoly.edu
ARMSTRONG, Kelli, J ... 617-552-0585 ... 232 B kelli.armstrong@bc.edu
ARMSTRONG, Kim ... 309-796-5006 ... 145 H armstrongk@bhc.edu
ARMSTRONG, Lee, F ... 334-844-5176 ... 1 F armstlf@auburn.edu
ARMSTRONG, Lori, B ... 410-704-3570 ... 228 E larmstrong@towson.edu
ARMSTRONG, Mary Beth ... 205-665-6720 ... 9 B armstrom@montevallo.edu
ARMSTRONG, Myeisha ... 760-757-2121 ... 57 E marmstrong@miracosta.edu
ARMSTRONG, Nancy, A ... 419-772-2251 ... 398 H n-armstrong@onu.edu
ARMSTRONG, Neal, E ... 512-232-3305 ... 505 D neal_armstrong@mail.utexas.edu
ARMSTRONG, Nicole ... 757-457-7170 ... 516 F nicole.armstrong@atlanticuniv.edu
ARMSTRONG, Pamla ... 580-559-5239 ... 407 J parmstro@ecok.edu
ARMSTRONG, Patricia, G ... 716-645-6136 ... 351 G pga2@buffalo.edu
ARMSTRONG, Peter ... 402-465-2153 ... 299 H parmstro@nebrwesleyan.edu
ARMSTRONG, Raul ... 787-840-2575 ... 565 A
ARMSTRONG, Rhonda ... 765-455-9343 ... 174 A rkarmstr@iuk.edu
ARMSTRONG, Scott ... 815-825-2086 ... 155 D scott.armstrong@kishwaukeecollege.edu
ARMSTRONG, Shane ... 310-377-5501 ... 56 F sarmstrong@marymountpv.edu
ARMSTRONG, Shelly ... 231-591-3825 ... 250 H armstros@ferris.edu
ARMSTRONG, Sherri ... 419-530-4842 ... 404 F sherri.armstrong@utoledo.edu
ARMSTRONG, Shirley ... 229-430-3511 ... 124 B sarmstrong@albanytech.edu
ARMSTRONG, Steve ... 620-223-2700 ... 193 A stevea@fortscott.edu
ARMSTRONG, Steven, M ... 920-832-6769 ... 548 B steven.m.armstrong@lawrence.edu
ARMSTRONG, Suzanne ... 757-221-7647 ... 518 A smarmstrong@wm.edu
ARMSTRONG, Terri ... 541-880-2287 ... 416 D armstrong@klamathcc.edu
ARMSTRONG, Thom, M ... 760-252-2411 ... 30 H tarmstrong@barstow.edu
ARMSTRONG, Thomas, J ... 307-532-8202 ... 556 C tom.armstrong@ewc.wy.edu
ARMSTRONG, William, L ... 303-963-3350 ... 82 C warmstrong@ccu.edu
ARMSTRONG-WILLIAMS, Dlynn ... 706-864-1869 ... 134 G dfarmstrong@northgeorgia.edu
ARMUSEWICZ, Allison ... 716-614-6238 ... 344 C aarmusewicz@niagaracc.suny.edu
ARN, Diana ... 501-977-2001 ... 25 G arn@uaccm.edu
ARNDT, Steven, A ... 920-424-0220 ... 551 E arndt@uwosh.edu
ARNDT, Wayne, S ... 732-987-2237 ... 310 C arndt@georgian.edu
ARNELL, Terri, J ... 941-359-7592 ... 116 B tarnell@ringling.edu
ARNER, Thomas ... 802-828-2800 ... 515 E arnert@ccv.edu
ARNESON, Rosemary ... 540-654-1000 ... 525 D rarneso3@umw.edu
ARNETT, Brad, K ... 770-484-1204 ... 133 G lru@lru.edu
ARNETT, Caleb ... 816-322-0110 ... 279 D caleb.arnett@calvary.edu
ARNETT, David ... 417-833-2551 ... 279 E darnett@cbcag.edu
ARNETT, Harold ... 785-442-6125 ... 193 F harnett@highlandcc.edu
ARNETT, Jennifer ... 415-476-4998 ... 75 A jarnett@support.ucsf.edu
ARNETT, Kathy ... 417-833-2551 ... 279 E karnett@cbcag.edu
ARNETT, Ron, W ... 606-474-3151 ... 201 D rarnett@kcu.edu
ARNIE, Karen ... 704-337-2374 ... 376 A arniek@queens.edu
ARNN, III, Larry, P ... 517-607-2301 ... 252 C president@hillsdale.edu
ARNO, Marlene ... 716-851-1431 ... 333 B arno@ecc.edu
ARNO, Rachel ... 617-588-1354 ... 231 C rarno@bfit.edu
ARNOLD, Becky, P ... 802-656-2010 ... 514 H becky.arnold@uvm.edu
ARNOLD, Carolyn ... 510-723-6965 ... 39 C carnold@chabotcollege.edu
ARNOLD, Christina ... 616-234-3532 ... 251 E carnold@grcc.edu
ARNOLD, Clinton, E ... 562-903-4816 ... 31 A clinton.arnold@biola.edu
ARNOLD, David ... 770-423-6203 ... 133 A
ARNOLD, David ... 575-492-2124 ... 321 H darnold@usw.edu
ARNOLD, Donna, C ... 619-482-6371 ... 71 D darnold@swccd.edu
ARNOLD, George, F ... 920-686-6138 ... 550 H george.arnold@sl.edu
ARNOLD, Harvey, E ... 772-462-6210 ... 111 B harnold@irsc.edu
ARNOLD, J. David ... 309-467-6322 ... 151 B arnold@eureka.edu
ARNOLD, Jane ... 412-536-1786 ... 432 H jane.arnold@laroche.edu
ARNOLD, Jeanne, J ... 616-331-3296 ... 251 F arnoljea@gvsu.edu
ARNOLD, Jeff (Dean) ... 262-472-1922 ... 553 A arnoldd@uww.edu
ARNOLD, Jim ... 415-485-9506 ... 42 B jim.arnold@marin.edu
ARNOLD, John ... 325-236-7408 ... 500 G john.arnold@tstc.edu
ARNOLD, Joseph ... 657-278-3256 ... 35 B jarnold@fullerton.edu
ARNOLD, Joshua ... 706-233-7233 ... 137 A jarnold@shorter.edu
ARNOLD, Julie ... 419-448-2953 ... 391 F jarnold3@heidelberg.edu
ARNOLD, Kelley, M ... 912-583-2241 ... 126 F karnold@bpc.edu
ARNOLD, Kelley, M ... 912-583-3263 ... 126 F karnold@bpc.edu
ARNOLD, Kenneth, L ... 707-256-3331 ... 58 F karnold@napavalley.edu
ARNOLD, Lois ... 989-774-3911 ... 249 C arnol1lr@cmich.edu
ARNOLD, Lorene ... 260-399-7700 ... 181 A larnold@sf.edu
ARNOLD, Lorin ... 856-256-4290 ... 314 A arnold@rowan.edu
ARNOLD, Mary, M ... 651-641-8268 ... 263 A arnold@csp.edu
ARNOLD, Melody ... 575-492-2102 ... 321 H marnold@usw.edu
ARNOLD, Michael, A ... 302-831-1195 ... 96 I marnold@udel.edu
ARNOLD, Nancy ... 615-297-7545 ... 467 A arnoldn@aquinascollege.edu
ARNOLD, Philip, M ... 518-255-5228 ... 354 E arnoldpm@cobleskill.edu
ARNOLD, Robert ... 815-836-5488 ... 156 F arnoldro@lewisu.edu
ARNOLD, Robert ... 765-983-1217 ... 171 E boba@earlham.edu
ARNOLD, Ronald, M ... 312-935-6646 ... 162 G rarnold@robertmorris.edu
ARNOLD, Sally ... 978-232-2029 ... 234 D sarnold@endicott.edu
ARNOLD, Shirley, E ... 828-884-8329 ... 362 H arnoldse@brevard.edu
ARNOLD, Stephen ... 409-984-6249 ... 501 C stephen.arnold@lamarpa.edu
ARNOLD, Sue ... 281-487-1170 ... 499 B sarnold@txchiro.edu
ARNOLD, Tai ... 518-587-2100 ... 355 G tai.arnold@esc.edu
ARNOLD, Tisha ... 870-575-8946 ... 25 B arnoldt@uapb.edu
ARNOLD, III, W. Ellis ... 501-450-1223 ... 22 A arnold@hendrix.edu
ARNONE, Harriet ... 516-686-7517 ... 343 D harnone@nyit.edu
ARNOULD, Karen, A ... 810-762-3344 ... 259 C karnould@umflint.edu
ARNST, Scott ... 810-762-3123 ... 259 C sarnst@umflint.edu
ARNUM, Waynette ... 860-906-5125 ... 91 C warnum@ccc.commnet.edu
ARNZEN, Diane ... 636-481-3282 ... 283 D darnzen@jeffco.edu
AROCHO, Miguel ... 787-890-2681 ... 566 H miguel.arocho1@upr.edu
AROMANDO, Drew, C ... 609-896-5178 ... 313 F aromando@rider.edu
ARON, Lester ... 973-972-4321 ... 316 C aronle@umdnj.edu
ARONBERG, Susan ... 561-912-2166 ... 107 B saronberg@evergladesuniversity.edu
ARONSON, Donna ... 507-457-6900 ... 271 B daronson@smumn.edu
ARONSON, Ed ... 541-881-5875 ... 420 E earonson@tvcc.cc
ARONSON, Linda ... 508-849-3458 ... 230 C laronson@annamaria.edu
ARONSON, Roberta, C ... 412-396-1818 ... 428 D aronson@duq.edu
ARORA, Alka ... 805-893-2920 ... 75 B alka.arora@sa.ucsb.edu
ARORA SINGH, Alka ... 623-845-3968 ... 15 H alka.arora.singh@gcmail.maricopa.edu
AROS, Jesse ... 361-570-4186 ... 504 A arosj@uhv.edu
AROZCO, Holly ... 714-816-0366 ... 73 B holly.arozco@trident.edu
ARP, Alissa ... 541-552-8173 ... 419 A arpa@sou.edu
ARP, Dan ... 541-737-2331 ... 418 F dan.arp@oregonstate.edu
ARP, Mary ... 217-641-4200 ... 154 I marp@jwcc.edu
ARP, William ... 225-771-3092 ... 214 I william_arp@subr.edu
ARPEY, Sharon, A ... 518-580-5590 ... 351 B sarpey@skidmore.edu
ARPINO, Donald ... 617-879-7899 ... 238 B darpino@massart.edu
ARPS, Joyce ... 903-593-8311 ... 499 D jarps@texascollege.edu
ARQUETTE, Mary ... 419-824-3969 ... 395 E marquette@lourdes.edu
ARRA, Linda, N ... 610-330-5115 ... 433 B arral@lafayette.edu
ARRAMBIDE, J. Mike ... 719-884-5000 ... 86 J jmarrambide@nbc.edu
ARREDONDO, Marisol ... 714-628-7339 ... 39 F arredond@chapman.edu
ARREDONDO, Patricia ... 414-227-3326 ... 551 D arredond@uwm.edu
ARREDONDO, Patricia ... 414-229-4503 ... 551 D arredond@uwm.edu
ARRICK, Laurie ... 231-876-3112 ... 248 A laurie.arrick@baker.edu
ARRIGO, Paul ... 281-425-6447 ... 489 M parrigo@lee.edu
ARRILLAGA MONTALVO, Sonia ... 787-763-6700 ... 562 D sarrillaga@se-pr.edu
ARRINGTON, Cedric ... 256-372-5254 ... 1 A cedric.arrington@aamu.edu
ARRINGTON, Doris, B ... 860-906-5085 ... 91 C darrington@ccc.commnet.edu
ARRINGTON, Harriette ... 757-925-6302 ... 528 A harrington@pdc.edu
ARRINGTON, Jeff ... 325-674-6802 ... 478 I arringtonj@acu.edu
ARRINGTON, Michelle ... 601-266-6698 ... 277 F michelle.arrington@usm.edu
ARRINGTON, Pamela ... 334-241-9592 ... 8 A parrington@troy.edu
ARRINGTON, Teresa, R ... 662-685-4771 ... 273 E tarrington@bmc.edu
ARRINGTON-JONES, Angela ... 773-291-6297 ... 147 G aarrington@ccc.edu
ARRIOLA, Benjamin ... 915-778-4001 ... 495 B
ARROCHA, Ashley ... 831-647-4128 ... 57 F ashley.arrocha@miis.edu
ARROSSA, Monty, J ... 208-732-6267 ... 143 E marrossa@csi.edu
ARROYO, Cruz ... 253-964-4688 ... 537 B carroyo@stmartin.edu
ARROYO, Enrique ... 787-841-2000 ... 565 B
ARROYO, Ethel ... 847-233-7700 ... 160 D earroyo@nc.edu
ARROYO, Gladys ... 787-279-1912 ... 563 D garroyo@bayamon.inter.edu
ARROYO, Ivonne, D ... 787-257-7323 ... 565 G iarroyo@suagm.edu
ARROYO, Luz ... 561-273-6500 ... 118 A larroyovazquez@southuniversity.edu
ARRUDA, Yvonne, D ... 401-865-2480 ... 453 H yarruda@providence.edu
ARSHADI, Nasser ... 314-516-5899 ... 291 D arshadi@umsl.edu
ARSTEIN, Mark ... 208-426-3277 ... 142 I markarstein@boisestate.edu
ARTALE, Maureen, P ... 607-436-3216 ... 353 E artalemp@oneonta.edu
ARTBAUER, Michael ... 216-687-3544 ... 388 D m.artbauer@csuohio.edu
ARTEAGA, Joseph ... 805-546-3205 ... 43 I joseph_arteaga@cuesta.edu
ARTEAGA, Patricia ... 973-748-9000 ... 307 H patricia_arteaga@bloomfield.edu
ARTEAGA, Yudit ... 305-892-7044 ... 112 A yudit.arteaga@jwu.edu
ARTEAGA-JOHNSON, Craig ... 909-621-8142 ... 63 A craig.arteagajohnson@pomona.edu
ARTECONA, Sarah, N ... 305-284-6100 ... 122 I sartecona@miami.edu
ARTER, Neil ... 405-425-5906 ... 409 E neil.arter@oc.edu
ARTERIAN, Hannah ... 315-443-9580 ... 357 C arterian@syr.edu
ARTHO, Donna ... 936-294-3101 ... 501 D artho@shsu.edu
ARTHUR, Alcott, S ... 410-951-4156 ... 228 B aarthur@coppin.edu
ARTHUR, Christon ... 269-471-3405 ... 247 D christon@andrews.edu
ARTHUR, Dave ... 512-476-2772 ... 481 C finaid@austingrad.edu
ARTHUR, Gwendolynne ... 508-793-7384 ... 233 B garthur@clarku.edu
ARTHUR, Jeff ... 757-671-7171 ... 518 H
ARTHUR, Mark ... 405-789-7661 ... 412 E mark.arthur@swcu.edu
ARTHUR, Salinda ... 912-478-5253 ... 131 E sarthur@georgiasouthern.edu
ARTHUR, Virginia ... 651-793-1920 ... 267 A virginia.arthur@metrostat.edu
ARTIBISE, Alan ... 956-882-8266 ... 505 E alan.artibise@utb.edu
ARTILES LEON, Noel ... 787-265-3877 ... 567 F director.oiip@upr.edu
ARTIM, Amanda ... 814-536-5168 ... 424 D amanda@crbc.net
ARTIM, Amanda ... 814-536-5168 ... 424 E amanda@crbc.net
ARTIM, Michael ... 814-536-5168 ... 424 D martim@crbc.net
ARTIM, Michael ... 814-536-5168 ... 424 E martim@crbc.net
ARTIS, Christine ... 718-933-6700 ... 341 G cartis@monroecollege.edu
ARTIS, Frederick, D ... 918-595-7898 ... 412 H fdartis@tulsacc.edu
ARTIS, Lori ... 618-468-3200 ... 156 E lartis@lc.edu
ARTLEY, James ... 904-731-4949 ... 106 D jartley@cci.edu
ARTMAN, Richard, B ... 608-796-3001 ... 553 C rbartman@viterbo.edu
ARTSON, Bradley ... 310-476-9777 ... 28 G bartson@ajula.edu
ARUL, Jebapriya ... 863-667-5086 ... 118 F jfarul@seu.edu
ARUNACHALAM, Vairam ... 573-882-3225 ... 291 B arunachalam@missouri.edu
ARVELO, Wildolfo ... 603-427-7602 ... 304 B warvelo@ccsnh.edu
ARVIN, Ann ... 650-498-6227 ... 71 G aarvin@stanford.edu
ARVIZU, Mimi ... 408-848-4840 ... 48 C marvizu@gavilan.edu
ARZOLA, Fernando ... 646-378-6150 ... 344 G fernando.arzola@nyack.edu
ASAMOAH, Yaw, A ... 724-357-2280 ... 442 F osebo@iup.edu
ASARO, Diane, C ... 773-508-2543 ... 157 C dasaro@luc.edu
ASATO, Susan ... 760-757-2121 ... 57 E sasato@miracosta.edu

ATWOOD, Lorraine 802-831-1204 515 B latwood@vermontlaw.edu
ATWOOD, Roy, A 208-882-1566 144 C dratwood@nsa.edu
AU, Peggy 510-628-8038 54 B peggyau@lincolnuca.edu
AU, Sau Fong 718-951-5476 326 F sau@brooklyn.cuny.edu
AUBELE, Emily 814-676-6591 442 C eaubele@clarion.edu
AUBERGER, Tammy 435-613-5240 512 A tammy.auberger@usu.edu
AUBIN, Mary Ann 314-768-1718 283 G aubin@kenrick.edu
AUBRECHT, Donald 724-589-2222 448 B daubrecht@thiel.edu
AUBRET, Maryliz 787-780-0070 560 H maubret@caribbean.edu
AUBREY, Leonard 516-686-1100 343 D laubrey@nyit.edu
AUBUT, Irene 603-271-6077 304 F iaubut@ccsnh.edu
AUCLAIR, Billye, W 508-849-3359 230 C bauclair@annamaria.edu
AUCOIN, Judi, F 205-726-2728 6 G jfaucoin@samford.edu
AUCOIN, Toni 337-262-5962 211 K taucoin@acadiana.edu
AUDAS, Jean Paul 405-325-2395 413 C jaudas@ou.edu
AUDETTE, Bert 207-948-9277 219 H baudette@unity.edu
AUDUS, Kenneth, L 785-864-3591 197 B audus@ku.edu
AUDYATIS, Todd 508-531-2690 237 D taudyatis@bridgew.edu
AUER, Margaret 313-993-1090 258 G auerme@udmercy.edu
AUER, Matthew 812-855-3550 173 E mauer@indiana.edu
AUERBACH, Michael 843-953-5991 457 B auerbachmh@cofc.edu
AUGENSPEIN, Amee 260-459-4567 175 C aaugenspein@ibcfortwayne.edu
AUGHENBAUGH, Barbara 410-837-5719 229 A baughenbaugh@ubalt.edu
AUGMAN, JR., William, J 937-376-2946 401 A
AUGOSTINI, Christopher, L 202-687-7330 98 D cla4@georgetown.edu
AUGSBURGER, Arol, R 312-949-7700 152 E aaugsburger@ico.edu
AUGSBURGER, Lance, A 515-964-0601 185 A augsburgerl@faith.edu
AUGUST, Bonne 718-260-5560 328 D baugust@citytech.cuny.edu
AUGUST-SCHWARTZ, Suzanne 510-869-6511 64 J saugustschwartz@samuelmerritt.edu
AUGUSTE, Wadner 212-749-2802 339 I wauguste@msmnyc.edu
AUGUSTIN, Monica, L 408-554-6908 68 C mlaugustin@scu.edu
AUGUSTINE, Lisa 440-365-5222 395 D
AUGUSTINE, Robert, M 217-581-2220 150 E rmaugustine@eiu.edu
AUGUSTINE-PLAISANCE, Lu-Ann 718-409-7302 356 C laugustine@sunymaritime.edu
AUGUSTINE-PLAISANCE, LuAnn 718-409-7304 356 C laugustine@sunymaritime.edu
AUGUSTUS, Edward 508-793-2011 233 C eaugustu@holycross.edu
AULD, Sandra 908-709-7030 316 B auld@ucc.edu
AULET, Maria, J 787-765-1915 564 D mjaulet@inter.edu
AULL, JR., Zeke 251-460-6609 9 D zaull@usouthal.edu
AULT, Allen 859-622-3565 200 J allen.ault@eku.edu
AULT, Brian 410-857-2262 224 C bault@mcdaniel.edu
AULT, Jill, K 530-226-4103 69 H jault@simpsonu.edu
AUM, Seok Joo 213-487-0110 45 D provost@dula.edu
AUMAN, Timothy, L 336-758-5210 380 C aumantl@wfu.edu
AUMANN, Trish 636-422-2244 289 B paumann@stlcc.edu
AUNE, Jeff 952-446-4152 263 C aunej@crown.edu
AUNE, Regina, C 956-326-2574 497 D regina.aune@tamiu.edu
AUNGST, Donald 563-425-5286 189 G aungstd@uiu.edu
AURE, Aaron 605-688-6195 466 C aaron.aure@sdstate.edu
AURICCHIO, Gail 516-739-1545 343 C gail@nyctcm.edu
AURICCHIO, Michele 518-464-8804 333 E mauricchio@excelsior.edu
AURIEMMA, Lisa 207-859-1233 219 G libdir@thomas.edu
AURORA, Rosleen 818-785-2726 38 K
AUSBAND, Avrohom 718-601-3523 361 L
AUSBORN, Dawn 910-630-7610 367 B dausborn@methodist.edu
AUSBORN, Scot 312-935-4232 154 A icsw.librarian@gmail.com
AUSBURY, Brad 417-862-9533 282 A bausbury@globaluniversity.edu
AUSEL, Jill 412-365-1244 425 C jausel@chatham.edu
AUSEN, Orrin, J 507-344-7350 261 C oausen@blc.edu
AUSMUS, Ryan 620-225-0186 192 E rausmus@dc3.edu
AUST, Kandyce 860-768-2409 95 B aust@hartford.edu
AUSTAD, Dianne, M 319-368-6464 187 H daustad@mtmercy.edu
AUSTER, Julie 914-395-2365 350 C jauster@sarahlawrence.edu
AUSTIN, Aaron, L 316-284-5324 191 C aaustin@bethelks.edu
AUSTIN, Alvin 704-378-1110 366 A aaustin@jcsu.edu
AUSTIN, Anne 870-612-2058 25 E anne.austin@uaccb.edu
AUSTIN, April 404-270-5153 138 B aprila@spelman.edu
AUSTIN, Beth 816-604-3182 285 D beth.austin@mcckc.edu
AUSTIN, Brian 865-471-3273 467 G baustin@cn.edu
AUSTIN, Charles 803-705-4967 455 D austinc@benedict.edu
AUSTIN, Chris 270-247-8521 204 G caustin@midcontinent.edu
AUSTIN, Dale, F 616-395-7950 252 D austin@hope.edu
AUSTIN, Deborah 717-264-4141 452 C daustin@wilson.edu
AUSTIN, Diane 617-243-2124 236 A daustin@lasell.edu
AUSTIN, Dominica 404-799-4500 126 H doaustin@brownmackie.edu
AUSTIN, Faires 334-386-7180 3 G faustin@faulkner.edu
AUSTIN, James 760-757-2121 57 E jaustin@miracosta.edu
AUSTIN, James 802-387-6786 513 G jaustin@landmark.edu
AUSTIN, Janice 574-289-7001 176 E jaustin@ivytech.edu
AUSTIN, Joseph, M 207-780-5158 220 G austin@usm.maine.edu
AUSTIN, Kelly, M 570-385-6001 440 D kma24@psu.edu
AUSTIN, L. Bruce 847-214-7366 150 F baustin@elgin.edu
AUSTIN, Laurie 718-960-8706 327 C laurie.austin@lehman.cuny.edu
AUSTIN, Laurie 425-739-8200 535 H laurie.austin@lwtc.edu
AUSTIN, Marlisa 502-213-5073 202 F marlisa.austin@kctcs.edu
AUSTIN, Michael 316-942-4291 195 F austinm@newmanu.edu
AUSTIN, Robert, C 806-371-5024 479 G rcaustin@actx.edu
AUSTIN, Suzanne, E 205-934-6290 8 F seaustin@uab.edu
AUSTIN, Tiffany 845-675-4581 344 G tiffany.austin@nyack.edu
AUSTIN, Timothy, R 508-793-2541 233 C taustin@holycross.edu
AUSTIN, Tracey, M 603-526-3886 303 G taustin@colby-sawyer.edu
AUSTIN, William 908-689-7618 317 C will@warren.edu
AUTREY, Denny 713-634-0011 495 G dautrey@swbts.edu
AUTRY, Timothy, J 803-535-5549 456 D tautry@claflin.edu
AUVENSHINE, Donnie 325-649-8408 488 C dauvenshine@hputx.edu
AUXIER, David 941-363-7218 118 J auxierd@scf.edu
AVALONE, Valarie, L 585-292-3021 341 H vavalone@monroecc.edu
AVALOS, Juan 949-582-4566 70 F javalos@saddleback.edu
AVALOS, Natalie 818-767-0888 79 H natalie.avalos@woodbury.edu
AVALOS, Yesenia 773-838-7984 147 H yavalos@ccc.edu
AVALOS-SÁNCHEZ, Javier 787-993-8863 567 B javier.avalos@upr.edu
AVANT, Cheryl 573-681-5162 283 I avantc@lincolnu.edu
AVANT, Jacqueline 678-260-3538 137 A javant@shorter.edu
AVANT, Linda 918-293-4678 410 E linda.avant@okstate.edu
AVANT, Toni, D 662-915-7174 277 D tavant@olemiss.edu
AVEILLE, Candido 305-821-3333 109 B caveille@mm.fnc.edu
AVELLANET, Maida 813-879-6000 107 A mavellanet@cci.edu
AVENDANO, John 815-802-8110 155 A president@kcc.edu
AVENT, Sherri, M 336-334-7973 378 A avent@ncat.edu
AVERILL, Kristine 503-495-2900 19 A kristine.averill@phoenix.edu
AVERILL, Leslie 802-651-5907 513 C averill@champlain.edu
AVERILL, Sue 330-672-2220 393 D saveril2@kent.edu
AVERRE, Amy 207-941-7187 218 A averrea@husson.edu
AVERSA, Ann 212-854-5561 323 E aaversa@barnard.edu
AVERY, Alice, M 203-371-7927 94 B averya@sacredheart.edu
AVERY, Annalea 208-524-3000 143 G annalea.avery@my.eitc.edu
AVERY, Annette 417-873-7312 281 D aavery@drury.edu
AVERY, Barbara 323-259-2661 59 I bavery@oxy.edu
AVERY, Brigid 616-632-2494 247 E brigid.avery@aquinas.edu
AVERY, Donald 478-289-2015 129 B davery@ega.edu
AVERY, Earl, L 781-891-2907 231 D eavery@bentley.edu
AVERY, Faith 513-721-7944 391 D favery@gbs.edu
AVERY, James 731-661-5329 477 B javery@uu.edu
AVERY, Joshua 513-721-7944 391 D javery@gbs.edu
AVERY, Kathy 918-293-4988 410 E kathy.avery@okstate.edu
AVERY, Lisa 509-533-3694 533 C
AVERY, Margery, L 585-567-9350 336 B margery.avery@houghton.edu
AVERY, Michael, R 513-721-7944 391 D president@gbs.edu
AVERY, Paula 310-377-5501 56 F pavery@marymountpv.edu
AVERY, Reginald, S 410-951-3838 228 B ravery@coppin.edu
AVERY, Robert, H 401-254-3236 454 C ravery@rwu.edu
AVERY, Susan 508-289-2500 246 E savery@whoi.edu
AVERY, Teresa 501-337-5000 21 D tavery@coto.edu
AVILÉS-GONZÁLEZ, Arturo 787-993-0000 566 G arturo.aviles@upr.edu
AVILÉS-GONZÁLEZ, Arturo 787-993-8850 567 B arturo.aviles@upr.edu
AVILA, Arcadio 562-860-2451 39 A aavila@cerritos.edu
AVILA, Celi 915-532-3737 508 H cavila@westerntech.edu
AVILA, Glenna 661-255-1050 32 F glenna@calarts.edu
AVILA, Lauri 928-428-8915 14 B lauri.avila@eac.edu
AVILA, Linda, C 310-794-0691 74 C lcavila@saa.ucla.edu
AVILA, Mike 909-607-9224 40 F mike.avila@cgu.edu
AVILA, Pedro 559-934-2128 78 C pedroavila@whccd.edu
AVILA, Susan 510-594-3661 32 C savila@cca.edu
AVILA, Vince 785-864-4036 197 B vavila1@ku.edu
AVILES, Angel 787-780-5134 564 H aaviles@nuc.edu
AVILES, Carmen 787-744-1060 564 F cre_caguas@mechtech.edu
AVILES, Gladys, M 248-204-4123 254 B gaviles@ltu.edu
AVILES, José 302-831-8123 96 I javiles@udel.edu
AVILES, José, E 787-265-3767 567 F finanzaz@uprm.edu
AVILES-FERRAN, Jeanette 787-620-2040 560 D javiles@aupr.edu
AVILES FONT, Juan 787-896-2252 562 B javiles@edpcollege.edu
AVILLION, Dianne 850-729-4901 114 A avilliond@nwfsc.edu
AVISSAR, Roni 305-421-4000 122 I avissar@miami.edu
AVITABLE, Mathew 718-270-7424 352 D mavitable@downstate.edu
AW, Fanta 202-885-3357 97 D fanta@american.edu
AWAKUNI, Gene, I 808-454-4750 141 H giawakun@hawaii.edu
AWBREY, Susan, M 248-370-2193 256 G awbrey@oakland.edu
AWBREY, Susan, M 248-370-4955 256 G awbrey@oakland.edu
AWE, Jacqueline 912-358-3114 136 G awej@savannahstate.edu
AWN, Peter 212-854-1932 330 F pja3@columbia.edu
AWOLAJU, Tafa 508-678-2811 239 B tafa.awolaju@bristolcc.edu
AWOLOLA, Oluyemi 727-725-2688 106 F yemi@cci.edu
AWUAH, Agatha 315-498-2500 345 D awuaha@sunyocc.edu
AWUAH, Emmanuel 315-498-7270 345 D awuahe@sunyocc.edu
AXELRAD, Albert, S 617-824-8036 234 B albert_axelrad@emerson.edu
AXELROD, Larry 604-482-5510 144 H laxelrod@adler.edu
AXELROTH, Elie, N 805-756-2511 33 I eaxelrot@calpoly.edu
AXELSON, Sara, L 307-766-5123 556 H saxelson@uwyo.edu
AXLER, David 570-504-9635 425 F
AXLER, Sheldon 415-338-1571 37 B axler@sfsu.edu
AXLUND, Martin 307-755-2169 557 B maxlund@wyotechstaff.edu
AXTELL, Denise 530-242-7770 69 D daxtell@shastacollege.edu
AXTELL, Richard, D 859-238-5342 199 G rick.axtell@centre.edu
AXTELL, Thomas, B 309-341-7212 155 F taxtell@knox.edu
AXTELL PAULSEN, Marijane 303-784-8045 85 M mpaulsen@jiu.edu
AXTMANN, Peter 413-565-1000 230 G paxtmann@baypath.edu
AXTON, Faith, M 660-263-3900 279 F fma@cccb.edu
AYALA, Adriana 408-273-2677 58 G aayala@nhu.edu
AYALA, Aurea 787-250-1912 563 G aayala@metro.inter.edu
AYALA, Benjamin 787-864-2222 563 F benaya@inter.edu
AYALA, Carlos 707-664-2132 37 D dean.education@sonoma.edu
AYALA, Carmen 787-761-0640 566 F decanaasuntosacademicos@utcpr.edu
AYALA, Eddie 787-279-1912 563 D eayala@bayamon.inter.edu
AYALA, Gladys, M 914-594-4498 343 F gladys_ayala@nymc.edu
AYALA, Israel 787-891-0925 563 A iayala@aguadilla.inter.edu
AYALA, Javier, I 585-292-3672 341 H jayala5@monroecc.edu
AYALA, Mary 575-562-2421 318 B mary.ayala@enmu.edu
AYALA, Paul 210-805-5863 504 B peayala@uiwtx.edu
AYALA, Ramon 787-250-1912 563 G rayala@metro.inter.edu
AYALA, Roberto 787-265-5413 567 F roberto.ayala@uprm.edu
AYALA RICE, Maggie 773-907-4041 147 D mrice19@ccc.edu
AYALA-ROGERS, Anikka 281-425-6337 489 M aayala@lee.edu
AYARS, Barbara, L 302-477-2210 97 B blayars@widener.edu
AYBAR, Jose, M 773-838-7511 147 H jaybar@ccc.edu
AYCOCK, Greg 951-739-7802 63 K greg.aycock@norcocollege.edu
AYDELOTT, Carla 541-684-7241 417 F caydelott@nwcu.edu
AYER, Bernice 270-686-4518 203 B bernice.ayer@kctcs.edu
AYERS, Albert, B 508-588-9100 240 A
AYERS, Beth 707-654-1186 33 C bookstore@csum.edu
AYERS, Edward, L 804-289-8102 525 E eayers@richmond.edu
AYERS, Frank 928-777-3800 14 C ayersf@erau.edu
AYERS, Irene 847-969-4928 145 D iayers@argosy.edu
AYERS, Irene 312-777-7630 145 C iayers@argosy.edu
AYERS, Keith 251-460-6211 9 D kayers@usouthal.edu
AYERS, Michael 718-758-8127 326 F mrayers@brooklyn.cuny.edu
AYERS, Michael, V 336-734-7478 370 F mayers@forsythtech.edu
AYERS, Nancy, A 208-467-8542 144 E naayers@nnu.edu
AYERS, Shari, L 614-235-4136 402 G sayers@tlsohio.edu

AYERS, Tom 810-762-9787 253 C
tayers@kettering.edu
AYERS, W. Bruce 606-589-3001 203 D
bruce.ayers@kctcs.edu
AYERS, William, J 302-857-1814 96 G
ayers@dtcc.edu
AYERSMAN, David, J 304-256-0281 543 A
dayersman@newriver.edu
AYEWOH, Michael 610-436-3592 444 A
mayewoh@wcupa.edu
AYI, Richard, S 712-279-3149 189 A
ayirs@stlukescollege.edu
AYLESBURY, Tom 626-568-8850 53 D
AYLMER, Francoise 503-725-5037 418 G
francoise@pdx.edu
AYLOR, James, H 434-924-3310 525 F
jha@virginia.edu
AYLOR, Jerri 806-457-4200 486 I
jaylor@fpctx.edu
AYLOR, Pete 864-587-4229 461 D
aylorp@smcsc.edu
AYLWARD, Robert, R 307-766-4860 556 H
raylward@uwyo.edu
AYLWARD, Sarah, D 662-846-4709 273 H
sdeason@deltastate.edu
AYMER, Albert 704-636-6823 365 D
AYNES, Danny 541-917-4822 416 I
aynesd@linnbenton.edu
AYON, Violet, R 714-808-4793 59 C
vayon@nocccd.edu
AYOOB, Kenneth 707-826-4491 36 E
kpa1@humboldt.edu
AYRAVAINEN, Eija 212-772-4878 327 E
eija.ayravainen@hunter.cuny.edu
AYRE, Joyce 406-377-9447 294 B
ayre@dawson.edu
AYRE, Joyce 406-377-9421 294 B
ayre@dawson.edu
AYRE-BOGGS, Rebecca 810-766-4044 248 C
rebecca.boggs@baker.edu
AYRES, Angel 617-989-4159 245 F
ayresa@wit.edu
AYRES, Christina, M 573-458-0101 281 E
cmayres@eastcentral.edu
AYRES, Dana 214-768-2841 495 A
dwayres@smu.edu
AYRES, Gary 618-468-3000 156 E
glayres@lc.edu
AYRES, Ted, D 316-978-6791 198 A
ted.ayres@wichita.edu
AYRES, Thomas, E 434-971-3301 557 G
thomas.e.ayres.mil@mail.mil
AYTCH, Keith 408-270-6450 67 C
keith.aytch@evc.edu
AYUSO, Jesus, M 787-257-0000 567 C
jesus.ayuso@upr.edu
AZADIAN, Patrick 626-873-2113 58 C
pazadian@mtsierra.edu
AZAIR, Cheryl 310-824-1586 26 D
cheryl@cherylazair.com
AZAR, Dimitri 312-996-3500 167 B
dazar@uic.edu
AZAR, Eve 908-835-2335 317 C
azar@warren.edu
AZAR, James, A 401-254-3124 454 C
jazar@rwu.edu
AZARI, Cynthia 951-222-8000 63 I
cynthia.azari@rcc.edu
AZARI, Cynthia 951-222-8155 64 A
AZCUNAGA, Cecilia 401-949-2820 453 F
cazcunaga@inteducators.org
AZDELL, Grant, L 804-752-7266 523 C
gazdell@rmc.edu
AZEBEOKHAI, I. Charles 678-915-7485 137 G
cazebeok@spsu.edu
AZEKE, Mercy 732-571-4409 311 E
mazeke@monmouth.edu
AZEVEDO, Bethany 559-730-3786 42 D
bethanya@cos.edu
AZEVEDO, Mario 601-979-8836 274 G
mario.j.azevedo@jsums.edu
AZHAND, Hamid, U 909-537-5136 36 B
hazhand@csusb.edu
AZIZ, Jihad, N 804-828-6200 526 B
jnaziz@vcu.edu
AZIZ, Kareem 410-276-0306 226 D
kaziz@host.sdc.edu
AZKOUL, Emilie 616-222-1447 250 A
emilie.azkoul@cornerstone.edu
AZLIN WRIGHT, Taisha 714-816-0366 73 B
taisha.wright@trident.edu
AZUR, Stephanie, A 610-841-3333 441 D
sazur@psb.edu
AZURE, Jackie 406-768-3213 294 D
jazure@fpcc.edu
AZURE, Tracy 701-477-7862 383 F
tazure@tm.edu
AZZIZ, Ricardo 706-721-2301 130 D
president@georgiahealth.edu

B

BAADE, K.Austin 262-691-5550 555 E
kbaade@wctc.edu
BAAK, Melanie 207-221-8754 218 C
mbaak@kaplan.edu
BAALMAN, Roger 307-766-1121 556 H
baalman@uwyo.edu
BAAR, Rachael 270-831-9803 202 D
rachael.baar@kctcs.edu
BAART, Aaron 712-722-6079 184 C
abaart@dordt.edu
BAAS, John 712-722-6020 184 C
jbaas@dordt.edu
BABA, Marietta 517-355-6675 255 A
mbaba@msu.edu
BABALIS, Eva 718-779-1430 346 B
ebabalis@mail.plazacollege.edu
BABASHANIAN, Mark, R 757-446-6000 518 G
babashmr@evms.edu
BABB, Brian 386-506-4457 104 F
babbb@daytonastate.edu
BABB, Brian, T 386-506-4457 104 F
babbb@daytonastate.edu
BABB, Mike 847-925-6825 151 G
mbabb@harpercollege.edu
BABB, Phillip 619-702-9400 33 A
phillip.babb@cibu.edu
BABB, Randy 719-389-6379 82 D
randy.babb@coloradocollege.edu
BABBITT, Jeff 585-567-9211 336 B
jeff.babbitt@houghton.edu
BABBITT, Steven 516-463-5019 335 G
steven.babbitt@hofstra.edu
BABBITT, Terry 505-277-8392 321 C
tbabbitt@unm.edu
BABCOCK, Bernie 541-881-5706 420 E
bbabcock@tvcc.cc
BABCOCK, Whit 513-556-4603 403 D
whit.babcock@uc.edu
BABEL, Thomas 630-515-3029 149 B
tbabel@devry.edu
BABER, James 740-264-5591 390 F
jbaber@egcc.edu
BABER, Karen 309-796-5362 145 H
baberk@bhc.edu
BABESHOFF, Ruth 714-628-4775 63 G
babeshoff_ruth@sccollege.edu
BABETZ, Jeffrey 843-863-7921 456 B
jbabetz@csuniv.edu
BABICH-SPECK, Kimberly 216-987-4000 389 B
kimberly.babich-speck@tri-c.edu
BABICK-SAQUI, Christine 219-866-6177 179 D
cbs@saintjoe.edu
BABIKI, Aleco 602-350-6525 413 A
BABIN, Louis 225-752-4233 209 C
lbabin@iticollege.edu
BABINGTON, Cynthia 765-658-4270 171 B
cbabington@depauw.edu
BABINGTON, Lynn 203-254-4150 92 H
lbabington@fairfield.edu
BABIZE, Mollie 413-369-4044 233 E
babize@csld.edu
BABYAK, Joyce 440-775-8534 397 G
joyce.babyak@oberlin.edu
BACA, Amy 575-538-6145 321 I
bacaamym@wnmu.edu
BACA, Denise 619-235-2049 46 N
dbaca@fidm.edu
BACA, Kim 505-424-2351 318 D
kbaca@iaia.edu
BACA, Max 505-454-3117 318 J
mbaca@nmhu.edu
BACA, Randy 254-298-8582 496 D
randy.baca@templejc.edu
BACA, W. Bradley 970-943-2186 89 E
bbaca@western.edu
BACARISSE, Charles 281-649-3428 487 H
cbacarisse@hbu.edu
BACCAR, Cindy 503-725-5533 418 G
baccarc@pdx.edu
BACCHETTA, Aldo 816-802-3334 283 E
abacchetta@kcai.edu
BACCI, Diana, S 610-341-5854 428 E
dbacci@eastern.edu
BACCI, Nancy 973-748-9000 307 H
nancy_bacci@bloomfield.edu
BACH, Bert, C 423-439-4219 473 F
bachb@etsu.edu
BACH, Bill 208-888-1505 19 A
bill.bach@phoenix.edu
BACH, Bruce 215-641-6519 436 G
bbach@mc3.edu
BACH, Carol Anne 615-547-1200 468 B
cbach@cumberland.edu
BACH, Craig 215-571-3608 427 H
bachcn@drexel.edu
BACH, Larry, C 612-343-4703 270 A
lcbach@northcentral.edu
BACH, Lee 248-476-1122 254 G
lbach@mispp.edu
BACHAND, Donald, J 989-964-4296 257 G
dbachand@svsu.edu
BACHARACH, Valerie, S 724-439-4900 434 A
vbacharach@laurel.edu
BACHAS, Leonidas, G 305-284-4117 122 I
bachas@miami.edu
BACHELER, Linda 239-590-1212 119 B
lbachele@fgcu.edu
BACHLE, Lori 402-552-3100 297 B
BACHMAN, Gary 517-586-3001 249 D
gbachman@cleary.edu
BACHMANN, Christopher 618-468-3100 156 E
cbachman@lc.edu
BACHMANN, Kirk, T 312-944-0882 156 D
BACHMANN, Robin 714-895-8382 41 C
rbachmann@gwc.cccd.edu
BACHMEIER, James 616-331-2188 251 F
bachmeij@gvsu.edu
BACHMEIER, John 715-836-5189 551 A
bachmejg@uwec.edu
BACHOO, Richard, R 860-832-1776 90 G
bachoor@ccsu.edu
BACHOVCHIN, Jeffery, J 610-660-1676 446 C
bachovch@sju.edu
BACHRACH, Beverly 305-623-2355 117 A
bbachrach@stu.edu
BACHRATY, James, J 716-839-8461 331 F
jbachrat@daemen.edu
BACINO, Angie 602-337-3044 12 I
abacino@brownmackie.edu
BACK, Andy 610-526-6027 430 D
aback@harcum.edu
BACK, Richard 315-312-2285 354 A
richard.back@oswego.edu
BACKELS, Kelsey, K 717-872-3122 443 D
kelsey.backels@millersville.edu
BACKER, Carol 800-782-2422 33 E
cbacker@mail.cnuas.edu
BACKLIN, William, W 641-422-4326 188 A
backwil@niacc.edu
BACKLUND, Mary, I 845-758-7472 323 D
backlund@bard.edu
BACKMAN, Kelli 402-481-8698 296 I
kelli.backman@bryanlgh.org
BACKMAN, Stephen, M 251-343-8200 6 F
stephen.backman@remingtoncollege.edu
BACKOFEN, Susan 304-929-1329 541 H
sbackofen@mountainstate.edu
BACKOS, Dean 734-487-4428 250 F
dbackos@emich.edu
BACKSCHEIDER,
Nickolas, A 334-844-4512 1 F
backsni@auburn.edu
BACKUS, Adrian 609-497-7837 312 F
faith.fish@ptsem.edu
BACKUS, Bruce, D 314-935-9882 292 I
backusb@wustl.edu
BACKUS, Robert, H 607-746-4677 355 F
backusrh@delhi.edu
BACON, Arthur, D 314-505-7104 280 D
bacona@csl.edu
BACON, Curt 541-552-6487 419 A
bacon@sou.edu
BACON, Jack 610-892-1007 441 C
jbacon@pit.edu
BACON, Judith 312-939-0111 150 D
judy@eastwest.edu
BACON, Karen 212-340-7700 361 M
kbacon@yu.edu
BACON, Pamela 210-458-6551 506 D
pamela.bacon@utsa.edu
BACON, Patricia 765-658-4181 171 B
patbacon@depauw.edu
BACOTE, Le Roy, H 434-848-9603 524 B
lbacote@saintpauls.edu
BACOTE, LeRoy 434-848-1848 524 B
lbacote@saintpauls.edu
BACZA, Gerald 304-367-4632 543 B
gerald.bacza@pierpont.edu
BACZEWSKI, Philip, C 940-565-3886 504 D
baczewski@unt.edu
BADAL, Amy, A 570-577-1638 423 E
amy.badal@bucknell.edu
BADAL, Robert, S 701-252-3467 381 C
badal@jc.edu
BADALYAN, Anna 213-763-7064 55 D
badalya@lattc.edu
BADE, Michael 415-502-6460 75 A
michael.bade@ucsf.edu
BADE, Robert, E 727-816-3356 114 F
badeb@phcc.edu
BADE, William, D 217-786-2326 157 B
bill.bade@llcc.edu
BADEAUX, Stephanie 985-543-4120 211 A
BADENHAUSEN, Richard 801-832-2460 512 G
rbadenhausen@westminstercollege.edu
BADERMAN, Barbara 602-943-2311 19 B
barb.baderman@west.edu
BADGER, Ellen, H 607-777-2510 351 F
ebadger@binghamton.edu
BADGER, Nancy 423-425-4438 477 F
nancy-badger@utc.edu
BADGLEY, Joseph, L 304-766-3252 542 J
jbadgley@kvctc.edu
BADGLEY, Margaret 509-963-3958 532 C
badgleym@cwu.edu
BADILLO, Ricardo 787-891-0925 563 A
rbadillo@aguadilla.inter.edu
BADILLO, Toni 915-831-2164 486 G
mbadill4@epcc.edu
BADINELLI, Sigrid 415-433-9200 68 F
sbadinelli@saybrook.edu
BADOLATO, Greg 617-266-1400 231 E
BADOLATO, Michael 978-762-4000 240 D
mbadolat@northshore.edu
BADOVINAC, Amanda 406-496-4828 296 A
abadovinac@mtech.edu
BADOVINAC, Amanda 406-496-4828 296 B
abadovinac@mtech.edu
BADOVINAC, John 406-496-4249 296 A
jbadovinac@mtech.edu
BADOVINAC, John, C 406-496-4249 296 B
jbadovinac@mtech.edu
BAEHR, Marie 319-399-8616 183 F
mbaehr@coe.edu
BAEHRE-KOLOVANI, Edna 757-822-1050 528 G
ekolovani@tcc.edu
BAENEN, Michael 617-627-3300 245 C
michael.baenen@tufts.edu
BAENNINGER, MaryAnn 320-363-5505 262 F
csbpres@csbsju.edu
BAER, Candace 401-454-6426 454 B
cbaer@risd.edu
BAER, Catherine, E 845-437-5401 359 F
cabaer@vassar.edu
BAER, Eugen 315-781-3300 335 F
baer@hws.edu
BAER, Karim 415-575-6176 32 G
kbaer@ciis.edu
BAER, Natasha 763-433-1707 265 G
natasha.baer@anokaramsey.edu
BAER, Robert 203-857-7369 92 C
rbaer@ncc.commnet.edu
BAERBOCK, Ben, J 414-410-4050 546 G
bjbaerbock@stritch.edu
BAERWALD, Bonnie 920-929-2131 554 G
bbaerwald@morainepark.edu
BAESLACK, III, William, A 216-368-4346 386 F
william.baeslack@case.edu
BAESSLER, Laura 937-382-6661 405 I
laura_baessler@wilmington.edu
BAETHKE, Mark 515-965-7312 183 H
mdbaethke@dmacc.edu
BAEZ, Ada 787-285-5457 562 F
abaez4@hccpr.edu
BAEZ, Annecy 718-289-5868 326 E
annecy.baez@bcc.cuny.edu
BAEZ, Estebania 787-864-2222 563 F
ebaez@inter.edu
BAEZ, Jose 787-746-1400 562 E
jbaez@huertas.edu
BAEZ, Mirna 787-753-0039 564 E
BAEZ MILAN, Tony 724-653-2183 427 G
tbaez@dec.edu
BAEZA-ORTEGO, Gilda 575-538-6350 321 I
baesaortegog@wnmu.edu
BAFFA, Joe 714-556-3610 77 B
joe.baffa@vanguard.edu
BAFFORD-BUBEL,
Karen, M 585-266-0430 333 D
karen.baffordbubel@cci.edu
BAGADIONG, Neil, S 812-374-5154 176 A
nbagadio@ivytech.edu
BAGALE, Edward, J 313-593-5140 259 B
ebagale@umich.edu
BAGBY, Crystal 360-676-2772 535 K
cbagby@nwic.edu
BAGBY, Don 254-710-8200 482 A
don_bagby@baylor.edu
BAGDAZIAN, Robert, A 805-525-4417 72 I
rbagdazian@thomasaquinas.edu
BAGEANT, Laura 410-704-2636 228 E
lbageant@towson.edu
BAGEL, George 770-534-6265 126 E
gbagel@brenau.edu
BAGEL, Jeffrey 716-851-1991 333 A
bagel@ecc.edu
BAGENTS, Bill 256-766-6610 4 C
bbagents@hcu.edu
BAGG, Eva 562-938-4736 54 E
ebagg@lbcc.edu
BAGG, Mary Beth 317-788-3220 180 F
bagg@uindy.edu
BAGGER, Jonathan 410-516-3355 223 F
bagger@jhu.edu
BAGGER, Jonathan, A 410-516-3355 223 F
bagger@jhu.edu
BAGGETT, Cody 217-641-4360 154 I
cbaggett@jwcc.edu
BAGGIO, Bobbe, G 215-951-1238 432 I
baggio@lasalle.edu
BAGGOT, Joseph 507-222-4075 261 G
jbaggot@carleton.edu
BAGGOTT, Martin, J 618-453-2341 165 B
jbaggott@siu.edu
BAGGS, Adam 817-257-6814 499 C
a.baggs@tcu.edu
BAGGS, David 843-863-7513 456 B
dbaggs@csuniv.edu
BAGGSON, Gulizar 479-619-2203 22 H
gbaggson@nwacc.edu
BAGILEO, Nick, J 202-526-3799 99 D
BAGLEY, David, K 585-395-2122 352 F
dbagley@brockport.edu

BAGLEY, Elizabeth ... 404-471-6339 ... 123 I ebagley@agnesscott.edu
BAGLEY, Jo, K ... 817-515-4507 ... 496 C jo.bagley@tccd.edu
BAGLEY, Michelle ... 360-992-2472 ... 532 F mbagley@clark.edu
BAGLEY, Pat ... 931-372-3149 ... 474 B pbagley@tntech.edu
BAGLEY, Rod ... 715-833-6480 ... 553 H rbagley1@cvtc.edu
BAGLEY, Vera, L ... 301-322-0801 ... 225 F vbagley@pgcc.edu
BAGNALL, James ... 928-428-8414 ... 14 B jim.bagnall@eac.edu
BAGNELL, Philip, C ... 423-439-6315 ... 473 F bagnell@etsu.edu
BAGNELL, William ... 252-328-6858 ... 377 E bagnellw@ecu.edu
BAGNO, Sherry ... 847-578-3262 ... 163 C sherry.bagno@rosalindfranklin.edu
BAGNOLI, Joseph, P ... 641-269-3600 ... 185 D bagnolij@grinnell.edu
BAGRANOFF, Nancy, A ... 804-289-8550 ... 525 E nbagrano@richmond.edu
BAGSTAD, Kristi ... 563-588-6314 ... 183 E kristi.bagstad@clarke.edu
BAGWELL, Andrea ... 202-274-5400 ... 100 A abagwell@udc.edu
BAGWELL, Elizabeth ... 828-251-6525 ... 378 D bbagwell@unca.edu
BAGWELL, Jack ... 803-327-8021 ... 463 H bagwell@yorktech.edu
BAGWELL, Linda ... 817-598-6274 ... 508 F lbagwell@wc.edu
BAGWELL, Lydia ... 575-527-7560 ... 319 G lbagwell@nmsu.edu
BAHAMONDE, Manuel, E ... 787-284-1912 ... 564 A mbahamon@ponce.inter.edu
BAHAR, Sonya ... 314-516-7150 ... 291 D bahars@umsl.edu
BAHARANYI, Ntam ... 334-727-8659 ... 8 B nbaharanyi@tuskegee.edu
BAHK, Solomon ... 213-385-2322 ... 79 I
BAHL, Katie ... 563-588-6510 ... 183 E katie.bahl@clarke.edu
BAHLS, Steven, C ... 309-794-7208 ... 145 E stevenbahls@augustana.edu
BAHNEMAN, Molly ... 651-846-1514 ... 269 C molly.bahneman@saintpaul.edu
BAHNEY, Steve ... 217-245-1488 ... 156 B steve.bahney@doc.illinois.gov
BAHR, Christine, M ... 618-537-6810 ... 158 A cmbahr@mckendree.edu
BAHR, Christopher ... 979-230-3119 ... 482 D christopher.bahr@brazosport.edu
BAHR, Janet ... 918-456-5511 ... 409 A bahr@nsuok.edu
BAHR, Paul ... 716-677-9500 ... 325 A pcbahr@bryantstratton.edu
BAI, Yifeng ... 973-748-9000 ... 307 H yifeng_bai@bloomfield.edu
BAIA, Larissa ... 603-524-3207 ... 304 C lbaia@ccsnh.edu
BAICK, Seung-Ju ... 770-279-0507 ... 130 A seungju@bellsouth.net
BAIER, Henry, D ... 734-764-3402 ... 259 A hbaier@umich.edu
BAIER, Kris ... 360-383-3003 ... 540 A kbaier@whatcom.ctc.edu
BAIER, Valerie, A ... 570-326-3761 ... 440 L vbaier@pct.edu
BAIERL, Kenneth, W ... 574-520-4560 ... 174 E kbaierl@iusb.edu
BAIGENT, Peter ... 631-632-6700 ... 352 C peter.baigent@stonybrook.edu
BAIGENT, Peter, M ... 631-632-6700 ... 352 C peter.baigent@stonybrook.edu
BAILES, Loretta ... 773-907-4418 ... 147 D lcanett-bailes@ccc.edu
BAILEY, Aileen, M ... 240-895-4338 ... 226 A ambailey@smcm.edu
BAILEY, Alison ... 309-438-2947 ... 153 D baileya@ilstu.edu
BAILEY, Ann ... 662-325-3555 ... 275 F housing@saffairs.msstate.edu
BAILEY, Anthony ... 213-740-6324 ... 76 F arbailey@usc.edu
BAILEY, Barbara ... 708-763-6529 ... 162 E barbara.bailey@resu.edu
BAILEY, Birdie, I ... 256-765-4311 ... 9 C bibailey@una.edu
BAILEY, Bliss ... 334-844-3500 ... 1 F bailebn@auburn.edu
BAILEY, Cassandra, L ... 310-258-8772 ... 56 E cbailey8@lmu.edu
BAILEY, Cassy ... 785-594-8484 ... 190 F cassy.bailey@bakeru.edu
BAILEY, Cheryl ... 701-355-8180 ... 383 H cbailey@mail.cdln.lib.nd.us
BAILEY, Chris, C ... 570-372-4149 ... 447 E baileycj@susqu.edu
BAILEY, Christopher, C ... 360-442-2101 ... 535 I cbailey@lowercolumbia.edu
BAILEY, Clint ... 252-328-2606 ... 377 E baileyrc@ecu.edu
BAILEY, Darlene ... 816-415-5943 ... 293 C baileyd@william.jewell.edu
BAILEY, David ... 303-361-7381 ... 83 K david.bailey@ccaurora.edu
BAILEY, David, C ... 574-631-2487 ... 180 G bailey.77@nd.edu
BAILEY, Dennis, A ... 850-644-8136 ... 119 D dbailey@fsu.edu
BAILEY, Dexter ... 631-632-4490 ... 352 C dexter.bailey@stonybrook.edu
BAILEY, Dixon ... 325-734-3651 ... 500 G dixon.bailey@tstc.edu
BAILEY, Donald Russell ... 401-865-1188 ... 453 H drbailey@providence.edu
BAILEY, Donna ... 800-818-2261 ... 304 I dbailey@dwc.edu
BAILEY, Dudley (Skip), L ... 585-292-2833 ... 341 H dbailey@monroecc.edu
BAILEY, Ed ... 231-995-1215 ... 256 D ebailey@nmc.edu
BAILEY, Gary ... 616-538-2330 ... 251 D gbailey@gbcol.edu
BAILEY, Georgianna ... 248-213-1610 ... 250 E gbailey@devry.edu
BAILEY, Guy ... 806-742-2121 ... 502 A guy.bailey@ttu.edu
BAILEY, Guy ... 205-348-5103 ... 8 E president@ua.edu
BAILEY, Helen ... 423-869-6387 ... 470 E hbailey@lmunet.edu
BAILEY, Howard, E ... 270-745-2791 ... 208 A howard.bailey@wku.edu
BAILEY, Jana, K ... 606-539-4234 ... 207 C jana.bailey@ucumberlands.edu
BAILEY, Jane ... 203-596-4638 ... 93 G jbailey@post.edu
BAILEY, Janet ... 304-462-4102 ... 544 A janet.bailey@glenville.edu
BAILEY, Janice ... 765-459-0561 ... 176 C jabailey@ivytech.edu
BAILEY, Janie ... 870-633-4480 ... 21 F jbailey@eacc.edu
BAILEY, Jaye ... 203-392-5552 ... 90 I baileyj10@southernct.edu
BAILEY, Jeff ... 870-972-3077 ... 20 D jbailey@astate.edu
BAILEY, Jeremy ... 330-339-3391 ... 394 A jbailey4@kent.edu
BAILEY, Jessica, H ... 601-984-6300 ... 277 E jhbailey@umc.edu
BAILEY, Jessica, M ... 336-750-3277 ... 380 B baileyjm@wssu.edu
BAILEY, John ... 217-479-7047 ... 157 F john.bailey@mac.edu
BAILEY, John ... 808-675-3458 ... 140 D baileyj@byuh.edu
BAILEY, Joseph, A ... 585-345-6900 ... 334 F jabailey@genesee.edu
BAILEY, Judith, A ... 802-485-2065 ... 514 C judyb@norwich.edu
BAILEY, Julie ... 305-809-3179 ... 108 I julie.bailey@fkcc.edu
BAILEY, Julie ... 432-264-5030 ... 488 B jbailey@howardcollege.edu
BAILEY, Kathy ... 864-977-7170 ... 460 A kim.bailey@ngu.edu
BAILEY, Kelly ... 805-525-4417 ... 72 I kbailey@thomasaquinas.edu
BAILEY, Kelly ... 724-738-4223 ... 443 F kelly.bailey@sru.edu
BAILEY, Ken ... 409-740-4400 ... 497 F baileyk@tamug.edu
BAILEY, Kevin ... 850-474-2214 ... 121 D baileyk@uwf.edu
BAILEY, Kim ... 816-322-0110 ... 279 D kim.bailey@calvary.edu
BAILEY, Lisa ... 909-652-6532 ... 39 E lisa.bailey@chaffey.edu
BAILEY, Maggie ... 619-849-2535 ... 62 L maggiebailey@pointloma.edu
BAILEY, Mara, Z ... 402-465-2222 ... 299 H mbailey@nebrwesleyan.edu
BAILEY, Margaret, A ... 803-934-3192 ... 459 G mbailey@morris.edu
BAILEY, Mark ... 909-621-8219 ... 62 H mark_bailey@pitzer.edu
BAILEY, Mark ... 205-853-1200 ... 5 C mbailey@jeffstateonline.com
BAILEY, Mark, L ... 214-841-3676 ... 485 F mbailey@dts.edu
BAILEY, Marvin ... 317-447-6601 ... 172 I marvin.bailey@harrison.edu
BAILEY, Mary, H ... 910-672-1390 ... 377 G mhbailey@uncfsu.edu
BAILEY, Mary Kaye ... 702-651-4362 ... 302 E mary.kaye.bailey@csn.edu
BAILEY, Michael, L ... 804-342-1497 ... 530 A mbailey@vuu.edu
BAILEY, Michelle ... 563-441-4152 ... 184 H
BAILEY, Mike ... 620-417-1019 ... 196 F mike.bailey@sccc.edu
BAILEY, Neil ... 478-289-2162 ... 129 B nabailey@ega.edu
BAILEY, Patricia, A ... 870-508-6102 ... 20 E pbailey@asumh.edu
BAILEY, Patrick, X ... 504-865-3434 ... 213 F pbailey@loyno.edu
BAILEY, Paul ... 678-466-4377 ... 127 D paulbailey@clayton.edu
BAILEY, Peter, A ... 302-295-1191 ... 97 C peter.a.bailey@wilmu.edu
BAILEY, JR., Philip, S ... 805-756-2226 ... 33 I pbailey@calpoly.edu
BAILEY, Richard ... 281-998-6150 ... 494 A richard.bailey@sjcd.edu
BAILEY, Richard, L ... 717-361-1181 ... 428 F baileyrl@etown.edu
BAILEY, Robyn ... 847-635-1444 ... 160 F rbailey@oakton.edu
BAILEY, Scott ... 706-272-4435 ... 128 C sbailey@daltonstate.edu
BAILEY, Shannon ... 330-339-3391 ... 394 A smbailey@kent.edu
BAILEY, Stephanie ... 615-963-7245 ... 474 A sbaile11@tnstate.edu
BAILEY, Steve ... 434-381-6110 ... 524 K sbailey@sbc.edu
BAILEY, Stuart, A ... 512-492-3033 ... 480 F sbailey@aoma.edu
BAILEY, Teresa ... 757-825-3693 ... 528 F baileyt@tncc.edu
BAILEY, Terry ... 706-272-2611 ... 128 C tbailey@daltonstate.edu
BAILEY, Thelathia, B ... 803-313-7042 ... 462 D tbailey@mailbox.sc.edu
BAILEY, William ... 252-493-7434 ... 372 H wbailey@email.pittcc.edu
BAILEY, William, D ... 814-393-2306 ... 442 B wbailey@clarion.edu
BAILEY-AYE, Regena ... 785-654-2416 ... 190 D rbailey@allencc.edu
BAILEY CLARK, Denise ... 301-934-7724 ... 222 C dbclark@csmd.edu
BAILEY-FOUGNIER, Dennis ... 831-479-6317 ... 31 I debailey@cabrillo.edu
BAILEY-JONES, Rachel ... 585-389-5139 ... 342 D rjones3@naz.edu
BAILEY-OCHOA, Celia ... 409-772-8909 ... 507 C cebailey@utmb.edu
BAILIN, Debra, M ... 802-626-6210 ... 515 G debra.bailin@lyndonstate.edu
BAILLIE, Harold ... 570-941-7520 ... 450 C harold.baillie@scranton.edu
BAILLIE, Joan, M ... 856-351-2601 ... 315 A baillie@salemcc.edu
BAILLIE, Thomas ... 206-543-5050 ... 539 A tbaillie@uw.edu
BAILO, Carole Anne ... 480-212-1704 ... 18 C
BAILON, Kathy ... 213-624-1200 ... 46 L kbailon@fidm.edu
BAILY, Michael ... 906-487-7276 ... 251 A michael.baily@finlandia.edu
BAILY, Scott ... 970-491-7655 ... 83 F scott.baily@colostate.edu
BAIMA, Thomas, A ... 847-566-6401 ... 167 F tbaima@usml.edu
BAIN, Andrew, C ... 410-951-4231 ... 228 B acbain@coppin.edu
BAIN, Daniel ... 251-809-1551 ... 5 B daniel.bain@jdcc.edu
BAIN, Donald, E ... 585-385-8010 ... 348 F dbain@sjfc.edu
BAIN, Jeff, N ... 931-363-9872 ... 471 A jbain@martinmethodist.edu
BAIN, Ken ... 202-274-5072 ... 100 A kbain@udc.edu
BAIN, Michael, L ... 404-669-2097 ... 136 B michael.bain@point.edu
BAINES, Moses ... 318-357-3162 ... 211 B
BAINES, Walt ... 480-245-7965 ... 14 J walt.baines@ibconline.edu
BAINTER, Bradley ... 309-298-1808 ... 168 C bl-bainter@wiu.edu
BAIR, Ava ... 719-336-1574 ... 86 B ava.bair@lamarcc.edu
BAIR, Ginny, V ... 218-477-2581 ... 267 F ginny.bair@mnstate.edu
BAIR, Miles, C ... 309-556-3134 ... 153 F mbair@iwu.edu
BAIR, Susanne, P ... 716-878-4324 ... 353 A bairsp@buffalostate.edu
BAIRD, David, L ... 714-895-8125 ... 41 C dbaird@gwc.cccd.edu
BAIRD, Davis ... 508-793-7673 ... 233 B dbaird@clarku.edu
BAIRD, Debra ... 256-216-6617 ... 1 E debra.baird@athens.edu
BAIRD, Denise, M ... 317-738-8270 ... 171 F dbaird@franklincollege.edu
BAIRD, Jeffrey ... 215-951-2620 ... 444 D bairdj@philau.edu
BAIRD, Karen ... 312-322-1720 ... 165 E kbaird@spertus.edu
BAIRD, Kathy ... 707-256-7168 ... 58 F kbaird@napavalley.edu
BAIRD, Lynn, N ... 208-885-6534 ... 144 G lbaird@uidaho.edu
BAIRD, Phil ... 701-255-3285 ... 383 G pbaird@uttc.edu
BAIRD, Robert ... 276-466-7911 ... 529 D robertbaird@vic.edu
BAIRD, Teresa ... 325-649-8308 ... 488 C bookstore@hputx.edu
BAIRD, Timothy, R ... 724-847-6490 ... 429 H trbaird@geneva.edu
BAISDEN, Emma, L ... 304-896-7402 ... 543 C emma.baisden@southernwv.edu
BAITMAN, Clay, L ... 618-235-2700 ... 165 D clay.baitman@swic.edu
BAITY, Deborah, A ... 831-656-2480 ... 558 A dbaity@nps.edu
BAITY, Kristie, F ... 336-734-7051 ... 370 F kbaity@forsythtech.edu
BAJOIE, Diane, E ... 504-568-4810 ... 213 A dbajoi@lsuhsc.edu
BAJOR, William ... 201-200-3409 ... 312 B wbajor@njcu.edu
BAJUSZIK, Pattie, A ... 724-287-8711 ... 423 G pattie.bajuszik@bc3.edu
BAK, Doug ... 719-846-5513 ... 88 F doug.bak@trinidadstate.edu
BAKARI, Sentwali ... 515-271-2835 ... 184 D sentwali.bakari@drake.edu
BAKAS, Joanna ... 617-850-1280 ... 235 F jbakas@hchc.edu
BAKEMEIR, Emily, P ... 203-432-4440 ... 96 A emily.bakemeir@yale.edu
BAKER, Adria ... 713-348-6095 ... 493 C abaker@rice.edu
BAKER, Alvin, D ... 606-326-2422 ... 201 F abaker00016@kctcs.edu
BAKER, Amy ... 573-288-6493 ... 280 I abaker@culver.edu
BAKER, Barbara ... 970-521-6611 ... 86 K barbara.baker@njc.edu
BAKER, Barry ... 407-823-2564 ... 120 B barry.baker@ucf.edu
BAKER, Barry ... 989-686-9346 ... 250 D bgbaker@delta.edu
BAKER, Barry, A ... 425-235-5839 ... 537 A bbaker@rtc.edu
BAKER, Ben, J ... 256-765-4278 ... 9 C bjbaker@una.edu
BAKER, Bill ... 405-422-1282 ... 411 G bakerb@redlandscc.edu
BAKER, Bill ... 434-239-3500 ... 522 B
BAKER, Brent ... 817-598-6275 ... 508 F bbaker@wc.edu
BAKER, Brent, A ... 765-641-4072 ... 169 E babaker@anderson.edu
BAKER, Brian ... 812-749-1212 ... 178 H bbaker@oak.edu
BAKER, III, Brooks, H ... 205-934-4427 ... 8 F bbaker@uab.edu
BAKER, Bruce ... 603-427-7604 ... 304 B bbaker@ccsnh.edu
BAKER, Carrie, B ... 850-873-3565 ... 110 H cbaker@gulfcoast.edu
BAKER, Chad ... 717-299-7702 ... 448 A baker@stevenscollege.edu
BAKER, Connie ... 805-654-6400 ... 77 F cbaker@vcccd.edu
BAKER, Credence ... 254-968-9050 ... 497 A cbaker@tarleton.edu
BAKER, Crystal ... 812-237-2215 ... 173 B crystal.baker@indstate.edu
BAKER, David ... 715-836-2542 ... 551 A bakerda@uwec.edu
BAKER, David, A ... 541-737-3871 ... 418 F david.baker@oregonstate.edu
BAKER, David, E ... 312-567-3561 ... 153 C bakerd@iit.edu
BAKER, Dawn ... 503-760-3131 ... 414 F dawn@birthingway.edu
BAKER, Debbie ... 307-382-1611 ... 557 A dbaker@wwcc.wy.edu
BAKER, Don ... 408-924-7820 ... 37 C don.baker@sjsu.edu
BAKER, Donald, B ... 401-825-2134 ... 453 D dbaker@ccri.edu
BAKER, Donna ... 816-584-6847 ... 287 E donna.baker@park.edu
BAKER, Douglas, D ... 208-885-6448 ... 144 G provost@uidaho.edu
BAKER, Dyann, J ... 860-701-5016 ... 93 E baker_dy@mitchell.edu
BAKER, Eliott, G ... 724-738-2010 ... 443 F eliott.baker@sru.edu
BAKER, Elisha (Bear) ... 907-786-1050 ... 10 H crbaker@uaa.alaska.edu
BAKER, Elizabeth ... 860-231-5319 ... 95 D ebaker@usj.edu
BAKER, Elizabeth ... 252-222-6216 ... 369 A bakere@carteret.edu
BAKER, Erma, A ... 540-654-2043 ... 525 D ebaker@umw.edu

BAKER, Fred 501-450-1362 22 A baker@hendrix.edu
BAKER, Gail 402-554-2232 301 A gbaker@unomaha.edu
BAKER, Gordon 678-466-4334 127 D gordonbaker@clayton.edu
BAKER, Greg 808-981-2790 140 F gbaker@hicom.edu
BAKER, Hilary 818-677-7750 35 F hilary.baker@csun.edu
BAKER, Hunter 731-661-5519 477 B hbaker@uu.edu
BAKER, Jackie 507-457-6695 271 B jbaker@smumn.edu
BAKER, James 307-686-0254 556 F jbaker@sheridan.edu
BAKER, James, P 417-836-8501 286 C jbaker@missouristate.edu
BAKER, Janet 610-740-3765 425 A jlbaker@cedarcrest.edu
BAKER, Jeff 619-644-7108 49 C jeff.baker@gcccd.edu
BAKER, Jeffrey 503-297-5544 417 G jbaker@ocac.edu
BAKER, Jeffrey, A 704-687-8457 379 A jbaker88@uncc.edu
BAKER, Jennifer 417-823-3469 289 I jbaker@forest.edu
BAKER, Jill 619-388-2803 65 G jbaker@sdccd.edu
BAKER, Jill 304-457-6337 540 E bakersj@ab.edu
BAKER, Jim 817-272-2261 505 C jimbaker@uta.edu
BAKER, Jo Nell 909-593-3511 75 E jbaker@laverne.edu
BAKER, Joe 262-524-7319 546 H jrbaker@carrollu.edu
BAKER, John, E 301-295-3028 558 D john.baker@usuhs.edu
BAKER, John, T 508-856-5538 237 C john.baker@umassmed.edu
BAKER, Johnny 256-835-5463 3 J jbaker@gadsdenstate.edu
BAKER, Joseph, J 610-499-4151 97 B jjbaker@widener.edu
BAKER, Joseph, J 610-499-4151 451 F jjbaker@widener.edu
BAKER, Josita, L 405-466-2980 408 G jlbaker@langston.edu
BAKER, Joyce 740-695-9500 385 B jbaker@belmontcollege.edu
BAKER, Judy 650-949-7388 47 H bakerjudy@foothill.edu
BAKER, Julie 419-423-2211 385 J jbaker@brownmackie.edu
BAKER, Karen, M 817-257-5566 499 C k.baker@tcu.edu
BAKER, Kelvin 954-486-7728 122 H
BAKER, Ken 937-320-2600 390 D kbaker@devry.edu
BAKER, Larry 406-994-6752 295 C lbaker@montana.edu
BAKER, Lee, D 919-684-3465 364 C ldbaker@duke.edu
BAKER, Linda 906-487-3381 255 B lpbaker@mtu.edu
BAKER, Lori 540-857-6067 529 B lbaker@virginiawestern.edu
BAKER, Marilyn 816-271-4200 286 G mbaker3@missouriwestern.edu
BAKER, Matt 660-562-1219 287 B mcbaker@nwmissouri.edu
BAKER, Matt 215-951-2870 444 D bakerm@philau.edu
BAKER, Matthew 660-562-1219 287 B mcbaker@nwmissouri.edu
BAKER, Maureen 402-844-7258 299 I maureen@northeast.edu
BAKER, Megan 847-330-0040 150 A mbaker6@devry.edu
BAKER, Melanie 540-636-2900 517 K melaniebaker@christendom.edu
BAKER, Michael 907-564-8259 10 D mbaker@alaskapacific.edu
BAKER, Michael, F 508-856-3040 237 C michael.baker@umassmed.edu
BAKER, Mike 859-442-1153 202 B mike.baker@kctcs.edu
BAKER, Molly 815-288-5511 164 B bakerm@svcc.edu
BAKER, Monica 928-226-4262 13 F monica.baker@coconino.edu
BAKER, Nancy 203-932-7307 95 C nbaker@newhaven.edu
BAKER, Nancy 704-636-6882 365 D nbaker@hoodseminary.edu
BAKER, Nancy, L 319-335-5867 182 F nancy-l-baker@uiowa.edu
BAKER, Natalie 404-880-6879 127 C nbaker@cau.edu
BAKER, Natasha 937-512-4636 401 J natasha.baker@sinclair.edu
BAKER, Neal 765-983-1355 171 E bakerne@earlham.edu
BAKER, Nelson 404-894-8920 130 F nelson.baker@pe.gatech.edu
BAKER, Nick 989-275-5000 253 E nick.baker@kirtland.edu
BAKER, Pamela, J 207-786-6066 217 C pbaker@bates.edu
BAKER, Patricia, L 985-447-0924 211 G pbaker@ltc.edu
BAKER, Paul, K 803-780-1007 463 C pbaker@voorhees.edu
BAKER, Pearl 606-539-4211 207 C pearl.baker@ucumberlands.edu
BAKER, Quincee 701-627-4638 381 B qbaker@fbcc.bia.edu
BAKER, Richard, A 713-743-8834 503 D rabaker4@central.uh.edu
BAKER, Robert 320-629-5118 268 E bakerr@pinetech.edu
BAKER, Robert 617-984-1642 243 H bbaker@quincycollege.edu
BAKER, Robert 518-631-9862 358 H bakerr@uniongraduatecollege.edu
BAKER, Robert, D 972-238-6174 485 D rbaker1@dcccd.edu
BAKER, Robert, T 336-758-5224 380 C bakerrt@wfu.edu
BAKER, Robin, E 503-554-2101 415 I rbaker@georgefox.edu
BAKER, Russell, D 317-921-4313 175 I rbaker80@ivytech.edu
BAKER, Ruth, E 410-334-2815 229 E rbaker@worwic.edu
BAKER, Sallie 828-835-4202 374 F sbaker@tricountycc.edu
BAKER, Sally, A 207-859-4609 217 G sabaker@colby.edu
BAKER, Sam 912-478-5047 131 E s_baker@georgiasouthern.edu
BAKER, Sandi, J 770-531-6408 133 C sbaker@laniertech.edu
BAKER, Sandy 951-222-8000 63 I sandy.baker@rcc.edu
BAKER, Sandy 951-222-8408 64 A sandy.baker@rcc.edu
BAKER, Sarah 207-288-5015 217 H sbaker@coa.edu
BAKER, Sarah 910-672-1185 377 G sbaker@uncfsu.edu
BAKER, Scott, R 740-427-5148 394 C bakersr@kenyon.edu
BAKER, Shane 919-761-2285 377 A sbaker@sebts.edu
BAKER, Stephen 212-353-4131 331 A baker@cooper.edu
BAKER, Stephen, N 401-874-4980 454 E majorbaker@uri.edu
BAKER, Steve 619-644-7155 49 C steve.baker@gcccd.edu
BAKER, Steven 561-803-2223 114 C steven_baker@pba.edu
BAKER, Susan, D 585-292-2124 341 H sbaker@monroecc.edu
BAKER, Suzanne 828-227-7127 380 A sbaker@wcu.edu
BAKER, Thomas, N 315-267-2900 354 C bakertn@potsdam.edu
BAKER, Timothy 670-234-3690 560 B timothyb@nmcnet.edu
BAKER, Todd 716-896-0700 359 H bakert@villa.edu
BAKER, Val 863-297-1000 115 C vbaker@polk.edu
BAKER, Wayne 432-335-6574 492 A wbaker@odessa.edu
BAKER, William, H 864-488-4600 459 B wbaker@limestone.edu
BAKER, William, P 602-386-4112 11 G william.baker@arizonachristian.edu
BAKER, Winston 936-468-2601 496 B bakerwa@sfasu.edu
BAKER, Wren 660-562-1212 287 B wbaker@nwmissouri.edu
BAKER-WATSON, Stevie 765-658-6075 171 B steviebaker-watson@depauw.edu
BAKEWELL-SACHS, Susan 609-771-3032 308 F sbakewel@tcnj.edu
BAKHIT, Izzeldin 267-256-0210 99 G izzeldin.bakhit@strayer.edu
BAKHIT, Norm 574-535-7507 171 G nbakhit@goshen.edu
BAKK, Kelly 218-749-7765 266 I k.bakk@mr.mnscu.edu
BAKKE, Andrea 703-812-4757 520 J abakke@leland.edu
BAKKE, Lisa 702-651-4211 302 E lisa.bakke@csn.edu
BAKKE, Ray 360-927-5744 531 D rayb@bgu.edu
BAKKEN, Jeffrey 309-677-3997 146 C jbakken@bradley.edu
BAKKEN, Turina, R 608-246-6516 554 D bakken@madisoncollege.org
BAKKER, Cornelia, E 847-543-2464 148 B cbakker@clcillinois.edu
BAKKER, Joseph 850-599-3197 118 L joseph.bakker@famu.edu
BAKKUM, Barclay 312-949-7013 152 E bbakkum@ico.edu
BAKKUM, Christine, S 608-785-8951 551 C cbakkum@uwlax.edu
BAKOWSKI, Tracy, L 302-739-4052 96 D tbakowsk@dtcc.edu
BAKR, Abu 401-874-4860 454 E abubakrmail@uri.edu
BAKSH-JARRETT, Gail 718-482-5116 328 B gailbj@lagcc.cuny.edu
BAKST, M, S 248-968-3360 260 E
BAKST, Y 248-968-3360 260 E
BAKY, John, S 215-951-1286 432 I baky@lasalle.edu
BALA, Devi 480-517-8343 16 B devi.bala@riosalado.edu
BALABAN, Michael 845-431-8044 332 D michael.balaban@sunydutchess.edu
BALACEK, Patti 608-785-9201 555 F balacekp@westerntc.edu
BALACHANDRAN, Elizabeth 224-293-5682 100 I ebalachandran@aiuonline.edu
BALAGOUR, Nina 215-612-6600 432 C n_balagour@chicareers.com
BALANOFF, Janet 407-823-1336 120 B janet.balanoff@ucf.edu
BALAS, E. Andrew 706-721-2621 130 D andrew.balas@georgiahealth.edu
BALAS, Heather 724-589-2014 448 B hbalas@thiel.edu
BALASCO, Vincent 401-825-1179 453 D vbalasco@ccri.edu
BALASKA, Rosanne 315-733-2300 359 C
BALASKI, Keith 612-659-6842 267 B keith.balaski@minneapolis.edu
BALASON, Severo 708-974-5346 159 B balasonjrs@morainevalley.edu
BALBACH, Donna, M 812-357-6525 180 A dbalbach@saintmeinrad.edu
BALCH, Angela 432-685-4508 491 A abalch@midland.edu
BALCH, Bradley 812-237-2919 173 B brad.balch@indstate.edu
BALCH, Glenna 512-404-4828 481 D gbalch@austinseminary.edu
BALCH, Maggie 781-736-3600 232 F balch@brandeis.edu
BALCH, Marcus 254-867-2254 500 F marcus.balch@tstc.edu
BALCH, Pamela, M 304-473-8181 545 G balch@wvwc.edu
BALD, Tim 920-403-3030 550 F tim.bald@snc.edu
BALDACCI, June 207-581-2695 220 A baldacci@maine.edu
BALDASARE, Paul 910-277-5660 376 C baldasar@sapc.edu
BALDASTY, Gerald, J 206-543-7468 539 A baldasty@uw.edu
BALDERAS, Maggie 805-966-3888 31 D mbalderas@brooks.edu
BALDERRAMA, Sylvia 845-437-5700 359 F sybalderrama@vassar.edu
BALDESCHWIELER, Karen 415-813-6024 58 J kbaldeschwieler@new.edu
BALDIN, Antoinette 419-995-8887 392 K baldin.a@rhodesstate.edu
BALDINI, Fred 916-278-7256 36 A baldinif@csus.edu
BALDONADO, Hernando 713-718-5069 487 I nandy.baldonado@hccs.edu
BALDONEDO, Claudia 718-482-5236 328 B claudiab@lagcc.cuny.edu
BALDREE, Megan 325-793-4801 490 H baldree.megan@mcm.edu
BALDRIDGE, Amanda 580-371-2371 408 I abaldridge@mscok.edu
BALDRIDGE, Patricia, M 215-951-2851 444 D baldridgep@philau.edu
BALDRIDGE, Susan 802-443-5391 514 A scbaldridge@middlebury.edu
BALDUCCI, Laureen 650-949-7463 47 H balduccilaureen@foothill.edu
BALDUS, Lisa 507-281-7771 268 I lisa.baldus@roch.edu
BALDWIN, Alphonso 847-543-2113 148 B abaldwin@clcillinois.edu
BALDWIN, Anne, E 585-245-5547 353 C baldwina@geneseo.edu
BALDWIN, Beatrice 225-342-6950 215 D beatrice.baldwin@la.gov
BALDWIN, Bobbie 901-448-5623 477 E bbaldwi2@uthsc.edu
BALDWIN, Bryan 508-531-2609 237 D bbaldwin@bridgew.edu
BALDWIN, Chad 307-766-2929 556 H cbaldwin@uwyo.edu
BALDWIN, Charlene 714-532-7747 39 F baldwin@chapman.edu
BALDWIN, Christine, A 714-850-4800 90 A baldwin@taftu.edu
BALDWIN, Darin 334-745-6437 7 D dbaldwin@suscc.edu
BALDWIN, David, N 508-626-4645 238 A dbaldwin@framingham.edu
BALDWIN, Deborah, J 501-569-3296 24 E djbaldwin@ualr.edu
BALDWIN, Gail 601-643-8322 273 G gail.baldwin@colin.edu
BALDWIN, Hazel, N 434-223-6117 519 G hbaldwin@hsc.edu
BALDWIN, Jackie 856-227-7200 308 D jbaldwin@camdencc.edu
BALDWIN, James, L 814-362-7602 449 B jlb20@pitt.edu
BALDWIN, Joelle 616-632-2076 247 E baldwjoe@aquinas.edu
BALDWIN, Karen 205-348-3393 8 E kbaldwin@advance.ua.edu
BALDWIN, Linda 909-594-5611 58 A lbaldwin@mtsac.edu
BALDWIN, Mary Sue 205-726-4097 6 G msbaldwi@samford.edu
BALDWIN, R. Chad 636-584-6609 281 E rcbaldwin@eastcentral.edu
BALDWIN, Robert, D 301-784-5000 221 B rbaldwin@allegany.edu
BALDWIN, Sarah 503-554-2321 415 I sbaldwin@georgefox.edu
BALDWIN, Stan 601-925-3321 275 C sbaldwin@mc.edu
BALDWIN, Thomas 218-281-8340 271 E tbaldwin@umn.edu
BALDWIN, Troy 504-816-4504 209 A tbaldwin@dillard.edu
BALDWIN, Veria 606-589-3018 203 D cookie.baldwin@kctcs.edu
BALDWIN, William 212-678-3052 357 G wjb12@tc.columbia.edu
BALDWIN-DIMEO, Caren 603-526-3714 303 G cbaldwin-dimeo@colby-sawyer.edu
BALDYGO, Robert 540-234-9261 526 D baldygor@brcc.edu
BALENTINE, Kim 417-626-1234 287 C kbalentine@occ.edu
BALES, John, G 760-480-8474 78 J bales@wscal.edu
BALES, John Anthony 208-885-5953 144 G jbales@uidaho.edu
BALES, Kay 765-285-5344 169 G kbales@bsu.edu
BALES, Michael 276-964-7323 528 E michael.bales@sw.edu
BALES, William, J 615-898-5818 473 G joe.bales@mtsu.edu
BALESTRERI, Teresa, A 314-516-5002 291 D tkb@umsl.edu
BALFOUR, Alan 404-894-3380 130 F alan.balfour@coa.gatech.edu
BALFOUR, David 802-773-5900 513 D david.balfour@csj.edu
BALGAS, Diana 510-885-3983 34 E diana.balgas@csueastbay.edu
BALGE, Daniel, N 507-354-8221 264 K balgedn@mlc-wels.edu
BALIK, Daniel, J 651-696-6265 264 J balik@macalester.edu
BALINT, Bill 724-357-4000 442 F wsbalint@iup.edu
BALISTRERI, Rebecca 414-847-3262 549 B beckybalistreri@miad.edu
BALISTRERI-CLARKE, Margaret, R 608-663-2212 547 F balistr@edgewood.edu
BALKCOM, Paris 312-980-9200 154 B pbalkcom@iadtchicago.edu
BALL, Charles 574-239-8318 172 M cball@hcc-nd.edu
BALL, Daniel, W 864-388-8300 459 A dball@lander.edu
BALL, Dave 319-296-4204 185 F david.ball@hawkeyecollege.edu
BALL, Deborah, L 734-647-1637 259 A dball@umich.edu
BALL, Diane 239-513-1122 111 A dball@hodges.edu
BALL, Don 330-494-6170 402 B dball@starkstate.edu
BALL, Donald 352-365-3532 112 J balld@lscc.edu
BALL, Drexel, B 803-535-5263 456 D dball@claflin.edu
BALL, Elizabeth 573-875-7403 280 A eqball@ccis.edu
BALL, Gerald, D 828-689-1242 366 I gball@mhc.edu
BALL, James, D 410-386-8192 221 G jball@carrollcc.edu
BALL, Jason 561-297-3440 119 A jball@fau.edu
BALL, Jennifer 502-495-1040 200 C jball@daymarcollege.edu
BALL, John 504-568-4500 213 A jball@lsuhsc.edu

BALL, Karen .... 559-791-2420 .... 53 A
kball@portervillecollege.edu
BALL, Karen .... 717-720-4050 .... 441 E
kball@passhe.edu
BALL, Kathy .... 304-384-6009 .... 543 G
bonner@concord.edu
BALL, Kenneth .... 703-993-1500 .... 519 E
kball@gmu.edu
BALL, Kevin .... 330-941-1560 .... 406 F
keball@ysu.edu
BALL, Kim .... 704-894-2521 .... 363 I
kiball@davidson.edu
BALL, Margaret, A .... 405-208-5060 .... 410 A
mball@okcu.edu
BALL, Margaret, T .... 718-817-3010 .... 334 C
mball@fordham.edu
BALL, Michael .... 859-246-6512 .... 201 H
michael.ball@kctcs.edu
BALL, Molly, A .... 309-457-2323 .... 158 H
maball@monmouthcollege.edu
BALL, Monte .... 330-339-3391 .... 394 A
mball15@kent.edu
BALL, Sam .... 253-833-9111 .... 534 H
sball@greenriver.edu
BALL, Scott .... 423-236-2881 .... 473 B
sball@southern.edu
BALL, Shelley .... 865-471-3235 .... 467 G
sball@cn.edu
BALL, Terri .... 913-367-6204 .... 193 F
tball@highlandcc.edu
BALL, Terri .... 913-367-6204 .... 193 G
tball@highlandcc.edu
BALL, Terry .... 801-422-2736 .... 509 H
terry_ball@byu.edu
BALL, Thomas, G .... 724-458-2163 .... 430 B
tgball@gcc.edu
BALL, Travis .... 903-886-5060 .... 498 B
travis.ball@tamuc.edu
BALL, William, S .... 513-558-0026 .... 403 D
william.s.ball@uc.edu
BALL-DAVIS, Marsha .... 860-906-5127 .... 91 C
mball-davis@ccc.commnet.edu
BALL-PARKER, Gayle .... 310-243-2801 .... 34 D
gball@csudh.edu
BALL-WILLIAMSON,
Carrie .... 662-862-8123 .... 274 E
cbball@iccms.edu
BALLA, Ruth Ann .... 305-237-3702 .... 113 H
rballa@mdc.edu
BALLABAN, David, C .... 610-921-7256 .... 421 E
dballaban@alb.edu
BALLAGH DE TOVAR,
Jane .... 913-621-8791 .... 192 F
jane@donnelly.edu
BALLAM, Gary, O .... 816-654-7562 .... 283 F
gballam@kcumb.edu
BALLANCE, Ronald, J .... 757-671-7171 .... 518 H
administration@ecpi.edu
BALLANTINE, Clay .... 413-559-5590 .... 235 C
BALLANTYNE, Sherri .... 425-564-2229 .... 531 G
sballant@bellevuecollege.edu
BALLANTYNE, Trina .... 201-216-8165 .... 315 E
tballant@stevens.edu
BALLARD, Carol .... 334-670-3182 .... 8 A
csupri@troy.edu
BALLARD, Carol .... 863-680-6236 .... 109 E
cballard@flsouthern.edu
BALLARD, Chris .... 217-362-6419 .... 158 G
cballard@millikin.edu
BALLARD, Donna .... 662-476-5054 .... 274 B
dballard@eastms.edu
BALLARD, Gail .... 231-876-3145 .... 248 A
gail.ballard@baker.edu
BALLARD, Glenda .... 903-223-3073 .... 498 F
glenda.ballard@tamut.edu
BALLARD, Jennifer .... 870-512-7861 .... 20 F
jennifer_ballard@asun.edu
BALLARD, Jennifer .... 503-883-2509 .... 416 H
jballard@linfield.edu
BALLARD, Jill, M .... 814-362-5091 .... 449 B
jballard@pitt.edu
BALLARD, Katie .... 270-686-4529 .... 203 B
katie.ballard@kctcs.edu
BALLARD, Lowell, W .... 630-752-5222 .... 168 H
lowell.ballard@wheaton.edu
BALLARD, Margaret .... 617-745-3876 .... 234 A
margaret.ballard@enc.edu
BALLARD, Phillip .... 870-862-8131 .... 23 G
pballard@southark.edu
BALLARD, Robin .... 309-694-8511 .... 152 C
rballard@icc.edu
BALLARD, Steve .... 870-543-5910 .... 23 H
sballard@seark.edu
BALLARD, Steve .... 252-328-6212 .... 377 E
chancellor@ecu.edu
BALLARD, Terri .... 412-536-1251 .... 432 H
terri.ballard@laroche.edu
BALLARD, William, H .... 419-772-2020 .... 398 H
b-ballard@onu.edu
BALLARD, William, P .... 802-656-2240 .... 514 H
william.ballard@uvm.edu
BALLARD GORMAN,
Shannon .... 518-244-3142 .... 348 A
ballas@sage.edu

BALLARD-THROWER,
Rhea .... 202-806-8047 .... 98 E
rballard@law.howard.edu
BALLARINI, John .... 262-554-6110 .... 549 A
jaballarini@yahoo.com
BALLATE, Henry .... 954-322-4460 .... 112 C
ballateh@jmvu.edu
BALLENGEE, Greg, A .... 740-351-3574 .... 401 I
gballengee@shawnee.edu
BALLENGER, Nicole .... 307-766-4286 .... 556 H
nicoleb@uwyo.edu
BALLENGER, P, J .... 256-824-6565 .... 8 G
john.ballenger@uah.edu
BALLENTINE, Angela .... 252-492-2061 .... 374 G
ballentine@vgcc.edu
BALLENTINE, Howard .... 302-736-2529 .... 97 A
ballentine@wesley.edu
BALLENTINE, John .... 803-799-9082 .... 461 A
jballentine@southuniversity.edu
BALLER, Jim .... 304-214-8960 .... 543 D
jballer@wvncc.edu
BALLESTEROS, E. Michael 207-974-4869 .... 218 H
mballesteros@emcc.edu
BALLESTEROS, Victor .... 972-438-6932 .... 492 E
vballesteros@parkercc.edu
BALLEW, Marcy .... 903-875-7335 .... 491 C
marcy.ballew@navarrocollege.edu
BALLIET, Emil .... 817-461-8741 .... 480 H
eballiet@abconline.org
BALLING, John, D .... 503-370-6004 .... 421 D
jballing@willamette.edu
BALLINGER, Jamie .... 207-859-1102 .... 219 G
ballingerj@thomas.edu
BALLINGER, Kevin .... 714-432-5531 .... 41 D
sballinger@occ.cccd.edu
BALLINGER, Marcia .... 440-365-5222 .... 395 D
BALLINGER, Philip .... 206-221-2305 .... 539 A
philipba@uw.edu
BALLINGER, Stacy .... 423-614-8630 .... 470 C
sballinger@leeuniversity.edu
BALLOM, Kenneth .... 217-333-2121 .... 167 D
ballom@illinois.edu
BALLOU, Dawn .... 617-732-2077 .... 241 C
dawn.ballou@mcphs.edu
BALLOU, Kathryn .... 913-344-6084 .... 190 F
kathryn.ballou@bakeru.edu
BALLOU, Trenna .... 435-722-6900 .... 510 N
trenna@ubatc.edu
BALLS, Jennifer .... 252-789-0219 .... 371 H
jballs@martincc.edu
BALMER, Shannon .... 541-684-7222 .... 417 F
sbalmer@nwcu.edu
BALMER, Stephanie .... 717-245-1287 .... 427 F
balmers@dickinson.edu
BALMOS, Donald .... 254-299-8602 .... 490 G
dbalmos@mclennan.edu
BALOG, John, A .... 904-256-7067 .... 111 L
jbalog@ju.edu
BALOG, Scott .... 850-201-8632 .... 122 A
balogs@tcc.fl.edu
BALOGA, Monica .... 321-674-7397 .... 108 H
mbaloga@fit.edu
BALOGH, Deborah Ware .... 317-788-3212 .... 180 F
dbalogh@uindy.edu
BALOGUN, Joseph, A .... 773-995-3987 .... 146 G
ja-balogun@csu.edu
BALOGUN, Lateef .... 252-536-7253 .... 371 B
balogunl@halifaxcc.edu
BALON, Michelle .... 352-365-3576 .... 112 J
balonm@lscc.edu
BALOUBI, Desire' .... 919-546-8307 .... 376 F
dbaloubi@shawu.edu
BALOUGH, Sandra, A .... 814-472-3151 .... 446 B
sbalough@francis.edu
BALRAM, Arlette .... 212-686-9040 .... 360 F
abalram@woodtobecoburn.edu
BALSA, Carmen, A .... 787-257-0000 .... 567 C
carmen.balsa@upr.edu
BALSAM, Carl, E .... 773-244-5610 .... 159 H
cbalsam@northpark.edu
BALSAMO, Michael .... 586-445-7141 .... 254 C
balsamom@macomb.edu
BALSANO, Gregory, R .... 562-903-4708 .... 31 A
greg.balsano@biola.edu
BALSEIRO, Wanda .... 787-878-5475 .... 563 B
wbalseiro@arecibo.inter.edu
BALSER, Deborah, B .... 314-516-5146 .... 291 D
balserd@umsl.edu
BALSER, Jeffrey .... 615-322-2151 .... 478 A
jeff.balser@vanderbilt.edu
BALSER, Jeffrey, R .... 615-936-3030 .... 478 A
jeff.balser@vanderbilt.edu
BALSER, Rose .... 920-748-8137 .... 550 D
bookstore@ripon.edu
BALSER, Teresa, C .... 352-392-1961 .... 120 C
tcbalser@ufl.edu
BALSLEY, Richard .... 229-317-6930 .... 128 D
rich.balsley@darton.edu
BALTES, Mary .... 813-935-5700 .... 116 A
marybaltes@remingtoncollege.edu
BALTHAZARD, Pierre .... 716-375-2200 .... 348 C
pbalthaz@sbu.edu
BALTIMORE, Lester .... 516-877-3142 .... 322 A
baltimore@adelphi.edu

BALTRUS, Susan, C .... 207-795-2846 .... 217 F
baltruss@cmhc.org
BALTZLEY, Dennis .... 602-978-7751 .... 18 H
dennis.baltzley@thunderbird.edu
BALZA, Stephen, J .... 507-354-8221 .... 264 K
balzasj@mlc-wels.edu
BALZANO, Wanda .... 336-758-4455 .... 380 C
balzanow@wfu.edu
BALZER, Brenda .... 443-334-2176 .... 226 E
bbalzer@stevenson.edu
BALZER, Jackie .... 503-725-5249 .... 418 G
jbalzer@pdx.edu
BALZER, William .... 419-372-0623 .... 385 E
wbalzer@bgsu.edu
BALZER, William, K .... 419-372-0623 .... 385 F
wbalzer@bgsu.edu
BAMBARA, Cynthia, S .... 301-784-5000 .... 221 B
cbambara@allegany.edu
BAMBERGER, Gregory .... 610-683-4095 .... 443 A
gbamberg@kutztown.edu
BAMBHROLIA, Savita .... 609-586-4800 .... 311 B
bambhros@mccc.edu
BAMBINA, Antonia, D .... 812-461-5357 .... 181 B
adbambina@usi.edu
BAME, Kevin .... 618-453-2474 .... 165 B
kbame@siu.edu
BAME, Shirley .... 208-524-3000 .... 143 G
shirley.bame@my.eitc.edu
BAMFORD, Carol, M .... 515-263-6129 .... 185 C
cbamford@grandview.edu
BAMFORD, Penny .... 510-869-6744 .... 64 J
pbamford@samuelmerritt.edu
BAMONTE, Paul .... 718-409-7254 .... 356 C
pbamonte@sunymaritime.edu
BANA, Mark .... 303-914-6220 .... 87 G
mark.bana@rrcc.edu
BANACH, Michael .... 718-940-5584 .... 349 A
mbanach@sjcny.edu
BANACH, Patricia, S .... 860-465-5000 .... 90 H
banachp@easternct.edu
BANAHAN, Richard .... 314-644-9766 .... 288 I
rbanahan@stlcc.edu
BANAS, Paul .... 425-889-5234 .... 536 C
paul.banas@northwestu.edu
BANASZAK, Larry .... 614-823-1693 .... 400 H
lbanaszak@otterbein.edu
BANASZAK, Lori .... 253-589-5788 .... 532 G
lori.banaszak@cptc.edu
BANASZAK HOLL,
Mark, M .... 734-763-1290 .... 259 A
mbanasza@umich.edu
BANAVAR, Jayanth, R .... 301-405-2316 .... 227 B
banavar@umd.edu
BANBURY, Doug .... 740-392-6868 .... 396 I
mbanbury@mvnu.edu
BANDA, Magda .... 708-656-8000 .... 159 D
magna.banda@morton.edu
BANDAS, Mark .... 615-322-6400 .... 478 A
mark.bandas@vanderbilt.edu
BANDAS, Raul .... 787-758-2525 .... 567 G
raul.bandas@upr.edu
BANDELIN, Janis, M .... 864-294-2191 .... 458 E
janis.bandelin@furman.edu
BANDO, Chris .... 609-201-8767 .... 65 D
BANDOIAN, Nancy .... 617-989-4476 .... 245 F
bandoiann@wit.edu
BANDRE, Mark .... 785-594-8420 .... 190 F
mark.bandre@bakeru.edu
BANDS, Kathleen .... 301-696-3400 .... 223 C
bands@hood.edu
BANDSTRA, Travis .... 708-239-4854 .... 166 C
travis.bandstra@trnty.edu
BANDURSKI, Jeff, J .... 262-243-5700 .... 547 C
jeffrey.bandurski@cuw.edu
BANDY, Chad .... 703-376-6091 .... 19 A
chad.bandy@phoenix.edu
BANDY, JR., John, M .... 404-413-4600 .... 131 G
jbandy@gsu.edu
BANDY, Kanoe .... 661-763-7779 .... 72 E
kbandy@taftcollege.edu
BANDY, Kenneth .... 704-463-1360 .... 375 F
kenneth.bandy@fsmail.pfeiffer.edu
BANDY, Mark .... 515-727-2100 .... 187 A
mbandy@hamiltonia.edu
BANDY-NEAL, LaMel .... 615-327-6767 .... 471 C
lbneal@mmc.edu
BANDYOPADHYAY,
Santanu .... 714-484-7311 .... 59 D
sbandyopadhyay@cypresscollege.edu
BANERJEE, Nantoo .... 269-471-6615 .... 252 A
banerjee@andrews.edu
BANERJI, Debashish .... 323-663-2167 .... 76 B
BANES, Edna, J .... 804-355-0671 .... 525 A
ebanes@upsem.edu
BANESS KING, Deborah ... 708-456-0300 .... 166 F
dbanessk@triton.edu
BANEY, Mary Ellen .... 412-396-6575 .... 428 D
baney@duq.edu
BANEY, Todd .... 704-922-6485 .... 370 G
baney.todd@gaston.edu
BANG, Barbara .... 701-671-2277 .... 382 G
barbara.bang@ndscs.edu
BANG, Sam .... 626-584-5398 .... 48 B
sbang@fuller.edu

BANGASSER, Karen .... 605-331-6684 .... 466 E
karen.bangasser@usiouxfalls.edu
BANGASSER, Kathy .... 815-599-3448 .... 152 B
kathy.bangasser@highland.edu
BANGASSER, Susan .... 909-384-8650 .... 65 C
sbangasser@sbccd.cc.ca.us
BANGERT, Darci, M .... 515-574-1035 .... 185 I
bangert@iowacentral.edu
BANGERT, Stephanie .... 510-869-6512 .... 64 J
sbangert@samuelmerritt.edu
BANGERT-DROWNS,
Robert .... 518-442-4988 .... 351 E
rbangert@uamail.albany.edu
BANICK, Gabrielle .... 608-757-6320 .... 553 G
gbanick@blackhawk.edu
BANISTER, Mickey, D .... 405-425-5200 .... 409 E
mickey.banister@oc.edu
BANISTER, Stephen .... 701-858-3855 .... 382 A
stephen.banister@minotstateu.edu
BANKART, Charles, A .... 785-864-3617 .... 197 B
cbankart@ku.edu
BANKEN, Mary Jo .... 573-882-6211 .... 291 B
bankenm@missouri.edu
BANKER, Bonnie .... 859-858-3511 .... 198 E
bonnie.banker@asbury.edu
BANKER, Joe .... 417-626-1234 .... 287 C
banker.joe@occ.edu
BANKER, Tollie .... 330-339-3391 .... 394 A
tbanker@kent.edu
BANKEY, Michael .... 567-661-7735 .... 400 I
michael_bankey@owens.edu
BANKHEAD, Brad .... 970-945-8691 .... 82 G
BANKIRER, Marcia .... 303-292-0015 .... 84 C
m.bankirer@denverschoolofnursing.edu
BANKIRER, Marcia .... 303-248-2701 .... 29 F
mbankirer@argosy.edu
BANKOLE-MEDINA,
Katherine .... 410-951-3431 .... 228 B
kbankole@coppin.edu
BANKS, Cerri .... 413-538-2481 .... 242 D
cbanks@mtholyoke.edu
BANKS, Christopher .... 213-613-2200 .... 70 H
christopher_banks@sciarc.edu
BANKS, Dacia, L .... 315-684-6289 .... 354 F
banksdl@morrisville.edu
BANKS, Darrell, L .... 859-233-8207 .... 207 A
dbanks@transy.edu
BANKS, Deborah .... 662-254-3335 .... 276 B
dbanks@mvsu.edu
BANKS, Heather, R .... 260-982-5306 .... 177 H
hrbanks@manchester.edu
BANKS, Ivan .... 610-399-2271 .... 442 A
ivan.banks@cheyney.edu
BANKS, Julie, M .... 937-229-3233 .... 404 A
jbanks1@udayton.edu
BANKS, Kathryn, M .... 252-638-7367 .... 370 A
banksk@cravencc.edu
BANKS, Kay .... 803-321-5146 .... 459 H
kay.banks@newberry.edu
BANKS, Kevin .... 443-885-3527 .... 224 E
kevin.banks@morgan.edu
BANKS, Kevin, M .... 813-974-6677 .... 121 A
kevinbanks@usf.edu
BANKS, Kimberly .... 904-256-7501 .... 111 L
kbanks@ju.edu
BANKS, Larry .... 801-274-3280 .... 512 F
larry.banks@wgu.edu
BANKS, Lynne .... 814-472-3002 .... 446 B
lbanks@francis.edu
BANKS, M. Katherine .... 979-845-7203 .... 497 E
k-banks@tamu.edu
BANKS, Marcus .... 510-869-8692 .... 64 J
mbanks@samuelmerritt.edu
BANKS, Mary .... 239-590-1172 .... 119 B
mbanks@fgcu.edu
BANKS, McRae .... 336-334-5338 .... 379 B
mcbanks@uncg.edu
BANKS, Melissa .... 912-443-3380 .... 136 H
mbanks@savannahtech.edu
BANKS, Michael .... 816-604-6544 .... 285 A
michael.banks@mcckc.edu
BANKS, Michelle, R .... 901-678-2713 .... 474 C
mbanks@memphis.edu
BANKS, Nicole, P .... 561-862-4310 .... 114 D
banksn@palmbeachstate.edu
BANKS, Pat, A .... 404-627-2681 .... 126 D
pat.banks@beulah.org
BANKS, Ronald .... 502-597-5948 .... 203 G
ron.banks@kysu.edu
BANKS, Sharon, S .... 304-766-3078 .... 544 F
banksss@wvstateu.edu
BANKS, Wayne .... 870-574-4493 .... 24 A
wbanks@sautech.edu
BANKS, Yvonne, R .... 651-631-5221 .... 270 B
yrbanks@nwc.edu
BANKS-DEAVER,
Yolanda, E .... 919-530-6204 .... 378 B
ybanks@nccu.edu
BANKSTON, Marsha .... 805-893-8653 .... 75 B
marsha.bankston@sa.ucsb.edu
BANKSTON, Patrick .... 219-980-6562 .... 174 B
pbanks@iun.edu
BANKSTON, Tony .... 309-556-3031 .... 153 F
iwuadmit@iwu.edu
BANKY, Lori .... 281-899-1240 .... 492 I

BARLOW, Jerry, N .... 504-282-4455 .... 213 H
jbarlow@nobts.edu
BARLOW, Jill, M .... 978-468-7111 .... 235 B
jbarlow@gcts.edu
BARLOW, John .... 207-326-2485 .... 219 D
john.barlow@mma.edu
BARLOW, Justin .... 678-839-5000 .... 139 A
jbarlow@westga.edu
BARLOW, Kevin .... 281-283-3065 .... 503 E
barlowk@uhcl.edu
BARLOW, Linda .... 903-693-2067 .... 492 C
lbarlow@panola.edu
BARLOW, Marlene, T .... 215-968-8000 .... 423 F
barlowm@bucks.edu
BARLOW, Michael .... 270-706-8614 .... 202 A
michael.barlow@kctcs.edu
BARLOW, Steve .... 307-855-2143 .... 556 B
barlow@cwc.edu
BARLOW, Thomas, M .... 813-879-6000 .... 107 A
tbarlow@cci.edu
BARLOW, William .... 440-775-8273 .... 397 G
bill.barlow@oberlin.edu
BARLOW-KELLEY, Jill .... 207-288-5015 .... 217 H
jbk@coa.edu
BARLOWE, Jamie .... 419-530-2413 .... 404 F
jamie.barlowe@utoledo.edu
BARNA, Adrienne, M .... 703-993-2380 .... 519 E
abarna@gmu.edu
BARNA, Peter .... 718-636-3744 .... 346 D
provost@pratt.edu
BARNABY, Mike .... 218-855-8039 .... 265 J
mbarnaby@clcmn.edu
BARNARD, Cheryl, A .... 860-231-5267 .... 95 D
cbarnard@usj.edu
BARNARD, Melinda .... 707-664-3236 .... 37 D
melinda.barnard@sonoma.edu
BARNARD, Monica .... 806-720-7232 .... 490 F
monica.barnard@lcu.edu
BARNARD, Susan .... 201-447-7938 .... 307 E
sbarnard@bergen.edu
BARNARD, Tom .... 217-351-2582 .... 161 C
tbarnard@parkland.edu
BARNDS, W. Kent .... 309-794-7314 .... 145 E
wkentbarnds@augustana.edu
BARNER, John, C .... 812-488-2362 .... 180 E
jb295@evansville.edu
BARNES, Abigail .... 303-975-5029 .... 89 H
abarnes@westwood.edu
BARNES, Amy .... 540-458-8920 .... 530 D
abarnes@wlu.edu
BARNES, Andre .... 415-239-3151 .... 40 C
abarnes@ccsf.edu
BARNES, Andrew .... 718-636-3570 .... 346 D
awbarnes@pratt.edu
BARNES, April .... 859-622-3855 .... 200 J
april.barnes@eku.edu
BARNES, Brian, M .... 907-474-7649 .... 10 I
bmbarnes@alaska.edu
BARNES, Carolyn .... 940-898-3456 .... 502 D
cbarnes@twu.edu
BARNES, Cheryl .... 404-756-4006 .... 125 D
cbarnes@atlm.edu
BARNES, Clarence, D .... 509-313-3404 .... 534 F
barnes@jepson.gonzaga.edu
BARNES, Dan .... 312-662-4041 .... 144 H
barnes@adler.edu
BARNES, David, M .... 402-449-2809 .... 297 H
gupres@graceu.edu
BARNES, Edwin, A .... 909-869-3020 .... 33 J
eabarnes@csupomona.edu
BARNES, Elizabeth, A .... 248-689-8282 .... 259 E
bbarnes@walshcollege.edu
BARNES, Emanuel .... 601-877-6147 .... 272 F
ebarnes@alcorn.edu
BARNES, Fred .... 310-665-6968 .... 60 B
fbarnes@otis.edu
BARNES, Gary, W .... 806-651-2095 .... 499 A
gbarnes@mail.wtamu.edu
BARNES, George .... 601-885-7002 .... 274 C
gebarnes@hindscc.edu
BARNES, Harold, B .... 815-224-0450 .... 153 E
harold_barnes@ivcc.edu
BARNES, III, James, H .... 651-638-6230 .... 261 D
j-barnes@bethel.edu
BARNES, Jeffrey .... 951-552-8639 .... 31 J
jbarnes@calbaptist.edu
BARNES, John .... 831-459-2973 .... 75 C
barnes@ucsc.edu
BARNES, John, J .... 920-403-3255 .... 550 F
john.barnes@snc.edu
BARNES, Julianna .... 619-660-4301 .... 49 B
julianna.barnes@gcccd.edu
BARNES, Karen .... 601-925-3241 .... 275 C
misscoll@bkstr.com
BARNES, Katharine, T .... 401-863-1914 .... 453 B
katharine_barnes@brown.edu
BARNES, Kathleen .... 978-232-2292 .... 234 D
kbarnes@endicott.edu
BARNES, Kelly .... 706-295-6842 .... 131 B
kbarnes@gntc.edu
BARNES, Kenneth, J .... 716-851-1157 .... 333 A
barnesk@ecc.edu
BARNES, Kimberly .... 989-386-6622 .... 255 C
kbarnes@midmich.edu
BARNES, Korinne .... 718-636-3600 .... 346 D
BARNES, Melissa .... 360-538-4095 .... 534 G
mbarnes@ghc.edu
BARNES, Mia .... 765-289-2291 .... 176 B
mbarnes3@ivytech.edu
BARNES, Michael, W .... 918-631-2359 .... 413 F
michael-barnes@utulsa.edu
BARNES, Patty .... 281-487-1170 .... 499 B
pbarnes@txchiro.edu
BARNES, Peter .... 404-727-0419 .... 129 D
peter.barnes@emory.edu
BARNES, Randall .... 619-388-3488 .... 65 F
rbarnes@sdccd.edu
BARNES, Randall .... 619-388-3523 .... 65 F
rbarnes@sdccd.edu
BARNES, Rita .... 931-372-3797 .... 474 B
ritabarnes@tntech.edu
BARNES, Rosalyn .... 404-752-1735 .... 134 E
rbarnes@msm.edu
BARNES, Russell .... 713-348-4350 .... 493 C
rcb@rice.edu
BARNES, Scott .... 434-797-8409 .... 526 G
sbarnes@dcc.vccs.edu
BARNES, Scott .... 435-797-2060 .... 511 E
scott.barnes@usu.edu
BARNES, Sharon, E .... 817-257-7095 .... 499 C
s.barnes@tcu.edu
BARNES, Shelly .... 219-785-5279 .... 179 A
sbarnes@pnc.edu
BARNES, Solita, K .... 670-284-5698 .... 560 B
solitab@nmcnet.edu
BARNES, Ted .... 254-295-4678 .... 504 C
tbarnes@umhb.edu
BARNES, Tina .... 859-291-0800 .... 200 A
tbarnes@daymarcollege.edu
BARNES, Wilson, C .... 678-915-5481 .... 137 G
wbarnes@spsu.edu
BARNES PHARR, Cindy .... 480-732-7093 .... 15 E
cindy.barnes.pharr@cgc.edu
BARNES-RHOADES,
Dianne .... 434-848-1805 .... 524 B
drhoades@saintpauls.edu
BARNES-TEAMER, Toya .... 504-816-4916 .... 209 A
tbteamer@dillard.edu
BARNES WHYTE, Susan .... 503-883-2517 .... 416 H
swhyte@linfield.edu
BARNET, John .... 914-961-8313 .... 349 I
jbarnet@svots.edu
BARNETT, Alan .... 660-359-3948 .... 287 A
abarnett@mail.ncmissouri.edu
BARNETT, Alan .... 731-286-3259 .... 475 B
barnett@dscc.edu
BARNETT, Amy .... 765-998-5565 .... 180 B
ambarnett@tayloru.edu
BARNETT, Beth .... 201-684-7529 .... 313 C
bbarnett@ramapo.edu
BARNETT, Carrie .... 801-281-7630 .... 510 M
carrie.barnett@stevenshenager.edu
BARNETT, Charlie .... 662-720-7375 .... 276 C
cbarnett@nemcc.edu
BARNETT, Cynthia .... 920-403-3057 .... 550 F
cynthia.barnett@snc.edu
BARNETT, Gina .... 415-565-4614 .... 74 A
barnettg@uchastings.edu
BARNETT, Howard .... 918-594-8001 .... 410 D
howard.barnett@okstate.edu
BARNETT, JR., Howard, G .... 918-594-8000 .... 410 G
BARNETT, Jacqualine .... 717-720-4038 .... 442 A
jbarnett@paisshe.edu
BARNETT, Jahnae, H .... 573-592-4216 .... 293 D
jbarnett@williamwoods.edu
BARNETT, James, R .... 850-474-2005 .... 121 D
jbarnett@uwf.edu
BARNETT, Jay .... 606-337-1142 .... 199 H
jbarnett@ccbbc.edu
BARNETT, Kimberly .... 719-502-2012 .... 87 B
kimberly.barnett@ppcc.edu
BARNETT, Larry, E .... 619-260-7777 .... 76 D
larryb@sandiego.edu
BARNETT, Margaret, J .... 540-868-7123 .... 527 C
mbarnett@lfcc.edu
BARNETT, Michael .... 803-754-4100 .... 457 D
BARNETT, Mike .... 785-328-4251 .... 192 I
mbarnett@fhsu.edu
BARNETT, Nicole .... 256-551-5211 .... 4 J
nicole.barnett@drakestate.edu
BARNETT, Robert .... 810-766-6878 .... 259 C
rbarnett@umflint.edu
BARNETT, Sharon .... 660-359-3948 .... 287 A
sbarnett@mail.ncmissouri.edu
BARNETT, Theresa .... 903-463-8753 .... 487 C
tbarnett@grayson.edu
BARNETT, Timothy, L .... 217-206-6581 .... 167 C
barnett.timothy@uis.edu
BARNETTE, Andrew .... 724-925-4047 .... 451 E
barnettea@wccc.edu
BARNETTE, Annette .... 304-462-4115 .... 544 A
annette.barnette@glenville.edu
BARNETTE, F. Gary .... 229-317-6728 .... 128 D
gary.barnette@darton.edu
BARNETTE, Jennifer, C .... 334-683-2313 .... 5 G
jbarnette@marionmilitary.edu
BARNETTE, Lindsey .... 256-761-6415 .... 7 G
lbarnette@talladega.edu
BARNETTE, Vivian, D .... 336-334-7727 .... 378 A
vdbarnet@ncat.edu
BARNEY, Alfred .... 678-891-2360 .... 131 C
alfred.barney@gpc.edu
BARNEY, Carl .... 800-972-5149 .... 510 C
BARNEY, James, N .... 317-916-7827 .... 175 K
jbarney6@ivytech.edu
BARNEY, Patti .... 954-201-7520 .... 102 E
pbarney@broward.edu
BARNEY, Rick .... 502-585-9911 .... 206 D
rbarney@spalding.edu
BARNHART, Amy .... 937-775-5721 .... 406 C
amy.barnhart@wright.edu
BARNHART, Bruce .... 724-938-4407 .... 441 G
barnhart@calu.edu
BARNHART, Mary Jo .... 724-437-4600 .... 441 B
mbarnhart@piht.edu
BARNHART, Mitch .... 859-257-8015 .... 207 D
mbarn@uky.edu
BARNHART, Ross .... 719-549-3365 .... 87 F
ross.barnhart@pueblocc.edu
BARNHART, Roy, R .... 724-852-3241 .... 451 B
rbarnhar@waynesburg.edu
BARNHART, Terry, L .... 671-735-5571 .... 559 E
terry.barnhart@guamcc.edu
BARNHILL, Carol .... 870-972-2028 .... 20 D
cbarnhil@astate.edu
BARNHILL, Holly .... 310-689-3200 .... 42 H
hbarnhill@kaplan.edu
BARNHILL, John .... 850-644-1224 .... 119 D
jbarnhill@admin.fsu.edu
BARNHILL, Kristopher, C .. 864-488-4602 .... 459 B
kbarnhill@limestone.edu
BARNHILL, Rob, M .... 262-243-5700 .... 547 C
rob.barnhill@cuw.edu
BARNHILL, Tapp .... 802-254-6370 .... 515 E
barnhilt@ccv.edu
BARNHOUSE, Richard .... 608-262-3786 .... 553 B
richard.barnhouse@uwc.edu
BARNITZ, LaTrobe .... 814-676-6591 .... 442 C
lbarnitz@clarion.edu
BARNUM, Martin .... 847-566-6401 .... 167 F
mbarnum@usml.edu
BARNWELL, Larry .... 864-977-7161 .... 460 A
larry.barnwell@ngu.edu
BARNWELL, Vollie .... 828-251-6700 .... 378 D
vbarnwel@unca.edu
BARON, Joshua, D .... 845-575-3000 .... 340 B
josh.baron@marist.edu
BARON, Kit .... 626-396-2322 .... 29 I
BARON, Melissa, M .... 724-946-7927 .... 451 C
baronmm@westminster.edu
BARON, Sara .... 757-352-4182 .... 523 E
sbaron@regent.edu
BARON, Stephanie .... 425-640-1049 .... 533 I
stephanie.baron@edcc.edu
BARON, Stuart .... 302-622-8000 .... 96 B
BARONAK, William, M .... 304-336-8061 .... 544 D
wbaronak@westliberty.edu
BARONE, OSF,
Ann Carmen .... 419-824-3703 .... 395 E
acarmen@lourdes.edu
BARONE, Janet .... 703-237-6200 .... 521 G
BARONE, Joseph .... 732-445-5215 .... 314 C
jbarone@pharmacy.rutgers.edu
BARONE, Michael .... 716-673-3323 .... 352 A
michael.barone@fredonia.edu
BARONIO, Lisa Birley .... 940-565-2010 .... 504 D
lisa.baronio@unt.edu
BAROODY, Daniel, A .... 607-735-1870 .... 332 I
dbaroody@elmira.edu
BAROUDI, George .... 516-299-3790 .... 338 E
george.baroudi@liu.edu
BARQUINERO, James, M .. 203-365-4763 .... 94 B
barquineroj@sacredheart.edu
BARQUINERO, Jim .... 203-365-4763 .... 94 B
barquineroj@sacredheart.edu
BARR, Ann .... 503-352-7200 .... 419 E
ann.barr@pacificu.edu
BARR, Carol, A .... 413-545-6330 .... 236 F
cbarr@provost.umass.edu
BARR, Jared .... 813-988-5131 .... 108 A
barrj@floridacollege.edu
BARR, Julia, R .... 304-462-4114 .... 544 A
julia.barr@glenville.edu
BARR, K. Jill .... 410-455-1337 .... 227 D
jbarr@umbc.edu
BARR, Kevin .... 812-237-3600 .... 173 B
kevin.barr@indstate.edu
BARR, Krispin, W .... 336-721-2627 .... 376 E
krispin.barr@salem.edu
BARR, Mary, G .... 812-877-8258 .... 179 B
mary.g.barr@rose-hulman.edu
BARR, Peter, B .... 304-462-4110 .... 544 A
peter.barr@glenville.edu
BARR, Robin .... 386-506-4473 .... 104 F
barrr@daytonastate.edu
BARR, Rodena .... 303-256-9306 .... 85 L
rbarr@jwu.edu
BARR, Sarah .... 402-465-2193 .... 299 H
sbarr@nebrwesleyan.edu
BARR, Suzy .... 843-574-6181 .... 461 G
suzy.barr@tridenttech.edu
BARR, Victor .... 865-974-2196 .... 477 D
vbarr@utk.edu
BARRACLOUGH, Diana .... 610-499-4153 .... 451 F
dbarraclough@widener.edu
BARRAM, Dirk .... 503-554-2822 .... 415 I
dbarram@georgefox.edu
BARRANTES, Jane .... 408-554-5416 .... 68 C
jbarrantes@scu.edu
BARRANTES, Laura .... 301-431-5401 .... 225 B
lbarrantes@nlc.edu
BARRAR, Elena .... 610-558-5516 .... 437 D
barrare@neumann.edu
BARRAS, Janet .... 678-359-5022 .... 132 A
janetb@gdn.edu
BARRATT, Marguerite .... 202-994-6130 .... 98 C
barratt@gwu.edu
BARREDA, Albert .... 956-882-7575 .... 505 E
albert.barreda@utb.edu
BARREE, Zita, M .... 434-223-6265 .... 519 G
zbarree@hsc.edu
BARREIRO, Antonio .... 303-256-9314 .... 85 L
tbarreiro@jwu.edu
BARRENTINE, Debra, A .... 256-228-6001 .... 6 A
barrentined@nacc.edu
BARRENTINE, Roger, A .... 636-481-3106 .... 283 D
rbarrent@jeffco.edu
BARRERA, Adriana, D .... 213-891-2081 .... 54 F
barrerad@laccd.edu
BARRERA, Merrynoll .... 408-934-4900 .... 49 K
merrynoll_barrera@heald.edu
BARRERA, Rosa .... 316-284-5241 .... 191 C
rbarrera@bethelks.edu
BARRERA, Steve, V .... 210-458-4249 .... 506 D
steve.barrera@utsa.edu
BARRETO, Mary Jo .... 803-323-2233 .... 463 E
mannm@winthrop.edu
BARRETO, Sandra .... 787-761-0640 .... 566 F
asistenciaeconomica@cbp.edu
BARRETO, Wanda .... 787-758-2480 .... 567 G
wanda.barreto@upr.edu
BARRETT, Barbara .... 602-978-7200 .... 18 H
barbara.barrett@thunderbird.edu
BARRETT, Bill .... 657-278-2425 .... 35 B
bbarrett@fullerton.edu
BARRETT, Brian, D .... 817-515-6960 .... 496 C
brian.barrett@tccd.edu
BARRETT, Carolyn .... 904-256-7090 .... 111 L
cbarret@ju.edu
BARRETT, Christina .... 413-236-2112 .... 239 A
BARRETT, David .... 620-242-0412 .... 195 C
barrettd@mcpherson.edu
BARRETT, David .... 860-509-9519 .... 93 A
dbarrett@hartsem.edu
BARRETT, Dawn .... 617-879-7100 .... 238 B
dawn.barrett@massart.edu
BARRETT, Denise .... 662-846-1967 .... 200 K
denise.barrett@frontier.edu
BARRETT, James .... 715-836-3887 .... 551 A
barretjd@uwec.edu
BARRETT, Joan .... 417-447-6914 .... 287 D
barrettj@otc.edu
BARRETT, John .... 770-426-2616 .... 133 E
jbarrett@life.edu
BARRETT, Juanita .... 773-244-4892 .... 159 H
jbarrett@northpark.edu
BARRETT, Karinda .... 850-201-6209 .... 122 A
barrettk@tcc.fl.edu
BARRETT, Kim, E .... 858-534-6655 .... 74 F
graduatedean@ucsd.edu
BARRETT, Laura .... 919-344-2517 .... 124 G
laura.barrett@armstrong.edu
BARRETT, Lawrence, M .... 207-974-4691 .... 218 H
lbarrett@emcc.edu
BARRETT, Leah, A .... 585-395-2772 .... 352 F
lbarrett@brockport.edu
BARRETT, Linda .... 620-242-0457 .... 195 C
barrettl@mcpherson.edu
BARRETT, Linda .... 401-874-2509 .... 454 E
lindab@uri.edu
BARRETT, Mark .... 978-837-5075 .... 242 A
barrettm@merrimack.edu
BARRETT, Michael .... 850-644-1768 .... 119 D
mgbarrett@admin.fsu.edu
BARRETT, Nancy .... 928-777-3713 .... 14 C
nancy.barrett@erau.edu
BARRETT, Pam, J .... 770-534-6176 .... 126 E
pbarrett@brenau.edu
BARRETT, Robert, T .... 803-536-8980 .... 460 G
rbarrett1@scsu.edu
BARRETT, Rosemary .... 845-341-4200 .... 345 E
rosemary.barrett@sunyorange.edu
BARRETT, Sarah .... 781-768-7162 .... 244 A
sarah.barrett@regiscollege.edu
BARRETT, Stephen .... 817-735-2261 .... 504 E
stephen.barrett@unthsc.edu
BARRETT, Susan .... 215-596-7626 .... 450 B
s.barrett@usciences.edu
BARRETT, Thomas .... 312-467-2317 .... 146 F
tbarrett@thechicagoschool.edu
BARRETT, Valoree .... 785-227-3380 .... 191 B
barrettv@bethanylb.edu
BARRETT, William .... 657-278-2115 .... 35 B
bbarrett@fullerton.edu

BARRICK, Mary Grace ... 707-476-4264 ... 42 C
marygrace-barrick@redwoods.edu
BARRIE, John ... 845-848-7500 ... 332 B
john.barrie@dc.edu
BARRIENTOS, Joseph ... 808-544-0267 ... 140 G
jbarrientos@hpu.edu
BARRIER, Jeremy ... 256-766-6610 ... 4 C
jbarrier@hcu.edu
BARRIERA, Heriberto ... 787-279-1912 ... 563 D
hbarriera@bayamon.inter.edu
BARRILLEAUX, Allayne ... 985-448-4011 ... 216 A
laynie.barrilleaux@nicholls.edu
BARRINGER, Judy ... 212-659-7215 ... 338 A
BARRINGTON, Ruth, A ... 401-825-2184 ... 453 D
rbarrington@ccri.edu
BARRIOS, Eric ... 787-766-1717 ... 565 I
ca_ebarrios@suagm.edu
BARRIOS, Eugenio ... 212-220-1266 ... 326 D
ebarrios@bmcc.cuny.edu
BARRIOS, Francisco ... 573-651-2154 ... 289 K
fbarrios@semo.edu
BARRIS, Julie ... 814-472-3012 ... 446 B
jbarris@francis.edu
BARRISH, David, J ... 804-523-5934 ... 527 A
dbarrish@reynolds.edu
BARRITT, Eric, D ... 248-364-6150 ... 256 G
barritt@oakland.edu
BARRON, Alexandra, L ... 512-464-8878 ... 493 E
alexb@stedwards.edu
BARRON, Brad, E ... 864-294-2033 ... 458 E
brad.barron@furman.edu
BARRON, Bruce ... 909-382-4091 ... 65 A
BARRON, Caulyne ... 602-648-5750 ... 14 A
cbarron@dunlap-stone.edu
BARRON, Dave ... 334-670-3657 ... 8 A
wdbarron@troy.edu
BARRON, David ... 918-343-7852 ... 411 H
dbarron@rsu.edu
BARRON, Dianne ... 334-670-3189 ... 8 A
dlbarron@troy.edu
BARRON, Eric, J ... 850-644-1085 ... 119 D
ebarron@fsu.edu
BARRON, Glenda, O ... 254-298-8600 ... 496 D
glenda.barron@templejc.edu
BARRON, Katie ... 970-542-3108 ... 86 G
katie.barron@morgancc.edu
BARRON, Maria, V ... 954-308-2180 ... 101 C
mbarron@aii.edu
BARRON, Michael ... 319-335-1548 ... 182 F
michael-barron@uiowa.edu
BARRON, Robert, E ... 847-970-4800 ... 167 F
rectorusml@usml.edu
BARROS, Michael ... 808-845-9135 ... 142 B
mbarros@hawaii.edu
BARROSO, Diana ... 305-593-1223 ... 102 H
dbarroso@albizu.edu
BARROTT, Jim ... 423-697-3211 ... 474 D
BARROW, Carla ... 229-225-5077 ... 138 A
cbarrow@southwestgatech.edu
BARROW, Christine, E ... 301-322-0419 ... 225 F
barowce@pgcc.edu
BARROW, Deborah, L ... 940-397-4212 ... 491 B
debbie.barrow@mwsu.edu
BARROW, Jerry ... 706-369-5763 ... 125 C
jbarrow@athenstech.edu
BARROW, Linda, M ... 770-531-6331 ... 133 C
lbarrow@laniertech.edu
BARROW, Lisa ... 252-527-6223 ... 371 G
lbarrow@lenoircc.edu
BARROWS, Barbara ... 641-585-8143 ... 189 I
barbara.barrows@waldorf.edu
BARROWS, David ... 217-206-6530 ... 167 C
barrows.david@uis.edu
BARROWS, Karen, A ... 585-475-2396 ... 347 G
karen.barrows@rit.edu
BARROWS, Karen, A ... 585-475-2396 ... 347 G
kab7050@rit.edu
BARROWS, Mert ... 620-223-2700 ... 193 A
mertb@fortscott.edu
BARROWS, Robert ... 617-228-2241 ... 239 C
rbarrows@bhcc.mass.edu
BARRRIS, Brad ... 706-236-2272 ... 126 C
bbarris@berry.edu
BARRUS, Kent, L ... 208-496-7205 ... 143 A
barrusk@byui.edu
BARRY, A. David ... 337-482-6219 ... 216 D
dbarry@louisiana.edu
BARRY, Ann Marie ... 847-635-1699 ... 160 F
annmarie@oakton.edu
BARRY, Christine ... 713-525-3156 ... 505 A
cbarry@stthom.edu
BARRY, Donna, M ... 973-655-4361 ... 311 F
barryd@mail.montclair.edu
BARRY, Ernie ... 214-768-2004 ... 495 A
ebarry@smu.edu
BARRY, Jeannette ... 402-375-7466 ... 299 G
jebarry1@wsc.edu
BARRY, Joanne ... 607-753-2302 ... 353 B
joanne.barry@cortland.edu
BARRY, John ... 254-710-1412 ... 482 A
john_barry@baylor.edu
BARRY, Julie ... 614-947-6065 ... 391 B
barryj@franklin.edu
BARRY, Kevin, G ... 302-295-1170 ... 97 C
kevin.g.barry@wilmu.edu
BARRY, Laura ... 201-559-3504 ... 310 B
barryl@felician.edu
BARRY, Lisa ... 303-280-7491 ... 84 G
lbarry@devry.edu
BARRY, Liz ... 858-566-1200 ... 44 B
lbarry@disd.edu
BARRY, Theresa ... 262-524-7334 ... 546 H
tbarry@carrollu.edu
BARRY, Thomas, E ... 214-768-4320 ... 495 A
tbarry@smu.edu
BARSAM, Steven, N ... 636-529-0000 ... 288 D
snbarsam@slchcmail.com
BARSKY, David ... 760-750-4329 ... 36 C
djbarsky@csusm.edu
BARTA, Barbara ... 614-234-1788 ... 396 H
bbarta@mccn.edu
BARTA, Gary ... 319-335-9435 ... 182 F
gary-barta@uiowa.edu
BARTA, Jennifer ... 402-878-2380 ... 298 E
jbarta@littlepriest.edu
BARTA, Lou ... 217-641-4215 ... 154 I
lbarta@jwcc.edu
BARTA, Sharon ... 510-261-8500 ... 61 G
sharon.barta@patten.edu
BARTANEN, Kristine, M ... 253-879-3205 ... 538 H
acadvp@pugetsound.edu
BARTEAU, Mark, A ... 302-831-4007 ... 96 I
barteau@udel.edu
BARTEE, Robert, D ... 402-559-4203 ... 300 H
bbartee@unmc.edu
BARTEL, Alexa ... 843-383-8126 ... 457 A
abartel@coker.edu
BARTEL, Brad ... 615-898-2953 ... 473 G
brad.bartel@mtsu.edu
BARTEL, Kyle, J ... 580-774-3705 ... 412 F
kyle.bartel@swosu.edu
BARTEL, LeRoy ... 972-825-4827 ... 495 F
lbartel@sagu.edu
BARTEL, Steven, J ... 605-256-5146 ... 465 I
steve.bartel@dsu.edu
BARTEL, Tonia ... 660-831-4105 ... 286 F
bartelt@moval.edu
BARTELL, William ... 605-331-6703 ... 466 E
bill.bartell@usiouxfalls.edu
BARTELMAY, Ryan ... 312-752-2454 ... 155 C
ryan.bartelmay@kendall.edu
BARTELS, Dennis ... 614-416-6200 ... 385 G
dbartels@bradfordschoolcolumbus.edu
BARTELS, Jean ... 912-478-5258 ... 131 E
jbartels@georgiasouthern.edu
BARTELS, Marilyn ... 800-955-2527 ... 282 D
mbartels@grantham.edu
BARTELS, Paige ... 802-440-4336 ... 513 A
pbartels@bennington.edu
BARTELS, Richard ... 606-337-1164 ... 199 H
rbartels@ccbbc.edu
BARTELS, Roy ... 325-574-7629 ... 508 I
rbartels@wtc.edu
BARTELS, Sharon, J ... 770-962-7580 ... 132 D
sbartels@gwinnetttech.edu
BARTELS, Suzanne, M ... 860-701-5155 ... 93 E
bartels_s@mitchell.edu
BARTELSON, Gretchen, G ... 712-324-5061 ... 188 C
gbartelson@nwicc.edu
BARTELT, Andrew, H ... 314-505-7013 ... 280 D
bartelta@csl.edu
BARTFIELD, Joel ... 518-262-7302 ... 322 D
bartfi@mail.amc.edu
BARTGES, Ellyn ... 320-308-0125 ... 269 A
elbartges@stcloudstate.edu
BARTH, Brad ... 701-671-2131 ... 382 G
brad.barth@ndscs.edu
BARTH, Christopher ... 845-938-3833 ... 559 A
christopher.barth@usma.edu
BARTH, Cynthia ... 410-225-4223 ... 224 B
cbarth@mica.edu
BARTH, Doug ... 785-594-4526 ... 190 F
doug.barth@bakeru.edu
BARTH, Michael ... 406-496-4233 ... 296 B
mbarth@mtech.edu
BARTH, Richard, P ... 410-706-7794 ... 227 C
rbarth@ssw.umaryland.edu
BARTH, Rick ... 205-665-6239 ... 9 B
rbarth@montevallo.edu
BARTHA, Jaimee ... 847-628-2514 ... 154 K
jbartha@judsonu.edu
BARTHELEMY, Jennifer ... 618-544-8657 ... 152 H
barthelemyj@iecc.edu
BARTHELL, John ... 405-974-2481 ... 413 B
jbarthell@uco.edu
BARTHELMAS, Frederick ... 518-587-2100 ... 355 G
rick.barthlemas@esc.edu
BARTHELMES, David ... 810-762-3324 ... 259 C
dwbarth@umflint.edu
BARTHOLMEY, Theresa ... 660-263-3900 ... 279 F
tbart@cccb.edu
BARTHOLOMEW, Nanette ... 757-826-1883 ... 516 K
registrar@bethel-college.com
BARTHOLOMEW, Sandra ... 434-947-8142 ... 523 B
sbartholomew@randolphcollege.edu
BARTHOLOMEW-FEIS,
Dixee ... 712-749-2131 ... 183 C
bartholomew@bvu.edu
BARTINI, Michael, D ... 207-725-3146 ... 217 E
mbartini@bowdoin.edu
BARTKOVICH, Jeffrey, P ... 585-292-3018 ... 341 H
jbartkovich@monroecc.edu
BARTKOWSKI, Anna ... 831-582-3332 ... 35 E
abartkowski@csumb.edu
BARTL, Noelle ... 575-562-2412 ... 318 B
noelle.bartl@enmu.edu
BARTLE, Gamin ... 973-408-3106 ... 309 E
gbartle@drew.edu
BARTLE, John, R ... 402-554-3989 ... 301 A
jbartle@unomaha.edu
BARTLEBAUGH, Brenda, P 318-797-5009 ... 213 D
brenda.bartlebaugh@lsus.edu
BARTLETT, Anita ... 580-628-6233 ... 409 B
anita.bartlett@north-ok.edu
BARTLETT, Annemarie, M ... 610-660-1299 ... 446 C
abartlet@sju.edu
BARTLETT, Beth ... 828-251-6506 ... 378 D
bbartlet@unca.edu
BARTLETT, Julia ... 913-234-0758 ... 191 J
julia.bartlett@cleveland.edu
BARTLETT, Kimberly ... 714-484-7104 ... 59 D
kbartlett@cypresscollege.edu
BARTLETT, Leeanna ... 214-828-8353 ... 497 C
lbartlett@bcd.tamhsc.edu
BARTLETT, Phil ... 802-773-5900 ... 513 D
phil.bartlett@csj.edu
BARTLETT, Raymond ... 713-743-8780 ... 503 C
rbartlett@uh.edu
BARTLETT, Rebecca ... 802-258-9226 ... 513 H
rbartlet@marlboro.edu
BARTLETT, Stacy ... 706-385-1100 ... 136 B
stacy.bartlett@point.edu
BARTLETT, Walter, C ... 336-599-1181 ... 372 G
bartlew@piedmontcc.edu
BARTLEY, Mary, E ... 515-961-1511 ... 189 C
mimi.bartley@simpson.edu
BARTLEY, Patricia, A ... 773-256-0717 ... 157 D
pbartley@lstc.edu
BARTLEY, Ron ... 843-921-6901 ... 460 B
rbartley@netc.edu
BARTLING, Kaitlyn ... 641-648-4611 ... 186 C
kaitlyn.bartling@iavalley.edu
BARTNETT, Jane ... 718-409-7277 ... 356 C
jbartnett@sunymaritime.edu
BARTO, Christopher, T ... 212-752-1530 ... 338 C
christopher.barto@limcollege.edu
BARTOL, Michelle, M ... 814-641-3432 ... 432 A
bartolm@juniata.edu
BARTOLD, Melissa ... 312-225-1700 ... 152 E
mbartold@ico.edu
BARTOLI, Andrea ... 703-993-4453 ... 519 E
abartoli@gmu.edu
BARTOLINI, Brian, J ... 401-865-1554 ... 453 H
bbartoli@providence.edu
BARTOLO, Tony ... 423-478-6208 ... 474 E
tbartolo@clevelandstatecc.edu
BARTOLOMEI, Francisco ... 787-751-0178 ... 565 F
fjbartolomei@suagm.edu
BARTOLOTTA, Charles ... 631-451-4790 ... 356 E
bartolc@sunysuffolk.edu
BARTOLOZZI, Richard ... 847-735-6016 ... 155 G
bartolozzi@lakeforest.edu
BARTON, Aimee ... 216-791-5000 ... 388 C
aimee.barton@case.edu
BARTON, Bill ... 912-871-1690 ... 135 D
bbarton@ogeecheetech.edu
BARTON, Carissa ... 303-745-6244 ... 84 H
cbarton@cci.edu
BARTON, Carolina ... 949-214-3093 ... 43 C
carolina.barton@cui.edu
BARTON, Charles "Lennie" 919-760-8375 ... 367 A
bartonl@meredith.edu
BARTON, Connie ... 530-242-7719 ... 69 D
cbarton@shastacollege.edu
BARTON, David ... 660-284-4800 ... 282 G
BARTON, Delores ... 404-270-5376 ... 138 B
dbarton@spelman.edu
BARTON, Gayle ... 413-542-2000 ... 230 A
gbarton@amherst.edu
BARTON, George ... 915-747-5640 ... 506 B
gbarton@utep.edu
BARTON, J. Mark ... 479-394-7622 ... 23 E
mbarton@rmcc.edu
BARTON, Jacqueline, K ... 626-395-3646 ... 32 H
jkbarton@caltech.edu
BARTON, John, D ... 248-218-2026 ... 257 D
jbarton@rc.edu
BARTON, Kyle ... 409-766-1100 ... 507 C
kbarton@utmb.edu
BARTON, Laurence ... 610-526-1301 ... 422 A
laurence.barton@theamericancollege.edu
BARTON, Mary ... 940-565-2085 ... 504 D
mary.barton@unt.edu
BARTON, Michelle ... 760-744-1150 ... 61 D
mbarton@palomar.edu
BARTON, Nancy ... 203-837-8588 ... 91 A
bartonn@wcsu.edu
BARTON, Pat ... 678-466-4185 ... 127 D
patbarton@clayton.edu
BARTON, Patricia ... 510-136-1220 ... 50 H
barton@hnu.edu
BARTON, Sarah ... 304-865-6034 ... 541 J
sarah.barton@ovu.edu
BARTON, Todd ... 727-726-1153 ... 103 I
toddbarton@clearwater.edu
BARTOW, Dean ... 307-778-1154 ... 556 E
dbartow@lccc.wy.edu
BARTOW, Margaret ... 440-525-7096 ... 394 F
mbartow@lakelandcc.edu
BARTRAM, Lydia ... 561-297-0180 ... 119 A
lbartram@fau.edu
BARTSCH, Jonathan ... 617-236-8800 ... 234 G
jbartsch@fisher.edu
BARTSCH, Kathy, R ... 512-471-2302 ... 505 D
kbartsch@po.utexas.edu
BARTSCHER, Patricia, B ... 415-338-2998 ... 37 B
pattyb@sfsu.edu
BARTUS, Thomas, J ... 609-258-7720 ... 312 G
tbartus@princeton.edu
BARWICK, Daniel, W ... 620-331-4100 ... 193 I
dbarwick@indycc.edu
BARZACCHINI, Mike ... 847-925-6510 ... 151 G
mbarzacc@harpercollege.edu
BASCH, Hersch ... 718-438-1002 ... 340 G
BASCIANO, Peter ... 706-667-4829 ... 125 G
pbasciano@aug.edu
BASEL, Barbara ... 605-773-3455 ... 465 F
barbara.basel@sdbor.edu
BASER, Ric, N ... 918-595-7980 ... 412 H
rbaser@tulsacc.edu
BASFORD, Jerry, L ... 801-581-7793 ... 511 C
jbasford@sa.utah.edu
BASFORD, Stacey, L ... 315-386-7204 ... 355 E
basfords@canton.edu
BASH, Cassaundra ... 574-936-8898 ... 169 D
cassaundra.bash@ancilla.edu
BASH, Tamela, S ... 419-772-2027 ... 398 H
t-bash@onu.edu
BASH, Todd ... 806-743-7382 ... 502 B
todd.bash@ttuhsc.edu
BASHAM, Robert ... 660-626-2395 ... 278 D
rbasham@atsu.edu
BASHANT, Wendy ... 941-487-4250 ... 120 A
wbashant@ncf.edu
BASHARA, Teri ... 318-678-6000 ... 209 I
tbashara@bpcc.edu
BASHAW, Edward ... 479-968-0490 ... 20 G
ebashaw@atu.edu
BASHAW, Pat ... 501-279-4315 ... 21 H
pbashaw@harding.edu
BASHFORD, Joanne ... 305-237-7445 ... 113 H
jbashfor@mdc.edu
BASHFORD, Mike ... 870-574-4480 ... 24 A
mbashfor@sautech.edu
BASILE, Carole, G ... 314-516-5109 ... 291 D
basilec@umsl.edu
BASILE, Elizabeth ... 718-368-4539 ... 328 A
ebasile@kbcc.cuny.edu
BASINGER, Randall, G ... 717-796-5375 ... 436 D
rbasinge@messiah.edu
BASINGER, Scott, F ... 713-798-4100 ... 481 H
scottb@bcm.edu
BASINSKI, Judith, B ... 716-878-4011 ... 353 A
basinsjb@buffalostate.edu
BASIRATMAND, Mehran ... 561-297-0230 ... 119 A
mehran@fau.edu
BASKETT, Carolyn, R ... 816-604-1166 ... 284 H
carolyn.baskett@mcckc.edu
BASKIN, Richard ... 678-359-5018 ... 132 A
rbaskin@gdn.edu
BASKIN, William ... 914-251-6485 ... 354 D
bill.baskin@purchase.edu
BASKO, Aaron, M ... 410-543-6161 ... 228 D
ambasko@salisbury.edu
BASLER, Julie ... 303-369-5151 ... 87 D
julie.basler@plattcolorado.edu
BASLER, Mike ... 314-744-5331 ... 285 J
baslerm@mobap.edu
BASLER, Sandra, K ... 636-481-3298 ... 283 D
sbasler@jeffco.edu
BASLER, Thomas, G ... 843-792-9211 ... 459 D
basler@musc.edu
BASLEY, Carolyn ... 312-935-4556 ... 162 G
cbasley@robertmorris.edu
BASNIGHT, Beth ... 617-323-6662 ... 241 F
beth_basnight@mspp.edu
BASOM, Richard ... 717-361-4762 ... 428 F
basomr@etown.edu
BASRI, Gibor ... 510-642-7294 ... 73 H
vcei@berkeley.edu
BASS, Brenda ... 319-273-2221 ... 182 G
brenda.bass@uni.edu
BASS, Charles ... 619-260-4819 ... 76 D
charlesb@sandiego.edu
BASS, Chris ... 909-607-6999 ... 40 F
chris.bass@cuc.edu
BASS, Donna ... 334-222-6591 ... 5 F
dbass@lbwcc.edu
BASS, Harry, S ... 252-335-3189 ... 377 F
hsbass@mail.ecsu.edu
BASS, Jimmy ... 910-962-4292 ... 379 D
bassj@uncw.edu
BASS, Mary, T ... 252-823-5166 ... 370 D
bassm@edgecombe.edu

BASS, Scott, A ... 202-885-2127 ... 97 D
provost@american.edu
BASS, Wanda, S ... 334-493-3573 ... 5 F
wsbass@lbwcc.edu
BASSANO, Theodore ... 610-607-6265 ... 445 C
tbassano@racc.edu
BASSEL, Cynthia, B ... 214-648-2510 ... 507 E
cynthia.bassel@utsouthwestern.edu
BASSETT, Cheryl ... 810-762-0553 ... 255 G
cheryl.bassett@edtech.mcc.edu
BASSETT, Claire, M ... 713-798-4712 ... 481 H
bassett@bcm.edu
BASSETT, Don ... 989-275-5000 ... 253 E
don.bassett@kirtland.edu
BASSETT, Dorothy, E ... 412-396-5839 ... 428 D
bassettd@duq.edu
BASSETT, Heidi, M ... 972-860-7255 ... 484 I
hbassett@dcccd.edu
BASSETT, Joanne ... 901-333-5020 ... 476 B
jbassett@southwest.tn.edu
BASSETT, John, E ... 509-865-8600 ... 535 A
bassett_j@heritage.edu
BASSETT, Mary ... 630-889-6527 ... 159 F
mbassett@nuhs.edu
BASSETT, Matthew, D ... 315-445-4450 ... 338 B
bassetmd@lemoyne.edu
BASSETT, Robert ... 714-997-6715 ... 39 F
bassett@chapman.edu
BASSETT, Susan ... 412-268-8555 ... 424 J
susanb@andrew.cmu.edu
BASSETTE, Lorraine, P ... 301-322-0524 ... 225 F
lbasssette@pgcc.edu
BASSETTE, Lynda, D ... 607-436-2407 ... 353 E
bassetld@oneonta.edu
BASSETTI, Mimi ... 215-572-2941 ... 422 C
bassetti@arcadia.edu
BASSHAM, Donna ... 417-255-7243 ... 286 D
donnabassham@missouristate.edu
BASSHAM, Kathy ... 817-598-6427 ... 508 F
kbassham@wc.edu
BASSHAM, Mia, W ... 570-740-0420 ... 435 C
mbassham@luzerne.edu
BASSI, Susan, E ... 309-556-3151 ... 153 F
sbassi@iwu.edu
BASSI-COOK, Teresa ... 724-838-4295 ... 447 C
bassi@setonhill.edu
BASSINGER, Donnie ... 828-726-2286 ... 368 G
dbassinger@cccti.edu
BASSO, Sharon, K ... 610-758-4156 ... 434 E
sbr2@lehigh.edu
BASSO, Susan ... 814-863-6188 ... 438 G
smb43@psu.edu
BAST, Carrie ... 330-325-6718 ... 397 D
cbast@neomed.edu
BASTECKI-PEREZ, Victoria 215-641-6482 ... 436 G
vbasteck@mc3.edu
BASTIAN, Joni ... 618-537-6555 ... 158 A
jjbastian@mckendree.edu
BASTIN, Judy ... 316-322-3235 ... 191 G
jbastin@butlercc.edu
BASTIN, Stephanie ... 502-597-6878 ... 203 G
stephanie.bastin@kysu.edu
BASTION, Tamela ... 570-662-4857 ... 443 C
tbastion@mansfield.edu
BASTIONY, Peter ... 305-949-9500 ... 106 B
pbastiony@cci.edu
BASTON, Michael ... 718-482-5180 ... 328 B
mbaston@lagcc.cuny.edu
BASU, Andra, M ... 610-921-7634 ... 421 E
abasu@alb.edu
BASU, Raj ... 918-594-8016 ... 410 G
raj.basu@okstate.edu
BASUALDO, Maria ... 607-778-5030 ... 324 G
basualdomi@sunybroome.edu
BATAILLON, Pamela ... 402-559-9567 ... 300 H
pdbataillon@unmc.edu
BATAYEH, Ed ... 248-349-5454 ... 259 E
ed.batayeh@walshcollege.edu
BATCHELDER, Kathy ... 330-684-8944 ... 403 C
ksbatch@uakron.edu
BATCHELDER, Rick ... 518-562-4106 ... 329 C
rick.batchelder@clinton.edu
BATCHELLER, Tamara ... 313-578-0436 ... 258 G
batchets@udmercy.edu
BATCHELOR, Gerald ... 731-425-2619 ... 475 C
gbatchelor@jscc.edu
BATCHELOR, Susan ... 618-545-3331 ... 155 B
sbatchelor@kaskaskia.edu
BATCHELOR, Susan ... 215-955-2867 ... 448 C
susan.mcfadden@jefferson.edu
BATCHELOR, William, D ... 334-844-3209 ... 1 F
wdb0007@auburn.edu
BATE, Carol ... 315-229-5906 ... 349 E
cbate@stlawu.edu
BATE, Jeff ... 801-375-5125 ... 510 J
jbate@rmuohp.edu
BATE, Joel, C ... 208-732-6836 ... 143 E
jbate@csi.edu
BATELL, Sue, S ... 608-796-3380 ... 553 C
ssbatell@viterbo.edu
BATEMAN, Bethany ... 877-638-8573 ... 387 B
bbateman@chancelloru.edu
BATEMAN, Bradley, W ... 740-587-6243 ... 389 I
batemanb@denison.edu
BATEMAN, Heather ... 269-749-7189 ... 257 A
hbateman@olivetcollege.edu
BATEMAN, Linda ... 260-665-4124 ... 180 D
batemanl@trine.edu
BATEMAN, JR., Rick ... 337-491-2641 ... 212 E
rick.bateman@sowela.edu
BATEMAN, William, K ... 989-837-4448 ... 256 E
batemanw@northwood.edu
BATENHORST, Jim Ann ... 806-894-9611 ... 494 G
jbatenho@southplainscollege.edu
BATENHORST, Mandy ... 580-349-1396 ... 410 B
mandyb@opsu.edu
BATES, Alan ... 256-840-4129 ... 7 A
abates@snead.edu
BATES, Becky ... 612-332-3361 ... 261 A
bbates@aii.edu
BATES, Brad, J ... 513-529-7286 ... 396 E
batesbj@muohio.edu
BATES, Brent ... 660-596-7252 ... 290 B
bbates@sfccmo.edu
BATES, Brian ... 408-924-6518 ... 37 C
brian.bates@sjsu.edu
BATES, Carol ... 318-678-6000 ... 209 I
cbates@bpcc.edu
BATES, Carol ... 906-487-7258 ... 251 A
carol.bates@finlandia.edu
BATES, Damien ... 928-317-5892 ... 12 A
damien.bates@azwestern.edu
BATES, Deborah ... 740-389-4636 ... 395 H
batesd@mtc.edu
BATES, Doug ... 931-372-3408 ... 474 B
dbates@tntech.edu
BATES, Evola, C ... 225-771-4680 ... 214 H
evola_bates@sus.edu
BATES, Janice ... 610-647-4400 ... 431 C
jbates@immaculata.edu
BATES, Jennifer ... 315-279-5646 ... 337 K
jbates@mail.keuka.edu
BATES, Jennifer ... 503-777-7289 ... 420 A
batesj@reed.edu
BATES, Joan ... 423-478-6205 ... 474 E
jbates@clevelandstatecc.edu
BATES, Julie ... 501-660-1002 ... 20 B
jbates@asusystem.edu
BATES, Leslie ... 937-769-1345 ... 384 A
lbates@antioch.edu
BATES, Lynette ... 909-558-4561 ... 54 D
lbates@llu.edu
BATES, Mark, R ... 440-775-8477 ... 397 G
mark.bates@oberlin.edu
BATES, Mary Lou, W ... 518-580-5588 ... 351 B
mbates@skidmore.edu
BATES, Michael ... 731-426-7560 ... 470 B
mbates@lanecollege.edu
BATES, Michael, D ... 816-235-6910 ... 291 C
batesmd@umkc.edu
BATES, Mike ... 503-375-7003 ... 415 F
mbates@corban.edu
BATES, Pamela ... 859-246-6335 ... 201 H
pamela.bates@kctcs.edu
BATES, Patrick, M ... 585-292-2820 ... 341 H
pbates@monroecc.edu
BATES, Ren ... 859-246-4605 ... 201 H
ren.bates@kctcs.edu
BATES, Starnell ... 803-822-3235 ... 459 E
batess@midlandstech.edu
BATES, Suzanne ... 330-263-2365 ... 388 F
sbates@wooster.edu
BATES, Tom ... 281-756-3561 ... 479 F
tbates@alvincollege.edu
BATES, Tom ... 360-416-7745 ... 538 D
tom.bates@skagit.edu
BATES, Winfrey ... 270-858-6501 ... 203 C
winfrey.bates@kctcs.edu
BATES-LEE, Cheryl, A ... 757-823-8323 ... 522 E
cabates-lee@nsu.edu
BATESON, Mark ... 740-654-6711 ... 400 C
batesonm@ohio.edu
BATH, Michael, J ... 906-227-2151 ... 256 C
mbath@nmu.edu
BATHE, David, A ... 765-269-5600 ... 176 D
dbathe@ivytech.edu
BATIC, Marjorie ... 317-955-6150 ... 177 I
mbatic@marian.edu
BATIE, Larry ... 205-929-1517 ... 5 H
lbatie@miles.edu
BATIG, Miria, T ... 216-361-2741 ... 387 B
mbatig@chancelloru.edu
BATISTA, Adrian ... 440-775-8472 ... 397 G
adrian.batista@oberlin.edu
BATISTA, Angela, E ... 812-464-1862 ... 181 B
BATISTA, Jorge ... 347-964-8600 ... 324 C
jbatista@boricuacollege.edu
BATKIN, Norton ... 845-758-7598 ... 323 D
batkin@bard.edu
BATSON, Barbara ... 479-575-2806 ... 24 C
bbatson@uark.edu
BATSON, James ... 847-925-6340 ... 151 G
jbatson@harpercollege.edu
BATSON, Judy ... 540-351-1513 ... 527 C
jbatson@lfcc.edu
BATSON, Marie ... 251-442-2370 ... 9 A
mbatson@umobile.edu
BATSON, Rebecca ... 302-857-7887 ... 96 C
rbatson@desu.edu
BATSON-BOREL, Dawn ... 305-626-3150 ... 109 A
dawn.batson@fmuniv.edu
BATT, Ellen ... 208-459-5814 ... 143 D
ebatt@collegeofidaho.edu
BATT, Marylou ... 617-349-8564 ... 236 B
mbatt@lesley.edu
BATTA, Rajan ... 716-645-2771 ... 351 G
seasdean@eng.buffalo.edu
BATTAGLIA, Janet, M ... 540-464-7213 ... 529 F
battagliajm@vmi.edu
BATTAGLINO, Lisa ... 508-531-1347 ... 237 D
lbattaglino@bridgew.edu
BATTALORA, Elizabeth ... 318-473-6459 ... 212 I
ebattalora@lsua.edu
BATTEN, Glenn, T ... 910-277-5556 ... 376 C
battengt@sapc.edu
BATTEN, Melissa ... 843-349-5228 ... 458 H
melissa.batten@hgtc.edu
BATTEN-MICKENS,
Meloyde ... 202-651-5337 ... 98 B
meloyde.batten-mickens@gallaudet.edu
BATTERSBY, Gerard ... 313-883-8552 ... 257 E
battersby.gerard@shms.edu
BATTERSON, Brett ... 312-431-2391 ... 163 B
bbatterson@roosevelt.edu
BATTERSON, Bruce ... 402-872-2224 ... 299 F
bbatterson@peru.edu
BATTISTA, Elizabeth ... 718-855-3661 ... 336 D
ebattista@idc.edu
BATTISTA, Vincent, C ... 718-855-3661 ... 336 D
vcbattista@idc.edu
BATTISTE, Doris ... 340-693-1121 ... 568 E
dbattis@live.uvi.edu
BATTISTE, Leilani ... 415-241-2294 ... 40 C
lbattist@ccsf.edu
BATTISTEL, George ... 503-768-7807 ... 416 G
georgeb@lclark.edu
BATTISTELLA, Diane ... 630-829-6415 ... 145 G
dbatistella@ben.edu
BATTISTI, Francis ... 607-778-5138 ... 324 G
BATTLE, Bruce ... 661-362-3432 ... 41 I
bruce.battle@canyons.edu
BATTLE, Donna ... 919-546-8491 ... 376 F
dbattle@shawu.edu
BATTLE-BRYANT, Rebecca 803-535-1231 ... 460 C
battle-bryantr@octech.edu
BATTLE-MERCER, Delois ... 252-536-7242 ... 371 B
mercerd@halifaxcc.edu
BATTLES, Denise ... 970-351-2877 ... 89 B
denise.battles@unco.edu
BATTLES, Denise ... 910-962-3389 ... 379 D
battlesd@uncw.edu
BATTRAW, Danny ... 928-428-8605 ... 14 B
danny.battraw@eac.edu
BATTURS, Beth Anne ... 410-777-7352 ... 221 C
babatturs@aacc.edu
BATTY, Philip ... 616-331-8648 ... 251 F
battyp@gvsu.edu
BATTY-HERBERT,
Kimberly ... 863-784-7329 ... 117 J
battyhek@southflorida.edu
BATY, David ... 860-412-7317 ... 92 D
dbaty@qvcc.commnet.edu
BAUBLITZ, Ivan ... 219-757-7907 ... 171 D
ibaublitz@devry.edu
BAUDER, Sarah, J ... 301-314-8279 ... 227 B
sbauder@umd.edu
BAUDRY, Michel ... 909-706-8271 ... 78 I
mbaudry@westernu.edu
BAUER, C. Jon ... 636-584-6501 ... 281 E
bauerj@eastcentral.edu
BAUER, Cynthia, M ... 414-288-7343 ... 548 F
cindy.bauer@marquette.edu
BAUER, Daniel, C ... 314-367-8700 ... 288 F
daniel.bauer@stlcop.edu
BAUER, Daniel, L ... 502-272-8240 ... 198 H
dbauer@bellarmine.edu
BAUER, Deb ... 401-949-2820 ... 453 F
BAUER, Don ... 620-365-5116 ... 190 D
bauer@allencc.edu
BAUER, Frank ... 724-938-5717 ... 441 G
bauer_f@calu.edu
BAUER, Jackie ... 320-308-5486 ... 269 B
jbauer@sctcc.edu
BAUER, James ... 989-729-3403 ... 248 F
jim.bauer@baker.edu
BAUER, James ... 313-664-7412 ... 249 E
jbauer@collegeforcreativestudies.edu
BAUER, James, M ... 305-284-2270 ... 122 I
jbauer@miami.edu
BAUER, James, R ... 503-370-6112 ... 421 D
jbauer@willamette.edu
BAUER, Jan, L ... 847-543-2750 ... 148 B
jbauer@clcillinois.edu
BAUER, Jason, K ... 515-263-2887 ... 185 C
jbauer@grandview.edu
BAUER, Jody ... 215-751-8060 ... 426 B
jbauer@ccp.edu
BAUER, John ... 678-915-7334 ... 137 G
jbauer@spsu.edu
BAUER, Kent ... 970-542-3111 ... 86 G
kent.bauer@morgancc.edu
BAUER, Kimberly, P ... 404-413-0728 ... 131 G
kimbauer@gsu.edu
BAUER, Lori ... 215-572-2970 ... 422 C
bauerl@arcadia.edu
BAUER, Mary Claire ... 518-629-7309 ... 336 C
m.bauer@hvcc.edu
BAUER, Michelle ... 217-732-3155 ... 156 I
mbauer@lincolncollege.edu
BAUER, Patrick ... 847-925-6827 ... 151 G
pbauer@harpercollege.edu
BAUER, Sarah ... 415-338-2174 ... 37 B
sbauer@sfsu.edu
BAUER, Thomas ... 928-523-6126 ... 16 I
thomas.bauer@nau.edu
BAUER, Thomas, G ... 805-565-6043 ... 79 A
tbauer@westmont.edu
BAUER, Tom ... 650-358-6782 ... 67 E
bauert@smccd.edu
BAUER, Warren, K ... 515-574-1120 ... 185 I
bauer@iowacentral.edu
BAUER-LEVESQUE,
Angela ... 617-682-1551 ... 234 E
abauer-levesque@eds.edu
BAUGH, Anita, G ... 320-308-5936 ... 269 B
abaugh@sctcc.edu
BAUGH, Frank ... 601-318-6772 ... 278 C
frank.baugh@wmcarey.edu
BAUGH, J. Thomas ... 423-869-3611 ... 470 E
BAUGH, Robbie ... 940-668-7731 ... 491 E
rbaugh@nctc.edu
BAUGHER, Kathy ... 615-248-1320 ... 476 G
kbaugher@trevecca.edu
BAUGHMAN, Leslie, C ... 214-692-8080 ... 480 I
baughmal@aii.edu
BAUGHMAN, Patricia ... 936-261-1944 ... 496 G
pabaughman@pvamu.edu
BAUHS, Timothy ... 312-369-7054 ... 148 D
tbauhs@colum.edu
BAUM, Christina ... 203-392-5760 ... 90 I
baumc1@southernct.edu
BAUM, Courtney ... 724-805-2253 ... 446 E
courtney.baum@email.stvincent.edu
BAUM, Cynthia, G ... 410-627-7859 ... 272 C
cynthia.baum@waldenu.edu
BAUM, Cynthia, G ... 443-627-7859 ... 272 C
cynthia.baum@waldenu.edu
BAUM, Daniel, B ... 410-777-2011 ... 221 C
dbbaum@aacc.edu
BAUM, Robert ... 724-805-2590 ... 446 E
bob.baum@email.stvincent.edu
BAUM, Robin ... 914-594-4882 ... 343 F
robin_baum@nymc.edu
BAUM-HAYES, Elyse ... 631-423-0483 ... 350 G
ehayes@icseminary.edu
BAUMAL, Robert ... 978-656-3244 ... 240 B
baumalr@middlesex.mass.edu
BAUMAN, Dallas ... 631-632-6974 ... 352 C
dallas.bauman@stonybrook.edu
BAUMAN, David ... 218-723-6179 ... 262 G
dbauman@css.edu
BAUMAN, Jerry ... 312-996-2497 ... 167 B
jbauman@uic.edu
BAUMAN, Joel ... 386-822-7100 ... 121 F
jbauman@stetson.edu
BAUMANN, Anita, M ... 814-472-3902 ... 446 B
abaumann@francis.edu
BAUMANN, Benjamin ... 508-678-2811 ... 239 B
ben.baumann@bristolcc.edu
BAUMANN, Erick ... 708-524-5054 ... 150 C
ebauman@dom.edu
BAUMANN, Joseph ... 815-455-8915 ... 157 H
jbaumann@mchenry.edu
BAUMANN, Julianne, D ... 607-735-1806 ... 332 I
jbaumann@elmira.edu
BAUMANN, Robert ... 913-684-2741 ... 558 F
robert.baumann@leavenworth.army.mil
BAUMANN, Terry ... 727-726-1153 ... 103 I
terrybaumann@clearwater.edu
BAUMER, Terry ... 317-274-2016 ... 174 D
tebaumer@iupui.edu
BAUMERT, Karen, D ... 208-732-6279 ... 143 E
kbaumert@csi.edu
BAUMET, Robert, L ... 716-878-5304 ... 353 A
baumetrl@buffalostate.edu
BAUMGAERTNER, Jill, P ... 630-752-5060 ... 168 H
jill.baumgaertner@wheaton.edu
BAUMGARDNER, Brice, D 573-629-3279 ... 282 E
bbaumgardner@hlg.edu
BAUMGARDNER, Deidra ... 317-738-8189 ... 171 F
dbaumgardner@franklincollege.edu
BAUMGARDNER, Michael . 518-244-2207 ... 348 A
baumgm@sage.edu
BAUMGARDNER, Waylon . 951-343-4876 ... 31 J
wbaumgardner@calbaptist.edu
BAUMGART, Reilly ... 618-262-8641 ... 153 A
baumgartr@iecc.edu
BAUMGARTEN, Bobbie ... 214-637-3530 ... 508 D
bbaumgarten@wadecollege.edu
BAUMGARTEN, Whitney ... 414-256-1272 ... 549 D
mmc-bookstore@mtmary.edu
BAUMGARTNER, Bruce ... 814-732-2776 ... 442 E
bbaumgartner@edinboro.edu
BAUMGARTNER,
Carolyn, G ... 419-530-5812 ... 404 F
carolyn.baumgartner@utoledo.edu

BAUMGARTNER, David, A 319-335-1023 .... 182 F david-baumgartner@uiowa.edu
BAUMGARTNER, Eric, T ... 419-772-2372 .... 398 H e-baumgartner@onu.edu
BAUMLER, Scott 319-368-6460 .... 187 H sbaumler@mtmercy.edu
BAUN, Dan 507-537-6978 .... 269 E dan.baun@smsu.edu
BAUN, Jeffrey, S 610-359-5315 .... 426 G jbaun@dccc.edu
BAURAIN, Thomas, S 816-322-0110 .... 279 D thomas.baurain@calvary.edu
BAUS, Amy 563-589-3132 .... 189 F abaus@dbq.edu
BAUSHKE, Ken 270-745-3056 .... 208 A ken.baushke@wku.edu
BAUSILI, Mark, T 716-878-4907 .... 353 A bausilmt@buffalostate.edu
BAUSINGER, Patricia, E .... 570-321-4049 .... 435 D baus@lycoming.edu
BAUSLER, Katie 907-796-6530 ...... 11 A katie.bausler@uas.alaska.edu
BAUSMAN, Marvin, D 812-426-2865 .... 177 C
BAUSS, Celia, N 864-592-4754 .... 461 C baussc@sccsc.edu
BAUSTISTA PERTUZ, Sofia 718-817-0664 .... 334 C spertuz@fordham.edu
BAUTISTA, Renato, J 973-275-5891 .... 310 F renato.bautista@shu.edu
BAUTSCH, Jack 206-934-3655 .... 537 D jack.bautsch@seattlecolleges.edu
BAVA, Brian 208-459-5319 .... 143 D bbava@collegeofidaho.edu
BAVERO, Gary, S 973-642-8460 .... 315 C gary.bavero@shu.edu
BAWCOM, Amy 254-526-1264 .... 482 H amy.bawcom@ctcd.edu
BAWCOM, Jerry, G 254-295-4500 .... 504 C jbawcom@umhb.edu
BAWOROWSKY, John 415-257-1334 .... 45 C john.baworowsky@dominican.edu
BAX, John 573-341-6999 .... 291 E baxj@mst.edu
BAXTER, Agnes 919-546-8212 .... 376 F abaxter@shawu.edu
BAXTER, Barbara, C 870-733-6722 .... 22 E bbaxter@midsouthcc.edu
BAXTER, Donna 910-755-7336 .... 368 F baxterd@brunswickcc.edu
BAXTER, Ginny 562-938-4634 .... 54 E gbaxter@lbcc.edu
BAXTER, James, E 717-221-1300 .... 430 E jebaxter@hacc.edu
BAXTER, Jessica, M 703-323-3288 .... 527 F jbaxter@nvcc.edu
BAXTER, Keith 580-745-2250 .... 412 C kbaxter@se.edu
BAXTER, Ken, A 309-467-6420 .... 151 B kabaxter@eureka.edu
BAXTER, Marty, A 859-246-6239 .... 201 H marty.baxter@kctcs.edu
BAXTER, Pat 212-229-8947 .... 342 E baxterp@newschool.edu
BAXTER, Richard, L 706-507-8043 .... 127 G baxter_richard@columbusstate.edu
BAXTER, Robert 402-878-2380 .... 298 E bbaxter@littlepriest.edu
BAXTER, Steven 360-452-9277 .... 536 G sbaxter@pencol.edu
BAY, Jonathan 801-601-4912 .... 509 F jtbay@argosy.edu
BAY, Stella 520-206-2622 .... 17 H sbay@pima.edu
BAYARD, SJ, Mike 206-296-6052 .... 538 B bayardm@seattleu.edu
BAYER, Hermann 757-493-6000 .... 99 G
BAYER, Richard, L 865-974-2105 .... 477 D rbayer@utk.edu
BAYERL, Sue 320-308-2111 .... 269 A sjbayerl@stcloudstate.edu
BAYLES, Kenneth 402-559-4945 .... 300 H kbayles@unmc.edu
BAYLES, Robert 209-462-8777 .... 52 I
BAYLESS, Rita 970-945-8691 .... 82 G
BAYLESS, Robert 816-802-3399 .... 283 E rbayless@kcai.edu
BAYLIS, Gordon 270-745-6733 .... 208 A gordon.baylis@wku.edu
BAYLOR, Bridget 540-234-9261 .... 526 D baylorb@brcc.edu
BAYLOR, Gail 828-298-3325 .... 380 D gbaylor@warren-wilson.edu
BAYLOR, Jeffrey, S 605-677-5759 .... 465 G jeffrey.baylor@usd.edu
BAYLOR, Martin 956-665-2121 .... 506 C baylormv@utpa.edu
BAYLOR, Monique 610-399-2343 .... 442 A mbaylor@cheyney.edu
BAYLOR, Oronde 954-499-9746 .... 104 J obaylor@devry.edu
BAYLY, Warwick, M 509-335-5581 .... 539 D wmb@wsu.edu
BAYNE, Deann 308-635-6018 .... 299 E dbayne@csc.edu
BAYNE, Doug 509-527-4253 .... 539 B doug.bayne@wwcc.edu
BAYNE, Suzanne 423-472-7141 .... 474 E sbayne@clevelandstatecc.edu
BAYNHAM, Donald 972-860-7119 .... 484 I baynham@dcccd.edu
BAYNUM, Thomas, B 309-796-5001 .... 145 H baynumt@bhc.edu
BAYONA, Maribel 787-753-6335 .... 562 G mbayona@icprjc.edu
BAYOUMI, Magdy, A 337-482-6147 .... 216 D mab@louisiana.edu
BAYRON, Ivonne 787-738-2161 .... 567 D ivone.bayron@upr.edu
BAYS, Katherine 814-536-5168 .... 424 E kbays@crbc.net
BAYS, Sherri, A 575-538-6150 .... 321 I bayss@wnmu.edu
BAYS, Steven 509-533-3570 .... 533 C stevenb@spokanefalls.edu
BAYSAL, Oktay 757-683-3787 .... 522 F obaysal@odu.edu
BAYTCH, Karen 617-349-8726 .... 236 B kbaytch@lesley.edu
BAYTO, Tammy 478-274-7852 .... 135 C tbayto@oftc.edu
BAYUK, Mary Ellen 814-898-6351 .... 439 F meb5@psu.edu
BAYUSIK, Linda 203-332-5085 .... 91 E lbayusik@hcc.commnet.edu
BAZAN, Teresita 512-223-7950 .... 481 B tbazan@austincc.edu
BAZAN, Yamilet 951-785-2100 .... 53 E ybazan@lasierra.edu
BAZANT, Robert, S 724-222-5330 .... 438 F rbazant@penncommercial.edu
BAZAR, Leon 361-593-2258 .... 498 D kulgb000@tamuk.edu
BAZARNIC, Steve 301-784-5000 .... 221 B sbazarnic@allegany.edu
BAZEMORE, Dennis 910-893-1540 .... 362 J bazemored@campbell.edu
BAZEMORE, Haywood, M . 803-705-4321 .... 455 D bazemoreh@benedict.edu
BAZIJIAN, Rosann, V 336-334-3418 .... 379 B rvbazirj@uncg.edu
BAZIL, Ted 914-961-8313 .... 349 I ted@svots.edu
BAZIL, Theodore 914-961-8313 .... 349 I tbazil@svots.edu
BAZIN, Angela 860-465-0147 .... 90 H bazina@easternct.edu
BAZLEY, Lisa 740-587-6526 .... 389 I bazleyl@denison.edu
BAZLUKE, Francine, T 802-656-8585 .... 514 H francine.bazluke@uvm.edu
BAZZELL, Darrell 608-263-2467 .... 550 J dbazzell@vc.wisc.edu
BEA, David 520-206-4519 .... 17 H dbea@pima.edu
BEACH, Aaron, T 231-995-1342 .... 256 D abeach@nmc.edu
BEACH, Gary 541-737-2815 .... 418 F gary.beach@oregonstate.edu
BEACH, Lorraine 512-231-2500 .... 486 A lbeach@devry.edu
BEACH, Nancy, S 540-365-4262 .... 519 C nbeach@ferrum.edu
BEACH, Natalie 503-399-5105 .... 414 J natalie.beach@chemeketa.edu
BEACHAM, David, M 864-597-4206 .... 463 G beachamdm@wofford.edu
BEACHLER, Judith 916-691-7205 .... 56 B beachlj@crc.losrios.edu
BEACHNAU, Andrew, J 616-331-2120 .... 251 F beachnaa@gvsu.edu
BEACHY, Randy 574-257-3319 .... 169 I beachyr@bethelcollege.edu
BEACON, John 812-237-3560 .... 173 B john.beacon@indstate.edu
BEADENKOPF, Scott 610-361-5327 .... 437 D beadenks@neumann.edu
BEADLE, Paul 724-832-1050 .... 448 F pbeadle@triangle-tech.edu
BEAGHAN, John, W 248-370-2445 .... 256 G beaghan@oakland.edu
BEAGLE, Deborah 734-384-4202 .... 255 D dbeagle@monroeccc.edu
BEAGLE, Donald 704-461-6740 .... 362 F donaldbeagle@bac.edu
BEAHON, Mary Ann 573-592-1127 .... 293 D mbeahon@williamwoods.edu
BEAIL, Linda 619-849-2408 .... 62 L lindabeail@pointloma.edu
BEAKES, Ben 304-357-4849 .... 542 A benbeakes@ucwv.edu
BEAL, Alvin (Chip) 715-394-8297 .... 552 F abeal@uwsuper.edu
BEAL, Billy 601-484-8765 .... 275 A bbeal@meridiancc.edu
BEAL, Jack 203-254-4000 .... 92 H jwbeal@fairfield.edu
BEAL, Jason 801-957-4205 .... 512 D jason.beal@slcc.edu
BEAL, Jennifer 515-244-4221 .... 181 F bealj@aib.edu
BEAL, Judy 617-521-2139 .... 244 F judy.beal@simmons.edu
BEAL, Stephen 510-594-3630 .... 32 C sbeal@cca.edu
BEAL, Tawny 925-439-2181 .... 43 G tbeal@losmedanos.edu
BEALE, Charles, L 302-831-8107 .... 96 I cbeale@udel.edu
BEALE, Connie, L 973-761-9401 .... 315 B concetta.beale@shu.edu
BEALE, Rita, W 804-819-4906 .... 526 C rwbeale@vccs.edu
BEALES, Sharon 215-619-7472 .... 436 G sbeales@mc3.edu
BEALL, Jim 912-583-3257 .... 126 F jbeall@bpc.edu
BEALS, Linda, M 937-327-6374 .... 406 B lbeals@wittenberg.edu
BEAM, Carla 907-786-1359 .... 10 G carla.beam@alaska.edu
BEAM, Donny 423-493-4100 .... 476 E security@tntemple.edu
BEAM, John 510-464-3474 .... 62 D jbeam@peralta.edu
BEAM, Julie 574-257-8715 .... 169 I julie.beam@bethelcollege.edu
BEAM, Linda 415-485-9340 .... 42 B linda.beam@marin.edu
BEAM, Linda 310-660-3401 .... 45 E lbeam@elcamino.edu
BEAM, Marc 530-242-7670 .... 69 D mbeam@shastacollege.edu
BEAM, Ruthanne 865-573-4517 .... 469 L rubeam@johnsonu.edu
BEAM, Tony 864-977-2008 .... 460 A tony.beam@ngu.edu
BEAMAN, Lorraine 916-638-1616 .... 50 A lorraine_beaman@heald.edu
BEAMAN, Patricia, L 716-839-8538 .... 331 F pbeaman@daemen.edu
BEAMAN, Riley 910-576-6222 .... 372 D beamanr@montgomery.edu
BEAMAN, Warren, J 503-517-1050 .... 421 B wbeaman@warnerpacific.edu
BEAMER, Sarah 276-326-4294 .... 516 L sbeamer@bluefield.edu
BEAMON, Cynthia 919-546-8476 .... 376 F cbeamon@shawu.edu
BEAMON, Cynthia 434-848-9603 .... 524 B cbeamon@saintpauls.edu
BEAMON, Stanley 312-850-7038 .... 147 F sbeamon3@ccc.edu
BEAMON, Vincent, L 252-335-3299 .... 377 F vlbeamon@mail.ecsu.edu
BEAN, Al 207-780-5588 .... 220 G albean@usm.maine.edu
BEAN, Athena 325-649-8810 .... 488 C abean@hputx.edu
BEAN, Becky 803-938-3728 .... 462 G beanjr@uscsumter.edu
BEAN, Carlena 207-941-7064 .... 218 A beanc@husson.edu
BEAN, Christopher, A 540-665-4553 .... 524 E cbean@su.edu
BEAN, Debra 858-642-8109 .... 58 I dbean@nu.edu
BEAN, Ethelle, S 605-256-5205 .... 465 I ethelle.bean@dsu.edu
BEAN, Gary 315-792-7106 .... 356 B gary.bean@sunyit.edu
BEAN, James, C 541-346-3186 .... 419 B provost@uoregon.edu
BEAN, Melissa, M 208-524-3000 .... 143 G melissa.bean@my.eitc.edu
BEAN, Miho, S 603-641-4145 .... 306 D miho.bean@unh.edu
BEAN, Norma, P 713-313-4420 .... 500 B bean_np@tsu.edu
BEAN, Paul 785-242-5200 .... 178 I
BEAN, Paul 785-242-5200 .... 17 B
BEAN, Paul 785-242-5200 .... 196 A
BEAN, Paul 785-242-5200 .... 195 I paul.bean@ottawa.edu
BEAN, Paul 785-242-5200 .... 549 H
BEAN, Phyllis 610-902-8546 .... 424 B pbean@cabrini.edu
BEAN, Shirley 206-878-3710 .... 535 B sbean@highline.edu
BEAN, Steve 218-322-2351 .... 266 G steve.bean@itascacc.edu
BEANE, Marian, E 704-687-7746 .... 379 A mebeane@uncc.edu
BEARCE, Jacqueline, S 413-542-2354 .... 230 A jsbearce@amherst.edu
BEARCE, John 702-651-7454 .... 302 E john.bearce@csn.edu
BEARD, Aileen 218-723-6000 .... 262 G abeard@css.edu
BEARD, Casey 541-278-5838 .... 414 G cbeard@bluedd.edu
BEARD, John, P 843-349-6441 .... 456 G johnb@coastal.edu
BEARD, Lisa 407-843-3984 .... 110 E lbeard@fortiscollege.edu
BEARD, Lori 614-221-7770 .... 396 B
BEARD, Mary, A 716-851-1675 .... 333 B beard@ecc.edu
BEARD, Rebecca 432-335-6404 .... 492 A bbeard@odessa.edu
BEARD, Richard, L 717-867-6363 .... 434 C rbeard@lvc.edu
BEARD, Russell 425-564-4200 .... 531 G russ.beard@bellevuecollege.edu
BEARD, Scott 304-876-5370 .... 544 C sbeard@shepherd.edu
BEARD, Timothy, L 727-816-3413 .... 114 F beardt@phcc.edu
BEARDMORE, Kevin 270-686-4504 .... 203 B kevin.beardmore@kctcs.edu
BEARDMORE, Melissa, A .. 410-777-2532 .... 221 C mabeardmore@aacc.edu
BEARDSLEE, Bill 603-899-4188 .... 305 A beardsleeb@franklinpierce.edu
BEARDSLEY, Kathleen 215-572-2838 .... 422 C beardsley@arcadia.edu
BEARE, Paul 559-278-0210 .... 35 A pbeare@csufresno.edu
BEARMAN, Alan 785-670-1855 .... 197 F alan.bearman@washburn.edu
BEARROWS, Thomas, R 217-333-0563 .... 167 A bearrows@uillinois.edu
BEARROWS, Thomas, R 312-996-7762 .... 167 B bearrows@uillinois.edu
BEARS TAIL, Daryl 701-255-3285 .... 383 G dbearstail@uttc.edu
BEARSS, Carrie 810-989-5501 .... 257 H cbearss@sc4.edu
BEARY, Richard 407-823-5242 .... 120 B richard.beary@ucf.edu
BEASCA, Jeffrey 714-533-3946 .... 37 E jeffb@calums.edu
BEASIMER, Linda, M 845-431-8979 .... 332 D beasimer@sunydutchess.edu
BEASLEY, Beth, M 217-544-6464 .... 163 H
BEASLEY, Dan, S 901-678-2438 .... 474 C dbeasley@memphis.edu
BEASLEY, David 870-972-2085 .... 20 D dbeasley@astate.edu
BEASLEY, David 870-972-2088 .... 20 D dbeasley@astate.edu
BEASLEY, Jack, D 757-446-5035 .... 518 G beaslejd@evms.edu
BEASLEY, Lori 405-974-3371 .... 413 B lbeasley@uco.edu
BEASLEY, Pete 352-629-1941 .... 115 I pete.beasley@rasmussen.edu
BEASLEY, Susan, S 434-832-7742 .... 526 E beasleys@cvcc.vccs.edu
BEATA, Anthony 239-280-2577 .... 101 I tony.beata@avemaria.edu
BEATRICE, Jonelle 330-941-1450 .... 406 F jabeatrice@ysu.edu
BEATSON, Bonnie 808-235-7374 .... 142 F beatson@hawaii.edu
BEATTIE, George, A 218-723-6562 .... 262 G gbeattie@css.edu
BEATTIE, Linda 502-585-9911 .... 206 D lbeattie@spalding.edu
BEATTIE, Martha, J 603-646-2258 .... 304 J martha.j.beattie@dartmouth.edu
BEATTY, Anthony 859-257-8200 .... 207 D abeat2@uky.edu
BEATTY, Del 435-652-7514 .... 512 B beatty@dixie.edu
BEATTY, Fred 334-241-5477 .... 8 A fbeatty@troy.edu
BEATTY, Heather, P 336-841-9309 .... 365 C hbeatty@highpoint.edu
BEATTY, Jaye 760-630-1555 .... 52 J jbeatty@kaplan.edu
BEATTY, Kimberly, A 817-515-5636 .... 496 C kimberly.beatty@tccd.edu
BEATTY, Krista, M 740-593-4330 .... 399 G mccallum@ohio.edu
BEATTY, Lisa, L 563-588-8000 .... 184 I lbeatty@emmaus.edu
BEATTY, Paul 406-496-4198 .... 296 A pbeatty@mtech.edu
BEATTY, Paul, V 406-496-4198 .... 296 B pbeatty@mtech.edu
BEATTY, Robert 856-256-4025 .... 314 A beatty@rowan.edu
BEATTY, Scott 207-741-5832 .... 219 A sbeatty@smccme.edu
BEATTY, Susan 503-725-5061 .... 418 G susan.beatty@pdx.edu
BEATTY, Tracy 269-965-3931 .... 253 B beattyt@kellogg.edu
BEATY, Katherine, M 309-677-3107 .... 146 C kbeaty@bradley.edu
BEATY, Vivian 313-845-9663 .... 252 B vbeaty@hfcc.edu
BEAUCHAMP, Becky 405-878-5420 .... 412 A

BEAUCHAMP, Denise 610-526-6665 430 D dbeauchamp@harcum.edu

BEAUCHAMP, CSC, E. William 503-943-7101 420 G beaucham@up.edu

BEAUCHAMP, Eddie 678-407-5381 130 C ebeauchamp@ggc.edu

BEAUCHAMP, Mary Jo 812-749-1399 178 H mbeauchamp@oak.edu

BEAUCHAMP, Nancy, F 205-853-1200 5 C nbeauchamp@jeffstateonline.com

BEAUCHAMP, Robin, L 401-254-3244 454 C rbeauchamp@rwu.edu

BEAUDIN, Giselda 407-646-2466 116 D gbeaudin@rollins.edu

BEAUDOIN, Amy, L 606-679-8501 203 C amy.beaudoin@kctcs.edu

BEAUDOIN, Susan 518-381-1327 350 E beaudose@sunysccc.edu

BEAUDRY, Sharon, L 603-526-3741 303 G sbeaudry@colby-sawyer.edu

BEAUGH, Richard 985-549-2000 216 C richard.beaugh@selu.edu

BEAUJON, Francis 530-257-6181 53 H fbeaujon@lassencollege.edu

BEAULIEU, Adrian, G 401-865-2114 453 H abeaulie@providence.edu

BEAULIEU, Ellen 617-928-4790 242 E ebeaulieu@mountida.edu

BEAULIEU, Gary, R 317-940-9624 170 F gbeaulie@butler.edu

BEAUMONT, Karen 413-528-7293 230 F karen@simons-rock.edu

BEAUMONT, Marilyn 252-493-7340 372 H mbeaumont@email.pittcc.edu

BEAUPRE, Judy 312-410-8998 146 F jbeaupre@tcsedsystem.edu

BEAUPRE, Walter 302-736-2436 97 A security@wesley.edu

BEAUPRE WHITE, Renee 802-287-8376 513 F beauprer@greenmtn.edu

BEAUPRE', Eugene, L 513-745-4271 406 E beaupre@xavier.edu

BEAUREGARD, Amy 410-644-6400 226 G

BEAUREGARD, Debbie 603-228-1541 306 E dbeauregard@piercelaw.edu

BEAUREGARD, Jill 320-589-6036 271 G beaureja@morris.umn.edu

BEAUREGARD, Kathy 269-387-3061 260 C kathy.beauregard@wmich.edu

BEAUREGARD, Michael 954-587-7100 113 E michael.beauregard@medvance.edu

BEAUREGARD, Michelle 401-232-6722 453 C mbeaureg@bryant.edu

BEAUREGARD, Stephen 508-565-1375 245 A sbeauregard@stonehill.edu

BEAUVAIS, Laura 401-874-4341 454 E beauvais@uri.edu

BEAVER, James 541-552-6093 419 A beaverj@sou.edu

BEAVER, Jeff, S 864-388-8208 459 A jbeaver@lander.edu

BEAVER, John 979-209-7300 482 C john.beaver@blinn.edu

BEAVER, Marie 573-592-4260 293 D mbeaver@williamwoods.edu

BEAVER, Mark, P 804-758-6764 528 C mbeaver@rappahannock.edu

BEAVER, Shirley 515-643-6615 187 F sbeaver@mercydesmoines.org

BEAVERS, Bobby, J 937-512-2748 401 J bobby.beavers@sinclair.edu

BEAVERS, Dennis 314-264-1580 478 B dennis.beavers@vatterott-college.edu

BEAVERS, Dennis 316-264-1580 168 A dennis.beavers@vatterott-college.edu

BEAVERS, Dennis 314-264-1580 405 D dennis.beavers@vatterott-college.edu

BEAVERS, Dennis 314-264-1580 292 C dennis.beavers@vatterott-college.edu

BEAVERS, Dennis 314-264-1580 292 B dennis.beavers@vatterott.edu

BEAVERS, Dennis 314-264-1500 292 D dennis.beavers@vatterott-college.edu

BEAVERS, Dennis 314-264-1580 292 F dennis.beavers@vatterot-college.edu

BEAVERS, Dennis 314-264-1580 292 H dennis.beavers@vatterott-college.edu

BEAVERS, Dennis 314-264-1580 292 G dennis.beavers@vatterott-college.edu

BEAVERS, Dennis 314-264-1580 301 C dennis.beavers@vatterott-college.edu

BEAVERS, Dennis 314-264-1580 189 H dennis.beavers@vatterott-college.edu

BEAVERS, Dennis 314-264-1580 414 A dennis.beavers@vatterott-college.edu

BEAVERS, Dennis 314-264-1580 414 B dennis.beavers@vatterott-college.edu

BEAVERS, Judy 517-321-0242 251 G jbeavers@glcc.edu

BEAVERS, Philip, E 517-321-0242 251 G pbeavers@glcc.edu

BEAZER, Ken 435-865-8354 511 D beazer@suu.edu

BEBBER, Glenda, H 704-233-8242 380 F gbebber@wingate.edu

BEBEE, Richard 202-274-7050 100 A rbebee@udc.edu

BEBENSEE, Mark, A 843-953-5156 456 C mark.bebensee@citadel.edu

BECENTI, Delores 505-786-4104 318 I dbecenti@navajotech.edu

BECERRA, Cynthia 209-478-0800 50 K cbecerra@humphreys.edu

BECERRA, Gilbert 361-698-2474 485 G gbecerra@delmar.edu

BECERRA, Rosina 310-206-7411 74 C rbecerra@conet.ucla.edu

BECERRA-BARCKHOLTZ, Beatriz 956-882-8292 505 E beatriz.becerra@utb.edu

BECERRA-FERNANDEZ, Irma 305-348-2000 119 C irma.fernandez@fiu.edu

BECHARD, Matthew 785-243-1435 192 A mbechard@cloud.edu

BECHER, Amy 724-589-2182 448 B abecher@thiel.edu

BECHER, Eric 606-218-5282 207 F ericbecher@upike.edu

BECHER, Gregory, J 805-525-4417 72 I gbecher@thomasaquinas.edu

BECHERER, Bob 618-468-3700 156 E rbecherer@lc.edu

BECHERER, Jack, J 815-921-4003 162 H j.becherer@rockvalleycollege.edu

BECHILL, Cynthia 248-457-2746 252 E cbechill@iadtdetroit.com

BECHTEL, Brian 816-604-3036 285 D brian.bechtel@mcckc.edu

BECHTEL, Janice, L 419-783-2444 389 H jbechtel@defiance.edu

BECHTEL-WHERRY, Lori, J 814-949-5012 438 I ljb3@psu.edu

BECHTOLD, Brad 864-294-3166 458 E brad.bechtold@furman.edu

BECK, Alissa 513-244-4892 388 E alissa_beck@mail.msj.edu

BECK, Anne, D 313-664-7473 249 E abeck@collegeforcreativestudies.edu

BECK, Barbara, E 518-580-5800 351 B bbeck@skidmore.edu

BECK, Carina 406-994-4353 295 C cbeck@montana.edu

BECK, Cherie 517-371-5140 258 F beckc@cooley.edu

BECK, Deborah 803-777-3957 462 A dbeck@gwm.sc.edu

BECK, Deborah, C 803-777-3957 462 A dbeck@sc.edu

BECK, Erika 702-992-2500 302 G erika.beck@nsc.edu

BECK, Fred 904-620-2900 120 D fbeck@unf.edu

BECK, Gerald, L 208-732-6601 143 E jbeck@csi.edu

BECK, Jeff 319-352-8491 189 J jeff.beck@wartburg.edu

BECK, Jen 512-245-2152 501 F jb32@txstate.edu

BECK, Jennifer 225-768-1779 214 C jbeck@ololcollege.edu

BECK, Jill 920-832-6525 548 B jill.beck@lawrence.edu

BECK, Joan 773-256-0756 157 D jbeck@lstc.edu

BECK, Jocelyn, M 610-799-1155 434 D jbeck@lccc.edu

BECK, John 517-750-1200 258 D jbeck@arbor.edu

BECK, Julie 417-268-6004 278 J jbeck@gobbc.edu

BECK, Kenneth, L 606-474-3135 201 D kbeck@kcu.edu

BECK, Lynn 209-946-2680 76 A lbeck@pacific.edu

BECK, Margaret, Z 941-752-5597 118 J beckm@scf.edu

BECK, Marilyn, C 256-306-2555 2 D mcb@calhoun.edu

BECK, Maryann, M 334-833-4522 4 E mbeck@huntingdon.edu

BECK, Maureen, A 443-334-2231 226 E mbeck@stevenson.edu

BECK, Morgan 620-223-2700 193 A morganb@fortscott.edu

BECK, Pam 567-661-7334 400 I pamela_back@owens.edu

BECK, Rhonda 859-257-4758 207 D rsbeck0@uky.edu

BECK, Richard 918-343-7615 411 H rbeck@rsu.edu

BECK, Robin, H 215-898-7581 448 J beck@isc.upenn.edu

BECK, Ronda 517-371-5140 258 F beckr@cooley.edu

BECK, Stacie 480-423-6536 16 C stacie.beck@scottsdalecc.edu

BECK-DUDLEY, Caryn 850-644-3090 119 D cbeckdudley@cob.fsu.edu

BECK-LITTLE, Rebecca 704-406-4358 364 E rbeck-little@gardner-webb.edu

BECKAGE, Cathy 570-702-8990 431 L cbeckage@johnson.edu

BECKEL, Dave 740-389-6786 399 D beckel.1@osu.edu

BECKEMEYER, Wendy, C 412-397-5255 445 H beckemeyer@rmu.edu

BECKENHAUER, Charles, D 254-710-3821 482 A charles_beckenhauer@baylor.edu

BECKER, Amber 859-442-1147 202 B amber.becker@kctcs.edu

BECKER, Barbara 817-272-3071 505 C bbecker@uta.edu

BECKER, Bart 425-564-3081 531 G bart.becker@bellevuecollege.edu

BECKER, Brian 815-753-8980 160 B bbecker@niu.edu

BECKER, Carol 212-854-9847 330 F cbecker@columbia.edu

BECKER, Charles, P 304-384-5190 543 G beckerc@concord.edu

BECKER, Christopher, F 714-703-1900 42 I cbecker@concorde.edu

BECKER, Dennis, M 303-871-3897 89 A dbecker@du.edu

BECKER, Elizabeth, M 708-209-3020 148 E elizabeth.becker@cuchicago.edu

BECKER, Frederick, W 570-326-3761 440 L fbecker@pct.edu

BECKER, J. Thomas 215-951-2945 444 D beckert@philau.edu

BECKER, Janet 740-654-6711 400 C becker@ohio.edu

BECKER, Janine 570-408-8009 452 A janine.becker@wilkes.edu

BECKER, Jeffrey 209-946-3986 76 A jbecker@pacific.edu

BECKER, Jim 812-855-4884 173 E jambecke@indiana.edu

BECKER, Jonathan 845-758-7378 323 D jbecker@bard.edu

BECKER, Joyce, D 573-651-2189 289 K jbecker@semo.edu

BECKER, Joyce, K 443-352-4031 226 E jbecker@stevenson.edu

BECKER, Karen 815-802-8405 155 A kbecker@kcc.edu

BECKER, Karl, D 215-222-4200 445 G kbecker@walnuthillcollege.edu

BECKER, Kurt 718-260-3608 346 C kbecker@poly.edu

BECKER, Larry 951-785-2460 53 E lbecker@lasierra.edu

BECKER, Linda 402-486-2507 300 C libecker@ucollege.edu

BECKER, Lois, S 904-256-7030 111 L lbecker1@ju.edu

BECKER, Mark, P 404-413-1300 131 G mbecker@gsu.edu

BECKER, Mary 507-457-1503 271 B mbecker@smumn.edu

BECKER, Maureen 540-458-8913 530 D mbecker@wlu.edu

BECKER, Mike 925-439-2181 43 G mbecker@losmedanos.edu

BECKER, Pete, D 708-209-3092 148 E pete.becker@cuchicago.edu

BECKER, Raymond 215-567-7080 422 D rbecker@aii.edu

BECKER, Richard, A 561-868-3137 114 D beckerr@palmbeachstate.edu

BECKER, Roger 402-872-2218 299 F rbecker@peru.edu

BECKER, Ron 201-761-6415 314 F rbecker@spc.edu

BECKER, S. Ann 321-674-7327 108 H abecker@fit.edu

BECKER, Sheila, R 563-556-5110 188 B beckers@nicc.edu

BECKER, Stefan 718-960-8764 327 C stefan.becker@lehman.cuny.edu

BECKER, Tom 402-486-2511 300 C tobecker@ucollege.edu

BECKER-GORBY, Sherry 304-434-8000 542 I sherrybg@eastern.wvnet.edu

BECKER-RICHARDS, Joicy 609-497-7900 312 F joicy.becker@ptsem.edu

BECKETT, Alice 415-503-6251 66 A abeckett@sfcm.edu

BECKETT, Keith 330-263-2500 388 F kbeckett@wooster.edu

BECKETT, Thomas, A 203-432-1414 96 A thomas.beckett@yale.edu

BECKFORD, John, S 864-294-2007 458 E john.beckford@furman.edu

BECKHORN, Roy 916-568-3190 55 J beckhor@losrios.edu

BECKLER, Bob 863-638-1019 123 D pastorbob@slwcog.com

BECKLER, Larry 843-525-8282 461 E lbeckler@tcl.edu

BECKLEY, Clark 913-234-0609 191 J clark.beckley@cleveland.edu

BECKLEY, David, L 662-252-2491 276 G dlbeckley@rustcollege.edu

BECKLEY, Gemma 662-252-8000 276 G gbeckley@rustcollege.edu

BECKLEY, Greg 805-654-6486 77 F gbeckley@vcccd.edu

BECKMAN, Ann 407-847-8966 107 I ann.beckman@fcc.edu

BECKMAN, Connie, L 570-662-4831 443 C cbeckman@mansfield.edu

BECKMAN, Donald, C 503-370-6315 421 D dbeckman@willamette.edu

BECKMAN, John 212-998-6848 344 B john.beckman@nyu.edu

BECKMAN, Nancy 773-481-8525 147 I nbeckman@ccc.edu

BECKMAN, Phyllis 225-359-9206 209 J pbeckman@catc.edu

BECKMAN, Sydney 865-545-5302 470 E sydney.beckman@lmunet.edu

BECKMANN, Terry, J 207-786-8339 217 C tbeckman@bates.edu

BECKNER, JR., James 276-656-0281 527 G jbeckner@patrickhenry.edu

BECKNER, Scott 478-445-5800 130 B scott.beckner@gcsu.edu

BECKS, Crystal 661-654-3012 34 A cbecks@csub.edu

BECKSTED, Scott, M 315-470-4992 355 A smbeckst@esf.edu

BECKSTRAND, Kennan, T 585-292-5627 325 C ktbeckstrand@bryantstratton.edu

BECKSTROM, Brian, A 319-352-8217 189 J brian.beckstrom@wartburg.edu

BECKSTROM, Robert, A 440-365-5222 395 D

BECKSTROM, Ronald 651-793-1889 267 A ronald.beckstrom@metrostate.edu

BECKUM, Randy 913-971-3461 195 D rbeckum@mnu.edu

BECKWITCH, Peter 517-437-7341 252 C peter.beckwitch@hillsdale.edu

BECKWITH, Cynthia, A 909-621-8512 49 F cynthia_beckwith@hmc.edu

BECKWITH, James 802-447-6319 514 F jbeckwith@svc.edu

BECKWITH, James 802-447-6342 514 F jbeckwith@svc.edu

BECKWITH, Robert 510-466-7269 62 E rbeckwith@peralta.edu

BECKWITH, Ryan 661-395-4266 52 L ryan.beckwith@bakersfieldcollege.edu

BECKWITH, Steven V, W 510-987-9436 73 G steven.beckwith@ucop.edu

BECVAR, Laurie, J 605-677-6926 465 G laurie.becvar@usd.edu

BECVAR, Laurie, J 605-677-6287 465 G laurie.becvar@usd.edu

BEDARD, Martha 505-277-4241 321 C mbedard@unm.edu

BEDARD, Richard, F 413-205-3532 229 G richard.bedard@aic.edu

BEDASHI, Allan, M 304-336-5100 544 D abedashi@westliberty.edu

BEDDALL, Tina 559-278-2191 35 A tina_beddall@csufresno.edu

BEDDARD, Wesley 252-940-6226 368 C wesleyb@beaufortccc.edu

BEDDOW, Lucinda 256-306-2784 2 D lmb@calhoun.edu

BEDELL, Frank 803-754-4100 457 D

BEDENBAUGH, Diana, L 864-488-4589 459 B dbedenbaugh@limestone.edu

BEDFORD, Allen 267-502-2567 423 C allen.bedford@brynathyn.edu

BEDFORD, April 504-280-1278 213 E awhatley@uno.edu

BEDFORD, John 405-208-5322 410 A jbedford@okcu.edu

BEDFORD, Laura 315-792-3179 359 E lbedford@utica.edu

BEDFORD, Norm 702-774-8000 302 I norm.bedford@unlv.edu

BEDI, Param, S 570-577-1557 423 E param.bedi@bucknell.edu

BEDICS, Stuart 610-282-1100 427 A stuart.bedics@desales.edu

BEDINI, Ken 860-465-5247 90 H bedini@easternct.edu

BEDITZ, Stephen 518-956-8120 351 E sbeditz@uamail.albany.edu

BEDNAR, Cynthia 610-436-2231 444 A cbednar@wcupa.edu

BEDNAR, Jean 847-628-2087 154 K jean.bednar@judsonu.edu

BEDNARZ, Bridgette 254-968-9271 497 A bednarz@tarleton.edu

BEDNEY, Elynda, A 269-471-6040 247 D bedney@andrews.edu

BEDOYA, Theresa 410-225-2434 224 B tbedoya@mica.edu

BEDTKE, James 507-457-1458 271 B jbedtke@smumn.edu

BEDWELL, Pamela .... 478-757-2666.... 133 H
pamela.bedwell@maconstate.edu
BEE, Allan, C .... 530-898-6322...... 34 C
abee@csuchico.edu
BEE, Patsy .... 304-424-8200.... 545 C
patsy.bee@mail.wvu.edu
BEE, Richard .... 562-903-4728...... 31 A
richard.e.bee@biola.edu
BEE, Timothy, S .... 520-621-1737...... 18 L
timbee@email.arizona.edu
BEEBE, Barbara, R .... 301-784-5000.... 221 B
bbeebe@allegany.edu
BEEBE, Craig .... 504-865-3579.... 213 F
cwbeebe@loyno.edu
BEEBE, Gayle, D .... 805-565-6024...... 79 A
president@westmont.edu
BEEBE, Norman .... 413-775-1333.... 239 E
beebe@gcc.mass.edu
BEEBE, Robert, D .... 909-593-3511...... 75 E
rbeebe@laverne.edu
BEEBE, Rose .... 304-424-8286.... 545 C
rose.beebe@mail.wvu.edu
BEECH, Amanda .... 661-255-1050...... 32 F
BEECH, JR., Derrick .... 404-756-5294.... 134 E
dbeech@msm.edu
BEECH, Glenn, J .... 412-675-9163.... 439 I
gxb2@psu.edu
BEECHAM, Sarah .... 706-649-1858.... 128 A
sbeecham@columbustech.edu
BEECHER, Brian .... 847-214-7595.... 150 F
bbeecher@elgin.edu
BEECHING, Angela Myles . 617-585-1118.... 242 I
angela.beeching@necmusic.edu
BEEKE, Joel, R .... 616-977-0599.... 257 B
BEEKMAN, Emily .... 212-243-5150.... 334 E
registrar@gts.edu
BEEKMAN, William, R .... 517-353-9818.... 255 A
beekman@msu.edu
BEELEN, Joan .... 616-957-6027.... 249 B
jrb44@calvinseminary.edu
BEELER, Jeremy .... 908-835-2301.... 317 C
jbeeler@warren.edu
BEELER, Shannon .... 720-855-6014...... 85 B
shannonb@heritage-education.com
BEEMAN, Greg .... 845-675-4417.... 344 G
greg.beeman@nyack.edu
BEEMAN, Robert .... 651-523-2326.... 264 A
rbeemanjr01@hamline.edu
BEEMER, Elizabeth .... 937-376-6444.... 387 A
ebeemer@centralstate.edu
BEEMER, Matthew .... 904-596-2473.... 122 D
mbeemer@tbc.edu
BEEMER, Pamela .... 847-467-1466.... 160 E
p-beemer@northwestern.edu
BEEN, Sharon, A .... 501-882-8836...... 20 C
sabeen@asub.edu
BEENE, Connie .... 913-768-1900.... 191 D
cbeene@brownmackie.edu
BEENK, Rose .... 775-831-1314.... 303 E
rbeenk@sierranevada.edu
BEER, Bernard .... 212-960-5353.... 346 F
beer@yu.edu
BEER, Linda .... 507-389-7351.... 269 D
linda.beer@southcentral.edu
BEER, Patrick .... 478-387-4720.... 131 A
BEER, Richard .... 360-486-8784.... 537 B
jrbeer@stmartin.edu
BEERS, David .... 253-879-3902.... 538 H
dbeers@pugetsound.edu
BEERS, George, S .... 650-949-7077...... 47 H
beersgeorge@foothill.edu
BEERS, Josh .... 717-560-8240.... 433 D
jbeers@lbc.edu
BEERS, Maggie .... 415-338-3613...... 37 B
mbeers@sfsu.edu
BEERS, Peter .... 717-560-8267.... 433 D
pbeers@lbc.edu
BEERS, Robert .... 406-657-1124.... 296 C
robert.beers@rocky.edu
BEERS, Stephen, T .... 479-524-7252...... 22 C
sbeers@jbu.edu
BEERS, Susan .... 714-992-7046...... 59 E
sbeers@fullcoll.edu
BEERY, Kevin, E .... 610-917-1401.... 450 E
kebeery@vfcc.edu
BEERY, Wendy .... 610-917-1429.... 450 E
wmbeery@vfcc.edu
BEESON, Duane, L .... 712-707-7116.... 188 D
beeson@nwciowa.edu
BEESON, Patricia, E .... 412-624-4223.... 449 A
beeson@pitt.edu
BEESON, Teresa .... 740-774-6300.... 389 D
tbeeson@daymargroup.edu
BEETS, A. Ray .... 319-296-4042.... 185 F
aurel.beets@hawkeyecollege.edu
BEETS, Shannon .... 775-831-1314.... 303 E
sbeets@sierranevada.edu
BEEZHOLD, Philip, D .... 616-526-6481.... 249 A
pdb2@calvin.edu
BEG, Christina .... 216-397-1998.... 392 L
cbeg@jcu.edu
BEGANY, James .... 724-357-2220.... 442 F
jbegany@iup.edu
BEGAY, Darryl, R .... 928-724-6698...... 13 L
darbegay@dinecollege.edu
BEGAY, Janice .... 785-749-8419.... 193 D
janice.begay@bie.edu
BEGAY, Karen, F .... 520-626-9809...... 18 L
kfbegay@email.arizona.edu
BEGAY, Precilla .... 505-863-7527.... 321 D
pbegay@gallup.unm.edu
BEGIN, Gene .... 781-239-4512.... 230 E
gbegin@babson.edu
BEGIN-RICHARDSON,
Janet .... 508-831-5060.... 246 F
jbrich@wpi.edu
BEGLEY, John, B .... 270-384-8505.... 204 D
begleyj@lindsey.edu
BEGLEY, Mary Ann .... 415-338-2722...... 37 B
begley@sfsu.edu
BEGLEY, Teresa, J .... 812-374-5127.... 176 A
tbegley@ivytech.edu
BEGLEY, Thomas .... 518-276-2525.... 347 D
begley@rpi.edu
BEGLINGER, Claire, M ...... 262-524-7242.... 546 H
cbegling@carrollu.edu
BEHAN, C. Joseph .... 315-655-7284.... 325 H
jbehan@cazenovia.edu
BEHAN KRAUS,
Carolyn, A .... 203-773-8521...... 90 C
cbehan@albertus.edu
BEHAUNEK, Luke .... 515-961-1562.... 189 C
luke.behaunek@simpson.edu
BEHE, Phil .... 252-399-6528.... 362 E
pbehe@barton.edu
BEHEN, Joseph .... 312-499-4272.... 164 C
jbehen@saic.edu
BEHLING, Laura, L .... 317-940-9278.... 170 F
lbehling@butler.edu
BEHM, Bonnie Lee .... 610-519-6456.... 450 H
bonnie.behm@villanova.edu
BEHM, Mark, E .... 410-704-2151.... 228 E
mbehm@towson.edu
BEHM, Rhonda, K .... 651-641-8894.... 263 A
rbehm@csp.edu
BEHN, Julie, J .... 408-944-6121...... 61 A
julie.behn@palmer.edu
BEHR, Fred, C .... 507-786-3636.... 271 C
behr@stolaf.edu
BEHR, John .... 914-961-8313.... 349 I
jbehr@svots.edu
BEHR, Kate, E .... 914-337-9300.... 330 G
kate.behr@concordia-ny.edu
BEHR, Richard, A .... 239-590-7399.... 119 B
rbehr@fgcu.edu
BEHRE, William .... 609-771-2797.... 308 F
behre@tcnj.edu
BEHRENDT, William, M ..... 214-648-6342.... 507 E
william.behrendt@utsouthwestern.edu
BEHRENS, Ann .... 217-228-5432.... 161 F
behrens@quincy.edu
BEHRENS, James .... 516-572-7700.... 342 C
james.behrens@ncc.edu
BEHRENS, Kim .... 559-791-2322...... 53 A
kbehrens@portervillecollege.edu
BEHRENS, Troy, T .... 214-768-2288.... 495 A
tbehrens@smu.edu
BEHRMAN, William .... 407-569-1307.... 107 I
president@fcc.edu
BEHUL, Paula .... 561-297-3004.... 119 A
pbehul@fau.edu
BEHUNEK, Sarah .... 303-458-3535...... 87 I
sbehunek@regis.edu
BEIDLEMAN, David, C .... 717-361-1493.... 428 F
beidlemand@etown.edu
BEIER, Nancy, A .... 410-777-2834.... 221 C
nabeier@aacc.edu
BEIERSCHMITT, Bill .... 918-338-8030.... 411 H
bbeierschmitt@rsu.edu
BEIKIRCH, Dale .... 432-685-5539.... 491 A
dbeikirch@midland.edu
BEIL, Cheryl .... 202-994-6712...... 98 C
cbeil@gwu.edu
BEIL, Don .... 202-651-5005...... 98 B
don.beil@gallaudet.edu
BEILBY, Rod .... 530-741-6838...... 80 K
rbeilby@yccd.edu
BEINHOFF, Lisa .... 575-835-5615.... 319 A
lbeinhoff@admin.nmt.edu
BEIRNE, Chris .... 706-385-1120.... 136 B
chris.beirne@point.edu
BEIRNE, Jay .... 617-578-7170.... 244 D
jbeirne@sbboston.com
BEISWANGER, Robert, C ... 716-839-8218.... 331 F
rbeiswan@daemen.edu
BEITEL, Amy .... 724-463-0222.... 424 D
abeitel@crbc.net
BEITEL, Leland .... 443-334-2838.... 226 E
lbeitel@stevenson.edu
BEITEY, George .... 619-388-7860...... 65 H
gbeitey@sdccd.edu
BEITL, Thomas, R .... 330-972-8643.... 403 B
tbeitl@uakron.edu
BEITNER, Veronica .... 616-632-2458.... 247 E
beitnver@aquinas.edu
BEITTEL, Lisa, B .... 508-421-5913.... 237 C
lisa.beittel@umassmed.edu
BEITZEL, Vernon, L .... 540-464-7211.... 529 F
beitzelvl@vmi.edu
BEJAR, Elizabeth .... 305-348-2151.... 119 C
elizabeth.bejar@fiu.edu
BEJNAROWICZ, Ewa .... 312-553-3193.... 147 C
ebejnarowicz@ccc.edu
BEJOU, David .... 252-335-3311.... 377 F
dbejou@mail.ecsu.edu
BEKKEN, Joseph .... 208-769-3368.... 144 D
jmbekken@nic.edu
BEKRITSKY, Brett .... 845-848-7405.... 332 B
brett.bekritsky@dc.edu
BELAND, Thomas .... 802-773-5900.... 513 D
tom.beland@csj.edu
BELANGER, OFM,
Brian, C .... 518-783-5047.... 350 I
bbelanger@siena.edu
BELANGER, David, J .... 413-585-2530.... 244 G
dbelange@smith.edu
BELANGER, Elise .... 617-296-8300.... 235 J
elise_belanger@laboure.edu
BELANGER, Kathleen .... 502-447-1000.... 206 F
kbelanger@spencerian.edu
BELANGER, Lisa .... 860-768-4666...... 95 B
belanger@hartford.edu
BELARDO, Lynette .... 212-686-9244.... 322 G
BELAUSKAS, August, J ...... 847-566-6401.... 167 F
gbelauskas@usml.edu
BELCASTRO, David .... 614-236-6771.... 386 E
dbelcast@capital.edu
BELCHER, Alan .... 704-463-3452.... 375 F
alan.belcher@fsmail.pfeiffer.edu
BELCHER, C. Gary .... 512-313-3000.... 483 K
charles.belcher@concordia.edu
BELCHER, Carol .... 843-574-6230.... 461 G
carol.belcher@tridenttech.edu
BELCHER, Chris .... 918-495-6529.... 411 C
cbelcher@oru.edu
BELCHER, David, O .... 828-227-7100.... 380 A
dbelcher@wcu.edu
BELCHER, Elizabeth, M ...... 304-929-5464.... 543 A
ebelcher@newriver.edu
BELCHER, Keith, E .... 912-279-5922.... 127 E
kbelcher@ccga.edu
BELCHER, Larry .... 765-998-5381.... 180 B
lwbelcher@taylor.edu
BELCHER, Michael .... 209-946-2537...... 76 A
mbelcher@pacific.edu
BELCHER, Michael .... 978-934-3929.... 237 B
michael_belcher@uml.edu
BELCHER, Nicholas .... 617-850-1297.... 235 F
nbelcher@hchc.edu
BELCHER, Tim .... 540-365-4366.... 519 C
tbelcher@ferrum.edu
BELCHER, Trevor .... 415-738-8042...... 58 J
BELD, Jo, M .... 507-786-3910.... 271 C
beld@stolaf.edu
BELDAN, Chris .... 717-290-8755.... 433 F
cbeldan@lancasterseminary.edu
BELDEN, Eric .... 330-490-7337.... 405 F
ebelden@walsh.edu
BELDON, William .... 360-992-2103.... 532 F
wbeldon@clark.edu
BELEN-NAZARIO, Lillian ... 787-620-2040.... 560 D
lbelen@aupr.edu
BELETTE, Magdiel .... 305-593-1223.... 102 H
mbelette@albizu.edu
BELEW, Paul, D .... 214-648-6062.... 507 E
paul.belew@utsouthwestern.edu
BELEW, Valerie, S .... 615-353-3342.... 475 E
valerie.belew@nscc.edu
BELFIELD, Sherri .... 704-378-1032.... 366 A
sbelfield@jcsu.edu
BELFIORE, Phil, J .... 814-824-2268.... 436 C
pbelfiore@mercyhurst.edu
BELIN, Jackie .... 908-526-1200.... 313 D
jbelin@raritanval.edu
BELINSKI, Victor .... 909-594-5611...... 58 A
vbelinski@mtsac.edu
BELINSKY, Joseph .... 330-339-3391.... 394 A
jbelinsky@kent.edu
BELISLE, William, R .... 504-284-5539.... 214 J
wbelisle@suno.edu
BELK, Adria .... 229-248-2530.... 126 A
abelk@bainbridge.edu
BELK, Peter .... 913-469-8500.... 194 B
pbelk@jccc.edu
BELK, Wesley, C .... 864-429-8728.... 463 A
wcbelk@mailbox.sc.edu
BELKIN, Betsey .... 440-646-8184.... 405 B
bbelkin@ursuline.edu
BELKIN, Michelle .... 561-273-6500.... 118 A
mbelkin@southuniversity.edu
BELKNAP, Peggy .... 928-536-6231...... 17 A
peggy.belknap@npc.edu
BELKO, Dawn .... 763-424-0715.... 268 B
dbelko@nhcc.edu
BELL, Aimee .... 440-826-2071.... 384 K
abell@bw.edu
BELL, Amy .... 870-743-3000...... 22 G
abell@northark.edu
BELL, Angela .... 304-558-1112.... 543 E
abell@hepc.wvnet.edu
BELL, Barrett .... 815-226-3372.... 163 A
bbell@rockford.edu
BELL, Brett .... 619-388-7810...... 65 H
bbell@sdccd.edu
BELL, Chris .... 940-552-6291.... 507 F
cbell@vernoncollege.edu
BELL, Christopher A, R .... 207-768-9511.... 220 F
chris.bell@umpi.edu
BELL, Claudia .... 617-369-3619.... 244 E
cbell@smfa.edu
BELL, Corinne .... 802-387-6863.... 513 G
corinnebell@landmark.edu
BELL, Damon .... 909-384-8992...... 65 C
dbell@sbccd.cc.ca.us
BELL, Daniel, R .... 304-462-4132.... 544 A
dan.bell@glenville.edu
BELL, Danielle .... 803-321-5128.... 459 H
danielle.bell@newberry.edu
BELL, David, D .... 614-823-1300.... 400 H
dbell@otterbein.edu
BELL, Dean .... 312-322-1791.... 165 E
dbell@spertus.edu
BELL, Debbie .... 910-277-5554.... 376 C
belldebb@sapc.edu
BELL, Deborah .... 863-784-7251.... 117 J
belld@southflorida.edu
BELL, Denise .... 850-973-9481.... 113 K
belld@nfcc.edu
BELL, Denise .... 508-793-2397.... 233 C
dbell@holycross.edu
BELL, Elaine .... 313-993-1588.... 258 G
belles@udmercy.edu
BELL, Genniver .... 850-561-2989.... 118 L
genniver.bell@famu.edu
BELL, Geraldine .... 205-929-1715........ 5 H
gbell@mail.miles.edu
BELL, Glenn .... 310-314-6064...... 30 A
BELL, Glenn, R .... 251-380-3099........ 7 E
bell@shc.edu
BELL, Gregory, J .... 570-321-4395.... 435 D
bell@lycoming.edu
BELL, Gretchen, M .... 336-599-1181.... 372 G
bellg@piedmontcc.edu
BELL, Harold .... 404-270-5269.... 138 B
hbell@spelman.edu
BELL, Hershey .... 814-866-6641.... 433 C
hbell@lecom.edu
BELL, Jacquelin .... 619-388-3428...... 65 F
jbell@sdccd.edu
BELL, Jeff, W .... 903-923-3221.... 500 E
jeff.bell@tstc.edu
BELL, Jennifer .... 856-256-4410.... 314 A
bellj@rowan.edu
BELL, Jenny .... 205-665-6565........ 9 B
jbell8@montevallo.edu
BELL, John, D .... 801-422-3037.... 509 H
john_bell@byu.edu
BELL, Jorge .... 415-550-4416...... 40 C
jbell@ccsf.edu
BELL, Jorge .... 415-239-3382...... 40 C
jbell@ccsf.edu
BELL, Julie .... 217-228-5432.... 161 F
bellju@quincy.edu
BELL, Juliette, B .... 410-651-6101.... 227 E
jbbell@umes.edu
BELL, Karen .... 617-266-1400.... 231 E
BELL, Kathleen .... 317-931-2305.... 170 H
kbell@cts.edu
BELL, Kathleen .... 651-779-3438.... 266 A
kathy.bell@century.edu
BELL, Kelli .... 740-593-4797.... 399 G
bellk@ohio.edu
BELL, Kelly, A .... 864-662-6064.... 455 C
kbell@andersonuniversity.edu
BELL, Lauren, C .... 804-752-7268.... 523 C
lbell@rmc.edu
BELL, Leia .... 860-727-6967...... 92 I
lbell@goodwin.edu
BELL, Leia .... 860-512-2903...... 91 F
lbell@mcc.commnet.edu
BELL, Lillie, F .... 318-357-6171.... 216 B
bell@nsula.edu
BELL, Lisa, G .... 859-246-6564.... 201 H
lisag.bell@kctcs.edu
BELL, Lynn .... 334-556-2223........ 4 A
lbell@wallace.edu
BELL, Marcus, V .... 803-376-5700.... 455 B
mbell@allenuniversity.edu
BELL, Margaret, G .... 410-857-2203.... 224 C
mbell@mcdaniel.edu
BELL, Marjorie .... 617-964-1100.... 230 B
mbell@ants.edu
BELL, Marty .... 217-228-5432.... 161 F
bellma@quincy.edu
BELL, Matt .... 317-921-4206.... 175 I
mpbell@ivytech.edu
BELL, Melleta .... 432-837-8388.... 501 E
mbell@sulross.edu
BELL, Michael .... 617-573-8120.... 245 B
mbell1@suffolk.edu
BELL, Mike .... 907-796-6140...... 11 A
mike.bell@uas.alaska.edu
BELL, Norma, G .... 205-853-1200........ 5 C
ngbell@jeffstateonline.com

BELL, Pam 314-264-1852 478 B
pam.bell@vatterott-college.edu

BELL, Pam 314-264-1852 301 C
pam.bell@vatterott-college.edu

BELL, Pam 314-264-1852 168 A
pam.bell@vatterott-college.edu

BELL, Pam 314-264-1852 405 D
pam.bell@vatterott-college.edu

BELL, Pam 314-264-1852 292 F
pam.bell@vatterott-college.edu

BELL, Pam 314-264-1852 292 B
pam.bell@vatterott.edu

BELL, Pam 314-264-1852 292 C
pam.bell@vatterott-college.edu

BELL, Pam 314-264-1852 292 G
pam.bell@vatterott-college.edu

BELL, Pam 314-264-1852 292 H
pam.bell@vatterott-college.edu

BELL, Pam 314-264-1852 189 H
pam.bell@vatterott-college.edu

BELL, Pam 334-833-4570 4 E
0377mgr@fheg.follett.com

BELL, Pam 904-620-2372 120 D
pbell@unf.edu

BELL, Pam 314-264-1852 414 A
pam.bell@vatterott-college.edu

BELL, Pam 314-264-1852 414 B
pam.bell@vatterott-college.edu

BELL, Pamela 314-587-2433 283 H

BELL, Patty 903-983-8678 489 I
pbell@kilgore.edu

BELL, Paul 405-325-4411 413 C
pbell@ou.edu

BELL, Rebecca 432-685-4556 491 A
rbell@midland.edu

BELL, Richard, S 803-938-3715 462 G
richbell@uscsumter.edu

BELL, Robert, H 626-585-7205 61 F
rhbell@pasadena.edu

BELL, Robert, H 626-585-7071 61 F
rhbell@pasadena.edu

BELL, Robert, W 864-379-8885 458 A
rbell@erskine.edu

BELL, Roberta 615-322-4359 478 A
roberta.bell@vanderbilt.edu

BELL, Ruffin 610-399-2240 442 A
rbell@cheyney.edu

BELL, Rusty 214-637-3530 508 D
rbell@wadecollege.edu

BELL, Scott 907-474-6265 10 I
svbell2@alaska.edu

BELL, Sharon, B 401-874-2378 454 E
sbbell@mail.uri.edu

BELL, Sheree 636-481-3119 283 D
sbell6@jeffco.edu

BELL, Steed 785-242-5200 195 I
steed.bell@ottawa.edu

BELL, Stephen 847-543-2238 148 B
sbell@clcillinois.edu

BELL, Stephen 610-558-5549 437 D
bells@neumann.edu

BELL, Steven, K 724-847-6530 429 H
skbell@geneva.edu

BELL, Stuart, R 225-578-1519 212 H
sbell@lsu.edu

BELL, Tommy 260-481-5443 174 C
belljt@ipfw.edu

BELL, Trudy 805-546-3206 43 I
tbell@cuesta.edu

BELL, Zoe 302-736-2566 97 A
bell@wesley.edy

BELL ADAMS, Sandra 718-262-2363 329 A
sadams@york.cuny.edu

BELL-GARRISON,
Eileen, K 509-313-6533 534 F
bellgarrison@gonzaga.edu

BELL-JOHNSON, Lilly 870-584-4471 25 C
lbell@cccua.edu

BELLACK, Janis, P 617-726-8002 242 B
jbellack@mghihp.edu

BELLAFIORE, April 508-678-2811 239 B
april.bellafiore@bristolcc.edu

BELLAH, Eric 865-981-8225 471 B
eric.bellah@maryvillecollege.edu

BELLAIRS, Bart 985-549-2253 216 C
bart.bellairs@selu.edu

BELLALTA, Maria 617-262-5000 231 G
maria.bellalta@the-bac.edu

BELLAMEY, Tim, H 618-634-3219 164 E
timb@shawneecc.edu

BELLAMY, Antoinette, P 910-630-7257 367 B
abellamy@methodist.edu

BELLAMY, Reagan 509-682-6445 539 E
rbellamy@wvc.edu

BELLAMY, Sandra 212-694-1000 324 C
sbellamy@boricuacollege.edu

BELLAMY, Timothy, R 919-530-5326 378 B
timothy.bellamy@nccu.edu

BELLANCA, Rose 734-973-3491 259 F
rbellanca@wccnet.edu

BELLANTI, Dorothy 716-829-7775 332 E
bellanti@dyc.edu

BELLARDINE, Louis 212-851-0623 330 F
lbellardine@columbia.edu

BELLAS, Peter 661-362-3144 41 I
peter.bellas@canyons.edu

BELLATTI, Tom 918-495-7018 411 C
tbellatti@oru.edu

BELLAVANCE, Leslie 607-871-2412 322 E
bellavance@alfred.edu

BELLAVIA, Rand 716-829-7616 332 E
bellavia@dyc.edu

BELLE, Walton, M 804-257-5885 530 A

BELLE-ISLE,
G. Christopher 585-292-2271 341 H
cbelleisle@monroecc.edu

BELLEFEUILLE, Kate 315-498-2291 345 D

BELLEFEUILLE, Barbara 574-807-7250 169 I
belleb@bethelcollege.edu

BELLER, Wendy 217-228-5432 161 F
bellewe@quincy.edu

BELLFIELD, Nicole 813-880-8064 111 D
nbellfield@online.academy.edu

BELLICINI, Pierre, A 814-866-8121 433 C
pbellicini@lecom.edu

BELLINA, Amy 732-571-3586 311 E
abellina@monmouth.edu

BELLING, Karen 630-752-5021 168 H
karen.belling@wheaton.edu

BELLINGER, Larry, L 214-828-8322 497 C
lbellinger@bcd.tamhsc.edu

BELLIVEAU, Cynthia, L 802-656-3890 514 H
cynthia.belliveau@uvm.edu

BELLMAN, Ben 740-420-5933 398 D

BELLO, Chippi 503-594-3099 415 A
chippi@clackamas.edu

BELLO, Diane 631-632-6175 352 C
diane.bello@stonybrook.edu

BELLO-BRUNSON,
Jane, M 219-464-6769 181 C
jane.bellobrunson@valpo.edu

BELLOLI, Ronald 928-724-6676 13 L
rbelloli@dinecollege.edu

BELLONA, Steven, J 315-859-4502 334 H
sbellona@hamilton.edu

BELLONI, Francis, L 914-594-4110 343 F
francis_belloni@nymc.edu

BELLOWS, Charlene, M 508-831-5577 246 F
cbellows@wpi.edu

BELLOWS, Kathryn, S 202-687-5867 98 D
bellowsk@georgetown.edu

BELLSOM, Lou 773-380-6880 168 F
lbellsom@westwood.edu

BELLUCCI, Anthony 973-642-8094 315 C
anthony.bellucci@shu.edu

BELLUCCI, Debbie 413-755-4334 241 B
dbellucci@stcc.edu

BELLUCCI, Keith 617-732-2145 241 C
keith.bellucci@mcphs.edu

BELLUM, Kim 605-882-5284 464 E
bellumk@lakeareatech.edu

BELMODIS, Cassie 503-399-5159 414 J
cassie.belmodis@chemeketa.edu

BELOBRAJDIC, Scott 618-650-2298 165 C
sbelobr@siue.edu

BELOTE, David, J 731-881-7525 477 G
dbelote@utm.edu

BELOTE, Eve 757-789-1767 526 H
ebelote@es.vccs.edu

BELOTE, Faith, D 757-594-7618 517 L
faith.belote@cnu.edu

BELOTE, Michael, R 478-301-2850 134 A
michael.r.belote@mercer.edu

BELOW, Debbie 573-651-2590 289 K
dbelow@semo.edu

BELSITO, Paul 508-767-7321 230 D
pbelsito@assumption.edu

BELSKY, Jeff 412-809-5100 444 G
belsky.jeff@pti.edu

BELSTRA, James, E 708-239-4720 166 C
jim.belstra@trnty.edu

BELTON, Ada, A 803-705-4327 455 D
beltona@benedict.edu

BELTON, Annie, R 803-536-8406 460 G
zs_abelton@scsu.edu

BELTON, Dean 601-928-6213 275 E
dean.belton@mgccc.edu

BELTON, Gale 404-297-9522 131 D
beltong@gptc.org

BELTON, Ray, L 318-670-9312 215 A
rbelton@susla.edu

BELTRAN, Cherie 254-647-1414 492 G
cbeltran@rangercollege.edu

BELTRAN, Dulce 305-237-2222 113 H
dbeltran@mdc.edu

BELTRAN, Fernando 209-667-3108 36 D
fbeltran@csustan.edu

BELTRAN, JD 415-351-3530 65 I
jdbeltran@sfai.edu

BELTRAN, Philip 408-554-5082 68 C
pjbeltran@scu.edu

BELWOOD, Marilyn 660-831-4085 286 F
belwoodmf@moval.edu

BELYEA, Daniel 207-974-4664 218 H
dbelyea@emcc.edu

BELYEA, Elizabeth 916-691-7367 56 B
belyeae@crc.losrios.edu

BELZER, Rita, A 716-270-5355 333 B
belzer@ecc.edu

BEMBRY, Walter 785-784-5225 189 G
bembry@uiu.edu

BEMELEN, Jeff 303-871-3256 89 A
jbemelen@du.edu

BEMIS, Carol 574-807-7370 169 I
bemisc@bethelcollege.edu

BEMIS, Scot, R 781-736-4464 232 F
bemis@brandeis.edu

BEMUS, Melissa, L 920-748-8112 550 D
bemusm@ripon.edu

BENAICHA, Hedi 401-456-8053 454 A
hbenaicha@ric.edu

BENALLY, Rebecca, M 928-724-6610 13 L
benallym@dinecollege.edu

BENALLY, Steven 505-786-4110 318 I
sbenally@navajotech.edu

BENALLY, Suzanne 303-546-3523 86 H
sbenally@naropa.edu

BENANAV, Jay 612-330-1792 261 B
benanav@augsburg.edu

BENARD, Jane 502-863-8437 201 A
jane_benard@georgetowncollege.edu

BENARD, Mary 760-757-2121 57 E
mbenard@miracosta.edu

BENARD, Rich, S 440-510-1112 386 C
rsbenard@bryantstratton.edu

BENATAN, Ethan 503-699-6325 416 J
ebenatan@marylhurst.edu

BENAVIDES, Adolfo 254-968-9350 497 A
benavides@tarleton.edu

BENAVIDES, Elma, F 512-863-1441 496 A
benavide@southwestern.edu

BENAVIDES, Lewis 940-898-3555 502 D
lbenavides@twu.edu

BENAVIDES-FRANKE,
Joanna 361-825-6052 498 C
joanna.benavides-franke@tamucc.edu

BENAVIDEZ, Max 909-621-8099 40 G
max.benavidez@cmc.edu

BENBOW, Camilla, P 615-322-8407 478 A
camilla.benbow@vanderbilt.edu

BENCA, Melissa 212-774-4860 340 C
mbenca@mmm.edu

BENCH, Patricia 661-763-7757 72 E
pbench@taftcollege.edu

BENCHIMOL, Daniel 212-875-4633 323 C
dbenchimol@bankstreet.edu

BENCHOFF, Bryan 740-593-0061 399 G
benchoff@ohio.edu

BENDAPUDI, Neeli 785-864-7573 197 B
neeli@ku.edu

BENDECK, Yvette 281-283-3022 503 E
bendeck@uhcl.edu

BENDELE, Jennifer 419-227-3141 404 D
jennifer@unoh.edu

BENDER, Claire, E 507-284-3293 262 E
bender.claire@mayo.edu

BENDER, David 610-396-6090 439 B
dsb@psu.edu

BENDER, David, L 989-837-4374 256 E
bender@northwood.edu

BENDER, George 412-396-4895 428 D
benderg@duq.edu

BENDER, James, E 651-631-5493 270 B
jebender@nwc.edu

BENDER, Jennie, M 606-474-3226 201 D
jbender@kcu.edu

BENDER, Joe 812-855-6017 173 E
jbender@bncollege.com

BENDER, Judith, A 201-360-4279 310 E
jbender@hccc.edu

BENDER, Judy 585-475-4315 347 G
jebpsn@rit.edu

BENDER, Karla 713-718-8247 487 I
karla.bender@hccs.edu

BENDER, Kathy 859-371-9393 198 G
kbender@beckfield.edu

BENDER, Laurie 732-224-2059 308 A
lbender@brookdalecc.edu

BENDER, Michael 203-325-4351 90 D

BENDER, Rick 432-685-4529 491 A
rbender@midland.edu

BENDER, Starr, S 407-303-1631 100 G
starr.bender@adu.edu

BENDER, Stephanie 443-518-4256 223 D
sbender@howardcc.edu

BENDER, Thomas, B 504-866-7426 214 A
librarian@nds.edu

BENDER, Trudy 928-524-7324 17 A
trudy.bender@npc.edu

BENDER, Virginia 201-761-6023 314 F
vbender@spc.edu

BENDER, Yaakov 718-868-2300 323 G

BENDERS, Alison 614-251-4730 398 F
bendersa@ohiodominican.edu

BENDICKSON, Mary 813-253-7210 110 M
mbendickson@hccfl.edu

BENDIKAS, Kristina 413-662-5526 238 C
k.bendikas@mcla.edu

BENDOLPH, Arthur 904-470-8151 105 G
a.bendolph@ewc.edu

BENDYNA, OP, Mary 615-297-7545 467 A
srmary@aquinascollege.edu

BENECKI, Anita 716-896-0700 359 H
benecki@villa.edu

BENEDETTI, Brian 253-864-3235 536 H
bbenedetti@pierce.ctc.edu

BENEDETTO, Mark 605-331-6684 466 E
mark.benedetto@usiouxfalls.edu

BENEDETTO, Robert 510-559-2540 60 E
rbenedetto@gtu.edu

BENEDETTO, Robert 510-649-2540 60 G
rbenedetto@gtu.edu

BENEDETTO, Robert 510-649-2540 48 J
rbenedetto@gtu.edu

BENEDETTO, William 845-431-8096 332 D
benedett@sunydutchess.edu

BENEDICK, Marijean 330-941-3515 406 F
mbenedik@ysu.edu

BENEDICT, Christine 608-663-2294 547 F
cbenedict@edgewood.edu

BENEDICT, David 727-376-6911 122 E
david.benedict@trinitycollege.edu

BENEDICT, Dow 304-876-5393 544 C
dbenedic@shepherd.edu

BENEDICT, Dwight 202-651-5064 98 B
dwight.benedict@gallaudet.edu

BENEDICT, Jody, C 585-385-8322 348 F
jbenedict@sjfc.edu

BENEDICT, Mike, A 563-884-5753 61 A
mike.benedict@palmer.edu

BENEDICT, Mike, A 563-884-5753 114 E
mike.benedict@palmer.edu

BENEDICT, Mike, A 563-884-5753 188 E
mike.benedict@palmer.edu

BENEDICT, Nancy 608-363-2380 546 E
benedict@beloit.edu

BENEDICT, Neil, F 607-587-4371 355 C
benedinf@alfredstate.edu

BENEDICT, Russel, K 208-496-1910 143 A
benedictr@byui.edu

BENEDICT-AUGUSTINE,
Amy 607-436-2534 353 E
amy.benedict-augustine@oneonta.edu

BENEDIKTSON, Dale, T 918-631-2547 413 F
dale-benediktson@utulsa.edu

BENEFIELD, Lazelle 405-271-2420 413 D
lazelle-benefield@ouhsc.edu

BENEKE, Ginny 858-642-8357 58 I
gbeneke@nu.edu

BENEKE, Thomas, J 515-574-1050 185 I
beneke@iowacentral.edu

BENESCH, Susan 719-549-2187 83 H
susan.benesch@colostate-pueblo.edu

BENFANTI, William, J 716-878-5557 353 A
benfanwj@buffalostate.edu

BENFATTI, Angela 719-384-6834 87 A
angela.benfatti@ojc.edu

BENFER, Beverly, J 610-799-1591 434 D
bbenfer@lccc.edu

BENFER, Pamela, A 570-577-1616 423 E
pam.benfer@bucknell.edu

BENFEY, Christopher 413-538-2372 242 D
cbenfey@mtholyoke.edu

BENFIELD, John, S 843-377-2147 456 A
jbenfield@charlestonlaw.edu

BENFORD, Gladys 870-575-8405 25 B
benfordg@uapb.edu

BENFORD, James, R 810-762-9899 253 C
jbenford@kettering.edu

BENGFORT, Randall, R 443-518-4720 223 D
rbengfort@howardcc.edu

BENGINIA, Francis, A 610-330-5090 433 B
benginif@lafayette.edu

BENGOCHEA, Harry 787-844-8991 568 A
harry.bengochea@upr.edu

BENGSTON, Carl 562-860-2451 39 A
cbengston@cerritos.edu

BENGTSON, John 559-244-5957 72 A
john.bengtson@scccd.edu

BENHAM, Maenette 808-956-0980 141 G
mbenham@hawaii.edu

BENISH, Allan 732-247-5241 312 A
abenish@nbts.edu

BENISH, Amy, L 262-554-2010 158 E
albenish@aol.com

BENISH, Amy, L 262-554-2010 549 A
albenish@aol.com

BENITEZ, Hubert 516-918-3615 324 E
hbenitez@bcl.edu

BENITZ-HODGE, Grissel 808-735-4852 140 E
ghodge@chaminade.edu

BENJAMIN, Arthur 817-557-3337 101 D
abenjamin@atienterprises.edu

BENJAMIN, Bill 727-873-4199 121 C
benjamin@mail.usf.edu

BENJAMIN, Bruce, A 918-561-8260 410 D
bruce.benjamin@okstate.edu

BENJAMIN, Eric, V 931-598-1241 472 L
ebenjami@sewanee.edu

BENJAMIN, Gregory 610-399-2419 442 A
gbenjamin@cheyney.edu

BENJAMIN, Helen 925-229-6820 43 D
hbenjamin@4cd.edu

BENJAMIN, Jodi 402-941-6102 298 I
benjamin@midlandu.edu

BENJAMIN, Mary, E .... 870-575-8475...... 25 B
benjaminm@uapb.edu
BENJAMIN, Robert .... 617-745-3595.... 234 A
robert.j.benjamin@enc.edu
BENJAMIN, Robert .... 574-239-8362.... 172 M
rbenjamin@hcc-nd.edu
BENJAMIN, Tritobia, H ...... 202-806-7040...... 98 E
tbenjamin@howard.edu
BENJAMIN, William .... 805-546-3129...... 43 I
william_benjamin@cuesta.edu
BENKE, Jack .... 573-592-5555.... 293 B
jack.benke@westminster-mo.edu
BENKE, Meg .... 518-587-2100.... 355 G
president@esc.edu
BENKE, Robin, P .... 276-328-0151.... 525 G
rpb@wise.edu
BENKOV, Edith .... 619-594-6111...... 37 A
ebenkov@mail.sdsu.edu
BENMERGUI, Diana .... 212-960-5274.... 346 F
benmergui@yu.edu
BENMERGUI, Diana .... 212-960-5277.... 361 M
benmergui@yu.edu
BENN, Sherri .... 512-245-2278.... 501 F
sb17@txstate.edu
BENNATTS, Denise .... 253-833-9111.... 534 H
dbennatts@greenriver.edu
BENNECKE, Margie .... 708-237-5050.... 160 D
mbennecke@nc.edu
BENNER, Brent, W .... 813-253-6211.... 123 A
bbenner@ut.edu
BENNETT, Albert, F .... 949-824-5315...... 74 B
abennett@uci.edu
BENNETT, Amy .... 317-955-6768.... 177 I
abennett@marian.edu
BENNETT, Ashley .... 903-927-3222.... 509 E
abennett@wileyc.edu
BENNETT, Barbara .... 956-364-4697.... 500 D
barb.bennett@.tstc.edu
BENNETT, Barbara, L .... 401-598-2838.... 453 E
bbennett@jwu.edu
BENNETT, Beth .... 417-823-3450.... 289 I
bbennett@forest.edu
BENNETT, Blaine .... 830-591-7275.... 495 D
blaine.bennett@swtjc.cc.tx.us
BENNETT, Bobby .... 434-947-8109.... 523 B
bbennett@randolphcollege.edu
BENNETT, Cameron, D ...... 253-535-7150.... 536 E
bennetcd@plu.edu
BENNETT, Carolyn .... 516-876-3203.... 353 D
bennettc@oldwestbury.edu
BENNETT, Carrie .... 973-748-9000.... 307 H
carrie_bennett@bloomfield.edu
BENNETT, Cathy .... 740-695-9500.... 385 B
cbennett@belmontcollege.edu
BENNETT, Cheryl .... 218-322-2360.... 266 G
cheryl.bennett@itascacc.edu
BENNETT, Chris .... 765-998-4574.... 180 B
chbennett@taylor.edu
BENNETT, Christina, L .... 973-642-8818.... 315 C
christina.bennett@shu.edu
BENNETT, Christopher .... 440-375-7000.... 394 E
cbennett@lec.edu
BENNETT, Craig .... 540-351-1517.... 527 C
cbennett@lfcc.edu
BENNETT, Daniel, P .... 906-487-2216.... 255 B
dpbennet@mtu.edu
BENNETT, David, A .... 606-474-3256.... 201 D
dbennett@kcu.edu
BENNETT, Dean .... 208-769-3366.... 144 D
dean_bennett@nic.edu
BENNETT, Derwin .... 518-255-5836.... 354 E
bennetdd@cobleskill.edu
BENNETT, Douglas .... 714-432-5126...... 41 D
dbennett@occ.cccd.edu
BENNETT, Drew, A .... 417-255-7900.... 286 C
drewbennett@missouristate.edu
BENNETT, Elbert .... 870-575-8504...... 25 B
bennette@uapb.edu
BENNETT, Elizabeth, C .... 949-824-7982...... 74 B
bennette@uci.edu
BENNETT, Eric .... 212-659-7290.... 338 A
ebennett@tkc.edu
BENNETT, Gene .... 870-780-1201...... 20 A
gbennett@smail.anc.edu
BENNETT, Helen .... 270-686-4285.... 199 B
helen.bennett@brescia.edu
BENNETT, Holly .... 740-695-9500.... 385 B
hbennett@belmontcollege.edu
BENNETT, James .... 913-288-7259.... 194 C
jbennett@kckcc.edu
BENNETT, Jamie .... 213-613-2200...... 70 H
jamie_bennett@sciarc.edu
BENNETT, Janis, A .... 304-766-3010.... 544 F
bennetja@wvstateu.edu
BENNETT, Jeff .... 863-638-2910.... 123 E
bennettjd@webber.edu
BENNETT, Jeff .... 615-383-1340.... 469 A
jbennett@fwbbc.edu
BENNETT, Jeff, D .... 910-277-5738.... 376 C
bennettjd@sapc.edu
BENNETT, Jo Ann .... 205-226-4670........ 2 B
jbennett@bsc.edu
BENNETT, Joan, W .... 732-932-9375.... 314 B
profmycogirl@yahoo.com
BENNETT, JoAnn .... 937-327-6185.... 406 B
jbennett@wittenberg.edu
BENNETT, Josh .... 406-447-6932.... 295 A
josh.bennett@umhelelna.edu
BENNETT, Karen .... 520-515-5417...... 13 E
bennettk@cochise.edu
BENNETT, Kerrie .... 401-874-5053.... 454 E
kbennett@uri.edu
BENNETT, Kim .... 260-665-4438.... 180 D
bennettk@trine.edu
BENNETT, Lea, S .... 662-685-4771.... 273 E
lbennett@bmc.edu
BENNETT, Linda .... 870-612-2020...... 25 E
linda.bennett@uaccb.edu
BENNETT, Linda, L .... 570-577-1149.... 423 E
linda.bennett@bucknell.edu
BENNETT, Linda L, M .... 812-464-1756.... 181 B
bennettl@usi.edu
BENNETT, Lori .... 805-378-1445...... 77 D
lbennett@vcccd.edu
BENNETT, Marcia, M .... 405-271-2332.... 413 D
marcia-bennett@ouhsc.edu
BENNETT, Marquis, L .... 570-450-3067.... 439 K
mlb44@psu.edu
BENNETT, Maybelle, T .... 202-806-4771...... 98 E
mbennett@research.howard.edu
BENNETT, Michael, J .... 727-341-3012.... 116 H
bennett.michael@spcollege.edu
BENNETT, Michelle .... 325-942-2246.... 480 E
michelle.bennett@angelo.edu
BENNETT, Mitchell .... 214-333-5139.... 484 D
mitch@dbu.edu
BENNETT, Patricia .... 850-729-4901.... 114 A
bennettp@nwfsc.edu
BENNETT, Patrick .... 614-947-6836.... 391 B
bennettp@franklin.edu
BENNETT, Peter .... 860-297-2080...... 94 E
peter.bennett@trincoll.edu
BENNETT, Rashad .... 954-923-4440.... 112 H
registrar@keycollege.edu
BENNETT, Rene .... 816-604-5412.... 285 B
rene.bennett@mcckc.edu
BENNETT, Richard .... 678-915-7443.... 137 G
rbennett@spsu.edu
BENNETT, Rick .... 408-855-5232...... 78 F
rick.bennett@wvm.edu
BENNETT, Robby .... 334-876-9228........ 4 B
rbennett@wccs.edu
BENNETT, Rodger .... 972-860-4802.... 484 G
rpbfape@dcccd.edu
BENNETT, Rodney, D .... 706-542-3564.... 138 G
bennettr@uga.edu
BENNETT, Samuel .... 806-742-6666.... 502 A
sam.bennett@ttu.edu
BENNETT, Sari, M .... 603-862-4285.... 306 C
sari.bennett@unh.edu
BENNETT, Scott .... 904-620-2002.... 120 D
sbennett@unf.edu
BENNETT, Shannon .... 919-546-8512.... 376 F
sbennett@shawu.edu
BENNETT, Sherri .... 870-838-2945...... 20 A
sbennett@smail.anc.edu
BENNETT, Sonja .... 803-535-5668.... 456 D
sbennett@claflin.edu
BENNETT, Stephen, R .... 507-933-7526.... 263 J
sbennett@gustavus.edu
BENNETT, Susan, A .... 240-895-4336.... 226 A
sabennett@smcm.edu
BENNETT, Tanya Lynn .... 973-408-3718.... 309 E
tbennett@drew.edu
BENNETT, Temple .... 706-357-5281.... 125 C
tbennett@athenstech.edu
BENNETT, Todd .... 404-364-8329.... 135 E
tbennett1@oglethorpe.edu
BENNETT-CAMPBELL,
Bonnie, L .... 815-224-0481.... 153 E
bonnie_campbell@ivcc.edu
BENNETT-WILLIAMS,
Emma .... 843-953-3989.... 456 C
ebennett@citadel.edu
BENNETTS, Lori .... 715-682-1824.... 549 F
lbennetts@northland.edu
BENNIE, Roanna .... 805-922-6966...... 26 L
rbennie@hancockcollege.edu
BENNIE, Scott .... 949-794-9090...... 71 F
sbennie@stanbridge.edu
BENNIGHOFF, James .... 254-710-6500.... 482 A
james_bennighoff@baylor.edu
BENNING, Tom .... 314-529-9304.... 284 C
tbenning@maryville.edu
BENNINGER, Paul .... 336-917-5460.... 376 E
paul.benninger@salem.edu
BENNINGTON, Cheryl .... 304-336-8049.... 544 D
cbennington@westliberty.edu
BENNION, Paul .... 208-459-5841.... 143 D
pbennion@collegeofidaho.edu
BENOIT, Andy .... 337-482-6474.... 216 D
ajbenoit@louisiana.edu
BENOIT, Anthony .... 617-588-1324.... 231 C
abenoit@bfit.edu
BENOIT, Barbara, Z .... 508-767-7387.... 230 D
bz.benoit@assumption.edu
BENOIT, Debra .... 985-493-2563.... 216 A
debi.benoit@nicholls.edu
BENOIT, Doug .... 714-432-5605...... 41 D
dbenoit@occ.cccd.edu
BENOIT, Joseph, N .... 605-668-1514.... 464 G
joseph.benoit@mtmc.edu
BENOIT, Kate .... 828-726-2375.... 368 G
kbenoit@cccti.edu
BENOIT, Pam .... 740-593-2600.... 399 G
benoit@ohio.du
BENOIT, Thomas .... 325-793-3869.... 490 H
tbenoit@mcm.edu
BENOIT, Tom .... 828-398-7200.... 368 B
tbenoit@abtech.edu
BENOIT, Twana .... 337-948-0239.... 212 C
twana.benoit@ltc.edu
BENOIT, Tyra .... 707-524-1519...... 68 E
tbenoit@santarosa.edu
BENOLIEL, Avraham .... 718-339-1090.... 361 H
abben@mindspring.com
BENOLIEL, Haim .... 718-339-1090.... 361 H
mikdashmelech@verizon.net
BENOLKEN, Julie .... 651-450-3622.... 266 F
jbenolk@inverhills.edu
BENSE, Judy, A .... 850-474-2200.... 121 D
jbense@uwf.edu
BENSEL, Terry .... 814-332-3391.... 421 F
tbensel@allegheny.edu
BENSEN, Steven, P .... 701-788-4761.... 381 H
steven.bensen@mayvillestate.edu
BENSHOFF, John, J .... 618-453-7300.... 165 B
jbenshof@siu.edu
BENSINK, Michael .... 508-678-2811.... 239 B
michael.bensink@bristolcc.edu
BENSLEY, James, S .... 231-995-1034.... 256 D
jbensley@nmc.edu
BENSON, Bill .... 541-962-3241.... 418 C
wbenson@eou.edu
BENSON, Brenda .... 310-434-4433...... 68 D
benson_brenda@smc.edu
BENSON, Bruce, D .... 303-860-5600...... 88 G
officeofthepresident@cu.edu
BENSON, Bryan, E .... 903-233-3809.... 490 A
bryanbenson@letu.edu
BENSON, Carrie, R .... 412-578-8776.... 424 I
crbenson@carlow.edu
BENSON, Daniel .... 507-389-6838.... 267 E
daniel.benson@mnsu.edu
BENSON, Dawn .... 406-275-4985.... 296 D
dawn_benson@skc.edu
BENSON, Duane .... 712-274-5133.... 187 G
bensond@morningside.edu
BENSON, Ella .... 757-424-0333.... 233 A
ella.benson@cambridgecollege.edu
BENSON, Erin, V .... 207-768-9453.... 220 F
erin.benson@umpi.edu
BENSON, George .... 843-953-5500.... 457 B
bensong@cofc.edu
BENSON, Greg .... 435-613-5294.... 512 A
greg.benson@usu.edu
BENSON, Gus .... 859-622-3636.... 200 J
gus.benson@eku.edu
BENSON, Holly .... 334-277-3390........ 3 E
holly.benson@vc.edu
BENSON, Jerry .... 540-568-3429.... 520 H
bensonaj@jmu.edu
BENSON, Joe .... 205-348-4566........ 8 E
joe.benson@ua.edu
BENSON, Joe .... 303-871-4521...... 89 A
joebenso@du.edu
BENSON, Kristin .... 651-846-2882...... 29 F
kbenson@argosy.edu
BENSON, Kristin .... 651-846-3412.... 260 I
kbenson@argosy.edu
BENSON, Matt, A .... 423-775-7295.... 467 F
matt.benson@bryan.edu
BENSON, Michael, T .... 435-586-7702.... 511 D
benson@suu.edu
BENSON, Mindy .... 435-586-7763.... 511 D
benson@suu.edu
BENSON, Neal, L .... 304-462-4117.... 544 A
neal.benson@glenville.edu
BENSON, Patricia .... 610-626-6142.... 430 D
pbenson@harcum.edu
BENSON, Paul, H .... 937-229-2601.... 404 A
pbenson1@udayton.edu
BENSON, Peter .... 203-287-3017...... 93 F
paier.admin@snet.net
BENSON, Richard .... 540-231-9752.... 529 G
deaneng@vt.edu
BENSON, Robert, M .... 865-882-4553.... 476 A
bensonrm@roanestate.edu
BENSON, Robin .... 918-647-1344.... 407 E
rbenson@carlalbert.edu
BENSON, Ruthann, E .... 608-785-8116.... 551 C
rbenson@uwlax.edu
BENSON, Samantha .... 910-879-5567.... 368 D
sbenson@bladencc.edu
BENSON, Stephanie, G .... 706-355-5112.... 125 C
sbenson@athenstech.edu
BENSON, Stephen, M .... 304-929-5486.... 543 A
sbenson@newriver.edu
BENSON, Suzie .... 509-682-6505.... 539 E
sbenson@wvc.edu
BENSON, Terra .... 520-206-4640...... 17 H
tbenson@pima.edu
BENSON, Todd .... 503-251-5726.... 421 A
tbenson@uws.edu
BENSON, Vaughn .... 402-375-7245.... 299 G
vabenso1@wsc.edu
BENSON, Wade, M .... 706-379-3111.... 140 A
wadeb@yhc.edu
BENSON-NICOL, Nancy ..... 479-979-1307...... 26 A
nbenson@ozarks.edu
BENSON-TYUS, Hasanna ... 202-462-2101...... 99 A
benson@iwp.edu
BENSTON, Kimberly .... 610-896-1014.... 430 G
kbenston@haverford.edu
BENT, Lauren .... 978-837-5250.... 242 A
BENTE, James .... 630-942-2409.... 148 A
bentej@cod.edu
BENTIVEGNA, Saverio, S .. 914-594-3368.... 343 F
saverio_bentivegna@nymc.edu
BENTLEY, Dean .... 404-727-6039.... 129 D
dean.bentley@emory.edu
BENTLEY, Gloria, A .... 563-588-7027.... 187 C
gloria.bentley@loras.edu
BENTLEY, Jane .... 708-974-5703.... 159 B
jane.bentley@morainevalley.edu
BENTLEY, Pamela .... 270-706-8731.... 202 A
pamela.bentley@kctcs.edu
BENTLEY, Sarah .... 512-492-3034.... 480 F
sbentley@aoma.edu
BENTLEY, Tony .... 309-347-5448.... 146 D
abentley@sandurg.edu
BENTLEY-COLTHART,
Nicki .... 304-472-8488.... 545 G
bentley-colthart@wvwc.edu
BENTON, Andrew, K .... 310-506-4451...... 61 H
andrew.benton@pepperdine.edu
BENTON, Debra, M .... 740-593-4260.... 399 G
bentond@ohio.edu
BENTON, James .... 828-659-0444.... 372 B
jimbenton@mcdowelltech.edu
BENTON, Katherine .... 405-382-9263.... 412 B
k.benton@sscok.edu
BENTON, Patrena, N .... 757-727-5000.... 519 H
patrena.benton@hamptonu.edu
BENTON, Ronald, W .... 303-963-3221...... 82 C
rbenton@ccu.edu
BENTON, Sherry .... 352-392-1575.... 120 C
benton@counsel.ufl.edu
BENTON, Tonya .... 206-878-3710.... 535 B
tbenton@highline.edu
BENTON-MESTAS, Andrea . 719-587-8333...... 80 L
andrea@adams.edu
BENTSON, Kenneth .... 505-454-3080.... 318 J
kbentson@nmhu.edu
BENTZ, Hank .... 812-265-2580.... 177 A
hbentz@ivytech.edu
BENULIS, Joan, R .... 585-385-8010.... 348 F
jbenulis@sjfc.edu
BENVENGER, Deborah, A .. 215-871-6711.... 444 C
admissions@pcom.edu
BENVENISTE,
Lawrence, M .... 404-727-6377.... 129 D
larry_benveniste@bus.emory.edu
BENVENUTTI, Mary Beth ... 510-748-2211...... 62 C
mbenvenutti@peralta.edu
BENVENUTTI-TORO,
Evelyn .... 787-751-1912.... 564 C
ebenven@inter.edu
BENWAY, Elizabeth .... 508-830-5086.... 238 D
ebenway@maritime.edu
BENWAY, Jennifer .... 617-349-8498.... 236 B
jbenway@lesley.edu
BENWELL, Deirdre .... 509-527-2066.... 539 C
deirdre.benwell@wallawalla.edu
BENZ, Deborah .... 507-457-5069.... 269 G
dbenz@winona.edu
BENZ, Kathleen .... 661-362-3032...... 41 I
kathleen.benz@canyons.edu
BENZEL, Brian, L .... 509-777-3208.... 540 C
bbenzel@whitworth.edu
BEODEKER, Robert .... 631-548-2514.... 356 F
beodekr@sunysuffolk.edu
BEOKU-BETTS,
Josephine, A .... 561-297-2057.... 119 A
beokubet@fau.edu
BEQUETTE, Angela, L .... 919-866-5394.... 374 H
albequette@waketech.edu
BEQUETTE, Barry .... 601-877-6137.... 272 F
bequette@alcorn.edu
BEQUETTE, Lori .... 704-355-3920.... 363 D
lori.bequette@carolinascollege.edu
BERALDI, JR., Thomas, F . 603-645-9695.... 305 I
t.beraldi@snhu.edu
BERAN, Connie .... 512-313-3000.... 483 K
connie.beran@concordia.edu
BERAN, Paul, B .... 479-788-7007...... 24 D
paul.beran@uafs.edu
BERAN, Wayne, B .... 361-570-4811.... 504 A
beranw@uhv.edu
BERARD, Wayne-Daniel, S 508-213-2121.... 243 E
wayne-daniel.berard@nichols.edu
BERARDI, William .... 508-678-2811.... 239 B
william.berardi@bristolcc.edu
BERBERET, James, M .... 815-599-3406.... 152 B
jim.berberet@highland.edu
BERCIER, Diane .... 701-477-7862.... 383 F
dbercier1@tm.edu

BERENBACK, Steven 401-454-6156 454 B sberenba@risd.edu

BERENBAUM, Devorah 718-645-0536 341 D mirrer@thejnet.com

BERENBAUM, Osher 917-645-0536 341 D mirrer@thejnet.com

BERENBAUM, Rachel 718-645-0536 341 D mirrer@thejnet.com

BERENDT, Sherri 312-427-2737 154 H 6berendt@jmls.edu

BERENSON, Jennifer, K 540-375-2204 523 G berenson@roanoke.edu

BERENSON, Jerry, A 610-526-5160 423 D jberenso@brynmawr.edu

BERESFORD, Jack, F 619-594-5204 37 A jack.beresford@sdsu.edu

BEREZNIAK, Ronald 941-756-0690 433 C rberezniak@lecom.edu

BERG, Alicia, M 312-369-7102 148 D aberg@colum.edu

BERG, Amy 607-753-5942 353 B amy.berg@cortland.edu

BERG, Dale 520-326-1600 17 J

BERG, Denise 570-662-4853 443 C dberg@mansfield.edu

BERG, Diana 952-888-4777 270 C dberg@nwhealth.edu

BERG, Eric 218-723-6630 262 G eberg@css.edu

BERG, Gary 805-437-8580 34 B gary.berg@csuci.edu

BERG, Jane 641-683-4253 185 G jane.berg@indianhills.edu

BERG, Jerry 815-394-5058 163 A jberg@rockford.edu

BERG, Joanne, E 608-262-3964 550 J jeberg@em.wisc.edu

BERG, Joel, H 206-543-5980 539 A joelberg@uw.edu

BERG, John 215-972-2007 440 J jberg@pafa.edu

BERG, John, A 314-935-7311 292 I jberg@wustl.edu

BERG, Kevin 509-682-6815 539 E kberg@wvc.edu

BERG, Linda, K 651-290-6321 272 E linda.berg@wmitchell.edu

BERG, Luciane 337-550-1308 212 J

BERG, Michele 386-323-8025 105 I michele.berg@erau.edu

BERG, Michele 386-323-8025 105 H michele.berg@erau.edu

BERG, Paula 701-228-5451 382 E paula.berg@dakotacollege.edu

BERG, Richard, R 717-290-8704 433 F rberg@lancasterseminary.edu

BERG, Roger 913-621-8744 192 F rberg@donnelly.edu

BERG, Scott, M 413-748-3859 244 H sberg@springfieldcollege.edu

BERG, Shelton, G 305-284-2241 122 I sberg@miami.edu

BERG, Stacey, L 832-824-4588 481 H sberg@bcm.edu

BERG, Tamara 507-457-5460 269 G tberg@winona.edu

BERG, Terry 806-371-5008 479 G tlberg@actx.edu

BERGAMO, Anne, M 856-691-8600 309 B abergamo@cccnj.edu

BERGAN, Maureen 251-380-3498 7 E mbergan@shc.edu

BERGANDI, Cherrie 715-833-6483 553 H cbergandi@cvtc.edu

BERGEN, Lori 414-288-3588 548 F lori.bergen@marquette.edu

BERGEN, Michael 718-951-5186 326 F mbergen@brooklyn.cuny.edu

BERGEN, Randy 618-664-7000 151 F president@greenville.edu

BERGER, Amy, C 818-677-2932 35 F amy.berger@csun.edu

BERGER, Aron 845-426-3276 360 H ydm@thejnet.com

BERGER, Brandi 706-233-7205 137 A bberger@shorter.edu

BERGER, David 212-960-5253 361 M dberger@yu.edu

BERGER, Edward, E 620-665-3505 193 H bergere@hutchcc.edu

BERGER, Patrice 402-472-5425 300 G pberger1@unl.edu

BERGER, Pearl 212-960-5363 361 M berger@yu.edu

BERGER, Pearl 212-960-5344 346 F dpearl@yu.edu

BERGER, Scott 320-762-4475 265 F scottb@alextech.edu

BERGER, Susan, A 315-655-7126 325 H sberger@cazenovia.edu

BERGER, Susan, A 315-655-7122 325 H sberger@cazenovia.edu

BERGER, Vance, J 423-775-7212 467 F bergerva@bryan.edu

BERGER-SWEENEY, Joanne, E 617-627-3864 245 C joanne.berger-sweeney@tufts.edu

BERGERON, Bette 618-650-3350 165 C bberger@siue.edu

BERGERON, Brad 312-332-0707 166 B

BERGERON, Iva, G 217-786-2792 157 B iva.bergeron@llcc.edu

BERGERON, Jack 517-483-1478 254 A bergerj@lcc.edu

BERGERON, Katherine 401-863-2573 453 B katherine_bergeron@brown.edu

BERGERON, Mindy 925-969-3385 52 C bergeron@jfku.edu

BERGERON, Stephanie, W 248-689-8282 259 E sbergeron@walshcollege.edu

BERGERS, Barbara 616-331-3255 251 F bergersb@gvsu.edu

BERGERSON, Catherine 239-489-9206 105 F mcbergerson@edison.edu

BERGES, Cherry, L 270-824-8677 202 G cherry.berges@kctcs.edu

BERGESON, Daniel 507-222-5992 261 G dbergeso@carleton.edu

BERGESON, John 651-638-6112 261 D j-bergeson@bethel.edu

BERGESON, Rachel 631-632-6740 352 C rachel.bergeson@stonybrook.edu

BERGFELD, Julie 314-529-9620 284 C jbergfeld@maryville.edu

BERGFELD, Steve 708-216-6648 157 C sbergfeld@luc.edu

BERGGREN, Jeffrey, C 260-359-4016 173 A jberggren@huntington.edu

BERGGREN, Kent, E 208-524-3000 143 G kent.berggren@my.eitc.edu

BERGGREN, Marie, N 510-287-3306 73 G marie.berggren@ucop.edu

BERGGREN, Stacey, L 208-467-8994 144 E

BERGH, David 802-635-1200 515 F david.bergh@jsc.edu

BERGH, Thomas, K 715-394-8081 552 F tbergh@uwsuper.edu

BERGHOFF, Carolyn 312-225-6288 167 G cberghoff@vandercook.edu

BERGHOLZ, John 312-261-3871 159 E john.bergholz@nl.edu

BERGHORN, George 517-483-1319 254 A berghorg@lcc.edu

BERGIN, Bonita, M 707-545-3647 30 I

BERGKAMP, Sheila 620-227-9201 192 E sbergkamp@dc3.edu

BERGLAND, Arne 805-493-3152 33 B bergland@clunet.edu

BERGLER, Michael 949-214-3187 43 C michael.bergler@cui.edu

BERGMAN, Beverly 478-471-2721 133 H beverly.bergman@maconstate.edu

BERGMAN, Bruce 308-535-3676 298 H bergmanb@mpcc.edu

BERGMAN, Dave 606-539-4167 207 C dave.bergman@ucumberlands.edu

BERGMAN, Matthew 217-228-5432 161 F bergmma@quincy.edu

BERGMAN, Stephanie 616-988-1000 249 F

BERGMAN, JR., William, T 215-204-6550 447 H william.bergman@temple.edu

BERGMANN, Hans 203-582-8960 93 H hans.bergmann@quinnipiac.edu

BERGMANN, Michelle 541-440-4620 420 F michelle.bergmann@umpqua.edu

BERGMANN, Ronald 718-960-8421 327 C ron.bergmann@lehman.cuny.edu

BERGMANN, Ronald, F 310-243-3720 34 D rbergmann@csudh.edu

BERGMANN, Tom 847-947-5516 159 E tbergmann@nl.edu

BERGMANN LOIZECEUX, Elizabeth 617-353-2000 232 E

BERGMEIER, Tyler 603-752-1113 304 H tbergmeier@ccsnh.edu

BERGQUIST, Viola 320-308-5177 269 B vbergquist@sctcc.edu

BERGREN, Rebecca, A 717-337-6866 429 I rbergren@gettysburg.edu

BERGRUD, Erik 816-584-6412 287 E erik.bergrud@park.edu

BERGSTROM, Chip 617-217-9070 231 A cbergstrom@baystate.edu

BERGSTROM, Paula 870-574-4488 24 A pbergstr@sautech.edu

BERGSTROM, Scott, J 208-496-1136 143 A bergstroms@byui.edu

BERGSTROM, Tracey 361-582-2535 508 B tracey.bergstrom@victoriacollege.edu

BERGUM, Mike 765-983-1483 171 E bergumi@earlham.edu

BERHE, Annette 901-435-1351 470 D annette.berhe@loc.edu

BERICH, Anthony 724-836-9949 449 C acb62@pitt.edu

BERINGER, Connie 650-738-4202 67 H beringer@smccd.edu

BERISH, Michele 718-409-6079 356 C mberish@sunymaritime.edu

BERK, Alvin 718-270-1763 352 D alvin.berk@downstate.edu

BERK, Anne-Marie, P 217-424-3593 158 G aberk@millikin.edu

BERK, Bradford, C 585-275-3407 359 B bradford_berk@urmc.rochester.edu

BERK, Steven, L 806-743-3000 502 B steven.berk@ttuhsc.edu

BERKELAND, Rondell 218-723-7033 262 G rberkela@css.edu

BERKELEY, Fred 706-385-1459 136 B fred.berkeley@point.edu

BERKEY, Dennis, D 508-831-5200 246 F dberkey@wpi.edu

BERKEY, Dolores 814-269-2082 449 D berkey@pitt.edu

BERKHEIMER, Eric, J 410-677-6553 228 D ejberkheimer@salisbury.edu

BERKHOF, Robert, A 616-526-6091 249 A berk@calvin.edu

BERKICH, Carla 361-825-2703 498 C carla.berkich@tamucc.edu

BERKMAN, Jennifer, R 410-543-6262 228 D jrberkman@salisbury.edu

BERKMAN, Ronald, M 216-687-3544 388 D ronald.berkman@csuohio.edu

BERKNER, Paul, D 207-859-4460 217 G pberkner@colby.edu

BERKO, Andrew 516-671-0379 360 B aberko@webb-institute.edu

BERKOFF, Lyudmila 312-777-7620 145 C lberkoff@argosy.edu

BERKOW, Daniel 209-667-3381 36 D dberkow@csustan.edu

BERKOWITZ, Bobbie 212-305-3582 330 F bb2509@columbia.edu

BERKOWITZ, Justin 386-267-0565 104 E director@daytonacollege.edu

BERLETH, Frank 570-454-6172 435 G frank.berleth@mccann.edu

BERLEY, Susan 820-652-0636 372 B susanberley@mcdowelltech.edu

BERLIN, Robert, Y 781-736-3720 232 F drb@brandeis.edu

BERLIN, Tom, J 304-457-6352 540 E berlintj@ab.edu

BERLINER, Donna 630-942-2475 148 A berliner@cod.edu

BERLINER, Herman, A 516-463-5402 335 G herman.a.berliner@hofstra.edu

BERLINER, Thomas 847-628-1520 154 K tberliner@judsonu.edu

BERLYN, Mark, A 314-516-6515 291 D berlynm@umsl.edu

BERMAN, Audrey 510-869-6129 64 J aberman@samuelmerritt.edu

BERMAN, Doug 978-837-5053 242 A bermand@merrimack.edu

BERMAN, Harris 617-636-2177 245 C harris.berman@tufts.edu

BERMAN, Joel 954-262-2130 114 B jb@nsu.nova.edu

BERMAN, Larry, S 404-413-5570 131 G larryberman@gsu.edu

BERMAN, Lou Ann 903-566-7052 506 E lberman@uttyler.edu

BERMAN, Marc 619-961-4271 72 J mberman@tjsl.edu

BERMAN, Mark, A 518-782-6957 350 I mberman@siena.edu

BERMAN, Mark, R 413-205-3008 229 G mark.berman@aic.edu

BERMAN, Mary Jane 513-529-1943 396 E bermanmj@muohio.edu

BERMAN, Michael 805-437-2099 34 B michael.berman@csuci.edu

BERMAN, Morris, S 714-449-7455 70 G mberman@scco.edu

BERMAN, Paul, S 202-994-6288 98 C pberman@law.gwu.edu

BERMAN, Paula 617-277-3915 232 D

BERMAN-MARTIN, Gail, L 508-999-8660 237 A gberman@umassd.edu

BERMANN, Todd 706-864-1450 134 G tberrman@northgeorgia.edu

BERMINGHAM, Jack 206-878-3710 535 B jberming@highline.edu

BERMONT, Becky 401-454-6918 454 B bbermont@risd.edu

BERMUDEZ, Angela 432-837-8193 501 E bermudez@sulross.edu

BERMUDEZ, Jose Luis 979-845-5141 497 E jbermudez@tamu.edu

BERMUDEZ, Megan 610-921-7510 421 E mbermudez@alb.edu

BERMUDEZ, Pedro 787-786-3030 560 G pbermudez@ucb.edu.pr

BERMUDEZ, Shaila 910-221-2224 364 F

BERMUDEZ VARGAS, Sixto 787-878-4146 567 A sixto.bermudez1@upr.edu

BERNA, Francis, J 215-951-1346 432 I berna@lasalle.edu

BERNABE, Arnaldo 718-518-6888 327 D abernabe@hostos.cuny.edu

BERNAD, Manuel, A 858-499-0202 41 G manuelb@coleman.edu

BERNADELLE, Guary 815-967-7300 162 I bernadelle@rockfordcareercollege.edu

BERNAL, Deanna 818-785-2726 38 K

BERNAL, Diego 210-486-2275 479 D dbernal@alamo.edu

BERNAL, Elena 781-283-1000 245 E

BERNAL-OLSON, Patricia 937-229-4211 404 A pbernalolson1@udayton.edu

BERNARD, Bill 212-924-5900 357 B wbernard@swedishinstitute.edu

BERNARD, Christophe 310-314-6036 30 A

BERNARD, David, K 314-921-9290 292 A dbernard@ugst.edu

BERNARD, Dee 651-450-3522 266 F dbernar@inverhills.edu

BERNARD, Frances 518-438-3111 340 A franb@mariacollege.edu

BERNARD, Kacey 610-341-1481 428 E kbernard@eastern.edu

BERNARD, Kacey 610-341-1389 438 D kbernard@eastern.edu

BERNARD, Liza 610-896-1181 430 G lbernard@haverford.edu

BERNARD, Marcella, J 207-859-4342 217 G mbernard@colby.edu

BERNARD, Marjorie, P 412-578-8880 424 I mpbernard@carlow.edu

BERNARD, Nancy, M 334-844-4744 1 F bernanm@auburn.edu

BERNARD, Nesta 202-238-2340 98 E nbernard@howard.edu

BERNARD, Pamela 919-684-3955 364 C pamela.bernard@duke.edu

BERNARD, Philip 617-989-4162 245 F bernardp@wit.edu

BERNARD, Richard 405-974-3493 413 B rbernard1@uco.edu

BERNARD, Sarah, J 207-786-8211 217 C sbernard@bates.edu

BERNARD, Sue 207-768-2786 218 J

BERNARD, Thomas 413-662-5205 238 C t.bernard@mcla.edu

BERNARD, Vicki 314-340-5112 282 F bernardv@hssu.edu

BERNARD, William, A 906-227-2920 256 C wbernard@nmu.edu

BERNARDI, Robert 985-448-4794 216 A rob.bernardi@nicholls.edu

BERNARDINO, Maria 209-954-5065 66 D mbernardino@deltacollege.edu

BERNARDIS, Tim 406-638-3113 294 E tim@lbhc.edu

BERNARDO, Daniel 509-335-4561 539 D bernardo@wsu.edu

BERNARDO, Lisa, M 209-667-3094 36 D lbernardo@csustan.edu

BERNARDO, Peter, R 216-397-4217 392 L pbernardo@jcu.edu

BERNARDO, Sandra 714-338-1303 30 B sbernardo@aii.edu

BERNARDO-SOUSA, Marie 401-598-1754 453 E mbernardo@jwu.edu

BERNAS, Judith, A 602-827-2017 18 L jbernas@email.arizona.edu

BERNAUER, Edmund 808-521-2288 141 B dean@orientalmedicine.edu

BERNDT, Michael 952-358-8498 268 A michael.berndt@normandale.edu

BERNE, Robert 212-998-2283 344 B bob.berne@nyu.edu

BERNECKER, Kim 972-825-4634 495 F kbernecker@sagu.edu

BERNECKI, Richard 716-827-2417 358 D berneckir@trocaire.edu

BERNEL, Liz 219-785-5719 179 A ebernel@pnc.edu

BERNER, Albert, J 973-618-3660 308 C aberner@caldwell.edu

BERNER, JR., Howard, E 314-275-3514 161 E howard.berner@principia.edu

BERNER, Nancy 931-598-1172 472 L nberner@sewanee.edu

BERNET, Glenn, H 417-865-2811 281 G bernetg@evangel.edu

BERNEY, Jan 360-438-4513 537 B jberney@stmartin.edu

BERNHARD, Andrew 503-654-8000 419 F abernhard@pioneerpacific.edu

BERNHARD, Mark, C 812-464-1829 181 B mbernhard@usi.edu

BERNHARD, Robert, J 574-631-3902 180 G bernhard.9@nd.edu

BERNHARDSON, Bonnie 218-879-0828 266 C bonnie@fdltcc.edu

BERNHARDSON, Mark 218-879-0703 266 C mbernhar@fdltcc.edu

BERNICK, Lee 702-895-1068 302 I
lee.bernick@unlv.edu
BERNIER, Joseph 401-454-6394 454 B
jbernier01@risd.edu
BERNIER, Julie, N 603-535-2230 307 A
jbernier@plymouth.edu
BERNOTSKY, Lorraine 610-425-7447 444 A
lbernotsky@wcupa.edu
BERNSTEIN, Aimee 718-409-5979 356 C
abernstein@sunymaritime.edu
BERNSTEIN, Alan 229-333-5870 139 C
abernste@valdosta.edu
BERNSTEIN, David 845-406-4308 361 B
BERNSTEIN, Melissa 801-581-3386 511 C
melissa.bernstein@law.utah.edu
BERNSTEIN, Melvin 617-373-4160 243 F
BERNSTEIN, Michael 504-865-5261 215 C
mbernstein@tulane.edu
BERNSTEIN, Pamela 603-880-8308 306 A
tmc@thomasmorecollege.edu
BERNSTEIN, Robin 402-557-7300 296 H
robin.bernstein@bellevue.edu
BERNSTEIN, Walter, B 203-837-8600 91 A
bernsteinw@wcsu.edu
BERNTSON, Joan, L 218-751-8670 270 D
joanberntson@oakhills.edu
BEROL, Peter, J 484-581-1272 428 E
pjberol@eastern.edu
BERON-HUDSON, Toni, A 562-985-4134 35 C
tberon@csulb.edu
BERONA, David 603-535-2817 307 A
daberona@plymouth.edu
BEROTTE JOSEPH,
Carole, M 718-289-5151 326 E
president@bcc.cuny.edu
BERQUAM, Lori 608-263-5700 550 J
lberquam@studentlife.wisc.edu
BERQUIST, Gina 503-255-0332 417 C
ginab@multnomah.edu
BERRIDGE, Bob 773-256-0783 157 D
bberridg@lstc.edu
BERRIOS, Eric 251-343-7227 3 D
eric.berrios@vc.edu
BERRIOS, Iris 787-743-7979 565 H
BERRIOS, Jose 787-751-0178 565 H
ac_jberrios@suagm.edu
BERRIOS, Marianne 787-852-1430 562 F
mberrios@hccpr.edu
BERRIOS, William 212-592-2000 350 F
wberrios@sva.edu
BERROL, Jerry, M 718-260-5800 328 D
jberrol@citytech.cuny.edu
BERRY, Brian 870-612-2014 25 E
brian.berry@uaccb.edu
BERRY, Carolynn 336-750-2110 380 B
berryc@wssu.edu
BERRY, Chad 859-985-3490 199 A
chad_berry@berea.edu
BERRY, Charles, W 214-828-8208 497 C
cberry@bcd.tamhsc.edu
BERRY, Clay 870-508-6124 20 E
cberry@asumh.edu
BERRY, David 765-269-5426 176 D
dberry19@ivytech.edu
BERRY, Dewayne 817-598-6227 508 F
dberry@wc.edu
BERRY, Donald, K 251-442-2203 9 A
dberry@umobile.edu
BERRY, Donna 559-638-3641 72 C
donn.berry@reedleycollege.edu
BERRY, Dwight 954-563-5899 101 F
BERRY, Edgar, L 229-430-4742 124 A
edgar.berry@asurams.edu
BERRY, Evan 772-462-7945 111 B
eberry@irsc.edu
BERRY, Fred 414-277-7324 549 C
berry@msoe.edu
BERRY, J. William 972-721-5226 503 B
berry@udallas.edu
BERRY, Jacob 617-521-2027 244 F
jacob.berry@simmons.edu
BERRY, Joanne 603-427-7609 304 B
jberry@ccsnh.edu
BERRY, Joe 501-882-4407 20 C
jlberry@asub.edu
BERRY, John 740-366-9395 386 H
berry.19@osu.edu
BERRY, John 740-366-9395 399 E
berry.19@osu.edu
BERRY, Joyce 970-491-6675 83 F
joyce.berry@colostate.edu
BERRY, Kathy 760-355-6215 51 A
kathy.berry@imperial.edu
BERRY, Larry 423-614-8086 470 C
lberry@leeuniversity.edu
BERRY, Laura 870-743-3000 22 G
lberry@northark.edu
BERRY, Laurie, M 812-468-2000 181 B
lberry@usi.edu
BERRY, Linda 510-981-2933 62 B
lberry@peralta.edu
BERRY, Linda, C 708-209-3209 148 E
linda.berry@cuchicago.edu
BERRY, Mark, E 843-953-7645 457 B
berrym@cofc.edu
BERRY, Mildred 305-626-1444 109 A
mberry@fmuniv.edu
BERRY, Mimi 585-389-2505 342 D
mberry3@naz.edu
BERRY, Molly 217-362-6410 158 G
mberry@millikin.edu
BERRY, Richard, A 936-468-2707 496 B
rberry@sfasu.edu
BERRY, Rick 757-683-3109 522 F
rberry@odu.edu
BERRY, Robert, L 904-620-2851 120 D
robert.berry@unf.edu
BERRY, Ronald 318-342-1100 216 E
rberry@ulm.edu
BERRY, Scott, A 260-359-4006 173 A
sberry@huntington.edu
BERRY, Scott, D 864-488-4525 459 B
sberry@limestone.edu
BERRY, Sharon, L 618-650-3839 165 C
shaberr@siue.edu
BERRY, Steven, M 785-827-5541 194 F
steve.berry@kwu.edu
BERRY, Trey 870-235-4004 23 I
tcberry@saumag.edu
BERRY, Yvonne 603-513-5215 306 E
yvonne.berry@law.unh.edu
BERRYHILL, Cathy 505-747-2194 320 A
cathyb@nnmc.edu
BERRYHILL, Jimmilea 706-842-0341 472 G
jberryhill@ogs.edu
BERRYMAN, Dan, C 509-313-6827 534 F
berryman@gonzaga.edu
BERRYMAN, Davis 405-491-6680 412 D
dberryma@snu.edu
BERRYMAN, Joanne 502-585-9911 206 D
jberryman@spalding.edu
BERRYMAN, Theresa 847-543-2890 148 B
tberryman@clcillinois.edu
BERRYMAN, Treva, G 615-366-4411 473 D
treva.berryman@tbr.edu
BERS, Trudy, H 847-635-1894 160 F
tbers@oakton.edu
BERSANO, Jacquelyn, A 815-740-5045 167 E
jbersano@stfrancis.edu
BERSCHBACK, Richard 248-689-8282 259 E
rberschb@walshcollege.edu
BERSHAD, Carolyn 607-753-4728 353 B
carolyn.bershad@cortland.edu
BERSI, Janna 310-243-3161 34 D
jbersi@csudh.edu
BERSON, Gail 508-286-8251 246 B
gberson@wheatonma.edu
BERT, Daryl, W 540-432-4101 518 F
daryl.bert@emu.edu
BERTCH, Dennis 269-488-4468 253 A
dbertch@kvcc.edu
BERTEAUX, Susan 508-830-5035 238 D
sberteaux@maritime.edu
BERTHELSEN, Mike 612-624-6837 272 A
berth004@umn.edu
BERTHELSEN, Rita 712-325-3356 186 F
rberthelsen@iwcc.edu
BERTHIAUME, Joe 940-898-3676 502 D
jberthiaume@twu.edu
BERTHIAUME, Peter, L 603-526-3675 303 G
pberthia@colby-sawyer.edu
BERTI, David, M 617-422-7215 243 B
dberti@nesl.edu
BERTINI, Kristine 207-780-5180 220 G
bertini@usm.maine.edu
BERTOCCHI, Bonnie, M 775-445-4450 303 B
bonnieb@wnc.edu
BERTOLI, Jim 812-877-8359 179 B
bertoli@rose-hulman.edu
BERTOLINE, Gary, R 765-494-2552 178 J
bertoline@purdue.edu
BERTOLINI, Leonard 815-836-5244 156 F
bertolle@lewisu.edu
BERTOLINO, Joseph, A 802-626-6404 515 G
joseph.bertolino@lyndonstate.edu
BERTOLUCCI, Linda 619-644-7799 49 C
linda.bertolucci@gcccd.edu
BERTONE, Genevieve 310-434-3911 68 D
bertone_genevieve@smc.edu
BERTOZZI, Nicholas 603-577-6640 304 I
bertozzi@dwc.edu
BERTRAM, Bob 207-780-4546 220 G
rbertram@usm.maine.edu
BERTRAM, Brian 517-264-7676 258 B
bbertram@sienaheights.edu
BERTRAM, Robert, G 585-292-2626 341 H
rbertram@monroecc.edu
BERTRAN, Lourdes 787-728-1515 568 D
lbertran@sagrado.edu
BERTRAND, Andre, E 404-215-2717 134 D
abertran@morehouse.edu
BERTSCH, Lynda 701-858-3360 382 A
lynda.bertsch@minotstateu.edu
BERTSOS, Daniel 937-775-4172 406 C
dan.bertsos@wright.edu
BERUBE, Eric 661-763-7720 72 E
eberube@taftcollege.edu
BERUBE, Patricia 413-572-5415 238 F
pberube@wsc.ma.edu
BERUBE, Virginia 406-377-9404 294 B
vberube@dawson.edu
BERUMEN, Yvonne 310-954-4250 57 H
yberumen@msmc.la.edu
BERUTO, Wendy 303-530-2100 81 I
wberutto@bcmt.org
BERWICK, Robert 202-408-2400 99 G
BERZAS, Elizabeth 225-768-1706 214 C
eberzas@ololcollege.edu
BERZINS, Martin 801-581-8224 511 C
mb@cs.utah.edu
BESANA, GianMario 312-362-5554 149 A
gbesana@depaul.edu
BESANCON, David 228-896-2522 275 E
david.besancon@mgccc.edu
BESAW, Gary 800-567-2344 547 A
gbesaw@menominee.edu
BESEDA, Michael 925-631-4277 64 F
mbeseda@stmarys-ca.edu
BESEDA, Michael, G 925-631-4277 64 F
mbeseda@stmarys-ca.edu
BESENYEI, Alicia 304-384-6313 543 G
abesenyei@concord.edu
BESHARA, John 330-941-3527 406 F
jbeshara@ysu.edu
BESHEARS, Susan 870-612-2133 25 E
susan.beshears@uaccb.edu
BESKID, Novella 803-777-0958 462 A
novella@sc.edu
BESNARD, Pamela 212-229-5662 342 E
besnardp@newschool.edu
BESPALEC, Dale, A 414-464-9777 553 E
dbespalec@wspp.edu
BESPALOV, Oleg 408-223-6471 67 B
oleg.bespalov@sjeccd.org
BESS, Janie 617-349-8542 236 B
iss@lesley.edu
BESS, Reginald, A 803-934-3181 459 G
rbess@morris.edu
BESS, Vivian, E 301-736-3631 224 A
vbess@msbbcs.edu
BESSE, Susan, M 978-468-7111 235 B
sbesse@gcts.edu
BESSER, Pamela 502-213-2616 202 F
pam.besser@kctcs.edu
BESSETTE, Jamie 205-665-6230 9 B
jbessette@montevallo.edu
BESSEY, Dean 207-948-9232 219 H
dbessey@unity.edu
BESSIE, Joseph, D 360-438-4310 537 B
jbessie@stmartin.edu
BESSLER, Joseph 918-610-8303 411 D
joe.bessler@ptstulsa.edu
BEST, Georgia 802-443-2258 514 A
best@middlebury.edu
BEST, Jason 206-876-6100 538 A
jbest@theseattleschool.edu
BEST, Mark, W 252-638-7247 370 A
bestm@cravencc.edu
BEST, Mickey 972-860-8201 484 H
mbest@dcccd.edu
BEST, Neil, A 724-847-6643 429 H
nabest@geneva.edu
BEST, Rebecca 218-855-8143 265 J
rbest@clcmn.edu
BEST, Robert 864-455-7992 462 F
BEST, Roger, J 660-543-8597 290 H
best@ucmo.edu
BEST, Sandra, M 912-358-4194 136 G
bestsm@savannahstate.edu
BEST, Sharon 386-752-1822 108 G
sharon.best@fgc.edu
BEST, Trinda 760-252-2411 30 H
tbest@barstow.edu
BESTE, Jeff 937-766-7858 386 G
bestej@cedarville.edu
BESTER, Barbara 651-523-2204 264 A
bbester@hamline.edu
BESTOCK, Donna, J 650-738-4121 67 H
bestock@smccd.edu
BESTUL, Michael 216-397-4261 392 L
mbestul@jcu.edu
BETANCOURT, Cybel 787-279-1912 563 D
cbetancourt@bayamon.inter.edu
BETANCOURT, Gladys 787-743-7979 565 H
ut-gbetancou@suagm.edu
BETECK, Ellis, B 410-651-6621 227 E
ebbeteck@umes.edu
BETH, Amy 201-447-7999 307 E
abeth@berger.edu
BETHANCOURT, Phillip 502-897-4205 206 C
pbethancourt@sbts.edu
BETHEA, Edward 843-661-8060 458 B
ed.bethea@fdtc.edu
BETHEL, Charles, N 304-877-6428 540 G
registrar@abc.edu
BETHKE, Jeffrey 312-362-6986 149 A
jbethke@depaul.edu
BETHKE-GOMEZ, Jesse 651-793-1805 267 A
jesse.bethkegomez@metrostate.edu
BETHMAN, Brenda 816-235-1643 291 C
bethmanb@umkc.edu
BETHSCHEIDER, John 281-756-5601 479 F
jbethscheider@alvincollege.edu
BETHSCHEIDER, John 281-756-3619 479 F
jbethschei@alvincollege.edu
BETHUNE, Andrew, J 989-964-4071 257 G
ajbethune@svsu.edu
BETHUNE, Lawrence, E 617-266-1400 231 E
BETHUNE-WALKER,
Nicole 813-664-4260 105 A
nbethune-walker@devry.edu
BETIT, Brent 802-387-6797 513 G
bbetit@landmark.edu
BETKER, Pam 303-762-6898 84 D
pam.betker@denverseminary.edu
BETORI, John 567-661-7575 400 I
john_betori@owens.edu
BETROLS, Lance 717-245-4711 558 G
BETSCHART, Joseph, V 503-845-3406 417 A
joseph.betschart@mtangel.edu
BETSEY, Charles 202-806-6800 98 E
cbetsey@howard.edu
BETSWORTH, Deborah 262-551-5725 546 I
dbetsworth@carthage.edu
BETTENCOURT, Patrick 209-575-6149 80 H
bettencourtp@mjc.edu
BETTING, Laurie 701-777-6055 381 F
laurie.betting@und.edu
BETTINGER, Lewis 608-342-1221 552 B
bettingerl@uwplatt.edu
BETTISON-VARGA, Lori 909-621-8148 69 A
president@scrippscollege.edu
BETTS, Albert 856-256-4200 314 A
betts@rowan.edu
BETTS, Diane 870-574-4560 24 A
dbetts@sautech.edu
BETTS, Keith 912-344-2514 124 G
keith.betts@armstrong.edu
BETTS, Kristen 912-344-3532 124 G
kristen.betts@armstrong.edu
BETTS, Russell 312-567-3800 153 C
betts@iit.edu
BETTS, Todd 402-557-7278 296 H
todd.betts@bellevue.edu
BETZ, Bridget, K 573-341-4282 291 E
berry@mst.edu
BETZ, Don 405-974-2311 413 B
betz@uco.edu
BETZ, Erica 610-398-5300 434 F
ebetz@lincolntech.com
BETZ, Jon 505-566-3505 320 D
betzj@sanjuancollege.edu
BETZ, Kimberly 651-690-8890 270 L
kkbetz@stkate.edu
BETZ, Leslie 309-556-3161 153 F
iwureg@iwu.edu
BETZ, Norma 732-255-0400 312 D
nbetz@ocean.edu
BETZ, Randy 757-569-6064 528 A
rbetz@pdc.edu
BETZ-BOGOLY, Cynthia 973-748-9000 307 H
cynthia_betz-bogoly@bloomfield.edu
BETZIG, Kaylen 262-691-5198 555 E
kbetzig@wctc.edu
BEU, Pat 605-394-1999 466 B
pat.beu@sdsmt.edu
BEUKELMAN, Doug, D 712-707-7121 188 D
dougb@nwciowa.edu
BEUSS, Ben 360-538-4082 534 G
bbeus@ghc.edu
BEUSSMAN, Victoria 507-786-3325 271 C
beussman@stolaf.edu
BEUTEL, Charles, M 815-740-5037 167 E
cbeutel@stfrancis.edu
BEUTLER, Randy, L 580-774-3766 412 F
randy.beutler@swosu.edu
BEVAN, Larry 724-222-5330 438 F
lbevan@penncommercial.edu
BEVERAGE, JR.,
Morris, W 440-525-7118 394 F
mbeverage@lakelandcc.edu
BEVERIDGE, Thomas 805-565-6017 79 A
tbeverid@westmont.edu
BEVERLY, Aleza, D 765-641-4251 169 E
adbeverly@anderson.edu
BEVERLY, Nancy, M 423-652-4728 470 A
nmbeverly@king.edu
BEVERLY, Pearlie 254-710-6939 482 A
pearl_beverly@baylor.edu
BEVERLY, Roger, D 423-585-2620 476 D
roger.beverly@ws.edu
BEVERSLUIS, Claudia 616-526-6102 249 A
cbeversl@calvin.edu
BEVILACQUA, Linda 305-899-3010 101 M
lbevilacqua@mail.barry.edu
BEVILLE, Jill 336-334-4013 379 B
jmbeville@uncg.edu
BEVINS, P. Scott 276-376-1066 525 G
pb8q@uvawise.edu
BEWSEY, Jeff 828-227-7322 380 A
bewsey@wcu.edu
BEY, George, J 601-974-1385 275 B
beygj@millsaps.edu
BEY, Laura 617-521-2181 244 F
laura.bey@simmons.edu

BEYAR, Renee 860-434-5232 93 D rbeyar@lymeacademy.edu
BEYDLER, Julie 970-542-3126 86 G julie.beydler@morgancc.edu
BEYER, Bryan 803-754-4100 457 D
BEYER, David 425-388-9573 534 C dbeyer@everettcc.edu
BEYER, Kirk, D 507-933-6075 263 J kbeyer@gustavus.edu
BEYER, Paul, N 443-997-5600 223 F pbeyer@jhu.edu
BEYER, Richard Allen 304-243-2233 546 A president@wju.edu
BEYER-HERMSEN, Leslie 740-389-6786 399 D beyer-hermsen.1@osu.edu
BEYER HOUPT, Julia 740-587-6636 389 I houpt@denison.edu
BEYL, Caula 865-974-7303 477 D cbeyl@utk.edu
BEYL, Tracy 717-396-7833 440 K tbeyl@pcad.edu
BEYROUTY, Craig 970-491-6274 83 F craig.beyrouty@colostate.edu
BEZA, Mary 573-681-5561 283 I bezam@lincolnu.edu
BEZBATCHENKO, Ann, E 312-915-8902 157 C abezbat@luc.edu
BEZET, Jared 561-912-1211 107 B jbezet@evergladesuniversity.edu
BEZJIAN, Ilene 626-812-3085 30 G ibezjian@apu.edu
BEZOTTE, Christine 607-735-1852 332 I cbezotte@elmira.edu
BHADA, Farokh 401-232-6005 453 C fbhada@bryant.edu
BHANDARI, Rohinton 415-955-2027 27 A mbhandari@alliant.edu
BHANDARI, Rupa 415-565-8909 74 A bhandari@uchastings.edu
BHARGAVA, Vivek 601-877-6450 272 F vivek@alcorn.edu
BHARUCHA, Jamshed 212-353-4240 331 A president@cooper.edu
BHATIA, Tarun 415-955-2006 27 A tbhatia@alliant.edu
BHATTACHARYA, Debasis 808-984-3631 142 E debasisb@hawaii.edu
BHATTACHARYA, Somnath 561-297-3629 119 A sbhatt@fau.edu
BHATTACHARYA, Somnath 561-297-3638 119 A sbhatt@fau.edu
BIA, Johnson 520-206-5001 17 H jbia@pima.edu
BIAFORA, Frank 727-873-4292 121 C fbiafora@mail.usf.edu
BIAGAS, Lisa 732-987-2286 310 C biagasl@georgian.edu
BIAGIOTTI, Eugene 610-647-4400 431 C ebiagiotti@immaculata.edu
BIALEK, Steve 414-277-7364 549 C bialek@msoe.edu
BIALK, Kathy 304-696-2281 544 B bialkk@marshall.edu
BIANCAMANO, John 860-679-1145 95 A jbiancamano@uchc.edu
BIANCAMANO, John, J 740-593-2626 399 G biancama@ohio.edu
BIANCHI, Amy, M 617-333-2236 233 F abianchi@curry.edu
BIANCHI, Ashley 901-843-3810 472 K bianchia@rhodes.edu
BIANCHI, Julius 805-493-3483 33 B bianchi@clunet.edu
BIANCHI, Mark 732-987-2678 310 C bianchim@georgian.edu
BIANCO, Amy 845-848-4065 332 B amy.bianco@dc.edu
BIASELLA, Tina 330-499-9600 393 I tbiasell@kent.edu
BIBB, Shawn 408-924-1500 37 C shawn.bibb@sjsu.edu
BIBBENS, Matthew, G 909-607-8966 40 G matthew.bibbens@cmc.edu
BIBBS, Mary 510-574-1103 44 F mbibbs@devry.edu
BIBEAU, Shelley 651-846-1683 269 C shelley.bibeau@saintpaul.edu
BIBEAU, Susan 860-701-5000 93 E bibeau_s@mitchell.edu
BIBI, Khalid, W 716-888-8293 325 F bibi@canisius.edu
BIBLE, Doug 501-205-8453 21 C dbible@cbc.edu
BIBLE, J. Brice 740-597-3246 399 G bibleb@ohio.edu
BICAK, Charles, J 308-865-8209 300 F bicakc@unk.edu
BICE, Cynthia 636-949-4618 283 J cbice@lindenwood.edu
BICE, Diane, K 810-762-7491 253 C dbice@kettering.edu
BICE, JR., Gary, L 716-673-3341 352 A gary.bice@fredonia.edu
BICE, Patricia 914-251-6360 354 D patricia.bice@purchase.edu
BICHARA, Kamal 330-339-3391 394 A kbichara@kent.edu
BICHEL, Rebecca 817-272-1413 505 C rbichel@uta.edu
BICKEL, Linda, S 573-681-5489 283 I bickell@lincolnu.edu
BICKEL, Sarah, L 928-523-6116 16 I sarah.bickel@nau.edu
BICKEL, Teri 301-846-2446 222 G tbickel@frederick.edu
BICKELL, Kris 203-576-4851 94 F ubonline@bridgeport.edu
BICKERS, Eugene, N 213-740-1114 76 F bickers@usc.edu
BICKFORD, David 480-557-1946 19 A david.bickford@phoenix.edu
BICKFORD, Deborah, J 937-229-2245 404 A dbickford1@udayton.edu
BICKFORD, George 312-553-5896 147 C gbickford@ccc.edu
BICKFORD, Jeffrey 978-556-3745 240 E jbickford@necc.mass.edu
BICKFORD, Sonja 406-791-5389 296 F sbickford01@ugf.edu
BICKING, Michael, D 610-436-3478 444 A mbicking@wcupa.edu
BICKLEY, Carol, A 803-321-5124 459 H carol.bickley@newberry.edu
BICKNELL, Brian 617-588-1365 231 C bbicknell@bfit.edu
BICKSLER, Leslie 304-647-6279 544 E lbicksler@osteo.wvsom.edu
BIDDAR, Patricia, S 908-709-7509 316 B biddar@ucc.edu
BIDDINGS-MURO, Regina, D 219-989-2323 178 K reginab@purduecal.edu
BIDDINGS-MURO, Regina, D 219-989-2552 178 K reginab@purduecal.edu
BIDDISCOMBE, John, S 860-685-2895 95 E jbiddiscombe@wesleyan.edu
BIDDLE, Chris 615-226-3990 472 A cbiddle@nadcedu.com
BIDDY, Scott 510-642-7374 73 H fsb@berkeley.edu
BIDOGLIO, Ana 714-459-1106 78 H abidoglio@wsulaw.edu
BIDWELL, Lorena, L 269-471-6124 247 D lorena@andrews.edu
BIEBER, Ann, D 610-799-1581 434 D abieber@lccc.edu
BIEBER, Deborah 773-256-3000 158 B dbieber@meadville.edu
BIEBER, Kori 541-956-7196 420 B kbieber@roguecc.edu
BIEBIGHAUSER, Victor, K 334-395-8800 7 B vbiebighauser@southuniversity.edu
BIEBIGHAUSER, Victor, K 334-395-8800 137 D vbiebighauser@southuniversity.edu
BIEBUYCK, Bill 563-588-6405 183 E bill.biebuyck@clarke.edu
BIEBUYCK, Brent 586-445-7119 254 C biebuyckb@macomb.edu
BIEGEL, Peter, J 904-632-3131 109 F pbiegel@fscj.edu
BIEGEN, M. Sharon 314-516-5711 291 D sharon_biegen@umsl.edu
BIEHN, Christopher 607-274-3115 336 G cbiehn@ithaca.edu
BIEL, Alan 814-732-2856 442 E abiel@edinboro.edu
BIELEC, John 215-895-1434 427 H jbielec@drexel.edu
BIELECK, Sara 937-224-0061 395 B sbieleck@swcollege.net
BIELECKI, Donald, P 716-286-8679 344 D dpb@niagara.edu
BIELEN, Paul 707-524-1608 68 E pbielen@santarosa.edu
BIELER, Glenn, M 410-516-8631 223 F gbieler1@jhu.edu
BIELMAN, Jess 503-517-1140 421 B jbielman@warnerpacific.edu
BIELSKI, Bradley, A 859-344-3305 206 I bradley.bielski@thomasmore.edu
BIELSKI, Olen 413-572-8178 238 F obielski@wsc.ma.edu
BIENENFELD, Sheila 408-924-5300 37 C sheila.bienenfeld@sjsu.edu
BIENERT, Bonnie 847-628-2083 154 K bbienert@judsonu.edu
BIENFANG, Kim 763-433-1483 265 G kim.bienfang@anokaramsey.edu
BIENZ, Richard 260-399-7700 181 A rbienz@sf.edu
BIER, Alice, G 718-951-5189 326 F abier@brooklyn.cuny.edu
BIER, Debbie 412-521-6200 445 I debbie.bier@rosedaletech.org
BIER, Jill 815-825-2086 155 D jill.bier@kishwaukeecollege.edu
BIERBAUER, Charles 803-777-4105 462 A bierbauer@sc.edu
BIERLICH, Sue 714-432-5562 41 D sbierlich@occ.cccd.edu
BIERMA, Lyle, D 616-957-6605 249 B lbierma@calvinseminary.edu
BIERMAN, Derek 402-844-7060 299 I derek@norteast.edu
BIERMAN, Scott 608-363-2201 546 E biermans@beloit.edu
BIERMAN, Steve 417-447-8856 287 D biermans@otc.edu
BIERMANN, Mark, L 319-352-8284 189 J mark.biermann@wartburg.edu
BIERMANN, Theodore 734-432-5515 254 D tbiermann@madonna.edu
BIERNACKI, Steve 505-566-3284 320 D biernackis@sanjuancollege.edu
BIERNBAUM, Dana 309-298-1800 168 C dm-biernbaum@wiu.edu
BIERNBAUM, John 309-298-3320 168 C j-biernbaum@wiu.edu
BIERYLA, John 570-389-4297 441 F jbieryla@bloomu.edu
BIES, James, B 605-274-4124 464 A jim.bies@augie.edu
BIESECKER, James 717-337-6700 429 I jbieseck@gettysburg.edu
BIETZ, Gordon 423-236-2801 473 B bietz@southern.edu
BIGARD, Heather 217-854-3231 146 A heather.bigard@blackburn.edu
BIGAS-GONZALEZ, Jenniffer 787-834-5151 565 D jbigas@email.pucpr.edu
BIGBY, Angela, D 702-968-2046 303 D abigby@roseman.edu
BIGCRANE, Mike 406-275-4789 296 D mike_bigcrane@skc.edu
BIGELOW, Holly 507-280-3509 268 I holly.bigelow@roch.edu
BIGELOW, Scott 910-521-6351 379 C scott.bigelow@uncp.edu
BIGELOW, Susan 307-674-6446 556 F sbigelow@sheridan.edu
BIGGANE, Michael, J 716-851-1416 333 B biggane@ecc.edu
BIGGER, Kimberly 870-248-4000 21 A kim.bigger@blackrivertech.edu
BIGGER, Roberta, H 864-597-4040 463 G biggerrh@wofford.edu
BIGGERS, Carla, D 409-944-1200 486 K cbiggers@gc.edu
BIGGERS, Darlene 281-283-3000 503 E biggers@uhcl.edu
BIGGERS, Leisa 310-660-3593 45 E lbiggers@elcamino.edu
BIGGERSTAFF, Debra 814-827-4422 450 A biggers@pitt.edu
BIGGERSTAFF, Patrick 704-233-8247 380 F dpbigg@wingate.edu
BIGGIO, Nancy 205-726-4267 6 G ncbiggio@samford.edu
BIGGS, Becca 503-821-8892 419 D beca@pnca.edu
BIGGS, Bonnie 206-726-5045 533 D bbiggs@cornish.edu
BIGGS, Deborah, L 989-774-7547 249 C biggs1dl@cmich.edu
BIGGS, Jocelyn 704-216-6001 366 G jbiggs@livingstone.edu
BIGGS, Kristen 231-843-5875 260 B
BIGGS, Patsy 501-370-4002 19 D patsy.biggs@arkansasbaptist.edu
BIGGS, Sheila 260-480-4223 176 F sbiggs@ivytech.edu
BIGGS, Shirley, A 803-535-5268 456 D sbiggs@claflin.edu
BIGGS, Sue, A 325-670-1314 487 F sbiggs@hsutx.edu
BIGGS, Susan 802-447-6389 514 F sbiggs@svc.edu
BIGHAM, William, L 937-766-7810 386 G bbigham@cedarville.edu
BIGLIENI, Lindy 417-269-3083 280 G admissions@coxcollege.edu
BIGNEY, Tracy 207-973-3234 219 I bigney@maine.edu
BIHL, Andy 304-461-3210 541 H abihl@mountainstate.edu
BIHLMEYER, Earl, F 504-988-1930 215 C ebihlme@tulane.edu
BIKLEN, Douglas, P 315-443-4751 357 C dpbiklen@syr.edu
BILACH, Matt 480-994-9244 18 F
BILBRUCK, Tom 661-362-3235 41 I tom.bilbruck@canyons.edu
BILDER, Kevin 480-517-8464 16 B kevin.bilder@riosalado.edu
BILDERBACK, Rebecca 620-365-5116 190 D bilderback@allencc.edu
BILELLA, Jamieson, A 973-655-4352 311 F bilellaj@mail.montclair.edu
BILES, Deron 817-923-1921 495 G dbiles@swbts.edu
BILGER, Cindy, L 570-577-1631 423 E cbilger@bucknell.edu
BILGER, Jackie 570-321-4309 435 D bilger@lycoming.edu
BILGIN, Deniz 831-242-5291 557 F deniz.bilgin@monterey.army.mil
BILIONIS, Louis, D 513-556-0121 403 D louis.bilionis@uc.edu
BILLARD, Edmund Thomas 623-572-3220 16 E ebillard@midwestern.edu
BILLARD, Trisha 516-876-3053 353 D billardt@oldwestbury.edu
BILLEAUDEAU, Kim, A 337-262-5300 216 D kimberlyb@louisiana.edu
BILLEAUX, David 361-825-2393 498 C david.billeaux@tamucc.edu
BILLECI, Celesta 805-893-3437 75 B celesta.billeci@sa.ucsb.edu
BILLEN, Isabelle 405-733-7356 411 I ibillen@rose.edu
BILLER, Gary, M 309-298-1814 168 C gm-biller@wiu.edu
BILLERMAN, John 740-374-8716 405 G jbillerman@wscc.edu
BILLHARTZ, Scott, L 618-537-6869 158 A slbillhartz@mckendree.edu
BILLI, John, E 734-936-5214 259 A jbilli@umich.edu
BILLIE, Marie, H 410-651-7502 227 E mhbillie@umes.edu
BILLIG, Michael 717-291-4152 429 F michael.billig@fandm.edu
BILLINGS, Amanda 812-330-6064 175 J abillings7@ivytech.edu
BILLINGS, Amanda 214-648-2344 507 E amanda.billings@utsouthwestern.edu
BILLINGS, Bob 360-596-5353 538 E bbillings@spscc.ctc.edu
BILLINGS, Chuck 415-485-3263 45 C cbillings@dominican.edu
BILLINGS, Debra 810-766-4278 247 G debra.billings@baker.edu
BILLINGS, Frank 516-572-8160 342 C frank.billings@ncc.edu
BILLINGS, Patricia, L 206-934-6739 537 F patricia.billings@seattlecolleges.edu
BILLINGSLEY, Anna, B 540-654-1055 525 D abilling@umw.edu
BILLINGSLEY, Dale, B 502-852-5209 207 E dbbill01@louisville.edu
BILLINGSLEY, Linda 318-487-7630 209 F billingsley@lacollege.edu
BILLINGSLEY, Tiffany 870-633-4480 21 F tbillingsley@eacc.edu
BILLINGTON, Paul 808-791-5232 140 B pbillington@argosy.edu
BILLINGTON, Suzanne K, L 208-885-5867 144 G suzib@uidaho.edu
BILLITTIER, Anthony 716-829-8124 332 E billitti@dyc.edu
BILLMAN, Kathleen 773-256-0770 157 D kbillman@lstc.edu
BILLMAN, Rhonda 330-287-1213 399 A billman.36@osu.edu
BILLS, Andy 336-841-4538 365 C abills@highpoint.edu
BILLS, Joyce 918-465-1777 408 A jbills@eosc.edu
BILLS, Linda, G 814-332-3362 421 F linda.bills@allegheny.edu
BILLS-WINDT, Caryn, A 312-413-8145 167 B cabw@uic.edu
BILLUPS, Vory 404-225-4474 125 E vbillups@atlantatech.edu
BILLY, Beth 251-809-1555 5 B beth.billy@jdcc.edu
BILLY, George, J 516-773-5501 558 I billyg@usmma.edu
BILMONT, John 415-241-2230 40 C jbilmont@ccsf.edu
BILODEAU, Denise 978-232-2102 234 D bilodeau@endicott.edu
BILODEAU, Gene 970-824-1103 82 H gene.bilodeau@cncc.edu
BILODEAU, Ken 401-454-6371 454 B kbilodea@risd.edu
BILODEAU, Rick 415-276-8199 19 A rick.bilodeau@phoenix.edu
BILOTTA, Barbara, J 716-880-2265 340 D barbara.bilotta@medaille.edu
BILOTTA, Leone 610-917-1483 450 E l_bilotta@vfcc.edu
BILSKY, Edward 207-602-2707 221 A ebilsky@une.edu
BILSKY, Steven 215-898-6121 448 J athdir@pobox.upenn.edu
BILYEU, David, D 541-383-7563 414 I dbilyeu@cocc.edu
BIMONTE-YERGANIAN, Maria 203-582-3446 93 H maria.bimonte@quinnipiac.edu

BIMROSE, Irene 309-692-4092 158 D
ibimrose@midstate.edu

BINA, Shawn 218-235-2170 269 F
s.bina@vcc.edu

BINA, III, William, F 478-301-5570 134 A
bina_wf@mercer.edu

BINARD, Kris 303-404-5103 85 A
kris.binard@frontrange.edu

BINAU, Brad, A 614-235-4136 402 G
bbinau@tlsohio.edu

BINDER, George 985-867-2229 214 G
gbinderfinaid@sjasc.edu

BINDER, Jan 602-285-7869 16 A
jan.binder@pcmail.maricopa.edu

BINDER, Rich 602-216-3129 480 G
rbinder@gmail.com

BINDER, Richard 602-216-3129 11 F
rbinder@argosy.edu

BINDER, Ronald, S 814-362-7630 449 B
binder@pitt.edu

BINDEWALD, Kurt 504-865-3226 213 F
kjbindew@loyno.edu

BINEK, Gordy 701-224-5697 382 D
gordon.binek@bismarckstate.edu

BINESH, Behzad 714-744-7099 39 F
binesh@chapman.edu

BINFORD, Gail 406-247-3000 295 F
gbinford@msubillings.edu

BING, Richard 212-998-2391 344 B
richard.bing@nyu.edu

BINGAMON, Cindy 314-837-6777 288 C
cbingamon@slcconline.edu

BINGEL, Laurie, A 618-235-2700 165 D
laurie.bingel@swic.edu

BINGER, LeAnn, M 804-862-6247 523 F
lbinger@rbc.edu

BINGER, Nancy 847-628-2510 154 K
nbinger@judsonu.edu

BINGHAM, C. Sam 864-503-5073 463 B
sbingham@uscupstate.edu

BINGHAM, Charlotte 806-742-3627 502 A
charlotte.bingham@ttu.edu

BINGHAM, Charlotte 806-742-3627 502 B
charlotte.bingham@ttu.edu

BINGHAM, Daniel 406-444-6800 295 A
daniel.bingham@umhelena.edu

BINGHAM,
James (Jim), L 913-588-4900 197 C
jbingham@kumc.edu

BINGHAM, Jean, M 312-567-5077 153 C
bingham@iit.edu

BINGHAM, Jeff 405-425-5152 409 E
jeff.bingham@oc.edu

BINGHAM, Nelson 765-983-1205 171 E
nelsonb@earlham.edu

BINGHAM, Nelson 765-983-1211 171 E
nelsonb@earlham.edu

BINGHAM, Rachel 801-524-8129 510 E
rbingham@ldsbc.edu

BINGHAM, Roger, B 812-374-5222 176 A
rbingham@ivytech.edu

BINGHAM, Rosie, P 901-678-2114 474 C
rbingham@memphis.edu

BINGHAM, Thomas, R 808-956-6460 141 G
bingham@hawaii.edu

BINION, Jim 940-552-6291 507 F
jbinion@vernoncollege.edu

BINK, Cynthia 718-260-5030 328 D
cbink@citytech.cuny.edu

BINKERD, James 707-638-5883 73 A
jim.binkerd@tu.edu

BINKLEY, Yildiz, B 615-963-5212 474 A
ybinkley@tnstate.edu

BINKOWSKI, Marcella 215-637-7700 431 A
smbinkowski@holyfamily.edu

BINNEY, Craig 508-565-1107 245 A
cbinney@stonehill.edu

BINNICKER, Paul 816-833-0524 282 C
binnicke@graceland.edu

BINNICKER, Paul 816-833-0524 185 B
binnicke@graceland.edu

BINNS, Andrew, N 215-898-7225 448 J
provost-ed@upenn.edu

BINSFELD, Douglas 651-450-3370 266 F
dbinsfe@inverhills.edu

BINSTOCK, Alvin, G 701-483-2328 381 G
alvin.binstock@dickinsonstate.edu

BINSTOCK, Neal, F 412-397-6290 445 H
binstock@rmu.edu

BINTNER, Leslie 515-244-4221 181 F
bintnerl@aib.edu

BIO, Cathy 808-984-3277 142 E
cbio@hawaii.edu

BIONDI, SJ, Lawrence 314-977-7777 289 C
biondi@slu.edu

BIOTEAU, Cynthia, A 801-957-4226 512 D
cbioteau@slcc.edu

BIR, Chad 317-955-6040 177 I
cbir@marian.edu

BIRBERICK, Anne 815-753-0494 160 B
annie@niu.edu

BIRCH, Andrea, C 770-718-5325 126 E
abirch@brenau.edu

BIRCH, Barbara 212-960-5373 361 M
birch@yu.edu

BIRCH, Brian 801-863-8361 511 F
brian.birch@uvu.edu

BIRCH, Esther 301-736-3631 224 A
esther.birch@msbbcs.edu

BIRCH, Laura, A 217-420-6661 158 G
lbirch@millikin.edu

BIRCHAK, Chris 713-221-8007 503 F
birchakc@uhd.edu

BIRCHARD, Michael 763-424-0850 268 B
mbirchard@nhcc.edu

BIRCHWOOD, Rachel 845-451-1459 331 E
r_birchw@culinary.edu

BIRCKBICHLER, Carrie, J 724-738-2150 443 F
carrie.birckbichler@sru.edu

BIRCKHEAD, Barry, D 678-915-4102 137 G
bbirckhe@spsu.edu

BIRD, Brandon 206-726-5024 533 D
bbird@cornish.edu

BIRD, Craig 210-924-4338 481 G
craig.bird@bua.edu

BIRD, Eric 617-879-7878 238 B
ebird@massart.edu

BIRD, Lee, E 405-744-5328 410 C
lee.bird@okstate.edu

BIRD, Lori 419-267-1266 397 E
lbird@northweststate.edu

BIRD, Lyly 909-537-7096 36 B
lbird@csusb.edu

BIRD, Nicole 909-868-4227 44 K
nbird@devry.edu

BIRD, Su Ann 229-931-2110 137 C
sbird@southgatech.edu

BIRD, SuAnn 229-931-2110 137 C
sbird@southgatech.edu

BIRD, Veronica 610-917-1422 450 E
rabird@vfcc.edu

BIRDINE, Phil 580-477-7700 414 C
phil.birdine@wosc.edu

BIRDSALL, Lynne 802-586-7711 514 G
lbirdsall@sterlingcollege.edu

BIRDSELL, David 646-660-6700 326 C
david.birdsell@baruch.cuny.edu

BIRDSONG, Jeff 918-540-6348 408 J
jbirdsong@neo.edu

BIRDSONG, Ronnie 575-562-4490 318 B
ronnie.birdsong@enmu.edu

BIRDWELL, Cindy, A 517-264-7194 258 B
cbirdwell@sienaheights.edu

BIRDWHISTELL, Terry, P 859-257-1466 207 D
tlbird@uky.edu

BIRELINE, David 949-214-3209 43 C
david.bireline@cui.edu

BIREN, Susan, J 781-736-3451 232 F
birren@brandeis.edu

BIRGE, Benjamin 301-985-7682 227 F
bbirge@umuc.edu

BIRGE, James, F 603-899-4129 305 A
birgej@franklinpierce.edu

BIRGE, Susan, N 203-254-4000 92 H
sbirge@fairfield.edu

BIRGEN, Mariah, H 319-352-8565 189 J
mariah.birgen@wartburg.edu

BIRGEN, Mike 606-626-2681 466 A
mike.birgen@northern.edu

BIRGENEAU, Robert, J 510-642-7464 73 H
chancellor@berkeley.edu

BIRINGER, Bobbi 312-261-3550 159 E
bobbi.biringer@nl.edu

BIRK, Michelle, L 618-235-2700 165 D
michelle.birk@swic.edu

BIRKE, Richard 503-370-6046 421 D
rbirke@willamette.edu

BIRKEDAHL, Patrice 510-659-6208 59 J
pbirkedahl@ohlone.edu

BIRKEDAHL, Walter 510-659-6216 59 J
wbirkedahl@ohlone.edu

BIRKENHOLTZ, Kenneth, I 515-961-1512 189 C
ken.birkenholtz@simpson.edu

BIRKHEAD, Clarence 704-337-2532 376 A
birkheadc@queens.edu

BIRKHEAD, Kathryn 479-986-4052 22 H
kbirkhead@nwacc.edu

BIRKHEAD, Mary 610-282-1100 427 A
mary.birkhead@desales.edu

BIRKHOLZ, Amberleigh 708-209-3629 148 E
amberleigh.birkholz@cuchicago.edu

BIRKNER, Linda, M 501-977-2006 25 G
birkner@uaccm.edu

BIRKY, Ian, T 610-758-3880 434 E
itb0@lehigh.edu

BIRMINGHAM, John 630-353-9010 149 B
jbirmingham@devry.edu

BIRMINGHAM, Jolene 312-226-6294 156 G
jbirmingham@lexingtoncollege.edu

BIRMINGHAM, Stacy, G 724-458-3841 430 B
sgbirmingham@gcc.edu

BIRNBACH, David, J 305-284-2002 122 I
dbirnbach@miami.edu

BIRNBAUM, Ben 617-552-3353 232 B
ben.birnbaum@bu.edu

BIRNBAUM, David 510-987-9725 75 B
david.birnbaum@ucop.edu

BIRNBAUM, Roger 323-856-7600 28 E

BIRO, Susan 410-386-8419 221 G
sbiro@carrollcc.edu

BIRON, Jackie 510-780-4500 53 J
jbiron00@lifewest.edu

BIRON, Louise 518-255-5532 354 E
bironl@cobleskill.edu

BIROS, Demetra 425-739-8315 535 H
demetra.biros@lwtc.edu

BIROS, Janice 215-895-2200 427 H
jan.biros@drexel.edu

BIRRINGER, Charles, E 920-924-3420 554 G
cbirringer@morainepark.edu

BIRX, Donald, L 814-898-6160 439 F
dlb69@psu.edu

BISAHA, Andrew 619-275-4700 46 K
andrew182@aol.com

BISARYA, Alvin 312-553-2500 147 B
abisarya@ccc.edu

BISBEY, CDP, Michele 412-536-1255 432 H
michele.bisbey@laroche.edu

BISCH, Debbie 620-227-9209 192 E
debbieb@dc3.edu

BISCHOFF, Jeannette 916-660-7000 69 F
jbischoff@sierracollege.edu

BISCHOFF, Margaretha 956-872-8310 494 H
etybuh@southtexascollege.edu

BISCHOFF, Richard, W 216-368-5445 386 F
richard.bischoff@case.edu

BISCONTI, Ursula 941-694-1122 307 F
uhn@berkeleycollege.edu

BISCONTI, Ursula 914-694-1122 323 H
uhn@berkeleycollege.edu

BISESE, Stephen, D 804-289-8615 525 E
sbisese@richmond.edu

BISESI, Linda 415-565-4645 74 A
bisesil@uchastings.edu

BISH, Courtney, D 315-386-7120 355 E
bish@canton.edu

BISH, Kevin 859-858-2272 198 D

BISHARA, Heather 561-297-4159 119 A
hbishara@fau.edu

BISHEL, Mary, A 219-785-5204 179 A
mbishel@pnc.edu

BISHOP, Angalynn 361-698-1255 485 G
abishop3@delmar.edu

BISHOP, Carol 518-255-5520 354 E
bishopcm@cobleskill.edu

BISHOP, Carol, M 607-746-4582 355 F
bishopcm@delhi.edu

BISHOP, Catherine 405-325-1543 413 C
cbishop@ou.edu

BISHOP, Catherine, F 405-325-1543 413 D
cbishop@ou.edu

BISHOP, Christine, C 850-729-4901 114 A
bishopc@nwfsc.edu

BISHOP, Christopher 888-384-0849 27 G
cjbishop@allied.edu

BISHOP, Christopher 970-675-3251 82 H
christopher.bishop@cncc.edu

BISHOP, David 806-785-9285 508 E
bishop@wbu.edu

BISHOP, Donald 574-631-7505 180 G
dbishop1@nd.edu

BISHOP, Eric 909-652-6290 39 E
eric.bishop@chaffey.edu

BISHOP, Eric 928-524-7400 17 A
eric.bishop@npc.edu

BISHOP, George 850-872-3803 110 H
gbishop@gulfcoast.edu

BISHOP, Ginger 828-328-7335 366 E
ginger.bishop@lr.edu

BISHOP, Indra 619-260-7898 76 D
ibishop@sandiego.edu

BISHOP, Jack 509-963-1914 532 C
bishopj@cwu.edu

BISHOP, Jeffrey 314-977-6663 289 C
jbisho12@slu.edu

BISHOP, Jim 260-484-4400 170 A
jbishop@brownmackie.edu

BISHOP, Kristin 276-656-0315 527 G
kbishop@patrickhenry.edu

BISHOP, Kristy, A 816-604-1165 284 H
kristy.bishop@mcckc.edu

BISHOP, Lewis 540-986-1800 522 D
lbishop@national-college.edu

BISHOP, Lisa, J 812-888-4274 181 D
bishop@vinu.edu

BISHOP, Mary 305-593-1223 102 H
mbishop@albizu.edu

BISHOP, Mauri 202-885-8526 100 C
mbishop@wesleyseminary.edu

BISHOP, Nancy 803-778-6638 455 G
bishopnw@cctech.edu

BISHOP, Nathaniel, L 540-985-8484 520 I
nlbishop@jchs.edu

BISHOP, Patty 925-631-4793 64 F
pbishop@stmarys-ca.edu

BISHOP, Paul 805-965-0581 68 B
pwbishop@sbcc.edu

BISHOP, Phil 206-876-6100 538 A
pbishop@theseattleschool.edu

BISHOP, Rex 706-754-7790 135 A
rbishop@northgatech.edu

BISHOP, Richard 860-832-2201 90 G
bishopr@ccsu.edu

BISHOP, Robert 510-780-4500 53 J
rbishop@lifewest.edu

BISHOP, Robert 414-288-6591 548 F
robert.bishop@marquette.edu

BISHOP, Sandy 715-365-4564 555 A
sbishop@nicoletcollege.edu

BISHOP, Selah 904-470-8220 105 G
selah.bisho0911@ewc.edu

BISHOP, Shane 406-377-9421 294 B
sbishop@dawson.edu

BISHOP, Shannon 828-694-1717 368 E
s_bishop@blueridge.edu

BISHOP, Steve 417-447-8152 287 D
bishops@otc.edu

BISHOP, Steve 601-276-3701 277 B
bishop@smcc.edu

BISHOP, Terri 510-848-0177 19 A
terri.bishop@apollogrp.edu

BISHOP, Wesley, T 504-286-5325 214 J
wbishop@suno.edu

BISHOP, William 504-861-5431 213 F
wgbishop@loyno.edu

BISHOP, Wilsie, S 423-439-4811 473 F
bishopws@etsu.edu

BISHOP STUART, Aimee 419-251-1802 395 I
aimee.bishopstuart@mercycollege.edu

BISKUP, Susan 570-408-4355 452 A
susan.biskup@wilkes.edu

BISKUPIAK, Walter, H 406-447-5420 293 G
bbiskupi@carroll.edu

BISLEY, Deanna 800-567-2344 547 A
dbisley@menominee.edu

BISMARK, Jeanie 870-235-4078 23 I
mjbismark@saumag.edu

BISSELL, Michelle 304-204-4096 542 J
mbissell@kvctc.edu

BISSELL, Sally, B 419-783-2350 389 H
sbissell@defiance.edu

BISSELL, Sandra 315-781-3312 335 F
bissell@hws.edu

BISSELL PAULSON, Lisa 707-965-7362 60 I
lpaulson@puc.edu

BISSET, Matthew, S 727-864-8222 105 E
bissetms@eckerd.edu

BISSET, William, J 718-862-7200 339 H
william.bisset@manhattan.edu

BISSETTE, Callie 252-399-6336 362 E
cbissette@barton.edu

BISSEY, Bret, S 973-972-8093 316 C
bisseybs@umdnj.edu

BISSONETTE, Bonita, S 715-675-3331 555 B
bissonet@ntc.edu

BISWAS, Harun 678-466-4240 127 D
harunbiswas@clayton.edu

BITIKOFER, Scott 407-646-2121 116 D
sbitikofer@rollins.edu

BITNER, Hannah 816-322-0110 279 D
hannah.bitner@calvary.edu

BITNER, Teddy 816-322-0110 279 D
teddy.bitner@calvary.edu

BITTENBENDER, David 206-934-7792 537 D
david.bittenbender@seattlecolleges.edu

BITTERBAUM, Erik, J 607-753-2201 353 B
erik.bitterbaum@cortland.edu

BITTERSFELD, Y 718-692-0208 361 F

BITTINGER, Dale 410-455-2278 227 D
bittinger@umbc.edu

BITTLE, Carolyn 910-410-1751 373 B
carolynb@richmondcc.edu

BITTORF, David, C 240-500-2000 223 A
bittorfd@hagerstowncc.edu

BITZER, Steve 715-682-4591 555 G
steve.bitzer@witc.edu

BIVENS, Leon, J 410-651-6681 227 E
ljbivens@umes.edu

BIXBY, Bill 724-589-2130 448 B
hbixby@thiel.edu

BIXBY, David, E 626-815-5334 30 G
dbixby@apu.edu

BIXBY, John, L 305-284-2211 122 I
jbixby@miami.edu

BIXEL, Gil 850-484-1575 115 B
gbixel@pensacolastate.edu

BIXLER, Cindy 386-226-7959 105 H
cynthia.bixler@erau.edu

BIXLER, Donald 618-453-2411 165 B
ombuds@siu.edu

BIXLER, Kirk, J 317-738-8801 171 F
kbixler@franklincollege.edu

BIZON, Walter, G 248-204-3020 254 B
wbizon@ltu.edu

BJELLAND, David 320-762-4407 265 F
davidb@alextech.edu

BJERKE, Jean 909-593-3511 75 E
jbjerke@laverne.edu

BJERKLIE, Joseph, R 207-834-8621 220 D
joseph.bjerklie@maine.edu

BJOKNE, Daniel, H 515-964-0601 185 A
bjokned@faith.edu

BJORGO, Lori 512-892-2835 483 D

BJORK, Ross 662-915-7546 277 D
rbjork@olemiss.edu

BJORKLUND, Robert, B .... 651-638-6396 .... 261 D
robert-bjorklund@bethel.edu

BJORKMAN, David, J .... 561-297-0113 .... 119 A
dbjorkm1@fau.edu

BJORKMAN, Karen .... 419-530-7842 .... 404 F
karen.bjorkman@utoledo.edu

BJORLAND, Kirk .... 641-784-5110 .... 185 B
kdbjorla@graceland.edu

BJORN, Thorr, D .... 401-874-5245 .... 454 E
tbjorn@uri.edu

BJUR, Richard .... 775-784-4040 .... 303 A
bjur@unr.edu

BLACK, Aaron .... 314-392-2292 .... 285 J
blacka@mobap.edu

BLACK, Adam .... 801-863-6378 .... 511 F
blackad@uvu.edu

BLACK, Angel .... 303-837-0825 .... 81 F
ablack@aii.edu

BLACK, Anita .... 510-436-2411 .... 62 E
ablack@peralta.edu

BLACK, Annette .... 313-496-2744 .... 259 G
ablack1@wcccd.edu

BLACK, Bettye, R .... 405-466-3294 .... 408 G
brblack@langston.edu

BLACK, Britt .... 630-752-5072 .... 168 H
britt.black@wheaton.edu

BLACK, Chesley .... 980-598-1050 .... 365 I
chesley.black@jwu.edu

BLACK, Christopher, B .... 260-422-5561 .... 173 C
cbblack@indianatech.edu

BLACK, David, R .... 610-341-5890 .... 438 D
dblack@eastern.edu

BLACK, David, R .... 610-341-5890 .... 428 E
drblack@eastern.edu

BLACK, Dennis, R .... 716-645-2982 .... 351 G
dblack@buffalo.edu

BLACK, Diane .... 251-442-2209 .... 9 A
dblack@umobile.edu

BLACK, Dorothy .... 731-352-4000 .... 467 E
blackd@bethelu.edu

BLACK, Eliza, E .... 803-934-3264 .... 459 G
eblack@morris.edu

BLACK, Ellen .... 843-349-5211 .... 458 H
ellen.black@hgtc.edu

BLACK, Heather .... 412-365-1281 .... 425 C
hblack@chatham.edu

BLACK, James .... 802-635-1298 .... 515 F
james.black@jsc.edu

BLACK, Jane .... 740-695-9500 .... 385 B
jblack@belmontcollege.edu

BLACK, Jason .... 205-726-3673 .... 6 G
jjblack@samford.edu

BLACK, Jeff .... 410-972-3303 .... 225 G
jeffrey.black@sjca.edu

BLACK, Jerry, D .... 937-775-2411 .... 406 C
jerry.black@wright.edu

BLACK, John .... 478-471-2712 .... 133 H
john.black@maconstate.edu

BLACK, John Paul .... 252-527-6223 .... 371 G
jblack@lenoircc.edu

BLACK, Joshua .... 423-614-8370 .... 470 C
jblack@leeuniversity.edu

BLACK, Joshua .... 864-941-8540 .... 460 D
black.j@ptc.edu

BLACK, Kedric .... 801-863-8536 .... 511 F
kedric.black@uvu.edu

BLACK, Laurie .... 802-258-3273 .... 514 E
laurie.black@worldlearning.org

BLACK, Lendley, C .... 218-726-7106 .... 271 F
chan@d.umn.edu

BLACK, Linda .... 970-351-1638 .... 89 B
linda.black@unco.edu

BLACK, Lynda, K .... 336-838-6148 .... 375 C
lynda.black@wilkescc.edu

BLACK, Lynn, C .... 308-398-7400 .... 297 A
lblack@cccneb.edu

BLACK, Mark .... 615-966-5709 .... 470 F
mark.black@lipscomb.edu

BLACK, Maryann .... 919-668-3792 .... 364 C
maryann.black@duke.edu

BLACK, Michael .... 404-894-2486 .... 130 F
mike.black@housing.gatech.edu

BLACK, Michael .... 805-922-6966 .... 26 L
mblack@pcpa.org

BLACK, Michael, E .... 210-567-7103 .... 507 A
blackm@uthscsa.edu

BLACK, Nanette .... 801-274-3280 .... 512 F
nanette.black@wgu.edu

BLACK, Rochelle, A .... 248-370-3682 .... 256 G
black@oakland.edu

BLACK, Rose Ann .... 718-779-1430 .... 346 B
rblack@plazacollege.edu

BLACK, Shaun, C .... 315-445-4569 .... 338 B
blacksc@lemoyne.edu

BLACK, Sul .... 803-705-4334 .... 455 D
blacks@benedict.edu

BLACK, Tanja .... 864-429-8728 .... 463 A
trblack@mailbox.sc.edu

BLACK, Thomas .... 650-723-1550 .... 71 G
thomas.black@stanford.edu

BLACK, Timothy, R .... 541-346-5023 .... 419 B
timblack@uoregon.edu

BLACK, Wilhemena .... 305-284-3064 .... 122 I
wblack@miami.edu

BLACK, William, N .... 215-204-4760 .... 447 H
william.black@temple.edu

BLACK-ARIAS, Maxinee .... 404-237-7573 .... 126 B
mblackarias@bauder.edu

BLACK CONE, Anne .... 802-223-6324 .... 514 B
anne.blackcone@neci.edu

BLACK-GOLD, Tonia .... 704-637-4393 .... 363 E
tblackgo@catawba.edu

BLACKABY, Leslie .... 509-574-6806 .... 540 D
lblackaby@yvcc.edu

BLACKBOURN, Richard, L .... 662-325-3717 .... 275 F
rlb277@msstate.edu

BLACKBURN, Alison, A .... 617-627-6272 .... 245 C
alison.blackburn@tufts.edu

BLACKBURN, Cheryl .... 425-388-9572 .... 534 C
cblackburn@everettcc.edu

BLACKBURN, David .... 716-286-8405 .... 344 D
deb@niagara.edu

BLACKBURN, J. Blair .... 214-333-5122 .... 484 D
blair@dbu.edu

BLACKBURN, James .... 315-279-5215 .... 337 K
jblackbu@mail.keuka.edu

BLACKBURN, John, D .... 217-732-3155 .... 156 I
jblackburn@lincolncollege.edu

BLACKBURN, Judith, S .... 410-706-2949 .... 227 C
jblackburn@umaryland.edu

BLACKBURN, Kristi, V .... 310-233-4044 .... 54 I
blackbkv@lahc.edu

BLACKBURN, Steven .... 860-509-9560 .... 93 A
sblackburn@hartsem.edu

BLACKBURN, Terri .... 208-467-8673 .... 144 E
tblackburn@nnu.edu

BLACKBURN-SMITH, Jefferson .... 614-823-1031 .... 400 H
jblackburnsmith@otterbein.edu

BLACKER, James .... 540-374-4310 .... 99 G
james.blacker@strayer.edu

BLACKHURST, Anne, E .... 218-477-2415 .... 267 F
blackhurst@mnstate.edu

BLACKKETTER, Donald, M .... 406-496-4129 .... 296 B
dblack@mtech.edu

BLACKLAW, Stuart .... 734-973-3488 .... 259 F
sblacklaw@wccnet.edu

BLACKMAN, Don .... 954-446-6192 .... 100 I
dblackman@aiufl.edu

BLACKMAN, Ronda .... 828-277-5521 .... 376 H
rblackman@southcollegenc.edu

BLACKMAN, Sharon, L .... 214-378-1748 .... 484 F
sblackman@dcccd.edu

BLACKMON, Bruce .... 910-410-1723 .... 373 B
bblackmon@richmondcc.edu

BLACKMON, Chianti .... 301-447-6932 .... 225 A
blackmon@msmary.edu

BLACKMON, Luke .... 843-863-8004 .... 456 B
lblackmon@csuniv.edu

BLACKMON, Mark .... 765-983-1416 .... 171 E
blackma@earlham.edu

BLACKMON, Terry, W .... 731-426-7601 .... 470 B
tblackmon@lanecollege.edu

BLACKMON, Velma, B .... 252-335-3294 .... 377 F
vbblackmon@mail.ecsu.edu

BLACKNEY, Kenneth .... 215-895-1505 .... 427 H
ksb@drexel.edu

BLACKSHEAR, Jim .... 505-863-7639 .... 321 D
jblackshear@gallup.unm.edu

BLACKSHEAR, Regina .... 314-340-3502 .... 282 F
blackshear@hssu.edu

BLACKSHIRE-BELAY, Carol, A .... 303-546-3588 .... 86 H
cblackshire-belay@naropa.edu

BLACKSMITH, Lourdes .... 630-466-7900 .... 168 B
lblacksmith@waubonsee.edu

BLACKSMITH, Robin .... 206-546-4503 .... 538 C
rblacksmith@shoreline.edu

BLACKSTAD, Ana .... 425-352-8359 .... 532 B
ablackstad@cascadia.edu

BLACKSTON, Barbara .... 931-221-6163 .... 473 E
blackstonb@apsu.edu

BLACKSTON, Michael .... 559-438-4222 .... 49 I
michael_blackston@heald.edu

BLACKSTONE, Tondelaya .... 410-951-4265 .... 228 B
tblackstone@coppin.edu

BLACKWELDER, Mary, B .... 414-955-8323 .... 548 G
blackwel@mcw.edu

BLACKWELDER, Tom .... 509-527-2113 .... 539 C
tom.blackwelder@wallawalla.edu

BLACKWELL, Amy .... 864-294-3496 .... 458 E
amy.blackwell@furman.edu

BLACKWELL, Ann .... 601-266-4568 .... 277 F
ann.blackwell@usm.edu

BLACKWELL, Billie Jo .... 908-852-1400 .... 308 E
blackwellb@centenarycollege.edu

BLACKWELL, Courtney .... 212-799-5000 .... 337 H

BLACKWELL, David .... 870-584-4471 .... 25 C
dblackwell@cccua.edu

BLACKWELL, David .... 859-257-8939 .... 207 D
dblackwell@uky.edu

BLACKWELL, Deborah .... 704-355-5970 .... 363 D
debbie.blackwell@carolinascollege.edu

BLACKWELL, Erik .... 757-499-7900 .... 517 D
emblackwell@bryantstratton.edu

BLACKWELL, Jeannine .... 859-257-3629 .... 207 D
jblack@uky.edu

BLACKWELL, Joyce .... 336-517-2154 .... 362 G
jblackwell@bennett.edu

BLACKWELL, Mary, D .... 623-845-3305 .... 15 H
m.blackwell@gcmail.maricopa.edu

BLACKWELL, Melanie .... 760-948-1947 .... 66 I
melanie.blackwell@sjvc.edu

BLACKWELL, Michael .... 803-754-4100 .... 457 D

BLACKWELL, Samuel .... 803-780-1239 .... 463 C
blackwell@voorhees.edu

BLACKWELL, Scott .... 601-266-4783 .... 277 F
edward.blackwell@usm.edu

BLACKWOOD, Clay .... 425-640-1233 .... 533 I
clay.blackwood@edcc.edu

BLACKWOOD, James .... 706-880-8050 .... 133 B
jblackwood@lagrange.edu

BLACKWOOD, Jothany, L .... 559-442-4600 .... 72 B
jothany.blackwood@fresnocitycollege.edu

BLACKWOOD, Kathy .... 650-358-6790 .... 67 E
blackwoodk@smccd.edu

BLACKWOOD, Phyllis .... 254-299-8659 .... 490 G
pblackwood@mclennan.edu

BLACKWOOD, Rodney, B .... 806-720-7402 .... 490 F
rod.blackwood@lcu.edu

BLADE, Michelle .... 415-749-4523 .... 65 I
mblade@sfai.edu

BLADES, Dawn .... 845-257-3171 .... 352 B
bladesd@newpaltz.edu

BLAES, Ziuta .... 337-521-8896 .... 211 J
ziuta.blaes@southlouisiana.edu

BLAESING, Ron .... 334-244-3758 .... 1 G
rblaesin@aum.edu

BLAGDAN, Donna .... 760-872-2000 .... 43 K
dblagdan@deepsprings.edu

BLAGG, Oneida .... 978-934-3565 .... 237 B
oneida_blagg@uml.edu

BLAGG, Rosalyn, R .... 870-508-6128 .... 20 E
rblagg@asumh.edu

BLAGUSZEWSKI, Edward, F .... 413-545-0444 .... 236 F
edblag@admin.umass.edu

BLAHA, Heather .... 216-916-7497 .... 394 B
hblaha@kent.edu

BLAHNIK, Brent .... 920-465-2190 .... 551 B
blahnikb@uwgb.edu

BLAHNIK, Jeff .... 262-472-1440 .... 553 A
blahnikj@uww.edu

BLAHNIK, Sheryl .... 217-875-7200 .... 162 F
sblahnik@richland.edu

BLAICH, Charles, F .... 765-361-6311 .... 181 E
blaichc@wabash.edu

BLAIFEDER, Mark .... 212-217-4020 .... 333 F
mark_blaifeder@fitnyc.edu

BLAIN, Judy .... 931-221-7691 .... 473 E
blainj@apsu.edu

BLAINE, Louise .... 641-673-1038 .... 190 C
blainel@wmpenn.edu

BLAINE-WALLACE, William .... 207-786-8272 .... 217 C
wblainew@bates.edu

BLAIR, Andrew, R .... 412-624-5749 .... 449 A
blair@pitt.edu

BLAIR, Anothony, L .... 717-866-5775 .... 429 A
ablair@evangelical.edu

BLAIR, Brian .... 202-885-2842 .... 97 D
bblair@american.edu

BLAIR, Christine .... 903-693-2075 .... 492 C
cblair@panola.edu

BLAIR, Cinnamon .... 505-277-1806 .... 321 C
cblair@salud.unm.edu

BLAIR, David, A .... 512-428-1286 .... 493 E
davidab@stedwards.edu

BLAIR, Jean .... 845-938-3615 .... 559 A
jean.blair@usma.edu

BLAIR, Jeff .... 614-251-4735 .... 398 F
blairj@ohiodominican.edu

BLAIR, John, P .... 270-745-6520 .... 208 A
jp.blair@wku.edu

BLAIR, Kimberly, P .... 540-365-4211 .... 519 C
kblair@ferrum.edu

BLAIR, Larry .... 415-749-4560 .... 65 I
lblair@sfai.edu

BLAIR, Linda .... 502-447-1000 .... 206 F
lblair@spencerian.edu

BLAIR, Marilou, C .... 716-851-1411 .... 333 B
blair@ecc.edu

BLAIR, Maureen .... 309-438-8611 .... 153 D
meblair@ilstu.edu

BLAIR, Michael, R .... 563-387-1040 .... 187 D
blairmic@luther.edu

BLAIR, Natalie .... 785-826-2642 .... 194 E
nblair@sal.ksu.edu

BLAIR, Ray .... 413-755-4868 .... 241 B
rblair@stcc.edu

BLAIR, Rob, M .... 806-894-9611 .... 494 G
rblair@southplainscollege.edu

BLAIR, Sylvia .... 410-386-8411 .... 221 G
sblair@carrollcc.edu

BLAIR, Thomas .... 770-216-2960 .... 132 F
tblair@ict-ils.edu

BLAIR, Thomas, S .... 540-375-2235 .... 523 G
blair@roanoke.edu

BLAIR, Timothy, V .... 610-436-2739 .... 444 A
tblair@wcupa.edu

BLAIR, Wendell .... 312-553-5662 .... 147 C
wblair@ccc.edu

BLAIR, Wray .... 301-687-4201 .... 228 C
wnblair@frotburg.edu

BLAIS, Edward, J .... 207-778-7033 .... 220 C
edward.blais@maine.edu

BLAIS, Roger, N .... 918-631-2554 .... 413 F
roger-blais@utulsa.edu

BLAISDELL, Kathryn .... 413-538-2291 .... 242 D
kblaisde@mtholyoke.edu

BLAISING, Craig, A .... 817-923-1921 .... 495 G
cblaising@swbts.edu

BLAKE, Alan .... 603-271-8904 .... 304 F
ablake@ccsnh.edu

BLAKE, Ben .... 860-465-5283 .... 90 H
blakeb@easternct.edu

BLAKE, Ben .... 740-392-6868 .... 396 I
ben.blake@mvnu.edu

BLAKE, Charles, E .... 901-322-0120 .... 466 G

BLAKE, Christopher R, L .... 319-368-6464 .... 187 H
cblake@mtmercy.edu

BLAKE, Darcy .... 650-543-3901 .... 57 B
dblake@menlo.edu

BLAKE, David, M .... 619-260-4594 .... 76 D
dblake@sandiego.edu

BLAKE, Diane, T .... 518-388-6104 .... 358 G
blaked@union.edu

BLAKE, Ira .... 570-389-4308 .... 441 F
iblake@bloomu.edu

BLAKE, James, E .... 203-392-5457 .... 90 I
blakej2@southernct.edu

BLAKE, John .... 907-474-5188 .... 10 I
jeblake@alaska.edu

BLAKE, Joi .... 650-738-4333 .... 67 H
blakej@smccd.edu

BLAKE, Karen .... 203-575-8269 .... 92 A
kblake@nvcc.commnet.edu

BLAKE, Katherine, H .... 781-891-2074 .... 231 D
kblake@bentley.edu

BLAKE, Larry .... 859-572-1907 .... 205 H
blakel1@nku.edu

BLAKE, Lisa .... 309-341-5282 .... 146 D
lblake@sandburg.edu

BLAKE, Lori .... 325-670-5896 .... 487 F
lblake@hsutx.edu

BLAKE, M. Brian .... 305-284-2211 .... 122 I

BLAKE, Paul .... 231-591-3030 .... 250 H
blakep@ferris.edu

BLAKE, Peg .... 707-826-3361 .... 36 E
plb91@humboldt.edu

BLAKE, Richard, D .... 214-841-3767 .... 485 F
rblake@dts.edu

BLAKE, Robert, C .... 202-994-6870 .... 98 C
rblake@gwu.edu

BLAKE, Scott .... 906-487-7242 .... 251 A
scott.blake@finlandia.edu

BLAKE, Susan, N .... 770-499-3576 .... 133 A
sblake@kennesaw.edu

BLAKE, Sylvia .... 914-831-2704 .... 339 C
sylvia.blake@liu.edu

BLAKE, Sylvia .... 914-831-2704 .... 339 D
sylvia.blake@liu.edu

BLAKE, William, J .... 330-941-2086 .... 406 F
wjblake@ysu.edu

BLAKEFIELD, Mary .... 765-973-8522 .... 173 F
mblakefie@iue.edu

BLAKELEY, Jane .... 575-562-2425 .... 318 B
jane.blakeley@enmu.edu

BLAKELEY, Mary Ann .... 440-525-7119 .... 394 F
mblakeley@lakelandcc.edu

BLAKELY, Craig, H .... 979-862-4445 .... 497 B
blakely@srph.tamhsc.edu

BLAKELY, Curtis .... 765-966-2656 .... 176 H
cblakely@ivytech.edu

BLAKELY, Dee .... 618-634-3247 .... 164 E
deeb@shawneecc.edu

BLAKELY, Edie .... 360-992-2239 .... 532 F
eblakely@clark.edu

BLAKELY, Robert .... 205-226-4918 .... 2 B
rblakely@bsc.edu

BLAKELY, Zeledith .... 252-638-1587 .... 370 A
blakelyz@cravencc.edu

BLAKEMORE, Donna .... 415-338-1042 .... 37 B
donnab@sfsu.edu

BLAKEMORE, Jerry, D .... 815-753-1000 .... 160 B

BLAKEMORE, Patricia .... 401-739-5000 .... 453 G
pblakemore@neit.edu

BLAKENEY, Erin .... 425-352-8307 .... 532 B
eblakeney@cascadia.edu

BLAKENEY, Sara .... 704-337-2536 .... 376 A
blakeneys@queens.edu

BLAKESLEE, Jim .... 920-929-2114 .... 554 G
jblakeslee@morainepark.edu

BLAKEY, Linda, S .... 734-973-3536 .... 259 F
blakey@wccnet.edu

BLAKLEY, Jackie .... 864-646-1305 .... 461 F
jblakle1@tctc.edu

BLAKLEY, Ramon .... 361-593-2315 .... 498 D
ramon.blakley@tamuk.edu

BLAKNEY, Rob .... 972-825-4643 .... 495 F
rblakney@sagu.edu

BLALOCK, Glenn .... 225-768-1754 .... 214 C
glenn.blalock@ololcollege.edu

BLALOCK, Rebecca .... 256-533-8434 .... 3 C
rebecca.blalock@vc.edu

BLALOCK, Rebecca .... 561-304-3466 .... 468 J

BLALOCK, Reed .... 318-767-2603 .... 212 I
rblalock@lsua.edu

BLALOCK, Tim 270-247-8521 204 G
tblalock@midcontinent.edu
BLALOCK, III, W. Ben 307-766-3948 556 H
bblalock@uwyo.edu
BLANCEAGLE, Glory, A 203-576-4506 94 F
gblancea@bridgeport.edu
BLANCHARD, Andrew 972-883-2273 506 A
ablanch@utdallas.edu
BLANCHARD, Barbara 619-644-7104 49 C
barbara.blanchard@gcccd.edu
BLANCHARD, Donald 212-431-2836 343 E
dblanchard@nyls.edu
BLANCHARD, Gina, A 740-392-6868 396 I
gina.blanchard@mvnu.edu
BLANCHARD, Gordon 847-578-3232 163 C
gordon.blanchard@rosalindfranklin.edu
BLANCHARD, John 907-796-6340 11 A
john.blanchard@uas.alaska.edu
BLANCHARD, John 212-749-2802 339 I
jblanchard@msmnyc.edu
BLANCHARD, Jon 207-893-6604 219 F
jblanchard@sjcme.edu
BLANCHARD, Joyce 207-621-3403 220 B
joyceb@maine.edu
BLANCHARD, Joyce 207-621-3191 220 B
joyceb@maine.edu
BLANCHARD, Kendall, A 229-928-1360 131 F
kendall.blanchard@gsw.edu
BLANCHARD, Loren 504-520-7525 217 A
lblancha@xula.edu
BLANCHARD, Marsha, L 573-888-0513 289 K
mblanchard@semo.edu
BLANCHARD, Myrtho 202-274-5946 100 A
mblanchard@udc.edu
BLANCHARD, Nicholas, R 410-651-3777 227 E
nrblanchard@umes.edu
BLANCHARD, Scott 802-322-1640 513 E
scott.blanchard@goddard.edu
BLANCHARD, Teri, L 740-427-5181 394 C
blanchard@kenyon.edu
BLANCHETT, Wanda, J 816-235-2231 291 C
blanchettw@umkc.edu
BLANCHETTE, David, M 401-456-8009 454 A
dblanchette@ric.edu
BLANCHETTE, Diane, F 401-341-2135 454 D
blanched@salve.edu
BLANCHETTE, Nick 715-675-3331 555 B
blanchet@ntc.edu
BLANCO, Julio 661-654-3450 34 A
jblanco@csub.edu
BLANCO, Mark, E 914-337-9300 330 G
mark.blanco@concordia-ny.edu
BLAND, Byron 650-433-3814 61 B
bbland@paloaltou.edu
BLAND, Constance 662-254-3421 276 B
cgbland@mvsu.edu
BLAND, Earl 913-971-3617 195 D
ebland@mnu.edu
BLAND, Glenda 256-378-2004 2 E
gbland@cacc.edu
BLAND, James 937-393-3431 402 A
jbland@sscc.edu
BLAND, John, D 704-687-5822 379 A
jdbland@uncc.edu
BLAND, Terry 662-562-3271 276 D
tbland@northwestms.edu
BLANDA, Diane, M 401-874-2024 454 E
dblanda@advance.uri.edu
BLANDFORD, David, K 989-463-7147 247 B
blandford@alma.edu
BLANDING, Bruce 731-424-3520 475 C
bblanding@jscc.edu
BLANDON, Darwin 423-493-4328 476 E
helpdesk@tntemple.edu
BLANEY, Tari 614-287-5021 389 A
tblaney@cscc.edu
BLANK, Bonnie 415-451-2819 66 B
bblank@sfts.edu
BLANK, Brian, B 414-410-4079 546 G
bbblank@stritch.edu
BLANK, Dave, L 336-278-6705 364 D
dblank@elon.edu
BLANK, Karen, J 212-854-2024 323 E
kblank@barnard.edu
BLANK, Kenneth, J 215-204-6875 447 H
kenneth.blank@temple.edu
BLANK DOUCETTE,
Margot 858-566-1200 44 B
m.blank@disd.edu
BLANKE, Raymond 405-733-7306 411 I
rblanke@rose.edu
BLANKEMEIER, David 254-298-8291 496 D
david.blankemeier@templejc.edu
BLANKENBAKER, Zarina 972-238-6025 485 D
zblankenbaker@dcccd.edu
BLANKENBEUHLER, Carla 304-204-4093 542 J
cblankenbeuhler@kvctc.edu
BLANKENHORN, Stacie 503-359-1082 419 E
bookstore@pacificu.edu
BLANKENSHIP, Anne 850-644-0170 119 D
ablankenship@fsu.edu
BLANKENSHIP, Barbara 601-857-3232 274 C
bsblankenship@hindscc.edu
BLANKENSHIP, Betsy 740-389-6786 399 D
blankenship.5@osu.edu
BLANKENSHIP, Bruce, A 304-457-6220 540 E
blankenshipba@ab.edu
BLANKENSHIP, Bryan 859-858-2228 198 D
BLANKENSHIP, Candice 870-762-3137 20 A
cblankenship@smail.anc.edu
BLANKENSHIP, Casey 804-862-6161 523 F
cblankenship@rbc.edu
BLANKENSHIP, Daniel, J 219-866-6154 179 D
djb@saintjoe.edu
BLANKENSHIP, Donna 937-512-2907 401 J
donna.blankenship@sinclair.edu
BLANKENSHIP, Eugene 918-781-7220 407 B
blankenshipe@bacone.edu
BLANKENSHIP, Karen 281-476-1850 493 H
karen.blankenship@sjcd.edu
BLANKENSHIP, Lise 956-665-2529 506 C
blankenship@utpa.edu
BLANKENSHIP, Mark 859-252-0361 204 B
mblankenship@lextheo.edu
BLANKENSHIP, Mary, R 276-326-4556 516 L
rblankenship@bluefield.edu
BLANKENSHIP, Mike 601-856-5400 274 D
mblankenship@holmescc.edu
BLANKENSHIP, Tim 404-471-5465 123 I
tblankenship@agnesscott.edu
BLANKENSHIP, Vince 903-923-2002 486 F
vblankenship@etbu.edu
BLANKENSTEIN, Beth 603-271-1754 304 F
bblankenstein@ccsnh.edu
BLANKINSHIP, Blair 410-837-5714 229 A
bblankinship@ubalt.edu
BLANKMEYER, Bonnie, L 210-567-2691 507 A
blankmeyer@uthscsa.edu
BLANKS, Janet 561-297-2230 119 A
blanks@ccs.fau.edu
BLANSETT, Dewey 662-329-7396 276 A
dblansett@oe.muw.edu
BLANSETT, H. Wayne 662-846-4150 273 H
wblanset@deltastate.edu
BLANTON, Amanda 864-646-1501 461 F
ablanton@tctc.edu
BLANTON, Buffy 270-444-9676 200 G
bblanton@daymarcollege.edu
BLANTON, Carmen 910-755-7332 368 F
blantonc@brunswickcc.edu
BLANTON, Jason 606-783-9361 204 I
j.blanton@moreheadstate.edu
BLANTON, Jay 859-257-6605 207 D
jay.blanton@uky.edu
BLANTON, Libby 434-736-2044 528 D
libby.blanton@southside.edu
BLANTON, Ryan 918-463-2931 407 H
ryan.blanton@connorsstate.edu
BLANTON, Shannon 901-678-5044 474 C
sblanton@memphis.edu
BLANTON, Sharon 503-725-6246 418 G
sblanton@pdx.edu
BLANTON, Wynn 614-882-2551 390 L
BLAPPERT, Gerald 985-732-6640 211 A
BLASE, Kristen 603-428-2226 305 D
kblase@nec.edu
BLASHAK, Ted 248-675-3800 247 F
BLASIG, Jerry, A 402-557-7075 296 H
jerry.blasig@bellevue.edu
BLASINGAME, David, T 314-935-5850 292 I
david_blasingame@wustl.edu
BLASS, Tammy 323-226-6511 55 G
tblass@dhs.lacounty.gov
BLASSINGAME, Susan 806-720-7602 490 F
susan.blassingame@lcu.edu
BLATCHLEY, Richard, L 651-631-5321 270 B
rlblatchley@nwc.edu
BLATHERWICK, Steve 856-227-7200 308 D
sblatherwick@camdencc.edu
BLATTNER, Nancy 973-618-3217 308 C
nblattner@caldwell.edu
BLAU, Kathy 620-276-9598 193 C
kathy.blau@gcccks.edu
BLAU, Phil 740-351-3137 401 I
pblau@shawnee.edu
BLAUSTEIN, Marilyn, H 413-545-0941 236 F
blaustein@oirp.umass.edu
BLAUWKAMP, Christi 760-366-3791 43 H
cblauwkamp@cmccd.edu
BLAYLOCK, Benny 318-342-1600 216 E
blaylock@ulm.edu
BLAYLOCK, John, V 402-844-7292 299 I
johnb@northeast.edu
BLAYLOCK, Vicki 601-635-2111 274 A
vblaylock
BLAZE, Douglas 865-974-2521 477 D
blaze@utk.edu
BLAZEJOWSKI, Carol, A 973-655-3031 311 F
blazejowskic@mail.montclair.edu
BLAZIS, Enoch 507-786-3002 271 C
blazis@stolaf.edu
BLEDSOE, Chad 828-448-6048 375 B
cbledsoe@wpcc.edu
BLEDSOE, Christopher 212-998-2040 344 B
christopher.bledsoe@nyu.edu
BLEDSOE, Kelly 478-757-5140 139 E
kbledsoe@wesleyancollege.edu
BLEDSOE, Lisa 971-722-5852 419 G
lbledsoe@pcc.edu
BLEDSOE, Martin 231-591-5000 250 H
bledsoem@ferris.edu
BLEDSOE, Mary, C 865-694-6415 475 G
mcbledsoe@pstcc.edu
BLEDSOE, W. Craig 615-966-1789 470 F
craig.bledsoe@lipscomb.edu
BLEEKE, Fred 314-505-7257 280 D
bleekef@csl.edu
BLEEKER, Joshua, J 214-841-3653 485 F
jbleeker@dts.edu
BLEEKER, Justin 866-323-0233 63 D
BLEICHER, Joe 860-253-3050 91 B
jbleicher@asnuntuck.edu
BLEICKEN, Linda, M 912-344-2535 124 G
linda.bleicken@armstrong.edu
BLEIFIELD, Elaina 763-424-0868 268 B
ebleifield@nhcc.edu
BLENIS, Brian, G 610-861-1344 437 A
bblenis@moravian.edu
BLETHYN, Teresa, P 540-375-2308 523 G
blethyn@roanoke.edu
BLEVINS, Anita, F 423-478-7021 472 H
ablevins@ptseminary.edu
BLEVINS, Cecilia 419-627-8345 398 B
cblevins@ohiobusinesscollege.edu
BLEVINS, Elizabeth 740-351-3112 401 I
eblevins@shawnee.edu
BLEVINS, Emmett 606-326-2027 201 F
emmett.blevins@kctcs.edu
BLEVINS, Karen, J 606-326-2063 201 F
karen.blevins@kctcs.edu
BLEVINS, Lori 336-249-8186 370 B
lblevins@davidsonccc.edu
BLEVINS, Melissa 877-442-0505 89 C
melissa.blevins@rockies.edu
BLEVINS, Robert 601-318-6155 278 C
robert.blevins@wmcarey.edu
BLEVINS, Ryan 219-464-5413 181 C
ryan.blevins@valpo.edu
BLEVINS, Sandra, J 865-573-4517 469 L
sblevins@johnsonu.edu
BLEW, Denise, M 610-758-3179 434 E
dmb3@lehigh.edu
BLEWETT, John 505-224-4138 317 K
jblewett@cnm.edu
BLEY, Maya 973-290-4223 308 G
mbley@cse.edu
BLEY-VROMAN, Robert 808-956-8516 141 G
vroman@hawaii.edu
BLEYMAIER, Gene 408-924-1200 37 C
gene.bleymaier@sjsu.edu
BLEZIEN, Paul 916-577-2200 79 G
pblezien@jessup.edu
BLICE, Taylor, G 412-578-8712 424 I
blicetg@carlow.edu
BLICHARZ, Marcia 609-771-2848 308 F
blicharz@tcnj.edu
BLIESE, James, D 715-675-3331 555 B
bliese@ntc.edu
BLIESE, Richard 651-641-3211 264 H
rbliese@luthersem.edu
BLIFFEN, John 901-375-4400 471 G
johnbliffen@midsouthcc.org
BLIGEN, Erica 615-525-2813 467 B
ebligen@argosy.edu
BLIGH, Kate 206-878-3710 535 B
kbligh@highline.edu
BLILEY, Sean 814-732-1304 442 E
sbliley@edinboro.edu
BLINKA, Sonja 409-933-8474 483 F
sblinka@com.edu
BLINN, Robert 618-545-3244 155 B
rblinn@kaskaskia.edu
BLISS, Chris 415-703-9545 32 C
cbliss@cca.edu
BLISS, Emily, J 910-962-1112 379 D
blisse@uncw.edu
BLISS, Frances 413-265-2314 233 D
blissf@elms.edu
BLISS, Lawrence 510-885-2139 34 E
lawrence.bliss@csueastbay.edu
BLISS, Lucia 315-866-0300 335 D
blisslm@herkimer.edu
BLISS, Michael, B 808-675-3705 140 D
blissm@byuh.edu
BLISS, Patricia, J 315-445-4141 338 B
blisspj@lemoyne.edu
BLISS, Robert, M 314-516-6874 291 D
rmbliss@umsl.edu
BLISS, Steve 912-525-5167 136 F
sbliss@scad.edu
BLISS-FURR, Carol 617-541-5394 241 A
cbliss@rcc.mass.edu
BLISSERT, Julie, H 315-312-2265 354 A
julie.blissert@oswego.edu
BLITT, William, J 972-377-1730 483 H
bblitt@collin.edu
BLITZ, Phebe 480-461-7000 15 I
phebe.blitz@mesacc.edu
BLITZ, Y 248-968-3360 260 E
BLITZER, Donna, M 831-459-3983 75 C
dblitzer@ucsc.edu
BLIVEN, Gail 651-690-6845 270 L
gnbliven@stkate.edu
BLIZZARD, Mary 304-558-4614 542 H
mblizzard@wvctcs.org
BLOCH, Bobbie 304-326-1358 541 K
bbloch@salemu.edu
BLOCK, Derryl 815-753-6155 160 B
dblock@niu.edu
BLOCK, Gene, D 310-825-2151 74 C
chancellor@conet.ucla.edu
BLOCK, Jayme, E 410-543-6156 228 D
jeblock@salisbury.edu
BLOCK, Jeff 406-447-6958 295 A
jeff.block@umhelena.edu
BLOCK, Ken, W 419-772-2036 398 H
k-block@onu.edu
BLOCK, Murray 518-608-8336 333 E
mblock@excelsior.edu
BLOCK, Peggy 270-534-3464 203 E
peggy.block@kctcs.edu
BLOCK, Regina, M 815-740-5047 167 E
rblock@stfrancis.edu
BLOCKER, Bill 832-252-4604 483 C
bill.blocker@cbshouston.edu
BLOCKER, Peggy, J 303-765-3114 85 D
pblocker@iliff.edu
BLOCKER, Robert, L 203-432-4160 96 A
robert.blocker@yale.edu
BLOCKSIDGE, Charles 412-237-4476 425 H
cblocksidge@ccac.edu
BLODGETT, Bruce, M 315-255-1743 325 G
blodgett@cayuga-cc.edu
BLODGETT, Martha Lee 850-474-2712 121 D
mblodget@uwf.edu
BLODGETT, Patricia, A 603-358-2280 306 G
pblodget@keene.edu
BLODGETT, Steve 507-786-3316 271 C
blodgett@stolaf.edu
BLOECHLE, Michael 217-206-7757 167 C
bloechle.michael@uis.edu
BLOEM, Russell, J 616-526-6651 249 A
rjb42@calvin.edu
BLOEMENDAAL, Mark, R 712-707-7127 188 D
markb@nwciowa.edu
BLOEMENDAAL-GRUETT,
Joan 320-629-5116 268 E
gruettj@pinetech.edu
BLOEMKER, Geraldine, A 610-499-4107 451 F
gabloemker@widener.edu
BLOHM, Jason 402-941-6435 298 I
blohm@midlandu.edu
BLOHM, John, I 804-828-2343 526 B
jiblohm@vcu.edu
BLOHOWIAK, Shelly 847-578-8355 163 C
shelly.blohowiak@rosalindfranklin.edu
BLOK, Tamara, L 818-767-0888 79 H
tamara.blok@woodbury.edu
BLOMBERG, Thomas 850-644-7365 119 D
tgblomberg@aol.com
BLOME, Christian 812-888-4313 181 D
cblome@vinu.edu
BLOMENKAMP, Jean 402-375-7389 299 G
jeblome1@wsc.edu
BLOMGREN, Richard 828-298-3325 380 D
rickb@warren-wilson.edu
BLOMQUIST, Eric 212-817-7150 327 B
eblomquist@gc.cuny.edu
BLOMQUIST, Mickel 801-818-8900 510 I
mikelb@provocollege.edu
BLOMQUIST, William, A 317-274-3976 174 D
blomquis@iupui.edu
BLONDE, Mitchell, P 517-264-7146 258 B
mblonde@sienaheights.edu
BLONDIN, Mark 401-739-5000 453 G
mblondin@neit.edu
BLONDIN, Monica, M 508-831-5469 246 F
mmlucey@wpi.edu
BLONIARZ, Peter 518-956-8240 351 E
pbloniarz@uamail.albany.edu
BLOOD, Janet 207-974-4606 218 H
jblood@emcc.edu
BLOOD, Rick 802-241-2520 515 C
rick.blood@vsc.edu
BLOODGOOD, Jane 785-587-2800 195 A
janebloodgood@matc.net
BLOOM, Bill 505-925-8595 321 G
wbloom@unm.edu
BLOOM, Joel 973-596-3102 312 C
joel.s.bloom@njit.edu
BLOOM, John, S 214-841-3590 485 F
jbloom@dts.edu
BLOOM, Richard 928-777-3837 14 C
richard.bloom@erau.edu
BLOOM, Steven 617-243-2440 236 A
sbloom@lasell.edu
BLOOM, Sue Ann 814-827-4472 450 A
sbloom@pitt.edu
BLOOM, Vicki 574-520-4448 174 E
vdbloom@iusb.edu
BLOOMBERG, Sandra 201-200-3321 312 B
sbloomberg@njcu.edu
BLOOMBERG, Steven 405-682-7814 409 F
smbloomberg@occc.edu
BLOOMER, Dennis, L 864-488-4561 459 B
dbloomer@limestone.edu
BLOOMFIELD, Stewart 212-938-5540 355 B
sbloomfield@sunyopt.edu

BLOOMFIELD, Susan, R .... 919-866-5452 .... 374 H srbloomfield@waketech.edu
BLOOMFIELD-MARTINEZ, Amber .... 913-621-8733 .... 192 F amber@donnelly.edu
BLOOMINGDALE, Mary, E 641-422-4351 .... 188 A bloommar@niacc.edu
BLOSS, Kim, K .... 870-235-4055 .... 23 I kkbloss@saumag.edu
BLOSSER, Joseph, D .... 336-841-9000 .... 365 C jblosser@highpoint.edu
BLOSSER, Kim .... 540-868-7111 .... 527 C kblosser@lfcc.edu
BLOSSOM, Dudley .... 212-752-1530 .... 338 C dudley.blossom@limcollege.edu
BLOUIN, Robert, A .... 919-966-1122 .... 378 E bob_blouin@unc.edu
BLOUNT, Brian, K .... 804-355-0671 .... 525 A bblount@upsem.edu
BLOUNT, Cameron .... 662-562-3354 .... 276 D cblount@northwestms.edu
BLOUNT, Joanna .... 574-936-8898 .... 169 D joanna.blount@ancilla.edu
BLOUNT, Nicole .... 404-880-8710 .... 127 C nblount@cau.edu
BLOUNT, Rhonda .... 912-449-7531 .... 139 D rblount@waycross.edu
BLOUNT, Sally, E .... 847-491-2840 .... 160 E sallyblount@kellogg.northwestern.edu
BLOW, Felicia .... 757-569-6791 .... 528 A fblow@pdc.edu
BLOW, Trevor .... 954-783-7339 .... 106 J tblow@cci.edu
BLOWERS, Kelsy .... 218-683-8543 .... 268 C kelsy.blowers@northlandcollege.edu
BLOXOM, Donald, R .... 318-797-5267 .... 213 D don.bloxom@lsus.edu
BLOYED, Carolyn .... 541-962-3519 .... 418 C cbloyed@eou.edu
BLOZOWSKY, Jason .... 570-454-6172 .... 435 G jason.blozowsky@mccann.edu
BLUE, Damon, A .... 323-563-4856 .... 39 G damonblue@cdrewu.edu
BLUE, Debbie .... 405-878-2028 .... 409 D debbie.blue@okbu.edu
BLUE, Deborah, G .... 559-244-5901 .... 72 A deborah.blue@scccd.edu
BLUE, Lynn .... 616-331-2035 .... 251 F bluel@gvsu.edu
BLUESTONE, Jeffrey, A .... 415-476-4451 .... 75 A jeff.bluestone@ucsf.edu
BLUESTONE, Leslie .... 215-641-6529 .... 436 G lbluesto@mc3.edu
BLUM, Christopher .... 603-880-8308 .... 306 A cblum@thomasmorecollege.edu
BLUM, Robert .... 817-272-2771 .... 505 C rwblum@uta.edu
BLUM, Susan .... 631-444-8250 .... 352 C susan.blum@stonybrook.edu
BLUM, Thomas, L .... 914-395-2203 .... 350 C tblum@sarahlawrence.edu
BLUMBERG, Audrey, S .... 516-877-3159 .... 322 A blumberg@adelphi.edu
BLUMBERG, Bruce, K .... 803-938-3838 .... 462 G bruceb@uscsumter.edu
BLUMBERG, Elizabeth .... 781-239-2762 .... 239 G eblumberg@massbay.edu
BLUMBERG, James, J .... 734-384-4249 .... 255 D jblumberg@monroeccc.edu
BLUME, Jane .... 360-752-8472 .... 531 H jblume@btc.ctc.edu
BLUME, Steven, W .... 800-431-8488 .... 29 C sblume@aptc.edu
BLUME, Thomas .... 605-394-2251 .... 466 B thomas.blume@sdsmt.edu
BLUME, Travis, A .... 260-422-5561 .... 173 C tablume@indianatech.edu
BLUMENFELD, Jessica .... 563-763-2702 .... 114 E jessica.blumenfeld@palmer.edu
BLUMENSTEIN, Robert .... 610-282-1100 .... 427 A robert.blumenstein@desales.edu
BLUMENTHAL, Bernard, G 215-951-1201 .... 432 I blumenth@lasalle.edu
BLUMENTHAL, Eric .... 503-251-5715 .... 421 A eblumenthal@uws.edu
BLUMENTHAL, George, R . 831-459-2058 .... 75 C chancellor@ucsc.edu
BLUMENTHAL, Jon .... 651-604-4101 .... 265 B
BLUMENTHAL, Marjory, S 202-687-6400 .... 98 D blumentm@georgetown.edu
BLUMER, Lindsay .... 920-748-8316 .... 550 D blumerl@ripon.edu
BLUMHARDT, Jon .... 808-845-9125 .... 142 B jon@hcc.hawaii.edu
BLUMREICH, Jim .... 920-498-5701 .... 555 C jim.blumreich@nwtc.edu
BLUNDELL, Keith .... 361-582-2535 .... 508 B keith.blundell@victoriacollege.edu
BLUNT, Grace .... 508-767-7172 .... 230 D gblunt@assumption.edu
BLUNT, Lisa .... 406-874-6214 .... 294 F bluntl@milescc.edu
BLUNT, Shelly, B .... 812-465-7020 .... 181 B sblunt@usi.edu
BLUST, Robert .... 414-288-7004 .... 548 F roby.blust@marquette.edu
BLUTREICH, Peter .... 336-750-3471 .... 380 B housing@wss.edu
BLY, Marie .... 603-752-1113 .... 304 H mbly@ccsnh.edu
BLYSKAL, Karen .... 732-255-0400 .... 312 D kblyskal@ocean.edu
BLYTHE, Gretchen, S .... 816-604-2251 .... 285 C gretchen.blythe@mcckc.edu
BLYTHE, Janett .... 270-534-3079 .... 203 E janett.blythe@kctcs.edu
BLYTHE, Tina .... 617-262-5000 .... 231 G tina.blythe@the-bac.edu
BLYTHE-SMITH, Karen .... 256-549-8357 .... 3 J ksmith@gadsdenstate.edu
BOADA, Maria .... 412-291-6247 .... 422 E mboada@aii.edu
BOAL, John, R .... 574-372-5100 .... 171 H boaljr@grace.edu
BOALS-GILBERT, Beverly .. 870-972-3052 .... 20 D bboals@astate.edu
BOARD, A. Jill .... 760-384-6212 .... 52 M jboard@cerrocoso.edu
BOARD, Christine .... 216-987-3467 .... 389 B christine.board@tri-c.edu
BOARD, Steve .... 920-206-2371 .... 548 D steve.board@mbbc.edu
BOARDLEY, Thomaice .... 301-860-3394 .... 228 A tboardley@bowiestate.edu
BOARDLEY SUBER, Dianne .... 919-516-4200 .... 376 D dbsuber@st-aug.edu
BOARDMAN, Gregory, E ... 650-725-1808 .... 71 G gboardman@stanford.edu
BOAT, Thomas, F .... 513-558-7333 .... 403 D thomas.boat@uc.edu
BOATMUN, Tim .... 580-745-2370 .... 412 C tboatmun@se.edu
BOATRIGHT, Jeremiah .... 325-574-6572 .... 508 I
BOATRIGHT-WELLS, Sue Ella .... 276-523-7489 .... 527 D sboatright@me.vccs.edu
BOATWRIGHT, Betty, R .... 803-536-8556 .... 460 G bboatwright@scsu.edu
BOATWRIGHT, Cassie .... 850-484-1778 .... 115 B cboatwright@pensacolastate.edu
BOATWRIGHT, Tamara .... 678-359-5259 .... 132 A tamarab@gdn.edu
BOATWRIGHT, Wally .... 843-383-8088 .... 457 A wboatwright@coker.edu
BOAZ, Matthew, L .... 513-529-7157 .... 396 E boazml@muohio.edu
BOB-PENNYPACKER, Beaulah .... 928-524-7326 .... 17 A beaulah.bob-pennypacker@npc.edu
BOBAK, Karen, A .... 315-568-3864 .... 342 H kbobak@nycc.edu
BOBART, David .... 410-837-4331 .... 229 A dbobart@ubalt.edu
BOBB, June .... 718-997-5780 .... 328 E june.bobb@qc.cuny.edu
BOBBETT, Tricia .... 417-667-8181 .... 280 E tbobbett@cottey.edu
BOBBIN, Michael, J .... 904-256-7055 .... 111 L mbobbin@ju.edu
BOBBIN, Steffi .... 617-559-8640 .... 235 E sbobbin@hebrewcollege.edu
BOBBITT, David .... 951-571-6341 .... 63 J david.bobbitt@mvc.edu
BOBBITT, David .... 951-372-7157 .... 63 K david.bobbitt@norcocollege.edu
BOBBITT, Donald, R .... 501-686-2505 .... 24 B president@uasys.edu
BOBICH, Marni .... 909-607-8533 .... 62 H marni_bobich@pitzer.edu
BOBINSKI, Michael, A .... 513-745-3414 .... 406 E bobinski@xavier.edu
BOBINSKY, Steven .... 928-777-4210 .... 14 C steven.bobinsky@erau.edu
BOBO, David .... 205-853-1200 .... 5 C dbobo@jeffstateonline.com
BOBROWSKI, Paul .... 937-229-3349 .... 404 A pbobrowski1@udayton.edu
BOCCHICCHIO, Rebecca .... 916-660-8000 .... 69 F rbocchicchio@sierracollege.edu
BOCCHINFUSO-COHEN, Rita .... 559-278-2381 .... 35 A ritab@csufresno.edu
BOCCHINO, Bud .... 713-798-2195 .... 481 H bocchino@bcm.edu
BOCCIA, Lenore .... 215-222-4200 .... 445 G lboccia@walnuthillcollege.edu
BOCHTE, Bill .... 785-826-2601 .... 194 E bochw001@k-state.edu
BOCIAN, David, F .... 951-827-2304 .... 74 E vpap@ucr.edu
BOCIAN, Terry, M .... 616-632-2475 .... 247 E bociater@aquinas.edu
BOCK, Jim .... 610-328-8529 .... 447 F jbock1@swarthmore.edu
BOCK, Lisa, L .... 336-862-7986 .... 373 A llbock@randolph.edu
BOCK, Mike .... 260-665-4878 .... 180 D bockm@trine.edu
BOCK, Wendy .... 309-796-5180 .... 145 H bockw@bhc.edu
BOCKMAN, Edward .... 847-543-2259 .... 148 B ebockman@clcillinois.edu
BOCZER, Amy .... 203-254-4000 .... 92 H aboczer@fairfield.edu
BODDIE-LAVAN, Jeanine .. 334-244-3610 .... 1 G jblavan@aum.edu
BODDY, Michael .... 314-252-3132 .... 281 F mboddy@eden.edu
BODE, Brian .... 913-288-7667 .... 194 C bbode@kckcc.edu
BODE, Lori .... 636-949-4925 .... 283 J lbode@lindenwood.edu
BODEN, Alison .... 609-258-6244 .... 312 G aboden@princeton.edu
BODEN, Janet .... 773-256-0744 .... 157 D jboden@lstc.edu
BODEN, Michael .... 845-431-8952 .... 332 D michael.boden@sunydutchess.edu
BODENBENDER, Laura .... 608-822-2315 .... 555 D lbodenbender@swtc.edu
BODIE, Cindy, H .... 336-315-8660 .... 363 C cbodie@carolinagrad.edu
BODIE, Darryl, A .... 336-315-8660 .... 363 C dbodie@carolinagrad.edu
BODIN, Susan .... 804-627-5300 .... 517 A
BODINE, Jordan .... 575-492-2143 .... 321 H jbodine@usw.edu
BODISON, Sacared, A .... 301-314-8091 .... 227 B sbodison@umd.edu
BODMAN, Andrew, R .... 909-537-5024 .... 36 B abodman@csusb.edu
BODNAR, Richard .... 718-997-5191 .... 328 E richard.bodnar@qc.edu
BODONI, June .... 978-867-4217 .... 235 A june.bodoni@gordon.edu
BODRATTI, Robert .... 518-828-4181 .... 330 E bodratti@sunycgcc.edu
BODRI, Michael .... 706-864-1958 .... 134 G msbodri@northgeorgia.edu
BODUR, Niyazi .... 516-686-7724 .... 343 D nbodur@nyit.edu
BODVARSSON, Orn .... 320-308-2225 .... 269 A obbodvarsson@stcloudstate.edu
BODY, Dorothy, H .... 814-732-5555 .... 442 E dbody@edinboro.edu
BOE, Eugene .... 218-739-3375 .... 264 I eboe@lbs.edu
BOECKERMANN, Gabriele . 513-569-1550 .... 387 G gabriele.boeckermann@cincinnatistate.edu
BOEDEKER, Katrina .... 260-399-7700 .... 181 A kboedeker@sf.edu
BOEDEKER, Sherri .... 641-423-2530 .... 186 J sboedeker@kaplan.edu
BOEDER, John, C .... 507-354-8221 .... 264 K boederjc@mlc-wels.edu
BOEGEL, Tom .... 415-239-3360 .... 40 C tboegel@ccsf.edu
BOEH, Scott .... 405-271-2359 .... 413 D scott-boeh@ouhsc.edu
BOEH, Thomas .... 559-244-5641 .... 35 A tboeh@csufresno.edu
BOEHLER, Ted .... 714-241-6209 .... 41 B tboehler@coastlin.edu
BOEHLER, Ted .... 714-241-6213 .... 41 B tboehler@coastline.edu
BOEHLER, Ted .... 714-241-6143 .... 41 B tboehler@coastline.edu
BOEHM, Beth, A .... 502-852-3975 .... 207 E baboeh01@louisville.edu
BOEHM, Christopher .... 205-552-1222 .... 3 A chris.boehm@ecacolleges.com
BOEHM, Christopher, H .... 610-921-7700 .... 421 E cboehm@alb.edu
BOEHM, JR., Edward, G ... 570-945-8500 .... 432 E edward.boehm@keystone.edu
BOEHM, J, J .... 989-964-4055 .... 257 G jjboehm@svsu.edu
BOEHM, Michael .... 574-284-4610 .... 179 F mboehm@saintmarys.edu
BOEHM, Michael, J .... 614-292-5881 .... 398 I boehm.1@osu.edu
BOEHMAN, Joseph, R .... 804-289-8000 .... 525 E jboehman@richmond.edu
BOEHME, Brian .... 740-364-9535 .... 386 H bboehmer@newark.ohio-state.edu
BOEHME, Michael, J .... 320-234-8509 .... 268 G mike.boehme@ridgewater.edu
BOEHMER, Bob .... 478-289-2027 .... 129 B bboehmer@ega.edu
BOEHNE, Cheryl .... 618-545-3184 .... 155 B cboehne@kaskaskia.edu
BOEHNE, Rhonda .... 618-545-3022 .... 155 B rboehne@kaskaskia.edu
BOEHNINGER, Candice .... 740-593-4100 .... 399 G boeningc@ohio.edu
BOEHNKE, Barbara .... 716-888-2937 .... 325 F boehnkeb@canisius.edu
BOEKER, Cathy .... 979-830-4455 .... 482 C cboeker@blinn.edu
BOELE, Erin .... 599-278-2345 .... 35 A eboele@csufresno.edu
BOELK, Nicole .... 989-729-3435 .... 248 F nicole.boelk@baker.edu
BOENKER, Norma .... 260-399-7700 .... 181 A nboenker@sf.edu
BOER, Larry .... 708-239-4608 .... 166 C larry.boer@trnty.edu
BOERBOOM, Chris .... 701-231-7867 .... 382 B chris.boerboom@ndsu.edu
BOERGER, Leah .... 859-371-9393 .... 198 G lboerger@beckfield.edu
BOERGERMANN, Gary .... 918-343-7625 .... 411 H gboergermann@rsu.edu
BOERNER, Anne .... 503-297-5544 .... 417 G aboerner@ocac.edu
BOERSIG, Pam .... 612-332-3361 .... 261 A pboersig@aii.edu
BOERSMA, Paul, H .... 616-395-7145 .... 252 D boersma@hope.edu
BOERST, Connie .... 920-433-6622 .... 546 D connie.boerst@bellincollege.edu
BOES, Heather .... 763-231-3160 .... 264 C hboes@herzing.edu
BOESCH, Donald, F .... 410-221-2001 .... 227 A boesch@umces.edu
BOESDORFER, Nancy, A ... 217-443-8856 .... 148 G nboes@dacc.edu
BOETSCH, Larry .... 540-458-8145 .... 530 D lboetsch@wlu.edu
BOETTCHER, Marlene, F .... 719-384-6824 .... 87 A marlene.boettcher@ojc.edu
BOETTGER, Jennifer .... 319-895-4153 .... 183 G jboettger@cornellcollege.edu
BOEVINGLOH, Linda .... 636-481-3488 .... 283 D lboeving@jeffco.edu
BOEZAART, Arn .... 616-331-6905 .... 251 F boezaara@gvsu.edu
BOGAGE, Alan .... 410-386-8339 .... 221 G abogage@carrollcc.edu
BOGAN, Gerri .... 706-821-8262 .... 135 G gbogan@paine.edu
BOGAN, Ivory .... 601-984-1400 .... 277 E bogan@umc.edu
BOGAN, Jeffrey, S .... 706-864-7999 .... 134 G jboggan@northgeorgia.edu
BOGAN, Jeremy .... 518-454-5155 .... 330 C boganj@strose.edu
BOGAN, Kim .... 619-849-2481 .... 62 L kimbogan@pointloma.edu
BOGAN, Yolanda .... 850-599-3145 .... 118 L yolanda.bogan@famu.edu
BOGAR, Teresa .... 512-444-8082 .... 499 E library@texastcm.edu
BOGART, Denise .... 229-333-5709 .... 139 C dbogart@valdosta.edu
BOGART, Marti, S .... 630-637-5355 .... 159 G msbogart@noctrl.edu
BOGART, William, T .... 865-981-8101 .... 471 B tom.bogart@maryvillecollege.edu
BOGATSKI, Anatole .... 510-780-4500 .... 53 J abogatski@lifewest.edu
BOGDAN, Sharon .... 410-532-5332 .... 225 D sbogdan@ndm.edu
BOGDANOVICH, Holly .... 562-860-2451 .... 39 A hbogdanovich@cerritos.edu
BOGDONOFF, Malinda .... 530-741-6700 .... 80 I
BOGEN, Janice, M .... 215-503-4335 .... 448 C janice.bogen@jefferson.edu
BOGER, John, C .... 919-962-4417 .... 378 E jcboger@email.unc.edu
BOGER-HAWKINS, Caitlin 860-738-6441 .... 92 B cboger-hawkins@nwcc.commnet.edu
BOGERT, Brian .... 570-408-4015 .... 452 A brian.bogert@wilkes.edu
BOGGAN, Laura, K .... 423-652-4707 .... 470 A lkboggan@king.edu
BOGGER, Tommy .... 757-823-2004 .... 522 E tlbogger@nsu.edu
BOGGESS, Kendra .... 304-384-5241 .... 543 G kendra@concord.edu
BOGGIE, Mark .... 520-515-5451 .... 13 E boggiem@cochise.edu
BOGGIO, P, J .... 508-213-2483 .... 243 E pamela.boggio@nichols.edu
BOGGS, Allan .... 937-775-3224 .... 406 C allan.boggs@wright.edu
BOGGS, Beverly .... 931-221-6540 .... 473 E boggsb@apsu.edu
BOGGS, Bonnie, B .... 734-384-4268 .... 255 D bboggs@monroeccc.edu
BOGGS, Doyle, W .... 864-597-4182 .... 463 G boggsdw@wofford.edu
BOGGS, Emily .... 740-774-6300 .... 389 D eboggs@daymarcollege.edu
BOGGS, Gretchen, M .... 410-250-1088 .... 227 E contedoc@ezy.net
BOGGS, Jill .... 260-665-4122 .... 180 D boggsj@trine.edu
BOGGS, John .... 281-998-6150 .... 494 B john.boggs@sjcd.edu
BOGGS, Larry .... 662-862-8252 .... 274 E laboggs@iccms.edu
BOGGS, Paul, R .... 903-233-3981 .... 490 A paulboggs@letu.edu

BOGGS, Rainie ... 859-253-3637 ... 200 K rainie.boggs@frontier.edu
BOGGS, Tex ... 310-578-1080 ... 28 L tboggs1@antioch.edu
BOGH, Wayne ... 909-389-3309 ... 65 B wbogh@craftonhills.edu
BOGHOSIAN, Bruce, M ... 510-987-9452 ... 28 H
BOGLE, Barry, J ... 915-831-7116 ... 486 G bbogle@epcc.edu
BOGLE, Darcy ... 661-763-7889 ... 72 E dbogle@taftcollege.edu
BOGLE, Yvonne ... 413-782-1594 ... 246 A ybogle@wne.edu
BOGLEY, John, W ... 509-527-5979 ... 540 B bogleyj@whitman.edu
BOGNER, Drew ... 516-678-5000 ... 341 F dbogner@molloy.edu
BOGNER, John ... 479-788-7051 ... 24 D john.bogner@uafs.edu
BOGOMILSKY, Moshe ... 718-434-0784 ... 325 I
BOGOMOLNY, Robert, L ... 410-837-4866 ... 229 A rbogomolny@ubalt.edu
BOGORAD, Deborah ... 845-434-5750 ... 357 A dbogorad@sullivan.suny.edu
BOGRIS, Claudia ... 973-655-3291 ... 311 F bogrisc@mail.montclair.edu
BOGUSLAWSKI, OP, Steven ... 202-495-3831 ... 99 C president@dhs.edu
BOHACH, Gregory ... 662-325-3006 ... 275 F gbohach@dafvm.msstate.edu
BOHACZ, Candy ... 269-467-9945 ... 251 B cbohacz@glenoaks.edu
BOHAKER, Linda, A ... 618-374-5495 ... 161 E linda.bohaker@principia.edu
BOHAM, Kenneth, A ... 828-726-2211 ... 368 G kboham@cccti.edu
BOHAN, David ... 973-378-9801 ... 315 B david.bohan@shu.edu
BOHAN, Ken ... 562-907-4261 ... 79 F kbohan@whittier.edu
BOHANNON, Betsy ... 859-622-1500 ... 200 J betsy.bohannon@eku.edu
BOHANON, Janet ... 770-531-6315 ... 133 C jbohanon@laniertech.edu
BOHASKA, Chris ... 410-225-2490 ... 224 B cbohaska@mica.edu
BOHLANDER, Brad ... 970-491-6621 ... 83 E brad.bohlander@colostate.edu
BOHLEKE, Briant ... 717-334-6286 ... 435 A bbohleke@ltsg.edu
BOHLEKE, Chuck ... 434-961-5348 ... 528 B cbohleke@pvcc.edu
BOHLEN, Charles ... 719-846-5541 ... 88 F charles.bohlen@trinidadstate.edu
BOHLMAN, Bonnie, G ... 701-483-2370 ... 381 G bonnie.bohlman@dickinsonstate.edu
BOHN, Bill ... 541-506-6090 ... 415 C bbohn@cgcc.cc.or.us
BOHN, Michael, R ... 303-492-7930 ... 88 H mike.bohn@colorado.edu
BOHN, Nicole ... 415-405-3583 ... 37 B nbohn@sfsu.edu
BOHNEN, Evan ... 740-376-4446 ... 395 G evan.bohnen@marietta.edu
BOHNENBLUST, Delyna ... 620-421-6700 ... 194 G delynab@labette.edu
BOHNET, Sandra ... 269-488-4409 ... 253 A sbohnet@kvcc.edu
BOHNETT, Sally ... 419-251-8985 ... 395 I sally.bohnett@mercycollege.edu
BOHNSACK, Jennifer ... 602-331-7500 ... 12 B jbohnsack@aii.edu
BOHNY, David ... 973-618-3440 ... 308 C dbohny@caldwell.edu
BOHREN, Karen ... 231-591-2607 ... 250 H bksferrisstate@bncollege.com
BOICE, Daniel ... 563-876-3353 ... 184 B dboice@dwci.edu
BOIES, Brandy ... 540-868-7161 ... 527 C bboies@lfcc.edu
BOIES, Chris ... 540-868-7129 ... 527 C cboies@lfcc.edu
BOIKE, Kristine ... 763-424-0964 ... 268 B kboike@nhcc.edu
BOILINI, Laura, L ... 386-312-4199 ... 116 F lauraboilini@sjrstate.edu
BOISE, Craig ... 216-687-2300 ... 388 D c.boise@law.csuohio.edu
BOISEN, Beth ... 715-232-1695 ... 552 E boisenb@uwstout.edu
BOISJOLY, Russell, P ... 716-673-4813 ... 352 A russell.boisjoly@fredonia.edu
BOISSEAU, Tracey, J ... 765-494-1494 ... 178 J
BOISSELLE, Dave ... 757-352-4757 ... 523 E daviboi@regent.edu
BOISSELLE, Vincent ... 315-781-3549 ... 335 F boisselle@hws.edu
BOISSONEAULT, Susan ... 508-678-2811 ... 239 B susan.boissoneault@bristolcc.edu
BOISVERT, David ... 603-897-8502 ... 305 F dboisvert@rivier.edu
BOISVERT, Marie ... 360-491-4700 ... 537 B
BOITNOTT, Tina ... 903-886-5110 ... 498 B tina.boitnott@tamuc.edu
BOJAR, Anthea, L ... 414-410-4006 ... 546 G albojar@stritch.edu
BOKHARI, Kelly ... 262-595-2597 ... 552 A bokhari@uwp.edu
BOKOWSKI, Debrah ... 503-534-4038 ... 416 J dbokowski@marylhurst.edu
BOKSAN, George ... 610-861-1421 ... 437 A megjb01@moravian.edu
BOKTOR, Monir ... 949-794-9090 ... 71 F mboktor@stanbridge.edu
BOLA, William ... 207-206-2365 ... 221 A wbola@une.edu
BOLA, William ... 207-602-2365 ... 221 A wbola@une.edu
BOLAND, Carolyn ... 513-244-4717 ... 388 E carolyn_boland@mail.msj.edu
BOLAND, Catherine ... 928-350-4001 ... 17 K cboland@prescott.edu
BOLAND, Kristine ... 419-783-2469 ... 389 H kboland@defiance.edu
BOLAND, Mary, G ... 808-956-8522 ... 141 G mgboland@hawaii.edu
BOLAND, Mary Kate ... 610-647-4400 ... 431 C mboland@immaculata.edu
BOLAND, Patrick, O ... 203-857-7032 ... 92 C pboland@ncc.commnet.edu
BOLAND-CHASE, Ann ... 590-961-4728 ... 435 F chase@marywood.edu
BOLDEN, Errol ... 410-951-3542 ... 228 B ebolden@coppin.edu
BOLDEN, John ... 313-496-2536 ... 259 G jbolden1@wcccd.edu
BOLDER, Catherine, M ... 973-972-4855 ... 316 C bolder@umdnj.edu
BOLDMAN, Denise ... 937-484-1243 ... 405 A dboldman@urbana.edu
BOLDREY, Penny ... 989-358-7297 ... 247 C boldreyp@alpenacc.edu
BOLDT, Amy ... 505-254-7575 ... 320 I
BOLDT, Deborah ... 505-428-1704 ... 320 E deborah.boldt@sfcc.edu
BOLDT, William ... 702-895-5895 ... 302 I william.boldt@unlv.edu
BOLDUC, Darlene, R ... 802-626-6490 ... 515 G darlene.bolduc@lyndonstate.edu
BOLDUC, Michael, C ... 561-237-7180 ... 113 D mbolduc@lynn.edu
BOLEK, Catherine ... 410-651-6714 ... 227 E csbolek@umes.edu
BOLEMAN, Roger, P ... 320-589-6150 ... 271 G bolemarp@morris.umn.edu
BOLEN, III, Robert ... 304-929-1405 ... 541 H bobbolen@mountainstate.edu
BOLENDER, Melanie ... 740-366-1351 ... 386 H
BOLES, Jessica ... 580-559-5539 ... 407 J jboles@ecok.edu
BOLEY, Paula ... 765-289-2291 ... 176 B pboley@ivytech.edu
BOLGER, Eric ... 417-690-2278 ... 279 J bolger@cofo.edu
BOLHOUSE, Lana ... 405-878-2081 ... 409 D lana.bolhouse@okbu.edu
BOLICK-FLOSS, Annie ... 707-826-3341 ... 36 E amb2@humboldt.edu
BOLIG, Kimberly, L ... 570-326-3761 ... 440 L kbolig@pct.edu
BOLIN, Alexis ... 408-848-4742 ... 48 C 0282mgr@fheg.follett.com
BOLIN-REECE, Mary, C ... 859-257-8701 ... 207 D mcreec01@uky.edu
BOLING, Charles ... 276-739-2514 ... 529 A cboling@vhcc.edu
BOLING, Cindy ... 405-974-2547 ... 413 B cboling@uco.edu
BOLING, Gena ... 573-876-7106 ... 290 C gboling@stephens.edu
BOLISH, Jennifer ... 651-905-3428 ... 261 E jbolish@browncollege.edu
BOLL, Jackie ... 714-992-7040 ... 59 E jboll@fullcoll.edu
BOLL, Julie ... 217-228-5432 ... 161 F bollju@quincy.edu
BOLLARD, Kathleen ... 303-860-5600 ... 88 G kathleen.bollard@cu.edu
BOLLEN, Kathryn, A ... 585-785-1228 ... 334 A bollenka@flcc.edu
BOLLENBACH, Evelyn ... 405-945-3317 ... 410 F
BOLLERER, Fred ... 202-639-1736 ... 98 A fbollerer@corcoran.org
BOLLIER, John, H ... 203-432-6754 ... 96 A john.bollier@yale.edu
BOLLIG, Nicole ... 785-587-2800 ... 195 A nicolefischer@matc.net
BOLLING, Phyllis ... 973-596-3420 ... 312 C phyllis.bolling@njit.edu
BOLLING, Ricky ... 276-523-7480 ... 527 D rbolling@mecc.vccs.edu
BOLLING-CLAY, Sharon ... 770-394-8300 ... 125 A dbolling@aii.edu
BOLLINGER, Bruce ... 701-231-6177 ... 382 B bruce.bollinger@ndsu.edu
BOLLINGER, Gary ... 402-486-2502 ... 300 C gabollin@ucollege.edu
BOLLINGER, Lee, C ... 212-854-9970 ... 330 F bollinger@columbia.edu
BOLLINGER, Mary ... 603-888-1311 ... 305 F mbollinger@rivier.edu
BOLLINGER, Richard ... 903-223-3068 ... 498 F rbolinger@tamut.edu
BOLLINGER, Robert, D ... 218-755-4147 ... 265 I rbollinger@bemidjistate.edu
BOLLMAN, Lois ... 612-659-6305 ... 267 B lois.bollman@minneapolis.edu
BOLLMAN-DALANSKY, Terri, L ... 814-641-3424 ... 432 A bollmat@juniata.edu
BOLLMANN, Janice, A ... 314-286-4805 ... 287 G jabollmann@ranken.edu
BOLMAN, Dave ... 602-383-8228 ... 18 K dbolman@uat.edu
BOLMIDA, Peter ... 937-512-3028 ... 401 J peter.bolmida@sinclair.edu
BOLOWSKI, Mary ... 201-200-3041 ... 312 B mbolowski@njcu.edu
BOLSINGER, Judith, A ... 412-578-6027 ... 424 I bolsingerja@carlow.edu
BOLSTER, Jeff ... 619-849-2480 ... 62 L jeffbolster@pointloma.edu
BOLT, Barb ... 814-868-9900 ... 428 I barbb@erieit.edu
BOLT, Carolyn ... 212-517-0454 ... 340 C cbolt@mmm.edu
BOLT, Dave ... 559-925-3222 ... 78 D davebolt@whccd.edu
BOLT, Gary ... 630-844-6878 ... 145 F gbolt@aurora.edu
BOLT, Gita ... 504-861-2657 ... 213 F gbolt@loyno.edu
BOLT, Tracy, L ... 443-334-2270 ... 226 E tbolt@stevenson.edu
BOLTE, Jenny, L ... 540-674-3652 ... 527 E jbolte@nr.edu
BOLTE, Michael ... 831-459-2991 ... 75 C bolte@ucolick.org
BOLTON, Cathy ... 940-552-6291 ... 507 F cbolton@vernoncollege.edu
BOLTON, David ... 417-328-1538 ... 290 A dbolton@sbuniv.edu
BOLTON, Denny, G ... 336-841-9202 ... 365 C ebolton@highpoint.edu
BOLTON, JR., Glenn Allen ... 414-955-8704 ... 548 G abolton@mcw.edu
BOLTON, Harry ... 707-654-1192 ... 33 C hbolton@csum.edu
BOLTON, Lance ... 719-502-2200 ... 87 B lance.bolton@ppcc.edu
BOLTON, Melenie ... 256-378-2047 ... 2 E mbolton@cacc.edu
BOLTON, Sarah, R ... 413-597-4171 ... 246 D sarah.r.bolton@williams.edu
BOLTON, Stanley ... 803-822-3523 ... 459 E boltons@midlandstech.edu
BOLTON, Tama ... 831-477-3548 ... 31 I tabolton@cabrillo.edu
BOLTON, Tonya, D ... 870-759-4130 ... 26 B tbolton@wbcoll.edu
BOLTZ, Fran ... 716-286-8751 ... 344 D fboltz@niagara.edu
BOLYAI, Stephen ... 973-720-2233 ... 317 D bolyais@wpunj.edu
BOLYARD, Adrienne, M ... 206-726-5021 ... 533 D abolyard@cornish.edu
BOMAN, Margaret ... 717-948-6020 ... 439 J myb9@psu.edu
BOMAN, Victoria ... 205-247-8837 ... 7 F vbowen@stillman.edu
BOMBA, Jody, L ... 909-593-3511 ... 75 E jbomba@laverne.edu
BOMBERGER, Sherry ... 717-757-1100 ... 452 J sherry.bomberger@yti.edu
BOMERSBACH, Bob ... 212-280-1428 ... 358 I bbomersbach@uts.columbia.edu
BOMOTTI, Gerry ... 702-895-3571 ... 302 I gerry.bomotti@unlv.edu
BONA, Dennis ... 269-965-3931 ... 253 B bonad@kellogg.edu
BONA, Mike ... 706-245-7226 ... 129 C mbona@ec.edu
BONACCI, Andrew ... 413-572-5394 ... 238 F abonacci@wsc.ma.edu
BONACIC, Patricia ... 310-900-1600 ... 45 F bonacic_v@compton.edu
BONAGURO, John, A ... 270-745-7003 ... 208 A john.bonaguro@wku.edu
BONAHUE, Edward ... 352-381-3822 ... 117 F ed.bohahue@sfcollege.edu
BONANDO, John, S ... 724-738-2728 ... 443 F john.bonando@sru.edu
BONANNO, Barbara ... 726-926-8924 ... 335 E bbonnano@hilbert.edu
BONANNO, Janice, M ... 617-228-2436 ... 239 C jbonanno@bhcc.mass.edu
BONANNO, Joseph ... 812-855-4440 ... 173 E jbonanno@indiana.edu
BONANNO, Steve ... 304-293-8676 ... 545 A steve.bonanno@mail.wvu.edu
BONANO, Anthony ... 718-260-3915 ... 346 C abonano@poly.edu
BONAPARTE, Donna ... 781-239-6434 ... 230 E dbonaparte@babson.edu
BONAPARTE, Wallace, T ... 843-792-1568 ... 459 D bonaparw@musc.edu
BONAPARTE, Wilma ... 414-297-7396 ... 554 F bonaparw@matc.edu
BONCUORE, Cheryl ... 312-752-2646 ... 155 C cheryl..boncuore@kendall.edu
BOND, Bill, E ... 406-756-3818 ... 294 C bbond@fvcc.edu
BOND, Bradley ... 815-753-9403 ... 160 B bbond@niu.edu
BOND, Cheryl ... 601-947-4201 ... 275 E cheryl.bond@mgccc.edu
BOND, Cindy, R ... 208-732-6454 ... 143 E cbond@csi.edu
BOND, Emma ... 601-426-6346 ... 277 A ebond@southeasternbaptist.edu
BOND, Inge ... 408-741-2166 ... 78 G inge.bond@westvalley.edu
BOND, Jan ... 419-289-5054 ... 384 G jbond1@ashland.edu
BOND, Kathy, E ... 337-475-5613 ... 215 G kbond@mcneese.edu
BOND, Martha ... 315-781-3780 ... 335 F mbond@hws.edu
BOND, Meredith, R ... 216-687-9321 ... 388 D m.bond40@csuohio.edu
BOND, Peter ... 972-883-2301 ... 506 A pbond@utdallas.edu
BOND, Roy, L ... 972-391-1087 ... 484 I roybond@dcccd.edu
BOND, Sandra ... 540-831-5248 ... 523 A smbond@radford.edu
BOND, Susan, E ... 610-359-1222 ... 426 G sbond@dccc.edu
BOND, Toney ... 910-296-2505 ... 371 E tbond@jamessprunt.edu
BONDAVALLI, Bonnie ... 815-836-5242 ... 156 F bondavbo@lewisu.edu
BONDAVALLI, Bruno ... 773-878-3439 ... 163 F bbondavalli@staugustine.edu
BONDI, Tony ... 626-229-1300 ... 53 I
BONDS, Dorothea ... 214-648-7500 ... 507 E dorothea.bonds@utsouthwestern.edu
BONDS, Jess ... 209-478-0800 ... 50 K jbonds@humphreys.edu
BONDS, Nell ... 870-743-3000 ... 22 G nbonds@northark.edu
BONDS, Thomas ... 662-862-8131 ... 274 E tabonds@iccms.edu
BONDS, TJ ... 770-394-8300 ... 125 A tbonds@aii.edu
BONDUM, Victoria ... 315-228-7481 ... 329 G vbondum@colgate.edu
BONDURANT, Derrith ... 903-566-7444 ... 506 E dbondurant@uttyler.edu
BONDURANT, Glenda, P ... 252-246-1333 ... 375 D gbondurant@wilsoncc.edu
BONDURANT, William, S ... 606-474-3234 ... 201 D bbondurant@kcu.edu
BONE, Andrew ... 503-399-6593 ... 414 J andrew.bone@chemeketa.edu
BONE, Don ... 215-573-3444 ... 448 J donbone@upenn.edu
BONEBRIGHT, Terri ... 765-658-4359 ... 171 B tbone@depauw.edu
BONELLI, Vicky ... 618-544-8657 ... 152 H bonelliv@iecc.edu
BONES, Rafael ... 413-572-8277 ... 238 F rbones@wsc.ma.edu
BONEWALD, Karen, I ... 603-526-3748 ... 303 G kbonewald@colby-sawyer.edu
BONEWITZ, Stan ... 512-313-3000 ... 483 K stan.bonewitz@concordia.edu
BONEZ, Allison ... 317-955-6080 ... 177 I abonez@marian.edu
BONFANTI, Philip ... 662-325-8853 ... 275 F pgb13@msstate.edu
BONFIGLIO, Robert, A ... 585-245-5618 ... 353 C bonfig@geneseo.edu
BONGARD, Joseph, W ... 610-785-6271 ... 446 A jbongard@scs.edu
BONGARTEN, Bruce, C ... 315-470-6510 ... 355 A bcbongarten@esf.edu
BONGARTZ, Michael ... 816-235-1515 ... 291 C bongartzm@umkc.edu
BONGO, Catherine, N ... 973-655-7137 ... 311 F bongoc@mail.montclair.edu
BONI, Bethyn ... 315-568-3252 ... 342 H bboni@nycc.edu
BONI, M. Sharon ... 304-367-0205 ... 543 H sharon.boni@fairmontstate.edu
BONICELLI, Paul ... 757-352-4320 ... 523 E pbonicelli@regent.edu
BONIFER, Duane ... 270-384-8043 ... 204 D boniferd@lindsey.edu
BONIFORTI, Alfredo, H ... 561-237-7173 ... 113 D aboniforti@lynn.edu
BONIFORTI, Chris, G ... 561-237-7163 ... 113 D cboniforti@lynn.edu

BONILLA, Ana, O ... 787-841-2000 ... 565 B
abonilla@pucpr.edu
BONILLA, Angelita ... 973-353-1494 ... 314 E
bonillan@andromeda.rutgers.edu
BONILLA, Anie ... 954-492-5353 ... 103 F
abonilla@citycollege.edu
BONILLA, Charles ... 312-369-8611 ... 148 D
cbonilla@colum.edu
BONILLA, Diana ... 818-364-7699 ... 55 A
bonilldi@lamission.edu
BONILLA, J. C ... 718-260-3201 ... 346 C
jbonilla@poly.edu
BONILLA, Kathleen ... 559-489-2221 ... 72 B
kathy.bonilla@fresnocitycollege.edu
BONILLA, Mary Kay ... 406-771-5123 ... 295 G
mbonilla@msugf.edu
BONILLA, Matthew, F ... 212-346-1200 ... 345 F
mbonilla@pace.edu
BONILLA, Ray ... 979-458-6000 ... 496 F
rbonilla@tamus.edu
BONILLA, Victor ... 787-892-4675 ... 564 B
vicbonil@sg.inter.edu
BONILLA-RODRIGUEZ,
Victor ... 787-725-6500 ... 561 A
vbonilla@albizu.edu
BONIN, Charles, G ... 207-768-9550 ... 220 F
charles.bonin@umpi.edu
BONINE, Dan ... 319-296-4223 ... 185 F
dan.bonine@hawkeyecollege.edu
BONINI, Robin ... 906-487-7225 ... 251 A
robin.bonini@finlandia.edu
BONK, Kenneth, J ... 540-831-5332 ... 523 A
kjbonk@radford.edu
BONK, Sharon, B ... 617-588-1356 ... 231 C
sbonk@bfit.edu
BONK, Theresa, A ... 412-339-6020 ... 440 C
tab19@psu.edu
BONKOWSKI, Marie ... 517-841-4528 ... 248 D
marie.bonkowski@baker.edu
BONN, Cynthia, L ... 401-874-7100 ... 454 E
deanofadmission@uri.edu
BONN, Robert, R ... 262-551-5942 ... 546 I
rbonn@carthage.edu
BONNE, Connie ... 563-441-2450 ... 186 I
cbonne@kucampus.edu
BONNEAU, Elizabeth ... 508-849-3459 ... 230 C
ebonneau@annamaria.edu
BONNER, A. Frank ... 704-406-4236 ... 364 E
fbonner@gardner-webb.edu
BONNER, Beverly, J ... 865-882-4550 ... 476 A
bonner@roanestate.edu
BONNER, Davita ... 386-481-2143 ... 102 C
bonnerd@cookman.edu
BONNER, Debera ... 804-524-5276 ... 529 H
dbonner@vsu.edu
BONNER, Gloria, L ... 615-898-2622 ... 473 G
gloria.bonner@mtsu.edu
BONNER, Hugh, W ... 315-464-6560 ... 352 E
bonnerh@upstate.edu
BONNER, James ... 215-572-2187 ... 422 C
bonner@arcadia.edu
BONNER, John, B ... 425-276-9520 ... 534 C
jbonner@everettcc.edu
BONNER, Judd ... 951-343-4256 ... 31 J
jbonner@calbaptist.edu
BONNER, Judy, L ... 205-348-4892 ... 8 E
judy.bonner@ua.edu
BONNER, Julia ... 414-229-4716 ... 551 D
jbonner@uwm.edu
BONNER, Paula, E ... 608-262-9630 ... 550 J
pbonner@waastaff.com
BONNER, Sirius ... 360-992-2355 ... 532 F
sbonner@clark.edu
BONNER, Thomas, P ... 651-696-6295 ... 264 J
bonner@macalester.edu
BONNER, William, L ... 803-754-3950 ... 463 F
BONNER, Yahosh ... 308-641-6608 ... 301 D
bonnerk@wncc.edu
BONNET, Larissa, B ... 307-674-6446 ... 556 F
lbonnet@sheridan.edu
BONNETT, Steve ... 319-363-0481 ... 186 H
BONNETTE, Clarence ... 803-793-5248 ... 457 F
bonnettec@denmarktech.edu
BONNETTE, Margaree ... 803-793-5175 ... 457 F
bonnettem@denmarktech.edu
BONNETTE, Thomas ... 802-860-2705 ... 513 C
bonnette@champlain.edu
BONNEY-BAKER, Janet ... 901-572-2446 ... 467 C
janet.bonney@bchs.edu
BONNIN, Linda ... 901-678-2843 ... 474 C
lmichael@memphis.edu
BONNIN, Linda, H ... 901-678-2843 ... 474 C
lmichael@memphis.edu
BONNSTETTER, Bret ... 847-925-6224 ... 151 G
bbonnste@harpercollege.edu
BONO, John ... 831-459-4747 ... 75 C
jbono@ucsc.edu
BONOFIGLIO, Carrie ... 517-338-3314 ... 249 D
cbono@cleary.edu
BONONES, Patrick ... 404-471-6396 ... 123 I
pbonones@agnesscott.edu
BONSANG, Stacy ... 781-595-6768 ... 236 C
sbonsang@mariancourt.edu
BONSIGNORE, Diana ... 770-650-3000 ... 99 G
BONSIGNORE, Francis ... 516-299-3017 ... 339 A
francis.bonsignore@liu.edu
BONTA, Anthony ... 305-899-3653 ... 101 M
abonta@mail.barry.edu
BONTATIBUS, Donna ... 860-343-5805 ... 91 G
dbontatibus@mxcc.commnet.edu
BONTE, Troy ... 724-503-1001 ... 451 A
tbonte@washjeff.edu
BONTINELLI, Stasi ... 303-751-8700 ... 81 H
bontinelli@bel-rea.com
BONTRAGER, Cindy, A ... 785-532-6767 ... 194 D
cab@ksu.edu
BONTRAGER, Katherine, A 859-572-6132 ... 205 H
bontragerk1@nku.edu
BONTRAGER, Kimberlee ... 423-869-6314 ... 470 E
kimberlee.bontrager@lmunet.edu
BONUCHI, Molly, A ... 308-635-6112 ... 301 D
bonuchim@wncc.edu
BONURA, Dominick ... 432-264-3752 ... 488 B
dbonura@howardcollege.edu
BONURA, Kimberlee ... 612-338-7224 ... 272 C
kimberlee.bonura@waldenu.edu
BONURA, Rocky ... 310-660-3670 ... 45 E
abonura@elcamino.edu
BONVENUTO, Chris ... 310-434-4508 ... 68 D
bonvenuto_chris@smc.edu
BONVILLAIN, Thomas ... 985-449-7173 ... 216 A
tom.bonvillain@nicholls.edu
BONVILLIAN, Gary ... 229-226-1621 ... 138 C
gbonvillian@thomasu.edu
BONVILLIAN, William, B ... 202-789-1828 ... 241 D
BOOBER, Ed ... 304-876-5374 ... 544 C
eboober@shepherd.edu
BOOCKER, David ... 402-554-2338 ... 301 A
dboocker@unomaha.edu
BOODROOKAS, George, J 209-575-6498 ... 80 H
boodrookasg@yosemite.cc.ca.us
BOOG, Melissa, M ... 410-543-6330 ... 228 D
mmboog@salisbury.edu
BOOHER, Doug ... 812-855-9529 ... 173 E
dbooher@indiana.edu
BOOHER, Mark ... 805-922-6966 ... 26 L
mbooher@pcpa.org
BOOK, Cheryl, A ... 612-343-4163 ... 270 A
cabook@northcentral.edu
BOOK, Connie ... 336-278-5661 ... 364 D
cbook@elon.edu
BOOK, Wes ... 612-343-4143 ... 270 A
wcbook@northcentral.edu
BOOKER, Kevin ... 404-653-7893 ... 134 D
kbooker@morehouse.edu
BOOKER, Marc ... 602-557-4609 ... 19 A
marc.booker@phoenix.edu
BOOKER, Marc ... 205-934-2420 ... 8 F
mbooker@uab.edu
BOOKER, Mary ... 909-621-8205 ... 63 A
mary.booker@pomona.edu
BOOKER, Sid ... 814-732-2810 ... 442 E
sbooker@edinboro.edu
BOOKER, Steve ... 407-646-2395 ... 116 D
sbooker@rollins.edu
BOOKER, Tyka ... 512-786-4484 ... 508 C
tyka.booker@vc.edu
BOOKMAN, Douglas ... 800-672-3060 ... 376 G
BOOKMEYER, Paul, G ... 816-942-8400 ... 278 I
paul.bookmeyer@avila.edu
BOOKOUT, James ... 334-670-3617 ... 8 A
jbookout@troy.edu
BOOKOUT, Jeff ... 870-358-8614 ... 20 F
jeff_bookout@asun.edu
BOOKWALTER, Robert ... 304-696-6703 ... 544 B
bookwalt@marshall.edu
BOOM, Bill ... 320-363-3996 ... 271 A
bboom@csbsju.edu
BOOMS, Carole ... 734-432-5811 ... 254 D
cbooms@madonna.edu
BOONE, Christine, R ... 803-536-8449 ... 460 G
cboone@scsu.edu
BOONE, Dan ... 615-248-1251 ... 476 G
dboone@trevecca.edu
BOONE, Debbie ... 334-291-4927 ... 2 F
debbie.boone@cv.edu
BOONE, J. Allen ... 901-843-3760 ... 472 K
boone@rhodes.edu
BOONE, John, B ... 919-866-5923 ... 374 H
jbboone@waketech.edu
BOONE, Katherine, B ... 410-455-3768 ... 227 D
kboone@umbc.edu
BOONE, Kathleen, C ... 716-839-8301 ... 331 F
kboone@daemen.edu
BOONE, LaShanda, R ... 314-340-3301 ... 282 F
boonel@hssu.edu
BOONE, Loren ... 320-308-3151 ... 269 A
ljboone@stcloudstate.edu
BOONE, Lynn ... 870-338-6474 ... 25 D
BOONE, Phil ... 325-674-2659 ... 478 I
phil.boone@acu.edu
BOONE, Rebecca ... 318-357-5621 ... 216 B
booner@nsula.edu
BOONE, Tracie ... 704-272-5324 ... 374 A
tboone@spcc.edu
BOONSTRA, Brenda ... 706-776-0103 ... 136 A
bboonstra@piedmont.edu
BOOP, David ... 219-866-6116 ... 179 D
dboop@saintjoe.edu
BOOR, Kathryn, J ... 607-255-3111 ... 331 B
kjb4@cornell.edu
BOORD, Peggy, L ... 904-632-3251 ... 109 F
pboord@fscj.edu
BOOREN, Diane ... 303-457-2757 ... 84 J
dbooren@cci.edu
BOOROM, Richard ... 303-923-4222 ... 81 E
rboorom@argosy.edu
BOOROS, Deborah ... 610-282-1100 ... 427 A
deborah.booros@desales.edu
BOOS, Jean ... 843-355-4167 ... 463 D
boosj@wiltech.edu
BOOS, Manfred, B ... 708-209-3088 ... 148 E
manfred.boos@cuchicago.edu
BOOSINGER, Timothy, R ... 334-844-5771 ... 1 F
provost@auburn.edu
BOOSTER, Richard ... 541-683-5141 ... 416 A
dbooster@gutenberg.edu
BOOTH, Ann ... 304-367-4047 ... 543 H
ann.booth@fairmontstate.edu
BOOTH, Austin ... 716-645-0983 ... 351 G
abooth@buffalo.edu
BOOTH, Bradley, W ... 202-685-2387 ... 557 I
bradley.booth@ndu.edu
BOOTH, Charlotte ... 262-646-6529 ... 549 E
cbooth@nashotah.edu
BOOTH, Derrick ... 916-484-8361 ... 56 A
boothd@arc.losrios.edu
BOOTH, Eric ... 512-313-3000 ... 483 K
eric.booth@concordia.edu
BOOTH, George, E ... 302-855-1662 ... 96 E
gbooth@dtcc.edu
BOOTH, James, M ... 713-525-6960 ... 505 A
booth@stthom.edu
BOOTH, Jane, E ... 212-854-0286 ... 330 F
jeb@gc.columbia.edu
BOOTH, Julie ... 530-541-4660 ... 53 G
booth@ltcc.edu
BOOTH, Kim ... 435-613-5207 ... 512 A
kim.booth@usu.edu
BOOTH, LaQuita ... 334-229-4124 ... 1 C
lbooth@alasu.edu
BOOTH, Margaret ... 419-372-9950 ... 385 E
boothmz@bgsu.edu
BOOTH, Melanie ... 503-636-3941 ... 416 J
mbooth@marylhurst.edu
BOOTH, Paige ... 512-448-8429 ... 493 E
paigeb@stedwards.edu
BOOTH, Richard ... 618-374-5127 ... 161 E
richard.booth@principia.edu
BOOTH, Ronnie, L ... 864-646-1773 ... 461 F
rlbooth@tctc.edu
BOOTH, Scott ... 614-947-6592 ... 391 B
booths@franklin.edu
BOOTH, Susan, A ... 573-629-3002 ... 282 E
sbooth@hlg.edu
BOOTH, Susan, L ... 540-224-4640 ... 520 I
slbooth1@jchs.edu
BOOTH, Terry, L ... 803-778-6624 ... 455 G
boothtl@cctech.edu
BOOTHBY, Mandy ... 712-749-2123 ... 183 C
boothbym@bvu.edu
BOOTHBY, Rebecca ... 318-342-1982 ... 216 E
ulm@campuscornerinc.com
BOOTHE, Alan ... 334-242-7710 ... 8 A
aboothe@troy.edu
BOOTHE, Diane ... 208-426-1611 ... 142 I
dianeboothe@boisestate.edu
BOOTHE, Jason ... 435-652-7526 ... 512 B
boothe@dixie.edu
BOOTHE, M. Shane ... 832-252-4646 ... 483 C
shane.boothe@cbshouston.edu
BOOTMAN, Lyle ... 520-626-1657 ... 18 L
bootman@pharmacy.arizona.edu
BOOZER, Andrew ... 803-461-3296 ... 459 C
andrew.boozer@lr.edu
BOPKO, Patricia ... 909-652-6152 ... 39 E
patricia.bopko@chaffey.edu
BOPP, Ruthane, I ... 847-735-5025 ... 155 G
bopp@lakeforest.edu
BOQUET, Elizabeth ... 203-254-4000 ... 92 H
eboquet@fairfield.edu
BOQUET, OSB,
Gregory, M ... 985-867-2232 ... 214 G
rector@sjasc.edu
BOQUETTE, Troy ... 810-762-0243 ... 255 G
troy.boquette@mcc.edu
BORASI, Raffaella ... 585-275-3950 ... 359 B
raffaella.borasi@rochester.edu
BORAWSKI, Judy ... 414-258-4810 ... 549 D
borawskj@mtmary.edu
BORCHERS, Mitch ... 913-469-8500 ... 194 B
mborchers@jccc.edu
BORCHERS, Patrick, J ... 402-280-3009 ... 297 F
borchers@creighton.edu
BORCHERS, Timothy, A ... 218-477-2764 ... 267 F
tim.borchers@mnstate.edu
BORCK, Pat ... 478-471-2865 ... 133 H
pat.borck@maconstate.edu
BORDEAUX, Lionel ... 605-856-5880 ... 465 C
lionel.bordeaux@sintegleska.edu
BORDEAUX, Lynette ... 605-856-5880 ... 465 C
lynette.bordeaux@sintegleska.edu
BORDELON, Deborah ... 708-534-8396 ... 151 E
dbordelon@govst.edu
BORDELON, Kristi ... 407-628-6275 ... 122 C
kbordelon@teu.edu
BORDEN, David, S ... 512-223-7738 ... 481 B
dborden@austincc.edu
BORDEN, John, S ... 212-875-4603 ... 323 C
jborden@bankstreet.edu
BORDEN, M. Paige ... 407-823-4765 ... 120 B
paige.borden@ucf.edu
BORDEN, Oliver ... 505-566-3490 ... 320 D
bordeno@sanjuancollege.edu
BORDEN, Robert ... 216-421-7467 ... 388 A
rborden@cia.edu
BORDEN, Sid ... 256-352-8213 ... 10 A
sid.borden@wallacestate.edu
BORDEN, Susan ... 410-626-2506 ... 225 G
susan.borden@sjca.edu
BORDEN, Vic ... 812-855-9893 ... 173 E
vborden@indiana.edu
BORDER, Debra ... 402-481-3804 ... 296 I
dborder@bryanlgh.org
BORDERS, Gayle, P ... 606-679-8501 ... 203 C
gayle.borders@kctcs.edu
BORDERS, Marianne ... 803-981-7320 ... 463 H
borders@sctechsystem.edu
BORDIN, Cristina, L ... 512-464-8893 ... 493 E
cristinb@stedwards.edu
BORELLI, Alyssa ... 425-637-1010 ... 532 E
aborelli@cityu.edu
BOREN, Carla ... 816-584-6317 ... 287 E
carla.boren@park.edu
BOREN, David, L ... 405-325-3916 ... 413 C
dboren@ou.edu
BOREN, J. B ... 806-352-5207 ... 508 E
borenjb@wbu.edu
BOREN, Laura ... 918-456-5511 ... 409 A
borenld@nsuok.edu
BORER, Jim ... 763-424-0736 ... 268 B
jborer@nhcc.edu
BORER, Ralph (Sam), J ... 402-557-7355 ... 296 H
sam.borer@bellevue.edu
BORES, Gerald ... 503-552-2007 ... 417 D
gbores@ncnm.edu
BORG, Mary, O ... 904-620-2649 ... 120 D
mborg@unf.edu
BORGE, Keith ... 914-654-5552 ... 330 B
kborge@cnr.edu
BORGER, Patricia, A ... 414-229-3013 ... 551 D
pborger@uwm.edu
BORGES, Dan ... 831-477-5220 ... 31 I
daborges@cabrillo.edu
BORGES, Eduardo ... 281-649-3299 ... 487 H
eborges@hbu.edu
BORGES, Michael ... 510-276-3888 ... 38 I
mborges@carrington.edu
BORGMAN, Cathleen, M ... 203-254-4081 ... 92 H
cborgman@fairfield.edu
BORGMAN, Kenneth, L ... 989-463-7314 ... 247 B
borgman@alma.edu
BORGMANN-INGWERSEN,
Marian ... 402-465-2415 ... 299 H
mborgman@nebrwesleyan.edu
BORGOGNONI, Mary, E ... 716-286-8352 ... 344 D
meb@niagara.edu
BORGSMILLER, Stephen ... 573-472-3210 ... 289 K
BORGSTROM, Karen ... 603-513-5189 ... 306 E
karen.borgstrom@law.unh.edu
BORGUS, Donna ... 585-389-2471 ... 342 D
dborgus8@naz.edu
BORICH, Joe ... 419-448-3014 ... 402 E
borichj@tiffin.edu
BORIS, Barbara, A ... 610-409-3605 ... 450 D
bboris@ursinus.edu
BORIS, Patricia, A ... 716-673-3131 ... 352 A
patricia.boris@fredonia.edu
BORJESSON, Peggy ... 503-399-2537 ... 414 J
peggy.borjesson@chemeketa.edu
BORK, Ronald ... 402-643-7475 ... 297 D
ron.bork@cune.edu
BORKOWSKI, Donald, V ... 207-725-3947 ... 217 E
dborkows@bowdoin.edu
BORKOWSKI, Ellen, Y ... 518-388-6293 ... 358 G
borkowse@union.edu
BORLAND, James ... 312-777-8661 ... 153 B
jborland@aii.edu
BORLANDOE, Janice, M ... 718-270-6046 ... 328 C
jborlandoe@mec.cuny.edu
BORN, Bill ... 574-535-7543 ... 171 G
billjb@goshen.edu
BORN, Brad ... 316-284-5239 ... 191 C
bborn@bethelks.edu
BORNEMANN, Jeffrey ... 414-955-8793 ... 548 G
jbornema@mcw.edu
BORNER, John ... 315-792-7530 ... 356 B
john.borner@sunyit.edu
BORNHEIMER, Mary, E ... 618-537-6524 ... 158 A
mebornheimer@mckendree.edu
BORNSTEIN, Eva ... 718-960-8232 ... 327 C
eva.bornstein@lehman.cuny.edu
BORNSTEIN, Leah, L ... 928-226-4100 ... 13 F
leah.bornstein@coconino.edu
BORNUS, Susan ... 651-523-2929 ... 264 A
sbornus@hamline.edu

BOUTTE, Gwen 504-671-5091 210 F gboutt@dcc.edu
BOUTTE, Kimberly 925-288-5800 49 H kimberly_boutte@heald.edu
BOUTWELL, Ashli 334-556-2226 4 A aboutwell@wallace.edu
BOUTWELL, Gale, M 417-873-7211 281 D gboutwel@drury.edu
BOUZARD, Ramona, S 319-352-8217 189 J ramona.bouzard@wartburg.edu
BOUZEK, Jeff 515-643-3180 187 F jbouzek@mercydesmoines.org
BOVA, Breda 505-277-7611 321 C bova@unm.edu
BOVA, Paul 802-485-2079 514 C pbova@norwich.edu
BOVE, Elena, M 310-338-2885 56 E ebove@lmu.edu
BOVE, Laurence 330-490-7123 405 F lbove@walsh.edu
BOVE, Maria 802-773-5900 513 D maria.bove@csj.edu
BOVEE, Jerry 801-626-7738 511 G jerrybovee@weber.edu
BOVEE, Valerie, J 507-354-8221 264 K boveevj@mlc-wels.edu
BOVIA, Marilyn 419-473-2700 389 C mmbovia@daviscollege.edu
BOW, Bryce 407-569-1343 107 I bryce.bow@fcc.edu
BOWAB, Lynn 978-681-0800 241 E bowab@mslaw.edu
BOWALKOWSKI, Brian 800-567-2344 547 A bkowalkowski@menominee.edu
BOWDEN, Anita 508-854-4206 240 F anitab@qcc.mass.edu
BOWDEN, Dorothy, J 256-533-7387 3 C dorothy.bowden@vc.edu
BOWDEN, Ron 903-434-8157 491 F rbowden@ntcc.edu
BOWDEN, Russ 707-527-4262 68 E rbowden@santarosa.edu
BOWDEN, Vicky 626-815-2110 30 G vbowden@apu.edu
BOWDICH, William 505-925-8851 321 G bbowdich@unm.edu
BOWDLER, Michelle, D 617-627-3766 245 C michelle.bowdler@tufts.edu
BOWE, Adraenne 212-817-7020 327 B abowe1@gc.cuny.edu
BOWE, Debbie 352-854-2322 103 K bowed@cf.edu
BOWE, Derek 256-726-7186 6 C dbowe@oakwood.edu
BOWE, Erik, R 770-499-3360 133 A ebowe@kennesaw.edu
BOWE, Mona 574-284-4587 179 F mbowe@saintmarys.edu
BOWELL, Daniel 765-998-5241 180 B dnbowell@taylor.edu
BOWEN, Alyncia 614-234-5177 396 H abowen@mccn.edu
BOWEN, Anne 360-383-3323 540 A abowen@whatcom.ctc.edu
BOWEN, Blannie, E 814-863-7494 438 G bxb1@psu.edu
BOWEN, Brian 585-475-2411 347 G
BOWEN, Bruce 801-626-6006 511 G babowen@weber.edu
BOWEN, Candice 303-492-6893 88 H candice.bowen@colorado.edu
BOWEN, Carmen 818-766-8151 42 J cbowen@concordecareercolleges.com
BOWEN, Corey, J 410-651-8100 227 E cjbowen@umes.edu
BOWEN, Gilbert, C 910-962-3123 379 D bowengc@uncw.edu
BOWEN, James 405-789-7661 412 E james.bowen@swcu.edu
BOWEN, Jamey 864-225-7653 458 C jameybowen@forrestcollege.edu
BOWEN, Janine 410-337-6460 222 I jbowen@goucher.edu
BOWEN, John 713-743-0209 503 D jbowen@uh.edu
BOWEN, John, J 401-598-1900 453 E jbowen@jwu.edu
BOWEN, Jose, A 214-768-2880 495 A jabowen@smu.edu
BOWEN, Julie 806-291-3470 508 E bowenj@wbu.edu
BOWEN, Kara 701-228-5432 382 E kara.bowen@dakotacollege.edu
BOWEN, Karen 336-599-1181 372 G bowenk@piedmontcc.edu
BOWEN, Laura 704-484-4106 369 E bowen@clevelandcc.edu
BOWEN, Laura 678-359-5585 132 A laurab@gdn.edu
BOWEN, Lauren, L 216-397-4374 392 L bowen@jcu.edu
BOWEN, Maxine 662-254-3578 276 B mrbowen@mvsu.edu
BOWEN, Patricia, A 606-693-5000 203 F pbowen@kmbc.edu
BOWEN, Rachel 610-526-6157 430 D rbowen@harcum.edu
BOWEN, Robin, E 978-665-3421 237 E rbowen@fitchburgstate.edu
BOWEN, Roxanne 423-585-6806 476 D roxanne.bowen@ws.edu
BOWEN, Samuel, J 320-222-6090 268 G sam.bowen@ridgewater.edu
BOWEN, Sharon, G 931-540-2548 475 A sbowen@columbiastate.edu
BOWEN, Sherri, W 336-734-7200 370 F sbowen@forsythtech.edu
BOWEN, Stephen, H 404-784-8300 129 D sbowen@emory.edu
BOWEN, Susan 229-317-6747 128 D susan.bowen@darton.edu
BOWEN, Susan 609-586-4800 311 B bowens@mccc.edu
BOWEN, Tamara 410-857-2223 224 C tbowen@mcdaniel.edu
BOWEN, Terry 410-386-8494 221 G tbowen@carrollcc.edu
BOWEN, Tom 901-678-5395 474 C tmbowen1@memphis.edu
BOWEN, W. Ann 423-585-6892 476 D ann.bowen@ws.edu
BOWENS, Ollie 662-252-8000 276 G obowens@rustcollege.edu
BOWENS, Pacey 870-762-3116 20 A pbowens@smail.anc.edu
BOWENS GELLMAN, Laura Lee 973-290-4410 308 G lbowens@cse.edu
BOWER, Beth, A 978-542-7757 238 E bbower@salemstate.edu
BOWER, David, A 812-464-1918 181 B bower@usi.edu
BOWER, Eric 216-791-5000 388 C eric.bower@case.edu
BOWER, Jami 678-839-6464 139 A jbower@westga.edu
BOWER, Marco 305-593-1223 102 H mbower@albizu.edu
BOWER, Mike 701-662-1501 382 F mike.bower@lrsc.edu
BOWER, Mike 567-661-7200 400 I mike_bower@owens.edu
BOWER, Shirley 585-475-5034 347 G slbwml@rit.edu
BOWER, SCC, Theresa 973-543-6528 307 B acslibrary@acs350.org
BOWERS, Amanda 407-628-6265 122 C abowers@teu.edu
BOWERS, Blake 360-992-2938 532 F bbowers@clark.edu
BOWERS, Bonnie 602-331-7500 12 B bbowers@aii.edu
BOWERS, David, A 212-938-5666 355 B dbowers@sunyopt.edu
BOWERS, David, D 619-239-0391 37 F dbowers@cwsl.edu
BOWERS, David, G 734-929-9095 249 D dbowers@cleary.edu
BOWERS, Dianne 770-531-6360 133 C dbowers@laniertech.edu
BOWERS, Gayln, K 707-965-6231 60 I gbowers@puc.edu
BOWERS, J. Betsy 850-474-2637 121 D bbowers@uwf.edu
BOWERS, Jane 212-237-8801 327 F jbowers@jjay.cuny.edu
BOWERS, John 270-745-4278 208 A john.bowers@wku.edu
BOWERS, John 206-934-3727 537 D john.bowers@seattlecolleges.edu
BOWERS, John 304-326-1341 541 K jbowers@salemu.edu
BOWERS, Karen 209-473-5200 50 E karen_bowers@heald.edu
BOWERS, Kathy 417-626-1234 287 C kbowers@occ.edu
BOWERS, Kevin 618-544-8657 152 H bowersk@iecc.edu
BOWERS, Lynn 773-380-6786 164 D lynn.bowers@seabury.edu
BOWERS, Marilyn, R 423-585-2633 476 D marilyn.bowers@ws.edu
BOWERS, Marilyn, R 423-318-2776 476 D marilyn.bowers@ws.edu
BOWERS, Maryanne, D 267-620-4870 422 C bowersm@arcadia.edu
BOWERS, Michael, E 864-587-4220 461 D bowersme@smcsc.edu
BOWERS, Paul, E 330-569-5453 391 G bowerspe@hiram.edu
BOWERS, Richard 817-598-6213 508 F rbowers@wc.edu
BOWERS, Rodney 321-674-8080 108 H rbowers@fit.edu
BOWERS, Stephanie 360-650-2055 539 F stephanie.bowers@wwu.edu
BOWERS, Steven, P 904-632-3218 109 F sbowers@fscj.edu
BOWERSOCK, Allison, H 540-985-9943 520 I ahbowersock@jchs.edu
BOWERSOCK, Gary 303-273-3330 83 B gbowerso@mines.edu
BOWES, William 860-493-0251 90 F bowesw@ct.edu
BOWIE, DeWayne 337-482-6287 216 D dkbowie@louisiana.edu
BOWIE, Jalonna 913-234-0681 191 J jalonna.bowie@cleveland.edu
BOWIE, John 207-755-5432 218 G jbowie@cmcc.edu
BOWIE, Linda 410-951-3915 228 B lbowie@coppin.edu
BOWIE, Lois 903-593-8311 499 D lbowie@texascollege.edu
BOWIE, Michelle 202-884-9611 99 H bowiem@trinitydc.edu
BOWIE, Staci, A 843-349-2227 456 G sbowie@coastal.edu
BOWKER, Janet, L 814-732-2544 442 E bowker@edinboro.edu
BOWLAN, Ronald, E 215-503-7268 448 C ron.bowlan@jefferson.edu
BOWLES, Adam 618-842-3711 152 G bowlesa@iecc.edu
BOWLES, Anita, K 864-587-4221 461 D bowlesa@smcsc.edu
BOWLES, Crystal 918-293-5274 410 E crystal.bowles@okstate.edu
BOWLES, Diane 704-378-1202 366 A dbowles@jcsu.edu
BOWLES, Dympna 212-217-4050 333 F dympna_bowles@fitnyc.edu
BOWLES, James, H 270-824-8588 202 G james.bowles@kctcs.edu
BOWLES, Janis 706-507-8800 127 G bowles_janis@columbusstate.edu
BOWLES, Michele 904-632-3132 109 F mbowles@fscj.edu
BOWLES, Ronald 214-333-5316 484 D ronb@dbu.edu
BOWLES, Ulisa 910-672-1411 377 G ubowles@uncfsu.edu
BOWLIN, Stephanie 909-469-5383 78 I sbowlin@westernu.edu
BOWLING, Doug 513-569-1752 387 G doug.bowling@cincinnatistate.edu
BOWLING, John, C 815-939-5221 161 A jbowling@olivet.edu
BOWLING, Karen 304-929-1327 541 H kbowling@mountainstate.edu
BOWLING, Lee 859-236-6991 205 B
BOWLING, Thomas, L 301-687-4311 228 C tbowling@frostburg.edu
BOWLUS, Robin 419-358-3453 385 D bowlusr@bluffton.edu
BOWMAN, Alan 518-631-9890 358 H bowmanr@uniongraduatecollege.edu
BOWMAN, JR., C. Alvin 309-438-5677 153 D abowman@ilstu.edu
BOWMAN, Chris 405-425-5161 409 E chris.bowman@oc.edu
BOWMAN, Corey, L 660-543-4114 290 H bowman@ucmo.edu
BOWMAN, David, B 214-459-8490 494 C
BOWMAN, Denvy, A 614-236-6908 386 E dbowman@capital.edu
BOWMAN, Don 413-572-8410 238 F dbowman@westfield.ma.edu
BOWMAN, Donald, R 941-752-5301 118 J bowmand@scf.edu
BOWMAN, Gail 859-985-3774 199 A bowmang@berea.edu
BOWMAN, Gina 870-972-2250 20 D gbowman@astate.edu
BOWMAN, Helen, Y 215-895-2803 427 H helen.y.bowman@drexel.edu
BOWMAN, Jane 336-838-6142 375 C jane.bowman@wilkescc.edu
BOWMAN, John 301-687-4211 228 C jbowman@frostburg.edu
BOWMAN, Judith, M 757-683-3260 522 F jbowman@odu.edu
BOWMAN, Kevin 808-687-7032 140 G kbowman@hpu.edu
BOWMAN, Marjorie 937-775-2933 406 C marjorie.bowman@wright.edu
BOWMAN, Melanie 816-604-4155 285 E melanie.bowman@mcckc.edu
BOWMAN, Michael 510-659-6064 59 J mbowman@ohlone.edu
BOWMAN, Nelson, E 936-261-1550 496 G nebowman@pvamu.edu
BOWMAN, Pam 662-685-4771 273 E pbowman@bmc.edu
BOWMAN, Pamela, L 309-298-1971 168 C pl-bowman@wiu.edu
BOWMAN, Paul 435-797-1042 511 E paul.bowman@usu.edu
BOWMAN, Richard 781-239-5298 230 E rbowman@babson.edu
BOWMAN, Robert 575-624-7158 318 C robert.bowman@roswell.enmu.edu
BOWMAN, Ron 239-513-1122 111 A rbowman@hodges.edu
BOWMAN, Ruby 317-917-3357 178 A rbowman@martin.edu
BOWMAN, Scott 612-874-3677 265 C scott_bowman@mcad.edu
BOWMAN, Teri, A 660-543-4900 290 H tbowman@ucmo.edu
BOWMAN, Ty 562-860-2451 39 A tbowman@cerritos.edu
BOWNE, Andy 616-234-3932 251 E abowne@grcc.edu
BOWNE, Kristine 626-396-2474 29 I kristine.bowne@artcenter.edu
BOWNES, Michael, A 205-348-8341 8 D mbownes@uasystem.ua.edu
BOWRING, Kelly 610-785-6287 446 A kbowring@scs.edu
BOWRON, Steve 507-433-0695 268 H steve.bowron@riverland.edu
BOWSER, Christopher 641-683-5155 185 G chris.bowser@indianhills.edu
BOWSER, Robert 724-357-3077 442 F robert.bowser@iup.edu
BOWSER, Steve 404-270-5326 138 B sbowser@spelman.edu
BOWYER, Donald 870-972-3053 20 D dbowyer@astate.edu
BOWYER, Karen, A 731-286-3300 475 B kbowyer@dscc.edu
BOWYER, Roger 937-529-2201 403 A rogerbowyer@united.edu
BOWYER, Tom 573-518-2110 285 I
BOX, Jay 859-256-3100 201 E jay.box@kctcs.edu
BOX, Jean, A 205-726-2565 6 G jabox@samford.edu
BOX, Margaret 325-942-2335 480 E
BOX, Thomas, W 206-281-2108 537 H twb@spu.edu
BOXTON, Kenneth 510-869-6967 64 J kboxton@samuelmerritt.edu
BOYAR, Virginia 530-541-4660 53 G boyar@ltcc.edu
BOYATT, Ed 951-785-2266 53 E eboyatt@lasierra.edu
BOYCE, Eric 828-251-6710 378 D eboyce@unca.edu
BOYCE, Glenn, F 662-472-2312 274 D gboyce@holmescc.edu
BOYCE, Lynn 405-224-3140 413 E lboyce@usao.edu
BOYCE, Mary 831-582-3952 35 E mboyce@csumb.edu
BOYCE, Richard, D 812-877-8443 179 B richard.boyce@rose-hulman.edu
BOYCE, Robert 301-687-4043 228 C rjboyce@frostburg.edu
BOYCHUK, Paul 818-785-2726 38 K
BOYD, Angela 757-727-5328 519 H angela.boyd@hamptonu.edu
BOYD, Betsy, A 541-346-0946 419 B eaboyd@uoregon.edu
BOYD, Bill 910-323-5614 363 A billboyd@carolinabiblecollege.org
BOYD, Brian 407-823-3016 120 B brian.boyd@ucf.edu
BOYD, Carla, L 218-726-8795 271 F clboyd@d.umn.edu
BOYD, Carla, M 217-443-8753 148 G cboyd@dacc.edu
BOYD, Catherine, C 843-953-1826 457 B boydc@cofc.edu
BOYD, Chrispher 336-770-3323 379 E boydc@uncsa.edu
BOYD, Clarence 918-495-7704 411 C cbody@oru.edu
BOYD, Cristine 330-325-6673 397 D cboyd@neomed.edu
BOYD, Cynthia 770-426-2756 133 E cboyd@life.edu
BOYD, Cynthia, E 312-942-5496 163 D cynthia_e_boyd@rush.edu
BOYD, Danielle 618-634-3298 164 E danielleb@shawneecc.edu
BOYD, David, L 714-850-4800 72 F boyd@taftu.edu
BOYD, Deborah 615-966-6263 470 F deborah.boyd@lipscomb.edu
BOYD, Debra 803-323-2220 463 E
BOYD, Ernest 731-426-7531 470 B eboyd@lanecollege.edu
BOYD, Franette 803-535-5237 456 D fboyd@claflin.edu
BOYD, Frank, A 309-556-3255 153 F fboyd@iwu.edu
BOYD, Gary 304-357-4704 542 A garyboyd@ucwv.edu
BOYD, Gerald, L 240-629-7841 222 G glboyd@frederick.edu
BOYD, Heather 303-273-3221 83 B heather.boyd@is.mines.edu
BOYD, JR., James, I 707-965-7203 60 I jboyd@puc.edu

BOYD, Jean Ellen ..... 618-634-3240 .... 164 E jeanb@shawneecc.edu
BOYD, Jeff ..... 847-214-7900 .... 150 F jboyd@elgin.edu
BOYD, Jody ..... 207-974-4633 .... 218 H jboyd@emcc.edu
BOYD, John ..... 405-682-7501 .... 409 F jboyd@occc.edu
BOYD, John, C ..... 828-765-7351 .... 372 A jboyd@mayland.edu
BOYD, Karen ..... 309-796-5225 .... 145 H boydk@bhc.edu
BOYD, Karen, O ..... 314-576-5923 .... 291 D boyd@umsl.edu
BOYD, Kathleen ..... 401-341-2374 .... 454 D boydk@salve.edu
BOYD, Keith ..... 312-942-2694 .... 163 D keith_boyd@rush.edu
BOYD, Kelly, R ..... 731-426-7533 .... 470 B kboyd@lanecollege.edu
BOYD, Ken ..... 912-443-3015 .... 136 H kboyd@savannahtech.edu
BOYD, Kim ..... 918-495-7108 .... 411 C kboyd@oru.edu
BOYD, Linda, D ..... 617-732-2800 .... 241 C linda.boyd@mcphs.edu
BOYD, Lonnie ..... 620-229-6136 .... 196 G lonnie.boyd@sckans.edu
BOYD, Margaret, E ..... 816-604-1326 .... 284 H margaret.boyd@mcckc.edu
BOYD, Margaret, M ..... 207-859-4312 .... 217 G mbboyd@colby.edu
BOYD, Mary, K ..... 619-260-4545 .... 76 D deanboyd@sandiego.edu
BOYD, Michael ..... 706-754-7807 .... 135 A mboyd@northgatech.edu
BOYD, Michael, J ..... 563-588-7024 .... 187 C michael.boyd@loras.edu
BOYD, Nick ..... 530-283-0202 .... 47 B nboyd@frc.edu
BOYD, Robert ..... 559-278-4480 .... 35 A robert_boyd@csufresno.edu
BOYD, Robert ..... 980-598-1906 .... 365 I robert.boyd@jwu.edu
BOYD, III, Samuel ..... 314-264-1000 .... 292 D samuel.boyd@vatterott.edu
BOYD, Sharon, H ..... 910-962-7769 .... 379 D boyds@uncw.edu
BOYD, Stephanie ..... 502-220-4444 .... 200 K stephanie.boyd@frontier.edu
BOYD, Steve ..... 970-945-8691 .... 82 G
BOYD, Steven ..... 916-484-8030 .... 56 A boyds@arc.losrios.edu
BOYD, Susan ..... 586-445-7408 .... 254 C boyds@macomb.edu
BOYD, Terry ..... 614-947-6140 .... 391 B boydt@franklin.edu
BOYD, Thomas ..... 303-273-3247 .... 83 B tboyd@mines.edu
BOYD, Todd, T ..... 580-774-3782 .... 412 F todd.boyd@swosu.edu
BOYD-PUGH, Jennifer, N .. 305-899-4057 .... 101 M jboydpugh@mail.barry.edu
BOYD-SCOTLAND, Joann .. 803-793-5100 .... 457 F boydscotland@denmarktech.edu
BOYD-STEWART, Ann ..... 412-365-1258 .... 425 C aboydstewart@chatham.edu
BOYDEN, Kenneth ..... 718-982-2224 .... 327 A kenneth.boyden@csi.cuny.edu
BOYDSTUN, Morris ..... 479-394-7622 .... 23 E mboydstun@rmcc.edu
BOYE-BEAMAN, Joni ..... 989-964-4062 .... 257 G jbb@svsu.edu
BOYENS, Kathy, R ..... 815-939-5211 .... 161 A kboyens@olivet.edu
BOYER, Bruce ..... 508-565-1380 .... 245 A bboyer@stonehill.edu
BOYER, Bruce, E ..... 573-875-7251 .... 280 A beboyer@ccis.edu
BOYER, Charles, D ..... 559-278-2061 .... 35 A cboyer@csufresno.edu
BOYER, Debra, A ..... 617-228-2403 .... 239 C dboyer@bhcc.mass.edu
BOYER, Gary ..... 315-279-5296 .... 337 K gboyer@mail.keuka.edu
BOYER, Jeff ..... 409-740-4503 .... 497 F boyerj@tamug.edu
BOYER, John, W ..... 773-702-8576 .... 166 G jwboyer@uchicago.edu
BOYER, Larry ..... 252-328-6514 .... 377 E boyerl@ecu.edu
BOYER, Mary ..... 215-702-4541 .... 444 B mboyer@pbu.edu
BOYER, Mary Jo ..... 610-450-6524 .... 426 G mboyer@dccc.edu
BOYER, Pat ..... 505-661-4688 .... 321 E patboyer@unm.edu
BOYER, Patricia ..... 505-661-4692 .... 321 E patboyer@unm.edu
BOYER, Paul, J ..... 413-597-4181 .... 246 D paul.j.boyer@williams.edu
BOYER, Raymond, E ..... 701-231-6539 .... 382 B ray.boyer@ndsu.edu
BOYER, Scott ..... 717-560-8271 .... 433 D sboyer@lbc.edu
BOYER, Suzanne, L ..... 410-777-2045 .... 221 C slboyer1@aacc.edu
BOYER-OWENS, Linda ..... 210-485-0230 .... 479 A lboyer-owens@alamo.edu
BOYES, Jerry, S ..... 716-878-6533 .... 353 A boyesjs@buffalostate.edu
BOYETT, Chad ..... 912-287-5808 .... 135 F cboyett@okefenokeetech.edu
BOYETT, James, C ..... 501-362-1125 .... 20 C jcboyett@heberspring.asub.edu
BOYETTE, Alan, J ..... 336-334-5494 .... 379 B alan_boyette@uncg.edu
BOYETTE, Barbara, G ..... 336-316-2825 .... 365 A boyettebg@guilford.edu
BOYETTE, Don, L ..... 252-246-1275 .... 375 D dboyette@wilsoncc.edu
BOYETTE, Rick ..... 903-823-3274 .... 496 E ricky.boyette@texarkanacollege.edu
BOYETTE, Sandra, C ..... 336-758-6082 .... 380 C boyette@wfu.edu
BOYE', Stephanie ..... 617-369-3618 .... 244 E sboye@smfa.edu
BOYKIN, Coretta ..... 251-578-1313 .... 6 E cboykin@rstc.edu
BOYKIN, Deborah ..... 757-221-3178 .... 518 A boykin@wm.edu
BOYKIN, III, George, H ..... 919-516-4888 .... 376 D ghboykin@st-aug.edu
BOYKIN, Karen ..... 215-780-1420 .... 446 G kboykin@salus.edu
BOYKIN, Melinda ..... 216-368-3245 .... 386 F melinda.boykin@case.edu
BOYKIN, Regena ..... 601-635-2111 .... 274 A rboykin@eccc.edu
BOYKIN, Ted ..... 570-586-2400 .... 422 G tboykin@bbc.edu
BOYLAN, Ellen ..... 570-348-6203 .... 435 F eboylan@marywood.edu
BOYLAN, Erin ..... 607-753-2517 .... 353 B erin.boylan@cortland.edu
BOYLAN, Joyce ..... 626-873-2111 .... 58 C
BOYLAN, Peter, J ..... 478-387-4776 .... 131 A
BOYLAN, Stanley, L ..... 212-463-0400 .... 358 B stanley.boylan@touro.edu
BOYLE, Ann, M ..... 618-650-3779 .... 165 C aboyle@siue.edu
BOYLE, Antonio ..... 803-536-7186 .... 460 G aboyle@scsu.edu
BOYLE, Brian ..... 251-442-2287 .... 9 A bboyle@umobile.edu
BOYLE, Christine ..... 215-968-8058 .... 423 F boylec@bucks.edu
BOYLE, Ellen ..... 518-438-3111 .... 340 A eboyle@mariacollege.edu
BOYLE, Jane, M ..... 973-655-2131 .... 311 F boylej@mail.montclair.edu
BOYLE, Jeff ..... 828-395-1456 .... 371 D jboyle@isothermal.edu
BOYLE, Jill ..... 970-945-8691 .... 82 G
BOYLE, JoAnne, W ..... 724-838-4211 .... 447 C boyle@setonhill.edu
BOYLE, John ..... 914-347-3910 .... 360 E john.boyle@sunywcc.edu
BOYLE, Kevin ..... 973-618-3372 .... 308 C kboyle@caldwell.edu
BOYLE, Lori ..... 619-239-0391 .... 37 F lboyle@cwsl.edu
BOYLE, Mary-Ellen ..... 508-793-7671 .... 233 B mboyle@clarku.edu
BOYLE, Mike, A ..... 615-898-2177 .... 473 G mike.boyle@mtsu.edu
BOYLE, Nuala ..... 585-389-2670 .... 342 D nboyle5@naz.edu
BOYLE, Patrick, M ..... 773-508-7070 .... 157 C pboyle@luc.edu
BOYLE, Rebecca ..... 716-827-2559 .... 358 D boyler@trocaire.edu
BOYLE, Richard ..... 713-221-8065 .... 503 F boyler@uhd.edu
BOYLE, Richard, A ..... 636-949-4477 .... 283 J rboyle@lindenwood.edu
BOYLE, Susan, A ..... 330-569-5119 .... 391 G boylesa@hiram.edu
BOYLE, Taggart ..... 617-984-1771 .... 243 H tboyle@quincycollege.edu
BOYLES, Bob ..... 618-842-3711 .... 152 G boylesr@iecc.edu
BOYLES, Dixon ..... 252-940-6223 .... 368 C dixonb@beaufortccc.edu
BOYLES, Elinda, C ..... 740-351-3005 .... 401 I eboyles@shawnee.edu
BOYLES, Joel ..... 662-562-3240 .... 276 D jboyles@northwestms.edu
BOYLES, Rhonda, J ..... 210-434-6711 .... 492 B rjboyles@lake.ollusa.edu
BOYLES, Robin ..... 662-846-4804 .... 273 H rboyles@deltastate.edu
BOYMELGREEN, Shaya ..... 718-434-0784 .... 325 I
BOYNTON, Andrew, C ..... 617-552-4107 .... 232 B andy.boynton@bc.edu
BOYNTON, Robert, A ..... 973-596-3441 .... 312 C robert.boynton@njit.edu
BOYS, Kevin, S ..... 937-393-3431 .... 402 A kboys@sscc.edu
BOYUM, Paula ..... 425-564-2265 .... 531 G paula.boyum@bellevuecollege.edu
BOYUM-BREEN, Trenda ..... 651-793-1521 .... 267 A trenda.boyumbreen@metrostate.edu
BOZARTH, Diane ..... 573-288-6473 .... 280 I dbozarth@culver.edu
BOZARTH, Peggy, I ..... 270-707-3844 .... 202 E peggy.bozarth@kctcs.edu
BOZEMAN, Carlyn ..... 937-512-2781 .... 401 J carlyn.bozeman@sinclair.edu
BOZEMAN, Joseph, C ..... 443-885-3017 .... 224 E joseph.bozeman@morgan.edu
BOZIC, Christy ..... 765-455-9375 .... 174 A cbozic@purdue.edu
BOZINSKI, Glenn ..... 570-674-6434 .... 436 F gbozinsk@misericordia.edu
BOZYLINSKY, Garrett, A ..... 401-874-4599 .... 454 E garry@uri.edu
BOZZUTO, Victoria ..... 203-285-2408 .... 91 D vbozzuto@gwcc.commnet.edu
BRAATEN, Beth ..... 719-590-6758 .... 83 J bbraaten@coloradotech.edu
BRAATEN, Jennifer, L ..... 540-365-4202 .... 519 C jbraaten@ferrum.edu
BRAATEN, Pamela, K ..... 701-788-4773 .... 381 H pamela.braaten@mayvillestate.edu
BRAATZ, Jay ..... 312-362-7561 .... 149 A jbraatz@depaul.edu
BRABAZON, Jodi ..... 215-574-9600 .... 431 B jbrabazon@hussianart.edu
BRABHAM, Sherry, F ..... 212-217-4020 .... 333 F sherry_brabham@fitnyc.edu
BRABHAM, Susan, S ..... 803-938-3795 .... 462 G brabhams@uscsumter.edu
BRABOY, John, R ..... 812-288-8878 .... 178 E macfs@mindspring.com
BRACCI, Steven ..... 310-689-3200 .... 42 H sbracci@kaplan.edu
BRACCIA, Daniel ..... 914-674-7379 .... 340 F dbraccia@mercy.edu
BRACCIANO, Susan ..... 816-271-4214 .... 286 G braccian@missouriwestern.edu
BRACE, Liz ..... 828-298-3325 .... 380 D gathering@warren-wilson.edu
BRACE, Simon ..... 704-847-5600 .... 377 B sbrace@ses.edu
BRACEY, Carol ..... 951-343-4456 .... 31 J cbracey@calbaptist.edu
BRACEY, Gerald ..... 228-897-7101 .... 278 C jerry.bracey@wmcarey.edu
BRACEY, Taylor ..... 563-344-1500 .... 183 B tbracey@brownmackie.edu
BRACEY, W. Earl ..... 309-298-1900 .... 168 C we-bracey@wiu.edu
BRACK, Jonathan, M ..... 215-572-3878 .... 451 D jbrack@wts.edu
BRACK, Tiffany ..... 219-769-3321 .... 170 C tabrack@brownmackie.edu
BRACKEN, Damien, S ..... 617-266-1400 .... 231 E
BRACKEN, Gary ..... 816-415-7871 .... 293 C brackeng@william.jewell.edu
BRACKEN, James ..... 330-672-2962 .... 393 D jbracke1@kent.edu
BRACKEN, Larry ..... 850-484-1705 .... 115 B lbracken@pensacolastate.edu
BRACKEN, Lisa ..... 803-778-6652 .... 455 G brackenlm@cctech.edu
BRACKER, Beverly ..... 619-961-4235 .... 72 J bbracker@tjsl.edu
BRACKETT, Andrew ..... 973-618-3519 .... 308 C abrackett@caldwell.edu
BRACKETT, Edmund ..... 816-584-6588 .... 287 E edmund.brackett@park.edu
BRACKETT, Geoffrey, L ..... 845-575-3000 .... 340 B geoffrey.brackett@marist.edu
BRACKETT, Jan ..... 207-725-3142 .... 217 E jbracket@bowdoin.edu
BRACKETT, Robert ..... 708-563-1577 .... 153 C rbrackett@iit.edu
BRACKIN, Chad ..... 225-578-4736 .... 212 G cmb@lsu.edu
BRACKLEY, Paul ..... 312-329-4225 .... 159 A paul.brackley@moody.edu
BRACKNELL, Ann ..... 205-391-2958 .... 6 I abracknell@sheltonstate.edu
BRACY, Marion ..... 504-520-7507 .... 217 A mbracy@xula.edu
BRADAC, John, P ..... 607-274-3365 .... 336 G jbradac@ithaca.edu
BRADACH, Carmen ..... 218-749-7743 .... 269 F c.bradach@mr.mnscu.edu
BRADACH, Carmen ..... 218-749-7743 .... 266 I c.bradach@mr.mnscu.edu
BRADBERRY, J. Chris ..... 402-280-2950 .... 297 F jcbradberry@creighton.edu
BRADBERRY, Richard ..... 443-885-3488 .... 224 E richard.bradberry@morgan.edu
BRADBURY, Boyd, L ..... 218-477-2095 .... 267 F bradbury@mnstate.edu
BRADBURY, Guy ..... 252-633-4464 .... 367 F gbradbury@moc.edu
BRADBURY JONES, Mary 503-675-3963 .... 416 J mjones@marylhurst.edu
BRADDER, Kelley, L ..... 515-961-1621 .... 189 C kelley.bradder@simpson.edu
BRADDIX, D'Andre ..... 314-516-5205 .... 291 D braddixd@umsl.edu
BRADDLEE, ... 914-674-7262 .... 340 F bradlee@mercy.edu
BRADDS, Nancy ..... 407-569-1160 .... 107 I nancy.bradds@fcc.edu
BRADEN, Jeffery, P ..... 919-515-2468 .... 378 C jeff_braden@ncsu.edu
BRADEN, SJ, Michael, L ..... 201-761-6014 .... 314 F mbraden@spc.edu
BRADEN, Sandra ..... 313-664-7471 .... 249 E sbraden@collegeforcreativestudies.edu
BRADFIELD, Brett ..... 605-331-6712 .... 466 E brett.bradfield@usiouxfalls.edu
BRADFIELD, Carol ..... 407-303-9585 .... 100 G carol.bradfield@adu.edu
BRADFIELD, Glynis ..... 269-471-3432 .... 252 A glynisb@andrews.edu
BRADFIELD, Katrina ..... 731-661-5346 .... 477 B kbradfie@uu.edu
BRADFIELD, Murray ..... 770-671-1200 .... 124 F mbradfield@argosy.edu
BRADFIELD, Terry ..... 202-885-8631 .... 100 C tbradfield@wesleyseminary.edu
BRADFORD, SR., Corey, S ..... 936-261-2150 .... 496 G csbradford@pvamu.edu
BRADFORD, Frances, C ..... 757-221-7802 .... 518 A fcbrad@wm.edu
BRADFORD, James ..... 615-322-2316 .... 478 A james.w.bradford@vanderbilt.edu
BRADFORD, Jerry ..... 256-233-8278 .... 1 E jerry.bradford@athens.edu
BRADFORD, Lawrence ..... 323-953-4000 .... 54 H bradfoll@lacitycollege.edu
BRADFORD, Linda ..... 205-247-8001 .... 7 F lbradford@stillman.edu
BRADFORD, Margaret ..... 541-956-7088 .... 420 B mbradford@roguecc.edu
BRADFORD, Michele ..... 256-439-6837 .... 3 J mbradford@gadsdenstate.edu
BRADFORD, Nicole ..... 817-515-4507 .... 496 C nicole.bradford@tccd.edu
BRADFORD, Peggy ..... 410-462-8001 .... 221 E pbradford@bccc.edu
BRADFORD, Robert ..... 706-721-0822 .... 130 D rbradford@georgiahealth.edu
BRADFORD, Sarah, E ..... 423-439-8304 .... 473 F bradfors@etsu.edu
BRADFORD, Susan, E ..... 713-942-3436 .... 505 A bradfords@stthom.edu
BRADFORD-PERRY, Emma ..... 225-771-4990 .... 214 I emma_perry@subr.edu
BRADFORD ROUSE, Teri ..... 805-565-7255 .... 79 A tbradfordrouse@westmont.edu
BRADIN, Bernice ..... 617-349-8685 .... 236 B bbradin@lesley.edu
BRADLEY, Alan ..... 615-297-7545 .... 467 A alanb@aquinascollege.edu
BRADLEY, Alice ..... 704-290-5832 .... 374 A abradley@spcc.edu
BRADLEY, Brenda ..... 712-274-6400 .... 190 B brenda.bradley@witcc.edu
BRADLEY, Carol, B ..... 863-667-5026 .... 118 F cbradly@seu.edu
BRADLEY, Colleen ..... 610-436-2128 .... 444 A cbradley@wcupa.edu
BRADLEY, Dale, R ..... 304-367-4692 .... 543 B dale.bradley@pierpont.edu
BRADLEY, Daniel, J ..... 812-237-4000 .... 173 B president@indstate.edu
BRADLEY, David, M ..... 713-221-8610 .... 503 F bradleyd@uhd.edu
BRADLEY, Dennis, J ..... 814-732-1030 .... 442 E bradley@edinboro.edu
BRADLEY, George, C ..... 706-821-8230 .... 135 G gbradley@paine.edu
BRADLEY, Jacquline ..... 707-468-3110 .... 57 A jbradley@mendocino.edu
BRADLEY, Jane ..... 641-782-1338 .... 189 E bradley@swcciowa.edu
BRADLEY, Jane ..... 802-322-1652 .... 513 E jane.bradley@goddard.edu
BRADLEY, Jennifer ..... 319-398-4913 .... 187 B jbradley@kirkwood.edu
BRADLEY, Jennifer ..... 808-734-9890 .... 141 J jbradley@hawaii.edu
BRADLEY, JoAnn ..... 718-270-4418 .... 352 D jbradley@downstate.edu
BRADLEY, Joseph ..... 410-617-5780 .... 223 I jbradley@loyola.edu
BRADLEY, Judy ..... 606-218-5253 .... 207 F judybradley@upike.edu
BRADLEY, Julie ..... 972-758-3821 .... 483 H jbradley@collin.edu
BRADLEY, Kathy ..... 717-337-6960 .... 429 I kbradley@gettysburg.edu
BRADLEY, Kevin, L ..... 812-265-2580 .... 177 A kbradley@ivytech.edu

BRADLEY, Leah, J .... 502-895-3411.... 204 F
lbradley@lpts.edu
BRADLEY, Marcy, K .... 607-871-2350.... 322 E
bradlemk@alfred.edu
BRADLEY, Mark .... 360-882-2200...... 48 E
markbradley@ggbts.edu
BRADLEY, Martha, S .... 801-585-3582.... 511 C
martha.bradley@utah.edu
BRADLEY, Monica .... 318-274-6118.... 215 E
bradleym@gram.edu
BRADLEY, Monty, E .... 614-823-1409.... 400 H
mbradley@otterbein.edu
BRADLEY, Natalie .... 707-256-7372...... 58 F
nbradley@napavalley.edu
BRADLEY, Nedra .... 601-484-8674.... 275 A
nbradley@meridiancc.edu
BRADLEY, Patrick, J .... 660-543-4515.... 290 H
pbradley@ucmo.edu
BRADLEY, Paul, A .... 651-631-5592.... 270 B
pabradley@nwc.edu
BRADLEY, Robert, E .... 850-644-0797.... 119 D
rbradley@fsu.edu
BRADLEY, Robert, J .... 302-292-3838...... 96 F
bradley@dtcc.edu
BRADLEY, Roger .... 386-267-0565.... 104 E
director@daytonacollege.edu
BRADLEY, Ryan .... 918-343-7782.... 411 H
ryanbradley@rsu.edu
BRADLEY, Tanya, W .... 802-626-6218.... 515 G
tanya.bradley@lyndonstate.edu
BRADLEY, Tess .... 610-341-5827.... 428 E
tbradley@eastern.edu
BRADLEY, Winifred .... 850-484-2014.... 115 B
wbradley@pensacolastate.edu
BRADLEY-DOPPES, Peg ..... 303-871-3399...... 89 A
pbd@du.edu
BRADLEY-HASTY, Barbara 252-536-7203.... 371 B
hastyba@halifaxcc.edu
BRADSHAW, Amelia, M ..... 804-523-5867.... 527 A
abradshaw@reynolds.edu
BRADSHAW, Boyd .... 636-227-2100.... 284 B
boyd.bradshaw@logan.edu
BRADSHAW, Brent .... 972-279-6511.... 479 H
bbradshaw@amberton.edu
BRADSHAW, Debra .... 816-268-5472.... 286 I
dlbradshaw@nts.edu
BRADSHAW, Felicia .... 202-231-3354.... 557 J
felicia.bradshaw@dodiis.mil
BRADSHAW, Gail .... 708-534-4124.... 151 E
gbradshaw@govst.edu
BRADSHAW, Gayle .... 530-541-4660...... 53 G
bradshaw@ltcc.edu
BRADSHAW, George .... 909-594-5611...... 58 A
gbradshaw@mtsac.edu
BRADSHAW, John, F .... 919-572-1625.... 362 C
jbradshaw@apexsot.edu
BRADSHAW, Ken .... 270-534-3169.... 203 E
ken.bradshaw@kctcs.edu
BRADSHAW, Kenny .... 901-448-5661.... 477 E
kbradsh1@uthsc.edu
BRADSHAW, Kim .... 704-355-5584.... 363 D
kim.bradshaw@carolinascollege.edu
BRADSHAW, Marjorie .... 913-234-0607.... 191 J
marjorie.bradshaw@cleveland.edu
BRADSHAW, Michael .... 601-477-4120.... 274 H
michael.bradshaw@jcjc.edu
BRADSHAW, Sheryl .... 903-813-2444.... 481 A
sbradshaw@austincollege.edu
BRADSHAW, Steve .... 706-295-6934.... 131 B
sbradshaw@gntc.edu
BRADSHAW, Susan .... 352-854-2322.... 103 K
bradshas@cf.edu
BRADSHAW, William .... 215-204-7759.... 447 H
william.bradshaw@temple.edu
BRADSHAW, Wilson, G .... 239-590-1055.... 119 B
president@fgcu.edu
BRADSHAW, York .... 410-951-1288.... 228 B
ybradshaw@coppin.edu
BRADSHER, Carl .... 434-791-5646.... 516 G
cbradshe@averett.edu
BRADSHER, Judy, S .... 336-599-1181.... 372 G
bradshj@piedmontcc.edu
BRADT, Jeremy .... 815-599-3486.... 152 B
jeremy.bradt@highland.edu
BRADT, Kay .... 785-594-8414.... 190 F
kay.bradt@bakeru.edu
BRADY, Brac .... 207-255-1290.... 220 E
bracb@maine.edu
BRADY, Carolyn, M .... 610-861-5342.... 437 H
cbrady@northampton.edu
BRADY, Christian .... 814-865-2631.... 438 G
cmb44@psu.edu
BRADY, Claire .... 352-435-6308.... 112 J
bradyc@lscc.edu
BRADY, David, M .... 203-576-4589...... 94 F
dbrady@bridgeport.edu
BRADY, Elizabeth, A .... 415-442-7813...... 48 F
ebrady@ggu.edu
BRADY, Henry .... 510-642-5116...... 73 H
hbrady@econ.berkeley.edu
BRADY, James .... 509-533-3660.... 533 C
jimb@spokanefalls.edu
BRADY, Jill .... 706-864-1760.... 134 G
jebrady@northgeorgia.edu
BRADY, Kathleen .... 314-977-8173.... 289 C
bradyk@slu.edu
BRADY, Kevin .... 985-549-2001.... 216 C
kevin.brady@selu.edu
BRADY, Linda, P .... 336-334-5266.... 379 B
lpbrady@uncg.edu
BRADY, Linda Beth .... 512-313-3000.... 483 K
lindabeth.brady@concordia.edu
BRADY, Michael .... 608-363-2200.... 546 E
bradym@beloit.edu
BRADY, Reginald .... 323-953-4287...... 54 H
bradyr@lacitycollege.edu
BRADY, Steven .... 315-464-4510.... 352 E
bradys@upstate.edu
BRADY, Steven, D .... 314-984-7640.... 289 A
sbrady@stlcc.edu
BRADY, Tara .... 781-768-7238.... 244 A
tara.brady@regiscollege.edu
BRADY, Thomas, F .... 219-785-5740.... 179 A
tfbrady@pnc.edu
BRADY, Todd .... 731-661-6566.... 477 B
tbrady@uu.edu
BRAENDEL, Carly .... 828-669-8012.... 367 E
cbraendel@montreat.edu
BRAEUTIGAM, Ronald, R .. 847-491-7040.... 160 E
braeutigam@northwestern.edu
BRAGG, Dallas .... 704-806-7171.... 541 H
dbragg@mountainstate.edu
BRAGG, Mark, S .... 423-439-4137.... 473 F
bragg@etsu.edu
BRAGG, Martin, E .... 805-756-2511...... 33 I
mbragg@calpoly.edu
BRAGG, Michael, B .... 217-333-2150.... 167 D
mbragg@illinois.edu
BRAGG, Nancy, S .... 540-665-4538.... 524 E
nbragg@su.edu
BRAGG, Rachel .... 304-929-1545.... 541 H
rbragg@mountainstate.edu
BRAGG, Sadie .... 212-220-8320.... 326 D
sbragg@bmcc.cuny.edu
BRAHA, Habtu .... 410-951-3447.... 228 B
hbraha@coppin.edu
BRAHA, Habtu .... 410-951-3014.... 228 B
hbraha@coppin.edu
BRAHAMS, Teri, T .... 865-694-6476.... 475 G
tbrahams@pstcc.edu
BRAHM, Gary .... 949-753-4774...... 31 B
chancellor@brandman.edu
BRAIDER, Christopher .... 303-492-3261...... 88 H
christopher.braider@colorado.edu
BRAIDES, Cheryl .... 215-612-6600.... 432 C
cbraides@chicareers.com
BRAILEY, David, J .... 860-701-7739...... 93 E
brailey_d@mitchell.edu
BRAILOFSKY, Yosef .... 845-362-3053.... 323 F
BRAILOW, David, G .... 317-738-8017.... 171 F
dbrailow@franklincollege.edu
BRAIM, Barry .... 413-775-1311.... 239 E
braim@gcc.mass.edu
BRAINARD, Mark, T .... 302-454-3917...... 96 F
brainard@dtcc.edu
BRAINARD, Nancy .... 918-495-7119.... 411 C
nbrainard@oru.edu
BRAINERD, Marian, J .... 937-775-5588.... 406 C
marian.brainerd@wright.edu
BRAISHER, Mark, H .... 405-912-9013.... 408 D
mbraisher@hc.edu
BRAITMAN, Keli .... 816-501-4122.... 288 A
keli.braitman@rockhurst.edu
BRAKEFIELD, Jean Ann ...... 843-349-2846.... 456 G
jeanann@coastal.edu
BRAKKE, David, F .... 540-568-3508.... 520 H
brakkedf@jmu.edu
BRALY, JR., Cliff .... 336-272-7102.... 364 G
bralyc@greensboro.edu
BRAMANTE, Paula .... 617-951-2350.... 242 G
paula.bramante@necb.edu
BRAMBILA, Albert .... 760-921-5447...... 61 C
abrambila@paloverde.edu
BRAMBLETT, Jeff .... 800-955-2527.... 282 D
jbramblett@grantham.edu
BRAMBLETT, Sandra, J ...... 404-894-8874.... 130 F
sandi.bramblett@irp.gatech.edu
BRAME, Tracey .... 616-301-6800.... 258 F
bramet@cooley.edu
BRAMLAGE, Jenell .... 419-227-3141.... 404 D
bramlage@unoh.edu
BRAMLAGE, SC, Nancy ...... 513-244-4844.... 388 E
nancy_bramlage@mail.msj.edu
BRAMLET-HECKER, Gwen . 319-277-0220.... 186 H
BRAMLETT, Nancy .... 816-303-7828.... 279 K
nbramlett@kc.coloradotech.edu
BRAMLETT, Rebecca .... 919-962-4388.... 378 E
rebecca_bramlett@unc.edu
BRAMMELL, Keith .... 606-326-2426.... 201 F
keith.brammell@kctcs.edu
BRAMMER, Erika .... 423-652-6301.... 470 A
ebrammer@king.edu
BRAMUCCI, Robert, S .... 949-582-4577...... 70 D
rbramucci@socccd.edu
BRAMWELL, Bevil .... 540-338-2700.... 517 G
frbramwell@cdu.edu
BRANAN, Jean .... 858-598-1200...... 30 D
jbranan@aii.edu
BRANCA, Matthew, P .... 570-326-3761.... 440 L
mbranca@pct.edu
BRANCAMP, William, M .... 601-977-0960.... 278 A
william.brancamp@vc.edu
BRANCATO, Marco .... 781-239-2571.... 239 G
mbrancato@massbay.edu
BRANCH, Craig .... 540-891-3007.... 526 I
cbranch@germanna.edu
BRANCH, Deborah, G .... 252-335-3271.... 377 F
dgbranch@mail.ecsu.edu
BRANCH, Gary .... 256-395-2211........ 7 D
gbranch@suscc.edu
BRANCH, Gary, L .... 251-580-2202........ 5 A
gbranch@faulknerstate.edu
BRANCH, Kevin .... 404-215-7902.... 134 D
kbranch@morehouse.edu
BRANCH, Miquon .... 619-321-3010...... 29 G
mbranch@argosy.edu
BRANCH, Teresa, S .... 406-243-5225.... 294 I
teresa.branch@umontana.edu
BRANCH-FRAPPIER,
Michele .... 803-754-4100.... 457 D
BRANCH-GRIFFIN,
Rebecca .... 804-524-5674.... 529 H
rbgriffi@vsu.edu
BRANCHEAU, Carrie .... 303-753-6046...... 88 B
BRANCHINI, Ann, Z .... 860-383-5204...... 92 E
abranchini@trcc.commnet.edu
BRANCOLINI, Kristine .... 310-338-4593...... 56 E
kbrancol@lmu.edu
BRAND, Amy .... 601-553-3455.... 275 A
abrand@meridiancc.edu
BRAND, David .... 910-678-8307.... 370 E
brandd@faytechcc.edu
BRAND, Frederick .... 609-984-1588.... 316 A
fbrand@tesc.edu
BRAND, Jeffrey, S .... 415-422-6304...... 76 E
brandj@usfca.edu
BRAND, Jonathan .... 319-895-4324.... 183 G
jbrand@cornellcollege.edu
BRAND, Latricia .... 503-768-7743.... 416 G
lbrand@lclark.edu
BRAND, Richard .... 865-981-8011.... 471 B
richard.brand@maryvillecollege.edu
BRAND, Ronald .... 609-894-9311.... 308 B
rbrand@bcc.edu
BRANDAU-HYNEK, Ann .... 608-785-9585.... 555 F
brandauhyneka@westerntc.edu
BRANDEBERRY, Shari .... 419-434-4245.... 406 A
registrar@winebrenner.edu
BRANDEBURG, Rosanne ... 352-365-3515.... 112 J
brandebr@lscc.edu
BRANDEBURY, Amy .... 812-488-2155.... 180 E
ab288@evansville.edu
BRANDEL, Rick, L .... 928-523-6696...... 16 I
rick.brandel@nau.edu
BRANDENBURG, Aurelia ... 859-985-3173.... 199 A
aurelia_brandenburg@berea.edu
BRANDENBURG, Mark, C . 843-953-5252.... 456 C
mark.brandenburg@citadel.edu
BRANDES, Derek .... 253-833-9111.... 534 H
dbrandes@greenriver.edu
BRANDES, Derek .... 509-544-4914.... 532 H
dbrandes@columbiabasin.edu
BRANDES, Gregory .... 310-689-3200...... 42 H
gbrandes@kaplan.edu
BRANDES, Rand .... 828-328-7077.... 366 E
rand.brandes@lr.edu
BRANDFORD-CALVO,
Dania, C .... 401-874-2018.... 454 E
brandford@uri.edu
BRANDIMORE, Merry Jo .. 989-964-4289.... 257 G
mjbrand@svsu.edu
BRANDING, Celeste, E ...... 630-844-7520.... 145 F
cbrandin@aurora.edu
BRANDON, Alonzo, C .... 757-683-3421.... 522 F
abrandon@odu.edu
BRANDON, Dave, E .... 217-424-3612.... 158 G
dbrandon@millikin.edu
BRANDON, David, A .... 734-764-9416.... 259 A
dabran@umich.edu
BRANDON, Deborah, L ...... 909-869-3427...... 33 J
dlbrandon@csupomona.edu
BRANDON, Eileen .... 706-721-2515.... 130 D
ebrandon@georgiahealth.edu
BRANDON, Elvis .... 615-230-3375.... 476 C
elvis.brandon@volstate.edu
BRANDON, Eric .... 828-328-7301.... 366 E
eric.brandon@lr.edu
BRANDON, John, R .... 419-289-5034.... 384 G
jbrandon@ashland.edu
BRANDON, Kevin .... 708-209-3127.... 148 E
kevin.brandon@cuchicago.edu
BRANDON, Lisa, K .... 618-537-6865.... 158 A
lkbrandon@mckendree.edu
BRANDON, Maureen .... 970-247-7264...... 84 K
brandon_m@fortlewis.edu
BRANDON, Sonia .... 970-248-1884...... 82 F
sbrandon@coloradomesa.edu
BRANDSEN, Cheryl .... 616-526-8538.... 249 A
brac@calvin.edu
BRANDSTETTER, Mike .... 253-680-7229.... 531 F
mbrandstetter@bates.ctc.edu
BRANDT, Allan, M .... 617-496-1464.... 235 D
brandt@fas.harvard.edu
BRANDT, Barry, M .... 712-707-7284.... 188 D
brandt@nwciowa.edu
BRANDT, Elaine .... 573-897-5000.... 284 A
BRANDT, Jay, J .... 561-237-7947.... 113 D
jbrandt@lynn.edu
BRANDT, John .... 540-261-4478.... 524 H
john.brandt@svu.edu
BRANDT, John .... 731-661-5015.... 477 B
jbrandt@uu.edu
BRANDT, Martin .... 631-420-2333.... 356 A
martin.brandt@farmingdale.edu
BRANDT, Thompson, A ..... 815-599-3450.... 152 B
thompson.brandt@highland.edu
BRANDT, Troy, A .... 515-574-1985.... 185 I
brandt@iowacentral.edu
BRANDT, William .... 973-278-5400.... 307 F
wab@berkeleycollege.edu
BRANDT, William .... 973-278-5400.... 323 H
wab@berkeleycollege.edu
BRANDT, William, A .... 724-946-6216.... 451 C
brandtwa@westminster.edu
BRANDT-RAUF, Paul .... 312-996-5939.... 167 B
pwb1@uic.edu
BRANDT STOVER,
Cynthia .... 510-430-2380...... 57 D
cbrandtstover@mills.edu
BRANHAM, Celeste .... 207-778-7087.... 220 C
cbranham@maine.edu
BRANHAM, Holly, L .... 307-532-8303.... 556 C
holly.branham@ewc.wy.edu
BRANHAM, Keith .... 574-289-7001.... 176 E
kbranham2@ivytech.edu
BRANHAM, LaTonya .... 937-376-6611.... 387 A
lbranham@centralstate.edu
BRANHAM, Lorraine .... 315-443-3627.... 357 C
lbranham@syr.edu
BRANHAM, Pamela .... 516-678-5000.... 341 F
pbranham@molloy.edu
BRANIGAN, David .... 814-863-9150.... 438 G
deb7@psu.edu
BRANKLE, Steve .... 479-524-7209...... 22 C
sbrankle@jbu.edu
BRANNAN, Angie, R .... 262-524-7335.... 546 H
abrannan@carrollu.edu
BRANNAN, Colleen, E .... 607-436-2748.... 353 E
brannace@oneonta.edu
BRANNEN, Andy .... 912-287-5858.... 135 F
abrannen@okefenokeetech.edu
BRANNER, Wade, H .... 540-464-7253.... 529 F
brannerwh@vmi.edu
BRANNOCK, Kathleen .... 518-783-2919.... 350 I
kbrannock@siena.edu
BRANNON, Brandi .... 940-552-6291.... 507 F
bbrannon@vernoncollege.edu
BRANNON, Jennifer .... 478-934-3352.... 134 B
jbrannon@mgc.edu
BRANNON, Jennifer .... 478-374-6221.... 134 B
jbrannon@mgc.edu
BRANNON, Melanie .... 704-357-8020.... 362 D
mbrannon@aii.edu
BRANNON, T. Porter .... 718-482-5148.... 328 B
tpbrannon@lagcc.cuny.edu
BRANNON, Tony, L .... 270-809-3328.... 205 A
tbrannon@murraystate.edu
BRANSFORD, Denise, A .... 312-341-2040.... 163 B
dbrandsford@roosevelt.edu
BRANSKY, David .... 805-654-6400...... 77 F
dbransky@vcccd.edu
BRANSON, Cathy .... 606-487-3148.... 202 C
cathy.branson@kctcs.edu
BRANSON, David .... 207-775-3052.... 218 E
dbranson@meca.edu
BRANSON, Lisa .... 703-414-4029.... 518 C
lbranson@devry.edu
BRANSON, Mark .... 312-662-4121.... 144 H
mbranson@adler.edu
BRANSON, Mark .... 336-249-8186.... 370 B
mbranson@davidsonccc.edu
BRANSON, Salinda Jo .... 309-649-6217.... 165 F
jo.branson@src.edu
BRANSON, Walter, J .... 260-481-6804.... 174 C
branson@ipfw.edu
BRANSTETTER, Jeffrey, C .. 402-280-2709.... 297 F
jbranstetter@creighton.edu
BRANSTETTER, Marie .... 913-288-7211.... 194 C
marie@kckcc.edu
BRANT, Christine .... 734-432-5620.... 254 D
cbrant@madonna.edu
BRANT, David .... 310-506-4730...... 61 H
david.brant@pepperdine.edu
BRANT, Felicia .... 202-274-5000.... 100 A
fbrant@udc.edu
BRANT, Joseph .... 410-234-4640.... 225 E
BRANT, Keith, E .... 925-631-4219...... 64 F
keb5@stmarys-ca.edu
BRANT, Kelly .... 419-772-2073.... 398 H
k-brant@onu.edu
BRANTLEY, Brenda .... 318-678-6000.... 209 I
bbrantley@bpcc.edu
BRANTLEY, Clarence, E ..... 248-341-2101.... 256 F
cebrantl@oaklandcc.edu
BRANTLEY, Clinton .... 478-757-5138.... 139 E
cbrantley@wesleyancollege.edu

BRENNEMAN, James, E .... 574-535-7180 .... 171 G president@goshen.edu
BRENNEMANN, Kyle, R .. 573-629-3008 .... 282 E kbrennemann@hlg.edu
BRENNEN, David .... 859-257-8319 .... 207 D dabr223@uky.edu
BRENNER, David, A .... 858-534-1501 .... 74 F dbrenner@ucsd.edu
BRENNER, Mark .... 602-557-2030 .... 19 A mark.brenner@apollogrp.edu
BRENNER, Paul .... 212-237-8968 .... 327 F pbrenner@jjay.cuny.edu
BRENNER-BUDER, Barbara .... 415-451-2817 .... 66 B bbrenner@sfts.edu
BRENNER-SCOTTI, Laura .. 609-984-1141 .... 316 A lbrennerscotti@tesc.edu
BRENT, Alicia .... 831-647-6541 .... 57 F alicia.brent@miis.edu
BRENT, Daniel .... 617-323-6662 .... 241 F dan_brent@mspp.edu
BRENTLINGER, Dustin .... 419-448-2062 .... 391 F dbrentli@heidelberg.edu
BRENTON, Angela .... 828-227-7495 .... 380 A academicaffairsoffice@wcu.edu
BRENTON, George, W .... 410-857-2714 .... 224 C gbrenton@mcdaniel.edu
BRENTON, Robin, A .... 410-857-2297 .... 224 C rbrenton@mcdaniel.edu
BRENZEL, Jeffrey .... 203-432-9321 .... 96 A jeff.brenzel@yale.edu
BRESCIANI, Dean .... 701-231-7211 .... 382 B dean.bresciani@ndsu.edu
BRESEE, Mikel .... 313-664-7421 .... 249 E mbresee@collegeforcreativestudies.edu
BRESEMAN, Mark, D .... 920-832-6519 .... 548 B mark.d.breseman@lawrence.edu
BRESHEARS, Pearlene .... 417-328-1729 .... 290 A pbreshears@sbuniv.edu
BRESKO, Lynn .... 336-256-1283 .... 379 B lynn_bresko@uncg.edu
BRESLAUER, George, W .... 510-642-1961 .... 73 H bresl@berkeley.edu
BRESLAUER, Kenneth, J .... 732-445-3956 .... 314 B kjbdna@rci.rutgers.edu
BRESLER, Pieter .... 317-805-1785 .... 541 K pbresler@salemu.edu
BRESLIN, Beau .... 518-580-5705 .... 351 B bbreslin@skidmore.edu
BRESLIN, Eileen, T .... 210-567-5800 .... 507 A breslin@uthscsa.edu
BRESLIN, Kathleen, A .... 610-359-5131 .... 426 G kbreslin@dccc.edu
BRESLIN, Lisa .... 410-857-2225 .... 224 C lbreslin@mcdaniel.edu
BRESLIN, Thomas .... 305-348-2304 .... 119 C thomas.breslin@fiu.edu
BRESNAHAN, Carol .... 407-646-2355 .... 116 D cbresnahan@rollins.edu
BRESSETTE, Andrew .... 706-236-2229 .... 126 C abressette@berry.edu
BRESSI-STOPPE, Elizabeth 215-895-1104 .... 450 B ebs@usciences.edu
BRESSINGTON, Cheryl .... 308-865-8655 .... 300 F bressingtonc@unk.edu
BRESSINGTON, Cheryl .... 308-865-8388 .... 300 F bressingtonc@unk.edu
BRESSLER, Coleen .... 402-844-7006 .... 299 I coleen@northeast.edu
BRESSLER, Darlene .... 765-677-2147 .... 175 B darlene.bressler@indwes.edu
BRESSLER, Gregory, W .... 973-655-5457 .... 311 F bresslerg@mail.montclair.edu
BRESSO, Michele .... 661-336-5041 .... 52 K mbresso@kccd.edu
BRETL, Jim .... 402-280-2722 .... 297 F bretlj@creighton.edu
BRETT, Anne .... 417-269-3402 .... 280 G abrett@coxcollege.edu
BRETT, Jennifer .... 203-576-4122 .... 94 F acup@bridgeport.edu
BRETTI, Anthony .... 912-478-5966 .... 131 E tbretti@georgiasouthern.edu
BRETTSCHNEIDER, Marla, B .... 603-862-4676 .... 306 C marla.brettschneider@unh.edu
BRETZ, Brenda, K .... 717-245-1587 .... 427 F bretz@dickinson.edu
BREUDER, Robert, L .... 630-942-2200 .... 148 A breuder@cod.edu
BREUER, Catherine, L .... 952-358-8243 .... 268 A catherine.breuer@normandale.edu
BREVETT, Renford A, B .... 484-365-7213 .... 434 H rbrevett@lincoln.edu
BREW, Alan .... 715-682-1329 .... 549 F abrew@northland.edu
BREWER, Brent .... 269-782-1411 .... 258 C bbrewer01@swmich.edu
BREWER, Clay .... 618-985-3741 .... 154 G claybrewer@jalc.edu
BREWER, Craig .... 415-955-2011 .... 27 A cbrewer@alliant.edu
BREWER, Dawn, M .... 812-888-4225 .... 181 D dbrewer@vinu.edu
BREWER, Deborah .... 716-614-5911 .... 344 C dbrewer@niagaracc.suny.edu
BREWER, Jane, T .... 843-549-6314 .... 462 E jtbrewer@mailbox.sc.edu
BREWER, Janet .... 501-760-4313 .... 22 F jbrewer@npcc.edu
BREWER, Janet, L .... 765-641-4272 .... 169 E jlbrewer@anderson.edu
BREWER, Jason .... 386-763-2781 .... 114 E jason.brewer@palmer.edu
BREWER, Jerry, T .... 803-777-4172 .... 462 A jerry-brewer@sc.edu
BREWER, Jim, L .... 870-460-1074 .... 25 A brewer@uamont.edu
BREWER, John .... 801-863-8320 .... 511 F brewerjc@uvu.edu
BREWER, JR., John, B .... 301-447-5280 .... 225 A brewer@msmary.edu
BREWER, Kristina .... 260-665-4161 .... 180 D brewerk@trine.edu
BREWER, Michael, H .... 484-664-3400 .... 437 C brewer@muhlenberg.edu
BREWER, Michelle .... 318-678-6017 .... 209 I mbrewer@bpcc.edu
BREWER, Nathan .... 618-664-6752 .... 151 F nathan.brewer@greenville.edu
BREWER, Patricia .... 513-487-1182 .... 402 I patricia.brewer@myunion.edu
BREWER, Randy .... 404-627-2681 .... 126 D randy.brewer@beulah.org
BREWER, Reta .... 785-832-8622 .... 193 D reta.brewer@bie.edu
BREWER, Rick .... 843-863-7505 .... 456 B rbrewer@csuniv.edu
BREWER, Robert, W .... 336-272-7102 .... 364 G rbrewer@greensboro.edu
BREWER, Ryan .... 205-329-7865 .... 3 A ryan.brewer@ecacolleges.com
BREWER, Stacey .... 864-596-9050 .... 457 E stacey.brewer@converse.edu
BREWER, Susan .... 870-460-1050 .... 25 A brewers@uamont.edu
BREWER, Theresa .... 617-427-0060 .... 241 A tbrewer@rcc.mass.edu
BREWER, Tim .... 704-878-3205 .... 372 C tbrewer@mitchellcc.edu
BREWINGTON, Donald, E .. 512-505-3054 .... 488 D debrewington@htu.edu
BREWIS, Greg, W .... 253-535-7430 .... 536 E brewisgw@plu.edu
BREWSTER, Carrie .... 925-631-4643 .... 64 F cbrewste@stmarys-ca.edu
BREWSTER, Edward .... 360-538-4000 .... 534 G brewster@ghc.edu
BREWSTER, Geoffrey .... 918-610-8303 .... 411 D geoffrey.brewster@ptstulsa.edu
BREWSTER, Twania .... 312-850-7035 .... 147 F tbrewster3@ccc.edu
BREY, Amanda .... 805-966-3888 .... 31 D amanda.brey@brooks.edu
BREZEL, Allen .... 404-872-3593 .... 125 F abrezel@johnmarshall.edu
BREZINA, Jennifer .... 661-362-5919 .... 41 I jennifer.brezina@canyons.edu
BREZINA, Kate .... 401-456-8086 .... 454 A kbrezina@ric.edu
BREZINSKI, Donald .... 603-645-9688 .... 305 I d.brezinski@snhu.edu
BREZLER, Kristin, D .... 301-766-3681 .... 223 G kbrezler@kaplan.edu
BRHEL, Richard, D .... 216-432-8965 .... 387 B rbhel@chancelloru.edu
BRIA, Jeff .... 301-431-5410 .... 225 B jbria@nlc.edu
BRIAN, Thomas, J .... 918-631-2200 .... 413 F thomas-brian@utulsa.edu
BRIANT, Clyde, L .... 401-863-7408 .... 453 B clyde_briant@brown.edu
BRIAR-LAWSON, Katharine .... 518-442-5324 .... 351 E kbriarlawson@uamail.albany.edu
BRIARE, Bill .... 503-594-3110 .... 415 A billb@clackamas.edu
BRICE, Albie .... 919-761-2100 .... 377 A abrice@sebts.edu
BRICE, Diane .... 806-371-5028 .... 479 G kdbrice@actx.edu
BRICE, Michelle .... 312-662-4113 .... 144 H mbrice@adler.edu
BRICE, Ruth .... 610-399-2033 .... 442 A rbrice@cheyney.edu
BRICELAND, Cynthia .... 724-503-1001 .... 451 A cbriceland@washjeff.edu
BRICHER, Gary .... 860-297-2331 .... 94 E gary.bricher@trincoll.edu
BRICK, George .... 575-624-8023 .... 319 C brick@nmmi.edu
BRICK, III, Harold (Ben), B .... 402-449-2893 .... 297 H gu-library@graceu.edu
BRICK, Robert .... 979-209-7206 .... 482 C rbrick@blinn.edu
BRICK, Susan, H .... 509-527-5790 .... 540 B bricksh@whitman.edu
BRICKER, Angela .... 570-286-3058 .... 436 B ab@mccannschool.com
BRICKER, J. Douglas .... 412-396-6361 .... 428 D bricker@duq.edu
BRICKER, Susan .... 805-654-6457 .... 77 F sbricker@vcccd.edu
BRICKETTO, Matthew, M ... 610-436-3301 .... 444 A mbricketto@wcupa.edu
BRICKHOUSE, Nancy .... 302-831-2101 .... 96 I nbrick@udel.edu
BRICKHOUSE, Wendy, W .. 252-335-0821 .... 369 G wbrickhouse@albemarle.edu
BRICKLE, Colleen .... 952-358-8158 .... 268 A colleen.brickle@normandale.edu
BRICKMAN, Larry .... 937-484-1359 .... 405 A lbrickman@urbana.edu
BRICKNER-WOOD, Larry .. 603-862-1165 .... 306 C larry.brickner-wood@unh.edu
BRIDDELL, Jocelyn .... 860-439-2834 .... 92 G jocelyn.briddell@conncoll.edu
BRIDGE, Claire .... 909-621-8148 .... 69 A claire.bridge@scrippscollege.edu
BRIDGE, David .... 660-562-1181 .... 287 B dbridge@nwmissouri.edu
BRIDGE, Louise .... 801-863-8689 .... 511 F bridgelo@uvu.edu
BRIDGEMAN, Doris .... 601-977-7836 .... 277 C dbridgeman@tougaloo.edu
BRIDGEMAN, Robert .... 352-638-9761 .... 102 B bbridgeman@beaconcollege.edu
BRIDGENS, Marc, E .... 570-326-3761 .... 440 L mbridgen@pct.edu
BRIDGEO, Kim .... 978-837-5938 .... 242 A kim.bridgeo@merrimack.edu
BRIDGER, Donald .... 303-458-4206 .... 87 I dbridger@regis.edu
BRIDGERS, Amy .... 252-399-6397 .... 362 E abbridgers@barton.edu
BRIDGES, Avie .... 714-564-6910 .... 63 F bridges_avie@sac.edu
BRIDGES, Barbara .... 818-785-2726 .... 38 K
BRIDGES, Carl .... 740-753-3591 .... 391 H bridges_c@hocking.edu
BRIDGES, Ceil, L .... 870-235-4079 .... 23 I clbridges@saumag.edu
BRIDGES, Clarence, E .... 312-413-5946 .... 167 B cbridges@uic.edu
BRIDGES, Craig .... 218-723-4822 .... 262 G cbridges@css.edu
BRIDGES, Daniel .... 323-343-3080 .... 35 D dbridges@cslanet.calstatela.edu
BRIDGES, Darryl, L .... 843-661-1225 .... 458 D dbridges@fmarion.edu
BRIDGES, David .... 229-391-5050 .... 123 H dbridges@abac.edu
BRIDGES, Deborah, K .... 504-280-6173 .... 213 E dkbridge@uno.edu
BRIDGES, Dennis .... 309-556-3345 .... 153 F dbridges@iwu.edu
BRIDGES, George, S .... 509-527-5132 .... 540 B bridges@whitman.edu
BRIDGES, Joey .... 704-406-4647 .... 364 E jbridges@gardner-webb.edu
BRIDGES, John, H .... 508-457-1313 .... 242 F jbridges@ngs.edu
BRIDGES, Kermit, S .... 972-825-4652 .... 495 F president@sagu.edu
BRIDGES, LaDonna .... 508-626-4906 .... 238 A lbridges@framingham.edu
BRIDGES, Martin .... 910-410-1818 .... 373 B mwbridges@richmondcc.edu
BRIDGES, Rebecca .... 972-708-7547 .... 487 B rebecca_bridges@gial.edu
BRIDGES, Ruth .... 254-298-8309 .... 496 D ruth.bridges@templejc.edu
BRIDGES, Shelton .... 502-451-0815 .... 206 H sbridges@sullivan.edu
BRIDGES, Shelton .... 502-451-0815 .... 206 G sbridges@sullivan.edu
BRIDGES, Steven, J .... 812-465-7048 .... 181 B sjbridge@usi.edu
BRIDGES, Tharsteen .... 334-874-5700 .... 2 H tbridges@ccal.edu
BRIDGES, Vernon, D .... 818-947-2541 .... 55 E bridgevd@lavc.edu
BRIDGMAN, Christa, L .... 828-298-3325 .... 380 D cbridgma@warren-wilson.edu
BRIDGMON, Phillip .... 918-456-5511 .... 409 A bridgmon@nsuok.edu
BRIDWELL, Virginia .... 425-564-2198 .... 531 G virginia.bridwell@bellevuecollege.edu
BRIELL, Scott, A .... 770-538-4706 .... 126 E sbriell@brenau.edu
BRIEN, Jane .... 845-758-4294 .... 323 D brien@bard.edu
BRIER, Bonnie .... 212-998-4095 .... 344 B bonnie.brier@nyu.edu
BRIER, Stephen, F .... 503-370-6022 .... 421 D sbrier@willamette.edu
BRIERE, Donna .... 603-752-1113 .... 304 H dbriere@ccsnh.edu
BRIGDON, Beth, P .... 706-721-9667 .... 130 D bbrigdon@georgiahealth.edu
BRIGGANCE, Richard .... 615-963-5171 .... 474 A rbriggance@tnstate.edu
BRIGGS, Baily .... 903-923-3217 .... 500 E baily.briggs@tstc.edu
BRIGGS, Betty, S .... 903-510-2371 .... 503 A bbri@tjc.edu
BRIGGS, Catherine .... 609-894-9311 .... 308 B cbriggs@bcc.edu
BRIGGS, Cordell .... 951-571-6320 .... 64 A cordell.briggs@rcc.edu
BRIGGS, Cordell .... 951-571-6150 .... 63 J cordell.briggs@mvc.edu
BRIGGS, Darcy .... 303-797-5623 .... 81 D darcy.briggs@arapahoe.edu
BRIGGS, De Armond .... 641-472-1162 .... 187 E dbriggs@mum.edu
BRIGGS, Douglas, S .... 540-636-2900 .... 517 K dougb@christendom.edu
BRIGGS, Jackie .... 507-453-2743 .... 267 C jbriggs@southeastmn.edu
BRIGGS, Jeff .... 785-628-4200 .... 192 I jbriggs@fhsu.edu
BRIGGS, Jennifer .... 812-429-1433 .... 177 C jbriggs@ivytech.edu
BRIGGS, Jerryl .... 937-376-6387 .... 387 A jbriggs@centralstate.edu
BRIGGS, Julie, A .... 585-245-5616 .... 353 C briggsja@geneseo.edu
BRIGGS, Karen .... 662-476-5041 .... 274 B kbriggs@eastms.edu
BRIGGS, Karen, M .... 215-670-9230 .... 438 E kmbriggs@peirce.edu
BRIGGS, Kennon .... 919-807-7100 .... 367 I briggsk@nccommunitycolleges.edu
BRIGGS, LaNae, R .... 803-786-3856 .... 457 C lrbriggs@columbiasc.edu
BRIGGS, LaVerne .... 804-524-5011 .... 529 H lbriggs@vsu.edu
BRIGGS, Lawrence .... 509-359-6685 .... 533 H lbriggs@ewu.edu
BRIGGS, Lynn .... 509-359-2227 .... 533 H lbriggs@ewu.edu
BRIGGS, Mary, K .... 276-944-6836 .... 519 A mkbriggs@ehc.edu
BRIGGS, Michelle, A .... 570-321-4190 .... 435 D briggs@lycoming.edu
BRIGGS, Patricia .... 802-831-1234 .... 515 B dmyette@vermontlaw.edu
BRIGGS, Pertrina .... 630-743-0695 .... 168 E pbriggs@westwood.edu
BRIGGS, Peter, F .... 517-353-1720 .... 255 A pbriggs@msu.edu
BRIGGS, Sarah, F .... 517-629-0244 .... 247 A sbriggs@albion.edu
BRIGGS, Stephen, R .... 706-236-2281 .... 126 C sbriggs@berry.edu
BRIGGS, Susan .... 406-683-7031 .... 294 J s_briggs@umwestern.edu
BRIGGS, Thyra .... 909-607-4408 .... 49 F thyra_briggs@hmc.edu
BRIGGS, William .... 657-278-3355 .... 35 B wbriggs@fullerton.edu
BRIGGS KITTREDGE, Cynthia .... 512-472-4133 .... 494 F cynthia.kittredge@ssw.edu
BRIGHAM, Allegra .... 662-329-7148 .... 276 A abrigham@vpura.muw.edu
BRIGHAM, Bettie Ann .... 610-341-5823 .... 428 E bbrigham@eastern.edu
BRIGHAM, David, R .... 215-972-2056 .... 440 J skesskler@pafa.edu
BRIGHAM, Jeffrey .... 617-964-1100 .... 230 B
BRIGHT, Brett, O .... 903-923-3240 .... 500 E brett.bright@tstc.edu
BRIGHT, Caroline, O .... 240-895-3000 .... 226 A cobright@smcm.edu
BRIGHT, Harry .... 641-472-1178 .... 187 E hbright@mum.edu
BRIGHT, James (Phillip) .... 731-881-7845 .... 477 G pbright@utm.edu
BRIGHT, Jessica .... 512-313-3000 .... 483 K jessica.bright@concordia.edu
BRIGHT, Kristina .... 573-592-4257 .... 293 D kbright@williamwoods.edu
BRIGHT, Marvin, L .... 757-822-1180 .... 528 G mlbright@tcc.edu
BRIGHT, Phillip .... 304-766-3322 .... 544 F pbright@wvstateu.edu
BRIGHT, Sarah .... 636-481-3218 .... 283 D sbright@jeffco.edu
BRIGHT, Steve .... 434-544-8208 .... 521 B bright@lynchburg.edu
BRIGHTBILL, Ashley, E .... 330-287-7507 .... 399 A brightbill.10@osu.edu
BRILEY, Brantley .... 252-527-6223 .... 371 G bbriley@lenoircc.edu
BRILEY, Jana .... 912-478-1652 .... 131 E janawms@georgiasouthern.edu
BRILEY, Terry .... 615-966-5714 .... 470 F terry.briley@lipscomb.edu
BRILL, Ann .... 309-341-7130 .... 155 F abrill@knox.edu
BRILL, Ann, M .... 785-864-4755 .... 197 B abrill@ku.edu

BRONK, Leslie ... 612-977-4222 ... 261 F
leslie.bronk@capella.edu
BRONK, Lisa ... 315-792-3006 ... 359 E
lbronk@utica.edu
BRONNER, Gwethalyn ... 847-543-2685 ... 148 B
gbronner@clcillinois.edu
BRONNER, Jennifer ... 740-826-8131 ... 397 A
jbronner@muskingum.edu
BRONSON, Jennifer ... 412-365-1862 ... 425 C
jbronson@chatham.edu
BRONSTEIN, Chaim ... 212-960-5400 ... 346 F
bronstein@yu.edu
BRONSTEIN, Ken ... 360-383-3359 ... 540 A
kbronstein@whatcom.ctc.edu
BRONSTEIN, Susan ... 716-338-1035 ... 337 E
susanbronstein@mail.sunyjcc.edu
BROOK, Raymond ... 540-986-1800 ... 205 D
rbrook@national-college.edu
BROOKBANK, Julie ... 605-995-3026 ... 464 F
julie.brookbank@mitchelltech.edu
BROOKE, Judith ... 321-674-8053 ... 108 H
jbrooke@fit.edu
BROOKE, Patrick, T ... 630-752-5126 ... 168 H
patrick.brooke@wheaton.edu
BROOKER, Nancy ... 330-287-1302 ... 399 A
brooker.1@osu.edu
BROOKER, Paulita ... 704-463-7302 ... 375 F
paulita.brooker@fsmail.pfeiffer.edu
BROOKER, Sarah ... 717-564-4112 ... 432 B
sbrooker@kaplan.edu
BROOKET, Jenn ... 517-264-7159 ... 258 B
jbrooket@sienaheights.edu
BROOKEY, Lauren, F ... 918-595-7977 ... 412 H
lbrookey@tulsacc.edu
BROOKNER, Laurie ... 415-565-8813 ... 74 A
brookner@uchastings.edu
BROOKS, Anthony, M ... 919-530-6298 ... 378 B
abrooks@nccu.edu
BROOKS, Beth ... 206-878-3710 ... 535 B
bbrooks@highline.edu
BROOKS, Beth, A ... 708-763-6975 ... 162 E
beth.brooks@resu.edu
BROOKS, Billie, K ... 304-710-3141 ... 542 K
hendersb@mctc.edu
BROOKS, Bob ... 325-670-1426 ... 487 F
bob.brooks@hsutx.edu
BROOKS, Bryan ... 972-825-4821 ... 495 F
bbrooks@sagu.edu
BROOKS, Carlton ... 719-502-2003 ... 87 B
carlton.brooks@ppcc.edu
BROOKS, Carolyn ... 323-856-7742 ... 28 E
cbrooks@afi.com
BROOKS, Charles ... 803-705-4358 ... 455 D
brooksc@benedict.edu
BROOKS, Chris ... 800-422-2418 ... 102 A
cbrooks@baymedical.org
BROOKS, Cindy, L ... 610-799-1121 ... 434 D
cbrooks@lccc.edu
BROOKS, Craig ... 719-336-1674 ... 86 B
craig.brooks@lamarcc.edu
BROOKS, Cynthia ... 615-963-7410 ... 474 A
cbrooks@tnstate.edu
BROOKS, Dana, D ... 304-293-8026 ... 545 A
dbrooks@mail.wvu.edu
BROOKS, Danny, K ... 205-226-4699 ... 2 B
dbrooks@bsc.edu
BROOKS, Darlene, D ... 901-843-3901 ... 472 K
brooksd@rhodes.edu
BROOKS, DeeAnna ... 803-323-2225 ... 463 E
brooksd@winthrop.edu
BROOKS, Delores, J ... 708-974-5376 ... 159 B
brooks@morainevalley.edu
BROOKS, II, Earl, D ... 260-665-4101 ... 180 D
brookse@trine.edu
BROOKS, Fred ... 252-451-8233 ... 372 E
fbrooks@nash.cc.nc.us
BROOKS, Gail ... 562-951-4455 ... 33 H
gbrooks@calstate.edu
BROOKS, Gene ... 605-575-2030 ... 466 E
gene.brooks@usiouxfalls.edu
BROOKS, Glee, R ... 530-226-4188 ... 69 H
gbrooks@simpsonu.edu
BROOKS, II, H. Gordon ... 337-482-6224 ... 216 D
gbrooks@louisiana.edu
BROOKS, Henry, M ... 410-651-6206 ... 227 E
hmbrooks@umes.edu
BROOKS, James ... 386-481-2716 ... 102 C
brooksj@cookman.edu
BROOKS, James, J ... 541-346-7057 ... 419 B
brooksja@uoregon.edu
BROOKS, James, W ... 317-805-1730 ... 541 K
jwb@salemu.edu
BROOKS, Jane ... 219-785-5657 ... 179 A
jbrooks@pnc.edu
BROOKS, Jason ... 620-341-5481 ... 192 G
jbrooks5@emporia.edu
BROOKS, Jessica, P ... 680-488-2471 ... 560 C
jessicab@palau.edu
BROOKS, John ... 678-466-4232 ... 127 D
johnbrooks@clayton.edu
BROOKS, John, I ... 910-672-1060 ... 377 G
jibrooks@uncfsu.edu
BROOKS, Julia ... 503-223-2245 ... 416 F
jbrooks@westernculinary.com
BROOKS, Juliette ... 201-692-7050 ... 310 A
juliette_brooks@fdu.edu
BROOKS, Justin, P ... 619-239-0391 ... 37 F
jbrooks@cwsl.edu
BROOKS, Keith ... 410-706-7131 ... 227 C
kbrooks@umaryland.edu
BROOKS, Kent ... 307-268-2703 ... 556 A
kbrooks@caspercollege.edu
BROOKS, Krista ... 217-732-3168 ... 156 H
kjbrooks@lincolnchristian.edu
BROOKS, L. Rayburn ... 864-941-8301 ... 460 D
brooks.r@ptc.edu
BROOKS, Larry ... 701-228-5457 ... 382 E
larry.brooks@dakotacollege.edu
BROOKS, Laura ... 410-234-4559 ... 225 E
BROOKS, Lois ... 541-737-0739 ... 418 F
lois.brooks@oregonstate.edu
BROOKS, Lyvette ... 215-751-8046 ... 426 B
lbrooks@ccp.edu
BROOKS, Madelene ... 252-222-6224 ... 369 A
brooksm@carteret.edu
BROOKS, Marilyn, A ... 804-257-5846 ... 530 A
mabrooks2@vuu.edu
BROOKS, Mark ... 229-931-2246 ... 137 C
mbrooks@southgatech.edu
BROOKS, Mark, D ... 270-901-1117 ... 201 I
mark.brooks@kctcs.edu
BROOKS, Monica ... 304-696-6474 ... 544 B
brooks@marshall.edu
BROOKS, Nancy, S ... 515-294-8757 ... 182 E
nsbrook@iastate.edu
BROOKS, Patricia ... 662-621-4168 ... 273 F
pbrooks@coahomacc.edu
BROOKS, Paul ... 972-825-4616 ... 495 F
pbrooks@sagu.edu
BROOKS, Randy, M ... 217-424-6205 ... 158 G
rbrooks@millikin.edu
BROOKS, Robert ... 617-928-4602 ... 242 E
rbrooks@mountida.edu
BROOKS, Roger, L ... 860-439-2030 ... 92 G
roger.brooks@conncoll.edu
BROOKS, Roger, L ... 804-289-8491 ... 525 E
rbrooks@richmond.edu
BROOKS, Ronnie ... 615-963-5671 ... 474 A
rbrooks6@tnstate.edu
BROOKS, Sandra, L ... 606-474-3247 ... 201 D
bookstore@kcu.edu
BROOKS, Sean ... 410-951-3455 ... 228 B
sbrooks@coppin.edu
BROOKS, Sherry ... 906-635-2216 ... 253 H
sbrooks@lssu.edu
BROOKS, Sherry, L ... 906-635-2216 ... 253 H
sbrooks1@lssu.edu
BROOKS, Steven ... 407-345-2800 ... 104 K
sbrooks2@devry.edu
BROOKS, Susan, H ... 704-687-5770 ... 379 A
sbrooks@uncc.edu
BROOKS, Telaekah ... 202-884-9519 ... 99 H
brookst@trinitydc.edu
BROOKS, Tim ... 303-871-3030 ... 89 A
tim.brooks@du.edu
BROOKS, Tim ... 617-627-3986 ... 245 C
tim.brooks@tufts.edu
BROOKS, Tom ... 828-339-4202 ... 374 C
tbrooks@southwesterncc.edu
BROOKS, Tyrone, W ... 208-885-5255 ... 144 G
tyroneb@uidaho.edu
BROOKS, Vera ... 410-462-8500 ... 221 E
vbrooks@bccc.edu
BROOKS, Walter ... 609-586-4800 ... 311 B
brooksw@mccc.edu
BROOKS, Wanda ... 504-816-4039 ... 209 A
wbrooks@dillard.edu
BROOKS, Wendy ... 989-358-7299 ... 247 C
brooksw@alpenacc.edu
BROOKS, Wesley, H ... 319-352-8260 ... 189 J
wes.brooks@wartburg.edu
BROOKS BLAIR, Sarah, D ... 937-529-2201 ... 403 A
sblair@united.edu
BROOKSHIRE, Kathy ... 601-484-8612 ... 275 A
kbrooksh@meridiancc.edu
BROOKSHIRE, Sue ... 252-940-6328 ... 368 C
sueb@beaufortccc.edu
BROOM, Cheryl ... 760-795-2121 ... 57 E
cbroom@miracosta.edu
BROOM, Mahailier, L ... 318-670-9345 ... 215 A
mbroom@susla.edu
BROOMALL, James, K ... 302-831-2795 ... 96 I
jbroom@udel.edu
BROOME, Charlene ... 704-272-5447 ... 374 A
cbroome@spcc.edu
BROOME, JR., David, E ... 704-687-5732 ... 379 A
debroome@uncc.edu
BROOME, Marion, E ... 317-274-1486 ... 174 D
mbroome@iupui.edu
BROOMHEAD, Keiko ... 617-989-4034 ... 245 F
broomheadk@wit.edu
BROPHY, Ann ... 314-968-6922 ... 292 J
annbrophy26@webster.edu
BROPHY, George ... 860-768-4608 ... 95 B
brophy@hartford.edu
BROPHY, Michael, S ... 310-377-5501 ... 56 F
mbrophy@marymountpv.edu
BROPHY, JR., William, E ... 256-824-6144 ... 8 G
william.brophy@uah.edu
BRORSON, Susan ... 218-281-8186 ... 271 E
sbrorson@umn.edu
BROSCHART, Jim ... 607-431-4026 ... 335 A
broschartj@hartwick.edu
BROSCHEIT, James ... 303-556-2886 ... 88 J
james.broscheit@ucdenver.edu
BROSIUS, Jo ... 859-622-2474 ... 200 J
jo.brosius@eku.edu
BROSKE, Kathleen, M ... 920-924-2139 ... 554 G
kbroske@morainepark.edu
BROSKI, Annette ... 315-792-5411 ... 341 E
abroski@mvcc.edu
BROSKY, Lisa ... 502-213-2400 ... 202 F
lisa.brosky@kctcs.edu
BROSNAN, Joseph, S ... 215-489-2203 ... 426 H
joseph.brosnan@delval.edu
BROSNIHAN, Kathleen ... 508-626-4575 ... 238 A
kbrosnihan@framingham.edu
BROSSEAU, Gayle ... 323-265-8973 ... 54 G
brossegd@elac.edu
BROSSETTE, Alicia ... 214-768-2030 ... 495 A
abrosset@smu.edu
BROSSMANN, William, D ... 517-321-0242 ... 251 G
wbrossmann@glcc.edu
BROSTROM, Nathan, E ... 510-987-9029 ... 73 G
nathan.brostrom@ucop.edu
BROSZ, Jeff ... 952-545-2000 ... 270 G
jeff.brosz@rasmussen.edu
BROTHERS, Gregory, A ... 713-646-1888 ... 494 I
gbrothers@stcl.edu
BROTHERS, James, F ... 937-229-2829 ... 404 A
jbrothers1@udayton.edu
BROTHERS, M. Elaine ... 260-399-7700 ... 181 A
ebrothers@sf.edu
BROTHERS, Wes ... 740-477-7757 ... 398 D
wbrothers@ohiochristian.edu
BROTHERTON, Thomas, S ... 712-852-5224 ... 186 A
tbrotherton@iowalakes.edu
BROTHWELL, Debbie ... 510-885-4135 ... 34 E
debbie.brothwell@csueastbay.edu
BROUCEK, Willard ... 605-626-2401 ... 466 A
broucekw@northern.edu
BROUDE, Nancy ... 617-587-5585 ... 242 H
brouden@neco.edu
BROUDER, Gerald, T ... 573-875-7200 ... 280 A
gbrouder@ccis.edu
BROUGH, Amy, F ... 860-297-5315 ... 94 E
amy.brough@trincoll.edu
BROUGHTON, Nancy ... 218-879-0837 ... 266 C
sam@fdltcc.edu
BROUGHTON, Phyllis, J ... 252-789-0247 ... 371 H
pbroughton@martincc.edu
BROUGHTON, Sandy, S ... 732-255-0400 ... 312 D
sbroughton@ocean.edu
BROUILLETTE,
Domenick, R ... 816-604-1370 ... 284 H
domenick.brouillette@mcckc.edu
BROUK, Judy ... 636-422-2240 ... 289 B
jbrouk@stlcc.edu
BROUK, Susan ... 660-263-4110 ... 286 H
susanbr@macc.edu
BROUNK, Thomas, M ... 314-935-5955 ... 292 I
tom_brounk@wustl.edu
BROUSSARD, Camille ... 212-431-2354 ... 343 E
cbroussard@nyls.edu
BROUSSARD, Michael ... 337-550-1292 ... 212 J
BROUSSARD, William ... 225-771-3170 ... 214 I
will_broussard@subr.edu
BROUWER, Peter, S ... 315-267-2515 ... 354 C
brouweps@potsdam.edu
BROUWERS, Mariette ... 541-737-2131 ... 418 F
mariette.brouwers@oregonstate.edu
BROWDER, Steven, K ... 317-738-8301 ... 171 F
sbrowder@franklincollege.edu
BROWER, Aaron ... 608-262-5246 ... 550 J
ambrower@wisc.edu
BROWER, Bob ... 619-849-2216 ... 62 L
bobbrower@pointloma.edu
BROWER, Laura ... 805-654-6460 ... 77 F
lbrower@vcccd.edu
BROWER, Paul, O ... 508-213-2271 ... 243 E
paul.brower@nichols.edu
BROWER, Pearl, K ... 907-852-3333 ... 10 F
pearl.brower@ilisagvik.edu
BROWER, Roderick ... 910-678-8232 ... 370 E
browerr@faytechcc.edu
BROWN, A, R ... 718-982-2335 ... 327 A
aramona.brown@csi.cuny.edu
BROWN, Aaron ... 951-222-8789 ... 64 A
aaron.brown@rcc.edu
BROWN, Adrienne ... 912-358-4166 ... 136 G
brownad@savannahstate.edu
BROWN, Albert, F ... 740-588-1210 ... 407 A
abrown@zanestate.edu
BROWN, Alfreda ... 330-672-2442 ... 393 D
abbrown@kent.edu
BROWN, Alistair ... 630-620-2101 ... 160 C
abrown@seminary.edu
BROWN, Amy ... 704-463-3046 ... 375 F
amy.brown@fsmail.pfeiffer.edu
BROWN, Amy, L ... 607-746-4584 ... 355 F
brownal@delhi.edu
BROWN, Andrea ... 435-652-7595 ... 512 B
abrown@dixie.edu
BROWN, Angela, C ... 254-968-9128 ... 497 A
abrown@tarleton.edu
BROWN, Angela, P ... 731-425-2347 ... 475 C
abrown@jscc.edu
BROWN, Angelo ... 770-916-3704 ... 128 G
abrown9@devry.edu
BROWN, Anne ... 617-228-3267 ... 239 C
abrown@bhcc.mass.edu
BROWN, Ansel, E ... 919-530-7477 ... 378 B
browna@nccu.edu
BROWN, Anthony ... 252-335-3277 ... 377 F
abrown@mail.ecsu.edu
BROWN, Arlene ... 256-840-4171 ... 7 A
abrown@snead.edu
BROWN, Arthur, E ... 212-217-3650 ... 333 F
arthur_brown@fitnyc.edu
BROWN, B, T ... 252-536-7256 ... 371 B
brownbt@halifaxcc.edu
BROWN, Barry ... 617-928-4502 ... 242 E
barrybrown@mountida.edu
BROWN, Bernetta, H ... 252-335-3596 ... 377 F
bhbrown@mail.ecsu.edu
BROWN, Beth ... 229-420-8000 ... 133 B
egbrown@lagrange.edu
BROWN, Bill ... 386-752-1822 ... 108 G
bill.brown@fgc.edu
BROWN, Bill ... 913-469-8500 ... 194 B
bbrown@jccc.edu
BROWN, Bill ... 863-638-7228 ... 123 D
bill.brown@warner.edu
BROWN, Bill ... 919-760-2367 ... 367 A
brownw@meredith.edu
BROWN, Bill ... 417-328-1601 ... 290 A
bbrown@sbuniv.edu
BROWN, Bob ... 903-886-5024 ... 498 B
bob.brown@tamuc.edu
BROWN, Bobbie ... 806-742-3661 ... 502 A
bobbie.brown@ttu.edu
BROWN, Bonita, J ... 336-334-4244 ... 379 B
bjbrown3@uncg.edu
BROWN, Braden ... 405-382-9277 ... 412 B
b.brown@sscok.edu
BROWN, Brandon ... 706-821-8233 ... 135 G
bbrown@paine.edu
BROWN, Breighan ... 269-782-1294 ... 258 C
bbrown02@swmich.edu
BROWN, Brenda ... 309-796-4815 ... 145 H
brownb@bhc.edu
BROWN, Brenda, L ... 478-988-6851 ... 134 C
bbrown@middlegatech.edu
BROWN, Brent, K ... 801-581-3003 ... 511 C
brent.brown@osp.utah.edu
BROWN, Brian ... 315-364-3207 ... 360 D
bbrown@wells.edu
BROWN, JR., Buck, F ... 864-379-8805 ... 458 A
brown@erskine.edu
BROWN, Calvin ... 205-348-5966 ... 8 E
cbrown@alumni.ua.edu
BROWN, Canter ... 478-825-6156 ... 129 F
brownc@fvsu.edu
BROWN, JR., Canter ... 478-825-6156 ... 129 F
brownc@fvsu.edu
BROWN, Carl ... 614-947-6080 ... 391 B
brownca@franklin.edu
BROWN, Carlton, E ... 404-880-8566 ... 127 C
cbrown@cau.edu
BROWN, Carly ... 412-747-7800 ... 99 G
BROWN, Carmen ... 803-584-3446 ... 462 E
cdbrown@mailbox.sc.edu
BROWN, Carmhiel, J ... 215-955-8051 ... 448 C
carmhiel.brown@jeffersonhospital.org
BROWN, Carol ... 860-701-5068 ... 93 E
brown_c@mitchell.edu
BROWN, Carol ... 559-791-2316 ... 53 A
cbrown@portervillecollege.edu
BROWN, Carol ... 901-333-4462 ... 476 B
cbrown@southwest.tn.edu
BROWN, Carol, J ... 309-341-7980 ... 155 F
cbrown@knox.edu
BROWN, Carolanne ... 561-803-2050 ... 114 C
carolanne_brown@pba.edu
BROWN, Carolyn, H ... 252-399-6357 ... 362 E
chbrown@barton.edu
BROWN, Carolyn, S ... 816-604-1204 ... 284 H
carolyn.brown@mcckc.edu
BROWN, Carolyn, S ... 801-524-8160 ... 510 E
cs-brown@ldsbc.edu
BROWN, Carrie ... 936-468-3971 ... 496 B
brownch@sfasu.edu
BROWN, Carrie ... 713-348-4428 ... 493 C
carrie.c.brown@rice.edu
BROWN, Cassandra ... 205-226-4643 ... 2 B
clbrown@bsc.edu
BROWN, Cathy, R ... 850-474-3127 ... 121 D
cbrown@uwf.edu
BROWN, Chad ... 740-588-1260 ... 407 A
cbrown@zanestate.edu
BROWN, Charity ... 559-453-2236 ... 48 A
charityb@fresno.edu
BROWN, Charlene ... 406-791-5271 ... 296 F
cbrown02@ugf.edu

BROWN, Charles 502-456-6773 206 H cbrown@sullivan.edu
BROWN, Charles 915-532-3737 508 H cbrown@westerntech.edu
BROWN, Charles, L 561-297-3988 119 A clbrown@fau.edu
BROWN, Charles, R 410-455-2207 227 D chbrown@umbc.edu
BROWN, Cheryl-Ann 321-674-7581 108 H cbrown@fit.edu
BROWN, Chris 408-924-1950 37 C chris.brown@sjsu.edu
BROWN, Christopher 949-376-6000 53 F cbrown@lagunacollege.edu
BROWN, Christopher 919-962-1000 377 C csbrown@northcarolina.edu
BROWN, Christopher, D 570-577-3164 423 E chris.brown@bucknell.edu
BROWN, Christopher, M 517-355-6509 255 A brownc28@msu.edu
BROWN, Christy, L 414-229-4461 551 D clb52@uwm.edu
BROWN, Cindy 417-455-5540 280 H cbrown@crowder.edu
BROWN, Clarence 909-594-5611 58 A cbrown@mtsac.edu
BROWN, Clay 870-460-1028 25 A browncl@uamont.edu
BROWN, Constance 212-854-2011 323 E cbrown@barnard.edu
BROWN, Constance 516-561-0050 325 E
BROWN, Cynthia 706-754-7714 135 A cbrown@northgatech.edu
BROWN, Cynthia, F 413-662-5242 238 C c.brown@mcla.edu
BROWN, Cynthia, L 508-213-2215 243 E cindy.brown@nichols.edu
BROWN, Dale 308-535-8112 298 H brownd@mpcc.edu
BROWN, Dan 502-863-7035 201 A dan_brown@georgetowncollege.edu
BROWN, Danene 619-660-4674 49 B danene.brown@gcccd.edu
BROWN, Daniel 806-291-3575 508 E brownd@wbu.edu
BROWN, Daniel 512-245-3579 501 F sp15@txstate.edu
BROWN, Daniel, E 808-974-7468 141 F dbrown@hawaii.edu
BROWN, Daniel, W 203-582-8927 93 H daniel.brown@quinnipiac.edu
BROWN, Danielle 407-275-9696 103 C
BROWN, Danita 203-857-7004 92 C dbrown@ncc.commnet.edu
BROWN, Danita, M 765-494-1239 178 J dmbrown@purdue.edu
BROWN, Darlene 215-248-7158 425 D brown@chc.edu
BROWN, Darryl 301-295-3412 558 D darryl.brown@usuhs.edu
BROWN, David 352-638-9721 102 B dbrown@beaconcollege.edu
BROWN, David 910-668-7731 491 E dbrown@nctc.edu
BROWN, David 262-691-5346 555 E dbrown@wctc.edu
BROWN, David 617-369-3870 244 E dbrown@smfa.edu
BROWN, David 314-434-4044 280 F david.brown@covenantseminary.edu
BROWN, OSB, David 704-461-6733 362 F davidbrown@bac.edu
BROWN, David, H 845-437-5315 359 F brown@vassar.edu
BROWN, Deanie 217-206-6222 167 C brown.deanie@uis.edu
BROWN, Debbi 808-984-3204 142 E debbi@hawaii.edu
BROWN, Deborah 352-588-7560 116 G deborah.brown02@saintleo.edu
BROWN, Deborah 512-863-1944 496 A brownd@southwestern.edu
BROWN, Deborah 615-217-9347 468 D dbrown@daymarinstitute.edu
BROWN, Delbert, W 585-245-5566 353 C brown@geneseo.edu
BROWN, Dennis 281-425-6300 489 M dbrown@lee.edu
BROWN, DeShanna 404-270-5128 138 B dbrown56@spelman.edu
BROWN, Diane, M 484-365-8055 434 H dbrown@lincoln.edu
BROWN, Dina 978-556-3701 240 E dbrown@necc.mass.edu
BROWN, Dolly 813-621-0041 106 C dbrown@cci.edu
BROWN, Dolores, M 262-524-7133 546 H docampo@carrollu.edu
BROWN, Dominique 602-557-8050 19 A dominique.brown@apollogrp.edu
BROWN, Donna 479-248-7236 21 G registrar@ecollege.edu
BROWN, Donna 660-626-2790 278 D dbrown@atsu.edu
BROWN, Donna 412-372-3900 424 F director2@careerta.edu
BROWN, Donna, L 218-477-2721 267 F donna.brown@mnstate.edu
BROWN, Donnie 806-291-3596 508 E brownd@wbu.edu
BROWN, Doug, M 505-277-6148 321 C browndm@mgt.unm.edu
BROWN, Drew 914-674-7385 340 F dbrown@mercy.edu
BROWN, Eleanor, J 718-855-3661 336 D ebrown@idc.edu
BROWN, Elizabeth, A 312-329-4141 159 A elizabeth.brown@moody.edu
BROWN, Eric, A 843-355-4170 463 D browne@wiltech.edu
BROWN, Erica 205-226-4733 2 B ebrown@bsc.edu
BROWN, Erin 360-442-2131 535 I mbrown@lowercolumbia.edu
BROWN, JR., Ermen 701-766-1342 381 A ermen.brown@littlehoop.edu
BROWN, Ethel 678-891-2526 131 C ebrown@gpc.edu
BROWN, Ethel, M 404-413-1300 131 G ebrown@gsu.edu
BROWN, Evelyn 731-426-7532 470 B ebrown@lanecollege.edu
BROWN, Faith 802-322-1616 513 E faith.brown@goddard.edu
BROWN, Felicia 252-335-3642 377 F fdbrown@mail.ecsu.edu
BROWN, Fletcher 860-628-4751 93 C fbrown@lincolncollegene.edu
BROWN, Fran 248-476-1122 254 G fbrown@mispp.edu
BROWN, Francis, H 801-581-8767 511 C fbrown@mines.utah.edu
BROWN, Frank 850-201-8499 122 A brownf@tcc.fl.edu
BROWN, Frankie, M 316-978-3065 198 A frankie.brown@wichita.edu
BROWN, Fred 970-339-6640 81 A fred.brown@aims.edu
BROWN, Gary 503-725-9149 418 G browng@pdx.edu
BROWN, Gary 814-824-2036 436 C gbrown@mercyhurst.edu
BROWN, Gary 608-785-9167 555 F browng@westerntc.edu
BROWN, Gary, L 919-530-7466 378 B gbrown@nccu.edu
BROWN, Genevieve 936-294-1101 501 D brown@shsu.edu
BROWN, Geoffrey 315-268-7633 329 B gbrown@clarkson.edu
BROWN, Giles 903-463-8620 487 C browng@grayson.edu
BROWN, Greg 760-366-5290 43 H gbrown@cmccd.edu
BROWN, Gregory, N 212-854-2003 323 E gbrown@barnard.edu
BROWN, Guilbert, L 703-993-8743 519 E gbrowne@gmu.edu
BROWN, H. David 816-271-4327 286 G browndav@missouriwestern.edu
BROWN, Heather 213-477-2966 57 H hbrown@msmc.la.edu
BROWN, Hilrie 615-383-4848 478 F hbrown@watkins.edu
BROWN, Isiah, D 713-313-1318 500 B brownid@tsu.edu
BROWN, J. Kevin 863-784-7424 117 J kevin.brown@southflorida.edu
BROWN, J.J 828-262-2060 377 D brownjj1@appstate.edu
BROWN, Jack 859-371-9393 198 G jbrown@beckfield.edu
BROWN, Jacqueline, L 301-322-0918 225 F jbrown@pgcc.edu
BROWN, James 508-854-4324 240 F jbrown@qcc.mass.edu
BROWN, James 570-389-4410 441 F jbrown@bloomu.edu
BROWN, James 570-662-4805 443 C jbrown@mansfield.edu
BROWN, James, C 315-792-3001 359 E jbrown@utica.edu
BROWN, James, W 319-895-4485 183 G jbrown@cornellcollege.edu
BROWN, James, W 757-455-5730 530 C bbrown@vwc.edu
BROWN, Jane, B 617-373-4810 243 F
BROWN, Janet, M 219-464-5289 181 C janet.brown@valpo.edu
BROWN, Janice 301-846-2485 222 G jbrown@frederick.edu
BROWN, Jasmin, K 910-630-7034 367 B jabrown@methodist.edu
BROWN, Jeff 828-250-2350 378 D jbrown@unca.edu
BROWN, Jeff 801-832-2900 512 G jbrown@westminstercollege.edu
BROWN, Jeffrey, D 573-629-3015 282 E jbrown@hlg.edu
BROWN, Jeffrey, S 757-594-7053 517 L jsbrown@cnu.edu
BROWN, Jen 631-273-5112 338 F jen.brown@liu.edu
BROWN, Jennifer 785-738-9085 195 G jbrown@ncktc.edu
BROWN, Jennifer, A 617-287-5420 236 G jennifer.brown@umb.edu
BROWN, Jeremy 970-248-1962 82 F jbrown@coloradomesa.edu
BROWN, Jeremy, D 631-244-3200 332 C president@dowling.edu
BROWN, Jerri 928-350-2113 17 K jbrown@prescott.edu
BROWN, Jesse, M 260-359-4028 173 A jbrown@huntington.edu
BROWN, Jessyca 254-659-7818 487 G jbrown@hillcollege.edu
BROWN, Jim 770-229-3455 137 F jbrown@sctech.edu
BROWN, JoAnn 318-670-6651 215 A jwarren@susla.edu
BROWN, Joann 318-274-6153 215 E brownj@gram.edu
BROWN, Joanna 413-552-2253 239 F jbrown@hcc.edu
BROWN, Joanne 409-832-2956 500 I jcbrown@lit.edu
BROWN, Johanna 810-762-0409 255 G johanna.brown@mcc.edu
BROWN, John 404-962-3206 139 B john.brown@usg.edu
BROWN, John 619-482-6320 71 D jbrown@swccd.edu
BROWN, John 215-489-2413 426 H john.brown@delval.edu
BROWN, John, H 706-507-8800 127 G brown_john9@columbusstate.edu
BROWN, John-Michael 314-837-6777 288 C jbrown@slcconline.edu
BROWN, Jonathan 206-878-3710 535 B jbrown@highline.edu
BROWN, Joseph 910-246-4957 373 H brownj@sandhills.edu
BROWN, Joseph, D 903-923-2277 486 F jbrown@etbu.edu
BROWN, Joyce 443-885-3015 224 E joyce.brown@morgan.edu
BROWN, Joyce, F 212-217-4000 333 F joyce_brown@fitnyc.edu
BROWN, JT 563-588-7810 187 C jt.brown@loras.edu
BROWN, Judi 360-475-7700 536 D jbrown@olympic.edu
BROWN, Julia 662-472-9011 274 D jubrown@holmescc.edu
BROWN, Julie 651-255-6111 271 D jbrown@unitedseminary.edu
BROWN, June, E 918-631-2584 413 F june-brown@utulsa.edu
BROWN, Karen 607-962-9221 331 C kbrown7@corning-cc.edu
BROWN, Karen 432-839-8697 501 E kbrown2@sulross.edu
BROWN, Karen, A 607-436-2524 353 E brownka@oneonta.edu
BROWN, Kate 603-899-1090 305 A 0212mgr@fhet.follett.com
BROWN, Kathie 814-677-1322 428 A occ@dbcollege.com
BROWN, Kathleen 502-776-1443 206 B
BROWN, Kathleen, M 574-284-4557 179 F kbrown@saintmarys.edu
BROWN, Kathryn, A 814-677-1322 428 C occ@dbcollege.com
BROWN, Kathryn, F 612-624-3533 272 A brown059@umn.edu
BROWN, Katrina, M 307-674-6446 556 F kbrown@sheridan.edu
BROWN, Keith 440-365-5222 395 D
BROWN, Keith, A 318-342-5422 216 E kbrown@ulm.edu
BROWN, Keith, A 205-853-1200 5 C kbrown@jeffstateonline.com
BROWN, Kelly 405-224-3140 413 E kbrown@usao.edu
BROWN, Kendal, N 712-290-8737 433 F kbrown@lancasterseminary.edu
BROWN, Kennard, D 901-448-4797 477 E kbrown@uthsc.edu
BROWN, Kenneth 509-777-4486 540 C kbrown@whitworth.edu
BROWN, Kent 573-635-4971 283 I kentbrown@molawcenter.com
BROWN, Kevin 215-572-2854 422 C brownka@arcadia.edu
BROWN, Kevin 541-784-5149 185 B brown@graceland.edu
BROWN, Kevin 843-349-5398 458 H kevin.brown@hgtc.edu
BROWN, Kevin 423-236-2874 473 B kbrown@southern.edu
BROWN, Kevin, A 919-866-5475 374 H kabrown@waketech.edu
BROWN, Kevin, H 425-637-1010 532 E khbrown@cityu.edu
BROWN, Kim 940-668-7731 491 E kbrown@nctc.edu
BROWN, Kim, S 757-455-3275 530 C kbrown@vwc.edu
BROWN, Kimberly, A 630-515-6044 158 F kbrown@midwestern.edu
BROWN, Kimberly, S 850-474-2200 121 D kimbrown@uwf.edu
BROWN, Kristen 626-395-8395 32 H kbrown@caltech.edu
BROWN, Kristen, C 336-272-7102 364 G kristen.brown@greensboro.edu
BROWN, Kristy 317-738-8051 171 F kbrown@franklincollege.edu
BROWN, Kyle 315-386-7164 355 E brownk@canton.edu
BROWN, Laura, J 815-455-3700 157 H lbrown@mchenry.edu
BROWN, Laura, S 607-255-5180 331 B lsb7@cornell.edu
BROWN, Lauren 704-357-8020 362 D laubrown@aii.edu
BROWN, Lawrence 334-277-3390 3 E lawrence.brown@vc.edu
BROWN, LeAnn 763-576-4784 265 H lbrown@anokatech.edu
BROWN, LeeAnn 304-473-8160 545 G brown_l@wvwc.edu
BROWN, Leon, R 804-706-5020 527 B lbrown@jtcc.edu
BROWN, JR., Leonard, E 717-245-1736 427 F brownl@dickinson.edu
BROWN, Levy 252-527-6223 371 G lbrown@lenoircc.edu
BROWN, Lewis 605-688-4161 466 C lewis.brown@sdstate.edu
BROWN, Linda 660-359-3948 287 A lbrown@mail.ncmissouri.edu
BROWN, Linda 580-628-6240 409 B linda.brown@north-ok.edu
BROWN, Linda, J 218-299-4206 262 I linbrown@cord.edu
BROWN, Lindsey 406-265-4190 295 E lindsey.brown@msun.edu
BROWN, Lisa 563-441-4016 184 H lbrown@eicc.edu
BROWN, Lisa, M 216-397-4184 392 L lmbrown@jcu.edu
BROWN, Llatetra, D 443-518-4766 223 D llatetrabrown@howardcc.edu
BROWN, Lori, A 973-313-6132 315 B lori.brown@shu.edu
BROWN, Lougene 706-507-8902 127 G brown_lougene@columbusstate.edu
BROWN, Lucille 203-285-2114 91 D lbrown@gwcc.commnet.edu
BROWN, Luther 662-846-4312 273 H lbrown@deltastate.edu
BROWN, Lynn 207-893-6603 219 F lbrown@sjcme.edu
BROWN, Lynn, M 904-620-2115 120 D lmbrown@unf.edu
BROWN, Lynne 212-998-2350 344 B lynne.brown@nyu.edu
BROWN, II, M.Christopher 601-877-6100 272 F president@alcorn.edu
BROWN, Mae, W 858-534-3156 74 F mbrown@ucsd.edu
BROWN, Manning 570-586-2400 422 G mbrown@bbc.edu
BROWN, Marcia, W 973-353-5541 314 E mwbrown@andromeda.rutgers.edu
BROWN, Marcus 217-875-7200 162 F mbrown@richland.edu
BROWN, Margie 318-397-6128 210 J mabrown@myneltc.edu
BROWN, Margo 904-819-6474 107 C mbrown@flagler.edu
BROWN, Marinell 859-442-1120 202 B marinell.brown@kctcs.edu
BROWN, Mark 712-324-5061 188 C mbrown@nwicc.edu
BROWN, Mark, C 703-247-2500 99 G mbrown@strayer.edu
BROWN, Mark, I 608-743-4526 553 G mbrown55@blackhawk.edu
BROWN, Marnika 616-632-2455 247 E brownmar@aquinas.edu
BROWN, Marsha, D 206-934-5136 537 F marsha.brown@seattlecolleges.edu
BROWN, Mary 504-988-7800 215 C mwbrown@tulane.edu
BROWN, Mary 217-544-6464 163 H
BROWN, Mary, L 864-596-9094 457 E mary.brown@converse.edu
BROWN, Mary Lee 215-898-7260 448 J marylb@pobox.upenn.edu
BROWN, Matthew, S 405-744-9164 410 C brownms@okstate.edu

BROWN, Melanie, A ... 386-312-4202 ... 116 F
melaniebrown@sjrstate.edu
BROWN, Melissa ... 412-809-5100 ... 444 G
brown.melissa@pti.edu
BROWN, Melvin, L ... 973-353-5872 ... 314 E
melbrown@rci.rutgers.edu
BROWN, Merri ... 215-248-6323 ... 435 B
mbrown@ltsp.edu
BROWN, Merv, R ... 208-496-2010 ... 143 A
brownme@byui.edu
BROWN, Michael ... 928-717-7709 ... 19 C
michael.brown@yc.edu
BROWN, Michael, E ... 202-994-6241 ... 98 C
brownm@gwu.edu
BROWN, Michael, J ... 765-361-6384 ... 181 E
BROWN, Michael, T ... 805-893-2944 ... 75 B
michael.brown@els.ucsb.edu
BROWN, Michaela ... 910-672-1287 ... 377 G
mbrown38@uncfsu.edu
BROWN, Michele ... 847-635-1724 ... 160 F
mbrown@oakton.edu
BROWN, Michelle ... 435-283-7127 ... 512 C
michelle.brown@snow.edu
BROWN, Mike ... 574-936-8898 ... 169 D
mike.brown@ancilla.edu
BROWN, Mike ... 903-463-8772 ... 487 C
mbrown@grayson.edu
BROWN, Mikell ... 804-594-1509 ... 527 B
mbrown@jtcc.edu
BROWN, Mindy ... 503-594-3041 ... 415 A
mindyb@clackamas.edu
BROWN, Monte ... 919-684-0317 ... 364 C
monte.brown@duke.edu
BROWN, Naima ... 352-395-5648 ... 117 F
naima.brown@sfcollege.edu
BROWN, Nancy, B ... 423-318-2709 ... 476 D
nancy.brown@ws.edu
BROWN, Nicci, C ... 704-233-8126 ... 380 F
brown@wingate.edu
BROWN, Nicole ... 708-802-7750 ... 151 C
nbrown@foxcolleg.edu
BROWN, Nicole, R ... 417-625-3137 ... 286 B
brown-n@mssu.edu
BROWN, Norman ... 202-319-5044 ... 97 E
brownn@cua.edu
BROWN, O. Ted ... 270-809-6937 ... 205 A
obrown@murraystate.edu
BROWN, Pamela ... 718-260-5008 ... 328 D
pbrown@citytech.cuny.edu
BROWN, Pamela ... 843-574-6246 ... 461 G
pamela.brown@tridenttech.edu
BROWN, Pamela, J ... 740-593-2583 ... 399 G
brownp@ohio.edu
BROWN, Pamela, S ... 217-228-5520 ... 146 B
pbrown@brcn.edu
BROWN, Patricia, R ... 716-839-8484 ... 331 F
pbrown@daemen.edu
BROWN, Patrick ... 253-680-7014 ... 531 F
pbrown@bates.ctc.edu
BROWN, Patty ... 423-697-2437 ... 474 D
BROWN, Paul ... 254-659-7860 ... 487 G
pbrown@hillcollege.edu
BROWN, Paul, M ... 404-880-8790 ... 127 C
pbrown@cau.edu
BROWN, Paul, P ... 856-225-6005 ... 314 D
peyton@camden.rutgers.edu
BROWN, Paul, R ... 740-588-1200 ... 407 A
pbrown@zanestate.edu
BROWN, Paul, R ... 610-758-6725 ... 434 E
prb207@lehigh.edu
BROWN, Paula ... 972-438-6932 ... 492 E
pbrown@parkercc.edu
BROWN, Peg, A ... 319-296-4283 ... 185 F
peg.brown@hawkeyecollege.edu
BROWN, Perry ... 406-243-4689 ... 294 I
perry.brown@umontana.edu
BROWN, Peter, M ... 914-594-4560 ... 343 F
peter_brown@nymc.edu
BROWN, Philip, R ... 207-768-2708 ... 218 J
pbrown@nmcc.edu
BROWN, Phillip ... 219-989-2240 ... 178 K
brown@purduecal.edu
BROWN, Phillip, M ... 618-650-3415 ... 165 C
phbrown@siue.edu
BROWN, Quiana ... 281-998-6150 ... 494 B
quiana.brown@sjcd.edu
BROWN, Quincy, D ... 706-880-8297 ... 133 B
qbrown@lagrange.edu
BROWN, R. McKenna ... 804-828-8471 ... 526 B
mbrown@vcu.edu
BROWN, Rachel ... 215-204-7981 ... 447 H
rachel.brown@temple.edu
BROWN, Rae Linda ... 310-338-5217 ... 56 E
raelinda.brown@lmu.edu
BROWN, Randy ... 408-848-4852 ... 48 C
rbrown@gavilan.edu
BROWN, Ray ... 573-592-5238 ... 293 B
ray.brown@westminster-mo.edu
BROWN, Raymond, A ... 610-527-0200 ... 445 J
bbrown@rosemont.edu
BROWN, Raymond, A ... 817-257-7490 ... 499 C
r.brown@tcu.edu
BROWN, Rebecca ... 214-333-5426 ... 484 D
rebeccab@dbu.edu
BROWN, Rebekkah, L ... 484-664-3247 ... 437 C
rbrown@muhlenberg.edu
BROWN, Renee, D ... 419-559-2367 ... 402 D
rbrown@terra.edu
BROWN, Reynolda ... 386-481-2602 ... 102 C
brownr@cookman.edu
BROWN, Rhodella ... 386-506-3969 ... 104 F
brownr@daytonastate.edu
BROWN, Rhonda ... 708-534-4044 ... 151 E
rbrown11@govst.edu
BROWN, Rhonda, L ... 215-204-7303 ... 447 H
rhonda.brown@temple.edu
BROWN, Richard ... 423-425-4393 ... 477 F
richard-brown@utc.edu
BROWN, Richard ... 856-415-2205 ... 310 D
rbrown@gccnj.edu
BROWN, Richard, B ... 801-581-6912 ... 511 C
brown@coe.utah.edu
BROWN, Richard, W ... 530-226-4728 ... 69 H
rbrown@simpsonu.edu
BROWN, Ricky ... 252-493-7423 ... 372 H
rbrown@email.pittcc.edu
BROWN, Robert ... 312-553-6029 ... 147 C
rbrown@ccc.edu
BROWN, Robert ... 410-386-8224 ... 221 G
rbrown@carrollcc.edu
BROWN, Robert, A ... 617-353-2200 ... 232 E
rabrown@bu.edu
BROWN, Robert, C ... 479-968-0237 ... 20 G
rcbrown@atu.edu
BROWN, Robert, C ... 216-368-4306 ... 386 F
robert.c.brown@case.edu
BROWN, Robert, K ... 918-781-7218 ... 407 B
brownr@bacone.edu
BROWN, Robert, L ... 803-981-7375 ... 463 H
rbrown@yorktech.edu
BROWN, Robert, M ... 251-460-6151 ... 9 D
rbrown@usouthal.edu
BROWN, Robin, C ... 970-491-2682 ... 83 F
robin.brown@colostate.edu
BROWN, Rock ... 406-265-3765 ... 295 E
rock.brown@msun.edu
BROWN, Rodney ... 972-773-8650 ... 464 H
BROWN, Rodney, J ... 801-422-3963 ... 509 H
rod_brown@byu.edu
BROWN, Roger ... 901-435-1535 ... 470 D
roger_brown@loc.edu
BROWN, Roger, G ... 423-425-4141 ... 477 F
roger-brown@utc.edu
BROWN, Roger, H ... 617-266-1400 ... 231 E
BROWN, Ron ... 254-295-4517 ... 504 C
rbrown@umhb.edu
BROWN, Ronald, C ... 512-245-2205 ... 501 F
rb04@txstate.edu
BROWN, Ronald, H ... 919-516-4859 ... 376 D
rhbrown@st-aug.edu
BROWN, Ronald, T ... 313-577-2200 ... 260 A
rtbrown@wayne.edu
BROWN, Rosann ... 814-641-3133 ... 432 A
brownr@juniata.edu
BROWN, Russ ... 772-462-6004 ... 111 B
rbrown@irsc.edu
BROWN, Sabrina ... 434-395-2021 ... 521 A
browncs2@longwood.edu
BROWN, Samuel ... 203-575-8022 ... 92 A
sbrown@nvcc.commnet.edu
BROWN, Sandra ... 858-534-3526 ... 74 F
BROWN, Sandra ... 605-668-1555 ... 464 G
sbrown@mtmc.edu
BROWN, Scott ... 513-785-3227 ... 396 F
brownsj3@muohio.edu
BROWN, Shanita ... 615-327-6223 ... 471 C
sbrown@mmc.edu
BROWN, Shannon ... 828-726-2288 ... 368 G
sbrown@cccti.edu
BROWN, Sharon, A ... 610-625-7847 ... 437 A
mesab01@moravian.edu
BROWN, Sharon, S ... 937-778-7821 ... 390 G
sbrown@edisonohio.edu
BROWN, Shelley ... 330-490-7134 ... 405 F
sbrown@walsh.edu
BROWN, Shirley, F ... 828-652-0676 ... 372 B
shirleyb@mcdowelltech.edu
BROWN, Shondae ... 256-395-2211 ... 7 D
sbrown@suscc.edu
BROWN, Simon ... 215-751-8039 ... 426 B
sbrown@ccp.edu
BROWN, Sloane ... 918-540-6393 ... 408 J
scbrown@neo.edu
BROWN, Stacy ... 305-534-7050 ... 122 B
stacyb@talmudicu.edu
BROWN, Stan ... 229-317-6721 ... 128 D
stan.brown@darton.edu
BROWN, Stephan ... 352-588-8331 ... 116 G
stephan.brown@saintleo.edu
BROWN, Stephanie ... 954-262-7456 ... 114 B
browstep@nsu.nova.edu
BROWN, Stephanie ... 417-447-2653 ... 287 D
browns@otc.edu
BROWN, Stephen, E ... 248-204-2300 ... 254 B
sbrown@ltu.edu
BROWN, Stephen, G ... 530-221-4275 ... 69 C
sbrown@shasta.edu
BROWN, Stephen, W ... 949-812-7445 ... 27 C
BROWN, Stephen, W ... 304-442-3105 ... 545 D
stephen.brown@mail.wvu.edu
BROWN, Steve ... 724-805-2534 ... 446 E
steve.brown@email.stvincent.edu
BROWN, Steve ... 202-639-1764 ... 98 A
sbrown@corcoran.org
BROWN, Steve ... 570-586-2400 ... 422 G
sbrown@bbc.edu
BROWN, Steve, D ... 423-439-4841 ... 473 F
browsd02@etsu.edu
BROWN, Steven ... 202-541-5205 ... 100 B
sbrown@wtu.edu
BROWN, Steven ... 802-287-8912 ... 513 F
browns@greenmtn.edu
BROWN, Steven, F ... 601-484-0221 ... 275 F
sb1812@meridian.msstate.edu
BROWN, Steven, L ... 304-710-3141 ... 542 K
brown175@mctc.edu
BROWN, Sue, A ... 918-595-7884 ... 412 H
sbrown3@tulsacc.edu
BROWN, Sue, C ... 309-655-2206 ... 163 G
sue.c.brown@osfhealthcare.org
BROWN, Susan ... 802-860-2754 ... 513 C
brown@champlain.edu
BROWN, Susan ... 509-359-6403 ... 533 H
sbrown@ewu.edu
BROWN, Susan, M ... 859-233-8225 ... 207 A
subrown@transy.edu
BROWN, Sylvia ... 252-744-6422 ... 377 E
brownsy@ecu.edu
BROWN, T. Rhett ... 704-233-8022 ... 380 F
rhbrown@wingate.edu
BROWN, Tammy ... 225-359-9207 ... 209 J
tbrown@catc.edu
BROWN, Tanasha ... 225-216-8103 ... 209 H
brownt@mybrcc.edu
BROWN, Ted ... 516-299-2229 ... 339 A
ted.brown@liu.edu
BROWN, Ted, R ... 931-363-9802 ... 471 A
tbrown@martinmethodist.edu
BROWN, Teresa ... 404-225-4700 ... 125 E
tbrown@atlantatech.edu
BROWN, Teresa ... 615-230-3377 ... 476 C
teresa.brown@volstate.edu
BROWN, Teresa, L ... 401-456-8240 ... 454 A
tlbrown@ric.edu
BROWN, Terrence ... 901-751-8453 ... 471 F
tbrown@mabts.edu
BROWN, Terry ... 304-327-4191 ... 543 F
tbrown@bluefieldstate.edu
BROWN, Terry ... 262-595-2261 ... 552 A
terry.brown@uwp.edu
BROWN, Therese ... 303-404-5535 ... 85 A
therese.brown@frontrange.edu
BROWN, Thomas ... 702-651-4002 ... 302 E
thomas.brown@csn.edu
BROWN, Thomas ... 540-231-3787 ... 529 G
tbrown@vt.edu
BROWN, Thomas, W ... 507-933-7005 ... 263 J
brownie@gustavus.edu
BROWN, Tim ... 843-574-6424 ... 461 G
tim.brown@tridenttech.edu
BROWN, Timothy ... 616-392-8555 ... 260 D
tim.brown@westernsem.edu
BROWN, Trachanda ... 215-242-7989 ... 425 D
browntt@chc.edu
BROWN, Travis ... 954-446-6169 ... 100 I
tbrown@aiufl.edu
BROWN, Venessa ... 618-482-6912 ... 165 C
vbrown@siue.edu
BROWN, Venessa ... 618-650-5867 ... 165 C
vbrown@siue.edu
BROWN, Vicki, R ... 540-985-9784 ... 520 I
vrbrown@jchs.edu
BROWN, Victor ... 609-894-9311 ... 308 B
vbrown@bcc.edu
BROWN, Victor ... 937-298-3399 ... 394 D
victor.brown@kcma.edu
BROWN, Violet ... 610-896-1000 ... 430 G
vbrown@haverford.edu
BROWN, Walter ... 909-868-4004 ... 44 K
wbrown@devry.edu
BROWN, Walter, E ... 412-648-3185 ... 449 A
walter.brown@ia.pitt.edu
BROWN, Wanda, C ... 336-633-0286 ... 373 A
wcbrown@randolph.edu
BROWN, Warren ... 206-934-5481 ... 537 E
warren.brown@seattlecolleges.edu
BROWN, Wes ... 912-260-4221 ... 137 B
wes.brown@sgc.edu
BROWN, Wes, S ... 912-260-4430 ... 137 B
wes.brown@sgc.edu
BROWN, Wilfred, E ... 805-893-4155 ... 75 B
wbrown@housing.ucsb.edu
BROWN, William ... 571-334-2600 ... 29 F
wbrown@argosy.edu
BROWN, William ... 520-494-5340 ... 13 D
william.brown@centralaz.edu
BROWN, William, E ... 937-766-7900 ... 386 G
bbrown@cedarville.edu
BROWN, William, H ... 704-894-2143 ... 363 I
wibrown@davidson.edu
BROWN, William, J ... 717-867-6180 ... 434 C
wbrown@lvc.edu
BROWN, William (Bill) ... 859-846-5358 ... 204 H
bbrown@midway.edu
BROWN, Willie, T ... 256-539-0834 ... 4 F
deanac@hbc1.edu
BROWN, Willie, T ... 256-539-0834 ... 4 F
deaninst@hbc1.edu
BROWN, Winston, D ... 504-520-7577 ... 217 A
wbrown@xula.edu
BROWN, Yvette ... 305-899-3600 ... 101 M
ybrown@mail.barry.edu
BROWN, Zachary ... 607-431-4547 ... 335 A
brownz@hartwick.edu
BROWN, Zachary, M ... 309-692-4092 ... 158 D
zbrown@midstate.edu
BROWN-BULLOCH, Lynn ... 843-661-8141 ... 458 B
lynn.brown-bulloch@fdtc.edu
BROWN-CORNELIUS,
Denise ... 502-272-8270 ... 198 H
dbrowncornelius@bellarmine.edu
BROWN-GUILLORY,
Elizabeth ... 713-313-1180 ... 500 B
brown_guillorye@tsu.edu
BROWN-HART, Denise ... 910-672-1856 ... 377 G
dbrownhart@uncfsu.edu
BROWN-HAYWOOD,
Felicia, L ... 717-948-6180 ... 439 J
flb1@psu.edu
BROWN MARSDEN,
Margaret ... 972-721-5245 ... 503 B
mebrown@udallas.edu
BROWN MORRIS, Kelly ... 404-756-8951 ... 134 E
kbrownmorris@msm.edu
BROWN-NEVERS,
Michelle, H ... 215-898-7233 ... 448 J
mbnevers@sfs.upenn.edu
BROWN-SOW, Lynette ... 215-751-8859 ... 426 B
lbrown@ccp.edu
BROWN-WADE, Glenda ... 205-929-1404 ... 5 H
plac@mail.miles.edu
BROWN-WELTY, Sharon ... 559-278-2448 ... 35 A
sharonb@csufresno.edu
BROWN WRIGHT, Lynda .. 404-413-2574 ... 131 G
lwright39@gsu.edu
BROWN-WRIGHT, Lynda .. 859-323-6589 ... 207 D
lynda.brownwright@uky.edu
BROWNBACK, H, O ... 618-235-2700 ... 165 D
h.brownback@swic.edu
BROWNE, Brian ... 718-990-2762 ... 348 G
browneb@stjohns.edu
BROWNE, Dorothy, C ... 757-823-8668 ... 522 E
dcbrowne@nsu.edu
BROWNE, Doug ... 620-417-1201 ... 196 F
doug.browne@sccc.edu
BROWNE, Jennifer ... 631-287-8304 ... 339 B
jennifer.browne@liu.edu
BROWNE, Joan, M ... 202-806-7513 ... 98 E
jmbrowne@howard.edu
BROWNE, Kevin, M ... 312-996-4350 ... 167 B
kbrowne@uic.edu
BROWNE, Kevin, M ... 209-228-4567 ... 74 D
kbrowne@ucmerced.edu
BROWNE, Nancy, E ... 305-595-9500 ... 100 F
nancy@amcollege.edu
BROWNE, Pamela ... 386-481-2858 ... 102 C
brownep@cookman.edu
BROWNE, Patrick ... 503-256-3180 ... 421 A
pbrowne@uws.edu
BROWNE, Richard, M ... 305-595-9500 ... 100 F
richard@amcollege.edu
BROWNE, Timm ... 562-907-4211 ... 79 F
tbrowne@whittier.edu
BROWNELL, Claire ... 303-871-4876 ... 89 A
cbrownel@du.edu
BROWNELL, Jennifer ... 336-506-4140 ... 368 A
jennifer.brownell@alamancecc.edu
BROWNELL, Lauren ... 318-342-6787 ... 216 E
brownell@ulm.edu
BROWNELL, Winifred, E ... 401-874-4101 ... 454 E
winnie@uri.edu
BROWNER, Stephanie ... 212-229-5100 ... 342 E
browners@newschool.edu
BROWNIE, Ronald ... 605-626-2568 ... 466 A
ronald.brownie@northern.edu
BROWNING, David, A ... 214-860-2015 ... 485 A
dbrowning@dcccd.edu
BROWNING, Debbie ... 740-245-7209 ... 404 E
browning@rio.edu
BROWNING, Douglas, D ... 301-846-2458 ... 222 G
dbrowning@frederick.edu
BROWNING, Eric ... 740-392-6868 ... 396 I
eric.browning@mvnu.edu
BROWNING, Gari ... 510-659-6200 ... 59 J
gbrowning@ohlone.edu
BROWNING, John ... 619-594-6648 ... 37 A
browning@mail.sdsu.edu
BROWNING, Julie ... 713-348-2575 ... 493 C
jmb@rice.edu
BROWNING, Katherine ... 301-387-3097 ... 222 H
katherine.browning@garrettcollege.edu
BROWNING, Marguerite ... 909-621-8125 ... 49 F
maggie_browning@hmc.edu
BROWNING, Mark ... 208-769-3316 ... 144 D
mark_browning@nic.edu
BROWNING, Midge ... 618-374-5776 ... 161 E
midge.browning@principia.edu

BRYANT, Brenda 313-927-1502 254 E
bbryant@marygrove.edu
BRYANT, Brenda 540-887-7220 521 C
bbryant@mbc.edu
BRYANT, Bruce, K 425-637-1010 532 E
brucebryant@cityu.edu
BRYANT, Carlton, G 800-782-2422 33 E
cbryant@mail.cnuas.edu
BRYANT, Cherie 207-741-5726 219 A
cbryant@smccme.edu
BRYANT, Clint 706-737-1626 125 G
cbryant@aug.edu
BRYANT, Daniel, C 740-376-4718 395 G
dan.bryant@marietta.edu
BRYANT, David, A 580-349-1302 410 B
dbryant@opsu.edu
BRYANT, David, A 407-303-9305 100 G
david.bryant@adu.edu
BRYANT, Debbie 870-460-1034 25 A
bryant@uamont.edu
BRYANT, Felicia 856-227-7200 308 D
fbryant@camdencc.edu
BRYANT, Fred 361-593-3922 498 D
kffcb00@tamuk.edu
BRYANT, Gerald 417-447-7553 287 D
bryantg@otc.edu
BRYANT, Jack 405-422-1256 411 G
bryantj@redlandscc.edu
BRYANT, III, James, S 803-535-1330 460 C
bryantj@octech.edu
BRYANT, Jay 602-978-7294 18 H
jay.bryant@thunderbird.edu
BRYANT, John 309-556-3449 153 F
jbryant@iwu.edu
BRYANT, Joy, L 864-644-5385 461 B
jbryant@swu.edu
BRYANT, Karen 618-842-3711 152 G
bryantk@iecc.edu
BRYANT, Kashina 207-513-3602 218 C
kabryant@kaplan.edu
BRYANT, Kevin 503-517-1220 421 B
kmbryant@warnerpacific.edu
BRYANT, Kimberly 215-895-1121 450 B
k.bryant@usciences.edu
BRYANT, Kinney 405-425-5155 409 E
kinney.bryant@oc.edu
BRYANT, Leisa 662-325-7353 275 F
lbryant@audit.msstate.edu
BRYANT, Leonora, C 336-433-5570 378 A
leonora@ncat.edu
BRYANT, Lori 702-933-9700 301 H
lbryant4@devry.edu
BRYANT, Margie 202-687-3698 98 D
bryantm@georgetown.edu
BRYANT, Matthew 706-419-1651 128 B
bryant@covenant.edu
BRYANT, Micki 714-564-6079 63 F
bryant_micki@sac.edu
BRYANT, Morgan 601-925-3354 275 C
mbryant@mc.edu
BRYANT, Paul 309-467-6377 151 B
pbryant@eureka.edu
BRYANT, Penny, J 314-367-8700 288 F
penny.bryant@stlcop.edu
BRYANT, Randal, E 412-268-8821 424 J
randy.bryant@cs.cmu.edu
BRYANT, Scott 903-923-2173 486 F
sbryant@etbu.edu
BRYANT, Sharon 312-850-7090 147 F
sbryant6@ccc.edu
BRYANT, Sheila, M 931-221-7178 473 E
bryantsm@apsu.edu
BRYANT, Stephanie 417-836-4408 286 C
stephaniebryant@missouristate.edu
BRYANT, Stephanie 803-754-4100 457 D
BRYANT, Steve 601-583-4100 273 A
BRYANT, Susan, V 949-824-6296 74 B
svbryant@uci.edu
BRYANT, Theresa 757-822-1184 528 G
tbryant@tcc.edu
BRYANT, Tim 513-244-4504 388 E
tim_bryant@mail.msj.edu
BRYANT, Toni 830-792-7229 494 E
tlbryant@schreiner.edu
BRYANT, Vickie 817-461-8741 480 H
vbryant@abconline.org
BRYANT, William, C 208-524-3000 143 G
bill.bryant@my.eitc.edu
BRYANT-WEBB, Jocelyn 410-951-3922 228 B
jbryant@coppin.edu
BRYCE, Jeanne 928-428-8261 14 B
jeanne.bryce@eac.edu
BRYCE, Mark 928-428-8231 14 B
mark.bryce@eac.edu
BRYD, John 803-323-3374 463 E
brydj@winthrop.edu
BRYDEN, David, L 336-841-9101 365 C
dbryden@highpoint.edu
BRYDGES, Bruce 315-267-2484 354 C
brydgebc@potsdam.edu
BRYDON, Lucinda, C 607-746-4603 355 F
brydonlm@delhi.edu
BRYDON, Marria, L 405-878-5416 412 A
mlbrydon@stgregorys.edu
BRYENTON, John 270-686-4615 203 B
john.bryenton@kctcs.edu
BRYLINSKY, Jody 269-387-2314 260 C
jody.brylinsky@wmich.edu
BRYNE, Kathryn 617-243-2176 236 A
kbryne@lasell.edu
BRYNTESON, Susan 302-831-2231 96 I
susanb@udel.edu
BRYSON, Barbara 713-348-5151 493 C
bwbryson@rice.edu
BRYSON, Cynthia 713-771-5336 132 F
cbryson@ict-ils.edu
BRYSON, J. Richard 740-389-4636 395 H
brysonr@mtc.edu
BRYSON, Lance 717-477-1451 443 E
jlbrys@ship.edu
BRYSON, Suzanne 828-251-6128 378 D
sbryson@unca.edu
BRYSON, Terri 256-890-4703 2 D
tbb@calhoun.edu
BRZEZINSKI, Michael, A 765-494-9399 178 J
mbrzezinski@purdue.edu
BRZEZINSKI, Steve 937-769-1855 384 B
sbrzezinski@antioch.edu
BRZORAD, John 828-328-7606 366 E
john.brzorad@lr.edu
BRZOZOWSKI, Samantha 615-383-4848 478 F
sbrzozowski@watkins.edu
BUBB, Kevin 517-483-9764 254 A
bubbk@lcc.edu
BUBLITZ, Josh 507-453-2735 267 C
jbublitz@southeastmn.edu
BUBNOVA, Elena 775-673-8239 302 H
ebubnova@tmcc.edu
BUCARO, S. Ted 937-229-4122 404 A
sbucaro1@udayton.edu
BUCCILLI, Michael 203-285-2144 91 D
mbuccilli@gwcc.commnet.edu
BUCELL, Michael 814-732-2252 442 E
bucell@edinboro.edu
BUCHA, Edward, R 724-738-2183 443 F
edward.bucha@sru.edu
BUCHANAN, Carrie 970-943-2101 89 E
cbuchanan@western.edu
BUCHANAN, Dave 262-595-2404 552 A
dave.buchanan@uwp.edu
BUCHANAN, Deborah, B 731-426-7552 470 B
dbuchanan@lanecollege.edu
BUCHANAN, Doug 806-742-2121 502 A
douglas.buchanan@ttu.edu.
BUCHANAN, Harvey 850-644-3444 119 D
buchanan@otc.fsu.edu
BUCHANAN, Janelle, M 806-720-7476 490 F
janelle.buchanan@lcu.edu
BUCHANAN, Jennifer, N 850-644-6876 119 D
jbuchanan@admin.fsu.edu
BUCHANAN, Kyrel, L 256-765-4328 9 C
kbuchanan@una.edu
BUCHANAN, Linda, R 319-385-6284 186 E
linda.buchanan@iwc.edu
BUCHANAN, Pam 251-442-2372 9 A
pbuchanan@umobile.edu
BUCHANAN, Pamela 828-227-7640 380 A
pbuchanan@wcu.edu
BUCHANAN, Richard 801-878-1400 303 D
rbuchanan@roseman.edu
BUCHANAN, Rollie, O 516-876-4873 353 D
buchananr@oldwestbury.edu
BUCHANAN, Saundra 541-506-6050 415 C
sbuchanan@cgcc.cc.or.us
BUCHANAN, Sharmane 954-446-6137 100 I
sbuchanan@aiufl.edu
BUCHANAN, Susan, M 509-527-5183 540 B
buchansm@whitman.edu
BUCHANAN, Tenielle 615-966-5264 470 F
tenielle.buchanan@lipscomb.edu
BUCHANAN, Thomas 307-766-4121 556 H
tombuch@uwyo.edu
BUCHANAN, Timothy, M 724-938-5887 441 G
buchanan@calu.edu
BUCHANAN, Tony 407-301-4928 478 H
tony.buchanan@earthlink.net
BUCHANAN, Trey 512-313-3000 483 K
trey.buchanan@concordia.edu
BUCHELI, Hernan 650-508-3512 59 H
hbucheli@ndnu.edu
BUCHER, John, E 440-775-6727 397 G
john.bucher@oberlin.edu
BUCHER, Karen, H 540-868-7132 527 C
kbucher@lfcc.edu
BUCHER, Oskar 541-684-7273 417 F
oskar@nwcu.edu
BUCHHEIT, Peter, J 814-362-7670 449 B
pjb4@pitt.edu
BUCHHOLTZ, Gina 701-224-5702 382 D
gina.buchholtz@bismarckstate.edu
BUCHHOLZ, Richard 405-422-6204 411 G
richard.buchholz@redlandscc.edu
BUCHHOLZ, Robert 336-278-5500 364 D
rbuchholz@elon.edu
BUCHHOLZ, Ron 262-472-1498 553 A
buchholr@uww.edu
BUCHHOLZ, Stephen 605-394-4034 466 F
stephen.buchholz@wdt.edu
BUCHMAN, Ashley 870-358-8636 20 F
ashley_buchman@asun.edu
BUCHMAN, Irene 212-217-4590 333 F
irene_buchman@fitnyc.edu
BUCHMAN, Lorne, M 626-396-2301 29 I
lorne.buchman@artcenter.edu
BUCHOLC, Stanley 978-665-3215 237 E
sbucholc@fitchburgstate.edu
BUCHOLZ, Jan 253-964-6519 536 H
jbucholz@pierce.ctc.edu
BUCHWALD, Adam 503-768-7227 416 G
buchwald@lclark.edu
BUCHWALD, Rosalinda 626-914-8897 40 B
rbuchwald@citruscollege.edu
BUCHWALDER, Mary, P 937-229-3131 404 A
mbuchwalder1@udayton.edu
BUCK, A. Scott 252-328-6910 377 E
bucka@ecu.edu
BUCK, Charles 208-292-1737 144 G
buck@uidaho.edu
BUCK, James, E 978-393-3431 402 A
jbuck@sscc.edu
BUCK, John 314-968-7030 292 J
buckjh@webster.edu
BUCK, Katherine 973-290-4204 308 G
kbuck@cse.edu
BUCK, Kavin 503-821-8942 419 D
kbuck@pnca.edu
BUCK, Kevan, C 918-631-3245 413 F
kevan-buck@utulsa.edu
BUCK, Marilyn, M 765-285-3716 169 G
mbuck@bsu.edu
BUCK, Mark 630-353-7049 149 B
mbuck@devry.edu
BUCK, Ryan 718-951-5000 326 F
ryanbuck@brooklyn.cuny.edu
BUCK, Sylvia, T 812-488-2724 180 E
sb79@evansville.edu
BUCK, Yolanda 804-524-5297 529 H
ybuck@vsu.edu
BUCKALEW, Leslie 209-588-5107 80 G
buckalewl@yosemite.edu
BUCKALEW, Thomas, D 205-652-3581 9 E
db@uwa.edu
BUCKER, Robert 818-677-2246 35 F
robert.bucker@csun.edu
BUCKHAULTS, Tex 806-874-3571 483 A
tex.buckhaults@clarendoncollege.edu
BUCKHAULTS, Tresea, L 318-342-5240 216 E
buckhaults@ulm.edu
BUCKHOLZ, Mark 575-234-9215 319 F
mbuckhol@nmsu.edu
BUCKI, SJ, John, P 315-445-4110 338 B
buckijp@lemoyne.edu
BUCKINGHAM, David, E 757-455-3273 530 C
debuckingham@vwc.edu
BUCKINGHAM, Paul 808-675-3518 140 D
buckingp@byuh.edu
BUCKINGHAM, Stacy 618-985-3741 154 G
stacybuckingham@jalc.edu
BUCKIUS, Richard, O 765-494-6209 178 J
rbuckius@purdue.edu
BUCKLA, Robert, J 414-410-4201 546 G
rjbuckla@stritch.edu
BUCKLAND, Stephen 513-721-7944 391 D
sbuckland@gbs.edu
BUCKLER, Carol 212-431-2182 343 E
carol.buckler@nyls.edu
BUCKLES, Beverly, J 909-558-4528 54 D
bbuckles@llu.edu
BUCKLES, Dale 270-706-8431 202 A
dale.buckles@kctcs.edu
BUCKLES, Eric 541-383-7216 414 I
ebuckles@cocc.edu
BUCKLES, Gregory, B 802-443-3000 514 A
deanofadmissions@middlebury.edu
BUCKLEW, Kathy 863-297-1016 115 C
kbucklew@polk.edu
BUCKLEY, Alison 302-855-1607 96 E
abuckley@dtcc.edu
BUCKLEY, Alison 443-518-4133 223 D
abuckley@howardcc.edu
BUCKLEY, Chris 910-893-1208 362 J
buckley@campbell.edu
BUCKLEY, Cindy 719-502-3100 87 B
cindy.buckley@ppcc.edu
BUCKLEY, Cornelius, M 805-525-4417 72 I
cbuckley@thomasaquinas.edu
BUCKLEY, Cynthia, S 405-466-3202 408 G
csbuckley@langston.edu
BUCKLEY, Emily 913-621-8731 192 F
ebuckley@donnelly.edu
BUCKLEY, Gerard 585-475-6317 347 G
gbuckley@ntid.rit.edu
BUCKLEY, Gregory, A 312-341-3376 163 B
gbuckley@roosevelt.edu
BUCKLEY, Irene 914-674-7308 340 F
ibuckley@mercy.edu
BUCKLEY, Jeanne 215-572-4019 422 C
buckleyj@arcadia.edu
BUCKLEY, Jennifer 630-844-6155 145 F
jbuckley@aurora.edu
BUCKLEY, Jerry 619-388-7350 65 H
jbuckley@sdccd.edu
BUCKLEY, JoBeth 765-983-1645 171 E
jebuckl07@earlham.edu
BUCKLEY, John, M 302-857-1200 96 G
jbuckley@dtcc.edu
BUCKLEY, John, W 718-817-4000 334 C
buckley@fordham.edu
BUCKLEY, Larry 909-384-8298 65 C
lbuckley@sbccd.cc.ca.us
BUCKLEY, Linda 415-338-3376 37 B
lbuckley@sfsu.edu
BUCKLEY, Marcus 518-454-5216 330 C
buckleym@strose.edu
BUCKLEY, Mary 314-966-3000 284 E
maryb@metrobusinesscollege.edu
BUCKLEY, Merdis, F 903-927-3312 509 E
mfbuckley@wileyc.edu
BUCKLEY, Neil, G 617-735-9866 234 C
buckley@emmanuel.edu
BUCKLEY, Noah 541-737-4411 418 F
osuadmit@oregonstate.edu
BUCKLEY, Patricia 518-458-5444 330 C
buckleyp@strose.edu
BUCKLEY, Peter, F 706-721-2231 130 D
pbuckley@georgiahealth.edu
BUCKLEY, Sally, A 617-333-2374 233 F
sbuckley@curry.edu
BUCKLEY, Stephanie 310-506-4893 61 H
stephanie.buckley@pepperdine.edu
BUCKLEY, Susan, C 319-335-3558 182 F
susan-buckley@uiowa.edu
BUCKLIN, Carolyn 515-643-6744 187 F
cbucklin@mercydesmoines.org
BUCKMAN, Cathy, M 574-520-4451 174 E
cmbuckma@iusb.edu
BUCKMAN, Kenneth 956-665-3461 506 C
buckman@utpa.edu
BUCKMAN, Ty 937-327-7924 406 B
tbuckman@wittenberg.edu
BUCKNER, Barbara 706-507-8505 127 G
buckner_barbara@columbusstate.edu
BUCKNER, Ben 614-837-4088 405 C
BUCKNER, Carole 213-252-5100 26 C
BUCKNER, Connie, S 828-398-7701 368 B
cbuckner@abtech.edu
BUCKNER, Patrice 912-478-3326 131 E
pbuckner@georgiasouthern.edu
BUCKNER, R. Ty 336-316-2248 365 A
rbuckner@guilford.edu
BUCKNER, Ramona 918-647-1320 407 E
rbuckner@carlalbert.edu
BUCKNER, Tina 417-667-8181 280 E
tbuckner@cottey.edu
BUCKRIDGE, Brett 215-637-7700 431 A
bbuckridge@holyfamily.edu
BUCY, Brandon, R 540-458-8651 530 D
bucyb@wlu.edu
BUDD, Carla 307-382-1832 557 A
cbudd@wwcc.wy.edu
BUDD, Deborah 510-981-2850 62 B
dbudd@peralta.edu
BUDD, Frank, C 843-953-5640 457 B
buddf@cofc.edu
BUDD, Jordan 603-513-5122 306 E
jordan.budd@law.unh.edu
BUDD KEPLER, Patricia 617-627-3427 245 C
pkeple01@tufts.edu
BUDDE, Bruce 309-694-5477 152 C
bbudde@icc.edu
BUDDE, Jill 641-683-5165 185 G
jbudde@indianhills.edu
BUDDE, Mitzi, J 703-461-1756 522 I
mbudde@vts.edu
BUDDEN, Chris 303-352-6911 84 A
chris.budden@ccd.edu
BUDERUS, Julie 970-339-6583 81 A
julie.buderus@aims.edu
BUDESCU, Gila 212-327-8054 347 H
gbudescu@rockefeller.edu
BUDJAC, Susan 715-422-5319 554 E
sue.budjac@mstc.edu
BUDKOWSKI, Dennis 740-389-4636 395 H
budkowskid@mtc.edu
BUDWIG, Nancy 508-793-7673 233 B
nbudwig@clarku.edu
BUDZILOWICZ, Mary 610-902-8352 424 B
mbudzy@cabrini.edu
BUDZYNSKI, John 312-949-7020 152 E
jbudzynski@ico.edu
BUECHELE, Angela, K 937-229-2941 404 A
abuechele1@udayton.edu
BUECHELE, Thomas 312-899-7420 164 C
tbuechele@saic.edu
BUECHER, Timothy, K 812-465-1136 181 B
tbuecher@usi.edu
BUECHNER, Marybeth 916-558-2512 56 D
buechnm@scc.losrios.edu
BUEHLER, Lesley 510-742-3126 59 J
lbuehler@ohlone.edu
BUEHLER, Maria 215-596-8855 450 B
m.buehler@usciences.edu
BUEHRER, Anna, R 309-649-6255 165 F
anna.buehrer@src.edu
BUEHRER, Danielle 912-260-4419 137 B
danielle.buehrer@sgc.edu

BUEKENS, Pierre .... 504-988-5397.... 215 C
sphaward@tulane.edu
BUEL, Kevin, A .... 845-675-4597.... 344 G
kevin.buel@nyack.edu
BUELL, Katie .... 630-829-6128.... 145 G
kbuell@ben.edu
BUENGER, Kathy .... 715-346-3812.... 552 D
kbuenger@uwsp.edu
BUENTELLO, Michael .... 713-525-3589.... 505 A
buentem@stthom.edu
BUENTELLO, Rachel, L ...... 361-593-4068.... 498 D
rachel.buentello@tamuk.edu
BUERSTER, Tara .... 618-393-2982.... 152 F
buerstert@iecc.edu
BUETTNER, Kathryn, A ...... 815-753-9504.... 160 B
kbuettner@niu.edu
BUFANO, Suzanne .... 843-953-6799.... 456 C
suzanne.bufano@citadel.edu
BUFF, Stacy .... 828-652-0663.... 372 B
stacybuff@mcdowelltech.edu
BUFFINGTON, Brenda .... 615-230-3494.... 476 C
brenda.buffington@volstate.edu
BUFFINGTON, Chelsea ...... 575-835-5780.... 319 A
cbuffington@admin.nmt.edu
BUFFINGTON, Dale, A ...... 818-779-8053...... 53 B
dbuffington@kingsuniversity.edu
BUFFINGTON, Sean, T ...... 215-717-6380.... 448 I
president@uarts.edu
BUFFINTON, Keith, W .... 570-577-3711.... 423 E
keith.buffinton@bucknell.edu
BUFFONE, Nancy .... 413-545-2554.... 236 F
buffone@admin.umass.edu
BUFFUM, Don .... 662-325-2861.... 275 F
dbuffum@procurement.msstate.edu
BUFFUM, Kathy, H .... 732-255-0400.... 312 D
kbuffum@ocean.edu
BUFORD, David .... 601-979-3950.... 274 G
david.s.buford@jsums.edu
BUFORD, N. Lynn .... 662-846-4155.... 273 H
lbuford@deltastate.edu
BUFORD, Shannon .... 573-334-9181.... 284 E
shannon@metrobusinesscollege.edu
BUGAIGHIS, Elizabeth .... 610-332-6272.... 437 H
ebugaighis@northampton.edu
BUGAJSKI, Tricia .... 260-399-7700.... 181 A
tbugajski@sf.edu
BUGAY, David, P .... 949-582-4699...... 70 D
dbugay@socccd.edu
BUGBEE, David .... 707-826-3626...... 36 E
drb7001@humboldt.edu
BUGBEE, Susan, H .... 619-260-2888...... 76 D
bugbee@sandiego.edu
BUGG, Elmer .... 323-241-5388...... 55 C
buggea@lasc.edu
BUGG, Gary, D .... 859-238-5535.... 199 G
gary.bugg@centre.edu
BUGGLIN, Tracy .... 740-826-8142.... 397 A
tbugglin@muskingum.edu
BUGGS, Richard .... 415-575-6116...... 32 G
rbuggs@ciis.edu
BUGGY, Gerard .... 340-693-1568.... 568 E
gbuggy@live.uvi.edu
BUGGY, James .... 864-455-7992.... 462 F
BUGOS, Michelle, L .... 309-649-6209.... 165 F
michelle.bugos@src.edu
BUHKS, Ephraim .... 718-261-5800.... 324 D
ebuhks@bramsonort.edu
BUHL, David, V .... 989-463-7143.... 247 B
buhldv@alma.edu
BUHL, Pat .... 651-450-3536.... 266 F
pbuhl@inverhills.edu
BUHL, Patti .... 918-456-5511.... 409 A
buhl@nsuok.edu
BUHLER, David, L .... 801-321-7103.... 511 B
dbuhler@utahsbr.edu
BUHLER, Douglas .... 517-355-0232.... 255 A
buhler@msu.edu
BUHLER, Mary Ann .... 785-539-3571.... 195 B
mabuhler@mccks.edu
BUHR, Connie .... 319-296-4281.... 185 F
connie.buhr@hawkeyecollege.edu
BUHRMAN, Robert, A .... 607-255-3732.... 331 B
rab8@cornell.edu
BUHROW, William, C .... 503-554-2340.... 415 I
bbuhrow@georgefox.edu
BUI, Vincent .... 650-325-5621...... 64 G
vincent.bui@stpatricksseminary.org
BUICE, Shawn .... 518-355-4000.... 471 F
sbuice@mabts.edu
BUISMAN, Kevin .... 507-389-6111.... 267 E
kevin.buisman@mnsu.edu
BUISSON, Renee .... 508-767-7331.... 230 D
rbuisson@assumption.edu
BUITER, Mike .... 864-242-5100.... 455 E
BUIZZARD, Nicholas .... 410-296-5350.... 226 I
BUJAK, Jeanette, K .... 704-233-8149.... 380 F
jbujak@wingate.edu
BUJOLD, James .... 218-285-2253.... 268 F
jbujold@rrcc.mnscu.edu
BUKER, Jennifer .... 807-859-1319.... 219 G
pr@thomas.edu
BUKOWIECKI, Richard .... 562-860-2451...... 39 A
rbukowiecki@cerritos.edu
BUKOWSKI, Bruce, J .... 410-293-2934.... 559 B
bukowski@usna.edu
BUKOWSKI, Joseph, E .... 740-695-9500.... 385 B
bukowski@belmontcollege.edu
BUKOWSKI, Tamzin .... 320-762-4415.... 265 F
tamzinb@alextech.edu
BULAONG, Grace, F .... 201-200-3027.... 312 B
gbulaong@njcu.edu
BULETTE, Nancy .... 415-458-3708...... 45 C
nancy.bulette@dominican.edu
BULEY, Paula Marie .... 603-897-8202.... 305 F
pbuley@rivier.edu
BULGER, Nancy, A .... 765-494-7929.... 178 J
bulger@purdue.edu
BULGER, Stephanie .... 313-496-2878.... 259 G
sbulger1@wcccd.edu
BULIK, Lou Anne .... 610-499-4458.... 451 F
labulik@widener.edu
BULL, Inger .... 719-227-8280...... 82 D
inger.bull@coloradocollege.edu
BULL, Kam .... 530-895-2376...... 31 H
bullka@butte.edu
BULL, Nancy .... 860-486-6092...... 94 G
nancy.bull@uconn.edu
BULL, Sharon, I .... 208-467-8609.... 144 E
sibull@nnu.edu
BULL, Vivian .... 973-408-3100.... 309 E
president@drew.edu
BULLARD, Robert, D .... 713-313-6849.... 500 B
bullardrd@tsu.edu
BULLARD, Robert, E .... 310-506-4101...... 61 H
bob.bullard@pepperdine.edu
BULLARD, Roland, N .... 919-516-4234.... 376 D
rnbullard@st-aug.edu
BULLARD, Sam, F .... 337-482-6841.... 216 D
sfb@louisiana.edu
BULLARD, Steven .... 936-468-3304.... 496 B
bullardsh@sfasu.edu
BULLARD-DILLARD, Rebecca .... 803-535-5243.... 456 D
rdillard@claflin.edu
BULLEN, James .... 305-821-3333.... 109 B
jbulle@mm.fnc.edu
BULLEN, James .... 305-821-3333.... 109 C
jbullen@mm.fnc.edu
BULLER, Jeff .... 561-799-8579.... 119 A
jbuller@fau.edu
BULLINGER, Cheryl .... 605-721-5213.... 464 H
cbullinger@national.edu
BULLINGHAM, Bree .... 212-517-0532.... 340 C
bbullingham@mmm.edu
BULLINGTON, Tena .... 256-233-8243........ 1 E
tena.bullington@athens.edu
BULLINS, Nancy .... 336-633-0256.... 373 A
ndbullins@randolph.edu
BULLION, Keith .... 304-326-1262.... 541 K
kbullion@salemu.edu
BULLIS, John .... 315-792-5307.... 341 E
jbullis@mvcc.edu
BULLIS, Michael, D .... 541-346-3405.... 419 B
bullism@uoregon.edu
BULLOCK, Barbara, A .... 219-981-4275.... 174 B
babulloc@iun.edu
BULLOCK, Barbara, J .... 937-775-3759.... 406 C
barbara.bullock@wright.edu
BULLOCK, Brian .... 610-519-4070.... 450 H
brian.bullock@villanova.edu
BULLOCK, Charles .... 408-924-2900...... 37 C
charles.bullock@sjsu.edu
BULLOCK, Debbie .... 484-365-8096.... 434 H
dbullock@lincoln.edu
BULLOCK, Galen .... 213-763-7210...... 55 D
bullockgw@lattc.edu
BULLOCK, James .... 704-337-2316.... 376 A
bullockj@queens.edu
BULLOCK, Jeffrey, F .... 563-589-3223.... 189 F
jbullock@dbq.edu
BULLOCK, Jim .... 304-865-6116.... 541 J
jim.bullock@ovu.edu
BULLOCK, John, D .... 858-499-0202...... 41 G
jbullock@coleman.edu
BULLOCK, Josh, B .... 920-924-3229.... 554 G
jbullock@morainepark.edu
BULLOCK, Linda, C .... 281-283-2574.... 503 E
bullock@uhcl.edu
BULLOCK, Michael .... 413-236-1602.... 239 A
mbullock@berkshirecc.edu
BULLOCK, Quintin, B .... 518-381-1304.... 350 E
bullocqb@sunysccc.edu
BULLOCK, Steven .... 402-941-6200.... 298 I
bullock@midlandu.edu
BULLPITT, Dorna .... 360-596-5209.... 538 E
dbullpitt@spscc.ctc.edu
BULLS, Derald .... 903-785-7661.... 492 D
dbulls@parisjc.edu
BULLS, W. Kenneth .... 336-750-2921.... 380 B
bullswk@wssu.edu
BULLUCK, Bruce .... 256-551-5210........ 4 J
bruce.bulluck@drakestate.edu
BULONE, Phil .... 813-889-3484.... 111 C
pbulone@academy.edu
BULOW, Daniel .... 708-524-6780.... 150 C
dbulow@dom.edu
BULT, Tracy .... 219-757-6132.... 179 C
BULTEMA, Christine .... 231-777-5237.... 248 E
christine.bultema@baker.edu
BULTEMA, Ron .... 937-512-2506.... 401 J
ron.bultema@sinclair.edu
BULTMAN, James, E .... 616-395-7780.... 252 D
bultmanj@hope.edu
BULZONI, Donna, R .... 570-422-3485.... 442 D
dbulzoni@po-box.esu.edu
BUMBACO, Domimick .... 914-674-3061.... 340 F
dbumbaco@mercy.edu
BUMGARDNER, Lydia, R .. 212-870-1233.... 344 A
registrarlb@nyts.edu
BUMPUS, Julie, A .... 706-236-2207.... 126 C
jbumpus@berry.edu
BUNCE, Larry .... 816-235-1045.... 291 C
buncel@umkc.edu
BUNCH, Joan .... 419-251-1722.... 395 I
joan.bunch@mercycollege.edu
BUNCH, Kirsten, H .... 828-694-1809.... 368 E
kristenb@blueridge.edu
BUNCH, Martha, M .... 336-272-7102.... 364 G
bunchm@greensboro.edu
BUNCH, Meredith, N .... 309-692-4092.... 158 D
mbunch@midstate.edu
BUNCH, Thomas, G .... 817-202-6207.... 495 E
buncht@swau.edu
BUNCH, Wes .... 828-327-7000.... 369 B
wbunch@cvcc.edu
BUNCH, Wilma, C .... 417-269-3051.... 280 G
wbunch@coxcollege.edu
BUNDALO, Katherine .... 414-382-6398.... 546 B
kathy.bundalo@alverno.edu
BUNDERS, Lisa .... 603-899-4237.... 305 A
BUNDRICK, David, R .... 417-865-2811.... 281 G
bundrickd@evangel.edu
BUNDY, Barbara .... 213-624-1200...... 46 L
bbundy@fidm.edu
BUNDY, Bradley, M .... 513-529-4029.... 396 E
bundybm@muohio.edu
BUNDY, James, A .... 203-432-1505...... 96 A
james.bundy@yale.edu
BUNDY, Lewis .... 510-217-4716...... 29 H
lbundy@argosy.edu
BUNDY, O. Keith .... 605-256-5146.... 465 I
keith.bundy@dsu.edu
BUNDY, III, O. Richard .... 802-656-2010.... 514 H
rich.bundy@uvm.edu
BUNDY, Penny .... 269-387-2000.... 260 C
penny.bundy@wmich.edu
BUNGE, Sacha .... 415-338-2204...... 37 B
sbunge@sfsu.edu
BUNIS, David, A .... 781-736-3993.... 232 F
dbunis@brandeis.edu
BUNKER, Laurel .... 651-638-6372.... 261 D
l-bunker@bethel.edu
BUNKOWSKE, Heidi .... 619-388-3911...... 65 F
hbunkows@sdccd.edu
BUNN, Dumont, C .... 478-988-6800.... 134 C
dbunn@middlegatech.edu
BUNN, Sandra, J .... 912-279-5965.... 127 E
sbunn@ccga.edu
BUNNELL, Brian .... 951-343-4350...... 31 J
bbunnell@calbaptist.edu
BUNNELL, David .... 620-235-4878.... 196 C
dbunnell@pittstate.edu
BUNNELL, Robin .... 541-888-7339.... 420 C
rbunnell@socc.edu
BUNNELL, Tom .... 603-228-1541.... 306 E
tom.bunnell@law.unh.edu
BUNNELL-RHYNE, Melinda, A .... 301-369-2800.... 221 F
melindabunnell@capitol-college.edu
BUNNING, Galen, B .... 785-227-3380.... 191 B
bunningg@bethanylb.edu
BUNTEN, Margie, J .... 714-895-8315...... 41 C
mbunten@gwc.cccd.edu
BUNTEN, Tricia .... 218-726-6995.... 271 F
tbunten@d.umn.edu
BUNTING, Cheryl .... 602-749-4542...... 13 K
cbunting@devry.edu
BUNTON, Tim, M .... 217-443-8780.... 148 G
tbunton@dacc.edu
BUNYARD, Magen .... 903-923-2325.... 486 F
mbunyard@etbu.edu
BUNYI, Beth .... 760-630-1555...... 52 J
bbunyi@kaplan.edu
BUOL, Deborah, L .... 563-589-3223.... 189 F
dbuol@dbq.edu
BUONO, Lisa .... 805-493-3663...... 33 B
llbuono@callutheran.edu
BUOSCIO, Amy .... 708-237-5050.... 160 D
abuoscio@nc.edu
BURAK, Deborah .... 610-861-4137.... 437 H
dburak@northampton.edu
BURAK, Marshall, J .... 510-628-8016...... 54 B
mburak@lincolnuca.edu
BURBA, Randy .... 714-997-6763...... 39 F
burba@chapman.edu
BURBANTE, Gilberto .... 985-448-4208.... 216 A
gilberto.burbante@nicholls.edu
BURCH, Beth .... 503-253-3443.... 417 H
bburch@ocom.edu
BURCH, Brad .... 630-652-8375.... 149 C
bburch@devry.edu
BURCH, C. Vicki .... 731-668-7240.... 478 G
vicki.burch@wtbc.edu
BURCH, Carl .... 501-450-1377...... 22 A
burch@hendrix.edu
BURCH, Chuck, S .... 704-406-4342.... 364 E
cburch@gardner-webb.edu
BURCH, Doug .... 801-622-1573.... 510 K
doug.burch@stevenshenager.edu
BURCH, Franki .... 704-406-4724.... 364 E
fburch@gardner-webb.edu
BURCH, John .... 270-789-5015.... 199 F
jrburch@campbellsville.edu
BURCH, John .... 850-201-8535.... 122 A
burchj@tcc.fl.edu
BURCH, Rhonda .... 812-866-7014.... 172 A
burch@hanover.edu
BURCH, Susan .... 406-756-3839.... 294 C
sburch@fvcc.edu
BURCH, Terese, A .... 815-395-5088.... 163 E
terriburch@sacn.edu
BURCH-SIMS, G. Pamela .. 615-963-7437.... 474 A
psims@tnstate.edu
BURCHAM, Daniel .... 231-591-3578.... 250 H
burchamd@ferris.edu
BURCHAM, David, W .... 310-258-5404...... 56 E
david.burcham@lmu.edu
BURCHAM, CFRE, Timothy, R .... 859-256-3100.... 201 E
tim.burcham@kctcs.edu
BURCHARD, Bob, P .... 573-875-7410.... 280 A
rpburchard@ccis.edu
BURCHARD, Elizabeth, B ... 802-443-5201.... 514 A
eboudah@middlebury.edu
BURCHARD, Eric .... 740-593-1804.... 399 G
burchard@ohio.edu
BURCHARD, Faye, C .... 573-875-7400.... 280 A
fcburchard@ccis.edu
BURCHETT, Amy .... 432-264-5063.... 488 B
aburchett@howardcollege.edu
BURCHETT, Bonnie, L .... 423-439-4446.... 473 F
bonnie@etsu.edu
BURCHETT, Lance .... 501-686-5987...... 24 F
leburchett@uams.edu
BURCHFIELD, Bill .... 814-868-9900.... 428 I
burchfield@erieit.edu
BURCHFIELD, James .... 406-243-5521.... 294 I
james.burchfield@umontana.edu
BURCHFIELD, Nettie, L ...... 985-549-2068.... 216 C
nburchfield@selu.edu
BURCHILL, John, K .... 785-827-5541.... 194 F
john@kwu.edu
BURD, Barbara .... 843-349-2401.... 456 G
bburd@coastal.edu
BURD, Gail, D .... 520-626-4099...... 18 L
gburd@email.arizona.edu
BURDA, Bradley .... 541-885-1180.... 418 E
bradley.burda@oit.edu
BURDA, Ed .... 304-457-6238.... 540 E
burdaep@ab.edu
BURDEN, Kathlyn .... 770-229-3328.... 137 F
kburden@sctech.edu
BURDEN, Paul .... 708-342-3360.... 150 B
pburden@devry.edu
BURDEN, Regina .... 931-393-1691.... 475 D
rburden@mscc.edu
BURDEN, Velma .... 912-478-5421.... 131 E
vburden@georgiasouthern.edu
BURDETTE, David, A .... 989-774-3334.... 249 C
burde1da@cmich.edu
BURDETTE, Ilona .... 859-336-5082.... 206 A
iburdette@sccky.edu
BURDGE, Amber .... 620-431-2820.... 195 E
aburdge@neosho.edu
BURDICK, Evelyn, P .... 708-209-3259.... 148 E
evelyn.burdick@cuchicago.edu
BURDICK, Jack .... 937-395-8112.... 394 D
jack.burdick@kcma.edu
BURDICK, Jonathan .... 585-275-6805.... 359 B
jonathan.burdick@rochester.edu
BURDICK, Mary Ellen .... 315-684-6461.... 354 F
burdicme@morrisville.edu
BURDICK, MaryEllen .... 315-792-7342.... 356 B
maryellen.burdick@sunyit.edu
BURDICK, Phil .... 847-925-6183.... 151 G
pburdick@harpercollege.edu
BURDICK, Rebekah .... 864-231-2073.... 455 C
rburdick@andersonuniversity.edu
BURDOWSKI, Allen .... 718-489-5324.... 348 E
aburdowski@sfc.edu
BURDSALL, Dawn, M .... 610-660-1333.... 446 C
dburdsal@sju.edu
BURDUE, JoEllen .... 414-277-7117.... 549 C
burdue@msoe.edu
BURDZINSKI, Donna, R ...... 727-816-3767.... 114 F
burdzid@phcc.edu
BURDZINSKI, Kenneth, R . 727-816-3412.... 114 F
burdzink@phcc.edu
BURFORD, Kristina .... 501-450-1362...... 22 A
burford@hendrix.edu
BURG, James .... 260-481-4146.... 174 C
burgj@ipfw.edu
BURG, Mary, G .... 785-864-3131.... 197 B
mburg@ku.edu
BURGARD, Bambi .... 816-802-3455.... 283 E
bburgard@kcai.edu

BURGARD, Jim, E ... 504-280-6698 ... 213 E
jburgard@uno.edu
BURGAY, Stephen, P ... 617-353-1168 ... 232 E
burgay@bu.edu
BURGDORF, Barry, D ... 512-499-4563 ... 505 B
bburgdorf@utsystem.edu
BURGE, Dale ... 620-241-0723 ... 191 I
dale.burge@centralchristian.edu
BURGE, Legand, L ... 334-727-8976 ... 8 B
lburge@tuskegee.edu
BURGENER, Kelly, T ... 208-496-1140 ... 143 A
burgenerk@byui.edu
BURGER, Arnold ... 615-329-8516 ... 468 I
aburger@fisk.edu
BURGER, Avrohom ... 516-295-5700 ... 361 N
BURGER, Cindy, L ... 717-766-2511 ... 436 D
cburger@messiah.edu
BURGER, Edward ... 254-710-6212 ... 482 A
edward_burger@baylor.edu
BURGER, Lisa ... 701-777-4463 ... 381 F
lisa.burger@und.edu
BURGER, Michael ... 334-244-3380 ... 1 G
mburger1@aum.edu
BURGER, Rosemary ... 570-340-6054 ... 435 F
burger@marywood.edu
BURGES, Jena ... 707-826-4192 ... 36 E
jb139@humboldt.edu
BURGESON, John ... 320-308-3081 ... 269 A
jcburgeson@stcloudstate.edu
BURGESON, Sharron ... 760-921-5444 ... 61 C
sharron.burgeson@paloverde.edu
BURGESS, Aaron ... 513-244-8677 ... 387 E
aaron.burgess@ccuniversity.edu
BURGESS, Barbara ... 409-882-3342 ... 501 B
bobbie.burgess@lsco.edu
BURGESS, Brenda, K ... 580-774-3015 ... 412 F
brenda.burgess@swosu.edu
BURGESS, Charlotte, G ... 909-748-8281 ... 76 C
char_burgess@redlands.edu
BURGESS, Dale ... 404-270-2919 ... 128 I
dburgess@devry.edu
BURGESS, Dawn ... 619-388-7681 ... 65 H
dburgess@sdccd.edu
BURGESS, Debbie ... 910-521-6279 ... 379 C
debbie.burgess@uncp.edu
BURGESS, Douglas ... 513-556-9900 ... 403 D
douglas.burgess@uc.edu
BURGESS, Duncan ... 206-934-6882 ... 537 F
duncan.burgess@seattlecolleges.edu
BURGESS, Ed ... 913-758-3033 ... 558 F
burgesse@leavenworth.army.mil
BURGESS, Jay ... 603-428-2254 ... 305 D
jburgess@nec.edu
BURGESS, Karen ... 864-239-5301 ... 455 F
kaburgess@brownmackie.edu
BURGESS, Marrlee ... 585-389-2884 ... 342 D
mburges4@naz.edu
BURGESS, Melissa ... 213-613-2200 ... 70 H
melissa_burgess@sciarc.edu
BURGESS, Nancy, E ... 301-583-7011 ... 225 F
burgesne@pgcc.edu
BURGESS, Norma ... 615-966-6146 ... 470 F
norma.burgess@lipscomb.edu
BURGESS, Shane, C ... 520-621-7621 ... 18 L
sburgess@cals.arizona.edu
BURGESS, Terrence ... 619-388-3453 ... 65 F
tburgess@sdccd.edu
BURGESS, Timothy, P ... 706-542-1361 ... 138 G
timb@uga.edu
BURGESS, Valerie ... 603-880-8308 ... 306 A
vburgess@thomasmorecollege.edu
BURGETT, Paul, J ... 585-274-3326 ... 359 B
pburgett@admin.rochester.edu
BURGETT, Shelley, J ... 606-679-8501 ... 203 C
shelly.burgett@kctcs.edu
BURGGRAF, JR., Thomas, F ... 970-641-2237 ... 89 E
tburggraf@western.edu
BURGGRAFF, Dennis ... 727-726-1153 ... 103 I
dennisburggraff@clearwater.edu
BURGGRAFF, Lucy ... 800-672-3060 ... 376 G
BURGGRAFF, Philip ... 727-726-1153 ... 103 I
philipburggraff@clearwater.edu
BURGGREN, Warrewn ... 940-565-2550 ... 504 D
warren.burggren@unt.edu
BURGHARDT, Sheila ... 435-613-5550 ... 512 A
sheila.burghardt@usu.ed
BURGHART, Michael ... 707-826-3512 ... 36 E
msb39@humboldt.edu
BURGHER, Karl ... 812-237-8449 ... 173 B
karl.burgher@indstate.edu
BURGHER, Louis, W ... 402-552-2586 ... 297 B
burgherlouis@clarksoncollege.edu
BURGIE-BRYANT, Willette ... 484-384-2942 ... 428 E
wburgie@eastern.edu
BURGIE-BRYANT, Willette, A ... 484-384-2942 ... 438 D
wburgie@eastern.edu
BURGIN, Brent ... 803-313-7063 ... 462 D
wbburgin@sc.edu
BURGIN, Jeffery ... 256-372-5233 ... 1 A
jeffery.burgin@aamu.edu
BURGIN, Vicki ... 251-442-2269 ... 9 A
vburgin@umobile.edu
BURGMAN, Raymonda ... 941-487-4225 ... 120 A
rburgman@ncf.edu
BURGMEIER, Julie ... 563-588-6374 ... 183 E
julie.bergmeier@clarke.edu
BURGNER, Ryan, C ... 308-635-6798 ... 301 D
burgnerr@wncc.edu
BURGOS, Ana, R ... 787-258-1501 ... 561 F
aburgos@columbiaco.edu
BURGOS, Henry ... 860-906-5007 ... 91 C
hburgos@ccc.commnet.edu
BURGOS, Irma ... 920-424-3080 ... 551 E
burgos@uwosh.edu
BURGOS, Jorge ... 787-720-4476 ... 566 D
decanatoestudiantes@colmizpa.edu
BURGOS, Jose, L ... 787-728-1515 ... 568 D
jburgos@sagrado.edu
BURGOS, Maida ... 305-821-3333 ... 109 B
mburgos@mm.fnc.edu
BURGOS, Maida ... 305-821-3333 ... 109 C
mburgos@mm.fnc.edu
BURGOS, Michael ... 858-642-8207 ... 58 I
mburgos@nu.edu
BURHENN, Herbert ... 423-425-4635 ... 477 F
herbert-burhenn@utc.edu
BURI, David ... 360-359-4958 ... 533 H
dburi@ewu.edu
BURIK, Larry ... 909-607-2226 ... 62 H
larry_burik@pitzer.edu
BURISH, Thomas, G ... 574-631-6631 ... 180 G
burish.2@nd.edu
BURK, Ann, M ... 308-432-6311 ... 299 E
aburk@csc.edu
BURK, Brandon ... 479-394-7622 ... 23 E
bburk@rmcc.edu
BURK, Jan ... 972-721-5221 ... 503 B
jburk@udallas.edu
BURK, Jill ... 254-968-9089 ... 497 A
burk@tarleton.edu
BURK, Kelly ... 765-983-1501 ... 171 E
burkke@earlham.edu
BURK, Thomas ... 973-328-5037 ... 309 A
tburk@ccm.edu
BURKARD, Donald, C ... 843-953-1432 ... 457 B
burkardd@cofc.edu
BURKE, OSB, Adrian ... 812-357-6515 ... 180 A
aburke@saintmeinrad.edu
BURKE, Andrew, J ... 575-527-7650 ... 319 G
aburke@nmsu.edu
BURKE, Barbara ... 718-260-5173 ... 328 D
bburke@citytech.cuny.edu
BURKE, Barbara ... 831-647-3513 ... 57 F
barbara.burke@miis.edu
BURKE, Barbara, A ... 217-581-2319 ... 150 E
baburke2@eiu.edu
BURKE, Brenda, L ... 804-828-7372 ... 526 B
blburke@vcu.edu
BURKE, Brian, E ... 414-277-7266 ... 549 C
burke@msoe.edu
BURKE, Brian, W ... 413-545-2204 ... 236 F
bwburke@external.umass.edu
BURKE, Carson ... 330-923-9959 ... 390 J
cburke@fortiscollege.edu
BURKE, Christy ... 740-376-4708 ... 395 G
christy.burke@marietta.edu
BURKE, Clarence ... 919-572-1625 ... 362 C
cburke@apexsot.edu
BURKE, Colleen ... 215-572-2785 ... 422 C
burkec@arcadia.edu
BURKE, Connie ... 617-739-1700 ... 243 A
conburke@aii.edu
BURKE, Dale ... 808-544-9394 ... 140 G
dburke@hpu.edu
BURKE, David ... 626-812-3016 ... 30 G
dburke@apu.edu
BURKE, Debbie ... 918-587-6789 ... 413 A
dburke@twsweld.com
BURKE, Debra ... 325-574-7988 ... 508 I
dburke@wtc.edu
BURKE, Derek, A ... 252-398-6369 ... 363 G
burked@chowan.edu
BURKE, Diane, M ... 315-279-5688 ... 337 K
dburke@mail.keuka.edu
BURKE, Donald, S ... 412-624-3001 ... 449 A
donburke@pitt.edu
BURKE, Ellen ... 607-735-1774 ... 332 I
eburke@elmira.edu
BURKE, Genevieve ... 312-752-2174 ... 155 C
genevieve.burke@kendall.edu
BURKE, George ... 216-687-3910 ... 388 D
g.burke@csuohio.edu
BURKE, Greg ... 318-357-5251 ... 216 B
burkeg@nsula.edu
BURKE, Heather ... 562-427-0861 ... 44 H
hburke@devry.edu
BURKE, Ingrid ... 307-766-5080 ... 556 H
burke@uwyo.edu
BURKE, Janice, P ... 215-503-9606 ... 448 C
janice.burke@jefferson.edu
BURKE, Jeanmarie, R ... 315-568-3869 ... 342 H
jburke@nycc.edu
BURKE, Joe ... 620-421-6700 ... 194 G
joeburke@labette.edu
BURKE, John ... 724-852-3307 ... 451 B
jburke@waynesburg.edu
BURKE, John ... 845-848-4079 ... 332 B
john.burke@dc.edu
BURKE, John ... 513-727-3232 ... 396 G
BURKE, Jonathan ... 949-376-6000 ... 53 F
jburke@lagunacollege.edu
BURKE, Jonathan, L ... 816-604-6620 ... 285 A
jon.burke@mcckc.edu
BURKE, Joseph, D ... 256-228-6001 ... 6 A
burkej@nacc.edu
BURKE, Joy ... 570-662-4804 ... 443 C
jburke@mansfield.edu
BURKE, Judith, A ... 765-285-1847 ... 169 G
jmoore@bsu.edu
BURKE, Keri ... 503-883-2269 ... 416 H
kburke@linfield.edu
BURKE, Kevin, L ... 704-337-2542 ... 376 A
burkek@queens.edu
BURKE, Kimberly, G ... 601-974-1250 ... 275 B
burkekg@millsaps.edu
BURKE, Kristin ... 617-824-8608 ... 234 B
kristin_burke@emerson.edu
BURKE, Larry, R ... 541-485-1780 ... 417 E
larryburke@newhope.edu
BURKE, JR., Lewis ... 270-901-1033 ... 201 I
lewis.burke@kctcs.edu
BURKE, Mary ... 508-747-0400 ... 243 H
mburke@quincycollege.edu
BURKE, Matthew ... 617-928-4500 ... 242 E
mburke@mountida.edu
BURKE, Melinda, W ... 520-621-3557 ... 18 L
melinda.burke@al.arizona.edu
BURKE, Mia ... 808-853-1040 ... 141 C
miab@pacrim.edu
BURKE, Michael, L ... 414-297-6320 ... 554 F
burkem@matc.edu
BURKE, Michael, P ... 617-495-1546 ... 235 D
mikeburke@fas.harvard.edu
BURKE, Morgan, J ... 765-494-3189 ... 178 J
mjb@purdue.edu
BURKE, Peggy ... 773-325-4605 ... 149 A
pburke@depaul.edu
BURKE, Peggy, Y ... 716-375-2394 ... 348 C
pyburke@sbu.edu
BURKE, Peggy, Y ... 716-375-2370 ... 348 C
pyburke@sbu.edu
BURKE, Scott, M ... 404-413-2088 ... 131 G
sburke@gsu.edu
BURKE, Sharon ... 570-945-8175 ... 432 E
sharon.burke@keystone.edu
BURKE, Sharon, T ... 603-899-4077 ... 305 A
burkes@franklinpierce.edu
BURKE, Ted ... 508-541-1774 ... 233 G
tburke@dean.edu
BURKE, Tom, J ... 661-336-5117 ... 52 K
tburke@kccd.edu
BURKE, Tracie, L ... 901-321-3357 ... 467 I
tburke@cbu.edu
BURKE, William ... 570-454-6172 ... 435 G
william.burke@mccann.edu
BURKE, William, R ... 570-941-7887 ... 450 C
william.burke@scranton.edu
BURKE-KELLY, Kathleen ... 818-719-6408 ... 55 B
kbk@piercecollege.edu
BURKERT, Amy, L ... 412-268-8494 ... 424 J
ak11@andrew.cmu.edu
BURKES, Kate ... 479-619-4299 ... 22 H
kburkes@nwacc.edu
BURKETT, Holly, L ... 865-981-5302 ... 475 G
hlburkett@pstcc.edu
BURKETT, Nancy ... 610-328-8651 ... 447 F
nburket1@swarthmore.edu
BURKETT, Norvel ... 865-974-3181 ... 477 D
nburkett@utk.edu
BURKEY, Daniel, E ... 402-280-2131 ... 297 F
dburkey@creighton.edu
BURKHALTER, James ... 806-742-1452 ... 502 A
j.burkhalter@ttu.edu
BURKHALTER, Shelia ... 410-837-4271 ... 229 A
sburkhalter@ubalt.edu
BURKHAMMER, Jerry, L ... 304-462-4114 ... 544 A
jerry.burkhammer@glenville.edu
BURKHARDT, Lou Ann ... 312-461-0600 ... 145 A
lburkhardt@aaart.edu
BURKHARDT, Paul ... 928-350-3210 ... 17 K
pburkhardt@prescott.edu
BURKHARDT, Robert ... 256-216-6660 ... 1 E
robert.burkhardt@athens.edu
BURKHARDT, Thomas, E ... 937-229-4333 ... 404 A
tburkhardt1@udayton.edu
BURKHART, Dan ... 406-657-1104 ... 296 C
burkhard@rocky.edu
BURKHART, Jenny ... 859-858-2318 ... 198 D
BURKHART, Patricia ... 954-492-5353 ... 103 F
pburkhart@citycollege.edu
BURKHEAD, Ann, E ... 724-847-6737 ... 429 H
aeburkhe@geneva.edu
BURKHOLDER, Brian, M ... 540-432-4132 ... 518 F
brian.burkholder@emu.edu
BURKHOLDER, Mary, E ... 419-783-2360 ... 389 H
mburkholder@defiance.edu
BURKHOLDER, Robert, C ... 215-503-6249 ... 448 C
robert.burkholder@jefferson.edu
BURKINK, Timothy, J ... 308-865-8342 ... 300 F
burkinktj@unk.edu
BURKMAN, Roger ... 502-585-9911 ... 206 D
rburkman@spalding.edu
BURKMAN, Tom, A ... 612-343-4748 ... 270 A
taburkma@northcentral.edu
BURKOS, Rivka ... 718-261-5800 ... 324 D
rburkos@bramsonort.edu
BURKS, Barry, L ... 336-334-7995 ... 378 A
blburks@ncat.edu
BURKS, Brent ... 254-295-4514 ... 504 C
bburks@umhb.edu
BURKS, Bryan ... 501-279-4240 ... 21 H
bburks@harding.edu
BURKS, David, B ... 501-279-4274 ... 21 H
president@harding.edu
BURKS, David, B ... 501-279-4274 ... 469 C
president@harding.edu
BURKS, Eric ... 785-738-9057 ... 195 G
eburks@ncktc.edu
BURKS, Laura ... 334-580-2144 ... 5 A
lburks@faulknerstate.edu
BURKS, Scott, A ... 502-852-4661 ... 207 E
scott.burks@louisville.edu
BURKS, Sid ... 909-652-6840 ... 39 E
sid.burks@chaffey.edu
BURKS, Suzanne, M ... 405-744-5458 ... 410 C
suzanne.burks@okstate.edu
BURKS, Valerie, C ... 407-582-1373 ... 123 B
vburks1@valenciacollege.edu
BURKUM, Karen, J ... 315-268-6576 ... 329 B
kburkum@clarkson.edu
BURLESON, Burt ... 254-710-3517 ... 482 A
burt_burleson@baylor.edu
BURLESON, Susan ... 336-249-8186 ... 370 B
sdburl@davidsonccc.edu
BURLEW, Elizabeth ... 315-655-7375 ... 325 H
eburlew@cazenovia.edu
BURLEW, Jon ... 606-679-8501 ... 203 C
jon.burlew@kctcs.edu
BURLEW, Lynette ... 318-473-6401 ... 212 I
lburlew@lsua.edu
BURLEY, Virginia ... 909-594-5611 ... 58 A
vburley@mtsac.edu
BURLINGAME, Kathy ... 218-846-3769 ... 267 D
kathy.burlingame@minnesota.edu
BURLINGAME, Kathy ... 218-749-7730 ... 266 I
k.burlingame@mr.mnscu.edu
BURLINGAME, Sherry ... 708-456-0300 ... 166 F
sburling@triton.edu
BURLINGHAM, Kay, A ... 847-866-3988 ... 151 D
kay.burlingham@garrett.edu
BURMA, William, H ... 515-263-2975 ... 185 C
bburma@grandview.edu
BURMAN, Tom ... 307-766-2292 ... 556 H
tburman@uwyo.edu
BURMASTER, Elizabeth ... 715-365-4415 ... 555 A
eburmaster@nicoletcollege.edu
BURMEISTER, James, E ... 701-788-4793 ... 381 H
james.burmeister@mayvillestate.edu
BURN, Killara ... 413-549-4600 ... 235 C
BURNAM, Paul ... 740-363-1146 ... 396 A
pburnam@mtso.edu
BURNAM, Scott, M ... 937-778-7849 ... 390 G
sburnam@edisonohio.edu
BURNE, Mary ... 617-739-1700 ... 243 A
mburne@aii.edu
BURNER, Emily ... 540-545-7334 ... 524 E
eburner@su.edu
BURNES, Michael ... 706-236-2245 ... 126 C
mburnes@berry.edu
BURNETT, Alex ... 718-631-6044 ... 328 F
aburnett@qcc.cuny.edu
BURNETT, Brian ... 719-255-3210 ... 88 I
bburnett@uccs.edu
BURNETT, Catherine, G ... 713-646-1831 ... 494 I
cburnett@stcl.edu
BURNETT, Daniel, C ... 606-679-8501 ... 203 C
danielc.burnett@kctcs.edu
BURNETT, Daniel, L ... 601-366-8880 ... 278 B
dburnett@wbs.edu
BURNETT, JR., Donald, L ... 208-885-4977 ... 144 G
dburnett@uidaho.edu
BURNETT, Eric ... 208-882-1566 ... 144 C
eburnett@moscow.com
BURNETT, Eric ... 208-882-1566 ... 144 C
eburnett@nsa.edu
BURNETT, Jeff ... 417-865-2811 ... 281 G
burnettj@evangel.edu
BURNETT, Jim, W ... 828-448-3100 ... 375 B
jburnett@wpcc.edu
BURNETT, John ... 361-593-4758 ... 498 D
john.burnett@tamuk.edu
BURNETT, Linda, G ... 409-882-3998 ... 501 B
linda.burnett@lsco.edu
BURNETT, Lori, W ... 229-430-6443 ... 124 A
lori.burnett@asurams.edu
BURNETT, Marc ... 931-372-3411 ... 474 B
mburnett@tntech.edu
BURNETT, Mark ... 206-296-6110 ... 538 B
markb@seattleu.edu
BURNETT, Mary, R ... 816-501-4555 ... 288 A
mary.burnett@rockhurst.edu
BURNETT, Maurice ... 213-763-7358 ... 55 D
burnetml@lattc.edu

BURNETT, Michael, F .... 225-578-5748.... 212 H
vocbur@lsu.edu
BURNETT, Myra .... 404-270-5027.... 138 B
mburnett@spelman.edu
BURNETT, Sharron, T .... 731-426-7645.... 470 B
sburnett@lanecollege.edu
BURNETT, Tod, A .... 949-582-4722...... 70 F
tburnett@saddleback.edu
BURNETT-ANDRUS,
Sonya .... 903-927-3351.... 509 E
sburnett-andrus@wileyc.edu
BURNETTE, Cindy .... 270-745-2755.... 208 A
cindy.burnette@wku.edu
BURNETTE, Colette, P .... 253-840-8421.... 536 H
cburnette@pierce.ctc.edu
BURNETTE, Daarel .... 937-376-6201.... 387 A
dburnette@centralstate.edu
BURNETTE, George .... 336-770-3259.... 379 E
burnetteg@uncsa.edu
BURNETTE, JR., Glen, G ... 910-521-6201.... 379 C
glen.burnette@uncp.edu
BURNETTE, Janet, K .... 828-339-4242.... 374 C
janet@southwesterncc.edu
BURNETTE, Janet, K .... 828-339-4250.... 374 C
janet@southwesterncc.edu
BURNETTE, Marcia .... 256-726-7484........ 6 C
mburnette@oakwood.edu
BURNETTE, Richard .... 850-644-1532.... 119 D
rburnette@admin.fsu.edu
BURNETTE, Sheryl, L .... 423-439-4230.... 473 F
burnetts@etsu.edu
BURNETTE, Stephanie .... 321-433-7271.... 102 D
burnettes@brevardcc.edu
BURNETTE, Teri .... 919-546-2677.... 376 F
tburnette@shawu.edu
BURNEY, Andrea .... 434-797-8458.... 526 G
aburney@dcc.vccs.edu
BURNEY, Brenda, D .... 931-540-2582.... 475 A
bburney1@columbiastate.edu
BURNEY, John .... 402-826-8221.... 297 G
john.burney@doane.edu
BURNEY, Linda .... 910-879-5519.... 368 D
lburney@bladencc.edu
BURNEY, Louise .... 601-974-1101.... 275 B
burnesl@millsaps.edu
BURNEY, Rolanda, C .... 410-651-7800.... 227 E
rcburney@umes.edu
BURNHAM, Don .... 601-856-5400.... 274 D
dburnham@holmescc.edu
BURNHAM, Mark, A .... 517-353-9000.... 255 A
mburnham@msu.edu
BURNHAM, Willette, S .... 843-792-2146.... 459 D
burnham@musc.edu
BURNIM, Mickey, L .... 301-860-3555.... 228 A
mlburnim@bowiestate.edu
BURNLEY, Christopher, L .. 434-947-8114.... 523 B
cburnley@randolphcollege.edu
BURNLEY, Lawrence, A ..... 509-777-4215.... 540 C
lburnley@whitworth.edu
BURNLEY, Linda .... 646-888-6639.... 339 E
lburnley@sloankettering.edu
BURNNETT, Susan .... 415-451-2864...... 66 B
sburnnett@sfts.edu
BURNS, Allison, L .... 570-963-2505.... 440 G
alb140@psu.edu
BURNS, Andrew .... 970-247-7180...... 84 K
burns_a@fortlewis.edu
BURNS, Anita .... 518-464-8545.... 333 E
aburns@excelsior.edu
BURNS, Barb .... 314-392-2362.... 285 J
burnsba@mobap.edu
BURNS, Barbara .... 478-757-3602.... 133 H
barbara.burns@maconstate.edu
BURNS, Beth .... 419-755-4324.... 397 C
burns.152@osu.edu
BURNS, Betty .... 812-749-1237.... 178 H
bburns@oak.edu
BURNS, Bob .... 617-627-3783.... 245 C
bob.burns@tufts.edu
BURNS, Candace .... 973-720-2138.... 317 D
burnsc@wpunj.edu
BURNS, Carl, F .... 573-341-4292.... 291 E
carlb@mst.edu
BURNS, Carla .... 973-408-3560.... 309 E
cburns@drew.edu
BURNS, Carolyn .... 415-808-3000...... 50 D
carolyn_burns@heald.edu
BURNS, Cathy .... 918-343-7538.... 411 H
cburns@rsu.edu
BURNS, Connie .... 610-799-1740.... 434 D
cburns1@lccc.edu
BURNS, Daniel, A .... 219-785-5377.... 179 A
dburns@pnc.edu
BURNS, Donna .... 909-594-5611...... 58 A
dburns@mtsac.edu
BURNS, Elizabeth .... 315-312-4100.... 354 A
elizabeth.burns@oswego.edu
BURNS, Gordon, G .... 336-838-6112.... 375 C
gordon.burns@wilkescc.edu
BURNS, J. Joseph .... 617-552-3273.... 232 B
john.burns@bc.edu
BURNS, Jacquelyn .... 307-855-2150.... 556 B
jburns@cwc.edu
BURNS, James, R .... 617-552-1603.... 232 B
james.burns.3@bc.edu
BURNS, Janie .... 731-352-4000.... 467 E
burnsj@bethelu.edu
BURNS, Jeffrey, S .... 804-752-7367.... 523 C
jburns@rmc.edu
BURNS, Jennifer, A .... 412-365-1849.... 425 C
jburns@chatham.edu
BURNS, Joseph, A .... 607-255-4843.... 331 B
deanoffaculty-mailbox@cornell.edu
BURNS, Karen, S .... 713-525-2124.... 505 A
burns@stthom.edu
BURNS, Kathleen .... 508-678-2811.... 239 B
kathleen.burns@bristolcc.edu
BURNS, Kevin, J .... 757-823-8381.... 522 E
kburns@nsu.edu
BURNS, Kristen .... 703-658-4304.... 517 K
krisburns@christendom.edu
BURNS, Lawrence, J .... 419-530-1228.... 404 F
lawrence.burns2@utoledo.edu
BURNS, Lita .... 208-769-3481.... 144 D
lita_burns@nic.edu
BURNS, Marie-Elaine .... 408-288-3191...... 67 D
marie-elaine.burns@sjcc.edu
BURNS, Mark, A .... 816-604-1550.... 284 H
mark.burns@mcckc.edu
BURNS, Marvin .... 405-466-6150.... 408 G
mburns@langston.edu
BURNS, Matthew .... 585-275-4085.... 359 B
matthew.burns@rochester.edu
BURNS, Max .... 678-359-5015.... 132 A
mburns@gdn.edu
BURNS, Nancy .... 408-260-0208...... 47 D
sjadmissions@fivebranches.edu
BURNS, Patrick .... 970-491-1833...... 83 F
patrick.burns@colostate.edu
BURNS, Patrick .... 928-776-2055...... 19 C
patrick.burns@yc.edu
BURNS, Pauletta .... 256-306-2598........ 2 D
pburns@calhoun.edu
BURNS, Paulette .... 817-257-7650.... 499 C
p.burns@tcu.edu
BURNS, Peter, S .... 716-926-8895.... 335 E
pburns@hilbert.edu
BURNS, Randy .... 270-384-8170.... 204 D
burnsr@lindsey.edu
BURNS, Raymond .... 715-634-4790.... 547 J
rburns@lco-college.edu
BURNS, Sara .... 425-739-8185.... 535 H
sunny.burns@lwtc.edu
BURNS, Sarah, H .... 704-233-8128.... 380 F
shburns@wingate.edu
BURNS, Scott .... 619-594-6018...... 37 A
sburns@mail.sdsu.edu
BURNS, Shawn, G .... 806-651-2300.... 499 A
sburns@mail.wtamu.edu
BURNS, Sonya, L .... 270-824-1823.... 202 G
sonyal.burns@kctcs.edu
BURNS, Stephanie .... 504-733-0074.... 209 B
sburns@nor.herzing.edu
BURNS, Steve .... 909-915-3762...... 29 G
riburns@argosy.edu
BURNS, Sunny .... 425-352-8255.... 532 B
sburns@cascadia.edu
BURNS, Susan .... 712-274-5388.... 187 G
burns@morningside.edu
BURNS, Thomas .... 716-286-8580.... 344 D
tburns@niagara.edu
BURNS, Thomas, D .... 615-460-6400.... 467 D
thomas.burns@belmont.edu
BURNS, Wendy .... 651-523-2235.... 264 A
wburns@hamline.edu
BURNS, William .... 701-231-7671.... 382 B
william.burns@ndsu.edu
BURNS, Yvonne .... 210-829-3900.... 504 B
yburns@uiwtx.edu
BURNSIDE, Alphonso .... 305-626-3668.... 109 A
aburnsid@fmuniv.edu
BURNSIDE, Michael .... 404-225-4448.... 125 E
mburnside@atlantatech.edu
BURPEE, Howard .... 207-741-5527.... 219 A
hburpee@smccme.edu
BURR, Donna .... 805-966-3888...... 31 D
dburr@brooks.edu
BURR, Jason, H .... 864-597-4381.... 463 G
burrjh@wofford.edu
BURR, Mei Mei .... 859-572-7559.... 205 H
burri@nku.edu
BURR, O.D .... 916-568-3048...... 55 J
burro@losrios.edu
BURR, Stephen .... 313-883-8623.... 257 E
burr.stephen@shms.edu
BURRAGE, Marie .... 212-817-7209.... 327 B
mburrage@gc.cuny.edu
BURRELL, Becky .... 419-995-8331.... 392 K
burrell.b@rhodesstate.edu
BURRELL, Daniel .... 414-297-7043.... 554 F
burrelld@matc.edu
BURRELL, James .... 229-430-4646.... 124 A
james.burrell@asurams.edu
BURRELL, Michael .... 580-371-2371.... 408 I
mburrell@mscok.edu
BURRELL, Michael, K .... 912-871-1645.... 135 D
mburrell@ogeecheetech.edu
BURRELL, Ray .... 919-735-5151.... 375 A
rayb@waynecc.edu
BURRELL, Steve .... 912-478-1294.... 131 E
sburrell@georgiasouthern.edu
BURRELL, Tamara .... 704-337-2498.... 376 A
burrellt@queens.edu
BURRELL, Todd, C .... 618-650-3705.... 165 C
tburrel@siue.edu
BURRER, Dennis, J .... 903-923-3252.... 500 E
dennis.burrer@tstc.edu
BURRER, Jarod, K .... 304-877-6428.... 540 G
jarod.burrer@abc.edu
BURRIGHT, John .... 913-288-7240.... 194 C
jburright@kckcc.edu
BURRILL, Cecelia .... 805-973-1240...... 39 H
cburrill@chartercollege.edu
BURRILL, Jennifer, R .... 269-471-6601.... 247 D
burrillj@andrews.edu
BURRIS, David .... 530-283-0202...... 47 B
dburris@frc.edu
BURRIS, Deborah, J .... 314-516-5695.... 291 D
dburris@umsl.edu
BURRIS, Janssen .... 225-214-1947.... 214 C
janssen.burris@ololcollege.edu
BURRIS, Kendra .... 806-743-2786.... 502 B
kendra.burris@ttuhsc.edu
BURRIS, Rolanda .... 847-628-1069.... 154 K
rburris@judsonu.edu
BURRISS, Annie, H .... 706-721-0252.... 130 D
ahburriss@georgiahealth.edu
BURROS, Carolyn .... 417-823-3454.... 289 I
cburros@forest.edu
BURROUGHS, Brenda .... 734-995-4678.... 249 G
burrob@cuaa.edu
BURROUGHS, Cynthia ...... 501-370-5337...... 23 B
cburroughs@philander.edu
BURROUGHS, W. Jeffrey .. 808-675-3923.... 140 D
burrougj@byuh.edu
BURROUGHS-DAVIS,
Robin .... 603-526-3752.... 303 G
rdavis@colby-sawyer.edu
BURROW, Jack .... 256-306-2545........ 2 D
jburrow@calhoun.edu
BURROW, Jeanavon .... 706-865-2134.... 138 E
jburrow@truett.edu
BURROWS, Angie .... 570-372-4120.... 447 E
burrowsa@susqu.edu
BURROWS, Carmen .... 757-825-2939.... 528 F
burrowsc@tncc.edu
BURROWS, David .... 920-832-6528.... 548 B
david.burrows@lawrence.edu
BURROWS, SC,
Joanne, M .... 563-588-6385.... 183 E
joanne.burrows@clarke.edu
BURROWS-SCHUMACHER,
Molly, A .... 563-588-4981.... 187 C
molly.burrowsschumacher@loras.edu
BURRUS, Ken .... 509-533-7220.... 533 A
kburrus@ccs.spokane.edu
BURRUS, Ken .... 509-533-7220.... 533 B
ken.burrus@ccs.spokane.edu
BURRUS, Ken .... 509-533-3630.... 533 C
kburrus@ccs.spokane.edu
BURRUS, Patricia .... 252-399-6417.... 362 E
pburrus@barton.edu
BURRUSS, John, W .... 713-798-6265.... 481 H
jburruss@bcm.edu
BURSAVICH, Gregory, F .... 336-316-2841.... 365 A
bursavichgf@guilford.edu
BURSI, Lee .... 217-786-2446.... 157 B
lee.bursi@llcc.edu
BURSON, Max .... 316-295-5521.... 193 B
mburson@friends.edu
BURSTEIN, Mark .... 609-258-3112.... 312 G
burstein@princeton.edu
BURSTYN, Yaakov .... 305-534-7050.... 122 B
BURSZTYN, Jacob .... 732-367-1060.... 307 G
jbursztyn@bmg.edu
BURT, Bruce, E .... 937-229-2131.... 404 A
bburt1@udayton.edu
BURT, Cecil .... 601-554-5506.... 276 E
jcburt@prcc.edu
BURT, Charles .... 617-745-3725.... 234 A
charles.burt@enc.edu
BURT, DeAnna .... 231-777-5244.... 248 E
deanna.burt@baker.edu
BURT, Jennifer, A .... 435-586-1997.... 511 D
burt@suu.edu
BURT, Mickey, G .... 563-884-5451.... 188 E
mickey.burt@palmer.edu
BURT, Mickey, G .... 563-884-5451.... 114 E
mickey.burt@palmer.edu
BURT, Mickey, G .... 563-884-5451...... 61 A
mickey.burt@palmer.edu
BURT, R. Andrew .... 563-441-4303.... 184 H
aburt@eicc.edu
BURT, R.J .... 360-867-6568.... 534 D
burtr@evergreen.edu
BURT, Theresa, E .... 215-926-2010.... 447 H
theresa.burt@temple.edu
BURT, Yolanda .... 216-687-2246.... 388 D
y.burt@csuohio.edu
BURT-GRACIK, Melissa ..... 619-849-2253...... 62 L
melissaburtgracik@pointloma.edu
BURTCH, Polly .... 314-968-6954.... 292 J
burtch@webster.edu
BURTIS, Brett, K .... 307-674-6446.... 556 F
bburtis@sheridan.edu
BURTIS, Karen, B .... 307-674-6446.... 556 F
kburtis@sheridan.edu
BURTLEY, Harold .... 219-980-6778.... 174 B
hburtley@iun.edu
BURTNER, Jeff, R .... 540-338-1776.... 522 G
BURTON, Adam .... 951-343-4286...... 31 J
aburton@calbaptist.edu
BURTON, Alan .... 580-745-2731.... 412 C
aburton@se.edu
BURTON, Becky .... 770-962-7580.... 132 D
bburton@gwinnetttech.edu
BURTON, Ben .... 317-921-4712.... 175 I
bburton@ivytech.edu
BURTON, Brian, K .... 360-650-3896.... 539 F
brian.burton@wwu.edu
BURTON, Caroyn .... 434-381-6510.... 524 K
cburton@sbc.edu
BURTON, Christopher, E .... 713-743-5666.... 503 D
ceburton@central.uh.edu
BURTON, Chuck .... 817-531-5813.... 502 C
cburton@txwes.edu
BURTON, Clen .... 225-675-8270.... 211 F
cburton@rpcc.edu
BURTON, Crompton, B .... 740-376-4704.... 395 G
hub.burton@marietta.edu
BURTON,
Crompton (Hub), B .... 740-376-4402.... 395 G
hub.burton@marietta.edu
BURTON, Dan .... 513-244-8167.... 387 E
dan.burton@ccuniversity.edu
BURTON, Donald, N .... 602-648-5750...... 14 A
dburton@dunlap-stone.edu
BURTON, E. James .... 615-898-2764.... 473 G
jim.burton@mtsu.edu
BURTON, Elizabeth .... 610-399-2427.... 442 A
eburton@cheyney.edu
BURTON, Gene .... 765-285-1832.... 169 G
gburton@bsu.edu
BURTON, Gregory, A .... 973-761-9362.... 315 B
gregory.burton@shu.edu
BURTON, Heather .... 540-868-7201.... 527 C
hburton@lfcc.edu
BURTON, Homer .... 270-247-8521.... 204 G
hburton@midcontinent.edu
BURTON, Jennus, L .... 928-523-2708...... 16 I
jennus.burton@nau.edu
BURTON, Lisa .... 256-551-3136........ 4 J
lisa.burton@drakestate.edu
BURTON, Liz .... 541-962-3359.... 418 C
eburton@eou.edu
BURTON, Lonnie .... 806-291-3635.... 508 E
burtonl@wbu.edu
BURTON, Marjorie .... 440-775-5782.... 397 G
marjorie.burton@oberlin.edu
BURTON, Pam .... 303-762-6948...... 84 D
pam.burton@denverseminary.edu
BURTON, Patrice .... 708-596-2000.... 164 H
pburton@ssc.edu
BURTON, Raymond, A .... 804-523-5374.... 527 A
rburton@reynolds.edu
BURTON, Robert .... 808-984-3245.... 142 E
reburton@hawaii.edu
BURTON, Terrance .... 508-999-8664.... 237 A
tburton@umassd.edu
BURTON, Timothy, P .... 516-877-3385.... 322 A
burton@adelphi.edu
BURTON, JR., Velmer, S .. 662-915-5526.... 277 D
vsburton@olemiss.edu
BURTON, Wayne, M .... 978-762-4000.... 240 D
wburton@northshore.edu
BURTON-GOSS, Sadie .... 781-239-6334.... 230 E
sburtongoss@babson.edu
BURTON-GRAHAM, Laura 410-337-6439.... 222 I
lburtong@goucher.edu
BURTT, Edward, H .... 740-368-3886.... 400 G
ehburtt@owu.edu
BURWELL, Elissia .... 903-730-4890.... 489 C
elissia_burwell@jarvis.edu
BURWELL, Tim, H .... 828-262-2070.... 377 D
burwellth@appstate.edu
BURY, Sandra .... 309-677-2808.... 146 C
sandy@bradley.edu
BURZACHECHI, Nancilee .... 412-237-8182.... 425 H
nancilee@ccac.edu
BURZICHELLI, Dominick ..... 856-415-2292.... 310 D
dburzichelli@gccnj.edu
BURZINSKI, Jody .... 620-421-6700.... 194 G
jodyb@labette.edu
BUSALACCHI, James .... 509-963-1202.... 532 C
busalacchij@cwu.edu
BUSAM, Leah .... 513-745-4892.... 406 E
BUSBOOM, Margo .... 402-461-7494.... 298 A
mbusboom@hastings.edu
BUSBY, Adam .... 707-967-2404...... 43 J
a_busby@culinary.edu
BUSBY, Bruce .... 260-481-6140.... 174 C
busbyb@ipfw.edu
BUSBY, Michael .... 615-963-7631.... 474 A
mbusby@tnstate.edu
BUSBY, Roy .... 940-367-4927.... 504 D
busby@unt.edu

BUSBY, Sheryl ...... 559-453-2312 ...... 47 K
sheryl.busby@fresno.edu
BUSBY, Teresa ...... 601-446-1211 .... 273 G
teresa.busby@colin.edu
BUSCH, C. Lawrence ...... 419-772-2362 .... 398 H
c-busch@onu.edu
BUSCH, Caroline, C ...... 804-752-7300 .... 523 C
cbusch@rmc.edu
BUSCH, Crystal ...... 651-846-3409 .... 260 I
cbusch@argosy.edu
BUSCH, Gregory ...... 419-755-4570 .... 397 C
gbusch@ncstatecollege.edu
BUSCH, Mary, E ...... 317-788-3303 .... 180 F
busch@uindy.edu
BUSCH, Mary Beth ...... 304-424-8271 .... 545 C
marybeth.busch@mail.wvu.edu
BUSCH, Marybeth ...... 419-755-4549 .... 397 C
mbusch@ncstatecollege.edu
BUSCH, Nancy ...... 718-817-4400 .... 334 C
busch@fordham.edu
BUSCHART, W. David ...... 303-762-6907 ...... 84 D
david.buschart@denverseminary.edu
BUSCHE, Donald ...... 949-582-4625 ...... 70 F
dbusche@saddleback.edu
BUSCHER, Frank ...... 901-321-3230 .... 467 I
fbuscher@cbu.edu
BUSCHMAN, John, E ...... 973-761-9005 .... 315 B
john.buschman@shu.edu
BUSCHUR, Carol ...... 513-475-3600 .... 200 L
cbuschur@galencollege.edu
BUSE, Beth, H ...... 651-201-1799 .... 265 E
beth.buse@so.mnscu.edu
BUSE, Jon ...... 319-398-5584 .... 187 B
jbuse@kirkwood.edi
BUSE, Kathleen ...... 973-618-3411 .... 308 C
kbuse@caldwell.edu
BUSE, William ...... 212-799-5000 .... 337 H
BUSEL, Yaakov ...... 732-985-6533 .... 313 A
BUSER, Boyd, R ...... 606-218-5411 .... 207 F
boydbuser@upike.edu
BUSER, David ...... 619-388-7663 ...... 65 H
dbuser@sdccd.edu
BUSH, Carolyn ...... 606-436-5721 .... 202 C
carolyn.bush@kctcs.edu
BUSH, Cathy ...... 440-525-7112 .... 394 F
cbush@lakelandcc.edu
BUSH, David ...... 435-797-1012 .... 511 E
david.bush@usu.edu
BUSH, David ...... 972-825-4888 .... 495 F
dbush@sagu.edu
BUSH, Edward ...... 951-222-8837 ...... 64 A
BUSH, Elizabeth ...... 770-394-8300 .... 125 A
ebush@aii.edu
BUSH, Gary ...... 256-372-4747 ...... 1 A
gary.bush@aamu.edu
BUSH, Gary, W ...... 678-915-5501 .... 137 G
gbush@spsu.edu
BUSH, Jean ...... 940-565-2055 .... 504 D
jean.bush@unt.edu
BUSH, Jeffrey, A ...... 504-862-8385 .... 215 C
jbush@tulane.edu
BUSH, Jim ...... 509-865-8570 .... 535 A
bush_j@heritage.edu
BUSH, Katherine ...... 845-437-5900 .... 359 F
kabush@vassar.edu
BUSH, Keith ...... 218-751-8670 .... 270 D
it@oakhills.edu
BUSH, Kristen ...... 540-231-6994 .... 529 G
khbush@vt.edu
BUSH, Lisa, F ...... 828-398-7202 .... 368 B
lbush@abtech.edu
BUSH, Lonica ...... 409-933-8413 .... 483 F
lbush@com.edu
BUSH, Michael ...... 805-986-5813 ...... 77 E
mbush@vcccd.edu
BUSH, Rachel ...... 229-732-5962 .... 124 E
rachelbush@andrewcollege.edu
BUSH, Robert ...... 318-473-6414 .... 212 I
rbush@lsua.edu
BUSH, Tim ...... 520-319-3300 ...... 12 J
tbush@brownmackie.edu
BUSHER, Edward, J ...... 937-429-8922 .... 387 H
bushere@clarkstate.edu
BUSHER, Edward, J ...... 937-328-6095 .... 387 H
bushere@clarkstate.edu
BUSHEY, Jane ...... 480-245-7930 ...... 14 J
jane.bushey@ibconline.edu
BUSHEY, Stephanie ...... 516-463-6853 .... 335 G
stephanie.bushey@hofstra.edu
BUSHMAN, David ...... 301-447-8399 .... 225 A
bushman@msmary.edu
BUSHMAN, Edward ...... 414-297-6641 .... 554 F
bushmane@matc.edu
BUSHNELL, Elizabeth, J ...... 260-982-5242 .... 177 H
ejbushnell@manchester.edu
BUSHNELL, Lynn, M ...... 203-582-8651 ...... 93 H
lynn.bushnell@quinnipiac.edu
BUSHNELL, Rebecca, W ...... 215-898-7320 .... 448 J
bushnell@falcon.sas.upenn.edu
BUSHNELL, Ryan ...... 517-321-0242 .... 251 G
rbushnell@glcc.edu
BUSHONG, Sara ...... 419-372-2856 .... 385 E
sbushon@bgsu.edu
BUSHWAY, Deb ...... 612-977-4149 .... 261 F
deb.bushway@capella.edu
BUSHWAY, Deborah ...... 612-977-4149 .... 261 F
deborah.bushway@capella.edu
BUSIC, David ...... 816-268-5400 .... 286 I
lkneely@nts.edu
BUSKEY, Cynthia ...... 404-880-8550 .... 127 C
cbuskey@cau.edu
BUSROE, Andrew ...... 606-368-6113 .... 198 C
andrewbusroe@alc.edu
BUSS, Brian ...... 920-735-5792 .... 554 A
buss@fvtc.edu
BUSS, Daryl, D ...... 608-263-6716 .... 550 J
bussd@svm.vetmed.wisc.edu
BUSS, James ...... 405-208-5273 .... 410 A
jbuss@okcu.edu
BUSS, Marney ...... 734-487-1300 .... 250 F
mbuss@emich.edu
BUSSANI, Nancy ...... 408-924-1120 ...... 37 C
nancy.bussani@sjsu.edu
BUSSARD, Patsy, G ...... 276-964-7332 .... 528 E
pat.bussard@sw.edu
BUSSE, Dan ...... 850-484-1158 .... 115 B
dbusse@pensacolastate.edu
BUSSELL, Helena ...... 817-531-4405 .... 502 C
hbussell@txwes.edu
BUSSELL, Paige ...... 903-468-3209 .... 498 B
paige.bussell@tamuc.edu
BUSSELL, Rachelle ...... 909-558-4544 ...... 54 D
rbussell@llu.edu
BUSSERT, Ronald ...... 918-594-8004 .... 410 G
ron.bussert@okstate.edu
BUSSEY, Brenda ...... 508-929-8455 .... 238 G
bbussey@worcester.edu
BUSSEY, Tosha ...... 404-527-4520 .... 126 I
tbussey@carver.edu
BUSTA, Joseph, F ...... 251-460-7616 ...... 9 D
jbusta@usouthal.edu
BUSTAMANTE, Camilla ...... 505-747-5454 .... 320 A
cbustamante@nnmc.edu
BUSTAMANTE, Chris ...... 480-517-8118 ...... 16 B
chris.bustamente@riosalado.edu
BUSTARD, James ...... 217-351-2211 .... 161 C
jbustard@parkland.edu
BUSTILLO, Pamela ...... 408-273-2696 ...... 58 G
pbustillo@nhu.edu
BUSTOS, Phillip ...... 505-224-4741 .... 317 K
pbustos@cnm.edu
BUSTROM, Carla ...... 612-977-5302 .... 261 F
carla.bustrom@capella.edu
BUSZEK, Thomas ...... 269-687-5641 .... 258 C
tbuszek@swmich.edu
BUTALA, Dick ...... 612-977-5770 .... 261 F
richard.butala@capella.edu
BUTCHER, Alva ...... 253-879-3394 .... 538 H
abutcher@pugetsound.edu
BUTCHER, Claudette ...... 918-293-5256 .... 410 E
claudette.butcher@okstate.edu
BUTCHER, Fred, R ...... 304-293-1536 .... 545 A
fbutcher@hsc.wvu.edu
BUTCHER, Michael ...... 912-279-5815 .... 127 E
mbutcher@ccga.edu
BUTCHER, Phil ...... 713-942-3409 .... 505 A
butchep@stthom.edu
BUTCHER, Sean ...... 706-233-7491 .... 137 A
sbutcher@shorter.edu
BUTCHER, Thomas, A ...... 616-331-2067 .... 251 F
butchert@gvsu.edu
BUTCHER, Tina ...... 706-507-8265 .... 127 G
butcher_tina@columbusstate.edu
BUTCHER, Tom ...... 513-721-7944 .... 391 D
tbutcher@gbs.edu
BUTDORFF, Carla ...... 419-747-5401 .... 397 C
196mgr@fheg.follett.com
BUTIN, Dan ...... 978-837-5338 .... 242 A
dan.butin@merrimack.edu
BUTKOVICH, Michelle ...... 248-204-2111 .... 254 B
mbutkovic@ltu.edu
BUTLER, Adam ...... 615-269-9900 .... 469 M
abutler@kaplan.edu
BUTLER, Allen, P ...... 815-455-8999 .... 157 H
abutler@mchenry.edu
BUTLER, Ann ...... 910-592-8081 .... 373 G
abutler@sampsoncc.edu
BUTLER, Barbara ...... 707-664-2397 ...... 37 D
barbara.butler@sonoma.edu
BUTLER, Beautrice ...... 210-486-2300 .... 479 D
bbutler@alamo.edu
BUTLER, Becky ...... 214-333-5106 .... 484 D
beckyb@dbu.edu
BUTLER, Bruce, D ...... 713-500-3369 .... 506 F
bruce.d.butler@uth.tmc.edu
BUTLER, Bryant ...... 601-968-5930 .... 273 C
bbutler@belhaven.edu
BUTLER, Cass ...... 816-221-1300 .... 281 B
cbutler@devry.edu
BUTLER, Connie ...... 402-643-7332 .... 297 D
connie.butler@cune.edu
BUTLER, D. Martin ...... 816-268-5421 .... 286 I
dbutler@nts.edu
BUTLER, Doze ...... 225-771-3660 .... 214 I
doze_butler@subr.edu
BUTLER, Frank, A ...... 859-257-1841 .... 207 D
fbutler@uky.edu
BUTLER, Gillian ...... 530-752-2000 ...... 73 I
gbutler@ucdavis.edu
BUTLER, Greg ...... 601-477-4113 .... 274 H
greg.butler@jcjc.edu
BUTLER, Greg, L ...... 412-291-6456 .... 422 E
gbutler@aii.edu
BUTLER, H. Julene ...... 801-422-2905 .... 509 H
julene_butler@byu.edu
BUTLER, Harry, P ...... 248-204-3925 .... 254 B
hbutler@ltu.edu
BUTLER, Heidi ...... 610-861-5453 .... 437 H
hbutler@northampton.edu
BUTLER, Jack ...... 931-372-3227 .... 474 B
jbutler@tntech.edu
BUTLER, Janice, R ...... 570-577-3973 .... 423 E
janice.butler@bucknell.edu
BUTLER, Jay ...... 718-405-3417 .... 330 A
jay.butler@mountsaintvincent.edu
BUTLER, Jennifer ...... 708-656-8000 .... 159 D
jennifer.butler@morton.edu
BUTLER, Joan ...... 202-495-3830 ...... 99 C
secretary@dhs.edu
BUTLER, Joan ...... 972-825-4650 .... 495 F
jbutler@sagu.edu
BUTLER, Joe ...... 254-442-5113 .... 482 I
joe.butler@cisco.edu
BUTLER, SJ, John, T ...... 617-552-2257 .... 232 B
john.butler@bc.edu
BUTLER, Johnnella, E ...... 404-270-5021 .... 138 B
jebutler@spelman.edu
BUTLER, Kathleen ...... 860-231-5322 ...... 95 D
kbutler@usj.edu
BUTLER, Kathleen, P ...... 325-235-7311 .... 500 G
kathleen.butler@tstc.edu
BUTLER, Kathy ...... 304-558-0261 .... 543 E
butler@hepc.wvnet.edu
BUTLER, Ken ...... 484-664-3126 .... 437 C
butler@muhlenberg.edu
BUTLER, Kevin ...... 704-337-2253 .... 376 A
butlerk@queens.edu
BUTLER, Kevin, S ...... 520-417-4007 ...... 13 E
butlerk@cochise.edu
BUTLER, Kim, I ...... 515-263-2841 .... 185 C
maintenance@grandview.edu
BUTLER, LeRoy ...... 419-824-3938 .... 395 E
lbutler@lourdes.edu
BUTLER, Markisha ...... 912-427-1969 .... 124 C
mbutler@altamahatech.edu
BUTLER, Mary Edith ...... 630-466-7900 .... 168 B
mbutler@waubonsee.edu
BUTLER, Michael ...... 909-469-5534 ...... 78 I
mbutler@westernu.edu
BUTLER, Patrick, B ...... 319-335-3565 .... 182 F
patrick-butler@uiowa.edu
BUTLER, Paul, C ...... 856-225-6637 .... 314 D
pbutler@camden.rutgers.edu
BUTLER, Peter, W ...... 312-942-8801 .... 163 D
peter_butler@rush.edu
BUTLER, Randy ...... 903-593-8311 .... 499 D
rbutler@texascollege.edu
BUTLER, Rebecca ...... 937-512-2500 .... 401 J
rebecca.butler@sinclair.edu
BUTLER, Rebecca ...... 937-512-3351 .... 401 J
rebecca.butler@sinclair.edu
BUTLER, Renee ...... 718-482-5292 .... 328 B
rbutler@lagcc.cuny.edu
BUTLER, Rhonda ...... 440-510-1112 .... 386 C
rybulter@bryantstratton.edu
BUTLER, Robert ...... 707-256-7625 ...... 58 F
rbutler@napavalley.edu
BUTLER, Robert ...... 310-900-1600 ...... 45 F
butler_r@compton.edu
BUTLER, Roxanna ...... 405-682-1611 .... 409 F
rbutler@occc.edu
BUTLER, Shai ...... 518-337-2306 .... 330 C
butlers@strose.edu
BUTLER, Sharon ...... 517-884-0101 .... 255 A
sbutler@msu.edu
BUTLER, Shirley ...... 843-349-5218 .... 458 H
shirley.butler@hgtc.edu
BUTLER, Susan ...... 203-576-4133 ...... 94 F
susanb@bridgeport.edu
BUTLER, Susie ...... 337-521-8913 .... 211 J
susie.butler@southlouisiana.edu
BUTLER, Terry ...... 216-987-3287 .... 389 B
terry.butler@tri-c.edu
BUTLER, Thomas, E ...... 361-582-2560 .... 508 B
tom.butler@victoriacollege.edu
BUTLER, Timothy, J ...... 215-951-2744 .... 444 D
butlert@philau.edu
BUTLER, Wendy ...... 303-837-0825 ...... 81 F
wlbutler@aii.edu
BUTLER, William, E ...... 214-860-2057 .... 485 A
wbutler@dcccd.edu
BUTLER-PURRY, Karen, L ...... 979-845-3628 .... 497 E
klbutler@tamu.edu
BUTNER, Dustie ...... 405-382-9525 .... 412 B
d.butner@sscok.edu
BUTRUM, Michael ...... 660-263-3900 .... 279 F
michaelb@cccb.edu
BUTT, Allen ...... 909-537-3180 ...... 36 B
abutt@csusb.edu
BUTTAFARRO, JR.,
Thomas ...... 716-375-2155 .... 348 C
tbuttafa@sbu.edu
BUTTENSCHON, Marianne 315-792-5631 .... 341 E
mbuttenschon@mvcc.edu
BUTTER, Karen ...... 415-476-8293 ...... 75 A
karen.butter@ucsf.edu
BUTTERBAUGH, Randy, R ...... 318-797-5116 .... 213 D
randy.butterbaugh@lsus.edu
BUTTERFIELD, Kevin ...... 804-289-8942 .... 525 E
kbutterf@richmond.edu
BUTTERFIELD, Patricia ...... 509-324-7332 .... 533 H
pbutter@wsu.edu
BUTTERFIELD, Patricia ...... 509-324-7332 .... 539 D
pbutter@wsu.edu
BUTTERMORE, Jim ...... 724-964-8811 .... 437 E
jbuttermore@ncstrades.edu
BUTTERS, Penny ...... 509-533-3527 .... 533 C
penny.butters@spokanefalls.edu
BUTTERWORTH, Sandra ...... 248-476-1122 .... 254 G
sbutterworth@mispp.edu
BUTTITTA, Deborah ...... 818-386-5659 ...... 62 F
buttitta@pgi.edu
BUTTLEMAN, Kurt ...... 206-934-4111 .... 537 C
kurt.buttleman@seattlecolleges.edu
BUTTON, Kyle, C ...... 323-343-3060 ...... 35 D
kbutton@cslanet.calstatela.edu
BUTTREY, Michael ...... 509-865-8505 .... 535 A
buttrey_m@heritage.edu
BUTTRY, Tonya ...... 573-334-6825 .... 289 J
tbuttry@sehosp.org
BUTTS, III, Calvin, O ...... 516-876-3160 .... 353 D
buttsc@oldwestbury.edu
BUTTS, Carl ...... 407-673-7406 .... 113 C
cbutts@lincolntech.com
BUTTS, Elvin ...... 910-892-3178 .... 365 B
ebutts@heritagebiblecollege.edu
BUTTS, Jeffrey ...... 212-237-8486 .... 327 F
jbutts@jjay.cuny.edu
BUTTS, Matthew, T ...... 330-337-4259 .... 393 H
mbutts@kent.edu
BUTTS, Sue ...... 251-981-3771 ...... 2 G
sue.butts@columbiasouthern.edu
BUTTS WILLIAMS,
Barbara ...... 612-977-5458 .... 261 F
barbara.buttswilliams@capella.edu
BUTTRUM, Deborah ...... 405-422-1262 .... 411 G
buttrumd@redlandscc.edu
BUTVILAS, George ...... 906-487-2303 .... 255 B
gjbutvil@mtu.edu
BUTWELL, Justin ...... 845-575-3000 .... 340 B
justin.butwell@marist.edu
BUTY, Carlene ...... 206-296-6100 .... 538 B
cbuty@seattleu.edu
BUTZINE, Craig, S ...... 724-938-1675 .... 441 G
BUUCK, Thomas ...... 260-399-7700 .... 181 A
tbuuck@sf.edu
BUXBAUM, Amy ...... 814-269-7991 .... 449 D
buxbaum@pitt.edu
BUXBAUM, Hannah ...... 812-855-4350 .... 173 E
hbuxbaum@indiana.edu
BUXBAUM, Howard ...... 973-748-9000 .... 307 H
howard_buxbaum@bloomfield.edu
BUXTON, Barry, M ...... 828-898-8785 .... 366 D
buxtonb@lmc.edu
BUXTON, Carolyn ...... 330-263-2631 .... 388 F
cbuxton@wooster.edu
BUXTON, Jasmine ...... 256-372-5615 ...... 1 A
jasmine.buxton@aamu.edu
BUXTON, Ralph, W ...... 212-220-1432 .... 326 D
rbuxton@bmcc.cuny.edu
BUXTON, Robert, E ...... 423-478-7703 .... 472 H
rbuxton@ptseminary.edu
BUXTON, Sheldon ...... 918-335-6291 .... 411 B
sbuxton@okwu.edu
BUXTON-HAMEL,
Kimberly ...... 303-256-9320 ...... 85 L
kbuxton@jwu.edu
BUYEA, James ...... 518-327-6099 .... 345 H
jbuyea@paulsmiths.edu
BUYOK, Albert ...... 970-339-6683 ...... 81 A
albert.buyok@aims.edu
BUYSSE, Jim ...... 951-222-8789 ...... 63 I
jim.buysse@rcc.edu
BUZANSKI, Catherine ...... 716-880-2179 .... 340 D
catherine.buzanski@medaille.edu
BUZHARDT, Landee ...... 803-321-5106 .... 459 H
landee.buzhardt@newberry.edu
BUZZELL, Sidney, S ...... 303-963-3421 ...... 82 C
sbuzzell@ccu.edu
BUZZELLI, OSB, Aaron, N 724-532-7961 .... 446 F
aaron.buzzelli@email.stvincent.edu
BUZZELLI, Andrew ...... 210-883-1190 .... 504 B
optometry@uiwtx.edu
BYARD, Brenda, K ...... 540-868-7208 .... 527 C
bbyard@lfcc.edu
BYARS, Delanda ...... 270-866-1302 .... 199 C
dbyars@brownmackie.edu
BYARS, Don ...... 936-261-1057 .... 496 G
dobyars@pvamu.edu
BYARS, Lauretta, F ...... 936-261-2120 .... 496 G
lfbyars@pvamu.edu
BYARS, Roger, D ...... 713-313-1814 .... 500 B
byarsrd@tsu.edu
BYARS, Susan ...... 239-590-7980 .... 119 B
sbyars@fgcu.edu
BYAS, Renee ...... 713-718-7514 .... 487 I
renee.byas@hccs.edu

C

CAIRE, Cynthia, D 504-865-3388 213 F caire@loyno.edu
CAIRES, Matthew 406-994-2826 295 C mcaires@montana.edu
CAIRNS, James 412-237-3024 425 H jcairns@ccac.edu
CAIRNS, Janet 918-631-3101 413 F janet-cairns@utulsa.edu
CAIRNS, Jill 207-834-7602 220 D jillb@maine.edu
CAIRNS, Leslie 918-631-2365 413 F leslie-cairns@utulsa.edu
CAIRNS, Michael 415-433-9200 68 F mcairns@saybrook.edu
CAIRNS, Michael, A 231-591-3770 250 H cairnsm@ferris.edu
CAIRO, Jim, R 504-568-4246 213 A jcairo@lsuhsu.edu
CAIROL, Miguel 718-260-5600 328 D mcairol@citytech.cuny.edu
CAIRY, Timothy, J 610-499-1193 451 F tjcairy@widener.edu
CAISON, Anthony, M 919-866-6101 374 H amcaison@waketech.edu
CAJAYON, Felicito 213-891-2056 54 F cajayof@email.laccd.edu
CAL, John 305-348-4001 119 C john.cal@fiu.edu
CALA, Catherine 330-941-3119 406 F cacala@ysu.edu
CALABRESE, Nancy 410-626-2553 225 G nancy.calabrese@sjca.edu
CALABRESE, Walter 252-444-0739 370 A calabresew@cravencc.edu
CALABRIA, Patrick 631-420-2400 356 A patrick.calabria@farmingdale.edu
CALABRO, Richard 505-224-3565 317 K rcalabro@cnm.edu
CALABRO, Stephen 239-939-4766 118 I scalabro@swfc.edu
CALAF, Jorge 787-279-1912 563 D jcalaf@bayamon.inter.edu
CALAIS, Debra 337-482-6199 216 D dcalais@louisiana.edu
CALAMAI, Anthony, G 828-262-3078 377 D calamaiag@appstate.edu
CALAMAIO, Caprice 913-234-0733 191 J caprice.calamaio@cleveland.edu
CALAMARE, Susan, S 617-422-7387 243 B scalamare@nesl.edu
CALAME, Catherine 516-299-2719 339 A catherine.calame@liu.edu
CALAME, Wanda 334-683-2304 5 G wcalame@marionmilitary.edu
CALAMETTI, Jeffrey, D 251-442-2242 9 A jcalametti@umobile.edu
CALAMIA, John, J 504-865-3946 213 F calamia@loyno.edu
CALANDRELLA, Drew 530-898-6131 34 C dcalandrella@csuchico.edu
CALAPA, Joseph, P 508-626-4523 238 A joec@framingham.edu
CALARESO, Jack, P 508-849-3333 230 C jcalareso@annamaria.edu
CALARESO, Joe 305-595-9500 100 F admissions@amcollege.edu
CALAWAY, Terry, A 913-469-8500 194 B tcalaway@jccc.edu
CALCADO, Antonio 732-445-2166 314 B acalcado@facilities.rutgers.edu
CALCAGNI, Thomas 406-994-4571 295 C tcalcagni@montana.edu
CALCAGNINO, Josephine, A 414-425-8300 550 E jcalcagnino@shst.edu
CALDARELLO, Beth 816-941-4030 281 A bcaldarello@devry.edu
CALDAS, Vicente 516-364-0808 343 A itsupport@nycollege.edu
CALDERBANK, Robert 919-668-2728 364 C natscidean@duke.edu
CALDERON, Ann Marie 615-230-3401 476 C annmarie.calderon@volstate.edu
CALDERON, Axel 787-753-6000 562 G acalderon@icprjc.edu
CALDERON, Hermes 787-780-0070 560 H hcalderon@caribbean.edu
CALDERON, Janet 407-303-6108 100 G janet.calderon@adu.edu
CALDERON, Larry, A 954-262-7552 114 B lc@nsu.nova.edu
CALDERON, Nancy 408-554-2397 68 C ntcalderon@scu.edu
CALDERON, Raoul 641-472-7000 187 E rcalderon@mum.edu
CALDERON, Sara 215-248-7384 435 B scalderon@ltsp.edu
CALDERON, Sonny 818-733-2600 59 A
CALDERSON, Carl 619-201-8780 65 D carl.calderson@sdcc.edu
CALDON, Heather 760-252-2411 30 H hcaldon@barstow.edu
CALDWELL, Adonna 901-572-2592 467 C adonna.caldwell@bchs.edu
CALDWELL, Agnes 517-265-5161 246 H acaldwell@adrian.edu
CALDWELL, Angela 870-248-4000 21 A angelac@blackrivertech.edu
CALDWELL, Avery 619-684-8794 59 B acaldwell@newschoolarch.edu
CALDWELL, Brinda, W 828-398-7134 368 B bcaldwell@abtech.edu
CALDWELL, Cheryl 417-255-7960 286 D cherylcaldwell@missouristate.edu
CALDWELL, Daniel 601-318-6115 278 C daniel.caldwell@wmcarey.edu
CALDWELL, David 508-286-3403 246 B dcaldwel@wheatoncollege.edu
CALDWELL, David 970-351-2707 89 B david.caldwell@unco.edu
CALDWELL, David 615-248-1311 476 G dcaldwell@trevecca.edu
CALDWELL, Diana 574-936-8898 169 D diana.caldwell@ancilla.edu
CALDWELL, Gail 256-726-7024 6 C gcaldwell@oakwood.edu
CALDWELL, Getchel 910-672-1661 377 G gcaldwel@uncfsu.edu
CALDWELL, Helen 704-378-1014 366 A hcaldwell@jcsu.edu
CALDWELL, Hollie 303-369-5151 87 D hollie.caldwell@plattcolorado.edu
CALDWELL, Jacqueline, H 918-631-2691 413 F jacqueline-caldwell@utulsa.edu
CALDWELL, James 303-280-7411 84 G jcaldwell@devry.com
CALDWELL, James 215-780-1306 446 G jcaldwell@salus.edu
CALDWELL, Janet 615-327-6851 471 C jcaldwell@mmc.edu
CALDWELL, Jeff 405-733-7395 411 I jcaldwell@rose.edu
CALDWELL, Jodi, K 912-478-5541 131 E jodic@georgiasouthern.edu
CALDWELL, Joyce 262-879-0200 549 H
CALDWELL, Lin, D 310-434-4200 68 D caldwell_lin@smc.edu
CALDWELL, Linda 251-580-2247 5 A lcaldwell@faulknerstate.edu
CALDWELL, Michael 559-278-3027 35 A mcaldwell@csufresno.edu
CALDWELL, Mike 801-832-2592 512 G mcaldwell@westminstercollege.edu
CALDWELL, Nina 314-529-9485 284 C ncaldwell@maryville.edu
CALDWELL, Patrice 575-562-2315 318 B patrice.caldwell@enmu.edu
CALDWELL, Percy 318-274-4101 215 E caldwellp@gram.edu
CALDWELL, Sandra 307-382-1720 557 A scaldwell@wwcc.wy.edu
CALDWELL, Sandy 307-382-1720 557 A scaldwel@wwcc.wy.edu
CALDWELL, Stefanie 312-935-4558 162 G scaldwell@robertmorris.edu
CALDWELL, Susan 606-589-0310 203 D susan.caldwell@kctcs.edu
CALDWELL, Vicki 704-878-3206 372 C vcaldwell@mitchellcc.edu
CALDWELL, Wayne 253-680-7464 531 F wcaldwell@bates.ctc.edu
CALE, Lynn 252-446-0436 370 D calel@edgecombe.edu
CALE, JR., William, G 256-765-4211 9 C wgcale@una.edu
CALEB, Peter 212-749-2802 339 I library@msmnyc.edu
CALENDA, Marianne 717-361-1196 428 F calendam@etown.edu
CALERO, Pamela 352-873-5808 103 K calerop@cf.edu
CALERO, Teofilo 773-878-2998 163 F tcalero@staugustine.edu
CALFAS, Karen, J 858-822-7552 74 F kcalfas@ucsd.edu
CALFEE, Laura 512-499-8787 503 C lcalfee@uh.edu
CALHOUN, Alan 413-545-2671 236 F calhoun@uhs.umass.edu
CALHOUN, Barbara, S 770-423-6258 133 A bcalhoun@kennesaw.edu
CALHOUN, Chris 202-806-1082 98 E chris.calhoun@howard.edu
CALHOUN, Deborah, C 803-934-3216 459 G dcalhoun@morris.edu
CALHOUN, Larry 478-289-2250 137 E lcalhoun@southeasterntech.edu
CALHOUN, Larry, D 423-439-2068 473 F calhoun@etsu.edu
CALHOUN, Linda 270-686-4400 203 B linda.calhoun@kctcs.edu
CALHOUN, M.Grace 773-508-7465 157 C athdir@luc.edu
CALHOUN, Mary Lynne 704-687-8992 379 A mlcalhou@uncc.edu
CALHOUN, Matthew 602-222-9300 11 H mcalhoun@arizonacollege.edu
CALHOUN, Matthew 601-276-3718 277 B mattc@smcc.edu
CALHOUN, Paul 518-580-5590 351 B pcalhoun@skidmore.edu
CALHOUN, Ralph 901-435-1276 470 D ralph_calhoun@loc.edu
CALHOUN, Sandy 970-491-6321 83 F sandy.calhoun@colostate.edu
CALHOUN, Thomas 601-979-7036 274 G thomas.c.calhoun@jsums.edu
CALHOUN, JR., Thomas, C 256-765-4709 9 C tcalhoun@una.edu
CALHOUN, Thomas, G 703-993-2541 519 E tcalhou2@gmu.edu
CALHOUN, Tony 731-426-7658 470 B tcalhoun@lanecollege.edu
CALHOUN, Valerie, A 717-290-8713 433 F vcalhoun@lancasterseminary.edu
CALHOUN, W. Rochelle 518-580-5760 351 B rcalhoun@skidmore.edu
CALHOUN-BROWN, Allison 404-413-2067 131 G acalhounbrown@gsu.edu
CALHOUN-FRENCH, Diane 502-213-2120 202 F diane.calhoun-french@kctcs.edu
CALI, Tim 773-697-2419 149 D tcali@devry.edu
CALIENDO, Amy, A 215-670-9114 438 E aacaliendo@peirce.edu
CALIENDO, Evelyn 847-467-3622 160 E evelyn-caliendo@northwestern.edu
CALIFF, Robert, M 919-668-8820 364 C calif001@mc.duke.edu
CALILAN, Kimo 707-864-7104 70 A james.calilan@solano.edu
CALINGO, Luis 818-767-0888 79 H luis.calingo@woodbury.edu
CALIXTO, Alfredo 773-878-3569 163 F acalixto@staugustine.edu
CALIXTO, Jeanette 510-436-1134 50 H calixto@hnu.edu
CALIZO, Lee 410-455-1754 227 D calizo@umbc.edu
CALKINS, Gregory 513-529-3020 396 E calkingp@muohio.edu
CALL, Christopher, D 805-565-6023 79 A ccall@westmont.edu
CALL, Diane 718-631-6222 328 F dcall@qcc.cuny.edu
CALL, Gregory, S 413-542-2334 230 A gscall@amherst.edu
CALL, Patrick, N 307-766-3179 556 H pcall@uwyo.edu
CALL, Tyler 801-627-8451 510 H callt@owatc.edu
CALL, Vickie, G 336-838-6146 375 C vickie.call@wilkescc.edu
CALLAGHAN, Aloysius, R 651-962-5777 272 B arcallaghan@stthomas.edu
CALLAGHAN, James 740-826-8121 397 A jamesc@muskingum.edu
CALLAGHAN, Karen, A 305-899-3401 101 M kcallaghan@mail.barry.edu
CALLAGHAN, Mary Ellen 914-633-2067 336 E mcallaghan@iona.edu
CALLAHAN, Brianne, S 508-213-2218 243 E brianne.callahan@nichols.edu
CALLAHAN, Candice 718-779-1430 346 B info@plazacollege.edu
CALLAHAN, IV, Charles 718-779-1430 346 B ccc4@plazacollege.edu
CALLAHAN, III, Charles, E 718-779-1430 346 B cec3@plazacollege.edu
CALLAHAN, SR., Charles, E 718-779-1430 346 B cec@plazacollege.edu
CALLAHAN, Cheryl, M 336-334-5099 379 B cmcallah@uncg.edu
CALLAHAN, Christopher 602-496-5012 11 J christopher.callahan@asu.edu
CALLAHAN, Clara, A 215-955-6983 448 C clara.callahan@jefferson.edu
CALLAHAN, Colleen 843-208-8258 462 C ccallaha@uscb.edu
CALLAHAN, Denise 503-370-6397 421 D dcallaha@willamette.edu
CALLAHAN, Edward 781-736-4240 232 F ecallaha@brandeis.edu
CALLAHAN, Elizabeth, K 718-779-1430 346 B ekc@plazacollege.edu
CALLAHAN, Frank 617-879-7263 238 B fcallahan@massart.edu
CALLAHAN, Joseph 559-442-8201 72 A joe.callahan@scccd.edu
CALLAHAN, Josh 707-826-6124 36 E jc115@humboldt.edu
CALLAHAN, Joy, T 919-209-2027 371 F jtcallahan@johnstoncc.edu
CALLAHAN, Laurie, F 703-284-1648 521 D laurie.callahan@marymount.edu
CALLAHAN, Margaret 414-288-3812 548 F margaret.callahan@marquette.edu
CALLAHAN, Mary 617-258-6432 241 D
CALLAHAN, Mary 323-953-4000 54 H callahm@lacitycollege.edu
CALLAHAN, Michael 805-654-6344 77 F mcallahan@vcccd.edu
CALLAHAN, Michael 419-227-3141 404 D macallah@unoh.edu
CALLAHAN, North 914-337-9300 330 G north.callahan@concordia-ny.edu
CALLAHAN, Patricia 978-762-4000 240 D tcallaha@northshore.edu
CALLAHAN, Patrick, F 914-251-6435 354 D patrick.callahan@purchase.edu
CALLAHAN, Paul, J 330-972-6166 403 B pcallah@uakron.edu
CALLAHAN, Phyllis 513-529-4432 396 E callahp@muohio.edu
CALLAHAN, Robert 319-368-6462 187 H rcallahan@mtmercy.edu
CALLAHAN, Timothy 617-236-8880 234 G tcallahan@fisher.edu
CALLAHAN, Timothy, C 425-602-3110 531 E tcallaha@bastyr.edu
CALLAN, Mike 314-246-7559 292 J mikecallan@webster.edu
CALLAN, Terrance, D 513-231-2223 384 H tcallan@athenaeum.edu
CALLAWAY, Cynthia 757-825-2725 528 F callawayc@tncc.edu
CALLAWAY, Karen, L 715-852-1365 553 H kcallaway@cvtc.edu
CALLAWAY, MaryKatherine 225-578-6144 212 H mkc@lsu.edu
CALLEN, Bruce 417-873-7546 281 D bcallen@drury.edu
CALLEN, Patricia, A 304-296-8282 545 F pcallen@wvjc.com
CALLEN, Patricia, A 724-437-4600 441 B pcallen@wvjc.com
CALLENDER, David, L 409-772-1902 507 C dcallender@utmb.edu
CALLIER, Theodore 504-816-4018 209 A tcallier@dillard.edu
CALLIHAN, Donna 660-359-3948 287 A dcallihan@mail.ncmissouri.edu
CALLIS, Keith 843-863-7133 456 B kcallis@csuniv.edu
CALLISON, Daniel, J 812-855-1538 174 D callison@indiana.edu
CALLOWAY, Dwight 707-864-7176 70 A dwight.calloway@solano.edu
CALLOWAY, Margaret 301-295-3383 558 D margaret.calloway@usuhs.edu
CALLOWAY, Terence 931-221-7786 473 E callowayt@apsu.edu
CALLUZZO, Vincent 914-633-2256 336 E vcalluzzo@iona.edu
CALLWOOD-BRATHWAITE, Denise 305-626-1415 109 A denise.callwood-brathwaite@fmuniv.eedu
CALME, Paul, H 513-745-3142 406 E calme@xavier.edu
CALMENSON, Susan, P 612-874-3756 265 C susan_calmenson@mcad.edu
CALMES, Daphne 323-563-4816 39 G daphnecalmes@cdrewu.edu
CALMESE, Carlotta, V 608-243-4270 554 D ccalmese@madisoncollege.org
CALO, Andrew 617-296-8300 235 J andrew_calo@laboure.edu
CALO, Balbina 212-472-1500 343 G bcalo@nysid.edu
CALOGRIDES, JR., Thomas 757-822-7335 528 G tcalogrides@tcc.edu
CALOTE, Robin 805-654-6460 77 F rcalote@vcccd.edu
CALOVINI, Susan 336-721-2617 376 E susan.calovini@salem.edu
CALPIN, Fran 570-945-8170 432 E fran.calpin@keystone.edu
CALTABIANO, Ronald 317-940-8652 170 F rcalt@butler.edu
CALUS-MCLAIN, Martha 503-352-2764 419 E martha@pacificu.edu
CALVANESE, Linda, K 251-343-8200 6 F linda.calvanese@remingtoncollege.edu
CALVERT, Carolyn, A 325-793-3808 490 H ccalvert@mcm.edu
CALVERT, Deb 651-290-6310 272 E deb.calvert@wmitchell.edu
CALVERT, Lisa, D 765-494-1704 178 J lcalvert@purdue.edu
CALVERT, Maxine 405-422-1466 411 G calvertm@redlandscc.edu
CALVERT, Ned 903-923-2120 486 F ncalvert@etbu.edu
CALVERT, Raymond, J 727-816-3418 114 F calverr@phcc.edu
CALVIN, Allen 650-433-3802 61 B acalvin@paloaltou.edu
CALVIN, Dennis, D 814-865-4028 438 G ifa@psu.edu
CALVIN, Larry 504-520-7537 217 A lcalvin@xula.edu

CAMPER, Diane ... 731-286-3338 ... 475 B camper@dscc.edu
CAMPER, Yolanda ... 318-342-3306 ... 216 E camper@ulm.edu
CAMPERI, Marcelo, F ... 415-422-6496 ... 76 E camperi@usfca.edu
CAMPFIELD, Ruth ... 817-598-6388 ... 508 F rcampfield@wc.edu
CAMPION, James, R ... 518-828-4181 ... 330 E campion@sunycgcc.edu
CAMPION, William, J ... 254-647-3234 ... 492 G bcampion@rangercollege.edu
CAMPO, Carlos ... 757-352-4015 ... 523 E ccampo@regent.edu
CAMPO, Juan, E ... 805-893-3945 ... 75 B jcampo@religion.ucsb.edu
CAMPO, Kathy ... 516-299-2503 ... 338 E kathy.campo@liu.edu
CAMPO, Regina, Z ... 717-337-6207 ... 429 I rcampo@gettysburg.edu
CAMPOS, Becky ... 714-997-6943 ... 39 F bcampos@chapman.edu
CAMPOS, Darcie, R ... 708-534-5000 ... 151 E dcampos@govst.edu
CAMPOS, Diana ... 575-234-9227 ... 319 F dcampos@nmsu.edu
CAMPOS, Jesus ... 956-872-8330 ... 494 H jhcampos@southtexascollege.edu
CAMPOS, Joseph ... 980-598-1101 ... 365 I joseph.campos@jwu.edu
CAMPOS, Lisa ... 928-523-5677 ... 16 I lisa.campos@nau.edu
CAMPOS, Luis ... 505-224-4565 ... 317 K lcampos@cnm.edu
CAMPOS, Pete ... 505-454-2501 ... 318 F pcampos@luna.edu
CAMPOS, Tammie ... 575-646-3616 ... 319 D tcampos@nmsu.edu
CAMPOS, Tom ... 210-486-0606 ... 479 E tcampos1@alamo.edu
CAMUTI, Alice ... 931-372-3232 ... 474 B acamuti@tntech.edu
CANACARIS, Diana ... 865-981-8198 ... 471 B diana.canacaris@maryvillecollege.edu
CANADA, Allison, M ... 410-334-2918 ... 229 E acanada@worwic.edu
CANADA, Britt ... 325-574-7671 ... 508 I bcanada@wtc.edu
CANADA, Greg ... 415-565-4885 ... 74 A canadag@uchastings.edu
CANADA, Mark ... 910-521-6431 ... 379 C mark.canada@uncp.edu
CANADAY, John ... 719-384-6819 ... 87 A john.canaday@ojc.edu
CANADAY, Joseph ... 215-596-7524 ... 450 B j.canaday@usciences.edu
CANADAY, William ... 937-708-5755 ... 405 H wcanaday@wilberforce.edu
CANALES, Angel ... 787-766-1717 ... 565 I acanales7@suagm.edu
CANALES, Carmen, I ... 336-758-3256 ... 380 C ccanales@wfu.edu
CANALES, Jason, G ... 413-662-5413 ... 238 C jason.canales@mcla.edu
CANALES, Jo Ann ... 361-825-3884 ... 498 C joann.canales@tamucc.edu
CANALES, Luis ... 270-809-4152 ... 205 A lcanales@murraystate.edu
CANALS, Alex ... 718-933-6700 ... 341 G acanals@monroecollege.edu
CANARD, Gregory, M ... 920-923-8583 ... 548 E gmcanard78@marianuniversity.edu
CANAS, Carlos ... 305-626-3698 ... 109 A carlos.canas@fmuniv.edu
CANAS, Renee ... 702-579-3544 ... 302 A rcanas@kaplan.edu
CANAVAN, Terry ... 631-499-7100 ... 338 D tcanavan@libi.edu
CANCEL, Jimmy ... 787-250-1912 ... 563 G jcancel@metro.inter.edu
CANCEL, Olga ... 787-754-8000 ... 566 E ocancel@pupr.edu
CANCEL-PEREZ, Magda, A ... 787-620-2040 ... 560 D mcancel@aupr.edu
CANCETTY, Alba ... 718-289-5889 ... 326 E alba.cancetty@bcc.cuny.edu
CANCHOLA, Rebecca ... 915-779-8031 ... 483 J rcanchola@computercareercenter.com
CANCILLA, Devon ... 303-991-1575 ... 81 B
CANCILLA, Mike ... 256-549-8311 ... 3 J mcancilla@gadsdenstate.edu
CANDEE, Kate ... 920-923-8727 ... 548 E kcandee@marianuniversity.edu
CANDELARIA, J. Randel ... 336-734-7216 ... 370 F jcandelaria@forsythtech.edu
CANDELARIA, Rene ... 210-733-0777 ... 489 F
CANDELARIO, Angela ... 787-743-7979 ... 565 H ut_acandelar@suagm.edu
CANDELAS, Saul, C ... 915-831-2354 ... 486 G scandel8@epcc.edu
CANDIA, Patricia ... 361-664-2981 ... 483 B candia@coastalbend.edu
CANDIDO, Jacqueline, P ... 215-898-0728 ... 448 J candido@sas.upenn.edu
CANDIELLO, Mario ... 410-532-5389 ... 225 D mcandiello@ndm.edu
CANDIOTTI, Alan ... 973-408-3362 ... 309 E acandiot@drew.edu
CANDLER, Brandy ... 812-298-2286 ... 177 D bcandler@ivytech.edu
CANDLER, George, B ... 212-327-7801 ... 347 H candler@rockefeller.edu
CANDREVA, Anne, M ... 412-578-6043 ... 424 I amcandreva@carlow.edu
CANDREVA, Anne, M ... 412-578-6043 ... 424 I candrevaam@carlow.edu
CANEDAY, Lois ... 651-757-4031 ... 262 H lcaneday@cva.edu
CANEDO, Agnes, F ... 509-963-3049 ... 532 C canedoa@cwu.edu
CANEIRO-LIVINGSTON, Graciela ... 563-588-6406 ... 183 E graciela.caneiro-livingston@clarke.edu
CANEPA, Janet, A ... 203-254-4280 ... 92 H jcanepa@fairfield.edu
CANEPA, Thomas ... 513-556-2495 ... 403 D tom.canepa@uc.edu
CANEPI, Karen ... 702-968-2033 ... 303 D kcanepi@roseman.edu
CANER, Emir ... 706-865-2134 ... 138 E ecaner@truett.edu
CANER, Ergun ... 817-461-8741 ... 480 H ecaner@abconline.org
CANFIELD, Anne ... 816-802-3426 ... 283 E acanfield@kcai.edu
CANFIELD, Cheri ... 847-233-7700 ... 160 D ccanfield@nc.edu
CANFIELD, Kathleen ... 847-925-6283 ... 151 G kcanfiel@harpercollege.edu
CANFIELD, Merle ... 607-753-5565 ... 353 B merle.canfield@cortland.edu
CANFIELD, Michael ... 703-284-1512 ... 521 D michael.canfield@marymount.edu
CANGI, Ellen ... 813-253-7995 ... 110 M ecangi@hccfl.edu
CANHAM, Drew ... 254-299-8692 ... 490 G dcanham@mclennan.edu
CANHAM, Raymond, P ... 972-238-6248 ... 485 D canham@dcccd.edu
CANIA, Lisa, M ... 315-229-5585 ... 349 E lcania@stlawu.edu
CANICK, Simon ... 651-290-6301 ... 272 E simon.canick@wmitchell.edu
CANIDA, II, Robert, L ... 910-522-5790 ... 379 C canida@uncp.edu
CANIGLIA, Alan ... 717-291-4168 ... 429 F alan.caniglia@fandm.edu
CANIGLIA, Alan, S ... 717-291-3985 ... 429 F alan.caniglia@fandm.edu
CANIZARES, Claude, R ... 617-253-3206 ... 241 D
CANNADA, JR., Robert, C ... 601-923-1600 ... 276 F rcannada@rts.edu
CANNADA, JR., Robert, C ... 704-366-5066 ... 376 B rcannada@rts.edu
CANNADAY, Billy, K ... 434-982-5207 ... 525 F bkc2p@virginia.edu
CANNADAY SAULNY, Helen ... 202-994-6710 ... 98 C saulnyh@gwu.edu
CANNADY, Sonya, Y ... 919-516-4482 ... 376 D sycannady@st-aug.edu
CANNADY-SMITH, Allison ... 253-879-3450 ... 538 H acannadysmith@pugetsound.edu
CANNAN, Erin ... 845-758-7454 ... 323 D cannan@bard.edu
CANNELL, Stephen ... 269-488-4241 ... 253 A scannell@kvcc.edu
CANNEY, Catherine, E ... 978-665-3181 ... 237 E ccanney@fitchburgstate.edu
CANNEY, Jane, W ... 651-962-6120 ... 272 B jwcanney@stthomas.edu
CANNICI, James, P ... 972-883-2575 ... 506 A cannici@utdallas.edu
CANNIFF, James, F ... 617-228-2435 ... 239 C jfcanniff@bhcc.mass.edu
CANNING, Fran ... 603-513-5171 ... 306 E fran.canning@law.unh.edu
CANNING, Ian ... 401-598-4405 ... 453 E icanning@jwu.edu
CANNING, John, B ... 401-232-6020 ... 453 C jcanning@bryant.edu
CANNING, Marcia, J ... 415-476-5003 ... 75 A mcanning@legal.ucsf.edu
CANNING, Mary ... 415-442-7885 ... 48 F mcanning@ggu.edu
CANNING, Patricia ... 215-248-7144 ... 425 D canningp@chc.edu
CANNON, Blake ... 870-612-2057 ... 25 E blake.cannon@uaccb.edu
CANNON, Brenda ... 931-393-1546 ... 475 D bcannon@mscc.edu
CANNON, Bunnie ... 225-578-0302 ... 212 H bcannon@lsu.edu
CANNON, Chris ... 251-460-6933 ... 9 D ccannon@usouthal.edu
CANNON, Danita ... 912-287-5806 ... 135 F dcannon@okefenokeetech.edu
CANNON, Donald, G ... 334-291-4981 ... 2 F glen.cannon@cv.edu
CANNON, Gordon ... 601-266-5116 ... 277 F gordon.cannon@usm.edu
CANNON, Gregory ... 845-575-3000 ... 340 B greg.cannon@marist.edu
CANNON, Jamie ... 530-895-2400 ... 31 H cannonja@butte.edu
CANNON, Jason ... 256-840-4150 ... 7 A jcannon@snead.edu
CANNON, Katherine ... 508-793-7499 ... 233 B kcannon@clarku.edu
CANNON, Leslie ... 254-659-7505 ... 487 G lcannon@hillcollege.edu
CANNON, Marsha ... 205-652-3517 ... 9 E mac@uwa.edu
CANNON, Mary ... 740-392-6868 ... 396 I mary.cannon@mvnu.edu
CANNON, Michael ... 202-685-3927 ... 557 I michael.cannon@ndu.edu
CANNON, Michael, R ... 314-935-5152 ... 292 I michael_cannon@wustl.edu
CANNON, Rebecca ... 225-768-0810 ... 214 C rebecca.cannon@ololcollege.edu
CANNON, Richard, J ... 603-862-2232 ... 306 C dick.cannon@unh.edu
CANNON, Sharon ... 610-399-2057 ... 442 A scannon@cheyney.edu
CANNON, Sharon ... 432-335-5150 ... 502 B sharon.cannon@ttuhsc.edu
CANNON, Sondra ... 732-224-2695 ... 308 A scannon@brookdalecc.edu
CANNON, Steve ... 214-648-6709 ... 507 E steve.cannon@ustouthwestern.edu
CANNON, Thomas ... 727-726-1153 ... 103 I tomcannon@clearwater.edu
CANNON, Tonya ... 706-385-1460 ... 136 B tonya.cannon@point.edu
CANNON, Tyrone, H ... 415-422-6167 ... 76 E cannont@usfca.edu
CANNON SMITH, Elizabeth ... 413-542-2031 ... 230 A alumni@amherst.edu
CANNY, Eric ... 386-822-8166 ... 121 F ecanny@stetson.edu
CANO, Mary ... 915-566-9621 ... 508 G mcano@westerntech.edu
CANO, Mary ... 915-566-9621 ... 508 H mcano@westerntech.edu
CANO, Mary ... 956-380-8128 ... 493 D mcano@riogrande.edu
CANON, Susan ... 507-786-3647 ... 271 C canon@stolaf.edu
CANON, Sybil ... 662-560-1103 ... 276 D srcanon@northwestms.edu
CANONICA, James ... 856-227-7200 ... 308 D jcanonica@camdencc.edu
CANOUGH, Corrine, M ... 585-785-1469 ... 334 A canoucm@flcc.edu
CANOY, Eugenio ... 408-274-7900 ... 67 C eugenio.canoy@evc.edu
CANOY, Robert, W ... 704-406-4395 ... 364 E rcanoy@gardner-webb.edu
CANT, David ... 714-241-6224 ... 41 B dcant@coastline.edu
CANT, Karen ... 714-484-7313 ... 59 D kcant@cypresscollege.edu
CANTALL, Nathaniel ... 803-765-6023 ... 455 B ncantall@allenuniversity.edu
CANTALUPA, Kathy ... 617-951-2350 ... 242 G kathy.cantalupa@necb.edu
CANTANIO, Teri, T ... 215-702-4422 ... 444 B tcatanio@pbu.edu
CANTARELLA, Theresa, C ... 718-390-4350 ... 348 G cantaret@stjohns.edu
CANTARERO, Maritza ... 408-741-2429 ... 78 G maritza.cantarero@westvalley.edu
CANTELON, Janet ... 509-574-4937 ... 540 D jcantelon@yvcc.edu
CANTER, Bridget ... 270-534-3088 ... 203 E bridget.canter@kctcs.edu
CANTER, John ... 614-947-6556 ... 391 B jcanter@franklin.edu
CANTERBURY, Jay ... 419-434-4076 ... 404 B canterbury@findlay.edu
CANTERBURY, Mary Ann ... 601-643-8414 ... 273 G maryann.canterbury@colin.edu
CANTERINO, Patricia ... 610-647-4400 ... 431 C pcanterino@immaculata.edu
CANTINE, Stephen ... 309-438-5637 ... 153 D scantin@ilstu.edu
CANTLEY, Shelby, D ... 765-641-4292 ... 169 E sdcantley@anderson.edu
CANTO-WILLIAMS, Loretta ... 925-439-2181 ... 43 G lcantowilliams@losmedanos.edu
CANTOR, Darlene ... 305-892-7066 ... 112 A darlene.cantor@jwu.edu
CANTOR, Larry ... 256-824-6203 ... 8 G larry.contor@uah.edu
CANTOR, Nancy ... 315-443-2235 ... 357 C ncantor@syr.edu
CANTOR, Ronald, G ... 207-741-5501 ... 219 A
CANTRELL, Andra, R ... 817-598-6260 ... 508 F acantrell@wc.edu
CANTRELL, Betsy ... 678-717-3941 ... 129 G bcantrell@gsc.edu
CANTRELL, Carol ... 212-229-5671 ... 342 E cantrelc@newschool.edu
CANTRELL, Chuck ... 423-425-4363 ... 477 F chuck-cantrell@utc.edu
CANTRELL, Danny, R ... 304-766-4183 ... 544 F dcantrel@wvstateu.edu
CANTRELL, Fred ... 352-213-4380 ... 120 C fhc@ufl.edu
CANTRELL, Hampton ... 310-338-2893 ... 56 E hampton.cantrell@lmu.edu
CANTRELL, Jill ... 770-531-6303 ... 133 C cantrell@laniertech.edu
CANTRELL, Pierce ... 979-845-2072 ... 496 F p-cantrell@tamu.edu
CANTRELL, JR., Pierce, E ... 979-845-2072 ... 497 E p-cantrell@tamu.edu
CANTRELL, Rhonda ... 316-942-4291 ... 195 F cantrellr@newmanu.edu
CANTRELL, Sharon ... 787-743-7979 ... 565 H scantrel@suagm.edu
CANTU, Benjamin ... 903-923-3375 ... 500 E benjamin.cantu@tstc.edu
CANTU, Charles ... 210-436-3320 ... 493 F ccantu@stmarytx.edu
CANTU, Martha ... 956-665-2147 ... 506 C cantum@utpa.edu
CANTU, Tony ... 559-489-2212 ... 72 B tony.cantu@fresnocitycollege.edu
CANTU, Valeriano ... 870-862-8131 ... 23 G vcantu@southark.edu
CANTWELL, Chris ... 618-393-2982 ... 152 F cantwellc@iecc.edu
CANTWELL, Linda ... 405-491-6324 ... 412 D lcantwel@snu.edu
CANTWELL, Linda ... 405-491-6324 ... 412 D
CANTY, Joan ... 817-531-4404 ... 502 E jcanty@txwes.edu
CANUETTE, JR., William (Bill) ... 910-296-2449 ... 371 E wcanuette@jamessprunt.edu
CAO, Nina ... 773-907-4473 ... 147 D ncao@ccc.edu
CAPACCIO, John ... 707-826-3451 ... 36 E capaccio@humboldt.edu
CAPALBO, Tony ... 815-455-8569 ... 157 H tcapalbo@mchenry.edu
CAPALDI, Elizabeth, D ... 480-965-1224 ... 11 J betty.capaldi@asu.edu
CAPALDO, Patricia ... 212-556-0002 ... 337 J
CAPANI, Peter ... 817-923-8459 ... 483 G peter.capani@fishermore.edu
CAPASSO, Ruth ... 330-499-9600 ... 393 I rcapasso@kent.edu
CAPASSO, Susan ... 203-576-5481 ... 94 C scapasso@stvincentscollege.edu
CAPDEVILLE, Michelle ... 413-755-4454 ... 241 B capdeville@stcc.edu
CAPE, Jane, A ... 937-328-6038 ... 387 H capej@clarkstate.edu
CAPE, Robert, E ... 843-953-6402 ... 457 B caper@cofc.edu
CAPECI, Jonathan ... 610-917-1433 ... 450 E jcapeci@vfcc.edu
CAPEHART, Robin, C ... 304-336-8000 ... 544 D wlpres@westliberty.edu
CAPELA, Michael ... 661-763-7768 ... 72 E mcapela@taftcollege.edu
CAPELL, Carey, M ... 843-953-6847 ... 456 C carey.capell@citadel.edu
CAPELLE, Rosita, V ... 692-625-3291 ... 560 A taklib@yahoo.com
CAPELLI, Joe ... 928-776-2184 ... 19 C joe.capelli@yc.edu
CAPELLI, Stephen, L ... 410-334-2813 ... 229 E scapelli@worwic.edu
CAPELO, Jenny ... 509-682-6662 ... 539 E jcapelo@wvc.edu
CAPENER, Don ... 904-256-7431 ... 111 L dcapene@ju.edu
CAPERS, Meggin ... 610-341-5902 ... 428 E mcapers@eastern.edu
CAPEZZUTO, Donna ... 740-699-2490 ... 400 B capezzuto@ohio.edu
CAPILOUTO, Eli ... 859-257-1701 ... 207 D elic@uky.edu
CAPISCIOLTO, Ken ... 616-222-3000 ... 253 F kcapisciolto@kuyper.edu
CAPISTRANO, Marites ... 216-781-9400 ... 388 B mcapis@cie-wc.edu
CAPLAN, Frances, J ... 412-397-6868 ... 445 H caplan@rmu.edu
CAPO, Leslie, L ... 504-568-4806 ... 213 A lcapo@lsuhsc.edu
CAPO, Nicholas, P ... 217-245-3010 ... 152 D ncapo@ic.edu
CAPOBIANCO, Lorraine ... 203-837-8301 ... 91 A capobiancol@wcsu.edu
CAPOBIANCO, Patrick ... 617-327-6777 ... 241 F patrick_capobianco@mspp.edu
CAPONE, Lucien ... 828-250-3835 ... 378 D scapone@unca.edu
CAPONI, Kimberly ... 630-466-7900 ... 168 B kcaponi@waubonsee.edu

CARLSON, Dylana ... 309-341-5230 ... 146 D dcarlson@sandburg.edu
CARLSON, Gerald, P ... 337-482-6678 ... 216 D gcarlson@louisiana.edu
CARLSON, Herbert, F ... 724-738-2545 ... 443 F herbert.carlson@sru.edu
CARLSON, Jean ... 914-831-0416 ... 330 D jcarlson@cw.edu
CARLSON, Jeffrey ... 708-524-6814 ... 150 C jcarlson@dom.edu
CARLSON, Jim ... 406-586-3585 ... 294 G jim.carlson@montanabiblecollege.edu
CARLSON, Jon, C ... 216-707-8076 ... 394 B jcarlson@kent.edu
CARLSON, Karen, A ... 218-299-3734 ... 262 I carlsonk@cord.edu
CARLSON, Kathleen ... 773-298-3305 ... 163 I carlson@sxu.edu
CARLSON, Kenna Lee ... 402-486-2503 ... 300 C kecarlso@ucollege.edu
CARLSON, Kerri ... 612-659-6204 ... 267 B kerri.carlson@minneapolis.edu
CARLSON, Kurt ... 919-497-3325 ... 366 H kcarlson@louisburg.edu
CARLSON, Libby, L ... 662-846-4268 ... 273 H lcarlson@deltastate.edu
CARLSON, Malinda, L ... 217-245-3011 ... 152 D mcarlson@ic.edu
CARLSON, Nancy ... 303-914-6389 ... 87 G nancy.carlson@rrcc.edu
CARLSON, Neil ... 616-526-6420 ... 249 A nec4@calvin.edu
CARLSON, Paul ... 815-802-8652 ... 155 A pcarlson@kcc.edu
CARLSON, Paul ... 323-953-4000 ... 54 H carlsopr@lacitycollege.edu
CARLSON, Paula, J ... 507-786-3632 ... 271 C carlsonp@stolaf.edu
CARLSON, Rich ... 402-486-2508 ... 300 C ricarlso@ucollege.edu
CARLSON, Rosa, F ... 559-791-2316 ... 53 A rcarlson@portervillecollege.edu
CARLSON, Rose ... 505-287-6622 ... 319 H rcarlson@nmsu.edu
CARLSON, Stanley, E ... 563-884-5684 ... 188 E stan.carlson@palmer.edu
CARLSON, Steve ... 920-206-2342 ... 548 D steve.carlson@mbbc.edu
CARLSON, Steven, T ... 574-372-5100 ... 171 H carlsost@grace.edu
CARLSON, Tracey ... 423-614-6000 ... 470 C tcarlson@leeuniversity.edu
CARLSON HURST, Marjorie, F ... 330-471-8244 ... 395 F mcarlson@malone.edu
CARLSTROM, Lester, H ... 773-244-5597 ... 159 H lcarlstrom@northpark.edu
CARLTON, LeAnn, K ... 816-654-7213 ... 283 F lcarlton@kcumb.edu
CARLTON, Melanie ... 870-584-4471 ... 25 C mcarlton@cccua.edu
CARLTON, William "Bee" ... 912-279-5892 ... 127 E wcarlton@ccga.edu
CARLUCCI, Carl ... 832-842-5550 ... 503 D ccarlucci@uh.edu
CARLUCCI, Carl, P ... 832-842-5550 ... 503 C ccarlucci@uh.edu
CARMACK, Connie, K ... 540-375-2230 ... 523 G carmack@roanoke.edu
CARMACK, Lance ... 937-255-6565 ... 557 C lance.carmack@afit.edu
CARMAN, Kevin, R ... 225-578-4201 ... 212 H zocarm@lsu.edu
CARMEL, Julie ... 508-929-8754 ... 238 G jcarmel@worcester.edu
CARMEN, Beth Anne ... 614-236-6211 ... 386 E bcarmen@capital.edu
CARMEN, Kim ... 318-675-5000 ... 213 B kcarme@lsuhsc.edu
CARMER, Gregory, W ... 978-867-4012 ... 235 A greg.carmer@gordon.edu
CARMICAL, Beth ... 910-272-3343 ... 373 D bcarmical@robeson.edu
CARMICHAEL, Ann, C ... 803-584-3446 ... 462 E anncar@mailbox.sc.edu
CARMICHAEL, Beverly ... 920-465-2074 ... 551 B carmichb@uwgb.edu
CARMICHAEL, Brenda ... 620-343-4600 ... 192 H bcarmichael@fhtc.edu
CARMICHAEL, Georgia ... 713-718-5466 ... 487 I georgia.carmichael@hccs.edu
CARMICHAEL, John ... 360-867-6100 ... 534 D carmichj@evergreen.edu
CARMICHAEL, Matt ... 530-752-5350 ... 73 I mecarmichael@ucdavis.edu
CARMICHAEL, Paul ... 860-343-5787 ... 91 G pcarmichael@mxcc.commnet.edu
CARMICHAEL, Peggy ... 304-214-8901 ... 543 D pcarmichael@wvncc.edu
CARMICHAEL, Stacy ... 228-896-2503 ... 275 E stacy.carmichael@mgccc.edu
CARMINE, Kevin ... 718-319-7965 ... 327 D kcarmine@hostos.cuny.edu
CARMODY, Margaret ... 877-246-9388 ... 150 B mcarmody@devry.edu
CARMODY, Patricia ... 507-537-6206 ... 269 E patricia.carmody@smsu.edu
CARMODY, Richard ... 805-922-6966 ... 26 L rcarmody@hancockcollege.edu
CARMONA, Gloria ... 760-355-6244 ... 51 A gloria.carmona@imperial.edu
CARMONA, José, I ... 787-875-4150 ... 565 I jocarmona@suagm.edu
CARNAGHI, Jan ... 317-955-6154 ... 177 I jcarnaghi@marian.edu
CARNAGHI, Jill, E ... 314-935-5022 ... 292 I jill.carnaghi@wustl.edu
CARNAGHI, John, R ... 850-644-4444 ... 119 D jcarnaghi@admin.fsu.edu
CARNAGHI, Laura ... 859-282-9999 ... 204 C lcarnaghi@lincolntech.com
CARNAHAN, Allison, G ... 260-422-5561 ... 173 C gcarnahan@indianatech.edu
CARNAHAN, Scott ... 503-883-2229 ... 416 H scarnah@linfield.edu
CARNAROLI, Craig ... 215-898-6693 ... 448 J carnarol@pobox.upenn.edu
CARNDUFF, Dagmar, L ... 414-847-3211 ... 549 B dagmarcarnduff@miad.edu
CARNE, Kim ... 906-786-5802 ... 248 I carnek@baycollege.edu
CARNE, Linda, P ... 804-752-3103 ... 523 C lindacarne@rmc.edu
CARNEGIE, Kay ... 503-399-5058 ... 414 J kay.carnegie@chemeketa.edu
CARNES, Kathy, M ... 252-493-7220 ... 372 H kcarnes@email.pittcc.edu
CARNES, Peter ... 508-565-1206 ... 245 A pcarnes@stonehill.edu
CARNEVALE, David ... 562-907-4284 ... 79 F dcarneva@whittier.edu
CARNEY, Bruce ... 919-962-2198 ... 378 E bruce@unc.edu
CARNEY, Conferlete ... 727-712-5742 ... 116 H carney.conferlete@spcollege.edu
CARNEY, Diane, E ... 412-291-6250 ... 422 E dcarney@aii.edu
CARNEY, Edward ... 856-227-7200 ... 308 D ecarney@camdencc.edu
CARNEY, Gary ... 610-861-1300 ... 437 A carneyg@moravian.edu
CARNEY, Ginny ... 218-335-4200 ... 264 G ginny.carney@lltc.edu
CARNEY, Kathleen ... 508-793-3371 ... 233 C kcarney@holycross.edu
CARNEY, Kay ... 415-451-2835 ... 66 B kcarney@sfts.edu
CARNEY, Leslie ... 407-646-2266 ... 116 D lcarney@rollins.edu
CARNEY, Leslie ... 407-646-1528 ... 116 D lcarney@rollins.edu
CARNEY, OSF, Margaret ... 716-375-2222 ... 348 C mcarney@sbu.edu
CARNEY, Martin ... 216-421-7424 ... 388 A mcarney@cia.edu
CARNEY, Paul ... 314-968-6974 ... 292 J paulcarney89@webster.edu
CARNEY, Sheila, A ... 412-578-6424 ... 424 I carneysa@carlow.edu
CARNEY, Tim ... 513-244-4426 ... 388 E tim_carney@mail.msj.edu
CARNEY, Timothy ... 202-319-5619 ... 97 E carneyt@cua.edu
CARNEY-DEBORD, Nan ... 740-587-6428 ... 389 I carneydebord@denison.edu
CARNEY-HALL, Karla ... 309-556-3111 ... 153 F dstudent@iwu.edu
CARNLEY, Raymond ... 864-833-8006 ... 460 E rcarnley@presby.edu
CARNWATH, Thomas ... 215-717-6640 ... 448 I tcarnwath@uarts.edu
CARNZ, Scott ... 206-239-2320 ... 531 B scarnz@aii.edu
CARO, Enrique ... 305-820-5003 ... 118 D ecaro@sec.edu
CARO, Jessica ... 787-832-6000 ... 562 G jcaro@icprjc.edu
CARO, Mary Ellen ... 609-984-1130 ... 316 A mcaro@tesc.edu
CAROL, Claudia, C ... 512-448-8538 ... 493 E claudiac@stedwards.edu
CAROLAN, Tammy ... 563-425-5337 ... 189 G carolant@uiu.edu
CAROLLO, Ann ... 858-795-5321 ... 67 I acarollo@sandfordburnham.org
CAROLLO, Chris ... 203-332-5078 ... 91 E ccarollo@hcc.commnet.edu
CARON, Christina ... 207-992-1939 ... 218 A caroncb@husson.edu
CARON, Linda ... 937-775-2225 ... 406 C linda.caron@wright.edu
CARONA, Charles ... 214-333-5200 ... 484 D charlesc@dbu.edu
CARONE, Joseph ... 567-661-7190 ... 400 I joseph_carone@owens.edu
CAROTHERS, Amy ... 775-784-6620 ... 303 A acarothers@unr.edu
CAROTHERS, Harry, G ... 303-963-3228 ... 82 C hcarothers@ccu.edu
CAROTHERS, John ... 775-784-1394 ... 303 A jcarothers@adv.unr.edu
CAROTHERS, Michael ... 703-257-5515 ... 516 I
CARP, Richard, M ... 925-631-4443 ... 64 F rmcarp@gmail.com
CARPENTER, Amanda ... 804-706-5189 ... 527 B acarpenter@jtcc.edu
CARPENTER, Amber, L ... 419-772-2012 ... 398 H a-carpenter@onu.edu
CARPENTER, Andrew ... 312-589-7472 ... 150 G acarpenter@ellis.edu
CARPENTER, Barbara ... 225-771-2613 ... 214 I carp.subr@aol.com
CARPENTER, Bobbi ... 434-381-6156 ... 524 K bcarpenter@sbc.edu
CARPENTER, Carolyn, A ... 573-629-3116 ... 282 E carolyn.carpenter@hlg.edu
CARPENTER, Courtney ... 757-221-4000 ... 518 A cmcarp@wm.edu
CARPENTER, Courtney, M ... 757-221-2001 ... 518 A cmcarp@wm.edu
CARPENTER, Dale ... 828-227-7311 ... 380 A carpenter@wcu.edu
CARPENTER, Dale, E ... 260-982-5393 ... 177 H decarpenter@manchester.edu
CARPENTER, Dana ... 225-771-2394 ... 214 I dana_carpenter@subr.edu
CARPENTER, David ... 478-929-6700 ... 133 H david.carpenter@maconstate.edu
CARPENTER, Debra ... 281-283-2150 ... 503 E carpenter@uhcl.edu
CARPENTER, Dennis, D ... 843-953-6922 ... 456 C denny.carpenter@citadel.edu
CARPENTER, Dianna, M ... 816-604-2230 ... 285 C dianna.carpenter@mcckc.edu
CARPENTER, Donnie ... 254-298-8460 ... 496 D donnie.carpenter@templejc.edu
CARPENTER, Dorynda ... 417-865-2811 ... 281 G carpenterd@evangel.edu
CARPENTER, Earl ... 310-506-4700 ... 61 H earl.carpenter@pepperdine.edu
CARPENTER, Ginny ... 708-239-4703 ... 166 C ginny.carpenter@trnty.edu
CARPENTER, Heather ... 617-236-8800 ... 234 G hcarpenter@fisher.edu
CARPENTER, Julia ... 405-691-3800 ... 408 H jcarpenter@macu.edu
CARPENTER, Julie ... 831-656-3054 ... 558 A jcarpenter@nps.edu
CARPENTER, Kathryn, H ... 312-996-8974 ... 167 B khc@uic.edu
CARPENTER, Katie ... 406-238-7390 ... 296 C katie.carpenter@rocky.edu
CARPENTER, Kenneth ... 505-277-4032 ... 321 C carpenk@unm.edu
CARPENTER, Kenneth ... 225-578-5863 ... 212 H kenc@lsu.edu
CARPENTER, Kenneth ... 435-613-5752 ... 512 A ken.carpenter@usu.edu
CARPENTER, Kimberly ... 323-241-5321 ... 55 C carpenkc@lasc.edu
CARPENTER, Larry ... 423-614-8440 ... 470 C lcarpenter@leeuniversity.edu
CARPENTER, Linda, M ... 814-641-3111 ... 432 A carpenl@juniata.edu
CARPENTER, Lisa ... 808-566-2411 ... 140 G lcarpenter@hpu.edu
CARPENTER, Marla ... 336-770-3337 ... 379 E carpem@uncsa.edu
CARPENTER, Mary, V ... 731-881-7070 ... 477 G maryc@utm.edu
CARPENTER, Michael ... 757-823-8104 ... 522 E mcarpenter@nsu.edu
CARPENTER, Mike ... 402-826-6781 ... 297 G mike.carpenter@doane.edu
CARPENTER, Monica, S ... 828-682-7315 ... 372 A mscarpenter@mayland.edu
CARPENTER, Patricia, A ... 207-778-7091 ... 220 C patc@maine.edu
CARPENTER, Paula ... 217-234-5217 ... 156 B pcarpent@lakeland.cc.il.us
CARPENTER, Richard ... 832-813-6515 ... 490 E richard.carpenter@lonestar.edu
CARPENTER, Robert ... 423-323-0259 ... 475 F rccarpenter@northeaststate.edu
CARPENTER, Rosalie ... 386-822-7348 ... 121 F rcarpent@stetson.edu
CARPENTER, Sally ... 630-637-5148 ... 159 G sacarpenter@noctrl.edu
CARPENTER, Scott ... 541-881-5773 ... 420 E scarpent@tvcc.cc
CARPENTER, Stan ... 512-245-2150 ... 501 F sc33@txstate.edu
CARPENTER, Stan ... 402-471-2505 ... 299 D scarpenter@nscs.edu
CARPENTER, Van ... 715-324-6900 ... 549 G van.carpenter@ni.edu
CARPENTER, Wayne, D ... 413-782-1565 ... 246 A wcarpent@wne.edu
CARPENTER, Wendi, B ... 718-409-7271 ... 356 C wcarpenter@sunymaritime.edu
CARPENTER-DAVIS, Cheryl ... 816-604-6630 ... 285 A cheryl.carpenter@mcckc.edu
CARPENTER-HUBIN, Julie ... 614-292-5915 ... 398 I carpenter-hubin.16@osu.edu
CARPENTER-WILLIAMS, Oshunda ... 815-802-8513 ... 155 A owilliams@kcc.edu
CARPI, Anthony ... 212-237-8944 ... 327 F acarpi@jjay.cuny.edu
CARPINELLI, Richard ... 304-442-3158 ... 545 D richard.carpinelli@mail.wvu.edu
CARPIO, Eric ... 719-587-7802 ... 80 L ecarpio@adams.edu
CARPIO, Joseph ... 505-346-2324 ... 321 B joseph.carpio@bie.edu
CARPIO, Joseph ... 505-346-2361 ... 321 B joseph.carpio@bie.edu
CARR, Bonnie, J ... 813-253-7006 ... 110 M bcarr@hccfl.edu
CARR, Charles ... 940-397-4748 ... 491 B charles.carr@mwsu.edu
CARR, Dennis ... 541-463-5583 ... 416 E carrd@lanecc.edu
CARR, Diane ... 803-738-7754 ... 459 E carrd@midlandstech.edu
CARR, Diane, M ... 973-761-7491 ... 310 F diane.carr@shu.edu
CARR, Frances ... 229-317-6744 ... 128 D frances.carr@darton.edu
CARR, Gary ... 864-644-5013 ... 461 B gcarr@swu.edu
CARR, James, W ... 501-279-4406 ... 21 H carr@harding.edu
CARR, Jeffrey ... 619-849-2415 ... 62 L jeffreycarr@pointloma.edu
CARR, Jeffrey ... 215-972-7623 ... 440 J jcarr@pafa.edu
CARR, Jessica ... 505-348-3700 ... 464 H jcarr@national.edu
CARR, Jill ... 419-372-2843 ... 385 E jcarr2@bgsu.edu
CARR, John ... 404-364-8439 ... 135 E jcarr1@oglethorpe.edu
CARR, Karen, A ... 315-786-2404 ... 337 F kcarr@sunyjefferson.edu
CARR, Karin ... 518-454-5113 ... 330 C carrk@strose.edu
CARR, Larry ... 617-989-4256 ... 245 F carrl@wit.edu
CARR, Lawrence ... 408-924-1166 ... 37 C larry.carr@sjsu.edu
CARR, Leslie ... 661-362-3100 ... 41 I leslie.carr@canyons.edu
CARR, Nancy ... 315-498-2834 ... 345 D
CARR, Nicole, T ... 251-460-6475 ... 9 D ncarr@jaguar1.usouthal.edu
CARR, Norma ... 801-957-4083 ... 512 D norma.carr@slcc.edu
CARR, Ricki ... 208-376-7731 ... 142 H rcarr@boisebible.edu
CARR, Robert ... 601-877-6141 ... 272 F rcarr@alcorn.edu
CARR, Rodger ... 281-283-2900 ... 503 E carr@uhcl.edu
CARR, Rosalie ... 336-315-8660 ... 363 C rcarr@carolinagrad.edu
CARR, Shannon ... 509-359-6582 ... 533 H scarr@ewu.edu
CARR, Sherrean ... 408-848-4757 ... 48 C scarr@gavilan.edu
CARR, Thomas, F ... 607-962-9223 ... 331 C carr_tom@corning-cc.edu
CARR, Tunya ... 816-600-3900 ... 464 H
CARR, William, D ... 256-782-5328 ... 4 L bcarr@jsu.edu
CARR ROBINETT, Angie ... 816-501-4541 ... 288 A angie.carr@rockhurst.edu
CARRADINE, Tania ... 504-671-5155 ... 210 F tcarra@dcc.edu
CARRAFIELLO, Susan ... 937-775-2660 ... 406 C susan.carrafiello@wright.edu
CARRANCO, Emilio ... 512-245-2161 ... 501 F ec05@txstate.edu
CARRANO, Jean, B ... 803-938-3708 ... 462 G jeabrown@uscsumter.edu
CARRANZA, Mike ... 956-872-3420 ... 494 H mcarranz@southtexascollege.edu
CARRARO, Frances ... 940-397-8948 ... 491 B frances.carraro@mwsu.edu
CARRASCO, Ed ... 407-330-7020 ... 100 H
CARRASCO, Hector ... 719-549-2696 ... 83 H hector.carrasco@colostate-pueblo.edu
CARRASQUILLO, Iris, N ... 787-850-9363 ... 567 E iris.carrasquillo@upr.edu
CARRAWAY, Carl ... 803-738-7624 ... 459 E carrawayc@midlandstech.edu
CARRAWAY, Jay ... 252-527-6223 ... 371 G jcarraway@lenoircc.edu
CARRAWAY, Kevin ... 252-328-6434 ... 377 E carrawayc@ecu.edu
CARRAWAY, Pauline ... 757-352-4007 ... 523 E paulcar@regent.edu
CARREIRA, Robert ... 520-515-5370 ... 13 E carreirar@cochise.edu
CARREIRO, Manuel, C ... 203-582-8721 ... 93 H manuel.carreiro@quinnipiac.edu

CARTER, Linda ... 816-604-3081 ... 285 D
linda.carter@mcckc.edu
CARTER, Linda ... 606-539-4230 ... 207 C
linda.carter@ucumberlands.edu
CARTER, Linda ... 336-334-5696 ... 379 B
linda_carter@uncg.edu
CARTER, Linnie, S ... 717-780-2321 ... 430 E
lscarter@hacc.edu
CARTER, Lisa ... 617-427-0060 ... 241 A
ljenkins@rcc.mass.edu
CARTER, Luther, F ... 843-661-1210 ... 458 D
lcarter@fmarion.edu
CARTER, Malika ... 701-777-4259 ... 381 F
malika.carter@und.edu
CARTER, Mark ... 660-596-7221 ... 290 B
mcarter@sfccmo.edu
CARTER, Matt, R ... 901-761-1356 ... 469 C
mrcarter@hst.edu
CARTER, Max, L ... 336-316-2445 ... 365 A
mcarter@guilford.edu
CARTER, Melody ... 478-825-6959 ... 129 F
carterm0@fvsu.edu
CARTER, Melody ... 478-825-6397 ... 129 F
carterm0@fvsu.edu
CARTER, Michael ... 270-789-5001 ... 199 F
mvcarter@campbellsville.edu
CARTER, Michael ... 661-255-1050 ... 32 F
mcarter@calarts.edu
CARTER, Michael ... 937-512-2975 ... 401 J
michael.carter@sinclair.edu
CARTER, Michele ... 254-526-1668 ... 482 H
michele.carter@ctcd.edu
CARTER, Michele, G ... 317-278-2665 ... 174 D
CARTER, Mike ... 918-495-7150 ... 411 C
mcarter@oru.edu
CARTER, Natasha ... 706-396-7591 ... 135 G
ncarter@paine.edu
CARTER, Niaomi ... 703-878-2800 ... 99 G
CARTER, Nichole ... 978-632-6600 ... 240 C
n_carter@mwcc.mass.edu
CARTER, Nick ... 617-964-1100 ... 230 B
ncarter@ants.edu
CARTER, Parris ... 937-708-5611 ... 405 H
pcarter@wilberforce.edu
CARTER, Patricia ... 305-626-3190 ... 109 A
pcarter@fmuniv.edu
CARTER, Petrina ... 434-791-5629 ... 516 G
pcarter@averett.edu
CARTER, Phillip ... 615-547-1307 ... 468 B
pcarter@cumberland.edu
CARTER, R. Daphne ... 843-661-1188 ... 458 D
rcarter@fmarion.edu
CARTER, R. Lee ... 919-508-2049 ... 380 E
rlcarter@peace.edu
CARTER, Richard ... 309-298-2501 ... 168 C
r-carter@wiu.edu
CARTER, Richard ... 309-298-1929 ... 168 C
r-carter@wiu.edu
CARTER, Richard ... 651-641-8271 ... 263 A
carter@csp.edu
CARTER, Richard, E ... 858-642-8110 ... 58 I
rcarter@nu.edu
CARTER, Ronald, L ... 909-558-4542 ... 54 D
rcarter@llu.edu
CARTER, Ronald, L ... 704-378-1006 ... 366 A
rcarter@jcsu.edu
CARTER, Rosalyn, Y ... 954-762-5640 ... 119 A
rcarter@fau.edu
CARTER, Sandra ... 864-225-7653 ... 458 C
sandracarter@forrestcollege.edu
CARTER, Saundra, M ... 202-274-5531 ... 100 A
scarter@udc.edu
CARTER, Shawna, M ... 608-246-6249 ... 554 D
smcarter@madisoncollege.org
CARTER, Sheila ... 312-369-7994 ... 148 D
scarter@colum.edu
CARTER, Shirley ... 336-887-3000 ... 366 C
scarter@laureluniversity.edu
CARTER, Shirley, P ... 336-315-8660 ... 363 C
scarter@carolinagrad.edu
CARTER, Shree ... 714-556-3610 ... 77 B
scarter@vanguard.edu
CARTER, Spencer, D ... 269-471-3395 ... 247 D
scarter@andrews.edu
CARTER, Steven ... 310-577-3000 ... 80 E
scarter@yosan.edu
CARTER, Steven ... 215-935-3879 ... 451 D
scarter@wts.edu
CARTER, Susan ... 503-699-3338 ... 416 J
scarter@marylhurst.edu
CARTER, Tamara ... 573-642-2251 ... 293 D
tammy.carter@williamwoods.edu
CARTER, Taysha ... 479-619-4396 ... 22 H
tcarter@nwacc.edu
CARTER, Tiffany ... 773-291-6317 ... 147 G
tcarter63@ccc.edu
CARTER, Tom ... 256-331-5263 ... 6 B
tom.carter@nwscc.edu
CARTER, Virginia, M ... 610-359-5394 ... 426 G
gcarter@dccc.edu
CARTER, Warrick, L ... 312-369-7200 ... 148 D
wcarter@colum.edu
CARTER, William, E ... 713-718-8708 ... 487 I
william.carter@hccs.edu
CARTER, William, M ... 412-648-1401 ... 449 A
wmc4@pitt.edu
CARTER, Yolanda ... 502-863-7967 ... 201 A
yolanda_carter@georgetowncollege.edu
CARTER, Zina ... 979-532-6417 ... 509 D
zinac@wcjc.edu
CARTER-CHAPMAN,
Renee, M ... 907-786-6486 ... 10 H
anrmc@uaa.alaska.edu
CARTER-COLEY, Stacey ... 919-718-7213 ... 369 C
scarter@cccc.edu
CARTER-STEVENS, Marilyn 718-862-7958 ... 339 H
marilyn.carter@manhattan.edu
CARTER-TELLISON,
Katrina ... 561-237-7210 ... 113 D
kcarter-tellison@lynn.edu
CARTHELL, Sidney, G ... 270-809-6836 ... 205 A
scarthell@murraystate.edu
CARTIER, Jolie, L ... 619-239-0391 ... 37 F
jcartier@cwsl.edu
CARTIER, Missy, M ... 559-323-2100 ... 66 C
mcartier@sjcl.edu
CARTIER, Mose ... 410-951-3636 ... 228 B
mcartier@coppin.edu
CARTLEDGE, Maureen ... 210-486-7173 ... 479 D
mcartledge@alamo.edu
CARTLEDGE, Vince, E ... 740-284-5191 ... 391 A
vcartledge@franciscan.edu
CARTMELL, Brandy, D ... 731-881-7050 ... 477 G
bcartmel@utm.edu
CARTMILL, Larry ... 816-942-5474 ... 282 H
larryc@heritage-education.com
CARTMILL, Mark ... 859-985-3922 ... 199 A
cartmillm@berea.edu
CARTNAL, Ryan ... 805-546-3946 ... 43 I
rcartnal@cuesta.edu
CARTNEY, Michael ... 605-882-5284 ... 464 E
cartneym@lakeareatech.edu
CARTOLANO, Joseph ... 718-631-6231 ... 328 F
jcartolano@qcc.cuny.edu
CARTON, Shirley ... 702-651-7341 ... 302 E
shirley.carton@csn.edu
CARTSONIS, George, A ... 248-341-2122 ... 256 F
gacartso@oaklandcc.edu
CARTWRIGHT, Alexander ... 716-645-3321 ... 351 G
vpr@buffalo.edu
CARTWRIGHT, Cindy ... 716-664-5100 ... 337 D
cindycartwright@jamestownbusinesscollege.edu
CARTWRIGHT, Peggy ... 909-652-6115 ... 39 E
peggy.cartwright@chaffey.edu
CARTWRIGHT, Rhonda, D . 512-448-8403 ... 493 E
rhondac@stedwards.edu
CARTWRIGHT, Rick, E ... 260-399-7700 ... 181 A
rcartwright@sf.edu
CARTY, Karenann ... 718-933-6700 ... 341 G
kcarty@monroecollege.edu
CARTY, Raymond, W ... 573-629-3265 ... 282 E
rcarty@hlg.edu
CARULLO, Susan, H ... 843-792-2071 ... 459 D
carullos@musc.edu
CARUSO, Anne-Marie ... 617-989-4174 ... 245 F
carusoa@wit.edu
CARUSO, David, A ... 603-283-2436 ... 303 F
dcaruso1@antioch.edu
CARUSO, Elizabeth, S ... 585-395-2414 ... 352 F
lcaruso@brockport.edu
CARUSO, Janet ... 516-572-7599 ... 342 C
janet.caruso@ncc.edu
CARUSO, Kelly ... 337-948-0333 ... 212 C
kcaruso@ltc.edu
CARUSO, Matt ... 908-737-0580 ... 311 A
mcaruso@kean.edu
CARUSO, Michael ... 903-510-2420 ... 503 A
mcar@tjc.edu
CARUSO, Michele, E ... 985-448-4081 ... 216 A
michele.caruso@nicholls.edu
CARUTHERS, Janet ... 573-875-7372 ... 280 A
jaocaruthers@ccis.edu
CARVAJAL, Augusto ... 787-780-0070 ... 560 H
acarvajal@caribbean.edu
CARVAJAL, Jane ... 703-414-4095 ... 518 C
jcarvajal@devry.edu
CARVAJAL, Richard ... 229-248-2510 ... 126 A
richard.carvajal@bainbridge.edu
CARVALHO, Susan ... 859-257-1565 ... 207 D
carvalho@uky.edu
CARVER, Barbara ... 516-364-0808 ... 343 A
bcarver@nycollege.edu
CARVER, Curt ... 404-962-3300 ... 139 B
curt.carver@usg.edu
CARVER, David, S ... 402-559-7276 ... 300 H
dcarver@unmc.edu
CARVER, Deborah, A ... 541-346-1892 ... 419 B
dcarver@uoregon.edu
CARVER, Doris, W ... 336-599-1181 ... 372 G
carverd@piedmontcc.edu
CARVER, Greg ... 912-279-5980 ... 127 E
gcarver@ccga.edu
CARVER, Helen ... 561-842-8324 ... 113 B
hcarver@lincolntech.com
CARVER, Jerelene ... 919-546-8525 ... 376 F
jcarver@shawu.edu
CARVER, Keith ... 865-974-0782 ... 477 C
carverk@tennessee.edu
CARVER, Matthew, J ... 716-880-2288 ... 340 D
matthew.j.carver@medaille.edu
CARVER, Nancy, G ... 973-655-7410 ... 311 F
carvern@mail.montclair.edu
CARVER, Peta ... 208-459-5180 ... 143 D
pcarver@collegeofidaho.edu
CARVER, Petra ... 208-459-5180 ... 143 D
pcarver@collegeofidaho.edu
CARVER, II, William, S ... 252-451-8328 ... 372 E
bcarver@nash.cc.nc.us
CARWEIN, Vicky, L ... 260-481-6103 ... 174 C
chancellor@ipfw.edu
CARWILE, Eunice, W ... 434-223-6144 ... 519 G
ecarwile@hsc.edu
CARY, Janelle ... 715-365-4439 ... 555 A
jcary@nicoletcollege.edu
CARY, Wendy, M ... 315-697-8200 ... 359 C
wcary@uscny.edu
CASADA, Tracy, L ... 606-679-8501 ... 203 C
tracy.casada@kctcs.edu
CASADOS, Felicia ... 505-287-6624 ... 319 H
fcasados@nmsu.edu
CASALE, Franklyn, M ... 305-628-6663 ... 117 A
fcasale@stu.edu
CASALEGNO, Gina ... 412-268-2075 ... 424 J
ginac@andrew.cmu.edu
CASAMENTO, Charlene ... 860-832-0033 ... 90 G
casamentoc@ccsu.edu
CASAMENTO, Laura ... 315-792-3219 ... 359 E
lcasamento@utica.edu
CASANOVA, Matthew ... 718-997-4433 ... 328 E
matthew.casanova@qc.cuny.edu
CASANOVER, D. Scott ... 314-264-1740 ... 292 G
scottc@vatterot-college.edu
CASANOVER, Scott ... 314-264-1740 ... 414 A
scott.casanover@vatterott-college.edu
CASANOVER, Scott ... 316-264-1740 ... 168 A
scott.casanover@vatterott-college.edu
CASANOVER, Scott ... 314-264-1740 ... 292 H
scott.casanover@vatterott-college.edu
CASANOVER, Scott ... 314-264-1740 ... 414 B
scott.casanover@vatterott-college.edu
CASANOVER, Scott ... 314-264-1740 ... 478 B
scott.casanover@vatterott-college.edu
CASANOVER, Scott ... 314-264-1740 ... 292 F
scott.casanover@vatterott-college.edu
CASANOVER, Scott ... 314-264-1740 ... 301 C
scott.casanover@vatterott-college.edu
CASANOVER, Scott ... 314-264-1740 ... 405 D
scott.casanover@vatterott-college.edu
CASARES, Nicole, A ... 360-417-6219 ... 536 G
ncasares@pencol.edu
CASAREZ, Melissa ... 269-749-7163 ... 257 A
mcasarez@olivetcollege.edu
CASAS, Alexander ... 305-348-1657 ... 119 C
alexander.casas@fiu.edu
CASCAMO, John ... 805-546-3973 ... 43 I
john_cascamo@cuesta.edu
CASCARDI, Anthony ... 510-642-5396 ... 73 H
ajcascardi@berkeley.edu
CASCIERO, Albert, J ... 202-274-6034 ... 100 A
acasciero@udc.edu
CASCINO, Terrence ... 507-284-3268 ... 262 D
cascino.terrence@mayo.edu
CASCINO, Terrence ... 507-538-0554 ... 262 B
tcascino@mayo.edu
CASCIO, Joe ... 310-434-4840 ... 68 D
cascio_joe@smc.edu
CASCIONE, Gregory ... 313-993-1250 ... 258 G
casciogl@udmercy.edu
CASE, Daniel ... 601-643-8385 ... 273 G
daniel.case@colin.edu
CASE, David ... 601-635-2111 ... 274 A
dcase@eccc.edu
CASE, Deborah ... 775-445-3270 ... 303 B
cased3@wnc.edu
CASE, SJ, Frank, E ... 509-313-6112 ... 534 F
casef@gonzaga.edu
CASE, Harold ... 405-682-1611 ... 409 F
hcase@occc.edu
CASE, Jackie, L ... 919-866-5649 ... 374 H
jlcase@waketech.edu
CASE, Jim ... 657-278-3121 ... 35 B
jcase@fullerton.edu
CASE, Jim ... 432-837-8036 ... 501 E
jcase@sulross.edu
CASE, Jimmy ... 432-837-8368 ... 501 E
jcase@sulross.edu
CASE, Joe, P ... 413-542-2296 ... 230 A
financialaid@amherst.edu
CASE, Judd ... 509-359-2532 ... 533 H
jcase@ewu.edu
CASE, Laura, M ... 865-981-8102 ... 471 B
laura.case@maryvillecollege.edu
CASE, Mark, R ... 203-837-8657 ... 91 A
casem@wcsu.edu
CASE, Mary ... 312-996-2716 ... 167 B
marycase@uic.edu
CASE, Michael ... 260-982-5431 ... 177 H
mcase@manchester.edu
CASE, Michael, A ... 607-587-3535 ... 355 C
casema@alfredstate.edu
CASE, Ron ... 856-415-2257 ... 310 D
rcase@gccnj.edu
CASE, Tom ... 907-786-1800 ... 10 H
chancellor@uaa.alaska.edu
CASE, Verna, M ... 704-894-2327 ... 363 I
vecase@davidson.edu
CASE-KING, Barbara ... 970-248-1266 ... 82 F
bking@coloradomesa.edu
CASEBEER, Clarice ... 417-967-5466 ... 290 E
CASEBEER, James ... 928-523-6080 ... 16 I
james.casebeer@nau.edu
CASEBOLT, Paul ... 813-988-5131 ... 108 A
admissions@floridacollege.edu
CASEL, Michael ... 610-896-1000 ... 430 G
mcasel@haverford.edu
CASEY, Barbara, A ... 413-597-4979 ... 246 D
barbara.a.casey@williams.edu
CASEY, Becky ... 334-876-9271 ... 4 B
bcasey@wccs.edu
CASEY, Brian, W ... 765-658-4220 ... 171 B
briancasey@depauw.edu
CASEY, Carol, E ... 901-843-3815 ... 472 K
casey@rhodes.edu
CASEY, Catherine ... 212-998-1245 ... 344 B
catherine.casey@nyu.edu
CASEY, Christopher ... 518-445-3332 ... 322 C
ccase@albanylaw.edu
CASEY, Deborah ... 253-833-9111 ... 534 H
dcasey@greenriver.edu
CASEY, Donald, E ... 773-325-7256 ... 149 A
dcasey@depaul.edu
CASEY, Gary, S ... 248-341-2034 ... 256 F
gscaey@oaklandcc.edu
CASEY, George, C ... 510-780-4500 ... 53 J
gcasey@lifewest.edu
CASEY, Janet ... 518-580-8111 ... 351 B
jcasey@skidmore.edu
CASEY, Jenn ... 803-461-3297 ... 459 C
jennifer.casey@lr.edu
CASEY, Joanne ... 518-445-2332 ... 322 C
jcase@albanylaw.edu
CASEY, Ken ... 270-707-3884 ... 202 E
ken.casey@kctcs.edu
CASEY, Kevin ... 207-941-7123 ... 218 A
caseyk@husson.edu
CASEY, Lawrence, J ... 607-871-2123 ... 322 E
casey@alfred.edu
CASEY, Lucas, J ... 515-263-6195 ... 185 C
lcasey@grandview.edu
CASEY, Mary, M ... 508-286-3464 ... 246 B
mcasey@wheatonma.edu
CASEY, Michael ... 501-450-3106 ... 25 H
mcasey@uca.edu
CASEY, Michael, T ... 518-580-5660 ... 351 B
mcasey@skidmore.edu
CASEY, Randy ... 414-297-7872 ... 554 F
caseyr@matc.edu
CASEY, Roger, N ... 410-857-2222 ... 224 C
presoffice@mcdaniel.edu
CASEY, Sandra, M ... 518-783-2314 ... 350 I
scasey@siena.edu
CASEY, Terry ... 256-782-5492 ... 4 L
tcasey@jsu.edu
CASEY, Timothy ... 800-962-7682 ... 293 A
tcasey@wma.edu
CASEY, Tom, R ... 843-953-8235 ... 457 B
caseyt@cofc.edu
CASEY, Warren ... 501-279-4056 ... 21 H
casey@harding.edu
CASEY, William, F ... 631-423-0483 ... 350 G
wcasey@icseminary.edu
CASEY-WHITEMAN,
Patricia, A ... 410-777-2776 ... 221 C
pacaseywhiteman@aacc.edu
CASH, Arlene ... 404-270-5186 ... 138 B
acash@spelman.edu
CASH, Erin ... 859-280-1249 ... 204 B
ecash@lextheo.edu
CASH, James, D ... 847-866-3926 ... 151 D
james.cash@garrett.edu
CASH, Keith ... 812-855-4286 ... 173 E
kcash@indiana.edu
CASH, Robert ... 405-878-2353 ... 409 D
robert.cash@okbu.edu
CASH, Teresa, Y ... 501-977-2009 ... 25 G
cash@uaccm.edu
CASHBURLESS, Martha, D 330-823-2838 ... 404 C
cashbumd@mountunion.edu
CASHEL, Malorie ... 417-625-9669 ... 286 B
cashel-m@mssu.edu
CASHEN, Therese ... 540-338-2700 ... 517 G
tcashen@cdu.edu
CASHIO, Cathy ... 409-740-4830 ... 497 F
cashioc@tamug.edu
CASHMAN, Jesse ... 612-330-1644 ... 261 B
cashman@augsburg.edu
CASHMAN, Laurie ... 312-341-3518 ... 163 B
lcashman@roosevelt.edu
CASHMAN, Richard ... 914-606-8501 ... 360 E
richard.cashman@sunywcc.edu
CASHWELL, Debbie ... 910-410-1803 ... 373 B
debbiec@richmondcc.edu
CASHWELL, Michael, B ... 804-355-0671 ... 525 A
mcashwell@upsem.edu
CASIELLO, Andrew, R ... 757-683-5314 ... 522 F
acasiell@odu.edu

CAUSEY, Brian, C .... 336-633-4165 .... 373 A
bccausey@randolph.edu

CAUSEY, Bruce .... 256-306-2569 .... 2 D
bcausey@calhoun.edu

CAUSEY, Joy .... 229-317-6886 .... 128 D
joy.causey@darton.edu

CAUSEY, Katherine .... 901-435-1259 .... 470 D
katherine_causey@loc.edu

CAUSEY, Mary Frances .... 928-350-1112 .... 17 K
mcausey@prescott.edu

CAUWELS, Beth .... 805-565-6101 .... 79 A
bcauwels@westmont.edu

CAVACO, Frank .... 617-964-1100 .... 230 B
fcavaco@ants.edu

CAVALIER, Donald, R .... 218-281-8585 .... 271 E
cavalier@umn.edu

CAVALIER, Philip Acree .... 309-467-6301 .... 151 B
pcavalier@eureka.edu

CAVALIERI, Correne .... 718-779-1430 .... 346 B
ccavalieri@plazacollege.edu

CAVALIERI, Cristina, G .... 215-503-9496 .... 448 C
cristina.cavalieri@jefferson.edu

CAVALIERI, Thomas, A .... 856-566-6996 .... 316 I
cavalita@umdnj.edu

CAVALLARO, Claire .... 657-278-4021 .... 35 B
ccavallaro@fullerton.edu

CAVALLARO, Gregory, M .. 540-464-7328 .... 529 F
gcav@vmiaa.org

CAVALLARO, Vito .... 212-938-5500 .... 355 B
vito@sunyopt.edu

CAVALLI, Mario .... 914-606-6844 .... 360 E
mario.cavalli@sunywcc.edu

CAVALLO, Susana .... 773-508-2760 .... 157 C
scavall@luc.edu

CAVALLUZZI, Marty, R .... 425-640-1557 .... 533 I
marty.cavalluzzi@edcc.edu

CAVALUZZI, Joseph .... 201-689-7639 .... 307 E
jcavaluzzi@bergen.edu

CAVAN, John, J .... 434-949-1003 .... 528 D
john.cavan@southside.edu

CAVANAGH, David .... 802-635-1289 .... 515 F
david.cavanagh@jsc.edu

CAVANAGH, Stephen .... 413-545-5093 .... 236 F
dean@nursing.umass.edu

CAVANAUGH, Amy .... 503-943-7201 .... 420 G
cavanaug@up.edu

CAVANAUGH, Brian .... 716-829-7878 .... 332 E
cavanaub@dyc.edu

CAVANAUGH, SSJ,
Cecelia, J .... 215-753-3623 .... 425 D
ccavanau@chc.edu

CAVANAUGH, Erica .... 701-766-1305 .... 381 A
erica.cavanaugh@littleloop.edu

CAVANAUGH, John, C .... 717-720-4010 .... 441 E
jcavanaugh@passhe.edu

CAVANAUGH, Kyle .... 919-684-2826 .... 364 C
kyle.cavanaugh@duke.edu

CAVANAUGH, Mary Anne . 803-641-3563 .... 462 B
maryanc@usca.edu

CAVANAUGH, Patricia .... 802-451-7588 .... 513 H
pcavanaugh@marlboro.edu

CAVANAUGH, Patrick, D ... 209-946-2345 .... 76 A
pcavanaugh@pacific.edu

CAVAZOS, Cyndi .... 210-434-6711 .... 492 B
cacavazos@lake.ollusa.edu

CAVAZOS, Hector, G .... 956-326-2347 .... 497 D
hectorg.cavazos@tamiu.edu

CAVAZOS, Henry .... 409-772-3004 .... 507 C
hcavazos@utmb.edu

CAVAZOS, Lisa .... 956-364-4050 .... 500 D
lisa.cavazos@tstc.edu

CAVAZOS, Rebecca .... 956-664-4680 .... 494 H
beckyc@southtexascollege.edu

CAVENAUGH, Andy .... 910-296-2480 .... 371 E
acavenaugh@jamessprunt.edu

CAVENDISH, John, M .... 317-573-8984 .... 541 K
jcavendish@salemu.edu

CAVENY, Deanna, M .... 843-953-5527 .... 457 B
cavenys@cofc.edu

CAVIN, JR., Elmo, M .... 806-743-3080 .... 502 B
elmo.cavin@ttuhsc.edu

CAVINS-TULL, Kathryn .... 817-257-7820 .... 499 C
k.cavins@tcu.edu

CAVIS, Mark .... 906-487-7315 .... 251 A
mark.cavis@finlandia.edu

CAVITT, Deborah .... 817-531-4298 .... 502 C
dcavitt@txwes.edu

CAWLEY, Steve .... 305-284-3515 .... 122 I
s.cawley@miami.edu

CAWOOD, J. Scott .... 215-702-4281 .... 444 B
scawood@pbu.edu

CAWTHON, Donald, L .... 254-968-9227 .... 497 A
cawthon@tarleton.edu

CAWTHON, James .... 574-936-8898 .... 169 D
jim.cawthon@ancilla.edu

CAYEA, Cynthia .... 516-364-0808 .... 343 A
library@nycollege.edu

CAYER, Cynthia, B .... 860-832-1741 .... 90 G
cayerc@ccsu.edu

CAYLOR, Deborah, Z .... 540-458-8730 .... 530 D
dcaylor@wlu.edu

CAYWOOD, Janet .... 620-278-4280 .... 196 H
jcaywood@sterling.edu

CAZALET, JR., David, J .... 606-679-8501 .... 203 C
david.cazalet@kctcs.edu

CAZAUBON, Steve .... 504-762-3050 .... 210 F
scazau@dcc.edu

CAZZETTA, Vinnie .... 845-341-4726 .... 345 E
vinnie.cazzetta@sunyorange.edu

CEARLEY, Anna .... 619-684-8791 .... 59 B
acearley@newschoolarch.edu

CEASAR, Ted .... 760-355-6312 .... 51 A
ted.ceasar@imperial.edu

CEBALLOS, Adis .... 213-251-3636 .... 29 J
aceballos@aii.edu

CEBELAK, Jane, P .... 772-462-7544 .... 111 B
jcebelak@irsc.edu

CEBRICK, Daniel, T .... 570-208-5870 .... 432 G
dtcebric@kings.edu

CEBRZYNSKI, Gerard, J .... 847-735-5104 .... 155 G
cebrzynski@lakeforest.edu

CECALA, Diana .... 843-349-5207 .... 458 H
dianna.cecala@hgtc.edu

CECCANECCHIO, Domenic . 215-895-1554 .... 427 H
dc444@drexel.edu

CECCHINI, Bernard .... 315-568-3127 .... 342 H
bcecchini@nycc.edu

CECCHINI, Dan .... 541-383-7700 .... 414 I
dcecchini@cocc.edu

CECERE, Janice .... 973-748-9000 .... 307 H
janice_cecere@bloomfield.edu

CECERO, Diane, M .... 585-292-2108 .... 341 H
dcecero@monroecc.edu

CECH, John .... 406-444-0314 .... 294 H
jcech@montana.edu

CECIL, Amy .... 336-721-2618 .... 376 E
amy.cecil@salem.edu

CECIL, Dale .... 270-686-4239 .... 199 B
dale.cecil@brescia.edu

CECIL, David, J .... 859-233-8239 .... 207 A
financialaid@transy.edu

CECIL, Jackie .... 606-886-3863 .... 201 G
jackie.cecil@kctcs.edu

CECIL, Jamie, N .... 717-867-6228 .... 434 C
cecil@lvc.edu

CECIL, Kristine .... 303-871-2412 .... 89 A
kristine.cecil@du.edu

CECIL, Patrick, A .... 502-895-3411 .... 204 F
pcecil@lpts.edu

CEDAR, Leslie .... 512-471-3800 .... 505 D
cedar@alumni.utexas.edu

CEDEL, Thomas .... 512-313-3000 .... 483 K
thomas.cedel@concordia.edu

CEDENO, Derena .... 717-394-6211 .... 426 C
dcedeno@csb.edu

CEDENO, Derena .... 717-764-9550 .... 426 D
dcedeno@csb.edu

CEDERGREN, Cindy .... 218-683-8611 .... 268 C
cindy.cedergren@northlandcollege.edu

CEDERHOLM, Annette .... 256-840-4142 .... 7 A
acederholm@snead.edu

CEDILLO, Arnulfo .... 415-485-9375 .... 42 B
arnulfo.cedillo@marin.edu

CEDRONE, David, C .... 617-994-6904 .... 236 D
dmcedrone@bhe.mass.edu

CEGLES, Victor .... 562-985-8527 .... 35 C
vcegles@csulb.edu

CEJA, Jared .... 909-652-6561 .... 39 E
jared.ceja@chaffey.edu

CELENTANA, Marc .... 609-771-2247 .... 308 F
mcelent@tcnj.edu

CELHAY, Lilia .... 510-464-3215 .... 62 D
lcelhay@peralta.edu

CELIAN, Doris .... 734-487-0324 .... 250 F
dcelian@emich.edu

CELL, Paul, M .... 973-655-5123 .... 311 F
cellp@mail.montclair.edu

CELLA, Barbara .... 925-439-2181 .... 43 G
bcella@losmedanos.edu

CELLEMME, Patricia .... 518-292-1710 .... 348 A
cellep@sage.edu

CELLEMME, Sharon .... 704-290-5244 .... 374 A
scellemme@spcc.edu

CELLI, David, S .... 570-389-4882 .... 441 F
dcelli@bloomu.edu

CELLI, Lorraine .... 516-299-3134 .... 338 E
lorraine.celli@liu.edu

CELLINI, Roger .... 909-748-8020 .... 76 C
roger_cellini@redlands.edu

CELLINI, Todd .... 912-201-8007 .... 137 D
tcellini@southuniversity.edu

CELTEK, Serkan .... 956-872-5584 .... 494 H
sbceltek@southtexascollege.edu

CEMAN, Jamie .... 920-424-2442 .... 551 E
cemanj@uwosh.edu

CEN, Luozhu .... 530-879-4050 .... 31 H
cenlu@butte.edu

CENCICH, John .... 724-938-4187 .... 441 G
cencich@calu.edu

CENCIUS, Joel, F .... 414-410-4203 .... 546 G
jfcencius@stritch.edu

CENKL, Pavel .... 802-586-7711 .... 514 G
pcenkl@sterlingcollege.edu

CENSER, Jack, R .... 703-993-1253 .... 519 E
jcenser@gmu.edu

CENSOR, Yerachmiel .... 845-356-7064 .... 361 E

CENTENO, Barbara .... 210-458-4037 .... 506 D
barbara.centeno@utsa.edu

CENTER, Mark, R .... 210-434-6711 .... 492 B
mrcenter@lake.ollusa.edu

CENTKO, John .... 218-333-6613 .... 268 D
johnb.centko@ntcmn.edu

CENTOPANTI,
Anthony (Tony) .... 203-857-7131 .... 92 C
acentopant@ncc.commnet.edu

CEO, Nicolette .... 516-678-5000 .... 341 F
nceo@molloy.edu

CEPEDA, Rita .... 408-270-6402 .... 67 B
chancellor.office@sjeccd.org

CEPEDA, Rosaline .... 670-234-5498 .... 560 B
rosalinec@nmcnet.edu

CEPEDA-BENITO, Antonio . 979-845-4274 .... 497 E
acepeda@tamu.edu

CEPEDA-BENITO, Antonio . 802-656-3166 .... 514 H
antonio.cepeda-benito@uvm.edu

CEPPI, Matthew .... 760-750-4040 .... 36 C
mceppi@csusm.edu

CEPPOS, Jerry .... 225-578-9294 .... 212 H
jceppos@lsu.edu

CEPRIANO, Lucia .... 631-420-2003 .... 356 A
lucia.cepriano@farmingdale.edu

CEPULL, Jeff .... 215-951-2516 .... 444 D
cepullj@philau.edu

CERCHIO, Bob .... 573-651-2297 .... 289 K
rcerchio@semo.edu

CERCONE, Charles .... 517-371-5140 .... 258 F
cerconec@cooley.edu

CERDA, Jenny .... 208-426-1156 .... 142 I
jennycerda@boisestate.edu

CERDA, Manuel .... 210-486-4111 .... 479 B
mcerda9@alamo.edu

CERES, Joanne, T .... 252-493-7208 .... 372 H
jceres@email.pittcc.edu

CERES, Sharon .... 252-493-7561 .... 372 H
sceres@email.pittcc.edu

CEREZO, Juan, E .... 718-862-7328 .... 339 H
juan.cerezo@manhattan.edu

CEREZO, Sabrina .... 718-951-5622 .... 326 F
scerezo@brooklyn.cuny.edu

CERILLI, Annette .... 401-232-6323 .... 453 C
acerilli@bryant.edu

CERINO, Michael, H .... 864-488-4564 .... 459 B
mcerino@limestone.edu

CERISE, Fred, P .... 225-578-8886 .... 212 G
fcerise@lsu.edu

CERNECH, John, C .... 402-280-2775 .... 297 F
jcer@creighton.edu

CERNOCH, Jeff .... 281-756-3539 .... 479 F
jcernoch@alvincollege.edu

CERNY, Glenn .... 734-462-4400 .... 258 A
gcerny@schoolcraft.edu

CERNY, Kirk, R .... 765-494-0764 .... 178 J
kcerny@purdue.edu

CERONE, Daniel, P .... 336-272-7102 .... 364 G
dcetrone@greensboro.edu

CERTA, Len .... 914-923-2847 .... 345 F
lcerta@pace.edu

CERVANTES, Augustin .... 408-273-2751 .... 58 G
acervantes@nhu.edu

CERVANTES, Cecillia Y, M 763-488-2414 .... 266 D
cecillia.cervantes@hennepintech.edu

CERVANTES, Javier .... 773-508-3335 .... 157 C
jcervantes@luc.edu

CERVANTES, Juana .... 915-779-8031 .... 483 J
jcervantes@computercareercenter.com

CERVANTES, Margaret .... 432-264-5009 .... 488 B
mcervantes@howardcollege.edu

CERVANTES, Mike .... 361-592-9335 .... 498 D
mike.cervantes@tamuk.edu

CERVANTES, Philip .... 972-438-6932 .... 492 E
pcervantes@parkercc.edu

CERVANTES, Richard .... 575-835-5675 .... 319 A
rcervantes@admin.nmt.edu

CERVASIO, Nancy .... 480-557-2100 .... 19 A
nancy.cervasio@phoenix.edu

CERVELLI, Janice, A .... 520-621-6751 .... 18 L
jcervell@email.arizona.edu

CERVENY, Alan .... 402-472-9531 .... 300 G
acerveny2@unl.edu

CERVENY, Mike, J .... 319-895-4357 .... 183 G
mcerveny@cornellcollege.edu

CERVENY, Terri .... 518-262-8043 .... 322 D
cervent@mail.amc.edu

CERVINI, John .... 517-607-2670 .... 252 C
john.cervini@hillsdale.edu

CERVONE, Frank .... 219-989-8185 .... 178 K
fcervone@purduecal.edu

CERVONKA, Daniel .... 203-576-2399 .... 94 F
cervonka@bridgeport.edu

CERZA, Donna .... 570-208-5868 .... 432 G
donnacerza@kings.edu

CESAR, Welson .... 318-487-7157 .... 209 F
cesar@lacollege.edu

CESARANO, Betty .... 505-473-6117 .... 320 F
betty.cesarano@santafeuniversity.edu

CESAREO, Francesco, C .... 508-767-7321 .... 230 D
fcesareo@assumption.edu

CESARIO, David, R .... 617-287-6200 .... 236 G
david.cesario@umb.edu

CESCA, Michele .... 657-278-4869 .... 35 B
mcesca@fullerton.edu

CESCO-CANCIAN, Fulvio .... 732-255-0400 .... 312 D
fcesco-cancian@ocean.edu

CESMEBASI, Erol .... 201-216-5576 .... 315 E
ecesmeba@stevens.edu

CESPEDES, Germán .... 787-751-0160 .... 561 H
gcespedes@cmpr.pr.gov

CESSNA, Tammy .... 859-858-2306 .... 198 D

CESTERO, Nicolle, M .... 413-205-3800 .... 229 G
nicolle.cestero@aic.edu

CESTERO, Vilmaris .... 787-600-4427 .... 568 C
vilmaris.cestero@upr.edu

CETIN, Matt .... 814-866-8132 .... 433 C
mcettin@lecom.edu

CETINKAYA, Coskun .... 832-230-5555 .... 491 D

CEVALLOS, F. Javier .... 610-683-4102 .... 443 A
cevallos@kutztown.edu

CEZAR, Henrique .... 802-635-1297 .... 515 F
henrique.cezar@jsc.edu

CHA, Jason .... 805-565-6132 .... 79 A
jacha@westmont.edu

CHAAPEL, Barbara, A .... 609-497-7760 .... 312 F
comm-pub@ptsem.edu

CHABALA, William, S .... 570-662-4695 .... 443 C
wchabala@mansfield.edu

CHABOT, Lisabeth .... 607-274-3182 .... 336 G
lchabot@ithaca.edu

CHABOTAR, Kent, J .... 336-316-2146 .... 365 A
chabotar@guilford.edu

CHACKO, Abraham .... 408-541-0100 .... 41 E
achacko@cogswell.edu

CHACONA, Julie, A .... 814-732-1779 .... 442 E
jchacona@edinboro.edu

CHACONIS, Alexis .... 718-260-5250 .... 328 D
achaconis@citytech.cuny.edu

CHADDOCK, Diane .... 269-782-1276 .... 258 C
dchaddock@swmich.edu

CHADEN, Caryn .... 312-362-8885 .... 149 A
cchaden@depaul.edu

CHADWELL, Faye .... 541-737-3411 .... 418 F
faye.chadwell@oregonstate.edu

CHADWICK, Becky, J .... 313-317-1534 .... 252 B
bchadwick@hfcc.edu

CHADWICK, D. Gregory .... 252-737-7030 .... 377 E
chadwickg@ecu.edu

CHADWICK, Jennifer .... 706-867-2885 .... 134 G
jchadwick@northgeorgia.edu

CHADWICK, Matthew .... 757-352-4826 .... 523 E
mchadwick@regent.edu

CHADWICK, Scott .... 513-745-3838 .... 406 E
chadwicks@xavier.edu

CHAFEE, Julie .... 508-929-8770 .... 238 G
jchaffee1@worcester.edu

CHAFFEE, Alecia .... 417-626-1234 .... 287 C
chaffee.alecia@occ.edu

CHAFFEE, Cynthia .... 312-567-3084 .... 153 C
cchaffee@iit.edu

CHAFFEE, Reta .... 603-513-1350 .... 306 F
reta.chaffee@granite.edu

CHAFFIN, Debbie .... 256-765-4297 .... 9 C
dkchaffin@una.edu

CHAFFIN, Jacquline .... 973-761-9354 .... 315 B
jacquline.chaffin@shu.edu

CHAFIN, Kristal, L .... 260-359-4290 .... 173 A
kchafin@huntington.edu

CHAFIN-EVANS, Karen, S . 606-218-5606 .... 207 F
karenevans@upike.edu

CHAGNON-BURKE,
Veronique .... 212-355-1501 .... 326 A

CHAH, Namyoung .... 323-731-2383 .... 60 H
nchah@psuca.edu

CHAHIN, T. Jaime .... 512-245-3333 .... 501 F
tc03@txstate.edu

CHAI, Lin .... 407-888-8689 .... 108 B
lchai@fcim.edu

CHAIREZ, Gladys .... 575-527-7664 .... 319 G
gchairez@nmsu.edu

CHAIRSELL, Christine .... 971-722-4005 .... 419 G
christine.chairsell@pcc.edu

CHAISSON, Breck .... 985-858-5805 .... 210 G
breck.chaisson@fletcher.edu

CHAITOVSKY, Myron, B .... 718-780-7906 .... 324 F
myron.chaitovsky@brooklaw.edu

CHAKRABORTY, Dave .... 805-437-8496 .... 34 B
dave.chakraborty@csuci.edu

CHAKRIN, Lewis .... 201-684-7377 .... 313 C
lchakrin@ramapo.edu

CHALEUNPHONH, Seuth .. 812-941-2319 .... 175 A
schaleun@ius.edu

CHALFIN, Marc, J .... 201-559-6034 .... 310 B
chalfinm@felician.edu

CHALFIN, Susan, M .... 201-559-3564 .... 310 B
chalfins@felician.edu

CHALFONTE, Barb .... 413-755-4465 .... 241 B
blchalfonte@stcc.edu

CHALK, Gregg .... 508-541-1668 .... 233 G
gchalk@dean.edu

CHALK, Rebecca .... 410-276-0306 .... 226 D
rchalk@host.sdc.edu

CHALKER, Grace .... 330-823-2674 .... 404 C
chalkegb@mountunion.edu

CHALKER, Peggy .... 937-695-0751 .... 402 A
pchalker@sscc.edu

CHALLENGER, Susan .... 781-283-2335 .... 245 E
schallen@wellesley.edu

CHALLIS, Don .... 201-291-1111 .... 307 F
edc@berkeleycollege.edu

CHAPMAN, Robyn, F 828-327-7000 369 B
rchapman@cvcc.edu

CHAPMAN, Ronald, K 801-422-8157 509 H
ronald_chapman@byu.edu

CHAPMAN, Sharon, H 803-938-3810 462 G
hamptons@uscsumter.edu

CHAPMAN, Susan, E 508-929-8034 238 G
schapman@worcester.edu

CHAPMAN, Tim 503-253-3443 417 H
tchapman@ocom.edu

CHAPMAN, Warren 312-369-7390 148 D
wchapman@colum.edu

CHAPP, Belena 215-568-4515 436 H
bchapp@moore.edu

CHAPPELL, Cindy 619-849-2531 62 L
cindychappell@pointloma.edu

CHAPPELL, David 910-362-7073 368 H
dchappell@cfcc.edu

CHAPPELL, Dorothy, F 630-752-5627 168 H
dorothy.chappell@wheaton.edu

CHAPPELL, Jean, M 304-710-3141 542 K
jean.chappell@mctc.edu

CHAPPELL, Julie 540-887-7225 521 C
jchappel@mbc.edu

CHAPPELL, Marilyn, J 818-779-8047 53 B
mchappell@kingsuniversity.edu

CHAPPELL, Paul, G 818-779-8259 53 B
pchappell@kingsuniversity.edu

CHAPPELL-WILLIAMS,
Lynette 607-255-3976 331 B
lc75@cornell.edu

CHAPUT, JR., Maury, L 410-777-2324 221 C
mlchaput@aacc.edu

CHARD, David, J 214-768-5465 495 A
dchard@smu.edu

CHARDKOFF, Richard, B 318-342-1540 216 E
chardkoff@ulm.edu

CHARETTE, Reno 406-657-2011 295 D
rcharette@msubillings.edu

CHARGIN, Jan 408-848-4724 48 C
jbchargin@gavilan.edu

CHARLAP, Wendy 732-729-3752 309 C
wcharlap@devry.edu

CHARLES, Curtis 910-672-2247 377 G
ccharles@uncfsu.ed

CHARLES, Cynthia 504-816-4263 209 A
ccharles@dillard.edu

CHARLES, Harvey 928-523-1308 16 I
harvey.charles@nau.edu

CHARLES, Jeffrey, R 408-554-4607 68 C
jcharles@scu.edu

CHARLES, Joanne 740-351-3560 401 I
jcharles@shawnee.edu

CHARLES, Kerry 706-771-4146 125 H
kcharles@augustatech.edu

CHARLES, Kevin, E 603-862-1098 306 C
kevin.charles@unh.edu

CHARLES, Kristin 415-239-3677 40 C
kcharles@ccsf.edu

CHARLES, Olivier 205-652-3579 9 E
ocharles@uwa.edu

CHARLESTON, Kathleen 217-353-2024 161 C
kcharleston@parkland.edu

CHARLIER, Hara 276-739-2429 529 A
hcharlier@vhcc.edu

CHARLSON, Elaine, M 713-743-9103 503 C
echarlson@uh.edu

CHARLSON, Elaine, M 713-743-9103 503 D
echarlson@uh.edu

CHARLTON, John 202-685-4242 557 I
charltonj@ndu.edu

CHARLTON, Patricia, A 702-651-5667 302 E
patty.charlton@csn.edu

CHARMOLI, Audrey 231-876-3100 248 A
audrey.charmoli@baker.edu

CHARNECO,
Maria del Pilar 787-766-1717 565 I
um_mcharneco@suagm.edu

CHARNEY, Dennis, S 212-241-5674 342 B

CHARNEY, Len 617-262-5000 231 G
len.charney@the-bac.edu

CHARNOW, Rebecca 212-749-2802 339 I
rcharnow@msmnyc.edu

CHAROENSIRI, Kanitta 540-231-5313 529 G
charkx@vt.edu

CHARON, Joseph 413-662-5284 238 C
joseph.charon@mcla.edu

CHARPENTIER, Heather 518-743-2342 355 D
charpentierh@sunyacc.edu

CHARPENTIER, Jennifer 262-564-2866 554 B
charpentierj@gtc.edu

CHARRIEZ, Ivette 787-878-6000 562 G
icharriez@icprjc.edu

CHARRIEZ, Mayra 787-764-0000 568 B
mayra.charriez@upr.edu

CHARRON, Michael 507-457-1606 271 B
mcharron@smumn.edu

CHARTER, Caryn 734-487-3090 250 F
ccharter@emich.edu

CHARTIER, Lark 337-482-6243 216 D
lark@louisiana.edu

CHARTON, Jacques 415-485-3227 45 C
charton@dominican.edu

CHARUHAS, Mary, S 847-543-2402 148 B
mcharuhas@clcillinois.edu

CHARVILLE, Mark, R 419-372-0638 385 F
markrc@bgsu.edu

CHASE, Anne 859-985-3266 199 A
anne_chase@berea.edu

CHASE, Brian 818-710-4439 55 B
chaseb@piercecollege.edu

CHASE, Bruce, W 540-831-5278 523 A
bchase@radford.edu

CHASE, Cheryl 641-269-3450 185 D
chaseche@grinnell.edu

CHASE, David 203-857-7058 92 C
dchase@ncc.commnet.edu

CHASE, David, D 509-527-4261 539 B
david.chase@wwcc.edu

CHASE, David, T 973-267-9404 313 B

CHASE, Diane 407-823-6197 120 B
diane.chase@ucf.edu

CHASE, Dina 626-585-7878 61 F
dmchase@pasadena.edu

CHASE, Geoffrey, W 619-594-2873 37 A
gchase@mail.sdsu.edu

CHASE, Gregory, M 336-734-7246 370 F
gchase@forsythtech.edu

CHASE, Horace, W 731-425-2610 475 C
hchase@jscc.edu

CHASE, John 323-663-2167 76 B

CHASE, Marilyn, O 317-788-2192 180 F
chase@uindy.edu

CHASE, Mary, E 402-280-2162 297 F
marychase@creighton.edu

CHASE, Mary Jane 801-832-2301 512 G
mjchase@westminstercollege.edu

CHASE, MaryEtta 801-957-4799 512 D
maryetta.chase@slcc.edu

CHASE, Michael 602-749-4539 13 K
mchase@devry.edu

CHASE, Michael, K 423-775-7327 467 F
mchase5606@bryan.edu

CHASE, Michelle 715-682-1811 549 F
mchase@northland.edu

CHASE, Patricia, A 304-293-5101 545 A
pachase@hsc.wvu.edu

CHASE, Ryan 480-517-8314 16 B
ryan.chase@riosalado.edu

CHASE PADULA, Allison 401-254-3793 454 C
achasepadula@rwu.edu

CHASIS, Jocelyn 410-455-3636 227 D
jocelyn_chasis@umbc.edu

CHASON, Foster 423-585-2681 476 D
foster.chason@ws.edu

CHASTAIN, Andrea, J 913-288-7270 194 C
chastain@kckcc.edu

CHASTAIN, Clint 678-359-5733 132 A
clintc@gdn.edu

CHASTAIN, Lesa, M 417-268-6091 278 J
ir@gobbc.edu

CHASTAIN, Lisa 478-934-3082 134 B
lchastain@mgc.edu

CHASTAIN, Stephanie, M 724-983-2846 440 E
smm45@psu.edu

CHASTAIN, Wes 828-837-6810 374 F
wchastain@tricountycc.edu

CHASTANT, Jane 713-623-2040 480 J
jchastant@aii.edu

CHASTEEN, Michael, D 864-833-8477 460 E
mchasteen@presby.edu

CHASZAR, Mark 432-837-8189 501 E
mchaszar@sulross.edu

CHATAS, Geoffrey 614-292-9232 398 I
chatas.1@osu.edu

CHATELAIN, Rose, D 504-568-4802 213 A
rtowns@lsuhsc.edu

CHATFIELD, Brenda, L 785-890-3641 195 H
bchatfield@nwktc.edu

CHATHAM, April 214-692-8080 480 I
achatham@aii.edu

CHATHAM, David, W 864-833-8299 460 E
dchatham@presby.edu

CHATMAN, Cheryl, T 651-603-6151 263 A
chatman@csp.edu

CHATMAN, Jesse 901-435-1470 470 D
jesse_chatman@loc.edu

CHATMAN, Robert 803-536-7200 460 G
zs_rchatman@scsu.edu

CHATMAN, Stephanie 601-979-2100 274 G
stephanie.i.chatman@jsums.edu

CHATMON, Angelo, V 804-257-5856 530 A
achatmon@vuu.edu

CHATTERJEE, Achala 909-384-8904 65 C
achatterjee@sbccd.cc.ca.us

CHATTERJEE-SUTTON,
Eva 802-440-4330 513 A
ecs@bennington.edu

CHATTERTON, Jim 603-623-0313 305 E
jimchatterton@nhia.edu

CHATTERTON, Marina 415-749-4587 65 I
mchatterton@sfai.edu

CHATTERTON, Stephen, A 208-282-2515 143 H
chatstep@isu.edu

CHATTIN, Duane, H 812-888-4164 181 D
dchattin@vinu.edu

CHATY, Karen 707-468-3065 57 A
kchaty@mendocino.edu

CHAUHDRI, Aamer 502-456-6509 206 G
achauhdri@sctd.edu

CHAUNCEY, Linda 206-934-4386 537 E
linda.chauncey@seattlecolleges.edu

CHAURET, Christian 765-455-9371 174 A
cchauret@iuk.edu

CHAUVIN, Marc 985-732-6640 211 A

CHAVARIA, Fred 415-239-3174 40 C
fchavari@ccsf.edu

CHAVES, William 509-359-2347 533 H
wchaves@ewu.edu

CHAVEZ, April 575-769-4061 318 A
april.chavez@clovis.edu

CHAVEZ, Chris 404-270-2718 128 I
cchavez2@devry.edu

CHAVEZ, Connie 575-461-4413 318 G
conniec@mesalands.edu

CHAVEZ, Conrad, L 970-247-7464 84 K
chavez_c@fortlewis.edu

CHAVEZ, Dennis, J 607-777-2428 351 F
dchavez@binghamton.edu

CHAVEZ, Ernest 505-224-4639 317 K
emchavez@cnm.edu

CHAVEZ, Gloriann 909-384-8665 65 C
gchavez@sbccd.cc.ca.us

CHAVEZ, Gloriann 909-389-3248 65 B
gchavez@sbccd.cc.ca.us

CHAVEZ, Guadalupe 956-872-3499 494 H
gchavez@southtexascollege.edu

CHAVEZ, Israel 563-588-8000 184 I
ichavez@emmaus.edu

CHAVEZ, Lisa, M 323-343-3500 35 D
lchavez@cslanet.calstatela.edu

CHAVEZ, Mario, J 308-635-6186 301 D
chavezm@wncc.edu

CHAVEZ, Mary 719-549-3280 87 F
mary.chavez@pueblocc.edu

CHAVEZ, Michael 661-654-3181 34 A
mchavez14@csub.edu

CHAVEZ, Michael 432-685-4507 491 A
mchavez@midland.edu

CHAVEZ, Miguel 330-490-7341 405 F
mchavez@walsh.edu

CHAVEZ, Olga 915-831-3322 486 G
ochave30@epcc.edu

CHAVEZ, Orquedia 916-649-2400 31 F

CHAVEZ, Ruby 214-459-2230 480 G
rvchavez@gmail.com

CHAVIANO-MORAN,
Rosa, M 973-972-1103 316 D
chaviaro@umdnj.edu

CHAVIRA, Jessica 325-235-7342 500 G
jessica.chavira@tstc.edu

CHAVIRA, Rejoice 909-389-3456 65 B
rchavira@craftonhills.edu

CHAVIS, Donna 843-921-6907 460 B
dchavis@netc.edu

CHAVIS, Gordon 407-823-3004 120 B
gordon.chavis@ucf.edu

CHAVIS, Kimberly 773-602-5501 147 E
kboyd@ccc.edu

CHAVIS, Linda 317-789-8264 171 A
lchavis@crossroads.edu

CHAVIS, Tim 248-204-3700 254 B
tchavis@ltu.edu

CHAVOUS, Warren 803-584-3446 462 E
chavousg@mailbox.sc.edu

CHAWKIN, Ken 641-472-4037 187 E
kchawkin@mum.edu

CHAYA, Ramon, C 585-345-6999 334 F
rcchaya@genesee.edu

CHEAGLE, Dorothy, S 803-934-3227 459 G
dcheagle@morris.edu

CHEAL, Catheryn, L 248-370-4566 256 G
cheal@oakland.edu

CHEATEM, Michelle 410-617-5171 223 I
micheatem@loyola.edu

CHEATHAM, Frank 270-789-5231 199 F
fdcheatham@campbellsville.edu

CHEATHAM, George 703-284-1560 521 D
george.cheatham@marymount.edu

CHEATHAM, Kathy 205-329-7853 3 A
kathy.cheatham@ecacolleges.com

CHEBATOR, Paul, J 617-552-3470 232 B
paul.chebator@bc.edu

CHECCHIO, Debbie 276-326-4243 516 L
dchecchio@bluefield.edu

CHECCI, Peg 802-793-0728 514 B
peg.checci@neci.edu

CHECCIO, Albert, R 213-740-2211 76 F
checcio@usc.edu

CHECHOWICH, Faye 765-998-4571 180 B
fychechow@taylor.edu

CHECK, Andrea, G 260-422-5561 173 C
agcheck@indianatech.edu

CHECKETTS, Max, L 808-675-3455 140 D
checkettsm@byuh.edu

CHECKOVICH, Irene, C 508-531-1231 237 D
icheckovich@bridgew.edu

CHECKOVICH, Peter, G 304-260-4380 542 G
pcheckov@blueridgectc.edu

CHECOV, Elissa 770-962-7580 132 D
echecov@gwinnetttech.edu

CHEE, Kathleen 808-544-0292 140 G
kchee@hpu.edu

CHEEK, Claude 516-299-3780 338 E
claude.cheek@liu.edu

CHEEK, Claude 516-299-3780 338 G
claude.cheek@liu.edu

CHEEK, Debbie, Q 843-921-6945 460 B
dcheek@netc.edu

CHEEK, Jimmy, G 865-974-3265 477 D
chancellor@utk.edu

CHEEK, JR., Lee 678-717-3688 129 G
lcheek@gsc.edu

CHEEK, Sherrie 662-472-2312 274 D
scheek@holmescc.edu

CHEEKS, Roger 757-352-4486 523 E
rogeche@regent.edu

CHEERS, Karen, T 276-739-2490 529 A
kcheers@vhcc.edu

CHEESEBRO, Dorothy 336-770-3321 379 E
cheesebrod@uncsa.edu

CHEESEMAN, Valerie 757-822-1994 528 G
vcheeseman@tcc.edu

CHEETHAM, William, C 315-445-4400 338 B
cheethwc@lemoyne.edu

CHEKWA, Emmanuel 205-929-1459 5 H
echekwa@miles.edu

CHELBERG, Gene 415-405-3728 37 B
chelberg@sfsu.edu

CHELETTE, Newton 661-722-6300 28 K
nchelette@avc.edu

CHELINE, OSB, Paschal 503-845-3269 417 A
paschal.cheline@mtangel.edu

CHELLMAN, Laura, G 715-836-5954 551 A
chellmlg@uwec.edu

CHELNICK, Robert 773-975-1295 549 A
krisbob1@cs.com

CHELNICK, Robert 773-975-1295 158 E
krisbob1@cs.com

CHELSEN, Paul, O 630-752-5026 168 H
paul.chelsen@wheaton.edu

CHEMA, Thomas, V 330-569-5120 391 G
chematv@hiram.edu

CHEMERINSKY, Erwin 949-824-7722 74 B
echemerinsky@law.uci.edu

CHEMSAK, Stephen 212-343-1234 341 B
schemsak@mcny.edu

CHEN, Bill 626-571-8811 77 A
billchen@uwest.edu

CHEN, Chau-Kuang 615-327-6848 471 C
ckchen@mmc.edu

CHEN, Chunju 262-472-1276 553 A
chenc@uww.edu

CHEN, Daxing (Michael) 210-431-5009 493 F
mchen@stmarytx.edu

CHEN, Desiree 630-617-3033 150 H
chend@elmhurst.edu

CHEN, Ekron 626-571-5110 54 C
ekron@les.edu

CHEN, Hui-Ling 603-222-4203 305 G
hchen@anselm.edu

CHEN, Jack 516-877-3334 322 A
jchen@adelphi.edu

CHEN, Jane 212-472-1500 343 G
jchen@nysid.edu

CHEN, Jie 208-885-6244 144 G
jiechen@uidaho.edu

CHEN, Julie 978-934-2226 237 B
julie_chen@uml.edu

CHEN, Karen 323-731-2383 60 H
esl@psuca.edu

CHEN, Liana 408-260-0208 47 D
accounting@fivebranches.edu

CHEN, Mary M, Y 302-454-3968 96 F
mchen@dtcc.edu

CHEN, May, K 510-981-2820 62 B
mchen@peralta.edu

CHEN, Megan 909-594-5611 58 A
mchen@mtsac.edu

CHEN, Nellie 212-349-4330 334 G
nchen@globe.edu

CHEN, Sheying 212-346-1555 345 F
schen@pace.edu

CHEN, Steve 518-629-7311 336 C
s.chen@hvcc.edu

CHEN, Tracy 617-327-6777 241 F
tracy_chen@mspp.edu

CHEN, Tsuey-Hwa 612-977-5732 261 F
tsuey-hwa.chen@capella.edu

CHEN, Wen-Hsin 617-989-4029 245 F
chenw@wit.edu

CHEN, Xiangming 860-297-5170 94 E
xiangming.chen@trincoll.edu

CHEN, Xueying 334-291-4979 2 F
xueying.chen@cv.edu

CHEN, Yanping 703-516-0035 525 C
yanping.chen@umtweb.edu

CHEN, Yemeng 516-739-1545 343 C
president@nyctcm.edu

CHEN, Yong-Zhuo 814-362-7633 449 B
yong@pitt.edu

CHEN-ORTEGA, Cathy 303-546-3517 86 H
cchenortega@naropa.edu

CHENAIL, Ronald 954-262-5389 114 B
ron@nsu.nova.edu

CHENAULT, Shirley .... 817-598-6337.... 508 F
chenault@wc.edu
CHENAULT, Venida .... 785-830-2770.... 193 D
venida.chenault@bie.edu
CHENCO, William .... 610-917-1430.... 450 E
bachenco@vfcc.edu
CHENETTE, Jonathan .... 845-437-5300.... 359 F
jochenette@vassar.edu
CHENEVERT, Peter, S .... 207-859-5530.... 217 G
pschenev@colby.edu
CHENEVERT, Renee .... 727-873-4475.... 121 C
rcheneve@mail.usf.edu
CHENEY, Christine .... 775-784-4345.... 303 A
cheney@unr.edu
CHENEY, John .... 413-542-2331.... 230 A
jycheney@amherst.edu
CHENEY, Susan .... 630-888-3500.... 161 G
susan.cheney@rasmussen.edu
CHENEY, Victor .... 904-819-6213.... 107 C
vcheney@flagler.edu
CHENG, Alex .... 662-915-7407.... 277 D
acheng@olemiss.edu
CHENG, Rita .... 618-453-2341.... 165 B
rcheng@siu.edu
CHENG, Stephen Z, D .... 330-972-7500.... 403 B
cheng@uakron.edu
CHENG, Wayne .... 714-533-1495...... 70 B
waynecheng@southbaylo.edu
CHENG, Yan .... 954-763-9840.... 101 G
dean@atom.edu
CHENGER, Geoffrey, L .... 304-788-6970.... 545 B
glchenger@mail.wvu.edu
CHENIER, Spencer .... 202-806-5857...... 98 E
schenier@howard.edu
CHENOWETH, Candace, A . 262-472-1592.... 553 A
chenowec@uww.edu
CHENOWETH, Gregg .... 815-939-5213.... 161 A
gchenowe@olivet.edu
CHENOWETH, Kevin .... 740-699-2335.... 400 B
chenowet@ohio.edu
CHERAGHI, S. Hossein ..... 413-782-1272.... 246 A
cheraghi@wne.edu
CHERECK, Deborah, T .... 541-346-6005.... 419 B
dchereck@uoregon.edu
CHEREWICK, Daniel, P ...... 248-341-2011.... 256 F
dpchere@oaklandcc.edu
CHERI, Ferd .... 217-228-5432.... 161 F
cherife@quincy.edu
CHERIYAN, Ajith .... 631-370-3300.... 350 D
acheriyan@sbmelville.edu
CHERMAK, Jerry .... 954-262-4419.... 114 B
chermack@nsu.nova.eduu
CHERMONTE, Debra, J .... 440-775-8411.... 397 G
debra.chermonte@oberlin.edu
CHERN, James .... 973-746-2323.... 311 F
chernj@mail.montclair.edu
CHERNAK, Robert, A .... 202-994-7210...... 98 C
rac@gwu.edu
CHERNOW, Barbara .... 631-632-6340.... 352 C
barbara.chernow@stonybrook.edu
CHERREY, Cynthia .... 609-258-3000.... 312 G
CHERREY, Cynthia .... 504-865-5180.... 215 C
ccherrey@tulane.edu
CHERRIN, Bruce, E .... 505-277-1740.... 321 C
cherrin@unm.edu
CHERRINGTON, R. Brent ... 801-524-8190.... 510 E
rb-cherrington@ldsbc.edu
CHERRY, Brian .... 906-227-1823.... 256 C
bcherry@nmu.edu
CHERRY, Charles, D .... 252-335-3593.... 377 F
cdcherry@mail.ecsu.edu
CHERRY, Christal, M .... 404-527-7718.... 132 G
ccherry@itc.edu
CHERRY, Christopher, R .... 715-394-8580.... 552 F
rcherry@uwsuper.edu
CHERRY, Evonne .... 254-647-3234.... 492 G
echerry@rangercollege.edu
CHERRY, Jewel, B .... 336-734-7297.... 370 F
jcherry@forsythtech.edu
CHERRY, Mark .... 321-433-7031.... 102 D
cherrym@brevardcc.edu
CHERRY, Michelle .... 305-809-3237.... 108 I
michelle.cherry@fkcc.edu
CHERRY, Stephanie .... 319-296-2320.... 185 F
stephanie.cherry@hawkeyecollege.edu
CHERUBIN, Daniel .... 212-772-4161.... 327 E
dcherubi@hunter.cuny.edu
CHERUBINI, Angela .... 914-395-2567.... 350 C
acherubini@sarahlawrence.edu
CHERUBINO, Thomas .... 908-709-7546.... 316 B
cherubino@ucc.edu
CHESBROUGH, Ronald ...... 636-922-8380.... 288 B
rchesbrough@stchas.edu
CHESLEY, Laurie .... 616-234-4230.... 251 E
lchesley@grcc.edu
CHESNEY, Alan, P .... 410-778-7706.... 229 D
achesney2@washcoll.edu
CHESNEY, Linda, H .... 718-262-5119.... 329 A
chesney@york.cuny.edu
CHESNEY, Scott .... 603-862-1870.... 306 C
scott.chesney@unh.edu
CHESNEY, Thom, D .... 972-860-4809.... 484 G
CHESNUT, Robert, W .... 217-581-2125.... 150 E
rwchesnut@eiu.edu
CHESSER, Jerald .... 909-941-9158...... 33 J
jwchesser@csupomona.edu
CHESSER, Ron .... 501-760-4230...... 22 F
rchesser@npcc.edu
CHESSER, Trace .... 502-459-3535.... 206 H
tchesser@sullivan.edu
CHESSON, JR., Andrew, L 318-675-5000.... 213 B
achess@lsuhsc.edu
CHESTER, Ann, M .... 304-293-1651.... 545 A
achester@hsc.wvu.edu
CHESTER, Brandi .... 870-248-4000...... 21 A
brandic@blackrivertech.edu
CHESTER, Cathie, L .... 607-871-2300.... 322 E
fchester@alfred.edu
CHESTER, Claudia .... 925-969-3108...... 52 C
cchester@jfku.edu
CHESTER, Steven .... 860-343-5864...... 91 G
schester@mxcc.commnet.edu
CHESTER, Timothy, M .... 706-542-3145.... 138 G
tchester@uga.edu
CHESTERFIELD,
Alverne, W .... 410-651-6253.... 227 E
awchesterfield@umes.edu
CHESTERFIELD, Gail .... 765-289-2291.... 176 B
gchester@ivytech.edu
CHESTERMAN, Gregg .... 760-366-5294...... 43 H
gchesterman@cmccd.edu
CHESTNUT, Jacki, L .... 612-874-3729.... 265 C
jacki_chestnut@mcad.edu
CHEUNG, Alvin .... 916-631-8108...... 33 F
CHEUNG, Enos .... 718-939-5100.... 338 D
echeung@libi.edu
CHEUNG, Lillian .... 651-631-0204.... 260 H
lcheung@aaaom.edu
CHEVALIER,
Jim Langstraat .... 971-722-2913.... 419 G
jim.langstraat@pcc.edu
CHEVALIER, JR., Joseph .. 404-756-5773.... 134 E
jchevalier@msm.edu
CHEVES, Brad, E .... 214-768-2667.... 495 A
bcheves@smu.edu
CHEW, Catherine .... 252-638-7200.... 370 A
chewc@cravencc.edu
CHEW, Dan .... 925-288-5800...... 49 H
dan_chew@heald.edu
CHEW, Kenneth .... 812-237-3939.... 173 B
kenneth.chew@indstate.edu
CHEYDLEUR, James .... 714-459-1139...... 78 H
jcheydleur@wsulaw.edu
CHEZUM, Kelly, O .... 315-268-4483.... 329 B
chezumk@clarkson.edu
CHI, Selina .... 323-265-8154...... 54 G
chiss@elac.edu
CHIA, Samuel .... 214-841-3956.... 485 F
schia@dts.edu
CHIABOTTI, Stephen, D ..... 334-953-5155.... 558 C
stephen.chiabotti@maxwell.af.mil
CHIACCHIERINI, Chris ...... 503-253-3443.... 417 H
cc@ocom.edu
CHIAL, Sally .... 612-977-5299.... 261 F
sally.chial@capella.edu
CHIANG, Amber .... 661-395-4251...... 52 L
amchiang@bakersfieldcollege.edu
CHIAPPETTA, Anthony .... 202-319-5623...... 97 E
chiappetta@cua.edu
CHIAPPINI, Thomas, A ...... 330-494-6170.... 402 B
tchiappini@starkstate.edu
CHIARA, Mary Jo, B .... 718-940-5574.... 349 A
mchiara@sjcny.edu
CHIARAMONTE, Susan ...... 877-248-6724...... 14 I
schiaramonte@hmu.edu
CHIARAVALLE, Paul .... 312-369-7363.... 148 D
pchiaravalle@colum.edu
CHICHESTER, Susan, E ...... 585-245-5577.... 353 C
sue@geneseo.edu
CHICKERING, F. William .... 609-896-5111.... 313 F
wchickering@rider.edu
CHICKONOSKI, Andrea ..... 734-487-2360.... 250 F
achicko1@emich.edu
CHICOINE, David, L .... 605-688-4111.... 466 C
david.chicoine@sdstate.edu
CHIELLI, Jack, A .... 570-408-4770.... 452 A
jack.chielli@wilkes.edu
CHIEVES, Kevin .... 912-443-5491.... 136 H
kchieves@savannahtech.edu
CHIGAWA, Steven .... 808-235-7457.... 142 F
chigawa@hawaii.edu
CHIGOGIDZE, Alex .... 718-982-2430.... 327 A
alex.chigogidze@csi.cuny.edu
CHIGOS, Lisa .... 619-961-4326...... 72 J
lchigos@tjsl.edu
CHIGWEDERE, Shingai ...... 972-929-9390.... 486 D
schigwedere@devry.edu
CHIH, Lo-Li .... 808-974-7595.... 141 F
loli@hawaii.edu
CHIKUNI, Ticha .... 859-336-5082.... 206 A
tichachikuni@sccky.edu
CHIKWEM, John, O .... 484-365-8253.... 434 H
jchikwem@lincoln.edu
CHIKWINYA, Mary .... 253-566-5127.... 538 F
mchikwinya@tacomacc.edu
CHILCOTE, Paul .... 419-289-5771.... 384 G
pchilcot@ashland.edu
CHILD, Elizabeth .... 202-884-9238...... 99 H
childe@trinitydc.edu
CHILDERS, Amber .... 501-337-5000...... 21 D
amber@coto.edu
CHILDERS, Camille .... 316-978-3620.... 198 A
camille.childers@wichita.edu
CHILDERS, Joseph .... 951-827-4302.... 74 E
joseph.childers@ucr.edu
CHILDERS, Karen .... 909-389-3392...... 65 B
kchilder@craftonhills.edu
CHILDERS, Steven, L .... 407-366-9493.... 115 K
schilders@rts.edu
CHILDRESS, Bates .... 802-773-5900.... 513 D
bates.childress@csj.edu
CHILDRESS, Herb .... 617-262-5000.... 231 G
herb.childress@the-bac.edu
CHILDRESS, Jamie .... 919-718-7336.... 369 C
jchildress@cccc.edu
CHILDRESS, Jamie, P .... 336-386-3279.... 374 E
childressj@surry.edu
CHILDRESS, John .... 615-322-2631.... 478 A
john.childress@vanderbilt.edu
CHILDRESS, Layton .... 417-447-8102.... 287 D
childrel@otc.edu
CHILDRESS, Thomas, C .... 704-637-4394.... 363 E
tchildre@catawba.edu
CHILDREY, Cynthia, A .... 928-523-5021...... 16 I
cynthia.childrey@nau.edu
CHILDREY, Lauren, T .... 336-272-7102.... 364 G
lauren.childrey@greensboro.edu
CHILDS, David, E .... 304-877-6428.... 540 G
david.childs@abc.edu
CHILDS, Debbie .... 325-649-8054.... 488 C
dchilds@hputx.edu
CHILDS, Dena .... 870-543-5959...... 23 H
dchilds@seark.edu
CHILDS, Kimberly, M .... 936-468-2805.... 496 B
kchilds@sfasu.edu
CHILDS, Linda, J .... 304-877-6428.... 540 G
linda.childs@abc.edu
CHILDS, Liz .... 801-863-8460.... 511 F
childsli@uvu.edu
CHILDS, Paige .... 864-941-8688.... 460 D
childs.p@ptc.edu
CHILDS, Randal, V .... 919-530-5264.... 378 B
rchilds@nccu.edu
CHILDS, Richard, G .... 410-864-4274.... 226 B
rchilds@stmarys.edu
CHILDS, Sidney .... 419-372-2677.... 385 E
sidneyc@bgsu.edu
CHILDS, Susan, T .... 919-508-2033.... 380 E
schilds@peace.edu
CHILDS, Tim .... 269-687-5651.... 258 C
tchilds@swmich.edu
CHILES, Rebecca .... 318-795-2392.... 213 D
rebecca.chiles@lsus.edu
CHILICKI, Stacy .... 207-216-4312.... 219 C
schilicki@yccc.edu
CHILLO, Joseph .... 617-730-7019.... 243 D
joseph.chillo@newbury.edu
CHILTON, Bette .... 815-825-2086.... 155 D
bette.chilton@kishwaukeecollege.edu
CHILTON, Bruce, D .... 845-758-7335.... 323 D
chilton@bard.edu
CHILTON, Tutii .... 680-488-2471.... 560 C
tutiichilton@gmail.com
CHIMENTI, Vito, R .... 215-670-9297.... 438 E
vrchimenti@peirce.edu
CHIMERA, Anthony .... 312-662-4031.... 144 H
achimera@adler.edu
CHIN, Calvin .... 646-557-4552.... 327 F
chin@jjay.cuny.edu
CHIN, Deborah .... 203-932-7020...... 95 C
dchin@newhaven.edu
CHIN, Elaine .... 408-924-3601...... 37 C
elaine.chin@sjsu.edu
CHIN, Jean, E .... 706-542-8715.... 138 G
jchin@uhs.uga.edu
CHIN, Penny, J .... 516-876-3137.... 353 D
chinp@oldwestbury.edu
CHIN, Sonia .... 619-849-2958...... 62 L
soniachin@pointloma.edu
CHIN, Steve .... 718-488-1389.... 338 G
steve.chin@liu.edu
CHIN, Steven .... 856-256-5300.... 314 A
chin@rowan.edu
CHIN, Yu Chul .... 714-517-1945...... 30 J
president@buc.edu
CHIN KEE FATT, Camille .. 718-780-7963.... 324 F
camille.chinkeefatt@brooklaw.edu
CHINARIS, Tim .... 334-386-7214.......... 3 G
tchinaris@faulkner.edu
CHINDEMI, Craig, T .... 716-888-8208.... 325 F
chindemc@canisius.edu
CHINETTI, Peter .... 617-964-1100.... 230 B
pchinetti@ants.edu
CHING, David, M .... 310-233-4091...... 54 I
chingdm@lahc.edu
CHING, Yee .... 408-260-8868...... 47 D
sjclinic@fivebranches.edu
CHING-BUSH, Elizabeth ..... 863-680-3949.... 109 E
echingbush@flsouthern.edu
CHING-RAPPA, Myrtle .... 808-956-4399.... 141 G
chingrapp@hawaii.edu
CHINN, Dorrienne .... 206-934-6869.... 537 F
dorrienne.chinn@seattlecolleges.edu
CHINN-JOINTER, June .... 901-435-1500.... 470 D
june_chinn-jointer@loc.edu
CHINNASWAMY, Sainath .. 508-678-2811.... 239 B
sainath.chinnaswamy@bristolcc.edu
CHINNAVASO, Michael ..... 510-883-7159...... 45 B
mchinnavaso@dspt.edu
CHINNIAH, Nim .... 773-702-8118.... 166 G
nim.chinniah@uchicago.edu
CHINNICI, OFM, Joseph ... 510-848-5232...... 47 I
jchinnici@fst.edu
CHINWAH, Lovette .... 937-376-6453.... 387 A
lchinwah@centralstate.edu
CHIODO, Gary .... 503-494-8801.... 418 D
okuboj@ohsu.edu
CHIOU, Sophia .... 740-245-7226.... 404 E
schiou@rio.edu
CHIPMAN, Nelson .... 412-392-4306.... 445 A
nchipman@pointpark.edu
CHIPMAN, Stephanie .... 217-245-3030.... 152 D
stephanie.chipman@ic.edu
CHIPMAN, Sue .... 478-471-2732.... 133 H
sue.chipman@maconstate.edu
CHIPPS, Michael, R .... 402-844-7054.... 299 I
michaelc@northeast.edu
CHIPREAN, Kristina, B .... 724-738-2052.... 443 F
kristina.chiprean@sru.edu
CHIQUITO, Yug Fon .... 626-529-8246...... 60 F
ychiquito@pacificoaks.edu
CHIRCO, Nicole .... 248-340-0600.... 247 I
nicole.chirco@baker.edu
CHIRPICH, MaryJo .... 218-755-2040.... 265 I
mchirpich@bemidjistate.edu
CHISEM, Lori .... 205-929-3409........ 5 E
lchisem@lawsonstate.edu
CHISHOLM, Arnett .... 734-973-3540.... 259 F
achisholm@wccnet.edu
CHISHOLM, Barbara .... 334-727-8535........ 8 B
chisholm@mytu.tuskegee.edu
CHISHOLM, Brendan, H .... 508-856-4031.... 237 C
brendan.chisholm@umassmed.edu
CHISHOLM, Bruce .... 336-599-1181.... 372 G
chishob@piedmontcc.edu
CHISHOLM, Douglas, W .... 937-766-7992.... 386 G
chisd@cedarville.edu
CHISHOLM, Konami .... 510-217-4717...... 29 H
kochisholm@argosy.edu
CHISHOLM, Mark, P .... 505-277-5115.... 321 C
markchis@unm.edu
CHISHOLM, Michael, T ..... 503-725-2500.... 418 G
chisholm@pdx.edu
CHISHOLM, Pam .... 802-828-2800.... 515 E
chisholp@ccv.edu
CHISHOLM- BURNS,
Marie .... 901-448-8026.... 477 E
mchisho3@uthsc.edu
CHISLER, Christi, R .... 909-869-3805...... 33 J
crchisler@csupomona.edu
CHISMAR, William, G .... 808-956-8866.... 141 G
chismar@hawaii.edu
CHISOLM, Roxanne .... 662-472-2312.... 274 D
rchisolm@holmescc.edu
CHISOM, Brian, T .... 540-375-2259.... 523 G
chisom@roanoke.edu
CHISSOE, David, H .... 405-789-7661.... 412 E
david.chissoe@swcu.edu
CHISUM, Virginia, E .... 432-335-6415.... 492 A
vchisum@odessa.edu
CHITRE, Manoj .... 909-607-9828...... 40 F
manoj.chitre@cgu.edu
CHITTIM, Del .... 863-667-5008.... 118 F
dchittim@seu.edu
CHITWOOD, Ashley .... 504-671-6607.... 210 F
achitw@dcc.edu
CHITWOOD, Charles .... 405-491-6455.... 412 D
cchitwood@snu.edu
CHITWOOD, James .... 847-969-4915...... 29 F
jchitwood@argosy.edu
CHITWOOD, Linda .... 662-915-7621.... 277 D
lchitwoo@olemiss.edu
CHIU, Edward .... 978-934-4814.... 237 B
edward_chiu@uml.edu
CHIU, Yuwen .... 415-282-7600...... 28 B
yuwenchiu@actcm.edu
CHIUDIONI, Kathy .... 317-813-2320.... 175 D
kchiudioni@ibcindianapolis.edu
CHLIWNIAK, Luba .... 520-206-7100...... 17 H
lchliwniak@pima.edu
CHMURA, Michael .... 781-239-4549.... 230 E
mchmura@babson.edu
CHMURA, Thomas, J .... 617-287-4087.... 236 E
tchmura@umassp.edu
CHO, Hyun Sung .... 770-279-0507.... 130 A
revdrcho@gcuniv.edu
CHO, Karen .... 808-235-7404.... 142 F
kcho@hawaii.edu
CHO, Katherine H, S .... 213-413-9500...... 71 B
dean@scusoma.edu
CHO, Ruth .... 562-926-1023...... 63 B
ruthsangacho@gmail.com
CHOATE, Brad, E .... 479-575-6800...... 24 C
choate@uark.edu
CHOATE, Edward .... 417-836-6616.... 286 C
edchoate@missouristate.edu
CHOATE, Jim .... 319-398-7612.... 187 B
jchoate@kirkwood.edu

CHOATE, Michael, J .... 972-883-2943 .... 506 A
mchoate@utdallas.edu
CHOATE, Regina .... 575-492-2774 .... 319 B
rchoate@nmjc.edu
CHOBOT, Karen, M .... 701-671-2385 .... 382 G
karen.chobot@ndscs.edu
CHOCKLEY, Cheri .... 573-635-6600 .... 284 F
cheri@metrobusinesscollege.edu
CHOCKLEY, Randy .... 573-635-6600 .... 284 F
chockrl@metrobusinesscollege.edu
CHODOSH, Hiram .... 801-581-6571 .... 511 C
chodoshh@law.utah.edu
CHOE, Peter .... 770-279-0507 .... 130 A
peterchoe85@gmail.com
CHOI, Andrew .... 714-822-0006 .... 37 E
tkd@calums.edu
CHOI, Anthony .... 714-822-8541 .... 37 E
anthonychoi@calumn.edu
CHOI, Bo Yoon .... 213-487-0110 .... 45 D
officemanager@dula.edu
CHOI, David .... 910-221-2224 .... 364 F
CHOI, Henry .... 714-533-1495 .... 70 B
advising@southbaylo.edu
CHOI, Jason .... 323-643-0301 .... 28 D
CHOI, Jeff .... 937-708-5512 .... 405 H
jchoi@wilberforce.edu
CHOI, Kyunam .... 714-525-0088 .... 48 I
qchoi3@yahoo.com
CHOI, Mun .... 860-486-4037 .... 94 G
mun.choi@uconn.edu
CHOI, Sun Hee .... 718-639-3975 .... 130 A
eastersun@hanmail.net
CHOI, Sun Young .... 213-385-2322 .... 79 I
CHOI, Susan .... 856-227-7200 .... 308 D
schoi@camdencc.edu
CHOICE, Thomas, L .... 815-825-2086 .... 155 D
tom.choice@kishwaukeecollege.edu
CHOJNICKI, Linda, M .... 413-782-1315 .... 246 A
lchojnic@wne.edu
CHOLETTE, Beth, K .... 585-245-5716 .... 353 C
cholette@geneseo.edu
CHOLICK, Fred, A .... 785-532-6266 .... 194 D
fcholick@ksu.edu
CHOMA, Michael .... 724-339-7542 .... 437 F
thedean@teacher.com
CHOMIAK, Renee DeLong . 562-860-2451 .... 39 A
rdlchomiak@cerritos.edu
CHONCEK, Christopher .... 412-392-3905 .... 445 A
cchoncek@pointpark.edu
CHONG, Bruce .... 912-201-8106 .... 137 D
bchong@southuniversity.edu
CHONG, Frank .... 707-527-4431 .... 68 E
fchong@santarosa.edu
CHONG, James, D .... 770-279-0507 .... 130 A
jamesdc@gcuniv.edu
CHONG, Jocelyn .... 310-434-4547 .... 68 D
chong_jocelyn@smc.edu
CHONG, Philip .... 800-782-2422 .... 33 E
pchong@mail.cnuas.edu
CHONG, Philip .... 800-782-2422 .... 33 E
pchong@prodigy.net
CHONG, Salvacion .... 808-942-1000 .... 141 D
salvacion.chong@remingtoncollege.edu
CHONKO, Arthur, J .... 740-587-6456 .... 389 I
chonko@denison.edu
CHOO, Jeff .... 617-327-6777 .... 241 F
jeff_choo@mspp.edu
CHOO, Tae Cheong .... 213-381-2221 .... 64 I
tchoo@samra.edu
CHOONOO, John .... 646-312-2196 .... 326 C
john.choonoo@baruch.cuny.edu
CHOPKA, John, A .... 717-796-4780 .... 436 D
jchopka@messiah.edu
CHOPP, Rebecca, S .... 610-328-8314 .... 447 F
rchopp1@swarthmore.edu
CHORBAJIAN, Gil .... 518-694-7394 .... 322 B
gil.chorbajian@acphs.edu
CHORNEY, Doris .... 215-965-4051 .... 436 H
dchorney@moore.edu
CHOROSZY, Melisa, N .... 775-784-6181 .... 303 A
choroszy@admin.unr.edu
CHOTTINER, Gregg .... 212-217-3400 .... 333 F
gregg_chottiner@fitnyc.edu
CHOU, Lexer .... 808-455-0248 .... 142 D
achou@hawaii.edu
CHOU, Victoria .... 312-996-5641 .... 167 B
vchou@uic.edu
CHOW, Fred .... 408-741-2635 .... 78 G
fred.chow@westvalley.edu
CHOW, Raymond .... 650-358-6742 .... 67 E
chow@smccd.edu
CHOW, Timothy .... 812-877-8910 .... 179 B
timothy.chow@rose-hulman.edu
CHOWDHURY, Faruque .... 908-737-3300 .... 311 A
fchowdhu@kean.edu
CHOWEN, Jodi .... 808-675-3260 .... 140 D
jodi.chowen@byuh.edu
CHOWN, David .... 563-425-5284 .... 189 G
chownd@uiu.edu
CHOWN, Deborah .... 413-775-1832 .... 239 E
chown@gcc.mass.edu
CHOWNING, John, E .... 270-789-5520 .... 199 F
jechowning@campbellsville.edu

CHOY, Jonathan .... 562-903-4742 .... 31 A
jonathan.choy@biola.edu
CHOY, Lance, M .... 650-723-1983 .... 71 G
lchoy@stanford.edu
CHREST, Erin .... 410-225-2493 .... 224 B
echrest@mica.edu
CHRESTAY, Joan, F .... 610-660-1226 .... 446 C
joan.chrestay@sju.edu
CHRESTMAN, Charles, V ... 910-272-3230 .... 373 D
cchrestman@robeson.edu
CHRISMAN, Dana .... 319-208-5017 .... 189 D
dchrisman@scciowa.edu
CHRISMAN, Rick .... 518-580-8340 .... 351 B
rchrisma@skidmore.edu
CHRISNER, Carl .... 417-862-9533 .... 282 A
cchrisner@globaluniversity.edu
CHRISOPE, Linda .... 314-392-2231 .... 285 J
chrislc@mobap.edu
CHRISPENS, Pamela .... 951-785-2002 .... 53 E
pchrispe@lasierra.edu
CHRIST, Andrew .... 201-200-3191 .... 312 B
achrist@njcu.edu
CHRIST, Brad .... 541-552-6451 .... 419 A
christb@sou.edu
CHRIST, Carol, T .... 413-585-2100 .... 244 G
cchrist@smith.edu
CHRIST, Sharon .... 717-771-4048 .... 440 H
sem1@psu.edu
CHRIST, Suzanne .... 618-545-3069 .... 155 B
schrist@kaskaskia.edu
CHRISTAL, Melodie, E .... 785-670-1876 .... 197 F
melodie.christal@washburn.edu
CHRISTALDI, Antoinette .... 610-526-1382 .... 422 A
antoinette.christaldi@theamericancollege.edu
CHRISTEL, Mark, A .... 330-263-2483 .... 388 F
mchristel@wooster.edu
CHRISTENBERRRY, Reid, J .... 678-891-2830 .... 131 C
reid.christenberry@gpc.edu
CHRISTENBURY, Elizabeth, S .... 704-894-2700 .... 363 I
bechristenbury@davidson.edu
CHRISTENER, Louise .... 805-378-1407 .... 77 D
lchristener@vcccd.edu
CHRISTENSEN, Amanda, J 812-288-8878 .... 178 E
CHRISTENSEN, Angela .... 612-659-6229 .... 267 B
angela.christensen@minneapolis.edu
CHRISTENSEN, April .... 660-263-3900 .... 279 F
aprilc@cccb.edu
CHRISTENSEN, Barbara, W .... 650-574-6560 .... 67 E
christensen@smccd.edu
CHRISTENSEN, Bill .... 641-472-1156 .... 187 E
bchristensen@mum.edu
CHRISTENSEN, Charles .... 419-448-3268 .... 402 E
christensenc@tiffin.edu
CHRISTENSEN, Dale, A .... 214-828-8250 .... 497 C
dchristensen@bcd.tamhsc.edu
CHRISTENSEN, Edward .... 732-263-5500 .... 311 E
echriste@monmouth.edu
CHRISTENSEN, Holly .... 912-510-3303 .... 127 E
hchristensen@ccga.edu
CHRISTENSEN, Jeffrey, T .. 217-333-1216 .... 167 D
jchriste@illinois.edu
CHRISTENSEN, John, E .... 402-554-2311 .... 301 A
johnchristensen@unomaha.edu
CHRISTENSEN, Jolene, D .. 507-933-7538 .... 263 J
jolene@gustavus.edu
CHRISTENSEN, Kathleen, E .... 512-223-1909 .... 481 B
kchriste@austincc.edu
CHRISTENSEN, Kay .... 208-282-5482 .... 143 H
chrikay@isu.edu
CHRISTENSEN, Keith, J .... 563-387-1506 .... 187 D
chriskei@luther.edu
CHRISTENSEN, Laure .... 816-584-6810 .... 287 E
laure.christensen@park.edu
CHRISTENSEN, Lisa, M .... 802-258-9259 .... 513 H
lmchrist@marlboro.edu
CHRISTENSEN, Marc .... 214-768-3051 .... 495 A
dean@engr.smu.edu
CHRISTENSEN, Matt .... 707-256-3343 .... 58 F
mchristensen@napavalley.edu
CHRISTENSEN, Nicolette, D .... 215-572-2901 .... 422 C
christen@arcadia.edu
CHRISTENSEN, Rocky .... 660-263-3900 .... 279 F
rockyc@cccb.edu
CHRISTENSEN, Rocky .... 660-263-3900 .... 279 F
CHRISTENSEN, Scott .... 972-438-6932 .... 492 E
schstnsn@parkercc.edu
CHRISTENSEN, Stephen .... 949-214-3198 .... 43 C
stephen.christensen@cui.edu
CHRISTENSEN, Tracie .... 310-794-2308 .... 74 C
traciec@support.ucla.edu
CHRISTENSEN, William .... 435-652-7887 .... 512 B
christenb@dixie.edu
CHRISTENSON, John, N .... 401-841-2266 .... 558 B
CHRISTENSON, Larry .... 478-445-5160 .... 130 B
larry.christenson@gcsu.edu
CHRISTENSON, Marybeth .. 320-629-5115 .... 268 E
christensonm@pinetech.edu
CHRISTENSON, Mike .... 612-659-6499 .... 267 B
mike.christenson@minneapolis.edu

CHRISTENSON, Timothy, J .... 571-557-4594 .... 557 J
timothy.christenson2@dodiis.mil
CHRISTENSON-JONES, Marybeth .... 763-576-4706 .... 265 H
mchristenson@anokatech.edu
CHRISTIAN, Beth .... 570-389-4102 .... 441 F
bchristi@bloomu.edu
CHRISTIAN, Clayton, T .... 406-444-0374 .... 294 H
cchristian@montana.edu
CHRISTIAN, Donal .... 718-270-6081 .... 328 C
dchristian@mec.cuny.edu
CHRISTIAN, Donald .... 512-313-3000 .... 483 K
donald.christian@concordia.edu
CHRISTIAN, Donald, P .... 845-257-3288 .... 352 B
president@newpaltz.edu
CHRISTIAN, Eric .... 340-693-1491 .... 568 E
echrist@live.uvi.edu
CHRISTIAN, Linda .... 800-962-7682 .... 293 A
lchristian@wma.edu
CHRISTIAN, Sonya .... 541-463-5120 .... 416 E
christians@lanecc.edu
CHRISTIAN, Susan, C .... 609-895-5768 .... 313 F
christian@rider.edu
CHRISTIAN DARK, Okianer .... 202-806-8000 .... 98 E
okianer.c.dark@howard.edu
CHRISTIANO, Patricia .... 914-674-7622 .... 340 F
pchristiano@mercy.edu
CHRISTIANO, Susan .... 518-736-3622 .... 334 D
schristi@fmcc.suny.edu
CHRISTIANSEN, Claudia .... 620-431-2820 .... 195 E
cchristiansen@neosho.edu
CHRISTIANSEN, David, J .. 814-898-6160 .... 439 F
djc21@psu.edu
CHRISTIANSEN, Douglas ... 615-322-6702 .... 478 A
douglas.christiansen@vanderbilt.edu
CHRISTIANSEN, Jeanne, M .... 208-885-7941 .... 144 G
jeannec@uidaho.edu
CHRISTIANSEN, Kari .... 218-855-8060 .... 265 J
kchristi@clcmn.edu
CHRISTIANSEN, Kayla .... 903-589-4061 .... 490 D
kchristiansen@ionmorris.edu
CHRISTIE, Cynthia, L .... 203-582-3656 .... 93 H
cynthia.christie@quinnipiac.edu
CHRISTIE, Marla .... 828-726-2203 .... 368 G
mchristie@cccti.edu
CHRISTIE, N. Bradley .... 864-379-8872 .... 458 A
nbc@erskine.edu
CHRISTIE, Pamela, L .... 989-837-4212 .... 256 E
christie@northwood.edu
CHRISTIE, Ray, L .... 989-774-7062 .... 249 C
chris2r@cmich.edu
CHRISTIE, Tori .... 712-325-3276 .... 186 F
tchristie@iwcc.edu
CHRISTIENSEN, Jared .... 847-317-8159 .... 166 E
jchristen@tiu.edu
CHRISTISON, Dominic .... 610-799-1560 .... 434 D
dchristison@lccc.edu
CHRISTMAN, Harold (Bud), G .... 828-689-1102 .... 366 I
bchristman@mhc.edu
CHRISTMAN, Pamela .... 401-456-8838 .... 454 A
pchristman@ric.edu
CHRISTMAN, Paul .... 307-268-2633 .... 556 A
pchristman@caspercollege.edu
CHRISTMAN, Rick .... 740-474-7217 .... 398 D
CHRISTMAN, Vanessa .... 610-526-6594 .... 423 D
vchristma@brynmawr.edu
CHRISTMANN, Dan .... 505-287-6673 .... 319 H
tazman1@nmsu.edu
CHRISTMAS, Erica, G .... 803-938-3851 .... 462 G
mcleodeg@uscsumter.edu
CHRISTMON, Kenneth, C .. 260-481-6605 .... 174 C
christmk@ipfw.edu
CHRISTNER, Richard .... 231-591-2163 .... 250 H
christnr@ferris.edu
CHRISTOFFERSON, Kimberlee, K .... 724-946-7247 .... 451 C
christkk@westminster.edu
CHRISTOFFERSON, Martin, G .... 607-844-8222 .... 357 I
christm@tc3.edu
CHRISTOPHER, Andrea, D . 717-749-6138 .... 440 B
axc8@psu.edu
CHRISTOPHER, Curtis .... 740-420-2847 .... 398 D
cchristopher@ohiochristian.edu
CHRISTOPHER, Dan .... 518-631-9843 .... 358 H
christopherd@uniongraduatecollege.edu
CHRISTOPHER, Greg, T .... 417-268-6009 .... 278 J
gchristopher@gobbc.edu
CHRISTOPHER, Gregory, A .... 419-372-7052 .... 385 E
gachris@bgsu.edu
CHRISTOPHER, Jennifer .... 201-360-4061 .... 310 E
jchristopher@hccc.edu
CHRISTOPHER, Mario .... 312-332-0707 .... 166 B
CHRISTOPHER, Marv .... 707-654-1050 .... 33 C
mchristopher@csum.edu
CHRISTOPHER, Renny .... 805-437-8994 .... 34 B
renny.christopher@csuci.edu
CHRISTOPHER, Robert .... 563-333-6260 .... 188 F
christopherrobert@sau.edu

CHRISTOPHER, Ronald, J . 716-880-2485 .... 340 D
ronald.j.christopher@medaille.edu
CHRISTOPHER-HICKS, Joann .... 410-951-3933 .... 228 B
jchristopher-hicks@coppin.edu
CHRISTOPHERSON, Carolyn .... 831-459-4886 .... 75 C
carolync@ucsc.edu
CHRISTOPHERSON, Karen 707-468-3091 .... 57 A
kchristo@mendocino.edu
CHRISTOPHERSON, Michelle .... 218-281-8679 .... 271 E
mchristo@umn.edu
CHRISTOPHERSON, Neal, J .... 509-527-5056 .... 540 B
christnj@whitman.edu
CHRISTY, Benjamin, C .... 716-878-6326 .... 353 A
christy@buffalostate.edu
CHRISTY, David, P .... 805-756-2705 .... 33 I
dchristy@calpoly.edu
CHRISTY, Gregory, E .... 712-707-7100 .... 188 D
president@nwciowa.edu
CHRISTY, John, R .... 256-961-7763 .... 8 G
john.christy@uah.edu
CHRISTY, Jon, A .... 563-387-1016 .... 187 D
chrijo01@luther.edu
CHRISTY, Kathy .... 417-447-6963 .... 287 D
christyk@otc.edu
CHRISTY, Michelle, D .... 617-324-9022 .... 241 D
CHRITE, E. LaBrent .... 973-655-4304 .... 311 F
chritee@mail.montclair.edu
CHRONISTER, Lynne .... 251-460-6333 .... 9 D
lchronister@usouthal.edu
CHRUSZCZYK, Cynthia, A . 305-899-3125 .... 101 M
cchruszczyk@mail.barry.edu
CHRYSANTHOU, Juanita .. 832-813-6504 .... 490 E
juanita.chrysanthou@lonestar.edu
CHRYSSIS, George, C .... 617-588-1300 .... 231 C
gchryssis@bfit.edu
CHRZASTEK, OP, Brian .... 202-495-3842 .... 99 C
bchrzastek@dhs.edu
CHU, Don .... 760-750-4311 .... 36 C
dchu@csusm.edu
CHU, Dragon .... 512-444-8082 .... 499 E
CHU, Jason, Y .... 425-558-0299 .... 533 G
jchu@digipen.edu
CHUA, Nate .... 641-844-5473 .... 186 D
nate.chua@iavalley.edu
CHUCHIAK, John, F .... 417-836-5425 .... 286 C
johnchuchiak@missouristate.edu
CHUDNOFSKY, Robert .... 707-778-3628 .... 68 E
rchudnofsky@santarosa.edu
CHUDNOVSKY, Marina .... 847-324-5588 .... 169 A
CHUDY, Beverly .... 716-926-8940 .... 335 E
bchudy@hilbert.edu
CHUK, Bonnie .... 617-236-8800 .... 234 G
bchuk@fisher.edu
CHUKS, Samuel .... 251-405-7021 .... 2 C
schuks@bishop.edu
CHULVICK, Charles, E .... 908-526-1200 .... 313 D
cchulvic@raritanval.edu
CHUMAN, Jerilyn .... 949-582-4573 .... 70 F
jchuman@saddleback.edu
CHUMLEY, Heidi .... 913-588-7201 .... 197 C
hchumley@kumc.edu
CHUMLEY, Josh .... 443-896-5115 .... 19 A
josh.chumley@phoenix.edu
CHUN, Edna .... 336-334-5167 .... 379 B
e_chun@uncg.edu
CHUN, Leanne .... 808-455-0676 .... 142 D
leannech@hawaii.edu
CHUN, Patrick .... 561-297-3199 .... 119 A
pchun@fau.edu
CHUNG, Bernie .... 610-896-1106 .... 430 G
bchung@haverford.edu
CHUNG, Byron .... 415-865-0198 .... 30 E
bchung@aii.edu
CHUNG, Chih-Ming (Ryan) .... 815-226-4186 .... 163 A
cchung@rockford.edu
CHUNG, Christina .... 661-362-3127 .... 41 I
christina.chung@canyons.edu
CHUNG, Jae Young .... 323-731-2383 .... 60 H
jychung@psuca.edu
CHUNG, Jaeyeon, L .... 847-866-3877 .... 151 D
jaeyeon.chung@garrett.edu
CHUNG, Jin .... 213-252-5100 .... 26 C
CHUNG, Munghwa .... 213-381-2221 .... 64 I
mchung@samra.edu
CHUNG, Peggy .... 718-779-1430 .... 346 B
pchung@plazacollege.edu
CHUNG, Rhea .... 213-763-7149 .... 55 D
chungj@lattc.edu
CHUNG, Sean .... 240-684-2542 .... 227 F
enroll@umuc.edu
CHUNG, Silvan .... 808-845-9404 .... 142 B
silvan@hawaii.edu
CHUNG, Wing-Kit .... 971-722-4250 .... 419 G
wchung@pcc.edu
CHUNG-HOON, Tanise .... 801-422-2577 .... 509 H
tanise@byu.edu
CHUNN, Robert, P .... 813-253-7260 .... 110 M
rchunn@hccfl.edu
CHUPP, Tim .... 616-222-3000 .... 253 F
tchupp@kuyper.edu

CLARK, Dennis 815-802-8606 155 A dclark@kcc.edu
CLARK, Diana 269-782-2110 258 C dclark@swmich.edu
CLARK, Diane 318-371-3035 211 C dclark@ltc.edu
CLARK, Donald 207-602-2274 221 A dclark@une.edu
CLARK, Donald, A 417-836-5509 286 C donclark@missouristate.edu
CLARK, Douglas, E 540-365-4551 519 C dclark@ferrum.edu
CLARK, Douglas, R 951-785-2244 53 E dclark@lasierra.edu
CLARK, E. Culpepper 706-542-1704 138 G cully@uga.edu
CLARK, Ed 507-389-6651 267 E edmund.clark@mnsu.edu
CLARK, Elizabeth 617-541-5332 241 A eclark@rcc.mass.edu
CLARK, Frank, A 252-492-2061 374 G clark@vgcc.edu
CLARK, Frank, C 843-792-2211 459 D clarkf@musc.edu
CLARK, Fred 508-531-6189 237 D fred.clark@bridgew.edu
CLARK, G. Reynolds 412-624-4200 449 A clark@pitt.edu
CLARK, Gail 765-987-1439 171 E clarkga@earlham.edu
CLARK, Gary, C 405-744-6384 410 C gary.clark@okstate.edu
CLARK, Gary, E 864-294-3460 458 E gary.clark@furman.edu
CLARK, Gaye 910-410-1804 373 B agclark@richmondcc.edu
CLARK, Geno 706-396-8118 135 G gclark@paine.edu
CLARK, George 509-963-2323 532 C clarkg@cwu.edu
CLARK, Ginger 813-253-7022 110 M gclark@hccfl.edu
CLARK, Harold, E 504-286-5119 214 J hclark@suno.edu
CLARK, Helen 252-446-0436 370 D clarkh@edgecombe.edu
CLARK, Irvin 912-358-3118 136 G clarki@savannahstate.edu
CLARK, III, Irvin, T 301-846-2565 222 G iclark@frederick.edu
CLARK, J. Milton 909-537-5032 36 B mclark@csusb.edu
CLARK, Jack 205-329-7900 3 A jack.clark@vc.edu
CLARK, Jacqueline 256-439-6831 3 J jhenderson@gadsdenstate.edu
CLARK, Jacqueline 718-262-5213 329 A jclark@york.cuny.edu
CLARK, James 763-576-4797 265 H jclark@anokatech.edu
CLARK, James, A 334-844-4765 1 F clarkj3@auburn.edu
CLARK, James, L 816-322-0110 279 D president@calvary.edu
CLARK, James, T 304-336-8043 544 D clarkj@westliberty.edu
CLARK, Jamie, K 740-588-1222 407 A jclark@zanestate.edu
CLARK, Jane, E 301-405-2437 227 B jeclark@umd.edu
CLARK, Janet 812-535-5182 179 E jclark@smwc.edu
CLARK, Jeanian 540-868-7122 527 C jclark@lfcc.edu
CLARK, Jeffrey, A 909-593-3511 75 E jclark@laverne.edu
CLARK, Jeffrey, A 518-580-5929 351 B jclark@skidmore.edu
CLARK, Jennifer, R 312-915-7819 157 C jclark7@luc.edu
CLARK, Jerry 601-984-5012 277 E jclark@umc.edu
CLARK, Jill 712-325-3285 186 F jclark@iwcc.edu
CLARK, Jim 859-622-1509 200 J james.clark@eku.edu
CLARK, Jimmy 479-979-1484 26 A jclark@ozarks.edu
CLARK, Joan 914-633-2046 336 E jclark@iona.edu
CLARK, Joanne 405-466-3489 408 G jclark@langston.edu
CLARK, John 603-577-6529 304 I clark@dwc.edu
CLARK, John, D 404-413-5057 131 G johnclark@gsu.edu
CLARK, John, L 419-372-0657 385 F jlclark@bgsu.edu
CLARK, John, P 603-535-2750 307 A jpclark@plymouth.edu
CLARK, John, S 865-694-6601 475 G jclark@pstcc.edu
CLARK, Justin 806-742-2020 502 A justin.clark@ttu.edu.
CLARK, Karen 254-299-8689 490 G kclark@mclennan.edu
CLARK, Karen 574-520-4845 174 E kbclark@iusb.edu
CLARK, Karen 765-973-8257 173 F krclark@iue.edu
CLARK, Karen 918-465-1814 408 A kclark@eosc.edu
CLARK, Kathleen 808-543-8022 140 G kclark@hpu.edu
CLARK, Kay 615-366-4411 473 D kay.clark@tbr.edu
CLARK, Kellie, E 708-709-3725 161 D kclark@prairiestate.edu
CLARK, Kim 814-868-9900 428 I clarkk@erieit.edu
CLARK, Kim, B 208-496-1111 143 A clarkk@byui.edu
CLARK, Kimbrely 334-229-6859 1 C kclark@alasu.edu
CLARK, Kira 303-530-2100 81 I dclark@bcmt.org
CLARK, Kristin 714-432-5765 41 D kclark@occ.cccd.edu
CLARK, Kyle 806-742-4250 502 A kyle.clark@ttu.edu
CLARK, Kym 432-264-5124 488 B kclark@howardcollege.edu
CLARK, L. Nathan, N 775-856-2266 301 G nclark@ccnn4u.com
CLARK, Laron, J 757-727-5356 519 H laron.clark@hamptonu.edu
CLARK, Lawrence, S 910-962-7301 379 D clarkl@uncw.edu
CLARK, Leanna 303-315-7734 88 J leanna.clark@ucdenver.edu
CLARK, Lela 910-521-6262 379 C lela.clark@uncp.edu
CLARK, Lesa, C 757-683-4406 522 F lclark@odu.edu
CLARK, Linda, J 360-442-2100 535 I lclark@lowercolumbia.edu
CLARK, Lloyd 502-863-7074 201 A lloyd_clark@georgetowncollege.edu
CLARK, Loretta 615-383-3230 467 A clarkl@dominicancampus.org
CLARK, Lynne 718-262-2698 329 A lclark@york.cuny.edu
CLARK, Margie 517-483-1461 254 A clarkm@lcc.edu
CLARK, Marilyn 909-599-5433 54 A mclark@lifepacific.edu
CLARK, Marlin 801-957-4004 512 D marlin.clark@slcc.edu
CLARK, Martin 937-395-8607 394 D martin.clark@khnetwork.org
CLARK, Mary 501-977-2011 25 G clark@uaccm.edu
CLARK, MaryAnn 516-299-2486 339 A maryann.clark@liu.edu
CLARK, OSB, Matthew 985-867-2245 214 G mrclark@sjasc.edu
CLARK, Michael 910-521-6815 379 C michael.clark@uncp.edu
CLARK, Michael 570-321-4249 435 D clark@lycoming.edu
CLARK, Michael, P 949-824-4501 74 B mpclark@uci.edu
CLARK, Nancy, L 225-578-2735 212 H nclark@lsu.edu
CLARK, Naoma 940-397-4544 491 B naoma.clark@mwsu.edu
CLARK, Nathaniel 323-357-3674 39 G nathanielclark@cdrewu.edu
CLARK, Nick 662-476-5075 274 B nclark@eastms.edu
CLARK, Nigel, N 304-293-6437 545 A nigel.clark@mail.wvu.edu
CLARK, Pam 989-686-9225 250 D pamelaclark@delta.edu
CLARK, Patricia 757-455-3221 530 C phclark@vwc.edu
CLARK, Paul, E 610-921-7708 421 E pclark@alb.edu
CLARK, Phillip 727-736-5082 117 G phillip_clark@schiller.edu
CLARK, R. Kent 559-278-5333 35 A rkclark@csufresno.edu
CLARK, R. Yvette 617-873-0171 233 A yvette.clark@cambridgecollege.edu
CLARK, Richard 925-522-7777 38 C raclark@carrington.edu
CLARK, Richard 404-894-1940 130 F rick.clark@admiss.gatech.edu
CLARK, Richard 702-895-1469 302 I richard.clark@unlv.edu
CLARK, Rick 562-907-4986 79 F rclark@whittier.edu
CLARK, Rob 585-275-4151 359 B rclark@rochester.edu
CLARK, Robert 404-880-6623 127 C rclark@cau.edu
CLARK, Robert, A 207-941-7138 218 A clarkr@husson.edu
CLARK, Robert, E 940-397-4179 491 B robert.clark@mwsu.edu
CLARK, II, Robert, E 410-293-7005 559 B rclarkii@usna.edu
CLARK, Robert, M 913-897-8400 197 B rmclark@ku.edu
CLARK, Rodney 508-678-2811 239 B
CLARK, Ron 309-649-6303 165 F ronald.clark@src.edu
CLARK, Ron, M 972-238-6277 485 D rclark@dcccd.edu
CLARK, S. Kay 615-366-4411 473 D kay.clark@tbr.edu
CLARK, III, Samuel, J 910-630-7020 367 B sclark@methodist.edu
CLARK, Sandra, G 443-412-2342 223 B sclark@harford.edu
CLARK, Sara, M 417-836-6105 286 C saraclark@missouristate.edu
CLARK, Sarah 619-201-8702 65 D sarah.clark@sdcc.edu
CLARK, Scott 415-451-2833 66 B sclark@sfts.edu
CLARK, Scott 415-482-1816 45 C scott.clark@dominican.edu
CLARK, Shani 229-317-6926 128 D shani.clark@darton.edu
CLARK, Shaun 870-584-4471 25 C sclark@cccua.edu
CLARK, Stanley, A 530-226-4133 69 H sclark@simpsonu.edu
CLARK, Stant 317-788-3998 180 F sclark@uindy.edu
CLARK, Steve 541-737-4875 418 F steve.clark@oregonstate.edu
CLARK, Steven, P 773-244-5773 159 H sclark@northpark.edu
CLARK, Sunny 415-452-5384 40 C sclark@ccsf.edu
CLARK, Susan, B 601-984-1290 277 E sbclark2@umc.edu
CLARK, Tabitha 773-947-6309 157 G tclark@mccormick.edu
CLARK, Tampa, J 903-586-2518 489 B acadean@jacksonville-college.edu
CLARK, Teresa 615-966-5859 470 F teresa.clark@lipscomb.edu
CLARK, Terri 501-779-1196 19 D terri.clark@arkansasbaptist.edu
CLARK, Thomas, N 309-298-1949 168 C tn-clark@wiu.edu
CLARK, Todd 317-632-5553 177 G tclark@lincolntech.com
CLARK, Todd 909-469-5473 78 I tclark@westernu.edu
CLARK, Todd 276-944-6529 519 A tclark@ehc.edu
CLARK, Tony 402-935-9400 299 A tclark@nechristian.edu
CLARK, Veronica 205-247-8018 7 F vclark@stillman.edu
CLARK, Victoria 425-822-8266 536 C victoria.clark@northwestu.edu
CLARK, Vincent, W 718-960-8539 327 C vincent.clark@lehman.cuny.edu
CLARK, Wanda 336-887-3000 366 C wclark@laureluniversity.edu
CLARK, Wayne 501-450-1263 22 A clark@hendrix.edu
CLARK, Wayne, N 208-496-2510 143 A clarkw@byui.edu
CLARK, Wendell 706-880-8060 133 B wclark@lagrange.edu
CLARK, Whitney 419-995-8436 399 B clark.1961@osu.edu
CLARK, William 330-684-8772 403 C bclark3@uakron.edu
CLARK, William 856-351-2602 315 A clark@salemcc.edu
CLARK-ARTIS, Roslyn, C 304-929-1375 541 H rartis@mountainstate.edu
CLARK-BETANCOURT, Tammy 217-443-8778 148 G tbetancourt@dacc.edu
CLARK-EVANS, Barbara 913-288-7504 194 C bclark@kckcc.edu
CLARK JOHNSON, Virginia, L 701-231-8211 382 B virginia.clark@ndsu.edu
CLARK-KAISER, Mary 616-632-2489 247 E clarkmar@aquinas.edu
CLARK-TALLEY, Christine 703-993-8757 519 E cclarkta@gmu.edu
CLARK-WHITE, Patricia 949-753-4774 31 B
CLARKBERG, Marin, E 607-255-9101 331 B mec30@cornell.edu
CLARKE, Adrienne 215-968-8461 423 F clarka@bucks.edu
CLARKE, Ann 315-443-5889 357 C anclarke@syr.edu
CLARKE, Ann 617-670-4421 234 G aclarke@fisher.edu
CLARKE, Anthony 910-410-1855 373 B ajclarke@richmondcc.edu
CLARKE, Arlene 770-962-7580 132 D aclarke@gwinnetttech.edu
CLARKE, Cara 606-759-7141 203 A cara.clarke@kctcs.edu
CLARKE, Claudia 607-778-5220 324 G clarkeck@sunybroome.edu
CLARKE, Clifford, M 260-482-9171 176 F cclarke@ivytech.edu
CLARKE, Cyril 541-737-2098 418 F cyril.clarke@oregonstate.edu
CLARKE, Ed 570-372-4114 447 E clarkeed@susqu.edu
CLARKE, JR., Harold 305-623-1452 109 A harold.clarke@fmuniv.edu
CLARKE, III, Irvine 540-568-3049 520 H clarkelx@jmu.edu
CLARKE, James 718-488-1657 338 G james.clarke@liu.edu
CLARKE, Jennifer 315-268-3826 329 B jclarke@clarkson.edu
CLARKE, Josh 731-661-5139 477 B jclarke@uu.edu
CLARKE, Karen 713-743-0945 503 C kbclarke@uh.edu
CLARKE, Karen, B 713-743-0945 503 D kbclarke@uh.edu
CLARKE, Kathleen, D 914-337-9300 330 G kathleen.clarke@concordia-ny.edu
CLARKE, Kathy 916-348-4689 45 I kclarke@epic.edu
CLARKE, Kenneth 602-787-7106 15 J ken.clarke@paradisevalley.edu
CLARKE, Kenneth, J 607-255-6002 331 B kic2@cornell.edu
CLARKE, Kevin 516-773-5754 558 I clarkek@usmma.edu
CLARKE, Lanette 406-758-6328 294 D lclark@fpcc.edu
CLARKE, Lisa 718-357-0500 349 F lclarke@edaff.com
CLARKE, Malanie 212-621-4101 327 F maclarke@jjay.cuny.edu
CLARKE, Marcus 919-546-8314 376 F mclarke@shawu.edu
CLARKE, Maryellen 910-272-3324 373 D mclarke@robeson.edu
CLARKE, Patrick 435-586-5479 511 D clarke@suu.edu
CLARKE, III, Robert, S 864-379-8775 458 A clarke@erskine.edu
CLARKE, Ryan 601-635-2111 274 A rclarke@eccc.edu
CLARKE, Shari 304-696-4676 544 B clarkes@marshall.edu
CLARKE, Sonia 985-858-5861 210 G sonia.clarke@fletcher.edu
CLARKSON, Bobbie 423-636-7300 477 A bclarkson@tusculum.edu
CLARKSON, Kris, R 814-641-3152 432 A clarksk@juniata.edu
CLARKSON, Nancy, E 585-785-1344 334 A clarksne@flcc.edu
CLARKSON, Priscilla, M 413-577-3902 236 F dean@honors.umass.edu
CLARKSON, Sallie 843-349-2448 456 G sallie@coastal.edu
CLARKSON, Sarah, M 814-641-3161 432 A clarkss@juniata.edu
CLARKSON, William 610-917-1477 450 E wmclarkson@vfcc.edu
CLARY, Christine 802-654-2548 514 D cclary@smcvt.edu
CLARY, Dean 309-649-6316 165 F dean.clary@src.edu
CLARY, Donnie, O 252-398-6250 363 G claryd@chowan.edu
CLARY, Gail 229-931-2318 137 C gclary@southgatech.edu
CLARY, Joshua 405-878-5152 412 A jrclary@stgregorys.edu
CLARY, Laurie 360-538-4009 534 G lclary@ghc.edu
CLARY, Michael, T 901-843-3940 472 K clary@rhodes.edu
CLARY, Neeley 740-774-7200 400 A claryn@ohio.edu
CLARY, Nicholas 802-654-2390 514 D nclary@smcvt.edu
CLARY, Robert 276-656-0208 527 G bclary@patrickhenry.edu
CLARY, Tia 806-720-7313 490 F tia.clary@lcu.edu
CLASS, Richard, T 212-472-1500 343 G rclass@nysid.edu
CLASSEN, Terry, L 715-836-5278 551 A classetl@uwec.edu
CLASSICK, Bede 360-438-4392 537 B fr_bede@stmartin.edu
CLATTERBUCK, Glen 217-479-7015 157 F glen.clatterbuck@mac.edu
CLATTERBUCK, Nanette 616-632-2973 247 E clattnan@aquinas.edu
CLATWORTHY, James, C 417-268-6600 278 J jclatworthy@gobbc.edu

CLAUD, Ashlee, B 540-831-5017 523 A
aclaud@radford.edu
CLAUDIO, Linette 787-766-1717 565 I
lclaudio@suagm.edu
CLAUNCH, Jacqueline 210-486-4900 479 B
jclaunch@alamo.edu
CLAUNCH, Jacqueline 210-486-4908 479 A
jclaunch@alamo.edu
CLAUSEN, Alan, G 319-277-2490 185 F
alan.clausen@hawkeyecollege.edu
CLAUSEN, Dave 530-251-8826 53 H
dclausen@lassencollege.edu
CLAUSEN, Doris 201-216-5189 315 E
doris.clausen@stevens.edu
CLAUSEN, Edwin, G 716-839-8210 331 F
eclausen@daemen.edu
CLAUSEN, Greg 712-325-3228 186 F
gclausen@iwcc.edu
CLAUSEN, Heather 402-844-7334 299 I
heatherc@northeast.edu
CLAUSEN, Janice 661-654-3360 34 A
jclausen@csub.edu
CLAUSER, Lisa 573-518-2129 285 I
lisac@mineralarea.edu
CLAUSON, Kathleen, M 641-784-5064 185 B
clauson@graceland.edu
CLAUSS, James, J 206-543-7444 539 A
uwhonors@uw.edu
CLAUSS, Karl 610-690-5707 447 F
kclauss1@swarthmore.edu
CLAUSSEN, Ann, E 610-861-1492 437 A
meaec01@moravian.edu
CLAUSSEN, Linda, C 540-674-3614 527 E
lclaussen@nr.edu
CLAUSSEN, Nicole 701-662-1568 382 F
nicole.claussen@lrsc.edu
CLAVERIE, Mark 518-587-2100 355 G
mark.claverie@esc.edu
CLAVILLE, Michelle 757-727-5239 519 H
michelle.claville@hamptonu.edu
CLAVIR, Kenneth, R 949-214-3080 43 C
ken.clavir@cui.edu
CLAVIR, Pamela 949-214-3133 43 C
pam.clavir@cui.edu
CLAWSON, Mellisa, A 207-778-7168 220 C
mellisa.clawson@maine.edu
CLAXTON, Brenda 432-264-5612 488 B
bclaxton@howardcollege.edu
CLAXTON, Patricia 325-574-7607 508 I
pclaxton@wtc.edu
CLAY, Aileen 603-206-8175 304 D
aclay@ccsnh.edu
CLAY, Antoinette, M 732-255-0400 312 D
aclay@ocean.edu
CLAY, Daniel 573-882-8524 291 B
clayda@missouri.edu
CLAY, David, S 641-269-3500 185 D
clayd@grinnell.edu
CLAY, Doreen 818-710-2510 55 B
claydj@piercecollege.edu
CLAY, Doug 216-325-6934 387 B
dclay@chancelloru.edu
CLAY, George, W 864-656-0723 456 E
gclay@clemson.edu
CLAY, Gladys 904-470-8087 105 G
gladys.clay@ewc.edu
CLAY, John, L 256-539-0834 4 F
president@hbc1.edu
CLAY, Karen 541-962-3792 418 C
karen.clay@eou.edu
CLAY, Makeba 301-934-2251 222 C
CLAY, Martyn 813-757-2110 110 M
mclay6@hccfl.edu
CLAY, Melanie, N 678-839-0627 139 A
melaniec@westga.edu
CLAY, Mercedes 419-783-2362 389 H
mclay@defiance.edu
CLAY, Patricia 304-896-1408 543 C
patricia.clay@southernwv.edu
CLAY, Patrick, G 816-654-7650 283 F
pclay@kcumb.edu
CLAY, Peggy 405-271-2033 413 D
peggy-clay@ouhsc.edu
CLAY, Philip, N 508-831-5201 246 F
pclay@wpi.edu
CLAY, Rex, J 704-922-6243 370 G
clay.rex@gaston.edu
CLAY, Sandra 912-583-3247 126 F
sclay@bpc.edu
CLAY, Sharon 913-758-6108 197 D
sharon.clay@stmary.edu
CLAY, Terry, M 410-777-2305 221 C
tmclay@aacc.edu
CLAY, Tira, H 404-962-2999 139 H
CLAY, Vonda 812-330-6040 175 J
vclay@ivytech.edu
CLAY BAUGH, Barbara 928-776-2359 19 C
barbara.claybaugh@yc.edu
CLAYBORNE, Hannah 502-272-8070 198 H
hclayborne@bellarmine.edu
CLAYBORNE, Staci, G 618-235-2700 165 D
staci.clayborne@swic.edu
CLAYBORNE SCOTT, Monica 731-426-7523 470 B
mclayborne@lanecollege.edu
CLAYBROOK, Jennifer, D 706-880-8032 133 B
jclaybrook@lagrange.edu
CLAYCOMB, Donald, M 573-897-5000 284 A
CLAYDEN, Jon 323-860-1188 58 E
jonc@mi.edu
CLAYMAN, Ralph, V 949-824-5926 74 B
rclayman@uci.edu
CLAYMORE, Charles (Tex) 320-762-4419 265 F
texc@alextech.edu
CLAYPOLE, Rita 304-263-6262 541 F
rclaypole@martinsburginstitute.edu
CLAYPOOL, Joe 859-323-5445 207 D
joclay2@uky.edu
CLAYTON, Carolyn 859-858-2210 198 D
CLAYTON, Carrie 903-566-7184 506 E
cclayton@uttyler.edu
CLAYTON, Dana 812-488-2500 180 E
dc26@evansville.edu
CLAYTON, Donald, E 314-286-0106 292 I
claytond@wustl.edu
CLAYTON, Gene, T 910-630-7011 367 B
gclayton@methodist.edu
CLAYTON, Jack, A 304-842-8269 543 H
jclayton@fairmontstate.edu
CLAYTON, Jan, L 918-595-7902 412 H
jclayton@tulsacc.edu
CLAYTON, Janet, S 803-934-3246 459 G
jclayton@morris.edu
CLAYTON, Jason 859-858-3511 198 E
jason.clayton@asbury.edu
CLAYTON, Jay, B 724-653-2202 427 G
jclayton@dec.edu
CLAYTON, Jeffrey, A 954-492-5353 103 F
jclayton@citycollege.edu
CLAYTON, John 316-942-4291 195 F
claytonj@newmanu.edu
CLAYTON, John 417-447-2667 287 D
claytonj@otc.edu
CLAYTON, Kirk 757-490-1241 516 B
kclayton@auto.edu
CLAYTON, Philip 909-447-2521 40 H
pclayton@cst.edu
CLAYTON, Rita 717-815-1615 452 G
rclayton@ycp.edu
CLAYTON, Taffye, B 919-962-6962 378 E
taffye@unc.edu
CLAYTON, Tiffany 610-921-7795 421 E
tclayton@alb.edu
CLAYTON, Vicki 206-726-5006 533 D
vclayton@cornish.edu
CLEAR, Todd, R 973-353-3311 314 E
tclear@rutgers.edu
CLEARFIELD, Michael 707-638-5982 73 A
michael.clearfield@tu.edu
CLEARMAN, Josh 253-833-9111 534 H
jclearman@greenriver.edu
CLEARY, Brian 860-512-2613 91 F
bcleary@mcc.commnet.edu
CLEARY, Charles 860-255-3403 92 F
ccleary@txcc.commnet.edu
CLEARY, CSC, Hugh 508-565-1487 245 A
hcleary@stonehill.edu
CLEARY, Lynn 315-464-5387 352 E
clearyl@upstate.edu
CLEARY, Michael, J 575-234-9220 319 F
mcleary@nmsu.edu
CLEARY, Paul, C 203-785-2867 96 A
paul.cleary@yale.edu
CLEARY, Thomas 210-485-0500 479 A
tcleary1@alamo.edu
CLEARY, Thomas, R 619-260-4659 76 D
tcleary@sandiego.edu
CLEARY, Tim 802-468-1458 515 D
tim.cleary@castleton.edu
CLEAVER, Lloyd 660-626-2191 278 D
lcleaver@atsu.edu
CLEAVES, Laura 800-818-2261 304 I
lcleaves@dwc.edu
CLEBSCH, Bill 650-725-0056 71 G
clebsch@stanford.edu
CLECKLER, Steven 205-970-9239 7 C
scleckler@sebc.edu
CLEEK, Linda, L 812-464-1863 181 B
lcleek@usi.edu
CLEEK, Stu 805-565-6029 79 A
scleek@westmont.edu
CLEERE, Ashley 706-778-8500 136 A
acleere@piedmont.edu
CLEGG, Earl, L 801-581-7028 511 C
eclegg@bookstore.utah.edu
CLEGG, Melody 208-524-3000 143 G
melody.clegg@my.eitc.edu
CLELAND, Colleen 734-995-7325 249 G
clelac@cuaa.edu
CLEM, Randy 916-558-2424 56 D
clemrj@scc.losrios.edu
CLEM, Tyler 513-772-9888 398 G
tyler.clem@omw.edu
CLEMENS, Bonnie 909-607-3679 40 E
bonnie_clemens@cuc.claremont.edu
CLEMENS, John 229-391-4870 123 H
jclemens@abac.edu
CLEMENS, Michael, B 818-779-8040 53 B
mclemens@kingsuniversity.edu
CLEMENS, Michael, B 818-779-8453 53 B
mclemens@kingsuniversity.edu
CLEMENS, Michael, B 818-779-8040 53 B
mclemens@kingsuniversity.edu
CLEMENS, Patrick, J 414-410-4839 546 G
pjclemens@stritch.edu
CLEMENS, Tom 612-977-5269 261 F
tom.clemens@capella.edu
CLEMENT, Brian 860-548-2468 94 A
clemeb@rpi.edu
CLEMENT, Carrie 802-728-1513 516 A
cclement@vtc.vsc.edu
CLEMENT, Gregory 978-632-6600 240 C
g_clement@mwcc.mass.edu
CLEMENT, James, A 205-726-2395 6 G
jaclemen@samford.edu
CLEMENT, Linda, M 301-314-8430 227 B
lclement@umd.edu
CLEMENT, Mercedes 386-506-3440 104 F
clemenm@daytonastate.edu
CLEMENT, Richard 435-797-2631 511 E
richard.clement@usu.edu
CLEMENT, Wayne 504-394-7744 214 B
wclement@olhcc.edu
CLEMENT O'BRIEN, Karen 802-442-5427 514 F
kcob@svc.edu
CLEMENTS, Charlotte, S 334-683-5110 5 D
cclements@judson.edu
CLEMENTS, Christine 262-472-1343 553 A
clementc@uww.edu
CLEMENTS, Dede 541-888-7351 420 C
dclements@socc.edu
CLEMENTS, Gary 252-527-6223 371 G
gclements@lenoircc.edu
CLEMENTS, Geri 478-553-2066 135 B
gclememts@oftc.edu
CLEMENTS, James, P 304-293-5531 545 A
jim.clements@mail.wvu.edu
CLEMENTS, Lee Ann, J 904-256-7300 111 L
lclemen@ju.edu
CLEMENTS, Maureen, K 214-647-8505 489 L
CLEMENTS, Stephen, K 859-858-3511 198 E
steve.clements@asbury.edu
CLEMENTS, Tommy 276-523-7431 527 D
tclements@me.vccs.edu
CLEMETSEN, Bruce 541-917-4806 416 I
clemetb@linnbenton.edu
CLEMMER, Greg 704-233-8000 380 F
clemmer@wingate.edu
CLEMMER, Greg, R 704-849-2132 380 F
clemmer@wingate.edu
CLEMMER, Robert 540-234-9261 526 D
clemmerr@brcc.edu
CLEMMONS, Raechelle 920-403-3866 550 F
raechelle.clemmons@snc.edu
CLEMMONS, Sarah 850-718-2213 103 D
clemmonss@chipola.edu
CLEMO, Lorrie, A 315-312-2290 354 A
lorrie.clemo@oswego.edu
CLEMONS, Brian 816-415-7802 293 C
clemonsb@william.jewell.edu
CLEMONS, Cheryl 270-686-4250 199 B
cheryl.clemons@brescia.edu
CLEMONS, Chuck 352-395-5202 117 F
chuck.clemons@sfcollege.edu
CLEMONS, Lai-L 620-229-6168 196 G
lai-l.clemons@sckans.edu
CLEMONS, Lorenzo 312-850-7167 147 F
lclemons4@ccc.edu
CLEMONS, Quinn 941-554-1565 101 A
lclemons@arogsy.edu
CLEMONS, Tammy 859-985-3524 199 A
clemonst@berea.edu
CLENDENEN, Mike 252-493-7645 372 H
mclendenen@email.pittcc.edu
CLENDENIN, Larry 505-984-6060 320 C
admissions@sjcsf.edu
CLENDINNING, David 304-766-3239 544 F
bdclendinning@wvstateu.edu
CLENNON, Hopeton, C 610-861-1411 437 A
chclennon@moravian.edu
CLERE, Ray 502-863-8122 201 A
ray_clere@georgetowncollege.edu
CLERKIN, Elizabeth 440-775-8450 397 G
liz.clerkin@oberlin.edu
CLEROU, Diane 559-244-5970 72 A
diane.clerou@scccd.edu
CLESCERI, Michael 815-479-7833 157 H
mclesceri@mchenry.edu
CLEVELAND, SR., Alvin, A 334-872-2533 6 H
aclevesr@aol.com
CLEVELAND, Andrew 651-846-1733 269 C
andrew.cleveland@saintpaul.edu
CLEVELAND, Arthur 951-343-4215 31 J
acleveland@calbaptist.edu
CLEVELAND, Ashley 913-234-0648 191 J
ashley.cleveland@cleveland.edu
CLEVELAND, III, Carl, S 913-234-0600 191 J
carl.clevelandiii@cleveland.edu
CLEVELAND, Charles, E 509-527-5158 540 B
clevelan@whitman.edu
CLEVELAND, Debbie 360-442-2241 535 I
dcleveland@lowercolumbia.edu
CLEVELAND, Iesha, M 919-536-7202 370 C
clevelai@durhamtech.edu
CLEVELAND, Loreen 801-840-4800 510 A
lcleveland@cci.edu
CLEVELAND, Reginald 731-426-7595 470 B
rcleveland@lanecollege.edu
CLEVENGER, Brian 217-206-6709 167 C
clevenger.brian@uis.edu
CLEVENGER, Julie 217-786-2365 157 B
julie.clevenger@llcc.edu
CLEVENGER, Khris 309-438-3200 153 D
kcleven@ilstu.edu
CLEVENGER, Timothy, R 541-346-2104 419 B
trc@uoregon.edu
CLEVENTURE, Sarah 423-652-4715 470 A
scleventure@king.edu
CLEVERING, Peter 708-239-4770 166 C
peter.clevering@trnty.edu
CLIATT, Cass 717-291-3981 429 F
cass.cliatt@fandm.edu
CLICK, Ben, A 240-895-4253 226 A
baclick@smcm.edu
CLICK, Sally, E 317-940-9854 170 F
sclick@butler.edu
CLICK, Stanley 606-759-7141 203 A
stanley.click@kctcs.edu
CLICK, Stanley, W 606-783-1538 203 A
stanley.click@kctcs.edu
CLICKNER, David 518-629-8068 336 C
d.clickner@hvcc.edu
CLIFFORD, Christopher 205-934-8229 8 F
cbcliff@uab.edu
CLIFFORD, Joan 518-244-2410 348 A
cliffj3@sage.edu
CLIFFORD, Patrick 732-235-8544 317 A
cliffopr@umdnj.edu
CLIFFORD, Paul 252-328-6072 377 E
cliffordp@ecu.edu
CLIFT, Carla 256-551-3120 4 J
carla.clift@drakestate.edu
CLIFT, Edward 818-767-0888 79 H
edward.clift@woodbury.edu
CLIFTON, Gaye, B 336-342-4261 373 E
cliftong@rockinghamcc.edu
CLIFTON, Mary 315-472-6603 325 D
mclifton@bryantstratton.edu
CLIFTON, Mary 315-652-6500 324 L
mclifton@bryantstratton.edu
CLIFTON, Maurice 570-504-7000 425 F
CLINARD, Rhonda 931-363-9820 471 A
rclinard@martinmethodist.edu
CLINDANIEL, Steven 602-944-3335 11 D
sclindaniel@aicag.edu
CLINE, Cathie 870-633-4480 21 F
ccline@eacc.edu
CLINE, Dave 678-915-7495 137 G
dcline@spsu.edu
CLINE, Elizabeth 330-325-6498 397 D
ecline@neomed.edu
CLINE, Gina 321-433-7000 102 D
clineg@brevardcc.edu
CLINE, Glen, E 607-587-3917 355 C
clinege@alfredstate.edu
CLINE, Glenda 765-966-2656 176 H
gcline@ivytech.edu
CLINE, J. Robert 864-231-2077 455 C
bcline@andersonuniversity.edu
CLINE, Jack 240-477-9505 197 B
jackcline@ku.edu
CLINE, Josepth 775-784-1740 303 A
cline@unr.edu
CLINE, Joshua 276-326-4208 516 L
jcline@bluefield.edu
CLINE, Kimberly, R 914-674-7307 340 F
kcline@mercy.edu
CLINE, Laurel 610-796-8317 421 G
laurel.cline@alvernia.edu
CLINE, Patricia 931-553-0071 471 I
patricia.cline@miller-motte.com
CLINE, Robert, J 814-871-5615 429 G
cline001@gannon.edu
CLINE, Tamara 530-283-0202 47 B
tcline@frc.edu
CLINE, Thomas, G 847-491-5608 160 E
t-cline@northwestern.edu
CLINE, Tricia 785-628-4091 192 I
tcline@fhsu.edu
CLINGMAN, A. Michele 575-492-2545 319 B
mclingman@nmjc.edu
CLINK, Wendy 954-201-7533 102 E
wclink@broward.edu
CLINTON, Adele 956-364-4302 500 D
adele.clinton@tstc.edu
CLINTON, Antwan, D 202-238-2661 98 E
aclinton@howard.edu
CLINTON, Christine, M 814-886-6380 437 B
cclinton@mtaloy.edu
CLINTON, Don 903-693-2055 492 C
dclinton@panola.edu

CLINTON, Francene .... 413-755-6306.... 241 B
clinton@stcc.edu
CLINTON, John .... 405-974-3773.... 413 B
jclinton@uco.edu
CLINTON, John .... 717-477-1377.... 443 E
jeclin@sufoundation.org
CLINTON, Joseph .... 845-848-7700.... 332 B
joseph.clinton@dc.edu
CLINTON, Linda, T .... 903-886-5139.... 498 B
linda.clinton@tamuc.edu
CLINTON, Ron .... 903-434-8186.... 491 F
rclinton@ntcc.edu
CLINTON-JONES,
Karen, A .... 716-878-6210.... 353 A
joneska@buffalostate.edu
CLIPPERTON, Ken .... 402-941-6268.... 298 I
clipperton@midlandu.edu
CLIPPINGER, David, C .... 860-444-8393.... 558 H
david.c.clippinger@uscga.edu
CLISH, Colleen .... 651-523-2468.... 264 A
cclish01@hamline.edu
CLITES, Mona .... 301-784-5000.... 221 B
mclites@allegany.edu
CLOCK, Joyce .... 218-733-5930.... 266 H
j.clock@lsc.edu
CLODFELTER, Elaine .... 704-272-5302.... 374 A
eclodfelter@spcc.edu
CLODFELTER, JR.,
Roger, D .... 336-841-9156.... 365 C
rclodfel@highpoint.edu
CLOETE, Marion, E .... 619-239-0391...... 37 F
mcloete@cwsl.edu
CLOKEY, Michael .... 505-428-1214.... 320 E
michael.clokey@sfccc.edu
CLONINGER, Mindy, E ...... 620-235-4241.... 196 C
mcloning@pittstate.edu
CLOONAN, Michele .... 617-521-2806.... 244 F
michele.cloonan@simmons.edu
CLOOS, Kevin, P .... 716-673-3452.... 352 A
kevin.cloos@fredonia.edu
CLOPTON, John, D .... 319-296-4004.... 185 F
john.clopton@hawkeyecollege.edu
CLOSE, Cathy .... 715-232-1235.... 552 E
closec@uwstout.edu
CLOSE, Cindy .... 330-494-6170.... 402 B
cclose@starkstate.edu
CLOSE, Steve .... 443-334-2690.... 226 E
sclose@stevenson.edu
CLOSTERMAN, Jane, E .... 573-882-2411.... 291 A
clostermanj@umsystem.edu
CLOTFELTER, James, H ..... 336-334-5426.... 379 B
james_clotfelter@uncg.edu
CLOTT, Christopher .... 815-740-3395.... 167 E
cclott@stfrancis.edu
CLOUD, Andy .... 432-837-8179.... 501 E
wacloud@sulross.edu
CLOUD, Chris .... 212-220-8021.... 326 D
ccloud@bmcc.cuny.edu
CLOUD, Rodney .... 334-387-3877........ 1 D
rodneycloud@amridgeuniversity.edu
CLOUD, Sybil .... 850-718-2223.... 103 D
clouds@chipola.edu
CLOUD, Yvonne .... 870-245-5299...... 22 I
cloudy@obu.edu
CLOUGH, Kenneth .... 518-438-3111.... 340 A
kclough@mariacollege.edu
CLOUGH, Lisa .... 505-661-4695.... 321 E
lclough@unm.edu
CLOUGH, Susan .... 970-542-3127...... 86 G
susan.clough@morgancc.edu
CLOUGH, JR., Victor, W ... 804-333-6705.... 528 C
vclough@rappahannock.edu
CLOUGHERTY, Helen .... 832-813-6514.... 490 E
helen.clougherty@lonestar.edu
CLOUGHERTY, Robert .... 518-587-2100.... 355 G
robert.clougherty@esc.edu
CLOUNCH, Teresa .... 785-594-8473.... 190 F
teresa.clounch@bakeru.edu
CLOUSE, Andrew, D .... 814-886-6480.... 437 B
aclouse@mtaloy.edu
CLOUSE, Christine .... 623-572-3286...... 16 E
cclous@midwestern.edu
CLOUSE, Cindy, D .... 606-679-8501.... 203 C
cindy.clouse@kctcs.edu
CLOUSE, Dave .... 731-989-6019.... 469 B
dclouse@fhu.edu
CLOUSE, Jim, W .... 432-837-8777.... 501 E
jclouse@sulross.edu
CLOUTIER BYLAND,
Tammy .... 816-235-1208.... 291 C
cloutiert@umkc.edu
CLOVER, Richard, D .... 502-852-3297.... 207 E
richard.clover@louisville.edu
CLOW, Todd .... 517-437-7341.... 252 C
todd.clow@hillsdale.edu
CLOW, William, T .... 309-298-1552.... 168 C
wt-clow@wiu.edu
CLOWERS, Laurie, C .... 919-866-5929.... 374 H
lcclowers@waketech.edu
CLOYD, J. Timothy .... 501-450-1351...... 22 A
cloyd@hendrix.edu
CLUBB, Patricia, L .... 512-232-7742.... 505 D
pclubb@mail.utexas.edu
CLUBB, Sandy Hatfield ...... 515-271-2889.... 184 D
sandra.clubb@drake.edu
CLUFF, Richard .... 480-461-7095...... 15 I
richard.cluff@mcmail.maricopa.edu
CLULOW, Frank .... 603-752-1113.... 304 H
fclulow@ccsnh.edu
CLUNIS, Tamara, T .... 806-371-5429.... 479 G
ttclunis@actx.edu
CLUSS, Bob .... 802-443-5025.... 514 A
rcluss@middlebury.edu
CLUTE, Richard .... 815-479-7588.... 157 H
rclute@mchenry.edu
CLUTTER, Archie .... 402-472-7084.... 300 G
aclutter2@unl.edu
CLUTTER, Michael, L .... 706-542-4741.... 138 G
mclutter@warnell.uga.edu
CLUTTER, Sam .... 724-357-2141.... 442 F
samuel.clutter@iup.edu
CLYBURN, Michael .... 423-869-6223.... 470 E
michael.clyburn@lmunet.edu
CLYBURN, Michael, A .... 860-701-6727.... 558 H
michael.a.clyburn@uscg.mil
CLYDE, William .... 718-862-7303.... 339 H
william.clyde@manhattan.edu
CLYDE, JR., William .... 516-299-2241.... 339 A
william.clyde@liu.edu
CLYMAR, Linda .... 717-394-6211.... 426 C
lclymar@csb.edu
CLYMER, Patrick, L .... 671-735-5561.... 559 E
gcc.registrar@guamcc.edu
CLYMER, Ron .... 203-575-8044...... 92 A
rclymer@nvcc.commnet.edu
COACHMAN, Kenneth .... 205-929-1457........ 5 H
kcoachman@mail.miles.edu
COAKLEY, Jim .... 615-226-3990.... 472 A
jcoakley@nadcedu.com
COAKLEY, Toni .... 580-477-7751.... 414 C
toni.coakley@wosc.edu
COALTER, Milton, J .... 804-355-0671.... 525 A
jcoalter@upsem.edu
COAN, Barbara .... 817-515-3010.... 496 C
barbara.coan@tccd.edu
COAN, John .... 413-265-2275.... 233 D
coanj@elms.edu
COARTNEY, Jorge, W .... 540-831-7802.... 523 A
jcoartne@radford.edu
COASH, Julia .... 203-773-8973...... 90 C
jcoash@albertus.edu
COAT, Christopher .... 814-827-4470.... 450 A
coat@pitt.edu
COATE, Letitia .... 707-664-2836...... 37 D
letitia.coate@sonoma.edu
COATES, James .... 708-596-2000.... 164 H
jcoates@ssc.edu
COATES, Jo Ann .... 724-480-3401.... 426 A
joann.coates@ccbc.edu
COATES, Thomas, E .... 716-878-6114.... 353 A
coateste@buffalostate.edu
COATES, Tom .... 906-635-6670.... 253 H
tcoates@lssu.edu
COATIE, Robert, M .... 305-348-2436.... 119 C
coatier@fiu.edu
COATNEY, Margie .... 573-592-1194.... 293 D
margie.coatney@williamwoods.edu
COATS, Carol .... 580-745-2134.... 412 C
ccoats@se.edu
COATS, Jeffrey .... 334-347-2623........ 3 F
jcoats@escc.edu
COATS, Rhonda .... 360-596-5231.... 538 E
rcoats@spscc.ctc.edu
COATSWORTH, John .... 212-854-2404.... 330 F
jhc2125@columbia.edu
COAUETTE, Chad .... 320-762-4403.... 265 F
chadc@alextech.edu
COAUETTE, Chad .... 763-576-4707.... 265 H
ccoauette@anokatech.edu
COAXUM, Thomas .... 256-372-8876........ 1 A
thomas.coaxum@aamu.edu
COAXUM, Tom .... 704-216-6328.... 366 G
tcoaxum@livingstone.edu
COBALLES-VEGA, Carmen . 718-518-6611.... 327 D
ccvega@hostos.cuny.edu
COBANE, Craig .... 270-745-2081.... 208 A
craig.cobane@wku.edu
COBANOGLU, Cihan .... 941-359-4200.... 121 B
COBARRUBIAS, Maria .... 201-200-2349.... 312 B
mcobarrubias@njcu.edu
COBAS, Antonio .... 954-499-9873.... 104 J
acobas@devry.edu
COBB, Beverly .... 937-298-3399.... 394 D
beverly.cobb@kcma.edu
COBB, Charles .... 270-706-8566.... 202 A
charles.cobb@kctcs.edu
COBB, Charles, G .... 828-262-7825.... 377 D
cobbcg@appstate.edu
COBB, Cindy .... 303-861-1151...... 84 B
ccobb@concorde.edu
COBB, Edythe .... 901-435-1731.... 470 D
edythe_cobb@loc.edu
COBB, James .... 931-372-3234.... 474 B
jimcobb@tntech.edu
COBB, Katharine .... 646-660-6660.... 326 C
katharine.cobb@baruch.cuny.edu
COBB, Kathy .... 321-433-7100.... 102 D
cobbk@brevardcc.edu
COBB, Keith .... 714-484-7116...... 59 D
kcobb@cypresscollege.edu
COBB, Kim, S .... 256-549-8236........ 3 J
kcobb@gadsdenstate.edu
COBB, Larry .... 334-229-4844........ 1 C
cobb@alasu.edu
COBB, Lisa .... 615-547-1304.... 468 B
lcobb@cumberland.edu
COBB, Myreon, K .... 419-434-4544.... 404 B
mcobb@findlay.edu
COBB, P. Denise .... 618-650-5609.... 165 C
pcobb@siue.edu
COBB, Stephen, H .... 270-809-3391.... 205 A
scobb@murraystate.edu
COBB, Steve .... 907-786-4878...... 10 H
ansrc@uaa.alaska.edu
COBIAN, Oscar .... 323-241-5328...... 55 C
cobianom@lasc.edu
COBLE, Bridgette .... 303-556-3664...... 86 F
bcoble@msudenver.edu
COBLE, Tammi .... 252-222-6081.... 369 A
coblet@carteret.edu
COBLENTZ, Pablo .... 208-426-1616.... 142 I
pablocoblentz@boisestate.edu
COBLER, Paula .... 361-570-4350.... 504 A
coblerp@uhv.edu
COBURN, Danielle .... 205-853-1200........ 5 C
dcoburn@jeffstateonline.com
COBURN, Kari, C .... 702-895-3771.... 302 I
kari@nevada.edu
COBURN, Kevin .... 802-287-8926.... 513 F
commsgmc@greenmtn.edu
COBURN, Mary, B .... 850-644-5590.... 119 D
mcoburn@fsu.edu
COBURN, Oakley, H .... 864-597-4300.... 463 G
coburnoh@wofford.edu
COCA, John .... 505-454-3405.... 318 J
johncoca@nmhu.edu
COCCHIARELLA, Frank, L .. 603-535-2260.... 307 A
frankc@plymouth.edu
COCCO-MITTEN, Melissa ... 415-503-6231...... 66 A
mcocco@sfcm.edu
COCHRAN, Angela .... 269-965-3931.... 253 B
cochrana@kellogg.edu
COCHRAN, Barry, A .... 260-359-4035.... 173 A
bcochran@huntington.edu
COCHRAN, Bob .... 503-594-6790.... 415 A
bobc@clackamas.edu
COCHRAN, Connie, L .... 713-313-7606.... 500 B
cochrancl@tsu.edu
COCHRAN, Daniel, J .... 574-239-8409.... 172 M
dcochran@hcc-nd.edu
COCHRAN, Douglas .... 541-737-4085.... 418 F
career.services@oregonstate.edu
COCHRAN, Edward, E .... 724-503-1001.... 451 A
ecochran@washjeff.edu
COCHRAN, Gerardine .... 727-816-3190.... 114 F
cochran@phcc.edu
COCHRAN, Geri .... 336-770-1457.... 379 E
cochrang@uncsa.edu
COCHRAN, Glenn .... 508-626-4636.... 238 A
gcochran@framingham.edu
COCHRAN, Jeanne .... 619-849-2513...... 62 L
jeannecochran@pointloma.edu
COCHRAN, Jerome .... 412-624-4247.... 449 A
cochran@pitt.edu
COCHRAN, Kevin .... 860-231-5238...... 95 D
kcochran@usj.edu
COCHRAN, Linda .... 601-923-1661.... 276 F
lcochran@rts.edu
COCHRAN, Mark, J .... 501-686-2540...... 24 B
mjcochran@uasys.edu
COCHRAN, Maryjo .... 334-670-3869........ 8 A
macochran@troy.edu
COCHRAN, Monica, J .... 304-367-4711.... 543 H
monica.cochran@fairmontstate.edu
COCHRAN, Nancy .... 303-871-6986...... 89 A
nancy.cochran@du.edu
COCHRAN, Philip, L .... 317-274-2481.... 174 D
plcochra@iupui.edu
COCHRAN, Raylene .... 850-478-8496.... 115 A
COCHRAN, Richard, M .... 989-774-6421.... 249 C
cochr1rm@cmich.edu
COCHRAN, Rodney .... 423-869-7101.... 470 E
rodney.cochran@lmunet.edu
COCHRAN, III, Sam, V ...... 319-335-7294.... 182 F
sam-cochran@uiowa.edu
COCHRAN, Scott .... 864-597-4261.... 463 G
cochranws@wofford.edu
COCHRAN, Susan, E .... 207-778-7200.... 220 C
cochran@maine.edu
COCHRAN, Teri .... 918-456-5511.... 409 A
cochrant@nsuok.edu
COCHRAN, Theodore, J ...... 770-423-6212.... 133 A
tcochran@kennesaw.edu
COCHRAN, Thomas .... 901-321-3381.... 467 I
tcochran@cbu.edu
COCHRANE, Ashley .... 859-985-3605.... 199 A
cochranea@berea.edu
COCHRANE, Camille, P ..... 205-391-2284........ 6 I
ccochrane@sheltonstate.edu
COCHRANE, John, T .... 319-895-4230.... 183 G
jcochrane@cornellcollege.edu
COCHRANE, Kerry .... 312-662-4237.... 144 H
kcochrane@adler.edu
COCKE, Paul .... 360-650-3350.... 539 F
paul.cocke@wwu.edu
COCKER, James, B .... 845-368-7208.... 350 A
COCKERILL, Ryan .... 815-836-5250.... 156 F
cockerry@lewisu.edu
COCKETT, Noelle, E .... 435-797-2201.... 511 E
noelle.cockett@usu.edu
COCKLEY, Anne .... 859-846-5408.... 204 H
acockley@midway.edu
COCKLIN, Joel .... 419-434-4250.... 406 A
jcocklin@winebrenner.edu
COCKRELL, David .... 719-384-6884...... 87 A
david.cockrell@ojc.edu
COCKRELL, Phillip .... 662-329-7352.... 276 A
pcockrell@ss.muw.edu
COCKRELL, Tarah .... 620-421-6700.... 194 G
tarahc@labette.edu
COCKROFT, Don .... 850-436-8444.... 123 C
don.cockroft@vc.edu
COCKRUM, Larry, L .... 606-539-4214.... 207 C
larry.cockrum@ucumberlands.edu
COCO, Joseph .... 610-683-4831.... 443 A
coco@kutztown.edu
COCO, Karen .... 318-670-9324.... 215 A
kcoco@susla.edu
COCOZZOLI, Gary, R .... 248-204-3000.... 254 B
gcocozzol@ltu.edu
CODDING, Amparo .... 201-447-7133.... 307 E
acodding@bergen.edu
CODDINGTON, Andrew ...... 315-228-6921.... 329 G
acoddington@colgate.edu
CODJOE, Henry, M .... 706-272-4406.... 128 C
hcodjoe@daltonstate.edu
CODNER, Jackie .... 580-745-2810.... 412 C
jcodner@se.edu
CODNER, Renee .... 760-630-1555...... 52 J
rcodner@kaplan.edu
CODY, Denise .... 515-244-4221.... 181 F
codyd@aib.edu
CODY, Doni, S .... 910-576-6222.... 372 D
codyd@montgomery.edu
CODY, Ken .... 603-862-1622.... 306 B
ken.cody@usnh.edu
CODY, Martha .... 805-756-6770...... 33 I
mcody@calpoly.edu
CODY, Mary Ellen .... 203-285-2296...... 91 D
mcody@gwcc.commnet.edu
CODY, Michael, A .... 423-439-7881.... 473 F
codym@etsu.edu
CODY, Robert .... 508-362-2131.... 239 D
rcody@capecod.edu
CODY, Susan .... 770-274-5402.... 131 C
susan.cody@gpc.edu
COE, Bonnie, L .... 740-364-9509.... 386 H
bcoe@cotc.edu
COE, Cheri .... 978-921-4242.... 242 C
cheri.coe@montserrat.edu
COE, Douglas, A .... 406-496-4207.... 296 B
dcoe@mtech.edu
COE, Lea .... 229-931-2352.... 137 C
lcoe@southgatech.edu
COE-SMITH, Jane .... 208-282-2794.... 143 H
coesjane@isu.edu
COEHOORN, Joel .... 402-363-5603.... 301 E
jcoehoorn@york.edu
COEN, Mary Beth .... 740-284-5371.... 391 A
mbcoen@franciscan.edu
COEN, William .... 209-946-2148...... 76 A
bcoen@pacific.edu
COFER, Mildred .... 973-877-3468.... 309 H
cofer@essex.edu
COFER, Stacy .... 316-323-6729.... 191 G
scofer@butlercc.edu
COFFEE, Laura, F .... 336-342-4261.... 373 E
coffeel@rockinghamcc.edu
COFFELT, Karen .... 530-226-4166...... 69 H
1004mgr@fheg.follett.com
COFFEY, Amanda, A .... 717-796-5300.... 436 D
acoffey@messiah.edu
COFFEY, Laura .... 512-492-3021.... 480 F
lcoffey@aoma.edu
COFFEY, Patrick, J .... 414-277-7226.... 549 C
coffey@msoe.edu
COFFEY, Paul .... 312-899-5176.... 164 C
pcoffey@saic.edu
COFFEY, Ron, L .... 260-359-4029.... 173 A
rcoffey@huntington.edu
COFFEY, Suzanne, R .... 413-542-2274.... 230 A
scoffey@amherst.edu
COFFEY-GAY, Melissa .... 434-381-6131.... 524 K
mcoffey@sbc.edu
COFFIN, Deborah, J .... 303-492-8447...... 88 H
deb.coffin@colorado.edu
COFFIN, John .... 847-214-7950.... 150 F
jcoffin@elgin.edu
COFFIN, Lee, A .... 617-627-5275.... 245 C
lee.coffin@tufts.edu
COFFIN, Sheila .... 312-341-3530.... 163 B
scoffin@roosevelt.edu
COFFIN, William .... 410-293-2809.... 559 B
coffin@usna.edu

COLEMAN, David 508-270-4004 239 G dcoleman@massbay.edu
COLEMAN, Dayna, L 509-777-4565 540 C dcoleman@whitworth.edu
COLEMAN, Deborah, D 614-287-3670 389 A dcoleman@cscc.edu
COLEMAN, Denise 708-239-4706 166 C denise.coleman@trnty.edu
COLEMAN, Diane 206-934-3842 537 E diane.coleman@seattlecolleges.edu
COLEMAN, Don 423-354-2533 475 F dscoleman@northeaststate.edu
COLEMAN, Elizabeth 802-440-4300 513 A ecoleman@bennington.edu
COLEMAN, Ellen 302-736-2508 97 A colemael@wesley.edu
COLEMAN, F. Paul 607-431-4449 335 A colemanf@hartwick.edu
COLEMAN, Frances, N 662-325-7661 275 F fcoleman@library.msstate.edu
COLEMAN, Hardin 617-353-3213 232 E hardin@bu.edu
COLEMAN, James, S 804-828-1674 526 B jscoleman@vcu.edu
COLEMAN, Jamie 208-467-8768 144 E jcoleman@nnu.edu
COLEMAN, Jay, T 319-352-8264 189 J todd.coleman@wartburg.edu
COLEMAN, Jeff 435-797-1223 511 E jeff.coleman@usu.edu
COLEMAN, Joe 904-256-7550 111 L jcolema@ju.edu
COLEMAN, Joseph, L 386-481-2626 102 C colemanj@cookman.edu
COLEMAN, Joyce 815-280-2515 154 J jcoleman@jjc.edu
COLEMAN, Joyce 661-395-4614 52 L
COLEMAN, June 620-341-5407 192 G jcoleman@emporia.edu
COLEMAN, Karen, W 773-702-7770 166 G kwcoleman@uchicago.edu
COLEMAN, Keith 515-244-4221 181 F colemank@aib.edu
COLEMAN, Laura, L 906-786-5802 248 I colemanl@baycollege.edu
COLEMAN, Linda 610-519-4074 450 H linda.coleman@villanova.edu
COLEMAN, Lisa, M 617-495-1540 235 D lisa_coleman@harvard.edu
COLEMAN, Lynn, C 443-518-4918 223 D lcoleman@howardcc.edu
COLEMAN, Marion, A 717-358-7194 429 F marion.coleman@fandm.edu
COLEMAN, Mark, E 704-403-1754 362 I mark.coleman@carolinashealthcare.org
COLEMAN, Mary 617-349-8458 236 B mcolema5@lesley.edu
COLEMAN, Mary, E 718-289-5128 326 E mary.coleman@bcc.cuny.edu
COLEMAN, Mary Sue 734-764-6270 259 A marysuec@umich.edu
COLEMAN, Michael 313-664-7676 249 E mcoleman@collegeforcreativestudies.edu
COLEMAN, Michael, J 540-231-5530 529 G colemanm@vt.edu
COLEMAN, Mick 612-659-6107 267 B mick.coleman@minneapolis.edu
COLEMAN, Ray 561-686-6600 119 A colemanr@fau.edu
COLEMAN, Reggie 405-491-6366 412 D rcoleman@snu.edu
COLEMAN, Richard, A 812-888-4280 181 D rcoleman@vinu.edu
COLEMAN, Rob 562-907-4271 79 F rcoleman@whittier.edu
COLEMAN, S. Michelle 415-575-6160 32 G mcoleman@ciis.edu
COLEMAN, Sean 412-365-1164 425 C scoleman1@chatham.edu
COLEMAN, Stephen, F 607-735-1804 332 I scoleman@elmira.edu
COLEMAN, Steve 727-784-0003 103 B scoleman@cfi.edu
COLEMAN, Steve, B 864-941-8373 460 D coleman.s@ptc.edu
COLEMAN, Tammy 870-584-4471 25 C tcoleman@cccua.edu
COLEMAN, Teresa 912-538-3103 137 E tcoleman@southeasterntech.edu
COLEMAN, Tina, L 757-221-1791 518 A tina.coleman@wm.edu
COLEMAN, Tonya, R 678-359-5435 132 A tonya_c@gdn.edu
COLEMAN, Vicki 336-334-7782 378 A vcoleman@ncat.edu
COLEMAN-LEE, Barbara 973-972-8385 316 E leeba@umdnj.edu
COLEMER, Dena 507-389-7272 269 D dena.colemer@southcentral.edu
COLEN, Alan, H 913-288-7117 194 C acolen@kckcc.edu
COLENDA, Christopher, C 304-293-4511 545 A ccolenda@hsc.wvu.edu
COLES, Alicia 757-873-2423 521 E
COLES, Allen 803-705-4679 455 D colesa@benedict.edu
COLES, Jeff 618-468-4200 156 E jcoles@lc.edu
COLES, Julius 404-215-6040 134 D jcoles@morehouse.edu
COLES, Patricia 847-317-7033 166 E pcoles@tiu.edu
COLES, Roger, L 989-774-6099 249 C coles1rl@cmich.edu
COLEY, Karen 920-887-4426 554 G kcoley@morainepark.edu
COLEY, Kathryn, S 631-420-2400 356 A kathy.coley@farmingdale.edu
COLEY, Ron, T 510-643-1430 73 H rcoley@berkeley.edu
COLEY, Soraya 661-654-2154 34 A scoley@csub.edu
COLEY, Soraya 661-654-2136 34 A scoley@csub.edu
COLEY, Thomas, G 574-289-7001 176 E
COLFORD, Francis, X 973-972-7981 316 C colforfx@umdnj.edu
COLGAN, Dennis 206-878-3710 535 B dcolgan@highline.edu
COLGAN, OSB, Tobias 812-357-6981 180 A tcolgan@saintmeinrad.edu
COLGAN, SJ, Tom 716-888-2488 325 F colgant@canisius.edu
COLGAN, William 802-225-3342 514 B will.colgan@neci.edu
COLICCHIO, Damian 201-559-6021 310 B colicchiod@felician.edu
COLIJN, G. Jan 609-652-4542 313 E jan.colijn@stockton.edu
COLIP, Mark 312-949-7405 152 E mcolip@ico.edu
COLKER, Lee 412-291-6220 422 E lcolker@aii.edu
COLLA, JR., Stanley, A 607-871-2144 322 E colla@alfred.edu
COLLADA, Tere 305-237-1135 113 H mcollado@mdc.edu
COLLADO, Diosa 312-777-8584 153 B dcollado@aii.edu
COLLADO, Raquel 718-780-4565 338 G raquel.collado@liu.edu
COLLADO, Shirley 802-443-5382 514 A scollado@middlebury.edu
COLLAND, Ronna 724-836-9906 449 C rsc5@pitt.edu
COLLANTES, Contiza 510-574-1124 44 F ccollantes@devry.edu
COLLAR, Doug 419-448-2157 391 F dcollar@heidelberg.edu
COLLARD, Bruce 603-668-2211 305 I b.collard@snhu.edu
COLLAZO, Carmen 787-250-1912 563 G ccollazo@metro.inter.edu
COLLAZO, David 787-807-0575 564 F dcollazo@mechtech.edu
COLLAZO, Evelyn 787-738-2161 567 D evlyn.collazo@upr.edu
COLLAZO, Ivonne 787-284-1912 564 A icollazo@ponce.inter.edu
COLLAZO, Julio, A 787-758-2525 567 G julio.collazo@upr.edu
COLLAZO, Lydia 787-780-5134 564 G lcollazo@nationalcollegepr.edu
COLLAZO, Mariela 787-766-1717 565 I mcollazo@suagm.edu
COLLAZO, Shelciy 787-993-8876 567 B shelciy.collazo@upr.edu
COLLEN, Dan 707-826-3666 36 E dgc7001@humboldt.edu
COLLER, Barry, S 212-327-7490 347 H collerb@rockefeller.edu
COLLERAN, Jeanne 216-397-4460 392 L jcolleran@jcu.edu
COLLETTE, Mark 508-849-3462 230 C mcollette@annamaria.edu
COLLEY, Debra, A 716-286-8560 344 D dcolley@niagara.edu
COLLEY, Karen 312-413-2175 167 B karenc@uic.edu
COLLIE, Cynthia 336-506-4410 368 A cynthia.collie@alamancecc.edu
COLLIE, Pamela, J 276-328-0128 525 G pjc9w@uvawise.edu
COLLIE, Susan, A 501-882-8967 20 C sacollie@asub.edu
COLLIER, Adrienne 585-395-2109 352 F acollier@brockport.edu
COLLIER, Barbara 662-915-7275 277 D bcollier@olemiss.edu
COLLIER, Barbara 323-226-4911 55 G bcollier@dhs.lacounty.gov
COLLIER, Barry, S 317-940-8421 170 F bcollier@butler.edu
COLLIER, Billie 850-644-5054 119 D bcollier@mailer.fsu.edu
COLLIER, Bridget 312-341-2005 163 B bcollier@roosevelt.edu
COLLIER, Cindy 661-395-4281 52 L ccollier@bakersfieldcollege.edu
COLLIER, Diondrae 408-273-2688 58 G dcollier@nhu.edu
COLLIER, Douglas 253-752-2020 534 E accounting@faithseminary.edu
COLLIER, Elizabeth 615-361-7555 468 E ecollier@daymarinstitute.edu
COLLIER, Harvest, L 573-341-4390 291 E hcollier@mst.edu
COLLIER, Jackie 859-622-1260 200 J jackie.collier@eku.edu
COLLIER, Jay 402-375-7325 299 G jacolli1@wsc.edu
COLLIER, Jo 918-781-3353 407 B collierj@bacone.edu
COLLIER, John 850-410-6161 118 L john.collier@famu.edu
COLLIER, Kristen, L 937-327-7523 406 B kcollier@wittenberg.edu
COLLIER, Lisa 618-545-3081 155 B lcollier@kaskaskia.edu
COLLIER, Roger 918-449-6521 409 A collier@nsuok.edu
COLLIER, Scott 704-290-5872 374 A scollier@spcc.edu
COLLIER, Sharon 870-633-4480 21 F scollier@eacc.edu
COLLIER, Willyerd, R 479-575-4019 24 C wcollier@uark.edu
COLLIER-WHITE, Nelva, G 410-651-7700 227 E ngcollier@umes.edu
COLLIFLOWER, Natalie 406-638-3148 294 E stewartn@lbhc.edu
COLLIN, Lor 530-541-4660 53 G collin@ltcc.edu
COLLING, Lynnde 307-268-2247 556 A lcolling@caspercollege.edu
COLLINGWOD, Tracy 716-673-3327 352 A tracy.collingwood@fredonia.edu
COLLINS, Aaron 251-981-3771 2 G aaron.collins@columbiasouthern.edu
COLLINS, Amy 678-717-3824 129 G acollins@gsc.edu
COLLINS, Andrea 804-524-5973 529 H acollins@vsu.edu
COLLINS, Anthony, G 315-268-6444 329 B president@clarkson.edu
COLLINS, Brad, M 405-878-5102 412 A bmcollins@stgregorys.edu
COLLINS, Bryan 516-299-2847 339 A bryan.collins@liu.edu
COLLINS, Buddy 662-862-8271 274 E bacollins@iccms.edu
COLLINS, Candis 757-457-7176 516 F candis.collins@atlanticuniv.edu
COLLINS, Carissa 304-296-8282 545 F ccollins@wvjcmorgantown.edu
COLLINS, Carrie 215-596-8948 450 B c.collins@usciences.edu
COLLINS, Celeste 212-472-1500 343 G ccollins@nysid.edu
COLLINS, Chinneta 301-423-3600 99 G
COLLINS, Christine 337-491-2664 212 E christine.collins@sowela.edu
COLLINS, Darron 207-288-5015 217 H dcollins@coa.edu
COLLINS, David 501-279-4332 21 H dcollins@harding.edu
COLLINS, David, A 724-532-5089 446 E david.collins@email.stvincent.edu
COLLINS, David, D 423-439-5884 473 F collinsd@etsu.edu
COLLINS, David, L 937-512-2919 401 J david.collins@sinclair.edu
COLLINS, Dean, C 706-385-1094 136 B dean.collins@point.edu
COLLINS, Deborah 870-230-5000 21 I collind@hsu.edu
COLLINS, Debra 214-333-5213 484 D debra@dbu.edu
COLLINS, Debra 717-262-2010 452 C dcollins@wilson.edu
COLLINS, Dennis 617-253-5145 241 D
COLLINS, Derrick, K 773-995-3505 146 G dcollins@csu.edu
COLLINS, Diana 215-596-8815 450 B d.collins@usciences.edu
COLLINS, Elaine 616-331-6821 251 F collinel@gvsu.edu
COLLINS, Elizabeth 508-588-9100 240 A
COLLINS, Elizabeth 303-860-5600 88 G elizabeth.collins@cu.edu
COLLINS, Ellen 617-323-6662 241 F ellen_collins@mspp.edu
COLLINS, Ellen 402-552-6140 297 B collins@clarksoncollege.edu
COLLINS, Elsa, G 610-683-4101 443 A collins@kutztown.edu
COLLINS, Fuji 209-228-4331 74 D fcollins@ucmerced.edu
COLLINS, Gary 478-301-2970 134 A collins_g@mercer.edu
COLLINS, SJ, George 203-254-4050 92 H gcollins1@fairfield.edu
COLLINS, Gwen 606-436-5721 202 C gwen.collins@kctcs.edu
COLLINS, Jacqueline, F 207-795-2844 217 F collinja@cmhc.org
COLLINS, Jacqueline, M 410-651-6407 227 E jmcollins@umes.edu
COLLINS, James 916-558-2279 56 D collins@scc.losrios.edu
COLLINS, James, E 508-793-7443 233 B jcollins@clarku.edu
COLLINS, James, E 563-588-7103 187 C jim.collins@loras.edu
COLLINS, Jennifer 336-758-4900 380 C collinjm@wfu.edu
COLLINS, Jim 256-766-6610 4 C jcollins@hcu.edu
COLLINS, Johanna 770-407-1165 124 F jlcollins@argosy.edu
COLLINS, John 609-771-2167 308 F jcollins@tcnj.edu
COLLINS, John, D 727-816-3310 114 F collinj@phcc.edu
COLLINS, John, E 217-333-0610 167 D jcollins@admin.housing.uiuc.edu
COLLINS, Joseph 630-942-2690 148 A collinsj@cod.edu
COLLINS, Judy 620-231-3825 193 A judyc@fortscott.edu
COLLINS, Justin 580-349-1522 410 B jkcollins@opsu.edu
COLLINS, Kamari 413-755-4558 241 B kacollins@stcc.edu
COLLINS, Kathy 713-348-5147 493 C kcollins@rice.edu
COLLINS, Kevin 407-366-9493 115 K kcollins@rts.edu
COLLINS, Kristine 208-426-2484 142 I kcollin@boisestate.edu
COLLINS, L. Kay 812-279-8126 178 H dcollins@ocub.oak.edu
COLLINS, L. Victor 410-704-5059 228 E vcollins@towson.edu
COLLINS, Lance, R 607-255-9679 331 B lc246@cornell.edu
COLLINS, Larry 615-889-5520 472 J larry.collins@remingtoncollege.edu
COLLINS, Laverne 412-536-1059 432 H laverne.collins@laroche.edu
COLLINS, Leigh Ann 979-532-6520 509 D lacollins@wcjc.edu
COLLINS, Lisa 671-734-1812 559 F lcollins@piu.edu
COLLINS, Lori, G 904-632-5112 109 F lcollins@fscj.edu
COLLINS, M. Sue 218-471-0015 266 E scollins@nhed.edu
COLLINS, Marianne 845-687-5093 358 E collinsm@sunyulster.edu
COLLINS, Mark 781-736-4380 232 F collins@brandeis.edu
COLLINS, Mark, A 307-766-4196 556 H mcollin7@uwyo.edu
COLLINS, Mary 724-805-2564 446 E mary.collins@email.stvincent.edu
COLLINS, Mary, K 315-445-4791 338 B collinsm@lemoyne.edu
COLLINS, Mary Elizabeth 253-879-3237 538 H lcollins@pugetsound.edu
COLLINS, Matt 510-885-3692 34 E @csueastbay.edu
COLLINS, Michael 641-673-1393 190 C collinsm@wmpenn.edu
COLLINS, Michael 805-525-4417 72 I mcollins@thomasaquinas.edu
COLLINS, Michael 269-488-4255 253 A mcollins@kvcc.edu
COLLINS, Michael, F 508-856-8100 237 C michael.collins@umassmed.edu
COLLINS, Mike 562-938-4541 54 E mcollins@lbcc.edu
COLLINS, Mildred, D 615-327-6413 471 C mcollins@mmc.edu
COLLINS, Nichole 804-862-6268 523 F dcollins@rbc.edu
COLLINS, Nicole 207-948-9213 219 H ncollins@unity.edu
COLLINS, Patti-Ann 617-228-2027 239 C pcollins@bhcc.mass.edu
COLLINS, Paul 312-662-4448 144 H pcollins@adler.edu
COLLINS, Peggy, P 864-596-9019 457 E peggy.collins@converse.edu
COLLINS, Phil 706-864-1547 134 G jpcollins@northgeorgia.edu
COLLINS, Richard 661-654-2221 34 A rcollins6@csub.edu
COLLINS, Robert 504-816-4092 209 A rcollins@dillard.edu
COLLINS, Robert, K 662-325-2431 275 F rcollins@saffairs.msstate.edu
COLLINS, Roger 904-680-7717 107 J rcollins@fcsl.edu

CONLEY, Lanny ... 407-366-9493 ... 115 K
lconley@rts.edu
CONLEY, Laura, H ... 330-972-5793 ... 403 B
lhc1@uakron.edu
CONLEY, Mark ... 206-543-4139 ... 539 A
mconley@uw.edu
CONLEY, Marsha, A ... 717-866-5775 ... 429 A
mconley@evangelical.edu
CONLEY, Michael Anne ... 415-442-7281 ... 48 F
maconley@ggu.edu
CONLEY, Sean ... 802-258-9203 ... 513 H
sconley@marlboro.edu
CONLEY, Sonja ... 620-331-4100 ... 193 I
sconley@indycc.edu
CONLEY, Susanne, H ... 508-626-4926 ... 238 A
sconley@framingham.edu
CONLEY, Terry ... 580-581-2308 ... 407 D
tconley@cameron.edu
CONLEY, William, J ... 508-793-3423 ... 233 C
wjconley@holycross.edu
CONLEY, William, T ... 570-577-1101 ... 423 E
bill.conley@bucknell.edu
CONLIFFE, Marcia ... 863-297-1004 ... 115 C
mconliffe@polk.edu
CONLIN, Pam ... 214-768-3738 ... 495 A
pconlin@smu.edu
CONLOGUE, Jon ... 413-572-5572 ... 238 F
jconlogue@wsc.ma.edu
CONLON, Cindy, H ... 256-765-4206 ... 9 C
chconlon@una.edu
CONLON, Joanne ... 610-436-3506 ... 444 A
jconlon@wcupa.edu
CONLON, Kevin, J ... 614-222-6171 ... 388 G
kconlon@ccad.edu
CONLON, Trish ... 503-399-2339 ... 414 J
trish.conlon@chemeketa.edu
CONN, Annette, L ... 215-968-8048 ... 423 F
conna@bucks.edu
CONN, Brian ... 423-614-8621 ... 470 C
bconn@leeuniversity.edu
CONN, Bruce ... 706-236-1756 ... 126 C
bconn@berry.edu
CONN, C. Paul ... 423-614-8600 ... 470 C
pconn@leeuniversity.edu
CONN, Keith ... 757-464-4600 ... 530 H
deankconn@cie-wc.edu
CONN, Melinda ... 314-434-4044 ... 280 F
melinda.conn@covenantseminary.edu
CONN, Sam ... 678-915-3440 ... 137 G
sconn@spsu.edu
CONNAGHAN, Stephen ... 202-319-5055 ... 97 E
connaghan@cua.edu
CONNALLY, Sam ... 502-852-3698 ... 207 E
s0conn02@louisville.edu
CONNAUGHTON,
David, M ... 409-772-3446 ... 507 C
dmconnau@utmb.edu
CONNEELY, James ... 410-532-5300 ... 225 D
jconneely@ndm.edu
CONNELL, Bernadean ... 817-598-6350 ... 508 F
bconnell@wc.edu
CONNELL, Christopher ... 513-785-3171 ... 396 F
connellcm@muohio.edu
CONNELL, Dan ... 606-783-2005 ... 204 I
d.connell@moreheadstate.edu
CONNELL, Mary Kay ... 401-341-2262 ... 454 D
connellm@salve.edu
CONNELL, Matthew, J ... 570-688-2466 ... 437 H
mconnell@northampton.edu
CONNELL, Patrick ... 518-454-2833 ... 330 C
connellp@strose.edu
CONNELL, S. Jack ... 585-594-6200 ... 347 F
connell_jack@roberts.edu
CONNELL, Timothy ... 562-908-3413 ... 63 H
tconnell@riohondo.edu
CONNELLY, Carol ... 219-785-5267 ... 179 A
cconnelly@pnc.edu
CONNELLY, Edward, D ... 860-628-4751 ... 93 C
econnelly@lincolncollegene.edu
CONNELLY, Frank, P ... 304-243-2241 ... 546 A
fconnelly@wju.edu
CONNELLY, Krysti, H ... 618-537-6861 ... 158 A
khconnelly@mckendree.edu
CONNELLY, Laurie ... 509-359-2372 ... 533 H
lconnelly@ewu.edu
CONNELLY, Marjorie, M ... 434-395-2001 ... 521 A
connellymm@longwood.edu
CONNELLY, Philip ... 908-737-7000 ... 311 A
pconnell@kean.edu
CONNELLY-WEIDA,
Cecelia, A ... 610-799-1630 ... 434 D
cconnellyweida@lccc.edu
CONNELY, Anne ... 610-398-5300 ... 434 F
aconnely@lincolntech.com
CONNELY, Kristen ... 425-564-2388 ... 531 G
kristen.connely@bellevuecollege.edu
CONNER, Andrea ... 641-269-3708 ... 185 D
conneran@grinnell.edu
CONNER, Arabie ... 785-242-5200 ... 195 I
arabie.conner@ottawa.edu
CONNER, B. Renee ... 301-784-5000 ... 221 B
rconner@allegany.edu
CONNER, Charlene ... 214-333-5244 ... 484 D
charlene@dbu.edu

CONNER, Courtney, L ... 276-619-4317 ... 525 G
cconner@swcenter.edu
CONNER, Cynthia ... 713-221-8614 ... 503 F
connerc@uhd.edu
CONNER, David ... 806-894-9611 ... 494 G
dconner@southplainscollege.edu
CONNER, Deborah ... 843-349-2300 ... 456 G
dconner@coastal.edu
CONNER, Jamelle ... 727-341-3358 ... 116 H
conner.jamelle@spcollege.edu
CONNER, Laurence ... 860-701-5028 ... 93 E
conner_l@mitchell.edu
CONNER, Louis, M ... 931-540-2632 ... 475 A
lconner@columbiastate.edu
CONNER, Meg ... 828-565-4095 ... 371 C
mbconner@haywood.edu
CONNER, Michael ... 951-487-3440 ... 58 B
mconner@msjc.edu
CONNER, Phyllis ... 402-375-7510 ... 299 G
phconne1@wsc.edu
CONNER, Rita, D ... 828-694-1825 ... 368 E
ritac@blueridge.edu
CONNER, Shelly ... 559-244-5980 ... 72 A
shelly.conner@scccd.edu
CONNER, Susan ... 517-629-0221 ... 247 A
sconner@albion.edu
CONNER, Victor ... 619-201-8710 ... 65 D
victor.conner@sdcc.edu
CONNERS, John, R ... 607-844-8222 ... 357 I
connerj@tc3.edu
CONNERS, Mary Ann ... 732-906-4681 ... 311 D
mconners@middlesexcc.edu
CONNERTY, Denise, A ... 215-204-0720 ... 447 H
denise.connerty@temple.edu
CONNERY, Elizabeth, A ... 570-348-6200 ... 435 F
connery@marywood.edu
CONNETT, David ... 909-469-5264 ... 78 I
dconnett@westernu.edu
CONNIFF, Brian, P ... 570-941-7560 ... 450 C
brian.conniff@scranton.edu
CONNIRY, JR., Charles, J 503-554-6152 ... 415 I
cconniry@georgefox.edu
CONNOLE, Kim ... 701-627-4738 ... 381 B
kconno@fbcc.bia.edu
CONNOLLY, Adam ... 843-383-8050 ... 457 A
aconnolly@coker.edu
CONNOLLY, Ann Marie ... 313-883-8500 ... 257 E
connolly.annmarie@shms.edu
CONNOLLY, Dan ... 920-686-6163 ... 550 H
dan.connolly@sl.edu
CONNOLLY, Derry ... 858-653-6740 ... 52 D
CONNOLLY, Donna ... 401-841-6499 ... 558 B
CONNOLLY, Elizabeth, A ... 315-386-7325 ... 355 E
connolly@canton.edu
CONNOLLY, Jim ... 203-332-5088 ... 91 E
jconnolly@hcc.commnet.edu
CONNOLLY, John ... 718-409-5979 ... 356 C
jconnolly@sunymaritime.edu
CONNOLLY, Jon, H ... 307-674-6446 ... 556 F
jconnolly@sheridan.edu
CONNOLLY, Lettie ... 563-242-4023 ... 182 C
lettie.connolly@ashford.edu
CONNOLLY, Lidy ... 858-653-6740 ... 52 D
CONNOLLY, Lynn ... 720-279-8990 ... 85 C
lconnolly@csl.org
CONNOLLY, Meg ... 314-977-7121 ... 289 C
burnsmm@slu.edu
CONNOLLY, Melissa, A ... 516-463-4160 ... 335 G
melissa.a.connolly@hofstra.edu
CONNOLLY, Michael ... 320-363-3512 ... 271 A
mconnolly@csbsju.edu
CONNOLLY, Monika ... 949-582-4602 ... 70 F
mconnolly@saddleback.edu
CONNOLLY, Patricia, A ... 412-536-1243 ... 432 H
patricia.connolly@laroche.edu
CONNOLLY, Robert, P ... 617-287-7073 ... 236 E
rconnolly@umassp.edu
CONNOLLY, Shawn ... 973-655-5457 ... 311 F
connollys@mail.montclari.edu
CONNOLLY, Tara ... 515-964-6447 ... 183 H
tkconnolly@dmacc.edu
CONNON, Ryan ... 207-453-5141 ... 218 I
rconnon@kvcc.me.edu
CONNOR, Adele ... 914-395-2521 ... 350 C
aconner@sarahlawrence.edu
CONNOR, Caroline ... 415-869-2900 ... 235 G
caroline.connor@hult.edu
CONNOR, Catherine, H ... 610-519-4036 ... 450 H
catherine.connor@villanova.edu
CONNOR, David ... 251-580-2222 ... 5 A
dconnor@faulknerstate.edu
CONNOR, Edward, J ... 508-831-5286 ... 246 F
econnor@wpi.edu
CONNOR, Erin ... 207-513-3620 ... 218 C
econnor@kaplan.edu
CONNOR, Francis, P ... 260-399-7700 ... 181 A
fconnor@sf.edu
CONNOR, Joanne ... 856-256-4102 ... 314 A
connorj@rowan.edu
CONNOR, Joseph ... 518-445-3224 ... 322 C
jconn@albanylaw.edu
CONNOR, Nancy, J ... 253-535-7465 ... 536 E
connornj@plu.edu

CONNOR, Pat ... 812-855-1764 ... 173 E
connorp@indiana.edu
CONNOR, Rosie ... 435-283-7160 ... 512 C
rosie.connor@snow.edu
CONNOR, Terrence ... 214-768-4909 ... 495 A
connor@smu.edu
CONNOR, Terry, D ... 859-344-3308 ... 206 I
terry.connor@thomasmore.edu
CONNORS, Anne ... 207-453-5126 ... 218 I
aconnors@kvcc.me.edu
CONNORS, Chalese ... 940-898-2373 ... 502 D
cconnors@twu.edu
CONNORS, Cheryl, C ... 401-739-5000 ... 453 G
cconnors@neit.edu
CONNORS, Chris ... 727-864-8404 ... 105 E
connorce@eckerd.edu
CONNORS, Christine, M ... 617-266-1400 ... 231 E
CONNORS, John ... 215-596-8973 ... 450 B
j.connors@usciences.edu
CONNORS, Michael, W ... 773-371-5484 ... 146 E
mconnors@ctu.edu
CONNORS, Nancy, J ... 631-687-2658 ... 349 B
nconnors@sjcny.edu
CONNORS, Nancy, J ... 718-940-5580 ... 349 A
nconnors@sjcny.edu
CONNORS, Natalie ... 219-785-5498 ... 179 A
nconnors@pnc.edu
CONNORS, Patricia ... 718-488-1038 ... 338 G
patricia.connors@liu.edu
CONOLEY, Jane ... 805-893-3917 ... 75 B
jane-conoley@education.ucsb.edu
CONOLLY, Charlene ... 410-287-6060 ... 222 A
cconolly@cecil.edu
CONOVER, Dustin ... 307-382-1644 ... 557 A
dconover@wwcc.wy.edu
CONOVER, Monica, M ... 770-407-1088 ... 124 F
mconover@argosy.edu
CONOVER, Randall ... 937-328-6180 ... 387 H
conoverr@clarkstate.edu
CONOVER, Wheeler ... 606-589-3038 ... 203 D
wheeler.conover@kctcs.edu
CONRAD, Cecilia ... 909-621-8137 ... 63 A
cecilia.conrad@pomona.edu
CONRAD, Jeffrey ... 617-236-8800 ... 234 G
jconrad@fisher.edu
CONRAD, Jerry ... 202-319-5515 ... 97 E
conradj@cua.edu
CONRAD, Jillian ... 813-463-7157 ... 101 B
jrconrad@argosy.edu
CONRAD, Jon, B ... 610-861-1526 ... 437 A
jconrad@moravian.edu
CONRAD, Kari, M ... 570-577-1217 ... 423 E
kari.conrad@bucknell.edu
CONRAD, Karol, A ... 270-824-1741 ... 202 G
karol.conrad@kctcs.edu
CONRAD, Katie, A ... 859-846-5807 ... 204 H
kconrad@midway.edu
CONRAD, Kelly ... 641-683-5159 ... 185 G
kconrad@indianhills.edu
CONRAD, Larry, D ... 919-962-3444 ... 378 E
larry_conrad@unc.edu
CONRAD, Rebecca ... 207-775-3052 ... 218 E
bconrad@meca.edu
CONRAD, Robert, F ... 812-877-8334 ... 179 B
conrad@rose-hulman.edu
CONRAD, Scott ... 707-524-1553 ... 68 E
sconrad@santarosa.edu
CONRAD, Valarie ... 312-949-7304 ... 152 E
vconrad@ico.edu
CONROY, Mark ... 954-308-7400 ... 117 C
CONROY, Michele ... 610-902-8526 ... 424 B
michele.r.kennedy@cabrini.com
CONROY, Nina ... 212-237-8606 ... 327 F
nconroy@jjay.cuny.edu
CONROY, JR., Philip ... 802-728-1000 ... 516 A
pconroy@vtc.edu
CONROY, Shelley, F ... 214-820-3361 ... 482 A
shelley_conroy@baylor.edu
CONROY, Terry ... 254-867-2316 ... 500 F
terry.conroy@tstc.edu
CONROY, Timothy ... 207-974-4682 ... 218 H
tconroy@emcc.edu
CONSOLVO, Camille ... 541-962-3635 ... 418 C
cconsolv@eou.edu
CONSTABLE, Jean ... 830-372-8090 ... 499 F
jconstable@tlu.edu
CONSTANCE, Eric, F ... 315-786-2252 ... 337 F
econstance@sunyjefferson.edu
CONSTANT, David ... 225-578-2322 ... 212 H
mondavia1@lsu.edu
CONSTANTIN, Michael ... 225-216-8615 ... 209 H
constantinm@mybrcc.edu
CONSTANTINE, Carol ... 508-678-2811 ... 239 B
carol.constantine@bristolcc.edu
CONSTANTINE, Doris, F ... 512-448-8525 ... 493 E
dorisc@stedwards.edu
CONSTANTINE, Ruth, H ... 413-585-2200 ... 244 G
rconstan@smith.edu
CONSTANTINO, John ... 808-245-8245 ... 142 C
johncons@hawaii.edu
CONSTANTINO, Lisa ... 303-447-3846 ... 86 H
lconstantino@naropa.edu

CONSTANTINOU,
Constantia ... 718-409-7236 ... 356 C
cconstantinou@sunymaritime.edu
CONSTON, Marcia ... 704-330-6647 ... 369 D
marcia.conston@cpcc.edu
CONTANT, Cheryl ... 715-682-1675 ... 549 F
ccontant@northland.edu
CONTARDI, Heather ... 570-288-8400 ... 429 D
CONTARINO, Sue ... 847-925-6200 ... 151 G
scontari@harpercollege.edu
CONTE, Jeffrey ... 914-606-6795 ... 360 E
jeffrey.conte@sunywcc.edu
CONTE, Jeffrey, A ... 914-606-6795 ... 360 E
jeffrey.conte@sunywcc.edu
CONTE, John ... 214-637-3530 ... 508 D
jconte@wadecollege.edu
CONTE, Michael ... 973-972-1263 ... 316 D
contemi@umdnj.edu
CONTE, Millie ... 718-631-6222 ... 328 F
mconte@qcc.cuny.edu
CONTI, Delia, B ... 724-430-4142 ... 439 G
dbc3@psu.edu
CONTI, Erik ... 336-506-4201 ... 368 A
conti@alamancecc.edu
CONTOMANOLIS,
Emanuel ... 585-475-5464 ... 347 G
emcoce@rit.edu
CONTOMANOLIS, Laurel ... 585-275-3166 ... 359 B
laurel.contomanolis@rochester.edu
CONTOS, Tanya ... 617-850-1231 ... 235 F
tcontos@hchc.edu
CONTRELLA, R. Thomas ... 412-373-6400 ... 447 B
tcontrella@sanfordbrown.edu
CONTRELLA, R. Thomas ... 412-373-6400 ... 447 A
tcontrella@western-school.com
CONTRERAS, Adriana ... 210-485-0020 ... 479 A
acontreras81@alamo.edu
CONTRERAS, Beatriz, D ... 920-424-3377 ... 551 E
contrera@uwosh.edu
CONTRERAS, James ... 202-274-6053 ... 100 A
jcontreras@udc.edu
CONTRERAS, Lisa ... 312-935-6620 ... 162 G
lcontreras@robertmorris.edu
CONTRERAS, Raquel, J ... 864-656-2451 ... 456 E
rcontre@clemson.edu
CONTRERAS, JR.,
Sebastian ... 847-635-1756 ... 160 F
scontrer@oakton.edu
CONTRERAS, Sylvia ... 608-663-3278 ... 547 F
scontreras@edgewood.edu
CONVER, M. Kathleen ... 309-677-2242 ... 146 C
mkc@bradley.edu
CONVERSE, Kenneth, L ... 712-749-2101 ... 183 C
conversek@bvu.edu
CONVERSE, Sharon, K ... 248-341-2154 ... 256 F
skconver@oaklandcc.edu
CONVEY, Cynthia ... 562-860-2451 ... 39 A
cconvey@cerritos.edu
CONWAY, Cathy ... 847-317-8135 ... 166 E
cconway@tiu.edu
CONWAY, Cathy ... 580-745-2152 ... 412 C
cconway@se.edu
CONWAY, Charles ... 718-270-3049 ... 352 D
charles.conway@downstate.edu
CONWAY, Charlotte ... 269-471-6616 ... 252 A
charlott@andrews.edu
CONWAY, Christine, G ... 717-291-4083 ... 429 F
christine.conway@fandm.edu
CONWAY, David ... 607-431-4943 ... 335 A
conwayd@hartwick.edu
CONWAY, Dennis, S ... 518-580-5566 ... 351 B
dconway@skidmore.edu
CONWAY, Guy ... 813-974-5400 ... 121 A
gconway@usf.edu
CONWAY, Jayne ... 760-744-1150 ... 61 D
jconway@palomar.edu
CONWAY, Jean, L ... 972-860-7001 ... 484 I
jconway@dcccd.edu
CONWAY, Karen ... 901-321-3536 ... 467 I
kconway@cbu.edu
CONWAY, Sandra ... 727-873-4775 ... 121 C
sconway@mail.usf.edu
CONWAY, Sharon ... 301-891-4005 ... 229 B
sconway@wau.edu
CONWAY, Steven ... 409-740-4714 ... 497 F
conways@tamug.edu
CONWAY, Thomas ... 910-672-2501 ... 377 G
tconway@uncfsu.edu
CONWAY-TURNER,
Katherine ... 301-696-3623 ... 223 C
conwayturner@hood.edu
CONWAY-WELCH, Colleen 615-343-3243 ... 478 A
colleen.conway-welch@vanderbilt.edu
CONWELL, Betty ... 425-739-8215 ... 535 H
betty.conwell@lwtc.edu
CONYERS, Rhyan, M ... 859-233-8898 ... 207 A
rconyers@transy.edu
CONZA, Lisa ... 516-299-3810 ... 338 E
lisa.conza@liu.edu
CONZATTI, Maria ... 516-572-7600 ... 342 C
maria.conzatti@ncc.edu
CONZETT, Karen ... 563-242-4023 ... 182 C
karen.conzett@ashford.edu
COODY, Sue ... 817-598-6423 ... 508 F
scoody@wc.edu

COOGAN, Janet .... 563-441-4201 .... 184 H
jcoogan@eicc.edu
COOGAN, Jay .... 612-874-3737 .... 265 C
president@mcad.edu
COOK, Aaron .... 231-995-2914 .... 256 D
acook@nmc.edu
COOK, Adrienne .... 978-867-4238 .... 235 A
adrienne.cook@gordon.edu
COOK, Allen, P .... 203-576-4192 .... 94 F
acook@bridgeport.edu
COOK, Amber .... 814-871-7421 .... 429 G
cook0692@gannon.edu
COOK, Andrea, P .... 503-517-1212 .... 421 B
acook@warnerpacific.edu
COOK, Angela .... 207-780-5737 .... 220 G
adcook@usm.maine.edu
COOK, Arlene .... 229-248-2579 .... 126 A
acook@bainbridge.edu
COOK, Barbara .... 973-300-2263 .... 315 F
bcook@sussex.edu
COOK, Barbara Jo .... 770-467-6038 .... 137 F
bcook@sctech.edu
COOK, Bradley .... 435-586-7704 .... 511 D
bradcook@suu.edu
COOK, Brenda, A .... 334-683-2353 .... 5 G
bcook@marionmilitary.edu
COOK, Brian .... 510-602-6767 .... 34 E
brian.cook@csueastbay.edu
COOK, Brian .... 510-885-7504 .... 34 E
brian.cook@csueastbay.edu
COOK, Brian .... 440-525-7720 .... 394 F
bcook@lakelandcc.edu
COOK, Bruce .... 386-506-4417 .... 104 F
cookb@daytonastate.edu
COOK, Bruce .... 909-652-6721 .... 39 E
bruce.cook@chaffey.edu
COOK, Carey, W .... 208-467-8661 .... 144 E
cwcook@nnu.edu
COOK, Charles, M .... 713-718-5042 .... 487 I
charles.cook@hccs.edu
COOK, Chris .... 806-742-2136 .... 502 A
chris.cook@ttu.edu
COOK, Colleen, M .... 740-368-3145 .... 400 G
cmcook@owu.edu
COOK, Connie, S .... 540-985-8344 .... 520 I
cscook@jchs.edu
COOK, Constance, E .... 734-763-0159 .... 259 A
cecook@umich.edu
COOK, Darrell .... 202-885-3541 .... 97 D
dcook@american.edu
COOK, David .... 309-268-8181 .... 151 I
david.cook@heartland.edu
COOK, David .... 415-485-9405 .... 42 B
david.cook@marin.edu
COOK, David, E .... 218-722-4000 .... 263 E
davidc@dbumn.edu
COOK, Dawn .... 678-664-0515 .... 139 F
dawn.cook@westgatech.edu
COOK, Debra .... 918-335-6264 .... 411 B
dcook@okwu.edu
COOK, Denise .... 706-379-5237 .... 140 A
bdcook@yhc.edu
COOK, Donald .... 203-365-7649 .... 94 B
cookd@sacredheart.edu
COOK, Donelda .... 410-617-5171 .... 223 I
dcook@loyola.edu
COOK, Donna, L .... 575-439-3699 .... 319 E
dcook@nmsua.nmsu.edu
COOK, Donna, M .... 401-341-2435 .... 454 D
donna.cook@salve.edu
COOK, Earl .... 334-291-4966 .... 2 F
earl.cook@cv.edu
COOK, Elizabeth .... 770-391-6200 .... 128 H
ecook@devry.edu
COOK, Ellen, D .... 337-482-6306 .... 216 D
edcook@louisiana.edu
COOK, Elsie .... 510-567-6174 .... 72 D
drcook@sum.edu
COOK, Gary .... 580-371-2371 .... 408 I
gcook@mscok.edu
COOK, Gary, R .... 214-333-5130 .... 484 D
mitch@dbu.edu
COOK, Gary, W .... 770-484-1204 .... 133 G
lru@lru.edu
COOK, Greg .... 262-472-1077 .... 553 A
cookg@uww.edu
COOK, Howard, M .... 803-786-3343 .... 457 C
hcook@columbiasc.edu
COOK, Jason, D .... 979-845-2217 .... 497 E
jason.cook@tamu.edu
COOK, Jeffrey .... 657-278-4475 .... 35 B
jcook@exchange.fullerton.edu
COOK, Jenene .... 617-427-0060 .... 241 A
jcook@rcc.mass.edu
COOK, Jerry .... 918-456-5511 .... 409 A
COOK, Jessica .... 606-546-1229 .... 207 B
jcook@unionky.edu
COOK, Jessica .... 302-736-2435 .... 97 A
jessica.cook@wesley.edu
COOK, Jim .... 573-651-2206 .... 289 K
jcook@semo.edu
COOK, John .... 603-206-8009 .... 304 D
jcook@ccsnh.edu
COOK, John, C .... 540-985-8317 .... 520 I
jccook@jchs.edu
COOK, Jolane .... 870-777-5722 .... 25 F
jolane.cook@uacch.edu
COOK, Karen .... 650-723-2300 .... 71 G
kcook@stanford.edu
COOK, Karen, L .... 410-777-7370 .... 221 C
kcook@aacc.edu
COOK, Kathy .... 425-388-9273 .... 534 C
kcook@everettcc.edu
COOK, Ken .... 912-443-5796 .... 136 H
kcook@savannahtech.edu
COOK, Larry .... 909-389-3384 .... 65 B
lcook@craftonhills.edu
COOK, Lenora .... 620-276-9521 .... 193 C
lenora.cook@gcccks.edu
COOK, Les, P .... 906-487-2465 .... 255 B
lpcook@mtu.edu
COOK, Margaret .... 813-246-7600 .... 115 J
margaret.cook@rasmussen.edu
COOK, Mark .... 616-395-7833 .... 252 D
cook@hope.edu
COOK, Mary .... 713-222-5340 .... 503 F
cookm@uhd.edu
COOK, Melinda .... 617-670-4462 .... 234 G
mcook1@fisher.edu
COOK, Melinda .... 800-567-2344 .... 547 A
melcook@menominee.edu
COOK, Melissa .... 207-288-5015 .... 217 H
mcook@coa.edu
COOK, Michelle .... 405-208-5000 .... 410 A
michelle.cook@okcu.edu
COOK, Michelle .... 336-750-2184 .... 380 B
cookm@wssu.edu
COOK, Michelle, G .... 706-583-8195 .... 138 G
mgcook@uga.edu
COOK, Patrick .... 978-656-3134 .... 240 B
cookp@middlesex.mass.edu
COOK, Phil .... 423-614-8500 .... 470 C
pcook@leeuniversity.edu
COOK, Renee .... 407-569-1309 .... 107 I
renee.cook@fcc.edu
COOK, Rich .... 616-331-5841 .... 251 F
cookri@gvsu.edu
COOK, Royrickers .... 334-844-5700 .... 1 F
cookroy@auburn.edu
COOK, Sandra .... 619-594-5384 .... 37 A
scook@mail.sdsu.edu
COOK, Scott, A .... 304-336-8137 .... 544 D
cookscot@westliberty.edu
COOK, Sharon, L .... 972-860-7629 .... 484 I
scook@dcccd.edu
COOK, Stacy, A .... 408-864-8330 .... 47 G
cookstacy@deanza.edu
COOK, Tena .... 308-432-6263 .... 299 E
tcook@csc.edu
COOK, Terry .... 410-455-2939 .... 227 D
tcook@umbc.edu
COOK, Tim .... 360-992-2217 .... 532 F
tcook@clark.edu
COOK, Tom, G .... 304-327-4111 .... 543 F
tcook@bluefieldstate.edu
COOK, Toni .... 510-748-2135 .... 62 C
tcook@peralta.edu
COOK, Vicki .... 231-995-1144 .... 256 D
vcook@nmc.edu
COOK, Vickie .... 618-664-7081 .... 151 F
vickie.cook@greenville.edu
COOK, William .... 304-307-0716 .... 543 C
william.cook@southernwv.edu
COOK-FRANCIS,
Lynette, S .... 520-621-3772 .... 18 L
lynettec@email.arizona.edu
COOK-HUFFMAN,
Daniel, J .... 814-641-3151 .... 432 A
cookhud@juniata.edu
COOK-NOBLES, Robin .... 784-283-2839 .... 245 E
rcooknob@wellesley.edu
COOKE, Barbara .... 816-604-3308 .... 285 D
barbara.cooke@mcckc.edu
COOKE, Connie, F .... 716-878-4902 .... 353 A
cookecf@buffalostate.edu
COOKE, Diane .... 757-569-6712 .... 528 A
dcooke@pdc.edu
COOKE, Harry .... 704-922-6355 .... 370 G
cooke.harry@gaston.edu
COOKE, Jasper .... 706-737-1401 .... 125 G
jcooke@aug.edu
COOKE, Matthew .... 616-957-6076 .... 249 B
mkc071@calvinseminary.edu
COOKE, Peggy, S .... 248-370-2190 .... 256 G
cooke@oakland.edu
COOKE, Sunita .... 619-644-7100 .... 49 C
sunita.cooke@gcccd.edu
COOKER, Dianne .... 704-991-0282 .... 374 D
dcooker8019@stanly.edu
COOKMAN, John .... 972-825-4659 .... 495 F
jcookman@sagu.edu
COOKS, Owen, J .... 336-750-2855 .... 380 B
cooksoj@wssu.edu
COOKSEY, Beth .... 615-230-3560 .... 476 C
beth.cooksey@volstate.edu
COOKSEY, Gaye, M .... 972-881-5807 .... 483 H
gcooksey@collin.edu
COOKSEY, Lynita, M .... 870-972-3574 .... 20 D
lcooksey@astate.edu
COOKSEY, Lynita, M .... 870-972-2030 .... 20 D
lcooksey@astate.edu
COOKSEY, Marilyn .... 504-286-3275 .... 278 C
marilyn.cooksey@wmcarey.edu
COOKSON, Nancy, B .... 402-465-2117 .... 299 H
nbc@nebrwesleyan.edu
COOL, Michael .... 609-652-4607 .... 313 E
michael.cool@stockton.edu
COOL, Sharon .... 605-331-6760 .... 466 E
sharon.cool@usiouxfalls.edu
COOLE, Gloria, G .... 218-722-4000 .... 263 E
finaid@dbumn.edu
COOLEY, Alvin, L .... 973-353-5882 .... 314 E
alvin.cooley@rutgers.edu
COOLEY, Dennis, R .... 608-342-1182 .... 552 B
cooleyde@uwplatt.edu
COOLEY, Francis .... 203-287-3029 .... 93 F
paier.dean@snet.net
COOLEY, John .... 614-287-2501 .... 389 A
jcooley@cscc.edu
COOLEY, Marianne, B .... 784-283-3344 .... 245 E
mcooley@wellesley.edu
COOLEY, Meghan, M .... 309-794-7314 .... 145 E
meghancooley@augustana.edu
COOLEY, Mike .... 972-860-7871 .... 485 C
mcooley@dcccd.edu
COOLEY, Van .... 269-387-2969 .... 260 C
van.cooley@wmich.edu
COOLIDGE, Kimberly .... 850-436-8444 .... 123 C
kim.coolidge@vc.edu
COOLING, Mike .... 619-688-0800 .... 43 B
mcooling@concorde.edu
COOMAR, Parmeshwar .... 734-384-4209 .... 255 D
pcoomar@monroeccc.edu
COOMBE, Robert, D .... 303-871-2111 .... 89 A
chancellor@du.edu
COOMBS, Gary, F .... 619-201-8989 .... 70 J
gcoombs@shadowmountain.org
COOMBS, Matt .... 831-755-6725 .... 49 E
mcoombs@hartnell.edu
COOMBS, Robert .... 207-741-5569 .... 219 A
rcoombs@smccme.edu
COOMER, Roger .... 501-337-5000 .... 21 D
rcoomer@coto.edu
COOMER, Sue, B .... 270-384-8024 .... 204 D
coomers@lindsey.edu
COOMES, Judy .... 270-686-4532 .... 203 B
judy.coomes@kctcs.edu
COON, David, W .... 415-485-9502 .... 42 B
davidwain.coon@marin.edu
COON, Omayra .... 910-221-2224 .... 364 F
COON, Thomas, G .... 517-355-2308 .... 255 A
coontg@msu.edu
COONAN, Daniel .... 408-554-5344 .... 68 C
dcoonan@scu.edu
COONAN, Patrick, R .... 516-877-4511 .... 322 A
coonan@adelphi.edu
COONEN, Ned .... 847-214-7557 .... 150 F
ncoonen@elgin.edu
COONEY, Terry .... 410-704-2128 .... 228 E
tcooney@towson.edu
COONEY MINER,
Dianne, C .... 585-385-8472 .... 348 F
dcooney-miner@sjfc.edu
COONING, Peggy, J .... 615-248-1355 .... 476 G
pcooning@trevecca.edu
COONROD, Curtis, C .... 314-516-5211 .... 291 D
curt_coonrod@umsl.edu
COONS, Christopher .... 814-824-3125 .... 436 C
ccoons@mercyhurst.edu
COONS, Maria .... 847-925-6143 .... 151 G
mcoons@harpercollege.edu
COONS, Patrick .... 502-272-8056 .... 198 H
pcoons@bellarmine.edu
COONS, Robert, A .... 812-877-8246 .... 179 B
robert.a.coons@rose-hulman.edu
COOPEE, Scott, J .... 413-782-1246 .... 246 A
sjcoopee@wne.edu
COOPER, Alan .... 212-678-8065 .... 337 G
alcooper@jtsa.edu
COOPER, Amy, M .... 270-384-8053 .... 204 D
coopera@lindsey.edu
COOPER, Aneita .... 870-759-4184 .... 26 B
acooper@wbcoll.edu
COOPER, Ann, A .... 803-778-6636 .... 455 G
cooperaa@cctech.edu
COOPER, Anne, M .... 727-341-3323 .... 116 H
cooper.anne@spcollege.edu
COOPER, Annie, L .... 570-662-4381 .... 443 C
acooper@mansfield.edu
COOPER, Barbara, I .... 252-222-6225 .... 369 A
cooperb@carteret.edu
COOPER, Beverly .... 765-269-5200 .... 176 D
bcooper@ivytech.edu
COOPER, Brett .... 870-759-4107 .... 26 B
bcooper@wbcoll.edu
COOPER, Candace .... 704-878-3256 .... 372 C
ccooper@mitchellcc.edu
COOPER, Carlton .... 903-886-5568 .... 498 B
carlton.cooper@tamuc.edu
COOPER, Carrie .... 601-984-1117 .... 277 E
cecooper@umc.edu
COOPER, Carrie .... 757-221-3055 .... 518 A
clcooper@wm.edu
COOPER, Cary, W .... 409-772-2665 .... 507 C
ccooper@utmb.edu
COOPER, Colleen, M .... 386-822-7481 .... 121 F
cmcooper@stetson.edu
COOPER, Cynthia, L .... 585-292-3015 .... 341 H
ccooper@monroecc.edu
COOPER, David .... 773-777-4220 .... 160 D
dcooper@nc.edu
COOPER, David .... 401-841-3540 .... 558 B
COOPER, David, H .... 336-278-5900 .... 364 D
dcooper8@elon.edu
COOPER, Derek .... 215-368-5000 .... 422 I
dcooper@biblical.edu
COOPER, Donna .... 518-464-8632 .... 333 E
dcooper@excelsior.edu
COOPER, Doug .... 404-653-7882 .... 134 D
dacooper@morehouse.edu
COOPER, Ed .... 229-430-3577 .... 124 B
ecooper@albanytech.edu
COOPER, Erik .... 530-741-6605 .... 80 K
ecooper@yccd.edu
COOPER, Frank .... 609-771-2357 .... 308 F
cooper@tcnj.edu
COOPER, Franklin .... 406-638-3161 .... 294 E
cooperf@lbhc.edu
COOPER, Gail, S .... 626-585-7282 .... 61 F
gscooper@pasadena.edu
COOPER, Gayle .... 870-612-2004 .... 25 E
gayle.cooper@uaccb.edu
COOPER, Hortense .... 310-660-3492 .... 45 E
hcooper@elcamino.edu
COOPER, James .... 610-409-3698 .... 450 D
jcooper@ursinus.edu
COOPER, James, E .... 334-727-8011 .... 8 B
cooper@tuskegee.edu
COOPER, James, M .... 619-239-0391 .... 37 F
jcooper@cwsl.edu
COOPER, James, W .... 678-915-4986 .... 137 G
jcooper@spsu.edu
COOPER, Jeffrey .... 215-898-1388 .... 448 J
jeffcoop@upenn.edu
COOPER, Jennifer .... 404-233-3949 .... 136 D
jcooper@richmont.edu
COOPER, John, D .... 563-333-6480 .... 188 F
cooperjohnd@sau.edu
COOPER, Jorsene .... 757-727-5323 .... 519 H
jorsene.cooper@hamptonu.edu
COOPER, Karen .... 603-897-8508 .... 305 F
kcooper@rivier.edu
COOPER, Karen, S .... 650-723-0198 .... 71 G
karen.cooper@stanford.edu
COOPER, Karla .... 402-826-8111 .... 297 G
karla.cooper@doane.edu
COOPER, Katie .... 304-336-8131 .... 544 D
katie.mills@westliberty.edu
COOPER, Katrina .... 304-829-7437 .... 540 H
kcooper@bethanywv.edu
COOPER, Kelly .... 815-226-4022 .... 163 A
kcooper@rockford.edu
COOPER, Kenneth .... 845-758-7461 .... 323 D
cooper@bard.edu
COOPER, Kerrie, L .... 315-386-7616 .... 355 E
cooper@canton.edu
COOPER, Lisa, A .... 229-931-2921 .... 131 F
lcooper@gsw.edu
COOPER, Lisa, J .... 215-951-2940 .... 444 D
cooperl@philau.edu
COOPER, Margaret .... 815-802-8962 .... 155 A
mcooper@kcc.edu
COOPER, Marilee .... 806-457-4200 .... 486 I
mcooper@fpctx.edu
COOPER, Marina .... 410-704-2356 .... 228 E
mcooper@towson.edu
COOPER, Mark, E .... 740-368-3108 .... 400 G
mecooper@owu.edu
COOPER, Mary, K .... 434-223-6311 .... 519 G
mcooper@hsc.edu
COOPER, Mary-Beth .... 585-475-2267 .... 347 G
mbccooper@rit.edu
COOPER, MaryKay .... 210-999-7011 .... 502 E
marykay.cooper@trinity.edu
COOPER, Matthew .... 609-984-1140 .... 316 A
mcooper@tesc.edu
COOPER, Michael .... 401-232-6227 .... 453 C
mcooper@bryant.edu
COOPER, N. John .... 412-624-1164 .... 449 A
cooper@pitt.edu
COOPER, Nani Lou, S .... 864-488-4617 .... 459 B
ncooper@limestone.edu
COOPER, Natalie .... 215-871-6560 .... 444 C
nataliecoo@pcom.edu
COOPER, Patricia, A .... 808-956-7541 .... 141 G
pcooper@hawaii.edu
COOPER, R. Scott .... 267-502-2681 .... 423 C
rscott.cooper@brynathyn.edu
COOPER, Reginald .... 870-574-4504 .... 24 A
rcooper@sautech.edu
COOPER, Rick .... 251-981-3771 .... 2 G
rick.cooper@columbiasouthern.edu
COOPER, Robert, A .... 213-740-2101 .... 76 F
racooper@usc.edu

COOPER, Ruth .... 512-313-3000 .... 483 K
ruth.cooper@concordia.edu
COOPER, Shaun .... 575-646-6030 .... 319 D
scooper@nmsu.edu
COOPER, Stephanie .... 973-300-2161 .... 315 F
scooper@sussex.edu
COOPER, Stewart, E .... 219-464-5002 .... 181 C
stewart.cooper@valpo.edu
COOPER, Susan .... 657-278-1605 ...... 35 B
scooper@fullerton.edu
COOPER, Tami, L .... 580-327-8530 .... 409 C
tlcooper@nwosu.edu
COOPER, Tammi .... 254-295-4507 .... 504 C
tcooper@umhb.edu
COOPER, Tana .... 620-792-9241 .... 190 H
coopert@bartonccc.edu
COOPER, Tara, L .... 606-546-1241 .... 207 B
tcooper@unionky.edu
COOPER, Toya .... 805-565-6832 ...... 79 A
tcooper@westmont.edu
COOPER, Tracey, L .... 440-525-7230 .... 394 F
tcooper@lakelandcc.edu
COOPER-WHITE,
Michael, L .... 717-334-6286 .... 435 A
mcooper@ltsg.edu
COOPERIDER, Susan .... 740-368-3376 .... 400 G
skcooper@owu.edu
COOPERSTEIN, Robert .... 408-944-6009 ...... 61 A
robert.cooperstein@palmer.edu
COOPWOOD, SR.,
Kenneth .... 417-836-3736 .... 286 C
kcoopwood@missouristate.edu
COOROUGH, Randall .... 262-691-5168 .... 555 E
rcoorough@wctc.edu
COOTE, Polly .... 415-451-2853 ...... 66 B
pcoote@sfts.edu
COOTER, Raelynn .... 215-503-6595 .... 448 C
raelynn.cooter@jefferson.edu
COOTER, Robert, B .... 502-272-7992 .... 198 H
rcooter@bellarmine.edu
COOTS, Kevin .... 606-326-2064 .... 201 F
kevin.coots@kctcs.edu
COOZE, Frederick, E .... 252-638-7294 .... 370 A
coozef@cravencc.edu
COPANS, Ruth, S .... 518-580-5506 .... 351 B
rcopans@skidmore.edu
COPAS, Aimee .... 701-328-4136 .... 381 E
aimee.copas@ndus.edu
COPAS, Lisa .... 937-393-3431 .... 402 A
lcopas@sscc.edu
COPE, Glen, H .... 314-516-5373 .... 291 D
copeg@umsl.edu
COPE, Henry .... 843-574-6606 .... 461 G
henry.cope@tridenttech.edu
COPE, Marla .... 913-234-0687 .... 191 J
marla.cope@cleveland.edu
COPE, Matthew .... 251-626-3303 .... 8 C
mcope@ussa.edu
COPELAND, Alice .... 903-730-4890 .... 489 C
acopeland@jarvis.edu
COPELAND, Brian .... 616-331-2257 .... 251 F
copelabr@gvsu.edu
COPELAND, David, L .... 540-464-7218 .... 529 F
copelanddl@vmi.edu
COPELAND, Dawn .... 931-393-3022 .... 475 D
dcopeland@mscc.edu
COPELAND, Elaine, J .... 803-327-7402 .... 456 F
ecopeland@clintonjuniorcollege.edu
COPELAND, Jessica .... 719-389-7270 ...... 82 D
jessica.copeland@coloradocollege.edu
COPELAND, Judson .... 405-425-5129 .... 409 E
judson.copeland@oc.edu
COPELAND, Leigh .... 843-525-8231 .... 461 E
lcopeland@tcl.edu
COPELAND, Louise .... 651-290-6439 .... 272 E
louise.copeland@wmitchell.edu
COPELAND, Maura .... 912-478-7481 .... 131 E
mconley@georgiasouthern.edu
COPELAND, Nate .... 501-279-4126 ...... 21 H
nbcopeland@harding.edu
COPELAND, Robert .... 803-327-7402 .... 456 F
rcopeland@clintonjuniorcollege.edu
COPELAND, JR.,
Robert, M .... 803-327-7402 .... 456 F
rcopeland@clintonjuniorcollege.edu
COPELAND, Sandra .... 252-862-1225 .... 373 C
sandrac@roanokechowan.edu
COPELAND, Sarah .... 423-473-2368 .... 474 E
scopeland01@clevelandstatecc.edu
COPELAND, Therese, A ..... 812-374-5115 .... 176 A
tcopeland15@ivytech.edu
COPELAND-MORGAN,
Youlonda .... 310-825-2665 ...... 74 C
ycopeland-morgan@saonet.ucla.edu
COPELIN, Michele .... 806-874-3571 .... 483 A
michele.copelin@clarendoncollege.edu
COPENAGLE, Lily .... 503-517-7916 .... 420 A
copenagl@reed.edu
COPENHAVER, Bonny .... 931-393-1698 .... 475 D
bcopenhaver@mscc.edu
COPENHAVER, Lisa, A ...... 301-766-3646 .... 223 G
lcopenhaver@kaplan.edu
COPENHAVER, Michael .... 619-644-7000 ...... 49 C
michael.coppenhaver@gcccd.edu
COPES, Marcella .... 410-951-3990 .... 228 B
mcopes@coppin.edu
COPLER, Thomas, H .... 804-752-7263 .... 523 C
tcopler@rmc.edu
COPLES, Jimmy .... 404-270-2873 .... 128 I
jcoples@devry.edu
COPLEY, Jason .... 301-369-2800 .... 221 F
jcopley@capitol-college.edu
COPLIN, Kimberly, A .... 740-587-6469 .... 389 I
coplin@denison.edu
COPLIN, Louis .... 518-629-7348 .... 336 C
l.coplin@hvcc.edu
COPONITI, Mike .... 405-224-3140 .... 413 E
mcoponiti@usao.edu
COPONITI, Mike, D .... 405-224-3140 .... 413 E
mcoponiti@usao.edu
COPP, Joan .... 717-394-6211 .... 426 C
COPPARD, Victoria .... 239-513-1135 .... 123 F
vcoppard@wolford.edu
COPPENHAVER, Dorian, H 409-772-2665 .... 507 C
dcoppenh@utmb.edu
COPPERSMITH, Clifford, P 570-326-3761 .... 440 L
COPPI, Carla, E .... 618-453-7661 .... 165 B
ccoppi@siu.edu
COPPIN, Ann, M .... 787-780-0070 .... 560 H
acoppin@caribbean.edu
COPPINGER, Debbie .... 615-460-6474 .... 467 D
debbie.coppinger@belmont.edu
COPPLE, Chad .... 618-437-5321 .... 162 D
copplec@rlc.edu
COPPLE, James "Dean" ...... 865-694-6536 .... 475 G
jdcopple@pstcc.edu
COPPOLA, David, L .... 203-365-4809 ...... 94 B
coppolad@sacredheart.edu
COPPOLA, Joseph .... 559-437-5303 ...... 44 G
jcoppola@devry.edu
COPPOLA, Lynn .... 215-591-5753 .... 427 B
lcoppola@devry.edu
COPPOLA, Robert .... 978-837-5118 .... 242 A
robert.coppola@merrimack.edu
COPPOLA, Sandra .... 973-278-5400 .... 307 F
sec@berkeleycollege.edu
COPPOLA, Stephen, A .... 704-687-5965 .... 379 A
scoppola@uncc.edu
COPPOLA, Tim .... 813-889-3460 .... 111 C
tcoppola@academy.edu
COPPOLA, William .... 817-515-3001 .... 496 C
william.coppola@tccd.edu
CORA, Gladys .... 787-766-1717 .... 565 I
um_gcora@suagm.edu
CORAZZA, Anthony .... 718-368-5124 .... 328 A
acorazza@kbcc.cuny.edu
CORBA, David .... 586-286-2058 .... 254 C
corbad@macomb.edu
CORBALIS, Kathleen, J ...... 609-343-4907 .... 307 C
corbalis@atlantic.edu
CORBAT, Carol .... 318-473-6431 .... 212 I
ccorbat@lsua.edu
CORBETT, Andy .... 303-352-3032 ...... 84 A
andy.corbett@cccs.edu
CORBETT, Ann .... 207-621-3145 .... 220 B
annie@maine.edu
CORBETT, Idna, M .... 610-436-3416 .... 444 A
icorbett@wcupa.edu
CORBETT, Keith .... 605-688-4153 .... 466 C
keith.corbett@sdstate.edu
CORBETT, Kevin, J .... 785-864-4760 .... 197 B
kcorbett@ku.edu
CORBETT, Martin .... 315-781-3656 .... 335 F
corbett@hws.edu
CORBETT, Michele .... 619-849-2510 ...... 62 L
michelecorbett@pointloma.edu
CORBETT, Mickey .... 432-837-8059 .... 501 E
mcorbett@sulross.edu
CORBIN, Dana, M .... 972-860-8152 .... 484 H
dcorbin@dcccd.edu
CORBIN, Rebecca .... 609-894-9311 .... 308 B
rcorbin@bcc.edu
CORBIN, Thomas .... 802-443-5504 .... 514 A
corbin@middlebury.edu
CORBIN, Ty .... 804-523-5726 .... 527 A
tcorbin@reynolds.edu
CORBINE, Theresa, C .... 315-386-7448 .... 355 E
corbine@canton.edu
CORBITT, Sandra, K .... 540-338-1776 .... 522 G
CORBITT, Timothy .... 860-832-1629 ...... 90 G
corbitt@ccsu.edu
CORBITT, Timothy, J .... 315-268-2327 .... 329 B
tcorbitt@clarkson.edu
CORBLY, James .... 785-827-5541 .... 194 F
james.corbly@kwu.edu
CORBOY, Lynne .... 215-780-1394 .... 446 G
lcorboy@salus.edu
CORBOY, Lynne .... 215-780-1392 .... 446 G
lcorboy@salus.edu
CORCORAN, Janenne .... 410-386-8444 .... 221 G
jcorcoran@carrollcc.edu
CORCORAN, Jerry, M .... 815-224-0404 .... 153 E
jerry_corcoran@ivcc.edu
CORCORAN, Krista, L .... 417-268-6064 .... 278 J
kcorcoran@gobbc.edu
CORCORAN, Lisa .... 425-564-2302 .... 531 G
lisa.corcoran@bellevuecollege.edu
CORCORAN, Mary, C .... 617-552-8647 .... 232 B
mary.corcoran@bc.edu
CORCORAN, Sean .... 860-701-6022 ...... 93 E
corcoran_s@mitchell.edu
CORCORAN, William .... 201-612-5234 .... 307 E
wcorcoran@bergen.edu
CORCORAN, William, M .... 570-208-5846 .... 432 G
wmcorcor@kings.edu
CORDANO, Mark .... 607-274-3341 .... 336 G
mcordano@ithaca.edu
CORDANO, Mark .... 978-837-5000 .... 242 A
cordanom@merrimack.edu
CORDARY, John .... 281-283-2135 .... 503 E
cordary@uhcl.edu
CORDEIRO, Paula, A .... 619-260-4540 ...... 76 D
cordeiro@sandiego.edu
CORDEIRO, Wayne .... 808-853-1040 .... 141 C
CORDEIRO, Wayne .... 541-485-1780 .... 417 E
waynecordeiro@newhope.edu
CORDEIRO, William .... 805-437-8860 ...... 34 B
william.corderio@csuci.edu
CORDELL, Barbara .... 903-694-4003 .... 492 C
bcordell@panola.edu
CORDELL, David, J .... 425-640-1412 .... 533 I
dcordell@edcc.edu
CORDELL, Janice, K .... 563-387-1018 .... 187 D
cordellj@luther.edu
CORDELL, Joyce .... 915-831-6530 .... 486 G
jyamasak@cpcc.edu
CORDELL, Michelle .... 479-619-4361 ...... 22 H
mcordell@nwacc.edu
CORDELL, Peggy .... 706-295-6959 .... 131 B
pcordell@gntc.edu
CORDELL, Penny .... 706-272-4498 .... 128 C
pcordell@daltonstate.edu
CORDER, Colleen .... 503-552-1702 .... 417 D
ccorder@ncnm.edu
CORDERO, Damaris .... 787-751-0160 .... 561 H
dcordero@cmpr.gov.pr
CORDERO, Eunice .... 787-284-1912 .... 564 A
ecordero@ponce.inter.edu
CORDERO, Heather .... 847-317-7071 .... 166 E
hcordero@tiu.edu
CORDERO, Irma, L .... 787-740-1611 .... 566 C
irma.cordero@uccaribe.edu
CORDERO, Jose .... 787-758-2525 .... 567 G
jose.cordero6@upr.edu
CORDERO, Maggie .... 562-860-2451 ...... 39 A
mcordero@cerritos.edu
CORDERO, Zain .... 787-882-2065 .... 566 A
mis@unitecpr.net
CORDERO DE VIDAL,
Pilar .... 787-896-2252 .... 562 B
pcordero@edpcollege.edu
CORDERY, Simon .... 706-864-1819 .... 134 G
sdcordery@northgeorgia.edu
CORDES, Cynthia .... 773-481-8180 .... 147 I
ccordes@ccc.edu
CORDIA, Judith .... 775-445-3295 .... 303 B
cordiaj@wnc.edu
CORDLE, David, P .... 910-962-7232 .... 379 D
cordled@uncw.edu
CORDLE, Robbie, L .... 301-687-4403 .... 228 C
rcordle@frostburg.edu
CORDOVA, Damion .... 970-339-6656 ...... 81 A
damion.cordova@aims.edu
CORDOVA, Denise .... 775-682-6708 .... 303 A
dcordova@unr.edu
CORDOVA, Mitchell .... 239-590-7074 .... 119 B
mcordova@fgcu.edu
CORDOVA, Ryan .... 505-747-2288 .... 320 A
rcordova@nnmc.edu
CORDOVA, Tracy, H .... 417-667-8181 .... 280 E
tcordova@cottey.edu
CORDOVEZ, Maria .... 787-850-9345 .... 567 E
maria.cordovez@upr.edu
CORDRAY, JR., John, A ... 843-953-8259 .... 457 B
cordrayj@cofc.edu
CORDULACK, John .... 217-875-7200 .... 162 F
jcordula@richland.edu
CORDULACK, Tricia .... 217-875-7200 .... 162 F
tcordulack@richland.edu
CORE, Gordon .... 724-938-5985 .... 441 G
core@calu.edu
CORE, Justin .... 541-881-5781 .... 420 E
jcore@tvcc.cc
CORE, Ron .... 912-478-5491 .... 131 E
rcore@georgiasouthern.edu
COREN, Richard, H .... 401-825-2028 .... 453 D
rhcoren@ccri.edu
CORESSEL, James .... 419-783-2503 .... 389 H
jcoressel@defiance.edu
COREY, Barry, H .... 562-903-4701 ...... 31 A
president@biola.edu
COREY, Frederick, C .... 602-496-0624 ...... 11 J
frederick.corey@asu.edu
COREY, M, J .... 304-637-1344 .... 541 A
coreym@dewv.edu
COREY, Pat .... 765-269-5605 .... 176 D
pcorey@ivytech.edu
COREY, Steven, M .... 269-749-7642 .... 257 A
scorey@olivetcollege.edu
COREY, Timothy .... 570-586-2400 .... 422 G
tcorey@bbc.edu
CORGNATI, Bart .... 919-962-4592 .... 377 C
bbc@northcarolina.edu
CORIA, Elizabeth .... 562-908-3411 ...... 63 H
elizabeth.coria@riohondo.edu
CORIELL, Bruce .... 719-389-6638 ...... 82 D
bcoriell@coloradocollege.edu
CORINA, Laura .... 617-984-1713 .... 243 H
lcorina@quincycollege.edu
CORINO, Mark, A .... 973-618-3412 .... 308 C
mcorino@caldwell.edu
CORJAY, Marcy .... 704-216-7217 .... 373 F
marcy.corjay@rccc.edu
CORKERY, John, E .... 312-987-1426 .... 154 H
7corkery@jmls.edu
CORKILL, Jim, R .... 805-893-5882 ...... 75 B
jim.corkill@accounting.ucsb.edu
CORKRAN, Kenneth, F .... 508-541-1700 .... 233 G
kcorkran@dean.edu
CORKRUM, Dalia, L .... 509-527-5193 .... 540 B
corkrum@whitman.edu
CORKUM, David .... 617-552-4500 .... 232 B
david.corkum@bc.edu
CORLE, Trish .... 814-262-3841 .... 441 A
tcorle@pennhighlands.edu
CORLEY, Bruce .... 817-274-4284 .... 482 B
CORLEY, Charlene .... 314-768-1234 .... 282 J
CORLEY, Diane .... 512-463-1808 .... 500 H
diane.corley@tsus.edu
CORLEY, John, C .... 870-230-5179 ...... 21 I
corleyj@hsu.edu
CORLEY, Teresa .... 615-794-4254 .... 472 F
tcorley@omorecollege.edu
CORLEY, Thomas .... 785-242-5200 .... 195 I
thomas.corley@ottawa.edu
CORLEY, Tom .... 785-242-5200 .... 196 A
CORLEY, Tom .... 785-242-5200 .... 178 I
CORLEY, Tom .... 785-242-5200 ...... 17 B
CORLEY, Tom .... 785-242-5200 .... 549 H
CORLL, Thomas .... 432-685-5540 .... 491 A
tcorll@midland.edu
CORMACK, Barbara .... 530-283-0202 ...... 47 B
bcormack@frc.edu
CORMIER, Marilyn, E .... 802-654-2215 .... 514 D
mcormier@smcvt.edu
CORN, Melanie .... 510-594-3649 ...... 32 C
mcorn@cca.edu
CORNACCHIA, Eugene, J .. 201-761-6010 .... 314 F
ecornacchia@spc.edu
CORNEJO-DARCY, Silvia ... 619-216-6755 ...... 71 D
scornejo@swccd.edu
CORNEJO-DARCY, Silvia ... 619-216-6795 ...... 71 D
scornejo@swccd.edu
CORNELIA, Jim .... 712-274-5234 .... 187 G
cornelia@morningside.edu
CORNELISON, Nelle .... 509-527-2664 .... 539 C
nelle.cornelison@wallawalla.edu
CORNELIUS, Alice .... 602-286-8330 ...... 15 G
alice.cornelius@gwmail.maricopa.edu
CORNELIUS, Jerod, L .... 651-631-5320 .... 270 B
jlcornelius@nwc.edu
CORNELIUS, Michael .... 480-423-6573 ...... 16 C
michael.cornelius@scottsdalecc.edu
CORNELIUS, Tim .... 479-619-3117 ...... 22 H
tcornelius@nwacc.edu
CORNELIUS TAYLOR,
Carmen .... 406-353-2607 .... 293 E
ctaylor@mail.fbcc.edu
CORNELL, Brian .... 718-409-7381 .... 356 C
bcornell@sunymaritime.edu
CORNELL, Craig .... 740-597-3280 .... 399 G
cornellc@ohio.edu
CORNELL, Dennis .... 213-740-2111 ...... 76 F
dcornell@president.usc.edu
CORNELL, Dona, G .... 832-842-0949 .... 503 C
dhcornell@uh.edu
CORNELL, Dona, G .... 713-743-0949 .... 503 D
dhcornell@uh.edu
CORNELL, John .... 912-279-5703 .... 127 E
jcornell@ccga.edu
CORNELL, Kenneth, E .... 206-281-2405 .... 537 H
CORNELL, Starr .... 248-364-6160 .... 256 G
cornell2@oakland.edu
CORNELL, Stefanie .... 510-574-1211 ...... 44 F
scornell@devry.edu
CORNELL-POKU, Natasha . 212-353-4099 .... 331 A
natasha@cooper.edu
CORNELL-SCOTT, Andrea ... 540-887-7270 .... 521 C
ascott@mbc.edu
CORNER, William, T .... 616-526-6451 .... 249 A
wtc2@calvin.edu
CORNERO, Robert .... 732-571-3424 .... 311 E
rcornero@monmouth.edu
CORNETT, Jeff .... 317-921-4282 .... 175 K
jcornett29@ivytech.edu
CORNETT, Scott .... 606-368-6120 .... 198 C
scottcornett@alc.edu
CORNETT, Sherry, N .... 770-720-5543 .... 136 C
snc@reinhardt.edu
CORNFORD, Ernest, A .... 314-516-5092 .... 291 D
cornford@umsl.edu
CORNIA, Gary, C .... 801-422-4122 .... 509 H
gary_cornia@byu.edu
CORNIER, Wilfredo .... 787-841-2000 .... 565 B
wcornier@pucpr.edu

CORNILLE, Keith, T 608-246-6464 554 D kcornille@madisoncollege.org
CORNISH, Irene, K 315-859-4999 334 H icornish@hamilton.edu
CORNISH, Letitia 336-750-2132 380 B cornishl@wssu.edu
CORNMAN, Thomas, H 937-766-7770 386 G tcornman@cedarville.edu
CORNNER, Ryan 323-265-8967 54 G cornnerm@elac.edu
CORNOG, Evan, W 516-463-5213 335 G evan.cornog@hofstra.edu
CORNUE, Amy, L 315-684-6041 354 F cornueal@morrisville.edu
CORNWELL, Grant, H 330-263-2311 388 F gcornwell@wooster.edu
CORNWELL, Mona, L 828-398-7117 368 B mcornwell@abtech.edu
CORNWELL, Nancy 406-994-6654 295 C nancy.cornwell@montana.edu
CORNWELL, Phillip, J 812-877-8232 179 B cornwell@rose-hulman.edu
CORNWELL, Shirley, A 937-393-3431 402 A scornwell@sscc.edu
COROMINAS, Mike 954-262-8840 114 B coromina@nsu.nova.edu
CORONA, Nayeli 619-574-6909 60 D ncorona@pacificcollege.edu
CORONA, Paul 847-491-8570 160 E p-corona@northwestern.edu
CORONA, Stacie 530-898-5931 34 C scorona@csuchico.edu
CORONADO, Ricardo 817-515-5234 496 C ricardo.coronado@tccd.edu
CORPENING, Brian, K 405-271-2332 413 D brian-corpening@ouhsc.edu
CORPUS, Ben 646-312-4570 326 C ben.corpus@baruch.cuny.edu
CORR, Daniel, P 480-423-6317 16 C daniel.corr@scottsdalecc.edu
CORR, Marianne 574-631-6411 180 G mcorr1@nd.edu
CORRADETTI, Arthur 718-631-6344 328 F acorradetti@qcc.cuny.edu
CORRADO, Rebecca 212-217-4202 333 F rebecca_corrado@fitnyc.edu
CORRAL, David 661-654-2254 34 A corral-david@aramark.com
CORRAL-NAVA, Nita 915-831-2302 486 G ncorraln@epcc.edu
CORRALIZA-TORRES, Cruz 787-480-2386 561 E ccorraliza@sanjuancapital.com
CORRAN, Robert 802-656-3075 514 H robert.corran@uvm.edu
CORREA, Florinda 361-582-2516 508 B florinda.correa@victoriacollege.edu
CORREA, Leslie, H 808-544-0235 140 G lcorrea@hpu.edu
CORREA, Omar, G 309-457-2142 158 H correa@monmouthcollege.eduedu
CORREA, Peter 404-965-6542 124 D pecorrea@aiuniv.edu
CORREA, Santy 787-284-1912 564 A scorrea@ponce.inter.edu
CORREA, Sylvia 256-233-8116 1 E sylvia.correa@athens.edu
CORREDERA, Enrique 802-656-2005 514 H enrique.corredera@uvm.edu
CORREIA, Jorge 781-595-6768 236 C jcorreia@mariancourt.edu
CORRELL, Dennis, L 570-327-4761 440 L dcorrell@pct.edu
CORRELL, Jen 717-728-2362 425 B jencorrell@centralpenn.edu
CORRELL, Scott 715-232-2121 552 E corrells@uwstout.edu
CORRENTI, Bill 718-368-5066 328 A bcorrenti@kbcc.cuny.edu
CORRIE, Bruce, P 651-641-8226 263 A corrie@csp.edu
CORRIE, Rosie 575-769-4021 318 A rosie.corrie@clovis.edu
CORRIGAN, Boo 845-938-3701 559 A boo.corrigan@usma.edu
CORRIGAN, Deborah 518-438-3111 340 A debc@mariacollege.edu
CORRIGAN, Gary 567-661-2692 400 I gary_corrigan@owens.edu
CORRIGAN, Kevin 404-727-6460 129 D kcorrig@emory.edu
CORRIGAN, JR., Robert, F 713-798-6392 481 H corrigan@bcm.edu
CORRIGAN, Tom 617-217-9205 231 A tcorrigan@baystate.edu
CORRISS, Mary Jean 540-362-6332 520 A corrissmj@hollins.edu
CORSELLO, Chris, L 704-403-4336 362 I chris.corsello@carolinashealthcare.org
CORSENTINO, Leanne 719-549-3206 87 F leanne.corsentino@pueblocc.edu
CORSETTI, Dan 617-912-9125 232 C dcorsetti@bostonconservatory.edu
CORSO, Joseph 225-578-3312 212 G jacorso@lsu.edu
CORSO, Michael 973-300-2226 315 F mcorso@sussex.edu
CORSO, Teri 973-290-4266 308 G tcorso@cse.edu
CORSON, D.J 319-296-4292 185 F debra.corson@hawkeyecollege.edu
CORSON-RIKERT, Janet, L 607-255-3564 331 B jlc18@cornell.edu
CORTES, Chris 559-638-3641 72 C chris.cortes@reedleycollege.edu
CORTES, Dario 212-986-4343 323 H dario@berkeleycollege.edu
CORTES, Dario, A 973-278-5400 307 F dario@berkeleycollege.edu
CORTES, Edymariel 939-292-8918 568 C edymariel.cortes@upr.edu
CORTES, Elvia, E 202-231-5605 557 J elvia.cortes@dodiis.mil
CORTES, Felix 787-841-2000 565 B fcortes@pucpr.edu
CORTES, Frances 787-878-5475 563 B fcortes@arecibo.inter.edu
CORTES, Gloria 787-891-0925 563 A gcortes@aguadilla.inter.edu
CORTES, Graciela 503-845-3555 417 A graciela.cortes@mtangel.edu
CORTES, Reinaldo 352-323-3691 112 J cortesr@lscc.edu
CORTES, Tammy 831-813-6820 490 E tammy.a.cortes@lonestar.edu
CORTES-SUAREZ, Gina 305-237-6034 113 H gcortes@mdc.edu
CORTESE, Joseph 570-504-9641 425 F
CORTEZ, Jack 973-748-9000 307 H jack_cortez@bloomfield.edu
CORTEZ, Lori 989-386-6622 255 C lcortez@midmich.edu
CORTEZ, Marc 503-517-1876 421 C mcortez@westernseminary.edu
CORTEZ, Michelle 909-472-0646 29 D mcortez@argosy.edu
CORTEZ, Ray 956-721-5303 489 J rcortez@laredo.edu
CORTEZ, Ronald 805-893-8291 75 B ron.cortez@vcadmin.ucsb.edu
CORTEZ, Sandra, L 956-721-5374 489 J sandra.cortez@laredo.edu
CORTEZ-FARAH, Terre 619-684-8763 59 B tcortez@newschoolarch.edu
CORTHELL, Ronald 219-989-2401 178 K ronald.corthell@purduecal.edu
CORTI, Tom 631-420-2264 356 A tom.corti@farmingdale.edu
CORTILET-ALBRECHT, Carol 219-989-2507 178 K carol.cortilet-albrecht@purduecal.edu
CORTINAS, Debra 361-825-5743 498 C debra.cortinas@tamucc.edu
CORVERS, Shana 225-216-8031 209 H corverss@mybrcc.edu
CORVEY, Rebecca, J 478-471-2734 133 H rebecca.corvey@maconstate.edu
CORVIN, Clay, L 504-282-4455 213 H claycor@wbsn.com
CORVINGTON, Roland 314-977-3873 289 C rcorving@slu.edu
CORWIN, Cynthia 719-255-3696 88 I ccorwin@uccs.edu
CORY, Christopher 212-346-1117 345 F ccory@pace.edu
CORY, Gerald, A 888-488-4968 51 F
CORY, Jeff 845-675-4425 344 G jeff.cory@nyack.edu
CORYAT, Catherine, A 973-655-4199 311 F coryatc@mail.montclair.edu
COSBY, Glen 509-533-3576 533 C glenc@spokanefalls.edu
COSBY, Helen 334-876-9234 4 B hcosby@wccs.edu
COSBY, Kevin, W 502-776-1443 206 B
COSBY, Laura 268-488-4440 253 A lcosby@kvcc.edu
COSCIA, Paul 336-316-2395 365 A pcoscia@guilford.edu
COSDEN, Julie 239-280-2558 101 I julie.cosden@avemaria.edu
COSENTINO, Lauren 310-506-4397 61 H lauren.cosentino@pepperdine.edu
COSER, Pete 918-687-3299 407 B coserp@bacone.edu
COSEY, Arnel 504-671-5055 210 F acosey@dcc.edu
COSGROVE, John 570-662-4586 443 C jcosgrov@mansfield.edu
COSGROVE, John, J 314-539-5380 288 G jcosgrove@stlcc.edu
COSGROVE, Maryellen 678-717-3482 129 G mcosgrove@gsc.edu
COSIMO, Julie 630-829-6037 145 G jcosimo@ben.edu
COSKY, Alicia, C 630-844-5116 145 F acosky@aurora.edu
COSMATO, Charlie 540-831-6597 523 A ccosmato@radford.edu
COSO, Xuchitl 863-680-4390 109 E xcoso@flsouthern.edu
COSPER, Tracy 229-317-6838 128 D tracy.cosper@darton.edu
COSSICH, Marc 936-468-2608 496 B mcossich@sfasu.edu
COSSICH, Monique 936-468-2504 496 B cossichm@sfasu.edu
COSTA, Elizabeth, A 540-985-9701 520 I eacosta@jchs.edu
COSTA, Kathleen 925-866-1822 43 F kcosta@dvc.edu
COSTA, Linda, J 732-932-7743 314 B smeds@rci.rutgers.edu
COSTA, Maria, D 423-439-7737 473 F costa@etsu.edu
COSTA, JR., Richard, F 859-371-9393 198 G rcosta@beckfield.edu
COSTA, Xavier 617-373-3682 243 F
COSTA-BROWN, Darlene 508-531-2889 237 D dcosta@bridgew.edu
COSTANTINO, Andrea 716-645-2171 351 G costanti@buffalo.edu
COSTANTINO, Arthur 360-867-6296 534 D costanta@evergreen.edu
COSTANZA, Carl, F 847-635-1876 160 F costanza@oakton.edu
COSTANZA, Laina 334-387-3877 1 D lainacostanza@amridgeuniversity.edu
COSTANZO, Brian 570-961-7841 433 A costanzob@lackawanna.edu
COSTAS, Edda 787-284-1912 564 A ecostas@ponce.inter.edu
COSTAS, Pamela, G 773-508-6200 157 C pcostas@luc.edu
COSTELLO, Dana 410-225-2338 224 B dcostello@mica.edu
COSTELLO, Dennis 586-445-7318 254 C costellod@macomb.edu
COSTELLO, Eileen 978-632-6600 240 C e_costello@mwcc.mass.edu
COSTELLO, Georgia 618-235-2700 165 D georgia.costello@swic.edu
COSTELLO, Gregory, W 507-344-7305 261 C costello@blc.edu
COSTELLO, Jamie 617-879-7703 238 B jcostello@massart.edu
COSTELLO, Janice 860-727-6919 92 I jcostello@goodwin.edu
COSTELLO, Joan 651-450-3618 266 F jcostel@inverhills.edu
COSTELLO, SJ, John 312-518-7535 157 C jcoste2@luc.edu
COSTELLO, Kathryn 270-745-6208 208 A kathryn.costello@wku.edu
COSTELLO, Kevin 617-327-6777 241 F kevin_costello@mspp.edu
COSTELLO, Mary Elizabeth 973-761-9175 315 B maryelizabeth.costello@shu.edu
COSTELLO, Richard, J 219-989-2540 178 K richard.costello@purduecal.edu
COSTELLO, Rose, M 260-481-6677 174 C costellr@ipfw.edu
COSTIGAN, Harry 215-567-7080 422 D hcostigan@edmc.edu
COSTNER, Carl 828-652-0614 372 B carlc@mcdowelltech.edu
COSTON, Charlotte, M 716-851-1180 333 A coston@ecc.edu
COSTON, D.C 701-483-2326 381 G dc.coston@dickinsonstate.edu
COSTON, Linda 229-430-2751 124 B lcoston@albanytech.edu
COSTON, Robert, H 304-647-6574 543 A rcoston@newriver.edu
COSTON, Todd 661-395-4601 52 L tcoston@bakersfieldcollege.edu
COSTON-MCHUGH, Rose 856-227-7200 308 D rcoston-mchugh@camdencc.edu
COTA, Amalia 925-288-5800 49 H amalia_cota@heald.edu
COTA, Marco 909-384-8952 65 C mcota@sbccd.cc.ca.us
COTA, Susan, A 925-485-5206 39 B scota@clpccd.org
COTE, Deborah 413-236-1022 239 A dcote@berkshirecc.edu
COTE, John, C 810-766-4191 248 C john.cote@baker.edu
COTE, Matthew 207-513-3660 218 C mcote@kaplan.edu
COTE, Shannon 207-775-3052 218 E scote@meca.edu
COTE-BONANNO, Joanne, F 973-655-6234 311 F bonannoj@mail.montclair.edu
COTEY, Kathryn, M 414-276-5200 546 F kmcotey@bryantstratton.edu
COTGREAVE, Bruce 806-345-5565 479 G blcotgreave@actx.edu
COTHAM, Brian 559-278-2111 35 A bcotham@csufresno.edu
COTHERN, John, W 615-898-2852 473 G john.cothern@mtsu.edu
COTHERN, Richard 912-427-5824 124 C rcothern@altamahatech.edu
COTHERN, Susan, L 828-884-8373 362 H stromsbl@brevard.edu
COTHRAN, Rick 864-646-1701 461 F rcothran@tctc.edu
COTHRAN, Robbie 864-503-5145 463 B rcothran@uscupstate.edu
COTLEUR, Mary Elizabeth 216-373-5316 397 F mcotleur@ndc.edu
COTNET-KLINGLER, Amy 304-442-3183 545 D amy.cotner-klingler@mail.wvu.edu
COTNOIR, Kathleen 413-565-1209 230 G kcotnoir@baypath.edu
COTNOIR, Paul 508-373-9731 231 B paul.cotnoir@becker.edu
COTREL, Jack, R 423-439-6900 473 F cotrel@etsu.edu
COTRONEO, Keith, J 304-710-3141 542 K cotroneo@mctc.edu
COTSONES, Rena 815-753-0834 160 B rcotsones@niu.edu
COTSONIS, Joachim 617-850-1243 235 F jcotsonis@hchc.edu
COTTEN, Melinda 713-348-6200 493 C cotten@rice.edu
COTTER, Anita 310-825-1443 74 C acotter@registrar.ucla.edu
COTTER, Dan, J 802-258-9297 513 H dcotter@marlboro.edu
COTTER, Geri, E 402-465-2159 299 H gec@nebrwesleyan.edu
COTTER, James, W 517-355-6532 255 A cotterj@msu.edu
COTTER, Jeff 805-922-6966 26 L jcotter@hancockcollege.edu
COTTER, Mary, L 315-445-5441 338 B cottemal@lemoyne.edu
COTTER, Michael 914-594-3675 343 F michael_cotter@nymc.edu
COTTERMAN, Susan 740-389-4636 395 H cottermans@mtc.edu
COTTIER, Mary 210-486-2597 479 D mcottier@alamo.edu
COTTINGHAM, Carolyn 914-674-7459 340 F ccottingham@mercy.edu
COTTO, Evelyn 787-746-1400 562 E ecoto@huertas.edu
COTTO, Marguerite, C 231-995-1775 256 D mcotto@nmc.edu
COTTO, Saulo 787-844-8181 568 A saulo.cotto@upr.edu
COTTON, Beverly 603-668-2211 305 I b.cotton@snhu.edu
COTTON, Beverly 817-257-5710 482 E beverly.cotton@tcu.edu
COTTON, Dwight 859-336-5082 206 A dwightcotton@sccky.edu
COTTON, Fran 806-894-9611 494 G fcotton@southplainscollege.edu
COTTON, Roger, D 417-268-1000 278 H rcotton@agts.edu
COTTON, Sabrina 256-726-7408 6 C cotton@oakwood.edu
COTTON, Trae 336-750-3200 380 B cottontt@wssu.edu
COTTON KELLY, Montique, R 419-372-7673 385 E mcotton@bgsu.edu
COTTONE, John 607-753-2701 353 B john.cottone@cortland.edu
COTTONHAM, Patricia 337-482-6266 216 D patcottonham@louisiaiana.edu
COTTONHAM, Patricia, F 337-482-6276 216 D pattcottonham@louisiana.edu
COTTRELL, Angela 816-235-1407 291 C cottrella@umkc.edu
COTTRELL, Debbie 830-372-8002 499 F dcottrell@tlu.edu
COTTRELL, Debbie 254-295-5059 504 C dcottrell@umhb.edu
COTTRELL, Janet 802-865-6492 513 C cottrell@champlain.edu
COTTRELL, Karen, R 757-221-1166 518 A krcott@wm.edu
COTTRELL, Leslie 378-839-6452 139 A lcottrel@westga.edu
COTTRELL, Rick 800-962-7682 293 A rcottrell@wma.edu
COTTRELL, Stephen, E 662-325-8460 275 F wec3@msstate.edu
COTTRELL, Terrance, L 815-740-5041 167 E tcottrell@stfrancis.edu
COTTRILL, Chad 503-883-2506 416 H ccottril@linfield.edu
COTTRILL, F. Layton 304-696-6295 544 B cottrill@marshall.edu
COTTRILL, Gary, L 812-246-3301 177 B gcottril@ivytech.edu
COTTRILL, Tamra 540-863-2905 526 F tcottrill@dslcc.edu
COTY, Blake 229-732-5934 124 E blakecoty@andrewcollege.edu

COTY, Mark 941-782-5980 433 C mcoty@lecom.edu
COUCH, Alisha, M 740-368-3099 400 G amcouch@owu.edu
COUCH, Brett 513-785-3070 396 F couchbc@muohio.edu
COUCH, Carl 480-423-6161 16 C carl.couch@scottsdalecc.edu
COUCH, Charlie 970-351-2231 89 B charlie.couch@unco.edu
COUCH, Daryl, D 864-644-5328 461 B dcouch@swu.edu
COUCH, JR., Gene, C 336-506-4154 368 A gene.couch@alamancecc.edu
COUCH, Lisa 760-384-6288 52 M lcouch@cerrocoso.edu
COUCH, Michael 513-745-1000 406 E couch@xavier.edu
COUCH, Stephen, R 570-385-6001 440 D src@psu.edu
COUCH, Valerie 405-208-5440 410 A vcouch@okcu.edu
COUCHEY, Evangeline 845-675-4733 344 G evangeline.couchey@nyack.edu
COUCHON, William, D 607-735-1830 332 I dcouchon@elmira.edu
COUGHENOUR, Brenda 814-262-6434 441 A bcoughen@pennhighlands.edu
COUGHLIN, Devan 904-256-7054 111 L dcoughl1@ju.edu
COUGHLIN, Eileen, V 360-650-3839 539 F eileen.coughlin@wwu.edu
COUGHLIN, OFM, F. Edward 716-375-2032 348 C coughlin@sbu.edu
COUGHLIN, Kathleen 210-829-6012 504 B coughlin@uiwtx.edu
COUGHLIN, Kevin 239-489-9027 105 F kcoughlinr@edison.edu
COUGHLIN, Mary Ann 413-748-3959 244 H mcoughlin@springfieldcollege.edu
COUGHLIN, Richard 660-785-4038 290 G coughlin@truman.edu
COULOMBE, Jennifer, B 336-734-7723 370 F jcoulombe@forsythtech.edu
COULON, Richard 949-824-6510 74 B rcoulon@uci.edu
COULSTON, Susan 269-782-1396 258 C scoulston@swmich.edu
COULTER, Ann 641-782-1340 189 E coulter@swcciowa.edu
COULTER, Chris 719-389-6568 82 D chris.coulter@coloradocollege.edu
COULTER, Christy, M 724-847-5566 429 H cmcoulte@geneva.edu
COULTER, Cindy 828-327-7000 369 B ccoulter@cvcc.edu
COULTER, Cynthia 201-360-4722 310 E ccoulter@hccc.edu
COULTER, Kristin 512-313-3000 483 K kristin.coulter@concordia.edu
COULTER, Laurie 903-813-2900 481 A lcoulter@austincollege.edu
COULTER, Martha 802-468-1314 515 D martha.coulter@castleton.edu
COUNCE, Bamby 901-572-2853 467 C bamby.counce@bchs.edu
COUNCIL, Juanette 910-672-1208 377 G jcouncil@uncfsu.edu
COUNCIL, William 910-410-1823 373 B bcouncil@richmondcc.edu
COUNIHAN, Patricia, B 207-581-1359 220 A counihan@maine.edu
COUNTS, LaNeta 404-471-6483 123 I lcounts@agnesscott.edu
COURCHAINE, Jeff 714-892-7711 41 C jcourchaine@gwc.cccd.edu
COURSEY, Greg 912-583-3221 126 F gcoursey@bpc.edu
COURSEY, Martha 404-297-9522 131 D courseym@gptc.edu
COURTADE, Kay 515-271-1657 184 A kay.courtade@dmu.edu
COURTEMANCHE, Brian 978-927-2278 234 D bcourtem@endicott.edu
COURTEY, Susan 818-240-1000 48 D scourtey@glendale.edu
COURTLEY-TODD, Laura 305-628-6677 117 A lcourtle@stu.edu
COURTNEY, Andolyn, M 716-888-2780 325 F courtnea@canisius.edu
COURTNEY, Hugh 617-373-3232 243 F
COURTNEY, Jim 773-947-6285 157 G jcourtney@mccormick.edu
COURTNEY, Justin 419-772-2145 398 H j-courtney@onu.edu
COURTNEY, Regina, L 214-828-8235 497 C rcourtney@bcd.tamhsc.edu
COURTNEY, Sharon, P 504-988-3390 215 C sharonc@tulane.edu
COURTRIGHT, Caren 509-793-2038 531 I carenc@bigbend.edu
COURTRIGHT, Mary Beth 508-588-9100 240 A
COURTWAY, Tom 501-450-5286 25 H tcourtway@uca.edu
COURY, David 850-644-6031 119 D dpcoury@admin.fsu.edu
COUSIN, Dennis 504-520-7330 217 A dcousin@xula.edu
COUSSONS-READ, Mary 303-315-5821 88 J mary.coussons-read@ucdenver.edu
COUTILISH, Theodore, G 734-487-2483 250 F ted.coutilish@emich.edu
COUTTS, Chris 540-868-7083 527 C ccoutts@lfcc.edu
COUTTS, Kimberly 760-797-2121 57 E kcoutts@miracosta.edu
COUTURE, Barbara 575-646-2035 319 D president@nmsu.edu
COUTURE, Daniel, R 802-654-3243 514 D dcouture@smcvt.edu
COUTURE, Donna, L 978-232-2026 234 D dcouture@endicott.edu
COUTURE, Janelle 216-391-6937 387 B jcouture@chancelloru.edu
COUTURE, Richard 607-274-3225 336 G rcouture@ithaca.edu
COVAL, Scott 610-282-1100 427 A scott.coval@desales.edu
COVALT, Lindy 765-966-2656 176 H lcovalt@ivytech.edu
COVAR, Tom 864-388-8305 459 A tcovar@lander.edu
COVAULT, Pamela 785-242-2067 195 E pcovault@neosho.edu
COVE, Lorraine, D 617-573-8160 245 B lcove@acad.suffolk.edu
COVELLE, Fred 617-422-7205 243 B fcovelle@nesl.edu
COVELLI-KOVACH, Andrea 215-572-4014 422 C covelli@arcadia.edu
COVENEY, Kevin, C 410-778-7700 229 D kcoveney2@washcoll.edu
COVENEY, Michael, J 215-572-2943 422 C coveney@arcadia.edu
COVER, Michael, S 570-577-3348 423 E mike.cover@bucknell.edu
COVERDALE, Pat 423-236-2276 473 B plcoverdale@southern.edu
COVERS, Beth, A 810-762-9925 253 C bcovers@kettering.edu
COVERT, Carl 903-785-7661 492 D ccovert@parisjc.edu
COVERT, Sheree, S 319-352-8272 189 J sheree.covert@wartburg.edu
COVEY, Angie, E 540-674-3655 527 E acovey@nr.edu
COVEY, Becky 276-466-7192 529 D beckycovey@vic.edu
COVEY, Bruce 404-727-6223 129 D bcovey@emory.edu
COVEY, Douglass, F 404-413-1500 131 G dcovey@gsu.edu
COVILLE, Joanne 909-621-8211 69 A joanne.coville@scrippscollege.edu
COVINGTON, Bill, C 512-245-2314 501 F bc18@txstate.edu
COVINGTON, Dan 606-546-1285 207 B dcovin@unionky.edu
COVINGTON, Dean 870-307-7206 22 D dean.covington@lyon.edu
COVINGTON, Janet 713-348-6312 493 C jcov@rice.edu
COVINGTON, Kate 620-276-9642 193 C kate.covington@gcccks.edu
COVINGTON, Mary 919-966-9176 378 E mary_covington@unc.edu
COVINGTON, Sirena 312-225-6288 167 G scovington@vandercook.edu
COVINGTON, Valerie, L 757-455-3108 530 C vcovington@vwc.edu
COVINGTON-GRAHAM, Adrianne 405-945-3383 410 F
COVINO, Nicholas 617-327-6777 241 F nicholas_covino@mspp.edu
COVINO, William, A 559-278-2636 35 A wcovino@csufresno.edu
COVONE, Nicole 305-892-7043 112 A nicole.covone@jwu.edu
COWAN, Carole, A 978-656-3101 240 B cowanc@middlesex.mass.edu
COWAN, Cindy 864-977-2058 460 A cindy.cowan@ngu.edu
COWAN, David 507-389-2267 267 E david.cowan@mnsu.edu
COWAN, David, G 713-646-1729 494 I dcowan@stcl.edu
COWAN, Judith 803-327-7402 456 F jcowan@clintonjuniorcollege.edu
COWAN, Kenneth, H 402-559-4238 300 H kcowan@unmc.edu
COWAN, Marianne 207-786-6128 217 C mcowan@bates.edu
COWAN, Michael 931-372-3034 474 B mcowan@tntech.edu
COWAN, Vickie, M 718-862-7398 339 H vickie.cowan@manhattan.edu
COWARD, Bettye, R 662-685-4771 273 E bcoward@bmc.edu
COWARD, Raymond, T 435-797-1167 511 E raymond.coward@usu.edu
COWARD, William 814-536-5168 424 D bcoward@crbc.net
COWARD, William 814-536-5168 424 E bcoward@crbc.net
COWART, John 352-395-5513 117 F john.cowart@sfcollege.edu
COWART, Julian 406-470-2036 412 E julian.cowart@swcu.edu
COWART, Lisa 832-813-6780 490 E lisa.a.cowart@lonestar.edu
COWART, Lisa 803-323-2273 463 E cowartl@winthrop.edu
COWDREY, Scott 507-457-7800 271 B rcowdrey@smumn.edu
COWDREY, Terry, E 207-859-4802 217 G terry.cowdrey@colby.edu
COWELL, Aaron 419-473-2700 389 C aacowell@daviscollege.edu
COWELL, Edwin, A 410-543-6080 228 D eacowell@salisbury.edu
COWELL, JR., James, W 626-395-4464 32 H jcowell@caltech.edu
COWELL, Karen 661-722-6300 28 K kcowell@avc.edu
COWELL, Scott 870-512-7833 20 F scott_cowell@asun.edu
COWELL-OATES, June 314-454-8694 282 B jcowell-oates@bjc.org
COWEN, Scott, S 504-865-5201 215 C scowen@tulane.edu
COWEN, Sonia 417-667-8181 280 E scowen@cottey.edu
COWGER, John 701-594-8192 382 F john.cowger@lrsc.edu
COWGER, Tiffany 618-395-7777 152 F cowgert@iecc.edu
COWHEY, Peter, F 858-822-7523 74 F pcowhey@uscd.edu
COWIE, Anne 617-369-3659 244 E acowie@mfa.org
COWIE, Lettie 714-556-3610 77 B officevpbf@vanguard.edu
COWLES, Carol 847-214-7226 150 F ccowles@elgin.edu
COWLEY, Dave 435-797-1146 511 E dave.cowley@usu.edu
COWLEY, Julie, A 512-863-1720 496 A cowleyj@southwestern.edu
COWLING, William Richard 314-991-6200 279 H rcowling@chamberlain.edu
COWMAN, Mary 718-260-3054 346 C mcowman@poly.edu
COWMAN, Shaun, E 563-588-4990 187 C shaun.cowman@loras.edu
COWSER, Erin, K 985-549-5861 216 C erin.moore@selu.edu
COWSER YANCY, Dorothy 919-546-8300 376 F dyancy@shawu.edu
COX, Alan 336-725-8344 375 G coxa@pbc.edu
COX, Aleshia 731-265-1203 470 B acox@lanecollege.edu
COX, Barbara 850-599-3796 118 L barbara.cox@famu.edu
COX, Ben 254-867-3063 500 F ben.cox@tstc.edu
COX, Betty, B 713-313-4218 500 B cox_bb@tsu.edu
COX, Bobbie 704-406-4627 364 E bcox@gardner-webb.edu
COX, Cameron 253-964-6598 536 H cmcox@pierce.ctc.edu
COX, Carolyn 304-384-5237 543 G ccox@concord.edu
COX, Carolyn, S 240-500-2000 223 A coxc@hagerstowncc.edu
COX, Cathy 706-379-3111 140 A ccox@yhc.edu
COX, Charlene 219-464-5093 181 C charlene.cox@valpo.edu
COX, Cheryl 864-592-4613 461 C coxc@sccsc.edu
COX, Christopher 617-262-5000 231 G christopher.cox@the-bac.edu
COX, Christopher, N 360-650-3051 539 F chris.cox@wwu.edu
COX, Christopher, P 419-372-8932 385 E cpcox@bgsu.edu
COX, Chuck 417-865-2811 281 G coxc@evangel.edu
COX, Cleve, H 252-249-1851 372 F ccox@pamlicocc.edu
COX, Craig, A 805-482-2755 64 E rector@stjohnsem.edu
COX, Darryl 949-451-5435 70 E dcox@ivc.edu
COX, Dave 217-234-5376 156 B dcox5612@lakeland.cc.il.us
COX, Dave 509-533-7179 533 B dave.cox@scc.spokane.edu
COX, David, N 901-678-5344 474 C davidcox@memphis.edu
COX, Deborah, M 270-824-8609 202 G deborah.cox@kctcs.edu
COX, Dennis 949-214-3182 43 C dennis.cox@cui.edu
COX, Dennis 304-865-6081 541 J dennis.cox@ovu.edu
COX, Dennis, W 304-865-6081 541 J dennis.cox@ovu.edu
COX, Dianne 423-425-4677 477 F dianne-cox@utc.edu
COX, Donna 870-543-5968 23 H dcox@seark.edu
COX, Ed 845-431-8071 332 D
COX, Fran 662-472-2312 274 D fcox@holmescc.edu
COX, Frank 501-329-6811 22 A
COX, Geoffrey 415-955-2001 27 A gcox@alliant.edu
COX, Geoffrey 858-635-4000 27 E gcox@alliant.edu
COX, Gloria 940-565-3305 504 D gcox@unt.edu
COX, Gregg 561-237-7210 113 D gcox@lynn.edu
COX, Gregg, C 561-237-7210 113 D gcox@lynn.edu
COX, Helen 808-245-8210 142 C helencox@hawaii.edu
COX, J. P. Hap 540-375-2302 523 G cox@roanoke.com
COX, James 714-620-3700 29 F jcox@argosy.edu
COX, James, H 559-455-5572 32 A cccacademic@sbcglobal.net
COX, Jamie, S 256-766-6610 4 C jcox@hcu.edu
COX, Janet, L 513-529-6724 396 E coxjl@muohio.edu
COX, Jason 270-686-2111 199 B jason.cox@brescia.edu
COX, Jeffrey, W 585-475-7433 347 G jwccst@rit.edu
COX, Jennifer 503-228-6528 414 E
COX, Jesse 313-927-1404 254 E jcox@marygrove.edu
COX, John, L 508-362-2131 239 D jcox@capecod.edu
COX, Karen 508-854-4479 240 F karenc@qcc.mass.edu
COX, Kelly 803-786-3723 457 C kcox@columbiasc.edu
COX, Kenneth, M 540-831-7600 523 A kcox3@radford.edu
COX, Lane 205-348-8697 8 E lcox@fa.ua.edu
COX, Larry 270-686-6416 199 B larry.cox@brescia.edu
COX, Laurie 608-262-7890 550 J cox@studentlife.wisc.edu
COX, Leah 540-654-1263 525 D lcox@umw.edu
COX, Leana 970-675-3334 82 H leana.cox@cncc.edu
COX, Lisa 423-869-6722 470 E lisa.cox@lmunet.edu
COX, Lori 618-252-5400 164 I lori.cox@sic.edu
COX, Lynne 541-917-4848 416 I coxly@linnbenton.edu
COX, M. Ron 803-313-7101 462 D roncox@mailbox.sc.edu
COX, Mary 724-830-1027 447 C cox@setonhill.edu
COX, Matthew 828-884-8217 362 H coxma@brevard.edu
COX, Michael 806-291-3765 508 E coxm@wbu.edu
COX, Michele, D 804-289-8838 525 E mcox@richmond.edu
COX, Michele, J 503-838-8396 419 C coxm@wou.edu
COX, Paul 305-428-5700 113 I pcox@aii.edu
COX, Randall 903-785-7661 492 D rcox@parisjc.edu
COX, Richard 831-443-1700 50 C richard_cox@heald.edu
COX, JR., Richard 303-784-8264 85 M rcox@jiu.edu
COX, Robert 503-491-7374 417 B robert.cox@mhcc.edu
COX, Robert 212-220-8041 326 D rcox@bmcc.cuny.edu
COX, Robert 307-532-8218 556 C bob.cox@ewc.wy.edu
COX, Ryan 916-568-3101 55 J coxr@losrios.edu
COX, Sandra 936-633-5211 480 D scox@angelina.edu
COX, Sandra, K 217-581-3413 150 E skcox@eiu.edu

COX, Steve .... 740-245-7438 .... 404 E
scox@rio.edu
COX, Susan, S .... 610-606-4609 .... 425 A
sue@cedarcrest.edu
COX, Teri .... 414-256-1208 .... 549 D
coxt@mtmary.edu
COX, Terry .... 206-934-7798 .... 537 D
terry.cox@seattlecolleges.edu
COX, Tiffa .... 615-963-7494 .... 474 A
tcox9@tnstate.edu
COX, Traci, R .... 419-995-8040 .... 392 K
cox.t@rhodesstate.edu
COX, Virgil .... 704-922-6295 .... 370 G
cox.virgil@gaston.edu
COX, William .... 931-221-1400 .... 473 E
coxw@apsu.edu
COY, Katherine, C .... 417-836-5274 .... 286 C
kathycoy@missouristate.edu
COY, Marisue, S .... 270-852-3300 .... 204 A
marisuec@kwc.edu
COY-OGAN, Lynne .... 207-973-1077 .... 218 A
coyoganl@husson.edu
COYKENDALL, John .... 785-227-3380 .... 191 B
coykendallj@bethanylb.edu
COYLE, Beth .... 973-278-5400 .... 323 H
bmc@berkelycollege.edu
COYLE, Beth .... 973-278-5400 .... 307 F
bmc@berkeleycollege.edu
COYLE, Cheryl .... 704-357-8020 .... 362 D
cacoyle@aii.edu
COYLE, James .... 714-997-7074 ...... 39 F
coyle@chapman.edu
COYLE, John .... 814-886-6465 .... 437 B
jcoyle@mtaloy.edu
COYLE, Mark .... 208-426-1826 .... 142 I
markcoyle@boisestate.edu
COYLE, Philip .... 903-233-3200 .... 490 A
philipcoyle@letu.edu
COYLE, Philip, A .... 423-266-4574 .... 136 D
pcoyle@richmont.edu
COYNE, Anthony, M .... 803-938-3749 .... 462 G
acoyne@uscsumter.edu
COYNE, John, B .... 330-569-5284 .... 391 G
coynejb@hiram.edu
COYNE, John, M .... 724-264-1328 .... 430 B
jmcoyne@gcc.edu
COYNE, Michael .... 928-681-0800 .... 241 E
coyne@mslaw.edu
COYNE, Michael .... 570-372-4128 .... 447 E
coyne@susqu.edu
COYNE, Mildred .... 321-433-7145 .... 102 D
coynem@brevardcc.edu
COYNE, Sandi .... 413-565-1000 .... 230 G
scoyne@baypath.edu
COZART, Melissa .... 859-858-3511 .... 198 E
melissa.cozart@asbury.edu
COZART, Wayne .... 434-243-9041 .... 525 F
wdc9q@virginia.edu
COZBY, Jerry .... 918-456-5511 .... 409 A
cozby@nsuok.edu
COZZENS, David .... 307-766-3296 .... 556 H
dcozzens@uwyo.edu
COZZENS, Susan .... 404-894-5054 .... 130 F
susan.cozzens@iac.gatech.edu
COZZOCREA, Rebecca .... 518-736-3622 .... 334 D
rswart@fmcc.suny.edu
CRABB, Jenna, S .... 505-277-2531 .... 321 C
jennas@unm.edu
CRABB, Robert, J .... 612-625-6510 .... 272 A
rcrabb@umn.edu
CRABILL, Casey .... 908-526-1200 .... 313 D
ccrabill@raritanval.edu
CRABREE, Troy .... 425-637-1010 .... 532 E
troy.crabtree@cityu.edu
CRABTREE, Candace .... 617-928-4633 .... 242 E
ccrabtree@mountida.edu
CRABTREE, Charles .... 978-478-3400 .... 246 G
ccrabtree@zbc.edu
CRABTREE, David .... 541-683-5141 .... 416 A
dcrabtree@gutenberg.edu
CRABTREE, Deonna .... 417-833-2551 .... 279 E
dmcrabtree@cbcag.edu
CRABTREE, Gina, D .... 316-978-3672 .... 198 A
gina.crabtree@wichita.edu
CRABTREE, JR., John, A ... 317-789-8288 .... 171 A
jcrabtree@crossroads.edu
CRABTREE, Kacy .... 828-898-8739 .... 366 D
crabtreek@lmc.edu
CRABTREE, Peter .... 510-464-3218 ...... 62 D
pcrabtree@peralta.edu
CRABTREE, Robbin, D .... 203-254-4000 ...... 92 H
rcrabtree@fairfield.edu
CRABTREE, Sarah .... 859-371-9393 .... 198 G
scrabtree@beckfield.edu
CRABTREE, Shane .... 801-957-4571 .... 512 D
shane.crabtree@slcc.edu
CRACCO, Elizabeth .... 860-486-4705 ...... 94 G
elizabeth.cracco@uconn.edu
CRACKENBERG, Peter .... 503-554-2138 .... 415 I
pcrackenberg@georgefox.edu
CRADDOCK, Alden .... 314-529-6687 .... 284 C
acraddock@maryville.edu
CRADDOCK, Chris .... 903-983-8181 .... 489 I
ccraddock@kilgore.edu
CRADDOCK, Christie .... 304-776-6290 .... 541 B
CRADDOCK, Jackie .... 510-594-3612 ...... 32 C
jcraddock@cca.edu
CRADIT, James, D .... 618-453-7960 .... 165 B
dcradit@business.siu.edu
CRADY, Thomas, M .... 507-933-7676 .... 263 J
tcrady@gustavus.edu
CRAFA, Robert .... 718-409-7460 .... 356 C
rcrafa@sunymaritime.edu
CRAFT, Ann .... 304-829-7255 .... 540 H
acraft@bethanywv.edu
CRAFT, Edwin .... 662-846-4840 .... 273 H
ecraft@deltastate.edu
CRAFT, Jackie, T .... 276-739-2561 .... 529 A
jcraft@vhcc.edu
CRAFT, Stephen .... 205-665-6540 .... 9 B
scraft@montevallo.edu
CRAFT, Tonya .... 601-974-1200 .... 275 B
craftte@millsaps.edu
CRAFT, William .... 619-388-2990 ...... 65 G
wcraft@sdccd.edu
CRAFT, William, J .... 218-299-3000 .... 262 I
president@cord.edu
CRAFT, William, P .... 619-388-2799 ...... 65 G
wcraft@sdccd.edu
CRAFTON, Michael .... 678-466-4100 .... 127 D
michaelcrafton@clayton.edu
CRAFTON, Teresa .... 478-274-7833 .... 135 C
tcrafton@oftc.edu
CRAFTS, JR., Roger, C .... 781-292-2321 .... 234 H
roger.crafts@olin.edu
CRAGER, Cindy .... 609-626-3658 .... 313 E
cindy.crager@stockton.edu
CRAGO, David, C .... 419-772-2034 .... 398 H
d-crago@onu.edu
CRAHEN, Sherri, A .... 216-397-3010 .... 392 L
scrahen@jcu.edu
CRAIG, Barbara .... 269-695-2995 .... 253 G
craig@lakemichigancollege.edu
CRAIG, Chris .... 559-791-2365 ...... 53 A
ccraig@portervillecollege.edu
CRAIG, Chris, J .... 740-376-4857 .... 395 G
chris.craig@marietta.edu
CRAIG, Christopher, J .... 417-836-5215 .... 286 C
chriscraig@missouristate.edu
CRAIG, Clarissa .... 913-469-8500 .... 194 B
ccraig@jccc.edu
CRAIG, Dennis .... 914-251-6300 .... 354 D
dennis.craig@purchase.edu
CRAIG, Florence .... 617-541-3501 .... 241 A
fcraig@rcc.mass.edu
CRAIG, Gary .... 206-315-5825 .... 533 D
gcraig@cornish.edu
CRAIG, Harold .... 404-225-4488 .... 125 E
hcraig@atlantatech.edu
CRAIG, James .... 916-361-1660 ...... 38 G
jcraig@carrington.edu
CRAIG, Jayne .... 575-769-4031 .... 318 A
jayne.craig@clovis.edu
CRAIG, Jennifer .... 617-964-1100 .... 230 B
jcraig@ants.edu
CRAIG, Jo-Ann .... 910-362-7057 .... 368 H
jcraig@cfcc.edu
CRAIG, John .... 610-359-5297 .... 426 G
jcraig@dccc.edu
CRAIG, Johnny .... 219-844-0100 .... 177 E
jcraig@kaplan.edu
CRAIG, Kathryn, M .... 330-569-5131 .... 391 G
craigkm@hiram.edu
CRAIG, La Saundra .... 513-569-1532 .... 387 G
lasaundra.craig@cincinnatistate.edu
CRAIG, Martha, P .... 865-981-8167 .... 471 B
mardi.craig@maryvillecollege.edu
CRAIG, Marva .... 212-220-8131 .... 326 D
mcraig@bmcc.cuny.edu
CRAIG, Michael .... 816-501-4065 .... 288 A
michael.craig@rockhurst.edu
CRAIG, Paige .... 708-209-3509 .... 148 E
paige.craig@cuchicago.edu
CRAIG, Quiester .... 336-334-7632 .... 378 A
craigq@ncat.edu
CRAIG, Randy .... 323-241-5238 ...... 55 C
craigrs@lasc.edu
CRAIG, Sandy .... 618-262-8641 .... 153 A
craigs@iecc.edu
CRAIG, Sharon .... 830-372-8001 .... 499 F
scraig@tlu.edu
CRAIG, Stephanie, A .... 814-371-2090 .... 448 D
scraig@triangle-tech.edu
CRAIG, Timothy .... 716-829-8394 .... 332 E
craigt@dyc.edu
CRAIG, William, G .... 732-571-3427 .... 311 E
wcraig@monmouth.edu
CRAIG KUNG, Pang-Jen ... 919-878-9900 ...... 99 G
CRAIGIE, Ted, W .... 603-526-3717 .... 303 G
tcraigie@colby-sawyer.edu
CRAIN, B, J .... 979-862-7777 .... 497 E
bjcrain@tamu.edu
CRAIN, John, L .... 985-549-2280 .... 216 C
jcrain@selu.edu
CRAIN, Laura, J .... 607-871-2101 .... 322 E
crain@alfred.edu
CRAIN, Ronald, D .... 618-453-6214 .... 165 B
dcrain@siu.edu
CRAIN, Steve .... 620-242-0400 .... 195 C
CRAIN, Terry .... 618-985-3741 .... 154 G
terrycrain@jalc.edu
CRALL, Leslie, D .... 580-774-3282 .... 412 F
les.crall@swosu.edu
CRAM, Stanley .... 920-924-6431 .... 554 G
scram@morainepark.edu
CRAM-RAHLF, Shelly .... 563-288-6011 .... 184 G
scramrahlf@eicc.edu
CRAMB, Alan, W .... 312-567-3163 .... 153 C
cramb@iit.edu
CRAMER, Alicia .... 713-646-1808 .... 494 I
acramer@stcl.edu
CRAMER, Ann .... 951-343-4210 ...... 31 J
acramer@calbaptist.edu
CRAMER, Gregory, D .... 630-889-6536 .... 159 F
gcramer@nuhs.edu
CRAMER, Joel .... 317-738-8197 .... 171 F
jcramer@franklincollege.edu
CRAMER, Judith .... 260-481-6130 .... 174 C
cramerj@ipfw.edu
CRAMER, Patricia .... 614-236-6714 .... 386 E
pcramer@capital.edu
CRAMER, Paul .... 717-361-1400 .... 428 F
cramerp@etown.edu
CRAMER, Rick .... 607-729-1581 .... 331 G
rcramer@davisny.edu
CRAMER, Robert, G .... 608-342-1226 .... 552 B
cramerr@uwplatt.edu
CRAMER, Steven .... 574-257-3313 .... 169 I
cramers@bethelcollege.edu
CRAMER, Walter .... 203-837-8547 ...... 91 A
cramerw@wcsu.edu
CRAMPTON, Anne-Marie ... 719-336-1520 ...... 86 B
anne-marie.crampton@lamarcc.edu
CRAMPTON, Tom .... 810-762-0506 .... 255 G
thomas.crampto@mcc.edu
CRAMPTON, Troy, D .... 515-574-1114 .... 185 I
crampton@iowacentral.edu
CRANCE, Gina-Lyn .... 610-921-7611 .... 421 E
gcrance@alb.edu
CRANDALL, Brian .... 845-938-3327 .... 559 A
8uscc@usma.edu
CRANDALL, Connie .... 605-688-5148 .... 466 C
connie.crandall@sdstate.edu
CRANDALL, Donald, W .... 479-524-7150 ...... 22 C
dcrandal@jbu.edu
CRANDALL, James .... 530-242-7989 ...... 69 D
jcrandall@shastacollege.edu
CRANDALL, Larry .... 801-302-2800 .... 510 G
larry.crandall@neumont.edu
CRANDALL, Laura .... 315-470-4865 .... 355 A
ldcranda@esf.edu
CRANDALL, Paige .... 914-395-2575 .... 350 C
pcrandall@sarahlawrence.edu
CRANDALL, Stephen, S .... 607-871-2184 .... 322 E
fcrandall@alfred.edu
CRANDELL, Gale, M .... 989-386-6664 .... 255 C
gcrandell@midmich.edu
CRANE, Carol .... 480-732-7114 ...... 15 E
carol.crane@cgc.edu
CRANE, Crystal, D .... 714-895-8970 ...... 41 C
ccrane@gwc.cccd.edu
CRANE, Helen .... 432-837-8203 .... 501 E
hcrane@sulross.edu
CRANE, Jeff .... 270-384-8150 .... 204 D
cranej@lindsey.edu
CRANE, Melanie .... 303-581-9955 .... 320 G
mcrane@acupuncturecollege.edu
CRANE, Peter .... 203-432-5109 ...... 96 A
peter.crane@yale.edu
CRANE, Ramona .... 719-219-9636 ...... 82 B
rlsfattire@hotmail.com
CRANE, Rob, M .... 913-288-7283 .... 194 C
rcrane@kckcc.edu
CRANE, Robert .... 956-380-8100 .... 493 D
rcrane@riogrande.edu
CRANE, Ron .... 972-825-4818 .... 495 F
rcrane@sagu.edu
CRANE, Susan .... 914-337-9300 .... 330 G
susan.crane@concordia-ny.edu
CRANE, Susan, L .... 989-964-4350 .... 257 G
scrane@svsu.edu
CRANE-SMITH, Jeanne .... 913-288-7362 .... 194 C
jeannecs@kckcc.edu
CRANER, Marcia, R .... 607-777-6757 .... 351 F
mcraner@binghamton.edu
CRANER, Marcia, R .... 607-777-2054 .... 351 F
mcraner@binghamton.edu
CRANFORD, Bill .... 601-925-3283 .... 275 C
cranford@mc.edu
CRANFORD, Carolyn .... 903-813-2281 .... 481 A
ccranford@austincollege.edu
CRANFORD, Shannon .... 580-628-6229 .... 409 B
shannon.cranford@north-ok.edu
CRANFORD, Sondra .... 727-784-0003 .... 103 B
scranford@cfi.edu
CRANFORD, Timothy .... 912-358-4154 .... 136 G
cranfordt@savannahstate.edu
CRANHAM, John, B .... 919-508-2336 .... 380 E
jbcranham@peace.edu
CRANK, Robert .... 816-322-0110 .... 279 D
bob.crank@calvary.edu
CRANK, Robert .... 816-322-0110 .... 279 D
admissions@calvary.edu
CRANMER, Wendy, M .... 607-753-2302 .... 353 B
wendy.cranmer@cortland.edu
CRANMORE, Jill, A .... 217-443-8756 .... 148 G
jcranmore@dacc.edu
CRANSTON, Carey .... 708-444-4500 .... 151 C
CRANSTON, Carolyn .... 412-924-1375 .... 444 H
ccranston@pts.edu
CRANSTON, Pam .... 410-516-8993 .... 223 F
pcranston@jhu.edu
CRANWELL, Mary, E .... 732-987-2285 .... 310 C
cranwell@georgian.edu
CRAPANZANO, Vincent .... 845-398-4019 .... 349 H
vcrapanz@stac.edu
CRAPP, Michael .... 570-422-3595 .... 442 D
mcrapp@po-box.esu.edu
CRATER, Richard .... 570-504-7305 .... 425 F
CRATTY, Frederic .... 203-837-8665 ...... 91 A
crattyf@wcsu.edu
CRAVEN, Bryan, C .... 850-718-2375 .... 103 D
cravenb@chipola.edu
CRAVEN, Heather .... 973-328-5281 .... 309 A
hcraven@ccm.edu
CRAVEN, James, S .... 509-313-6137 .... 534 F
craven@gonzaga.edu
CRAVEN, Randy .... 423-236-2732 .... 473 B
rlcraven@southern.edu
CRAVER, Robert .... 303-369-5151 ...... 87 D
robert.craver@plattcolorado.edu
CRAVEY, Irene .... 903-923-3312 .... 500 E
irene.cravey@tstc.edu
CRAVO, Ana, M .... 201-761-6104 .... 314 F
acravo@spc.edu
CRAWFORD, Allison .... 615-794-4254 .... 472 F
acrawford@omorecollege.edu
CRAWFORD, Bill, E .... 806-354-6070 .... 479 G
wecrawford@actx.edu
CRAWFORD, Brenda .... 712-274-5606 .... 187 G
crawford@morningside.edu
CRAWFORD, Brian .... 304-336-8252 .... 544 D
bcrawford@westliberty.edu
CRAWFORD, Bruce .... 205-929-6312 .... 5 E
bcrawford@lawsonstate.edu
CRAWFORD, Bryan .... 719-562-7002 ...... 87 F
bryan.crawford@pueblocc.edu
CRAWFORD, Cardon, B .... 843-953-6966 .... 456 C
cardon.crawford@citadel.edu
CRAWFORD, Carol .... 215-728-4415 .... 438 B
carol.crawford@jevs.org
CRAWFORD, Catherine .... 903-923-2069 .... 486 F
ccrawford@etbu.edu
CRAWFORD, Cathy .... 260-399-7700 .... 181 A
ccrawford@sf.edu
CRAWFORD, Charlie .... 253-566-6005 .... 538 F
ccrawford@tacomacc.edu
CRAWFORD, Chris .... 785-628-4531 .... 192 I
ccrawfor@fhsu.edu
CRAWFORD, Clinton .... 718-270-5140 .... 328 C
crawford@mec.cuny.edu
CRAWFORD, David .... 970-521-6643 ...... 86 K
david.crawford@njc.edu
CRAWFORD, David .... 773-947-6250 .... 157 G
dcrawford@mccormick.edu
CRAWFORD, David, S .... 202-526-3799 ...... 99 D
CRAWFORD, Debbie .... 970-945-8691 ...... 82 G
CRAWFORD, Deborah .... 215-895-6203 .... 427 H
deborah.l.crawford@drexel.edu
CRAWFORD, Deena .... 601-266-4829 .... 277 F
deena.crawford@usm.edu
CRAWFORD, Derrick .... 760-750-4309 ...... 36 C
crawford@csusm.edu
CRAWFORD, Diane .... 919-546-8309 .... 376 F
dcrawford@shawu.edu
CRAWFORD, Doris, S .... 434-528-5276 .... 530 B
dorisscott@vul.edu
CRAWFORD, Forrest, C .... 801-626-7420 .... 511 G
fcrawford@weber.edu
CRAWFORD, Galen .... 513-562-6273 .... 384 D
gcrawford@artacademy.edu
CRAWFORD, Gene, L .... 570-577-1631 .... 423 E
gene.crawford@bucknell.edu
CRAWFORD, George, F .... 417-865-2811 .... 281 G
crawfordc@evangel.edu
CRAWFORD, Gregory, P .... 574-631-6456 .... 180 G
gregory_crawford@nd.edu
CRAWFORD, Holly .... 203-392-5237 ...... 90 I
crawfordh1@southernct.edu
CRAWFORD, Holly .... 585-273-4734 .... 359 B
hcrawford@admin.rochester.edu
CRAWFORD, Holly .... 509-963-3101 .... 532 C
crawfordh@cwu.edu
CRAWFORD, Iris .... 813-463-7139 .... 101 B
ncrawford@argosy.edu
CRAWFORD, Isiaah .... 206-296-6963 .... 538 B
crawford@seattleu.edu
CRAWFORD, J. Patrick .... 850-474-2426 .... 121 D
pat@uwf.edu
CRAWFORD, JR.,
James, E .... 423-585-6956 .... 476 D
james.crawford@ws.edu
CRAWFORD, Jane, T .... 386-312-4190 .... 116 F
janecrawford@sjrstate.edu

CRAWFORD, John .... 330-672-2760.... 393 D jcrawfor1@kent.edu
CRAWFORD, John, D .... 229-333-5339.... 139 C jdcrawford@valdosta.edu
CRAWFORD, John, P .... 716-880-2879.... 340 D jpc334@medaille.edu
CRAWFORD, Jonas .... 805-986-5870...... 77 E jcrawford@vcccd.edu
CRAWFORD, Kara .... 540-261-4102.... 524 H kara.crawford@svu.edu
CRAWFORD, Kathryn .... 605-394-1288.... 466 B kathryn.crawford@sdsmt.edu
CRAWFORD, Kevin .... 706-245-7226.... 129 C kcrawford@lifespring.net
CRAWFORD, Lelia .... 404-727-3300.... 129 D lcrawfo@emory.edu
CRAWFORD, Linden, G ..... 314-984-7609.... 289 A lcrawford@stlcc.edu
CRAWFORD, Malinda .... 406-756-3828.... 294 C mcrawfor@fvcc.edu
CRAWFORD, Matt .... 952-358-8454.... 268 A matt.crawford@normandale.edu
CRAWFORD, Missie .... 478-289-2172.... 129 B mcrawford@ega.edu
CRAWFORD, Nellie .... 757-727-5221.... 519 H nellie.crawford@hamptonu.edu
CRAWFORD, R. Scott .... 765-361-6355.... 181 E crawforr@wabash.edu
CRAWFORD, Ray Scott ...... 318-678-6000.... 209 I rcrawford@bpcc.edu
CRAWFORD, Rhia .... 828-765-7351.... 372 A rcrawford@mayland.edu
CRAWFORD, Ronald, W ..... 804-355-8135.... 516 J rcrawford@btsr.edu
CRAWFORD, Sabrina .... 425-637-1010.... 532 E scrawford@cityu.edu
CRAWFORD, Steve .... 661-362-2203...... 56 G scrawford@masters.edu
CRAWFORD, Steven, R ...... 740-587-5717.... 389 I crawfords@denison.edu
CRAWFORD, Teresa .... 863-784-7041.... 117 J teresa.crawford@southflorida.edu
CRAWFORD, Tim .... 254-295-4180.... 504 C tcrawford@umhb.edu
CRAWFORD, Valerie .... 309-268-8145.... 151 I val.crawford@heartland.edu
CRAWFORD, Valerie, S ...... 334-244-3667........ 1 G vsamuel@aum.edu
CRAWFORD, Virginia .... 601-266-5390.... 277 F virginia.crawford@usm.edu
CRAWFORD, Wilbur, O ...... 215-574-9600.... 431 B wcrawford@bs.edu
CRAWFORD, III, William, H .... 480-732-7309...... 15 E bill.crawford.iii@cgc.edu
CRAWLEY, Cathy .... 478-445-5149.... 130 B cathy.crawley@gcsu.edu
CRAWLEY, Deborah .... 610-558-5519.... 437 D cawleyd@neumann.edu
CRAWLEY, Todd, C .... 717-221-1300.... 430 E tcrawley@hacc.edu
CRAWMER, Martha .... 937-328-6031.... 387 H crawmerm@clarkstate.edu
CRAYS, Linda, L .... 713-500-2080.... 506 F linda.l.crays@uth.tmc.edu
CREA, Catharine .... 914-594-4480.... 343 F catharine_crea@nymc.edu
CREAGER, Carol .... 540-887-7310.... 521 C ccreager@mbc.edu
CREAGH, Curtis .... 573-681-5079.... 283 I creaghc@lincolnu.edu
CREAHAN, Patricia, H .... 716-888-2616.... 325 F creahan@canisius.edu
CREAKMAN, Melissa .... 304-896-7411.... 543 C melissa.creakman@southernwv.edu
CREAMER, Barry .... 214-818-1326.... 484 B bcreamer@criswell.edu
CREAMER, David .... 513-529-4225.... 396 E creamerd@muohio.edu
CREAMER, Deborah .... 303-765-3170...... 85 D dcreamer@iliff.edu
CREAMER, George .... 617-879-7163.... 238 B creamer@massart.edu
CREAMER, Stephen .... 978-762-4000.... 240 D screamer@northshore.edu
CREAMER, Tia .... 918-631-3244.... 413 F tia-creamer@utulsa.edu
CREASIA, Joan, L .... 865-974-7584.... 477 D jcreasia@utk.edu
CREASMAN, Alice, J .... 304-473-8440.... 545 G creasman_aj@wvwc.edu
CREASON, Paul .... 562-938-4171...... 54 E pcreason@lbcc.edu
CREASON, Rita, A .... 270-789-5233.... 199 F racreason@campbellsville.edu
CRECELIUS, Carolyn .... 573-518-2100.... 285 I kayc@mineralarea.edu
CRECELIUS, Kathryn, J ...... 443-997-2370.... 223 F kcrecelius@jhu.edu
CREDILLE, John .... 417-328-1606.... 290 A jcredille@sbuniv.edu
CREDLE, Sid, H .... 757-727-5361.... 519 H sid.credle@hamptonu.edu
CREECH, Bill .... 918-595-7888.... 412 H bcreech@tulsacc.edu
CREECH, Pat .... 918-540-6294.... 408 J pcreech@neo.edu
CREED, J. Bradley .... 205-726-2718........ 6 G jbcreed@samford.edu
CREED, Stephanie .... 501-882-4547...... 20 C sacreed@asub.edu
CREED-DIKEOGU, Gloria ... 785-242-5200.... 195 I creeddikeogu@ottawa.edu
CREEDON, James .... 215-204-1991.... 447 H james.creedon@temple.edu
CREEGER, Joan .... 704-216-3602.... 373 F joan.creeger@rccc.edu
CREEHAN, Dennis, W .... 304-457-6404.... 540 E creehandw@ab.edu
CREEHAN, Kenneth .... 314-968-6969.... 292 J creehan@webster.edu
CREEHAN, Richard, A .... 304-457-1700.... 540 E creehanra@ab.edu
CREEK, Fred, A .... 253-833-9111.... 534 H fcreek@greenriver.edu
CREEKMORE, Crystal .... 575-562-2175.... 318 B crystal.creekmore@enmu.edu
CREEL, Angie .... 928-344-7776...... 12 A angela.creel-erb@azwestern.edu
CREEL, Ronnie .... 334-670-3496........ 8 A rcreel@troy.edu
CREEL, Scott .... 615-248-1236.... 476 G screel@trevecca.edu
CREEL, Shane .... 361-593-2237.... 498 D randolph.creel@tamuk.edu
CREELY, Hilliary .... 724-357-2223.... 442 F hilliary.creely@iup.edu
CREER, John .... 636-949-4777.... 283 J jcreer@lindenwood.edu
CREFT, Dawn, H .... 407-303-7894.... 100 G dawn.creft@adu.edu
CREGAN, CSC, Mark, T ..... 508-565-1301.... 245 A presidentcregan@stonehill.edu
CREGGER, Crystal, Y .... 276-233-4762.... 529 C ccregger@wcc.vccs.edu
CREIGHTON, Clarinda .... 816-584-6833.... 287 E clarinda.creighton@park.edu
CREIGHTON, Grace .... 914-674-7369.... 340 F gcreighton@mercy.edu
CREIGHTON, Joanne, V ..... 610-896-1021.... 430 G jwankmil@haverford.edu
CREIGHTON, Karen .... 417-447-2601.... 287 D creightk@otc.edu
CREMEAN, Erin .... 419-627-8345.... 398 B ecremean@ohiobusinesscollege.edu
CREMER, Doug .... 530-895-2946...... 31 H cremerdo@butte.edu
CREMER, Douglas .... 818-767-0888...... 79 H douglas.cremer@woodbury.edu
CREMER, Phyllis, A .... 818-767-0888...... 79 H phyllis.cremer@woodbury.edu
CRENSHAW, Chris .... 601-266-4414.... 277 F christopher.crenshaw@usm.edu
CRENSHAW, Christine .... 405-744-5358.... 410 C christine.crenshaw@okstate.edu
CRENSHAW, Jan .... 281-998-6150.... 494 A jan.crenshaw@sjcd.edu
CRENSHAW, Karen .... 724-503-1001.... 451 A kcrenshaw@washjeff.edu
CREOLA, Thomas .... 772-398-9990.... 112 F tcreola@keisercollege.edu
CRERAR, Gregg .... 203-392-5518...... 90 I crerarg1@southernct.edu
CRESCENZO, Mario .... 212-650-5250.... 326 G mcrescenzo@ccny.cuny.edu
CRESON, Gadsby .... 901-272-5120.... 471 D gcreson@mca.edu
CRESPINO, Curt, J .... 816-235-1105.... 291 C crespinocj@umkc.edu
CRESPO, Jorge .... 787-751-0178.... 565 F ac_jcrespo@suagm.edu
CRESPO, Jorge, L .... 787-751-0178.... 565 F ac_jcrespo@suagm.edu
CRESPO, Lynn .... 864-455-7992.... 462 F lcrespo@bju.edu
CRESPO, Ricardo .... 787-751-1912.... 564 C rcrespo@inter.edu
CRESPO-KEBLER, Elizabeth .... 787-993-8864.... 567 B elizabeth.crespo1@upr.edu
CRESPO-LOPEZ, Sylvia ...... 212-237-8897.... 327 F sylopez@jjay.cuny.edu
CRESPY, Charles, T .... 989-774-2481.... 249 C cresp1ct@cmich.edu
CRESSWELL-YEAGER, Tiffany .... 610-285-5021.... 439 L tjc8@psu.edu
CREW, Dwayne .... 478-825-6200.... 129 F crewd@fvsu.edu
CREW, Robert .... 318-357-5800.... 216 B crew@nsula.edu
CREWELL, Don .... 626-395-6280...... 32 H dcrewell@caltech.edu
CREWS, Bradford, W .... 561-297-2190.... 119 A bcrews2@fau.edu
CREWS, Christopher, M ..... 812-941-2212.... 175 A cmcrews@ius.edu
CREWS, II, Lyen, C .... 859-846-5701.... 204 H lcrews@midway.edu
CREWS, Micah, R .... 423-652-4773.... 470 A mrcrews@king.edu
CREWS, Michele .... 617-879-2114.... 246 C mcrews@wheelock.edu
CREWS, Phyllis .... 703-709-5875.... 522 H pcrews@potomac.edu
CREWS, Ron .... 910-221-2224.... 364 F
CREWS, Sharon .... 205-929-6307........ 5 E sharon.crews@lawsonstate.edu
CREWS, William, O .... 415-380-1326...... 48 E billcrews@ggbts.edu
CREWS, Yolanda, M .... 804-524-5189.... 529 H ycrews@vsu.edu
CRIBBY, William .... 617-928-4021.... 242 E wcribby@mountida.edu
CRICK, James .... 502-451-0815.... 206 G jcrick@sullivan.edu
CRICK, James .... 502-451-0815.... 206 H jcrick@sullivan.edu
CRICKENBERGER, Leslie ... 706-583-2818.... 125 C lcrickenberger@athenstech.edu
CRICKENBERGER, Tamela . 434-592-3508.... 520 K tlcrickenberger@liberty.edu
CRIDER, Wayne .... 706-245-7226.... 129 C wcrider@ec.edu
CRILLEY, Bonnie .... 814-866-8144.... 433 C bcrilley@lecom.edu
CRILLY, Sam .... 405-912-9064.... 408 D scrilly@hc.edu
CRIM, Kim .... 717-846-5000.... 452 H
CRIMMIN, Nancy, P .... 508-767-7536.... 230 D ncrimmin@assumption.edu
CRIMMINS, Cindy .... 717-815-1216.... 452 G ccrimmins@ycp.edu
CRIMMINS, Kate .... 410-837-6135.... 229 A kcrimmins@ubalt.edu
CRIMMINS LECHOWICZ, Catherine .... 860-685-2841...... 95 E ccrimmins@wesleyan.edu
CRING, Christine, A .... 315-684-6079.... 354 F cringca@morrisville.edu
CRINITI, Stephen .... 304-243-2424.... 546 A scriniti@wju.edu
CRINO, Sally, E .... 563-333-6080.... 188 F crinosallye@sau.edu
CRISCI, David, A .... 570-340-6077.... 435 F dacrisci@marywood.edu
CRISLER, Pat .... 402-457-2759.... 298 G pcrisler@mccneb.edu
CRISMAN, Pam .... 217-234-5354.... 156 B pcrisman@lakeland.cc.il.us
CRISMAN, Steve .... 325-793-4601.... 490 H scrisman@mcm.edu
CRISMON, M. Lynn .... 512-471-3718.... 505 D lynn.crismon@austin.utexas.edu
CRISP, JR., Delmas, S ...... 910-630-7031.... 367 B dcrisp@methodist.edu
CRISP, Kathryn .... 615-904-8167.... 473 G kathy.crisp@mtsu.edu
CRISP, Whitney .... 229-931-2299.... 137 C wcrisp@southgatech.edu
CRISP, Winston, B .... 919-966-4045.... 378 E wbcrisp@email.unc.edu
CRISPELL, Brian .... 813-988-5131.... 108 A deanofstudents@floridacollege.edu
CRISPIN, Jon .... 251-981-3771........ 2 G jon.crispin@columbiasouthern.edu
CRISS, Art .... 845-569-3136.... 342 A art.criss@msmc.edu
CRISSINGER, Amy, S .... 605-256-5139.... 465 I amy.crissinger@dsu.edu
CRIST, Alan, N .... 608-263-4384.... 550 I acrist@uwsa.edu
CRIST, Diane, G .... 651-962-6765.... 272 B dgcrist@stthomas.edu
CRIST, William, J .... 337-482-2001.... 216 D wjc4092@louisiana.edu
CRIST, William, M .... 520-626-1197...... 18 L wcrist@email.arizona.edu
CRISTANTELLO, David, A .. 716-839-8212.... 331 F dcristan@daemen.edu
CRISTELLI, Bruno, P .... 409-772-1939.... 507 C bcristel@utmb.edu
CRISTELLO, Justin .... 859-442-1687.... 202 B justin.cristello@kctcs.edu
CRISTIANO KELLY, Patricia .... 215-955-1755.... 448 C patricia.kelly@jefferson.edu
CRISTOBAL, Nereida .... 787-620-2040.... 560 D ncristobal@aupr.edu
CRISTOBAL, Remy, B .... 671-735-2218.... 559 G remybc@uguam.uog.edu
CRISTOFARO, Theresa, R .. 856-225-6053.... 314 D terri.cristofaro@rutgers.edu
CRISWELL, John .... 972-860-7786.... 484 F jcriswell@dcccd.edu
CRITE, Ken .... 815-802-8222.... 155 A kcrite@kcc.edu
CRITEL-RATHJE, Dina .... 402-643-7396.... 297 D dina.critel-rathje@cune.edu
CRITES, Randall, W .... 304-473-8030.... 545 G crites@wvwc.edu
CRITES, Tammy, J .... 304-473-8186.... 545 G crites_t@wvwc.edu
CRITTENDEN, Barbara, J ... 641-782-1425.... 189 E crittenden@swcciowa.edu
CRITTENDEN, Steve .... 218-683-8565.... 268 C steve.crittenden@northlandcollege.edu
CROAT, Lisa .... 515-643-6720.... 187 F lcroat@mercydesmoines.org
CROCCO, Margaret .... 319-335-5380.... 182 F margaret-crocco@uiowa.edu
CROCE, Edward .... 210-434-6711.... 492 B ecroce@lake.ollusa.edu
CROCETTO, Ryan .... 215-596-8708.... 450 B r.crocetto@usciences.edu
CROCITTO, Peter .... 561-547-6000.... 112 G pcrocitto@keiseruniversity.edu
CROCK, Veronica .... 334-347-2623........ 3 F vcrock@escc.edu
CROCKER, Daniel .... 207-974-4623.... 218 H dcrocker@emcc.edu
CROCKER, Dennis .... 815-939-5391.... 161 A dcrocker@olivet.edu
CROCKER, Gilda .... 352-854-2322.... 103 K crockerg@cf.edu
CROCKER, Jane, S .... 856-415-2250.... 310 D jcrocker@gccnj.edu
CROCKER, Marjorie .... 706-419-1544.... 128 B crocker@covenant.edu
CROCKER, Rhonda .... 575-624-7382.... 318 C rhonda.crocker@roswell.enmu.edu
CROCKER, Richard, R .... 603-646-3350.... 304 J richard.r.crocker@dartmouth.edu
CROCKER, Robert, A .... 516-796-4800.... 342 H rcrocker@nycc.edu
CROCKER, Teresa .... 404-894-2500.... 130 F teresa.crocker@police.gatech.edu
CROCKER, Tillman .... 575-624-7486.... 318 C tillman.crocker@roswell.enmu.edu
CROCKER, W. Jack .... 941-752-5200.... 118 J crockej@scf.edu
CROCKETT, Bennie, R .... 601-318-6116.... 278 C crockett@wmcarey.edu
CROCKETT, Betty, P .... 410-543-6051.... 228 D bpcrockett@salisbury.edu
CROCKETT, Brian, S .... 540-464-7287.... 529 F briancrockett@vmiaa.org
CROCKETT, Charles, E .... 936-261-2653.... 496 G cecrockett@pvamu.edu
CROCKETT, Daniel, E .... 304-558-4618.... 543 E crockett@hepc.wvnet.edu
CROCKETT, Dave .... 217-581-6250.... 150 E dmcrockett@eiu.edu
CROCKETT, Deborah .... 207-947-4591.... 217 D dcrockett@bealcollege.edu
CROCKETT, Julie, A .... 303-458-3524...... 87 I jcrocket@regis.edu
CROCKETT, Michael .... 928-428-8215...... 14 B mike.crockett@eac.edu
CROCKETT, Samuel, T .... 301-776-3656.... 223 G scrockett@kaplan.edu
CROCKETT, William, P .... 410-706-3902.... 227 C bcrocket@umaryland.edu
CROCKETT-BELL, Sharon .... 210-486-2887.... 479 D scrockett-bell@alamo.edu
CROCKETT-BELL, Sharon .... 210-486-2886.... 479 D scrockett-bell@alamo.edu
CROCKFORD, Elizabeth, C . 603-526-3761.... 303 G bcrockford@colby-sawyer.edu
CROCKROM, SR., Charles 205-929-1447........ 5 H ccrockrom@miles.edu
CROCQUET, Marc .... 954-262-8842.... 114 B crocquet@nsu.nova.edu
CROFOOT-MORLEY, Deborah .... 713-525-3109.... 505 A crofoot@stthom.edu
CROFT, Lucy, S .... 904-620-2525.... 120 D lcroft@unf.edu
CROFT, Nicole .... 866-680-2756.... 510 F academicdean@midwifery.edu
CROFT, Russell .... 843-383-8081.... 457 A rcroft@coker.edu
CROFT, Twila .... 406-791-5308.... 296 F tcroft@ugf.edu
CROGHAN, David .... 301-846-2491.... 222 G dcroghan@frederick.edu
CROGHAN, John .... 315-859-4129.... 334 H jcroghan@hamilton.edu
CROLEY, Linda .... 386-752-1822.... 108 G linda.croley@fgc.edu
CROMARTY, Geoffrey .... 215-951-2970.... 444 D cromartyg@philau.edu
CROMBIE, Richard .... 651-635-8041.... 261 D r-crombie@bethel.edu
CROMEENS, Julie .... 325-738-3318.... 500 G julie.cromeens@abilene.tstc.edu
CROMER, Daniel .... 305-428-5909.... 113 I dcromer@aii.edu
CROMER, Steve .... 706-646-6234.... 137 F scromer@sctech.edu
CROMLEY, Brenda .... 570-389-4674.... 441 F bcromley@bloomu.edu
CROMWELL, Dennis .... 812-855-4717.... 173 E dcromwel@indiana.edu
CROMWELL, J. Randolph .. 731-352-4000.... 467 E cromwellr@bethelu.edu
CROMWELL, James .... 808-974-7414.... 141 F cromwell@hawaii.edu
CROMWELL, Ronald .... 256-233-8214........ 1 E ronald.cromwell@athens.edu

CRUTCHFIELD, Carla .... 501-337-5000 ...... 21 D
ccrutchfield@coto.edu
CRUTCHFIELD, Victor .... 901-448-7271 .... 477 E
vcrutchfield@uthsc.edu
CRUTSINGER, Christy .... 940-565-2550 .... 504 D
christy.crutsinger@unt.edu
CRUTSINGER, Gene .... 419-448-3383 .... 402 E
crutsingerg@tiffin.edu
CRUZ, Abraham .... 347-964-8600 .... 324 C
acruz@boricuacollege.edu
CRUZ, Anthony .... 513-569-1640 .... 387 G
anthony.cruz@cincinnatistate.edu
CRUZ, Beatriz .... 718-429-6600 .... 359 G
beatriz.cruz@vaughn.edu
CRUZ, Carmen, L .... 787-257-0000 .... 567 C
carmen.cruz3@upr.edu
CRUZ, Celestino .... 787-746-1400 .... 562 E
ccruz@huertas.edu
CRUZ, Erin .... 559-791-2332 ...... 53 A
ecruz@portervillecollege.edu
CRUZ, Esteban .... 217-786-2200 .... 157 B
esteban.cruz@llcc.edu
CRUZ, Felicita .... 787-834-9595 .... 566 B
fcruz@uaa.edu
CRUZ, Heather, A .... 716-851-1858 .... 333 A
cruzh@ecc.edu
CRUZ, Heidi .... 305-222-2815 .... 107 G
hcruz@careercollege.edu
CRUZ, Irma del Pilar .... 787-828-1319 .... 565 I
um_idelpilar@suagm.edu
CRUZ, Israel .... 787-264-1912 .... 564 B
icruz@sg.inter.edu
CRUZ, Jackie .... 831-755-6810 ...... 49 E
jcruz@hartnell.edu
CRUZ, Jaime .... 787-769-0007 .... 560 H
jacruz@carolina.caribbean.edu
CRUZ, Janet .... 615-794-4254 .... 472 F
jcruz@omorecollege.edu
CRUZ, Johnny .... 520-621-1877 ...... 18 L
cruzj@email.arizona.edu
CRUZ, Jose .... 956-872-3554 .... 494 H
jcruz@southtexascollege.edu
CRUZ, Lambert .... 602-386-4111 ...... 11 G
lambert.cruz@arizonachristian.edu
CRUZ, Larry .... 787-850-9342 .... 567 E
larry.cruz@upr.edu
CRUZ, Larry .... 787-850-9351 .... 567 E
larry.cruz@upr.edu
CRUZ, Lourdes .... 203-837-9202 ...... 91 A
cruzl@wcsu.edu
CRUZ, Luis, M .... 787-279-2250 .... 563 D
lcruz@bayamon.inter.edu
CRUZ, Mariela .... 787-620-2040 .... 560 D
marielacruz@aupr.edu
CRUZ, Martin .... 787-766-1717 .... 565 I
um_mcruzsa@suagm.edu
CRUZ, Monica .... 361-354-2258 .... 483 B
mcruz@coastalbend.edu
CRUZ, Nathaniel .... 718-518-4253 .... 327 D
ncruz@hostos.cuny.edu
CRUZ, Nereida .... 787-850-9328 .... 567 E
nereida.cruz@upr.edu
CRUZ, Octavio .... 408-270-6423 ...... 67 C
octavio.cruz@evc.edu
CRUZ, Olga .... 787-815-0000 .... 567 A
olga.cruz2@upr.edu
CRUZ, Oscar .... 787-786-3030 .... 560 G
oscruz@ucb.edu.pr
CRUZ, Pedro .... 787-738-2161 .... 567 D
pedro.cruz3@upr.edu
CRUZ, Robert .... 201-360-4051 .... 310 E
rcruz@hccc.edu
CRUZ, Rosa, E .... 787-848-1589 .... 564 I
rcruz@popac.edu
CRUZ, Rosalia .... 212-694-1000 .... 324 C
rcruz@boricuacollege.edu
CRUZ, Tony .... 760-744-1150 ...... 61 D
tcruz@palomar.edu
CRUZ, Villan .... 718-933-6700 .... 341 G
vcrux@monroecollege.edu
CRUZ, Zoraida .... 787-279-1912 .... 563 D
zcruz@bayamon.inter.edu
CRUZ BONILLA, Jessica .... 787-744-1060 .... 564 F
jecbo@mechtech.edu
CRUZ-CUEVAS, Oscar .... 787-786-4508 .... 561 I
ocruz@cedoc.edu
CRUZ GORRITZ, Carlos .... 787-709-4442 .... 564 F
ccruz@mechtech.edu
CRUZ-JIMENEZ, Iris .... 787-834-5151 .... 565 D
incruz@email.pucpr.edu
CRUZ-RICHMAN, Daisy ..... 718-270-7631 .... 352 D
dcruzrichman@downstate.edu
CRUZ SOTO, Bethzaida ...... 787-840-2575 .... 565 A
CRUZ-URIBE, Kathryn .... 831-582-4401 ...... 35 E
kcruz@csumb.edu
CRUZADO, Waded .... 406-994-2341 .... 295 C
president@montana.edu
CRYER, Byron, L .... 214-648-2590 .... 507 E
byron.cryer@utsouthwestern.edu
CRYLEN, Thomas .... 847-925-6169 .... 151 G
tcrylen@harpercollege.edu
CSIKOS, Andrew, M .... 814-269-7130 .... 449 D
csikos@pitt.edu

CUADRA, Darla .... 510-261-8500 ...... 61 G
darla.cuadra@patten.edu
CUADRADO-GARCÍA,
Héctor .... 787-993-8953 .... 567 B
hector.cuadrado@upr.edu
CUARON, Berta .... 760-744-1150 ...... 61 D
bcuaron@palomar.edu
CUARTA, Adrian .... 813-974-2750 .... 121 A
acuarta@admin.usf.edu
CUBANO, Luis, A .... 787-798-3001 .... 566 C
luis.cubano@uccaribe.edu
CUBAR, Janet .... 240-567-7356 .... 224 D
janet.cubar@montgomerycollege.edu
CUBBA, Stephanie .... 213-477-2766 ...... 57 H
scubba@msmc.la.edu
CUBBAGE, Alan, K .... 847-491-4886 .... 160 E
a-cubbage@northwestern.edu
CUBBERLEY, Frances, M ... 610-359-5141 .... 426 G
fcubberl@dccc.edu
CUBBIN, Michael .... 510-574-1100 ...... 44 F
mcubbin@devry.edu
CUBBINS, Elaine .... 520-383-8401 ...... 18 I
ecubbins@tocc.cc.az.us
CUBE, Joan .... 925-631-8317 ...... 64 F
jic2@stmarys-ca.edu
CUBELIC, Chuck .... 412-809-5100 .... 444 G
cubelic.chuck@pti.edu
CUBIT, James, R .... 847-735-5054 .... 155 G
cubit@lakeforest.edu
CUCCIA, Christopher .... 718-390-4094 .... 348 G
cucciac@stjohns.edu
CUCOLO, Anthony .... 717-245-4400 .... 558 G
CUCURELLA-ADORNO,
Ana, E .... 787-780-0070 .... 560 H
president@caribbean.edu
CUDDEBACK, Madelyne .... 617-994-6486 .... 245 B
mcuddeba@suffolk.edu
CUDDY, Colleen .... 212-746-6069 .... 360 C
czc2003@med.cornell.edu
CUDE, Ruth .... 361-354-2767 .... 483 B
rcude@coastalbend.edu
CUDHEA, Renee, M .... 518-489-7436 .... 340 A
srcudhea@mariacollege.edu
CUE, Elaine .... 270-886-1302 .... 199 C
rcue@brownmackie.edu
CUELLAR, Tina .... 409-772-1983 .... 507 C
ehcuella@utmb.edu
CUELLAR, Toni .... 254-298-8333 .... 496 D
toni.cuellar@templejc.edu
CUENIN, Walter .... 781-736-3574 .... 232 F
cuenin@brandeis.edu
CUERVO, Heydee .... 305-226-9999 .... 109 C
hcuervo@mm.fnc.edu
CUETO, Jose, M .... 787-780-0070 .... 560 H
jcueto@caribbean.edu
CUETO, Omar .... 787-279-1912 .... 563 D
ocueto@bayamon.inter.edu
CUEVAS, Felix, A .... 787-844-2750 .... 568 A
felix.cuevas@upr.edu
CUEVAS, Felix, A .... 787-844-8181 .... 568 A
felix.cuevas@upr.edu
CUEVAS, José .... 787-834-3718 .... 567 F
support@uprm.edu
CUFF, Michael .... 508-830-5037 .... 238 D
mcuff@maritime.edu
CUFFARI, Gina .... 216-447-8807 ...... 19 A
gina.cuffari@phoenix.edu
CUIMAN, Leonzo .... 718-270-1972 .... 352 D
lcuiman@downstate.edu
CUKANNA, Paul-James ..... 412-396-5002 .... 428 D
cukanna@duq.edu
CUKROWSKI, Ken, R .... 325-674-3700 .... 478 I
cukrowskik@acu.edu
CULATTA, Victor .... 408-795-5600 ...... 37 C
victor.culatta@sjsu.edu
CULBERSON, Roy .... 940-498-6282 .... 491 E
rculberson@nctc.edu
CULBERT, John .... 773-325-7954 .... 149 A
jculbert@depaul.edu
CULBERTSON, Charles, R . 540-828-5720 .... 517 B
cculbert@bridgewater.edu
CULBERTSON, Lindsay ...... 903-923-2072 .... 486 F
lculbertson@etbu.edu
CULBERTSON, Paul .... 717-764-9550 .... 426 D
pculbertson@csb.edu
CULBERTSON, JR.,
Rodney, A .... 704-366-5066 .... 376 B
rculbertson@rts.edu
CULBREATH, Geri .... 912-279-5761 .... 127 E
gculbreath@ccga.edu
CULBREATH, Jahan .... 937-376-6289 .... 387 A
jculbreath@centralstate.edu
CULBRETH, Paul .... 717-299-7763 .... 448 A
culbreth@stevenscollege.edu
CULHAM, Mark .... 405-789-7661 .... 412 E
mark.culham@swcu.edu
CULHAN, Timothy, P .... 859-238-5360 .... 199 G
tim.culhan@centre.edu
CULHANE, Marianne, B ..... 402-280-3154 .... 297 F
mculhane@creighton.edu
CULKOWSKI, Justin, F ...... 315-470-6632 .... 355 A
jfculkow@esf.edu
CULL, Cecelia .... 617-682-1525 .... 234 E
ccull@eds.edu

CULLARS, Kyle .... 478-445-1976 .... 130 B
kyle.cullars@gcsu.edu
CULLEN, Andrew .... 505-277-6465 .... 321 C
acullen@unm.edu
CULLEN, Daryl .... 415-282-7600 ...... 28 B
darylcullen@actcm.edu
CULLEN, Holly .... 225-578-3872 .... 212 H
hhouk@lsu.edu
CULLEN, Jim .... 503-493-6508 .... 415 E
jcullen@cu-portland.edu
CULLEN, Jim .... 570-961-7864 .... 433 A
cullenj@lakcawanna.edu
CULLEN, Kathleen .... 608-266-9399 .... 553 F
kathleen.cullen@wtcsystem.edu
CULLEN, Keith .... 334-244-3345 .... 1 G
kcullen1@aum.edu
CULLEN, Kevin .... 302-736-2442 ...... 97 A
cullenke@wesley.edu
CULLEN, Marie, D .... 330-941-1518 .... 406 F
mdcullen@ysu.edu
CULLEN, Matt .... 323-357-3438 ...... 39 G
mattcullen@cdrewu.edu
CULLEN, Richard, T .... 845-451-1300 .... 331 E
r_cullen@culinary.edu
CULLENBERG, Steven .... 951-827-2762 ...... 74 E
steven.cullenberg@ucr.edu
CULLER, Fred, B .... 304-883-2424 .... 543 A
fculler@newriver.edu
CULLER, Kevin, J .... 313-845-9755 .... 252 B
kjculler@hfcc.edu
CULLER, Lori, L .... 260-359-4213 .... 173 A
lculler@huntington.edu
CULLER, Valerie .... 734-384-4139 .... 255 D
vculler@monroeccc.edu
CULLERTON, Laura .... 303-369-5151 ...... 87 D
laura.cullerton@plattcolorado.edu
CULLEY, Christopher, M .... 614-292-0611 .... 398 I
culley.8@osu.edu
CULLEY, JR., W. Glenn ..... 434-223-6216 .... 519 G
gculley@hsc.edu
CULLIGAN, Rob .... 320-363-3388 .... 271 A
rculligan@csbsju.edu
CULLINAN, Carol .... 716-880-2211 .... 340 D
carol.cullinan@medaille.edu
CULLINAN, Mary .... 541-552-6111 .... 419 A
cullinanm@sou.edu
CULLINAN, Matthew, S ...... 336-758-3097 .... 380 C
cullinan@wfu.edu
CULLINAN, William .... 414-288-5053 .... 548 F
william.cullinan@marquette.edu
CULLINANE, Mary .... 508-565-3360 .... 245 A
stonehillbkstr@fheg.follett.com
CULLISON, Janet, L .... 443-518-4904 .... 223 D
jcullison@howardcc.edu
CULLITON, Pamela .... 314-529-9520 .... 284 C
pculliton@maryville.edu
CULLITON, Richard .... 860-685-2627 ...... 95 E
rculliton@wesleyan.edu
CULLNANE, Chris .... 601-968-8505 .... 273 C
ccullnane@belhaven.edu
CULLUM, Carol, J .... 910-362-7040 .... 368 H
ccullum@cfcc.edu
CULLUM, Charles .... 508-929-8038 .... 238 G
ccullum2@worcester.edu
CULLUM, Douglas .... 585-594-6331 .... 344 F
cullumd@nes.edu
CULLUMBER, Shari .... 317-931-3324 .... 170 H
scullumber@cts.edu
CULLUMS, Ron .... 740-654-6711 .... 400 C
cullums@ohio.edu
CULLUP, Michael .... 521-344-1403 ...... 19 A
michael.cullup@phoenix.edu
CULOTTA, Cheryl, C .... 518-327-6340 .... 345 H
cculotta@paulsmiths.edu
CULOTTA, Sheryl .... 860-685-2008 ...... 95 E
sculotta@wesleyan.edu
CULP, Kristin, J .... 937-328-6087 .... 387 H
culpk@clarkstate.edu
CULP, Mark, K .... 610-861-5301 .... 437 H
mculp@northampton.edu
CULPEPPER, Grady .... 404-756-4033 .... 125 D
gculpepper@atlm.edu
CULPEPPER, R. Alan .... 678-547-6471 .... 134 A
culpepper_ra@mercer.edu
CULPEPPER, Suzann .... 229-430-3510 .... 124 B
sculpepper@albanytech.edu
CULUM, Samra .... 208-732-6223 .... 143 E
sculum@csi.edu
CULVER, Dale .... 913-758-4372 .... 197 D
culverd@stmary.edu
CULVER, Jay .... 863-638-2947 .... 123 E
culverjr@webber.edu
CULVER, Jeff .... 303-256-9330 ...... 85 L
jculver@jwu.edu
CULVER, Richard, W .... 410-543-6017 .... 228 D
rwculver@salisbury.edu
CULVER, Sandi .... 907-786-1464 ...... 10 H
smculver@uaa.alaska.edu
CULVER, Terry .... 212-217-4109 .... 333 F
terry_culver@fitnyc.edu
CUMBERLAND, Denise .... 502-585-9911 .... 206 D
dcumberland@spalding.edu
CUMBIA, Doug .... 540-868-7235 .... 527 C
dcumbia@lfcc.edu

CUMBIE, Donna, L .... 252-222-6161 .... 369 A
dlc@carteret.edu
CUMBY, Rick .... 423-478-6226 .... 474 E
rcumby@clevelandstatecc.edu
CUMENS, Chris .... 270-901-1113 .... 201 I
chris.cumens@kctcs.edu
CUMINGS, Victoria .... 503-517-1012 .... 421 B
vcumings@warnerpacific.edu
CUMMING, Carrie .... 269-387-4300 .... 260 C
carrie.cumming@wmich.edu
CUMMING, Tammie .... 718-260-5007 .... 328 D
tcumming@citytech.cuny.edu
CUMMINGS, Alison .... 404-270-5344 .... 138 B
acummin3@spelman.edu
CUMMINGS, SSE,
Brian, J .... 802-654-2386 .... 514 D
bcummings@smcvt.edu
CUMMINGS, Carmen .... 850-599-3707 .... 118 L
carmen.cummings@famu.edu
CUMMINGS, Carmen, M ...... 386-312-4152 .... 116 F
carmencummings@sjrstate.edu
CUMMINGS, Corlis .... 678-466-4270 .... 127 D
corliscummings@clayton.edu
CUMMINGS, Cynthia .... 508-910-6402 .... 237 A
ccumings2@umassd.edu
CUMMINGS, Dee Dee .... 765-983-1513 .... 171 E
cummide@earlham.edu
CUMMINGS, Edmond, M .. 504-286-5258 .... 214 J
ecumming@suno.edu
CUMMINGS, Eric .... 615-547-1323 .... 468 B
ecummings@cumberland.edu
CUMMINGS, Helen .... 973-642-8380 .... 315 C
helen.cummings@shu.edu
CUMMINGS, Jeff .... 707-476-4100 ...... 42 C
jeff-cummings@redwoods.edu
CUMMINGS, Jim .... 270-745-5327 .... 208 A
jim.cummings@wku.edu
CUMMINGS, Jim .... 205-802-1200 .... 3 B
jim.cummings@vc.edu
CUMMINGS, Jonathan .... 304-293-7173 .... 545 A
jonathan.cumming@mail.wvu.edu
CUMMINGS, Joseph .... 718-489-5346 .... 348 E
jcummings@sfc.edu
CUMMINGS, Joyce .... 954-308-2177 .... 101 C
cummingsj@aii.edu
CUMMINGS, Kevin, R .... 914-594-4536 .... 343 F
webmaster@nymc.edu
CUMMINGS, Kris .... 253-964-6529 .... 536 H
kycummings@pierce.ctc.edu
CUMMINGS, Lisa .... 802-635-1382 .... 515 F
lisa.cummings@jsc.edu
CUMMINGS, Marge .... 606-337-1407 .... 199 H
mcummings@ccbbc.edu
CUMMINGS, Mary .... 724-852-3271 .... 451 B
mcumming@waynesburg.edu
CUMMINGS, Matthew .... 814-732-1333 .... 442 E
mcummings@edinboro.edu
CUMMINGS, Natalie, A ...... 317-788-3205 .... 180 F
cummingsn@uindy.edu
CUMMINGS, Owen .... 503-845-3547 .... 417 A
owen.cummings@mtangel.edu
CUMMINGS, Sara .... 617-824-8446 .... 234 B
sara_cummings@emerson.edu
CUMMINGS, Terrence, M .. 803-533-3721 .... 460 G
tcummings@scsu.edu
CUMMINGS, Tiffany, N ...... 434-381-6362 .... 524 K
tcummings@sbc.edu
CUMMINGS, Victor .... 707-527-4615 ...... 68 E
vcummings@santarosa.edu
CUMMINGS, Walter .... 404-756-4052 .... 125 D
wcummings@atlm.edu
CUMMINGS,
Wm. Theodore .... 281-283-3100 .... 503 E
cummings@uhcl.edu
CUMMINGS-DANSON,
Gail, L .... 518-580-5370 .... 351 B
gcumming@skidmore.edu
CUMMINS, Cheryl .... 662-846-4405 .... 273 H
ccummins@deltastate.edu
CUMMINS, David, J .... 330-972-8396 .... 403 B
dcummins@uakron.edu
CUMMINS, F. James .... 810-766-4250 .... 247 G
jim.cummins@baker.edu
CUMMINS, Jim .... 417-455-5538 .... 280 H
jimcummins@crowder.edu
CUMMINS, Richard .... 509-542-4869 .... 532 H
rcummins@columbiabasin.edu
CUMMINS, Stephen .... 630-942-3007 .... 148 A
cummins@cod.edu
CUMMISKEY, Raymond, V 636-481-3100 .... 283 D
rcummisk@jeffco.edu
CUMOLETTI, Susan, K .... 315-652-6500 .... 324 L
scumoletti@bryantstratton.edu
CUMPIANO, Barbarita .... 787-832-6000 .... 562 G
bcumpiano@icprjc.edu
CUNDALL, JR., Michael .... 336-285-2030 .... 378 A
mcundall@ncat.edu
CUNDARI, Alan .... 909-469-5670 ...... 78 I
acundari@westernu.edu
CUNDIFF, H. Lynn .... 928-757-0801 ...... 16 F
lcundiff@mohave.edu
CUNDIFF, Michael .... 314-984-7608 .... 289 A
mcundiff@stlcc.edu
CUNDIFF, Sarah .... 316-942-4291 .... 195 F
cundiffs@newmanu.edu

CUNEAZ, Jodi ... 810-766-4015 ... 248 C
jodi.cuneaz@baker.edu
CUNHA, Sonia ... 973-642-8743 ... 315 C
sonia.cunha@shu.edu
CUNNING, Catherine, A ... 973-378-2661 ... 310 F
catherine.cunning@shu.edu
CUNNING, Charles, J ... 864-488-4540 ... 459 B
cunning@limestone.edu
CUNNINGHAM, Al ... 912-443-5827 ... 136 H
acunningham@savannahtech.edu
CUNNINGHAM, Austin, J .. 972-883-2234 ... 506 A
cunning@utdallas.edu
CUNNINGHAM, Bruce, W . 919-684-9007 ... 364 C
bruce.cunningham@duke.edu
CUNNINGHAM, Carl, G ... 251-460-6895 ... 9 D
ccunningham@usouthal.edu
CUNNINGHAM, Cecelia ... 616-632-2816 ... 247 E
cunnicec@aquinas.edu
CUNNINGHAM, Chester, M ... 270-824-8699 ... 202 G
chet.cunningham@kctcs.edu
CUNNINGHAM, Dave ... 206-546-4595 ... 538 C
dcunningham@shoreline.edu
CUNNINGHAM, David ... 313-845-4106 ... 252 B
CUNNINGHAM, Diana, J ... 914-594-4200 ... 343 F
diana_cunningham@nymc.edu
CUNNINGHAM, Diane ... 270-707-3921 ... 202 E
diane.cunningham@kctcs.edu
CUNNINGHAM, Eddie ... 302-454-3922 ... 96 F
ecunning@dtcc.edu
CUNNINGHAM, Eric ... 573-875-7649 ... 280 A
ercunningham@ccis.edu
CUNNINGHAM, Gary ... 606-679-8501 ... 203 C
gary.cunningham@kctcs.edu
CUNNINGHAM, Jack, L ... 302-356-6921 ... 97 C
john.l.cunningham@wilmu.edu
CUNNINGHAM, James ... 630-617-3012 ... 150 H
james.cunningham@elmhurst.edu
CUNNINGHAM, James, E . 570-326-3761 ... 440 L
jcunning@pct.edu
CUNNINGHAM, Janet, L ... 580-327-8400 ... 409 C
jlcunningham@nwosu.edu
CUNNINGHAM, Joan ... 973-328-5340 ... 309 A
jcunningham@ccm.edu
CUNNINGHAM, John ... 404-270-5074 ... 138 B
jcunning@spelman.edu
CUNNINGHAM, John ... 774-455-7601 ... 236 E
jcunningham@umassonline.net
CUNNINGHAM, Joi, M ... 248-370-3496 ... 256 G
cunning3@oakland.edu
CUNNINGHAM, Julie ... 716-375-2301 ... 348 C
jcunning@sbu.edu
CUNNINGHAM, Karla, K ... 317-940-9570 ... 170 F
kcunning@butler.edu
CUNNINGHAM, Kathleen .. 610-606-4635 ... 425 A
ksglass@cedarcrest.edu
CUNNINGHAM, Kay ... 901-321-3430 ... 467 I
kay.cunningham@cbu.edu
CUNNINGHAM, Kevin, A .. 563-884-5898 ... 61 A
kevin.cunningham@palmer.edu
CUNNINGHAM, Kevin, A .. 563-884-5898 ... 114 E
kevin.cunningham@palmer.edu
CUNNINGHAM, Kevin, A .. 563-884-5898 ... 188 E
kevin.cunningham@palmer.edu
CUNNINGHAM, Khaneetah 314-513-4226 ... 288 H
kcunningham@stlcc.edu
CUNNINGHAM, Lawrence (Bubba), R ... 919-962-8200 ... 378 E
bubba@uncaa.unc.edu
CUNNINGHAM, Luana ... 318-487-7301 ... 209 F
cunningham@lacollege.edu
CUNNINGHAM, Marina ... 973-655-4499 ... 311 F
cunninghamm@mail.montclair.edu
CUNNINGHAM, Mark ... 404-756-4654 ... 125 D
mcunningham@atlm.edu
CUNNINGHAM, Mary ... 516-773-5398 ... 558 I
cunninghamm@usmma.edu
CUNNINGHAM, Michael ... 504-862-3308 ... 215 C
mcunnin1@tulane.edu
CUNNINGHAM, Michael ... 619-594-5259 ... 37 A
mcunningham@mail.sdsu.edu
CUNNINGHAM, Michael, A ... 419-995-8215 ... 399 B
cunningham.15@osu.edu
CUNNINGHAM, Michael, M ... 570-326-3761 ... 440 L
mcunning@pct.edu
CUNNINGHAM, Pam ... 724-852-3384 ... 451 B
pcunning@waynesburg.edu
CUNNINGHAM, Pat ... 719-389-6707 ... 82 D
pat.cunningham@coloradocollege.edu
CUNNINGHAM, Paul R, G 252-744-2201 ... 377 E
cunninghamp@ecu.edu
CUNNINGHAM, R. Michael ... 217-443-8831 ... 148 G
mcunningham@dacc.edu
CUNNINGHAM, Rose ... 201-360-4158 ... 310 E
rcunningham@hccc.edu
CUNNINGHAM, Sean ... 512-463-1808 ... 500 H
sean.cunningham@tsus.edu
CUNNINGHAM, Shannon .. 918-540-6272 ... 408 J
scunningham@neo.edu
CUNNINGHAM, Sheila ... 803-780-1266 ... 463 C
scunningham@voorhees.edu
CUNNINGHAM, Steven, D 815-753-6021 ... 160 B
cunningham@niu.edu
CUNNINGHAM, Todd ... 724-357-4000 ... 442 F
todd.cunningham@iup.edu
CUNNINGHAM, William, J 215-596-8535 ... 450 B
w.cunningham@usciences.edu
CUNZ, Leonard ... 908-852-1400 ... 308 E
cunzl@centenarycollege.edu
CUOMO, Michele ... 718-631-6344 ... 328 F
mcuomo@qcc.cuny.edu
CUOZZO, Frank ... 201-200-3173 ... 312 B
fcuozzo@njcu.edu
CUOZZO, Jenifer ... 202-685-3785 ... 557 I
cuozzoj@ndu.edu
CUP, Jo Beth ... 312-662-4101 ... 144 H
jcup@adler.edu
CUPP, Dondi, L ... 734-647-6079 ... 259 A
dcupp@umich.edu
CUPPARI, Antoinette ... 954-938-3083 ... 104 G
acuppari@keller.edu
CUPPER, Barbara ... 415-433-6691 ... 46 L
bcupper@fidm.edu
CUPPER, Barbara ... 415-675-5200 ... 47 A
bcupper@fidm.edu
CUPPLES, Thomas, B ... 302-356-6761 ... 97 C
thomas.b.cupples@wilmu.edu
CUPPS, Lowell ... 803-786-3686 ... 457 C
lcupps@columbiasc.edu
CUPRAK, Greg ... 610-436-3200 ... 444 A
gcuprak@wcupa.edu
CURAVO, Pam ... 419-824-3731 ... 395 E
pcuravo@lourdes.edu
CURBO, Billy, D ... 254-659-7701 ... 487 G
bdcurbo@hillcollege.edu
CURCHACK, Mark, P ... 215-572-4076 ... 422 C
curchacm@arcadia.edu
CURD, David ... 877-248-6724 ... 14 I
CURD, Michael ... 877-248-6724 ... 14 I
m.curd@hmu.edu
CURE, Nancy ... 972-860-8261 ... 484 H
ncure@dcccd.edu
CUREG, Sapphire ... 304-327-4512 ... 543 F
scureg@bluefieldstate.edu
CURET, Nahomy ... 787-257-7373 ... 565 G
ue_ncuret@suagm.edu
CURETON, Alan, S ... 651-631-5250 ... 270 B
ascureton@nwc.edu
CURETON, Archie, L ... 585-245-5731 ... 353 C
cureton@geneseo.edu
CURETON, Michael ... 513-556-4951 ... 403 D
michael.cureton@uc.edu
CURIN, Donna, B ... 312-915-6404 ... 157 C
dcurin@luc.edu
CURL, John ... 801-581-8788 ... 511 C
jcurl@sa.utah.edu
CURL, Timothy, D ... 859-371-9393 ... 198 G
tcurl@beckfield.edu
CURLEE, Michelle ... 406-477-6215 ... 294 A
mcurlee@cdkc.edu
CURLESS, Chris ... 805-893-4638 ... 75 B
chris.curless@purc.ucsb.edu
CURLEY, Greg, M ... 814-641-3521 ... 432 A
curleyg@juniata.edu
CURLEY, Lauren ... 781-239-2572 ... 239 G
lcurley@massbay.edu
CURLEY, Meredith ... 480-557-1588 ... 19 A
meredith.curley@phoenix.edu
CURLEY, Michael, J ... 508-831-6919 ... 246 F
mjcurley@wpi.edu
CURLEY, Russell, L ... 218-477-2565 ... 267 F
russell.curley@mnstate.edu
CURLEY, Thomas ... 413-236-2103 ... 239 A
tcurley@berkshirecc.edu
CURLL, Steve ... 814-371-2090 ... 448 D
scurll@triangle-tech.edu
CURNS, Jeannine ... 419-448-2111 ... 391 F
jcurns@heidelberg.edu
CURNUTT, Cindy ... 432-335-6601 ... 492 A
ccurnutt@odessa.edu
CURNUTT, Marlin, R ... 423-585-2690 ... 476 D
marlin.curnutt@ws.edu
CURRALL, Steven, C ... 530-752-4600 ... 73 I
scc@ucdavis.edu
CURRAN, Catherine ... 847-969-4901 ... 145 D
ccurran@argosy.edu
CURRAN, Daniel, J ... 937-229-4122 ... 404 A
president@udayton.edu
CURRAN, Diana, T ... 810-762-3150 ... 259 C
dtcurran@umflint.edu
CURRAN, James, W ... 404-727-8720 ... 129 D
jcurran@sph.emory.edu
CURRAN, Joanne, M ... 607-436-2541 ... 353 E
curranjm@oneonta.edu
CURRAN, Linda ... 303-678-3620 ... 85 A
linda.curran@frontrange.edu
CURRAN, Susan ... 401-232-6020 ... 453 C
scurran3@bryant.edu
CURRAN, Terrence, M ... 910-962-3876 ... 379 D
currant@uncw.edu
CURRAN, OSFS, Thomas, B ... 816-501-4250 ... 288 A
thomas.curran@rockhurst.edu
CURREN, Robert, A ... 407-303-9372 ... 100 G
robert.curren@adu.edu
CURRENT, Amy, L ... 563-589-0274 ... 190 A
acurrent@wartburgseminary.edu
CURRERI, Joseph ... 323-343-3700 ... 35 D
joseph.curreri@calstatela.edu
CURRERI, Michelle, S ... 401-874-4462 ... 454 E
michelle@uri.edu
CURREY, David ... 714-997-6789 ... 39 F
dcurrey@chapman.edu
CURREY, Pamela, A ... 804-828-2092 ... 526 B
pacurrey@vcu.edu
CURRIE, Catherine ... 401-232-6369 ... 453 C
ccurrie@bryant.edu
CURRIE, Dean, W ... 626-395-6275 ... 32 H
dean.currie@caltech.edu
CURRIE, Eunice, M ... 817-272-5554 ... 505 C
currie@uta.edu
CURRIE, Jacqueline ... 205-366-8894 ... 7 F
jcurrie@stillman.edu
CURRIE, John ... 785-532-6912 ... 194 D
ksuad@ksu.edu
CURRIE, John ... 215-887-5511 ... 451 D
jcurrie@wts.edu
CURRIE, Kevin, D ... 724-738-2082 ... 443 F
kevin.currie@sru.edu
CURRIE, Stephanie ... 716-286-8205 ... 344 D
sbc@niagara.edu
CURRIE, Tammy, H ... 757-221-1909 ... 518 A
thcurr@wm.edu
CURRIE, Thomas, W ... 704-337-2450 ... 525 A
tcurrie@upsem.edu
CURRIE, Walter James ... 691-320-2480 ... 559 D
jimc@comfsm.fm
CURRIER, Camile, W ... 318-342-5230 ... 216 E
currier@ulm.edu
CURRIER, Chuck ... 630-942-2790 ... 148 A
currier@cod.edu
CURRIER, Michelle, L ... 315-386-7228 ... 355 E
currierm@canton.edu
CURRIN, Alicia ... 903-886-5034 ... 498 B
alicia.currin@tamuc.edu
CURRIN, Bruce, A ... 402-472-3105 ... 300 G
bcurrin1@unl.edu
CURRIN, Catherine ... 252-789-0297 ... 371 H
ccurrin@martincc.edu
CURRIN, Thomas ... 678-915-7482 ... 137 G
tcurrin@spsu.edu
CURRISTINE, Eileen ... 609-343-6810 ... 307 C
ecurrist@atlantic.edu
CURRO, Margaret (Peg) ... 508-678-2811 ... 239 B
peg.curro@bristolcc.edu
CURRY, Anne ... 205-226-4904 ... 2 B
acurry@bsc.edu
CURRY, Bonita, P ... 517-353-3243 ... 255 A
curryb@msu.edu
CURRY, Carolyn ... 302-857-6060 ... 96 C
ccurry@desu.edu
CURRY, Charles, T ... 724-738-2002 ... 443 F
charles.curry@sru.edu
CURRY, Cynthia, S ... 304-367-4000 ... 543 H
cindy.curry@fairmontstate.edu
CURRY, Dean, C ... 717-766-2511 ... 436 D
dcurry@messiah.edu
CURRY, JR., H. Pete ... 717-337-6311 ... 429 I
pcurry@gettysburg.edu
CURRY, James ... 252-249-1851 ... 372 F
pbanks@pamlicocc.edu
CURRY, JR., James, L ... 770-720-5577 ... 136 C
jlc1@reinhardt.edu
CURRY, Janel ... 978-867-4063 ... 235 A
janel.curry@gordon.edu
CURRY, Jason ... 615-329-8582 ... 468 I
jcurry@fisk.edu
CURRY, Keith ... 310-900-1600 ... 45 F
curry_k@compton.edu
CURRY, Michael ... 252-789-0268 ... 371 H
mcurry@martincc.edu
CURRY, Michael, D ... 989-837-4758 ... 256 E
currym@northwood.edu
CURRY, Ralph, W ... 906-786-5802 ... 248 I
curryr@baycollege.edu
CURRY, Robert ... 662-252-8000 ... 276 G
rcurry@rustcollege.edu
CURRY, Ruby ... 314-513-4135 ... 288 H
rcurry@stlcc.edu
CURRY, Susan ... 319-384-5452 ... 182 F
sue-curry@uiowa.edu
CURRY, Terri, A ... 712-274-5257 ... 187 G
curryte@morningside.edu
CURRY, II, Theodore, H ... 517-353-5300 ... 255 A
thcurry@msu.edu
CURRY, Tina ... 252-536-7263 ... 371 B
curryt@halifaxcc.edu
CURRY, Valerie ... 310-531-9710 ... 29 E
vcurry@argosy.edu
CURRY, Vicki ... 620-365-5116 ... 190 D
curry@allencc.edu
CURRY, William, N ... 601-318-6103 ... 278 C
bill.curry@wmcarey.edu
CURRY DAMATO, Ellen, R 914-654-5854 ... 330 B
ecurry@cnr.edu
CURTIN, Brian ... 207-893-6670 ... 219 F
bcurtin@sjcme.edu
CURTIN, Caitlin, F ... 510-204-0700 ... 40 A
ccurtin@cdsp.edu
CURTIN, Kathleen, M ... 410-857-2259 ... 224 C
kcurtin@mcdaniel.edu
CURTIN, Michael, J ... 502-852-6166 ... 207 E
mjcurt01@louisville.edu
CURTIN, Valerie ... 406-447-6913 ... 295 A
valerie.curtin@umhelena.edu
CURTIS, Alicia ... 803-938-3742 ... 462 G
curtisam@uscsumter.edu
CURTIS, Allison ... 805-965-0581 ... 68 B
curtis@sbcc.edu
CURTIS, Alyce ... 617-928-4556 ... 242 E
acurtis@mountida.edu
CURTIS, Amy ... 207-879-8757 ... 218 B
CURTIS, Benjamin, J ... 607-735-1821 ... 332 I
bcurtis@elmira.edu
CURTIS, Carolyn, G ... 518-629-7204 ... 336 C
c.curtis@hvcc.edu
CURTIS, Christine, W ... 803-777-9516 ... 462 A
curtisch@sc.edu
CURTIS, Cynthia, A ... 615-460-6408 ... 467 D
cynthia.curtis@belmont.edu
CURTIS, Deborah, J ... 660-543-4116 ... 290 H
curtis@ucmo.edu
CURTIS, Deborah, J ... 309-438-5415 ... 153 D
djcurti@ilstu.edu
CURTIS, Deloris, Y ... 203-332-5102 ... 91 E
dcurtis@hcc.commnet.edu
CURTIS, Ed ... 301-552-1400 ... 229 C
ecurtis@bible.edu
CURTIS, Edison ... 928-724-6727 ... 13 L
ecurtis@dinecollege.edu
CURTIS, Elaine ... 931-540-2534 ... 475 A
bcurtis@columbiastate.edu
CURTIS, Jeanne, F ... 215-898-6300 ... 448 J
curtis@isc.upenn.edu
CURTIS, Jeffrey, H ... 540-464-7104 ... 529 F
curtisjh@vmi.edu
CURTIS, Jerri ... 301-295-3638 ... 558 D
jerri.curtis@usuhs.edu
CURTIS, John ... 910-410-1737 ... 373 B
jrcurtis@richmondcc.edu
CURTIS, Joseph ... 615-329-8773 ... 468 I
jcurtis@fisk.edu
CURTIS, K. Tyler ... 620-341-5440 ... 192 G
kcurtis2@emporia.edu
CURTIS, Kathleen, A ... 915-747-7201 ... 506 B
kacurtis@utep.edu
CURTIS, Kelly ... 310-377-5501 ... 56 F
kcurtis@marymountpv.edu
CURTIS, Kelly, T ... 864-488-4601 ... 459 B
kcurtis@limestone.edu
CURTIS, Mark ... 775-753-2265 ... 302 F
mark.curtis@gbcnv.edu
CURTIS, Marvin ... 574-520-4170 ... 174 E
mcurtis@iusb.edu
CURTIS, Matt ... 914-831-0313 ... 330 D
mcurtis@cw.edu
CURTIS, Monty, L ... 318-869-5042 ... 208 H
mcurtis@centenary.edu
CURTIS, Regina ... 413-775-1426 ... 239 E
curtis@gcc.mass.edu
CURTIS, Rick ... 406-243-2122 ... 294 I
rcurtis@mso.umt.edu
CURTIS, Robert ... 614-947-6127 ... 391 B
robert.curtis@franklin.edu
CURTIS, Santhia ... 404-752-1895 ... 134 E
scurtis@msm.edu
CURTIS, Seletha, R ... 314-286-4803 ... 287 G
srcurtis@ranken.edu
CURTIS, Stephen, M ... 215-751-8028 ... 426 B
scurtis@ccp.edu
CURTIS, Susan ... 336-517-2289 ... 362 G
scurtis@bennett.edu
CURTIS, Ted ... 330-972-6107 ... 403 B
curtis4@uakron.edu
CURTIS, Timothy ... 928-428-8220 ... 14 B
tim.curtis@eac.edu
CURTIS, Tina ... 606-759-7141 ... 203 A
tina.curtis@kctcs.edu
CURTIS-CHAVEZ, Mark ... 216-987-5137 ... 389 B
mark.curtis-chavez@tri-c.edu
CURTIS HANE, Audrey ... 316-942-4291 ... 195 F
hanea@newmanu.edu
CURTIS POWELL, Melissa 614-235-4136 ... 402 G
mcpowell@tlsohio.edu
CURTISS, Kathleen, M ... 603-283-2361 ... 303 F
kcurtiss@antioch.edu
CURTO, Stephen, A ... 732-224-2593 ... 308 A
scurto@brookdalecc.edu
CURVIN, Nicole ... 802-258-9261 ... 513 H
ncurvin@marlboro.edu
CUSACK, Kelly, J ... 419-372-0632 ... 385 F
kcusack@bgsu.edu
CUSACK, Kristen ... 303-360-4701 ... 83 K
kristen.cusack@ccaurora.edu
CUSACK, Mary ... 810-762-0474 ... 255 G
CUSEO, Vincent ... 323-259-2700 ... 59 I
admission@oxy.edu
CUSHMAN, Bob ... 509-527-2603 ... 539 C
bob.cushman@wallawalla.edu
CUSHMAN, Jenifer, S ... 814-641-3181 ... 432 A
cushmaj@juniata.edu
CUSHMAN, Ron ... 417-873-7323 ... 281 D
rcushman@drury.edu

CUSHMAN, Valerie, J 540-458-8702 530 D
vcushman@wlu.edu
CUSICK, Dianna 612-659-6319 267 B
dianna.cusick@minneapolis.edu
CUSICK, Eileen 413-755-4014 241 B
cusick@stcc.edu
CUSICK, Sherry 563-589-3721 189 F
scusick@dbq.edu
CUSKER, Anne 812-265-2580 177 A
acusker@ivytech.edu
CUSPARD, Lisa-Marie 510-580-6740 80 A
lcuspard@cci.edu
CUSSEN, Susan 845-451-1471 331 E
s_cussen@culinary.edu
CUSSON, Regina 860-486-0537 94 G
regina.cusson@uconn.edu
CUSTER, Cristeen 507-457-2569 269 G
ccuster@winona.edu
CUSTER, Laura 859-344-3314 206 I
laura.custer@thomasmore.edu
CUSTER, Mandi 740-654-6711 400 C
custera@ohio.edu
CUSTER, Rodney 605-642-6262 465 H
rod.custer@bhsu.edu
CUSUMANO, Siobhan 215-574-9600 431 B
scusumano@hussianart.edu
CUTAIA, Diana 617-879-2238 246 C
dcutaia@wheelock.edu
CUTCHIN, Claudine 812-749-1443 178 H
ccutchin@oak.edu
CUTCHIN, Jeff 618-395-7777 152 I
cutchinj@iecc.edu
CUTHBERT, James, E 585-594-6860 347 F
cuthbertj@roberts.edu
CUTIETTA, Robert, A 213-740-5389 76 F
musicdean@thornton.usc.edu
CUTLER, David, A 802-654-2653 514 D
dcutler@smcvt.edu
CUTLER, Jared 937-512-2789 401 J
jared.cutler@sinclair.edu
CUTLER, Jerry 302-831-2171 96 I
jcutler@udel.edu
CUTLER, Nancy 408-554-4915 68 C
ncutler@scu.edu
CUTLER, Sally, M 317-940-9742 170 F
scutler@butler.edu
CUTLIFF, Janice 270-843-6750 200 B
jcutliff@daymarcollege.edu
CUTLIP, Mark 304-696-3253 544 B
cutlipm@marshall.edu
CUTOLO, Chuck 516-572-7811 342 C
chuck.cutolo@ncc.edu
CUTONE, Joan 412-536-1079 432 H
joan.cutone@laroche.edu
CUTRELL, Kathy 336-887-3000 366 C
kcutrell@laureluniversity.edu
CUTRELL, Kel Lee 706-778-8500 136 A
kcutrell@piedmont.edu
CUTRELL, Lori 615-230-4834 476 C
lori.cutrell@volstate.edu
CUTRER, Emily 760-750-4050 36 C
ecutrer@csusm.edu
CUTRI, David 419-530-6294 404 F
david.cutri@utoledo.edu
CUTRIGHT, Patricia 509-963-1902 532 C
cutright@cwu.edu
CUTSHAW, Kathleen, D 808-956-9190 141 G
cutshaw@hawaii.edu
CUTSINGER, Ginger 269-965-3931 253 B
cutsingerg@kellogg.edu
CUTSPEC, John 828-251-6868 378 D
jcutspec@unca.edu
CUTTING, Alicia 603-206-8006 304 D
acutting@ccsnh.edu
CUTTING, Judy 903-875-7573 491 C
judy.cutting@navarrocollege.edu
CUTTING, Merrill, W 808-955-1500 141 A
merrill_cutting@heald.edu
CUTTINO, Robert, E 770-538-4749 126 E
rcuttino@brenau.edu
CUYKENDALL, Lora, L 503-494-8252 418 D
news@ohsu.edu
CUZZOLINO, Robert, G 215-871-6770 444 C
bob@pcom.edu
CVITKOVIC, Kimberly, F 269-660-8021 257 C
cvitkovick@millercollege.edu
CVITKOVIC, Vicky 847-543-6504 148 B
vcvitkovic@clcillinois.edu
CWALINA, Marianne, F 781-891-2129 231 D
mcwalina@bentley.edu
CYBORON, Robert 808-544-0215 140 G
rcyboron@hpu.edu
CYGAN, Brian 570-326-3761 440 L
blc1@pct.edu
CYLKE, Catherine 703-579-3572 302 A
CYNAR, Deana 908-852-1400 308 E
cynar@centenarycollege.edu
CYPHERS, Christopher, J 212-752-1530 338 C
christopher.cyphers@limcollege.edu
CYPHERS BENSON, Laura 530-242-7649 69 D
lbenson@shastacollege.edu
CYPRESS, Sharen 731-989-6986 469 B
scypress@fhu.edu
CYPRIAN, Alecia 504-816-4398 209 A
acyprian@dillard.edu
CYREE, Kendall, B 662-915-5820 277 D
kbcyree@olemiss.edu
CYRUS, Cynthia 615-322-4474 478 A
cynthia.j.cyrus@vanderbilt.edu
CYTERSKI-ACOSTA, Andrea 210-805-5864 504 B
cyterski@uiwtx.edu
CZAJKIEWICZ, Zbigniew 281-283-3703 503 E
czajkiewiez@uhcl.edu
CZAJKOWSKI, Joyce 608-822-2419 555 D
jczajkowski@swtc.edu
CZARAPATA, Paul 859-256-3100 201 E
paul.czarapata@kctcs.edu
CZARDA, Lawrence, D 336-272-7221 364 G
lczarda@greensboro.edu
CZARNIK, Mimi 414-382-6138 546 B
mimi.czarnik@alverno.edu
CZARNIK-NEIMEYER, Jake 920-686-6176 550 H
jake.czarnik-neimeyer@sl.edu
CZEKAJ, Sandra 219-785-5696 179 A
czekajs@pnc.edu
CZEKAJ, Walter, P 724-938-5244 441 G
czekaj@calu.edu
CZEKANSKI, Kathleen 215-951-1322 432 I
czekanski@lasalle.edu
CZERNIAK, Walter, L 815-753-0783 160 B
wczerniak@niu.edu
CZERWINSKI, Rick 540-887-7336 521 C
rczerwin@mbc.edu
CZERWINSKI-ALJETS, Sue 618-468-4800 156 E
sczerwin@lc.edu
CZOHARA, Cami 603-623-0313 305 E
cczohara@nhia.edu
CZUBATYJ, Anna 586-791-6610 248 B
czubatyj.anna@baker.edu
CZYZ, Vito 716-375-2525 348 C
vczyc@sbu.edu

D

DÁNILA, Alba 787-751-0160 561 H
adavila@cmpr.pr.gov
DÁVILA-LÓPEZ, Rafael, F 787-250-0000 566 G
rafael.davila4@upr.edu
DA GRACA, John 956-968-2132 498 D
j-dagraca@tamuk.edu
DAAKE, Mary 308-865-8501 300 F
daakem@unk.edu
DAAR, Karen 323-265-8723 54 G
daarkl@elac.edu
DABBELT, Katie 419-586-0388 406 D
katie.dabbelt@wright.edu
DABBS, Melinda 615-794-4254 472 F
meldabbs@omorecollege.edu
DABIRIAN, Amir 657-278-5000 35 B
adabirian@fullerton.edu
DABNEY, David, O 419-530-8776 404 F
david.dabney@utoledo.edu
DABNEY, Jerome 773-602-5252 147 E
jdabney@ccc.edu
DABOUB, Joel 817-735-2204 504 E
joel.daboub@unthsc.edu
DABOVAL, Jeanne, M 337-475-5508 215 G
jdaboval@mcneese.edu
DABROWIAK, Derek 219-980-7707 176 G
ddabrowiak@ivytech.edu
DABROWSKI, Jan 503-699-6275 416 J
jdabrowski@marylhurst.edu
DACAL, Anita, S 412-578-6343 424 I
dacalas@carlow.edu
DACANAY, Emelita 310-578-1080 28 L
edacanay@antiochla.edu
DACE, Karen, L 816-235-6704 291 C
dacek@umkc.edu
DACHELET, Derek 608-822-2417 555 D
ddachelet@swtc.edu
DACHILLE, Nancy 215-248-7048 425 D
ndachill@chc.edu
DACOSTA, Tracy, M 401-254-3541 454 C
tdacosta@rwu.edu
DACUS, Kent 951-343-4687 31 J
kdacus@calbaptist.edu
DADDONA, Mark 678-466-4070 127 D
markdaddona@clayton.edu
DADDONA, Sharon, N 860-727-6903 92 I
sdaddona@goodwin.edu
DADEZ, Edward 352-588-8206 116 G
ed.dadez@saintleo.edu
DADEZ, Teresa 352-588-8347 116 G
teresa.dadez@saintleo.edu
DAERIS, Deborah 207-780-5670 220 G
daeris@usm.maine.edu
DAFFER, Steve 405-733-7424 411 I
sdaffer@rose.edu
DAFFRON, Eric 201-684-7532 313 C
edaffron@ramapo.edu
DAFFRON, Jeanne 816-271-4234 286 G
daffron@missouriwestern.edu
DAFFRON, SJ, Justin 312-915-6406 157 C
jdaffro@luc.edu
DAFLER, James, E 724-946-7317 451 C
daflerje@westminster.edu
DAFOE, Robert, J 401-841-7008 558 B
DAGANAAR, Mark 913-469-8500 194 B
mdaganaar@jccc.edu
DAGAVARIAN, Debra 609-652-4514 313 E
dagavarian@stockton.edu
DAGES, John, R 202-994-5300 98 C
dages@gwu.edu
DAGG, Carrie 618-842-3711 152 G
daggc@iecc.edu
DAGG, Joey 304-876-5395 544 C
jdagg@shepherd.edu
DAGGETT, Natalie 575-769-4956 318 A
natalie.daggett@clovis.edu
DAGGETT, Paula 210-486-0224 479 E
pdaggett@alamo.edu
DAGOSTIN, Jean 334-983-3521 4 A
jdagostin@wallace.edu
DAGRADI, Linda 413-205-3270 229 G
linda.dagradi@aic.edu
DAGUE, Saralyn 304-829-7835 540 H
sdague@bethanywv.edu
DAHILL, Patricia 617-587-5632 242 H
dahillp@neco.edu
DAHL, Carolyn, C 205-348-6331 8 E
cdahl@ccs.ua.edu
DAHL, Christopher, C 585-245-5501 353 C
cdahl@geneseo.edu
DAHL, James, G 217-424-6285 158 G
jdahl@millikin.edu
DAHL, James, G 217-424-6284 158 G
jdahl@millikin.edu
DAHL, Margaret, W 706-583-8209 138 G
mwd@uga.edu
DAHL, Mark 503-768-7339 416 G
dahl@lclark.edu
DAHL, Nelson, D 715-422-5327 554 E
nelson.dahl@mstc.edu
DAHL, Noel 415-703-9537 32 C
ndahl@cca.edu
DAHL, Tracy 360-736-9391 532 D
tdahl@centralia.edu
DAHL, Wendy 206-268-4107 530 I
wdahl@antioch.edu
DAHLBERG, Albert, A 401-863-1885 453 B
albert_a_dahlberg@brown.edu
DAHLBERG, James 715-468-2815 555 G
jim.dahlberg@witc.edu
DAHLBERG, Margaret 701-845-7200 382 C
margaret.dahlberg@vcsu.edu
DAHLBERG, Steve 218-935-0417 272 D
sdahlberg@wetcc.edu
DAHLE, Tammi 205-665-6262 9 B
dahlet@montevallo.edu
DAHLE, Tammi, S 205-665-6262 9 B
dahlet@montevallo.edu
DAHLEN, Anne 651-385-6323 267 C
adahlen@southeastmn.edu
DAHLEN, David 507-284-2793 262 E
dahlen.david@mayo.edu
DAHLEN, David, L 507-284-2749 262 B
dahlen.david@mayo.edu
DAHLEN, David, L 507-284-4839 262 D
dahlen.david@mayo.edu
DAHLGREN, Jerod, T 716-878-5569 353 A
dahlgrjt@buffalostate.edu
DAHLIN, Jim 828-669-0012 367 E
jdahlin@montreat.edu
DAHLKE, Bobbie 763-576-4994 265 H
bdahlke@anokatech.edu
DAHLMAN, Chuck 303-964-3678 87 I
cdahlman@regis.edu
DAHLQUIST, Kent, R 610-683-4027 443 A
dahlquis@kutztown.edu
DAHLQUIST, Martin (Dick), R 402-449-2846 297 H
ddahlquist@graceu.edu
DAHLQUIST, Sally 651-450-3567 266 F
sdahlqu@inverhills.edu
DAHLSTRAND, John 785-670-1972 197 F
john.dahlstrand@washburn.edu
DAHLSTROM, Duane 320-308-5572 269 B
ddahlstrom@sctcc.edu
DAHLSTROM, Joe, F 361-572-6421 508 B
joe.dahlstrom@victoriacollege.edu
DAHLSTROM, Joe, F 361-570-4150 504 A
dahlstromj@uhv.edu
DAHLSTROM, Robert, E 512-232-6400 505 D
robert.dahlstrom@austin.utexas.edu
DAHLSTROM, Thomas 610-341-5898 438 D
tdahlstro@eastern.edu
DAHLSTROM, Thomas, A 610-341-5898 428 E
tdahlstr@eastern.edu
DAHLVANG, Donna, R 715-394-8393 552 F
ddahlva1@uwsuper.edu
DAHLVIG, Jolyn 509-777-3208 540 C
jdahlvig@whitworth.edu
DAHM, Lisa 713-646-1873 494 I
ldahm@stcl.edu
DAHMES, Victoria 504-398-2237 214 B
vdahmes@olhcc.edu
DAHSE, Winston 713-718-7564 487 I
winston.dahse@hccs.edu
DAHULICH, Michael 570-561-1818 446 D
mdahulich@stots.edu
DAI, Hai-Lung 215-204-3177 447 H
hai-lung.dai@temple.edu
DAI, Hai-Lung 215-204-9570 447 H
hai-lung.dai@temple.edu
DAI, Hai-Lung 215-204-4775 447 H
provost@temple.edu
DAIDLE, Heather 337-981-4010 214 E
heather.daidle@remingtoncollege.edu
DAIDONE, Angela 201-355-1309 310 B
daidonea@felician.edu
DAIEK, Deborah 734-462-4400 258 A
ddaiek@schoolcraft.edu
DAIGLE, Anna 337-491-2689 212 E
anna.daigle@sowela.edu
DAIGLE, Claire 415-641-1241 65 I
cdaigle@sfai.edu
DAIGLE, Darryl 985-380-2436 211 I
darryl.daigle@ltc.edu
DAIGLE, David 207-216-4410 219 C
ddaigle@yccc.edu
DAIGLE, Dick 757-490-1241 516 B
ddaigle@auto.edu
DAIGLE, Thomas 508-999-8708 237 A
tdaigle@umassd.edu
DAIL, Walter Ashley 252-493-7330 372 H
adail@email.pittcc.edu
DAILEY, Brian 910-962-3711 379 D
daileyb@uncw.edu
DAILEY, David 218-749-7772 266 I
d.dailey@mr.mnscu.edu
DAILEY, John, T 318-675-5000 213 B
jdaile@lsuhsc.edu
DAILEY, Suzanne, C 618-235-2700 165 D
suzanne.dailey@swic.edu
DAILEY, Tara 513-771-2424 385 I
tdailey@brownmackie.edu
DAILEY, Tim 541-888-7439 420 C
tdailey@socc.edu
DAILY, Cecilia (Jody) 765-459-0561 176 C
cdaily@ivytech.edu
DAILY, Daniel, R 605-677-5371 465 G
daniel.daily@usd.edu
DAILY, Hall, P 626-395-6256 32 H
hdaily@caltech.edu
DAILY, Paula 239-489-9111 105 F
pdaily@edison.edu
DAILY, Steve 765-459-0561 176 C
sdaily@ivytech.edu
DAIN, Benny 580-349-1564 410 B
bdain@opsu.edu
DAIS, Olga 718-262-2140 329 A
odais@york.cuny.edu
DAISEY, Mary Beth, B 856-225-6050 314 D
daisey@camden.rutgers.edu
DAISY, Joseph 691-320-2480 559 D
DAKE, Jean 423-425-4184 477 F
jean-dake@utc.edu
DAKOTA, Cherie 906-353-4628 253 D
cdakota@kbocc.org
DAKWAR, Mohammad 414-297-8087 554 F
dakwarmm@matc.edu
DALAGER, Jon 402-375-7030 299 G
jodalag1@wsc.edu
DALAVARIS, Christin 618-545-3000 155 B
cdalavaris@kaskaskia.edu
DALBEY, Mark 314-434-4044 280 F
mark.dalbey@covenantseminary.edu
DALBOW, Dawn, S 540-828-5310 517 B
ddalbow@bridgewater.edu
DALBY, Evelyn 760-795-6610 57 E
edalby@miracosta.edu
DALBY, John 815-836-5923 156 F
dalbyjo@lewisu.edu
DALE, Carroll, W 276-376-1081 525 G
cwd7q@wise.edu
DALE, Cheryl 601-318-6199 278 C
cheryl.dale@wmcarey.edu
DALE, Dianna 718-405-3227 330 A
dianna.dale@mountsaintvincent.edu
DALE, Elizabeth 215-895-2436 427 H
ead52@drexel.edu
DALE, Jean 402-375-7220 299 G
jedale1@wsc.edu
DALE, Kimberly 954-776-4476 112 E
kdale@keiseruniversity.edu
DALE, Louis 205-934-8762 8 F
ldale@uab.edu
DALE, Lynn, F 864-592-4833 461 C
dalel@sccsc.edu
DALE, Melissa 732-571-3598 311 E
mdale@monmouth.edu
DALE, Mike 270-745-6127 208 A
mike.dale@wku.edu
DALE, Paul 602-787-6610 15 J
paul.dale@paradisevalley.edu
DALE, Shanna 417-255-7255 286 D
shannadale@missouristate.edu
DALE, Terri 620-431-2800 195 E
tdale@neosho.edu
DALEN, Dean 218-683-8560 268 C
dean.dalen@northlandcollege.edu
DALENE, Jack 435-283-7130 512 C
jack.dalene@snow.edu

DALES, Sandra 910-695-3789 373 H daless@sandhills.edu
DALEY, Ben 619-398-4902 50 G
DALEY, Carol 540-338-2700 517 G cdaley@cdu.edu
DALEY, Deborah 405-280-1786 297 F deborahdaley@creighton.edu
DALEY, Elizabeth, M 213-740-2804 76 F edaley@cinema.usc.edu
DALEY, Karen 616-698-7111 250 C rdaley@davenport.edu
DALEY, Michael, D 716-673-3434 352 A michael.daley@fredonia.edu
DALEY, Miesha, V 773-995-3555 146 G mdaley@csu.edu
DALEY, Ron 606-487-3158 202 C ron.daley@kctcs.edu
DALEY, Thomas 617-353-2111 232 E tomdaley@bu.edu
DALGLISH, Lucy 301-405-2383 227 B
DALLA, Ronald 509-359-6566 533 H rdalla@ewu.edu
DALLAM, Colleen, C 410-334-2864 229 E cdallam@worwic.edu
DALLAS, David, W 785-827-5541 194 F dallas@kwu.edu
DALLEY, Annique 510-628-8023 54 B studentservices@lincolnuca.edu
DALLINGER, Deborah 925-788-9131 61 G deborah.dallinger@patten.edu
DALLMAN, Bruce, D 620-235-4365 196 C bdallman@pittstate.edu
DALLMAN, Sara, E 303-963-3147 82 C sdallman@ccu.edu
DALONZO, Beth 740-826-8137 397 A bdalonzo@muskingum.edu
DALPE, J. Kyle 775-673-7166 302 H kdalpe@tmcc.edu
DALRYMPLE, Ruth 210-486-2174 479 D
DALRYMPLE, Scott 518-464-8684 333 E sdalrymple@excelsior.edu
DALSING, Deirdre, L 608-342-1865 552 B dalsingd@uwplatt.edu
DALSKE, James 707-654-1070 33 C jdalske@csum.edu
DALTO, Diane 518-743-2337 355 D daltod@sunyacc.edu
DALTON, Ben 740-753-6516 391 H dalton_b@hocking.edu
DALTON, Brenda 404-270-5245 138 B bdalton@spelman.edu
DALTON, Brenda 972-860-4677 484 G bdalton@dcccd.edu
DALTON, Brett, A 864-656-2444 456 E dbrett@clemson.edu
DALTON, Brian, F 814-332-2102 421 F bdalton@allegheny.edu
DALTON, Cheri 432-335-6530 492 A cdalton@odessa.edu
DALTON, Dana, L 336-734-7369 370 F ddalton@forsythtech.edu
DALTON, Deborah 508-626-4698 238 A ddalton@framingham.edu
DALTON, Donna 802-626-6406 515 G donna.dalton@lyndonstate.edu
DALTON, James 845-938-2050 559 A 8ord@usma.edu
DALTON, Jennifer 304-473-8017 545 G haught_j@wvwc.edu
DALTON, John 765-973-8450 173 F jodalton@iue.edu
DALTON, Judith 215-572-4088 422 C daltonj@arcadia.edu
DALTON, Karen 909-447-2534 40 H kdalton@cst.edu
DALTON, Linda 510-885-4120 34 E linda.dalton@csueastbay.edu
DALTON, Liz 706-355-5025 125 C edalton@athenstech.edu
DALTON, Meghan 704-406-4255 364 E mdalton@gardner-webb.edu
DALTON, Thomas 518-464-8632 333 E tdalton@excelsior.edu
DALTON, William 225-216-8601 209 H daltonw@mybrcc.edu
DALTON-RANN, RaVonda 336-750-2046 380 B daltonrannr@wssu.edu
DALTON-RUSSELL, Belinda 270-534-3081 203 E belinda.dalton-russell@kctcs.edu
DALY, Adrian 216-791-5000 388 C adrian.daly@case.edu
DALY, Barbara, M 252-789-0234 371 H bdaly@martincc.edu
DALY, Carson 704-461-6728 362 F carsondaly@bac.edu
DALY, Christina 617-585-1103 242 I chris.daly@necmusic.edu
DALY, Cory 307-855-2186 556 B cdaly@cwc.edu
DALY, Debra 402-280-2424 297 F dldaly@creighton.edu
DALY, Jonathan, P 805-525-4417 72 I jdaly@thomasaquinas.edu
DALY, Kathleen, M 850-644-4453 119 D kdaly@fsu.edu
DALY, Lois, K 518-783-2306 350 I daly@siena.edu
DALY, Pamela 619-683-2446 44 M pdaly@devry.edu
DALY, Patrick 972-721-5145 503 B mpdaly@udallas.ede
DALY, Shawn, p 716-286-8050 344 D sdaly@niagara.edu
DALY-EIMER, Anne, M 856-691-8600 309 B adaly@cccnj.edu
DALY-WESTON, Marilyn 212-650-3995 327 E marilyn.daley-weston@hunter.cuny.edu
DALZELL, Beth 603-513-1332 306 F beth.dalzell@granite.edu
DALZELL, Douglas 410-951-3826 228 B ddalzell@coppin.edu
DAMAR, Andrea 212-343-1234 341 B adamar@mcny.edu
DAMATO, Harold 973-300-2201 315 F hdamato@sussex.edu
DAMAZO, Dennis, E 724-847-5678 429 H dedamazo@geneva.edu
DAMBERG, Paul 218-733-7607 266 H p.damberg@lsc.edu
DAMBROSIA, Pamela 718-261-5800 324 D pdambrosia@bramsonort.edu
DAME, Andrew 913-758-6126 197 D andrew.dame@stmary.edu
DAME, Robert 630-889-6515 159 F rdame@nuhs.edu
DAMERON, Paul 270-789-5059 199 F padameron@campbellsville.edu
DAMES, Christopher 314-516-6473 291 D cdames@umsl.edu
DAMEWOOD, Tony, M 402-552-6109 297 B damewood@clarksoncollege.edu
DAMHOFF, Russ 815-288-5511 164 B damhofr@svcc.edu
DAMIAN, Karen 802-387-6711 513 G kdamian@landmark.edu
DAMIANI, Glenn 505-224-3223 317 K gdamiani@cnm.edu
DAMIANI, Joel, J 716-851-1405 333 B damiani@ecc.edu
DAMIANI, Susan, M 718-990-7562 348 G damianis@stjohns.edu
DAMIANO, Ann, E 717-867-6077 434 C damiano@lvc.edu
DAMIANO, Fred 315-781-3955 335 F damiano@hws.edu
DAMICO, Debra, L 718-862-7213 339 H debra.damico@manhattan.edu
DAMM, SM, Frank 808-739-4645 140 E fdamm@chaminade.edu
DAMM, Richard, T 720-748-8322 550 D dammr@ripon.edu
DAMMER, Bob 310-434-4397 68 D dammer_bob@smc.edu
DAMMER, Linda 386-226-6396 105 I linda.dammer@erau.edu
DAMMINGER, Joanne 856-351-2707 315 A jdamminger@salemcc.edu
DAMMON, Robert 412-268-3696 424 J rd19@andrew.cmu.edu
DAMON, Brad 858-642-8318 58 I bdamon@nu.edu
DAMON, Jud 904-819-6252 107 C jdamon@flagler.edu
DAMON, Paula 712-279-5405 183 A paula.damon@briarcliff.edu
DAMON, Robert 507-288-4563 263 B bdamon@crossroadscollege.edu
DAMONE, Bob 619-574-6909 60 D bdamone@pacificcollege.edu
DAMORE, Gary, P 602-386-4156 11 G gary.damore@arizonachristian.edu
DAMOUR, Marion 954-535-8700 107 F mdamour@careercollege.edu
DAMPEER, Susan, C 574-284-4601 179 F sdampeer@saintmarys.edu
DAMPIER, Pat 843-383-8062 457 A pdampier@coker.edu
DAMPIER, Paula 770-297-5896 126 E pland@brenau.edu
DAMRON, Greg 706-721-9076 130 D gdamron@georgiahealth.edu
DAMRON, James 401-232-6261 453 C jdamron@bryant.edu
DAMRON, Kathy 785-864-7100 197 B mkdtopeka@aol.com
DAMRON, Ron 606-218-5224 207 F ronalddamron@upike.edu
DAMROW, Bobbi 715-675-3331 555 B damrow@ntc.edu
DAMSCHRODER, Matthew 309-556-3113 153 F orl@iwu.edu
DAMSKY, Sarah 212-650-5913 326 G sdamsky@ccny.cuny.edu
DANA, Robert, Q 207-581-1406 220 A rdana@maine.edu
DANA, Susan 406-994-1776 295 C sdana@montana.edu
DANAJOVITS, Joseph 860-738-6368 92 B jdanajovits@nwcc.commnet.edu
DANCE, Andrea 252-335-0821 369 G andrea_dance@albemarle.edu
DANCHISE, Roger, A 781-891-2274 231 D rdanchise@bentley.edu
DANCIK, Deborah, B 503-370-6561 421 D ddancik@willamette.edu
DANCY, Regina, M 704-636-6818 365 D rdancy@hoodseminary.edu
DANDAPANI, Ramaswami 719-255-3551 88 I rdan@eas.uccs.edu
DANDELAKE, George 904-470-8150 105 G g.dandelake@ewc.edu
DANDRIDGE, Horace 313-927-1555 254 E hdandridge@marygrove.edu
DANE, Francis, C 540-224-4515 520 I fcdane@jchs.edu
DANE, Jane, H 757-683-6702 522 F jhdane@odu.edu
DANE, Kathy 904-743-1122 112 B kdane@jones.edu
DANE, Kendra 651-290-6343 272 E kendra.dane@wmitchell.edu
DANE, Phil, W 731-881-7660 477 G pdane@utm.edu
DANEN, Todd 920-403-3943 550 F todd.danen@snc.edu
DANESH, Hamid 614-287-5912 389 A hdanesh@cscc.edu
DANFORD, Richard 740-376-4899 395 G richard.danford@marietta.edu
DANFORD, Robert, E 610-499-4087 451 F redanford@widener.edu
DANFORD, Tom 615-366-4451 473 D tom.danford@tbr.edu
DANFORTH, Meridith 972-860-4823 484 G mdanforth@dcccd.edu
DANG, Connie 616-331-2177 251 F dangc@gvsu.edu
DANGELO, Linda 617-732-2224 241 C linda.dangelo@mcphs.edu
DANGLER, Steven 607-753-2111 353 B steven.dangler@cortland.edu
DANHEISER, Priscilla, R 478-301-2089 134 A danheiser_p@mercer.edu
DANIEL, Andrea 706-355-5124 125 C adaniel@athenstech.edu
DANIEL, Arriana 404-225-4529 125 E adaniel@atlantatech.edu
DANIEL, Brett 903-675-6239 502 F daniel@tvcc.edu
DANIEL, David, E 972-883-2201 506 A dedaniel@utdallas.edu
DANIEL, Dean 940-855-4322 508 E danield@wbu.edu
DANIEL, Diane, B 434-949-1017 528 D diane.daniel@southside.edu
DANIEL, Elnora 757-727-5000 519 H elenora.daniel@hamptonu.edu
DANIEL, Floyd 501-279-4312 21 H rcoker@harding.edu
DANIEL, Kevin, S 719-587-7741 80 L ksdaniel@adams.edu
DANIEL, Larry 904-620-2520 120 D ldaniel@unf.edu
DANIEL, Linda 903-675-6350 502 F ldaniel@tvcc.edu
DANIEL, Lori 256-395-2211 7 D ldaniel@suscc.edu
DANIEL, Margaret 615-297-7545 467 A daniel@aquinascollege.edu
DANIEL, Mary 254-867-3363 500 F mary.daniel@tstc.edu
DANIEL, Meagan 630-829-1813 145 G mdaniel@ben.edu
DANIEL, Michael 251-981-3771 2 G michael.daniel@columbiasouthern.edu
DANIEL, Nancy 617-348-6513 245 D daniel@urbancollege.edu
DANIEL, Richard 915-747-8600 506 B rjdaniel@utep.edu
DANIEL, Robin, L 336-272-7102 364 G rdaniel@greensboro.edu
DANIEL, Sandra, D 229-931-2275 131 F sandra.daniel@gsw.edu
DANIEL, Sharlene 423-775-6596 472 G sdaniel@ogs.edu
DANIEL, Sherman 680-488-2471 560 C shermand1961@yahoo.com
DANIEL, Stephen, P 757-683-3093 522 F sdaniel@odu.edu
DANIEL, Steve 706-646-6168 137 F sdaniel@sctech.edu
DANIEL, Thomas, E 404-656-2211 139 B tom.daniel@usg.edu
DANIEL, Tim 701-483-2181 381 G tim.daniel@dickinsonstate.edu
DANIEL, W. John 205-934-3474 8 F wdaniel@uab.edu
DANIEL-ROBINSON, Kim 973-720-3766 317 D danielrobinsonk@wpunj.edu
DANIELL, Steven 817-531-4900 502 C sdaniell@txwes.edu
DANIELLE, Bob 253-943-3085 533 F rdanielle@devry.edu
DANIELS, Brooke 617-369-3605 244 E bdaniels@smfa.edu
DANIELS, Calvin 913-234-0710 191 J calvin.daniels@cleveland.edu
DANIELS, Clayton 912-279-5775 127 E cdaniels@ccga.edu
DANIELS, Debra, S 815-280-2207 154 J ddaniels@jjc.edu
DANIELS, Dennis, E 936-261-3085 496 G dedaniels@pvamu.edu
DANIELS, Dennis, E 936-261-5206 496 G dedaniels@pvamu.edu
DANIELS, Gerri, L 906-227-2650 256 C gdaniels@nmu.edu
DANIELS, Glynis, A 610-799-1936 434 D gdaniels@lccc.edu
DANIELS, Herman, G 850-872-3857 110 H hdaniels@gulfcoast.edu
DANIELS, III, Jack, E 323-241-5273 55 C danielje@lasc.edu
DANIELS, James 760-252-2411 30 H jdaniels@barstow.edu
DANIELS, Jennifer 949-376-6000 53 F jdaniels@lagunacollege.edu
DANIELS, Joel 740-397-9934 386 H jdaniels@cotc.edu
DANIELS, Jon, M 785-227-3380 191 B danielsj@bethanylb.edu
DANIELS, Judy 337-550-1218 212 J
DANIELS, Kathryn 206-726-5080 533 D kdaniels@cornish.edu
DANIELS, Kyle 585-266-0430 333 D kdaniels@cci.edu
DANIELS, LaMetrius 615-329-8598 468 I ldaniels@fisk.edu
DANIELS, Linda 404-962-3155 139 B linda.daniels@usg.edu
DANIELS, Lisa 518-464-8500 333 E ldaniels@excelsior.edu
DANIELS, Martin 425-637-1010 532 E mdaniels@cityu.edu
DANIELS, Matt 641-844-5708 186 D matt.daniels@iavalley.edu
DANIELS, Maurice, C 706-542-5424 138 G sswdean@uga.edu
DANIELS, Michael 828-448-3564 375 B mdaniels@wpcc.edu
DANIELS, Mildred, L 803-536-7171 460 G mdanie8@scsu.edu
DANIELS, Nettie 318-274-6142 215 E danielsn@gram.edu
DANIELS, Orangel, J 910-362-7129 368 H odaniels@cfcc.edu
DANIELS, Pat, E 252-451-8329 372 E pdaniels@nash.cc.nc.us
DANIELS, Patti, J 618-537-6936 158 A pjdaniels@mckendree.edu
DANIELS, Phil 573-592-5225 293 B phil.daniels@westminster-mo.edu
DANIELS, Randell, W 734-384-4224 255 D rdaniels@monroeccc.edu
DANIELS, Rebecca 315-229-5731 349 E rdaniels@stlawu.edu
DANIELS, Rochelle 803-822-3208 459 E danielsr@midlandstech.edu
DANIELS, Ronald, J 410-516-4170 223 F president@jhu.edu
DANIELS, Ronnie 606-573-3274 203 D ronnie.daniels@kctcs.edu
DANIELS, Ryan 414-847-3237 549 B ryandaniels@miad.edu
DANIELS, Sally 612-330-1525 261 B daniels@augsburg.edu
DANIELS, Scott 626-815-5441 30 G sdaniels@apu.edu
DANIELS, Shelia 386-822-7472 121 F sdaniels@stetson.edu
DANIELS, Terri 407-708-2126 117 H danielst@seminolestate.edu
DANIELS, Ursula 201-612-5355 307 E udaniels@bergen.edu
DANIELS, Wanda 251-405-7003 2 C wdaniels@bishop.edu
DANIELS, Wesley, J 843-383-8178 457 A wdaniels@coker.edu
DANIELSEN, Randy 480-219-6009 278 D rdanielsen@atsu.edu
DANIELSON, Amy 414-443-3637 549 D danielsa@mtmary.edu
DANIELSON, Chad 269-660-8021 257 C danielsonc@millercollege.edu
DANIELSON, David 530-879-4078 31 H danielsonda@butte.edu
DANIELSON, David, D 651-631-5329 270 B dddanielson@nwc.edu
DANIELSON, James 907-796-6534 11 A jedanielson@uas.alaska.edu
DANIELSON, Lisa, M 920-424-3007 551 E danielsn@uwosh.edu
DANIELSON, Mary Ann 402-280-2535 297 F maryanndanielson@creighton.edu

DANIELSON, Ronald, L ... 408-554-6813 ... 68 C
rdanielson@scu.edu
DANIELSON, Timothy ... 920-424-1037 ... 551 E
danielso@uwosh.edu
DANIEU, Paul, F ... 716-851-1856 ... 333 C
danieu@ecc.edu
DANIK, Stephen, R ... 724-480-3356 ... 426 A
steve.danik@ccbc.edu
DANILOWICZ, Bret, S ... 405-744-5663 ... 410 C
bret.danilowicz@okstate.edu
DANKEL, Richard ... 401-232-6117 ... 453 C
rdankel@bryant.edu
DANKO, James, M ... 317-940-9900 ... 170 F
jdanko@butler.edu
DANLEY, Charrita, D ... 757-727-5231 ... 519 H
charrita.danley@hamptonu.edu
DANLEY, Janet, V ... 509-758-1703 ... 539 B
janet.danley@wwcc.edu
DANLEY, Judy ... 336-841-9244 ... 365 C
jdanley@highpoint.edu
DANLEY, Stacy ... 334-229-4505 ... 1 C
sdanley@alasu.edu
DANNA, Debra ... 504-864-7550 ... 213 F
danna@loyno.edu
DANNA, John ... 716-851-1360 ... 333 B
danna@ecc.edu
DANNA, Stephen ... 518-792-5425 ... 354 B
dann1253@plattsburgh.edu
DANNECKER, Debra, A ... 414-277-7131 ... 549 C
schreite@msoe.edu
DANNECKER, Ronald ... 716-829-7600 ... 332 E
dannecrh@dyc.edu
DANNELLEY, Jenny ... 909-652-6231 ... 39 E
jenny.dannelley@chaffey.edu
DANNELLY, Jason ... 402-941-6545 ... 298 I
dannelly@midlandu.edu
DANNEN, Troy, A ... 319-273-2470 ... 182 G
troy.dannen@uni.edu
DANNENBAUM,
Martha, C ... 979-458-8300 ... 497 E
mdannenbaum@tamu.edu
DANNER, Jerry ... 601-979-2144 ... 274 G
jerry.l.danner@jsums.edu
DANNER-ODENWELDER,
Tracey ... 765-289-2291 ... 176 B
tdannerodenwel@ivytech.edu
DANOS, Paul ... 603-646-2460 ... 304 J
paul.danos@dartmouth.edu
DANSER, Dolores, A ... 717-245-1589 ... 427 F
danserd@dickinson.edu
DANSER, Jeff ... 407-582-5529 ... 123 B
jdanser@valenciacollege.edu
DANT, Kittridge ... 270-686-4508 ... 203 B
kitt.dant@kctcs.edu
DANT, Mary ... 618-545-3105 ... 155 B
mdant@kaskaskia.edu
DANTLEY, Scott, J ... 410-951-3828 ... 228 B
sdantley@coppin.edu
DANTSIN, Catherine ... 610-861-1509 ... 437 A
kdantsin@moravian.edu
DANVILLE, M. Lisa ... 860-679-2701 ... 95 A
danville@uchc.edu
DANZELL, Linda ... 508-678-2811 ... 239 B
linda.danzell@bristolcc.edu
DANZEY, Ida ... 310-434-4792 ... 68 D
danzey_ida@smc.edu
DANZY, Jamia ... 860-701-7708 ... 93 E
danzy_j@mitchell.edu
DAPICE-WONG, Stephanie ... 631-665-1600 ... 358 B
stephanie.wong@touro.edu
DARABI, Rachelle ... 417-836-8346 ... 286 C
rachelledarabi@missouristate.edu
DARAGAN, Patricia, A ... 860-444-8553 ... 558 H
patricia.a.daragan@uscga.edu
DARANDARI, H. Sam ... 314-516-6423 ... 291 D
darandarih@umsl.edu
DARBONE, Davidson ... 337-491-2888 ... 212 E
david.darbone@sowela.edu
DARBUT, Jeff ... 480-461-7382 ... 15 I
jeffrey.darbut@mcmail.maricopa.edu
DARBY, Barbara, A ... 904-766-6551 ... 109 F
bdarby@fscj.edu
DARBY, Cindy ... 318-678-6000 ... 209 I
cdarby@bpcc.edu
DARBY, Mary, A ... 225-771-5640 ... 214 I
magdarby@yahoo.com
DARCANGELO, Robin ... 707-864-7889 ... 70 A
robin.darcangelo@solano.edu
DARCY, Diane ... 718-482-5080 ... 328 B
ddarcy@lagcc.cuny.edu
DARCY, Kip ... 810-762-7331 ... 253 C
kdarcy@kettering.edu
DARDEN, Barbara ... 610-683-4484 ... 443 A
darden@kutztown.edu
DARDEN, Beth ... 618-634-3224 ... 164 E
bethda@shawneecc.edu
DARDEN, James ... 618-634-3325 ... 164 E
jamesda@shawneecc.edu
DARDEN, Mary ... 210-253-3264 ... 483 K
mary.darden@concordia.edu
DARDIS, Anne-Marie ... 703-416-1441 ... 520 C
amdardis@ipsciences.deu
DARDIS, Greg ... 503-675-3969 ... 416 J
gdardis@marylhurst.edu
DARE, Adebimpe ... 617-928-4763 ... 242 E
adare@mountida.edu
DARE, Donna ... 314-539-5288 ... 288 G
ddare@stlcc.edu
DARE, Stephen, A ... 518-388-6180 ... 358 G
dares@union.edu
DARGA, Richard ... 773-995-2378 ... 146 G
rdarga@csu.edu
DARIN, Mary, K ... 972-238-6230 ... 485 D
mkdarin@dcccd.edu
DARIN, Thomas, R ... 585-389-2830 ... 342 D
tdarin2@naz.edu
DARING, William ... 508-854-4415 ... 240 F
wdaring@qcc.mass.edu
DARLAGE, Larry, J ... 817-515-6200 ... 496 C
larry.darlage@tccd.edu
DARLING, Douglas, D ... 701-662-1506 ... 382 F
doug.darling@lrsc.edu
DARLING, Joshua, J ... 864-488-8219 ... 459 B
jdarling@limestone.edu
DARLINGTON, Carol ... 989-386-6625 ... 255 C
cdarlington@midmich.edu
DARNALL, Steve ... 707-826-4202 ... 36 E
wsd1@humboldt.edu
DARNALL BURKE, Randi ... 707-826-3361 ... 36 E
darnall@humboldt.edu
DARNELL, Darrell, L ... 202-994-1000 ... 98 C
ddarnell@gwu.edu
DARNELL, Meg ... 212-924-5900 ... 357 B
placement@swedishinstitute.edu
DARNELL, Meg ... 212-924-5900 ... 357 B
ce@swedishinstitute.edu
DARNELL, Roe ... 707-468-3071 ... 57 A
rdarnell@mendocino.edu
DAROCA, Laura ... 310-665-6895 ... 60 B
otisalum@otis.edu
DAROSKY, Renee ... 312-939-4975 ... 151 H
rdarosky@harrington.edu
DARR, Brandi ... 724-836-7167 ... 449 C
bsd@pitt.edu
DARR, Eric, D ... 717-901-5111 ... 430 F
edarr@harrisburgu.edu
DARR, Steven ... 863-638-7230 ... 123 D
steven.darr@warner.edu
DARRAH, SSJ, Mary ... 215-248-7031 ... 425 D
darrahm@chc.edu
DARRIGRAND, Denise, M ... 508-793-7423 ... 233 B
ddarrigrand@clarku.edu
DARRINGTON,
Jessyca, M ... 334-229-4894 ... 1 C
jdarrington@alasu.edu
DARROUGH, Kelvin ... 305-892-7639 ... 112 A
kdarrough@jwu.edu
DARROW, David ... 231-876-3126 ... 248 A
david.darrow@baker.edu
DARROW, David, W ... 937-229-4615 ... 404 A
ddarrow1@udayton.edu
DARROW, Karen ... 406-756-3900 ... 294 C
kdarrow@fvcc.edu
DARST, Robert ... 508-999-8989 ... 237 A
rdarst@umassd.edu
DARST, Valerie ... 660-263-4110 ... 286 H
valeried@macc.edu
DART, Greg ... 435-283-7154 ... 512 C
greg.dart@snow.edu
DART, Greg ... 435-613-5217 ... 512 A
greg.dart@usu.edu
DARVILLE, Dennis ... 919-761-2100 ... 377 A
ddarville@sebts.edu
DARVILLE, Robert, H ... 706-233-7335 ... 137 A
rdarville@shorter.edu
DARWIN, Mike ... 205-726-4241 ... 6 G
mdarwin@samford.edu
DAS, Dilip ... 410-951-6102 ... 228 B
ddas@coppin.edu
DAS, Pradeep, K ... 404-627-2681 ... 126 D
pradeep.das@beulah.org
DAS, Purna ... 219-785-5254 ... 179 A
pdas@pnc.edu
DASBURG, Deanne ... 828-884-8129 ... 362 H
dasburg@brevard.edu
DASENBROCK, Reed, W ... 808-956-8447 ... 141 G
rdasenbr@hawaii.edu
DASEY-MORALES,
Maureen ... 316-978-3440 ... 198 A
maureen.dasey-morales@witchita.edu
DASGUPTA, Nandini ... 510-869-8711 ... 64 J
ndasgupta@samuelmerritt.edu
DASHER, Glenn ... 256-824-6200 ... 8 G
dasherg@uah.edu
DASHER, Josh ... 912-287-5819 ... 135 F
jdasher@okefenokeetech.edu
DASHIELD, Richeleen ... 908-526-1200 ... 313 D
rdashield@raritanval.edu
DASILVA, Joseph ... 413-755-4889 ... 241 B
jdasilva@stcc.edu
DASINGER, Hank ... 334-285-5177 ... 4 K
hank.dasinger@istc.edu
DASTMOZD, Rassoul ... 651-846-1335 ... 269 C
rassoul.dastmozd@saintpaul.edu
DATEMA, Jay ... 212-343-1234 ... 341 B
jdatema@mcny.edu
DATHER, Julie ... 605-668-1525 ... 464 G
jdather@mtmc.edu
DATSKO, Robert, G ... 814-472-3006 ... 446 B
rdatsko@francis.edu
DATTA, Asoke ... 808-544-1106 ... 140 G
adatta@hpu.edu
DATTA, Sumana ... 979-845-6774 ... 497 E
sumad@tamu.edu
DATUIN, Bonnie Mae, M ... 671-735-5616 ... 559 E
bonniemae.datuin@guamcc.edu
DAUDISTEL, Howard ... 915-747-8533 ... 506 B
hdaudistel@utep.edu
DAUER, Eve ... 443-627-7587 ... 272 C
eve.dauer@waldenu.edu
DAUGHADAY, David ... 410-617-2349 ... 223 I
daughaday@loyola.edu
DAUGHERTY, Craig, A ... 740-427-5430 ... 394 C
daugherty@kenyon.edu
DAUGHERTY, Donna ... 706-295-6306 ... 130 E
ddaugher@highlands.edu
DAUGHERTY, Eleanor ... 773-702-5243 ... 166 G
ebd1@uchicago.edu
DAUGHERTY, Penny, J ... 541-346-2971 ... 419 B
penny@uoregon.edu
DAUGHERTY, Rex ... 918-293-4966 ... 410 E
rex.daugherty@okstate.edu
DAUGHERTY, Robert, C ... 216-361-2760 ... 387 B
rdaugherty@chancelloru.edu
DAUGHERTY, Robyn ... 479-524-7301 ... 22 C
rdaugherty@jbu.edu
DAUGHERTY, Tim ... 618-985-4872 ... 154 G
timdaugherty@jalc.edu
DAUGHERTY, Vernon, D ... 828-398-7220 ... 368 B
vdaugherty@abtech.edu
DAUGHETY, Kathy ... 252-399-6529 ... 362 E
kdaughety@barton.edu
DAUGHT, Gary ... 423-461-8799 ... 471 J
gfdaught@milligan.edu
DAUGHTERS, Kenneth, A ... 563-588-8000 ... 184 I
kdaughters@emmaus.edu
DAUGHTREY, III,
Thomas, W ... 910-630-7316 ... 367 B
tdaughtrey@methodist.edu
DAUGHTRY, Dee Dee, D ... 919-209-2066 ... 371 F
dddaughtry@johnstoncc.edu
DAULTON, Jonathan, G ... 864-242-5100 ... 455 E
DAUM, Sarah ... 909-594-5611 ... 58 A
sdaum@mtsac.edu
DAUN, Eugene ... 847-578-3252 ... 163 C
eugene.daun@rosalindfranklin.edu
DAUPHINAIS, Micahael ... 239-280-2505 ... 101 I
michael.dauphinais@avemaria.edu
DAUSEN, Peter, G ... 831-656-3037 ... 558 A
pgdausen@nps.edu
DAUTERIVE, Jerry ... 401-254-3444 ... 454 C
jdauterive@rwu.edu
DAUTREMONT-SMITH,
Julian ... 607-587-4011 ... 355 C
dautrej@alfredstate.edu
DAUWALDER, David, P ... 203-932-7267 ... 95 C
ddauwalder@newhaven.edu
DAVAR, David ... 212-678-6161 ... 337 G
dadavar@jtsa.edu
DAVAULT, Joey ... 405-733-7392 ... 411 I
jdavault@rose.edu
DAVELAAR, Kate ... 616-395-7145 ... 252 D
davelaark@hope.edu
DAVENPORT, A. Wade ... 610-607-6271 ... 445 C
wdavenport@racc.edu
DAVENPORT, Brenda ... 314-513-4248 ... 288 H
bdavenport@stlcc.edu
DAVENPORT, Daniel, D ... 208-885-6312 ... 144 G
dand@uidaho.edu
DAVENPORT, Darrien ... 717-815-6663 ... 452 G
ddavenp2@ycp.edu
DAVENPORT, Douglas ... 660-785-7200 ... 290 G
douglas@truman.edu
DAVENPORT, Elizabeth ... 773-702-8282 ... 166 G
ejld@uchicago.edu
DAVENPORT, Fiona, E ... 215-887-5511 ... 451 D
fdavenport@wts.edu
DAVENPORT, Floyd ... 785-670-2066 ... 197 F
floyd.davenport@washburn.edu
DAVENPORT, Holly ... 212-752-1530 ... 338 C
holly.davenport@limcollege.edu
DAVENPORT, Jeunet ... 414-278-7677 ... 547 D
jdavenport@devry.edu
DAVENPORT, Karen ... 914-964-4296 ... 329 D
DAVENPORT, Mary ... 651-846-1314 ... 269 C
mary.davenport@saintpaul.edu
DAVENPORT, Mary ... 507-433-0530 ... 268 H
mary.davenport@riverland.edu
DAVENPORT, Mike ... 270-824-8661 ... 202 G
mike.davenport@kctcs.edu
DAVENPORT, Mona ... 217-581-6690 ... 150 E
mydavenport@eiu.edu
DAVENPORT, Nancy ... 202-885-3200 ... 97 D
DAVENPORT, Richard ... 507-389-1111 ... 267 E
richard.davenport@mnsu.edu
DAVENPORT, Robert ... 405-585-5301 ... 409 D
robert.davenport@okbu.edu
DAVENPORT, Robin ... 910-630-7609 ... 367 B
rdavenport@methodist.edu
DAVENPORT, Robin ... 973-618-3905 ... 308 C
rdavenport@caldwell.edu
DAVENPORT, Sarah ... 940-552-6291 ... 507 F
sdavenport@vernoncollege.edu
DAVENPORT, Shirley ... 636-481-3333 ... 283 D
sdavenp1@jeffco.edu
DAVENPORT, Susan, C ... 609-984-1130 ... 316 A
sdavenport@tesc.edu
DAVENPORT, Thomas ... 270-706-8699 ... 202 A
tom.davenport@kctcs.edu
DAVENPORT, Zebulun, R ... 317-274-8990 ... 174 D
zrdavenp@iupui.edu
DAVENPORT-RAMIREZ,
Keisha ... 212-229-8996 ... 342 E
davenpok@newschool.edu
DAVES, Christine ... 612-874-3796 ... 265 C
christine_daves@mcad.edu
DAVEY, Cathleen ... 201-684-7612 ... 313 C
cdavey@ramapo.edu
DAVEY, Martha ... 307-855-2235 ... 556 B
mdavey@cwc.edu
DAVEY, Patricia, J ... 419-372-0710 ... 385 F
pdavey@bgsu.edu
DAVEY, Stephen ... 800-672-3060 ... 376 G
DAVID, Brenda, M ... 901-432-7735 ... 469 C
bdavid@hst.edu
DAVID, Garry ... 940-552-6291 ... 507 F
gdavid@vernoncollege.edu
DAVID, George ... 670-234-5498 ... 560 B
georged@nmcnet.edu
DAVID, Haven ... 940-552-6291 ... 507 F
hdavid@vernoncollege.edu
DAVID, Jacob ... 212-563-6647 ... 358 F
revjdavid@yahoo.com
DAVID, Karl, H ... 414-277-7372 ... 549 C
david@msoe.edu
DAVID, Kevin ... 918-595-7925 ... 412 H
k_david@tulsacc.edu
DAVID, Kim ... 713-798-4975 ... 481 H
kcotner@bcm.edu
DAVID, Kyle ... 774-455-7560 ... 236 E
kdavid@umassp.edu
DAVID, Linda, V ... 914-654-5286 ... 330 B
ldavid@cnr.edu
DAVID, Miriam ... 859-985-3212 ... 199 A
miriam_david@berea.edu
DAVID, Paula ... 508-793-7681 ... 233 B
pdavid@clarku.edu
DAVID, Richard ... 607-778-5199 ... 324 G
davidrc@sunybroome.edu
DAVID, Vivian ... 757-727-5331 ... 519 H
vivian.david@hamptonu.edu
DAVIDANN, Jon ... 808-544-0811 ... 140 G
jdavidann@hpu.edu
DAVIDHIZAR, Larry, J ... 312-329-4005 ... 159 A
larry.davidhizar@moody.edu
DAVIDOWITZ, Menachem ... 585-473-2810 ... 357 D
DAVIDS, Cheryl ... 828-339-7018 ... 374 C
c_davids@southwesterncc.edu
DAVIDSEN, Susanna ... 612-312-2500 ... 272 C
susanna.davidsen@waldenu.edu
DAVIDSON, Andrew, R ... 212-854-6313 ... 330 F
ard2@columbia.edu
DAVIDSON, Anthony ... 914-323-5315 ... 339 J
anthony.davidson@mville.edu
DAVIDSON, Brenda ... 252-399-6393 ... 362 E
bdavidso@barton.edu
DAVIDSON, Conrad ... 701-858-3159 ... 382 A
conrad.davidson@minotstateu.edu
DAVIDSON, Debbie ... 262-564-3422 ... 554 B
davidsond@gtc.edu
DAVIDSON, Dennis, W ... 704-637-4474 ... 363 E
ddavidso@catawba.edu
DAVIDSON, Donald ... 603-641-7287 ... 305 G
ddavidson@anselm.edu
DAVIDSON, Elsa Jean ... 212-749-2802 ... 339 I
studentlife@msmnyc.edu
DAVIDSON, Erin ... 817-598-6285 ... 508 F
edavidson@wc.edu
DAVIDSON, Georglyn, L ... 215-968-8251 ... 423 F
davidson@bucks.edu
DAVIDSON, J. Shane ... 325-670-1276 ... 487 F
jdsd@hsutx.edu
DAVIDSON, JaCenda ... 615-329-8712 ... 468 I
jdavidson@fisk.edu
DAVIDSON, James, A ... 410-827-5846 ... 222 B
jdavidson@chesapeake.edu
DAVIDSON, Jamie ... 702-895-3627 ... 302 I
jamie.davidson@unlv.edu
DAVIDSON, Janet ... 724-480-3395 ... 426 A
janet.davidson@ccbc.edu
DAVIDSON, John ... 870-508-6122 ... 20 E
jdavidson@asumh.edu
DAVIDSON, Jon ... 810-762-3300 ... 259 C
jdavidso@umflint.edu
DAVIDSON, Katrena, J ... 330-941-1712 ... 406 F
katrena.davidson@ysu.edu
DAVIDSON, Keith, S ... 410-651-6496 ... 227 E
kdavidson@umes.edu
DAVIDSON, Laura ... 919-760-8531 ... 367 A
davidsonl@meredith.edu
DAVIDSON, Laura-Lee ... 317-917-3628 ... 178 A
ldavidson@martin.edu
DAVIDSON, Leslie ... 413-528-7245 ... 230 F
leslied@simons-rock.edu

DAVIDSON, Leslie .... 540-665-5561.... 524 E
ldavids2@su.edu
DAVIDSON, Lynda, J .... 412-397-6801.... 445 H
davidson@rmu.edu
DAVIDSON, Michael .... 317-921-4538.... 175 K
mdavidson40@ivytech.edu
DAVIDSON, Nancy .... 605-274-5516.... 464 A
nancy.davidson@augie.edu
DAVIDSON, Sharon .... 718-262-2155.... 329 A
sdavid@york.cuny.edu
DAVIDSON, Stacy .... 719-389-6953...... 82 D
sdavidson@coloradocollege.edu
DAVIDSON, Steve .... 615-966-6280.... 470 F
steve.davidson@lipscomb.edu
DAVIDSON, Suellen .... 870-368-2059...... 23 A
sdavidson@ozarka.edu
DAVIDSON, Suzanne .... 212-431-2818.... 343 E
sdavidson@nyls.edu
DAVIDSON, Valerie, J .... 317-940-9281.... 170 F
vdavidso@butler.edu
DAVIDSON, Vicky, L .... 937-775-2587.... 406 C
vicky.davidson@wright.edu
DAVIDSON, Wayne, A .... 215-368-5000.... 422 I
wdavidson@biblical.edu
DAVIE, Karen .... 845-675-4608.... 344 G
karen.davie@nyack.edu
DAVIE, Keith, A .... 845-675-4770.... 344 G
keith.davie@nyack.edu
DAVIES, Ann .... 608-363-2667.... 546 E
daviesa@beloit.edu
DAVIES, Anna .... 818-710-4224...... 55 B
daviesa@piercecollege.edu
DAVIES, Becky .... 972-721-5206.... 503 B
bdavies@udallas.edu
DAVIES, Bobby .... 201-327-8877.... 309 G
bdavies@eastwick.edu
DAVIES, Dana .... 352-588-8283.... 116 G
dana.davies@saintleo.edu
DAVIES, David .... 601-266-4533.... 277 F
david.davies@usm.edu
DAVIES, Diana, K .... 609-258-2560.... 312 G
ddavies@princeton.edu
DAVIES, Glyn .... 310-206-8041...... 74 C
gdavies@ponet.ucla.edu
DAVIES, Haldene .... 340-693-1004.... 568 E
hdavies@live.uvi.edu
DAVIES, Herbert, O .... 402-559-5131.... 300 H
dele.davies@unmc.edu
DAVIES, Jeffrey .... 919-962-1591.... 377 C
jrd@northcarolina.edu
DAVIES, Mandy .... 916-660-7302...... 69 F
mdavies@sierracollege.edu
DAVIES, Marilyn, S .... 909-593-3511...... 75 E
mdavies@laverne.edu
DAVIES, Mark .... 405-208-5284.... 410 A
mdavies@okcu.edu
DAVIES, Mark, D .... 570-577-1019.... 423 E
mark.davies@bucknell.edu
DAVIES, Mark, Y .... 405-208-5284.... 410 A
mdavies@okcu.edu
DAVIES, Pamela, L .... 704-337-2216.... 376 A
daviesp@queens.edu
DAVIES, Paul .... 804-752-7399.... 523 C
pauldavies@rmc.edu
DAVIES, Peter .... 603-513-5255.... 306 E
peter.davies@law.unh.edu
DAVIES, Robert .... 541-962-3512.... 418 C
bob.davies@eou.edu
DAVIES, Susan .... 828-262-7244.... 377 D
daviess@appstate.edu
DAVIES, Susan .... 810-762-9927.... 253 C
sdavies@kettering.edu
DAVIES HADAWAY,
Meredith .... 410-778-7268.... 229 D
mhadaway2@washcoll.edu
DAVIES-WILSON, Dennis .. 505-661-4685.... 321 E
davies@unm.edu
DAVILA, Alfonso, L .... 787-751-0178.... 565 F
adavila@suagm.edu
DAVILA, David .... 361-825-2616.... 498 C
david.davila@tamucc.edu
DAVILA, Grace .... 713-221-8633.... 503 F
davilag@uhd.edu
DAVILA, Ivan, E .... 787-841-2000.... 565 B
idavila@pucpr.edu
DAVILA, Jaime .... 413-549-4600.... 235 C
DAVIN, Donna .... 706-290-2163.... 126 C
ddavin@berry.edu
DAVINO, Rich .... 508-626-4625.... 238 A
rdavino@framingham.edu
DAVIS, A. Alex .... 323-953-4000...... 54 H
alexanal@lacitycollege.edu
DAVIS, Adrienne, D .... 314-935-8583.... 292 I
adriennedavis@wustl.edu
DAVIS, Alan, B .... 205-853-1200........ 5 C
adavis@jeffstateonline.com
DAVIS, Alana .... 804-752-7227.... 523 C
adavis@rmc.edu
DAVIS, Albert .... 985-448-4090.... 216 A
albert.davis@nicholls.edu
DAVIS, Alison, H .... 912-525-4653.... 136 F
ahdavis@scad.edu
DAVIS, Amanda .... 916-558-2441...... 56 D
davisa@scc.losrios.edu
DAVIS, Amy .... 225-638-8613.... 210 A
agauthier@ltc.edu
DAVIS, Ana .... 617-879-7046.... 238 B
ana.davis@massart.edu
DAVIS, Andrea .... 314-340-3330.... 282 F
davisa@hssu.edu
DAVIS, Andrew, B .... 706-778-8500.... 136 A
ddavis@piedmont.edu
DAVIS, Anita, A .... 901-843-3889.... 472 K
adavis@rhodes.edu
DAVIS, Anthony .... 260-484-4400.... 170 A
adavis@brownmackie.edu
DAVIS, Anthony .... 713-646-1797.... 494 I
adavis@stcl.edu
DAVIS, Anthony, K .... 563-588-7205.... 187 C
anthony.davis@loras.edu
DAVIS, Barbara .... 419-251-1704.... 395 I
barbara.davis@mercycollege.edu
DAVIS, Barbara .... 614-222-4035.... 388 G
bdavis@ccad.edu
DAVIS, Becky .... 904-743-1122.... 112 B
bdavis@jones.edu
DAVIS, Benjamin, A .... 765-641-4101.... 169 E
badavis@anderson.edu
DAVIS, Bettye .... 870-512-7874...... 20 F
bettye_davis@asun.edu
DAVIS, Bob .... 415-239-3720...... 40 C
bdavis@ccsf.edu
DAVIS, Bob .... 417-823-3451.... 289 I
bdavis@forest.edu
DAVIS, Bonnie .... 207-221-4476.... 221 A
bdavis@une.edu
DAVIS, Bonnie, H .... 336-599-1181.... 372 G
davisb@piedmontcc.edu
DAVIS, Brad .... 408-741-2060...... 78 E
brad_davis@wvm.edu
DAVIS, Bradley .... 408-741-2668...... 78 G
bradley.davis@wvm.edu
DAVIS, Bradley .... 408-741-2060...... 78 G
bradley.davis@wvm.edu
DAVIS, Bradley, W .... 941-752-5388.... 118 J
davisb@scf.edu
DAVIS, Brenda .... 601-928-6381.... 275 E
brenda.davis2@mgccc.edu
DAVIS, Brian .... 816-584-6771.... 287 E
brian.davis@park.edu
DAVIS, Brian, E .... 330-972-5302.... 403 B
bdavis@uakron.edu
DAVIS, Bridget, K .... 256-533-7387........ 3 C
bridget.davis@vc.edu
DAVIS, Britt .... 910-893-1200.... 362 J
davisb@campbell.edu
DAVIS, Bruce .... 801-626-6789.... 511 G
brucedavis@weber.edu
DAVIS, Bryan .... 951-343-4721...... 31 J
bdavis@calbaptist.edu
DAVIS, C. Grant .... 334-844-4866........ 1 F
daviscg@auburn.edu
DAVIS, C. Scott .... 804-862-6456.... 523 F
sdavis@rbc.edu
DAVIS, Carenado .... 252-527-6223.... 371 G
cdavis@lenoircc.edu
DAVIS, Carol .... 309-647-6395.... 165 F
carol.davis@src.edu
DAVIS, Caroline .... 615-383-4848.... 478 F
cdavis@watkins.edu
DAVIS, Cassandra, E .... 973-761-7161.... 315 B
cassandra.davis@shu.edu
DAVIS, Catherine, C .... 609-497-7882.... 312 F
student.relations@ptsem.edu
DAVIS, Cathleen, M .... 937-775-5700.... 406 C
cathleen.davis@wright.edu
DAVIS, Charles, H .... 570-675-9221.... 440 F
chd11@psu.edu
DAVIS, Christopher .... 865-573-4517.... 469 L
cdavis@johnsonu.edu
DAVIS, Christopher, A .... 410-293-6381.... 559 B
cdavis@usna.edu
DAVIS, Chuck .... 206-934-4340.... 537 E
chuck.davis@seattlecolleges.edu
DAVIS, Cliff .... 417-447-2652.... 287 D
davisc@otc.edu
DAVIS, Connie .... 985-549-2094.... 216 C
cdavis@selu.edu
DAVIS, Coralynn, V .... 570-577-1380.... 423 E
coralynn.davis@bucknell.edu
DAVIS, Corby .... 360-676-2772.... 535 K
cdavis@nwic.edu
DAVIS, Curtis .... 404-215-2664.... 134 D
cdavis@morehouse.edu
DAVIS, Cynthia .... 240-684-2800.... 227 F
cynthia.davis@umuc.edu
DAVIS, D. Alan .... 870-235-5059...... 23 I
dadavis@saumag.edu
DAVIS, D. Scott .... 478-301-2110.... 134 A
davis_ds@mercer.edu
DAVIS, Daisy .... 404-297-9522.... 131 D
davisd@gptc.edu
DAVIS, Dale, P .... 605-256-5238.... 465 I
dale.davis@dsu.edu
DAVIS, Dana .... 478-757-3506.... 127 A
ddavis@centralgatech.edu
DAVIS, Dana .... 706-295-6366.... 130 E
ddavis@highlands.edu
DAVIS, Daniel, P .... 417-624-7070.... 284 D
danield@pcg.org
DAVIS, Danny .... 413-748-3532.... 244 H
ddavis@springfieldcollege.edu
DAVIS, Dave, D .... 504-247-1230.... 215 C
ddavis6@tulane.edu
DAVIS, David .... 601-974-1432.... 275 B
davisdc@millsaps.edu
DAVIS, David, B .... 845-368-7200.... 350 A
david.davis@use.salvationarmy.org
DAVIS, David, H .... 828-694-1845.... 368 E
daviddav@blueridge.edu
DAVIS, Debbie .... 828-627-4521.... 371 C
ddavis@haywood.edu
DAVIS, Debbie .... 859-257-8311.... 207 D
ddavis@email.uky.edu
DAVIS, Deborah .... 212-650-3162.... 327 E
deborah.davis@hunter.cuny.edu
DAVIS, Debra .... 419-530-8355.... 404 F
debra.davis@utoledo.edu
DAVIS, Debra, C .... 251-434-3410........ 9 D
ddavis@usouthal.edu
DAVIS, Deidra .... 207-326-2138.... 219 D
deidra.davis@mma.edu
DAVIS, Derek .... 816-268-5424.... 286 I
dldavis@nts.edu
DAVIS, Diana .... 513-244-4478.... 388 E
diana_davis@mail.msj.edu
DAVIS, Dianne, L .... 828-398-7841.... 368 B
ddavis@abtech.edu
DAVIS, Dirk .... 951-343-3905...... 31 J
ddavis@calbaptist.edu
DAVIS, Don .... 626-815-3828...... 30 G
ddavis@apu.edu
DAVIS, Donald, L .... 972-883-6176.... 506 A
don.davis@utdallas.edu
DAVIS, Donna .... 760-757-2121...... 57 E
ddavis@miracosta.edu
DAVIS, Donna .... 636-922-8300.... 288 B
ddavis@stchas.edu
DAVIS, Donna, J .... 415-422-6822...... 76 E
davisdj@usfca.edu
DAVIS, Dorothy .... 314-889-1475.... 281 I
ddavis@fontbonne.edu
DAVIS, Ed .... 530-741-6853...... 80 K
edavis@yccd.edu
DAVIS, Eddie .... 972-825-4686.... 495 F
edavis@sagu.edu
DAVIS, Eddie, J .... 979-847-8700.... 497 E
edavis@tamu.edu
DAVIS, Elizabeth .... 254-710-3601.... 482 A
elizabeth_davis@baylor.edu
DAVIS, Ellen .... 512-863-1571.... 496 A
davise@southwestern.edu
DAVIS, Ernie .... 903-693-1112.... 492 C
edavis@panola.edu
DAVIS, Evelyn .... 423-624-0077.... 467 H
evelynd@chattanoogacollege.edu
DAVIS, Faye .... 918-685-0724.... 407 B
davisf@bacone.edu
DAVIS, Frances .... 512-892-2640.... 495 C
DAVIS, Frederic, I .... 410-293-1586.... 559 B
fid@usna.edu
DAVIS, Gary .... 218-726-7572.... 271 F
gdavis@d.umn.edu
DAVIS, Gayle .... 916-961-8727...... 64 B
DAVIS, Gayle, R .... 616-331-2400.... 251 F
davisgr@gvsu.edu
DAVIS, Gilda .... 504-286-5176.... 214 J
gdavis@suno.edu
DAVIS, Glenda .... 214-379-5526.... 492 F
gdavis@pqc.edu
DAVIS, Glenn .... 330-672-3131.... 393 D
gdavis3@kent.edu
DAVIS, JR., Gordon .... 913-684-3443.... 558 F
gordon.davis@leavenworth.army.mil
DAVIS, Gregory .... 630-515-4554.... 149 B
gdavis@devry.edu
DAVIS, Gregory, A .... 757-823-8011.... 522 E
gadavis@nsu.edu
DAVIS, Gwenda, R .... 973-642-8803.... 315 C
gwenda.davis@shu.edu
DAVIS, Hazel .... 480-517-8273...... 16 B
hazel.davis@riosalado.edu
DAVIS, Heather .... 336-750-3350.... 380 B
davish@wssu.edu
DAVIS, Helane .... 518-445-2393.... 322 C
hdavi@albanylaw.edu
DAVIS, Henry .... 718-270-4985.... 328 C
hdavis@mec.cuny.edu
DAVIS, Henry, C .... 334-229-4401........ 1 C
hdavis@alasu.edu
DAVIS, Herbert, R .... 919-572-1625.... 362 C
hdavis@apexsot.edu
DAVIS, Hillel .... 212-960-5411.... 361 M
hdavis@yu.edu
DAVIS, Houston .... 404-962-3060.... 139 B
houston.davis@usg.edu
DAVIS, Howard .... 805-378-1457...... 77 D
hdavis@vcccd.edu
DAVIS, Howard .... 248-204-2316.... 254 B
hdavis@ltu.edu
DAVIS, Jack .... 540-231-6416.... 529 G
davisa@vt.edu
DAVIS, James .... 310-206-0011...... 74 C
jdavis@conet.ucla.edu
DAVIS, James .... 972-825-4803.... 495 F
jdavis@sagu.edu
DAVIS, James, A .... 515-294-0323.... 182 E
davis@iastate.edu
DAVIS, James Earl .... 215-204-8017.... 447 H
dean.ed@temple.edu
DAVIS, Janet .... 312-935-6805.... 162 G
jdavis@robertmorris.edu
DAVIS, Janice .... 229-931-2381.... 137 C
jdavis@southgatech.edu
DAVIS, Jef, C .... 330-941-2336.... 406 F
jcdavis05@ysu.edu
DAVIS, Jeff .... 423-493-4230.... 476 E
davisj@tntemple.edu
DAVIS, Jeff .... 912-871-1640.... 135 D
jdavis@ogeecheetech.edu
DAVIS, Jeff .... 936-468-3407.... 496 B
jhdavis@sfasu.edu
DAVIS, Jeff .... 541-757-8944.... 416 I
jeff.davis@linnbenton.edu
DAVIS, Jeffrey .... 706-864-1641.... 134 G
jldavis@northgeorgia.edu
DAVIS, Jeffrey, W .... 260-481-0739.... 174 C
davisj@ipfw.edu
DAVIS, Jenna .... 719-336-1589...... 86 B
jenna.davis@lamarcc.edu
DAVIS, Jennifer .... 302-831-2769...... 96 I
jjdavis@udel.edu
DAVIS, Jennifer, L .... 740-374-8716.... 405 G
jdavis@wscc.edu
DAVIS, Jermyn .... 719-389-6748...... 82 D
jermyn.davis@coloradocollege.edu
DAVIS, Jerold .... 212-592-2000.... 350 F
jdavis@sva.edu
DAVIS, Jerome .... 212-854-5017.... 330 F
jd2145@columbia.edu
DAVIS, Jerome .... 205-226-4848........ 2 B
jdavis@bsc.edu
DAVIS, Jerry, C .... 417-690-2470.... 279 J
pres@cofo.edu
DAVIS, Jessica .... 732-247-5241.... 312 A
jdavis@nbts.edu
DAVIS, Jim, L .... 701-477-7862.... 383 F
jdavis@tm.edu
DAVIS, Jimmy, H .... 731-661-5461.... 477 B
jdavis@uu.edu
DAVIS, Joan .... 214-333-6855.... 484 D
joan@dbu.edu
DAVIS, Joe, M .... 765-641-4084.... 169 E
jmdavis@anderson.edu
DAVIS, Joel .... 973-803-5000.... 315 D
jdavis@somerset.edu
DAVIS, John .... 540-423-9179.... 526 I
jmdavis@germanna.edu
DAVIS, John .... 626-873-2144...... 58 C
DAVIS, John .... 413-585-3000.... 244 G
jdavis@smith.edu
DAVIS, John .... 605-677-5341.... 465 G
john.davis@usd.edu
DAVIS, John .... 920-206-2371.... 548 D
jdavis@mbbc.edu
DAVIS, John .... 920-206-2332.... 548 D
john.davis@mbbc.edu
DAVIS, John, L .... 304-336-8024.... 544 D
jdavis@westliberty.edu
DAVIS, John, L .... 304-336-8337.... 544 D
jdavis@westliberty.edu
DAVIS, John, R .... 740-376-4390.... 395 G
john.davis@marietta.edu
DAVIS, Jon .... 843-863-7218.... 456 B
jdavis@csuniv.edu
DAVIS, Jonathan, M .... 802-626-6419.... 515 G
jonathan.davis@lyndonstate.edu
DAVIS, Judson, B .... 731-989-6023.... 469 B
jdavis@fhu.edu
DAVIS, Julia, T .... 478-301-2644.... 134 A
davis_jt@mercer.edu
DAVIS, Julianna .... 203-254-4030...... 92 H
jdavis@fairfield.edu
DAVIS, Julie .... 315-268-6713.... 329 B
davisju@clarkson.edu
DAVIS, Julie, A .... 207-778-7142.... 220 C
jadavis@maine.edu
DAVIS, June .... 910-296-2424.... 371 E
jdavis@jamessprunt.edu
DAVIS, Karan, P .... 850-718-2205.... 103 D
davisk@chipola.edu
DAVIS, Karen .... 805-493-3164...... 33 B
kdavis@clunet.edu
DAVIS, Karen .... 401-863-3377.... 453 B
karen_davis@brown.edu
DAVIS, Karen, S .... 937-393-3431.... 402 A
ksdavis@sscc.edu
DAVIS, Kathleen .... 207-893-7741.... 219 F
kdavis@sjcme.edu
DAVIS, Kathy .... 715-346-4193.... 552 D
kdavis@uwsp.edu
DAVIS, Kathy, K .... 207-768-9581.... 220 F
kathy.k.davis@umpi.edu
DAVIS, Katie .... 478-274-7775.... 135 C
kdavis@oftc.edu

DAVIS, Kelly ..... 479-968-0242 ..... 20 G kdavis@atu.edu

DAVIS, Kelly ..... 817-272-2194 ..... 505 C kdavis@uta.edu

DAVIS, Ken, R ..... 423-478-1131 ..... 472 H kdavis@ptseminary.edu

DAVIS, Kenneth ..... 212-659-8888 ..... 342 B

DAVIS, JR., Kenneth, M ..... 919-658-2502 ..... 367 F kdavis@moc.edu

DAVIS, Kerry ..... 904-819-6200 ..... 107 C kdavis@flagler.edu

DAVIS, Kim, D ..... 806-371-2912 ..... 479 G kddavis@actx.edu

DAVIS, Kimberly ..... 904-470-8000 ..... 105 G k.davis@ewc.edu

DAVIS, Kimely ..... 434-832-7627 ..... 526 E davisk@cvcc.vccs.edu

DAVIS, LaDonna ..... 301-937-8448 ..... 226 H ldavis@tesst.com

DAVIS, Larry ..... 903-223-3106 ..... 498 F larry.davis@tamut.edu

DAVIS, Larry, D ..... 501-977-2013 ..... 25 G davis@uaccm.edu

DAVIS, Larry, E ..... 412-624-6337 ..... 449 A ledavis@pitt.edu

DAVIS, Larry, J ..... 314-516-5606 ..... 291 D ldavis@umsl.edu

DAVIS, Laura ..... 913-758-6308 ..... 197 D davisl@stmary.edu

DAVIS, Laura ..... 859-280-1236 ..... 204 B ldavis@lextheo.edu

DAVIS, Laurie ..... 706-864-1763 ..... 134 G ldavis@northgeorgia.edu

DAVIS, Lee ..... 912-344-2535 ..... 124 G lee.davis@armstrong.edu

DAVIS, LeeAnn ..... 386-506-3404 ..... 104 F davisl@daytonastate.edu

DAVIS, Len, L ..... 516-876-3191 ..... 353 D davisl@oldwestbury.edu

DAVIS, Lily ..... 619-849-2524 ..... 62 L lilydavis@pointloma.edu

DAVIS, Linda ..... 617-879-2341 ..... 246 C ldavis@wheelock.edu

DAVIS, Linda ..... 810-989-5765 ..... 257 H ldavis@sc4.edu

DAVIS, Linda ..... 254-562-3848 ..... 491 C linda.davis@navarrocollege.edu

DAVIS, Linda, P ..... 386-822-7710 ..... 121 F ldavis@stetson.edu

DAVIS, Lisa ..... 202-687-3887 ..... 98 D davis1@georgetown.edu

DAVIS, Lois ..... 503-725-2320 ..... 418 G loisd@pdx.edu

DAVIS, Loren ..... 253-589-5771 ..... 532 G loren.davis@cptc.edu

DAVIS, Lori, A ..... 502-597-6414 ..... 203 G lori.davis@kysu.edu

DAVIS, LuAnn ..... 402-486-2503 ..... 300 C ludavis@ucollege.edu

DAVIS, M. Wayne ..... 251-460-6132 ..... 9 D wdavis@usouthal.edu

DAVIS, Maggie ..... 513-244-4630 ..... 388 E maggie_davis@mail.msj.edu

DAVIS, Malcolm ..... 713-743-0580 ..... 503 D mdavis@uh.edu

DAVIS, Marcellus ..... 763-433-1695 ..... 265 G marcellus.davis@anokaramsey.edu

DAVIS, Margaret ..... 845-368-7200 ..... 350 A margaret.davis@use.salvationarmy.org

DAVIS, Maria ..... 269-749-7643 ..... 257 A mdavis@olivetcollege.edu

DAVIS, Marie ..... 229-391-4988 ..... 123 H mdavis@abac.edu

DAVIS, Marie ..... 318-869-5013 ..... 208 H mdavis@centenary.edu

DAVIS, Marilyn, S ..... 217-424-6379 ..... 158 G mdavis@millikin.edu

DAVIS, Marjorie ..... 509-533-4152 ..... 533 C marjorie.davis@spokanefalls.edu

DAVIS, Mark ..... 310-506-4472 ..... 61 H mark.davis@pepperdine.edu

DAVIS, Marsha ..... 845-758-7433 ..... 323 D davis@bard.edu

DAVIS, Mary ..... 212-217-4300 ..... 333 F mary_davis@fitnyc.edu

DAVIS, Mary ..... 828-298-3325 ..... 380 D mdavis@warren-wilson.edu

DAVIS, Matthew ..... 402-557-7232 ..... 296 H matthew.davis@bellevue.edu

DAVIS, Matthew ..... 920-206-2310 ..... 548 D matthew.davis@mbbc.edu

DAVIS, Matthew ..... 920-261-9300 ..... 548 D mdavis@mbbc.edu

DAVIS, Matthew, D ..... 812-877-8421 ..... 179 B matthew.davis@rose-hulman.edu

DAVIS, Meagon ..... 478-757-3803 ..... 139 E mdavis@wesleyancollege.edu

DAVIS, Megan, W ..... 603-862-2450 ..... 306 C megan.davis@unh.edu

DAVIS, Melvin ..... 601-979-1400 ..... 274 G melvin.davis@jsums.edu

DAVIS, Michael ..... 770-381-7200 ..... 132 C

DAVIS, Michael, G ..... 985-448-4030 ..... 216 A mike.davis@nicholls.edu

DAVIS, Michelle ..... 434-544-8228 ..... 521 B davis@lynchburg.edu

DAVIS, Mike ..... 386-752-1822 ..... 108 G mike.davis@fgc.edu

DAVIS, Miles ..... 540-545-7253 ..... 524 E mdavis3@su.edu

DAVIS, Mitch ..... 251-442-2334 ..... 9 A mdavis@umobile.edu

DAVIS, Mitchel, W ..... 207-725-3930 ..... 217 E mwdavis@bowdoin.edu

DAVIS, Nan, M ..... 903-813-3000 ..... 481 A ndavis@austincollege.edu

DAVIS, Nancy ..... 413-265-2272 ..... 233 D davisn@elms.edu

DAVIS, Nancy ..... 619-644-7000 ..... 49 C nancy.davis@gcccd.edu

DAVIS, Nancy ..... 919-962-2011 ..... 378 E nancy_davis@unc.edu

DAVIS, Natalie ..... 601-643-8354 ..... 273 G natalie.davis@colin.edu

DAVIS, Ora ..... 334-387-3877 ..... 1 D oradavis@amridgeuniversity.edu

DAVIS, Pam ..... 423-746-5327 ..... 476 F pdavis@twcnet.edu

DAVIS, Pamela ..... 919-760-8360 ..... 367 A davisp@meredith.edu

DAVIS, Pamela, B ..... 216-368-2825 ..... 386 F pamela.davis@case.edu

DAVIS, Patricia ..... 972-860-8180 ..... 484 H pdavis@dcccd.edu

DAVIS, Patricia ..... 207-780-5911 ..... 220 G patdavis@usm.maine.edu

DAVIS, Patricia, A ..... 251-380-3063 ..... 7 E pdavis@shc.edu

DAVIS, Patrick ..... 772-546-5534 ..... 110 N patdavis@hsbc.edu

DAVIS, Patti ..... 410-386-8066 ..... 221 G pdavis@carrollcc.edu

DAVIS, Paul ..... 641-784-5422 ..... 185 B pjdavis@graceland.edu

DAVIS, Paul ..... 936-468-1111 ..... 496 B pdavis@sfasu.edu

DAVIS, Paula ..... 719-846-5680 ..... 88 F paula.davis@trinidadstate.edu

DAVIS, Paula ..... 609-343-5091 ..... 307 C pdavis@atlantic.edu

DAVIS, Peggy ..... 804-524-5030 ..... 529 H pdavis@vsu.edu

DAVIS, Pete, D ..... 608-342-1147 ..... 552 B davisp@uwplatt.edu

DAVIS, Phillip ..... 805-756-5301 ..... 33 I pdavis@calpoly.edu

DAVIS, Phillip, L ..... 612-659-6300 ..... 267 B phil.davis@minneapolis.edu

DAVIS, Rachelle ..... 301-387-3044 ..... 222 H rachelle.davis@garrettcollege.edu

DAVIS, Raeanne ..... 212-237-8604 ..... 327 F radavis@jjay.cuny.edu

DAVIS, Ralph ..... 770-426-2713 ..... 133 E rdavis@life.edu

DAVIS, Ralph, U ..... 843-661-1110 ..... 458 D rdavis@fmarion.edu

DAVIS, Rance ..... 315-229-5551 ..... 349 E rdavis@stlawu.edu

DAVIS, Randy ..... 502-213-2122 ..... 202 F randall.davis@kctcs.edu

DAVIS, Ray, J ..... 410-651-6083 ..... 227 E rjdavis@umes.edu

DAVIS, Rebecca ..... 361-593-3344 ..... 498 D koosr00@tamuk.edu

DAVIS, Rene ..... 202-872-4700 ..... 99 B rene@medtech.edu

DAVIS, Renee ..... 334-386-7230 ..... 3 G rdavis@faulkner.edu

DAVIS, Rhonda ..... 417-624-7070 ..... 284 D rdavis@messengercollege.edu

DAVIS, Richard ..... 317-931-2391 ..... 170 H ddavis@cts.edu

DAVIS, TOR, Richard ..... 740-283-6406 ..... 391 A rdavis@franciscan.edu

DAVIS, Richard, E ..... 954-262-1203 ..... 114 B redavis@nsu.nova.edu

DAVIS, Rick ..... 850-973-9492 ..... 113 K davisr@nfcc.edu

DAVIS, Rick ..... 662-246-6441 ..... 275 D rdavis@msdelta.edu

DAVIS, Rob ..... 612-874-3793 ..... 265 C rob_davis@mcad.edu

DAVIS, Robert, H ..... 303-492-7006 ..... 88 H robert.davis@colorado.edu

DAVIS, JR., Robert, W ..... 570-941-7500 ..... 450 C robert.davis@scranton.edu

DAVIS, Roger ..... 615-966-7161 ..... 470 F roger.davis@lipscomb.edu

DAVIS, Ron ..... 901-383-6712 ..... 99 G rnd@strayer.edu

DAVIS, Ron ..... 217-641-4500 ..... 154 I rmdavis@jwcc.edu

DAVIS, Rondell ..... 757-363-2121 ..... 516 H

DAVIS, Ruth ..... 718-855-3661 ..... 336 D rdavis@idc.edu

DAVIS, Sally ..... 404-752-1942 ..... 134 E sdavis@msm.edu

DAVIS, Sandie ..... 706-295-6339 ..... 130 E sdavis@highlands.edu

DAVIS, Sandra ..... 803-536-7067 ..... 460 G sdavis@scsu.edu

DAVIS, Sandra, L ..... 909-869-2289 ..... 33 J sldavis@csupomona.edu

DAVIS, Shane ..... 318-487-7181 ..... 209 F davis@lacollege.edu

DAVIS, Shara ..... 440-365-5222 ..... 395 D

DAVIS, Sharon ..... 513-569-1475 ..... 387 G sharon.davis@cincinnatistate.edu

DAVIS, Sharon ..... 214-860-8705 ..... 485 B sdavis@dcccd.edu

DAVIS, Sharon ..... 254-526-1346 ..... 482 H sharon.davis@ctcd.edu

DAVIS, Shauna, N ..... 804-523-2288 ..... 527 A sdavis01@ccwa.vccs.edu

DAVIS, Shelly ..... 207-893-7726 ..... 219 F sdavis@sjcme.edu

DAVIS, Sherri ..... 205-929-6357 ..... 5 E sdavis@lawsonstate.edu

DAVIS, Sherri ..... 606-672-2312 ..... 200 K sherri.davis@frontier.edu

DAVIS, Sherry ..... 254-659-7602 ..... 487 G sdavis@hillcollege.edu

DAVIS, Stan ..... 205-726-2366 ..... 6 G csdavis@samford.edu

DAVIS, Stefan, S ..... 317-274-8828 ..... 174 D ssdavis@iupui.edu

DAVIS, Stephen ..... 410-225-2355 ..... 224 B sdavis@mica.edu

DAVIS, Steve ..... 954-382-6531 ..... 122 F sdavis@tiu.edu

DAVIS, Steve ..... 304-357-4980 ..... 542 A stevedavis@ucwv.edu

DAVIS, Steven, J ..... 208-496-3305 ..... 143 A daviss@byui.edu

DAVIS, Stewart ..... 256-549-8202 ..... 3 J sdavis@gadsdenstate.edu

DAVIS, Stuart ..... 650-723-9406 ..... 71 G spdavis@stanford.edu

DAVIS, Sue ..... 225-768-1802 ..... 214 C sue.davis@ololcollege.edu

DAVIS, Sue, E ..... 330-941-2000 ..... 406 F sedavis@ysu.edu

DAVIS, Susan ..... 314-529-9340 ..... 284 C sdavis5@maryville.edu

DAVIS, Susan, H ..... 502-272-8217 ..... 198 H sdavis@bellarmine.edu

DAVIS, Susan, Y ..... 573-875-7210 ..... 280 A sydavis@ccis.edu

DAVIS, Suzanne, E ..... 315-268-6451 ..... 329 B daviss@clarkson.edu

DAVIS, Taishieka ..... 318-670-6415 ..... 215 A tdavis@susla.edu

DAVIS, Tamaria ..... 404-270-5002 ..... 138 B tkdavis@spelman.edu

DAVIS, Tammy ..... 325-574-7695 ..... 508 I tdavis@wtc.edu

DAVIS, Terry ..... 619-482-6561 ..... 71 D tdavis@swccd.edu

DAVIS, Thomas ..... 434-791-5651 ..... 516 G thom.davis@averett.edu

DAVIS, Thomas ..... 803-705-4687 ..... 455 D davist@benedict.edu

DAVIS, Thomas, A ..... 423-775-7205 ..... 467 F davisto@bryan.edu

DAVIS, Thomas, D ..... 517-353-6727 ..... 255 A tdd@msu.edu

DAVIS, Tiffany ..... 810-766-4277 ..... 247 G tiffany.davis@baker.edu

DAVIS, Tina ..... 859-622-3876 ..... 200 J tina.davis@eku.edu

DAVIS, Todd ..... 678-359-5061 ..... 132 A toddd@gdn.edu

DAVIS, Tom ..... 334-670-3196 ..... 8 A tomdavis@troy.edu

DAVIS, Tom ..... 954-545-4500 ..... 117 I registrar@sfbc.edu

DAVIS, Tom ..... 505-786-4113 ..... 318 I tdavis@navajotech.edu

DAVIS, Tom ..... 440-375-7170 ..... 394 E tdavis@lec.edu

DAVIS, Tommye Lou ..... 254-710-3750 ..... 482 A tommye_lou_davis@baylor.edu

DAVIS, Tracie, L ..... 574-289-7001 ..... 176 E tldavis@ivytech.edu

DAVIS, Tracy ..... 641-782-1434 ..... 189 E davis@swcciowa.edu

DAVIS, Tracy ..... 415-371-0002 ..... 60 A

DAVIS, Tyler ..... 843-574-5505 ..... 456 B tdavis@csuniv.edu

DAVIS, Wayne ..... 865-974-5321 ..... 477 D wtdavis@utk.edu

DAVIS, Wayne ..... 757-825-3513 ..... 528 F davisw@tncc.edu

DAVIS, Wendell, M ..... 919-530-6204 ..... 378 B wendell.davis@nccu.edu

DAVIS, Wendy ..... 520-515-3623 ..... 13 E davisw@cochise.edu

DAVIS, Wendy ..... 501-812-2273 ..... 23 C wdavis@pulaskitech.edu

DAVIS, Wesley ..... 701-477-7862 ..... 383 F wdavis1@tm.edu

DAVIS, William ..... 610-359-6500 ..... 426 G wdavis@dccc.edu

DAVIS AUSTIN, Patricia ..... 215-895-5844 ..... 427 H pda@drexel.edu

DAVIS-BLAKE, Alison ..... 734-764-1363 ..... 259 A alisondb@umich.edu

DAVIS-DUKES, Janet ..... 973-720-3096 ..... 317 D davisdukesj@wpunj.edu

DAVIS FREEMAN, Louisa, M ..... 413-755-4333 ..... 241 B ldavisfreeman@stcc.edu

DAVIS-FULMER, Deryl ..... 920-693-1231 ..... 554 C deryl.davisfulmer@gotoltc.edu

DAVIS-JOHNSON, Max ..... 208-426-3033 ..... 142 I maxdavisjohnson@boisestate.edu

DAVIS-MCFARLAND, Elise ..... 843-574-6010 ..... 461 G elise.davis-mcfarland@tridenttech.edu

DAVIS OCHI, Megan ..... 773-896-2400 ..... 146 H mdavis-ochi@ctschicago.edu

DAVIS-TARIQ, Alison, D ..... 757-823-2908 ..... 522 E adtariq@nsu.edu

DAVIS-VAN ATTA, David ..... 845-437-5276 ..... 359 F ddavisa@vassar.edu

DAVISON, Brent ..... 254-295-8642 ..... 504 C bdavison@umhb.edu

DAVISON, Dale ..... 602-978-7739 ..... 18 H dale.davison@thunderbird.edu

DAVISON, Don ..... 513-721-7944 ..... 391 D ddavison@gbs.edu

DAVISON, Frieda, M ..... 864-503-5610 ..... 463 B fdavison@uscupstate.edu

DAVISON, Ian, R ..... 989-774-1870 ..... 249 C davis1ir@cmich.edu

DAVISON, James ..... 412-924-1346 ..... 444 H jdavison@pts.edu

DAVISON, Kim, K ..... 972-985-3781 ..... 483 H kdavison@collin.edu

DAVISON, Rodney ..... 940-565-2592 ..... 504 D davison@union.admin.unt.edu

DAVISON, Ruth, L ..... 850-474-2217 ..... 121 D rdavison@uwf.edu

DAVISON, Vickie ..... 406-657-1005 ..... 296 C vicki.davison@rocky.edu

DAVISON-WILSON, Sandra ..... 616-451-2787 ..... 250 H davisons@ferris.edu

DAVISSON, Thomas, F ..... 502-451-0815 ..... 206 H tdavisson@sullivan.edu

DAVISSON, Thomas, F ..... 502-451-0815 ..... 206 G tdavisson@sullivan.edu

DAVITT, Alison ..... 410-225-4219 ..... 224 B adavitt@mica.edu

DAVITT, Jeffrey ..... 904-819-6489 ..... 107 C jdavitt@flagler.edu

DAVOLT, David ..... 208-376-7731 ..... 142 H ddavolt@boisebible.edu

DAVOLT, Victor, L ..... 303-458-4900 ..... 87 I vdavolt@regis.edu

DAVOUD, Mohammad ..... 912-478-7412 ..... 131 E mdavoud@georgiasouthern.edu

DAVROS, Harry ..... 214-637-3530 ..... 508 D hdavros@wadecollege.edu

DAVY, Catherine, A ..... 313-593-5030 ..... 259 B kdavy@umd.umich.edu

DAW, Meredith ..... 773-702-7040 ..... 166 G daw@uchicago.edu

DAW, Michael ..... 415-442-6682 ..... 48 F mdaw@ggu.edu

DAWE, Lloyd, A ..... 803-641-3338 ..... 462 B lloydd@usca.edu

DAWE, Richard, L ..... 870-368-7371 ..... 23 A rdawe@ozarka.edu

DAWES, Charles ..... 207-893-6621 ..... 219 F cdawes@sjcme.edu

DAWES, Doug ..... 701-845-7234 ..... 382 C doug.dawes@vcsu.edu

DAWES, Stephen ..... 864-294-3031 ..... 458 E steve.dawes@furman.edu

DAWKINS, Antoinette ..... 706-821-8145 ..... 135 G adawkins@paine.edu

DAWKINS, Eryn, J ..... 706-542-7912 ..... 138 G edawkins@uga.edu

DAWKINS, Kelly, T ..... 803-327-8047 ..... 463 H kdawkins@yorktech.edu

DAWKINS, Kemel, W ..... 973-353-5541 ..... 314 E kemeld@andromeda.rutgers.edu

DAWKINS, Lisa ..... 304-357-4374 ..... 542 A lisadawkins@ucwv.edu

DAWKINS, Nancy, A ..... 414-410-4007 ..... 546 G nadawkins@stritch.edu

DAWKINS, Norman ..... 212-431-2142 ..... 343 E ndawkins@nyls.edu

DAWKINS, Phyllis, W ..... 504-816-4368 ..... 209 A pdawkins@dillard.edu

DAWKINS, Rita ..... 704-330-6862 ..... 369 D rita.dawkins@cpcc.edu

DAWLEY, Anna Marie ..... 315-268-6475 ..... 329 B adawley@clarkson.edu

DAWLEY, Michael ..... 508-793-7578 ..... 233 B mdawley@clarku.edu

DAWN, Veliky ..... 252-536-7227 ..... 371 B velikyd@halifaxcc.edu

DAWSON, B. James ..... 423-869-6391 ..... 470 E james.dawson@lmunet.edu

DEANGELIS, Toni 719-846-5520 88 F toni.deangelis@trinidadstate.edu
DEANGELO, OFM CONV, Jude 202-319-5575 97 E deangelo@cua.edu
DEANGELO, Mary 413-748-3757 244 H mdeangelo@springfieldcollege.edu
DEANNA, Linda 312-996-4857 167 B ldeanna@uic.edu
DEANS, Beverly 919-735-5151 375 A bdeans@waynecc.edu
DEAR, Carley 601-857-3357 274 C carley.dear@hindscc.edu
DEARBORN, Philip, E 717-560-8233 433 D pdearborn@lbc.edu
DEARCORN, Casey 307-754-6084 556 G casey.dearcorn@northwestcollege.edu
DEARDURFF, Dayle 513-861-6400 402 I dayle.deardurff@myunion.edu
DEARSMAN, Matt 630-353-7049 149 B mdearsman@devry.edu
DEARSTYNE, JR., Kenneth, E 717-872-3475 443 D kenneth.dearstyne@millersville.edu
DEARTH, John, C 716-673-3251 352 A john.dearth@fredonia.edu
DEAS, Edwin 760-773-2511 42 A edeas@collegeofthedesert.edu
DEAS, M. Gary 334-347-2623 3 F gdeas@escc.edu
DEASE, Dennis, J 651-962-6500 272 B djdease@stthomas.edu
DEASE, Mary Ann 203-837-8248 91 A deasem@wcsu.edu
DEASON, Michael 972-860-4670 484 G mdeason@dcccd.edu
DEATHERAGE, Eric 417-455-5610 280 H ericdeatherage@crowder.edu
DEATHERAGE, Janet 312-915-6512 157 C jdeathe@luc.edu
DEATLEY, Janeen, S 937-393-3431 402 A jdeatley@sscc.edu
DEATON, Amy 931-221-6131 473 E deatona@apsu.edu
DEATON, Andrea, D 405-325-1646 413 C adeaton@ou.edu
DEATON, Brady, J 573-882-3387 291 B deatonb@missouri.edu
DEATON, Bruce 313-487-7017 209 F deaton@lacollege.edu
DEATON, Judy 949-675-4451 51 D interior_designer@msn.com
DEATON, Sharon 949-675-4451 51 D interior_designer@msn.com
DEATS, Jacqueline 714-997-6851 39 F deats@chapman.edu
DEATS, John 432-685-4726 491 A jdeats@midland.edu
DEAVER, Christy 828-339-4406 374 C christyd@southwesterncc.edu
DEAVER, Reekitta 252-527-6223 371 G rdeaver@lenoircc.edu
DEAVER, Robin 910-678-8484 370 E deaverr@faytechcc.edu
DEBARROS, Angelia 210-485-0374 479 A adebarros1@alamo.edu
DEBASIO, Nancy 816-995-2810 288 A nancy.debasio@researchcollege.edu
DEBASIO, Nancy, O 816-995-2815 287 H nancy.debasio@researchcollege.edu
DEBAUN, Amy 860-297-2305 94 E amy.debaun@trincoll.edu
DEBEAUCHAMP, Debbie 425-739-8232 535 H deborah.debeauchamp@lwtc.edu
DEBEER, Dean 718-779-1430 346 B ddb@plazacollege.edu
DEBELA, Kenesa 773-256-0716 157 D kdebela@lstc.edu
DEBENEDICTS, Elissa 217-757-1190 322 H edebenedicts@funeraleducation.org
DEBERNARDI, Maureen 617-779-4369 244 B admissionsandrecords@sjs.edu
DEBIAK, Lauren 816-501-4232 288 A lauren.debiak@rockhurst.edu
DEBIAS, Patti 773-256-0728 157 D pdebias@lstc.edu
DEBLASIO, Denise, M 973-655-4340 311 F deblasiod@mail.montclair.edu
DEBLOIS, Benjamin, A 910-755-7403 368 F debloisb@brunswickcc.edu
DEBOARD, John 580-581-2237 407 D jdeboard@cameron.edu
DEBOCK, Devin 918-293-4944 410 E devin.debock@okstate.edu
DEBOER, Katie 612-659-6306 267 B katie.deboer@minneapolis.edu
DEBOER, Keith 616-222-1247 250 A keith.deboer@cornerstone.edu
DEBOER-MORAN, Jason 651-641-8766 263 A moran@csp.edu
DEBOER-MORAN, Jason, T 651-641-8766 263 A moran@csp.edu
DEBONO, Chad 719-336-6660 86 B chad.debono@lamarcc.edu
DEBORD, Bonnie, H 770-720-5502 136 C bhd@reinhardt.edu
DEBOSE, Angela, W 813-974-4018 121 A awdebose@usf.edu
DEBOSE, Henry 804-524-5992 529 H hdebose@vsu.edu
DEBOSKEY, Brian 303-542-7000 464 H
DEBOW, Arthur 503-297-5544 417 G adebow@ocac.edu
DEBOWER, Lore 508-362-2131 239 D ldebower@capecod.edu
DEBRAGA, Angie 775-775-2231 302 F angie.debraga@gbcnv.edu
DEBRAGGIO, Michael, J 315-859-4654 334 H mdebragg@hamilton.edu
DEBRITO, Joannie, L 303-963-3378 82 C jdebrito@ccu.edu
DEBRIZZI, JR., Thomas, A 203-576-4690 94 F tdebriz@bridgeport.edu
DEBROCK, Larry 217-333-2747 167 D ldebrock@business.uiuc.edu
DEBRUM, David 692-625-6416 560 A ddebrum@cmi.edu
DEBUHR, Larry 812-866-6846 172 A debuhr@hanover.edu
DEBURE, Olivier 727-864-8421 105 E debureoc@eckerd.edu
DEBURRO, Jennifer 207-602-2132 221 A jdeburro@une.edu
DEBUS, Casey 307-532-8311 556 C casey.debus@ewc.wy.edu
DEBUSK, Frankie 423-636-7300 477 A fdebusk@tusculum.edu
DEBUSK, Lisa 907-277-1000 10 E contact@chartercollege.edu
DEC, Ted 631-687-5155 349 A tdec@sjcny.edu
DEC, Ted 631-687-5155 349 B tdec@sjcny.edu
DECAIRE, Maryann 847-578-8810 163 C maryann.decaire@rosalindfranklin.edu
DECAIRE, Maryann 847-578-3217 163 C maryann.decaire@rosalindfranklin.edu
DECALO, Ruth 212-678-8915 337 G rudecalo@jtsa.edu
DECAMILLIS, Susan 231-995-1014 256 D sdecamillis@nmc.edu
DECARBO, Diane, M 724-658-1938 423 G diane.decarbo@bc3.edu
DECARLO, Robert, L 516-877-3184 322 A decarlo@adelphi.edu
DECARVALHO, Fatima 973-655-7818 311 F decarvalhf@mail.montclair.edu
DECASTRO, John 936-294-2200 501 D jdecastro@shsu.edu
DECASTRO-SALLIS, Kishma 412-397-6238 445 H sallis@rmu.edu
DECATUR, Jane 508-626-4585 238 A jdecatur@framingham.edu
DECATUR, Sean 440-775-8410 397 G sean.decatur@oberlin.edu
DECATUR, William 401-454-6474 454 B wdecatur@risd.edu
DECELLE, Jerry, L 518-564-2082 354 B decellejl@plattsburgh.edu
DECENA, Peter 408-924-2222 37 C peter.decena@sjsu.edu
DECENZO, David, A 843-349-2001 456 G ddecenzo@coastal.edu
DECHANT, Bill 828-565-4027 371 C wmdechant@haywood.edu
DECHANT, Margaret 361-825-5952 498 C margaret.dechant@tamucc.edu
DECHARINTE, Janeen 815-838-0500 156 F decharja@lewisu.edu
DECHELLIS, Andrea 973-642-8092 315 C andrea.dechellis@shu.edu
DECHILLO, Neal 978-542-6630 238 E ndechillo@salemstate.edu
DECICCIO, Albert, C 802-447-6333 514 F adeciccio@svc.edu
DECICCO, Darlene 631-656-2134 334 B darlene.decicco@ftc.edu
DECINQUE, Gregory, T 716-338-1060 337 E gregdecinque@mail.sunyjcc.edu
DECK, Alisa 812-374-5129 176 A adeck@ivytech.edu
DECK, Joseph, G 210-434-6711 492 B jgdeck@lake.ollusa.edu
DECKER, Ann 772-462-7240 111 B adecker@irsc.edu
DECKER, Barbara, Q 515-643-6601 187 F bdecker@mercydesmoines.org
DECKER, Charles 810-989-2133 248 G charles.decker@baker.edu
DECKER, Charley 517-265-5161 246 H
DECKER, Christie 605-361-0200 464 B cdecker@sf.coloradotech.edu
DECKER, Christy 518-828-4181 330 E christy.decker@sunycgcc.edu
DECKER, David, R 614-947-6017 391 B deckerd@franklin.edu
DECKER, Diann 801-818-8900 510 I diann.decker@provocollege.edu
DECKER, Douglas 724-983-0700 434 B ddecker@laurel.edu
DECKER, Douglas, S 724-439-4900 434 A ddecker@laurel.edu
DECKER, Kim 334-244-3636 1 G kdecker@aum.edu
DECKER, Lisa, M 212-752-1530 338 C lisa.decker@limcollege.edu
DECKER, Nancy 724-983-0700 434 B ndecker@laurel.edu
DECKER, Nancy, M 724-439-4900 434 A ndecker@laurel.edu
DECKER, Pat 913-469-8500 194 B pdecker5@jccc.edu
DECKER, Paul, W 818-767-0888 79 H paul.decker@woodbury.edu
DECKER, Sheryl 574-237-0774 170 E sdecker@brownmackie.edu
DECKER, Stephanie 973-684-6868 312 E sdecker@pccc.edu
DECKER, Steven 715-468-2815 555 G steven.decker@witc.edu
DECKER, Susan 812-535-5138 179 E sdecker@smwc.edu
DECKER, Timothy 845-298-0755 332 D tdecker@sunydutchess.edu
DECLUE, Gary 217-641-4999 154 I declueg@jwcc.edu
DECLUE, Stephanie 816-415-7606 293 C declues@william.jewell.edu
DECMAN, Mike 815-740-3427 167 E mdecman@stfrancis.edy
DECOCK, Murray 315-228-7489 329 G mdecock@colgate.edu
DECOLFMACKER, Robert 207-985-7976 218 D robertdecolfmacker@landingschool.edu
DECONCILIS, Patricia, A 724-653-2213 427 G pdecon@dec.edu
DECONINCK, Lori 603-668-2211 305 I l.deconinck@snhu.edu
DECONNO, David 518-580-5719 351 B ddecanno@skidmore.edu
DECONTI, Katherine 860-297-2366 94 E katherine.deconti@trincoll.edu
DECONTI, Merlin, A 401-598-4700 453 E mdeconti@jwu.edu
DECORDOVA, Endia 860-512-2903 91 F edecordova@mcc.commnet.edu
DECOSTA, Jean 805-756-5198 33 I jdecosta@calpoly.edu
DECOSTA, Melvin 808-735-4792 140 E security@chaminade.edu
DECOSTER, Patrice 518-587-2100 355 G pat.decoster@esc.edu
DECOTEAU, Brian 701-255-3285 383 G bdecoteau@uttc.edu
DECOTEAU, Steve 701-477-7862 383 F sdecoteau@tm.edu
DECOUDREAUX, Alecia, A 510-430-2094 57 D adecoudreaux@mills.edu
DECOURCY, Alan 513-244-4487 388 E alan_decourcy@mail.msj.edu
DECOURSEY, Paul, A 515-574-1055 185 I decoursey@iowacentral.edu
DECOY, Dirk 740-695-9500 385 B ddecoy@belmontcollege.edu
DECRISTO, James 336-734-2862 379 E decristoj@uncsa.edu
DECROSTA, Tony 970-491-5793 83 F tony.decrosta@colostate.edu
DECUIR, Anthony 504-865-3039 213 F deancmfa@loyno.edu
DEDE, Brenda, S 814-393-2337 442 B bdede@clarion.edu
DEDECKER, Sherry 805-893-3713 75 B sherry.dedecker@library.ucsb.edu
DEDEO, Patrick 973-720-2224 317 D dedeop@wpunj.edu
DEDIEMAR, Jeanette 850-644-2466 119 D jdediemar@fsu.edu
DEDIOS, Paul 714-484-7335 59 D pdedios@cypresscollege.edu
DEDMAN, Tony 615-547-7610 468 B tdedman@cumberland.edu
DEDOMINICIS, H. Ken 202-319-6911 97 E dedominicis@cua.edu
DEDWYLDER, Jason 601-477-4240 274 H jason.dedwylder@jcjc.edu
DEE, Edward 718-779-1430 346 B edee@plazacollege.edu
DEE, Kay, C 812-877-8502 179 B dee@rose-hulman.edu
DEE, Shawn, G 336-334-4822 371 A sgdee@gtcc.edu
DEE, Tina 231-777-0660 256 A tina.dee@muskegoncc.edu
DEEB, Bassam 716-614-6240 344 C bdeeb@niagaracc.suny.edu
DEEB, Bassam, M 716-826-1200 358 D deebb@trocaire.edu
DEEDRICK, Gary, A 864-242-5100 455 E
DEEDS, Cher 330-684-8952 403 C cher@uakron.edu
DEEDS, Sarene 417-873-7869 281 D sdeeds@drury.edu
DEEDS, William, C 712-274-5103 187 G deeds@morningside.edu
DEEGAN, Robert, P 760-744-1150 61 D rdeegan@palomar.edu
DEEGAN, Rosemary, L 610-921-7202 421 E rdeegan@alb.edu
DEEGEN, Lynn 601-928-6212 275 E lynn.deegen@mgccc.edu
DEEHAN, Theresa, L 973-761-9746 315 B theresa.deehan@shu.edu
DEEK, Fadi, P 973-596-2997 312 C fadi.deek@njit.edu
DEEL, Connie 785-594-8362 190 F connie.deel@bakeru.edu
DEEL, Susan, M 989-463-7348 247 B deel@alma.edu
DEEM, Marie 412-536-1128 432 H marie.deem@laroche.edu
DEEMER, Kevin, L 440-964-4329 393 E kdeemer@kent.edu
DEEN, Candace 717-872-3771 443 D candace.deen@millersville.edu
DEEN, Michael 903-813-2306 481 A mdeen@austincollege.edu
DEER, Susan 845-574-4000 347 I
DEES, Andriel 715-425-3711 552 C andriel.dees@uwrf.edu
DEES, Andriel 715-425-3833 552 C andriel.dees@uwrf.edu
DEES, Charles 973-596-8293 312 C charles.dees@njit.edu
DEES, Margaret 904-680-7649 107 J mdees@fcsl.edu
DEESE, Nicole 318-869-5147 208 H ndeese@centenary.edu
DEESS, Eugene, P 973-596-3110 312 C deess@njit.edu
DEETER, Daniel, P 574-284-4543 179 F ddeeter@saintmarys.edu
DEETZ, Kristi, R 812-888-4358 181 D kdeetz@vinu.edu
DEFA, Dennis 406-994-3651 295 C dennis.defa@montana.edu
DEFALCO, Ron, E 713-718-7586 487 I ron.defalco@hccs.edu
DEFALUSSY, George 607-735-1978 332 I gdefalussy@elmira.edu
DEFATTA, Jerry 601-266-5013 277 F jerry.defatta@usm.edu
DEFEIS, Evelyn 973-684-5900 312 E edefeis@pccc.edu
DEFELICE, OSB, Jonathan, P 603-641-7010 305 G jdefelice@anselm.edu
DEFELICE, Robert, A 781-891-2256 231 D rdefelice@bentley.edu
DEFENDORF, Monica 607-962-9587 331 C mdefendo@corning-cc.edu
DEFEO, Gregory 412-809-5100 444 G defeo.greg@pti.edu
DEFEO, Joseph 203-254-4025 92 H jdefeo@fairfield.edu
DEFFENBACHER, Mark 559-453-2080 48 A mdeffen@fresno.edu
DEFFENBAUGH, Cynthia, B 804-289-8438 525 E cdeffenb@richmond.edu
DEFFKE, Cliff 303-280-7530 84 G cdeffke@devry.edu
DEFILIPPO, Eugene, B 617-552-4681 232 B gene.d@bc.edu
DEFOE, Darren 207-221-8727 218 C ddefoe@kaplan.edu
DEFOE, Richard 504-278-6230 211 E rdefoe@nunez.edu
DEFOOR, Keith 706-379-5156 140 A kdefoor@yhc.edu
DEFORD, J. Kevin 423-652-4859 470 A jkdeford@king.edu
DEFORE, Matt 205-726-4021 6 G mdefore@samford.edu
DEFOREST, Kristin, A 607-746-4590 355 F deforeka@delhi.edu
DEFRANCESCO, Joyce 724-589-2855 448 B jdefrancesco@thiel.edu
DEFRANCIS, Robert 304-214-8820 543 D rdefrancis@wvncc.edu
DEFRANCO, Agnes, L 713-743-2422 503 D aldefranco@central.uh.edu
DEFRANCO, Jeff 530-541-4660 53 G defranco@ltcc.edu
DEFRANCO, Thomas 860-486-3813 94 G thomas.defranco@uconn.edu
DEFRATES, Bruce 509-359-6329 533 H bdefrates@ewu.edu
DEFREECE, Michele, T 607-746-4652 355 F defreemt@delhi.edu
DEFREECE, Perri, D 607-746-4700 355 F defreepd@delhi.edu
DEFRIES, Brandi 507-457-1750 271 B bdefries@smumn.edu

DEGAIN, Sabrina 336-506-4161 368 A sabrina.degain@alamancecc.edu
DEGAISH, Ann 361-825-2612 498 C ann.degaish@tamucc.edu
DEGARMO, David, L 602-944-3335 11 D ddegarmo@aicag.edu
DEGATEGNO, Paul, J 610-892-1411 439 C pjd15@psu.edu
DEGAZON, Karen 212-938-5654 355 B kdegazon@sunyopt.edu
DEGEN, Bruno 718-270-6110 328 C bdegen@mec.cuny.edu
DEGEN, Charlotte 413-662-5231 238 C charlotte.degen@mcla.edu
DEGENEVIEVE, Barbara 312-899-1294 164 C
DEGENHART, Mary Louise 314-367-8700 288 F mary.degenhart@stlcop.edu
DEGEORGE, Christine, C 941-359-7645 116 B ccarnegi@ringling.edu
DEGER, Beth 937-328-6023 387 H degerb@clarkstate.edu
DEGERMAN, Roger, E 218-299-3645 262 I degerman@cord.edu
DEGESO, Melissa 407-277-0311 107 B mdegeso@evergladesuniversity.edu
DEGEUS, Marilyn, J 816-654-7262 283 F mdegeus@kcumb.edu
DEGIOIA, John (Jack), J 202-687-4134 98 D president@georgetown.edu
DEGIOVANNI, Kim 301-387-3040 222 H kim.degiovanni@garrettcollege.edu
DEGIOVINE, Christopher 518-454-5293 330 C frchris@strose.edu
DEGN, Jason 402-399-2431 297 C jdegn@csm.edu
DEGNAN, James, W 215-204-4643 447 H james.degnan@temple.edu
DEGNAN, Susan 218-262-6710 266 E susandegnan@hibbing.edu
DEGRAFFENREID, Pamela 828-227-7346 380 A degraffen@wcu.edu
DEGRANGE, Karen, A 812-877-8285 179 B karen.degrange@rose-hulman.edu
DEGRAW, Julie 419-358-3248 385 D degrawj@bluffton.edu
DEGROAT, Aziza 614-837-4088 405 C
DEGROAT, Kevin 718-405-3400 330 A kevin.degroat@mountsaintvincent.edu
DEGROFT, Michael 717-299-7796 448 A degroft@stevenscollege.edu
DEGROOTE, David, K 320-308-2192 269 A dkdegroote@stcloudstate.edu
DEHAAN, Laurens 415-433-9200 68 F ldehaan@saybrook.edu
DEHAEMERS, Jennifer 816-235-1143 291 C dehaemersj@umkc.edu
DEHAHN, Tracee 805-756-2586 33 I tdehahn@calpoly.edu
DEHART, Dan, J 818-779-8557 53 B ddehart@kingsuniversity.edu
DEHART, Joe 515-964-6279 183 H jcdehart@dmacc.edu
DEHART, Robert 402-363-5686 301 E bdehart@york.edu
DEHAVEN, Barbara 201-216-8762 315 E bdehaven@stevens.edu
DEHAVEN, James 269-353-1280 253 A jdehaven@kvcc.edu
DEHAVEN, Jane 515-244-4221 181 F dehavenj@aib.edu
DEHAYES, Donald, H 401-874-4410 454 E ddehayes@uri.edu
DEHLIN, Catherine, L 906-227-2420 256 C cdehlin@nmu.edu
DEHN, Paula 270-852-3117 204 A pdehn@kwc.edu
DEHNE, Nathan, D 920-565-1588 548 A dehnend@lakeland.edu
DEHOYOS, Diane, N 915-747-5601 506 B dndehoyos@utep.edu
DEI ROSSI, Gary 209-468-9155 72 G
DEI TOS, Nina Cecelia 570-504-9619 425 F
DEIBERT, Glenn 912-287-5827 135 F gdeibert@okefenokeetech.edu
DEICHEN, Michael, G 407-823-3702 120 B michael.deichen@ucf.edu
DEICHERT, Karen 724-480-3444 426 A karen.deichert@ccbc.edu
DEICHMANN, Wendy, J 937-529-2201 403 A wjdedwards@united.edu
DEIERLING, Tara 573-592-4248 293 D tdeierli@williamwoods.edu
DEIGHTON, Joe 251-380-3023 7 E jdeighton@shc.edu
DEIGNAN, Kathleen 609-258-5431 312 G kdeignan@princeton.edu
DEIKE, Randall 212-998-4553 344 B randall.deike@nyu.edu
DEIKE, Terri 903-233-3769 490 A terrideike@letu.edu
DEINNOCENTIIS, Maria 212-517-0482 340 C mdeinnocentiis@mmm.edu
DEIRTH, Sherry 812-330-6074 175 J sdeirth@ivytech.edu
DEITCHMAN, Jay 518-629-7567 336 C j.deitchman@hvcc.edu
DEITEMEYER, Kandi, W 252-335-0821 369 G kdeitemeyer@albemarle.edu
DEITRICK, Becky 570-372-4015 447 E deitrick@susqu.edu
DEITS, Will 805-986-5821 77 E wdeits@vcccd.edu
DEJESUS, Arnoldo 585-594-6140 347 F dejesus_arnoldo@roberts.edu
DEJESUS, Janie, A 814-371-2090 448 D jdejesus@triangle-tech.edu
DEJESUS, Javier 787-841-2000 565 B javier_dejesus@pucpr.edu
DEJESUS, Jose, L 787-250-1912 563 G jdejesus@metro.inter.edu
DEJESUS, Lisa 229-430-3504 124 B ldejesus@albanytech.edu
DEJESUS-RUEFF, Richard 585-385-8229 348 F rdejesus@sjfc.edu
DEJOHN, Fred 212-431-2881 343 E fdejohn@nyls.edu
DEJONG, Carol 616-395-7760 252 D cdejong@hope.edu
DEJONG, Chris 712-722-6070 184 C cdejong@dordt.edu
DEJONG, David, N 412-624-4228 449 A dejong@pitt.edu
DEJORGE, Alex, A 787-258-1501 561 F adejorge@columbiaco.edu
DEJORGE, Alex, R 787-743-4041 561 F ardejorge@columbiaco.edu
DEJTHAI, Eddie 239-280-2507 101 I eddie.dejthai@avemaria.edu
DEJULIO, Rosemary, A 718-817-3009 334 C dejulio@fordham.edu
DEJULIO, Thomas, E 718-817-3111 334 C tdejulio@fordham.edu
DEKAN, Doug, D 715-833-6238 553 H ddekan@cvtc.edu
DEKAY, Amy, M 716-880-2224 340 D amy.marie.dekay@medaille.edu
DEKAY, Todd 717-358-6021 429 F todd.dekay@fandm.edu
DEKKER, Jan 559-638-3641 72 C jan.dekker@reedleycollege.edu
DEKKER NETTLEMAN, Mary 605-357-1309 465 G med@usd.edu
DEKLOTZ, Steve 503-493-6286 415 E sdeklotz@cu-portland.edu
DEKOSKY, Steven, T 434-924-0311 525 F sd3zc@virginia.edu
DEKREY, Susan 845-437-7400 359 F sudekrey@vassar.edu
DEKRUIF, Kimberly 909-469-5342 78 I kdekruif@westernu.edu
DEKSHENIEKS, Craig 770-426-2833 133 E craig.dekshenieks@life.edu
DEL BALZO, Mary Beth 914-831-0463 330 D mdelbalzo@cw.edu
DEL BELLO, Wendy 281-756-3686 479 F wdelbello@alvincollege.edu
DEL BELLO, Wendy 281-756-3600 479 F wdelbello@alvincollege.edu
DEL CARMEN GIL, Maria 787-763-7005 561 H mcgil@cmpr.pr.gov
DEL CERRO, Gerardo 212-353-4321 331 A cerro@cooper.edu
DEL CONTE, Christopher 817-257-7710 499 C c.delconte@tcu.edu
DEL GIORNO, Julie 610-861-1361 437 A jdelgiorno@moravian.edu
DEL GIUDICE, Tristan, S 814-641-3390 432 A delgiut@juniata.edu
DEL NODAL, Diana 305-418-4220 115 D ddelnodal@pupr.edu
DEL PINO, Jennifer 515-961-1530 189 C jennifer.delpino@simpson.edu
DEL RIO-MORALES, Ricardo 787-725-6500 561 A consejoactivo@gmail.com
DEL ROSARIO, Dativa 510-436-2407 62 E ddelrosario@peralta.edu
DEL ROSARIO, Diana 216-987-5027 389 B diana.del-rosario@tri-c.edu
DEL SESTO, Lisa 312-322-1726 165 E ldelsesto@spertus.edu
DEL TONDO, Bruce 719-587-7227 80 L bdeltond@adams.edu
DEL TORO, Debra 210-829-6001 504 B ddeltoro@uiwtx.edu
DEL TORO, Edgar 787-664-0352 568 C edgar.deltoro@upr.edu
DEL VALLE, Deb 513-745-3877 406 E delvalle@xavier.edu
DEL VALLE, Wilfredo 787-863-2390 563 E wilfredo.delvalle@fajardo.inter.edu
DEL VECCHIO, Ron 218-281-8109 271 E dsvedars@umn.edu
DELA TEJA, Magdalena 817-515-6203 496 C magdalena.delateja@tccd.edu
DELABY, Lisa 530-895-2937 31 H delabyli@butte.edu
DELACH, Ruth 412-809-5100 444 G delach.ruth@pti.edu
DELAET, Lee 314-889-4539 281 I ldelaet@fontbonne.edu
DELAGUERRA, Christy 201-327-8877 309 G
DELAHAYA, Richard 615-963-5331 474 A rdelahay@tnstate.edu
DELAHOUSSAYE, Yasmin 213-891-2279 54 F delahoyj@email.laccd.edu
DELAHOYDE, Theresa 402-481-8843 296 I tdelahoyde@bryanlgh.org
DELAHUNT, Tom 515-271-2092 184 D tom.delahunt@drake.edu
DELAHUNTY, Jennifer 740-427-5778 394 C delahuntyj@kenyon.edu
DELAIN, Cindy 559-730-6265 42 D cindyd@cos.edu
DELALUE-KING, Shontay 401-232-6448 453 C sdelalue@bryant.edu
DELAND, Jane, S 202-885-8602 100 C jdeland@wesleyseminary.edu
DELAND, Robert 312-225-6288 167 G rdeland@vandercook.edu
DELANEY, Anne Marie 781-239-6481 230 E delaneya@babson.edu
DELANEY, Christopher 717-337-6235 429 I cdelaney@gettysburg.edu
DELANEY, Connie, J 612-624-1410 272 A delan108@umn.edu
DELANEY, Jeff 912-358-4400 136 G delaneyj@savannahstate.edu
DELANEY, John 423-425-4534 477 F john-delaney@utc.edu
DELANEY, John, A 904-620-2500 120 D jdelaney@unf.edu
DELANEY, John, T 412-648-1556 449 A jtd@pitt.edu
DELANEY, Kevin, J 310-338-5756 56 E kevin.delaney@lmu.edu
DELANEY, Melissa 510-841-9230 79 J mdelaney@wi.edu
DELANEY, Meredith 513-558-9964 403 E meredith.delaney@uc.edu
DELANEY, Peggy 831-459-4375 75 C pdelaney@ucsc.edu
DELANEY, Thomas 212-992-8851 344 B tom.delaney@nyu.edu
DELANEY, Timothy, J 740-284-5210 391 A tdelaney@franciscan.edu
DELANEY, Timothy, R 412-624-4216 449 A tdelaney@pitt.edu
DELANEY, Ute 845-752-3000 358 F registrar@uts.edu
DELANOY, Debra 845-687-5088 358 E delanoyd@sunyulster.edu
DELANSKY, Barbara 541-463-5337 416 E delanskyb@lanecc.edu
DELANY, Mary 530-752-1605 73 I medelaney@ucdavis.edu
DELAP, Joe 256-782-5004 4 L jdelap@jsu.edu
DELAP, Ronald 903-233-3900 490 A ronalddelap@letu.edu
DELARCO, Karen, R 484-664-3496 437 C delarco@muhlenberg.edu
DELAROSA, Antonio, S 765-641-4150 169 E asdelarosa@anderson.edu
DELAROSA, Sam 312-939-4975 151 H sdelarosa@harrington.edu
DELAROZ, Laura 415-865-0198 30 E mdelaroz@aii.edu
DELATE, John 914-251-6320 354 D john.delate@purchase.edu
DELAUTER, Leslie, J 215-898-5551 448 J collegehouses@pobox.upenn.edu
DELAWALLA, Noorali 562-860-2451 39 A ndelawalla@cerritos.edu
DELAY, Mary, G 210-567-2010 507 A delay@uthscsa.edu
DELBELSO, Debra 518-783-2339 350 I ddelbelso@siena.edu
DELBRIDGE, Kristina 518-587-2100 355 G kristina.delbridge@esc.edu
DELBUONO, Mary Gray 412-536-1300 432 H mary.delbuono@laroche.edu
DELCAMBRE, Ken 409-944-1314 486 K kdelcamb@gc.edu
DELCAMP, Erich 303-458-4050 87 I edelcamp@regis.edu
DELCAMP, Tom 215-222-4200 445 G tdelcamp@walnuthillcollege.edu
DELEMEESTER, Gregory, J 740-376-4630 395 G greg.delemeester@marietta.edu
DELENER, N.J 215-572-4691 422 C delenern@arcadia.edu
DELEO, Phyllis 203-777-2068 90 C pdeleo@albertus.edu
DELEON, Gilbert 210-530-9449 488 E
DELEON, Hilda 713-798-4612 481 H hildad@bcm.edu
DELEON, Javier 956-364-4562 500 D javier.deleon@tstc.edu
DELEON, Jerry 541-463-5870 416 E deleonj@lanecc.edu
DELEON, John 214-860-3673 485 B jdeleon@dcccd.edu
DELEON, Rocio 310-954-4025 57 H rdeleon@msmc.la.edu
DELEON, Rolando 262-691-5175 555 E rdeleon5@wctc.edu
DELEON, Verna 800-567-2344 547 A vdeleon@menominee.edu
DELEON, Zelma 940-565-3901 504 D zelma.deleon@unt.edu
DELEON GUERRERA, Neda, C 670-234-5498 560 B nedac@nmcnet.edu
DELEON GUERRERO, Galvin, S 670-234-5498 560 B galving@nmcnet.edu
DELERME, Leslie 740-368-3152 400 G ljdelerm@owu.edu
DELFORTE, Joseph, L 585-785-1227 334 A delforjl@flcc.edu
DELGADILLO, Carlos, E 509-527-4282 539 B carlos.delgadillo@wwcc.edu
DELGADO, Art 815-921-4092 162 H a.delgado@rockvalleycollege.edu
DELGADO, Fernando, P 715-425-3700 552 C fernando.delgado@uwrf.edu
DELGADO, Genobeba 305-231-3326 109 D gdelgado@mm.fnc.edu
DELGADO, Gilbert 954-965-7272 107 H gdelgado@careercollege.edu
DELGADO, Gilbert 954-732-6183 107 G gdelgado@careercollege.edu
DELGADO, Irene, R 718-409-5879 356 C idelgado@sunymaritime.edu
DELGADO, Jane Lee 212-220-1407 326 D jdelgado@bmcc.cuny.edu
DELGADO, Junior 413-572-5546 238 F jdelgado@wsc.ma.edu
DELGADO, Laura, M 787-765-4210 561 C
DELGADO, Luis, J 787-780-0070 560 H jdelgado@caribbean.edu
DELGADO, Maria, L 787-878-5475 563 B mdelgado@arecibo.inter.edu
DELGADO, Nydia 787-878-5475 563 B ndelgado@arecibo.inter.edu
DELGADO, Ricardo 636-949-4735 283 J rdelgado@lindenwood.edu
DELGADO, Steve 718-518-4314 327 D sdelgado@hostos.cuny.edu
DELGADO ALTIERI, Maria, E 787-896-2252 562 B mdelgado@edpcollege.edu
DELGADO-LIBRERO, M. Celeste 434-381-6334 524 K jys@sbc.edu
DELGAUDIO, Rose 562-938-4397 54 E rdelgaudio@lbcc.edu
DELGIORNO, Christopher, M 845-575-3000 340 B christopher.delgiorno@marist.edu
DELGIUDICE, Candice 619-201-8741 65 D candice.delgiudice@sdcc.edu
DELGIZZO, Kimberley 617-353-3590 232 E delgizzo@bu.edu
DELHOUSAYE, Darryl, L 602-850-8000 17 G ddelhousaye@phoenixseminary.edu
DELILE, John 207-453-5123 218 I jdelile@kvcc.me.edu
DELIN, Theresa, M 847-491-3293 160 E t-delin@northwestern.edu
DELIO, Vincent 518-956-8010 351 E vdelio@uamail.albany.edu
DELISA, Kenneth, J 860-465-5269 90 H delisak@easternct.edu
DELISI, Richard 732-932-7496 314 C richard.delisi@gse.rutgers.edu
DELISIO, Christopher, J 740-368-3324 400 G cjdelisi@owu.edu
DELISLE, David, W 315-268-6666 329 B delisle@clarkson.edu
DELIZIO, Carissa 603-899-4142 305 A delizioc@franklinpierce.edu
DELK, Kim 405-733-7979 411 I kdelk@rose.edu
DELKER, David 785-826-2963 194 E ddelker@k-state.edu
DELL, Erin, B 336-316-2196 365 A edell@guilford.edu
DELL, Jennifer 770-534-6164 126 E jdell@brenau.edu
DELL, Troy 301-687-4471 228 C tadell@frostburg.edu
DELLA POSTA, Joseph, B 315-445-4564 338 B dellapjb@lemoyne.edu
DELLA VOLPE, Angela 657-278-2024 35 B adellavolpe@fullerton.edu
DELLAMURA, Virginia, C 203-857-7311 92 C vdellamura@ncc.commnet.edu
DELLAPINA, Mario 718-960-8350 327 C mario.dellapina@lehman.cuny.edu
DELLAR, Dan 231-843-5985 260 B ddellar@westshore.edu
DELLAVECCHIA, Nancy, J 330-672-2444 393 D ndellave@kent.edu

DELLER, Jean ... 260-665-4100 ... 180 D
dellerj@trine.edu

DELLHIME, Roberta, G ... 909-748-8040 ... 76 C
roberta_dellhime@redlands.edu

DELLI CARPINI, Michael, X ... 215-898-4407 ... 448 J
dean@asc.upenn.edu

DELLICARPINI, Dominic ... 717-815-1231 ... 452 G
dcarpini@ycp.edu

DELLINGER, Dewey ... 704-922-6236 ... 370 G
dewey.dellinger@gaston.edu

DELLINGER, Janice ... 864-503-5771 ... 463 B
dellinger@uscupstate.edu

DELLINGER, Tim ... 731-424-2603 ... 475 C
tdellinger1@jscc.edu

DELLIVENERI, Richard ... 303-964-3656 ... 87 I
rdellive@regis.edu

DELLUTRI, Alexandra ... 708-237-5030 ... 160 D
adellutri@nc.edu

DELLWO, Sarah ... 406-447-6908 ... 295 A
sarah.dellwo@umhelena.edu

DELL'AQUILO, Bobbie ... 516-686-7851 ... 343 D
rdellaqu@nyit.edu

DELL'OMO, Gregory, G ... 412-397-6400 ... 445 H
dellomo@rmu.edu

DELL'OSA, Lydia, J ... 610-359-7322 ... 426 G
ldellosa@dccc.edu

DELMAR, Cindy ... 585-345-6813 ... 334 F
cmdelmar@genesee.edu

DELMAR, James ... 845-687-5278 ... 358 E
delmarj@sunyulster.edu

DELMONACO, JR., Rocco 202-687-7014 ... 98 D
rd254@georgetown.edu

DELNEGRO, Ann, L ... 302-855-1687 ... 96 E
delnegro@dtcc.edu

DELOATCH, Eugene ... 443-885-3231 ... 224 E
eugene.deloatch@eng.morgan.edu

DELOATCH, Lois ... 919-530-7856 ... 378 B
lois.deloatch@nccu.edu

DELOATCH, Sandra, J ... 757-823-8408 ... 522 E
provost@nsu.edu

DELOE, Mary ... 419-473-2700 ... 389 C
mdeloe@daviscollege.edu

DELONG, Allen, W ... 207-725-3536 ... 217 E
adelong2@bowdoin.edu

DELONG, Brian, C ... 610-799-1179 ... 434 D
bdelong2@lccc.edu

DELONG, Cliff ... 605-455-6079 ... 465 A
cdelong@olc.edu

DELONG, Mary Lou ... 617-552-3636 ... 232 B
marylou.delong@bc.edu

DELONG, Michael ... 501-812-2373 ... 23 C
mdelong@pulaskitech.edu

DELONG, Richard ... 810-766-4018 ... 247 G
richard.delong@baker.edu

DELONG, Shirley ... 610-799-1743 ... 434 D
sdelong3@lccc.edu

DELONGORIA, Maria ... 631-451-4174 ... 356 D
delongm@sunysuffolk.edu

DELONY, John ... 325-674-2784 ... 478 I
john.delony@acu.edu

DELORENZO, Dominick ... 423-893-2001 ... 478 D
dominick.delorenzo@vc.edu

DELORENZO, Donna ... 904-819-6255 ... 107 C
ddelorenzo@flagler.edu

DELORENZO, Michael ... 217-333-1300 ... 167 D
michaeld@illinois.edu

DELORENZO, Patricia ... 410-888-9048 ... 226 F
pdelorenzo@tai.edu

DELORENZO, Stephen, F ... 518-438-3111 ... 340 A
steved@mariacollege.edu

DELOREY, Mark, J ... 269-387-6005 ... 260 C
mark.delorey@wmich.edu

DELOS SANTOS, Maria Cecilia, H ... 671-735-5644 ... 559 E
studentsupportservices@guamcc.edu

DELOUISE, Tia ... 973-278-5400 ... 323 H
tdl@berkeleycollege.edu

DELOUISE, Tia ... 973-278-5400 ... 307 F
tdl@berkeleycollege.edu

DELOZIER, David ... 610-396-6056 ... 439 B
dcd11@psu.edu

DELP, Kevin ... 864-242-5100 ... 455 E

DELPHENICH, Pamela ... 617-253-1727 ... 241 D

DELPRETE, Angela ... 440-646-8371 ... 405 B
adelprete@ursuline.edu

DELUCA, Daryl ... 617-358-0700 ... 232 E
djdeluca@bu.edu

DELUCA, Eileen ... 239-985-2498 ... 105 F
ecduluca@edison.edu

DELUCA, Mary ... 443-840-5215 ... 222 D
mdeluca@ccbcmd.edu

DELUCA, Paul, M ... 608-262-1304 ... 550 J
pmdeluca@wisc.edu

DELUCA, Peter, L ... 805-525-4417 ... 72 I
pdeluca@thomasaquinas.edu

DELUCA, Tony ... 610-359-5110 ... 426 G
tdeluca@dccc.edu

DELUCA, Vincent, J ... 212-817-7500 ... 327 B
vdeluca@gc.cuny.edu

DELUCAS, Vicki ... 740-588-1441 ... 400 E
delucas@ohio.edu

DELUCCHI, Jennifer ... 916-568-3039 ... 55 J
deluccj@losrios.edu

DELUGACH, Harry, S ... 256-824-6614 ... 8 G
harry.delugach@uah.edu

DELUNAS, Linda ... 219-980-6643 ... 174 B
ldelunas@iun.edu

DELVECCHIO, Edie ... 201-200-3159 ... 312 B
edelvecchio@njcu.edu

DELVENTHAL, Bruce, W ... 518-564-3140 ... 354 B
delvenbw@plattsburgh.edu

DELVISCIO, Gregory ... 607-777-2175 ... 351 F
gregdelv@binghamton.edu

DELYSER, Susan ... 315-279-5247 ... 337 K
sdelyser@mail.keuka.edu

DELZEIT, Greg ... 785-442-6039 ... 193 F
gdelzeit@highlandcc.edu

DEMA, Anne, C ... 816-415-5912 ... 293 C
demaa@william.jewell.edu

DEMAIO, Charles, P ... 812-514-8446 ... 173 B
cdemaio@indstatefoundation.org

DEMAIO, Dennis ... 657-278-2900 ... 35 B
ddemaio@fullerton.edu

DEMARCO, Deborah ... 508-856-2903 ... 237 C
deborah.demarco@umassmed.edu

DEMARESKI, Roger ... 609-258-8022 ... 312 G
rogerd@princeton.edu

DEMAREST, David, F ... 650-724-8887 ... 71 G
demarest@stanford.edu

DEMAREST, Geralynn ... 518-828-4181 ... 330 E
demarest@sunycgcc.edu

DEMARK, Paul ... 707-476-4358 ... 42 C
paul-demark@redwoods.edu

DEMARKEY, Nina ... 714-484-7188 ... 59 D
ndemarkey@cypresscollege.edu

DEMARTE, Daniel ... 757-822-1061 ... 528 G
ddemarte@tcc.edu

DEMASTERS, Janice ... 314-991-6200 ... 279 H
jdemasters@chamberlain.edu

DEMATTEO, Jeanne ... 925-631-4123 ... 64 F
jdematte@stmarys-ca.edu

DEMAYO, Andrea ... 518-244-2427 ... 348 A
demaya@sage.edu

DEMBECK, Brian, B ... 443-997-3728 ... 223 F
bdembeck@jhu.edu

DEMBOSKY, Cassandra, C 607-255-3203 ... 331 B
ccd3@cornell.edu

DEMBOSKY, Deborah ... 910-630-7522 ... 367 B
driley@methodist.edu

DEMBY, Harod, C ... 919-516-4593 ... 376 D
hcdemby@st-aug.edu

DEMCIE, Christine ... 716-829-7688 ... 332 E
demciec@dyc.edu

DEMCZUK, Bernard ... 202-994-1000 ... 98 C
bdemczuk@gwu.edu

DEMEDEIROS, Joe ... 512-233-1443 ... 493 E
joed@stedwards.edu

DEMEIS, Debra ... 781-283-2322 ... 245 E
ddemeis@wellesley.edu

DEMELLO, Kenneth ... 509-533-3555 ... 533 C

DEMENT, Jennifer ... 503-491-7385 ... 417 B
jennifer.dement@mhcc.edu

DEMENT, Mary ... 870-762-3113 ... 20 A
mdement@smail.anc.edu

DEMENT, Paul ... 732-263-5679 ... 311 E
pdement@monmouth.edu

DEMERCHANT, Doug, B ... 630-752-5321 ... 168 H
doug.demerchant@wheaton.edu

DEMERITT, Linda, C ... 814-332-3393 ... 421 F
linda.demeritt@allegheny.edu

DEMERRITT, Stan ... 806-291-3415 ... 508 E
demerritt@wbu.edu

DEMERS, David ... 413-565-1000 ... 230 G
ddemers@baypath.edu

DEMERS, Mary ... 207-941-7131 ... 218 A
demersm@husson.edu

DEMERS, Paul ... 603-897-8537 ... 305 F
pdemers@rivier.edu

DEMERS, Susan, S ... 727-791-2501 ... 116 H
demers.susan@spcollege.edu

DEMERS, Suzanne ... 863-784-7041 ... 117 J
suzanne.demers@southflorida.edu

DEMERVE, Steeve ... 727-723-1037 ... 107 D

DEMES, Dennis ... 561-732-4424 ... 117 B
ddemes@svdp.edu

DEMETRIOU, Sophia ... 212-925-6625 ... 326 G
sdemetriou@ccny.cuny.edu

DEMETRULIAS, Diana ... 650-508-3494 ... 59 H
ddemetrulias@ndnu.edu

DEMIANCZYK, Jacquie ... 412-291-6286 ... 422 E
jdemianczyk@aii.edu

DEMICHAEL, Mark ... 765-677-2317 ... 175 B
mark.demichael@indwes.edu

DEMING, Elizabeth ... 229-430-3693 ... 124 B
edeming@albanytech.edu

DEMING, Els ... 253-840-8401 ... 536 H
edeming@pierce.ctc.edu

DEMING, Ronald ... 731-352-4232 ... 467 E
demingr@bethelu.edu

DEMIRCAY, Vuslat ... 619-684-8858 ... 59 B
vdemircay@newschoolarch.edu

DEMITH, Lindsey ... 727-725-2688 ... 106 F
ldemith@cci.edu

DEMITSAS, Yiani ... 260-422-5561 ... 173 C
jdemitsas@indianatech.edu

DEMLEITNER, Nora, V ... 540-458-8502 ... 530 D
demleitnern@wlu.edu

DEMMINGS, Elizabeth ... 765-658-4220 ... 171 B
betsydemmings@depauw.edu

DEMO, Tina ... 860-509-9549 ... 93 A
tdemo@hartsem.edu

DEMOSS, Brian ... 209-588-5222 ... 80 G
demossb@yosemite.edu

DEMOTT, Robin ... 309-341-5221 ... 146 D
rdemott@sandburg.edu

DEMPSEY, Connie ... 570-961-4692 ... 17 D
connie.dempsey@pennfoster.edu

DEMPSEY, Grace ... 909-537-5005 ... 36 B

DEMPSEY, Greg ... 206-934-5378 ... 537 F
greg.dempsey@seattlecolleges.edu

DEMPSEY, John, G ... 217-333-2500 ... 167 D
jgdempse@illinois.edu

DEMPSEY, John, R ... 910-695-3700 ... 373 H
dempseyj@sandhills.edu

DEMPSEY, JR ... 312-553-2500 ... 147 B
jdempsey@ccc.edu

DEMPSEY, Kelly, J ... 608-757-6328 ... 553 G
kdempsey@blackhawk.edu

DEMPSEY, Marianne ... 301-447-5330 ... 225 A
dempsey@msmary.edu

DEMPSEY, Michael ... 207-893-7891 ... 219 F
mdempsey@sjcme.edu

DEMPSEY, Michael ... 845-848-4058 ... 332 B
michael.dempsey@dc.edu

DEMPSEY, Patricia ... 410-972-4511 ... 225 G
patricia.dempsey@sjca.edu

DEMPSEY, Richard ... 972-883-2141 ... 506 A
rmdempsey@utdallas.edu

DEMPSEY, Robert ... 718-289-5705 ... 326 E
robert.dempsey@bcc.cuny.edu

DEMPSEY, Ron ... 816-415-5034 ... 293 C
dempseyr@william.jewell.edu

DEMPSEY, Ron, D ... 678-915-7351 ... 137 G
dempsey@spsu.edu

DEMPSEY, Sarah ... 269-927-6188 ... 253 G
sdempsey@lakemichigancollege.edu

DEMPSEY, Van, O ... 304-367-4241 ... 543 H
van.dempsey@fairmontstate.edu

DEMPSEY, Wayne, W ... 770-531-3116 ... 126 E
wdempsey@brenau.edu

DEMPSEY, William ... 610-683-4575 ... 443 A
dempsey@kutztown.edu

DEMPSTER, Douglas, J ... 512-471-9601 ... 505 D
ddempster@austin.utexas.edu

DEMROVSKY, Amy ... 303-797-5753 ... 81 D
amy.demrovsky@arapahoe.edu

DEMSKI, Gary ... 574-520-4457 ... 174 E
gdemski@iusb.edu

DEMURANT, Joanna ... 518-828-4181 ... 330 E
joanna.demurant@sunycgcc.edu

DEMUTH, Paul ... 651-423-8370 ... 266 B
paul.demuth@dctc.edu

DEN HARTOG, Douglas ... 510-783-2100 ... 49 J
ddenhartog@heald.edu

DENARD, Jeffrey, D ... 630-637-5142 ... 159 G
jddenard@noctrl.edu

DENARD, Letitia ... 404-270-5143 ... 138 B
ldenard@spelman.edu

DENARDO, Arlina, B ... 610-330-5055 ... 433 B
denardoa@lafayette.edu

DENARDO, John ... 312-413-8202 ... 167 B
jdenardo@uic.edu

DENARDO, Melissa, D ... 724-480-3439 ... 426 A
melissa.denardo@ccbc.edu

DENBOER, Marten ... 909-869-3443 ... 33 J
mdenboer@csupomona.edu

DENBOW, Gary, A ... 417-833-2551 ... 279 E
gdenbow@cbcag.edu

DENBY, Eric, N ... 434-924-4019 ... 525 F
end@virginia.edu

DENBY, Karlene ... 281-487-1170 ... 499 B
kdenby@txchiro.edu

DENDY, David ... 563-589-3618 ... 189 F
ddendy@dbq.edu

DENDY, Larry, C ... 252-493-7239 ... 372 H
ldendy@email.pittcc.edu

DENEEN, Linda ... 218-726-7588 ... 271 F
ldeneen@d.umn.edu

DENG, Yi ... 704-687-8450 ... 379 A
yi.deng@uncc.edu

DENHAM, Cynthia ... 256-840-4133 ... 7 A
cdenham@snead.edu

DENHAM, Kerrigann ... 217-757-1190 ... 322 H
kdenham@funeraleducation.org

DENHAM, Rena, B ... 541-956-7279 ... 420 B
rdenham@roguecc.edu

DENHAM, Scott, D ... 704-894-2855 ... 363 I
scdenham@davidson.edu

DENHART, Rich ... 608-663-2000 ... 548 C
rdenhart@mediainstitute.edu

DENHEETEN, Kathryn ... 989-775-4123 ... 257 F
denheeten.katy@sagchip.edu

DENHOLM, Jack ... 701-845-7160 ... 382 C
jack.denholm@vcsu.edu

DENIO, John ... 518-694-7263 ... 322 B
john.denio@acphs.edu

DENIO, John ... 401-232-6140 ... 453 C
jdenio@bryant.edu

DENIS, Alex ... 954-201-7405 ... 102 E
adenis@broward.edu

DENISON, Bronda ... 334-670-5843 ... 8 A
bdenison@troy.edu

DENKER, Audria ... 502-410-6200 ... 200 L
adenker@galencollege.edu

DENKER, Lee ... 402-554-2444 ... 301 A
ldenker@unomaha.edu

DENLINGER, Ann ... 919-508-2395 ... 380 E
adenlinger@peace.edu

DENLINGER, Tammy ... 574-372-5100 ... 171 H
denlintl@grace.edu

DENLY, David ... 620-229-6104 ... 196 G
david.denly@sckans.edu

DENMAN, Bob, G ... 501-569-3194 ... 24 E
bgdenman@ualr.edu

DENMAN, Ellie ... 601-977-0960 ... 278 A
ellie.denman@vc.edu

DENMARK, Robert, M ... 973-972-5410 ... 317 B
denmarrm@umdnj.edu

DENNA, Eric ... 801-581-3100 ... 511 C
eric.denna@utah.edu

DENNE, Cynthia, K ... 909-593-3511 ... 75 E
cdenne@laverne.edu

DENNEE, Mary Jo, R ... 716-851-1999 ... 333 A
dennee@ecc.edu

DENNEHY, Michael ... 972-860-4607 ... 484 G
mdennehy@dcccd.edu

DENNEY, Carolyn ... 509-527-2811 ... 539 C
carolyn.denney@wallawalla.edu

DENNEY, James ... 662-329-7462 ... 276 A
jdenney@vpaa.muw.edu

DENNEY, Karen ... 828-627-4546 ... 371 C
kdenney@haywood.edu

DENNEY, Martha ... 610-896-1232 ... 430 G
mdenney@haverford.edu

DENNING, CSC, John ... 508-565-1363 ... 245 A
jdenning@stonehill.edu

DENNING, Rusty ... 864-941-8417 ... 460 D
denning.r@ptc.edu

DENNIS, Anne ... 515-643-6640 ... 187 F
adennis@mercydesmoines.org

DENNIS, Anthony ... 513-861-6400 ... 402 I
tony.dennis@myunion.edu

DENNIS, Dave, D ... 319-363-8213 ... 187 H
ddennis@mtmercy.edu

DENNIS, Denise ... 973-748-9000 ... 307 H
denise_bane@bloomfield.edu

DENNIS, Diana ... 815-753-2111 ... 160 B
ddennis@niu.edu

DENNIS, Dixie ... 931-221-7414 ... 473 E
dennisdi@apsu.edu

DENNIS, Eric ... 316-448-3150 ... 464 H
edennis@national.edu

DENNIS, Jack ... 410-617-2444 ... 223 I
jdennis@loyola.edu

DENNIS, James, M ... 618-537-6936 ... 158 A
jdennis@mckendree.edu

DENNIS, Jeff ... 864-644-5521 ... 461 B
jdennis@swu.edu

DENNIS, Larry ... 850-644-5775 ... 119 D
ldennis@ci.fsu.edu

DENNIS, Peggy ... 419-372-8495 ... 385 E
fayed@bgsu.edu

DENNIS, Raymond, A ... 310-338-5994 ... 56 E
rdennis@lmu.edu

DENNIS, Roger, J ... 215-571-4755 ... 427 H
rjd45@drexel.edu

DENNIS, Sheryl ... 903-566-7222 ... 506 E
sdennis@uttyler.edu

DENNIS, Suzanne ... 718-780-7912 ... 324 F
suzanne.dennis@brooklaw.edu

DENNIS, Terry ... 863-680-3937 ... 109 E
vdennis@flsouthern.edu

DENNIS-PHILLIPS, Ruth ... 336-517-2207 ... 362 G
rdphillips@bennett.edu

DENNISON, Anne ... 207-775-3052 ... 218 E
adennison@meca.edu

DENNISON, Corley, F ... 304-696-2360 ... 544 B
dennisoc@marshall.edu

DENNISON, George ... 303-534-6290 ... 83 E
george.dennison@colostate.edu

DENNISON, Lyn ... 706-821-8253 ... 135 G
ldennison@paine.edu

DENNISON, Manifa ... 231-777-5261 ... 248 E
manifa.dennison@baker.edu

DENNISON, Marla, K ... 651-631-5395 ... 270 B
mkdennison@nwc.edu

DENNISON, Rodney ... 239-489-9248 ... 105 F
rdennison@edison.edu

DENNISON, T. Wayne ... 770-499-3151 ... 133 A
wdenniso@kennesaw.edu

DENNISTON, Julia, M ... 305-341-6600 ... 102 F
jdenniston@brownmackie.edu

DENNISTON, Mark ... 937-382-6661 ... 405 I
mark_denniston@wilmington.edu

DENNISTON, Marsha ... 605-331-6633 ... 466 E
marsha.denniston@usiouxfalls.edu

DENNISTON, Terry ... 423-425-4203 ... 477 F
terry-denniston@utc.edu

DENNY, David ... 503-699-6313 ... 416 J
ddenny@marylhurst.edu

DENON, Gregory ... 617-989-4112 ... 245 F
denong@wit.edu

DENSBERGER, Derek ... 714-556-3610 ... 77 B
ddensberger@vanguard.edu

DEUTER, Clayton 605-995-7132 464 F clayton.deuter@mitchelltech.edu

DEUTSCH, Gail, S 714-449-7459 70 G gdeutsch@scco.edu

DEUTSCH, Thomas, A 312-942-5567 163 D thomas_deutsch@rush.edu

DEUTSCH, Yeruchem 718-963-9770 359 A ed@utsb.org

DEVALL, Wendy 225-216-8503 209 H devallw@mybrcc.edu

DEVAN, Rhonda, K 828-694-1716 368 E r_devan@blueridge.edu

DEVANE, Larry, F 405-422-1260 411 G devanel@redlandscc.edu

DEVANEY, Barbara, J 207-768-9750 220 F barbara.devaney@umpi.edu

DEVANI, Jeani 617-217-9066 231 A jdevani@baystate.edu

DEVANTIER, Paul 314-505-7257 280 D devantierp@csl.edu

DEVAUGHN, Gerald 803-780-1265 463 C gdevaughn@voorhees.edu

DEVAULT, Sylvia, Y 812-488-2239 180 E sy5@evansville.edu

DEVAUX, April, A 585-785-1634 334 A devauxaa@flcc.edu

DEVEAU, Laura, A 617-353-3540 232 E ladeveau@bu.edu

DEVEAU, Shawn 409-772-9803 507 C sjdeveau@utmb.edu

DEVENNY, Marianne 815-455-8716 157 H mdevenny@mchenry.edu

DEVENS, Philip 401-232-6119 453 C revdev@bryant.edu

DEVER, Carolyn 615-322-2851 478 A carolyn.dever@vanderbilt.edu

DEVER, David 310-434-4384 68 D dever_david@smc.edu

DEVER, John, T 757-825-2711 528 F deverj@tncc.edu

DEVER, Michael, K 517-750-1200 258 D miked@arbor.edu

DEVER, Susan 310-900-1600 45 F dever_s@compton.edu

DEVEREAUX, Kent 206-726-5029 533 D kdevereaux@cornish.edu

DEVEREAUX, Martin, C 561-237-7151 113 D mdevereaux@lynn.edu

DEVERES, Georgette 909-621-8088 40 G georgette.deveres@cmc.edu

DEVERS, James 570-941-6267 450 C james.devers@sranton.edu

DEVERS, Monica 320-308-4894 269 A mcdevers@stcloudstate.edu

DEVERS-JONES, Caitlin 727-784-0003 103 B cdeversjones@cfi.edu

DEVERSE, Nancy 360-538-4030 534 G ndeverse@ghc.edu

DEVERTEUIL, Johanna 863-638-2914 123 E deverteuilj@webber.edu

DEVERY, Dennis 609-777-5693 316 A ddevery@tesc.edu

DEVESTERN, Diane 610-436-3511 444 A ddevestern@wcupa.edu

DEVICO, Barbara, F 617-287-7008 236 E bdevico@umassp.edu

DEVICTORIA, Carol 516-686-7476 343 D cdevicto@nyit.edu

DEVIER, David, H 937-328-6026 387 H devierd@clarkstate.edu

DEVILBISS, John, W 435-797-1358 511 E john.devilbiss@usu.edu

DEVILBISS, Mark, B 937-327-7808 406 B mdevilbiss@wittenberg.edu

DEVINCENTIS, Mark 585-340-9501 329 F mdevincentis@crcds.edu

DEVINE, Dennis 406-771-5140 295 G dennis.devine@msugf.edu

DEVINE, Flora, B 770-499-3562 133 A fdevine@kennesaw.edu

DEVINE, Frederick, R 336-316-2134 365 A fdevine@guilford.edu

DEVINE, Jane 718-482-5421 328 B jane@lagcc.cuny.edu

DEVINE, Linda, W 813-253-6203 123 A ldevine@ut.edu

DEVINE, Mary 218-846-3711 267 D mary.devine@minnesota.edu

DEVINE, Michelle 989-275-5000 253 E michelle.devine@kirtland.edu

DEVINE, Scott, W 240-895-4295 226 A swdevine@smcm.edu

DEVITO, Felix 508-588-9100 240 A

DEVITO, Jennifer 516-918-3628 324 E jdevito@bcl.edu

DEVITO, Paul, L 610-660-3261 446 C pdevito@sju.edu

DEVITO, William, J 215-951-1326 432 I devito@lasalle.edu

DEVITTO, John 704-272-5333 374 A jdevitto@spcc.edu

DEVIVO, Sharon, B 718-429-6600 359 G sharon.devivo@vaughn.edu

DEVLIN, Diane, M 617-627-5878 245 C diane.devlin@tufts.edu

DEVLIN, George, A 803-705-4417 455 D devling@benedict.edu

DEVLIN, Jeffrey 740-588-1242 407 A jdevlin@zanestate.ed

DEVLIN, Susan, L 860-701-5161 93 E devlin_s@mitchell.edu

DEVLIN, Thomas, C 510-642-3461 73 H tcd@berkeley.edu

DEVOE, Michele 973-618-3484 308 C mdevoe@caldwell.edu

DEVOE HEIDMAN, Sheila 520-515-5362 13 E heidmans@cochise.edu

DEVORE, Brett 563-425-5248 189 G devoreb@uiu.edu

DEVORE, Cynthia 651-793-1466 267 A cynthia.devore@metrostate.edu

DEVORE, Janice, G 217-424-3524 158 G jdevore@millikin.edu

DEVORE, Victor 619-660-4323 49 B victor.devore@gcccd.edu

DEVORE, William 847-543-2640 148 B bdevore@clcillinois.edu

DEVOS, Edward 617-327-6777 241 F edward_devos@mspp.edu

DEVOSS, David, V 270-809-2222 205 A public.safety@murraystate.edu

DEVRIES, Eileen, A 845-451-1323 331 E e_devrie@culinary.edu

DEVRIES, II, Henry, E 616-526-6148 249 A hdevries@calvin.edu

DEVRIES, Janet 307-268-2662 556 A jdevries@caspercollege.edu

DEVRIES, Kathleen 303-914-6326 87 G kathleen.devries@rrcc.edu

DEVRIES, Lora 712-722-6422 184 C ldevries@dordt.edu

DEVRIES, Warren, R 410-455-3270 227 D wdevries@umbc.edu

DEW, Beverley 804-594-1479 527 B bdew@jtcc.edu

DEW, John, R 334-670-5991 8 A jrdew@troy.edu

DEWAARD, Chad 573-277-6694 280 I cdewaard@culver.edu

DEWALD, Barb 712-707-7192 188 D bdewald@nwciowa.edu

DEWALD, Daryll 509-335-5548 539 D daryll.dewald@wsu.edu

DEWALD, Janice, P 214-828-8341 497 C jdewald@bcd.tamhsc.edu

DEWALT, Ardie 212-220-8141 326 D adewalt@bmcc.cuny.edu

DEWALT, Carol 603-668-6660 305 B

DEWALT, Marie 304-876-5299 544 C mdewalt@shepherd.edu

DEWAN, Craig 315-866-0300 335 D dewancp@herkimer.edu

DEWAN, Sue 518-464-8673 333 E sdewan@excelsior.edu

DEWBERRY, Angela 404-471-6306 123 I adewberry@agnesscott.edu

DEWBERRY, Angela, B 704-894-2227 363 I andewberry@davidson.edu

DEWBERRY, Thomas 541-683-5141 416 A cdewberry@gutenberg.edu

DEWBRE, Dane 806-894-9611 494 G ddewbre@southplainscollege.edu

DEWBRE, Jeri Ann 806-894-9611 494 G jdewbre@southplainscollege.edu

DEWEERTH, Jennifer 315-731-5818 341 E jdeweerth@mvcc.edu

DEWEES, Bridget 803-535-5793 456 D bdewees@claflin.edu

DEWEES, Deborah 360-560-3353 539 F deborah.dewees@wwu.edu

DEWEES, Julie 309-298-1800 168 C jk-dewees@wiu.edu

DEWEESE, Kass 580-477-7769 414 C kass.deweese@wosc.edu

DEWEESE, Sam 812-330-6260 175 J sdeweese@ivytech.edu

DEWET, Carol 717-291-3985 429 F carol.dewet@fandm.edu

DEWEY, Amy 610-526-1000 422 A amy.dewey@theamericancollege.edu

DEWEY, Barbara, I 814-865-0401 438 G bid1@psu.edu

DEWEY, Gregory 909-593-3511 75 E gdewey@laverne.edu

DEWEY, Gwen 206-264-9100 531 D gwend@bgu.edu

DEWEY, Marvin 620-278-4290 196 H mdewey@sterling.edu

DEWEY, Phyllis, K 716-926-8930 335 E pdewey@hilbert.edu

DEWEY, Susan 607-844-8222 357 I deweys@tc3.edu

DEWEY, Susan 501-977-2084 25 G dewey@uaccm.edu

DEWINE, Sue 812-866-7056 172 A dewine@hanover.edu

DEWINTER, Naomi 231-348-6618 256 B ndewinter@ncmich.edu

DEWIS, Rob 408-855-5327 78 F rob.dewis@wvm.edu

DEWITT, Bob 937-769-1852 384 A bdewitt@antioch.edu

DEWITT, Brenda, E 740-368-3329 400 G bedewitt@owu.edu

DEWITT, Charles, B 615-353-3346 475 E charles.dewitt@nscc.edu

DEWITT, Dan 502-897-4555 206 C ddewitt@sbts.edu

DEWITT, David 301-784-5000 221 B ddewitt@allegany.edu

DEWITT, Deborah, S 937-327-7001 406 B ddewitt@wittenberg.edu

DEWITT, Jean 713-221-5553 503 F dewittj@uhd.edu

DEWITT, Matt 314-837-6777 288 C mdewitt@slcconline.edu

DEWITT, Sara 206-393-3531 531 A sdewitt@argosy.edu

DEWITT, Siobhan, K 412-578-6651 424 I skdewitt@carlow.edu

DEWOLF, Sheridan 619-644-7158 49 C sheridan.dewolf@gcccd.edu

DEWOLF, William 617-824-8655 234 B william_dewolf@emerson.edu

DEWOLFE, Sandra 408-270-6448 67 C sandra.dewolfe@evc.edu

DEWOLFE, Sandra 408-274-7900 67 C sandra.dewolfe@evc.edu

DEWOODY, Susan 479-524-7371 22 C sdewoody@jbu.edu

DEWSNUP, Vicky 801-622-1569 510 K vicky.dewsnup@stevenshenager.edu

DEXTER, Ann 781-891-2640 231 D adexter@bentley.edu

DEXTER, Brian 509-542-4727 532 H bdexter@columbiabasin.edu

DEXTER, Karen, B 816-604-2217 285 C karen.dexter@mcckc.edu

DEXTER, Kathleen, A 207-621-3153 220 B dexter@maine.edu

DEXTER-HARRIS, Roz 904-632-3375 109 F rdexter@fscj.edu

DEXTER-WILSON, Elizabeth 251-380-3470 7 E edexterwilson@shc.edu

DEY, Farouk 412-268-2064 424 J fdey@andrew.cmu.edu

DEY, Kate 415-703-9575 32 C

DEYER, Carole, A 586-286-2147 254 C deyerc@macomb.edu

DEYOUNG, Gene 916-577-2200 79 G gdeyoung@jessup.edu

DEYOUNG, Michael 702-968-2006 303 D mdeyoung@roseman.edu

DEYOUNG, Paul 503-777-7290 420 A paul.deyoung@reed.edu

DEYOUNG, Renee 231-439-6347 256 B rdeyoung@ncmich.edu

DEZEMBER, Mary 575-835-5172 319 A dezember@nmt.edu

DEZENBERG, Maria 253-943-2800 533 F mdezenberg@devry.edu

DHANAK, Manhar 954-924-7242 119 A dhanak@fau.edu

DHANKHER, Veena 978-630-9597 240 C

DHAWAN, Atam, P 973-642-7664 312 C atam.p.dhawan

DHILLON, Upinder, S 607-777-2314 351 F dhillon@binghamton.edu

DHILLON, Vineeta 707-654-1086 33 C vdhillon@csum.edu

DHINGRA, Ashok 727-873-4287 121 C adhingra@mail.usf.edu

DHIR, Vijay, K 310-825-8507 74 C vdhir@seas.ucla.edu

DI DONATO, Ana 352-588-8992 116 G ana.didonato@saintleo.edu

DI FAVA, John 617-252-1703 241 D

DI GIACOMO, Michael 610-917-3949 450 E m_digiacomo@vfcc.edu

DI GUILIO, Raymond 916-484-8483 56 A diguilr@arc.losrios.edu

DI LELLO, Joseph 914-968-6200 349 D joseph.dilello@archny.org

DI LULLO, Trish 256-233-8184 1 E trish.dilullo@athens.edu

DI MARE, Lesley 719-549-2951 83 H presidentsoffice@colostate-pueblo.edu

DI NALLO, Benjamin 201-559-3507 310 B dinallob@felician.edu

DI NARDI, Jason 914-594-4668 343 F jason_dinardi@nymc.edu

DI NUCCI, Jo Ellen 208-426-1200 142 I jedinucc@boisestate.edu

DI PASQUALE, Ray 401-825-2188 453 D rmdipasquale@ccri.edu

DI RADDO, Colleen 302-736-2420 97 A diraddo@wesley.edu

DIAB, Dorey 330-494-6170 402 B ddiab@starkstate.edu

DIACON, Todd 330-672-8529 393 D tdiacon@kent.edu

DIAH, Max 516-773-5684 558 I diahm@usmma.edu

DIAL, Bill 303-914-6298 87 G bill.dial@rrcc.edu

DIAL, Cortez, K 804-524-5070 529 H cdial@vsu.edu

DIAL, Eugene, A 985-448-4021 216 A eugene.dial@nicholls.edu

DIAL, Sheila 407-226-6438 104 K sdial@devry.edu

DIAMOND, Alice 617-349-8550 236 B adiamond@lesley.edu

DIAMOND, Beverly, E 843-953-5528 457 B diamondb@cofc.edu

DIAMOND, Christopher, R 860-832-1934 90 G diamondchr@ccsu.edu

DIAMOND, Fred 626-914-8691 40 B fdiamond@citruscollege.edu

DIAMOND, Holly 313-845-9887 252 B hadiamond@hfcc.edu

DIAMOND, John, N 479-575-2000 24 C diamond@uark.edu

DIAMOND, Raymond, T 225-578-8846 213 C

DIAMOND BURROWAY, Sarah 606-326-2106 201 F sdiamondburrowa0001@kctc.edu

DIANA, Kate 952-888-4777 270 C kdiana@nwhealth.edu

DIANDA, Lisa 209-473-5217 50 E lisa_dianda@heald.edu

DIANGELO, JR., Joseph, A 610-660-1645 446 C jodiange@sju.edu

DIAS, James 518-956-8170 351 E jdias@uamail.albany.edu

DIAS, Margaret, S 508-999-8791 237 A mdias@umassd.edu

DIAS, Robert 408-270-6400 67 B robert.dias@sjeccd.org

DIAWARA, Patricia 719-549-3058 87 F patricia.diawara@pueblocc.edu

DIAZ, Aida 787-720-4476 566 D serviciocristiano@colmizpa.edu

DIAZ, Alfred 787-725-8120 562 C adiaz@eap.edu

DIAZ, Allison 980-598-1016 365 I allison.diaz@jwu.edu

DIAZ, Alphonso, V 765-494-9705 178 J avdiaz@purdue.edu

DIAZ, Amy 815-921-4283 162 H a.diaz@rockvalleycollege.edu

DIAZ, Andrea 401-254-3317 454 C adiaz@rwu.edu

DIAZ, Armando 210-567-0372 507 A diaza@uthscsa.edu

DIAZ, Carmen Marie 920-686-6372 550 H carmenmarie.diaz@sl.edu

DIAZ, Deborah 407-447-7300 110 A ddiaz@ftccollege.edu

DIAZ, Emiliano 916-278-3901 36 A diaz@csus.edu

DIAZ, Fernando 773-995-2259 146 G fdiaz@csu.edu

DIAZ, Francisco 973-720-3244 317 D diazf@wpunj.edu

DIAZ, Franco, L 787-284-1912 564 A fldiaz@ponce.inter.edu

DIAZ, Glenda 787-250-1912 563 G gdiaz@metro.inter.edu

DIAZ, Gloria 787-764-0000 568 B gloria.diaz5@upr.edu

DIAZ, J. Lionel 480-731-8233 15 D lionel.diaz@domail.maricopa.edu

DIAZ, Jackie 254-710-3805 482 A jackie_diaz@baylor.edu

DIAZ, Jacob 206-296-6155 538 B diazj@seattleu.edu

DIAZ, Janet 313-883-8696 257 E diaz.janet@shms.edu

DIAZ, Javier 787-834-9595 566 B jdiaz@uaa.edu

DIAZ, Jesus, A 787-751-0178 565 F ac_jdiaz@suagm.edu

DIAZ, Jo Ann 843-953-5580 457 B diazv@cofc.edu

DIAZ, Joel 805-986-5810 77 E jdiaz@vcccd.edu

DIAZ, Jorge 787-786-3030 560 G jdiaz@ucb.edu.pr

DIAZ, Joseph 801-957-4043 512 D joseph.diaz@slcc.edu

DIAZ, Leticia, M 321-206-5602 101 M ldiaz@mail.barry.edu

DIAZ, Linda 201-529-7461 313 C ldiaz@ramapo.edu

DIAZ, Lourdes 787-284-1912 564 A ldiaz@ponce.inter.edu

DIAZ, Maria, S 787-257-7373 565 G ue_mdiaz@suagm.edu

DIAZ, Mark 305-284-2862 122 I markdiaz@miami.edu

DIAZ, Mischelle, R 512-448-8404 493 E mischeld@stedwards.edu

DIAZ, Paula .... 312-935-3033 .... 162 G
pdiaz@robertmorris.edu
DIAZ, Ramonita .... 787-878-5475 .... 563 B
rdiaz@arecibo.inter.edu
DIAZ, Robert .... 212-220-8305 .... 326 D
rdiaz@bmcc.cuny.edu
DIAZ, Roberto .... 215-893-5252 .... 426 E
DIAZ, Russell .... 845-848-4048 .... 332 B
russell.diaz@dc.edu
DIAZ, Ruth, M .... 787-763-6700 .... 562 D
rmdiaz@se-pr.edu
DIAZ, Sam .... 570-504-9069 .... 425 F
DIAZ, Sharon, C .... 510-869-6512 .... 64 J
sdiaz@samuelmerritt.edu
DIAZ, Sonia .... 787-728-1515 .... 568 D
sdiaz@sagrado.edu
DIAZ, Tatiana, A .... 717-766-2511 .... 436 D
tdiaz@messiah.edu
DIAZ, Walter .... 956-665-3551 .... 506 C
diazwr@utpa.edu
DIAZ-ALONSO, Hernan ..... 213-613-2200 .... 70 H
hernan@sciarc.edu
DIAZ-BONACQUISTI, Judi 303-556-4498 .... 86 F
jbonacqu@msudenver.edu
DIAZ-DIAZ, Judith .... 787-993-8957 .... 567 B
judith.diaz2@upr.edu
DIAZ-HERRERA, Jorge, L .. 315-279-5201 .... 337 K
jdiazh@mail.keuka.edu
DIAZ-RODRIGUEZ,
Nereida .... 787-798-6732 .... 566 C
nereida.diaz@uccaribe.edu
DIBARI, Diane .... 415-955-2107 .... 27 F
ddibari@alliant.edu
DIBB, Andrew M, T .... 267-502-2582 .... 423 C
andrew.dibb@brynathyn.edu
DIBBERT, Douglas, S .... 919-962-7050 .... 378 E
doug_dibbert@unc.edu
DIBBINI, Murad .... 510-436-1430 .... 50 H
dibbini@hnu.edu
DIBBLE, Emily .... 617-228-2412 .... 239 C
dibble@bhcc.mass.edu
DIBELLO, Nan, M .... 716-686-7800 .... 355 G
nan.dibello@esc.edu
DIBENEDETTO, Eileen, M .. 212-854-7732 .... 323 E
edibened@barnard.edu
DIBENEDETTO, Steve .... 847-947-5409 .... 159 E
steve.dibenedetto@nl.edu
DIBIASIO, Daniel, A .... 419-772-2030 .... 398 H
d-dibiasio@onu.edu
DIBISCEGLIE, Lisa .... 973-618-3280 .... 308 C
ldibi@caldwell.edu
DIBLEY, Paula .... 704-216-3467 .... 373 F
paula.dibley@rccc.edu
DIBONIFAZIO, Susan .... 570-408-4000 .... 452 A
susan.dibonifazio@wilkes.edu
DIBRIGIDA, Vladimir .... 303-329-6355 .... 83 D
director@cstcm.edu
DIBRITO, Kyle, J .... 717-221-1300 .... 430 E
kjdibrit@hacc.edu
DICAMILLO, Thomas .... 520-494-5204 .... 13 D
tom.dicamillo@centralaz.edu
DICAPRIO, Deborah, A .... 845-575-3000 .... 340 B
deborah.dicaprio@marist.edu
DICARLO, Michael .... 318-257-2577 .... 215 F
miked@latech.edu
DICARLO, Sandra, V .... 419-372-0648 .... 385 F
sandrad@bgsu.edu
DICARO, Kim .... 313-496-2625 .... 259 G
kdicaro1@wcccd.edu
DICE, Douglas .... 989-463-7162 .... 247 B
dice@alma.edu
DICE, Frances .... 412-237-3064 .... 425 H
fdice@ccac.edu
DICESARE, Deborah, A .... 818-778-5522 .... 55 E
dicesad@lavc.edu
DICHRISTINA, Joseph, J ... 814-332-4356 .... 421 F
joseph.dichristina@allegheny.edu
DICK, Beth .... 231-777-0314 .... 256 A
DICK, Larry .... 956-380-8179 .... 493 D
ldick@riogrande.edu
DICK, Larry .... 956-380-8179 .... 493 D
personnel@riogrande.edu
DICK, Nancy .... 425-739-8228 .... 535 H
nancy.dick@lwtc.edu
DICKASON, John .... 909-447-2512 .... 40 H
jdickason@cst.edu
DICKENS, Brian, K .... 713-313-1379 .... 500 B
dickensbk@tsu.edu
DICKENS, Margaret, A .... 715-833-6419 .... 553 H
mdickens@cvtc.edu
DICKENS, Martha .... 828-398-7302 .... 368 B
mdickens@abtech.edu
DICKENS, Reginald .... 903-730-4890 .... 489 C
rdickens@jarvis.edu
DICKENS, Robert, E .... 775-784-1417 .... 303 A
robertd@unr.edu
DICKENS, Susan .... 651-779-3298 .... 266 A
susan.dickens@century.edu
DICKENS, Tony .... 419-720-6670 .... 401 C
tdickens@proskills.edu
DICKENSON, Debra, L .... 703-726-4200 .... 98 C
ddickens@gwu.edu
DICKER, James, W .... 610-330-5021 .... 433 B
dickerj@lafayette.edu
DICKERMAN,
Christopher, M .... 610-359-5302 .... 426 G
cdickerman@dccc.edu
DICKERMAN, Robert .... 413-755-4606 .... 241 B
dickerman@stcc.edu
DICKERSON, Bill .... 281-998-6150 .... 493 G
bill.dickerson@sjcd.edu
DICKERSON, Cathy, S .... 540-375-2262 .... 523 G
cdickerson@roanoke.edu
DICKERSON, Darby .... 806-742-3990 .... 502 A
DICKERSON, Dee Ann .... 918-647-1300 .... 407 E
ddickerson@carlalbert.edu
DICKERSON, Donna .... 903-566-7447 .... 506 E
ddickerson@uttyler.edu
DICKERSON, John .... 601-849-0112 .... 273 G
john.dickerson@colin.edu
DICKERSON, Larry .... 816-802-3363 .... 283 E
ldickerson@kcai.edu
DICKERSON, Mark .... 626-387-5763 .... 30 G
mdickerson@apu.edu
DICKERSON, Mary Ann .... 913-469-8500 .... 194 B
mdkerson@jccc.edu
DICKERSON, Shirley .... 936-468-4109 .... 496 B
sdickerson@sfasu.edu
DICKERSON, Valerie .... 208-377-8080 .... 143 C
vdickerson@carrington.edu
DICKERT, Gerry .... 409-984-6342 .... 501 C
DICKEY, Daryl .... 678-839-6534 .... 139 A
ddickey@westga.edu
DICKEY, Elbert, C .... 402-472-2966 .... 300 G
edickey1@unl.edu
DICKEY, Elizabeth, D .... 212-875-4595 .... 323 C
edickey@bankstreet.edu
DICKEY, Jennifer .... 313-664-7428 .... 249 E
jdickey@collegeforcreativestudies.edu
DICKEY, M. Thaxter .... 813-988-5131 .... 108 A
dickeyt@floridacollege.edu
DICKEY, Marilyn .... 850-201-6652 .... 122 A
dickeym@tcc.fl.edu
DICKEY, Matt .... 417-626-1234 .... 287 C
dickey.matt@occ.edu
DICKEY, Nancy, W .... 979-436-9100 .... 497 B
dickey@tamhsc.edu
DICKEY, Serita .... 281-998-6150 .... 494 A
serita.dickey@sjcd.edu
DICKEY, Todd, R .... 213-740-8184 .... 76 F
svpadmin@usc.edu
DICKEY, Wanda .... 813-988-5131 .... 108 A
library@floridacollege.edu
DICKEY, Wyman .... 904-269-7086 .... 110 C
wdickey@fortiscollege.edu
DICKHERBER, David .... 636-949-4907 .... 283 J
ddickherber@lindenwood.edu
DICKIE, Christopher .... 870-612-2048 .... 25 E
christopher.dickie@uaccb.edu
DICKINSON, Marjorie, M .. 530-752-2619 .... 73 I
mmdickinson@ucdavis.edu
DICKINSON, Mark, D .... 651-696-6278 .... 264 J
dickinsonm@macalester.edu
DICKINSON, Michael, B .... 607-255-9300 .... 331 B
mbd3@cornell.edu
DICKINSON, Patricia .... 304-766-3363 .... 544 F
dickinpa@wvstateu.edu
DICKINSON, Rosie, A .... 956-326-2202 .... 497 D
rosie@tamiu.edu
DICKMEYER, Nathan .... 718-482-6119 .... 328 B
ndickmeyer@lagcc.cuny.edu
DICKSON, Beverly .... 704-330-4119 .... 369 D
beverly.dickson@cpcc.edu
DICKSON, Brook, E .... 540-362-6287 .... 520 A
bdickson@hollins.edu
DICKSON, Chris, M .... 260-422-5561 .... 173 C
cmdickson@indianatech.edu
DICKSON, Eric .... 508-421-1400 .... 237 C
eric.dickson@umassmemorial.org
DICKSON, Janet .... 419-824-3704 .... 395 E
jdickson@lourdes.edu
DICKSON, Jo Carole .... 502-213-2411 .... 202 F
jocarole.dickson@kctcs.edu
DICKSON, John .... 727-873-4350 .... 121 C
jdickson@mail.usf.edu
DICKSON, John .... 202-639-1843 .... 98 A
jdickerson@corcoran.org
DICKSON, Nancy .... 724-480-3553 .... 426 A
nancy.dickson@ccbc.edu
DICKSON, Richard, P .... 504-865-5500 .... 215 C
rpd@tulane.edu
DICKSON, Risa .... 909-537-5029 .... 36 B
rdickson@csusb.edu
DICOLA, Rose Ann .... 412-237-6517 .... 425 H
rdicola@ccac.edu
DIDEROT, Dimanche .... 404-527-4520 .... 126 I
ddiderot@carver.edu
DIDIER, Kim .... 515-965-7064 .... 183 H
kmdidier@dmacc.edu
DIDION, John .... 714-480-7489 .... 63 E
didion_john@rsccd.edu
DIDION, Judy .... 419-517-8905 .... 395 E
jdidion@lourdes.edu
DIDONATO, Reylynda .... 720-859-7900 .... 81 C
DIDONNA, Diane .... 219-877-3100 .... 170 D
ddidonna@brownmackie.edu
DIEBEL, Carol .... 907-474-6939 .... 10 I
cediebel@alaska.edu
DIEBOLD, Ann .... 610-519-4560 .... 450 H
ann.diebold@villanova.edu
DIECKMAN, Stacy .... 402-844-7288 .... 299 I
stacyd@northeast.edu
DIECKMANN, Mike, F .... 850-474-2555 .... 121 D
michaeldieckmann@uwf.edu
DIECKMEYER, Diane .... 951-372-7199 .... 63 K
diane.dieckmeyer@norcocollege.edu
DIEDERICH, Nicole .... 419-434-4445 .... 404 B
diederich@findlay.edu
DIEDRCHS, Carol, P .... 614-292-6151 .... 398 I
diedrichs.1@0osu.edu
DIEDRICH, Gui .... 979-458-6000 .... 496 F
gdiedrich@tamus.edu
DIEDRICK, James, K .... 404-471-6102 .... 123 I
jdiedrick@agnesscott.edu
DIEDRIECH, Dan, C .... 314-516-4734 .... 291 D
diedriechd@umsl.edu
DIEFENDORF, Wendy .... 518-244-2443 .... 348 A
diefew@sage.edu
DIEHL, Bert .... 440-525-7140 .... 394 F
rdiehl@lakelandcc.edu
DIEHL, Dave .... 301-696-3800 .... 223 C
diehld@hood.edu
DIEHL, Hope, L .... 610-359-5333 .... 426 G
hdiehl@dccc.edu
DIEHL, Joan .... 570-348-6248 .... 435 F
1226mgr@pheg.follett.com
DIEHL, Melissa, M .... 570-577-3776 .... 423 E
melissa.diehl@bucknell.edu
DIEHL, Michele .... 215-646-7300 .... 430 C
diehl.m@gmc.edu
DIEHL, Randy, L .... 512-471-4141 .... 505 D
diehl@austin.utexas.edu
DIEHL, Shanda .... 360-992-2421 .... 532 F
sdiehl@clark.edu
DIEHL, Timothy .... 207-725-3716 .... 217 E
tdiehl@bowdoin.edu
DIEHM, Perry .... 913-971-3722 .... 195 D
pdiehm@mnu.edu
DIEKER, R. Joseph .... 319-895-4210 .... 183 G
jdieker@cornellcollege.edu
DIEKMANN, Beth .... 507-285-7259 .... 268 I
beth.diekmann@roch.edu
DIEM, Richard, A .... 210-458-6463 .... 506 D
richard.diem@utsa.edu
DIEMER, Gregory, M .... 715-346-2641 .... 552 D
gdiemer@uwsp.edu
DIEMER, Rene .... 215-248-6305 .... 435 B
registrar@ltsp.edu
DIEMER, Robert .... 352-588-8974 .... 116 G
robert.diemer@saintleo.edu
DIENER, Connie .... 920-923-7615 .... 548 E
cdiener@marianuniversity.edu
DIENER, Melissa .... 920-686-6146 .... 550 H
melissa.diener@sl.edu
DIENHART, Mark, C .... 651-962-6920 .... 272 B
mcdienhart@stthomas.edu
DIENNO, Michele .... 513-785-3251 .... 396 F
diennomm@muohio.edu
DIENST, Tom .... 907-796-6497 .... 11 A
tom.dienst@uas.alaska.edu
DIEPENBROCK, Amy .... 210-436-3102 .... 493 F
adiepenbrock@stmarytx.edu
DIERCKX, Heidi .... 607-735-1954 .... 332 I
hdierckx@elmira.edu
DIERENFIELD, Bruce, J ..... 716-888-2683 .... 325 F
derenfb@canisius.edu
DIERICKX, George .... 269-782-1207 .... 258 C
gdierickx@swmich.edu
DIERINGER, Deanna, L ..... 907-474-6629 .... 10 I
dldieringer@alaska.edu
DIERINGER, Dennis, D .... 770-484-1204 .... 133 G
lru@lru.edu
DIERINGER, Jerome, T .... 410-704-2516 .... 228 E
jdieringer@towson.edu
DIERINGER, Stephanie, L .. 619-298-1829 .... 71 C
DIERKS, David, R .... 319-335-3305 .... 182 F
david-dierks@uiowa.edu
DIERLAM, Lois .... 914-337-9300 .... 330 G
lois.dierlam@concordia-ny.edu
DIESMAN, Julie .... 765-459-0561 .... 176 C
jdiesman@ivytech.edu
DIETERLE, Sheila .... 719-336-1621 .... 86 B
sheila.dieterle@lamarcc.edu
DIETLIN, Lisa .... 847-925-6278 .... 151 G
ldietlin@harpercollege.edu
DIETRICH, Darryl .... 218-723-6165 .... 262 G
ddietric@css.edu
DIETRICH, David .... 330-287-1203 .... 399 A
dietrich.114@osu.edu
DIETRICH, John, F .... 321-433-7090 .... 102 D
dietrichj@brevardcc.edu
DIETRICH, Robert, C .... 570-326-3761 .... 440 L
rdietric@pct.edu
DIETRICH, Robin .... 540-887-7025 .... 521 C
rdietrich@mbc.edu
DIETRICH, Sandra .... 919-866-5674 .... 374 H
sldietrich@waketech.edu
DIETZ, Carol, P .... 216-397-4314 .... 392 L
cdietz@jcu.edu
DIETZ, Fred, K .... 270-809-2684 .... 205 A
fdietz@murraystate.edu
DIETZ, John .... 814-865-0965 .... 438 G
jld@psu.edu
DIETZ, Kenneth .... 502-852-6176 .... 207 E
kenneth.dietz@louisville.edu
DIETZ, Larry .... 309-438-2111 .... 153 D
ldietz@ilstu.edu
DIETZ, Pam .... 620-672-5641 .... 196 D
pamd@prattcc.edu
DIETZ, Sally .... 607-274-3385 .... 336 G
sdietz@ithaca.edu
DIETZ, Sidney .... 602-286-8290 .... 15 G
dietz@gatewaycc.edu
DIETZLER, Deborah, H .... 706-542-2251 .... 138 G
dietzler@uga.edu
DIEUDONNE', Jose' .... 706-385-1015 .... 136 B
jose.dieudonne@point.edu
DIEUGENIO, Richard, D .... 814-865-6563 .... 438 G
rxd2@psu.edu
DIEZ, Mary .... 414-382-6214 .... 546 B
mary.diez@alverno.edu
DIEZ, Nicole .... 305-899-3593 .... 101 M
ndiez@mail.barry.edu
DIEZ, Pam .... 225-216-8287 .... 209 H
diezp@mybrcc.edu
DIFABIO, Mark .... 386-226-7055 .... 105 I
mark.difabio@erau.edu
DIFELICIANTONIO,
Richard, G .... 610-409-3200 .... 450 D
rdifeliciantonio@ursinus.edu
DIFETERICI, Amanda .... 803-799-9082 .... 461 A
adifeterici@southuniversity.edu
DIFFEY, Cheryl .... 225-923-2524 .... 208 C
DIFFEY, Steve .... 662-472-2312 .... 274 D
sdiffey@holmescc.edu
DIFFIE, Rita Nell .... 432-685-4503 .... 491 A
rndiffie@midland.edu
DIFFILY, Michael, E .... 603-577-6000 .... 304 I
diffily@dwc.edu
DIFILIPO, Steve .... 410-287-1021 .... 222 A
sdifilipo@cecil.edu
DIFOLCO PARKER, Jane ... 334-844-4000 .... 1 F
jdp0035@auburn.edu
DIFRANCO, Heidi .... 803-641-3397 .... 462 B
heidid@usca.edu
DIFRANCO, Kathleen, J ..... 216-397-4291 .... 392 L
difranco@jcu.edu
DIFRONZO-HEITZER,
Nicola .... 610-647-4400 .... 431 C
ndifronzoheitzer@immaculata.edu
DIGBY, Annette .... 573-876-7213 .... 290 C
adigby@stephens.edu
DIGBY, Joan .... 516-299-2840 .... 339 A
joan.digby@liu.edu
DIGERLANDO, Rose .... 847-214-7635 .... 150 F
rdigerlando@elgin.edu
DIGGS, Charles .... 617-541-5310 .... 241 A
cdiggs@rcc.mass.edu
DIGGS, Michael .... 217-875-7200 .... 162 F
mdiggs@richland.edu
DIGIACOMO, Robert .... 631-656-2154 .... 334 B
rdigiacomo@ftc.edu
DIGIANFILIPPO, Denise ..... 602-787-6693 .... 15 J
denise.digianfilippo@paradisevalley.edu
DIGIORGIO, Anthony, J ..... 803-323-2225 .... 463 E
digiorgioa@winthrop.edu
DIGIRONIMO, Joseph .... 215-468-8800 .... 431 K
director@culinaryarts.edu
DIGMAN, Jo-Ann .... 314-539-5358 .... 288 G
jdigman1@stlcc.edu
DIGNAN WEIR, Joette .... 330-972-6401 .... 403 B
jdweir@uakron.edu
DIGRAZIA, Lauren .... 860-486-3903 .... 94 G
lauren.digrazia@uconn.edu
DIGREGORIO, Christian .... 570-348-6234 .... 435 F
digregorio@marywood.edu
DIGREGORIO, Theresa .... 716-614-6430 .... 344 C
digregor@niagaracc.suny.edu
DIGREORIO, Jeffrey .... 510-849-8283 .... 48 J
jdigreorio@gtu.edu
DIGUISEPPE, Steven, A ..... 717-872-3352 .... 443 D
steve.diguiseppe@millersville.edu
DIINA-DEMPSEY,
Stephanie, C .... 512-223-7736 .... 481 B
diina@austincc.edu
DIIORIO, Lisa .... 631-244-3220 .... 332 C
diioriol@dowling.edu
DIJULIA, Dominick, J .... 610-660-1707 .... 446 C
ddijulia@sju.edu
DIKEMAN, Scott .... 802-468-1214 .... 515 D
scott.dikeman@castleton.edu
DILAURO, Nanette .... 212-854-2154 .... 323 E
ndilauro@barnard.edu
DILBECK, Jack .... 270-706-8892 .... 202 A
jdilbeck0001@kctcs.edu
DILBECK, Joel .... 334-386-7259 .... 3 G
jdilbeck@faulkner.edu
DILDAY, Gwynne .... 773-702-6889 .... 166 G
egdilday@uchicago.edu
DILENO, Susan .... 440-826-2222 .... 384 K
sdileno@bw.edu
DILEO, Jeffrey .... 361-570-4201 .... 504 A
dileoj@uhv.edu
DILES, David .... 216-368-2866 .... 386 F
dxd87@case.edu

DILGER, Patrick 203-392-6586 90 I dilgerp1@southernct.edu
DILIBERTO, James, G 631-691-8733 336 F dilibertoj@idti.edu
DILIBERTO, John, G 631-691-8733 336 F johng@idti.edu
DILISIO, James 410-704-2125 228 E jdilisio@towson.edu
DILL, Anna Maria 541-962-3774 418 C adill@eou.edu
DILL, April 580-477-7710 414 C april.dill@wosc.edu
DILL, Bonnie, T 301-405-2095 227 B btdill@umd.edu
DILL, Gary 575-492-2123 321 H gdill@usw.edu
DILL, Herb 440-375-7555 394 E hdill@lec.edu
DILL, Jane, P 864-644-5404 461 B jdill@swu.edu
DILL, Julia 573-518-2261 285 I jdill@mineralarea.edu
DILL, Ken 864-644-5431 461 B kdill@swu.edu
DILL, Randy, G 208-732-6600 143 E rdill@csi.edu
DILL, Rosemary 662-621-4201 273 F rdill@coahomacc.edu
DILL, Stephen 617-879-2355 246 C sdill@wheelock.edu
DILLABOUGH, Daniel, J 619-260-2247 76 D dillaboughd@sandiego.edu
DILLANE, Robert, J 717-867-6060 434 C dillane@lvc.edu
DILLARD, Cara 804-440-1529 527 A cdillard@ccwa.vccs.edu
DILLARD, Glenn 501-279-4407 21 H gdillard@harding.edu
DILLARD, Maria, P 954-262-8051 114 B mdillard@nsu.nova.edu
DILLBECK, Michael 641-472-1187 187 E sdillbeck@mum.edu
DILLBECK, Susan 641-472-1187 187 E
DILLE, Wayne 641-628-5268 183 D dille@central.edu
DILLEMUTH, Jim 612-659-6600 267 B jim.dillemuth@minneapolis.edu
DILLENBERG, Jack 480-219-6081 278 D jdillenberg@atsu.edu
DILLENBURG, Brenda 715-389-7011 554 E brenda.dillenburg@mstc.edu
DILLER, Elizabeth 740-857-1311 401 F ediller@rosedale.edu
DILLER, Lisa, C 423-236-2417 473 B ldiller@southern.edu
DILLER, Tiffany 504-613-1507 19 A tiffany.diller@phoenix.edu
DILLET, Brigette 775-423-2254 303 B bdillet@wnc.edu
DILLINGHAM, Martin 615-383-4848 478 F mdillingham@watkins.edu
DILLINGHAM, Sabine 240-895-4192 226 A sldillingham@smcm.edu
DILLINGHAM, Tom 931-393-1756 475 D tdillingham@mscc.edu
DILLINGHAM-EVANS, Donna 435-652-7506 512 B dillingh@dixie.edu
DILLION, Diana 605-856-2355 465 C diana.dillion@sintegleska.edu
DILLMAN, David 903-813-3000 481 A ddillman@austincollege.edu
DILLMAN, Joanna 985-732-6640 211 A
DILLMAN, Rob 916-649-2400 31 F
DILLON, Anastacia 503-768-7095 416 G adillon@lclark.edu
DILLON, Andrew, P 512-471-3821 505 D adillon@ischool.utexas.edu
DILLON, Charles, T 231-843-5540 260 B ctdillon@westshore.edu
DILLON, Clotilde 212-594-4000 357 H cdillon@tcicollege.edu
DILLON, III, Cyrus, I 434-223-6197 519 G cdillon@hsc.edu
DILLON, Dawn, M 919-508-2005 380 E ddillon@peace.edu
DILLON, Francis, X 508-565-1344 245 A fdillon@stonehill.edu
DILLON, Glen 304-293-7206 545 A ghdillon@hsc.wvu.edu
DILLON, Howard 212-217-4040 333 F howard_dillon@fitnyc.edu
DILLON, James, S 717-720-4100 441 E jdillon@passhe.edu
DILLON, John 610-683-4002 443 A dillon@kutztown.edu
DILLON, Kendall 515-271-1661 184 A kendall.dillon@dmu.edu
DILLON, Mary Jane 904-819-6314 107 C dillonmj@flagler.edu
DILLON, Michael 410-455-2111 227 D midillon@umbc.edu
DILLON, Mike 573-592-4209 293 D mike.dillon@williamwoods.edu
DILLON, Paul 201-360-4631 310 E pdillon@hccc.edu
DILLON, R. Mark 630-752-5016 168 H mark.dillon@wheaton.edu
DILLON, Rick 304-384-5231 543 G rdillon@concord.edu
DILLON, Sarah 715-675-3331 555 B dillon@ntc.edu
DILLON, T. Kevin 713-500-3535 506 F kevin.dillon@uth.tmc.edu
DILLON, Thomas 419-434-5777 404 B dillon@findlay.edu
DILLON HOGAN, Kate 716-375-2128 348 C khogan@sbu.edu
DILLOW, Rhonda 618-634-3251 164 E rhondad@shawneecc.edu
DILLOW, Sarah, L 423-652-4739 470 A sldillow@king.edu
DILLSWORTH, Gary 716-926-8920 335 E gdillsworth@hilbert.edu
DILMORE, Donald, H 814-732-2779 442 E ddilmore@edinboro.edu
DILORENZO, Peter 856-227-7200 308 D pdilorenzo@camdencc.edu
DILORENZO, Thomas 205-934-5643 8 F tmd@uab.edu
DILORENZO, Vicki 518-694-7331 322 B vicki.dilorenzo@acphs.edu
DILS, Keith 724-738-2292 443 F keith.dils@sru.edu
DILUSTRO, John 252-398-6220 363 G dilusj@chowan.edu
DIMAGGIO, Jacqueline, R 864-250-8179 458 G jacqui.dimaggio@gvltec.edu
DIMAIO, Amy 408-453-9900 50 F adimaio@henley-putnam.edu
DIMAIO, Judith 516-686-7594 343 D jdimaio@nyit.edu
DIMARCO, Casey 518-694-7278 322 B casey.dimarco@acphs.edu
DIMARCO, Erin 302-356-6924 97 C erin.j.dimarco@wilmu.edu
DIMARCO, Scott, L 570-662-4672 443 C sdimarco@mansfield.edu
DIMARIA, Vince 216-987-2341 389 B vince.dimaria@tri-c.edu
DIMARIO, Joseph, X 847-578-8633 163 C joseph.dimario@rosalindfranklin.edu
DIMASI, Louis 802-654-2566 514 D ldimasi@smcvt.edu
DIMATTIA, Andrea 570-504-9634 425 F
DIMAURO, JR., Alfred 508-831-6678 246 F fred@wpi.edu
DIMENNA, Grey 732-571-3598 311 E gdimenna@monmouth.edu
DIMENT, Gregory, S 269-337-7149 252 K greg.diment@kzoo.edu
DIMICK, Jeffrey, A 304-865-6131 541 J jeffrey.dimick@ovu.edu
DIMINO, John, L 215-204-7276 447 H john.dimino@temple.edu
DIMINO, Laura 717-901-5139 430 F ldimino@harrisburgu.edu
DIMINO, Solweig 973-300-2215 315 F sdimino@sussex.edu
DIMITROV, Danielle, E 718-982-2250 327 A danielle.dimitrov@csi.cuny.edu
DIMKOVA, Dimitrina 703-323-5053 527 F ddimkova@nvcc.edu
DIMMITT, Al 816-604-4003 285 E al.dimmitt@mcckc.edu
DIMOLA, Anne 631-244-3020 332 C dimolaa@dowling.edu
DIMOLITSAS, Spiros 202-687-3730 98 D seniorvp@georgetown.edu
DIMON, Denise 619-260-6824 76 D dimon@sandiego.edu
DIMON, Donna, L 240-567-7290 224 D donna.dimon@montgomerycollege.edu
DIMOND, David 914-632-5400 341 G ddimond@monroecollege.edu
DINAN, Susan 973-720-3657 317 D dinans@wpunj.edu
DINANI, Thandiwe 714-556-3610 77 B thandiwe.dinani@vanguard.edu
DINARDO, N. John 215-895-2510 427 H dinardo@drexel.edu
DINDIAL-THOMPSON, Heidi 727-725-2688 106 F hdindialthompson@cci.edu
DINDOFFER, Tamara, L 517-750-1200 258 D tammyd@arbor.edu
DINE YOUNG, Katie 812-866-6842 172 A kdineyoung@hanover.edu
DINEEN, Elizabeth 413-565-1000 230 G edineen@baypath.edu
DINEGAR, Leonard 303-860-5600 88 G leonard.dinegar@cu.edu
DINELL, Brandon 585-720-0660 325 B bdinell@bryantstratton.edu
DINELLO, William, V 718-262-2350 329 A wdinello@york.cuny.edu
DINER, David 434-971-3303 557 G david.n.diner.mil@mail.mil
DINGER, Tim 479-524-7234 22 C tdinger@jbu.edu
DINGLE, Terry 843-661-8321 458 B terry.dingle@fdtc.edu
DINGLEY, Clare 320-589-6030 271 G strandcd@morris.umn.edu
DINGMAN, Brandie 518-381-1280 350 E dingmabm@sunysccc.edu
DINGMANN, Melissa 218-281-8576 271 E dingmann@umn.edu
DINIELLI, Michael 909-652-6904 39 E michael.dinielli@chaffey.edu
DINKEL, Georgianne 530-226-4727 69 H jdinkel@simpsonu.edu
DINKEL, M.L. (Mel) 909-621-8026 40 E mel_dinkel@cuc.claremont.edu
DINKEL, Shirley 785-670-1470 197 F shirley.dinkel@washburn.edu
DINKINS, Marva 910-879-5570 368 D mdinkins@bladencc.edu
DINKINS, Sandy, E 904-264-2172 116 C sdinkins@iws.edu
DINNAN, Matthew, A 203-254-4000 92 H madinnan@fairfield.edu
DINNDORF, Elizabeth, A 803-786-3178 457 C bdinndorf@columbiasc.edu
DINNDORF, Robert, J 608-246-6440 554 D rdinndorf@madisoncollege.org
DINNO, Christopher 707-664-2870 37 D christopher.dinno@sonoma.edu
DINSE, Jayne 507-389-7269 269 D jayne.dinse@southcentral.edu
DINTINO, Dennis 718-260-3770 346 C ddintino@poly.edu
DINUZZO, Theresa, M 904-620-2602 120 D tdinuzzo@unf.edu
DINWIDDIE, Mollie, D 660-543-4140 290 H dinwiddie@ucmo.edu
DION, Kent 406-377-9416 294 B kent_d@dawson.edu
DIONNE, Woody 802-635-1280 515 F woody.dionne@jsc.edu
DIORIO, Mary Ann 860-255-3474 92 F mdiorio@txcc.commnet.edu
DIPADOVA, Audra 949-582-4616 70 F adipadova@saddleback.edu
DIPADOVA-STOCKS, Laurie 816-559-5617 287 E laurie.dipadovastocks@park.edu
DIPALMA, Allen, A 412-624-7415 449 A dipalma@pitt.edu
DIPETRO, David 412-396-5140 428 D dipetro@duq.edu
DIPIERRO, John 269-965-3931 253 B dipierroj@kellogg.edu
DIPIETRO, Joe 865-974-2241 477 C utpresident@tennessee.edu
DIPIPPA, John, M 501-324-9434 24 E jmdipippa@ualr.edu
DIPIRO, Joseph, T 843-792-8450 459 D dipiroj@musc.edu
DIPIRO, Joseph, T 803-777-4151 462 A joseph.dipiro@sc.edu
DIPLOCK, Peter 860-486-2238 94 G peter.diplock@uconn.edu
DIPPEL, Kellie 970-824-1147 82 H kellie.dippel@cncc.edu
DIPPMAN, Terry 419-473-2700 389 C tdippman@daviscollege.edu
DIPUCCIO, Denise 910-962-7933 379 D dipucciod@uncw.edu
DIRADDO, Colleen 484-384-2943 438 D cdiraddo@eastern.edu
DIRE, James 808-245-8229 142 C dire@hawaii.edu
DIRECTOR, Stephen, W 617-373-2170 243 F
DIRIKER, Veronique, L 410-651-8142 227 E vdiriker@umes.edu
DIRK, Brian 440-375-7220 394 E bdirk@lec.edu
DIRKS, Nicholas, B 212-854-8296 330 F nbd7@columbia.edu
DIRKSCHNEIDER, Carla 402-552-6295 297 B dirkschneider@clarksoncollege.edu
DIRKSE, John 661-654-6181 34 A jdirkse@csub.edu
DIRKSEN, Carolyn 423-614-8118 470 C cdirksen@leeuniversity.edu
DIRKSEN, Dawn 866-323-0233 63 D
DIRLAM, David 513-487-3234 335 B ddirlam@huc.edu
DIRST, Eric 630-515-4510 149 B edirst@devry.edu
DISABATINO, Gail 864-656-2161 456 E gaild@clemson.edu
DISABATO, Sharyn 352-588-7438 116 G sharyn.disabato@saintleo.edu
DISAIA, Kenneth, F 401-598-2346 453 E kdisaia@jwu.edu
DISALVIO, Philip 617-287-7925 236 G philip.disalvio@umb.edu
DISALVO, Stephen 314-529-9521 284 C sdisalvo@maryville.edu
DISALVO, Steven, R 920-923-7617 548 E sdisalvo@marianuniversity.edu
DISANTI, Francis, J 610-660-1506 446 C disanti@sju.edu
DISATE, Nancy 303-861-1151 84 B ndisate@concorde.edu
DISCHINO, Maureen 617-989-4009 245 F dischinom@wit.edu
DISHMAN, Laurie 615-547-1278 468 B ldishman@cumberland.edu
DISHMAN, Leslie, B 985-448-4415 216 A leslie.dishman@nicholls.edu
DISHMAN, Marcie 919-718-7491 369 C mdishman@cccc.edu
DISHNER, Annette, H 252-451-8236 372 E adishner@nash.cc.nc.us
DISKIN, Becca, L 417-659-5422 286 B diskin-b@mssu.edu
DISKIN, Jon 510-666-8248 26 H jdiskin@aimc.edu
DISLA, Jessica 973-748-9000 307 H jessica_disla@bloomfield.edu
DISMUKES, JR., Tommy, G 334-833-4402 4 E tdismukes@huntingdon.edu
DISNEW, Carolyn 212-752-1530 338 C carolyn.disnew@limcollege.edu
DISORBO, Brenda 423-478-6215 474 E bdisorbo@clevelandstatecc.edu
DISPIGNO, OFM, Francis, J 716-375-2142 348 C
DISQUE, Carol 336-506-4138 368 A carol.disque@alamancecc.edu
DISS, Christina 503-883-2282 416 H cdiss@linfield.edu
DISTANISLAO, Mary 414-288-7040 548 F mary.distanislao@marquette.edu
DISTASI, Vincent, F 724-458-2116 430 B vfdistasi@gcc.edu
DISTEFANO, Ann, L 570-577-3200 423 E ann.distefano@bucknell.edu
DISTEFANO, Anthony, F 215-780-1420 446 G tdistefano@salus.edu
DISTEFANO, Dawn 516-572-7943 342 C dawn.distefano@ncc.edu
DISTEFANO, Jacqueline 845-257-3295 352 B distefaj@newpaltz.edu
DISTEFANO, Jennifer 603-668-2211 305 I j.distefano@snhu.edu
DISTEFANO, Phillip, P 303-492-8908 88 H phil.distefano@colorado.edu
DISTISO, Christopher 860-628-4751 93 C cdistiso@lincolncollegene.edu
DITCHFIELD, Dora 706-864-1951 134 G dditchfield@northgeorgia.edu
DITCHIK, Jill 718-270-2075 352 D jditchik@downstate.edu
DITHOMAS, Debbie 951-372-7879 63 K debbie.dithomas@norcocollege.edu
DITMAN, Mark 713-348-5441 493 C mditman@rice.edu
DITTBENNER, Richard 619-388-6914 65 E rdittben@sdccd.edu
DITTEMORE, Nancy 951-785-2300 53 E ndittemo@lasierra.edu
DITTMAN, Jeff 605-256-5229 465 I jeff.dittman@dsu.edu
DITTMAN, Judith, L 605-256-5177 465 I judy.dittman@dsu.edu
DITTMER, Amy 573-592-4313 293 D amy.dittmer@williamwoods.edu
DITTMER, Harold "Hal", E 916-447-5171 298 A hdittmer@wellhead.com
DITTO, John 815-288-5511 164 B dittoj@svcc.edu
DITTO, William, L 808-956-6451 141 G wditto@hawaii.edu
DITULIO, James, E 309-298-2453 168 C je-ditulio@wiu.edu
DITULLIO, Anthony 315-267-2135 354 C ditulija@potsdam.edu
DITZLER, Mauri, A 309-457-2127 158 H mditzler@monmouthcollege.edu
DIVELY, Mary Jo 412-268-9519 424 J mjdively@andrew.cmu.edu
DIVEN-BROWN, Laura 662-915-7175 277 D ldivenbr@olemiss.edu
DIVENS, Gary 856-338-1817 308 D gdivens@camdencc.edu
DIVERS, Debralee 419-372-0607 385 F divers@bgsu.edu
DIVERSI, Sarah 603-206-8004 304 D sdiversi@ccsnh.edu
DIVINE, Darren, D 702-651-5602 302 E darren.divine@csn.edu
DIVINE, David 409-933-8309 483 F ddivine@com.edu
DIVINO, Claudio 507-288-4563 263 B academic@crossroadscollege.edu
DIVINS, Howard 814-641-0440 428 A hcc@dbcollege.com
DIVITA, Brian 616-632-2929 247 E bjd002@aquinas.edu
DIVITA KOPACZ, Anne 312-893-7160 151 A akopacz@erikson.edu

DIVJAK, Robert .... 203-575-8235 ..... 92 A
rdivjak@nvcc.commnet.edu
DIX, Rachel, T .... 252-985-5175 .... 375 E
rdix@ncwc.edu
DIXEY, Mary .... 860-548-2487 ..... 94 A
dixeym@rpi.edu
DIXIT, Oolka .... 773-695-1000 .... 149 F
odixit@keller.edu
DIXON, Albert .... 415-841-4051 ..... 40 C
adixon@ccsf.edu
DIXON, Andre .... 484-365-7441 .... 434 H
adixon@lincoln.edu
DIXON, Ann .... 501-279-4349 ..... 21 H
adixon@harding.edu
DIXON, Barbara .... 914-251-6020 .... 354 D
barbara.dixon@purchase.edu
DIXON, Bradley .... 785-442-6028 .... 193 F
bdixon@highlandcc.edu
DIXON, Brenda .... 575-769-2811 .... 318 A
brenda.dixon@clovis.edu
DIXON, Bruce, W .... 606-474-3215 .... 201 D
bdixon@kcu.edu
DIXON, Carol .... 909-537-5250 ..... 36 B
cdixon@csusb.edu
DIXON, Carol, M .... 614-235-4136 .... 402 G
cdixon@tlsohio.edu
DIXON, Cathy .... 410-626-2548 .... 225 G
cathy.dixon@sjca.edu
DIXON, Chester, L .... 512-223-1222 .... 481 B
cdixon@austincc.edu
DIXON, Curtis .... 212-217-7777 .... 333 F
curtis_dixon@fitnyc.edu
DIXON, David .... 216-649-8700 .... 394 B
ddixon@kent.edu
DIXON, Diane .... 315-568-3065 .... 342 H
ddixon@nycc.edu
DIXON, Eddy .... 478-757-3508 .... 127 A
evd@centralgatech.edu
DIXON, Gentry .... 567-661-7617 .... 400 I
gentry_dixon@owens.edu
DIXON, Isaac .... 503-768-6239 .... 416 G
idixon@lclark.edu
DIXON, James .... 336-517-2225 .... 362 G
jdixon@bennett.edu
DIXON, Jeananne, F .... 540-674-3610 .... 527 E
jdixon@nr.edu
DIXON, Jenny .... 928-681-5656 ..... 16 F
jdixon@mohave.edu
DIXON, Jeri, L .... 630-801-7900 .... 168 B
jdixon@waubonsee.edu
DIXON, Jesse, L .... 715-836-3367 .... 551 A
dixonjl@uwec.edu
DIXON, John .... 843-661-1335 .... 458 D
jdixon@fmarion.edu
DIXON, Joyce .... 662-254-3425 .... 276 B
jadixon@msu.edu
DIXON, Kris .... 609-894-9311 .... 308 B
kdixon@bcc.edu
DIXON, Lloyd .... 937-708-5724 .... 405 H
ldixon@wilberforce.edu
DIXON, Martha, J .... 716-851-1939 .... 333 C
dixon@ecc.edu
DIXON, Michael, G .... 260-982-5000 .... 177 H
mgdixon@manchester.edu
DIXON, Patrick .... 870-972-2042 ..... 20 D
pdixon@astate.edu
DIXON, Paula .... 706-245-7226 .... 129 C
pdixon@ec.edu
DIXON, JR., Ralph, W .... 704-406-4253 .... 364 E
rdixon@gardner-webb.edu
DIXON, Richard .... 405-946-7799 .... 411 E
richardd@plattcollege.org
DIXON, Rick, L .... 660-543-4255 .... 290 H
dixon@ucmo.edu
DIXON, Robert .... 405-744-6512 .... 410 C
robert.dixon@okstate.edu
DIXON, Robert .... 312-413-1878 .... 167 B
robd@uic.edu
DIXON, Roger .... 478-471-2720 .... 133 H
roger.dixon@maconstate.edu
DIXON, Samuel .... 678-466-4200 .... 127 D
samdixon@clayton.edu
DIXON, Sandra .... 510-574-1231 ..... 44 F
sdixon@devry.edu
DIXON, Serafina Marie .... 734-432-5338 .... 254 D
sserafina@madonna.edu
DIXON, Sherry, N .... 662-685-4771 .... 273 E
sdixon@bmc.edu
DIXON, Siri .... 503-222-3225 .... 415 H
sdixon@cci.edu
DIXON, Sylvia .... 704-922-6475 .... 370 G
dixon.sylvia@gaston.edu
DIXON, Terry .... 251-981-3771 ..... 2 G
terry.dixon@columbiasouthern.edu
DIXON, William .... 270-831-9650 .... 202 D
bill.dixon@kctcs.edu
DIXSON, Mary .... 210-486-4937 .... 479 B
mdixson1@alamo.edu
DIZÉN, Mügé .... 217-351-2433 .... 161 C
mdizen@parkland.edu
DIZAZZO, Laura .... 206-934-5492 .... 537 E
laura.dizazzo@seattlecolleges.edu
DIZAZZO, Laura .... 253-833-9111 .... 534 H
lgriep@geenriver.edu
DIZINNO, Janet, B .... 210-436-3737 .... 493 F
jdizinno@stmarytx.edu
DJAFERIS, Theodore, E .... 413-545-6388 .... 236 F
djaferis@ecs.umass.edu
DJALALI, Chaden .... 319-335-2610 .... 182 F
chaden-djalali
DJIN, Yana .... 212-247-3434 .... 339 G
ydjin@mandl.edu
DLUGOS, James, S .... 207-893-7711 .... 219 F
jdlugos@sjcme.edu
DLUGOS, OSA, Raymond . 978-837-5130 .... 242 A
raymond.dlugos@merrimack.edu
DMITZAK, Amy, H .... 717-872-3586 .... 443 D
amy.dmitzak@millersville.edu
DMOCH, Jack, L .... 757-455-3114 .... 530 C
jdmoch@vwc.edu
DMYTRENKO, Suzanne .... 415-338-2823 ..... 37 B
suzanne@sfsu.edu
DO-NGUYEN,
Gigi Diemuyen .... 713-718-5058 .... 487 I
gigi.do@hccs.edu
DOAK, Bryan .... 928-344-7617 ..... 12 A
bryan.doak@azwestern.edu
DOAK, Greg .... 207-768-9571 .... 220 F
greg.doak@umpi.edu
DOAK, James, W .... 254-710-2222 .... 482 A
jim_doak@baylor.edu
DOAK, Josh .... 417-659-4460 .... 286 B
doak-j@mssu.edu
DOAK, Rebecca .... 330-823-2889 .... 404 C
doakaw@mountunion.edu
DOAK, Robert .... 773-380-6783 .... 164 D
bob.doak@seabury.edu
DOAN, Viet .... 701-231-5143 .... 382 B
viet.doan@ndsu.edu
DOANE, Christopher .... 502-852-6907 .... 207 E
doane@louisville.edu
DOANE, Dudley, J .... 434-982-3013 .... 525 F
djd4j@virginia.edu
DOANE, Dudley, J .... 434-924-6166 .... 525 F
djd4j@virginia.edu
DOANE, Paulann, T .... 307-268-2256 .... 556 A
pdoane@caspercollege.edu
DOBB, Linda, S .... 510-885-3711 ..... 34 E
linda.dobb@csueastbay.edu
DOBB, Linda, S .... 510-885-3664 ..... 34 E
linda.dobb@csueastbay.edu
DOBBELAAR, Henry .... 201-216-5340 .... 315 E
hdobbela@stevens.edu
DOBBELAERE, Arthur, G ... 630-515-7305 .... 158 F
adobbe@midwestern.edu
DOBBELAERE, Arthur, G ... 623-572-3400 ..... 16 E
adobbe@midwestern.edu
DOBBELMANN, Duncan .... 802-440-4400 .... 513 A
duncand@bennington.edu
DOBBERSTEIN, Trina .... 440-826-2111 .... 384 K
tdobbers@bw.edu
DOBBINS, Eric .... 816-802-3468 .... 283 E
edobbins@kcai.edu
DOBBINS, Kathleen .... 256-726-7266 ..... 6 C
dobbins@oakwood.edu
DOBBINS, Kenneth, W .... 573-651-2222 .... 289 K
president@semo.edu
DOBBS, Amanda .... 870-368-2013 ..... 23 A
adobbs@ozarka.edu
DOBBS, Paul .... 617-879-7105 .... 238 B
pauldobbs@massart.edu
DOBBS, Peggy .... 912-260-4238 .... 137 B
peggy.dobbs@sgc.edu
DOBBS, Ricky .... 903-886-5878 .... 498 B
ricky.dobbs@tamuc.edu
DOBELL, Daniel .... 570-662-4000 .... 443 C
ddobell@mansfield.edu
DOBELLE, Evan, S .... 413-572-5201 .... 238 F
edobelle@wsc.ma.edu
DOBI, Hanko, H .... 203-932-7191 ..... 95 C
hdobi@newhaven.edu
DOBISE, Michael .... 413-748-3880 .... 244 H
mdobise@springfieldcollegel.edu
DOBISH, Rodney, W .... 412-396-4781 .... 428 D
dobish@duq.edu
DOBKIN, Bethami .... 925-631-4408 ..... 64 F
bethami.dobkin4@stmarys-ca.edu
DOBKIN, David, P .... 609-258-3020 .... 312 G
ddobkin@princeton.edu
DOBLIN, Stephen, A .... 409-880-8398 .... 501 A
steve.doblin@lamar.edu
DOBMEYER, Ann .... 413-565-1000 .... 230 G
dobmeyer@baypath.edu
DOBRANSKY, Mary .... 402-557-7160 .... 296 H
mary.dobransky@bellevue.edu
DOBRIN, Allan, H .... 212-794-5305 .... 326 B
allan.dobrin@mail.cuny.edu
DOBRINA, Milena .... 773-697-2093 .... 149 D
mdobrina@devry.edu
DOBRINSKY, Herbert, C .... 212-960-0850 .... 361 M
dobrinsk@yu.edu
DOBROTA, Joseph .... 757-352-4140 .... 523 E
jdobrota@regent.edu
DOBROWSKI, Pauline .... 508-565-1290 .... 245 A
pdobrowski@stonehill.edu
DOBSON, Cheryl .... 417-625-9389 .... 286 B
dobson-c@mssu.edu
DOBSON, Cheryl .... 914-323-5177 .... 339 J
cheryl.dobson@mville.edu
DOBSON, Henry (Van), V .. 610-758-3774 .... 434 E
hvd211@lehigh.edu
DOBSON, James .... 410-234-4579 .... 225 E
DOBSON, Jennie, P .... 256-549-8263 ..... 3 J
jdobson@gadsdenstate.edu
DOBSON, Lark, T .... 301-322-0616 .... 225 F
ldobson@pgcc.edu
DOBSON, Lisa .... 910-592-8081 .... 373 G
ldobson@sampsoncc.edu
DOBSON-HOPKINS, Nina . 443-885-3130 .... 224 E
nina.hopkins@morgan.edu
DOBYNS, Kevin .... 904-743-1122 .... 112 B
kdobyns@jones.edu
DOCKEN, Lori .... 608-263-2571 .... 550 I
ldocken@uwsa.edu
DOCKENDORF, Amy, L .... 605-256-5130 .... 465 I
amy.dockendorf@dsu.edu
DOCKERY, Benjamin .... 502-897-4629 .... 206 C
bdockery@sbts.edu
DOCKERY, David, S .... 731-661-5180 .... 477 B
ddockery@uu.edu
DOCKERY, James, C .... 919-530-5214 .... 378 B
jcdockery@nccu.edu
DOCKERY, Sheila .... 910-879-5505 .... 368 D
sdockery@bladencc.edu
DOCKETY, Maribeth, B .... 302-855-1675 ..... 96 E
mdockety@dtcc.edu
DOCKING, Jeffrey, R .... 517-265-5161 .... 246 H
jdocking@adrian.edu
DOCKINS, Natalie, C .... 559-442-4600 ..... 72 B
natalie.culver-dockins@fresnocitycollege.edu
DOCKINS, Waynna .... 870-612-2009 ..... 25 E
waynna.dockins@uaccb.edu
DOCTOR, OFM, John .... 217-228-5432 .... 161 F
docotjo@quincy.edu
DOCUMET, Paola .... 305-237-4048 .... 113 H
pdocumet@mdc.edu
DODD, Carley .... 325-674-2223 .... 478 I
doddc@acu.edu
DODD, Linda, M .... 724-287-8711 .... 423 G
linda.dodd@bc3.edu
DODD, Shelley .... 307-766-4273 .... 556 H
shelley@uwyo.edu
DODD, William, M .... 956-882-3822 .... 505 E
william.dodd@utb.edu
DODDS, DeLoss .... 512-471-5757 .... 505 D
ddodds@mail.utexas.edu
DODDS, Gloria .... 706-649-1016 .... 128 A
gdodds@columbustech.edu
DODDS, Jerrilynn, D .... 914-395-2303 .... 350 C
jdodds@sarahlawrence.edu
DODDS, S. Curtis .... 530-226-4148 ..... 69 H
cdodds@simpsonu.edu
DODDS, Thomas, E .... 607-255-7445 .... 331 B
ted56@cornell.edu
DODENHOFF, Michelle .... 803-777-2070 .... 462 A
mdodenho@mailbox.sc.edu
DODGE, Barbara .... 920-693-1386 .... 554 C
barbara.dodge@gotoltc.edu
DODGE, Billie, S .... 410-778-7760 .... 229 D
bdodge2@washcoll.edu
DODGE, Brian, R .... 607-871-2154 .... 322 E
dodgeb@alfred.edu
DODGE, Cabot, W .... 978-468-7111 .... 235 B
DODGE, Carole, E .... 561-237-7915 .... 113 D
cdodge@lynn.edu
DODGE, Cynthia .... 636-573-9300 .... 286 E
cdodge@motech.edu
DODGE, Darla .... 775-445-4224 .... 303 B
dodge@wnc.edu
DODGE, Georgina .... 319-335-3565 .... 182 F
georgina-dodge@uiowa.edu
DODGE, Kevin .... 301-387-3328 .... 222 H
kevin.dodge@garrettcollege.edu
DODGE, Marvin .... 435-283-7200 .... 512 C
marvin.dodge@snow.edu
DODGE, Michelle .... 503-251-5710 .... 421 A
mdodge@uws.edu
DODGE, Norma Jean .... 620-417-1171 .... 196 F
normajean.dodge@sccc.edu
DODGE, Richard .... 954-262-3651 .... 114 B
dodge@nsu.nova.edu
DODGE, Ron .... 845-938-3999 .... 559 A
ron.dodge@usma.edu
DODGE, Wendy .... 201-447-7236 .... 307 E
wdodge@bergen.edu
DODGE-REYOME,
Nancy, M .... 315-267-2131 .... 354 C
dodgenm@potsdam.edu
DODGEN, Tom .... 972-241-3371 .... 484 E
tdodgen@dallas.edu
DODIER, Elizabeth .... 956-326-2412 .... 497 D
edodier@tamiu.edu
DODSON, Al .... 662-562-3308 .... 276 D
adodson@northwestms.edu
DODSON, Devin .... 909-868-4084 ..... 44 K
ddodson@devry.edu
DODSON, Don, C .... 408-554-4055 ..... 68 C
ddodson@scu.edu
DODSON, JR., Howard .... 202-806-7234 ..... 98 E
howard.dodson@howard.edu
DODSON, Jennifer .... 269-467-9945 .... 251 B
jdodson@glenoaks.edu
DODSON, Jerry .... 254-442-5152 .... 482 I
jerry.dodson@cisco.edu
DODSON, Jim .... 575-565-2154 .... 318 B
jim.dodson@enmu.edu
DODSON, Lloyd, R .... 312-329-4231 .... 159 A
ldodson@moody.edu
DODSON, Lorraine .... 301-846-2486 .... 222 G
ldodson@frederick.edu
DODSON, Shelley .... 765-973-8332 .... 173 F
midodson@iue.edu
DODSON, Victor, H .... 443-412-2416 .... 223 B
vdodson@harford.edu
DODSON, Wendy, B .... 910-695-3701 .... 373 H
dodsonw@sandhills.edu
DOEBBERT, Jan .... 320-762-4504 .... 265 F
jand@alextech.edu
DOEBLE, Gina .... 239-489-9029 .... 105 F
gdoeble@edison.edu
DOELL, Elaine .... 603-535-2618 .... 307 A
edoell@plymouth.edu
DOELLER, Kathleen .... 480-990-3773 ..... 15 C
DOEPKER, Joel .... 417-447-2655 .... 287 D
doepkerj@otc.edu
DOERFER, Carol .... 518-828-4181 .... 330 E
doerfer@sunycgcc.edu
DOERING, Douglas .... 207-775-3052 .... 218 E
doug@meca.edu
DOERING, Laura .... 515-294-1840 .... 182 E
ljdoeri@iastate.edu
DOERKSEN, Randall, C .... 316-295-5893 .... 193 B
doerksen@friends.edu
DOERNER, Kinchel .... 270-745-8794 .... 208 A
kinchel.doerner@wku.edu
DOERNER, Kinchel .... 605-688-4181 .... 466 C
kinchel.doerner@sdstate.edu
DOERPINGHAUS, Helen, I 803-777-2808 .... 462 A
doerp@sc.edu
DOERR, Gail .... 410-888-9048 .... 226 F
gdoerr@tai.edu
DOERR, Judith, E .... 520-515-5400 ..... 13 E
doerrj@cochise.edu
DOFFONEY, Leige .... 310-233-4021 ..... 54 I
doffonlc@lahc.edu
DOFFONEY, Ned .... 714-808-4797 ..... 59 C
ndoffoney@nocccd.edu
DOGBEVIA, Moses .... 402-461-7466 .... 298 A
mdogbevia@hastings.edu
DOGGETT, Jeffrey .... 978-837-5207 .... 242 A
doggettj@merrimack.edu
DOGGETT, Laine .... 240-895-4514 .... 226 A
ledoggett@smcm.edu
DOGONNIUCK, Theodore .. 516-773-5000 .... 558 I
dogonniuck@usmma.edu
DOHERTY, Arthur .... 541-278-5850 .... 414 G
adoherty@bluecc.edu
DOHERTY, Brian .... 941-487-4300 .... 120 A
bdoherty@ncf.edu
DOHERTY, Brian, E .... 413-265-2372 .... 233 D
dohertyb@elms.edu
DOHERTY, Dan .... 970-339-6336 ..... 81 A
dan.doherty@aims.edu
DOHERTY, Eileen .... 773-298-5060 .... 163 I
edoherty@sxu.edu
DOHERTY, Frank, J .... 540-568-6830 .... 520 H
dohertfj@jmu.edu
DOHERTY, Katherine .... 603-752-1113 .... 304 H
kdoherty@ccsnh.edu
DOHERTY, Kenneth .... 313-577-3756 .... 260 A
ac0578@wayne.edu
DOHERTY, Kevin .... 620-421-6700 .... 194 G
kevind@labette.edu
DOHERTY, Kevin .... 312-369-7162 .... 148 D
kdoherty@colum.edu
DOHERTY, Kristal .... 864-646-1795 .... 461 F
kdoherty@tctc.edu
DOHERTY, Mary Jane .... 781-768-7015 .... 244 A
mj.doherty@regiscollege.edu
DOHERTY, Paul .... 425-640-1713 .... 533 I
paul.doherty@edcc.edu
DOHERTY, Paula .... 360-417-6275 .... 536 G
pdoherty@pencol.edu
DOHERTY, Sharon .... 651-690-6783 .... 270 L
sldoherty@stkate.edu
DOHERTY, Steve .... 269-488-4442 .... 253 A
sdoherty@kvcc.edu
DOHMAN, Gloria .... 701-671-2619 .... 382 G
gloria.dohman@ndscs.edu
DOHNALIK, Judith .... 254-298-8600 .... 496 D
j.dohnalik@templejc.edu
DOIG, Kathleen .... 304-637-1359 .... 541 A
doigk@dewv.edu
DOIGUCHI, Farah .... 808-845-9120 .... 142 B
farah@hawaii.edu
DOKE, Tim .... 214-648-7144 .... 507 E
tim.doke@utsouthwestern.edu
DOKEY, Denise .... 225-768-0818 .... 214 C
denise.dokey@ololcollege.edu
DOKTOR, Caryn, G .... 212-799-5000 .... 337 H
DOLAK, James .... 970-491-4752 ..... 83 F
jim.dolak@colostate.edu
DOLAMORE, Joan .... 617-243-2497 .... 236 A
jdolamore@lasell.edu
DOLAN, Andrew, B .... 231-995-1019 .... 256 D
adolan@nmc.edu

DOLAN, Barbara .... 605-394-2649 .... 466 B
barbara.dolan@sdsmt.edu
DOLAN, Carol .... 912-358-4014 .... 136 G
dolanc@savannahstate.edu
DOLAN, Daniel .... 212-237-8900 .... 327 F
ddolan@jjay.cuny.edu
DOLAN, Donna, M .... 617-521-2111 .... 244 F
donna.dolan@simmons.edu
DOLAN, Gayle .... 617-277-3915 .... 232 D
DOLAN, Julie, L .... 203-254-4000 .... 92 H
jdolan@fairfield.edu
DOLAN, Linda .... 320-762-4439 .... 265 F
lindad@alextech.edu
DOLAN, Mary, K .... 315-267-4816 .... 354 C
dolanmk@potsdam.edu
DOLAN, Teresa, A .... 352-723-5800 .... 120 C
tdolan@dental.ufl.edu
DOLAN, Tina, M .... 781-283-3501 .... 245 E
cdolan@wellesley.edu
DOLANSKY, Brian, P .... 914-606-6284 .... 360 E
brian.dolansky@sunywcc.edu
DOLDER-ZIEKE, Beth, D .... 608-796-3828 .... 553 C
bdzieke@viterbo.edu
DOLDO, Frank .... 315-786-2250 .... 337 F
fdoldo@sunyjefferson.edu
DOLE, Karen, F .... 641-422-4327 .... 188 A
dolekare@niacc.edu
DOLE, Wanda .... 501-569-8803 .... 24 E
wvdole@ualr.edu
DOLHEIMER, Mary, E .... 717-815-1274 .... 452 G
mdolheim@ycp.edu
DOLIBER, Joy .... 561-237-7233 .... 113 D
jdoliber@lynn.edu
DOLINAY, Petro .... 215-885-2360 .... 435 E
pdolinay@manor.edu
DOLINSKY, Beverly .... 978-232-2194 .... 234 D
bdolinsk@endicott.edu
DOLINSKY, Claudia .... 305-593-1223 .... 102 H
cdolinsky@albizu.edu
DOLINSKY, Diane .... 570-702-8907 .... 431 L
ddolinsky@johnson.edu
DOLIVE, Mark .... 817-515-3083 .... 496 C
mark.dolive@tccd.edu
DOLIVE, Mark .... 817-515-2113 .... 496 C
mark.dolive@tccd.edu
DOLL, Caroline .... 805-437-3232 .... 34 B
caroline.doll@csuci.edu
DOLL, Cheryl, A .... 610-799-1087 .... 434 D
cdoll@lccc.edu
DOLL, Tammy .... 620-417-1131 .... 196 F
tammy.doll@sccc.edu
DOLLA, Marie .... 718-779-1430 .... 346 B
mdolla@plazacollege.edu
DOLLAR, Marek .... 513-529-4036 .... 396 E
dollarm@muohio.edu
DOLLAR, Mark, E .... 423-652-6320 .... 470 A
medollar@king.edu
DOLLARD, Heidi .... 413-545-6133 .... 236 F
hdollard@oit.umass.edu
DOLLARD, John, D .... 512-232-9205 .... 505 D
dollard@mail.utexas.edu
DOLLARD, Pam .... 608-890-1066 .... 553 B
pam.dollard@uwc.edu
DOLLASE, Beth .... 816-654-7282 .... 283 F
bdollase@kcumb.edu
DOLLENMAYER, Lisa .... 727-726-1153 .... 103 I
lisadollenmayer@clearwater.edu
DOLLHOPF, Mark, R .... 203-432-1941 .... 96 A
mark.dollhopf@yale.edu
DOLLING, David .... 202-994-6080 .... 98 C
dolling@gwu.edu
DOLLING, Lisa .... 201-216-5405 .... 315 E
ldolling@stevens.edu
DOLLY, Patricia, A .... 248-232-4500 .... 256 F
padolly@oaklandcc.edu
DOLLYHITE, Ronald .... 336-838-6281 .... 375 C
ronald.dollyhite@wilkescc.edu
DOLO, Bet .... 206-268-4002 .... 530 I
bdolo@antioch.edu
DOLSEN, David, H .... 620-229-6298 .... 196 G
david.dolsen@sckans.edu
DOMAN, Earle, F .... 417-836-5526 .... 286 C
earledoman@missouristate.edu
DOMAN-FLYGARE, Sarah . 651-450-3733 .... 266 F
sflygar@inverhills.edu
DOMANN, Jessica .... 713-942-5036 .... 505 A
domannj@sthom.edu
DOMAS, Matthew, S .... 662-562-3235 .... 276 D
gmdomas@northwestms.edu
DOMBROWSKI, Michael .... 716-614-5980 .... 344 C
mdombrowski@niagaracc.suny.edu
DOMBROWSKI, Teresa, A . 630-515-6479 .... 158 F
tdombr@midwestern.edu
DOMENECH, Manuel .... 432-335-5360 .... 502 B
manuel.domenech@ttuhsc.edu
DOMENITZ, Linda .... 860-906-5153 .... 91 C
ldomenitz@ccc.commnet.edu
DOMERACKI, Kristin .... 713-942-9505 .... 488 A
kdomeracki@hgst.edu
DOMES, Chris, E .... 703-284-1502 .... 521 D
chris.domes@marymount.edu
DOMHOLDT, Elizabeth .... 218-723-6012 .... 262 G
bdomhold@css.edu
DOMIANO, Sam .... 985-549-2282 .... 216 C
sdomiano@selu.edu
DOMIN, Greg .... 706-507-8704 .... 127 G
domin_gregory@columbusstate.edu
DOMINELLI, Angela .... 518-694-7333 .... 322 B
angela.dominelli@acphs.edu
DOMINGO, Jannette .... 212-237-8757 .... 327 F
jdomingo@jjay.cuny.edu
DOMINGUEZ, Carmen .... 305-237-3374 .... 113 H
cdoming3@mdc.edu
DOMINGUEZ, Carmen .... 661-362-3116 .... 41 I
carmen.dominguez@canyons.edu
DOMINGUEZ,
Jeronimo, C .... 505-277-2215 .... 321 C
dominguz@unm.edu
DOMINGUEZ, Joe .... 956-364-4341 .... 500 D
armando.dominguez@tstc.edu
DOMINGUEZ, Leo .... 432-837-8596 .... 501 E
leodo@sulross.edu
DOMINGUEZ, Leo, G .... 432-837-8033 .... 501 E
leodo@sulross.edu
DOMINGUEZ, Maria .... 575-538-6611 .... 321 I
dominguezm@wnmu.edu
DOMINGUEZ, Mary .... 831-755-6855 .... 49 E
mdomingu@hartnell.edu
DOMINGUEZ, Norberto .... 787-296-0453 .... 562 I
dominguez@inter.edu
DOMINIAK, Dorothy .... 773-256-0726 .... 157 D
ddominia@lstc.edu
DOMINIAK, Tracy .... 716-677-9500 .... 325 A
tdominiak@bryantstratton.edu
DOMINY, Michele .... 845-758-7420 .... 323 D
dominy@bard.edu
DOMINY, Robert .... 478-757-3579 .... 127 A
rdominy@centralgatech.edu
DOMKE-DAMONTE,
Darla, J .... 843-349-2129 .... 456 G
ddamonte@coastal.edu
DOMNICK, Krista, R .... 919-515-2866 .... 378 C
krdomnic@ncsu.edu
DOMPE, Rudy .... 818-719-6440 .... 55 B
domperf@piercecollege.edu
DOMPIERRE, Michael, B ... 636-922-8355 .... 288 B
mdompierre@stchas.edu
DOMZALSKI, James .... 570-740-0342 .... 435 C
jdomzalski@luzerne.edu
DOMZALSKI, Jim .... 570-740-0342 .... 435 C
jdomzalski@luzerne.edu
DONA, David .... 541-383-7222 .... 414 I
ddona@cocc.edu
DONAGHUE, Joanne .... 860-434-5232 .... 93 D
jdonaghue@lymeacademy.edu
DONAHOE, Patrick .... 406-994-4531 .... 295 C
uccpd@montana.edu
DONAHOO, David .... 434-592-3084 .... 520 K
ddonahoo@liberty.edu
DONAHUE, Amy .... 860-486-0636 .... 94 G
amy.donahue@uconn.edu
DONAHUE, Ann .... 740-366-9123 .... 399 E
donahue.5@osu.edu
DONAHUE, Ann, E .... 603-641-4123 .... 306 D
annie.donahue@unh.edu
DONAHUE, Bob .... 614-947-6010 .... 391 B
donahueb@franklin.edu
DONAHUE, Colin, J .... 818-677-2561 .... 35 F
colin.donahue@csun.edu
DONAHUE, Eileen, B .... 203-432-5850 .... 96 A
eileen.donahue@yale.edu
DONAHUE, Gabriel, M .... 973-290-4055 .... 308 G
gdonahue@cse.edu
DONAHUE, Gerard, J .... 610-660-1016 .... 446 C
gdonahue@sju.edu
DONAHUE, James, A .... 510-649-2410 .... 48 J
president@gtu.edu
DONAHUE, James, P .... 423-652-6002 .... 470 A
jpd@king.edu
DONAHUE, Janice, M .... 423-585-6921 .... 476 D
janice.donahue@ws.edu
DONAHUE, Linda, V .... 802-654-2563 .... 514 D
ldonahue@smcvt.edu
DONAHUE, Lorraine .... 814-262-3822 .... 441 A
ldonahue@pennhighlands.edu
DONAHUE, Lynne .... 401-739-5000 .... 453 G
ldonahue@neit.edu
DONAHUE, Mick .... 360-679-5333 .... 538 D
mick.donahue@skagit.edu
DONAHUE, Mick .... 360-416-7732 .... 538 D
mick.donahue@skagit.edu
DONAHUE, Nancy .... 865-694-6541 .... 475 G
ndonahue@pstcc.edu
DONAHUE, Patrick .... 812-855-4269 .... 173 E
donahued@indiana.edu
DONAHUE, Sally, C .... 617-495-1580 .... 235 D
sdonahue@fas.harvard.edu
DONAHUE, Sandy .... 207-948-9229 .... 219 H
sdonahue@unity.edu
DONAHUE, Tim .... 971-722-4338 .... 419 G
tdonahue@pcc.edu
DONALD, Samuel .... 850-599-2644 .... 118 L
samuel.donald@famu.edu
DONALDSON, Anthony .... 951-343-4841 .... 31 J
adonaldson@calbaptist.edu
DONALDSON, Charles .... 501-569-3328 .... 24 E
cwdonaldson@ualr.edu
DONALDSON, Charles, W . 501-569-3328 .... 24 E
cwdonaldson@ualr.edu
DONALDSON, Colleen .... 585-395-5118 .... 352 F
cdonalds@brockport.edu
DONALDSON, Dan .... 816-584-6846 .... 287 E
daniel.donaldson@park.edu
DONALDSON, Glen .... 618-546-5659 .... 156 B
glen.donaldson@doc.illinois.gov
DONALDSON, Janice, W ... 904-620-2476 .... 120 D
jdonalds@unf.edu
DONALDSON, Jennifer .... 858-598-1200 .... 30 D
jdonaldson@aii.edu
DONALDSON, Jody .... 319-398-7186 .... 187 B
jdonald@kirkwood.edu
DONALDSON, John, A .... 406-265-3520 .... 295 E
jdonaldson@msun.edu
DONALDSON, Lisa .... 970-204-8113 .... 85 A
lisa.donaldson@frontrange.edu
DONALDSON, Monde .... 251-414-2291 .... 7 E
mdonaldson@shc.edu
DONALDSON, Penny .... 785-442-6054 .... 193 F
pdonaldson@highlandcc.edu
DONALDSON, Scott .... 510-780-4500 .... 53 J
sdonalds@lifewest.edu
DONALDSON, Stewart .... 909-607-9013 .... 40 F
stewart.donaldson@cgu.edu
DONALDSON, Tracey .... 215-968-8091 .... 423 F
donaldso@bucks.edu
DONAT, Kim .... 309-268-8046 .... 151 I
kim.donat@heartland.edu
DONAT, Patricia .... 706-864-1840 .... 134 G
pldonat@northgeorgia.edu
DONATH, Ben .... 712-749-2181 .... 183 C
donath@bvu.edu
DONATO, CSC, John, J .... 503-943-8532 .... 420 G
donato@up.edu
DONATO, Matt .... 909-621-8519 .... 62 H
matthew_donato@pitzer.edu
DONATUCCI, Nancy .... 724-339-7542 .... 437 F
gradeservices@nbi.edu
DONAUDY, Tom .... 561-297-2663 .... 119 A
tdonaudy@fau.edu
DONAVANT, Lori, A .... 731-881-7815 .... 477 G
ldonavant@utm.edu
DONAVANT, Susan, H .... 804-752-7222 .... 523 C
sdonavan@rmc.edu
DONCASTER, Bill .... 617-349-8525 .... 236 B
wdoncast@lesley.edu
DONCEVIC, John, G .... 724-847-6692 .... 429 H
jgdoncev@geneva.edu
DONCHESKI, Michael .... 724-749-6050 .... 440 B
mad10@psu.edu
DONCITS, Diane .... 651-641-3472 .... 264 H
ddoncits@luthersem.edu
DONCSECZ, Joseph, J .... 814-865-1355 .... 438 G
jjd7@psu.edu
DONDERO, Eileen .... 239-590-7967 .... 119 B
edondero@fgcu.edu
DONEGAN, Helen .... 407-317-7725 .... 120 B
helen.donegan@ucf.edu
DONEGAN, John, P .... 734-487-3591 .... 250 F
jdonega1@emich.edu
DONELSON, Charlotte .... 307-855-2154 .... 556 B
donelson@cwc.edu
DONELSON, Rollin .... 336-334-5963 .... 379 B
rollin_donelson@uncg.edu
DONELSON, Tery .... 573-875-7490 .... 280 A
tldonelson@ccis.edu
DONESKY, Grant .... 206-726-5043 .... 533 D
gdonesky@cornish.edu
DONEY, J.R .... 620-417-1101 .... 196 F
jr.doney@sccc.edu
DONG, Suhua .... 717-337-6487 .... 429 I
sdong@gettysburg.edu
DONGES, James .... 812-855-3684 .... 173 E
jdonges@indiana.edu
DONHAM, Marilyn .... 734-973-3630 .... 259 F
mdonham@wccnet.edu
DONHARDT, Gary, L .... 901-678-2231 .... 474 C
donhardt@memphis.edu
DONIN, Robert, B .... 603-646-0101 .... 304 J
robert.b.donin@dartmouth.edu
DONINI, Joseph .... 845-398-4040 .... 349 H
jdonini@stac.edu
DONIUS, Mary Alice .... 914-654-5803 .... 330 B
mdonius@cnr.edu
DONKERSLOOT, Norman .. 616-392-8555 .... 260 D
norman@westernsem.edu
DONLAN, Ally .... 828-298-3325 .... 380 D
adonlan@warren-wilson.edu
DONLAN, Michael, J .... 757-446-5890 .... 518 G
donlanmj@evms.edu
DONLEY, Bob .... 515-281-3934 .... 182 D
bdonley@iastate.edu
DONLEY, Laurie .... 330-339-3391 .... 394 A
ldonley@kent.edu
DONN, Denise, C .... 209-954-5114 .... 66 D
dcdonn@deltacollege.edu
DONNA, Jerry, A .... 217-581-3714 .... 150 E
jdonna@eiu.edu
DONNAY, Brent .... 320-308-3039 .... 269 A
btdonnay@stcloudstate.edu
DONNELL, Dorothy .... 662-252-8400 .... 276 G
ddonnell@rustcollege.edu
DONNELL, Floyd, D .... 812-374-5223 .... 176 A
fdonnell@ivytech.edu
DONNELL, Kathy, S .... 951-487-3002 .... 58 B
kdonnell@msjc.edu
DONNELL, Richard, H .... 731-424-5883 .... 470 B
rdonnell@lanecollege.edu
DONNELL, Robert .... 314-264-1000 .... 292 D
robert.donnell@vatterott.edu
DONNELL, Shauna, H .... 479-968-0343 .... 20 G
sdonnell@atu.edu
DONNELLA, II, Joseph, A 717-337-6280 .... 429 I
donnella@gettysburg.edu
DONNELLAN, Barbara .... 617-369-3832 .... 244 E
bdonnellan@mfa.org
DONNELLY, Daniel .... 615-297-7545 .... 467 A
donnelly@aquinascollege.edu
DONNELLY, Eileen, G .... 302-356-6812 .... 97 C
eileen.g.donnelly@wilmu.edu
DONNELLY, Gloria .... 215-762-4943 .... 427 H
gd27@drexel.edu
DONNELLY, Jim .... 336-249-8186 .... 370 B
jdonnelly@davidsonccc.edu
DONNELLY, John .... 434-961-5205 .... 528 B
jdonnelly@pvcc.edu
DONNELLY, Liz .... 405-208-7910 .... 410 A
ldonnelly@okcu.edu
DONNELLY, Maureen, D ... 617-353-9159 .... 232 E
mdonnell@bu.edu
DONNELLY, Patrick, G .... 937-229-3334 .... 404 A
pdonnelly1@udayton.edu
DONNELLY, Sherri .... 518-445-2396 .... 322 C
sdonn@albanylaw.edu
DONNELLY, Shirley, A .... 714-895-8121 .... 41 C
sdonnelly@gwc.cccd.edu
DONNELLY, William, H .... 740-376-4701 .... 395 G
whdonnelly@sbcglobal.net
DONNELLY HAMILTON,
Ann .... 419-772-2729 .... 398 H
a-donnelly@onu.edu
DONOFF, R. Bruce .... 617-432-1401 .... 235 D
bruce_donoff@hms.harvard.edu
DONOFRIO, A. Steven .... 212-998-2362 .... 344 B
steven.donofrio@nyu.edu
DONOGHUE, Daniel, J .... 858-822-5155 .... 74 F
ddonoghue@ucsd.edu
DONOGHUE, Karen, A .... 203-254-4000 .... 92 H
kdonoghue@fairfield.edu
DONOHOE, John .... 617-824-8515 .... 234 B
john_donohoe@emerson.edu
DONOHOE, Nancy .... 312-935-6715 .... 162 G
ndonohoe@robertmorris.edu
DONOHOE, Neil .... 617-912-9143 .... 232 C
ndonohoe@bostonconservatory.edu
DONOHOE, Timothy .... 215-568-9215 .... 436 E
tdonohoe@phmc.org
DONOHUE, Beth .... 315-568-3115 .... 342 H
bdonohue@nycc.edu
DONOHUE, Darrell .... 207-326-4311 .... 219 D
darrell.donohue@mma.edu
DONOHUE, James .... 717-544-7743 .... 433 E
jdonohue2@lancastergeneralcollege.edu
DONOHUE, Mary .... 518-736-3622 .... 334 D
mdonohue@fmcc.suny.edu
DONOHUE, Michael .... 212-752-1530 .... 338 C
michael.donohue@limcollege.edu
DONOHUE, Patricia, C .... 609-586-4800 .... 311 B
donohuep@mccc.edu
DONOHUE, OSA,
Peter, M .... 610-519-8881 .... 450 H
peter.donohue@villanova.edu
DONOHUE-MENDOZA,
Michelle .... 408-741-2185 .... 78 G
michelle.donohue@westvalley.edu
DONOHUE-SMITH,
Maureen .... 607-735-1957 .... 332 I
mdonohuesmith@elmira.edu
DONOTO, Chris .... 847-317-8113 .... 166 E
cdonoto@tiu.edu
DONOVAN, Amy .... 888-227-3552 .... 261 F
amy.donovan@capella.edu
DONOVAN, Amy, E .... 978-468-7111 .... 235 B
adonovan@gcts.edu
DONOVAN, Celeste .... 620-417-1016 .... 196 F
celeste.donovan@sccc.edu
DONOVAN, Donald, T .... 713-798-3380 .... 481 H
ddonovan@bcm.edu
DONOVAN, Gary, L .... 320-589-6065 .... 271 G
donovang@morris.umn.edu
DONOVAN, Jaclyn .... 229-931-2222 .... 131 F
jaclyn.donovan@gsw.edu
DONOVAN, James, J .... 808-956-7301 .... 141 G
jdonovan@hawaii.edu
DONOVAN, Joan .... 607-844-8222 .... 357 I
donovaj@tc3.edu
DONOVAN, Joseph .... 978-542-6119 .... 238 E
jdonovan@salemstate.edu
DONOVAN, Joseph, W .... 215-951-1849 .... 432 I
donovan@lasalle.edu
DONOVAN, Kara .... 515-643-6604 .... 187 F
kscholten@mercydesmoines.org
DONOVAN, Kevin .... 716-896-0700 .... 359 H
kdonovan@villa.edu
DONOVAN, Mark .... 312-413-1401 .... 167 B
mdonovan@uic.edu

DOUGLAS, Delano 804-524-5214 529 H
ddouglas@vsu.edu
DOUGLAS, Derek 773-702-3627 166 G
drbdouglas@uchicago.edu
DOUGLAS, Diane, J 715-394-8218 552 F
ddougla2@uwsuper.edu
DOUGLAS, James, M 713-313-1122 500 B
douglasj@tsu.edu
DOUGLAS, Jeffrey, A 309-341-7491 155 F
jdouglas@knox.edu
DOUGLAS, Jim 508-213-2333 243 E
jim.douglas@nichols.edu
DOUGLAS, Katherine, P 607-962-9232 331 C
kdouglas@corning-cc.edu
DOUGLAS, Kelly, C 619-260-7974 76 D
kdouglas@sandiego.edu
DOUGLAS, Kimberly 626-395-6416 32 H
kdouglas@its.caltech.edu
DOUGLAS, Kris 765-677-2710 175 B
kris.douglas@indwes.edu
DOUGLAS, Kristen 678-664-0529 139 F
kristen.douglas@westgatech.edu
DOUGLAS, Laura 515-248-7206 183 H
lldouglas@dmacc.edu
DOUGLAS, Linda 919-843-9393 378 E
linda_douglas@unc.edu
DOUGLAS, Lisa 303-315-2769 88 J
lisa.douglas@ucdenver.edu
DOUGLAS, Malcolm, C 847-574-5166 156 A
mdouglas@lfgsm.edu
DOUGLAS, Mary 419-824-3880 395 E
mdouglas@lourdes.edu
DOUGLAS, Michelle 304-696-2597 544 B
douglasm@marshall.edu
DOUGLAS, Minnie, L 562-408-6969 26 I
DOUGLAS, Renee 231-591-2614 250 H
douglar3@ferris.edu
DOUGLAS, Renee 231-591-5968 250 H
douglar3@ferris.edu
DOUGLAS, Scott, C 828-398-7147 368 B
sdouglas@abtech.edu
DOUGLAS, Shawn 478-471-0779 133 H
shawn.douglas@maconstate.edu
DOUGLAS, Sherry, L 308-432-6230 299 E
sdouglas@csc.edu
DOUGLAS, Stephen, L 304-293-4731 545 A
stephen.douglas@mail.wvu.edu
DOUGLAS, Tanya 317-543-4895 178 A
tdouglas@martin.edu
DOUGLASS, Barbara 860-738-6406 92 B
bdouglass@nwcc.commnet.edu
DOUGLASS, Brent 540-887-7201 521 C
bdouglass@mbc.edu
DOUGLASS, Carolinda 815-753-0492 160 B
cdoug@niu.edu
DOUGLASS, Claudia, B 989-774-3631 249 C
dougl1cb@cmich.edu
DOUGLASS, David, A 503-370-6447 421 D
ddouglas@willamette.edu
DOUGLASS, Debbie 559-730-3736 42 D
debbied@cos.edu
DOUGLASS, Georgia 630-752-5515 168 H
georgia.douglass@wheaton.edu
DOUGLASS, James 507-433-0611 268 H
jdouglas@riverland.edu
DOUGLASS, Jill 505-428-1351 320 E
jill.douglass@sfcc.edu
DOUGLASS, Scott, R 302-831-2200 96 I
douglass@udel.edu
DOUGLIS, Evan 518-276-6460 347 D
douglis@rpi.edu
DOUILLARD, Paul 718-405-3258 330 A
paul.douillard@mountsaintvincent.edu
DOUKAS, Peter, H 215-707-4990 447 H
peter.doukas@temple.edu
DOULIS, Peter 215-871-6900 444 C
peterd@pcom.edu
DOUMA, Debbie 850-484-1193 115 B
ddouma@pensacolastate.edu
DOURLEIN, Peter 520-621-9414 18 L
dourlein@u.arizona.edu
DOUTHAT, James, E 570-321-4101 435 D
douthat@lycoming.edu
DOUTHIT, Tricia 303-273-3383 83 B
tdouthit@mines.edu
DOUTHITT, Robin, A 608-262-4847 550 J
douthitt@wisc.edu
DOVE, Bill 719-389-6384 82 D
william.dove@coloradocollege.edu
DOVE, Cathy, S 607-255-4914 331 B
csd3@cornell.edu
DOVE, Danyele 610-526-6047 430 D
ddove@harcum.edu
DOVE, John 606-886-3863 201 G
john.dove@kctcs.edu
DOVE, Robert, B 901-843-3800 472 K
dove@rhodes.edu
DOVE, Wendy 406-771-4399 295 G
wendy.dove@msugf.edu
DOVER, Gordon 901-272-6852 471 D
gdover@mca.edu
DOVI, John 703-821-8570 524 J
jdovi@stratford.edu
DOVI, Sharon 607-844-8222 357 I
dovis@tc3.edu
DOW, Dennis, C 650-508-3578 59 H
ddow@ndnu.edu
DOW, Larry 860-297-2157 94 E
larry.dow@trincoll.edu
DOW, Sarah 617-585-1296 242 I
sarah.dow@necmusic.edu
DOW, Steven, R 402-465-2255 299 H
sdow@nebrwesleyan.edu
DOW-MCDONALD, Jennifer 810-762-0533 255 G
jennifer.dow@mcc.edu
DOW-ROYER, Cathy, A 413-205-3262 229 G
cathy.dow-royer@aic.edu
DOW-SIMPSON, Evelyn 505-224-5217 317 K
evdow@cnm.edu
DOWD, Bonnie Ann 619-388-6975 65 E
bdowd@sdccd.edu
DOWD, Deirdre, M 516-876-3191 353 D
dowdd@oldwestbury.edu
DOWD, Dennis, C 214-333-5338 484 D
denny@dbu.edu
DOWD, John, P 843-661-1295 458 D
jdowd@fmarion.edu
DOWD, Julia, A 415-422-2531 76 E
dowd@usfca.edu
DOWD, Sarah 803-778-6668 455 G
dowdss@cctech.edu
DOWDEN, G. Blair 260-359-4050 173 A
bdowden@huntington.edu
DOWDEY, Don 432-837-8124 501 E
ddowdey@sulross.edu
DOWDLE, Deedie Kay 513-529-1809 396 E
dowdledk@muohio.edu
DOWDLE, Rita 662-562-3206 276 D
rbdowdle@northwestms.edu
DOWDY, Kathleen, B 806-371-5389 479 G
kbdowdy@actx.edu
DOWDY, Lawrence, A 610-436-6974 444 A
ldowdy@wcupa.edu
DOWDY, Mickey 252-328-9595 377 E
dowdym@ecu.edu
DOWDY, Phyllis 910-695-3739 373 H
dowdyp@sandhills.edu
DOWDY, Ronald 386-481-2031 102 C
dowdyr@cookman.edu
DOWE, Peter 585-395-2531 352 F
pdowe@brockport.edu
DOWELL, Chanda 309-854-1721 145 H
dowellc@bhc.edu
DOWELL, David 562-985-4128 35 C
ddowell@csulb.edu
DOWELL, Elise 212-678-8950 337 G
eldowell@jtsa.edu
DOWELL, Marcia, A 317-940-9257 170 F
mdowell@butler.edu
DOWELL, Marsha 864-503-5328 463 B
mdowell@uscupstate.edu
DOWER, Julia 603-542-7744 304 G
jdower@ccsnh.edu
DOWER, Karyn 209-381-6585 57 C
karyn.dower@mccd.edu
DOWLAND, Pam 812-357-6515 180 A
pdowland@saintmeinrad.edu
DOWLESS, Donald, V 706-233-7201 137 A
chimes@shorter.edu
DOWLING, Amy, S 570-321-4134 435 D
dowling@lycoming.edu
DOWLING, Denise 406-243-4001 294 I
denise.dowling@umontana.edu
DOWLING, Earl 630-942-3416 148 A
dowlinge@cod.edu
DOWLING, Joseph, B 714-895-8158 41 C
jdowling@gwc.cccd.edu
DOWLING, Victoria, A 618-537-2154 158 A
vadowling@mckendree.edu
DOWNES, Amanda 302-736-2318 97 A
downesam@wesley.edu
DOWNES, John 770-426-2646 133 E
jdownes@life.edu
DOWNES, Timothy 404-727-6532 129 D
timothy.downes@emory.edu
DOWNEY, Catherine 503-552-1761 417 D
cdowney@ncnm.edu
DOWNEY, James 412-924-1450 444 H
jdowney@pts.edu
DOWNEY, John 704-337-2227 376 A
downeyj@queens.edu
DOWNEY, John, A 540-234-9261 526 D
downeyj@brcc.edu
DOWNEY, Nancy 207-859-4503 217 G
ndowney@colby.edu
DOWNEY, Nora 610-785-6582 446 A
ndowney@scs.edu
DOWNEY, Robert, F 724-938-4299 441 G
downey_r@calu.edu
DOWNING, Amy 617-730-7174 243 D
amy.downing@newbury.edu
DOWNING, Andre 502-456-6509 206 G
adowning@sctd.edu
DOWNING, Arthur 646-312-1020 326 C
arthur.downing@baruch.cuny.edu
DOWNING, Charlotte, M 585-292-2000 341 H
DOWNING, Irvine 956-882-4238 505 E
irv.downing@utb.edu
DOWNING, Kimberly 513-556-5028 403 D
kimberly.downing@uc.edu
DOWNING, Lenora 540-986-1800 521 I
downing@ncbt.edu
DOWNING, Lenora 540-986-1800 541 I
ldowning@national-college.edu
DOWNING, Lenora, S 540-986-1800 521 J
downing@ncbt.edu
DOWNING, Lenora, S 540-986-1800 522 D
ldowning@national-college.edu
DOWNING, Michael 508-336-8700 453 E
mdowning@jwu.edu
DOWNING, Rossann 816-604-4071 285 E
rossann.downing@mcckc.edu
DOWNING, Sherry 513-862-2743 391 E
DOWNING, Stacey 501-370-5354 23 B
sdowning@philander.edu
DOWNING, Steve 317-955-6351 177 I
sdowning@marian.edu
DOWNING, Teresa 603-899-4105 305 A
downingt@franklinpierce.edu
DOWNS, Kim 802-443-5208 514 A
kdowns@middlebury.edu
DOWNS, Lisa 913-971-3380 195 D
ldowns@mnu.edu
DOWNS, Ronald, J 502-231-5221 204 E
rdowns@mylbc.us
DOWNS, Timothy, M 716-286-8342 344 D
downs@niagara.edu
DOWNS, Wil 812-237-4114 173 B
wil.downs@indstate.edu
DOWSE, Bruce 308-535-3605 298 H
dowseb@mpcc.edu
DOWSETT, Carol 989-729-3405 248 F
carol.dowsett@baker.edu
DOXEY, Scott, Y 540-261-8577 524 H
scott.doxey@svu.edu
DOXIE-DIXON, Eloise 504-520-7515 217 A
edixon@xula.edu
DOYAL, Renee 972-792-7450 486 E
rdoyal@devry.edu
DOYLE, Amanda 337-482-6730 216 D
amandad@louisiana.edu
DOYLE, Catherine 585-389-2123 342 D
cdoyle0@naz.edu
DOYLE, Cathleen, H 410-777-2902 221 C
chdoyle@aacc.edu
DOYLE, Christine, M 610-355-7151 426 G
cdoyle@dccc.edu
DOYLE, Christy 509-533-7295 533 B
christy.doyle@scc.spokane.edu
DOYLE, Clare 215-248-7071 425 D
doylec@chc.edu
DOYLE, Creig 603-535-2331 307 A
cwdoyle@plymouth.edu
DOYLE, Denise 210-283-6827 504 B
ddoyle@uiwtx.edu
DOYLE, Diana 303-797-5701 81 D
diana.doyle@arapahoe.edu
DOYLE, Duane 270-843-6750 200 B
ddoyle@daymarcollege.edu
DOYLE, Eileen 914-633-2483 336 E
edoyle@iona.edu
DOYLE, Gerald 312-567-5203 153 C
doyle@iit.edu
DOYLE, J. Griffin 706-542-8096 138 G
gdoyle@uga.edu
DOYLE, Janice, B 301-445-1901 227 A
jdoyle@usmd.edu
DOYLE, Jeanette, M 508-831-5260 246 F
jmdoyle@wpi.edu
DOYLE, Jeff 254-710-1011 482 A
jeff_doyle@baylor.edu
DOYLE, Leslie 314-889-4503 281 I
ldoyle@fontbonne.edu
DOYLE, Lori 215-895-2100 427 H
lori.n.doyle@drexel.edu
DOYLE, Mary 831-459-4906 75 C
mdoyle1@ucsc.edu
DOYLE, Michael, H 563-588-7823 187 C
michael.doyle@loras.edu
DOYLE, Patrick 970-248-1847 82 F
pdoyle@coloradomesa.edu
DOYLE, Sheila 607-777-3844 351 F
sdoyle@binghamton.edu
DOYNE, Diane 312-369-7524 148 D
ddoyne@colum.edu
DOZIER, Belinda 270-886-1302 199 C
bdozier@brownmackie.edu
DOZIER, Cheryl 912-358-4000 136 G
ssupresident@savannahstate.edu
DOZIER, Felicia 863-784-7231 117 J
dozierf@southflorida.edu
DOZIER, Jack 417-447-7570 287 D
dozierj@otc.edu
DOZIER, Luann, D 504-865-5794 215 C
ldozier@tulane.edu
DRABEK, Walter, J 716-888-8359 325 F
drabek@canisius.edu
DRABIER, Renee 817-735-2146 504 E
renee.drabier@unthsc.edu
DRABIK, Mary, A 954-545-4500 117 I
mdrabik@sfbc.edu
DRABIK, Thomas 954-545-4500 117 I
academics@sfbc.edu
DRAEGER, Darren 415-388-1133 48 E
darren.draeger@lifeway.com
DRAGAN, Kimberly 860-738-6418 92 B
kdragan@nwcc.commnet.edu
DRAGHI, Mary Kathleen 814-871-7430 429 G
draghi002@gannon.edu
DRAGO, Linda, S 412-396-5181 428 D
drago@duq.edu
DRAGONETTI, William 954-752-1414 108 J
wdragonetti@fmti.edu
DRAGOO, Lloyd 432-837-8614 501 E
ldragoo@sulross.edu
DRAHUS-CAPO, Deborah 787-751-3374 561 E
ddrahus@sanjuancapital.com
DRAIN, Cecil, B 804-828-7247 526 B
cbdrain@vcu.edu
DRAIN, Jerome 404-756-4443 125 D
jdrain@atlm.edu
DRAIN, Timothy, S 903-510-2458 503 A
tdra@tjc.edu
DRAKE, Autumn 405-912-9096 408 D
adrake@hc.edu
DRAKE, Brent, M 765-494-6136 178 J
bmdrake@purdue.edu
DRAKE, Carlene 909-558-4581 54 D
cdrake@llu.edu
DRAKE, Carolyn, C 559-244-2604 72 B
carolyn.drake@fresnocitycollege.edu
DRAKE, Charles, E 405-744-6494 410 C
cedrake@okstate.edu
DRAKE, Chris 972-273-3301 485 C
cdrake@dcccd.edu
DRAKE, Janet, M 701-845-7302 382 C
jan.drake@vcsu.edu
DRAKE, Jennifer, A 317-791-5704 180 F
jdrake@uindy.edu
DRAKE, Kay, L 859-238-5467 199 G
kay.drake@centre.edu
DRAKE, Linda, R 949-824-4016 74 B
lrdrake@uci.edu
DRAKE, Marianne 413-662-5224 238 C
m.drake@mcla.edu
DRAKE, Michael, V 949-824-5111 74 B
chancellor@uci.edu
DRAKE, Peter 212-966-0300 342 F
info@nyaa.edu
DRAKE, Ricky 334-229-5104 1 C
rdrake@alasu.edu
DRAKE, Roger, D 270-384-8040 204 E
draker@lindsey.edu
DRAKE, Steve 618-283-4170 156 B
DRAKE, Susan, K 217-243-9071 152 D
sdrake@ic.edu
DRAKE, Tom 575-769-4994 318 A
tom.drake@clovis.edu
DRAKE, Tonya, M 206-546-6910 538 C
tdrake@shoreline.edu
DRAKE-DEESE, Kent 603-358-2346 306 G
kdrakedeese@keene.edu
DRAKEFORD, Carolyn 803-705-4423 455 D
drakefordc@benedict.edu
DRAKULICH, J. Scott 973-877-3370 309 H
drakulich@essex.edu
DRALE, Christina, S 501-569-3204 24 E
csdrale@ualr.edu
DRANE, Kim 307-382-1645 557 A
kdrane-n@wwcc.wy.edu
DRANGMEISTER, Cheryl 505-428-1162 320 E
cheryl.drangmeister@sfcc.edu
DRAPEAU, Guy 860-297-4210 94 E
guy.drapeau@trincoll.edu
DRAPER, Ann 831-459-5358 75 C
ann@ucsc.edu
DRAPER, David 310-377-5501 56 F
ddraper@marymountpv.edu
DRAPER, David, E 419-434-4202 406 A
president@winebrenner.edu
DRAPER, Dennis 310-338-7504 56 E
ddraper@lmu.edu
DRAPER, Frances 303-492-7531 88 H
frances.draper@colorado.edu
DRAPER, James 603-358-2492 306 G
jdraper@keene.edu
DRAPER, Jeri 215-751-8199 426 B
jdraper@ccp.edu
DRAPER, Mary 727-726-1153 103 I
marydraper@clearwater.edu
DRAPER, Mary, C 727-726-1153 103 I
marydraper@clearwater.edu
DRAPER, Nancy, J 405-912-9024 408 D
ndraper@hc.edu
DRAPER, Randall, W 303-492-2695 88 H
randall.draper@colorado.edu
DRASKOVIC, Inez 585-785-1322 334 A
draskoi@flcc.edu
DRASS, Mike 302-736-2545 97 A
drassmi@wesley.edu
DRAUDE, Barbara, J 615-904-8189 473 G
barbara.draude@mtsu.edu

DRAUDT, Wayne, J .... 815-836-5235.... 156 F
draudtwa@lewisu.edu
DRAUGALIS, JoLaine .... 405-271-6484.... 413 D
jolaine-draugalis@ouhsc.edu
DRAUGHON, Bill .... 305-348-3961.... 119 C
draughon@fiu.edu
DRAUGHON, Katherine, A . 812-465-7107.... 181 B
kdraughon@usi.edu
DRAUS, David, A .... 612-330-1033.... 261 B
draus@augsburg.edu
DRAVES, Patricia, H .... 330-823-2690.... 404 C
dravesph@mountunion.edu
DRAYER, Kevin, S .... 315-255-1743.... 325 G
drayer@cayuga-cc.edu
DRAYFAHL, Perry, M .... 610-499-1291.... 451 F
pmdrayfahl@widener.edu
DRAYNA, Jonathan .... 414-425-8300.... 550 E
jdrayna@shst.edu
DRAYTON, Ronald .... 803-738-7606.... 459 E
draytonr@midlandstech.edu
DREBIN, Diane .... 360-992-2080.... 532 F
ddrebin@clark.edu
DREBLOW, Lewis, M .... 740-826-8050.... 397 A
dreblow@muskingum.edu
DRECKMAN, Lisa .... 417-833-2551.... 279 E
ldreckman@cbcag.edu
DREES, Betty, M .... 816-235-1808.... 291 C
dreesb@umkc.edu
DREES, Lynn .... 941-752-5428.... 118 J
dreesl@scf.edu
DREESSEN, Angela .... 309-694-5353.... 152 C
angela.dreessen@icc.edu
DREFFS, Daryl, A .... 603-668-2211.... 305 I
d.dreffs@snhu.edu
DREGER, Barb .... 920-735-4776.... 554 A
dreger@fvtc.edu
DREGIER, Denise, M .... 443-412-2428.... 223 B
ddregier@harford.edu
DREHER, John .... 404-627-2681.... 126 D
john.dreher@beulah.org
DREHER, Karolina .... 610-796-8218.... 421 G
karolina.dreher@alvernia.edu
DREHER, Melanie .... 312-942-7117.... 163 D
melanie_dreher@rush.edu
DREIBELBIS, Elizabeth, M . 717-846-5000.... 452 H
DREIBELBIS, John, A .... 717-846-5000.... 452 H
DREIFUSS, Susan, B .... 410-843-8852.... 272 C
susan.dreifuss@waldenu.edu
DREILING, Karolyn .... 913-758-3293.... 197 D
karolyn.dreiling@stmary.edu
DREISBACH, Joseph, H ..... 570-941-4760.... 450 C
joseph.dreisbach@scranton.edu
DREITH, Michael .... 618-985-2637.... 154 G
mikedreith@jalc.edu
DREITZ, Donetta .... 620-417-1061.... 196 F
donetta.dreitz@sccc.edu
DREITZLER, M. Sue .... 440-375-7255.... 394 E
sdreitzler@lec.edu
DRENKOW, Daniel, D .... 605-274-5251.... 464 A
dan.drenkow@augie.edu
DRENNEN, Carol, K .... 440-964-4234.... 393 E
cdrennen@kent.edu
DRENNEN, Michelle .... 859-341-5627.... 199 E
mdrennen@brownmackie.edu
DRENNON, Marsha, K .... 660-596-7223.... 290 B
mdrennon@sfccmo.edu
DRENTH, Lucy .... 215-489-2475.... 426 H
lucille.drenth@delval.edu
DRESCHER, Greg .... 845-451-2401.... 331 E
g_dresch@culinary.edu
DRESCHER, Kurt, W .... 978-468-7111.... 235 B
kdrescher@gcts.edu
DRESSANDER, Jan .... 701-349-3621.... 383 E
jandressander@trinitybiblecollege.edu
DRESSEL, Laurie .... 303-280-7653...... 84 G
lsein@devry.edu
DRESSELHAUS, Mark .... 316-942-4291.... 195 F
dresselhausm@newmanu.edu
DRESSEN, Dan .... 507-786-3962.... 271 C
dressen@stolaf.edu
DRESSER, Charles, E .... 312-329-4267.... 159 A
cdresser@moody.edu
DRESSER-RECKTENWALD,
Wendy .... 607-587-4025.... 355 C
dressews@alfredstate.edu
DRESSMAN, Michael, R .... 713-221-8003.... 503 F
dressmanm@uhd.edu
DREVON, CSC, Charles, D 574-239-8392.... 172 M
cdrevon@hcc-nd.edu
DREW, Dan .... 317-278-5323.... 174 D
drew@iupui.edu
DREW, Daniel, J .... 716-888-2569.... 325 F
drewd@canisius.edu
DREW, Don .... 405-425-5577.... 409 E
don.drew@oc.edu
DREW, John .... 617-827-6047.... 236 G
john.drew@umb.edu
DREW, Rus .... 706-568-2022.... 127 G
drew_rus@columbusstate.edu
DREW, Todd .... 402-872-2222.... 299 F
tdrew@peru.edu
DREWELOW, Lonna .... 319-368-6468.... 187 H
drewelow@mtmercy.edu
DREWENSKI, Shirley .... 708-596-2000.... 164 H
sdrewenski@ssc.edu
DREWETT, Jerry, S .... 318-257-2769.... 215 F
uajsd@latech.edu
DREWS, David .... 517-265-5161.... 246 H
ddrews@adrian.edu
DREXLER, Brad .... 610-796-8216.... 421 G
bradley.drexler@alvernia.edu
DREXLER, Brad .... 610-796-8376.... 421 G
brad.drexler@alvernia.edu
DREXLER, Jim .... 706-419-1408.... 128 B
drexler@covenant.edu
DREYER, Allen, R .... 570-586-2400.... 422 G
adreyer@bbc.edu
DREYER, Brenda .... 605-626-2552.... 466 A
brenda.dreyer@northern.edu
DREYER, CSC, Chris, J ..... 574-239-8383.... 172 M
cdreyer@hcc-nd.edu
DREYER, John, M .... 260-452-3139.... 170 J
john.dreyer@ctsfw.edu
DREYER, Thomas .... 978-934-4801.... 237 B
thomas_dreyer@uml.edu
DREYFUS, Lawrence, A ...... 816-235-2576.... 291 C
dreyfusl@umkc.edu
DREYFUS, Mark, B .... 757-671-7171.... 518 H
president@ecpi.edu
DREYFUSS, Simeon .... 503-699-3961.... 416 J
sdreyfuss@marylhurst.edu
DREYFUSS, Teresa .... 562-908-3403...... 63 H
tdreyfuss@riohondo.edu
DREYFUSS, Teresa .... 562-908-3404...... 63 H
tdreyfuss@riohondo.edu
DRICI, Zahia .... 309-556-3760.... 153 F
zdrici@iwu.edu
DRICKEY, Nancy .... 503-883-2201.... 416 H
ndricke@linfield.edu
DRIER, Tracy, M .... 715-833-6498.... 553 H
tdrier@cvtc.edu
DRIES, Kelly, J .... 414-410-4390.... 546 G
kjdries@stritch.edu
DRIES, Richard .... 414-297-6572.... 554 F
driesr@matc.edu
DRIESSNER, Johnnie .... 503-493-6549.... 415 E
jdriessner@cu-portland.edu
DRIFKA, Amy .... 612-977-5368.... 261 F
amy.drifka@capella.edu
DRIGGERS, Kimberly, A .... 910-277-5561.... 376 C
driggers@sapc.edu
DRIGGERS, Randy .... 504-282-4455.... 213 H
rdriggers@nobts.edu
DRILLING, Peter .... 716-652-8900.... 325 J
pdrilling@cks.edu
DRIMMER, Alan .... 480-557-1696...... 19 A
alan.drimmer@phoenix.edu
DRINAN, Helen, G .... 617-521-2070.... 244 F
helen.drinan@simmons.edu
DRINKARD, Gretchen .... 314-454-7055.... 282 B
gdrinkard@bjc.org
DRINKO, J. Randall .... 216-781-9400.... 388 B
instruct@cie-wc.edu
DRINKO, Randy .... 757-464-4600.... 530 H
instruct@cie-wc.edu
DRINKWATER, L. Ray .... 804-706-5064.... 527 B
ldrinkwater@jtcc.edu
DRISCOLL, Daniel, R .... 630-889-6542.... 159 F
ddriscoll@nuhs.edu
DRISCOLL,
Edward (Terry), C .... 757-221-3332.... 518 A
ecdris@wm.edu
DRISCOLL, Frederick .... 617-989-4135.... 245 F
driscollf@wit.edu
DRISCOLL, Karen .... 360-992-2260.... 532 F
kdriscoll@clark.edu
DRISCOLL, Laura .... 307-268-2733.... 556 A
ldriscoll@caspercollege.edu
DRISCOLL, Lisa .... 508-849-3398.... 230 C
ldriscoll@annamaria.edu
DRISCOLL, Lori .... 850-769-1551.... 110 H
ldriscoll@gulfcoast.edu
DRISCOLL, Marcy, P .... 850-644-6885.... 119 D
mdriscoll@fsu.edu
DRISCOLL, Marsha .... 218-755-3984.... 265 I
mdriscoll@bemidjistate.edu
DRISCOLL, Mary, C .... 716-375-7673.... 348 C
mdriscol@sbu.edu
DRISCOLL, Mary Erina .... 212-650-5302.... 326 G
DRISCOLL, Michael .... 410-837-4865.... 229 A
mdriscoll@ubalt.edu
DRISCOLL, Michael .... 724-357-2200.... 442 F
michael.driscoll@iup.edu
DRISCOLL, Micheline .... 718-368-5436.... 328 A
mdriscoll@kbcc.cuny.edu
DRISCOLL, Michelle .... 815-802-8524.... 155 A
mdriscoll@kcc.edu
DRISCOLL, JR., Robert, G 401-865-2090.... 453 H
rdriscol@providence.edu
DRISCOLL, Robert, L .... 770-720-5504.... 136 C
rld@reinhardt.edu
DRISCOLL, William .... 617-745-6704.... 234 A
william.driscoll@enc.edu
DRISKELL, Lavon .... 662-685-4771.... 273 E
ldriskell@bmc.edu
DRISKILL, Jerry .... 318-671-4001.... 214 F
DRISKO, Connie, L .... 706-721-2117.... 130 D
cdrisko@georgiahealth.edu
DRIVER, C. Berry .... 817-923-1921.... 495 G
bdriver@swbts.edu
DRIVER, Doug .... 970-943-7010...... 89 E
ddriver@western.edu
DRIVER, Louise .... 501-882-8845...... 20 C
oldriver@asub.edu
DRIVER-LINN, Erin .... 617-384-9033.... 235 D
erin_driver-linn@harvard.edu
DRNEK, James .... 216-687-3977.... 388 D
j.drnek@csuohio.edu
DROBNICKI, John .... 718-262-2025.... 329 A
drobnicki@york.cuny.edu
DRODDY, Jason .... 225-578-5745.... 212 H
jdroddy@lsu.edu
DROEGEMEIER, Kelvin ...... 405-325-3806.... 413 C
kkd@ou.edu
DROEL, Bill .... 708-974-5221.... 159 B
droel@morainevalley.edu
DROGE, Michael .... 816-584-6202.... 287 E
michael.droge@park.edu
DROKER, Stephanie .... 559-934-2221...... 78 C
stephaniedroker@whccd.edu
DROLETTE, Frances .... 781-736-8302.... 232 F
drolette@brandeis.edu
DROLL, Charlotte .... 570-389-4921.... 441 F
cdroll@bloomu.edu
DROMPP, Michael, R .... 901-843-3795.... 472 K
drompp@rhodes.edu
DRONE-SILVERS, Scott ...... 217-234-5338.... 156 B
dsilvers@lakeland.cc.il.us
DRONEY, Michael .... 330-494-6170.... 402 B
mdroney@starkstate.edu
DRONSFIELD, Shelli .... 304-876-5107.... 544 C
sdronsfi@shepherd.edu
DROOG, Sue .... 712-722-6017.... 184 C
sdroog@dordt.edu
DROPKIN, Keith .... 617-588-1363.... 231 C
kdropkin@bfit.edu
DROPKIN, Shelley .... 617-588-1302.... 231 C
sdropkin@bfit.edu
DROSS, Cindy .... 920-693-1385.... 554 C
cindy.dross@gotoltc.edu
DROST, Donald .... 732-906-2568.... 311 D
ddrost@middlesexcc.edu
DROST, Jim .... 641-673-1104.... 190 C
drostj@wmpenn.edu
DROUGHT, Joe .... 815-921-4353.... 162 H
i.drought@rockvalleycollege.edu
DROUIN, Amy .... 816-501-4628.... 288 A
amy.drouin@rockhurst.edu
DROUIN, Nancy .... 207-216-4434.... 219 C
ndrouin@yccc.edu
DROWN, Steven, A .... 530-754-6295...... 73 I
sadrown@ucdavis.edu
DRUCKER, David .... 508-541-1508.... 233 G
ddrucker@dean.edu
DRUCKER, Sheldon .... 201-692-2875.... 310 A
drucker@fdu.edu
DRUCKER, Sheldon .... 201-692-7100.... 310 A
drucker@fdu.edu
DRUCKREY, Melissa .... 601-979-2123.... 274 G
melissa.l.druckrey@jsums.edu
DRUDING, Marlene .... 856-225-6768.... 314 D
mdruding@camden.rutgers.edu
DRUEKE, Tim .... 803-323-2228.... 463 E
drueket@winthrop.edu
DRUGOVICH, Margaret, L . 607-431-4990.... 335 A
president@hartwick.edu
DRUIN, Cathy .... 502-456-6509.... 206 G
cdruin@sctd.edu
DRUMLUK, Sandy .... 607-844-8222.... 357 I
drumlus@tc3.edu
DRUMM, C. Scott .... 504-282-4455.... 213 H
sdrumm@nobts.edu
DRUMM, Kathy .... 704-330-6717.... 369 D
kathy.drumm@cpcc.edu
DRUMM, Kevin .... 607-778-5100.... 324 G
drummke@sunybroome.edu
DRUMM, Rene' .... 423-236-2766.... 473 B
rdrumm@southern.edu
DRUMMER, Carlee .... 847-635-1671.... 160 F
cdrummer@oakton.edu
DRUMMER, Carol, J .... 516-463-4876.... 335 G
carol.j.drummer@hofstra.edu
DRUMMER FRANCIS,
Raydora, S .... 315-470-4815.... 355 A
rsdrumme@esf.edu
DRUMMOND, Carl, N .... 260-481-5750.... 174 C
drummond@ipfw.edu
DRUMMOND, Darl, E .... 847-543-2048.... 148 B
ddrummond@clcillinois.edu
DRUMMOND, Gordon .... 480-212-1704...... 18 C
DRUMMOND, Jason, S ...... 660-543-4157.... 290 H
drummond@ucmo.edu
DRUMMOND, Jerri .... 401-454-6655.... 454 B
jdrummon@risd.edu
DRUMMOND, Lew .... 205-391-2347...... 6 I
ldrummondr@sheltonstate.edu
DRUMMOND, Marcy .... 213-763-7036...... 55 D
drummomj@lattc.edu
DRUMMOND, Mary Bea ... 918-594-8223.... 410 D
mary_bea.drummond@okstate.edu
DRUMMOND, Peter .... 847-574-5234.... 156 A
pdrummond@lfgsm.edu
DRUMMOND, Sarah, B ...... 617-964-1100.... 230 B
sdrummond@ants.edu
DRUMMY, Michael .... 714-997-6919...... 39 F
mdrummy@chapman.edu
DRURY, Joel .... 405-422-1257.... 411 G
druryj@redlandscc.edu
DRURY, Timothy .... 718-405-3239.... 330 A
timothy.drury@mountsaintvincent.edu
DRUSE, Rick .... 620-227-9264.... 192 E
rdruse@dc3.edu
DRUST, Kristin .... 215-335-0800.... 434 G
kdrust@lincolntech.com
DRY, Shana .... 803-313-7008.... 462 D
drysf@sc.edu
DRYDEN, Barbara .... 386-226-6300.... 105 H
dbfinaid@erau.edu
DRYE, Felix, M .... 919-536-7217.... 370 C
dryef@durhamtech.edu
DRYER, Christy .... 410-287-6060.... 222 A
cdryer@cecil.edu
DRYER, Norma .... 956-665-7021.... 506 C
dryern@utpa.edu
DRYER, Peter .... 276-326-4281.... 516 L
pdryer@bluefield.edu
DRYGAS, Emily .... 907-474-6631...... 10 I
emily.drygas@alaska.edu
DRZEWIECKI, Teresa .... 410-843-8506.... 272 C
teresa.drzewiecki@laureate.net
DU, Fang .... 330-829-8175.... 404 C
dufang@mountunion.edu
DUARTE, Angelina .... 415-485-9619...... 42 B
angelina.duarte@marin.edu
DUARTE, Ivette .... 305-348-2423.... 119 C
duartei@fiu.edu
DUARTE, Lamar .... 210-486-3600.... 479 C
pacsfa8@alamo.edu
DUARTE, Mark, A .... 671-735-2266.... 559 G
mduarte@uguam.uog.edu
DUARTE, Melanie .... 617-912-9160.... 232 C
mduarte@bostonconservatory.edu
DUBACH, John, F .... 413-545-2211.... 236 F
dubach@chancellor.umass.edu
DUBAK, Izabela .... 630-889-6576.... 159 F
idubak@nuhs.edu
DUBBINK, Mary, T .... 724-334-6041.... 440 C
mtd13@psu.edu
DUBE, CarolAnne .... 207-974-4817.... 218 H
cadube@emcc.edu
DUBEAU, Peter .... 410-225-2371.... 224 B
pdubeau@mica.edu
DUBEY, Steve .... 775-784-1331.... 303 A
sdubey@unr.edu
DUBIEL, Julia .... 805-962-8179...... 29 A
jdubiel@antioch.edu
DUBIEL, Mandy .... 517-629-0600.... 247 A
adubiel@albion.edu
DUBIN, Bruce .... 303-373-2008...... 88 C
DUBINSKY, Zalman .... 973-267-8005.... 313 B
zalmandubinsky@gmail.com
DUBLE, Troy .... 706-419-1122.... 128 B
duble@covenant.edu
DUBLON, Felice .... 312-629-6800.... 164 C
fdublon@saic.edu
DUBOIS, Arthur .... 203-575-8056...... 92 A
adubois@nvcc.commnet.edu
DUBOIS, Glenn .... 804-819-4903.... 526 C
gdubois@vccs.edu
DUBOIS, Keith .... 207-780-5250.... 220 G
dubois@usm.maine.edu
DUBOIS, Melinda, C .... 585-245-5736.... 353 C
dubois@geneseo.edu
DUBOIS, Philip, L .... 704-687-5729.... 379 A
pdubois@uncc.edu
DUBOIS, Priscilla, L .... 540-985-8491.... 520 I
pldubois@jchs.edu
DUBOIS, Raymond .... 713-792-6161.... 507 B
DUBOIS, Shelly .... 480-515-7648.... 149 B
sdubois@devry.edu
DUBOIS, Toni .... 714-992-7074...... 59 E
tdubois@fullcoll.edu
DUBOSE, Cheryl .... 843-355-4162.... 463 D
dubosec@wiltech.edu
DUBOSE, Lisa .... 567-661-7263.... 400 I
lisa_dubose@owens.edu
DUBOSE, Richard, A .... 270-745-5405.... 208 A
rick.dubose@wku.edu
DUBRAY, Kirsten .... 916-484-8175...... 56 A
dubrayk@arc.losrios.edu
DUBRAY, Robert, R .... 412-365-1641.... 425 C
rdubray@chatham.edu
DUBREUIL, Thomas .... 610-625-7051.... 437 A
DUBROY, Tashni .... 919-546-8274.... 376 F
tdubroy@shawu.edu
DUBUC-PEDERSEN,
Danielle .... 402-354-7259.... 299 C
danielle.dubuc-pedersen@methodistcollege.
edu
DUBUIS, Dina .... 734-432-5309.... 254 D
ddubuis@madonna.edu
DUBY, Paul, B .... 906-227-2670.... 256 C
pduby@nmu.edu

DUCHARME, Gaylene 406-338-5421 293 F gatk@bfcc.org
DUCHARME-WHITE, Sherri 414-955-4145 548 G sducharm@mail.mcw.edu
DUCHON, Maire, I 718-862-7166 339 H maire.duchon@manhattan.edu
DUCHSCHERER, Eric, D 315-267-2350 354 C duchsced@potsdam.edu
DUCIOAME, Lynn 940-397-4676 491 B lynn.ducioame@mwsu.edu
DUCK, Patricia, M 724-836-9689 449 C pmd1@pitt.edu
DUCKER, Dalia 415-955-2133 27 F ddoucker@alliant.edu
DUCKETT, Dwaine, B 510-987-0301 73 G dwaine.duckett@ucop.edu
DUCKETT, Randy, R 803-641-3487 462 B randyd@usca.edu
DUCKSWORTH, Stephanie 407-261-0319 108 D sducksworth@fcnh.com
DUCKWORTH, Brad 414-382-6323 546 B brad.duckworth@alverno.edu
DUCKWORTH, Cory, L 801-863-6158 511 F duckwoco@uvu.edu
DUCKWORTH, Latoya 573-681-5970 283 I duckworthl@lincolnu.edu
DUCKWORTH, Tony 918-444-3926 409 A duckwo01@nsuok.edu
DUCLOS-BARRETT, Victoria 401-341-2345 454 D duclosv@salve.edu
DUCOFFE, Robert 574-520-4133 174 E ducoffe@iusb.edu
DUCOTE, Melissa 318-345-9109 210 H mducote@ladelta.edu
DUCRAY, Sarah 202-651-5000 98 B sarah.ducray@gallaudet.edu
DUCUENNOIS, Sara 954-262-2103 114 B ducuenno@nsu.nova.edu
DUDA, Laura 570-504-1588 433 A dudal@lackawanna.edu
DUDA, Mark 570-961-7852 433 A dudam@lackawanna.edu
DUDA, Stephen 570-504-1734 433 A dudas@lackawanna.edu
DUDA, Teri 201-967-9667 307 F td@berkeleycollege.edu
DUDAK, Nancy, J 610-519-7300 450 H nancy.dudak@villanova.edu
DUDAS, Bertalan 814-866-8142 433 C bdudas@lecom.edu
DUDAS, Maryann 724-838-4275 447 C dudas@setonhill.edu
DUDAS, Philip 651-905-3542 261 E pdudas@browncollege.edu
DUDEK, Scott 305-573-1600 101 E sdudek@atienterprises.edu
DUDENHEFER, Diane 901-321-3545 467 I ddudenhe@cbu.edu
DUDGEON, David 305-899-3727 101 M ddudgeon@mail.barry.edu
DUDLEY, Brad, D 310-506-6825 61 H brad.dudley@pepperdine.edu
DUDLEY, Christopher, H 336-841-4530 365 C cdudley@highpoint.edu
DUDLEY, Deborah, L 315-267-2113 354 C dudleydl@potsdam.edu
DUDLEY, Erlene 573-592-4291 293 D edudley@williamwoods.edu
DUDLEY, Jacklyn, K 270-809-4126 205 A jdudley@murraystate.edu
DUDLEY, Jennifer 201-360-4646 310 E jdudley@hccc.edu
DUDLEY, Lavoyd, R 318-274-6227 215 E dudleyr@gram.edu
DUDLEY, Manuel 336-334-4822 371 A mcdudley@gtcc.edu
DUDLEY, JR., Phillip, L 402-469-1449 298 A pdudley@hastings.edu
DUDLEY, Sharese 219-980-6791 174 B shaadudl@iun.edu
DUDLEY, Valerie 610-660-1015 446 C vdudley@sju.edu
DUDLEY, Walter, T 540-458-8470 530 D wdudley@wlu.edu
DUDLEY, William, C 413-597-4352 246 D william.c.dudley@williams.edu
DUDLEY-ESHBACH, Janet, E 410-543-6011 228 D jdudleyeshbach@salisbury.edu
DUDT, Susan 770-426-2700 133 E sdudt@life.edu
DUENAS, Felicia 323-241-5376 55 C duenasmv@lasc.edu
DUENAS, Hector 305-273-4499 103 J hector@cbt.edu
DUERK, Jeffrey 216-368-3227 386 F duerk@case.edu
DUERKSEN, Deanne 620-947-3121 197 A deanned@tabor.edu
DUERWACHTER, Kathleen, A 608-796-3072 553 C kaduerwachter@viterbo.edu
DUESING, Jason, G 817-923-1921 495 G jduesing@swbts.edu
DUESTERHAUS, Molly 864-596-9614 457 E molly.duesterhaus@converse.edu
DUETT, Belinda, G 334-833-4519 4 E bduett@huntingdon.edu
DUEWEKE, Anne, T 269-337-7418 252 K anne.dueweke@kzoo.edu
DUEWEKE, Pauline 586-791-6610 248 B pauline.dueweke@baker.edu
DUFAULT-HUNTER, David 626-815-2022 30 G ddhunter@apu.edu
DUFF, Cathy 239-590-7043 119 B cduff@fgcu.edu
DUFF, Debra 414-256-1258 549 D duffd@mtmary.edu
DUFF, John, A 727-864-8318 105 E duffja@eckerd.edu
DUFF, Patricia 978-934-2369 237 B patricia_duff@uml.edu
DUFF, Rebecca 540-985-8246 520 I rduff@jchs.edu
DUFFEL-JONES, Mona 504-816-4024 209 A mduffeljones@dillard.edu
DUFFETT, Robert, G 605-995-2601 464 C roduffet@dwu.edu
DUFFEY, Patrick 903-813-2361 481 A pduffey@austincollege.edu
DUFFIE, James, E 561-868-3077 114 D duffiej@palmbeachstate.edu
DUFFIE, Robert 361-582-2469 508 B robert.duffie@victoriacollege.edu
DUFFOURC, Danielle 504-520-7563 217 A
DUFFY, Andrew 215-895-6468 427 H andrew.duffy@drexel.edu
DUFFY, Arwen 626-396-2311 29 I arwen.duffy@artcenter.edu
DUFFY, Brad 318-487-7222 209 F bduffy@lacollege.edu
DUFFY, Brian 215-972-2030 440 J bduffy@pafa.edu
DUFFY, Brian 901-320-9768 478 C bduffy@victory.edu
DUFFY, Cami 270-809-3155 205 A cduffy@murraystate.edu
DUFFY, Charles 707-468-3011 57 A cduffy@mendocino.edu
DUFFY, Christopher, L 215-670-9174 438 E cduffy@peirce.edu
DUFFY, Daniel 206-296-5550 538 B duffyd@seattleu.edu
DUFFY, Daniel 918-660-3090 413 D daniel-duffy@ouhsc.edu
DUFFY, Dolly 574-631-2788 180 G eduffy@nd.edu
DUFFY, James 717-337-6240 429 I jpduffy@gettysburg.edu
DUFFY, James, P 757-683-5421 522 F jduffy@odu.edu
DUFFY, Kristine 315-498-2222 345 D duffyk@sunyocc.edu
DUFFY, Larry, K 580-477-7705 414 C larry.duffy@wosc.edu
DUFFY, Michael 517-265-5161 246 H mduffy@adrian.edu
DUFFY, Pamela, A 619-239-0391 37 F pduffy@cwsl.edu
DUFFY, Rachelle, M 517-265-5161 246 H rduffy@adrian.edu
DUFFY, Susan 781-239-6425 230 E sduffy@babson.edu
DUFFY, Trent 740-699-2338 400 B duffyt@ohiou.edu
DUFFY, William 563-425-5354 189 G duffyw@uiu.edu
DUFNER, Jessie 406-874-6226 294 F dufnerj@milescc.edu
DUFORE, Timothy, R 330-972-7238 403 B tdufore@uakron.edu
DUFORT, Shirlee 518-736-3622 334 D shirlee.dufort@fmcc.suny.edu
DUFOUR, Graciela 815-836-5270 156 F dufourgr@lewisu.edu
DUFRESNE-REYES, Alice 408-848-4791 48 C adufresnereyes@gavilan.edu
DUGAN, Brendan, J 718-489-5416 348 E bdugan@sfc.edu
DUGAN, Christine, M 717-245-1180 427 F duganc@dickinson.edu
DUGAN, Donald 262-691-5309 555 E ddugan@wctc.edu
DUGAN, James 602-870-9222 13 K jdugan@devry.edu
DUGAN, Jim 480-515-7648 149 B jdugan@devry.edu
DUGAN, Melinda, E 215-887-5511 451 D mdugan@wts.edu
DUGAN, Michael 216-381-1680 397 F mdugan@ndc.edu
DUGAN, Robert 850-474-3135 121 D rdugan@uwf.edu
DUGAN, Robert, E 617-573-8536 245 B rdugan@suffolk.edu
DUGAN, Thomas, F 718-270-2626 352 D tdugan@downstate.edu
DUGAS, Ross, B 952-888-4777 270 C rdugas@nwhealth.edu
DUGATKIN, David 845-257-3802 352 B dugatkind@newpaltz.edu
DUGDALE, Kathy 218-733-5990 266 H k.dugdale@lsc.edu
DUGGAN, Christina 781-768-7228 244 A christina.duggan@regiscollege.edu
DUGGAN, Joseph 206-546-6949 538 C jduggan@shoreline.edu
DUGGAN, Michael, B 617-573-8468 245 B mduggan@suffolk.edu
DUGGAN, Roberta 707-826-5833 36 E duggan@humboldt.edu
DUGGAN, Sean 806-742-2661 502 A s.duggan@ttu.edu
DUGGAN, Theresa 516-299-2783 339 A theresa.duggan@liu.edu
DUGGAN-GOLD, Lori 516-877-3262 322 A duggangold@adelphi.edu
DUGGER, Jim 901-435-1680 470 D jim_dugger@loc.edu
DUGGER, Karen 410-704-5456 228 E kdugger@towson.edu
DUGUID, Stephanie 601-643-8341 273 G stephanie.duguid@colin.edu
DUHON, Gail 616-222-1431 250 A gail.duhon@cornerstone.edu
DUHON, Stacey 318-274-6120 215 E duhons@gram.edu
DUIGNAN, Kevin 845-398-4017 349 H kduignan@stac.edu
DUIN, Diane 406-896-5841 295 D dduin@msubillings.edu
DUISTERMARS, Blaine 712-325-3292 186 F bduistermars@iwcc.edu
DUJARDIAN, Tamara 407-628-5870 106 H tdujardian@cci.edu
DUKE, Charles, R 828-262-2234 377 D dukecr@appstate.edu
DUKE, Kenneth 828-884-8144 362 H dukekm@brevard.edu
DUKE, Lisa, A 770-423-6333 133 A lduke8@kennesaw.edu
DUKE, Lori 919-760-2291 367 A dukel@meredith.edu
DUKE, Phyllis 908-737-5000 311 A pduke@kean.edu
DUKE, Russell 626-650-2306 48 H
DUKE, Shalamon 310-287-4423 55 F dukesa@wlac.edu
DUKE, Steven 336-758-5938 380 C dukest@wfu.edu
DUKE, Susan, I 716-851-1169 333 A dukesi@ecc.edu
DUKE, Todd 765-973-8611 173 F mtduke@iue.edu
DUKES, Charlene, M 301-322-0400 225 F cdukes@pgcc.edu
DUKES, Gary 503-838-8221 419 C dukesg@wou.edu
DUKES, Kenya 919-878-9900 99 G
DUKES, Melinda 423-636-7305 477 A mdukes@tusculum.edu
DUKES, Michael 601-965-5980 273 C mdukes@belhaven.edu
DUKES, Mona, B 843-355-4121 463 D dukesm@wiltech.edu
DUKETT, William 724-503-1001 451 A wdukett@washjeff.edu
DULABAUM, Mary 847-628-2089 154 K mdulabaum@judsonu.edu
DULARDIAN, Garland 256-726-7005 6 C gdulan@oakwood.edu
DULAN, Silas 785-594-8364 190 F silas.dulan@bakeru.edu
DULANEY, Jeri 979-627-0286 482 C jeri.dulaney@blinn.edu
DULANEY, Malik 972-721-5064 503 B mdulaney@udallas.edu
DULANY, Ann 740-284-5254 391 A adulany@franciscan.edu
DULAY, Sarah 708-237-5050 160 D sdulay@nc.edu
DULEPSKI, Deborah, L 203-576-2388 94 F ddulepsk@bridgeport.edu
DULEY, Susan 818-299-5500 78 A sduley@westcoastuniversity.edu
DULEY, Victoria 518-562-4184 329 C victoria.duley@clinton.edu
DULGAR, Laura 623-935-8808 15 F laura.dulgar@estrellamountain.edu
DULIN, Bill 828-327-7000 369 B bdulin@cvcc.edu
DULIN, Scott 617-236-8800 234 G sdulin@fisher.edu
DULING, Ennis 802-468-1239 515 D ennis.duling@castleton.edu
DULING, Sandra 802-468-1396 515 D sandy.duling@castleton.edu
DULLEA, Robert 206-296-2590 538 B dullea@seattleu.edu
DUMANTAY, Danilo 691-320-2480 559 D comptroller@comfsm.fm
DUMAS, Brandon 225-771-3922 214 I brandon_dumas@subr.edu
DUMAS, Carrie, M 404-752-1733 134 E cdumas@msm.edu
DUMAS, Dan 502-897-4131 206 C ddumas@sbts.edu
DUMAS, Maureen 401-598-2350 453 E mdumas@jwu.edu
DUMAS, Roxanne 617-879-2208 246 C rdumas@wheelock.edu
DUMAUAL, Roberto 718-522-9073 323 B rdumaual@asa.edu
DUMAY, Harry, E 603-641-7100 305 G hdumay@anselm.edu
DUMESTRE, Marcel 612-728-5100 271 B mdumestr@smumn.edu
DUMKE, Alyce 920-735-5695 554 A dumke@fvtc.edu
DUMKE, David 715-346-4171 552 D ddumke@uwsp.edu
DUMM, Pamela 502-213-2109 202 F pamela.dumm@kctcs.edu
DUMMER, Robin, K 530-226-4733 69 H rdummer@simpsonu.edu
DUMONT, Cathy 207-859-1167 219 G alumni@thomas.edu
DUMONT, Ronald 201-692-2811 310 A ronald_dumont@fdu.edu
DUMONT, Sara, E 202-885-1321 97 D dumont@american.edu
DUMONTELLE, Janine 714-997-6553 39 F jpdumont@chapman.edu
DUMONTHIER, William, N 408-944-6062 61 A william.dumonthier@palmer.edu
DUMPSON, Kimberly, C 410-651-7773 227 E kdumpson@umes.edu
DUNAVANT, James, R 405-466-3579 408 G jrdunavant@langston.edu
DUNAWAY, Greg 662-325-2646 275 F dunaway@soc.msstate.edu
DUNAWAY, Greg, A 804-594-1430 527 B !lclair@jtcc.edu
DUNAWAY, Mary Kay 501-450-3183 25 H marykay@uca.edu
DUNBAR, Brenda 714-816-0366 73 B brenda.dunbar@trident.edu
DUNBAR, David, G 215-368-5000 422 I ddunbar@biblical.edu
DUNBAR, Dean 213-381-3333 53 C ddunbar@lac.edu
DUNBAR, Deirdre, M 262-554-2010 158 E midwestcollege@aol.com
DUNBAR, Deirdre, M 262-554-2010 549 A midwestcollege@aol.com
DUNBAR, Diana 805-654-6400 77 F ddunbar@vcccd.edu
DUNBAR, John 404-270-2716 128 I jdunbar@devry.edu
DUNBAR, Kristin 906-635-2625 253 H kdunbar@lssu.edu
DUNBAR, Nathan 503-517-1206 421 B ndunbar@warnerpacific.edu
DUNBAR, William 734-462-4400 258 A wdunbar@schoolcraft.edu
DUNBAR, William 773-975-1295 158 E ddunbarphd@aol.com
DUNBAR, William, J 262-554-2010 549 A dunbarphd@aol.com
DUNBAR-JACOB, Jaqueline 412-624-2400 449 A dunbar@pitt.edu
DUNCAN, Chris 937-327-7915 406 B cduncan@wittenberg.edu
DUNCAN, Darrell 615-966-6166 470 F darrell.duncan@lipscomb.edu
DUNCAN, David 417-626-1234 287 C duncan.david@occ.edu
DUNCAN, Dawn, B 212-217-4106 333 F dawn_duncan@fitnyc.edu
DUNCAN, Douglas, S 727-341-3246 116 H duncan.doug@spcollege.edu
DUNCAN, Frances 850-484-2230 115 B fduncan@pensacolastate.edu
DUNCAN, JR., Gene 717-299-7782 448 A duncan@stevenscollege.edu
DUNCAN, Geri 704-290-5221 374 A gduncan@spcc.edu
DUNCAN, Ian 727-726-1153 103 I ianduncan@clearwater.edu
DUNCAN, Jennifer 573-882-7560 291 B duncanjenn@missouri.edu
DUNCAN, Jennifer 610-917-1489 450 E jlduncan@vfcc.edu
DUNCAN, Jenny 918-293-5488 410 E jenny.duncan@okstate.edu
DUNCAN, Jerelyn, L 501-244-5130 19 D jerelyn.duncan@arkansasbaptist.edu
DUNCAN, Jim 901-843-3850 472 K duncanjb@rhodes.edu
DUNCAN, John, B 843-863-7955 456 B jduncan@csuniv.edu
DUNCAN, Laura, H 334-833-4069 4 E lduncan@huntingdon.edu

DURDEN, Tracey .... 734-432-5673 .... 254 D
tdurden@madonna.edu
DURDEN, William, G .... 717-245-1322 .... 427 F
durden@dickinson.edu
DUREE, Christopher .... 641-844-5720 .... 186 B
christopher.duree@iavalley.edu
DUREE, Christopher, A ...... 641-844-5720 .... 186 D
christopher.duree@iavalley.edu
DUREN, Andrew, M .... 708-974-5203 .... 159 B
duren@morainevalley.edu
DUREN, Deborah .... 573-876-7212 .... 290 C
debd@stephens.edu
DURETTE, Kristi .... 603-645-9780 .... 305 I
k.durette@snhu.edu
DURFEE, Carissa .... 617-989-4086 .... 245 F
durfeec@wit.edu
DURFEE, Mike .... 307-532-8346 .... 556 C
mike.durfee@ewc.wy.edu
DURFF, Beth, D .... 501-450-5200 ...... 25 H
bethd@uca.edu
DURFIELD, Jonathan .... 832-813-6615 .... 490 E
jonathan.durfield@lonestar.edu
DURGANS, Kenneth, B .... 317-278-3820 .... 174 D
kdurgans@iupui.edu
DURGIN, William .... 315-792-7200 .... 356 B
william.durgin@sunyit.edu
DURHAM, David, L .... 304-293-8220 .... 545 A
david.durham@mail.wvu.edu
DURHAM, Ed .... 410-287-1010 .... 222 A
edurham@cecil.edu
DURHAM, Gesele .... 414-229-3305 .... 551 D
gerdurham@uwm.edu
DURHAM, Jerry .... 319-226-2015 .... 182 A
durhamjd@ihs.org
DURHAM, John .... 252-328-6105 .... 377 E
durhamj@ecu.edu
DURHAM, John, R .... 610-519-7164 .... 450 H
john.durham@villanova.edu
DURHAM, Kimberly .... 954-262-8601 .... 114 B
durham@nova.edu
DURHAM, Lisa .... 704-378-1135 .... 366 A
ldurham@jcsu.edu
DURHAM, Lynn .... 404-894-8261 .... 130 F
lynn.durham@carnegie.gatech.edu
DURHAM, Rhonda .... 501-882-4442 ...... 20 C
rsdurham@asub.edu
DURHAM, Ron .... 559-278-4062 ...... 35 A
rdurham@csufresno.edu
DURHAM, Tammara .... 785-864-4060 .... 197 B
tdurham@ku.edu
DURHAM, Wes, T .... 812-465-7016 .... 181 B
wdurham@usi.edu
DURHAM, William, H .... 704-233-8218 .... 380 F
durham@wingate.edu
DURIN, Lynne .... 815-825-2086 .... 155 D
lynne.durin@kishwaukeecollege.edu
DURINGER, Robert, A .... 406-243-4662 .... 294 I
robert.duringer@umontana.edu
DURISH, Aubrey, L .... 815-740-5047 .... 167 E
adurish@stfrancis.edu
DURKEE, Katherine .... 813-253-7027 .... 110 M
kdurkee@hccfl.edu
DURKEE, Phillip, A .... 831-656-2517 .... 558 A
padurkee@nps.edu
DURKEE, Robert, K .... 609-258-6428 .... 312 G
durkee@princeton.edu
DURKIN, Karen .... 856-415-2284 .... 310 D
kdurkin@gccnj.edu
DURKIN, Rebecca .... 847-578-8351 .... 163 C
rebecca.durkin@rosalindfranklin.edu
DURKLE, Robert, F .... 937-229-4411 .... 404 A
rdurkle1@udayton.edu
DURLING, John .... 913-217-6462 ...... 19 A
john.durling@phoenix.edu
DURNEY, L. John .... 845-398-4116 .... 349 H
ldurney@stac.edu
DURNFORD, Ronald, R ..... 504-520-5031 .... 217 A
rdurnfor@xula.edu
DURNIN, Ellen .... 203-392-5356 ...... 90 I
durnine1@southernct.edu
DUROCHER, Becky, L .... 985-448-4510 .... 216 A
becky.leblanc-durocher@nicholls.edu
DUROCHER, Jennifer .... 203-773-8577 ...... 90 C
jdurocher@albertus.edu
DUROSS, Frank .... 315-792-5526 .... 341 E
fduross@mvcc.edu
DURR, David .... 501-812-2351 ...... 23 C
ddurr@pulaskitech.edu
DURR, Elaine .... 336-278-5229 .... 364 D
edurr@elon.edu
DURR, Elaine Jeanne .... 608-342-1176 .... 552 B
durrj@uwplatt.edu
DURR, Kimberly, H .... 618-650-2477 .... 165 C
kdurr@siue.edu
DURR, Michael .... 315-792-7340 .... 356 B
durrm1@sunyit.edu
DURRENCE, J. Larry .... 409-933-8271 .... 483 F
ldurrence@com.edu
DURRETT, Duane .... 940-627-2690 .... 508 F
ddurrett@wc.edu
DURSI, Joseph, F .... 914-594-4487 .... 343 F
joseph_dursi@nymc.edu
DURSI, Joseph, F .... 914-594-4234 .... 343 F
joseph_dursi@nymc.edu
DURSKY, Jill .... 641-673-1046 .... 190 C
durskyj@wmpenn.edu
DURSO, Thomas, W .... 610-921-7526 .... 421 E
tdurso@alb.edu
DURST, Devoiry .... 732-414-2834 .... 317 F
DURST, Maribeth .... 352-588-8244 .... 116 G
maribeth.durst@saintleo.edu
DURST, Steve .... 231-591-2254 .... 250 H
dursts@ferris.edu
DURY, Carl, G .... 615-353-3615 .... 475 E
carl.dury@nscc.edu
DURYEA, Amanda .... 518-327-6242 .... 345 H
aduryea@paulsmiths.edu
DUSENBURY, Renata .... 919-546-8252 .... 376 F
rdusenbury@shawu.edu
DUSENBURY, Renata .... 919-546-8395 .... 376 F
rdusenbury@shawu.edu
DUSHDUROVA, Valida .... 505-690-2671 .... 321 E
valida@unm.edu
DUSING, Roger .... 816-584-6386 .... 287 E
roger.dusing@park.edu
DUSSOURD, Ellen, A .... 716-645-2258 .... 351 G
dussourd@buffalo.edu
DUST, Nancy .... 870-368-2006 ...... 23 A
ndust@ozarka.edu
DUSTERHOFT, Bruce .... 407-569-1363 .... 107 I
bruce.dusterhoft@fcc.edu
DUTCHER, Debra .... 518-327-6082 .... 345 H
ddutcher@paulsmiths.edu
DUTCHER, Donald .... 315-866-0300 .... 335 D
dutcherdm@herkimer.edu
DUTCHER, James .... 518-255-5337 .... 354 E
dutchejm@cobleskill.edu
DUTCHER, Robin .... 802-828-2835 .... 515 E
dutcherr@ccu.edu
DUTKA, Mela .... 410-778-7752 .... 229 D
mdutka2@washcoll.edu
DUTLER, Sue .... 312-935-2210 .... 162 G
sdutler@robertmorris.edu
DUTREMBLE, Kathy .... 850-484-1630 .... 115 B
kdutremble@pensacolastate.eduedu
DUTREMBLE, Kathy .... 850-484-2076 .... 115 B
kdutremble@pensacolastate.edu
DUTRISAC, Gordon .... 425-558-0299 .... 533 G
gordon@digipen.edu
DUTSCHKE, Dennis .... 215-527-2901 .... 422 C
dutschkd@arcadia.edu
DUTTA, Debasish .... 217-333-6715 .... 167 D
ddutta@illinois.edu
DUTTA, Mitra .... 312-996-9450 .... 167 B
dutta@uic.edu
DUTTA, Soumitra .... 607-255-6418 .... 331 B
sd599@cornell.edu
DUTTO, Larry .... 559-730-3808 ...... 42 D
larryd@cos.edu
DUTTON, Colleen .... 972-883-2221 .... 506 A
colleen.dutton@utdallas.edu
DUTTON, Jill, M .... 517-780-4547 .... 248 D
jill.dutton@baker.edu
DUTTON, Mary Pat .... 913-758-6110 .... 197 D
registrar@stmary.edu
DUTTON, Shelley, A .... 703-284-1549 .... 521 D
shelley.dutton@marymount.edu
DUVAL, Derethia .... 415-338-2208 ...... 37 B
derethia@sfsu.edu
DUVAL, Michael, W .... 806-371-5159 .... 479 G
mwduval@actx.edu
DUVAL TSIOLES, Denise ... 312-935-4241 .... 154 A
dduval@icsw.edu
DUVALL, Helen .... 409-933-8482 .... 483 F
hduvall1@com.edu
DUWALL, John, E .... 304-293-7171 .... 545 A
john.duwall@mail.wvu.edu
DUZENSKI, Ted .... 706-595-0166 .... 125 H
tduzensk@augustatech.edu
DUZIK, David, B .... 402-465-2144 .... 299 H
dduzik@nebrwesleyan.edu
DUZIK, Don .... 712-274-6400 .... 190 B
don.duzik@witcc.edu
DUZINSKI, Jennifer .... 413-775-1813 .... 239 E
duzinskij@gcc.mass.edu
DVORACEK, Nick .... 920-424-7363 .... 551 E
dvoracek@uwosh.edu
DVORACSEK, Joe .... 727-341-6108 .... 116 H
dvoracsek.joe@spcollege.edu
DVORAK, Jerome .... 570-389-4216 .... 441 F
jdvorak@bloomufdn.org
DVORAK, Karen .... 505-747-2160 .... 320 A
karend@nnmc.edu
DVORAK, Robert .... 415-380-1358 ...... 48 E
robertdvorak@ggbts.edu
DVORAK, Susan .... 414-466-9777 .... 553 E
sdvorak@wspp.edu
DVORSKE, Tom .... 337-475-5510 .... 215 G
tdvorske@mcneese.edu
DWIGHT, Beverly, J .... 413-782-2210 .... 246 A
bdwight@wne.edu
DWIGHT SMITH, Denise ... 704-687-2231 .... 379 A
ddsmith@uncc.edu
DWIRE, Steven, W .... 518-454-5464 .... 330 C
dwires@strose.edu
DWORACZYK, Bill .... 214-768-3140 .... 495 A
billd@smu.edu
DWORAK, Joseph, V .... 651-638-6400 .... 261 D
j-dworak@bethel.edu
DWORKIN, James, B .... 219-785-5331 .... 179 A
jdworkin@pnc.edu
DWORSHAK, Lydia .... 701-483-2092 .... 381 G
lydia.dworshak@dickinsonstate.edu
DWYER, Gretchen, V .... 410-778-7811 .... 229 D
gdwyer2@washcoll.edu
DWYER, James, P .... 989-964-4209 .... 257 G
jdwyer@svsu.edu
DWYER, Katelyn .... 617-296-8300 .... 235 J
katelyn_dwyer@laboure.edu
DWYER, Ken .... 508-854-4579 .... 240 F
krd@qcc.mass.edu
DWYER, Patricia .... 302-736-2352 ...... 97 A
pdwyer@wesley.edu
DWYER, Sharon .... 805-648-8976 ...... 77 F
sdwyer@vcccd.edu
DWYER, Thomas .... 502-410-6200 .... 200 L
tdwyer@galencollege.edu
DWYER, JR., Thomas, L ... 401-598-1410 .... 453 E
tdwyer@jwu.edu
DWYER, Thomas, P .... 804-752-7244 .... 523 C
tdwyer@rmc.edu
DYAL, Donald .... 806-742-2261 .... 502 A
donald.dyal@ttu.edu
DYBATA, Christine .... 615-525-2805 .... 467 B
cdybata@argosy.edu
DYBDAHL, Tammy .... 303-753-6046 ...... 88 B
tdybdahl@rmcad.edu
DYBEN, Andrea .... 561-803-2062 .... 114 C
andrea_dyben@pba.edu
DYBICK, Thomas .... 413-205-3972 .... 229 G
thomas.dybick@aic.edu
DYBWAD, Peter .... 510-841-9230 ...... 79 J
pdybwad@wi.edu
DYCHES, David .... 435-283-7058 .... 512 C
david.dyches@snow.edu
DYCKMAN, Lise .... 415-575-6181 ...... 32 G
ldyckman@ciis.edu
DYE, Arthur .... 203-576-4605 ...... 94 F
adye@bridgeport.edu
DYE, Danny, L .... 502-231-5221 .... 204 E
ddye@mylbc.us
DYE, Hank, C .... 865-974-8184 .... 477 C
hank.dye@tennessee.edu
DYE, Joanna .... 309-796-5442 .... 145 H
dyej@bhc.edu
DYE, John .... 330-337-6403 .... 383 J
college@awc.edu
DYE, Larry .... 580-628-6217 .... 409 B
larry.dye@north-ok.edu
DYE, Michael .... 480-994-9244 ...... 18 F
michaeld@swiha.edu
DYE, Michael .... 940-397-4278 .... 491 B
michael.dye@mwsu.edu
DYE, Ryan, D .... 563-333-6389 .... 188 F
dyeryand@sau.edu
DYE, Teresa .... 651-730-5100 .... 263 G
tdye@globeuniversity.edu
DYER, Amelia, G .... 703-461-1724 .... 522 I
adyer@vts.edu
DYER, Chris .... 417-255-7255 .... 286 D
cdyer@missouristate.edu
DYER, Cynthia, M .... 515-961-1519 .... 189 C
cyd.dyer@simpson.edu
DYER, Duane .... 909-447-2596 ...... 40 H
ddyer@cst.edu
DYER, Edgar, L .... 843-349-2628 .... 456 G
dyer@coastal.edu
DYER, Esther, L .... 865-971-5216 .... 475 G
eldyer@pstcc.edu
DYER, Gail, A .... 401-865-2463 .... 453 H
gdyer@providence.edu
DYER, John, C .... 214-841-3588 .... 485 F
jdyer@dts.edu
DYER, John, C .... 214-841-3538 .... 485 F
jdyer@dts.edu
DYER, Karen .... 812-535-5101 .... 179 E
kdyer@smwc.edu
DYER, Kent .... 484-664-3140 .... 437 C
dyer@muhlenberg.edu
DYER, Kristyn, M .... 508-793-2418 .... 233 C
kdyer@holycross.edu
DYER, Peggy, D .... 918-595-8100 .... 412 H
pdyer@tulsacc.edu
DYER, Robin .... 704-484-4128 .... 369 E
dyer@clevelandcc.edu
DYER, Ruth .... 785-532-6224 .... 194 D
rdyer@ksu.edu
DYER, Steve .... 818-767-0888 ...... 79 H
steve.dyer@woodbury.edu
DYER, Tom .... 206-283-4500 ...... 29 F
tdyer@argosy.edu
DYER, Tom .... 206-393-3503 .... 531 A
tdyer@argosy.edu
DYERLY, Kevin .... 909-748-8482 ...... 76 C
kevin_dyerly@redlands.edu
DYERLY, Kevin, M .... 509-527-5778 .... 540 B
dyerlyk@whitman.edu
DYESS, Hubert .... 601-426-6346 .... 277 A
hdyess@southeasternbaptist.edu
DYJAK, Mary Lou .... 413-748-3271 .... 244 H
mdyjak@springfieldcollege.edu
DYKEMA, Mark .... 717-545-4747 .... 432 F
DYKENS, Amy .... 660-248-6213 .... 279 G
amdykens@centralmethodist.edu
DYKES, Allison .... 404-727-8878 .... 129 D
allison.dykes@emory.edu
DYKES, Bill, G .... 513-772-9888 .... 398 G
bill.dykes@omw.edu
DYKES, Danny .... 601-643-8403 .... 273 G
danny.dykes@colin.edu
DYKES, Donald, E .... 860-444-8213 .... 558 H
donald.e.dykes@uscga.edu
DYKES, JR., Jay .... 225-292-5464 .... 208 B
jay@dykeselec.com
DYKES, Jordin, L .... 225-292-5464 .... 208 B
jldykes@brc.edu
DYKSHOORN, Sharon .... 712-274-6400 .... 190 B
sharon.dykshoorn@witcc.edu
DYKSTRA, Arlen, R .... 314-392-2201 .... 285 J
adykstra@mobap.edu
DYKSTRA, Doug .... 808-235-7402 .... 142 F
dykstra@hawaii.edu
DYKSTRA, Frank .... 520-515-5311 ...... 13 E
poncho@cochise.edu
DYKSTRA, Joel .... 575-624-8203 .... 319 C
dykstra@nmmi.edu
DYKZEUL, Carin .... 503-682-3903 .... 419 F
cdykzeul@pioneerpacific.edu
DYLAK, Sandy .... 914-251-6953 .... 354 D
sandy.dylak@purchase.edu
DYMEK, Cheryle .... 270-707-3707 .... 202 E
cheryle.dymek@kctcs.edu
DYMENT, Christine .... 508-588-9100 .... 240 A
DYMOWSKI, Tom .... 210-829-3131 .... 504 B
dymowski@uiwtx.edu
DYMSKI, M, L .... 617-349-8208 .... 236 B
mld@lesley.edu
DYNAK, David .... 303-556-2611 ...... 88 J
david.dynak@ucdenver.edu
DYRUD, Lars .... 218-683-8616 .... 268 C
lars.dyrud@northlandcollege.edu
DYSARD, Nancy, J .... 443-412-2408 .... 223 B
ndysard@harford.edu
DYSSON, Melissa, J .... 217-245-3080 .... 152 D
mdyson@ic.edu
DZADOVSKY, Indira .... 321-433-5687 .... 102 D
dzadovskyi@brevardcc.edu
DZAU, Victor .... 919-684-2255 .... 364 C
victor.dzau@duke.edu
DZIADON, Ann, H .... 850-474-3063 .... 121 D
adziadon@uwf.edu
DZIAK, SJ, Ted .... 504-865-2304 .... 213 F
dziak@loyno.edu
DZIEDZIAK, Michael .... 610-341-1376 .... 428 E
mdziedzi@eastern.edu
DZIEKAN, Rebecca .... 585-343-0055 .... 334 F
rldziekan@genesee.edu
DZIESINSKI, Lori .... 989-356-9021 .... 247 C
dziesinl@alpenacc.edu
DZIEWATKOSKI, Julius, J . 740-264-5591 .... 390 F
jdziewatkoski@egcc.edu
DZIJA, Alan .... 718-270-3176 .... 352 D
alan.dzija@downstate.edu
DZIK, John, L .... 706-778-8500 .... 136 A
jdzik@piedmont.edu
DZIK, Marianne .... 815-224-0433 .... 153 E
marianne_dzik@ivcc.edu
DZINANKA, John, S .... 631-420-2017 .... 356 A
john.dzinanka@farmingdale.edu
DZUBAY, Tim .... 816-412-5502 .... 464 H
tdzubay@national.edu
DZUREC, Laura .... 330-672-8794 .... 393 D
ldzurec@kent.edu
DZWONKOWSKI,
David, R .... 315-470-6641 .... 355 A
drdzwonk@esf.edu
DÍAZ, Alina .... 787-250-0000 .... 566 G
alina.diaz@upr.edu
DÍAZ, Tania .... 787-720-1022 .... 560 F
recursos@atlanticcollege.edu
D'ABRAMO, Louis .... 662-325-7400 .... 275 F
ldabramo@grad.msstate.edu
D'ACIERNO, Michael .... 718-951-5150 .... 326 F
brooklyn@bkstore.com
D'AGOSTINO, Jennifer .... 518-587-2100 .... 355 G
jennifer.d'agostino@esc.edu
D'AGOSTINO, Thomas .... 315-781-3307 .... 335 F
tdagostino@hws.edu
D'AGOSTO, Danielle .... 914-251-6507 .... 354 D
danielle.dagosto@purchase.edu
D'AIELLO, Christina .... 212-875-4645 .... 323 C
cdaiello@bankstreet.edu
D'ALESSANDRI, Robert .... 570-504-7000 .... 425 F
D'ALESSANDRO, Marie, A 585-292-5627 .... 325 C
madalessandro@bryantstratton.edu
D'ALESSANDRO, Marie, A 585-292-5627 .... 325 B
madalessandro@bryantstratton.edu
D'ALLEGRO, Mary Lou .... 518-783-2307 .... 350 I
mdallegro@siena.edu
D'AMARO, Gina .... 516-918-3726 .... 324 E
gdamaro@bcl.edu
D'AMATO, Anthony .... 312-567-8821 .... 153 C
damato@iit.edu
D'AMBRA, Diane .... 401-598-1854 .... 453 E
ddambra@jwu.edu

D'AMBRA, Lauri ... 516-671-2213 ... 360 B ldambra@webb-institute.edu
D'AMBROSE, Martin ... 312-987-2396 ... 154 H 6dambrose@jmls.edu
D'AMBROSIO, Arnold ... 989-837-4205 ... 256 E dambrosio@northwood.edu
D'AMBROSIO, Rose ... 201-692-2706 ... 310 A rose_dambrosio@fdu.edu
D'AMICO, Catherine ... 702-968-1639 ... 303 D cdamico@roseman.edu
D'AMICO, Janna ... 517-265-5161 ... 246 H
D'AMICO, Joseph, L ... 480-966-5394 ... 19 A joseph.damico@phoenix.edu
D'AMOUR, Angela, L ... 805-565-6125 ... 79 A adamour@westmont.edu
D'AMOUR, Gene ... 504-520-5444 ... 217 A gdamour@xula.edu
D'ANGELO, Frank ... 928-771-4885 ... 19 C frank.dangelo@yc.edu
D'ANGELO, Greg ... 617-369-3633 ... 244 E gdangelo@smfa.edu
D'ANGELO, Kathryn, P ... 215-204-6545 ... 447 H kathryn.dangelo@temple.edu
D'ANGELO, Louann ... 415-572-5622 ... 238 F
D'ANIERI, Paul, J ... 352-392-0780 ... 120 C danieri@clas.ufl.edu
D'ANJOU, Sara ... 617-730-7059 ... 243 D sara.danjou@newbury.edu
D'ANNA, Debora ... 828-884-8159 ... 362 H debora.danna@brevard.edu
D'ANTONIO, Louis, S ... 203-285-2021 ... 91 D ldantonio@gwcc.commnet.edu
D'APRIX, Kathleen ... 718-779-1430 ... 346 B kdaprix@mail.plazacollege.edu
D'AQUINO, Erik ... 716-851-1588 ... 333 B daquino@ecc.edu
D'ARCANGELIS, Linda ... 518-271-3348 ... 340 E darcangelisl@gmail.com
D'ARCANGELIS, Linda ... 518-271-3285 ... 350 B
D'ARGENIO, John ... 518-783-2450 ... 350 I dargenio@siena.edu
D'ARRIGO, Diane ... 617-287-5052 ... 236 G diane.darrigo@umb.edu
D'ATTILIO, Michael ... 518-454-5115 ... 330 C dattilm@strose.edu
D'AVERSA, Robert ... 570-422-3324 ... 442 D robert.daversa@po-box.esu.edu
D'EATH, Kelly ... 256-549-8266 ... 3 J kdeath@gadsdenstate.edu
D'ELIA, Christopher ... 225-578-8574 ... 212 H cdelia@lsu.edu
D'EMIDIO CASTON, Marianne ... 805-962-8179 ... 29 A
D'HONDT, Steven, L ... 401-874-6808 ... 454 E dhondt@gso.uri.edu
D'IMPERIO, Pat ... 914-606-6846 ... 360 E pat.d'imperio@sunywcc.edu
D'LENA, Brandye ... 949-582-4680 ... 70 F bdlena@socccd.org
D'ORAZIO, Peter ... 610-565-1095 ... 452 B pdorazio@williamson.edu
D'OYLEY, Alicia ... 508-531-1214 ... 237 D alicia.doyley@bridgew.edu
D'SOUZA, Dinesh, J ... 212-659-7207 ... 338 A dinesh.dsouza@tkc.edu
D'URSO, Mary, D ... 610-785-6201 ... 446 A mdurso@scs.edu

E

EADDY, Mary ... 843-349-5341 ... 458 H mary.eaddy@hgtc.edu
EADES, Annmarie ... 404-752-8458 ... 134 E aeades@msm.edu
EADES, Tim ... 740-477-7456 ... 398 D tsharp@ohiochristian.edu
EADIE, Michael, J ... 716-888-2842 ... 325 F eadie@canisius.edu
EADS, Jessica, L ... 516-463-6318 ... 335 G jessica.l.eads@hofstra.edu
EADS, Linda, S ... 214-768-3754 ... 495 A leads@smu.edu
EADS, Sonja ... 606-759-7141 ... 203 A sonja.eads@kctcs.edu
EADY, Niya ... 404-225-4452 ... 125 E neady@atlantatech.edu
EAGAN, III, Aristide, C ... 504-762-3005 ... 210 F aeagan@dcc.edu
EAGAN, Dennis, K ... 513-231-2223 ... 384 H deagan@athenaeum.edu
EAGEN, Nancy ... 617-266-1400 ... 231 E
EAGLE, Robert ... 304-434-8000 ... 542 I reagle@eastern.wvnet.edu
EAGLE, Teresa ... 304-746-8924 ... 544 B thardman@marshall.edu
EAGLEN, Robert ... 330-325-6121 ... 397 D reaglen@neomed.edu
EAGLESON, Marcia ... 508-929-8965 ... 238 G meagleson@worcester.edu
EAGLIN, Ron ... 386-506-4176 ... 104 F eaglinr@daytonastate.edu
EAKER, C, W ... 972-721-5384 ... 503 B eaker@udallas.edu
EAKIN, J. Thomas ... 401-232-6046 ... 453 C teakin@bryant.edu
EAKIN, Richard, R ... 252-328-6373 ... 377 E eakinr@ecu.edu
EAKINS, Bill ... 308-535-3607 ... 298 H eakinsw@mpcc.edu
EAKINS, Lewis ... 256-726-7374 ... 6 C leakins@oakwood.edu
EAKINS, Stanley, G ... 252-328-6966 ... 377 E eakinss@ecu.edu
EAKINS, Valerie ... 260-480-4225 ... 176 F eakins@ivytech.edu
EALY, Edna ... 850-973-9474 ... 113 K ealye@nfcc.edu
EAMOE, Deborah ... 513-861-6400 ... 402 I deborah.eamoe@myunion.edu
EANES, Delores ... 276-656-0212 ... 527 G deanes@patrickhenry.edu
EANNACE, Maryrose ... 315-792-5301 ... 341 E meannace@mvcc.edu
EAPEN, Jacob ... 609-586-4800 ... 311 B eapenj@mccc.edu
EARDLEY, Larry ... 775-784-4901 ... 302 D larry_eardley@nshe.nevada.edu
EARHART, Doug ... 202-722-8100 ... 99 G
EARHEART-BROWN, Daniel, J ... 901-334-5809 ... 471 E jebrown@memphisseminary.edu
EARL, Renarde, D ... 336-734-7382 ... 370 F rearl@forsythtech.edu
EARL, Robert ... 212-854-7758 ... 323 E rearl@barnard.edu
EARLE, James, P ... 603-899-4162 ... 305 A earlejp@franklinpierce.edu
EARLE, James, V ... 412-648-1102 ... 449 A earle@pitt.edu
EARLE, Steven, R ... 562-903-4740 ... 31 A steve.earle@biola.edu
EARLE, Susan ... 626-650-2306 ... 48 H
EARLES, Bobbi, L ... 563-588-7120 ... 187 C bobbi.earles@loras.edu
EARLEY, P. Christopher ... 765-494-4366 ... 178 J pcearley@purdue.edu
EARLEY, Rita ... 828-765-7351 ... 372 A rearley@mayland.edu
EARLEY, Samantha ... 812-941-2342 ... 175 A searley@ius.edu
EARLS, C. Anthony ... 308-865-8519 ... 300 F earlsca@unk.edu
EARLS, Jim ... 859-336-5082 ... 206 A jearls@sccky.edu
EARLS, Jimmie ... 859-336-5082 ... 206 A jearls@sccky.edu
EARLS, Trisha ... 912-201-8107 ... 137 D tearls@southuniversity.edu
EARLY, Ida, H ... 314-935-5105 ... 292 I ida_early@wustl.edu
EARLY, Johnnie ... 419-530-1931 ... 404 F johnnie.early@utoledo.edu
EARLY, Lisa ... 410-951-3666 ... 228 B learly@coppin.edu
EARLY, Loretta ... 405-325-9222 ... 413 C learly@ou.edu
EARLY, Loretta, M ... 405-325-3287 ... 413 D loretta-early@ou.edu
EARLY, Margaret ... 510-869-1524 ... 64 J mearly@samuelmerritt.edu
EARLY, Matthew ... 404-727-2197 ... 129 D matthew.early@emory.edu
EARLY, Peter ... 409-933-8404 ... 483 F pearly@com.edu
EARLY, Robert ... 615-343-4601 ... 478 A robert.early@vanderbilt.edu
EARNEST, Meredyth ... 229-248-2596 ... 126 A meredyth.earnest@bainbridge.edu
EARNEST, Sarah ... 978-232-2458 ... 234 D searnest@endicott.edu
EARNS, Lane, R ... 920-424-2220 ... 551 E earns@uwosh.edu
EARP, Christy ... 336-838-6117 ... 375 C christy.earp@wilkescc.edu
EARSHEN, Susan, J ... 716-878-3042 ... 353 A earshesj@buffalostate.edu
EARST, John ... 850-599-3256 ... 118 L john.earst@famu.edu
EARVIN, Larry, L ... 512-505-3001 ... 488 D llearvin@htu.edu
EARWICKER, David ... 916-278-3668 ... 36 A earwicke@saclink.csus.edu
EASLEY, Carol ... 850-201-8481 ... 122 A easleyc@tcc.fl.edu
EASLEY, Mike ... 704-233-8999 ... 380 F m.easley@wingate.edu
EASON, Charles ... 707-864-3382 ... 70 A charles.eason@solano.edu
EASON, Cynthia, G ... 864-250-8601 ... 458 G cynthia.eason@gvltec.edu
EASON, Kevin ... 817-515-4430 ... 496 C kevin.eason@tccd.edu
EASON, Wayne ... 601-635-2111 ... 274 A weason@eccc.edu
EASSA, Emad ... 847-214-7885 ... 150 F eeassa@elgin.edu
EASSON, Donald, D ... 508-831-4993 ... 246 F deasson@wpi.edu
EAST, Ernie, L ... 231-995-1276 ... 256 D eeast@nmc.edu
EAST, Jody, L ... 641-422-4218 ... 188 A eastjody@niacc.edu
EAST, Patricia, A ... 319-296-4214 ... 185 F patricia.east@hawkeyecollege.edu
EASTBURN, Meredith ... 615-383-4848 ... 478 F meastburn@watkins.edu
EASTER, Benna ... 641-784-5372 ... 185 B easter@graceland.edu
EASTER, Jennifer, K ... 717-867-6335 ... 434 C easter@lvc.edu
EASTER, Joyce, B ... 757-455-2126 ... 530 C jeaster@vwc.edu
EASTER, Julian ... 480-677-7701 ... 13 D julian.easter@centralaz.edu
EASTER, Michael ... 573-518-2188 ... 285 I mreaster@mineralarea.edu
EASTER, Robert, A ... 217-333-3070 ... 167 A
EASTERLING, Cal ... 918-495-6538 ... 411 C ceasterling@oru.edu
EASTERLING, Cynthia ... 601-266-6579 ... 277 F cynthia.easterling@usm.edu
EASTERLING, Doug ... 847-925-6955 ... 151 G deasterl@harpercollege.edu
EASTERLING, Karen ... 810-767-4000 ... 248 C karen.easterling@baker.edu
EASTERLING, Karen ... 989-872-6000 ... 247 G karen.easterling@baker.edu
EASTERLING, Mayson ... 864-977-7055 ... 460 A mayson.easterling@ngu.edu
EASTERLING, III, William, E ... 814-865-6546 ... 438 G wee2@psu.edu
EASTERWOOD, Allyson ... 601-266-6986 ... 277 F allyson.easterwood@usm.edu
EASTHAM, Yvette ... 270-707-3731 ... 202 E yvette.eastham@kctcs.edu
EASTMAN, III, Donald, R ... 727-864-8211 ... 105 E deastman@eckerd.edu
EASTMAN, Douglas ... 802-635-1677 ... 515 F doug.eastman@jsc.edu
EASTMAN, Garrett ... 508-373-9709 ... 231 B garrett.eastman@becker.edu
EASTMAN, John ... 903-785-7661 ... 492 D jeastman@parisjc.edu
EASTMAN, Lori ... 518-580-5640 ... 351 B leastman@skidmore.edu
EASTMAN, Michael ... 260-982-5412 ... 177 H emeastman@manchester.edu
EASTMAN, Mindy, R ... 641-422-4363 ... 188 A eastmmin@niacc.edu
EASTON, Emily ... 312-369-7931 ... 148 D eeaston@colum.edu
EASTON, Mark ... 928-226-4284 ... 13 F mark.easton@coconino.edu
EASTON, Michelle ... 304-357-4879 ... 542 A michelleeaston@ucwv.edu
EASTON, Miwa ... 425-249-4751 ... 538 G miwa.easton@tlc.edu
EASTON, Shannon ... 518-608-8234 ... 333 E seaston@excelsior.edu
EASTON, Stephen, D ... 307-766-6416 ... 556 H seaston3@uwyo.edu
EASTRIDGE, Charlene ... 276-739-2461 ... 529 A ceastridge@vhcc.edu
EASTTORP, Karl ... 715-422-5326 ... 554 E karl.easttorp@mstc.edu
EASTTY, Michelle ... 907-822-3201 ... 10 B meastty@akbible.edu
EASTUS, Victoria ... 212-431-2870 ... 343 E veastus@nyls.edu
EASTWOOD, Candy ... 618-634-3231 ... 164 E candye@shawneecc.edu
EATHERTON, Janice ... 509-434-5063 ... 533 B janice.eatherton@ccs.spokane.edu
EATON, Arlinda ... 770-423-6117 ... 133 A aeaton4@kennesaw.edu
EATON, Carol ... 386-506-3000 ... 104 F carol.eaton@daytonastate.edu
EATON, Eric ... 803-533-3742 ... 460 G eaton1@scsu.edu
EATON, Frank ... 603-668-2211 ... 305 I f.eaton@snhu.edu
EATON, Harvill, C ... 615-547-1234 ... 468 B eaton@cumberland.edu
EATON, James, M ... 708-709-3570 ... 161 D jeaton@prairiestate.edu
EATON, Janet ... 903-927-3293 ... 509 E jeaton@wileyc.edu
EATON, Joyce, A ... 336-316-2146 ... 365 A jeaton@guilford.edu
EATON, Kelly, E ... 402-465-2438 ... 299 H kee@nebrwesleyan.edu
EATON, Kent ... 620-242-0506 ... 195 C eatonk@mcpherson.edu
EATON, Kevin ... 817-598-6270 ... 508 F keaton@wc.edu
EATON, L. David ... 845-257-3210 ... 352 B eatond@newpaltz.edu
EATON, Mark, A ... 636-584-6733 ... 281 E maeaton@eastcentral.edu
EATON, Randy ... 828-227-7338 ... 380 A jreaton@wcu.edu
EATON, Rob ... 208-496-1132 ... 143 A eatonr@byui.edu
EATON, Scott ... 859-572-5193 ... 205 H eatons@nku.edu
EATON, Stephanie ... 314-516-5765 ... 291 D stephanie@umsl.edu
EATON, Stephen, B ... 760-252-2411 ... 30 H seaton@barstow.edu
EATON, Timothy, W ... 405-912-9456 ... 408 D teaton@hc.edu
EATON-CLARKE, Germel ... 484-365-7205 ... 434 H geaton@lincoln.edu
EATON-CRAWFORD, Margaret ... 617-732-2132 ... 241 C margaret.eaton-crawford@mcphs.edu
EATON-NEEB, Rosalyn ... 507-786-3615 ... 271 C eatonnee@stolaf.edu
EATON-STULL, Yvonne, M 814-332-4368 ... 421 F yvonne.eatonstull@allegheny.edu
EATOUGH, Michael ... 508-999-8311 ... 237 A meatough@umassd.edu
EAVES, Betsy ... 318-869-5108 ... 208 H beaves@centenary.edu
EAVES, Ken ... 760-252-2411 ... 30 H keaves@barstow.edu
EAVES, Robert ... 803-934-3229 ... 459 G reaves@morris.edu
EAVES, Stephen ... 316-295-5849 ... 193 B stephen_eaves@friends.edu
EAVES-MCLENNAN, Kristi . 919-760-8455 ... 367 A eavesk@meredith.edu
EBBELING, Jason ... 860-701-5197 ... 93 E ebbeling_j@mitchell.edu
EBBERS, Susan ... 651-255-6108 ... 271 D sebbers@unitedseminary.edu
EBBERS, Susan ... 651-255-6143 ... 271 D sebbers@unitedseminary.edu
EBBERT, Deborah ... 215-248-7069 ... 425 D ebbertd@chc.edu
EBEID, Fred ... 262-595-2243 ... 552 A fred.ebeid@uwp.edu
EBEL, Jeffrey ... 618-545-3234 ... 155 B jebel@kaskaskia.edu
EBELTOFT, Gail ... 701-438-2530 ... 381 G gail.ebeltoft@dickinsonstate.edu
EBEN, Brian ... 712-279-1634 ... 183 A brian.eben@briarcliff.edu
EBENSTEIN, Lance ... 616-222-3000 ... 253 F lebenstein@kuyper.edu
EBER, John ... 773-298-3601 ... 163 I eber@sxu.edu
EBERHARDT, David ... 205-226-4731 ... 2 B deberhar@bsc.edu
EBERHARDT, Everett, V ... 703-323-3266 ... 527 F eeberhardt@nvcc.edu
EBERHARDT, Paul ... 641-648-4611 ... 186 C paul.eberhardt@iavalley.edu
EBERHARDT, Ronald, E ... 724-925-4071 ... 451 E eberhardtr@wccc.edu
EBERHART, Becky, J ... 847-866-3938 ... 151 D becky.eberhart@garrett.edu
EBERHART, Cathy ... 563-884-5114 ... 188 E cathy.eberhart@palmer.edu
EBERLE, Debra, A ... 812-941-2200 ... 175 A deberle@ius.edu
EBERLE, Jeanette ... 863-638-2978 ... 123 E eberleja@webber.edu
EBERLE, OSB, Peter ... 503-845-3304 ... 417 A peter.eberle@mtangel.edu
EBERLE, Sarah ... 512-313-3000 ... 483 K sarah.eberle@concordia.edu
EBERLEIN, Tim ... 800-342-7342 ... 14 G tim.eberlein@golfacademy.edu
EBERLY, John, M ... 717-780-2648 ... 430 E jmeberly@hacc.edu
EBERLY, Marian ... 973-300-2257 ... 315 F meberly@sussex.edu
EBERSOLD, E. Douglas ... 573-592-4339 ... 293 D doug.ebersold@williamwoods.edu
EBERSOLD, Julie, A ... 417-836-5654 ... 286 C julieebersold@missouristate.edu
EBERSOLE, Bradley, J ... 740-374-8716 ... 405 G bebersole@wscc.edu
EBERSOLE, Erin, R ... 610-647-4400 ... 431 C eebersole@immaculata.edu
EBERSOLE, John, F ... 518-464-8524 ... 333 E jebersole@excelsior.edu
EBERSOLE, Ken ... 978-867-4500 ... 235 A ken.ebersole@gordon.edu
EBERSOLE, Kenney ... 352-371-2833 ... 105 C academicdean@dragonrises.edu
EBERSOLE, Susan ... 212-749-2802 ... 339 I sebersole@msmnyc.edu
EBERSOLE, Tim ... 717-477-1218 ... 443 E tmeber@ship.edu
EBERT, Derry ... 303-963-3338 ... 82 C debert@ccu.edu
EBERT, James ... 607-436-2125 ... 353 E james.ebert @onenta.edu
EBERT, Sharon ... 570-961-7860 ... 433 A eberts@lackawanna.edu
EBERTZ, Susan J, S ... 563-589-0265 ... 190 A library@wartburgseminary.edu

EBNER, Timothy, J 801-581-5808 511 C
tebner@sa.utah.edu
EBNER-SMITH, Maria, E 248-370-4423 256 G
ebnersmi@oakland.edu
EBONG, Imeh, D 904-620-2700 120 D
i.ebong@unf.edu
EBRAHIMPOUR, Maling 727-873-4786 121 C
mebrahimpour@mail.usf.edu
EBSEN, David, W 541-885-1600 418 E
david.ebsen@oit.edu
EBSTEIN, Gemma, F 860-685-2535 95 E
gebstein@wesleyan.edu
EBY, Larry 302-225-6289 96 H
ebyl@gbc.edu
EBY, Tim, J 314-516-6765 291 D
ebyt@umsl.edu
ECCLES, John, G 434-544-8226 521 B
eccles@lynchburg.edu
ECCLES, Tom 845-758-7598 323 D
ccs@bard.edu
ECCLESTON, David 617-262-5000 231 G
david.eccleston@the-bac.edu
ECHANDI, Pura 787-786-3030 560 G
pechandi@ucb.edu.pr
ECHARD, B. J 580-559-5769 407 J
brajec@ecok.edu
ECHEGARAY, Luis 787-725-6500 561 A
lechegaray@sju.albizu.edu
ECHEVARRI, Richard 215-780-1410 446 G
rech@salus.edu
ECHEVARRIA, Agustin 787-763-5845 562 I
aecheva@inter.edu
ECHEVARRIA, Fabian 209-478-0800 50 K
ECHEVERRIA, John 802-831-1214 515 B
jecheverria@vermontlaw.edu
ECHOLS, Carolyn, J 410-276-0306 226 D
cechols@host.sdc.edu
ECHOLS, Connie, C 530-226-4178 69 H
cechols@simpsonu.edu
ECHOLS, Cynthia 414-443-3639 549 D
echolsc@mtmary.edu
ECHOLS, Mike 402-557-7851 296 H
mike.echols@bellevue.edu
ECHOLS, Steve 423-493-4100 476 E
ECHOLS TOBE, Dorothy 201-684-7621 313 C
dechols@ramapo.edu
ECK, Daniel, W 920-565-6589 548 A
eckdw@lakeland.edu
ECK, Debra 717-334-6286 435 A
deck@ltsg.edu
ECK, Don 503-654-8000 419 F
deck@pioneerpacific.edu
ECK, James, C 919-497-3201 366 H
jeck@louisburg.edu
ECK, Katherine, D 610-285-5057 439 L
kde1@psu.edu
ECK, Stephen 405-425-5118 409 E
stephen.eck@oc.edu
ECK, Tim 801-626-6352 511 G
teck@weber.edu
ECKARD, Shannon 704-504-5409 19 A
shannon.eckard@phoenix.edu
ECKARDT, Chip 715-836-2381 551 A
eckardpp@uwec.edu
ECKARDT, Jill 561-297-3904 119 A
jeckardt@fau.edu
ECKARDT, Michael, J 207-581-3465 220 A
michael.eckardt@maine.edu
ECKARDT, Paula, J 212-924-5900 357 B
peckardt@swedishinstitute.edu
ECKEL, Mark 317-789-8282 171 A
meckel@crossroads.edu
ECKEL, Terri 928-776-2129 19 C
terri.eckel@yc.edu
ECKELS, Robert, T 417-836-6865 286 C
bobeckels@missouristate.edu
ECKEN, Lou 989-463-7245 247 B
ecken@alma.edu
ECKER, Brian 717-264-4141 452 C
brian.ecker@wilson.edu
ECKERT, Gerald, C 717-872-3775 443 D
jerry.eckert@millersville.edu
ECKERT, Jason, C 937-229-2045 404 A
jeckert1@udayton.edu
ECKERT, Phyllis 702-579-3539 302 A
peckert@kaplan.edu
ECKERT, Thomas, C 608-757-7772 553 G
tom.eckert@blackhawk.edu
ECKLES, Robert 212-410-8480 343 B
reckles@nycpm.edu
ECKLES, Robert 212-410-8007 343 B
reckles@nycpm.edu
ECKLEY, Lloydean, M 512-245-2158 501 F
le11@txstate.edu
ECKLIN, Laura 707-256-7105 58 F
lecklin@napavalley.edu
ECKLUND, Timothy, R 716-878-3506 353 A
ecklunt r@buffalostate.edu
ECKMAN, John 503-725-5401 418 G
eckman@pdx.edu
ECKMAN, Steven 386-506-3180 104 F
eckmans@daytonastate.edu
ECKMAN, Steven, W 402-363-5621 301 E
seckman@york.edu

ECKRICH, Steve, E 541-737-4323 418 F
stevee@osubookstore.com
ECKSTEIN, Mark 716-829-8349 332 E
eckstein@dyc.edu
ECKSTEIN, Rebecca, R 740-368-3028 400 G
rreckste@owu.edu
ECONOMOU, James, S 310-825-7943 74 C
jeconomou@conet.ucla.edu
ECSEDY, Brenda 617-879-2225 246 C
becsedy@wheelock.edu
ECUNG, Antonia 559-791-2308 53 A
aecung@portervillecollege.edu
EDAMATSU, Phyllis, Y 302-857-7023 96 C
edamatsu@desu.edu
EDBURG, Lisa 573-518-2294 285 I
lisae@mineralarea.edu
EDDIE, Torrence 901-383-6501 99 G
EDDIE, Walter 914-632-5400 341 G
weddiel@monroecollege.edu
EDDINGER, Frederick, G 717-872-3275 443 D
frederick.eddinger@millersville.edu
EDDINGER, Pam 805-378-1407 77 D
peddinger@vcccd.edu
EDDINGER, Terry, W 336-315-8660 363 C
teddinger@carolinagrad.edu
EDDINGTON, Natalie, D 410-706-2176 227 C
neddingt@rx.umaryland.edu
EDDINS, Trevell 847-214-7391 150 F
teddins@elgin.edu
EDDINS-FOLENSBEE,
Florence, F 713-798-4768 481 H
florence@bcm.edu
EDDLEMAN, Bill 573-651-2062 289 K
weddleman@semo.edu
EDDLEMAN, Bill 573-651-2192 289 K
weddleman@semo.edu
EDDLEMAN, Donna, M 435-586-7710 511 D
eddleman@suu.edu
EDDY, Alex 513-244-8145 387 E
alex.eddy@ccuniversity.edu
EDDY, James, M 336-315-7317 379 B
jmeddy@uncg.edu
EDDY, Jean 401-454-6419 454 B
jeddy@risd.edu
EDDY, Laura, M 620-341-5465 192 G
leddy@emporia.edu
EDDY, Libby 907-474-7500 10 I
ofeddy@alaska.edu
EDDY, Rick 309-341-5234 146 D
reddy@sandburg.edu
EDDY, Walter, D 973-655-7894 311 F
eddyw@mail.montclair.edu
EDELBROCK, Craig, S 610-648-3202 439 H
cse1@psu.edu
EDELBROCK, Robert 877-442-0505 89 C
robert.edelbrock@rockies.edu
EDELEN, Charles 812-941-2400 175 A
cedelen@ius.edu
EDELMAN, David 805-898-2926 47 C
davidedelman@fielding.edu
EDELSON, Paul 631-632-7052 352 C
paul.edelson@stonybrook.edu
EDELSTEIN, Ronald, A 323-563-4980 39 G
ronaldedelstein@cdrewu.edu
EDEN, Bradford, L 219-464-5099 181 C
brad.eden@valpo.edu
EDEN, Gene, F 610-799-1146 434 D
geden@lccc.edu
EDEN, James, R 920-924-3317 554 G
jeden@morainepark.edu
EDEN, James, V 262-335-5705 554 G
jeden@morainepark.edu
EDEN, Karen, S 563-884-5613 188 E
karen.eden@palmer.edu
EDEN, Peter, A 802-387-6730 513 G
petereden@landmark.edu
EDENFIELD, Joe 757-569-6744 528 A
jedenfield@pdc.edu
EDENS, Byron 423-493-4288 476 E
edensb@tntemple.edu
EDENS, Gary 915-747-7471 506 B
gedens@utep.edu
EDENS, Michael, H 504-282-4455 213 H
medens@nobts.edu
EDENS, Mike 903-693-2021 492 C
medens@panola.edu
EDENS, Ruth 617-964-1100 230 B
redens@ants.edu
EDER, Sheila 973-972-5449 316 C
edersh@umdnj.edu
EDERER, Jeff 303-256-9400 85 L
jederer@jwu.edu
EDGAR, Kimberly, S 615-898-2622 473 G
kimberly.edgar@mtsu.edu
EDGAR, Paula 973-642-8593 315 C
paula.edgar@shu.edu
EDGAR, Wendy 952-446-4138 263 C
edgarw@crown.edu
EDGE, Jed 478-934-3138 134 B
jedge@mgc.edu
EDGE, Johnnie 478-553-2124 135 B
jedge@oftc.edu
EDGECOMBE, Nydia 718-518-4180 327 D
nedgecombe@hostos.cuny.edu

EDGERTON, Gary 317-940-9825 170 F
gedgerto@butler.edu
EDGERTON, Teresa 402-486-2540 300 C
teedgert@ucollege.edu
EDGETTE, Bill 903-813-2240 481 A
bedgette@austincollege.edu
EDGEWORTH, Lori 419-251-1614 395 I
lori.edgeworth@mercycollege.edu
EDGINGTON, Rick 580-628-6220 409 B
rick.edgington@north-ok.edu
EDGINGTON, Steve 714-879-3901 50 I
sedgington@hiu.edu
EDGREN, III, Gerald, R 920-924-3184 554 G
gedgren@morainepark.edu
EDICK, Nancy 402-554-2719 301 A
nedick@unomaha.edu
EDIDIN, Aron 941-487-4360 120 A
edidin@ncf.edu
EDIE, Shawn 781-768-7452 244 A
shawn.edie@regiscollege.edu
EDINBURGH, Mary 518-587-2100 355 G
mary.edinburgh@esc.edu
EDINGER, Denise 617-296-8300 235 J
denise_edinger@laboure.edu
EDINGER, Joan, B 318-257-3036 215 F
jedinger@latech.edu
EDINGTON, Mary 253-833-9111 534 H
medington@greenriver.edu
EDINGTON, Pamela 203-857-7309 92 C
pedington@ncc.commnet.edu
EDKINS, Ivonna 562-427-0861 44 H
iedkins@devry.edu
EDLEMAN, Dan 903-886-5126 498 B
daniel.edelman@tamuc.edu
EDLER, Thomas 314-454-8515 282 B
tedler@bjc.org
EDLESTON, Robert, J 785-587-2800 195 A
robertedleston@matc.net
EDLEY, JR., Christopher 510-642-6483 73 H
edley@berkeley.edu
EDLUND, Kristy 303-762-6886 84 D
kristy.edlund@denverseminary.edu
EDMAN, Neal, A 724-946-7110 451 C
nedman@westminster.edu
EDMAN, Patricia 612-374-5800 263 F
pedman@dunwoody.edu
EDMAN, Sally 712-707-7321 188 D
sedman@nwciowa.edu
EDMINSTER, Warren 270-809-3166 205 A
wedminster@murraystate.edu
EDMISTON, Joseph, R 412-675-9047 439 I
jre14@psu.edu
EDMOND, Steven 512-505-3130 488 D
ssedmond@htu.edu
EDMONDS, Charles, W 570-321-4347 435 D
edmonds@lycoming.edu
EDMONDS, Gail, N 410-337-6150 222 I
gedmonds@goucher.edu
EDMONDS, James, Q 731-989-6092 469 B
jedmonds@fhu.edu
EDMONDS, Kerry 540-362-6630 520 A
kedmonds@hollins.edu
EDMONDS, Lawson, C 205-652-3545 9 E
ledmonds@uwa.edu
EDMONDS, Mabel 253-589-5510 532 G
mabel.edmonds@cptc.edu
EDMONDS, Melody 931-668-7010 475 D
medmonds@mscc.edu
EDMONDS, Michelle, K 434-949-1006 528 D
michelle.edmonds@southside.edu
EDMONDS, Mike 719-389-6684 82 D
medmonds@coloradocollege.edu
EDMONDS, William, A 724-938-4404 441 G
edmonds@calu.edu
EDMONDSON, Angie, S 276-944-6108 519 A
aedmonds@ehc.edu
EDMONDSON, Charles, M 607-871-2101 322 E
edmondson@alfred.edu
EDMONDSON,
Melanie, M 443-334-2272 226 E
medmondson@stevenson.edu
EDMONDSON, Ricks 817-515-7726 496 C
ricks.edmondson@tccd.edu
EDMONDSON, William 814-871-7298 429 G
edmondso002@gannon.edu
EDMONSON, Frances 731-425-2654 475 C
fedmonson@jscc.edu
EDMONSON, Michele 661-362-3435 41 I
michele.edmonson@canyons.edu
EDMUNDS, Anne 314-246-8295 292 J
anneedmunds@webster.edu
EDMUNDS, Kate 831-459-3700 75 C
kmedmund@ucsc.edu
EDMUNDSON, John 928-314-9500 12 A
john.edmundson@azwestern.edu
EDNEY, Kristyn 972-761-6884 485 D
kkedney@dcccd.edu
EDNEY, Norris 601-877-6120 272 F
nedney@alcorn.edu
EDOUARD, Randall 607-777-2791 351 F
redouard@binghamton.edu
EDRICH, Terri 972-860-4825 484 G
tedrich@dcccd.edu
EDSALL, Denese 954-201-7502 102 E
dedsall@broward.edu

EDSALL, Paul 724-838-4236 447 C
edsall@setonhill.edu
EDSCORN, Steven, R 901-334-5812 471 E
sedscorn@memphisseminary.edu
EDSON, Deborah 757-822-7433 528 G
dedson@tcc.edu
EDSON, Rob 315-498-2097 345 D
edsonr@sunyocc.edu
EDSTROM, Julie, A 612-330-1740 261 B
edstrom@augsburg.edu
EDUARDO, Marcelo 601-925-3214 275 C
eduardo@mc.edu
EDWALDS-GILBERT,
Gretchen 909-607-2822 69 A
gretchen.edwalds-gilbert@scrippscollege.edu
EDWARDS, Alan, T 252-493-7777 372 H
aedwards@email.pittcc.edu
EDWARDS, Amy 217-333-3551 167 D
aledward@illinois.edu
EDWARDS, Ana 770-423-6200 133 A
aedwar50@kennesaw.edu
EDWARDS, Bahola 432-685-4520 491 A
bahola@midland.edu
EDWARDS, Bambi 252-638-7317 370 A
edwardsb@cravencc.edu
EDWARDS, Barbara 314-286-4870 287 G
bedwards@ranken.edu
EDWARDS, Barbara 303-556-4331 88 J
barbara.edwards@ucdenver.edu
EDWARDS, Benee 334-420-4291 7 H
btedwards@trenholmstate.edu
EDWARDS, Betty 334-420-4321 7 H
bedwards@trenholmstate.edu
EDWARDS, Betty 405-733-7380 411 I
eedwards@rose.edu
EDWARDS, Brad 803-321-5166 459 H
brad.edwards@newberry.edu
EDWARDS, Bruce 305-899-3050 101 M
bedwards@mail.barry.edu
EDWARDS, Bruce, L 419-372-7302 385 E
edwards@bgsu.edu
EDWARDS, Bud 765-658-4268 171 B
budedwards@depauw.edu
EDWARDS, Candace 410-386-8505 221 G
cedwards@carrollcc.edu
EDWARDS, Carlton, G 804-257-5851 530 A
cgedwards@vuu.edu
EDWARDS, Carol 806-742-0700 502 A
carol.edwards@ttu.edu
EDWARDS, Cathy 214-860-8685 485 B
cedwards@dcccd.edu
EDWARDS, Charles 630-844-3847 145 F
cedwards@aurora.edu
EDWARDS, JR., Charles 515-271-3194 184 D
charles.edwards@drake.edu
EDWARDS, JR., Charles 515-271-2871 184 D
charles.edwards@drake.edu
EDWARDS, Cynthia 404-297-9522 131 D
edwardsc@gptc.edu
EDWARDS, Danielle 515-244-4221 181 F
edwardsd@aib.edu
EDWARDS, David 903-875-7348 491 C
david.edwards@navarrocollege.edu
EDWARDS, David 732-906-2533 311 D
dedwards@middlesexcc.edu
EDWARDS, Denise, E 989-328-1226 255 E
denisee@montcalm.edu
EDWARDS, Dennis 417-269-8272 280 G
dennis.edwards@coxcollege.edu
EDWARDS, Donald 828-689-1246 366 I
dedwards@mhc.edu
EDWARDS, JR.,
Donald, A 334-395-8800 7 B
daedwards@southuniversity.edu
EDWARDS, Doreen 607-871-2422 322 E
dedwards@alfred.edu
EDWARDS, Dorothy, P 804-862-6274 523 F
dedwards@rbc.edu
EDWARDS, Elizabeth 662-862-8265 274 E
eedwards@iccms.edu
EDWARDS, Ellen 207-947-4591 217 D
eedwards@bealcollege.edu
EDWARDS, Frank 404-880-8672 127 C
fedwards@cau.edu
EDWARDS, Gary 661-362-2291 56 G
gedwards@masters.edu
EDWARDS, George 606-886-3863 201 G
george.edwards@kctcs.edu
EDWARDS, Germaine 504-671-5040 210 F
gedwar@dcc.edu
EDWARDS, Harry 562-903-4883 31 A
harry.edwards@biola.edu
EDWARDS, Ian, C 412-396-6204 428 D
edwards181@duq.edu
EDWARDS, Ishmell, H 662-252-8000 276 G
iedwards@rustcollege.edu
EDWARDS, James, L 765-641-4011 169 E
jedwards@anderson.edu
EDWARDS, Jan 719-227-8285 82 D
jan.edwards@coloradocollege.edu
EDWARDS, Jane 203-432-8680 96 A
jane.edwards@yale.edu
EDWARDS, Jeff 337-439-5765 208 J
jeff@deltatech.edu

EDWARDS, Jeff, E ... 517-750-1200 ... 258 D
jedwards@arbor.edu
EDWARDS, Jennifer ... 215-717-6366 ... 448 I
jedwards@uarts.edu
EDWARDS, Jennifer, T ... 254-968-9480 ... 497 A
jtedwards@tarleton.edu
EDWARDS, Jessica ... 423-746-5331 ... 476 F
jedwards@twcnet.edu
EDWARDS, John ... 949-451-5255 ... 70 E
jedwards@ivc.edu
EDWARDS, Jon ... 508-270-4102 ... 239 G
jedwards@massbay.edu
EDWARDS, Jon, N ... 814-827-4438 ... 450 A
edwards@pitt.edu
EDWARDS, Joyce, P ... 336-334-7755 ... 378 A
edwardsj@ncat.edu
EDWARDS, Jude ... 301-891-4092 ... 229 B
jedwards@wau.edu
EDWARDS, Judson ... 334-670-3989 ... 8 A
jcedwards@troy.edu
EDWARDS, Julie ... 417-447-8188 ... 287 D
edwardsj@otc.edu
EDWARDS, Karen ... 251-460-7092 ... 9 D
cedwards@usouthal.edu
EDWARDS, Karen, K ... 641-269-3703 ... 185 D
edwardsk@grinnell.edu
EDWARDS, Karin ... 860-885-5203 ... 92 E
kedwards@trcc.commnet.edu
EDWARDS, Kelly ... 406-657-1143 ... 296 C
kelly.edwards@rocky.edu
EDWARDS, Kevin, M ... 413-265-2448 ... 233 D
edwardskevin@elms.edu
EDWARDS, Laurie, L ... 712-324-5061 ... 188 C
ledwards@nwicc.edu
EDWARDS, Leanne ... 314-843-4200 ... 292 H
leanne.edwards@vatterott-college.edu
EDWARDS, Leslie, G ... 406-657-1032 ... 296 C
leslie.edwards@rocky.edu
EDWARDS, Lisa, K ... 718-270-6238 ... 328 C
ledwards@mec.cuny.edu
EDWARDS, Lorraine ... 201-684-7656 ... 313 C
ledwards@ramapo.edu
EDWARDS, Louis, W ... 713-313-6747 ... 500 B
edwards_lw@tsu.edu
EDWARDS, Mark ... 580-628-6240 ... 409 B
mark.edwards@north-ok.edu
EDWARDS, Mark, H ... 315-655-7334 ... 325 H
medwards@cazenovia.edu
EDWARDS, Marsha ... 503-594-3300 ... 415 A
marsha@clackamas.edu
EDWARDS, Mary ... 310-314-6154 ... 30 A
EDWARDS, Mary Louise ... 765-966-2656 ... 176 H
medwards14@ivytech.edu
EDWARDS, Melinda ... 256-352-8172 ... 10 A
melinda.edwards@wallacestate.edu
EDWARDS, Michael ... 641-673-2120 ... 190 C
edwardsm@wmpenn.edu
EDWARDS, Michael ... 713-718-7101 ... 487 I
michael.edwards@hccs.edu
EDWARDS, Michael ... 215-895-2311 ... 427 H
mte28@drexel.edu
EDWARDS, Michael, C ... 773-995-9544 ... 146 G
medwards@csu.edu
EDWARDS, Nigel ... 404-880-8151 ... 127 C
nedwards@cau.edu
EDWARDS, Pat ... 407-478-0500 ... 110 L
EDWARDS, Randy, K ... 828-262-2058 ... 377 D
edwardsrk@appstate.edu
EDWARDS, Richard ... 848-932-7821 ... 314 B
redwards@oldqueens.rutgers.edu
EDWARDS, Rick ... 828-395-1676 ... 371 D
redwards@isothermal.edu
EDWARDS, Robert ... 828-227-7321 ... 380 A
edwardsr@wcu.edu
EDWARDS, Ron ... 608-785-9552 ... 555 F
edwardsr@westerntc.edu
EDWARDS, Ronald ... 516-299-4236 ... 339 A
ronald.edwards@liu.edu
EDWARDS, Sandra, B ... 978-762-4000 ... 240 D
sedwards@northshore.edu
EDWARDS, Skip ... 336-249-8186 ... 370 B
sedwards@davidsonccc.edu
EDWARDS, Susie ... 316-322-3121 ... 191 G
sedwards@butlercc.edu
EDWARDS, TerCraig, D ... 336-734-7953 ... 370 F
tedwards@forsythtech.edu
EDWARDS, Thomas ... 207-859-1362 ... 219 G
edwardst@thomas.edu
EDWARDS, Tiffani ... 602-386-4103 ... 11 G
tiffani.eduwards@arizonachristian.edu
EDWARDS, Tim ... 205-652-3457 ... 9 E
tedwards@uwa.edu
EDWARDS, Tobi ... 337-893-4984 ... 212 B
tedwards@ltc.edu
EDWARDS, Valerie ... 802-635-1290 ... 515 F
valerie.edwards@jsc.edu
EDWARDS, Virjean ... 206-543-2100 ... 539 A
vedwards@uw.edu
EDWARDS, William ... 312-553-5926 ... 147 C
wedwards13@ccc.edu
EDWARDS, Willie ... 830-591-7222 ... 495 D
public.info@swtjc.cc.tx.us
EDWARDS, Zenobia ... 704-378-1300 ... 366 A
zedwards@jcsu.edu

EDWARDS- EVANS,
Nicole ... 601-979-2615 ... 274 G
nicole.e.evans@jsums.edu
EDWARDS-ALEXANDER,
Shoshanna ... 610-660-1140 ... 446 C
sedwards@sju.edu
EDWARDS LANGE, Sheila 206-543-2441 ... 539 A
sredward@uw.edu
EDWARDS SAUNDERS,
Abby ... 843-377-2413 ... 456 A
asaunders@charlestonlaw.edu
EDWIN, Judith ... 340-693-1152 ... 568 E
jedwin@live.uvi.edu
EFFORD, Lelia, A ... 305-626-3180 ... 109 A
laefford@fmuniv.edu
EFIRD, Barbara, M ... 919-508-2006 ... 380 E
befird@peace.edu
EFIRD, Sana ... 828-398-7176 ... 368 B
sefird@abtech.edu
EFTHYMIOU,
Lampeto (Betty) ... 718-631-6611 ... 328 F
lefthymiou@qcc.cuny.edu
EFTINK, Maria ... 314-889-4533 ... 281 I
meftink@fontbonne.edu
EFTINK, Maurice, R ... 662-915-5974 ... 277 D
eftink@olemiss.edu
EGAN, Brian ... 973-684-5999 ... 312 E
began@pccc.edu
EGAN, Carolyn ... 850-644-4440 ... 119 D
cegan@admin.fsu.edu
EGAN, James ... 734-973-3390 ... 259 F
jegan@wccnet.edu
EGAN, Jonathon ... 315-568-3311 ... 342 H
jegan@nycc.edu
EGAN, Maryan ... 239-590-1234 ... 119 B
megan@fgcu.edu
EGAN, Maureen, V ... 219-866-6123 ... 179 D
mo@saintjoe.edu
EGAN, Russi ... 760-921-5524 ... 61 C
regan@paloverde.edu
EGAN, Thomas ... 610-647-4400 ... 431 C
tegan@immaculata.edu
EGBE, Emmanuel ... 718-270-5170 ... 328 C
egbe@mec.cuny.edu
EGBELU, Pius, J ... 973-596-3314 ... 312 C
pius.j.egbelu@njit.edu
EGBERT, Jeb ... 949-783-4800 ... 78 A
jegbert@westcoastuniversity.edu
EGBERT, Jessica, D ... 801-375-5125 ... 510 J
jegbert@rmuohp.edu
EGBERT, Jessie, W ... 205-652-3535 ... 9 E
jwe@uwa.edu
EGBERT, Kay ... 214-828-8236 ... 497 C
kegbert@bcd.tamhsc.edu
EGDORF, Randall ... 217-641-4973 ... 154 I
regdorf@jwcc.edu
EGEBERG, Kenneth ... 860-486-4114 ... 94 G
kenneth.egeberg@uconn.edu
EGELAND, Hillary ... 845-434-5750 ... 357 A
hegeland@sullivan.suny.edu
EGELER, William, G ... 207-768-2792 ... 218 J
wegeler@nmcc.edu
EGENESS, Cynthia ... 651-690-6864 ... 270 L
cnegeness@stkate.edu
EGENREIDER, Michael ... 740-420-5926 ... 398 D
megenreider@ohiochristian.edu
EGERER, Sarah ... 706-233-4065 ... 126 C
segerer@berry.edu
EGGEBRAATEN, Allan ... 641-585-8174 ... 189 I
eggebraa@waldorf.edu
EGGENSPERGER, Martin ... 501-337-5000 ... 21 D
meggensperger@coto.edu
EGGERS, John, M ... 320-308-0121 ... 269 A
jmeggers@stcloudstate.edu
EGGERS, Judy, K ... 414-443-8857 ... 553 D
judy.eggers@wlc.edu
EGGERT, Bill ... 701-224-2623 ... 381 E
bill.eggert@ndus.edu
EGGLESTON, Anne-Marie .. 815-825-2086 ... 155 D
egglestn@kishwaukeecollege.edu
EGGLESTON, Kathryn, K ... 972-238-6364 ... 485 D
keggleston@dcccd.edu
EGGLESTON, Tami ... 618-537-6926 ... 158 A
teggleston@mckendree.edu
EGGLESTON, Theo ... 813-879-6000 ... 107 A
tegglest@cci.edu
EGGLESTON, Theresa ... 562-902-3390 ... 71 A
theresaeggleston@scuhs.edu
EGGLETON, Freida, K ... 270-745-5432 ... 208 A
freida.eggleton@wku.edu
EGITTO, Victor, T ... 323-259-2686 ... 59 I
egitto@oxy.edu
EGLE, Donald, K ... 540-568-5322 ... 520 H
egledk@jmu.edu
EGLSAER, Richard ... 936-294-1006 ... 501 D
eglsaer@shsu.edu
EGNOR, Clark ... 304-696-6265 ... 544 B
egnor3@marshall.edu
EGO, Brian ... 603-626-4972 ... 305 A
egob@franklinpierce.edu
EGSEGIAN, Randall, J ... 919-536-7230 ... 370 C
egsegianr@durhamtech.edu
EHARDT, Thomas ... 713-743-8750 ... 503 C
tehardt@uh.edu

EHARDT, Tom ... 713-743-5325 ... 503 D
tehardt@uh.edu
EHASZ, Maribeth ... 407-823-4372 ... 120 B
maribeth.ehasz@ucf.edu
EHEREDGE, Katherine, C ... 850-474-2766 ... 121 D
ketheredge@uwf.edu
EHLER, Gina, M ... 262-524-7247 ... 546 H
gehler@carrollu.edu
EHLERS, Chris ... 918-781-7233 ... 407 B
ehlersc@bacone.edu
EHLERS, Nancy, M ... 716-652-8900 ... 325 J
nehlers@cks.edu
EHLERS, Pam ... 405-744-8252 ... 410 C
pam.ehlers@okstate.edu
EHLERS, Susan ... 651-773-1705 ... 266 A
susan.ehlers@century.edu
EHLERT, Alycia ... 615-230-3214 ... 476 C
alycia.ehlert@volstate.edu
EHMANN, Daniel, R ... 302-454-3935 ... 96 F
ehmann@dtcc.edu
EHMEN, Stacy, L ... 217-443-8803 ... 148 G
stacy@dacc.edu
EHNES, Gary ... 406-791-5926 ... 296 F
gehnes01@ugf.edu
EHREN, Judith, A ... 914-594-4495 ... 343 F
judith_ehren@nymc.edu
EHRENFELD, A ... 718-236-1171 ... 346 J
EHRENFELD, S, B ... 718-236-1171 ... 346 J
EHRENKRANTZ, Dan ... 215-576-0800 ... 445 D
dehrenkrantz@rrc.edu
EHRESMAN, Judith, A ... 609-586-4800 ... 311 B
ehresmaj@mccc.edu
EHRLICH, Anne, R ... 818-767-0888 ... 79 H
anne.ehrlich@woodbury.edu
EHRLICH, Brian ... 321-674-8202 ... 108 H
behrlich@fit.edu
EHRLICH, Jonathan, D ... 828-298-3325 ... 380 D
jehrlich@warren-wilson.edu
EHRLICH, Margaret ... 770-274-5125 ... 131 C
margaret.ehrlich@gpc.edu
EHRLICH, Robert ... 660-626-2297 ... 278 D
rehrlich@atsu.edu
EHRMAN, Stephen, C ... 202-994-4026 ... 98 C
sehrmann@gwu.edu
EHRMANTRAUT, Dominic . 901-321-3286 ... 467 I
dehrmant@cbu.edu
EHRMANTRAUT, Jan ... 859-280-1232 ... 204 B
jehrmantraut@lextheo.edu
EIBECK, Pamela, A ... 209-946-2223 ... 76 A
president@pacific.edu
EICH, Aprile ... 651-846-3393 ... 260 I
aeich@argosy.edu
EICH, Melissa ... 413-775-1201 ... 239 E
eichm@gcc.mass.edu
EICHAS, Linda ... 321-433-7760 ... 102 D
eichasl@brevardcc.edu
EICHELBERGER, John ... 907-474-7229 ... 10 I
jceichelberger@alaska.edu
EICHELBERGER, Lisa ... 678-466-4900 ... 127 D
lisaeichelberger@clayton.edu
EICHELMAN, Sara ... 843-574-0101 ... 459 F
sara.eichel@miller-motte.net
EICHELROTH, Kathleen ... 508-929-8098 ... 238 G
keichelroth@worcester.edu
EICHENLAUB, Mark, P ... 618-235-2700 ... 165 D
mark.eichenlaub@swic.edu
EICHENSTEIN, Joseph ... 732-985-6533 ... 313 A
EICHER, Michael ... 614-292-9858 ... 398 I
eicher@osu.edu
EICHFIELD, Tara ... 912-287-5809 ... 135 F
teichfield@okefenokeetech.edu
EICHHORN, Edward ... 201-216-5214 ... 315 E
eeichhor@stevens.edu
EICHHORN, Gregory, E ... 610-921-7260 ... 421 E
geichhorn@alb.edu
EICHLER, Barry ... 212-960-5214 ... 361 M
eichler@yu.edu
EICHLER, Richard ... 212-854-2878 ... 330 F
re1@columbia.edu
EICHMANN, Lauren ... 505-473-6440 ... 320 F
lauren.eichmann@santafeuniversity.edu
EICHNER, Kevin ... 785-242-5200 ... 17 B
EICHNER, Kevin ... 785-242-5200 ... 196 A
EICHNER, Kevin ... 785-242-5200 ... 178 I
kevin.eichner@ottawa.edu
EICHNER, Kevin ... 785-242-5200 ... 549 H
EICHNER, Kevin, C ... 785-242-5200 ... 195 I
kevin.eichner@ottawa.edu
EICHOLTZ, Kristin ... 610-282-1100 ... 427 A
kristin.eicholtz@desales.edu
EICHORST, Christopher ... 509-777-4780 ... 540 C
ceichorst@whitworth.edu
EICHORST, Shawn ... 305-284-2673 ... 122 I
sme@miami.edu
EICK, Caroline ... 301-447-5632 ... 225 A
eick@msmary.edu
EICKHOLT, Marcia ... 419-227-3141 ... 404 D
marcia@unoh.edu
EICKMEIER, Valerie ... 317-920-2403 ... 174 D
veickmei@iupui.edu
EIDGAHY, Saeid ... 619-388-2795 ... 65 G
seidgahy@sdccd.edu
EIDSON, Kristi ... 812-429-1427 ... 177 C
keidson@ivytech.edu

EIDSON, Marshall ... 210-829-3866 ... 504 B
meidson@uiwtx.edu
EIDSON, Paul ... 714-841-6252 ... 29 B
EIDSON, Rebecca, W ... 864-646-1507 ... 461 F
reidson@tctc.edu
EIFLER, Chris ... 214-234-4850 ... 486 H
ceifler@cci.edu
EIGENBROOD, Rick ... 206-281-2710 ... 537 H
eigend@spu.edu
EIGENBROT, Edwin ... 215-885-2360 ... 435 E
eeigenbrot@manor.edu
EIGHMY, Taylor ... 806-742-3905 ... 502 A
taylor.eighmy@ttu.edu
EIKE, Claire ... 312-629-9379 ... 164 C
ceike@saic.edu
EIKENS, Anita ... 414-382-6343 ... 546 B
anita.eikens@alverno.edu
EILERING, Susan ... 217-479-7106 ... 157 F
susan.eilering@mac.edu
EILOLA, William ... 906-635-2757 ... 253 H
weilola@lssu.edu
EIMER, Greg, A ... 217-732-3155 ... 156 I
geimer@lincolncollege.edu
EIMERS, Mardy, T ... 573-882-3412 ... 291 B
eimersm@missouri.edu
EINHELLIG, Frank, E ... 417-836-5119 ... 286 C
frankeinhellig@missouristate.edu
EINOLF, Karl, W ... 301-447-5396 ... 225 A
einolf@msmary.edu
EINSPAHR, Kent ... 402-643-7315 ... 297 D
kent.einspahr@cune.edu
EINSTEIN, Heath ... 817-257-7490 ... 499 C
h.einstein@tcu.edu
EINSTEIN, Kristen ... 315-781-3700 ... 335 F
einstein@hws.edu
EINSTEIN, Richard ... 860-628-4751 ... 93 C
reinstein@lincolncollegene.edu
EIS, Linda ... 417-625-3797 ... 286 B
eis-l@mssu.edu
EISCH, Sheri ... 262-564-2720 ... 554 B
eischs@gtc.edu
EISELE, Chad ... 309-341-7280 ... 155 F
ceisele@knox.edu
EISEN, Arnold, M ... 212-678-8072 ... 337 G
areisen@jtsa.edu
EISEN, George ... 585-389-2370 ... 342 D
geisen1@naz.edu
EISEN, Jeffrey, M ... 919-658-7759 ... 367 F
jeisen@moc.edu
EISENBACH, Theresa ... 203-332-5013 ... 91 E
teisenbach@hcc.commnet.edu
EISENBARTH, Jeffrey ... 407-646-2117 ... 116 D
jeisenbarth@rollins.edu
EISENBARTH, Kathryn, L ... 503-352-2705 ... 419 E
eisenbak@pacificu.edu
EISENBEISER, Colleen, K .. 410-777-1963 ... 221 C
ckeisenbeiser@aacc.edu
EISENBERG, Eric ... 813-974-2804 ... 121 A
eisenberg@usf.edu
EISENBERG, Marty ... 660-785-7777 ... 290 G
martye@truman.edu
EISENBERGER, Shlomo ... 440-943-5300 ... 401 D
seisenberger@telshehsihdmi.net
EISENBERGER,
Yosef Yisioel ... 845-362-3053 ... 323 F
EISENHAUER, Joseph ... 313-993-1204 ... 258 G
eisenhjg@udmercy.edu
EISENHAUER, Walt ... 570-484-2168 ... 443 B
weisenha@lhup.edu
EISENHUTH, Wayne ... 507-222-4427 ... 261 G
weisenhu@carleton.edu
EISENMAN, Ann ... 563-244-7040 ... 184 F
aeisenman@eicc.edu
EISENMAN, Elaine ... 781-239-4355 ... 230 E
eeisenman@babson.edu
EISENMANN, Linda ... 508-286-8212 ... 246 B
eisenmann_linda@wheatonma.edu
EISENMENGER, Paul ... 847-317-7087 ... 166 E
peisenme@tiu.edu
EISENSTADT, Robert, C ... 318-342-1151 ... 216 E
eisenstadt@ulm.edu
EISENSTEIN, Laya ... 718-268-4700 ... 347 A
EISENSTEIN, Paul ... 614-823-1609 ... 400 H
peisenstein@otterbein.edu
EISENTRAGER, Pete ... 816-235-2665 ... 291 C
eisentragerp@umkc.edu
EISERLOH, Matt ... 972-438-6932 ... 492 E
meiserloh@parkercc.edu
EISGRUBER,
Christopher, L ... 609-258-3026 ... 312 G
eisgrube@princeton.edu
EISINGER, David, W ... 563-588-4992 ... 187 C
david.eisinger@loras.edu
EISINGER, Robert ... 912-525-5801 ... 136 F
reisinge@scad.edu
EISLER, David, L ... 231-591-2500 ... 250 H
eislerd@ferris.edu
EISMEIER, Elizabeth, A ... 845-437-5500 ... 359 F
eismeier@vassar.edu
EISNAUGLE, Eva ... 704-463-3424 ... 375 F
eva.eisnaugle@fsmail.pfeiffer.edu
EISNER, SND, Janet ... 617-735-9825 ... 234 C
president@emmanuel.edu

EITEL, Keith 817-923-1921 495 G keitel@swbts.edu
EITEL, Norine 660-626-2391 278 D neitel@atsu.edu
EITH, Gary, L 440-525-7084 394 F geith@lakelandcc.edu
EITT, Gretchen 703-526-5873 516 E geitt@argosy.edu
EJIAGA, Romanus 504-286-5384 214 J rejiaga@suno.edu
EJIGU, Gebeyehu 708-534-4120 151 E gejigu@govst.edu
EJIGU, Gebeyehu 708-534-8044 151 E gejigu@govst.edu
EKARD COLLINS, Megan 619-849-2298 62 L meganekardcollins@pointloma.edu
EKBOLM, Kathleen 508-541-1530 233 G deanbkstr@fheg.follett.com
EKE, Kenoye 318-274-2245 215 E
EKEY, William, M 443-412-2344 223 B bekey@harford.edu
EKKER, David 757-822-7287 528 G dekker@tcc.edu
EKSTROM, Rodney 603-535-2217 307 A raekstrom@plymouth.edu
EKURE, Ebuta 803-705-4431 455 D ekuree@benedict.edu
EL-AASSER, Mohamed, S 610-758-2981 434 E mse0@lehigh.edu
EL-BERMAWY, Mohamed 573-288-6344 280 I melbermawy@culver.edu
EL FATTAL, David 562-860-2451 39 A delfattal@cerritos.edu
EL-GAYAR, Omar, F 605-256-5799 465 I omar.el-gayar@dsu.edu
EL-HAGGAN, Ahmed 410-951-3850 228 B elhaggan@coppin.edu
EL-HAQQ, Mahdi 410-276-0306 226 D emahdi@host.sdc.edu
EL-HOUT, Eman 909-915-2100 29 K
EL MOHANDES, Ayman 402-559-4950 300 H aelmohandes@unmc.edu
EL-REWINI, Hesham 701-777-3412 381 F rewini@engr.und.edu
EL-SAYED, Jacqueline, A 810-762-7992 253 C jelsayed@kettering.edu
EL-SHAMAA, Mariam, N 740-427-5820 394 C elshamaam@kenyon.edu
EL SHAYEB, Tarek 270-745-4857 208 A tarek.elshayeb@wku.edu
ELACHI, Charles 818-354-5673 32 H charles.elachi@jpl.nasa.gov
ELAM, Becky 951-487-3011 58 B belam@msjc.edu
ELAM, Brandon 478-757-3408 127 A belam@centralgatech.edu
ELAM, Demar 334-387-3877 1 D demarelam@amridgeuniversity.edu
ELAM, Harry, J 650-723-2300 71 G helam@stanford.edu
ELAM, Jacqueline 661-255-1050 32 F jelam@calarts.edu
ELAM, John, W 614-825-6255 383 K jelam@aiam.edu
ELAM, Michael 318-487-5443 210 E melam@ltc.edu
ELAM, Richard, L 540-868-7042 527 C relam@lfcc.edu
ELAM, Terry 434-592-3966 520 K tlelam@liberty.edu
ELAM, Terry, D 706-771-4005 125 H telam@augustatech.edu
ELAND, Tom 612-659-6286 267 B thomas.eland@minneapolis.edu
ELANDER, Robin 805-962-8179 29 A relander@antioch.edu
ELBE, Joyce 845-848-7900 332 B joyce.elbe@dc.edu
ELBE, Michael 217-641-4300 154 I melbe@jwcc.edu
ELBEL, Jacqueline 972-438-6932 492 E jelbel@parkercc.edu
ELBERT, Dennis, J 701-777-2135 381 F delbert@business.und.edu
ELBOUSHI, Toni, C 323-563-5827 39 G tonielboushi@cdrewu.edu
ELBOW, Gary 806-742-2184 502 A gary.elbow@ttu.edu
ELCHANANI, Matanya 203-576-4322 94 F matanya@btidgeport.edu
ELDAYRIE, Elias, G 352-392-4577 120 C eldayrie@ufl.edu
ELDE, Robert, P 612-624-2244 272 A elde@umn.edu
ELDER, Anissa 404-816-4533 132 E aelder@atl.herzing.edu
ELDER, Connie 619-660-4400 49 B connie.elder@gcccd.edu
ELDER, Dana 509-359-6305 533 H delder@ewu.edu
ELDER, Darla 814-732-2743 442 E delder@edinboro.edu
ELDER, Eric 310-314-6101 30 A
ELDER, Laura 770-531-6318 133 C lelder@laniertech.edu
ELDER, Tom 903-823-3358 496 E thomas.elder@texarkanacollege.edu
ELDERT, John 617-266-1400 231 E
ELDERTON, R. Brian 215-951-1540 432 I elderton@lasalle.edu
ELDREDGE, Brad 406-756-3619 294 C beldredge@fvcc.edu
ELDREDGE, Shirley 423-472-7141 474 E seldredge@clevelandstatecc.edu
ELDRIDGE, Jon 541-552-6223 419 A eldridgj@sou.edu
ELDRIDGE, Jonathan 541-552-6223 419 A eldridgj@sou.edu
ELDRIDGE, Joseph, T 202-885-3336 97 D eldridg@american.edu
ELDRIDGE, Karen 865-981-8207 471 B karen.eldridge@maryvillecollege.edu
ELDRIDGE, Kim 479-524-7424 22 C keldridge@adm.jbu.edu
ELDRIDGE, Linda, P 859-846-5340 204 H leldridge@midway.edu
ELDRIDGE, Maurice, G 610-328-8312 447 F meldrid1@swarthmore.edu
ELDRIDGE, Paul 303-963-3093 82 C peldridge@ccu.edu
ELDRIDGE, Randy 610-527-0200 445 J reldridge@rosemont.edu
ELENICH, Richard 906-487-2763 255 B rjelenic@mtu.edu
ELEY, Curt 972-883-2270 506 A curt.eley@utdallas.edu
ELEY, Greg 765-998-5224 180 B greley@taylor.edu
ELFERDINK, William 828-884-8282 362 H elferdwa@brevard.edu
ELFRINK, Ann Marie 918-495-6001 411 C aelfrink@oru.edu
ELFRINK, Stephanie 314-529-9370 284 C selfrink@maryville.edu
ELGER, William, R 409-266-2006 507 C welger@utmb.edu
ELGINBEHI, Iman 845-434-5750 357 A ielginbehi@sullivan.suny.edu
ELGIRUS, Marie Lourdes 781-239-3140 239 G melgirus@massbay.edu
ELHINDI, Mohamed 608-785-8309 551 C melhindi@uwlax.edu
ELIADI, Carol 617-373-5680 241 C carol.eliadi@mcphs.edu
ELIAS, Ben 510-267-1340 44 I belias@devry.edu
ELIAS, Helen 619-388-3709 65 F helias@sdccd.edu
ELIAS, Stephanny, J 617-333-2010 233 F selias0104@curry.edu
ELIASSON-CREEK, Fia 253-833-9111 534 H feliasson-creek@greenriver.edu
ELICK, Cynthia, M 260-481-6204 174 C elick@ipfw.edu
ELICKER, Beth 207-775-3052 218 E belicker@meca.edu
ELICKER, Kreig 716-338-1040 337 E kreigelicker@mail.sunyjcc.edu
ELIPTICO, Frankie 670-234-5498 560 B frankiee@nmcnet.edu
ELIPTICO, Frankie, M 670-284-5498 560 B frankiee@nmcnet.edu
ELIQUE, Jose 702-895-3668 302 I chiefofpolice@unlv.edu
ELIZA, Lourdes 787-852-1430 562 F leliza@hccpr.edu
ELIZALDE, Velma 361-354-2304 483 B velmae@coastalbend.edu
ELIZALDE, Velma 361-354-2707 483 B velmae@coastalbend.edu
ELIZANDRO, John 516-686-7605 343 D jelizand@nyit.edu
ELIZER, Michelle 602-386-4115 11 G michelle.elizer@arizonachristian.edu
ELIZONDO, Laura, M 956-326-2213 497 D laura@tamiu.edu
ELIZONDO, Maria 956-664-4600 494 H marye@southtexascollege.edu
ELKESHK, Abed 718-405-3300 330 A abed.elkeshk@mountsaintvincent.edu
ELKIN, Rob 617-912-9112 232 C relkin@bostonconservatory.edu
ELKINGTON, John, A 808-675-3542 140 D elkingtj@byuh.edu
ELKINS, Becki, S 319-895-4595 183 G belkins@cornellcollege.edu
ELKINS, Donna 502-213-7112 202 F donna.elkins@kctcs.edu
ELKINS, Geoffrey, W 864-488-8347 459 B ekins-geoffrey@aramark.com
ELKINS, Jolene 910-672-1084 377 G jelkins@uncfsu.edu
ELKINS, Leah 513-241-4338 384 C leah.elkins@antonellicollege.edu
ELKINS, Mark 904-596-2445 122 D melkins@tbc.edu
ELKINS, Mary Jane 434-949-1063 528 D maryjane.elkins@southside.edu
ELKINS, Mary Jane 434-949-1051 528 D maryjane.elkins@southside.edu
ELKINS, Paula, S 706-886-6831 138 D pelkins@tfc.edu
ELKINS, Penny, L 678-547-6556 134 A elkins_pl@mercer.edu
ELKINS, Susan 931-372-3394 474 B selkins@tntech.edu
ELKINS, Vicki 580-477-7728 414 C vicki.elkins@wosc.edu
ELKS, Martha 404-752-1881 134 E melks@msm.edu
ELLARD, Mark 205-387-0511 2 A mellard@bscc.edu
ELLARD, Peter, C 518-783-2307 350 I pellard@siena.edu
ELLEFSEN, David 775-753-2385 302 F david.ellefsen@gbcnv.edu
ELLEFSON-KUEHN, Julie 847-925-6732 151 G jellefso@harpercollege.edu
ELLENBERG, George, B 850-474-2077 121 D gellenberg@uwf.edu
ELLENBERGER, Sheila, J 740-826-8260 397 A sheilaj@muskingum.edu
ELLENBURG, Phillip 615-966-6219 470 F phil.ellenburg@lipscomb.edu
ELLENS, S. Dean 630-617-3059 150 H ellenss@elmhurst.edu
ELLENS, Timothy, L 616-526-6475 249 A tje6@calvin.edu
ELLENSON, David 212-824-2201 335 B dellenson@huc.edu
ELLENSTEIN, Peter 620-331-4100 193 I pellenstein@ingefestival.org
ELLER, Greg 850-729-5332 114 A eller@nwfsc.edu
ELLER, Greg 901-321-3307 467 I geller@cbu.edu
ELLER, Warren, S 910-521-6637 379 C warren.eller@uncp.edu
ELLERMAN, Larry, M 318-342-5350 216 E ellerman@ulm.edu
ELLERTSON, Christopher, J 210-999-7207 502 E cellerts@trinity.edu
ELLERTSON, Shari 715-346-2385 552 D sellerts@uwsp.edu
ELLIBEE, Margaret 262-691-5207 555 E mellibee@wctc.edu
ELLIBEE, Margaret 501-812-2216 23 C
ELLIBEE, Margaret, A 262-691-5207 555 E mellibee@wctc.edu
ELLIEHAUSEN-SLOBOZIEN, Kathryn 717-291-4215 429 F kathy.elliehausenslobozien@fandm.edu
ELLIMAN, Don 303-315-7682 88 J chancellor@ucdenver.edu
ELLING, Wayne, H 206-281-2599 537 H elling@spu.edu
ELLINGER, Amanda, M 540-985-8206 520 I amellinger@jchs.edu
ELLINGER, John, M 419-372-2006 385 E johne@bgsu.edu
ELLINGHUYSEN, Scott 507-457-5696 269 G sellinghuysen@winona.edu
ELLINGHUYSEN, Scott 507-457-5050 269 G sellinghuysen@winona.edu
ELLINGSON, Mike 701-231-7307 382 B michael.ellingson@ndsu.edu
ELLINGSON, Scott, D 218-299-3004 262 I sellings@cord.edu
ELLINGTON, Jim 208-732-6605 143 E jellington@csi.edu
ELLINGTON, John 828-669-8012 367 E jellington@montreat.edu
ELLINGTON, Keri 317-738-8086 171 F kellington@franklincollege.edu
ELLINGTON, Michael, A 304-293-2702 545 A michael.ellington@mail.wvu.edu
ELLINGTON, Ross 850-645-6900 119 D wellington@admin.fsu.edu
ELLINOR, Ben 941-359-4200 121 B
ELLINWOOD, Dawn, M 802-654-2566 514 D dellinwood@smcvt.edu
ELLIOT, Autumn 406-265-3770 295 E autumn.elliot@msun.edu
ELLIOT, John 860-486-1361 94 G john.elliot@uconn.edu
ELLIOT BROWN, Karin, A 323-343-3820 35 D kbrown5@calstatela.edu
ELLIOTT, Angela, P 563-333-6339 188 F elliottangelap@sau.edu
ELLIOTT, Barbara 215-596-7558 450 B b.elliott@usciences.edu
ELLIOTT, Barbara, A 304-929-6727 543 A belliott@newriver.edu
ELLIOTT, Brian 503-588-9207 415 F belliott@corban.edu
ELLIOTT, Carolyn 713-500-3476 506 F carolyn.elliott@uth.tmc.edu
ELLIOTT, Charles 304-384-5334 543 G celliott@concord.edu
ELLIOTT, Clara 413-552-2219 239 F celliott@hcc.edu
ELLIOTT, Clifton, R 843-355-4138 463 D elliottr@wiltech.edu
ELLIOTT, Craig 510-869-6627 64 J celliott@samuelmerritt.edu
ELLIOTT, David 603-526-3718 303 G delliott@colby-sawyer.edu
ELLIOTT, David, R 570-340-6075 435 F delliott@marywood.edu
ELLIOTT, Diane 717-361-1198 428 F elliottd@etown.edu
ELLIOTT, Donna 920-735-5638 554 A elliott@fvtc.edu
ELLIOTT, Emily 603-752-1113 304 H eelliott@ccsnh.edu
ELLIOTT, Gregg 719-587-7011 80 L greggelliott@adams.edu
ELLIOTT, Heather 419-423-2211 385 J helliott@brownmackie.edu
ELLIOTT, Holly 205-391-2211 6 I helliott@sheltonstate.edu
ELLIOTT, Jacquelyn 870-743-3000 22 G jelliott@northark.edu
ELLIOTT, James 312-329-4166 159 A jim.elliott@moody.edu
ELLIOTT, James 304-367-4220 543 H rusty.elliott@fairmontstate.edu
ELLIOTT, Jeffrey 402-885-8228 300 H jeffrey.elliott@unmc.edu
ELLIOTT, Jeffrey 703-416-1441 520 C jelliott@ipsciences.edu
ELLIOTT, John, P 412-624-6127 449 A jelliott@cfo.pitt.edu
ELLIOTT, Julie 610-341-1583 428 E jelliott@eastern.edu
ELLIOTT, Justin 574-522-0397 172 D justin.elliott@harrison.edu
ELLIOTT, Kathy 405-744-4188 410 C kathy.elliott@okstate.edu
ELLIOTT, Ken 828-327-7000 369 B kelliott@cvcc.cedu
ELLIOTT, Kiersten 310-434-4173 68 D elliott_kiersten@smc.edu
ELLIOTT, Larry 802-786-6996 515 E elliottl@ccv.edu
ELLIOTT, Lynn 276-944-6117 519 A lelliott@ehc.edu
ELLIOTT, Marilyn 859-858-2033 198 D
ELLIOTT, Mark 330-499-9600 393 I mellio12@kent.edu
ELLIOTT, Melissa, J 940-552-6291 507 F mjelliott@vernoncollege.edu
ELLIOTT, Michael, S 870-297-4261 94 E michael.elliott@trincoll.edu
ELLIOTT, Patrick 607-777-2043 351 F pelliott@binghamton.edu
ELLIOTT, Peter, A 863-297-1081 115 C pelliott@polk.edu
ELLIOTT, Rennae 256-726-7533 6 C elliott@oakwood.edu
ELLIOTT, Richard 718-482-5501 328 B richard@lagcc.cuny.edu
ELLIOTT, Rita 815-226-3374 163 A relliott@rockford.edu
ELLIOTT, Rob 715-675-3331 555 B elliottr@ntc.edu
ELLIOTT, Scott, D 601-484-8619 275 A selliott@meridiancc.edu
ELLIOTT, Stanley, J 919-658-2502 367 F selliott@moc.edu
ELLIOTT, Tracy 941-752-5399 118 J elliott@scf.edu
ELLIOTT, Tracy, E 856-225-6324 314 D telliott@camden.rutgers.edu
ELLIOTT, Trish 602-387-7000 19 A trish.elliott@apollogrp.edu
ELLIOTT, Wyley 479-936-5174 22 H welliott@nwacc.edu
ELLIOTT CAIN, Pam 515-294-6218 182 E pelliott@iastate.edu
ELLIOTT-NELSON, Linda 928-344-7516 12 A linda.elliott-nelson@azwestern.edu
ELLIS, Annette, M 903-923-3313 500 E annette.ellis@tstc.edu
ELLIS, Barbara, J 336-256-7856 378 A ellis@ncat.edu
ELLIS, Bonnie 425-352-8125 532 B bellis@cascadia.edu
ELLIS, Bonny, R 717-780-2583 430 E brellis@hacc.edu
ELLIS, Brent 517-750-1200 258 D bellis@arbor.edu
ELLIS, Bret, R 801-626-7660 511 G bretellis@weber.edu
ELLIS, Brian 405-325-6211 413 C be@ou.edu
ELLIS, Bridget 252-399-6371 362 E bbellis@barton.edu
ELLIS, Butch 714-879-3901 50 I bellis@hiu.edu
ELLIS, Carl 206-934-2647 537 E carl.ellis@seattlecolleges.edu

ENGEBRETSON, Pam ... 651-779-3994 ... 266 A
pam.engebretson@century.edu
ENGEL, Cristi, L ... 402-461-5177 ... 298 F
ENGEL, Deidre ... 712-279-5448 ... 183 A
deidre.engel@briarcliff.edu
ENGEL, Heather ... 585-475-2627 ... 347 G
ncedar@rit.edu
ENGEL, John ... 706-721-4595 ... 130 D
jengel@georgiahealth.edu
ENGEL, Kirk ... 510-654-2934 ... 46 J
kengel@expression.edu
ENGEL, Richard, R ... 530-752-9960 ... 73 I
rrengel@ucdavis.edu
ENGEL, Shawna ... 901-272-5115 ... 471 D
sengel@mca.edu
ENGELBACH, Karl, M ... 530-754-7237 ... 73 I
kmengelbach@ucdavis.edu
ENGELBRECHT, Laci ... 217-479-7043 ... 157 F
laci.engelbrecht@mac.edu
ENGELBRECHT, Sharon ... 417-626-1234 ... 287 C
engelbrecht.sharon@occ.edu
ENGELBRIDE, Edward ... 518-320-1286 ... 351 D
edward.engelbride@suny.edu
ENGELEN, John, T ... 404-727-5311 ... 129 D
john.engelen@emory.edu
ENGELHARDT, Jon ... 254-710-3111 ... 482 A
jon_engelhardt@baylor.edu
ENGELHARDT, Kelli ... 406-791-5237 ... 296 F
kengelhardt01@ugf.edu
ENGELHART, Rene ... 916-646-2774 ... 64 J
rengelhart@samuelmerritt.edu
ENGELLANT, Roxanne ... 406-683-7305 ... 294 J
r_engellant@umwestern.edu
ENGELLS, Thomas ... 409-772-1503 ... 507 C
tengells@utmb.edu
ENGELMAN, Denisa, A ... 580-774-3212 ... 412 F
denisa.engelman@swosu.edu
ENGELMAN, Mark, D ... 580-774-3269 ... 412 F
mark.engelman@swosu.edu
ENGELMEYER, Renee ... 507-285-7183 ... 268 I
renee.engelmeyer@roch.edu
ENGELSEN, Karen ... 805-986-5847 ... 77 E
kengelsen@vcccd.edu
ENGEN, Stuart ... 701-671-2446 ... 382 G
stuart.engen@ndscs.edu
ENGER, Lee ... 217-228-5432 ... 161 F
engerle@quincy.edu
ENGERT, Lara ... 312-752-2130 ... 155 C
lara.engert@kendall.edu
ENGH, SJ, Michael, E ... 408-554-4100 ... 68 C
mengh@scu.edu
ENGH, Peter, M ... 508-213-2390 ... 243 E
peter.engh@nichols.edu
ENGLAND, A, W ... 313-593-5290 ... 259 B
england@umd.umich.edu
ENGLAND, David ... 225-768-1711 ... 214 C
david.england@ololcollege.edu
ENGLAND, David ... 615-966-6210 ... 470 F
david.england@lipscomb.edu
ENGLAND, David, C ... 860-255-3500 ... 92 F
dengland@txcc.commnet.edu
ENGLAND, Pamela ... 504-816-4871 ... 209 A
pengland@dillard.edu
ENGLAND, Robert, E ... 330-337-6403 ... 383 J
college@awc.edu
ENGLAND, Robert, E ... 330-337-6403 ... 383 J
reengland@awc.edu
ENGLAND, Sid ... 530-752-2432 ... 73 I
asengland@ucdavis.edu
ENGLAND, Tresa ... 970-675-3285 ... 82 H
tresa.england@cncc.edu
ENGLE, Chris ... 810-762-0242 ... 255 G
chris.engle@mcc.edu
ENGLE, Kevin, E ... 330-684-8948 ... 403 C
kengle@uakron.edu
ENGLE, Marcia, J ... 540-432-4148 ... 518 F
marcy.engle@emu
ENGLE, Patricia, A ... 810-762-9773 ... 253 C
pengle@kettering.edu
ENGLEBERT, Mary, F ... 828-262-6519 ... 377 D
englebertmf@appstate.edu
ENGLEBRECHT, JoAnn ... 940-898-2684 ... 502 D
jenglebrecht@twu.edu
ENGLEHARDT, Richard ... 606-693-5000 ... 203 F
ENGLERT, Mark, G ... 307-686-0254 ... 556 F
menglert@sheridan.edu
ENGLERT, Richard ... 215-204-7405 ... 447 H
president@temple.edu
ENGLERT, William, C ... 310-233-4301 ... 54 I
englerbc@lahc.edu
ENGLESTATTER, Pauline ... 301-447-5600 ... 225 A
englesta@msmary.edu
ENGLIN, Peter, D ... 515-294-5636 ... 182 E
penglin@iastate.edu
ENGLISH, Alison ... 714-556-3610 ... 77 B
aenglish@vanguard.edu
ENGLISH, Andrew ... 412-291-6423 ... 422 E
aenglish@aii.edu
ENGLISH, Anna ... 404-460-2462 ... 136 B
anna.english@point.edu
ENGLISH, Carl, J ... 716-372-7978 ... 345 C
cenglish@obi.edu
ENGLISH, Chris ... 828-694-1839 ... 368 E
chrise@blueridge.edu
ENGLISH, Claude ... 816-584-6492 ... 287 E
claude.english@park.edu
ENGLISH, David ... 309-794-7203 ... 145 E
davidenglish@augustana.edu
ENGLISH, Denise, K ... 352-365-3541 ... 112 J
englishd@lscc.edu
ENGLISH, Eva ... 406-353-2607 ... 293 E
eenglish@mail.fbcc.edu
ENGLISH, Evon ... 361-825-5787 ... 498 C
evon.english@tamucc.edu
ENGLISH, Herbert ... 301-696-3550 ... 223 C
english@hood.edu
ENGLISH, Hope ... 806-291-3430 ... 508 E
hope@wbu.edu
ENGLISH, John, R ... 785-532-5590 ... 194 D
jenglish@ksu.edu
ENGLISH, Linda ... 970-945-8691 ... 82 G
ENGLISH, Matthew ... 503-280-8516 ... 415 E
menglish@cu-portland.edu
ENGLISH, Millie ... 910-277-5227 ... 376 C
englishmb@sapc.edu
ENGLISH, Patricia ... 805-965-0581 ... 68 B
englishp@sbcc.edu
ENGLISH, Patry ... 407-708-2144 ... 117 H
englishp@seminolestate.edu
ENGLISH, Raymond, A ... 440-775-5666 ... 397 G
ray.english@oberlin.edu
ENGLISH, Suzanne ... 419-434-4425 ... 404 B
english@findlay.edu
ENGLISH, Suzanne ... 724-805-2660 ... 446 E
ENGLISH, Zachary ... 561-912-1211 ... 107 B
zenglish@evergladesuniversity.edu
ENGLISH-WHITMAN,
Shirley ... 603-899-1131 ... 305 A
engliss@franklinpierce.edu
ENGLN, Jay ... 719-389-6772 ... 82 D
jay.engln@coloradocollege.edu
ENGLUND, Melissa, M ... 215-895-6395 ... 427 H
englunmm@drexel.edu
ENGQUIST, John ... 218-751-8670 ... 270 D
johnengquist@oakhills.edu
ENGSTROM, Janet ... 708-732-7427 ... 200 K
janet.engstrom@frontier.edu
ENGSTROM, Royce, C ... 406-243-2311 ... 294 I
royce.engstrom@umontana.edu
ENICKS, Charles ... 706-721-9660 ... 130 D
cenicks@georgiahealth.edu
ENKE, Kathryn ... 320-363-5070 ... 262 F
kenke@csbsju.edu
ENLOE, Donald ... 303-871-2463 ... 89 A
denloe@du.edu
ENLOW, Todd ... 918-456-5511 ... 409 A
enlowm@nsuok.edu
ENNASSEF, Abdelilan ... 973-328-5155 ... 309 A
aennassef@ccm.edu
ENNEKING, Barbara, A ... 314-615-6902 ... 291 D
benneking@emergingtech.org
ENNEKING, Thomas ... 317-955-6010 ... 177 I
tenneking@marian.edu
ENNEN, Rita ... 701-483-2883 ... 381 G
rita.ennen@dickinsonstate.edu
ENNIS, Daniel ... 843-349-2746 ... 456 G
dennis@coastal.edu
ENNIS, Daniel, G ... 410-516-2373 ... 223 F
danielgennis@jhu.edu
ENNIS, Jackie ... 252-399-6571 ... 362 E
jennis@barton.edu
ENNIS, Kim ... 205-387-0511 ... 2 A
kennis@bscc.edu
ENNIS, Matt ... 941-752-5574 ... 118 J
ennism@scf.edu
ENNIST, Phyllis ... 937-529-2201 ... 403 A
pjennist@united.edu
ENNS-REMPEL, Kevin ... 559-453-2300 ... 48 A
kevin.enns.rempel@fresno.edu
ENOCH, Hollace, J ... 804-257-5841 ... 530 A
hjenoch@vuu.edu
ENOS, Elizabeth ... 781-239-2751 ... 239 G
eenos@massbay.edu
ENOS, Jonathan, C ... 717-291-3982 ... 429 F
jon.enos@fandm.edu
ENOS, Ronald ... 623-572-3270 ... 16 E
renosx@midwestern.edu
ENOS, Stacey ... 828-298-3325 ... 380 D
senos@warren-wilson.edu
ENRIGHT, Jacquelyn, K ... 301-369-2800 ... 221 F
jke@capitol-college.edu
ENRIGHT, John ... 213-613-2200 ... 70 H
john_enright@sciarc.edu
ENRIGHT, Judy ... 507-433-0636 ... 268 H
jenright@riverland.edu
ENRIGHT, Mia ... 508-531-1242 ... 237 D
menright@bridgew.edu
ENRIGHT, Patrick ... 973-328-5700 ... 309 A
penright@ccm.edu
ENRIQUEZ, Anita, B ... 671-735-2553 ... 559 G
abe@uguam.uog.edu
ENRIQUEZ, Igri ... 787-765-3560 ... 562 A
enriquez@edpcollege.edu
ENSEL, Julie ... 706-233-7308 ... 137 A
jensel@shorter.edu
ENSENBERGER, Matthew ... 847-925-6586 ... 151 G
mensenbe@harpercollege.edu
ENSER, Pamela, E ... 315-386-7042 ... 355 E
enserp@canton.edu
ENSEY, Dianne ... 806-457-4200 ... 486 I
densey@fpctx.edu
ENSING, Kim ... 805-922-6966 ... 26 L
kensing@hancockcollege.edu
ENSLE, Kay, E ... 814-676-6591 ... 442 C
kensle@clarion.edu
ENSLEY, Carol ... 916-278-7737 ... 36 A
censley@csus.edu
ENSLEY, Dana ... 706-379-5336 ... 140 A
ddensley@yhc.edu
ENSLEY, Kevin ... 817-923-1921 ... 495 G
kensley@swbts.edu
ENSLIN, Jonathan ... 262-472-1482 ... 553 A
enslinj@uww.edu
ENSMAN, JR., Richard, G ... 585-345-6809 ... 334 F
rgensman@genesee.edu
ENSOR, Pat ... 713-221-8011 ... 503 F
ensorp@uhd.edu
ENSWORTH, Scott, F ... 724-480-3364 ... 426 A
scott.ensworth@ccbc.edu
ENTERLINE, Keri ... 954-783-7339 ... 106 J
kenterline@cci.edu
ENTERS, David, T ... 262-243-5700 ... 547 C
dave.enters@cuw.edu
ENTESSARI, Abbass ... 305-623-1441 ... 109 A
aentessa@fmuniv.edu
ENTREKIN, Cindy ... 256-215-4251 ... 2 E
centrekin@cacc.edu
ENTRIKIN, Nicholas ... 574-631-5204 ... 180 G
entrikin.1@nd.edu
ENTRIKIN, Nicholas, J ... 310-825-4921 ... 74 C
nentrikin@international.ucla.edu
ENTRINGER, Chris, E ... 563-556-5110 ... 188 B
entringc@nicc.edu
ENTWISLE, Barbara ... 919-962-1319 ... 378 E
entwisle@unc.edu
ENTWISTLE, David, E ... 801-581-7480 ... 511 C
david.entwistle@hsc.utah.edu
ENTZ, Mary ... 515-791-1721 ... 183 H
mjentz@dmacc.edu
ENTZ, Ryan ... 316-323-6084 ... 191 G
rentz1@butlercc.edu
ENTZMINGER, Robert, L ... 501-450-1273 ... 22 A
entzminger@hendrix.edu
ENWEMEKA, Chukuka, S ... 414-229-4712 ... 551 D
enwemeka@uwm.edu
ENYARD, Richard ... 573-876-7172 ... 290 C
renyard@stephens.edu
ENYARD, Richard, K ... 217-581-3514 ... 150 E
ENYEDI, Alexander ... 269-387-4350 ... 260 C
alex.enyedi@wmich.edu
ENZ FINKEN, Kathleen ... 805-756-2186 ... 33 I
kensfink@calpoly.edu
ENZOR, Sharon, B ... 662-685-4771 ... 273 E
senzor@bmc.edu
EOFF, Shirley ... 325-942-2722 ... 480 E
shirley.eoff@angleo.edu
EPEMA, Michael ... 712-722-6080 ... 184 C
epema@dordt.edu
EPLAWY, Rick ... 440-375-7225 ... 394 E
replawy@lec.edu
EPLEY, David ... 520-795-0787 ... 11 I
president@asaom.edu
EPLING, Linda ... 859-246-6584 ... 201 H
linda.epling@kctcs.edu
EPLING, Rob ... 513-569-1557 ... 387 G
rob.epling@cincinnatistate.edu
EPP, Adam ... 425-889-5263 ... 536 C
adam.epp@northwestu.edu
EPP, Ken ... 503-517-1815 ... 421 C
kepp@westernseminary.edu
EPP, Stephanie Ann ... 309-438-2586 ... 153 D
saepp@ilstu.edu
EPPEHIMER, Trevor ... 704-636-6534 ... 365 D
teppehimer@hoodseminary.edu
EPPERHART, David, H ... 870-230-5146 ... 21 I
epperd@hsu.edu
EPPERLY, Ronald ... 276-656-0205 ... 527 G
repperly@patrickhenry.edu
EPPERSON, Annissa ... 913-758-6172 ... 197 D
eppersona@stmary.edu
EPPERSON, Doug ... 509-335-4582 ... 539 D
epperson@wsu.edu
EPPERSON, Douglas ... 805-756-2706 ... 33 I
dleppers@calpoly.edu
EPPERSON, II, Richard, P ... 434-223-6153 ... 519 G
repperson@hsc.edu
EPPERSON, Shonte ... 903-927-3260 ... 509 E
sepperson@wileyc.edu
EPPERSON, Steve ... 360-416-7771 ... 538 D
steve.epperson@skagit.edu
EPPES, Thomas, E ... 662-915-5315 ... 277 D
teppes@olemiss.edu
EPPICH, David ... 505-566-3318 ... 320 D
eppichd@sanjuancollege.edu
EPPINETTE, Chance, W ... 318-342-5021 ... 216 E
eppinette@ulm.edu
EPPINGER, Beth ... 479-788-7334 ... 24 D
beth.eppinger@uafs.edu
EPPLER, Michelle ... 402-557-7010 ... 296 H
michelle.eppler@bellevue.edu
EPPLEY, Doug ... 814-472-3017 ... 446 B
deppley@francis.edu
EPPLING, Chris ... 706-865-2134 ... 138 E
ceppling@truett.edu
EPPLING, Marcie, T ... 256-824-6443 ... 8 G
marcie.eppling@uah.edu
EPPS, Bruce ... 614-236-6461 ... 386 E
bepps@capital.edu
EPPS, Carol ... 864-596-9595 ... 457 E
carol.epps@converse.edu
EPPS, Joanne, A ... 215-204-8993 ... 447 H
joanne.epps@temple.edu
EPPS, Ronald ... 254-299-8647 ... 490 G
repps@mclennan.edu
EPPS, Valerie ... 202-274-5210 ... 100 A
vepps@udc.edu
EPSTEIN, Adam ... 314-965-8363 ... 285 F
EPSTEIN, Chaim, L ... 718-438-1002 ... 340 G
EPSTEIN, Joanne ... 352-335-2332 ... 100 D
EPSTEIN, Meryl ... 602-331-7500 ... 12 B
mepstein@aii.edu
EPSTEIN, Scott ... 616-554-5691 ... 250 C
sepstein@davenport.edu
EPSTEIN, Shelley ... 309-677-3260 ... 146 C
sepstein@bradley.edu
EPTING, Bert ... 706-291-5338 ... 137 A
bepting@shorter.edu
EPTING, James, B ... 864-977-7018 ... 460 A
jimmy.epting@ngu.edu
ERARDI, Lauren ... 203-582-3686 ... 93 H
lauren.erardi@quinnipiac.edu
ERARDI, Scott, M ... 860-832-2032 ... 90 G
erardis@ccsu.edu
ERARIO, Vince ... 678-264-8808 ... 133 E
vince.erario@life.edu
ERATO, Michael, J ... 414-425-8300 ... 550 E
merato@shst.edu
ERB, Brian, I ... 706-236-2234 ... 126 C
berb@berry.edu
ERB, Daniel, E ... 336-841-4595 ... 365 C
derb@highpoint.edu
ERB, Jennifer ... 610-799-1034 ... 434 D
0617mgr@sheg.follett.com
ERBERT, Daniel ... 970-339-6602 ... 81 A
daniel.erbert@aims.edu
ERBES, Fred, S ... 712-274-5168 ... 187 G
erbes@morningside.edu
ERBY, Betty, A ... 414-276-5200 ... 546 F
baerby@bryantstratton.edu
ERCHUL, James, C ... 612-330-1758 ... 261 B
erchul@augsburg.edu
ERCK, Lisa ... 916-631-8108 ... 33 F
ERCKERT, Joseph ... 215-489-2397 ... 426 H
joseph.erckert@delval.edu
ERDICE, Stephanie ... 717-477-7447 ... 443 E
smerdice@ship.edu
ERDMAN, Al ... 254-526-1331 ... 482 H
al.erdman@ctcd.edu
ERDMAN, Anne, C ... 269-927-8127 ... 253 G
erdman@lakemichigancollege.edu
ERDMAN, Howard ... 208-792-2456 ... 144 B
herdman@lcsc.edu
ERDMAN, Peg ... 928-532-6111 ... 17 A
peg.erdman@npc.edu
ERDMANN, David ... 407-646-2317 ... 116 D
derdmann@rollins.edu
ERDMANN, James ... 215-503-6595 ... 448 C
james.erdmann@jefferson.edu
ERDMANN, Joel ... 251-460-6101 ... 9 D
jerdmann@usouthal.edu
ERDMANN, Stephanie ... 800-567-2344 ... 547 A
serdamann@menominee.edu
ERECKSON, Stanley ... 303-964-5387 ... 87 I
sereckso@regis.edu
EREKSON, Charles, F ... 408-554-4533 ... 68 C
cerekson@scu.edu
EREKSON, David ... 703-526-5842 ... 29 F
derekson@argosy.edu
EREKSON, David ... 703-526-5842 ... 516 E
derekson@argosy.edu
EREKSON, Homer ... 817-257-7527 ... 499 C
h.erekson@tcu.edu
EREKSON, Thomas, L ... 309-298-2442 ... 168 C
tl-erekson@wiu.edu
EREVELLES, Winston ... 210-436-3996 ... 493 F
werevelles@stmarytx.edu
ERFAN, Shahir ... 718-482-5576 ... 328 B
serfan@lagcc.cuny.edu
ERFFMEYER, Kenneth ... 616-526-6097 ... 249 A
kde2@calvin.edu
ERGEN, Marlene ... 320-363-5282 ... 262 F
mergen@csbsju.edu
ERHAN, Ali ... 616-632-2819 ... 247 E
erhanali@aquinas.edu
ERICKSEN, Donald, O ... 651-631-5249 ... 270 B
doericksen@nwc.edu
ERICKSEN, Robert, B ... 310-825-1681 ... 74 C
bericksen@saonet.ucla.edu
ERICKSON, Ami, N ... 307-674-6446 ... 556 F
aerickson@sheridan.edu
ERICKSON, Christine ... 831-582-4091 ... 35 E
cherickson@csumb.edu
ERICKSON, Craig ... 952-358-8232 ... 268 A
craig.erickson@normandale.edu

ESTEP, Kimberly, K ... 615-353-3326 ... 475 E
kimberly.estep@nscc.edu

ESTEP, Leon, F ... 334-387-3877 ... 1 D
leonestep@amridgeuniversity.edu

ESTEP, Tim ... 704-337-2460 ... 376 A
estept@queens.edu

ESTEPP, J. Mark ... 276-964-7315 ... 528 E
mark.estepp@sw.edu

ESTER, Joyce, C ... 773-602-5000 ... 147 E

ESTERBERG, Kristin, G ... 978-542-6246 ... 238 E
kesterberg@salemstate.edu

ESTERHUIZEN, Amy, H ... 563-556-5110 ... 188 B
esterhuizena@portal.nicc.edu

ESTERS, Lorenzo ... 502-597-6822 ... 203 G
lorenzo.esters@kysu.edu

ESTES, Bill ... 678-839-6447 ... 139 A
bestes@westga.edu

ESTES, David, C ... 210-434-6711 ... 492 B
dcestes@lake.ollusa.edu

ESTES, Edward ... 757-479-3706 ... 517 H
eestes@baptistseminary.edu

ESTES, Eric ... 440-775-8462 ... 397 G
eric.estes@oberlin.edu

ESTES, Lane ... 205-226-4640 ... 2 B
lestes@bsc.edu

ESTES, Michael ... 601-984-1130 ... 277 E
mestes@umc.edu

ESTES, Susan ... 650-574-6404 ... 67 G
estes@smccd.edu

ESTES, Thomas ... 601-266-5005 ... 277 F
tom.estes@usm.edu

ESTES-LEWIS, Karyn ... 207-513-3640 ... 218 C
kestes@kaplan.edu

ESTESS, Larry, M ... 318-342-5205 ... 216 E
estess@ulm.edu

ESTESS, Larry, M ... 318-342-5140 ... 216 E
estess@ulm.edu

ESTEVEZ MARTINEZ, Jacqueline ... 212-938-5500 ... 355 B
jmartinez@sunyopt.edu

ESTEY, Diana, L ... 336-841-9205 ... 365 C
destey@highpoint.edu

ESTILL, Donna ... 620-223-2700 ... 193 A
donnae@fortscott.edu

ESTILL, Sandi, L ... 606-759-7141 ... 203 A
sandi.estill@kctcs.edu

ESTLACK, Scarlet ... 806-874-3571 ... 483 A
scarlet.estlack@clarendoncollege.edu

ESTOCK, Steven ... 575-562-2632 ... 318 B
steven.estock@enmu.edu

ESTRADA, Donna ... 985-858-5731 ... 210 G
donna.estrada@fletcher.edu

ESTRADA, George ... 530-242-7930 ... 69 D
gestrada@shastacollege.edu

ESTRADA, George ... 203-576-4330 ... 94 F
gestrada@bridgeport.edu

ESTRADA, James ... 860-832-2553 ... 90 G
james.estrada@ccsu.edu

ESTRADA, Maria ... 787-780-5134 ... 564 H
mestrada@nuc.edu

ESTRADA-HAMBY, Lisa ... 940-397-4076 ... 491 B
lisa.hamby@mwsu.edu

ESTRELLA, Fred ... 928-523-9998 ... 16 I
fred.estrella@nau.edu

ESTRELLADO, Michelle ... 213-251-3636 ... 29 J
mestrellado@aii.edu

ESTRELLADO, Michelles ... 310-752-4700 ... 30 A

ESTREMERA, Miguel, A ... 973-353-5089 ... 314 E
miguele@rutgers.edu

ESTRIDGE, Charles ... 614-837-4088 ... 405 C

ESTRIDGE, Gwen ... 303-300-8740 ... 81 L
gwen.estridge@collegeamerica.com

ESTRIN, Elena ... 212-349-4330 ... 334 G
eestrin@globe.edu

ESTRY, Douglas ... 517-353-5380 ... 255 A
estry@msu.edu

ETCHELLS, Timothy ... 802-443-5707 ... 514 A
tetchell@middlebury.edu

ETCHEMENDY, John, W ... 650-724-4074 ... 71 G
etch@stanford.edu

ETE, Sonia ... 310-360-8888 ... 26 G

ETESAMNIA, Hamid ... 909-748-8063 ... 76 C
hamid_etesamnia@redlands.edu

ETHIER, Richard ... 802-241-2520 ... 515 C
richard.ethier@vsc.edu

ETHINGTON, Robert ... 707-527-4573 ... 68 E
rethington@santarosa.edu

ETINGE, Elias ... 706-821-8302 ... 135 G
etinge@paine.edu

ETRE-PEREZ, Pam ... 505-224-3974 ... 317 K
petreperez@cnm.edu

ETSCHMAIER, Gale ... 619-594-1643 ... 37 A
gale.etschmaier@sdsu.edu

ETSE, Penselyn ... 691-320-2480 ... 559 D
petse@comfsm.fm

ETSITTY, Marie, R ... 928-724-6829 ... 13 L
metsitty@sinecollege.edu

ETTARO, Barbara ... 814-863-1030 ... 438 G
bxm7@psu.edu

ETTEMA, Robert ... 307-766-4253 ... 556 H
rettema@uwyo.edu

ETTER, Alan ... 202-274-5314 ... 100 A
aetter@udc.edu

ETTLE, Violeta ... 202-885-2720 ... 97 D
vi@american.edu

ETTLING, John ... 518-564-2010 ... 354 B
president_office@plattsburgh.edu

ETTORE, JD ... 620-223-2700 ... 193 A
jde@fortscott.edu

ETUALE, Mikaele ... 684-699-9155 ... 559 C
m.etuale@amsamoa.edu

EUBANK, Charlotte ... 573-840-9662 ... 290 F
ceubank@trcc.edu

EUBANK, Gary ... 937-529-2201 ... 403 A
geubank@united.edu

EUBANK, Jeff ... 215-702-4202 ... 444 B
jeubank@pbu.edu

EUBANK, Jeffrey, M ... 816-604-6645 ... 285 A
jeff.eubank@mcckc.edu

EUBANKS, Audrey, C ... 251-442-2218 ... 9 A
aeubanks@umobile.edu

EUBANKS, David, A ... 727-864-7888 ... 105 E
eubankda@eckerd.edu

EUBANKS, David, L ... 865-573-4517 ... 469 L
deubanks@johnsonu.edu

EUBANKS, Gail ... 912-443-5443 ... 136 H
geubanks@savannahtech.edu

EUBANKS, Gregory ... 205-247-8145 ... 7 F
geubanks@stillman.edu

EUBANKS, Karla, C ... 912-427-5899 ... 124 C
keubanks@altamahatech.edu

EUBANKS, Kathleen, L ... 508-999-8086 ... 237 A
keubanks@umassd.edu

EUBANKS, Philip, A ... 865-573-4517 ... 469 L
peubanks@johnsonu.edu

EUBANKS, Ranelle ... 870-460-1233 ... 25 A
eubanksr@uamont.edu

EUDY, Kim ... 619-260-7967 ... 76 D
keudy@sandiego.edu

EUDY, Kristina ... 704-991-0235 ... 374 D
keudy5611@stanly.edu

EULER, Tim ... 304-357-4363 ... 542 A
timueler@ucwv.edu

EULIANO, Guy ... 814-838-7673 ... 429 C
geuliano@fortisinstitute.edu

EUNICE, E, E ... 850-201-7000 ... 122 A
eunicee@tcc.fl.edu

EURE, Darius ... 252-335-3307 ... 377 F
deure@mail.ecsu.edu

EUSTROM, Jim ... 503-399-5076 ... 414 J
jim.eustrom@chemeketa.edu

EVAN, Joseph ... 570-208-5895 ... 432 G
josephevan@kings.edu

EVANCHIK, Michele ... 609-292-2108 ... 316 A
mevanchik@tesc.edu

EVANGELISTA, Joleen, M ... 671-735-5540 ... 559 E
materialsmanagement@guamcc.edu

EVANGELISTA, Nancy ... 607-871-2649 ... 322 E
fevangel@alfred.edu

EVANOVICH, Dolan ... 614-292-8835 ... 398 I
evanovich.1@osu.edu

EVANS, Alana ... 906-487-7358 ... 251 A
alana.evans@finlandia.edu

EVANS, Andrew ... 781-283-2305 ... 245 E

EVANS, Angela, J ... 770-423-6300 ... 133 A
aevans@kennesaw.edu

EVANS, Annette ... 706-542-7066 ... 138 G
amevans@uga.edu

EVANS, Atlas, D ... 617-726-5164 ... 242 B
aevans3@mghihp.edu

EVANS, Beth ... 718-990-6999 ... 348 G
evansb@stjohns.edu

EVANS, Beverly, A ... 717-815-1228 ... 452 G
behinger@ycp.edu

EVANS, Brian ... 559-253-2235 ... 27 B
bevans@alliant.edu

EVANS, Brian ... 502-863-8223 ... 201 A
brian_evans@georgetowncollege.edu

EVANS, Brian ... 502-863-8040 ... 201 A
brian_evans@georgetowncollege.edu

EVANS, Brian, K ... 801-422-3760 ... 509 H
brian_evans@byu.edu

EVANS, Carol, A ... 231-995-1705 ... 256 D
cevans@nmc.edu

EVANS, Carolyn, L ... 601-977-7764 ... 277 C
cevans@tougaloo.edu

EVANS, Cheryl ... 580-628-6201 ... 409 B
cheryl.evans@north-ok.edu

EVANS, Cheryl, O ... 585-385-8015 ... 348 F
cevans@sjfc.edu

EVANS, Chet ... 941-756-0690 ... 433 C
cevans@lecom.edu

EVANS, Damian ... 262-595-2540 ... 552 A
damian.evans@uwp.edu

EVANS, Dana ... 336-655-2137 ... 337 G
devans@psandl.com

EVANS, Dave ... 619-388-2737 ... 65 G
devans@sdccd.edu

EVANS, David ... 229-391-2647 ... 134 F
devans@moultrietech.edu

EVANS, David ... 972-273-3561 ... 485 C
devans@dcccd.edu

EVANS, David, R ... 712-749-2243 ... 183 C
evansd@bvu.edu

EVANS, Deborah, L ... 610-861-1340 ... 437 A
debevans@moravian.edu

EVANS, Denise ... 281-476-1878 ... 493 H
denise.evans@sjcd.edu

EVANS, Diane, T ... 936-261-2202 ... 496 G
dtevans@pvamu.edu

EVANS, Doree ... 252-222-6282 ... 369 A
evansd@carteret.edu

EVANS, Elizabeth, J ... 217-424-6335 ... 158 G
eevans@millikin.edu

EVANS, Eric, D ... 781-981-7000 ... 241 D

EVANS, Erik ... 570-389-4047 ... 441 F
eevans@bloomu.edu

EVANS, Frederick, M ... 803-516-4930 ... 460 G
fevans6@scsu.edu

EVANS, Gail ... 415-338-2206 ... 37 B
gevans@sfsu.edu

EVANS, George ... 618-545-2751 ... 155 B
gevans@kaskaskia.edu

EVANS, JR., Gilbert, L ... 386-312-4127 ... 116 F
gilbertevans@sjrstate.edu

EVANS, Gregory ... 815-455-8564 ... 157 H
gevans@mchenry.edu

EVANS, J. David ... 770-423-6194 ... 133 A
devans@kennesaw.edu

EVANS, Jack ... 706-721-3964 ... 130 D
jaevans@georgiahealth.edu

EVANS, Jack ... 813-253-7604 ... 110 M
jevans@hccfl.edu

EVANS, JR., Jack ... 972-524-3341 ... 495 H

EVANS, SR., Jack ... 972-524-3341 ... 495 H

EVANS, James, D ... 636-949-4900 ... 283 J
jevans@lindenwood.edu

EVANS, Jane ... 740-695-9500 ... 385 B
jevans@belmontcollege.edu

EVANS, Janet, D ... 412-392-3824 ... 445 A
jevans@pointpark.edu

EVANS, Janie ... 802-287-8203 ... 513 F
evansj@greenmtn.edu

EVANS, Jaylene ... 970-542-3168 ... 86 G
jaylene.evans@morgancc.edu

EVANS, Jeannette, H ... 315-684-6067 ... 354 F
evansjh@morrisville.edu

EVANS, Jeffrey, L ... 313-593-5110 ... 259 B
jlevan@umd.umich.edu

EVANS, Jennifer, M ... 717-867-6271 ... 434 C
jevans@lvc.edu

EVANS, Joe, W ... 405-224-3140 ... 413 E
jwevans@usao.edu

EVANS, Jon ... 714-459-1164 ... 78 H
jonevans@wsulaw.edu

EVANS, Joseph ... 410-706-8501 ... 227 C
jevans@af.umaryland.edu

EVANS, Joy ... 678-717-3800 ... 129 G
jevans@gsc.edu

EVANS, Julia ... 909-607-3689 ... 40 F
julia.evans@cgu.edu

EVANS, Julie ... 701-777-6345 ... 381 F
jae@und.edu

EVANS, K. James ... 814-362-7650 ... 449 B
kje2@pitt.edu

EVANS, Kamira ... 610-892-1566 ... 441 C
kevans@pit.edu

EVANS, Karen, V ... 610-921-7630 ... 421 E
kevans@alb.edu

EVANS, Karyn ... 937-393-3431 ... 402 A
kevans@sscc.edu

EVANS, Katherine ... 973-761-9500 ... 315 B
katherine.evans@shu.edu

EVANS, Kenneth ... 973-300-2350 ... 315 F
kevans@sussex.edu

EVANS, Kenneth, R ... 405-325-2070 ... 413 C
evansk@ou.edu

EVANS, Kim ... 802-831-1225 ... 515 B
kevans@vermontlaw.edu

EVANS, Lana ... 419-267-1225 ... 397 E
levans@northweststate.edu

EVANS, Laurie ... 313-664-1501 ... 249 E
levans@collegeforcreativestudies.edu

EVANS, Leigh ... 478-553-2054 ... 135 B
levans@oftc.edu

EVANS, Lexie ... 206-934-3890 ... 537 E
lexie.evans@seattlecolleges.edu

EVANS, Linda ... 803-641-3342 ... 462 B
lindae@usca.edu

EVANS, Lisa ... 828-398-7390 ... 368 B
levans@abtech.edu

EVANS, Lisa ... 513-569-1564 ... 387 G
lisa.evans@cincinnatistate.edu

EVANS, Liz ... 412-392-5945 ... 445 A
eevans@pointpark.edu

EVANS, III, Louis, D ... 713-221-2766 ... 503 F
evansl@uhd.edu

EVANS, Marion, W ... 251-626-3303 ... 8 C
mevans@ussa.edu

EVANS, Marisa, L ... 814-886-6336 ... 437 B
mevans@mtaloy.edu

EVANS, Mark ... 330-672-2972 ... 393 D
mevans@kent.edu

EVANS, Mark ... 845-938-5502 ... 559 A
mark.evans@usma.edu

EVANS, Mark ... 434-793-6822 ... 521 J
evans@ncbt.edu

EVANS, Mary ... 315-859-4668 ... 334 H
mevans@hamilton.edu

EVANS, Mercedes ... 617-879-7060 ... 238 B
msevans@massart.edu

EVANS, Michael ... 334-420-4302 ... 7 H
mevans@trenholmstate.edu

EVANS, Michael ... 812-855-9249 ... 173 E
mirevans@indiana.edu

EVANS, Michael ... 817-461-8741 ... 480 H
mevans@abconline.org

EVANS, Michael, L ... 806-743-2738 ... 502 B
michael.evans@ttuhsc.edu

EVANS, Mike ... 765-289-2291 ... 176 B
mevans@ivytech.edu

EVANS, Nicole ... 614-251-4603 ... 398 F
evansn@ohiodominican.edu

EVANS, Patrice ... 404-614-6337 ... 132 G
pevans@itc.edu

EVANS, Paul, N ... 608-262-6982 ... 550 J
paul.evans@housing.wisc.edu

EVANS, R. Gregory ... 912-478-2676 ... 131 E
rgevans@georgiasouthern.edu

EVANS, JR., R. Lee ... 334-844-8348 ... 1 F
evansrl@auburn.edu

EVANS, R. Scott ... 330-941-1585 ... 406 F
sevans@ysu.edu

EVANS, Renee ... 201-761-7806 ... 314 F
wknapp@spc.edu

EVANS, Richard, W ... 585-785-1300 ... 334 A
evansrw@flcc.edu

EVANS, Rick ... 818-677-2906 ... 35 F
rick.evans@csun.edu

EVANS, Robert ... 501-660-1000 ... 20 D
revans@astate.edu

EVANS, Robert ... 501-660-1001 ... 20 B
revans@asusystem.edu

EVANS, Robert ... 773-907-4817 ... 147 D
revans@ccc.edu

EVANS, Roberta ... 406-243-4911 ... 294 I
roberta.evans@umontana.edu

EVANS, Sam ... 773-947-6282 ... 157 G
sevans@mccormick.edu

EVANS, Sam ... 270-745-4664 ... 208 A
sam.evans@wku.edu

EVANS, Sarah ... 317-931-2377 ... 170 H
sevans@cts.edu

EVANS, Sharlotte ... 706-821-3965 ... 233 A
sharlotte.evans@cambridgecollege.edu

EVANS, Shirley ... 410-276-0306 ... 226 D
sevans@host.sdc.edu

EVANS, Sidney, S ... 540-458-8754 ... 530 D
sevans@wlu.edu

EVANS, Steve ... 281-425-6887 ... 489 M
sevans@lee.edu

EVANS, Susan ... 239-590-1057 ... 119 B
sevans@fgcu.edu

EVANS, Tabitha ... 409-882-3319 ... 501 B
tabitha.evans@lsco.edu

EVANS, Thomas ... 406-447-4401 ... 293 G
tevans@carroll.edu

EVANS, Thomas ... 973-408-3379 ... 309 E
tevans@drew.edu

EVANS, Thomas, A ... 515-281-6527 ... 182 D
taevans@iastate.edu

EVANS, Thomas, S ... 315-443-9732 ... 357 C
tevans02@syr.edu

EVANS, Thomas, W ... 812-246-3301 ... 177 B
tevans17@ivytech.edu

EVANS, Tonya ... 305-892-7551 ... 112 A
tonya.evans@jwu.edu

EVANS, Tracy, L ... 304-929-5480 ... 543 A
tevans@newriver.edu

EVANS, Valarie, J ... 919-536-7217 ... 370 C
evansv@durhamtech.edu

EVANS, W, F ... 804-257-5606 ... 530 A
wfevans@vuu.edu

EVANS, W. Franklin ... 803-536-7180 ... 460 G
wevans1@scsu.edu

EVANS, Warren ... 808-791-5200 ... 29 F
waevans@argosy.edu

EVANS, Warren ... 808-791-5200 ... 140 B
waevans@argosy.edu

EVANS, Wendy ... 570-955-1456 ... 433 A
evansw@lackawanna.edu

EVANS, William, G ... 816-501-4659 ... 288 A
bill.evans@rockhurst.edu

EVANS, Zina ... 352-392-1365 ... 120 C
zevans@ufl.edu

EVANS-DAILEY, Amber ... 218-281-8568 ... 271 E
evan0331@umn.edu

EVANS-DAME, Kimberly ... 315-792-5637 ... 341 E
kevans-dame@mvcc.edu

EVANS JONES, Cheryl ... 706-821-8324 ... 135 G
cevansjones@paine.edu

EVANS-PLANTS, Penny ... 706-232-5374 ... 126 C
peplants@berry.edu

EVARIAN, Jane ... 661-654-3035 ... 34 A
jevarian@csub.edu

EVASHEVSKI, Keith ... 307-766-2187 ... 556 H
keski@uwyo.edu

EVE, Debra ... 406-353-2607 ... 293 E
deve@mail.fbcc.edu

EVE, Stacey ... 406-791-5306 ... 296 F

EVELAND, Larry ... 651-290-6356 ... 272 E
larry.eveland@wmitchell.edu

FALCON-CHANDLER, Carole ... 406-353-2607 .... 293 E
cfalconc@mail.fbcc.edu
FALCONER, James ... 860-434-5232 ...... 93 D
jfalconer@lymeacademy.edu
FALCONETTI, Angela, M ... 540-857-6020 .... 529 B
afalconetti@virginiawestern.edu
FALCONI, Stefano ... 617-521-2877 .... 244 F
stefano.falconi@simmons.edu
FALDER, Mike ... 765-998-5538 .... 180 B
mcfalder@taylor.edu
FALDUTO, Ellen ... 330-263-2230 .... 388 F
efalduto@wooster.edu
FALE, Tauvela ... 684-699-9155 .... 559 C
t.fale@amsamoa.edu
FALER, Kurt ... 630-889-6463 .... 159 F
kfaler@nuhs.edu
FALERO, Mercy ... 787-480-2382 .... 561 E
mfalero@sanjuancapital.com
FALES, Michael, F ... 269-749-7624 .... 257 A
mfales@olivetcollege.edu
FALESE, Joseph, T ... 815-836-5275 .... 156 F
falesejo@lewisu.edu
FALGOUT, Katherine ... 985-380-2436 .... 211 I
katherine.falgout@ltc.edu
FALK, Adam, F ... 413-597-4233 .... 246 D
adam.f.falk@williams.edu
FALK, Dan ... 620-229-6267 .... 196 G
dan.falk@sckans.edu
FALK, Israel ... 845-356-7065 .... 361 E
FALK, Jessica ... 620-229-6155 .... 196 G
jessica.falk@sckans.edu
FALK, Joyce ... 619-849-2534 .... 62 L
joycefalk@pointloma.edu
FALK, Keith, L ... 920-923-8594 .... 548 E
kfalk@marianuniversity.edu
FALK, Stephanie, A ... 717-867-6696 .... 434 C
falk@lvc.edu
FALKE, Steve, J ... 814-863-0205 .... 438 G
sfalke@bncollege.com
FALKENBERG, Janice ... 414-297-8718 .... 554 F
falkenjm@matc.edu
FALKENBERG, Taunji ... 503-229-0492 .... 416 B
taunji_falkenberg@heald.edu
FALKENRATH, Rex ... 801-832-2588 .... 512 G
rfalkenrath@westminstercollege.edu
FALKENSTERN, Sharon ... 814-676-6591 .... 442 B
sfalkenstern@clarion.edu
FALKENSTIEN, Sarah, N ... 909-748-8044 ...... 76 C
sarah_falkenstien@redlands.edu
FALKIEWICZ, Linda, K ... 313-577-3550 .... 260 A
ab4753@wayne.edu
FALKNER, Jeff ... 641-784-5341 .... 185 B
falkner@graceland.edu
FALKNER, Thomas, M ... 410-857-2248 .... 224 C
tfalkner@mcdaniel.edu
FALKOWSKI, William, G ... 716-270-2942 .... 333 B
falkowski@ecc.edu
FALKS, Delisa, F ... 979-458-5311 .... 497 E
delisa@tamu.edu
FALL, Diane ... 309-796-4840 .... 145 H
falld@bhc.edu
FALL, Stephany ... 850-599-3203 .... 118 L
stephany.fall@famu.edu
FALLACARO, Anthony ... 203-596-4531 ...... 93 G
afallacaro@post.edu
FALLERT, Danelle ... 323-265-8797 ...... 54 G
fallerdj@elac.edu
FALLIN, Terri ... 417-667-8181 .... 280 E
tfallin@cottey.edu
FALLING, Cary ... 405-425-5290 .... 409 E
cary.falling@oc.edu
FALLING, Sali, K ... 765-285-5162 .... 169 G
sfalling@bsu.edu
FALLIS, Jennifer ... 516-726-5669 .... 558 I
fallisj@usmma.edu
FALLIS, Sue ... 925-631-4856 ...... 64 F
sfallis@stmarys-ca.edu
FALLO, Thomas, M ... 310-660-3111 ...... 45 E
tfallo@elcamino.edu
FALLON, Ann Marie ... 503-725-9423 .... 418 G
amfallon@pdx.edu
FALLON, Greg ... 973-684-5895 .... 312 E
gfallon@pccc.edu
FALLON, III, John, A ... 765-289-1241 .... 169 G
jafallon@bsu.edu
FALLON, Melissa, A ... 607-436-3368 .... 353 E
fallonma@oneonta.edu
FALLON, Patricia, C ... 617-521-2018 .... 244 F
patricia.fallon@simmons.edu
FALLON, Thomas ... 978-556-3866 .... 240 E
tfallon@necc.mass.edu
FALLONE, Deborah, A ... 914-323-5224 .... 339 J
deborah.fallone@mville.edu
FALLS, Meda ... 731-925-5722 .... 475 C
mfalls@jscc.edu
FALLS, Mike ... 704-484-4129 .... 369 E
fallsm@clevelandcc.edu
FALLS, Sarah ... 212-472-1500 .... 343 G
sfalls@nysid.edu
FALOTICO, Michael ... 312-777-7735 ...... 29 F
mfalotico@argosy.edu
FALSO, Frank ... 570-422-3333 .... 442 D
ffalso@esufoundation.org

FALTER, Ben ... 386-822-7201 .... 121 F
bfalter@stetson.edu
FALTYN, Timothy, W ... 918-463-2931 .... 407 H
FALVEY, Mary ... 323-343-4300 ...... 35 D
mfalvey@calstatela.edu
FALWELL, JR., Jerry ... 434-582-2957 .... 520 K
jlfjr@liberty.edu
FALWELL, Jonathan ... 434-582-2000 .... 520 K
jonfalwell@liberty.edu
FALWELL, Tyler ... 434-592-3095 .... 520 K
twfalwell2@liberty.edu
FALZERANO, Christine ... 718-260-3025 .... 346 C
cfalzera@poly.edu
FALZONE, Kris ... 219-981-4232 .... 174 B
kfalzone@iun.edu
FAMA, Melissa ... 978-632-6600 .... 240 C
m_fama@mwcc.mass.edu
FAMBLE, JR., Freddie ... 325-793-4906 .... 490 H
ffamble@mcm.edu
FAMULA, Michelle, S ... 530-752-2333 ...... 73 I
msfamula@ucdavis.edu
FAMULARE, Dominick, F ... 518-388-6168 .... 358 G
famularn@union.edu
FAN, Lori ... 309-677-2245 .... 146 C
llw@bradley.edu
FANCHER, Karen, J ... 503-255-0332 .... 417 C
kfancher@multnomah.edu
FANDOZZI, Melissa ... 518-828-4181 .... 330 E
melissa.fandozzi@sunycgcc.edu
FANEK, Sami ... 727-725-2688 .... 106 F
sfanek@cci.edu
FANEUFF, Ken ... 706-379-5202 .... 140 A
kfaneuff@yhc.edu
FANFANX, Lerick ... 617-745-3869 .... 234 A
lerick.fanfanx@enc.edu
FANG, John ... 310-453-8300 ...... 45 G
john@emperors.edu
FANGMEYER, Len, J ... 308-865-8555 .... 300 F
fangmeyerlj@unk.edu
FANNAN, Lisa, L ... 816-604-2314 .... 285 C
lisa.fannan@mcckc.edu
FANNER, Sjohonton ... 940-552-6291 .... 507 F
sfanner@vernoncollege.edu
FANNIN, John ... 269-782-1262 .... 258 C
jfannin@swmich.edu
FANNIN, Larry ... 801-878-1053 .... 303 D
lfannin@roseman.edu
FANNIN, William, R ... 432-552-2110 .... 507 D
fannin_w@utpb.edu
FANNING, Vivian ... 276-223-4777 .... 529 C
vfanning@wcc.vccs.edu
FANSHAW, Charles ... 202-685-3929 .... 557 I
fanshawc@ndu.edu
FANSLER, A. Gigi ... 217-732-3155 .... 156 I
gfansler@lincolncollege.edu
FANT, Charlotte ... 662-915-5059 .... 277 D
cfant@olemiss.edu
FANT, Gene ... 731-661-5520 .... 477 B
gfant@uu.edu
FANT, Greg ... 575-646-2127 .... 319 D
gfant@nmsu.edu
FANT, William, K ... 513-558-3326 .... 403 D
bill.fant@uc.edu
FANTE, Cheryl ... 352-854-2322 .... 103 K
fantec@cf.edu
FANTER, Jeff ... 317-921-4502 .... 175 I
jfanter@ivytech.edu
FANTINI, Beatriz ... 802-258-3343 .... 514 E
beatriz.fantini@worldlearning.org
FANTOZZI, Joseph ... 212-650-7865 .... 326 G
jfantozzi@ccny.cuny.edu
FANUTTI, Carol ... 716-827-2462 .... 358 D
fanuttic@trocaire.edu
FAOUR, Sheila ... 318-675-5000 .... 213 B
sfaour@lsuhsc.edu
FAOUR, William, G ... 423-624-0077 .... 467 H
billf@chattanoogacollege.edu
FARAHANI, Gohar ... 301-846-2451 .... 222 G
gfarahani@frederick.edu
FARAHI, Dawood ... 908-737-7000 .... 311 A
dfarahi@kean.edu
FARAKISH, Negar ... 908-412-3590 .... 316 B
negar.farakish@ucc.edu
FARAN, Ellen, W ... 617-253-4078 .... 241 D
FARANDA, John, P ... 909-621-8153 ...... 40 G
john.faranda@cmc.edu
FARARA, Joseph ... 802-635-1272 .... 515 F
joe.farara@jsc.edu
FARBANIEC, David ... 845-257-3196 .... 352 B
farbanid@newpaltz.edu
FARBROTHER, Barry ... 386-226-6817 .... 105 I
barry.farbrother@erau.edu
FARE, Bridget, M ... 412-396-6052 .... 428 D
fareb@duq.edu
FARELLA, Adriana ... 202-319-5300 ...... 97 E
farella@cua.edu
FARES, Ted ... 575-562-2511 .... 318 B
ted.fares@enmu.edu
FARFAN, Erika, M ... 740-427-5571 .... 394 C
farfane@kenyon.edu
FARHA, Darron, C ... 219-464-6702 .... 181 C
darron.farha@valpo.edu
FARHA, Nicholas ... 636-227-2100 .... 284 B
nicholas.farha@logan.edu

FARHANG, Ahad ... 718-951-5669 .... 326 F
afarhang@brooklyn.cuny.edu
FARIA, Geraldine ... 718-951-5214 .... 326 F
gfaria@brooklyn.cuny.edu
FARIA, Pamela ... 617-243-2221 .... 236 A
pfaria@lasell.edu
FARIAS, Antonio ... 860-701-6702 .... 558 H
antonio.farias@uscg.edu
FARIAS, Frank ... 520-621-6688 ...... 18 L
ffarias@email.arizona.edu
FARIAS, Jaime, D ... 915-831-2394 .... 486 G
jfarias@epcc.edu
FARIDIAN, Fred ... 909-884-8891 ...... 43 A
ffaridian@concorde.edu
FARINELLA, Nicole ... 312-935-6689 .... 162 G
nfarinella@robertmorris.edu
FARINHOLT, Phil ... 910-362-7014 .... 368 H
pfarinholt@cfcc.edu
FARINOS, Jose, L ... 772-462-7611 .... 111 B
jfarinos@irsc.edu
FARISH, Donald, J ... 401-254-3201 .... 454 C
FARISH, Guy ... 440-826-2478 .... 384 K
gfarish@bw.edu
FARKAS, Abraham ... 707-524-1508 ...... 68 E
afarkas@santarosa.edu
FARKAS, Scott, M ... 937-382-6661 .... 405 I
scott_farkas@wilmington.edu
FARLAND, William, H ... 970-491-7194 ...... 83 F
william.farland@colostate.edu
FARLEY, Barbara ... 612-330-1024 .... 261 B
farleyb@augsburg.edu
FARLEY, Christy ... 928-523-0185 ...... 16 I
christy.farley@nau.edu
FARLEY, Erik, S ... 745-587-6605 .... 389 I
farleye@denison.edu
FARLEY, Jean ... 617-296-8300 .... 235 J
jean_farley@laboure.edu
FARLEY, Jeff, A ... 724-480-3366 .... 426 A
jeff.farley@ccbc.edu
FARLEY, Jerry, B ... 785-670-1556 .... 197 F
jerry.farley@washburn.edu
FARLEY, Karen ... 563-336-3323 .... 184 E
kfarley@eicc.edu
FARLEY, Kay ... 785-670-1049 .... 197 F
kay.farley@washburn.edu
FARLEY, Kenneth ... 626-395-6005 ...... 32 H
farley@gps.caltech.edu
FARLEY, Lee ... 559-442-8231 ...... 72 B
lee.farley@fresnocitycollege.edu
FARLEY, Michael ... 704-971-8500 .... 363 F
FARLEY, Patrick ... 301-891-4551 .... 229 B
pfarley@wau.edu
FARLEY, Penelope, L ... 410-778-7224 .... 229 D
pfarley2@washcoll.edu
FARLEY, Susan ... 425-602-3354 .... 531 E
sfarley@bastyr.edu
FARLEY, Thomas, R ... 757-455-3263 .... 530 C
tfarley@vwc.edu
FARLEY, Tim ... 925-631-4830 ...... 64 F
tif5@stmarys-ca.edu
FARLEY, Troy ... 616-331-3311 .... 251 F
farleytr@gvsu.edu
FARMER, Anne ... 708-209-3237 .... 148 E
anne.farmer@cuchicago.edu
FARMER, Carla ... 417-667-8181 .... 280 E
cfarmer@cottey.edu
FARMER, David ... 910-695-3911 .... 373 H
farmerdj@sandhills.edu
FARMER, JR., John, J ... 973-353-5561 .... 314 E
jofarmer@andromeda.rutgers.edu
FARMER, Joyce ... 610-282-1100 .... 427 A
joyce.farmer@desales.edu
FARMER, Karla ... 620-223-2700 .... 193 A
karlaf@fortscott.edu
FARMER, Ken, R ... 513-721-7944 .... 391 D
kfarmer@gbs.edu
FARMER, Larry, G ... 704-637-4227 .... 363 E
lfarmer@catawba.edu
FARMER, Linda ... 541-684-4644 .... 419 F
lfarmer@pioneerpacific.edu
FARMER, Lindsey ... 910-695-3726 .... 373 H
farmerl@sandhills.edu
FARMER, Lorna ... 908-852-1400 .... 308 E
farmer@centenarycollege.edu
FARMER, Pam ... 864-977-7009 .... 460 A
pam.farmer@ngu.edu
FARMER, Patricia ... 603-358-2370 .... 306 G
pfarmer@keene.edu
FARMER, Patricia J, B ... 315-229-5265 .... 349 E
pfarmer@stlawu.edu
FARMER, Richard ... 617-578-7100 .... 244 D
rfarmer@sbboston.com
FARMER, Scott ... 337-482-5393 .... 216 D
sfarmer@louisiana.edu
FARMER, Stephen, M ... 919-966-3992 .... 378 E
smfarmer@email.unc.edu
FARMER, Steve ... 601-968-5929 .... 273 C
sfarmer@belhaven.edu
FARMER, Steve ... 419-227-3141 .... 404 D
wfarmer@unoh.edu
FARMER, Vickie, L ... 319-895-4243 .... 183 G
vfarmer@cornellcollege.edu
FARMER, William ... 323-464-2777 ...... 27 I
wfarmer@ca.aada.org

FARMER-NEAL, Rochonda ... 254-710-1453 .... 482 A
rochonda_farmer-neal@baylor.edu
FARMER NOONAN, Erin ... 617-735-9991 .... 234 C
farmer@emmanuel.edu
FARNESKI, Anna ... 201-684-6844 .... 313 C
afarnesk@ramapo.edu
FARNEY, Ashlee ... 312-922-1884 .... 157 E
afarney@maccormac.edu
FARNHAM, Bruce ... 619-660-4347 ...... 49 B
bruce.farnham@gcccd.edu
FARNHAM, Margaret, L ... 614-235-4136 .... 402 G
mfarnham@tlsohio.edu
FARNSWORTH, Briant, J ... 801-863-8006 .... 511 F
briant.farnsworth@uvu.edu
FARNSWORTH, Scott ... 928-776-2234 ...... 19 C
scott.farnsworth@yc.edu
FARNSWORTH, Ward ... 512-232-1322 .... 505 D
deansoffice@law.utexas.edu
FARO, Michael, E ... 585-594-6130 .... 347 F
farom@roberts.edu
FAROL, Dorothy ... 714-997-6611 ...... 39 F
farol@chapman.edu
FARQUHARSON, Janice, E ... 309-624-8980 .... 163 G
janice.farquharson@osfhealthcare.org
FARR, Betty ... 603-428-2480 .... 305 D
bfarr@nec.edu
FARR, C. Stephen ... 478-757-3700 .... 139 E
sfarr@wesleyancollege.edu
FARR, Harbin ... 912-449-7530 .... 139 D
hfarr@waycross.edu
FARR, Lamar ... 215-953-5999 ...... 99 G
lamar.farr@strayer.edu
FARR, Lum ... 318-368-3179 .... 210 K
lfarr@ltc.edu
FARR, Matthew ... 609-894-9311 .... 308 B
mfarr@bcc.edu
FARR, Pamela ... 912-287-5842 .... 135 F
pfarr@okefenokeetech.edu
FARR, Ralph, E ... 409-747-3810 .... 507 C
rfarr@utmb.edu
FARR, Sharon ... 573-288-6633 .... 280 I
sfarr@culver.edu
FARRA, Taline ... 617-587-5624 .... 242 H
farrat@neco.edu
FARRAND, Michael ... 423-775-6596 .... 472 G
mfarrand@ogs.edu
FARRAR, Barbara ... 262-595-2256 .... 552 A
farrar@uwp.edu
FARRAR, Carol ... 951-372-7017 ...... 63 K
carol.farrar@norcocollege.edu
FARRAR, James, D ... 540-458-8465 .... 530 D
jdfarrar@wlu.edu
FARRAR, Jazaer ... 708-596-2000 .... 164 H
jfouad-farrar@ssc.edu
FARRAR, Margaret, E ... 309-794-7313 .... 145 E
margaretfarrar@augustana.edu
FARRELL, Amy, E ... 717-245-1869 .... 427 F
farrell@dickinson.edu
FARRELL, Christina ... 610-558-5638 .... 437 D
farrellc@neumann.edu
FARRELL, Cynthia, H ... 724-589-2178 .... 448 B
cfarrell@thiel.edu
FARRELL, Gina ... 210-431-4377 .... 493 F
gfarrell@stmarytx.edu
FARRELL, Howard, M ... 940-397-4782 .... 491 B
howard.farrell@mwsu.edu
FARRELL, Jack ... 714-997-6983 ...... 39 F
jfarrell@chapman.edu
FARRELL, Jack ... 315-279-5434 .... 337 K
jferrell@mail.keuka.edu
FARRELL, Jack ... 315-279-5405 .... 337 K
jfarrell@mail.keuka.edu
FARRELL, OSA, Joseph, L ... 610-519-3546 .... 450 H
joseph.l.farrell@villanova.edu
FARRELL, Kathleen ... 914-251-6090 .... 354 D
kathleen.farrell@purchase.edu
FARRELL, Lauren, M ... 724-925-4079 .... 451 E
farrelll@wccc.edu
FARRELL, Lisa, M ... 636-584-6558 .... 281 E
lmfarrell@eastcentral.edu
FARRELL, Maggie ... 307-766-3224 .... 556 H
farrell@uwyo.edu
FARRELL, Mark ... 412-392-3879 .... 445 A
mfarrell@pointpark.edu
FARRELL, Martin, F ... 610-660-1225 .... 446 C
mfarrell@sju.edu
FARRELL, Mary Ellen ... 973-275-2293 .... 315 B
maryellen.farrell@shu.edu
FARRELL, Maureen ... 708-974-5788 .... 159 B
farrell@morainevalley.edu
FARRELL, Michael ... 716-851-1685 .... 333 A
farrell@ecc.edu
FARRELL, Mike, K ... 620-229-6286 .... 196 G
mike.farrell@sckans.edu
FARRELL, Nancy ... 413-265-2389 .... 233 D
farrelln@elms.edu
FARRELL, Pat ... 410-225-2367 .... 224 B
pfarrell@mica.edu
FARRELL, Patrick, V ... 610-758-3605 .... 434 E
pvf209@lehigh.edu
FARRELL, Phylene ... 413-236-5201 .... 239 A
pfarrell@berkshirecc.edu
FARRELL, R. Joel ... 202-685-2906 .... 557 I
robert.farrellii@ndu.edu

FEICHTER, Kathryn .... 330-966-5452.... 402 B
kfeichter@starkstate.edu
FEICK, Andrew .... 610-409-3598.... 450 D
afeick@ursinus.edu
FEIER, Julie .... 970-943-2061...... 89 E
jfeier@western.edu
FEIERSTEIN, Barry .... 301-502-8639...... 19 A
barry.feierstein@phoenix.edu
FEIERTAG, Jason .... 484-664-3140.... 437 C
feiertag@muhlenberg.edu
FEIGELSTOCK, Yitzchok ..... 516-225-4700.... 346 K
rcli@mlb.edu
FEIGENBAUM, Maurice .... 973-684-6036.... 312 E
mfeigenbaum@pccc.edu
FEIGERT, Kendra, M .... 717-867-6126.... 434 C
feigert@lvc.edu
FEIL, Hallie, L .... 308-635-6126.... 301 D
FEIL, Kevin, D .... 717-815-6818.... 452 G
kfeil@ycp.edu
FEILDS, Richard, A .... 404-527-4520.... 126 I
rfeilds@carver.edu
FEIN, Cheri .... 212-217-4700.... 333 F
cheri_fein@fitnyc.edu
FEIN, Gene .... 718-817-3900.... 334 C
fein@fordham.edu
FEIN, Jason .... 973-408-3648.... 309 E
jfein@drew.edu
FEIN, Michael, T .... 434-832-7751.... 526 E
feinm@cvcc.vccs.edu
FEIN, Oliver, T .... 212-746-4030.... 360 C
ofein@med.cornell.edu
FEINAUER, John .... 540-261-4091.... 524 H
john.feinauer@svu.edu
FEINBERG, David, T .... 310-267-9315...... 74 C
dfeinberg@mednet.ucla.edu
FEINER, Barbara, A .... 314-935-9842.... 292 I
barbara.a.feiner@wustl.edu
FEINERMAN, Frances .... 413-236-2102.... 239 A
ffeinerm@berkshirecc.edu
FEINGOLD, Marilyn .... 856-374-4932.... 308 D
mfeingold@camdencc.edu
FEINMAN, Shannon .... 434-949-1012.... 528 D
shannon.feinman@southside.edu
FEINSTEIN, Andrew, H .... 909-869-3464...... 33 J
andyf@csupomona.edu
FEINSTEIN, David .... 212-964-2830.... 340 H
FEINSTEIN, Jerald, L .... 301-548-5500...... 99 G
FEISTHAMEL, Kevin, P ...... 330-569-5952.... 391 G
FEITZ, David, A .... 801-321-7211.... 511 B
dfeitz@utahsbr.edu
FEKARIS, Cynthia .... 212-594-4000.... 357 H
cfekaris@tcicollege.edu
FEKE, Donald, L .... 216-368-4389.... 386 F
dlf4@case.edu
FEKETE, Michael .... 815-836-5549.... 156 F
feketemi@lewisu.edu
FELCH, Katrina .... 715-675-3331.... 555 B
felch@ntc.edu
FELD, Steven .... 610-902-8275.... 424 B
steven.feld@cabrini.edu
FELD-GORE, Jeffrey .... 503-768-7178.... 416 G
jfeldgore@lclark.edu
FELDBLUM, Miriam .... 909-621-8017...... 63 A
miriam.feldblum@pomona.edu
FELDER, Barbara, M .... 803-535-1218.... 460 C
felderb@octech.edu
FELDER, Luther .... 706-821-8295.... 135 G
lfelder@paine.edu
FELDER, Nigel .... 937-376-6566.... 387 A
nfelder@centralstate.edu
FELDER-DEAS, Altoya, A ... 803-934-3167.... 459 G
afdeas@morris.edu
FELDHAUS, Joseph, H ...... 513-745-3908.... 406 E
feldhausjl@xavier.edu
FELDHUES, Nicole .... 412-396-5675.... 428 D
feldhuesn@duq.edu
FELDHUS, Karima .... 949-451-5336...... 70 E
kfeldhus@ivc.edu
FELDMAN, Aharon .... 410-484-7200.... 225 C
FELDMAN, Barbara .... 201-200-3001.... 312 B
bfeldman@njcu.edu
FELDMAN, Barry .... 860-626-6803...... 94 G
barry.feldman@uconn.edu
FELDMAN, Cecile, A .... 973-972-4633.... 316 D
feldman@umdnj.edu
FELDMAN, Dan .... 781-736-8405.... 232 F
feldman@brandeis.edu
FELDMAN, Jacqueline .... 978-632-6600.... 240 C
j_feldman@mwcc.mass.edu
FELDMAN, Mary Jane .... 716-614-5926.... 344 C
feldman@niagaracc.suny.edu
FELDMAN, Rachelle .... 510-642-7117...... 73 H
FELDMAN, Robert, S .... 413-545-4173.... 236 F
feldman@sbs.umass.edu
FELDMAN, Stuart .... 212-851-1192.... 358 B
sfeldman@touro.edu
FELDMANN, Deborah .... 510-594-3606...... 32 C
dfeldmann@cca.edu
FELDMANN, Jacob .... 718-645-0536.... 341 D
FELDMEIER, Theresa .... 614-236-6813.... 386 E
tfeldmei@capital.edu
FELDSCHER, Donald .... 215-489-4978.... 426 H
donald.feldscher@delval.edu

FELDT, Tina .... 318-869-5424.... 208 H
tfeldt@centenary.edu
FELIBERTY, Victor, A .... 787-284-1912.... 564 A
vfeliber@ponce.inter.edu
FELICE, Susan .... 708-656-8000.... 159 D
susan.felice@morton.edu
FELICIANA, Jerrye, B .... 301-736-3631.... 224 A
jerrye.feliciana@msbbcs.edu
FELICIANO, Alberto .... 787-764-0000.... 568 B
alberto.feliciano@upr.edu
FELICIANO, Idali .... 517-265-5161.... 246 H
ifeliciano@adrian.edu
FELICIANO, Josean .... 787-786-3030.... 560 G
jfeliciano@ucb.edu.pr
FELICIANO, Orlando .... 847-317-8072.... 166 E
feliciano@tiu.edu
FELICIANO, Patsy .... 813-974-3827.... 121 A
pfelicia@admin.usf.edu
FELICIANO RIOS, Lynette . 787-265-3863.... 567 F
aeconomica@uprm.edu
FELIO, John, R .... 518-783-2471.... 350 I
jfelio@siena.edu
FELIU, Julio .... 787-841-2000.... 565 B
jfeliu@pucpr.edu
FELIX, Catherine .... 559-278-6715...... 35 A
cdfelix@csufresno.edu
FELIX-MATA, Bertha .... 559-934-2217...... 78 C
berthafelixmata@whccd.edu
FELIX-RODRIGUEZ,
Tamara .... 787-620-2040.... 560 D
tdrodriguez@aupr.edu
FELKER, Sharon .... 618-634-3270.... 164 E
sharonf@shawneecc.edu
FELKER, Sharon, M .... 303-963-3369...... 82 C
sfelker@ccu.edu
FELKNOR, Bruce .... 312-629-6128.... 164 C
bfelknor@saic.edu
FELL, Janet .... 732-923-4645.... 311 E
jfell@monmouth.edu
FELL, Katherine, R .... 419-434-4510.... 404 B
fell@findlay.edu
FELL, Stephanie .... 918-631-2241.... 413 F
stephanie-fell@utulsa.edu
FELLEGY, Anna .... 218-879-0878.... 266 C
afellegy@fdltcc.edu
FELLENBERG, William .... 201-200-3598.... 312 B
wfellenberg@njcu.edu
FELLINGER, Jennifer .... 360-491-4700.... 537 B
jfellinger@stmartin.edu
FELLMER, Jennine .... 641-472-1190.... 187 E
alumni@mum.edu
FELLOWS, Maureen, O .... 315-470-6621.... 355 A
mfellows@esf.edu
FELSER, Francis, J .... 716-250-7500.... 324 H
fjfelser@bryantstratton.edu
FELSKE, Julie, L .... 989-837-4436.... 256 E
felske@northwood.edu
FELSOVALYI, Erzsebet .... 973-748-9000.... 307 H
elizabeth_felsovalyi@bloomfield.edu
FELT, K.C .... 208-282-3755.... 143 H
feltkc@isu.edu
FELT, Suzanne .... 208-524-3000.... 143 G
suzanne.felt@my.eitc.edu
FELTES, Carol .... 212-327-8909.... 347 H
cfeltes@rockvax.rockefeller.edu
FELTMAN, Richard .... 718-951-5693.... 326 F
rfeltman@brooklyn.cuny.edu
FELTMANN, Charles .... 636-227-2100.... 284 B
charles.feltmann@logan.edu
FELTON, David, A .... 304-293-2521.... 545 A
david.felton@hsc.wvu.edu
FELTON, Herman .... 704-216-6044.... 366 G
hfelton@livingstone.edu
FELTON, James .... 828-227-2276.... 380 A
jafelton@wcu.edu
FELTON, Jennifer .... 712-749-2120.... 183 C
feltonj@bvu.edu
FELTON, Judith .... 860-343-5816...... 91 G
jfelton@mxcc.commnet.edu
FELTON, Rob .... 503-554-2129.... 415 I
rfelton@georgefox.edu
FELTON, Terence .... 630-466-7900.... 168 B
tfelton@waubonsee.edu
FELTS, Bennie, L .... 919-941-2920.... 375 F
bennie.felts@fsmail.pfeiffer.edu
FELTS, Ronald .... 661-726-1911...... 73 F
ron.felts@uav.edu
FELTY, Donna, H .... 423-652-4752.... 470 A
dhfelty@king.edu
FELTZ, Jason .... 325-793-6550.... 490 H
feltz.jason@mcm.edu
FELVER, Eric .... 518-327-6017.... 345 H
efelver@paulsmiths.edu
FEMINO, Donald .... 978-232-5201.... 234 D
dfemino@endicott.edu
FENDER, Donna .... 276-223-4729.... 529 C
dfender@wcc.vccs.edu
FENDERS, Nancy .... 207-941-7153.... 218 A
fendersn@husson.edu
FENDRICH, Carlotta .... 719-549-2904...... 83 H
carlotta.fendrich@colostate-pueblo.edu
FENESY, Kim .... 973-972-4440.... 316 D
fenesy@umdnj.edu
FENESY, Kim, E .... 973-972-1699.... 316 D
fenesy@umdnj.edu

FENG, Janet .... 281-649-3748.... 487 H
jfeng@hbu.edu
FENLASON, Laurie .... 413-585-2170.... 244 G
lfenlaso@smith.edu
FENN, Patricia .... 732-255-0400.... 312 D
pfenn@ocean.edu
FENNELL, Angelia .... 903-593-8311.... 499 D
afennell@texascollege.edu
FENNELL, Barbara .... 432-686-4250.... 491 A
bfennell@midland.edu
FENNELL, Catherine .... 610-896-1221.... 430 G
cfennell@haverford.edu
FENNELL, Catherine .... 610-527-0200.... 445 J
fennell@roesmont.edu
FENNELL, Craig .... 215-204-1492.... 447 H
craig.fennell@temple.edu
FENNELL, Dwight .... 903-593-8311.... 499 D
dfennell@texascollege.edu
FENNELL, Sabrina .... 716-839-8228.... 331 F
sfennell@daemen.edu
FENNELL, Sheena .... 740-753-6356.... 391 H
fennells@hocking.edu
FENNELL, Shirley .... 919-546-8227.... 376 F
sfennell@shawu.edu
FENNELL-MCGAY, Carolyn 803-793-5108.... 457 F
mcgayc@denmarktech.edu
FENNER-LEINO, Patti .... 715-682-1230.... 549 F
pfen-lei@northland.edu
FENNERN, Nicole .... 507-457-1781.... 271 B
nfennern@smumn.edu
FENNESSEY, Tom .... 715-394-8122.... 552 F
tfenness@uwsuper.edu
FENNING, Robert, L .... 757-683-3464.... 522 F
rfenning@odu.edu
FENSKE, David, E .... 215-895-2479.... 427 H
def23@drexel.edu
FENSKE, Susanne .... 262-691-5295.... 555 E
sfenske@wctc.edu
FENSTAD, Terry .... 413-572-5276.... 238 F
tfenstad@wsc.ma.edu
FENTER, Glen, F .... 870-733-6722...... 22 E
gfenter@midsouthcc.edu
FENTON, James, W .... 419-772-2070.... 398 H
j-fenton@onu.edu
FENTON, Mimi .... 828-227-7398.... 380 A
mfenton@wcu.edu
FENTON, Patrick .... 408-741-2056...... 78 G
pat.fenton@westvalley.edu
FENTON, Walter .... 618-664-6500.... 151 F
walter.fenton@greenville.edu
FENTON, William, E .... 502-272-8059.... 198 H
wfenton@bellarmine.edu
FENTON-MACE, Christina .. 570-945-8162.... 432 E
christina.mace@keystone.edu
FENTRESS, Connie .... 757-789-1728.... 526 H
cfentress@es.vccs.edu
FENTRESS, Craig, M .... 240-500-2000.... 223 A
fentressc@hagerstowncc.edu
FENTRESS, Lisa, I .... 757-455-3337.... 530 C
lfentress@vwc.edu
FENTRESS, Mike .... 360-752-8320.... 531 H
mfentress@btc.ctc.edu
FENTRESS, Viki, P .... 318-797-5234.... 213 D
viki.fentress@lsus.edu
FENVES, Gregory, L .... 512-471-1166.... 505 D
fenves@utexas.edu
FENWICK, Garland .... 540-423-9046.... 526 I
gfenwick@germanna.edu
FENWICK, Leslie, T .... 202-806-7340...... 98 E
lfenwick@howard.edu
FEOLA, Ralph, J .... 315-792-5444.... 341 E
rfeola@mvcc.edu
FERALDI, Corey .... 803-641-3280.... 462 B
coreyf@usca.edu
FERALDI, Patricia, A .... 716-673-3553.... 352 A
patricia.feraldi@fredonia.edu
FERBER, Maragaret, C .... 585-389-2020.... 342 D
mferber6@naz.edu
FERBRACHE, Jeanne .... 402-559-3937.... 300 H
jferbrache@unmc.edu
FERCH, John .... 907-822-3201...... 10 B
jferch@akbible.edu
FERCHLAND-PARELLA,
Joanne .... 619-594-6323...... 37 A
jparella@mail.sdsu.edu
FERDEN, Patricia .... 507-457-5330.... 269 G
pferden@winona.edu
FERDINAND, Amy .... 973-655-4367.... 311 F
ferdinanda@mail.montclair.edu
FEREBEE, Ryan, A .... 757-594-7033.... 517 L
ryan.ferebee@cnu.edu
FEREIRA, James, A .... 651-638-6300.... 261 D
j-fereira@bethel.edu
FERGASON, Linda .... 330-449-9600.... 393 I
lfergaso@kent.edu
FERGERSON, James .... 507-222-4292.... 261 G
jfergers@carleton.edu
FERGERSON, Nicole .... 775-831-1314.... 303 E
nferguson@sierranevada.edu
FERGUSON, Angela, M .... 704-403-1614.... 362 I
angela.ferguson@carolinashealthcare.org
FERGUSON, Annette .... 806-874-3571.... 483 A
annette.ferguson@clarendoncollege.edu
FERGUSON, Bennett .... 678-359-5023.... 132 A
benf@gdn.edu

FERGUSON, Charity, F .... 270-384-8100.... 204 D
fergusonc@lindsey.edu
FERGUSON, Chen .... 513-785-7703.... 396 F
fergusc@muohio.edu
FERGUSON, Christy .... 716-286-8345.... 344 D
clf@niagara.edu
FERGUSON, Cristie .... 903-693-2005.... 492 C
cferguson@panola.edu
FERGUSON, Darla .... 321-433-7080.... 102 D
fergusond@brevardcc.edu
FERGUSON, Devin .... 972-825-4700.... 495 F
dferguson@sagu.edu
FERGUSON, Douglas, J .... 610-359-7399.... 426 G
dferguson@dccc.edu
FERGUSON, F. Joel .... 831-459-2412...... 75 C
fjf@ucsc.edu
FERGUSON, Gail .... 940-397-4273.... 491 B
gail.ferguson@mwsu.edu
FERGUSON, Janice, Y .... 716-625-6300.... 324 K
jyferguson@bryantstratton.edu
FERGUSON, Jason .... 503-229-0492.... 416 B
jason_ferguson@heald.edu
FERGUSON, Jessame, E .... 410-857-2741.... 224 C
jferguson@mcdaniel.edu
FERGUSON, Joe, C .... 402-844-7236.... 299 I
joe@northeast.edu
FERGUSON, Joseph, S .... 361-570-4390.... 504 A
fergusonj@uhv.edu
FERGUSON, Judy .... 281-649-3450.... 487 H
jferguson@hbu.edu
FERGUSON, Julie .... 973-972-4640.... 316 F
fergusje@umdnj.edu
FERGUSON, Keith, D .... 615-353-3604.... 475 E
keith.ferguson@nscc.edu
FERGUSON, Ken .... 573-681-5265.... 283 I
fergusonk@lincolnu.edu
FERGUSON, Kimberly .... 404-270-5133.... 138 B
kfergu15@spelman.edu
FERGUSON, Larry .... 606-326-2232.... 201 F
larry.ferguson@kctcs.edu
FERGUSON, Larry, W .... 803-323-2216.... 463 E
fergusonl@winthrop.edu
FERGUSON, Lee .... 214-333-5363.... 484 D
lee@dbu.edu
FERGUSON, Lisa, M .... 740-283-6450.... 391 A
lferguson@franciscan.edu
FERGUSON, Lori .... 580-349-1566.... 410 B
lorif@opsu.edu
FERGUSON, Lorrie .... 540-863-2823.... 526 F
lferguson@dslcc.edu
FERGUSON, Nancy .... 513-727-3431.... 396 G
FERGUSON, Nicole .... 775-831-1314.... 303 E
nferguson@sierranevada.edu
FERGUSON, Noreen .... 248-204-3106.... 254 B
nferguson@ltu.edu
FERGUSON, Pamela .... 973-720-2615.... 317 D
fergusonp4@wpunj.edu
FERGUSON, Paul .... 912-478-7288.... 131 E
pferguson@georgiasouthern.edu
FERGUSON, Paul, W .... 207-581-1512.... 220 A
president@umaine.edu
FERGUSON, Randy, L .... 262-243-5700.... 547 C
randall.ferguson@cuw.edu
FERGUSON, Rebecca, C .... 419-372-8421.... 385 E
fergusb@bgsu.edu
FERGUSON, Renee .... 541-880-2234.... 416 D
ferguson@klamathcc.edu
FERGUSON, Richard, C .... 203-582-5350...... 93 H
richard.ferguson@quinnipiac.edu
FERGUSON, Richard, T .... 937-229-5400.... 404 A
dferguson1@udayton.edu
FERGUSON, Roberta .... 304-696-6632.... 544 B
fergusor@marshall.edu
FERGUSON, Rose, A .... 815-599-3402.... 152 B
rose.ferguson@highland.edu
FERGUSON, JR., Roy, W .. 540-828-5605.... 517 B
rferguso@bridgewater.edu
FERGUSON, Sarah .... 972-860-4854.... 484 G
sferguson@dcccd.edu
FERGUSON, Stephanie .... 540-887-7039.... 521 C
sferguson@mbc.edu
FERGUSON, Teresa, D .... 864-587-4003.... 461 D
fergusont@smcsc.edu
FERGUSON, Theressa .... 573-681-5128.... 283 I
fergusont@lincolnu.edu
FERGUSON, Thomas .... 614-231-3095.... 385 C
thomas.ferguson@bexley.edu
FERGUSON, Timothy .... 859-572-7770.... 205 H
fergusont2@nku.edu
FERGUSON, Tommy .... 903-589-4016.... 490 D
tferguson@lonmorris.edu
FERGUSON, Valerie .... 214-333-5113.... 484 D
valerie@dbu.edu
FERGUSON, Vicki .... 510-235-7800...... 43 E
vferguson@contracosta.edu
FERGUSON, Vicki .... 405-224-3140.... 413 E
facfergusonv@usao.edu
FERGUSON, Vincent .... 215-248-4665.... 435 B
vferguson@ltsp.edu
FERGUSON, William .... 315-228-7333.... 329 G
wferguson@colgate.edu
FERGUSON, William, L .... 864-379-8881.... 458 A
ferguson@erskine.edu

FIELDING, Chad .... 870-230-5081...... 21 I
fieldic@hsu.edu
FIELDING, Richard .... 619-421-6700...... 71 D
FIELDING, William .... 256-782-5773........ 4 L
fielding@jsu.edu
FIELDS, Ann .... 641-673-1076.... 190 C
fieldsa@wmpenn.edu
FIELDS, Ann, Z .... 901-722-3230.... 473 C
annfields@sco.edu
FIELDS, Beverly .... 806-457-4200.... 486 I
bfields@fpctx.edu
FIELDS, Brad .... 610-225-5032.... 428 E
bfields@eastern.edu
FIELDS, Christine .... 276-739-2426.... 529 A
cfields@vhcc.edu
FIELDS, Christopher .... 614-947-6803.... 391 B
fieldsc@franklin.edu
FIELDS, Darin, E .... 304-829-7313.... 540 H
dfields@bethanywv.edu
FIELDS, Dennis .... 717-545-4747.... 432 F
FIELDS, Edward .... 502-597-6163.... 203 G
edward.fields@kysu.edu
FIELDS, Gene .... 337-482-9246.... 216 D
gene.fields@louisiana.edu
FIELDS, Jay .... 803-793-5286.... 457 F
fieldsj@denmarktech.edu
FIELDS, Jeff .... 276-656-0222.... 527 G
jfields@patrickhenry.edu
FIELDS, John .... 229-430-4711.... 124 A
john.fields@asurams.edu
FIELDS, Lee, M .... 252-334-2080.... 367 C
lee.fields@macuniversity.edu
FIELDS, Leonard, B .... 563-562-3263.... 188 B
fieldsl@nicc.edu
FIELDS, M. Evelyn .... 803-536-4974.... 460 G
efields@scsu.edu
FIELDS, Marcia, C .... 573-840-9666.... 290 F
FIELDS, Marcia, C .... 573-840-9675.... 290 F
mfields@trcc.edu
FIELDS, Melea .... 562-902-3344..... 71 A
meleafields@scuhs.edu
FIELDS, Michael .... 707-668-5663..... 44 A
FIELDS, Peter .... 406-994-4221.... 295 C
pfields@msubobcats.com
FIELDS, Petra .... 704-991-0231.... 374 D
pfields7679@stanly.edu
FIELDS, Russell .... 775-784-6987.... 303 A
rfields@unr.edu
FIELDS, Stan, D .... 816-604-1578.... 284 H
stan.fields@mcckc.edu
FIELDS, Todd, E .... 972-881-5174.... 483 H
tfields@collin.edu
FIELDS, Valerie .... 803-536-4969.... 460 G
vfields1@scsu.edu
FIENE, Jay .... 909-537-5600...... 36 B
jfiene@csusb.edu
FIENE, John, L .... 402-554-3670.... 301 A
jfiene@unomaha.edu
FIENSY, David, A .... 606-474-3263.... 201 D
dfiensy@kcu.edu
FIERBAUGH, Lee .... 423-461-8719.... 471 J
lfierbaugh@milligan.edu
FIERKE, Kimberly .... 607-431-4000.... 335 A
FIERO, Diane .... 661-362-3424...... 41 I
diane.fiero@canyons.edu
FIERO, Tom, D .... 517-750-1200.... 258 D
tfiero@arbor.edu
FIFE, Jerry .... 615-343-6688.... 478 A
jerry.fife@vanderbilt.edu
FIFE, Kaaren .... 913-288-7281.... 194 C
kfife@kckcc.edu
FIFE, Linda, L .... 443-412-2377.... 223 B
lfife@harford.edu
FIFER, Tom .... 660-831-4219.... 286 F
fifert@moval.edu
FIFIELD, Mary, L .... 617-228-2400.... 239 C
mfifield@bhcc.mass.edu
FIFRICK, Heather .... 608-822-2366.... 555 D
hfifrick@swtc.edu
FIGA, Jan .... 217-245-3020.... 152 D
jan.figa@ic.edu
FIGARELLE, Thomas .... 406-771-4412.... 295 G
thomas.figarelle@msugf.edu
FIGARI, Charles, A .... 713-500-8400.... 506 F
charles.a.figari@uth.tmc.edu
FIGGS, Joel .... 785-243-1435.... 192 A
jfiggs@cloud.edu
FIGHERA, Christine .... 714-992-7025...... 59 E
cfighera@fullcoll.edu
FIGHERA, Joe .... 619-482-6446...... 71 D
jfighera@swccd.edu
FIGUEIRA, Russell, J .... 610-526-1200.... 422 A
russell.figueira@theamericancollege.edu
FIGUEREDO, Danilo, H ..... 973-748-9000.... 307 H
danilo_figueredo@bloomfield.edu
FIGUEROA, Ana, M .... 973-290-4434.... 308 G
afigueroa@cse.edu
FIGUEROA, Caroline .... 787-761-0640.... 566 F
oficialderegistroacademico@utcpr.edu
FIGUEROA, Eduardo .... 787-882-2065.... 566 A
FIGUEROA, Fernando .... 361-698-1205.... 485 G
ffigueroa@delmar.edu
FIGUEROA, Gema, C .... 787-738-2161.... 567 D
gema.figueroa@upr.edu
FIGUEROA, Jennifer, E ...... 570-577-1028.... 423 E
j.figueroa@bucknell.edu
FIGUEROA, Julio .... 787-257-7373.... 565 G
ue_jfigueroa@suagm.edu
FIGUEROA, Margarita .... 787-720-1022.... 560 F
admisiones@atlanticcollege.edu
FIGUEROA, Maria .... 787-725-6500.... 561 A
mafigueroa@albizu.edu
FIGUEROA, Maria, V .... 787-743-7979.... 565 H
ut_mfigueroa@suagm.edu
FIGUEROA, Mark .... 503-768-7676.... 416 G
figueroa@lclark.edu
FIGUEROA, Rachel .... 330-499-9600.... 393 I
rfiguero@kent.edu
FIGUEROA, Roberto .... 518-464-8800.... 333 E
rfigueroa@excelsior.edu
FIGUEROA, Samuel .... 787-738-2161.... 567 D
samuel.figueroa5@upr.edu
FIGUEROA, William .... 787-758-2525.... 567 G
william.figueroa2@upr.edu
FIIGUEROA, Ken .... 407-888-4000.... 113 A
kfigueroa@orlando.chefs.edu
FIKE, David, J .... 313-927-1208.... 254 E
dfike@marygrove.edu
FIKE, Esther .... 407-831-9816.... 103 E
efike@citycollege.edu
FIKE, Esther .... 954-492-5353.... 103 F
efike@citycollege.edu
FIKE, Janet .... 304-214-8837.... 543 D
jfike@wvncc.edu
FIKE, Jeffrey .... 540-828-5395.... 517 B
jfike@bridgewater.edu
FIKE, Linda, K .... 301-387-3049.... 222 H
linda.fike@garrettcollege.edu
FILAN, Sonia .... 480-461-7446...... 15 I
sonia.filan@mcmail.maricopa.edu
FILARDI, Salvatore .... 203-582-8800...... 93 H
salvatore.filardi@quinnipiac.edu
FILARDI, Salvatore .... 508-999-8058.... 237 A
sfilardi@umassd.edu
FILBRY, Sandra .... 516-463-4335.... 335 G
sandra.filbry@hofstra.edu
FILBY, Robert, G .... 740-284-5472.... 391 A
rfilby@franciscan.edu
FILE, Carter .... 620-665-3509.... 193 H
FILE, David, C .... 319-385-6245.... 186 E
dfile@iwc.edu
FILEMYR, Ann .... 505-424-2354.... 318 D
afilemyr@iaia.edu
FILIPIAK, Joseph, M .... 312-915-7671.... 157 C
jfilipi@luc.edu
FILIPP, Robert .... 773-442-5300.... 160 A
r-filipp@neiu.edu
FILIPPELLI, Karen, S .... 520-621-4789...... 18 L
filippek@email.arizona.edu
FILIPPIDIS, Barbara .... 512-448-8558.... 493 E
barbaraf@stedwards.edu
FILIPPONE, Anne .... 610-902-8407.... 424 B
anne.ferry@cabrini.edu
FILIPPONE, Gregg, S .... 716-851-1073.... 333 A
filipponeg@ecc.edu
FILIPPONE, Robin .... 716-270-5237.... 333 B
filippone@ecc.edu
FILLINGER, Barbara .... 734-973-3560.... 259 F
bfilling@wccnet.edu
FILLIPPI, Carolyn .... 315-229-5267.... 349 E
cfillippi@stlawu.edu
FILLNER, Russ .... 406-447-6917.... 295 A
russ.fillner@umhelena.edu
FILLPOT, Jim .... 909-652-6460...... 39 E
jim.fillpot@chaffey.edu
FILORAMO, Dorothy .... 845-848-7400.... 332 B
dorothy.filoramo@dc.edu
FILOSA, Bruce .... 718-951-5366.... 326 F
bfilosa@brooklyn.cuny.edu
FILOWSKI, Melissa .... 509-865-8544.... 535 A
filowski_m@heritage.edu
FILPUS-LUYCKX, Mary ...... 706-737-1492.... 125 G
mfilpusl@aug.edu
FILSON, Cori .... 518-580-5355.... 351 B
cfilson@skidmore.edu
FINALY, Roy .... 619-477-6310...... 73 D
rfinaly@usuniversity.edu
FINCANNON, Angie .... 765-998-5311.... 180 B
anfincann@taylor.edu
FINCH, Brian, K .... 860-444-8480.... 558 H
bryan.k.finch@uscg.mil
FINCH, Christopher .... 201-559-6084.... 310 B
finchc@felician.edu
FINCH, Daniel .... 419-720-6670.... 401 C
dfinch@proskills.edu
FINCH, Donald .... 608-249-6611.... 547 G
donnie@msn.herzing.edu
FINCH, Irene .... 207-741-5715.... 219 A
ifinch@smccme.edu
FINCH, J. Howard .... 205-726-2364........ 6 G
hfinch@samford.edu
FINCH, Jack, R .... 740-377-2520.... 402 F
jfinch1@zoominternet.net
FINCH, Judy .... 503-768-7328.... 416 G
finchj@lclark.edu
FINCH, Mary Ellen .... 314-529-9400.... 284 C
mfinch@maryville.edu
FINCH, Thomas .... 315-786-2235.... 337 F
tfinch@sunyjefferson.edu
FINCH, Tony .... 662-720-7304.... 276 C
tfinch@nemcc.edu
FINCH, Tracy .... 870-972-2031...... 20 D
tfinch@astate.edu
FINCHER, David, B .... 660-263-3900.... 279 F
academics@cccb.edu
FINCHER, Wade .... 501-882-8866...... 20 C
wade@asub.edu
FINCK, Kathleen .... 802-225-3258.... 514 B
kathleen.finck@neci.edu
FINCK, Konrad .... 312-329-4066.... 159 A
konrad.finck@moody.edu
FINDLEY, Brenda .... 706-867-2705.... 134 G
bkfindley@northgeorgia.edu
FINDLEY, Donna .... 478-387-4846.... 131 A
FINDLEY, Pamela, L .... 256-782-5151........ 4 L
pfindley@jsu.edu
FINDT, William .... 910-879-5502.... 368 D
wfindt@bladencc.edu
FINE, Ricka, K .... 410-777-1868.... 221 C
rkfine@aacc.edu
FINE, Robert .... 773-508-2398.... 157 C
rfine@luc.edu
FINEGAN, SC, Carol, M .... 718-405-3349.... 330 A
carol.finegan@mountsaintvincent.edu
FINEGAN, James, M .... 814-871-7681.... 429 G
finegan001@gannon.edu
FINEGAN, Kathleen .... 816-501-3621.... 278 I
kathleen.finegan@avila.edu
FINEGOLD, David, L .... 848-932-5935.... 314 B
dfinegold@oldqueens.rutgers.edu
FINEIS, Jill .... 802-586-7711.... 514 G
jfineis@sterlingcollege.edu
FINEMAN, Robert .... 206-934-3791.... 537 D
robert.fineman@seattlecolleges.edu
FINEO, Richard .... 860-632-3007...... 93 B
rfineo@holyapostles.edu
FINEOUT-OVERHOLT,
Ellen .... 903-923-2210.... 486 F
efineoutoverholt@etbu.edu
FINESILVER, Jennifer .... 317-632-5553.... 177 G
jfinesilver@lincolntech.com
FINFROCK, Randal, M .... 724-925-4060.... 451 E
finfrockr@wccc.edu
FINGADO, Marianne .... 415-264-6635...... 58 I
mfingado@nu.edu
FINGER, Eleanor .... 540-231-8893.... 529 G
efinger@vt.edu
FINGER, Mary .... 312-362-8666.... 149 A
mfinger@depaul.edu
FINK, Brenda .... 626-914-8830...... 40 B
bfink@citruscollege.edu
FINK, Charles, R .... 631-423-0483.... 350 G
cfink@icseminary.edu
FINK, Ernest .... 718-409-7341.... 356 C
efink@sunymaritime.edu
FINK, Gayle, M .... 301-860-3403.... 228 A
gfink@bowiestate.edu
FINK, Jonathan .... 503-725-9944.... 418 G
jon.fink@pdx.edu
FINK, Joseph, W .... 412-624-9510.... 449 A
fink@pitt.edu
FINK, Michael .... 909-652-6453...... 39 E
michael.fink@chaffey.edu
FINK, Michael .... 912-525-5879.... 136 F
mfink@scad.edu
FINK, Robert .... 262-595-2207.... 552 A
robert.fink@uwp.edu
FINKE, Barbara .... 816-802-3434.... 283 E
bfinke@kcai.edu
FINKE, John .... 317-955-6202.... 177 I
jfinke@marian.edu
FINKEL, Lee .... 602-557-1595...... 19 A
lee.finkel@phoenix.edu
FINKELMAN, Jay .... 213-615-7267.... 146 F
jfinkelman@thechicagoschool.edu
FINKELSTEIN, Barbara, E .. 508-588-9100.... 240 A
FINKELSTEIN, Eric, M .... 718-990-2417.... 348 G
finkelse@stjohns.edu
FINKELSTEIN, Larry, A ...... 617-373-2462.... 243 F
FINKELSTEIN, Monte .... 850-201-8488.... 122 A
finkelsm@tcc.fl.edu
FINKELSTEIN, Richard .... 540-654-1052.... 525 D
rfinkels@umw.edu
FINKENBINE, Roy .... 313-993-3250.... 258 G
finkenre@udmercy.edu
FINKS, Frederick, J .... 419-289-5050.... 384 G
ffinks@ashland.edu
FINLAY, Barbara, A .... 540-338-1776.... 522 G
FINLAY, Cheryl, S .... 412-383-4473.... 449 A
cfinlay@pitt.edu
FINLAYSON, Al .... 218-733-7613.... 266 H
a.finlayson@lsc.edu
FINLAYSON,
Alexander (Sandy) .... 215-572-3823.... 451 D
sfinlayson@wts.edu
FINLAYSON, Deborah .... 806-742-0502.... 502 A
deborah.finlayson@ttu.edu
FINLAYSON, Jeanne .... 508-565-1337.... 245 A
jfinlayson@stonehill.edu
FINLEY, Adam .... 817-598-8831.... 508 F
afinley@wc.edu
FINLEY, Heather .... 417-829-1422...... 19 A
heather.brown@phoenix.edu
FINLEY, James .... 479-899-6644...... 21 B
jfinley@bryancollege.com
FINLEY, Jane .... 251-442-2219........ 9 A
jfinley@umobile.edu
FINLEY, Jenna .... 970-351-2721...... 89 B
jenna.finley@unco.edu
FINLEY, Jennifer .... 828-277-5521.... 376 H
jfinley@southcollegenc.edu
FINLEY, Julius .... 360-779-9993.... 535 J
jfinley@ncad.edu
FINLEY, Lucinda, M .... 716-645-3594.... 351 G
finleylu@buffalo.edu
FINLEY, Michelle .... 918-495-6203.... 411 C
mfinley@oru.edu
FINLEY, Rebecca .... 215-503-9000.... 448 C
rebecca.finley@jefferson.edu
FINLEY, Tony .... 501-279-4242...... 21 H
tfinley@harding.edu
FINLEY, William, D .... 304-367-4842.... 543 H
william.finley@fairmontstate.edu
FINLINSON, Kitt .... 801-524-8165.... 510 E
kfinlin@ldsbc.edu
FINLINSON, Norm .... 801-422-4640.... 509 H
norm_finlinson@byu.edu
FINN, Alan .... 503-725-3649.... 418 G
finnal@pdx.edu
FINN, Alicia, A .... 603-641-7600.... 305 G
afinn@anselm.edu
FINN, Bob, D .... 509-313-6100.... 534 F
finn@gonzaga.edu
FINN, Edward, J .... 563-333-6289.... 188 F
finnedwardj@sau.edu
FINN, Erin .... 215-895-6712.... 427 H
emf332@drexel.edu
FINN, Eugene, J .... 330-672-6000.... 393 D
gfinn@kent.edu
FINN, John .... 330-263-2373.... 388 F
jfinn@wooster.edu
FINN, June .... 201-559-6037.... 310 B
finnj@felician.edu
FINN, Kevin .... 248-204-4100.... 254 B
kfinn@ltu.edu
FINN, Louise .... 410-617-5252.... 223 I
lafinn@loyola.edu
FINN, William .... 708-974-5727.... 159 B
finn@morainevalley.edu
FINN KENNEY, Rebecca ... 415-458-3720...... 45 C
rebecca.finnkenney@dominican.edu
FINN-SHERMAN, Miriam .. 781-768-7222.... 244 A
miriam.sherman@regiscollege.edu
FINNAN, Diane, P .... 908-852-1400.... 308 E
finnand@centenarycollege.edu
FINNEGAN, Barry .... 636-949-4455.... 283 J
bfinnegan@lindenwood.edu
FINNEGAN, Faye, A .... 563-588-7155.... 187 C
faye.finnegan@loras.edu
FINNEGAN, John .... 612-625-1179.... 272 A
finne001@umn.edu
FINNEGAN, Michael, S ..... 256-824-6480........ 8 G
michael.finnegan@uah.edu
FINNEGAN, Olya .... 414-443-8867.... 553 D
olya.finnegan@wlc.edu
FINNEL, Kristin, M .... 920-922-8611.... 554 G
kfinnel@morainepark.edu
FINNELL, Todd .... 760-355-6472...... 51 A
todd.finnell@imperial.edu
FINNELLY, Ryan, L .... 847-317-8145.... 166 E
rfinnell@tiu.edu
FINNEN, Mary .... 646-660-6549.... 326 C
mary.finnen@baruch.cuny.edu
FINNERTY, Mary Beth .... 518-782-6818.... 350 I
mfinnerty@siena.edu
FINNERTY, Pat .... 419-227-3141.... 404 D
pfinnert@unoh.edu
FINNERTY, Robert .... 585-475-4733.... 347 G
bob.finnerty@rit.edu
FINNEY, Andy .... 208-769-3266.... 144 D
andy_finney@nic.edu
FINNEY, David, F .... 802-860-2734.... 513 C
finney@champlain.edu
FINNEY, Howard, H .... 214-860-2202.... 485 A
hfinney@dcccd.edu
FINNEY, Janice .... 850-644-1328.... 119 D
jfinney@admin.fsu.edu
FINNEY, Lesley, M .... 717-361-1445.... 428 F
finneylm@etown.edu
FINNEY, Marc .... 434-848-1840.... 524 B
mfinney@saintpauls.edu
FINNEY, Sarah .... 206-296-6390.... 538 B
sfinney@seattleu.edu
FINNEY, Terry .... 870-972-2398...... 20 D
tfinney@astate.edu
FINNIGAN, Kristia, H .... 803-777-6727.... 462 A
finnigan@sc.edu
FINNIN, Meredith .... 212-752-1530.... 338 C
meredith.finnin@limcollege.edu
FINNING, Shannon .... 781-239-4309.... 230 E
sfinning@babson.edu
FINTON, Stephan .... 860-444-8500.... 558 H
stephan.p.finton@uscga.edu
FINUCANE, Margaret .... 216-397-1780.... 392 L
mfinucane@jcu.edu

FITZPATRICK, Jane .... 606-783-2053.... 204 I
j.fitzpatrick@moreheadstate.edu
FITZPATRICK, John, C ...... 718-429-6600.... 359 G
john.fitzpatrick@vaughn.edu
FITZPATRICK, M. Louise ... 610-519-4909.... 450 H
louise.fitzpatrick@villanova.edu
FITZPATRICK, SC,
Margaret, M .... 845-398-4013.... 349 H
mfitzpat@stac.edu
FITZPATRICK, Mary Anne .. 803-777-7798.... 462 A
fitzpatm@gwm.sc.edu
FITZPATRICK, Pat .... 718-390-3131.... 360 A
pfitzpat@wagner.edu
FITZPATRICK, Sharon .... 405-945-3292.... 410 F
FITZPATRICK, Susan .... 906-635-2831.... 253 H
sfitzpatrick@lssu.edu
FITZPATRICK, Timothy, J .. 352-392-2061.... 120 C
timf@ufl.edu
FITZPATRICK, Timothy, M . 860-444-8603.... 558 H
timothy.m.fitzpatrick@uscga.edu
FITZSIMMONS, Joanne ..... 518-445-2324.... 322 C
jfitz@albanylaw.edu
FITZSIMMONS, John .... 207-629-4000.... 218 F
jfitzsimmons@mccs.me.edu
FITZSIMMONS, Peter .... 408-270-6130...... 67 B
peter.fitzsimmons@sjeccd.org
FITZSIMMONS, Rodney ..... 520-748-9799...... 12 H
rfitzsimmons@brooklinecollege.edu
FITZSIMMONS, Stephanie . 732-224-2369.... 308 A
sfitzsimmons@brookdalecc.edu
FITZSIMMONS, Tracy .... 540-665-4505.... 524 E
tfitzsim@su.edu
FITZSIMMONS, Verna, M .. 785-826-2601.... 194 D
FITZSIMMONS, Verna, M .. 785-826-2601.... 194 E
vfitzsimmons@k-state.edu
FITZSIMMONS, William, R 617-495-1557.... 235 D
wrf@fas.harvard.edu
FITZSIMONS, Connie .... 310-660-3715...... 45 E
cfitzsimons@elcamino.edu
FITZSIMONS, Debra .... 949-582-4665...... 70 D
dfitzsimons@socccd.edu
FITZWATER, Valerie .... 972-825-5469.... 495 F
vfitzwater@sagu.edu
FIVECOAT, Frederick .... 610-892-1519.... 441 C
ffivecoat@pit.edu
FIX, John .... 256-824-6605........ 8 G
john.fix@uah.edu
FIXEN, Randall .... 701-662-1518.... 382 F
randy.fixen@lrsc.edu
FJELD, Laura, B .... 919-843-5844.... 377 C
lbfjeld@northcarolina.edu
FJORTOFT, Nancy, F .... 630-515-6072.... 158 F
nfjort@midwestern.edu
FLACHMANN, Michael ...... 661-654-2121...... 34 A
mflachmann@csub.edu
FLACK, Anna .... 631-451-4008.... 356 D
flacka@sunysuffolk.edu
FLACK, Bobby, L .... 301-447-5220.... 225 A
flack@msmary.edu
FLACK, Felecia, J .... 906-227-1272.... 256 C
fflack@nmu.edu
FLACK, Lisa .... 217-228-5432.... 161 F
flackli@quincy.edu
FLACK, Wayne, R .... 218-299-3362.... 262 I
flack@cord.edu
FLAD-JESION, Ann, M .... 920-565-1204.... 548 A
flad-jesionad@lakeland.edu
FLADELAND, Diane .... 701-355-8140.... 383 H
dflade@umary.edu
FLAGEL, Andrew .... 781-736-2005.... 232 F
aflagel@brandeis.edu
FLAGG, Aaron .... 860-768-5236...... 95 B
aflagg@hartford.edu
FLAGG, Mary .... 610-372-4721.... 445 C
mflagg@racc.edu
FLAGGERT, James .... 703-821-8570.... 524 J
jflaggert@stratford.edu
FLAGGS, Gladys .... 662-254-3603.... 276 B
gflaggs@mvsu.edu
FLAGLER, William .... 703-764-5043.... 527 F
wflagler@nvcc.edu
FLAGSTAD, Lois .... 605-642-6599.... 465 H
lois.flagstad@bhsu.edudu
FLAHARTY, Sue .... 910-938-6251.... 369 F
flahartys@coastalcarolina.edu
FLAHERTY, Eileen, P .... 716-851-1844.... 333 C
flaherty@ecc.edu
FLAHERTY, Jane .... 979-845-8588.... 497 E
jflaherty@tamu.edu
FLAHERTY, John .... 212-817-7769.... 327 B
jflaherty@gc.cuny.edu
FLAHERTY, Pamela .... 781-280-3631.... 240 B
flahertyp@middlesex.mass.edu
FLAHERTY, Richard, A .... 617-746-5412.... 244 B
FLAHERTY, Rob .... 785-594-8319.... 190 F
rob.flaherty@bakeru.edu
FLAHERTY-GOLDSMITH,
Linda .... 205-226-4923........ 2 B
lflahert@bsc.edu
FLAHIVE, Roger .... 973-328-5011.... 309 A
rflahive@ccm.edu
FLAIG, Sue .... 813-253-7132.... 110 M
sflaig@hccfl.edu
FLAIM, Lou .... 307-382-1616.... 557 A
lflaim@wwcc.wy.edu
FLAKE, Bryant .... 435-586-7725.... 511 D
flake@suu.edu
FLAKE, Forrest .... 801-422-3861.... 509 H
forrest_flake@byu.edu
FLAKE, Susan, R .... 704-272-5331.... 374 A
sflake@spcc.edu
FLAMER, LaTonya .... 336-517-2111.... 362 G
lflamer@bennett.edu
FLAMER, Thelma .... 202-231-2768.... 557 J
thelma.flamer@dodiis.mil
FLAMM, Mara .... 215-717-6621.... 448 I
mflamm@uarts.edu
FLAMMER, Rachel .... 716-888-2965.... 325 F
flammer@canisius.edu
FLANAGAN, Alyce .... 256-352-8295...... 10 A
alyce.malcolm@wallacestate.edu
FLANAGAN, Colleen .... 860-493-0261...... 90 F
flanaganc@ct.edu
FLANAGAN, Elizabeth, A ... 540-231-7676.... 529 G
betsyf@vt.edu
FLANAGAN, Hilary .... 216-397-4432.... 392 L
hflanagan@jcu.edu
FLANAGAN, J. Kelly .... 801-422-3142.... 509 H
kelly_flanagan@byu.edu
FLANAGAN, James .... 212-247-3434.... 339 G
jflanagan@mandl.edu
FLANAGAN, James, L .... 770-484-1204.... 133 G
lru@lru.edu
FLANAGAN, James, P .... 603-641-6025.... 305 G
jflanagan@anselm.edu
FLANAGAN, Jason .... 281-487-1170.... 499 B
jflanagan@txchiro.edu
FLANAGAN, Jeanne .... 518-485-3902.... 330 C
flanagaj@strose.edu
FLANAGAN, Jerry, E .... 802-654-3000.... 514 D
jflanagan@smcvt.edu
FLANAGAN, Joan .... 815-479-7884.... 157 H
jflanaga@mchenry.edu
FLANAGAN, John .... 973-642-8404.... 315 C
john.flanagan@shu.edu
FLANAGAN, Joseph, V .... 716-375-2302.... 348 C
jflan@sbu.edu
FLANAGAN, Justin .... 419-227-3141.... 404 D
jdglanag@unoh.edu
FLANAGAN, Kathleen .... 310-338-4482...... 56 E
flanagan@lmu.edu
FLANAGAN, Lawrence .... 203-932-7402...... 95 C
lflanagan@newhaven.edu
FLANAGAN, Lori .... 314-516-5661.... 291 D
flanagamlo@umsl.edu
FLANAGAN, Mary Jane ...... 989-774-3131.... 249 C
flana1mj@cmich.edu
FLANAGAN, Maureen, P .... 215-574-9600.... 431 B
mflanagan@hussianart.edu
FLANAGAN, Michael .... 610-399-2360.... 442 A
mflanagan@cheyney.edu
FLANAGAN, Scott .... 608-663-2294.... 547 F
sflanagan@edgewood.edu
FLANAGAN, Tim .... 707-476-4381...... 42 C
tim-flanagan@redwoods.edu
FLANAGAN, Timothy, J .... 508-626-4575.... 238 A
tflanagan@framingham.edu
FLANAGAN-HERSTEK,
Katherine, M .... 570-675-9225.... 440 F
kfh2@psu.edu
FLANARY, Barry .... 802-447-4312.... 514 F
bflanary@svc.edu
FLANDERS, Bruce .... 913-971-3568.... 195 D
blflanders@mnu.edu
FLANDERS, Lorene .... 678-839-6369.... 139 A
lflanders@westga.edu
FLANIGAN, Marjie .... 304-384-6035.... 543 G
mflanigan@concord.edu
FLANIGAN, Patricia .... 949-582-4365...... 70 F
pflanigan@saddleback.edu
FLANIGAN, Raaven .... 859-291-0800.... 200 A
rflanigan@daymarcollege.edu
FLANIGAN, JR.,
Robert, D .... 404-270-5072.... 138 B
rflaniga@spelman.edu
FLANIK, Greg, G .... 440-826-2700.... 384 K
gflanik@bw.edu
FLANNAGAN, Dorothy, A .. 210-458-6878.... 506 D
dorothy.flannagan@utsa.edu
FLANNELY, SC, Jean .... 718-405-3230.... 330 A
jean.flannely@mountsaintvincent.edu
FLANNERY, Brenda .... 507-389-9423.... 267 E
brenda.flannery@mnsu.edu
FLANNERY, Chad .... 618-252-5400.... 164 I
chad.flannery@sic.edu
FLANNERY, Katherine .... 215-951-2965.... 444 D
flanneryk@philau.edu
FLANNERY, Kathleen .... 620-231-7000.... 196 C
kflannery@pittstate.edu
FLANNERY, Maura, C .... 718-990-1860.... 348 G
flannerm@stjohns.edu
FLANNERY, Patrick .... 517-607-2239.... 252 C
patrick.flannery@hillsdale.edu
FLANNERY, Teresa (Terry) . 202-885-2163...... 97 D
flannery@american.edu
FLANZRAICH, Gerri .... 516-686-1158.... 343 D
gflanzra@nyit.edu
FLATEAU, John .... 718-270-5067.... 328 C
jflat@mec.cuny.edu
FLATHMAN, Christian .... 912-478-6397.... 131 E
cflathman@georgiasouthern.edu
FLATT, Bonnie .... 503-251-5712.... 421 A
bflatt@uws.edu
FLATTERY, Patrick .... 218-723-6042.... 262 G
pflatter@css.edu
FLAVIN, Stephen, P .... 508-831-5095.... 246 F
sflavin@wpi.edu
FLAX, Carol .... 419-772-2047.... 398 H
c-flax@onu.edu
FLAX, Christine .... 443-334-2639.... 226 E
cflax@stevenson.edu
FLAX-HYMAN, Cheryl, L ... 850-747-3215.... 110 H
cflax-hyman@gulfcoast.edu
FLEAGLE, Steven, R .... 319-384-0595.... 182 F
steve-fleagle@uiowa.edu
FLECHA, Gladys, E .... 787-852-1430.... 562 F
gflecha@hccpr.edu
FLECK, Lorraine .... 540-375-2299.... 523 G
fleck@roanoke.edu
FLECKENSTEIN,
Marilynn, P .... 716-286-8352.... 344 D
mpf@niagara.edu
FLECKENSTEIN, Susan, M . 810-762-9864.... 253 C
sflecken@kettering.edu
FLEENER, Harry .... 850-718-2310.... 103 D
fleenerh@chipola.edu
FLEENER, Jayne .... 919-515-5900.... 378 C
fleener@ncsu.edu
FLEENOR, Rick .... 606-539-4154.... 207 C
rick.fleenor@ucumberlands.edu
FLEET, Frances .... 419-448-3326.... 402 E
ffleet@tiffin.edu
FLEETWOOD, Janet .... 215-895-2141.... 427 H
janet.fleetwood@drexel.edu
FLEGE, Kelly, A .... 319-273-5885.... 182 G
kelly.flege@uni.edu
FLEISCHER, Stephen .... 323-343-4800...... 35 D
sfleischer@cslanet.calstatela.edu
FLEISCHER, Vicki .... 973-642-8512.... 315 C
vicki.fleischer@shu.edu
FLEISCHMAN, Jean .... 978-542-7765.... 238 E
jfleischman@salemstate.edu
FLEISCHMAN, Linda, M .... 315-279-5204.... 337 K
lfleisch@mail.keuka.edu
FLEISCHMANN, Kenneth ... 314-977-3948.... 289 C
fleiske@slu.edu
FLEIT, Jody .... 617-587-5511.... 242 H
fleitj@neco.edu
FLEITAS, Dionisio .... 214-333-5303.... 484 D
dion@dbu.edu
FLEMING, Allyson .... 615-327-6235.... 471 C
afleming@mmc.edu
FLEMING, Carol .... 828-398-7307.... 368 B
cfleming@abtech.edu
FLEMING, David .... 269-782-1201.... 258 C
dfleming@swmich.edu
FLEMING, Elizabeth .... 413-565-1000.... 230 G
lfleming@baypath.edu
FLEMING, Elizabeth, A .... 864-596-9050.... 457 E
betsy.fleming@converse.edu
FLEMING, Erika .... 305-428-5700.... 113 I
efleming@aii.edu
FLEMING, Graham, R .... 510-642-7540...... 73 H
vcrfleming@berkeley.edu
FLEMING, Honoree .... 802-468-1344.... 515 D
honoree.fleming@castleton.edu
FLEMING, J. Christopher ... 361-825-5934.... 498 C
christopher.fleming@tamucc.edu
FLEMING, James .... 605-642-6270.... 465 H
james.fleming@bhsu.edu
FLEMING, James .... 503-352-1510.... 419 E
jfleming@pacificu.edu
FLEMING, James, J .... 304-243-2224.... 546 A
jfleming@wju.edu
FLEMING, Jami .... 877-442-0505...... 89 C
jami.fleming@rockies.edu
FLEMING, Jennifer .... 479-498-6020...... 20 G
jfleming@atu.edu
FLEMING, Julie, C .... 770-720-5527.... 136 C
jcf@reinhardt.edu
FLEMING, Justin .... 507-786-3615.... 271 C
flemingj@stolaf.edu
FLEMING, Kay .... 618-985-3741.... 154 G
kayfleming@jalc.edu
FLEMING, Kevin .... 951-739-7880...... 63 K
kevin.fleming@norcocollege.edu
FLEMING, Kirsten .... 909-537-5300...... 36 B
FLEMING, Linda .... 814-871-7549.... 429 G
fleming006@gannon.edu
FLEMING, Maria .... 340-692-4183.... 568 E
mflemin@live.uvi.edu
FLEMING, Mark, J .... 610-861-1472.... 437 A
memjf01@moravian.edu
FLEMING, Michael .... 404-222-2588.... 134 D
mfleming@morehouse.edu
FLEMING, Mike, R .... 618-235-2700.... 165 D
mike.fleming@swic.edu
FLEMING, Nina .... 262-551-5800.... 546 I
nfleming@carthage.edu
FLEMING, Patricia, A .... 574-284-4575.... 179 F
pfleming@saintmarys.edu
FLEMING, Paul, C .... 504-864-7490.... 213 F
pcflemin@loyno.edu
FLEMING, Richard .... 443-550-6021.... 222 C
rfleming@csmd.edu
FLEMING, Rita .... 501-686-2920...... 24 B
rfleming@uasys.edu
FLEMING, Robert .... 617-824-8670.... 234 B
robert_fleming@emerson.edu
FLEMING, Saundra .... 773-878-4699.... 163 F
sfleming@staugustine.edu
FLEMING, Scott, S .... 202-687-3455...... 98 D
ssf2@georgetown.edu
FLEMING, Shannon .... 501-370-5378...... 23 B
sfleming@philander.edu
FLEMING, Sherie .... 256-378-2021........ 2 E
sfleming@cacc.edu
FLEMING, Siobhan .... 832-813-6764.... 490 E
siobhan.fleming@lonestar.edu
FLEMING, Stephen .... 404-894-5217.... 130 F
fleming@gatech.edu
FLEMING, Tom, O .... 310-338-2714...... 56 E
tfleming@lmu.edu
FLEMING, Trish .... 215-836-2222.... 422 B
tfleming@antonelli.edu
FLEMING, Vickie .... 919-497-3203.... 366 H
vfleming@louisburg.edu
FLEMING, William .... 919-962-4651.... 377 C
wafleming@northcarolina.edu
FLEMING, William .... 312-942-6832.... 163 D
bill_p_fleming@rush.edu
FLEMING, William, B .... 561-803-2001.... 114 C
william_fleming@pba.edu
FLEMION, Meg .... 419-434-4510.... 404 B
flemion@findlay.edu
FLEMMING, Joshua .... 518-736-3622.... 334 D
joshua.flemming@fmcc.suny.edu
FLEMMING, Sondra, G .... 214-860-2146.... 485 A
sflemming@dcccd.edu
FLENIKEN, Tracey .... 940-668-7731.... 491 E
tfleniken@nctc.edu
FLENNER, Ronald, W .... 757-446-5829.... 518 G
flennerw@evms.edu
FLENTJE, Mike .... 920-686-6137.... 550 H
mike.flentje@sl.edu
FLESHER, Van .... 615-383-4848.... 478 F
vflesher@watkins.edu
FLESHLER, David .... 216-368-2399.... 386 F
david.fleshler@case.edu
FLETCHER, Anthony, S .... 972-860-7645.... 484 I
anthonyfletcher@dcccd.edu
FLETCHER, Bill .... 615-898-2500.... 473 G
bill.fletcher@mtsu.edu
FLETCHER, Bridget .... 314-977-7778.... 289 C
fletchb@slu.edu
FLETCHER, Christopher ...... 305-809-3147.... 108 I
chrisopher.fletcher@fkcc.edu
FLETCHER, Cindy .... 832-556-4013.... 489 M
cpereza@lee.edu
FLETCHER, Courtney .... 402-559-4333.... 300 H
cfletcher@unmc.edu
FLETCHER, Heidi, L .... 410-532-5105.... 225 D
hfletcher@ndm.edu
FLETCHER, James, A .... 208-282-3540.... 143 H
fletjame@isu.edu
FLETCHER, Janice .... 617-243-2145.... 236 A
jfletcher@lasell.edu
FLETCHER, Jeff .... 573-897-5000.... 284 A
FLETCHER, John .... 252-328-5817.... 377 E
fletcherjo@ecu.edu
FLETCHER, Lance .... 617-262-5000.... 231 G
lance.fletcher@the-bac.edu
FLETCHER, Lynn .... 307-268-2211.... 556 A
lfletcher@caspercollege.edu
FLETCHER, Maria .... 208-282-5304.... 143 H
fletmari@isu.edu
FLETCHER, Randy .... 217-351-2236.... 161 C
rfletcher@parkland.edu
FLETCHER, Richard, L .... 440-826-2323.... 384 K
rfletche@bw.edu
FLETCHER, Scott .... 503-768-6001.... 416 G
graddean@lclark.edu
FLETCHER, Thomas .... 570-389-5161.... 441 F
tfletche@bloomu.edu
FLETCHER, Wesla .... 843-525-8293.... 461 E
wfletcher@tcl.edu
FLETCHER, William, A .... 352-846-3903.... 120 C
afletcher@ufl.edu
FLETCHER, William, A .... 843-953-5114.... 456 C
bill.fletcher@citadel.edu
FLEURIET, Cathy, A .... 512-245-8113.... 501 F
cf07@txstate.edu
FLEURY, Jane .... 518-631-9851.... 358 H
fleuryj@uniongraduatecollege.edu
FLEURY, Traci .... 704-971-8500.... 363 F
FLEWELLING, Colleen .... 570-372-4567.... 447 E
flewelling@susqu.edu
FLEWELLING, Colleen .... 570-372-4183.... 447 E
flewelling@susq.edu
FLICK, Kenneth .... 843-525-8238.... 461 E
kflick@tcl.edu
FLICK, Larry .... 541-737-0123.... 418 F
larry.flick@oregonstate.edu
FLICK, Matt .... 937-294-0592.... 401 H
flick@saa.edu

FLICKINGER, Catherine ..... 516-686-7792.... 343 D
cflickin@nyit.edu
FLICKINGER, Craig .... 734-432-5725.... 254 D
cflickinger@madonna.edu
FLIEGE, Cheryl .... 309-694-5599.... 152 C
cfliege@icc.edu
FLIER, Jeffrey, S .... 617-432-1501.... 235 D
jeffrey_flier@hms.harvard.edu
FLIKEID, Ben .... 651-730-5100.... 263 G
bflikeid@globeuniversity.edu
FLIKKEMA, Melvin, J .... 616-222-3000.... 253 F
mflikkema@kuyper.edu
FLINN, Amy .... 254-298-8364.... 496 D
alflinn@templejc.edu
FLINN, Darwin .... 413-528-7204.... 230 F
dflinn@simons-rock.edu
FLINN, Deborah .... 860-515-3873...... 90 E
FLINN, Gordon, B .... 530-226-4735...... 69 H
gflinn@simpsonu.edu
FLINN, Nancy .... 510-436-1054...... 50 H
flinn@hnu.edu
FLINN, Randal .... 219-866-6165.... 179 D
rflinn@saintjoe.edu
FLINN, Ronald, T .... 517-355-3366.... 255 A
flinn@msu.edu
FLINT, Aaron .... 603-645-9678.... 305 I
a.flint@snhu.edu
FLINT, Joe .... 773-380-6786.... 164 D
joe.flint@seabury.edu
FLINT, Juanita .... 972-860-4694.... 484 G
juanitazf@dcccd.edu
FLINTOFT, Rebecca .... 303-273-3050...... 83 B
rebecca.flintoft@is.mines.edu
FLINTON, JoElla .... 405-945-9106.... 410 F
FLIPPO, Angela, D .... 870-759-4117...... 26 B
aflippo@wbcoll.edu
FLIS, Denise .... 405-208-5848.... 410 A
dflis@okcu.edu
FLOCCHINI, Randy .... 775-674-7688.... 302 H
rflocchini@tmcc.edu
FLOCKEN, Lise .... 760-757-2121...... 57 E
lflocken@miracosta.edu
FLOHR, Robin .... 740-264-5591.... 390 F
rflohr@egcc.edu
FLOM, Sheldon .... 307-754-6284.... 556 G
sheldon.flom@northwestcollege.edu
FLOMENHAFT, Marion .... 516-678-5000.... 341 F
mflomenhaft@molloy.edu
FLOOD, Carolyn .... 731-352-4020.... 467 E
floodc@bethelu.edu
FLOOD, Cathy, T .... 920-923-8082.... 548 E
cflood@marianuniversity.edu
FLOOD, David .... 215-762-3699.... 427 H
david.flood@drexel.edu
FLOOD, Flora .... 256-726-7287...... 6 C
fflood@oakwood.edu
FLOOD, Pierre .... 323-563-4824...... 39 G
pierreflood@cdrewu.edu
FLOOD, Thomas .... 718-489-5443.... 348 E
thomasflood@sfc.edu
FLOOD, Tim .... 619-644-7653...... 49 C
tim.flood@gcccd.edu
FLOOD, Tim .... 619-644-7141...... 49 C
tim.flood@gcccd.edu
FLOOD, Timothy, J .... 920-929-2136.... 554 G
tflood@morainepark.edu
FLOOR, Gregory .... 617-850-1285.... 235 F
gfloor@hchc.edu
FLOR, Doug .... 706-880-8923.... 133 B
dflor@lagrange.edu
FLORA, Allen .... 301-696-3811.... 223 C
flora@hood.edu
FLORCZAK, Gregory, P ...... 716-880-2200.... 340 D
gregory.p.florczak@medaille.edu
FLORCZAK, Joan, E .... 203-576-4665...... 94 F
joan@bridgeport.edu
FLORENCE, Bob, K .... 816-604-6546.... 285 A
bob.florence@mcckc.edu
FLORENCE, Christopher ..... 314-434-4044.... 280 F
chris.florence@covenantseminary.edu
FLORENDO, Chava .... 541-552-6128.... 419 A
florendch@sou.edu
FLORENTINE, Dennis .... 908-835-2326.... 317 C
dflorentine@warren.edu
FLORER, Timothy, M .... 847-649-3980.... 149 H
tflorer@keller.edu
FLORES, Anthony .... 510-464-3592...... 62 D
aflores@peralta.edu
FLORES, Barbara .... 787-746-1400.... 562 E
bflores@huertas.edu
FLORES, Ben .... 915-747-5491.... 506 B
bflores@utep.edu
FLORES, Caren .... 510-783-2100...... 49 J
caren_flores@heald.edu
FLORES, Chio .... 509-335-9711.... 539 D
cflores@wsu.edu
FLORES, Cindy .... 318-676-7811.... 211 D
cflores@nwltc.edu
FLORES, Deanna, L .... 407-303-1851.... 100 G
deanna.flores@adu.edu
FLORES, Efrain .... 787-758-2525.... 567 G
efrain.flores@upr.edu
FLORES, Elizabeth .... 915-747-7872.... 506 B
lizaf@utep.edu
FLORES, Fatima .... 561-912-2166.... 107 B
fflores@evergladesuniversity.edu
FLORES, Fernando .... 915-831-6391.... 486 G
fernief@epcc.edu
FLORES, Greg .... 503-725-4971.... 418 G
gregory.flores@pdx.edu
FLORES, Gustavo .... 707-664-4388...... 37 D
gustavo.flores@sonoma.edu
FLORES, Hector .... 585-475-4476.... 347 G
hefgrad@rit.edu
FLORES, Henry .... 210-436-3214.... 493 F
hflores@stmarytx.edu
FLORES, Jacob, C .... 956-721-5148.... 489 J
jacob.flores@laredo.edu
FLORES, Javier .... 325-942-2047.... 480 E
javier.flores@angelo.edu
FLORES, Javier .... 307-382-1642.... 557 A
jflores@wwcc.wy.edu
FLORES, Jayne, T .... 671-735-5638.... 559 E
pio@guamcc.edu
FLORES, Kat .... 541-888-7293.... 420 C
kflores@socc.edu
FLORES, Kathy .... 253-680-7178.... 531 F
kflores@bates.ctc.edu
FLORES, Matt .... 512-245-2922.... 501 F
mgf20@txstate.edu
FLORES, Michael .... 210-486-3960.... 479 C
rflores@alamo.edu
FLORES, Mildred .... 787-780-0070.... 560 H
mflores@caribbean.edu
FLORES, Robert .... 909-599-5433...... 54 A
rflores@lifepacific.edu
FLORES, Roberto .... 863-453-6661.... 117 J
robert.flores@southflorida.edu
FLORES, Ruben .... 787-279-1912.... 563 D
rflores@bayamon.inter.edu
FLORES, Rudy .... 530-895-2429...... 31 H
floresru@butte.edu
FLORES, Sirio, J .... 718-982-3210.... 327 A
sirio.flores@csi.cuny.edu
FLORES, Susan .... 956-364-4443.... 500 D
susan.flores@tstc.edu
FLORES, William, V .... 713-221-8001.... 503 F
president@uhd.edu
FLORES-CHURCH, Adriana 562-860-2451...... 39 A
achurch@cerritos.edu
FLORES-MEDINA, Donna .. 505-454-5328.... 318 F
dflores@luna.edu
FLOREY, Nancy, E .... 717-361-1406.... 428 F
floreyne@etown.edu
FLORIAN, Greg, E .... 217-875-7200.... 162 F
gflorian@richland.edu
FLORIAN, James, S .... 520-621-1634...... 18 L
florianj@email.arizona.edu
FLORIAN, Robyn, L .... 517-750-1200.... 258 D
rflorian@arbor.edu
FLORIO, Charles, B .... 903-510-2261.... 503 A
cflo2@tjc.edu
FLORIO, SJ, Philip, J .... 718-817-4503.... 334 C
pflorio2@fordham.edu
FLOROS, John .... 785-532-6147.... 194 D
floros@ksu.edu
FLORY, Lowell .... 800-287-8822.... 169 H
florylo@bethanyseminary.edu
FLOT, Rob .... 847-735-5200.... 155 G
flot@lakeforest.edu
FLOTTE, Terence, R .... 508-856-8000.... 237 C
terry.flotte@umassmed.edu
FLOUHOUSE, Steve .... 606-326-2055.... 201 F
steve.flouhouse@kctcs.edu
FLOURNOY, Bonita .... 404-756-4025.... 125 D
bflournoy@atlm.edu
FLOURNOY, Jacob, W .... 501-686-2901...... 24 B
jwflournoy@uasys.edu
FLOWERS, Damon .... 734-677-5322.... 259 F
dflowers@wccnet.edu
FLOWERS, George .... 334-844-4700...... 1 F
flowegt@auburn.edu
FLOWERS, Joanne .... 615-256-1463.... 466 H
joanne.flowers@gmail.com
FLOWERS, Marshall .... 828-669-8012.... 367 E
mflowers@montreat.edu
FLOWERS, Paury .... 610-957-6149.... 447 F
pflower1@swarthmore.edu
FLOWERS, Robert .... 315-781-3827.... 335 F
flowers@hws.edu
FLOWERS, Robert .... 817-531-4461.... 502 C
rflowers@txwes.edu
FLOYD, Andrew .... 229-430-3983.... 124 A
andrew.floyd@asurams.edu
FLOYD, Arlene .... 330-941-2333.... 406 F
afloyd@ysu.edu
FLOYD, Brenda, L .... 940-898-3505.... 502 D
bfloyd@twu.edu
FLOYD, Carey .... 580-371-2371.... 408 I
cfloyd@mscok.edu
FLOYD, Charlsie .... 636-949-4909.... 283 J
cfloyd@lindenwood.edu
FLOYD, Cindy .... 619-574-6909...... 60 D
cmfloyd@pacificcollege.edu
FLOYD, Cynthia .... 334-291-4905...... 2 F
cynthia.floyd@cv.edu
FLOYD, David J, W .... 225-765-2437.... 212 H
rulife1@lsu.edu
FLOYD, Donna .... 510-235-7800...... 43 E
dfloyd@contracosta.edu
FLOYD, Elizabeth .... 864-225-7653.... 458 C
lizfloyd@forrestcollege.edu
FLOYD, Elson, S .... 509-335-4200.... 539 D
presidentsoffice@wsu.edu
FLOYD, Gregg, S .... 330-672-2422.... 393 D
gfloyd@kent.edu
FLOYD, James, J .... 909-621-8351...... 40 G
james.floyd@cmc.edu
FLOYD, Jennifer .... 606-539-4479.... 207 C
jennifer.floyd@ucumberlands.edu
FLOYD, Linda .... 706-295-6511.... 131 B
lfloyd@gntc.edu
FLOYD, Lydia .... 404-880-8454.... 127 C
lfloyd@cau.edu
FLOYD, Mark .... 541-737-4611.... 418 F
mark.floyd@oregonstate.edu
FLOYD, Polly, K .... 850-263-3261.... 101 L
pkfloyd@baptistcollege.edu
FLOYD, Richard .... 610-409-3200.... 450 D
rfloyd@ursinus.edu
FLOYD, Shirley .... 910-642-7141.... 374 B
sfloyd@sccnc.edu
FLOYD, Virgina .... 404-752-1953.... 134 E
vfloyd@msm.edu
FLUEGEMAN, Tere .... 949-582-4920...... 70 D
tfluegeman@socccd.edu
FLUELLEN, William .... 561-912-2166.... 107 B
wfluellen@evergladesuniversity.edu
FLUET, Gregoire, J .... 860-632-3010...... 93 B
rector@holyapostles.edu
FLUGUM, Deborah .... 818-677-2301...... 35 F
deborah.flugum@csun.edu
FLUHARTY, Steven, J .... 215-898-7236.... 448 J
vpr@pobox.upenn.edu
FLUKE, Donald, W .... 574-372-5100.... 171 H
dwfluke@grace.edu
FLUKE, Lauri, A .... 405-878-2020.... 409 D
lauri.fluke@okbu.edu
FLUKER, Zillah .... 334-229-5679...... 1 C
zfluker@alasu.edu
FLUNKER, Thomas, G .... 507-344-7577.... 261 C
tom.flunker@blc.edu
FLY, Jim .... 316-677-9400.... 197 G
jfly@watc.edu
FLYER, Robert .... 440-365-5222.... 395 D
FLYNN, Charles, L .... 718-405-3232.... 330 A
charles.flynn@mountsaintvincent.edu
FLYNN, Chris .... 540-231-6557.... 529 G
flynnc@vt.edu
FLYNN, Christie .... 253-964-6553.... 536 H
cflynn@pierce.ctc.edu
FLYNN, Jackie .... 412-391-7021.... 450 G
admissions@vettechinstitute.edu
FLYNN, Joan .... 410-617-5161.... 223 I
jflynn@loyola.edu
FLYNN, John, J .... 212-769-5055.... 347 E
FLYNN, Karen .... 203-932-7317...... 95 C
kflynn@newhaven.edu
FLYNN, Kathy, A .... 319-296-4218.... 185 F
kathleen.flynn@hawkeyecollege.edu
FLYNN, Kevin .... 781-239-2549.... 239 G
kflynn@massbay.edu
FLYNN, Linda .... 979-830-4251.... 482 C
lflynn@blinn.edu
FLYNN, Mari .... 570-945-8335.... 432 E
mari.flynn@keystone.edu
FLYNN, Maria .... 270-534-3140.... 203 E
maria.flynn@kctcs.edu
FLYNN, Marilyn, L .... 213-740-8311...... 76 F
mflynn@usc.edu
FLYNN, Mark .... 706-568-2080.... 127 G
flynn_mark@columbusstate.edu
FLYNN, Maura .... 716-926-8822.... 335 E
mflynn@hilbert.edu
FLYNN, Michael .... 716-685-9631.... 342 H
mflynn@nycc.edu
FLYNN, Monty .... 315-498-2538.... 345 D
flynnm@sunyocc.edu
FLYNN, Richard, B .... 413-748-3241.... 244 H
rflynn@springfieldcollege.edu
FLYNN, Stuart, D .... 602-827-2066...... 18 L
flynns@email.arizona.edu
FLYNN, Thomas, F .... 610-796-8203.... 421 G
tom.flynn@alvernia.edu
FLYNN, Thomas, V .... 505-565-1413.... 245 A
tflynn@stonehill.edu
FLYNN SAULNIER,
Christine .... 718-982-2315.... 327 A
christine.saulnier@csi.cuny.edu
FLYNT, Samuel .... 334-244-3270...... 1 G
sflynt@aum.edu
FLYTHE, Claud .... 434-848-6401.... 524 B
cflythe@saintpauls.edu
FOCARETO, Nicole .... 440-526-1660.... 405 D
nicole.focareto@vatterott-college.edu
FOCHT, Jeffrey, W .... 610-861-5434.... 437 H
jfocht@northampton.edu
FOCKLER, Debra .... 509-359-6348.... 533 H
dfockler@ewu.edu
FOECKLER, Michael, S ...... 540-636-2900.... 517 K
foeckler@christendom.edu
FOEHL, Brooks, L .... 413-597-4408.... 246 D
brooks.l.foehl@williams.edu
FOERST, Cara Herrick .... 973-642-8726.... 315 C
cara.foerst@shu.edu
FOERTSCH, James .... 701-774-4243.... 383 A
james.foertsch@willistonstate.edu
FOGARINO, Shirley .... 510-981-2852...... 62 B
sfogarino@peralta.edu
FOGARTY, John .... 850-644-1346.... 119 D
jfogarty@fsu.edu
FOGARTY, Raymond .... 401-232-6407.... 453 C
rfogarty@bryant.edu
FOGARTY, Thomas, J .... 717-221-1300.... 430 E
tjfogart@hacc.edu
FOGARTY, Timothy, P .... 814-393-2235.... 442 B
tfogarty@clarion.edu
FOGARTY, William .... 413-552-2221.... 239 F
bfogarty@hcc.edu
FOGEL, Henry .... 312-341-3782.... 163 B
hfogel@roosevelt.edu
FOGELGREN, John, A .... 302-454-3922...... 96 F
fogelgre@dtcc.edu
FOGERSON, Linda .... 760-757-2121...... 57 E
lfogerson@miracosta.edu
FOGERTY, Karen .... 617-912-9108.... 232 C
kfogerty@bostonconservatory.edu
FOGERTY, Rebecca, R .... 302-831-8065...... 96 I
bfogerty@udel.edu
FOGG, Christine .... 231-777-5239.... 248 E
christine.fogg@baker.edu
FOGG, Davina, K .... 509-527-4201.... 539 B
davina.fogg@wwcc.edu
FOGG, Neal .... 978-542-2495.... 238 E
neal.fogg@salemstate.edu
FOGG, Richard .... 785-587-2800.... 195 A
richardfogg@matc.net
FOGGS, Ranodore, M .... 618-537-6911.... 158 A
rmfoggs@mckendree.edu
FOGLE, Rick, A .... 724-836-9916.... 449 C
fogle@pitt.edu
FOGLEMAN, David .... 318-670-9590.... 215 A
dfogleman@susla.edu
FOHRMAN, Jonathan .... 619-388-2873...... 65 G
jfohrma@sdccd.edu
FOISY, Brian .... 701-858-3331.... 382 A
brian.foisy@minotstateu.edu
FOLBERG, Robert .... 248-370-3634.... 256 G
rfolberg@oakland.edu
FOLDA, Joe .... 719-549-2730...... 83 H
joe.folda@colostate-pueblo.edu
FOLDA, John, T .... 402-643-4052.... 300 A
sggs@stgregoryseminary.edu
FOLEY, Anne .... 312-369-7477.... 148 D
afoley@colum.edu
FOLEY, Beth .... 435-797-1437.... 511 E
beth.foley@usu.edu
FOLEY, Brian, P .... 703-822-6697.... 527 F
bfoley@nvcc.edu
FOLEY, C. Brad .... 541-346-5661.... 419 B
bfoley@uoregon.edu
FOLEY, Chris, J .... 317-274-0402.... 174 D
cfoley@iupui.edu
FOLEY, Cindy .... 310-544-6405...... 64 H
cindy.foley@usw.salvationarmy.org
FOLEY, Constance, L .... 724-738-2003.... 443 F
constance.foley@sru.edu
FOLEY, Don .... 907-474-7317...... 10 I
djfoley@alaska.edu
FOLEY, Erin .... 410-532-3586.... 225 D
efoley@ndm.edu
FOLEY, Erin .... 541-885-1013.... 418 E
erin.foley@oit.edu
FOLEY, Fred, J .... 215-951-1543.... 432 I
foley@lasalle.edu
FOLEY, Gary, A .... 803-535-1264.... 460 C
foleyg@octech.edu
FOLEY, Henry .... 814-865-6332.... 438 G
hcf2@psu.edu
FOLEY, Jeffrey, W .... 706-737-1445.... 125 G
jwfoley@aug.edu
FOLEY, Jeremy, N .... 352-375-4683.... 120 C
jeremy@gators.uaa.ufl.edu
FOLEY, John .... 508-793-7444.... 233 B
jfoley@clarku.edu
FOLEY, John .... 716-851-1114.... 333 A
foleyj@ecc.edu
FOLEY, Linda .... 402-354-7050.... 299 C
linda.foley@methodistcollege.edu
FOLEY, Lisa .... 530-541-4660...... 53 G
foley@ltcc.edu
FOLEY, Mark, R .... 251-442-2201...... 9 A
markfoley@umobile.edu
FOLEY, Michael .... 570-348-6233.... 435 F
foley@marywood.edu
FOLEY, Neil .... 845-341-4180.... 345 E
neil.foley@sunyorange.edu
FOLEY, Phyllis .... 615-230-4828.... 476 C
phyllis.foley@volstate.edu
FOLEY, Robert, A .... 978-665-3195.... 237 E
rfoley@fitchburgstate.edu
FOLEY, Ryan .... 912-688-6061.... 135 D
rfoley@ogeecheetech.edu
FOLEY, Thomas, P .... 814-886-6411.... 437 B
tfoley@mtaloy.edu

FOLEY, Tim .... 310-544-6461 .... 64 H
tim.foley@usw.salvationarmy.org
FOLEY, Timothy .... 251-626-3303 .... 8 C
tfoley@ussa.edu
FOLGER, Pamela, M .... 217-424-6294 .... 158 G
pmfolger@millikin.edu
FOLK, Joseph .... 330-499-9600 .... 393 I
jfolk@kent.edu
FOLKENDT, Kurt .... 858-513-9240 .... 182 C
research@ashford.edu
FOLKERT, Eva Dean .... 616-395-7956 .... 252 D
folkert@hope.edu
FOLKS, Kay .... 260-481-6103 .... 174 C
folksp@ipfw.edu
FOLKS, Lonnie .... 609-652-4877 .... 313 E
lonnie.folks@stockton.edu
FOLLICK, David .... 516-299-3389 .... 339 A
david.follick@liu.edu
FOLLICK, Edwin .... 714-533-1495 .... 70 B
edfollick@southbaylo.edu
FOLLICK, Edwin .... 714-533-3946 .... 37 E
efollick@calums.edu
FOLLINS, Craig .... 773-291-6313 .... 147 G
cfollins@ccc.edu
FOLLOSCO, David .... 818-710-2944 .... 55 B
follosd@piercecollege.edu
FOLSE, Victoria .... 309-556-3051 .... 153 F
vfolse@iwu.edu
FOLSOM, B. Kevin .... 214-874-3441 .... 485 F
kfolsom@dts.edu
FOLSOM, Scott, D .... 801-585-1158 .... 511 C
scott.folsom@dps.utah.edu
FOLT, Carol, L .... 603-646-2223 .... 304 J
carol.l.folt@dartmouth.edu
FOLTIN, Craig .... 216-987-4705 .... 389 B
craig.foltin@tri-c.edu
FOLZ, James .... 518-828-4181 .... 330 E
folz@sunycgcc.edu
FOMBELLE, Douglas, W .... 215-641-4801 .... 261 D
d-fombelle@bethel.edu
FONDETTO, Gina .... 973-642-8377 .... 315 C
gina.fondetto@shu.edu
FONDILLER, Jennifer .... 212-854-2817 .... 323 E
jfondill@barnard.edu
FONG, Bobby .... 610-409-3587 .... 450 D
bfong@ursinus.edu
FONG, Bruce, W .... 713-789-7771 .... 485 F
bfong@dts.edu
FONG, Donald .... 540-338-2700 .... 517 G
dfong@cdu.edu
FONG, Harry, M .... 408-554-4398 .... 68 C
hfong@scu.edu
FONG, Jennifer, C .... 818-947-2433 .... 55 E
fongjc@lavc.edu
FONG, Lindy .... 323-780-6738 .... 54 G
fonglw@elac.edu
FONG, Norman .... 916-631-8108 .... 33 F
FONG, Wyman .... 925-485-5261 .... 39 C
wfong@clpccd.org
FONG, Yaa-Yin .... 808-956-8259 .... 141 E
yaayin@hawaii.edu
FONGER, Ron .... 503-493-6510 .... 415 E
rfonger@cu-portland.edu
FONKEN, David .... 512-223-4606 .... 481 B
fonken@austincc.edu
FONS, August .... 575-492-2721 .... 319 B
afons@nmjc.edu
FONSECA, James, W .... 740-453-0762 .... 399 G
fonseca@ohio.edu
FONSECA, James, W .... 740-533-4600 .... 399 G
fonseca@ohio.edu
FONSECA, Mimi .... 503-517-1100 .... 421 B
mfonseca@warnerpacific.edu
FONT, Iris, J .... 787-740-4282 .... 566 C
iris.font@uccaribe.edu
FONTAINE, Christopher, W .... 903-233-4071 .... 490 A
chrisfontaine@letu.edu
FONTAINE, David .... 315-792-3050 .... 359 E
dsfontaine@utica.edu
FONTAINE, Deborah, C .... 757-823-8670 .... 522 E
dcfontaine@nsu.edu
FONTAINE, Dorrie, K .... 434-924-0141 .... 525 F
dkf2u@virginia.edu
FONTAINE, Mike .... 502-968-7191 .... 199 D
mfontaine@brownmackie.edu
FONTAINE, Yvette, M .... 619-260-7691 .... 76 D
yvettef@sandiego.edu
FONTANEZ, Eduardo .... 787-857-3600 .... 563 C
efontanez@br.inter.edu
FONTANILLA, Linda .... 805-546-3116 .... 43 I
linda_fontanilla@cuesta.edu
FONTANILLA, Linda .... 949-451-5214 .... 70 E
lfontanilla@ivc.edu
FONTANO, Dominick .... 718-390-3164 .... 360 A
dfontano@wagner.edu
FONTENETTE, Edward, J .... 870-575-8410 .... 25 B
fontenettee@uapb.edu
FONTENOT, Helen .... 504-398-2100 .... 214 B
hfontenot@olhcc.edu
FONTENOT, Janet, S .... 618-235-2700 .... 165 D
janet.fontenot@swic.edu
FONTENOT, Karen .... 985-549-2101 .... 216 C
kfontenot@selu.edu

FONTENOT, Patrick .... 210-486-4431 .... 479 B
pfontenot@alamo.edu
FONTES, Mary .... 218-793-2460 .... 268 C
mary.fontes@northlandcollege.edu
FONTEYN, Paul, J .... 802-287-8201 .... 513 F
fonteynp@greenmtn.edu
FONTHAM, Elizabeth .... 504-559-1388 .... 213 A
efonth@lsuhsc.edu
FONTOURA, Ana .... 914-654-5456 .... 330 B
afontoura@cnr.edu
FONTS, Raul, A .... 401-865-2754 .... 453 H
rfonts@providence.edu
FONVILLE, John, A .... 252-638-7220 .... 370 A
fonvillj@cravencc.edu
FONZO, Crescenzo .... 201-761-6402 .... 314 F
cfonzo@spc.edu
FOO, Lori .... 808-454-4742 .... 141 H
lori@uhwo.hawaii.edu
FOOSE, David .... 913-234-0650 .... 191 J
david.foose@cleveland.edu
FOOTE, Clarinda, L .... 870-307-7327 .... 22 D
clarinda.foote@lyon.edu
FOOTE, Jeffrey, C .... 518-255-5300 .... 354 E
footjc@cobleskill.edu
FOOTE, Joe, S .... 405-325-2721 .... 413 C
jfoote@ou.edu
FOOTE, Monica, W .... 718-939-5100 .... 338 D
mfoote@libi.edu
FOOTE, Rebecca, L .... 315-443-3765 .... 357 C
rlfoote@syr.edu
FOOTE, Tom, J .... 708-209-3142 .... 148 E
tom.foote@cuchicago.edu
FOOTER, Nancy .... 940-565-2717 .... 504 D
nfooter@unt.edu
FOPMA, Wes .... 712-722-6020 .... 184 C
wfopma@dordt.edu
FORAKER, Wayne .... 480-557-3285 .... 19 A
wayne.foraker@phoenix.edu
FORBES, Carol, M .... 612-330-1184 .... 261 B
forbes@augsburg.edu
FORBES, Cassie .... 828-765-7351 .... 372 A
cforbes@mayland.edu
FORBES, David .... 406-243-6670 .... 294 I
david.forbes@umontana.edu
FORBES, Don, L .... 320-363-2490 .... 262 F
dforbes@csbsju.edu
FORBES, Donald .... 320-363-2490 .... 271 A
dforbes@csbsju.edu
FORBES, Gerald .... 580-559-5208 .... 407 J
gforbes@ecok.edu
FORBES, J. Thomas .... 812-855-5394 .... 173 D
jtforbes@indiana.edu
FORBES, J.T .... 812-855-5700 .... 173 E
forbesjt@indiana.edu
FORBES, Karen, J .... 610-330-5005 .... 433 B
forbesk@lafayette.edu
FORBES, Kathryn, P .... 603-862-1505 .... 306 C
kathie.forbes@unh.edu
FORBES, Lindi, D .... 620-421-6700 .... 194 G
lindif@labette.edu
FORBES, Marcia, E .... 608-246-6607 .... 554 D
mforbes@madisoncollege.org
FORBES, Maribeth .... 781-595-6768 .... 236 C
mforbes@mariancourt.edu
FORBES, Robert, P .... 678-915-3291 .... 137 G
rforbes@spsu.edu
FORBES, Sharon .... 708-237-5050 .... 160 D
sforbes@nc.edu
FORBES, Shawna .... 313-496-2587 .... 259 G
sforbes1@wcccd.edu
FORBES, Suzetta, R .... 906-932-4231 .... 251 C
suef@gogebic.edu
FORBES, Tonya .... 919-866-5955 .... 374 H
tpforbes@waketech.edu
FORBES-BOYTE, Kari, L .... 605-256-5270 .... 465 I
kari.forbes-boyte@dsu.edu
FORBES ISAIS, Geraldine .... 505-277-2879 .... 321 C
gforbes@unm.edu
FORBES-VIERLING, Suzanne .... 909-915-3771 .... 29 G
sforbes-vierling@argosy.edu
FORBESS, Timothy .... 937-529-2201 .... 403 A
tforbess@united.edu
FORBIS, Brenda .... 912-344-2904 .... 124 G
brenda.forbis@armstrong.edu
FORBUSH, Dan .... 518-580-5746 .... 351 B
dforbush@skidmore.edu
FORCE, Bruce .... 918-293-5456 .... 410 E
bruce.force@okstate.edu
FORCE, Darcy .... 817-202-6629 .... 495 E
dforce@swau.edu
FORCH, Paul, J .... 434-924-3586 .... 525 F
pjf8t@virginia.edu
FORCINITO, Lorraine .... 262-524-7124 .... 546 H
lforcini@carrollu.edu
FORD, Amy .... 580-559-5725 .... 407 J
aford@ecok.edu
FORD, Beth .... 216-373-5351 .... 397 F
bford@ndc.edu
FORD, Brian .... 703-821-8570 .... 524 J
bford@stratford.edu
FORD, Bryant .... 410-225-4208 .... 224 B
bford@mica.edu
FORD, Carol .... 601-643-8626 .... 273 G
carol.ford@colin.edu

FORD, Charles, W .... 270-247-8521 .... 204 G
cford@midcontinent.edu
FORD, Charlotte .... 205-226-4740 .... 2 B
cford@bsc.edu
FORD, Daryl .... 617-349-8541 .... 236 B
dford@lesley.edu
FORD, Deborah, L .... 262-595-2211 .... 552 A
deborah.ford@uwp.edu
FORD, Dow .... 601-403-1214 .... 276 E
dford@prcc.edu
FORD, Duane, M .... 608-822-2300 .... 555 D
dford@swtc.edu
FORD, Gillian, F .... 814-332-2155 .... 421 F
gford@allegheny.edu
FORD, Glenn .... 870-633-4480 .... 21 F
gford@eacc.edu
FORD, III, Harrison .... 843-661-8231 .... 458 B
harrison.ford@fdtc.edu
FORD, James .... 503-682-3903 .... 419 F
jford@pioneerpacific.edu
FORD, Jean .... 734-384-4274 .... 255 D
jford@monroeccc.edu
FORD, Jeff .... 417-447-6930 .... 287 D
fordj@otc.edu
FORD, Jimmy .... 502-852-7155 .... 207 E
jimmy.ford@louisville.edu
FORD, John .... 985-448-4040 .... 216 A
john.ford@nicholls.edu
FORD, John .... 716-270-5735 .... 333 C
fordj@ecc.edu
FORD, Josanne .... 215-569-9215 .... 436 E
jford@phmc.org
FORD, Kari .... 940-668-7731 .... 491 E
kford@nctc.edu
FORD, Kathy .... 909-469-5542 .... 78 I
kford@westernu.edu
FORD, Kevan .... 216-325-6919 .... 387 B
kford@chancelloru.edu
FORD, Kim, R .... 202-274-7181 .... 100 A
kford@udc.edu
FORD, Kimberly .... 330-337-6403 .... 383 J
college@awc.edu
FORD, Lacy, K .... 803-777-2808 .... 462 A
ford@mailbox.sc.edu
FORD, Laura, C .... 309-794-7452 .... 145 E
lauraford@augustana.edu
FORD, Linda .... 918-610-8303 .... 411 D
linda.ford@ptstulsa.edu
FORD, Madeline .... 718-518-4211 .... 327 D
mford@hostos.cuny.edu
FORD, Mark, C .... 913-971-3614 .... 195 D
mford@mnu.edu
FORD, Mary .... 603-822-5432 .... 306 F
mary.ford@granite.edu
FORD, Mary, E .... 573-629-3046 .... 282 E
mford@hlg.edu
FORD, Michael .... 312-341-2098 .... 163 B
mford@roosevelt.edu
FORD, Michael, B .... 503-768-7000 .... 416 G
mford@lclark.edu
FORD, Michelle .... 802-764-2139 .... 514 B
michelle.ford@neci.edu
FORD, Nadine, Y .... 919-516-4128 .... 376 D
nford@st-aug.edu
FORD, Nancy .... 620-365-5116 .... 190 D
ford@allencc.edu
FORD, Pamela, R .... 318-257-3031 .... 215 F
prford@latech.edu
FORD, Ralph .... 908-709-7142 .... 316 B
ford@ucc.edu
FORD, Raquel .... 901-752-2625 .... 19 A
raquel.ford@phoenix.edu
FORD, Regina .... 714-484-7344 .... 59 D
rford@cypresscollege.edu
FORD, Ricky .... 662-720-7302 .... 276 C
rgford@nemcc.edu
FORD, Shelly .... 601-928-6222 .... 275 E
shelly.ford@mgccc.edu
FORD, Sylverna, V .... 901-678-2201 .... 474 C
sford@memphis.edu
FORD, Timothy .... 207-602-2334 .... 221 A
tford@une.edu
FORD, Tom, B .... 330-569-5954 .... 391 G
fordtb@hiram.edu
FORD, Victoria, A .... 740-376-4725 .... 395 G
vicki.ford@marietta.edu
FORD, W. Glenn .... 503-883-2458 .... 416 H
gford@linfield.edu
FORD, Wendy .... 330-494-6170 .... 402 B
wford@starkstate.edu
FORD, William .... 215-968-8285 .... 423 F
fordw@bucks.edu
FORD, William .... 407-628-5870 .... 106 H
wford@cci.edu
FORD FISHER, Margaret .... 713-718-8010 .... 487 I
margaret.fordfisher@hccs.edu
FORD-KEE, Dianthia .... 484-365-7391 .... 434 H
dfkee@lincoln.edu
FORDE, Althea .... 718-960-8066 .... 327 C
althea.forde@lehman.cuny.edu
FORDE, Dermot, M .... 419-372-9475 .... 385 E
dforde@bgsu.edu
FORDIS, JR., C. Michael .... 713-798-3395 .... 481 H
fordis@bcm.edu

FORDOSKI, Dori .... 814-371-2090 .... 448 D
dfordoski@triangle-tech.edu
FORDYCE, Richard, A .... 660-263-3900 .... 279 F
rfordyce@cccb.edu
FORE, Janet, S .... 574-284-5281 .... 179 F
jfore@saintmarys.edu
FORE, Marilyn .... 843-349-5208 .... 458 H
marilyn.fore@hgtc.edu
FOREMAN, Artie .... 601-635-2111 .... 274 A
aforeman@eccc.edu
FOREMAN, David, M .... 570-577-3200 .... 423 E
david.foreman@bucknell.edu
FOREMAN, Dorine, M .... 845-368-7202 .... 350 A
FOREMAN, Hank, T .... 828-262-7525 .... 377 D
foremanht@appstate.edu
FOREMAN, Karen, N .... 540-868-7109 .... 527 C
kforeman@lfcc.edu
FOREMAN, Pamela .... 804-257-5821 .... 530 A
pforeman@vuu.edu
FOREMAN, Ronald, R .... 845-368-7210 .... 350 A
FOREMAN, Todd, D .... 607-436-2081 .... 353 E
ârematd@oneonta.edu
FOREST, Laura Ann .... 334-844-6444 .... 1 F
laf0009@auburn.edu
FOREST, Rebecca .... 978-632-6600 .... 240 C
r_forest@mwcc.mass.edu
FOREST, Robert .... 610-647-4400 .... 431 C
rforest@immaculata.edu
FORESTELL, Paul .... 516-299-2701 .... 339 A
paul.forestell@liu.edu
FORESTER, Lyn .... 402-826-8631 .... 297 G
lyn.forester@doane.edu
FORESTER, Sherri, L .... 270-901-1115 .... 201 I
sherri.forester@kctcs.edu
FORESYTH, Jan .... 432-264-5051 .... 488 B
jforesyth@howardcollege.edu
FORGER, James .... 517-355-4583 .... 255 A
forger@msu.edu
FORGET, Robert, L .... 608-796-3012 .... 553 C
rlforget@viterbo.edu
FORGETTE, Adrienne, M .... 712-707-7077 .... 188 D
aforgett@nwciowa.edu
FORGEY, Glendon, S .... 903-675-6211 .... 502 F
forgey@tvcc.edu
FORGEY, Laura .... 612-359-6491 .... 261 B
forgey@augsburg.edu
FORINA, Olga .... 718-818-6470 .... 349 G
FORIST, Margery, E .... 989-328-1268 .... 255 E
margef@montcalm.edu
FORK, Patricia, A .... 614-235-4136 .... 402 G
pfork@tlsohio.edu
FORKUM, James .... 707-524-1849 .... 68 E
jforkum@santarosa.edu
FORLINES, Jon .... 615-383-1340 .... 469 A
jforlines@fwbbc.edu
FORLINES, Susan .... 615-383-1340 .... 469 A
susan@fwbbc.edu
FORMAN, Dan .... 212-960-0867 .... 346 F
forman@yu.edu
FORMAN, Daniel, T .... 212-960-0863 .... 361 M
forman@yu.edu
FORMAN, Fran .... 417-690-3223 .... 279 J
fforman@cofo.edu
FORMAN, Peter .... 201-692-9612 .... 310 A
forman@fdu.edu
FORMAN, Robert .... 718-990-7552 .... 348 G
honors@stjohns.edu
FORMAN, Robin .... 404-727-6062 .... 129 D
robin.forman@emory.edu
FORMAN, Scheherazade, W .... 301-322-0886 .... 225 F
formansw@pgcc.edu
FORNERIS, Glenda .... 815-802-8835 .... 155 A
gforneris@kcc.edu
FORNES, Yrenes .... 954-322-4460 .... 112 C
library@jmvu.edu
FORNEY, Judith .... 940-565-2436 .... 504 D
judith.forney@unt.edu
FORNEY, Phyllis .... 314-687-2900 .... 289 F
pforney@sbc-hazelwood.com
FOROUDASTAN, Hooshang .... 919-546-8323 .... 376 F
hooshang@shawu.edu
FORREN, Connor .... 434-381-6479 .... 524 K
cforren@sbc.edu
FORREST, Barb .... 218-793-2531 .... 268 C
barb.forrest@northlandcollege.edu
FORREST, Barbara .... 205-665-6055 .... 9 B
forrestb@montevallo.edu
FORREST, Christy .... 336-249-8186 .... 370 B
clforrest@davidsonccc.edu
FORREST, Cynthia .... 207-602-2372 .... 221 A
cforrest@une.edu
FORREST, Haegan .... 617-243-2165 .... 236 A
hforrest@lasell.edu
FORREST, Peg .... 602-386-4140 .... 11 G
peggy.forrest@arizonachristian.edu
FORREST, Seth .... 410-951-6183 .... 228 B
sforrest@coppin.edu
FORREST, Stephen, R .... 734-764-1185 .... 259 A
stevefor@umich.edu
FORRESTER, Don .... 540-785-5440 .... 526 A
donforrester@vbc.edu

FORRESTER, Jill, M .... 717-245-1669.... 427 F forrestj@dickinson.edu
FORRESTER, Joe, D .... 724-480-3400.... 426 A joe.forrester@ccbc.edu
FORRESTER, Michael, P .... 864-592-4805.... 461 C forresterm@sccsc.edu
FORRESTER, Nancy .... 423-354-2521.... 475 F nfforrester@northeaststate.edu
FORRESTER, Risa .... 405-425-5954.... 409 E risa.forrester@oc.edu
FORRISTER, Ann .... 517-264-3999.... 246 H
FORSHEE, Scott .... 406-657-2298.... 295 D sforshee@msubillings.edu
FORSMAN, Nadine .... 218-235-2154.... 269 F n.forsman@vcc.edu
FORSSTROM, Janice, M .... 978-762-4000.... 240 D jforsstr@northshore.edu
FORSTEN, Michele .... 718-260-5109.... 328 D mforsten@citytech.cuny.edu
FORSTER, Daniel .... 617-521-2031.... 244 F daniel.forster@simmons.edu
FORSTER, David .... 573-592-4381.... 293 D dforster@williamwoods.edu
FORSTER, Jerry .... 931-598-1260.... 472 L jforster@sewanee.edu
FORSTER, Leticia .... 434-832-7617.... 526 E forsterl@cvcc.vccs.edu
FORSTER, Marjorie .... 410-706-6631.... 227 C mforster@umaryland.edu
FORSTER, Michael .... 601-266-5253.... 277 F michael.forster@usm.edu
FORSTER, Patrick .... 503-821-8912.... 419 D patrick@pnca.edu
FORSTER, Stefanie .... 207-216-4321.... 219 C sforster@yccc.edu
FORSTROM, Katharine .... 308-432-6246.... 299 E kforstrom@csc.edu
FORSYTH, Anne, S .... 805-525-4417...... 72 I aforsyth@thomasaquinas.edu
FORSYTH, Ashley .... 215-545-1347.... 422 D aforsyth@aii.edu
FORSYTH, Melissa .... 606-886-3863.... 201 G melissa.forsyth@kctcs.edu
FORSYTHE, Christa .... 303-530-2100...... 81 I cforsythe@bcmt.org
FORSYTHE, George, B .... 573-592-5315.... 293 B barney.forsythe@westminster-mo.edu
FORSYTHE, Jacqueline ...... 660-626-2272.... 278 D jforsythe@atsu.edu
FORSYTHE, Mary, E .... 910-962-3154.... 379 D forsythem@uncw.edu
FORSYTHE, Micah .... 406-586-3585.... 294 G micah.forsythe@montanabiblecollege.edu
FORSYTHE, JR., Ronald, G .... 410-651-2272.... 227 E rgforsythe@umes.edu
FORT, Gregg .... 716-926-8790.... 335 E gfort@hilbert.edu
FORT, Rebecca, L .... 330-471-8313.... 395 F rfort@malone.edu
FORTE, Gregory .... 216-987-4294.... 389 B gregory.forte@tri-c.edu
FORTE, Joseph .... 316-942-4291.... 195 F fortej@newmanu.edu
FORTE, Paul, D .... 401-456-8224.... 454 A pforte@ric.edu
FORTE, Teresa (Terrie) .... 413-747-0204.... 233 A teresa.forte@cambridgecollege.edu
FORTE, Tyrone .... 718-262-2228.... 329 A tforte@york.cuny.edu
FORTE-PARNELL, Charlotte .... 661-722-6300...... 28 K cforteparnell@avc.edu
FORTENBERRY, Kimberly .. 813-880-8072.... 111 C kfortenberry@academy.edu
FORTHOFER, Scott .... 406-496-4500.... 296 B sforthofer@mtech.edu
FORTIN, Denis .... 269-471-3648.... 247 D fortind@andrews.edu
FORTIN, Jay .... 570-504-7000.... 425 F
FORTIN, Maurice, G .... 325-942-2222.... 480 E maurice.fortin@angelo.edu
FORTIN, Shelley .... 843-661-8110.... 458 B shelley.fortin@fdtc.edu
FORTIN-WAVRA, Marion ... 402-554-4800.... 301 A mfortin-wavra@unomaha.edu
FORTMAN, Susan .... 516-678-5000.... 341 F sfortman@molloy.edu
FORTMILLER, Dan .... 503-725-4446.... 418 G fortmid@pdx.edu
FORTMILLER, Dan .... 503-725-4446.... 418 G daniel.fortmiller@pdx.edu
FORTNER, James .... 404-894-7894.... 130 F james.fortner@business.gatech.edu
FORTNER, Martin .... 318-670-9322.... 215 A mfortner@susla.edu
FORTNER, Melissa .... 706-865-2134.... 138 E mfortner@truett.edu
FORTNER, Tom .... 601-984-1100.... 277 E tfortner@umc.edu
FORTON, Joseph .... 305-821-3333.... 109 C jforton@mm.fnc.edu
FORTON, Joseph .... 305-821-3333.... 109 D jforton@mm.fnc.edu
FORTON, Joseph .... 305-821-3333.... 109 B jforton@mm.fnc.edu
FORTOSIS, Robert .... 727-864-8252.... 105 E fortoscr@eckerd.edu
FORTSCH, Peggy .... 319-226-2031.... 182 A fortscps@ihs.org
FORTUNE, Beth .... 615-322-4234.... 478 A beth.fortune@vanderbilt.edu
FOS, Peter, J .... 504-280-5536.... 213 E president@uno.edu
FOSA, Richard .... 407-277-0311.... 107 B rfosa@evergladesuniversity.edu
FOSDYCK, Rick .... 641-683-5117.... 185 G rfosdyck@indianhills.edu
FOSHEE, Brian, E .... 901-843-3870.... 472 K foshee@rhodes.edu
FOSKEY, Becky .... 478-289-2104.... 129 B bfoskey@ega.edu
FOSKEY, Josh .... 478-934-3335.... 134 B jfoskey@mgc.edu
FOSS, Anna .... 413-499-4660.... 239 A afoss@berkshirecc.edu
FOSS, Jennifer, J .... 757-683-3132.... 522 F jfoss@odu.edu
FOSS, Lisa .... 320-308-4028.... 269 A lhfoss@stcloudstate.edu
FOSS, Marcia, J .... 701-845-7534.... 382 C marcia.foss@vcsu.edu
FOSS, Michael, C .... 413-755-4510.... 241 B mfoss@stcc.edu
FOSS, Pedar, W .... 765-658-4359.... 171 B pfoss@depauw.edu
FOSSEN, Linda .... 859-622-8835.... 200 J linda.fossen@eku.edu
FOSSEN, Linda .... 360-752-8440.... 531 H lfossen@btc.ctc.edu
FOSSUM, Dallas .... 701-671-2314.... 382 G dallas.fossum@ndscs.edu
FOSSUM, Scott .... 605-995-3025.... 464 F scott.fossum@mitchelltech.edu
FOSSUM, Tracy .... 507-786-3885.... 271 C fossum@stolaf.edu
FOSTER, Adrienne .... 310-287-4589...... 55 F fosteraa@wlac.edu
FOSTER, Alan .... 918-781-7285.... 407 B fostera@bacone.edu
FOSTER, Andrew .... 203-773-3059...... 90 C afoster@albertus.edu
FOSTER, Anita .... 859-336-5082.... 206 A afoster@sccky.edu
FOSTER, Anne .... 513-569-1898.... 387 G anne.foster@cincinnatistate.edu
FOSTER, Ben .... 972-524-3341.... 495 H
FOSTER, Blair, W .... 716-888-2990.... 325 F foster@canisius.edu
FOSTER, Brandi .... 406-444-0332.... 294 H bfoster@montana.edu
FOSTER, Brian, L .... 573-882-6596.... 291 B fosterbl@missouri.edu
FOSTER, Cherie, A .... 248-341-2117.... 256 F cafoster@oaklandcc.edu
FOSTER, Clark, M .... 518-564-2130.... 354 B fostercm@plattsburgh.edu
FOSTER, Collins .... 678-891-2320.... 131 C collins.foster@gpc.edu
FOSTER, Connie .... 270-745-2904.... 208 A connie.foster@wku.edu
FOSTER, Donald, W .... 614-823-1350.... 400 H dfoster@otterbein.edu
FOSTER, Donna .... 864-941-8430.... 460 D foster.d@ptc.edu
FOSTER, Eddie, D .... 252-638-3919.... 370 A fostere@cravencc.edu
FOSTER, Ellen .... 251-380-3460........ 7 E efoster@shc.edu
FOSTER, Felecia .... 901-435-1740.... 470 D felecia_foster@loc.edu
FOSTER, Gaines .... 225-578-8619.... 212 H dnfost@lsu.edu
FOSTER, Gretchen, K .... 308-635-6183.... 301 D fosterg2@wncc.edu
FOSTER, Isaac .... 646-378-6125.... 344 G isaac.foster@nyack.edu
FOSTER, Ivan, V .... 336-750-2830.... 380 B fosteriv@wssu.edu
FOSTER, Jacqueline .... 910-362-7019.... 368 H jfoster@cfcc.edu
FOSTER, James, D .... 256-533-7387........ 3 C jim.foster@vc.edu
FOSTER, James, E .... 503-554-2144.... 415 I jfoster@georgefox.edu
FOSTER, Janet .... 562-985-5459...... 35 C jfoster4@csulb.edu
FOSTER, Jeanie .... 858-653-3000...... 33 D
FOSTER, Joan, L .... 303-556-3215...... 86 F fosterjl@msudenver.edu
FOSTER, Joseph .... 859-622-1583.... 200 J joseph.foster@eku.edu
FOSTER, Julie .... 775-831-1314.... 303 E jfoster@sierranevada.edu
FOSTER, Karen .... 318-342-5220.... 216 E kfoster@ulm.edu
FOSTER, Kathryn, A .... 207-778-7256.... 220 C kfoster@maine.edu
FOSTER, Kay, S .... 256-549-8224........ 3 J kaysmith@gadsdenstate.edu
FOSTER, Keith .... 509-434-5275.... 533 A kfoster@ccs.spokane.edu
FOSTER, Keith .... 509-434-5275.... 533 B keith.foster@ccs.spokane.edu
FOSTER, Kelli .... 801-274-3280.... 512 F kelli.foster@wgu.edu
FOSTER, LaTonya .... 630-617-6466.... 150 H latonya.foster@elmhurst.edu
FOSTER, Linda .... 904-470-8012.... 105 G lefoster@ewc.edu
FOSTER, Mary Jane .... 203-576-4696...... 94 F mjfoster@bridgeport.edu
FOSTER, Mary Louise .... 402-844-7129.... 299 I marylouise@northeast.edu
FOSTER, Meezie .... 302-225-6235...... 96 H fosterm@gbc.edu
FOSTER, Melanie .... 512-637-5677.... 493 E seubookstore@texasbook.com
FOSTER, Michelle .... 319-208-5063.... 189 D mfoster@scciowa.edu
FOSTER, Nancy .... 231-876-3149.... 248 A nancy.foster@baker.edu
FOSTER, Nicola .... 212-346-1949.... 345 F nfoster@pace.edu
FOSTER, Rita, F .... 334-242-5645........ 9 C rffoster@una.edu
FOSTER, Robert, W .... 304-647-6290.... 544 E rfoster@osteo.wvsom.edu
FOSTER, Scot .... 510-869-6744...... 64 J sfoster@samuelmerritt.edu
FOSTER, Shannon .... 907-834-1632...... 11 B sfoster@pwscc.edu
FOSTER, Sharon .... 858-635-4858...... 27 E sfoster@alliant.edu
FOSTER, JR., Sidney, C .... 330-972-6102.... 403 B sfoster@uakron.edu
FOSTER, Stephen, P .... 937-775-2380.... 406 C stephen.foster@wright.edu
FOSTER, Tim .... 309-268-4908.... 156 I tfoster@lincolncollege.edu
FOSTER, Tim .... 970-248-1498...... 82 F tfoster@coloradomesa.edu
FOSTER, Timothy .... 717-757-1100.... 452 J tim.foster@yti.edu
FOSTER, Timothy, W .... 207-725-3228.... 217 E tfoster@bowdoin.edu
FOSTER, Yvonne .... 717-867-6161.... 434 C foster@lvc.edu
FOSTER BOYD, Marsha .... 313-831-5200.... 250 G mboyd@etseminary.edu
FOSTER CURTIS, Ellen ...... 708-534-8046.... 151 E efostercurtis@govst.edu
FOSTER-DAY, Emily .... 617-879-7016.... 238 B efoster-day@massart.edu
FOSTER GNAGE, Marie ..... 304-424-8200.... 545 C marie.gnage@mail.wvu.edu
FOSTER-JOHNSON, Lynn .. 603-646-1187.... 304 J lynn.foster-johnson@dartmouth.edu
FOSTER ZSIGA, Erin .... 207-786-6215.... 217 C efoster@bates.edu
FOSTNER, Jay, J .... 920-403-3169.... 550 F jay.fostner@snc.edu
FOTH, Rodney .... 252-492-2061.... 374 G fothr@vgcc.edu
FOTIS, Fred .... 614-247-6110.... 398 I ffotis@studentlife.osu.edu
FOTOUHI, Farshad .... 313-577-3776.... 260 A fotouhi@wayne.edu
FOUBERG, Erin .... 605-626-3456.... 466 A ehfouberg@northern.edu
FOUCART, Steve .... 417-836-5632.... 286 C stevefoucart@missouristate.edu
FOULKE, Bryce .... 407-569-1365.... 107 I financialaid@fcc.edu
FOULSHAM, Linda, M .... 828-262-2144.... 377 D foulshamlm@appstate.edu
FOUNTAIN, Barbara .... 707-864-4000...... 70 A barbara.fountain@solano.edu
FOUNTAIN, Barbara .... 707-864-7000...... 70 A barbara.fountain@solano.edu
FOUNTAIN, Cheryl, A .... 904-620-2496.... 120 D fountain@unf.edu
FOUNTAIN, James .... 918-628-3700.... 407 C jfountain@brownmackie.edu
FOUNTAIN, Jeffrey .... 702-579-3527.... 302 A jfountain@kaplan.edu
FOUNTAINE, Cynthia .... 618-453-8761.... 165 B fountaine@siu.edu
FOURMAN, Elizabeth .... 574-284-4584.... 179 F efourman@saintmarys.edu
FOURNIER, Jody .... 614-236-6445.... 386 E jfournie@capital.edu
FOURNIER, Marc .... 617-243-2291.... 236 A mfournier@lasell.edu
FOURNIER, Renee, K .... 860-701-5084...... 93 E fournier_r@mitchell.edu
FOURNIER, Robyn .... 714-556-3610...... 77 B rfournier@vanguard.edu
FOUST, Cynthia, R .... 580-774-7172.... 412 F cindy.foust@swosu.edu
FOUST, Dane, R .... 410-543-6080.... 228 D drfoust@salisbury.edu
FOUST, Jasper .... 478-757-3408.... 127 A jfoust@centralgatech.edu
FOUST, Karen, R .... 501-450-1362...... 22 A foust@hendrix.edu
FOUST, Pam .... 217-641-4956.... 154 I pfoust@jwcc.edu
FOUST, Sean .... 619-275-4700...... 46 K seanf@fashioncareerscollege.com
FOUT, Leslie, G .... 865-694-6529.... 475 G lgfout@pstcc.edu
FOUTCH, Tim .... 918-456-5511.... 409 A foutch@nsuok.edu
FOUTS, Paul .... 415-442-7026...... 48 F pfouts@ggu.edu
FOUTS, Shawn, M .... 806-335-4352.... 479 G smfounts@actx.edu
FOUTY, Dennis .... 832-842-4603.... 503 C dfouty@uh.edu
FOUTY, Dennis .... 832-842-4603.... 503 D dfouty@uh.edu
FOUTY, Jamie .... 509-527-4642.... 539 B jamie.fouty@wwcc.edu
FOWLE, Marilyn .... 940-397-4117.... 491 B marilyn.fowle@mwsu.edu
FOWLE, Teri .... 281-998-6151.... 493 G teri.fowle@sjcd.edu
FOWLER, Alex .... 508-999-8025.... 237 A afowler@umassd.edu
FOWLER, Angela .... 803-981-7339.... 463 H afowler@yorktech.edu
FOWLER, Carlton .... 816-604-4101.... 285 E carlton.fowler@mcckc.edu
FOWLER, Cass .... 386-506-3101.... 104 F fowlerma@daytonastate.edu
FOWLER, Craig .... 828-227-7282.... 380 A cfowler@wcu.edu
FOWLER, Craig .... 715-234-7082.... 555 G craig.fowler@witc.edu
FOWLER, David, G .... 601-815-1149.... 277 E dfowler@umc.edu
FOWLER, Deedy .... 269-927-8109.... 253 G fowlerd@lakemichigancollege.edu
FOWLER, Dwight .... 610-341-1388.... 428 E dfowler@eastern.edu
FOWLER, Gregory .... 603-668-2211.... 305 I g.fowler@snhu.edu
FOWLER, Gregory, T .... 928-523-1186...... 16 I gt.fowler@nau.edu
FOWLER, James .... 508-541-1547.... 233 G jfowler@dean.edu
FOWLER, Jeffrey .... 314-977-2849.... 289 C fowlerjl@slu.edu
FOWLER, Jeffrey, D .... 713-779-1110.... 494 D jfowler@sbhouston.com
FOWLER, Julie, H .... 903-983-8281.... 489 I jfowler@kilgore.edu
FOWLER, Kelly .... 559-489-2352...... 72 B kelly.fowler@fresnocitycollege.edu
FOWLER, Liesl, A .... 309-794-7211.... 145 E lieslfowler@augustana.edu
FOWLER, Lindi .... 864-977-7200.... 460 A lindi.fowler@ngu.edu
FOWLER, Lisa .... 678-891-2995.... 131 C lisa.fowler@gpc.edu
FOWLER, Lynn .... 941-487-4230.... 120 A lfowler@ncf.edu
FOWLER, Marc .... 616-222-1443.... 250 A marc.fowler@cornerstone.edu
FOWLER, Mary .... 269-927-8168.... 253 G fowler@lakemichigancollege.edu
FOWLER, Matt .... 618-262-8641.... 153 A fowlerm@iecc.edu
FOWLER, Mike .... 502-451-0815.... 206 H mfowler@sullivan.edu
FOWLER, Pamela, W .... 734-763-4119.... 259 A pfowler@umich.edu
FOWLER, Paul .... 404-727-0512.... 129 D pgfowle@emory.edu
FOWLER, Peter .... 617-989-4082.... 245 F fowlerp@wit.edu
FOWLER, Richard .... 315-472-6603.... 325 D rfowler@bryantstratton.edu
FOWLER, S. Kevin .... 903-510-2419.... 503 A kfow@tjc.edu
FOWLER, Sandra, S .... 334-683-5108........ 5 D sfowler@judson.edu
FOWLER, Sandy .... 530-674-9199...... 38 A sfowler@cambridge.edu
FOWLER, Shaanette .... 330-490-7320.... 405 F sfowler@walsh.edu
FOWLER, Tammy .... 870-972-3024...... 20 D tlfowler@astate.edu
FOWLER, Verna, M .... 800-567-2344.... 547 A vfowler@menominee.edu
FOWLER, Vivia, L .... 478-757-5229.... 139 E vfowler@wesleyancollege.edu
FOWLER, Walter, B .... 412-365-1105.... 425 C wfowler@chatham.edu
FOWLER-HILL, Sandra ...... 425-388-9216.... 534 C sfowler-hill@everettcc.edu
FOWLES, Erin .... 847-543-2375.... 148 B efowles@clcillinois.edu
FOWLES, Gareth .... 561-237-7601.... 113 D gfowles@lynn.edu

FOWLES, Michelle, R ... 818-947-2437 ... 55 E
fowlesmr@lavc.edu
FOWLKES, Bruce, M ... 309-467-6423 ... 151 B
bfowlkes@eureka.edu
FOWLKES, Carolyn, J ... 312-939-0111 ... 150 D
caroline@eastwest.edu
FOWLKES, Dane ... 903-923-2068 ... 486 F
dfowlkes@etbu.edu
FOWLKES, Deborah, W ... 303-492-8484 ... 88 H
deborah.fowlkes@colorado.edu
FOWLKES, Jeffrey, B ... 734-763-5882 ... 259 A
fowlkes@umich.edu
FOWLKES, Keith ... 276-376-4578 ... 525 G
jkf7e@uvawise.edu
FOX, Amanda ... 970-225-4860 ... 82 A
amanda.fox@collegeamerica.edu
FOX, Amanda, T ... 205-665-6038 ... 9 B
foxat@montevallo.edu
FOX, Andrea, D ... 404-752-1510 ... 134 E
afox@msm.edu
FOX, Anthony ... 989-386-6622 ... 255 C
aefox@midmich.edu
FOX, Brenda ... 903-463-8631 ... 487 C
foxb@grayson.edu
FOX, Carl ... 406-994-4145 ... 295 C
carl.fox1@montana.edu
FOX, Carole, M ... 512-463-1808 ... 500 H
carole.fox@tsus.edu
FOX, Chris ... 412-261-2647 ... 432 D
cfox@kaplan.edu
FOX, Christie, L ... 435-797-3940 ... 511 E
clfox@cc.usu.edu
FOX, Christina ... 415-869-2918 ... 235 G
christina.fox@hult.edu
FOX, Christopher ... 617-369-3894 ... 244 E
cfox@mfa.org
FOX, D. Jeff ... 208-732-6220 ... 143 E
jfox@csi.edu
FOX, Dan ... 303-273-3231 ... 83 B
dfox@mines.edu
FOX, David ... 937-708-5253 ... 405 H
dfox@wilberforce.edu
FOX, Debbie ... 225-768-1727 ... 214 C
deborah.fox@ololcollege.edu
FOX, Delcy ... 518-783-8300 ... 350 I
fox@siena.edu
FOX, Donnie, S ... 606-337-1530 ... 199 H
dfox@ccbbc.edu
FOX, Doug ... 615-226-3990 ... 472 A
dfox@nadcedu.com
FOX, Douglas ... 325-942-2333 ... 480 E
doug.fox@angelo.edu
FOX, Douglas ... 405-974-2649 ... 413 B
dfox@uco.edu
FOX, Jan, I ... 304-696-6671 ... 544 B
fox@marshall.edu
FOX, Jeanne ... 574-257-3386 ... 169 I
foxj@bethelcollege.edu
FOX, John ... 229-931-6884 ... 131 F
john.fox@gsw.edu
FOX, John, T ... 404-778-4432 ... 129 D
john_fox@emory.org
FOX, Karen ... 617-364-3510 ... 232 A
kfox@boston.edu
FOX, Karen, L ... 717-560-8254 ... 433 D
kfox@lbc.edu
FOX, Kelly, L ... 303-492-3224 ... 88 H
kelly.fox@colorado.edu
FOX, Krista ... 253-833-9111 ... 534 H
kfox@greenriver.edu
FOX, Linda, K ... 706-542-4879 ... 138 G
lkfox@uga.edu
FOX, Lori ... 212-678-3438 ... 357 G
lfox@exchange.tc.columbia.edu
FOX, Lynn ... 209-946-2421 ... 76 A
lfox@pacific.edu
FOX, Marie ... 650-949-6149 ... 47 G
foxmarie@fhda.edu
FOX, Mark ... 704-484-4104 ... 369 E
foxm@clevelandcc.edu
FOX, Mark ... 423-461-8760 ... 471 J
mpfox@milligan.edu
FOX, Mary David ... 864-503-5040 ... 463 B
mdfox@uscupstate.edu
FOX, OP, Mary Michael ... 615-297-7545 ... 467 A
srmmichael@aquinascollege.edu
FOX, Michael, J ... 757-221-1693 ... 518 A
mjfox1@wm.edu
FOX, Noah ... 617-364-3510 ... 232 A
nfox@boston.edu
FOX, P. Michael ... 585-395-2504 ... 352 F
mfox@brockport.edu
FOX, Pamela ... 540-887-7026 ... 521 C
pfox@mbc.edu
FOX, Pat ... 843-574-6307 ... 461 G
pat.fox@tridenttech.edu
FOX, Patricia ... 740-654-6711 ... 400 C
fox@ohio.edu
FOX, Phyllis ... 423-461-8708 ... 471 J
pfox@milligan.edu
FOX, Rebecca, M ... 305-284-4330 ... 122 I
rfox@miami.edu
FOX, Richard ... 718-368-4799 ... 328 A
rfox@kbcc.cuny.edu
FOX, Robert ... 502-852-6745 ... 207 E
bob.fox@louisville.edu
FOX, Robert ... 559-244-5905 ... 72 A
robert.fox@scccd.edu
FOX, Robert ... 215-468-8800 ... 431 K
admissions@culinaryarts.edu
FOX, BSG, Ronald, A ... 773-380-7041 ... 164 D
ron.fox@seabury.edu
FOX, Rusty ... 817-515-3015 ... 496 C
rusty.fox@tccd.edu
FOX, Sean ... 307-754-6102 ... 556 G
sean.fox@northwestcollege.edu
FOX, Shari ... 615-794-4254 ... 472 F
sfox@omorecollege.edu
FOX, Susan, E ... 804-355-0671 ... 525 A
sfox@upsem.edu
FOX, Thomas ... 909-706-3548 ... 78 I
tfox@westernu.edu
FOX, Timothy ... 410-617-2863 ... 223 I
tfox@loyola.edu
FOX, Todd ... 954-783-7339 ... 106 J
tfox@cci.edu
FOX, William ... 315-229-5892 ... 349 E
wfox@stlawu.edu
FOX, William, A ... 740-587-6271 ... 389 I
foxw@denison.edu
FOX-FORRESTER, Susan ... 432-837-8178 ... 501 E
sforrester@sulross.edu
FOXMAN, Michael, W ... 706-721-5632 ... 130 D
mfoxman@georgiahealth.edu
FOXMAN, Philip, R ... 814-332-5383 ... 421 F
phil.foxman@allegheny.edu
FOXMAN, Ruth ... 860-231-5221 ... 95 D
rfoxman@usj.edu
FOXWORTH, Jessica, L ... 601-877-6479 ... 272 F
jfoxworth@alcorn.edu
FOY, Morna ... 608-266-2449 ... 553 F
morna.foy@wtcsystem.edu
FOZARD, John, D ... 405-691-3800 ... 408 H
ecox@macu.edu
FOZARD, Jonathan ... 405-945-3284 ... 410 F
FRABONI, David, J ... 404-413-3405 ... 131 G
dfraboni@gsu.edu
FRADEN, Rena ... 860-297-2130 ... 94 E
rena.fraden@trincoll.edu
FRADKIN, Bernard ... 951-222-8038 ... 64 A
bernie.fradkin@rcc.edu
FRAGE, Gary ... 229-430-3593 ... 124 B
gfrage@albanytech.edu
FRAGNOLI, Kristen, M ... 585-292-3369 ... 341 H
kfragnoli@monroecc.edu
FRAGOSO, Marcos ... 210-805-3014 ... 504 B
fragoso@uiwtx.edu
FRAHER, Michael, P ... 845-437-5320 ... 359 F
mifraher@vassar.edu
FRAIER, Whitney ... 618-537-6813 ... 158 A
wlfraier@mckendree.edu
FRAILE, Pedro ... 787-727-3583 ... 568 D
pfraile@sagrado.edu
FRAILING, Mallory ... 517-265-5161 ... 246 H
FRAINIER, Janine, L ... 317-940-9228 ... 170 F
jfrainie@butler.edu
FRAIRE, John ... 509-335-5900 ... 539 D
jfraire@wsu.edu
FRAIRE, Virginia, M ... 512-223-6019 ... 481 B
vfraire@austincc.edu
FRALEY, Doug ... 606-487-3086 ... 202 C
doug.fraley@kctcs.edu
FRALEY, F. Allen ... 330-471-8237 ... 395 F
afraley@malone.edu
FRALIC, Bradley, W ... 216-368-2126 ... 386 F
bradley.fralic@case.edu
FRALICKER, Tamara ... 618-395-7777 ... 152 I
fralickert@iecc.edu
FRAME, Adrienne ... 850-644-2860 ... 119 D
aframe@admin.fsu.edu
FRAME, J. Davidson ... 703-516-0035 ... 525 C
davidson.frame@umtweb.edu
FRAME, Randall, L ... 484-384-2980 ... 438 D
rframe@eastern.edu
FRAMPTON, John ... 845-687-5288 ... 358 E
framptoj@sunyulster.edu
FRANCE, Kathleen ... 419-473-2700 ... 389 C
kfrance@daviscollege.edu
FRANCE, Lucy ... 406-243-5710 ... 294 I
lucy.france@umontana.edu
FRANCE, Melissa, H ... 918-631-2516 ... 413 F
melissa-france@utulsa.edu
FRANCE, Nancy ... 503-838-8327 ... 419 C
francen@wou.edu
FRANCHAK, Jan ... 513-244-4824 ... 388 E
jen_franchak@mail.msj.edu
FRANCHI, Gary ... 719-549-3053 ... 87 F
gary.franchi@pueblocc.edu
FRANCIES, Karen ... 281-649-3450 ... 487 H
kfrancies@hbu.edu
FRANCIOSI, Adrienne ... 617-243-2400 ... 236 A
afranciosi@lasell.edu
FRANCIS, Amy ... 419-783-2376 ... 389 H
afrancis@defiance.edu
FRANCIS, Billy ... 501-337-5000 ... 21 D
bfrancis@coto.edu
FRANCIS, Charles ... 559-442-4600 ... 72 B
charles.francis@fresnocitycollege.edu
FRANCIS, JR., D. Morgan ... 336-838-6102 ... 375 C
morgan.francis@wilkescc.edu
FRANCIS, Diana ... 219-473-4211 ... 170 G
dfrancis@ccsj.edu
FRANCIS, Donald ... 301-846-2435 ... 222 G
dfrancis@frederick.edu
FRANCIS, Eddie ... 214-376-1000 ... 492 F
FRANCIS, Gerald, L ... 336-278-7900 ... 364 D
francis@elon.edu
FRANCIS, Heather ... 972-825-4627 ... 495 F
hfrancis@sagu.edu
FRANCIS, James, M ... 630-617-3041 ... 150 H
jimf@elmhurst.edu
FRANCIS, Jeff ... 972-825-4731 ... 495 F
jfrancis@sagu.edu
FRANCIS, Jeffrey ... 918-631-2084 ... 413 F
jeffrey-francis@utulsa.edu
FRANCIS, Karen ... 603-623-0313 ... 305 E
kfrancis@nhia.edu
FRANCIS, Krista ... 360-417-6394 ... 536 G
kfrancis@pencol.edu
FRANCIS, Lance ... 706-385-1062 ... 136 B
lance.francis@point.edu
FRANCIS, Laurel ... 714-432-5670 ... 41 D
lfrancis@occ.cccd.edu
FRANCIS, Laurie ... 201-447-7117 ... 307 E
lfrancis@bergen.edu
FRANCIS, Leon ... 610-558-5584 ... 437 D
francisl@neumann.edu
FRANCIS, Lesa-Gaye ... 954-492-5353 ... 103 F
lgayefrancis@citycollege.edu
FRANCIS, Michael, R ... 801-863-8818 ... 511 F
francimi@uvu.edu
FRANCIS, Monty, E ... 214-860-2178 ... 485 A
mefrancis@dcccd.edu
FRANCIS, Norman, C ... 504-520-7541 ... 217 A
nfrancis@xula.edu
FRANCIS, Paige ... 479-619-4337 ... 22 H
pfrancis@nwacc.edu
FRANCIS, Patricia, L ... 607-436-2846 ... 353 E
francipl@oneonta.edu
FRANCIS, Randall ... 502-863-7962 ... 201 A
randall_francis@georgetowncollege.edu
FRANCIS, Robert ... 215-895-6966 ... 427 H
raf47@drexel.edu
FRANCIS, Robert ... 206-546-4797 ... 538 C
bfrancis@shoreline.edu
FRANCISCHETTI, Jessica ... 406-657-1041 ... 296 C
francisj@rocky.edu
FRANCISCO, Eva Lynn ... 904-819-6460 ... 107 C
efrancisco@flagler.edu
FRANCKO, David, A ... 205-348-8280 ... 8 E
dfrancko@ua.edu
FRANCO, Barry ... 843-574-6796 ... 461 G
barry.franco@tridenttech.edu
FRANCO, Darlery ... 201-360-4191 ... 310 E
dfranco@hccc.edu
FRANCO, Juan ... 402-472-3755 ... 300 G
jfranco2@unl.edu
FRANCO, Kerry ... 562-908-3476 ... 63 H
foundation@riohondo.edu
FRANCO, Maria ... 386-226-6225 ... 14 C
maria.franco@erau.edu
FRANCO, Maria ... 386-226-6225 ... 105 H
francom@erau.edu
FRANCO, Maria ... 386-226-6225 ... 105 I
maria.franco@erau.edu
FRANCO, Michael, R ... 410-225-2594 ... 224 B
mfranco@mica.edu
FRANCO, Onorina ... 575-538-6174 ... 321 I
francoo@wnmu.edu
FRANCO, Rita ... 209-478-0800 ... 50 K
rfranco@humphreys.edu
FRANCO, Robert ... 808-734-9514 ... 141 J
bfranco@hawaii.edu
FRANCO, Vivian ... 559-278-6111 ... 35 A
vivian_franco@csufresno.edu
FRANCOIS, K. Michael ... 936-261-1009 ... 496 G
kmfrancois@pvamu.edu
FRANCOIS-SEENY, Denise 610-861-5066 ... 437 H
dfrancois@northampton.edu
FRANCOS, Richard ... 516-463-6613 ... 335 G
richard.francos@hofstra.edu
FRANDSEN, Michael ... 517-629-0315 ... 247 A
mfrandsen@albion.edu
FRANGIONE, Amy ... 609-586-4800 ... 311 B
frangioa@mccc.edu
FRANK, Anthony, A ... 970-491-6211 ... 83 F
presofc@colostate.edu
FRANK, Brad ... 612-977-5736 ... 261 F
brad.frank@capella.edu
FRANK, Brian ... 727-341-4143 ... 116 H
frank.brian@spcollege.edu
FRANK, Brian ... 513-569-1579 ... 387 G
brian.frank@cincinnatistate.edu
FRANK, Christine, D ... 312-942-8735 ... 163 D
christine_frank@rush.edu
FRANK, David ... 541-346-4198 ... 419 B
dfrank@uoregon.edu
FRANK, Debra ... 609-771-3031 ... 308 F
frank@tcnj.edu
FRANK, Elaine ... 406-275-4972 ... 296 D
elaine_frank@skc.edu
FRANK, Greg ... 757-822-7260 ... 528 G
gfrank@tcc.edu
FRANK, Isabel ... 718-817-4602 ... 334 C
frank@fordham.edu
FRANK, Jonathan ... 312-793-7150 ... 151 A
jfrank@erikson.edu
FRANK, Karen, S ... 202-687-3432 ... 98 D
frankk@georgetown.edu
FRANK, Katherine ... 765-973-8521 ... 173 F
kpfrank@iue.edu
FRANK, Kristin ... 602-331-7500 ... 12 B
kfrank@aii.edu
FRANK, Linda ... 518-587-2100 ... 355 G
linda.frank@esc.edu
FRANK, Lisa ... 330-382-7429 ... 393 F
lfrank@kent.edu
FRANK, Marie ... 225-578-2307 ... 212 H
mfrank@lsu.edu
FRANK, Mary Lou ... 478-934-3019 ... 134 B
mlfrank@mgc.edu
FRANK, Penny, M ... 814-332-4311 ... 421 F
pfrank@allegheny.edu
FRANK, Richard ... 732-224-2753 ... 308 A
rfrank@brookdalecc.edu
FRANK, Robert ... 740-593-2850 ... 399 G
frank@ohio.edu
FRANK, Robert, G ... 505-277-2626 ... 321 C
unmpres@unm.edu
FRANK, Sandy, K ... 812-464-1762 ... 181 B
sfrank@usi.edu
FRANK, Shawn ... 828-328-7298 ... 366 E
shawn.frank@lr.edu
FRANK, Thomas, E ... 401-865-2723 ... 453 H
tfrank@providence.edu
FRANK, Vincent, P ... 717-901-5115 ... 430 F
vfrank@harrisburgu.edu
FRANK-ALSTON,
Melissa, M ... 706-771-4035 ... 125 H
mfalston@augustatech.edu
FRANKE, Mark, A ... 260-481-6258 ... 174 C
franke@ipfw.edu
FRANKEL, Bonnie ... 312-362-6760 ... 149 A
bfranke2@depaul.edu
FRANKEN, Kathy ... 319-232-6980 ... 189 G
frankenk@uiu.edu
FRANKEN, Lynn ... 724-589-2200 ... 448 B
lfranken@thiel.edu
FRANKENBURG, Doug ... 704-355-1549 ... 363 D
doug.frankenburg@carolinascollege.edu
FRANKIEL, Tamar ... 310-824-1586 ... 26 D
tfrankiel@gmail.com
FRANKL, Molly, E ... 605-394-2414 ... 466 B
molly.frankl@sdsmt.edu
FRANKLE, Barbara ... 901-435-1201 ... 470 D
barbara_frankle@loc.edu
FRANKLIN, Audrey ... 336-517-2247 ... 362 G
afranklin@bennett.edu
FRANKLIN, Brinley ... 860-486-0497 ... 94 G
brinley.franklin@uconn.edu
FRANKLIN, Carol ... 216-987-5504 ... 389 B
carol.franklin@tri-c.edu
FRANKLIN, Cheryl, P ... 340-692-4117 ... 568 E
cfrankl@live.uvi.edu
FRANKLIN, Geralyn ... 936-468-3101 ... 496 B
franklingm@sfasu.edu
FRANKLIN, Janice ... 334-229-4106 ... 1 C
franklin@alasu.edu
FRANKLIN, Joseph ... 575-835-5700 ... 319 A
jfranklin@admin.nmt.edu
FRANKLIN, K. Mike ... 406-447-5559 ... 293 G
mfranklin@carroll.edu
FRANKLIN, Karen ... 575-624-7138 ... 318 C
karen.franklin@roswell.enmu.edu
FRANKLIN, Kathy, C ... 434-528-5276 ... 530 B
kfranklin@vul.edu
FRANKLIN, Kim ... 803-786-3862 ... 457 C
kfranklin@columbiasc.edu
FRANKLIN, Laura ... 828-884-8112 ... 362 H
phillil@brevard.edu
FRANKLIN, Laura ... 831-646-4816 ... 57 G
lfranklin@mpc.edu
FRANKLIN, Laura, L ... 828-883-8112 ... 362 H
phillil@brevard.edu
FRANKLIN, Laurie ... 425-388-9035 ... 534 C
lfranklin@everettcc.edu
FRANKLIN, Loretta ... 703-414-4000 ... 518 C
lfranklin@devry.edu
FRANKLIN, Marshall, E ... 864-242-5100 ... 455 E
FRANKLIN, Reginald ... 575-624-8263 ... 319 C
franklin@nmmi.edu
FRANKLIN, Robert, M ... 404-215-2645 ... 134 D
rfranklin@morehouse.edu
FRANKLIN, Roschoune ... 323-856-7621 ... 28 E
rfranklin@afi.com
FRANKLIN, Scott ... 806-291-3745 ... 508 E
franklins@wbu.edu
FRANKLIN, Susan ... 402-461-7411 ... 298 A
sfranklin@hastings.edu
FRANKLIN, Teresa ... 918-587-6789 ... 413 A
tfranklin@twsweld.com
FRANKLIN, Truitt ... 706-886-6831 ... 138 D
tfranklin@tfc.edu
FRANKLIN, William ... 310-243-2828 ... 34 D
wfranklin@csudh.edu

FREILICH, Yosef .... 718-601-3523 .... 361 L
rabbifreilich@yahoo.com
FREITAG, Paul, A .... 612-343-4455 .... 270 A
pafreita@northcentral.edu
FREITAG, Thomas .... 215-641-6538 .... 436 G
tfreitag@mc3.edu
FREITAS, Frances Anne ..... 330-382-3805 .... 393 F
ffreitas@kent.edu
FREITAS, Rockne .... 808-956-6405 .... 141 E
rfreitas@hawaii.edu
FREJOSKY, Joe .... 423-493-4225 .... 476 E
frejosj@tntemple.edu
FREJOSKY, Joe .... 423-493-4220 .... 476 E
frejosj@tntemple.edu
FREJOSKY, Pam .... 423-493-4100 .... 476 E
frejosky@tntemple.edu
FREMONT, II, Ron, H ...... 909-869-4379 ..... 33 J
rfremont@csupomona.edu
FRENCH, Allyn .... 920-693-1871 .... 554 C
allyn.french@gotoltc.edu
FRENCH, Amy .... 270-686-6415 .... 199 B
amy.french@brescia.edu
FRENCH, Barbara .... 415-476-6296 ..... 75 A
bfrench@ucsf.edu
FRENCH, Daphne .... 912-260-4232 .... 137 B
daphne.french@sgc.edu
FRENCH, JR., George, T ..... 205-929-1428 .... 5 H
gtfrench@aol.com
FRENCH, Jeremiah .... 918-540-6113 .... 408 J
jerempf@neo.edu
FRENCH, Joy .... 303-724-2516 ..... 88 J
joy.french@ucdenver.edu
FRENCH, Marjie, M .... 210-458-4228 .... 506 D
marjie.french@utsa.edu
FRENCH, Mark .... 614-287-2810 .... 389 A
mfrench1@cscc.edu
FRENCH, Meghan, Q .... 212-346-1025 .... 345 F
mfrench@pace.edu
FRENCH, Paige .... 540-515-3749 .... 517 B
pfrench@bridgewater.edu
FRENCH, CSSP, Raymond . 412-396-4827 .... 428 D
french@duq.edu
FRENCH, Richard, G .... 781-283-3583 .... 245 E
rfrench@wellesley.edu
FRENCH, Robert, C .... 315-470-6511 .... 355 A
rcfrench@esf.edu
FRENCH, Stephanie .... 502-410-6200 .... 200 L
sfrench@galencollege.edu
FRENCH, William, R .... 609-497-7789 .... 312 F
bill.french@ptsem.edu
FRENDEWEY, JR., James . 906-487-2259 .... 255 B
jimf@mtu.edu
FRENDIAN, Michel .... 312-893-7145 .... 151 A
mfrendian@erikson.edu
FRENK, Julio .... 617-495-2936 .... 235 D
jfrenk@hsph.harvard.edu
FRENZEL, Michelle .... 218-755-2020 .... 265 I
mfrenzel@bemidjistate.edu
FRERE, Leslie .... 219-866-6116 .... 179 D
lfrere@saintjoe.edu
FRERICHS, Chris .... 515-961-1711 .... 189 C
chris.frerichs@simpson.edu
FRERIDGE, Jenifer .... 601-928-6288 .... 275 E
jenifer.freridge@mgccc.edu
FRESCH, Cathy .... 814-871-5842 .... 429 G
fresch001@gannon.edu
FRESCHETTE, Brigitte .... 701-662-1546 .... 382 F
brigitte.freschette@lrsc.edu
FRESH, Frederick .... 404-270-5185 .... 138 B
ffresh@spelman.edu
FRESHLY, Dana .... 406-771-4309 .... 295 G
dfreshly@msugf.edu
FRESHOUR, Brett .... 330-490-7171 .... 405 F
bfreshour@walsh.edu
FRESHWATER, Laurie, A ... 252-222-6281 .... 369 A
lap@carteret.edu
FRESHWATER, Thomas, A . 910-962-7673 .... 379 D
freshwatert@uncw.edu
FRESQUEZ, Anthony .... 605-455-6093 .... 465 A
afresquez@olc.edu
FRESQUEZ, Julie .... 951-343-4302 ..... 31 J
jfresque@calbaptist.edu
FREUND, Deborah, A .... 909-621-8025 ..... 40 F
debbie.freund@cgu.edu
FREW, Erin .... 719-549-2207 ..... 83 H
erin.frew@colostate-pueblo.edu
FREY, Angela .... 414-382-6206 .... 546 B
angela.frey@alverno.edu
FREY, Cathy .... 802-485-2327 .... 514 C
frey@norwich.edu
FREY, Don .... 360-736-9391 .... 532 D
dfrey@centralia.edu
FREY, Donald .... 402-280-2300 .... 297 F
donaldfrey@creighton.edu
FREY, Isabel, D .... 516-463-4779 .... 335 G
isabel.d.frey@hofstra.edu
FREY, Joan, L .... 502-410-6200 .... 200 L
jfrey@galencollege.edu
FREY, Len .... 870-972-3303 ..... 20 D
lfrey@astate.edu
FREY, Lori .... 717-264-4141 .... 452 C
lfrey@wilson.edu
FREY, Melissa .... 503-589-7652 .... 414 J
melissa.frey@chemeketa.edu
FREY, Ruth .... 773-380-6787 .... 164 D
ruth.frey@seabury.edu
FREY, Sandy .... 636-481-3348 .... 283 D
sfrey@jeffco.edu
FREYBURGER, James .... 912-201-8109 .... 137 D
jfreyburger@southuniversity.edu
FREYTAG, Carol .... 419-755-4214 .... 399 C
freytag.7@osu.edu
FREYTAG, Peter .... 303-373-2008 ..... 88 C
FREYTES, Diana .... 787-523-6000 .... 562 G
dfreytes@icprjc.edu
FREYTES, Elvin, R .... 212-966-0300 .... 342 F
elvin@nyaa.edu
FREYTES, Liza .... 787-279-1912 .... 563 D
lfreytes@bayamon.inter.edu
FRIAS, Frank .... 626-529-8064 ..... 60 F
ffrias@pacificoaks.edu
FRIAS, Mary Lou .... 508-531-1252 .... 237 D
mfrias@bridgew.edu
FRICK, Caroline .... 706-754-7722 .... 135 A
cfrick@northgatech.edu
FRICK, Hedwig (Hedy) ...... 937-484-1353 .... 405 A
hfrick@urbana.edu
FRICK, Jeffrey .... 920-403-3001 .... 550 F
jeffrey.frick@snc.edu
FRICK, Lillian, K .... 989-386-6605 .... 255 C
lfrick@midmich.edu
FRICKE, Bob .... 419-227-3141 .... 404 D
rlfricke@unoh.edu
FRICKE, David .... 732-906-2519 .... 311 D
dfricke@middlesexcc.edu
FRICKS, Brad .... 256-228-6001 .... 6 A
fricksb@nacc.edu
FRICKX, Gretchen .... 312-939-4975 .... 151 H
gfrickx@harrington.edu
FRID, Sarah .... 760-921-5469 ..... 61 C
sfrid@paloverde.edu
FRIDAY, Brenda .... 570-422-3534 .... 442 D
bfriday@po-box.esu.edu
FRIDAY-STROUD,
Shawnta .... 850-599-3565 .... 118 L
shawnta.friday-stroud@famu.edu
FRIDDELL, Melinda .... 229-226-1621 .... 138 C
mfriddell@thomasu.edu
FRIDGE, Rob .... 417-873-7527 .... 281 D
rfridge@drury.edu
FRIE, Vinetta .... 225-216-8504 .... 209 H
friev@mybrcc.edu
FRIEBEL, Thomas .... 718-368-6646 .... 328 A
tfriebel@kbcc.cuny.edu
FRIED, Barry, J .... 608-796-3811 .... 553 C
bjfried@viterbo.edu
FRIED, Linda, P .... 212-305-9300 .... 330 F
lpfried@columbia.edu
FRIED, Ray .... 325-235-7302 .... 500 G
ray.fried@tstc.edu
FRIED-GOODNIGHT,
Maud .... 856-691-8600 .... 309 B
mgoodnight@cccnj.edu
FRIEDBERG, Connie .... 412-809-5100 .... 444 G
friedberg.connie@pti.edu
FRIEDBERG, Susan, L .... 630-953-1300 .... 149 C
sfriedberg@devry.edu
FRIEDEL, Kristin, M .... 315-859-4637 .... 334 H
kfriedel@hamilton.edu
FRIEDENBERG, Samantha . 610-799-1754 .... 434 D
sfriedenberg@lccc.edu
FRIEDERICHS, Marla, J ...... 651-962-6151 .... 272 B
mjfriederich@stthomas.edu
FRIEDHOFF, Scott .... 330-263-2118 .... 388 F
sfriedhoff@wooster.edu
FRIEDKIN, Rebecca, J ...... 203-432-7085 ..... 96 A
rebecca.friedkin@yale.edu
FRIEDLANDER, Jack .... 805-965-0581 ..... 68 B
friedlan@sbcc.edu
FRIEDLEN, Karen .... 414-256-1203 .... 549 D
friedlek@mtmary.edu
FRIEDLINE, Patrick .... 312-329-4414 .... 159 A
patrick.friedline@moody.edu
FRIEDLY, Allison .... 651-846-1305 .... 269 C
allisonl.friedly@saintpaul.edu
FRIEDMAN, Aaron .... 612-626-3700 .... 272 A
alfried@umn.edu
FRIEDMAN, Aaron .... 612-626-4949 .... 272 A
alfried@umn.edu
FRIEDMAN, Al .... 425-388-9399 .... 534 C
afriedman@everettcc.edu
FRIEDMAN, Anita, S .... 757-683-5789 .... 522 F
asfriedm@odu.edu
FRIEDMAN, Avraham .... 847-982-2500 .... 152 A
friedman@htc.edu
FRIEDMAN, Beth .... 402-354-7236 .... 299 C
beth.friedman@methodistcollege.edu
FRIEDMAN, Daniel .... 206-616-2442 .... 539 A
dsfx@uw.edu
FRIEDMAN, Danielle .... 212-431-2843 .... 343 E
dfriedman@nyls.edu
FRIEDMAN, David .... 410-484-7200 .... 225 C
FRIEDMAN, Eric .... 201-360-4011 .... 310 E
efriedman@hccc.edu
FRIEDMAN, Frank .... 434-977-1620 .... 528 B
ffriedman@pvcc.edu
FRIEDMAN, Gary .... 309-438-2111 .... 153 D
gafried@ilstu.edu
FRIEDMAN, Jay, R .... 716-645-3313 .... 351 G
jf5@buffalo.edu
FRIEDMAN, Jill, D .... 314-935-5261 .... 292 I
jill.friedman@wustl.edu
FRIEDMAN, Joel .... 401-825-2003 .... 453 D
jafriedman@ccri.edu
FRIEDMAN, Judith Ann ...... 310-287-4244 ..... 55 F
friedmja@wlac.edu
FRIEDMAN, Larry, S .... 610-558-5522 .... 437 D
lfriedma@neumann.edu
FRIEDMAN, Lauren .... 203-575-8139 ..... 92 A
lfriedman@nvcc.commnet.edu
FRIEDMAN, Mark .... 573-681-5316 .... 283 I
friedmanm@lincolnu.edu
FRIEDMAN, Melissa .... 212-280-6001 .... 337 G
mefriedman@jtsa.edu
FRIEDMAN, Robert .... 212-960-5269 .... 346 F
friedman@yu.edu
FRIEDMAN, Robert .... 212-960-5269 .... 361 M
rfriedm2@yu.edu
FRIEDMAN, Scott .... 847-925-6266 .... 151 G
sfriedma@harpercollege.edu
FRIEDMAN, Stephen, J ..... 212-346-1097 .... 345 F
president@pace.edu
FRIEDMAN, William .... 312-369-7623 .... 148 D
bfriedman@colum.edu
FRIEDMAN, Yaakov .... 847-982-2500 .... 152 A
yfriedman@htc.edu
FRIEDMAN-LOMBARDO,
Jaclyn .... 973-655-7599 .... 311 F
friedmanlj@mail.montclair.edu
FRIEDMANN, Mina .... 212-217-3560 .... 333 F
mina_friedmann@fitnyc.edu
FRIEDNER, Julia .... 615-217-9347 .... 468 D
jfriedner@daymarinstitute.edu
FRIEDRICH, Brian, L .... 402-643-7364 .... 297 D
brian.friedrich@cune.edu
FRIEDRICH, Dan .... 605-256-5555 .... 465 I
dan.friedrich@dsu.edu
FRIEDRICH, Katherine .... 409-933-8150 .... 483 F
kfriedrich@com.edu
FRIEDRICHSEN,
Steven, W .... 909-706-3911 ..... 78 I
sfriedrichsen@westernu.edu
FRIEL, Kathern, R .... 302-573-5497 ..... 96 F
friel@dtcc.edu
FRIEL, Terri, L .... 312-281-3320 .... 163 B
tfriel@roosevelt.edu
FRIEL, Wm. Jake .... 724-287-8711 .... 423 G
jake.friel@bc3.edu
FRIEND, Dane .... 713-798-4300 .... 481 H
dfriend@bcm.edu
FRIEND, Dane, K .... 713-798-1544 .... 481 H
dfriend@bcm.edu
FRIEND, David .... 402-457-2770 .... 298 G
djfriend@mccneb.edu
FRIEND, Dean .... 717-846-5000 .... 452 H
FRIEND, Gwyn .... 312-362-6961 .... 149 A
gfriend@depaul.edu
FRIEND, Jennifer .... 937-461-5174 .... 396 C
jennifer.friend@staffmiamijacobs.edu
FRIEND, Joanie .... 314-539-5157 .... 288 G
jfriend4@stlcc.edu
FRIEND, Margaret .... 918-335-6238 .... 411 B
mfriend@okwu.edu
FRIEND, Vivian, M .... 727-816-3427 .... 114 F
friendv@phcc.edu
FRIERSON, Henry, T .... 352-392-6622 .... 120 C
hfrierson@ufl.edu
FRIERSON, Muriel .... 856-256-4367 .... 314 A
frierson@rowan.edu
FRIERY, Gary .... 281-998-6150 .... 494 A
gary.friery@sjcd.edu
FRIES, James .... 505-454-3269 .... 318 J
president_office@nmhu.edu
FRIES, Jane .... 970-542-3106 ..... 86 G
jane.fries@morgancc.edu
FRIESEKE, Mary .... 414-382-6098 .... 546 B
mary.frieseke@alverno.edu
FRIESEN, Gary .... 765-998-4965 .... 180 B
grfriesen@taylor.edu
FRIESEN, Jared .... 715-682-1290 .... 549 F
jfriesen@northland.edu
FRIESZ, Mary .... 701-224-5748 .... 382 D
mary.b.friesz@bismarckstate.edu
FRIGO, Daniel .... 651-213-4406 .... 264 B
dfrigo@hazelden.edu
FRIGO, Sandy .... 213-613-2200 ..... 70 H
sandy_frigo@sciarc.edu
FRIGO, Terence .... 312-567-8973 .... 153 C
frigo@iit.edu
FRIGOT, Pamela, J .... 724-738-2057 .... 443 F
pamela.frigot@sru.edu
FRINDELL TEUSCHER,
Karen .... 707-527-4377 ..... 68 E
kfrindell@santarosa.edu
FRIPPS, Kristina .... 610-892-1536 .... 441 C
kfripps@pit.edu
FRISBEE, Holly .... 212-966-0300 .... 342 F
hfrisbee@nyaa.edu
FRISBEE, Stephen .... 315-792-5399 .... 341 E
sfrisbee@mvcc.edu
FRISBIE, Kathy .... 970-542-3240 ..... 86 G
kathy.frisbie@morgancc.edu
FRISBIE, Lorene, E .... 269-660-8021 .... 257 C
frisbiel@millercollege.edu
FRISBY, Anthony .... 215-503-4990 .... 448 C
anthony.frisby@jefferson.edu
FRISCH, Edward, G .... 520-621-7766 ..... 18 L
frisch@arizona.edu
FRISCH, Kim .... 303-458-4909 ..... 87 I
kfrisch@regis.edu
FRISCH, Ronald, W .... 412-624-8030 .... 449 A
paurf5@pitt.edu
FRISCHE, Daniel, J .... 317-738-8049 .... 171 F
dfrische@franklincollege.edu
FRISINA, Warren .... 516-463-4783 .... 335 G
warren.frisina@hofstra.edu
FRISKICS, Scott .... 406-353-2607 .... 293 E
friskics@hotmail.com
FRISKO, Peter .... 215-895-1389 .... 427 H
peter.j.frisko@drexel.edu
FRISTAD, Erin .... 360-344-4100 .... 513 E
erin.fristad@goddard.edu
FRITCH, Jacque .... 800-962-7682 .... 293 A
jfritch@wma.edu
FRITCH, Margie .... 619-388-2789 ..... 65 G
mfritch@sdccd.edu
FRITCH, Todd, G .... 413-205-3449 .... 229 G
todd.fritch@aic.edu
FRITH, Deidre .... 334-347-2623 .... 3 F
dfrith@escc.edu
FRITHSEN, Donna .... 610-526-5159 .... 423 D
dfrithsen@brynmawr.edu
FRITSCH, John .... 609-894-9311 .... 308 B
jfritsch@bcc.edu
FRITSCH, Robert .... 619-388-7515 ..... 65 H
rfritsch@sdccd.edu
FRITSCHE, Teresa .... 570-422-3422 .... 442 D
tfritsche@po-box.esu.edu
FRITTS, Jack .... 630-829-6060 .... 145 G
jfritts@ben.edu
FRITZ, Dave .... 702-567-1920 .... 301 I
dafritz@cci.edi
FRITZ, David, A .... 816-604-2249 .... 285 C
david.fritz@mcckc.edu
FRITZ, Ethel .... 516-572-7124 .... 342 C
ethel.fritz@ncc.edu
FRITZ, Greg .... 402-941-6400 .... 298 I
gfrtiz@midlandu.edu
FRITZ, Greg .... 402-399-2407 .... 297 C
gfritz@csm.edu
FRITZ, Gretchen .... 570-348-6210 .... 435 F
gfritz@marywood.edu
FRITZ, John .... 410-455-6596 .... 227 D
fritz@umbc.edu
FRITZ, Lawrence, M .... 323-343-3820 ..... 35 D
lfritz@calstatela.edu
FRITZ, Lindsey .... 815-802-8628 .... 155 A
lfritz@kcc.edu
FRITZ, Sarah, B .... 608-246-6559 .... 554 D
fritz@madisoncollege.org
FRITZ, Stephen .... 806-742-1828 .... 502 A
steve.fritz@ttu.edu
FRITZ, Stephen, J .... 651-962-5901 .... 272 B
sjfritz@stthomas.edu
FRITZ, Thomas, R .... 814-472-3006 .... 446 B
tfritz@francis.edu
FRITZ, William, J .... 718-982-2400 .... 327 A
william.fritz@csi.cuny.edu
FRITZE, Barbara, B .... 717-337-6582 .... 429 I
bfritze@gettysburg.edu
FRITZE, Ronald .... 256-216-5524 .... 1 E
ron.fritze@athens.edu
FRIZADO, Joseph .... 419-372-7202 .... 385 E
frizado@bgsu.edu
FRIZZELL, D. Christine ...... 508-999-8648 .... 237 A
cfrizzell@umassd.edu
FRIZZELL, Douglas, K .... 513-244-4239 .... 388 E
doug_frizzell@mail.msj.edu
FRIZZELL, Robert .... 479-788-7205 ..... 24 D
robert.frizzell@uafs.edu
FROCK, Gemma .... 803-593-9231 .... 455 A
frockg@atc.edu
FRODSHAM, Dennis, W .... 334-683-5105 .... 5 D
dfrodsham@judson.edu
FRODYMA, Tina .... 773-298-3912 .... 163 I
frodyma@sxu.edu
FROEHLE, Paula, M .... 312-332-0707 .... 166 B
FROEHLICH-MUELLER,
Kerry, K .... 608-757-7654 .... 553 G
kfroehlich-mueller@blackhawk.edu
FROEMKE, Kenneth, M ...... 423-775-7249 .... 467 F
froemkke@bryan.edu
FROHARDT, Russell .... 512-448-8550 .... 493 E
russellf@stedwards.edu
FROHOFF, Katherine .... 816-501-4151 .... 288 A
katherine.frohoff@rockhurst.edu
FROHRIB, Patti .... 920-735-5611 .... 554 A
frohrib@fvtc.edu
FROLE, Angelo .... 740-203-8001 .... 389 A
afrole@cscc.edu
FROMAN, John .... 352-323-3697 .... 112 J
fromanj@lscc.edu
FROMING, William .... 650-433-3830 ..... 61 B
bfroming@paloaltou.edu
FROMMELT, Gene .... 940-552-6291 .... 507 F
gfrommelt@vernoncollege.edu

FROMMELT, Steve .... 816-604-1087 .... 284 H
steve.frommelt@mcckc.edu
FRONCZEK, Andrew, F ...... 216-397-4275 .... 392 L
afronczek@jcu.edu
FRONCZEK, Walter .... 708-994-5372 .... 159 B
fronczek@morainevalley.edu
FRONHEISER, Joey .... 434-832-7016 .... 526 E
fronheiserj@cvcc.vccs.edu
FRONK, Michael, R .... 386-822-7523 .... 121 F
mfronk@stetson.edu
FRONK, Peter .... 608-363-2375 .... 546 E
fronkp@beloit.edu
FRONTERA, Jose, A .... 787-841-2000 .... 565 B
jose_frontera@pucpr.edu
FRONTIERA, Charlene .... 650-574-6312 ..... 67 G
frontierac@smccd.edu
FRONZAGLIA, Shawn, G ... 412-268-4309 .... 424 J
sgfronza@andrew.cmu.edu
FRONZONI, Susan .... 570-674-6249 .... 436 F
sfronzon@misericordia.edu
FROOM, David .... 240-895-4228 .... 226 A
dfroom@smcm.edu
FROSLID JONES,
Karen, L .... 202-885-6155 ..... 97 D
kfroslid@american.edu
FROSS, Sharon .... 617-951-2350 .... 242 G
sharon.fross@necb.edu
FROST, Aimee .... 807-832-5303 .... 512 G
afrost@westminstercollege.edu
FROST, Carol .... 307-766-4121 .... 556 H
frost@uwyo.edu
FROST, Christopher .... 631-687-1271 .... 349 B
cfrost@sjcny.edu
FROST, Dana, L .... 864-644-5004 .... 461 B
dfrost@swu.edu
FROST, Eric .... 315-464-4393 .... 352 E
froste@upstate.edu
FROST, Jacque, L .... 765-494-7126 .... 178 J
frostj@purdue.edu
FROST, Judith .... 207-755-5265 .... 218 G
jfrost@cmcc.edu
FROST, Julia, H .... 479-979-1401 ..... 26 A
jfrost@ozarks.edu
FROST, Linda .... 859-622-1403 .... 200 J
linda.frost@eku.edu
FROST, Lorraine .... 909-537-5100 ..... 36 B
lfrost@csusb.edu
FROST, Mark .... 518-276-8246 .... 347 D
frostm@rpi.edu
FROST, Mark .... 518-783-4100 .... 350 I
mfrost@siena.edu
FROST, Mike .... 406-243-4711 .... 294 I
michael.frost@umontana.edu
FROST, Pamela .... 860-343-5793 ..... 91 G
pfrost@mxcc.commnet.edu
FROST, Richard, A .... 616-395-7800 .... 252 D
frost@hope.edu
FROST, Robert .... 530-938-5201 ..... 42 E
rfrost@siskiyous.edu
FROST, Stephanie .... 203-254-4030 ..... 92 H
sfrost@fairfield.edu
FROST, Vivian .... 620-252-7199 .... 192 B
vivianf@coffeyville.edu
FROSTMAN, Valerie .... 817-257-7513 .... 482 E
v.forstman@tcu.edu
FROUDE, Bill .... 859-572-5680 .... 205 H
froudew1@nku.edu
FROYD, Erin .... 954-515-4589 ..... 42 H
efroyd@kaplan.edu
FRUCHTHANDLER,
Abraham, H .... 718-377-0777 .... 346 G
FRUEH, Elizabeth .... 715-425-3737 .... 552 C
elizabeth.frueh@uwrf.edu
FRUEHLING, Christopher .. 402-461-7743 .... 298 A
cfruehling@hastings.edu
FRUITTICHER, Lee .... 678-359-5009 .... 132 A
leef@gdn.edu
FRUM, Jennifer, L .... 706-542-6126 .... 138 G
jfrum@uga.edu
FRUMKIN, Howard .... 206-543-2100 .... 539 A
frumkin@uw.edu
FRUMKIN, Jeffery, R .... 734-763-4551 .... 259 A
jfrumkin@umich.edu
FRUMKIN, Michael .... 407-823-6424 .... 120 B
michael.frumkin@ucf.edu
FRUMKIN, Steven .... 212-217-4330 .... 333 F
steven_frumkin@fitnyc.edu
FRUSH, Karen .... 919-668-3749 .... 364 C
frush002@mc.duke.edu
FRUTCHEY, Shelby .... 706-320-1266 ..... 19 A
shelby.frutchey@phoenix.edu
FRUZZETTI, Armida .... 775-674-7550 .... 302 H
afruzzetti@tmcc.edu
FRY, Angela .... 870-574-4523 ..... 24 A
afry@sautech.edu
FRY, Blake .... 715-425-3711 .... 552 C
blake.fry@uwrf.edu
FRY, Blake, W .... 715-425-3711 .... 552 C
blake.fry@uwrf.edu
FRY, Bobbye, G .... 210-829-6006 .... 504 B
fry@uiwtx.edu
FRY, Eldon, E .... 717-766-2511 .... 436 D
efry@messiah.edu
FRY, Jacy .... 605-256-5267 .... 465 I
jacy.fry@dsu.edu
FRY, John, A .... 215-895-2100 .... 427 H
jaf@drexel.edu
FRY, Matt .... 979-845-2217 .... 497 E
mattfry@tamu.edu
FRY, Pamela .... 405-744-7135 .... 410 C
pamela.fry@okstate.edu
FRY, Renae .... 763-493-0546 .... 268 B
rfry@nhcc.edu
FRY, Sally, V .... 304-367-4214 .... 543 H
sally.fry@fairmontstate.edu
FRY, Scott .... 918-825-4678 .... 410 E
scott.fry@okstate.edu
FRYATT, Rayann .... 302-736-2439 ..... 97 A
fryattra@wesley.edu
FRYDRYCH, Paul, M .... 978-762-4000 .... 240 D
pfrydryc@northshore.edu
FRYE, Curt .... 402-375-7200 .... 299 G
cufrye1@wsc.edu
FRYE, Deanne .... 843-383-8263 .... 457 A
dfrye@coker.edu
FRYE, Holly .... 304-876-5402 .... 544 C
FRYE, Jeffrey .... 419-434-4501 .... 404 B
frye@findlay.edu
FRYE, Joseph .... 502-272-3333 .... 198 H
jfrye@bellarmine.edu
FRYE, Karen .... 910-576-6222 .... 372 D
fryek@montgomery.edu
FRYE, Keener .... 307-766-4166 .... 556 H
hfry1@uwyo.edu
FRYE, Lela .... 352-395-5420 .... 117 F
lela.frye@sfcollege.edu
FRYER, Christopher .... 860-628-4751 ..... 93 C
cfryer@lincolncollegene.edu
FRYER, Robert .... 215-591-5729 .... 427 B
rfryer@devry.edu
FUCHKO, III, John, M ...... 404-962-3025 .... 139 B
john.fuchko@usg.edu
FUCHS, Kathleen, F .... 920-832-6574 .... 548 B
kathleen.f.fuchs@lawrence.edu
FUCHS, Monique .... 617-989-4513 .... 245 F
fuchsm@wit.edu
FUCHS, Nancy, J .... 612-374-5800 .... 263 F
nfuchs@dunwoody.edu
FUCHS, Tina, M .... 503-838-8220 .... 419 C
fuchst@wou.edu
FUCHS, W. Kent .... 607-255-2364 .... 331 B
provost@cornell.edu
FUCIARELLI, Alfred .... 229-333-5694 .... 139 C
affuciarelli@valdosta.edu
FUCIARELLI, Sue, E .... 229-333-5800 .... 139 C
semitchell@valdosta.edu
FUDA, Gary .... 254-526-1397 .... 482 H
gary.fuda@ctcd.edu
FUDALLY, Steve .... 218-733-7600 .... 266 H
s.fudally@lsc.edu
FUDGE, Denise, G .... 270-384-8203 .... 204 D
fudged@lindsey.edu
FUENTES, Angeles .... 831-582-4136 ..... 35 E
afuentes@csumb.edu
FUENTES, Carlos .... 787-766-1717 .... 565 I
um_mdelgado@suagm.edu
FUENTES, Jose, A .... 787-279-1912 .... 563 D
jfuentes@bayamon.inter.edu
FUENTES, Juanita .... 719-549-3255 ..... 87 F
juanita.fuentes@pueblocc.edu
FUENTES, Pablo .... 915-351-8100 .... 480 C
FUENTES, Ramon .... 787-257-7373 .... 565 G
ue_rfuentes@suagm.edu
FUENTES, Stephanie .... 303-753-6046 ..... 88 B
sfuentes@rmcad.edu
FUENTES-AFFLICK, Elena .. 415-476-1977 ..... 75 A
efuentes@sfghpeds.ucsf.edu
FUENTES-MARTIN, Mari ...... 956-882-5141 .... 505 E
marifuentes.martin@utb.edu
FUENTES-RUÍZ, Verónica .. 787-993-8916 .... 567 B
veronica.fuentes@upr.edu
FUENTEZ, Tammy .... 620-421-6700 .... 194 G
tammyf@labette.edu
FUERST, Mitchell .... 626-960-5046 ..... 59 F
FUERST, Nathan .... 860-486-3137 ..... 94 G
nathan.fuerst@uconn.edu
FUEST, Melissa .... 973-408-3695 .... 309 E
mfuest@drew.edu
FUGALE, Stephen .... 610-519-4400 .... 450 H
stephen.fugale@villanova.edu
FUGARD, Anne, S .... 904-620-1920 .... 120 D
anne.fugard@unf.edu
FUGATE, Amy .... 810-762-0237 .... 255 G
amy.fugate@mcc.edu
FUGATE, Mark .... 865-981-8145 .... 471 B
mark.fugate@maryvillecollege.edu
FUGATE, Megan, A .... 620-421-6700 .... 194 G
meganf@labette.edu
FUGATE, Wendy .... 814-838-7673 .... 429 C
wfugate@fortisinstitute.edu
FUGATE, Wesley (Wes) ...... 434-947-8000 .... 523 B
wfugate@randolphcollege.edu
FUGETT, Charlotte, A .... 520-206-7619 ..... 17 H
cfugett@pima.edu
FUGLIESE, Susan .... 617-731-7623 .... 243 G
sfugliese@pmc.edu
FUHER, Tanya .... 701-224-5524 .... 382 D
tanya.fuher@bismarckstate.edu
FUHR, Thomas, W .... 315-267-2166 .... 354 C
fuhrtw@potsdam.edu
FUHRMAN, Susan, H .... 212-678-3131 .... 357 G
susanf@tc.columbia.edu
FUHRMAN, Tim .... 509-793-2351 .... 531 I
timf@bigbend.edu
FUHRMANN, Jennifer .... 860-768-4296 ..... 95 B
fuhrmann@hartford.edu
FUJIMOTO, Andrew .... 808-983-4115 .... 140 H
andrewf@tokai.edu
FUJITA, Rich .... 307-268-3088 .... 556 A
rfujita@caspercollege.edu
FUJIYOSHI, Lois, M .... 808-933-1944 .... 141 F
lfujiyos@hawaii.edu
FUKS, Matt .... 605-697-5198 .... 466 C
matt.fuks@statealum.com
FULCHER, D. Keith .... 662-846-4708 .... 273 H
kfulcher@deltastate.edu
FULCHER, Kerry .... 619-849-2651 ..... 62 L
kerryfulcher@pointloma.edu
FULD, Kenneth .... 603-862-2062 .... 306 C
ken.fuld@unh.edu
FULDA, Henry .... 320-589-6060 .... 271 G
fuldah@morris.umn.edu
FULFORD, Lynda .... 805-493-3839 ..... 33 B
fulford@clunet.edu
FULFORD, Sherri .... 334-242-2688 .... 1 F
fulfosg@auburn.edu
FULFORD, William, J .... 251-460-7277 .... 9 D
hfulford@usouthal.edu
FULIGNI, Paul .... 618-650-2560 .... 165 C
pfulign@siue.edu
FULK, Scott .... 219-980-6792 .... 174 B
sfulk@iun.edu
FULK, Sheryl, E .... 812-877-8344 .... 179 B
sheryl.fulk@rose-hulman.edu
FULKERSON, Cathy .... 775-753-2009 .... 302 F
cathy.fulkerson@gbcnv.edu
FULKERSON,
Christopher, D .... 336-278-5055 .... 364 D
fulkers@elon.edu
FULKERSON, Tahita, M ..... 817-515-1002 .... 496 C
tahita.fulkerson@tccd.edu
FULKERSON, JR.,
William, J .... 919-684-8076 .... 364 C
fulke003@mc.duke.edu
FULL, Karen, A .... 810-762-7496 .... 253 C
kfull@kettering.edu
FULLAM, Deborah, R .... 717-867-6206 .... 434 C
fullam@lvc.edu
FULLEM, Wendy .... 973-300-2120 .... 315 F
wfullem@sussex.edu
FULLEMAN, Robert .... 973-720-2200 .... 317 D
fullemanr@wpunj.edu
FULLER, Barbara, J .... 276-964-7200 .... 528 E
barbara.fuller@sw.edu
FULLER, Brad .... 800-962-7682 .... 293 A
bfuller@wma.edu
FULLER, Cindy .... 217-424-6387 .... 158 G
cfuller@millikin.edu
FULLER, Dale .... 229-243-6436 .... 126 A
dale.fuller@bainbridge.edu
FULLER, Danielle .... 859-371-9393 .... 198 G
dfuller@beckfield.edu
FULLER, David .... 701-858-3300 .... 382 A
president@minotstateu.edu
FULLER, Edwin, W .... 607-274-3036 .... 336 G
efuller@ithaca.edu
FULLER, Elizabeth .... 508-774-0657 .... 231 B
betsy.fuller@becker.edu
FULLER, JR., Henry, M ..... 843-953-5185 .... 456 C
hank.fuller@citadel.edu
FULLER, Hester .... 802-888-1381 .... 515 E
hester.fuller@ccv.edu
FULLER, Janet .... 336-278-7729 .... 364 D
jfuller3@elon.edu
FULLER, Jerry, A .... 512-471-2866 .... 505 D
jfuller@austin.utexas.edu
FULLER, Jim .... 765-677-2090 .... 175 B
jim.fuller@indwes.edu
FULLER, Lana .... 217-234-5222 .... 156 B
lfuller@lakeland.cc.il.us
FULLER, Laurinda .... 562-985-4296 ..... 35 C
lfuller@csulb.edu
FULLER, Lois, J .... 610-499-4498 .... 451 F
ljfuller@widener.edu
FULLER, Mark .... 205-726-2711 .... 6 G
dmfuller@samford.edu
FULLER, Mark .... 303-753-6046 ..... 88 B
FULLER, Mark, A .... 413-545-5583 .... 236 F
dean@isenberg.umass.edu
FULLER, Mary, W .... 508-531-6141 .... 237 D
mfuller@bridgew.edu
FULLER, Michael .... 541-684-7248 .... 417 F
mfuller@nwcu.edu
FULLER, Mildred, K .... 757-823-2366 .... 522 E
mkfuller@nsu.edu
FULLER, Norine .... 213-624-1200 ..... 46 L
nfuller@fidm.edu
FULLER, Pam .... 480-557-1140 ..... 19 A
pam.fuller@apollogrp.edu
FULLER, Rex .... 509-359-7900 .... 533 H
rfuller@ewu.edu
FULLER, Robert .... 309-677-3283 .... 146 C
rcf@bradley.edu
FULLER, Roger, D .... 817-257-6122 .... 499 C
r.fuller@tcu.edu
FULLER, Sherry .... 515-961-1543 .... 189 C
sherry.fuller@simpson.edu
FULLER, Stephen .... 704-357-8020 .... 362 D
sfuller@aii.edu
FULLER, Tony .... 276-739-2575 .... 529 A
mmcbride@vhcc.edu
FULLER, Vivian .... 410-276-0306 .... 226 D
vfuller@host.sdc.edu
FULLER, Vivian, L .... 601-979-2360 .... 274 G
vivian.l.fuller@jsums.edu
FULLERTON, Darren, S ...... 417-625-3135 .... 286 B
fullerton-d@mssu.edu
FULLERTON, Fred, C .... 208-467-8530 .... 144 E
ffullerton@nnu.edu
FULLMAN, Joshua .... 402-363-5719 .... 301 E
jfullman@york.edu
FULLMER, Paul .... 717-867-6135 .... 434 C
fullmer@lvc.edu
FULMER, David .... 918-495-6549 .... 411 C
dfulmer@oru.edu
FULMER, Gregory, L .... 717-291-3993 .... 429 F
greg.fulmer@fandm.edu
FULMER, Hal .... 334-670-3112 .... 8 A
hfulmer@troy.edu
FULMER, Judy .... 334-670-3102 .... 8 A
jfulmer@troy.edu
FULMER, Shannon .... 214-692-8080 .... 480 I
sfulmer@aii.edu
FULMER, Terry .... 617-373-2000 .... 243 F
FULMORE, Robbin, S .... 757-683-3701 .... 522 F
rfulmore@odu.edu
FULOP, Timothy .... 814-886-6302 .... 437 B
tfulop@mtaloy.edu
FULP, Andrew .... 912-525-5000 .... 136 F
afulp@scad.edu
FULTON, Dean .... 360-752-8378 .... 531 H
dfulton@btc.ctc.edu
FULTON, Deborah, M .... 540-231-0735 .... 529 G
dfulton@vt.edu
FULTON, Delores .... 336-725-8344 .... 375 G
fultond@pbc.edu
FULTON, Donna .... 541-880-2233 .... 416 D
fulton@klamathcc.edu
FULTON, Erica .... 870-575-8491 ..... 25 B
fultone@uapb.edu
FULTON, Jodie .... 541-956-7200 .... 420 B
jfulton@roguecc.edu
FULTON, Kathy .... 254-298-8426 .... 496 D
kath.library@templejc.edu
FULTON, Richard .... 808-235-7443 .... 142 F
fulton@hawaii.edu
FULTON, Ronnie .... 941-744-1244 .... 108 C
FULTZ, Angela .... 606-759-7141 .... 203 A
angela.fultz@kctcs.edu
FULTZ, Larenda .... 731-286-3234 .... 475 B
fultz@dscc.edu
FUNDERBURK, Dana .... 618-664-7015 .... 151 F
dana.funderburk@greenville.edu
FUNDERBURK, Jerome ...... 704-216-6248 .... 366 G
jfunderburk@livingstone.edu
FUNG, Hsin-Ming .... 213-613-2200 ..... 70 H
ming@sciarc.edu
FUNG CHEN PENN,
Emma .... 684-699-9155 .... 559 C
e.fungchenpenn@amsamoa.edu
FUNIGIELLO, Tony .... 716-827-2481 .... 358 D
funigiello@trocaire.edu
FUNK, Carla .... 321-242-0737 .... 108 H
cfunk@fit.edu
FUNK, Chad .... 916-484-8401 ..... 56 A
funkc@arc.losrios.edu
FUNK, Cynthia .... 615-322-2750 .... 478 A
cindy.funk@vanderbilt.edu
FUNK, David .... 503-255-0332 .... 417 C
dfunk@multnomah.edu
FUNK, Nancy .... 530-242-7689 ..... 69 D
nfunk@shastacollege.edu
FUNK, Ruth .... 620-947-3121 .... 197 A
ruthf@tabor.edu
FUNK, Tracy .... 317-921-4371 .... 175 K
tfunk@ivytech.edu
FUNK-BAXTER, Kathryn ...... 361-825-2321 .... 498 C
kathryn.funk-baxter@tamucc.edu
FUNKE, Kathy, W .... 812-465-7050 .... 181 B
kfunke@usi.edu
FUQUA, Amy .... 605-642-6397 .... 465 H
amy.fuqua@bhsu.edu
FUQUA, Douglas .... 808-983-4138 .... 140 H
dfuqua@tokai.edu
FUQUA, Heather .... 502-447-1000 .... 206 F
hfuqua@spencerian.edu
FUQUA, JR., Jacques, L ... 334-244-3224 .... 1 G
jfuqua2@aum.edu
FUQUA, Jan, R .... 270-809-4049 .... 205 A
jfuqua@murraystate.edu
FUQUA, Stacy .... 432-552-2809 .... 507 D
fuqua_s@utpb.edu
FUQUAY, Melissa .... 757-352-4270 .... 523 E
mfuquay@regent.edu
FURBEE, Thomas, V .... 304-829-7749 .... 540 H
tfurbee@bethanywv.edu

FURDA, Eric, J 215-898-2886 448 J
furda@admissions.upenn.edu
FURE-SLOCUM, Carolyn 507-222-4003 261 G
cfureslo@carleton.edu
FURGAL, Charles, A 508-286-8213 246 B
cfurgal@wheatoncollege.edu
FURLANI, Thomas 716-645-7979 351 G
furlani@ccr.buffalo.edu
FURLONG, Bill 937-224-0061 395 B
bfurlong@swcollege.net
FURLONG, Deborah 920-465-2374 551 B
furlongd@uwgb.edu
FURLONG, Matthew 409-772-5113 507 C
mfurlong@utmb.edu
FURLONG, Scott 920-465-2336 551 B
furlongs@uwgb.edu
FURMAN, John, A 360-650-3496 539 F
john.furman@wwu.edu
FURNACE, Tina 708-237-5000 160 D
tfurnace@nc.edu
FURNER, Jennifer 315-279-5264 337 K
jfurner@mail.keuka.edu
FURNISH, Shearle 330-941-3409 406 F
sfurnish@ysu.edu
FURNSTAHL, Doug 218-235-2119 269 F
d.furnstahl@vcc.edu
FURQUERON, Cherry 432-264-5603 488 B
cfurqueron@howardcollege.edu
FURR, Kelia 205-726-4230 6 G
kfurr@samford.edu
FURR, Timothy, L 320-222-5735 268 G
tim.furr@ridgewater.edu
FURROW, Louise 626-815-5328 30 G
lfurrow@apu.edu
FURSE, Cynthia, M 801-581-7236 511 C
cfurse@ece.utah.edu
FURST, Michele 617-879-7366 238 B
mfurst@massart.edu
FURST-BOWE, Julie 618-650-2481 165 C
jfurstb@siue.edu
FURTADO, Maria 727-864-8331 105 E
furtadm@eckerd.edu
FURTAW, Paul 215-596-7570 450 B
p.furtaw@usciences.edu
FURTEK, Diane, H 413-205-3212 229 G
diane.furtek@aic.edu
FURTICK, Corrine 317-917-3329 178 A
cfurtick@martin.edu
FURTON, Kenneth 305-348-2866 119 C
kenneth.furton@fiu.edu
FURTWENGLER, Scott 281-998-6150 494 B
scott.furtwengler@sjcd.edu
FURUKAWA, Karen 707-527-4302 68 E
kfurukawa-schlereth@santarosa.edu
FURUKAWA, Tom 323-265-8669 54 G
furukat@elac.edu
FURUKAWA-SCHLERETH,
Laurence 707-664-2310 37 D
laurence.furukawa-schlereth@sonoma.edu
FURUSETH, Owen, J 704-687-1302 379 A
ojfuruse@uncc.edu
FURUSHIMA, Randall 808-853-1040 141 C
randallf@pacrim.edu
FURUTO, Brian 808-845-9123 142 B
bfuruto@hawaii.edu
FURUTO, Sandra 808-956-7487 141 E
yano@hawaii.edu
FURUYAMA, Ron 310-434-4370 68 D
furuyama_ron@smc.edu
FUSARO, Dennis 540-622-7676 523 D
dfusaro@rts.edu
FUSCHETTI, Deborah, M 863-784-7139 117 J
deborah.fuschetti@southflorida.edu
FUSCO, Cathy 415-433-9200 68 F
cfusco@saybrook.edu
FUSCO, David, J 814-641-3684 432 A
fusco@juniata.edu
FUSCO, Valerie 315-792-7111 356 B
valerie.fusco@sunyit.edu
FUSCO, William, J 707-664-2639 37 D
bill.fusco@sonoma.edu
FUSE-HALL, Rosalind 850-599-3225 118 L
rosalind.fuse-hall@famu.edu
FUSILIER, LaDonna 870-574-4519 24 A
lfusilier@sautech.edu
FUSS, Kevin, J 815-825-2086 155 D
kevin.fuss@kishwaukeecollege.edu
FUSSELL, Carl 408-554-4024 68 C
cfussell@scu.edu
FUSSELL, Paula, V 352-392-1075 120 C
pvarnes@ufl.edu
FUTCH, Lynn 912-871-1606 135 D
lfutch@ogeecheetech.edu
FUTHEY, Carol 970-248-1881 82 F
cfuthey@coloradomesa.edu
FUTHEY, Tracy 919-684-8111 364 C
futhey@duke.edu
FUTRELL, Norman 773-291-6279 147 G
nfutrell1@ccc.edu
FUTRELL, Tamara, Y 540-458-8766 530 D
tfutrell@wlu.edu
FUTRELLE, Carole 828-884-8280 362 H
futrelcw@brevard.edu
FUZY, Bob 864-587-4295 461 D
fuzyb@smcsc.edu
FYE, Christa, D 434-223-6324 519 G
cfye@hsc.edu
FYFE, Brenda, S 314-968-6913 292 J
fyfebr@webster.edu
FYFE, Dorothy, R 718-270-2258 352 D
dfyfe@downstate.edu
FYFE, John 415-442-6540 48 F
jfyfe@ggu.edu
FYFFE, Richard 641-269-3351 185 D
fyffe@grinnell.edu
FYFFE, Robert 937-775-3336 406 C
robert.fyffe@wright.edu
FYLES, Susan 415-485-3283 45 C
sfyles@dominican.edu
FYOCK, Debra, R 412-648-1458 449 A
dfyock@bc.pitt.edu

G

GAALSWYK, Terry, B 308-635-6103 301 D
gaalswy2@wncc.edu
GAARDER, David, K 972-883-6374 506 A
dkg053000@utdallas.edu
GABA, Barbara 908-965-6091 316 B
gaba@ucc.edu
GABBARD, Billie, J 727-816-3116 114 F
gabbarb@phcc.edu
GABBARD, Clinton 269-927-8120 253 G
cgabbard@lakemichigancollege.edu
GABBARD, Jene 281-649-3747 487 H
vgabbard@hbu.edu
GABBARD, Kurt, A 512-404-4816 481 D
kgabbard@austinseminary.edu
GABBARD, Ruth 859-371-9393 198 G
rgabbard@beckfield.edu
GABBE, Steve, G 614-292-1200 398 I
gabbe.1@osu.edu
GABBERT, Jill 312-942-6302 163 D
jill_gabbert@rush.edu
GABBERT, Paula, S 864-294-2064 458 E
paula.gabbert@furman.edu
GABEHART, Alan, D 318-798-4117 213 D
alan.gabehart@lsus.edu
GABEL, Ann-Marie 562-938-4540 54 E
agabel@lbcc.edu
GABEL, Barb 419-448-2183 391 F
bgabel@heidelberg.edu
GABEL, Joan 573-882-6688 291 B
gabelj@missouri.edu
GABEL, Stephen, H 773-702-0790 166 G
sgabel@uchicago.edu
GABER, Sharon 479-575-2151 24 C
sgaber@uark.edu
GABERT, Glen, E 201-360-4003 310 E
ggabert@hccc.edu
GABERT, Susan, S 603-641-7231 305 G
sgabert@anselm.edu
GABIANELLI, Barbara, A 203-576-4134 94 F
bag@bridgeport.edu
GABIS, Mark 270-926-1188 200 B
mgabis@daymargroup.com
GABIS, Mark 270-926-1188 200 C
mgabis@daymargroup.com
GABIS, Mark 270-926-1188 389 D
mgabis@daymargroup.com
GABIS, Mark 270-926-1188 468 C
mgabis@daymargroup.com
GABIS, Mark, A 270-926-1188 468 E
mgabis@daymargroup.com
GABIS, Mark, A 270-926-1188 468 D
mgabis@daymargroup.com
GABIS, Mark, A 270-926-1188 389 G
mgabis@daymargroup.com
GABIS, Mark, A 270-926-1188 200 D
mgabis@daymargroup.com
GABIS, Mark, A 270-926-1188 200 F
mgabis@daymargroup.com
GABIS, Mark, A 270-926-1188 200 A
mgabis@daymargroup.com
GABIS, Mark, A 270-926-1188 200 G
mgabis@daymargroup.com
GABIS, Mark, A 270-926-1188 200 H
mgabis@daymargroup.com
GABIS, Mark, A 270-926-1188 200 E
mgabis@daymargroup.com
GABLE, Carol 315-229-5563 349 E
cgable@stlawu.edu
GABLE, Marsha 714-564-6230 63 F
gable_marsha@sac.ed
GABONAY, Paul, W 317-788-3290 180 F
gabonay@uindy.edu
GABOURY, Mario 203-932-7253 95 C
mgaboury@newhaven.edu
GABOVITCH, Rhonda 508-678-2811 239 B
rhonda.gabovitch@bristolcc.edu
GABRIEL, George, E 703-323-3129 527 F
ggabriel@nvcc.edu
GABRIEL, Lisa 281-283-3032 503 E
gabriel@uhcl.edu
GABRIEL, Rochelle 973-748-9000 307 H
rochelle_gabriel@bloomfield.edu
GABRIELE, Carol 508-849-3380 230 C
cgabriele@annamaria.edu
GABRIELE, Gary, A 610-519-5860 450 H
gary.gabriele@villanova.edu
GABRIELSE, Ken 405-878-2305 409 D
ken.gabrielse@okbu.edu
GABRIELSON, Kerry 719-846-5643 88 F
kerry.gabrielson@trinidadstate.edu
GABRIELSON, Linda 802-828-2800 515 E
linda.gabrielson@ccv.edu
GABY, Dennis 714-449-7459 70 G
dgaby@scco.edu
GACHETTE, Yves, M 716-878-4521 353 A
gachetym@buffalostate.edu
GACHUPIN, Raymond 505-346-2354 321 B
allen.gachupin@bie.edu
GACIOCH, Dennis, M 860-768-4007 95 B
gacioch@hartford.edu
GACKENHEIMER, Lois, M 561-683-1400 100 E
GACKLE, Joel 714-556-3610 77 B
joel.gackle@vanguard.edu
GACSEH, Mary 573-364-8464 284 G
mary@metrobusinesscollege.edu
GADBERRY, Brad 770-531-6319 133 C
bgadberry@laniertech.edu
GADD, Dale 574-807-7322 169 I
gaddd@bethelcollege.edu
GADD, Elisabeth 864-646-1812 461 F
egadd@tctc.edu
GADD, Keeley 859-623-8956 205 G
kgadd@educorp.edu
GADD ZIRILLO, Bethany 330-382-7430 393 F
bgadd@kent.edu
GADDE, Sandee, A 989-463-7146 247 B
gadde@alma.edu
GADDIE, Faith 717-396-7833 440 K
fgaddie@pcad.edu
GADDIS, Glendi 210-999-7011 502 E
ggaddis@trinity.edu
GADDIS, Phil 507-457-1888 271 B
pgaddis@smumn.edu
GADDY, Margo, H 910-576-6222 372 D
gaddym@montgomery.edu
GADDY, Stoney 307-674-6446 556 F
sgaddy@sheridan.edu
GADDY, Tina 312-341-3558 163 B
tgaddy@roosevelt.edu
GADIKIAN, Randolph Lee 716-673-3181 352 A
randolph.gadikian@fredonia.edu
GADSBY, Peter 845-758-7457 323 D
gadsby@bard.edu
GADSON, John 478-445-4467 130 B
john.gadson@gcsu.edu
GADSON, Mark, P 610-409-3000 450 D
GADZINSKI, James, G 906-227-2971 256 C
jgadzins@nmu.edu
GAEDE, Rhonda, K 256-824-6573 8 G
rhonda.gaede@uah.edu
GAEKLE, Robert 219-785-5220 179 A
rgaekle@pnc.edu
GAER-CARLTON, Kathy 509-963-1211 532 C
gaerk@cwu.edu
GAERTE, Phyllis, E 585-567-9620 336 B
phyllis.gaerte@houghton.edu
GAERTNER, Gregory 312-329-4125 159 A
greg.gaertner@moody.edu
GAERTNER, Ursula 605-455-6035 465 A
ugaertner@olc.edu
GAETA, Alexa 404-471-6423 123 I
agaeta@agnesscott.edu
GAETA, James 512-863-1259 496 A
gaetaj@southwestern.edu
GAETA, Michael 503-253-3443 417 H
president@ocom.edu
GAETJENS, Stuart 931-393-1663 475 D
ssgaetjens@mscc.edu
GAETZ, Ivan 719-389-6070 82 D
ivan.gaetz@coloradocollege.edu
GAETZ, Ivan, K 303-458-3556 87 I
igaetz@regis.edu
GAFFNER, Lori 618-664-7120 151 F
lori.gaffner@greenville.edu
GAFFNEY, Dick 910-221-2224 364 F
GAFFNEY, FSC, James 815-836-5230 156 F
brjgaff@lewisu.edu
GAFFNEY, Kevin 610-921-7520 421 E
kgaffney@alb.edu
GAFFNEY, Michelle 330-823-7288 404 C
gaffnemi@mountunion.edu
GAFFNEY, II, Paul, G 732-571-3402 311 E
president@monmouth.edu
GAFFNEY, Paul, J 512-863-1379 496 A
gaffneyp@southwestern.edu
GAFFNEY, Phillip 706-204-2201 130 E
pgaffney@highlands.edu
GAFFNEY, Tiffany, D 401-865-2191 453 H
tgaffne1@providence.edu
GAFFNEY, Tony 407-851-2525 106 K
tgaffney@cci.edu
GAGAN, Kelly 585-389-2411 342 D
kgagan8@naz.edu
GAGE, Adrian 508-929-8563 238 G
agage@worcester.edu
GAGE, Amy 651-690-6829 270 L
agage@stkate.edu
GAGE, Brent 205-934-4073 8 F
bgage@uab.edu
GAGE, Chris 812-866-7028 172 A
gage@hanover.edu
GAGE, Chris 972-883-2055 506 A
ccg034000@utdallas.edu
GAGE, Colin, C 816-235-1430 291 C
gagec@umkc.edu
GAGE, David 315-781-3734 335 F
gage@hws.edu
GAGE, J. Scott 978-837-5468 242 A
j.scott.gage@merrimack.edu
GAGE, Jeannie 361-825-2332 498 C
jeannie.gage@tamucc.edu
GAGE, Julia, A 401-841-6535 558 B
GAGE, Kathryn 405-974-2361 413 B
kgage@uco.edu
GAGE, Ryan 503-961-6200 418 A
rgage@pioneerpacific.edu
GAGE, Warren 954-771-0376 112 I
wgage@knoxseminary.edu
GAGLIANO, Richard 414-277-7228 549 C
gagliano@msoe.edu
GAGNE PENDLETON, Lori 860-515-3858 90 E
lpendleton@charteroak.edu
GAGNER, Michael, J 608-757-7754 553 G
mgagner@blackhawk.edu
GAGNIER, Rick, R 509-865-8663 535 A
gagnier_r@heritage.edu
GAGNON, Ann, M 603-358-2000 306 G
agagnon@keene.edu
GAGNON, Carol, A 207-221-8710 218 C
cagagnon@kaplan.edu
GAGNON, Craig, L 920-832-6587 548 B
craig.l.gagnon@lawrence.edu
GAGNON, Karen 712-274-5159 187 G
gagnon@morningside.edu
GAGNON, Paula 207-216-4318 219 C
pgagnon@yccc.edu
GAGNON, Roberta 269-965-3931 253 B
gagnonr@kellogg.edu
GAHAGANS, Steve 479-575-6626 24 C
steveg@uark.edu
GAHAN, Mick 402-457-2402 298 G
mgahan@mccneb.edu
GAHL, Leslie, L 260-982-5256 177 H
llgahl@manchester.edu
GAHM, Jamie, L 815-224-0428 153 E
jamie_gahm@ivcc.edu
GAHMAN, Debora 215-699-5700 433 G
dgahman@lsb.edu
GAI, Dennis, E 516-572-7222 342 C
dennis.gai@ncc.edu
GAIER, Mary 937-512-2163 401 J
mary.gaier@sinclair.edu
GAIKO, Sylvia 270-745-8985 208 A
sylvia.gaiko@wku.edu
GAILEY, Kim 970-943-3140 89 E
kgailey@western.edu
GAILEY, Susan Coia 617-266-1400 231 E
GAILLAT, Ana 269-467-9945 251 B
agaillat@glenoaks.edu
GAILLIARD, Gary 817-735-2210 504 E
gary.gailliard@unthsc.edu
GAILOR, Kathleen 845-451-1302 331 E
k_gailor@culinary.edu
GAINER, Nancy, S 443-518-4073 223 D
ngainer@howardcc.edu
GAINES, Chad 660-248-6228 279 G
cgaines@centralmethodist.edu
GAINES, David, J 512-863-1494 496 A
gainesd@southwestern.edu
GAINES, Deborah 973-655-3123 311 F
gainesd@mail.montclair.edu
GAINES, James, R 808-956-7490 141 E
gaines@hawaii.edu
GAINES, John 615-936-2811 478 A
john.gaines@vanderbilt.edu
GAINES, JR., Larry, R 856-225-6174 314 D
gaines@camden.rutgers.edu
GAINES, JR., Leonard 518-381-1283 350 E
gaineslg@sunysccc.edu
GAINES, Randy 208-282-2872 143 H
gainrand@isu.edu
GAINES, Rhonda 405-273-5331 408 B
rgaines@familyoffaithcollege.edu
GAINES, Shivaun, P 973-655-7648 311 F
gainess@mail.montclair.edu
GAINES, Steven, D 805-893-4339 75 B
gaines@bren.ucsb.edu
GAINEY, Karen, W 864-488-4504 459 B
kgainey@limestone.edu
GAINOR, Birma 803-786-3856 457 C
bmgainor@columbiasc.edu
GAINSBOROUGH, Juliet 781-891-2868 231 D
jgainsborough@bentley.edu
GAISBAUER,
Mary Catherine 765-494-7536 178 J
mcgaisbauer@purdue.edu
GAITAN, Deborah 210-486-4454 479 B
dgaitan@alamo.edu
GAITAN, Maria 707-527-4431 68 E
mgaitan@santarosa.edu
GAITHER, Karen, L 313-993-1700 258 G
gaither@udmercy.edu

GANIO, John ... 845-687-5092 ... 358 E
ganioj@sunyulster.edu
GANN, Alexander ... 516-367-6890 ... 329 E
ganna@cshl.edu
GANN, John ... 903-223-3114 ... 498 F
john.gann@tamut.edu
GANN, Johnny ... 254-647-3234 ... 492 G
jgann@rangercollege.edu
GANN, Michael ... 662-846-4675 ... 273 H
mgann@deltastate.edu
GANN, Pamela, B ... 909-621-8111 ... 40 G
pamela.gann@cmc.edu
GANN, Robert ... 310-660-3015 ... 45 E
bgann@elcamino.edu
GANN, Sandra, K ... 336-342-4261 ... 373 E
ganns@rockinghamcc.edu
GANNAWAY, Anne, A ... 563-333-6283 ... 188 F
gannawayannem@sau.edu
GANNETT-MALICK, Lynn .. 205-970-9218 ... 7 C
lynngm@sebc.edu
GANNON, Debbie, K ... 515-263-6020 ... 185 C
dgannon@grandview.edu
GANNON, James, G ... 414-410-4151 ... 546 G
jggannon@stritch.edu
GANNON, Kim ... 512-245-2371 ... 501 F
kg33@txstate.edu
GANNON, Marcy ... 301-934-7560 ... 222 C
marcyg@csmd.edu
GANNON, Susan ... 908-737-3461 ... 311 A
sgannon@kean.edu
GANS, Nancy ... 775-850-0700 ... 302 C
ngans@morrison.neumont.edu
GANSBERG, Alan, L ... 818-401-1032 ... 42 F
agansberg@columbiacollege.edu
GANSCHOW, Darby ... 605-677-6623 ... 465 G
darby.ganschow@usd.edu
GANSKE, Kathryn, M ... 540-678-4381 ... 524 E
kganske@su.edu
GANSZ, David ... 937-778-7951 ... 390 G
dgansz@edisonohio.edu
GANT, Jocelind, E ... 814-393-2109 ... 442 B
jgant@clarion.edu
GANT, Patricia ... 415-485-9414 ... 42 B
patricia.gant@marin.edu
GANTENBEIN, Tony ... 320-629-5159 ... 268 E
gantenbeint@pinetech.edu
GANTHER, Sonya ... 608-796-3930 ... 553 C
sganther@viterbo.edu
GANTMAN, Amy ... 310-665-6851 ... 60 B
agantman@otis.edu
GANTNER, Christine, M ... 920-424-3414 ... 551 E
gantner@uwosh.edu
GANTNER, Myrna ... 678-839-6445 ... 139 A
mgantner@westga.edu
GANTT, Aubra, J ... 817-515-7778 ... 496 C
aubra.gantt@tccd.edu
GANTT, Bernard ... 718-289-5887 ... 326 E
bernard.gantt@bcc.cuny.edu
GANTT, Kevin ... 913-758-6230 ... 197 D
ganttk@stmary.edu
GANTT, Rachel ... 505-473-6678 ... 320 F
rachel.gantt@santafeuniversity.edu
GANZEL, Toni ... 502-852-5192 ... 207 E
toni.ganzel@louisville.edu
GAONA, Selin ... 816-604-4190 ... 285 E
selin.gaona@mcckc.edu
GARAFOLA, David ... 972-438-6932 ... 492 E
dgarafola@parkercc.edu
GARAND, Bob ... 843-661-8326 ... 458 B
bob.garand@fdtc.edu
GARANZINI, SJ,
Michael, J ... 312-915-6400 ... 157 C
mgaranz@luc.edu
GARAVASO, Pieranno ... 320-589-6250 ... 271 G
garavapf@morris.umn.edu
GARAWITZ, Amy ... 212-229-5662 ... 342 E
garawita@newschool.edu
GARAY, Stephanie ... 910-962-3188 ... 379 D
garays@uncw.edu
GARBACZ-SYNDER, Amy .. 912-344-3118 ... 124 G
amy.synder@armstrong.edu
GARBADE, Henry ... 843-208-8087 ... 462 C
hgarbade@uscb.edu
GARBARINO, James ... 816-444-0669 ... 288 A
bookstore@rockhurst.edu
GARBART, Hadley ... 410-225-2231 ... 224 B
hgarbart@mica.edu
GARBE, John ... 585-389-2038 ... 342 D
jgarbe6@naz.edu
GARBE, Theresa ... 423-461-8718 ... 471 J
tmgarbe@milligan.edu
GARBER, Alan, M ... 617-496-5100 ... 235 D
alan_garber@harvard.edu
GARBER, Barbara ... 415-351-3538 ... 65 I
bgarber@sfai.edu
GARBER, Christopher, W ... 260-982-5027 ... 177 H
cwgarber@manchester.edu
GARBER, Darrell ... 610-683-4253 ... 443 A
garber@kutztown.edu
GARBER, Gail ... 860-486-5519 ... 94 G
gail.garber@uconn.edu
GARBER, Gena ... 641-628-5156 ... 183 D
garberg@central.edu
GARBER, Kevin, S ... 913-971-3275 ... 195 D
ksgarber@mnu.edu
GARBER, Philip ... 847-214-7285 ... 150 F
pgarber@elgin.edu
GARBER, Sandy ... 928-776-2117 ... 19 C
sandy.garber@yc.edu
GARBER BAX, Sharlene ... 660-543-4114 ... 290 H
bax@ucmo.edu
GARBINI, Dennis, J ... 973-761-9011 ... 315 B
dennis.garbini@shu.edu
GARBIOGLU, Ibrahim ... 412-323-2323 ... 425 H
igarbioglu@ccac.edu
GARCEAU, Linda, R ... 423-439-4289 ... 473 F
garceaul@etsu.edu
GARCES, Gabriel ... 407-447-7300 ... 110 A
ggarces@ftccollege.edu
GARCIA, A. Ramon ... 719-549-2149 ... 83 H
aramon.garcia@colostate-pueblo.edu
GARCIA, Abigail ... 602-331-7500 ... 12 B
GARCIA, Adam ... 775-784-4689 ... 303 A
adam_garcia@police.unr.edu
GARCIA, Adrienne ... 813-253-7014 ... 110 M
agarcia@hccfl.edu
GARCIA, Aida ... 787-725-6500 ... 561 A
agarcia@sju.albizu.edu
GARCIA, Al ... 212-349-4330 ... 334 G
agarcia@globe.edu
GARCIA, Albert ... 916-558-2337 ... 56 D
garciaaj@scc.losrios.edu
GARCIA, Alberto ... 787-848-0810 ... 568 A
alberto.garcia3@upr.edu
GARCIA, Alexandra ... 210-434-6711 ... 492 B
amgarcia08@lake.ollusa.edu
GARCIA, Alfredo ... 505-260-6180 ... 318 J
a_garcia@nmhu.edu
GARCIA, Alice ... 708-709-3519 ... 161 D
agarcia@prairiestate.edu
GARCIA, Amarillys ... 787-746-1400 ... 562 E
agarcia@huertas.edu
GARCIA, Andrea ... 707-638-5272 ... 73 A
andrea.garcia@tu.edu
GARCIA, Angelica ... 925-631-4165 ... 64 F
mag6@stmarys-ca.edu
GARCIA, Ava, M ... 671-735-5527 ... 559 E
gccavp@guamcc.edu
GARCIA, Bernardo ... 305-821-3333 ... 109 D
navarrob@mm.fnc.edu
GARCIA, Bob ... 989-463-7299 ... 247 B
garciab@alma.edu
GARCIA, Brenda, W ... 575-439-3697 ... 319 E
brenda@nmsua.nmsu.edu
GARCIA, Brett ... 540-261-4503 ... 524 H
brett.garcia@svu.edu
GARCIA, Carlos ... 210-829-2717 ... 504 B
cagarci9@uiwtx.edu
GARCIA, Carol ... 718-779-1430 ... 346 B
cgarcia@plazacollege.edu
GARCIA, Carol ... 307-674-6446 ... 556 F
cgarcia@sheridan.edu
GARCIA, Caroline, M ... 520-621-3900 ... 18 L
cmgarcia@email.arizona.edu
GARCIA, Cathy ... 619-594-4723 ... 37 A
cgarcia@mail.sdsu.edu
GARCIA, Christian ... 305-284-5451 ... 122 I
christian@miami.edu
GARCIA, Christina ... 626-914-8825 ... 40 B
cmgarcia@citruscollege.edu
GARCIA, Dan, D ... 806-651-2031 ... 499 A
ddgarcia@mail.wtamu.edu
GARCIA, Daniel ... 810-762-9752 ... 253 C
dgarcia@kettering.edu
GARCIA, David ... 330-672-1001 ... 393 D
tgarcia5@kent.edu
GARCIA, Delia ... 305-348-3598 ... 119 C
garciade@fiu.edu
GARCIA, Della ... 602-243-8124 ... 16 D
della.garcia@smcmail.maricopa.edu
GARCIA, Diana ... 630-743-0680 ... 168 E
dgarcia@westwood.edu
GARCIA, Elena ... 787-780-0070 ... 560 H
egarcia@caribbean.edu
GARCIA, Eliezer ... 787-786-3030 ... 560 G
egarcia@ucb.edu.pr
GARCIA, Elizabeth ... 860-439-2624 ... 92 G
elizabeth.garcia@conncoll.edu
GARCIA, Elizabeth ... 610-282-1100 ... 427 A
elizabeth.garcia@desales.edu
GARCIA, JR., Enrique ... 361-698-1293 ... 485 G
egarcia@delmar.edu
GARCIA, Eva ... 787-264-1912 ... 564 B
egarcia@sg.inter.edu
GARCIA, Florence ... 406-768-6300 ... 294 D
fgarcia@fpcc.edu
GARCIA, Frances ... 787-786-2412 ... 566 C
frances.garcia@uccaribe.edu
GARCIA, Gerard ... 973-972-3251 ... 316 C
garciage@umdnj.edu
GARCIA, Gilda ... 940-565-2711 ... 504 D
ggarcia@unt.edu
GARCIA, Gladys ... 661-654-3485 ... 34 A
ggarcia32@csub.edu
GARCIA, Helen ... 915-566-9621 ... 508 H
hgarcia@westerntech.edu
GARCIA, Irma ... 718-489-5490 ... 348 E
igarcia@sfc.edu
GARCIA, Janet, K ... 605-221-3234 ... 464 D
jgarcia@kilian.edu
GARCIA, Joann ... 760-252-2411 ... 30 H
jgarcia@barstow.edu
GARCIA, Joe ... 312-996-9450 ... 167 A
jggarcia@uic.edu
GARCIA, Joe ... 210-784-1203 ... 498 E
jgarcia@tamusa.tamus.edu
GARCIA, Jorge ... 831-443-1700 ... 50 C
jorge_garcia@heald.edu
GARCIA, Jorge ... 787-779-2500 ... 561 D
ccat@coqui.edu
GARCIA, Joyce ... 323-265-8732 ... 54 G
garciajb@elac.edu
GARCIA, Juan ... 956-364-4604 ... 500 D
juan.garcia@tstc.edu
GARCIA, Juan, B ... 575-439-3717 ... 319 E
jbgarcia@nmsua.nmsu.edu
GARCIA, Juliet, V ... 956-882-8201 ... 505 E
president@utb.edu
GARCIA, Julio ... 408-273-2690 ... 58 G
jgarcia@nhu.edu
GARCIA, Kellie ... 661-654-3206 ... 34 A
kgarcia@csub.edu
GARCIA, Kim, L ... 408-274-6700 ... 67 B
kim.garcia@sjeccd.org
GARCIA, Leslie ... 503-494-5657 ... 418 D
cedma@ohsu.edu
GARCIA, Louie ... 415-276-0198 ... 30 E
lgarcia@aii.edu
GARCIA, Luis ... 787-285-5457 ... 562 F
lgarcia@hccpr.edu
GARCIA, Maria ... 305-595-9500 ... 100 F
registrar@amcollege.edu
GARCIA, Melissa ... 956-721-5189 ... 489 J
melissagarcia@laredo.edu
GARCIA, Myra ... 718-390-3121 ... 360 A
myra.garcia@wagner.edu
GARCIA, Orlando ... 305-348-3357 ... 119 C
orlando.garcia@fiu.edu
GARCIA, Oscar, S ... 830-591-7330 ... 495 D
o_garcia@swtjc.cc.tx.us
GARCIA, Pete ... 305-348-0504 ... 119 C
pete.garcia@fiu.edu
GARCIA, Peter ... 925-685-1230 ... 43 F
pgarcia@dvc.edu
GARCIA, Racquel ... 212-247-3434 ... 339 G
GARCIA, Raul ... 847-635-1637 ... 160 F
rgarcia@oakton.edu
GARCIA, Rene ... 305-237-3519 ... 113 H
rgarcia@mdc.edu
GARCIA, Rick ... 310-338-6047 ... 56 E
rgarcia@lmu.edu
GARCIA, Rick ... 817-515-5292 ... 496 C
rick.garcia@tccd.edu
GARCIA, Robert, P ... 214-860-2064 ... 485 A
rgarcia1@dcccd.edu
GARCIA, Roberto ... 719-389-6348 ... 82 D
rgarcia@coloradocollege.edu
GARCIA, Ron ... 505-454-3251 ... 318 J
garcia_rs@nmhu.edu
GARCIA, Rosemarie, M ... 505-428-1201 ... 320 E
rosemarie.garcia@sfcc.edu
GARCIA, Rudy ... 505-224-4342 ... 317 K
rudyg@cnm.edu
GARCIA, Sandra ... 713-221-8001 ... 503 F
garcias@uhd.edu
GARCIA, Sarah ... 208-769-3341 ... 144 D
sarah_garcia@nic.edu
GARCIA, Skip ... 312-413-5473 ... 167 B
jggarcia@uic.edu
GARCIA, Stella ... 956-364-4030 ... 500 D
stella.garcia@tstc.edu
GARCIA, Steve ... 760-245-4271 ... 77 H
steve.garcia@vvc.edu
GARCIA, Steven, N ... 909-621-8030 ... 40 F
steve.garcia@cgu.edu
GARCIA, Sunshine ... 805-437-3776 ... 34 B
sunshine.garcia@csuci.edu
GARCIA, Susan, P ... 740-587-6592 ... 389 I
garcia@denison.edu
GARCIA, Tania ... 805-437-8452 ... 34 B
tania.garcia@csuci.edu
GARCIA, Tary ... 787-264-1912 ... 564 B
tdgarcia@sg.inter.edu
GARCIA, Teresa ... 319-208-1920 ... 189 D
tgarcia@scciowa.edu
GARCIA, Val ... 661-763-7945 ... 72 E
vgarcia@taftcollege.edu
GARCIA, Veronica ... 858-642-8265 ... 58 I
vgarcia@nu.edu
GARCIA, Veronica ... 971-722-7800 ... 419 G
veronica.garcia6@pcc.edu
GARCIA, Veronica ... 956-882-4322 ... 505 E
veronica.m.garcia@utb.edu
GARCIA, Vonda ... 760-750-4852 ... 36 C
vgarcia@csusm.edu
GARCIA, William ... 973-596-5320 ... 312 C
william.garcia@njit.edu
GARCIA, Yessika ... 212-686-9040 ... 360 F
ygarcia@woodtobecoburn.edu
GARCIA, Zeke ... 505-863-7522 ... 321 D
egarcia@gallup.unm.edu
GARCIA-ANOYO, Lemuel .. 512-404-4809 ... 481 D
lemgarr@hotmail.com
GARCIA-HILLS, Rosemarie 708-209-3257 ... 148 E
rosemarie.garcia@cuchicago.edu
GARCIA-LUNA, Marisa ... 817-515-4742 ... 496 C
marisa.garcialuna@tccd.edu
GARCIA-MARENKO,
Emilio ... 269-471-3375 ... 252 A
egm@andrews.edu
GARCIA-MARENKO,
Emilio ... 269-471-3375 ... 247 D
egm@andrews.edu
GARCIA-MILLER, Maria ... 209-478-0800 ... 50 K
mgarcia@humphreys.edu
GARCIA ORTEGA, Ismael .. 787-945-7013 ... 562 C
decanoadministracion@eap.edu
GARCIA-REYES, Ana, I ... 718-518-4313 ... 327 D
agreyes@hostos.cuny.edu
GARCIA VAN DE GRIEK,
Jessica ... 615-966-5210 ... 470 F
jessica.vandegriek@lipscomb.edu
GARCON, Reginald ... 410-888-9048 ... 226 F
rgarcon@tai.edu
GARCÍA, Maria ... 210-341-1366 ... 491 G
mgarcia@ost.edu
GARCÍA, Mildred ... 657-278-3456 ... 35 B
presidentgarcia@fullerton.edu
GARD, Evelyn ... 203-285-2065 ... 91 D
egard@gwcc.commnet.edu
GARD, Krista, L ... 718-990-6749 ... 348 G
mcgowank@stjohns.edu
GARDEA, Oscar, M ... 415-338-2897 ... 37 B
omgardea@sfsu.edu
GARDELLA, Patrick ... 859-858-2130 ... 198 D
GARDI, Kerri ... 610-683-4647 ... 443 A
gardi@kutztown.edu
GARDIAL, Sarah ... 319-335-0866 ... 182 F
sarah-gardial@uiowa.edu
GARDIER PATERSON,
Mary, T ... 570-340-6018 ... 435 F
paterson@marywood.edu
GARDIN, Carey, C ... 920-923-7617 ... 548 E
cgardin@marianuniversity.edu
GARDIN, T. Hershel ... 248-414-6900 ... 254 F
thgardin@mji.edu
GARDINER, Arthur, Z ... 603-448-2445 ... 305 C
GARDINER, Duane ... 361-593-2170 ... 498 D
duane.gardiner@tamuk.edu
GARDINER, Jane, W ... 910-630-7158 ... 367 B
jgardiner@methodist.edu
GARDNER, Amanda ... 276-944-6922 ... 519 A
agardner@ehc.edu
GARDNER, Andy ... 704-484-4041 ... 369 E
gardner@clevelandcc.edu
GARDNER, Beth ... 304-252-9547 ... 542 B
GARDNER, Betina ... 859-622-1778 ... 200 J
betina.gardner@eku.edu
GARDNER, Brian ... 314-529-9387 ... 284 C
bgardner@maryville.edu
GARDNER, Brian ... 770-407-1046 ... 467 B
bgardner@argosy.edu
GARDNER, Brian ... 770-407-1046 ... 124 F
bgardner@argosy.edu
GARDNER, Brian ... 503-554-2112 ... 415 I
gardnerb@georgefox.edu
GARDNER, Butch ... 501-279-4110 ... 21 H
bgardner@harding.edu
GARDNER, Butch ... 501-279-4454 ... 21 H
bgardner@harding.edu
GARDNER, Clinton, D ... 928-541-7777 ... 16 H
president@ncu.edu
GARDNER, Craig ... 801-957-4601 ... 512 D
craig.gardner@slcc.edu
GARDNER, David ... 315-364-3229 ... 360 D
dgardner@wells.edu
GARDNER, David, M ... 785-864-0229 ... 197 B
gardner@ku.edu
GARDNER, Denise ... 865-974-4373 ... 477 D
d.gardner@utk.edu
GARDNER, Dinelia ... 201-559-6154 ... 310 B
gardnerd@felician.edu
GARDNER, Dorothy ... 252-451-8300 ... 372 E
dgardner@nash.cc.nc.us
GARDNER, Doug ... 701-530-9600 ... 383 B
doug.gardner@rasmussen.edu
GARDNER, Gail, A ... 518-458-5336 ... 330 C
gardnerg@strose.edu
GARDNER, Greg ... 405-682-7534 ... 409 F
ggardner@occc.edu
GARDNER, Guy, S ... 610-565-0999 ... 452 B
ggardner@williamson.edu
GARDNER, Gwendolyn, S .. 704-894-2597 ... 363 I
gwgardner@davidson.edu
GARDNER, James ... 660-359-3948 ... 287 A
jgardner@mail.ncmissouri.edu
GARDNER, Jeanne, W ... 719-549-3308 ... 87 F
jeanne.gardner@pueblocc.edu
GARDNER, Jeff ... 231-348-6624 ... 256 B
jgardner@ncmich.edu
GARDNER, Jessica ... 847-574-5266 ... 156 A
jgardner@lfgsm.edu
GARDNER, Jill, M ... 304-788-6901 ... 545 B
jlgardner@mail.wvu.edu
GARDNER, John ... 206-780-6213 ... 531 C
john.gardner@bgi.edu

GARY, Susan ... 704-337-2305 ... 376 A garys@queens.edu
GARY, SR., William, H ... 703-323-2399 ... 527 F wgary@nvcc.edu
GARZA, Cutberto ... 617-552-3260 ... 232 B bert.garza@bc.edu
GARZA, Felipe ... 361-593-2611 ... 498 D felipe.garza@tamuk.edu
GARZA, Fena ... 713-718-7748 ... 487 I fena.garza@hccs.edu
GARZA, Kim ... 509-793-2010 ... 531 I kimg@bigbend.edu
GARZA, Lanette ... 210-486-3731 ... 479 C lgarza@alamo.edu
GARZA, Lori ... 512-892-2640 ... 495 C
GARZA, Noemi ... 956-872-2681 ... 494 H ngarza24@southtexascollege.edu
GARZA, Nora, R ... 956-721-5868 ... 489 J nrgarza@laredo.edu
GARZA, Raul ... 703-556-8888 ... 524 C
GARZA, Rebecca, J ... 214-860-2618 ... 485 A rgarza@dcccd.edu
GARZA, Robert ... 210-486-3930 ... 479 C rgarza@alamo.edu
GARZA, Sergio, D ... 956-326-2674 ... 497 D sgarza@tamiu.edu
GARZA, JR., Victor ... 408-274-7900 ... 67 C victor.garza@evc.edu
GARZA, Wanda ... 956-872-2770 ... 494 H wgarza@southtexascollege.edu
GARZA-RODERICK, Jessie 209-833-7900 ... 66 D jgarza-roderick@deltacollege.edu
GASAWAY, Debbie ... 870-460-1622 ... 25 A gasaway@uamont.edu
GASAWAY, R. Clinton ... 765-361-6375 ... 181 E gasawayc@wabash.edu
GASCHK, Kenneth, K ... 262-243-5700 ... 547 C ken.gaschk@cuw.edu
GASH, William, H ... 910-521-6271 ... 379 C william.gash@uncp.edu
GASIOR, Donna ... 773-298-3165 ... 163 I gasior@sxu.edu
GASKELL, Carolyn ... 509-527-2133 ... 539 C carolyn.gaskell@wallawalla.edu
GASKILL, Gayle ... 651-690-6857 ... 270 L ggaskill@stkate.edu
GASKIN, Beth ... 912-525-5806 ... 136 F egaskin@scad.edu
GASKIN, Evelyn ... 480-927-0000 ... 19 A evelyn.gaskin@phoenix.edu
GASKIN, Lori ... 805-730-4011 ... 68 B lgaskin@sbcc.edu
GASKIN-FITCHUE, Leah ... 937-376-2946 ... 401 A lfitchue@payne.edu
GASKINS, Frances ... 252-527-6223 ... 371 G fgaskins@lenoircc.edu
GASKINS, Laverne, L ... 229-333-5351 ... 139 C llgaskin@valdosta.edu
GASKINS, Leebrian, E ... 956-326-2310 ... 497 D lgaskins@tamiu.edu
GASOSKE, Betsy ... 314-434-4044 ... 280 F registrar@covenantseminary.edu
GASPAR, Leigh ... 781-891-2874 ... 231 D lgaspar@bentley.edu
GASPAR, Timothy ... 419-383-5858 ... 404 F terry.gaspar@utoledo.edu
GASPAR JARVIS, Donna ... 207-602-2461 ... 221 A dgaspar@une.edu
GASPARIAN, Albert ... 714-895-8334 ... 41 C agasparian@gwc.cccd.edu
GASPARRO, Paul ... 216-987-2004 ... 389 B paul.gasparro@tri-c.edu
GASPER, Joseph ... 570-740-0372 ... 435 C jgasper@luzerne.edu
GASPER, William ... 213-763-7043 ... 55 D gasperw@lattc.edu
GASPER, William ... 617-638-4590 ... 232 E wgasper@bu.edu
GASQUE, Jeanne, F ... 727-816-3213 ... 114 F gasquej@phcc.edu
GASS, C. Michael ... 240-895-3115 ... 226 A cmgass@smcm.edu
GASSAWAY, Kathy ... 530-938-5200 ... 42 E gassaway@siskiyous.edu
GASSEAU, Michelle ... 617-243-2150 ... 236 A mgaseau@lasell.edu
GASSEL, Robert, K ... 313-593-5410 ... 259 B bgassel@umd.umich.edu
GASSER, Heather ... 208-885-6616 ... 144 G hgasser@uidaho.edu
GASSER, Ray ... 208-885-6571 ... 144 G rgasser@uidaho.edu
GASSER, Stephanie ... 520-325-0123 ... 18 G registrar@theartcenter.edu
GASSNER, Sheila ... 573-681-5084 ... 283 I gassners@lincolnu.edu
GASSNER, Taryn, E ... 302-857-1829 ... 96 D tgassner@dtcc.edu
GASSON, Grant ... 602-850-8000 ... 17 G ggasson@phoenixseminary.edu
GAST, Alice, P ... 610-758-3156 ... 434 E apg206@lehigh.edu
GAST, Kristen ... 770-962-7580 ... 132 D kgast@gwinnetttech.edu
GAST, Steve ... 712-279-1707 ... 183 A steve.gast@briarcliff.edu
GASTENVELD, Paula, M ... 434-736-2085 ... 528 D paula.gastenveld@southside.edu
GASTEVICH, Donna ... 414-256-1217 ... 549 D gastevid@mtmary.edu
GASTON, Aracelis ... 787-832-6000 ... 562 G agaston@icprjc.edu
GASTON, Carmen ... 503-943-8506 ... 420 G kwong@up.edu
GASTON, David ... 785-864-3624 ... 197 B adgaston@ku.edu
GASTON, Della, J ... 336-342-4261 ... 373 E gastond@rockinghamcc.edu
GASTON, Garrett ... 216-649-8800 ... 394 B ggaston@kent.edu
GASTON, John, C ... 229-333-5832 ... 139 C jgaston@valdosta.edu
GASTON, Kenneth ... 410-651-7550 ... 227 E klgaston@umes.edu
GASTON, Lori ... 704-894-2208 ... 363 I logaston@davidson.edu
GASTON, Neely ... 704-527-9909 ... 235 B ngaston@gcts.edu
GASTON-MARSH, Latonia, D ... 716-878-4618 ... 353 A marshld@buffalostate.edu
GATCH, Denise, D ... 941-752-5325 ... 118 J gatch@scf.edu
GATCHELL, Michael, D ... 864-294-2475 ... 458 E mike.gatchell@furman.edu
GATELY, Kevin ... 781-280-3225 ... 240 B gatelyk@middlesex.mass.edu
GATELY, Kevin ... 603-897-8232 ... 305 F kgately@rivier.edu
GATES, Amanda ... 617-585-1100 ... 242 I amanda.gates@necmusic.edu
GATES, Anne ... 216-421-7463 ... 388 A agates@cia.edu
GATES, Cynthia, K ... 405-585-5255 ... 409 D cynthia.gates@okbu.edu
GATES, Geoffrey ... 602-749-4541 ... 13 K ggates@devry.edu
GATES, Kathryn, F ... 662-915-7206 ... 277 D kfg@olemiss.edu
GATES, Leigh ... 312-939-4975 ... 151 H lgates@harrington.edu
GATES, Lori ... 503-842-8222 ... 420 D gates@tillamookbay.cc
GATES, Pamela, S ... 989-774-3342 ... 249 C gates1ps@cmich.edu
GATES, Reginald ... 817-515-5001 ... 496 C reginald.gates@tccd.edu
GATES, Robert ... 570-389-4015 ... 441 F rgates@bloomu.edu
GATES, Sheila, R ... 301-766-3677 ... 223 G sgates@kaplan.edu
GATES, Steve ... 479-936-5168 ... 22 H sgates@nwacc.edu
GATES, William, R ... 831-656-2754 ... 558 A bgates@nps.edu
GATES BLACK, Joy ... 817-515-5006 ... 496 C joy.gatesblack@tccd.edu
GATES-MILINER, Elaine ... 619-574-6909 ... 60 D egates@pacificcollege.edu
GATEWOOD, Algie ... 971-722-5302 ... 419 G agatewoo@pcc.edu
GATEWOOD, David ... 949-451-5650 ... 70 E dgatewood@ivc.edu
GATEWOOD-JASHO, Gay-linn ... 404-880-8892 ... 127 C gjasho@cau.edu
GATHARD, James ... 718-933-6700 ... 341 G jgathard@monroecollege.edu
GATHERS, Avis ... 803-793-5241 ... 457 F gathersa@denmarktech.edu
GATHII, James ... 518-445-3304 ... 322 C jgath@albanylaw.edu
GATHINGS, Kimberly ... 662-329-7138 ... 276 A kgathings@acadsupp.muw.edu
GATHJE, Pete ... 901-334-5832 ... 471 E pgathje@memphisseminary.edu
GATHMAN, Allen ... 573-651-2682 ... 289 K agathman@semo.edu
GATHRO, Richard ... 202-220-1300 ... 344 G richard.gathro@nyack.edu
GATLEY, Ian ... 973-596-3220 ... 312 C ian.gatley@njit.edu
GATLIN, Greg ... 617-573-8428 ... 245 B ggatlin@suffolk.edu
GATLIN, Kerry, P ... 256-765-4401 ... 9 C kpgatlin@una.edu
GATLIN, Lavonne ... 256-765-4787 ... 9 C lgatlin@una.edu
GATO, Stacy ... 207-221-4208 ... 221 A sgato@une.edu
GATRELL, Jay ... 812-237-3087 ... 173 B jay.gatrell@indstate.edu
GATTA, George ... 631-451-4611 ... 356 D gattag@sunysuffolk.edu
GATTA, John, J ... 931-598-1248 ... 472 L jogatta@sewanee.edu
GATTAS, Joyce, M ... 619-594-5124 ... 37 A gattas@mail.sdsu.edu
GATTEN, Jeffrey ... 661-255-1050 ... 32 F jgatten@calarts.edu
GATTERDAM, Hans ... 817-272-3275 ... 505 C hgatt@uta.edu
GATTI, Robert, M ... 614-823-1250 ... 400 H rgatti@otterbein.edu
GATTIN, Tom ... 870-230-5135 ... 21 I gattint@hsu.edu
GATTON, Pam ... 903-983-8207 ... 489 I pgatton@kilgore.edu
GATTON, Philip, S ... 618-453-4172 ... 165 B philg@pso.siu.edu
GATTON, Steven, J ... 903-233-4466 ... 490 A stevegatton@letu.edu
GATTY, Janie ... 724-335-5336 ... 438 A director@oaa.edu
GATZKE, Donald ... 817-272-2801 ... 505 C gatzke@uta.edu
GAUBATZ, Noreen ... 205-226-4671 ... 2 B ngaubatz@bsc.edu
GAUBATZ, Ronnie ... 314-529-9536 ... 284 C rgaubatz@maryville.edu
GAUBERT, Judith ... 985-867-2240 ... 214 G jgaubert@sjasc.edu
GAUCHAT, Urs, P ... 973-596-3079 ... 312 C urs.p.gauchat@njit.edu
GAUCHEL, Steph, L ... 617-627-4640 ... 245 C steph.gauchel@tufts.edu
GAUDINO, James, L ... 509-963-2111 ... 532 C gaudino@cwu.edu
GAUDIO, Arthur, R ... 413-782-2201 ... 246 A agaudio@law.wne.edu
GAUDIO, Melissa ... 570-408-4358 ... 452 A melissa.gaudio@wilkes.edu
GAUGH, Sherri ... 505-566-4007 ... 320 D gaughs@sanjuancollege.edu
GAUGHAN, Cheryl ... 619-849-2499 ... 62 L cherylgaughan@pointloma.edu
GAUGHF, Natalie, W ... 601-815-4236 ... 277 E nwgaughf1@umc.edu
GAUL, Julie, M ... 412-578-6042 ... 424 I gauljm@carlow.edu
GAUL, Veera ... 401-598-1001 ... 453 E vgual@jwu.edu
GAULDEN, JR., Corbett, F 325-942-2337 ... 480 E corbett.gaulden@angelo.edu
GAULT, Brian, C ... 601-923-1671 ... 276 F bgault@rts.edu
GAULT, Carrie, J ... 724-458-2134 ... 430 B cjgault@gcc.edu
GAULT, Kevin ... 727-726-1153 ... 103 I kevingault@clearwater.edu
GAULT, Ron ... 931-393-1582 ... 475 D rgault@mscc.edu
GAULT, Sandra ... 816-235-6234 ... 291 C gaults@umkc.edu
GAUME, Curtis, C ... 716-888-2300 ... 325 F gaume@canisius.edu
GAUMONT, Suzanne ... 408-554-4642 ... 68 C sgaumont@scu.edu
GAUNA, Lucy ... 210-486-4408 ... 479 B lgauna5@alamo.edu
GAUNT, John, C ... 785-864-4281 ... 197 B jgaunt@ku.edu
GAUNT, Marianne, I ... 732-932-7505 ... 314 B gaunt@rci.rutgers.edu
GAUNT, Victoria, F ... 410-864-4234 ... 226 B vgaunt@stmarys.edu
GAURMER, Terry ... 303-458-1629 ... 87 I tgaurmer@regis.edu
GAUS, Gregory, J ... 623-572-3400 ... 16 E ggausx@midwestern.edu
GAUS, Gregory, J ... 630-515-7307 ... 158 F ggausx@midwestern.edu
GAUSE, William, C ... 973-972-7697 ... 316 F gausewc@umdnj.edu
GAUSS, Nancy ... 970-943-2053 ... 89 E ngauss@western.edu
GAUSVIK, Tom, E ... 706-542-2621 ... 138 G tgausvik@uga.edu
GAUT, LaDonna ... 903-923-2477 ... 509 E ldgaut@wileyc.edu
GAUTHIER, Laureen ... 802-225-3205 ... 514 B laureen.gauthier@neci.edu
GAUTHIER, Raymond, C ... 503-682-3903 ... 419 F rgauthier@pioneerpacific.edu
GAUTIER, Ed, E ... 985-549-2064 ... 216 C egautier@selu.edu
GAUTNEY, Michael, B ... 256-765-4274 ... 9 C mbgautney@una.edu
GAUTSCHI, David ... 212-636-6111 ... 334 C gautschi@fordham.edu
GAUVIN, Keith ... 203-596-4612 ... 93 G kgauvin@post.edu
GAVAL, Kathleen, D ... 610-660-1204 ... 446 C kgaval@sju.edu
GAVALETZ, Tami ... 618-374-5187 ... 161 E tami.gavaletz@principia.edu
GAVANUS, Michael ... 215-248-7163 ... 425 D gavanusmi@chc.edu
GAVAZZI, Stephen, M ... 419-755-4221 ... 399 C gavazzi.1@osu.edu
GAVER, Bob ... 402-363-5721 ... 301 E bagaver@york.edu
GAVIN, Carrie ... 850-599-3076 ... 118 L carrie.gavin@famu.edu
GAVIN, Jack ... 732-571-3536 ... 311 E gavin@monmouth.edu
GAVIN, M. F. Chip ... 207-973-3335 ... 219 I chip.gavin@maine.edu
GAVIN, Michael ... 414-297-6760 ... 554 F gavinmj@matc.edu
GAVIN, Mike ... 828-395-1295 ... 371 D mgavin@isothermal.edu
GAVIN, Todd ... 803-822-3233 ... 459 E gavint@midlandstech.edu
GAVIN-WILLIAMS, Barbara ... 908-709-7511 ... 316 B gavin@ucc.edu
GAVLICK, Christopher ... 914-251-6916 ... 354 D christopher.gavlick@purchase.edu
GAVLIK, Deborah ... 567-661-7510 ... 400 I deborah_gavlik@owens.edu
GAW, Kevin, E ... 404-413-1835 ... 131 G kgaw@gsu.edu
GAWEHN, Julie ... 575-562-2115 ... 318 B julie.gawehn@enmu.edu
GAWEL, Gary, P ... 912-478-0268 ... 131 E gpgawel@georgiasouthern.edu
GAWELEK, Mary Ann ... 724-838-4216 ... 447 C gawelek@setonhill.edu
GAWENDA, Matt ... 312-922-1884 ... 157 E mgawenda@maccormac.edu
GAWLIK, Gail ... 815-740-5041 ... 167 E ggawlik@stfrancis.edu
GAWRONSKI, JR., Michael ... 845-341-4284 ... 345 E michael.gawronski@sunyorange.edu
GAWTHROP, Larry ... 810-762-0235 ... 255 G larry.gawthrop@mcc.edu
GAY, Bob ... 212-229-5150 ... 342 E gayr@newschool.edu
GAY, Cliff ... 478-289-2025 ... 129 B cgay@ega.edu
GAY, John ... 410-386-8434 ... 221 G jgay@carrollcc.edu
GAY, Judith, R ... 215-751-8355 ... 426 B jgay@ccp.edu
GAY, Kathleen ... 318-678-6000 ... 209 I kgay@bpcc.edu
GAYESKI, Diane ... 607-274-3895 ... 336 G gayeski@ithaca.edu
GAYHART, Terri ... 414-297-6663 ... 554 F gayhartt@matc.edu
GAYLE, Barbara, M ... 608-796-3080 ... 553 C bmgayle@viterbo.edu
GAYLE, Ruth, R ... 215-965-4002 ... 436 H rgayle@moore.edu
GAYLEN, Nancy, I ... 217-424-6244 ... 158 G ngaylen@millikin.edu
GAYLOR, Sue, S ... 570-321-4219 ... 435 D gaylor@lycoming.edu
GAYMER, Dawn ... 269-387-4200 ... 260 C dawn.gaymer@wmich.edu
GAYMON, Denise ... 256-551-1710 ... 4 J denise.gaymon@drakestate.edu
GAYMON, Joffery ... 843-208-8118 ... 462 C jofferyb@mailbox.sc.edu
GAYNOR, Deborah ... 717-264-4141 ... 452 C dgaynor@wilson.edu
GAYNOR, Dona, E ... 321-674-8102 ... 108 H dgaynor@fit.edu
GAYNOR, Julie ... 940-397-4353 ... 491 B julie.gaynor@mwsu.edu
GAYNOR, Kimberly ... 281-649-3025 ... 487 H kgaynor@hbu.edu
GAYNOR, Michael ... 610-519-4000 ... 450 H michael.gaynor@villanova.edu
GAYNOR, Suzanne ... 607-431-4670 ... 335 A gaynors@hartwick.edu
GAYTON, Linda ... 973-684-6104 ... 312 E lgayton@pccc.edu
GAZA, Roberto ... 305-223-4561 ... 116 E rgaza@sjvcs.edu
GAZTAMBIDE, Fernando ... 787-265-3866 ... 567 F fernando.gaztambide@upr.edu
GAZZALE, Bob ... 323-856-7600 ... 28 E
GBADEGESIN, Segun ... 202-806-6700 ... 98 E sgbadegesin@howard.edu
GBENEDIO, Pender ... 803-750-2510 ... 99 G pender.gbenedio@strayer.edu
GEADELMANN, Patricia, L 319-273-6144 ... 182 G patricia.geadelmann@uni.edu
GEAGHAN, Tom ... 216-687-4745 ... 388 D t.geaghan@csuohio.edu
GEALT, Michael ... 501-569-3545 ... 24 E magealt@ualr.edu
GEAR, Jill ... 419-434-4429 ... 404 B gear@findlay.edu
GEAR, Lisa, L ... 213-738-6834 ... 71 E admissions@swlaw.edu
GEARAN, Mark, D ... 315-781-3309 ... 335 F gearan@hws.edu
GEARHART, G. David ... 479-575-4148 ... 24 C gdgearh@uark.edu
GEARHART, Gregory, L ... 717-691-6007 ... 436 D gearhart@messiah.edu
GEARHART, Rob ... 607-274-1909 ... 336 G rgearhart@ithaca.edu

GEARHART, Trevor ... 715-324-6900 ... 549 G trevor.gearhart@ni.edu
GEARHART, William, H ... 401-456-8200 ... 454 A wgearhart@ric.edu
GEARIN, Christopher, A ... 314-434-2212 ... 282 I
GEARY, Colette ... 914-654-5363 ... 330 B cgeary@cnr.edu
GEARY, Gregg ... 808-956-7205 ... 141 G geary@hawaii.edu
GEARY, Leslie, H ... 203-576-4625 ... 94 F lgeary@bridgeport.edu
GEARY, Melanie ... 303-534-6290 ... 83 E melanie.geary@colostate.edu
GEARY, JR., Raymond, R ... 814-362-5198 ... 449 B rgeary@pitt.edu
GEARY, Wes ... 303-404-5024 ... 85 A wes.geary@frontrange.edu
GEASE, Eleanor ... 202-885-8650 ... 100 C egease@wesleyseminary.edu
GEASEY, David, W ... 607-436-3314 ... 353 E geaseydw@oneonta.edu
GEASON, Robin ... 985-447-0924 ... 211 G rgeason@ltc.edu
GEBB, Billie Anne ... 859-253-3637 ... 200 K billieanne.gebb@frontier.edu
GEBEL, Karen ... 319-296-2320 ... 185 F karen.gebel@hawkeyecollege.edu
GEBER, David ... 212-749-2802 ... 339 I dgeber@msmnyc.edu
GEBHARD, Susan ... 336-917-5783 ... 376 E susan.gebhard@salem.edu
GEBHARDT, Charles ... 402-643-7411 ... 297 D charles.gebhardt@cune.edu
GEBHARDT, Virginia ... 660-263-4110 ... 286 H virginig@macc.edu
GEBHART, Daniel, L ... 260-481-6322 ... 174 C gebhartd@ipfw.edu
GEBHART, Jennifer, L ... 937-775-5611 ... 406 C jennifer.gebhart@wright.edu
GEDDES, Eva, R ... 845-368-7200 ... 350 A eva.geddes@use.salvationarmy.org
GEDDES, Leonard ... 828-328-7024 ... 366 E leonard.geddes@lr.edu
GEDDES, Wesley ... 845-368-7200 ... 350 A wesley.geddes@use.salvationarmy.org
GEDDINGS, Scarlet ... 803-535-1243 ... 460 C geddingss@octech.edu
GEDDIS, Janet ... 610-558-5540 ... 437 D geddisj@neumann.edu
GEDEON, Tai ... 973-642-8744 ... 315 C tai-gedeo@shu.edu
GEDNALSKE, Julie ... 605-331-6683 ... 466 E julie.gednalske@usiouxfalls.edu
GEE, Albert, R ... 936-261-1730 ... 496 G argee@pvamu.edu
GEE, Billy ... 706-272-4461 ... 128 C bgee@daltonstate.edu
GEE, Carmelita ... 708-763-6941 ... 162 E carmelita.gee@resu.edu
GEE, E. Gordon ... 614-292-2424 ... 398 I gee.2@osu.edu
GEE, Henry ... 408-274-7900 ... 67 C henry.gee@evc.edu
GEE, Henry ... 562-908-3489 ... 63 H hgee@riohondo.edu
GEE, Jean ... 406-243-5370 ... 294 I jean.gee@umontana.edu
GEE, Jeffrey, S ... 434-223-6164 ... 519 G jgee@hsc.edu
GEE, Terry ... 619-594-2853 ... 37 A tgee@mail.sdsu.edu
GEEHAN, Margaret, M ... 518-629-7117 ... 336 C m.geehan@hvcc.edu
GEENEN, Patricia ... 414-382-6258 ... 546 B pat.geenen@alverno.edu
GEENENS, Dave ... 913-360-7633 ... 191 A dgeenens@benedictine.edu
GEER, Anne, R ... 585-385-8070 ... 348 F ageer@sjfc.edu
GEER, Lyn ... 703-330-5398 ... 540 F lgeer@apus.edu
GEER, Nathan ... 503-375-7010 ... 415 F ngeer@corban.edu
GEFELL, Michele, D ... 315-786-2271 ... 337 F mgefell@sunyjefferson.edu
GEFFERT, Bryn ... 413-542-2212 ... 230 A bgeffert@amherst.edu
GEFFNER, Linda, O ... 860-231-5208 ... 95 D lgeffner@usj.edu
GEGENHEIMER BALDASSARO, Sarah ... 202-994-5152 ... 98 C sarahgb@gwu.edu
GEGG-LAPLUME, Tamara ... 314-968-6982 ... 292 J laplume@webster.edu
GEGGIE, Steven ... 847-317-8178 ... 166 E sgeggie@tiu.edu
GEHEBER, Leah ... 225-768-1746 ... 214 C lgeheber@ololcollege.edu
GEHLER, Jan, L ... 480-423-6310 ... 16 C jan.gehler@scottsdalecc.edu
GEHLHAR, Jim ... 252-328-4829 ... 377 E gehlhar@ecu.edu
GEHLHAUSEN, Keith ... 812-488-2943 ... 180 E kg77@evansville.edu
GEHLING, William ... 617-627-3232 ... 245 C bill.gehling@tufts.edu
GEHR, Theresa ... 614-287-2642 ... 389 A tgehr@cscc.edu
GEHRELS, David ... 903-586-5261 ... 490 D dgehrels@lonmorris.edu
GEHRET, Steve ... 423-636-5096 ... 477 A sgehret@tusculum.edu
GEHRICH, Michael, D ... 317-381-6000 ... 181 D mgehrich@vinu.edu
GEHRING, Dale ... 701-858-3375 ... 382 A dale.gehring@minotstateu.edu
GEHRKE, Deb ... 715-232-2312 ... 552 E gehrked@uwstout.edu
GEHRLS, Janet ... 563-441-2455 ... 186 I jgehrls@kucampus.edu
GEHRMAN-ROTTIER, Laura ... 715-346-3811 ... 552 D lgehrman@uwsp.edu
GEIB, Bethany ... 740-857-1311 ... 401 F bgeib@rosedale.edu
GEIB, Christine ... 215-643-8458 ... 430 C geib.c@gmc.edu
GEIER, Cathy ... 202-884-9545 ... 99 H geierc@trinitydc.edu
GEIER, Connie ... 605-626-2415 ... 466 A geierc@northern.edu
GEIER, Nikki ... 620-276-9531 ... 193 C nikki.geier@gcccks.edu
GEIER, Peter, E ... 614-292-2635 ... 398 I geier.10@osu.edu
GEIGER, Andy ... 414-229-5669 ... 551 D geigera@uwm.edu
GEIGER, Don ... 920-693-1378 ... 554 C don.geiger@gotoltc.edu
GEIGER, Haley ... 414-326-2336 ... 547 B hgeiger@ccon.edu
GEIGER, Jim ... 937-327-7430 ... 406 B jgeiger@wittenberg.edu
GEIGER, Martha ... 513-558-0087 ... 403 E geigerml@ucmail.uc.edu
GEIGER, Robin ... 502-597-7014 ... 203 G robin.geiger@kysu.edu
GEIGER, William ... 903-566-7081 ... 506 E wgeiger@uttyler.edu
GEIGLE, Michele, Z ... 727-736-5082 ... 117 G michele_geigle@schiller.edu
GEIL, Carol ... 641-844-5747 ... 186 D carol.geil@iavalley.edu
GEILING, Betty, C ... 914-337-9300 ... 330 G elizabeth.geiling@concordia-ny.edu
GEILING, Bryan, K ... 610-989-1351 ... 450 F bgeiling@vfmac.edu
GEIMAN, Michelle ... 614-251-4597 ... 398 F geimanm@ohiodominican.edu
GEIMER, Jill ... 312-332-0707 ... 166 B
GEIRBOLINI, Rafael ... 787-769-9965 ... 567 C rafael.gierbolini@upr.edu
GEISER, Jeff ... 575-562-2153 ... 318 B jeff.geiser@enmu.edu
GEISER, Laura ... 314-977-2543 ... 289 C geiserla@slu.edu
GEISLER, Michael ... 802-443-5275 ... 514 A geisler@middlebury.edu
GEISLER, Norman, L ... 951-698-6389 ... 77 G
GEISSLER, Gregory, J ... 303-556-6819 ... 86 F ggeissle@msudenver.edu
GEIST, Alan ... 937-766-7768 ... 386 G geista@cedarville.edu
GEIST, Betsy ... 206-268-4904 ... 530 I bgeist@antioch.edu
GEIST, Edward, V ... 203-576-4956 ... 94 F edwgeist@bridgeport.edu
GELAYE, Enku ... 413-254-2300 ... 236 F egelaye@stuaf.umass.edu
GELBKE, Konrad ... 517-355-9671 ... 255 A gelbke@nscl.msu.edu
GELCH, Deborah ... 617-243-2390 ... 236 A dgelch@lasell.edu
GELDART, David ... 617-369-3230 ... 244 E dgeldart@mfa.org
GELDENHUYS, Tammie ... 620-331-4100 ... 193 I tgeldenhuys@indycc.edu
GELDER, Alvern ... 616-957-6045 ... 249 B af094@calvinseminary.edu
GELDER, Minna ... 503-589-7870 ... 414 J minna.gelder@chemeketa.edu
GELDWORTH, Lipa ... 718-853-8500 ... 358 A
GELERNTER, Mark ... 303-556-5938 ... 88 J mark.gelernter@ucdenver.edu
GELETA, Nomsa ... 814-732-2724 ... 442 E ngeleta@edinboro.edu
GELFAND, Jack ... 315-312-2888 ... 354 A jack.gelfand@oswego.edu
GELFAND, M ... 732-364-1220 ... 307 D
GELFER, Miriam ... 617-682-1518 ... 234 E mgelfer@eds.edu
GELFMAN, Arnold, J ... 732-224-2749 ... 308 A agelfman@brookdalecc.edu
GELINAS, Cynthia, B ... 803-641-3609 ... 462 B cindyg@usca.edu
GELINAS, Cynthia, B ... 803-641-2841 ... 462 B cindyg@usca.edu
GELINAS, David ... 704-894-2698 ... 363 I dagelinas@davidson.edu
GELL, Barry ... 518-255-5440 ... 354 E gellbf@cobleskill.edu
GELLE, Mark ... 507-786-3294 ... 271 C gelle@stolaf.edu
GELLER, Jack ... 218-281-8248 ... 271 E gelle045@umn.edu
GELLER, L. Randy ... 541-346-3082 ... 419 B rgeller@uoregon.edu
GELLER, Mark ... 800-371-6105 ... 16 G mark@nationalparalegal.edu
GELLER, Mary, A ... 320-363-5601 ... 262 F mgeller@csbsju.edu
GELLES, Richard, J ... 215-898-5511 ... 448 J gelles@sp2.upenn.edu
GELLIN, Marcia, A ... 716-851-1113 ... 333 A gellin@ecc.edu
GELLMAN-DANLEY, Barbara ... 740-245-7205 ... 404 E bdanley@rio.edu
GELMAN, Sheldon, R ... 212-960-0820 ... 361 M srgelman@yu.edu
GELO, Daniel, J ... 210-458-4359 ... 506 D daniel.gelo@utsa.edu
GELOSO, Lauren ... 914-674-7231 ... 340 F lgeloso@mercy.edu
GELSINGER, Sue ... 610-372-4721 ... 445 C sgelsinger@racc.edu
GELTCH, Wendy ... 863-297-1083 ... 115 C wgeltch@polk.edu
GELVIN, Karen ... 316-323-6915 ... 191 G kgelvin@butlercc.edu
GELY, Gilda, G ... 616-234-3920 ... 251 E ggely@grcc.edu
GEMME, Terese ... 203-392-5499 ... 90 I gemmet1@southernct.edu
GEMPERLINE, Paul ... 252-328-6012 ... 377 E gemperlinep@ecu.edu
GEMPESAW, Bobby ... 513-529-6721 ... 396 E gempescm@muohio.edu
GENANDT, James ... 620-431-2820 ... 195 E jgenandt@neosho.edu
GENAO, Janet ... 813-879-6000 ... 107 A jgenao@cci.edu
GENARD, Daniel, J ... 757-683-3090 ... 522 F dgenard@odu.edu
GENCO, Rosemarie ... 973-720-2107 ... 317 D gencor@wpunj.edu
GENDERNALIK-COOPER, Mary, L ... 540-654-1000 ... 525 D mgendern@umw.edu
GENDRON, Josee ... 530-242-7574 ... 69 D jgendron@shastacollege.edu
GENECIN, Paul ... 203-432-0076 ... 96 A paul.genecin@yale.edu
GENEGA, Paul ... 973-748-9000 ... 307 H paul_genega@bloomfield.edu
GENELIN, Nancy ... 507-389-7228 ... 269 D nancy.genelin@southcentral.edu
GENERALS, Donald ... 609-586-4800 ... 311 B generald@mccc.edu
GENESE, Carol ... 718-933-6700 ... 341 G cgenese@monroecollege.edu
GENET, Robert ... 717-846-5000 ... 452 H
GENGARO, Nicholas ... 973-642-8859 ... 315 C nicholas.gengaro@shu.edu
GENNA, Angela ... 602-285-7357 ... 16 A angela.genna@pcmail.maricopa.edu
GENNARO, Gwen ... 719-255-3153 ... 88 I ggennaro@uccs.edu
GENNARO, Susan ... 617-552-4250 ... 232 B susan.gennaro@bc.edu
GENO, Rita, B ... 802-468-1203 ... 515 D rita.geno@castleton.edu
GENOUS, Zandra ... 847-543-2420 ... 148 B zgenous@clcillinois.edu
GENOVESE, JR., Louis ... 973-877-3040 ... 309 H genovese@essex.edu
GENSHAFT, Judy, L ... 813-974-2791 ... 121 A jgensha@usf.edu
GENSLER, Charlotte ... 505-224-4551 ... 317 K cgensler@cnm.edu
GENSON, Barrett ... 239-590-1520 ... 119 B bgenson@fgcu.edu
GENTHNER, Patricia ... 585-389-2002 ... 342 D pgenthn5@naz.edu
GENTHON, Paulette ... 402-556-4456 ... 300 D info@ucha.com
GENTILE, Dina, M ... 610-789-6700 ... 445 B dgentile@prismcareerinstitute.edu
GENTILE, James ... 301-431-5454 ... 225 B jgentile@nlc.edu
GENTILE, Kathy, J ... 314-516-6383 ... 291 D gentilek@umsl.edu
GENTILE, Patricia ... 609-463-4507 ... 307 C pgentile@atlantic.edu
GENTILE, Sam, A ... 702-458-9650 ... 303 C
GENTILLON, Jeanne ... 626-529-8079 ... 60 F jgentillon@pacificoaks.edu
GENTLES, Lori ... 415-405-2650 ... 37 B lgentles@sfsu.edu
GENTLEWARRIOR, Sabrina ... 508-531-1429 ... 237 D sgentlewarrior@bridgew.edu
GENTNER, Lisa, K ... 812-246-3301 ... 177 B lgentner@ivytech.edu
GENTRY, Bradley, D ... 217-786-2278 ... 157 B brad.gentry@llcc.edu
GENTRY, Jerry, H ... 270-831-9622 ... 202 D jerry.gentry@kctcs.edu
GENTRY, Jodi, D ... 352-392-4626 ... 120 C jodi-gentry@ufl.edu
GENTRY, Margaret ... 315-859-4615 ... 334 H mgentry@hamilton.edu
GENTRY, Richard, E ... 956-326-2325 ... 497 D rgentry@tamiu.edu
GENTRY, Susan ... 252-335-0821 ... 369 G susan_gentry@albemarle.edu
GENTRY, Vickie ... 318-357-6288 ... 216 B gentry@nsula.edu
GENTRY, W. Marichal ... 203-432-2907 ... 96 A marichal.gentry@yale.edu
GENTRY-BARTH, Danielle ... 513-585-0359 ... 387 D danielle.gentry-barth@thechristhospital.com
GENTRY-EPLEY, Beth ... 816-415-5946 ... 293 C gentry-epleyb@william.jewell.edu
GENTRY-WRIGHT, Susan, C ... 864-833-8100 ... 460 E sgentry-w@presby.edu
GENTSCH, James ... 205-652-3361 ... 9 E jgentsch@uwa.edu
GENTUL, Jack ... 973-596-3466 ... 312 C jack.gentul@njit.edu
GENTZLER, Randall ... 410-617-2345 ... 223 I rdgentzler@loyola.edu
GENUA, Kathy ... 516-918-3626 ... 324 E kgenua@bcl.edu
GENUNG, Bruce ... 760-750-7305 ... 36 C bgenung@csusm.edu
GEOCARIS, Diane, F ... 949-824-2880 ... 74 B dfgeocar@uci.edu
GEOFFRION-SCANNELL, Kathryn ... 978-837-5211 ... 242 A geoffrionsck@merrimack.edu
GEOGHEGAN, Jeffrey, P ... 860-679-3162 ... 95 A geoghegan@uchc.edu
GEOGHEGAN, Michael ... 513-569-1586 ... 387 G michael.geoghegan@cincinnatistate.edu
GEORGALLIS, Christine ... 352-588-8464 ... 116 G christine.georgallis@saintleo.edu
GEORGE, Abraham ... 706-507-8111 ... 127 G george_abraham@columbusstate.edu
GEORGE, Archie, A ... 208-885-7995 ... 144 G archie@uidaho.edu
GEORGE, Carol, S ... 937-766-7900 ... 386 G georgec@cedarville.edu
GEORGE, Charles ... 903-785-7661 ... 492 D cgeorge@parisjc.edu
GEORGE, Chris ... 303-871-4883 ... 89 A chris.george@du.edu
GEORGE, Christi ... 205-652-3840 ... 9 E cjw@uwa.edu
GEORGE, Dennis, K ... 270-745-3570 ... 208 A dennis.george@wku.edu
GEORGE, Douglas, J ... 716-652-8900 ... 325 J dgeorge@cks.edu
GEORGE, Ellen ... 309-999-4580 ... 152 C egeorge@icc.edu
GEORGE, Francis ... 847-566-6401 ... 167 F
GEORGE, Gene ... 316-322-3338 ... 191 G ggeorge@butlercc.edu
GEORGE, Janice, S ... 620-421-6700 ... 194 G janicec@labette.edu
GEORGE, Laura ... 617-873-0170 ... 233 A laura.george@cambridgecollege.edu
GEORGE, LePra ... 312-589-7431 ... 150 G lgeorge@ellis.edu
GEORGE, Lynda ... 859-257-3172 ... 207 D lgeorge@uky.edu
GEORGE, Maggie ... 928-724-6669 ... 13 L mlgeorge@dinecollege.edu
GEORGE, Marie, A ... 610-902-8200 ... 424 B marie.a.george@cabrini.edu
GEORGE, Mertha, V ... 601-877-6154 ... 272 F mgeorge@alcorn.edu
GEORGE, Michael ... 419-517-8990 ... 395 E mgeorge@lourdes.edu
GEORGE, Michel ... 503-768-7850 ... 416 G mgeorge@lclark.edu
GEORGE, Monique ... 646-660-6590 ... 326 C monique.george@baruch.cuny.edu
GEORGE, JR., Orlando, J ... 302-739-4053 ... 96 D pres@dtcc.edu
GEORGE, Pamela ... 216-397-1908 ... 392 L pgeorgemerrill@jcu.edu
GEORGE, Philip, J ... 315-445-4644 ... 338 B georgepj@lemoyne.edu
GEORGE, R. Dillard ... 757-683-4156 ... 522 F rdgeorge@odu.edu
GEORGE, Robert ... 941-756-0690 ... 433 C rgeorge@lecom.edu
GEORGE, Russell ... 970-675-3201 ... 82 H russell.george@cncc.edu
GEORGE, Sandra, B ... 562-951-4700 ... 33 H sgeorge@calstate.edu
GEORGE, Sarah, B ... 801-581-6927 ... 511 C sgeorge@umnh.utah.edu
GEORGE, Sharon, A ... 603-641-7084 ... 305 G sgeorge@anselm.edu

GEORGE, Susan 304-473-8080 545 G
george@wvwc.edu
GEORGE, Tami, B 910-272-3541 373 D
tgeorge@robeson.edu
GEORGE, Thomas 678-891-2500 131 C
thomas.george@gpc.edu
GEORGE, Thomas, F 314-516-5252 291 D
tfgeorge@umsl.edu
GEORGE, Timothy, F 205-726-2632 6 G
tfgeorge@samford.edu
GEORGE, Tom 253-680-7080 531 F
tgeorge@bates.ctc.edu
GEORGE, Varghese, T 706-721-0801 130 D
vgeorge@georgiahealth.edu
GEORGE, Viji, D 914-337-9300 330 G
viji.george@concordia-ny.edu
GEORGE, W. Michael 205-348-7219 8 E
michael.george@ua.edu
GEORGE, William, D 570-577-1228 423 E
wdgeorge@bucknell.edu
GEORGE-TAYLOR,
Mosunmola 423-697-2552 474 D
GEORGENES, George 617-850-1317 235 F
gag@hchc.edu
GEORGES, Anthony, C 314-516-5508 291 D
tony_georges@umsl.edu
GEORGESON, Lance 425-249-4752 538 G
lance.georgeson@tlc.edu
GEORGIOPOULOS,
Michael 407-823-5338 120 B
michaelg@ucf.edu
GEORGIOU, Tina 212-343-1234 341 B
tgeorgiou@mcny.edu
GEPHART, JR.,
George, W 215-895-2000 427 H
GEPPI, Steve 410-386-8524 221 G
sgeppi@carrollcc.edu
GERA, Holly, P 973-655-5234 311 F
gerah@mail.montclair.edu
GERAC, Anna 802-728-1586 516 A
agerac@vtc.edu
GERACI, Richard, V 575-624-8400 319 C
cmdt@nmmi.edu
GERAGHTY, Patricia, L 414-288-3423 548 F
patricia.geraghty@marquette.edu
GERALD, Trudy 619-388-3522 65 F
tgerald@sdccd.edu
GERAMI, Keyvan 314-286-3670 287 G
kgerami@ranken.edu
GERARD, Ada 916-638-1616 50 A
ada_gerard@heald.edu
GERARD, Debra 714-480-7450 63 E
gerard_debra@rsccd.edu
GERARD, Phillip, R 864-242-5100 455 E
GERASSIMIDES, Gus 859-985-3158 199 A
gus_gerassimides@berea.edu
GERATY, Brent G, T 269-471-6530 247 D
bgeraty@andrews.edu
GERBASI, Iris 714-997-6676 39 F
gerbasi@chapman.edu
GERBER, Brian 229-333-5925 139 C
blgerber@valdosta.edu
GERBER, Cheryl 724-946-7102 451 C
gerberca@westminster.edu
GERBER, Elizabeth, L 815-599-3421 152 B
liz.gerber@highland.edu
GERBER, Joanna 310-578-1080 28 L
jgerber@antiochla.edu
GERBER, Linda 971-722-4357 419 G
linda.gerber@pcc.edu
GERBER, Michael, A 718-780-7923 324 F
michael.gerber@brooklaw.edu
GERBERRY, Jeffrey 614-947-6007 391 B
jeffrey.gerberry@franklin.edu
GERBOTH, Karen, L 937-327-6141 406 B
kgerboth@wittenberg.edu
GERBSCH, Julie 912-344-2600 124 G
julie.gerbsch@armstrong.edu
GERCH, Sheila 914-674-7339 340 F
sgersh@mercy.edu
GERDA, Joe 661-362-3452 41 I
joe.gerda@canyons.edu
GERDEMAN, Penny 419-434-4558 404 B
gerdeman@findlay.edu
GERDES, Darin 843-574-3220 456 B
dgerdes@csuniv.edu
GERDES, Neil, W 773-256-3000 158 B
ngerdes@meadville.edu
GERDES, Neil, W 773-896-2400 146 H
ngerdes@ctschicago.edu
GERDICH, Michael 724-805-2895 446 E
michael.gerdich@email.stvincent.edu
GERDING, Melissa, D 610-519-4044 450 H
melissa.gerding@villanova.edu
GERDRUM, Kacie 541-684-7288 417 F
kgerdrum@nwcu.edu
GERE, Nicholas 207-602-2011 221 A
ngere@une.edu
GEREAUX, Teresa, T 540-375-2282 523 G
gereaux@roanoke.edu
GEREMIA, Kenneth 413-528-7291 230 F
kgeremia@simons-rock.edu
GERENA, Elizabeth 787-850-9301 567 E
elizabeth.gerena@upr.edu

GERETY, RSM, Jane 401-341-2337 454 D
jane.gerety@salve.edu
GERETY, Mason 928-523-2012 16 I
mason.gerety@nau.edu
GERHARD, Karen 563-588-6444 183 E
karen.gerhard@clarke.edu
GERHARDT, Mark 605-995-7174 464 F
mark.gerhardt@mitchelltech.edu
GERHARDT, Winifred 440-826-2222 384 K
wgerhard@bw.edu
GERHART, Phillip, M 812-488-2651 180 E
pg3@evansville.edu
GERHARTER, Janelle 402-844-7063 299 I
janelle@northeast.edu
GERIG, Bev 541-917-4857 416 I
gerigb@linnbenton.edu
GERIGUIS, David 951-785-2002 53 E
dgerigui@lasierra.edu
GERIK, Debbie 254-659-7704 487 G
debgerik@hillcollege.edu
GERING, Jon 660-785-4248 290 G
jgering@truman.edu
GERITY, Patrick, E 724-925-4219 451 E
gerityk@wccc.edu
GERITY, Peter, F 575-835-5227 319 A
vpaa@admin.nmt.edu
GERKEN, Keith 907-796-6496 11 A
william.gerken@uas.alaska.edu
GERKEN, Robert 484-664-3110 437 C
rgerken@muhlenberg.edu
GERKEN, Stacey 715-346-3553 552 D
sgerken@uwsp.edu
GERKIN, David 623-845-4762 15 H
david.gerkin@gcmail.maricopa.edu
GERKIN, Jeffrey, G 865-974-3131 477 D
jgerkin@utk.edu
GERKO, Danielle 814-262-3825 441 A
dgerko@pennhighlands.edu
GERL, Beth, R 410-871-3199 224 C
bgerl@mcdaniel.edu
GERLACH, David, M 315-386-7082 355 E
gerlach@canton.edu
GERLACH, Jeanne, M 817-272-5476 505 C
gerlach@uta.edu
GERLICA, Reg 313-845-9605 252 B
rgerlica@hfcc.edu
GERLICH, Bella 907-474-7224 10 I
bkgerlich@alaska.edu
GERLING, Angela 573-592-5245 293 B
angela.gerling@westminster-mo.edu
GERMAIN, George, F 989-328-1275 255 E
georgeg@montcalm.edu
GERMAN, Dana, B 610-921-7225 421 E
dgerman@alb.edu
GERMAN, Deborah 407-266-1000 120 B
deborah.german@ucf.edu
GERMAN, Lisa 256-352-8306 10 A
lisa.german@wallacestate.edu
GERMAN, JR.,
Robert (Chip) 717-871-5844 443 D
robert.german@millersville.edu
GERMANO, William 212-353-4274 331 A
germano@cooper.edu
GERMANY, Sylvia 256-726-8218 6 C
germany@oakwood.edu
GERN, William, A 307-766-5353 556 H
willger@uwyo.edu
GERNAND, Peg 812-280-7271 178 I
peg.gernand@ottawa.edu
GERNAND, Peg 812-280-7271 195 I
peg.gernand@ottawa.edu
GERNERT, Maureen, C 203-837-8266 91 A
gernertm@wcsu.edu
GERNES, Todd, S 508-565-1840 245 A
tgernes@stonehill.edu
GERRITY, Nancy 405-682-7587 409 F
ngerrity@occc.edu
GERROW, Robin 419-372-8589 385 E
robstan@bgsu.edu
GERRY, Thomas 518-828-4181 330 E
gerry@sunycgcc.edu
GERSEY, Martin, L 574-520-5522 174 E
mgersey@iusb.edu
GERSH, Geniene, M 269-387-1000 260 C
geniene.m.gersh@wmich.edu
GERSHEN, Jay, A 330-325-6263 397 D
president@neomed.edu
GERSHON, I. Richard 662-915-6900 277 D
igershon@olemiss.edu
GERSHOWITZ, Whitney 804-862-6461 523 F
wgershowitz@rbc.edu
GERSICH, Frank 309-457-2119 158 H
fgersich@monmouthcollege.edu
GERST, Bernard 410-704-3383 228 E
bgerst@towson.edu
GERSTEIN, Dean 909-607-9406 40 F
dean.gerstein@cgu.edu
GERSTER, Patrick 408-298-2181 67 D
patrick.gerster@sjcc.edu
GERSZEWSKI,
Raymond, H 701-788-4770 381 H
ray.gerszewski@mayvillestate.edu
GERTS, John 231-843-5850 260 B
jkgerts@westshore.edu

GERTSMAN, Josh 253-833-9111 534 H
jgerstman@greenriver.edu
GERTSON, Katherine 212-799-5000 337 H
GERTZ, Genie 510-659-6272 59 J
ggertz@ohlone.edu
GERTZ, Tanya, M 563-387-1536 187 D
gertta01@luther.edu
GERVAIS, Carly 504-278-6421 211 E
cgervais@nunez.edu
GERVASI, Robert 217-228-5432 161 F
gervasi@quincy.edu
GERVIN, Dennis 209-588-5115 80 G
gervind@yosemite.edu
GERZINA, Holly 330-325-6740 397 D
hgerzina@neomed.edu
GESO, Cristina, A 215-895-1674 427 H
cag58@drexel.edu
GESSELL, Donna 706-864-1528 134 G
dgessell@northgeorgia.edu
GESSFORD, Sheryl 916-485-6045 56 A
gessfos@arc.losrios.edu
GESSLER, Klaus 845-431-8939 332 D
gessler@sunydutchess.edu
GESSNER, David 715-836-5182 551 A
gessnedp@uwec.edu
GESSNER, James, C 570-389-4105 441 F
jgessner@bloomu.edu
GESSNER, James, R 218-722-4000 263 E
jimg@dbumn.edu
GESTRINE, Beverley 360-736-9391 532 D
bgestrine@centralia.edu
GESTRING, Sheila 605-677-5255 465 G
sheila.gestring@usd.edu
GETCHELL, Stephanie, L 919-530-7824 378 B
getchells@nccu.edu
GETSOM, Denise 304-793-6845 544 E
dgetson@osteo.wvsom.edu
GETTER, Angela 662-254-3490 276 B
angela.getter@mvsu.edu
GETTING, Kris, A 651-962-6168 272 B
kagetting@stthomas.edu
GETTY, Larry, R 785-628-4513 192 I
lgetty@fhsu.edu
GETZ, Dan 715-634-4790 547 J
dgetz@lco-college.edu
GETZ, Karen 724-266-3838 448 H
kgetz@tsm.edu
GETZ, Kathleen, A 312-915-6115 157 C
kgetz@luc.edu
GETZ, Roger 302-736-2455 97 A
getz@wesley.edu
GETZEN, Bruce 808-245-8355 142 C
bgetzen@hawaii.edu
GEU, Thomas 605-677-5443 465 G
thomas.geu@usd.edu
GEUDER, Maridith, W 662-325-7454 275 F
geuderm@ur.msstate.edu
GEWISSLER, Laura 732-987-2425 310 C
gewisslerl@georgian.edu
GEYE, Trina 254-968-9400 497 A
geye@tarleton.edu
GEYER, Dennis 916-278-3901 36 A
dgeyer@csus.edu
GEYER, Enid 518-262-5586 322 D
geyere@mail.amc.edu
GEYER, Enid 518-262-6008 322 D
geyere@mail.amc.edu
GEYER, Jonathan 304-829-7645 540 H
jgeyer@bethanywv.edu
GEYER, Mariann 412-392-3805 445 A
mgeyer@pointpark.edu
GHADIALI, Khushroo 575-234-9414 319 F
khushroo@nmsu.edu
GHAHRAMANI, Saeed 413-782-1218 246 A
sghahram@wne.edu
GHAN, Landon 417-268-6113 278 J
lghan@gobbc.edu
GHAN, Mark 775-445-4237 303 B
mark_ghan@wnc.edu
GHANEM, Salma, I 989-774-1885 249 C
ghane1si@cmich.edu
GHANNADIAN, F. Frank 813-253-6221 123 A
fghannadian@ut.edu
GHARAHBAGHIAN,
Mohsen 858-499-0202 41 G
mohseng@coleman.edu
GHARAKHANIAN, Anahid 213-738-6786 71 E
academicaffairs@swlaw.edu
GHARIB, Morteza 626-395-6365 32 H
vpr@caltech.edu
GHAZARIAN, Esther, A 781-768-7280 244 A
esther.ghazarian@regiscollege.edu
GHAZVINI, Mariam 510-592-9688 59 G
mariam@npu.edu
GHEE, Harry 910-323-5614 363 A
GHILANI, Mary 570-740-0456 435 C
mghilani@luzerne.edu
GHILZAI, Naushad 818-299-5500 78 A
nghilzai@westcoastuniversity.edu
GHIO, Frederick, W 401-456-8201 454 A
fghio@ric.edu
GHISELLI, Nina 415-955-2164 27 F
nghiselli@alliant.edu

GHOLKAR, Girija, V 212-678-8023 337 G
gigholkar@jtsa.edu
GHOLSON, Shari 270-534-3372 203 E
shari.gholson@kctcs.edu
GHOLSTON, Brandon 770-394-8300 125 A
bgholston@aii.edu
GHORAYEB, Samir 409-984-6484 501 C
samir.ghorayeb@lamarpa.edu
GHORI, Aisha 312-467-2309 146 F
aghori@thechicagoschool.edu
GHOSH, Jayati 415-485-3238 45 C
jayati.ghosh@domincan.edu
GHOSH, Sibdas 415-482-3583 45 C
sibdas.ghosh@dominican.edu
GHOUS, Mostafa 707-864-7000 70 A
mostafa.ghous@solano.edu
GHRIGA, Mohammed 718-488-1159 338 G
mohammed.ghriga@liu.edu
GIACCHETTI, Richard 408-554-4982 68 C
rgiacchetti@scu.edu
GIACCHINO, Mike 305-949-9500 106 B
mgiacchino@cci.edu
GIACOBBE, Jeff 973-655-5373 311 F
giacobbej@mail.montclair.edu
GIACOMELLI, Marie, A 217-793-4201 162 G
mgiacomelli@robertmorris.edu
GIACOMINO, Dennis 419-267-1356 397 E
dgiacomino@northweststate.edu
GIACONA, Nick 505-984-6110 320 C
ngiacona@sjcsf.edu
GIAMARTINO, Gary, A 618-650-3823 165 C
ggiamar@siue.edu
GIAMBELLUCA, Russell 209-667-3077 36 D
rgiambelluca@csustan.edu
GIAMBRA, Leonard, M 860-701-6679 558 H
leonard.m.giambra@uscg.mil
GIAMPAOLI, Michael, J 203-576-4168 94 F
gmichael@bridgeport.edu
GIAMPAPA, Heather 215-780-1391 446 G
hgiampapa@salus.edu
GIAMPIETRO, Michael 413-565-1000 230 G
mgiampietro@baypath.edu
GIANCHETTA, Larry, D 406-243-4831 294 I
larry.gianchetta@business.umt.edu
GIANCOLI, Adriana, F 607-735-1855 332 I
agiancoli@elmira.edu
GIANETTI, Natalie 517-750-1200 258 D
ngianetti@arbor.edu
GIANNATTASIO, Joseph 305-428-5700 113 I
giannatj@aii.edu
GIANNET, Stanley, M 352-797-5001 114 F
giannes@phcc.edu
GIANNETTI, Kevin 718-855-3661 336 D
kgiannetti@idc.edu
GIANNINI, Tula 718-636-3702 346 D
tgiannin@pratt.edu
GIANNOTTI, Louis, J 410-293-1400 559 B
giannott@usna.edu
GIANOTTI, Margaret 541-278-5775 414 G
mgianotti@bluecc.edu
GIANOUSSOPOULOS,
Denise 310-665-6962 60 B
dgianoussopoulos@otis.edu
GIAQUINTO, Thomas 518-244-4547 348 A
giaqut@sage.edu
GIARDINA, Dolores 610-436-2728 444 A
dgiardina@wcupa.edu
GIARDINA, Nancy 616-331-2400 251 F
giardinn@gvsu.edu
GIARDINA, Richard 510-261-8500 61 G
richard.giardina@patten.edu
GIARRUSSO, Denise, J 904-632-5007 109 F
dgiarrus@fscj.edu
GIARRUSSO, John 518-956-8090 351 E
jgiarrusso@uamail.albany.edu
GIAUQUE, Margie, T 218-755-2038 265 I
mgiauque@bemidjistate.edu
GIBB, Julie 309-341-5242 146 D
jgibb@sandburg.edu
GIBB, Katharine 864-503-5444 463 B
kgibb@uscupstate.edu
GIBBEL, Mark 646-660-6067 326 C
mark.gibbel@baruch.cuny.edu
GIBBENS, Charlie, E 915-747-5352 506 B
cegibbens@utep.edu
GIBBENS, Susan 860-512-3680 91 F
sgibbens@mcc.commnet.edu
GIBBINS, Debbie 713-646-1889 494 I
dgibbins@stcl.edu
GIBBONS, Arthur 845-758-7442 323 D
gibbons@bard.edu
GIBBONS, Charlie 334-229-4250 1 C
cgibbons@alasu.edu
GIBBONS, Dennis 315-792-5361 341 E
dgibbons@mvcc.edu
GIBBONS, Earl, F 360-650-3308 539 F
earl.gibbons@wwu.edu
GIBBONS, Jeremy 802-447-4696 514 F
jgibbons@svc.edu
GIBBONS, Kari 630-829-6306 145 G
kgibbons@ben.edu
GIBBONS, Michael 540-261-4371 524 H
michael.gibbons@svu.edu
GIBBONS, Michael, P 570-348-6221 435 F
gibbons@marywood.edu

GILL, Allison ... 978-837-5174 ... 242 A
gilla@merrimack.edu

GILL, Ann, M ... 970-491-5421 ... 83 F
ann.gill@colostate.edu

GILL, Anne, M ... 617-989-4193 ... 245 F
gilla@wit.edu

GILL, Barbara, A ... 301-314-8350 ... 227 B
bgill@umd.edu

GILL, Barbara, J ... 850-201-6570 ... 122 A
gillb@tcc.fl.edu

GILL, Chris, G ... 509-313-3827 ... 534 F
gill@its.gonzaga.edu

GILL, D. Christopher ... 573-288-6322 ... 280 I
cgill@culver.edu

GILL, Dennis ... 541-881-5915 ... 420 E
dgill@tvcc.cc

GILL, Diane, E ... 717-531-4103 ... 440 A
deg9@psu.edu

GILL, Jamie, W ... 727-864-8337 ... 105 E
gilljw@eckerd.edu

GILL, Janet ... 712-274-6400 ... 190 B
janet.gill@witcc.edu

GILL, Jeffery, A ... 574-372-5100 ... 171 H
gillja@grace.edu

GILL, Keith ... 202-885-3001 ... 97 D
gill@american.edu

GILL, Lanae ... 313-993-1230 ... 258 G
gilla@udmercy.edu

GILL, Lee, A ... 330-972-7522 ... 403 B
lee16@uakron.edu

GILL, Michele ... 308-345-8119 ... 298 H
gillm@mpcc.edu

GILL, Michele ... 308-345-3600 ... 298 H
gillm@mpcc.edu

GILL, Nancy ... 805-437-8456 ... 34 B
nancy.gill@csuci.edu

GILL, Nicholas ... 207-216-4467 ... 219 C
ngill@yccc.edu

GILL, Rebecca ... 828-884-8233 ... 362 H
rebecca.gill@brevard.edu

GILL, Robert ... 301-624-2719 ... 222 G
bgill@frederick.edu

GILL, Russell ... 480-515-7648 ... 149 B
rgill@devry.edu

GILL, Ruth ... 410-334-2928 ... 229 E
rgill@worwic.edu

GILL, Sandra ... 630-829-6216 ... 145 G
sgill@ben.edu

GILL, Sean, P ... 860-444-8201 ... 558 H
sean.p.gill@uscg.mil

GILL, Steven ... 609-258-3466 ... 312 G
sgill@princeton.edu

GILL, Tom ... 503-338-2368 ... 415 B
tgill@clatsopcc.edu

GILL-JACOBSON, Roseanne ... 419-824-3829 ... 395 E
rgill-jacobson@lourdes.edu

GILLAHAN, Sheilah ... 731-286-3316 ... 475 B
gillahan@dscc.edu

GILLAN, Christine ... 302-858-5475 ... 96 E
cgillan1@dtcc.edu

GILLAN, Maria ... 973-684-5904 ... 312 E
mgillan@pccc.edu

GILLARD, Natalie ... 575-461-4413 ... 318 G
natalieg@mesalands.edu

GILLARDI, Michael ... 401-598-1450 ... 453 E
mgillardi@jwu.edu

GILLASPIE, Ray ... 270-824-8592 ... 202 G
ray.gillaspie@kctcs.edu

GILLE, Chaudron ... 678-717-3835 ... 129 G
cgille@gsc.edu

GILLECE, Nancy, E ... 301-696-3710 ... 223 C
gillece@hood.edu

GILLELAND, Drew ... 541-552-6319 ... 419 A
gilliland@sou.edu

GILLEN, Ann ... 209-946-2135 ... 76 A
agillen@pacific.edu

GILLEN, Dan ... 319-296-4268 ... 185 F
daniel.gillen@hawkeyecollege.edu

GILLEN, Edward ... 203-582-8471 ... 93 H
edward.gllen@quinnipiac.edu

GILLEN, Jonathan ... 541-881-5842 ... 420 E
jgillen@tvcc.cc

GILLEN-CARYL, Shawn ... 315-498-2537 ... 345 D
gillencs@sunyocc.edu

GILLER, Patricia ... 312-777-8562 ... 153 B
pgiller@aii.edu

GILLES, Barbara, L ... 412-578-6123 ... 424 I
gillesbl@carlow.edu

GILLESPIE, Bart ... 678-839-6582 ... 139 A
bgillesp@westga.edu

GILLESPIE, SJ, C. Kevin ... 610-660-1200 ... 446 C
cgillesp@sju.edu

GILLESPIE, Christine ... 215-968-8718 ... 423 F
gillespi@bucks.edu

GILLESPIE, David, M ... 301-687-4396 ... 228 C
dgillespie@frostburg.edu

GILLESPIE, Donald, A ... 718-817-3190 ... 334 C
gillespie@fordham.edu

GILLESPIE, Gregory ... 928-717-7778 ... 19 C
greg.gillespie@yc.edu

GILLESPIE, Joseph, E ... 610-558-5641 ... 437 D
gillespj@neumann.edu

GILLESPIE, Maggie ... 570-389-4950 ... 441 F
mgillesp@bloomu.edu

GILLESPIE, Melanie ... 864-644-5504 ... 461 B
mlgillespie@swu.edu

GILLESPIE, Michael ... 212-220-8323 ... 326 D
mgillespie@bmcc.cuny.edu

GILLESPIE, Nancy, N ... 260-399-7700 ... 181 A
ngillespie@sf.edu

GILLESPIE, Pamela ... 212-650-7271 ... 326 G
prgcc@ccny.cuny.edu

GILLESS, J. Keith ... 510-642-7171 ... 73 H
gilless@berkeley.edu

GILLETT, Charisse, L ... 859-252-0361 ... 204 B
cgillett@lextheo.edu

GILLETT, William ... 603-668-2211 ... 305 I
w.gillett@snhu.edu

GILLETTE, Donna ... 207-947-4591 ... 217 D
dgillette@bealcollege.edu

GILLETTE, Emily ... 203-365-7671 ... 94 B
gillettee@sacredheart.edu

GILLETTE, Jack ... 617-349-8401 ... 236 B
jgillett@lesley.edu

GILLETTE, Kimberly ... 218-282-8442 ... 271 E
gillette@umn.edu

GILLETTE, Lynn ... 775-831-7509 ... 303 E
lgillette@sierranevada.edu

GILLETTE, Maureen, D ... 773-442-5500 ... 160 A
m-gillette@neiu.edu

GILLETTE, Susan ... 410-706-5353 ... 227 C
sgillett@umaryland.edu

GILLETTE, Vivian ... 701-255-3285 ... 383 G
vgillette@uttc.edu

GILLEY, Michael ... 276-523-2400 ... 527 D
mgilley@me.vccs.edu

GILLIAM, Cynthia ... 832-813-6512 ... 490 E
cynthia.f.gilliam@lonestar.edu

GILLIAM, JR., Franklin, D ... 310-206-7568 ... 74 C
fgilliam@conet.ucla.edu

GILLIAM, Janice, H ... 423-323-0201 ... 475 F
jhgilliam@northeaststate.edu

GILLIAM, Jerry ... 270-707-3741 ... 202 E
jerry.gilliam@kctcs.edu

GILLIAM, Kevin, E ... 616-538-2330 ... 251 D
kgilliam@gbcol.edu

GILLIAM, Michael ... 615-361-7555 ... 468 E
mgilliam@daymarinstitute.edu

GILLIAM, Thomas, J ... 850-484-1690 ... 115 B
tgilliam@pensacolastate.edu

GILLIAM, Tom ... 850-484-1500 ... 115 B
tgilliam@pensacolastate.edu

GILLICK, Megan ... 410-617-2290 ... 223 I
mgillick@loyola.edu

GILLIES, Cheryl ... 661-255-1050 ... 32 F
cgillies@calarts.edu

GILLIGAN, Patrick, K ... 740-427-5643 ... 394 C
gilliganp@kenyon.edu

GILLIGAN, Thomas, J ... 402-466-4774 ... 297 G
thomas.gilligan@doane.edu

GILLIGAN, Thomas, W ... 512-471-5058 ... 505 D
dean.gilligan@mccombs.utexas.edu

GILLIGAN, William ... 617-824-8190 ... 234 B
william_gilligan@emerson.edu

GILLILAND, Christie ... 253-833-9111 ... 534 H
cgilliland@greenriver.edu

GILLILAND, Jane, A ... 607-587-3979 ... 355 C
gillilja@alfredstate.edu

GILLIN, Gary ... 507-537-6253 ... 269 E
gary.gillin@smsu.edu

GILLING RAYNOR, Beatrice ... 718-951-6545 ... 326 F
braynor@brooklyn.cuny.edu

GILLINGWATER, Danielle ... 510-574-1100 ... 44 F
dgillingwater@devry.edu

GILLIS, Arthur ... 225-771-5050 ... 214 I
arthur_gillis@subr.edu

GILLIS, Chester ... 202-687-4259 ... 98 D
gillisc@georgetown.edu

GILLIS, Graham ... 501-450-3181 ... 25 H
ggillis@uca.edu

GILLIS, Ida ... 219-980-6853 ... 174 B
ilgillis@iun.edu

GILLIS, Rick, D ... 414-955-6333 ... 548 G
rgillis@mcw.edu

GILLISPIE, Charley, E ... 219-464-5215 ... 181 C
charley.gillispie@valpo.edu

GILLISS, Buster ... 701-224-5512 ... 382 D
buster.gilliss@bismarckstate.edu

GILLISS, Catherine ... 919-684-3786 ... 364 C
catherine.gilliss@duke.edu

GILLMAN, Patricia ... 660-596-7379 ... 290 B
pgillman@sfccmo.edu

GILLMAN, Rick ... 219-464-6718 ... 181 C
rick.gillman@valpo.edu

GILLMING, Kenneth, D ... 617-364-3510 ... 232 A
kgillming@boston.edu

GILLOOLY, Patrick ... 617-258-9276 ... 241 D
pgill@mit.edu

GILLUM, Danny ... 620-227-9269 ... 192 E
dgillum@dc3.edu

GILLUM, Debra ... 574-257-3369 ... 169 I
gillumd@bethelcollege.edu

GILLUS, Raynaldo ... 937-376-6205 ... 387 A
rgillus@centralstate.edu

GILMAN, Frederick, J ... 412-268-5124 ... 424 J
gilman@andrew.cmu.edu

GILMAN, Jean ... 314-977-3415 ... 289 C
jgilman2@slu.edu

GILMAN, Josephine ... 301-387-3091 ... 222 H
josephine.gilman@garrettcollege.edu

GILMAN, Mary, A ... 864-597-4010 ... 463 G
gilmanaf@wofford.edu

GILMAN, Regis ... 828-227-7397 ... 380 A
rgilman@wcu.edu

GILMAN, Roger ... 360-650-3681 ... 539 F
roger.gilman@wwu.edu

GILMAN, Sarah, S ... 808-455-0497 ... 141 H
sgilman@hawaii.edu

GILMAN, Sharon ... 520-515-5382 ... 13 E
gilmans@cochise.edu

GILMARTIN, Maureen, A ... 410-827-5842 ... 222 B
mgilmartin@chesapeake.edu

GILMARTIN, Michael ... 831-646-4039 ... 57 G
mgilmartin@mpc.edu

GILMER, Elizabeth ... 478-289-2037 ... 129 B
egilmer@ega.edu

GILMER, Francene ... 859-257-1564 ... 207 D
fgi222@uky.edu

GILMER, Garrett ... 419-372-2081 ... 385 E
ggilmer@bgsu.edu

GILMER, Larry ... 910-843-5304 ... 367 G

GILMER, Randy, G ... 276-328-0312 ... 525 G
rgg8z@uvawise.edu

GILMER, Shannon ... 404-237-7573 ... 126 B
sgilmer@bauder.edu

GILMORE, Becky ... 913-360-7578 ... 191 A
bgilmore@benedictine.edu

GILMORE, Calvin, L ... 336-272-7102 ... 364 G
gilmorec@greensboro.edu

GILMORE, Dan ... 856-256-4684 ... 314 A
gilmore@rowan.edu

GILMORE, David ... 401-254-3843 ... 454 C
dgilmore@rwu.edu

GILMORE, Denise ... 620-431-2820 ... 195 E
dgilmore@neosho.edu

GILMORE, Don ... 661-362-2811 ... 56 G
dgilmore@masters.edu

GILMORE, Elizabeth ... 575-758-8914 ... 318 H
info@midwiferycollege.org

GILMORE, George ... 603-535-2846 ... 307 A
gtgilmore@plymouth.edu

GILMORE, Grover, C ... 216-368-2270 ... 386 F
gcg@case.edu

GILMORE, Jennifer, D ... 812-888-5332 ... 181 D
jgilmore@vinu.edu

GILMORE, John, W ... 609-497-7705 ... 312 F
john.gilmore@ptsem.edu

GILMORE, Kevin, P ... 913-971-3294 ... 195 D
kgilmore@mnu.edu

GILMORE, Laurie, A ... 518-438-3111 ... 340 A
laurieg@mariacollege.edu

GILMORE, Maureen ... 585-266-0430 ... 333 D
mgilmore@cci.edu

GILMORE, Rick ... 816-271-4226 ... 286 G
gilmore@missouriwestern.edu

GILMORE, Rick ... 816-271-4527 ... 286 G
gilmore@missouriwestern.edu

GILMORE, Robert ... 914-323-5357 ... 339 J
robert.gilmore@mville.edu

GILMORE, Robert, F ... 203-576-4649 ... 94 F
rgilmore@bridgeport.edu

GILMORE, Sherri ... 802-485-2001 ... 514 C
sgilmore@norwich.edu

GILMOUR, Allan ... 313-577-2230 ... 260 A
allan.gilmour@wayne.edu

GILMOUR, Davie, J ... 570-320-2400 ... 438 G
djg120@psu.edu

GILMOUR, Davie Jane ... 570-326-3761 ... 440 L
dgilmour@pct.edu

GILNER, David ... 513-487-3273 ... 335 B
dgilner@huc.edu

GILNETT, Jennifer, J ... 206-281-2974 ... 537 H
jgilnett@spu.edu

GILOT, Sandra ... 973-618-3353 ... 308 C
sgilot@caldwell.edu

GILOTH, Copper, F ... 413-545-4833 ... 236 F
giloth@oit.umass.edu

GILPATRICK, Russell ... 623-572-3804 ... 16 E
rgilpa@midwestern.edu

GILPIN, Sue ... 309-268-8139 ... 151 I
sue.gilpin@heartland.edu

GILRAIN, Tim ... 267-234-2028 ... 19 A
tim.gilrain@phoenix.edu

GILROY, Janice ... 914-606-6610 ... 360 E
janice.gilroy@sunywcc.edu

GILROY, Maryellen ... 518-783-2328 ... 350 I
mgilroy@siena.edu

GILSON, David ... 216-791-5000 ... 388 C
david.gilson@case.edu

GILSON, Ken ... 562-903-4870 ... 31 A
ken.gilson@biola.edu

GILSON, William, C ... 505-662-0339 ... 321 E
wgilson@unm.edu

GILSRUD, Linda, J ... 218-755-3966 ... 265 I
lgilsrud@bemidjistate.edu

GILSRUD, Tim ... 218-755-2220 ... 265 I
tgilsrud@bemidjistate.edu

GILSTRAP, Don ... 316-978-3586 ... 198 A
don.gilstrap@wichita.edu

GILTZ, Scott ... 503-594-3440 ... 415 A
scottg@clackamas.edu

GILYARD, Reginald ... 714-997-6684 ... 39 F

GIMA, Wesley, T ... 671-735-3025 ... 559 E
wesley.gima@guamcc.edu

GIMENEZ, Clara ... 802-831-1323 ... 515 B
cgimenez@vermontlaw.edu

GIN, David ... 510-430-3264 ... 57 D
dgin@mills.edu

GINDELE, Linda, K ... 513-556-1301 ... 403 D
linda.gindele@uc.edu

GINDER, Amy ... 775-445-3240 ... 303 B
aginder@wnc.edu

GINDER, Bernice ... 732-445-1749 ... 314 B
ginder@rutgers.edu

GINDER, Greg ... 317-955-6018 ... 177 I
gginder@marian.edu

GINDER, Terry ... 212-217-4260 ... 333 F
terry_ginder@fitnyc.edu

GINES, Joan, E ... 801-585-9144 ... 511 C
joan.gines@utah.edu

GINES, Scott ... 361-593-2414 ... 498 D
david.gines@tamuk.edu

GINEVAN, Douglas, W ... 207-786-6093 ... 217 C
dginevan@bates.edu

GINGERELLA, David ... 978-556-3924 ... 240 E
dgingerella@necc.mass.edu

GINGERICH, Jeffrey ... 610-902-8302 ... 424 B
jpg722@cabrini.edu

GINGERICH, Orval, J ... 612-330-1383 ... 261 B
gingerio@augsburg.edu

GINGERICH, Samuel ... 605-773-3455 ... 465 F
samg@sdbor.edu

GINGERICH, Willard, P ... 973-655-4383 ... 311 F
gingerichw@mail.montclair.edu

GINGRAS, Gregory ... 510-869-1589 ... 64 J
ggingras@samuelmerritt.edu

GINNETTI, Philip, E ... 814-732-2729 ... 442 E
provost@edinboro.edu

GINNEY, Monica ... 859-344-3346 ... 206 I
monica.ginney@thomasmore.edu

GINSBERG, Mark, R ... 703-993-2004 ... 519 E
mginsber@gmu.edu

GINSBERG, Rick ... 785-864-4297 ... 197 B
ginsberg@ku.edu

GINSBURG, Charles, M ... 214-648-8597 ... 507 E
charles.ginsburg@utsouthwestern.edu

GINSBURG, John ... 314-968-7105 ... 292 J
ginsbujo@webster.edu

GINSPARG, Elie ... 847-982-2500 ... 152 A
ginsparg@htc.edu

GINTER, Earl ... 706-542-7575 ... 138 G
eginter@uga.edu

GINTER, Judy ... 912-344-3231 ... 124 G
judy.ginter@armstrong.edu

GINTHER, John ... 253-680-7123 ... 531 F
jginther@bates.ctc.edu

GINTHER, Randy ... 325-649-8036 ... 488 C
rginther@hputx.edu

GINZBERG, Michael, J ... 202-885-1985 ... 97 D
ginzberg@aeerican.edu

GINZBERG, Michael, J ... 212-960-0845 ... 361 M
mginzber@yu.edu

GIOGLIO, Thomas ... 570-422-3642 ... 442 D
tgioglio@po-box.esu.edu

GIOIELLI, Brian ... 612-874-3787 ... 265 C
bgioielli@mcad.edu

GIORDANI, Robert ... 410-704-2096 ... 228 E
rgiordani@towson.edu

GIORDANO, Anthony ... 617-422-7286 ... 243 B
agiordano@nesl.edu

GIORDANO, Chris ... 567-661-7129 ... 400 I
christopher_giordano@owens.edu

GIORDANO, George ... 315-268-7722 ... 329 B
ggiordan@clarkson.edu

GIORDANO, Matthew ... 716-896-0700 ... 359 H
giordano@villa.edu

GIORDANO, Nick ... 575-538-6109 ... 321 I

GIORDANO, Sandra, M ... 610-861-1487 ... 437 A
mesmg02@moravian.edu

GIORGIO, Cynthia, R ... 951-827-7884 ... 74 E
cynthia.giorgio@ucr.edu

GIORLANDO, Michael ... 504-864-7787 ... 213 F
giorland@loyno.edu

GIOVANINI, Mike ... 626-284-2777 ... 27 D
mgiovanini@alliant.edu

GIOVANNELLI, Joseph ... 718-951-5116 ... 326 F
jgiovannelli@brooklyn.cuny.edu

GIOVANNELLI, Tony ... 724-964-8811 ... 437 E
tgiovannelli@ncstrades.edu

GIOVANNINI, Eugene ... 602-286-8008 ... 15 G
e.giovannini@gwmail.maricopa.edu

GIOVANNINI, Joanne ... 570-288-8400 ... 429 D

GIPP, David ... 701-255-3285 ... 383 G
dmgipp@aol.com

GIPP, Freda ... 785-749-8407 ... 193 D
freda.gipp@bie.edu

GIPSON, Amy ... 573-876-7111 ... 290 C
agipson@stephens.edu

GIPSON, William ... 215-898-0809 ... 448 J
wgipson@exchange.upenn.edu

GIRARD, Christine, L ... 480-970-0000 ... 18 E
c.girard@scnm.edu

GIRARD, Don ... 310-434-4287 ... 68 D
girard_donald@smc.edu

GIRARD, Matthew ... 617-369-3871 ... 244 E
mgirard@smfa.edu

GLORIA SAWYER, Rita ..... 323-563-4922 ..... 39 G ritasawyer@cdrewu.edu
GLOSSER, Wade, W ..... 816-654-7717 ..... 283 F bglosser@kcumb.edu
GLOSTER, Sandra ..... 803-780-1019 ..... 463 C sdgloster@voorhees.edu
GLOTZBACH, Philip, A ..... 518-580-5700 ..... 351 B pglotzba@skidmore.edu
GLOVEN, Greta ..... 303-765-3109 ..... 85 D ggloven@iliff.edu
GLOVER, Charles ..... 215-702-4301 ..... 444 B bookstore@pbu.edu
GLOVER, David ..... 757-727-5259 ..... 519 H david.glover@hamptonu.edu
GLOVER, Devon, H ..... 208-524-3000 ..... 143 G devon.glover@my.eitc.edu
GLOVER, Diane, F ..... 919-718-7231 ..... 369 C dglover@cccc.edu
GLOVER, Glenda, B ..... 601-979-2411 ..... 274 G glenda.b.glover@jsums.edu
GLOVER, Jamie, L ..... 580-581-2987 ..... 407 D jglover@cameron.edu
GLOVER, Joseph ..... 352-392-2404 ..... 120 C jglover@aa.ufl.edu
GLOVER, Joseph, M ..... 812-941-2028 ..... 175 A joglover@ius.edu
GLOVER, Nathaniel ..... 904-470-8010 ..... 105 G n.glover@ewc.edu
GLOVER, Paula ..... 660-263-4110 ..... 286 H paulag@macc.edu
GLOVER, Shirley ..... 478-988-6890 ..... 134 C sglover@middlegatech.edu
GLOVER-BROWN, Michelle ..... 516-876-2787 ..... 353 D brownmi@oldwestbury.edu
GLOWKA, Arthur, W ..... 770-720-5628 ..... 136 C awg@reinhardt.edu
GLUCK, Daniel ..... 916-577-2200 ..... 79 G dgluck@jessup.edu
GLUCK, Scott ..... 412-392-4205 ..... 445 A sgluck@pointpark.edu
GLUCKOWSKY, Moshe, M ..... 718-774-3430 ..... 325 I
GLUSKER, Marjorie ..... 914-606-6585 ..... 360 E marge.glusker@sunywcc.edu
GLYNN, Amy, C ..... 413-545-8500 ..... 236 F aglynn@admin.umass.edu
GLYNN, Christine, L ..... 414-410-4083 ..... 546 G clglynn@stritch.edu
GLYNN, Graham ..... 914-674-7125 ..... 340 F gglynn@mercy.edu
GLYNN, Joan, M ..... 336-272-7710 ..... 364 G joan.glynn@greensboro.edu
GLYNN, John, B ..... 414-410-4313 ..... 546 G jbglynn@stritch.edu
GLYNN, Patrick, M ..... 314-434-2212 ..... 282 I pglynn@hickeycollege.edu
GMEINER, Rebecca ..... 678-466-4145 ..... 127 D rebeccagmeiner@clayton.edu
GMELCH, Walter, H ..... 415-422-2108 ..... 76 E whgmelch@usfca.edu
GMYS, Joshua ..... 724-836-7496 ..... 449 C upgalum@pitt.edu
GNADE, Bruce ..... 972-883-6636 ..... 506 A gnade@utdallas.edu
GNADINGER, Cindy, G ..... 502-272-8259 ..... 198 H cgnadinger@bellarmine.edu
GNAGE, David, C ..... 717-749-6061 ..... 440 B dcg12@psu.edu
GNAN, Peter, D ..... 708-209-3192 ..... 148 E pete.gnan@cuchicago.edu
GNASSO, Emil, A ..... 610-758-3200 ..... 434 E emg3@lehigh.edu
GNECCO, Donald ..... 706-776-0117 ..... 136 A dgnecco@piedmont.edu
GNIADY, Carol ..... 504-762-5498 ..... 210 F cgniad@dcc.edu
GNIEWEK, Julie, A ..... 920-923-8080 ..... 548 E jagniewek78@marianuniversity.edu
GNIOT, Phillip ..... 606-783-2097 ..... 204 I p.gniot@moreheadstate.edu
GOAD, Philip ..... 256-766-6610 ..... 4 C pgoad@hcu.edu
GOAD, William ..... 405-425-1870 ..... 409 E bill.goad@oc.edu
GOAN, Bradley, L ..... 859-233-8300 ..... 207 A bgoan@transy.edu
GOBAR, Angela ..... 601-979-0663 ..... 274 G angela.m.gobar@jsums.edu
GOBBI, Laura ..... 510-430-2112 ..... 57 D lgobbi@mills.edu
GOBBLE, Sheryl ..... 619-388-7428 ..... 65 H sgobble@sdccd.edu
GOBEN, Allen ..... 309-268-8100 ..... 151 I allen.goben@heartland.edu
GOBER, Chris, G ..... 636-922-8211 ..... 288 B cgober@stchas.edu
GOBER, T. Kale ..... 870-230-5072 ..... 21 I gobertk@hsu.edu
GOBLE, Daniel ..... 203-837-8851 ..... 91 A gobled@wcsu.edu
GOBLE, David, S ..... 843-953-7691 ..... 456 C
GOBLET, Lois, E ..... 518-255-5524 ..... 354 E gobletle@cobleskill.edu

GOCHENAUR, Heather, K .. 260-982-5873 ..... 177 H hkgochenaur@manchester.edu
GOCHENAUR, Jack, A ..... 260-982-5245 ..... 177 H jagochenaur@manchester.edu
GOCHNAUER, Richard, D .. 302-356-6795 ..... 97 C richard.d.gochnauer@wilmu.edu
GOCIAL, Tammy ..... 314-529-6893 ..... 284 C tgocial@maryville.edu
GOCKE, Philip ..... 417-833-2551 ..... 279 E pgocke@cbcag.edu
GOCKEN, Drew ..... 515-965-7120 ..... 183 H rdgocken@dmacc.edu
GOCKLEY, Daniel, L ..... 304-367-4216 ..... 543 H dan.gockley@fairmontstate.edu
GODAR, Mark, E ..... 641-269-3300 ..... 185 D godar@grinnell.edu
GODBOLD, Heidi ..... 719-638-6580 ..... 84 I hgodbold@cci.edu
GODBOUT, Muriel ..... 315-364-3356 ..... 360 D mgodbout@wells.edu
GODDARD, Deanna ..... 507-457-2493 ..... 269 G dgoddard@winona.edu
GODDARD, Diane, H ..... 785-864-4904 ..... 197 B dgoddard@ku.edu
GODDARD, Robert ..... 802-773-5900 ..... 513 D robert.goddard@csj.edu
GODDARD, Scott, D ..... 304-637-1352 ..... 541 A goddards@dewv.edu
GODDING, Jesse ..... 972-825-4811 ..... 495 F jgodding@sagu.edu
GODEK, Jim ..... 949-376-6000 ..... 53 F jgodek@lagunacollege.edu
GODENZI, Alberto, A ..... 617-552-6399 ..... 232 B alberto.godenzi@bc.edu
GODES, Iris ..... 508-854-4260 ..... 240 F igodes@qcc.mass.edu
GODFREY, Abby ..... 215-591-5700 ..... 427 B agodfrey@devry.edu
GODFREY, Blanton ..... 919-515-6500 ..... 378 C blanton_godfrey@ncsu.edu
GODFREY, Christian, J ..... 208-524-3000 ..... 143 G christian.godfrey@my.eitc.edu
GODFREY, Christine ..... 415-257-1365 ..... 45 C christine.godfrey@dominican.edu
GODFREY, Eric ..... 206-543-0128 ..... 539 A egodfrey@uw.edu
GODFREY, Herbert, G ..... 570-208-5834 ..... 432 G hggodfre@kings.edu
GODFREY, Robert ..... 928-524-7431 ..... 17 A robert.godfrey@npc.edu
GODFREY, W. Robert ..... 760-480-8474 ..... 78 J bvansolkema@wscal.edu
GODFREY-DAWSON, Angela, R ..... 252-335-0821 ..... 369 G adawson@albemarle.edu
GODIN, Normand ..... 951-222-8307 ..... 64 A
GODIN, Roger, A ..... 717-291-3989 ..... 429 F roger.godin@fandm.edu
GODINA, Estela ..... 312-226-6294 ..... 156 G busofc1@lexingtoncollege.edu
GODINO, Trish ..... 603-271-6984 ..... 304 F tgodino@ccsnh.edu
GODLESKI, Christopher ..... 315-652-6500 ..... 324 L cmgodleski@bryantstratton.edu
GODLESKI, Mark, G ..... 315-445-4520 ..... 338 B godlesmg@lemoyne.edu
GODLEY, Linda ..... 601-304-4300 ..... 272 F godley@alcorn.edu
GODO, James ..... 630-637-5809 ..... 159 G jwgodo@noctrl.edu
GODSEY, Jim ..... 507-288-4563 ..... 263 B library@crossroadscollege.edu
GODSEY, R. Kirby ..... 478-330-5609 ..... 134 A godsey_rk@mercer.edu
GODWIN, Angeline, D ..... 276-656-0201 ..... 527 G agodwin@patrickhenry.edu
GODWIN, Donald, R ..... 619-260-4588 ..... 76 D donald.godwin@sandiego.edu
GODWIN, Jack ..... 916-278-6686 ..... 36 A jgodwin@csus.edu
GODWIN, Joseph, H ..... 616-331-2400 ..... 251 F godwinj@gvsu.edu
GODWIN, Michael, R ..... 662-325-1332 ..... 275 F mgodwin@utc.msstate.edu
GODWIN, Ronald, S ..... 434-582-7600 ..... 520 K rgodwin@liberty.edu
GODWIN, Wendell ..... 580-559-5274 ..... 407 J wgodwin@ecok.edu
GODZWA, Alicia ..... 540-362-6660 ..... 520 A agodzwa@hollins.edu
GOEB, Rick, A ..... 218-755-4022 ..... 265 I rgoeb@bemidjistate.edu
GOEBEL, Jeffrey, D ..... 218-477-2069 ..... 267 F goebelj@mnstate.edu
GOEBEL, Ken ..... 603-358-2378 ..... 306 G kgoebel@keene.edu
GOEBEL, Rob ..... 217-228-5432 ..... 161 F goebero@quincy.edu
GOECKER, James, A ..... 812-877-8894 ..... 179 B james.goecker@rose-hulman.edu
GOEDDE, Tony, G ..... 419-434-4556 ..... 404 B goedde@findlay.edu
GOEDEKE, Allen ..... 336-841-9191 ..... 365 C agoedeke@highpoint.edu

GOEDERT, JoAnn ..... 301-445-1921 ..... 227 A sansbury@usmd.edu
GOEL, Meeta ..... 970-945-8691 ..... 82 G
GOELDNER, Jason ..... 715-365-4534 ..... 555 A jgoeldner@nicoletcollege.edu
GOELLNER, Marilyn ..... 814-732-1778 ..... 442 E mgoellner@edinboro.edu
GOELOE-ALSTON, Hendrina ..... 718-270-1191 ..... 352 D hgoeloe-alston@downstate.edu
GOELZHAUSER, Michael, J ..... 812-464-1717 ..... 181 B mjgoelzh@usi.edu
GOEN, Jennifer ..... 239-590-1020 ..... 119 B jgoen@fgcu.edu
GOEPPINGER, Kathleen, H 630-515-7300 ..... 158 F drgoeppinger@midwestern.edu
GOEPPINGER, Kathleen, H 623-572-3400 ..... 16 E drgoeppinger@midwestern.edu
GOERING, Doug ..... 907-474-7730 ..... 10 I djgoering@alaska.edu
GOERING, Fred ..... 316-284-5250 ..... 191 C fgoering@bethelks.edu
GOERING, Wynn ..... 505-863-7650 ..... 321 D lmraz@gallup.unm.edu
GOERING, Wynn, M ..... 505-277-0896 ..... 321 C wgoering@unm.edu
GOERTEMILLER, Paul ..... 903-510-2389 ..... 503 A pgoe@tjc.edu
GOERTLER, Reed ..... 707-638-5259 ..... 73 A reed.goertler@tu.edu
GOERTZ, Christine ..... 563-884-5159 ..... 188 E christine.goertz@palmer.edu
GOERTZ, Christine, G ..... 563-884-5159 ..... 61 A christine.goertz@palmer.edu
GOERTZ, Christine, G ..... 563-884-5159 ..... 114 E christine.goertz@palmer.edu
GOERTZEN, Leroy ..... 253-759-6104 ..... 415 F lgoertzen@nbs.edu
GOERTZEN, Ryan ..... 918-836-6886 ..... 412 G rgoertzen@mail.spartan.edu
GOERZEN, Les ..... 316-284-5261 ..... 191 C lgoerzen@bethelks.edu
GOETHE, Corey ..... 989-386-6622 ..... 255 C cgoethe@midmich.edu
GOETSCH, Lori, A ..... 785-532-7402 ..... 194 D lgoetsch@ksu.edu
GOETSCHIUS, Susan, C ..... 607-871-2170 ..... 322 E goetschius@alfred.edu
GOETZ, Bruce, P ..... 303-273-3225 ..... 83 B bgoetz@mines.edu
GOETZ, Michael, A ..... 414-847-3305 ..... 549 B mikegoetz@miad.edu
GOETZE, David ..... 810-989-5761 ..... 257 H dpgoetze@sc4.edu
GOETZMAN, David ..... 719-587-7820 ..... 80 L degoetzm@adams.edu
GOEWERT, Ed ..... 618-374-5109 ..... 161 E ed.goewert@principia.edu
GOFF, Allen ..... 836-686-1444 ..... 106 E agoff@cci.edu
GOFF, Anton ..... 301-860-3571 ..... 228 A agoff@bowiestate.edu
GOFF, Catherine ..... 509-359-6362 ..... 533 H cgoff@ewu.edu
GOFF, David ..... 303-724-7304 ..... 88 J david.goff@ucdenver.edu
GOFF, David, W ..... 870-236-6901 ..... 21 E dgoff@crc.edu
GOFF, Gary ..... 865-882-4501 ..... 476 A goffdg@roanestate.edu
GOFF, Karen ..... 732-987-2601 ..... 310 C kgoff@georgian.edu
GOFF, Kathleen ..... 413-542-2226 ..... 230 A kgoff@amherst.edu
GOFF, Michelle ..... 478-289-2095 ..... 129 B mgoff@ega.edu
GOFF, Patricia, A ..... 401-865-1031 ..... 453 H pgoff@providence.edu
GOFF, Susan ..... 707-468-3131 ..... 57 A sgoff@mendocino.edu
GOFF-CREWS, Kimberly, M ..... 203-432-6602 ..... 96 A kimberly.goff-crews@yale.edu
GOFFNETT, Chris ..... 989-386-6622 ..... 255 C cgoffnett@midmich.edu
GOFORTH, Craig ..... 828-689-1405 ..... 366 I cgoforth@mhc.edu
GOGGIN, Megan ..... 312-226-6294 ..... 156 G pr@lexingtoncollege.edu
GOGGIN, Trudi ..... 708-524-6824 ..... 150 C tgoggin@dom.edu
GOGNAT, Tim ..... 937-327-7457 ..... 406 B tgognat@wittenberg.edu
GOGOL, Miriam ..... 914-674-3033 ..... 340 F mgogol@mercy.edu
GOGUE, Jay ..... 334-844-4650 ..... 1 F president@auburn.edu
GOH, Phan ..... 408-260-0208 ..... 47 D sjextension@fivebranches.edu
GOHLKE, Brian, B ..... 608-757-7773 ..... 553 G bgohlke@blackhawk.edu
GOHMANN, Jennifer ..... 502-585-9911 ..... 206 D jgohmann@spalding.edu

GOHN, Sherry ..... 360-442-2216 ..... 535 I sgohn@lowercolumbia.edu
GOIN, Jay ..... 972-385-1055 ..... 19 A jay.goin@phoenix.edu
GOIN, JR., Randy, A ..... 850-245-0466 ..... 118 K randy.goin@flbog.edu
GOINES, Shirley, M ..... 479-968-0399 ..... 20 G sgoines@atu.edu
GOINGS, Amy ..... 253-589-5782 ..... 532 G amy.goings@cptc.edu
GOINGS, Eric ..... 918-335-6257 ..... 411 B egoings@okwu.edu
GOINS, David ..... 409-882-3367 ..... 501 B david.goins@lsco.edu
GOINS, Deb ..... 740-374-8716 ..... 405 G dgoins@wscc.edu
GOINS, Jessica, D ..... 864-488-4590 ..... 459 B jgoins@limestone.edu
GOINS, Scott, E ..... 337-475-5329 ..... 215 G sgoins@mcneese.edu
GOKE, Evelyn ..... 906-487-7272 ..... 251 A evelyn.goke@finlandia.edu
GOKE-PARIOLA, Abiodun . 704-337-2492 ..... 376 A g-p@queens.edu
GOKEL, George, W ..... 314-516-5321 ..... 291 D gokelg@umsl.edu
GOLABEK, Sue ..... 843-208-8144 ..... 462 C sgolabek@uscb.edu
GOLBA, Gina ..... 816-802-3397 ..... 283 E ggolba@kcai.edu
GOLD, Cheryl ..... 727-864-8058 ..... 105 E goldcc@eckerd.edu
GOLD, Donna ..... 207-288-5015 ..... 217 H dgold@coa.edu
GOLD, Ellen ..... 734-487-1107 ..... 250 F ellen.gold@emich.edu
GOLD, Harriet, B ..... 270-384-8017 ..... 204 D goldh@lindsey.edu
GOLD, Jeffrey ..... 419-383-5320 ..... 404 F jeffrey.gold@utoledo.edu
GOLD, Jeffrey, P ..... 419-383-4243 ..... 404 F jeffrey.gold@utoledo.edu
GOLD, Kathleen, E ..... 802-626-4860 ..... 515 G kathleen.gold@lyndonstate.edu
GOLD, Kim ..... 828-395-1663 ..... 371 D kgold@isothermal.edu
GOLD, Mark ..... 718-951-5861 ..... 326 F mark@brooklyn.cuny.edu
GOLD, Marla, J ..... 215-762-7091 ..... 427 H mjg32@drexel.edu
GOLD, Steven, J ..... 714-816-0366 ..... 73 B steven.gold@trident.edu
GOLD, Victor, J ..... 213-736-1062 ..... 56 E victor.gold@lls.edu
GOLDAMMER, Diana ..... 605-995-2160 ..... 464 C digoldam@dwu.edu
GOLDBERG, Barbara ..... 818-947-2647 ..... 55 E goldbeba@lavc.edu
GOLDBERG, Brian ..... 401-454-6134 ..... 454 B bgoldber@risd.edu
GOLDBERG, Daryl ..... 909-941-9410 ..... 62 J dgoldberg@plattcollege.edu
GOLDBERG, Donald ..... 310-660-3200 ..... 45 E dgoldberg@elcamino.edu
GOLDBERG, Ellen, J ..... 630-844-5147 ..... 145 F egoldbrg@aurora.edu
GOLDBERG, Glenn ..... 904-819-6305 ..... 107 C ggoldberg@flagler.edu
GOLDBERG, Jane, F ..... 360-538-4005 ..... 534 G jgoldber@ghc.edu
GOLDBERG, Jeanette ..... 603-668-2211 ..... 305 I j.goldberg@snhu.edu
GOLDBERG, Jeffrey, B ..... 520-621-6594 ..... 18 L jgoldberg@arizona.edu
GOLDBERG, Jerold, S ..... 216-368-3266 ..... 386 F jsg@case.edu
GOLDBERG, Joy ..... 865-882-4659 ..... 476 A goldbergjt@roanestate.edu
GOLDBERG, Marc ..... 503-491-7019 ..... 417 B marc.goldberg@mhcc.edu
GOLDBERG, Robert ..... 646-981-4500 ..... 358 B rgoldberg@touro.edu
GOLDBERG, Susan ..... 302-477-2005 ..... 97 B slgoldberg@widener.edu
GOLDBERG, Velda ..... 201-761-6033 ..... 314 F vgoldberg@spc.edu
GOLDBERGBELLE, Jonathan ..... 217-206-6678 ..... 167 C goldbergbelle.jonathan@uis.edu
GOLDBLATT, Elizabeth ..... 415-282-7600 ..... 28 B elizabethgoldblatt@actcm.edu
GOLDEN, Alan, J ..... 570-662-4046 ..... 443 C agolden@mansfield.edu
GOLDEN, Andrew, K ..... 609-258-4136 ..... 312 G agolden@princeton.edu
GOLDEN, Anne ..... 402-826-6795 ..... 297 G anne.golden@doane.edu
GOLDEN, Beverley ..... 903-566-7303 ..... 506 E bgolden@uttyler.edu
GOLDEN, Bryan, A ..... 229-391-5060 ..... 123 H bgolden@abac.edu
GOLDEN, Carolyn ..... 334-244-3369 ..... 1 G cgolden2@aum.edu
GOLDEN, Cheryl ..... 901-435-1429 ..... 470 D cheryl_golden@loc.edu

GONZALEZ, Fernando ... 787-884-6000 ... 562 G
fgonzalez@icprjc.edu
GONZALEZ, Francisco ... 787-891-0925 ... 563 A
fgonzale@aguadilla.inter.edu
GONZALEZ, George ... 281-998-6150 ... 493 G
george.gonzalez@sjcd.edu
GONZALEZ, Gerardo ... 812-856-8001 ... 173 E
gonzalez@indiana.edu
GONZALEZ, Gladys ... 305-626-3677 ... 109 A
gladys.gonzalez@fmuniv.edu
GONZALEZ, Griselda ... 212-217-4000 ... 333 F
griselda_gonzalez@fitnyc.edu
GONZALEZ, Hector ... 609-894-9311 ... 308 B
hgonzalez@bcc.edu
GONZALEZ, Herman ... 623-845-3562 ... 15 H
herman.gonzalez@gcmail.maricopa.edu
GONZALEZ, J, E ... 727-873-4716 ... 121 C
jegon@mail.usf.edu
GONZALEZ, Jaime ... 787-620-2040 ... 560 D
trodriguez@aupr.edu
GONZALEZ, James ... 973-972-9797 ... 316 C
gonzalj1@umdnj.edu
GONZALEZ, Jean ... 714-867-5009 ... 70 C
GONZALEZ, Jeffery ... 305-348-2731 ... 119 C
jeff@fiu.edu
GONZALEZ, Jemilis ... 787-882-2065 ... 566 A
recursoshumanos@unitecpr.net
GONZALEZ, Jorge ... 323-259-2634 ... 59 I
jgonzale@oxy.edu
GONZALEZ, Jose ... 914-323-5445 ... 339 J
jose.gonzalez@mville.edu
GONZALEZ, Judith ... 787-766-1717 ... 565 I
jugonzalez@suagm.edu
GONZALEZ, Karen ... 787-766-1717 ... 565 I
um_kgonzalez@suagm.edu
GONZALEZ, Linda ... 915-831-2566 ... 486 G
lgonz265@epcc.edu
GONZALEZ, Lizbeth ... 603-882-6923 ... 304 E
lgonzalez@ccsnh.edu
GONZALEZ, Lori ... 574-252-8526 ... 169 I
lori.gonzalez@bethelcollege.edu
GONZALEZ, Lori, S ... 828-262-2070 ... 377 D
gonzalezls@appstate.edu
GONZALEZ, Luis ... 724-357-2330 ... 442 F
luis.gonzalez@iup.edu
GONZALEZ, Luz ... 559-278-3013 ... 35 A
luz_gonzalez@csufresno.edu
GONZALEZ, Mari, G ... 787-743-7979 ... 565 H
mggonzalez@suagm.edu
GONZALEZ, Maria ... 305-273-4499 ... 103 J
registrar@cbt.edu
GONZALEZ, Marilyn ... 787-882-2065 ... 566 A
secretaria_ejecutiva@unitecpr.net
GONZALEZ, Marisol ... 787-264-1912 ... 564 B
margonza@sg.inter.edu
GONZALEZ, Mary ... 361-593-2494 ... 498 D
kamlp00@tamuk.edu
GONZALEZ, Mauricio ... 904-620-2600 ... 120 D
mgonzale@unf.edu
GONZALEZ, Moe ... 512-444-8082 ... 499 E
faid@texastcm.edu
GONZALEZ, Monica, D ... 787-723-4481 ... 561 B
mgonzalez@ceaprc.edu
GONZALEZ, Nichole ... 716-375-2572 ... 348 C
ngonzalez@sbu.edu
GONZALEZ, Noelia ... 209-667-3337 ... 36 D
ngonzalez@csustan.edu
GONZALEZ, Patricia ... 787-250-1912 ... 563 G
pgonzalez@metro.inter.edu
GONZALEZ, R. Louie ... 219-932-3600 ... 176 G
lgonzale@ivytech.edu
GONZALEZ, Raul, D ... 818-947-2606 ... 55 E
gonzalrd@lavc.edu
GONZALEZ, Reina, M ... 787-840-8108 ... 568 A
reina.gonzalez@upr.edu
GONZALEZ, Reyes ... 414-256-1228 ... 549 D
gonzaler@mtmary.edu
GONZALEZ, Roberto ... 310-434-4912 ... 68 D
gonzalez_roberto@smc.edu
GONZALEZ, Rocelia, T ... 904-620-2870 ... 120 D
rrgonz@unf.edu
GONZALEZ, Rosa ... 787-891-0925 ... 563 A
rgonzale@aguadilla.inter.edu
GONZALEZ, Ruben, L ... 516-876-3275 ... 353 D
gonzalezr@oldwestbury.edu
GONZALEZ, Rudy ... 210-212-6080 ... 495 G
rgonzalez@swbts.edu
GONZALEZ, Ruth ... 860-738-6315 ... 92 B
rgonzalez@nwcc.commnet.edu
GONZALEZ, Sandra ... 787-882-2065 ... 566 A
GONZALEZ, Sara ... 407-277-0311 ... 107 B
sgonzalez@evergladesuniversity.edu
GONZALEZ, Sarai ... 787-746-1400 ... 562 E
sgonzalez@huertas.edu
GONZALEZ, Saraliz ... 787-857-3600 ... 563 C
sgonzalez@br.inter.edu
GONZALEZ, Sergio, M ... 305-284-4111 ... 122 I
smgonzalez@miami.edu
GONZALEZ, Sophia ... 210-486-2247 ... 479 D
fklein@alamo.edu
GONZALEZ, Stacy ... 515-244-2209 ... 348 A
gonzas@sage.edu
GONZALEZ, Thomasa ... 609-652-4724 ... 313 E
t.gonzalez@stockton.edu

GONZALEZ, Tina ... 212-799-5000 ... 337 H
GONZALEZ, Urania ... 787-720-1022 ... 560 F
administracion@atlanticcollege.edu
GONZALEZ, Virginia ... 787-743-7979 ... 565 H
ut_vgonzalez@suagm.edu
GONZALEZ, Yanira ... 787-891-0925 ... 563 A
ygonzalezz@aguadilla.inter.edu
GONZALEZ-BAEZ,
Marilucy ... 787-751-1912 ... 564 C
marigonza@inter.edu
GONZALEZ DE SCOLLARD,
Edith ... 212-817-7520 ... 327 B
egonzalez@gc.cuny.edu
GONZALEZ-GENERALS,
Joann ... 973-618-3589 ... 308 C
jgonzalez@caldwell.edu
GONZALEZ-LIMA, Erika ... 512-505-3044 ... 488 D
egonzalez-lima@htu.edu
GONZALEZ-MORENO,
Adriana ... 619-275-4700 ... 46 K
adriana@fashioncareerscollege.com
GONZALEZ NIEVES,
Rosa, E ... 787-896-2252 ... 562 B
rgonzalez@edpcollege.edu
GONZALEZ-SCARANO,
Francisco ... 210-567-4432 ... 507 A
scarano@uthscsa.edu
GONZALEZ VELEZ,
Adelino ... 787-725-8120 ... 562 C
agonzalez0021@eap.edu
GOOCH, Cheryl Renee ... 484-365-7664 ... 434 H
cgooch@lincoln.edu
GOOCH, Cynthia ... 402-457-2649 ... 298 G
cgooch@mccneb.edu
GOOCH, Gene ... 254-299-8679 ... 490 G
ggooch@mclennan.edu
GOOCH, Janet ... 660-785-4383 ... 290 G
jquinzek@truman.edu
GOOCH, Mary, E ... 936-261-1066 ... 496 G
megooch@pvamu.edu
GOOD, Barry ... 406-243-7811 ... 294 I
barry.good@umontana.edu
GOOD, Barry ... 406-243-7851 ... 295 B
barry.good@umontana.edu
GOOD, Chad ... 847-543-2477 ... 148 B
cgood@clcillinois.edu
GOOD, Claire ... 859-622-1721 ... 200 J
claire.good@eku.edu
GOOD, Glenn ... 352-392-3261 ... 120 C
GOOD, Jennifer ... 334-244-3481 ... 1 G
jgood@aum.edu
GOOD, Joseph, C ... 843-792-4063 ... 459 D
goodj@musc.edu
GOOD, Julie ... 505-428-1653 ... 320 E
julie.good@sfcc.edu
GOOD, Kathy ... 864-596-9622 ... 457 E
kathy.good@converse.edu
GOOD, Laura, E ... 330-823-6050 ... 404 C
goodle@mountunion.edu
GOOD, Michael, L ... 352-273-7500 ... 120 C
mgood@ufl.edu
GOOD, Rhonda ... 717-337-6015 ... 429 I
rgood@gettysburg.edu
GOOD, Rhonda, L ... 717-766-2511 ... 436 D
rgood@messiah.edu
GOOD, William ... 309-854-1831 ... 145 H
goodb@bhc.edu
GOOD LUCK, Aldean ... 406-638-3118 ... 294 E
goodluckav@lbhc.edu
GOODACRE, Charles, J ... 909-558-4683 ... 54 D
cgoodacre@llu.edu
GOODALE, Brian ... 518-587-2100 ... 355 G
brian.goodale@esc.edu
GOODALL, Debbie ... 816-604-5280 ... 285 B
debbie.goodall@mcckc.edu
GOODARZI, Shirin, M ... 410-777-2148 ... 221 C
smgoodarzi@aacc.edu
GOODCUFF, Esther ... 516-877-3681 ... 322 A
goodcuff@adelphi.edu
GOODE, Debbie ... 580-581-2255 ... 407 D
debbieg@cameron.edu
GOODE, Gail ... 513-772-9888 ... 398 G
gail.goode@omw.edu
GOODE, Greg, J ... 812-237-7778 ... 173 B
greg.goode@indstate.edu
GOODE, Greg, J ... 425-602-3006 ... 531 E
ggoode@bastyr.edu
GOODE, Greg, R ... 785-309-3100 ... 196 E
GOODE, Mark ... 714-432-5898 ... 41 D
mgoode@occ.cccd.edu
GOODE, Tammy ... 423-585-6845 ... 476 D
tammy.goode@ws.edu
GOODE, Tracy ... 229-317-6929 ... 128 D
tracy.goode@darton.edu
GOODELL-LACKEY,
Shirley, J ... 802-654-2586 ... 514 D
sgoodell-lackey@smcvt.edu
GOODEN, Charles, H ... 314-340-5030 ... 282 F
goodenc@hssu.edu
GOODEN, Winston, E ... 626-584-5501 ... 48 B
gooden@fuller.edu
GOODER, Kellee ... 307-532-8336 ... 556 C
kellee.gooder@ewc.wy.edu
GOODFELLOW, Sandy ... 615-383-1340 ... 469 A
alex@fwbbc.edu

GOODGAME, Henry ... 404-215-2658 ... 134 D
hgoodgame@morehouse.edu
GOODHAND, Melony ... 501-686-5670 ... 24 F
mjgoodhand@uams.edu
GOODHEART, Harriet, K ... 610-660-1532 ... 446 C
hgoodhea@sju.edu
GOODHUE, Bill ... 607-436-2532 ... 353 E
goodhucw@oneonta.edu
GOODHUE, Robert, M ... 617-287-5624 ... 236 E
rgoodhue@umassp.edu
GOODHUE LYNCH, Mary . 508-588-9100 ... 240 A
GOODIN, Ruth ... 925-439-2181 ... 43 G
rgoodin@losmedanos.edu
GOODING, Betsy ... 903-434-8137 ... 491 F
bgooding@ntcc.edu
GOODING, Marjory ... 626-395-8808 ... 32 H
marjory.gooding@caltech.edu
GOODING, Mary, B ... 229-333-7444 ... 139 C
mbgooding@valdosta.edu
GOODLING, Barry, G ... 717-796-5064 ... 436 D
bgoodlin@messiah.edu
GOODLING, Eileen, J ... 716-338-1025 ... 337 E
eileengoodling@mail.sunyjcc.edu
GOODLIVE, Kathy ... 707-476-4151 ... 42 C
kathy-goodlive@redwoods.edu
GOODMAN, Brent, S ... 805-756-2204 ... 33 I
bgoodman@calpoly.edu
GOODMAN, Brittney, G ... 218-477-2923 ... 267 F
brittney.goodman@mnstate.edu
GOODMAN, Clay ... 623-935-8456 ... 15 F
clay.goodman@estrellamountain.edu
GOODMAN, Debbie ... 229-225-3978 ... 138 A
dgoodman@southwestgatech.edu
GOODMAN, Elizabeth, A ... 636-227-2100 ... 284 B
elizabeth.goodman@logan.edu
GOODMAN, George, A ... 636-227-2100 ... 284 B
george.goodman@logan.edu
GOODMAN, Grayson ... 407-303-1631 ... 100 G
grayson.goodman@adu.edu
GOODMAN, Guy ... 309-694-8970 ... 152 C
ggoodman@icc.edu
GOODMAN, Jacque ... 641-844-7106 ... 186 D
jacque.goodman@iavalley.edu
GOODMAN, Jacque ... 641-844-5640 ... 186 B
jacque.goodman@iavalley.edu
GOODMAN, Jacqueline, K 315-267-2116 ... 354 C
goodmajk@potsdam.edu
GOODMAN, James ... 808-455-0228 ... 142 D
goodmanj@hawaii.edu
GOODMAN, Jeremy ... 781-292-2373 ... 234 H
jeremy.goodman@olin.edu
GOODMAN, Jerry, C ... 713-798-7234 ... 481 H
jgoodman@bcm.edu
GOODMAN,
John (Chris), C ... 812-246-3301 ... 177 B
jgoodman17@ivytech.edu
GOODMAN, Julie ... 308-432-6487 ... 299 E
jgoodman@csc.edu
GOODMAN, Larry, J ... 312-942-7073 ... 163 D
larry_j_goodman@rush.edu
GOODMAN, Lena, C ... 920-433-6638 ... 546 D
lena.goodman@bellincollege.edu
GOODMAN, Marc, P ... 310-506-4670 ... 61 H
marc.goodman@pepperdine.edu
GOODMAN, Michael ... 504-865-5725 ... 215 C
mgoodman@tulane.edu
GOODMAN, Patricia ... 859-442-1173 ... 202 B
patricia.goodman@kctcs.edu
GOODMAN, Patricia ... 603-882-6923 ... 304 E
pgoodman@ccsnh.edu
GOODMAN, Rachel ... 641-472-7000 ... 187 E
rgoodman@mum.edu
GOODMAN, Richard, H ... 503-494-5078 ... 418 D
goodmanr@ohsu.edu
GOODMAN, Robert, M ... 848-932-3600 ... 314 C
execdean@cook.rutgers.edu
GOODMAN, Sharon ... 910-410-1734 ... 373 B
sharong@richmondcc.edu
GOODMAN, Steven ... 315-464-6563 ... 352 E
goodmans@upstate.edu
GOODMAN, Sylvia ... 405-789-6400 ... 412 D
sgoodman@snu.edu
GOODMAN, Timothy, D ... 478-289-2034 ... 129 B
goodman@ega.edu
GOODMAN, Veronica ... 803-535-5540 ... 456 D
vgoodman@claflin.edu
GOODMAN, William, L ... 651-638-6400 ... 261 D
w-goodman@bethel.edu
GOODMAN, Willie ... 404-527-5735 ... 132 G
wgoodman@itc.edu
GOODNER, Jason ... 229-732-5929 ... 124 E
jasongoodner@andrewcollege.edu
GOODNOUGH, Doug ... 517-264-7141 ... 258 B
dgoodnou@sienaheights.edu
GOODNOW, Jean ... 989-686-9201 ... 250 D
jeangoodnow@delta.edu
GOODRICH, Blaine ... 517-841-4522 ... 248 D
blaine.goodrich@baker.edu
GOODRICH, Curtis Jason .. 409-880-8305 ... 501 A
jason.goodrich@lamar.edu
GOODRICH, Deborah, J ... 607-587-4215 ... 355 C
goodridj@alfredstate.edu
GOODRICH, James, A ... 323-343-2800 ... 35 D
jgoodri7@calstatela.edu

GOODRICH, Joy, P ... 804-354-5210 ... 530 A
jgoodrich@vuu.edu
GOODRICH, Larry ... 972-825-4820 ... 495 F
lgoodrich@sagu.edu
GOODRICH, Lynda ... 360-650-3109 ... 539 F
lynda.goodrich@wwu.edu
GOODRICH, Mark ... 415-338-2723 ... 37 B
goodrich@sfsu.edu
GOODRICH PELLETIER,
Monica ... 508-213-2108 ... 243 E
monica.goodrich-pelletier@nichols.edu
GOODROW, Thomas ... 860-253-3032 ... 91 B
tgoodrow@asnuntuck.edu
GOODRUM, OP,
Mary Cecilia ... 615-297-7545 ... 467 A
srmcecilia@aquinascollege.edu
GOODSON, Holly ... 706-721-7544 ... 130 D
hgoodson@georgiahealth.edu
GOODSON, Kenneth ... 903-434-8260 ... 491 F
kgoodson@ntcc.edu
GOODSON, Leigh ... 918-561-1400 ... 410 D
leigh.goodson@okstate.edu
GOODSTEIN, Eban ... 845-758-7067 ... 323 D
ebangood@bard.edu
GOODSTEIN, Lynne ... 860-486-4223 ... 94 G
lynne.goodstein@uconn.edu
GOODSTEIN, Richard, E ... 864-656-3311 ... 456 E
GOODWIN, Alan ... 805-493-3573 ... 33 B
agoodwin@clunet.edu
GOODWIN, Ann ... 860-685-2200 ... 95 E
agoodwin@wesleyan.edu
GOODWIN, Anna ... 540-362-6223 ... 520 A
agoodwin@hollins.edu
GOODWIN, Candace ... 773-929-8500 ... 149 D
cgoodwin@devry.edu
GOODWIN, Cheryl ... 206-876-6100 ... 538 A
cgoodwin@theseattleschool.edu
GOODWIN, Christy ... 251-578-1313 ... 6 E
cgoodwin@rstc.edu
GOODWIN, Cindi, J ... 336-633-4475 ... 373 A
cjgoodwin@randolph.edu
GOODWIN, David ... 205-726-2337 ... 6 G
dbgoodwi@samford.edu
GOODWIN, Dennis ... 303-797-5801 ... 81 D
dennis.goodwin@arapahoe.edu
GOODWIN, Doug ... 904-363-6221 ... 117 D
GOODWIN, Douglas ... 618-344-5600 ... 164 A
douglas.goodwin@sbc-collinsville.com
GOODWIN, Erika, A ... 937-382-6661 ... 405 I
erika_goodwin@wilmington.edu
GOODWIN, Jennifer ... 516-299-3759 ... 338 E
jennifer.goodwin@liu.edu
GOODWIN, Jennifer ... 903-823-3200 ... 496 E
jennifer.goodwin@texarkanacollege.edu
GOODWIN, Jerome ... 919-530-6739 ... 378 B
jgoodwin@nccu.edu
GOODWIN, Ken ... 971-722-4980 ... 419 G
kgoodwin@pcc.edu
GOODWIN, Kristine, C ... 401-865-2144 ... 453 H
kgoodwi2@providence.edu
GOODWIN, Larry ... 218-723-6033 ... 262 G
lgoodwin@css.edu
GOODWIN, Laura ... 303-315-2105 ... 88 J
laura.goodwin@ucdenver.edu
GOODWIN, Mark ... 972-721-4068 ... 503 B
mgoodwin@udallas.edu
GOODWIN, Mary Ann ... 509-533-3820 ... 533 C
maryanng@spokanefalls.edu
GOODWIN, Michael ... 802-447-6343 ... 514 F
mgoodwin@svc.edu
GOODWIN, Michelle ... 301-934-7635 ... 222 C
michellg@csmd.edu
GOODWIN, Mike ... 541-737-3288 ... 418 F
mike.goodwin@oregonstate.edu
GOODWIN, Naomi ... 310-243-3303 ... 34 D
ngoodwin@csudh.edu
GOODWIN, Robert ... 240-684-2476 ... 227 F
graddean@umuc.edu
GOODWIN, Stephen, D ... 859-846-5782 ... 204 H
sgoodwin@midway.edu
GOODWIN, Steve ... 413-545-2766 ... 236 F
sgoodwin@cns.umass.edu
GOODWIN, Valerie, A ... 716-372-7978 ... 345 C
vgoodwin@obi.edu
GOODWIN, Virginia ... 317-543-3672 ... 178 A
vgoodwin@martin.edu
GOODWIN, Wayne ... 601-979-2522 ... 274 G
wayne.goodwin@jsums.edu
GOODWIN, Wendell, B ... 919-866-5148 ... 374 H
wbgoodwin@waketech.edu
GOODWIN, Whittington ... 281-649-3238 ... 487 H
wgoodwin@hbu.edu
GOODYEAR, Jack ... 214-333-5238 ... 484 D
jackg@dbu.edu
GOOKIN, Kathleen ... 502-410-6200 ... 200 L
kgookin@galencollege.edu
GOOLSBY, Bethany ... 901-448-8212 ... 477 E
bgoolsby@uthsc.edu
GOOLSBY, Edwin, G ... 727-816-3264 ... 114 F
goolsbe@phcc.edu
GOON, Arthur ... 203-932-7005 ... 95 C
agoon@newhaven.edu
GOON, Arthur, D ... 201-559-6049 ... 310 B
goona@felician.edu

GOVE, Marilyn .... 949-480-4131 .... 69 J
mgove@soka.edu
GOVE, Ryan, K .... 913-588-6681 .... 197 C
rgove@kumc.edu
GOVEA, Hector .... 432-552-2740 .... 507 D
govea_h@utpb.edu
GOVEA, Sam .... 972-860-4216 .... 484 G
sgovea@dcccd.edu
GOVER, Bruce .... 606-679-8501 .... 203 C
bruce.gover@kctcs.edu
GOVERT, OSF,
Mary Evelyn .... 260-399-7700 .... 181 A
mgovert@sf.edu
GOVINDAN, Indira .... 201-692-2060 .... 310 A
govindan@fdu.edu
GOVITZ, Leanne .... 989-686-9490 .... 250 D
leannegovitz@delta.edu
GOVITZ, Scott .... 989-386-6624 .... 255 C
sgovitz@midmich.edu
GOVONI, Mark .... 215-951-2700 .... 444 D
govonim@philau.edu
GOW, Joe .... 608-785-8004 .... 551 C
jgow@uwlax.edu
GOWDY, Lisa .... 517-780-4567 .... 248 D
lisa.gowdy@baker.edu
GOWER, J. Michael .... 212-960-5475 .... 361 M
gower@yu.edu
GOWER, Michael, E .... 615-898-2540 .... 473 G
mike.gower@mtsu.edu
GOWER, Paula .... 405-585-5410 .... 409 D
paula.gower@okbu.edu
GOWER, Paula .... 405-682-1611 .... 409 F
pgower@occc.edu
GOWER, Stephanie .... 205-453-6300 .... 99 G
GOWN, Jacob .... 310-476-9777 .... 28 G
jgown@ajula.edu
GOWRON, Leah .... 831-647-3558 .... 57 F
leah.gowron@miis.edu
GOYAK, Antone .... 715-324-6900 .... 549 G
antone.goyak@ni.edu
GOYETTE, Barbara .... 410-295-5554 .... 225 G
barbara.goyette@sjca.edu
GOYETTE, Dan .... 414-382-6040 .... 546 B
dan.goyette@alverno.edu
GOYETTE, Kelly .... 859-344-3619 .... 206 I
kelly.goyette@thomasmore.edu
GOZON, Richard, C .... 215-955-6617 .... 448 C
richard.gozon@jefferson.edu
GOZUM, Allan .... 630-829-6418 .... 145 G
agozum@ben.edu
GOZZO, James .... 518-694-7255 .... 322 B
james.gozzo@acphs.edu
GRAAGE, Eric .... 401-454-6525 .... 454 B
egraage@risd.edu
GRABAN, Jennifer, L .... 812-488-1178 .... 180 E
jg54@evansville.edu
GRABE, William .... 928-523-4340 .... 16 I
william.grabe@nau.edu
GRABER, David .... 402-375-7257 .... 299 G
dagrabe1@wsc.edu
GRABER, Doug .... 620-947-3121 .... 197 A
dougg@tabor.edu
GRABER, Thomas .... 570-208-5900 .... 432 G
thomasgraber@kings.edu
GRABER, Tony .... 316-284-5233 .... 191 C
tgraber@bethelks.edu
GRABLE, Lynda .... 478-445-7305 .... 130 B
lynda.grable@gcsu.edu
GRABOIS, Neil .... 212-229-5400 .... 342 E
graboisn@newschool.edu
GRABOWSKA, Lynette .... 605-367-6122 .... 466 D
lynette.grabowska@southeasttech.edu
GRABOWSKI, Janice, T .... 724-925-4123 .... 451 E
grabowskij@wccc.edu
GRABOWSKI, John, F .... 410-777-2231 .... 221 C
jfgrabowski@aacc.edu
GRABOWSKI, Mark .... 417-328-1556 .... 290 A
mgrabowski@sbuniv.edu
GRABOWSKI, Rod .... 813-974-8848 .... 121 A
rgrabowski@admin.usf.edu
GRABUS, Scott .... 215-572-8515 .... 422 C
grabuss@arcadia.edu
GRACA, Michael .... 508-286-3503 .... 246 B
mgraca@wheatonma.edu
GRACA, Thomas, J .... 972-860-7218 .... 484 I
tomgraca@dcccd.edu
GRACE, Chris .... 562-903-4708 .... 31 A
chris.grace@biola.edu
GRACE, Coy, F .... 870-633-4480 .... 21 F
cgrace@eacc.edu
GRACE, Dennis .... 239-280-1613 .... 101 I
dennis.grace@avemaria.edu
GRACE, Ellen .... 561-868-3135 .... 114 D
gracee@palmbeachstate.edu
GRACE, Gary, S .... 319-352-8276 .... 189 J
gary.grace@wartburg.edu
GRACE, Glenda .... 718-518-4154 .... 327 D
ggrace@hostos.cuny.edu
GRACE, Michelle, M .... 847-543-2274 .... 148 B
mgrace@clcillinois.edu
GRACE, Nabil, F .... 248-204-2500 .... 254 B
ngrace@ltu.edu
GRACE, Patricia .... 218-879-0819 .... 266 C
pgrace@fdltcc.edu

GRACE, Ted, W .... 618-453-4485 .... 165 B
tgrace@siu.edu
GRACIA, Hector .... 787-780-0070 .... 560 H
graciah@caribbean.edu
GRACIA, Jessica, L .... 508-565-1301 .... 245 A
jlgracia@stonehill.edu
GRACIA, Susan .... 617-521-2076 .... 244 F
susan.gracia@simmons.edu
GRACIA, Zaida .... 787-728-1515 .... 568 D
zgracia@sagrado.edu
GRACIE, Larry, W .... 252-249-1851 .... 372 F
lgracie@pamlicocc.edu
GRACYALNY, David .... 410-225-2220 .... 224 B
dgracyal@mica.edu
GRACYK, June .... 440-684-6083 .... 405 B
jgracyk@ursuline.edu
GRADOWSKI, Charles .... 484-365-7404 .... 434 H
cgradowski@lincoln.edu
GRADY, Amber .... 870-512-7890 .... 20 F
amber_grady@asun.edu
GRADY, Bruce .... 919-546-8574 .... 376 F
bgrady@shawu.edu
GRADY, Carole .... 453-879-4802 .... 512 B
grady@dixie.edu
GRADY, Christine .... 815-753-1311 .... 160 B
cgrady@niu.edu
GRADY, David, L .... 319-335-3114 .... 182 F
david-grady@uiowa.edu
GRADY, Dennis, O .... 540-831-7163 .... 523 A
dgrady4@radford.edu
GRADY, Donald .... 815-753-1811 .... 160 B
dgrady@niu.edu
GRADY, J. Thomas .... 508-678-2811 .... 239 B
tom.grady@bristolcc.edu
GRADY, Janet, L .... 814-269-2078 .... 449 D
jgrady@pitt.edu
GRADY, Lynne .... 706-379-3111 .... 140 A
lbgrady@yhc.edu
GRADY, Paul .... 310-233-4112 .... 54 I
gradyp@lahc.edu
GRADY, Rayford .... 804-745-2444 .... 517 C
rlgrady@bryantstratton.edu
GRADY, Sarah .... 718-409-7262 .... 356 C
sgrady@sunymaritime.edu
GRADY, Suzanne .... 845-257-3245 .... 352 B
gradys@newpaltz.edu
GRADY, OSF, Thomas .... 718-489-5367 .... 348 E
tgrady@sfc.edu
GRAEBERT, James, K .... 414-288-3048 .... 548 F
james.graebert@marquette.edu
GRAEF, Stephen, T .... 330-363-5361 .... 384 J
tgraef@aultman.com
GRAEM, David .... 903-675-6364 .... 502 F
dgraem@tvcc.edu
GRAESSER, William .... 765-966-2656 .... 176 H
bgraesse@ivytech.edu
GRAF, Bob .... 651-696-6280 .... 264 J
rgraf@macalester.edu
GRAF, Debby .... 208-376-7731 .... 142 H
dgraf@boisebible.edu
GRAF, Elizabeth .... 219-866-6195 .... 179 D
bethg@saintjoe.edu
GRAF, Nancy .... 316-295-5888 .... 193 B
ngraf@friends.edu
GRAFF, Irene .... 310-660-3515 .... 45 E
igraff@elcamino.edu
GRAFF, Irene .... 310-660-3593 .... 45 F
igraff@elcamino.edu
GRAFF, Jonathan .... 575-624-8291 .... 319 C
graff@nmmi.edu
GRAFFAM, JoAnn, K .... 417-625-3072 .... 286 B
graffam-j@mssu.edu
GRAFFICE, Anne .... 330-823-2030 .... 404 C
graffiaz@mountunion.edu
GRAFTON, David .... 215-248-6347 .... 435 B
dgrafton@ltsp.edu
GRAFTON, Ken .... 701-231-7655 .... 382 B
k.grafton@ndsu.edu
GRAFTON, Steve, C .... 734-763-9730 .... 259 A
sgrafton@umich.edu
GRAGG, JR., Derrick, L .... 734-487-1050 .... 250 F
derrick.gragg@emich.edu
GRAGG, T. Dewayne .... 903-875-7376 .... 491 C
dewayne.gragg@navarrocollege.edu
GRAHAM, Amanda .... 619-201-8711 .... 65 D
amanda.graham@sdcc.edu
GRAHAM, Amie, E .... 757-594-7672 .... 517 L
amie.graham@cnu.edu
GRAHAM, Angela .... 540-863-2806 .... 526 F
agraham@dslcc.edu
GRAHAM, Archie .... 414-297-6870 .... 554 F
grahama@matc.edu
GRAHAM, Bernard .... 570-408-4280 .... 452 A
bernard.graham@wilkes.edu
GRAHAM, Bruce .... 312-996-1040 .... 167 B
bgraham@uic.edu
GRAHAM, Carlos .... 573-681-5971 .... 283 I
grahamc@lincolnu.edu
GRAHAM, Catherine .... 310-338-2753 .... 56 E
cgraham@lmu.edu
GRAHAM, Charles, W .... 405-325-2444 .... 413 C
cwgraham@ou.edu
GRAHAM, Christina, L .... 814-362-7654 .... 449 B
cgraham5@pitt.edu

GRAHAM, Christine .... 941-907-2262 .... 107 B
chgraham@evergladesuniversity.edu
GRAHAM, Chuck .... 352-335-2332 .... 100 D
GRAHAM, David .... 305-892-7022 .... 112 A
david.graham@jwu.edu
GRAHAM, Deborah, L .... 314-516-4165 .... 291 D
gramhamdeb@umsl.edu
GRAHAM, Duncan .... 510-748-2301 .... 62 C
dgraham@peralta.edu
GRAHAM, Frances, D .... 919-530-6738 .... 378 B
fdgraham@nccu.edu
GRAHAM, Jack .... 970-491-3350 .... 83 F
jack.graham@colostate.edu
GRAHAM, James, F .... 660-543-4279 .... 290 H
graham@ucmo.edu
GRAHAM, Janielle .... 773-995-2067 .... 146 G
jgraham@csu.edu
GRAHAM, Jay .... 214-818-1311 .... 484 B
jgraham@criswell.edu
GRAHAM, Jean .... 251-580-2293 .... 5 A
jgraham@faulknerstate.edu
GRAHAM, Jeanne .... 906-932-4231 .... 251 C
jeanneg@gogebic.edu
GRAHAM, Jeffrey .... 956-665-2112 .... 506 C
grahamja@utpa.edu
GRAHAM, Jennifer .... 254-298-8592 .... 496 D
jennifer.graham@templejc.edu
GRAHAM, Joan, E .... 585-475-6079 .... 347 G
jegirp@rit.edu
GRAHAM, Joe, A .... 574-372-5100 .... 171 H
grahamja@grace.edu
GRAHAM, Joe, M .... 704-233-8148 .... 380 F
graham@wingate.edu
GRAHAM, John .... 845-938-5868 .... 559 A
john.graham@usma.edu
GRAHAM, III, John .... 412-346-2100 .... 444 E
jgrahamiii@pia.edu
GRAHAM, John, D .... 812-855-1432 .... 173 E
grahamjd@indiana.edu
GRAHAM, John, M .... 512-471-4716 .... 505 D
john.graham@athletics.utexas.edu
GRAHAM, John-Bauer .... 256-782-5255 .... 4 L
jgraham@jsu.edu
GRAHAM, Kathleen .... 570-577-3200 .... 423 E
kathy.graham@bucknell.edu
GRAHAM, Keith .... 570-740-0307 .... 435 C
kgraham@luzerne.edu
GRAHAM, Kevin .... 321-674-8111 .... 108 H
kgraham@fit.edu
GRAHAM, Kevin, C .... 217-425-4663 .... 158 G
kgraham@millikin.edu
GRAHAM, Kim .... 805-922-6966 .... 26 L
kgraham@hancockcollege.edu
GRAHAM, Ladd .... 818-299-5500 .... 78 A
lgraham@westcoastuniversity.edu
GRAHAM, LeRoy .... 802-443-5770 .... 514 A
leroyg@middlebury.edu
GRAHAM, JR., Louis, W .... 617-253-2808 .... 241 D
GRAHAM, Margaret, P .... 434-223-6167 .... 519 G
bgraham@hsc.edu
GRAHAM, MariAnn .... 651-962-5000 .... 272 B
magraham@stthomas.edu
GRAHAM, Mark, R .... 276-944-6104 .... 519 A
mgraham@ehc.edu
GRAHAM, Mary, S .... 601-928-6280 .... 275 E
mary.graham@mgccc.edu
GRAHAM, Melody .... 319-368-6482 .... 187 H
melody@mtmercy.edu
GRAHAM, SJ, Michael, J .... 513-745-3502 .... 406 E
GRAHAM, Mickey .... 580-477-7782 .... 414 C
mckey.graham@wosc.edu
GRAHAM, Nancy, D .... 724-847-6550 .... 429 H
ngraham@geneva.edu
GRAHAM, Nicole .... 305-892-7554 .... 112 A
nicole.graham@jwu.edu
GRAHAM, Philip .... 858-795-5210 .... 67 I
pgraham@sandfordburnham.org
GRAHAM, Robert, J .... 724-852-3456 .... 451 B
rgraham@waynesburg.edu
GRAHAM, Roy .... 803-934-3298 .... 459 G
roygraham@morris.edu
GRAHAM, Sandra .... 414-382-6366 .... 546 B
sandra.graham@alverno.edu
GRAHAM, Stephanie .... 608-663-4861 .... 547 F
srgraham@edgewood.edu
GRAHAM, Stephanie .... 909-607-6722 .... 49 F
stephanie_graham@hmc.edu
GRAHAM, Stephen, A .... 973-761-9011 .... 315 B
stephen.graham@shu.edu
GRAHAM, Steven, W .... 573-884-3360 .... 291 A
grahams@umsystem.edu
GRAHAM, Susie .... 812-330-6247 .... 175 J
sgraham31@ivytech.edu
GRAHAM, Tamara, L .... 302-477-2037 .... 97 B
tlgraham@widener.edu
GRAHAM, Terri .... 402-461-7431 .... 298 A
tgraham@hastings.edu
GRAHAM, Troy .... 901-320-9763 .... 478 C
tgraham@victory.edu
GRAHAM, William, A .... 617-495-4513 .... 235 D
wgraham@hds.harvard.edu
GRAHAM, Wray .... 901-375-4400 .... 471 G
wraygraham@midsouthcc.org

GRAHAM-CORNELL,
Michael .... 203-254-4088 .... 92 H
mgraham-cornell@fairfield.edu
GRAHAM-HANDLEY, Tad .... 212-625-6000 .... 323 A
GRAHAM-ROBEY, Judith .... 617-228-3296 .... 239 C
jgraham@bhcc.mass.edu
GRAINGER, Kristen .... 503-370-6209 .... 421 D
kgrainge@willamette.edu
GRAJEK, Michael, A .... 330-569-5272 .... 391 G
grajekma@hiram.edu
GRAMBERG, Anne-Katrin .... 334-844-4026 .... 1 F
gramban@auburn.edu
GRAMENZ, Gary .... 559-453-2291 .... 48 A
gary.gramenz@fresno.edu
GRAMLICH, Nicole .... 314-768-7806 .... 286 A
ngramlich@missouricollege.com
GRAMLING, Jennifer .... 865-251-1800 .... 473 A
jgramling@southcollegetn.edu
GRAMLING, Keith, E .... 504-865-3240 .... 213 F
gramling@loyno.edu
GRAMLING, P.J .... 325-649-8406 .... 488 C
pgramling@hputx.edu
GRAMLING, Tim .... 719-590-6797 .... 83 J
GRAMMER, Jill .... 303-444-0202 .... 86 H
jgrammer@naropa.edu
GRAMMER, Robert .... 615-460-6417 .... 467 D
robert.grammer@belmont.edu
GRAMS, Ed, J .... 574-289-7001 .... 176 E
egrams@ivytech.edu
GRAMS, Kathyrn .... 678-839-6552 .... 139 A
kgrams@westga.du
GRAMS, Mary Ann .... 210-784-1000 .... 498 E
mgrams@tamusa.tamus.edu
GRAN, Donald, F .... 386-763-2651 .... 114 E
donald.gran@palmer.edu
GRAN, Tracey .... 651-690-6566 .... 270 L
tlgran@stkate.edu
GRANA, Joe .... 714-879-3901 .... 50 I
jgrana@hiu.edu
GRANADE, Ray .... 870-245-5121 .... 22 I
granade@obu.edu
GRANADO, Esequiel .... 956-665-2701 .... 506 C
zeke@utpa.edu
GRAÑADOS, Alex .... 661-362-2626 .... 56 G
agranados@masters.edu
GRANADOS, Patricia .... 708-456-0300 .... 166 F
pgranado@triton.edu
GRANATA, Brian .... 215-572-2194 .... 422 C
granatab@arcadia.edu
GRANATOWSKI, Doris .... 480-212-1704 .... 18 C
GRANBERRY,
Jacqueline, M .... 601-857-3363 .... 274 C
jgranberry@hindscc.edu
GRANBERRY-RUSSELL,
Paulette .... 517-353-3922 .... 255 A
prussell@msu.edu
GRAND PRE, Paul, D .... 914-337-9300 .... 330 G
paul.grandpre@concordia-ny.edu
GRANDALL, Jerolyn, R .... 608-785-9576 .... 555 F
grandallj@westerntc.edu
GRANDCHAMP,
Michael, N .... 401-341-2142 .... 454 D
grandchm@salve.edu
GRANDE, Joseph .... 507-284-3796 .... 262 D
grande.joseph@mayo.edu
GRANDES, Jayne, M .... 848-932-3980 .... 314 B
grandes@rutgers.edu
GRANDGEORGE, Cindy .... 661-362-3420 .... 41 I
cindy.grandgeorge@canyons.edu
GRANDILLO, Michael, A .... 920-565-1204 .... 548 A
grandilloma@lakeland.edu
GRANDINETTI, Faon .... 708-456-0300 .... 166 F
fgrandin@triton.edu
GRANDINETTI, Margie .... 610-606-4636 .... 425 A
mlgrandi@cedarcrest.edu
GRANDNER, Deborah, F .... 301-314-7343 .... 227 B
dgrandne@umd.edu
GRANDVILLE, Fran .... 215-785-0111 .... 440 I
GRANDY, E. Ann .... 757-683-4132 .... 522 F
egrandy@odu.edu
GRANEY, Carol .... 215-717-6281 .... 448 I
graney@uarts.edu
GRANEY-MULHOLLAND,
Michael .... 925-969-3319 .... 52 C
mgraney@jfku.edu
GRANFIELD, Cathy .... 414-955-8566 .... 548 G
mcw@matthewsstores.com
GRANGER, Earl, T .... 757-221-1188 .... 518 A
earl.granger@wm.edu
GRANGER, Gary .... 503-771-1112 .... 420 A
ggranger@reed.edu
GRANGER, Heidi .... 703-993-2349 .... 519 E
hgranger@gmu.edu
GRANGER, Jennifer .... 617-243-2430 .... 236 A
jgranger@lasell.edu
GRANGER, Jill .... 434-381-6166 .... 524 K
granger@sbc.edu
GRANGER, Joey .... 601-984-1199 .... 277 E
jgranger@umc.edu
GRANGER, Ron .... 307-855-2105 .... 556 B
rgranger@cwc.edu
GRANGER, Vern .... 614-292-3324 .... 398 I
GRANHOLD, Kevin, B .... 713-500-3624 .... 506 F
kevin.b.granhold@uth.tmc.edu

GRANITTO, Joseph .... 516-299-4002.... 339 A
joseph.granitto@liu.edu
GRANLUND, Shirley, M .... 952-446-4112.... 263 C
granlunds@crown.edu
GRANNY, John .... 440-834-3735.... 393 G
jgranny@kent.edu
GRANT, Alan .... 540-231-4152.... 529 G
algrant@vt.edu
GRANT, Andrew .... 212-824-2294.... 335 B
agrant@huc.edu
GRANT, Andrew .... 330-490-7334.... 405 F
agrant@walsh.edu
GRANT, Andrew, D .... 419-372-3905.... 385 E
agrant@bgsu.edu
GRANT, Armada .... 443-885-3195.... 224 E
armada.grant@morgan.edu
GRANT, Barry .... 860-512-3403...... 91 F
bgrant@mcc.commnet.edu
GRANT, Beth, A .... 813-988-5131.... 108 A
registrar@floridacollege.edu
GRANT, Bob .... 937-775-2771.... 406 C
bob.grant@wright.edu
GRANT, Bradford, C .... 202-806-7420...... 98 E
bcgrant@howard.edu
GRANT, Brian, T .... 315-268-6480.... 329 B
bgrant@clarkson.edu
GRANT, Brid .... 860-486-3016...... 94 G
brid.grant@uconn.edu
GRANT, Bud .... 563-333-6419.... 188 F
grantrobert@sau.edu
GRANT, Christy .... 402-354-7077.... 299 C
christy.grant@methodistcollege.edu
GRANT, Dale, E .... 308-432-6202.... 299 E
dgrant@csc.edu
GRANT, Debby .... 956-665-2500.... 506 C
debbygrant@utpa.edu
GRANT, Deborah, L .... 504-865-5210.... 215 C
dgrant@tulane.edu
GRANT, Diane .... 717-764-9550.... 426 C
dgrant@csb.edu
GRANT, Donna .... 504-286-5040.... 214 J
dgrant@suno.edu
GRANT, Edward, B .... 989-774-3105.... 249 C
grant1eb@cmich.edu
GRANT, Gary .... 817-735-3013.... 504 E
gary.grant@unthsc.edu
GRANT, George .... 616-331-6850.... 251 F
grantg@gvsu.edu
GRANT, James .... 660-263-4110.... 286 H
jamesg@macc.edu
GRANT, Jeff .... 229-245-3852.... 139 C
jgrant@valdosta.edu
GRANT, Jessie .... 740-351-3549.... 401 I
jgrant@shawnee.edu
GRANT, Jordan, L .... 206-281-2469.... 537 H
grantj@spu.edu
GRANT, Keith .... 513-671-1920.... 198 G
kgrant@beckfield.edu
GRANT, Kizuwanda .... 214-379-5500.... 492 F
kgrant@pqc.edu
GRANT, Kizuwanda .... 214-379-5407.... 492 F
kgrant@pqc.edu
GRANT, Louise, G .... 207-941-7176.... 219 E
grantl@nescom.edu
GRANT, Lyman, W .... 512-223-3352.... 481 B
lgrant@austincc.edu
GRANT, Marta .... 254-526-1302.... 482 H
ctc.international@ctcd.edu
GRANT, Marvin .... 904-470-8892.... 105 G
marvin.grant@ewc.edu
GRANT, Mary .... 912-525-6131.... 136 F
mgrant@scad.edu
GRANT, Mary, E .... 317-788-3581.... 180 F
mgrant@uindy.edu
GRANT, Mary, K .... 413-662-5201.... 238 C
mary.grant@mcla.edu
GRANT, Michael .... 212-592-2000.... 350 F
mgrant@sva.edu
GRANT, Michelle .... 904-332-0910.... 110 K
GRANT, Ralph, T .... 973-803-5000.... 315 D
rgrant@somerset.edu
GRANT, Richard .... 207-859-1106.... 219 G
careerdir@thomas.edu
GRANT, Robert .... 816-501-4418.... 288 A
bob.grant@rockhurst.edu
GRANT, S. G .... 607-777-7329.... 351 F
sggrant@binghamton.edu
GRANT, Sabrina .... 973-720-2754.... 317 D
grants@wpunj.edu
GRANT, Sharone, V .... 410-651-6597.... 227 E
svgrant@umes.edu
GRANT, Steve .... 229-430-4623.... 124 A
steve.grant@asurams.edu
GRANT, Tameiko .... 904-264-9122.... 106 I
GRANT, Terry .... 304-724-3700.... 540 F
tgrant@apus.edu
GRANT, Terry, H .... 605-394-1204.... 466 B
terry.grant@asu.edu
GRANT, Velvet, L .... 757-683-3159.... 522 F
vlgrant2@odu.edu
GRANT BAHAN, Rebecca .. 314-889-4509.... 281 I
rgrantbahan@fontbonne.edu
GRANVILLE, Andrea, L ...... 212-752-1530.... 338 C
andrea.granville@limcollege.edu
GRAPES, Jody .... 212-353-4160.... 331 A
grapes@cooper.edu
GRAPPO, Ann Marie .... 212-217-3900.... 333 F
ann_grappo@fitnyc.edu
GRASKY, Staci .... 207-741-5515.... 219 A
sgrasky@smccme.edu
GRASSADONIA, Jane, M .. 814-886-6472.... 437 B
jgrassadonia@mtaloy.edu
GRASSEL, OSB, Martin ..... 503-845-3326.... 417 A
martin.grassel@mtangel.edu
GRASSEL, Nancy .... 605-642-6545.... 465 H
nancy.grassel@bhsu.edu
GRASSETTI, J. Vincent .... 413-755-4061.... 241 B
vgrassetti@stcc.edu
GRASSI, Suna, K .... 617-636-2917.... 245 C
suna.grassi@tufts.edu
GRASSINI, Dennis, J .... 401-825-2151.... 453 D
dgrassini@ccri.edu
GRASSO, Domenico .... 802-656-2918.... 514 H
domenico.grasso@uvm.edu
GRASSO, Maureen .... 706-425-2933.... 138 G
mgrasso@uga.edu
GRATE, Sheresa .... 918-333-6830.... 411 B
sgrate@okwu.edu
GRATEROLE-ROSARIO,
Agustin .... 787-993-8886.... 567 B
agustin.graterole@upr.edu
GRATTAN, Matthew .... 518-381-1314.... 350 E
grattamj@sunysccc.edu
GRATTON, John .... 575-234-9210.... 319 F
jgratton@nmsu.edu
GRATZ, Robert, D .... 512-245-2121.... 501 F
rg02@txstate.edu
GRATZ, Robin, J .... 260-982-5063.... 177 H
rjgratz@manchester.edu
GRATZ, T, R .... 360-736-9391.... 532 D
trgratz@centralia.edu
GRAU, Frances .... 787-720-1022.... 560 F
fgrau@atlanticcollege.edu
GRAU, Isidro .... 713-221-8494.... 503 F
graui@uhd.edu
GRAU, Leeann .... 740-389-4636.... 395 H
graul@mtc.edu
GRAU, Monica, C .... 607-436-2255.... 353 E
graumc@oneonta.edu
GRAUBART, Steven .... 202-274-5221.... 100 A
sgraubart@udc.edu
GRAUMAN, Gregory .... 202-855-6063...... 97 D
grauman@american.edu
GRAUMLICH, Lisa .... 206-221-0907.... 539 A
graumlic@uw.edu
GRAUNKE, Jan .... 920-686-6180.... 550 H
jan.graunke@sl.edu
GRAUPE, Frank .... 212-749-2802.... 339 I
fgraupe@msmnyc.edu
GRAVDAHL, Jeanette .... 605-698-3966.... 465 E
jgravdahl@swc.tc
GRAVEL, Matthew .... 413-755-4623.... 241 B
mgravel@stcc.edu
GRAVELY, Archer, R .... 828-232-5118.... 378 D
gravely@unca.edu
GRAVENBERG, Eric .... 510-436-2478...... 62 E
egravenberg@peralta.edu
GRAVER, Mark .... 812-537-4010.... 177 A
mgraver@ivytech.edu
GRAVES, Aaron .... 919-684-6571.... 364 C
aaron.graves@duke.edu
GRAVES, Becky .... 256-352-8159...... 10 A
becky.graves@wallacestate.edu
GRAVES, Ben .... 270-247-8521.... 204 G
bgraves@midcontinent.edu
GRAVES, Bettye .... 601-979-2803.... 274 G
betty.r.graves@jsums.edu
GRAVES, Billy, J .... 910-962-3761.... 379 D
gravesb@uncw.edu
GRAVES, Diane, J .... 210-999-8121.... 502 E
diane.graves@trinity.edu
GRAVES, Finley .... 940-565-3097.... 504 D
gravesf@unt.edu
GRAVES, Frank .... 254-299-8126.... 490 G
fgraves@mclennan.edu
GRAVES, Harold, B .... 719-884-5000...... 86 J
hbgraves@nbc.edu
GRAVES, James, E .... 801-581-8537.... 511 C
james.graves@hsc.utah.edu
GRAVES, Jessica .... 937-294-0592.... 401 H
jessica@saa.edu
GRAVES, Kimberley .... 808-735-4787.... 140 E
kimberley.graves@chaminade.edu
GRAVES, Larry .... 608-262-9652.... 553 B
larry.graves@uwc.edu
GRAVES, Lisa .... 785-825-5422.... 191 E
lgraves@brownmackie.edu
GRAVES, Loreatha, D .... 336-334-7551.... 378 A
loretha@ncat.edu
GRAVES, Marcene .... 540-535-3461.... 524 E
mgraves@su.edu
GRAVES, Matt .... 208-792-2247.... 144 B
mlgraves@lcsc.edu
GRAVES, Michele .... 425-640-1513.... 533 I
mgraves@edcc.edu
GRAVES, Patricia, A .... 989-686-9218.... 250 D
pagraves@delta.edu
GRAVES, Peter, E .... 512-463-1808.... 500 H
peter.graves@tsus.edu
GRAVES, Randy, K .... 269-471-3854.... 247 D
gravesr@andrews.edu
GRAVES, Rita .... 318-357-5178.... 216 B
gravesr@nsula.edu
GRAVES, Robbie .... 731-661-5008.... 477 B
rgraves@uu.edu
GRAVES, Robert .... 413-528-7316.... 230 F
rgraves@simons-rock.edu
GRAVES, Robert .... 217-333-1660.... 167 D
rbgraves@illinois.edu
GRAVES, Sara, J .... 256-824-6064........ 8 G
sara.graves@uah.edu
GRAVES, Susan .... 270-534-3155.... 203 E
susan.graves@kctcs.edu
GRAVES, Veronica .... 301-736-3631.... 224 A
veronica.graves@msbbcs.edu
GRAVES, William, T .... 318-342-1010.... 216 E
GRAVETT, Erika .... 478-825-6301.... 129 F
gravette@fvsu.edu
GRAVIETTE, Kimberly, K .... 402-461-7387.... 298 A
kgraviette@hastings.edu
GRAVITT, Michael .... 816-472-4852.... 283 E
mgravitt@kcai.edu
GRAVLEY, John .... 913-667-5700.... 191 H
jgravley@cbts.edu
GRAVO, Daniel .... 330-244-4752.... 405 F
dgravo@walsh.edu
GRAY, Aaron .... 816-531-5223.... 280 C
GRAY, Alicia .... 409-882-3343.... 501 B
alicia.gray@lsco.edu
GRAY, Anita .... 260-359-4063.... 173 A
agray@huntington.edu
GRAY, Ashley .... 225-675-8270.... 211 F
agray@rpcc.edu
GRAY, Bo .... 828-835-4222.... 374 F
bgray@tricountycc.edu
GRAY, Charlotte .... 417-777-5062.... 279 A
cgray@texascountytech.edu
GRAY, Charlotte .... 417-967-5466.... 290 E
GRAY, Christopher .... 309-694-5132.... 152 C
christopher.gray@icc.edu
GRAY, Corey .... 402-643-3651.... 297 D
corey.gray@cune.edu
GRAY, Craig .... 336-316-2020.... 365 A
graycr@guilford.edu
GRAY, Cynthia, B .... 608-363-2024.... 546 E
graycb@beloit.edu
GRAY, David .... 575-624-8078.... 319 C
david@nmmi.edu
GRAY, David, E .... 502-895-3411.... 204 F
dgray@lpts.edu
GRAY, David, J .... 814-865-6574.... 438 G
djg36@psu.edu
GRAY, David, R .... 540-868-7154.... 527 C
dgray@lfcc.edu
GRAY, David, R .... 610-989-1203.... 450 F
dgray@vfmac.edu
GRAY, David, W .... 615-898-2414.... 473 G
david.gray@mtsu.edu
GRAY, Deborah .... 229-225-4087.... 138 A
dgray@southwestgatech.edu
GRAY, Donna .... 501-205-8805...... 21 C
dgray@cbc.edu
GRAY, Douglass, P .... 410-827-5830.... 222 B
dgray@chesapeake.edu
GRAY, Erin .... 312-567-3720.... 153 C
grayi@iit.edu
GRAY, Gary .... 907-474-7780...... 10 I
GRAY, Gary .... 406-657-2282.... 295 D
ggray@msubillings.edu
GRAY, Gary, E .... 618-235-2700.... 165 D
gary.gray@swic.edu
GRAY, Gary, W .... 714-449-7481...... 70 G
ggray@scco.edu
GRAY, Glenn .... 920-465-2040.... 551 B
grayg@uwgb.edu
GRAY, Gregory .... 951-222-8804...... 64 A
GRAY, Gregory, S .... 334-727-8011........ 8 B
gsgray@tuskegee.edu
GRAY, Gregory, W .... 951-222-8800...... 63 I
greg.gray@rcc.edu
GRAY, J. Ian .... 517-355-0306.... 255 A
gray@msu.edu
GRAY, III, James, A .... 252-985-5140.... 375 E
jgray@ncwc.edu
GRAY, Jeff .... 478-387-4781.... 131 A
GRAY, Jeffrey .... 515-271-1506.... 184 A
jeffrey.gray@dmu.edu
GRAY, Jeffrey, L .... 718-817-4750.... 334 C
gray@fordham.edu
GRAY, Jennifer, L .... 518-255-5408.... 354 E
institutionalresearch@cobleskill.edu
GRAY, Joe .... 615-547-1255.... 468 B
jgray@cumberland.edu
GRAY, John, C .... 302-295-1139.... 97 C
john.c.gray@wilmu.edu
GRAY, Karol .... 919-962-3795.... 378 E
kkgray@unc.edu
GRAY, Kelly .... 419-755-4823.... 397 C
kgray@ncstatecollege.edu
GRAY, Kenneth, D .... 304-293-5811.... 545 A
ken.gray@mail.wvu.edu
GRAY, Kilen .... 502-895-3411.... 204 F
kgray@lpts.edu
GRAY, Kimberly, F .... 706-729-2328.... 125 G
kgray@aug.edu
GRAY, Kristen .... 706-778-0100.... 136 A
kgray@piedmont.edu
GRAY, Kristen .... 616-395-7945.... 252 D
gray@hope.edu
GRAY, Leah .... 731-425-2606.... 475 C
lgray@jscc.edu
GRAY, Linda .... 903-589-4024.... 490 D
lgray@lonmorris.edu
GRAY, Lisa, G .... 410-546-6390.... 228 D
lggray@salisbury.edu
GRAY, Lydia, E .... 718-862-7231.... 339 H
lydia.gray@manhattan.edu
GRAY, Martha, D .... 607-274-3164.... 336 G
mgray@ithaca.edu
GRAY, Maryann, J .... 310-825-5573...... 74 C
mgray@conet.ucla.edu
GRAY, Megan .... 419-251-1784.... 395 I
megan.gray@mercycollege.edu
GRAY, Michael .... 606-546-1390.... 207 B
mwgray@unionky.edu
GRAY, Michaelle .... 580-371-2371.... 408 I
mgray@mscok.edu
GRAY, Nancy .... 480-342-4053.... 262 E
gray.nancy@mayo.edu
GRAY, Nancy, O .... 540-362-6321.... 520 A
presoffc@hollins.edu
GRAY, Nyree .... 213-738-6871...... 71 E
deanofstudents@swlaw.edu
GRAY, Rebecca .... 254-968-9473.... 497 A
rgray@tarleton.edu
GRAY, Rebecca .... 843-953-5633.... 457 B
grayrj@cofc.edu
GRAY, Reginald .... 214-379-5409.... 492 F
rgray@pqc.edu
GRAY, Richard, D .... 860-486-3455...... 94 G
richard.gray@uconn.edu
GRAY, Robert, R .... 804-257-5842.... 530 A
rrgray@vuu.edu
GRAY, Sandra, C .... 859-858-3511.... 198 E
president@asbury.edu
GRAY, Sarah .... 309-649-6265.... 165 F
sarah.gray@src.edu
GRAY, Shaun .... 207-741-5580.... 219 A
sgray@smccme.edu
GRAY, Sheryl .... 865-471-3240.... 467 G
sgray@cn.edu
GRAY, Shonda .... 443-885-3430.... 224 E
shonda.gray@morgan.edu
GRAY, Susan .... 478-289-2027.... 129 B
sgray@ega.edu
GRAY, Taylor, C .... 702-651-7627.... 302 E
taylor.gray@csn.edu
GRAY, Tim .... 319-208-5022.... 189 D
tgray@scciowa.edu
GRAY, Toni .... 806-354-6083.... 479 G
tbgray@actx.edu
GRAY, Warren .... 606-589-3070.... 203 D
warren.gray@kctcs.edu
GRAY, Warren, S .... 401-865-1602.... 453 H
wgray@providence.edu
GRAY, Wilbur, E .... 717-728-2511.... 425 B
billgray@centralpenn.edu
GRAY, William .... 417-777-5062.... 279 A
bgray@texascountytech.edu
GRAY-DEVINE, Sherry .... 580-371-2371.... 408 I
GRAY-LACKEY, Denise ...... 502-213-7202.... 202 F
denise.graylackey@kctcs.edu
GRAY-LITTLE, Bernadette ... 785-864-3131.... 197 B
graylittle@ku.edu
GRAY PAYTON, Pamela .... 619-260-4681...... 76 D
grayp@sandiego.edu
GRAY-REED, Diane .... 626-529-8451...... 60 F
dgray-reed@pacificoaks.edu
GRAYBEAL, Clay .... 207-221-4509.... 221 A
cgraybeal@une.edu
GRAYBEAL, Jerry, G .... 801-626-8114.... 511 G
jgraybeal@weber.edu
GRAYBEAL, Susan, E .... 423-354-2471.... 475 F
segraybeal@northeaststate.edu
GRAYS, Shantay .... 713-718-5053.... 487 I
shantay.grays@hccs.edu
GRAYSON, Chinester .... 334-874-5700........ 2 H
cgrayson@ccal.edu
GRAYSON, Denise, R .... 605-256-5152.... 465 I
denise.grayson@dsu.edu
GRAYSON, Lorenzo .... 251-405-7170........ 2 C
lgrayson@bishop.edu
GRAYSON, Paul .... 212-774-0727.... 340 C
pgrayson@mmm.edu
GRAZIANO, Joanne .... 516-299-2999.... 339 A
joanne.graziano@liu.edu
GRAZIANO, Vincent, S ...... 412-391-6710.... 423 B
vgraziano@bradfordpittsburgh.edu
GRAZIOTTI, Michael .... 305-892-5374.... 112 A
michael.graziotti@jwu.edu
GRBOVIC, Vesna .... 312-777-8668.... 153 B
vgrbovic@aii.edu
GREAF, Eileen .... 330-941-2364.... 406 F
egreaf@ysu.edu
GREALISH, William .... 617-578-7178.... 244 D
wgrealish@sbboston.com

GREANEY, KC 707-521-7940 68 E kgreaney@santarosa.edu
GREAR, Nancy, C 585-389-2801 342 D ngrear2@naz.edu
GREASLEY, Philip 859-257-3381 207 D greasle@uky.edu
GREATHOUSE, Jan 615-248-7782 476 G jgreathouse@trevecca.edu
GREATHOUSE, Jane 507-389-7408 269 D jane.greathouse@southcentral.edu
GREAVES, Christopher 718-997-3930 328 E christopher.greaves@qc.cuny.edu
GREB, Christine 215-951-2808 444 D grebc@philau.edu
GREBEL, David, A 817-257-7130 499 C d.grebel@tcu.edu
GREBING, Karen 573-651-2433 289 K kgrebing@semo.edu
GRECO, Anne 215-751-8217 426 B agreco@ccp.edu
GRECO, Carol 804-627-5300 517 A
GRECO, Frank, M 412-365-1133 425 C greco@chatham.edu
GRECO, Gary 860-738-6397 92 B ggreco@nwcc.commnet.edu
GRECO, Joseph 610-543-2500 99 G
GRECO, Juneann 570-340-6004 435 F greco@marywood.edu
GRECO, Michelle 504-671-6001 210 F mgreco@dcc.edu
GRECO, Peter 925-631-4747 64 F peter.greco2@stmarys-ca.edu
GRECO, Sal 516-299-3796 338 E sal.greco@liu.edu
GREDEN, Leigh 734-487-7048 250 F lgreden@emich.edu
GREDER, Darcy, L 309-556-3541 153 F dgreder@iwu.edu
GREDY, John, W 937-766-3200 386 G jgredy@cedarville.edu
GREEAR, Marisa 360-442-2391 535 I mgreear@lowercolumbia.edu
GREEN, Allen 914-395-2249 350 C agreen@sarahlawrence.edu
GREEN, Alus 201-360-4047 310 E agreen@hccc.edu
GREEN, Amber 619-644-7631 49 C amber.green@gcccd.edu
GREEN, Amy 931-540-2764 475 A amy.green@columbiastate.edu
GREEN, Andrew 516-773-5587 558 I greena@usmma.edu
GREEN, Andy 256-782-5268 4 L agreen@jsu.edu
GREEN, Anita 313-593-5190 259 B ujima@umd.umich.edu
GREEN, Ann, F 828-694-1709 368 E anng@blueridge.edu
GREEN, Audrey 661-362-3424 41 I audrey.green@canyons.edu
GREEN, Barbara, C 626-395-6351 32 H barbarag@caltech.edu
GREEN, Betti 315-781-3600 335 F bgreen@hws.edu
GREEN, Bevley, W 251-460-6188 9 D bwgreen@usouthal.edu
GREEN, Carla 804-527-1000 99 G
GREEN, Carla, D 913-288-7273 194 C cgreen@kckcc.edu
GREEN, Carol 903-233-4010 490 A carolgreen@letu.edu
GREEN, Carol 253-840-8419 536 H cgreen@pierce.ctc.edu
GREEN, Cathy 603-513-5101 306 E cathy.green@law.unh.edu
GREEN, Charles, D 319-335-5026 182 F charles-green@uiowa.edu
GREEN, Chris 859-985-3727 199 A greenchr@berea.edu
GREEN, Christopher 805-546-3902 43 I cgreen@cuesta.edu
GREEN, Clarence 660-562-1254 287 B cgreen@nwmissouri.edu
GREEN, JR., Clarence 660-562-1127 287 B cgreen@nwmissouri.edu
GREEN, Constance, C 503-842-8222 420 D green@tillamookbay.cc
GREEN, Danny 919-760-8026 367 A greend@meredith.edu
GREEN, David, A 217-786-2406 157 B david.green@llcc.edu
GREEN, David, M 818-947-2679 55 E greendm@lavc.edu
GREEN, Denise, O 989-774-3700 249 C green1do@cmich.edu
GREEN, Don 657-278-2413 35 B dgreen@fullerton.edu
GREEN, Donald 616-643-5737 250 H greend@ferris.edu
GREEN, Donald 231-591-2548 250 H greend@ferris.edu
GREEN, Donald 973-290-4290 308 G security@cse.edu
GREEN, JR., Donald, W 904-632-3105 109 F dgreen@fscj.edu
GREEN, Donna 562-985-8403 35 C dgreen4@csulb.edu
GREEN, Ed 408-855-5021 78 F ed.green@wvm.edu
GREEN, Elaine 215-248-7063 425 D greene@chc.edu
GREEN, Eleanor, M 979-845-5051 497 E emgreen@tamu.edu
GREEN, Ellen, R 806-371-5131 479 G ergreen@actx.edu
GREEN, Finley, L 423-652-4865 470 A flgreen@king.edu
GREEN, Gary, M 336-734-7200 370 F ggreen@forsythtech.edu
GREEN, Hope 773-380-6840 168 F hgreen@westwood.edu
GREEN, Jean, M 217-228-5432 161 F greenje@quincy.edu
GREEN, Jeff, W 256-549-8317 3 J jgreen@gadsdenstate.edu
GREEN, Jeffrey 312-662-4401 144 H jgreen@adler.edu
GREEN, Jennifer 909-621-8000 49 F jgreen@hmc.edu
GREEN, Jennifer, K 434-395-2944 521 A mailto:greenjk@longwood.edu
GREEN, Jenny 607-729-1581 331 G jgreen@davisny.edu
GREEN, Jerry 718-817-4170 334 C jgreen@fordham.edu
GREEN, Jim 360-992-2408 532 F jgreen@clark.edu
GREEN, Joel 626-584-5298 48 B cats@fuller.edu
GREEN, John, C 610-683-4114 443 A jgreen@kutztown.edu
GREEN, Jonathan, D 309-556-3101 153 F provost@iwu.edu
GREEN, Joyce 803-536-8551 460 G jgreen@scsu.edu
GREEN, Judith 201-684-7523 313 C jgreen2@ramapo.edu
GREEN, Julia 207-941-7129 218 A greenj@husson.edu
GREEN, Karen 336-517-2159 362 G kagreen@bennett.edu
GREEN, Karen 484-664-3182 437 C green@muhlenberg.edu
GREEN, Keith, A 717-901-5123 430 F kgreen@harrisburgu.edu
GREEN, Kristina 207-893-7998 219 F kgreen@sjcme.edu
GREEN, Kurt 530-541-4660 53 G green@ltcc.edu
GREEN, Lillie, F 757-727-5057 519 H lillie.green@hamptonu.edu
GREEN, Lisa 315-792-3736 359 E lcgreen@utica.edu
GREEN, Lorry 864-977-7124 460 A lorry.green@ngu.edu
GREEN, Mark, A 618-235-2700 165 D mark.green@swic.edu
GREEN, Mary 269-965-3931 253 B greenm@kellogg.edu
GREEN, Mary Beth 334-222-6591 5 F mbgreen@lbwcc.edu
GREEN, Mary Jo 715-422-5504 554 E maryjo.green@mstc.edu
GREEN, Matthew 805-546-3924 43 I mgreen@cuesta.edu
GREEN, Matthew 845-688-1568 358 E greenm@sunyulster.edu
GREEN, Melanie, H 804-627-5300 517 A
GREEN, Melissa 567-429-3535 400 I melissa_green3@owens.edu
GREEN, Michael, R 717-867-6208 434 C mgreen@lvc.edu
GREEN, Michael, S 518-629-4554 336 C m.green@hvcc.edu
GREEN, Mike 615-966-6000 470 F mike.green@lipscomb.edu
GREEN, Moishe 845-352-5852 360 H
GREEN, Monica 951-372-7082 63 K monica.green@norcocollege.edu
GREEN, Myrtes 205-929-6305 5 E mdgreen@lawsonstate.edu
GREEN, Nancy, L 765-966-2656 176 H ngreen12@ivytech.edu
GREEN, Nichol 601-928-6264 275 E nichol.green@mgccc.edu
GREEN, O. Jerome 501-374-6305 23 F
GREEN, Paul 509-327-2443 19 A paul.green@phoenix.edu
GREEN, Paula 626-914-8873 40 B pgreen@citruscollege.edu
GREEN, Paula, L 508-849-3344 230 C pgreen@annamaria.edu
GREEN, Rachel, T 904-819-6223 107 C rgreen@flagler.edu
GREEN, Ragan 478-275-7865 135 C rgreen@oftc.edu
GREEN, Ramona 903-223-3058 498 F ramona.green@tamut.edu
GREEN, Ray 903-468-3005 498 B raymond.green@tamuc.edu
GREEN, Rebecca 760-355-6499 51 A becky.green@imperial.edu
GREEN, Rhonda, T 209-575-6664 80 H greenr@yosemite.cc.ca.us
GREEN, Robert, L 540-464-7321 529 F greenrl@vmi.edu
GREEN, Ronald, F 843-953-7416 456 C ron.green@citadel.edu
GREEN, Ronnie 402-472-2871 300 E rgreen@nebraska.edu
GREEN, Ronnie, D 402-472-2871 300 G rgreen2@unl.edu
GREEN, Ruvain 845-352-5852 360 H
GREEN, Sandy, B 864-488-8348 459 B sgreen@limestone.edu
GREEN, Satasha 516-686-7706 343 D
GREEN, Sean-Michael 845-575-3800 340 B sean-michael.green@marist.edu
GREEN, Sharon, F 318-670-9337 215 A sgreen@susla.edu
GREEN, Shirley 602-787-6604 15 J shirley.green@paradisevalley.edu
GREEN, Stanton 732-571-3419 311 E sgreen@monmouth.edu
GREEN, Susan 802-635-1308 515 F susan.green@jsc.edu
GREEN, Tim 256-549-8601 3 J tgreen@gadsdenstate.edu
GREEN, Timothy, M 615-248-1387 476 G tgreen@trevecca.edu
GREEN, Tracey 315-498-2532 345 D
GREEN, Tracy 804-523-5789 527 A tgreen@reynolds.edu
GREEN, Vannessa 718-951-5842 326 F vgreen@brooklyn.cuny.edu
GREEN, Wandra, B 816-235-1601 291 C greenwb@umkc.edu
GREEN, Wayne 334-974-5700 2 H wgreen@ccal.edu
GREEN, William 423-614-8240 470 C wgreen@leeuniversity.edu.edu
GREEN, William, S 305-284-2006 122 I wgreen@miami.edu
GREEN-QUARLES, Ryanne 916-361-1660 38 G rgreen@carrington.edu
GREEN WARE, Nikisha 601-979-1472 274 G nikisha.g.ware@jsums.edu
GREENAN, Jennie 309-692-4092 158 D jgreenan@midstate.edu
GREENAN, Linda 202-687-5677 98 D greenanl@georgetown.edu
GREENBAUM, Michael, B 212-678-8800 337 G migreenbaum@jtsa.edu
GREENBAUM, Steve 215-885-2360 435 E sgreenbaum@manor.edu
GREENBERG, Barbara, L 973-972-1796 316 D greenbbl@umdnj.edu
GREENBERG, Erik 703-376-6150 19 A erik.greenberg@phoenix.edu
GREENBERG, Jeffrey 215-591-5738 427 B jgreenberg@devry.edu
GREENBERG, Judith, G 617-422-7245 243 B jgreenberg@nesl.edu
GREENBERG, Kenneth, S 617-573-8265 245 B kgreenbe@suffolk.edu
GREENBERG, Mark, L 215-895-2200 427 H mlg25@drexel.edu
GREENBERG, Raymond, S 843-792-2211 459 D greenber@musc.edu
GREENBERG, Roberta 718-933-6700 341 G rgreenbe@monroecollege.edu
GREENBERG, Scott, B 508-626-4550 238 A sgreenberg@framingham.edu
GREENBERG, Stephen, B 713-798-8878 481 H stepheng@bcm.edu
GREENBERG, Wendy 610-409-3329 450 D wgreenberg@ursinus.edu
GREENBERG, Yeshaya 305-534-7050 122 B
GREENBLATT, Kathy 410-225-2219 224 B greenblatt@mica.edu
GREENE, Barbara 704-484-4040 369 E greeneb@clevelandcc.edu
GREENE, Brent, D 715-425-4891 552 C brent.d.greene@uwrf.edu
GREENE, D. Gayle 919-532-5522 374 H dggreene@waketech.edu
GREENE, David, A 773-702-1377 166 G davidgreene@uchicago.edu
GREENE, Doug 641-782-1324 189 E greene@swcciowa.edu
GREENE, Gail 865-471-3532 467 G ggreene@cn.edu
GREENE, Gloria 256-824-6000 8 G gloria.green@uah.edu
GREENE, Heidi 302-736-2300 97 A greene@cchs.k12.de.us
GREENE, James 202-319-5247 97 E greene@cua.edu
GREENE, James 386-506-4429 104 F greenej@daytonastate.edu
GREENE, Jane, D 864-379-8715 458 A
GREENE, Jeff, W 606-474-3298 201 D jgreene@kcu.edu
GREENE, Jessica, A 617-552-3111 232 B jessica.greene.2@bc.edu
GREENE, John, W 615-322-2426 478 A john.greene@vanderbilt.edu
GREENE, Joseph, J 401-598-1038 453 E jgreene@jwu.edu
GREENE, Karen, L 614-234-5685 396 H kgreene@mccn.edu
GREENE, Ken, S 252-334-2019 367 C ken.greene@macuniversity.edu
GREENE, Kenneth 973-443-8084 310 A greene@fdu.edu
GREENE, Lori, A 773-508-3079 157 C lgreene@luc.edu
GREENE, M. Dwaine 910-893-1211 362 J greene@campbell.edu
GREENE, Marcia 239-590-7781 119 B mgreene@fgcu.edu
GREENE, Marisol 505-454-3499 318 J mgreene@nmhu.edu
GREENE, Mark 808-983-4163 140 H mgreene@tokai.edu
GREENE, Mark 307-766-2474 556 H mgreene@uwyo.edu
GREENE, Mike 480-732-7146 15 E mike.greene@cgc.edu
GREENE, Moshe 516-239-9002 350 H
GREENE, Patricia 843-521-4117 462 C pagreene@uscb.edu
GREENE, Perry 516-877-4041 322 A greene@adelphi.edu
GREENE, Randy 201-216-8761 315 E rgreene@stevens.edu
GREENE, Roger 212-410-8147 343 B rgreene@nycpm.edu
GREENE, Rose Lynn 727-784-0003 103 B rgreene@careerpathtraining.com
GREENE, Ryan 206-296-6260 538 B greener@seattleu.edu
GREENE, Shelley, W 336-629-2758 373 A swgreene@randolph.edu
GREENE, Steve 918-495-7040 411 C sgreene@oru.edu
GREENE, Thomas 530-541-4660 53 G greene@ltcc.edu
GREENE, Thomas, G 503-943-7107 420 G greene@up.edu
GREENE, Thomas Christopher 802-828-8613 515 A thomas.greene@vcfa.edu
GREENE, Timothy, J 269-387-2378 260 C tim.greene@wmich.edu
GREENE, Tom 718-636-3787 346 D tgreene@pratt.edu
GREENE, Tommy 704-484-4084 369 E greene@clevelandcc.edu
GREENE, Travis 641-269-3700 185 D greenet@grinnell.edu
GREENE, Vanessa 616-395-7800 252 D greene@hope.edu
GREENE-CORVEE, Judi 413-775-1387 239 E green-corveej@gcc.mass.edu
GREENE-RAINEY, Velva 484-365-7335 434 H vgrainey@lincoln.edu
GREENER, Gary, J 213-738-6834 71 E ggreener@swlaw.edu
GREENFELD, Shia 718-782-7070 359 A swg@utsny.edu
GREENFIELD, Brenda, T 315-470-6683 355 A bgreenfield@esf.edu
GREENFIELD, Derek 601-877-6700 272 F dgreenfield@alcorn.edu
GREENFIELD, Helga 404-270-5053 138 B hgreenfield@spelman.edu
GREENFIELD, Helga 404-270-6425 138 B hgreenfield@spelman.edu
GREENFIELD, Ilene 201-291-1111 323 H igl@berkeleycollege.edu
GREENFIELD, Meg 504-278-6424 211 E mgreenfield@nunez.edu
GREENFIELD, Wendy, M 610-526-5221 423 D wgreenfi@brynmawr.edu
GREENGART, Eli 410-484-7200 225 C
GREENHALGH, Jill 651-779-3338 266 A jill.greenhalgh@century.edu
GREENHALGH, Mark 714-992-7042 59 E mgreenhalgh@fullcoll.edu
GREENHAW, David, M 314-918-2620 281 F dgreenhaw@eden.edu
GREENHAW, Eric 479-524-7285 22 C egreenhaw@jbu.edu
GREENHOUSE, Jeremy 413-755-4524 241 B jgreenhouse@stcc.edu
GREENING, Doug, J 936-294-1910 501 D ppl_djg@shsu.edu
GREENING, Kris 870-743-3000 22 G kgreening@northark.edu
GREENIP, Jeffrey 305-892-7002 112 A jeff.greenip@jwu.edu
GREENLAW, David, E 407-303-7894 100 G dave.greenlaw@adu.edu

GREENLEAF, Katherine ...... 207-780-5920.... 220 G kgreenleaf@usm.maine.edu
GREENLEE, Carmen, M ..... 207-725-3286.... 217 E cgreenle@bowdoin.edu
GREENLEE, Daniel, D .... 906-487-2436.... 255 B ddgreen@mtu.edu
GREENLEE, Lisa .... 580-477-7702.... 414 C lisa.greenlee@wosc.edu
GREENLEE, Richard .... 740-695-1720.... 399 G greenlee@ohio.edu
GREENLEE, Richard .... 740-588-1435.... 400 E greenlee@ohio.edu
GREENLEE, Richard, W ...... 740-699-2494.... 400 B greenlee@ohio.edu
GREENO, Jimmie .... 215-972-2303.... 440 J jgreeno@pafa.edu
GREENSLADE, Ernestine .... 978-556-3862.... 240 E egreenslade@necc.mass.edu
GREENSPAN, Richard .... 713-348-6920.... 493 C rgreenspan@rice.edu
GREENSTEIN, Arlene, T ..... 978-542-6324.... 238 E agreenstein@salemstate.edu
GREENSTEIN, David .... 212-353-4198.... 331 A davidg@cooper.edu
GREENSTREET, Robert, C .. 414-229-4016.... 551 D bobg@uwm.edu
GREENUP, Troy .... 562-907-4287...... 79 F greenup@whittier.edu
GREENWADE, Gabrielle ...... 281-487-1170.... 499 B ggreenwade@txchiro.edu
GREENWALD, J. Patrick .... 716-888-8216.... 325 F greenwal@canisius.edu
GREENWALD, Nicole .... 206-876-6100.... 538 A ngreenwald@theseattleschool.edu
GREENWALD, Richard .... 718-940-5900.... 349 A rgreenwald@sjcny.edu
GREENWALD, Richard .... 973-408-3327.... 309 E rgreenwald@drew.edu
GREENWALT, Riane, B .... 618-650-2852.... 165 C rgreenw@siue.edu
GREENWAY, Janet .... 605-995-7136.... 464 F janet.greenway@mitchelltech.edu
GREENWAY, Kimberly .... 256-765-4248........ 9 C kagreenway@una.edu
GREENWAY, Lidell .... 229-468-2240.... 139 I lidell.greenway@wiregrass.edu
GREENWELL, James, A ..... 302-857-1070...... 96 G jgreenw@dtcc.edu
GREENWELL, Joseph, D .... 415-338-3885...... 37 B joey@sfsu.edu
GREENWELL, Randall .... 309-649-6251.... 165 F randy.greenwell@src.edu
GREENWOOD, Anita .... 978-934-4605.... 237 B anita_greenwood@uml.edu
GREENWOOD, Gail .... 423-472-7141.... 474 E ggreenwood@clevelandstatecc.edu
GREENWOOD, M. R. C .... 808-956-9704.... 141 E mrcgreenwood@hawaii.edu
GREENWOOD, Mark, D ...... 641-422-4395.... 188 A greenmar@niacc.edu
GREENWOOD, Paul, G .... 207-859-4776.... 217 G pggreenw@colby.edu
GREENWOOD, Scott .... 541-737-2351.... 418 F scott.greenwood@oregonstate.edu
GREENY, Erik .... 707-664-2563...... 37 D erik.greeny@sonoma.edu
GREER, Bobby, T .... 864-488-8251.... 459 B bgreer@limestone.edu
GREER, Christine, G .... 906-227-1700.... 256 C cgreer@nmu.edu
GREER, Colleen .... 218-755-2988.... 265 I cgreer@bemidjistate.edu
GREER, Irina .... 843-470-8393.... 461 E igreer@tcl.edu
GREER, James .... 325-793-4882.... 490 H jgreer@mcm.edu
GREER, Jody .... 260-665-4105.... 180 D greerj@trine.edu
GREER, Karla, J .... 972-860-7173.... 484 I kgreer@dcccd.edu
GREER, Kevin .... 417-626-1234.... 287 C greer.kevin@occ.edu
GREER, Kimberly .... 507-389-5717.... 267 E kimberly.greer@mnsu.edu
GREER, Linda, L .... 704-922-6266.... 370 G greer.linda@gaston.edu
GREER, M. Bradley .... 864-429-8728.... 463 A greerm@mailbox.sc.edu
GREER, Michael, A .... 814-886-6425.... 437 B mgreer@mtaloy.edu
GREER, Rebecca, M .... 540-224-4696.... 520 I rmgreer@jchs.edu
GREER, Sandra, C .... 510-430-2096...... 57 D sgreer@mills.edu
GREER, Sheree, D .... 606-474-3186.... 201 D sgreer@kcu.edu
GREER, William, B .... 423-461-8710.... 471 J bgreer@milligan.edu
GREER, JR., William, T ..... 757-455-3215.... 530 C wtgreer@vwc.edu
GREFFENSTEET-MOON, Cheryl .... 409-740-4418.... 497 F cgreffens@tamug.edu
GREGERSON, Robert .... 912-344-2617.... 124 G robert.gregerson@armstrong.edu
GREGG, Amy .... 808-933-0720.... 141 F agregg@hawaii.edu
GREGG, Carol, M .... 989-463-7231.... 247 B gregg@alma.edu
GREGG, Cody .... 956-872-2528.... 494 H cgregg@southtexascollege.edu
GREGG, Daniel .... 706-754-7728.... 135 A dgregg@northgatech.edu
GREGG, Gerald, A .... 503-943-7161.... 420 G gregg@up.edu
GREGG, Heidi .... 973-300-2232.... 315 F hgregg@sussex.edu
GREGG, Karla .... 417-447-6966.... 287 D greggk@otc.edu
GREGG, Mary, D .... 601-266-5001.... 277 F mary.gregg@usm.edu
GREGG, Michael, J .... 818-779-8040...... 53 B lpyun@kingsuniversity.edu
GREGG, Michael, J .... 818-779-8503...... 53 B mgregg@kingsuniversity.edu
GREGG, Patti .... 678-891-2571.... 131 C patricia.gregg@gpc.edu
GREGG, Robert, S .... 609-652-4505.... 313 E robert.gregg@stockton.edu
GREGG, Thomas, W .... 724-458-3795.... 430 B twgregg@gcc.edu
GREGG, Virginia .... 518-276-6524.... 347 D greggv@rpi.edu
GREGOIRE, David, P .... 518-564-2090.... 354 B gregoidp@plattsburgh.edu
GREGOIRE, Nicole .... 617-746-1990.... 235 G nicole.gregoire@hult.edu
GREGOIRE, JR., Paul, E .... 504-282-4455.... 213 H pgregoire@nobts.edu
GREGOIRE, Ronald, J .... 217-786-2243.... 157 B ron.gregoire@llcc.edu
GREGOIRE, Tom .... 614-292-9426.... 398 I gregoire.5@osu.edu
GREGOR, Ray .... 715-682-1680.... 549 F rgregor@northland.edu
GREGORI-GAHAN, Heidi .. 812-465-1248.... 181 B gahan@usi.edu
GREGORI ZEHEL, Renee ... 570-961-4715.... 435 F rzehel@marywood.edu
GREGOROWICZ, Stephen .. 609-586-4800.... 311 B gregoros@mccc.edu
GREGORY, Annette, K .... 512-414-9820.... 481 B agregory@austincc.edu
GREGORY, Brent .... 662-246-6302.... 275 D bgregory@msdelta.edu
GREGORY, Carolyn .... 216-368-5276.... 386 F carolyn.gregory@case.edu
GREGORY, Charles .... 630-829-6009.... 145 G cgregory@ben.edu
GREGORY, Christopher ...... 508-626-4510.... 238 A cgregory@framingham.edu
GREGORY, Dan .... 320-308-4932.... 269 A ddgregory@stcloudstate.edu
GREGORY, Darlene .... 334-386-7108........ 3 G dgregory@faulkner.edu
GREGORY, David .... 606-783-5100.... 204 I d.gregory@moreheadstate.edu
GREGORY, David, B .... 615-366-4430.... 473 D david.gregory@tbr.edu
GREGORY, David, D .... 413-585-3770.... 244 G dgregory@smith.edu
GREGORY, Denise .... 740-351-3182.... 401 I dgregory@shawnee.edu
GREGORY, Ellen, D .... 859-846-6046.... 204 H egregory@midway.edu
GREGORY, J. Roy .... 931-221-7127.... 473 E gregoryr@apsu.edu
GREGORY, Jack, L .... 931-363-9816.... 471 A jgregory@martinmethodist.edu
GREGORY, John .... 330-823-2280.... 404 C gregorjl@mountunion.edu
GREGORY, John, H .... 207-581-1609.... 220 A jgregory@maine.edu
GREGORY, Lisa .... 217-875-7200.... 162 F lgregory@richland.edu
GREGORY, Mark .... 503-725-3281.... 418 G gregorym@pdx.edu
GREGORY, Melissa .... 240-567-7320.... 224 D melissa.gregory@montgomerycollege.edu
GREGORY, Michelle .... 503-491-7210.... 417 B michelle.gregory@mhcc.edu
GREGORY, Richard .... 281-618-5508.... 490 E richard.b.gregory@lonestar.edu
GREGORY, Stephen .... 740-351-3259.... 401 I sgregory@shawnee.edu
GREGORY, Thomas, L .... 434-223-6161.... 519 G tgregory@hsc.edu
GREGORY, Tom, F .... 570-326-3761.... 440 L tgregory@pct.edu
GREGORY, Travis .... 760-355-6212...... 51 A travis.gregory@imperial.edu
GREGORY, Trisha .... 301-687-4201.... 228 C tgregory@frostburg.edu
GREGORYK, Michael, D .... 909-594-5611...... 58 A mgregoryk@mtsac.edu
GREIFE, Alice, L .... 660-543-4450.... 290 H greife@ucmo.edu
GREIFE, Steve, B .... 816-604-2221.... 285 C steve.greife@mcckc.edu
GREIG, Carl .... 903-223-3062.... 498 F carl.greig@tamut.edu
GREIG, Judith, M .... 650-508-3503...... 59 H jgreig@ndnu.edu
GREIL, Stan .... 405-733-7488.... 411 I sgreil@rose.edu
GREIM, Jeffrey .... 413-565-1000.... 230 G jgreim@baypath.edu
GREINER, A. Cathleen .... 805-546-3122...... 43 I anna_greiner@cuesta.edu
GREINER, Jodi .... 641-673-1047.... 190 C greinerj@wmpenn.edu
GREINER, Stephen .... 606-436-5721.... 202 C steve.greiner@kctcs.edu
GREINKE, Gary, A .... 805-893-2218...... 75 B gary.greinke@ia.ucsb.edu
GREISOFE, Jennifer .... 516-299-4053.... 339 A jennifer.greisofe@liu.edu
GRELL, Vince .... 602-387-7000...... 19 A vince.grell@apollogrp.edu
GRELL, Vince .... 602-557-1937...... 19 A vince.grell@phoenix.edu
GRELLE, Elaine .... 978-837-5947.... 242 A grellee@merrimack.edu
GRELLE, Michael .... 660-543-4116.... 290 H grelle@ucmo.edu
GRELLSON, Mona, S .... 651-631-5390.... 270 B msgrellson@nwc.edu
GREMILLION, Henry .... 504-619-8500.... 213 A hgremi@lsuhsc.edu
GREMMELS, Gillian (Jill), S .... 704-894-2160.... 363 I jigremmels@davidson.edu
GREMMELS, Luther .... 205-652-3768........ 9 E gremmels@uwa.edu
GRENA, Eileen, A .... 302-477-2102...... 97 B eagrena@widener.edu
GRENDA, Katherine .... 586-445-7315.... 254 C grendak@macomb.edu
GRENDER, Teresa .... 606-368-6044.... 198 C teresagrender@alc.edu
GRENNAN, Jon .... 845-434-5750.... 357 A jgrennan@sullivan.suny.edu
GRENNAN, Kim .... 619-961-4291...... 72 J kimg@tjsl.edu
GRENNIER, Dana .... 414-277-6765.... 549 C grennier@msoe.edu
GRENON, Jamie .... 401-254-4847.... 454 C jgrenon@rwu.edu
GRENOT, Teresa .... 707-826-3441...... 36 E teresa.grenot@humboldt.edu
GRENOT-SCHEYER, Marquita .... 562-985-4513...... 35 C mgrenot@csulb.edu
GREPPIN, Monica .... 615-366-4417.... 473 D monica.greppin@tbr.edu
GRESE, Susan .... 734-995-7457.... 249 G greses@cuaa.edu
GRESH, Charles, E .... 215-951-1539.... 432 I gresh@lasalle.edu
GRESHAM, Gwen .... 870-743-3000...... 22 G gweng@northark.edu
GRESHAM, Jerry .... 731-881-7250.... 477 G jgresham@utm.edu
GRESHAM, John .... 314-768-1889.... 283 G gresham@kenrick.edu
GRESHAM, Loren, P .... 405-491-6300.... 412 D lgresham@snu.edu
GRESHAM, Mary, H .... 716-645-6640.... 351 G gsedean@buffalo.edu
GRESHAM, Susan .... 812-535-5121.... 179 E sgresham@smwc.edu
GRESS, Michael .... 812-888-4506.... 181 D mgress@vinu.edu
GRESSETT, Chris .... 305-644-1171.... 104 D cgressett@dademedical.edu
GRESSLEY, Jerry, A .... 260-359-4052.... 173 A jgressley@huntington.edu
GRETCH, Jim .... 406-791-5320.... 296 F jgretch@ugf.edu
GREUFE, Sandra .... 641-648-4611.... 186 C sandra.greufe@iavalley.edu
GREULICH, William .... 760-245-4271...... 77 H bill.greulich@vvc.edu
GREVE, Debbie .... 620-235-4206.... 196 C dgreve@pittstate.edu
GREVESEN, Chris .... 732-729-3701.... 309 C cgrevesen@devry.edu
GREVILLE, Liza, J .... 814-362-5121.... 449 B greville@pitt.edu
GREVING, John .... 402-465-2486.... 299 H jgreving@nebrwesleyan.edu
GREWAL, Dilawar .... 718-390-3239.... 360 A dilawar.grewal@wagner.edu
GREWAL, Harpal, S .... 803-535-5202.... 456 D hgrewal@claflin.edu
GREY, Kimberly .... 314-392-2241.... 285 J grey@mobap.edu
GREY, Margaret .... 203-785-2393...... 96 A margaret.grey@yale.edu
GREYDANUS, John .... 541-737-9099.... 418 F john.greydanus@oregonstate.edu
GRGURICH, Stephanie .... 952-838-1870.... 263 D sgrgurich@devry.edu
GRIBBEN, Les .... 212-817-7000.... 327 B lgribben@gc.cuny.edu
GRIBBIN, David .... 478-289-2047.... 129 B dgribbin@ega.edu
GRIBBIN, Kathy .... 574-257-3416.... 169 I gribbik@bethelcollege.edu
GRIBBIN, William, G .... 434-582-2466.... 520 K wgribbin@liberty.edu
GRIBBLE, Kari .... 608-663-2305.... 547 F kgribble@edgewood.edu
GRIBBLE, Shannon, L .... 301-687-4161.... 228 C slgribble@frostburg.edu
GRIBBONS, Barry .... 661-362-5500...... 41 I barry.gribbons@canyons.edu
GRIBOU, Julius, M .... 210-458-4110.... 506 D julius.gribou@utsa.edu
GRICE, Len .... 870-733-6743...... 22 E lgrice@midsouthcc.edu
GRICE, Sharon .... 319-895-4215.... 183 G sgrice@cornellcollege.edu
GRICE, Sharon .... 319-895-4167.... 183 G sgrice@cornellcollege.edu
GRICE, Vivian, D .... 803-641-3550.... 462 B viviang@usca.edu
GRIEGER, Ingrid .... 914-633-2038.... 336 E igrieger@iona.edu
GRIEGO, Brenda .... 702-968-1619.... 303 D bgriego@roseman.edu
GRIEGO, Elizabeth, B .... 209-946-2365...... 76 A egriego@pacific.edu
GRIER, Douglas, L .... 630-466-7900.... 168 B dgrier@waubonsee.edu
GRIER, Ed, A .... 804-827-0072.... 526 B egrier@vcu.edu
GRIER, Frank, O .... 334-833-4005........ 4 E fgrier@huntingdon.edu
GRIER, Judith, M .... 757-789-1753.... 526 H jgrier@es.vccs.edu
GRIER, Tricia, S .... 334-833-4534........ 4 E tgrier@huntingdon.edu
GRIESBACH, Scott .... 715-232-2131.... 552 E griesbachs@uwstout.edu
GRIESSE, Sarah .... 612-330-1489.... 261 B griesse@augsburg.edu
GRIEVE, Cathy .... 303-871-2397...... 89 A cgrieve@du.edu
GRIEVE, Kim .... 419-824-3834.... 395 E kgrieve@lourdes.edu
GRIEVE, Kimberly .... 605-677-5331.... 465 G kimberly.grieve@nsd.edu
GRIFFENBERG, Bill .... 843-661-8261.... 458 B bill.griffenberg@fdtc.edu
GRIFFES, Michael .... 910-843-5304.... 367 G
GRIFFES, Michelle Rae .... 910-843-5304.... 367 G
GRIFFETH, Hank .... 478-757-3510.... 127 A hgriffeth@centralgatech.edu
GRIFFEY, David .... 201-761-7106.... 314 F dgriffey@spc.edu
GRIFFIN, Adrian .... 718-260-5050.... 328 D agriffin@citytech.cuny.edu
GRIFFIN, Archie .... 614-292-9820.... 398 I griffin@ohiostatealumni.org
GRIFFIN, Barbara .... 202-806-2100...... 98 E bgriffin@howard.edu
GRIFFIN, Brent .... 715-324-6900.... 549 G brent.griffin@ni.edu
GRIFFIN, Brian .... 919-658-7763.... 367 F bgriffin@moc.edu
GRIFFIN, Bruce .... 510-659-6514...... 59 J bgriffin@ohlone.edu
GRIFFIN, Cathy .... 908-526-1200.... 313 D cgriffin@raritanval.edu
GRIFFIN, Charles Andrew .. 928-523-8555...... 16 I andrew.griffin@nau.edu
GRIFFIN, Clifton, P .... 410-548-3894.... 228 D cpgriffin@salisbury.edu
GRIFFIN, D. Joseph .... 617-373-2121.... 243 F
GRIFFIN, Dale, M .... 405-878-2377.... 409 D dale.griffin@okbu.edu
GRIFFIN, Daniel .... 706-886-6831.... 138 D dgriffin@tfc.edu
GRIFFIN, David .... 425-637-1010.... 532 E dgriffin@cityu.edu
GRIFFIN, Deborah .... 510-659-6151...... 59 J dgriffin@ohlone.edu
GRIFFIN, Dennis .... 614-825-6255.... 383 K dgriffin@aiam.edu
GRIFFIN, Donitha .... 334-876-9302........ 4 B dgriffin@wccs.edu
GRIFFIN, Doris .... 559-244-2680...... 72 B doris.griffin@scccd.edu
GRIFFIN, Elaine .... 615-966-5818.... 470 F elaine.griffin@lipscomb.edu
GRIFFIN, Ellen .... 415-338-1666...... 37 B elleng@sfsu.edu
GRIFFIN, SR., Ervin, V .... 252-536-7217.... 371 B griffine@halifaxcc.edu
GRIFFIN, Gary .... 815-939-5296.... 161 A ggriffin@olivet.edu
GRIFFIN, Jacquelyn, H ...... 864-977-7081.... 460 A jackie.griffin@ngu.edu
GRIFFIN, James .... 401-598-1563.... 453 E jgriffin@jwu.edu

GRIFFIN, Janie 503-491-6701 417 B
janie.griffin@mhcc.edu

GRIFFIN, Jeff, D 504-816-8018 213 H
jgriffin@nobts.edu

GRIFFIN, Jennie 601-979-2522 274 G
jennie.b.griffin@jsums.edu

GRIFFIN, Jo 405-425-5119 409 E
jo.griffin@oc.edu

GRIFFIN, Joan 805-493-3555 33 B
griffin@clunet.edu

GRIFFIN, Joel 864-941-8446 460 D
griffin.j@ptc.edu

GRIFFIN, Joseph, E 530-226-4157 69 H
jgriffin@simpsonu.edu

GRIFFIN, Karen 813-253-7002 110 M
kgriffin@hccfl.edu

GRIFFIN, Larry 901-375-4400 471 G
larrygriffin@midsouthcc.org

GRIFFIN, Lee, G 225-578-3811 212 H
lgriffin@lsufoundation.org

GRIFFIN, Leslie 662-846-4400 273 H
lgriffin@deltastate.edu

GRIFFIN, Linner 252-328-1418 377 E
griffinl@ecu.edu

GRIFFIN, Lisa 229-217-4144 134 F
lgriffin@moultrietech.edu

GRIFFIN, Lori 253-912-3633 536 H
lgriffin@pierce.ctc.edu

GRIFFIN, Lynn 843-383-8071 457 A
lgriffin@coker.edu

GRIFFIN, Mark 973-353-1458 314 E
markg@andromeda.rutgers.edu

GRIFFIN, Matthew 678-915-4288 137 G
jgriffin@spsu.edu

GRIFFIN, Michael 415-575-6154 32 G
admissions@ciis.edu

GRIFFIN, Michael 305-899-2900 101 M
mgriffin@mail.barry.edu

GRIFFIN, Michael 212-636-6520 334 C
mgriffinl@fordham.edu

GRIFFIN, Michael, D 256-824-5677 8 G
michael.griffin@uah.edu

GRIFFIN, Patricia 610-660-1266 446 C
pgriffin@sju.edu

GRIFFIN, Patricia, L 785-628-5377 192 I
pgriffin@fhsu.edu

GRIFFIN, Patrick 845-431-8924 332 D
griffin@sunydutchess.edu

GRIFFIN, Patsy 770-531-6326 133 C
pgriff@laniertech.edu

GRIFFIN, Paul, F 315-684-6081 354 F
griffipf@morrisville.edu

GRIFFIN, Randy, R 541-881-5595 420 E
rgriffin@tvcc.cc

GRIFFIN, Rick 619-644-7868 49 C
rick.griffin@gcccd.edu

GRIFFIN, Sallie 601-877-6377 272 F
sgriffin@alcorn.edu

GRIFFIN, Susan 513-745-3311 406 E
0565mgr@fheg.follett.com

GRIFFIN, Tamara 870-612-2022 25 E
tamara.griffin@uaccb.edu

GRIFFIN, Teresa 330-490-7503 405 F
tgriffin@walsh.edu

GRIFFIN, Terrie, E 434-528-5276 530 B
tgriffin@vul.edu

GRIFFIN, Thomas, H 919-515-5036 378 C
thgriffi@ncsu.edu

GRIFFIN, Tim 719-502-2320 87 B
tim.griffin@ppcc.edu

GRIFFIN, Timothy 201-216-5325 315 E
tgriffin@stevens.edu

GRIFFIN, Walt, R 864-488-4616 459 B
wgriffin@limestone.edu

GRIFFIN, William 910-678-8564 370 E
griffinw@faytechcc.edu

GRIFFIN-DONALDSON, Michelle 513-569-1515 387 G
michelle.donaldson@cincinnstate.edu

GRIFFIS, Frank 817-515-5209 496 C
frank.griffis@tccd.edu

GRIFFIS, Mary, E 660-543-4359 290 H
griffis@ucmo.edu

GRIFFITH, Becki, S 281-425-6399 489 M
bgriffit@lee.edu

GRIFFITH, Debbie 828-232-5066 378 D
dgriffit@unca.edu

GRIFFITH, Denise 618-634-3277 164 E
deniseg@shawneecc.edu

GRIFFITH, Dennis, J 330-369-3200 402 H
tbcmail@tbc-trumbullbusiness.com

GRIFFITH, Dennis, R 937-393-3431 402 A
dgriffith@soucc.sscc.edu

GRIFFITH, Dennison, W 614-222-3220 388 G
dgriffith@ccad.edu

GRIFFITH, Doris 559-244-2680 72 A
doris.griffith@scccd.edu

GRIFFITH, Howard 703-448-3393 523 D
hgiffith@rts.edu

GRIFFITH, Ivelaw, L 718-262-2780 329 A
provost@york.cuny.edu

GRIFFITH, Jeffrey 505-272-2321 321 C
jkgriffith@salud.unm.edu

GRIFFITH, John 610-526-5160 423 D
jgriffith@brynmawr.edu

GRIFFITH, Jolene 641-782-1456 189 E
griffith@swcciowa.edu

GRIFFITH, Kathy 740-392-6868 396 I
kathy.griffity@mvnu.edu

GRIFFITH, Kippi, R 512-448-8405 493 E
kippig@stedwards.edu

GRIFFITH, Larry 765-361-6212 181 E
griffitl@wabash.edu

GRIFFITH, Larry, K 724-847-6585 429 H
lkgriffith@geneva.edu

GRIFFITH, Mark 716-829-7551 332 E
griffith@dyc.edu

GRIFFITH, Maxine, F 212-854-6524 330 F
mfg30@columbia.edu

GRIFFITH, Mike 541-880-2244 416 D
griffith@klamathcc.edu

GRIFFITH, Roger, D 304-647-6563 543 A
rgriffith@newriver.edu

GRIFFITH, Ross, A 336-758-5244 380 C

GRIFFITH, Sally 847-925-6793 151 G
sgriffit@harpercollege.edu

GRIFFITH, Steven, J 515-961-1720 189 C
steve.griffith@simpson.edu

GRIFFITHS, Andy 207-288-5015 217 H
agriffiths@coa.edu

GRIFFITHS, Fredrick 413-542-2123 230 A
ftgriffiths@amherst.edu

GRIFFITHS, Geoffrey 217-351-2273 161 C
ggriffiths@parkland.edu

GRIFFITHS, Jose-Marie 401-232-6060 453 C
jgriffiths@bryant.edu

GRIFFITHS, Kelly, A 334-683-2372 5 G
kgriffiths@marionmilitary.edu

GRIFFITHS, Slade 620-441-6584 192 D
griffiths@cowley.edu

GRIFFUS, Randall 706-272-4440 128 C
rgriffus@daltonstate.edu

GRIGG, Daniel, J 336-334-4822 371 A
djgrigg@gtcc.edu

GRIGG, Eddie, G 704-334-6882 367 H
egrigg@nlts.edu

GRIGGS, Carmen, S 617-912-9121 232 C
cgriggs@bostonconservatory.edu

GRIGGS, Cindy 859-371-9393 198 G
cgriggs@beckfield.edu

GRIGGS, Deborah 334-420-4260 7 H
dgriggs@trenholmstate.edu

GRIGGS, Donald, R 843-953-5540 457 B
griggsd@cofc.edu

GRIGGS, Gary, B 831-459-2464 75 C
griggs@es.ucsc.edu

GRIGGS, Judith, R 412-396-6661 428 D
griggs@duq.edu

GRIGGS, Michelle 815-394-5112 163 A
mgriggs@rockford.edu

GRIGGS, Robert, J 218-755-2097 265 I
rgriggs@bemidjistate.edu

GRIGGS, Ronald, K 740-427-5632 394 C
griggs@kenyon.edu

GRIGGS, Tanya 510-869-6131 64 J
tgriggs@samuelmerritt.edu

GRIGGS, Thomas, J 906-786-5802 248 I
griggst@baycollege.edu

GRIGGS-GRIFFIN, Ebony 859-344-4069 206 I
ebony.griggs-griffin@thomasmore.edu

GRIGSBY, Beth 712-279-5504 183 A
beth.grigsby@briarcliff.edu

GRIGSBY, Bryon, L 540-665-4525 524 E
bgrigsby@su.edu

GRIGSBY, Lindle, D 972-860-7199 484 I
lgrigsby@dcccd.edu

GRIGSBY, Mark 918-540-6275 408 J
mgrigsby@neo.edu

GRIJALVA, Luis-Pablo 936-261-9300 496 G
lpgrijalva@pvamu.edu

GRIJALVA, Sara 575-835-5133 319 A
sjgrijalva@admin.nmt.edu

GRILL, Joshua, L 570-577-3200 423 E
josh.grill@bucknell.edu

GRILL, Stephen, A 574-372-5100 171 H
grillsa@grace.edu

GRILLI, Eugene, P 330-941-1331 406 F
epgrilli@ysu.edu

GRILLO, Mary Ann 212-226-5500 323 A
mgrillo@aii.edu

GRILLO, Robert 305-348-2738 119 C
robert.grillo@fiu.edu

GRILLOT, Larry, R 405-325-3821 413 C
lrgrillot@ou.edu

GRILLOT, Suzette, R 405-325-6003 413 C
sgrillot@ou.edu

GRIM, Sandy 304-384-5290 543 G
counseling_center@concord.edu

GRIMES, Charles, R 330-471-8438 395 F
cgrimes@malone.edu

GRIMES, Debbie, J 205-391-2233 6 I
dgrimes@sheltonstate.edu

GRIMES, Deborah 252-527-6223 371 G
dgrimes@lenoircc.edu

GRIMES, Donnie 606-539-4197 207 C
donnie.grimes@ucumberlands.edu

GRIMES, Judith 816-271-5991 286 G
grimes@missouriwestern.edu

GRIMES, Judy 816-271-5991 286 G
grimes@missouriwestern.edu

GRIMES, Kathryn 952-885-5436 270 C
kgrimes@nwhealth.edu

GRIMES, Larry 304-829-7420 540 H
lgrimes@bethanywv.edu

GRIMES, Lee 956-872-7271 494 H
lgrimes@southtexascollege.edu

GRIMES, Mark 812-749-1368 178 H
mgrimes@oak.edu

GRIMES, Paul 620-235-4598 196 C
paul.grimes@pittstate.edu

GRIMES, Robert 212-636-6300 334 C
rgrimes@fordham.edu

GRIMES, Robert (Bud), D 731-881-7615 477 G
bgrimes@utm.edu

GRIMES, Steve 918-540-6226 408 J
sgrimes@neo.edu

GRIMES, Terri, A 815-599-3514 152 B
terri.grimes@highland.edu

GRIMES, Therese 814-269-7043 449 D
tgrimes@pitt.edu

GRIMES, Tresmaine 914-633-2206 336 E
tgrimes@iona.edu

GRIMES, William, S 512-505-3021 488 D
wsgrimes@htu.edu

GRIMLEY, Janet 206-934-5488 537 E
janet.grimley@seattlecolleges.edu

GRIMM, Carol, M 218-477-2327 267 F
grimm@mnstate.edu

GRIMM, Dan 954-731-8880 104 B

GRIMM, Gary 503-370-6814 421 D
ggrimm@willamette.edu

GRIMM, Keith 503-370-6210 421 D
kgrimm@willamette.edu

GRIMM, Randy 816-322-0110 279 D
randy.grimm@calvary.edu

GRIMM, Rich 731-661-5102 477 B
rgrimm@uu.edu

GRIMM, Robert, J 610-683-4120 443 A
grimm@kutztown.edu

GRIMM, Tony 815-935-4992 161 A
tgrimm@olivet.edu

GRIMMER, Karen, D 618-374-5152 161 E
karen.grimmer@principia.edu

GRIMMER, Kevin, M 315-792-7520 356 B
grimmek@sunyit.edu

GRIMMER, Nick 315-792-7110 356 B
nick.grimmer@sunyit.edu

GRIMMETT, Branden 507-786-3268 271 C
grimmett@stolaf.edu

GRIMSHAW-CLARK, Maria 315-312-4416 354 A
maria.grimshaw@oswego.edu

GRIMSLEY, Deloris 973-877-3056 309 H
dgrimsle@essex.edu

GRIMSLEY, Linda 229-430-4635 124 A
linda.grimsley@asurams.edu

GRIMSON, W. Eric, L 617-253-9742 241 D

GRINDE, Jane 701-788-4647 381 H
jane.grinde@mayvillestate.edu

GRINDELL, Monique 503-352-1566 419 E
grindelm@pacificu.edu

GRINNAN, Susan 804-706-5035 527 B
sgrinnan@jtcc.edu

GRINNELL, Jimmy, E 704-687-4585 379 A
jegrinne@uncc.edu

GRINNELL, Mike 509-542-4898 532 H
mgrinnell@columbiabasin.edu

GRINO, Placido 713-798-8085 481 H
grino@bcm.edu

GRINSTEAD, Joshua 212-312-4330 332 A
jgrinstead@devry.edu

GRIPP, Kristine 216-791-5000 388 C
kristine.gripp@case.edu

GRIPPIN, Margaret 518-255-5516 354 E
grippim@cobleskill.edu

GRISCOM, William, E 717-299-7722 448 A
griscom@stevenscollege.edu

GRISHAM, Bob 360-438-4372 537 B
bgrisham@stmartin.edu

GRISHAM, Elizabeth 417-255-7240 286 D
elizabethgrisham@missouristate.edu

GRISHAM, Linda 781-239-3147 239 G
lgrisham@massbay.edu

GRISI, Mark, P 215-968-8391 423 F
grisim@bucks.edu

GRISSETT, Jendia 334-386-7264 3 G
jgrissett@faulkner.edu

GRISSOM, Cytha, D 717-477-1444 443 E
cdgris@ship.edu

GRISSOM, Randy 505-428-1252 320 E
randy.grissom@sfcc.edu

GRISWOLD, Al 206-934-5482 537 E
alfred.griswold@seattlecolleges.edu

GRISWOLD, Anna, M 814-863-0507 438 G
amg5@psu.edu

GRISWOLD, Emmett 229-430-3396 124 B
egriswold@albanytech.edu

GRISWOLD, Mac 713-348-6163 493 C
griswold@rice.edu

GRISWOLD, Richard, M 617-262-5000 231 G
richard.griswold@the-bac.edu

GRISWOLD, William 334-285-5177 4 K
bill.griswold@istc.edu

GRITTON, Mark 559-934-2455 78 C
markgritton@whccd.edu

GRITZAN, Walt 330-339-3391 394 A
wgritzan@kent.edu

GRIZANTI, Vincent 716-896-0700 359 H
vgrizanti@villa.edu

GRIZZLE, Debra, F 706-245-7226 129 C
dgrizzle@ec.edu

GRIZZLE, Jeff 870-512-7866 20 F
jeff_grizzle@asun.edu

GRIZZLE, Jerry, W 575-624-8001 319 C
supt@nmmi.edu

GROAT, Gary 415-380-1330 48 E
garygroat@ggbts.edu

GROBINS, Mary Alice 360-416-7719 538 D
maryalice.grobins@skagit.edu

GRODE-HANKS, Carol 605-995-7103 464 F
carol.grode-hanks@mitchelltech.edu

GROELING, Jeff 260-744-8746 180 B
jfgroeling@taylor.edu

GROENER, Michael 323-259-2646 59 I
groenerm@oxy.edu

GROENINGER, Sandra 847-543-2345 148 B
sgroeninger@clcillinois.edu

GROENWALD, Susan, L 630-512-8900 279 H
sgroenwald@chamberlain.edu

GROESBECK, John 417-625-9348 286 B
groesbeck-j@mssu.edu

GROFF, Keith 614-947-6122 391 B
groffk@franklin.edu

GROFF, Rodney 717-728-2258 425 B
rodgroff@centralpenn.edu

GROGAN, Anne 617-349-8155 236 B
agrogan@lesley.edu

GROGAN, Fred, L 816-604-2044 285 C
fred.grogan@mcckc.edu

GROGAN, Rita 408-855-5072 78 F
rita.grogan@wvm.edu

GROGAN LAVIN, Bernadette 718-990-1980 348 G
lavinb@stjohns.edu

GROGG, Sam, L 516-877-4125 322 A
sgrogg@adelphi.edu

GROH, Sara 315-228-6134 329 G
sgroh@colgate.edu

GROH BECK, Genelle 507-457-1421 271 B
ggroh@smumn.edu

GROHMAN, Adam 516-299-2256 339 A
adam.grohman@liu.edu

GROLEAU, Dan 715-365-4450 555 A
dgroleau@nicoletcollege.edu

GROLEAU, Ron, W 815-224-0482 153 E
ron_groleau@ivcc.edu

GROMAN, Beth 260-399-7700 181 A
bgroman@sf.edu

GROMATZKY, Steven 913-360-7511 191 A
sgromatzky@benedictine.edu

GRONA, Marion 940-552-6291 507 F
mgrona@vernoncollege.edu

GRONBECK-TEDESCO, Susan 785-864-6161 197 B
slgt@ku.edu

GRONDAHL, Mary, M 518-454-5150 330 C
grondahm@strose.edu

GRONER, Steve 618-532-2049 155 B
sgroner@kaskaskia.edu

GRONNIGER, Eileen, C 785-442-6010 193 F
egronniger@highlandcc.edu

GRONO, Anthony 718-817-4943 334 C
grono@fordham.edu

GROOM, David 503-255-0332 417 C
dgroomjr@multnomah.edu

GROOME, Jean, M 336-734-7292 370 F
jgroome@forsythtech.edu

GROOMS, Craig 814-732-2761 442 E
eup_admissions@edinboro.edu

GROOMS, David 808-984-3376 142 E
grooms@hawaii.edu

GROOMS, Jean, M 843-792-3433 459 D
groomsj@musc.edu

GROOMS, Jerri, H 931-540-2538 475 A
jgrooms@columbiastate.edu

GROOP, Judith, M 717-691-6035 436 D
jgroop@messiah.edu

GROOTERS, Stacy 508-565-1324 245 A
sgrooters@stonehill.edu

GROOVER, Brenda 417-864-7220 281 H
bgroover@cci.edu

GROOVER, Diane 520-206-4592 17 H
dgroover@pima.edu

GROOVER, Joann, V 803-938-3789 462 G
groover@vm.sc.edu

GROOVER, John 912-486-7602 135 D
jgroover@ogeecheetech.edu

GROOVER, R. Edwin 404-669-2065 136 B
eddie.groover@point.edu

GROPEN, Laura 760-744-1150 61 D
lgropen@palomar.edu

GROPP, Douglas, M 214-528-8600 492 H

GROPP, Jonathan 864-622-6011 455 C
jgropp@andersonuniversity.edu

GROPPER, Idania, R 904-620-1707 120 D
igropper@unf.edu

GROPPER, Nancy 212-875-4703 323 C ngropper@bankstreet.edu
GRORUD, Kelly 608-663-2200 547 F kgrorud@edgewood.edu
GROS, Kathy, R 504-865-3552 213 F kgros@loyno.edu
GROSBY, Karen 954-262-5716 114 B grosby@nsu.nova.edu
GROSETH, Jaynee 406-994-2401 295 C jgroseth@montana.edu
GROSETH, Rolf, S 406-657-2300 295 D rolf.groseth@msubillings.edu
GROSHANS, David, E 308-635-6105 301 D groshans@wncc.edu
GROSHONG, Matt 425-564-5608 531 G matt.groshon@bellevuecollege.edu
GROSLAND, David, E 515-574-1149 185 I grosland@iowacentral.edu
GROSOVSKY, Andrew 617-287-5775 236 G andrew.grosovsky@umb.edu
GROSPITCH, Eric 816-235-8955 291 C grospitche@umkc.edu
GROSS, Anne 303-871-3382 89 A agross@du.edu
GROSS, Barbara, L 818-677-2121 35 F barbara.gross@csun.edu
GROSS, Bernard, M 301-459-8686 226 D rbernard@host.sdc.edu
GROSS, Bill 605-274-4311 464 A bill.gross@augie.edu
GROSS, Carla, E 717-691-6027 436 D cgross@messiah.edu
GROSS, Daryl, J 315-443-8705 357 C djgross@syr.edu
GROSS, Dolores 915-831-2122 486 G dgross2@epcc.edu
GROSS, Jim 507-285-7256 268 I jim.gross@roch.edu
GROSS, Laura 518-255-5626 354 E grossll@cobleskill.edu
GROSS, Mary Margaret 610-861-1350 437 A registrar@moravian.edu
GROSS, Michael 508-362-2131 239 D mgross@capecod.edu
GROSS, Michael 732-987-2373 310 C gross@georgian.edu
GROSS, Michelle, R 410-951-3610 228 B mgross@coppin.edu
GROSS, Monika 301-860-4091 228 A mgross@bowiestate.edu
GROSS, Natalie 914-337-0700 350 C ngross@sarahlawrence.edu
GROSS, Peter 503-251-5709 421 A pgross@uws.edu
GROSS, Richard 614-251-4567 398 F grossr@ohiodominican.edu
GROSS, Scott 606-436-5721 202 C scott.gross@kctcs.edu
GROSS, Susan 212-431-2888 343 E sgross@nyls.edu
GROSS, Tim 770-426-2611 133 E tim.gross@life.edu
GROSS, Tim, A 208-467-8959 144 E tagross@nnu.edu
GROSS METHNER, Sara, E 651-962-5000 272 B gross6968@stthomas.edu
GROSSBERG, Richard 718-951-5296 326 F richardg@brooklyn.cuny.edu
GROSSE, Mike 502-456-0004 206 G mgrosse@sullivan.edu
GROSSE, Mike 502-451-0815 206 H mgrosse@sullivan.edu
GROSSET, Jane, M 215-751-8085 426 B jgrosset@ccp.edu
GROSSI, OSB, Anthony 724-537-4554 446 E anthony.grossi@email.stvincent.edu
GROSSI, Deann 312-777-8665 153 B dgrossi@aii.edu
GROSSINGER, Harvey 202-651-5000 98 B harvey.grossinger@gallaudet.edu
GROSSKOPF, John 850-973-1601 113 K grosskopfj@nfcc.edu
GROSSMAN, Alan 201-200-3344 312 B agrossman@njcu.edu
GROSSMAN, Brian 425-235-7836 537 A bgrossman@rtc.edu
GROSSMAN, Claudio 202-274-4004 97 D grossman@american.edu
GROSSMAN, Divina 508-999-8004 237 A chancellor@umassd.edu
GROSSMAN, Joshua, M 240-895-4367 226 A jmgrossman@smcm.edu
GROSSMAN, LuAnn 605-331-6738 466 E luann.grossman@usiouxfalls.edu
GROSSMAN, Miriam 845-425-1370 345 B
GROSSMAN, Richard, G 603-535-2425 307 A rggrossman@plymouth.edu
GROSSMAN, Ruth 732-414-2834 317 F ytcbks@gmail.com
GROSZ, Dale 701-671-2188 382 G dale.grosz@ndscs.edu
GROSZ, Ken 701-228-5431 382 E ken.grosz@dakotacollege.edu
GROSZ, Kenneth 701-228-5431 382 A ken.grosz@dakotacollege.edu
GROTGEN, John 229-333-5940 139 C jgrotgen@valdosta.edu
GROTH, Cary 775-784-6900 303 A cgroth@unr.edu
GROTH, Sue 360-442-2110 535 I sgroth@lowercolumbia.edu
GROTHE, Malcom, P 206-934-6808 537 F malcolm.grothe@seattlecolleges.edu
GROTHOUS, Tom 419-227-3141 404 D trgrot@unoh.edu
GROTRIAN, James 402-457-2335 298 G jgrotrian@mccneb.edu
GROUSOSKY, David, P 412-396-6699 428 D grousosk@duq.edu
GROUT, David 574-372-5100 171 H groutd@grace.edu
GROUT, John 706-236-2233 126 C jgrout@berry.edu
GROVE, Dana 913-469-8500 194 B dgrove@jccc.edu
GROVE, Daryl 563-425-5311 189 G groved@uiu.edu
GROVE, Doug 714-556-3610 77 B dgrove@vanguard.edu
GROVE, Helen 937-512-2522 401 J helen.grove@sinclair.edu
GROVE, Kathryne 303-871-7436 89 A kathryne.grove@du.edu
GROVE, Kathy, M 641-422-4382 188 A grovekat@niacc.edu
GROVE, Laurie 717-396-7188 448 A grove@stevenscollege.edu
GROVE, Luke, J 515-574-1062 185 I grove@iowacentral.edu
GROVE, Russell 208-376-7731 142 H russellg@boisebible.edu
GROVE, Shannon, D 814-886-6391 437 B sgrove@mtaloy.edu
GROVE, Susan, M 972-860-7040 484 I sgrove@dcccd.edu
GROVE-MARKWOOD, Robert 207-942-6781 217 B rgrove-markwood@bts.edu
GROVER, Arthur 215-951-1300 432 I grover77@lasalle.edu
GROVER, Barbara 801-957-4434 512 D barbara.grover@slcc.edu
GROVER, Carol, N 315-279-5252 337 K cgrover@mail.keuka.edu
GROVER, Herbert 806-291-1118 508 E groverh@wbu.edu
GROVER, James 636-978-7488 292 E
GROVER, Rajiv 901-678-3633 474 C rgrover@memphis.edu
GROVER-BISKER, Edna 573-341-6170 291 E egroverb@mst.edu
GROVER-ROOSA, Janice 307-382-1701 557 A jgrover@wwcc.wy.edu
GROVES, Allen, W 434-924-7429 525 F awg8vd@virginia.edu
GROVES, Betsy, A 508-856-2265 237 C betsy.groves@umassmed.edu
GROVES, Danford, F 910-272-3335 373 D dgroves@robeson.edu
GROVES, Denise 254-968-9121 497 A registrar@tarleton.edu
GROVES, Denise 432-837-8432 501 E dgroves@sulross.edu
GROVES, Doris 309-438-2343 153 D dfgrove@ilstu.edu
GROVES, Eric 619-849-2520 62 L ericgroves@pointloma.edu
GROVES, Greg 318-397-6167 210 J ggroves@myneltc.edu
GROVES, Jason 325-674-2646 478 I jason.groves@acu.edu
GROVES, Jay 309-438-5631 153 D jrgrove@ilstu.edu
GROVES, Jeffrey 909-621-8122 49 F groves@hmc.edu
GROVES, Kathleen, H 585-395-2317 352 F kgroves@brockport.edu
GROVES, Kathy 573-592-1106 293 D kathy.groves@williamwoods.edu
GROVES, Mike 970-245-8101 85 H mgrove@intelliteccollege.edu
GROVES, Monica, R 651-631-5380 270 B mrgroves@nwc.edu
GROVES, Robert 517-884-1008 255 A grovesr@msu.edu
GROVES, Robert, M 202-687-6400 98 D provost@georgetown.edu
GROVES, Tami 415-282-7600 28 B tamigroves@actcm.edu
GROW, David 801-274-3280 512 F dgrow@wgu.edu
GROWDEN, Melissa, A 517-264-7614 258 B mgrowden@sienaheights.edu
GROWDON, James, F 610-785-6252 446 A jgrowdon@scs.edu
GROWNEY, Kathy 603-668-2211 305 I k.growney@snhu.edu
GROWNS, Richard, O 501-977-2024 25 G growns@uaccm.edu
GROZA, Adam 415-380-1448 48 E adamgroza@ggbts.edu
GRUBB, Autumn 252-638-2039 370 A grubbc@cravencc.edu
GRUBB, David 504-286-5343 214 J dgrubb@suno.edu
GRUBB, Derek 970-542-3158 86 G derek.grubb@morgancc.edu
GRUBB, Geoffrey, J 419-824-3818 395 E ggrubb@lourdes.edu
GRUBB, Lillie 620-223-2700 193 A lillieg@fortscott.edu
GRUBE, Dave 616-222-1412 250 A dave.grube@cornerstone.edu
GRUBE, M. Marshall 423-439-4219 473 F grube@etsu.edu
GRUBE, Sean 816-501-4843 288 A sean.grube@rockhurst.edu
GRUBER, Carol 215-646-7300 430 C gruber.c@gmc.edu
GRUBER, Christopher, J 704-894-2710 363 I chgruber@davidson.edu
GRUBER, Donna 419-434-4540 404 B gruber@findlay.edu
GRUBER, Thomas 504-671-6480 210 F tgrube@dcc.edu
GRUBY, Elizabeth 773-878-3752 163 F egruby@staugustine.edu
GRUEN, Kris 802-322-1721 513 E kris.gruen@goddard.edu
GRUENDLER, Donny 323-860-1188 58 E donnyg@mi.edu
GRUENDYKE, Randall 765-998-5205 180 B rngruendyke@taylor.edu
GRUENIG, Gwen 907-450-8190 10 G gdgruenig@alaska.edu
GRUENING, Jennifer 309-677-4939 146 C jgruening@bradley.edu
GRUENING, Kyle 715-365-4481 555 A gruening@nicoletcollege.edu
GRUENLOH, Gwen 719-336-1572 86 B gwen.gruenloh@lamarcc.edu
GRUETT, Jon 314-968-6903 292 J gruettjo@webster.edu
GRUETZEMACHER, Richard, R 423-425-4007 477 F richard-gruetzemacher@utc.edu
GRUGEL, Kenneth, E 814-393-2315 442 B kgrugel@clarion.edu
GRUHLER, Sarah 360-992-2406 532 F sgruhler@clark.edu
GRUICHICH, Dawn 480-732-7050 15 E dawn.gruichich@cgc.edu
GRULKE, Kimmi 928-226-4343 13 F kimmi.grulke@coconino.edu
GRUMBLES, Owen Kent 336-316-2499 365 A grumblesok@gulford.edu
GRUMET, Barbara 718-260-5345 328 D bgrumet@citytech.cuny.edu
GRUNBLATT, Akiva 718-268-4700 347 A
GRUND, Faye 419-520-2602 384 G fgrund@ashland.edu
GRUND, Vernon 406-243-4621 294 I vernon.grund@umontana.edu
GRUNDBERG, Andy 202-639-1847 98 A agrundberg@corcoran.org
GRUNDEN, Jennifer, J 302-857-1040 96 G jgrunden@dtcc.edu
GRUNDER, John 831-647-6512 57 F john.grunder@miis.edu
GRUNDER, Mark 989-358-7317 247 C grunderm@alpenacc.edu
GRUNDHAUSER, Tony 651-523-2219 264 A agrundhauser01@hamline.edu
GRUNDIG, John 863-680-6212 109 E jgrundig@flsouthern.edu
GRUNDY, Diane, H 724-458-2049 430 B dhgrundy@gcc.edu
GRUNDY, Jeffrey, W 973-596-2451 312 C jeffrey.w.grundy@njit.edu
GRUNDY, Marc, A 423-236-2834 473 B magrundy@southern.edu
GRUNER, Bradley, W 702-651-5920 302 E bradley.gruner@csn.edu
GRUNER, Celeste, A 704-216-3459 373 F celeste.gruner@rccc.edu
GRUNINGER, Sandra 212-686-9040 360 F sgruninger@woodtobecoburn.edu
GRUNOW, Tamie, L 989-686-9042 250 D tlgrunow@delta.edu
GRUNTMEIR, Laura 405-422-1253 411 G gruntmeirl@redlandscc.edu
GRUNWALD, Gerald 215-503-8982 448 C gerald.grunwald@jefferson.edu
GRUNWALD, James, R 507-354-8221 264 K grunwajr@mlc-wels.edu
GRUS, Shannon, M 636-584-6505 281 E smgrus@eastcentral.edu
GRUSHINSKI, Alberta 570-945-8373 432 E alberta.grushinski@keystone.edu
GRUSKA, Julie 320-363-3395 271 A jgruska@csbsju.edu
GRUSKA, Julie, E 320-363-3395 262 F jgruska@csbsju.edu
GRUSZKA, William 404-413-4469 131 G billgruszka@gsu.edu
GRUVER, Barry, L 609-497-7705 312 F barry.gruver@ptsem.edu
GRUVER, Wendy 903-886-5140 498 B wendy.gruver@tamuc.edu
GRUWELL, Mark, A 712-362-0439 186 A mgruwell@iowalakes.edu
GRZESIAK, Michael, P 724-503-1001 451 A mgrzesiak@washjeff.edu
GRZYBOWSKI, Mark, J 815-224-0437 153 E mark_grzybowski@ivcc.edu
GSCHWEND, Richard 217-875-7200 162 F rqschwend@richland.edu
GSTALDER, Steven 203-773-0129 90 C sgstalder@albertus.edu
GUADAGNINO, Beatrice 954-545-4500 117 I cfo@sfbc.edu
GUADAGNINO, Joseph 954-545-4500 117 I jguadagnino@sfbc.edu
GUADALUPE, Ana, R 787-764-0000 566 G anlupe@uprrp.edu
GUADALUPE, Ana, R 787-763-3877 568 B rectoria@uprrp.edu
GUADALUPE, Sarahi 787-769-9965 567 C sarahi.guadalupe@upr.edu
GUADALUPE, Yvonne 787-766-1717 565 I yguadalupe@suagm.edu
GUADAMUZ, Tatiana 510-261-8500 61 G tatiana.gaudamuz@patten.edu
GUAGLIANONE, Curtis 509-865-8530 535 A guaglianone_c@heritage.edu
GUAJARDO, Dan 918-495-7703 411 C dguajardo@oru.edu
GUAL, Karen 954-382-6441 122 F kgual@tiu.edu
GUALTIERI, Karen 845-574-4226 347 I kgualtie@sunyrockland.edu
GUAN, Sharon 773-325-7726 149 A xguan@depaul.edu
GUANCI-THERRIEN, Patricia 603-641-7202 305 G pguanci@anselm.edu
GUANG, Virginia 787-743-4041 561 F vguang@columbiaco.edu
GUARASCI, Richard 718-390-3131 360 A guarasci@wagner.edu
GUARDINO, Richard, V 516-463-4069 335 G richard.v.guardino@hofstra.edu
GUARIGLIA, Carolyn, L 315-255-1743 325 G guarigliac@cayuga-cc.edu
GUARIGLIA, Daniel, M 716-286-8431 344 D dmg@niagara.edu
GUASCONI, Joseph 973-378-2643 315 B joseph.guasconi@shu.edu
GUAY, Roger 207-947-4591 217 D rguay@bealcollege.edu
GUAY, Sheila 401-323-6324 453 C sguay@bryant.edu
GUBAN, Philip 440-943-7600 401 G pguban@dioceseofcleveland.org
GUBBINS, Jean, E 216-368-5557 386 F jeg2@case.edu
GUBLER, Seth 435-652-7571 512 B sgubler@dixie.edu
GUC, Jeremy 248-689-8282 259 E jguc@walshcollege.edu
GUCKERT, Donald, J 319-335-1201 182 F don-guckert@uiowa.edu
GUDBRANSON, Margaret 216-421-8016 388 A mgudbranson@cia.edu
GUDENA, Chandragupta 432-837-8702 501 E cgudena@sulross.edu
GUDMUNDSON, Donald 970-351-2764 89 B donald.gudmundson@unco.edu
GUEDEA CARRENO, Lisa, G 574-535-7425 171 G lisagc@goshen.edu
GUELICH, Julie 952-358-8156 268 A julie.guelich@normandale.edu
GUEMPEL, Stephen 337-550-1301 212 J
GUENARD, Erik, M 906-932-4231 251 C erikg@gogebic.edu
GUENARD, Hayward 985-448-4479 216 A hayward.guenard@nicholls.edu
GUENGERICH, Colleen 575-835-5525 319 A cguengerich@admin.nmt.edu
GUENTER-SCHLESINGER, Sue 360-650-3307 539 F sue.guenter-schlesinger@wwu.edu
GUENTHER, Thomas 847-543-2264 148 B tguenther@clcillinois.edu
GUERIN, David 318-257-4854 215 F dguerin@latech.edu
GUERIN, Fae 908-835-2302 317 C guerin@warren.edu
GUERIN, Keith 908-526-1200 313 D kguerin@raritanval.edu
GUERIN, Michael, W 909-869-3065 33 J mguerin@csupomona.edu
GUERIN, Thomas, B 513-556-2389 403 D tom.guerin@uc.edu

GUERRA, Blanca 210-567-2621 507 A
guerrabe@uthscsa.edu
GUERRA, Dahlia 956-665-2175 506 C
guerrad@utpa.edu
GUERRA, Elizabeth 909-469-5418 78 I
guerra@westernu.edu
GUERRA, Esmeralda 956-665-2100 506 C
engd5dc@utpa.edu
GUERRA, Juan, M 512-245-2820 501 F
jg76@txstate.edu
GUERRA, Luis 510-436-1516 50 H
guerra@hnu.edu
GUERRA, Manuel 503-365-4684 414 J
manuel.guerra@chemeketa.edu
GUERRA, Michael 510-628-8031 54 B
mguerra@lincolnuca.edu
GUERRA, Michael 209-575-6867 80 H
guerram@mjc.edu
GUERRA, Olivia 972-860-8065 484 H
oguerra@dcccd.edu
GUERRA, Ron 336-841-9363 365 C
rguerra@highpoint.edu
GUERRA, Sabra 254-968-9770 497 A
sguerra@tarleton.edu
GUERREIRO, Mario, H 417-268-1000 278 H
mguerreiro@agts.edu
GUERRERO, Alfred, A 310-287-4314 55 F
guerreraa@wlac.edu
GUERRERO, Bertha, M 671-735-5638 559 E
boardoftrustees@guamcc.edu
GUERRERO, Blas 925-439-2181 43 G
bguerrero@losmedanos.edu
GUERRERO, Carmen 805-986-5824 77 E
cguerrero@vcccd.edu
GUERRERO, Daniel, G 310-206-6382 74 C
dguerrero@athletics.ucla.edu
GUERRERO, Dolores 361-593-4410 498 D
dolores.guerrero@tamuk.edu
GUERRERO, Jennifer 609-984-1588 316 A
jguerrero@tesc.edu
GUERRERO, John 670-234-5498 560 B
johng@nmcnet.edu
GUERRERO, Sherrie, L 909-652-6131 39 E
sherrie.guerrero@chaffey.edu
GUERRERO, Tammy 219-989-2675 178 K
guerrero@purduecal.edu
GUERRERO, Tim 303-464-2320 87 H
tguerrero@redstone.edu
GUERRETTE, Leslie, R 207-834-7550 220 D
leslieg@maine.edu
GUERRIERI, Joe 213-763-3683 55 D
guerrierij@lattc.edu
GUERRIERI, Rose, A 330-675-8866 393 J
rguerrie@kent.edu
GUERRIERO, Franco 740-654-6711 400 C
guerrief@ohio.edu
GUERRIERO, Steven 215-248-7022 425 D
guerrieros@chc.edu
GUERRIERO, Steven 215-248-7120 425 D
guerrieros@chc.edu
GUERRIERO, William 480-732-7012 15 E
william.guerriero@cgc.edu
GUERRISI, Theresa, L 717-780-2576 430 E
tlguerri@hacc.edu
GUERRY, Sara 980-598-1007 365 I
sara.guerry@jwu.edu
GUERTIN, Donna 413-565-1000 230 G
dguertin@baypath.edu
GUESS, Melissa 660-359-3948 287 A
mguess@mail.ncmissouri.edu
GUEST, Denise 540-891-3040 526 I
dguest@germanna.edu
GUEST, James 402-472-7488 300 G
jguest2@unl.edu
GUEST, James 845-368-7200 350 A
james.guest@use.salvationarmy.org
GUEST, Joshua 662-472-2312 274 D
jguest@holmescc.edu
GUETERSLOH, Ryan 510-885-3690 34 E
ryan.guetersloh@csueastbay.edu
GUETTI, Joan 973-761-9018 315 B
joan.guetti@shu.edu
GUEUERRA, Jonathan 305-809-3204 108 I
jonathan.gueuerra@fkcc.edu
GUEVARA, Christine 505-473-6652 320 F
christine.guevara@santafeuniversity.edu
GUEVARA, Julia 616-331-2400 251 F
guevaraj@gvsu.edu
GUEVARA, Yamil 813-663-0100 99 G
GUFFEY, Larry, D 256-228-6001 6 A
ldguffey@nacc.edu
GUFFEY, Paula, J 606-679-8501 203 C
paula.guffey@kctcs.edu
GUFFEY, Ryan 636-949-4475 283 J
rguffey@lindenwood.edu
GUGELCHUK, Gary 909-469-5381 78 I
gugelchuk@westernu.edu
GUGENHEIMER, Yirmiya 718-853-8500 358 A
GUGERTY, SSND,
Catherine 410-617-2997 223 I
cgugerty@loyola.edu
GUGGENHEIM, Joan 609-586-4800 311 B
guggenhj@mccc.edu
GUGGENMOS, Karl, J 401-598-2244 453 E
kguggenmos@jwu.edu
GUGLIELMO, B. Joseph 415-476-8010 75 A
guglielmoj@pharmacy.ucsf.edu
GUGLIELMO, David 757-822-1177 528 G
dguglielomo@tcc.edu
GUGLIELMONI, Mark, J 203-254-4080 92 H
mguglielmoni@fairfield.edu
GUICHARD-ASHBROOK,
Danielle 617-253-3795 241 D
GUIDA, Nancy, J 212-431-2325 343 E
nguida@nyls.edu
GUIDO, Deana 252-451-8244 372 E
dguido@nash.cc.nc.us
GUIDO, Diane 626-812-3034 30 G
dguido@apu.edu
GUIDO, OP, Joseph, J 401-865-2687 453 H
jguido@providence.edu
GUIDRY, Stephen 954-783-7339 106 J
sguidry@cci.edu
GUILBAULT, Melodi 863-638-7122 123 D
melodi.guilbault@warner.edu
GUILBAULT, Susie 909-607-7821 40 F
susie.guilbault@cgu.edu
GUILBE, Robert 718-782-2200 324 C
rguilbe@boricuacollege.edu
GUILBEAULT, Nancy, G 612-330-1169 261 B
guilbeau@augsburg.edu
GUILBERT, Debra, A 740-368-3394 400 G
daguilbe@owu.edu
GUILD, Richard, L 920-403-3216 550 F
rick.guild@snc.edu
GUILER, Douglas 352-365-3526 112 J
guilerd@lscc.edu
GUILER, Jeff 614-236-6508 386 E
jguiler@capital.edu
GUILFOIL, Kacey 818-386-5606 62 F
kguilfoil@pgi.edu
GUILFOILE, Patrick, G 218-755-2016 265 I
pguilfoile@bemidjistate.edu
GUILFORD, Arthur, M 941-359-4340 121 A
aguilford@sar.usf.edu
GUILFORD, Arthur, M 941-359-4200 121 B
GUILFORD, Renate, H 703-993-2299 519 E
rguilfor@gmu.edu
GUILIANO, Edward 516-686-7650 343 D
edwardg@nyit.edu
GUILLAUME, JR.,
Alfred, J 574-520-4183 174 E
guillaum@iusb.edu
GUILLEN, George 281-283-3950 503 E
guillen@uhcl.edu
GUILLEN, Patrick 310-243-3893 34 D
pguillen@csudh.edu
GUILLETTE, Natalie, L 802-656-4183 514 H
natalie.guillette@uvm.edu
GUILLIANI, Melissa 787-766-1717 565 I
mguilliani@suagm.edu
GUILLIOM, Allison 313-577-2230 260 A
dy9063@wayne.edu
GUILLIOT, Jessie 650-543-3896 57 B
jguilliot@menlo.edu
GUILLORY, Angela 225-578-2171 212 H
angelagu@lsu.edu
GUILLORY, Ann, V 201-559-6154 310 B
guillorya@felician.edu
GUILLORY, Justin 360-676-2772 535 K
jguillory@nwic.edu
GUILLORY, Sharon, E 337-475-5748 215 G
eguillory@mcneese.edu
GUILLORY, Tonya, L 202-806-5990 98 E
tguillory@howard.edu
GUILMETTE, Ronald 978-837-5555 242 A
ronald.guilmette@merrimack.edu
GUILMETTE, Winfield, L 610-409-3591 450 D
wguilmette@ursinus.edu
GUIM, George 408-273-2765 58 G
gguim@nhu.edu
GUIMOND, Kathy, A 505-277-1933 321 C
kguimo@unm.edu
GUINAN, JR., Mark, A 607-871-2909 322 E
guinan@alfred.edu
GUINAN, Mary 702-895-5090 302 I
mary.guinan@unlv.edu
GUINARA, Angel 713-780-9777 480 A
info@acaom.edu
GUINN, Raines 303-457-2757 84 J
rguinn@cci.edu
GUINN, Stephen 913-667-5700 191 H
sguinn@cbts.edu
GUINN, Traci, L 989-774-3945 249 C
guinn1tl@cmich.edu
GUION, John 916-278-7322 36 A
jguion@csus.edu
GUION, Kent 706-721-9265 130 D
wguion@georgiahealth.edu
GUISEPPI, Lori 407-478-0500 110 L
lorig@orl.herzing.edu
GUITER, Kristin 202-639-1867 98 A
kguiter@corcoran.org
GUIZADO, Roy 909-469-5445 78 I
roygpac@westernu.edu
GUKENBERGER, Vickie 630-942-8425 148 A
gukenbergerv@cod.edu
GUKICH, Doris, B 863-638-7261 123 D
doris.gukich@warner.edu
GULARTE, Mary Anne 562-860-2451 39 A
mgularte@cerritos.edu
GULAS, Charles 314-529-9625 284 C
cgulas@maryville.edu
GULDBRANDSEN, Thad 603-535-2525 307 A
tcguldbrandsen@plymouth.edu
GULEBIAN, Bryan 404-870-8980 139 G
GULEFF, Virginia 707-468-3014 57 A
vguleff@mendocino.edu
GULICK, Joseph, G 217-333-3303 167 D
ggulick@illinois.edu
GULINO, Tracy 858-566-1200 44 B
tgulino@disd.edu
GULLATT, David 318-257-3712 215 F
gullattd@latech.edu
GULLEDGE, Jim, E 704-463-3366 375 F
jim.gulledge@fsmail.pfeiffer.edu
GULLETT, J. Dan 731-286-3237 475 B
gullett@dscc.edu
GULLETT, J. Dan 731-286-3327 475 B
gullett@dscc.edu
GULLEY, Cheryl 615-383-4848 478 F
cgulley@watkins.edu
GULLEY, Jeff 260-484-4400 170 A
jgulley@brownmackie.edu
GULLEY, Lawrence 662-254-3306 276 B
gulley@mvsu.edu
GULLEY, S. Beverly 773-298-3221 163 I
gulley@sxu.edu
GULLEY, Shawn, M 504-286-5348 214 J
sgulley@suno.edu
GULLEY, Yancey 706-355-5175 125 C
ygulley@athenstech.edu
GULLICKSON, Janet 509-533-3535 533 A
janet.gullickson@spokanefalls.edu
GULLICKSON, Janet 509-533-3535 533 C
janet.gullickson@spokanefalls.edu
GULLICKSON, Marcia, A 563-387-1400 187 D
gullicma@luther.edu
GULLION, Christy, D 202-624-1424 539 A
cgullion@uw.edu
GULLO, Safawo 256-726-7054 6 C
sgullo@oakwood.edu
GULLY, Constance, G 314-340-3321 282 F
gullyc@hssu.edu
GULSTAD, Rita 660-248-6211 279 G
rgulstad@centralmethodist.edu
GUM, Tory 847-628-2082 154 K
tgum@judsonu.edu
GUMA, Susan 914-395-2374 350 C
sguma@sarahlawrence.edu
GUMBRIS, Janet 508-531-1246 237 D
jgumbris@bridgew.edu
GUMBS, Jean 718-270-6434 328 C
jgumbs@mec.cuny.edu
GUMBS, Marva 202-994-6495 98 C
mgumbs@gwu.edu
GUMM, Eric 325-674-2000 478 I
gummj@acu.edu
GUMPPER, Marianne, L 203-254-4184 92 H
mgumpper@fairfield.edu
GUMZ, Diane 503-777-7560 420 A
diane.gumz@reed.edu
GUNBY, Stephanie 404-816-4533 132 E
sgunby@atl.herzing.edu
GUNDEN, Randy 574-535-7007 171 G
randygg@goshen.edu
GUNDERMAN, Lisa 501-977-2025 25 G
gunderman@uaccm.edu
GUNDERSEN, Ryan 702-579-3548 302 A
rgundersen@kaplan.edu
GUNDERSON, Garth, M 208-496-3000 143 A
gundersong@byui.edu
GUNDERSON, Gayle, C 303-963-3252 82 C
ggunderson@ccu.edu
GUNDERSON, Greg 314-968-5911 292 J
greggunderson86@webster.edu
GUNDERSON, Jeff 415-749-4559 65 I
jgunderson@sfai.edu
GUNDERSON, Shirley 402-399-2435 297 C
sgunderson@csm.edu
GUNDRUM, Peggy 847-214-7399 150 F
pgundrum@elgin.edu
GUNEL, Esther, L 734-487-3116 250 F
egunel@emich.edu
GUNKEL, John 973-353-5213 314 E
jgunkel@andromeda.rutgers.edu
GUNN, Cathy 606-783-2162 204 I
c.gunn@moreheadstate.edu
GUNN, Daniel, P 207-778-7276 220 C
dpgunn@maine.edu
GUNN, E. Anthony 336-342-4261 373 E
gunnt@rockinghamcc.edu
GUNN, George, A 530-221-4275 69 C
ggunn@shasta.edu
GUNN, Karen 801-957-4366 512 D
karen.gunn@slcc.edu
GUNN, Michael, C 605-394-2414 466 B
michael.gunn@sdsmt.edu
GUNN, Rebecca 704-406-2118 364 E
rgunn@gardner-webb.edu
GUNN, Stanley, T 512-223-1200 481 B
sgunn@austincc.edu
GUNN, Tim 972-438-6932 492 E
tgunn@parkercc.edu
GUNNELS, Robert 870-574-4541 24 A
rgunnels@sautech.edu
GUNNER, Jeanne 714-744-7627 39 F
gunner@chapman.edu
GUNNING, Kathleen 570-372-4320 447 E
gunning@susqu.edu
GUNNING, Mary Jo 570-961-4724 435 F
gunning@marywood.edu
GUNNINK, Brett 406-994-2111 295 C
bgunnink@montana.edu
GUNNOE, JR., Charles 616-632-2151 247 E
gunnocha@aquinas.edu
GUNS, Michael 608-663-6714 547 F
mguns@edgewood.edu
GUNSALUS, Robert 408-551-1691 68 C
rgunsalus@scu.edu
GUNSOLLEY, Joanne 785-227-3380 191 B
gunsolleyj@bethanylb.edu
GUNTER, Deby 406-771-4392 295 G
dgunter@msugf.edu
GUNTER, Ellen 334-291-4918 2 F
ellen.gunter@cv.edu
GUNTER, Gail, P 662-329-7333 276 A
ggunter@library.muw.edu
GUNTER, Joan 985-549-2301 216 C
joan.gunter@selu.edu
GUNTER, Kathy 334-244-3343 1 G
kgunter1@aum.edu
GUNTER, Mary 479-968-0398 20 G
mgunter@atu.edu
GUNTER, Michael 870-850-4826 23 H
mgunter@seark.edu
GUNTER, Pat 541-956-7158 420 B
pgunter@roguecc.edu
GUNTER, Randy 910-576-6222 372 D
gunterr@montgomery.edu
GUNTER, Steve 828-765-7351 372 A
sgunter@mayland.edu
GUNTER-SMITH,
Pamela, J 973-408-3073 309 E
pgunter@drew.edu
GUNTHER, Janet 270-707-3833 202 E
janet.gunther@kctcs.edu
GUNTHORPE, Sydney 505-224-3824 317 K
sydney@cnm.edu
GUNTHORPE, Sydney, D 505-224-4427 317 K
sydney@cnm.edu
GUO, Lan 816-415-5032 293 C
guol@william.jewell.edu
GUPCHUP, Gireesh, V 618-650-5153 165 C
ggupchu@siue.edu
GUPTA, Mahendra, R 314-935-6344 292 I
guptam@wustl.edu
GUPTA, Sunil 212-346-8449 326 D
sbgupta@bmcc.cuny.edu
GURA, Daniel, T 813-253-6277 123 A
dgura@ut.edu
GURANOWSKI, Vicki 212-217-4100 333 F
vicki_guranowski@fitnyc.edu
GUREK, Shannon, D 413-542-2802 230 A
sdqurek@amherst.edu
GURLAND, Jerome, S 413-782-1508 246 A
jgurland@wne.edu
GURLER, Dan 415-575-6125 32 G
dgurler@ciis.edu
GURNON, R, G 508-830-5001 238 D
rgurnon@maritime.edu
GURROLA, Jeannette 909-607-8632 40 F
jeanette.gurrola@cgu.edu
GURROLA, Virginia 559-791-2222 53 A
vgurrola@portervillecollege.edu
GURSKIS, Daniel, A 973-655-5104 311 F
gurskisd@mail.montclair.edu
GUSSIN, Louise 410-888-9048 226 F
lgussin@tai.edu
GUST, Jonathan 610-519-6508 450 H
jonathan.gust@villanova.edu
GUSTAFS, Anita, O 864-833-8233 460 E
agustafs@presby.edu
GUSTAFSON, Crandon 617-262-5000 231 G
crandon.gustafson@the-bac.edu
GUSTAFSON, Donna, J 812-877-8275 179 B
donna.gustafson@rose-hulman.edu
GUSTAFSON, Eric 508-626-4012 238 A
egustafson1@framingham.edu
GUSTAFSON, Eric, T 704-847-5600 377 B
egustafson@ses.edu
GUSTAFSON, Liz 510-580-6715 80 A
lgustafson@cci.edu
GUSTAFSON, Peter, A 812-877-8230 179 B
peter.a.gustafson@rose-hulman.edu
GUSTAFSON, Ralph 651-638-6122 261 D
r-gustafson@bethel.edu
GUSTAFSON, Rita 661-654-3405 34 A
rgustafson@csub.edu
GUSTAFSON, Thomas, J 802-656-4450 514 H
thomas.gustafson@uvm.edu
GUSTAFSON, William 516-299-2824 339 A
william.gustafson@liu.edu
GUSTAVSON, David, B 318-795-4279 213 D
david.gustavson@lsus.edu

HADLEY, Pamela ... 610-399-2260 ... 442 A
phadley@cheyney.edu
HADLEY TORRES, Nola ... 510-981-2935 ... 62 B
nhadley@peralta.edu
HADLOCK, Eddie, L ... 940-668-7731 ... 491 E
ehadlock@nctc.edu
HADLOCK, Heather ... 214-333-5340 ... 484 D
heather@dbu.edu
HADRA, Becky, L ... 301-784-5000 ... 221 B
bhadra@allegany.edu
HADSELL, Heidi ... 860-509-9502 ... 93 A
hadsell@hartsem.edu
HADWICK, Jim ... 775-850-0700 ... 302 C
jhadwick@morrison.neumont.edu
HADWIN, Julie ... 803-584-3446 ... 462 E
jhadwin@mailbox.sc.edu
HAEFNER, Jeremy, A ... 585-475-6399 ... 347 G
jahpro@rit.edu
HAEFNER, Ronald, I ... 920-748-8320 ... 550 D
haefnerr@ripon.edu
HAEFNER, Stephen, R ... 570-326-3761 ... 440 L
shaefner@pct.edu
HAEGER, John, D ... 928-523-3232 ... 16 I
john.haeger@nau.edu
HAEGER, Loredana ... 801-957-6321 ... 512 D
loredana.haeger@slcc.edu
HAEHL, Sherry, L ... 910-814-5582 ... 362 J
haehl@campbell.edu
HAELEN, Robert ... 518-320-1100 ... 351 D
HAESLOOP, Mary ... 650-508-3651 ... 59 H
mhaesloop@ndnu.edu
HAEUSER, Patricia, N ... 928-523-7777 ... 16 I
patricia.haeuser@nau.edu
HAFELI, Mary ... 845-257-3860 ... 352 B
hafelim@newpaltz.edu
HAFER, Greg ... 417-626-1234 ... 287 C
ghafer@occ.edu
HAFFAR, Warren ... 215-572-4094 ... 422 C
haffarw@arcadia.edu
HAFFEY, Jim ... 662-226-0830 ... 274 D
jhaffey@holmescc.edu
HAFFNER, Christopher, D ... 904-819-6225 ... 107 C
haffnerc@flagler.edu
HAFFORD, Patrick ... 617-989-4870 ... 245 F
haffordp@wit.edu
HAFKEMEYER, Susan, P ... 563-588-7769 ... 187 C
sue.hafkemeyer@loras.edu
HAFNER, Arthur, W ... 765-285-5277 ... 169 G
ahafner@bsu.edu
HAFNER, JR., David, T ... 808-956-4636 ... 141 G
hafner@hawaii.edu
HAFNER, Donald, L ... 617-552-4173 ... 232 B
donald.hafner@bc.edu
HAFNER, Greg ... 641-673-2168 ... 190 C
hafnerg@wmpenn.edu
HAFNER, Lars, A ... 941-752-5201 ... 118 J
hafnerl@scf.edu
HAFT, Jennifer ... 702-992-2354 ... 302 G
jennifer.haft@nsc.edu
HAFT, Tami ... 208-769-7729 ... 144 D
tami_haft@nic.edu
HAGAN, Abdalla, F ... 903-927-3343 ... 509 E
afhagan@wileyc.edu
HAGAN, Bruce ... 949-451-5254 ... 70 E
bhagan@ivc.edu
HAGAN, G. Michael ... 605-336-6588 ... 465 D
gmhagan@sfseminary.edu
HAGAN, Linda ... 248-689-8282 ... 259 E
lhagan@walshcollege.edu
HAGAN, Michael ... 217-351-2457 ... 161 C
mhagan@parkland.edu
HAGAN, Rick ... 619-260-4624 ... 76 D
rhagan@sandiego.edu
HAGAN, Waldon ... 757-822-1227 ... 528 G
whagan@tcc.edu
HAGAN, Willie, J ... 310-243-3301 ... 34 D
presidenthagan@csudh.edu
HAGANS, Elbert ... 606-487-3178 ... 202 C
elbert.hagans@kctcs.edu
HAGANS, Karen ... 419-289-5067 ... 384 G
khagans@ashland.edu
HAGANS, Lori, R ... 405-878-2708 ... 409 D
lori.hagans@okbu.edu
HAGARA, Kimberly ... 409-747-3277 ... 507 C
kkhagara@utmb.edu
HAGBERG, Stewart ... 801-818-8900 ... 510 I
stewarth@provocollege.edu
HAGE, Gloria ... 734-487-1055 ... 250 F
ghage@emich.edu
HAGEDORN, Christine ... 215-968-8034 ... 423 F
hagedorn@bucks.edu
HAGEDORN, Valerie, A ... 412-531-4433 ... 426 F
info@deantech.edu
HAGEMAN, James, H ... 989-774-3094 ... 249 C
hagem1jh@cmich.edu
HAGEMAN, Kristin ... 651-773-1780 ... 266 A
kristin.hageman@century.edu
HAGEMANN, Ryan ... 541-346-5767 ... 418 B
ryan_hagemann@ous.edu
HAGEMEYER, Gwen ... 812-535-5285 ... 179 E
ghagemeyer@smwc.edu
HAGEN, Berta ... 218-285-2207 ... 268 F
bhagen@rrcc.mnscu.edu

HAGEN, Cheryl, M ... 734-462-4400 ... 258 A
chagen@schoolcraft.edu
HAGEN, Gary, D ... 701-788-4754 ... 381 H
gary.hagen@mayvillestate.edu
HAGEN, Lauralee ... 253-535-7203 ... 536 E
hagen@plu.edu
HAGEN, Mike ... 641-683-5243 ... 185 G
michael.hagen@indianhills.edu
HAGEN, Patrick ... 608-647-6186 ... 553 B
patrick.hagen@uwc.edu
HAGEN, Peter ... 609-652-4504 ... 313 E
hagenp@stockton.edu
HAGEN, Randi ... 904-819-6322 ... 107 C
rhagen@flagler.edu
HAGEN, Stan ... 503-838-8174 ... 419 C
hagens@wou.edu
HAGEN, Susan ... 205-226-4660 ... 2 B
shagen@bsc.edu
HAGENBAUGH, Stacie ... 413-585-2582 ... 244 G
shagenba@smith.edu
HAGENBUCH, Brian ... 607-431-4518 ... 335 A
hagenbuchb@hartwick.edu
HAGER, Amy ... 660-263-4110 ... 286 H
amyh@macc.edu
HAGER, Melissa ... 609-652-4295 ... 313 E
melissa.hager@stockton.edu
HAGER, Michael, A ... 319-273-2382 ... 182 G
michael.hager@uni.edu
HAGER, Tim ... 515-964-6409 ... 183 H
tjhager@dmacc.edu
HAGERMAN, Brandi, F ... 336-633-0213 ... 373 A
bfhagerman@randolph.edu
HAGERMAN, Elizabeth, M ... 812-877-1511 ... 179 B
HAGERMANN, P. Donald ... 302-356-6844 ... 97 C
p.donald.hagermann@wilmu.edu
HAGERTY, Michael ... 617-266-1400 ... 231 E
HAGG, Scott ... 707-826-4400 ... 36 E
skh7001@humboldt.edu
HAGGANS, Mary, S ... 417-667-8181 ... 280 E
mhaggans@cottey.edu
HAGGARD, Bill ... 828-251-6474 ... 378 D
bhaggard@unca.edu
HAGGARD, Cynthia ... 785-442-6002 ... 193 F
chaggard@highlandcc.edu
HAGGARD, David, L ... 423-775-7207 ... 467 F
david.haggard@bryan.edu
HAGGERTY, Christina ... 815-455-8727 ... 157 H
chaggerty@mchenry.edu
HAGGERTY, Dennis ... 609-894-9311 ... 308 B
dhaggert@bcc.edu
HAGGERTY, Gary ... 617-266-1400 ... 231 E
HAGGERTY, Janet, A ... 918-631-2304 ... 413 F
janet-haggerty@utulsa.edu
HAGGINS, Debra, L ... 757-727-5340 ... 519 H
debra.haggins@hamptonu.edu
HAGGINS, Tanya ... 216-201-9025 ... 394 G
HAGGRAY, M. Annette ... 443-412-2244 ... 223 B
ahaggray@harford.edu
HAGGRAY, Shelby, M ... 202-885-8614 ... 100 C
shaggray@wesleyseminary.edu
HAGHIGHI, Shawn ... 636-949-4726 ... 283 J
shaghighi@lindenwood.edu
HAGLER, James ... 478-471-2778 ... 133 H
james.hagler@maconstate.edu
HAGON, Sean, P ... 617-585-1100 ... 242 I
sean.hagon@necmusic.edu
HAGOVSKY, Beth ... 610-660-1072 ... 446 C
bhagovsk@sju.edu
HAGSTROM, Steven, W ... 817-515-5186 ... 496 C
steven.hagstrom@tccd.edu
HAGUE, Barth, A ... 316-978-6288 ... 198 A
barth.hague@wichita.edu
HAGUE, Stephen, T ... 410-323-6211 ... 222 F
sthague@faiththeological.org
HAH, Megan ... 626-289-7719 ... 26 K
HAHKA, Curt ... 906-487-7380 ... 251 A
curt.hahka@finlandia.edu
HAHN, Jacqueline ... 808-981-2790 ... 140 F
HAHN, Kathy ... 828-328-7402 ... 366 E
kathy.hahn@lr.edu
HAHN, Kelli ... 269-927-6701 ... 253 G
khahn@lakemichigancollege.edu
HAHN, Marc ... 207-602-2340 ... 221 A
mhahn@une.edu
HAHN, Marc, B ... 816-654-7203 ... 283 F
HAHN, Mary Joan ... 509-313-4220 ... 534 F
hahn@gonzaga.edu
HAHN, Norman, P ... 757-825-2952 ... 528 F
hahnn@tncc.edu
HAHN, Roger ... 816-268-5412 ... 286 I
rlhahn@nts.edu
HAHN, Sarah ... 212-650-7060 ... 326 G
shahn@ccny.cuny.edu
HAHN, Stephen ... 973-720-2565 ... 317 D
hahns@wpunj.edu
HAHN, Terence ... 312-777-8705 ... 153 B
thahn@aii.edu
HAHS, Sharon, K ... 773-442-5400 ... 160 A
s-hahs@neiu.edu
HAID, William, R ... 858-534-5448 ... 74 F
whaid@ucsd.edu
HAIDER, Rita ... 740-351-3127 ... 401 I
rhaider@shawnee.edu

HAIDLE, Shirley, J ... 208-467-8523 ... 144 E
sjhaidle@nnu.edu
HAIGHT, Donald ... 707-638-5270 ... 73 A
donald.haight@tu.edu
HAIGHT, Larry, L ... 530-226-4110 ... 69 H
lhaight@simpsonu.edu
HAIGLER, Anna, D ... 803-536-7047 ... 460 G
ahaigler@scsu.edu
HAIL, Amy ... 207-221-4228 ... 221 A
ahail@une.edu
HAIL, Joyce ... 501-569-3110 ... 24 E
jahail@ualr.edu
HAILE, Bob, A ... 309-649-6331 ... 165 F
bob.haile@src.edu
HAILE, Christine, E ... 518-956-8080 ... 351 E
chaile@uamail.albany.edu
HAILE, Gregory, A ... 954-201-7410 ... 102 E
ghaile@broward.edu
HAILEY, Maryann ... 903-875-7305 ... 491 C
maryann.hailey@navarrocollege.edu
HAILEY, Robert, C ... 504-862-8064 ... 215 C
rhailey@tulane.edu
HAILU, Elias ... 713-313-7879 ... 500 B
hailu_ex@tsu.edu
HAIN, C. Stuart ... 610-328-8575 ... 447 F
chain1@swarthmore.edu
HAIN, Judith, E ... 973-655-5293 ... 311 F
hainj@mail.montclair.edu
HAIN, Peggy, S ... 402-465-2137 ... 299 H
phain@nebrwesleyan.edu
HAIN, Tom ... 432-552-2782 ... 507 D
hain_t@utpb.edu
HAINAJ, Rosa ... 440-365-5222 ... 395 D
HAINES, Chris ... 602-285-7800 ... 16 A
HAINES, Chris ... 602-243-8000 ... 16 D
chris.haines@smcmail.maricopa.edu
HAINES, Chuck ... 805-893-8541 ... 75 B
chuck.haines@bap.ucsb.edu
HAINES, Ena ... 212-678-3486 ... 357 G
ena@tc.columbia.edu
HAINES, Gerald, C ... 240-500-2000 ... 223 A
hainesg@hagerstowncc.edu
HAINES, Malcolm ... 757-727-5477 ... 519 H
malcolm.haines@hamptonu.edu
HAINES, Terry ... 913-266-8601 ... 17 B
HAINES, Terry ... 913-266-8601 ... 195 I
terry.haines@ottawa.edu
HAINES, Terry ... 913-266-8601 ... 196 A
HAINES, Terry ... 913-266-8601 ... 178 I
donna.levene@ottawa.edu
HAINES, Terry ... 913-266-8601 ... 549 H
HAINEY, Dale, E ... 817-202-6519 ... 495 E
haineyd@swau.edu
HAINGRAY, Donald ... 585-567-9287 ... 336 B
donald.haingray@houghton.edu
HAINLINE, Benjamin ... 580-628-6250 ... 409 B
ben.hainline@north-ok.edu
HAINSTOCK, Brian ... 215-717-6614 ... 448 I
bhainstock@uarts.edu
HAIR, Shannon ... 434-797-8495 ... 526 G
shair@dcc.vccs.edu
HAIRSTON, Creasie ... 312-996-3219 ... 167 B
cfh@uic.edu
HAIRSTON, Demond ... 704-463-3408 ... 375 F
demond.hairston@fsmail.pfeiffer.edu
HAIRSTON, Gregory, G ... 336-750-2125 ... 380 B
hairstong@wssu.edu
HAIRSTON, Jewel, E ... 804-524-5871 ... 529 H
jhairston@vsu.edu
HAIRSTON, Lathan ... 870-862-8131 ... 23 G
lhairston@southark.edu
HAIRSTON, Marie ... 415-565-4703 ... 74 A
hairston@uchastings.edu
HAIRSTON, Tali ... 206-281-2455 ... 537 H
tali@spu.edu
HAISCH, Craig ... 503-883-2217 ... 416 H
chaisch@linfield.edu
HAISEN, Michael ... 808-735-4785 ... 140 E
mhaisen@chominade.edu
HAISLETT, Judith ... 575-562-2221 ... 318 B
judith.haislett@enmu.edu
HAISLIP, Jackie, F ... 252-789-0259 ... 371 H
jhaislip@martincc.edu
HAISMA, Dale ... 616-632-3037 ... 247 E
haismdal@aquinas.edu
HAITCH, Russell ... 800-287-8822 ... 169 H
haitcru@bethanyseminary.edu
HAITH, Carolyn ... 213-738-6705 ... 71 E
registrar@swlaw.edu
HAJEK, Laurel, A ... 312-987-1404 ... 154 H
6hajek@jmls.edu
HAJELA, Prabhat ... 518-276-6624 ... 347 D
hajelap@rpi.edu
HAJEWSKI, Vicki ... 715-394-8241 ... 552 F
vhajewsk@uwsuper.edu
HAJJAR, David, P ... 212-746-6900 ... 360 C
dphajjar@med.cornell.edu
HAJOVSKY, Ted ... 979-209-7211 ... 482 C
thajovsky@blinn.edu
HAKA, Clifford, H ... 517-355-2341 ... 255 A
hakac@msu.edu
HAKANSON, David ... 205-726-2032 ... 6 G
dhakanson@samford.edu
HAKE, Stephen, R ... 540-338-1776 ... 522 G

HAKER, Catherine, A ... 518-454-5158 ... 330 C
hakerc@strose.edu
HAKIM, George ... 810-762-3223 ... 259 C
heohak@umflint.edu
HAKIM, Iman, A ... 520-626-7083 ... 18 L
ihakim@email.arizona.edu
HAKKAKIAN, Eliyahu ... 410-484-7200 ... 225 C
HAKKENBERG, Michael, A ... 540-375-2379 ... 523 G
hakkenberg@roanoke.edu
HAKL, Roberta, H ... 605-667-5651 ... 465 G
roberta.hakl@usd.edu
HAKLIN, Joseph, R ... 765-361-6233 ... 181 E
haklinj@wabash.edu
HAKODA, Kensuke ... 785-827-5541 ... 194 F
hakoda@kwu.edu
HALAKAN, Cathy ... 518-262-4019 ... 322 D
halakac@mail.amc.edu
HALARIS, Dimitris ... 914-633-2649 ... 336 E
dhalaris@iona.edu
HALASZ, Thomas ... 803-777-3971 ... 462 A
halasztj@mailbox.sc.edu
HALAUFIA, Patty ... 435-797-2053 ... 511 E
patty.halaufia@usu.edu
HALBERSTADT, Joseph ... 718-438-1002 ... 340 G
yhalberstadt@yeshivanet.com
HALBERT, Jay ... 325-942-2355 ... 480 E
jay.halbert@angelo.edu
HALBERT, Martin ... 940-565-3025 ... 504 D
martin.halbert@unt.edu
HALBROOK, David, W ... 540-338-1776 ... 522 G
HALCOMB, Jonda ... 361-698-1218 ... 485 G
jhalcomb@delmar.edu
HALDAR, Fran ... 330-339-3391 ... 394 A
fhaldar@kent.edu
HALDEMAN, Pam ... 310-954-4366 ... 57 H
phaldeman@msmc.la.edu
HALE, Barry ... 903-923-2020 ... 486 F
bhale@etbu.edu
HALE, Brian ... 334-683-2367 ... 5 G
bhale@marionmilitary.edu
HALE, Christi ... 580-349-1556 ... 410 B
chale@opsu.edu
HALE, David ... 315-228-7422 ... 329 G
dhale@colgate.edu
HALE, Debra, A ... 802-626-6492 ... 515 G
debra.hale@lyndonstate.edu
HALE, Duke ... 704-847-5600 ... 377 B
dhale@ses.edu
HALE, Ed ... 478-445-3350 ... 130 B
ed.hale@gcsu.edu
HALE, Georgia ... 479-788-7721 ... 24 D
georgia.hale@uafs.edu
HALE, Jeffery, L ... 918-540-6201 ... 408 J
jhale@neo.edu
HALE, Jerold ... 313-593-5490 ... 259 B
jlhale@umd.umich.edu
HALE, Kara, B ... 620-431-2820 ... 195 E
khale@neosho.edu
HALE, Kathleen ... 207-948-9169 ... 219 H
khale@unity.edu
HALE, Kathy, M ... 816-604-1022 ... 284 H
kathy.hale@mcckc.edu
HALE, Kenneth ... 216-987-4251 ... 389 B
kenneth.hale@tri-c.edu
HALE, Mark ... 717-564-4112 ... 432 B
mhale@kaplan.edu
HALE, Melva, P ... 270-843-6750 ... 200 B
mhale@daymarcollege.edu
HALE, Nora, M ... 704-847-5600 ... 377 B
nhale@ses.edu
HALE, Nori ... 785-242-5200 ... 195 I
nori.hale@ottawa.edu
HALE, Philip, P ... 312-915-6494 ... 157 C
phale@luc.edu
HALE, Steve ... 415-241-2255 ... 40 C
shale@ccsf.edu
HALE, Susie ... 863-784-7232 ... 117 J
susie.hale@southflorida.edu
HALE, Ted ... 860-906-5053 ... 91 C
thale@ccc.commnet.edu
HALE, Timothy ... 315-312-2378 ... 354 A
timothy.hale@oswego.edu
HALE, Zoe, M ... 831-656-2511 ... 558 A
zmhale@nps.edu
HALE-SMITH, Margaret ... 269-467-9945 ... 251 B
mhalesmith@glenoaks.edu
HALER, Jennifer ... 317-573-8946 ... 541 K
jhaler@salemu.edu
HALES, Christie, C ... 434-949-1068 ... 528 D
christie.hales@southside.edu
HALEVY, Julia ... 617-262-5000 ... 231 G
julia.halevy@the-bac.edu
HALEY, Brian ... 916-660-7202 ... 69 F
bhaley@sierracollege.edu
HALEY, Donna ... 678-839-6438 ... 139 A
dhaley@westga.edu
HALEY, Gene ... 863-784-7112 ... 117 J
ghaley@neboo.com
HALEY, John, R ... 315-445-4689 ... 338 B
haleyjr@lemoyne.edu
HALEY, Ken ... 903-785-7661 ... 492 D
khaley@parisjc.edu
HALEY, Randy ... 337-392-3102 ... 216 B
haley@nsula.edu

HALLER, Bryan .... 212-220-8013 .... 326 D
bhaller@bmcc.cuny.edu
HALLER, Hal .... 770-484-1204 .... 133 G
library@lru.edu
HALLER, James, P .... 864-587-4208 .... 461 D
hallerje@smcsc.edu
HALLER, John, G .... 610-660-1305 .... 446 C
jhaller@sju.edu
HALLER, John, R .... 320-308-5922 .... 269 B
jhaller@sctcc.edu
HALLERAN, Donna .... 608-265-3443 .... 550 J
dhalleran@vc.wisc.edu
HALLERAN, Michael .... 757-221-1993 .... 518 A
halleran@wm.edu
HALLETT, David .... 503-399-5172 .... 414 J
david.hallett@chemeketa.edu
HALLETT, Tom .... 708-209-3350 .... 148 E
tom.hallett@cuchicago.edu
HALLGREN, Martyne .... 402-557-7199 .... 296 H
martyne.hallgren@bellevue.edu
HALLICK, Lesley, M .... 503-352-2123 .... 419 E
president@pacificu.edu
HALLIDAY, Chris .... 660-626-2800 .... 278 D
challiday@atsu.edu
HALLIDAY, Nancy, E .... 516-463-5740 .... 335 G
nancy.halliday@hofstra.edu
HALLIDAY, Robert, M .... 315-792-3122 .... 359 E
rhalliday@utica.edu
HALLIGAN, Meg, F .... 563-333-6311 .... 188 F
halliganmegf@sau.edu
HALLIS, John .... 205-665-6512 .... 9 B
hallisj@montevallo.edu
HALLISEY, L. Ann .... 510-204-0716 .... 40 A
ahallisey@cdsp.edu
HALLLSMITH, George .... 216-987-4854 .... 389 B
george.hallsmith@tri-c.edu
HALLMAN, Janet, S .... 253-879-8620 .... 538 H
jhallman@pugetsound.edu
HALLMAN, Raymond .... 215-248-7007 .... 425 D
hallmanr@chc.edu
HALLMARK, James .... 979-458-6070 .... 496 F
jhallmark@tamus.edu
HALLORAN, Beth .... 641-269-3200 .... 185 D
halloran@grinnell.edu
HALLORAN, Florence .... 770-962-7580 .... 132 D
fhalloran@gwinnetttech.edu
HALLORAN, Sybil, C .... 804-828-6125 .... 526 B
schallor@vcu.edu
HALLORAN, Tom .... 781-595-6768 .... 236 C
thalloran@mariancourt.edu
HALLQUIST, Carrie, L .... 715-833-6670 .... 553 H
challquist1@cvtc.edu
HALLSTROM, Lilian .... 808-543-8088 .... 140 G
lhallstrom@hpu.edu
HALLSTROM, Peggy .... 605-626-3011 .... 466 A
hallstrp@northern.edu
HALLUM, Ann .... 415-338-2231 .... 37 B
glider@sfsu.edu
HALMON, Judy .... 803-793-5170 .... 457 F
holmanj@denmarktech.edu
HALOMAN, Barbara .... 314-595-3400 .... 278 F
HALONEN, Jane, S .... 850-474-2688 .... 121 D
jhalonen@uwf.edu
HALPERIN, Edward, C .... 914-594-4900 .... 343 F
edward_halperin@nymc.edu
HALPERIN, Michael .... 607-735-1895 .... 332 I
registrar@elmira.edu
HALPERIN, William, E .... 973-972-4422 .... 317 A
halperwe@umdnj.edu
HALPERN, Avrohom .... 516-239-9002 .... 350 H
HALPERN, Daphne .... 212-650-3733 .... 327 E
HALPERN, Jane, L .... 410-704-2466 .... 228 E
jhalpern@towson.edu
HALPERN, Linda, C .... 540-568-2852 .... 520 H
halperlc@jmu.edu
HALPERN, Mike .... 208-769-3310 .... 144 D
mike_halpern@nic.edu
HALPIN, Eamon .... 318-473-6545 .... 212 I
ehalpin@lsua.edu
HALPIN, Eamon .... 318-427-4469 .... 212 I
ehalpin@lsua.edu
HALPIN-ROBBINS,
Kathleen .... 413-565-1000 .... 230 G
khrobbins@baypath.edu
HALSEY, Cindy .... 843-470-8396 .... 461 E
chalsey@tcl.edu
HALSEY, Glenn .... 307-755-9820 .... 557 B
ghalsey@wyotechstaff.edu
HALSEY, Mark, D .... 845-758-7267 .... 323 D
halsey@bard.edu
HALSEY, Robert .... 781-239-4347 .... 230 E
halsey@babson.edu
HALSEY, Timothy .... 805-966-3888 .... 31 D
timothy.halsey@brooks.edu
HALSMER, Dominic .... 918-495-6004 .... 411 C
dhalsmer@oru.edu
HALSTEAD, Barbara .... 407-582-3250 .... 123 B
bhalstead@valenciacollege.edu
HALSTEAD, John, R .... 585-395-2361 .... 352 F
halstead@brockport.edu
HALSTEAD, Joyce .... 229-225-5062 .... 138 A
jhalstead@southwestgatech.edu
HALSTEAD, Lois, A .... 312-942-7117 .... 163 D
lois_a_halstead@rush.edu

HALSTEAD, Michele .... 845-257-3295 .... 352 B
halsteam@newpaltz.edu
HALSTEAD, Sarah .... 541-684-7250 .... 417 F
khalstead@nwcu.edu
HALSTED, Steve .... 406-771-4367 .... 295 G
shalsted@msugf.edu
HALTER, Robert .... 317-274-7746 .... 174 D
rhalter@iupui.edu
HALTERMAN, Lauren, C .... 410-827-5818 .... 222 B
lhalterman@chesapeake.edu
HALTERMAN, Rick .... 423-236-2871 .... 473 B
halterman@southern.edu
HALTTUNEN, Lynda .... 760-744-1150 .... 61 D
lhalttunen@palomar.edu
HALUSCHAK, Rich .... 626-396-2308 .... 29 I
rich.haluschak@artcenter.edu
HALUSHKA, Lisa .... 248-751-7800 .... 258 F
halushkl@cooley.edu
HALUSHKA, Perry, V .... 843-792-3012 .... 459 D
halushpv@musc.edu
HALUSKA, Jan .... 423-236-2738 .... 473 B
haluska@southern.edu
HALUZAK, Jennifer, L .... 414-955-8246 .... 548 G
jhaluzak@mcw.edu
HALVERSON, Andrea, R .... 651-631-5121 .... 270 B
arhalverson@nwc.edu
HALVERSON, Tom, L .... 605-256-5165 .... 465 I
tom.halverson@dsu.edu
HALVERSTADT, David .... 360-538-4234 .... 534 G
dhalverst@ghc.edu
HALVORSON, Daisy .... 605-668-1566 .... 464 G
dhalvorson@mtmc.edu
HALVORSON, J. Derek .... 706-419-1117 .... 128 B
derek.halvorson@covenant.edu
HALVORSON, Paula .... 785-460-5497 .... 192 C
paula.halvorson@colbycc.edu
HALVORSON, Stephen, J .... 704-366-5066 .... 376 B
shalvorson@rts.edu
HALVORSON, Terry .... 715-425-3265 .... 552 C
terry.n.halvorson@uwrf.edu
HALVORSON, Terry, N .... 715-425-3265 .... 552 C
terry.n.halvorson@uwrf.edu
HAM, Carol Ann .... 229-317-6734 .... 128 D
carolann.ham@darton.edu
HAM, Clay .... 217-732-3168 .... 156 H
cham@lincolnchristian.edu
HAM, Frederic .... 321-674-7318 .... 108 H
fmh@fit.edu
HAM, Gary .... 978-762-4000 .... 240 D
gham@northshore.edu
HAM, Karen, L .... 315-267-2344 .... 354 C
hamkl@potsdam.edu
HAM, Marsha, K .... 203-932-7386 .... 95 C
mham@newhaven.edu
HAM, Paige .... 919-735-5151 .... 375 A
peham@waynecc.edu
HAM, Scott, D .... 317-940-8112 .... 170 F
sdham@butler.edu
HAMADA, Larisa .... 562-985-8256 .... 35 C
larisa.hamada@csulb.edu
HAMAKER, Michelle .... 308-865-8517 .... 300 F
hamakerm@unk.edu
HAMAN, Linda .... 636-227-2100 .... 284 B
linda.haman@logan.edu
HAMANN, Andrew .... 507-529-2789 .... 268 I
andrew.hamann@roch.edu
HAMANN, Dick, T .... 407-708-2258 .... 117 H
hamannd@seminolestate.edu
HAMANN, Gregory, J .... 541-917-4200 .... 416 I
hamanng@linnbenton.edu
HAMANN, Julie, A .... 419-372-0669 .... 385 F
jrogers@bgsu.edu
HAMANN, Melanie .... 573-840-9767 .... 290 F
mhamann@trcc.edu
HAMBERGER, Barnett .... 212-998-2310 .... 344 B
bwh1@nyu.edu
HAMBEY, Anthony .... 205-226-4850 .... 2 B
ahambey@bsc.edu
HAMBLEN, Jon .... 916-660-7382 .... 69 F
jhamblen@sierracollege.edu
HAMBLIN, Carolyn .... 928-875-9116 .... 16 F
chamblin@mohave.edu
HAMBLIN, Veronica .... 660-263-3900 .... 279 F
vhamblin@cccb.edu
HAMBLIN-FOX, Jeannie .... 765-966-2656 .... 176 H
jhamblin@ivytech.edu
HAMBLING, William .... 574-284-4552 .... 179 F
whamblin@saintmarys.edu
HAMBLY, Raine .... 714-432-5628 .... 41 D
rhambly@occ.cccd.edu
HAMBRICH, Uriia .... 601-979-2911 .... 274 G
uriia.hambrich@jsums.edu
HAMBRIGHT, M. Karen .... 912-279-5879 .... 127 E
khambright@ccga.edu
HAMBROCK, Daniel .... 651-793-1712 .... 267 A
daniel.hambrock@metrostate.edu
HAMBURG, Gail .... 509-793-2002 .... 531 I
gailh@bigbend.edu
HAMBURG, Gary .... 773-834-2059 .... 166 A
ghamburg@ttic.edu
HAMBURG, Jo Ann .... 845-341-4903 .... 345 E
joann.hamburg@sunyorange.edu
HAMBURGER, Daniel .... 630-725-1930 .... 149 B
dhamburger@devry.edu

HAMBY, Dale .... 717-901-5100 .... 430 F
dhamby@harrisburgu.edu
HAMBY, Dan .... 270-707-3790 .... 202 E
dan.hamby@kctcs.edu
HAMBY, David .... 918-343-7771 .... 411 H
dhamby@rsu.edu
HAMBY, Edwina, H .... 615-329-8768 .... 468 I
ehamby@fisk.edu
HAMBY, Eileen .... 386-506-3939 .... 104 F
hambye@daytonastate.edu
HAMBY, Karen, G .... 205-726-2643 .... 6 G
kghamby@samford.edu
HAMEL, Carolyn .... 508-999-8032 .... 237 A
chamel@umassd.edu
HAMEL, Dale, M .... 508-626-4580 .... 238 A
dhamel@framingham.edu
HAMEL, James .... 978-665-3584 .... 237 E
jhamel@fitchburgstate.edu
HAMEL, John .... 617-573-8460 .... 245 B
jhamel@suffolk.edu
HAMEL, Kayte .... 815-825-2086 .... 155 D
kayte.hamel@kishwaukeecollege.edu
HAMEL, Thomas .... 847-635-1660 .... 160 F
thamel@oakton.edu
HAMELINE, Walter .... 718-390-3488 .... 360 A
whamelin@wagner.edu
HAMEN, Laurie, M .... 630-637-5155 .... 159 G
lahamen@noctrl.edu
HAMER, Ronald, J .... 518-454-2060 .... 330 C
hamerj@strose.edu
HAMES, Anne .... 731-352-4066 .... 467 E
hamesa@bethelu.edu
HAMES, Becky .... 731-352-4046 .... 467 E
hamesb@bethelu.edu
HAMIL, Bobby .... 678-466-4050 .... 127 D
bobbyhamil@clayton.edu
HAMILL, Anne .... 410-837-5753 .... 229 A
ahamill@ubalt.edu
HAMILL, Jonathan, T .... 334-649-5000 .... 557 E
HAMILL, Paul, J .... 607-274-1326 .... 336 G
hamill@ithaca.edu
HAMILL, Robert, P .... 740-392-6868 .... 396 I
robert.hamill@mvnu.edu
HAMILTON, Alice .... 785-442-6025 .... 193 F
ahamilton@highlandcc.edu
HAMILTON, Allana, R .... 423-279-7632 .... 475 F
arhamilton@northeaststate.edu
HAMILTON, Amanda, B .... 253-535-7667 .... 536 E
hawkinab@plu.edu
HAMILTON, Barbara .... 870-837-4003 .... 24 A
bhamilto@sautech.edu
HAMILTON, Barbara .... 601-318-6524 .... 278 C
barbara.hamilton@wmcarey.edu
HAMILTON, Ben .... 912-583-3280 .... 126 F
bhamilton@bpc.edu
HAMILTON, Bill .... 850-484-1304 .... 115 B
bhamilton@pensacolastate.edu
HAMILTON, Billy Jo .... 813-974-3039 .... 121 A
bjhamilton@usf.edu
HAMILTON, Bob .... 412-237-3108 .... 425 H
rhamilton@ccac.edu
HAMILTON, Carolyn, K .... 707-965-7500 .... 60 I
ckhamilton@puc.edu
HAMILTON, Cecilia .... 305-348-2560 .... 119 C
cecilia.hamilton@fiu.edu
HAMILTON, Charlene .... 337-482-6243 .... 216 D
personnel@louisiana.edu
HAMILTON, Cheresa, Y .... 904-620-2455 .... 120 D
chamilto@unf.edu
HAMILTON, Cheryl .... 336-917-5329 .... 376 E
cheryl.hamilton@salem.edu
HAMILTON, Donna, B .... 301-405-9354 .... 227 B
dhamil@umd.edu
HAMILTON, Dwight .... 616-331-2242 .... 251 F
hamiltdw@gvsu.edu
HAMILTON, JR., Elbert .... 713-629-8940 .... 508 A
HAMILTON, Eldrie .... 318-274-6321 .... 215 E
hamiltoneb@gram.edu
HAMILTON, Eric .... 843-574-6272 .... 461 G
eric.hamilton@tridenttech.edu
HAMILTON, Ethan .... 619-849-2621 .... 62 L
ethanhamilton@pointloma.edu
HAMILTON, Eugene, J .... 989-964-4069 .... 257 G
hamilton@svsu.edu
HAMILTON, Fred .... 212-226-5500 .... 323 A
fhamilton@aii.edu
HAMILTON, Gary .... 909-869-4426 .... 33 J
gahamilton@csupomona.edu
HAMILTON, Glenn .... 708-524-6795 .... 150 C
hamilton@dom.edu
HAMILTON, Glenn .... 980-598-1925 .... 365 I
glenn.hamilton@jwu.edu
HAMILTON, Glenn, R .... 859-858-3511 .... 198 E
glenn.hamilton@asbury.edu
HAMILTON, Jackie .... 314-918-2627 .... 281 F
jhamilton@eden.edu
HAMILTON, Janet .... 409-984-6354 .... 501 C
janet.hamilton@lamarpa.edu
HAMILTON, Jeff .... 910-576-6222 .... 372 D
hamiltonj@montgomery.edu
HAMILTON, Jeff .... 740-351-3263 .... 401 I
jhamilton@shawnee.edu
HAMILTON, Judy .... 714-556-3610 .... 77 B
jhamilton@vanguard.edu

HAMILTON, Kate .... 517-264-7142 .... 258 B
khamilton@sienaheights.edu
HAMILTON, Kathleen .... 718-260-3792 .... 346 C
hamilton@poly.edu
HAMILTON, Kathleen, M .... 607-733-7177 .... 332 H
khamilton@ebi-college.com
HAMILTON, Kerry-Ann .... 202-238-2338 .... 98 E
k_hamilton@howard.edu
HAMILTON, Kevin .... 501-975-6060 .... 23 B
khamilton@philander.edu
HAMILTON, Kevin .... 585-345-6950 .... 334 F
kphamilton@genesee.edu
HAMILTON, Larry .... 702-895-1229 .... 302 I
larry.hamilton@unlv.edu
HAMILTON, Laura .... 585-271-3657 .... 348 B
lhamilton@stbernards.edu
HAMILTON, Laura, Y .... 832-252-4612 .... 483 C
laura.hamilton@cbshouston.edu
HAMILTON, Lesley .... 512-492-3040 .... 480 F
lhamilton@aoma.edu
HAMILTON, Lisa .... 724-503-1001 .... 451 A
lhamilton@washjeff.edu
HAMILTON, Margaret .... 856-227-7200 .... 308 D
mhamilton@camdencc.edu
HAMILTON, Marty .... 423-236-2806 .... 473 B
mlhamil@southern.edu
HAMILTON, Mary Jane .... 361-825-2649 .... 498 C
mary.hamilton@tamucc.edu
HAMILTON, Maryanne .... 563-386-3570 .... 185 E
HAMILTON, Matt .... 405-325-8481 .... 413 C
mhamilton@ou.edu
HAMILTON, Melodi .... 909-558-4567 .... 54 D
mbhamilton@llu.edu
HAMILTON, Michael, E .... 865-974-1224 .... 477 D
mhamilton@tennessee.edu
HAMILTON, Michelle .... 262-551-6000 .... 546 I
mhamilton@carthage.edu
HAMILTON, Mike .... 205-226-7790 .... 2 B
mhamilto@bsc.edu
HAMILTON, Monica .... 863-638-2775 .... 123 D
monica.hamilton@warner.edu
HAMILTON, Neil, W .... 651-962-4886 .... 272 B
nwhamilton@stthomas.edu
HAMILTON, Pat .... 605-721-5200 .... 464 H
phamilton@national.edu
HAMILTON, Patti .... 845-451-1458 .... 331 E
p_hamilt@culinary.edu
HAMILTON, Rhoda .... 281-899-1240 .... 492 I
HAMILTON, Richard .... 360-442-2263 .... 535 I
rhamilton@lowercolumbia.edu
HAMILTON, Rick .... 601-477-4025 .... 274 H
rick.hamilton@jcjc.edu
HAMILTON, Robert .... 802-735-2612 .... 322 B
robert.hamilton@acphs.edu
HAMILTON, Roy .... 219-989-2779 .... 178 K
hamilton@purduecal.edu
HAMILTON, Scott .... 276-523-7469 .... 527 D
shamilton@me.vccs.edu
HAMILTON, Shaan .... 651-846-1694 .... 269 C
shaan.hamilton@saintpaul.edu
HAMILTON, Susan .... 425-352-8583 .... 532 B
shamilton@cascadia.edu
HAMILTON, Sylvia .... 609-984-7188 .... 316 A
shamilton@tesc.edu
HAMILTON, Theresa .... 601-857-3250 .... 274 C
thhamilton@hindscc.edu
HAMILTON, Wallace, O .... 405-789-7661 .... 412 E
wallace.hamilton@swcu.edu
HAMILTON, Wayne, T .... 802-626-6410 .... 515 G
wayne.hamilton@lyndonstate.edu
HAMILTON, William, P .... 803-536-7060 .... 460 G
whamilton@scsu.edu
HAMILTON-CHANDLER,
Beverly .... 609-258-6355 .... 312 G
hamilton@princeton.edu
HAMILTON-DAVIS, Jody .... 919-546-8415 .... 376 F
jhamiltondavis@shawu.edu
HAMILTON-GOLDEN,
Barbara .... 201-447-7113 .... 307 E
bagolden@bergen.edu
HAMILTON SLANE,
Sandra .... 530-242-7669 .... 69 D
sslane@shastacollege.edu
HAMINGTON, Maurice, F .... 303-556-8441 .... 86 F
mhamingt@msudenver.edu
HAMLET, Michael .... 931-221-7179 .... 473 E
hamletm@apsu.edu
HAMLETT, Adele .... 916-660-7160 .... 69 F
ahamlett@sierracollege.edu
HAMLETT, Melvin, R .... 731-426-7539 .... 470 B
hamlett@lanecollege.edu
HAMLETT, Willie .... 626-815-3890 .... 30 G
whamlett@apu.edu
HAMLIN, Kelly .... 828-652-0629 .... 372 B
khamlin@mcdowelltech.edu
HAMLIN, Lyn .... 201-200-3525 .... 312 B
lhamlin@njcu.edu
HAMM, Annette .... 609-652-4325 .... 313 E
annette.hamm@stockton.edu
HAMM, Bradley, J .... 847-491-2045 .... 160 E
bradely.hamm@northwestern.edu
HAMM, Jeff .... 870-230-5377 .... 21 I
hammj@hsu.edu
HAMM, Jolene, D .... 540-365-4219 .... 519 C
jdhamm@ferrum.edu

HANLON, Christopher 610-921-7264 421 E chanlon@alb.edu
HANLON, Erin 617-296-8300 235 J erin_hanlon@laboure.edu
HANLON, Joyce 617-730-7074 243 D joyce.hanlon@newbury.edu
HANLON, Philip, J 734-764-9292 259 A hanlon@umich.edu
HANLON, Rob 479-936-5116 22 H rhanlon@nwacc.edu
HANN, Julia 478-445-1549 130 B julia.hann@gcsu.edu
HANNA, Alexis 440-375-7214 394 E ahanna@lec.edu
HANNA, Bashar, W 215-489-2324 426 H bashar.hanna@delval.edu
HANNA, C. Phil 270-384-8102 204 D hannap@lindsey.edu
HANNA, Jeffery, G 540-458-8459 530 D jhanna@wlu.edu
HANNA, Kimberly 575-461-4413 318 G kimberlyh@mesalands.edu
HANNA, Laura 817-531-4480 502 C lhanna@txwes.edu
HANNA, Mae 513-732-5332 403 E hannamh@email.uc.edu
HANNA, Mark 806-371-5401 479 G mlhanna@actx.edu
HANNA, Michael 315-781-3574 335 F hanna@hws.edu
HANNA, Nancy 323-563-4960 39 G nhanna@cdrewu.edu
HANNA, Peter 562-947-8755 71 A peterhanna@scuhs.edu
HANNA, Roger 970-675-3212 82 H roger.hanna@cncc.edu
HANNA, Sean 585-275-2354 359 B sean.hanna@rochester.edu
HANNABURY, Stephen, P 781-292-2401 234 H stephen.hannabury@olin.edu
HANNAFIN, Robert 516-299-2210 339 A robert.hannafin@liu.edu
HANNAH, Andrew 773-702-7876 166 G ashannah@uchicago.edu
HANNAH, Marcus 334-876-9360 4 B mhannah@wccs.edu
HANNAH, Mary 218-751-8670 270 D registrar@oakhills.edu
HANNAH, Roddy 570-586-2400 422 G rhannah@bbc.edu
HANNAH, Russ 870-972-3303 20 D rhannah@astate.edu
HANNAHS, Mitch 618-544-8657 152 H hannahsm@iecc.edu
HANNAM, Paula, A 610-799-1718 434 D phannam@lccc.edu
HANNAM, Susan, E 724-738-2982 443 F susan.hannam@sru.edu
HANNAN, Michael 814-732-2460 442 E hannan@edinboro.edu
HANNAN, Steven, M 419-289-5007 384 G shannan@ashland.edu
HANNAR, Christine 636-949-4965 283 J channar@lindenwood.edu
HANNEMAN, Richard 402-457-2739 298 G rhanneman@mccneb.edu
HANNER, Mary Beth 518-464-8500 333 E mhanner@excelsior.edu
HANNIGAN, Jennifer 903-675-6327 502 F jhannigan@tvcc.edu
HANNIGAN, Jim 610-566-1776 452 B jhannigan@williamson.edu
HANNIGAN, Terence 718-862-8000 339 H terence.hannigan@manhattan.edu
HANNO, Barbara 406-586-3585 294 G barbara.hanno@montanabiblecollege.edu
HANNO, Dennis 781-239-5660 230 E dhanno@babson.edu
HANNON, Bernard 765-285-1186 169 G bmhannon@bsu.edu
HANNON, Charles 724-503-1001 451 A channon@washjeff.edu
HANNON, Jim, M 563-333-6359 188 F hannonjamesm@ambrose.sau.edu
HANNON, Kristin 330-966-5459 402 B khannon@starkstate.edu
HANNON, Patrick, K 678-664-0527 139 F pat.hannon@westgatech.edu
HANNON, Ron 408-848-4895 48 C rhannon@gavilan.edu
HANNUM, Judy, A 508-793-2431 233 C jhannum@holycross.edu
HANOFEE, Rose 845-434-5750 357 A rhanofee@sullivan.suny.edu
HANOLD, John, W 814-863-0768 438 G jhh6@psu.edu
HANOUSEK, Mandy 208-885-5369 144 G hanousek@uidaho.edu
HANRAHAN, Susan, N 870-972-3112 20 D hanrahan@astate.edu
HANRAHAN, Thomas 718-399-4308 346 D hanrahan@pratt.edu
HANRAHAN, Thomas, M 717-867-6030 434 C hanrahan@lvc.edu
HANS, John 651-905-3474 261 E jhans@browncollege.edu
HANSBURY, Kevin 302-736-2586 97 A hansbuke@wesley.edu
HANSEL, Marie, C 708-709-3766 161 D mhansel@prairiestate.edu
HANSEL, Sheila 713-646-1799 494 I shansel@stcl.edu
HANSELL, Phyllis 973-761-9015 315 B phyllis.hansell@shu.edu
HANSEN, Allan 310-287-4307 55 F hansenas@wlac.edu
HANSEN, Andrew, C 307-766-4286 556 H hansen@uwyo.edu
HANSEN, Anne, P 775-445-3235 303 B anne@wnc.edu
HANSEN, Beverly 262-564-3160 554 B hansenb@gtc.edu
HANSEN, Carl, F 707-826-3731 36 E ch1@humboldt.edu
HANSEN, Carl, K 575-624-8011 319 C hansenc@nmmi.edu
HANSEN, Cheryl 503-534-4005 416 J chansen@marylhurst.edu
HANSEN, Chris 423-236-2915 473 B chansen@southern.edu
HANSEN, Christian 203-576-4642 94 F registrar@bridgeport.edu
HANSEN, Corinne 605-642-6215 465 H corinne.hansen@bhsu.edu
HANSEN, Courtney 719-208-3800 464 H
HANSEN, D. Alton 208-496-3303 143 A hansena@byui.edu
HANSEN, David 843-574-6021 461 G david.hansen@tridenttech.edu
HANSEN, David 605-367-7568 465 F dhansen@sdbor.edu
HANSEN, Douglas 801-957-4084 512 D douglas.hansen@slcc.edu
HANSEN, Dwight 605-642-6146 465 H dwight.hansen@bhsu.edu
HANSEN, Eileen 515-643-6612 187 F ehansen@mercydesmoines.org
HANSEN, Eric 978-665-4095 237 E ehansen@fitchburgstate.edu
HANSEN, Erica, L 516-671-7373 360 B ehansen@webb-institute.edu
HANSEN, Ginger 828-898-8944 366 D hanseng@lmc.edu
HANSEN, Gregg 978-468-7111 235 B ghansen@gcts.edu
HANSEN, Heather 907-564-8275 10 D hhansen@alaskapacific.edu
HANSEN, James 706-886-6831 138 D jhansen@tfc.edu
HANSEN, James, R 334-844-5860 1 F honors@auburn.edu
HANSEN, Jessica 515-244-4221 181 F hansenj@aib.edu
HANSEN, Jim 909-384-8958 65 C jhansen@sbccd.cc.ca.us
HANSEN, Julie 641-673-1096 190 C hansenj@wmpenn.edu
HANSEN, Kathy 909-537-5142 36 B hansen@csusb.edu
HANSEN, Kaylyn, L 580-327-8439 409 C klhansen@nwosu.edu
HANSEN, Kenneth 402-559-5301 300 H hansenkl@unmc.edu
HANSEN, Kent, A 909-558-2644 54 D khansen@claysonlaw.com
HANSEN, Kevin 801-626-8022 511 G khansen@weber.edu
HANSEN, Kinsey 432-264-5127 488 B khansen@howardcollege.edu
HANSEN, Lauren 262-551-5816 546 I lhansen@carthage.edu
HANSEN, Linda, L 406-768-6331 294 D lhansen@fpcc.edu
HANSEN, Lynn 407-823-2362 120 B lynn.hansen@ucf.edu
HANSEN, Marianne, W 509-777-4347 540 C mhansen@whitworth.edu
HANSEN, Mary Mincer 515-271-1424 184 A mary.hansen@dmu.edu
HANSEN, Matt, B 563-333-6258 188 F hansenmattb@sau.edu
HANSEN, Patricia 212-774-0748 340 C phansen@mmm.edu
HANSEN, Peter 210-436-3324 493 F phansen@stmarytx.edu
HANSEN, Richard 513-861-6400 402 I richard.hansen@myunion.edu
HANSEN, Ted, P 440-510-1112 386 C tphansen@bryantstratton.edu
HANSEN, Terry 432-264-5160 488 B thansen@howardcollege.edu
HANSEN, Tiffany 619-574-6909 60 D thansen@pacificcollege.edu
HANSEN, Timothy, J 408-962-6400 30 F thansen@aii.edu
HANSEN, Timothy, R 847-578-8734 163 C tim.hansen@rosalindfranklin.edu
HANSEN, Troy 314-513-4267 288 H thansen@stlcc.edu
HANSEN, Vagn, K 256-765-4288 9 C vkhansen@una.edu
HANSEN-KIEFFER, Kristin, M 717-796-5234 436 D khansen@messiah.edu
HANSEN-MCCRORY, Heidi 434-381-6164 524 K hmccrory@sbc.edu
HANSHEW, Daniel, S 304-877-6428 540 G dan.hanshew@abc.edu
HANSMAN, Erin, M 573-592-1116 293 D ehansman@williamwoods.edu
HANSOM, Connie 615-297-7545 467 A hansomc@aquinascollege.edu
HANSON, Andrew 208-792-2218 144 B ahanson@lcsc.edu
HANSON, Barbara 281-476-1501 493 H barbara.hanson@sjcd.edu
HANSON, Brenda 406-756-3812 294 C bhanson@fvcc.edu
HANSON, Catherine 979-230-3632 482 D catherine.hanson@brazosport.edu
HANSON, Charles, D 810-762-7812 253 C chanson@kettering.edu
HANSON, Christina, R 717-766-2511 436 D chanson@messiah.edu
HANSON, Christy, L 651-696-6332 264 J chanson5@macalester.edu
HANSON, Clint 603-880-8308 306 A tmc@thomasmorecc.edu
HANSON, Daniel 402-872-2239 299 F dhanson@peru.edu
HANSON, David, W 804-828-6116 526 B dwhanson@vcu.edu
HANSON, Denise 319-226-2012 182 A hansondl@ihs.org
HANSON, Gail, S 202-885-3484 97 D gsher@american.edu
HANSON, Gary, A 310-506-4607 61 H gary.hanson@pepperdine.edu
HANSON, Glenn 910-642-7141 374 B ghanson@sccnc.edu
HANSON, Hans, M 515-271-2222 184 D hans.hanson@drake.edu
HANSON, Janet, K 715-394-8014 552 F jhanson@uwsuper.edu
HANSON, Jenifer, A 319-368-6469 187 H jhanson@mtmercy.edu
HANSON, Karen 612-625-0051 272 A karhan@umn.edu
HANSON, Kent 507-433-0607 268 H kent.hanson@riverland.edu
HANSON, Kent 218-793-2461 268 C kent.hanson@northlandcollege.edu
HANSON, Kirk, O 408-554-7898 68 C kohanson@scu.edu
HANSON, Kristina 281-487-1170 499 B khanson@txchiro.edu
HANSON, Laurie, R 563-336-3351 184 E lhanson@eicc.edu
HANSON, Linda 507-389-2986 267 E linda.hanson@mnsu.edu
HANSON, Linda, N 651-523-2202 264 A president@hamline.edu
HANSON, Lisa 309-341-5212 146 D lhanson@sandburg.edu
HANSON, Melissa, S 901-321-3399 467 I mhanson@cbu.edu
HANSON, Patricia 701-777-4361 381 F pat.hanson@und.edu
HANSON, Paula 361-593-2897 498 D p-hanson@tamuk.edu
HANSON, Richard, A 218-755-2011 265 I rhanson@bemidjistate.edu
HANSON, Rick, D 816-501-4275 288 A rick.hanson@rockhurst.edu
HANSON, Sara 402-354-7111 299 C sara.hanson@methodistcollege.edu
HANSON, Shirley, M 701-788-4767 381 H shirley.m.hanson@mayvillestate.edu
HANSON, Stephen, E 757-221-3590 518 A sehanson@wm.edu
HANSON, Steven, J 425-235-2235 537 A shanson@rtc.edu
HANSON, Susan 909-469-5329 78 I shanson@westernu.edu
HANSON, Susanah 724-266-3838 448 H shanson@tsm.edu
HANSON, Terry, L 432-264-5015 488 B tlhanson@howardcollege.edu
HANSON HEGG, Breanne 651-523-2012 264 A bhansonhegg01@hamline.edu
HANSON HUBER, Tonya 952-358-8213 268 A tonya.huber@normandale.edu
HANSTEIN, Andrea 714-992-7014 59 E ahanstein@fullcoll.edu
HANTEN, Joan 360-475-7120 536 D jhanten@olympic.edu
HANTZ, Joan 406-477-6215 294 A jhantz@cdkc.edu
HANTZSCHEL, Linda, J 516-463-6903 335 G linda.j.hantzschel@hofstra.edu
HANUSA, Matt 503-296-7468 415 G mhanusa@devry.edu
HANUSCIN, R. Douglas 419-755-4871 397 C dhanusci@ncstatecollege.edu
HANYPSIAK, Krista, L 716-645-3020 351 G klh5@buffalo.edu
HANZLIK, Gilbertt 804-524-3698 529 H ghanzik@vsu.edu
HANZLIK, Jodie, R 970-491-6817 83 F jodie.hanzlik@colostate.edu
HAO, Lan 626-914-8521 40 B lhao@citruscollege.edu
HAPEMAN, Barbara 570-961-7837 433 A hapemanb@lackawanna.edu
HAPPE, Doyle 713-529-2778 482 G happe@paralegal.edu
HAPPOLD, Jennifer 402-844-7045 299 I jennifer@northeast.edu
HAPSMITH, Linda, M 907-474-1849 10 I lhapsmith@alaska.edu
HARADA, Margaret 425-564-2064 531 G maggie.harada@bellevuecollege.edu
HARAPNUIK, Dwayne 325-674-2833 478 I dkh09a@acu.edu
HARB, Sam 337-363-2197 212 A sharb@acadiana.edu
HARBAUGH, Martha 314-529-9360 284 C mharbaugh@maryville.edu
HARBER, Dan 507-433-0609 268 H dharber@riverland.edu
HARBER, Debra, J 540-654-2468 525 D dharber@umw.edu
HARBER, Linda 703-993-2600 519 E lharber@gmu.edu
HARBERT, Robert, E 706-419-1116 128 B harbert@covenant.edu
HARBIN, Alicia 303-464-2340 87 H aharbin@redstone.edu
HARBIN, Bien 334-874-5700 2 H bharbin@ccal.edu
HARBIN, Eddie 580-745-2843 412 C eharbin@se.edu
HARBIN, Samuel, L 215-368-7538 424 C sharbin@cbs.edu
HARBIN, Suzanne 256-352-8144 10 A suzanne.harbin@wallacestate.edu
HARBISON, Amanda 205-391-5878 6 I aharbison@sheltonstate.edu
HARBISON, John 909-335-8863 42 G jharbison@cccollege.edu
HARBOUT, Ellen, K 740-427-5121 394 C harboute@kenyon.edu
HARDASH, Peter 714-480-7340 63 E hardash_peter@rsccd.edu
HARDAWAY, Patricia, L 937-708-5704 405 H phardaway@wilberforce.edu
HARDAWAY, Rex 404-727-4332 129 D rex.hardaway@emory.edu
HARDAWAY, Thelria 615-963-5137 474 A thardaway@tnstate.edu
HARDCASTLE, Bob 610-359-5182 426 G bhardcastle@dccc.edu
HARDCASTLE, Louis, B 770-484-1204 133 G lru@lru.edu
HARDECKE, John, M 636-584-6656 281 E hardecj@eastcentral.edu
HARDEE, Jerry 770-426-2775 133 E jhardee@life.edu
HARDEE, Judy 843-349-5212 458 H judy.hardee@hgtc.edu
HARDEE, Teresa 850-599-3211 118 L teresa.hardee@famu.edu
HARDEE, Terrence 856-691-8600 309 B thardee@cccnj.edu
HARDEE, Tim 803-778-6640 455 G hardeebt@cctech.edu
HARDEMAN, Patricia, R 478-757-5192 139 E phardeman@wesleyancollege.edu
HARDEN, Audrey 407-447-7300 110 A aharden@ftccollege.edu
HARDEN, Erica 478-553-2068 135 B eharden@oftc.edu
HARDEN, Jim 906-487-7307 251 A jim.harden@finlandia.edu
HARDEN, Mark 617-427-7293 235 B mharden@gcts.edu
HARDEN, Robert 972-825-4814 495 F rharden@sagu.edu
HARDEN, Ronald, W 916-348-4689 45 I rharden@epic.edu
HARDEN, Thomas, K 920-465-2207 551 B hardent@uwgb.edu
HARDEN-ABE, Yoshiko 206-878-3710 535 B yharden@highline.edu
HARDEN SMITH, Lisa 336-770-3314 379 E smithl@uncsa.edu
HARDER, James, M 419-358-3324 385 D harderj@bluffton.edu
HARDER, Maria, D 605-256-5129 465 I maria.harder@dsu.edu
HARDER, Mike 254-867-3940 500 C mike.harder@systems.tstc.edu
HARDER, Natalie 337-521-8953 211 J natalie.harder@southlouisiana.edu
HARDERS, Michael 770-423-6533 133 A mharders@kennesaw.edu

HARNISH, Eric .... 661-362-3400 ...... 41 I
eric.harnish@canyons.edu
HARNUM, Donald, P .... 609-896-5054 .... 313 F
harnum@rider.edu
HAROLD, Martin .... 858-653-6740 ...... 52 D
HARP, Brittaney .... 859-371-9393 .... 198 G
bharp@beckfield.edu
HARP, Debbie .... 606-539-4259 .... 207 C
debbie.harp@ucumberlands.edu
HARP, Deborah .... 312-893-7114 .... 151 A
dharp@erikson.edu
HARP, Jeff .... 405-974-2800 .... 413 B
jharp@uco.edu
HARP, John, W .... 319-895-4234 .... 183 G
jharp@cornellcollege.edu
HARP-STEPHENS, Becky ... 859-246-6498 .... 201 H
becky.harp@kctcs.edu
HARPER, Allyson, R .... 612-874-3775 .... 265 C
allyson_harper@mcad.edu
HARPER, Cheri .... 502-895-3411 .... 204 F
charper@lpts.edu
HARPER, David .... 229-209-5239 .... 124 E
dahar@andrewcollege.edu
HARPER, David .... 828-298-3325 .... 380 D
dharper@warren-wilson.edu
HARPER, David .... 937-229-2973 .... 404 A
dharper1@udayton.edu
HARPER, Deborah .... 607-274-3136 .... 336 G
dharper@ithaca.edu
HARPER, Derry .... 850-245-0466 .... 118 K
derry.harper@flbog.edu
HARPER, Donna, L .... 540-568-3705 .... 520 H
harperdl@jmu.edu
HARPER, Doreen, C .... 205-934-5360 ...... 8 F
dcharper@uab.edu
HARPER, E. Royster .... 734-764-5132 .... 259 A
harperer@umich.edu
HARPER, Elizabeth .... 703-323-3398 .... 527 F
eharper@nvcc.edu
HARPER, Heather .... 615-230-3519 .... 476 C
heather.harper@volstate.edu
HARPER, Jane .... 765-269-5640 .... 176 D
jharper@ivytech.edu
HARPER, Jane .... 817-515-5391 .... 496 C
jane.harper@tccd.edu
HARPER, Janice, A .... 919-530-5216 .... 378 B
jharper@nccu.edu
HARPER, Jimmy .... 423-614-8420 .... 470 C
jharper@leeuniversity.edu
HARPER, Joann .... 706-245-7226 .... 129 C
jharper@ec.edu
HARPER, Katherine .... 304-766-3142 .... 544 F
harperkl@wvstateu.edu
HARPER, Kristin .... 205-226-4720 ...... 2 B
kharper@bsc.edu
HARPER, Larisa .... 740-588-1252 .... 407 A
lharper@zanestate.edu
HARPER, Lisa .... 405-974-2553 .... 413 B
lharper@uco.edu
HARPER, Lisa, D .... 859-858-3511 .... 198 E
lisa.harper@asbury.edu
HARPER, Lisa, M .... 903-510-2147 .... 503 A
lhar@tjc.edu
HARPER, Loretta, F .... 801-585-0928 .... 511 C
loretta.harper@utah.edu
HARPER, Marjoree .... 318-678-6000 .... 209 I
mharper@bpcc.edu
HARPER, Mary, J .... 812-464-1767 .... 181 B
mjharper@usi.edu
HARPER, Mary Ann .... 501-337-5000 ...... 21 D
mharper@coto.edu
HARPER, Norma .... 706-233-7268 .... 137 A
nharper@shorter.edu
HARPER, Ollie .... 601-979-2260 .... 274 G
ollie.l.harper@jsums.edu
HARPER, Pam .... 270-706-8434 .... 202 A
pam.harper@kctcs.edu
HARPER, Patricia .... 816-654-7162 .... 283 F
pharper@kcumb.edu
HARPER, Randy .... 870-574-4590 ...... 24 A
rharper@sautech.edu
HARPER, Rhonda .... 214-210-4079 .... 169 B
HARPER, Robert .... 559-278-2482 ...... 35 A
roberth@csufresno.edu
HARPER, Robert .... 903-593-8311 .... 499 D
rharper@texascollege.edu
HARPER, Rosie .... 601-977-7818 .... 277 C
rharper@tougaloo.edu
HARPER, Sandra, S .... 225-768-1710 .... 214 C
sandra.harper@ololcollege.edu
HARPER, Vernon .... 610-436-1000 .... 444 A
vharper@wcupa.edu
HARPER, Yolanda .... 901-320-9700 .... 478 C
yharper@victory.edu
HARPER HAGAN, Mary, T 718-990-2505 .... 348 G
harperm@stjohns.edu
HARPER-MARINICK,
Maria .... 480-731-8101 ...... 15 D
maria.harper@domail.maricopa.edu
HARPEST, Todd, R .... 419-783-2312 .... 389 H
tharpest@defiance.edu
HARPHAM, Jennifer .... 757-822-1360 .... 528 G
jharpham@tcc.edu
HARPINE, Layne .... 252-444-7289 .... 370 A
harpinel@cravencc.edu
HARPS, Trynette Lottie .... 231-777-0559 .... 256 A
trynette.lottie-harps@muskegoncc.edu
HARPST, Steve .... 845-341-4230 .... 345 E
steve.harpst@sunyorange.edu
HARPSTER, G. F. (Jody) .... 717-477-1030 .... 443 E
gfharp@ship.edu
HARR, Jon, P .... 423-323-0231 .... 475 F
jpharr@northeaststate.edu
HARR, Kathleen .... 785-354-5853 .... 190 F
kharr@stormontvail.org
HARR, Lois .... 718-862-7142 .... 339 H
lois.harr@manhattan.edu
HARRADINE, Andy, A .... 315-267-3011 .... 354 C
andy@potsdam.edu
HARRAH, Scott .... 301-784-5000 .... 221 B
sharrah@allegany.edu
HARRAL, Judy .... 361-825-2495 .... 498 C
judy.harral@tamucc.edu
HARRAL, Kevin .... 650-949-7223 ...... 47 H
harralkevin@foothill.edu
HARRAR, William, R .... 570-389-4255 .... 441 F
wharrar@bloomu.edu
HARREL, Erin .... 239-489-9300 .... 105 F
HARRELL, Brandan .... 229-931-2801 .... 137 C
bharrell@southgatech.edu
HARRELL, Bryant, L .... 860-727-6756 ...... 92 I
bharrell@goodwin.edu
HARRELL, Charlie, R .... 252-823-5166 .... 370 D
harrellc@edgecombe.edu
HARRELL, Diana .... 512-245-1555 .... 501 F
dh32@txstate.edu
HARRELL, Frank (Doug) .... 504-865-5352 .... 215 C
fharrel@tulane.edu
HARRELL, Ivan, L .... 410-777-2830 .... 221 C
ilharrell@aacc.edu
HARRELL, Jerry, H .... 317-921-4447 .... 175 K
jeharrel@ivytech.edu
HARRELL, Lee .... 740-368-3052 .... 400 G
jlharrell@owu.edu
HARRELL, P. Randy .... 252-398-6209 .... 363 G
harrer@chowan.edu
HARRELL, Pamela, J .... 919-209-2048 .... 371 F
pjharrell@johnstoncc.edu
HARRELL, Ronald .... 270-706-8580 .... 202 A
ron.harrell@kctcs.edu
HARRELL, Wanda .... 423-585-6976 .... 476 D
wanda.harrell@ws.edu
HARRELSON, Jerry, W .... 336-316-2333 .... 365 A
jharrelson@guilford.edu
HARRELSON, Laura .... 407-888-4000 .... 113 A
lharrelson@orlando.chefs.edu
HARRES, JR., Burt, H .... 727-816-3490 .... 114 F
harresb@phcc.edu
HARREYS, M. Seamus .... 617-373-4095 .... 243 F
HARRI, Ed .... 360-383-3220 .... 540 A
eharri@whatcom.ctc.edu
HARRI, Robert .... 563-387-2103 .... 187 D
harrro01@luther.edu
HARRICK, Kristie .... 205-970-9244 ...... 7 C
kharrick@sebc.edu
HARRIENDORF, SC,
Cecilia .... 718-405-3215 .... 330 A
cecilia.harriendorf@mountsaintvincent.edu
HARRIGAN, Maureen .... 410-234-4520 .... 225 E
HARRIGAN, Theresa, A .... 617-552-3430 .... 232 B
theresa.harrigan@bc.edu
HARRIGER, Sherill .... 863-638-7235 .... 123 D
sherill.harriger@warner.edu
HARRILL, Thad .... 828-395-1624 .... 371 D
tharrill@isothermal.edu
HARRIMAN, Mark .... 661-654-2496 ...... 34 A
mharriman@csub.edu
HARRIMAN, Mark .... 661-654-2635 ...... 34 A
mharriman@csub.edu
HARRIMAN, Scott .... 207-454-1012 .... 219 B
sharriman@wccc.me.edu
HARRING, Kathleen, E .... 484-664-3424 .... 437 C
harring@muhlenberg.edu
HARRING-HENDON,
Janice .... 773-442-4000 .... 160 A
j-harringhendon@neiu.edu
HARRINGTON, Anne, E .... 603-641-7465 .... 305 G
aharrington@anselm.edu
HARRINGTON, Antivan .... 407-843-3984 .... 110 E
aharrington@fortiscollege.edu
HARRINGTON, Bonnie .... 215-751-8253 .... 426 B
bharrington@ccp.edu
HARRINGTON, Daphne .... 617-521-2754 .... 244 F
daphne.harrington@simmons.edu
HARRINGTON, David .... 603-641-7020 .... 305 G
dharrington@anselm.edu
HARRINGTON, CM,
Donald, J .... 718-990-6301 .... 348 G
pres@stjohns.edu
HARRINGTON, James .... 540-887-7333 .... 521 C
jharring@mbc.edu
HARRINGTON, James, W . 253-692-5646 .... 539 A
jwh@uw.edu
HARRINGTON, Janet .... 617-670-4413 .... 234 G
jharrington@fisher.edu
HARRINGTON, John, D .... 207-768-9585 .... 220 F
john.harrington@umpi.edu
HARRINGTON, Kristen .... 617-879-2260 .... 246 C
kharrington@wheelock.edu
HARRINGTON,
L. Katharine .... 213-740-7849 ...... 76 F
vpap@usc.edu
HARRINGTON, Lynn .... 708-974-5704 .... 159 B
harrington@morainevalley.edu
HARRINGTON, Mary, M .... 662-915-7387 .... 277 D
ccmary@olemiss.edu
HARRINGTON, Melissa .... 406-496-4108 .... 296 A
mharrington@mtech.edu
HARRINGTON, Melissa .... 406-496-4108 .... 296 B
mharrington@mtech.edu
HARRINGTON, Melody .... 405-878-5310 .... 412 A
maharrington@stgregorys.edu
HARRINGTON, Michael .... 631-420-2053 .... 356 A
michael.harrington@farmingdale.edu
HARRINGTON, Pamela .... 401-454-6318 .... 454 B
pharring@risd.edu
HARRINGTON, Paul .... 651-641-3216 .... 264 H
pharrington001@luthersem.edu
HARRINGTON, Robert .... 417-625-3191 .... 286 B
harrington-r@mssu.edu
HARRINGTON, Sharon .... 704-330-1437 .... 366 A
sharrington@jcsu.edu
HARRINGTON, Shawn, M . 860-231-5314 ...... 95 D
sharrington@usj.edu
HARRINGTON, Sherre Lee 706-236-2285 .... 126 C
sharrington@berry.edu
HARRINGTON, Thea .... 570-945-8516 .... 432 E
thea.harrington@keystone.edu
HARRINGTON, Thomas .... 504-280-1154 .... 213 E
trharrin@uno.edu
HARRINGTON, Thomas .... 520-206-4772 ...... 17 H
teharrington@pima.edu
HARRINGTON WILSON,
Alice, E .... 585-292-2304 .... 341 H
awilson@monroecc.edu
HARRIS, Allatia .... 281-459-7140 .... 494 A
allatia.harris@sjcd.edu
HARRIS, Amelia, J .... 276-376-4557 .... 525 G
ajh7a@uvawise.edu
HARRIS, Andrew .... 603-358-2772 .... 306 G
aharris5@keene.edu
HARRIS, Andrew, M .... 940-565-2055 .... 504 D
aharris@unt.edu
HARRIS, Angela .... 706-272-4476 .... 128 C
aharris@daltonstate.edu
HARRIS, Anjour, B .... 804-828-2021 .... 526 B
abharris@vcu.edu
HARRIS, Ann .... 573-681-5074 .... 283 I
harrisa@lincolnu.edu
HARRIS, Ann .... 503-725-4441 .... 418 G
harrisa@pdx.edu
HARRIS, Anne .... 510-885-4602 ...... 34 E
anne.harris@csueastbay.edu
HARRIS, Anthony .... 610-341-5840 .... 428 E
aharris8@eastern.edu
HARRIS, April .... 256-824-6085 ...... 8 G
april.harris@uah.edu
HARRIS, Benjamin, G .... 812-246-3301 .... 177 B
bharris88@ivytech.edu
HARRIS, Bennie, L .... 615-966-5687 .... 470 F
bennie.harris@lipscomb.edu
HARRIS, Bernice .... 303-556-3786 ...... 84 A
bernice.harris@ccd.edu
HARRIS, Beth .... 203-287-3023 ...... 93 F
paierartlibrary@snet.net
HARRIS, Beth, A .... 773-702-7243 .... 166 G
ba-harris@uchicago.edu
HARRIS, Bethany, W .... 434-949-1007 .... 528 D
bethany.harris@southside.edu
HARRIS, Betsy, A .... 207-768-2791 .... 218 J
bharris@nmcc.edu
HARRIS, Beverly .... 620-331-4100 .... 193 I
bharris@indycc.edu
HARRIS, Beverly Jo .... 304-734-6601 .... 542 H
jharris@bridgemont.edu
HARRIS, Brenda .... 325-670-1262 .... 487 F
bharris@hsutx.edu
HARRIS, Brent .... 254-295-8642 .... 504 C
bharris@umhb.edu
HARRIS, Brice, W .... 916-568-3021 ...... 55 J
harrisbw@losrios.edu
HARRIS, Camille .... 312-939-4975 .... 151 H
charris@harrington.edu
HARRIS, Carolyn .... 866-621-0124 ...... 89 C
carolyn.harris@rockies.edu
HARRIS, Celia, D .... 781-736-3015 .... 232 F
cdharris@brandeis.edu
HARRIS, Charles .... 334-420-4232 ...... 7 H
charris@trenholmstate.edu
HARRIS, Charles, S .... 434-791-5701 .... 516 G
csharris@averett.edu
HARRIS, Charlotte .... 937-775-2821 .... 406 C
charlotte.harris@wright.edu
HARRIS, Charlotte, M .... 205-348-6690 ...... 8 E
charris@fa.ua.edu
HARRIS, Chelsy .... 719-502-3033 ...... 87 B
chelsy.harris@ppcc.edu
HARRIS, Chris .... 949-214-3169 ...... 43 C
chris.harris@cui.edu
HARRIS, Chris .... 440-375-7000 .... 394 E
charris1@lec.edu
HARRIS, Chris .... 601-635-2111 .... 274 A
charris@eccc.edu
HARRIS, Chriss .... 419-755-4753 .... 397 C
charris@ncstatecollege.edu
HARRIS, Christina .... 215-568-9215 .... 436 E
chharris@phmc.org
HARRIS, Clark .... 810-762-0500 .... 255 G
clark.harris@mcc.edu
HARRIS, Clayton .... 216-987-4325 .... 389 B
clayton.harris@tri-c.edu
HARRIS, Cliff .... 313-664-7403 .... 249 E
charris@collegeforcreativestudies.edu
HARRIS, Craig .... 716-926-8888 .... 335 E
charris@hilbert.edu
HARRIS, Craig .... 540-857-6479 .... 529 B
charris@virginiawestern.edu
HARRIS, D. Steve .... 229-317-6780 .... 128 D
steve.harris@darton.edu
HARRIS, Dan, I .... 414-277-7230 .... 549 C
harris@msoe.edu
HARRIS, Darrell, A .... 904-264-2172 .... 116 C
dharris@iws.edu
HARRIS, David .... 501-812-2205 ...... 23 C
dharris@pulaskitech.edu
HARRIS, David .... 718-268-4700 .... 347 A
HARRIS, David, J .... 269-660-8021 .... 257 C
harrisd@millercollege.edu
HARRIS, David, P .... 909-558-7600 ...... 54 D
dpharris@llu.edu
HARRIS, David, R .... 617-627-3310 .... 245 C
david.harris@tufts.edu
HARRIS, David, W .... 505-277-7520 .... 321 C
dwharris@unm.edu
HARRIS, DaVonne .... 574-535-7000 .... 171 G
HARRIS, Debbie .... 804-751-9191 .... 524 A
dharris@rsht.edu
HARRIS, Delphia .... 901-435-1380 .... 470 D
delphia_harris@loc.edu
HARRIS, Denise .... 716-926-8727 .... 335 E
dharris@hilbert.edu
HARRIS, Dennis .... 405-422-1283 .... 411 G
harrisd@redlandscc.edu
HARRIS, Dina .... 574-520-4131 .... 174 E
dlharris@iusb.edu
HARRIS, Duncan .... 307-766-4110 .... 556 H
dharris@uwyo.edu
HARRIS, Erica .... 606-539-4250 .... 207 C
erica.harris@ucumberlands.edu
HARRIS, SR., Forrest, E .... 615-256-1463 .... 466 H
harrisfe@abcnash.edu
HARRIS, Freda, J .... 608-262-6423 .... 550 I
fharris@uwsa.edu
HARRIS, G. Duncan .... 860-512-3203 ...... 91 F
gharris@mcc.commnet.edu
HARRIS, Gail .... 423-746-5208 .... 476 F
gharris@twcnet.edu
HARRIS, Gheretta, R .... 248-341-2081 .... 256 F
grharris@oaklandcc.edu
HARRIS, Greg .... 770-426-2836 .... 133 E
gharris@life.edu
HARRIS, Greg .... 503-584-7153 .... 414 J
greg.harris@chemeketa.edu
HARRIS, Gregory .... 617-573-8406 .... 245 B
gharris@suffolk.edu
HARRIS, Gregory .... 803-533-3740 .... 460 G
gharri17@scsu.edu
HARRIS, Gregory, C .... 704-378-1101 .... 366 A
gcharris@jcsu.edu
HARRIS, Helen .... 225-216-8089 .... 209 H
harrish@mybrcc.edu
HARRIS, Hubert, B .... 804-524-8989 .... 529 H
hharris@vsu.edu
HARRIS, Hugh, W .... 610-330-5330 .... 433 B
harrish@lafayette.edu
HARRIS, James .... 903-593-8311 .... 499 D
jharris@texascollege.edu
HARRIS, III, James, T .... 610-499-4101 ...... 97 B
jtharris@widener.edu
HARRIS, III, James, T .... 610-499-4101 .... 451 F
jtharris@widener.edu
HARRIS, Janet, Y .... 601-984-4113 .... 277 E
jyharris@umc.edu
HARRIS, Jay, H .... 260-481-6785 .... 174 C
harrishj@ipfw.edu
HARRIS, Jerrold, R .... 570-389-4129 .... 441 F
jharris@bloomu.edu
HARRIS, Jerry .... 307-778-1280 .... 556 E
jharris@lccc.wy.edu
HARRIS, Jo-Anne .... 610-399-2247 .... 442 A
jharris@cheyney.edu
HARRIS, Joel, C .... 843-953-6841 .... 456 C
joel.harris@citadel.edu
HARRIS, John .... 515-961-1626 .... 189 C
john.harris@simpson.edu
HARRIS, John .... 903-923-2181 .... 486 F
jharris@etbu.edu
HARRIS, John, D .... 979-830-4151 .... 482 C
jharris@blinn.edu
HARRIS, Joseph .... 601-426-6346 .... 277 A
jharris@southeasternbaptist.edu
HARRIS, Judy .... 252-493-7252 .... 372 H
jharris@email.pittcc.edu
HARRIS, Kathy .... 618-544-8657 .... 152 H
harrisk@iecc.edu

HARTFORD, Linda .... 920-498-6937.... 555 C
linda.hartford@nwtc.edu
HARTFORD, Sharon, M ..... 509-527-4323.... 539 B
sharon.hartford@wwcc.edu
HARTGE, Steve, P .... 314-286-3669.... 287 G
sphartge@ranken.edu
HARTHORN, Karen, M ...... 651-962-6353.... 272 B
kmharthorn@stthomas.edu
HARTIG, Jeanne .... 312-567-3000.... 153 C
jhartig@iit.edu
HARTIGAN, Ellen .... 718-631-6351.... 328 F
ehartigan@qcc.cuny.edu
HARTIGAN, William, J ...... 401-865-2166.... 453 H
hartigan@providence.edu
HARTIN, Linda, A .... 334-222-6591........ 5 F
lhartin@lbwcc.edu
HARTING, William .... 317-955-6015.... 177 I
bharting@marian.edu
HARTING, William .... 317-955-6016.... 177 I
bharting@marian.edu
HARTKE, Emily .... 217-234-5259.... 156 B
ehartke@lakeland.cc.il.us
HARTLEROAD, LeAnn .... 618-393-2982.... 152 F
hartleroadl@iecc.edu
HARTLESS, Sharon .... 434-582-7600.... 520 K
shartles@liberty.edu
HARTLEY, Brian .... 618-664-6821.... 151 F
brian.hartley@greenville.edu
HARTLEY, Carolyn .... 219-980-6971.... 174 B
cjhartle@iun.edu
HARTLEY, Christina .... 401-454-6794.... 454 B
chartley@risd.edu
HARTLEY, Christopher .... 617-682-1532.... 234 E
chartley@eds.edu
HARTLEY, Gary .... 916-608-6500...... 56 C
HARTLEY, Greg, L .... 916-348-4689...... 45 I
ghartley@epic.edu
HARTLEY, Lorraine .... 216-987-2424.... 389 B
lorraine.hartley@tri-c.edu
HARTLEY, Meredith .... 504-861-5888.... 213 F
mhartley@loyno.edu
HARTLEY, Rebecca .... 205-665-6360........ 9 B
hartleyrs@montevallo.edu
HARTLEY, Stacey, M .... 419-372-0719.... 385 F
staceyh@bgsu.edu
HARTLEY, Stephanie, J ...... 601-923-1657.... 276 F
shartley@rts.edu
HARTLEY, William .... 972-721-5194.... 503 B
whartley@udallas.edu
HARTLEY, William, B .... 714-772-3330...... 28 J
whar838361@aol.com
HARTMAN, Brandi, P .... 864-488-4606.... 459 B
bhartman@limestone.edu
HARTMAN, Bryan, G .... 518-564-3824.... 354 B
hartmabg@plattsburgh.edu
HARTMAN, Cheryl, J .... 605-221-3100.... 464 D
chartman@kilian.edu
HARTMAN, Christine, M .... 717-337-6276.... 429 I
chartman@gettysburg.edu
HARTMAN, Dean, A .... 706-880-8246.... 133 B
dhartman@lagrange.edu
HARTMAN, Eric, G .... 931-598-1229.... 472 L
ehartman@sewanee.edu
HARTMAN, Freda .... 480-557-3049...... 19 A
freda.hartman@phoenix.edu
HARTMAN, Jackie, L .... 785-532-6221.... 194 D
jlh1980@ksu.edu
HARTMAN, James, P .... 215-951-2966.... 444 D
hartmanj@philau.edu
HARTMAN, Joel, L .... 407-823-6778.... 120 B
joel.hartman@ucf.edu
HARTMAN, Joseph .... 972-825-4774.... 495 F
jhartman@sagu.edu
HARTMAN, Kenneth .... 215-895-0501.... 427 H
kenneth.e.hartman@drexel.edu
HARTMAN, Laurie .... 315-792-7400.... 356 B
laurie.hartman@sunyit.edu
HARTMAN, Luke .... 540-432-4000.... 518 F
luke.hartman@emu.edu
HARTMAN, Nancy .... 513-244-8447.... 387 E
nancy.hartman@ccuniversity.edu
HARTMAN, Nathan .... 859-344-3602.... 206 I
nathan.hartman@thomasmore.edu
HARTMAN, Robert .... 740-477-7843.... 398 D
rhartman@ohiochristian.edu
HARTMAN, Robin .... 714-879-3901...... 50 I
rhartman@hiu.edu
HARTMAN, Sherry, L .... 208-467-8588.... 144 E
slhartman@nnu.edu
HARTMANN, Anita .... 907-474-7231...... 10 I
amharmann@alaska.edu
HARTMANN, Bruce .... 630-466-7900.... 168 B
bhartmann@waubonsee.edu
HARTMANN, Kimberly .... 636-227-2100.... 284 B
kimberly.hartmann@logan.edu
HARTMANN, Patricia .... 414-382-6072.... 546 B
pat.hartmann@alverno.edu
HARTMANN, Shari .... 714-459-1120...... 78 H
shartmann@wsulaw.edu
HARTMANN, Wendy .... 636-584-6712.... 281 E
wahartm@eastcentral.edu
HARTNER, Joseph .... 610-606-4631.... 425 A
jhartner@cedarcrest.edu

HARTNETT, Deborah .... 212-650-8638.... 326 G
dhartnett@ccny.cuny.edu
HARTOG, John .... 712-324-5066.... 188 C
jhartog@nwicc.edu
HARTOG, II, John .... 515-964-0601.... 185 A
hartogj2@faith.edu
HARTOG, William, M .... 540-458-8710.... 530 D
bhartog@wlu.edu
HARTON, George .... 301-552-1400.... 229 C
gharton@bible.edu
HARTON, Mary Kay .... 928-344-7580...... 12 A
marykay.harton@azwestern.edu
HARTS, Stanley, H .... 910-962-3057.... 379 D
hartss@uncw.edu
HARTSFIELD, LaTanya .... 404-237-7573.... 126 B
lhartsfield@bauder.edu
HARTSOCK, James .... 240-629-7902.... 222 G
jhartsock@frederick.edu
HARTSOE, Janice .... 678-717-3822.... 129 G
jhartsoe@gsc.edu
HARTUNG, Jason .... 661-362-2207...... 56 G
jhartung@masters.edu
HARTVIGSEN, Jake .... 941-487-4150.... 120 A
jhartvigsen@ncf.edu
HARTWELL, Robert, E .... 516-877-4231.... 322 A
hartwell@adelphi.edu
HARTZ, James .... 270-686-4630.... 203 B
jim.hartz@kctcs.edu
HARTZ, Jan .... 949-753-4774...... 31 B
hartz@brandman.edu
HARTZ, Jason, M .... 517-265-5161.... 246 H
shelfer@adrian.edu
HARTZ, Wayne .... 603-358-2220.... 306 G
whartz@keene.edu
HARTZEL, Ruth Ann .... 724-847-5673.... 429 H
rhartzel@geneva.edu
HARTZLER, Christi .... 407-823-4663.... 120 B
christi.hartzler@ucf.edu
HARTZLER, Murray, G .... 843-661-1237.... 458 D
mhartzler@fmarion.edu
HARTZOG, Gail, C .... 850-718-2342.... 103 D
hartzogg@chipola.edu
HARVELL, Leah .... 808-942-1000.... 141 D
careers.hnl.cs@remingtoncollege.edu
HARVENER, Lisa .... 586-791-6610.... 248 B
lisa.harvener@baker.edu
HARVEY, Addie .... 901-435-1704.... 470 D
addie_harvey@loc.edu
HARVEY, Barron, H .... 202-806-1500...... 98 E
bharvey@howard.edu
HARVEY, Brian, J .... 417-864-7220.... 281 H
bharvey@cci.edu
HARVEY, Bryan, C .... 413-545-6238.... 236 F
harvey@provost.umass.edu
HARVEY, David .... 941-487-4511.... 120 A
dharvey@ncf.edu
HARVEY, David, T .... 765-658-4359.... 171 B
harvey@depauw.edu
HARVEY, Diana .... 801-957-4278.... 512 D
diana.harvey@slcc.edu
HARVEY, Gayle, S .... 217-581-3511.... 150 E
gsharvey@eiu.edu
HARVEY, Iris, E .... 330-672-7882.... 393 D
iharvey1@kent.edu
HARVEY, Jenny .... 540-234-9261.... 526 D
harveyj@brcc.edu
HARVEY, Joe .... 407-847-8966.... 107 I
joe.harvey@fcc.edu
HARVEY, John .... 803-754-4100.... 457 D
HARVEY, John .... 325-793-4751.... 490 H
jharvey@mcm.edu
HARVEY, Keith .... 218-744-7522.... 266 I
k.harvey@mr.mnscu.edu
HARVEY, Kelly .... 252-536-7219.... 371 B
harveyk@halifaxcc.edu
HARVEY, Kim, M .... 636-481-3207.... 283 D
kharvey@jeffco.edu
HARVEY, Laurie .... 516-686-7711.... 343 D
lharve05@nyit.edu
HARVEY, Leah .... 651-793-1333.... 267 A
leah.harvey@metrostate.edu
HARVEY, Leah .... 651-793-1777.... 267 A
leah.harvey@metrostate.edu
HARVEY, Linda .... 718-780-7966.... 324 F
linda.harvey@brooklaw.edu
HARVEY, Lydia .... 907-564-8218...... 10 D
lydiah@alaskapacific.edu
HARVEY, Marcus .... 816-604-4121.... 285 E
marcus.harvey@mcckc.edu
HARVEY, Maria .... 601-979-2107.... 274 G
maria.l.harvey@jsums.edu
HARVEY, Mary, J .... 773-702-8806.... 166 G
mharvey@uchicago.edu
HARVEY, Pauline .... 907-442-3400...... 10 I
pharvey1@alaska.edu
HARVEY, Peter, W .... 509-527-5145.... 540 B
harvey@whitman.edu
HARVEY, Richard, C .... 304-367-4395.... 543 H
richard.harvey@fairmontstate.edu
HARVEY, Roberta .... 856-256-5140.... 314 A
harvey@rowan.edu
HARVEY, Sarah, J .... 260-359-4010.... 173 A
sharvey@huntington.edu

HARVEY, Scott .... 864-646-1556.... 461 F
sharvey@tctc.edu
HARVEY, Shannon, S .... 717-337-3855.... 430 E
ssharvey@hacc.edu
HARVEY, Steven .... 603-645-9611.... 305 I
s.harvey@snhu.edu
HARVEY, Stewart, A .... 207-581-2638.... 220 A
stewarth@maine.edu
HARVEY, Stu .... 405-682-7849.... 409 F
sharvey@occc.edu
HARVEY, Valtroud .... 410-923-4500...... 99 G
valtroud.harvey@strayer.edu
HARVEY, William, B .... 336-334-7757.... 378 A
wbharvey@ncat.edu
HARVEY, William, R .... 757-727-5231.... 519 H
presidentsoffice@hamptonu.edu
HARVEY-JACOBS, Pam .... 920-465-2111.... 551 B
harveyp@uwgb.edu
HARVEY-LEE, Peggy, A ...... 585-292-2252.... 341 H
pharvey-lee@monroecc.edu
HARVEY-PATE, Cheryl .... 248-457-2765.... 252 E
HARVEY-SAHAK, Judy, B . 909-621-8973...... 69 A
judy.harveysahak@scrippscollege.edu
HARVEY-SMITH, Alicia, B . 410-462-8302.... 221 E
abharvey-smith@bccc.edu
HARVIN, Lillian .... 510-869-8785...... 64 J
lharvin@samuelmerritt.edu
HARVIN, Peter, B .... 864-231-2017.... 455 C
pharvin@andersonuniversity.edu
HARVITH, John .... 412-624-4380.... 449 A
harvith@pitt.edu
HARWARD, Brian .... 814-332-3027.... 421 F
bharward@allegheny.edu
HARWOOD, Debra .... 704-991-0206.... 374 D
dharwood5544@stanly.edu
HARWOOD, Scott .... 518-891-2915.... 344 E
sharwood@nccc.edu
HASAN, Zia .... 803-535-5219.... 456 D
hasan@claflin.edu
HASBROUCK, Norman, G .. 724-938-1561.... 441 G
hasbrouck@calu.edu
HASELDEN, Gregory, W .... 864-379-8812.... 458 A
haselden@erskine.edu
HASELOFF, Gregory, K ...... 859-858-3511.... 198 E
greg.haseloff@asbury.edu
HASELTON, Blake .... 502-852-5597.... 207 E
blake.haselton@louisville.edu
HASENOEHRL, Mary .... 208-792-2458.... 144 B
mlhasenoehrl@lcsc.edu
HASFURTHER, Victor .... 435-879-4801.... 512 B
hasfurther@dixie.edu
HASH, Jennifer .... 303-722-5724...... 86 C
jhash@lincolntech.com
HASH, Joseph .... 707-476-4212...... 42 C
joe-hash@redwoods.edu
HASHEMIPOUR,
Mohammad .... 516-364-0808.... 343 A
HASHIMOTO, Brenna .... 808-956-2974.... 141 E
hbrenna@hawaii.edu
HASINGER, Guenther .... 808-956-8566.... 141 G
hasinger@hawaii.edu
HASKA, Christine, M .... 831-656-3411.... 558 A
cmhaska@nps.edu
HASKAJ, Tatjana .... 617-588-1358.... 231 C
thaskaj@bfit.edu
HASKAMP, Misty .... 573-875-7582.... 280 A
mrhaskamp@ccis.edu
HASKELL, Benjamin, E .... 207-941-7176.... 219 E
haskellb@nescom.edu
HASKELL, Heather .... 602-275-7133...... 18 A
heather.haskell@rsiaz.edu
HASKELL, Richard .... 781-239-3191.... 239 G
rhaskell@massbay.edu
HASKETT, Tammy .... 828-227-7222.... 380 A
haskett@wcu.edu
HASKEY, Glennita .... 928-724-6723...... 13 L
ghaskey@dinecollege.edu
HASKINS, Brenda .... 985-448-4518.... 216 A
brenda.haskins@nicholls.edu
HASKINS, Casi .... 561-912-1211.... 107 B
chaskins@evergladesuniversity.edu
HASKINS, Dana, R .... 972-860-7269.... 484 I
drhaskins@dcccd.edu
HASKINS, Dennis, E .... 931-363-9889.... 471 A
dhaskins@martinmethodist.edu
HASKINS, Eileen, T .... 401-598-1035.... 453 E
ehaskins@jwu.edu
HASKINS, Jamie .... 573-592-5262.... 293 B
jamie.haskins@westminster-mo.edu
HASKINS, Mike .... 843-953-6461.... 457 B
haskinsm@cofc.edu
HASKINS, Nena .... 574-936-8898.... 169 D
nena.haskins@ancilla.edu
HASKINS, Richard .... 412-392-8097.... 445 A
rhaskins@pointpark.edu
HASKVITZ, Esther .... 518-244-4590.... 348 A
haskev@sage.edu
HASL, Rudolph, C .... 619-961-4215...... 72 J
hasl@tjsl.edu
HASLAG, Daniel .... 573-592-5282.... 293 B
dan.haslag@westminster-mo.edu
HASLAM, Laurie .... 980-598-1312.... 365 I
laurie.haslam@jwu.edu
HASLANGER, Sally .... 617-253-8844.... 241 D

HASLEM, Lori .... 309-341-7214.... 155 F
lhaslem@knox.edu
HASLER, Paul .... 715-346-3059.... 552 D
phasler@uwsp.edu
HASLIM, Hue .... 602-429-1078...... 19 B
hue.haslim@west.edu
HASLUND, Steve .... 281-487-1170.... 499 B
shaslund@txchiro.edu
HASS, Marjorie .... 903-813-3001.... 481 A
mhass@austincollege.edu
HASSAN, Nidia .... 903-510-2883.... 503 A
nhas@tjc.edu
HASSAN, Sharon, E .... 301-322-0749.... 225 F
hassanse@pgcc.edu
HASSEL, George, E .... 610-499-4182.... 451 F
gehassel.sr@widener.edu
HASSELER, Susan .... 605-274-4113.... 464 A
susan.hasseler@augie.edu
HASSELL, Adalecia .... 787-841-2000.... 565 B
ahassell@pucpr.edu
HASSELL, Coletta .... 678-891-2455.... 131 C
coletta.hassell@gpc.edu
HASSELL, Dayna .... 973-748-9000.... 307 H
dayna_hassell@bloomfield.edu
HASSELTINE, Donald .... 507-222-4199.... 261 G
dhasseltine@carleton.edu
HASSENZAHL, David .... 412-365-1842.... 425 C
dhassenzahl@chatham.edu
HASSETT, A. Tracy .... 508-831-5473.... 246 F
thassett@wpi.edu
HASSINGER, Steven .... 717-728-2262.... 425 B
stevehassinger@centralpenn.edu
HASSLER, Ardoth .... 202-687-1973...... 98 D
hasslera@georgetown.edu
HASSON, Amy, S .... 410-548-3316.... 228 D
ashasson@salisbury.edu
HASSON, Eileen .... 631-420-2369.... 356 A
hassone@farmingdale.edu
HASTAD, Doug, N .... 262-524-7246.... 546 H
dhastad@carrollu.edu
HASTED, Grigor .... 517-437-7341.... 252 C
grigor.hasted@hillsdale.edu
HASTIE, John .... 607-778-5196.... 324 G
hastiejt@sunybroome.edu
HASTINGS, Dana, M .... 785-532-6221.... 194 D
dhasting@ksu.edu
HASTINGS, Daniel, E .... 617-253-6056.... 241 D
HASTINGS, Destiny .... 641-423-2530.... 186 H
HASTINGS, Destiny .... 641-423-2530.... 186 J
dehastings@kaplan.edu
HASTINGS, Donald, B .... 518-580-5768.... 351 B
dhasting@skidmore.edu
HASTINGS, Edward, T .... 610-361-5293.... 437 D
hastinge@neumann.edu
HASTINGS, Jan .... 818-401-1030...... 42 F
jhastings@columbiacollege.edu
HASTINGS, Janel, H .... 909-607-8191...... 49 F
janel_hastings@hmc.edu
HASTINGS, Jennifer, D .... 253-879-2460.... 538 H
jhastings@pugetsound.edu
HASTINGS, Kevin, J .... 309-341-7438.... 155 F
khasting@knox.edu
HASTINGS, Michael, M .... 207-581-1484.... 220 A
mhastings@maine.edu
HASTINGS, Nancy .... 312-329-4415.... 159 A
nancy.hastings@moody.edu
HASTINGS, Rebecca .... 425-352-8256.... 532 B
rhastings@cascadia.edu
HASTINGS, Susan .... 651-255-6120.... 271 D
shastings@unitedseminary.edu
HASTINGS-CANDELORO,
Valerie, J .... 302-225-6246...... 96 H
hastinv@gbc.edu
HASTINGS-SHEPPARD,
Lisa, C .... 302-739-4623...... 96 D
lhasting@dtcc.edu
HATAIER, Maria .... 212-678-3779.... 357 G
mrt2112@tc.columbia.edu
HATANAKA, Janice .... 562-985-5252...... 35 C
jhatanak@csulb.edu
HATCH, Adam .... 808-544-0839.... 140 G
ahatch@hpu.edu
HATCH, Barbara .... 781-239-2629.... 239 G
bhatch@massbay.edu
HATCH, Blaine .... 928-524-7440...... 17 A
blaine.hatch@npc.edu
HATCH, SHCJ,
Jeanne Marie .... 610-527-0200.... 445 J
jhatch@rosemont.edu
HATCH, Jennifer .... 717-764-9550.... 426 D
jhatch@csb.edu
HATCH, Joy, A .... 804-819-4990.... 526 C
jhatch@vccs.edu
HATCH, Mark .... 719-389-6805...... 82 D
mhatch@coloradocollege.edu
HATCH, Mary .... 847-214-7421.... 150 F
mhatch@elgin.edu
HATCH, Nathan, O .... 336-758-5211.... 380 C
hatch@wfu.edu
HATCH, Paul .... 218-262-6731.... 266 E
paulhatch@hibbing.edu
HATCHER, Barb .... 540-365-4231.... 519 C
bhatcher@ferrum.edu
HATCHER, Betty, K .... 252-638-3745.... 370 A
hatcherb@cravencc.edu

HATCHER, Brian 410-617-5026 223 I bhatcher@loyola.edu
HATCHER, George 919-546-8353 376 F ghatcher@shawu.edu
HATCHER, Kevin, L 909-537-5011 36 B khatcher@csusb.edu
HATCHER, Lisa, M 304-929-6737 543 A lhatcher@newriver.edu
HATCHER, Oeida 434-544-8344 521 B hatcher@lynchburg.edu
HATCHER, Robert 212-817-7020 327 B rhatcher@gc.cuny.edu
HATCHER, Wayne 870-248-4000 21 A wayne.hatcher@blackrivertech.edu
HATER, Karen 407-646-2345 116 D khater@rollins.edu
HATFIELD, Amy 360-475-7841 536 D ahatfield@olympic.edu
HATFIELD, Barbara, S 318-473-6446 212 I bhatfield@lsua.edu
HATFIELD, Chad 914-961-8313 349 I hatfield@svots.edu
HATFIELD, Heather 865-539-7331 475 G hrhatfield@pstcc.edu
HATFIELD, Karen 352-588-8460 116 G karen.hatfield@saintleo.edu
HATFIELD, Mark 662-720-7270 276 C mahatfield@nemcc.edu
HATFIELD, Renee 503-222-3225 415 H rhatfiel@cci.edu
HATFIELD, Sharon, L 540-985-8263 520 I slhatfield@jchs.edu
HATFIELD, Tish 419-995-8230 392 K hatfield.t@rhodesstate.edu
HATHAWAY, Brent 307-766-4194 556 H bhathaway@uwyo.edu
HATHAWAY, Gretchel, L 518-388-8327 358 G hathawag@union.edu
HATHAWAY, Jeffrey 516-463-6750 335 G jeffrey.hathaway@hofstra.edu
HATHAWAY, Joel 314-434-4044 280 F joel.hathaway@covenantseminary.edu
HATHAWAY, Karry, L 443-412-2401 223 B khathaway@harford.edu
HATHAWAY, Kristin 231-876-3118 248 A kristin.hathaway@baker.edu
HATHAWAY, Nick 405-325-3916 413 C nhathaway@ou.edu
HATHAWAY, Tom 513-569-1493 387 G tom.hathaway@cincinnatistate.edu
HATHAWAY, William 757-352-4294 523 E willhat@regent.edu
HATHAWAY-CLARK, Bill 303-458-4066 87 I whathawa@regis.edu
HATHCOCK, Michele 828-398-7203 368 B mhathcock@abtech.edu
HATHCOTE, Jan, M 706-542-4907 138 G hathcote@uga.edu
HATHMAN, Laurie, E 816-501-4144 288 A laurie.hathman@rockhurst.edu
HATHORN, Janine, M 540-458-8671 530 D jhathorn@wlu.edu
HATMAN, Lonnie 360-596-5300 538 E lhatman@spscc.ctc.edu
HATNEY, Taura 706-396-7606 135 G thatney@paine.edu
HATRAK, Gregory 914-961-8313 349 I ghatrak@svots.edu
HATTAUER, Edward, A 718-990-6384 348 G hattauee@stjohns.edu
HATTAWAY, Trey 903-983-8218 489 I thattaway@kilgore.edu
HATTEBERG, Gregory, A 214-841-3704 485 F alumni@dts.edu
HATTEN, Angie 309-692-4092 158 D ahatten@midstate.edu
HATTEN, LaRue 504-286-3275 278 C larue.hatten@wmcarey.edu
HATTER, John, L 812-374-5119 176 A jhatter@ivytech.edu
HATTERMAN, Dawn, K 816-604-3223 285 D
HATTERMANN, Troy 309-694-5156 152 C troy.hattermann@icc.edu
HATTLESTAD, Neil, W 501-450-3122 25 H neilh@uca.edu
HATTMAN, Melissa 314-516-5708 291 D hattmanm@umsl.edu
HATTO, Susan 989-328-1254 255 E susanf@montcalm.edu
HATTON, John 314-577-8600 289 C hattonjf@slu.edu
HATTON, Karl 270-247-8521 204 G khatton@midcontinent.edu
HATTON, Martin 662-329-7138 276 A mhatton@as.muw.edu
HATTON, Martin 662-329-7110 276 A mhatton@as.muw.edu
HATTON, Nora 859-336-5082 206 A nhatton@sccky.edu
HATUEY, Josie 617-348-6507 245 D hatuey@urbancollege.edu
HATZENBUEHLER, Linda 208-282-4899 143 H hatzlind@isu.edu
HAU, Hoang 562-907-4244 79 F hhau@whittier.edu
HAUB, Mark 865-251-1800 473 A mhaub@southcollegetn.edu
HAUCK, Gary 989-328-1234 255 E garyh@montcalm.edu
HAUCK, Steven 605-882-5284 464 E haucks@lakeareatech.edu
HAUF, Todd 701-483-2570 381 G todd.hauf@dickinsonstate.edu
HAUG, Ericka 218-299-3250 262 I haug@cord.edu
HAUG, Marsha, L 610-436-3411 444 A mhaug@wcupa.edu
HAUGABROOK, Adrian, K 617-879-2008 246 C ahaugabrook@wheelock.edu
HAUGE, Todd, W 410-293-1600 559 B hauge@usna.edu
HAUGEN, Catherine (Kate) 701-231-7052 382 B kate.haugen@ndsu.edu
HAUGEN, Daniel 612-861-7554 260 G haugen@alfredadler.edu
HAUGEN, Diane, M 608-796-3001 553 C dmhaugen@viterbo.edu
HAUGEN, Dolores 253-566-6090 538 F dhaugen@tacomacc.edu
HAUGEN, Donna, M 516-572-7809 342 C donna.haugen@ncc.edu
HAUGEN, Doris 847-628-1510 154 K dhaugen@judsonu.edu
HAUGEN, Doug 530-938-5295 42 E haugend@siskiyous.edu
HAUGEN, Jay 314-977-2350 289 C haugenjp@slu.edu
HAUGEN, Nancy 510-869-6511 64 J nhaugen@samuelmerritt.edu
HAUGEN, Regina 270-384-8300 204 D haugenr@lindsey.edu
HAUGHIE, Jennifer, A 240-500-2000 223 A fisherj@hagerstowncc.edu
HAUGHT, Kenneth 701-483-2330 381 G ken.haught@dickinsonstate.edu
HAUGHT, Paul, A 901-321-3579 467 I phaught@cbu.edu
HAUGHTON, Chantaye 410-276-0306 226 D chaughton@host.sdc.edu
HAUGSLAND, Judy, M 414-410-4202 546 G jmhaugsland@stritch.edu
HAUK, Gary, S 404-727-6021 129 D gary.hauk@emory.edu
HAUKE, Raymond, A 620-341-5173 192 G rhauke@emporia.edu
HAULOTTE, Erin 847-947-5491 159 E erin.haulotte@nl.edu
HAUPERT, Vincent, D 260-359-4089 173 A vhaupert@huntington.edu
HAURY, Clifford, W 434-961-5380 528 B chaury@pvcc.edu
HAUS, David 304-327-4155 543 F dhaus@bluefieldstate.edu
HAUS, Teri 970-943-2196 89 E thaus@western.edu
HAUSAM, Wiley 914-251-6196 354 D wiley.hausam@purchase.edu
HAUSAMMANN, Marilyn 617-495-8635 235 D marilyn_hausammann@harvard.edu
HAUSCARRIAGUE, Elizabeth 925-685-1230 43 F ehauscarriague@dvc.edu
HAUSCHILDT, Jim 816-932-6739 289 D jhaushildt@saintlukescollege.edu
HAUSE, Jeffrey 402-280-3581 297 F jeffreyhause@creighton.edu
HAUSER, Carol 513-529-3131 396 E hauserca@muohio.edu
HAUSER, Chuck 252-940-6371 368 C chuckh@beaufortccc.edu
HAUSER, John 336-838-6149 375 C john.hauser@wilkescc.edu
HAUSER, Joseph, H 901-722-3228 473 C jhauser@sco.edu
HAUSER, LuAnn 620-431-2820 195 E lhauser@neosho.edu
HAUSER, Robert 217-244-2807 167 D r-hauser@illinois.edu
HAUSER, Stephen 215-702-4217 444 B shauser@pbu.edu
HAUSER, Stephen, C 608-246-2101 554 D shauser@madisoncollege.org
HAUSFATHER, Sam 314-529-9466 284 C shausfather@maryville.edu
HAUSKNECHT, Robert 708-456-0300 166 F rhauskne@triton.edu
HAUSLER, Jackie 716-827-4347 358 D hauslerj@trocaire.edu
HAUSMAN, Amy 973-290-4214 308 G bookstore@cse.edu
HAUSMANN, Tom, L 608-796-3860 553 C tlhausmann@viterbo.edu
HAUSS, Kevin 212-237-8512 327 F khauss@jjay.cuny.edu
HAUSSLER, Alicia 308-398-7335 297 A ahaussler@cccneb.edu
HAUVER, Dottie 508-793-2327 233 C dhauver@holycross.edu
HAVEARD, Melanie, J 850-474-2540 121 D mhaveard@uwf.edu
HAVELKA, Ted 212-594-4000 357 H thavelka@tcicollege.edu
HAVELY, Candace 319-296-4229 185 F candace.havely@hawkeyecollege.edu
HAVENS, Brandi 806-874-3571 483 A brandi.havens@clarendoncollege.edu
HAVENS, Luisa, M 915-747-5890 506 B lmhavens@utep.edu
HAVERKAMP, Hans 802-635-1335 515 F hans.haverkamp@jsc.edu
HAVERLACK, Sandra, J 540-863-2822 526 F shaverlack@dslcc.edu
HAVERLY, Mark 660-596-7407 290 B mhaverly@sfccmo.edu
HAVERSAT, Walt 803-799-9082 461 A whaversat@southuniversity.edu
HAVERSTICK, III, Henry, W 718-780-7906 324 F henry.haverstick@brooklaw.edu
HAVERTY, April 414-955-4844 548 G ahaverty@mcw.edu
HAVERTY, Dan 574-239-8350 172 M dhaverty@hcc-nd.edu
HAVHOLM, Karen, G 715-836-3405 551 A havholkg@uwec.edu
HAVIG, Dee 307-754-6412 556 G dee.havig@northwestcollege.edu
HAVILAND, Bobbie 620-365-5116 190 D haviland@allencc.edu
HAVIS, Allan 858-534-4004 74 F ahavis@ucsd.edu
HAVIS, Joe 217-424-6251 158 G jhavis@millikin.edu
HAVLOVIC, Stephen, J 607-587-3913 355 C havlovics@alfredstate.edu
HAVRAN, Natalie, M 609-652-4384 313 E natalie.havran@stockton.edu
HAWES, Heather 404-270-5068 138 B hhawes@spelman.edu
HAWES, Matthew 315-866-0300 335 D hawesmr@herkimer.edu
HAWGOOD, Samuel 415-476-2342 75 A sam.hawgood@ucsf.edu
HAWK, Jeanine 415-355-2000 27 A jhawk@alliant.edu
HAWK, Linda 760-750-4950 36 C lhawk@csusm.edu
HAWK, Thomas, R 215-751-8029 426 B thawk@ccp.edu
HAWK, Tricia 785-227-3380 191 B hawkt@bethanylb.edu
HAWKES, Peter 570-422-3494 442 D phawkes@po-box.esu.edu
HAWKEY, Christina 928-344-1723 12 A christina.hawkey@azwestern.edu
HAWKEY, Earl, W 402-472-2025 300 G ehawkey1@unl.edu
HAWKEY, Philip, A 909-593-3511 75 E phawkey@laverne.edu
HAWKIN, Chris 541-463-5547 416 E hawkinc@lanecc.edu
HAWKINS, Andre 772-462-7100 111 B ahawkins@irsc.edu
HAWKINS, Angela 415-476-5997 75 A angela.hawkins@ucsf.edu
HAWKINS, Audrey 903-675-6357 502 F ahawkins@tvcc.edu
HAWKINS, Ben 910-893-1380 362 J hawkinsb@campbell.edu
HAWKINS, Billy, C 256-761-6212 7 G bhawkins@talladega.edu
HAWKINS, Carson 731-661-5018 477 B chawkins@uu.edu
HAWKINS, Charles 951-487-3073 58 B chawkins@msjc.edu
HAWKINS, Cheryl 734-462-4400 258 A chawkins@schoolcraft.edu
HAWKINS, Christie 405-744-4244 410 C christie.hawkins@okstate.edu
HAWKINS, Daryl 610-341-5822 428 E dhawkins@eastern.edu
HAWKINS, DeLores 515-964-6514 183 H dwhawkins@dmacc.edu
HAWKINS, Don 205-970-9213 7 C dhawkins@sebc.edu
HAWKINS, Donna 215-646-7300 430 C hawkins.d@gmc.edu
HAWKINS, Greg 901-986-5969 273 C stlife@belhaven.edu
HAWKINS, Irene 302-857-6261 96 C ihawkins@desu.edu
HAWKINS, JR., Jack 334-670-3200 8 A jhawkins@troy.edu
HAWKINS, Jacqueline 270-706-8538 202 A jhawkins0045@kctcs.edu
HAWKINS, James, M 850-599-3379 118 L james.hawkins@famu.edu
HAWKINS, JoAnn 443-518-4974 223 D jhawkins@howardcc.edu
HAWKINS, John 802-862-9616 513 B jhawkins@burlington.edu
HAWKINS, Jonathan 615-547-1239 468 B jhawkins@cumberland.edu
HAWKINS, Julia 606-783-5189 204 I j.hawkins@moreheadstate.edu
HAWKINS, Katherine 540-831-6514 523 A khawkins3@radford.edu
HAWKINS, Lewis 770-394-8300 125 A rhawkins@aii.edu
HAWKINS, Marcia 606-546-1211 207 B mhawkins@unionky.edu
HAWKINS, Mark 312-362-5562 149 A mhawkin1@depaul.edu
HAWKINS, Mary, B 402-557-7005 296 H mary.hawkins@bellevue.edu
HAWKINS, Mary, M 303-871-4758 89 A mhawkins@du.edu
HAWKINS, Mel 865-471-3246 467 G mhawkins@cn.edu
HAWKINS, JR., Melvin 803-822-3592 459 E hawkinsm@midlandstech.edu
HAWKINS, Michele 561-297-3245 119 A mhawkins@fau.edu
HAWKINS, Mike 816-414-3700 285 H registrar@mbts.edu
HAWKINS, Patricia 404-965-8118 124 D phawkins@aiuniv.edu
HAWKINS, Paul, M 386-312-4134 116 F mikehawkins@sjrstate.edu
HAWKINS, Regina 312-553-2500 147 B rhawkins@ccc.edu
HAWKINS, Robert, S 706-542-2277 138 G rhawkins@uga.edu
HAWKINS, Ronald, E 434-592-4030 520 K rehawkin@liberty.edu
HAWKINS, Susan 206-296-6090 538 B shawkins@seattleu.edu
HAWKINS, Tara 775-673-7206 302 H thawkins@tmcc.edu
HAWKINS, Vernon, L 922-860-4221 484 G vhawkins@dcccd.edu
HAWKINS, Warren, H 903-927-3390 509 E whawkins@wileyc.edu
HAWKINS, William 203-837-8509 91 A hawkinsw@wcsu.edu
HAWKINS, William 860-231-5405 95 D bhawkins@usj.edu
HAWKINSON, Kenneth 309-298-1066 168 C ks-hawkinson@wiu.edu
HAWKS, Kathy 651-361-3450 265 A khawks@mcnallysmith.edu
HAWKS, Nicole 617-353-2230 232 E nhawkes@bu.edu
HAWKS, Sue, W 910-642-7141 374 B shawks@sccnc.edu
HAWKSHEAD, Richard 404-965-6574 124 D rhawkshead@aiuniv.edu
HAWLEY, Dennis, W 570-577-1911 423 E dennis.hawley@bucknell.edu
HAWLEY, Donna, J 316-978-3015 198 A donna.hawley@wichita.edu
HAWLEY, Dwight 630-620-2129 160 C dhawley@seminary.edu
HAWLEY, Eric 435-797-8146 511 E eric.hawley@usu.edu
HAWLEY, Harold 843-349-5279 458 H harold.hawley@hgtc.edu
HAWLEY, Katie 802-865-6424 513 C hawley@champlain.edu
HAWLEY, Kent 217-641-4570 154 I khawley@jwcc.edu
HAWLEY, Michael, E 314-286-4846 287 G mehawley@ranken.edu
HAWLEY, Michelle 323-343-5969 35 D mhawley@calstatela.edu
HAWLEY, Stephanie 512-223-7637 481 B shawley@austincc.edu
HAWLEY, Thomas 605-626-2524 466 A thawley@northern.edu
HAWLEY, Thomas, A 231-843-5803 260 B tahawley@westshore.edu
HAWN, Sherry 973-877-3000 309 H
HAWN, Sherry 212-343-1234 341 B shawn@mcny.edu
HAWORTH, Karen 847-947-5246 159 E khaworth@nl.edu
HAWORTH-HOEPPNER, Susan 616-632-2974 247 E haworsus@aquinas.edu
HAWS, Pamela, M 817-272-3365 505 C haws@uta.edu
HAWSEY, David, S 276-944-6133 519 A dhawsey@ehc.edu
HAWSEY, Vicki 256-352-8180 10 A vicki.hawsey@wallacestate.edu
HAWTHORNE, Camille 724-946-7110 451 C hawthorc@westminster.edu
HAWTHORNE, Marge 740-695-9500 385 B mhawthor@belmontcollege.edu
HAWTHORNE, Mary Jane 731-352-4046 467 E hawthornemj@bethelu.edu
HAWTIN, Mary, L 810-989-5546 257 H mhawtin@sc4.edu
HAWXHURST, Joan 269-337-7384 252 K joan.hawxhurst@kzoo.edu
HAXTON, Lori 660-626-2236 278 D lhaxton@atsu.edu

HAY, April .... 812-237-2020 .... 173 B
april.hay@indstate.edu
HAY, George .... 312-467-2560 .... 146 F
ghay@tcsedsystem.edu
HAY, Judy .... 406-771-5133 .... 295 G
jhay@msugf.edu
HAY, Kuni .... 408-741-2052 ...... 78 G
kuni.hay@westvalley.edu
HAY, Michael, D .... 503-491-7211 .... 417 B
michael.hay@mhcc.edu
HAY, Sharon, L .... 401-865-2750 .... 453 H
sharhay@providence.edu
HAY, William .... 605-856-5880 .... 465 C
william.hay@sintegleska.edu
HAYASHI, Adam .... 847-635-1862 .... 160 F
ahayashi@oakton.edu
HAYASHIDA, Peter, A .... 951-827-5203 ...... 74 E
peter.hayashida@ucr.edu
HAYDEN, Brian .... 724-480-3460 .... 426 A
brian.hayden@ccbc.edu
HAYDEN, Cathy, C .... 601-857-3322 .... 274 C
cchayden@hindscc.edu
HAYDEN, Dolph .... 918-293-4809 .... 410 E
dolph.hayden@okstate.edu
HAYDEN, Donna, G .... 601-877-6182 .... 272 F
dhayden@alcorn.edu
HAYDEN, Hart .... 803-822-3676 .... 459 E
haydenh@midlandstech.edu
HAYDEN, John, D .... 215-836-2222 .... 422 B
john.hayden@antonelli.edu
HAYDEN, Julie, M .... 619-201-8964 ...... 70 J
jmhayden@socalsem.edu
HAYDEN, Roger .... 410-704-2487 .... 228 E
rhayden@towson.edu
HAYDEN, Ruby .... 425-739-8208 .... 535 H
ruby.hayden@lwtc.edu
HAYDEN-MILES, Marie ..... 631-420-2012 .... 356 A
marie.hayden-miles@farmingdale.edu
HAYDEN-MILES, Marie ..... 631-420-2171 .... 356 A
marie.hayden-miles@farmingdale.edu
HAYDN, Stephanie .... 907-564-8346 ...... 10 D
shaydn@alaskapacific.edu
HAYDOCK, Joseph .... 559-297-4500 ...... 51 C
jhaydock@it-email.com
HAYDON, Darrell .... 510-885-2749 ...... 34 E
darrell.haydon@csueastbay.edu
HAYE, Erin .... 207-216-4311 .... 219 C
ehaye@yccc.edu
HAYE, Melissa .... 304-327-4145 .... 543 F
mhaye@bluefieldstate.edu
HAYEK, Cheryl .... 800-955-2527 .... 282 D
chayek@grantham.edu
HAYEN, Christopher .... 518-388-6911 .... 358 G
hayenc@union.edu
HAYES, Ann, C .... 717-867-6416 .... 434 C
hayes@lvc.edu
HAYES, Ann, K .... 573-651-2552 .... 289 K
ahayes@semo.edu
HAYES, Anne, M .... 610-566-1776 .... 452 B
ahayes@williamson.edu
HAYES, Becky .... 912-201-8029 .... 137 D
bhayes@southuniversity.edu
HAYES, Billy .... 251-981-3771 .... 2 G
billy.hayes@columbiasouthern.edu
HAYES, Blair .... 301-985-7940 .... 227 F
diversity-initiatives@umuc.edu
HAYES, Charlene, M .... 410-516-8113 .... 223 F
chayes13@jhu.edu
HAYES, Chuck .... 810-762-0501 .... 255 G
chuck.hayes@mcc.edu
HAYES, Clint, R .... 606-679-8501 .... 203 C
clint.hayes@kctcs.edu
HAYES, Collette, M .... 302-454-3959 ...... 96 F
cmhayes@dtcc.edu
HAYES, Connie .... 434-947-8116 .... 523 B
chayes@randolphcollege.edu
HAYES, Dale .... 772-462-7809 .... 111 B
dhayes@irsc.edu
HAYES, Dan .... 434-791-7252 .... 516 G
dhayes@averett.edu
HAYES, Daniel, J .... 315-267-2147 .... 354 C
hayesdj@potsdam.edu
HAYES, David, M .... 518-388-6233 .... 358 G
hayesd@union.edu
HAYES, Debra, L .... 330-972-7210 .... 403 B
dlhayes@uakron.edu
HAYES, Denise .... 909-621-8355 ...... 40 E
denise_hayes@cuc.claremont.edu
HAYES, Diane .... 802-831-1308 .... 515 B
dhayes@vermontlaw.edu
HAYES, Erik, Z .... 812-877-8230 .... 179 B
erik.hayes@rose-hulman.edu
HAYES, Gaye .... 229-928-1273 .... 131 F
gaye.hayes@gsw.edu
HAYES, Gaynelle, H .... 409-944-1206 .... 486 K
ghayes@gc.edu
HAYES, George .... 212-431-2837 .... 343 E
ghayes@nyls.edu
HAYES, Greg .... 816-235-1015 .... 291 C
hayesgr@umkc.edu
HAYES, Homer, M .... 903-510-3203 .... 503 A
bhay2@tjc.edu
HAYES, Ingrid .... 256-824-6857 .... 8 G
ingrid.hayes@uah.edu
HAYES, Jack .... 401-863-2972 .... 453 B
HAYES, Jeannie .... 606-242-0309 .... 203 D
jhayes0114@kctcs.edu
HAYES, Jeff .... 678-359-5008 .... 132 A
jeff@gdn.edu
HAYES, Jeff .... 863-638-1426 .... 123 D
jeff.hayes@warner.edu
HAYES, Jennifer .... 360-475-7106 .... 536 D
jhayes@olympic.edu
HAYES, Jerry .... 413-572-5260 .... 238 F
jhayes@wsc.ma.edu
HAYES, Jessica .... 516-299-1451 .... 339 A
jessica.hayes@liu.edu
HAYES, Jessica .... 516-299-2480 .... 339 A
jessica.hayes@liu.edu
HAYES, Joanne .... 541-440-4600 .... 420 F
joanne.hayes@umpqua.edu
HAYES, Joe .... 907-474-7081 ...... 10 I
uaf-fyalum@alaska.edu
HAYES, Joe, F .... 864-977-1367 .... 460 A
joe.hayes@ngu.edu
HAYES, John .... 352-392-1784 .... 120 C
hayesj@ufl.edu
HAYES, Julie, C .... 413-545-4169 .... 236 F
jhayes@hfa.umass.edu
HAYES, Kelly .... 631-656-2157 .... 334 B
khayes@ftc.edu
HAYES, Lance, R .... 512-448-8750 .... 493 E
lanceh@stedwards.edu
HAYES, Linda .... 650-306-3353 ...... 67 F
lhayes@smccd.edu
HAYES, Linda .... 513-862-3571 .... 391 E
HAYES, Marshall .... 815-825-2086 .... 155 D
marshall.hayes@kishwaukeecollege.edu
HAYES, Michelle .... 603-862-1370 .... 306 C
michelle.hayes@unh.edu
HAYES, Mike .... 423-614-8406 .... 470 C
mhayes@leeuniversity.edu
HAYES, Nancy, K .... 415-338-2521 ...... 37 B
nkhayes@sfsu.edu
HAYES, Paul, S .... 423-439-4213 .... 473 F
hayes@etsu.edu
HAYES, Phebe, A .... 337-482-6829 .... 216 D
phayes@louisiana.edu
HAYES, Ray .... 205-348-8343 .... 8 D
crhayes@uasystem.ua.edu
HAYES, Rhonda, M .... 252-335-3103 .... 377 F
rmhayes@mail.ecsu.edu
HAYES, Richard, L .... 251-380-2738 .... 9 D
rlhayes@usouthal.edu
HAYES, Rob .... 617-266-1400 .... 231 E
HAYES, Robin, A .... 501-882-8936 ...... 20 C
rahayes@asub.edu
HAYES, Samantha .... 270-852-3130 .... 204 A
shays@kwc.edu
HAYES, Sandra, J .... 207-725-3770 .... 217 E
shayes@bowdoin.edu
HAYES, Sandra, L .... 408-554-1784 ...... 68 C
shayes@scu.edu
HAYES, Stephanie, A .... 804-524-5997 .... 529 H
shayes@vsu.edu
HAYES, Suzanne .... 518-587-2100 .... 355 G
suzanne.hayes@esc.edu
HAYES, Theresa .... 323-464-2777 ...... 27 I
thayes@ca.aada.org
HAYES, Valerie, O .... 814-732-2167 .... 442 E
vhayes@edinboro.edu
HAYES, Wendy .... 937-376-6470 .... 387 A
whayes@centralstate.edu
HAYES, William .... 336-750-2142 .... 380 B
hayeswl@wssu.edu
HAYES-MORRISON, Ruth . 352-371-2833 .... 105 C
admissions@dragonrises.edu
HAYGOOD, Jennifer .... 919-807-7100 .... 367 I
haygoodj@nccommunitycolleges.edu
HAYHURST, David, T .... 619-594-6061 ...... 37 A
hayhurst@engineering.sdsu.edu
HAYHURST, Neil .... 225-216-8169 .... 209 H
hayhurstn@mybrcc.edu
HAYLER, David, E .... 828-262-8635 .... 377 D
haylerd@appstate.edu
HAYLOCK, Ryan .... 706-291-2121 .... 137 A
rhaylock@shorter.edu
HAYMAN, Gregory .... 916-558-2544 ...... 56 D
haymang@scc.losrios.edu
HAYMET, Anthony, D .... 858-534-2827 ...... 74 F
thaymet@ucsd.edu
HAYNER, Kate .... 510-869-4780 ...... 64 J
khayner@samuelmerritt.edu
HAYNER, Leon .... 407-646-2649 .... 116 D
lhayner@rollins.edu
HAYNER, Stephen, A .... 404-687-4514 .... 127 F
hayners@ctsnet.edu
HAYNES, Alexis .... 315-279-5674 .... 337 K
ahaynes@mail.keuka.edu
HAYNES, Amy, M .... 330-684-8932 .... 403 C
hamy@uakron.edu
HAYNES, Angela, N .... 919-516-4065 .... 376 D
anhaynes@st-aug.edu
HAYNES, Brian .... 678-466-5433 .... 127 D
brianhaynes@clayton.edu
HAYNES, Calvin .... 816-279-7000 .... 278 E
faid@acot.edu
HAYNES, Carl, E .... 607-844-8222 .... 357 I
haynesc@tc3.edu
HAYNES, Carolyn .... 513-529-2021 .... 396 E
haynesca@muohio.edu
HAYNES, Carolyn, A .... 513-529-6722 .... 396 E
haynesca@muohio.edu
HAYNES, David, A .... 540-985-4020 .... 520 I
dahaynes@jchs.edu
HAYNES, David, S .... 906-227-2242 .... 256 C
dhaynes@nmu.edu
HAYNES, Douglas, M .... 949-824-2798 ...... 74 B
dhaynes@uci.edu
HAYNES, Hal .... 701-483-2090 .... 381 G
hal.haynes@dickinsonstate.edu
HAYNES, John, G .... 806-743-7387 .... 502 B
john.g.haynes@ttuhsc.edu
HAYNES, John, K .... 404-215-2609 .... 134 D
jhaynes@morehouse.edu
HAYNES, Karen, S .... 760-750-4040 ...... 36 C
pres@csusm.edu
HAYNES, Lisa .... 616-331-7204 .... 251 F
haynesl@gvsu.edu
HAYNES, Martha, B .... 906-227-2610 .... 256 C
haynes@nmu.edu
HAYNES, Pamela, J .... 336-888-9055 .... 365 C
phaynes@highpoint.edu
HAYNES, Patricia, A .... 636-922-8427 .... 288 B
phaynes@stchas.edu
HAYNES, Penny, A .... 518-381-1374 .... 350 E
haynespa@sunysccc.edu
HAYNES, Peter, F .... 225-578-9903 .... 212 H
pfhaynes@vetmed.lsu.edu
HAYNES, Sandra .... 303-556-2978 ...... 86 F
hayness@msudenver.edu
HAYNES, Scot .... 904-264-9122 .... 106 I
HAYNES, Scott .... 870-245-5220 ...... 22 I
hayness@obu.edu
HAYNES, Stephanie, C .... 304-637-1335 .... 541 A
hayness@dewv.edu
HAYNES, Susan .... 325-649-8043 .... 488 C
shaynes@hputx.edu
HAYNES, Thomas .... 850-599-3491 .... 118 L
thomas.haynes@famu.edu
HAYNES, Tina .... 704-216-4561 .... 373 F
tina.haynes@rccc.edu
HAYNES, Victoria .... 816-995-2831 .... 287 H
victoria.haynes@researchcollege.edu
HAYNIE, Glenda, D .... 804-333-6719 .... 528 C
ghaynie@rappahannock.edu
HAYNIE, Janice .... 910-672-1211 .... 377 G
jhaynie@uncfsu.edu
HAYNIE, Todd .... 928-428-8320 ...... 14 B
todd.haynie@eac.edu
HAYS, Antoinette, M .... 781-768-7122 .... 244 A
antoinette.hays@regiscollege.edu
HAYS, Cheryl, M .... 412-268-6382 .... 424 J
chays@andrew.cmu.edu
HAYS, Christi .... 703-821-8570 .... 524 J
chays@stratford.edu
HAYS, Danny .... 870-245-5526 ...... 22 I
haysd@obu.edu
HAYS, Ina, R .... 636-584-6565 .... 281 E
haysir@eastcentral.edu
HAYS, Joel .... 602-386-4127 ...... 11 G
joel.hays@arizonachristian.edu
HAYS, Karen .... 732-906-2515 .... 311 D
khays@middlesexcc.edu
HAYS, Larry .... 314-529-9390 .... 284 C
lhays@maryville.edu
HAYS, Laura .... 580-349-1354 .... 410 B
lola@opsu.edu
HAYS, Mark .... 918-293-5130 .... 410 E
mark.hays@okstate.edu
HAYS, Regina, M .... 618-650-3324 .... 165 C
rmhays@siue.edu
HAYS, Rex .... 913-469-8500 .... 194 B
rhays@jccc.edu
HAYS, Richard .... 919-660-3411 .... 364 C
richard.hays@duke.edu
HAYS, Stacie .... 712-274-5254 .... 187 G
hays@morningside.edu
HAYS, Wm. Randy .... 859-238-5471 .... 199 G
randy.hays@centre.edu
HAYS-MUSSOINI,
Stephanie .... 765-973-8331 .... 173 F
HAYSBERT, JoAnn .... 757-727-5693 .... 519 H
joann.haysbert@hamptonu.edu
HAYTER, Christopher, A .... 614-823-1348 .... 400 H
chayter@otterbein.edu
HAYTER, Richard .... 972-721-5227 .... 503 B
rhayter@udallas.edu
HAYTER, Sonya .... 417-269-3469 .... 280 G
shayter@coxcollege.edu
HAYTON, Heather .... 336-316-2397 .... 365 A
hhayton@guilford.edu
HAYWARD, Craig .... 949-451-5766 ...... 70 E
chayward@ivc.edu
HAYWARD, Dawn .... 215-646-7300 .... 430 C
hayward.d@gmc.edu
HAYWARD, Jayanne .... 717-867-6321 .... 434 C
hayward@lvc.edu
HAYWARD, John .... 419-251-1314 .... 395 I
john.hayward@mercycollege.edu
HAYWARD, Lisa .... 425-235-7873 .... 537 A
lhayward@rtc.edu
HAYWARD, Maysa .... 732-255-0400 .... 312 D
mhayward@ocean.edu
HAYWARD-WYZIK, Lisa ... 603-542-7744 .... 304 G
lwyzik@ccsnh.edu
HAYWOOD, Carl .... 210-829-3935 .... 504 B
carl@uiwtx.edu
HAYWOOD, Chanta .... 919-530-7395 .... 378 B
chaywood@nccu.edu
HAYWOOD, Jerry .... 478-825-6211 .... 129 F
haywoodj@fvsu.edu
HAYWOOD, Michele .... 910-576-6222 .... 372 D
haywoodm@montgomery.edu
HAYWOOD, Zina .... 262-564-3104 .... 554 B
haywoodz@gtc.edu
HAYWORTH, Kimberly, K .. 517-750-1200 .... 258 D
kimh@arbor.edu
HAZAM, Bruce .... 207-288-5015 .... 217 H
bhazam@coa.edu
HAZARD, Laurie, L .... 401-232-6746 .... 453 C
lhazard@bryant.edu
HAZARD, Victor, A .... 859-257-3754 .... 207 D
vahaz2@uky.edu
HAZEL, Julie .... 719-502-3005 ...... 87 B
julie.hazel@ppcc.edu
HAZEL, Marianne .... 814-768-3401 .... 443 B
mhazel@lhup.edu
HAZELBAKER, Nicole .... 406-683-7900 .... 294 J
n_hazelbaker@umwestern.edu
HAZELKORN, Michael .... 912-279-5720 .... 127 E
mhazelkorn@ccga.edu
HAZELTON, Janet .... 802-468-1208 .... 515 D
janet.hazelton@castleton.edu
HAZELWOOD, Renita .... 336-386-3392 .... 374 E
hazelwoodr@surry.edu
HAZELWOOD, Rhonda, L .. 336-386-3397 .... 374 E
hazelwoodr@surry.edu
HAZEN, Ian .... 315-268-6439 .... 329 B
ihazen@clarkson.edu
HAZEN, Verna, J .... 585-475-5520 .... 347 G
vjhsfa@rit.edu
HAZEN, Virginia, S .... 603-646-2451 .... 304 J
virginia.s.hazen@dartmouth.edu
HAZLETT, Brian .... 410-704-2588 .... 228 E
bhazlett@towson.edu
HAZLETT, Margaret, L .... 207-725-3490 .... 217 E
mhazlett@bowdoin.edu
HAZZARD, Douglas .... 904-256-7100 .... 111 L
dhazzar@ju.edu
HAZZARD, Mike .... 270-706-8686 .... 202 A
mikew.hazzard@kctcs.edu
HAZZARD, Nancy, J .... 315-498-2119 .... 345 D
hazzardn@sunyocc.edu
HAZZARD, Terry .... 251-405-7285 .... 2 C
thazzard@bishop.edu
HE, Huot .... 301-548-5500 ...... 99 G
HE, Yuxin .... 512-454-1188 .... 480 F
info@aoma.edu
HEACOCK, Maureen .... 937-769-1846 .... 384 B
mheacock@antioch.edu
HEACOCK, Ronald, C .... 518-743-2237 .... 355 D
heacockr@sunyacc.edu
HEAD, Elizabeth .... 904-620-2111 .... 120 D
ehead@unf.edu
HEAD, Elizabeth, M .... 904-620-2111 .... 120 D
ehead@unf.edu
HEAD, Janet .... 801-333-8100 .... 509 K
HEAD, Linda .... 832-813-6816 .... 490 E
linda.head@lonestar.edu
HEAD, Robert, L .... 815-226-4010 .... 163 A
rhead@rockford.edu
HEAD, Steve .... 281-618-5440 .... 490 E
steve.head@lonestar.edu
HEADING-GRANT,
Wanda, R .... 802-656-8426 .... 514 H
wanda.heading-grant@uvm.edu
HEADINGS, Ronald .... 419-358-3660 .... 385 D
headingsr@bluffton.edu
HEADLEY, Larry .... 816-414-3700 .... 285 H
lheadley@mbts.edu
HEADLEY, Sarah .... 501-205-8811 ...... 21 C
sheadley@cbc.edu
HEADRICK, Darrell, L .... 804-752-7374 .... 523 C
dheadric@rmc.edu
HEADRICK, Dennis .... 402-323-3427 .... 300 B
dheadric@southeast.edu
HEADRICK, Robert .... 479-248-7236 ...... 21 G
bheadrick@ecollege.edu
HEADY, Nancy .... 325-649-8069 .... 488 C
nheady@hputx.edu
HEAFNER, Lori .... 843-349-7871 .... 458 H
lori.heafner@hgtc.edu
HEAGLE, Leanne .... 937-255-6565 .... 557 C
leanne.heagle@afit.edu
HEALD, James, W .... 414-955-4400 .... 548 G
jheald@mcw.edu
HEALEY, Maureen .... 219-866-6161 .... 179 D
HEALEY, Stephen, E .... 203-576-4271 ...... 94 F
healey@bridgeport.edu
HEALEY, Tom .... 810-762-0417 .... 255 G
thomas.healey@mcc.edu
HEALY, Amy .... 518-255-5111 .... 354 E
healyak@cobleskill.edu

HEALY, Diane 312-942-6849 163 D diane_healy@rush.edu
HEALY, Gayle 518-629-7326 336 C g.healy@hvcc.edu
HEALY, James 508-856-2007 237 C james.healy@umassmed.edu
HEALY, John 210-832-2198 504 B jhealy@uiwtx.edu
HEALY, Kevin 612-338-6537 261 B healyk@augsburg.edu
HEALY, Mary 812-749-1277 178 H mhealy@oak.edu
HEALY, Patrick, J 203-582-8643 93 H patrick.healy@quinnipiac.edu
HEALY, Paul, F 215-717-6161 448 I phealy@uarts.edu
HEALY, Rose Mary 973-278-5400 307 F rmh@berkeleycollege.edu
HEALY, Rose Mary 973-278-5400 323 H rmh@berkeleycollege.edu
HEALY, William, L 863-680-4140 109 E whealy@flsouthern.edu
HEANEY, Roma, E 313-593-5353 259 B rheaney@umich.edu
HEAP, Jeffrey 815-280-2401 154 J jheap@jjc.edu
HEARD, Al 323-563-9326 39 G alvinheard@cdrewu.edu
HEARD, JR., Ernest, W 615-460-6424 467 D ernest.heard@belmont.edu
HEARD, Jeanne, K 501-686-5572 24 F heardjeannek@uams.edu
HEARD, John 660-626-2397 278 D jheard@atsu.edu
HEARD, Michael 229-217-4207 134 F mheard@moultrietech.edu
HEARD, Pamela, K 973-353-5805 314 E pkheard@andromeda.rutgers.edu
HEARD-JOHNSON, Cessa 206-934-6749 537 F cessa.heard.johnson@seattlecolleges.edu
HEARIN, Rick 301-314-7236 227 B rhearin@umd.edu
HEARIT, Keith, M 269-387-2394 260 C keith.hearit@wmich.edu
HEARN, Deyna 310-434-4435 68 D hearn_deyna@smc.edu
HEARN, Kevin 716-286-8405 344 D khearn@niagara.edu
HEARN, JR., Robert, W 302-855-1684 96 E rhearn@dtcc.edu
HEARN, Sabrina, B 205-934-9176 8 D shearn@uasystem.ua.edu
HEARNS, Rene 814-732-1052 442 E rhearns@edinboro.edu
HEAROD, Marguerite 405-382-9950 412 B m.hearod@sscok.edu
HEARON, Michael 678-731-0555 19 A michael.hearon@phoenix.edu
HEARTFIELD, Judy 254-526-1472 482 H judy.heartfield@ctcd.edu
HEARTLEIN, Karrie 309-341-7340 155 F kheartle@knox.edu
HEARTT, Justine 916-278-5992 36 A hearttj@csus.edu
HEASLEY, Ronald, P 717-361-1558 428 F heasleyrp@etown.edu
HEASTON, Amy 912-344-2505 124 G amy.heaston@armstrong.edu
HEASTON, Fran 305-558-9500 105 J
HEATER, Margaret 585-343-0055 334 F meheater@genesee.edu
HEATH, Aaron 816-322-0110 279 D aaron.heath@calvary.edu
HEATH, Ann 610-647-4400 431 C aheath@immaculata.edu
HEATH, Bill 863-638-2953 123 E heathwl@webber.edu
HEATH, Bob 417-626-1234 287 C heath.bob@occ.edu
HEATH, Cheryl, A 307-674-6446 556 F cheath@sheridan.edu
HEATH, David, A 212-938-5650 355 B dheath@sunyopt.edu
HEATH, Diann 785-825-5422 191 E dheath@brownmackie.edu
HEATH, Erin, L 651-628-3323 270 B elheath@nwc.edu
HEATH, Fred, M 512-495-4350 505 D fheath@austin.utexas.edu
HEATH, Gregory 616-538-2330 251 D gheath@gbcol.edu
HEATH, Hildy 415-405-4256 37 B hheath@sfsu.edu
HEATH, Jason 502-897-4106 206 C jheath@sbts.edu
HEATH, Jeffrey, D 864-242-5100 455 E
HEATH, Joan, L 512-245-2133 501 F jh06@txstate.edu
HEATH, Kathy 207-326-2339 219 D kathy.heath@mma.edu
HEATH, Kerri 310-506-7586 61 H kerri.heath@pepperdine.edu
HEATH, Marie 904-470-8141 105 G
HEATH, Mary-Teresa 518-828-4181 330 E mary-teresa.heath@sunycgcc.edu
HEATH, Raymond, P 570-348-6246 435 F heath@marywood.edu
HEATH, Richard, C 410-777-2204 221 C rcheath@aacc.edu
HEATH, Robert 205-366-8851 7 F rheath@stillman.edu
HEATH, Susan, D 801-832-2283 512 G sheath@westminstercollege.edu
HEATH-THORNTON, Debra 610-225-5055 428 E dheath@eastern.edu
HEATHERLY, David, L 910-938-6789 369 F heatherlyd@coastalcarolina.edu
HEATON, Dennis 641-472-7000 187 E dheaton@mum.edu
HEATON, Karick 801-302-2879 510 G karick.heaton@neumont.edu
HEATON, Monica 563-425-5773 189 G heatonm@uiu.edu
HEATON, Scott 209-946-2541 76 A sheaton@pacific.edu
HEATON, Tim 605-688-5117 466 C tim.heaton@sdstate.edu
HEATON, JR., William 714-449-7464 70 G wheaton@scco.edu
HEATON-DUNLAP, Anne 650-543-3804 57 B adunlap@menlo.edu
HEATOR, Martin 734-462-4400 258 A mheator@schoolcraft.edu
HEATWOLE, Deirdre 774-455-7300 236 G dheatwole@umassp.edu
HEATWOLE, Deirdre 617-287-5324 236 E dheatwole@umassp.edu
HEAVENER, Mac 904-596-2400 122 D macheavener@tbc.edu
HEBARD, John 907-474-6831 10 I jahebard@alaska.edu
HEBBARD, Don 972-279-6511 479 H dhebbard@amberton.edu
HEBBARD, Matthew 956-872-2147 494 H mshebbar@southtexascollege.edu
HEBDON, Catherine 907-277-1000 10 E contact@chartercollege.edu
HEBERER, Janet 402-844-7021 299 I janet@northeast.edu
HEBERLE, Julia, F 610-921-7581 421 E jheberle@alb.edu
HEBERLING, Michael 810-766-4374 247 G mike.heberling@baker.edu
HEBERT, Anglea 985-858-5709 210 G angela.hebert@fletcher.edu
HEBERT, Barbara, B 985-549-3894 216 C bhebert@selu.edu
HEBERT, Carol 318-487-5443 210 E chebert@ltc.edu
HEBERT, Carolyn 860-515-3880 90 E chebert@charteroak.edu
HEBERT, Debborah 707-654-1182 33 C dhebert@csum.edu
HEBERT, Helen, D 336-334-5371 379 B helen_dennison@uncg.edu
HEBERT, Jaimie 936-294-1001 501 D hebert@shsu.edu
HEBERT, Joseph 281-998-6150 494 B joseph.hebert@sjcd.edu
HEBERT, Mark 502-852-3133 207 E mark.hebert@louisville.edu
HEBERT, Rudolph 413-572-5699 238 F rudy@wsc.ma.edu
HEBERT, Sally 505-925-8502 321 G shebert@unm.edu
HEBERT, III, Stanley 510-885-4238 34 E stanley.hebert@csueastbay.edu
HECHT, Boruch 973-267-9404 313 B boruch.hecht@gmail.com
HECHT, George, E 541-346-2290 419 B ghecht@uoregon.edu
HECHT, Laura 661-654-2124 34 A lhecht@csub.edu
HECHT, Pinchas 718-645-0536 341 D phecht@thejnet.com
HECK, Barbara, H 410-778-7805 229 D bheck2@washcoll.edu
HECK, Catherine, J 740-283-6498 391 A check@franciscan.edu
HECK, Paul 773-878-3194 163 F pheck@staugustine.edu
HECK, Thomas, R 701-252-3467 381 C theck@jc.edu
HECK, Traci 918-595-8634 412 H theck@tulsacc.edu
HECKAMAN, Daniel, A 218-477-2300 267 F daniel.heckaman@mnstate.edu
HECKAMAN, Judith, M 717-560-8278 433 D jheckaman@lbc.edu
HECKARD, Bonnie 734-462-4400 258 A bheckard@schoolcraft.edu
HECKEL, David 704-463-3124 375 F david.heckel@fsmail.pfeiffer.edu
HECKELER, Dave 775-850-0700 302 C dheckeler@morrison.neumont.edu
HECKENDORN, Miles, J 320-308-3453 269 A mjheckendorn@stcloudstate.edu
HECKENLAIBLE, Anna 605-331-6651 466 E anna.heckenlaible@usiouxfalls.edu
HECKER, Jeffrey, E 207-581-1954 220 A jhecker@maine.edu
HECKER, Laurel, A 340-692-3160 568 E lhecker@live.uvi.edu
HECKERT, L. Randall 330-471-8280 395 F rheckert@malone.edu
HECKLER, Mark, A 219-464-5115 181 C mark.heckler@valpo.edu
HECKMAN, Mary Ellen 610-372-4721 445 C mheckman@racc.edu
HECKMAN, Richard, A 717-245-1308 427 F heckman@dickinson.edu
HECTOR, Gerald 704-378-1190 366 A ghector@jcsu.edu
HEDAYAT, Nasser 407-582-3326 123 B nhedayat@valenciacollege.edu
HEDBERG, Nancy 503-375-7010 415 F nhedberg@corban.edu
HEDBERG, Rick 701-858-3042 382 A rick.hedberg@minotstateu.edu
HEDBERG, Ulf 202-250-2642 98 B ulf.hedberg@gallaudet.edu
HEDDERICK, Malgorzata 617-253-9358 241 D
HEDDLESTON, George 937-775-7098 406 C george.heddleston@wright.edu
HEDDLESTON, Patrick, D 330-823-6572 404 C heddlepd@mountunion.edu
HEDEEN, Deborah, L 208-282-2783 143 H hededebo@isu.edu
HEDEEN, Paul 734-384-4152 255 D phedeen@monroeccc.edu
HEDGE, Clarence, A 405-466-3419 408 G cahedge@langston.edu
HEDGE, Dennis 605-688-6197 466 C dennis.hedge@sdstate.edu
HEDGECOCK, Wally 210-524-2100 19 A wally.hedgecock@phoenix.edu
HEDGEMAN, Denita 901-435-1729 470 D denita_hedgeman@loc.edu
HEDGER, Mark 417-268-6023 278 J mhedger@gobbc.edu
HEDGES, Amy, M 859-371-9393 198 G ahedges@beckfield.edu
HEDGES, Denise, C 417-667-8181 280 E dhedges@cottey.edu
HEDGES, Douglas 609-343-4911 307 C hedges@atlantic.edu
HEDGES, Jerris, R 808-692-0881 141 G jerris@hawaii.edu
HEDGES, Mark, C 270-852-3242 204 A mhedges@kwc.edu
HEDGES, Mimi 573-442-2211 290 C mhedges@stephens.edu
HEDGES, Tammy, L 901-678-5314 474 C thedges@memphis.edu
HEDLIN, Carol 907-796-6016 11 A carol.hedlin@uas.alaska.edu
HEDLUN, Randy 417-862-9533 282 A rhedlun@globaluniversity.edu
HEDLUND, Joyce, B 207-454-1001 219 B jhedlund@wccc.me.edu
HEDLUND, Paul, H 785-827-5541 194 F paul.hedlund@kwu.edu
HEDMAN, Shawn 507-537-6292 269 E shawn.hedman@smsu.edu
HEDRICK, Erica 978-927-2217 234 D ehedrick@endicott.edu
HEDRICK, Jennifer 303-457-2757 84 J jhedrick@cci.edu
HEDRICK, Van 940-668-7347 491 E vhedrick@nctc.edu
HEEKE, JR., David 989-774-3046 249 C heeke1dw@cmich.edu
HEEN, Shellee 808-544-0290 140 G sheen@hpu.edu
HEENAN, Christine 617-495-1703 235 D christine_heenan@harvard.edu
HEENAN, Elizabeth, A 215-951-1240 432 I heenan@lasalle.edu
HEER, Angela 816-501-3727 278 I angela.heer@avila.edu
HEEREN, Matthew 660-626-2064 278 D mheeren@atsu.edu
HEERMAN, Heather 508-565-1325 245 A hheerman@stonehill.edu
HEERMANN, Keith 417-862-9533 282 A kheermann@globaluniversity.edu
HEERSINK, Heather 719-587-7759 80 L heather_heersink@adams.edu
HEETER-BASS, Janet, A 740-826-8080 397 A jheeter@muskingum.edu
HEETLAND, David, L 847-866-3970 151 D david.heetland@garrett.edu
HEFFELFINGER, Sara 928-777-3710 14 C heffels@erau.edu
HEFFELFINGER, Scott 610-372-4721 445 C sheffelfinger@racc.edu
HEFFERIN, Cathy, D 336-633-0208 373 A cdhefferin@randolph.edu
HEFFERNAN, Gloria, C 315-445-5438 338 B heffergc@lemoyne.edu
HEFFERNAN, Robert, J 848-932-7305 314 B heffernan@instlres.rutgers.edu
HEFFERNAN, Thomas, J 561-237-7270 113 D theffernan@lynn.edu
HEFFLEY, David, P 215-699-5700 433 G dheffley@lsb.edu
HEFFNER, David, B 570-321-4278 435 D heffner@lycoming.edu
HEFFRON, Jay 949-480-4028 69 J heffron@soka.edu
HEFLEY, Jacqueline, D 512-404-4826 481 D jhefley@austinseminary.edu
HEFLIN, David 605-361-0200 464 B dheflin@ctuonline.edu
HEFLIN, Sherry 717-815-1257 452 G sheflin@ycp.edu
HEFNER, David, S 706-721-6569 130 D dhefner@georgiahealth.edu
HEGARTY, Kevin, P 512-471-1422 505 D hegarty@mail.utexas.edu
HEGARTY, Staci 815-534-3300 162 A staci.hegarty@rasmussen.edu
HEGDE, Raju 909-389-3362 65 B rhegde@craftonhills.edu
HEGEDUS, George, C 610-799-1132 434 D ghegedus@lccc.edu
HEGEDUS, Mary Ellen 574-239-8391 172 M mhegedus@hcc-nd.edu
HEGEL, Barbara 907-796-6457 11 A barbara.hegel@uas.alaska.edu
HEGEMAN, Diane 303-797-5702 81 D diane.hegeman@arapahoe.edu
HEGGEMEYER, Terri 402-844-7263 299 I roseann@northeast.edu
HEGLAND, Paul, R 262-551-5858 546 I paul@carthage.edu
HEGMAN, John, P 404-471-6109 123 I jhegman@agnesscott.edu
HEGRANES, Colleen 651-690-8844 270 L cahegranes@stkate.edu
HEGYES, Louis, L 610-799-1575 434 D admissions@lccc.edu
HEICHELBECK, Tamie 618-664-7000 151 F tamie.heichelbeck@greenville.edu
HEIDA, Debbie 706-236-2207 126 C dheida@berry.edu
HEIDBREDER, Kay, K 540-231-6293 529 G heidbred@vt.edu
HEIDE, Gale 406-586-3585 294 G gale.heide@montanabiblecollege.edu
HEIDEL, Wie 409-740-4547 497 F heidelw@tamug.edu
HEIDEMAN, Carl, E 616-395-7670 252 D heideman@hope.edu
HEIDEN, Jill 843-661-8003 458 B jill.heiden@fdtc.edu
HEIDER, Cindy 816-271-4364 286 G heider@missouriwestern.edu
HEIDER, Donald, B 312-915-6548 157 C dheider@luc.edu
HEIDER, Mary Jane 585-345-6813 334 F mjheider@genesee.edu
HEIDERMAN, JR., Donald, L 812-265-2580 177 A dheiderm@ivytech.edu
HEIDERMAN, Paula 812-537-4010 177 A pheiderm@ivytech.edu
HEIDICK, Venesa, A 979-845-1059 497 E vheidick@tamu.edu
HEIDINGSFIELD, Michael, J 512-499-4688 505 B mheidingsfield@utsystem.edu
HEIDKE, Stephen 314-392-2372 285 J heidkesj@mobap.edu
HEIDRICH, Mark, W 240-895-4208 226 A mwheidrich@smcm.edu
HEIDRICK, Judy 785-738-9058 195 G jheidrick@ncktc.edu
HEIDT, Loretta, A 701-483-2314 381 G loretta.heidt@dickinsonstate.edu
HEIDTKE, Staci, L 715-836-5358 551 A heidtksl@uwec.edu
HEIER, Greg 402-826-8583 297 G greg.heier@doane.edu
HEIFETZ, Harry, S 262-554-2010 549 A harryh.21stcentury@rcn.com
HEIFETZ, Harry, S 262-554-2010 158 E harryh.21stcentury@rcn.com
HEIFNER, Bryan 432-335-6512 492 A bheifner@odessa.edu
HEIGH, Lorraine 301-552-1400 229 C lheigh@bible.edu
HEIGHES, Robert 734-487-1222 250 F rheighes@emich.edu
HEIGHT, Linda, L 248-204-2128 254 B lheight@ltu.edu
HEIGLE, Christopher, A 870-633-4480 21 F cheigle@eacc.edu
HEIKEL, Karen 920-424-1463 551 E heikelk@uwosh.edu
HEIKKILA, Christina 910-362-7000 368 H
HEIL, Elissa 479-979-1338 26 A eheil@ozarks.edu
HEIL, Lina 619-388-2759 65 G lheil@sdccd.edu

HEIL, Marti 812-855-7137 173 E heilm@indiana.edu
HEIL, Mary Colleen 717-396-7833 440 K mcheil@pcad.edu
HEILEMAN, Gregory 505-277-2611 321 C heileman@unm.edu
HEILGEIST, Peter, J 435-586-7732 511 D heilgeist@suu.edu
HEILKE, Thomas, W 785-864-8040 197 B heilke@ku.edu
HEILLE, Gregory 314-256-8881 278 G heille@ai.edu
HEILMAN, Carl, R 620-792-9301 190 H heilmanc@bartonccc.edu
HEILMAN, Timothy Bruce 804-204-1209 516 J theilman@btsr.edu
HEILMAN, Valerie 701-228-5437 382 E valerie.heilman@dakotacollege.edu
HEILSTEDT, Martin, R 425-235-2369 537 A mheilstedt@rtc.edu
HEIM, Peggy, M 610-799-1532 434 D pheim@lccc.edu
HEIMAN, Kelly, J 262-524-7695 546 H kheiman@carrollu.edu
HEIMAN, Scott, R 608-246-6018 554 D sheiman@madisoncollege.org
HEIMANN, Anne 402-481-3908 296 I anne.heimann@bryanlgh.org
HEIMANN, B. Sue 419-289-5324 384 G sheimann@ashland.edu
HEIMARCK, Heather 617-262-5000 231 G heather.heimarck@the-bac.edu
HEIMBROCK, Kimberly 859-572-5139 205 H heimbrockk@nku.edu
HEIMBURGER, David 314-977-2233 289 C dheimbu1@slu.edu
HEIMEL, Theres 952-944-0080 263 I theimel@nti.edu
HEIMERL, Marc, D 920-923-8796 548 E mdheimerl78@marianuniversity.edu
HEIMMERMANN, Dan 662-329-7142 276 A dheimmermann@vpaa.muw.edu
HEIMOVITZ, Issac 718-438-1002 340 G
HEIN, Audrey, D 563-333-6364 188 F heinaudreyd@sau.edu
HEIN, Barbara 607-778-5222 324 G heinbg@sunybroome.edu
HEIN, Beth, A 715-852-1380 553 H bhein1@cvtc.edu
HEIN, Candy 956-326-4483 497 D candy.hein@tamiu.edu
HEIN, Gail 908-709-7610 316 B hein@ucc.edu
HEIN, Holly, A 207-948-9244 219 H hein@unity.edu
HEIN, Sherril 909-948-7582 67 A sherrilh@sjvc.edu
HEIN, Steven, M 912-478-0831 131 E shein@georgiasouthern.edu
HEINDL, Michael, J 601-928-6234 275 E michael.heindl@mgccc.edu
HEINEMAN, Pete 402-557-7146 296 H pete.heineman@bellevue.edu
HEINEMAN, William 978-556-3327 240 E wheineman@necc.mass.edu
HEINEMANN, Brian 760-366-5278 43 H bheinemann@cmccd.edu
HEINEMANN, Dovid 732-367-4259 311 C
HEINEMANN, Ken 813-935-5700 116 A kenheinemann@remingtoncollege.edu
HEINEN, Judith 313-927-1256 254 E jheinen@marygrove.edu
HEINEN, Terry 615-230-3227 476 C terry.heinen@volstate.edu
HEININGER, Carole 610-789-6700 445 B cheininger@prismcareerinstitute.edu
HEINLEIN, Chester 609-894-9311 308 B cheinlei@bcc.edu
HEINOLD, Sandra 361-570-4286 504 A heinolds@uhv.edu
HEINRICH, Carl 913-469-8500 194 B heinrich@jccc.edu
HEINRICH, George, F 973-972-4631 316 C heinrich@umdnj.edu
HEINRICH, George, F 973-972-4631 316 F heinrige@umdnj.edu
HEINRICH, Heike 216-687-2051 388 D h.heinrich@csuohio.edu
HEINRICH, Mark, A 205-391-5880 6 I mheinrich@sheltonstate.edu
HEINRICH, Matt, W 816-501-4064 288 A matt.heinrich@rockhurst.edu
HEINRICH, Peggy 847-214-6911 150 F pheinrich@elgin.edu
HEINRICH, Sam 916-577-2200 79 G sheinrich@jessup.edu
HEINRICHS, Abby 262-551-6100 546 I ahanna@carthage.edu
HEINS, Donald 607-962-9264 331 C dheins1@corning-cc.edu
HEINSELMAN, Gregg, M 715-425-4444 552 C gregg.heinselman@uwrf.edu
HEINSOHN, Lori 701-224-5690 382 D lori.heinsohn@bismarckstate.edu

HEINTZ, Barbara, B 808-933-3116 141 F bheintz@hawaii.edu
HEINTZ, David 860-628-4751 93 C dheintz@lincolncollegene.edu
HEINTZ, Jill 315-792-5584 341 E jheintz@mvcc.edu
HEINTZE, Michael, R 512-245-1977 501 F mh63@txstate.edu
HEINTZELMAN, Jonathan, R 312-915-7262 157 C jheintz@luc.edu
HEINZ, Anne, K 303-492-2202 88 H anne.heinz@colorado.edu
HEINZ, Heidi 217-854-3231 146 A hhein@blackburn.edu
HEINZ, Kartha 206-876-6100 538 A facilities@theseattleschool.edu
HEINZEN, Kathleen, M 920-832-6561 548 B kathleen.m.heinzen@lawrence.edu
HEINZMAN, Mary, B 563-333-6241 188 F heinzmanmaryb@sau.edu
HEISER, Andrew 712-274-5493 187 G heiser@morningside.edu
HEISER, Gregory, M 405-325-3221 413 C gheiser@ou.edu
HEISEY, Donald 252-493-7289 372 H dheisey@email.pittcc.edu
HEISEY, Nancy 540-432-4141 518 F nancy.heisey@emu.edu
HEISEY, Terry, M 717-866-5775 429 A theisey@evangelical.edu
HEISLER, John, F 614-885-5585 401 B jheisler@pcj.edu
HEISSERER, Gary 641-784-5265 185 B heissere@graceland.edu
HEISSERER, Nick 218-855-8038 265 J nheisserer@clcmn.edu
HEIST, Daniel, P 814-865-1359 438 G dph3@psu.edu
HEIST, Richard 386-226-6634 105 H richard.heist@erau.edu
HEITHAUS, Peter, A 314-516-5809 291 D peter_heithaus@umsl.edu
HEITKEMPER, Mary 509-313-4231 534 F heitkemper@gonzaga.edu
HEITMILLER, Janet 713-221-8678 503 F heitmillerj@uhd.edu
HEITZ, Tim 717-560-8211 433 D theitz@lbc.edu
HEITZENRATER, Kim, D 931-598-1121 472 L kheitzen@sewanee.edu
HEITZMANN, Dennis, E 814-865-0966 438 G deh8@psu.edu
HEJL, Cindy 303-556-4741 86 F hejlc@msudenver.edu
HEKKEL, Jerry 206-726-5111 533 D jhekkel@cornish.edu
HELBERT, Lee, A 708-709-3639 161 D lhelbert@prairiestate.edu
HELBIG, Tuesdi 270-745-3250 208 A tuesdi.helbig@wku.edu
HELBING, Shirley 570-702-8918 431 L shelbing@johnson.edu
HELBLE, Joseph 603-646-2238 304 J joseph.helble@dartmouth.edu
HELD, Jeffrey 607-733-2300 359 C jheld@uscny.edu
HELD, Steve 636-227-2100 284 B steve.held@logan.edu
HELDT, Kim 812-749-1218 178 H kheldt@oak.edu
HELEKAR, Andrea 213-624-1200 46 L ahelekar@fidm.edu
HELENS, Joyce, M 320-308-5017 269 B jhelens@sctcc.edu
HELFGOT, Steven 480-731-8098 15 D steve.helfgot@domail.maricopa.edu
HELFRICH, Christine 301-846-2518 222 G chelfrich@frederick.edu
HELFRICH, Glenda 806-743-2986 502 B glenda.helfrich@ttuhsc.edu
HELFRICH, Stephen, P 812-464-1782 181 B shelfric@usi.edu
HELGERSON, Carolyn 605-221-3108 464 D chelgerson@kilian.edu
HELGESEN, Paul 978-867-4730 235 A paul.helgesen@gordon.edu
HELGESEN, Pete 913-360-7476 191 A phelgesen@benedictine.edu
HELGESON, Danyel 507-433-0526 268 H danyel.helgeson@riverland.edu
HELGESON, Richard, J 731-881-7380 477 G helgeson@utm.edu
HELIS, James 516-773-5348 558 I helisj@usmma.edu
HELLA, Lori, L 989-774-7194 249 C hella1ll@cmich.edu
HELLAND, Karen 541-888-7212 420 C khelland@socc.edu
HELLENBRAND, Harry 818-677-2957 35 F harry.hellenbrand@csun.edu
HELLER, Adam 623-245-4600 18 J aheller@uti.edu
HELLER, Caren, A 212-746-5767 360 C cah2021@med.cornell.edu

HELLER, Carrie 765-973-8404 173 F hellerc@iue.edu
HELLER, Donald, E 517-355-1734 255 A dheller@msu.edu
HELLER, James 262-595-2455 552 A james.heller@uwp.edu
HELLER, Joshua, W 585-785-1335 334 A hellerjw@flcc.edu
HELLER, Leonard, E 859-218-6512 207 D lehell2@uky.edu
HELLER, Tracy 858-635-4763 27 E theller@alliant.edu
HELLER, William 727-873-4979 121 C wheller@mail.usf.edu
HELLER-ROSS, Holly 518-564-5180 354 B hellerhb@plattsburgh.edu
HELLER-STERN, Miriam 310-476-9777 28 G mstern@ajula.edu
HELLERSTEIN, Laurel 978-232-2153 234 D lhellers@endicott.edu
HELLERUD, Nancy 314-246-7440 292 J nancyhellerud@webster.edu
HELLESON, Connie 503-777-7705 420 A chelleson@reed.edu
HELLIE, Thomas 503-883-2408 416 H thellie@linfield.edu
HELLIGE, Joseph 310-338-2733 56 E jhellige@lmu.edu
HELLING, Mary Kay 605-688-4173 466 C mary.helling@sdstate.edu
HELLING, Nathan, M 605-336-6588 465 D nhelling@sfseminary.edu
HELLMERS, Nathan, J 919-508-2303 380 E njhellmers@peace.edu
HELLMICH, David, M 859-246-4649 201 H david.hellmich@kctcs.edu
HELLMUND, Paul, C 413-369-4044 233 E hellmund@csld.edu
HELLUMS, Duane 502-410-6200 200 L dhellums@galencollege.edu
HELLWIG, Beth, A 715-836-5992 551 A hellwiba@uwec.edu
HELLYER, Brenda 281-998-6100 493 G brenda.hellyer@sjcd.edu
HELM, Darlene 225-359-9218 209 J dhelm@catc.edu
HELM, Hunt, C 502-272-8046 198 H hhelm@bellarmine.edu
HELM, Jennifer 304-724-3700 540 F jhelm@apus.edu
HELM, Jonathan, C 254-710-8824 482 A jonathan_helm@baylor.edu
HELM, Karen, P 919-515-6648 378 C karen_helm@ncsu.edu
HELM, Lloyd, L 503-255-0332 417 C lhelm@multnomah.edu
HELM, Marlene, M 859-846-5726 204 H mhelm@midway.edu
HELM, Peyton, R 484-664-3125 437 C pres@muhlenberg.edu
HELM, Ron, C 870-368-2027 23 A rhelm@ozarka.edu
HELM, Scott 641-782-1481 189 E helm@swcciowa.edu
HELM, Steve 540-831-5471 523 A shelm@radford.edu
HELM, Thomas 603-668-2211 305 I t.helm@snhu.edu
HELMAN, Jay, W 970-943-2114 89 E jhelman@western.edu
HELMBRECHT, Lena 912-260-4314 137 B lena.helmbrecht@sgc.edu
HELMBURGER, David 314-977-2233 289 C heimbu1@slu.edu
HELMER, Robert, C 440-826-2424 384 K rhelmer@bw.edu
HELMER, Shannon 610-799-1857 434 D shelmer@lccc.edu
HELMICH, Doris 520-494-5200 13 D doris.helmich@centralaz.edu
HELMICK, Michael, S 336-342-4261 373 E
HELMICK, Sarah 330-675-8961 393 J shelmick@kent.edu
HELMICK, Tom 724-852-3210 451 B thelmick@waynesburg.edu
HELMING, Jay 202-685-3909 557 I jay.helming@ndu.edu
HELMS, Bryan 229-732-5946 124 E bryanhelms@andrewcollege.edu
HELMS, Chris 828-765-7351 372 A chelms@mayland.edu
HELMS, Doris, R 864-656-3243 456 E biol110@clemson.edu
HELMS, Jim 812-537-4010 177 A jhelms@ivytech.edu
HELMS, Lance 912-538-3207 137 E lhelms@southeasterntech.edu
HELMS, Mark 704-330-6127 369 D mark.helms@cpcc.edu
HELMS, Sherrie 912-583-3206 126 F shelms@bpc.edu
HELMS, Steve 334-222-6591 5 F shelms@lbwcc.edu

HELMSING, Debra, F 260-665-4240 180 D helmsingd@trine.edu
HELMSTETTER, Donald, W 651-641-8227 263 A helmstetter@csp.edu
HELMUS, D. Mark 317-940-9332 170 F mhelmus@butler.edu
HELOU, Ibrahim (Abe) 909-593-3511 75 E ahelou@laverne.edu
HELSABECK, Hank 503-554-2143 415 I hhelsabeck@georgefox.edu
HELSEL, Dennis 252-398-6484 363 G helsel@chowan.edu
HELSEN, Michael, L 231-777-5206 248 E mike.helsen@baker.edu
HELSETH, Joe 423-697-2606 474 D
HELSHAM, Irene 684-699-9155 559 C i.helsham@amsamoa.edu
HELSPER, Nancy 320-589-6012 271 G helsper@morris.umn.edu
HELTON, Karen 903-927-3369 509 E khelton@wileyc.edu
HELTON, Kasey 678-915-3998 137 G khelton@spsu.edu
HELTON, Patti 303-871-3289 89 A phelton@du.edu
HELTON, Richard, E 812-888-4208 181 D president@vinu.edu
HELTON, Tom 706-507-8909 127 G helton_tom@columbusstate.edu
HELTON, Tonja 813-620-1446 110 D
HELTSLEY, Susan, D 360-438-4534 537 B sheltsley@stmartin.edu
HELVERING, Christal, R 765-641-4205 169 E crhelvering@anderson.edu
HELVEY, Pam 417-864-7220 281 H
HELVY, Eric 256-761-6277 7 G ehelvy@talladega.edu
HELWICK, Christine 562-951-4500 33 H chelwick@calstate.edu
HELWIG, Christine, A 518-629-7343 336 C c.helwig@hvcc.edu
HELWIG, Daniel, S 717-815-1502 452 G dhelwig@ycp.edu
HELWIG, Denice 707-826-3300 36 E dh7003@humboldt.edu
HELWIG, Susan, M 570-674-6368 436 F shelwig@misericordia.edu
HEMANS, Peter 828-694-1723 368 E peterh@blueridge.edu
HEMBREE, Lois, D 620-421-6700 194 G loish@labette.edu
HEMESATH, Michael 320-363-2882 271 A sjpresident@csbsju.edu
HEMINGWAY, Sally, A 478-757-5212 139 E shemingway@wesleyancollege.edu
HEMLICK, Lisa, M 610-341-5830 428 E lhemlick@eastern.edu
HEMMASI, Harriette 401-863-2162 453 B harriette_hemmasi@brown.edu
HEMMING, Erik G, C 414-229-4201 551 D hemmingc@aux.uwm.edu
HEMMINGER, John, C 949-824-5796 74 B jchemmin@uci.edu
HEMMINGSEN, Jens 614-236-6105 386 E jhemming@capital.edu
HEMMITT, Ernita 404-880-6128 127 C ehemmitt@cau.edu
HEMMITT, Ernita 404-880-6701 127 C ehemmitt@cau.edu
HEMPE, Laura, J 414-410-4194 546 G ljhempe@stritch.edu
HEMPEL, Lamont, C 909-748-8589 76 C monty_hempel@redlands.edu
HEMPHILL, Brian, O 304-766-3111 544 F bhemphill@wvstateu.edu
HEMPHILL, Constance 704-334-6882 367 H chemphill@nlts.edu
HEMPHILL, Michael, R 318-869-5104 208 H mhemphill@centenary.edu
HEMPHILL, Teale 719-336-1591 86 B teale.hemphill@lamarcc.edu
HEMPHILL, Valory 800-438-6932 492 E vhemphill@parkercc.edu
HEMPSTEAD, Laurie, A 518-381-1271 350 E hempstla@sunysccc.edu
HEMRICK, Robert, D 731-425-2636 475 C dhemrick@jscc.edu
HEMSEY, Charles 516-796-4800 342 H chemsey@nycc.edu
HENAHAN, David 518-587-2100 355 G david.henahan@esc.edu
HENAN, Carmen 505-424-2302 318 D chenan@iaia.edu
HENARD, Kevin 817-760-5831 487 G khenard@hillcollege.edu
HENAULT, Cheri 860-701-5052 93 E henault_c@mitchell.edu
HENBERG, Marvin 208-459-5502 143 D
HENCHY, Dolores 201-355-1133 310 B henchyd@felician.edu
HENCK, Anita 626-815-5348 30 G hwilliams@apu.edu
HENDEE, Helen 706-737-1442 125 G hhendee@aug.edu

HENRY, Dolph 865-981-8141 471 B
dolph.henry@maryvillecollege.edu

HENRY, Donna, P 239-590-7156 119 B
dhenry@fgcu.edu

HENRY, Frank 406-395-4313 296 E
fghenry_9@hotmail.com

HENRY, Jamie 618-544-8657 152 H
henryj@iecc.edu

HENRY, Janis 404-965-6504 124 D
jhenry@aiuniv.edu

HENRY, Jeffery 406-395-4875 296 E
jhenry@stonechild.edu

HENRY, Jennifer 314-529-9552 284 C
jhenry@maryville.edu

HENRY, Jerlynn 505-786-4180 318 I
jhenry@navajotech.edu

HENRY, Jerry 903-223-3012 498 F
jerry.henry@tamut.edu

HENRY, Jon 207-621-3000 220 B
jhenry@maine.edu

HENRY, Jonathan 727-726-1153 103 I
jonathanhenry@clearwater.edu

HENRY, Katie 501-450-5007 25 H
khenry@uca.edu

HENRY, Kelly, K 585-292-5627 325 B
kkhenry@bryantstratton.edu

HENRY, Kelly, K 585-292-5627 325 C
kkhenry@bryantstratton.edu

HENRY, Kevin, C 717-866-5775 429 A
khenry@evangelical.edu

HENRY, Kim 318-676-7811 211 D
ksnider@nwltc.edu

HENRY, Kim 712-325-3445 186 F
khenry@iwcc.edu

HENRY, Larry 701-477-7862 383 F
lhenry@tm.edu

HENRY, Linda 913-360-7500 191 A
lhenry@benedictine.edu

HENRY, Marci 970-521-6617 86 K
marci.henry@njc.edu

HENRY, Margaret 303-871-3740 89 A
mhenry@du.edu

HENRY, Margaret Rose 302-888-5284 96 F
mrhenry@dtcc.edu

HENRY, Matthew 903-233-3510 490 A
matthewhenry@letu.edu

HENRY, Melanie 985-380-2436 211 I
melanie.henry@ltc.edu

HENRY, Melody 406-395-4313 296 E
mrbhenry@hotmail.com

HENRY, Melody 903-434-8148 491 F
mhenry@ntcc.edu

HENRY, Nick 706-272-4435 128 C
nhenry@daltonstate.edu

HENRY, Patrick, J 304-336-8250 544 D
phenry@westliberty.edu

HENRY, Philip, W 717-477-1481 443 E
pwhenr@ship.edu

HENRY, Raylean 615-366-3917 473 D
raylean.henry@tbr.edu

HENRY, Rita 402-554-2779 301 A
rhenry@unomaha.edu

HENRY, Robert, H 405-208-5032 410 A
rhenry@okcu.edu

HENRY, Ronnie 229-317-6700 128 D
ronnie.henry@darton.edu

HENRY, Ronnie, A 229-317-6700 128 D
ronnie.henry@darton.edu

HENRY, Shannon, B 336-750-2020 380 B
henrysb@wssu.edu

HENRY, Susan, P 802-865-4422 515 E
henrys@ccv.edu

HENRY, TOR, Terence 740-283-6216 391 A
thenry@franciscan.edu

HENRY, Terrence 914-674-7607 340 F
thenry@mercy.edu

HENRY, Thad 704-463-3034 375 F
thad.henry@fsmail.pfeiffer.edu

HENRY, Veronica 631-420-2622 356 A
veronica.henry@farmingdale.edu

HENRY-CROWE, Susan 404-727-6226 129 D
shenryc@emory.edu

HENRY-DAVENPORT,
Jannette 706-821-8636 135 G
jhenrydavenport@paine.edu

HENRY-MITCHELL, Kim 856-691-8600 309 B
kmitchell@cccnj.edu

HENRY-QUINN, Barbara 877-442-0505 89 C
barbara.henry-quinn@rockies.edu

HENRY ROBINSON,
Shanelle 914-773-3775 345 F
shenryrobinson@pace.edu

HENSAL, Nathan 815-599-3599 152 B
nathan.hensal@highland.edu

HENSCHEL, Paul, D 440-525-7060 394 F
phenschel@lakelandcc.edu

HENSEL, Chester 610-876-7300 451 F
cahensel@widener.edu

HENSGEN, Brian, C 217-442-3044 148 G
bhensgen@dacc.edu

HENSHAW, Debbie 706-649-1888 128 A
dhenshaw@columbustech.edu

HENSHAW, Rodney, N 515-271-3993 184 D
rod.henshaw@drake.edu

HENSLER, Douglas, A 316-978-3200 198 A
doug.hensler@wichita.edu

HENSLER, Gary 903-463-8650 487 C
henslerg@grayson.edu

HENSLEY, Bridgette, C 608-785-8073 551 C
bhensley@uwlax.edu

HENSLEY, Frances, S 304-696-6690 544 B
hensleyf@marshall.edu

HENSLEY, Glenn, S 540-224-6752 520 I
gshensley@jchs.edu

HENSLEY, Kimberly, S 815-753-8494 160 B
khensley@niu.edu

HENSLEY, Linda 619-421-6700 71 D
lhensley@swccd.edu

HENSLEY, Mary 512-223-7618 481 B
mhensley@austincc.edu

HENSLEY, Michele, R 540-432-4139 518 F
michele.hensley@emu.edu

HENSLEY, Mike 704-216-3651 373 F
mike.hensley@rccc.edu

HENSLEY, Ron 417-255-7255 286 D
ronhensley@missouristate.edu

HENSLEY, Sarah, L 304-367-4692 543 B
sarah.hensley@pierpont.edu

HENSLEY, Scott 580-745-3198 412 C
shensley@se.edu

HENSLEY, Shane 810-989-2107 248 G
shane.hensley@baker.edu

HENSLEY, Stephen, W 304-696-2269 544 B
hensley@marshall.edu

HENSLEY, Wanda, F 501-977-2028 25 G
hensley@uaccm.edu

HENSON, Brandi 405-682-1611 409 F
bhenson@occc.edu

HENSON, Emily 618-252-5400 164 I
emily.henson@sic.edu

HENSON, Greg 630-705-8250 160 C
ghenson@seminary.edu

HENSON, Jackie 614-251-4548 398 F
hensonj2@ohiodominican.edu

HENSON, Jena 312-752-2182 155 C
jena.henson@kendall.edu

HENSON, Joel 805-482-2755 64 E
jhenson@stjohnsem.edu

HENSON, Kevin 650-574-6581 67 G
hensonk@smccd.edu

HENSON, Mark 618-985-3741 154 G
markhenson@jalc.edu

HENSON, Pamella, A 314-935-5277 292 I
hensonp@wustl.edu

HENSON, Rob 812-426-2865 177 C
rhenson@wvutech.edu

HENSON, Scott 706-721-4416 130 D
shenson@georgiahealth.edu

HENSON, Travis 618-545-3177 155 B
thenson@kaskaskia.edu

HENSON-WILLIAMS,
Paula 253-864-3229 536 H
phenson@pierce.ctc.edu

HENSRUD, Faith 715-394-8449 552 F
fhensrud@uwsuper.edu

HENSRUD, Faith, C 715-394-8455 552 F
fhensrud@uwsuper.edu

HENSS, Mark 217-206-7796 167 C
henss.mark@uis.edu

HENTHORN, Janet 312-235-3507 164 F
j.henthorn@shimer.edu

HENTHORNE, Michael 541-737-2416 418 F
michael.henthorne@oregonstate.edu

HENTON, June, M 334-844-4790 1 F
hentoju@auburn.edu

HENTSCHEL, Alain, R 386-312-4302 116 F
alainhentschel@sjrstate.edu

HENTZ, Herbert, E 413-775-1809 239 E
hentz@gcc.mass.edu

HENZEL, JR., John, R 706-245-7226 129 C
jhenzel@ec.edu

HENZY, John 856-415-2106 310 D
jhenzy@gccnj.edu

HEO, Chan 714-517-1945 30 J
chieffinancial@buc.edu

HEOS, Pamela 517-371-5140 258 F
heosp@cooley.edu

HEPBURN, Deborah, G 814-371-2090 448 G
dhepburn@triangle-tech.edu

HEPBURN, Deborah, G 814-371-2090 448 F
dhepburn@triangle-tech.edu

HEPBURN, Valerie 912-279-5705 127 E
president@ccga.edu

HEPERI, Vernon, L 801-422-4771 509 H
vernon_heperi@byu.edu

HEPHNER-LABANC,
Brandi 662-915-5050 277 D
bhl@olemiss.edu

HEPLER, Lisa, L 814-393-2229 442 B
lhepler@clarion.edu

HEPLER, Meghan, E 570-321-4231 435 D
hepler@lycoming.edu

HEPLER, Robin 614-222-6163 388 G
rhepler@ccad.edu

HEPNER, Mickey 405-974-2809 413 B
mhepner@uco.edu

HEPPNER, Angela 417-624-7070 284 D
aheppner@messengercollege.edu

HEPPNER, Harold, H 406-353-2607 293 E
hheppner@mail.fbcc.edu

HEPPNER, Keith 956-380-8171 493 D
kheppner@riogrande.edu

HERALD, John 606-886-3863 201 G
john.herald@kctcs.edu

HERALD, Sara, B 305-899-3080 101 M
sherald@mail.barry.edu

HERB, Amanda, K 740-374-8716 405 G
aherb@wscc.edu

HERBERT, Derek 970-521-6714 86 K
derek.herbert@njc.edu

HERBERT, George, E 319-335-3179 182 F
george-herbert@uiowa.edu

HERBERT, Jim 678-915-6824 137 G
jherbert@spsu.edu

HERBERT, Mike 541-888-7705 420 C
mherbert@socc.edu

HERBERT, Nancy 870-633-4480 21 F
nherbert@eacc.edu

HERBERT-ASHTON,
Marilyn, J 540-857-6372 529 B
mherbert-ashton@virginiawestern.edu

HERBERTZ, Anita 317-955-6021 177 I
aherbertz@marian.edu

HERBKERSMAN, Neil 937-512-2524 401 J
neil.herbkersman@sinclair.edu

HERBRAND, Laurie 209-228-2741 74 D
lherbrand@ucmerced.edu

HERBST, Adam 320-363-3819 271 A
aherbst@csbsju.edu

HERBST, Chet 208-792-2240 144 B
cgherbst@lcsc.edu

HERBST, Daniel 480-732-7120 15 E
daniel.herbst@cgc.edu

HERBST, Gordon, J 814-732-2585 442 E
herbst@edinboro.edu

HERBST, Jeffrey 315-228-7444 329 G
jherbst@colgate.edu

HERBST, Joel 561-297-3970 119 A
jherbst1@fau.edu

HERBST, John, H 859-257-5781 207 D
herbst@uky.edu

HERBST, Susan 860-486-2337 94 G
president@uconn.edu

HERBST, Susan 860-486-2337 95 A
president@uconn.edu

HERCHMER, Janice 716-896-0700 359 H
jherchmer@villa.edu

HERCULES, Tim 314-977-3434 289 C
hercultp@slu.edu

HERDEA, Eve 312-662-4403 144 H
eherdea@adler.edu

HERDLICK, Michael 419-448-3582 402 E
herdlickm@tiffin.edu

HERDLICK, Mike 419-448-3421 402 E
herdlickm@tiffin.edu

HERDLITZKA, Roxana 740-753-7032 391 H
herdlitzka_r@hocking.edu

HEREDIA, Deborah 706-771-4027 125 H
dheredia@augustatech.edu

HEREFORD, Taylor 912-449-7510 139 D
thereford@waycross.edu

HERENCIA, Ada 787-844-8181 568 A
ada.herencia@upr.edu

HERENDEEN, Steve, A 260-422-5561 173 C
saherendeen@indianatech.edu

HERGAN, Mark, J 443-352-4400 226 E
mhergan@stevenson.edu

HERGENROTHER,
Diane, S 718-990-1428 348 G
hergenrd@stjohns.edu

HERGERT, Erin 719-549-3226 87 F
erin.hergert@pueblocc.edu

HERGERT, Travis, J 641-422-4990 188 A
hergetra@niacc.edu

HERGOTT, Lori 402-461-7370 298 A
lhergott@hastings.edu

HERINGER, David, L 870-307-7290 22 D
david.heringer@lyon.edu

HERLIHY, James, E 205-665-6600 9 B
herlihyj@montevallo.edu

HERLIHY, Joseph, M 617-552-2855 232 B
joseph.herlihy@bc.edu

HERLITZKE, Mary Ann 608-789-6080 555 F
herlitzkem@westerntc.edu

HERMAN, Amber 336-838-6292 375 C
amber.herman@wilkescc.edu

HERMAN, Anne 503-352-2777 419 E
hermana@pacificu.edu

HERMAN, Annette 435-797-1158 511 E
annette.herman@usu.edu

HERMAN, Arthur 724-459-9500 452 E

HERMAN, Barbara, B 817-257-7855 499 C
b.herman@tcu.edu

HERMAN, Catherine 518-956-8151 351 E
cherman@uamail.albany.edu

HERMAN, David 907-277-1000 10 E
david.herman@chartercollege.edu

HERMAN, David, E 716-673-3271 352 A
david.herman@fredonia.edu

HERMAN, Fran 248-414-6900 254 F
fherman@mji.edu

HERMAN, Harry 516-678-5000 341 F
hherman@molloy.edu

HERMAN, Harvey 605-856-5880 465 C
harvey.herman@sintegleska.edu

HERMAN, Janet 618-842-3711 152 G
hermanj@iecc.edu

HERMAN, Jeanne 330-941-2264 406 F
jmherman@ysu.edu

HERMAN, Jeff, M 863-667-5249 118 F
jmherman@seu.edu

HERMAN, Jennifer 716-286-8186 344 D
jherman@niagara.edu

HERMAN, Karen, D 507-538-0162 262 B
herman.karen@mayo.edu

HERMAN, Rick 951-222-8384 64 A
rick.herman@rcc.edu

HERMAN, Sharon, S 816-654-7177 283 F
sherman@kcumb.edu

HERMAN-BARLOW, Janet 440-365-5222 395 D

HERMANCE, Patricia 302-736-0403 97 A
hermance@ccs.k12.de.us

HERMANN-ARTIM, Diane 802-388-5371 515 E

HERMANNY, Danielle, E 503-943-8715 420 G
hermannd@up.edu

HERMANO, Mara 401-454-6336 454 B
mhermano@risd.edu

HERMANSEN, Beckie 435-283-7346 512 C
beckie.hermansen@snow.edu

HERMANSON, Dean, E 480-423-6390 16 C
dean.hermanson@scottsdalecc.edu

HERMANSON, Steve 605-668-1500 464 G
shermanson@mtmc.edu

HERMES, John 405-425-1815 409 E
john.hermes@oc.edu

HERMES, Joseph 312-996-3490 167 B
jhermes@uic.edu

HERMES, Wayne, J 970-247-7432 84 K
hermes_w@fortlewis.edu

HERMON, Vada 620-227-9213 192 E
vhermon@dc3.edu

HERMOSILLO, Gilbert 760-757-2121 57 E
ghermosillo@miracosta.edu

HERMSEN, Albert, G 313-577-4982 260 A
ahermsen@wayne.edu

HERMSEN, Cindy, L 248-370-3370 256 G
hermsen@oakland.edu

HERNÁNDEZ-CRUZ,
Carmen 787-850-0000 566 G
carmen.hernandez1@upr.edu

HERN, Marcia, J 502-852-8300 207 E
m.hern@louisville.edu

HERNANDEZ, Abraham 956-882-8281 505 E
abraham.hernandez@utb.edu

HERNANDEZ, Albert 303-765-3183 85 D
ahernandez@iliff.edu

HERNANDEZ, Alex 915-831-6383 486 G
aherna78@epcc.edu

HERNANDEZ, Ana 813-974-4041 121 A
ahernandez@usf.edu

HERNANDEZ, Ana 787-764-0000 568 B
ana.hernandez@upr.edu

HERNANDEZ, Annette 717-560-8240 433 D
ahernandez@lbc.edu

HERNANDEZ, Arnold 208-459-5868 143 D
ahernandez@collegeofidaho.edu

HERNANDEZ, Arthur 361-825-2661 498 C
art.hernandez@tamucc.edu

HERNANDEZ, Ayana, D 919-530-7266 378 B
ahernandez@nccu.edu

HERNANDEZ, Carlos 940-565-3231 504 D
carlos.hernandez@unt.edu

HERNANDEZ, Carmen, H 787-850-9375 567 E
carmen.hernandez@upr.edu

HERNANDEZ, Cathy 602-286-8028 15 G
cathleen.hernandez@gwmail.maricopa.edu

HERNANDEZ, Christine 916-558-2438 56 D
hernana2@scc.losrios.edu

HERNANDEZ, Christine 787-786-3030 560 G
chernandez@ucb.edu.pr

HERNANDEZ, Daisy 801-840-4800 510 A
dhernandez@cci.edu

HERNANDEZ, David 805-565-6164 79 A
dhernand@westmont.edu

HERNANDEZ, Dino, M 248-204-2306 254 B
dhernande@ltu.edu

HERNANDEZ, Edwin 787-881-1212 565 B
edwin_hernandez@pucpr.edu

HERNANDEZ, Eliza 210-486-4913 479 B
ehernandez716@alamo.edu

HERNANDEZ, Emmanuel 787-257-7373 565 G
ehernande@suagm.edu

HERNANDEZ, Felix 805-922-6966 26 L
fhernandez@hancockcollege.edu

HERNANDEZ, Francisco 787-840-8894 568 A
francisco.hernandez7@upr.edu

HERNANDEZ, Francisco, J 808-956-3290 141 G
fjh@hawaii.edu

HERNANDEZ, Frank 847-214-7442 150 F
fhernandez@elgin.edu

HERNANDEZ, Frank 432-552-2120 507 D
hernandez_f@utpb.edu

HERNANDEZ, Grace 806-742-2121 502 A
grace.hernandez@ttu.edu

HERNANDEZ, Harry 787-738-2161 567 D
harry.hernandez2@upr.edu

HERNANDEZ, Ilsamar 787-751-0160 561 H
ihernandez@cmpr.pr.gov

HESS MOLL, Sandra 815-455-8987 157 H
smoll@mchenry.edu

HESSE, Allison 714-556-3610 77 B
allison.hesse@vanguard.edu

HESSE, Carla 510-642-5195 73 H
chesse@berkeley.edu

HESSE, Cindy 303-360-4752 83 K
cindy.hesse@ccaurora.edu

HESSE-BIBER, Sharlene 617-552-4130 232 B
sharlene.hesse-biber@bc.edu

HESSEE, Jennifer 918-540-6250 408 J
jennifer.hessee@neo.edu

HESSELBERG, Bonnie 941-752-5530 118 J
hesselb@scf.edu

HESSELL, Debra 617-578-7100 244 D
dhessell@sbboston.com

HESSELRODE, Betsy 731-989-6021 469 B
bhesselrode@fhu.edu

HESSLER, James 231-591-3947 250 H
hesslej@ferris.edu

HESSLER, Robert, L 308-635-6030 301 D
hesslerr@wncc.edu

HESSMANN, Steven, L 724-983-2907 440 E
sxh46@psu.edu

HESTAND, Phil 870-972-2318 20 D
phestand@astate.edu

HESTER, Barry, C 318-670-6414 215 A
bhester@susla.edu

HESTER, Brenda 606-337-4524 199 H
bhester@ccbbc.edu

HESTER, Clyda 740-377-2520 402 F
clydasteacup@windstream.net

HESTER, Colleen 217-479-7025 157 F
president@mac.edu

HESTER, D. Jean 503-821-8926 419 D
jhester@pnca.edu

HESTER, David 502-895-3411 204 F
dhester@lpts.edu

HESTER, Kerri 916-660-7603 69 F
khester@sierracollege.edu

HESTER, Kevin 615-844-5000 469 A
khester@fwbbc.edu

HESTER, Lynda 252-473-2264 369 G
lynda_hester@albemarle.edu

HESTER, Malcolm 606-337-1114 199 H
mhester@ccbbc.edu

HESTER, Mary 620-242-0487 195 C
hesterm@mcpherson.edu

HESTER, Michael, D 678-839-0626 139 A
mhester@westga.edu

HESTER, Ranan 501-279-4331 21 H
rhester@harding.edu

HESTER, Ray 252-536-7250 371 B
hesterr@halifaxcc.edu

HESTER, Susan 919-530-7601 378 B
shester@nccu.edu

HESTNESS, Gregory, S 612-626-4734 272 A
hestness@umn.edu

HESTON, Dave 602-850-8000 17 G
dheston@phoenixseminary.edu

HESTON, Grant 407-823-5988 120 B
grant.heston@ucf.edu

HETH, Justin 630-752-5022 168 H
justin.heth@wheaton.edu

HETHERINGTON, Kathleen, B 443-518-4820 223 D
khetherington@howardcc.edu

HETHERINGTON, Vincent, J 216-707-8004 394 B
vjh@kent.edu

HETRICK, Barbara 904-620-2560 120 D
barbara.hetrick@unf.edu

HETRICK, Janice 215-637-7700 431 A
jhetrick@holyfamily.edu

HETRICK, Lori, J 864-488-4610 459 B
lhetrick@limestone.edu

HETTLEMAN, Thomas 410-617-1120 223 I
tdhettleman@loyola.edu

HETTRICK, Allyson 828-298-3325 380 D
ahettrick@warren-wilson.edu.edu

HETU, Marcel 559-334-2960 78 C
marcelhetu@whccd.edu

HETZEL, Bob 608-785-6491 551 C
bhetzel@uwlax.edu

HETZEL, June 562-903-6000 31 A
june.hetzel@bioloa.edu

HETZEL, Sandra 718-818-6470 349 G

HEU, Nancy 808-235-7435 142 F
heu@hawaii.edu

HEUBLER, Deborah, T 808-956-0768 141 G
dhuebler@hawaii.edu

HEUER, John, J 215-898-6884 448 J
heuer@hr.upenn.edu

HEUER, Kathy 651-757-4061 262 H
kheuer@cva.edu

HEUER, Mychael 360-867-6189 534 D
heuermy@evergreen.edu

HEUER, Timothy 773-508-3254 157 C
theuer@luc.edu

HEUGEL, Jim 425-889-4098 536 C
jim.heugel@northwestu.edu

HEULITT, Ken 312-329-2070 159 A
ken.heulitt@moody.edu

HEUPEL, Jaelee 808-983-4187 140 H
jae@tokai.edu

HEURING, Curt 609-771-3269 308 F
heuring@tcnj.edu

HEURING, Michael 406-243-2022 294 I
michael.heuring@umontana.edu

HEUSER, Laura 732-224-2259 308 A
kheuser@brookdalecc.edu

HEUSNER, Warren 718-270-6048 328 C
wheusner@mec.cuny.edu

HEUTON, Mary Ellen 304-696-6603 544 B
heuton@marshall.edu

HEVERON, Eileen 858-642-8106 58 I
eheveron@nu.edu

HEVRON, Danelle 617-544-8657 152 H
hevrond@iecc.edu

HEWELL, Sherry, D 270-824-8666 202 G
sherry.hewell@kctcs.edu

HEWERDINE, Kevin, L 812-877-8184 179 B
kevin.l.hewerdine@rose-hulman.edu

HEWES, Colleen 425-739-8244 535 H
colleen.hewes@lwtc.edu

HEWES, Pollyanne 207-947-4591 217 D
phewes@bealcollege.edu

HEWETSON, Hank 812-855-1763 173 E
hhewetso@indiana.edu

HEWETT, James, E 712-749-2248 183 C
hewettj@bvu.edu

HEWETT, Kelly 410-334-2908 229 E
khewett@worwic.edu

HEWETT, Lamar 803-549-6314 462 E
dlhewett@mailbox.sc.edu

HEWITT, Bradley, L 618-650-2871 165 C
bhewitt@siue.edu

HEWITT, Dawn 718-262-2060 329 A
hewittd@york.cuny.edu

HEWITT, Emma 712-274-6400 190 B
emma.hewitt@witcc.edu

HEWITT, Gordon, J 315-859-4084 334 H
ghewitt@hamilton.edu

HEWITT, JR., Harold, W 714-997-6815 39 F
hewitt@chapman.edu

HEWITT, Janine 860-509-9520 93 A

HEWITT, Mark, S 781-736-2010 232 F
mhewitt@brandeis.edu

HEWITT, Maureen, A 312-935-4235 154 A
mhewitt@icsw.edu

HEWITT, Michael 718-951-5131 326 F
mhewitt@brooklyn.cuny.edu

HEWITT, Nathaniel 903-923-2404 509 E
nhewitt@wileyc.edu

HEWITT, Rene 816-331-5700 287 F
rhewitt@pcitraining.edu

HEWITT, Russ 402-826-8295 297 G
russ.hewitt@doane.edu

HEWITT, Stephany 843-574-6922 461 G
stephany.hewitt@tridenttech.edu

HEWITT BOYD, Kimberly 612-624-9547 272 A
boyd009@umn.edu

HEWITT-CLARKE, Gail 301-295-1667 558 D
gail.hewitt-clarke@usuhs.edu

HEWLETT, Fannie 423-697-4456 474 D

HEWLETT, Peggy 803-777-3861 462 A
peggy.hewlett@sc.edu

HEWLETT, Rod 402-557-7125 296 H
rod.hewlett@bellevue.edu

HEXTER, Ralph, J 530-752-4964 73 I
provost@ucdavis.edu

HEY, Jeanne 207-602-2371 221 A
jhey@une.edu

HEYDARI, Shahryar 706-778-8500 136 A
sheydari@piedmont.edu

HEYER, Cary, R 608-246-6443 554 D
cheyer@madisoncollege.org

HEYER, Doreen, E 213-738-6801 71 E
academicadmin@swlaw.edu

HEYING, Lori 319-363-8213 187 H
lheying@mtmercy.edu

HEYING, Steve 210-829-6023 504 B
lindaw@uiwtx.edu

HEYMAN, George 585-271-3657 348 B
gheyman@stbernards.edu

HEYMAN, Jeffrey 510-466-7369 62 A
jheyman@peralta.edu

HEYMAN, Jeffrey 510-436-2419 62 E
jheyman@peralta.edu

HEYMAN, Lawrence, A 610-785-6235 446 A
lheyman@scs.edu

HEYNDERICKX, Roy, F 360-438-4307 537 B
president@stmartin.edu

HEYNING, Katharina, E 262-472-1101 553 A
heyningk@uww.edu

HEYWARD, Elijah 703-812-4757 520 J
eheyward@leland.edu

HEYWARD, ILene 340-693-1101 568 E
iheyward@live.uvi.edu

HEYWARD, Kerry, L 404-413-0500 131 G
kheyward@gsu.edu

HEYWARD, Loretta 912-358-3049 136 G
heywardl@savannahstate.edu

HIATT, Aaron 415-433-9200 68 F
ahiatt@saybrook.edu

HIATT, Jim 615-248-1256 476 G
jhiatt@trevecca.edu

HIATT, Jon 605-331-6636 466 E
jon.hiatt@usiouxfalls.edu

HIBBARD, Kristine 904-264-9122 106 I
khibbard@cci.edu

HIBBARD, Steve, V 262-243-5700 547 C
steve.hibbard@cuw.edu

HIBBERD, Grover 502-863-8091 201 A
grover_hibberd@georgetowncollege.edu

HIBBS, Joseph, L 856-691-8600 309 B
jhibbs@cccnj.edu

HIBBS, Randy 920-206-2318 548 D
rhibbs@mbbc.edu

HIBBS, Thomas, S 254-710-7689 482 A
thomas_hibbs@baylor.edu

HIBLER, Dirk 904-819-6336 107 C
dhibler@flagler.edu

HIBNER, Lisa 225-216-8244 209 H
hibnerl@mybrcc.edu

HICE, Muriel 269-488-4410 253 A
mhice@kvcc.edu

HICHWA, Richard, D 319-335-2106 182 F
richard-hichwa@uiowa.edu

HICKE, Linda 847-467-4490 160 E
l-hicke@northwestern.edu

HICKEY, Bill 320-363-5480 262 F
whickey@csbsju.edu

HICKEY, Catherine, M 508-999-8182 237 A
chickey@umassd.edu

HICKEY, David 513-569-1448 387 G
david.hickey@cincinnatistate.edu

HICKEY, Dean 508-373-9520 231 B
dean.hickey@becker.edu

HICKEY, Diane 678-891-2304 131 C
diane.hickey@gpc.edu

HICKEY, Eric 559-278-2803 27 B
ehickey@alliant.edu

HICKEY, Jay 401-841-6515 558 B

HICKEY, John, M 253-879-3203 538 H
hickey@pugetsound.edu

HICKEY, Lynn 210-458-4444 506 D
lynn.hickey@utsa.edu

HICKEY, Melissa 845-675-4424 344 G
melissa.hickey@nyack.edu

HICKEY, JR., Robert, E 937-775-3326 406 C
robert.hickey@wright.edu

HICKEY, Thomas, F 312-915-7796 157 C
thickey@luc.edu

HICKMAN, Carla 314-889-1416 281 I
chickman@fontbonne.edu

HICKMAN, Heather 415-749-4540 65 I
hhickman@sfai.edu

HICKMAN, Melissa 317-931-2311 170 H
mhickman@cts.edu

HICKMAN, Randall 586-445-7866 254 C
hickmanr@macomb.edu

HICKMAN, Thomas, N 803-323-2129 463 E
hickmant@winthrop.edu

HICKMAN, Tim 909-558-4532 54 D
thickman@llu.edu

HICKMAN, Tom 701-671-2354 382 G
tom.hickman@ndscs.edu

HICKMAN, Tracy 386-752-1822 108 G
tracy.hickman@fgc.edu

HICKMAN, Wesley, T 803-777-3478 462 A
whickman@mailbox.sc.edu

HICKOX, Chad, E 206-934-5201 537 F
chad.hickox@seattlecolleges.edu

HICKOX, Charles 859-622-6605 200 J
charles.hickox@eku.edu

HICKS, Ali 505-565-1290 245 A
ahicks@stonehill.edu

HICKS, Barbara 928-541-7777 16 H
bhicks@ncu.edu

HICKS, Brenda, D 620-229-6387 196 G
brenda.hicks@sckans.edu

HICKS, Brian, A 336-734-7191 370 F
bhicks@forsythtech.edu

HICKS, Bruce 310-287-4307 55 F
hicksbr@wlac.edu

HICKS, Bryan 256-372-4014 1 A
byran.hicks@aamu.edu

HICKS, Cheryl 816-414-3700 285 H
chicks@mbts.edu

HICKS, Dale, A 813-974-9232 121 A
dhicks1@usf.edu

HICKS, David, L 610-292-9852 445 E
bishophicks@comcast.net

HICKS, Deanita 870-762-3146 20 A
dhicks@smail.anc.edu

HICKS, Debbie, L 757-455-3338 530 C
dlhicks@vwc.edu

HICKS, Dennis 765-973-8456 173 F
dehicks@iue.edu

HICKS, Douglas 315-228-7222 329 G
dhicks@colgate.edu

HICKS, Ed 334-386-7309 3 G
ehicks@faulkner.edu

HICKS, Elena 410-617-2251 223 I
ehicks@loyola.edu

HICKS, Elizabeth, M 617-253-4090 241 D

HICKS, Geoffrey 434-832-7641 526 E
hicksg@cvcc.vccs.edu

HICKS, George 740-588-1379 407 A
ghicks@zanestate.edu

HICKS, J. David 423-652-4782 470 A
jdhicks@king.edu

HICKS, Janine, M 815-740-2272 167 E
jhicks@stfrancis.edu

HICKS, Jim 423-425-4246 477 F
jim-hicks@utc.edu

HICKS, Jimmy 691-320-2480 559 D
jhicks@comfsm.fm

HICKS, Jud 806-457-4200 486 I
jhicks@fpctx.edu

HICKS, Julia 860-685-2100 95 E
jhicks@wesleyan.edu

HICKS, Kathleen 406-275-4969 296 D
kathleen_hicks@skc.edu

HICKS, Kelly 918-343-7553 411 H
kellyhicks@rsu.edu

HICKS, Kenneth 215-248-7103 425 D
hicksk@chc.edu

HICKS, Larry 919-962-5401 378 E
larry_hicks@unc.edu

HICKS, LaTosha 828-726-2705 368 G
lhicks@cccti.edu

HICKS, Lawrence 313-593-5380 259 B
hickslg@umd.umich.edu

HICKS, Loretta 404-297-9522 131 D
hicksl@gptc.edu

HICKS, Marcus 404-297-9522 131 D
hicksm@gptc.edu

HICKS, Michael 706-821-8350 135 G
mhicks@paine.edu

HICKS, Michael, G 574-284-4719 179 F
mhicks@saintmarys.edu

HICKS, Minora 803-327-7402 456 F
mhicks@clintonjuniorcollege.edu

HICKS, Mona, L 561-803-2174 114 C
mona_hicks@pba.edu

HICKS, Nancy, W 609-652-4693 313 E
nancy.hicks@stockton.edu

HICKS, Ramona 314-977-5028 289 C
rhicks1@slu.edu

HICKS, Renardo, L 803-376-5700 455 B
rhicks@allenuniversity.edu

HICKS, Renee, G 985-493-2556 216 A
renee.hicks@nicholls.edu

HICKS, Ronald 847-566-6401 167 F
rhicks@usml.edu

HICKS, Sara 978-837-5502 242 A
hickss@merrimack.edu

HICKS, Scott, M 434-592-4808 520 K
smhicks@liberty.edu

HICKS, Stacey 209-384-6100 57 C
stacey.hicks@mccd.edu

HICKS, Timothy, J 315-859-4790 334 H
thicks@hamilton.edu

HICKS, Virginia 304-876-5712 544 C
vhicks@shepherd.edu

HICKS, Wanda 706-355-5160 125 C
whicks@athenstech.edu

HICKS-GOLDSTEIN, Regan 302-454-3998 96 F
regan@dtcc.edu

HICKSON, Cheryl, E 443-412-2129 223 B
chickson@harford.edu

HICSWA, Stefani, G 406-874-6158 294 F
hicswas@milescc.edu

HIDALGO, Jeannie 305-220-4120 115 F
hrdir@ptcmatt.com

HIDALGO, Lisa 985-858-5729 210 G
lisa.hidalgo@fletcher.edu

HIDALGO, Maria 505-424-2317 318 D
mhidalgo@iaia.edu

HIDY, Steve 952-888-4777 270 C
shidy@nwhealth.edu

HIEDEMAN, Ann 701-671-2904 382 G
ann.hiedeman@ndscs.edu

HIEL, Edwin 619-388-3036 65 F
ehiel@sdccd.edu

HIEMENZ, Karen, A 320-308-5017 269 B
khiemenz@sctcc.edu

HIEMER, Linda 866-621-0124 89 C
linda.hiemer@rockies.edu

HIEMSTRA, Tricia 805-893-2489 75 B
tricia.hiemstra@hr.ucsb.edu

HIERONYMUS, Bob 208-882-1566 144 C
bobh@nsa.edu

HIERS, Richard 314-434-4044 280 F
richard.hiers@covenantseminary.edu

HIESIGER, Linda 413-585-2231 244 G
lhiesige@smith.edu

HIETALA, David 507-431-2250 268 H
david.hietala@riverland.edu

HIETALA, Robert 406-994-5523 295 C
robert.hietala@montana.edu

HIETAPELTO, Amy, B 773-442-6100 160 A
a-hietapelto@neiu.edu

HIETSCH, Stephen, C 717-245-1891 427 F
hietschs@dickinson.edu

HIETT, David 617-746-1990 235 G
david.hiett@hult.edu

HIETT, Jim 615-230-3350 476 C
jim.hiett@volstate.edu

HIGA, Jane, H 805-565-6028 79 A
jhiga@westmont.edu

HIGA, Milton 808-734-9572 141 J
miltonh@hawaii.edu

HIGASHI, Guy 808-853-1040 141 C

HILLESHEIM, Gwen 312-752-2000 155 C
gwen.hillesheim@kendall.edu

HILLIAR, Mara, M 804-594-1570 527 B
mhilliar@jtcc.edu

HILLIARD, Aaron 231-777-0447 256 A
aaronhilliard@muskegoncc.edu

HILLIARD, Beth 859-256-3100 201 E
beth.hilliard@kctcs.edu

HILLIARD, Colette 903-675-6306 502 F
chilliard@tvcc.edu

HILLIARD, Danny, C 405-325-0311 413 C
dhilliard@ou.edu

HILLIARD, Dianne 775-445-3288 303 B
dianne@wnc.edu

HILLIARD, Ericka 706-868-2010 19 A
ericka.hilliard@phoenix.edu

HILLIARD, Mark 615-794-4254 472 F
mhilliard@omorecollege.edu

HILLIS, Vicki, B 419-372-0651 385 F
vickih@bgsu.edu

HILLMAN, Brenda 925-631-4457 64 F
bhillman@stmarys-ca.edu

HILLMAN, Greg 601-426-6346 277 A
ghillman@southeasternbaptist.edu

HILLMAN, Melinda 865-481-2000 476 A
hillmanmk@roanestate.edu

HILLMAN, Michel 701-328-2965 381 E
michel.hillman@ndus.edu

HILLS, Fred 254-299-8000 490 G
fhills@mclennan.edu

HILLS, Jim 206-546-4634 538 C
jhills@shoreline.edu

HILLS, Warren 269-387-3895 260 C
warren.hills@wmich.edu

HILLSTOCK, Laurie 864-644-5038 461 B
lhillstock@swu.edu

HILLYER, Jill 336-334-4079 379 B
jill_hillyer@uncg.edu

HILPERT, John, M 662-846-4000 273 H
jhilpert@deltastate.edu

HILSABECK, Alison 847-947-5065 159 E
ahilsabeck@nl.edu

HILT, Elizabeth 650-433-3818 61 B
ehilt@paloaltou.edu

HILTE, Ken 719-502-2140 87 B
ken.hilte@ppcc.edu

HILTERBRAN, Stephen 870-543-5907 23 H
shilterbran@seark.edu

HILTON, Adriel 563-425-5221 189 G
hiltona@uiu.edu

HILTON, Carol 949-582-4872 70 F
chilton@saddleback.edu

HILTON, Don 254-647-3234 492 G
dhilton@rangercollege.edu

HILTON, III, Earl, M 336-334-7686 378 A
hiltone@ncat.edu

HILTON, Eric 610-399-2000 442 A
ehilton@cheyney.edu

HILTON, James, L 434-924-1432 525 F
jlh5mc@virginia.edu

HILTON, Linda 802-241-2520 515 C
hiltonl@lsc.vsc.edu

HILTON, Linwood 404-752-1663 134 E
lhilton@msm.edu

HILTON, Richard, H 315-697-2300 359 C
rhilton@uscny.edu

HILTON, Robert, C 479-979-1203 26 A
rchilton@mail.ozarks.edu

HILTON, Stacey 928-717-7775 19 C
stacey.hilton@yc.edu

HILTONSMITH, Lisa 631-420-2245 356 A
lisa.hiltonsmith@farmingdale.edu

HILTS, Deb, B 607-431-4171 335 A
hiltsd@hartwick.edu

HILVO, Wendy 414-326-2337 547 B
wendy.hilvo@ccon.edu

HILYER, Billy, D 334-386-7103 3 G
bhilyer@faulkner.edu

HIMARIOS, Daniel 817-272-2881 505 C
himarios@uta.edu

HIMBEAULT-TAYLOR,
Simone 734-764-5132 259 A
shtaylor@umich.edu

HIMBER, David 212-960-5330 361 M
himber@yu.edu

HIMES, A.C. (Buddy) 936-468-2801 496 B
himesac@sfasu.edu

HIMLER, Kim, A 724-925-4116 451 E
himlerk@wccc.edu

HIMLEY, Margaret, R 315-443-1137 357 C
mrhimley@syr.edu

HIMMELBERGER,
Stacey, J 315-859-4416 334 H
shimmelb@hamilton.edu

HIMMELMAN, Ken 802-440-4312 513 A
khimmelman@bennington.edu

HIMMELSTEIN, Amos 323-259-1347 59 I
himmelstein@oxy.edu

HIMSEL, Christian 262-243-5700 547 C
christian.himsel@cuw.edu

HIMSTEDT, Lucy 812-488-2625 180 E
lh133@evansville.edu

HINCH, Virginia 509-359-2329 533 H
vhinch@ewu.edu

HINCHEE, Jeanne 423-697-4721 474 D

HINCK, Shelly, S 989-774-3951 249 C
hinck1ss@cmich.edu

HINCKER, Larry 540-231-5396 529 G
hincker@vt.edu

HINCKLEY, Richard 702-651-7488 302 E
richard.hinckley@csn.edu

HIND, Jonathan, T 315-859-4116 334 H
jhind@hamilton.edu

HINDELEH, Nitsa 314-392-2319 285 J
hindeleh@mobap.edu

HINDERS, Sally 208-769-3349 144 D
sally_hinders@nic.edu

HINDES, Victoria 408-741-2020 78 G
victoria.hindes@westvalley.edu

HINDIN, Patricia, K 973-972-4211 316 H
hindinpk@umdnj.edu

HINDS, Blayne, E 405-962-1620 408 G
behinds@langston.edu

HINDS, M. Ray 813-988-5131 108 A
hindsr@floridacollege.edu

HINDS, Randy, C 770-423-6755 133 A
rhinds@kennesaw.edu

HINDS, Steven 479-619-2220 22 H
schinds1@nwacc.edu

HINDUS, Myra 617-266-1400 231 E

HINE, James 415-502-3037 75 A
jhine@finance.ucsf.edu

HINE, Mark, L 434-592-3240 520 K
mhine@liberty.edu

HINE, Suzanne, A 423-746-5205 476 F
shine@twcnet.edu

HINE, Terry 203-576-5072 94 C
thine@stvincentscollege.edu

HINE, William, C 217-581-6644 150 E
wchine@eiu.edu

HINES, Alexander 507-457-5597 269 G
ahines@winona.edu

HINES, Bonnie 318-473-6438 212 I
hines@lsua.edu

HINES, Bradford 414-297-6990 554 F
hinesbe@matc.edu

HINES, Clay, T 919-866-5699 374 H
cthines@waketech.edu

HINES, Cory 214-333-5628 484 D
coryh@dbu.edu

HINES, Craig 312-662-4111 144 H
chines@adler.edu

HINES, DeAnna, J 404-413-1350 131 G
djhines@gsu.edu

HINES, Deborah-Harmon 508-856-2444 237 C
deborah-harmon.hines@umassmed.edu

HINES, Elizabeth, E 724-946-7031 451 C
ehines@westminster.edu

HINES, Florence, W 410-857-2273 224 C
fhines@mcdaniel.edu

HINES, Jean, C 804-289-8181 525 E
jhines@richmond.edu

HINES, Joseph 908-497-4363 316 B
joseph.hines@ucc.edu

HINES, Kenneth, D 919-658-7783 367 F
dhines@moc.edu

HINES, Lara 314-392-2242 285 J
robeyl@mobap.edu

HINES, Mark 978-934-4000 237 B
mark_hines@uml.edu

HINES, Mary, E 412-578-6123 424 I
hinesme@carlow.edu

HINES, Michelle 661-763-7870 72 E
mhines@taftcollege.edu

HINES, Nancy, A 563-333-6377 188 F
hinesnancya@sau.edu

HINES, Nancy, G 509-777-4638 540 C
nhines@whitworth.edu

HINES, Odessa 919-546-8268 376 F
ohines@shawu.edu

HINES, Patti 619-574-6909 60 D
phines@pacificcollege.edu

HINES, Resche 773-995-2549 146 G
rhines@csu.edu

HINES, Ruth 617-427-0600 241 A
rhines@rcc.mass.edu

HINES, JR., Samuel, M 843-953-5007 456 C
sam.hines@citadel.edu

HINES-FRITTS,
Mary Lou, A 816-235-1107 291 C
hinesml@umkc.edu

HINEY, Delaine, S 712-362-0428 186 A
dhiney@iowalakes.edu

HINEY, Karen 980-598-1705 365 I
karen.hiney@jwu.edu

HINGELBERG, Julie 313-664-7494 249 E
julieh@collegeforcreativestudies.edu

HINKEN, Michele 415-458-3726 45 C
michele.hinken@dominican.edu

HINKLE, Adrian 405-789-7661 412 E
adrian.hinkle@swcu.edu

HINKLE, Ana 907-834-1623 11 B
ahinkle@pwscc.edu

HINKLE, Barbara 724-838-4206 447 C
hinkle@setonhill.edu

HINKLE, Barbara, C 724-838-4206 447 C
hinkle@setonhill.edu

HINKLE, Bernadette 610-436-2961 444 A
bhinkle@wcupa.edu

HINKLE, Charles, R 407-823-6432 120 B
rhinkle@ucf.edu

HINKLE, Keith 310-506-4893 61 H
keith.hinkle@pepperdine.edu

HINKLE, Lance 405-744-5237 410 C
lance.hinkle@okstate.edu

HINKLE, M, L 620-665-3526 193 H
hinklem@hutchcc.edu

HINKLE, Sandy, L 573-651-2250 289 K
shinkle@semo.edu

HINKLEY, Lisa 847-735-5235 155 G
hinkley@lakeforest.edu

HINKLEY, Richard 434-592-3077 520 K
rdhinkle@liberty.edu

HINMAN, David 253-680-7713 531 F
dhinman@bates.ctc.edu

HINNEN, Jack 205-226-4761 2 B
jhinnen@bsc.edu

HINNEN, Marsha 251-981-3771 2 G
marsha.hinnen@columbiasouthern.edu

HINNERS, Gordon 828-689-1208 366 I
ghinners@mhc.edu

HINOJOSA, Gilberto 301-322-0656 225 F
hinojogx@pgcc.edu

HINOJOSA, Maggie 956-665-2321 506 C
hinojosam@utpa.edu

HINRICHS, Jay 970-351-2362 89 B
jay.hinrichs@unco.edu

HINRICHS, Kathleen 620-223-2700 193 A
kathleenh@fortscott.edu

HINRICHS, Mark 520-318-2700 12 C
mhinrichs@aii.edu

HINSHAW, Ada Sue 301-295-9002 558 D
adasue.hinshaw@usuhs.edu

HINSHAW, Dana 620-665-3322 193 H
hinshawd@hutchcc.edu

HINSHAW, Garrett, D 828-327-7000 369 B
ghinshaw@cvcc.edu

HINSHAW, Lynn 828-898-3473 366 D
hinshawl@lmc.edu

HINSON, Bobby 850-201-6071 122 A
hinsonb@tcc.fl.edu

HINSON, Danny 865-471-3310 467 G
dhinson@cn.edu

HINSON, David 704-991-0183 374 D
hinsonld@stanly.edu

HINSON, David, J 501-450-1340 22 A

HINSON, Dianne, B 919-747-0007 374 H
dbhinson@waketech.edu

HINSON, Jane 478-445-4546 130 B
jane.hinson@gcsu.edu

HINTERLONG, James, E 804-828-1036 526 B
jehinterlong@vcu.edu

HINTON, Amy, E 601-426-6346 277 A
ahinton@southeasternbaptist.edu

HINTON, Billy, C 713-500-8444 506 F
william.c.hinton@uth.tmc.edu

HINTON, Cheryl 443-352-4489 226 E
chinton@stevenson.edu

HINTON, Don 435-652-7651 512 B
hinton@dixie.edu

HINTON, H. Scott 435-797-2776 511 E
hinton@engineering.usu.edu

HINTON, John, A 252-398-6376 363 G
hintoj@chowan.edu

HINTON, Mary 845-569-3190 342 A
mary.hinton@msmc.edu

HINTON, Neil 740-753-7212 391 H
hinton_n@hocking.edu

HINTON, Shannon 281-476-1501 493 H
shannon.hinton@sjcd.edu

HINTON-DOYLE, June 516-678-5000 341 F
jhinton-doyle@molloy.edu

HINTON-RIVERA, Jake 928-524-7662 17 A
jake.hinton-rivera@npc.edu

HINTY, Danny 614-222-3224 388 G
dhinty@ccad.edu

HINTZ, Carol 816-235-1621 291 C
hintzc@umkc.edu

HINTZ, Debra 704-406-3973 364 E
dhintz@gardner-webb.edu

HINTZ, Nancy 920-748-8346 550 D

HINTZ, Sharon 908-835-2356 317 C
hintz@warren.edu

HINZ, Chuck 319-398-5511 187 B
chinz@kirkwood.edu

HINZ, Chuck 319-398-5574 187 B
chinz@kirkwood.edu

HINZ, James 770-593-2257 132 B
jahinz@yahoo.com

HINZ, Laurence, A 505-473-6234 320 F
president@santafeuniversity.edu

HINZMAN, Larry 907-474-7331 10 I
ldhinzman@alaska.edu

HIPES, Mark 276-326-4340 516 L
mhipes@bluefield.edu

HIPOL, Ana 408-848-4720 48 C
ahipol@gavilan.edu

HIPOLITO, Veronica 928-226-4334 13 F
veronica.hipolito@coconino.edu

HIPONIA, Lorenzo, S 202-231-8785 557 J
lorenzo.hiponia@dodiis.mil

HIPP, Joye, G 803-786-3178 457 C
joyehipp@columbiasc.edu

HIPP, Kathleen 603-577-6659 304 I
hipp@dwc.edu

HIPPLE, Andrew 717-757-1100 452 J
andy.hipple@yti.edu

HIPPLER, Stanley 337-475-5181 215 G
stan@mcneese.edu

HIPPOLITE WRIGHT,
Debbie 808-675-3799 140 D
debbie.hippolite.wright@byuh.edu

HIPPS, OSB, Norman, W 724-805-2271 446 E
norman.hipps@email.stvincent.edu

HIPPS, Suzanne 602-243-8153 16 D
suzanne.hipps@smcmail.maricopa.edu

HIRA, Labh 515-294-4077 182 E
lhira@foundation.iastate.edu

HIRA, Tahira, K 515-294-2042 182 E
tkhira@iastate.edu

HIRAK, Joe 802-728-1283 516 A

HIRALDO, Rafael 787-863-2390 563 E
rafael.hiraldo@fajardo.inter.edu

HIRAMOTO, Patti 831-582-3366 35 E
phiramoto@csumb.edu

HIRD, Lon 605-367-7284 466 D
lon.hird@southeasttech.edu

HIRDLER, Joy, L 707-965-6232 60 I
jhirdler@puc.edu

HIRE, Jack 740-587-5698 389 I
hire@denison.edu

HIRE, Lynn 913-621-8707 192 F
lhire@donnelly.edu

HIRLEMAN, E. Daniel 209-228-4021 74 D
dhirleman@ucmerced.edu

HIRNEISEN, Deborah 610-917-2003 450 E
dghirneisen@vfcc.edu

HIRNER, Leo, J 816-604-4501 284 H
leo.hirner@mcckc.edu

HIROKAWA, Randy 808-974-7300 141 F
randyh@hawaii.edu

HIROKO, Tezuko 269-927-8100 253 G
tezuko@lakemichigancollege.edu

HIRSCH, Andrew, H 570-577-3698 423 E
andy.hirsch@bucknell.edu

HIRSCH, Brian 210-999-8330 502 E
brian.hirsch@trinity.edu

HIRSCH, Deborah 617-928-4730 242 E
dhirsch@mountida.edu

HIRSCH, Deborah 408-554-4113 68 C
dhirsch@scu.edu

HIRSCH, Deborah 563-876-3353 184 B
dhirsch@dwci.edu

HIRSCH, Glenn 612-624-4390 272 A

HIRSCH, Jerry, A 413-782-1247 246 A
jhirsch@wne.edu

HIRSCH, Linda, R 563-333-6296 188 F
hirschlindar@sau.edu

HIRSCH, Michael, L 512-505-3125 488 D
mlhirsch@htu.edu

HIRSCH, Michele 718-489-5202 348 E
mhirsch@sfc.edu

HIRSCH, Robert 941-405-1500 433 C
rhirsch@lecom.edu

HIRSCH, Samuel 215-751-8160 426 B
shirsch@ccp.edu

HIRSCH, Tom 641-472-1170 187 E
thirsch@mum.edu

HIRSCHBECK, Denise, R 314-935-5320 292 I
dhirschbeck@wustl.edu

HIRSCHFIELD, Michael, T 262-472-1633 553 A
hirschfm@uww.edu

HIRSCHY, Margaret 419-434-4260 406 A
hirschym@findlay.edu

HIRSH, Barbara 215-576-0800 445 D
bhirsh@rrc.edu

HIRSH, Deborah, D 714-438-4707 41 A
dhirsh@mail.cccd.edu

HIRSH, Dennis 614-891-5030 398 A

HIRSHMAN, Elliot 619-594-5201 37 A
presidents.office@sdsu.edu

HIRSHON, Arnold 216-368-5292 386 F
arnold.hirshon@case.edu

HIRST, Martha, K 718-990-3250 348 G
hirstm@stjohns.edu

HIRST, Thomas, M 845-451-1904 331 E
t_hirst@culinary.edu

HIRT, E. Jill 610-861-5421 437 H
jhirt@northampton.edu

HIRTLE, Christopher 413-572-5455 238 F
chirtle@wsc.ma.edu

HIRTZEL, Lucas, R 573-629-3011 282 E
lhirtzel@hlg.edu

HIRTZINGER, Debbie, A 937-778-7961 390 G
dhirtzinger@edisonohio.edu

HISAMOTO, Masashi 773-834-2500 166 A
hisamoto@ttic.edu

HISCANO, Lisa 908-965-2358 316 B
hiscano@ucc.edu

HISE, Paul 806-720-7279 490 F
paul.hise@lcu.edu

HISER, Larry, R 740-376-4665 395 G
larry.hiser@marietta.edu

HISEY, Richard, M 617-266-1400 231 E

HISKES, Anne 616-331-8655 251 F
hiskesa@gvsu.edu

HISKEY, Robert, M 419-586-0381 406 D robert.hiskey@wright.edu
HISLE, W. Lee 860-439-2650 92 G wlhis@conncoll.edu
HISLOP, Charli 888-384-0849 27 G charli@allied.edu
HISRICH, Matt 765-983-1523 171 E hisrima@earlham.edu
HISS, Nancy 503-699-6242 416 J nhiss@marylhurst.edu
HISSONG, Kimberly 315-229-5837 349 E khissong@stlawu.edu
HISTAND, James, L 574-535-7456 171 G jimlh@goshen.edu
HISTAND, Phillip, C 541-737-9355 418 F phillip.histand@oregonstate.edu
HITCH, Elizabeth, J 801-321-7122 511 B ehitch@utahsbr.edu
HITCHCOCK, Cheryl, Y 443-885-3535 224 E cheryl.hitchcock@morgan.edu
HITCHCOCK, Claude, E 443-885-3938 224 E claude.hitchcock@morgan.edu
HITCHCOCK, Eloise 615-547-1351 468 B ehitchcock@cumberland.edu
HITCHCOCK, Susan 607-255-5147 331 B sh54@cornell.edu
HITCHCOCK, Walter, T 575-624-8183 319 C hitchcock@nmmi.edu
HITCHELL, Dan 314-968-7442 292 J danhitchell51@webster.edu
HITE, Carl 423-478-6200 474 E chite@clevelandstatecc.edu
HITE, Elinor 312-662-4415 144 H ehite@adler.edu
HITE, Joe 940-552-6291 507 F jhite@vernoncollege.edu
HITE, Patrick 214-768-2146 495 A phite@smu.edu
HITE, Robert, D 415-442-7058 48 F bhite@ggu.edu
HITE, Trudy, E 302-356-6965 97 C trudy.e.hite@wilmu.edu
HITES, Michael 217-244-0102 167 A hites@uillinois.edu
HITESMAN, Bill 402-461-2400 297 A bhitesman@cccneb.edu
HITLIN, Amy 919-760-8521 367 A hitlina@meredith.edu
HITT, John, C 407-823-1823 120 B john.hitt@ucf.edu
HITT, Richard, J 863-784-7036 117 J richard.hitt@southflorida.edu
HITTENBERGER, Jeff 714-556-3610 77 B officeoftheprovost@vanguard.edu
HITTLE, Dennis, M 309-794-7370 145 E dennishittle@augustana.edu
HITZ, Randy 503-725-4697 418 G hitz@pdx.edu
HITZEL, Joan 515-244-4221 181 F hitzelj@aib.edu
HITZEMAN, John 936-294-1900 501 D pur_jch@shsu.edu
HIXON, Jennifer 413-565-1000 230 G jhixon@baypath.edu
HIXSON, Carla 701-224-5580 382 D carla.hixson@bismarckstate.edu
HIXSON, Carol 727-873-4400 121 C carol.hixson@nelson.usf.edu
HIXSON, Jana 254-710-1421 482 A jana_hixson@baylor.edu
HIXSON, John 479-619-4341 22 H jhixson@nwacc.edu
HIXSON, Paul 217-244-6227 167 D pch@mx.uillinois.edu
HIYANE-BROWN, Kathi 360-383-3330 540 A khiyane-brown@whatcom.ctc.edu
HJELLUM, Wilma 402-457-2723 298 G whjellum@mccneb.edu
HLADEK, Thomas 718-482-5510 328 B tomhl@lagcc.cuny.edu
HLADIO, Patricia, A 724-738-2044 443 F patricia.hladio@sru.edu
HLADIS, Jirka 303-245-4702 86 H jirka@naropa.edu
HLAVIN, Karen 847-543-2384 148 B khlavin@clcillinois.edu
HLINAK, Matthew, J 708-524-6812 150 C mhlinak@dom.edu
HLINKA, Karen 270-534-3236 203 E karen.hlinka@kctcs.edu
HLUBB, Emma 931-424-7366 471 A ehlubb@martinmethodist.edu
HLUBB, James, R 931-424-7379 471 A jhlubb@martinmethodist.edu
HMIELEWSKI, Christopher 507-537-7984 269 E christopher.hmielewski@smsu.edu
HMIELEWSKI, Thomas 715-682-1208 549 F thmielewski@northland.edu
HO, Co 714-992-7020 59 E cho@fullcoll.edu
HO, David 402-457-2716 298 G dho@mccneb.edu
HO, John, T 716-645-3786 351 G proho@buffalo.edu
HO, Peggy 773-442-5143 160 A k-ho1@neiu.edu
HO, Sam 408-298-2181 67 B sam.ho@sjeccd.org
HO, Sandra 603-427-7614 304 B sho@ccsnh.edu
HOABY, Candy 402-354-7137 299 C candance.hoaby@methodistcollege.edu
HOADLEY, Diane 715-836-2500 551 A hoadled@uewc.edu
HOAG, David 847-317-7128 166 E dhoag@tiu.edu
HOANG, Linh 808-734-9570 141 J lhoang@hawaii.edu
HOANG, Minh-Ha 619-260-4506 76 D hoangm@sandiego.edu
HOAR, Robert 608-785-8039 551 C rhoar@uwlax.edu
HOARD, David 601-979-2282 274 G david.hoard@jsums.edu
HOARE, William, D 262-551-6200 546 I whoare@carthage.edu
HOBAN, Elizabeth 973-328-5160 309 A ehoban@ccm.edu
HOBAN, Kristi, M 817-257-7803 499 C k.hoban@tcu.edu
HOBAN, Patricia, K 503-370-6206 421 D phoban@willamette.edu
HOBAN, Patricia, K 503-375-5477 421 D phoban@willamette.edu
HOBAN, Theresa, M 315-568-3216 342 H thoban@nycc.edu
HOBAUGH, Greg 215-572-3848 451 D ghobaugh@wts.edu
HOBBIE, Lawrence 516-877-3165 322 A hobbie@adelphi.edu
HOBBS, Bruce, R 208-496-3110 143 A hobbsb@byui.edu
HOBBS, Clinton, G 706-379-3111 140 A clinth@yhc.edu
HOBBS, Evelyn 575-527-7630 319 G erhobbs@nmsu.edu
HOBBS, Harriet 910-879-5516 368 D hhobbs@bladencc.edu
HOBBS, Jeanie 817-598-6267 508 F hobbs@wc.edu
HOBBS, Jeffrey 714-432-5725 41 D jhobbs@occ.cccd.edu
HOBBS, Jeremy 415-351-3536 65 I jhobbs@sfai.edu
HOBBS, Lynn, E 478-934-3012 134 B lhobbs@mgc.edu
HOBBS, Marcia, B 270-809-2196 205 A mhobbs4@murraystate.edu
HOBBS, Nancy, A 734-764-7254 259 A hobbsn@umich.edu
HOBBS, Pamelia, C 336-599-1181 372 G hobbsp@piedmontcc.edu
HOBBS, Patrick, E 973-642-8750 315 C patrick.hobbs@shu.edu
HOBBS, Patrick, J 973-642-8750 315 B patrick.hobbs@shu.edu
HOBBS, Phillip, M 205-853-1200 5 C mhobbs@jeffstateonline.com
HOBBS, Rose 518-438-3111 340 A roseh@mariacollege.edu
HOBBS, Valerie 303-581-9955 320 G vhobbs@acupuncturecollege.edu
HOBBS, Valerie 303-581-9955 88 E
HOBBY, Angela 229-333-5365 139 I angela.hobby@wiregrass.edu
HOBBY-MEARS, Michelle 949-480-4134 69 J mhobby@soka.edu
HOBERMAN, Chaim 516-225-4700 346 K
HOBIN, Caron, T 413-565-1000 230 G chobin@baypath.edu
HOBIN, Gail 617-287-5310 236 G gail.hobin@umb.edu
HOBLER, Billie, J 419-586-0324 406 D bj.hobler@wright.edu
HOBLER, Dean 419-227-3141 404 D dahobler@unoh.edu
HOBLET, Kent, H 662-325-1418 275 F hoblet@cvm.msstate.edu
HOBLICK, Dave 303-753-6046 88 B dhoblick@rmcad.edu
HOBSON, James 703-284-1617 521 D bing.hobson@marymount.edu
HOBSON, Lynn, M 620-341-5267 192 G lhobson@emporia.edu
HOBSON, Paula Lee 775-674-7686 302 H phobson@tmcc.edu
HOBSON, Sheila 301-860-3451 228 A shobson@bowiestate.edu
HOBSON, Tricia 405-422-1263 411 G hobsont@redlandscc.edu
HOBYAK, Michael, S 215-785-0111 440 I
HOCHANADEL, Gery 972-438-6932 492 E ghochanadel@parkercc.edu
HOCHMAN, Carey 206-322-6100 536 I chochman@pmi.edu
HOCHSCHILD, Joshua 301-447-7435 225 A hochschild@msmary.edu
HOCHSTEIN, Dale 201-761-7827 314 F dhochstein@spc.edu
HOCHSTETLER, Char 574-535-7541 171 G chardh@goshen.edu
HOCK, Amy 402-471-2505 299 D ahock@nscs.edu
HOCK, Carl, E 856-566-6066 316 E hock@umdnj.edu
HOCK, Carl, E 856-566-6066 316 I hock@umdnj.edu
HOCK, Joan 215-489-2975 426 H joan.hock@delval.edu
HOCKENBERRY, Frederick 301-846-2544 222 G fhockenberry@frederick.edu
HOCKENHULL, Benjamin, R 512-448-8688 493 E ben@stedwards.edu
HOCKENSMITH, William 805-922-6966 26 L whockensmith@hancockcollege.edu
HOCKETT, Anne, B 336-633-0218 373 A abhockett@randolph.edu
HOCKING, Eileen 860-231-5308 95 D ehocking@usj.edu
HOCKMAN, Joan 814-371-2090 448 D jhockman@triangle-tech.edu
HOCKSTRA, Dale 650-543-3874 57 B dhockstra@menlo.edu
HOCQUARD, Stephen, L 989-964-4081 257 G shoc@svsu.edu
HOCUTT, Kirby 806-742-3355 502 A kirby.hocutt@ttu.edu
HOCUTT, Martha 205-652-3675 9 E mhocutt@uwa.edu
HODGE, Bobby 720-859-7900 81 C
HODGE, Brad, K 215-670-9210 438 E bkhodge@peirce.edu
HODGE, David 978-478-3400 246 G dhodge@zbc.edu
HODGE, David 334-291-4928 2 F david.hodge@cv.edu
HODGE, David 513-529-2345 396 E president@muohio.edu
HODGE, Derek, M 703-323-3267 527 F dhodge@nvcc.edu
HODGE, Doug 731-286-3359 475 B hodge@dscc.edu
HODGE, Evelyn 334-229-4139 1 C ehodge@alasu.edu
HODGE, Gary, B 972-881-5897 483 H ghodge@collin.edu
HODGE, Hortencia 559-438-4222 49 I hortencia_hodge@heald.edu
HODGE, Jimmer 218-262-6705 266 E jimmerhodge@hibbing.edu
HODGE, Johnesa 313-496-2796 259 G jdimick1@wcccd.edu
HODGE, Kevin 214-234-4850 486 H khodge@cci.edu
HODGE, Marilyn 757-822-7244 528 G mhodge@tcc.edu
HODGE, Michel, A 718-262-2707 329 A mahodge@york.cuny.edu
HODGE, Mike 314-264-1740 292 B mike.hodge@vatterott.edu
HODGE, Mildred 860-885-2344 92 E mhodge@trcc.commnet.edu
HODGE, Tiffani 404-523-8520 138 B thodge3@spelman.edu
HODGE, Wendy 860-701-5166 93 E hodge_w@mitchell.edu
HODGE-HENRY, Harriet 617-282-9798 279 I harriet@techmission.org
HODGEN, Danielle 509-527-4301 539 B danielle.hodgen@wwcc.edu
HODGES, Carolyn, R 865-974-3694 477 D chodges@utk.edu
HODGES, Christopher 215-893-5262 426 E christopher.hodges@curtis.edu
HODGES, Dale, B 269-471-3321 247 D dbhodges@andrews.edu
HODGES, Daniel, K 540-365-4365 519 C dhodges@ferrum.edu
HODGES, Dawn 770-229-3293 137 F dhodges@sctech.edu
HODGES, Elaine 843-661-8020 458 B elaine.hodges@fdtc.edu
HODGES, Greg 276-656-0213 527 G ghodges@patrickhenry.edu
HODGES, Heath 918-463-2931 407 H heath.hodges@connorsstate.edu
HODGES, James 510-885-3957 34 E james.hodges@csueastbay.edu
HODGES, Jeff 540-362-6503 520 A jhodges@hollins.edu
HODGES, Jill 906-487-3310 255 B jhodges@mtu.edu
HODGES, Jimmy 256-352-8229 10 A jimmy.hodges@wallacestate.edu
HODGES, Kimberly, S 860-701-5000 93 E hodges_k@mitchell.edu
HODGES, Nathan, L 270-901-1111 201 I nathan.hodges@kctcs.edu
HODGES, Omega 828-298-3325 380 D ohodges@warren-wilson.edu
HODGES, Rhonda 276-656-0256 527 G rhodges@patrickhenry.edu
HODGES, Richard, A 215-898-4050 448 J rhodges@sas.upenn.edu
HODGES, Ricky, C 336-734-7272 370 F rhodges@forsythtech.edu
HODGES, Stacey 601-276-3708 277 B slee@smcc.edu
HODGES, Stephen 617-746-1990 235 G stephen.hodges@hult.edu
HODGES, Tim 785-594-8365 190 F tim.hodges@bakeru.edu
HODGES, Tina 731-352-4032 467 E hodgest@bethelu.edu
HODGES, Victoria 317-805-1788 541 K vhodges@salemu.edu
HODGES, Zachary 713-718-5721 487 I zachary.hodges@hccs.edu
HODGES MOORE, Sue 859-572-5349 205 H moores4@nku.edu
HODGINS, Diane, W 850-729-6485 114 A hodginsd@nwfsc.edu
HODGINS, Randy 206-221-5670 539 A rhodgins@uw.edu
HODGSON, Regina 813-879-6000 107 A rhodgson@cci.edu
HODNETT, James 478-387-4715 131 A
HODOWANEC, Michael 610-372-4721 445 C mhodowanec@racc.edu
HODOWNES, Stephen 603-645-9730 305 I s.hodownes@snhu.edu
HODSDON, Roger 626-815-5080 30 G rhodsdon@apu.edu
HODSON, Andrea 603-283-2363 303 F ahodson@antioch.edu
HODSON, J. Bradford 620-235-4757 196 C bhodson@pittstate.edu
HODSON, Luke 859-985-3503 199 A hodsonl@berea.edu
HODUM, Robert 931-372-3888 474 B rhodum@tntech.edu
HOEBER, Mark, S 716-851-1413 333 C hoeber@ecc.edu
HOECK, Andreas 303-715-3218 88 D
HOEF, Ted 314-968-6980 292 J hoeftl@webster.edu
HOEFER, Michael, T 770-394-8300 125 A mhoefer@aii.edu
HOEFLER, William 479-968-0353 20 G whoeflerjr@atu.edu
HOEFT, Robert 217-333-9480 167 D rhoeft@illinois.edu
HOEG, Portia 814-332-3350 421 F phoeg@allegheny.edu
HOEGE, Jennifer, L 608-246-6220 554 D jlhoege@madisoncollege.org
HOEHLEIN, Rebecca 619-275-4700 46 K rebecca@fashioncareerscollege.com
HOEHN, Alex, J 718-990-2998 348 G hoehna@stjohns.edu
HOEHNER, Robert 314-505-7170 280 D hoehnerr@csl.edu
HOEHNKE, Diane 414-443-8627 553 D diane.hoehnke@wlc.edu
HOEKSTRA, Erik 712-722-6002 184 C erik.hoekstra@dordt.edu
HOEKSTRA, Jack 866-323-0233 63 D
HOEKSTRA, Jonathan 254-867-4892 500 C jonathan.hoekstra@systems.tstc.edu
HOEKSTRA, Steven, J 785-827-5541 194 F hoekstr@kwu.edu
HOEL, Aaron 301-687-3101 228 C ahoel@frostburg.edu
HOEL, Monica, S 276-944-6126 519 A mshoel@ehc.edu
HOELLEN, Kathy, L 803-981-7150 463 H khoellen@yorktech.edu
HOELSCHER, Ronda 325-793-4857 490 H hoelscher.ronda@mcm.edu
HOELTING, Floyd, B 512-471-8631 505 D floydh@austin.utexas.edu
HOELTZEL, Susan 718-960-8731 327 C susan.hoeltzel@lehman.cuny.edu
HOEMANN, D. Lee 360-867-6300 534 D hoemannl@evergreen.edu
HOEPFER, Maureen, G 717-780-1157 430 E mhoepfer@hacc.edu
HOEPPNER, Stephen, A 651-962-6949 272 B sahoeppner@stthomas.edu
HOERITZ, Kim 412-396-6213 428 D hoeritzk@duq.edu
HOERSCH, Alice, L 215-951-1010 432 I hoersch@lasalle.edu
HOERSCH, Kathy 619-425-3200 62 G khoersch@pmi.edu
HOERST, Barbara 215-951-1386 432 I hoerst@lasalle.edu
HOERTH, Richard 920-693-1237 554 C rich.hoerth@gotoltc.edu
HOETING, Mark 870-972-3033 20 D mhoeting@astate.edu
HOEVET, Suzy 712-279-5408 183 A suzy.hoevet@briarcliff.edu

HOEWING, Rodney, E .... 217-333-2034.... 167 D rhoewing@illinois.edu
HOEY, John, T .... 508-999-8027.... 237 A jhoey@umassd.edu
HOFEMANN, Neva .... 408-273-2718...... 58 G nhofemann@nhu.edu
HOFER, OP, Andrew .... 202-495-3861...... 99 C ahofer@dhs.edu
HOFER, Jeanie, H .... 573-341-4208.... 291 E jeanie@mst.edu
HOFER, Linda .... 605-995-2956.... 464 C lihofer@dwu.edu
HOFER, Philip .... 909-593-3511...... 75 E phofer@laverne.edu
HOFER, Titus, W .... 479-248-7236...... 21 G titus@ecollege.edu
HOFF, Andrew .... 559-278-4004...... 35 A andrewh@csufresno.edu
HOFF, Andrew .... 559-278-3936...... 35 A andrewh@csufresno.edu
HOFF, Darren .... 763-433-1159.... 265 G darren.hoff@anokaramsey.edu
HOFF, Dianne .... 678-839-6570.... 139 A dhoff@westga.edu
HOFF, Kathy .... 614-257-5013.... 390 B khoff@devry.edu
HOFF, Reno, R .... 503-375-7000.... 415 F rhoff@corban.edu
HOFFACKER, Thomas, E ... 270-809-2146.... 205 A thoffacker@murraystate.edu
HOFFARD, Dwight .... 618-985-3741.... 154 G dwighthoffard@jalc.edu
HOFFBAUER, Claudia .... 509-574-4612.... 540 D choffbauer@yvcc.edu
HOFFBERG, Michael, C ..... 610-519-4264.... 450 H michael.hoffberg@villanova.edu
HOFFER, Wallace, C .... 330-966-5450.... 402 B whoffer@starkstate.edu
HOFFMAN, A, P .... 334-556-2225........ 4 A ahoffman@wallace.edu
HOFFMAN, Agnes .... 503-725-5502.... 418 G hoffmana@pdx.edu
HOFFMAN, Angela .... 859-336-5082.... 206 A ahoffman@sccky.edu
HOFFMAN, Barbara .... 319-399-8540.... 183 F bhoffman@coe.edu
HOFFMAN, Barbara .... 419-372-2120.... 385 E bahoffm@bgsu.edu
HOFFMAN, Bart .... 714-564-6800...... 63 F hoffman_bart@sac.edu
HOFFMAN, Beth .... 301-687-4101.... 228 C bhoffman@frostburg.edu
HOFFMAN, Brad .... 513-244-4230.... 388 E brad_hoffman@mail.msj.edu
HOFFMAN, Bryce, T .... 518-564-2090.... 354 B bhoff003@plattsburgh.edu
HOFFMAN, Carolyn, F .... 301-322-0561.... 225 F hoffmacf@pgcc.edu
HOFFMAN, Cheryl, A .... 309-833-6021.... 165 F cheryl.hoffman@src.edu
HOFFMAN, David .... 540-665-5457.... 524 E dhoffman@su.edu
HOFFMAN, Deborah .... 813-935-5700.... 116 A deborahhoffman@remingtoncollege.edu
HOFFMAN, Derek, M .... 717-872-3820.... 443 D derek.hoffman@millersville.edu
HOFFMAN, Donna .... 909-384-8987...... 65 C dhoffman@sbccd.cc.ca.us
HOFFMAN, Ed .... 402-471-2505.... 299 D ehoffman@nscs.edu
HOFFMAN, Erin .... 847-735-5207.... 155 G hoffman@lakeforest.edu
HOFFMAN, Gail .... 212-854-1079.... 330 F gh2116@columbia.edu
HOFFMAN, Heather .... 404-270-2700.... 128 I hhoffman@devry.edu
HOFFMAN, Jeffrey .... 626-396-2325...... 29 I jeffrey.hoffman@artcenter.edu
HOFFMAN, Jeffrey, L .... 315-255-1743.... 325 G foundation@cayuga-cc.edu
HOFFMAN, Joseph, M ...... 301-687-4120.... 228 C jhoffman@frostburg.edu
HOFFMAN, Kathy, S .... 716-851-1832.... 333 C hoffman@ecc.edu
HOFFMAN, Larry .... 914-395-2384.... 350 C lhoffman@sarahlawrence.edu
HOFFMAN, Linda .... 585-594-6400.... 347 F hoffman_linda@roberts.edu
HOFFMAN, Lorraine, B ...... 530-898-6231...... 34 C lbhoffman@csuchico.edu
HOFFMAN, Louis .... 410-484-7200.... 225 C clhoffman@westshore.edu
HOFFMAN, Marcia, K .... 570-577-1631.... 423 E marcia.hoffman@bucknell.edu
HOFFMAN, Marion, S .... 850-488-2447.... 120 C marionh@ufl.edu
HOFFMAN, Martin .... 609-894-9311.... 308 B mhoffman@bcc.edu
HOFFMAN, Mary .... 719-587-7372...... 80 L mchoffma@adams.edu
HOFFMAN, Melissa .... 402-354-7212.... 299 C melissa.hoffman@methodistcollege.edu
HOFFMAN, Michael .... 716-375-2530.... 348 C mhoffman@sbu.edu
HOFFMAN, Michael .... 605-995-3022.... 464 F mike.hoffman@mitchelltech.edu
HOFFMAN, Micki, D .... 636-584-6532.... 281 E mdhoffma@eastcentral.edu
HOFFMAN, Mika .... 518-464-8773.... 333 E mhoffman@excelsior.edu
HOFFMAN, Neil, J .... 414-847-3210.... 549 B neilhoffman@miad.edu
HOFFMAN, Patricia, A .... 916-285-9468...... 51 E
HOFFMAN, Paula .... 320-629-5180.... 268 E hoffmanp@pinetech.edu
HOFFMAN, Peter .... 912-877-1906.... 124 G peter.hoffman@armstrong.edu
HOFFMAN, Robert .... 507-389-5566.... 267 E robert.hoffman@mnsu.edu
HOFFMAN, Robyn .... 740-374-8716.... 405 G rhoffman@wscc.edu
HOFFMAN, Sandra .... 856-415-2220.... 310 D shoffma2@gccnj.edu
HOFFMAN, Sharon, L .... 802-287-8215.... 513 F hoffmans@greenmtn.edu
HOFFMAN, Steven, A .... 859-236-6688.... 199 G steven.hoffman@centre.edu
HOFFMAN, Thomas .... 507-453-2770.... 267 C thoffman@southeastmn.edu
HOFFMAN, Wendy .... 859-846-5364.... 204 H whoffman@midway.edu
HOFFMAN-JOHNSON, Gail .... 989-686-9291.... 250 D gailhoffman@delta.edu
HOFFMANN, Len .... 563-589-0322.... 190 A lhoffmann@wartburgseminary.edu
HOFFMANN, Lowell .... 731-286-3307.... 475 B hoffmann@dscc.edu
HOFFMANN, Mark .... 701-777-2492.... 381 F mark.hoffmann@und.edu
HOFFMANN, Pauline .... 716-375-2578.... 348 C hoffmann@sbu.edu
HOFFMANN, Phylis .... 501-205-8813...... 21 C phoffmann@cbc.edu
HOFFMANN, Susie .... 785-670-1643.... 197 F susie.hoffmann@washburn.edu
HOFFMANN HARDING, Erin .... 574-631-7394.... 180 G eharding@nd.edu
HOFFMANS, Kim .... 805-378-1459...... 77 D khoffmans@vcccd.edu
HOFFMASTER, Linda, L ..... 717-764-9550.... 426 D lhoffmaster@csb.edu
HOFFMEYER, Tom .... 254-710-1561.... 482 A tom_hoffmeyer@baylor.edu
HOFFNUNG, Michele .... 203-582-8903...... 93 H michele.hoffnung@quinnipiac.edu
HOFFSIS, Glen, F .... 352-392-2213.... 120 C hoffsisg@vetmed.ufl.edu
HOFMANN, Glenn .... 978-837-5306.... 242 A glenn.hofmann@merrimack.edu
HOFMANN, Jacqueline ...... 406-243-7908.... 295 B jacqueline.hofmann@umontana.edu
HOFMEYER, Karna .... 712-324-5061.... 188 C khofmeyer@nwicc.edu
HOFNER, Amyjo .... 617-262-5000.... 231 G amyjo.hofner@the-bac.edu
HOFRENNING, Dan .... 507-786-3128.... 271 C dhofrenn@stolaf.edu
HOFRENNING, Ilene .... 508-626-4900.... 238 A ihofrenning@framingham.edu
HOFSTEDT, Petra .... 715-682-1983.... 549 F phofstedt@northland.edu
HOFSTETTER, Dale .... 513-745-8308.... 403 F hofsteda@uc.edu
HOFSTETTER, Martha, J .... 302-857-1124...... 96 G mhofste1@dtcc.edu
HOFSTETTER, Shirley, A .... 636-584-6704.... 281 E sahofste@eastcentral.edu
HOFSTETTER, Thomas, F ... 410-706-2069.... 227 C thofs001@umaryland.edu
HOFTIEZER, David .... 609-984-1164.... 316 A dhoftiezer@tesc.edu
HOGAN, Amy .... 785-242-5200.... 195 I amy.hogan@ottawa.edu
HOGAN, Andrea .... 203-582-5215...... 93 H andrea.hogan@quinnipiac.edu
HOGAN, Andrea .... 203-932-7338...... 95 C ahogan@newhaven.edu
HOGAN, Beverly, W .... 601-977-7730.... 277 C bhogan@tougaloo.edu
HOGAN, Bill .... 206-296-5451.... 538 B hoganw@seattleu.edu
HOGAN, Carrie .... 518-783-2554.... 350 I chogan@siena.edu
HOGAN, Cheryl .... 231-843-5864.... 260 B clhogan@westshore.edu
HOGAN, Christopher .... 617-287-6800.... 236 G christopher.hogan@umb.edu
HOGAN, Dave .... 334-386-7152........ 3 G dhogan@faulkner.edu
HOGAN, Heather .... 440-775-8410.... 397 G heather.hogan@oberlin.edu
HOGAN, Jennifer .... 810-767-2150.... 259 C jhogan@umflint.edu
HOGAN, Joan, P .... 828-448-6041.... 375 B jhogan@wpcc.edu
HOGAN, John, A .... 812-374-5115.... 176 A jhogan@ivytech.edu
HOGAN, John, T .... 401-865-2676.... 453 H jhogan@providence.edu
HOGAN, Judith .... 781-280-3816.... 240 B hoganj@middlesex.mass.edu
HOGAN, Kay .... 850-973-9422.... 113 K hogank@nfcc.edu
HOGAN, Lesley .... 253-833-9111.... 534 H lhogan@greenriver.edu
HOGAN, Marianna .... 212-431-2173.... 343 E mhogan@nyls.edu
HOGAN, Martha, A .... 972-238-6210.... 485 D mhogan@dcccd.edu
HOGAN, Pamela .... 603-668-2211.... 305 I p.hogan@snhu.edu
HOGAN, Pat .... 910-362-7009.... 368 H phogan@cfcc.edu
HOGAN, Patrick, J .... 301-445-1927.... 227 A pjhogan@usmd.edu
HOGAN, Paul .... 603-271-6426.... 304 F phogan@ccsnh.edu
HOGAN, Phyllis, E .... 317-466-2121.... 173 C pehogan@indianatech.edu
HOGAN, Robert .... 773-843-4524.... 147 H rhogan@ccc.edu
HOGAN, Roseann .... 903-886-5926.... 498 B roseann.hogan@tamuc.edu
HOGAN, Sean .... 847-543-2419.... 148 B shogan@clcillinois.edu
HOGAN, CSSP, Sean .... 412-396-5069.... 428 D hogan@duq.edu
HOGAN, Susan, S .... 413-597-4204.... 246 D susan.s.hogan@williams.edu
HOGAN, Terrence .... 319-273-2332.... 182 G terry.hogan@uni.edu
HOGAN, Tracy .... 415-482-3507...... 45 C tracy.hogan@dominican.edu
HOGAN, William .... 907-786-4407...... 10 H whhogan@uaa.alaska.edu
HOGARTH, William, T .... 727-873-4151.... 121 C whogarth@mail.usf.edu
HOGARTH-SMITH, Heather .... 340-693-1151.... 568 E hhogart@live.uvi.edu
HOGARTY, Lisa .... 617-495-1512.... 235 D lisa_hogarty@harvard.edu
HOGEBOOM, Cindi .... 510-261-8500...... 61 G cindi.hogeboom@patten.edu
HOGELAND, Beth .... 541-917-4211.... 416 I hogelab@linnbenton.edu
HOGENCAMP, Kelly .... 909-621-8273...... 69 A registrar@ad.scrippscol.edu
HOGENSON, Deborah .... 952-888-4777.... 270 C dhogenson@nwhealth.edu
HOGG, James, E .... 770-207-3130.... 125 C jhogg@athenstech.edu
HOGG, Matt .... 215-572-3838.... 451 D mhogg@wts.edu
HOGG, Michael .... 504-862-8495.... 215 C mhogg@tulane.edu
HOGGARD, Jonathan .... 516-686-7516.... 343 D
HOGGE, Jane Curley .... 410-617-2131.... 223 I jchogge@loyola.edu
HOGLUND, Carol .... 307-778-1281.... 556 E choglund@lccc.wy.edu
HOGLUND, Susan .... 740-826-8081.... 397 A shoglund@muskingum.edu
HOGREFE, Richard .... 909-389-3205...... 65 B rhogrefe@craftonhills.edu
HOGSETT, Denise .... 304-696-2370.... 544 B hogsettd@marshall.edu
HOGUE, Belinda .... 334-727-8763........ 8 B bahoque@mytu.tuskegee.edu
HOGUE, Eileen .... 719-502-2419...... 87 B eileen.hogue@ppcc.edu
HOGUE, Eric .... 916-577-1801...... 79 G ehogue@jessup.edu
HOGUE, Jeffery, H .... 417-328-1591.... 290 A jhogue@sbuniv.edu
HOGUE, Stacey, L .... 501-569-3318...... 24 E slhogue@ualr.edu
HOGUE, William, F .... 803-777-0707.... 462 A hogue@sc.edu
HOHBERG, Tonian .... 213-624-1200...... 46 L thohberg@fidm.edu
HOHENBERG, Pierre .... 212-998-2212.... 344 B pierre.hohenberg@nyu.edu
HOHENSTEIN, Janet, M ...... 218-477-2956.... 267 F hohenst@mnstate.edu
HOHIEMER, Victoria .... 270-686-4512.... 203 B vickie.hohiemer@kctcs.edu
HOHL, Kathleen .... 414-297-6208.... 554 F hohlk@matc.edu
HOHMAN, Adam .... 260-982-5228.... 177 H arhohman@manchester.edu
HOHMANN, Mark .... 502-585-9911.... 206 D mhohmann@spalding.edu
HOI, Samuel .... 310-665-6935...... 60 B shoi@otis.edu
HOILES, Thomas .... 440-834-3734.... 393 G thoiles@kent.edu
HOILMAN, Sandra, K .... 828-448-6025.... 375 B shoilman@wpcc.edu
HOING, Joe, W .... 479-979-1321...... 26 A jhoing@ozarks.edu
HOINS, Dennis .... 315-279-5251.... 337 K dhoins@mail.keuka.edu
HOIT, Marc, I .... 919-515-0141.... 378 C mark_hoit@ncsu.edu
HOJAN-CLARK, Jane .... 414-229-6300.... 551 D jhojan@uwm.edu
HOJAN-FIGGE, Elizabeth, M .... 262-554-2010.... 549 A mwcfinancialaid@aol.com
HOKE, Mary .... 210-829-3982.... 504 B mhoke@uiwtx.edu
HOL, Dick .... 509-533-8018.... 533 B dick.hol@ccs.spokane.edu
HOL, Dick .... 509-533-8013.... 533 A dhol@ccs.spokane.edu
HOLAK, Susan, L .... 718-982-2464.... 327 A susan.holak@csi.cuny.edu
HOLAWAY, Rick .... 615-966-6133.... 470 F rick.holaway@lipscomb.edu
HOLBERG, Connie .... 315-786-2402.... 337 F cholberg@sunyjefferson.edu
HOLBERT, Carolyn .... 704-216-3750.... 373 F carolyn.holbert@rccc.edu
HOLBERT, Woodrow .... 734-995-7598.... 249 G woodrow.holbert@cuaa.edu
HOLBROOK, Adam .... 937-393-3431.... 402 A aholbrook@sscc.edu
HOLBROOK, Carl .... 334-347-2623........ 3 F cholbrook@escc.edu
HOLBROOK, Catherine .... 508-531-1276.... 237 D cholbrook@bridgew.edu
HOLBROOK, Christine .... 413-552-2299.... 239 F cholbrook@hcc.edu
HOLBROOK, Eddie .... 704-484-5338.... 369 E holbrook@clevelandcc.edu
HOLBROOK, Jennifer .... 870-230-5275...... 21 I holbroj@hsu.edu
HOLBROOK, Karen .... 813-974-5481.... 121 A kholbrook@research.usf.edu
HOLBROOK, Mary Anne .... 276-466-7887.... 529 D maryanneholbrook@vic.edu
HOLBROOK, Peter, J .... 414-410-4004.... 546 G pjholbrook@stritch.edu
HOLBROOK MIMS, Mary . 903-785-7661.... 492 D mmims@parisjc.edu
HOLBROOKS, Johnnie, L .. 432-837-8100.... 501 E johnnieh@sulross.edu
HOLCOMB, Carole .... 404-471-6348.... 123 I cholcomb@agnesscott.edu
HOLCOMB, David .... 254-295-4184.... 504 C dholcomb@umhb.edu
HOLCOMB, Donna .... 440-834-3737.... 393 G dholcomb@kent.edu
HOLCOMB, Gay, L .... 859-858-3511.... 198 E gay.holcomb@asbury.edu
HOLCOMB, Grant .... 585-276-8902.... 359 B gholcomb@mag.rochester.edu
HOLCOMB, J. David .... 713-798-4613.... 481 H jholcomb@bcm.edu
HOLCOMB, Jeffrey, R .... 605-367-8355.... 466 D jeff.holcomb@southeasttech.edu
HOLCOMB, Mark .... 815-939-5236.... 161 A mholcomb@olivet.edu
HOLCOMB, Nancy .... 724-589-2155.... 448 B nholcomb@thiel.edu
HOLCOMB, Richard, E .... 248-341-2054.... 256 F reholcomb@oaklandcc.edu
HOLCOMB, Todd, R .... 308-635-6101.... 301 D holcombt@wncc.edu
HOLCOMBE, Annalisa, A .... 801-832-2551.... 512 G aholcombe@westminstercollege.edu
HOLCOMBE, Robert .... 864-429-8728.... 463 A reholcom@mailbox.sc.edu
HOLDA, William, M .... 903-983-8100.... 489 I bholda@kilgore.edu
HOLDEN, Camille .... 928-757-0838...... 16 F cholden@mohave.edu
HOLDEN, Dave .... 618-664-6750.... 151 F dave.holden@greenville.edu
HOLDEN, Eileen .... 863-297-1098.... 115 C eholden@polk.edu
HOLDEN, Elaine, P .... 704-637-4402.... 363 E epholden@catawba.edu
HOLDEN, Howard .... 610-902-8240.... 424 B howard.holden@cabrini.edu
HOLDEN, John .... 312-362-7165.... 149 A jholden2@depaul.edu
HOLDEN, Joseph, M .... 951-698-6389...... 77 G
HOLDEN, Larry .... 615-327-6339.... 471 C lholden@mmc.edu
HOLDEN, Nina .... 313-664-7864.... 249 E nholden@collegeforcreativestudies.edu
HOLDEN, Ronnie, E .... 410-651-6229.... 227 E reholden@umes.edu
HOLDEN, Scott, A .... 212-799-5000.... 337 H
HOLDEN, Wesley .... 772-546-5534.... 110 N wesleyholden@hsbc.edu
HOLDEN-DUFFY, Cheryl ... 410-651-6460.... 227 E clduffy@umes.edu
HOLDEN-HUCHTON, Patricia .... 940-898-2401.... 502 D pholdenhuchton@twu.edu
HOLDER, Ann, H .... 936-294-1613.... 501 D lib_ahh@shsu.edu

HOLMES, Sharon, N .... 920-924-6326.... 554 G
sholmes@morainepark.edu
HOLMES, Susan .... 956-364-4107.... 500 D
susan.holmes@tstc.edu
HOLMES, Terrell .... 302-857-6375...... 96 C
tholmes@desu.edu
HOLMES, Tiffany .... 312-345-3760.... 164 C
tholmes@saic.edu
HOLMES, Wanda .... 662-621-4853.... 273 F
wholmes@coahomacc.edu
HOLMES, Wendy .... 845-341-4662.... 345 E
wendy.holmes@sunyorange.edu
HOLMES, William .... 859-622-1478.... 200 J
william.holmes@eku.edu
HOLMGREN, Janet, L .... 510-261-8500...... 61 G
janet.holmgren@patten.edu
HOLMGREN, Marilyn .... 605-721-5275.... 464 H
mholmgren@national.edu
HOLMGREN, Richard, A .... 814-332-2898.... 421 F
richard.holmgren@allegheny.edu
HOLMQUIST, David .... 562-903-4886...... 31 A
dave.holmquist@biola.edu
HOLMQUIST, Eric .... 712-279-5435.... 183 A
eric.holmquist@briarcliff.edu
HOLMQUIST, Jake .... 718-862-7449.... 339 H
jake.holmquist@manhattan.edu
HOLMSTROM, Kevin .... 701-224-5776.... 382 D
kevin.holmstrom@bismarckstate.edu
HOLNESS, Lansford .... 303-975-5024...... 89 H
lholness@westwood.edu
HOLODICK, Nicholas, A .... 570-208-5895.... 432 G
naholodi@kings.edu
HOLOMAN, Christopher, L 716-926-8854.... 335 E
choloman@hilbert.edu
HOLOPIREK, Darnell .... 620-792-9367.... 190 H
holopirekd@bartonccc.edu
HOLOWICKI, Linda .... 708-209-3170.... 148 E
linda.holowicki@cuchicago.edu
HOLPER, Mark .... 651-779-5834.... 266 A
mark.holper@century.edu
HOLS, Eric .... 703-284-1601.... 521 D
eric.hols@marymount.edu
HOLSCLAW, Mick .... 916-568-3017...... 55 J
holsclm@losrios.edu
HOLSCLAW, Scott .... 870-245-5129...... 22 I
holsclaws@obu.edu
HOLSCLAW, Sheila, K .... 859-846-5310.... 204 H
sholsclaw@midway.edu
HOLSENBECK, Daniel .... 407-823-2387.... 120 B
daniel.holsenbeck@ucf.edu
HOLSINGER, Kent .... 860-486-2182...... 94 G
kent.holsinger@uconn.edu
HOLSINGER-FUCHS,
Pamela .... 715-232-2639.... 552 E
holsinger-fuchsp@uwstout.edu
HOLSOPPLE, Heather .... 517-265-5161.... 246 H
hholsopple@adrian.edu
HOLST, Tim .... 218-726-7571.... 271 F
tholst@umn.edu
HOLSTAD, Deb .... 320-308-3277.... 269 B
dholstad@sctcc.edu
HOLSTAD, Deb, A .... 320-308-3227.... 269 B
dholstad@sctcc.edu
HOLSTEIN, David .... 561-868-3004.... 114 D
holsteid@palmbeachstate.edu
HOLSTEN, Robert, D .... 252-246-1258.... 375 D
rholsten@wilsoncc.edu
HOLSTER, Melissa .... 617-228-2271.... 239 C
mholster@bhcc.mass.edu
HOLSTINE, Tammy .... 304-357-4383.... 542 A
tammyholstine@ucwv.edu
HOLSTON, Tavarez .... 229-217-4202.... 134 F
tholston@moultrietech.edu
HOLSTON, William .... 336-841-9221.... 365 C
bookstor@highpoint.edu
HOLT, Amy .... 575-562-2467.... 318 B
amy.holt@enmu.edu
HOLT, Brooke .... 479-619-4298...... 22 H
bholt@nwacc.edu
HOLT, Bruce .... 865-981-8035.... 471 B
bruce.holt@maryvillecollege.edu
HOLT, Chad .... 252-398-6298.... 363 G
holtch@chowan.edu
HOLT, Christine .... 703-257-6664.... 527 F
chholt@nvcc.edu
HOLT, Debbie .... 859-246-6286.... 201 H
debbie.holt@kctcs.edu
HOLT, Dennis .... 573-986-6888.... 289 K
dholt@semo.edu
HOLT, Diann .... 757-822-1069.... 528 G
dholt@tcc.edu
HOLT, Jerry .... 219-785-5200.... 179 A
jholt@pnc.edu
HOLT, Jim .... 956-548-8776.... 505 E
jim.holt@utb.edu
HOLT, Joseph .... 559-651-2500...... 66 E
HOLT, Joseph, L .... 410-778-7201.... 229 D
jholt2@washcoll.edu
HOLT, Lynda .... 518-608-8171.... 333 E
lholt@excelsior.edu
HOLT, Raymond .... 229-931-2001.... 137 C
rholt@southgatech.edu
HOLT, Roslyn, J .... 318-670-6436.... 215 A
rholt@susla.edu
HOLT, Russ .... 925-439-2181...... 43 G
rholt@losmedanos.edu
HOLT, Wilford .... 334-420-4400........ 7 H
wholt@trenholmstate.edu
HOLTE, Terri .... 404-237-7573.... 126 B
tholte@khec.com
HOLTEN, Kathryn .... 803-323-2275.... 463 E
holtenk@winthrop.edu
HOLTER, Joan .... 218-723-6041.... 262 G
jholer@css.edu
HOLTER, Sherer .... 509-963-2111.... 532 C
holters@cwu.edu
HOLTFRETER, David .... 217-875-7200.... 162 F
dholt@richland.edu
HOLTGREN, Shawn .... 574-257-3344.... 169 I
holtgrs@bethelcollege.edu
HOLTHAUS, Barbara .... 217-641-4104.... 154 I
bholthaus@jwcc.edu
HOLTHOUSER, David, M .... 704-894-2220.... 363 I
daholthouser@davidson.edu
HOLTMANN, Ruth Ann .... 314-421-0949.... 290 D
holtmann@siba.edu
HOLTMEIER, Kelly .... 920-498-6384.... 555 C
kelly.holtmeier@nwtc.edu
HOLTON, Simone .... 802-387-6753.... 513 G
sholton@landmark.edu
HOLTROP, Stephen, D .... 260-359-4166.... 173 A
sholtrop@huntington.edu
HOLTSCHNEIDER,
Dennis, H .... 312-362-8890.... 149 A
president@depaul.edu
HOLTZ, Barry .... 212-678-8030.... 337 G
baholtz@jtsa.edu
HOLTZ, Daniel, F .... 320-222-5205.... 268 G
daniel.holtz@ridgewater.edu
HOLTZ, Eddie .... 712-325-3426.... 186 F
eholtz@iwcc.edu
HOLTZCLAW, Barry .... 510-204-0745...... 40 A
bholtzclaw@cdsp.edu
HOLTZCLAW, Mike .... 510-659-6191...... 59 J
mholtzclaw@ohlone.edu
HOLWAY, Carla, A .... 610-648-3258.... 439 H
cah1@psu.edu
HOLWICK, Jana .... 440-375-7252.... 394 E
jholwick@lec.edu
HOLYCROSS, Robert, L ..... 205-652-3601........ 9 E
rlh@uwa.edu
HOLZ-CLAUSE, Mary .... 860-486-4792...... 94 G
mary.holz-clause@uconn.edu
HOLZBERLEIN, Anne .... 405-974-2770.... 413 B
aholzberlein@uco.edu
HOLZEM, Madeline .... 608-785-8013.... 551 C
mholzem@uwlax.edu
HOLZEMER, William, L ..... 973-353-5149.... 314 E
holzemer@andromeda.rutgers.edu
HOLZEMER, William, L ..... 732-932-1770.... 314 C
holzemer@andromeda.rutgers.edu
HOLZER, Charlotte .... 718-871-6187.... 358 B
charloth@touro.edu
HOLZER, Marc .... 973-353-5268.... 314 E
mholzer@rutgers.edu
HOLZHEUSER, Christina ..... 361-825-5975.... 498 C
christina.holzheuser@tamucc.edu
HOLZMAN, Terri .... 920-748-8351.... 550 D
holzmant@ripon.edu
HOM, Kevin .... 718-260-5525.... 328 D
khom@citytech.cuny.edu
HOMAN, David .... 847-233-7700.... 160 D
dhoman@nc.edu
HOMAN, Elizabeth .... 240-567-7970.... 224 D
elizabeth.homan@montgomerycollege.edu
HOMAN, J. Michael .... 507-284-9595.... 262 D
HOMAN, J. Michael .... 507-284-9595.... 262 B
homan.michael@mayo.edu
HOMAN, Patricia .... 513-875-3344.... 387 C
patricia.homan@chatfield.edu
HOMAN, Richard, V .... 215-762-3500.... 427 H
homan-richardv@drexel.edu
HOMAN, Richard, V .... 757-446-5800.... 518 G
homanrv@evms.edu
HOMAN, Thomas .... 218-723-2214.... 262 G
thoman@css.edu
HOMANN, Gordon .... 617-912-9154.... 232 C
ghomann@bostonconservatory.edu
HOMBURGER, John, R .... 518-564-2130.... 354 B
homburjr@plattsburgh.edu
HOMEIER, Debra, L .... 906-227-2092.... 256 C
dhomeier@nmu.edu
HOMER, Jessica .... 781-768-7049.... 244 A
jessica.homer@regiscollege.edu
HOMESLEY, Diane .... 678-839-6582.... 139 A
dhomesley@westga.edu
HOMIAK, JR., Albert, J ..... 302-831-7285...... 96 I
homiak@udel.edu
HOMKOW, Gary .... 516-572-7304.... 342 C
gary.homkow@ncc.edu
HOMOLKA, Karen, K .... 217-245-3094.... 152 D
khomolk@ic.edu
HOMSHER, Betsy, E .... 810-762-9540.... 253 C
bhomsher@kettering.edu
HOMSTED, Gillian .... 800-862-9616.... 513 B
ghomsted@burlington.edu
HONABACH, Dennis .... 859-572-6406.... 205 H
honabachd1@nku.edu
HONAKER, Evelyn, J .... 423-585-6972.... 476 D
evelyn.honaker@ws.edu
HONAKER, Everett .... 276-591-5699.... 524 G
HONAN, Molly .... 617-735-9876.... 234 C
honanm@emmanuel.edu
HONDROS, Jack .... 610-526-1445.... 422 A
jack.hondros@theamericancollege.edu
HONDROS, Linda .... 614-508-7203.... 392 A
HONEA, Adam .... 480-557-1659...... 19 A
adam.honea@phoenix.edu
HONEA, Scott .... 979-436-0900.... 497 B
shonea@tamhsc.edu
HONECK, Sara .... 913-588-5170.... 197 C
shoneck@kumc.edu
HONEGAN, Rhonda .... 404-270-5075.... 138 B
rhonegan@spelman.edu
HONEGGER, Rose .... 337-482-6819.... 216 D
oia@louisiana.edu
HONEMAN, Donald .... 508-793-7419.... 233 B
dhoneman@clarku.edu
HONEY, Delores .... 417-625-9696.... 286 B
honey-d@mssu.edu
HONEYCUTT, Alan .... 858-642-8190...... 58 I
ahoneycutt@nu.edu
HONEYCUTT, Tony, L .... 606-679-8501.... 203 C
tony.honeycutt@kctcs.edu
HONEYMAN, Ryan, C .... 937-778-7808.... 390 G
rhoneymanr@edisonohio.edu
HONEYWOOD, Omega .... 803-327-7402.... 456 F
ohoneywood@clintonjuniorcollege.edu
HONG, E-Sing .... 408-260-0208...... 47 D
chinesedoctoral@fivebranches.edu
HONG, Luoluo .... 808-974-7334.... 141 F
luoluo@hawaii.edu
HONG, Steven .... 323-464-2777...... 27 I
shong@ca.aada.org
HONG, Tran .... 951-343-3907...... 31 J
thong@calbaptist.edu
HONHOLT, Richard .... 616-222-1954.... 250 A
richard.honholt@cornerstone.edu
HONKE, Mary, J .... 402-844-7124.... 299 I
maryh@northeast.edu
HONNELL, Cherie .... 503-494-7800.... 418 D
regohsu@ohsu.edu
HONNELL, Cherie .... 503-494-7800.... 418 D
finaid@ohsu.edu
HONSBERGER, Dean .... 269-387-4280.... 260 C
dean.honsberger@wmich.edu
HONTS, Arlen .... 316-295-5800.... 193 B
ahonts@friends.edu
HOOD, Brent .... 919-735-5151.... 375 A
wbhood@waynecc.edu
HOOD, Donna .... 828-395-1404.... 371 D
dhood@isothermal.edu
HOOD, Gwendolyn, D .... 205-348-5855........ 8 E
ghood@aalan.ua.edu
HOOD, James .... 336-316-2462.... 365 A
jhood@guilford.edu
HOOD, Jean .... 817-272-5554.... 505 C
jmhood@uta.edu
HOOD, Jeremiah .... 312-521-6881...... 19 A
jeremiah.hood@phoenix.edu
HOOD, Jon .... 402-449-2928.... 297 H
jhood@graceu.edu
HOOD, Mary, D .... 408-554-2732...... 68 C
mhood@scu.edu
HOOD, Michael, J .... 724-357-2397.... 442 F
mhood@iup.edu
HOOD, Mike .... 903-233-4115.... 490 A
mikehood@letu.edu
HOOD, Nan, S .... 610-989-1456.... 450 F
nhood@vfmac.edu
HOOD, Pam .... 317-917-3370.... 178 A
phood@martin.edu
HOOD, Patricia .... 706-649-1883.... 128 A
phood@columbustech.edu
HOOD, Philip, R .... 217-245-3046.... 152 D
philip.hood@ic.edu
HOOD, Richard, J .... 318-342-1010.... 216 E
hood@ulm.edu
HOOD, Robert .... 650-306-3340...... 67 F
hoodr@smccd.edu
HOOD, Scott, W .... 207-725-3256.... 217 E
shood@bowdoin.edu
HOOD, Sonya .... 931-393-1765.... 475 D
shood@mscc.edu
HOOD, Steven .... 205-348-9364........ 8 E
shood1@sa.ua.edu
HOOD, Tim .... 815-599-3417.... 152 B
tim.hood@highland.edu
HOOD, W.C. (Chip) .... 864-656-3414.... 456 E
chip@clemson.edu
HOOGAKKER, John .... 540-458-8446.... 530 D
jhoogakker@wlu.edu
HOOGHART, Anne .... 517-264-7662.... 258 B
ahooghar@sienaheights.edu
HOOK, Amy .... 617-353-2399.... 232 E
amyhook@bu.edu
HOOK, Morgan .... 518-320-1311.... 351 D
morgan.hook@suny.edu
HOOK, Randall .... 540-828-5358.... 517 B
rhook@bridgewater.edu
HOOK, Rebecca .... 610-436-6973.... 444 A
rhook@wcupa.edu
HOOK, Sam .... 864-592-4630.... 461 C
hooks@sccsc.edu
HOOK, Talbort .... 808-455-0611.... 142 D
talbort@hawaii.edu
HOOKER, Brenda .... 773-995-2304.... 146 G
b-hooker@csu.edu
HOOKER, Dianna .... 406-638-3142.... 294 E
dianna@lbhc.edu
HOOKER, Mary Kaye .... 404-237-7573.... 126 B
mahooker@bauder.edu
HOOKER-HARING,
Christopher .... 484-664-3245.... 437 C
hookerh@muhlenberg.edu
HOOKS, Beth .... 919-735-5151.... 375 A
bhooks@waynecc.edu
HOOKS, Brenda .... 502-456-6504.... 206 H
bhooks@sullivan.edu
HOOKS, Gerald, D .... 478-289-2036.... 129 B
jhooks@ega.edu
HOOKS, Haley .... 229-317-6746.... 128 D
haley.hooks@darton.edu
HOOLE, Thomas .... 978-934-3509.... 237 B
thomas_hoole@uml.edu
HOOPER, Celia, R .... 336-334-5744.... 379 B
crhooper@uncg.edu
HOOPER, Debra, A .... 919-488-8500.... 366 F
dhooper@living-arts-college.edu
HOOPER, John .... 940-565-3858.... 504 D
john.hooper@unt.edu
HOOPER, Lynn .... 405-425-5157.... 409 E
lynn.looper@oc.edu
HOOPER, Robert, D .... 740-427-5109.... 394 C
hooperr@kenyon.edu
HOOPER, Stephanie, L .... 304-336-8990.... 544 D
stephanie.hooper@westliberty.edu
HOOPES, Clark, D .... 330-471-8427.... 395 F
choopes@malone.edu
HOOPES, Tom .... 913-360-7529.... 191 A
thoopes@benedictine.edu
HOOTEN, Al .... 936-294-1016.... 501 D
ahooten@shsu.edu
HOOTEN, Jon .... 909-447-2558...... 40 H
jhooten@cst.edu
HOOTEN, Michael .... 806-354-5589.... 502 B
michael.hooten@ttuhsc.edu
HOOTON, Linda, J .... 205-853-1200........ 5 C
lhooton@jeffstateonline.com
HOOTS, Cathy .... 336-750-2265.... 380 B
hoots@wssu.edu
HOOVER, Becky, J .... 330-972-6462.... 403 B
hoover@uakron.edu
HOOVER, Chris .... 620-341-5337.... 192 G
choover@emporia.edu
HOOVER, Christine .... 561-433-2330.... 118 B
HOOVER, Douglas .... 724-938-4096.... 441 G
hoover@calu.edu
HOOVER, James, W .... 214-841-3694.... 485 F
jhoover@dts.edu
HOOVER, Jean, B .... 717-262-2007.... 452 C
jhoover@wilson.edu
HOOVER, Jeffrey .... 717-560-8258.... 433 D
jhoover@lbc.edu
HOOVER, Jonathan .... 214-333-5821.... 484 D
jonh@dbu.edu
HOOVER, Kathleen .... 610-558-5560.... 437 D
hooverk@neumann.edu
HOOVER, Kevin .... 559-438-4222...... 49 I
kevin_hoover@heald.edu
HOOVER, Kim .... 601-984-6200.... 277 E
khoover@umc.edu
HOOVER, Linda .... 806-742-3031.... 502 A
linda.hoover@ttu.edu
HOOVER, Lisa .... 214-637-3530.... 508 D
lhoover@wadecollege.edu
HOOVER, Lisa, D .... 570-577-3757.... 423 E
lisa.hoover@bucknell.edu
HOOVER, Lorette, M .... 912-427-5800.... 124 C
lhoover@altamahatech.edu
HOOVER, Marissa .... 717-948-6316.... 439 J
mrg159@psu.edu
HOOVER, Myrna .... 850-644-6089.... 119 D
mhoover@fsu.edu
HOOVER, Nancy .... 503-699-6261.... 416 J
nhoover@marylhurst.edu
HOOVER, Nancy, Z .... 740-587-6629.... 389 I
hoover@denison.edu
HOOVER, Samantha .... 212-472-1500.... 343 G
shoover@nysid.edu
HOOVER, Sara .... 205-226-4989........ 2 B
shoover@bsc.edu
HOOVER, Tom .... 423-425-5300.... 477 F
tom-hoover@utc.edu
HOOVLER, David .... 412-237-4554.... 425 H
dhoovler@ccac.edu
HOOYMAN, Jamie .... 660-359-3948.... 287 A
jhooyman@mail.ncmissouri.edu
HOPE, Laura .... 909-652-6113...... 39 E
laura.hope@chaffey.edu
HOPE, Maury, M .... 515-294-0323.... 182 E
mmhope@iastate.edu
HOPE, Oral .... 212-431-2300.... 343 E
ohope@nyls.edu
HOPE, Thomas .... 407-646-1580.... 116 D
thope@rollins.edu

HOPEWELL, JR., Woodson, H 757-727-5303 519 H woodson.hopewell@hamptonu.edu
HOPEY, Christopher, E 978-837-5110 242 A christopher.hopey@merrimack.edu
HOPKINS, Amanda 407-646-2124 116 D ahopkins@rollins.edu
HOPKINS, Becky 323-343-3200 35 D bhopkins@cslanet.calstatela.edu
HOPKINS, Christi 620-242-0414 195 C hopkinsc@mcpherson.edu
HOPKINS, Darlene 910-630-7150 367 B dhopkins@methodist.edu
HOPKINS, David, R 937-775-2312 406 C david.hopkins@wright.edu
HOPKINS, Debbie 704-216-7211 373 F debbie.hopkins@rccc.edu
HOPKINS, Denise, C 718-990-1323 348 G hopkinsd@stjohns.edu
HOPKINS, Drew, W 609-984-3430 316 A dhopkins@tesc.edu
HOPKINS, Dustin 918-781-7400 407 B hopkinsd@bacone.edu
HOPKINS, Gena 260-459-4513 175 C ghopkins@ibcfortwayne.edu
HOPKINS, Glenn, W 662-915-7177 277 D ghopkins@olemiss.edu
HOPKINS, Hunter, H 412-261-2647 432 D hhopkins@kaplan.edu
HOPKINS, Jane, L 618-664-6600 151 F jane.hopkins@greenville.edu
HOPKINS, Jason 312-777-8651 153 B jkhopkins@aii.edu
HOPKINS, Jayne, S 270-384-8033 204 D hopkinsj@lindsey.edu
HOPKINS, Jim 405-224-3140 413 E jhopkins@usao.edu
HOPKINS, John 330-263-2082 388 F jhopkins@wooster.edu
HOPKINS, LC, John 703-416-1441 520 C jhopkins@ipsciences.edu
HOPKINS, Joseph 205-726-2778 6 G jhopkins@samford.edu
HOPKINS, Kathryn 870-777-5722 25 F kathryn.hopkins@uacch.edu
HOPKINS, Laurie, B 803-786-3669 457 C lhopkins@columbiasc.edu
HOPKINS, Marilyn 707-638-5276 73 A marilyn.hopkins@tu.edu
HOPKINS, Mark 706-236-2231 126 C mhopkins@berry.edu
HOPKINS, Melissa 910-277-5670 376 C hopkinsmc@sapc.edu
HOPKINS, Nicole 509-574-6870 540 D nhopkins@yvcc.edu
HOPKINS, Paulette 619-388-7813 65 H phopkins@sdccd.edu
HOPKINS, Robert, J 910-277-5008 376 C hopkinsb@sapc.edu
HOPKINS, Robert, P 212-353-4350 331 A bob@cooper.edu
HOPKINS, Ronald 281-998-6150 494 A ronald.hopkins@sjcd.edu
HOPKINS, Sara 615-248-1653 476 G shopkins@trevecca.edu
HOPKINS, Shelli 918-781-7344 407 B hopkinss@bacone.edu
HOPKINS, Shirley, L 804-523-5896 527 A shopkins@reynolds.edu
HOPKINS, T. Hampton 704-355-5585 363 D hampton.hopkins@carolinascollege.edu
HOPKINS, Thomas, F 540-464-7228 529 F hopkinstf@vmi.edu
HOPKINS, Tony 740-588-1409 407 A thopkins@zanestate.edu
HOPKINS, Tony 740-588-1409 400 E hopkint1@ohio.edu
HOPKINS, Willie 718-951-3166 326 F whopkins@brooklyn.cuny.edu
HOPKINS-BEST, Mary 715-232-2421 552 E hopkinsbestm@uwstout.edu
HOPKINS GROSS, Anne, M 802-447-6323 514 F ahopkinsgross@svc.edu
HOPP, Melissa 443-840-3176 222 D mhopp@ccbcmd.edu
HOPP, Susan 503-883-2278 416 H shopp@linfield.edu
HOPPA, Anthony, T 585-245-5516 353 C thoppa@geneseo.edu
HOPPE, Elizabeth 909-706-3497 78 I shoppe@westernu.edu
HOPPE, Heather 419-251-8989 395 I heather.hoppe@mercycollege.edu
HOPPE, Jim 651-696-6220 264 J hoppe@macalester.edu
HOPPE, Ken 870-236-6901 21 E khoppe@crc.edu
HOPPER, Darla 812-535-5110 179 E dhopper@smwc.edu
HOPPER, David, R 757-455-3415 530 C dhopper@vwc.edu
HOPPER, George, M 662-325-2953 275 F ghopper@cfr.msstate.edu
HOPPER, Jack 409-880-8741 501 A jack.hopper@lamar.edu
HOPPER, Karen, S 870-508-6110 20 E khopper@asumh.edu
HOPPER, Lisa 501-760-4241 22 F lhopper@npcc.edu
HOPPER, Marianne, F 512-448-8551 493 E marianh@stedwards.edu
HOPPER, William 305-626-3701 109 A william.hopper@fmuniv.edu
HOPPES, Cherron 415-442-6510 48 F choppes@ggu.edu
HOPPLE, Dennis, M 570-577-1201 423 E dennis.hopple@bucknell.edu
HOPPLE, Stephnie 928-541-7777 16 H shopple@ncu.edu
HOPPMANN, Richard, A 803-733-1531 462 A richard.hoppmann@uscmed.sc.edu
HOPSON, George, A 864-977-2194 460 A george.hopson@ngu.edu
HOPSON, Pamela, F 812-465-7188 181 B pfhopson@usi.edu
HOPWOOD, Dennis, T 509-527-5172 540 B hopwoodt@whitman.edu
HOPWOOD, Julie, D 207-581-1512 220 A julie.hopwood@maine.edu
HOR, Annie, Y 209-667-3709 36 D ahor@csustan.edu
HORADAN, Lloyd 478-553-2060 135 B lhoradan@oftc.edu
HORADAN, Lloyd 478-553-2060 135 C lhoradan@oftc.edu
HORAK, Janice 254-968-9075 497 A jhorak@tarleton.edu
HORAK, Janice 254-968-9890 497 A jhorak@tarleton.edu
HORAK, Maureen 413-662-5205 238 C m.horak@mcla.edu
HORAK, Michael, D 972-860-8344 484 I mhorak@dcccd.edu
HORAN, James, J 207-948-9263 219 H jhoran@unity.edu
HORAN, Kevin 925-866-1822 43 F khoran@srvc.net
HORAN, Maureen, T 814-375-4829 439 E mth12@psu.edu
HORAN, Michael, D 404-364-8322 135 E mhoran@oglethorpe.edu
HORAN, Thomas 909-607-9302 40 F thomas.horan@cgu.edu
HORAZDOVSKY, Bruce, F 507-284-3862 262 C horazdovsky.bruce@mayo.edu
HORBACEWICZ, Jill 212-463-0400 358 B jillh@touro.edu
HORGAN, Elizabeth 508-213-2289 243 E elizabeth.horgan@nichols.edu
HORGAN, Joan 518-454-5296 330 C horganj@strose.edu
HORGAN, Louise, M 732-224-2202 308 A lhorgan@brookdalecc.edu
HORGAN, Ralph, R 412-268-6156 424 J rh44@andrew.cmu.edu
HORINE, Troy 316-942-4291 195 F horinet@newmanu.edu
HORINEK, Jon 405-682-1611 409 F jhorinek@occc.edu
HORISSIAN, Kevork, T 570-577-3548 423 E kevork.horissian@bucknell.edu
HORMANN, Shana 206-268-5714 530 I shormann@antioch.edu
HORN, Allison 503-883-2323 416 H ahorn@linfield.edu
HORN, Brian, S 727-816-3458 114 F hornb@phcc.edu
HORN, Carla 717-757-1100 452 J carla.horn@yti.edu
HORN, Christy, A 605-394-1604 466 B christy.horn@sdsmt.edu
HORN, Cindy 231-591-5309 250 H hornc@ferris.edu
HORN, David, G 978-468-7111 235 B dhorn@gcts.edu
HORN, David, G 614-292-6359 398 I horn.5@osu.edu
HORN, George 912-478-2897 131 E ghorn@georgiasouthern.edu
HORN, Herman 512-245-2539 501 F hh18@txstate.edu
HORN, Jamie 334-386-7168 3 G jhorn@faulkner.edu
HORN, Jay 817-272-2355 505 C horn@uta.edu
HORN, John, F 215-898-7593 448 J horn3@pobox.upenn.edu
HORN, SJ, John, P 314-768-1891 283 G horn@kenrick.edu
HORN, Jonathon 419-995-8302 392 K horn.j@rhodesstate.edu
HORN, Kristin 717-728-2288 425 B kristinhorn@centralpenn.edu
HORN, Larry 713-623-2040 480 J lhorn@aii.edu
HORN, Larry, S 812-488-2775 180 E lh6@evansville.edu
HORN, Mark 479-788-7006 24 D mark.horn@uafs.edu
HORN, Michael 704-330-5963 369 D michael.horn@cpcc.edu
HORN, Paul 212-998-3228 344 B paul.horn@nyu.edu
HORN, Samuel, E 763-417-8250 262 A
HORN, Tammy 859-246-6637 201 H tammy.horn@kctcs.edu
HORN BUNK, Sheri 661-763-7936 72 E shornbunk@taftcollege.edu
HORNBEAK, Joe, N 405-466-3265 408 G jnhornbeak@langston.edu
HORNBECK, Billi 605-455-6037 465 A bhornbeck@olc.edu
HORNBERGER, Cynthia, A 785-670-1213 197 F cynthia.hornberger@washburn.edu
HORNBERGER, Lois 503-352-2240 419 E lhornberger@pacificu.edu
HORNBERGER, Rob 417-836-6444 286 C robhornberger@missouristate.edu
HORNBERGER, Tiffany 502-863-8027 201 A tiffany_hornberger@georgetowncollege.edu
HORNBUCKLE, Jami 606-783-2372 204 I j.hornbuckle@moreheadstate.edu
HORNBURG, Trisha, L 262-691-5446 555 E thornburg@wctc.edu
HORNDT, Christin 989-275-5000 253 E christin.horndt@kirtland.edu
HORNE, Arlene 678-839-4760 139 A ahorne@westga.edu
HORNE, Arthur, M 706-542-6446 138 G ahorne@uga.edu
HORNE, Cathy 704-272-5337 374 A chorne@spcc.edu
HORNE, Denise, M 252-246-1263 375 D dhorne@wilsoncc.edu
HORNE, Derek 850-599-3868 118 L derek.horne@famu.edu
HORNE, Hadie, C 252-246-1221 375 D hhorne@wilsoncc.edu
HORNE, J. Douglas 801-524-8110 510 E d-horne@ldsbc.edu
HORNE, Pamela, T 765-494-9116 178 J pamhorne@purdue.edu
HORNE, JR., Rex, M 870-245-5400 22 I president@obu.edu
HORNE, Rhonda 937-258-8251 392 B
HORNE, Robert 215-780-1313 446 G rhorne@salus.edu
HORNE, Valerie 601-403-1211 276 E vhorne@prcc.edu
HORNE, Walter 330-325-6558 397 D wih@neomed.edu
HORNER, Jeff 719-502-2011 87 B jeffrey.horner@ppcc.edu
HORNER, Jeffrey, T 423-798-7952 476 D jeff.horner@ws.edu
HORNER, Kenneth, R 931-540-2533 475 A khorner@columbiastate.edu
HORNER, Theresa 716-827-2485 358 D hornert@trocaire.edu
HORNER, Theresa, M 814-269-7001 449 D thorner@pitt.edu
HORNING, Kirsten 503-338-2341 415 B khorning@clatsopcc.edu
HORNS, Phyllis, N 252-744-2265 377 E hornsp@ecu.edu
HORNSBERGER, Bill 330-869-3600 385 H whornsberger@brownmackie.edu
HORNSBY, Jacob 415-518-5396 74 A hornsbyj@uchastings.edu
HORNSHUH KENT, Jan 541-485-1780 417 E jankent@newhope.edu
HOROWITZ, Anne, B 215-596-7518 450 B a.horowitz@usciences.edu
HOROWITZ, Avery 718-252-7800 358 B averymh@touro.edu
HOROWITZ, Boruch Avrohom 718-438-2018 346 I rcby26@aol.com
HOROWITZ, Elias 845-783-0833 359 D
HOROWITZ, Sam, L 904-264-2172 116 C shorowitz@iws.edu
HOROWITZ, Sara 212-678-8838 337 G sahorowitz@jtsa.edu
HORR, Stephen, J 207-221-8770 218 C shorr@kaplan.edu
HORRAS, Danielle 208-377-8080 143 C dhorras@carrington.edu
HORRELL, Jeffrey, L 603-646-2235 304 J jeffrey.l.horrell@dartmouth.edu
HORROCKS, Dianne, K 208-282-2592 143 H horrdian@isu.edu
HORSCH, Ellen, S 906-487-1737 255 B eshorsch@mtu.edu
HORSEY, Cheryl 215-641-5546 430 C horsey.c@gmc.edu
HORSEY, Dwight, G 717-872-3026 443 D dwight.horsey@millersville.edu
HORSLEY, Jeff, O 714-808-4822 59 C jhorsley@nocccd.edu
HORSLEY, Julia 252-536-7254 371 B horsleyj@halifaxcc.edu
HORSMAN, Karen 317-931-2315 170 H khorsman@cts.edu
HORST, Pamela 907-822-3201 10 B phorst@akbible.edu
HORSTMAN, Scott 281-476-1501 493 H scott.horstman@sjcd.edu
HORSTMEYER, Mark 708-974-5275 159 B horstmeyer@morainevalley.edu
HORTON, Amy 847-317-7152 166 E ahorton@tiu.edu
HORTON, C, R 864-488-4586 459 B chorton@limestone.edu
HORTON, Carol, R 626-914-8886 40 B chorton@citruscollege.edu
HORTON, Claudia 816-833-0524 185 B horton@graceland.edu
HORTON, Claudia, D 816-833-0524 282 C horton@graceland.edu
HORTON, Connie 310-506-4210 61 H connie.horton@pepperdine.edu
HORTON, Dan 414-382-6238 546 B dan.horton@alverno.edu
HORTON, Gretchen 503-253-3443 417 H ghorton@ocom.edu
HORTON, Howard, E 617-951-2350 242 G howard.horton@necb.edu
HORTON, Jana 251-575-8252 1 B jhorton@ascc.edu
HORTON, Jane, T 540-458-8401 530 D jhorton@wlu.edu
HORTON, Jason 317-299-6001 177 F
HORTON, Jeanine 918-495-7575 411 C jhorton@oru.edu
HORTON, Jeff 916-649-2400 31 F
HORTON, Joanne, M 804-594-1569 527 B jhorton@jtcc.edu
HORTON, Johnna 507-389-7223 269 D johnna.horton@southcentral.edu
HORTON, Joseph, M 603-641-7600 305 G jhorton@anselm.edu
HORTON, Kimberly 937-769-1837 384 B khorton2@antioch.edu
HORTON, Larry, N 650-725-3324 71 G larry.horton@stanford.edu
HORTON, Mac 251-380-2272 7 E horton@shc.edu
HORTON, Marshae 804-257-5742 530 A mthorton@vuu.edu
HORTON, Michele 850-471-4639 115 B mhorton@pensacolastate.edu
HORTON, Muriel 843-574-6138 461 G muriel.horton@tridenttech.edu
HORTON, Peter 412-536-1050 432 H peter.horton@laroche.edu
HORTON, Stanley, W 360-538-4051 534 G shorton@ghc.edu
HORTON, Steve 318-357-5851 216 B hortons@nsula.edu
HORTON, Steve 318-357-4330 216 B hortons@nsula.edu
HORTON, Susan 845-434-5750 357 A shorton@sullivan.suny.edu
HORTON, JR., Walter, E 330-325-6290 397 D wehj@neomed.edu
HORTON, JR., Walter, E 330-325-6499 397 D wehj@neomed.edu
HORVATH, Cathy 701-858-4444 382 A cathy.horvath@minotstateu.edu
HORVATH, Fran 831-656-2228 558 A rfhorvat@nps.edu
HORVATH, Karl 215-646-7300 430 C horvath.k@gmc.edu
HORVATH, Katherine, K 978-468-7111 235 B khorvath@gcts.edu
HORVATH, Michael 678-839-6445 139 A mhorvath@westga.edu
HORVATH, Rebecca, L 215-951-1898 432 I horvath@lasalle.edu
HORVATH, Virginia, S 716-673-3456 352 A virginia.horvath@fredonia.edu
HORWATH, Amy 814-536-5168 424 E ahorwath@crbc.net
HORWATH, Donna 303-963-3365 82 C dhorwath@ccu.edu
HORWITZ, Pamela 314-529-9418 284 C phorwitz@maryville.edu
HOSACK, Susan, E 314-935-5567 292 I sue.hosack@wustl.edu
HOSCH, Jason 504-278-6281 211 E jhosch@nunez.edu
HOSEA, Walter 865-251-1800 473 A whosea@southcollegetn.edu
HOSEI, Huan, F 671-735-5584 559 E adulteducation@guamcc.edu
HOSELTON, Steven, A 312-341-2442 163 B shoselton@roosevelt.edu
HOSENEY, Jason 573-840-9668 290 F jhoseney@trcc.edu
HOSENEY, Jason 651-450-3692 266 F jhosene@inverhills.edu
HOSHIKO, Carol 808-734-9568 141 J hoshiko@hawaii.edu
HOSKEY, Lisa 607-274-3011 336 G

HOSKIN, Marilyn .... 212-650-5700 .... 326 G
mhoskin@ccny.cuny.edu
HOSKINS, Deb .... 970-641-2237 .... 89 E
dhoskins@western.edu
HOSKINS, Phillip, J .... 573-882-2011 .... 291 A
hoskinsp@umsystem.edu
HOSKINS, Sheila .... 252-823-5166 .... 370 D
hoskinss@edgecombe.edu
HOSKINS, Steve .... 606-546-4151 .... 207 B
shoskins@unionky.edu
HOSKINSON, Buddy .... 859-223-9608 .... 206 E
bhoskinson@spencerian.edu
HOSKINSON, Heidi .... 316-295-5861 .... 193 B
heidi_hoskinson@friends.edu
HOSKOWITZ, Joel, M .... 410-386-8412 .... 221 G
jhoskowitz@carrollcc.edu
HOSPEDALES, Marcia .... 973-877-3353 .... 309 H
hospedales@essex.edu
HOSS, Cindy .... 620-665-3507 .... 193 H
hossc@hutchcc.edu
HOSS, Neal .... 760-750-4400 .... 36 C
nhoss@csusm.edu
HOSSAIN, Zakir .... 570-484-2136 .... 443 B
zhossain@lhup.edu
HOSSENLOPP, Jeanne .... 414-288-1532 .... 548 F
jeanne.hossenlopp@marquette.edu
HOSTEN-HAAS, Nicole .... 718-951-5671 .... 326 F
nicole@brooklyn.cuny.edu
HOSTER, Robert, L .... 570-577-3352 .... 423 E
bob.hoster@bucknell.edu
HOSTETLER, Bumper, R .... 812-888-4510 .... 181 D
bhostetler@vinu.edu
HOSTETLER, Chad .... 304-457-6320 .... 540 E
hostetlercs@ab.edu
HOSTETLER, James .... 570-577-1911 .... 423 E
jom.hostetler@bucknell.edu
HOSTETLER, Lori, J .... 812-888-4121 .... 181 D
lhostetler@vinu.edu
HOSTETLER, Theodore, J .... 434-947-8133 .... 523 B
thostetler@randolphcollege.edu
HOSTETLER, Timothy, J .... 423-775-7262 .... 467 F
hostetti@bryan.edu
HOSTETTER, Julie, M .... 800-287-8822 .... 169 H
hosteju@bethanyseminary.edu
HOSTETTER, Larry .... 270-686-4236 .... 199 B
larry.hostetter@brescia.edu
HOSTETTER, Steve, J .... 218-751-8670 .... 270 D
stevehostetter@oakhills.edu
HOSTINA, Michael .... 907-450-8080 .... 10 G
mike.hostina@alaska.edu
HOTALING, Diane, E .... 757-455-3216 .... 530 C
dhotaling@vwc.edu
HOTALING, Marcus, S .... 518-388-6161 .... 358 G
hotalinm@union.edu
HOTCHKISS, Carolyn .... 781-239-5528 .... 230 E
hotchkiss@babson.edu
HOTCHKISS, Charles .... 617-989-4831 .... 245 F
hotchkissc@wit.edu
HOTCHKISS, David .... 415-239-3000 .... 40 C
dhotchki@ccsf.edu
HOTCHKISS, Pat .... 520-515-5420 .... 13 E
hotchkis@cochise.edu
HOTEZ, Peter .... 713-798-4951 .... 481 H
hotez@bcm.edu
HOTTEL, Haven .... 910-893-1421 .... 362 J
hottelh@campbell.edu
HOTTEL, Timothy, L .... 901-448-6202 .... 477 E
thottel@uthsc.edu
HOTTON, Bob .... 661-362-2696 .... 56 G
bhotton@masters.edu
HOTZLER, Russell, K .... 718-260-5400 .... 328 D
rhotzler@citytech.cuny.edu
HOU, Feng .... 941-752-5694 .... 118 J
fengh@scf.edu
HOUBECK, JR., Robert, L .... 810-762-3410 .... 259 C
rhoubeck@umflint.edu
HOUCHINS, Shelia, E .... 270-745-4493 .... 208 A
shelia.houchins@wku.edu
HOUCK, Clarence, M .... 803-934-3235 .... 459 G
chouck@morris.edu
HOUCK, Keith, W .... 407-582-3465 .... 123 B
khouck@valenciacollege.edu
HOUCK, Laurie .... 330-263-2583 .... 388 F
lhouck@wooster.edu
HOUCK, Maureen, B .... 516-463-6745 .... 335 G
maureen.b.houck@hofstra.edu
HOUCK, Susan .... 803-738-7610 .... 459 E
houcks@midlandstech.edu
HOUDEK, Rob .... 605-642-6562 .... 465 H
robert.houdek@bhsu.edu
HOUDESHELL, Tara .... 740-366-9223 .... 386 H
thoudesh@cotc.edu
HOUFER, Michael .... 651-747-4085 .... 266 A
michael.houfer@century.edu
HOUGH, Bradley .... 636-227-2100 .... 284 B
brad.hough@logan.edu
HOUGH, John .... 304-724-3700 .... 540 F
jhough@apus.edu
HOUGH, Melanie .... 317-921-4823 .... 175 K
mhough11@ivytech.edu
HOUGH, Susan .... 916-278-7469 .... 36 A
shough@csus.edu
HOUGH, Tony .... 803-738-7695 .... 459 E
hought@midlandstech.edu
HOUGHTON, David, C .... 405-878-3254 .... 409 D
david.houghton@okbu.edu
HOUGHTON, James .... 212-799-5000 .... 337 H
HOUGHTON, Susan .... 510-659-6441 .... 59 J
shoughton@ohlone.edu
HOUGLAND, Dawm .... 312-341-3531 .... 163 B
dhougland@roosevelt.edu
HOUK, Christopher .... 270-686-4241 .... 199 B
chris.houk@brescia.edu
HOUK, Suzanne, N .... 724-458-2208 .... 430 B
snhouk@gcc.edu
HOULE, Linda .... 508-362-2131 .... 239 D
lhoule@capecod.edu
HOULE, Pamela .... 508-580-5550 .... 351 B
phoule@skidmore.edu
HOULETTE, Forrest .... 502-456-6504 .... 206 H
fhoulette@sullivan.edu
HOULIHAN, Briana .... 608-240-3601 .... 19 A
briana.houlihan@phoenix.edu
HOULIHAN, Janet, M .... 714-895-8307 .... 41 C
jhoulihan@gwc.cccd.edu
HOULIHAN, Robert .... 516-678-5000 .... 341 F
rhoulihan@molloy.edu
HOULIHAN, Timothy, J .... 718-489-5290 .... 348 E
thoulihan@sfc.edu
HOULKER, Megan .... 781-239-5264 .... 230 E
mhoulker@babson.edu
HOULT, Kevin .... 256-782-8122 .... 4 L
khoult@jsu.edu
HOUPIS, James .... 510-885-3711 .... 34 E
james.houpis@csueastbay.edu
HOUPT, Mark .... 217-732-3168 .... 156 H
mhoupt@lincolnchristian.edu
HOURIGAN, Gerard .... 216-987-4706 .... 389 B
gerard.hourigan@tri-c.edu
HOUSE, Antionette .... 434-848-6495 .... 524 B
ahouse@saintpauls.edu
HOUSE, Barbara, S .... 716-270-2662 .... 333 A
house@ecc.edu
HOUSE, Charles (Chuck) .... 408-541-0100 .... 41 E
HOUSE, Cheryl .... 520-206-4646 .... 17 H
chouse@pima.edu
HOUSE, Donald .... 334-649-5000 .... 557 E
HOUSE, J. Daniel .... 815-753-6002 .... 160 B
jhouse@niu.edu
HOUSE, Janice, M .... 805-546-3248 .... 43 I
jhouse@cuesta.edu
HOUSE, Jess .... 203-837-9500 .... 91 A
housej@wcsu.edu
HOUSE, Karen .... 603-358-2114 .... 306 G
khouse@keene.edu
HOUSE, Renee .... 732-247-5241 .... 312 A
rhouse@nbts.edu
HOUSE, Seymour .... 503-845-3507 .... 417 A
seymour.house@mtangel.edu
HOUSE, Steven, D .... 336-278-6647 .... 364 D
shouse@elon.edu
HOUSE, Vicki, D .... 325-670-5892 .... 487 F
vhouse@hsutx.edu
HOUSEKNECHT, Eric, T .... 215-368-5000 .... 422 I
rhouseknecht@biblical.edu
HOUSENICK, Joseph .... 570-408-4631 .... 452 A
joseph.housenick@wilkes.edu
HOUSER, David .... 310-578-1080 .... 28 L
dhouser@antioch.edu
HOUSER, Frieda .... 406-444-6570 .... 294 H
fhouser@montana.edu
HOUSER, Gary .... 530-242-7590 .... 69 D
ghouser@shastacollege.edu
HOUSER, Gerald, B .... 503-370-6413 .... 421 D
jhouser@willamette.edu
HOUSER, Janet .... 303-458-4174 .... 87 I
jhouser@regis.edu
HOUSER, Kay .... 910-642-7141 .... 374 B
khouser@sccnc.edu
HOUSER, Kristin .... 661-362-3245 .... 41 I
kristin.houser@canyons.edu
HOUSER, Samuel .... 717-291-4271 .... 429 F
sam.houser@fandm.edu
HOUSH, David, P .... 573-882-7703 .... 291 B
houshd@missouri.edu
HOUSHMAND, Ali, A .... 856-256-4100 .... 314 A
houshmand@rowan.edu
HOUSHOWER, Hans .... 419-358-3234 .... 385 D
houshowerh@bluffton.edu
HOUSKA, Nila .... 712-749-2233 .... 183 C
houskan@bvu.edu
HOUSKAMP, Beth .... 626-284-2777 .... 27 D
bhouskamp@alliant.edu
HOUSKER, Alissa, M .... 602-216-3132 .... 11 F
ahousker@argosy.edu
HOUSLEY, Harold .... 903-875-7307 .... 491 C
harold.housley@navarrocollege.edu
HOUSLEY, Heather, L .... 404-413-2070 .... 131 G
heatherh@gsu.edu
HOUSLEY, John .... 912-525-5080 .... 136 F
jhousley@scad.edu
HOUSLEY, La Royce .... 310-954-4191 .... 57 H
ldodd@msmc.la.edu
HOUSTON, A. Glen .... 281-283-3000 .... 503 E
houston@uhcl.edu
HOUSTON, Adam .... 760-921-5463 .... 61 C
ahouston@paloverde.edu
HOUSTON, Alan, C .... 858-534-2247 .... 74 F
ahouston@ucsd.edu
HOUSTON, Alexander .... 484-384-2986 .... 428 E
ahouston@eastern.edu
HOUSTON, Alexander, G .... 484-384-2986 .... 438 D
ahouston@eastern.edu
HOUSTON, Don .... 408-855-5428 .... 78 F
don.houston@wvm.edu
HOUSTON, Douglas, B .... 530-741-6700 .... 80 I
HOUSTON, Kristen .... 206-876-6100 .... 538 A
khouston@theseattleschool.edu
HOUSTON, M. Sue .... 419-372-5387 .... 385 E
shousto@bgsu.edu
HOUSTON, Michelle .... 631-499-7100 .... 338 D
mhouston@libi.edu
HOUSTON, Ned, R .... 802-586-7711 .... 514 G
nhouston@sterlingcollege.edu
HOUSTON, Pam .... 901-448-1164 .... 477 E
phouston@uthsc.edu
HOUSTON, Paul .... 404-894-3300 .... 130 F
paul.houston@cos.gatech.edu
HOUSTON, Richard .... 662-846-4694 .... 273 H
rhouston@deltastate.edu
HOUSTON, Teresa .... 662-846-4698 .... 273 H
thouston@deltastate.edu
HOUSTON, Teresa, L .... 601-635-6202 .... 274 A
thouston@eccc.edu
HOUSTON, Vinson .... 256-782-5993 .... 4 L
vhouston@jsu.edu
HOUSTON, Whitney, C .... 972-860-7396 .... 484 I
whitneyhouston@dcccd.edu
HOUSTON, William .... 662-621-4226 .... 273 F
whouston@coahomacc.edu
HOUSTON, Willie .... 937-376-6631 .... 387 A
whouston@centralstate.edu
HOUSTON-BLACK,
Barbaina, M .... 252-335-3279 .... 377 F
bmhouston-black@mail.ecsu.edu
HOUSTON-BROWN,
Clive, K .... 909-593-3511 .... 75 E
cio@laverne.edu
HOUTSMA, Lisa .... 605-336-4602 .... 464 H
lhoutsma@national.edu
HOVATTER, Angela, L .... 301-687-4301 .... 228 C
ahovatter@frostburg.edu
HOVDA, Ric, A .... 619-594-1424 .... 37 A
rhovda@mail.sdsu.edu
HOVELAND-BELDEN,
Connie .... 608-785-9877 .... 555 F
beldenc@westerntc.edu
HOVERSON, Sharon, R .... 218-299-4642 .... 262 I
hoverson@cord.edu
HOVERSTEN, Mark, E .... 208-885-5423 .... 144 G
hoverstm@uidaho.edu
HOVESTOL, Daniel .... 218-751-8670 .... 270 D
ohfinaid@oakhills.edu
HOVEY, Ann .... 714-992-7033 .... 59 E
ahovey@fullcoll.edu
HOVEY, Anne .... 714-992-7064 .... 59 E
ahovey@fullcoll.edu
HOVEY, Roger, S .... 308-635-6012 .... 301 D
rhovey@wncc.edu
HOWARD, Andrew .... 806-743-7103 .... 502 B
andrew.howard@ttuhsc.edu
HOWARD, Angela .... 708-342-3500 .... 150 B
ahoward@devry.edu
HOWARD, Angelita .... 404-627-2681 .... 126 D
angelita.howard@beulah.org
HOWARD, Barbara, C .... 352-365-3520 .... 112 J
howardb@lscc.edu
HOWARD, Barry .... 615-361-7555 .... 468 E
bhoward@daymarinstitute.edu
HOWARD, Burgwell .... 847-467-0301 .... 160 E
b-howard@northwestern.edu
HOWARD, Carol .... 828-298-3325 .... 380 D
choward@warren-wilson.edu
HOWARD, Catherine, W .... 804-828-8790 .... 526 B
choward@vcu.edu
HOWARD, Charles, L .... 215-898-8456 .... 448 J
choward@pobox.upenn.edu
HOWARD, Cheryl .... 617-521-2131 .... 244 F
cheryl.howard@simmons.edu
HOWARD, Christian .... 517-264-7133 .... 258 B
choward@sienaheights.edu
HOWARD, Christie .... 903-593-8311 .... 499 D
choward@texascollege.edu
HOWARD, Christopher, B .... 434-223-6110 .... 519 G
choward@hsc.edu
HOWARD, Cluster .... 606-436-5721 .... 202 C
cluster.howard@kctcs.edu
HOWARD, Dale, S .... 330-490-7303 .... 405 F
dhoward@walsh.edu
HOWARD, Dan .... 870-972-2030 .... 20 D
dhoward@astate.edu
HOWARD, Dan, J .... 303-556-2624 .... 88 J
dan.howard@ucdenver.edu
HOWARD, Debbie, M .... 912-449-7560 .... 139 D
dhoward@waycross.edu
HOWARD, Doris .... 415-503-6214 .... 66 A
finaid@sfcm.edu
HOWARD, Douglas, W .... 716-880-2240 .... 340 D
douglas.w.howard@medaille.edu
HOWARD, Drema, K .... 813-974-9718 .... 121 A
dhoward@usf.edu
HOWARD, Eddie, J .... 706-737-1609 .... 125 G
ehoward@aug.edu
HOWARD, Garth .... 313-927-1210 .... 254 E
hhoward@marygrove.edu
HOWARD, Gary, E .... 859-858-3511 .... 198 E
gary.howard@asbury.edu
HOWARD, Gena .... 610-921-7859 .... 421 E
ghoward@alb.edu
HOWARD, James .... 573-681-5275 .... 283 I
jhoward@nebook.com
HOWARD, Jane .... 620-792-9208 .... 190 H
howardj@bartonccc.edu
HOWARD, Jason .... 740-588-1442 .... 400 E
howardj2@ohio.edu
HOWARD, Jay, R .... 317-940-9874 .... 170 F
jrhoward@butler.edu
HOWARD, Jeff .... 325-235-7396 .... 500 G
jeff.howard@tstc.edu
HOWARD, Jennifer, L .... 425-388-9232 .... 534 C
jhoward@everettcc.edu
HOWARD, Jessica .... 971-722-6268 .... 419 G
jessica.howard@pcc.edu
HOWARD, Jim .... 541-349-7471 .... 417 F
jhoward@nwcu.edu
HOWARD, Jim .... 303-762-6941 .... 84 D
jim.howard@denverseminary.edu
HOWARD, Kasi .... 573-642-3361 .... 293 B
kasi.howard@westminster-mo.edu
HOWARD, Kate .... 901-678-2566 .... 474 C
mkhoward@memphis.edu
HOWARD, Katrina .... 912-427-5876 .... 124 C
khoward@altamahatech.edu
HOWARD, Kevin .... 478-825-6300 .... 129 F
howardk@fvsu.edu
HOWARD, Kimberly, A .... 802-656-4296 .... 514 H
kimberly.howard@uvm.edu
HOWARD, Lelia .... 267-502-2680 .... 423 C
lelia.howard@brynathyn.edu
HOWARD, Leon .... 662-252-8000 .... 276 G
lhoward@rustcollege.edu
HOWARD, Marciela .... 305-666-9242 .... 103 H
mhoward@citycollege.edu
HOWARD, Margaret .... 973-408-3071 .... 309 E
phoward@drew.edu
HOWARD, Martin, J .... 617-353-2290 .... 232 E
mjhoward@bu.edu
HOWARD, Mary Ann .... 478-757-5137 .... 139 E
mhoward@wesleyancollege.edu
HOWARD, Maureen .... 575-646-3221 .... 319 D
mhoward@nmsu.edu
HOWARD, Michael, W .... 617-324-8142 .... 241 D
HOWARD, Michele, M .... 704-687-0343 .... 379 A
mmhoward@uncc.edu
HOWARD, Michelle, L .... 989-774-7506 .... 249 C
howar1ml@cmich.edu
HOWARD, Patricia .... 913-345-8288 .... 197 D
howardp@stmary.edu
HOWARD, Philip .... 706-721-0909 .... 130 D
phoward@georgiahealth.edu
HOWARD, Phillip, D .... 404-215-2659 .... 134 D
phoward@morehouse.edu
HOWARD, Predita .... 478-934-3092 .... 134 B
phoward@mgc.edu
HOWARD, R. Keith .... 219-981-4452 .... 176 G
khoward@ivytech.edu
HOWARD, Randy, B .... 765-285-1033 .... 169 G
rbhoward@bsu.edu
HOWARD, Robert .... 252-536-4221 .... 371 B
howardr@halifaxcc.edu
HOWARD, Robert, P .... 919-344-2650 .... 124 G
robert.howard@armstrong.edu
HOWARD, Ronald .... 601-925-3203 .... 275 C
howard@mc.edu
HOWARD, Rosetta .... 662-621-4244 .... 273 F
rhoward@coahomacc.edu
HOWARD, Sandra .... 205-929-6397 .... 5 E
showard@lawsonstate.edu
HOWARD, Sarah, E .... 219-989-2367 .... 178 K
howard@purduecal.edu
HOWARD, Sharon, L .... 304-647-6369 .... 544 E
showard@osteo.wvsom.edu
HOWARD, Shawanda, M .... 504-286-5388 .... 214 J
showard@suno.edu
HOWARD, Steve .... 601-403-1219 .... 276 E
swhoward@prcc.edu
HOWARD, Susan, L .... 603-283-2367 .... 303 F
showard@antioch.edu
HOWARD, Tammy, M .... 414-410-4225 .... 546 G
tmhoward@stritch.edu
HOWARD, Tim .... 717-755-2300 .... 422 F
thoward@aii.edu
HOWARD, Traci, D .... 619-239-0391 .... 37 F
thoward@cwsl.edu
HOWARD, Trish .... 801-863-8440 .... 511 F
howardpa@uvu.edu
HOWARD, Walter, C .... 706-396-7639 .... 135 G
whoward@paine.edu
HOWARD, William .... 520-206-4568 .... 17 H
whoward@pima.edu
HOWARD, William, F .... 518-320-1100 .... 351 D
HOWARD, William, L .... 240-895-4388 .... 226 A
wlhoward@smcm.edu
HOWARD, Yaffa .... 215-635-7300 .... 430 A
yhoward@gratz.edu

HUBERT, Anthony 910-678-8244 370 E huberta@faytechcc.edu
HUBERT, Barbara 714-997-6940 39 F hubert@chapman.edu
HUBIN, David, R 541-346-3036 419 B hubin@uoregon.edu
HUBINGER, Amy, M 906-227-2626 256 C ahubinge@nmu.edu
HUBLER, Barbara 415-338-2611 37 B bhubler@sfsu.edu
HUBLER, Grant 541-956-7235 420 B grant@roguecc.edu
HUBREGTSE, Joyce 605-221-3113 464 D jhubregtse@kilian.edu
HUCH, Robert, E 540-261-8413 524 H bob.huch@svu.edu
HUCK, Jack, J 402-323-3415 300 B jhuck@southeast.edu
HUCKABA, Sam 850-644-4404 119 D shuckaba@fsu.edu
HUCKABAY, Sonia 559-791-2403 53 A shuckaba@portervillecollege.edu
HUCKABY, Hank, M 404-656-2202 139 B chancellor@usg.edu
HUCKEBY, Ed 405-789-7661 412 E ed.huckeby@swcu.edu
HUCKESTEIN, Jim 541-917-4331 416 I jim.huckestein@linnbenton.edu
HUCKESTEIN, Julie, A 503-399-6575 414 J julie.huckestein@chemeketa.edu
HUCKINS, Heather 603-535-2249 307 A hhuckins@plymouth.edu
HUCKMAN, Beverly, B 312-942-7093 163 D beverly_b_huckman@rush.edu
HUCKS, Cheri, A 864-592-4931 461 C hucksc@sccsc.edu
HUDACK, Jon 716-827-2547 358 D hudackj@trocaire.edu
HUDAK, DeDe 916-577-2305 79 G dhudak@jessup.edu
HUDAK, Jane, E 484-664-3300 437 C hudak@muhlenberg.edu
HUDAK, Randy 304-293-3944 545 A randy.hudak@mail.wvu.edu
HUDAK, Sharon 570-674-6295 436 F shudak@misericordia.edu
HUDDLESTON, Gwen 805-654-6388 77 F ghuddleston@vcccd.edu
HUDDLESTON, Mark, W 603-862-2450 306 C presidents.office@unh.edu
HUDDLESTON, Timothy 417-690-2209 279 J thuddleston@cofo.edu
HUDDY, Michael 207-834-7607 220 D michael.huddy@maine.edu
HUDEC, Susan 718-940-5854 349 A shudec@sjcny.edu
HUDEC, Susan 631-687-4594 349 B shudec@sjcny.edu
HUDELSON-PUTNAM, Cece 209-575-6131 80 H hudelsonputnam@mjc.edu
HUDGENS, Lisa 618-985-3741 154 G lisahudgens@jalc.edu
HUDGIN, Denise 419-251-1324 395 I denise.hudgin@mercycollege.edu
HUDGINS, Chris 702-895-0301 302 I chris.hudgins@unlv.edu
HUDGINS, Jim 870-460-1018 25 A hudgins@uamont.edu
HUDGINS, John, L 410-951-3528 228 B jhudgins@coppin.edu
HUDGINS, V. Lavoyed 859-985-3240 199 A hudginsv@berea.edu
HUDNUT-BEUMLER, James 615-343-3960 478 A james.hudnut-beumler@vanderbilt.edu
HUDOCK, Virginia, S 803-641-3310 462 B gingerh@usca.edu
HUDOK, Cynthia, K 304-367-4213 543 H cynthia.hudok@fairmontstate.edu
HUDSICK, Walter 425-352-8162 532 B whudsick@cascadia.edu
HUDSON, Angela 501-686-2504 24 B ahudson@uasys.edu
HUDSON, Bill 816-604-1453 284 H bill.hudson@mcckc.edu
HUDSON, Blake, W 423-285-1689 467 F blake.hudson@bryan.edu
HUDSON, Bobby 615-230-3445 476 C bobby.hudson@volstate.edu
HUDSON, David, D 714-895-8907 41 C dhudson@gwc.cccd.edu
HUDSON, Dean, A 214-828-8391 497 C dhudson@bcd.tamhsc.edu
HUDSON, Dean, P 843-349-2739 456 G dhudson@coastal.edu
HUDSON, Debra 270-247-8521 204 G dhudson@midcontinent.edu
HUDSON, Delaphine 562-907-4223 79 F dhudson@whittier.edu
HUDSON, Delores 256-372-5227 1 A delores.hudson@aamu.edu
HUDSON, Donald 812-488-2452 180 E dh104@evansville.edu
HUDSON, Donald 609-894-9311 308 B dhudson@bcc.edu
HUDSON, Earnest 828-227-7301 380 A ehudson@wcu.edu
HUDSON, Gregory 662-621-4153 273 F ghudson@coahomacc.edu
HUDSON, Harold 937-529-2201 403 A hhudson@united.edu
HUDSON, Jackie 205-929-1401 5 H jhudson@miles.edu
HUDSON, James, B 502-852-2234 207 E jbhuds01@louisville.edu
HUDSON, Jennifer, M 713-646-1899 494 I jhudson@stcl.edu
HUDSON, Jerry 806-742-3385 502 A jerry.hudson@ttu.edu
HUDSON, Karen 615-771-7821 478 H karen.hudson@williamsoncc.edu
HUDSON, Kathy 434-961-5446 528 B khudson@pvcc.edu
HUDSON, Keith 270-686-4261 199 B keith.hudson@brescia.edu
HUDSON, Lea Ann 404-471-6402 123 I lhudson@agnesscott.edu
HUDSON, Lyla 843-792-8721 459 D hudsonly@musc.edu
HUDSON, Marilyn 405-789-7661 412 E marilyn.hudson@swcu.edu
HUDSON, Mark, A 217-581-3923 150 E mahudson@eiu.edu
HUDSON, Maureen 781-280-3506 240 B hudsonm@middlesex.mass.edu
HUDSON, Melissa, A 530-226-4974 69 H mhudson@simpsonu.edu
HUDSON, Michael, J 630-637-5661 159 G mjhudson@noctrl.edu
HUDSON, Pam 417-455-5506 280 H phudson@crowder.edu
HUDSON, Pat 816-414-3700 285 H phudson@mbts.edu
HUDSON, Richard 502-585-9911 206 D rhudson@spalding.edu
HUDSON, Richard, B 479-575-7964 24 C rhudson@uark.edu
HUDSON, Robert 617-353-3710 232 E rhudson@bu.edu
HUDSON, Robert 252-399-6345 362 E rdhudson@barton.edu
HUDSON, Rodeny, B 803-535-5470 456 D rhudson@claflin.edu
HUDSON, Stacy 208-769-7819 144 D stacy_hudson@nic.edu
HUDSON, Tijuana, R 803-535-5197 456 D thudson@claflin.edu
HUDSON, Tim 870-972-3030 20 D timhudson@astate.edu
HUDSON, JR., William 850-599-3183 118 L william.hudson@famu.edu
HUDSON, William, B 608-342-1561 552 B hudsonw@uwplatt.edu
HUDSON-MACISAAC, Kelley 760-744-1150 61 D kmacisaac@palomar.edu
HUDSPETH, Donald 585-475-7077 347 G don@acmt.hr
HUDSPETH, Harvey, L 806-651-2116 499 A hhudspeth@mail.wtamu.edu
HUDSPETH, Larry 503-821-8943 419 D hudspeth@pnca.edu
HUDY, Karen 216-421-7321 388 A khudy@cia.edu
HUEBNER, Julie, A 630-752-5490 168 H julie.huebner@wheaton.edu
HUEBNER, Kathleen 215-780-1361 446 G kathyh@salus.edu
HUEBNER, Maryjo "MJ" 402-461-7398 298 A mjhuebner@hastings.edu
HUEBNER, Thomas 205-391-2999 6 I thuebner@sheltonstate.edu
HUEBOTTER, Chris 573-288-6542 280 I chuebotter@culver.edu
HUEBSCH, Pat 541-956-7163 420 B phuebsch@roguecc.edu
HUEFTLE, Theresa 216-432-8986 387 B thueftle@chancelloru.edu
HUEG, Kurt 650-949-7349 47 H huegkurt@foothill.edu
HUEGEL, Mary 978-232-2084 234 D mhuegel@endicott.edu
HUELSBECK, David, R 253-535-7645 536 E huelsdr@plu.edu
HUELSBECK, Tom, A 253-535-7200 536 E tom.huelsbeck@plu.edu
HUELSMAN, Shelly 620-227-9285 192 E shuelsman@dc3.edu
HUENEMANN, Kurt 419-448-2351 391 F keh@heidelberg.edu
HUENINK, Richard 262-551-6200 546 I rhuenink@carthage.edu
HUENNEKE, Laura 928-523-2230 16 I laura.huenneke@nau.edu
HUERTA, David 559-278-8400 35 A davidhu@csufresno.edu
HUERTA, Margie, C 575-527-7510 319 G marhuert@nmsu.edu
HUERTA, Patricia 312-362-8601 149 A phuerta@depaul.edu
HUERTAS, Carmelo, V 973-972-7551 316 C huertarv@umdnj.edu
HUERTAS, Mildred 787-257-7373 565 G ue_mhuertas@suagm.edu
HUERTAS, Orlando 305-626-3798 109 A orlando.huertas@fmuniv.edu
HUERTAS-BERMÚDEZ, Antonio 787-993-8862 567 B antonio.huertas@upr.edu
HUESER, Kyle 712-274-6400 190 B kyle.hueser@witcc.edu
HUESING, Alan 903-923-2172 486 F ahuesing@etbu.edu
HUESTON, Eddie, C 972-238-6170 485 D ehueston@dcccd.edu
HUEWITT, Jerri 404-297-9522 131 D huewittj@gptc.edu
HUEY, Lindley 617-253-6162 241 D
HUFF, Alexandra 617-369-3659 244 E ahuff@mfa.org
HUFF, Amy 931-393-1629 475 D ahuff@mscc.edu
HUFF, Betty 901-678-5218 474 C bjhuff@memphis.edu
HUFF, Dwayne 417-833-2551 279 E dhuff@cbcag.edu
HUFF, Eugene, C 925-229-6851 43 D ehuff@4cd.edu
HUFF, Glenda 325-649-8014 488 C ghuff@hputx.edu
HUFF, III, Joseph, E 409-944-1302 486 K jhuff@gc.edu
HUFF, Kim, R 803-535-1204 460 C huffk@octech.edu
HUFF, Lester 301-295-1210 558 D lester.huff@usuhs.edu
HUFF, Marie 828-227-7271 380 A mhuff@wcu.edu
HUFF, Scott 971-722-5573 419 G shuff@pcc.edu
HUFF, Thomas, F 804-827-5600 526 B tfhuff@vcu.edu
HUFF, Tim, T 405-744-5459 410 C tim.huff@okstate.edu
HUFFAKER, John 806-742-2155 502 A john.huffaker@ttu.edu
HUFFARD, Evertt, W 901-761-1352 469 C dean@hst.edu
HUFFARD, Lorri, M 276-223-4829 529 C lhuffard@wcc.vccs.edu
HUFFCUTT, Tom, G 715-833-6661 553 H thuffcutt@cvtc.edu
HUFFMAN, Debbie 940-668-4475 491 E dhuffman@nctc.edu
HUFFMAN, Don 312-662-4236 144 H dhuffman@adler.edu
HUFFMAN, Gerald 206-296-5869 538 B huffmanje@seattleu.edu
HUFFMAN, Jeffery 419-559-2257 402 D jhuffman01@terra.edu
HUFFMAN, Jessamine 256-840-4151 7 A jhuffman@snead.edu
HUFFMAN, Laurene, K 740-374-8716 405 G lhuffman@wscc.edu
HUFFMAN, Linda 573-518-2204 285 I lhuffman@mineralarea.edu
HUFFMAN, Lon 269-467-9945 251 B lhuffman@glenoaks.edu
HUFFMAN, Maggie 503-491-7145 417 B maggie.huffman@mhcc.edu
HUFFMAN, Mari, L 419-866-0261 402 C mlhuffman@stautzenberger.com
HUFFMAN, Monica, R 660-543-4106 290 H mhuffman@ucmo.edu
HUFFMAN, Pat 425-640-1002 533 I phuffman@edcc.edu
HUFFMAN, Rebecca 276-328-0139 525 G reg5a@uvawise.edu
HUFFMAN, Robin 260-399-7700 181 A rhuffman@sf.edu
HUFFMAN, Sherri, H 434-797-8576 526 G shuffman@dcc.vccs.edu
HUFFMAN, Tammy, S 740-588-1212 407 A thuffman@zanestate.edu
HUFFMAN, Virginia, A 212-327-8300 347 H huffman@rockefeller.edu
HUFFSTETLER, Edward, W 540-828-5332 517 B ehuffste@bridgewater.edu
HUFFT, Anita, G 229-333-5959 139 C ahufft@valdosta.edu
HUFNAGEL, Michele 724-503-1001 451 A mhufnagel@washjeff.edu
HUFSTETLER, Catrice 770-975-4000 127 B
HUFTALIN, Deneece 801-957-4285 512 D deneece.huftalin@slcc.edu
HUFTEL, Joe 715-246-6561 555 G joe.huftel@witc.edu
HUG-ENGLISH, Cheryl 775-784-6122 303 A cherylh@med.unr.edu
HUGETZ, Edward 713-743-3419 503 D ehugetz@uh.edu
HUGETZ, Edward, T 832-842-0543 503 C ehugetz@uh.edu
HUGGETT, Monica 212-799-5000 337 H
HUGGINS, Cynthia, E 207-255-1210 220 E chuggins@maine.edu
HUGGINS, Desiree 337-262-5962 211 K dhuggins@acadiana.edu
HUGGINS, Jonathan 706-236-2217 126 C jhuggins@berry.edu
HUGGINS, Regina, M 919-866-5408 374 H rmhuggins@waketech.edu
HUGHES, A. LeAnn 423-652-4706 470 A lhughes@king.edu
HUGHES, Angela 219-473-4227 170 G ahughes2@ccsj.edu
HUGHES, Ann 912-583-3230 126 F
HUGHES, B. Hilles 740-376-4645 395 G hilles.hughes@marietta.edu
HUGHES, Barbara, J 814-641-3311 432 A hughesb@juniata.edu
HUGHES, Bernice 229-391-5130 123 H bhughes@abac.edu
HUGHES, Billy 205-665-6130 9 B hugheswl@montevallo.edu
HUGHES, Bobbi, R 253-535-8268 536 E hughesbr@plu.edu
HUGHES, Bonnie 506-865-8588 535 A hughes_b@heritage.edu
HUGHES, C. Raymond 860-906-5012 91 C rhughes@ccc.commnet.edu
HUGHES, Charles, F 417-690-2211 279 J hughes@cofo.edu
HUGHES, Christine 617-824-8908 234 B christine_hughes@emerson.edu
HUGHES, Craig 716-839-8246 331 F
HUGHES, David 785-738-9008 195 G dhughes@ncktc.edu
HUGHES, David 207-780-4946 220 G dehughes@usm.maine.edu
HUGHES, David 501-760-4311 22 F dhughes@npcc.edu
HUGHES, Derek 701-845-7401 382 C derek.hughes@vcsu.edu
HUGHES, DeVetta 843-574-6199 461 G devetta.hughes@tridenttech.edu
HUGHES, Dianna 662-252-8000 276 G dr_hughes@rustcollege.edu
HUGHES, Ed 859-442-1175 202 B ed.hughes@kctcs.edu
HUGHES, Edwin 973-278-5400 307 F ejh@berkeleycollege.edu
HUGHES, Edwin 973-278-5400 323 H ejh@berkeleycollege.edu
HUGHES, Elizabeth 312-567-5045 153 C hughes@iit.edu
HUGHES, Elizabeth, B 417-690-2212 279 J ehughes@cofo.edu
HUGHES, Erinn 281-649-3213 487 H erhughes@hbu.edu
HUGHES, Ernie, T 225-771-3911 214 H ernie_hughes@sus.edu
HUGHES, Frank 605-274-4325 464 A frank.hughes@augie.edu
HUGHES, James, J 860-297-2376 94 E james.hughes@trincoll.edu
HUGHES, James, L 410-706-1935 227 C jhughes@umaryland.edu
HUGHES, James, W 848-932-2828 314 C jwhughes@rci.rutgers.edu
HUGHES, Jason 608-363-2137 546 E hughesj@beloit.edu
HUGHES, Jay 870-460-1053 25 A hughesj@uamont.edu
HUGHES, Jennifer 650-574-6118 67 G hughesj@smccd.edu
HUGHES, Jerry, M 660-543-4250 290 H hughes@ucmo.edu
HUGHES, Jim 620-235-4154 196 C jhughes@pittstate.edu
HUGHES, Joe Pat 580-371-2371 408 I jhughes@mscok.edu
HUGHES, John 661-362-2223 56 G jhughes@masters.edu
HUGHES, Jonathan 808-942-1000 141 D careers.hnl.rc@remingtoncollege.edu
HUGHES, Joseph, B 215-895-2210 427 H engineering@coe.drexel.edu
HUGHES, Joy, R 703-993-8728 519 E jhughes@gmu.edu
HUGHES, Karla 606-783-2002 204 I k.hughes@moreheadstate.edu
HUGHES, Kevin, M 757-594-7335 517 L kmhughes@cnu.edu
HUGHES, Laura 870-460-1454 25 A hughesl@uamont.edu
HUGHES, Laura 208-792-2224 144 B lhughes@lcsc.edu
HUGHES, Lecia 325-793-4998 490 H hughes.lecia@mcm.edu
HUGHES, Leslie 601-635-2111 274 A lhughes@eccc.edu
HUGHES, Linda 402-354-7049 299 C linda.hughes@methodistcollege.edu

HUGHES, Louise .... 870-612-2013...... 25 E
louise.hughes@uaccb.edu
HUGHES, Lucille .... 215-717-6144.... 448 I
lhughes@uarts.edu
HUGHES, Mark .... 301-925-3800.... 275 C
rmhughes@mc.edu
HUGHES, Mark .... 512-245-2501.... 501 F
mh66@txstate.edu
HUGHES, Marshall .... 617-541-5381.... 241 A
mhughes@rcc.mass.edu
HUGHES, Martha .... 972-273-3590.... 485 C
mhughes@dcccd.edu
HUGHES, Martin .... 616-222-1497.... 250 A
martin.hughes@cornerstone.edu
HUGHES, Mary, E .... 614-235-4136.... 402 G
mhughes@tlsohio.edu
HUGHES, Matthew .... 334-347-2623......... 3 F
mhughes@escc.edu
HUGHES, Melany .... 308-432-6415.... 299 E
mhughes@csc.edu
HUGHES, Michael .... 415-422-2465...... 76 E
hughesm@usfca.edu
HUGHES, Michael, J .... 740-351-3539.... 401 I
mhughes@shawnee.edu
HUGHES, Michelle .... 508-588-9100.... 240 A
HUGHES, Michelle .... 610-683-4822.... 443 A
hughes@kutztown.edu
HUGHES, Mike .... 231-591-2924.... 250 H
hughesm@ferris.edu
HUGHES, Mike, C .... 817-923-1921.... 495 G
mhughes@swbts.edu
HUGHES, Montaven .... 765-459-0561.... 176 C
mhughes@ivytech.edu
HUGHES, Myron .... 513-556-4344.... 403 D
myron.hughes@uc.edu
HUGHES, Nancy .... 405-224-3140.... 413 E
nhughes@usao.edu
HUGHES, Nancy, B .... 607-746-4573.... 355 F
hughesnb@delhi.edu
HUGHES, Peter, D .... 518-244-2200.... 348 A
hughep@sage.edu
HUGHES, Randy .... 361-593-3207.... 498 D
j.hughes@tamuk.edu
HUGHES, Robert .... 615-963-1836.... 474 A
rhughes@tnstate.edu
HUGHES, Robert, A .... 402-398-5527.... 296 G
robert.hughes@alegent.org
HUGHES, Ronald .... 586-445-7183.... 254 C
hughesr@macomb.edu
HUGHES, Sandra .... 843-863-7933.... 456 B
shughes@csuniv.edu
HUGHES, Scott .... 352-787-7660.... 102 B
shughes@beaconcollege.edu
HUGHES, Sherri, L .... 703-284-1550.... 521 D
sherri.hughes@marymount.edu
HUGHES, Stacy .... 312-915-6740.... 157 C
shughe2@luc.edu
HUGHES, Tamera, J .... 803-536-8106.... 460 G
thughes@scsu.edu
HUGHES, Tanya, G .... 432-335-6750.... 492 A
thughes@odessa.edu
HUGHES, Tom .... 928-776-2205...... 19 C
tom.hughes@yc.edu
HUGHES, Tom .... 800-962-7682.... 293 A
athletics@wma.edu
HUGHES, W. William .... 909-558-1300...... 54 D
bhughes@llu.edu
HUGHES HANDLEY,
Allyson .... 207-621-3403.... 220 B
allyson.handley@maine.edu
HUGHES HARRIS,
Cynthia .... 850-599-3818.... 118 L
cynthia.hughes@famu.edu
HUGHEY, Andrew, C .... 713-313-7470.... 500 B
hugheyac@tsu.edu
HUGHEY, Richard .... 831-459-4908...... 75 C
vpdue@ucsc.edu
HUGHEY, Willie, M .... 903-927-3211.... 509 E
wmhughey@wileyc.edu
HUGHLEY, Corine .... 229-430-3537.... 124 B
chughley@albanytech.edu
HUGHSTON, Patty .... 251-580-2101......... 5 A
phughston@faulknerstate.edu
HUGINE, JR., Andrew .... 256-372-5230......... 1 A
andrew.hugine@aamu.edu
HUGLE, Shelbie .... 859-246-6216.... 201 H
shelbie.hugle@kctcs.edu
HUGUENIN, Sanders .... 276-328-0120.... 525 G
jsh4ew@uvawise.edu
HUHRA, Lourdene .... 847-543-2514.... 148 B
lhuhra@clcillinois.edu
HUI, Andrew .... 215-702-4203.... 444 B
ahui@pbu.edu
HUI, Timothy, K .... 215-702-4377.... 444 B
thui@pbu.edu
HUIATT, Ron .... 724-938-5775.... 441 G
huiatt@calu.edu
HUIDEKOPER, Elizabeth .... 401-863-9400.... 453 B
elizabeth_huidekoper@brown.edu
HUISH, Darrel, S .... 651-201-1454.... 265 E
darrel.huish@so.mnscu.edu
HUISH, David .... 928-524-7888...... 17 A
david.huish@npc.edu
HUISKAMP, Julie, G .... 563-562-3263.... 188 B
huiskamj@nicc.edu
HUIZINGA, Dorota .... 657-278-4831...... 35 B
dhuizinga@fullerton.edu
HUKE, Theresa .... 610-361-5249.... 437 D
huket@neumann.edu
HUKILL, Lezlie .... 806-291-3446.... 508 E
lezlieh@wbu.edu
HUKOWICZ, Elizabeth .... 413-265-2360.... 233 D
hukowicze@elms.edu
HULBERT, Stephen, T .... 985-448-4003.... 216 A
stephen.hulbert@nicholls.edu
HULETT, Kevin .... 918-293-5476.... 410 E
kevin.hulett@okstate.edu
HULETT, Matt .... 505-277-0385.... 321 C
mhulett@unm.edu
HULIN, Alicia .... 337-521-8920.... 211 J
alicia.hulin@southlouisiana.edu
HULIN, Christopher, P .... 615-868-6503.... 471 H
chris.hulin@mtsa.edu
HULKE, Carla, J .... 507-354-8221.... 264 K
hulkecj@mlc-wels.edu
HULL, Brian .... 479-979-1421...... 26 A
bhull@ozarks.edu
HULL, Brooks, A .... 903-813-2419.... 481 A
bhull@austincollege.edu
HULL, Deborah .... 323-731-2383...... 60 H
dhull@psuca.edu
HULL, Edward, C .... 413-545-1964.... 236 F
ehull@gw.housing.umass.edu
HULL, James, L .... 419-755-4850.... 397 C
jhull@ncstatecollege.edu
HULL, Jim .... 217-234-5225.... 156 B
jhull17327@lakeland.cc.il.us
HULL, JR., Joe .... 843-953-5546.... 457 B
hulljj@cofc.edu
HULL, Judy, M .... 931-372-3491.... 474 B
jmhull@tntech.edu
HULL, Karla .... 229-333-5950.... 139 C
khull@valdosta.edu
HULL, Shawn .... 573-592-4389.... 293 D
shull@williamwoods.edu
HULL, Stephen, E .... 863-297-1026.... 115 C
shull@polk.edu
HULL, Teresa .... 909-652-7653...... 39 E
teresa.hull@chaffey.edu
HULL, Thomas, A .... 212-346-1200.... 345 F
HULLETT, Lisa .... 256-352-8267...... 10 A
lisa.hullett@wallacestate.edu
HULON, Jane .... 601-643-8310.... 273 G
jane.hulon@colin.edu
HULS, Jack .... 360-417-6246.... 536 G
jhuls@pencol.edu
HULSE, Debra .... 325-793-4761.... 490 H
hulse.debra@mcm.edu
HULSEBOSCH, Patricia .... 202-448-7036...... 98 B
patricia.hulsebosch@gallaudet.edu
HULSEY, Janet .... 706-419-1262.... 128 B
hulsey@covenant.edu
HULSEY, Tara .... 843-863-7075.... 456 B
thulsey@csuniv.edu
HULSEY, Timothy, L .... 804-828-1803.... 526 B
tlhulsey@vcu.edu
HULSMAN, J. Patrick .... 716-286-8771.... 344 D
phulsman@niagara.du
HULST, Mary .... 616-526-7617.... 249 A
msh4@calvin.edu
HULSTEIN, Pamela, L .... 712-722-6689.... 184 C
hulstein@dordt.edu
HULSTINE, Thomas .... 717-544-5395.... 433 E
tjhulsti@lancastergeneralcollege.edu
HULTBERG, Jane .... 207-288-5015.... 217 H
jhultberg@coa.edu
HULTIN, Jerry, M .... 718-260-3500.... 346 C
hultin@poly.edu
HULTIN, Steve, R .... 970-491-0007...... 83 F
steve.hultin@colostate.edu
HULTMAN, Ken .... 402-554-3514.... 301 A
khultman@unomaha.edu
HULTQUIST, Sharon, S ...... 260-480-4280.... 176 F
shultqui@ivytech.edu
HULTZ, Rachel .... 502-897-4121.... 206 C
rehultz@sbts.edu
HUMAN, Renee .... 281-998-6150.... 494 B
renee.human@sjcd.edu
HUMBERGER, Laura .... 406-994-4361.... 295 C
lhumberger@montana.edu
HUMBERT, Mark .... 315-312-2248.... 354 A
mark.humbert@oswego.edu
HUMBLE, Dina .... 562-938-4446...... 54 E
dhumble@lbcc.edu
HUME, Gary .... 615-230-3600.... 476 C
gary.hume@volstate.edu
HUME, Richard .... 631-420-2080.... 356 A
richard.hume@farmingdale.edu
HUMERICK, Rosalind, M .... 386-312-4212.... 116 F
rosalindhumerick@sjrstate.edu
HUMES, Cynthia .... 909-607-8713...... 40 G
cynthia.humes@cmc.edu
HUMESTON, Howard, D ...... 305-899-3139.... 101 M
dhumeston@mail.barry.edu
HUMISTON, Dolores, J ...... 509-777-4320.... 540 C
dhumiston@whitworth.edu
HUMME, Larryl .... 708-239-3977.... 166 C
larryl.humme@trnty.edu
HUMMEL, Paul .... 630-466-7900.... 168 B
phummel@waubonsee.edu
HUMMEL, Scott .... 601-318-6769.... 278 C
scott.hummel@wmcarey.edu
HUMMEL, Scott .... 601-318-6497.... 278 C
shummel@wmcarey.edu
HUMMER, Alissa .... 805-893-4091...... 75 B
alissa.hummer@planning.ucsb.edu
HUMMER, Jim .... 760-773-2561...... 42 A
jhummer@collegeofthedesert.edu
HUMMER, Judith, G .... 717-290-8718.... 433 F
jhummer@lancasterseminary.edu
HUMMERT, Mary Lee .... 785-864-4904.... 197 B
mlhummert@ku.edu
HUMMINGBIRD, Edward .. 505-922-6506.... 321 B
edward.hummingbird@bie.edu
HUMPHREY, Amy .... 865-471-2000.... 467 G
ahumphrey@cn.edu
HUMPHREY, Bonnie .... 660-831-4108.... 286 F
humphreyb@moval.edu
HUMPHREY, Christopher .. 404-237-7573.... 126 B
chhumphrey@bauder.edu
HUMPHREY, Dana, N .... 207-581-2213.... 220 A
danah@maine.edu
HUMPHREY, George, D ..... 520-626-7301........ 18 L
ghumphre@email.arizona.edu
HUMPHREY, George, E ...... 617-732-2292.... 241 C
george.humphrey@mcphs.edu
HUMPHREY, Kathy, W ...... 412-648-1006.... 449 A
kathyh@pitt.edu
HUMPHREY, Keith, B .... 520-621-7057........ 18 L
khumphre@email.arizona.edu
HUMPHREY, Laura .... 803-313-7066.... 462 D
humphrlb@mailbox.sc.edu
HUMPHREY, Lynn .... 208-426-2948.... 142 I
lynnhumphrey@boisestate.edu
HUMPHREY, Richard .... 423-775-6596.... 472 G
rhumphrey@ogs.edu
HUMPHREY, Scott .... 315-792-3835.... 359 E
shumphrey@utica.edu
HUMPHREY, Shawn .... 904-448-9499.... 118 C
HUMPHREY, Twila .... 719-502-2052...... 87 B
twila.humphrey@ppcc.edu
HUMPHREYS, Amy .... 309-268-8194.... 151 I
amy.humphreys@heartland.edu
HUMPHREYS, Bryce .... 509-882-7049.... 540 D
bhumphreys@yvcc.edu
HUMPHREYS, George, G ... 270-824-1723.... 202 G
george.humphreys@kctcs.edu
HUMPHREYS, Joe .... 361-485-4485.... 504 A
humphreysj@uhv.edu
HUMPHREYS, Melanie ...... 630-752-5941.... 168 H
melanie.humphreys@wheaton.edu
HUMPHREYS, Robert, G .... 209-478-0800...... 50 K
rgh@humphreys.edu
HUMPHREYS, JR.,
Robert, G .... 209-478-0800...... 50 K
rhumphreys@humphreys.edu
HUMPHRIES, Brian, L .... 651-286-7620.... 270 B
blhumphries@nwc.edu
HUMPHRIES, Corey .... 706-233-7231.... 137 A
chumphries@shorter.edu
HUMPHRIES, Evelyn .... 847-969-4983.... 145 D
ehumphries@argosy.edu
HUMPHRIES, Karl .... 903-875-7600.... 491 C
karl.humphries@navarrocollege.edu
HUMPHRIES, Kelly .... 864-250-7000...... 99 G
kyh@strayer.edu
HUMPHRIES, Lou .... 619-388-3473...... 65 F
lhumphri@sdccd.edu
HUMPHRIES, Tara .... 919-735-5151.... 375 A
tarah@waynecc.edu
HUMPRES, Patricia .... 714-484-7309...... 59 D
phumpres@cypresscollege.edu
HUNCHBERGER, Mary ...... 360-417-6535.... 536 G
mhunchberger@pencol.edu
HUNDERSMARCK,
Steven, F .... 260-422-5561.... 173 C
sfhundersmarck@indianatech.edu
HUNDLEY, Patrick .... 618-650-2345.... 165 C
phundle@siue.edu
HUNDRIESER, James .... 603-535-2240.... 307 A
jmhundrieser@plymouth.edu
HUNEYCUTT, Richy .... 252-527-6223.... 371 G
rhuneycutt@lenoircc.edu
HUNGER, Suzanne .... 406-447-6938.... 295 A
hungers@umhelena.edu
HUNGERFORD, Dan .... 740-376-4720.... 395 G
dan.hungerford@marietta.edu
HUNKER, Kurt .... 619-684-8787...... 59 B
khunker@newschoolarch.edu
HUNN, Martha, S .... 843-349-2962.... 456 G
mhunn@coastal.edu
HUNN, II, Marvin, T .... 214-841-3751.... 485 F
mhunn@dts.edu
HUNNEWELL, Lila .... 617-358-5220.... 232 E
lilawell@bu.edu
HUNNICUTT, Lew .... 806-648-1450.... 486 I
lunnicutt@fpctx.edu
HUNNICUTT, Marianne ...... 630-942-4306.... 148 A
hunnicutt@cod.edu
HUNNICUTT, Veronica .... 415-239-3762...... 40 C
vhunnicu@ccsf.edu
HUNSAKER, Deanna .... 660-626-2356.... 278 D
dhunsaker@atsu.edu
HUNSAKER, Miles .... 801-524-8108.... 510 E
mhunsaker@ldsbc.edu
HUNSBERGER, Gerald .... 607-431-4738.... 335 A
hunsbergerg@hartwick.edu
HUNSBERGER, Susan .... 208-459-5407.... 143 D
shunsberger@collegeofidaho.edu
HUNSICKER, Donald .... 617-262-5000.... 231 G
don.hunsicker@the-bac.edu
HUNSICKER, Jennie, I .... 610-398-5300.... 434 F
jhunsicker@lincolntech.com
HUNSINGER, Fred .... 215-340-8401.... 423 F
hunsinge@bucks.edu
HUNSINGER PATTEN,
Rachael .... 518-743-2243.... 355 D
pattenr@sunyacc.edu
HUNSUCKER, Jeremy .... 847-467-2152.... 160 E
jhunsucker@northwestern.edu
HUNSUCKER, Scott, E .... 704-233-8220.... 380 F
scotth@wingate.edu
HUNT, Alice .... 773-896-2400.... 146 H
ahunt@ctschicago.edu
HUNT, Altavese .... 803-327-7402.... 456 F
ahunt@clintonjuniorcollege.edu
HUNT, Cathy .... 270-831-9723.... 202 D
cathy.hunt@kctcs.edu
HUNT, Daphne .... 254-968-1852.... 497 A
djhunt@tarleton.edu
HUNT, Darla .... 606-759-7141.... 203 A
darla.hunt@kctcs.edu
HUNT, David, A .... 801-422-3868.... 509 H
david_hunt@byu.edu
HUNT, Delores .... 704-406-2361.... 364 E
dhunt@gardner-webb.edu
HUNT, Denise .... 760-921-5510...... 61 C
dhunt@paloverde.edu
HUNT, Dennis .... 812-866-7017.... 172 A
huntd@hanover.edu
HUNT, Gregory, K .... 570-340-6063.... 435 F
gkhunt@marywood.edu
HUNT, J. Steven .... 503-375-7591.... 415 F
shunt@corban.edu
HUNT, James, W .... 512-863-1567.... 496 A
huntj@southwestern.edu
HUNT, Jeffrey .... 808-235-7442.... 142 F
jwhunt@hawaii.edu
HUNT, Jennifer .... 617-912-9130.... 232 C
jhunt@bostonconservatory.edu
HUNT, Jill .... 270-809-3763.... 205 A
thunt2@murraystate.edu
HUNT, John .... 254-526-1402.... 482 H
john.hunt@ctcd.edu
HUNT, Judith, L .... 973-655-4301.... 311 F
huntjl@mail.montclair.edu
HUNT, Karen .... 937-327-6377.... 406 B
khunt@wittenberg.edu
HUNT, Lawrence .... 413-585-2260.... 244 G
lhunt@smith.edu
HUNT, Lisa, O .... 910-272-3501.... 373 D
lohunt@robeson.edu
HUNT, Lori .... 509-434-5004.... 533 A
lori.hunt@ccs.spokane.edu
HUNT, Louis, D .... 919-515-1428.... 378 C
ldhunt@ncsu.edu
HUNT, Mark .... 334-386-7140......... 3 G
mhunt@faulkner.edu
HUNT, Marsha, D .... 301-937-8448.... 226 H
mhunt@tesst.com
HUNT, Marvin .... 913-288-7659.... 194 C
mhunt@kckcc.edu
HUNT, Mary .... 312-226-6294.... 156 G
mhunt@lexingtoncollege.edu
HUNT, Melany, L .... 626-395-6249...... 32 H
hunt@caltech.edu
HUNT, Patricia .... 304-734-6611.... 542 H
phunt@bridgemont.edu
HUNT, Patricia .... 304-204-4097.... 542 J
phunt@kvctc.edu
HUNT, Patrick, G .... 240-895-4307.... 226 A
pghunt@smcm.edu
HUNT, Paul, M .... 517-432-4499.... 255 A
pmhunt@msu.edu
HUNT, Penelepe, C .... 312-413-2992.... 167 B
phunt@uic.edu
HUNT, Peter, G .... 434-949-1005.... 528 D
peter.hunt@southside.edu
HUNT, Rene .... 662-325-0610.... 275 F
rch2@its.msstate.edu
HUNT, Roe, B .... 803-535-5471.... 456 D
rhunt@claflin.edu
HUNT, Ruston .... 678-915-7338.... 137 G
rhunt@spsu.edu
HUNT, Rusty .... 336-249-8186.... 370 B
rthunt@davidsonccc.edu
HUNT, Ryan .... 513-569-1756.... 387 G
ryan.hunt@cincinnatistate.edu
HUNT, Sharon, P .... 336-272-7102.... 364 G
shunt@greensboro.edu
HUNT, Steven .... 910-521-6401.... 379 C
steven.hunt@uncp.edu
HUNT, Todd, A .... 407-582-1463.... 123 B
thunt3@valenciacollege.edu
HUNT, Virginia .... 570-504-7300.... 425 F
HUNT-BULL, Nicholas .... 603-668-2211.... 305 I
n.hunt-bull@snhu.edu

HUNT-CARTER, Pamela ..... 831-459-2749 ..... 75 C
phcarter@ucsc.edu
HUNT-SELLHORST, Sarah . 803-313-7458 .... 462 E
sehunt@mailbox.sc.edu
HUNTER, Amber, S .... 402-472-0671 .... 300 G
ahunter3@unl.edu
HUNTER, Barbara (Bobbie) 670-234-5498 .... 560 B
bobbieh@nmcnet.edu
HUNTER, Ben, D .... 317-940-9982 .... 170 F
bdhunter@butler.edu
HUNTER, Benita .... 773-838-7519 .... 147 H
bhunter@ccc.edu
HUNTER, Bill .... 850-201-6556 .... 122 A
hunterb@tcc.fl.edu
HUNTER, Bill .... 850-973-9448 .... 113 K
hunterb@nfcc.edu
HUNTER, Bonnie, L .... 219-464-5411 .... 181 C
bonnie.hunter@valpo.edu
HUNTER, Brandon .... 404-756-1652 .... 134 E
bhunter@msm.edu
HUNTER, Carolyn, A .... 513-585-2068 .... 387 D
carolyn.hunter@thechristcollege.edu
HUNTER, Charles .... 602-386-4133 ..... 11 G
chuck.hunter@arizonachristian.edu
HUNTER, Cynthia .... 941-752-5290 .... 118 J
hunterc@scf.edu
HUNTER, Donna, L .... 304-766-4146 .... 544 F
hunterdl@wvstateu.edu
HUNTER, Edith, T .... 212-280-1342 .... 358 I
ehunter@uts.columbia.edu
HUNTER, Gary .... 970-247-7224 ..... 84 K
ghunter@fortlewis.edu
HUNTER, Gayle .... 386-752-1822 .... 108 G
gayle.hunter@fgc.edu
HUNTER, Gerald, E .... 336-750-2703 .... 380 B
hunterge@wssu.edu
HUNTER, Ira .... 773-907-4800 .... 147 D
ihunter@ccc.edu
HUNTER, Jack, M .... 417-836-5636 .... 286 C
jackhunter@missouristate.edu
HUNTER, JR., Jairy, C ...... 843-863-7500 .... 456 B
jhunter@csuniv.edu
HUNTER, James, E .... 804-524-5997 .... 529 H
jhunter@vsu.edu
HUNTER, Jane .... 503-768-7446 .... 416 G
hunter@lclark.edu
HUNTER, Janet .... 563-387-2229 .... 187 D
hunterja@luther.edu
HUNTER, Janice .... 760-872-2000 ..... 43 K
jhunter@deepsprings.edu
HUNTER, Jeanne .... 814-375-4722 .... 439 E
jch20@psu.edu
HUNTER, Jim .... 952-446-4325 .... 263 C
hunterj@crown.edu
HUNTER, John .... 417-626-1234 .... 287 C
library@occ.edu
HUNTER, Joseph, A .... 781-292-2255 .... 234 H
joseph.hunter@olin.edu
HUNTER, Karen .... 903-923-2475 .... 509 E
khunter@wileyc.edu
HUNTER, Kim .... 870-245-5185 ..... 22 I
hunterk@obu.edu
HUNTER, Kim .... 513-244-4248 .... 388 E
kim_hunter@mail.msj.edu
HUNTER, Kymm .... 803-705-4519 .... 455 D
hunterk@benedict.edu
HUNTER, Larry, T .... 614-236-6641 .... 386 E
lhunter2@capital.edu
HUNTER, Lori .... 865-981-8121 .... 471 B
lori.hunter@maryvillecollege.edu
HUNTER, Lynn .... 508-270-4005 .... 239 G
lhunter@massbay.edu
HUNTER, Maria .... 480-994-9244 ..... 18 F
mariah@swiha.edu
HUNTER, Mark, A .... 805-756-5222 ..... 33 I
mhunter@calpoly.edu
HUNTER, Mary .... 925-969-3466 ..... 52 C
mhunter@jfku.edu
HUNTER, Melissa .... 931-221-7315 .... 473 E
hunterm@apsu.edu
HUNTER, Pam .... 760-773-2508 ..... 42 A
phunter@collegeofthedesert.edu
HUNTER, Patricia .... 425-739-8361 .... 535 H
patricia.hunter@lwtc.edu
HUNTER, Rebecca .... 508-793-7561 .... 233 B
rhunter@clarku.edu
HUNTER, Robert, D .... 325-674-2495 .... 478 I
hunterr@acu.edu
HUNTER, Rosemarie .... 801-972-3596 .... 511 C
r.hunter@partners.utah.edu
HUNTER, Steve .... 360-867-6310 .... 534 D
hunters@evergreen.edu
HUNTER, Susan .... 503-552-1512 .... 417 D
shunter@ncnm.edu
HUNTER, Susan, J .... 207-581-1547 .... 220 A
hunter@maine.edu
HUNTER, Susan, S .... 804-523-5375 .... 527 A
shunter@reynolds.edu
HUNTER, Tim, W .... 814-332-2755 .... 421 F
tim.hunter@allegheny.edu
HUNTER, Tracie .... 310-377-5501 ..... 56 F
thunter@marymountpv.edu
HUNTER, Vivian .... 434-848-1852 .... 524 B
vhunter@saintpauls.edu
HUNTER, W, B .... 602-850-8000 ..... 17 G
bhunter@phoenixseminary.edu
HUNTER-GOLDSWORTHY,
Heidi .... 570-484-2344 .... 443 B
hgh4845@lhup.edu
HUNTER HAYES, Tracey ... 484-365-7370 .... 434 H
thunterhayes@lincoln.edu
HUNTINGTON, Judith .... 914-654-5430 .... 330 B
president@cnr.edu
HUNTINGTON, Mark, W ... 260-982-5051 .... 177 H
mwhuntington@manchester.edu
HUNTINGTON, Robert .... 419-448-2202 .... 391 F
president@heidelberg.edu
HUNTLEY, Daniel .... 641-844-5670 .... 186 D
daniel.huntley@iavalley.edu
HUNTLEY, Deborah .... 989-964-4144 .... 257 G
dhuntley@svsu.edu
HUNTLEY, Edelma, D .... 828-262-2130 .... 377 D
huntleyed@appstate.edu
HUNTLEY, Kristy .... 860-628-4751 ..... 93 C
khuntley@lincolncollegene.edu
HUNTLEY, Steve, E .... 904-264-2172 .... 116 C
steve.huntley@iws.edu
HUNTLEY-SMITH, Jen .... 775-784-8262 .... 303 A
jhuntleysmith@unr.edu
HUNTOON, JR., David, H . 845-938-2610 .... 559 A
8sgs@usma.edu
HUNTOON, Jacqueline, E .. 906-487-2327 .... 255 B
jeh@mtu.edu
HUNTSINGER, Trish .... 828-395-1297 .... 371 D
thuntsing@isothermal.edu
HUNTSMAN, Deborah, C ... 330-672-3237 .... 393 D
dhuntsm1@kent.edu
HUNTSMAN, Kent .... 512-863-1235 .... 496 A
huntsmak@southwestern.edu
HUNTZE-ROONEY,
Deborah .... 408-288-3731 ..... 67 D
deborah.huntze@sjcc.edu
HUO, Xiaoming (Sharon) ... 931-372-3463 .... 474 B
xhuo@tntech.edu
HUOPPI, Jennifer .... 860-465-4357 ..... 90 H
huoppij@easternct.edu
HUOT, Anne, E .... 585-395-2651 .... 352 F
ahuot@brockport.edu
HUPFER, Mary, A .... 812-464-1627 .... 181 B
mhupfer@usi.edu
HUPKE, Doug .... 415-405-3824 ..... 37 B
dhupke@sfsu.edu
HUPP, Mark .... 419-755-5665 .... 397 C
mhupp@ncstatecollege.edu
HUPP, Stephen .... 304-424-8273 .... 545 C
stephen.hupp@mail.wvu.edu
HUPPE, Alicia, L .... 972-377-1749 .... 483 H
ahuppe@collin.edu
HUPPERT, Susan .... 515-271-1384 .... 184 A
susan.huppert@dmu.edu
HURD, Cathy .... 704-378-1181 .... 366 A
churd@jcsu.edu
HURD, Clifton .... 407-277-0311 .... 107 B
churd@evergladesuniversity.edu
HURD, James, R .... 850-474-2384 .... 121 D
jhurd@uwf.edu
HURD, Janice .... 501-279-4403 ..... 21 H
jhurd@harding.edu
HURD, Roy .... 707-546-4000 ..... 45 H
rhurd@empcol.edu
HURD, Sandra, N .... 315-443-1899 .... 357 C
snhurd@syr.edu
HURD, Sherie .... 707-546-4000 ..... 45 H
shurd@empcol.edu
HURD-MATOS, April .... 707-546-4000 ..... 45 H
ahurdmatos@empirecollege.com
HURDLE, Bill .... 478-757-4024 .... 139 E
bhurdle@wesleyancollege.edu
HURDLE-WINSLOW,
B. Lynn .... 252-335-0821 .... 369 G
lynnhw@albemarle.edu
HURLBERT, Janet, M .... 570-321-4082 .... 435 D
hurlbjan@lycoming.edu
HURLBUT, L, E .... 540-464-7292 .... 529 F
hurlbutle@vmi.edu
HURLEIGH, Barbara .... 718-405-3733 .... 330 A
barbara.hurleigh@mountsaintvincent.edu
HURLEY, Alicia .... 212-998-6859 .... 344 B
alicia.hurley@nyu.edu
HURLEY, Celia .... 919-718-7360 .... 369 C
churley@cccc.edu
HURLEY, Charles, T .... 574-631-7495 .... 180 G
hurley.32@nd.edu
HURLEY, Deanne .... 440-646-8320 .... 405 B
dhurley@ursuline.edu
HURLEY, Gail, A .... 814-865-5423 .... 438 G
gah5@psu.edu
HURLEY, James .... 606-218-5272 .... 207 F
jhurley@upike.edu
HURLEY, James, B .... 601-923-1630 .... 276 F
jhurley@rts.edu
HURLEY, James, M .... 847-491-4286 .... 160 E
j-hurley2@northwestern.edu
HURLEY, John .... 360-867-6500 .... 534 D
hurleyj@evergreen.edu
HURLEY, John, J .... 716-888-2100 .... 325 F
hurleyj@canisius.edu
HURLEY, Leah, A .... 214-648-7986 .... 507 E
leah.hurley@utsouthwestern.edu
HURLEY, Marja, M .... 860-679-3483 ..... 95 A
hurley@nso1.uchc.edu
HURLEY, Patricia .... 818-240-1000 ..... 48 D
phurley@glendale.edu
HURLEY, Richard, V .... 540-654-1301 .... 525 D
president@umw.edu
HURLEY, Rose .... 928-776-2211 ..... 19 C
rose.hurley@yc.edu
HURLEY, Sam .... 903-928-3288 .... 502 F
shurley@tvcc.edu
HURLEY, Tracy .... 210-784-2300 .... 498 E
thurley@tamusa.tamus.edu
HURLEY, Travis .... 417-626-1234 .... 287 C
hurley.travis@occ.edu
HURLEY, Wanda .... 601-635-2111 .... 274 A
whurley@eccc.edu
HURLIMANN, John .... 701-483-2166 .... 381 G
john.hurlimann@dickinsonstate.edu
HURRELL, Rockie .... 719-502-2007 ..... 87 B
rockie.hurrell@ppcc.edu
HURST, Carmen, A .... 765-269-5650 .... 176 D
churst@ivytech.edu
HURST, Carol, P .... 540-674-3611 .... 527 E
churst@nr.edu
HURST, Dan .... 727-726-1153 .... 103 I
danhurst@clearwater.edu
HURST, DeWayne .... 909-607-8509 ..... 40 F
dewayne.hurst@cgu.edu
HURST, Fred .... 928-523-6598 ..... 16 I
fred.hurst@nau.edu
HURST, James .... 574-520-4125 .... 174 E
jhurst@iusb.edu
HURST, Jason .... 850-718-2260 .... 103 D
hurstj@chipola.edu
HURST, Jeffrey, J .... 801-626-7256 .... 511 G
jhurst@weber.edu
HURST, Laura .... 610-660-1175 .... 446 C
lannhurs@sju.edu
HURST, Mark .... 423-585-2629 .... 476 D
mark.hurst@ws.edu
HURST, Richard, S .... 773-508-7465 .... 157 C
rhurst@luc.edu
HURST, Susan .... 870-245-5567 ..... 22 I
hursts@obu.edu
HURST, Thomas, R .... 410-864-3613 .... 226 B
thurst@stmarys.edu
HURST, Timothy .... 931-221-7671 .... 473 E
hurstt@apsu.edu
HURT, Lynn .... 540-857-6244 .... 529 B
lhurt@virginiawestern.edu
HURTADO, Geoffrey .... 414-229-5390 .... 551 D
ghurtado@uwm.edu
HURTADO, Jose .... 707-256-7225 ..... 58 F
jhurtado@napavalley.edu
HURTADO, Mike .... 626-914-8870 ..... 40 B
mhurtado@citruscollege.edu
HURTE, Vernon .... 757-221-2300 .... 518 A
vjhurt@wm.edu
HURTIG, Juliet, K .... 419-772-2032 .... 398 H
j-hurtig@onu.edu
HURWITZ, Donna .... 212-774-4801 .... 340 C
dhurwitz@mmm.edu
HURWITZ, T. Alan .... 202-651-5005 ..... 98 B
president@gallaudet.edu
HUSAIN, Naveed .... 718-997-3009 .... 328 E
naveed.husain@qc.cuny.edu
HUSAK, William .... 310-338-5940 ..... 56 E
whusak@lmu.edu
HUSBY, Kristin .... 303-975-5015 ..... 89 H
khusby@westwood.edu
HUSCHLE, Brian .... 218-683-8800 .... 268 C
brian.huschle@northlandcollege.edu
HUSEBY, Matthew .... 847-543-2575 .... 148 B
mhuseby@clcillinois.edu
HUSEIN, Lori, A .... 310-338-7552 ..... 56 E
lhusein@lmu.edu
HUSELTON, Ken .... 412-323-4000 .... 423 A
khuselton@mcg-btc.org
HUSHON, Kate .... 814-868-9900 .... 428 I
kateh@erieit.edu
HUSK, Mark, A .... 317-921-4723 .... 175 I
mhusk@ivytech.edu
HUSK, Stephanie .... 503-375-7010 .... 415 F
shusk@corban.edu
HUSKEY, Dana, K .... 336-342-4261 .... 373 E
huskeyd@rockinghamcc.edu
HUSKEY, Jeffrey .... 605-688-6895 .... 466 C
jeffrey.huskey@sdstate.edu
HUSKEY, Robin .... 903-983-8620 .... 489 I
rhuskey@kilgore.edu
HUSKINS, Steve .... 423-697-4466 .... 474 D
HUSMANN, Calvin, D .... 920-832-6517 .... 548 B
calvin.d.husmann@lawrence.edu
HUSS, H. Fenwick .... 404-413-7000 .... 131 G
hfhuss@gsu.edu
HUSS, Larry, F .... 803-754-4100 .... 457 D
HUSSAIN, Asif .... 718-368-6674 .... 328 A
ahussain@kbcc.cuny.edu
HUSSEY, LeighAnn .... 601-928-6225 .... 275 E
leighann.hussey@mgccc.edu
HUSSEY, Mark, A .... 979-862-4384 .... 497 E
mhussey@tamu.edu
HUSSON, James, J .... 617-552-3441 .... 232 B
james.husson@bc.edu
HUSSON, William, J .... 303-458-1844 ..... 87 I
whusson@regis.edu
HUST, Ryan .... 847-317-7152 .... 166 E
rhust@tiu.edu
HUSTED, David, S .... 972-881-5684 .... 483 H
dhusted@collin.edu
HUSTED, Jean, L .... 203-582-8645 ..... 93 H
jean.husted@quinnipiac.edu
HUSTED, Joy Lin .... 918-343-7545 .... 411 H
jhusted@rsu.edu
HUSTOLES, Carol L, J .... 269-387-1900 .... 260 C
carol.hustoles@wmich.edu
HUSTON, Gina .... 360-475-7766 .... 536 D
ghuston@olympic.edu
HUSTON, Jayne .... 724-830-4612 .... 447 C
huston@setonhill.edu
HUSTON, Richard .... 858-653-6740 ..... 52 D
HUSTON, Robert, H .... 304-766-3261 .... 544 F
hustonrh@wvstateu.edu
HUSTON, Susan, A .... 716-645-5300 .... 351 G
huston@buffalo.edu
HUSTON, William, D .... 859-336-5082 .... 206 A
whuston@sccky.edu
HUTCHCRAFT, Joy, D .... 309-438-8041 .... 153 D
jdhutch@ilstu.edu
HUTCHENS, Sue .... 513-562-8749 .... 384 D
shutchens@artacademy.edu
HUTCHENS, III,
William, H .... 304-293-5841 .... 545 A
whhutchens@mail.wvu.edu
HUTCHERSON, Annette .... 863-297-1039 .... 115 C
ahutcherson@polk.edu
HUTCHERSON, Cecil, L ...... 864-592-4693 .... 461 C
hutchersonc@sccsc.edu
HUTCHERSON, Cindy .... 812-265-2580 .... 177 A
chutcher@ivytech.edu
HUTCHERSON, Patricia, J . 318-274-3242 .... 215 E
jenkinsp@gram.edu
HUTCHESON, Christina ...... 618-437-5321 .... 162 D
hutchesonc@rlc.edu
HUTCHESON, Crystal .... 407-847-8966 .... 107 I
crystal.hutcheson@fcc.edu
HUTCHESON, Donna, R ...... 770-420-4421 .... 133 A
dhutches@kennesaw.edu
HUTCHESON, Patty, S .... 770-593-2257 .... 132 B
gjcfs@mindspring.com
HUTCHESON, Philip .... 615-966-5850 .... 470 F
philip.hutcheson@lipscomb.edu
HUTCHINGS, Hayden .... 864-596-9744 .... 457 E
hayden.hutchings@converse.edu
HUTCHINGS, Robert, L .... 512-471-3200 .... 505 D
rhutchings@austin.utexas.edu
HUTCHINS, Carin .... 832-813-6737 .... 490 E
carin.a.hutchins@lonestar.edu
HUTCHINS, Donald, L .... 410-276-0306 .... 226 D
dhutchins@host.sdc.edu
HUTCHINS, Greg .... 608-262-6151 .... 553 B
greg.hutchins@uwex.edu
HUTCHINS, James .... 859-291-0800 .... 200 A
jhutchins@daymarcollege.edu
HUTCHINS, Mark .... 931-372-3206 .... 474 B
mhutchins@tntech.edu
HUTCHINS, Mittie, D .... 903-923-3206 .... 500 E
mittie.hutchins@tstc.edu
HUTCHINS, Paul, C .... 910-592-8081 .... 373 G
phutchins@sampsoncc.edu
HUTCHINS, Terrel, F .... 269-488-4244 .... 253 A
thutchins@kvcc.edu
HUTCHINS, Thelma, J .... 304-367-4122 .... 543 H
thelma.hutchins@fairmontstate.edu
HUTCHINS, Thomas .... 931-221-7456 .... 473 E
hutchinst@apsu.edu
HUTCHINS, Wesley, D .... 336-757-3053 .... 370 F
whutchins@forsythtech.edu
HUTCHINSON, Adriane, W 847-543-2443 .... 148 B
ahutchinson@clcillinois.edu
HUTCHINSON, Andre .... 503-943-7371 .... 420 G
hutchina@up.edu
HUTCHINSON, Barbara, L . 717-780-2356 .... 430 E
blhutchi@hacc.edu
HUTCHINSON, Brian, A ...... 606-783-2088 .... 204 I
b.hutchinson@moreheadstate.edu
HUTCHINSON, Corrie .... 537-442-2211 .... 290 C
HUTCHINSON, Craig .... 207-780-4035 .... 220 G
craigh@usm.maine.edu
HUTCHINSON, Diane, L ...... 315-255-1743 .... 325 G
diane.hutchinson@cayuga-cc.edu
HUTCHINSON, Gayle, E ...... 530-898-6171 ..... 34 C
ghutchinson@csuchico.edu
HUTCHINSON, James .... 256-726-7145 .... 6 C
jhutchinson@oakwood.edu
HUTCHINSON, John .... 352-787-7660 .... 102 B
jhutchinson@beaconcollege.edu
HUTCHINSON, John, S .... 713-348-4996 .... 493 C
hutchinson@rice.edu
HUTCHINSON, Kathryn, T . 718-990-6820 .... 348 G
hutchink@stjohns.edu
HUTCHINSON, Lisa .... 215-248-6393 .... 435 B
lhutchinson@ltsp.edu
HUTCHINSON, Michael .... 501-370-5382 ..... 23 B
mhutchinson@philander.edu
HUTCHINSON, Natalie, N .. 641-628-5220 .... 183 D
hutchinsonn@central.edu

INGERSOLL, Julia .... 610-526-6132.... 430 D
jingersoll@harcum.edu
INGERSOLL, Pat .... 616-234-3869.... 251 E
pingerso@grcc.edu
INGHAM, Joanne .... 212-431-2876.... 343 E
jingham@nyls.edu
INGHRAM, Scott .... 304-384-5271.... 543 G
inghramcs@concord.edu
INGLE, Andrea .... 765-285-5974.... 169 G
akingle@bsu.edu
INGLE, Brooke .... 970-247-7421...... 84 K
bookstoremgr@fortlewis.edu
INGLE, Jeff, S .... 704-406-4654.... 364 E
jingle@gardner-webb.edu
INGLE, Kent .... 863-667-5002.... 118 F
kingle@seu.edu
INGLE, Pam .... 417-624-7070.... 284 D
pingle@messengercollege.edu
INGLE, Vernell .... 417-624-7070.... 284 D
vingle@messengercollege.edu
INGLES, Roger, D .... 740-368-3738.... 400 G
rdingles@owu.edu
INGLES, Susan, L .... 414-410-4236.... 546 G
slingles@stritch.edu
INGLI, Robin, C .... 651-523-2461.... 264 A
ringli@hamline.edu
INGLIS, Mark .... 216-421-7403.... 388 A
minglis@cia.edu
INGLISH, Darla .... 940-397-4321.... 491 B
darla.inglish@mwsu.edu
INGMIRE, Randall, L .... 785-539-3571.... 195 B
ringmire@mccks.edu
INGOLD, Barbara, S .... 815-740-3369.... 167 E
bingold@stfrancis.edu
INGOLD, Scott .... 305-284-4206.... 122 I
singold@miami.edu
INGOLFSLAND, Dennis ..... 952-446-4239.... 263 C
ingolfsland@crown.edu
INGRAHAM, Barry .... 207-768-2702.... 218 J
bingraham@nmcc.edu
INGRAHAM, Carolyn, K .... 706-737-1636.... 125 G
cingraha@aug.edu
INGRAHAM, Patricia .... 607-777-5572.... 351 F
pingraha@binghamton.edu
INGRAHAM, Timothy .... 978-468-7111.... 235 B
tingraham@gcts.edu
INGRAM, Archinya .... 803-327-7402.... 456 F
aingram@clintonjuniorcollege.edu
INGRAM, Beth .... 319-335-3565.... 182 F
beth-ingram@uiowa.edu
INGRAM, Beverly .... 318-487-7694.... 209 F
ingram@lacollege.edu
INGRAM, Charles, E .... 609-652-4381.... 313 E
charles.ingram@stockton.edu
INGRAM, Charlotte .... 276-466-7868.... 529 D
charlotteingram@vic.edu
INGRAM, Earl .... 334-670-3104........ 8 A
ingram@troy.edu
INGRAM, Geoff .... 951-785-2000...... 53 E
gingram@lasierra.edu
INGRAM, Gregory .... 301-891-4017.... 229 B
gingram@wau.edu
INGRAM, Iris .... 805-378-1412...... 77 D
iingram@vcccd.edu
INGRAM, J. Kevin .... 785-539-3571.... 195 B
kingram@mccks.edu
INGRAM, J. LaVelle .... 410-455-2472.... 227 D
jlavelle@umbc.edu
INGRAM, Jim .... 662-862-8047.... 274 E
jingram@iccms.edu
INGRAM, Joyce, A .... 850-644-7950.... 119 D
jingram@admin.fsu.edu
INGRAM, Lashawanda, T ... 315-386-7128.... 355 E
ingraml@canton.edu
INGRAM, Mike .... 423-746-5292.... 476 F
mingram@twcnet.edu
INGRAM, Ozzie .... 214-333-6875.... 484 D
ozzie@dbu.edu
INGRAM, Sherry .... 704-406-4303.... 364 E
singram@gardner-webb.edu
INGRAM, Shirley, M .... 956-872-5051.... 494 H
singram@southtexascollege.edu
INGRAM, Sue .... 417-255-7911.... 286 D
sueingram@missouristate.edu
INGRAM, Victoria, L .... 540-828-5393.... 517 B
vingram@bridgewater.edu
INGRAM, Wanda Rhea .... 334-244-3476........ 1 G
wingram4@aum.edu
INGRAM, William, G .... 919-536-7250.... 370 C
ingramb@durhamtech.edu
INGRAM-WALLACE,
Brenda, J .... 610-921-7585.... 421 E
bingramwallace@alb.edu
INGRASSIA, Maria .... 845-434-5750.... 357 A
mingrassia@sullivan.suny.edu
INGS, Margaret Ann .... 617-824-8299.... 234 B
margaret_ann_ings@emerson.edu
INIGO, Juan .... 787-841-2000.... 565 B
juan_inigo@pucpr.edu
INIGUEZ-JIMENEZ,
J. Alfredo .... 956-764-5798.... 489 J
ainiguez@laredo.edu
INKSTER, Larry .... 606-546-1233.... 207 B
linkster@unionky.edu

INMAN, Ann .... 812-866-7013.... 172 A
inmana@hanover.edu
INMAN, Barbara, L .... 757-727-5264.... 519 H
barbara.inman@hamptonu.edu
INMAN, Dean .... 870-862-8131...... 23 G
dinman@southark.edu
INMAN, Gerald .... 617-989-4252.... 245 F
inmang@wit.edu
INMAN, John, G .... 724-458-2176.... 430 B
jginman@gcc.edu
INMAN, Keith .... 502-852-6924.... 207 E
akinma01@louisville.edu
INMAN, Leigh .... 619-961-4278...... 72 J
glinman@tjsl.edu
INMAN, Linda, D .... 336-334-7708.... 378 A
ldinman@ncat.edu
INMAN, Lucille .... 707-546-4000...... 45 H
linman@empirecollege.com
INMAN, Marianne, E .... 660-248-6221.... 279 G
minman@centralmethodist.edu
INMAN, Stan, D .... 801-585-5028.... 511 C
sinman@sa.utah.edu
INNIS, Daniel, E .... 603-862-1983.... 306 C
dan.innis@unh.edu
INOA, Luis .... 845-437-5862.... 359 F
inoa@vassar.edu
INOKUCHI, Richard .... 650-738-4166...... 67 H
inokuchi@smccd.edu
INOSHITA, Lynn .... 808-845-9118.... 142 B
inoshita@hawaii.edu
INOUYE, Carolyn .... 805-986-5803...... 77 E
cinouye@vcccd.edu
INOUYE, Jon .... 949-794-9090...... 71 F
jinouye@stanbridge.edu
INOUYE, Susan, K .... 808-956-8155.... 141 E
susani@hawaii.edu
INOWAY-RONNIE, Eden ... 608-265-5975.... 550 J
etinoway@wisc.edu
INSANALLI, Dawn .... 914-637-2726.... 336 E
dinsanalli@iona.edu
INSCHO, Edward .... 706-721-5615.... 130 D
einscho@georgiahealth.edu
INSERTO, Fathiah .... 909-396-6090...... 32 I
INSKEEP, Tony, D .... 910-277-5079.... 376 C
inskeeptd@sapc.edu
INSLEE, Trish .... 316-978-3693.... 198 A
trish.inslee@wichita.edu
INSLER, Gayle, D .... 516-877-3167.... 322 A
insler@adelphi.edu
INSLEY, Andrea .... 206-587-3899.... 537 E
ainsley@sccd.ctc.edu
INSLEY, Lynn .... 201-216-8927.... 315 E
linsley@stevens.edu
INTEMANN, Gerald, W ...... 724-357-2219.... 442 F
gerald.intemann@iup.edu
INTILLE, Amy .... 617-989-4885.... 245 F
intillea@wit.edu
INTROCASO, CDP,
Candace .... 412-536-1204.... 432 H
cintrocaso@laroche.edu
INZER, Monica, C .... 315-859-4421.... 334 H
minzer@hamilton.edu
IOANNOU, Carin .... 336-770-3301.... 379 E
ioannouc@uncsa.edu
IOCANO, Lynn .... 302-857-6250...... 96 C
liocano@desu.edu
IODICE, Emilio .... 773-508-2760.... 157 C
eiodice@luc.edu
IOLI, Christine .... 412-809-5100.... 444 G
ioli.christine@pti.edu
IORG, Jeff .... 415-380-1322...... 48 E
jeffiorg@ggbts.edu
IORIO, Richard .... 800-342-7342...... 48 G
richard.iorio@golfacademy.edu
IORIO, Sharon .... 316-978-3301.... 198 A
sharon.iorio@wichita.edu
IOSSI, Lora .... 402-557-7343.... 296 H
lora.iossi@bellevue.edu
IPACH, Nichole .... 805-437-8893...... 34 B
nichole.ipach@csuci.edu
IPPINECA, Carey, L .... 607-735-1812.... 332 I
cippineca@elmira.edu
IPPOLITO, Andrew .... 201-692-2531.... 310 A
andrew_ippolito@fdu.edu
IRBY, Michele .... 573-651-5120.... 289 K
mirby@semo.edu
IRBY, Xaviere, J .... 334-874-5700........ 2 H
xirby@ccal.edu
IRELAND, Alan .... 336-750-2935.... 380 B
irelandag@wssu.edu
IRELAND, Chris, M .... 801-581-3402.... 511 C
cireland@deans.pharm.utah.edu
IRELAND, Jim, D .... 620-792-9339.... 190 H
irelandj@bartonccc.edu
IRGENS, Dana .... 763-433-1822.... 265 G
dana.irgens@anokaramsey.edu
IRICK, Troy, D .... 260-359-4066.... 173 A
tirick@huntington.edu
IRIS, Michael .... 908-852-1400.... 308 E
irism@centenarycollege.edu
IRISH, Allyson .... 617-521-2324.... 244 F
allyson.irish@simmons.edu
IRISH, Bridget .... 970-382-6940...... 84 K
irish_b@fortlewis.edu

IRISH, Edward, P .... 757-221-2425.... 518 A
epiris@wm.edu
IRIZARRY, Elba, T .... 787-264-1912.... 564 B
elbatirizarry@sg.inter.edu
IRIZARRY, Jose, R .... 787-296-1101.... 233 A
jose.irizarry@cambridgecollege.edu
IRIZARRY MERCADO,
Jose, R .... 787-763-6700.... 562 D
dririzarry@se-pr.edu
IRIZARY, Herminio .... 787-841-2000.... 565 B
hirizary@pucpr.edu
IRLA-CHESNEY, Kathy .... 603-862-2120.... 306 C
kathy.irla-chesney@unh.edu
IROFF, Jayson .... 954-201-7423.... 102 E
jiroff@broward.edu
IROFF, Steven .... 770-576-4498.... 136 E
IRUDAYAM, Irene .... 508-849-3410.... 230 C
iirudayam@annamaria.edu
IRVIN, Camilla .... 334-833-4577........ 4 E
cirvin@huntingdon.edu
IRVIN, Cynthia .... 904-680-7653.... 107 J
cirvin@fcsl.edu
IRVIN, Dale, T .... 212-870-1223.... 344 A
dirvin@nyts.edu
IRVIN, David .... 972-829-2150.... 464 H
IRVIN, Dexter .... 808-974-7762.... 141 F
ldirvin@hawaii.edu
IRVIN, Hal .... 540-231-7784.... 529 G
hirvin@vt.edu
IRVIN, Howard, J .... 510-723-6744...... 39 C
hirvin@chabotcollege.edu
IRVIN, Michael, E .... 864-503-5217.... 463 B
mirvin@uscupstate.edu
IRVIN, ValaRay .... 225-771-2480.... 214 I
valaray_irvin@subr.edu
IRVIN, Zoe, A .... 443-518-4742.... 223 D
zirvin@howardcc.edu
IRVINE, Angela .... 802-654-2396.... 514 D
airvine@smcvt.edu
IRVINE, David .... 518-262-5251.... 322 D
irvined@mail.amc.edu
IRVINE, Dianne .... 225-342-6950.... 215 D
dianne.irvinne@la.gov
IRVINE, Shelly .... 540-887-7367.... 521 C
sirvine@mbc.edu
IRVING, Jacqueline .... 610-341-5872.... 428 E
jirving@eastern.edu
IRVING, Jean, H .... 530-898-5944...... 34 C
jirving@csuchico.edu
IRVING, Merrill .... 847-635-2604.... 160 F
mirving@oakton.edu
IRWIN, Bonnie .... 217-581-2917.... 150 E
dbirwin@eiu.edu
IRWIN, Darci .... 616-222-1439.... 250 A
darci.irwin@cornerstone.edu
IRWIN, Dennis .... 740-593-1479.... 399 G
irwind@ohio.edu
IRWIN, Graham .... 513-583-5000.... 390 A
girwin@devry.edu
IRWIN, Holly .... 619-849-2706...... 62 L
hollyirwin@pointloma.edu
IRWIN, Joseph .... 404-894-0771.... 130 F
joe.irwin@alumni.gatech.edu
IRWIN, Kathy .... 810-762-0415.... 255 G
kathy.irwin@mcc.edu
IRWIN, Lorry .... 845-434-5750.... 357 A
lirwin@sullivan.suny.edu
IRWIN, Robert .... 864-578-8770.... 460 F
rirwin@sherman.edu
IRWIN, Suzy .... 903-823-3095.... 496 E
suzy.irwin@texarkanacollege.edu
IRWIN, Ursula .... 503-491-7469.... 417 B
ursula.irwin@mhcc.edu
IRWIN, William .... 570-208-5900.... 432 G
williamirwin@kings.edu
IRWIN-DEVITIS, Linda .... 757-683-3777.... 522 F
ldevitis@odu.edu
ISAAC, Bina .... 760-862-1333...... 42 A
bisaac@collegeofthedesert.edu
ISAAC, JR., Lawrence ...... 505-786-4172.... 318 I
lisaac@navajotech.edu
ISAAC, Mark .... 559-453-5516...... 47 K
mark.isaac@fresno.edu
ISAAC, Nancy .... 620-431-2820.... 195 E
nisaac@neosho.edu
ISAAC, Samantha .... 561-912-2166.... 107 B
sissac@evergladesuniversity.edu
ISAACS, Becky .... 580-559-5243.... 407 J
bisaacs@ecok.edu
ISAACS, Carol, B .... 260-481-6147.... 174 C
isaacs@ipfw.edu
ISAACS, Jerry .... 918-495-7750.... 411 C
jisaacs@oru.edu
ISAACS, Mona .... 859-622-1986.... 200 J
mona.isaacs@eku.edu
ISAACS, Yolanda .... 815-280-6691.... 154 J
yisaacs@jjc.edu
ISAACSON, Lyn, R .... 641-628-5266.... 183 D
isaacsonl@central.edu
ISAACSON, Melvin .... 212-346-1366.... 345 F
misaacson@pace.edu
ISAACSON, Michael, L ...... 605-642-6788.... 465 H
michael.isaacson@bhsu.edu

ISABELLE, Callista, S .... 484-664-3120.... 437 C
cisabelle@muhlenberg.edu
ISABELLE, Geoffrey, S .... 315-684-6070.... 354 F
isabelgs@morrisville.edu
ISACKMAN, Brigid, K .... 215-596-8701.... 450 B
b.isackman@usciences.edu
ISACSON, Barbara .... 973-748-9000.... 307 H
barbara_isacson@bloomfield.edu
ISAK, Misty .... 609-984-1588.... 316 A
misak@tesc.edu
ISAKOFF, Louis, A .... 757-352-2794.... 523 E
isakoff@regent.edu
ISBELL, Corey .... 785-738-9055.... 195 G
cisbell@ncktc.edu
ISBELL, Monica .... 336-506-4130.... 368 A
isbellm@alamancecc.edu
ISBELL, Teresa, S .... 214-860-2017.... 485 A
tisbell@dcccd.edu
ISCH, Larry, A .... 479-979-1420...... 26 A
laisch@ozarks.edu
ISEKENEGBE, Thomas, A .. 856-691-8600.... 309 B
thomasi@cccnj.edu
ISELI, Madeline .... 937-512-2510.... 401 J
madeline.iseli@sinclair.edu
ISELI, Madeline .... 937-512-2022.... 401 J
madeline.iseli@sinclair.edu
ISEMINGER, Ernie .... 909-621-8096...... 40 G
ernie.iseminger@cmc.edu
ISEMINGER, Jeff .... 507-389-2823.... 267 E
jeffrey.iseminger@mnsu.edu
ISENBERG, Jerold .... 847-982-2500.... 152 A
isenberg@htc.edu
ISENHOUR, John, L .... 770-423-6620.... 133 A
jisenhou@kennesaw.edu
ISENHOWER, Robert, W .... 864-587-4117.... 461 D
isenhowerb@smcsc.edu
ISERMANN, Sue, L .... 815-224-0408.... 153 E
sue_isermann@ivcc.edu
ISGETT, J. Samuel .... 864-877-3052.... 460 A
sam.isgett@ngu.edu
ISH, Cheryl, J .... 570-208-5855.... 432 G
cjish@kings.edu
ISHEE, Jimmy .... 940-898-2852.... 502 D
jishee@twu.edu
ISHERWOOD, J. Thomas .. 770-720-5502.... 136 C
jti@reinhardt.edu
ISHIDA, Yoshiharu .... 808-946-3773.... 140 C
ISHII, Susan .... 661-224-2923...... 44 J
sishii@devry.edu
ISHIMOTO, Lester .... 808-454-4700.... 141 H
lishimot@hawaii.edu
ISHIYAMA, Howard, J .... 412-536-1282.... 432 H
howard.ishiyama@laroche.edu
ISHMAEL, Amy .... 918-540-6212.... 408 J
aishmael@neo.edu
ISHOP, Kedra, B .... 512-475-7326.... 505 D
kedra.ishop@austin.utexas.edu
ISKRA, Theresa .... 571-371-5140.... 258 F
iskrat@cooley.edu
ISLE, Wendy .... 620-331-4100.... 193 I
wisle@indycc.edu
ISMAIL, Amid .... 215-707-2799.... 447 H
amid.ismail@temple.edu
ISMAIL, Shaik .... 503-883-2228.... 416 H
sismail@linfield.edu
ISOLA, Susan .... 724-836-7741.... 449 C
smi10@pitt.edu
ISOM, Roger .... 410-293-1881.... 559 B
isom@usna.edu
ISOMOTO, Robert, G .... 310-434-4201.... 68 D
isomoto_robert@smc.edu
ISOZAKI, Peggy .... 415-883-2211...... 42 B
peggy.isozaki@marin.edu
ISPIR, Sheri .... 401-598-1872.... 453 E
sispir@jwu.edu
ISRAEL, Adrienne, M .... 336-316-2181.... 365 A
aisrael@guilford.edu
ISRAEL, Cary, A .... 972-758-3801.... 483 H
cisrael@collin.edu
ISRAEL, Richard .... 714-556-3610...... 77 B
rich.israel@vanguard.edu
ISRAEL, Susan, H .... 860-515-3839...... 90 E
sisrael@charteroak.edu
ISSELMANN, Sandy .... 920-832-6541.... 548 B
sandy.isselmann@lawrence.edu
ISSOD, Cheryl .... 410-225-2310.... 224 B
cissod@mica.edu
ITALIANO, Christina .... 414-326-2306.... 547 B
christina.italiano@ccon.edu
ITO, Kimberly .... 281-648-0880.... 500 A
kito@tsb.edu
ITTLEMAN, Leona, R .... 413-755-4055.... 241 B
ittleman@stcc.edu
ITZHAKI, Rafael .... 714-816-0366...... 73 B
rafael.itzhaki@trident.edu
IULIANO, Robert, W .... 617-496-4179.... 235 D
robert_iuliano@harvard.edu
IUSO, Kenneth, J .... 732-445-2620.... 314 B
iuso@rci.rutgers.edu
IUSO, Kenneth, J .... 732-445-2620.... 314 C
iuso@rci.rutgers.edu
IVAN, Elaine, R .... 719-365-8291...... 86 E
IVANKOVIC, John .... 845-341-4190.... 345 E
john.ivankovic@sunyorange.edu

JACKSON, Robert .... 715-682-1207 .... 549 F rjackson@northland.edu
JACKSON, Robert, D .... 847-578-3248 .... 163 C robert.jackson@rosalindfranklin.edu
JACKSON, Roberta .... 212-463-0400 .... 358 B roberta.jackson@touro.edu
JACKSON, Ron .... 864-592-4817 .... 461 C jacksonr@sccsc.edu
JACKSON, Ronald .... 513-556-5858 .... 403 D ronald.jackson@uc.edu
JACKSON, Ronald, C .... 215-751-8876 .... 426 B rcjackson@ccp.edu
JACKSON, Rose Mary .... 501-882-8855 .... 20 C rmjackson@asub.edu
JACKSON, Rosemary .... 423-585-2614 .... 476 D rosemary.jackson@ws.edu
JACKSON, Sally .... 509-533-3123 .... 533 C sally.jackson@spokanefalls.edu
JACKSON, Shanna .... 615-790-4419 .... 475 A sjackson@columbiatate.edu
JACKSON, Sharon .... 561-273-6500 .... 118 A smjackson@southuniversity.edu
JACKSON, Sharon, S .... 804-752-3747 .... 523 C sjackson@rmc.edu
JACKSON, Shawn .... 740-389-6786 .... 399 D jackson.368@osu.edu
JACKSON, Sherry .... 904-256-7212 .... 111 L sjackso@ju.edu
JACKSON, Shirley, A .... 518-276-6211 .... 347 D president@rpi.edu
JACKSON, Starlene .... 919-718-7216 .... 369 C sjackson@cccc.edu
JACKSON, Stephanie .... 803-699-5096 .... 19 A stephanie.jackson@phoenix.edu
JACKSON, Susan .... 406-586-3585 .... 294 G susan.jackson@montanabiblecollege.edu
JACKSON, Suzanne .... 828-328-7080 .... 366 E suzanne.jackson@lr.edu
JACKSON, Tammy .... 651-687-9000 .... 270 I tammy.jackson@rasmussen.edu
JACKSON, Tanya .... 404-237-7573 .... 126 B tjackson@bauder.edu
JACKSON, JR., Thomas, H .... 706-542-8090 .... 138 G tjackson@uga.edu
JACKSON, Tim .... 713-348-4052 .... 493 C timothy.j.jackson@rice.edu
JACKSON, Tom .... 918-456-5511 .... 409 A jacks009@nsuok.edu
JACKSON, Tom .... 910-521-6883 .... 379 C tom.jackson@uncp.edu
JACKSON, JR., Tom .... 502-852-6933 .... 207 E trjack02@louisville.edu
JACKSON, Tondaleya .... 803-705-4479 .... 455 D jacksont@benedict.edu
JACKSON, Twana .... 304-929-6716 .... 543 A tjackson@newriver.edu
JACKSON, Tye .... 270-247-8521 .... 204 G tjackson@midcontinent.edu
JACKSON, Tyrone .... 228-896-2507 .... 275 E tyrone.jackson@mgccc.edu
JACKSON, Vera .... 601-979-2326 .... 274 G vera.j.jackson@jsums.edu
JACKSON, Vickie, G .... 405-466-3484 .... 408 G vgjackson@langston.edu
JACKSON, Vincent .... 213-763-7035 .... 55 D vjackson@lattc.edu
JACKSON, Wayne .... 407-823-2716 .... 120 B wayne.jackson@ucf.edu
JACKSON, Weldon .... 301-860-3462 .... 228 A wjackson@bowiestate.edu
JACKSON, Wendy .... 704-216-6158 .... 366 G wjackson@livingstone.edu
JACKSON, William .... 301-891-4133 .... 229 B news@wau.edu
JACKSON, Willie, J .... 334-727-8514 .... 8 B jacksonw@tuskegee.edu
JACKSON, Wilma .... 402-826-8620 .... 297 G wilma.jackson@doane.edu
JACKSON, Zena .... 972-273-3482 .... 485 C zjackson@dcccd.edu
JACKSON-ELMOORE, Cynthia .... 517-355-2326 .... 255 A jacks174@msu.edu
JACKSON-HAMMOND, Cynthia .... 937-376-6332 .... 387 A chammond@centralstate.edu
JACKSON HOLLOWAY, Melissa .... 919-530-6105 .... 378 B jacksonm@nccu.edu
JACKSON-LEE, Sophia .... 318-670-9355 .... 215 A slee@susla.edu
JACKSON THOMPSON, Karlene .... 718-488-1216 .... 338 G karlene.thompson@liu.edu
JACOB, Alan, B .... 509-777-3250 .... 540 C ajacob@whitworth.edu
JACOB, Antony .... 302-292-6100 .... 99 G antony.jacob@strayer.edu
JACOB, Craig .... 602-870-9222 .... 13 K cjacob@devry.edu
JACOB, Mary .... 805-893-3753 .... 75 B mary.jacob@sa.ucsb.edu
JACOB, Mary, J .... 805-893-3753 .... 75 B jacob-m@sa.ucsb.edu
JACOB, Travis .... 208-376-7731 .... 142 H tjacob@boisebible.edu
JACOBI, Judy, N .... 219-785-5593 .... 179 A jjacobi@pnc.edu
JACOBOWITZ, Chanie .... 732-367-1060 .... 307 G cjacobowitz@bmg.edu
JACOBOWITZ, Sharon .... 516-239-9002 .... 350 H
JACOBS, Alexandra, M .... 315-267-2918 .... 354 C jacobsam@potsdam.edu
JACOBS, Alice, M .... 217-443-8848 .... 148 G amjacobs@dacc.edu
JACOBS, Andrew, C .... 207-834-7671 .... 220 D andrew.jacobs@maine.edu
JACOBS, Bonita .... 706-864-1993 .... 134 G bjacobs@northgeorgia.edu
JACOBS, Bret .... 504-865-3979 .... 213 F bljacobs@loyno.edu
JACOBS, Bruce .... 812-855-5650 .... 173 E jacobsb@indiana.edu
JACOBS, Carol .... 937-294-6155 .... 393 C cjacobs2@kaplan.edu
JACOBS, Carolyn .... 413-585-7950 .... 244 G cjacobs@smith.edu
JACOBS, Charles .... 313-845-9607 .... 252 B cjacobs@hfcc.edu
JACOBS, Craig, M .... 610-892-1509 .... 441 C cjacobs@pit.edu
JACOBS, Dawn Ellen .... 951-343-4275 .... 31 J djacobs@calbaptist.edu
JACOBS, Dennis .... 408-554-4533 .... 68 C dcjacobs@scu.edu
JACOBS, Derya .... 412-397-3851 .... 445 H jacobs@rmu.edu
JACOBS, Holly, A .... 330-941-2340 .... 406 F hajacobs@ysu.edu
JACOBS, James .... 586-445-7241 .... 254 C jacobsj@macomb.edu
JACOBS, Jane .... 973-761-9181 .... 315 B jane.jacobs@shu.edu
JACOBS, Jeanne .... 305-237-5006 .... 113 H jfjacobs@mdc.edu
JACOBS, Jeff .... 701-224-5441 .... 382 D jeffrey.jacobs@bismarckstate.edu
JACOBS, Jim .... 415-476-0311 .... 75 A jim.jacobs@ucsf.edu
JACOBS, Jim .... 407-847-8966 .... 107 I jim.jacobs@fcc.edu
JACOBS, JR., John, O .... 334-844-9891 .... 1 F jacobjo@auburn.edu
JACOBS, Joshua, E .... 270-809-3763 .... 205 A jjacobs@murraystate.edu
JACOBS, Junoesque .... 601-977-7765 .... 277 C jjacobs@tougaloo.edu
JACOBS, Ken .... 785-628-4259 .... 192 I kjacobs@fhsu.edu
JACOBS, Kerri .... 617-824-8655 .... 234 B kerri_jacobs@emerson.edu
JACOBS, Kevin .... 303-315-2727 .... 88 J kevin.jacobs@ucdenver.edu
JACOBS, Kim .... 402-826-8111 .... 297 G kim.jacobs@doane.edu
JACOBS, Linda .... 517-265-5161 .... 246 H
JACOBS, Lloyd, A .... 419-530-2211 .... 404 F lloyd.jacobs@utoledo.edu
JACOBS, Lori, A .... 757-594-7961 .... 517 L lori.jacobs@cnu.edu
JACOBS, Mark .... 480-965-2354 .... 11 J mark.jacobs@asu.edu
JACOBS, Mary, R .... 513-875-3344 .... 387 C mary.jacobs@chatfield.edu
JACOBS, Pat .... 661-654-2483 .... 34 A pjacobs@csub.edu
JACOBS, Patricia .... 615-460-6490 .... 467 D patricia.jacobs@belmont.edu
JACOBS, Patti .... 617-327-6777 .... 241 F patti_jacobs@mspp.edu
JACOBS, Phillip .... 479-968-0320 .... 20 G pjacobs@atu.edu
JACOBS, Sarah .... 603-668-2211 .... 305 I s.jacobs@snhu.edu
JACOBS, Sheila .... 404-215-2675 .... 134 D sjacobs@morehouse.edu
JACOBS, Stan, G .... 432-685-6829 .... 491 A sjacobs@midland.edu
JACOBS, Steve .... 303-458-3560 .... 87 I jjacobs@regis.edu
JACOBS, Susan .... 978-921-4242 .... 242 C susan.jacobs@montserrat.edu
JACOBS, Tina .... 206-393-3545 .... 531 A tjacobs@argosy.edu
JACOBS, Todd .... 231-591-3817 .... 250 H jacobst@ferris.edu
JACOBS, Tracy .... 410-225-2378 .... 224 B tjacobs@mica.edu
JACOBS, Wayne .... 903-233-3860 .... 490 A waynejacobs@letu.edu
JACOBS ASTLE, Karen .... 215-503-1040 .... 448 C karen.astle@jefferson.edu
JACOBS ELSON, Claire .... 609-258-4131 .... 312 G celson@princeton.edu
JACOBSEN, Brandy .... 318-670-9371 .... 215 A bjacobsen@susla.edu
JACOBSEN, Cheryl, R .... 563-588-7107 .... 187 C cheryl.jacobsen@loras.edu
JACOBSEN, Jeffrey .... 406-994-3681 .... 295 C agdean@montana.edu
JACOBSEN, Jim .... 605-367-5461 .... 466 D jim.jacobsen@southeasttech.edu
JACOBSEN, Michael, V .... 801-863-8998 .... 511 F michael.jacobsen@uvu.edu
JACOBSEN, Paul, G .... 308-635-6144 .... 301 D jacobsen@wncc.edu
JACOBSEN, Richard, T .... 208-282-3134 .... 143 H jacorich@isu.edu
JACOBSEN, Stan .... 828-884-8381 .... 362 H jacobssf@brevard.edu
JACOBSMA, Kelly, G .... 616-395-7790 .... 252 D jacobsma@hope.edu
JACOBSMEYER, Adam, R .... 808-675-3368 .... 140 D adam.jacobsmeyer@byuh.edu
JACOBSMEYER, Tom, V .... 818-947-2336 .... 55 E jacobsmt@lavc.edu
JACOBSON, Adela .... 619-388-7356 .... 65 H ajacobson@sdccd.edu
JACOBSON, Adele .... 605-352-2662 .... 464 C adjacobs@dwu.edu
JACOBSON, Anne, D .... 804-828-1223 .... 526 B adjacobson@vcu.edu
JACOBSON, Beatrice, F .... 563-333-6100 .... 188 F jacobsonbeatricef@sau.edu
JACOBSON, Bert .... 815-802-8242 .... 155 A bjacobson@kcc.edu
JACOBSON, Betsy .... 218-733-7618 .... 266 H b.jacobson@lsc.edu
JACOBSON, Carl .... 302-831-6070 .... 96 I carlj@udel.edu
JACOBSON, Cynthia .... 620-365-5116 .... 190 D jacobson@allencc.edu
JACOBSON, Gabriel .... 585-567-9220 .... 336 B gabriel.jacobson@hougton.edu
JACOBSON, Gloria .... 773-298-3706 .... 163 I jacobson@sxu.edu
JACOBSON, Janet, L .... 712-274-5244 .... 187 G jacobson@morningside.edu
JACOBSON, John, E .... 765-285-5251 .... 169 G jejacobson@bsu.edu
JACOBSON, Kathy .... 231-777-5207 .... 248 E kathy.jacobson@baker.edu
JACOBSON, Larry, P .... 585-385-8256 .... 348 F ljacobson@sjfc.edu
JACOBSON, Mary .... 763-433-1315 .... 265 G mary.jacobson@anokaramsey.edu
JACOBSON, Renee, R .... 231-995-1256 .... 256 D jacobsr@nmc.edu
JACOBSON, Ron .... 718-817-1000 .... 334 C rjacobson@fordham.edu
JACOBSON, Shane, M .... 802-656-0518 .... 514 H shane.jacobson@uvm.edu
JACOBSON, Stacy .... 651-690-6526 .... 270 L ssjacobson@stkate.edu
JACOBSON, Steven .... 209-946-2331 .... 76 A sjacobson@pacific.edu
JACOBSON, Thomas .... 215-204-8421 .... 447 H jacobson.thomas@temple.edu
JACOBSON, Tim .... 952-995-1471 .... 266 D tim.jacobson@hennepintech.edu
JACOBSON, Timothy, K .... 262-691-5221 .... 555 E tjacobson9@wctc.edu
JACOBSON, Trisha .... 713-221-8141 .... 503 F jacobsonp@uhd.edu
JACOBSON, Vicky .... 203-576-5869 .... 94 C vjacobson@stvincentscollege.edu
JACOBSON-BERG, Judy .... 320-308-5096 .... 269 B jjacobsonberg@sctcc.edu
JACOBY, Brian .... 612-375-1900 .... 264 D bjacoby@ipr.edu
JACOBY, Robin, M .... 214-648-2288 .... 507 E robin.jacoby@utsouthwestern.edu
JACQUES, Ed .... 617-879-2446 .... 246 C ejacques@wheelock.edu
JACQUES, Kathleen, C .... 207-795-2858 .... 217 F jacqueka@cmhc.org
JACQUES, Lori .... 508-999-8025 .... 237 A ljacques@umassd.edu
JACQUES, Paul .... 323-856-7643 .... 28 E pjacques@afi.com
JACQUES, Theresa, K .... 906-487-2936 .... 255 B tjacques@mtu.edu
JACQUET, Roberta .... 610-902-8260 .... 424 B jacquet@cabrini.edu
JACQUEZ, Ricardo .... 575-646-2914 .... 319 D rjacquez@nmsu.edu
JADALLAH, Edward .... 843-349-2773 .... 456 G ejadalla@coastal.edu
JADHAV, Esther .... 859-858-3511 .... 198 E esther.jadhav@asbury.edu
JADLOS, Melissa .... 585-385-8164 .... 348 F mjadlos@sjfc.edu
JADUSHLEVER, Renee .... 510-430-2033 .... 57 D reneejad@mills.edu
JAECKEL, Andrea .... 734-487-3328 .... 250 F ajaeckel@emich.edu
JAECKEL, Roger .... 707-654-1127 .... 33 C rjaeckel@csum.edu
JAECKS, Steve .... 423-697-3397 .... 474 D
JAECQUES, Chad .... 660-831-4172 .... 286 F jaecquesc@moval.edu
JAEGER, Alberta .... 973-300-2176 .... 315 F ajaeger@sussex.edu
JAEGER, David .... 239-590-2315 .... 119 B djaeger@fgcu.edu
JAEGER, Lauren .... 716-839-8372 .... 331 F ljaeger@daemen.edu
JAEGER, Lois, A .... 507-344-7365 .... 261 C ljaeger@blc.edu
JAEGER, Naftalie .... 515-239-9002 .... 350 H
JAEGER, Steven, C .... 507-344-7330 .... 261 C sjaeger@blc.edu
JAEGER, Timothy, J .... 949-214-3179 .... 43 C tim.jaeger@cui.edu
JAEHNE, Dennis .... 408-924-5360 .... 37 C dennis.jaehne@sjsu.edu
JAEHNIG, Adrea .... 207-942-6781 .... 217 B ajaehnig@bts.edu
JAFARI, Marzie, A .... 718-960-8666 .... 327 C marzie.jafar@lehman.cuny.edu
JAFERIAN, Warren .... 978-232-2272 .... 234 D wjaferia@endicott.edu
JAFFE, David, L .... 561-237-7099 .... 113 D djaffe@lynn.edu
JAFFE, Hyla .... 603-668-2211 .... 305 I h.jaffe@snhu.edu
JAFFE, John, G .... 434-381-6139 .... 524 K jgjaffe@sbc.edu
JAFFE, Leslie, R .... 413-585-2806 .... 244 G ljaffe@smith.edu
JAFFE, Steven .... 562-947-8755 .... 71 A stevenjaffe@scuhs.edu
JAFFEE, Victoria .... 949-214-3042 .... 43 C victori.jaffe@cui.edu
JAFFER, Nori .... 212-986-4343 .... 323 H naj@berkeleycollege.edu
JAFFRAY, Shelly .... 714-564-6500 .... 63 F jaffray_shelly@sac.edu
JAFFRY, John-Herbert .... 636-227-2100 .... 284 B john.jaffry@logan.edu
JAGENDORF, Susan .... 518-255-5558 .... 354 E jagends@cobleskill.edu
JAGER, Donna .... 612-343-4488 .... 270 A dmjager@northcentral.edu
JAGER, Mark .... 503-280-8525 .... 415 E mjager@cu-portland.edu
JAGERS, J. Lee .... 214-382-3902 .... 485 F ljagers@dts.edu
JAGGER, Kathleen .... 859-233-8121 .... 207 A kjagger@transy.edu
JAGGERS, Charles, R .... 765-285-8261 .... 169 G cjaggers@bsu.edu
JAGGERS, Dametraus .... 419-755-4101 .... 399 C jaggers.7@osu.edu
JAGGERS, Karen .... 928-428-8308 .... 14 B karen.jaggers@eac.edu
JAGODZINSKI, Paul .... 928-523-2701 .... 16 I paul.jagodzinski@nau.edu
JAHAN, Mina .... 408-855-5360 .... 78 F mina.jahan@wvm.edu
JAHANGIR, Rashed .... 312-939-0111 .... 150 D rashed@eastwest.edu
JAHN, Bradley .... 208-377-8080 .... 143 C bjahn@carrington.edu
JAHN, Eric, G .... 732-235-6948 .... 316 G jahneg@umdnj.edu
JAHNKE, Eileen .... 920-403-3251 .... 550 F eileen.jahnke@snc.edu
JAHNKE, Tamera, S .... 417-836-5249 .... 286 C tamerajahnke@missouristate.edu
JAHR, Paul, K .... 478-445-5169 .... 130 B paul.jahr@gcsu.edu
JAIME, Victor .... 760-355-6219 .... 51 A victor.jaime@imperial.edu
JAIN, Arun .... 713-743-1422 .... 503 D ajain@uh.edu
JAIN, Madhu .... 312-939-0111 .... 150 D madhu@eastwest.edu
JAIN, Ravi .... 209-946-3066 .... 76 A rjain@pacific.edu
JAIS, Michele .... 570-450-3186 .... 439 K m5j@psu.edu
JAKUB, William .... 740-283-6366 .... 391 A wjakub@franciscan.edu
JAKUBIAK, Laura .... 770-537-5720 .... 139 F laura.jakubiak@westgatech.edu
JAKUBOW, Sandra .... 561-297-3534 .... 119 A sjakubow@fau.edu
JAKUBOWICZ, OFM, Gregory .... 518-783-2332 .... 350 I gregj@siena.edu
JAKUBOWSKI, Gerald .... 707-654-1020 .... 33 C gjakubowski@csum.edu
JAKUBS, Deborah .... 919-660-5800 .... 364 C deborah.jakubs@duke.edu
JALALI, Reza .... 207-753-6653 .... 220 G reza@usm.maine.edu
JALLOH, Pavi .... 201-556-2840 .... 309 D pjalloh@devry.edu
JALOMO, Romero .... 408-298-2181 .... 67 D romero.jalomo@sjcc.edu
JALOVICK, Mark, A .... 715-798-3525 .... 444 B wwc@pbu.edu
JAMASB, Shirin .... 302-856-9033 .... 96 E sjamasb@dtcc.edu

JAMBHEKAR, Sunil .... 941-782-5692.... 433 C
sjambhekar@lecom.edu
JAMEISON, Linda, C .... 864-833-8379.... 460 E
ljameison@presby.edu
JAMERSON, James .... 606-546-2553.... 207 B
jjamerson@unionky.edu
JAMERSON, Jill .... 602-749-4537...... 13 K
jjamerson@devry.edu
JAMERSON, Paula .... 903-983-8187.... 489 I
pjamerson@kilgore.edu
JAMES, A, D .... 334-727-8213........ 8 B
jamesad@mytu.tuskegee.edu
JAMES, Alicia .... 248-414-6900.... 254 F
ajames@mji.edu
JAMES, Ann .... 513-569-1512.... 387 G
ann.james@cincinnatistate.edu
JAMES, Arthur .... 972-860-4417.... 485 C
ajames@dcccd.edu
JAMES, Barbara .... 423-236-2942.... 473 B
bjames@southern.edu
JAMES, Bobby .... 870-777-5722...... 25 F
bobby.james@uacch.edu
JAMES, Brian .... 706-245-7226.... 129 C
bjames@ec.edu
JAMES, Bruce .... 501-975-6066...... 23 B
bjames@philander.edu
JAMES, Buckley .... 386-506-4414.... 104 F
jamesb@daytonastate.edu
JAMES, Carley .... 904-819-6459.... 107 C
cjames@flagler.edu
JAMES, Carmichael .... 404-799-4500.... 126 H
cejames@brownmackie.edu
JAMES, Catherine .... 269-965-3931.... 253 B
jamesc@kellogg.edu
JAMES, Charles .... 859-246-6393.... 201 H
charles.james@kctcs.edu
JAMES, Conley .... 718-270-6137.... 328 C
conley@mec.cuny.edu
JAMES, David .... 617-573-8148.... 245 B
djames@suffolk.edu
JAMES, Donna .... 701-845-7276.... 382 C
donna.james@vcsu.edu
JAMES, Frank, R .... 501-370-5212...... 23 B
fjames@philander.edu
JAMES, Glenn .... 210-829-3940.... 504 B
gjames@uiwtx.edu
JAMES, Glenn, W .... 931-372-6144.... 474 B
gjames@tntech.edu
JAMES, Henry, D .... 704-687-8454.... 379 A
hjames1@uncc.edu
JAMES, Hollis .... 423-236-2002.... 473 B
hjames@southern.edu
JAMES, Jacqueline .... 404-270-5111.... 138 B
jjames@spelman.edu
JAMES, Janet, C .... 972-238-6974.... 485 D
jjames@dcccd.edu
JAMES, Jesse, L .... 563-589-3214.... 189 F
jjames@dbq.edu
JAMES, Jessica, L .... 912-583-3262.... 126 F
jljames@bpc.edu
JAMES, John .... 502-585-9911.... 206 D
jjames@spalding.edu
JAMES, John .... 864-596-2067.... 457 E
john.james@converse.edu
JAMES, Joy, L .... 804-706-5214.... 527 B
jjames@jtcc.edu
JAMES, Judith .... 540-868-4075.... 527 C
jjames@lfcc.edu
JAMES, Kathy .... 325-649-8409.... 488 C
kjames@hputx.edu
JAMES, Kelly .... 815-394-5045.... 163 A
kjames@rockford.edu
JAMES, Larry, C .... 937-775-3494.... 406 C
larry.james@wright.edu
JAMES, Larry, G .... 509-335-5581.... 539 D
jameslg@wsu.edu
JAMES, Larry, K .... 501-450-3111...... 25 H
larryj@uca.edu
JAMES, Latisha .... 216-368-3909.... 386 F
latisha.james@case.edu
JAMES, Leroy, K .... 202-806-1073...... 98 E
l_k_james@howard.edu
JAMES, Linda .... 503-493-6456.... 415 E
lijames@cu-portland.edu
JAMES, Lori .... 860-832-2525...... 90 G
jamesloa@ccsu.edu
JAMES, Margaret .... 814-871-7238.... 429 G
james015@gannon.edu
JAMES, Mark, S .... 816-604-1011.... 284 H
mark.james@mcckc.edu
JAMES, Mary, C .... 724-946-7363.... 451 C
mjames@westminster.edu
JAMES, Melinda, L .... 630-466-7900.... 168 B
mjames@waubonsee.edu
JAMES, Michael .... 850-599-3560.... 118 L
michael.james@famu.edu
JAMES, Michael .... 360-676-2772.... 535 K
mjames@nwic.edu
JAMES, Michael, F .... 402-449-2817.... 297 H
mjames8054@graceu.edu
JAMES, Pansy .... 212-594-4000.... 357 H
pjames@tcicollege.edu
JAMES, Patricia .... 425-564-3152.... 531 G
patricia.james@bellevuecollege.edu
JAMES, Patricia .... 951-639-5440...... 58 B
pjames@msjc.edu
JAMES, Patrick .... 312-629-6600.... 164 C
pjames@saic.edu
JAMES, Patrick .... 601-974-1220.... 275 B
jamespg@millsaps.edu
JAMES, Penny .... 402-354-7225.... 299 C
penny.james@methodistcollege.edu
JAMES, Reginald .... 334-271-1670........ 6 D
rjames@princeinstitute.edu
JAMES, Richard, L .... 801-585-5690.... 511 C
rljames@usa.utah.edu
JAMES, Scott .... 978-542-6243.... 238 E
jscott@salemstate.edu
JAMES, Sean .... 661-395-4221...... 52 L
sjames@bakersfieldcollege.edu
JAMES, Sean, P .... 661-336-5165...... 52 K
sjames@kccd.edu
JAMES, Steven .... 865-981-8802.... 471 B
steven.james@maryvillecollege.edu
JAMES, Sujaya .... 404-527-4688.... 126 I
sjames@carver.edu
JAMES, Sujaya .... 404-527-4520.... 126 I
sjames@carver.edu
JAMES, Tessa .... 800-567-2344.... 547 A
tjames@menominee.edu
JAMES, Thomas .... 212-678-3050.... 357 G
james@tc.edu
JAMES, Timmy .... 256-331-6281........ 6 B
timmy.james@nwscc.edu
JAMES, Tracy .... 636-481-3187.... 283 D
tjames@jeffco.edu
JAMES, William, S .... 910-277-5062.... 376 C
jamesws@sapc.edu
JAMES-MOORE, Annette ... 901-272-5153.... 471 D
amoore@mca.edu
JAMES PRYOR, Jennifer ... 914-323-5299.... 339 J
jj.pryor@mville.edu
JAMES-WHIDBEE, Donna .. 252-335-3785.... 377 F
dmjameswidbee@mail.ecsu.edu
JAMESON, Deborah .... 800-818-2261.... 304 I
djameson@dwc.edu
JAMESON, Dennis .... 916-577-2200...... 79 G
djameson@jessup.edu
JAMESON, J, L .... 215-898-6796.... 448 J
ljameson@mail.med.upenn.edu
JAMESON, Maisha .... 510-464-3236...... 62 D
mjameson@peralta.edu
JAMESON, Sean .... 914-395-2494.... 350 C
sjameson@sarahlawrence.edu
JAMIESON, Leah, H .... 765-494-5346.... 178 J
lhj@purdue.edu
JAMIESON, Michelle, E ..... 724-287-8711.... 423 G
michelle.jamieson@bc3.edu
JAMIESON, Richard, J .... 216-368-3720.... 386 F
rjj@case.edu
JAMIESON-DRAKE, David . 919-684-3501.... 364 C
david.jamieson.drake@duke.edu
JAMIL, Hasan .... 713-313-1953.... 500 B
jamil_hx@tsu.edu
JAMISON, Calvin, D .... 972-883-2213.... 506 A
cjamison@utdallas.edu
JAMISON, Charles .... 610-409-3607.... 450 D
cjamison@ursinus.edu
JAMISON, David, L .... 412-397-6225.... 445 H
jamison@rmu.edu
JAMISON, J. Wesley .... 724-836-9940.... 449 C
jamison@pitt.edu
JAMISON, Kristin, E .... 217-245-3046.... 152 D
kristin.jamison@ic.edu
JAMISON, Matt .... 303-678-3845...... 85 A
matt.jamison@frontrange.edu
JAMISON, Steven, A .... 859-238-5455.... 199 G
steve.jamison@centre.edu
JAMISON, Todd, M .... 740-587-5712.... 389 I
jamisont@denison.edu
JAMMER, Veronica .... 281-476-1501.... 493 H
veronica.jammer@sjcd.edu
JAMROGOWICZ, John .... 843-574-6136.... 461 G
john.jamrogowicz@tridenttech.edu
JANAK, Bickram .... 443-885-3333.... 224 E
bickram.janak@morgan.edu
JANAK, Kenneth .... 817-257-5712.... 499 C
k.janak@tcu.edu
JANARO, Walter, A .... 540-636-2900.... 517 K
walter@christendom.edu
JANDA, Kenneth, C .... 949-824-6022...... 74 B
kcjanda@uci.edu
JANDOVITZ, Tom .... 301-846-2501.... 222 G
tjandovitz@frederick.edu
JANDRIS, Thomas .... 708-209-3597.... 148 E
thomas.jandris@cuchicago.edu
JANDT, Fred, E .... 909-473-8118...... 36 B
fjandt@csusb.edu
JANES, Brian .... 401-454-6651.... 454 B
bjanes@risd.edu
JANES, Sarah .... 281-998-6150.... 493 G
sarah.janes@sjcd.edu
JANESCH, Cynthia, D .... 570-577-3200.... 423 E
cindy.janesch@bucknell.edu
JANESKO, Lisa .... 724-437-4600.... 441 B
ljanesko@piht.edu
JANEY, Stephanie, C .... 617-541-5345.... 241 A
sjaney@rcc.mass.edu
JANG, Jeanie .... 562-903-4875...... 31 A
jeanie.jang@biola.edu
JANG, Michelle .... 714-533-1495...... 70 B
michelle@southbaylo.edu
JANIAK, Carola .... 909-793-4263...... 49 D
JANIK, Julie .... 972-721-4127.... 503 B
jjanik@udallas.edu
JANIS, Anita .... 707-465-2300...... 42 C
anita-janis@redwoods.edu
JANIS, Robert, J .... 312-362-8762.... 149 A
bjanis@depaul.edu
JANITZ, Suzanne .... 607-431-4244.... 335 A
janitzs@hartwick.edu
JANKE, Louise, L .... 608-785-8604.... 551 C
ljanke@uwlax.edu
JANKO, Karen .... 312-777-8666.... 153 B
kjanko@aii.edu
JANKOVIAK, Michael, W ... 989-386-6603.... 255 C
mjankoviak@midmich.edu
JANKOWSKI, Cheryl .... 440-934-3101.... 398 C
cjankowski@ohiobusinesscollege.edu
JANKOWSKI, Phillip, E ..... 219-785-5404.... 179 A
pjankowski@pnc.edu
JANKOWSKI, Stephen, E ... 618-650-2760.... 165 C
sjankow@siue.edu
JANKOWSKI-SMITH,
Shelli, M .... 617-373-2728.... 243 F
JANNE, Rex .... 979-845-4570.... 497 E
r-janne@tamu.edu
JANNEY, Dell Ann .... 573-288-6388.... 280 I
djanney@culver.edu
JANNEY, Suzanne, L .... 941-487-4110.... 120 A
janney@ncf.edu
JANNIK, Nancy .... 507-457-5010.... 269 G
njannik@winona.edu
JANNING, Michelle, Y .... 509-527-4952.... 540 B
janninmy@whitman.edu
JANOSIK, Daniel .... 704-847-5600.... 377 B
djanosik@ses.edu
JANOT, Melissa .... 617-349-8755.... 236 B
mjanot@lesley.edu
JANOVY, CJ .... 913-588-2598.... 197 C
cjanovy@kumc.edu
JANOWIAK, Diane, J .... 708-709-3603.... 161 D
djanowiak@prairiestate.edu
JANOWIAK, Steve .... 712-279-5494.... 183 A
steve.janowiak@briarcliff.edu
JANOWITZ, Deannie .... 213-381-2221...... 64 I
djanowitz@samra.edu
JANOWSKI, Barbara .... 575-874-4697...... 19 A
barbara.janowski@phoenix.edu
JANSEN, James .... 206-546-4651.... 538 C
jjansen@shoreline.edu
JANSEN, James, S .... 402-280-5589.... 297 F
jimjansen@creighton.edu
JANSEN, Mark .... 815-599-3455.... 152 B
mark.jansen@highland.edu
JANSEN, Sandy .... 865-974-6611.... 477 C
sjansen@utk.edu
JANSEN, Shelley .... 970-943-2616...... 89 E
sjansen@western.edu
JANSEN, Wendy .... 605-221-3100.... 464 D
wjansen@kilian.edu
JANSKY, Linda .... 603-897-8249.... 305 F
ljansky@rivier.edu
JANSMA, Pamela .... 817-272-3491.... 505 C
pjansma@uta.edu
JANSSEN, Jill, M .... 815-599-3412.... 152 B
jill.janssen@highland.edu
JANSSEN, Michelle .... 859-985-3007.... 199 A
janssenm@berea.edu
JANSSON, Jimilea .... 580-628-6771.... 409 B
jimilea.jansson@north-ok.edu
JANTO, Armund, M .... 414-277-7126.... 549 C
janto@msoe.edu
JANULIS, Jeffrey .... 773-481-8816.... 147 I
jjanulis@ccc.edu
JANUS, Eric, S .... 651-290-6310.... 272 E
eric.janus@wmitchell.edu
JANUSZESKI, Carol, A .... 512-448-8414.... 493 E
carolj@stedwards.edu
JANUTOLO, D. Blake .... 765-641-4541.... 169 E
dbjanutolo@anderson.edu
JANVIER, Kathy, A .... 302-454-3973...... 96 F
kathy.janvier@dtcc.edu
JANVIER, Patricia .... 317-578-7353.... 178 G
JANZ, Curtis .... 405-425-5358.... 409 E
curtis.janz@oc.edu
JANZ, Kenneth .... 507-457-2299.... 269 G
kjanz@winona.edu
JANZEN, Amy .... 405-425-5907.... 409 E
amy.janzen@oc.edu
JANZEN, Dennis .... 559-453-2000...... 48 A
djanzen@fresno.edu
JANZEN, Scott .... 574-296-6213.... 169 C
registrar@ambs.edu
JANZER, Todd .... 215-785-0111.... 440 I
JAQUES, Kate .... 916-484-8654...... 56 A
jaquesk@arc.losrios.edu
JARA, Mike .... 803-641-3254.... 462 B
mikej@usca.edu
JARACZEWSKI, John .... 262-595-2591.... 552 A
john.jaraczewski@uwp.edu
JARAMILLO, Fernan .... 507-222-4301.... 261 G
fjaramil@carleton.edu
JARAMILLO, Ray .... 806-665-8801.... 483 A
ray.jaramillo@clarendoncollege.edu
JARAMILLO FLEMING,
Melissa .... 575-835-5880.... 319 A
mjaramillo@admin.nmt.edu
JARBOE, Dan .... 870-245-5591...... 22 I
jarboed@obu.edu
JARDINE, Daniel .... 607-777-2365.... 351 F
djardine@binghamton.edu
JARED, Tim .... 864-622-6011.... 455 C
tjared@andersonuniversity.edu
JARETT, Sadie .... 334-874-5700........ 2 H
sjarret@ccal.edu
JARGO, Jeralyn .... 651-779-3235.... 266 A
jeralyn.jargo@century.edu
JARICH, Amy .... 510-642-3175...... 73 H
JARLEY, Paul .... 407-823-2181.... 120 B
pjarley@bus.ucf.edu
JARMAN, Chet .... 252-940-6241.... 368 C
chetj@beaufortccc.edu
JARMIN MILLER,
Catherine .... 503-883-2494.... 416 H
cjarmin@linfield.edu
JARMUZ, Nick .... 312-935-2005.... 162 G
njarmuz@robertmorris.edu
JARNAGIN, Lea .... 657-278-3211...... 35 B
ljarnagin@fullerton.edu
JARNAGIN, Missy .... 805-437-3282...... 34 B
missy.jarnagin@csuci.edu
JAROSZ, John .... 402-354-7065.... 299 C
john.jarosz@methodistcollege.edu
JAROSZ, Jonathan .... 810-424-5486.... 259 C
jarosz@umflint.edu
JAROT, Lisa .... 847-628-1572.... 154 K
ljarot@judsonu.edu
JARR, William .... 770-426-2632.... 133 E
wdjarr@life.edu
JARRELL, Bruce, E .... 410-706-2304.... 227 C
brucejarrell@som.umaryland.edu
JARRELL, Camille, L .... 337-373-0011.... 212 D
cjarrell@lct.edu
JARRELL, Michelle .... 205-391-2328........ 6 I
mjarrell@sheltonstate.edu
JARRELL, Sasha .... 850-729-5363.... 114 A
jarrells@nwfsc.edu
JARRELL, Sheila .... 928-776-2188...... 19 C
sheila.jarrell@yc.edu
JARRETT, Jessica .... 918-335-6334.... 411 B
founders@okwu.edu
JARRETT, Juan, A .... 413-545-0360.... 236 F
jjarrett@admin.umass.edu
JARRETT, Kathy .... 413-565-1000.... 230 G
kjarrett@baypath.edu
JARRETT, Robert .... 713-221-8191.... 503 F
jarrettr@uhd.edu
JARRETT, Tasha .... 773-602-5258.... 147 E
JARRETT-HORTIS,
Frances, L .... 864-503-5195.... 463 B
fjarrett-hortis@uscupstate.edu
JARRY, Timothy .... 508-793-2515.... 233 C
tjarry@holycross.edu
JARSTFER, Amiel .... 423-869-6203.... 470 E
amiel.jarstfer@lmunet.edu
JARVIE, Greg, I .... 330-672-9494.... 393 D
gjarvie@kent.edu
JARVIS, Jeffrey, A .... 419-227-3141.... 404 D
jjarvis@unoh.edu
JARVIS, Keith .... 307-532-8255.... 556 C
keith.jarvis@ewc.wy.edu
JARVIS, Sam .... 610-841-3333.... 441 D
sjarvis@psb.edu
JARVIS, Shelli, W .... 703-323-3074.... 527 F
sjarvis@nvcc.edu
JARZABSKI, Kerri, P .... 413-782-1312.... 246 A
kjarzabs@wne.edu
JASHINSKI, Michelle, L .... 814-371-2090.... 448 D
mjashinski@triangle-tech.edu
JASIENIECKI, Darren .... 219-473-4292.... 170 G
djasieniecki@ccsj.edu
JASIEWICZ, James .... 574-289-7001.... 176 E
jjasiewicz1@ivytech.edu
JASINSKI, John .... 660-562-1110.... 287 B
johnj@nwmissouri.edu
JASMAN, Troy .... 712-274-6400.... 190 B
troy.jasman@witcc.edu
JASON, Greer .... 718-817-3080.... 334 C
jason@fordham.edu
JASON, Hoerr, U .... 610-921-7221.... 421 E
jhoerr@alb.edu
JASS, Lori .... 651-635-8084.... 261 D
l-jass@bethel.edu
JASTORFF, Mark .... 303-556-8320...... 86 F
mjastorf@msudenver.edu
JASTORFF, Michael .... 605-642-6279.... 465 H
michael.jastorff@bhsu.edu
JASUR, Angela .... 631-420-2717.... 356 A
angela.jasur@farmingdale.edu
JASWAL, Faisal .... 425-564-6151.... 531 G
fjaswal@bellevuecollege.edu
JASZCZAK, John .... 215-637-7700.... 431 A
jaszczak@holyfamily.edu
JASZKA, Michael, S .... 716-286-8343.... 344 D
msj@niagara.edu

JATTKOWSKI-HUDSON, Anna, J ... 815-226-3392 ... 163 A ajattkowski-hudson@rockford.edu
JATULIS, Viltis, A ... 805-525-4417 ... 72 I vjatulis@thomasaquinas.edu
JAUNARAJS, Imants ... 740-593-2909 ... 399 G jaunaraj@ohio.edu
JAURIGUI, Leroy ... 952-446-4181 ... 263 C jauriguil@crown.edu
JAURON, Les ... 530-895-2266 ... 31 H jauronle@butte.edu
JAVAHERIPOUR, G, H ... 760-245-4271 ... 77 H gh.javaheripour@vvc.edu
JAVARIZ, Gerardo ... 787-890-2681 ... 566 H gerardo.javariz@upr.edu
JAVIER, Byron, A ... 312-850-7140 ... 147 F bjavier@ccc.edu
JAVIER, Maria Dolorez ... 831-755-6752 ... 49 E mjavier@hartnell.edu
JAVOR, Seta ... 818-767-0888 ... 79 H seta.javor@woodbury.edu
JAVOREK, Mary, E ... 216-397-4943 ... 392 L javorek@jcu.edu
JAVOROSKI, Alan ... 715-422-5402 ... 554 E al.javoroski@mstc.edu
JAWORSKI, Bernie ... 909-607-3647 ... 40 F bernie.jaworski@cgu.edu
JAX, John ... 608-785-8805 ... 551 C jjax@uwlax.edu
JAY, Andrea ... 305-348-7347 ... 119 C andrea.jay@fiu.edu
JAYARAMAN, Ruki ... 312-505-0705 ... 29 F rjayaraman@argosy.edu
JAYASURIYA, Kumara ... 219-785-5201 ... 179 A kjayasur@pnc.edu
JAYAWICKREMA, Arosha .. 860-768-4276 ... 95 B jaya@hartford.edu
JAYE, Marilyn ... 617-559-8642 ... 235 E mjaye@hebrewcollege.edu
JAYNE, Billie Jo ... 315-279-5684 ... 337 K bjjayne@keuka.edu
JAYNE, Joanne ... 718-429-6600 ... 359 G joanne.jayne@vaughn.edu
JAYNE, Lorrie ... 828-298-3325 ... 380 D ljayne@warren-wilson.edu
JAYNES, D. Thomas ... 919-536-7207 ... 370 C jaynest@durhamtech.edu
JAYNES, Kathy ... 406-265-4147 ... 295 E kjaynes@msun.edu
JAYNES, Lorene ... 406-771-4305 ... 295 G ljaynes@msugf.edu
JAZDZEWSKI, Richard, L .. 262-472-1305 ... 553 A jazdzewr@uww.edu
JAZWIECKI, Gabrielle, E ... 203-837-8281 ... 91 A jazwieckig@wcsu.edu
JAZZABI, Monica ... 323-343-3342 ... 35 D mjazzabi@cslanet.calstatela.edu
JEAN, Kevin, J ... 919-658-7750 ... 367 F kjean@moc.edu
JEAN, Libby ... 269-749-7655 ... 257 A ljean@olivetcollege.edu
JEAN, Martin, D ... 203-432-9681 ... 96 A martin.jean@yale.edu
JEAN-LOUIS, Linda ... 516-877-3321 ... 322 A registrar@adelphi.edu
JEAN-LOUIS, Patrick ... 617-541-5388 ... 241 A pjeanlouis@rcc.mass.edu
JEAN-MARIE, Cherisna ... 615-687-6904 ... 466 H abclibrary2011@gmail.com
JEAN-PIERRE, Paul ... 718-631-6314 ... 328 F pjean-pierre@qcc.cuny.edu
JEANCAKE, Chris ... 912-427-1958 ... 124 C cjeancake@altamahatech.edu
JEANES, Opey ... 919-734-8585 ... 367 F ojeanes@moc.edu
JEANES, Opey, D ... 919-734-8585 ... 367 F ojeanes@moc.edu
JEANPIERRE, Letha ... 408-864-8976 ... 47 G jeanpierreletha@deanza.edu
JEANRENAUD, Stephane ... 704-366-5066 ... 376 B sjeanrenaud@rts.edu
JEBALI, Lisa ... 978-837-5109 ... 242 A lisa.jebali@merrimack.edu
JEBSEN, Chris ... 419-358-3254 ... 385 D jebsenc@bluffton.edu
JECH, Sue ... 507-433-0610 ... 268 H sue.jech@riverland.edu
JEELANI, Shaik ... 334-727-8970 ... 8 B jeelanis@mytu.tuskegee.edu
JEFFCOAT, Harold, G ... 217-424-6208 ... 158 G hjeffcoat@millikin.edu
JEFFERS, Brenda, R ... 217-544-6464 ... 163 H
JEFFERS, Karen ... 918-595-7441 ... 412 H kjeffers@tulsacc.edu
JEFFERSON, Adriene ... 772-462-7606 ... 111 B ajeffers@irsc.edu
JEFFERSON, Arthur ... 601-979-2484 ... 274 G arthur.jefferson@jsums.edu
JEFFERSON, Barbie, F ... 864-597-4237 ... 463 G jeffersonbf@wofford.edu
JEFFERSON, Curtis ... 352-395-5175 ... 117 F curtis.jefferson@sfcollege.edu
JEFFERSON, Debrah ... 773-995-3586 ... 146 G djeffers@csu.edu
JEFFERSON, Doug ... 817-598-6247 ... 508 F djefferson@wc.edu
JEFFERSON, Henry ... 606-759-7141 ... 203 A henry.jefferson@kctcs.edu
JEFFERSON, Jeff ... 870-574-4499 ... 24 A jjeffers@sautech.edu
JEFFERSON, Jennifer ... 603-641-4156 ... 306 D jennifer.jefferson@unh.edu
JEFFERSON, Joy ... 757-727-4012 ... 519 H joy.jefferson@hamptonu.edu
JEFFERSON, Karyl ... 360-676-2772 ... 535 K kjefferson@nwic.edu
JEFFERSON, Michael ... 707-965-7080 ... 60 I mjeffereson@puc.edu
JEFFERSON, Patrick ... 323-241-5280 ... 55 C jefferpd@lasc.edu
JEFFERSON, Richard, P ... 617-552-3334 ... 232 B richard.jefferson@bc.edu
JEFFERSON, Sharon ... 850-201-8490 ... 122 A jefferss@tcc.fl.edu
JEFFERSON, Sheri ... 704-216-6010 ... 366 G sjefferson@livingstone.edu
JEFFERSON, Shirley ... 802-831-1333 ... 515 B sjefferson@vermontlaw.edu
JEFFERSON, Vivian ... 409-880-8188 ... 500 I vgjefferson@lit.edu
JEFFERSON, Willie ... 803-780-1049 ... 463 C williej@voorhees.edu
JEFFERY, Charles, F ... 623-845-4001 ... 15 H charles.jeffery@gcmail.maricopa.edu
JEFFERY, Jack ... 740-774-7200 ... 400 A jefferyj@ohio.edu
JEFFERY, James, E ... 570-586-2400 ... 422 G jjeffery@bbc.edu
JEFFERY, James, R ... 269-471-3481 ... 247 D jimjeff@andrews.edu
JEFFERY, John, A ... 610-660-1060 ... 446 C jjeffery@sju.edu
JEFFERY, Kathryn ... 916-558-2100 ... 56 D jefferk@scc.losrios.edu
JEFFERY, Penny ... 936-468-4008 ... 496 B
JEFFES, Annette, S ... 413-662-5416 ... 238 C annette.jeffes@mcla.edu
JEFFORD, Janet, L ... 860-727-6904 ... 92 I jjefford@goodwin.edu
JEFFRESS, Conway, A ... 734-462-4400 ... 258 A jeffress@schoolcraft.edu
JEFFREY, David ... 763-576-4725 ... 265 H djeffrey@anokatech.edu
JEFFREY, David, K ... 540-568-7044 ... 520 H jeffredk@jmu.edu
JEFFREY, Don ... 334-983-6556 ... 8 A djeffr@troy.edu
JEFFREY, Don ... 334-670-3365 ... 8 A djeffr@troy.edu
JEFFREY, Dorothy ... 816-322-0110 ... 279 D dorothy.filsinger@calvary.edu
JEFFREY, Douglas ... 517-607-2518 ... 252 C doug.jeffrey@hillsdale.edu
JEFFREY, Douglas ... 517-437-7341 ... 252 C doug.jeffrey@hillsdale.edu
JEFFREY, Russell ... 512-313-3000 ... 483 K russell.jeffrey@concordia.edu
JEFFRIES, Frankie ... 901-435-1530 ... 470 D frankie_jeffries@loc.edu
JEFFRIES, John ... 410-455-2386 ... 227 D jeffries@umbc.edu
JEFFRIES, Mammie ... 904-470-8055 ... 105 G m.jeffries@ewc.edu
JEFFRIES, Rosemary ... 732-987-2252 ... 310 C jeffries@georgian.edu
JEFFRIES, Shellie ... 616-632-2130 ... 247 E jeffrmic@aquinas.edu
JEFFRIES, Susan, K ... 580-327-8570 ... 409 C skjeffries@nwosu.edu
JEFFRION, William ... 504-520-6780 ... 217 A wjeffrio@xula.edu
JEFFS, Madeline ... 509-542-4765 ... 532 H mjeffs@columbiabasin.edu
JEFIMENKO, Otto ... 219-981-4291 ... 174 B ojefimen@iun.edu
JEFREMOW, George ... 212-217-4420 ... 333 F george_jefremow@fitnyc.edu
JEHNINGS, Marcia ... 860-512-2703 ... 91 F mjehnings@mcc.commnet.edu
JEKA, Mary, R ... 617-627-4220 ... 245 C mary.jeka@tufts.edu
JELENIC, Susan ... 216-265-3151 ... 386 D smjelenic@bryantstratton.edu
JELINAK, Micah ... 734-207-9581 ... 255 F mjelinak@mts.edu
JELINEK, John, A ... 312-329-4185 ... 159 A john.jelinek@moody.edu
JELLEMA, Jon, A ... 616-331-2400 ... 251 F jellemaj@gvsu.edu
JELLERSON, George ... 804-862-6212 ... 523 F gjellerson@rbc.edu
JELLISON, Rebecca ... 269-782-1241 ... 258 C rjellison@swmich.edu
JELLY, Katherine ... 518-587-2100 ... 355 G katherine.jelly@esc.edu
JEMIOLA, Richard ... 757-352-4028 ... 523 E richjem@regent.edu
JEMISON, Henry ... 501-370-5365 ... 23 B hjemison@philander.edu
JEMISON, Jan ... 415-565-4723 ... 74 A jemisonj@uchastings.edu
JEN, Ezbon ... 707-524-1591 ... 68 E ejen@santarosa.edu
JENAL, Robert, E ... 508-856-3892 ... 237 C robert.jenal@umassmed.edu
JENCKS, Doyle ... 580-477-7736 ... 414 C doyle.jencks@wosc.edu
JENDA, Overtoun ... 334-844-4184 ... 1 F jendaov@auburn.edu
JENE, Beverly ... 802-322-1650 ... 513 E beverly.jene@goddard.edu
JENERETTE, Kim ... 937-766-3640 ... 386 G kimjenerette@cedarville.edu
JENETTE, Brian ... 213-381-3333 ... 53 C bjenette@lac.edu
JENIK, Jeff ... 803-641-3455 ... 462 B jeffj@usca.edu
JENIOUS, Anita ... 615-322-4075 ... 478 A anita.jenious@vanderbilt.edu
JENKINS, Allen ... 718-933-6700 ... 341 G ajenkins@monroecollege.edu
JENKINS, Anne ... 252-737-1133 ... 377 E jenkinsa@ecu.edu
JENKINS, Anthony, L ... 410-651-2200 ... 227 E aljenkins@umes.edu
JENKINS, Ashley ... 617-739-1700 ... 243 A ajenkins@aii.edu
JENKINS, Betty, A ... 803-705-4808 ... 455 D jenkinsb@benedict.edu
JENKINS, Bobby ... 580-349-1376 ... 410 B bjenkins@opsu.edu
JENKINS, Bonita ... 706-771-4019 ... 125 H bjenkins@augustatech.edu
JENKINS, Brandon ... 919-735-5151 ... 375 A bmjenkins@waynecc.edu
JENKINS, Brian ... 657-278-2423 ... 35 B bjenkins@fullerton.edu
JENKINS, Briar ... 580-477-7700 ... 414 C briar.jenkins@wosc.edu
JENKINS, Bryan ... 919-807-7100 ... 367 I jenkinsb@nccommunitycolleges.edu
JENKINS, Carolyn ... 404-237-7573 ... 126 B cjenkins@bauder.edu
JENKINS, Carri, P ... 801-422-1166 ... 509 H carri_jenkins@byu.edu
JENKINS, Cheryl, S ... 919-760-8338 ... 367 A jenkinsc@meredith.edu
JENKINS, Darlene ... 575-562-2321 ... 318 B darlene.jenkins@enmu.edu
JENKINS, Debbie ... 503-594-3002 ... 415 A debbiej@clackamas.edu
JENKINS, Deborah, D ... 410-334-2904 ... 229 E djenkins@worwic.edu
JENKINS, Debra ... 262-524-7120 ... 546 H djenkins@carrollu.edu
JENKINS, Edward ... 205-781-7471 ... 5 H
JENKINS, G. Scott ... 336-334-7006 ... 378 A gsjenkin@ncat.edu
JENKINS, Gerald ... 440-525-7248 ... 394 F gjenkins@lakelandcc.edu
JENKINS, H.E ... 512-313-3000 ... 483 K he.jenkins@concordia.edu
JENKINS, Helen ... 713-646-1887 ... 494 I hjenkins@stcl.edu
JENKINS, J. Marshall ... 706-236-2259 ... 126 C mjenkins@berry.edu
JENKINS, Jacqueline, D ... 302-454-3916 ... 96 F jjenkins@dtcc.edu
JENKINS, Jan ... 479-968-0456 ... 20 G ejenkins@atu.edu
JENKINS, Jane, E ... 614-235-4136 ... 402 G jjenkins@tlsohio.edu
JENKINS, Jeffrey, L ... 812-877-8209 ... 179 B jenkins@rose-hulman.edu
JENKINS, Jessika ... 281-873-0262 ... 483 I j.jenkins@commonwealth.edu
JENKINS, Jim ... 909-594-5611 ... 58 A jjenkins@mtsac.edu
JENKINS, SR., Jimmy, R .. 704-216-6098 ... 366 G jjenkins@livingstone.edu
JENKINS, John ... 404-527-4520 ... 126 I jjenkins@carver.edu
JENKINS, John, B ... 312-280-3500 ... 153 B jbjenkins@aii.edu
JENKINS, CSC, John, I ... 574-631-3903 ... 180 G jenkins.1@nd.edu
JENKINS, Katrina, E ... 217-245-3060 ... 152 D katrina.jenkins@ic.edu
JENKINS, Kevin ... 870-307-7220 ... 22 D kevin.jenkins@lyon.edu
JENKINS, Lidia ... 415-241-2286 ... 40 C ljenkins@ccsf.edu
JENKINS, Malia ... 619-201-8728 ... 65 D malia.jenkins@sdcc.edu
JENKINS, Mark ... 713-348-4966 ... 493 C jenky@rice.edu
JENKINS, Matt ... 304-263-0979 ... 542 C
JENKINS, Max, A ... 405-878-5141 ... 412 A majenkins@stgregorys.edu
JENKINS, Mike ... 903-983-8189 ... 489 I mjenkins@kilgore.edu
JENKINS, Murner ... 318-670-9351 ... 215 A mjenkins@ssla.edu
JENKINS, Paul ... 513-244-4351 ... 388 E paul_jenkins@mail.msj.edu
JENKINS, Richard, J ... 701-858-3299 ... 382 A dick.jenkins@minotstateu.edu
JENKINS, Robert ... 713-500-3334 ... 506 F robert.jenkins@uth.tmc.edu
JENKINS, Rod ... 972-708-7321 ... 487 B rod_jenkins@gial.edu
JENKINS, Roger, L ... 513-529-1799 ... 396 E roger.jenkins@muohio.edu
JENKINS, Ronald ... 973-972-3469 ... 316 F jenkinjw@umdnj.edu
JENKINS, Ronnie, D ... 620-229-6356 ... 196 G ronnie.jenkins@sckans.edu
JENKINS, Scott ... 810-762-0502 ... 255 G scott.jenkins@mcc.edu
JENKINS, Shantelle, K ... 610-957-5700 ... 426 G sjenkins@dccc.edu
JENKINS, Sharon ... 575-439-3806 ... 319 E djenkins@nmsua.nmsu.edu
JENKINS, Sonja ... 478-988-6800 ... 134 C sjenkins@middlegatech.edu
JENKINS, Stephen ... 541-962-3553 ... 418 C stephen.jenkins@eou.edu
JENKINS, Sterling ... 719-296-6106 ... 87 F sterling.jenkins@pueblocc.edu
JENKINS, Steve ... 619-201-8720 ... 65 D steve.jenkins@sdcc.edu
JENKINS, Steven ... 740-392-6868 ... 396 I steven.jenkins@mvnu.edu
JENKINS, Sylvia ... 708-974-5201 ... 159 B jenkins@morainevalley.edu
JENKINS, Tara, F ... 508-854-4249 ... 240 F tarafj@qcc.mass.edu
JENKINS, Terry ... 217-641-4960 ... 154 I tjenkins@jwcc.edu
JENKINS, Timothy, S ... 219-464-5411 ... 181 C tim.jenkins@valpo.edu
JENKINS, Vanessa, C ... 757-823-8173 ... 522 E vcjenkins@nsu.edu
JENKINS, William, L ... 225-578-2111 ... 212 G wljenk@lsu.edu
JENKINS, William, L ... 225-578-6977 ... 212 H wljenk@lsu.edu
JENKINS-CARTER, D'Lonika ... 510-567-6174 ... 72 D djenkins@sum.edu
JENKINS-MONROE, Valata ... 415-955-2112 ... 27 F vmonroe@alliant.edu
JENKINS-SCOTT, Jackie ... 617-879-2161 ... 246 C jjenkins-scott@wheelock.edu
JENKS, Debra ... 414-277-4516 ... 549 C jenks@msoe.edu
JENKS, Paul ... 402-486-2536 ... 300 C pajenks@ucollege.edu
JENLINK, Christee ... 918-449-6000 ... 409 A jenlink@nsuok.edu
JENNEMAN, Eugene, A ... 231-995-1572 ... 256 D ejenneman@nmc.edu
JENNERJOHN, Julie ... 906-487-7352 ... 251 A julie.jennerjohn@finlandia.edu
JENNESS, Valerie ... 949-824-6094 ... 74 B jenness@uci.edu
JENNETT, Charles ... 804-828-0190 ... 526 B cjennett@vcu.edu
JENNETTE, Judy ... 252-940-6326 ... 368 C judyj@beaufortccc.edu
JENNINGS, Arbolina, L ... 713-313-7661 ... 500 B jennings_al@tsu.edu
JENNINGS, Barbara ... 641-844-5522 ... 186 B barb.jennings@iavalley.edu
JENNINGS, Bret ... 256-765-4658 ... 9 C nmjennings@una.edu
JENNINGS, Charla ... 870-743-3000 ... 22 G charlam@northark.edu
JENNINGS, Charles ... 209-954-5040 ... 66 D cjennings@deltacollege.edu
JENNINGS, Chris ... 213-624-1200 ... 46 L cjennings@fidm.edu
JENNINGS, Christal ... 610-225-5102 ... 428 E cjenning@eastern.edu
JENNINGS, David, C ... 845-675-4616 ... 344 G david.jennings@nyack.edu
JENNINGS, Denise ... 510-981-5014 ... 62 B djennings@peralta.edu
JENNINGS, Donna ... 630-353-9069 ... 149 B djennings@devry.edu
JENNINGS, George-Harold 973-408-3392 ... 309 E gjenning@drew.edu
JENNINGS, John, L ... 903-813-2410 ... 481 A jjennings@austincollege.edu
JENNINGS, Lindsay ... 817-923-8459 ... 483 G lindsay.jennings@fishermore.edu
JENNINGS, Patricia, L ... 302-295-1163 ... 97 C pattie.l.jennings@wilmu.edu
JENNINGS, Rita, O ... 252-335-0821 ... 369 G rjennings@albemarle.edu
JENNINGS, Robert, R ... 484-365-7400 ... 434 H rjennings@lincoln.edu
JENNINGS, Ross ... 253-833-9111 ... 534 H rjennings@greenriver.edu

JOHNS, Xenia ... 770-228-7348 ... 137 F xjohns@sctech.edu
JOHNS-LAUDERDALE, Wendy ... 985-549-5544 ... 216 C wjohns@selu.edu
JOHNSEN, David, C ... 319-335-7144 ... 182 F david-johnsen@uiowa.edu
JOHNSEN, John, H ... 315-792-3120 ... 359 E jjohnsen@utica.edu
JOHNSON, Abe ... 972-548-6677 ... 483 H ajohnson@collin.edu
JOHNSON, Alan, D ... 812-482-3030 ... 181 D ajohnson@vinu.edu
JOHNSON, JR., Albert, D . 580-581-2999 ... 407 D ajohnson@cameron.edu
JOHNSON, Alex ... 412-237-4413 ... 425 H ajohnson@ccac.edu
JOHNSON, Alex, F ... 617-726-8008 ... 242 B ajohnson@mghihp.edu
JOHNSON, Alice ... 502-597-6343 ... 203 G alice.johnson@kysu.edu
JOHNSON, Alice ... 210-486-0902 ... 479 E ajohnson235@alamo.edu
JOHNSON, Alisa ... 207-948-9203 ... 219 H ajohnson@unity.edu
JOHNSON, Allan ... 202-806-5042 ... 98 E ajohnson@howard.edu
JOHNSON, Allen ... 951-343-4477 ... 31 J ajohnson@calbaptist.edu
JOHNSON, Amy ... 610-861-1304 ... 437 A johnsona@moravian.edu
JOHNSON, Anderson ... 909-607-8235 ... 40 F andy.johnson@cgu.edu
JOHNSON, Andre ... 510-885-3769 ... 34 E andre.johnson@csueastbay.edu
JOHNSON, Andrea ... 870-236-6901 ... 21 E ajohnson@crc.edu
JOHNSON, Andrew ... 559-453-2317 ... 47 K andy.johnson@fresno.edu
JOHNSON, Andy ... 912-260-4430 ... 137 B andy.johnson@sgc.edu
JOHNSON, Angela ... 216-987-4213 ... 389 B angela.johnson@tri-c.edu
JOHNSON, Anna ... 740-753-6553 ... 391 H johnson_a@hocking.edu
JOHNSON, Anna ... 312-427-2737 ... 154 H 6johnson@jmls.edu
JOHNSON, Anne ... 313-927-1209 ... 254 E ajohnson@marygrove.edu
JOHNSON, Anne ... 651-450-3642 ... 266 F ajohnson@inverhills.edu
JOHNSON, Annette, M ... 906-786-5802 ... 248 I johnsona@baycollege.edu
JOHNSON, Annie ... 213-624-1200 ... 46 L ajohnson@fidm.edu
JOHNSON, Arvid ... 708-524-6465 ... 150 C ajohnson@dom.edu
JOHNSON, Barbara ... 609-777-4351 ... 316 A bjohnson@tesc.edu
JOHNSON, Barbara, G ... 412-578-6021 ... 424 I johnsonbg@carlow.edu
JOHNSON, Barbara, L ... 308-865-8205 ... 300 F johnsonbl@unk.edu
JOHNSON, Barbara, L ... 802-656-4490 ... 514 H barbara.johnson@uvm.edu
JOHNSON, Barry ... 704-406-4440 ... 364 E bjohnson@gardner-webb.edu
JOHNSON, Belinda ... 401-863-3476 ... 453 B belinda_johnson@brown.edu
JOHNSON, Ben ... 325-670-1252 ... 487 F bjohnson@hsutx.edu
JOHNSON, Bernard ... 973-754-7192 ... 312 E bjohnson@pccc.edu
JOHNSON, Bernice, D ... 919-530-7370 ... 378 B bjohnson@nccu.edu
JOHNSON, Beth Ann, H ... 203-392-5250 ... 90 I johnsonb3@southernct.edu
JOHNSON, Betsy ... 567-661-7883 ... 400 I betsy_johnson@owens.edu
JOHNSON, Bonnie ... 641-673-1036 ... 190 C johnsonb@wmpenn.edu
JOHNSON, Bonnie ... 815-394-5047 ... 163 A bonjohnson@rockford.edu
JOHNSON, Brad ... 770-938-4711 ... 133 D
JOHNSON, Brad ... 325-649-8025 ... 488 C bjohnson@hputx.edu
JOHNSON, Brad ... 901-751-8453 ... 471 F bjohnson@mabts.edu
JOHNSON, Brad, W ... 903-434-8102 ... 491 F bjohnson@ntcc.edu
JOHNSON, Bradley ... 859-858-3511 ... 198 E bjohnson@asbury.edu
JOHNSON, Brandon ... 816-501-2400 ... 278 I brandon.johnson@avila.edu
JOHNSON, Brenda ... 812-855-3403 ... 173 E johnbren@indiana.edu
JOHNSON, Brenda ... 510-981-2830 ... 62 B bjohnson@peralta.edu
JOHNSON, Brenda, R ... 510-780-4500 ... 53 J bjohnson@lifewest.edu
JOHNSON, Bret ... 210-826-1000 ... 487 D bjohnson@hallmarkcollege.edu
JOHNSON, Brian ... 931-221-7992 ... 473 E johnsonb@apsu.edu
JOHNSON, Brian, D ... 208-885-6246 ... 144 G johnsonb@uidaho.edu
JOHNSON, Brian, M ... 570-326-3761 ... 440 L bmj2@pct.edu
JOHNSON, Brian, T ... 219-464-6732 ... 181 C brian.johnson1@valpo.edu
JOHNSON, Brodie, I ... 901-320-9700 ... 478 C bjohnson@victory.edu
JOHNSON, Bryan, M ... 205-726-4036 ... 6 G bmjohnso@samford.edu
JOHNSON, C. Lynn ... 320-222-5208 ... 268 G lynn.johnson@ridgewater.edu
JOHNSON, Calvin ... 870-575-8471 ... 25 B johnsonc@uapb.edu
JOHNSON, Calvin, M ... 334-844-4546 ... 1 F johncal@auburn.edu
JOHNSON, Candace ... 810-766-4109 ... 248 C candace.johnson@baker.edu
JOHNSON, Carl ... 847-317-8138 ... 166 E cjohnson@tiu.edu
JOHNSON, Carl ... 303-871-3111 ... 89 A cdjohnson@du.edu
JOHNSON, Carl, E ... 704-687-7217 ... 379 A cjohns1@uncc.edu
JOHNSON, Carol ... 606-783-2022 ... 204 I c.johnson@moreheadstate.edu
JOHNSON, Carol ... 651-690-6650 ... 270 L cpjohnson@stkate.edu
JOHNSON, Carol ... 704-878-3225 ... 372 C cjohnson@mitchellcc.edu
JOHNSON, Carol, B ... 386-481-2075 ... 102 C johnsonc@cookman.edu
JOHNSON, Casie ... 507-453-2663 ... 267 C cjohnson@southeastmn.edu
JOHNSON, Catherine, W ... 336-506-4237 ... 368 A johnsonc@alamancecc.edu
JOHNSON, Cathi ... 901-334-5811 ... 471 E chjohnson@memphisseminary.edu
JOHNSON, Cecelia ... 931-540-2762 ... 475 A cjohnson@columbiastate.edu
JOHNSON, Cel ... 619-260-7878 ... 76 D cel@sandiego.edu
JOHNSON, Celestine ... 765-459-0561 ... 176 C cjohnson@ivytech.edu
JOHNSON, Charlene, M ... 803-536-7243 ... 460 G cmjohnson@scsu.edu
JOHNSON, Charles ... 706-272-4434 ... 128 C cdjohnson@daltonstate.edu
JOHNSON, JR., Charles, R ... 812-888-4262 ... 181 D provost@vinu.edu
JOHNSON, Charlie ... 405-974-2315 ... 413 B chjohnson@uco.edu
JOHNSON, Charlotte ... 870-584-4471 ... 25 C cjohnson@cccua.edu
JOHNSON, Charlotte, H ... 603-646-2243 ... 304 J charlotte.h.johnson@dartmouth.edu
JOHNSON, Chauncy ... 307-268-2025 ... 556 A cjohnson
JOHNSON, Cheri, L ... 785-827-5541 ... 194 F kcherib@kwu.edu
JOHNSON, Cheryl ... 618-545-3091 ... 155 B cjohnson@kaskaskia.edu
JOHNSON, Chris ... 478-757-3400 ... 127 A cjjohnson@centralgatech.edu
JOHNSON, Chris ... 303-762-6924 ... 84 D chris.johnson@denverseminary.edu
JOHNSON, Chris ... 434-592-3017 ... 520 K cjohnson@liberty.edu
JOHNSON, Chris ... 425-235-2352 ... 537 A cjohnson@rtc.edu
JOHNSON, Christana ... 304-876-5453 ... 544 C cjohns12@shepherd.edu
JOHNSON, Christine ... 509-434-5006 ... 533 B christine.johnson@ccs.spokane.edu
JOHNSON, Christine ... 509-434-5006 ... 533 A cjohnson@ccs.spokane.edu
JOHNSON, Christine, P ... 941-309-4731 ... 116 B cjohnso4@ringling.edu
JOHNSON, Christopher ... 203-254-4332 ... 92 H cjohnson@fairfield.edu
JOHNSON, Christopher, P ... 208-885-6126 ... 144 G cjohnson@uidaho.edu
JOHNSON, Cindi Beth ... 651-255-6137 ... 271 D cbjohnson@unitedseminary.edu
JOHNSON, Cindy ... 620-235-4185 ... 196 C cjohnso1@pittstate.edu
JOHNSON, Cindy, K ... 816-604-1011 ... 284 H cindy.johnson@mcckc.edu
JOHNSON, Clara, E ... 757-594-8801 ... 517 L clara.johnson@cnu.edu
JOHNSON, Classie, O ... 601-877-6333 ... 272 F alcorn@bkstr.com
JOHNSON, JR., Clyde ... 443-552-1659 ... 224 B cjohnson01@mica.edu
JOHNSON, Colleen ... 916-608-6500 ... 56 C
JOHNSON, Cornelia ... 302-454-3944 ... 96 F cornelia@dtcc.edu
JOHNSON, Corry ... 912-449-7540 ... 139 D cjohnson@waycross.edu
JOHNSON, Craig ... 813-253-7051 ... 110 M cjohnson@hccfl.edu
JOHNSON, Craig ... 870-972-2852 ... 20 D crjohnso@astate.edu
JOHNSON, Craig ... 773-244-5637 ... 159 H crjohnson@northpark.edu
JOHNSON, Croslena ... 864-646-1568 ... 461 F cjohnso5@tctc.edu
JOHNSON, Curtis ... 501-244-5111 ... 19 D curtis.johnson@arkansasbaptist.edu
JOHNSON, Cuthrell ... 336-750-2230 ... 380 B johnsonc@wssu.edu
JOHNSON, Cynthia ... 360-486-8131 ... 537 B cjohnson@stmartin.edu
JOHNSON, D. Nichole ... 614-236-6945 ... 386 E njohnson@capital.edu
JOHNSON, Dacia ... 218-736-1512 ... 267 D dacia.johnson@minnesota.edu
JOHNSON, Dale ... 510-780-4500 ... 53 J djohnson@lifewest.edu
JOHNSON, Daniel ... 701-662-1515 ... 382 F dan.johnson@lrsc.edu
JOHNSON, Daniel ... 803-584-3446 ... 462 E johns943@mailbox.sc.edu
JOHNSON, Daniel ... 360-475-7441 ... 536 D djohnson@olympic.edu
JOHNSON, Daniel ... 918-456-5511 ... 409 A johnso89@nsuok.edu
JOHNSON, Daniel, R ... 203-582-8930 ... 93 H dan.johnson@quinnipiac.edu
JOHNSON, Daniel, W ... 414-443-8952 ... 553 D daniel.johnson@wlc.edu
JOHNSON, Darren ... 518-381-1320 ... 350 E johnsod@sunysccc.edu
JOHNSON, Daryl ... 651-793-1227 ... 267 A daryl.johnson@metrostate.edu
JOHNSON, Daryl ... 651-793-1303 ... 267 A daryl.johnson@metrostate.edu
JOHNSON, Dave ... 503-375-7021 ... 415 F djohnson@corban.edu
JOHNSON, David ... 716-338-1002 ... 337 E davejohnson@mail.sunyjcc.edu
JOHNSON, David ... 606-368-6031 ... 198 C davidjohnson@alc.edu
JOHNSON, David ... 602-240-3284 ... 48 E davidjohnson@ggbts.edu
JOHNSON, David ... 812-855-8908 ... 173 E dj44@indiana.edu
JOHNSON, David ... 256-824-6288 ... 8 G david.johnson@uah.edu
JOHNSON, David ... 650-306-3336 ... 67 F johnsond@smccd.edu
JOHNSON, David, A ... 330-494-6170 ... 402 B djohnson@starkstate.edu
JOHNSON, David, J ... 513-745-3202 ... 406 E johnsond8@xavier.edu
JOHNSON, David, N ... 919-209-2050 ... 371 F dnjohnson@johnstoncc.edu
JOHNSON, Deborah ... 419-251-1327 ... 395 I deborah.johnson@mercycollege.edu
JOHNSON, Deborah, R ... 414-410-4222 ... 546 G drjohnson@stritch.edu
JOHNSON, Debra ... 318-274-2560 ... 215 E johnsond@gram.edu
JOHNSON, Debra, J ... 540-985-8492 ... 520 I djjohnson@jchs.edu
JOHNSON, Deirdra, G ... 410-334-2902 ... 229 E djohnson@worwic.edu
JOHNSON, Denis ... 913-971-3279 ... 195 D ddjohnson@mnu.edu
JOHNSON, Dennis ... 719-549-3035 ... 87 F dennis.johnson@pueblocc.edu
JOHNSON, Dennis ... 314-889-1452 ... 281 I djohnson@fontbonne.edu
JOHNSON, Deshawn ... 248-204-2117 ... 254 B djohnson@ltu.edu
JOHNSON, DeWayne ... 213-637-1376 ... 79 D dejohnson@westwood.edu
JOHNSON, Dexter ... 425-564-4261 ... 531 G dexter.johnson@bellevuecollege.edu
JOHNSON, Diana ... 479-936-5135 ... 22 H djohnson@nwacc.edu
JOHNSON, Diane ... 518-828-4181 ... 330 E diane.johnson@sunycgcc.edu
JOHNSON, Diane, S ... 515-263-6149 ... 185 C djohnson@grandview.edu
JOHNSON, Donna ... 845-431-8682 ... 332 D djohnson@sunydutchess.edu
JOHNSON, Donnie ... 419-448-3438 ... 402 E johnsond@tiffin.edu
JOHNSON, Doris ... 972-524-3341 ... 495 H
JOHNSON, Doris, W ... 803-705-4536 ... 455 D johnsond@benedict.edu
JOHNSON, Douglas, P ... 207-581-1392 ... 220 A douglasj@maine.edu
JOHNSON, Earl ... 918-631-3142 ... 413 F earl-johnson@utulsa.edu
JOHNSON, Edward ... 716-829-7636 ... 332 E
JOHNSON, Edwin ... 406-243-2995 ... 294 I edwin.johnson@umontana.edu
JOHNSON, Elise ... 586-498-4119 ... 254 C johnsonem@macomb.edu
JOHNSON, Elizabeth, J ... 415-422-6534 ... 76 E johnson@usfca.edu
JOHNSON, Eric ... 318-487-7134 ... 209 F ejohnson@lacollege.edu
JOHNSON, Eric ... 219-464-5085 ... 181 C eric.johnson@valpo.edu
JOHNSON, Eric ... 402-844-7299 ... 299 I paulsb@northeast.edu
JOHNSON, Eric, A ... 330-777-2070 ... 403 B ejohnson@upakron.com
JOHNSON, Eric, C ... 617-627-5484 ... 245 C eric.johnson@tufts.edu
JOHNSON, Eric, W ... 985-549-3860 ... 216 C ejohnson@selu.edu
JOHNSON, Erica ... 404-270-5189 ... 138 B esjohnson@spelman.edu
JOHNSON, Erie ... 760-379-5001 ... 52 M eriejohn@cerrocoso.edu
JOHNSON, Estelle ... 605-668-1363 ... 464 G ejohnson@mtmc.edu
JOHNSON, Eva, R ... 253-535-7159 ... 536 E johnsoer@plu.edu
JOHNSON, Ezra ... 916-577-2200 ... 79 G
JOHNSON, Fatima, R ... 585-245-5620 ... 353 C johnsonf@geneseo.edu
JOHNSON, Faye, R ... 229-226-1621 ... 138 C fjohnson@thomasu.edu
JOHNSON, Floretha, J ... 636-922-8365 ... 288 B fjohnson@stchas.edu
JOHNSON, Francie, H ... 757-823-9159 ... 522 E fhjohnson@nsu.edu
JOHNSON, Frank ... 620-947-3121 ... 197 A frankj@tabor.edu
JOHNSON, Frank ... 404-756-4013 ... 125 D frankjohnson@atlm.edu
JOHNSON, Freddie, L ... 404-756-4442 ... 125 D fjohnson@atlm.edu
JOHNSON, Frederick ... 412-392-6132 ... 445 A fjohnson@pointpark.edu
JOHNSON, Fredrick, P ... 443-412-2407 ... 223 B frjohnson@harford.edu
JOHNSON, G. David ... 251-460-6261 ... 9 D djohnson@usouthal.edu
JOHNSON, Gary ... 704-878-3250 ... 372 C gjohnson@mitchellcc.edu
JOHNSON, Gary, K ... 815-224-0378 ... 153 E gary_johnson@ivcc.edu
JOHNSON, George ... 336-279-9237 ... 364 D gjohnson8@elon.edu
JOHNSON, George ... 937-376-2946 ... 401 A gjohnson@payne.edu
JOHNSON, Georgene, T ... 740-374-8716 ... 405 G gjohnson@wscc.edu
JOHNSON, Gerry ... 502-213-7276 ... 202 F gerald.johnson@kctcs.edu
JOHNSON, Ginger ... 928-776-2119 ... 19 C ginger.johnson@yc.edu
JOHNSON, Glen ... 276-739-2467 ... 529 A gjohnson@vhcc.edu
JOHNSON, Glenn ... 304-929-1495 ... 541 H gjohnson@mountainstate.edu
JOHNSON, Gloria ... 615-963-7518 ... 474 A gjohnson@tnstate.edu
JOHNSON, Gloria ... 972-860-7001 ... 484 I gloriajohnson@dcccd.edu
JOHNSON, Gordon, L ... 270-745-6455 ... 208 A gordon.johnson@wku.edu
JOHNSON, Gralon ... 601-877-6111 ... 272 F gralon@alcorn.edu
JOHNSON, Gregg ... 520-239-5275 ... 19 A gregg.johnson@phoenix.edu
JOHNSON, Gregory, A ... 562-988-2278 ... 28 I gjohnson@auhs.edu
JOHNSON, Gregory, W ... 757-221-3952 ... 518 A gwjohnson@wm.edu
JOHNSON, Harold ... 940-898-3130 ... 502 D hjohnson@twu.edu
JOHNSON, Henry, J ... 617-348-6353 ... 245 D johnson@urbancollege.edu
JOHNSON, Howard, C ... 718-270-5010 ... 328 C hcjohnson@mec.cuny.edu
JOHNSON, Irma ... 502-597-6634 ... 203 G irma.johnson@kysu.edu
JOHNSON, J. Lee ... 517-264-7108 ... 258 B ljohnson@sienaheights.edu
JOHNSON, J. Theodore ... 704-233-8105 ... 380 F tjohnson@wingate.edu
JOHNSON, J.I ... 405-466-3260 ... 408 G jijohnson@langston.edu
JOHNSON, Jacqueline ... 320-589-6020 ... 271 G jrjohnso@morris.umn.edu
JOHNSON, James ... 620-235-4389 ... 196 C jjohnson@pittstate.edu
JOHNSON, James, E ... 727-816-3340 ... 114 F johnsoj@phcc.edu
JOHNSON, James, F ... 215-898-2173 ... 448 J johnsonj@isc.upenn.edu
JOHNSON, James, J ... 507-453-2721 ... 267 C jjohnson@southeastmn.edu
JOHNSON, James, K ... 651-286-7773 ... 270 B jkjohnson2@nwc.edu
JOHNSON, James, M ... 630-752-5113 ... 168 H james.johnson@wheaton.edu
JOHNSON, James, R ... 610-519-4300 ... 450 H james.johnson@villanova.edu
JOHNSON, James, R ... 717-477-1373 ... 443 E jrjohnson@ship.edu
JOHNSON, Janet, L ... 812-464-1928 ... 181 B jljohnson@usi.edu

JOHNSON, Jason .... 580-628-6240.... 409 B
jason.johnson@north-ok.edu
JOHNSON, Jason, L .... 970-491-6270...... 83 F
jason.johnson@colostate.edu
JOHNSON, Jean .... 785-594-8384.... 190 F
jean.johnson@bakeru.edu
JOHNSON, Jean .... 773-838-7544.... 147 H
jjohnson2@ccc.edu
JOHNSON, Jean .... 202-994-3725...... 98 C
sonjej@gwumc.edu
JOHNSON, Jean, A .... 319-399-8561.... 183 F
jjohnson@coe.edu
JOHNSON, Jeffrey, C .... 561-237-7333.... 113 D
jjohnson@lynn.edu
JOHNSON, Jeffrey, W .... 515-294-6561.... 182 E
jjohnsn@iastate.edu
JOHNSON, Jennifer .... 559-442-8281...... 72 B
jennifer.johnson@fresnocitycollege.edu
JOHNSON, Jenny .... 731-989-6378.... 469 B
jjohnson@fhu.edu
JOHNSON, Jerrold .... 563-387-1865.... 187 D
johnsjer@luther.edu
JOHNSON, Jerry .... 812-866-7364.... 172 A
johnsonj@hanover.edu
JOHNSON, Jerry .... 214-821-5433.... 484 B
jjohnson@criswell.edu
JOHNSON, Jerry, B .... 903-813-2271.... 481 A
jbjohnson@austincollege.edu
JOHNSON, Jeryl .... 843-863-8080.... 456 B
jjohnson@csuniv.edu
JOHNSON, Jill .... 501-760-4324...... 22 F
jjohnson@npcc.edu
JOHNSON, Jill, R .... 864-587-4232.... 461 D
johnsoj@smcsc.edu
JOHNSON, Jo .... 309-796-5005.... 145 H
johnsonjo@bhc.edu
JOHNSON, Jo Ann .... 580-559-5246.... 407 J
jajohnsn@ecok.edu
JOHNSON, Jodi, S .... 706-272-4475.... 128 C
jjohnson@daltonstate.edu
JOHNSON, John, F .... 708-209-3004.... 148 E
john.johnson@cuchicago.edu
JOHNSON, John, J .... 361-698-1269.... 485 G
jjohnson@delmar.edu
JOHNSON, John, P .... 386-226-6200.... 105 H
john.p.johnson@erau.edu
JOHNSON, John, P .... 386-226-6200.... 105 I
john.p.johnson@erau.edu
JOHNSON, John, P .... 386-226-6200...... 14 C
john.p.johnson@erau.edu
JOHNSON, Jonathan .... 706-529-6752.... 128 C
jljohnson@daltonstate.edu
JOHNSON, Joseph, F .... 804-342-3896.... 530 A
jfjohnson@vuu.edu
JOHNSON, Joyce .... 951-639-5439...... 58 B
jajohnso@msjc.edu
JOHNSON, Judy .... 309-438-7611.... 153 D
jjohns4@ilstu.edu
JOHNSON, Julie .... 801-462-1056...... 29 F
jljohnson@argosy.edu
JOHNSON, Julie .... 360-736-9391.... 532 D
jjohnson@centralia.edu
JOHNSON, Julie, A .... 901-678-3951.... 474 C
juljohn@memphis.edu
JOHNSON, Julie, H .... 920-748-8772.... 550 D
johnsonj@ripon.edu
JOHNSON, K-Lee .... 215-769-3128.... 428 E
kjohnso2@eastern.edu
JOHNSON, Karen .... 623-572-3291...... 16 E
kjohns@midwestern.edu
JOHNSON, Karen .... 906-487-7348.... 251 A
karen.johnson@finlandia.edu
JOHNSON, Karen .... 507-457-5300.... 269 G
kjohnson@winona.edu
JOHNSON, Karen .... 402-354-7038.... 299 C
karen.johnson@methodistcollege.edu
JOHNSON, Karen, A .... 574-284-4571.... 179 F
kjohnson@saintmarys.edu
JOHNSON, Karen, D .... 630-515-7268.... 158 F
kjohns@midwestern.edu
JOHNSON, Karen, L .... 607-871-2346.... 322 E
kjohnson@alfred.edu
JOHNSON, Katherine, M ... 727-816-3400.... 114 F
johnsonk@phcc.edu
JOHNSON, Kathleen .... 219-785-5288.... 179 A
kjohnso@pnc.edu
JOHNSON, Kathleen .... 404-215-2660.... 134 D
kljohnso@morehouse.edu
JOHNSON, Kathleen, L ...... 651-696-6551.... 264 J
johnsonkl@macalester.edu
JOHNSON, Kathryn .... 901-333-5172.... 476 B
ktjohnson@southwest.tn.edu
JOHNSON, Kathryn, B .... 315-268-3943.... 329 B
kjohnson@clarkson.edu
JOHNSON, Kathy .... 269-488-4223.... 253 A
kjohnson@kvcc.edu
JOHNSON, Kathy .... 317-278-0033.... 174 D
kjohnso@iupui.edu
JOHNSON, Kathy .... 954-492-5353.... 103 F
kjohnson@citycollege.edu
JOHNSON, Kathy, J .... 605-642-6512.... 465 H
kathy.johnson@bhsu.edu
JOHNSON, Kathy, Y .... 615-230-3580.... 476 C
kathy.y.johnson@volstate.edu
JOHNSON, Kaytie .... 215-965-4052.... 436 H
kjohnson@moore.edu
JOHNSON, Keith .... 785-242-5200.... 195 I
keith.johnson@ottawa.edu
JOHNSON, Keith .... 270-706-8413.... 202 A
keith.johnson@kctcs.edu
JOHNSON, Keith .... 408-855-5457...... 78 F
keith.johnson@wvm.edu
JOHNSON, Keith .... 701-671-2218.... 382 G
keith.johnson@ndscs.edu
JOHNSON, Kelley .... 760-245-4271...... 77 H
kelley.johnson@vvc.edu
JOHNSON, Kelly .... 312-362-5067.... 149 A
kjohnson@depaul.edu
JOHNSON, Kellye .... 405-789-7661.... 412 E
kellye.johnson@swcu.edu
JOHNSON, Ken, L .... 214-860-2113.... 485 A
kenljohnson@dcccd.edu
JOHNSON, Kenneth .... 740-593-2247.... 399 G
johnsok9@ohio.edu
JOHNSON, Kent, M .... 319-273-2122.... 182 G
kent.johnson@uni.edu
JOHNSON, Kent, R .... 219-785-5249.... 179 A
kjohnson@pnc.edu
JOHNSON, Kersten .... 605-677-6713.... 465 G
kersten.johnson@usd.edu
JOHNSON, Kevin, R .... 530-752-0243...... 73 I
krjohnson@ucdavis.edu
JOHNSON, Kim .... 319-398-5525.... 187 B
kjohnso@kirkwood.edu
JOHNSON, Kim .... 714-556-3610...... 77 B
officevpem@vanguard.edu
JOHNSON, Kirk .... 712-274-5116.... 187 G
johnson@morningside.edu
JOHNSON, Kirk .... 509-963-1866.... 532 C
johnsonk@cwu.edu
JOHNSON, Kris .... 520-319-3300...... 12 J
kkjohnson@brownmackie.edu
JOHNSON, Kristie .... 802-773-5900.... 513 D
kristie.johnson@csj.edu
JOHNSON, Landy, C .... 580-767-7666.... 230 D
lajohnson@assumption.edu
JOHNSON, LaRhonda, K .... 252-514-6715.... 370 A
johnsonl@cravencc.edu
JOHNSON, Larry .... 601-977-7758.... 277 C
ljohnson@tougaloo.edu
JOHNSON, Larry .... 706-272-4571.... 128 C
ljohnson@daltonstate.edu
JOHNSON, Larry .... 870-236-6901...... 21 E
ljohnson@crc.edu
JOHNSON, Larry .... 202-685-2128.... 557 I
johnsonl@ndu.edu
JOHNSON, Latasha .... 312-850-7016.... 147 F
ljohnson02@ccc.edu
JOHNSON, LaTrina .... 317-632-5553.... 177 G
ljohnson@lincolntech.com
JOHNSON, Laura .... 870-574-4513...... 24 A
ljohnson@sautech.edu
JOHNSON, Lawrence, J ..... 513-556-2321.... 403 D
lawrence.johnson@uc.edu
JOHNSON, Lawrence, J ..... 513-556-2322.... 403 D
lawrence.johnson@uc.edu
JOHNSON, Lea .... 518-438-3111.... 340 A
ljohnson@mariacollege.edu
JOHNSON, Leda .... 623-935-8868...... 15 F
leda.johnson@estrellamountain.edu
JOHNSON, Lee .... 816-483-9600.... 289 E
lee.johnson@spst.edu
JOHNSON, Lena, H .... 757-455-3116.... 530 C
ljohnson@vwc.edu
JOHNSON, Lennor .... 773-697-2179.... 149 D
ljohnson2@devry.edu
JOHNSON, Les .... 218-281-8345.... 271 E
ljohnson@umn.edu
JOHNSON, Levester .... 317-940-9381.... 170 F
ljohnson@butler.edu
JOHNSON, Linda .... 501-337-5000...... 21 D
lindaj@coto.edu
JOHNSON, Linda .... 802-773-5900.... 513 D
linda.johnson@csj.edu
JOHNSON, Lisa .... 617-287-6020.... 236 G
lisa.johnson@umb.edu
JOHNSON, Lisa .... 615-327-6407.... 471 C
ljohnson@mmc.edu
JOHNSON, Lisa .... 757-825-2728.... 528 F
johnsonl@tncc.edu
JOHNSON, Lisa .... 423-636-7305.... 477 A
ljohnson@tusculum.edu
JOHNSON, Lisa .... 701-858-3494.... 381 E
lisa.a.johnson@ndus.edu
JOHNSON, Lisa, A .... 252-335-0821.... 369 G
lajohnson@albemarle.edu
JOHNSON, Lisa, D .... 413-585-4905.... 244 G
ldjohnso@smith.edu
JOHNSON, Lois, M .... 717-720-4122.... 441 E
ljohnson@passhe.edu
JOHNSON, Lonnie .... 816-271-4417.... 286 G
johnsonl@missouriwestern.edu
JOHNSON, Lori .... 615-230-3526.... 476 C
lori.johnson@volstate.edu
JOHNSON, Lori .... 503-297-5544.... 417 G
ljohnson@ocac.edu
JOHNSON, Louise, N .... 215-248-6321.... 435 B
ljohnson@ltsp.edu
JOHNSON, Lucia .... 972-860-8016.... 484 H
ljohnson@dcccd.edu
JOHNSON, Lynda, K .... 770-423-6033.... 133 A
ljohnson@kennesaw.edu
JOHNSON, Lynn .... 970-491-1550...... 83 F
lynn.johnson@colostate.edu
JOHNSON, Lynn .... 631-632-6151.... 352 C
lynn.johnson@stonybrook.edu
JOHNSON, Lynne .... 907-796-6416...... 11 A
lynne.johnson@uas.alaska.edu
JOHNSON, Maggie .... 972-708-7415.... 487 B
admissions@gial.edu
JOHNSON, Marc .... 763-422-6112.... 265 G
marc.johnson@anokaramsey.edu
JOHNSON, Marc .... 775-784-4805.... 303 A
marc.johnson@unr.edu
JOHNSON, Marco .... 661-726-1911...... 73 F
marco.johnson@uav.edu
JOHNSON, Marguerite .... 617-732-2277.... 241 C
peg.johnson@mcphs.edu
JOHNSON, Marianne, H .... 215-699-5700.... 433 G
mjohnson@lsb.edu
JOHNSON, Marie, D .... 802-656-5700.... 514 H
marie.johnson@uvm.edu
JOHNSON, Marjorie, R ...... 206-281-2650.... 537 H
mjohnson@spu.edu
JOHNSON, Mark .... 425-235-2352.... 537 A
mark.johnson@rtc.edu
JOHNSON, Mark .... 248-218-2080.... 257 D
mjohnson@rc.edu
JOHNSON, Mark .... 314-889-1467.... 281 I
mjohnson@fontbonne.edu
JOHNSON, Mark, R .... 919-735-5151.... 375 A
mrjohnson@waynecc.edu
JOHNSON, Mark, S .... 202-806-6270...... 98 E
mark.johnson@howard.edu
JOHNSON, Marsha .... 404-816-4533.... 132 E
mjohnson@atl.herzing.edu
JOHNSON, Marshel .... 501-337-5000...... 21 D
mjohnson@coto.edu
JOHNSON, Martha .... 847-628-1513.... 154 K
mjohnson@judsonu.edu
JOHNSON, Martha .... 252-473-5936.... 369 G
martha_johnson@albemarle.edu
JOHNSON, Mary .... 910-678-8372.... 370 E
johnsoma@faytechcc.edu
JOHNSON, Mary .... 507-453-2745.... 267 C
mjohnson@southeastmn.edu
JOHNSON, Mary .... 618-262-8641.... 153 A
johnsonm@iecc.edu
JOHNSON, Mary Jean .... 419-358-3272.... 385 D
johnsonmj@bluffton.edu
JOHNSON, Matthew .... 701-349-3621.... 383 E
mjohnson@trinitybiblecollege.edu
JOHNSON, Matthew .... 661-835-1111...... 67 K
JOHNSON, McCeil, J .... 312-261-3935.... 159 E
mjohnson@nl.edu
JOHNSON, McMillan, H ..... 540-375-5205.... 523 G
johnson@roanoke.edu
JOHNSON, Melanie .... 937-224-0061.... 395 B
mjohnson@swcollege.net
JOHNSON, Melissa .... 701-671-2520.... 382 G
melissa.j.johnson@ndscs.edu
JOHNSON, Melody .... 479-979-1219...... 26 A
mjohnson@ozarks.edu
JOHNSON, Merrill, L .... 503-554-2411.... 415 I
mjohnson@georgefox.edu
JOHNSON, Michael .... 206-268-4106.... 530 I
mjohnson@antioch.edu
JOHNSON, Michael .... 218-322-2401.... 266 G
mike.johnson@itascacc.edu
JOHNSON, Michael .... 660-562-1212.... 287 B
mikej@nwmissouri.edu
JOHNSON, Michael, C .... 214-860-2167.... 485 A
mcjohnson@dcccd.edu
JOHNSON, Michael, D .... 646-962-4953.... 360 C
mdj2002@qatar-med.cornell.edu
JOHNSON, Michael, D .... 607-255-2000.... 331 B
mdj27@cornell.edu
JOHNSON, Michael, D .... 407-823-1911.... 120 B
michael.johnson@ucf.edu
JOHNSON, Michael, J .... 717-245-1019.... 427 F
johnsomi@dickinson.edu
JOHNSON, Michael, J .... 913-684-3357.... 558 F
michael.johnson@leavenworth.army.mil
JOHNSON, Michael, L .... 270-824-8567.... 202 G
michael.johnson@kctcs.edu
JOHNSON, Michele .... 253-864-3100.... 536 H
mjohnson@pierce.ctc.edu
JOHNSON, Michelle .... 626-969-3434...... 30 G
mmjohnson@apu.edu
JOHNSON, Michelle .... 309-796-5370.... 145 H
johnsonm@bhc.edu
JOHNSON, Michelle, C ...... 610-892-1253.... 439 C
mlc286@psu.edu
JOHNSON, Mike .... 503-352-2871.... 419 E
johnsong@pacificu.edu
JOHNSON, Mike .... 479-575-6601...... 24 C
mrj03@uark.edu
JOHNSON, Mike .... 405-878-2013.... 409 D
mike.johnson@okbu.edu
JOHNSON, Mildred .... 540-231-6267.... 529 G
mildredj@vt.edu
JOHNSON, Mimi .... 334-420-4243........ 7 H
mjohnson@trenholmstate.edu
JOHNSON, Mindy .... 816-604-4339.... 285 E
mindy.johnson@mcckc.edu
JOHNSON, Mitchell .... 336-334-4822.... 371 A
mjohnson@gtcc.edu
JOHNSON, Molly, B .... 785-227-3380.... 191 B
johnsonm@bethanylb.edu
JOHNSON, Monir .... 763-488-2415.... 266 D
monir.johnson@hennepintech.edu
JOHNSON, Monty .... 218-631-7812.... 267 D
monty.johnson@minnesota.edu
JOHNSON, Myra, B .... 828-395-1300.... 371 D
mjohnson@isothermal.edu
JOHNSON, Nancy .... 606-886-3863.... 201 G
nancy.johnson@kctcs.edu
JOHNSON, Nancy .... 903-875-7385.... 491 C
nancy.johnson@navarrocollege.edu
JOHNSON, Nancy, N .... 713-646-1751.... 494 I
njohnson@stcl.edu
JOHNSON, Nathan .... 616-538-2330.... 251 D
njohnson@gbcol.edu
JOHNSON, Nial, L .... 309-677-2333.... 146 C
nial@bradley.edu
JOHNSON, Nick .... 801-818-8900.... 510 I
nick.johnson@provocollege.edu
JOHNSON, Nikita .... 773-291-6200.... 147 G
njohnson@ccc.edu
JOHNSON, JR., P. Kelly ... 919-508-2329.... 380 E
pkjohnsonjr@peace.edu
JOHNSON, Pam .... 256-835-5456........ 3 J
pjohnson@gadsdenstate.edu
JOHNSON, Pam .... 215-591-5786.... 427 B
pjohnson4@devry.edu
JOHNSON, Pamela .... 651-523-2207.... 264 A
pjohnson19@hamline.edu
JOHNSON, Pamela .... 903-233-4459.... 490 A
pamjohnson@letu.edu
JOHNSON, Pamela, D .... 937-766-7765.... 386 G
johnsonp@cedarville.edu
JOHNSON, Patrice .... 340-693-1058.... 568 E
pjohnso@live.uvi.edu
JOHNSON, Patricia, A .... 607-254-1590.... 331 B
paj5@cornell.edu
JOHNSON, Patrick .... 240-567-5288.... 224 D
patrick.johnson@montgomerycollege.edu
JOHNSON, Paul .... 478-757-2641.... 133 H
paul.johnson@maconstate.edu
JOHNSON, Paul, C .... 480-965-9235...... 11 J
paul.c.johnson@asu.edu
JOHNSON, III, Paul, C ..... 803-313-7100.... 462 E
johnsopc@mailbox.sc.edu
JOHNSON, III, Paul, C ..... 803-313-7003.... 462 D
pcjohnson3@sc.edu
JOHNSON, Paula "Tendai" 919-719-5060.... 376 F
tejohnson@shawu.edu
JOHNSON, Paulette .... 314-644-9228.... 288 I
pjohnson@stlcc.edu
JOHNSON, Paulette .... 256-726-7250........ 6 C
pjohnson@oakwood.edu
JOHNSON, Peg .... 505-428-1506.... 320 E
peg.johnson@sfcc.edu
JOHNSON, Peggy .... 281-283-3007.... 503 E
johnsonp@uhcl.edu
JOHNSON, Penny .... 408-855-5195...... 78 F
penny.johnson@wvm.edu
JOHNSON, Peter, B .... 701-777-4317.... 381 F
peter.johnson@und.edu
JOHNSON,
Pharris D. (PJ) .... 404-253-3111.... 136 F
pjohnson@scad.edu
JOHNSON, Philip .... 906-487-7201.... 251 A
philip.johnson@finlandia.edu
JOHNSON, Philip, M .... 503-255-0332.... 417 C
pjohnson@multnomah.edu
JOHNSON, Phillip .... 205-391-2665........ 6 I
pjohnson@sheltonstate.edu
JOHNSON, Phillip, A .... 574-631-8338.... 180 G
johnson.30@nd.edu
JOHNSON, Phyllis, E .... 701-777-6736.... 381 F
phyllis.e.johnson@research.und.edu
JOHNSON, Ralph .... 256-372-5221........ 1 A
ralph.johnson@aamu.edu
JOHNSON, Ralph .... 864-977-2077.... 460 A
ralph.johnson@ngu.edu
JOHNSON, Ralph, F .... 706-542-7369.... 138 G
rfj@uga.edu
JOHNSON, Raymond .... 801-333-8100.... 509 K
JOHNSON, Rebecca .... 770-467-6037.... 137 F
rajohnson@sctech.edu
JOHNSON, Rebecca .... 541-322-3100.... 418 F
rebecca.johnson@osucascades.edu
JOHNSON, Rebecca, D ...... 203-932-7176...... 95 C
rjohnson@newhaven.edu
JOHNSON, Reginald .... 773-291-6348.... 147 G
rjohnson244@ccc.edu
JOHNSON, Renita, A .... 804-329-8456.... 530 A
rajohnson@vuu.edu
JOHNSON, Rhonda .... 510-885-3419...... 34 E
rhonda.johnson@csueastbay.edu
JOHNSON, Rhonda .... 817-598-6283.... 508 F
rjohnson@wc.edu
JOHNSON, Richard .... 870-236-6901...... 21 E
rjohnson@crc.edu

JOHNSON, Richard, A .... 864-597-4090.... 463 G
johnsonra@wofford.edu
JOHNSON, Richard, G .... 805-756-1281..... 33 I
rjohnson@calpoly.edu
JOHNSON, Richard, W .... 315-268-7718.... 329 B
rjohnson@clarkson.edu
JOHNSON,
Richard (Rick), L .... 913-588-5179.... 197 C
rjohnso1@kumc.edu
JOHNSON, Rick .... 239-590-7072.... 119 B
rjohnson@wgcu.edu
JOHNSON, Rick .... 806-651-2080.... 499 A
rjohnson@mail.wtamu.edu
JOHNSON, Rita .... 828-328-7235.... 366 E
rita.johnson@lr.edu
JOHNSON, Robert .... 225-922-2800.... 209 G
rjohnson@lctcs.edu
JOHNSON, Robert .... 916-691-7390..... 56 B
johnsor@crc.losrios.edu
JOHNSON, Robert .... 516-773-5755.... 558 I
johnsonr@usmma.edu
JOHNSON, Robert, E .... 913-667-5700.... 191 H
rjohnson@cbts.edu
JOHNSON, Robert, E .... 508-373-1900.... 231 B
robert.johnson@becker.edu
JOHNSON, Robert, E .... 704-687-8242.... 379 A
robejohn@uncc.edu
JOHNSON, Robert, L .... 973-972-4538.... 316 F
rjohnson@umdnj.edu
JOHNSON, JR.,
Robert, M .... 901-843-3745.... 472 K
johnsonb@rhodes.edu
JOHNSON, Roberta, L .... 515-294-0109.... 182 E
rljohns@iastate.edu
JOHNSON, Rodney .... 803-934-3226.... 459 G
johnsonrod@morris.edu
JOHNSON, Rodney .... 937-766-4114.... 386 G
johnsnr@cedarville.edu
JOHNSON, Roger .... 870-248-4000..... 21 A
rogerj@blackrivertech.edu
JOHNSON, Roger .... 218-733-5935.... 266 H
r1.johnson@lsc.edu
JOHNSON, Ronald .... 713-500-3455.... 506 F
ronald.johnson@uth.tmc.edu
JOHNSON, Ronald, A .... 713-313-7922.... 500 B
johnsonra@tsu.edu
JOHNSON, Ronald, D .... 701-231-8804.... 382 B
ronald.d.johnson@ndsu.edu
JOHNSON, Ronald, W .... 310-206-0404..... 74 C
rojohnso@saonet.ucla.edu
JOHNSON, Rose .... 828-627-4516.... 371 C
rjohnson@haywood.edu
JOHNSON, Ruben .... 972-860-8160.... 484 H
rjohnson@dcccd.edu
JOHNSON, Rushton .... 404-225-4444.... 125 E
rjohnson@atlantatech.edu
JOHNSON, Ryan .... 501-205-8815..... 21 C
rjohnson@cbc.edu
JOHNSON, Ryan .... 765-289-2291.... 176 B
rjohnson@ivytech.edu
JOHNSON, Sabrina, C .... 540-654-1046.... 525 D
sjohnson@umw.edu
JOHNSON, Samuel .... 215-568-9215.... 436 E
sjohnson@phmc.org
JOHNSON, Sandra .... 661-726-1911..... 73 F
sandra.johnson@uav.edu
JOHNSON, Sandra .... 212-243-5150.... 334 E
sjohnson@gts.edu
JOHNSON, Sandra .... 516-463-6933.... 335 G
sandra.johnson@hofstra.edu
JOHNSON, Sara .... 315-265-9260.... 329 B
clarkson@bkstr.com
JOHNSON, Sara .... 517-264-7185.... 258 B
sjohnson@sienaheights.edu
JOHNSON, Sara .... 662-862-8050.... 274 E
scjohnson@iccms.edu
JOHNSON, Sara, S .... 803-786-3029.... 457 C
sjohnson@columbiasc.edu
JOHNSON, Sarah .... 303-837-0825..... 81 F
sljohnson@aii.edu
JOHNSON, Scherry, F .... 972-883-2105.... 506 A
sjohnson@utdallas.edu
JOHNSON, Scott .... 336-838-6141.... 375 C
scott.johnson@wilkescc.edu
JOHNSON, Scott .... 309-438-2251.... 153 D
sdjohns@ilstu.edu
JOHNSON, Scott .... 701-228-5474.... 382 E
scott.johnson@dakotacollege.edu
JOHNSON, Scott, L .... 716-878-5906.... 353 A
johnsosl@buffalostate.edu
JOHNSON, Sean .... 707-664-2790..... 37 D
sean.johnson@sonoma.edu
JOHNSON, Serena .... 704-290-5844.... 374 A
sjohnson@spcc.edu
JOHNSON, Sharon .... 903-468-8707.... 498 B
sharon.johnson@tamuc.edu
JOHNSON, Sheila .... 765-289-2291.... 176 B
sjohnson@ivytech.edu
JOHNSON, Sheila .... 731-668-7240.... 478 G
sheila.johnson@wtbc.edu
JOHNSON, Sheila, G .... 405-744-6321.... 410 C
sheila.johnson@okstate.edu
JOHNSON, Shelia .... 304-327-4040.... 543 F
sjohnson@bluefieldstate.edu
JOHNSON, Sherie .... 410-951-3846.... 228 B
shejohnson@coppin.edu
JOHNSON, Sherrick, L ...... 706-771-4008.... 125 H
sjohnson@augustatech.edu
JOHNSON, Sonia .... 870-236-6901..... 21 E
sjohnson@crc.edu
JOHNSON, Sonja .... 616-331-6811.... 251 F
johnsoso@gvsu.edu
JOHNSON, Stacey .... 718-939-5100.... 338 D
sjohnson@libi.edu
JOHNSON, Stefanie .... 407-303-9498.... 100 G
stefanie.johnson@adu.edu
JOHNSON, Stephanie .... 410-455-1517.... 227 D
sjohn@umbc.edu
JOHNSON, Stephen .... 560-860-2451..... 39 A
sjohnson@cerritos.edu
JOHNSON, Stephen .... 325-674-3791.... 478 I
stephan.johnson@acu.edu
JOHNSON, Stephen .... 817-923-1921.... 495 G
sjohnson@swbts.edu
JOHNSON, Stephen, P .... 607-255-9029.... 331 B
spj2@cornell.edu
JOHNSON, Steve .... 503-552-2001.... 417 D
sjohnson@ncnm.edu
JOHNSON, Steve .... 800-422-2418.... 102 A
sjohnson@baymedical.org
JOHNSON, Steve .... 913-360-7415.... 191 A
stevej@benedictine.edu
JOHNSON, Steve .... 504-280-6303.... 213 E
sgjohnso@uno.edu
JOHNSON, Steve .... 435-652-7544.... 512 B
johnsons@dixie.edu
JOHNSON, Steven .... 212-346-1835.... 345 F
sjohnson@pace.edu
JOHNSON, Steven .... 989-774-4000.... 249 C
JOHNSON, Steven .... 215-489-2905.... 426 H
steven.johnson@delval.edu
JOHNSON, Steven, C .... 208-885-7372.... 144 G
stevejohnson@uidaho.edu
JOHNSON, Steven, D .... 607-436-3592.... 353 E
johnsosd@oneonta.edu
JOHNSON, Steven, L .... 212-346-1835.... 345 F
sjohnson@pace.edu
JOHNSON, Steven, L .... 973-655-7677.... 311 F
johnsonst@mail.montclair.edu
JOHNSON, Steven, L .... 937-512-2525.... 401 J
steven.lee.johnson@sinclair.edu
JOHNSON, Susan .... 805-652-5536..... 77 C
sjohnson@vcccd.edu
JOHNSON, Susan .... 513-244-4503.... 388 E
susan_johnson@mail.msj.edu
JOHNSON, Susie .... 863-784-7108.... 117 J
susie.johnson@southflorida.edu
JOHNSON, Sylvester, C .... 504-865-5300.... 215 C
sylj@tulane.edu
JOHNSON, Sylvia, M .... 847-543-2404.... 148 B
cps086@clcillinois.edu
JOHNSON, Tammy .... 304-696-3161.... 544 B
johnson73@marshall.edu
JOHNSON, Ted .... 847-543-2247.... 148 B
tjohnson@clcillinois.edu
JOHNSON, Ted .... 858-822-5949..... 74 F
edjohnson@ucsd.edu
JOHNSON, Teisha .... 312-949-7407.... 152 E
tjohnson@ico.edu
JOHNSON, Teresa .... 731-286-3226.... 475 B
johnson@dscc.edu
JOHNSON, Terri .... 248-213-1614.... 149 B
tjohnson@devry.edu
JOHNSON, Terry .... 816-414-3763.... 285 H
tjohnson@mbts.edu
JOHNSON, Terry, L .... 937-382-6661.... 405 I
terry_johnson@wilmington.edu
JOHNSON, Theodore, T .... 973-596-3140.... 312 C
johnson@njit.edu
JOHNSON, Thomas .... 323-343-3480..... 35 D
tjohnson@cslanet.calstatela.edu
JOHNSON, Thomas .... 712-325-3227.... 186 F
tjohnson@iwcc.edu
JOHNSON, Thomas, A ...... 903-510-2950.... 503 A
tjoh@tjc.edu
JOHNSON, Thomasine ...... 202-319-6065..... 97 E
johnsotn@cua.edu
JOHNSON, Tim .... 318-487-7118.... 209 F
tjohnson@lacollege.edu
JOHNSON, Tim, P .... 937-766-7777.... 386 G
johnsont@cedarville.edu
JOHNSON, Timothy .... 336-334-5636.... 379 B
tjjohns3@uncg.edu
JOHNSON, Timothy .... 617-731-7116.... 243 G
johnsontim@pmc.edu
JOHNSON, Tina .... 615-898-5910.... 473 G
ntjohnso@mtsu.edu
JOHNSON, Tobe .... 404-653-7886.... 134 D
tjohnson@morehouse.edu
JOHNSON, Todd .... 757-683-3462.... 522 F
tjohnso@odu.edu
JOHNSON, Tom .... 314-246-7975.... 292 J
thomasjohnson18@webster.edu
JOHNSON, Tom .... 910-221-2224.... 364 F
JOHNSON, Tom .... 425-249-4766.... 538 G
tom.johnson@tlc.edu
JOHNSON, Tonjanita .... 631-632-4418.... 352 C
tonjanita.johnson@stonybrook.edu
JOHNSON, Tony .... 903-983-8102.... 489 I
tjohnson@kilgore.edu
JOHNSON, Tony, W .... 843-953-5871.... 456 C
tony.johnson@citadel.edu
JOHNSON, Tonya, L .... 678-359-5011.... 132 A
tonyaj@gdn.edu
JOHNSON, Tracey .... 618-634-3271.... 164 E
traceyj@shawneecc.edu
JOHNSON, Tracie .... 615-383-4848.... 478 F
tjohnson@watkins.edu
JOHNSON, Travis .... 704-334-6882.... 367 H
tjohnson@nlts.edu
JOHNSON, Troy .... 940-565-4602.... 504 D
tjohnson@unt.edu
JOHNSON, Trygve, D .... 616-395-7145.... 252 D
johnsont@hope.edu
JOHNSON, Tyron, S .... 407-582-1344.... 123 B
tjohnson@valenciacollege.edu
JOHNSON, Vermelle, J ...... 803-535-5417.... 456 D
vjohnson@claflin.edu
JOHNSON, Vicki, M .... 731-989-6095.... 469 B
vjohnson@fhu.edu
JOHNSON, Victoria, D .... 504-865-5591.... 215 C
victoria@tulane.edu
JOHNSON, W. Stephen ..... 731-989-6632.... 469 B
sjohnson@fhu.edu
JOHNSON, Walter .... 864-977-7068.... 460 A
walter.johnson@ngu.edu
JOHNSON, Walter .... 601-979-2522.... 274 G
walter.l.johnson@jsums.edu
JOHNSON, Warner, O .... 412-397-6409.... 445 H
johnsonw@rmu.edu
JOHNSON, Wayne, E .... 704-406-4331.... 364 E
wjohnson@gardner-webb.edu
JOHNSON, Wendy .... 225-675-8270.... 211 F
wjohnson@rpcc.edu
JOHNSON, Wendy .... 937-393-3431.... 402 A
wjohnson@sscc.edu
JOHNSON, William, H .... 203-254-4000..... 92 H
wjohnson@fairfield.edu
JOHNSON, William, L .... 313-927-1226.... 254 E
wjohnson@marygrove.edu
JOHNSON, Yvonne, J .... 314-984-7665.... 289 A
yjohnson@stlcc.edu
JOHNSON-BAILEY,
Juanita .... 706-542-2846.... 138 G
jjb@uga.edu
JOHNSON-BLAKE,
Deborah .... 404-225-4491.... 125 E
djohnsonblake@atlantatech.edu
JOHNSON-CRAFT, Shirley . 928-757-0857..... 16 F
sjohnsoncraft@mohave.edu
JOHNSON-CRAMER,
Michael, E .... 570-577-1756.... 423 E
m.johnson-cramer@bucknell.edu
JOHNSON-FANNIN,
Arcelia .... 210-883-1015.... 504 B
johnsonf@uiwtx.edu
JOHNSON HADLEY,
Erma, C .... 817-515-5201.... 496 C
erma.johnson-hadley@tccd.edu
JOHNSON-HAWKINS,
Alma .... 818-710-2911..... 55 B
JOHNSON-HOUSTON,
Debbie, L .... 337-475-5716.... 215 G
djohnsonhouston@mcneese.edu
JOHNSON-KINCAID,
Denise .... 812-429-1430.... 177 C
ajohnson@ivytech.edu
JOHNSON-ODIM, Cheryl .. 708-524-6813.... 150 C
cjohnson-odim@dom.edu
JOHNSON RENVALL,
Poppy .... 505-224-4435.... 317 K
pjohnsonrenvall@cnm.edu
JOHNSON-ROSS, Debora .. 410-386-4632.... 224 C
djohnson@mcdaniel.edu
JOHNSON-SHAHEED,
Karen .... 301-860-3555.... 228 A
kshaheed@bowiestate.edu
JOHNSON-TAYLOR,
Don, W .... 803-321-5112.... 459 H
don.johnson-taylor@newberry.edu
JOHNSON-WEEKS,
Demetria .... 713-313-7940.... 500 B
weeks_dj@tsu.edu
JOHNSON-WHATLEY,
Jeanne .... 404-270-2803.... 128 I
jjohnson-whatley@devry.edu
JOHNSON WILLIAMS,
Nikki .... 540-362-6217.... 520 A
nwilliams@hollins.edu
JOHNSON-WILLIAMS,
Shawn .... 608-663-2312.... 547 F
johnson@edgewood.edu
JOHNSRUD, Courtney .... 406-771-4387.... 295 G
cjohnsrud@msugf.edu
JOHNSRUD, Jason, C .... 202-462-2101..... 99 A
admissions@iwp.edu
JOHNSRUD, Linda, K .... 808-956-7075.... 141 E
johnsrud@hawaii.edu
JOHNSTON, Alysia .... 620-251-7700.... 192 B
alysiaj@coffeyville.edu
JOHNSTON, Amy, J .... 260-480-4255.... 176 F
ajohnston18@ivytech.edu
JOHNSTON, Andrew, J ...... 615-460-6407.... 467 D
andrew.johnston@belmont.edu
JOHNSTON, Angela .... 330-263-2313.... 388 F
ajohnston@wooster.edu
JOHNSTON, Bonnie .... 415-451-2812..... 66 B
bjohnston@sfts.edu
JOHNSTON, Brian .... 216-373-5252.... 397 F
bjohnston@ndc.edu
JOHNSTON, Brian, A .... 202-319-6425..... 97 E
johnston@cua.edu
JOHNSTON, Cheryl, L .... 724-847-6577.... 429 H
cljohnst@geneva.edu
JOHNSTON, Christine, D ... 309-457-2327.... 158 H
cjohnsto@monmouthcollege.edu
JOHNSTON, Daniel .... 402-354-7080.... 299 C
dan.johnston@methodistcollege.edu
JOHNSTON, Danielle .... 702-992-2621.... 302 G
danielle.johnston@nsc.edu
JOHNSTON, Daryl .... 352-271-2905.... 117 F
daryl.johnston@sfcollege.edu
JOHNSTON, Deborah .... 907-564-8204..... 10 D
debj@alaskapacific.edu
JOHNSTON, Dexter, L .... 310-434-4549..... 68 D
johnston_dexter@smc.edu
JOHNSTON, Dusty, R .... 940-552-6291.... 507 F
drj@vernoncollege.edu
JOHNSTON, E. Bubby .... 601-635-2111.... 274 A
bjohnston@eccc.edu
JOHNSTON, Emily .... 251-460-6231...... 9 D
ejohnsto@usouthal.edu
JOHNSTON, F. Bruce .... 870-307-7247..... 22 D
bruce.johnston@lyon.edu
JOHNSTON, Gordon, T ...... 573-840-9654.... 290 F
gordonj@trcc.edu
JOHNSTON, James .... 940-397-4594.... 491 B
james.johnston@mwsu.edu
JOHNSTON, James, K .... 219-989-2232.... 178 K
johnston@purduecal.edu
JOHNSTON, Jed .... 402-826-8604.... 297 G
jed.johnston@doane.edu
JOHNSTON, Jeff .... 574-520-4454.... 174 E
jjohnsto@iusb.edu
JOHNSTON, Jeff .... 219-980-6937.... 174 B
jjohnsto@iusb.edu
JOHNSTON, Jeffrey .... 907-747-7704..... 11 A
jeff.johnston@uas.alaska.edu
JOHNSTON, Jessica .... 847-866-3921.... 151 D
jessica.johnston@garrett.edu
JOHNSTON, Jobyna .... 563-425-5279.... 189 G
johnstonj@uiu.edu
JOHNSTON, John .... 212-217-3600.... 333 F
john_johnston@fitnyc.edu
JOHNSTON, John, E .... 517-265-5161.... 246 H
jjohnston@adrian.edu
JOHNSTON, Judy .... 502-895-3411.... 204 F
jjohnston@lpts.edu
JOHNSTON, Julie, L .... 530-251-8820..... 53 H
jjohnston@lassencollege.edu
JOHNSTON, Kara .... 303-256-9682..... 85 L
kjohnston@jwu.edu
JOHNSTON, Kathy .... 620-421-6700.... 194 G
kathyj@labette.edu
JOHNSTON, Kathy .... 636-481-3280.... 283 D
kjohnsto@jeffco.edu
JOHNSTON, Kerrie .... 978-934-3948.... 237 B
kerrie_johnston@uml.edu
JOHNSTON, Kimberly .... 309-672-5583.... 158 C
kajohnston@methodistcol.edu
JOHNSTON, Kimberly .... 540-654-1618.... 525 D
kjohnston@umw.edu
JOHNSTON, Laine .... 360-383-3126.... 540 A
ljohnston@whatcom.ctc.edu
JOHNSTON, Larry .... 620-276-9559.... 193 C
larry.johnston@gcccks.edu
JOHNSTON, Matthew .... 661-835-1111..... 67 J
JOHNSTON, Matthew .... 805-922-8256..... 67 M
JOHNSTON, Matthew .... 805-967-9677..... 67 L
JOHNSTON, Matthew .... 805-339-2999..... 68 A
JOHNSTON, Michelle .... 203-392-6501..... 90 I
johnstonm2@southerct.edu
JOHNSTON, Michelle .... 205-665-6392...... 9 B
johnstonmr@montevallo.edu
JOHNSTON, Michelle .... 231-591-3648.... 250 H
michelle_johnston@ferris.edu
JOHNSTON, Miriam, K .... 214-692-8080.... 480 I
kjohnston@aii.edu
JOHNSTON, Pamela .... 210-999-7507.... 502 E
pamela.johnston@trinity.edu
JOHNSTON, Paul, E .... 207-859-4252.... 217 G
pejohnst@colby.edu
JOHNSTON, Paul, R .... 812-374-5156.... 176 A
pjohnston6@ivytech.edu
JOHNSTON, Peter .... 508-588-9100.... 240 A
JOHNSTON, Raschelle .... 816-414-3700.... 285 H
financialaid@mbts.edu
JOHNSTON, Robert, C .... 315-445-4321.... 338 B
johnstrc@lemoyne.edu
JOHNSTON, Robin .... 850-201-8580.... 122 A
johnstor@tcc.fl.edu
JOHNSTON, Roxanne .... 585-395-2309.... 352 F
rjohnsto@brockport.edu
JOHNSTON, Sally .... 702-651-5664.... 302 E
sally.johnston@csn.edu

JOHNSTON, Sandra ... 815-455-9793 ... 157 H
sjohnston@mchenry.edu
JOHNSTON, Sandra ... 386-752-1822 ... 108 G
sandra.johnston@fgc.edu
JOHNSTON, Susan ... 703-784-2884 ... 557 H
susan.johnston@usmc.mil
JOHNSTON, Thomas, C ... 207-941-7176 ... 219 E
thom@nescom.edu
JOHNSTON, Tim ... 760-245-4271 ... 77 H
tim.johnston@vvc.edu
JOHNSTON, Tim ... 903-434-8175 ... 491 F
tjohnston@ntcc.edu
JOHNSTON, Timothy ... 313-927-1650 ... 254 E
tjohnston@marygrove.edu
JOHNSTON, Timothy, D ... 336-334-5607 ... 379 B
johnston@uncg.edu
JOHNSTON, William ... 715-232-1184 ... 552 E
johnstonw@uwstout.edu
JOHNSTON, William, N ... 302-736-2508 ... 97 A
wnj@wesley.edu
JOHNSTON, William, S ... 406-243-5211 ... 294 I
bill.johnston@umontana.edu
JOHNSTON-ORTIZ, Eric ... 575-624-7121 ... 318 C
eric.johnston-ortiz@roswell.enmu.edu
JOHNSTON-O'CONNOR,
Elizabeth ... 203-932-7139 ... 95 C
ejohnstonoconnor@newhaven.edu
JOHNSTON-ROBLEDO,
Ingrid ... 716-673-4708 ... 352 A
ingrid.johnston-robledo@fredonia.edu
JOINER, Erin ... 502-897-4206 ... 206 C
ejoiner@sbts.edu
JOINER, Haywood ... 318-473-6466 ... 212 I
hjoiner@lsua.edu
JOINER, Karen ... 360-442-2861 ... 535 I
kjoiner@lowercolumbia.edu
JOINER, Steve ... 615-966-7141 ... 470 F
steve.joiner@lipscomb.edu
JOINER, Wayne ... 919-546-8251 ... 376 F
wjoiner@shawu.edu
JOINES, Pete ... 678-284-4700 ... 129 A
pjoines@devry.edu
JOKELA, Roxana ... 402-559-4385 ... 300 H
rjokela@unmc.edu
JOKERST-HARTER, Jill ... 314-367-8700 ... 288 F
jill.harter@stlcop.edu
JOLER-LABBE, Michelle ... 207-859-1240 ... 219 G
hr@thomas.edu
JOLINE, Mary Lou ... 717-560-8215 ... 433 D
mjoline@lbc.edu
JOLIVETTE, Thomas ... 651-641-3528 ... 264 H
tjolivet@luthersem.edu
JOLLEY, Bryan ... 563-425-5666 ... 189 G
jolleyb@uiu.edu
JOLLEY, Courtney ... 410-617-5025 ... 223 I
cjolley@loyola.edu
JOLLEY, JR., Edward, B ... 912-358-3000 ... 136 G
jolleye@savannahstate.edu
JOLLEY, Kassandra ... 404-270-5323 ... 138 B
kjolley@spelman.edu
JOLLEY, Kate ... 707-527-4413 ... 68 E
kjolley@santarosa.edu
JOLLEY, Rick ... 864-587-4260 ... 461 D
jolleyr@smcsc.edu
JOLLEY, Tammy ... 870-612-2027 ... 25 E
tammy.jolley@uaccb.edu
JOLLIFFE, Vicki, M ... 724-439-4900 ... 434 A
vjolliffe@laurel.edu
JOLLY, Connie ... 843-574-6150 ... 461 G
connie.jolly@tridenttech.edu
JOLLY, James ... 607-431-4000 ... 335 A
JOLLY, Jim, L ... 256-549-8256 ... 3 J
jjolly@gadsdenstate.edu
JOLLY, Julia, A ... 916-558-2407 ... 56 D
jollyj@scc.losrios.edu
JOLLY, Laura, D ... 706-583-0690 ... 138 G
ljolly@uga.edu
JOLLY, Lawson ... 352-588-8354 ... 116 G
lawson.jolly@saintleo.edu
JOLLY, Melody ... 714-850-4800 ... 72 F
jolly@taftu.edu
JOLLY, Michael ... 719-846-5691 ... 88 F
michael.jolly@trinidadstate.edy
JOLLY, Randy ... 903-468-8175 ... 498 B
randy.jolly@tamuc.edu
JOLLY, Richard, C ... 432-685-4523 ... 491 A
rjolly@midland.edu
JOLLY-SMITH, Sue ... 662-329-7175 ... 276 A
sjolly@edhs.muw.edu
JOLMAN, Leslie ... 231-777-5251 ... 248 E
leslie.jolman@baker.edu
JOLY, Jennifer ... 303-937-4232 ... 82 E
jjoly@chu.edu
JOLY, Maureen, S ... 610-285-5039 ... 439 L
msj13@psu.edu
JONAS-MORRISON, Carol 719-502-3383 ... 87 B
carol.jonas-morrison@ppcc.edu
JONES, Aaron ... 417-873-7301 ... 281 D
aaronjones@drury.edu
JONES, Al ... 405-974-2775 ... 413 B
ajones63@uco.edu
JONES, Albert, W ... 570-484-2322 ... 443 B
ajones@lhup.edu
JONES, Alesia, M ... 250-934-5321 ... 8 F
amjones@uab.edu

JONES, Allison ... 323-953-4000 ... 54 H
jonessa@lacitycollege.edu
JONES, Allison ... 918-495-6912 ... 411 C
ajones@oru.edu
JONES, Almarie ... 856-415-2154 ... 310 D
ajones@gccnj.edu
JONES, Alvena ... 903-927-3318 ... 509 E
ajones@wileyc.edu
JONES, Amanda ... 260-482-9171 ... 176 F
ajones@ivytech.edu
JONES, Amy ... 425-889-7823 ... 536 C
amy.jones@northwestu.edu
JONES, Amy, J ... 712-749-2101 ... 183 C
jonesa@bvu.edu
JONES, Andrew, C ... 714-438-4888 ... 41 A
ajones@mail.cccd.edu
JONES, Anita ... 513-771-2424 ... 385 I
asjones@brownmackie.edu
JONES, Anthony ... 256-761-8571 ... 7 G
amjones@talladega.edu
JONES, Anthony ... 615-329-8665 ... 468 I
ajones@fisk.edu
JONES, April ... 704-330-6190 ... 369 D
april.jones@cpcc.edu
JONES, Art ... 605-642-6245 ... 465 H
art.jones@bhsu.edu
JONES, Barbara ... 870-862-8131 ... 23 G
brjones@southark.edu
JONES, Barbara ... 859-257-2936 ... 207 D
bwjones@uky.edu
JONES, Barbara ... 601-484-8804 ... 275 A
bjones@meridiancc.edu
JONES, Barbara ... 513-529-4631 ... 396 E
jonesb2@muohio.edu
JONES, Barbara, E ... 607-746-4440 ... 355 F
jonesbe@delhi.edu
JONES, Beatrice ... 215-751-8266 ... 426 B
bjones@ccp.edu
JONES, Ben ... 440-775-8624 ... 397 G
ben.jones@oberlin.edu
JONES, Benjamin ... 570-662-4383 ... 443 C
bjones@mansfield.edu
JONES, Bert ... 804-819-4920 ... 526 C
bjones@vccs.edu
JONES, Beverly ... 512-863-1527 ... 496 A
jonesb@southwestern.edu
JONES, Bill ... 209-543-7000 ... 52 G
bjones@kaplancollege.edu
JONES, III, Bob ... 864-242-5100 ... 455 E
JONES, Bobby ... 662-476-5016 ... 274 B
bjones@eastms.edu
JONES, Bobby, G ... 870-230-5090 ... 21 I
jonesb@hsu.edu
JONES, Bonnie ... 941-359-4200 ... 121 B
JONES, Bonnie ... 678-717-3616 ... 129 G
bjones@gsc.edu
JONES, Bonnie ... 903-923-2229 ... 486 F
bjones@etbu.edu
JONES, Brad ... 606-546-1629 ... 207 B
bjones@unionky.edu
JONES, Brad ... 317-738-8033 ... 171 F
bjones@franklincollege.edu
JONES, Brenda ... 281-922-3403 ... 494 B
brenda.jones@sjcd.edu
JONES, Brenda ... 414-847-3231 ... 549 B
brendajones@miad.edu
JONES, Brian ... 310-544-6442 ... 64 H
brian.jones@usw.salvationarmy.org
JONES, Brian ... 813-879-6000 ... 107 A
brjones@cci.edu
JONES, Brian ... 507-389-2422 ... 267 E
brian.jones@mnsu.edu
JONES, Brinda, A ... 843-661-1131 ... 458 D
bjones@fmarion.edu
JONES, Britt, E ... 325-670-1317 ... 487 F
brittj@hsutx.edu
JONES, Bronte ... 410-626-2514 ... 225 G
bronte.jones@sjca.edu
JONES, Candace, L ... 919-497-3237 ... 366 H
cjones@louisburg.edu
JONES, Carl ... 318-357-4254 ... 216 B
jonesc@nsula.edu
JONES, Carl ... 404-880-8787 ... 127 C
cjones@cau.edu
JONES, JR., Carnell ... 508-999-8618 ... 237 A
cjones@umassd.edu
JONES, Carol ... 706-272-4545 ... 128 C
cjones@daltonstate.edu
JONES, Carol, F ... 478-988-6800 ... 134 C
cjones@middlegatech.edu
JONES, Carolyn, D ... 973-655-5194 ... 311 F
jonesc@mail.montclair.edu
JONES, Carolyn, J ... 412-924-1404 ... 444 H
cjones@pts.edu
JONES, Carolyn, K ... 812-888-4176 ... 181 D
cjones@vinu.edu
JONES, Catherine ... 815-479-7752 ... 157 H
cjones@mchenry.edu
JONES, Cathy ... 240-567-5321 ... 224 D
cathy.jones@montgomerycollege.edu
JONES, Cathy ... 704-330-1461 ... 366 A
cjones2@jcsu.edu
JONES, Cecelia, K ... 903-593-8311 ... 499 D
ckjones@texascollege.edu

JONES, Celeste ... 330-494-6170 ... 402 B
cjones@starkstate.edu
JONES, Charles, E ... 270-745-3253 ... 208 A
charles.jones2@wku.edu
JONES, Cheri ... 530-541-4660 ... 53 G
jones@ltcc.edu
JONES, Cherryl ... 573-681-5042 ... 283 I
jonesc@lincolnu.edu
JONES, Chris ... 606-589-3003 ... 203 D
chris.jones@kctcs.edu
JONES, Chris ... 740-857-1311 ... 401 F
cjones@rosedale.edu
JONES, Chrissy ... 509-533-3743 ... 533 C
chrissy.davis@spokanefalls.edu
JONES, Christa ... 617-348-6503 ... 245 D
jones@urbancollege.edu
JONES, Christopher ... 978-867-4500 ... 235 A
chris.jones@gordon.edu
JONES, Clayton, H ... 662-915-7431 ... 277 D
chj1@olemiss.edu
JONES, Cliff ... 870-733-6731 ... 22 E
cejones@midsouthcc.edu
JONES, Clifton ... 803-648-6851 ... 462 B
JONES, Courtney ... 405-382-9204 ... 412 B
c.jones@sscok.edu
JONES, Cravor ... 304-327-4016 ... 543 F
cjones@bluefieldstate.edu
JONES, Cynthia, F ... 860-486-2265 ... 94 G
cynthia.f.jones@uconn.edu
JONES, D.B ... 215-895-1267 ... 427 H
d.b.jones@drexel.edu
JONES, Dan ... 714-241-6221 ... 41 B
djones@coastline.edu
JONES, Dan ... 903-886-5011 ... 498 B
dan.jones@tamuc.edu
JONES, Dan, L ... 828-262-3180 ... 377 D
jonesdl@appstate.edu
JONES, Daniel ... 315-792-7234 ... 356 B
daniel.jones@sunyit.edu
JONES, Daniel, W ... 662-915-7111 ... 277 D
chancllr@olemiss.edu
JONES, Danielle ... 484-365-8048 ... 434 H
djones@lincoln.edu
JONES, Danneal ... 305-626-3711 ... 109 A
danneal.jones@fmuniv.edu
JONES, Danny, L ... 601-977-7870 ... 277 C
dljones@tougaloo.edu
JONES, Danson ... 979-532-6975 ... 509 D
jonesd@wcjc.edu
JONES, Darcy ... 814-824-2233 ... 436 C
djones@mercyhurst.edu
JONES, Darin ... 801-832-2573 ... 512 G
djones@westminstercollege.edu
JONES, Darnell ... 816-501-4117 ... 288 A
darnell.jones@rockhurst.edu
JONES, Darren ... 501-977-2191 ... 25 G
jones@uaccm.edu
JONES, Darren ... 301-736-3631 ... 224 A
darren.jones@msbbcs.edu
JONES, Darryl ... 914-654-5522 ... 330 B
djones@cnr.edu
JONES, David ... 507-389-2121 ... 267 E
david.jones@mnsu.edu
JONES, David ... 908-852-1400 ... 308 E
jonesd@centenarycollege.edu
JONES, David ... 908-852-1400 ... 308 E
djones@centenarycollege.edu
JONES, David ... 650-725-3334 ... 71 G
david.jones@stanford.edu
JONES, David ... 904-256-7267 ... 111 L
djones1@ju.edu
JONES, David ... 251-809-1592 ... 5 B
david.jones@jdcc.edu
JONES, David, R ... 301-784-5000 ... 221 B
djones@allegany.edu
JONES, Debbie ... 415-808-3000 ... 50 D
debbie_jones@heald.edu
JONES, Deborah ... 757-727-5251 ... 519 H
deborah.jones@hamptonu.edu
JONES, Deborah, A ... 859-238-5286 ... 199 G
deb.jones@centre.edu
JONES, Debra ... 360-752-8313 ... 531 H
djones@btc.ctc.edu
JONES, Deneese ... 515-271-3623 ... 184 D
deneese.jones@drake.edu
JONES, Dennis ... 510-436-1049 ... 50 H
jones@hnu.edu
JONES, Dennis, H ... 256-766-6610 ... 4 C
djones@hcu.edu
JONES, Dennis, L ... 727-341-3152 ... 116 H
jones.dennisl@spcollege.edu
JONES, Diana ... 641-784-5412 ... 185 B
dianaj@graceland.edu
JONES, Dianna ... 781-768-7291 ... 244 A
dianna.jones@regiscollege.edu
JONES, DiOnetta ... 617-253-9602 ... 241 D
JONES, Don ... 617-585-1154 ... 242 I
don.jones@necmusic.edu
JONES, Donald ... 860-768-4751 ... 95 B
djones@hartford.edu
JONES, Donald, A ... 502-371-8330 ... 198 F
djones@ata.edu
JONES, Donald, E ... 803-754-4100 ... 457 D

JONES, Dorothy, D ... 904-743-1122 ... 112 B
vjones@jones.edu
JONES, Doug ... 910-893-1235 ... 362 J
jones@campbell.edu
JONES, Douglas, W ... 805-565-6048 ... 79 A
vpfinance@westmont.edu
JONES, Eduardo ... 312-850-7230 ... 147 F
erjones@ccc.edu
JONES, Edward ... 704-461-6848 ... 362 F
edwardjones@bac.edu
JONES, JR., Edward ... 202-274-7441 ... 100 A
ejones@udc.edu
JONES, Eli ... 225-578-5297 ... 212 H
elijones@lsu.edu
JONES, Elizabeth, R ... 404-413-3003 ... 131 G
bethjones@gsu.edu
JONES, Ellen ... 251-343-8200 ... 6 F
ellen.jones@remingtoncollege.edu
JONES, Ellen ... 517-483-9871 ... 254 A
jonese14@lcc.edu
JONES, Elliot ... 248-218-2036 ... 257 D
ejones@rc.edu
JONES, Elwin ... 251-981-3771 ... 2 G
elwin.jones@columbiasouthern.edu
JONES, Eric ... 312-915-7452 ... 157 C
ejones6@luc.edu
JONES, Eric ... 641-628-5249 ... 183 D
jonese@central.edu
JONES, Eric, C ... 860-444-8286 ... 558 H
eric.c.jones@uscg.mil
JONES, Erica ... 910-592-8081 ... 373 G
ejones@sampsoncc.edu
JONES, Erica ... 406-683-7511 ... 294 J
e_jones@umwestern.edu
JONES, Ericka, D ... 512-505-3040 ... 488 D
edjones@htu.edu
JONES, Faye ... 615-353-3556 ... 475 E
faye.jones@nscc.edu
JONES, Frances ... 309-677-2646 ... 146 C
fjc@bradley.edu
JONES, Garry ... 407-679-0100 ... 110 F
gjones@fullsail.com
JONES, Garry ... 662-243-2643 ... 274 B
gjones@eastms.edu
JONES, Gary ... 618-252-5400 ... 164 I
gary.jones@sic.edu
JONES, Gena ... 806-743-2865 ... 502 B
gena.jones@ttuhsc.edu
JONES, Geoffrey ... 952-358-8191 ... 268 A
geoffrey.jones@normandale.edu
JONES, George, A ... 606-759-7141 ... 203 A
george.jones@kctcs.edu
JONES, Gerald ... 334-386-7600 ... 3 G
gjones@faulkner.edu
JONES, Geraldine ... 724-938-4407 ... 441 G
jones_gm@calu.edu
JONES, Gina ... 803-323-2194 ... 463 E
jonesg@winthrop.edu
JONES, Gladys, J ... 601-977-7821 ... 277 C
gjones@tougaloo.edu
JONES, Glendell ... 870-230-5091 ... 21 I
president@hsu.edu
JONES, Glenn ... 973-720-2950 ... 317 D
jonesg13@wpunj.edu
JONES, Glenna, S ... 815-224-0230 ... 153 E
glenna_jones@ivcc.edu
JONES, Gloria ... 803-323-3900 ... 463 E
jonesg@winthrop.edu
JONES, Grace, S ... 860-383-5201 ... 92 E
gjones@trcc.commnet.edu
JONES, Gwen ... 937-512-4294 ... 401 J
gwen.jones@sinclair.edu
JONES, Gwendolyn ... 937-512-2509 ... 401 J
gwendolyn.jones@sinclair.edu
JONES, Harold ... 903-675-6256 ... 502 F
hjones@tvcc.edu
JONES, Harold, P ... 205-934-5149 ... 8 F
jonesh@uab.edu
JONES, Harriett, S ... 706-821-8219 ... 135 G
hjones@paine.edu
JONES, Ingrid ... 561-297-3959 ... 119 A
ijones7@fau.edu
JONES, J. Pernell ... 610-341-5948 ... 428 E
pjones1@eastern.edu
JONES, J. Preston ... 954-262-5127 ... 114 B
prestonj@nova.edu
JONES, J. Robert ... 706-649-1837 ... 128 A
bjones@columbustech.edu
JONES, Jacquelyn, K ... 573-882-4097 ... 291 B
jonesjk@missouri.edu
JONES, James ... 843-863-7665 ... 456 B
jjones@csuniv.edu
JONES, JR., James, F ... 860-297-2086 ... 94 E
james.f.jones@trincoll.edu
JONES, James, M ... 812-888-5555 ... 181 D
jjones@vinu.edu
JONES, James, V ... 716-888-2475 ... 325 F
jones11@canisius.edu
JONES, Jane, M ... 423-439-4211 ... 473 F
jonesj@etsu.edu
JONES, Janet ... 256-331-5310 ... 6 B
janetj@nwscc.edu
JONES, Janet ... 732-445-6127 ... 314 B
jbjones@rutgers.edu

JONES, Janet .... 937-512-2514.... 401 J
janet.jones@sinclair.edu
JONES, Jay .... 870-460-1022...... 25 A
jonesj@uamont.edu
JONES, Jayne, W .... 479-968-0400...... 20 G
jjones@atu.edu
JONES, Jean .... 814-732-2981.... 442 E
jjones@edinboro.edu
JONES, Jeannine .... 541-343-1641.... 417 F
jjones@nwcu.edu
JONES, Jeff .... 574-520-4252.... 174 E
jones427@iusb.edu
JONES, Jeffrey .... 570-422-3833.... 442 D
jjones@po-box.esu.edu
JONES, Jeffrey, A .... 724-847-6512.... 429 H
jajones@geneva.edu
JONES, Jennifer .... 815-455-8770.... 157 H
jjones@mchenry.edu
JONES, Jennifer .... 606-546-1205.... 207 B
jjones@unionky.edu
JONES, Jennifer .... 201-200-3005.... 312 B
jjones@njcu.edu
JONES, Jenny .... 859-246-6653.... 201 H
jenny.jones@kctcs.edu
JONES, Jenny .... 704-687-7799.... 379 A
jenny.jones@uncc.edu
JONES, Jenny, E .... 512-542-7834.... 497 B
jjones@tamhsc.edu
JONES, Jessica .... 815-921-4755.... 162 H
j.jones@rockvalleycollege.edu
JONES, Jessica, S .... 252-246-1216.... 375 D
jjones@wilsoncc.edu
JONES, Jim .... 706-721-0011.... 130 D
jjones@georgiahealth.edu
JONES, Jim .... 325-670-1207.... 487 F
jjones@hsutx.edu
JONES, Jimmie .... 501-907-6670...... 23 C
jjones@pulaskitech.edu
JONES, Jimmie, L .... 513-785-3283.... 396 F
jonesjl@muohio.edu
JONES, Jimmy .... 202-806-1280...... 98 E
jimmy.jones@howard.edu
JONES, JoAnna .... 252-492-2061.... 374 G
jonesj@vgcc.edu
JONES, John .... 662-254-3435.... 276 B
john.jones@mvsu.edu
JONES, John .... 765-677-2387.... 175 B
john.jones@indwes.edu
JONES, John .... 530-251-8877...... 53 H
jjones@lassencollege.edu
JONES, John, D .... 803-786-3966.... 457 C
jdjones@columbiasc.edu
JONES, John, P .... 520-621-1112...... 18 L
jpjones@email.arizona.edu
JONES, John, R .... 479-788-7912...... 24 D
john.jones@uafs.edu
JONES, John, S .... 772-546-5534.... 110 N
johnjones@hsbc.edu
JONES, John Raymond ...... 815-753-6100.... 160 B
jrjones@niu.edu
JONES, Johnny, D .... 410-651-6215.... 227 E
jdjones@umes.edu
JONES, Jon .... 417-268-6110.... 278 J
jjones@gobbc.edu
JONES, Joree .... 334-291-4913....... 2 F
joree.jones@cv.edu
JONES, Joseph .... 773-244-5648.... 159 H
jjones@northpark.edu
JONES, Joyce .... 706-737-1411.... 125 G
jjones@aug.edu
JONES, Judy .... 870-245-5578...... 22 I
jonesj@obu.edu
JONES, Judy .... 979-532-6561.... 509 D
judyj@wcjc.edu
JONES, June .... 352-854-2322.... 103 K
jonesj@cf.edu
JONES, Karen .... 828-395-1429.... 371 D
kjones@isothermal.edu
JONES, Karen .... 717-815-1787.... 452 G
kjones@ycp.edu
JONES, Karen, B .... 843-953-5773.... 457 B
jonesk@cofc.edu
JONES, Karen, S .... 478-289-2012.... 129 B
kjones@ega.edu
JONES, Katherine .... 919-735-5151.... 375 A
kathyj@waynecc.edu
JONES, Kathryn .... 803-705-4865.... 455 D
jonesk@benedict.edu
JONES, Kathryn, C .... 870-972-3027...... 20 D
kjones@astate.edu
JONES, Katie .... 413-565-1000.... 230 G
kjones@baypath.edu
JONES, Katrina .... 812-330-6042.... 175 J
katjones@ivytech.edu
JONES, Ken .... 818-767-0888...... 79 H
ken.jones@woodbury.edu
JONES, Ken, A .... 918-595-7029.... 412 H
kjones@tulsacc.edu
JONES, Kenneth, E .... 662-252-8000.... 276 G
kjones@rustcollege.edu
JONES, Kent .... 256-228-6001....... 6 A
jonesk@nacc.edu
JONES, Kevin, M .... 919-530-5436.... 378 B
kjones151@nccu.edu

JONES, Kim .... 731-668-7240.... 478 G
kim.jones@wtbc.edu
JONES, Kim .... 903-823-3004.... 496 E
kim.jones@texarkanacollege.edu
JONES, Kim .... 361-593-2187.... 498 D
krkdy00@tamuk.edu
JONES, Kona .... 217-875-7200.... 162 F
kona@richland.edu
JONES, Kristen .... 406-756-3894.... 294 C
kjones@fvcc.edu
JONES, Kushi .... 951-343-4344...... 31 J
kjones@calbaptist.edu
JONES, Lance .... 307-268-2672.... 556 A
ljones@caspercollege.edu
JONES, Larry, H .... 931-598-1187.... 472 L
ljones@sewanee.edu
JONES, Larry, W .... 662-329-7282.... 276 A
ljones@its.muw.edu
JONES, Laura, B .... 734-764-7423.... 259 A
laurabj@umich.edu
JONES, Laurel .... 408-855-5122...... 78 F
laurel.jones@wvm.edu
JONES, Laurene .... 609-586-4800.... 311 B
jonesl@mccc.edu
JONES, Laurie, S .... 706-568-2005.... 127 G
jones_laurie@columbusstate.edu
JONES, Lee, H .... 757-499-7900.... 517 D
lejones@bryantstratton.edu
JONES, Leslie .... 985-448-4325.... 216 A
leslie.jones@nicholls.edu
JONES, Lewis .... 304-327-4161.... 543 F
ljones@bluefieldstate.edu
JONES, Linda, E .... 607-871-2767.... 322 E
jones@alfred.edu
JONES, Linda, M .... 254-968-9104.... 497 A
ljones@tarleton.edu
JONES, Linda Kay .... 575-538-6133.... 321 I
jonesl6@wnmu.edu
JONES, Lirse .... 973-720-2101.... 317 D
jonesl@wpunj.edu
JONES, Lisa .... 845-257-3216.... 352 B
jonesl@newpaltz.edu
JONES, Lisa .... 801-832-2237.... 512 G
ljones@westminstercollege.edu
JONES, Lisa, R .... 785-670-1712.... 197 F
lisa.jones@washburn.edu
JONES, Marcia .... 678-466-4250.... 127 D
marciajones@clayton.edu
JONES, Marcia, A .... 913-588-4876.... 197 C
mjones@kumc.edu
JONES, Marcus .... 318-357-5701.... 216 B
marcusj@nsula.edu
JONES, Margaret .... 914-422-4043.... 345 F
mjones@pace.edu
JONES, Marian .... 704-378-1074.... 366 A
myjones@jcsu.edu
JONES, Mark, W .... 540-362-6363.... 520 A
jonesmw@hollins.edu
JONES, Marvin, L .... 410-651-6144.... 227 E
mljones@umes.edu
JONES, Mary .... 805-654-6346...... 77 F
mjones@vcccd.edu
JONES, Mary .... 870-575-8461...... 25 B
jonesm@uapb.edu
JONES, Mary .... 405-491-6609.... 412 D
mjones@snu.edu
JONES, Mary, C .... 502-213-2200.... 202 F
maryc.jones@kctcs.edu
JONES, Mary, O .... 814-371-6920.... 428 A
mainc@dbcollege.com
JONES, Matteel .... 843-525-8216.... 461 E
mjones@tcl.edu
JONES, Mattie .... 386-752-1822.... 108 G
mattie.jones@fgc.edu
JONES, Maurice .... 510-748-2234.... 62 C
majones@peralta.edu
JONES, Megan .... 423-323-0201.... 475 F
majones@northeaststate.edu
JONES, Melanie, E .... 803-327-8012.... 463 H
mjones@yorktech.edu
JONES, Melinda, L .... 901-678-2690.... 474 C
mljones6@memphis.edu
JONES, Melissa, A .... 910-678-8474.... 370 E
jonesma@faytechcc.edu
JONES, Melvin .... 304-766-3061.... 544 F
mjones55@wvstateu.edu
JONES, Michelle, M .... 570-321-4031.... 435 D
jones@lycoming.edu
JONES, Mike .... 601-925-3819.... 275 C
jones01@mc.edu
JONES, Mike .... 325-649-8830.... 488 C
mjones@hputx.edu
JONES, Monique .... 312-935-2003.... 162 G
mqjones@robertmorris.edu
JONES, Murel, M .... 252-335-3944.... 377 F
mmjones@mail.ecsu.edu
JONES, Nancy .... 610-399-2000.... 442 A
njones@cheyney.edu
JONES, Nancy, A .... 816-654-7039.... 283 F
njones@kcumb.edu
JONES, Nancy, L .... 804-524-5976.... 529 H
nljones@vsu.edu
JONES, Nate .... 407-708-2148.... 117 H
jonesn@seminolestate.edu

JONES, Ned, J .... 518-783-2423.... 350 I
jones@siena.edu
JONES, Nicholas, P .... 410-516-4050.... 223 F
npjones@jhu.edu
JONES, Nolan .... 972-825-7970.... 495 F
nojones@sagu.edu
JONES, Norman .... 256-372-8653........ 1 A
norman.jones@aamu.edu
JONES, Norman .... 215-489-2491.... 426 H
robert.yapsuga@delval.edu
JONES, Pamela .... 225-771-5763.... 214 I
pamela_jones@subr.edu
JONES, Pamela .... 972-241-3371.... 484 E
pjones@dallas.edu
JONES, Pamela, R .... 716-880-2451.... 340 D
pamela.r.jones@medaille.edu
JONES, Para, M .... 330-494-6170.... 402 B
pjones@starkstate.edu
JONES, Patricia .... 301-736-3631.... 224 A
patricia.jones@msbbcs.edu
JONES, Patricia .... 863-297-1025.... 115 C
pjones@polk.edu
JONES, Patricia, C .... 636-227-2100.... 284 B
patricia.jones@logan.edu
JONES, Patrick .... 518-464-8500.... 333 E
pjones@excelsior.edu
JONES, Patty .... 727-341-3141.... 116 H
jones.patty@spcollege.edu
JONES, Paul, A .... 478-445-5148.... 130 B
paul.jones@gcsu.edu
JONES, Peter .... 215-204-2044.... 447 H
peter.jones@temple.edu
JONES, Phil .... 772-546-5534.... 110 N
philjones@hsbc.edu
JONES, Philip .... 717-245-1740.... 427 F
jonesph@dickinson.edu
JONES, JR., Philip, M .... 704-687-0514.... 379 A
pmjones@uncc.edu
JONES, Pocahantas .... 252-862-1222.... 373 C
jonesp@roanokechowan.edu
JONES, R. Channing .... 910-272-3600.... 373 D
cjones@robeson.edu
JONES, Randall, F .... 214-648-6846.... 507 E
randall.jones@utsouthwestern.edu
JONES, Randy .... 302-857-6230...... 96 C
ljones@desu.edu
JONES, Randy .... 805-565-7048...... 79 A
rjones@westmont.edu
JONES, Rauchelle .... 281-283-2536.... 503 E
jonesrau@uhcl.edu
JONES, Rene .... 870-733-6722...... 22 E
rjones@midsouthcc.edu
JONES, Renee, P .... 910-277-5331.... 376 C
jonesrp@sapc.edu
JONES, Renwick .... 205-366-8885....... 7 F
rjones@stillman.edu
JONES, Richard .... 718-270-5128.... 328 C
richardj@mec.cuny.edu
JONES, Richard .... 856-256-4040.... 314 A
jonesri@rowan.edu
JONES, Rilla, C .... 662-720-7411.... 276 C
rjones@nemcc.edu
JONES, Robert .... 303-762-6913...... 84 D
robert.jones@denverseminary.edu
JONES, Robert .... 401-232-6027.... 453 C
rjones10@bryant.edu
JONES, Robert, A .... 317-788-3304.... 180 F
rjones@uindy.edu
JONES, Robert, H .... 304-293-4611.... 545 A
robert.jones@mail.wvu.edu
JONES, Robert, J .... 612-624-3533.... 272 A
jones012@umn.edu
JONES, Robert, P .... 915-831-3112.... 486 G
rjones35@epcc.edu
JONES, Robert, R .... 239-732-3753.... 105 F
rrjones@edison.edu
JONES, Robin .... 575-769-4921.... 318 A
robin.jones@clovis.edu
JONES, Rockwell, F .... 740-368-3000.... 400 G
rfjones@owu.edu
JONES, Roger .... 704-461-6665.... 362 F
rogerjones@bac.edu
JONES, Ron .... 714-564-6319...... 63 F
jones_ron@sac.edu
JONES, Ronald, L .... 901-272-5100.... 471 D
rjones@mca.edu
JONES, Rosalie, I .... 215-596-8697.... 450 B
r.jones@usciences.edu
JONES, Rose .... 256-331-5313....... 6 B
jonesr@nwscc.edu
JONES, Roslyn, M .... 716-851-1693.... 333 C
jonesm@ecc.edu
JONES, Sam .... 601-477-4038.... 274 H
sam.jones@jcjc.edu
JONES, Sam .... 850-729-4929.... 114 A
joness@nwfsc.edu
JONES, Samuel, B .... 843-953-6367.... 457 B
jonessa@cofc.edu
JONES, Samuel, E .... 757-221-2565.... 518 A
sejone@wm.edu
JONES, Samuel, T .... 731-989-6992.... 469 B
sjones@fhu.edu
JONES, Sandra .... 870-743-3000...... 22 G
sjones@northark.edu

JONES, Sarah, L .... 540-464-7667.... 529 F
jonessl10@vmi.edu
JONES, Scott .... 765-455-9380.... 174 A
scotjone@iuk.edu
JONES, Serene .... 212-280-1403.... 358 I
sjones@uts.columbia.edu
JONES, Shannon .... 803-799-9082.... 461 A
sjones@southuniversity.edu
JONES, Sharon .... 503-943-7314.... 420 G
joness@up.edu
JONES, Shawn .... 562-860-2451...... 39 A
sjones@cerritos.edu
JONES, Sheba .... 312-662-4131.... 144 H
sjones@adler.edu
JONES, Sheila .... 570-389-4027.... 441 F
sjones@bloomu.edu
JONES, Sheri .... 610-861-5451.... 437 H
sjones@northampton.edu
JONES, Sherra .... 201-216-5700.... 315 E
sherra.jones@stevens.edu
JONES, Sherry .... 317-554-8300.... 170 B
shejones@brownmackie.edu
JONES, Sherry .... 216-987-3237.... 389 B
sherry.jones@tri-c.edu
JONES, Sloan, W .... 678-717-3836.... 129 G
sjones@gsc.edu
JONES, Stacey .... 479-788-7302...... 24 D
stacey.jones@uafs.edu
JONES, Stanley .... 229-333-5727.... 139 C
sjones@valdosta.edu
JONES, Stanton, L .... 630-752-5004.... 168 H
stanton.jones@wheaton.edu
JONES, Stephen .... 864-242-5100.... 455 E
JONES, Stephen .... 937-484-1300.... 405 A
sjones@urbana.edu
JONES, Stephen, M .... 801-422-8271.... 509 H
stephen_jones@byu.edu
JONES, Stephen, W .... 330-569-5128.... 391 G
jonessw@hiram.edu
JONES, Steve .... 904-826-0084.... 122 J
sjones@usa.edu
JONES, Steven .... 323-343-3830...... 35 D
sjones@calstatela.edu
JONES, Stuart .... 434-791-7110.... 516 G
sdjones@averett.edu
JONES, Stuart .... 435-586-7775.... 511 D
jones@suu.edu
JONES, Sue .... 936-633-3209.... 480 D
sjones@angelina.edu
JONES, Susan .... 573-592-1107.... 293 D
susan.jones@williamwoods.edu
JONES, Susan, H .... 703-993-2446.... 519 E
shjones@gmu.edu
JONES, Susan, Y .... 909-594-5611...... 58 A
sjones@mtsac.edu
JONES, Tami .... 606-783-2080.... 204 I
t.jones@moreheadstate.edu
JONES, Tamica .... 404-880-8126.... 127 C
tjones@cau.edu
JONES, Tara .... 706-233-7337.... 137 A
tjones@shorter.edu
JONES, Teresa .... 225-216-8053.... 209 H
jonest@mybrcc.edu
JONES, Terri .... 253-566-5352.... 538 F
tjones@tacomacc.edu
JONES, Thomas .... 765-998-5204.... 180 B
thjones@taylor.edu
JONES, Thomas, H .... 704-406-4369.... 364 E
tjones@gardner-webb.edu
JONES, Tim .... 850-245-0466.... 118 K
tim.jones@flbog.edu
JONES, Tim .... 870-230-5117...... 21 I
jonest@hsu.edu
JONES, Tim .... 501-812-2760...... 23 C
thjones@pulaskitech.edu
JONES, Tim .... 334-493-3573....... 5 F
twjones@lbwcc.edu
JONES, Tim .... 412-536-1139.... 432 H
tim.jones@laroche.edu
JONES, Timothy Paul .... 502-897-4347.... 206 C
tjones@sbts.edu
JONES, Tina, N .... 205-652-3497....... 9 E
tnj@uwa.edu
JONES, Todd .... 515-964-6242.... 183 H
tgjones@dmacc.edu
JONES, Todd .... 706-295-6339.... 130 E
tjones@highlands.edu
JONES, Todd .... 215-751-8167.... 426 B
tjones@ccp.edu
JONES, Tom, O .... 870-759-4101...... 26 B
tjones@wbcoll.edu
JONES, Tony .... 312-899-5136.... 164 C
tonyjones@saic.edu
JONES, Tony .... 804-706-5235.... 527 B
tjones@jtcc.edu
JONES, Trevor, H .... 410-334-2828.... 229 E
tjones@worwic.edu
JONES, V. Dale .... 434-223-6116.... 519 G
djones@hsc.edu
JONES, Valerie .... 704-290-5862.... 374 A
vjones@spcc.edu
JONES, Vanessa .... 252-492-2061.... 374 G
jonesv@vgcc.edu

JONES, Verma 870-575-8476 25 B
jonesv@uapb.edu
JONES, Virgil, E 507-933-7449 263 J
vjones@gustavus.edu
JONES, Virginia 972-273-3171 485 C
vjones@dcccd.edu
JONES, W. Terrell 814-865-5906 438 G
wtj1@psu.edu
JONES, Walter 562-908-3467 63 H
walter.jones@riohondo.edu
JONES, Wayne, E 607-777-2144 351 F
wjones@binghamton.edu
JONES, Wendy 325-674-2359 478 I
jonesw@acu.edu
JONES, William 706-880-8257 133 B
wjones@lagrange.edu
JONES, William 765-269-5199 176 D
wjones4@ivytech.edu
JONES, William, H 803-754-4100 457 D
JONES, Wilma 718-982-4001 327 A
wilma.jones@csi.cuny.edu
JONES, Winfred 318-274-6344 215 E
jones@gram.edu
JONES, Yolanda 622-254-3528 276 B
yjones@mvsu.edu
JONES, Yvette, M 504-865-5259 215 C
yjones@tulane.edu
JONES-HARRIS, Lisa 313-845-9610 252 B
ljones-harris@hfcc.edu
JONES-HENDRICKSON,
Simon, B 340-692-4020 568 E
sjonesh@live.uvi.edu
JONES JOHNSON,
Yosette 212-817-7700 327 B
yjonesjohnson@gc.cuny.edu
JONES-NAGLE, Jessica 516-686-7915 343 D
jjonesna@nyit.edu
JONES-SCHENK, Jan 801-274-3280 512 F
jjonesschenk@wgu.edu
JONES SCHWEITZER,
Sharon 210-999-8406 502 E
sjones@trinity.edu
JONES-SEARLE, Donna 860-253-3030 91 B
djones-searle@asnuntuck.edu
JONES-VARNELL,
Karla (Page) 252-672-1751 370 A
jonesp@cravencc.edu
JONES WATKINS, Brenda 708-456-0300 166 F
bwatkins@triton.edu
JONES-WILCOX, Youlanda 731-286-3265 475 B
ywilcox@dscc.edu
JONES-WILCOX, Youlanda 731-286-3346 475 B
ywilcox@dscc.edu
JONES-WILCOX, Youlanda 731-286-3345 475 B
ywilcox@dscc.edu
JONES-WOODIN, Beryl, R 718-780-7957 324 F
beryl.jones@brooklaw.edu
JONESHILL, Nancy 870-236-6901 21 E
njoneshill@crc.edu
JONG-EBOT, William 305-626-3162 109 A
wjebot@fmuniv.edu
JONGEWARD, David, W 503-255-0332 417 C
jongeward@multnomah.edu
JONGSMA KNAUSS,
Sonya 712-722-6024 184 C
sjknauss@dordt.edu
JONSE, Paula 903-813-2059 481 A
pjonse@austincollege.edu
JONTE-PACE, Diane, E 408-554-4751 68 C
djontepace@scu.edu
JORDAHL, Nanette, J 715-425-0699 552 C
nanette.j.jordahl@uwrf.edu
JORDAHL, Ronald, I 704-847-5600 377 B
rjordahl@ses.edu
JORDAN, A. Dane 704-233-8026 380 F
djordan@wingate.edu
JORDAN, Amanda 276-326-4263 516 L
ajordan@bluefield.edu
JORDAN, Amber 706-295-6768 131 B
ajordan@gntc.edu
JORDAN, Andy 803-593-9231 455 A
jordana@atc.edu
JORDAN, Angela 312-935-2002 162 G
ajordan@robertmorris.edu
JORDAN, Angela 843-661-8341 458 B
angela.jordan@fdtc.edu
JORDAN, Ann 918-610-8303 411 D
ann.jordan@ptstulsa.edu
JORDAN, Augustus 802-443-5382 514 A
jordan@middlebury.edu
JORDAN, Austina 706-245-7226 129 C
ajordan@ec.edu
JORDAN, Belva Brown 918-610-8303 411 D
belva.jordan@ptstulsa.edu
JORDAN, Ben 256-395-2211 7 D
benjordan@suscc.edu
JORDAN, Carol, W 704-337-2400 376 A
jordanc@queens.edu
JORDAN, Cherly 256-395-2211 7 D
cjordan@suscc.edu
JORDAN, Corey 315-386-7319 355 E
jordanc@canton.edu
JORDAN, Dave 443-518-3801 223 D
djordan@howardcc.edu
JORDAN, Diane 573-334-9181 284 E
diane@metrobusinesscollege.edu
JORDAN, Donald, K 212-650-7278 326 G
djordan@aol.com
JORDAN, Edward, K 386-312-4083 116 F
edwardjordan@sjrstate.edu
JORDAN, Ellen 919-658-7755 367 F
ejordan@moc.edu
JORDAN, Ellen, S 919-658-7755 367 F
ejordan@moc.edu
JORDAN, Gillian 207-581-7700 220 B
gillian@maine.edu
JORDAN, Gregory, D 423-652-4784 470 A
gdjordan@king.edu
JORDAN, Harold 404-752-1506 134 E
hjordan@msm.edu
JORDAN, Herb 251-405-7135 2 C
hjordan@bishop.edu
JORDAN, Holly 254-526-1128 482 H
holly.jordan@ctcd.edu
JORDAN, Jack 517-780-4561 248 D
jack.jordan@baker.edu
JORDAN, Jeffrey, C 206-281-2123 537 H
jordaj2@spu.edu
JORDAN, John 425-889-7788 536 C
john.jordan@northwestu.edu
JORDAN, Judy, G 615-547-1249 468 B
jjordan@cumberland.edu
JORDAN, Katina 877-442-0505 89 C
katina.jordan@rockies.edu
JORDAN, Katrina 513-556-3471 403 D
katrina.jordan@uc.edu
JORDAN, Kimberly, L 678-839-6421 139 A
kjordan@westga.edu
JORDAN, Larry, W 301-736-3631 224 A
larry.jordan@msbbcs.edu
JORDAN, Laurel 802-443-5626 514 A
ljordan@middlebury.edu
JORDAN, Lorrie 714-628-4933 63 G
jordan_lorrie@sccollege.edu
JORDAN, Lucille, A 603-882-6923 304 E
ljordan@ccsnh.edu
JORDAN, Mary, V 423-439-4211 473 F
jordanm@etsu.edu
JORDAN, Megan, K 781-283-3795 245 E
mjordan@wellesley.edu
JORDAN, Michael 864-977-7058 460 A
mike.jordan@ngu.edu
JORDAN, Michael, J 252-823-5166 370 D
jordanm@edgecombe.edu
JORDAN, Michael, R 304-637-1311 541 A
jordanm@dewv.edu
JORDAN, Nancy, E 908-526-1200 313 D
njordan@raritanval.edu
JORDAN, Pamela 405-271-2118 413 D
pamela-jordan@ouhsc.edu
JORDAN, Percy 409-984-6335 501 C
jordanpj@lamarpa.edu
JORDAN, Peter 817-515-4501 496 C
peter.jordan@tccd.edu
JORDAN, Richard 806-354-5401 502 B
richard.jordan@ttuhsc.edu
JORDAN, Ronald, P 401-874-5003 454 E
ronjordan@uri.edu
JORDAN, Sabrina 215-222-4200 445 G
sjordan@walnuthillcollege.edu
JORDAN, Sandra 803-641-3434 462 B
JORDAN, Stephen, M 303-556-3022 86 F
smjordan@msudenver.edu
JORDAN, Susan 870-862-8131 23 G
sjordan@southark.edu
JORDAN, Terry, J 601-977-7720 277 C
tjordan@tougaloo.edu
JORDAN, Tiffany 918-587-6789 413 A
JORDAN, Timothy, G 603-283-2362 303 F
tjordan@antioch.edu
JORDAN, Tuajuanda, C 503-768-7100 416 G
casdean@lclark.edu
JORDAN, Tyrone 248-526-2627 249 C
jorda1t@cmich.edu
JORDAN-SMITH, Barbara 518-445-2380 322 C
bjord@albanylaw.edu
JORDAN WAGNER,
James 931-372-3372 474 B
jordanwagner@tntech.edu
JORDANO, Mark 814-871-7438 429 G
jordan001@gannon.edu
JORDEN, Steven 660-626-2529 278 D
sjorden@atsu.edu
JORDON, Christina 863-638-2944 123 E
cmjordon@webber.edu
JORDRE, Todd 605-626-3005 466 A
todd.jordre@northern.edu
JORDT, Mary 406-756-3362 294 C
mjordt@fvcc.edu
JORE, Katie 715-346-3710 552 D
kjore@uwsp.edu
JORGE, Milagros 405-466-3427 408 G
mjorge@langston.edu
JORGENSEN, Colleen 303-914-6241 87 G
colleen.jorgensen@rrcc.edu
JORGENSEN, Harlan, R 712-707-7333 188 D
harlan@nwciowa.edu
JORGENSEN, Janice, E 701-788-4762 381 H
janice.jorgensen@mayvillestate.edu
JORGENSEN, Jennifer 402-826-8261 297 G
jennifer.jorgensen@doane.edu
JORGENSEN, Jerry 816-584-6445 287 E
jerry.jorgensen@park.edu
JORGENSEN, Laurie 630-942-2755 148 A
jorgensenl@cod.edu
JORGENSEN, Lin 727-864-8886 105 E
jorgenly@eckerd.edu
JORGENSEN, Michael 435-283-7262 512 C
michael.jorgensen@snow.edu
JORGENSEN, Mike 712-279-5396 183 A
mike.jorgensen@briarcliff.edu
JORGENSEN, Patti 920-735-5649 554 A
jorgensp@fvtc.edu
JORGENSEN, Rita 516-299-2445 339 A
rita.jorgensen@liu.edu
JORGENSEN, Ronald, A 712-274-5128 187 G
jorgensenr@morningside.edu
JORGENSEN, Stephen, R 573-882-6227 291 B
jorgensens@missouri.edu
JORGENSEN-FUNK,
Sandy 619-594-5220 37 A
jorgens1@mail.sdsu.edu
JORGENSON, Cheryl, K 405-325-3681 413 C
cjorgenson@ou.edu
JORGENSON, Donald 701-662-1521 382 F
donald.jorgenson@lrsc.edu
JORGENSON, Evelyn, E 660-263-4110 286 H
evelynj@macc.edu
JORGENSON, Jan 360-538-4243 534 G
jjorgens@ghc.edu
JORGENSON, Jo 480-517-8538 16 B
jo.jorgenson@riosalado.edu
JORGENSON, Millard, C 309-556-3066 153 F
bjorgens@iwu.edu
JORNS, Jody 620-672-5641 196 D
jodyj@prattcc.edu
JOSAY, Ashley 724-838-7832 447 C
josay@setonhill.edu
JOSCHKO, Brian 309-677-1002 146 C
bjoschko@bradley.edu
JOSE, Jorge 317-856-1079 173 D
jjv@iu.edu
JOSE, Jorge 812-856-2408 173 E
jjv@indiana.edu
JOSE, Juana Clare 520-383-8401 18 I
jjose@tocc.cc.az.us
JOSE, Robert, O 617-373-5877 243 F
JOSEPH, Barba, A 212-650-5435 326 G
barba@ccny.cuny.edu
JOSEPH, Beatriz 210-481-3936 479 C
ijospeh@alamo.edu
JOSEPH, Bernice 907-474-5860 10 I
bmjoseph@alaska.edu
JOSEPH, JR., Cheney, C 225-578-8491 213 C
JOSEPH, Daniel, P 410-951-3549 228 B
djoseph@coppin.edu
JOSEPH, Dayle, F 401-874-2766 454 E
dayle@uri.edu
JOSEPH, Gerard 217-206-6724 167 C
joseph.gerard@uis.edu
JOSEPH, Jann 734-487-1414 250 F
jjosep10@emich.edu
JOSEPH, Josh 212-960-0083 361 M
josh.joseph@yu.edu
JOSEPH, Michael 219-464-6896 181 C
michael.joseph@valpo.edu
JOSEPH, Mitch 937-484-1262 405 A
jmjoseph@urbana.edu
JOSEPH, Noson 718-601-3523 361 L
noson.jo@juno.com
JOSEPH, Pamela, K 419-995-8284 399 B
joseph.122@osu.edu
JOSEPH, Patricia, A 484-365-8259 434 H
joseph@lincoln.edu
JOSEPH, Richard 617-746-1990 235 G
richard.joseph@hult.edu
JOSEPH, Sonya, F 407-582-4994 123 B
sjoseph@valenciacollege.edu
JOSEPH, Stephen, M 724-287-8711 423 G
steve.joseph@bc3.edu
JOSEPH, Susan 423-697-3136 474 D
JOSEPH, Wendy 253-589-5822 532 G
wendy.joseph@cptc.edu
JOSEPH-COLLINS, Gina 413-565-1000 230 G
gjcollins@baypath.edu
JOSEPH DENLEY,
Tristan, M 931-221-7676 473 E
denleyt@apsu.edu
JOSEPH MATTISON, Sue 920-465-2050 551 B
mattisons@uwgb.edu
JOSEPHS, Nadine, W 412-291-6298 422 E
njosephs@aii.edu
JOSEPHSON, David 973-655-6956 311 F
josephsond@mail.montclair.edu
JOSEY, Peige 334-222-6591 5 F
pjosey@lbwcc.edu
JOSHEE, Jeet 562-985-4106 35 C
jeet.joshee@csulb.edu
JOSHEE, Jeet 562-985-8330 35 C
jeet.joshee@csulb.edu
JOSHI, Anupama 310-243-2046 34 D
ajoshi@csudh.edu
JOSLIN, Dennis, A 402-354-7257 299 C
dennis.joslin@methodistcollege.edu
JOSLIN, Marshal, V 903-923-3320 500 E
marshal.joslin@tstc.edu
JOSLIN, Mike 661-362-3260 41 I
michael.joslin@canyons.edu
JOSLIN, Monica 413-662-5242 238 C
m.joslin@mcla.edu
JOST, Bruce 502-213-7264 202 F
bruce.jost@kctcs.edu
JOST, Jenifer 402-941-6241 298 I
jostj@midlandu.edu
JOST, Lynn 559-453-2311 47 K
lynn.jost@fresno.edu
JOST, Patricia, A 812-888-4225 181 D
pjost@vinu.edu
JOST, Robert 386-226-6142 105 I
robert.jost@erau.edu
JOST, Steve, A 301-860-4212 228 A
sjost@bowiestate.edu
JOTHEN, Karen, G 651-690-6666 270 L
kgjothen@stkate.edu
JOURDAN, Nan 717-846-5000 452 H
JOURDENAIS, Renee 831-647-4182 57 F
renee.jourdenais@miis.edu
JOVANOVICH, Donna 804-594-1576 527 B
djovanovich@jtcc.edu
JOVELL, Kristi 802-865-5728 513 C
kjovell@champlain.edu
JOWERS, Angel 205-652-3547 9 E
ajowers@uwa.edu
JOWI, Doreen 570-389-5247 441 F
djowi@bloomu.edu
JOY, Darrell 314-843-4200 292 H
darrell.joy@vatterott-college.edu
JOY, Frank 505-428-1225 320 E
frank.joy@sfcc.edu
JOY, John 937-393-3431 402 A
jjoy@sscc.edu
JOY, John, A 734-384-4226 255 D
jjoy@monroeccc.edu
JOYAL, Jessica 802-225-3318 514 B
jessica.joyal@neci.edu
JOYCE, Charles 740-284-5327 391 A
cjoyce@franciscan.edu
JOYCE, David, C 828-884-8264 362 H
president@brevard.edu
JOYCE, Erin 785-594-8413 190 F
erin.joyce@bakeru.edu
JOYCE, Gerard 610-282-1100 427 A
gerard.joyce@desales.edu
JOYCE, Jane 617-349-8785 236 B
ajoyce5@lesley.edu
JOYCE, Kelly 757-221-2466 518 A
kajoyc@wm.edu
JOYCE, Kevin 239-280-1531 101 I
kevin.joyce@avemaria.edu
JOYCE, Kevin 914-674-7775 340 F
kjoyce@mercy.edu
JOYCE, Kimberly, L 302-739-3732 96 D
kimjoyce@dtcc.edu
JOYCE, Mahlia 410-857-2791 224 C
mjoyce@mcdaniel.edu
JOYCE, Marguerite, P 281-579-9977 273 C
mjoyce@belhaven.edu
JOYCE, Mary 228-896-2517 275 E
mary.joyce@mgccc.edu
JOYCE, Michael, A 508-830-5050 238 D
mjoyce@maritime.edu
JOYCE, Paul 208-885-6338 144 G
joyce@uidaho.edu
JOYCE, Ronald, A 860-297-2361 94 E
ronald.joyce@trincoll.edu
JOYCE, Teresa, M 770-423-6023 133 A
tjoyce@kennesaw.edu
JOYCE-BRADY, Jean 617-732-2178 241 C
jean.joyce-brady@mcphs.edu
JOYE, Teresa 510-649-2410 48 J
tjoye@gtu.edu
JOYNER, David, M 814-865-1086 438 G
dmj14@psu.edu
JOYNER, James, N 540-464-7096 529 F
joynerjm@vmi.edu
JOYNER, Jennifer 706-507-8956 127 G
joyner_jennifer@columbusstate.edu
JOYNER, Jill 704-847-5600 377 B
jjoyner@ses.edu
JOYNER, Joseph 757-822-1530 528 G
jjoyner@tcc.edu
JOYNER, Laurie, M 937-327-7916 406 B
ljoyner@wittenberg.edu
JOYNER, SR., Stephen 704-330-1406 366 A
sjoyner@jcsu.edu
JOYNER, Stephen, E 718-951-5114 326 F
sjoyner@brooklyn.cuny.edu
JOYNER-GRAHAM, JoAnn 718-270-4832 328 C
jjoyner@mec.cuny.edu
JOYNTON, Olin 989-358-7246 247 C
joyntono@alpenacc.edu
JOZAITIS, Judy 217-786-2200 157 B
judy.jozaitis@llcc.edu

JROSKI, Linda, L .... 610-330-5017 .... 433 B
jroskil@lafayette.edu
JUARBE, Lorraine .... 787-763-6425 .... 562 I
ljuarbe@inter.edu
JUARBE, Myriam .... 787-720-4476 .... 566 D
asistenciaeconomica@colmizpa.edu
JUAREZ, Benjamin .... 617-353-3334 .... 232 E
bjuarez@bu.edu
JUAREZ, David .... 210-434-6711 .... 492 B
djuarez4090@lake.ollusa.edu
JUAREZ, Elisa .... 520-494-5426 .... 13 D
elisa.juarez@centralaz.edu
JUAREZ, Reina .... 858-534-3755 .... 74 F
rjuarez@ucsd.edu
JUBIE, Kathie .... 218-879-0808 .... 266 C
kjubie@fdltcc.edu
JUCHEMS, Jane, J .... 319-352-8521 .... 189 J
jane.juchems@wartburg.edu
JUCHNIEWICZ, Tarcilia, M 201-559-6086 .... 310 B
JUCHT, Craig .... 605-221-3110 .... 464 D
cjucht@kilian.edu
JUCKIEWICZ, Robert, W .... 516-463-6900 .... 335 G
robert.w.juckiewicz@hofstra.edu
JUDD, Cristle Collins .... 207-725-3578 .... 217 E
cjudd@bowdoin.edu
JUDD, Deborah .... 304-876-5287 .... 544 C
djudd@shepherd.edu
JUDD, Kimberly .... 802-387-6723 .... 513 G
kjudd@landmark.edu
JUDD, Maureen .... 617-726-6069 .... 242 B
mjudd@mghihp.edu
JUDD, Summer .... 731-989-6662 .... 469 B
sjudd@fhu.edu
JUDD, T. Randy .... 435-652-7641 .... 512 B
judd@dixie.edu
JUDD, Tim .... 270-789-5027 .... 199 F
tmjudd@campbellsville.edu
JUDE, China .... 718-997-2795 .... 328 E
china.jude@qc.cuny.edu
JUDGE, Jeff .... 952-358-7272 .... 268 A
jeff.judge@normandale.edu
JUDGE, Joseph .... 609-896-5121 .... 313 F
jjudge@rider.edu
JUDGE, Kathleen, M .... 757-455-3298 .... 530 C
kjudge@vwc.edu
JUDGE, Laurie, L .... 765-641-3787 .... 169 E
lljudge@anderson.edu
JUDGE, Mark .... 321-253-2929 .... 106 H
mjudge@cci.edu
JUDGE, Mark, W .... 321-253-2929 .... 106 G
mjudge@cci.edu
JUDGE, Peter .... 803-323-2160 .... 463 E
judgep@winthrop.edu
JUDGE, William .... 617-682-1553 .... 234 E
wjudge@eds.edu
JUDKINS, Fred .... 334-727-8011 .... 8 B
fjudkins@mytu.tuskegee.edu
JUDSON, Shartrisse .... 706-396-8150 .... 135 G
sjudson@paine.edu
JUDY, Joyce, M .... 802-828-2800 .... 515 E
judyj@ccv.edu
JUDY, Thomas, L .... 775-784-6662 .... 303 A
tomj@unr.edu
JUE, Jeffrey, K .... 215-887-5511 .... 451 D
jjue@wts.edu
JUEDES, Scott .... 781-283-1000 .... 245 E
JUGGANAIKLOO,
M. Spalding .... 208-496-7009 .... 143 A
jugganaikloos@byui.edu
JUHL, Lavonne .... 501-812-2293 .... 23 C
ljuhl@pulaskitech.edu
JUKOSKI, Mary Ellen .... 860-701-5027 .... 93 E
jukoski_m@mitchell.edu
JULIA, Jake .... 847-491-2912 .... 160 E
jjulia@northwestern.edu
JULIAN, Augusta, A .... 859-246-6501 .... 201 H
augusta.julian@kctcs.edu
JULIAN, Carol .... 386-822-7738 .... 121 F
cjulian@stetson.edu
JULIAN, Charity .... 812-749-1235 .... 178 H
cjulian@oak.edu
JULIAN, Elizabeth, A .... 706-771-4049 .... 125 H
ejulian@augustatech.edu
JULIAN, James, R .... 617-287-7050 .... 236 E
jjulian@umassp.edu
JULIAN, Leisa .... 765-285-1104 .... 169 G
lijulian@bsu.edu
JULIAN, Tijuana, S .... 417-873-7215 .... 281 D
tjulian@drury.edu
JULIAN, Tracey .... 423-636-7300 .... 477 A
tjulian@tusculum.edu
JULIEN, Earlye, A .... 563-884-5476 .... 188 E
earlye.julien@palmer.edu
JULIEN, Heidi .... 205-348-4610 .... 8 E
hjulien@slis.ua.edu
JULIEN-MOLINEAUX,
Gabrielle .... 410-888-9048 .... 226 F
gjulien-molineaux@tai.edu
JULIN, Paul .... 315-268-7718 .... 329 B
pjulin@clarkson.edu
JULIO, Elizabeth .... 906-353-4600 .... 253 D
liz@kbocc.org
JULIO, Liz .... 906-353-4600 .... 253 D
liz@kbocc.org
JULIUS, David .... 815-967-7322 .... 162 I
djulius@rockfordcareercollege.edu
JULIUS, James .... 760-757-2121 .... 57 E
jjulius@miracosta.edu
JULIUS, Peg .... 319-398-1274 .... 187 B
peg.julius@kirkwood.edu
JULIUS, Peg .... 319-398-1274 .... 187 B
pjulius@kirkwood.edu
JUMP, Jonathan, D .... 740-362-3440 .... 396 A
jjump@mtso.edu
JUMPER, Barbara .... 202-274-5140 .... 100 A
bjumper@udc.edu
JUMPER, G. Robin .... 850-263-3261 .... 101 L
grjumper@baptistcollege.edu
JUMPS, Tressa .... 623-845-3809 .... 15 H
tressa.jumps@gcmail.maricopa.edu
JUNE, Jan, J .... 585-785-1273 .... 334 A
juneje@flcc.edu
JUNE, Jane .... 508-854-4517 .... 240 F
janej@qcc.mass.edu
JUNE, Vincent .... 678-891-2300 .... 131 C
vincent.june@gpc.edu
JUNEJA, Renu .... 219-464-6880 .... 181 C
renu.juneja@valpo.edu
JUNG, Barnabas .... 415-371-0002 .... 60 A
JUNG, Holly .... 512-313-3000 .... 483 K
holly.jung@concordia.edu
JUNG WHANG, Eui .... 323-643-0301 .... 28 D
JUNGKUNTZ, David .... 360-752-8355 .... 531 H
djungkun@btc.ctc.edu
JUNGO, Rene .... 918-293-5026 .... 410 E
rene.jungo@okstate.edu
JUNISBAI, Barbara .... 909-607-7304 .... 62 H
barbara_junisbai@pitzer.edu
JUNKER, Linda, K .... 301-447-5306 .... 225 A
junker@msmary.edu
JUNKER, Tercio, B .... 317-937-9336 .... 170 H
tjunker@cts.edu
JUNKERMAN, Charles, L .. 650-723-6866 .... 71 G
clj@stanford.edu
JUNKIN, Lawrence .... 410-857-2256 .... 224 C
cjunkin@mcdaniel.edu
JUNN, Ellen .... 408-924-2400 .... 37 C
ellen.junn@sjsu.edu
JUNOR, Bill .... 914-251-6460 .... 354 D
bill.junor@purchase.edu
JURASEK, Richard, T .... 716-880-2202 .... 340 D
richard.t.jurasek@medaille.edu
JURASINSKI, OSBM,
M. Cecilia .... 215-885-2360 .... 435 E
scecilia@manor.edu
JURENOVICH, David, M .... 210-829-6007 .... 504 B
davidj@uiwtx.edu
JURGELA, Linda .... 617-735-9920 .... 234 C
jurgela@emmanuel.edu
JURGENS, Ronald .... 800-567-2344 .... 547 A
rjurgens@menominee.edu
JURGENS, William, K .... 321-674-8032 .... 108 H
bjurgens@fit.edu
JURICH, Tom .... 502-852-5732 .... 207 E
jurich@louisville.edu
JURICK, Donna, M .... 512-448-8412 .... 493 E
donnaj@stedwards.edu
JURMA, William .... 308-865-8521 .... 300 F
jurmaw@unk.edu
JUSKEVICE, Leigh .... 207-948-9208 .... 219 H
ljuskevice@unity.edu
JUSKIEWICZ,
Mary Kathryn .... 802-728-1319 .... 516 A
mjuskiewicz@vtc.edu
JUSSEAUME, Richard .... 330-490-7102 .... 405 F
rjusseaume@walsh.edu
JUSTER, Fern, R .... 914-594-4507 .... 343 F
fern_juster@nymc.edu
JUSTICE, Brooke .... 270-901-1001 .... 201 I
brooke.justice@kctcs.edu
JUSTICE, Gary .... 606-218-5294 .... 207 F
garyjustice@upike.edu
JUSTICE, George .... 573-884-4178 .... 291 B
justiceg@missouri.edu
JUSTICE, Joshua .... 276-376-4514 .... 525 G
jvj6e@uvawise.edu
JUSTICE, Katherine .... 281-283-2160 .... 503 E
justice@uhcl.edu
JUSTICE, Lorraine .... 585-475-5436 .... 347 G
lxjpgd@rit.edu
JUSTICE, Melinda .... 606-886-3863 .... 201 G
melinda.justice@kctcs.edu
JUSTICE, Stephen, C .... 949-451-5212 .... 70 E
cjustice@ivc.edu
JUSTICE, Teresa, R .... 803-323-2460 .... 463 E
justicet@winthrop.edu
JUSTIZ, Manuel, J .... 512-471-7255 .... 505 D
mjustiz@mail.utexas.edu
JUSTUS, Cynthia .... 304-929-1668 .... 541 H
cjustus@mountainstate.edu
JUTT, Kathy .... 260-484-4400 .... 170 A
kjutt@brownmackie.edu
JUUSELA, Kari .... 617-266-1400 .... 231 E
JWANIER, David .... 610-740-3790 .... 425 A
djwanier@cedarcrest.edu

K

KAANOI, Aulani .... 808-739-8394 .... 140 E
akaanoi@chaminade.edu
KAASA, Teri, L .... 919-536-7249 .... 370 C
kaasat@durhamtech.edu
KAATRUDE, Peter, B .... 409-984-6216 .... 501 C
peter.kaatrude@lamarpa.edu
KAAZ, Barry .... 785-460-5429 .... 192 C
barry.kaaz@colbycc.edu
KAAZ, Lisa .... 408-741-2065 .... 78 G
lisa.kaaz@westvalley.edu
KABALA, Heather .... 724-836-9885 .... 449 C
hlk3@pitt.edu
KABAT LENSCH, Ellen .... 563-336-3331 .... 184 E
ekabat@eicc.edu
KABBAZ, Michael, S .... 513-529-2075 .... 396 E
mkabbaz@muohio.edu
KABETZKE, Donald .... 214-333-5305 .... 484 D
donaldk@dbu.edu
KABISATPATHY, Ashok .... 803-793-5105 .... 457 F
kabisatpathya@denmarktech.edu
KABISATPATHY,
Bijayalaxmi .... 803-793-5196 .... 457 F
kabisatpathyk@denmark.edu
KACEY, Debra .... 828-398-2512 .... 376 H
dkacey@southcollegenc.edu
KACHEL, Tim .... 701-252-3467 .... 381 C
kachel@jc.edu
KACHUR, John .... 412-434-6626 .... 428 D
bksduquesne@bncollege.com
KACZMAREK, Christine .... 518-580-5813 .... 351 B
ckaczmar@skidmore.edu
KACZOR, Adrian .... 561-912-2166 .... 107 B
akaczor@evergladesuniversity.edu
KACZOROWSKI, Robert .... 856-227-7200 .... 308 D
rkaczorowski@camdencc.edu
KACZVINSKY, Don .... 318-257-4805 .... 215 F
dkaczv@latech.edu
KADA, Solange .... 707-256-7186 .... 58 F
skada@napavalley.edu
KADAVY, Matthew, T .... 402-465-2323 .... 299 H
mtk@nebrwesleyan.edu
KADDEN, Jerome, H .... 410-484-7200 .... 225 C
KADEL, Andrew .... 212-243-5150 .... 334 E
kadel@gts.edu
KADEL, Jim .... 740-351-3270 .... 401 I
jkadel@shawnee.edu
KADIR, Susan .... 561-868-3389 .... 114 D
kadirs@palmbeachstate.edu
KADISH, Alan .... 212-463-0400 .... 73 A
alan.kadish@touro.edu
KADISH, Alan .... 212-463-0400 .... 72 K
alan.kadish@touro.edu
KADISH, Alan .... 212-463-0400 .... 358 B
alan.kadish@touro.edu
KADISH, Steven, N .... 603-646-2715 .... 304 J
steven.n.kadish@dartmouth.edu
KADLIK, MaryLou .... 207-602-2306 .... 221 A
mkadlik@une.edu
KADUC, Maria .... 701-671-2616 .... 382 G
maria.kaduc@ndscs.edu
KAECHELE, Judith .... 203-254-4000 .... 92 H
jkaechele@fairfield.edu
KAEGI, Keli, A .... 413-597-4233 .... 246 D
keli.a.kaegi@williams.edu
KAESER, Martha .... 636-227-2100 .... 284 B
martha.kaeser@logan.edu
KAESS, Almabeth .... 719-384-6821 .... 87 A
almabeth.kaess@ojc.edu
KAFATOS, Menas .... 714-289-2048 .... 39 F
kafatos@chapman.edu
KAFELE, Fatima .... 718-488-1014 .... 338 G
fatima.kafele@liu.edu
KAFER, August .... 304-424-8210 .... 545 C
augie.kafer@mail.wvu.edu
KAFF, Pinches .... 718-854-2290 .... 323 I
rabbikaff@bhsy.org
KAFTAN, John .... 315-792-3102 .... 359 E
jkaftan@utica.edu
KAGAN, Aaron .... 303-629-8200 .... 90 B
KAGAN, Aleksandra .... 718-261-5800 .... 324 D
akagan@bramsonort.edu
KAGAN, Israel .... 303-629-8200 .... 90 B
KAGOL, Phillip .... 651-636-3305 .... 270 E
phillip.kagol@rasmussen.edu
KAHALAS, Harvey .... 312-906-6596 .... 153 C
kahalas@stuart.iit.edu
KAHALAS, Judith .... 617-427-0060 .... 241 A
jkahalas@rcc.mass.edu
KAHAN, Miriam .... 818-299-5500 .... 78 A
mkahan@westcoastuniversity.edu
KAHKEDJIAN, George .... 480-731-8102 .... 15 D
george.kahkedjian@domail.maricopa.edu
KAHKOLA, Shane .... 606-337-1512 .... 199 H
skahkola@ccbbc.edu
KAHL, Michael, D .... 585-389-2890 .... 342 D
mkahl6@naz.edu
KAHLE, David, J .... 617-627-3435 .... 245 C
david.kahle@tufts.edu
KAHLE, Lisa .... 607-753-5793 .... 353 B
lisa.kahle@cortland.edu
KAHLER, James, W .... 808-853-1040 .... 141 C
jimk@pacrim.edu
KAHLER, Josephine .... 304-357-4835 .... 542 A
josephinekahler@ucwv.edu
KAHLER, Kari, L .... 231-995-1228 .... 256 D
kkahler@nmc.edu
KAHLER, Ken .... 413-545-2619 .... 236 F
umass@bkstr.com
KAHLER, Lewis .... 315-792-5537 .... 341 E
lkahler@mvcc.edu
KAHLER, Mark .... 731-661-5543 .... 477 B
mkahler@uu.edu
KAHLER, William .... 619-239-0391 .... 37 F
wkahler@cwsl.edu
KAHLIG, Charla .... 254-295-5436 .... 504 C
ckahlig@umhb.edu
KAHN, Alfred .... 281-283-2600 .... 503 E
kahn@uhcl.edu
KAHN, Amy .... 877-798-0584 .... 89 C
amy.kahn@rockies.edu
KAHN, Amy .... 585-395-2126 .... 352 F
akahn@brockport.edu
KAHN, Avi .... 718-382-8702 .... 361 C
KAHN, Carrie, W .... 716-270-5167 .... 333 A
kahn@ecc.edu
KAHN, Fito .... 512-472-4133 .... 494 F
fito.kahn@ssw.edu
KAHN, Henry .... 415-476-1683 .... 75 A
henry.kahn@ucsf.edu
KAHN, James, R .... 212-746-0463 .... 360 C
jkahn@med.cornell.edu
KAHN, Jay, V .... 603-358-2000 .... 306 G
jkahn@keene.edu
KAHN, Lance, W .... 252-399-6388 .... 362 E
lwkahn@barton.edu
KAHN, Patricia .... 732-224-2061 .... 308 A
pkahn@brookdalecc.edu
KAHN, Robert .... 718-482-5073 .... 328 B
bobkahn@lagcc.cuny.edu
KAHN, Shirley, S .... 205-934-0177 .... 8 F
kahn@uab.edu
KAHN-JETTER, Zella .... 360-491-4700 .... 537 B
zkahnjetter@stmartin.edu
KAHOL, Pawan .... 620-235-4223 .... 196 C
pkahol@pittstate.edu
KAHOL, Pawan .... 417-836-5335 .... 286 C
kaholpawan@missouristate.edu
KAHR, Audra .... 610-606-4630 .... 425 A
ajhoffma@cedarcrest.edu
KAHRIG, Tammy .... 513-745-4845 .... 406 E
kahrigt@xavier.edu
KAHRL, Sarah, H .... 740-427-5154 .... 394 C
kahrls@kenyon.edu
KAHWAJIAN, Z. Greg .... 626-873-2181 .... 58 C
KAIDEN, Drew .... 718-488-1249 .... 338 G
drew.kaiden@liu.edu
KAIL, Pam .... 870-933-7903 .... 20 B
pkail@asusystem.edu
KAIN, Douglas .... 209-384-6344 .... 57 C
kain.d@mccd.edu
KAIN, Kassi .... 509-313-4100 .... 534 F
kain@gonzaga.edu
KAINTH, Pritpal .... 516-876-3207 .... 353 D
kainthp@oldwestbury.edu
KAIO, Christopher .... 713-221-8430 .... 503 F
kaioc@uhd.edu
KAIRIS, Rob .... 330-499-9600 .... 393 I
rkairis@kent.edu
KAISER, Chris, A .... 617-253-4500 .... 241 D
KAISER, David, M .... 305-237-7445 .... 113 H
dkaiser@mdc.edu
KAISER, Dick .... 605-394-2351 .... 466 B
dick.kaiser@sdsmt.edu
KAISER, Farley .... 651-675-4700 .... 264 F
fkaiser@msp.chefs.edu
KAISER, Joyce .... 716-827-2445 .... 358 D
kaiserj@trocaire.edu
KAISER, Kenneth, H .... 215-204-6545 .... 447 H
ken.kaiser@temple.edu
KAISER, Larry .... 215-707-8773 .... 447 H
larry.kaiser@temple.edu
KAISER, Larry, R .... 215-707-8773 .... 447 H
larry.kaiser@temple.edu
KAISER, Nancy .... 618-468-3315 .... 156 E
nkaiser@lc.edu
KAISER, William .... 209-575-6835 .... 80 H
kaiserw@yosemite.cc.ca.us
KAISRLIK, Linda .... 407-628-5870 .... 106 H
lkaisrlik@cci.edu
KAIVOLA, Karen .... 386-822-7726 .... 121 F
kkaivola@stetson.edu
KAJIWARA, Robert .... 808-245-8236 .... 142 C
kajiwara@hawaii.edu
KAJSTURA, Alex .... 520-206-2111 .... 17 H
akajstura@pima.edu
KAKAR, Casandra .... 602-285-7607 .... 16 A
casandra.kakar@pcmail.maricopa.edu
KAKKURI, David .... 239-590-1425 .... 119 B
dkakkuri@fgcu.edu
KAKOULIDIS, Sofia .... 516-463-6810 .... 335 G
sofia.kakoulidis@hofstra.edu
KAKUGAWA-LEONG,
Alyson, Y .... 808-974-7642 .... 141 F
alyson@hawaii.edu
KALAFATIS, Lara, A .... 216-368-4244 .... 386 F
lara.kalafatis@case.edu

KALANI BEYER, Carl ... 626-529-8417 ... 60 F kbeyer@pacificoaks.edu
KALANTZIS, Mary ... 217-333-0960 ... 167 D kalantzi@illinois.edu
KALB, John, M ... 214-768-3895 ... 495 A jmkalb@smu.edu
KALBERER, Neal ... 701-355-8222 ... 383 H nkalberer@umary.edu
KALBFLEISCH, Gary ... 206-546-5813 ... 538 C garyk@shoreline.edu
KALBFLEISCH, Pamela ... 708-209-3164 ... 148 E pamela.kalbfleisch@cuchicago.edu
KALBFLEISCH, Pamela ... 949-214-3286 ... 43 C pamela.kalbfleisch@cui.edu
KALBRENER, Kristen ... 508-910-6503 ... 237 A kkalbrener@umassd.edu
KALDAHL, Tim ... 402-554-2762 ... 301 A tkaldahl@unomaha.edu
KALDENBERG, Tom ... 319-398-5561 ... 187 B tom.kaldenberg@kirkwood.edu
KALDIS, Paula ... 978-681-0800 ... 241 E paulad@mslaw.edu
KALDOR, Teresa ... 310-506-4375 ... 61 H mariateresa.taningco@pepperdine.edu
KALE, Kathy ... 408-554-5021 ... 68 C kkale@scu.edu
KALEMBA, Lena ... 815-455-8581 ... 157 H lkalemba@mchenry.edu
KALER, Eric, W ... 612-626-1616 ... 272 A upres@umn.edu
KALER, Robin ... 217-333-5010 ... 167 D rkaler@illinois.edu
KALERT, David ... 210-341-1366 ... 491 G dkalert@ost.edu
KALEVITCH, Maria, V ... 412-397-4020 ... 445 H kalevitch@rmu.edu
KALFAYAN, Stephanie ... 650-725-2788 ... 71 G kalfayan@stanford.edu
KALIAN, Heidi ... 703-658-4304 ... 517 K kalian@christendom.edu
KALICKI, Scott ... 603-524-3207 ... 304 C skalicki@ccsnh.edu
KALINA, Steve ... 208-321-8800 ... 143 B skalina@brownmackie.edu
KALINOWSKI, Teresa ... 716-851-1051 ... 333 A kalinowski@ecc.edu
KALINOWSKI, Teresa ... 716-270-5112 ... 333 B kalinowski@ecc.edu
KALIONZES, Jane ... 619-594-1982 ... 37 A jkalionz@mail.sdsu.edu
KALIS, Michelle ... 860-231-5229 ... 95 D mkalis@usj.edu
KALISA, Marie-Chantal ... 402-472-3747 ... 300 G mkalisa2@unl.edu
KALIVITIS, Chrissy ... 504-733-0074 ... 209 B ckalivitis@nor.herzing.edu
KALK, Jonathan ... 808-245-8272 ... 142 C kalk@hawaii.edu
KALKBRENNER, John ... 641-269-4300 ... 185 D kalkbren@grinnell.edu
KALKBRENNER, Suzanne, K ... 518-629-4530 ... 336 C s.kalkbrenner@hvcc.edu
KALKHORAN, Iraj ... 718-260-3619 ... 346 C iraj@poly.edu
KALKWARF, Kenneth, L ... 210-567-3160 ... 507 A kalkwarf@uthscsa.edu
KALLIERIS, Nick, C ... 847-543-2476 ... 148 B nkallieris@clcillinois.edu
KALLIN, Robert ... 717-337-6301 ... 429 I rkallin@gettysburg.edu
KALLINA, Wendy ... 478-387-4746 ... 131 A
KALLSEN, Tammy ... 970-521-6730 ... 86 K tammy.kallsen@njc.edu
KALM, Stephen ... 406-243-4970 ... 294 I stephen.kalm@umontana.edu
KALMANOWITZ, Osher ... 718-645-0536 ... 341 D mirrer@thejnet.com
KALMBACH, Charles, F ... 609-497-7991 ... 312 F charles.kalmbach@ptsem.edu
KALOOSTIAN, Damita ... 602-243-8021 ... 16 D damita.kaloostian@smcmail.maricopa.edu
KALOUPEK, W. Thomas ... 540-231-6221 ... 529 G kals@vt.edu
KALOUS, Annie ... 641-648-4611 ... 186 C annie.kalous@iavalley.edu
KALOUSEK, Kay ... 480-219-6111 ... 278 D kkalousek@atsu.edu
KALOYEROS, Alain ... 518-442-4533 ... 351 E akaloyeros@uamail.albany.edu
KALPAKGIAN, Mark ... 858-653-6740 ... 52 D
KALSBEEK, David, H ... 312-362-8706 ... 149 A dkalsbee@depaul.edu
KALSKI, Lynn ... 940-696-8752 ... 507 F lkalski@vernoncollege.edu
KALSOW, Susan ... 712-749-2250 ... 183 C kalsow@bvu.edu
KALTCHEV, Matey ... 414-277-7544 ... 549 C kaltchev@msoe.edu
KALTEFLEITER, Caroline ... 607-753-4203 ... 353 B caroline.kaltefleiter@cortland.edu
KALTENBAUGH, Louise ... 504-286-5019 ... 214 J lkaltenb@suno.edu
KALTHOFF, Theodore, J ... 501-882-8830 ... 20 C tjkalthoff@asub.edu
KALU, Mma ... 919-546-8350 ... 376 F mkalu@shawu.edu
KALUSH, Paul ... 213-738-6818 ... 71 E accounting@swlaw.edu
KAMAHELE, Ron ... 907-786-4680 ... 10 H afrck@uaa.alaska.edu
KAMALI, Reza ... 209-667-3153 ... 36 D rkamali@csustan.edu
KAMATH, Cecile, E ... 843-792-2252 ... 459 D kamath@musc.edu
KAMATH, Kiran ... 925-439-2181 ... 43 G kkamath@losmedanos.edu
KAMATH, Shyam ... 925-631-8674 ... 64 F sjk3@stmarys-ca.edu
KAMEDA, Stephen ... 808-984-3517 ... 142 E skameda@hawaii.edu
KAMENETSKIY, Boris ... 212-349-4330 ... 334 G borisk@globe.edu
KAMENETSKY, Shmuel ... 215-473-1212 ... 447 G talmudicalyeshiva@yahoo.com
KAMENETSKY, Sholom ... 215-477-1000 ... 447 G talmudicalyeshvia@yahoo.com
KAMIAB, Jane ... 336-770-3297 ... 379 E kamiabj@uncsa.edu
KAMIENIECKI, Sheldon ... 831-459-3212 ... 75 C sk1@ucsc.edu
KAMIKAWA, Julie ... 414-258-4810 ... 549 D kamikawj@mtmary.edu
KAMINSHINE, Steven, J ... 404-413-9040 ... 131 G skaminshine@gsu.edu
KAMINSKI, Charles ... 413-236-2105 ... 239 A ckaminsk@berkshirecc.edu
KAMINSKI, Donald ... 304-243-2000 ... 546 A
KAMINSKI, Janice, M ... 724-480-3423 ... 426 A jan.kaminski@ccbc.edu
KAMINSKI, Linda ... 509-574-4635 ... 540 D lkaminski@yvcc.edu
KAMINSKI, Marie ... 414-847-3334 ... 549 B mkaminski@miad.edu
KAMINSKI, Nancy ... 651-213-4175 ... 264 B graduateschool@hazelden.edu
KAMINSKY, Frances, R ... 203-596-4580 ... 93 G fkaminsky@post.edu
KAMIONKOWSKI, Tamar ... 215-576-0800 ... 445 D tkamionkowski@rrc.edu
KAMIS, Ingrida ... 313-664-7462 ... 249 E ikamis@collegeforcreativestudies.edu
KAMISHER, Lisa ... 617-731-7190 ... 243 G lkamisher@pmc.edu
KAMLET, Lee ... 203-582-3641 ... 93 H lee.kamlet@quinnipiac.edu
KAMLET, Mark, S ... 412-268-6684 ... 424 J kamlet@andrew.cmu.edu
KAMM, Judy ... 781-891-2867 ... 231 D jkamm@bentley.edu
KAMMERZELL, Joan ... 360-752-8436 ... 531 H jkammerz@btc.ctc.edu
KAMMERZELL, Sharyl ... 509-335-2636 ... 539 D sharyl.kammerzell@wsu.edu
KAMOCHE, Njambi ... 847-925-6764 ... 151 G nkamoche@harpercollege.edu
KAMPF, Stephen ... 419-372-7485 ... 385 E skampf@bgsu.edu
KAMPS, Anne ... 920-498-6367 ... 555 C anne.kamps@nwtc.edu
KAMPS, Larissa ... 866-323-0233 ... 63 D
KAMUSIKIRI, Sandra ... 909-537-5058 ... 36 B skamusik@csusb.edu
KAMWITHI, Gina ... 419-755-4711 ... 397 C gkamwithi@ncstatecollege.edu
KAN-SHAGHAGHI, Kazem ... 704-886-6500 ... 99 G kazem.khan-shaghaghi@strayer.edu
KANACH, Nancy, A ... 609-258-5524 ... 312 G nkanach@princeton.edu
KANAMORI, Yasuko ... 412-731-8690 ... 445 F ykanamori@rpts.edu
KANAREK, Berel ... 914-736-1500 ... 345 A
KANAREK, E ... 914-736-1500 ... 345 A
KANAREK, Robin ... 617-627-5902 ... 245 C robin.kanarek@tufts.edu
KANDEL, David ... 636-949-4970 ... 283 J dkandel@lindenwood.edu
KANDEL, Sally, A ... 330-672-7901 ... 393 D skandel@kent.edu
KANDER, Ron ... 215-951-2970 ... 444 D kanderr@philau.edu
KANDUS-FISHER, Christopher ... 386-822-7200 ... 121 F ckandus@stetson.edu
KANE, Andrew ... 609-258-3469 ... 312 G kane@princeton.edu
KANE, Barry, S ... 212-854-1458 ... 330 F barry@columbia.edu
KANE, Bob ... 954-438-8882 ... 112 K
KANE, JR., Edward ... 518-437-4570 ... 351 E ekane@uamail.albany.edu
KANE, Elizabeth ... 201-761-6046 ... 314 F ekane@spc.edu
KANE, Gerald, J ... 434-924-4274 ... 525 F gjk5y@virginia.edu
KANE, James ... 713-221-8236 ... 503 F kanej@uhd.edu
KANE, Janet ... 610-647-4400 ... 431 C jkane@immaculata.edu
KANE, Jeffrey ... 516-299-2917 ... 338 E jeffrey.kane@liu.edu
KANE, Jesse ... 605-256-5124 ... 465 I jesse.kane@dsu.edu
KANE, Kara, M ... 716-880-2884 ... 340 D kara.m.kane@medaille.edu
KANE, Kevin, M ... 610-660-3020 ... 446 C kevin.kane@sju.edu
KANE, Luanne ... 763-433-1297 ... 265 G luanne.kane@anokaramsey.edu
KANE, Marion, J ... 352-323-3617 ... 112 J kanem@lscc.edu
KANE, Melissa ... 951-222-8589 ... 64 A melissa.kane@rcc.edu
KANE, Melissa ... 951-222-8589 ... 63 I melissa.kane@rcc.edu
KANE, Michael ... 281-476-1501 ... 493 H michael.kane@sjcd.edu
KANE, Sara, F ... 863-638-7602 ... 123 D sara.kane@warner.edu
KANE, Scott, D ... 401-456-8391 ... 454 A skane@ric.edu
KANE, Teresa, L ... 336-841-9166 ... 365 C tkane@highpoint.edu
KANE, Terrence ... 607-777-5014 ... 351 F tkane@binghamton.edu
KANE, Thomas ... 401-254-3531 ... 454 C tkane@rwu.edu
KANE, Thomas, F ... 570-674-6223 ... 436 F tkane@misericordia.edu
KANE, Thomas, W ... 781-891-2340 ... 231 D tkane@bentley.edu
KANE, Tim ... 352-323-3680 ... 112 J kanet@lscc.edu
KANE, Vicki ... 281-476-1501 ... 493 H vicki.kane@sjcd.edu
KANE-MUNRO, Ellen ... 312-915-6195 ... 157 C emunro@luc.edu
KANELOS, Gwen, E ... 708-209-3101 ... 148 E gwen.kanelos@cuchicago.edu
KANGAS, Christie ... 319-273-2281 ... 182 G christie.kangas@uni.edu
KANIA, Edward, A ... 704-894-2125 ... 363 I edkania@davidson.edu
KANIPE, H. Dean ... 828-652-0634 ... 372 B deank@mcdowelltech.edu
KANIS, David, R ... 773-995-2339 ... 146 G dkanis@csu.edu
KANJIRATHINKAL, Mathew ... 563-876-3353 ... 184 B mathewk@dwci.edu
KANKE, Frederick, W ... 936-639-1301 ... 480 D fkanke@angelina.edu
KANN, Stephanie, J ... 847-808-8444 ... 168 I skann@worshamcollege.com
KANNAN, Jack ... 919-735-5151 ... 375 A jek@waynecc.edu
KANNENWISCHER, Susan, E ... 614-236-6511 ... 386 E skannenwischer@capital.edu
KANNON, Gavindarajan ... 478-825-6320 ... 129 F kannong@fvsu.edu
KANNWISCHER, Kelly ... 714-556-3610 ... 77 B officevpua@vanguard.edu
KANOSKY, Joe, M ... 815-599-3513 ... 152 B joe.kanosky@highland.edu
KANOTZ, Ashley ... 304-829-7411 ... 540 H akanotz@bethanywv.edu
KANTARDJIEFF, Katherine ... 760-750-7204 ... 36 C kkantard@csusm.edu
KANTER, Connie ... 206-296-6148 ... 538 B kanterc@seattleu.edu
KANTER, Joshua ... 847-982-2500 ... 152 A jkanter@htc.edu
KANTNER, Joanne ... 815-825-2086 ... 155 D joanne.kantner@kishwaukeecollege.edu
KANTNER, Michael ... 856-256-4566 ... 314 A kantner@rowan.edu
KANTOR, Ali ... 617-521-1038 ... 244 F ali.kantor@simmons.edu
KANTOR, Rebecca ... 303-315-6343 ... 88 J rebecca.kantor@ucdenver.edu
KANU, Andrew ... 804-524-5769 ... 529 H akanu@vsu.edu
KAO, Monica ... 628-448-0023 ... 51 G vp-admin@itsla.edu
KAOUDIS, Kathy ... 303-914-6341 ... 87 G kathy.koaudis@rrcc.edu
KAPADIA, Malika ... 585-389-2887 ... 342 D mkapadi1@naz.edu
KAPARTHI, Shashidhar ... 319-273-3050 ... 182 G shashi.kaparthi@uni.edu
KAPCSOS, Kathy ... 610-861-5499 ... 437 H kkapcsos@northampton.edu
KAPFER, Mark ... 563-336-3315 ... 184 E mkapfer@eicc.edu
KAPITAN, James ... 219-769-3321 ... 170 C jkapitan@brownmackie.edu
KAPLAN, Anne, C ... 815-753-9503 ... 160 B akaplan@niu.edu
KAPLAN, Barbara, E ... 937-382-6661 ... 405 I barbara_kaplan@wilmington.edu
KAPLAN, John ... 650-433-3806 ... 61 B jkaplan@paloaltou.edu
KAPLAN, John, A ... 315-267-2222 ... 354 C kaplanja@potsdam.edu
KAPLAN, Jonathan, A ... 612-312-2456 ... 272 C jonathan.kaplan@waldenu.edu
KAPLAN, Karen, K ... 713-500-3045 ... 506 F karen.k.kaplan@uth.tmc.edu
KAPLAN, Leonard, I ... 973-596-3638 ... 312 C leonard.i.kaplan@njit.edu
KAPLAN, Richard ... 617-732-2808 ... 241 C richard.kaplan@mcphs.edu
KAPLAN, Ronald, S ... 847-578-8840 ... 163 C ronald.kaplan@rosalindfranklin.edu
KAPLAN, Shelley ... 781-239-5840 ... 230 E skaplan1@babson.edu
KAPLAN, Steven, H ... 203-932-7276 ... 95 C skaplan@newhaven.edu
KAPLINSKY, Yoheved ... 212-799-5000 ... 337 H
KAPLOWITZ, Craig ... 847-628-1126 ... 154 K ckaplowitz@judsonu.edu
KAPOOR, Pushap, R ... 617-984-1775 ... 243 H pkapoor@quincycollege.edu
KAPP, Alisha ... 217-854-3231 ... 146 A alisha.kapp@blackburn.edu
KAPPAS, Constance ... 309-796-4845 ... 145 H kappasc@bhc.edu
KAPPEL, Stephanie ... 304-829-7133 ... 540 H skappel@bethanywv.edu
KAPPLAN, Bethany ... 727-726-1153 ... 103 I bethanykaplan@clearwater.edu
KAPPUS, Sheryl, S ... 254-659-7501 ... 487 G skappus@hillcollege.edu
KAPRIVE, Mark ... 561-803-2542 ... 114 C mark_kaprive@pba.edu
KAPTAIN, Laurence ... 225-578-9959 ... 212 H kaptain@lsu.edu
KAPTIK, Michael, W ... 808-956-8177 ... 141 G kaptik@hawaii.edu
KAPUR, Anup ... 484-384-2931 ... 438 D akapur@eastern.edu
KAPUR, Bobby ... 713-798-4951 ... 481 H kapur@bcm.edu
KARABETSOS, Michael, L ... 517-264-7109 ... 258 B mkarabet@sienaheights.edu
KARAHADIAN, Milton ... 619-849-2649 ... 62 L miltonkarahadian@pointloma.edu
KARAM, Robert ... 318-473-6475 ... 212 I rkaram@lsua.edu
KARAMAN, Ana ... 415-422-6136 ... 76 E takaraman@usfca.edu
KARAMARGIN, C.J ... 520-206-4850 ... 17 H ckaramargin@pima.edu
KARAMOL, Mark ... 567-661-7988 ... 400 I mark_karamol@owens.edu
KARANJA, Benson, M ... 404-627-2681 ... 126 D benson.karanja@beulah.org
KARANJA, Peter ... 404-627-2681 ... 126 D peter.karanja@beulah.org
KARAS, Gregory ... 617-912-9146 ... 232 C gkaras@bostonconservatory.edu
KARAS, Gregory ... 617-236-8800 ... 234 G gkaras@fisher.edu
KARAS, Jane, A ... 406-756-3800 ... 294 C jkaras@fvcc.edu
KARAS, Jennifer ... 303-871-6793 ... 89 A jkaras@du.edu
KARAS, Tara ... 941-487-5001 ... 120 A tkaras@ncf.edu
KARAS, Tim ... 408-855-5167 ... 78 F tim.karas@wvm.edu
KARASINSKI, Tracy ... 401-825-2402 ... 453 D tkarasinski@ccri.edu
KARBHARI, Vistasp ... 256-824-6335 ... 8 G vistasp.karbhari@uah.edu
KARBOWSKI, Suzane ... 308-635-6067 ... 301 D karbowsk@wncc.edu
KARCHER, Jeff ... 715-346-3901 ... 552 D jkarcher@uwsp.edu
KARCHER, Steve ... 859-985-3130 ... 199 A steve_karcher@berea.edu
KARDAN, Sal ... 213-621-2200 ... 41 F
KARGBO, Mariatu ... 703-212-7410 ... 519 F
KARGES, Teri ... 843-863-7050 ... 456 B tkarges@csuniv.edu
KARICKHOFF, Kelly ... 765-459-0561 ... 176 C karickhoff@ivytech.edu
KARICKHOFF, Michael ... 765-459-0561 ... 176 C mkarickh@ivytech.edu
KARIM, Anwar ... 903-886-5550 ... 498 B anwar.karim@tamuc.edu
KARIM, Mohammad, A ... 757-683-3460 ... 522 F mkarim@odu.edu
KARIMKHANI, Denise ... 254-295-4636 ... 504 C karimkhani@umhb.edu
KARIMPOR, Mehdi ... 562-408-6969 ... 26 I
KARIMPOUR, Mehdi ... 562-408-6969 ... 26 I
KARIUKI, Cheryl ... 601-629-3568 ... 272 F cheryl@alcorn.edu
KARKI, Bhagbat ... 716-888-2336 ... 325 F karkib@canisius.edu
KARL, Debbie ... 325-734-3640 ... 500 G debbie.karl@tstc.edu

KARLBERG, Anne Marie .... 360-383-3302 .... 540 A
amkarlberg@whatcom.ctc.edu

KARLET, Herbert, J .... 304-710-3141 .... 542 K
karlet@mctc.edu

KARLIN, Angela, L .... 660-543-4040 .... 290 H
karlin@ucmo.edu

KARLIN, Barbara, H .... 415-442-7882 .... 48 F
bkarlin@ggu.edu

KARLIN, Bree .... 928-505-3314 .... 16 F
bkarlin@mohave.edu

KARLIN, Craig, E .... 785-628-4408 .... 192 I
ckarlin@fhsu.edu

KARLIN, Jane .... 212-824-2212 .... 335 B
jkarlin@huc.edu

KARLIN, Lisa, M .... 785-628-4232 .... 192 I
lkarlin@fhsu.edu

KARLOFF, Michael .... 402-461-7473 .... 298 A
mkarloff@hastings.edu

KARLOUTSOS, James, D .... 617-850-1290 .... 235 F
jkarloutsos@hchc.edu

KARLSSON, Anette .... 216-687-2558 .... 388 D
a.karlsson@csuohio.edu

KARMANOVA, Tatiana .... 909-537-3986 .... 36 B
tkarma@csusb.edu

KARMIS, Beth .... 312-949-7415 .... 152 E
bkarmis@ico.edu

KARNES, Melinda Ann .... 716-673-3717 .... 352 A
melinda.karnes@fredonia.edu

KARNES, Michael, S .... 585-753-3700 .... 341 H
mkarnes@monroecc.edu

KARNES, Susan, J .... 816-415-5973 .... 293 C
armstrongs@william.jewell.edu

KARNES, Valerie .... 760-384-6258 .... 52 M
vkarnes@cerrocoso.edu

KARNS, Jennifer, E .... 703-416-1441 .... 520 C
jkarns@ipsciences.edu

KARNS, Julie, A .... 609-896-5016 .... 313 F
karns@rider.edu

KARNS, Leslie .... 801-878-1402 .... 303 D
lkarns@roseman.edu

KAROL, Diana .... 903-510-2127 .... 503 A
dkar@tjc.edu

KAROLLE-BERG, Julia .... 216-397-4193 .... 392 L
jkarolle@jcu.edu

KARON, Judith, S .... 218-726-7161 .... 271 F
jkaron@d.umn.edu

KAROW, Thomas, R .... 312-341-3512 .... 163 B
tkarow@roosevelt.edu

KARP, Adam .... 916-484-8050 .... 56 A
karpa@arc.losrios.edu

KARP, David .... 518-580-5779 .... 351 B
dkarp@skidmore.edu

KARP, Emily .... 212-237-8488 .... 327 F
ekarp@jjay.cuny.edu

KARP, Jeff .... 913-234-0634 .... 191 J
jeff.karp@cleveland.edu

KARP, Robert, M .... 518-564-4106 .... 354 B
karprm@plattsburgh.edu

KARP, Roberta .... 518-891-2915 .... 344 E
bkarp@nccc.edu

KARPALO, Nikolay .... 610-526-6012 .... 430 D
facilities@harcum.edu

KARPEL, Michael .... 760-252-2411 .... 30 H
mkarpel@barstow.edu

KARPER, Barbara, M .... 315-445-4530 .... 338 B
karperbm@lemoyne.edu

KARPF, Michael .... 859-323-5126 .... 207 D
mkarpf@uky.edu

KARPOVICH, Jeff, A .... 336-841-9011 .... 365 C
jkarpovi@highpoint.edu

KARPP, Edward .... 818-240-1000 .... 48 D
ekarpp@glendale.edu

KARR, Charles, L .... 205-348-6400 .... 8 E
ckarr@eng.ua.edu

KARR, Forrest .... 906-227-1826 .... 256 C
fkarr@nmu.edu

KARR, Mary .... 414-256-1251 .... 549 D
karrm@mtmary.edu

KARR, Susan .... 281-351-3644 .... 490 E
susan.karr@lonestar.edu

KARRICK, Cathy .... 618-545-3182 .... 155 B
ckarrick@kaskaskia.edu

KARRIKER, W. Keith .... 864-833-8220 .... 460 E
kkarriker@presby.edu

KARRY, Cathy .... 626-396-2321 .... 29 I
cathy.karry@artcenter.edu

KARRY, Cathy .... 313-664-7677 .... 249 E
ckarry@collegeforcreativestudies.edu

KARSHMER, Judith .... 415-422-2959 .... 76 E
jfkarshmer@usfca.edu

KARSON, Kimberly, M .... 330-972-7608 .... 403 B
kmorgan@uakron.edu

KARSTEN, Paul .... 206-517-4541 .... 537 G
pkarsten@siom.edu

KARSTEN, Peter .... 989-729-3431 .... 248 F
pete.karsten@baker.edu

KARSTEN, Suzanne .... 773-477-4822 .... 60 D
skarsten@pacificcollege.edu

KARTHAUSER, Patricia, F .... 402-465-2551 .... 299 H
pkart@nebrwesleyan.edu

KARTJE, Jean, V .... 630-942-4516 .... 148 A
kartjej@cod.edu

KARVIA, Nick .... 714-992-7009 .... 59 E
nkarvia@fullcoll.edu

KARWOCKI, Michele .... 603-271-7140 .... 304 F
mkarwocki@ccsnh.edu

KARWOWSKI, Sharon .... 607-844-8222 .... 357 I
karwows@tc3.edu

KASARGOD, Sameer .... 443-896-5108 .... 19 A
sameer.kasargod@phoenix.edu

KASBOHM, Kristine, E .... 716-888-8407 .... 325 F
kasbohmk@canisius.edu

KASCENSKA, John, R .... 802-626-6346 .... 515 G
john.kascenska@lyndonstate.edu

KASDIN, Robert .... 212-854-9967 .... 330 F
rk2052@columbia.edu

KASDORF, Michael .... 217-234-5431 .... 156 B
mkasdorf@lakeland.cc.il.us

KASE, Robert .... 815-740-3367 .... 167 E
rkase@stfrancis.edu

KASE, Ronald .... 201-684-7287 .... 313 C
rkase@ramapo.edu

KASEM, Shahed .... 773-481-3730 .... 160 D
skasem@nc.edu

KASEY, Jay, D .... 614-293-9701 .... 398 I
kasey.3@osu.edu

KASEY, Tina .... 270-686-2110 .... 199 B
tina.kasey@brescia.edu

KASH, Elizabeth, F .... 516-877-3247 .... 322 A
kash@adelphi.edu

KASHACK, Susan .... 707-664-2122 .... 37 D
susan.kashack@sonoma.edu

KASHIMA, Stephanie .... 408-741-2119 .... 78 G
stephanie.kashima@westvalley.edu

KASHIWADA, Keith .... 808-734-9578 .... 141 J
kashiwad@hawaii.edu

KASHYAP, Rajiv .... 973-720-2964 .... 317 D
kashyapr@wpunj.edu

KASIMATIS, Margaret .... 310-338-3790 .... 56 E
mkasimat@lmu.edu

KASKEL, Beth .... 216-373-5182 .... 397 F
bkaskel@ndc.edu

KASKEL, Roberta .... 504-865-3835 .... 213 F
rekaskel@loyno.edu

KASLER, Brian .... 217-757-1190 .... 322 H
bkasler@funeraleducation.org

KASLYN, SJ, Robert, J .... 202-319-5492 .... 97 E
kaslyn@cua.edu

KASPARI, Brenda .... 701-355-8130 .... 383 H
bkaspari@umary.edu

KASPER, Chet .... 906-248-8431 .... 248 H
ckasper@bmcc.edu

KASPER, Lisa, A .... 973-655-6911 .... 311 F
kasperl@mail.montclair.edu

KASPRZAK, Ken .... 847-947-5575 .... 159 E
kkasprzak@nl.edu

KASSA, Adane .... 231-777-0332 .... 256 A
adane.kassa@muskegoncc.edu

KASSA, Zewdnesh .... 973-877-3107 .... 309 H
zkassa@essex.edu

KASSEBAUM, Denise .... 303-724-7100 .... 88 J
denise.kassebaum@ucdenver.edu

KASSEL, Sarah .... 541-552-6127 .... 419 A
kassels@sou.edu

KASSIMIR, Ronald .... 212-229-8947 .... 342 E
kassimir@newschool.edu

KASSNER, Scott .... 805-893-8000 .... 75 B
skassner@ltsc.ucsb.edu

KASSON, Jeff .... 614-823-1876 .... 400 H
jkasson@otterbein.edu

KASTAN, Shira .... 305-284-2618 .... 122 I
skastan@miami.edu

KASTER, James, D .... 540-458-8720 .... 530 D
jdkaster@wlu.edu

KASTERN, Amanda, A .... 443-412-2345 .... 223 B
akastern@harford.edu

KASTNER, Marc, A .... 617-253-8900 .... 241 D

KASTOR, Lisa .... 330-263-2496 .... 388 F
lkastor@wooster.edu

KASUNIC, Lisa .... 330-966-5460 .... 402 B
lkasunic@starkstate.edu

KASVINSKY, Peter, J .... 330-941-3091 .... 406 F
pjkasvinsky@ysu.edu

KASYAN, Linda .... 910-362-7054 .... 368 H
lkasyan@cfcc.edu

KATCHER, Marcie .... 516-773-5863 .... 558 I
katcherm@usmma.edu

KATCHMAR, Paul .... 314-792-5510 .... 341 E
pkatchmar@mvcc.edu

KATEHI, Linda, P .... 530-752-2065 .... 73 I
chancellor@ucdavis.edu

KATEMAN, Mike .... 573-875-7563 .... 280 A
mwkateman@ccis.edu

KATEN-BAHENSKY, Donna .... 608-263-8025 .... 550 J
dkaten-bahensky@uwhealth.org

KATER, Charles .... 816-584-6567 .... 287 E
charles.kater@park.edu

KATER, Sue .... 480-731-8121 .... 15 D
sue.kater@domail.maricopa.edu

KATES, Donald .... 215-780-1240 .... 446 G
don@salus.edu

KATES, Jonathan, A .... 434-924-3721 .... 525 F
jak7g@virginia.edu

KATES, Kenneth .... 319-356-3155 .... 182 F
ken-kates@uiowa.edu

KATHMAN, Mary Jo .... 513-862-2743 .... 391 E

KATHOL, Diane .... 402-481-8847 .... 296 I
diane.kathol@bryanlgh.org

KATHOL, Lyle, J .... 402-844-7215 .... 299 I
lylek@northeast.edu

KATHURIA, Navneet .... 713-798-4951 .... 481 H
kathuria@bcm.edu

KATINAS, James .... 617-850-1303 .... 235 F
jkatinas@hchc.edu

KATIP, William, J .... 574-372-5100 .... 171 H
bill.katip@grace.edu

KATIS, David, J .... 814-393-1997 .... 442 B
dkatis@clarion.edu

KATKANANT, Chanida .... 201-360-4014 .... 310 E
ckatkanant@hccc.edu

KATO, Stephen .... 908-709-7045 .... 316 B
kato@ucc.edu

KATOS, Demetrios .... 617-850-1253 .... 235 F
dkatos@hchc.edu

KATOSANG, Dahlia, M .... 680-488-2471 .... 560 C
dahliapcc@palaunet.com

KATRENICZ, Laura .... 570-740-0384 .... 435 C
lkatrenicz@luzerne.edu

KATS, Lee .... 310-506-4501 .... 61 H
lee.kats@pepperdine.edu

KATSCHKE, Richard, N .... 414-955-4748 .... 548 G
rkatschk@mcw.edu

KATSIAFICAS, Charles .... 909-621-8016 .... 63 A
charles.katsiaficas@pomona.edu

KATSILOMETES, Bessie .... 208-373-1708 .... 143 H
katsbess@isu.edu

KATSKY, Patricia .... 805-969-3626 .... 60 J
pkatsky@pacifica.edu

KATSOULEAS, Thomas .... 919-660-5386 .... 364 C
tom.katsouleas@duke.edu

KATT, Donald, C .... 845-687-5050 .... 358 E
kattd@sunyulster.edu

KATTELMANN, Dean .... 605-688-4136 .... 466 C
dean.kattelmann@sdstate.edu

KATTERMAN, Sharon .... 708-974-5271 .... 159 B
katterman@morainevalley.edu

KATZ, Avi .... 800-371-6105 .... 16 G
avi@nationalparalegal.edu

KATZ, Ben .... 617-928-4777 .... 242 E
bkatz@mountida.edu

KATZ, Bernard .... 718-782-7070 .... 359 A
bkatz@utsny.edu

KATZ, Brit .... 601-974-1200 .... 275 B
katzrb@millsaps.edu

KATZ, Clifford, H .... 401-874-4402 .... 454 E
chkatz@uri.edu

KATZ, Craig .... 201-200-3022 .... 312 B
ckatz@njcu.edu

KATZ, Daniel .... 301-431-5402 .... 225 B
dkatz@nlc.edu

KATZ, Edward, J .... 828-250-3872 .... 378 D
ekatz@unca.edu

KATZ, Elya .... 718-941-8000 .... 341 A

KATZ, Harry, C .... 607-255-3230 .... 331 B
hck2@cornell.edu

KATZ, Helen .... 309-268-8173 .... 151 I
helen.mckay-katz@heartland.edu

KATZ, Jeffrey .... 270-745-6311 .... 208 A
jeffrey.katz@wku.edu

KATZ, Jeffrey .... 845-758-7501 .... 323 D
katz@bard.edu

KATZ, Jonathan, N .... 626-395-4068 .... 32 H
jkatz@caltech.edu

KATZ, Louis, H .... 202-994-6600 .... 98 C
lkatz@gwu.edu

KATZ, Martin, J .... 303-871-6301 .... 89 A
mkatz@du.edu

KATZ, Matthew .... 909-469-5567 .... 78 I
mkatz@westernu.edu

KATZ, Milton .... 816-802-3373 .... 283 E
mkatz@kcai.edu

KATZ, Paul .... 856-361-2800 .... 314 A
katzp@rowan.edu

KATZ, Saul, W .... 718-368-5051 .... 328 A
bkatz@kbcc.cuny.edu

KATZENMEYER, Scott .... 216-781-9400 .... 388 B
scottk@cie-wc.edu

KATZENMEYER, Scott .... 757-464-4600 .... 530 H
instruct@cie-wc.edu

KATZMAN, Carol .... 212-854-5768 .... 323 E
ckatzman@barnard.edu

KATZMAN, Gerald .... 518-694-7298 .... 322 B
gerald.katzman@acphs.edu

KAUCHER, Ellie .... 800-877-4723 .... 233 A
ellie.kaucher@cambridgecollege.edu

KAUFFMAN, Brad .... 803-799-9082 .... 137 D
bkauffman@southuniversity.edu

KAUFFMAN, Dana .... 703-323-3750 .... 527 F
tkauffman@nvcc.edu

KAUFFMAN, JR., John, M .... 910-893-1776 .... 362 J
kauffmanj@campbell.edu

KAUFFMAN, Peg .... 717-872-3402 .... 443 D
peg.kauffman@millersville.edu

KAUFFMAN, Steve .... 312-369-7383 .... 148 D
skauffman@colum.edu

KAUFFMAN, Wendy .... 910-695-3814 .... 373 H
kauffmanw@sandhills.edu

KAUFFMAN, William, R .... 314-977-3719 .... 289 C
kauffman@slu.edu

KAUFMAN, Angela .... 817-257-7830 .... 499 C
a.kaufman@tcu.edu

KAUFMAN, Daniel, J .... 678-407-5001 .... 130 C
dkaufman@ggc.edu

KAUFMAN, Donald, E .... 812-888-5343 .... 181 D
dkaufman@vinu.edu

KAUFMAN, Geof .... 253-680-7105 .... 531 F
gkaufman@bates.ctc.edu

KAUFMAN, Helena .... 507-222-4349 .... 261 G
hkaufman@carleton.edu

KAUFMAN, Kris, A .... 716-878-3000 .... 353 A
kaufmaka@buffalostate.edu

KAUFMAN, Lon .... 312-413-3450 .... 167 B
lkaufman@uic.edu

KAUFMAN, Norman .... 561-297-3061 .... 119 A
nkaufman@fau.edu

KAUFMAN, Patty .... 517-841-4528 .... 248 D
patty.kaufman@baker.edu

KAUFMAN, Paula .... 217-333-0790 .... 167 D
ptk@illinois.edu

KAUFMAN, Paulette .... 303-751-8700 .... 81 H
kaufman@bel-rea.com

KAUFMAN, Robert .... 724-836-9898 .... 449 C

KAUFMAN, Steven .... 734-462-4400 .... 258 A
skaufman@schoolcraft.edu

KAUFMAN-OSBORN, Timothy .... 509-527-5397 .... 540 B
kaufmatv@whitman.edu

KAUFMANN, Marta .... 215-968-8242 .... 423 F
kaufmann@bucks.edu

KAUFMANN, Nancy, K .... 636-529-0000 .... 288 D
nkaufmann@slchcmail.com

KAUFMANN, Sandra .... 516-876-2715 .... 353 D
kaufmanns@oldwestbury.edu

KAUGARS, Karlis .... 607-436-3663 .... 353 E
karlis.kaugars@oneonta.edu

KAUKE, Donna .... 815-599-3688 .... 152 B
donna.kauke@highland.edu

KAUKUS, Arlene, F .... 716-645-2231 .... 351 G
arleneks@buffalo.edu

KAUL, Gitanjali .... 561-297-1333 .... 119 A
gkaul@fau.edu

KAUL, Terri, S .... 262-243-5700 .... 547 C
terri.kaul@cuw.edu

KAUNITZ, Carol .... 732-255-0400 .... 312 D
ckaunitz@ocean.edu

KAUR, Kuldeep .... 530-741-6700 .... 80 I

KAUS, Annette .... 575-835-5333 .... 319 A
akaus@admin.nmt.edu

KAUS, Cheryl .... 609-652-4512 .... 313 E
cheryl.kaus@stockton.edu

KAUSHAL, Janice .... 312-935-4852 .... 162 G
jkaushal@robertmorris.edu

KAUSHANSKY, Kenneth .... 631-444-9011 .... 352 C
kenneth.kashansky@stonybrook.edu

KAUSHIK, Suresh, C .... 334-420-4244 .... 7 H
skaushik@trenholmstate.edu

KAUTZ, Barbara, K .... 413-748-3222 .... 244 H
bkautz@springfieldcollege.edu

KAUTZ, III, John .... 561-803-2084 .... 114 C
john_kautz@pba.edu

KAUTZ DE ARANGO, Kathy .... 610-341-5870 .... 428 E
kkautz2@eastern.edu

KAVALIER, Barbara .... 408-298-2181 .... 67 D

KAVANAGH, Kathy, J .... 914-594-4487 .... 343 F
kathy_johnston@nymc.edu

KAVANAGH, Kenneth .... 239-590-7007 .... 119 B
kavanagh@fgcu.edu

KAVANAUGH, Maria, A .... 508-565-1331 .... 245 A
mkavanaugh@stonehill.edu

KAVANAUGH, Michael .... 714-484-7108 .... 59 D
mkavanaugh@cypresscollege.edu

KAVANAUGH, Steven .... 610-896-1141 .... 430 G
skavanau@haverford.edu

KAVERMAN, Don .... 314-340-3534 .... 282 F
kavermad@hssu.edu

KAVOURIS, John .... 312-369-8646 .... 148 D
jkavouris@colum.edu

KAVRAN, Elizabeth .... 440-449-2015 .... 405 B
ekavran@ursuline.edu

KAWA, Steve .... 714-628-4717 .... 63 G
kawa_steve@sccollege.edu

KAWAII, Toi .... 415-808-3000 .... 50 D
toi_kawaii@heald.edu

KAWAKAMI, Alice, K .... 323-343-3950 .... 35 D
akawaka@calstatela.edu

KAWAMOTO, Judy .... 401-232-6046 .... 453 C
jkawamot@bryant.edu

KAWANNA, JR., Ronald .... 708-596-2000 .... 164 H
rkawanna@ssc.edu

KAY, Bill .... 800-533-3378 .... 138 F
bkay@uofa.edu

KAY, Carol .... 915-831-2854 .... 486 G
ckay@epcc.edu

KAY, Christine, M .... 337-475-5243 .... 215 G
ckay@mcneese.edu

KAY, James, F .... 609-497-7815 .... 312 F
academic.dean@ptsem.edu

KAY, Kent .... 314-539-5291 .... 288 G
kentkay@stlcc.edu

KAY, R. David .... 570-327-4770 .... 440 L
dkay@pct.edu

KAY, Sabrina .... 213-355-7777 .... 47 J

KAY, Steve, A .... 858-534-4281 ...... 74 F
skay@ucsd.edu
KAY, Steve, A .... 213-740-2531 ...... 76 F
dean@dornsife.usc.edu
KAYE, David .... 209-956-1240 ...... 38 J
dkaye@carrington.edu
KAYE, Deborah, M .... 904-620-2881 .... 120 D
dkaye@unf.edu
KAYE, Ted .... 925-424-1013 ...... 39 D
tkaye@laspositascollege.edu
KAYLOR, Alice, J .... 724-537-4566 .... 446 E
alice.kaylor@email.stvincent.edu
KAYLOR, Sean, P .... 845-575-3000 .... 340 B
sean.kaylor@marist.edu
KAYNAMA, Shohreh .... 410-704-3342 .... 228 E
skaynama@towson.edu
KAYNARD, Meryl .... 718-997-5725 .... 328 E
meryl.kaynard@qc.cuny.edu
KAYNE, Susan, W .... 212-346-1200 .... 345 F
skayne@pace.edu
KAYS, Brenda .... 704-991-0220 .... 374 D
bkays2651@stanly.edu
KAYS, Vernon .... 314-984-7388 .... 289 A
vkays@stlcc.edu
KAYSEN-LUZBETAK,
Angie .... 815-280-6679 .... 154 J
akaysen@jjc.edu
KAZANECKI-KEMPTER,
Diane .... 631-420-2065 .... 356 A
KAZANJIAN, Victor, H .... 781-283-2685 .... 245 E
vkazanji@wellesley.edu
KAZARIAN, Julie .... 508-929-8650 .... 238 G
jkazarian@worcester.edu
KAZDA, Kathleen .... 262-691-5464 .... 555 E
kkazda@wctc.edu
KAZEE, Thomas, A .... 812-488-2151 .... 180 E
president@evansville.edu
KAZEN, James, D .... 210-567-0390 .... 507 A
kazen@uthscsa.edu
KAZEROUNIAN, Kazem ..... 860-486-2221 ...... 94 G
kazem.kazerounian@uconn.edu
KAZIN, Robert .... 315-859-4340 .... 334 H
rkazin@hamilton.edu
KAZLO WATSON, Jaime ... 518-562-4161 .... 329 C
jaime.kazlo@clinton.edu
KAZMAREK, Robin .... 386-822-7315 .... 121 F
rkazmare@stetson.edu
KAZMIR, Darin .... 361-582-2417 .... 508 B
darin.kazmir@victoriacollege.edu
KAZUMA, Clement .... 680-488-2471 .... 560 C
KEA, Jerry .... 707-642-8188 ...... 70 A
thomas.kea@solano.edu
KEACH, Troy .... 507-266-4077 .... 262 E
keach.troy@mayo.edu
KEADY, Thomas, J .... 617-552-6795 .... 232 B
thomas.keady@bc.edu
KEAGY, Thomas, A .... 215-951-1042 .... 432 I
keagy@lasalle.edu
KEAL, Aaron, J .... 620-421-6700 .... 194 G
aaronk@labette.edu
KEALA, David .... 808-675-3572 .... 140 D
david.keala@byuh.edu
KEALEY, Michelle, L .... 814-393-2352 .... 442 B
mkealey@clarion.edu
KEAN, Betsy .... 415-338-2687 ...... 37 B
bkean@sfsu.edu
KEAN, Cheryl .... 269-471-3288 .... 247 D
kean@andrews.edu
KEAN, Linda .... 781-239-4284 .... 230 E
kean@babson.edu
KEANE, James .... 631-851-6520 .... 356 G
keanej@sunysuffolk.edu
KEANE-DAWES,
Jennifer, M .... 410-651-6507 .... 227 E
jmkeanedawes@umes.edu
KEAR, Dennis, J .... 417-836-5254 .... 286 C
denniskear@missouristate.edu
KEARNEY, Anne, E .... 315-445-4195 .... 338 B
kearneae@lemoyne.edu
KEARNEY, Catherine .... 209-468-9155 ...... 72 G
KEARNEY, Janice .... 870-575-8283 ...... 25 B
kearneyj@uapb.edu
KEARNEY, John .... 570-504-7000 .... 425 F
KEARNEY, Joseph, D .... 414-288-1955 .... 548 F
joseph.kearney@marquette.edu
KEARNEY, Margaret .... 585-275-9093 .... 359 B
margaret.kearney@rochester.edu
KEARNS, Amy .... 505-473-6318 .... 320 F
amy.kearns@santafeuniversity.edu
KEARNS, Joanne .... 973-328-5044 .... 309 A
jkearns@ccm.edu
KEARNS, Kevin, P .... 716-673-3335 .... 352 A
kevin.kearns@fredonia.edu
KEARNS, Michael .... 928-757-0801 ...... 16 F
mkearns@mohave.edu
KEARNS, Tom .... 765-983-1200 .... 171 E
kearnto@earlham.edu
KEARNS-BARRETT,
Marybeth .... 508-793-2448 .... 233 C
mkearns@holycross.edu
KEAS, Lenora .... 361-698-1208 .... 485 G
lkeas@delmar.edu
KEASEY, Rosemary, C .... 724-287-8711 .... 423 G
rosemary.keasey@bc3.edu

KEASLER, Robert, L .... 859-238-5451 .... 199 G
robert.keasler@centre.edu
KEASLING, Diane .... 423-461-8968 .... 471 J
dlkeasling@milligan.edu
KEAST, Cindy .... 620-665-3565 .... 193 H
keastc@hutchcc.edu
KEATHLEY, Kenneth .... 919-761-2435 .... 377 A
kkeathley@sebts.edu
KEATHLEY, Naymond .... 254-710-2657 .... 482 A
naymond_keathley@baylor.edu
KEATING, Dana .... 618-252-5400 .... 164 I
dana.keating@sic.edu
KEATING, Frederick .... 856-415-2100 .... 310 D
fkeating@gccnj.edu
KEATING, Jeff .... 909-469-5205 ...... 78 I
jkeating@westernu.edu
KEATING, Joe .... 740-588-1396 .... 400 E
keatingj@ohio.edu
KEATING, Joe .... 740-588-1383 .... 407 A
jkeating@zanestate.edu
KEATING, Kathy .... 616-234-4953 .... 251 E
kkeating@grcc.edu
KEATING, MaryJo .... 860-297-5110 ...... 94 E
maryjo.keating@trincoll.edu
KEATING, Patrick, C .... 605-256-5222 .... 465 I
pat.keating@dsu.edu
KEATING, Patrick, J .... 617-552-3255 .... 232 B
patrick.keating@bc.edu
KEATING, Richard, S .... 413-782-1473 .... 246 A
rkeating@wne.edu
KEATING, Sarah .... 570-945-8112 .... 432 E
sarah.keating@keystone.edu
KEATING, Scott, A .... 215-702-4391 .... 444 B
skeating@pbu.edu
KEATON, Angela .... 423-636-7300 .... 477 A
akeaton@tusculum.edu
KEATON, Kim .... 304-461-3209 .... 541 H
kkeaton@mountainstate.edu
KEATS, Patrick .... 540-636-2900 .... 517 K
pkeats@christendom.edu
KEATY, Anthony .... 781-899-5500 .... 231 F
akeaty@blessedjohnxxiii.edu
KEBAETSE, Masego .... 484-384-2968 .... 438 D
mkebaets@eastern.edu
KEBISEK, Kris .... 503-297-5544 .... 417 G
kkebisek@ocac.edu
KECHICHIAN,
Avedis (Avo) .... 909-593-3511 ...... 75 E
akechichian@laverne.edu
KECK, Amy .... 630-375-8260 .... 162 G
akeck@robertmorris.edu
KECK, David, A .... 434-223-6269 .... 519 G
dkeck@hsc.edu
KECK, Eric .... 802-917-2674 .... 514 B
eric.keck@neci.edu
KECK, Kathleen, A .... 518-327-6223 .... 345 H
kkeck@paulsmiths.edu
KECK, Kay .... 269-965-3931 .... 253 B
keckk@kellogg.edu
KECK, Michael .... 315-279-5267 .... 337 K
mkeck@mail.keuka.edu
KECK, III, Ray, M .... 956-326-2320 .... 497 D
president@tamiu.edu
KECK, Sara, E .... 573-629-3014 .... 282 E
skeck@hlg.edu
KECSKÉS, Gary .... 630-466-7900 .... 168 B
gkecskes@waubonsee.edu
KEDROSKI, Cristie .... 850-729-5357 .... 114 A
kedroskc@nwfsc.edu
KEDROWSKI, Jeff .... 630-617-3042 .... 150 H
jeffk@elmhurst.edu
KEDSKI, Cathy .... 508-830-5042 .... 238 D
ckedski@maritime.edu
KEEBAUGH, Joseph, E .... 920-433-6631 .... 546 D
joe.keebaugh@bellincollege.edu
KEEBLE, Mike .... 913-588-1443 .... 197 C
rkeeble@kumc.edu
KEEBLER, David .... 805-654-6354 ...... 77 F
dkeebler@vcccd.edu
KEECH, Brian .... 215-895-2100 .... 427 H
brian.keech@drexel.edu
KEEDY, Thomas, E .... 765-361-6227 .... 181 E
keedyt@wabash.edu
KEEFE, Kathleen, A .... 724-925-4101 .... 451 E
keefek@wccc.edu
KEEFE, Kevin .... 973-328-5064 .... 309 A
kkeefe@ccm.edu
KEEFE, Maureen .... 617-879-7705 .... 238 B
mkeefe@massart.edu
KEEFE, Maureen, R .... 801-581-8262 .... 511 C
maureen.keefe@nurs.utah.edu
KEEFE, Terri, K .... 610-799-1580 .... 434 D
tkeefe@lccc.edu
KEEFE, Thomas, W .... 972-721-5203 .... 503 B
KEEFE, Tim .... 480-732-7033 ...... 15 E
tim.keefe@cgc.edu
KEEFE, Timothy, C .... 603-535-2206 .... 307 A
timk@plymouth.edu
KEEFER, Elizabeth .... 216-368-4286 .... 386 F
elizabeth.keefer@case.edu
KEEFER, Gary, B .... 724-773-3556 .... 439 A
gbk3@psu.edu
KEEFER, Joey .... 405-946-7799 .... 411 F
joeyk@plattcollege.org

KEEFER, Michael, R .... 814-393-1610 .... 442 B
mkeefer@cuf-inc.org
KEEFER, Sue .... 719-384-6882 ...... 87 A
sue.keefer@ojc.edu
KEEGAN, Kim .... 603-206-8005 .... 304 D
kkeegan@ccsnh.edu
KEEGAN, Michael .... 605-394-2336 .... 466 B
michael.keegan@sdsmt.edu
KEEGAN, Thomas .... 360-416-7997 .... 538 D
thomas.keegan@skagit.edu
KEEHLWETTER, F. Stanley . 724-458-2142 .... 430 B
fskeehlwetter@gcc.edu
KEEHNER, Julia, A .... 304-473-8440 .... 545 G
keehner@wvwc.edu
KEEL, Brooks, A .... 912-478-5211 .... 131 E
bkeel@georgiasouthern.edu
KEEL, Kimberly .... 803-323-2211 .... 463 E
keelk@winthrop.edu
KEELER, Anne, B .... 540-828-5386 .... 517 B
akeeler@bridgewater.edu
KEELER, Chuck .... 860-701-5254 ...... 93 E
keeler_c@mitchell.edu
KEELER, John, T .... 412-624-7605 .... 449 A
keeler@pitt.edu
KEELER, Joseph .... 408-848-4715 ...... 48 C
jkeeler@gavilan.edu
KEELER, Richard .... 951-222-8211 ...... 64 A
richard.keeler@rcc.edu
KEELEY, Brian .... 360-383-3375 .... 540 A
bkeeley@whatcom.ctc.edu
KEELEY, Eileen, M .... 704-894-2422 .... 363 I
eikeeley@davidson.edu
KEELS, Carl .... 301-736-3631 .... 224 A
genekeels@aol.com
KEELY, Donna, J .... 802-626-6344 .... 515 G
donna.keely@lyndonstate.edu
KEEN, Cathy .... 352-395-5829 .... 117 F
cathy.keen@sfcollege.edu
KEEN, Hubert .... 631-420-2239 .... 356 A
hubert.keen@farmingdale.edu
KEEN, Kathryn .... 432-335-6412 .... 492 A
kkeen@odessa.edu
KEEN, Larry .... 910-678-8321 .... 370 E
keenl@faytechcc.edu
KEEN, Russell .... 912-478-1583 .... 131 E
russellkeen@georgiasouthern.edu
KEEN, Suzanne, P .... 540-458-8400 .... 530 D
keens@wlu.edu
KEENAN, Claudia .... 757-446-5208 .... 518 G
keenance@evms.edu
KEENAN, Claudine .... 609-652-3593 .... 313 E
claudine.keenan@stockton.edu
KEENAN, Kathleen .... 617-879-7065 .... 238 B
kkeenan@massart.edu
KEENAN, Robert .... 518-631-9848 .... 358 H
keenanr@uniongraduatecollege.edu
KEENAN, Ruth .... 281-998-6104 .... 493 G
ruth.keenan@sjcd.edu
KEENE, David .... 859-276-4357 .... 206 H
dkeene@sullivan.edu
KEENE, Sheila .... 515-244-4221 .... 181 F
sheilak@aib.edu
KEENER, Barb .... 419-755-4539 .... 397 C
bkeener@ncstatecollege.edu
KEENER, Donna, L .... 940-565-4346 .... 504 D
dkeener@unt.edu
KEENER, Gary, S .... 540-863-2900 .... 526 F
gkeener@dslcc.edu
KEENER, John, F .... 434-947-8367 .... 523 B
jkeener@randolphcollege.edu
KEENER, Roger, E .... 716-375-2354 .... 348 C
rkeener@sbu.edu
KEENEY, Donald .... 512-472-4133 .... 494 F
donald.keeney@ssw.edu
KEENEY, Leroy, M .... 717-815-1360 .... 452 G
lkeeney@ycp.edu
KEENEY, Madonna .... 815-599-3449 .... 152 B
madonna.keeney@highland.edu
KEENEY, Mary Ellen, R ...... 518-587-2100 .... 355 G
maryellen.keeney@esc.edu
KEENEY, Robert .... 919-536-7201 .... 370 C
keeneyr@durhamtech.edu
KEENUM, Mark, E .... 662-325-3221 .... 275 F
president@msstate.edu
KEEP, John .... 609-771-3255 .... 308 F
keep@tcnj.edu
KEEPERS, Beverly, C .... 502-585-7121 .... 206 D
bkeepers@spalding.edu
KEES, Tedd, C .... 517-321-0242 .... 251 G
tkees@glcc.edu
KEESE, Russelle .... 256-761-6132 .... 7 G
rkeese@talladega.edu
KEESECKER, Barbara, A ..... 301-766-3636 .... 223 G
bkeesecker@kaplan.edu
KEESLING, Donna .... 765-993-1341 .... 171 E
keesldo@earlham.edu
KEETER, Brian, C .... 334-844-4650 .... 1 F
bck0001@auburn.edu
KEETER, Howell, W .... 417-690-2370 .... 279 J
hkeeter@cofo.edu
KEETER, Tara .... 252-536-6223 .... 371 B
keetert@halifaxcc.edu
KEETON, Cheryl, L .... 919-866-5611 .... 374 H
clkeeton@waketech.edu

KEETON, James, E .... 601-984-1010 .... 277 E
jkeeton@umc.edu
KEETON, Kristi .... 913-971-3544 .... 195 D
kkeeton@mnu.edu
KEETON, Tim .... 913-971-3607 .... 195 D
tkeeton@mnu.edu
KEGEL, Gregory .... 406-265-3740 .... 295 E
kegel@msun.edu
KEGELMAN, Nancy .... 732-224-2221 .... 308 A
nkegelman@brookdalecc.edu
KEGLER, Jason .... 620-431-2820 .... 195 E
jkegler@neosho.edu
KEHL, Maria .... 760-922-8714 ...... 61 C
mkehl@paloverde.edu
KEHLE, Paul .... 315-781-3304 .... 335 F
kehle@hws.edu
KEHLER, Bill .... 406-657-1140 .... 296 C
kehlerb@rocky.edu
KEHOE, Clare .... 718-940-5579 .... 349 A
ckehoe@sjcny.edu
KEHOE, Clare .... 718-940-5579 .... 349 B
ckehoe@sjcny.edu
KEHOE, Joseph .... 925-631-4286 ...... 64 F
jkehoe@stmarys-ca.edu
KEHOE, Robert, J .... 585-395-2226 .... 352 F
rkehoe@brockport.edu
KEHOE, Sharon, A .... 208-882-2536 .... 144 G
skehoe@uidaho.edu
KEHRBERG, Robert .... 828-227-7028 .... 380 A
rkehrberg@wcu.edu
KEHRER, Sharon, K .... 636-227-2100 .... 284 B
sharon.kehrer@logan.edu
KEHRES, Larry, T .... 330-823-4880 .... 404 C
kehreslt@mountunion.edu
KEIFER, SuzAnne .... 972-882-7520 .... 498 B
suzanne.keifer@tamuc.edu
KEIFFER, Connie .... 304-734-6606 .... 542 H
ckeiffer@bridgemont.edu
KEIGHER, Craig .... 815-802-8402 .... 155 A
ckeigher@kcc.edu
KEILERS, Vikki .... 903-233-4141 .... 490 A
vikkikeilers@letu.edu
KEILITZ, Craig, D .... 336-841-9057 .... 365 C
ckeilitz@highpoint.edu
KEILLER, James, B .... 404-627-2681 .... 126 D
james.keiller@beulah.org
KEILLOR, Robin .... 503-352-2081 .... 419 E
keillor@pacificu.edu
KEILSON, Suzanne .... 410-617-2608 .... 223 I
skeilson@loyola.edu
KEIM, Barbara .... 636-922-8573 .... 288 B
bkeim@stchas.edu
KEIM, Barry, A .... 772-462-4705 .... 111 B
bkeim@irsc.edu
KEIM, Howard .... 620-327-8233 .... 193 E
howardk@hesston.edu
KEIN, Chris .... 207-948-9283 .... 219 H
ckein@unity.edu
KEIRN, Christy, C .... 870-508-6107 ...... 20 E
ckeirn@asumh.edu
KEIRSTEAD, Carol, A .... 864-242-5100 .... 455 E
KEISER, Arthur .... 954-776-4476 .... 112 E
artk@keiseruniversity.edu
KEISER, Pamela, G .... 570-577-1238 .... 423 E
pamela.keiser@bucknell.edu
KEISER, Sue, T .... 662-915-7111 .... 277 D
stkeiser@olemiss.edu
KEISER, Thomas .... 757-479-3706 .... 517 H
tkeiser@baptistseminary.edu
KEISLER, Ruben .... 501-337-5000 ...... 21 D
rkeisler@coto.edu
KEISLING, Bruce, L .... 502-897-4807 .... 206 C
bkeisling@sbts.edu
KEISLING, Kristin .... 765-289-2291 .... 176 B
kkeisling@ivytech.edu
KEISTER, Shaun, B .... 530-754-4438 ...... 73 I
sbkeister@ucdavis.edu
KEITA, Alma, G .... 229-931-2708 .... 131 F
alma.keita@gsw.edu
KEITES, Jim .... 352-395-5536 .... 117 F
jim.keites@sfcollege.edu
KEITGES, David .... 513-529-5623 .... 396 E
dkeitges@muohio.edu
KEITH, C. David .... 478-301-5639 .... 134 A
keith_cd@mercer.edu
KEITH, Colleen, P .... 864-587-4236 .... 461 D
keithc@smcsc.edu
KEITH, Dana, S .... 205-348-4530 .... 8 E
dkeith@fa.ua.edu
KEITH, Edwin, M .... 662-325-2513 .... 275 F
ekeith@saffairs.msstate.edu
KEITH, Heather .... 908-709-7514 .... 316 B
keith@ucc.edu
KEITH, Jamie, L .... 352-392-1358 .... 120 C
jlkeith@ufl.edu
KEITH, Jeffrey .... 813-626-8008 ...... 99 G
jeffrey.keith@strayer.edu
KEITH, Jeffrey, D .... 801-422-4331 .... 509 H
jeff_keith@byu.edu
KEITH, Joe .... 704-825-6272 .... 370 G
keith.joe@gaston.edu
KEITH, Lisa, M .... 706-233-7250 .... 137 A
lkeith@shorter.edu

KEITH, Marcia .... 219-473-4375.... 170 G
mkeith@ccsj.edu
KEITH, Nancy .... 806-291-3766.... 508 E
keithn@wbu.edu
KEITH, Paul, D .... 832-252-4603.... 483 C
paul.keith@cbshouston.edu
KEITH, Paula, S .... 618-536-3471.... 165 A
pkeith@siu.edu
KEITH, Shelby, C .... 318-797-5221.... 213 D
shelby.keith@lsus.edu
KEITH, Shena .... 312-915-7283.... 157 C
smcnama@luc.edu
KEIZS, Marcia, V .... 718-262-2350.... 329 A
mkeizs@york.cuny.edu
KELAHER, James, E .... 713-798-7880.... 481 H
jkelaher@bcm.edu
KELCHNER, Dana .... 660-596-7250.... 290 B
dkelchner@sfccmo.edu
KELCHNER, Loretta, L .... 660-263-3900.... 279 F
lkelchner@cccb.edu
KELCHNER, Mark .... 660-596-7402.... 290 B
mkelchner@sfccmo.edu
KELEDEI, Raymond, F .... 401-841-6594.... 558 B
KELEMAN, Frank .... 517-629-0236.... 247 A
fkeleman@albion.edu
KELEMEN, Mary, E .... 206-546-4733.... 538 C
mkelemen@shoreline.edu
KELEMEN, Paul .... 972-273-3590.... 485 C
pkelemen@dcccd.edu
KELIN, Shebon .... 303-861-1151...... 84 B
skelin@concorde.edu
KELL, Christine .... 814-866-8169.... 433 C
ckell@lecom.edu
KELL, Gwen .... 707-256-7335...... 58 F
gkell@napavalley.edu
KELLAM, James, W .... 410-651-6174.... 227 E
jwkellam@umes.edu
KELLAR, Deborah .... 303-762-6881...... 84 D
debbie.kellar@denverseminary.edu
KELLAR, Katharine, E .... 724-653-2221.... 427 G
kkellar@dec.edu
KELLAR, Michelle .... 641-628-7523.... 183 D
kellarm@central.edu
KELLAR, Patricia, L .... 570-208-5845.... 432 G
plkellar@kings.edu
KELLARIS, William .... 540-338-1776.... 522 G
KELLEHER, Audrey .... 877-804-1424.... 273 C
akelleher@belhaven.edu
KELLEHER, Erin, C .... 978-665-3151.... 237 E
ekelleher@fitchburgstate.edu
KELLEHER, Maureen, E .... 617-373-2333.... 243 F
KELLEHER, Paul, D .... 212-749-2802.... 339 I
pkelleher@msmnyc.edu
KELLEHER, William, J .... 413-782-1288.... 246 A
bkelleher@wne.edu
KELLEN, Jim .... 251-405-7086...... 2 C
jkellen@bishop.edu
KELLEN, Vincent, J .... 859-257-3609.... 207 D
vkellen@uky.edu
KELLENBENZ, Joe .... 215-780-1402.... 446 G
jkellenbenz@salus.edu
KELLEPOURIS, Nikos .... 913-971-3687.... 195 D
nskellepouris@mnu.edu
KELLER, Alison .... 248-218-2268.... 257 D
akeller@rc.edu
KELLER, Bill .... 718-368-5028.... 328 A
bkeller@kbcc.cuny.edu
KELLER, Bruce .... 215-572-2922.... 422 C
kellerb@arcadia.edu
KELLER, Chaim, D .... 773-463-7738.... 165 H
KELLER, Charlotte .... 928-757-0852...... 16 F
ckeller@mohave.edu
KELLER, Christopher, J .... 570-389-4740.... 441 F
ckeller@bloomu.edu
KELLER, Cindy .... 276-656-0337.... 527 G
ckeller@patrickhenry.edu
KELLER, David .... 248-218-2150.... 257 D
dkeller@rc.edu
KELLER, Donald, G .... 716-829-7675.... 332 E
kellerd@dyc.edu
KELLER, Harrison .... 512-232-8277.... 505 D
harrison.keller@austin.utexas.edu
KELLER, Heather .... 573-288-6570.... 280 I
hkeller@culver.edu
KELLER, James .... 650-306-3238...... 67 F
kellerj@smccd.edu
KELLER, Joe .... 661-362-2226...... 56 G
jkeller@masters.edu
KELLER, John .... 413-265-2210.... 233 D
kellerj@elms.edu
KELLER, John, C .... 319-335-2142.... 182 F
john-keller@uiowa.edu
KELLER, Jonathan .... 617-994-6941.... 236 D
jkeller@bhe.mass.edu
KELLER, Kara .... 828-398-7870.... 368 B
kkeller@abtech.edu
KELLER, Kathleen .... 402-474-5315.... 298 C
kkeller@kaplanuniversity.edu
KELLER, Kerri, D .... 785-532-6506.... 194 D
kdkeller@ksu.edu
KELLER, Kristina .... 320-308-5538.... 269 B
kkeller@sctcc.edu
KELLER, Linda, B .... 270-852-3110.... 204 A
lkeller@kwc.edu
KELLER, Lise, K .... 336-334-5243.... 379 B
lise_keller@uncg.edu
KELLER, Marlon, D .... 215-699-5700.... 433 G
mkeller@lsb.edu
KELLER, Mary .... 732-255-0400.... 312 D
mkeller@ocean.edu
KELLER, Michael, A .... 650-723-5553...... 71 G
michael.keller@stanford.edu
KELLER, Michael, J .... 605-677-5455.... 465 G
mike.keller@usd.edu
KELLER, Mike .... 325-236-8253.... 500 G
mike.keller@tstc.edu
KELLER, Peter .... 570-662-4804.... 443 C
pkeller@mansfield.edu
KELLER, Rebecca .... 518-262-8105.... 322 D
kellerr@mail.amc.edu
KELLER, Robert .... 970-491-5679...... 83 F
robert.keller@colostate.edu
KELLER, Robert, G .... 513-529-7000.... 396 E
kellerrg@muohio.edu
KELLER, Scott .... 815-280-2775.... 154 J
skeller@jjc.edu
KELLER, Scott .... 610-358-4547.... 437 D
kellersc@neumann.edu
KELLER, Stephen, H .... 413-755-4440.... 241 B
keller@stcc.edu
KELLER, Susan .... 714-459-1141...... 78 H
skeller@wsulaw.edu
KELLER, Tammy, S .... 270-686-4246.... 199 B
tammy.keller@brescia.edu
KELLER, Thomas .... 636-227-2100.... 284 B
thomas.keller@logan.edu
KELLER, Travis .... 740-392-6868.... 396 I
travis.keller@mvnu.edu
KELLER, Wayne .... 818-240-1000...... 48 D
wkeller@glendale.edu
KELLER-RABER, Candace .. 407-355-4809.... 104 K
ckeller-raber@devry.edu
KELLERER, Eric, J .... 208-467-8350.... 144 E
ejkellerer@nnu.edu
KELLERHOUSE, James .... 518-445-3209.... 322 C
jkell@albanylaw.edu
KELLERSBERGER, Gail .... 713-221-8047.... 503 F
kellersbergerg@uhd.edu
KELLETT, Chris .... 206-726-5180.... 533 D
ckellett@cornish.edu
KELLETT, Earle .... 706-233-7821.... 137 A
ekellett@shorter.edu
KELLETT, Lucas, C .... 207-778-7344.... 220 C
luke.kellett@maine.edu
KELLEY, Amber, L .... 512-223-2012.... 481 B
amberk@austincc.edu
KELLEY, Aundrea .... 617-994-6979.... 236 D
akelley@bhe.mass.edu
KELLEY, Bev .... 620-241-0723.... 191 I
bev.kelley@centralchristian.edu
KELLEY, Brenda .... 334-214-4815...... 2 F
brenda.kelley@cv.edu
KELLEY, JR., Charles, S ... 504-282-4455.... 213 H
ckelley@nobts.edu
KELLEY, Cindy .... 304-766-3248.... 542 J
ckelley@kvctc.edu
KELLEY, Danny, R .... 926-261-3180.... 496 G
drkelley@pvamu.edu
KELLEY, Debbie, D .... 417-625-9805.... 286 B
kelley-d@mssu.edu
KELLEY, Ella .... 225-771-4845.... 214 I
ella_kelley@aol.com
KELLEY, Ella .... 225-771-2360.... 214 I
ella_kelley@subr.edu
KELLEY, Gary, D .... 806-651-3451.... 499 A
gkelley@mail.wtamu.edu
KELLEY, Gary, F .... 978-232-2048.... 234 D
gkelley@endicott.edu
KELLEY, Gloria .... 704-330-6441.... 369 D
gloria.kelley@cpcc.edu
KELLEY, Holly .... 904-743-1122.... 112 B
hkelley@jones.edu
KELLEY, James, W .... 336-633-0049.... 373 A
jwkelley@randolph.edu
KELLEY, Jan .... 541-485-1780.... 417 E
jankelley@newhope.edu
KELLEY, Jane .... 518-737-3622.... 334 D
jkelley@fmcc.suny.edu
KELLEY, Jeanne .... 617-353-3565.... 232 E
jkelley@bu.edu
KELLEY, Katherine, M .... 423-439-4224.... 473 F
kelleyk@etsu.edu
KELLEY, Kathleen .... 860-253-3011...... 91 B
kkelley@asnuntuck.edu
KELLEY, Kelvin, J .... 325-670-5898.... 487 F
kjkelley@hsutx.edu
KELLEY, Kevin .... 417-328-1536.... 290 A
kkelley@sbuniv.edu
KELLEY, Kim .... 706-754-7726.... 135 A
kkelley@northgatech.edu
KELLEY, Kimberly .... 309-268-8057.... 151 I
kim.kelley@heartland.edu
KELLEY, Kimberly .... 262-595-2553.... 552 A
kelleyk@uwp.edu
KELLEY, Larry .... 252-985-5281.... 375 E
lkelley@ncwc.edu
KELLEY, Laurie, C .... 503-943-8332.... 420 G
kelleyl@up.edu
KELLEY, Lawrence, R .... 805-756-2171...... 33 I
lkelley@calpoly.edu
KELLEY, Lisa .... 859-622-2101.... 200 J
lisa.kelley@eku.edu
KELLEY, Marie, N .... 225-768-1789.... 214 C
mkelley@ololcollege.edu
KELLEY, Meredith .... 530-898-4113...... 34 C
makelley@csuchico.edu
KELLEY, Michael .... 402-280-2733.... 297 F
michaelk@creighton.edu
KELLEY, Mildred .... 972-860-4195.... 484 G
mkelley1@dcccd.edu
KELLEY, Richard, D .... 631-656-2130.... 334 B
rkelley@ftc.edu
KELLEY, Ritch .... 570-586-2400.... 422 G
rkelley@bbc.edu
KELLEY, Robert, O .... 701-777-2121.... 381 F
robert.kelley@und.edu
KELLEY, Rosa .... 646-312-2050.... 326 C
rosa.kelley@baruch.cuny.edu
KELLEY, Scott, C .... 512-499-4560.... 505 B
skelley@utsystem.edu
KELLEY, Susan .... 717-531-5665.... 440 A
sqk6@psu.edu
KELLEY, Sylvia .... 541-552-6127.... 419 A
kelleysy@sou.edu
KELLEY, Thomas .... 508-626-4614.... 238 A
tkelley@framingham.edu
KELLEY, Todd .... 262-551-5900.... 546 I
tkelley@carthage.edu
KELLEY, Tom .... 301-934-7822.... 222 C
tkelley@csmd.edu
KELLEY, Zachary .... 315-655-7174.... 325 H
jzkelley@cazenovia.edu
KELLEY-WINDERS,
Anna Faye .... 228-897-4360.... 275 E
annafaye.kelley@mgccc.edu
KELLIHER, Marsha, C .... 512-448-8593.... 493 E
marshak@stedwards.edu
KELLLY, Sarah, M .... 937-327-7800.... 406 B
smkelly@wittenberg.edu
KELLO, Christopher .... 209-228-4104...... 74 D
ckello@ucmerced.edu
KELLOGG, Angie .... 715-346-4323.... 552 D
akellogg@uwsp.edu
KELLOGG, Dan .... 715-346-2046.... 552 D
dkellogg@uwsp.edu
KELLOGG, Gary .... 530-221-4275...... 69 C
gkellogg@shasta.edu
KELLOGG, John .... 612-625-3387.... 272 A
j-kell@umn.edu
KELLOGG, Leslie .... 269-927-8167.... 253 G
souden@lakemichigancollege.edu
KELLOGG, Magy .... 802-831-1232.... 515 B
mkellogg@vermontlaw.edu
KELLOGG, Magy .... 802-831-1265.... 515 B
mkellogg@vermontlaw.edu
KELLOGG, Tonia .... 405-585-5802.... 409 D
tonia.kellogg@okbu.edu
KELLOGG-BRADLEY,
Polly .... 507-288-4563.... 263 B
pkelloggbradley@crossroadscollege.edu
KELLOGG PITTMAN,
Tiffany .... 804-204-1218.... 516 J
tpittman@btsr.edu
KELLOUGH, Stephen, B .... 630-752-5087.... 168 H
stephen.kellough@wheaton.edu
KELLY, Alan, J .... 516-463-5027.... 335 G
alan.j.kelly@hofstra.edu
KELLY, Anita .... 484-664-3178.... 437 C
akelly@muhlenberg.edu
KELLY, Anna .... 401-739-5000.... 453 G
akelly@neit.edu
KELLY, Annice .... 312-369-8171.... 148 D
akelly@colum.edu
KELLY, Audrey .... 908-737-7000.... 311 A
aukelly@kean.edu
KELLY, OSB, Augustine .... 603-641-7250.... 305 G
akelly@anselm.edu
KELLY, Barbara .... 334-386-7299...... 3 G
bkelly@faulkner.edu
KELLY, Benji .... 270-789-5211.... 199 F
jbkelly@campbellsville.edu
KELLY, Bill .... 570-702-8984.... 431 L
bkelly@johnson.edu
KELLY, Brendan, B .... 850-474-2332.... 121 D
bkelly@uwf.edu
KELLY, Brian .... 508-541-1622.... 233 G
bkelly@dean.edu
KELLY, Brian .... 805-525-4417...... 72 I
bkelly@thomasaquinas.edu
KELLY, Brian .... 510-780-4500...... 53 J
KELLY, Cassandra .... 503-228-6528.... 414 E
KELLY, Chris .... 620-235-4122.... 196 C
ckelly@pittstate.edu
KELLY, OSB, David .... 724-805-2644.... 446 E
david.kelly@email.stvincent.edu
KELLY, Dennis, M .... 610-902-8554.... 424 B
dmk323@cabrini.edu
KELLY, Diane .... 312-225-6288.... 167 G
dkelly@vandercook.edu
KELLY, Donald .... 901-272-5796.... 471 D
dkelly@mca.edu
KELLY, Edward, J .... 423-439-8550.... 473 F
kellye@etsu.edu
KELLY, Eleanor, A .... 302-477-2273...... 97 B
eakelly@widener.edu
KELLY, Evelyn .... 252-527-6223.... 371 G
ekelly@lenoircc.edu
KELLY, Gary, E .... 781-891-2360.... 231 D
gkelly@bentley.edu
KELLY, George .... 610-282-1100.... 427 A
george.kelly@desales.edu
KELLY, George, N .... 615-327-6800.... 471 C
gkelly@mmc.edu
KELLY, Grace, A .... 802-654-2568.... 514 D
gkelly@smcvt.edu
KELLY, Hank .... 740-420-5924.... 398 D
hkelly@ohiochristian.edu
KELLY, Heather, A .... 302-831-2021...... 96 I
hkelly@udel.edu
KELLY, Jack .... 617-732-2143.... 241 C
jack.kelly@mcphs.edu
KELLY, Jack .... 717-262-2013.... 452 C
jkelly@wilson.edu
KELLY, James .... 650-543-3860...... 57 B
jkelly@menlo.edu
KELLY, RET., James .... 401-841-3674.... 558 B
KELLY, Jamie .... 617-989-4668.... 245 F
kellyj8@wit.edu
KELLY, Jane .... 585-389-2320.... 342 D
jkelly5@naz.edu
KELLY, Janet, H .... 478-988-6800.... 134 C
jkelly@middlegatech.edu
KELLY, Jeff .... 515-964-6630.... 183 H
jjkelly@dmacc.edu
KELLY, Jeffrey, M .... 443-352-4012.... 226 E
jkelly@stevenson.edu
KELLY, Jennifer .... 516-686-1254.... 343 D
jkelly16@nyit.edu
KELLY, Jennifer .... 412-261-2647.... 432 D
jennifer.kelly@kaplan.edu
KELLY, JR., John, W .... 864-656-3015.... 456 E
jkelly@clemson.edu
KELLY, Judith .... 518-454-5211.... 330 C
kellyj@strose.edu
KELLY, Karen .... 334-291-4938...... 2 F
karen.kelly@cv.edu
KELLY, Kathryn .... 973-596-3305.... 312 C
kelly@njit.edu
KELLY, Kathy .... 513-244-4418.... 388 E
kathy_kelly@mail.msj.edu
KELLY, Kevin .... 413-545-0222.... 236 F
kk@admissions.umass.edu
KELLY, Kevin .... 207-221-8732.... 218 C
kkelly@kaplan.edu
KELLY, Kevin, P .... 860-701-5079...... 93 E
kelly_k@mitchell.edu
KELLY, Kevin, R .... 937-229-3557.... 404 A
kellyker@udayton.edu
KELLY, Kristi .... 815-836-5332.... 156 F
kellykr@lewisu.edu
KELLY, Leslie, E .... 207-834-7522.... 220 D
lesliek@maine.edu
KELLY, Lois, M .... 805-756-5893...... 33 I
lkelly@calpoly.edu
KELLY, Louise .... 615-230-3400.... 476 C
louise.kelly@volstate.edu
KELLY, Lyn .... 585-475-2946.... 347 G
lyn.kelly@rit.edu
KELLY, M. Genevra .... 864-833-2820.... 460 E
gkelly@presby.edu
KELLY, Marcia, J .... 603-646-3113.... 304 J
marcia.j.kelly@dartmouth.edu
KELLY, DC, Margaret, J .... 718-990-6470.... 348 G
kellymj@stjohns.edu
KELLY, Margaret, S .... 215-637-7700.... 431 A
mkelly@holyfamily.edu
KELLY, Marisa .... 607-274-3113.... 336 G
provost@ithaca.edu
KELLY, Marjorie .... 518-743-2257.... 355 D
kellym@sunyacc.edu
KELLY, Mark .... 269-927-8100.... 253 G
mkelly@lakemichigancollege.edu
KELLY, Mark .... 312-369-7650.... 148 D
mkelly@colum.edu
KELLY, Mark, L .... 864-294-2151.... 458 E
mark.kelly@furman.edu
KELLY, Mary Ellen .... 413-775-1335.... 239 E
kelly@gcc.mass.edu
KELLY, Mary Knopp .... 914-674-7809.... 340 F
mkkelly@mercy.edu
KELLY, Matt .... 614-287-2437.... 389 A
mkelly@cscc.edu
KELLY, Matthew .... 740-364-9644.... 386 H
mkelly@cotc.edu
KELLY, Matthew .... 908-852-1400.... 308 E
kellym@centenarycollege.edu
KELLY, Maureen .... 617-879-7365.... 238 B
mkelly@massart.edu
KELLY, Michael .... 810-762-0455.... 255 G
michael.kelly@mcc.edu
KELLY, Michelle .... 608-663-3256.... 547 F
registrar@edgewood.edu
KELLY, Mike .... 970-339-6509...... 81 A
mike.kelly@aims.edu
KELLY, Mike .... 360-538-4011.... 534 G
mkelly@ghc.edu

KENNON, John (Gil) 573-518-2127 285 I
gil@mineralarea.edu
KENNON, Paul 314-340-3351 282 F
kennonp@hssu.edu
KENNY, Cathleen 845-569-3210 342 A
cathleen.kenny@msmc.edu
KENNY, Dan 810-985-7000 248 G
dan.kenny@baker.edu
KENNY, Ed, N 540-863-2880 526 F
ekenny@dslcc.edu
KENNY, Eddie 352-588-8994 116 G
edmond.kenny@saintleo.edu
KENNY, Keith (Dallas) 308-865-8246 300 F
kennyd2@unk.edu
KENNY, Kevin 925-288-5800 49 H
kevin_kenny@heald.edu
KENNY, Maureen, E 617-552-4030 232 B
maureen.kenny@bc.edu
KENNY, Mike 219-473-4341 170 G
mkenny@ccsj.edu
KENNY, Robert 732-987-2416 310 C
kennyr@georgian.edu
KENNY, Shirley 706-737-1440 125 G
KENT, Caryn 518-244-2391 348 A
kentc@sage.edu
KENT, David 414-277-7350 549 C
kent@msoe.edu
KENT, Jonathan 607-431-4116 335 A
kentj@hartwick.edu
KENT, Leigh 360-992-2101 532 F
lkent@clark.edu
KENT, Linda 425-249-4758 538 G
linda.kent@tlc.edu
KENT, Ronald, H 313-577-3398 260 A
ad0831@wayne.edu
KENT, Tom 518-793-5250 355 D
kentt@sunyacc.edu
KENT-DAVIS, Linda, S 401-456-8031 454 A
lkent@ric.edu
KENT-HUMMEL, Deena 937-769-1851 384 B
dkent@antioch.edu
KENTON, Jay 541-737-3646 418 B
jay_kenton@ous.edu
KENTOPP, Timothy 803-780-1219 463 C
tkentopp@voorhees.edu
KENWORTHY, Anne, H 901-321-4213 467 I
akenwort@cbu.edu
KENYON, Charles, B 716-878-4618 353 A
kenyoncb@buffalostate.edu
KENYON, Kevin, S 765-285-8988 169 G
kkenyon@bsu.edu
KENYON, Steven 508-678-2811 239 B
steve.kenyon@bristolcc.edu
KENYON, JR., Thomas, W 732-235-9619 316 C
kenyontw@umdnj.edu
KENZOR, Jennifer 812-877-8217 179 B
jennifer.seddelmeyer@rose-hulman.edu
KEOHANE, Edward, J 508-856-2900 237 C
edward.keohane@umassmed.edu
KEOHANE, Ellen, J 508-793-2477 233 C
ekeohane@holycross.edu
KEON, Thomas, L 219-989-2203 178 K
thomas.keon@purduecal.edu
KEOUGH, Edward 718-862-7178 339 H
edward.keough@manhattan.edu
KEOUGH, Patrick, J 252-222-6257 369 A
pjk@carteret.edu
KEOUGH, Vicki, A 708-216-3582 157 C
vkeough@luc.edu
KEPHART, Kevin 605-688-5642 466 C
kevin.kephart@sdstate.edu
KEPHAS, Kalwin 691-370-3191 559 D
dirksa@comfsm.fm
KEPIC, Paul 214-570-0100 509 A
pkepic@westwood.edu
KEPIC, Paul 817-547-9600 509 B
pkepic@westwood.edu
KEPLAN, Cary 415-808-3000 50 D
cary_kaplan@heald.edu
KEPPLE, JR., Thomas, R 814-641-3101 432 A
kepplet@juniata.edu
KEPPLER, Kurt, J 225-578-3607 212 H
kkeppler@lsu.edu
KEPPNER, Dana 217-228-5432 161 F
keppnda@quincy.edu
KERBAUGH, Jon 303-837-0825 81 F
KERBS, Nancy 417-667-8181 280 E
nkerbs@cottey.edu
KERBUSCH, William 440-826-2233 384 K
bkerbusc@bw.edu
KERBY, Debra 660-785-4346 290 G
dkerby@truman.edu
KERDA, Stephen, J 202-231-3068 557 J
stephen.kerda@dodiis.mil
KERDOLFF, Russell, A 859-572-6455 205 H
kerdolff@nku.edu
KERESTLY, Ed 325-674-2546 478 I
ed.kerestly@acu.edu
KERFELD, Sally 320-222-5977 268 G
sally.kerfeld@ridgewater.edu
KERICH, Julie, A 717-358-4743 429 F
julie.kerich@fandm.edu
KERKAERT, Debra 507-537-6093 269 E
deb.kerkaert@smsu.edu

KERKER, R. Michael 512-471-2694 505 D
mkerker@austin.utexas.edu
KERKHOFF, Tom 217-540-3555 156 B
tkerkhof@lakeland.cc.il.us
KERLEY, Jim 850-872-3800 110 H
jkerley@gulfcoast.edu
KERLIN, Julia, M 404-413-1405 131 G
jkerlin1@gsu.edu
KERLIN, Matthew, S 205-726-2825 6 G
mskerlin@samford.edu
KERLIN, Scott 415-433-9200 68 F
skerlin@saybrook.edu
KERMAN, Lucy, E 215-895-2123 427 H
lucy.e.kerman@drexel.edu
KERMAN, Ron 615-297-7545 467 A
kermanr@aquinascollege.edu
KERMES, Anita 916-278-6082 36 A
anita.kermes@csus.edu
KERN, Philip, A 859-323-3775 207 D
philip.kern@uky.edu
KERN, Ralph, M 208-496-9510 143 A
kernr@byui.edu
KERN-SIMIRENKO, Cheryl 330-972-7495 403 B
cks7@uakron.edu
KERNAGIS, Ken 505-566-3299 320 D
kernagisk@sanjuancollege.edu
KERNAN, William 503-838-8154 419 C
kernanb@wou.edu
KERNEK, Lee 407-823-3812 120 B
lee.kernek@ucf.edu
KERNER, Kelly 207-725-3808 217 E
kkerner@bowdoin.edu
KERNER, Kelly, K 207-725-3808 217 E
kkerner@bowdoin.edu
KERNER, Martha 608-262-0063 550 J
mkerner@bussvc.wisc.edu
KERNICK, Rhonda 432-264-5101 488 B
rkernick@howardcollege.edu
KERNIN, Richard, P 716-286-8044 344 D
rpk@niagara.edu
KERNS, Connie, M 620-792-9273 190 H
kernsc@bartonccc.edu
KERNS, John 858-598-1200 30 D
jkerns@aii.edu
KERNS, Michael 209-954-5632 66 D
mkerns@deltacollege.edu
KERP, Lauri 860-444-8308 558 H
bookstore@uscga.edu
KERR, Andre 864-592-4774 461 C
kerra@sccsc.edu
KERR, Anne, B 863-680-4100 109 E
akerr@flsouthern.edu
KERR, Barbara 360-992-2921 532 F
bkerr@clark.edu
KERR, Chad 620-241-0723 191 I
chad.kerr@centralchristian.edu
KERR, Colleen 206-219-2408 539 D
colleen.kerr@wsu.edu
KERR, Greg 620-278-4217 196 H
gkerr@sterling.edu
KERR, James, M 419-995-8890 399 B
kerr.63@osu.edu
KERR, John 251-414-3203 7 E
jkerr@shc.edu
KERR, Johnathan, C 706-886-6831 138 D
jkerr@tfc.edu
KERR, Jon 360-442-2531 535 I
jkerr@lowercolumbia.edu
KERR, Marcus 817-531-4237 502 C
mkerr@txwes.edu
KERR, Mary, E 216-368-2544 386 F
mary.kerr@case.edu
KERR, Samuel 605-721-5214 464 H
skerr@national.edu
KERR, Shelly, K 541-346-3227 419 B
skerr@uoregon.edu
KERR, Steve 216-391-6937 387 B
skerr@chancelloru.edu
KERR, Steve 801-626-7587 511 G
skerr1@weber.edu
KERR, Steven 216-391-6937 387 B
cuprovost@chancelloru.edu
KERRICK, Sandra 804-751-9191 524 A
skerrick@rsht.edu
KERRIGAN, John, E 408-554-4968 68 C
jekerrigan@scu.edu
KERRIGAN, JR., John, F 503-883-2443 416 H
kerrigan@linfield.edu
KERRIGAN, Patrick, G 608-796-3041 553 C
pgkerrigan@viterbo.edu
KERRIS, Debra 941-554-1553 101 A
dkerris@argosy.edu
KERSCHNER, Joseph, E 414-955-8213 548 G
jkerschner@mcw.edu
KERSCHNER-TAPPAN,
Alexis 505-224-4669 317 K
akerschner@cnm.edu
KERSENBROCK,
Angela, M 407-708-2483 117 H
kersenbrocka@seminolestate.edu
KERSEY, Elizabeth, A 757-683-3152 522 F
ekersey@odu.edu
KERSEY-MATUSIAK,
Gloria 215-637-7700 431 A
gkmatusiak@holyfamily.edu

KERSEY OTTO, Sarah 734-487-0400 250 F
sarah.otto@emich.edu
KERSH, Rogan 336-758-3128 380 C
kersh@wfu.edu
KERSHAW, Mara 503-491-7219 417 B
mara.kershaw@mhcc.edu
KERSTEN, David, J 716-847-8370 325 J
dkersten@buffalodiocese.org
KERSTEN, Davide, W 773-244-6214 159 H
dwkersten@northpark.edu
KERSTEN, James, B 515-574-1132 185 I
kersten@iowacentral.edu
KERSTETTER, Philip, P 919-658-7746 367 F
pkerstetter@moc.edu
KERSTIENS, Michael, J 812-941-2596 175 A
mjkersti@ius.edu
KERSTING, Monica, R 218-299-4557 262 I
kersting@cord.edu
KERWIN, Bill 714-241-6323 41 B
bkerwin@coastline.edu
KERWIN, Cornelius, M 202-885-2121 97 D
president@american.edu
KERWIN, Mark 617-369-3281 244 E
mkerwin@mfa.org
KERWOOD, Jennifer 413-236-2188 239 A
jkerwood@berkshirecc.edu
KESERAUSKIS,
Elizabeth, M 618-650-3605 165 C
ekesera@siue.edu
KESICKI, Michael 814-871-5873 429 G
kesicki001@gannon.edu
KESLER, Michael 802-773-5900 513 D
michael.kesler@csj.edu
KESSELMAN, Harvey 609-652-4514 313 E
harvey.kesselman@stockton.edu
KESSENICH, Raymond, J 319-363-8213 187 H
rkessenich@mtmercy.edu
KESSIN, Janet 212-799-5000 337 H
KESSINGER, Kevin, S 765-658-4175 171 B
kevinkessinger@depauw.edu
KESSLER, Gene 219-473-4299 170 G
gkessler@ccsj.edu
KESSLER, Jeanne, D 785-670-1629 197 F
jeanne.kessler@washburn.edu
KESSLER, Jeffrey, A 516-877-3660 322 A
kessler@adelphi.edu
KESSLER, Karen 850-484-1673 115 B
kkessler@pensacolastate.edu
KESSLER, Nevin, E 919-515-3226 378 C
nevin_kessler@ncsu.edu
KESSLER, Richard 212-580-0210 342 E
kesslerr@newschool.edu
KESSLER, Susan, B 386-312-4021 116 F
susankessler@sjrstate.edu
KESSLER, Suzanne 914-251-6600 354 D
suzanne.kessler@purchase.edu
KESTEN, Philip, R 408-554-4311 68 C
pkesten@scu.edu
KESTER, Chris 618-664-6735 151 F
chris.kester@greenville.edu
KESTER, Karen, A 941-752-5329 118 J
kesterk@scf.edu
KESTER, Kelly 360-383-3245 540 A
kkester@whatcom.ctc.edu
KESTER, Lori 303-556-2906 84 A
lori.kester@ccd.edu
KESTER-MABON, Eric 701-228-5621 382 E
eric.kester-mabon@dakotacollege.edu
KESTERSON, Ronald, L 865-694-6608 475 G
rkesterson@pstcc.edu
KESTERSON, Sean, K 989-774-7865 249 C
keste1sk@cmich.edu
KESTNER, Laura, F 414-288-7424 548 F
laura.kestner@marquette.edu
KETCHAM, Kelly 509-682-6865 539 E
kketcham@wvc.edu
KETCHESON, Kathi, A 503-725-3432 418 G
ketchesonk@pdx.edu
KETCHUM, Deann 206-393-3530 531 A
dketchum@argosy.edu
KETCHUM, Deann, M 206-393-3530 531 A
dketchum@argosy.edu
KETCHUM, William 678-915-7479 137 G
wketchum@spsu.edu
KETELS, Margo 563-589-3131 189 F
mketels@dbq.edu
KETNER, Annette 619-260-2925 76 D
aketner@sandiego.edu
KETO, Stephen, W 919-515-9224 378 C
steve_keto@ncsu.edu
KETTEMAN, Paul, G 615-383-1340 469 A
gketteman@fwbbc.edu
KETTENACKER, Vicki 314-984-7729 289 A
vkettenacker@stlcc.edu
KETTENBEIL, Ken 313-593-5555 259 B
kketten@umich.edu
KETTER, Jason 610-683-4112 443 A
ketter@give2ku.org
KETTERER, John, J 256-782-5303 4 L
jkettere@jsu.edu
KETTERER, Patricia 212-237-8516 327 F
pketterer@jjay.cuny.edu
KETTERING, III, Rocky 210-436-3138 493 F
rkettering@stmarytx.edu

KETTERMAN, Dave, V 417-667-8181 280 E
dketterman@cottey.edu
KETTERMAN, Jesse 301-687-4226 228 C
jketterman@frostburg.edu
KETTL, Donald, F 301-405-6355 227 B
kettl@umd.edu
KETTLEWELL, Charles, L 214-648-3606 507 E
charles.kettlewell@utsouthwestern.edu
KETTNER, Valrey, V 701-231-9608 382 B
val.kettner@ndsu.edu
KETTNER-POLLEY, Rick 617-759-1700 243 A
rketner-polley@aii.edu
KETTS, Amy 636-651-1600 289 F
aketts@sbc-fenton.com
KETTY, Sanjay 330-494-1214 386 A
snketty@brownmackie.edu
KETTYLE, William, M 617-253-1774 241 D
KEUFFEL, Elizabeth 603-641-7203 305 G
ekeuffel@anselm.edu
KEUP, Mike 309-677-2677 146 C
mkeup@bradley.edu
KEVIL, Tim 903-875-7443 491 C
tim.kevil@navarrocollege.edu
KEY, Charlet 309-796-5143 145 H
keyc@bhc.edu
KEY, Chris 404-327-8787 129 E
KEY, Dan 641-844-5741 186 D
dan.key@iavalley.edu
KEY, Danny 704-233-8025 380 F
dkey@wingate.edu
KEY, Elizabeth 801-832-2202 512 G
ekey@westminstercollege.edu
KEY, Henry 908-709-7151 316 B
key@ucc.edu
KEY, John 205-652-5456 9 E
jkey@uwa.edu
KEY, Rand 832-813-6522 490 E
rand.key@lonestar.edu
KEY, Roby, V 817-257-7706 499 C
r.key@tcu.edu
KEY, Ronald 678-278-1378 131 C
ronald.key@gpc.edu
KEY, Spencer 607-729-1581 331 G
skey@davisny.edu
KEY, Stacy 479-979-1360 26 A
skey@ozarks.edu
KEY, Stan, R 859-257-8907 207 D
stan.key@uky.edu
KEYES, Beth, H 937-229-3769 404 A
bkeyes@udayton.edu
KEYES, Danny 318-628-4342 210 C
dkeyes@ltc.edu
KEYES, James, R 802-443-5523 514 A
jkeyes@middlebury.edu
KEYES, Judy 617-287-6300 236 G
judy.keyes@umb.edu
KEYES, Robert 575-234-9216 319 F
rkeyes@nmsu.edu
KEYS, Carolyn 909-594-5611 58 A
ckeys@mtsac.edu
KEYS, James, A 910-843-5304 367 G
KEYS, Margo, A 715-858-1825 553 H
mkeys@cvtc.edu
KEYS, Marina 503-845-3550 417 A
marina.keys@mtangel.edu
KEZIRIAN, Wayne, M 401-598-1900 453 E
wkezirian@jwu.edu
KHACHATRYAN, Davit 949-451-5326 70 E
dkhachatryan@ivc.edu
KHADANGA, Dave 334-386-7113 3 G
dkhadanga@faulkner.edu
KHADIVAR, Jennifer 219-769-6418 19 A
jennifer.khadivar@phoenix.edu
KHALDEN, Jeff 817-598-6485 508 F
jkhalden@wc.edu
KHALEEL, Tasneem 406-657-2177 295 D
tkhaleel@msubillings.edu
KHALSA, Barbara 480-517-8131 16 B
barbara.khalsa@riosalado.edu
KHAN, Akhande 330-941-3394 406 F
askhan@ysu.edu
KHAN, Ali, A 252-335-3291 377 F
aakhan@mail.ecsu.edu
KHAN, Andrea 816-802-3466 283 E
akhan@kcai.edu
KHAN, Kamran 713-348-3500 493 C
kamran@rice.edu
KHAN, M. Wasiullah 312-939-0111 150 D
chancellor@eastwest.edu
KHAN, Muhammad 510-574-1241 44 F
mkhan99@devry.edu
KHAN, Rehan 617-373-2752 243 F
KHAN-MARCUS, Zaveeni 805-893-8411 75 B
zaveeni.khan-marcus@sa.ucsb.edu
KHANDKE, Kailash 864-294-3316 458 E
kailash.khandke@furman.edu
KHANEJA, Gurvinder 973-684-6741 312 E
gkhaneja@pccc.edu
KHANI, Anthony 212-243-5150 334 E
khani@gts.edu
KHANNA, Pradeep 217-333-9525 167 D
pkhanna@illinois.edu
KHANNA, Ranjana 919-668-2548 364 C
rkhanna@duke.edu

KIM, Samuel 770-279-0507 130 A
38317muel@hanmail.net
KIM, SamYoung 770-279-0507 130 A
chsyk30@hotmail.com
KIM, Sang Jo 714-535-3886 70 B
sjkim@southbaylo.edu
KIM, Shalom, Y 213-481-1313 69 E
KIM, Soo Jin 770-279-0507 130 A
soojinkim@bellsouth.net
KIM, Uriah 860-509-9516 93 A
ukim@hartsem.edu
KIM, Young 703-663-8088 517 E
KIM, Young Hwan 770-638-1383 130 A
yhkim30024@yahoo.com
KIM, Young Jun 770-638-1383 130 A
humbleofman@yahoo.co.kr
KIM, Yun 310-453-8300 45 G
yun@emperors.edu
KIM, Yun 570-422-3856 442 D
ykim@po-box.esu.edu
KIM, Zukweon 323-731-2383 60 H
KIMATA, Stephen, A 434-924-4293 525 F
sak@virginia.edu
KIMBALL, Amber, M 919-508-2028 380 E
amkimball@peace.edu
KIMBALL, Cathy 904-731-4949 106 D
ckimball@cci.edu
KIMBALL, Christopher 805-493-3100 33 B
ckimball@clunet.edu
KIMBALL, Curtis 603-668-2211 305 I
c.kimball@snhu.edu
KIMBALL, Elmer 802-654-0505 515 E
elmer.kimball@ccv.edu
KIMBALL, Jon 617-521-2411 244 F
jon.kimball@simmons.edu
KIMBALL, Joseph 814-824-2559 436 C
jkimball@mercyhurst.edu
KIMBALL, Kevin 541-383-7209 414 I
kekimball@cocc.edu
KIMBARK, Kris 409-933-8131 483 F
kkimbark@com.edu
KIMBERLING, C. Ronald 312-777-7735 145 C
ckimberling@argosy.edu
KIMBERLING, Charles, L 413-662-5099 238 C
charles.kimberling@mcla.edu
KIMBERLING, Charles, R 847-969-4915 145 D
ckimberling@argosy.edu
KIMBERLING, Renee 951-222-8150 64 A
renee.kimberling@rcc.edu
KIMBLE, Darius, Z 903-927-3316 509 E
dkimble@wileyc.edu
KIMBLE, James, A 419-372-0680 385 F
jkimble@bgsu.edu
KIMBRO, K. Sean 919-530-7025 378 B
kkimbro@nccu.edu
KIMBROUGH, Michael, J 913-288-7161 194 C
kimbr@kckcc.edu
KIMBROUGH, Scott 904-256-7118 111 L
skimbro@ju.edu
KIMBROUGH, Walter, M 504-816-4640 209 A
wkimbrough@dillard.edu
KIMBROW, Terry 501-205-8904 21 C
tkimbrow@cbc.edu
KIMES, Althea 757-352-4047 523 E
akimes@regent.edu
KIMES, Gene 254-295-4608 504 C
gkimes@umhb.edu
KIMMEL, Howard, S 973-596-3574 312 C
howard.kimmel@njit.edu
KIMMEL, Margaret 207-786-6328 217 C
mkimmel@bates.edu
KIMMEL, Rhonda 262-595-2281 552 A
rhonda.kimmel@uwp.edu
KIMMEL, William 212-229-5762 342 E
kimmelw@newschool.edu
KIMMELBLATT, Rachel 518-629-7736 336 C
r.kimmelblatt@hvcc.edu
KIMMELMAN, Eric 518-736-3622 334 D
ekimmelm@fmcc.suny.edu
KIMMELMAN, Scott 772-462-7760 111 B
skimmelm@irsc.edu
KIMMENS, Randy 480-731-8202 15 D
randy.kimmens@domail.maricopa.edu
KIMMERLE, Robert, S 518-580-5733 351 B
bkimmerl@skidmore.edu
KIMMERLY, Ian 415-641-1241 65 I
ikimmerly@sfai.edu
KIMMINS, William, P 516-876-3179 353 D
kimminsw@oldwestbury.edu
KIMMITT, Francis 423-493-4260 476 E
kimmittf@tntemple.edu
KIMREY, Donna 704-991-0285 374 D
dkimrey5073@stanly.edu
KIMREY, Phil 205-726-2736 6 G
ppkimrey@samford.edu
KIMS, Erdene 718-933-6700 341 G
ekims@monroecollege.edu
KIMSEY, James 520-494-5200 13 D
jim.kimsey@centralaz.edu
KIMSEY, Phillip 706-295-6350 130 E
pkimsey@highlands.edu
KIMURA, Keiko 408-298-2181 67 D
keiko.kimura@sjcc.edu
KIMURA, Melissa 562-947-8755 71 A
melissakimura@scuhs.edu
KINANE, Denis, F 215-898-1038 448 J
dean@dental.upenn.edu
KINANE, Michael, G 516-876-3212 353 D
kinanem@oldwestbury.edu
KINANE, Michael, G 516-876-3162 353 D
kinanem@oldwestbury.edu
KINARD, Sylvia 718-270-6936 328 C
skinard@mec.cuny.edu
KINARD, Trent 803-584-3446 462 E
tkinard@mailbox.sc.edu
KINARD, Zeolean, F 864-941-8688 460 D
kinard.z@ptc.edu
KINCADE, Luis 432-264-5092 488 B
wkincade@howardcollege.edu
KINCAID, Brenda 704-922-6247 370 G
kincaid.brenda@gaston.edu
KINCAID, Paul, K 417-836-5139 286 C
paulkincaid@missouristate.edu
KINCAID, Rachel, A 504-280-7049 213 E
rakincai@uno.edu
KINCAID, Ramona 808-245-8336 142 C
rkincaid@hawaii.edu
KINCAID, Scott, A 317-940-9700 170 F
kincaid@butler.edu
KINCAID, Tim 419-559-2211 402 D
tkincaid@terra.edu
KINCAID, William 317-931-2330 170 H
bkincaid@cts.edu
KINCAID, Zach, O 434-381-6262 524 K
zkincaid@sbc.edu
KINCHEN, Thomas, A 850-263-3261 101 L
takinchen@baptistcollege.edu
KINCHERLOW-MARTIN,
Janet 256-306-2561 2 D
jkm@calhoun.edu
KIND, Jule 765-677-2980 175 B
jule.kind@indwes.edu
KIND, Larry 715-675-3331 555 B
kind@ntc.edu
KIND-KEPPEL, Heather 217-875-7200 162 F
hkindkep@richland.edu
KINDE, Haragewen 909-384-8265 65 C
hkinde@sbccd.cc.ca.us
KINDE, Wayne 858-695-8587 50 J
wkinde@horizoncollege.org
KINDER, Angie, M 304-260-4380 542 G
akinder@blueridgectc.edu
KINDER, L. Chad 580-774-7036 412 F
chad.kinder@swosu.edu
KINDERS, Mark 405-974-5560 413 B
mkinders@uco.edu
KINDL, Christine 724-938-5492 441 G
kindl@calu.edu
KINDLE, Carolyn 618-634-3364 164 E
carolynk@shawneecc.edu
KINDLE, Derek 202-806-2864 98 E
dkindle@howard.edu
KINDLE, Joan 847-925-6738 151 G
jkindle@harpercollege.edu
KINDRED, Cheryl 480-545-8755 12 G
KINEAVY, Jacqueline 973-684-6300 312 E
jkineavy@pccc.edu
KINERSON, Sara 802-635-1257 515 F
sara.kinerson@jsc.edu
KINES, Teresa 336-249-8186 370 B
tkines@davidsonccc.edu
KINESKEY, Jessica 407-628-5870 106 H
jkineskey@cci.edu
KING, Adrienne 304-442-3131 545 D
adrienne.king@mail.wvu.edu
KING, Alex, H 515-294-2770 182 E
alexking@ameslab.gov
KING, Amanda 601-266-5000 277 F
amanda.king@usm.edu
KING, Amy 815-306-2600 162 C
amy.king@rasmussen.edu
KING, Amy 303-871-7420 89 A
KING, Amy, L 304-457-6354 540 E
kingal@ab.edu
KING, Andrew, B 618-650-2197 165 C
andking@siue.edu
KING, Andrew, R 914-968-6200 349 D
sjsds@archny.org
KING, Angelynn 207-255-1234 220 E
angelynn.king@maine.edu
KING, B, J 423-439-4414 473 F
kingbj@etsu.edu
KING, Barbara 405-682-1611 409 F
bking@occc.edu
KING, Barbara, E 570-408-4107 452 A
barbara.king@wilkes.edu
KING, Baron 215-702-4224 444 B
baronking@pbu.edu
KING, Becky, L 254-710-4566 482 A
becky_king@baylor.edu
KING, Beverly 910-521-6295 379 C
beverly.king@uncp.edu
KING, Bill 530-541-4660 53 G
king@ltcc.edu
KING, Brad 501-569-3400 24 E
cbking@ualr.edu
KING, Brad 435-613-5246 512 A
brad.king@usu.edu
KING, Brenda, M 304-336-8076 544 D
kingbren@westliberty.edu
KING, Brent 713-500-7863 506 F
brent.king@uth.tmc.edu
KING, Brian 831-479-6302 31 I
brking@cabrillo.edu
KING, Bruce 510-235-7800 43 E
bking@contracosta.edu
KING, Bruce 507-786-3334 271 C
kingb@stolaf.edu
KING, Carol, S 570-586-2400 422 G
cking@bbc.edu
KING, Carole 202-884-9120 99 H
kingc@trinitydc.edu
KING, Carolee 409-772-1904 507 C
caaking@utmb.edu
KING, Carolee 409-772-8738 507 C
caaking@utmb.edu
KING, Caroline 941-907-2262 107 B
caking@evergladesuniversity.edu
KING, Charles, G 423-652-4700 470 A
gregking1@king.edu
KING, Charles, W 540-568-6434 520 H
kingcw@jmu.edu
KING, Cheryl 301-295-3045 558 D
cheryl.king@usuhs.edu
KING, Christopher 956-665-2221 506 C
kingca@utpa.edu
KING, Christy 407-708-2103 117 H
kingc@seminolestate.edu
KING, Chuck 303-753-6046 88 B
cking@rmcad.edu
KING, Chula, G 850-474-3135 121 D
cking@uwf.edu
KING, Curt 413-662-5062 238 C
curt.king@mcla.edu
KING, Cynthia 202-651-5865 98 B
cynthia.king@gallaudet.edu
KING, Cynthia, L 610-861-5510 437 H
cking@northampton.edu
KING, Cynthia, P 617-726-2947 242 B
cking@mghihp.edu
KING, D. Wayne 859-238-5550 199 G
wayne.king@centre.edu
KING, Dan 617-327-6777 241 F
dan_king@mspp.edu
KING, David 315-312-3692 354 A
david.king@oswego.edu
KING, David 706-721-2856 130 D
daking@georgiahealth.edu
KING, David, A 541-737-2676 418 F
ecampus@oregonstate.edu
KING, David, A 540-432-4440 518 F
david.king@emu.edu
KING, David, A 330-471-8121 395 F
dking@malone.edu
KING, David, S 203-582-3213 93 H
david.king@quinnipiac.edu
KING, David, W 805-565-6036 79 A
dking@westmont.edu
KING, Deanna 812-298-2205 177 D
dking@ivytech.edu
KING, Deborah 870-338-6474 25 D
KING, Deborah 252-399-6306 362 E
dking@barton.edu
KING, Dee 248-204-2127 254 B
dking@ltu.edu
KING, Denise 636-922-8698 288 B
dking@stchas.edu
KING, Denise 423-472-7141 474 E
dking05@clevelandstatecc.edu
KING, Dennis 785-628-4291 192 I
dking@fhsu.edu
KING, Diane 603-427-7630 304 B
djking@ccsnh.edu
KING, Don 508-999-8575 237 A
dking@umassd.edu
KING, Donald (Jr.) 765-285-1478 169 G
jking@bsu.edu
KING, Donna 606-783-2000 204 I
d.king@moreheadstate.edu
KING, Donna 903-463-8735 487 C
donnaking@grayson.edu
KING, Dottie 812-535-5296 179 E
president@smwc.edu
KING, Duane 918-596-2710 413 F
duane-king@utulsa.edu
KING, E. Thayne 918-456-5511 409 A
king21@nsuok.edu
KING, Eddie 843-208-8135 462 C
eking@uscb.edu
KING, Edward, M 617-353-9095 232 E
eking@bu.edu
KING, Elizabeth 316-978-3510 198 A
elizabeth.king@witchita.edu
KING, Elizabeth 636-949-4975 283 J
eking@lindenwood.edu
KING, Elizabeth, C 513-558-8547 403 D
elizabeth.king@uc.edu
KING, Elston, H 504-286-5197 214 J
eking@suno.edu
KING, Fred, L 304-293-4611 545 A
fking@mail.wvu.edu
KING, Gordon, B 617-557-1520 245 B
gking@suffolk.edu
KING, Greg 305-341-6600 102 F
grking@brownmackie.edu
KING, Greg 423-236-2983 473 B
gking@southern.edu
KING, Gregory 330-823-2282 404 C
kinggl@mountunion.edu
KING, JR., H. Lee 434-223-7258 519 G
lking@hsc.edu
KING, Hazel 910-892-3178 365 B
hking@heritagebiblecollege.edu
KING, Herbert 651-773-1794 266 A
herbert.king@century.edu
KING, J. D 402-935-9400 299 A
jdking@nechristian.edu
KING, Jackie, E 585-275-1051 359 B
jking@admin.rochester.edu
KING, James 615-336-4470 473 D
james.king@tbr.edu
KING, CSC, James, B 574-631-7800 180 G
king.61@nd.edu
KING, Janice 530-754-1388 73 I
janking@ucdavis.edu
KING, Janice 775-753-2361 302 F
janice.king@gbcnv.edu
KING, Jeannie 704-337-2509 376 A
kingj@queens.edu
KING, Jeff 706-764-3530 131 B
jking@gntc.edu
KING, Jennifer 413-559-5427 235 C
KING, Jerry 903-675-6210 502 F
jking@tvcc.edu
KING, Jessica 303-975-5016 89 H
jking@westwood.edu
KING, Jim 318-257-2445 215 F
king@latech.edu
KING, Jim 254-295-4644 504 C
jking@umhb.edu
KING, Jim, M 318-257-2445 215 F
king@latech.edu
KING, Joan 509-335-9681 539 D
joank@wsu.edu
KING, Jodie 215-248-7004 425 D
kingj@chc.edu
KING, Joe 334-244-3600 1 G
jking25@aum.edu
KING, John 218-726-8821 271 F
jking@d.umn.edu
KING, John, C 806-720-7211 490 F
john.king@lcu.edu
KING, John, J 401-254-3042 454 C
jjking@rwu.edu
KING, John, M 617-552-4445 232 B
john.king.2@bc.edu
KING, John, W 423-652-4832 470 A
jwking@king.edu
KING, Jovanna, J 864-656-0663 456 E
jovanna@clemson.edu
KING, Joy, S 512-505-3015 488 D
jsking@htu.edu
KING, Julie, A 803-786-3871 457 C
juking@columbiasc.edu
KING, Karen, D 423-439-5654 473 F
kingk@etsu.edu
KING, Katherine 949-480-4161 69 J
kking@soka.edu
KING, Katie 405-491-6350 412 D
kking@snu.edu
KING, Kelli, B 574-535-7563 171 G
kellibk@goshen.edu
KING, Kim 765-459-0561 176 C
kking@ivytech.edu
KING, Kim 773-896-2400 146 H
kking@ctschicago.edu
KING, Kimberly 425-558-0299 533 G
kimking@digipen.edu
KING, Kristin 267-502-2579 423 C
kristin.king@brynathyn.edu
KING, Kristy 251-343-8200 6 F
kristy.king@remingtoncollege.edu
KING, Kristyn 815-394-5061 163 A
kking@rockford.edu
KING, Kwanna 918-463-2931 407 H
kwanna.king@connorsstate.edu
KING, L. Dianne 864-231-2026 455 C
ldking@andersonuniversity.edu
KING, Laura 870-512-7850 20 F
laura_king@asun.edu
KING, Laura, C 814-393-1926 442 B
lking@clarion.edu
KING, Laura, M 651-201-1732 265 E
laura.king@so.mnscu.edu
KING, Leslie 770-426-2757 133 E
lking@life.edu
KING, Libby 423-869-6358 470 E
libby.king@lmunet.edu
KING, Linda 304-367-4081 543 B
linda.king@pierpont.edu
KING, Linda, L 541-346-2966 419 B
llking@uoregon.edu

KIRKLIN, Kathleen 916-608-6500 56 C
KIRKMAN, Duane 828-328-7028 366 E
duane.kirkman@lr.edu
KIRKMAN, Sue 805-585-8077 31 E
sue.kirkman@brooks.edu
KIRKMAN, Susan 805-690-7601 31 D
sue.kirkman@brooks.edu
KIRKPATRICK, Brett, A 409-772-2371 507 C
bkirkpat@utmb.edu
KIRKPATRICK, Dana 510-436-1601 50 H
kirkpatrick@hnu.edu
KIRKPATRICK, Holly, R 215-572-4475 422 C
kirkpath@arcadia.edu
KIRKPATRICK, Judith, A 315-792-3122 359 E
jkirkpatrick@utica.edu
KIRKPATRICK, Kenneth, J 765-658-4141 171 B
kjkirk@depauw.edu
KIRKPATRICK, Laura 931-363-9864 471 A
lkirkpatrick@martinmethodist.edu
KIRKPATRICK, Lindsey 918-561-8468 410 D
lindsey.kirkpatrick@okstate.edu
KIRKPATRICK, Lisa, L 512-448-8408 493 E
lisak@stedwards.edu
KIRKPATRICK, Mac 864-388-8398 459 A
mkirkpat@lander.edu
KIRKPATRICK, Nancy 317-955-6223 177 I
nkirkpatrick@marian.edu
KIRKPATRICK, R. James 517-355-4473 255 A
cnsdean@msu.edu
KIRKPATRICK, Stephen 516-876-3156 353 D
kirkpatricks@oldwestbury.edu
KIRKPATRICK, Stephen 901-321-4036 467 I
skirkpat@cbu.edu
KIRKSEY, Jason 405-744-9154 410 C
jason.kirksey@okstate.edu
KIRKSEY, Jeff 585-567-9561 336 B
jeff.kirksey@houghton.edu
KIRKSEY, Jennifer 740-593-1804 399 G
kirkseyj@ohio.edu
KIRKSEY, Kirk, A 214-645-8404 507 E
kirk.kirksey@utsouthwestern.edu
KIRKTON, Vicki, S 574-535-7376 171 G
vickysk@goshen.edu
KIRKWOOD, Rod 863-686-1444 106 E
rkirkwoo@cci.edu
KIRKWOOD, Rod 813-621-0041 106 C
rkirkwoo@cci.edu
KIRKWOOD, Valerie 509-793-2371 531 I
valeriek@bigbend.edu
KIRKWOOD, William, G 423-439-4219 473 F
kirkwood@etsu.edu
KIRMER, Lisa 620-343-4600 192 H
lkirmer@fhtc.edu
KIRNAN, Jack, V 267-341-3373 431 A
jkirnan@holyfamily.edu
KIRSCH, Lloyd 480-990-3773 15 C
KIRSCH, OSB, Myron 724-805-2111 446 E
myron.kirsch@email.stvincent.edu
KIRSCH, Rodney, P 814-863-4826 438 G
rpk6@psu.edu
KIRSCHENMANN,
Sandra, G 916-325-4600 427 H
sandra.g.kirschenmann@drexel.edu
KIRSCHLING, Jane, M 859-323-6533 207 D
janek@uky.edu
KIRSCHNER, Kelly 727-864-8965 105 E
kirschkm@eckerd.edu
KIRSH, Bruce, M 603-899-4080 305 A
kirshb@franklinpierce.edu
KIRSHMAN, David 510-594-3688 32 C
dkirshman@cca.edu
KIRSTEIN, Frank, W 716-888-8361 325 F
kirstein@canisius.edu
KIRSTEIN, Kurt 425-637-1010 532 E
kdkirstein@cityu.edu
KIRSTEN, Jan 732-255-0400 312 D
jkirsten@ocean.edu
KIRTLAND, James, L 419-289-5012 384 G
jkirtlan@ashland.edu
KIRTLEY, Adam, M 509-522-4449 540 B
kirtleam@whitman.edu
KIRTLEY, Brad, J 931-221-7561 473 E
kirtleyb@apsu.edu
KIRTLEY, Karen 304-696-3328 544 B
kirtley@marshall.edu
KIRTMAN, Janet 212-346-1700 345 F
jkirtman@pace.edu
KIRVES, Carol 270-707-3751 202 E
carol.kirves@kctcs.edu
KIRWAN, William 301-445-1901 227 A
bkirwan@usmd.edu
KIRWIN, Margaret 518-454-5160 330 C
kirwinm@strose.edu
KISELICA, Mark 609-771-2100 308 F
kiselica@tcnj.edu
KISELYUK, Ella 212-817-7701 327 B
ekiselyuk@gc.cuny.edu
KISER, Dan 828-328-7154 366 E
dan.kiser@lr.edu
KISER, Holly 817-531-4495 502 C
hkiser@txwes.edu
KISER, Joseph, B 276-328-0143 525 G
jbk5b@uvawise.edu
KISER, Kristy 276-328-0220 525 G
kej5c@uvawise.edu
KISER, Lee 828-448-6707 375 B
lkiser@wpcc.edu
KISER, Leonard, R 336-734-7313 370 F
lkiser@forsythtech.edu
KISER, Lyda, C 540-869-0623 527 C
lkiser@lfcc.edu
KISER, Michael, D 207-859-4356 217 G
mdkiser@colby.edu
KISER, Ronnie 276-964-7221 528 E
ronnie.kiser@sw.edu
KISER, Sara, B 334-683-5104 5 D
skiser@judson.edu
KISH-GOODLING,
Donna, M 484-664-3479 437 C
kishgood@muhlenberg.edu
KISNER, Dawn 410-287-1025 222 A
dkisner@cecil.edu
KISPERT, Craig, G 206-281-2536 537 H
ckispert@spu.edu
KISPERT, John, J 843-661-1110 458 D
jkispert@fmarion.edu
KISS, Elizabeth 404-471-6280 123 I
president@agnesscott.edu
KISS, Nikki 920-693-1136 554 C
nikki.kiss@gotoltc.edu
KISSACK, Heather 254-659-7731 487 G
hkissack@hillcollege.edu
KISSEL, Anthony 352-588-8991 116 G
anthony.kissel@saintleo.edu
KISSEL, Karen 708-534-4054 151 E
kkissel@govst.edu
KISSELL, Joseph 570-389-4263 441 F
jkissell@bloomu.edu
KISSICK, Sharon 910-521-6298 379 C
sharon.kissick@uncp.edu
KISSIS, Leonora 718-951-5861 326 F
lkissis@brooklyn.cuny.edu
KISSLING, Paul 972-241-3371 484 E
pkissling@dallas.edu
KIST, Jennifer, S 814-269-7049 449 D
jskist@pitt.edu
KIST, Tom 732-729-3813 309 C
tkist@devry.edu
KISTLER, Kevin 661-362-3025 41 I
kevin.kistler@canyons.edu
KISTLER, Kevin 209-381-6489 57 C
kevin.kistler@mccd.edu
KISTLER, Ron 580-928-5533 412 F
ron.kistler@swosu.edu
KISTNER, Warren 309-556-3071 153 F
wkistner@iwu.edu
KITAJIMA, Lorraine, N 650-949-7243 47 H
kitajimalorraine@fhda.edu
KITCHEN, Augusta 803-780-1159 463 C
akitchen@voorhees.edu
KITCHEN, Cheryl 419-772-2220 398 H
c-kitchen@onu.edu
KITCHEN, Clifford 719-549-3121 87 F
clifford.kitchen@pueblocc.edu
KITCHEN, Darrell, B 937-327-7002 406 B
dkitchen@wittenberg.edu
KITCHEN, James, R 619-594-5211 37 A
jkitchen@mail.sdsu.edu
KITCHEN, Janie 606-326-2163 201 F
janie.kitchen@kctcs.edu
KITCHEN, Kimberly 814-641-3114 432 A
kitchek@juniata.edu
KITCHEN, Mark 307-754-6405 556 G
mark.kitchen@northwestcollege.edu
KITCHEN, Steve 678-915-3929 137 G
skitchen@spsu.edu
KITCHEN, Todd 479-619-4232 22 H
tkitchen@nwacc.edu
KITCHENS, Angie 706-737-1469 125 G
akitchens@aug.edu
KITCHENS, Joann 701-662-1502 382 F
joann.kitchens@lrsc.edu
KITCHENS, Joseph, H 770-720-5966 136 C
jhk@reinhardt.edu
KITCHENS, Larry 870-236-6901 21 E
lkitchens@crc.edu
KITCHENS, Larry, E 817-257-7121 499 C
l.kitchens@tcu.edu
KITCHENS, Penny 478-553-2060 135 B
pkitchens@oftc.edu
KITCHENS, Ronnie 601-426-6346 277 A
rkitchens@southeasternbaptist.edu
KITCHENS, Tempie 770-233-6170 137 F
tkitchens@sctech.edu
KITCHINGS, Dorcas, A 803-822-3584 459 E
kitchingsd@midlandstech.edu
KITCHNER, Russell 304-724-3700 540 F
rkitchner@apus.edu
KITE, Bruce 575-646-2446 319 D
bkite@nmsu.edu
KITE, Joy, A 608-822-2319 555 D
jkite@swtc.edu
KITEI, Susan, C 610-758-3870 434 E
sck0@lehigh.edu
KITHCART, Jane 845-687-5111 358 E
kithcarj@sunyulster.edu
KITSON, Clair 423-236-2918 473 B
cjkitson@southern.edu
KITTEL, Jane 715-675-3331 555 B
kittelj@ntc.edu
KITTELL, Gary 315-464-4448 352 E
kittelg@upstate.edu
KITTINGER, Fred 407-823-1208 120 B
fred.kittinger@ucf.edu
KITTLE, Aaron, P 304-457-6342 540 E
kittleap@ab.edu
KITTLE, Paul 336-841-9107 365 C
pkittle@highpoint.edu
KITTO, Kathleen 360-650-5929 539 F
kathleen.kitto@wwu.edu
KITTS, Kenneth, D 910-521-6224 379 C
ken.kitts@uncp.edu
KIVEL, Andy 925-685-1230 43 F
akivel@dvc.edu
KIVETZ, Robert 212-998-4611 344 B
rsk1@nyu.edu
KIYOSAKI, Donna 808-454-4742 141 H
donnafay@hawaii.edu
KIYOSHI, Jack, O 670-234-5498 560 B
jackk@nmcnet.edu
KIZINA, Terrence, R 814-871-5759 429 G
kizina002@gannon.edu
KJARTANSON, Mary 619-221-2144 65 H
mkjartan@sdccd.edu
KJONAAS, Wayne 970-247-7525 84 K
kjonaas_w@fortlewis.edu
KLAAS, Alan 928-692-3085 16 F
aklaas@mohave.edu
KLAAS, Carlene 312-362-8146 149 A
cklaas@depaul.edu
KLAAS, Daniel 702-369-9944 301 F
KLABECHEK, IV, John 262-551-5911 546 I
jklabechek@carthage.edu
KLACIK, Michael 402-474-5315 298 C
mklacik@kaplanuniversity.edu
KLADIVKO, Deborah 803-641-3577 462 B
debk@usca.edu
KLAFFKE, David 208-467-8641 144 E
dklaffke@nnu.edu
KLAG, Michael, J 410-955-3540 223 F
mklag@jhsph.edu
KLAGGE, Jay 480-446-5022 19 A
jay.klagge@phoenix.edu
KLAHR, Sabine 801-581-8876 511 C
s.klahr@ic.utah.edu
KLAIBER, Robert 207-221-8750 218 C
rklaiber@kaplan.edu
KLAICH, Daniel, J 775-784-4901 302 D
chancellor@nevada.edu
KLAPERMAN MORROW,
Carol 212-998-4798 344 B
carol.morrow@nyu.edu
KLAPHAAK, Kirk, K 812-941-2445 175 A
kklapha@ius.edu
KLAPPER, Robert 770-729-8400 125 B
KLASEN, James 617-588-1344 231 C
jklasen@bfit.edu
KLASKO, Stephen, K 813-974-2196 121 A
sklasko@health.usf.edu
KLASS, Stephen, P 413-597-3118 246 D
stephen.p.klass@williams.edu
KLAUBER, James, S 270-686-4508 203 B
james.klauber@kctcs.edu
KLAUDER, Mark, J 802-447-6322 514 F
mklauder@svc.edu
KLAUS, Allen, R 210-434-6711 492 B
arklaus@lake.ollusa.edu
KLAUS, Byron, D 417-268-1000 278 H
bklaus@agts.edu
KLAUS, Chad, L 609-258-5498 312 G
klaus@princeton.edu
KLAUS, Dennis 801-957-4250 512 D
dennis.klaus@slcc.edu
KLAUS, John Mark 814-472-3391 446 B
jklaus@francis.edu
KLAUS, Katie 920-433-6651 546 D
katie.klaus@bellincollege.edu
KLAUSA, Jon 773-256-0784 157 D
jklausa@lstc.edu
KLAUSER, Patricia, A 203-371-7978 94 B
klauserp@sacredheart.edu
KLAUSMEYER, Robert 573-875-7304 280 A
rklausmeyer@ccis.edu
KLAWE, Maria, M 909-921-8120 49 F
klawe@hmc.edu
KLAWITTER, Christina 608-363-2660 546 E
klawitterc@beloit.edu
KLAWUNN, Margaret, M 401-863-1800 453 B
margaret_klawunn@brown.edu
KLAY, Kathy, A 937-328-6085 387 H
klayk@clarkstate.edu
KLCO, JoEllen 330-499-9600 393 I
jklco@kent.edu
KLEBE, Kelli 719-255-3417 88 I
kklebe@uccs.edu
KLEBESADEL, Shirley 715-232-2190 552 E
klebesadels@uwstout.edu
KLEDZIK, Eric 321-674-8107 108 H
ekledzik@fit.edu
KLEE, Dane 815-455-8763 157 H
dklee@mchenry.edu
KLEE, John 606-759-7141 203 A
john.klee@kctcs.edu
KLEEMAN, Beverly, S 509-777-4548 540 C
bkleeman@whitworth.edu
KLEEN, Betty 985-448-4191 216 A
betty.kleen@nicholls.edu
KLEI, Thomas, R 225-578-7696 212 H
tklei@lsu.edu
KLEICH, Tammie 308-635-6072 301 D
kleicht@wncc.edu
KLEIN, Andrew, O 508-849-3313 230 C
aklein@annamaria.edu
KLEIN, Andrew, R 317-274-4417 174 D
anrklein@iupui.edu
KLEIN, Barb 641-648-4611 186 C
barb.klein@iavalley.edu
KLEIN, Barbara, A 410-269-5087 227 C
bklein@umaryland.edu
KLEIN, Bob, P 518-783-2432 350 I
rklein@siena.edu
KLEIN, Cynthia 412-809-5100 444 G
klein.cynthia@pti.edu
KLEIN, David, A 434-223-6129 519 G
dklein@hsc.edu
KLEIN, Eileen 512-223-5766 481 B
eklein@austincc.edu
KLEIN, Gary, L 608-796-3074 553 C
glklein@viterbo.edu
KLEIN, James 541-552-6114 419 A
kleinj@sou.edu
KLEIN, James, W 301-766-3671 223 G
jklein@kaplan.edu
KLEIN, Janie 925-631-4572 64 F
mminguil@stmarys-ca.edu
KLEIN, Jason, D 605-336-6588 465 D
jklein@sfseminary.edu
KLEIN, Jim 502-456-6508 206 H
jklein@sullivan.edu
KLEIN, Joanne, R 240-895-4251 226 A
jrklein@smcm.edu
KLEIN, John, E 434-947-8140 523 B
jklein@randolphcollege.edu
KLEIN, June 650-433-3849 61 B
jklein@paloaltou.edu
KLEIN, Marjorie, S 814-332-5910 421 F
marjorie.klein@allegheny.edu
KLEIN, Mendel 718-384-5460 361 I
KLEIN, Michael 631-370-3300 350 D
mklein@sbmelville.edu
KLEIN, Michael 718-368-5087 328 A
mklein@kbcc.cuny.edu
KLEIN, Michelle, W 504-866-7426 214 A
finance@nds.edu
KLEIN, Paul 415-749-4589 65 I
paulklein@sfai.edu
KLEIN, Sandy, L 701-483-2371 381 G
sandy.klein@dickinsonstate.edu
KLEIN, Scott 812-866-7061 172 A
klein@hanover.edu
KLEIN, Shelley 661-763-7711 72 E
sklein@taftcollege.edu
KLEIN, Steve 503-352-2822 419 E
kleinsk@pacificu.edu
KLEIN, Steven, J 765-361-6253 181 E
kleins@wabash.edu
KLEIN, Susan 816-802-3435 283 E
sklein@kcai.edu
KLEIN, Terry 715-468-2815 555 G
terry.klein@witc.edu
KLEIN-ROBARTS, Rowena 630-515-3005 149 G
rklein-robarts@keller.edu
KLEIN-WHEATON, Kristin 716-270-4432 333 C
kleinwheaton@ecc.edu
KLEINDL, Brad 816-584-6308 287 E
brad.kleindl@park.edu
KLEINE, Patricia, A 715-836-2320 551 A
kleinepa@uwec.edu
KLEINER, Stephen 513-772-9888 398 G
stephen.kleiner@omw.edu
KLEINERT, Edward 216-987-3244 389 B
edward.kleinert@tri-c.edu
KLEINFELD, Ira, H 203-932-7063 95 C
ikleinfeld@newhaven.edu
KLEINHANS, Randy 574-372-5100 171 H
kleinhrp@grace.edu
KLEINKAUFMAN, Dovid 718-327-7600 360 I
yfr1@verizon.net
KLEINMAN, Ilene 201-447-7160 307 E
ikleinman@bergen.edu
KLEINMAN, Kent 607-255-9110 331 B
aapdean@cornell.edu
KLEINMAN, Naftaly 212-343-1234 341 B
nkleinman@mcny.edu
KLEINMAN, Yisroel 718-853-8500 358 A
KLEINPETER, Jennifer 225-675-8270 211 F
jkleinpeter@rpcc.edu
KLEINSORGE, Ilene, K 541-737-6024 418 F
ilene.kleinsorge@bus.oregonstate.edu
KLEINTOP, Douglas 610-660-1219 446 C
dkleinto@sju.edu
KLEINWORTH, Tom 713-798-6297 481 H
tklein@bcm.edu
KLEM, Janikke 408-924-1143 37 C
janikke.klem@sjsu.edu

KNIGHT, Sheri 620-343-4600 192 H
sknight@fhtc.edu
KNIGHT, Sherry 989-774-7326 249 C
knigh1s@cmich.edu
KNIGHT, Steven, H 601-318-6111 278 C
steve.knight@wmcarey.edu
KNIGHT, Tim 870-245-5216 22 I
knightt@obu.edu
KNIGHT, Tim 202-884-9133 99 H
knightt@trinitydc.edu
KNIGHT, Unita 910-296-2460 371 E
uknight@jamessprunt.edu
KNIGHT, W. Hal 423-439-7627 473 F
knighth@etsu.edu
KNIGHT, Wendy, S 563-557-8271 188 B
knightw@nicc.edu
KNIGHTON, Denise 662-915-7792 277 D
denisek@olemiss.edu
KNIGHTON, Diana, W 205-929-1442 5 H
diana@mail.miles.edu
KNIPE, Robert, G 585-345-6969 334 F
rgknipe@genesee.edu
KNIPLE, Jeffrey 410-617-2032 223 I
jwkniple@loyola.edu
KNIPPLE, Robert, W 814-269-2080 449 D
knipple@pitt.edu
KNIPSCHIELD, Debbie 253-833-9111 534 H
dknipschield@greenriver.edu
KNISELY, Bertie 610-861-1345 437 A
bertiek@moravian.edu
KNISPEL, Todd 406-377-9413 294 B
knispelt@dawson.edu
KNISS, Fred, L 540-432-4105 518 F
fred.kniss@emu.edu
KNOBEL, Dale, T 740-587-6281 389 I
knobel@denison.edu
KNOBEL, David 954-535-8820 107 G
dknobel@careercollege.edu
KNOBLAUCH, Laura 309-438-8658 153 D
lmknobl@ilstu.edu
KNOBLICH, Julie, A 620-792-9275 190 H
knoblichj@bartonccc.edu
KNOCH, Daniel, L 517-437-7341 252 C
dan.knoch@hillsdale.edu
KNOCHE, Charlotte, M 651-641-8240 263 A
knoche@csp.edu
KNODELL, Jane, E 802-656-1417 514 H
jane.knodell@uvm.edu
KNODLE-BRAGIEL, Lisa 503-883-2214 416 H
lbragiel@linfield.edu
KNOEBEL, Ann, G 210-999-7601 502 E
aknoebel@trinity.edu
KNOEBEL, Thomas, L 414-425-8300 550 E
tknoebel@shst.edu
KNOELL, Karen 605-995-2647 464 C
kaknoell@dwu.edu
KNOETTGEN, Suzi 785-243-1435 192 A
sknoettgen@cloud.edu
KNOFF, Gregory 313-664-7650 249 E
gknoff@collegeforcreativestudies.edu
KNOKE, Luke 317-845-0300 178 B
lknoke@medtechcollege.edu
KNOLL, Joseph 617-824-8112 234 B
joseph_knoll@emerson.edu
KNOLL, Kathy 575-562-2611 318 B
kathy.knoll@enmu.edu
KNOLLMAN, Paul, L 734-384-4282 255 D
pknollman@monroeccc.edu
KNOOR, Robert 616-957-6039 249 B
rknoor@calvinseminary.edu
KNOP, Joachim, W 202-994-6506 98 C
knop@gwu.edu
KNOP-COX, Barbara 405-422-1401 411 G
knopcoxb@redlandscc.edu
KNORR, Joseph 301-447-5271 225 A
knorr@msmary.edu
KNORR, Stephen, C 573-882-2726 291 A
knorrs@umsystem.edu
KNORR, Walter 312-413-9097 167 A
wknorr@uillinois.edu
KNORTZ, Geraldine 802-654-2200 514 D
gknortz@smcvt.edu
KNOST, Julie 812-855-7559 173 E
jknost@indiana.edu
KNOST, Julie 812-855-7559 173 D
knost@indiana.edu
KNOTHE, Thomas, E 608-796-3360 553 C
teknothe@viterbo.edu
KNOTT, Allan 214-860-8531 485 B
aknott@dcccd.edu
KNOTT, Cindy 928-541-7777 16 H
cknott@ncu.edu
KNOTT, Gregory 305-237-0825 113 H
gknott@mdc.edu
KNOTT, Jack, H 213-740-0350 76 F
jhknott@usc.edu
KNOTT, Kevin 217-351-2239 161 C
kknott@parkland.edu
KNOTT, Ronald 812-357-6544 180 A
rknott@saintmeinrad.edu
KNOTT, Toni 559-456-2777 27 B
tknott@alliant.edu
KNOTT, William 616-222-1918 250 A
bill.knott@cornerstone.edu
KNOTTS, Bradley 815-226-3398 163 A
bknotts@rockford.edu
KNOTTS, Cecil 318-357-5965 216 B
knottsc@nsula.edu
KNOTTS, David 636-798-2166 283 J
dknotts@lindenwood.edu
KNOTTS, Debby 505-277-5765 321 C
debby@unm.edu
KNOUFF, Christine 859-341-5627 199 E
cknouff@brownmackie.edu
KNOUSE, Christine 717-262-2016 452 C
cknouse@wilson.edu
KNOWLES, Aaron 407-712-1424 19 A
aaron.knowles@phoenix.edu
KNOWLES, Daniel, M 212-746-6464 360 C
dknowles@med.cornell.edu
KNOWLES, Harley 423-746-5201 476 F
hknowles@twcnet.edu
KNOWLES, J. Geoff 765-269-5681 176 D
jknowles5@ivytech.edu
KNOWLES, J. Geoff 765-269-5681 176 D
jknowles5@ivytech.edy
KNOWLES, John 239-687-5402 101 H
jknowles@avemarialaw.edu
KNOWLES, Kriss 847-214-7819 150 F
kknowles@elgin.edu
KNOWLES, Monica 360-992-2904 532 F
mknowles@clark.edu
KNOWLES, Susan 315-268-6633 329 B
sknowles@clarkson.edu
KNOWLTON, Douglas, D 651-201-1652 265 E
douglas.knowlton@so.mnscu.edu
KNOWLTON, Eloise 508-767-7487 230 D
eknowlton@assumption.edu
KNOX, Chrisanne 925-685-1230 43 F
cknox@dvc.edu
KNOX, George, C 620-421-6700 194 G
georgek@labette.edu
KNOX, Jan, H 336-841-9641 365 C
jknox@highpoint.edu
KNOX, Linda 219-989-2337 178 K
linda.knox@purduecal.edu
KNOX, Marg 512-322-3774 505 B
mknox@utsystem.edu
KNOX, Pamela 615-366-4411 473 D
pamela.knox@tbr.edu
KNOX, Ronnie 256-233-8186 1 E
ronnie.knox@athens.edu
KNOX, Ruth, A 478-757-5212 139 E
rknox@wesleyancollege.edu
KNOX, Teresa 918-298-8200 407 F
KNOX, Teresa, L 918-610-0027 407 G
tknox@communitycarecollege.edu
KNOX, Teresa, L 918-610-0027 411 A
tknox@communitycarecollege.edu
KNUDSEN, Alice 510-430-2350 57 D
aknudsen@mills.edu
KNUDSEN, H. Peter 406-496-4395 296 B
pknudsen@mtech.edu
KNUDSEN, J. Todd 562-902-3358 71 A
toddknudsen@scuhs.edu
KNUDSEN, Kjell 218-726-7281 271 F
kknudsen@d.umn.edu
KNUDSEN, Ross 208-376-7731 142 H
rknudsen@boisebible.edu
KNUDSON, Kari 701-224-5604 382 D
kari.l.knudson@bismarckstate.edu
KNUDSON, Paula, M 608-785-8150 551 C
pknudson@uwlax.edu
KNUDSON-CARL, Tara 402-399-2449 297 C
tknudsoncarl@csm.edu
KNUESEL, Rita 320-363-5503 271 A
rknuesel@csbsju.edu
KNUESEL, Rita 320-363-5503 262 F
rknuesel@csbsju.edu
KNUEVE, Donald, S 419-783-2581 389 H
dknueve@defiance.edu
KNUTEL, Phillip, G 781-891-3422 231 D
pknutel@bentley.edu
KNUTH, Barbara, A 607-255-5864 331 B
bak3@cornell.edu
KNUTSEN, John, D 510-883-2073 45 B
jknutsen@dspt.edu
KNUTSON, Craig 405-208-5000 410 A
crknutson@okcu.edu
KNUTSON, Julie 734-487-0427 250 F
jknutson@emich.edu
KNUTSON, Karen 320-363-5922 262 F
kknutson@csbsju.edu
KNUTSON, Karen, G 320-363-5922 271 A
kknutson@csbsju.edu
KNUTSON, Sherry 415-749-4571 65 I
sknutson@sfai.edu
KNUTZEN, Gary 360-416-7714 538 D
gary.knutzen@skagit.edu
KNUTZEN, Kathleen 661-654-2210 34 A
kknutzen@csub.edu
KO, Jeanne 212-472-1500 343 G
jko@nysid.edu
KO, Vivien 323-343-2730 35 D
vko@calstatela.edu
KO, Winston, T 530-754-8918 73 I
ko@lsdo.ucdavis.edu
KOAL, Penny 360-596-5227 538 E
pkoal@spscc.ctc.edu
KOAN, Mark 602-285-7855 16 A
mark.koan@pcmail.maricopa.edu
KOBALLA, Thomas 912-478-5648 131 E
tkoballa@georgiasouthern.edu
KOBAYASHI, Frank 408-741-2117 78 G
frank.kobayashi@westvalley.edu
KOBAYASHI, JR., Paul, Y 808-956-7161 141 E
pyk@hawaii.edu
KOBAYASHI, Vivian 408-541-0100 41 E
vkobayashi@cogswell.edu
KOBERNA, Sharon 480-517-8220 16 B
sharon.koberna@riosalado.edu
KOBES, Patricia 845-574-4280 347 I
pkobes@sunyrockland.edu
KOBLER, Wendy 256-372-8344 1 A
wendy.kobler@aamu.edu
KOBOLAKIS, Evan 201-612-5499 307 E
ekobolakis@bergen.edu
KOBRITZ, Richard 818-345-7921 42 F
rkobritz@columbiacollege.edu
KOBULNICKY, Paul, J 330-941-3675 406 F
pjkobulnicky@ysu.edu
KOBUS, Lee 732-255-0400 312 D
lkobus@ocean.edu
KOBYLSKI, Janet 570-408-4501 452 A
janet.kobylski@wilkes.edu
KOCAR, Deb 617-349-8800 236 B
ugadm@lesley.edu
KOCER, Ken 605-668-1589 464 G
kkocer@mtmc.edu
KOCH, Amelia 617-266-1400 231 E
KOCH, Bill 252-328-6166 377 E
kochb@ecu.edu
KOCH, Connie 314-362-6289 282 B
ckoch@bjc.org
KOCH, Dennis 903-886-5796 498 B
dennis.koch@tamuc.edu
KOCH, Don 618-634-3289 164 E
donk@shawneecc.edu
KOCH, Erec 212-772-5195 327 E
erkoch@hunter.cuny.edu
KOCH, James 651-638-6415 261 D
j-koch@bethel.edu
KOCH, Jennifer 716-888-2235 325 F
koch25@canisius.edu
KOCH, Jo Ann 770-394-8300 125 A
jkoch@aii.edu
KOCH, Keith 612-977-5322 261 F
keith.koch@capella.edu
KOCH, Kelly 989-386-6639 255 C
kkoch@midmich.edu
KOCH, Linda, D 570-484-2022 443 B
lkoch@lhup.edu
KOCH, Lindsey 361-570-4136 504 A
kochl@uhv.edu
KOCH, Paul 831-459-5861 75 C
plkoch@ucolick.ort
KOCH, Paul 563-333-6212 188 F
kochpaulc@sau.edu
KOCH, Paul, C 563-333-6196 188 F
kochpaulc@sau.edu
KOCH, Robert 657-278-2638 35 B
rkoch@fullerton.edu
KOCH, Susan 217-206-6634 167 C
koch@uis.edu
KOCH, Susan 217-206-6634 167 A
koch@uis.edu
KOCH, Thomas, L 520-621-2448 18 L
tlkoch@email.arizona.edu
KOCHAN, Roman 562-985-4047 35 C
rkochan@csulb.edu
KOCHANCZYK, Kristin 617-262-5000 231 G
kristin.kochanczyk@the-bac.edu
KOCHANEK, Lea 210-341-1366 491 G
lkochanek@ost.edu
KOCHARD, Dale, A 610-758-5801 434 E
dak304@lehigh.edu
KOCHARD, Lawrence, E 434-924-4245 525 F
lek8e@virginia.edu
KOCHER, Andy, M 317-788-3493 180 F
akocher@uindy.edu
KOCHER, Betty, A 269-387-2360 260 C
betty.kocher@wmich.edu
KOCHER, Bruce 269-488-4205 253 A
bkocher@kvcc.edu
KOCHER, Charles 856-691-8600 309 B
ckocher@cccnj.edu
KOCHER, Craig, T 804-289-8500 525 E
ckocher@richmond.edu
KOCHER, Edward, W 412-396-6082 428 D
kocher@duq.edu
KOCHERA, Melissah 203-596-4652 93 G
mkochera@post.edu
KOCHEVAR, Brenda 218-749-0314 266 I
b.kochevar@mr.mnscu.edu
KOCHEVAR, Deborah 508-887-4700 245 C
deborah.kochevar@tufts.edu
KOCHIEN, Kenneth, G 603-526-3627 303 G
kkochien@colby-sawyer.edu
KOCHIN, Frank, S 314-516-6311 291 D
kochinf@umsl.edu
KOCHIS, Stephen, J 845-575-3000 340 B
stephen.kochis@marist.edu
KOCHON, Barbara 413-565-1000 230 G
bkochon@baypath.edu
KOCIAN, Bryce 979-532-6308 509 D
brycek@wcjc.edu
KOCIAN, Justin 402-494-2311 299 B
jkocian@thenicc.edu
KOCICH, Dennis 979-830-4160 482 C
dkocich@blinn.edu
KOCIOLEK, Patrick 303-492-8464 88 H
patrick.kociolek@colorado.edu
KOCK, Kathryn 989-774-6995 249 C
koch1ke@cmich.edu
KOCOUR, Bruce 865-471-3240 467 G
bkocour@cn.edu
KOCZON, Lenore 701-858-3310 382 A
lenore.koczon@minotstateu.edu
KODAMA, Be-Jay 808-739-8526 140 E
bkodama@chaminade.edu
KODAT, Catherine 215-717-6260 448 I
ckodat@uarts.edu
KODER, Tim 419-372-7706 385 E
tkoder@bgsu.edu
KODNER-WENZEL, Andrea 952-358-8469 268 A
andrea.kodner-wenzel@normandale.edu
KOEBEL, Dave 402-457-2391 298 G
dkoebel@mccneb.edu
KOECHIG, Donna 541-463-5307 416 E
koechigd@lanecc.edu
KOEGEL, Warren 256-782-5368 4 L
wkoegel@jsu.edu
KOEGLER, Jason, W 304-336-8302 544 D
jkoegler@westliberty.edu
KOEHLER, Al 636-922-8452 288 B
alkoehler@stchas.edu
KOEHLER, David 308-635-6021 301 D
koehlerd@wncc.edu
KOEHLER, Donna 253-589-5588 532 G
donna.koehler@cptc.edu
KOEHLER, John 406-791-5330 296 F
jkoehler01@ugf.edu
KOEHLER, Kory 281-998-6150 494 A
kory.koehler@sjcd.edu
KOEHLER, Larry 810-232-8153 255 G
larry.koehler@mcc.edu
KOEHLER, Martha, K 813-253-7007 110 M
mkoehler@hccfl.edu
KOEHLER, Randy 513-244-8449 387 E
randy.koehler@ccuniversity.edu
KOEHN, David 918-444-2186 409 A
koehn@nsuok.edu
KOEHN, Effie, F 406-243-6413 294 I
effie.koehn@umontana.edu
KOEHN, Jack 224-293-5961 83 J
KOEHN, Michelle 316-226-2002 182 A
koehnml@ihs.org
KOEHN, Suzie 307-855-2148 556 B
suzie@cwc.edu
KOEHNKE, Paul 704-330-6121 369 D
paul.koehnke@cpcc.edu
KOELBL, James 207-221-4701 221 A
jkoelbl@une.edu
KOELKER, June 817-257-7106 499 C
j.koelker@tcu.edu
KOELLEIN, David 615-794-4254 472 F
dkoellein@omorecollege.edu
KOELLER, Martin, E 973-761-9782 315 B
martin.koeller@shu.edu
KOELLIKER, Marilynn 785-670-1450 197 F
marilynn.koelliker@washburn.edu
KOELTZOW, Dawn 309-677-2510 146 C
dkoeltzow@bradley.edu
KOENIG, Eric 415-476-4318 75 A
ekoenig@ucsf.edu
KOENIG, Jerry, L 317-921-4491 175 K
jkoenig@ivytech.edu
KOENIG, Jim 815-836-5206 156 F
koenigji@lewisu.edu
KOENIG, Jim 320-363-5563 271 A
jkoenig@csbsju.edu
KOENIG, Jim, J 320-363-5563 262 F
jkoenig@csbsju.edu
KOENIG, Pam 405-382-9202 412 B
p.koenig@sscok.edu
KOENIG-GRIFFIN, Karen 636-584-6575 281 E
kgriffin@eastcentral.edu
KOENIG SEGUIN, Chris 313-927-1221 254 E
cseguin@marygrove.edu
KOENIGSKNECHT, Cindy, J 734-462-4400 258 A
cchampne@schoolcraft.edu
KOEP, Jeffrey 702-895-4210 302 I
jeffrey.koep@unlv.edu
KOEPKE, Andrea 419-434-4677 404 B
koepke@findlay.edu
KOEPKE, Mark 701-252-3467 381 C
mkoepke@jc.edu
KOEPP, Gary, W 440-775-6648 397 G
gary.koepp@oberlin.edu
KOEPPEL, Edmund 516-572-7126 342 C
edmund.koeppel@ncc.edu
KOEPPEN, Bruce 203-528-5301 93 H
bruce.koeppen@quinnipiac.edu

KOERBER, Brent 614-236-7167 386 E
bkoerber@capital.edu
KOERMER, Kelly, A 410-777-7432 221 C
kkoermer@aacc.edu
KOERNER, Mari, E 602-543-6352 11 J
mari.koerner@asu.edu
KOERNER, Mark 513-244-8112 387 E
mark.koerner@ccuniversity.edu
KOESER, Bryan 920-693-1731 554 C
bryan.koeser@gotoltc.edu
KOETT, Kevin 606-783-2014 204 I
k.koett@moreheadstate.edu
KOETTING, Sandy 573-681-5071 283 I
koettings@lincolnu.edu
KOETZNER, John 707-468-3000 57 A
jkoetzne@mendocino.edu
KOEVEN, Gary, J 435-652-7770 512 B
koeven@dixie.edu
KOFFLER, Jeromy 503-943-7470 420 G
koffler@up.edu
KOFRON, Cheryl, L 563-884-5670 188 E
cheryl.kofron@palmer.edu
KOGA, Laura, A 815-740-5084 167 E
lkoga@stfrancis.edu
KOGA, Sheryl 415-955-2011 27 A
skoga@alliant.edu
KOGA, Sheryl 415-442-7859 48 F
skoga@ggu.edu
KOGAN, Alexander 212-327-8001 347 H
kogana@rockefeller.edu
KOGAN, Linda 719-255-3757 88 I
lkogan@uccs.edu
KOGER, Ron, R 678-915-3720 137 G
rkoger@spsu.edu
KOGUT, Leonard, V 276-964-7500 528 E
len.kogut@sw.edu
KOHAN, Eileen, B 213-740-5679 76 F
kohan@usc.edu
KOHL, Erin, K 920-565-1256 548 A
kohlek@lakeland.edu
KOHL, Jay 732-932-4716 314 B
jkohl@aps.rutgers.edu
KOHL, John 978-934-2108 237 B
john_kohl@uml.edu
KOHL, Marie 315-792-5340 341 E
mkohl@mvcc.edu
KOHL, Troy 920-735-5766 554 A
kohlt@fvtc.edu
KOHLER, David, L 253-535-7380 536 E
kohlerdl@plu.edu
KOHLER, Donald 712-325-3262 186 F
dkohler@iwcc.edu
KOHLER, Lynn 813-287-6700 104 M
lkohler@devry.edu
KOHLI, Cathy, L 419-995-8060 392 K
kohli.c@rhodesstate.edu
KOHLMEYER, Bill 503-399-6505 414 J
bill.kohlmeyer@chemeketa.edu
KOHN, David 845-341-4388 345 E
david.kohn@sunyorange.edu
KOHN, Don 310-314-6078 30 A
KOHN, Gregory, N 406-657-1160 296 C
greg.kohn@rocky.edu
KOHN, Jerome 631-656-2185 334 B
jkohn@ftc.edu
KOHN, Marilyn, F 212-678-8997 337 G
makohn@jtsa.edu
KOHN, Melissa 920-236-6100 554 A
kohn@fvtc.edu
KOHN, Paul 404-385-3708 130 F
paul.kohn@ssc.gatech.edu
KOHN, Shayeh 718-327-7600 360 I
yfr1@verizon.net
KOHN SANDERS,
Courtney 708-534-5000 151 E
csanders5@govst.edu
KOHNEN-CAHALL, Nan 513-569-5807 387 G
nan.cahall@cincinnatistate.edu
KOHNKE, Maria 805-493-3105 33 B
kohnke@clunet.edu
KOHR, Lesa, J 585-594-6966 347 F
kohrl@roberts.edu
KOHRMAN, Robert 313-577-2001 260 A
dt9443@wayne.edu
KOHRS, Becky 402-471-2505 299 D
bkohrs@nscs.edu
KOIVISTO, Rex 503-255-0332 417 C
rexk@multnomah.edu
KOJIMA, Glenn, Y 714-449-7465 70 G
gkojima@scco.edu
KOJIRO, Angela 239-687-5332 101 H
amkojiro@avemarialaw.edu
KOK, Cynthia 616-526-6125 249 A
ckok@calvin.edu
KOK, John, H 712-722-6210 184 C
jkok@dordt.edu
KOKAJKO, Hillary, C 336-841-9118 365 C
hkokajko@highpoint.edu
KOKER, John, J 920-424-1210 551 E
koker@uwosh.edu
KOKER, Michelle 612-624-2941 272 A
koker@umn.edu
KOKINOVA, Margarita, D 330-325-6333 397 D
mkokinov@neomed.edu
KOKOLSKYJ, Lydia, D 215-881-7399 438 H
ldk143@psu.edu
KOKOLUS, Cait 610-785-6280 446 A
ckokolus@scs.edu
KOKOLUS, John 717-361-1411 428 F
kokolusj@etown.edu
KOKONAS, Georgios 914-961-8313 349 I
gkokonas@svots.edu
KOKORUDA, George, S 214-648-0100 507 E
george.kokoruda@utsouthwestern.edu
KOKOSKA, Stephen 570-389-4713 441 F
skokoska@bloomu.edu
KOKX-TEMPLET, Ann 281-998-6150 493 G
ann.kokx-templet@sjcd.edu
KOLACINSKI, John 213-484-8850 31 G
KOLAJO, Ebenezer 678-839-6449 139 A
ekolajo@westga.edu
KOLANDER, John, D 414-443-8863 553 D
john.kolander@wlc.edu
KOLATCH, John, P 570-577-1592 423 E
john.kolatch@bucknell.edu
KOLB, Daniel 812-357-6566 180 A
dkolb@saintmeinrad.edu
KOLB, Gary 618-453-4308 165 B
gkolb@siu.edu
KOLB, John, E 518-276-2122 347 D
kolbj@rpi.edu
KOLB, Susan 605-455-6051 465 A
sheathershaw@olc.edu
KOLBE, Donald, A 262-595-2228 552 A
donald.kolbe@uwp.edu
KOLBE, Rick 859-572-5551 205 H
kolber1@nku.edu
KOLCHARNO, Julia 570-504-9614 425 F
KOLCHEVSKA, Natasha 505-277-2611 321 C
nakol@unm.edu
KOLENBRANDER, Kirk, D 617-253-3365 241 D
KOLENDA, Richard 315-312-2246 354 A
richard.kolenda@oswego.edu
KOLENOVIC, Zeke 212-472-1500 343 G
zkolenovic@nysid.edu
KOLESAR, James, G 413-597-4233 246 D
james.g.kolesar@williams.edu
KOLESAR-LYNCH,
Marilyn, K 972-860-4181 484 G
mklynch@dcccd.edu
KOLHOFF, Kathleen 684-699-9155 559 C
k.kolhoff@amsamoa.edu
KOLIMAGA, Karen 978-632-6600 240 C
k_kolimaga@mwcc.mass.edu
KOLINS, Craig 971-722-6182 419 G
ckolins@pcc.edu
KOLISZ, Karin 219-757-6132 179 C
KOLLAR, Kristen 216-791-5000 388 C
kristen.kollar@case.edu
KOLLAR, Lisa 386-226-7068 105 H
lisa.kollar@erau.edu
KOLLAR, OSB, Rene 724-805-2343 446 E
rene.kollar@email.stvincent.edu
KOLLATH, Carissa 402-844-7159 299 I
carissa@northeast.edu
KOLLBAUM, Kristin, E 712-324-5061 188 C
kkollbaum@nwicc.edu
KOLLER, Rebecca, H 402-472-3917 300 E
rkoller@nebraska.edu
KOLLIEN, Mike 989-358-7339 247 C
kollienm@alpenacc.edu
KOLLIGIAN, John 609-258-3285 312 G
jkjr@princeton.edu
KOLLMEYER, Will 662-862-8274 274 E
wakollmeyer@iccms.edu
KOLLOCK, Chenita, R 410-651-8045 227 E
crkollock@umes.edu
KOLLROSS, Crystal 626-585-7759 61 F
cakollross@pasadena.edu
KOLMAN, Mark 740-427-5000 394 C
kolmanm@kenyon.edu
KOLODZEJSKI, Sue 301-552-1400 229 C
skolodzejski@bible.edu
KOLODZIEJSKI, Gwynne 610-796-8325 421 G
gwynne.kolodziejski@alvernia.edu
KOLOMITZ, Kara 781-768-7055 244 A
kara.kolomitz@regiscollege.edu
KOLOVIC, Alia 312-980-9293 154 B
akolovic@iadtchicago.edu
KOLPACK, Bryce 715-675-3331 555 B
kolpack@ntc.edu
KOLVOORD, Robert 540-568-2752 520 H
kolvoora@jmu.edu
KOM, Sheila 208-792-2288 144 B
sheilak@lcsc.edu
KOMACEK, Stanley 724-938-4407 441 G
komacek@calu.edu
KOMACK, Julie 781-239-2661 239 G
jkomack@massbay.edu
KOMANECKY, Sharon 912-449-7600 139 D
skomanecky@waycross.edu
KOMANECKY, Sharon, K 912-449-7600 139 D
skomanecky@waycross.edu
KOMARNY, Phil 724-830-1850 447 C
komarny@setonhill.edu
KOMDAT, Mark 845-687-5051 358 E
komdatm@sunyulster.edu
KOMEIJI, Kalowena 808-454-4873 141 H
kalowena@hawaii.edu
KOMORA, Melissa 518-244-2325 348 A
komorm@sage.edu
KOMOTO, Cary 952-358-8428 268 A
cary.komoto@normandale.edu
KOMP, Chuck 715-365-4537 555 A
ckomp@nicoletcollege.edu
KOMPARE, Lou 440-365-5222 395 D
KOMPEL, John, F 508-767-7350 230 D
jkompel@assumption.edu
KOMPELIEN, Ken 701-671-2297 382 G
ken.kompelien@ndscs.edu
KOMUNIECKI, Patricia, R 419-530-4968 404 F
patricia.komuniecki@utoledo.edu
KONAN, Denise, E 808-956-6570 141 G
konan@hawaii.edu
KONANGI, Vijaya 216-687-3588 388 D
v.konangi@csuohio.edu
KONARSKI, Len 617-287-5519 236 G
len.konarski@umb.edu
KONCSOL, Carol 848-932-7454 314 B
koncsol@oldqueens.rutgers.edu
KONCZAL, Timothy, J 330-672-9192 393 D
tkonczal@kent.edu
KONDA, Kevin, J 316-978-3490 198 A
kevin.konda@wichita.edu
KONDO, Shareese 501-370-5279 23 B
skondo@philander.edu
KONDRACH, Carol, S 609-895-5196 313 F
kondrach@rider.edu
KONDRAK, Mark 651-523-2512 264 A
mkondrak01@hamline.edu
KONDRAT, Mary Ellen 785-864-4720 197 B
maryek@ku.edu
KONDRATENKO, Svetlana 619-298-1829 71 C
KONDRATH, William 617-682-1510 234 E
bkondrath@eds.edu
KONECNY, Lise' 419-267-1262 397 E
lkonecny@northweststate.edu
KONEN, Judee, L 402-461-7434 298 A
jkonen@hastings.edu
KONESCO, Jason, T 317-447-6022 172 C
jason.konesco@harrison.edu
KONESCO, Jason, T 317-447-6022 172 J
jason.konesco@harrison.edu
KONESCO, Jason, T 317-447-6022 172 I
jason.konesco@harrison.edu
KONESCO, Jason, T 317-447-6022 172 F
jason.konesco@harrison.edu
KONESCO, Jason, T 317-447-6022 172 D
jazon.konesco@harrison.edu
KONESCO, Jason, T 317-447-6022 172 G
jason.konesco@harrison.edu
KONESCO, Jason, T 317-447-6022 172 H
jason.konesco@harrison.edu
KONESCO, Jason, T 317-447-6022 172 E
jason.konesco@harrison.edu
KONESCO, Jason, T 317-447-6022 172 K
jason.konesco@harrison.edu
KONESCO, Jason, T 317-447-6022 172 B
jason.konesco@harrison.edu
KONESCO, Jason, T 317-447-6022 172 L
jason.konesco@harrison.edu
KONG, Xiangping 609-626-6025 313 E
xiangping.kong@stockton.edu
KONIG, Angela, A 641-422-1521 188 A
angela.konig@iwd.iowa.gov
KONIG, Michael 413-565-1000 230 G
mkonig@baypath.edu
KONIG, Susan 212-772-4070 327 E
skonig@hunter.cuny.edu
KONING, Shawnn 951-343-4224 31 J
skoning@calbaptist.edu
KONKLE, Lance, R 716-851-1868 333 A
konkle@ecc.edu
KONKLE, Thomas, E 812-888-4451 181 D
tkonkle@vinu.edu
KONKOLESKI, RJ 740-695-9500 385 B
rkonkoleski@belmontcollege.edu
KONKOLY, Thomas, H 440-826-3460 384 K
tkonkoly@bw.edu
KONKOTH, Shanthi 212-247-3434 339 G
skonkoth@mandl.edu
KONNY, Sharon 847-214-7260 150 F
skonny@elgin.edu
KONO, Kim 971-722-4387 419 G
kim.kono@pcc.edu
KONOPACKE, Michael 989-729-3353 248 F
michael.konopacke@baker.edu
KONOPKA, Daniel 914-633-2069 336 E
dkonopka@iona.edu
KONOPKA, Joseph 732-729-3901 309 C
jkonopka@devry.edu
KONOPSKI, Michael, J 716-286-8721 344 D
mjk@niagara.edu
KONRAD, Jim 847-491-8121 160 E
j-konrad@northwestern.edu
KONSCHAK, Norma 218-683-8613 268 C
norma.konschak@northlandcollege.edu
KONSTALID, Daniel, T 717-337-6200 429 I
dkonstal@gettysburg.edu
KONUWA, Alfred, B 530-661-5712 80 J
akonuwa@yccd.edu
KONWERSKI, Peter, A 202-994-7210 98 C
peterk@gwu.edu
KONYA, Jeffrey 661-654-2200 34 A
jkonya@csub.edu
KONYAOLE, Cedric 501-370-5336 23 B
cronyaole@philander.edu
KONZ, Jeff 828-251-6570 378 D
jkonz@unca.edu
KONZEM, Gail 785-227-3380 191 B
konzemg@bethanylb.edu
KONZEM, Richard 816-501-4854 288 A
richard.konzem@rockhurst.edu
KOO, James 714-525-0088 48 I
KOOB, Sondra 215-785-0111 440 I
KOOHANG, Alex 478-471-2801 133 H
alex.koohang@maconstate.edu
KOOI, Jana 904-633-8322 109 F
janakooi@fscj.edu
KOOI, Janeen, W 260-982-5219 177 H
jwkooi@manchester.edu
KOOI, Shelly 219-464-5212 181 C
shelly.kooi@valpo.edu
KOOIMAN, Florence 219-864-2400 178 F
fkooiman@midamerica.edu
KOOK, Kathleen 510-649-2465 48 J
kkook@gtu.edu
KOON, Ann, M 740-264-5591 390 F
akoon@egcc.edu
KOON, Chi 718-270-6107 328 C
chi@mec.cuny.edu
KOON, J. Michael 304-214-8967 543 D
mkoon@wvncc.edu
KOONCE, Kenneth, L 225-578-2080 212 H
kkoonce@lsu.edu
KOONTZ, David 562-903-4760 31 A
dave.koontz@biola.edu
KOONTZ, Sondra 316-284-5341 191 C
skoontz@bethelks.edu
KOONZ, Peter 518-454-5182 330 C
koonzp@strose.edu
KOOP, Stuart 510-436-1250 50 H
koop@hnu.edu
KOOP LIECHTY, Dan 574-535-7002 171 G
dankl@goshen.edu
KOOPMAN, Jan 402-643-7341 297 D
alumni@cune.edu
KOOPMANS, Sue, M 573-875-7668 280 A
smkoopmans@ccis.edu
KOOPMANS, Tina, M 340-693-1540 568 E
tkoopma@live.uvi.edu
KOOTI, John 717-477-1435 443 E
jgkooti@ship.edu
KOPACH, Christopher, M 520-241-6482 18 L
ckopach@email.arizona.edu
KOPACK, David 213-381-3333 53 C
dkopack@lac.edu
KOPAS, Michael 973-408-3609 309 E
mkopas@drew.edu
KOPELOWITZ, Seymour 216-464-4050 394 H
skopelowitz@siegalcollege.edu
KOPENEC, Rose, M 414-425-8300 550 E
rkopenec@shst.edu
KOPERA, Ken 864-646-1770 461 F
kkopera@tctc.edu
KOPERSKI, Kate 716-286-8288 344 D
kjk@niagara.edu
KOPERSKI, Mike 415-442-7082 48 F
mkoperski@ggu.edu
KOPF, Gregory, S 913-945-6636 197 C
gkopf@kumc.edu
KOPICKO, Ronald, L 517-750-1200 258 D
rkopicko@arbor.edu
KOPISCHKE, Kevin 320-762-4404 265 F
kevink@alextech.edu
KOPLOWITZ, Stephan 661-255-1050 32 F
skoplowitz@calarts.edu
KOPONEN, Glenn 845-675-4691 344 G
glenn.koponen@nyack.edu
KOPP, Courtney, A 515-574-1020 185 I
kopp@iowacentral.edu
KOPP, Mark, W 864-242-5100 455 E
KOPP, Stephen, J 304-696-2300 544 B
kopp@marshall.edu
KOPP, Sue 503-517-1032 421 B
skopp@warnerpacific.edu
KOPP, Will 614-287-2412 389 A
wkopp@cscc.edu
KOPPEL, Roberta, K 401-874-5177 454 E
bkoppel@uri.edu
KOPPEL, Sheree 502-456-6509 206 G
skoppel@sctd.edu
KOPPELL, Jonathan 602-496-0402 11 J
koppel@asu.edu
KOPPER, Beverly 262-472-1672 553 A
kopperb@uww.edu
KOPPI, Steve 413-538-2081 242 D
skoppi@mtholyoke.edu
KOPTEROS, Michelle, C 773-883-7279 158 E
kopter15@hotmail.com
KORAN, Noel 541-552-6522 419 A
korann@sou.edu
KORB, Christine 503-699-3361 416 J
ckorb@maryhurst.edu

KORB, Judy 913-469-8500 194 B jkorb@jccc.edu
KORB, Leigh, S 662-846-4000 273 H lkorb@deltastate.edu
KORB, Leslie 270-384-8030 204 D korbl@lindsey.edu
KORB, Scott 906-635-2032 253 H skorb@lssu.edu
KORB, Scott, M 906-635-2032 253 H skorb@lssu.edu
KORB-NICE, Jobe, S 206-281-2564 537 H jobe@spu.edu
KORBEL, Linda 847-635-1952 160 F lkorbel@oakton.edu
KORBER, Stephanie 814-269-7074 449 D korber@pitt.edu
KORCAN-BUZZA, Andrea, L 724-847-6603 429 H akorcanb@geneva.edu
KORD, JoLanna 620-341-6839 192 G jkord@emporia.edu
KORDENBROCK, Jeffrey 859-344-3321 206 I jeff.kordenbrock@thomasmore.edu
KOREEN, Michael 952-358-7007 268 A michael.koreen@normandale.edu
KOREN, Christina 814-886-6407 437 B ckoren@mtaloy.edu
KORETOFF, Lisa, A 336-334-4822 371 A lakoretoff@gtcc.edu
KOREY, Eileen 330-972-8589 403 B korey@uakron.edu
KOREY-SMITH, Kristin 808-235-7361 142 F ksmith@hawaii.edu
KORF, Abraham 305-673-5664 123 G rabbikorf@hotmail.com
KORF, Benzion 305-653-8770 123 G bkorf@lecfl.com
KORFIATIS, George, P 201-216-5263 315 E gkorfiat@stevens.edu
KORINEK, Clare, M 312-915-7235 157 C ckorine@luc.edu
KORINKE, Kim 805-378-1463 77 D kkorinke@vcccd.edu
KORIS, Carol 305-913-2104 112 A carol.koris@jwu.edu
KORMAN, Thomas, P 517-750-1200 258 D tkorman@arbor.edu
KORN, Benjamin 801-957-4247 512 D benjamin.korn@slcc.edu
KORN, Jane 509-313-3700 534 F jkorn@lawschool.gonzaga.edu
KORNBERG, Judith 212-986-4343 323 H jdk@berkeleycollege.edu
KORNBERG, Judith 973-278-5400 307 F
KORNBERG, Mindy 206-685-4730 539 A mindyk@uw.edu
KORNBERG, Sir Hans 617-353-4020 232 E hlk@bu.edu
KORNBLUH, Mark 859-257-1246 207 D kornbluh@uky.edu
KORNBLUH, Rebecca 909-621-8000 62 H rebecca_kornbluh@cucmail.claremont.edu
KORNEGAY, Anne 804-758-6731 528 C akornegay@rappahannock.edu
KORNEGAY, Arthur 910-296-2575 371 E akornegay@jamessprunt.edu
KORNEGAY, Barbara, R 919-658-7756 367 F bkornegay@moc.edu
KORNEGAY, Carolyn, T 405-466-3411 408 G ctkornegay@langston.edu
KORNEGAY, Jeffrey 910-879-5574 368 D jeffkornegay@bladencc.edu
KORNEGAY, Jeri, S 260-982-5285 177 H jskornegay@manchester.edu
KORNEGAY, Joy 919-735-5151 375 A jkornegay@waynecc.edu
KORNER, Barbara, O 814-865-2591 438 G bok2@psu.edu
KORNFELD, Harriet, S 617-724-6399 242 B hkornfeld@mghihp.edu
KORNIEWICZ, Denise 701-777-4555 381 F denise.korniewicz@und.edu
KORNKVEN, Kelly 701-788-4816 381 H kelly.kornkven@mayvillestate.edu
KORNMILLER, Brenda, L 740-374-8716 405 G bkornmiller@wscc.edu
KORNOWSKI, Andrew 502-213-4162 202 F andrew.kornowski@kctcs.edu
KORNUTA, Halyna 858-653-6740 52 D
KOROCH, Greg, A 269-927-8161 253 G koroch@lakemichigancollege.edu
KOROMA, Ibrahim, H 202-274-5415 100 A ikoroma@udc.edu
KOROMA, Joseph 559-934-2306 78 C josephkoroma@whccd.edu
KOROPCHAK, John 618-453-4550 165 B koropcha@siu.edu
KOROPCHAK, John, A 618-453-4551 165 B koropcha@siu.edu
KORPELA, Doreen 906-487-7201 251 A doreen.korpela@finlandia.edu
KORPI, Ray 360-992-2932 532 F rkorpi@clark.edu
KORPICS, Wayne 419-423-2211 385 J wkorpics@brownmackie.edu
KORR, Wynne, S 217-333-2261 167 D wkorr@illinois.edu
KORSCHGEN, Ann, J 573-882-7651 291 B korschgena@missouri.edu
KORSE-DEVLIN, Allison 661-362-3648 41 I allison.devlin@canyons.edu
KORSTAD, Donna 509-542-4401 532 H dkorstad@columbiabasin.edu
KORSTAD, John 918-495-6942 411 C jkorstad@oru.edu
KORTE, Andi 910-695-3767 373 H kortea@sandhills.edu
KORTUS, Matt 952-446-4160 263 C kortusm@crown.edu
KORVAS, Ronald 407-646-2174 116 D rkorvas@rollins.edu
KORVER, Bill 910-323-5614 363 A
KORWITTS, Kayte 312-980-4822 154 B kkorwitts@iadtchicago.edu
KORYCANSKY, Kevin 202-462-2101 99 A korycansky@iwp.edu
KORZAN, Loren 419-227-3141 404 D lkorzan@unoh.edu
KORZINEK, Sue 616-331-2035 251 F korzines@gvsu.edu
KOSAK, Robbee 412-268-2136 424 J rkosak@andrew.cmu.edu
KOSANOVIC, David 614-251-4512 398 F kosanovd@ohiodominican.edu
KOSBOTH, Michele 617-243-2227 236 A mkosboth@lasell.edu
KOSCHMEDER, Douglas 563-387-1167 187 D registrar@luther.edu
KOSEL, Paul 402-554-2648 301 A pkosel@unomaha.edu
KOSELUK, William 805-893-5252 75 B william.koseluk@ic.ucsb.edu
KOSH, Jamie 814-472-3372 446 B jkosh@francis.edu
KOSHEWA, Angela, D 502-852-6981 207 E adkosh01@louisville.edu
KOSHORK, Lori 206-726-5027 533 D lkoshork@cornish.edu
KOSHUT, Thomas, M 256-824-6100 8 G tom.koshut@uah.edu
KOSHUTE, Daniel 814-472-3222 446 B dkoshute@francis.edu
KOSIEWICZ, Lisa 415-422-2710 76 E lkosiewicz@usfca.edu
KOSIN, Mary 570-740-0395 435 C mkosin@luzerne.edu
KOSINSKI, Mark 203-285-2077 91 D mkosinski@gwcc.commnet.edu
KOSINSKI, Melissa 419-473-2700 389 C mkosinski@daviscollege.edu
KOSINSKI, Ross 623-572-3329 16 E rkosin@midwestern.edu
KOSINSKY, James, A 708-209-3519 148 E jim.kosinsky@cuchicago.edu
KOSKI, Lynne, D 402-844-7036 299 I lynne@northeast.edu
KOSKOSKI, Scott 412-365-1650 425 C skoskoski@chatham.edu
KOSLOSKI, James 516-877-3974 322 A kosloski@adelphi.edu
KOSLOSKY, Jill 620-252-7295 192 B jillk@coffeyville.edu
KOSLOW-MARTIN, Jodi 630-844-7510 145 F jkoslow@aurora.edu
KOSMER, Mary, K 920-923-8089 548 E mkkosmer09@marianuniversity.edu
KOSMOSKI, Kathleen 912-486-7409 135 D kkosmoski@ogeecheetech.edu
KOSOWSKY, Vicki 812-535-5216 179 E vkosowsk@smwc.edu
KOSS, Michelle 734-462-4400 258 A mkoss@schoolcraft.edu
KOSSE, Glenn, F 502-272-8328 198 H gkosse@bellarmine.edu
KOSSEFF, Christopher, O 973-972-4866 316 C kosseff@umdnj.edu
KOSSES, Jennifer 617-732-2866 241 C jennifer.kosses@mcphs.edu
KOSSUTH, Joanne 781-292-2431 234 H joanne.kossuth@olin.edu
KOST, Carrie 920-686-6141 550 H carrie.kost@sl.edu
KOSTELL, Stacey 217-333-0302 167 D skostell@illinois.edu
KOSTELNIK, Marjorie 402-472-2913 300 G mkostelnik2@unl.edu
KOSTER, Ed 605-668-1367 464 G edward.koster@mtmc.edu
KOSTRAB, Lynn, M 330-569-5109 391 G kostrablm@hiram.edu
KOSTRUBANIC, Robert, M 260-481-6196 174 C kostrubr@ipfw.edu
KOSTRZEWA, Waldemar 203-575-8297 92 A wkostrzewa@nvcc.commnet.edu
KOSTYUKOV, Victoria 718-522-9073 323 B victoria_kostyukov@asa.edu
KOTAGAL, Nirmala 507-285-7143 268 I nirmala.kotagal@roch.edu
KOTAJARVI, Kathy 920-693-1163 554 C kathy.kotajarvi@gotoltc.edu
KOTARSKI, Beth 610-328-8058 447 F bkotars1@swarthmore.edu
KOTARSKI, Vida 317-955-6203 177 I vidako@marian.edu
KOTCAMP, Butch 740-351-3429 401 I bkotcamp@shawnee.edu
KOTECKI, Kathy 406-657-1660 295 D kkotecki@msubillings.edu
KOTESKEY, Kerri 406-791-5207 296 F kkoteskey01@ugf.edu
KOTH, Tara 402-449-2831 297 H tkoth@graceu.edu
KOTHE, Alison 765-361-6027 181 E kothea@wabash.edu
KOTHENBEUTEL, Nancy 563-336-3328 184 E nkothenbeutel@eicc.edu
KOTILA, Paul, M 603-899-4303 305 A kotilapm@franklinpierce.edu
KOTKIN, Laura 718-281-5144 328 F lkotkin@qcc.cuny.edu
KOTLER, A. Malkiel 732-367-1060 307 G
KOTLER, Aaron 732-367-1060 307 G akotler@bmg.edu
KOTLER, Yitzchok, S 732-367-1060 307 G
KOTLIKOFF, Michael, I 607-253-3771 331 B mik7@cornell.edu
KOTLINSKI, Michael, J 717-337-6363 429 I mkotlinski@gettysburg.edu
KOTOWICZ, Keith, A 414-847-3301 549 B keithkotowicz@miad.edu
KOTSAKIS, Ted 360-992-2936 532 F tkotsakis@clark.edu
KOTSIOPULOS, Peter 308-698-5270 300 F pkotsiopulos@nufoundation.org
KOTSIOPULOS, Peter 308-865-8474 300 F pkotsiopulos@nufoundation.org
KOTTAS, Kathy 620-792-9355 190 H kottask@bartonccc.edu
KOTTER, Ronald, L 812-888-4124 181 D rkotter@vinu.edu
KOTTICH, Sarah 402-399-2427 297 C skottich@csm.edu
KOTTON, Stevenson 692-625-4931 560 A
KOTUBEY, Jordan 248-457-2739 252 E
KOTULSKI, Bob, L 417-268-6036 278 J bkotulski@gobbc.edu
KOUA, Deb 515-965-7025 183 H dkkoua@dmacc.edu
KOUBEK, Richard 225-578-5701 212 H rkoubek@lsu.edu
KOUCOUMARIS, John, S 740-695-9500 385 B jkoucoum@belmontcollege.edu
KOUDELIK-JONES, Rachelle 540-857-6187 529 B rkoudelikjones@virginiawestern.edu
KOUDOU, Nick 816-559-6182 287 E nick.koudou@park.edu
KOUGH, Katherine 717-262-2006 452 C kkough@wilson.edu
KOUKARI, Ray 262-619-6712 554 B koukarir@gtc.edu
KOUKOLA, Christine, H 573-882-4523 291 B koukolac@missouri.edu
KOULIK, Chester 845-451-1347 331 E c_koulik@culinary.edu
KOUMARIANOS, Dee 603-577-6570 304 I ykoumarianos@dwc.edu
KOURIS, Demitris 817-257-7727 499 C d.kouris@tcu.edu
KOURY, Kevin, A 724-938-4125 441 G koury@calu.edu
KOUSEN, Sandra 219-981-1111 176 G skousen@ivytech.edu
KOUTSOUTIS, Kalli 718-429-6600 359 G kalli.koutsoutis@vaughn.edu
KOUTSOVITIS, Christopher, S 914-337-9300 330 G christopher.koutsovitis@concordia-ny.edu
KOVAC, Jason 913-469-8500 194 B jasonkovac@jccc.edu
KOVAC, John 412-809-5100 444 G kovac.john@pti.edu
KOVAC, Matt 724-287-8711 423 G matt.kovac@bc3.edu
KOVACH, Kathy 912-427-1963 124 C kkovach@altamahatech.edu
KOVACH-ALLEN, Katharina, E 585-345-6831 334 F kekovachallen@genesee.edu
KOVACICH, Christine 330-325-6551 397 D ckovacich@neomed.edu
KOVACS, Anita, A 863-784-7123 117 J anita.kovacs@southflorida.edu
KOVACS, Charles 941-359-7650 116 B ckovacs@ringling.edu
KOVACS, Mark, C 315-792-3025 359 E mkovacs@utica.edu
KOVAL, Volga 707-826-4143 36 E volga.koval@humboldt.edu
KOVALA, Irene 623-845-3012 15 H irene.kovala@gcmail.maricopa.edu
KOVALCHICK, Ann 515-271-2345 184 D ann.kovalchick@drake.edu
KOVALCIK, Andrew, B 412-648-0233 449 A kandrew@pitt.edu
KOVANES, Tera, D 540-654-1042 525 D tkovanes@umw.edu
KOVATCH, John, E 330-972-6922 403 B kovatch@uakron.edu
KOVATCH, Richard, A 434-982-5166 525 F rak3e@virginia.edu
KOVATCHITCH, Marian 315-798-8125 348 D mkovatch@secon.edu
KOVERMAN, Robert 312-369-6543 148 D rkoverman@colum.edu
KOVEROLA, Catherine 617-349-8317 236 B koverola@lesley.edu
KOVIC, Hong Yu 860-383-5284 92 E hkovic@trcc.commnet.edu
KOVLER, Allen 518-828-4181 330 E kovler@sunycgcc.edu
KOWAL, Donna, M 585-395-5400 352 F dkowal@brockport.edu
KOWALCHUK, Elizabeth 785-864-3661 197 B kowalchu@ku.edu
KOWALESKI, Curt 920-403-3117 550 F curt.kowaleski@snc.edu
KOWALEWSKI, John, L 801-626-7212 511 G jkowalewski@weber.edu
KOWALEWSKY, Lyn 989-358-7280 247 C kowalewl@alpenacc.edu
KOWALIK, Thomas 607-777-2792 351 F kowalik@binghamton.edu
KOWALSKI, Beth 614-251-4576 398 F kowalskb@ohiodominican.edu
KOWALSKI, JR., Edward, J 315-255-1743 325 G kowalskie@cayuga-cc.edu
KOWALSKI, Gerard, J 706-542-8318 138 G kowalski@uga.edu
KOWALSKI, JR., Jonathan, V 414-277-4510 549 C kowalski@msoe.edu
KOWALSKI, Karl 907-450-8383 10 I karl.kowalski@alaska.edu
KOWALSKI, Karl 907-450-8383 10 G karl.kowalski@alaska.edu
KOWALSKI, Melanie 570-504-1583 433 A kowalskim@lackawanna.edu
KOWALSKI, Timothy, J 540-231-4000 518 I
KOWAR, Pamela 860-255-3603 92 F pkowar@txcc.commnet.edu
KOWEEK, Joan 518-828-4181 330 E joan.koweek@sunycgcc.edu
KOWICH, Colleen 816-271-5650 286 G ckowich@missouriwestern.edu
KOWICH, Debra, A 734-764-0304 259 A dkowich@umich.edu
KOWNACKI, James 570-484-2460 443 B jkownack@lhup.edu
KOWPAK, Corinne 207-216-4399 219 C ckowpak@yccc.edu
KOWTA, Mayumi 805-437-3107 34 B mayumi.kowta@csuci.edu
KOYE, Diane 609-984-1110 316 A dkoye@tesc.edu
KOYZIS, Anthony 304-336-8004 544 D akoyzis@westliberty.edu
KOZACHYN, Karen 610-359-5362 426 G kkozachy@dccc.edu
KOZACZKA, Stanley 315-655-7132 325 H skozaczka@cazenovia.edu
KOZAK, Diane 907-786-4513 10 H andhk1@uaa.alaska.edu
KOZAK, Gregory 847-574-5194 156 A gkozak@lfgsm.edu
KOZAK, Laura, A 410-706-8138 227 C lkoza001@umaryland.edu
KOZAKIEWICZ, Patricia 201-684-7610 313 C pkozakie@ramapo.edu
KOZEL, Anj 612-332-3361 261 A akozel@aii.edu
KOZERACKI, Carol 818-710-4108 55 B kozaraca@piercecollege.edu
KOZIATEK, Caroline 203-932-7479 95 C ckoziatek@newhaven.edu
KOZIEK, Timothy, J 708-709-3702 161 D tkoziek@prairiestate.edu
KOZIK, Bob 518-631-9881 358 H kozikr@uniongraduatecollege.edu
KOZIKOWSKI, Mitch 724-938-5706 441 G kozikowski@calu.edu
KOZIL, Cindy, T 508-541-1552 233 G ckozil@dean.edu
KOZIMOR, Renee 847-635-1761 160 F rkozimor@oakton.edu
KOZISEK, Kelly, L 541-737-4261 418 F kelly.kozisek@oregonstate.edu
KOZISEK, Sue 402-421-7410 298 J
KOZLOWSKI, Gerald, F 972-860-7143 484 I geraldkozlowski@dcccd.edu
KOZLOWSKI, Jerry, A 585-345-6999 334 F jakozlowski@genesee.edu

KOZLOWSKI, Lynn, T .... 716-829-3434 .... 351 G sphhp@buffalo.edu
KOZLOWSKI, Marjorie .... 847-925-6523 .... 151 G mkozlows@harpercollege.edu
KOZLOWSKI, Michelle .... 559-934-2240 .... 78 B michellekozlowski@whccd.edu
KOZOJED, Bob, J .... 701-788-4872 .... 381 H bob.kozojed@mayvillestate.edu
KOZOMAN, Robert .... 312-362-6695 .... 149 A bkozoman@depaul.edu
KOZUMA, Hikaru .... 215-898-4340 .... 448 J kozuma@exchange.upenn.edu
KRAAL, Steven, A .... 512-475-6976 .... 505 D sakraal@mail.utexas.edu
KRACKER, Christie .... 330-263-2498 .... 388 F ckracker@wooster.edu
KRACKOW, Michael, S .... 540-224-4478 .... 520 I mskrackow@jchs.edu
KRAEMER, David .... 212-678-8075 .... 337 G dakraemer@jtsa.edu
KRAEMER, Ronald, D .... 574-631-9700 .... 180 G kraemer.5@nd.edu
KRAEUCHI, Bob .... 314-719-8024 .... 281 I rkraeuch@fontbonne.edu
KRAFT, Deborah .... 443-334-2689 .... 226 E dkraft@stevenson.edu
KRAFT, Gary, L .... 402-472-3609 .... 300 G gary.kraft@uln.edu
KRAFT, Jeffrey .... 708-524-6294 .... 150 C jkraft@dom.edu
KRAFT, John .... 912-344-2589 .... 124 G john.kraft@armstrong.edu
KRAFT, John .... 352-392-2398 .... 120 C john.kraft@cba.ufl.edu
KRAFT, Kathy .... 701-627-4738 .... 381 B kkraft@fbcc.bia.edu
KRAFT, Patricia .... 912-279-5858 .... 127 E pkraft@ccga.edu
KRAFT, Paul .... 541-881-5599 .... 420 E pkraft@tvcc.cc
KRAFT, Ronald, D .... 707-256-7160 .... 58 F rkraft@napavalley.edu
KRAFT, Walter .... 734-487-6895 .... 250 F walter.kraft@emuch.edu
KRAFT-MEYER, Kelly .... 434-381-6205 .... 524 K kraft_meyer@sbc.edu
KRAGE O'CONNER, Bridget .... 920-403-3007 .... 550 F bridget.oconnor@snc.edu
KRAGT, Donna .... 616-234-4040 .... 251 E dkragt@grcc.edu
KRAGULJEVIC, Nev .... 520-494-5471 .... 13 D nev.kraguljevic@centralaz.edu
KRAHE, Sharon, A .... 814-871-7670 .... 429 G krahe@gannon.edu
KRAHL, Tracy .... 312-362-5577 .... 149 A tkrahl@depaul.edu
KRAIMER, Paul .... 651-905-3509 .... 261 E pkraimer@browncollege.edu
KRAISINGER, Jodi .... 724-836-9942 .... 449 C kraising@pitt.edu
KRAJEWSKA, Monika .... 805-898-2905 .... 47 C mkrajewska@fielding.edu
KRAJNIAK, Chris, A .... 262-554-2010 .... 158 E chriskrajn@aol.com
KRAJNIAK, Chris, A .... 262-554-2010 .... 549 A chriskrajn@aol.com
KRAJNIK, Michelle .... 802-258-3280 .... 514 E michelle.krajnik@worldlearning.org
KRAKLAU, Laura .... 269-927-8198 .... 253 G kraklau@lakemichigancollege.edu
KRAKOFF, Steve, P .... 419-372-7127 .... 385 E skrakof@bgsu.edu
KRAKORA, Edward, M .... 419-289-5401 .... 384 G ekrakora@ashland.edu
KRAKORA, Julie, M .... 815-740-3415 .... 167 E jkrakora@stfrancis.edu
KRAKOWSKY, Robin .... 303-256-9462 .... 85 L rkrakowsky@jwu.edu
KRAKOWSKY, Robin .... 401-598-1411 .... 453 E rkrakowsky@jwu.edu
KRAL, Kathy .... 678-839-6585 .... 139 A kkral@westga.edu
KRAL, Martin, J .... 309-298-1838 .... 168 C mj-kral@wiu.edu
KRALEVICH, Richard, C .... 302-857-1754 .... 96 D richardk@dtcc.edu
KRALICEK, James .... 816-531-5223 .... 280 C jkralicek@concordecareercolleges.com
KRALL, Jason .... 412-578-6152 .... 424 I jkrall@carlow.edu
KRALL, Jim .... 479-524-7145 .... 22 C jkrall@jbu.edu
KRALL, Julia .... 304-876-5526 .... 544 C jkrall@shepherd.edu
KRALL, Lisi .... 607-753-4827 .... 353 B lisi.krall@cortland.edu
KRALLMAN, Denise, A .... 513-529-7095 .... 396 E krallmda@muohio.edu
KRAM, Lauri .... 425-640-1522 .... 533 I lkram@edcc.edu
KRAMBUHL, Scott .... 541-917-4722 .... 416 I krambus@linnbenton.edu
KRAMER, Alan .... 860-913-2032 .... 92 I akramer@goodwin.edu
KRAMER, Arthur .... 201-200-3073 .... 312 B akramer@njcu.edu
KRAMER, Benjamin .... 540-674-3600 .... 527 E bkramer@nr.edu
KRAMER, Bruce, H .... 651-962-4425 .... 272 B bhkramer@stthomas.edu
KRAMER, Cathy .... 828-298-3325 .... 380 D service@warren-wilson.edu
KRAMER, Chris .... 217-234-5475 .... 156 B ckramer@lakeland.cc.il.us
KRAMER, Eric .... 413-528-7476 .... 230 F ekramer@simons-rock.edu
KRAMER, Eugene .... 513-745-8318 .... 403 F eugene.kramer@uc.edu
KRAMER, Jill .... 317-921-4569 .... 175 I jkramer5@ivytech.edu
KRAMER, John .... 305-220-4120 .... 115 F acadir@ptcmatt.com
KRAMER, Kathleen, A .... 619-260-6832 .... 76 D kramer@sandiego.edu
KRAMER, Kathleen, R .... 717-270-6310 .... 430 E krkramer@hacc.edu
KRAMER, Kirk, A .... 810-989-5503 .... 257 H kkramer@sc4.edu
KRAMER, Kyle .... 812-357-6678 .... 180 A kkramer@saintmeinrad.edu
KRAMER, Lisa .... 563-243-4023 .... 182 C lisa.kramer@ashford.edu
KRAMER, Mark .... 757-825-2815 .... 528 F kramerm@tncc.edu
KRAMER, Matt .... 617-327-6777 .... 241 F matt_kramer@mspp.edu
KRAMER, Monte .... 605-773-3455 .... 465 F montek@sdbor.edu
KRAMER, Nancy .... 319-226-2040 .... 182 A kramerna@ihs.org
KRAMER, Nancy .... 773-907-4443 .... 147 D nkramer@ccc.edu
KRAMER, Nikki, A .... 920-923-8142 .... 548 E nakramer22@marianuniversity.edu
KRAMER, Pamela .... 239-687-5305 .... 101 H pkramer@avemarialaw.edu
KRAMER, Scott, E .... 270-852-3286 .... 204 A scottkr@kwc.edu
KRAMER, Steve .... 620-223-2700 .... 193 A stevek@fortscott.edu
KRAMER, Sue .... 610-902-8781 .... 424 B susan.m.kramer@cabrini.edu
KRAMER, Terry .... 781-239-2431 .... 239 G tkramer1@massbay.edu
KRAMER, Thomas A, M .... 773-702-9800 .... 166 G tkramer@uchicago.edu
KRAMER-ERTEL, Pamela .... 570-422-3377 .... 442 D pkramer@po-box.esu.edu
KRAMER-JEFFERSON, Kate .... 301-846-2409 .... 222 G kkramerjefferson@frederick.edu
KRAMLICH, Carol .... 209-478-0800 .... 50 K ckramlich@humphreys.edu
KRAMP, Julie .... 620-792-9278 .... 190 H krampj@bartonccc.edu
KRAMPF, Harry .... 507-389-6315 .... 267 E harry.krampf@mnsu.edu
KRAN, Paul .... 212-678-4106 .... 357 G kran@tc.columbia.edu
KRANE, Barbara .... 954-969-9771 .... 108 F barbaraw@steinerleisure.com
KRANE, Maria, C .... 402-280-2221 .... 297 F mkrane@creighton.edu
KRANSBERGER, M. Elizabeth (Beth) .... 619-961-4330 .... 72 J bkransberger@tjsl.edu
KRANTZ, Margaret .... 812-866-7126 .... 172 A krantzm@hanover.edu
KRANTZ, Susan, E .... 504-280-6268 .... 213 E skrantz@uno.edu
KRANZLER, Michael .... 212-960-5277 .... 346 F kranzler@yu.edu
KRANZLER, Michael .... 212-960-5277 .... 361 M kranzler@yu.edu
KRAPF, Audrey .... 631-420-2009 .... 356 A audrey.krapf@farmingdale.edu
KRAPF, Keith .... 618-985-3741 .... 154 G keithkrapf@jalc.edu
KRAPOHL, Robert, H .... 847-317-4004 .... 166 E rkrapohl@tiu.edu
KRAPPES, Frank .... 970-491-5105 .... 83 F louis.krappes@colostate.edu
KRASOWSKI, Marilyn .... 651-846-1363 .... 269 C marilyn.krasowski@saintpaul.edu
KRATKY, Rita .... 406-247-3000 .... 295 F rkratky@cot.msubillings.edu
KRATKY, Rita .... 406-247-3019 .... 295 D rkratky@msubillings.edu
KRATOCHVIL, Bob .... 925-439-2181 .... 43 G bkratochvil@losmedanos.edu
KRATOCHVIL, Charles, P .... 530-752-1996 .... 73 I cpkratochvil@ucdavis.edu
KRATOCHVIL, Christopher .... 402-559-8490 .... 300 H ckrotoch@unmc.edu
KRATOCHVIL, Richard .... 617-951-2350 .... 242 G richard.kratochvil@necb.edu
KRATTENMAKER, Tom .... 503-768-7975 .... 416 G tkratt@lclark.edu
KRATZ, JR., Charles, E .... 570-941-4008 .... 450 C charles.kratz@scranton.edu
KRATZ, David .... 212-966-0300 .... 342 F info@nyaa.edu
KRATZ, Dennis .... 972-883-2984 .... 506 A dkratz@utdallas.edu
KRATZ, Ken .... 504-568-4970 .... 213 A kkratz@lsuhsc.edu
KRATZER, David .... 352-392-1265 .... 120 C kratzerd@ufl.edu
KRATZKE, William, P .... 901-678-3221 .... 474 C wkratzke@memphis.edu
KRAUS, Brian .... 615-230-3428 .... 476 C brian.kraus@volstate.edu
KRAUS, Edwin .... 719-632-7626 .... 85 G ekraus@intellitec.edu
KRAUS, Jeffrey .... 718-390-3254 .... 360 A jkraus@wagner.edu
KRAUS, Jeffrey .... 718-390-3173 .... 360 A jkraus@wagner.edu
KRAUS, John .... 417-865-2811 .... 281 G krausj@evangel.edu
KRAUS, John, D .... 603-862-2411 .... 306 C john.kraus@unh.edu
KRAUS, Kevin .... 563-387-1005 .... 187 D krauske@luther.edu
KRAUS, Larry .... 818-719-6420 .... 55 B krausl@piercecollege.edu
KRAUS, Laura .... 512-444-8082 .... 499 E administrator@texastcm.edu
KRAUS, Marcy .... 585-275-2354 .... 359 B marcy.kraus@rochester.edu
KRAUS, Pamela .... 410-263-2371 .... 225 G pamela.kraus@sjca.edu
KRAUS, William .... 440-525-7000 .... 394 F wkraus@lakelandcc.edu
KRAUS, William .... 330-972-2416 .... 403 B wkraus@uakron.edu
KRAUSE, Ann Marie .... 715-422-5421 .... 554 E annmarie.krause@mstc.edu
KRAUSE, Aric .... 801-832-2627 .... 512 G akrause@westminstercollege.edu
KRAUSE, Barbara, L .... 518-580-5700 .... 351 B bkrause@skidmore.edu
KRAUSE, Carolyn .... 513-861-6400 .... 402 I carolyn.krause@myunion.edu
KRAUSE, Chris .... 254-710-6672 .... 482 A chris_krause@baylor.edu
KRAUSE, David, H .... 708-524-6994 .... 150 C dkrause@dom.edu
KRAUSE, David, R .... 210-436-3141 .... 493 F dkrause@stmarytx.edu
KRAUSE, Deborah .... 314-918-2587 .... 281 F dkrause@eden.edu
KRAUSE, Greg .... 580-628-6760 .... 409 B greg.krause@north-ok.edu
KRAUSE, Jyl .... 309-467-6322 .... 151 B jkrause@eureka.edu
KRAUSE, Karen .... 507-457-5632 .... 269 G kkrause@winona.edu
KRAUSE, Karen .... 817-272-3561 .... 505 C kkrause@uta.edu
KRAUSE, Kassy .... 423-236-2900 .... 473 B kkrause@southern.edu
KRAUSE, Kate .... 505-277-2631 .... 321 C kkrause@unm.edu
KRAUSE, Laura .... 802-440-4714 .... 513 A lkrause@bennington.edu
KRAUSE, Mark .... 402-935-9400 .... 299 A mkrause@nechristian.edu
KRAUSHAAR, Robert .... 518-320-1278 .... 351 D robert.kraushaar@suny.edu
KRAUSS, Jeremy .... 508-929-8090 .... 238 G jkrauss@worcester.edu
KRAUTH, Stephanie .... 573-592-5240 .... 293 B stephanie.krauth@westminster-mo.edu
KRAVAS, Connie .... 206-685-1980 .... 539 A ckravas@uw.edu
KRAVCAK, Jamison .... 215-643-8458 .... 430 C kravcak.j@gmc.edu
KRAVETZ, Joanne .... 310-314-6124 .... 30 A
KRAWITZ, Ira .... 212-650-7581 .... 326 G ikrawitz@ccny.cuny.edu
KRAWITZ, Natalie .... 573-882-3611 .... 291 A krawitzn@umsystem.edu
KRAY, Helga .... 909-537-5185 .... 36 B hkray@csusb.edu
KRAYNACK, Justin .... 570-408-4550 .... 452 A justin.kraynack@wilkes.edu
KRAYNAK, Carrie .... 724-964-8811 .... 437 E ckraynak@ncstrades.edu
KREAGH, CM, Kevin .... 716-286-8400 .... 344 D kreagh@niagara.edu
KREBS, Julianne .... 937-393-3431 .... 402 A jkrebs@sscc.edu
KREBS, Katharine .... 607-777-2150 .... 351 F kkrebs@binghamton.edu
KREBS, Paul, R .... 505-925-5510 .... 321 C pkrebs@unm.edu
KREBS, Paula .... 508-531-2169 .... 237 D pkrebs@bridgew.edu
KREBS, Phil .... 530-741-6700 .... 80 I
KREBS, Stephanie, R .... 813-253-6204 .... 123 A srkrebs@ut.edu
KRECH, Donald, A .... 570-577-1242 .... 423 E donald.krech@bucknell.edu
KRECKE, Kathryn .... 602-978-7034 .... 18 H kathryn.kreke@thunderbird.edu
KREHBIEL, Brenda .... 620-242-0415 .... 195 C krehbieb@mcpherson.edu
KREHBIEL, Erika, M .... 773-442-4223 .... 160 A e-krehbiel@neiu.edu
KREHBIEL, Lee .... 479-788-7304 .... 24 D lee.krehbiel@uafs.edu
KREIDER, Paul, K .... 304-293-4841 .... 545 A paul.kreider@mail.wvu.edu
KREIDLER, Daniel .... 815-280-1524 .... 154 J dkreidle@jjc.edu
KREIDLER, Mickie, L .... 605-256-5100 .... 465 I mickie.kreidler@dsu.edu
KREIDLER, Steve .... 405-974-2251 .... 413 B skreidler@uco.edu
KREIN, Joanie .... 614-221-7770 .... 396 B
KREINER, Thane .... 408-551-6058 .... 68 C tkreiner@scu.edu
KREISBERG, Melinda .... 304-336-8065 .... 544 D mkreisberg@westliberty.edu
KREISBERG, Robert .... 304-336-8062 .... 544 D kreisbob@westliberty.edu
KREISER, Valerie .... 610-740-3785 .... 425 A valerie@cedarcrest.edu
KREITL, Bethany .... 206-296-6082 .... 538 B kreitlb@seattleu.edu
KREITZ, Patricia .... 925-631-4525 .... 64 F pak2@stmarys-ca.edu
KREITZER, Joseph, L .... 651-962-6032 .... 272 B jlkreitzer@stthomas.edu
KREJCI, Janet .... 309-438-7400 .... 153 D jkrejci@ilstu.edu
KREJCI, Mark, J .... 218-299-3001 .... 262 I krejci@cord.edu
KREJCI, Teresa .... 641-782-1336 .... 189 E tkrejci@swcciowa.edu
KREKE, Toni, L .... 660-543-4069 .... 290 H kreke@ucmo.edu
KREMENEK, Amy .... 315-498-7252 .... 345 D kremenea@sunyocc.edu
KREMENS, Zdzislaw .... 860-832-1801 .... 90 G kremensz@ccsu.edu
KREMER, Edward .... 913-288-7111 .... 194 C ekremer@kckcc.edu
KREMER, Peter, W .... 502-272-8334 .... 198 H pkremer@bellarmine.edu
KREMER, Steve .... 860-486-2933 .... 94 G steven.kremer@uconn.edu
KREMER, Timothy .... 563-589-3396 .... 189 F finaid@univ.dbq.edu
KREMINSKI, Richard .... 719-549-2340 .... 83 H rick.kreminski@colostate-pueblo.edu
KREMS, Ruth .... 860-906-5141 .... 91 C rkrems@ccc.commnet.edu
KRENDL, Kathy, A .... 614-823-1420 .... 400 H kkrendl@otterbein.edu
KRENT, Harold, J .... 312-906-5010 .... 153 C hkrent@kentlaw.edu
KRENTZ, Kenneth, L .... 252-335-0821 .... 369 G kkrentz@albemarle.edu
KRENTZ, Shelby .... 859-815-7648 .... 202 B shelby.krentz@kctcs.edu
KREPPS, Pamela .... 814-827-4401 .... 450 A krepps@pitt.edu
KRESCH, Thomas .... 570-389-4748 .... 441 F tkresch@bloomu.edu
KRESL-HOTZ, Peggie .... 307-778-1258 .... 556 E peggiekreslhotz@lccc.wy.edu
KRESS, Anne, M .... 585-292-2100 .... 341 H akress@monroecc.edu
KRESS, Cathann, A .... 515-294-5390 .... 182 E cathann@iastate.edu
KRESS, Debra, G .... 512-475-8029 .... 505 D debra.kress@austin.utexas.edu
KRESS, Jacqueline .... 732-987-2729 .... 310 C kressj@georgian.edu
KRESS, Lisa, P .... 785-864-3911 .... 197 B lpkress@ku.edu
KRESS, Michael .... 718-982-2350 .... 327 A michael.kress@csi.cuny.edu
KRESS, Ruth .... 812-357-6561 .... 180 A rkress@saintmeinrad.edu
KRESSAL, Linda .... 828-835-4288 .... 374 F lkressal@tricountycc.edu
KRETA, Steve .... 707-654-1019 .... 33 C skreta@csum.edu
KRETSCHMER, Mark .... 805-525-4417 .... 72 I mkretschmer@thomasaquinas.edu
KRETSCHMER, Mark, R .... 805-525-4417 .... 72 I mkretschmer@thomasaquinas.edu
KREUZMAN, Henry, B .... 330-263-2008 .... 388 F hkreuzman@wooster.edu
KREVH, Janet, M .... 216-397-4349 .... 392 L jkrevh@jw.edu
KREY, Maria .... 425-637-1010 .... 532 E mariakrey@city.edu
KREY, Philip, D .... 215-248-6310 .... 435 B pkrey@ltsp.edu
KRHIN, Daniel, J .... 920-748-8394 .... 550 D krhind@ripon.edu

KRICHMAR, Lee 562-860-2451 39 A
lkrichmar@cerritos.edu
KRICKX, Guido 916-278-3583 36 A
krickx@csus.edu
KRIDELBAUGH, Linda 541-888-7402 420 C
lkridelbaugh@socc.edu
KRIEB, Dennis 618-468-4300 156 E
dkrieb@lc.edu
KRIEBEL, Denise A, T 765-641-4133 169 E
dakriebel@anderson.edu
KRIEBEL, Richard, M 215-871-6527 444 C
rickk@pcom.edu
KRIEDER, Eric, W 330-972-5303 403 B
ewk@uakron.edu
KRIEG, Katherine 225-490-1674 214 C
kkrieg@ololcollege.edu
KRIEG, Randall 207-893-6641 219 F
rkrieg@sjcme.edu
KRIEGER, Nora 973-748-9000 307 H
nora_krieger@bloomfield.edu
KRIEGER, Rob 973-748-9000 307 H
rob_krieger@bloomfield.edu
KRIEGERMEIER, Pat 815-455-8726 157 H
pkriegermeier@mchenry.edu
KRIEGH, Debbie 541-881-5805 420 E
dkriegh@tvcc.cc
KRIEPS, Kevin 219-473-4330 170 G
kkrieps@ccsj.edu
KRIER, Jacob, C 507-344-7519 261 C
jake.krier@blc.edu
KRIER, Joe 715-232-1334 552 E
krierj@uwstout.edu
KRIESE, Theresa 605-995-2621 464 C
thkriese@dwu.edu
KRIETSCH, Gary 707-826-4111 36 E
gdk7001@humboldt.edu
KRIKAU, Paul 574-520-5805 174 E
pkrikau@iusb.edu
KRIKORIAN, Gregory, H 717-867-6238 434 C
krikoria@lvc.edu
KRIM, Lisa 202-687-7004 98 D
kriml@georgetown.edu
KRIMMEL, Bob, S 814-472-3276 446 B
bkrimmel@francis.edu
KRIMMEL, J. Thomas 781-292-2291 234 H
thomas.krimmel@olin.edu
KRIMPELBEIN, Kristi 715-232-2441 552 E
krimpelbeink@uwstout.edu
KRIPPEL, Nancy, F 770-534-6119 126 E
nkrippel@brenau.edu
KRISAK, Wendy 610-282-1100 427 A
wendy.krisak@desales.edu
KRISE, Thomas, W 253-535-7101 536 E
tkrise@plu.edu
KRISHNAMURTHY, K 573-341-4154 291 E
kkrishna@mst.edu
KRISHNAMURTI, Praveen 414-256-0238 549 D
krishnap@mtmary.edu
KRISHNAN, G, V 713-221-8478 503 F
krishnang@uhd.edu
KRISHNAN, Kris 201-360-4771 310 E
kkrishnan@hccc.edu
KRISHNAN, Ramayya 412-268-2159 424 J
rk2x@andrew.cmu.edu
KRISLOV, Marvin 440-775-8400 397 G
marvin.krislov@oberlin.edu
KRISS, George 618-537-6425 158 A
gnkriss@mckendree.edu
KRISS, OSF, M. Elise 260-399-7700 181 A
ekriss@sf.edu
KRISTENSEN, Douglas, A 308-865-8208 300 F
kristensend@unk.edu
KRISTENSEN, Sheryl 309-692-4092 158 D
skristensen@midstate.edu
KRISTOF, Leslie 954-382-5303 19 A
leslie.kristof@phoenix.edu
KRISTOFCO, Clare, M 858-534-6861 74 F
ckristofco@uscd.edu
KRISTOFCO, Clare, M 858-534-6861 74 F
ckristofco@ucsd.edu
KRISTOFF, Tricia 904-819-6311 107 C
tkristoff@flagler.edu
KRITIKOS, Mike 773-907-4777 147 D
mkritikos@ccc.edu
KRITSCHER, Matt 510-723-6716 39 C
mkritscher@chabotcollege.edu
KRIVDA, Ronald, A 724-925-4278 451 E
krivdar@wccc.edu
KRIVESTI, Robin 740-593-2665 399 G
krivesti@ohio.edu
KRIVOSKI, James, F 610-330-5200 433 B
krivoskj@lafayette.edu
KRNA, Karan 800-955-2527 282 D
kkrna@grantham.edu
KROB, Adam 504-865-5026 215 C
akrob@tulane.edu
KROB, Jay, C 785-827-5541 194 F
jayk@kwu.edu
KROBER, Alfred, C 585-594-6501 347 F
krobera@roberts.edu
KROBER, Kent 314-516-4115 291 D
kroberk@umsl.edu
KROBOTH, Patricia, D 412-624-3270 449 A
pkroboth@pitt.edu
KROC, Richard, J 520-621-8543 18 L
kroc@email.arizona.edu
KROEGER, Laura 859-442-1177 202 B
laura.kroeger@kctcs.edu
KROEGER, Lillian 254-526-1114 482 H
admissions.registrar@ctcd.edu
KROEKER, Dean 620-241-0770 191 I
dean.kroeker@centralchristian.edu
KROENING, Mike 507-453-2752 267 C
mkroening@southeastmn.edu
KROENKE, Joel 800-567-2344 547 A
jkroenke@menominee.edu
KROENKE, Paul 309-677-2325 146 C
pkroenke@bradley.edu
KROEZE, Nicholas, V 616-222-3000 253 F
nvk@kuyper.edu
KROGER, John 503-777-7500 420 A
krogerj@reed.edu
KROGH, Nancy 208-885-2020 144 G
nkrogh@uidaho.edu
KROGH, Nancy, A 208-885-2020 144 G
nkrogh@uidaho.edu
KROGH-JESPERSEN,
Mary-Beth 570-963-2539 440 G
mik2@psu.edu
KROGMAN, Mark, A 207-741-5629 219 A
mkrogman@smccme.edu
KROH, Lynne 417-862-9533 282 A
enroll@globaluniversity.edu
KROH, JR., Robert, C 215-951-1315 432 I
kroh@lasalle.edu
KROHN, Paul 630-617-3142 150 H
paulk@elmhurst.edu
KROLL, Charles 617-850-1222 235 F
ckroll@hchc.edu
KROLL, John, R 773-702-1941 166 G
xjrk@uchicago.edu
KROLL, Mark 956-882-7304 505 E
mark.kroll@utb.edu
KROLOFF, Reed 248-645-3301 250 B
rkroloff@cranbrook.edu
KROM, Bethany 507-284-3293 262 E
krom.bethany@mayo.edu
KRONCKE, Charles 513-244-4273 388 E
charles_kroncke@mail.msj.edu
KRONDAK, Anita, M 913-288-7274 194 C
akrondak@kckcc.edu
KRONEMAN, Ann 517-483-1604 254 A
kronemaa@lcc.edu
KRONENBURGER, John 630-942-3614 148 A
kronenburgerj@cod.edu
KRONENFIELD, Michael 480-219-6091 278 D
mkronenfield@atsu.edu
KRONSTEIN, Krista 330-263-2498 388 F
kkronstein@wooster.edu
KROOK, Darrell 603-668-2211 305 I
d.krook@snhu.edu
KROOK, Scott 507-285-7205 268 I
scott.krook@roch.edu
KROPF, Kevin 785-594-8327 190 F
kevin.kropf@bakeru.edu
KROPFF, Robert 330-972-7048 403 B
bobk@uakron.edu
KROPP, Vicky 989-358-7317 247 C
kroppv@alpenacc.edu
KROPP-ANDERSON,
Pamela 207-973-1048 218 A
kroppandersonp@husson.edu
KROSCH, Brandon 651-255-6136 271 D
bkrosch@unitedseminary.edu
KROTSENG, Martha, V 304-327-4000 543 F
mkrotseng@bluefieldstate.edu
KROTZER, Mary Jane 205-366-8929 7 F
mkrotzer@stillman.edu
KROUT, Robin 513-771-2424 385 I
rkrout@brownmackie.edu
KROVI, Ravi 330-972-7442 403 B
krovi@uakron.edu
KRSTIC, Miroslav 858-534-5556 74 F
mkrstic@ucsd.edu
KRUCHOWSKI, Gary 218-733-7649 266 H
g.kruchowski@lsc.edu
KRUCZEK, Thomas 561-237-7458 113 D
tkruczek@lynn.edu
KRUDOP, James, D 334-382-2133 5 F
jkrudop@lbwcc.edu
KRUEGER, Bryon, D 651-631-5392 270 B
bdkrueger@nwc.edu
KRUEGER, Cheryl 937-775-2556 406 C
cheryl.krueger@wright.edu
KRUEGER, Cindy 419-267-1233 397 E
ckrueger@northweststate.edu
KRUEGER, Conrad 210-486-0915 479 E
ckrueger@alamo.edu
KRUEGER, James, M 314-516-6539 291 D
jimkrueger@umsl.edu
KRUEGER, Jim 402-399-2332 297 C
jkrueger@csm.edu
KRUEGER, Joni 605-274-4015 464 A
joni.krueger@augie.edu
KRUEGER, Justin 815-226-4006 163 A
jkrueger@rockford.edu
KRUEGER, Karl 215-248-6330 435 B
kkrueger@ltsp.edu
KRUEGER, Kurt, J 949-214-3194 43 C
kurt.krueger@cui.edu
KRUEGER, Mablene 312-935-6645 162 G
mkrueger@robertmorris.edu
KRUEGER, Mary, M 419-372-8034 385 E
mkruege@bgsu.edu
KRUFT, Sherre 831-647-4123 57 F
sherre.kruft@miis.edu
KRUG, Bryce 314-918-2568 281 F
bkrug@eden.edu
KRUG, Christopher 858-642-8145 58 I
ckrug@nu.edu
KRUG, Sheila, R 620-229-6368 196 G
sheila.krug@sckans.edu
KRUG, Stefan 617-521-3929 244 F
stefan.krug@simmons.edu
KRUGER, Darrell 309-438-3006 153 D
dpkruge@ilstu.edu
KRUGER, Michael, J 704-366-5066 376 B
mkruger@rts.edu
KRUGMAN, Richard, D 303-724-0882 88 J
richard.krugman@ucdenver.edu
KRUHLY, Leslie, L 215-898-7005 448 J
kruhly@pobox.upenn.edu
KRUKONES, James, H 216-397-4762 392 L
jkrukones@jcu.edu
KRUKOWSKA, Justyna 510-883-2071 45 B
jkrukowska@dspt.edu
KRULAK, Charles, C 205-226-4620 2 B
ckrulak@bsc.edu
KRULL, Kimberly 785-243-1435 192 A
kkrull@cloud.edu
KRULL, Lucille 503-251-6115 539 C
lucy.krull@wallawalla.edu
KRULY, Kenneth, C 716-888-3755 325 F
krulyk@canisius.edu
KRUMHANSL, Ezra 502-585-9911 206 D
ekrumhansl@spalding.edu
KRUMM, Brenda, L 620-431-2820 195 E
bkrumm@neosho.edu
KRUMMRICH, Philip 606-783-2726 204 I
s.faulkner@moreheadstate.edu
KRUMPE, Keith 828-250-3880 378 D
kkrumpe@unca.edu
KRUMWIEDE, Robert 218-726-7560 271 F
tkrumw@d.umn.edu
KRUPANSKY, Sharla 270-534-3275 203 E
sharla.krupansky@kctcs.edu
KRUPICA, Glen 217-854-3231 146 A
glen.krupica@blackburn.edu
KRUPICA, Suzanne 217-854-3231 146 A
suzanne.krupica@blackburn.edu
KRUPKA, Moshe 212-463-0400 358 B
moshe.krupka@touro.edu
KRUPP, Jason 727-341-3050 116 H
krupp.jason@spcollege.edu
KRUPP, Robert, A 503-517-1838 421 C
rakrupp@westernseminary.edu
KRUPSKI, Eric, A 617-422-7232 243 B
ekrupski@nesl.edu
KRUSE, Emily 563-588-6436 183 E
emily.kruse@clarke.edu
KRUSE, Janetta 817-598-6391 508 F
jkruse@wc.edu
KRUSE, Joe 920-686-6233 550 H
joe.kruse@sl.edu
KRUSE, Kristen 541-962-3512 418 C
kristen.kruse@eou.edu
KRUSE, Mary 517-264-7112 258 B
mkruse@sienaheights.edu
KRUSE, Tom, D 563-588-4948 187 C
tom.kruse@loras.edu
KRUSE, Tracy, L 563-562-3263 188 B
kruset@nicc.edu
KRUSE, Valerie 386-226-6339 105 H
krusev@erau.edu
KRUSEE, Kelly 310-377-5501 56 F
kkrusee@marymountpv.edu
KRUSEMARK, Stacy, L 605-256-5127 465 I
stacy.krusemark@dsu.edu
KRUSEN, Cynthia 978-840-0176 240 C
c_krusen@mwcc.mass.edu
KRUSHINSKI, Lynn 570-702-8955 431 L
lkrushinski@johnson.edu
KRUSLING, James 818-240-1000 48 D
krusling@glendale.edu
KRUSNIAK, Bryan 660-626-2364 278 D
bkrusniak@atsu.edu
KRUTKY, Judith, B 440-826-2257 384 K
jkrutky@bw.edu
KRUTZ, Ellen 610-519-4237 450 H
ellen.lacorte@villanova.edu
KRUZEL, Douglas 734-973-3497 259 F
kruzel@wccnet.edu
KRYGEL, Barbara 586-791-6610 248 B
barbara.krygel@baker.edu
KRYSHAK, Michael 916-649-2400 31 F
kryshak@aiu.edu
KRYSIAK, Richard 405-744-7147 410 C
rick.krysiak@okstate.edu
KRYSTOSEK, Brooke 503-493-6454 415 E
bkrystosek@cu-portland.edu
KRZAK, Chris 909-593-3511 75 E
ckrzak@laverne.edu
KRZYSTOFIAK, Susan 716-645-2642 351 G
krzystof@buffalo.edu
KRZYWICKI, Tricia 617-327-6777 241 F
tricia_krzywicki@mspp.edu
KRZYZANOWSKI, SSND,
Georgeann 414-258-4810 549 D
krzyzag@mtmary.edu
KRZYZKOWSKI, Karen 215-489-2309 426 H
karen.kay@delval.edu
KSENDZOVSKY, Yelena 440-449-1700 384 I
faid@atsinstitute.edu
KTUL, Kathy 252-492-2061 374 G
ktul@vgcc.edu
KUA, Kenway, L 808-675-3565 140 D
kuak@byuh.edu
KUAN, Jeffrey 973-408-3258 309 E
jkuan@drew.edu
KUANG, Connie 909-931-7599 79 C
ckuang@westwood.edu
KUBA, Jodie, M 808-956-3993 141 G
jodiek@hawaii.edu
KUBA, Michael 304-473-8090 545 G
kuba_m@wvwc.edu
KUBA, Shawn, M 304-473-8560 545 G
kuba_s@wvwc.edu
KUBACAK, James 254-299-8608 490 G
jkubacak@mclennan.edu
KUBASEK, Stephen 352-588-8254 116 G
stephen.kubasek@saintleo.edu
KUBASKA, Julie 914-594-4550 343 F
julie_kubaska@nymc.edu
KUBAT, Laural 507-389-7219 269 D
laural.kubat@southcentral.edu
KUBAT, Robert, A 765-494-6133 178 J
rkubat@purdue.edu
KUBB, Richard 314-529-9606 284 C
rkubb@maryville.edu
KUBE, Thomas, A 480-314-2102 18 D
KUBEJA, Judy 814-732-2729 442 E
kubeja@edinboro.edu
KUBERSKI, Chris 618-437-5321 162 D
kuberski@rlc.edu
KUBERSKY, Edward 201-559-6117 310 B
kuberskye@felician.edu
KUBIC, Craig 816-414-3700 285 H
ckubic@mbts.edu
KUBINAK, Lois, A 610-921-7612 421 E
lkubinak@alb.edu
KUBO, Takeo 408-288-3733 67 D
takeo.kubo@sjcc.edu
KUBOW, Steven 908-737-0300 311 A
skubow@kean.edu
KUCERA, Kevin 734-487-2390 250 F
kkucera@emich.edu
KUCHARSKI, Chris 570-961-7856 433 A
kucharskic@lackawanna.edu
KUCHENREUTHER, Brad 360-254-3282 534 B
KUCIA, John, F 513-745-3997 406 E
kucia@xavier.edu
KUCINSKI, Nancy 325-670-1298 487 F
nkicinski@hsutx.edu
KUCK, Ann 208-459-5826 143 D
akuck@collegeofidaho.edu
KUCKO, Jane 817-257-7473 499 C
j.kucko@tcu.edu
KUCYNDA, Steve 660-596-7282 290 B
skucynda@sfccmo.edu
KUCZEWSKI, Mark, G 708-327-9200 157 C
mkuczew@lumc.edu
KUDLAC, John 412-392-3920 445 A
jkudlac@pointpark.edu
KUDLIK, Richard 714-241-6150 41 B
rkudlik@coastline.edu
KUDRAVETZ, Douglas 202-885-3283 97 D
doug@american.edu
KUEBLER, Alan, S 314-935-5727 292 I
alan_kuebler@wustl.edu
KUEBLER, Elizabeth, D 630-617-3069 150 H
betsyk@elmhurst.edu
KUEFNER, Michael 479-899-6928 22 H
mkuefner@nwacc.edu
KUEHL, William 405-878-5161 412 A
wmkuehl@stgregorys.edu
KUEHLER, Robert 303-837-2112 88 G
robert.kuehler@cu.edu
KUEHN, Lisa 620-252-7137 192 B
lisak@coffeyville.edu
KUEHNER, Megan, R 904-620-2523 120 D
mkuehner@unf.edu
KUEKER, Victoria 847-628-1569 154 K
vkueker@judsonu.edu
KUENNEN, Daniel, S 410-651-6183 227 E
dskuennen@umes.edu
KUENSTLER, Donna 432-837-8361 501 E
dkuenstl@sulross.edu
KUERBIS, Matt 503-223-2245 416 F
mkuerbis@westernculinary.com
KUERZI, Kenneth 856-256-4138 314 A
kuerzi@rowan.edu
KUFFELL, Lorne 205-348-7205 8 E
lkuffel@ua.edu
KUGA, Donna, J 724-773-3939 439 A
djk3@psu.edu

KUGELMANN DEKAT, Laurie .... 972-721-5322 .... 503 B ldekat@udallas.edu
KUGLER, Angela .... 425-558-0299 .... 533 G akugler@digipen.edu
KUGLER, Sharon .... 203-432-1128 .... 96 A sharon.kugler@yale.edu
KUHL, Colleen, M .... 563-588-7650 .... 187 C colleen.kuhl@loras.edu
KUHL, Jennifer, A .... 631-244-3273 .... 332 C kuhlj@dowling.edu
KUHL, Sara .... 262-472-1194 .... 553 A kuhls@uww.edu
KUHLHORST, Michelle .... 260-399-7700 .... 181 A mkuhlhorst@sf.edu
KUHLMAN, Ann .... 203-432-2305 .... 96 A ann.kuhlman@yale.edu
KUHLMAN, Gregory .... 718-951-5174 .... 326 F kuhlman@brooklyn.cuny.edu
KUHLMANN, Diana, E .... 620-341-5304 .... 192 G dkuhlman@emporia.edu
KUHN, Bill .... 952-446-4227 .... 263 C kuhnb@crown.edu
KUHN, Charles .... 301-447-5244 .... 225 A ckuhn@msmary.edu
KUHN, Helen .... 217-245-3013 .... 152 D registrar@ic.edu
KUHN, Jeffrey, J .... 608-259-2957 .... 554 D jjkuhn@madisoncollege.org
KUHN, Kathryn, A .... 414-955-8217 .... 548 G kkuhn@mcw.edu
KUHN, Kevin .... 601-477-4106 .... 274 H kevin.kuhn@jcjc.edu
KUHN, Robert .... 814-824-2104 .... 436 C rkuhnn@mercyhurst.edu
KUHN, Sean .... 937-433-3410 .... 390 I
KUHN, Stephen .... 262-524-7132 .... 546 H skuhn@carrollu.edu
KUHNS, Heather, L .... 610-799-1584 .... 434 D hkuhns@lccc.edu
KUHR, Krista .... 407-215-9707 .... 110 L kkuhr@orl.herzing.edu
KUHR, Peggy .... 406-243-2311 .... 294 I peggy.kuhr@umontana.edu
KUIPER, Jeff .... 507-537-6225 .... 269 E kuiperjb@smsu.edu
KUIPERS, David .... 229-931-2001 .... 137 C dkuipers@southgatech.edu
KUJAWA, Edward .... 415-485-3245 .... 45 C ekujawa@dominican.edu
KUJAWA, Lisa, R .... 248-204-2403 .... 254 B lkujawa@ltu.edu
KUJAWA, Rose Marie .... 734-432-5315 .... 254 D srosemarie@madonna.edu
KUJAWA, Thomas .... 920-465-2300 .... 551 B kujawat@uwgb.edu
KUJAWA, Tricia, A .... 217-786-2211 .... 157 B tricia.kujawa@llcc.edu
KUJOVICH, Gil .... 802-831-1327 .... 515 B gkujovich@vermontlaw.edu
KUKAINIS, Maris .... 856-227-7200 .... 308 D mkukainis@camdencc.edu
KUKER, Ronald .... 937-529-2201 .... 403 A rkuker@united.edu
KUKOR, Jerome, J .... 732-932-2721 .... 314 C kukor@aesop.rutgers.edu
KUKREJA, Anil .... 504-520-7652 .... 217 A akukreja@xula.edu
KUKUK, Karen, S .... 248-370-3500 .... 256 G kukuk@oakland.edu
KUKULIES, Emily Ann .... 808-845-9219 .... 142 B emily@hcc.hawaii.edu
KULA, Jarrod .... 909-599-5433 .... 54 A jkula@lifepacific.edu
KULAGA, Jon, S .... 859-858-3511 .... 198 E jon.kulaga@asbury.edu
KULAWIAK, Ted .... 630-645-4341 .... 149 B tkulawiak@devry.edu
KULBICKI, OFM CONV, Timothy, A .... 410-864-3602 .... 226 B tkulbicki@stmarys.edu
KULBISKI, Neil .... 785-594-4791 .... 190 F neil.kulbiski@bakeru.edu
KULCZYCKI, Michael .... 630-652-8235 .... 149 C mkulczycki@devry.edu
KULESZA, Darrell .... 508-541-1864 .... 233 G dkulesza@dean.edu
KULHOWVICK, John, P .... 802-654-2445 .... 514 D jkulhowvick@smcvt.edu
KULICH, James .... 630-617-6472 .... 150 H jimk@elmhurst.edu
KULICK, Liz, M .... 215-968-8123 .... 423 F kulicke@bucks.edu
KULICK, Steven, W .... 315-445-4560 .... 338 B kulicksw@lemoyne.edu
KULICS, Jennifer .... 330-672-9494 .... 393 D jkulics@kent.edu
KULIG, Nicole, V .... 617-708-3504 .... 241 A nkulig@rcc.mass.edu
KULKARNI, Mukund, S .... 717-948-6105 .... 439 J msk5@psu.edu
KULL, Michael .... 219-989-2231 .... 178 K mjkull@purduecal.edu
KUMAR, Chandra .... 606-326-2008 .... 201 F chandra.kumar@kctcs.edu
KUMAR, Mukul .... 617-619-1900 .... 235 G mukul.kumar@hult.edu
KUMAR, Neeraj .... 312-341-3587 .... 163 B neeraj.kumar@roosevelt.edu
KUMAR, Senthil, B .... 909-396-6090 .... 32 I
KUMAR, Shashi .... 516-773-5357 .... 558 I kumars@usmma.edu
KUMAR, Sunil .... 773-702-1680 .... 166 G sunil.kumar@chicagobooth.edu
KUMAR, Sunil .... 646-386-6481 .... 346 C skumar@poly.edu
KUMAR, Thulasi .... 573-341-4954 .... 291 E tkchr@mst.edu
KUMARASAMY, Sundar .... 937-229-3725 .... 404 A sundar@udayton.edu
KUMASAKA, S. Mikiko .... 801-581-8151 .... 511 C s.mikiko.kumasaka@utah.edu
KUMM, David .... 402-643-7222 .... 297 D david.kumm@cune.edu
KUMNICK, Stephen .... 860-231-5363 .... 95 D skumnick@usj.edu
KUMPF, Robert .... 732-255-0400 .... 312 D rkumpf@ocean.edu
KUNA, Gerri .... 701-858-3497 .... 382 A gerri.kuna@minotstateu.edu
KUNCE, Kim, M .... 708-709-3684 .... 161 D kkunce@prairiestate.edu
KUNCL, Ralph, W .... 909-748-8390 .... 76 C ralph_kuncl@redlands.edu
KUNDELL, Ken, F .... 410-543-6043 .... 228 D kfkundell@salisbury.edu
KUNERT, Charles .... 503-493-6538 .... 415 E ckunert@cu-portland.edu
KUNG, Susanna .... 212-594-4000 .... 357 H skung@tcicollege.edu
KUNIYOSHI, Tammy .... 808-956-3028 .... 141 G tammyk@hawaii.edu
KUNKEL, Bruce .... 619-849-2571 .... 62 L brucekunkel@pointloma.edu
KUNKEL, Cheryl, A .... 859-371-9393 .... 198 G ckunkel@beckfield.edu
KUNKEL, Glenn .... 510-261-8500 .... 61 G glenn.kunkel@patten.edu
KUNKEL, Karl .... 620-235-4684 .... 196 C kkunkel@pittstate.edu
KUNKEL, Lilith, R .... 330-337-4215 .... 393 H lkunkel@kent.edu
KUNKEL, Marita .... 503-352-1401 .... 419 E marita.kunkel@pacificu.edu
KUNKEL, Sharon, L .... 518-276-6233 .... 347 D kunkes@rpi.edu
KUNKEL, Thomas .... 920-403-3165 .... 550 F thomas.kunkel@snc.edu
KUNKO, Bill .... 575-492-2501 .... 319 B bkunko@nmjc.edu
KUNKO, Christina .... 575-492-2782 .... 319 B ckunko@nmjc.edu
KUNNAPAS, Tiia .... 404-270-2903 .... 128 I tkunnapas@devry.edu
KUNSMANN, Jill, F .... 414-847-3335 .... 549 B jillkunsmann@miad.edu
KUNSTLE, Rozann, R .... 719-637-0600 .... 81 K rkunstle@collegeamerica.edu
KUNTZ, Daniel .... 805-493-3855 .... 33 B kuntz@clunet.edu
KUNTZ, F. Douglas .... 570-321-4116 .... 435 D kuntz@lycoming.edu
KUNTZ, Jason, A .... 717-867-6231 .... 434 C kuntz@lvc.edu
KUNTZ, John .... 973-300-2231 .... 315 F jkuntz@sussex.edu
KUNTZ, Lisa, M .... 610-398-5300 .... 434 F lkuntz@lincolntech.com
KUNTZ, Robert .... 805-565-7263 .... 79 A bkuntz@westmont.edu
KUNTZ, Wayne .... 228-897-3878 .... 275 E wayne.kuntz@mgccc.edu
KUNTZELMAN, Ken .... 928-344-7699 .... 12 A kenneth.kuntzelman@azwestern.edu
KUNZ, Kent .... 208-241-2900 .... 143 H kunzkent@isu.edu
KUNZE, Joel .... 563-425-5259 .... 189 G kunzej@uiu.edu
KUO, Ling Ling .... 626-571-8811 .... 77 A linglingk@uwest.edu
KUO, Thomas, K .... 541-737-4331 .... 418 F kent.kuo@oregonstate.edu
KUO, Wai-Lan .... 512-444-8082 .... 499 E administrator@texastcm.edu
KUPCZYNSKI, Bonnie, L .... 218-722-4000 .... 263 E bonniek@dbumn.edu
KUPEC, Matthew, G .... 919-962-0329 .... 378 E matt_kupec@unc.edu
KUPER, Jane, T .... 605-274-4110 .... 464 A jane.kuper@augie.edu
KUPER, Tom .... 713-623-2040 .... 480 J tkuper@aii.edu
KUPERMAN, Eli .... 732-367-1060 .... 307 G ekuperman@bmg.edu
KUPERSHTEYN, Jacob .... 212-349-4330 .... 334 G jkupershteyn@globe.edu
KUPERSMITH, Peter, A .... 215-489-2254 .... 426 H peter.kupersmith@delval.edu
KUPETZ, Denise .... 303-256-9648 .... 85 L dkupetz@jwu.edu
KUPKA, Alyssa .... 312-362-6585 .... 149 A akupka@depaul.edu
KUPP, Terry, L .... 315-255-1743 .... 325 G terry.kupp@cayuga-cc.edu
KUPPINGER, Karen .... 585-389-2100 .... 342 D kkuppin9@naz.edu
KURAPATI, Raaj .... 907-474-5866 .... 10 I rkurapati@alaska.edu
KURITA, Katsura .... 410-234-4540 .... 225 E
KURKOWSKI, Bridget .... 712-749-2235 .... 183 C kurkowskib@bvu.edu
KURLAND, Michael .... 860-486-0744 .... 94 G michael.kurland@uconn.edu
KURLINSKI, Susan .... 253-943-3164 .... 533 F skurlinski@devry.edu
KURN, Seth, A .... 401-739-5000 .... 453 G skurn@neit.edu
KUROKAWA, Linda .... 760-757-2121 .... 57 E lkorokawa@miracosta.edu
KUROWSKI, Mark .... 630-829-6029 .... 145 G mkurowski@ben.edu
KURPIUS, David .... 225-578-1948 .... 212 H kurpius@lsu.edu
KURTINITIS, Sandra, L .... 443-840-1015 .... 222 D skurtinitis@ccbcmd.edu
KURTYKA, Steve .... 973-761-9454 .... 315 B steve.kurtyka@shu.edu
KURTZ, Andrew, J .... 419-372-0710 .... 385 F kurtzj@bgsu.edu
KURTZ, Diane, L .... 517-750-1200 .... 258 D dkurtz@arbor.edu
KURTZ, Edward, J .... 810-766-4224 .... 247 G ed.kurtz@baker.edu
KURTZ, Eldon .... 540-432-4390 .... 518 F kurtze@emu.edu
KURTZ, Henry, A .... 901-678-3067 .... 474 C kkurtz@memphis.edu
KURTZ, Jan .... 503-777-7578 .... 420 A kurtzj@reed.edu
KURTZ, Maija .... 719-549-3014 .... 87 F maija.kurtz@pueblocc.edu
KURTZ, Polly .... 970-351-1890 .... 89 B polly.kurtz@unco.edu
KURTZ, Rebecca .... 740-695-9500 .... 385 B bkurtz@belmontcollege.edu
KURTZ, Rick .... 231-591-3667 .... 250 H rick_kurtz@ferris.edu
KURTZ, Rick, S .... 989-774-3436 .... 249 C kurtz1rs@cmich.edu
KURTZ, Scott .... 812-476-6000 .... 172 E scott.kurtz@harrison.edu
KURTZ, Steve .... 573-518-2146 .... 285 I skurtz@mineralarea.edu
KURTZ, Terri .... 361-572-6463 .... 508 B terri.kurtz@victoriacollege.edu
KURTZ, Terry, J .... 440-826-3170 .... 384 K tkurtz@bw.edu
KURTZ, William .... 269-749-7700 .... 257 A bkurtz@olivetcollege.edu
KURUVILLA, Mohan .... 281-649-3325 .... 487 H mkuruvilla@hbu.edu
KURZ, Matt .... 309-556-3181 .... 153 F mkurz@iwu.edu
KURZ, Richard .... 817-735-2323 .... 504 E richard.kurz@unthsc.edu
KUSANO, Ellen, I .... 808-974-7499 .... 141 F ekusano@hawaii.edu
KUSCH, Josh .... 303-963-3463 .... 82 C jkusch@ccu.edu
KUSE, Tammy .... 815-836-5216 .... 156 F kuseta@lewisu.edu
KUSER, Janet .... 617-236-8800 .... 234 G jkuser@fisher.edu
KUSH, Michael .... 914-337-9300 .... 330 G michael.kush@concordia-ny.edu
KUSHIBAB, Debbie .... 623-935-8812 .... 15 F debbie.kushibab@estrellamountain.edu
KUSHIGIAN, Elise, J .... 317-940-9620 .... 170 F ekushigi@butler.edu
KUSHINO, Karen .... 773-697-2002 .... 149 D kkushino@devry.edu
KUSHMEREK, Michael .... 978-665-3441 .... 237 E mkushmerek@fitchburgstate.edu
KUSHNER, Cathy .... 518-464-8543 .... 333 E ckushner@excelsior.edu
KUSHNER, Melissa .... 610-607-6212 .... 445 C mkushner@racc.edu
KUSNIERZ, Zbigniew .... 708-763-1251 .... 162 E zbigniew.kusnierz@resu.edu
KUSPA, Adam .... 713-798-4951 .... 481 H akuspa@bcm.edu
KUSS, Vincent .... 315-464-4361 .... 352 E kussv@upstate.edu
KUSSE, Debra .... 585-475-3947 .... 347 G dskpur@rit.edu
KUSSMAN, Kevin .... 360-992-2356 .... 532 F kkussman@clark.edu
KUSTER, Brian .... 270-745-2037 .... 208 A brian.kuster@wku.edu
KUSTRA, Robert, W .... 208-426-1491 .... 142 I bobkustra@boisestate.edu
KUSZYNSKI, Lawrence, J .. 352-854-2322 .... 103 K larry.kuszynski@cf.edu
KUTATELADZE, Andrei .... 303-871-2693 .... 89 A akutatel@du.edu
KUTCH, Keith .... 443-334-2090 .... 226 E kkutch@stevenson.edu
KUTCHNER, Wendy .... 215-204-7357 .... 447 H wendy.kutchner@temple.edu
KUTI, Morakinyo .... 937-376-6547 .... 387 A mkuti@centralstate.edu
KUTLER, Ken .... 607-274-3209 .... 336 G kkutler@ithaca.edu
KUTNER, Sender .... 847-982-2500 .... 152 A kutner@htc.edu
KUTNICK, Jerry, M .... 215-635-7300 .... 430 A jkutnick@gratz.edu
KUTTENKULER, Scott .... 870-460-1110 .... 25 A kuttenkuler@uamont.edu
KUTZ, Ellen, M .... 330-490-7302 .... 405 F ekutz@walsh.edu
KUWASAKI, L. Michelle .... 206-878-3710 .... 535 B mkuwasaki@highline.edu
KUWITZKY, Chris .... 405-325-5161 .... 413 C ckuwitzky@ou.edu
KUYKENDALL, Francis .... 870-862-8131 .... 23 G fkuykendall@southark.edu
KUYKENDALL, John .... 870-575-8498 .... 25 B kuykendallj@uapb.edu
KUYKENDALL, Randy .... 915-532-3737 .... 508 H rkuykendall@westerntech.edu
KUYKENDALL, Todd .... 575-769-4919 .... 318 A todd.kuykendall@clovis.edu
KUZAK, Michael, J .... 906-227-1126 .... 256 C mkuzak@nmu.edu
KUZMA, George .... 718-862-7362 .... 339 H george.kuzma@manhattan.edu
KUZMA, Lynn .... 207-780-4347 .... 220 G kuzma@usm.maine.edu
KUZUOKA, Gina .... 502-588-7185 .... 206 D gkuzuoka@spalding.edu
KUZYK, Chelsey .... 253-943-3070 .... 533 F ckuzyk@devry.edu
KVAAL, Kimberly, L .... 415-422-6732 .... 76 E klkvaal@usfca.edu
KVAM, Robert, A .... 765-285-5495 .... 169 G rkvam@bsu.edu
KVISTAD, Gregg, O .... 303-871-2966 .... 89 A gkvistad@du.edu
KWAN, Cecilia .... 213-763-7088 .... 55 D kwancw@lattc.edu
KWAN, Phoebe .... 415-338-6810 .... 37 B pkwan@sfsu.edu
KWANBUNBUMPEN, Ada . 504-286-5244 .... 214 J akwanbun@suno.edu
KWESKIN, Amy, B .... 314-935-5608 .... 292 I amy.b.kweskin@wustl.edu
KWIATKOWSKI, Amy .... 602-943-2311 .... 19 B amy.kwiatkowski@west.edu
KWIECHIEN, Garth .... 775-784-1641 .... 303 A gkwiechien@unr.edu
KWOK, Borree .... 910-893-1460 .... 362 J kwokb@campbell.edu
KWOLEK-FOLLAND, Angel .... 352-392-4792 .... 120 C akf@aa.ufl.edu
KWON, David .... 213-738-0712 .... 70 B kwon@southbaylo.edu
KWONG, Joanne .... 212-854-2037 .... 323 E jkwong@barnard.edu
KYLE, Lorrie .... 407-646-1540 .... 116 D lkyle@rollins.edu
KYLE, Michael .... 507-786-3025 .... 271 C kylem@stolaf.edu
KYLE, Paul .... 913-469-8500 .... 194 B pkyle@jccc.edu
KYLE, Penelope, W .... 540-831-5401 .... 523 A pwkyle@radford.edu
KYLE, Roberta .... 508-929-8130 .... 238 G rkyle@worcester.edu
KYLE, Sherry, L .... 989-386-6601 .... 255 C skyle@midmich.edu
KYLE, Theresa .... 310-660-3281 .... 45 E tkyle@elcamino.edu
KYLES, Vanessa, M .... 251-809-1516 .... 5 B vanessa.kyles@jdcc.edu
KYPRIOS, Linda .... 972-881-5726 .... 483 H lkyprios@collin.edu
KYSOR, Darwin, V .... 814-641-3351 .... 432 A kysord@juniata.edu
KYTE, Richard, L .... 608-796-3704 .... 553 C rlkyte@viterbo.edu
KYZER, Melany .... 405-789-6400 .... 412 D mkyzer@snu.edu

L

LÓPEZ, José .... 787-850-9376 .... 567 E jose.lopez33@upr.edu
LÓPEZ GARRIGA, Juan .... 787-265-3828 .... 567 F juan.lopez16@upr.edu
LÓPEZ-NUNCI, Adrián .... 787-250-0000 .... 566 G adrian.lopeznunci@upr.edu
LA BRANCHE, Mark, D .... 919-497-3226 .... 366 H mdl@louisburg.edu

LA BRIE, Mary Anne .... 603-623-0313.... 305 E
maryannelabrie@nhia.edu
LA CHAPELLE, Jacqueline . 337-550-1282.... 212 J
LA DUKE, John, C .... 308-865-8518.... 300 F
ladukejc@unk.edu
LA FOEUR, Mary Ann .... 703-416-1441.... 520 C
mlafoeur@ipsciences.edu
LA PERLA-MORALES,
Joann .... 732-906-2517.... 311 D
jlaperla@middlesexcc.edu
LA PLANTE, Brian .... 518-445-2381.... 322 C
blapl@albanylaw.edu
LA POINT, Kristine, L .... 773-975-1295.... 158 E
krisbob1@cs.com
LA POINT, Kristine, L .... 262-975-1295.... 549 A
krisbob1@cs.com
LA RUE, Lacie .... 541-737-4218.... 418 F
lacie.larue@oregonstate.edu
LA SERNA, Jennifer .... 559-730-3823...... 42 D
jenniferl@cos.edu
LAACKMAN, Donald, J ...... 312-553-5901.... 147 C
dlaackman@ccc.edu
LAAGER, Melinda .... 912-427-5835.... 124 C
mlaager@altamahatech.edu
LAAKSO, Kathleen .... 901-843-3885.... 472 K
laakso@rhodes.edu
LAANAN, Frankie, S .... 671-735-2444.... 559 G
laanan@uguam.uog.edu
LABAO, Nida .... 562-947-8755...... 71 A
nidalabao@scuhs.edu
LABARBERA, Mark .... 219-464-6894.... 181 C
mark.labarbera@valpo.edu
LABARBERA, Paul .... 845-758-7819.... 323 D
labarbera@bard.edu
LABAT, Tony .... 415-641-1241...... 65 I
tlabat@sfai.edu
LABATE, William .... 310-206-7323...... 74 C
labate@ats.ucla.edu
LABAUGH, Amy, R .... 208-496-9810.... 143 A
labaugha@byui.edu
LABAUVE-MAHER, Laura .. 847-925-6522.... 151 G
llabauve@harpercollege.edu
LABBADIA, Gail .... 860-253-3015...... 91 B
glabbadia@asnuntuck.edu
LABE, Dorothy .... 610-896-4923.... 430 G
dlabe@haverford.edu
LABE, Paul, E .... 443-412-2291.... 223 B
plabe@harford.edu
LABEFF, Toni .... 903-434-8105.... 491 F
tlabeff@ntcc.edu
LABELLE, Alyssa .... 603-271-7731.... 304 F
alabelle@ccsnh.edu
LABELLE-HAMER, Nettie ... 907-474-6167...... 10 I
nettie.labellehamer@alaska.edu
LABINE, Nancy .... 423-478-6227.... 474 E
nlabine@clevelandstatecc.edu
LABKOWSKI, Zalman .... 718-434-0784.... 325 I
LABOE, Mark .... 773-325-4004.... 149 A
mlaboe@depaul.edu
LABOE, Timothy .... 313-883-8556.... 257 E
laboe.timothy@shms.edu
LABONTE, Gene, R .... 978-542-6542.... 238 E
glabonte@salemstate.edu
LABONTE, Kim .... 618-650-2789.... 165 A
klabont@siue.edu
LABONTE, Robert .... 978-632-6600.... 240 C
r_labonte@mwcc.mass.edu
LABORDO, Darwin .... 909-869-2008...... 33 J
dlabordo@csupomona.edu
LABOY, Lilliam .... 787-284-1912.... 564 A
llaboy@ponce.inter.edu
LABOY, Rafael .... 787-720-4476.... 566 D
relacionespublicas@colmizpa.edu
LABRANCHE, Michael .... 504-398-2241.... 214 B
mlabranche@olhcc.edu
LABRIE, John, G .... 617-373-2400.... 243 F
LABRIE, SJ, Joseph .... 310-338-5238...... 56 E
jlabrie@lmu.edu
LABRIE, Lori, A .... 713-313-7040.... 500 B
labrie_la@tsu.edu
LABRIE, Lynn .... 928-317-6178...... 12 A
lynn.labrie@azwestern.edu
LABRIE, Mary Anne .... 603-623-0313.... 305 E
mlabrie@nhia.edu
LABRIOLA, Elisabeth, S ..... 860-439-2064...... 92 G
elisabeth.labriola@conncoll.edu
LABRON, Wendy .... 617-735-9778.... 234 C
labronw@emmanuel.edu
LABROSSE, Tonya, B .... 603-899-4097.... 305 A
labrosset@franklinpierce.edu
LABRUZZO, Anne .... 928-350-4006...... 17 K
alabruzzo@prescott.edu
LABUDE, Mark, S .... 318-342-3610.... 216 E
labude@ulm.edu
LABYAK, Gregory .... 618-545-3015.... 155 B
glabyak@kaskaskia.edu
LACEK, Steven .... 304-896-7357.... 543 C
steven.lacek@southernwv.edu
LACEY, Aaron .... 314-264-1802.... 301 C
aaron.lacey@vatterott-college.edu
LACEY, Aaron .... 314-264-1802.... 168 A
aaron.lacey@vatterott-college.edu
LACEY, Aaron .... 314-264-1802.... 414 B
aaron.lacey@vatterott-college.edu
LACEY, Aaron .... 314-264-1802.... 292 H
aaron.lacey@vatterott-college.edu
LACEY, Aaron .... 314-264-1802.... 292 F
aaron.lacey@vatterott-college.edu
LACEY, Aaron .... 314-264-1802.... 405 D
aaron.lacey@vatterott-college.edu
LACEY, Linda .... 575-646-5746.... 319 D
lacey@nmsu.edu
LACEY, Pete .... 810-989-5561.... 257 H
placey@sc4.edu
LACEY, R. Alton .... 314-392-2355.... 285 J
president@mobap.edu
LACEY-HAUN, Lora .... 816-235-1700.... 291 C
lacey-haunc@umkc.edu
LACH, Peter .... 304-367-4219.... 543 H
peter.lach@fairmontstate.edu
LACHANCE, Andrea .... 607-753-5430.... 353 B
andrea.lachance@cortland.edu
LACHANCE, Beatrice .... 615-547-1244.... 468 B
blachance@cumberland.edu
LACHANCE, Elizabeth, A .... 585-385-8410.... 348 F
llachance@sjfc.edu
LACHANCE, Laurie, G .... 207-859-1201.... 219 G
president@thomas.edu
LACHAPELLE, Laurie .... 978-762-4000.... 240 D
llachape@northshore.edu
LACHER, Candis .... 509-793-2063.... 531 I
candyl@bigbend.edu
LACHUT, Darlene, M .... 804-745-2444.... 517 C
dmlachut@bryantstratton.edu
LACIEN, Mark .... 219-989-2579.... 178 K
lacien@purduecal.edu
LACK, Paul, D .... 443-334-2205.... 226 E
cvanrensselaer@stevenson.edu
LACKEY, Charles .... 956-882-6552.... 505 E
charles.lackey@utb.edu
LACKEY, David, A .... 570-586-2400.... 422 G
dlackey@bbc.edu
LACKEY, Fred, G .... 251-442-2482........ 9 A
LACKEY, Mary Lou .... 209-946-2011...... 76 A
LACKEY, Miles .... 515-294-2220.... 182 E
mlackey@iastate.edu
LACKEY, Polly, R .... 806-291-3702.... 508 E
lackeyp@wbu.edu
LACKEY, Russell, L .... 515-263-6004.... 185 C
rlackey@grandview.edu
LACKEY, Sharon .... 803-321-5113.... 459 H
sharon.lackey@newberry.edu
LACKMAN, Vickie .... 253-680-7180.... 531 F
vlackman@bates.ctc.edu
LACKNER, Andrew .... 985-871-6201.... 215 C
alackner@tulane.edu
LACKNER, Elisabeth .... 718-631-6279.... 328 F
elackner@qcc.cuny.edu
LACOUR, Debra, R .... 979-830-4130.... 482 C
debra.lacour@blinn.edu
LACOUR, Joseph .... 318-670-9378.... 215 A
jlacour@susla.edu
LACOUR, Mary .... 985-549-2244.... 216 C
mlacour@selu.edu
LACOUR, Melissa .... 504-671-6219.... 210 F
mlacou@dcc.edu
LACOURSE, Michael .... 858-642-8107...... 58 I
mlacourse@nu.edu
LACOURSE, Peter, W .... 231-995-1198.... 256 D
placourse@nmc.edu
LACOURSE, William .... 410-455-2598.... 227 D
lacourse@umbc.edu
LACOVARA, Vincent, A ...... 202-319-6735...... 97 E
lacovara@cua.edu
LACRO, Erika .... 808-845-9225.... 142 B
lacro@hawaii.edu
LACROIX, Michael, J .... 402-280-2217.... 297 F
lacroix@creighton.edu
LACROIX, Roland, J .... 207-581-4053.... 220 A
roland.j.lacroix@maine.edu
LACY, Charles, F .... 702-968-2016.... 303 D
clacy@roseman.edu
LACY, Gary .... 914-948-6206.... 355 G
gary.lacy@esc.edu
LACY, Linda, L .... 562-860-2451...... 39 A
llacy@cerritos.edu
LACY, Russell .... 503-255-0332.... 417 C
rlacy@multnomah.edu
LACY, William, B .... 530-752-6376...... 73 I
wblacy@ucdavis.edu
LADAGE, Marcia .... 816-932-6742.... 289 D
mladage@saintlukescollege.edu
LADAS, Lori .... 406-447-5426.... 293 G
ladas@carroll.edu
LADD, Jack .... 432-552-2170.... 507 D
ladd_j@utpb.edu
LADD, Sheilah, M .... 802-626-6697.... 515 G
sheilah.ladd@lyndonstate.edu
LADD, Susan, K .... 515-271-3048.... 184 D
susan.ladd@drake.edu
LADE, Becky .... 515-271-1485.... 184 A
becky.lade@dmu.edu
LADENDECKER, Rob .... 213-388-9950...... 46 E
LADERMAN, Michael, S ...... 305-899-3189.... 101 M
mladerman@mail.barry.edu
LADEWIG, Patricia, A .... 303-458-1843...... 87 I
pladewig@regis.edu
LADHA, Amin .... 734-973-3400.... 259 F
amin@wccnet.edu
LADISCH, Christine, M ...... 765-494-8210.... 178 J
ladischc@purdue.edu
LADITKA, Doug .... 330-263-2310.... 388 F
dladitka@wooster.edu
LADITKA, Robyn .... 330-263-2545.... 388 F
rladitka@wooster.edu
LADNER, Barbara .... 304-766-4113.... 544 F
ladnerbe@wvstateu.edu
LADNER, Gayle .... 985-732-6640.... 211 A
LADNER, Hilda .... 320-589-6095.... 271 G
hladner@morris.umn.edu
LADNER, Marilyn .... 352-854-2322.... 103 K
ladnerm@cf.edu
LADNER, Pam .... 228-497-7642.... 275 E
pamela.ladner@mgccc.edu
LADNER-MATHIS, Jocelyn 216-987-4537.... 389 B
jocelyn.ladner-mathis@tri-c.edu
LADREW, Tammy .... 540-868-7056.... 527 C
tladrew@lfcc.edu
LADUCA, Bonnie .... 651-690-8664.... 270 L
bsladuca@stkate.edu
LADUCER, Wanda .... 701-477-7862.... 383 F
wladucer@tm.edu
LADUSAW, William .... 831-459-2696...... 75 C
humdean@ucsc.edu
LAEL, Robert .... 217-206-7020.... 167 C
lael.robert@uis.edu
LAFAILLE, Pierre-Carly ...... 972-929-6777.... 486 D
plafaille@devry.edu
LAFATA-JOHNSON,
Paulette .... 219-980-6769.... 174 B
plafataj@iun.edu
LAFAVE, Alan .... 605-626-2497.... 466 A
lafavea@northern.edu
LAFAYETTE, Jack .... 610-921-6652.... 421 E
jlafayette@alb.edu
LAFERLA, Chris .... 712-325-3293.... 186 F
claferla@iwcc.edu
LAFEVER, Michael .... 716-827-2491.... 358 D
lafeverm@trocaire.edu
LAFEVER, Steven, D .... 316-978-3070.... 198 A
steve.lafever@wichita.edu
LAFFERTY, Carolyn .... 732-255-0400.... 312 D
clafferty@ocean.edu
LAFFERTY, T. Kevin .... 813-258-7456.... 123 A
klafferty@ut.edu
LAFFERTY, William, J .... 717-337-6912.... 429 I
wlaffert@gettysburg.edu
LAFFEY, Brian .... 312-567-3677.... 153 C
blaffey1@iit.edu
LAFFITTE, Ron .... 864-587-4002.... 461 D
laffitter@smcsc.edu
LAFLAMME, Janet .... 207-893-7755.... 219 F
jlaflamm@sjcme.edu
LAFLAMME, Martha .... 603-752-1113.... 304 H
mlaflamme@ccsnh.edu
LAFLASH, Debra, A .... 508-854-4551.... 240 F
dal@qcc.mass.edu
LAFLEN, Jody .... 206-934-5566.... 537 E
jody.laflen@seattlecolleges.edu
LAFLEUR, Joyce .... 616-632-2106.... 247 E
laflejoy@aquinas.edu
LAFLEUR, Joyce, L .... 616-632-2106.... 247 E
laflejoy@aquinas.edu
LAFOND, Robert .... 215-637-7700.... 431 A
rlafond@holyfamily.edu
LAFONTAINE, Joni .... 701-477-7862.... 383 F
jlafontaine@tm.edu
LAFORGE, Catherine .... 603-668-2211.... 305 I
c.laforge@snhu.edu
LAFORGE, Daniel .... 207-948-9287.... 219 H
dlaforge@unity.edu
LAFORGIA, John .... 507-284-2073.... 262 B
laforgia.john@mayo.edu
LAFORGIA, John, W .... 507-284-2073.... 262 D
LAFRANCE, Mark .... 617-243-2178.... 236 A
mlafrance@lasell.edu
LAFUZE, Alice .... 765-983-1677.... 171 E
lafuzal@earlham.edu
LAGASSE, Ray .... 701-777-6438.... 381 F
raymond.lagasse@und.edu
LAGATTA, James, J .... 518-629-4523.... 336 C
j.lagatta@hvcc.edu
LAGATTA, Regina .... 518-255-5524.... 354 E
lagattrm@cobleskill.edu
LAGATTA, Regina, M .... 607-746-4556.... 355 F
lagattrm@delhi.edu
LAGEORGE, Lisa .... 661-362-2205...... 56 G
llageorge@masters.edu
LAGER, Carol .... 360-752-8323.... 531 H
clager@btc.ctc.edu
LAGESON, David .... 541-962-3114.... 418 C
dlageson@eou.edu
LAGGNER, Laurie .... 802-586-7711.... 514 G
llaggner@sterlingcollege.edu
LAGRANGE, Janet .... 337-521-8900.... 211 J
janet.lagrange@southlouisiana.edu
LAGRANGE, Linda .... 505-454-3578.... 318 J
lagrange_l@nmhu.edu
LAGRANGE, Teresa .... 216-523-7402.... 388 D
t.lagrange@csuohio.edu
LAGRASSA, Michael .... 508-999-9180.... 237 A
mlagrassa@umassd.edu
LAGROW, Patricia .... 405-974-3371.... 413 B
plagrow@uco.edu
LAGUARDIA, John, A .... 330-972-5328.... 403 B
jlaguardia@uakron.edu
LAGUERRE, Jowel, C .... 707-864-7112...... 70 A
jowel.laguerre@solano.edu
LAGUERRE-BROWN,
Caroline .... 410-516-8075.... 223 F
clbrown@jhu.edu
LAGUNA, Robert .... 512-492-3010.... 480 F
rlaguna@aoma.edu
LAHANN, Mary .... 928-777-3803...... 14 C
mary.lahann@erau.edu
LAHARGOUE, Brian .... 785-841-9640.... 196 B
LAHART, Amy .... 570-674-6340.... 436 F
alahart@misericordia.edu
LAHART, Edward .... 570-504-7000.... 425 F
LAHER, Ronald .... 610-527-0200.... 445 J
rlaher@rosemont.edu
LAHEY, John, L .... 203-582-8700...... 93 H
john.lahey@quinnipiac.edu
LAHM, Chris .... 417-626-1234.... 287 C
lahm.chris@occ.edu
LAHM, Terry, D .... 614-236-6800.... 386 E
tlahm@capital.edu
LAHR, Sheri, K .... 580-327-8550.... 409 C
sklahr@nwosu.edu
LAI, Chun .... 215-572-3850.... 451 D
clai@wts.edu
LAI, Mary, M .... 516-299-2502.... 338 E
mary.lai@liu.edu
LAI HING, Kenneth .... 256-726-7112........ 6 C
laihing@oakwood.edu
LAIBLE, Jim .... 815-967-7307.... 162 I
jlaible@rockfordcareercollege.edu
LAIDACKER, Crystal .... 972-241-3371.... 484 E
claidacker@dallas.edu
LAING, Katherine .... 217-333-1086.... 167 A
klaing@illinois.edu
LAING-IDLE, Michelle, L ... 704-357-8020.... 362 D
mlaing@aii.edu
LAINO, Nicholas .... 315-866-0300.... 335 D
lainonf@herkimer.edu
LAIPSON, Peter .... 413-528-7239.... 230 F
plaipson@simons-rock.edu
LAIR, Patrick .... 651-423-8399.... 266 B
pat.lair@dctc.edu
LAIRD, Allan .... 208-459-5151.... 143 D
alaird@collegeofidaho.edu
LAIRD, Brenda .... 307-778-1372.... 556 E
blaird@lcccfoundation.edu
LAIRD, Kim .... 903-468-3039.... 498 B
kim.laird@tamuc.edu
LAIRD, Richard .... 321-433-7032.... 102 D
lairdr@brevardcc.edu
LAIRD, Stephen .... 660-626-2701.... 278 D
slaird@atsu.edu
LAIRD, William, G .... 312-915-7803.... 157 C
wlaird@luc.edu
LAIRMORE, Michael, D ..... 530-752-1361...... 73 I
mdlairmore@ucdavis.edu
LAJAUNIE, Carol .... 800-962-7682.... 293 A
clajaunie@wma.edu
LAJAUNIE, Ronald, P .... 337-482-6235.... 216 D
rpl7290@louisiana.edu
LAJEUNESSE, Mary Ellen .. 518-629-7292.... 336 C
m.lajeunesse@hvcc.edu
LAJINESS, Todd .... 313-883-8501.... 257 E
lajiness.todd@shms.edu
LAJUBUTU, Oyebanjo .... 410-951-3494.... 228 B
olajubutu@coppin.edu
LAKE, Amber .... 641-673-1078.... 190 C
lakea@wmpenn.edu
LAKE, Diana .... 360-475-7831.... 536 D
dlake@olympic.edu
LAKE, Doris, J .... 270-831-9617.... 202 D
doris.lake@kctcs.edu
LAKE, Gashaw .... 502-597-6117.... 203 G
gashaw.lake@kysu.edu
LAKE, James, G .... 334-683-2300........ 5 G
jlake@marionmilitary.edu
LAKE, Jeannine .... 816-204-2158...... 19 A
jeannine.lake@phoenix.edu
LAKE, Kathy .... 231-591-2113.... 250 H
lakek@ferris.edu
LAKE, Kathy .... 414-382-6084.... 546 B
kathy.lake@alverno.edu
LAKE, Marjean .... 801-524-8163.... 510 E
mlake@ldsbc.edu
LAKE, Michael, P .... 850-644-2478.... 119 D
mlake@admin.fsu.edu
LAKE, Stephanie, S .... 919-866-5927.... 374 H
sslake@waketech.edu
LAKE, Todd .... 615-460-6628.... 467 D
todd.lake@belmont.edu
LAKE, Tracy .... 860-231-5447...... 95 D
tlake@usj.edu
LAKE-KING, Shirley .... 340-693-1400.... 568 E
sking@live.uvi.edu
LAKEN, Elizabeth, A .... 815-740-3372.... 167 E
elaken@stfrancis.edu

LAKEN, Michael, J ... 630-515-6148 ... 158 F mlaken@midwestern.edu
LAKETA, Dave ... 815-740-3464 ... 167 E dlaketa@stfrancis.edu
LAKEY, John ... 308-865-8427 ... 300 F lakeyj@unk.edu
LAKIN, Lyn ... 785-594-4590 ... 190 F lyn.lakin@bakeru.edu
LAKIS, James ... 570-321-4141 ... 435 D lakis@lycoming.edu
LAKSO, James, J ... 814-641-3121 ... 432 A lakso@juniata.edu
LAKURIQI, Elona ... 215-951-2186 ... 444 D lakuriqie@philau.edu
LALIBERTE, Jean ... 334-670-3608 ... 8 A jlaliber@troy.edu
LALIBERTE, Michael, R ... 414-229-1122 ... 551 D lalibert@uwm.edu
LALJIANI, Karen ... 972-273-3392 ... 485 C klaljiani@dcccd.edu
LALLY, Jay ... 321-674-8225 ... 108 H jlally@fit.edu
LALLY, Mary ... 617-573-8430 ... 245 B mlally@suffolk.edu
LALLY, Shiela ... 617-236-8800 ... 234 G slally@fisher.edu
LALOR, Melinda, M ... 205-934-8420 ... 8 F mlalor@uab.edu
LALOVIC-HAND, Mira ... 856-256-4146 ... 314 A lalovic-hand@rowan.edu
LALUZERNE, Joseph ... 651-638-6879 ... 261 D j-laluzerne@bethel.edu
LALUZERNE, Shannon, S ... 920-923-7661 ... 548 E slaluzerne@marianuniversity.edu
LAM, Felix ... 212-650-8173 ... 326 G flam@ccny.cuny.edu
LAM, Kenneth ... 718-420-4164 ... 360 A kenneth.lam@wagner.edu
LAM, Lap-Pun ... 509-335-4553 ... 539 D lap-pun.lam@wsu.edu
LAM, Minh ... 510-466-7262 ... 62 A mlam@peralta.edu
LAM, Nathan ... 310-824-1586 ... 26 D
LAM, Simon, Y ... 415-338-2541 ... 37 B slam@sfsu.edu
LAM YUEN, Peteru ... 684-699-9155 ... 559 C p.lamyuen@amsamoa.edu
LAMADANIE, Mahmoud ... 318-274-7798 ... 215 E lamadaniem@gram.edu
LAMADE, Dawn ... 706-379-3526 ... 140 A dlamade@yhc.edu
LAMADRID, Eduardo ... 787-766-1912 ... 562 I elamadrid@inter.edu
LAMADRID, Edward ... 773-477-4822 ... 60 D elamadrid@pacificcollege.edu
LAMADRID, Edward ... 888-729-4811 ... 161 B
LAMADRID, Lucas ... 704-461-6724 ... 362 F lucaslamadrid@bac.edu
LAMADRID, Lupe ... 225-578-1221 ... 212 H glamadrid@lsu.edu
LAMAIR, Louis ... 808-942-1000 ... 141 D
LAMANNA, Paul, A ... 716-851-1469 ... 333 B lamanna@ecc.edu
LAMANTIA, Paul ... 207-255-1305 ... 220 E paul.lamantia@maine.edu
LAMAR, Charlene ... 912-688-6039 ... 135 D clamar@ogeecheetech.edu
LAMAR, Chris ... 317-788-3399 ... 180 F lamarc@uindy.edu
LAMAR, Sharmaine ... 610-690-5675 ... 447 F slamar1@swarthmore.edu
LAMAR, Sondra ... 479-788-7025 ... 24 D sondra.lamar@uafs.edu
LAMARCHE, Paul ... 609-258-4999 ... 312 G lamarche@princeton.edu
LAMARRE, Wayne ... 207-602-2412 ... 221 A wlamarre@une.edu
LAMAS, Carmen ... 215-951-1209 ... 432 I lamas@lasalle.edu
LAMAS, Frank ... 817-272-6080 ... 505 C lamas@uta.edu
LAMATTINA, Lina ... 585-345-6999 ... 334 F lmlamattina@genesee.edu
LAMB, Bill ... 319-398-5509 ... 187 B blamb@kirkwood.edu
LAMB, Colin ... 620-276-9640 ... 193 C colin.lamb@gcccks.edu
LAMB, Craig ... 765-269-5870 ... 176 D clamb@ivytech.edu
LAMB, David ... 716-829-7652 ... 332 E kavinokytheater@dyc.edu
LAMB, Duane ... 205-348-8092 ... 8 E dlamb@fa.ua.edu
LAMB, Jeffrey ... 707-864-7000 ... 70 A jeffrey.lamb@solano.edu
LAMB, Jimmie ... 972-825-4636 ... 495 F jlamb@sagu.edu
LAMB, John, C ... 414-288-1671 ... 548 F john.lamb@marquette.edu
LAMB, Keith ... 940-397-4291 ... 491 B keith.lamb@mwsu.edu
LAMB, Kevin, D ... 740-376-4712 ... 395 G kevin.lamb@marietta.edu
LAMB, Linda ... 315-866-0300 ... 335 D lamblc@herkimer.edu
LAMB, Martha ... 508-286-3905 ... 246 B mlamb@wheatonma.edu
LAMB, Marybeth ... 781-768-7147 ... 244 A marybeth.lamb@regiscollege.edu
LAMB, Melissa ... 912-427-5841 ... 124 C mlamb@altamahatech.edu
LAMB, Michael ... 706-649-1821 ... 128 A mlamb@columbustech.edu
LAMB, Sophie, A ... 785-827-5541 ... 194 F sophie.lamb@kwu.edu
LAMB, Stephan ... 805-756-6509 ... 33 I slamb@calpoly.edu
LAMB, Sue ... 757-388-2900 ... 524 D
LAMB, Susan, E ... 925-685-1230 ... 43 F slamb@dvc.edu
LAMBA, Sandy ... 209-473-5200 ... 50 E sandy_lamba@heald.edu
LAMBE, Joan ... 212-772-5462 ... 327 E joan.lambe@hunter.cuny.edu
LAMBERT, Ame ... 802-860-2784 ... 513 C alambert@champlain.edu
LAMBERT, Angela ... 304-327-4480 ... 543 F alambert@bluefieldstate.edu
LAMBERT, Collin ... 312-329-4290 ... 159 A collin.lambert@moody.edu
LAMBERT, Connie ... 509-963-1411 ... 532 C lambertc@cwu.edu
LAMBERT, Elaine, J ... 570-326-3761 ... 440 L elambert@pct.edu
LAMBERT, Elizabeth, A ... 607-735-1825 ... 332 I elambert@elmira.edu
LAMBERT, James ... 419-372-9970 ... 385 E jlamber@bgsu.edu
LAMBERT, Kathryn, C ... 856-566-6972 ... 316 I lambertkc@umdnj.edu
LAMBERT, Kevin ... 606-633-3305 ... 203 D kevin.lambert@kctcs.edu
LAMBERT, Kim, D ... 315-792-3341 ... 359 E klambert@utica.edu
LAMBERT, Lake ... 478-301-2915 ... 134 A lambert_l@mercer.edu
LAMBERT, Lee, D ... 206-546-4551 ... 538 C llambert@shoreline.edu
LAMBERT, Leo, M ... 336-278-7900 ... 364 D lambert@elon.edu
LAMBERT, Leslie, T ... 540-365-4206 ... 519 C llambert@ferrum.edu
LAMBERT, Linda ... 360-383-3295 ... 540 A llambert@whatcom.ctc.edu
LAMBERT, Lori, A ... 513-745-3203 ... 406 E lambert@xavier.edu
LAMBERT, Mark, A ... 540-985-9031 ... 520 I malambert@jchs.edu
LAMBERT, Matthew ... 315-786-2271 ... 337 F mlambert@sunyjefferson.edu
LAMBERT, Matthew, T ... 202-687-4636 ... 98 D mtl6@georgetown.edu
LAMBERT, Patrick ... 845-398-4396 ... 349 H plambert@stac.edu
LAMBERT, Peggy, E ... 330-287-1376 ... 399 A lambert.133@osu.edu
LAMBERT, Rebecca ... 479-524-7493 ... 22 C blambert@jbu.edu
LAMBERT, Sara ... 423-775-6596 ... 472 G slambert@ogs.edu
LAMBERT, Stacey ... 617-327-6777 ... 241 F stacey_lambert@mspp.edu
LAMBETH, Christopher ... 513-721-7944 ... 391 D clambeth@gbs.edu
LAMBIE-SIMPSON, Yasmin ... 650-543-3976 ... 57 B ylambie-simpson@menlo.edu
LAMBLA, Kenneth, A ... 704-687-0090 ... 379 A kalambla@uncc.edu
LAMBORGHINI, Nita ... 978-556-3818 ... 240 E nlamborghini@necc.mass.edu
LAMBORN, Alan ... 970-491-6614 ... 83 F alan.lamborn@colostate.edu
LAMBORN, John, E ... 765-361-6327 ... 181 E lambornj@wabash.edu
LAMBRAKIS, Christine ... 602-286-8227 ... 15 G christine.lambrakis@gwmail.maricopa.edu
LAMBRECHT, Anne, K ... 989-463-7225 ... 247 B lambrechtak@alma.edu
LAMBRECHT, Jennifer ... 763-424-0909 ... 268 B jsummer-lambrecht@nhcc.edu
LAMBRECHT, John ... 708-456-0300 ... 166 F jlambrec@triton.edu
LAMBRECHT, Michael ... 541-962-3516 ... 418 C mlambrecht@eou.edu
LAMBRECHT, Tom ... 740-753-6196 ... 391 H lambrecht_t@hocking.edu
LAMBRECHTSEN, Karen ... 916-577-2200 ... 79 G klambrechtsen@jessup.edu
LAMBRIGHT, Jonathan ... 912-358-3269 ... 136 G lambrij@savannahstate.edu
LAMBROS, Mary Ann ... 410-225-2262 ... 224 B mlambros@mica.edu
LAME BULL, Crystal ... 509-865-8653 ... 535 A lamebull_c@heritage.edu
LAMENS, Georgia-Lynn ... 631-687-4534 ... 349 B glamens@sjcny.edu
LAMERSON, Cindy ... 581-803-2013 ... 114 C cynthia_lamerson@pba.edu
LAMHAOUAR, Said ... 718-429-6600 ... 359 G said.lamhaouar@vaughn.edu
LAMICA, Victoria ... 925-485-5287 ... 39 C vlamica@clpccd.cc.ca.us
LAMIMAN, Lynne ... 972-708-7536 ... 487 B
LAMINACK, Jackie ... 713-646-1800 ... 494 I jlaminack@stcl.edu
LAMIRAND, Hershel ... 405-271-2200 ... 413 D hershel-lamirand@ouhsc.edu
LAMKIN, Corbet, J ... 870-574-4501 ... 24 A clamkin@sautech.edu
LAMKIN, Fletcher, M ... 785-827-5541 ... 194 F fletcher.lamkin@kwu.edu
LAMM, Deborah, L ... 252-823-5166 ... 370 D lammd@edgecombe.edu
LAMM, Edward ... 920-403-3005 ... 550 F edward.lamm@snc.edu
LAMM, Gary ... 254-295-4545 ... 504 C glamm@umhb.edu
LAMM, Norman ... 212-960-5280 ... 346 F lamm@yu.edu
LAMM, Peggy ... 970-248-1020 ... 82 F plamm@coloradomesa.edu
LAMMERS, Keith ... 215-780-1260 ... 446 G keith@salus.edu
LAMMERS, Kim ... 419-783-2563 ... 389 H klammers@defiance.edu
LAMMERS, Michael ... 503-699-6252 ... 416 J mlammers@marylhurst.edu
LAMMERS, Paul ... 605-668-1544 ... 464 G plammers@mtmc.edu
LAMMERS, Shelley ... 402-844-7282 ... 299 I shelley@northeast.edu
LAMMLE, Gretchen ... 860-628-4751 ... 93 C glammle@lincolncollegene.edu
LAMMONS, Anthony ... 951-343-4217 ... 31 J alammons@calbaptist.edu
LAMOE, Jeff, P ... 913-684-2905 ... 558 F jeff.lamoe@leavenworth.army.mil
LAMONICA, P. Raymond ... 225-578-0335 ... 212 G plamoni@lsu.edu
LAMONT, Wanda ... 914-964-4296 ... 329 D
LAMONTAGNE, Gregory ... 716-614-6450 ... 344 C glamontagne@niagaracc.suny.edu
LAMONTAGNE, Michael ... 253-833-9111 ... 534 H mlamontagne@greenriver.edu
LAMONTAGNE, Ramona ... 815-836-5291 ... 156 F lamontra@lewisu.edu
LAMONTAGNE, Susan ... 413-572-5425 ... 238 F slamontagne@wsc.ma.edu
LAMOREAUX, Barbara ... 330-287-1214 ... 399 A lamoreaux.1@osu.edu
LAMOREAUX, Marilyn ... 435-652-7502 ... 512 B lamoreaux@dixie.edu
LAMORTE, Debra ... 212-998-6411 ... 344 B debra.lamorte@nyu.edu
LAMORTE, JR., Louis, A ... 215-951-1075 ... 432 I lamorte@lasalle.edu
LAMOTHE, Ida, M ... 508-541-1624 ... 233 G ilamothe@dean.edu
LAMOTHE, Viviane ... 510-235-7800 ... 43 E vlamothe@contracosta.edu
LAMOTT, Eric, E ... 651-641-8729 ... 263 A lamott@csp.edu
LAMOTTE, Steve ... 302-736-2485 ... 97 A steve.lamotte@wesley.edu
LAMOUNTAIN, Kevin ... 602-759-2258 ... 11 H klamountain@arizonacollege.edu
LAMP, Joel ... 904-256-7400 ... 111 L jlamp@ju.edu
LAMPARELLI, Kimberly ... 518-458-5354 ... 330 C lamparek@strose.edu
LAMPE, Gregory, P ... 608-263-1794 ... 553 B greg.lampe@uwc.edu
LAMPHERE, Amy ... 630-844-5467 ... 145 F lamphere@aurora.edu
LAMPHERE, Scott ... 617-243-2115 ... 236 A slamphere@lasell.edu
LAMPHERE, Sue ... 740-363-1146 ... 396 A slamphere@mtso.edu
LAMPKIN, Alison ... 706-802-5473 ... 130 E alampkin@highlands.edu
LAMPKIN, Patricia, M ... 434-924-7984 ... 525 F pml@virginia.edu
LAMPKIN-WILLIAMS, Ann ... 313-593-5321 ... 259 B lampkin@umd.umich.edu
LAMPKIN-WILLIAMS, Ann ... 313-593-5390 ... 259 B lampkin@umd.umich.edu
LAMPKINS, Larry ... 270-247-8521 ... 204 G llampkins@midcontinent.edu
LAMPLEY, Paul, C ... 662-252-8000 ... 276 G plampley@rustcollege.edu
LAMPONE, Rosalie ... 501-312-0007 ... 23 D rosalie.lampone@remingtoncollege.edu
LAMPUS, Rita ... 239-513-1122 ... 111 A rlampus@hodges.edu
LAMWERS, Linda, L ... 610-436-3405 ... 444 A llamwers@wcupa.edu
LAMY, Patrick, J ... 973-748-9000 ... 307 H patrick_lamy@bloomfield.edu
LAN, Larry ... 407-888-8689 ... 108 B
LANA, Peter ... 585-389-2344 ... 342 D plana0@naz.edu
LANAGAN, Keni ... 865-981-8308 ... 471 B keni.lanagan@maryvillecollege.edu
LANASA, Steven, M ... 913-621-6070 ... 192 F slanasa@donnelly.edu
LANCASTER, Adrianna ... 580-559-5368 ... 407 J alancaster@ecok.edu
LANCASTER, Beth ... 864-596-9704 ... 457 E beth.lancaster@converse.edu
LANCASTER, Carol ... 202-687-0468 ... 98 D lancastc@georgetown.edu
LANCASTER, James ... 626-852-6403 ... 40 B jlancaster@citruscollege.edu
LANCASTER, Lindsay ... 405-733-7311 ... 411 I llancaster@rose.edu
LANCASTER, Loren ... 406-874-6171 ... 294 F lancastral@milescc.edu
LANCASTER, Sydney ... 440-365-5222 ... 395 D
LANCE, Ann, H ... 507-284-2915 ... 262 D
LANCE, Charlene ... 330-684-8755 ... 403 C clance@uakron.edu
LANCE, Charles, A ... 828-669-8012 ... 367 E clance@montreat.edu
LANCE, Danette ... 303-784-8045 ... 85 M dlance@jiu.edu
LANCHESTER, Judy ... 209-588-5366 ... 80 G lanchesterj@yosemite.cc.ca.us
LAND, Lauren ... 870-245-5283 ... 22 I landl@obu.edu
LAND, Mark ... 812-855-0850 ... 173 D mdland@iu.edu
LAND, Matt ... 260-665-4143 ... 180 D landm@trine.edu
LAND, Mitch ... 757-352-4916 ... 523 E mland@regent.edu
LAND, Patricia ... 941-637-5656 ... 105 F pland@edison.edu
LAND, Paul, W ... 410-543-6105 ... 228 D pwland@salisbury.edu
LAND, Sabrina ... 773-821-4976 ... 146 G sland20@csu.edu
LAND, Steven, J ... 423-478-7702 ... 472 H president@ptseminary.edu
LANDAU, Barbara ... 410-516-8094 ... 223 F landau@jhu.edu
LANDE, Richard ... 507-457-5045 ... 269 G rlande@winona.edu
LANDEN, Robyn ... 307-268-2362 ... 556 A rlanden@caspercollege.edu
LANDEN, William ... 307-268-2667 ... 556 A blanden@caspercollege.edu
LANDER, Beth ... 215-885-2360 ... 435 E blander@manor.edu
LANDER, Harry, M ... 212-746-5979 ... 360 C hmlander@med.cornell.edu
LANDER, Laura ... 413-565-1000 ... 230 G llander@baypath.edu
LANDER, Maria ... 704-290-5267 ... 374 A mlander@spcc.edu
LANDERS, Joanne ... 216-421-7327 ... 388 A jlanders@cia.edu
LANDERS, Mary ... 816-501-4199 ... 288 A mary.landers@rockhurst.edu
LANDERS, Sharon ... 615-771-7821 ... 478 H sharon.landers@williamsoncc.edu
LANDERS, Stephanie ... 313-993-1549 ... 258 G landerss@udmercy.edu
LANDERS, Thomas, L ... 405-325-2621 ... 413 C landers@ou.edu
LANDERS, Timothy, M ... 585-343-0055 ... 334 F tmlanders@genesee.edu
LANDES, Marie, C ... 540-665-4516 ... 524 E mlandes@su.edu
LANDEY, Sena ... 765-983-1468 ... 171 E landse@earlham.edu
LANDGAARD, Jodi ... 507-372-3403 ... 267 G jodi.landgaard@mnwest.edu
LANDGRAF, Tanya ... 712-749-2212 ... 183 C landgraft@bvu.edu
LANDGREN, Peter ... 513-556-3737 ... 403 D peter.landgren@uc.edu
LANDIS, Ann ... 229-226-1621 ... 138 C alandis@thomasu.edu
LANDIS, Justin ... 517-264-7172 ... 258 B jlandis@sienaheights.edu
LANDIS, SCC, Marie Cecelia ... 973-543-6528 ... 307 B spmcl@juno.com
LANDIS, Shirley, A ... 215-951-2717 ... 444 D landiss@philau.edu
LANDMAN, Bruce ... 678-839-5190 ... 139 A landman@westga.edu
LANDON, Jennifer ... 603-645-9724 ... 305 I j.landon@snhu.edu
LANDPHAIR, Juliette, L ... 804-289-8468 ... 525 E jlandpha@richmond.edu
LANDREBE, Robert, S ... 978-468-7111 ... 235 B blandrebe@gcts.edu
LANDRITH, J. Wayne ... 864-977-7017 ... 460 A wayne.landrith@ngu.edu
LANDRON, Carmen, T ... 787-620-2040 ... 560 D clandron@aupr.edu

LANDRUM, Fred 606-487-3181 202 C fred.landrum@kctcs.edu
LANDRUM, Katherine, S 601-974-1502 275 B landrks@millsaps.edu
LANDRUM, Kay 616-222-1402 250 A kay.landrum@cornerstone.edu
LANDRUM, Kay 817-598-6499 508 F klandrum@wc.edu
LANDRUM, Kristin 276-656-0259 527 G klandrum@patrickhenry.edu
LANDRUM, Paul 575-538-6488 321 I landrump@wumu.edu
LANDRUM, Thomas, S 706-542-2002 138 G tlandrum@uga.edu
LANDRUM, Treina 318-342-5305 216 E landrum@ulm.edu
LANDRUM, Wes 704-922-6462 370 G landrum.wes@gaston.edu
LANDRUM-SIMS, Alonzetta 334-347-2623 3 F alandrum-sims@escc.edu
LANDRY, Abbie 318-357-4403 216 B landry@nsula.edu
LANDRY, Bill 843-574-6745 461 G bill.landry@tridenttech.edu
LANDRY, Cara 225-675-8270 211 F clandry@rpcc.edu
LANDRY, Debbie 918-456-5511 409 A landry@nsuok.edu
LANDRY, Fred 318-869-5136 208 H flandry@centenary.edu
LANDRY, James 310-338-2833 56 E james.landry@lmu.edu
LANDRY, Karen 425-267-0153 534 C klandry@everettcc.edu
LANDRY, Lisa, C 337-482-5430 216 D ldlandry@louisiana.edu
LANDRY, Lisa, L 337-482-6471 216 D housing@louisiana.edu
LANDRY, Madelaine 337-550-1257 212 J
LANDRY, Mark 228-497-7809 275 E mark.landry@mgccc.edu
LANDRY, Patrick 337-482-6402 216 D pml@louisiana.edu
LANDRY, Ruth 337-482-5811 216 D rwl@louisiana.edu
LANDRY, Shawntel, D 214-210-4050 169 B
LANDRY, Stephen 973-275-2299 315 B stephen.landry@shu.edu
LANDRY, Valencia, V 225-308-4590 208 B vvessel@brc.edu
LANDSAW, Christy 918-456-5511 409 A landsaw@nsuok.edu
LANDSMARK, Theodore, C 617-262-5000 231 G ted.landsmark@the-bac.edu
LANDSTROM, Corey 563-387-1020 187 D clandstrom@luther.edu
LANDWEHR, Brynn 630-844-7861 145 F landwehr@aurora.edu
LANDWER, Allan, J 325-670-2222 487 F alandwer@hsutx.edu
LANE, Amy 715-232-1469 552 E lanea@uwstout.edu
LANE, Austin 936-273-7222 490 E austin.lane@lonestar.edu
LANE, Barbara 573-329-5160 283 I laneb@lincolnu.edu
LANE, Charles, E 213-740-3649 76 F clane@caps.usc.edu
LANE, David 207-621-3448 220 B dlane@maine.edu
LANE, David, H 410-234-4848 225 E
LANE, Deborah 205-348-8089 8 E dlane@ur.ua.edu
LANE, Deborah 405-744-6384 410 C debbie.lane@okstate.edu
LANE, Diane, C 410-287-6060 222 A dlane@cecil.edu
LANE, Diane, L 217-362-6416 158 G dlane@millikin.edu
LANE, Edwin, H 816-415-7643 293 C lanee@william.jewell.edu
LANE, Eric 516-463-5854 335 G eric.lane@hofstra.edu
LANE, Iris 810-989-2374 248 G iris.lane@baker.edu
LANE, Jennifer 808-675-4971 140 D jennifer.lane@byuh.edu
LANE, Jill 678-466-4194 127 D jilllane@clayton.edu
LANE, Jill 618-468-4900 156 E jlane@lc.edu
LANE, Kelly 859-344-3386 206 I kelly.lane@thomasmore.edu
LANE, Kelly 617-369-3631 244 E klane@mfa.org
LANE, Kimberly 216-373-5290 397 F klane@ndc.edu
LANE, Laura 248-476-1122 254 G llane@mispp.edu
LANE, Marguerite 516-678-5000 341 F mlane@molloy.edu
LANE, Mark 808-455-0213 142 D marklane@hawaii.edu
LANE, Mary 363-334-4822 371 A mslane@gtcc.edu
LANE, Matt 304-776-6290 541 B mlane@cci.edu
LANE, Natalie 307-382-1673 557 A nlane@wwcc.wy.edu
LANE, Nicole 724-222-5330 438 F nlane@penncommercial.edu
LANE, Phyllis 360-867-6034 534 D lanep@evergreen.edu
LANE, Robert, J 515-961-1417 189 C bob.lane@simpson.edu
LANE, Roberta 847-578-8309 163 C roberta.lane@rosalindfranklin.edu
LANE, Russ 402-557-7452 296 H russ.lane@bellevue.edu
LANE, Shelese 404-270-5110 138 B sjlane@spelman.edu
LANE, Tamara 806-743-2300 502 B tamara.lane@ttuhsc.edu
LANE, Thomas 989-686-9298 250 D thlane@delta.edu
LANE COBB, Michelle 252-789-0244 371 H mlane@martincc.edu
LANE-MARTIN, Tanya 585-345-6800 334 F tmlanemartin@genesee.edu
LANEY, Jo 575-562-2677 318 B jo.laney@enmu.edu
LANEY, Mary, A 386-312-4069 116 F maryannelaney@sjrstate.edu
LANEY, Miriam 803-778-7825 455 G laneymt@cctech.edu
LANFEAR, Jeffery 773-325-8308 149 A jlanfear@depaul.edu
LANG, Anita 201-216-5163 315 E alang@stevens.edu
LANG, Ashley 319-352-8486 189 J ashley.lang@wartburg.edu
LANG, Carol 215-204-8231 447 H carol.lang@temple.edu
LANG, Celine 321-674-7111 108 H celine@fit.edu
LANG, Christine 843-574-6162 461 G chris.lang@tridenttech.edu
LANG, Cyndi 574-520-4490 174 E clang@iusb.edu
LANG, Donna 409-740-4409 497 F langd@tamug.edu
LANG, Heather 303-581-9955 320 G heather@acupuncturecollege.edu
LANG, Heather 971-722-4532 419 G heather.lang@pcc.edu
LANG, Jennifer 718-780-0383 324 F jennifer.lang@brooklaw.edu
LANG, Kathy, J 414-288-1782 548 F kathy.lang@marquette.edu
LANG, Mandy 715-422-5446 554 E mandy.lang@mstc.edu
LANG, Melissa, W 757-446-6054 518 G langmw@evms.edu
LANG, Paul, L 906-227-2920 256 C plang@nmu.edu
LANG, Sherrie 210-486-2252 479 D slang14@alamo.edu
LANG, Stephen, W 432-837-8061 501 E slang@sulross.edu
LANGAN, Sally 920-498-5688 555 C sally.langan@nwtc.edu
LANGAN, Terrence, G 651-962-6001 272 B tglangan@stthomas.edu
LANGDON, Deb 740-389-4636 395 H langdond@mtc.edu
LANGDON, Lucas, O 270-686-4336 199 B lucas.langdon@brescia.edu
LANGDON, Rita 516-299-2334 339 A rita.langdon@liu.edu
LANGDON, Steven, D 515-643-6716 187 F slangdon@mercydesmoines.org
LANGDON, Tennille 660-831-4157 286 F langdont@moval.edu
LANGE, Andrea, G 410-778-7776 229 D alange2@washcoll.edu
LANGE, Chris, J 414-410-4207 546 G cjlange@stritch.edu
LANGE, Christine, M 941-359-7594 116 B clange@ringling.edu
LANGE, Dan 541-278-5891 414 G dlange@bluecc.edu
LANGE, Douglas, J 606-218-5988 207 F douglaslange@upike.edu
LANGE, Janet 309-677-2523 146 C lange@bradley.edu
LANGE, Karen 307-778-1204 556 E klange@lccc.wy.edu
LANGE, Karen, M 651-962-6050 272 B kmlange@stthomas.edu
LANGE, Lisa 606-218-5216 207 F lisalange@upike.edu
LANGE, Mindy, W 717-691-6024 436 D mlange@messiah.edu
LANGE, Peter 919-684-2631 364 C peter.lange@duke.edu
LANGE, Rob 757-594-8070 517 L robert.lange@cnu.edu
LANGE, Steven 320-629-5155 268 E langes@pinetech.edu
LANGE, Tom, J 715-831-7285 553 H tlange8@cvtc.edu
LANGE, Tyana 765-455-9217 174 A tylange@iuk.edu
LANGEMO, Bree 719-502-3008 87 B bree.langemo@ppcc.edu
LANGENBACHER, Mark 808-942-1000 141 D mark.langenbacher@remingtoncollege.edu
LANGENBACK, Timothy 941-752-5342 118 J langent@scf.edu
LANGENSTEIN, Deborah 980-598-1205 365 I deborah.langenstein@jwu.edu
LANGER, Nathan 218-723-6010 262 G nlanger@css.edu
LANGER, Peter 617-287-5611 236 G peter.langer@umb.edu
LANGERUD, Steven 765-658-4280 171 B stevelangarud@depauw.edu
LANGEVIN, John 207-602-2549 221 A jlangevin@une.edu
LANGFERMAN, Neil 317-955-6759 177 I nlangferman@marian.edu
LANGFORD, Allison 417-328-2093 290 A alangford@sbuniv.edu
LANGFORD, David 201-692-9867 310 A david_langford@fdu.edu
LANGFORD, Debra 304-876-5216 544 C dlangfor@shepherd.edu
LANGFORD, George, M 315-443-3949 357 C glangfor@syr.edu
LANGFORD, Harold (Hal), P 903-886-5189 498 B hal.langford@tamuc.edu
LANGFORD, James, D 325-674-2855 478 I langford@acu.edu
LANGFORD, Joel, C 770-720-5585 136 C jcl@reinhardt.edu
LANGFORD, Mike 828-328-7302 366 E mike.langford@lr.edu
LANGFORD, Pam 909-537-5008 36 B plangfor@csusb.edu
LANGFORD, Pamela 909-537-7454 36 B plangfor@csusb.edu
LANGHAM, Gay 601-643-8307 273 G gay.langham@colin.edu
LANGHAM, Julie 706-595-0166 125 H jlangham@augustatech.edu
LANGHAM, Lynda 936-468-2503 496 B llangham@sfasu.edu
LANGIS, Gayle 207-893-7850 219 F glangis@sjcme.edu
LANGKILDE, Jared 480-461-7396 15 I jared.langkilde@mcmail.maricopa.edu
LANGLAND, Elizabeth 602-543-4506 11 J elizabeth.langland@asu.edu
LANGLAND, Meg 573-592-5381 293 B meg.langland@westminster-mo.edu
LANGLEY-TURNBAUGH, Samantha 207-780-5361 220 G langley@usm.maine.edu
LANGLEY, Amy 256-840-4185 7 A alangley@snead.edu
LANGLEY, Angie 662-720-7249 276 C alangle@nemcc.edu
LANGLEY, Dawn 336-599-1181 372 G langled@piedmontcc.edu
LANGLEY, Dorothy 903-730-4890 489 C dorothy_langley@jarvis.edu
LANGLEY, Goldie 614-947-6509 391 B langleyg@franklin.edu
LANGLEY, Harry 304-896-7412 543 C harry.langley@southernwv.edu
LANGLEY, Harry, M 724-938-1523 441 G langley@calu.edu
LANGLEY, Janet 602-286-8017 15 G janet.langley@gwmail.maricopa.edu
LANGLEY, Janet, R 601-974-1134 275 B langljr@millsaps.edu
LANGLEY, Pamela 603-271-7150 304 F plangley@ccsnh.edu
LANGLEY, Winston 617-287-5600 236 G winston.langley@umb.edu
LANGLIE, Mary, L 516-876-3175 353 D langliem@oldwestbury.edu
LANGLOIS, John 508-767-7045 230 D jlanglois@assumption.edu
LANGLOIS, Judith, H 512-232-3600 505 D jlanglois@austin.utexas.edu
LANGLOIS, Mary Ann 716-888-2103 325 F langloim@canisius.edu
LANGMADE, Mary 612-343-4776 270 A malangma@northcentral.edu
LANGOLF, Judi 810-989-2138 248 G judi.langolf@baker.edu
LANGREHR, Andrew 314-984-7679 289 A alangrehr@stlcc.edu
LANGRELL, Ron 253-680-7103 531 F rlangrell@bates.ctc.edu
LANGRIDGE, Nick 540-568-3197 520 H langrinl@jmu.edu
LANGSETH, Kay 402-461-7300 298 A klangseth@hastings.edu
LANGSETH, Roger 507-535-3309 263 B
LANGSETH, Roger, W 507-288-4563 263 B rlangseth@crossroadscollege.edu
LANGSTAFF, Kris, A 606-474-3153 201 D klangstaff@kcu.edu
LANGSTON, II, Bill, C 863-680-4209 109 E blangston@flsouthern.edu
LANGSTON, Carol 501-812-2211 23 C clangston@pulaskitech.edu
LANGSTON, Diane 706-295-6357 130 E dlangston@highlands.edu
LANGSTON, Ginna, V 918-631-2641 413 F ruth-langston@utulsa.edu
LANGSTON, Nancy, F 804-828-5174 526 B nlangston@vcu.edu
LANGSTON, Randall 970-351-2881 89 B randall.langston@unco.edu
LANGSTON, Randall 585-395-2772 352 F rlangsto@brockport.edu
LANGSTON-SMITH, Sanette 601-977-4458 277 C slsmith@tougaloo.edu
LANGSTRAAT, Nate 360-383-3350 540 A nlangstraat@whatcom.ctc.edu
LANGTEAU, Paula 715-735-4339 553 B paula.langteau@uwc.edu
LANGUTH, Christine 860-383-5211 92 E clanguth@trcc.commnet.edu
LANHAM, Allen, K 217-581-6061 150 E aklanham@eiu.edu
LANHAM, Heather 937-778-7803 390 G hlanham@edisonohio.edu
LANHAM, Jeff 740-245-7485 404 E jlanham@rio.edu
LANIAK, Timothy, S 704-527-9909 235 B tlaniak@gcts.edu
LANIER, Amy, S 803-786-3927 457 C alanier@columbiasc.edu
LANIER, Carolyn 203-837-8277 91 A lanierc@wcsu.edu
LANIER, Gregory, W 850-474-2934 121 D glanier@uwf.edu
LANIER, Marilyn 415-405-3838 37 B mlanier@sfsu.edu
LANIER, Percy 205-929-1665 5 H plani@mail.miles.edu
LANIER, Stephen, M 843-792-2211 459 D lanier@musc.edu
LANIER, William 406-265-4117 295 E wjlanier@msun.edu
LANIUS, Karin 740-389-6786 399 D lanius.1@osu.edu
LANKA, Greg 330-494-6170 402 B glanka@starkstate.edu
LANKER, Jason 716-926-8933 335 E jlanker@hilbert.edu
LANKES, Susan 716-652-8900 325 J slankes@cks.edu
LANKFORD, Donna, W 706-385-1017 136 B donna.lankford@point.edu
LANKFORD, Eric 740-374-8716 405 G elankford@wscc.edu
LANKFORD, Peggy 575-538-6629 321 I lankfordp@wnmu.edu
LANKFORD, Timothy 303-923-4233 81 E tlankford@argosy.edu
LANN, Jennifer 802-387-4767 513 G jlann@landmark.edu
LANN, Patti 318-676-7811 211 D plann@nwltc.edu
LANNERT, Mary 406-447-6944 295 A mary.lannert@umhelena.edu
LANNING, Gale 507-453-1443 267 C glanning@southeastmn.edu
LANNING, Patrick 503-399-5144 414 J patrick.lanning@chemeketa.edu
LANNING, Stephanie 620-227-9409 192 E slg@dc3.edu
LANNON, SJ, Timothy, R 402-280-2770 297 F tlannon@creighton.edu
LANNUTTI, Pamela 215-951-1935 432 I lannuttip@lasalle.edu
LANOUE, David 706-568-2056 127 G lanoue_david@columbusstate.edu
LANOUETTE, Ruth, M 920-832-6528 548 B ruth.m.lanouette@lawrence.edu
LANPHEAR, Joel 989-774-7547 249 C lanph1jh@cmich.edu
LANPHER, Jill 802-225-3306 514 B jill.lanpher@neci.edu
LANPHER, Jim 803-754-4100 457 D
LANSER, Michael 920-693-1123 554 C michael.lanser@gotoltc.edu
LANSWERK, Marcy 507-284-9387 262 E landswerk.marcy@mayo.edu
LANTAGNE, Douglas, O 802-656-2990 514 H doug.lantagne@uvm.edu
LANTING, Mark 815-802-8709 155 A mlanting@kcc.edu
LANTIS, Jeffrey, S 517-437-7341 252 C jeff.lantis@hillsdale.edu

LANTZ, Dona .... 215-568-4012.... 436 H
dlantz@moore.edu
LANTZ, Glen .... 563-588-6784.... 183 E
glen.lantz@clarke.edu
LANTZ, James, D .... 989-328-1220.... 255 E
jlantz@montcalm.edu
LANTZ, Mary Jan .... 409-944-1281.... 486 K
mlantz@gc.edu
LANTZ, Susan .... 570-577-1601.... 423 E
susan.lantz@bucknell.edu
LANTZY, Robert .... 719-638-6580...... 84 I
rlantzy@cci.edu
LANUZZA, Jerry .... 980-598-1434.... 365 I
jerry.lanuzza@jwu.edu
LANZA-KADUCE, Linda ..... 352-395-5493.... 117 F
linda.lanza-kaduce@sfcollege.edu
LANZALACO, Joseph, M ... 585-385-8367.... 348 F
jlanzalaco@sjfc.edu
LANZI, Lesley .... 518-736-3622.... 334 D
lesley.lanzi@fmcc.suny.edu
LANZILLO, Lee-Ann .... 617-349-8875.... 236 B
llanzill@lesley.edu
LANZILLO, Susan .... 508-626-4534.... 238 A
slanzillo@framingham.edu
LANZILOTTI, Salvatore ...... 808-734-9520.... 141 J
ssl@hawaii.edu
LANZONE, Peggie .... 602-371-1188...... 17 B
LAOS, Joel .... 303-762-6903...... 84 D
joel.laos@denverseminary.edu
LAP, James .... 718-260-5565.... 328 D
jlap@citytech.cuny.edu
LAPAGLIA, Karen .... 814-838-7673.... 429 C
klapaglia@fortisinstitute.edu
LAPALOMBARA, Catherine 301-322-0414.... 225 F
lapalocx@pgcc.edu
LAPAZ, Dan .... 262-524-7343.... 546 H
dlapaz@carrollu.edu
LAPENNA, Alan, G .... 860-444-8322.... 558 H
alan.g.lapenna@uscg.mil
LAPERUTA, Domenick .... 718-960-8593.... 327 C
domenick.laperuta@lehman.cuny.edu
LAPHAM, Steve .... 301-891-4161.... 229 B
slapham@wau.edu
LAPIDUS, Chaim, D .... 410-484-7200.... 225 C
cdl@nirc.edu
LAPIDUS, Richard, S .... 909-869-2400...... 33 J
rslapidus@csupomona.edu
LAPIER, Terry .... 561-381-4990.... 102 G
LAPIERRE, Jonathan .... 617-879-2427.... 246 C
jlapierre@wheelock.edu
LAPINSKAS, Connie, L .... 765-494-7537.... 178 J
clapinsk@purdue.edu
LAPINSKI, Jason .... 216-373-6352.... 397 F
jlapinski@ndc.edu
LAPLACE, Bobbi .... 412-536-1087.... 432 H
bobbi.laplace@laroche.edu
LAPLANTE, Glenn .... 802-287-8236.... 513 F
laplanteg@greenmtn.edu
LAPLANTE, Kim .... 920-498-5487.... 555 C
kim.laplante@nwtc.edu
LAPLANTE, Larry .... 207-768-2707.... 218 J
llaplante@nmcc.edu
LAPOINTE, Gregory .... 207-621-3240.... 220 B
glapointe@maine.edu
LAPOINTE, Laurence .... 860-465-5113...... 90 H
lapointel@easternct.edu
LAPOMARDO, Elaine .... 617-873-0274.... 233 A
elaine.lapomardo@cambridgecollege.edu
LAPORTE, Diana, M .... 518-564-2537.... 354 B
laportdm@plattsburgh.edu
LAPORTE, Laura .... 518-736-3622.... 334 D
llporte@fmcc.suny.edu
LAPORTE, Sally .... 323-464-2777...... 27 I
library@ca.aada.org
LAPORTE, Sandra .... 312-567-5199.... 153 C
laporte@iit.edu
LAPP, Katherine, N .... 617-495-9877.... 235 D
katie_lapp@harvard.edu
LAPPIN, Joan .... 330-339-3391.... 394 A
jlappin@kent.edu
LAPPLE, James, H .... 212-327-8371.... 347 H
james.lapple@rockefeller.edu
LAPRADE, Kimberly .... 602-639-7500...... 14 H
LAPRADE, Susan .... 508-854-4368.... 240 F
susanl@qcc.mass.edu
LAPREY, Patricia .... 973-408-3618.... 309 E
plaprey@drew.edu
LAPREZIOSA, Mark .... 215-572-2833.... 422 C
laprezim@arcadia.edu
LAPRISE, John, P .... 423-585-6882.... 476 D
john.laprise@ws.edu
LAQUEY, Karen .... 806-291-3526.... 508 E
laqueyk@wbu.edu
LARA, Cynthia .... 210-999-8290.... 502 E
clara@trinity.edu
LARA, Dan .... 541-917-4741.... 416 I
larad@linnbenton.edu
LARA, Ernest .... 623-935-8010...... 15 F
ernie.lara@estrellamountain.edu
LARA, Helen .... 213-613-2200...... 70 H
helen_lara@sciarc.edu
LARA, Susan .... 432-552-2600.... 507 D
lara_s@utpb.edu
LARAR, Barbara .... 877-338-0006.... 521 E
LARCOM, Geoffrey .... 734-487-4400.... 250 F
glarcom@emich.edu
LARD, Carter .... 718-270-1133.... 352 D
clard@downstate.edu
LAREAU, Joel .... 417-447-7551.... 287 D
lareauj@otc.edu
LAREAU, Martin .... 708-596-2000.... 164 H
mlareau@ssc.edu
LAREY, Keith, L .... 903-813-2431.... 481 A
klarey@austincollege.edu
LARGE, Donald, L .... 334-844-4650........ 1 F
largedl@auburn.edu
LARGENT, Elizabeth .... 701-277-3889.... 383 C
betty.largent@rasmussen.edu
LARGENT, Liz .... 405-682-7834.... 409 F
llargent@occc.edu
LARGENT, Michael .... 205-329-7900...... 14 G
mike.largent@ecacolleges.com
LARGENT, Michael .... 205-329-7945........ 3 A
mike.largent@ecacolleges.com
LARGENT, Michael .... 205-329-7900.... 110 G
mike.largent@ecacolleges.com
LARGENT, Michael .... 205-329-7900...... 48 G
mike.largent@ecacolleges.com
LARGENT, Michael .... 205-329-7900.... 458 F
mike.largent@ecacolleges.com
LARGENT, Trudy .... 510-466-7296...... 62 E
tlargent@peralta.edu
LARIA, Miriam .... 201-200-3484.... 312 B
mlaria@njcu.edu
LARIMORE, Marla .... 620-251-7700.... 192 B
marlal@coffeyville.edu
LARIOS, Liza .... 718-631-6356.... 328 F
llarios@qcc.cuny.edu
LARK, Catherine .... 603-646-2441.... 304 J
catherine.lark@dartmouth.edu
LARKIN, Bob .... 775-770-2528...... 19 A
robert.larkin@phoenix.edu
LARKIN, Carla, M .... 785-827-5541.... 194 F
carla@kwu.edu
LARKIN, Conal .... 203-575-8173...... 92 A
clarkin@nvcc.commnet.edu
LARKIN, Jon .... 541-962-3740.... 418 C
jlarkin@eou.edu
LARKIN, Kim .... 813-879-6000.... 107 A
klarkin@cci.edu
LARKIN, Linda .... 860-515-3841...... 90 E
llarkin@charteroak.edu
LARKIN, Linda .... 716-338-1125.... 337 E
lindalarkin@mail.sunyjcc.edu
LARKIN, SSJ,
Mary Josephine .... 215-248-7055.... 425 D
mjlarkin@chc.edu
LARKIN, Michael, F .... 512-448-8452.... 493 E
michaell@stedwards.edu
LARKIN, Thomas, F .... 413-748-3458.... 244 H
tlarkin@springfieldcollege.edu
LARKIN, Willie .... 443-885-3035.... 224 E
willie.larkin@morgan.edu
LARKIN-BEENE, Bridgett ... 815-280-2476.... 154 J
blarkin@jjc.edu
LARNER, Eve .... 914-606-6562.... 360 E
eve.larner@sunywcc.edu
LAROBINA, Michael, D ...... 203-371-7859...... 94 B
larobinam@sacredheart.edu
LAROCCA MEYER,
Theresa .... 718-940-5820.... 349 A
tlaroccameyer@sjcny.edu
LAROCCA MEYER,
Theresa .... 631-687-4513.... 349 B
tlaroccameyer@sjcny.edu
LAROCHELLE, Josee .... 408-924-1550...... 37 C
josee.larochelle@sjsu.edu
LAROCHELLE, Therese .... 603-897-8241.... 305 F
tlarochelle@rivier.edu
LAROCQUE, Monique .... 207-780-5422.... 220 G
mlarocque@usm.maine.edu
LAROCQUE, Sandra .... 701-477-7862.... 383 F
salrocqu@tm.edu
LAROSA, Angela .... 607-778-5187.... 324 G
larosaam@sunybroome.edu
LAROSA, George, P .... 631-420-2170.... 356 A
larosa@farmingdale.edu
LAROSEE, Howie .... 617-879-7938.... 238 B
hlarosee@massart.edu
LARRABEE, Kate .... 607-274-1082.... 336 G
klarrabee@ithaca.edu
LARRABEE, Stephanie, D ... 207-255-1203.... 220 E
steph@maine.edu
LARSEN, Chris .... 417-690-2373.... 279 J
larsen@cofo.edu
LARSEN, Dianna .... 360-475-7208.... 536 D
LARSEN, Eric .... 765-983-1893.... 171 E
larseer@earlham.edu
LARSEN, Erin .... 651-423-8433.... 266 B
erin.larsen@dctc.edu
LARSEN, Geri .... 410-532-5866.... 225 D
glarsen@ndm.edu
LARSEN, Jacque .... 208-524-3000.... 143 G
jacque.larsen@my.eitc.edu
LARSEN, Jacque .... 540-423-9050.... 526 I
jlarsen@germanna.edu
LARSEN, Jay, A .... 605-688-4695.... 466 C
jay.larsen@sdstate.edu
LARSEN, Jennifer .... 402-559-4837.... 300 H
jlarsen@unmc.edu
LARSEN, Jon-Erik .... 503-352-7221.... 419 E
larsenj@pacificu.edu
LARSEN, Juliana, P .... 801-626-6459.... 511 G
jlarsen@weber.edu
LARSEN, Katrina .... 715-425-3350.... 552 C
katrina.larsen@uwrf.edu
LARSEN, Kerstin .... 609-258-9289.... 312 G
klarsen@princeton.edu
LARSEN, Kevin, W .... 252-334-2009.... 367 C
kevin.larsen@macuniversity.edu
LARSEN, Kevin, W .... 252-334-2044.... 367 C
kevin.larsen@macuniversity.edu
LARSEN, Kristina, L .... 858-534-3133...... 74 F
klarseni@ucsd.edu
LARSEN, Lauralyn .... 707-778-3930...... 68 E
llarsen@santaorsa.edu
LARSEN, Naomi .... 865-471-3471.... 467 G
nlarsen@cn.edu
LARSEN, Philip .... 727-726-1153.... 103 I
phillarsen@clearwater.edu
LARSEN, III, Randolph, K . 240-895-4597.... 226 A
rklarsen@smcm.edu
LARSEN, Robert .... 507-537-7150.... 269 E
robert.larsen@smsu.edu
LARSEN, Ron .... 406-994-4371.... 295 C
ronl@montana.edu
LARSEN, Ronald, L .... 412-624-5139.... 449 A
rlarsen@pitt.edu
LARSEN, Susan .... 435-283-7317.... 512 C
susan.larsen@snow.edu
LARSEN, Tina .... 402-935-9400.... 299 A
tlarsen@nechristian.edu
LARSEN, Tom, A .... 402-844-7138.... 299 I
toml@northeast.edu
LARSEN, Whitney .... 540-261-4504.... 524 H
whitney.larsen@svu.edu
LARSEN-REUTER, Karen .... 937-294-6155.... 393 C
kreuter@kaplan.edu
LARSON, Ann .... 513-529-5040.... 396 E
ann.larson@muohio.edu
LARSON, Barb .... 308-398-7359.... 297 A
blarson@cccneb.edu
LARSON, Barbara .... 813-253-7015.... 110 M
blarson2@hccfl.edu
LARSON, Bruce, R .... 507-284-8541.... 262 B
larson.bruce@mayo.edu
LARSON, Carol .... 763-576-4710.... 265 H
clarson@anokatech.edu
LARSON, Carol .... 434-961-6546.... 528 B
clarson@pvcc.edu
LARSON, Craig .... 763-424-0733.... 268 B
clarson@nhcc.edu
LARSON, Cynthia .... 619-261-7245...... 29 F
clarson-daugherty@argosy.edu
LARSON, Dale, C .... 214-841-3624.... 485 F
dlarson@dts.edu
LARSON, Daniel, J .... 814-865-9591.... 438 G
djl18@psu.edu
LARSON, Daniel, L .... 309-341-7492.... 155 F
dlarson2@knox.edu
LARSON, Daniel, P .... 315-255-1743.... 325 G
daniel.larson@cayuga-cc.edu
LARSON, Debra .... 618-537-6816.... 158 A
dlarson@mckendree.edu
LARSON, Debra .... 805-756-2131...... 33 I
dslarson@calpoly.edu
LARSON, Don, A .... 858-534-0386...... 74 F
dlarson@ucsd.edu
LARSON, Donna .... 503-338-2440.... 415 B
dlarson@clatsopcc.edu
LARSON, Doreen .... 304-367-4933.... 543 B
doreen.larson@pierpont.edu
LARSON, Dottie .... 765-269-5612.... 176 D
dlarson@ivytech.edu
LARSON, Elaine, E .... 859-238-5365.... 199 G
e.larson@centre.edu
LARSON, Gary, N .... 630-752-5990.... 168 H
gary.larson@wheaton.edu
LARSON, Gayle .... 651-423-8395.... 266 B
gayle.larson@dctc.edu
LARSON, Gloria, C .... 781-891-2101.... 231 D
glarson@bentley.edu
LARSON, Jon, H .... 732-255-0330.... 312 D
jlarson@ocean.edu
LARSON, Joyce .... 603-535-2806.... 307 A
jlarson@plymouth.edu
LARSON, Kalynn .... 435-652-7535.... 512 B
larson@dixie.edu
LARSON, Keith .... 423-636-7305.... 477 A
klarson@tusculum.edu
LARSON, Kenneth, J .... 765-269-5660.... 176 D
klarson@ivytech.edu
LARSON, Kent, D .... 208-282-2981.... 143 H
larskent@isu.edu
LARSON, Lisa .... 952-488-2465.... 266 D
lisa.larson@hennepintech.edu
LARSON, Lisa, M .... 319-895-4219.... 183 G
llarson@cornellcollege.edu
LARSON, Lois .... 651-793-1414.... 267 A
lois.larson@metrostate.edu
LARSON, Matthew .... 860-486-2616...... 94 G
matthew.larson@uconn.edu
LARSON, Mike .... 515-244-4221.... 181 F
larsonm@aib.edu
LARSON, Nathan .... 303-300-8740...... 81 L
nathan.larson@collegeamerica.edu
LARSON, Paul, V .... 805-565-6286...... 79 A
plarson@westmont.edu
LARSON, Phyllis .... 507-786-3004.... 271 C
larsonph@stolaf.edu
LARSON, Phyllis .... 507-786-3744.... 271 C
larsonph@stolaf.edu
LARSON, Rachel, S .... 507-933-7446.... 263 J
rlarson@gustavus.edu
LARSON, Richard .... 559-934-2705...... 78 C
richardlarson@whccd.edu
LARSON, Rick .... 952-446-4190.... 263 C
larsonr@crown.edu
LARSON, Rob, K .... 563-387-1568.... 187 D
larsro01@luther.edu
LARSON, Robert .... 701-224-2498.... 381 E
robert.l.larson@ndus.edu
LARSON, Rodney .... 207-941-7122.... 218 A
larsonr@husson.edu
LARSON, Ross .... 262-551-5812.... 546 I
rlarson@carthage.edu
LARSON, Sandy .... 229-931-2450.... 137 C
slarson@southgatech.edu
LARSON, Stacey .... 312-225-6288.... 167 G
slarson@vandercook.edu
LARSON, Steve .... 912-525-4781.... 136 F
slarson@scad.edu
LARSON, Steve .... 406-756-3821.... 294 C
slarson@fvcc.edu
LARSON, Susan .... 575-562-2211.... 318 B
susan.larson@enmu.edu
LARSON, Susan .... 913-971-3698.... 195 D
slarson@mnu.edu
LARSON, Susan .... 706-355-5034.... 125 C
slarson@athenstech.edu
LARSON, Thomas, R .... 423-652-4765.... 470 A
trlarson@king.edu
LARSON, Trina .... 480-732-7222...... 15 E
trina.larson@cgc.edu
LARSON-COONEY, Kim, K 303-797-5723...... 81 D
kim.larson-cooney@arapahoe.edu
LARSON DIAZ, Mary .... 806-742-2121.... 502 A
mary.diaz@ttu.edu
LARTEY, Charles, R .... 330-471-8469.... 395 F
clartey@malone.edu
LARUE, Clint .... 405-425-5191.... 409 E
clint.larue@oc.edu
LARUE, David .... 330-724-1600.... 383 I
dlarue@akroninstitute.com
LARUE, Rita .... 215-895-1534.... 427 H
larue@drexel.edu
LARVICK, Steve .... 541-552-6594.... 419 A
larvick@sou.edu
LASALDE-DOMINICCI,
José, A .... 787-250-0000.... 566 G
jose.lasalde@upr.edu
LASALLE, Patti .... 214-768-7660.... 495 A
plasalle@smu.edu
LASANEN, Raymond, E ...... 906-487-2510.... 255 B
relasane@mtu.edu
LASCANO, Rey .... 432-552-2108.... 507 D
lascano_r@utpb.edu
LASCEK-SPEAKMAN,
Natalie .... 717-396-7833.... 440 K
nlascek@pcad.edu
LASCH, Jacqueline, D .... 407-582-3302.... 123 B
jlasch@valenciacollege.edu
LASER KIGER, Amy .... 540-234-9261.... 526 D
kigera@brcc.edu
LASEY, Brian .... 479-968-0261...... 20 G
blasey@atu.edu
LASH, Gail, D .... 937-708-5734.... 405 H
glash@wilberforce.edu
LASH, Jeff .... 330-494-6170.... 402 B
jlash@starkstate.edu
LASH, Jonathan .... 413-559-5521.... 235 C
president@hampshire.edu
LASH, Julie .... 317-274-2548.... 174 D
jlash@iupui.edu
LASHAWAY, Robert, V .... 406-994-2001.... 295 C
rvl@facilities.montana.edu
LASHBROOK, Jeffrey, T ..... 585-395-5028.... 352 F
jlashbro@brockport.edu
LASHBROOK, Velma, J ...... 612-330-1229.... 261 B
lashbroo@augsburg.edu
LASHER, John .... 315-792-7265.... 356 B
john.lasher@sunyit.edu
LASHIN-CUREWITZ,
Sandy .... 508-373-9529.... 231 B
sandy.curewitz@becker.edu
LASHLEY, Bob .... 405-425-5120.... 409 E
bob.lashley@oc.edu
LASHLEY, Brian, R .... 860-465-5306...... 90 H
lashleyb@easternct.edu
LASHLEY, Edwin, L .... 410-543-6007.... 228 D
ellashley@salisbury.edu
LASHLEY, Jeffery .... 660-263-4110.... 286 H
jeffl@macc.edu
LASHLEY, Kent .... 405-733-7490.... 411 I
klashley@rose.edu
LASHLEY, Marsha .... 660-831-4115.... 286 F
lashleym@moval.edu

LASHLEY, Sarah, E ... 859-238-5573 ... 199 G sarah.lashley@centre.edu
LASHURE, Faith ... 630-466-7900 ... 168 B flashure@waubonsee.edu
LASICH, Deb ... 303-273-3097 ... 83 B dlasich@mines.edu`
LASIEWSKI, Doreen ... 401-739-5000 ... 453 G dlasiewski@neit.edu
LASITER, Paul, B ... 310-506-4497 ... 61 H paul.lasiter@pepperdine.edu
LASKA-NIXON, Diane ... 508-767-7026 ... 230 D dlaska@assumption.edu
LASKARIS, Maria ... 603-646-2604 ... 304 J maria.laskaris@dartmouth.edu
LASKARIS, Theodore ... 802-860-2757 ... 513 C
LASKE, Lori, L ... 719-587-7867 ... 80 L lllaske@adams.edu
LASKER, Y. Mayer ... 718-377-0777 ... 346 G
LASKOWSKI-SACHNOFF, Marilyn ... 732-906-2502 ... 311 D mlaskowski-sachnoff@middlesexcc.edu
LASKY, Melodee, S ... 732-932-7402 ... 314 B mlasky@rci.rutgers.edu
LASLEY, Roger ... 507-222-4289 ... 261 G rlasley@carleton.edu
LASLEY, Steven, T ... 615-460-6404 ... 467 D steve.lasley@belmont.edu
LASNIER, George ... 304-442-3355 ... 545 D george.lasnier@mail.wvu.edu
LASSEIGNE, Craig ... 972-929-9313 ... 486 D classeigne@devry.edu
LASSEN, Gregg ... 409-880-8395 ... 501 A gregg.lassen@lamar.edu
LASSILA, Deborah, L ... 906-487-3112 ... 255 B dlassila@mtu.edu
LASSITER, Donald, L ... 910-630-7081 ... 367 B lassiter@methodist.edu
LASSITER, Fred ... 614-251-4513 ... 398 F lassitef@ohiodominican.edu
LASSITER, Jack ... 870-460-1020 ... 25 A lassiter@uamont.edu
LASSITER, Pamela ... 920-424-0330 ... 551 E lassitep@uwosh.edu
LASSITER, JR., Wright, L ... 214-378-1601 ... 484 F wlassiter@dcccd.edu
LASSLEY, Joan, K ... 559-323-2100 ... 66 C jlassley@sjcl.edu
LASSNER, David, K ... 808-956-3501 ... 141 E david@hawaii.edu
LASSNER, Jennifer ... 319-335-2123 ... 182 F jennifer-lassner@uiowa.edu
LASTER, Jill, L ... 817-257-7790 ... 499 C j.laster@tcu.edu
LASTINGER, Michael ... 304-293-6955 ... 545 A michael.lastinger@mail.wvu.edu
LASTORIA, Michael, D ... 585-567-9622 ... 336 B michael.lastoria@houghton.edu
LASTRA, Sarai ... 787-743-7979 ... 565 H ut_slastra@suagm.edu
LASURE, Keith ... 864-941-8687 ... 460 D lasure.k@ptc.edu
LATANE, Jane ... 520-383-8401 ... 18 I jlatane@tocc.cc.az.us
LATCHAW HIRSH, Sharon 610-527-0200 ... 445 J shirsh@rosemont.edu
LATCHUM, Lucy, L ... 757-594-7702 ... 517 L llatchum@cnu.edu
LATCOVICH, Mark, A ... 440-943-7600 ... 401 G mal@dioceseofcleveland.org
LATERRA BELLINO, Frank 718-940-5852 ... 349 A flaterra@sjcny.edu
LATERRA BELLINO, Frank 631-687-1247 ... 349 B flaterra@sjcny.edu
LATHAM, Adrienne ... 615-329-8632 ... 468 I alatham@fisk.edu
LATHAM, Amy ... 662-562-3201 ... 276 D a_latham@northwestms.edu
LATHAM, Angela ... 708-534-4376 ... 151 E alatham@govst.edu
LATHAM, Brenda ... 209-381-6410 ... 57 C latham.b@mccd.edu
LATHAM, Clara ... 940-397-4757 ... 491 B clara.latham@mwsu.edu
LATHAM, Eric ... 937-484-1346 ... 405 A elatham@urbana.edu
LATHAM, Karen, K ... 701-323-6734 ... 381 D klatham@mohs.org
LATHAM, Linda, H ... 334-734-7582 ... 370 F llatham@forsythtech.edu
LATHAM, Marilae ... 618-664-7110 ... 151 F marilae.latham@greenville.edu
LATHAM, Mark ... 912-260-4300 ... 137 B mark.latham@sgc.edu
LATHAM, Mark ... 802-831-1226 ... 515 B mlatham@vermontlaw.edu
LATHAM, Michael ... 718-817-4700 ... 334 C latham@fordham.edu
LATHAM, Sarah, C ... 205-726-4502 ... 6 G sclatham@samford.edu
LATHAM, Sarah, V ... 256-782-5276 ... 4 L slatham@jsu.edu
LATHAM, Tricia ... 580-477-7725 ... 414 C tricia.latham@wosc.edu

LATHROP, Sam ... 217-228-5432 ... 161 F lathrsa@quincy.edu
LATIF, Niaz ... 219-989-3251 ... 178 K nlatif@purduecal.edu
LATIGO, Ben ... 603-577-6610 ... 304 I blatigo@dwc.edu
LATIMER, Dewana ... 731-425-2624 ... 475 C dlatimer@jscc.edu
LATIMER, Loretta ... 904-470-8100 ... 105 G m.latimer@ewc.edu
LATIMER, Tanisha ... 864-941-8363 ... 460 D latimer.t@ptc.edu
LATIMORE, Debra ... 919-546-8223 ... 376 F dlatimore@shawu.edu
LATIMORE, Leatrice, D ... 504-284-5435 ... 214 J llatimor@suno.edu
LATIMORE, Nancy, J ... 717-361-1407 ... 428 F latimonj@etown.edu
LATIN, Quintin ... 256-761-6221 ... 7 G qlatin@talladega.edu
LATINO, Jennifer, A ... 910-814-5577 ... 362 J latinoj@campbell.edu
LATINVILLE, Darlene ... 213-624-1200 ... 46 L dlatinville@fidm.edu
LATIOLAIS, Perry ... 281-487-1170 ... 499 B platiolais@txchiro.edu
LATO, Tracy ... 314-768-1845 ... 283 G lato@kenrick.edu
LATORELLA, Jacqueline ... 813-253-6219 ... 123 A jlatorella@ut.edu
LATORRE, Daria ... 610-796-8264 ... 421 G daria.latorre@alvernia.edu
LATORTUE, Paul ... 787-751-7410 ... 568 B prlatortue@aol.com
LATOUF, Christina ... 646-660-6114 ... 326 C christina.latouf@baruch.cuny.edu
LATOUR, Bill ... 217-641-4290 ... 154 I blatour@jwcc.edu
LATOUR, Mickey, A ... 618-453-2469 ... 165 B mlatour@siu.edu
LATOUR, Terry, S ... 814-393-2343 ... 442 B tlatour@clarion.edu
LATSHAW, Todd, M ... 717-867-6330 ... 434 C latshaw@lvc.edu
LATTA, Bruce, J ... 410-293-1801 ... 559 B latta@usna.edu
LATTA, Marcia, S ... 765-658-4212 ... 171 B mlatta@depauw.edu
LATTA, Mark, A ... 402-280-2860 ... 297 F marklatta@creighton.edu
LATTA, Stanley ... 814-865-5423 ... 438 G sxl1@psu.edu
LATTEN, Erin ... 507-453-1462 ... 267 C elatten@southeastmn.edu
LATTER, George ... 619-849-2317 ... 62 L georgelatter@pointloma.edu
LATTER, Gerald ... 212-327-8925 ... 347 H latter@rockefeller.edu
LATTIMORE, Dan, L ... 901-678-2991 ... 474 C dlattimr@memphis.edu
LATTIMORE, John ... 704-484-4020 ... 369 E lattimorej@clevelandcc.edu
LATTIMORE, Mark ... 478-825-6296 ... 129 F lattimorem@fvsu.edu
LATTIMORE, Michael, P ... 973-353-1670 ... 314 E mikelatt@andromeda.rutgers.edu
LATTIMORE, Vergel, L ... 704-636-6168 ... 365 D vlattimore@hoodseminary.edu
LATTING, John ... 404-727-6036 ... 129 D john.latting@emory.edu
LATUSZEK, Doty, A ... 260-422-5561 ... 173 C dalatuszek@indianatech.edu
LATZ, Gil ... 317-278-1265 ... 174 D glatz@iupui.edu
LATZ, Gil ... 503-725-5350 ... 418 G latzg@pdx.edu
LAU, Allison ... 206-878-3710 ... 535 B alau@highline.edu
LAU, Bradley, A ... 503-554-2312 ... 415 I blau@georgefox.edu
LAU, Danny ... 678-717-3779 ... 129 G dlau@gsc.edu
LAU, Jason ... 415-485-9316 ... 42 B jason.lau@marin.edu
LAU, John ... 760-355-6235 ... 51 A john.lau@imperial.edu
LAU, Kimberly ... 831-459-2418 ... 75 C lau@ucsc.edu
LAU, Lawrence ... 310-577-3000 ... 80 E lau@yosan.edu
LAU, Stuart ... 808-956-8010 ... 141 G stuartl@hawaii.edu
LAUB, James, A ... 561-803-2302 ... 114 C james_laub@pba.edu
LAUB, Jeffrey, W ... 434-832-7707 ... 526 E laubj@cvcc.vccs.edu
LAUB, Joe ... 212-484-1108 ... 327 F jlaub@jjay.cuny.edu
LAUB, Marty ... 312-935-4245 ... 154 A
LAUB, Richard ... 970-223-2669 ... 85 E rlaub@ibmc.edu
LAUBAUCH, Harold ... 954-262-1303 ... 114 B harold@nsu.nova.edu

LAUBE, Irene, H ... 919-536-7211 ... 370 C laubei@durhamtech.edu
LAUBE, Philip ... 740-826-8101 ... 397 A plaube@muskingum.edu
LAUBER, Nick ... 816-331-5700 ... 287 F nlauber@pcitraining.edu
LAUBERSHEIMER, David, E ... 217-786-2240 ... 157 B david.laubersheimer@llcc.edu
LAUDE, David, A ... 512-471-6176 ... 505 D dalaude@mail.utexas.edu
LAUDER, Frank ... 617-873-0137 ... 233 A finaid@cambridgecollege.edu
LAUDER, Sue, M ... 978-665-3314 ... 237 E slauder@fitchburgstate.edu
LAUDERBACK, Cindy ... 360-417-6233 ... 536 G clauderback@pencol.edu
LAUER, Andrew, J ... 212-790-0310 ... 361 M andrewlauer@yu.edu
LAUER, Bonnie ... 570-740-0734 ... 435 C blauer@luzerne.edu
LAUER, Brenda ... 970-521-6713 ... 86 K brenda.lauer@njc.edu
LAUER, John ... 719-389-6618 ... 82 D jlauer@coloradocollege.edu
LAUER, Jonathan, D ... 717-766-2511 ... 436 D jlauer@messiah.edu
LAUER, Larry, D ... 817-257-7808 ... 499 C l.lauer@tcu.edu
LAUERMAN, Meg ... 402-472-0088 ... 300 G mlauerman1@unl.edu
LAUFENBERG, Helen ... 608-822-2308 ... 555 D hlaufenberg@swtc.edu
LAUFENBERG, Linda, J ... 563-588-6385 ... 183 E linda.laufenberg@clarke.edu
LAUFER, Marilyn ... 334-844-1486 ... 1 F laufema@auburn.edu
LAUFFENBURGER, Linda, M ... 937-327-7811 ... 406 B llauffenburger@wittenberg.edu
LAUGEL, JoAnn, E ... 812-488-2364 ... 180 E jl25@evansville.edu
LAUGHLIN, Ed ... 978-478-3400 ... 246 G elaughlin@zbc.edu
LAUGHLIN, Frederick, L ... 231-995-1197 ... 256 D flaughlin@nmc.edu
LAUGHLIN, Janet ... 434-791-5630 ... 516 G jlaughlin@averett.edu
LAUGHLIN, Judith ... 724-938-4430 ... 441 G laughlin@calu.edu
LAUGHLIN, Karen, L ... 850-644-2740 ... 119 D klaughlin@admin.fsu.edu
LAUGHLIN, Larry, W ... 301-295-3016 ... 558 D larry.laughlin@usuhs.edu
LAUGHLIN, Lynn ... 217-732-3168 ... 156 H llaughli@lincolnchristian.edu
LAUGHLIN, Michelle ... 605-361-0200 ... 464 B mlaughlin@sf.coloradotech.edu
LAUGHLIN, Patricia ... 312-567-3827 ... 153 C plaughli@iit.edu
LAUGHLIN, Ronda ... 360-752-8334 ... 531 H rlaughlin@btc.ctc.edu
LAUGHLIN, Russ ... 817-645-3921 ... 495 E laughlinr@swau.edu
LAUGHLIN, Sherry ... 601-318-6170 ... 278 C slaughlin@wmcarey.edu
LAUGHRAN, Patrick ... 508-626-4357 ... 238 A plaughran@framingham.edu
LAUGHREY, James, C ... 202-231-3351 ... 557 J james.laughrey@dodiis.mil
LAUGHTER, Ray ... 832-813-6621 ... 490 E ray.laughter@lonestar.edu
LAUGHTER, Terry ... 910-277-5223 ... 376 C laughterth@sapc.edu
LAUGHTON, John ... 609-771-2278 ... 308 F jlaughto@tcnj.edu
LAUINGER, Curt ... 605-394-4034 ... 466 F curt.lauinger@wdt.edu
LAUN, Tracye ... 925-609-6650 ... 38 F tlaun@carrington.edu
LAUNDRY, William, D ... 518-564-2280 ... 354 B laundrwd@plattsburgh.edu
LAUNIUS, Michael ... 509-963-3612 ... 532 C launiusm@cwu.edu
LAURANZON, Anne Marie 804-752-7317 ... 523 C alauranz@rmc.edu
LAURENCE, David ... 928-776-7666 ... 19 C david.laurence@yc.edu
LAURENT, Joyce ... 574-257-3365 ... 169 I laurenj@bethelcollege.edu
LAURENT, Robert ... 574-257-3353 ... 169 I laurenb@bethelcollege.edu
LAURENT, Timothy ... 406-791-5302 ... 296 F tlaurent01@ugf.edu
LAURENZ, Jamie ... 575-562-2312 ... 318 B jamie.laurenz@enmu.edu
LAURENZI, Kellie, L ... 412-397-5201 ... 445 H laurenzi@rmu.edu
LAURETANO, Angela ... 914-632-5400 ... 341 G alauretano@monroecollege.edu
LAURIA, Dorothy, M ... 203-582-8258 ... 93 H dorothy.lauria@quinnipiac.edu
LAURIA, James ... 412-809-5100 ... 444 G lauria.james@pti.edu

LAURIE, Sean ... 516-678-5000 ... 341 F slaurie@molloy.edu
LAURIN, Janet ... 714-533-3946 ... 37 E jlaurin@calums.edu
LAURITZEN, Rhonda ... 801-627-8388 ... 510 H lauritzr@owatc.edu
LAURSEN, Gary ... 907-474-6295 ... 10 I galaursen@alaska.edu
LAUSCH, Mark, C ... 608-243-4508 ... 554 D mlausch@madisoncollege.org
LAUSELL, Ana, C ... 787-891-0925 ... 563 A amelon@aguadilla.inter.edu
LAUTERBACH, Lisa ... 734-487-1118 ... 250 F lisa.lauterbach@emich.edu
LAUTERBACK, Evelyn ... 419-586-0329 ... 406 D evelyn.lauterback@wright.edu
LAUTH, Thomas, P ... 706-542-2059 ... 138 G tplauth@uga.edu
LAUX, Carolyn ... 850-729-5360 ... 114 A lauxc@nwfsc.edu
LAUX, Dan ... 402-461-7301 ... 298 A dlaux@hastings.edu
LAUZON CLABO, Laurie ... 617-643-0605 ... 242 B llauzonclabo@mghihp.edu
LAVALLA, Daniel, N ... 215-368-5000 ... 422 I dlavalla@biblical.edu
LAVALLEE, David ... 518-320-1251 ... 351 D david.lavallee@suny.edu
LAVANIA, Ambrish ... 803-793-5263 ... 457 F lavaniaa@denmarktech.edu
LAVELLE, Helen ... 312-942-2030 ... 163 D helen_lavelle@rush.edu
LAVELLI, Lucinda ... 352-392-0207 ... 120 C llavelli@arts.ufl.edu
LAVENDER, Carol ... 281-649-3300 ... 487 H clavender@hbu.edu
LAVENDER, Earl ... 615-966-5834 ... 470 F earl.lavender@lipscomb.edu
LAVENDER, Julie ... 989-275-5000 ... 253 E julie.lavender@kirtland.edu
LAVENDER, Melissa ... 850-747-3211 ... 110 H mlavender@gulfcoast.edu
LAVENDER, Michael, K ... 828-652-0681 ... 372 B michaell@mcdowelltech.edu
LAVERNIA, Enrique, J ... 530-752-0554 ... 73 I lavernia@ucdavis.edu
LAVERRIERE, Robert, J ... 937-255-6234 ... 557 C robert.laverriere@afit.edu
LAVERY, Jim ... 740-389-4636 ... 395 H laveryj@mtc.edu
LAVERY, Roger ... 765-285-6000 ... 169 G rlavery@bsu.edu
LAVES, Beth ... 270-745-1900 ... 208 A beth.laves@wku.edu
LAVIAL, Pierre ... 772-466-4822 ... 101 J pierre.lavial@aviator.edu
LAVIGNA, Lisa ... 518-608-8252 ... 333 E llavigna@excelsior.edu
LAVIGNA, Robert ... 608-890-3888 ... 550 J rlavigna@ohr.wisc.edu
LAVIGNE, JR., F. Travis ... 985-858-5706 ... 210 G travis.lavigne@fletcher.edu
LAVIGNE, Robert, W ... 508-213-2217 ... 243 E robert.lavigne@nichols.edu
LAVILLA, Joe ... 415-865-0198 ... 30 E jlavilla@aii.edu
LAVIN, Aisha ... 706-667-4170 ... 125 G alavin@aug.edu
LAVIN, Marjorie, W ... 518-587-2100 ... 355 G marjorie.lavin@esc.edu
LAVIN, Thomas, J ... 401-456-8094 ... 454 A tlavin@ric.edu
LAVINE, Danielle, R ... 207-942-6781 ... 217 B dlavine@bts.edu
LAVINE, Steven, D ... 661-255-1050 ... 32 F slavine@calarts.edu
LAVIOLETTE, Marc ... 239-590-7891 ... 119 B mlaviole@fgcu.edu
LAVISTA, Daniel, J ... 213-891-2201 ... 54 F preid@email.laccd.edu
LAVIT, Daniel, A ... 270-809-2160 ... 205 A dlavit@murraystate.edu
LAVITT, Melissa ... 208-426-3776 ... 142 I melissalavitt@boisestate.edu
LAVOIE, Chuck ... 802-468-1250 ... 515 D chuck.lavoie@castleton.edu
LAVOIE, Kathleen, H ... 518-564-3150 ... 354 B lavoiekh@plattsburgh.edu
LAVOIE, Lisa ... 860-255-3805 ... 92 F
LAVORATA, Christina, M ... 304-367-4101 ... 543 H chris.lavorata@fairmontstate.edu
LAW, Christina ... 631-632-6280 ... 352 C christina.law@stonybrook.edu
LAW, John, W ... 630-844-5438 ... 145 F jlaw@aurora.edu
LAW, Mary Conley ... 360-438-4356 ... 537 B marylaw@stmartin.edu
LAW, Melinda ... 980-598-1004 ... 365 I melinda.law@jwu.edu
LAW, Nancy ... 903-983-8101 ... 489 I nlaw@kilgore.edu
LAW, William, D ... 727-341-3241 ... 116 H law.bill@spcollege.edu

LEAP, Terri 636-651-3290 279 B
tleap@brownmackie.edu
LEAR, Doug 603-899-4123 305 A
leard@franklinpierce.edu
LEAR, Shelly 315-781-3388 335 F
lear@hws.edu
LEAREY, Fred 301-387-3100 222 H
fred.learey@garrettcollege.edu
LEARN, Linda 570-702-8956 431 L
llearn@johnson.edu
LEARNED, Betsy, P 401-254-3625 454 C
blearned@rwu.edu
LEARNED, Betty Ann 508-588-9100 240 A
LEARY, Alison 212-998-4217 344 B
alison.leary@nyu.edu
LEARY, Carol, A 413-565-1000 230 G
cleary@baypath.edu
LEARY, Dennis 252-335-3388 377 F
deleary@mail.ecsu.edu
LEARY, Diane 508-565-1307 245 A
dleary@stonehill.edu
LEARY, James 508-856-8200 237 C
james.leary@umassmed.edu
LEARY, Robert 503-255-0332 417 C
rleary@multnomah.edu
LEARY, Thomas, P 570-740-0388 435 C
tleary@luzerne.edu
LEARY, JR., Thomas, S 213-821-6251 76 F
lear442@usc.edu
LEARY, Tim 206-296-6160 538 B
tleary@seattleu.edu
LEAS, Terry 509-793-2001 531 I
terryl@bigbend.edu
LEATH, Randy 325-794-4407 482 I
randy.leath@cisco.edu
LEATH, Steven 515-294-2042 182 E
sleath@iastate.edu
LEATHERBARROW, Ronald 360-383-3230 540 A
rleatherbarrow@whatcom.ctc.edu
LEATHERBURY, Maurice 817-272-2271 505 C
leatherbury@uta.edu
LEATHERMAN, Dale 870-759-4124 26 B
dleatherman@wbcoll.edu
LEATHERS, Barb 309-268-8148 151 I
barb.leathers@heartland.edu
LEATHERS, Debra, L 213-738-6814 71 E
advancement@swlaw.edu
LEATHERS, Ed, C 972-881-5142 483 H
eleathers@collin.edu
LEATHERS, Evelyn 903-927-3386 509 E
eleathers@wileyc.edu
LEATHERS, Evelyn 919-546-8368 376 F
eleathers@shawu.edu
LEATHERS, Walt 509-467-1727 535 C
wleather@interface.edu
LEATHERWOOD, Cynthia, D 205-247-8038 7 F
cleatherwood@stillman.edu
LEATHERWOOD, Laura 828-565-4220 371 C
lbleatherwood@haywood.edu
LEAU, Michael 684-699-9155 559 C
m.leau@amsamoa.edu
LEAVER, Harold, L 989-964-4047 257 G
hlleaver@svsu.edu
LEAVER, Walt 615-966-7653 470 F
walt.leaver@lipscomb.edu
LEAVITT, Andrew 706-864-2873 134 G
ajleavitt@northgeorgia.edu
LEAVITT, Lorretta 619-594-6420 37 A
lleavitt@mail.sdsu.edu
LEAVITT, Mary, E 812-246-3301 177 B
mleavitt@ivytech.edu
LEAVITT, Stephen, C 518-388-6116 358 G
leavitts@union.edu
LEBAR, Peter, M 814-332-5369 421 F
pete.lebar@allegheny.edu
LEBBE, Duane 504-568-4832 213 A
dlebbe@lsuhsc.edu
LEBEAU, Bryan 913-758-6115 197 D
lebeau87@stmary.edu
LEBEAU, Mandie, A 617-422-7499 243 B
mlebeau@nesl.edu
LEBEAU, Michael 205-226-4719 2 B
mlebeau@bsc.edu
LEBEDEFF, Alex 510-659-6263 59 J
alebedeff@ohlone.edu
LEBEL, Paul 701-777-2167 381 F
paul.lebel@und.edu
LEBER, Frank, W 312-329-4388 159 A
fleber@moody.edu
LEBER, Sally 740-368-3080 400 G
ssleber@owu.edu
LEBERIS, Elisa, M 630-752-5566 168 H
elisa.leberis@wheaton.edu
LEBESCH, Anna, M 386-312-4061 116 F
annalebesch@sjrstate.edu
LEBESCO, Kathleen 212-774-4861 340 C
klebesco@mmm.edu
LEBHERZ, Joe 301-682-8315 225 A
lebherz@msmary.edu
LEBICA, John 508-362-2131 239 D
jlebica@capecod.edu
LEBIODA, Ed 805-437-8547 34 B
ed.lebioda@csuci.edu
LEBLANC, Ann 757-352-4222 523 E
aleblanc@regent.edu
LEBLANC, Barbara 603-641-7243 305 G
bleblanc@anselm.edu
LEBLANC, Bruce 309-796-5431 145 H
leblancb@bhc.edu
LEBLANC, Debbie 207-947-4591 217 D
dleblanc@bealcollege.edu
LEBLANC, Elva, C 817-515-7750 496 C
elva.leblanc@tccd.edu
LEBLANC, Erica 310-434-4227 68 D
leblanc_erica@smc.edu
LEBLANC, Jacqueline 212-752-1530 338 C
jacqueline.leblanc@limcollege.edu
LEBLANC, Jerry, L 337-482-6235 216 D
jerrylukeleblanc@louisiana.edu
LEBLANC, Nina 337-439-5765 208 J
nina@deltatech.edu
LEBLANC, Paul 603-645-9631 305 I
p.leblanc@snhu.edu
LEBLANC, Robert 713-525-3540 505 A
leblancr@stthom.edu
LEBLANC, Thomas, J 305-284-3356 122 I
leblanc@miami.edu
LEBLANC, William 401-825-2225 453 D
leblanc@ccri.edu
LEBLEU BURNS, Michele 408-864-8218 47 G
lebleuburnsmichele@deanza.edu
LEBO, Cathy, J 410-516-4107 223 F
lebo@jhu.edu
LEBO, Nikki 765-269-5483 176 D
nlebo@ivytech.edu
LEBO, Russ 559-734-9000 66 E
russl@sjvc.edu
LEBON, Nathalie 717-337-6781 429 I
nlebon@gettysburg.edu
LEBRON, Maria 312-226-6294 156 G
finaid@lexingtoncollege.edu
LEBRON, Nestor, A 787-864-2222 563 F
nalebron@inter.edu
LEBRUN, Kathy 512-472-4133 494 F
kathy.lebrun@ssw.edu
LEBSOCK, Gale 760-384-6215 52 M
glebsock@cerrocoso.edu
LECHEHEB, Kamel 718-488-1082 338 G
kamel.lecheheb@liu.edu
LECHKO, Amy 440-646-8336 405 B
alechko@ursuline.edu
LECHLER, Terry 254-299-8652 490 G
tlechler@mclennan.edu
LECHNER, David 402-472-2191 300 E
dlechner@nebraska.edu
LECHOWSKI, Piotr 312-372-4900 149 E
plechowski@devry.edu
LECHTENBERG, Melanie 217-641-4310 154 I
mlechtenberg@jwcc.edu
LECHTENBERG, Victor 765-494-9095 178 J
vll@purdue.edu
LECK, Kathleen, M 847-574-5196 156 A
kleck@lfgsm.edu
LECKERMAN, Natalie 215-780-1315 446 G
nleckerman@salus.edu
LECKONBY, Larry, W 843-953-5030 456 C
larry.leckonby@citadel.edu
LECKRONE, Michael, J 260-982-5004 177 H
mjleckrone@manchester.edu
LECLAIR, Jane 518-608-8256 333 E
jleclair@excelsior.edu
LECLERC, Robin 248-204-2203 254 B
rleclerc@ltu.edu
LECOMPTE, Pier 787-844-8181 568 A
pier.lecompte@upr.edu
LECOUNT, Heidi 919-760-8633 367 A
lecounth@meredith.edu
LECOURT, Nancy 707-965-6234 60 I
LECRONE, Jeffrey, L 570-321-4112 435 D
lecrone@lycoming.edu
LEDBETTER, Beverly, E 401-863-9900 453 B
beverly_ledbetter@brown.edu
LEDBETTER, Bonnie 251-343-8200 6 F
bonnie.ledbetter@remingtoncollege.edu
LEDBETTER, Cathy 678-946-1103 130 E
cledbetter@highlands.edu
LEDBETTER, Kate 828-669-8012 367 E
kledbetter@montreat.edu
LEDBETTER, Kim, M 828-652-0602 372 B
kims@mcdowelltech.edu
LEDBETTER, Lisa 704-216-3620 373 F
lisa.ledbetter@rccc.edu
LEDBETTER, Mary, L 828-659-6001 372 B
maryl@mcdowelltech.edu
LEDBETTER, Neal 251-442-2429 9 A
nledbetter@umobile.edu
LEDBETTER, Sam 256-549-8690 3 J
sledbetter@gadsdenstate.edu
LEDBETTER, William, B 828-652-0674 372 B
bradl@mcdowelltech.edu
LEDDY, Michael 401-341-2195 454 D
mike.leddy@salve.edu
LEDERER, Benjamin 718-851-0183 347 B
LEDERMANN, Stacy, A 585-385-8142 348 F
sledermann@sjfc.edu
LEDESMA, Amadeo 575-527-7530 319 G
amadeol@nmsu.edu
LEDESMA, Mark 206-726-5028 533 D
mledesma@cornish.edu
LEDESMA, Stefanie 575-439-3711 319 E
sledesma@nmsua.nmsu.edu
LEDFORD, Greg 828-765-7351 372 A
gledford@mayland.edu
LEDFORD, Howard 706-335-9337 133 C
hledford@laniertech.edu
LEDFORD, Julia 270-686-4627 203 B
julia.ledford@kctcs.edu
LEDFORD, Julie 360-736-9391 532 D
jledford@centralia.edu
LEDFORD, Kristin 304-766-3206 542 J
kledford@kvctc.edu
LEDFORD, Laura 217-362-6499 158 G
lledford@millikin.edu
LEDFORD, Randy 336-249-8186 370 B
rledford@davidsonccc.edu
LEDFORD, Robert 407-971-5010 117 H
ledford@seminolestate.edu
LEDFORD, Terry 864-941-8559 460 D
ledford.t@ptc.edu
LEDFORD, Tommy, R 828-765-7351 372 A
tledford@mayland.edu
LEDMAN, Robert 520-383-8401 18 I
rledman@tocc.cc.az.us
LEDONNE, Patricia, N 540-375-2500 523 G
ledonne@roanoke.edu
LEDONNE, Peter 201-447-7159 307 E
pledonne@bergen.edu
LEDOUX, Michael, W 610-499-4345 451 F
mwledoux@widener.edu
LEDUC, Don 517-371-5140 258 F
leducd@cooley.edu
LEDUC, Paul, D 518-564-2090 354 B
leducpd@plattsburgh.edu
LEDVINA, Anne 205-226-7722 2 B
aledvina@bsc.edu
LEDWIN, Richard 323-259-2613 59 I
ledwin@oxy.edu
LEDY, Ann 651-757-4007 262 H
aledy@cva.edu
LEDYARD, Christopher, L 740-283-6437 391 A
cledyard@franciscan.edu
LEE, Alberta, G 585-292-2106 341 H
alee@monroecc.edu
LEE, Allisha 270-707-3958 202 E
allisha.lee@kctcs.edu
LEE, Amanda 910-362-7475 368 H
alee@cfcc.edu
LEE, Amy, H 510-464-3124 62 D
ahlee@peralta.edu
LEE, IHM, Andrea, J 651-690-6525 270 L
ajlee@stkate.edu
LEE, Andrew 908-737-4850 311 A
jilee@kean.edu
LEE, Angelo, C 615-327-6223 471 C
aclee@mmc.edu
LEE, Ann, B 812-941-2356 175 A
alee@ius.edu
LEE, Barbara 831-646-4014 57 G
blee@mpc.edu
LEE, Benjamin, G 605-336-6588 465 D
benlee@sfseminary.edu
LEE, Bert 410-276-0306 226 D
blee@host.sdc.edu
LEE, Beth, I 714-879-3901 50 I
bilee@hiu.edu
LEE, Bo Min 714-527-0691 46 A
LEE, Brenda 419-530-7730 404 F
brenda.lee@utoledo.edu
LEE, Brian, K 626-395-6307 32 H
brian.lee@caltech.edu
LEE, Carla 314-340-3307 282 F
leec@hssu.edu
LEE, Catherine 910-362-7033 368 H
clee@cfcc.edu
LEE, Catherine 334-844-1350 1 F
leecath@auburn.edu
LEE, Charley 714-527-0691 46 A
LEE, Chenetta 334-876-9303 4 B
chenetta.lee@wccs.edu
LEE, Chow 510-574-1281 44 F
clee@devry.edu
LEE, Chris 270-706-8622 202 A
chris.lee@kctcs.edu
LEE, Christopher 804-819-4685 526 C
clee@vccs.edu
LEE, Cindy 352-588-8869 116 G
cindy.lee@saintleo.edu
LEE, Crystal 225-675-8270 211 F
clee@rpcc.edu
LEE, Curtis 253-964-6595 536 H
clee@pierce.ctc.edu
LEE, D. Lynn 443-412-2258 223 B
llee@harford.edu
LEE, Dana 914-594-4567 343 F
dana_lee@nymc.edu
LEE, Darin, N 208-496-2311 143 A
leed@byui.edu
LEE, David 303-273-3155 83 B
dlee@mines.edu
LEE, David, C 706-542-5969 138 G
dclee@uga.edu
LEE, David, D 270-745-5204 208 A
david.lee@wku.edu
LEE, David, Y 703-333-5904 530 E
LEE, Dean 870-972-3880 20 D
deanlee@astate.edu
LEE, Debra, A 330-471-8406 395 F
dlee@malone.edu
LEE, Delores 310-243-3691 34 D
dslee@csudh.edu
LEE, Dennis 229-225-5087 138 A
dlee@southwestgatech.edu
LEE, Dewain 907-786-1214 10 H
aydos@uaa.alaska.edu
LEE, Diana 405-491-6310 412 D
dlee@snu.edu
LEE, Diane, M 410-455-2859 227 D
dlee@umbc.edu
LEE, Donald, E 252-493-7262 372 H
dlee@email.pittcc.edu
LEE, Donna, A 404-471-6391 123 I
dlee@agnesscott.edu
LEE, Donzell 601-877-6122 272 F
dlee@alcorn.edu
LEE, Donzell 601-877-3920 272 F
dlee@alcorn.edu
LEE, Doug 724-852-3630 451 B
dlee@waynesburg.edu
LEE, Elaine 808-454-4793 141 H
elainel@hawaii.edu
LEE, Elwyn, C 832-842-5090 503 D
eclee@uh.edu
LEE, Eric 617-973-1101 245 B
elee@suffolk.edu
LEE, Eungjo 770-279-0507 130 A
eunjol@hotmail.com
LEE, Frieda 415-338-2356 37 B
friedale@sfsu.edu
LEE, Giljae 218-726-6832 271 F
glee@umn.edu
LEE, Gloria 203-392-5200 90 I
leeg1@southernct.edu
LEE, Grayce 504-468-2900 215 B
drlee@southwest.edu
LEE, Harlan 425-564-2212 531 G
harlan.lee@bellevuecollege.edu
LEE, Herbert 831-459-2351 75 C
vpaa@ucsc.edu
LEE, Hesseung 215-965-4017 436 H
hlee@moore.edu
LEE, Ho Woo 770-279-0507 130 A
howlee21@hotmail.com
LEE, Humphrey 256-331-5214 6 B
hlee@nwscc.edu
LEE, Ingrid 928-226-4315 13 F
ingrid.lee@coconino.edu
LEE, Irene 907-277-1000 10 E
contact@chartercollege.edu
LEE, J. Steve 251-442-2390 9 A
slee@umobile.edu
LEE, Jane 513-785-3045 396 F
leeje1@muohio.edu
LEE, Jay 970-521-6607 86 K
jay.lee@njc.edu
LEE, Joel 512-651-4730 464 H
LEE, John 707-826-3961 36 E
john.lee@humboldt.edu
LEE, Jonathan 310-233-4471 54 I
leej@lahc.edu
LEE, Jonathan 860-509-9556 93 A
jlee@hartsem.edu
LEE, Jonathan, E 540-375-2237 523 G
jelee@roanoke.edu
LEE, Joni, C 501-569-3186 24 E
jclee@ualr.edu
LEE, Kathleen, F 317-921-4967 175 K
klee@ivytech.edu
LEE, Katrina, K 919-658-2502 367 F
klee@moc.edu
LEE, Keum Hee 213-385-2322 79 I
LEE, Kevin 620-862-5252 190 G
kevin.lee@barclaycollege.edu
LEE, Kim 601-923-1681 276 F
klee@rts.edu
LEE, Kyu, H 253-752-2020 534 E
revkhlee@faithseminary.edu
LEE, Larry 361-698-1700 485 G
llee@delmar.edu
LEE, Larry, K 814-332-2324 421 F
larry.lee@allegheny.edu
LEE, Laura 864-225-7653 458 C
lauralee@forrestcollege.edu
LEE, Leon 212-226-7300 346 E
llee@pbcny.edu
LEE, Linda, J 414-288-7206 548 F
linda.j.lee@marquette.edu
LEE, Linda, S 657-725-7789 71 G
lslee@stanford.edu
LEE, Lisa 714-533-3946 37 E
lisa@calums.edu
LEE, Lisa 212-410-8032 343 B
llee@nycpm.edu
LEE, Lisa 610-328-8402 447 F
llee2@swarthmore.edu
LEE, Lyann 808-942-1000 141 D

LEIKER, Robert, D ..... 619-265-0107 ..... 62 K
rleiker@platt.edu
LEIMBACH, Bill ..... 410-337-6138 ..... 222 I
bleimbach@goucher.edu
LEIMBACH, Bridget, S ..... 410-386-8032 ..... 221 G
bleimbach@carrollcc.edu
LEIMBEK, Melissa ..... 763-424-0946 ..... 268 B
mleimbek@nhcc.edu
LEIMER, Christina ..... 559-278-3906 ..... 35 A
cleimer@csufresno.edu
LEIMER, Jennifer ..... 601-928-6211 ..... 275 E
jennifer.leimer@mgccc.edu
LEIN, Laura ..... 734-764-5347 ..... 259 A
leinl@umich.edu
LEINBERRY, Beth ..... 401-841-4448 ..... 558 B
LEINEN, Margaret ..... 772-465-2400 ..... 119 A
mleinen@fau.edu
LEININGER, Earl ..... 704-406-3522 ..... 364 E
eleininger@gardner-webb.edu
LEININGER, Jeffrey ..... 708-209-3470 ..... 148 E
jeffrey.leininger@cuchicago.edu
LEINWALL, Checka ..... 814-827-4469 ..... 450 A
leinwall@pitt.edu
LEINWEBER, Laura ..... 619-849-2856 ..... 62 L
lauraleinweber@pointloma.edu
LEIPERTZ, Rosemary ..... 724-339-7542 ..... 437 F
financialaid@nbi.edu
LEIPHEIMER, John ..... 724-589-2212 ..... 448 B
jleipheimer@thiel.edu
LEISINGER, Scott, C ..... 319-352-8495 ..... 189 J
scott.leisinger@wartburg.edu
LEISSNER, Lance ..... 903-589-4039 ..... 490 D
lleissner@lonmorris.edu
LEIST, Terry ..... 406-994-4361 ..... 295 C
tleist@montana.edu
LEISTIKOW, Patricia ..... 218-322-2403 ..... 266 G
patricia.leistikow@itascacc.edu
LEITE, Randy ..... 740-593-9336 ..... 399 G
leite@ohio.edu
LEITER, Dena ..... 908-709-7027 ..... 316 B
leiter@ucc.edu
LEITHNER STAUFFER,
Andrea, C ..... 570-577-1331 ..... 423 E
andrea.leithner.stauffer@bucknell.edu
LEITNAKER, Gary, E ..... 785-532-6277 ..... 194 D
geleit@ksu.edu
LEITNER, Jennifer ..... 603-882-6923 ..... 304 E
jleitner@ccsnh.edu
LEITNER, Lewis ..... 609-652-4298 ..... 313 E
lewis.leitner@stockton.edu
LEITSON, Cynthia ..... 216-987-3510 ..... 389 B
cynthia.leitson@tri-c.edu
LEITZEL, Thomas, C ..... 843-525-8247 ..... 461 E
tleitzel@tcl.edu
LEIVAS, Chris ..... 925-685-1230 ..... 43 F
cleivas@dvc.edu
LEJA, Ann ..... 651-793-1376 ..... 267 A
ann.leja@metrostate.edu
LEJTER, Nelly ..... 603-428-2217 ..... 305 D
nlejter@nec.edu
LEKANG, Laurie ..... 701-671-2871 ..... 382 G
laurie.lekang@ndscs.edu
LELAND, Chris ..... 405-733-7350 ..... 411 I
cleland@rose.edu
LELAND, Dorothy ..... 209-228-4417 ..... 74 D
chancellor@ucmerced.edu
LELAND, Mary ..... 916-558-2198 ..... 56 D
lelandm@scc.losrios.edu
LELAND, Melinda, T ..... 276-739-2548 ..... 529 A
mleland@vhcc.edu
LELAND, Ted ..... 209-946-2392 ..... 76 A
tleland@pacific.edu
LELCHOOK, Heather ..... 970-667-4611 ..... 81 A
heather.lelchook@aims.edu
LELE, Pradeep ..... 281-618-7123 ..... 490 E
pradeep.m.lele@lonestar.edu
LELIAERT, Deborah, S ..... 940-565-2108 ..... 504 D
leliaert@unt.edu
LELIK, Mary ..... 312-996-3254 ..... 167 B
lelik@uic.edu
LELNER, Larry ..... 315-279-5235 ..... 337 K
lehner@mail.keuka.edu
LELONG, Kristine, D ..... 504-865-3858 ..... 213 F
klelong@loyno.edu
LELOUDIS, James, L ..... 919-843-7754 ..... 378 E
leloudis@unc.edu
LEMA, Barbara ..... 508-286-8206 ..... 246 B
blema@wheatoncollege.edu
LEMAHIEU, Dan ..... 847-735-5083 ..... 155 G
lemahieu@lakeforest.edu
LEMAHIEU, Keith ..... 219-864-2400 ..... 178 F
klemahieu@midamerica.edu
LEMAIRE, Renee ..... 334-222-6591 ..... 5 F
rlemaire@lbwcc.edu
LEMANN, Nicholas ..... 212-854-6056 ..... 330 F
nl2124@columbia.edu
LEMANSKI, Larry ..... 903-886-5018 ..... 498 B
larry.lemanski@tamuc.edu
LEMASTER, Charles ..... 254-647-3214 ..... 492 G
clemaster@rangercollege.edu
LEMASTER, Courtney ..... 270-852-3107 ..... 204 A
LEMASTER, J. Michael ..... 937-258-8251 ..... 392 B
LEMASTERS, Michael ..... 724-357-2696 ..... 442 F
michael.lemasters@iup.edu

LEMASTERS, Phil ..... 325-793-3898 ..... 490 H
plemasters@mcm.edu
LEMASTERS, Rosanna ..... 740-695-1720 ..... 400 B
stclair@ohio.edu
LEMAY, Aaron ..... 936-294-3899 ..... 501 D
caaronlemay@shsu.edu
LEMAY, Eileen ..... 563-589-0300 ..... 190 A
elemay@wartburgseminary.edu
LEMAY, Elaine ..... 510-869-6739 ..... 64 J
elemay@samuelmerritt.edu
LEMAY, Jerret ..... 315-312-2237 ..... 354 A
jerret.lemay@oswego.edu
LEMAY, Mitch ..... 415-485-9467 ..... 42 B
mitchell.lemay@marin.edu
LEMBKE, Roberta ..... 507-786-3097 ..... 271 C
lembke@stolaf.edu
LEMBO, Vincent, J ..... 617-373-2157 ..... 243 F
LEMBURG, Mary ..... 713-718-8505 ..... 487 I
mary.lemburg@hccs.edu
LEMCOE, Diane ..... 908-526-1200 ..... 313 D
dlemcoe@raritanval.edu
LEMERY, Cynthia ..... 518-327-6399 ..... 345 H
clemery@paulsmiths.edu
LEMESHOW, Stanley, A ..... 614-247-8196 ..... 398 I
lemeshow.1@osu.edu
LEMIERE, Donna ..... 617-928-4519 ..... 242 E
dlemiere@mountida.edu
LEMIESZ, Linda ..... 212-353-4115 ..... 331 A
lemiesz@cooper.edu
LEMIEUX, Carlene, P ..... 207-893-7754 ..... 219 F
clemieux@sjcme.edu
LEMING, Heidi ..... 912-279-5970 ..... 127 E
hleming@ccga.edu
LEMISH, Dafna, P ..... 618-453-7708 ..... 165 B
gkolb@siu.edu
LEMKE, Angela ..... 276-376-4517 ..... 525 G
aml7u@uvawise.edu
LEMKE, Chris ..... 616-222-1360 ..... 250 A
chris.lemke@cornerstone.edu
LEMKE, Gregory, J ..... 218-477-5869 ..... 267 F
greg.lemke@mnstate.edu
LEMKE, Steve, W ..... 504-282-4455 ..... 213 H
slemke@nobts.edu
LEMLEY, David ..... 310-506-4275 ..... 61 H
david.lemley@pepperdine.edu
LEMMA, Paulette ..... 860-832-2364 ..... 90 G
lemma@ccsu.edu
LEMME, Gary, D ..... 334-844-4444 ..... 1 F
gdl0003@aces.edu
LEMMER, Nick ..... 507-457-6649 ..... 271 B
nlemmer@smumn.edu
LEMMON, John ..... 650-508-3605 ..... 59 H
jlemmon@ndnu.edu
LEMMONS, Crystal ..... 417-625-9394 ..... 286 B
lemmons-c@mssu.edu
LEMOINE, Sandra, M ..... 318-342-1235 ..... 216 E
slemoine@ulm.edu
LEMON, Jason ..... 619-260-4585 ..... 76 D
jasonlemon@sandiego.edu
LEMON, Jason ..... 402-474-5315 ..... 298 C
jlemon@kaplanuniversity.edu
LEMON, Ronald, E ..... 304-896-7425 ..... 543 C
ronald.lemon@southernwv.edu
LEMON, William, J ..... 314-824-2002 ..... 291 D
lemonj@umsl.edu
LEMOND, Charles ..... 901-843-3890 ..... 472 K
lemond@rhodes.edu
LEMONIS, Samuel ..... 601-857-3204 ..... 274 C
splemonis@hindscc.edu
LEMONNIER, Janet ..... 973-642-8724 ..... 315 C
janet.wagman-lemonnier@shu.edu
LEMONS, James ..... 434-832-7680 ..... 526 E
lemonsj@cvcc.vccs.edu
LEMONS, L. Jay ..... 570-372-4130 ..... 447 E
supres@susqu.edu
LEMUEL, Robert, L ..... 989-964-4393 ..... 257 G
lemuel@svsu.edu
LEMURA, Linda, M ..... 315-445-4312 ..... 338 B
lemuralm@lemoyne.edu
LEMUS, Maria De Jesus ..... 773-371-5453 ..... 146 E
mlemus@ctu.edu
LENA, Hugh, F ..... 401-865-2155 ..... 453 H
hlena@providence.edu
LENAHAN, Robert ..... 631-632-6350 ..... 352 C
robert.lenahan@stonybrook.edu
LENARD, Mary ..... 262-595-2644 ..... 552 A
mary.lenard@uwp.edu
LENCHAK, Timothy, A ..... 563-876-3353 ..... 184 B
tlenchak@dwci.edu
LENCZOWSKI, John ..... 202-462-2101 ..... 99 A
lenczowski@iwp.edu
LENDIO, Darolyn ..... 808-956-9901 ..... 141 E
lendio@hawaii.edu
LENFEST, Richard ..... 413-572-5405 ..... 238 F
rlenfest@wsc.ma.edu
LENGERICH, Shannon ..... 847-925-6889 ..... 151 G
slengeri@harpercollege.edu
LENHARDT, Rachel ..... 712-325-3282 ..... 186 F
rlenhardt@iwcc.edu
LENHARDT, Steven ..... 617-994-6928 ..... 236 D
slenhardt@bhe.mass.edu
LENIG, Joni, L ..... 931-540-2752 ..... 475 A
jlenig@columbiastate.edu

LENIHAN, Bernard ..... 908-709-7605 ..... 316 B
lenihan@ucc.edu
LENIHAN, Gerald ..... 973-642-8252 ..... 315 C
gerald.lenihan@shu.edu
LENKER, Michael ..... 509-533-8280 ..... 533 B
mike.lenker@scc.spokane.edu
LENNEMAN, Marc ..... 406-447-4336 ..... 293 G
mlenneman@carroll.edu
LENNERTZ, Reid ..... 239-590-7960 ..... 119 B
rlennert@fgcu.edu
LENNEY, Raina ..... 202-885-5936 ..... 97 D
lenney@american.edu
LENNIE, Peter ..... 585-275-5931 ..... 359 B
lennie@rochester.edu
LENNIHAN, Louise ..... 212-817-7280 ..... 327 B
llennihan@gc.cuny.edu
LENNO, Chip ..... 408-924-1177 ..... 37 C
chip.lenno@sjsu.edu
LENNON, Gerald, P ..... 610-758-3165 ..... 434 E
gpl0@lehigh.edu
LENNON, John ..... 845-848-4061 ..... 332 B
john.lennon@dc.edu
LENNOX, Marybeth ..... 802-287-8238 ..... 513 F
lennoxmb@greenmtn.edu
LENO, Leah ..... 218-879-0813 ..... 266 C
leah@fdltcc.edu
LENO, Melissa ..... 218-733-5903 ..... 266 H
m.leno@lsc.edu
LENO, Tom ..... 701-224-5497 ..... 382 D
thomas.leno@bismarckstate.edu
LENON, Mary Jane ..... 401-865-2566 ..... 453 H
mjlenon@providence.edu
LENORE-JENKINS, Shani ..... 314-529-9350 ..... 284 C
slenore@maryville.edu
LENROW, Jon ..... 215-670-9359 ..... 438 E
jlenrow@peirce.edu
LENSING, Peggy ..... 563-387-1015 ..... 187 D
lensinpe@luther.edu
LENSINK, Scott ..... 217-234-5222 ..... 156 B
slensink@lakeland.cc.il.us
LENSMEYER, Kris ..... 573-592-5319 ..... 293 B
kris.lensmeyer@westminster-mo.edu
LENT, Scott ..... 903-223-3087 ..... 498 F
scott.lent@tamut.edu
LENTING, Amy ..... 312-225-6288 ..... 167 G
alenting@vandercook.edu
LENTINI, James, P ..... 513-529-6010 ..... 396 E
james.lentini@muohio.edu
LENTINO, Nicholas ..... 860-727-6765 ..... 92 I
nlentino@goodwin.edu
LENTNER, Nikolaus ..... 914-251-6070 ..... 354 D
nikolaus.lentner@purchase.edu
LENTO, Joseph ..... 718-260-5430 ..... 328 D
jlento@citytech.cuny.edu
LENTSCH, Michael ..... 515-964-6216 ..... 183 H
mjlentsch@dmacc.edu
LENTSNER, Dina ..... 614-236-6952 ..... 386 E
dlentsne@capital.edu
LENTZ, Alice ..... 828-726-2234 ..... 368 G
alentz@cccti.edu
LENTZ, Heather ..... 605-995-7227 ..... 464 F
heather.lentz@mitchelltech.edu
LENTZ, Lynette ..... 402-375-7241 ..... 299 G
lylentz1@wsc.edu
LENWAY, Stefanie, A ..... 517-355-8377 ..... 255 A
lenway@msu.edu
LENZ, Christopher ..... 323-343-3237 ..... 35 D
clenz@cslanet.calstatela.edu
LENZ, Joseph ..... 515-271-3939 ..... 184 D
joe.lenz@drake.edu
LENZ, Mary ..... 320-762-4648 ..... 265 F
maryl@alextech.edu
LENZ, Patrick, J ..... 510-987-9101 ..... 73 G
patrick.lenz@ucop.edu
LENZ, Suzanne ..... 603-623-0313 ..... 305 E
suzannelenz@nhia.edu
LENZI, John ..... 413-545-2313 ..... 236 F
jlenzi@registrar.umass.edu
LENZI, Patrick ..... 610-436-1048 ..... 444 A
plenzi@wcupa.edu
LEO, Donald, J ..... 571-858-3002 ..... 529 G
donleo@vt.edu
LEON, Aixa ..... 787-738-2161 ..... 567 D
aixa.leon@upr.edu
LEON, Christine ..... 714-241-6257 ..... 41 B
cleon@coastline.edu
LEON, Dante, J ..... 425-235-5831 ..... 537 A
dleon@rtc.edu
LEON, Gloria ..... 914-606-6744 ..... 360 E
gloria.leon@sunywcc.edu
LEON, Juan, C ..... 787-844-8812 ..... 568 A
juan.leon1@upr.edu
LEON, Wayne ..... 203-932-7416 ..... 95 C
wleon@newhaven.edu
LEON GUERRERO,
Barbara, B ..... 671-735-5519 ..... 559 E
csi@guamcc.edu
LEON GUERRERO,
Deborah, D ..... 671-735-2585 ..... 559 G
deborah@uguam.uog.edu
LEONARD, Brenda ..... 704-330-6626 ..... 369 D
brenda.leonard@cpcc.edu
LEONARD, David, M ..... 540-458-8752 ..... 530 D
dleonard@wlu.edu

LEONARD, Debbie ..... 305-809-3203 ..... 108 I
debbie.leonard@fkcc.edu
LEONARD, III, Edward, F ..... 785-227-3380 ..... 191 B
president@bethanylb.edu
LEONARD, Gloria, J ..... 314-516-5362 ..... 291 D
gloria_leonard@umsl.edu
LEONARD, Jesse, W ..... 814-641-3162 ..... 432 A
leonarj@juniata.edu
LEONARD, Joseph, G ..... 202-296-5254 ..... 98 C
gleonard@gwu.edu
LEONARD, Katie ..... 570-702-8925 ..... 431 L
kleonard@johnson.edu
LEONARD, Katy ..... 205-226-4647 ..... 2 B
kleonard@bsc.edu
LEONARD, Kevin, M ..... 585-292-5627 ..... 325 C
kmleonard@bryantstratton.edu
LEONARD, Kimberly ..... 618-453-2466 ..... 165 B
kleonard@siu.edu
LEONARD, Nora ..... 757-388-2900 ..... 524 D
LEONARD, Patricia, L ..... 910-962-3117 ..... 379 D
leonard@uncw.edu
LEONARD, Patricia, Y ..... 810-989-5523 ..... 257 H
pleonard@sc4.edu
LEONARD, OSFS, Peter ..... 610-282-1100 ..... 427 A
peter.leonard@desales.edu
LEONARD, Robert ..... 256-824-2233 ..... 8 G
robert.leonard@uah.edu
LEONARD, Steve ..... 317-738-8316 ..... 171 F
sleonard@franklincollege.edu
LEONARD, Susan ..... 435-613-5230 ..... 512 A
susan.leonard@usu.edu
LEONARD, Thomas, C ..... 510-642-3773 ..... 73 H
toml@berkeley.edu
LEONARD, Tim ..... 214-768-4465 ..... 495 A
tleonard@smu.edu
LEONARD, Vee ..... 239-590-1101 ..... 119 B
vleonard@fgcu.edu
LEONARD, William ..... 617-735-9883 ..... 234 C
leonard@emmanuel.edu
LEONARD-HINDS,
Hannah ..... 404-237-7573 ..... 126 B
hleonardhinds@bauder.edu
LEONARD-RAY, Pamela ..... 843-574-6411 ..... 461 G
pamela.leonard-ray@tridenttech.edu
LEONARD-ROCK, Pearl ..... 608-663-2256 ..... 547 F
prock@edgewood.edu
LEONE, Therese, M ..... 510-430-2228 ..... 57 D
tmleone@mills.edu
LEONHARDT, Chuck ..... 970-351-1890 ..... 89 B
charles.leonhardt@unco.edu
LEONOR, JR., Samuel, E ..... 951-785-2090 ..... 53 E
sleonor@lasierra.edu
LEOPARD, David ..... 706-379-3111 ..... 140 A
LEOPARD, Tim ..... 205-348-8157 ..... 8 E
tleopard@fa.ua.edu
LEOPARDI, Dino ..... 607-844-8222 ..... 357 I
leopard@tc3.edu
LEOPOLD, Lillian ..... 619-482-6564 ..... 71 D
lleopold@swccd.edu
LEOUSIS, Kim ..... 251-442-2290 ..... 9 A
kleousis@umobile.edu
LEPAGE, Bob ..... 413-755-4477 ..... 241 B
rglepage@stcc.edu
LEPAGE, Francoise ..... 415-485-3284 ..... 45 C
flepage@dominican.edu
LEPAGE, G. Peter ..... 607-255-4146 ..... 331 B
gpl3@cornell.edu
LEPAGE, Greg ..... 425-739-8108 ..... 535 H
greg.lepage@lwtc.edu
LEPAGE, Joe ..... 512-863-1915 ..... 496 A
lepagej@southwestern.edu
LEPAGE, Sharon ..... 808-440-4263 ..... 140 E
slepage@chaminade.edu
LEPLEY, Pamela, D ..... 804-828-6057 ..... 526 B
pdlepley@vcu.edu
LEPOWSKY, Steven ..... 860-679-4885 ..... 95 A
lepowsky@nso2.uchc.edu
LEPPANEN, Hannu ..... 906-487-7285 ..... 251 A
hannu.leppanen@finlandia.edu
LEPPERT, Glenn, W ..... 620-862-5252 ..... 190 G
registrar@barclaycollege.edu
LEPUS, Jennifer ..... 410-455-3751 ..... 227 D
jlepus@umbc.edu
LERBINGER, Jan ..... 617-585-1284 ..... 242 I
jan.lerbinger@necmusic.edu
LERCH, Carol ..... 508-929-8119 ..... 238 G
clerch@worcester.edu
LERCH, Derek ..... 530-283-0202 ..... 47 B
dlerch@frc.edu
LERCH, Maureen, T ..... 330-684-8951 ..... 403 C
mlerch@uakron.edu
LERENBERG, Marsha ..... 816-604-4565 ..... 285 E
marsha.lerenberg@mcckc.edu
LERER, Nava ..... 516-877-3236 ..... 322 A
lerer@adelphi.edu
LERER, Seth ..... 858-534-6270 ..... 74 F
slerer@ucsd.edu
LERMAN, Linda ..... 203-857-7211 ..... 92 C
llerman@ncc.commnet.edu
LERMAN, Steven ..... 202-994-6510 ..... 98 C
lerman@gwu.edu
LERME, Keith ..... 502-456-6504 ..... 206 H
klerme@sullivan.edu

LEWALLEN, Willard, C ...... 831-755-6900 ...... 49 E
wlewallen@hartnell.edu
LEWANDOWSKI, John ...... 313-845-9620 .... 252 B
jjlewandowski@hfcc.edu
LEWANDOWSKI,
Joseph, D ...... 660-543-4633 .... 290 H
lewandowski@ucmo.edu
LEWANDOWSKI, Kenneth . 814-944-5643 .... 452 J
ken.lewandowski@yti.edu
LEWELLEN, Mary ...... 765-289-2291 .... 176 B
mlewelle@ivytech.edu
LEWELLEN, Mary ...... 765-289-2291 .... 176 B
mlewellen@ivytech.edu
LEWELLEN, Phyllis ...... 928-776-2190 ...... 19 C
phyllis.lewellen@yc.edu
LEWELLEN, Randy ...... 903-983-8130 .... 489 I
rlewellen@kilgore.edu
LEWICKI, Denise ...... 860-628-4751 ...... 93 C
dlewicki@lincolncollegene.edu
LEWICKI, Donald, C ...... 814-362-7660 .... 449 B
lewicki@pitt.edu
LEWIN, Harris, A ...... 530-754-7764 ...... 73 I
lewin@ucdavis.edu
LEWIN, Lisa, M ...... 414-410-4230 .... 546 G
lmlewin@stritch.edu
LEWIN, Luis, E ...... 765-494-7395 .... 178 J
luislewin@purdue.edu
LEWIN, Ross ...... 301-405-4772 .... 227 B
LEWIS, Albert ...... 708-974-5407 .... 159 B
lewisjra@morainevalley.edu
LEWIS, Alex, O ...... 405-962-1663 .... 408 G
aolewis@langston.edu
LEWIS, Alisha ...... 870-584-4471 ...... 25 C
alewis@cccua.edu
LEWIS, Ann ...... 208-769-7812 .... 144 D
ann_lewis@nic.edu
LEWIS, Annabelle ...... 706-771-4171 .... 125 H
alewis@augustatech.edu
LEWIS, April ...... 864-596-9040 .... 457 E
april.lewis@converse.edu
LEWIS, Beverly, N ...... 336-734-7512 .... 370 F
blewis@forsythtech.edu
LEWIS, Bill ...... 505-566-3339 .... 320 D
lewisb@sanjuancollege.edu
LEWIS, Bill, E ...... 314-434-2212 .... 282 I
LEWIS, Blaine, D ...... 330-823-7365 .... 404 C
lewisbd@mountunion.edu
LEWIS, Brian ...... 765-677-2188 .... 175 B
brian.lewis@indwes.edu
LEWIS, Brien ...... 704-637-4414 .... 363 E
wblewis@catawba.edu
LEWIS, Bruce ...... 847-491-4933 .... 160 E
balewis@northwestern.edu
LEWIS, C. Jasper ...... 870-235-4065 ...... 23 I
cjlewis@saumag.edu
LEWIS, Carol, E ...... 907-474-7083 ...... 10 I
celewis@alaska.edu
LEWIS, Carolyn ...... 256-372-5690 ...... 1 A
carolyn.lewis@aamu.edu
LEWIS, Carolyn ...... 201-559-3560 .... 310 B
lewisc@felician.edu
LEWIS, Cassandra, B ...... 601-877-3905 .... 272 F
cblewis@alcorn.edu
LEWIS, Charles, R ...... 256-782-5003 ...... 4 L
LEWIS, Christopher ...... 517-371-5140 .... 258 F
lewisch@cooley.edu
LEWIS, Cindy ...... 805-493-3199 ...... 33 B
clewis@clunet.edu
LEWIS, Craig ...... 425-388-9031 .... 534 C
clewis@everettcc.edu
LEWIS, Crissy ...... 864-578-8770 .... 460 F
clewis@sherman.edu
LEWIS, Daniel, G ...... 925-631-4616 ...... 64 F
dlewis@stmarys-ca.edu
LEWIS, Daphne ...... 704-216-3463 .... 373 F
daphne.lewis@rccc.edu
LEWIS, David ...... 801-281-7630 .... 510 M
david.lewis@stevenshenager.edu
LEWIS, David, A ...... 808-675-4783 .... 140 D
david.lewis@byuh.edu
LEWIS, David, E ...... 585-275-5240 .... 359 B
david.lewis@rochester.edu
LEWIS, David, R ...... 802-356-6824 ...... 97 C
david.r.lewis@wilmu.edu
LEWIS, David, W ...... 317-274-0462 .... 174 D
dlewis@iupui.edu
LEWIS, Dawanna ...... 713-221-8974 .... 503 F
lewisd@uhd.edu
LEWIS, Debra ...... 415-485-9326 ...... 42 B
debra.lewis@marin.edu
LEWIS, Dewey, H ...... 910-938-6225 .... 369 F
lewisd@coastalcarolina.edu
LEWIS, Donald ...... 651-641-3262 .... 264 H
dlewis@luthersem.edu
LEWIS, Donald, E ...... 205-916-2800 ...... 4 D
donl@bhm.herzing.edu
LEWIS, Donald, M ...... 651-523-2941 .... 264 A
dlewis02@gw.hamline.edu
LEWIS, Donna ...... 601-925-3967 .... 275 C
dlewis@mc.edu
LEWIS, Donna, M ...... 304-647-6566 .... 543 A
dlewis@newriver.edu
LEWIS, Doris ...... 269-965-3931 .... 253 B
lewisd@kellogg.edu
LEWIS, Dusty ...... 575-624-7328 .... 318 C
dusty.lewis@roswell.enmu.edu
LEWIS, E. Charles ...... 817-202-6720 .... 495 E
lewis@swau.edu
LEWIS, Earl ...... 404-727-6055 .... 129 D
earl.lewis@emory.edu
LEWIS, Earnestine ...... 434-949-1064 .... 528 D
earnestine.lewis@southside.edu
LEWIS, Eleanor ...... 717-867-6302 .... 434 C
lewis@lvc.edu
LEWIS, Eva ...... 423-697-2659 .... 474 D
LEWIS, Felicia ...... 502-597-6286 .... 203 G
felicia.lewis@kysu.edu
LEWIS, Fred ...... 423-279-7665 .... 475 F
fdlewis@northeaststate.edu
LEWIS, Georj ...... 219-980-6824 .... 174 B
gllewis@iun.edu
LEWIS, Gillian, O ...... 206-546-4780 .... 538 C
glewis@shoreline.edu
LEWIS, Goldene ...... 718-270-6121 .... 328 C
goldene@mec.cuny.edu
LEWIS, Gregory ...... 804-257-5750 .... 530 A
gelewis@vuu.edu
LEWIS, Gregory, V ...... 661-824-2977 ...... 58 H
LEWIS, Hal, M ...... 312-322-1715 .... 165 E
LEWIS, III, Henry ...... 305-626-3600 .... 109 A
henry.lewis@fmuniv.edu
LEWIS, Hosea ...... 334-229-6810 ...... 1 C
hlewis@alasu.edu
LEWIS, Jack, M ...... 540-674-3601 .... 527 E
jlewis@nr.edu
LEWIS, Jacyn ...... 415-955-2038 ...... 27 A
jlewis@alliant.edu
LEWIS, James, E ...... 206-934-5157 .... 537 F
james.lewis@seattlecolleges.edu
LEWIS, III, James, E ...... 812-941-2430 .... 175 A
lewisjae@ius.edu
LEWIS, Jan ...... 541-737-4605 .... 418 B
jan_lewis@ous.edu
LEWIS, Jan, P ...... 253-535-7283 .... 536 E
lewisjp@plu.edu
LEWIS, Jan Ellen ...... 973-353-5213 .... 314 E
janlewis@andromeda.rutgers.edu
LEWIS, Jane, L ...... 209-946-2125 ...... 76 A
jlewis@pacific.edu
LEWIS, Jeanne ...... 609-652-4201 .... 313 E
jeanne.lewis@stockton.edu
LEWIS, Jeannie, M ...... 559-323-2100 ...... 66 C
jlewis@sjcl.edu
LEWIS, Jennifer ...... 619-660-4670 ...... 49 B
jennifer.lewis@gcccd.edu
LEWIS, Jerry ...... 817-272-0979 .... 505 C
jerrylewis@uta.edu
LEWIS, Jim ...... 817-272-2584 .... 505 C
jimlewis@uta.edu
LEWIS, Jim ...... 806-743-2530 .... 502 B
jim.lewis@ttuhsc.edu
LEWIS, Jim, D ...... 704-637-4720 .... 363 E
jdlewis@catawba.edu
LEWIS, John ...... 518-464-8560 .... 333 E
jlewis@excelsior.edu
LEWIS, John, C ...... 801-422-2533 .... 509 H
john_lewis@byu.edu
LEWIS, John, H ...... 901-448-2745 .... 477 E
jlewis51@uthsc.edu
LEWIS, John, L ...... 815-753-0936 .... 160 B
jlewis@niu.edu
LEWIS, Joi ...... 510-430-2130 ...... 57 D
jlewis@mills.edu
LEWIS, Joi ...... 612-659-6700 .... 267 B
joi.lewis@minneapolis.edu
LEWIS, Joseph, S ...... 949-824-8792 ...... 74 B
jslewis@uci.edu
LEWIS, Judith ...... 716-829-7776 .... 332 E
lewisj@dyc.edu
LEWIS, Judith, H ...... 914-323-5279 .... 339 J
judith.lewis@mville.edu
LEWIS, Karen ...... 615-327-6262 .... 471 C
klewis@mmc.edu
LEWIS, Katherine, P ...... 570-340-6094 .... 435 F
kplewis@marywood.edu
LEWIS, Kathie ...... 559-730-3826 ...... 42 D
kathiel@cos.edu
LEWIS, Kayli ...... 407-277-0311 .... 107 B
kalewis@evergladesuniversity.edu
LEWIS, Keisha ...... 205-929-1810 ...... 5 H
klewis@miles.edu
LEWIS, Kenneth ...... 706-396-8102 .... 135 G
klewis@paine.edu
LEWIS, JR., Kenneth, A ...... 252-492-2061 .... 374 G
lewis@vgcc.edu
LEWIS, Kenneth, D ...... 803-536-7132 .... 460 G
kdlewis@scsu.edu
LEWIS, Kent ...... 270-852-3289 .... 204 A
klewis@kwc.edu
LEWIS, Leontye ...... 910-672-1265 .... 377 G
llewis8@uncfsu.edu
LEWIS, Leslie ...... 607-274-3533 .... 336 G
llewis@ithaca.edu
LEWIS, Linda, E ...... 870-543-5906 ...... 23 H
llewis@seark.edu
LEWIS, Lindsey, C ...... 781-891-2551 .... 231 D
llewis@bentley.edu
LEWIS, Lisa ...... 860-486-2240 ...... 94 G
lisa.lewis@uconn.edu
LEWIS, Lisa ...... 805-898-4010 ...... 47 C
llewis@fielding.edu
LEWIS, Lori ...... 410-857-2250 .... 224 C
llewis@mcdaniel.edu
LEWIS, Lori ...... 336-917-5577 .... 376 E
lori.lewis@salem.edu
LEWIS, Lynn ...... 864-646-1437 .... 461 F
llewis@tctc.edu
LEWIS, Lynn ...... 434-381-6106 .... 524 K
llewis@sbc.edu
LEWIS, Mark ...... 325-674-2867 .... 478 I
mark.lewis@acu.edu
LEWIS, Marsha, L ...... 716-829-2533 .... 351 G
ubnursingdean@buffalo.edu
LEWIS, Mary ...... 651-641-8892 .... 263 A
lewis@csp.edu
LEWIS, Mary ...... 772-462-7444 .... 111 B
mlewis@irsc.edu
LEWIS, Michael ...... 785-749-8451 .... 193 D
michael.lewis@bie.edu
LEWIS, Michael ...... 614-251-4589 .... 398 F
lewism2@ohiodominican.edu
LEWIS, Michele ...... 406-353-2607 .... 293 E
mlewis@mail.fbcc.edu
LEWIS, Nichole, R ...... 919-516-5082 .... 376 D
nrlewis@st-aug.edu
LEWIS, Nora, E ...... 215-746-1172 .... 448 J
nlewis@sas.upenn.edu
LEWIS, Orlando ...... 803-376-4746 .... 455 B
olewis@allenuniversity.edu
LEWIS, Pamela ...... 765-459-0561 .... 176 C
plewis@ivytech.edu
LEWIS, Phil ...... 405-425-5560 .... 409 E
phil.lewis@oc.edu
LEWIS, Preston ...... 325-942-2248 .... 480 E
preston.lewis@angelo.edu
LEWIS, Rebecca ...... 585-245-5546 .... 353 C
lewis@geneseo.edu
LEWIS, Rebecca, B ...... 423-439-6155 .... 473 F
bakerr@etsu.edu
LEWIS, Richard ...... 330-325-2511 .... 397 D
rwl@neomed.edu
LEWIS, Richard ...... 928-350-1307 ...... 17 K
rlewis@prescott.edu
LEWIS, Rita, F ...... 704-461-6726 .... 362 F
ritalewis@bac.edu
LEWIS, Rob ...... 859-985-3323 .... 199 A
lewisro@berea.edu
LEWIS, Robin ...... 606-326-2423 .... 201 F
robin.lewis@kctcs.edu
LEWIS, Rosalyn ...... 318-247-0430 .... 215 E
lewisros@gram.edu
LEWIS, S. Kay ...... 206-543-6107 .... 539 A
sklewis@uw.edu
LEWIS, Scott ...... 801-506-4030 ...... 19 A
scott.lewis@phoenix.edu
LEWIS, Shaun, M ...... 504-286-5292 .... 214 J
slewis@suno.edu
LEWIS, Shelia ...... 619-477-6310 ...... 73 D
slewis@usuniveristy.edu
LEWIS, Shirley ...... 707-864-7000 ...... 70 A
shirley.lewis@solano.edu
LEWIS, Steven ...... 207-942-6781 .... 217 B
slewis@bts.edu
LEWIS, Susan ...... 325-674-2024 .... 478 I
lewiss@acu.edu
LEWIS, Susan, A ...... 617-262-5000 .... 231 G
susan.lewis@the-bac.edu
LEWIS, Ted, A ...... 865-694-6523 .... 475 G
talewis@pstcc.edu
LEWIS, Terry, W ...... 731-881-7890 .... 477 G
tlewis@utm.edu
LEWIS, Thomas ...... 443-287-9900 .... 223 F
tomlewis@jhu.edu
LEWIS, Thomas, C ...... 404-413-1404 .... 131 G
tomlewis@gsu.edu
LEWIS, Tiffany ...... 619-683-2727 ...... 64 D
LEWIS, Tiffany ...... 765-677-2102 .... 175 B
tiffany.lewis@indwes.edu
LEWIS, Tim, D ...... 402-363-5638 .... 301 E
tim.lewis@york.edu
LEWIS, Tresha ...... 513-745-5671 .... 403 F
tresha.lewis@uc.edu
LEWIS, Trevor ...... 305-626-3750 .... 109 A
trevor.lewis@fmuniv.edu
LEWIS, Urick ...... 610-526-6032 .... 430 D
ulewis@harcum.edu
LEWIS, Victoria ...... 831-479-6406 ...... 31 I
vilewis@cabrillo.edu
LEWIS, Vivian ...... 585-273-2760 .... 359 B
vivian.lewis@rochester.edu
LEWIS, Walter ...... 518-587-2100 .... 355 G
walter.lewis@esc.edu
LEWIS, William, A ...... 601-403-1201 .... 276 E
wlewis@prcc.edu
LEWIS, SR., William, T ...... 540-231-3811 .... 529 G
wtlewis@vt.edu
LEWIS-BOYD, Janice ...... 313-593-5200 .... 259 B
jckboyd@umd.umich.edu
LEWIS-BRIM, Cathy ...... 863-638-7241 .... 123 D
cathy.lewis-brim@warner.edu
LEWIS-JASPER, Vera ...... 409-944-1496 .... 486 K
vlewis@gc.edu
LEWIS LOGUE, Judith ...... 619-260-4720 ...... 76 D
jllogue@sandiego.edu
LEWIS-MOTTS, Irene ...... 330-494-6170 .... 402 B
imotts@starkstate.edu
LEWIS SAULO, Mileva ...... 650-292-5579 ...... 64 J
msaulo@samuelmerritt.edu
LEWIS-THOMAS, Janice ...... 256-726-7840 ...... 6 C
jthomas@oakwood.edu
LEWIS-WHITE, Yasmin ...... 202-885-8552 .... 100 C
ylwhite@wesleyseminary.edu
LEWIT, Jonathan, D ...... 845-257-3130 .... 352 B
lewit@newpaltz.edu
LEWKIEWICZ, Debra ...... 845-434-5750 .... 357 A
dlewkiew@sullivan.suny.edu
LEWTER, Andy ...... 865-981-8215 .... 471 B
andy.lewter@maryvillecollege.edu
LEWTHWAITE,
Barbara-Jayne ...... 908-852-1400 .... 308 E
lewthwaiteb@centenarycollege.edu
LEWTON, John, C ...... 260-480-4212 .... 176 F
clewton@ivytech.edu
LEWY, MariLynn, J ...... 941-752-5384 .... 118 J
lewym@scf.edu
LEX, Andrea, A ...... 301-322-0723 .... 225 F
lexaa@pgcc.edu
LEXOW, Les ...... 636-227-2100 .... 284 B
les.lexow@logan.edu
LEYBA, Cindy ...... 505-661-4686 .... 321 E
cleyba@unm.edu
LEYBA, Marylou ...... 415-239-3291 ...... 40 C
mleyba@ccsf.edu
LEYDEN, John, J ...... 401-865-2390 .... 453 H
jleyden@providence.edu
LEYDON, Betty ...... 609-258-5601 .... 312 G
betty@princeton.edu
LEYDON, John ...... 919-962-4908 .... 377 C
jleydon@northcarolina.edu
LEYDON, Pamela, F ...... 904-819-6423 .... 107 C
pleydon@flagler.edu
LEYKAM, Scott ...... 503-943-7117 .... 420 G
leykam@up.edu
LEYSER, Becky ...... 510-549-4704 ...... 71 I
bleyser@sksm.edu
LEYSTER, Susan ...... 360-438-4381 .... 537 B
leysters@stmartin.edu
LEYVA-PUEBLA, Ricardo .. 206-934-6455 .... 537 F
ricardo.leyva-puebla@seattlecolleges.edu
LEZAK JANOW, Roseann .. 860-509-9501 ...... 93 A
rlezak@hartsem.edu
LE'I, Emilia ...... 684-699-9155 .... 559 C
e.lei@amsamoa.edu
LI, Al ...... 314-434-4044 .... 280 F
al.li@covenantseminary.edu
LI, Benn ...... 212-924-5900 .... 357 B
bli@swedishinstitute.edu
LI, Christine ...... 212-650-6850 .... 326 G
cli@sci.ccny.cuny.edu
LI, Joanne ...... 937-775-4859 .... 406 C
joanne.li@wright.edu
LI, Kevin ...... 773-481-8250 .... 147 I
kli@ccc.edu
LI, Luchen ...... 812-877-8810 .... 179 B
li2@rose-hulman.edu
LI, Ming ...... 740-593-1889 .... 399 G
lim1@ohio.edu
LI, Peter, B ...... 330-972-6493 .... 403 B
peter8@uakron.edu
LI, Rui ...... 610-430-4959 .... 444 A
rli@wcupa.edu
LI, Shao ...... 512-444-8082 .... 499 E
LI, Sheng ...... 714-533-1495 ...... 70 B
sli@southbaylo.edu
LI, Xin ...... 425-558-0299 .... 533 G
xli@digipen.edu
LI, Yan ...... 415-355-1601 ...... 28 B
yanli@actcm.edu
LI, Yi ...... 937-775-2611 .... 406 C
yi.li@wright.edu
LI, Zhan ...... 925-631-4604 ...... 64 F
zgl1@stmarys-ca.edu
LI-BUGG, Cherry ...... 707-527-4392 ...... 68 E
wli-bugg@santarosa.edu
LI-CHEN, Wei ...... 626-529-8461 ...... 60 F
wlichen@pacificoaks.edu
LIANG, Bryan, A ...... 619-239-0391 ...... 37 F
bliang@cwsl.edu
LIANG, John Paul ...... 713-780-9777 .... 480 A
info@acaom.edu
LIANG, Mark ...... 714-564-6040 ...... 63 F
liang_mark@sac.edu
LIANG, Sherry ...... 510-628-8027 ...... 54 B
controller@lincolnuca.edu
LIAO-TROTH, Matthew ...... 478-445-4715 .... 130 B
matthew.liao@gcsu.edu
LIBBERTON, Larry ...... 563-242-4023 .... 182 C
larry.libberton@ashford.edu
LIBBY, Betsy ...... 207-755-5334 .... 218 G
blibby@cmcc.edu
LIBBY, Elizabeth ...... 847-735-6011 .... 155 G
libby@lakeforest.edu
LIBBY, John ...... 240-567-7951 .... 224 D
john.libby@montgomerycollege.edu

LINDENMEYER, Kriste 856-225-2809 314 D
kriste.lindenmeyer@camden.rutgers.edu

LINDENMEYER, Mark, L 410-617-2576 223 I
lindenmeyer@loyola.edu

LINDENMEYR, Adele 610-519-7090 450 H
adele.lindenmeyr@villanova.edu

LINDENMUTH, Susan, E 610-799-1151 434 D
slindenmuth@lccc.edu

LINDER, Chad 717-815-1346 452 G
clinder@ycp.edu

LINDER, Cynthia 912-287-4098 135 F
clinder@okefenokeetech.edu

LINDER, Jim 402-554-2373 300 E
jlinder@nebraska.edu

LINDER, Keith, D 602-496-0789 11 J
keith.linder@asu.edu

LINDER, Mark 256-765-4397 9 C
mdlinder@una.edu

LINDER, Vincent, P 517-586-3007 249 D
vlinder@cleary.edu

LINDGREN, Dianne 828-339-4268 374 C
diannel@southwesterncc.edu

LINDGREN, Katherine, S 423-425-4646 477 F
kay-lindgren@utc.edu

LINDGREN, Rita 701-224-5427 382 D
rita.lindgren@bismarckstate.edu

LINDGREN, Robert, R 804-752-7211 523 C
rlindgren@rmc.edu

LINDGREN, Sheri 414-464-9777 553 E
sherilindgren@wspp.edu

LINDGREN, Teresa 606-783-2449 204 I
t.lindgren@moreheadstate.edu

LINDKE, Bernice 734-487-2390 250 F
bernice.lindke@emich.edu

LINDLEY, Carolyn, V 847-491-8557 160 E
c-lindley@northwestern.edu

LINDLEY, Georgia 662-325-1810 275 F
georgia@saffairs.msstate.edu

LINDLEY, Patricia 620-235-4132 196 C
plindley@pittstate.edu

LINDLEY, Robert 405-974-2929 413 B
rlindley@uco.edu

LINDLEY, Stu 314-744-7623 285 J
lindleys@mobap.edu

LINDNER, Bill 850-644-7572 119 D
blindner@campus.fsu.edu

LINDNER, Hollie, M 208-467-8531 144 E
hmlindner@nnu.edu

LINDNER, Janet, E 203-432-2188 96 A
janet.lindner@yale.edu

LINDNER, JoEllen 605-298-5852 465 B
joellen.lindner@presentation.edu

LINDNER, Rosalyn, A 716-878-6939 353 A
lindera@buffalostate.edu

LINDNER, Susan 718-262-2272 329 A
slindner@york.cuny.edu

LINDO, Patricia 860-512-3100 91 F
plindo@mcc.commnet.edu

LINDON, Jeniffer 606-436-5721 202 C
jennifer.lindon@kctcs.edu

LINDQUIST, Brian 480-557-1221 19 A
brian.lindquist@phoenix.edu

LINDQUIST, Cynthia, A 701-766-4055 381 A
president@littlehoop.edu

LINDQUIST, Joyce 970-207-4500 89 D
joycel@uscareerinstitute.edu

LINDQUIST, Kathy 918-335-6234 411 B
klindquist@okwu.edu

LINDQUIST, Kimberly 734-384-4101 255 D
klindquist@monroeccc.edu

LINDSAY, Cecile 562-985-4128 35 C
clindsay@csulb.edu

LINDSAY, Charles, W 267-502-2549 423 C
charles.lindsay@brynathyn.edu

LINDSAY, Creighton 503-845-3508 417 A
creighton.lindsay@mtangel.edu

LINDSAY, D. Michael 978-867-4800 235 A
president@gordon.edu

LINDSAY, Dane 619-388-7823 65 H
dlindsay@sdccd.edu

LINDSAY, Dawn 410-777-2222 221 C

LINDSAY, Dennis 541-684-7253 417 F
dennisl@nwcu.edu

LINDSAY, Doug 907-564-8287 10 D
dlindsay@alaskapacific.edu

LINDSAY, Elise 216-368-2517 386 F
exl4@case.edu

LINDSAY, Gloria, A 540-857-7583 529 B
glindsay@virginiawestern.edu

LINDSAY, John 401-232-6154 453 C
jlindsay@bryant.edu

LINDSAY, Jonathan 614-222-3234 388 G
jlindsay@ccad.edu

LINDSAY, Kristen 419-448-2301 391 F
klindsay@heidelberg.edu

LINDSAY, Larry 765-677-2103 175 B
larry.lindsay@indwes.edu

LINDSAY, Laura, F 225-578-1248 212 H
aclind@lsu.edu

LINDSAY, Shawn 417-626-1234 287 C
lindsay.shawn@occ.edu

LINDSAY, Terry 773-244-4588 159 H
tlindsay@northpark.edu

LINDSAY, Twila 410-923-4585 99 G
twila.lindsay@strayer.edu

LINDSETH, Becky 218-683-8630 268 C
becky.lindseth@northlandcollege.edu

LINDSETH, Becky 218-793-2476 268 C
becky.lindseth@northlandcollege.edu

LINDSETH, Paul, G 218-755-4143 265 I
plindseth@bemidjistate.edu

LINDSEY, April 336-887-3000 366 C
alindsey@laureluniversity.edu

LINDSEY, Beverly 662-846-4648 273 H
blindsey@deltastate.edu

LINDSEY, Bruce, M 314-935-6200 292 I
blindsey@wustl.edu

LINDSEY, Candice 903-566-7221 506 E
clindsey@uttyler.edu

LINDSEY, DeLois 860-768-5122 95 B
lindsey@hartford.edu

LINDSEY, Earlene 205-652-3528 9 E
elindsey@uwa.edu

LINDSEY, Greg 612-625-9505 272 A
linds301@umn.edu

LINDSEY, John 336-887-3000 366 C
jlindsey@laureluniversity.edu

LINDSEY, Larry, J 989-837-4376 256 E
larryl@northwood.edu

LINDSEY, Lee 707-476-4100 42 C
lee-lindsey@redwoods.edu

LINDSEY, Patrick, O 313-577-4228 260 A
cz5360@wayne.edu

LINDSEY, Shannon 785-628-4462 192 I
sdlindsey@fhsu.edu

LINDSEY-LLOYD, Karen 601-925-3901 275 C
lloyd@mc.edu

LINDSLEY, Bonnie, G 419-372-0677 385 F
blindsl@bgsu.edu

LINDSTAEDT, William 415-502-2422 75 A
bill.lindstaedt@ucsf.edu

LINDSTROM, Richard 559-442-8277 72 B
richard.lindstrom@fresnocitycollege.edu

LINDSTROM, Ryan 801-863-8303 511 F
lindstry@uvu.edu

LINDTORTH, Scott, A 919-684-0539 364 C
scott.lindroth@duke.edu

LINDUSKA, Kim 515-964-6628 183 H
kjlinduska@dmacc.edu

LINDVALL, Sherie, J 651-638-6233 261 D
s-lindvall@bethel.edu

LINEBACK, Pamela 513-745-5720 403 F
pamela.lineback@uc.edu

LINEBAUGH, Craig, W 202-994-0724 98 C
cline@gwu.edu

LINEBAUGH, Jonathan 954-771-0376 112 I

LINEBERG, Kimberly 304-260-4380 542 G
klineberg@blueridgectc.edu

LINEBERGER, Marilyn 404-880-8049 127 C
mlineberger@cau.edu

LINEBERGER, Susanne, B 386-312-4050 116 F
susannelineberger@sjrstate.edu

LINEBURG, Robert 540-831-5228 523 A
rlineburg@radford.edu

LINEHAN, Rob 765-998-4905 180 B
rblinehan@taylor.edu

LINEHAN, Sarah, J 518-743-2263 355 D
linehans@sunyacc.edu

LINEMAN, Hope 814-676-6591 442 C
hlineman@clarion.edu

LINENBERG, Harry 215-591-5735 427 B
hlinenberg@devry.edu

LINER, Andrea, H 903-510-2405 503 A
alin2@tjc.edu

LINFANTE, Felix 973-877-2538 309 H
linfante@essex.edu

LINFANTE, Patrick 973-761-9328 315 B
patrick.linfante@shu.edu

LING, Jack, T 937-229-2541 404 A
jling1@udayton.edu

LINGEFELT, Jeff 803-938-3784 462 G
jdlingef@uscsumter.edu

LINGEN, BVM, Joan 563-588-6406 183 E
joan.lingen@clarke.edu

LINGENFELTER, Michelle 330-382-7415 393 F
mweekley@kent.edu

LINGENFELTER, Shelly 330-337-4267 393 H
mweekley@kent.edu

LINGER, Frederick, S 740-427-5250 394 C
lingerf@kenyon.edu

LINGER, JR., Jerry 859-371-9393 198 G
jlinger@beckfield.edu

LINGERFELT, Harley, W 405-878-5100 412 A
hwlingerfelt@stgregorys.edu

LINGLE, Ronald, K 910-938-6211 369 F
lingler@coastalcarolina.edu

LINGO, Melissa, L 386-763-2783 114 E
melissa.lingo@palmer.edu

LINGRELL, Scott 678-839-6423 139 A
slingrel@westga.edu

LINGUA, Jane 310-954-4132 57 H
jlingua@msmc.la.edu

LINHART, Lisa 303-762-6980 84 D
lisa.linhart@denverseminary.edu

LINHOST, Donald 314-977-2479 289 C
dcassens@slu.edu

LINIO, Richard 413-205-3502 229 G
richard.linio@aic.edu

LINIO, Rick 304-442-3104 545 D
rick.linio@mail.wvu.edu

LINK, Harvey 701-671-2112 382 G
harvey.link@ndscs.edu

LINK, Hilary 212-854-7517 323 E
hlink@barnard.edu

LINK, Johnson 864-656-7389 456 E
jwl@clemson.edu

LINK, Laura 612-874-3700 265 C
laura_link@mcad.edu

LINK, Lisa 616-222-1426 250 A
lisa.link@cornerstone.edu

LINK, Rebecca, C 717-815-1336 452 G
rlink@ycp.edu

LINK, Robert 419-434-4528 404 B
link@findlay.edu

LINK, Rosemary, J 515-961-1615 189 C
rosemary.link@simpson.edu

LINKINS, Arthur 903-334-6650 498 F
arthur.linkins@tamut.edu

LINKOFF, Debbie 440-449-1700 384 I
debbie.linkoff@atsinstitute.edu

LINN, Brent 901-375-4400 471 G
brentlinn@midsouthcc.org

LINN, Cindy 740-588-1547 400 E
linnc@ohio.edu

LINN, Jackie 785-826-2607 194 E
jdean@k-state.edu

LINN, Joseph, G 785-628-4222 192 I
jlinn@fhsu.edu

LINN, Reid, J 540-568-6131 520 H
linnrj@jmu.edu

LINN, Richard, T 716-827-4351 358 D
linnr@trocaire.edu

LINN, Timon 410-626-6931 225 G
timon.linn@sjca.edu

LINNANE, SJ, Brian, F 410-617-2201 223 I
president@loyola.edu

LINNE, Gil 860-628-4751 93 C
glinne@lincolncollegene.edu

LINNEBUR, Michael 316-942-4291 195 F
linneburm@newmanu.edu

LINNEHAN, JR., James, F 978-656-3151 240 B
linnehanj@middlesex.mass.edu

LINNELL, Allen 267-502-2798 423 C
allen.linnell@brynathyn.edu

LINNENBURGER, Jane, C 309-677-2515 146 C
jane@bradley.edu

LINNEVERS, David 831-582-3094 35 E
dlinnevers@csumb.edu

LINNEY, Jean, A 610-519-4606 450 H
jean.linney@villanova.edu

LINO, Paulette 510-723-2665 39 C
plino@chabotcollege.edu

LINOS, Megan, W 812-465-1061 181 B
mwlinos@usi.edu

LINRUD, JoAnn 701-858-3110 382 A
joann.linrud@minotstateu.edu

LINSCHEID, David 316-284-5251 191 C
dlin@bethelks.edu

LINSENBIGLER, John 865-573-4517 469 L
jlinsen@johnsonu.edu

LINSKY, Faith 603-283-2163 303 F
flinsky@antioch.edu

LINSON, Marci 417-690-2636 279 J
linson@cofo.edu

LINSON, Phil 323-856-7792 28 E
plinson@afi.com

LINTHICUM, David 410-287-6060 222 A
dlinthicum@cecil.edu

LINTHICUM, Glen 615-248-1243 476 G
glinthicum@trevecca.edu

LINTON, Leon, E 847-229-9595 164 G

LINTON, Meg 310-665-6907 60 B
mlinton@otis.edu

LINTON, Pamela 212-752-1530 338 C
pamela.linton@limcollege.edu

LINTON, Peggy 334-493-3573 5 F
plinton@lbwcc.edu

LINTS, Richard 978-468-7111 235 B
rlints@gcts.edu

LINZER, Daniel, I 847-491-5117 160 E
dlinzer@northwestern.edu

LINZEY, Scott 912-525-5100 136 F
slinzey@scad.edu

LINZMEYER, Kathryn 510-723-6751 39 C
klinzmeyer@chabotcollege.edu

LINZY, Nancy 314-513-4433 288 H
nlinzy@stlcc.edu

LIPAN, Petruta 314-977-3571 289 C
lipanp@slu.edu

LIPE, Leslie 503-338-2450 415 B
llipe@clatsopcc.edu

LIPHART, Jodi 904-826-0084 122 J
jliphart@usa.edu

LIPHART, Kristin 715-682-1496 549 F
kliphart@northland.edu

LIPIEC, Susan 216-373-5211 397 F
slipiec@ndc.edu

LIPINSKI, Barbara 805-962-8179 29 A
blipinski@antioch.edu

LIPINSKI, Marion, A 410-706-0025 227 C
mlipinski@umaryland.edu

LIPINSKI, Tomas, A 317-278-2376 174 D
tlipinsk@iupui.edu

LIPIRA, Pat 417-625-9394 286 B
lipira-p@mssu.edu

LIPKEY, Debra 202-651-5000 98 B
debra.lipkey@gallaudet.edu

LIPKIN, Michael 845-574-4466 347 I
mlipkin@sunyrockland.edu

LIPMAN, Howard 305-348-6298 119 C
howard.lipman@fiu.eduu

LIPMAN, Sheryl, H 901-678-2155 474 C
slipman@memphis.edu

LIPMAN, Steven 617-266-1400 231 E

LIPOLD, Tony 949-582-4547 70 F
tlipold@saddleback.edu

LIPORTO, Charles 603-513-1354 306 F
charles.liporto@granite.edu

LIPP, Dawn 317-554-8326 170 B
dlipp@brownmackie.edu

LIPP, Evan, E 508-767-7285 230 D
elipp@assumption.edu

LIPP, Jeanne 303-300-8740 81 L
jeanne.lipp@collegeamerica.com

LIPPARD, Rodney 704-216-3686 373 F
rodney.lippard@rccc.edu

LIPPARD, Rodney, U 252-399-6501 362 E
relippard@barton.edu

LIPPE, Karen, M 561-868-3735 114 D
lippek@palmbeachstate.edu

LIPPENS, Susan, M 419-866-0261 402 C
smlippens@stautzenberger.com

LIPPERT, Rebecca, M 215-887-5511 451 D
rlippert@wts.edu

LIPPERT, Wendy, S 717-766-2511 436 D
wlippert@messiah.edu

LIPPIELLO, Stephen 304-214-8809 543 D
slippiello@wvncc.edu

LIPPIN, Carol, A 732-987-2360 310 C
lippin@georgian.edu

LIPPINCOTT, Andi 315-279-5313 337 K
alippinc@keuka.edu

LIPPINCOTT, Doug 315-279-5641 337 K
dlippinc@mail.keuka.edu

LIPPMAN, Fred 954-262-1508 114 B
flippman@nsu.nova.edu

LIPPMAN, Stuart 212-463-0400 358 B
stuartl@touro.edu

LIPSCHUTZ, Ronnie 831-459-3275 75 C
rligsch@ucsc.edu

LIPSCOMB, Benjamin 585-567-9374 336 B
benjamin.lipscomb@houghton.edu

LIPSCOMB, Donnie 423-869-6353 470 E
donnie.lipscomb@lmunet.edu

LIPSCOMB, Natasha 704-216-3622 373 F
natasha.lipscomb@rccc.edu

LIPSCOMB, Sharyon 225-578-8833 212 G
slipsc1@lsu.edu

LIPSETT, Teresa 787-743-7979 565 H

LIPSHITZ, Rita 773-973-0241 152 A
lipshitz@htc.edu

LIPSKIER, Hershel 973-267-9404 313 B

LIPTAK, M. Victoria 818-767-0888 79 H
vic.liptak@woodbury.edu

LIPTON, Jeffrey 303-492-7523 88 H
lipton@colorado.edu

LIPTON, Jeffrey 631-656-2122 334 B
jlipton@ftc.edu

LIPTON, Mitchell 212-353-4121 331 A
lipton@cooper.edu

LIRA, Juan, R 956-326-2601 497 D
jlira@tamiu.edu

LIRA, Ken 760-776-7428 42 A
klira@collegeofthedesert.edu

LIRLEY, Sean 719-336-1543 86 B
sean.lirley@lamarcc.edu

LISBOA, Sandra 787-738-2161 567 D
sandra.lisboa@upr.edu

LISCHKA, Rosemary, L 913-288-7246 194 C
rlischka@kckcc.edu

LISENBY, Sadie 901-321-3527 467 I
slisenby@cbu.edu

LISI, Peter 860-768-2446 95 B
lisi@hartford.edu

LISK, III, Earl, B 419-372-0644 385 F
elisk@bgsu.edu

LISKO, Adele 816-941-0430 281 A
alisko@devry.edu

LISKOV, Barbara 617-253-5886 241 D

LISLE, Kristy 352-323-3630 112 J
lislek@lscc.edu

LISS, Donna 660-785-4163 290 G
dliss@truman.edu

LISS, Ron 505-428-1301 320 E
ron.liss@sfcc.edu

LIST, Kathleen, L 941-359-7587 116 B
klist@ringling.edu

LISTER, Basil, M 816-604-6748 285 A
basil.lister@mcckc.edu

LISTER, Carole, B 864-597-4230 463 G
listercb@wofford.edu

LISTER, Charlotte, T 302-857-1290 96 G
clister@dtcc.edu

LOCKE, Heidi 503-821-8972 419 D
hlocke@pnca.edu
LOCKE, Helen 949-451-5364 70 E
vlocke@ivc.edu
LOCKE, Jason, C 607-255-4099 331 B
jcl31@cornell.edu
LOCKE, Lisa 517-629-0206 247 A
llocke@albion.edu
LOCKE, Mamie, E 757-727-5400 519 H
mamie.locke@hamptonu.edu
LOCKE, Mary, G 772-462-4702 111 B
mlocke@irsc.edu
LOCKE, Pamela 559-438-4222 49 I
pamela_locke@heald.edu
LOCKERBY, Thomas, P 617-552-9076 232 B
thomas.lockerby@bc.edu
LOCKETT, JR., Eugene, D 301-985-7330 227 F
cfo@umuc.edu
LOCKETT, Nora 276-326-4237 516 L
nlockett@bluefield.edu
LOCKETT, Tina 724-266-3838 448 H
tlockett@tsm.edu
LOCKETT, Tom 217-224-0600 168 A
tom.lockett@vatterott-college.edu
LOCKHART, Anne, A 318-342-5426 216 E
lockhart@ulm.edu
LOCKHART, Elaine 828-726-2241 368 G
elockhart@cccti.edu
LOCKHART, Heidi 909-594-5611 58 A
hlockhart@mtsac.edu
LOCKHART, Janet 310-506-4301 61 H
janet.lockhart@pepperdine.edu
LOCKHART, Janet, M 915-831-2676 486 G
jlockha2@epcc.edu
LOCKHART, Kristin 612-624-0594 272 A
lockhart@umn.edu
LOCKHART, Marcella, F 615-256-1463 466 H
mlockhart@abcnash.edu
LOCKHART, Tom 651-255-6113 271 D
tlockhart@unitedseminary.edu
LOCKLEAR, Amy 409-933-8229 483 F
alocklear@com.edu
LOCKLEAR, William, L 910-272-3304 373 D
wlocklea@robeson.edu
LOCKLEAR, Zoe 910-775-4041 379 C
zoe.locklear@uncp.edu
LOCKREM, Michael 605-688-6161 466 C
michael.lockrem@sdstate.edu
LOCKRIDGE, Gail 641-683-5151 185 G
dlockrid@indianhills.edu
LOCKRIDGE, Jeanne 312-893-7140 151 A
jlockridge@erikson.edu
LOCKTON, Barry 559-453-2089 48 A
bhl@fresno.edu
LOCKWARD, Ana, C 516-678-5000 341 F
alockward@molloy.edu
LOCKWOOD, Catherine 312-935-6640 162 G
clockwood@robertmorris.edu
LOCKWOOD, Charles, J 614-292-2600 398 I
lockwood.59@osu.edu
LOCKWOOD, Daniel, R 503-255-0332 417 C
dlockwood@multnomah.edu
LOCKWOOD, Lawrence, J 319-335-0217 182 F
larry-lockwood@uiowa.edu
LOCKWOOD, Susan 334-291-4975 2 F
susan.lockwood@cv.edu
LOCOCO, Nina 406-447-4388 293 G
nlococo@carroll.edu
LOCURTO, Chuck 401-232-6196 453 C
clocurto@bryant.edu
LOCUST, JR., Jonathan, E 419-207-5504 384 G
jlocust@ashland.edu
LOCUST, Wayne 860-486-1463 94 G
wayne.locust@uconn.edu
LODDER, Diane, E 919-866-5198 374 H
delodder@waketech.edu
LODGE, Danielle 478-757-5205 139 E
dlodge@wesleyancollege.edu
LODGE, Danielle 478-757-5180 139 E
dlodge@wesleyancollege.edu
LODGE, Helen 417-667-8181 280 E
hlodge@cottey.edu
LODGE, John, G 847-566-6401 167 F
jlodge@usml.edu
LODOVICO, John 860-255-3420 92 F
jlodovico@txcc.commnet.edu
LOE, Meika 315-228-7546 329 G
mloe@colgate.edu
LOEB, Elizabeth, C 870-633-4480 21 F
eloeb@eacc.edu
LOEB, Mara, C 318-342-3678 216 E
loeb@ulm.edu
LOEDING, David 808-934-2705 142 A
loeding@hawaii.edu
LOEFFEL, Linda, L 414-443-8842 553 D
linda.loeffel@wlc.edu
LOEFFELHOLZ, Mary 617-373-4774 243 F
LOEHER, Larry, L 310-825-9149 74 C
lloeher@ucla.edu
LOEHFELM, Courtney 303-797-5914 81 D
courtney.loehfelm@arapahoe.edu
LOEHRING, Michael 208-885-6163 144 G
loehring@uidaho.edu
LOENDOWSKI, Ken 814-944-5643 452 I

LOERA, Daniel, L 909-593-3511 75 E
dloera@laverne.edu
LOERS, Deborah, L 319-352-8745 189 J
deb.loers@wartburg.edu
LOESCH, Richard 847-578-3225 163 C
rick.loesch@rosalindfranklin.edu
LOESCHER-JUNGE, Lou 913-588-5278 197 C
ljunge@kumc.edu
LOESCHKE, Maravene, S 410-704-2356 228 E
presidentsoffice@towson.edu
LOESER, Diane 614-236-6159 386 E
dloeser@capital.edu
LOESSBERG-ZAHL, Robert, J 530-304-8847 73 I
rjloessb@ucdavis.edu
LOESSIN, Bruce, A 216-368-4352 386 F
bruce.loessin@case.edu
LOETTERLE, Jon 402-461-7424 298 A
jloetterle@hastings.edu
LOETZ, Devon 443-627-7511 272 C
devon.loetz@laureate.net
LOEWEN, Carrie 503-847-2557 421 A
cloewen@uws.edu
LOEWEN, Howard, J 626-584-5304 48 B
hloewen@fuller.edu
LOEWEN, Steve 620-343-4600 192 H
sloewen@fhtc.edu
LOEWENSTEIN, Gaither 562-938-4127 54 E
gloewenstein@lbcc.edu
LOEWENSTEIN, Karna 712-325-3400 186 F
kloewenstein@iwcc.edu
LOEWY, Michael 415-955-2149 27 F
mloewy@alliant.edu
LOF, Gregory 617-724-6313 242 B
glof@mghihp.edu
LOFFLER, Alicia 847-491-4647 160 E
a-loffler@kellogg.northwestern.edu
LOFFREDO, Deborah 518-580-5790 351 B
dloffredo@skidmore.edu
LOFFREDO, Joe 585-475-2829 347 G
jjlrgr@rit.edu
LOFFREDO, Vince 913-588-4698 197 C
vloffredo@kumc.edu
LOFGREN, Richard 859-323-5220 207 D
lofgren@uky.edu
LOFLAND, Jessica 580-349-1362 410 B
jlofland@opsu.edu
LOFLIN, Gene 828-398-7240 368 B
williamgloflin@abtech.edu
LOFQUIST, Vicki 651-795-1810 267 A
vicki.lofquist@metrostate.edu
LOFSTEAD, Rebecca, B 304-293-9358 545 A
becky.lofstead@mail.wvu.edu
LOFT, Jan 507-537-6218 269 E
jan.loft@smsu.edu
LOFTHOUSE, David, R 951-785-2938 53 E
dlofthou@lasierra.edu
LOFTIN, Lynn 580-559-5252 407 J
lloftin@ecok.edu
LOFTIN, R. Bowen 979-845-2217 497 E
president@tamu.edu
LOFTON, Antwan 202-806-6077 98 E
antwan.lofton@howard.edu
LOFTUS, Bill 863-638-2941 123 E
loftuswj@webber.edu
LOFTUS, Edna, A 910-277-5256 376 C
eaol@sapc.edu
LOFTUS, Edward, J 570-577-1458 423 E
edward.loftus@bucknell.edu
LOFTUS, James, P 414-410-4003 546 G
jploftus@stritch.edu
LOFTUS, Kate 262-472-1392 553 A
loftusk@uww.edu
LOFTUS, Marie 718-933-6700 341 G
mloftus@monroecollege.edu
LOFTUS, Robert 508-929-8017 238 G
frrob@worcester.edu
LOFTUS, Roger 507-786-3068 271 C
loftus@stolaf.edu
LOFTUS-BERLIN, Eileen 973-278-5400 323 H
eml@berkeleycollege.edu
LOGAN, Barry 207-725-3290 217 E
blogan@bowdoin.edu
LOGAN, Bert 971-722-4490 419 G
bert.logan@pcc.edu
LOGAN, David, A 401-254-4509 454 C
dlogan@law.rwu.edu
LOGAN, Elaine 313-593-5400 259 B
loganem@umd.umich.edu
LOGAN, Erin 405-682-7821 409 F
elogan@occc.edu
LOGAN, Ethan 806-742-1480 502 A
ethan.logan@ttu.edu
LOGAN, Gary 210-999-7306 502 E
glogan@trinity.edu
LOGAN, Irene, F 804-524-5902 529 H
ilogan@vsu.edu
LOGAN, Linda 269-749-6669 257 A
llogan@olivetcollege.edu
LOGAN, Lori 817-531-6571 502 C
llogan@txwes.edu
LOGAN, Mark 562-860-2451 39 A
mlogan@cerritos.edu
LOGAN, Mike 712-274-6400 190 B
mike.logan@witcc.edu

LOGAN, Renita, G 910-938-6145 369 F
loganr@coastalcarolina.edu
LOGAN, Robin 210-829-3933 504 B
rlogan@uiwtx.edu
LOGAN, Ruth 585-594-6260 347 F
loganr@roberts.edu
LOGAN, Sarah 325-942-2259 480 E
sarah.logan@angelo.edu
LOGAN, Shannon 212-229-5687 342 E
logans@newschool.edu
LOGAN, Steve 214-768-2422 495 A
loganse@smu.edu
LOGAN, Timothy, M 254-710-6665 482 A
tim_logan@baylor.edu
LOGAN, Tonya 740-264-5591 390 F
tlogan@egcc.edu
LOGAN, Traci, A 781-891-3472 231 D
tlogan@bentley.edu
LOGAN, Vanessa 602-243-8046 16 D
vanessa.logan@smcmail.maricopa.edu
LOGAN-BENNETT, Lorie 410-704-2386 228 E
lloganbennett@towson.edu
LOGEL, Mark, J 812-488-2941 180 E
ml44@evansville.edu
LOGGAN, Todd 503-251-2836 421 A
tloggan@uws.edu
LOGGINS, Jeff 662-254-3325 276 B
jloggins@mvsu.edu
LOGGINS, Penny 706-778-8500 136 A
ploggins@piedmont.edu
LOGIE, Bryan 912-201-6021 137 D
blogie@southuniversity.edu
LOGSDON, Michael 301-387-3333 222 H
michael.logsdon@garrettcollege.edu
LOGSDON, Paul 417-865-2811 281 G
logsdonp@evangel.edu
LOGSDON, Paul, M 419-772-2180 398 H
p-logsdon@onu.edu
LOGSDON, Penelope 270-706-8649 202 A
penelope.logsdon@kctcs.edu
LOGSDON-CONRADSEN, Susan 706-236-5494 126 C
sconradsen@berry.edu
LOGSTON, Susan, E 203-285-2187 91 D
slogston@gwcc.commnet.edu
LOGUE, Alexandra 212-794-5414 326 B
academicaffairs@mail.cuny.edu
LOGUE, Christin 423-614-8415 470 C
clogue@leeuniversity.edu
LOGUE, Mary 805-565-6251 79 A
mlogue@westmont.edu
LOGUE, Rose, M 814-393-2223 442 B
rlogue@clarion.edu
LOGUE, Susan 618-536-5535 165 B
slogue@siu.edu
LOH, Wallace, D 301-405-1000 227 B
wdloh@umd.edu
LOHDEN, Bethany, L 636-584-6503 281 E
lohdenb@eastcentral.edu
LOHIDE, Kurtis, D 707-654-1000 33 C
klohide@csum.edu
LOHMANN, Steven, L 580-327-8406 409 C
sllohmann@nwosu.edu
LOHR, Joel 209-946-2325 76 A
jlohr@pacific.edu
LOHRENZ, Steven 508-910-6353 237 A
slohrenz@umassd.edu
LOHRI-POSEY, Brenda 740-695-9500 385 B
bposey@belmontcollege.edu
LOHRMEYER, Robert 208-792-2225 144 B
rlohrmey@lcsc.edu
LOHSANDT, Marie, A 605-256-5122 465 I
marie.lohsandt@dsu.edu
LOHSE, MaryPat 617-349-8669 236 B
mlohse@lesley.edu
LOHSTROH, Tracy 618-634-3203 164 E
tracyl@shawneecc.edu
LOILAND, Cheri 253-680-7206 531 F
cloiland@bates.ctc.edu
LOILAND, Sharon 701-777-3178 381 F
sharon.loiland@und.edu
LOISEAU, Marvin 617-588-1337 231 C
mloiseau@bfit.edu
LOISELLE, Helene 407-582-1701 123 B
hloiselle@valenciacollege.edu
LOIZZO, Joseph, A 740-284-7217 391 A
jloizzo@franciscan.edu
LOJKO, Frank 435-652-7511 512 B
lojko@dixie.edu
LOKEY, Cheryl, P 318-323-2889 208 G
cheryl.lokey@careertc.edu
LOKEY, Pat 480-423-6653 16 C
pat.lokey@scottsdalecc.edu
LOKKEN, Jay, M 608-785-8017 551 C
jlokken@uwlax.edu
LOKKEN, Pamela, S 314-935-5752 292 I
lokken@wustl.edu
LOKMAN, Lawrence, H 310-825-9045 74 C
llokman@support.ucla.edu
LOKUTA, Sharon 260-422-5561 173 C
slokuta@indianatech.edu
LOLATTE, Richard, J 203-773-8501 90 C
rjlolatte@albertus.edu
LOLLAR, Cay 662-862-8032 274 E
cllollar@iccms.edu

LOMANTO, Susan, M 973-972-5332 316 E
lomanto@umdnj.edu
LOMAS, Mark 704-499-9200 99 G
LOMAX, Terri, L 919-515-2117 378 C
terri_lomax@ncsu.edu
LOMBARD, Amy 724-938-4418 441 G
lombard@calu.edu
LOMBARD, Anne, E 315-470-6658 355 A
aelombard@esf.edu
LOMBARD, Gary, A 405-682-7810 409 F
glombard@occc.edu
LOMBARD, J. Anthony 423-478-7716 472 H
alombard@ptseminary.edu
LOMBARD, Karen, L 515-574-1140 185 I
lombard@iowacentral.edu
LOMBARDI, George, J 203-371-7989 94 B
lombardig@sacredheart.edu
LOMBARDI, Mark 314-529-9330 284 C
president@maryville.edu
LOMBARDI, Phillip 401-232-6374 453 C
plombard@bryant.edu
LOMBARDI, Ryan 740-593-2561 399 G
lombardi@ohio.edu
LOMBARDO, Joann 860-486-5519 94 G
joann.lombardo@uconn.edu
LOMBARDO, John 631-851-6225 356 D
lombarj@sunysuffolk.edu
LOMBARDO, Michael 503-777-7542 420 A
lombardm@reed.edu
LOMBARDO, Pam 805-893-2040 75 B
pam.lombardo@ehs.ucsb.edu
LOMBARDO, Roberto 386-506-3159 104 F
lombarr@daytonastate.edu
LOMBARDO, Tony 225-578-5603 212 H
lombardo@lsu.edu
LOMBELLA, James 860-253-3048 91 B
jlombella@asnuntuck.edu
LOMELI, Cristina 818-386-5608 62 F
clomeli@pgi.edu
LOMELINO, Josh 615-794-4254 472 F
jlomelino@omorecollege.edu
LOMENA, Sandra 305-821-3333 109 B
slomena@mm.fnc.edu
LOMETTI, Guy 718-405-3343 330 A
guy.lometti@mountsaintvincent.edu
LOMONACO, Barbara 859-233-8215 207 A
blomonaco@transy.edu
LONABOCKER, Louise, M 617-552-3300 232 B
louise.lonabocker@bc.edu
LONDA, Ivan 212-962-0002 342 G
ilonda@nyci.edu
LONDON, Howard 508-531-1295 237 D
hlondon@bridgew.edu
LONDON, Manuel 631-632-8304 352 C
manuel.london@stonybrook.edu
LONDON, Michael 415-422-4400 76 E
melondon@usfca.edu
LONDON-JONES, Emily 504-520-7517 217 A
LONE HILL, Karen 605-455-6100 465 A
klonehill@olc.edu
LONEKER, Ronald 973-290-4235 308 G
rloneker@cse.edu
LONERGAN, Dennis 718-862-7349 339 H
dennis.lonergan@manhattan.edu
LONERGAN, Joel, C 256-824-6414 8 G
joel.lonergan@uah.edu
LONERGAN, Penny 913-758-6111 197 D
longergan@stmary.edu
LONERGAN, Peter, E 716-880-2177 340 D
peter.e.lonergan@medaille.edu
LONERGAN, Thomas 616-698-7111 250 C
tlongeran1@davenport.edu
LONEY, Carl, E 937-327-7307 406 B
cloney@wittenberg.edu
LONEY, Teresa, A 816-604-1517 284 H
teresa.loney@mcckc.edu
LONG, Amanda 813-621-0041 106 C
along@cci.edu
LONG, Andrew 970-521-6652 86 K
andrew.long@njc.edu
LONG, Andrew 360-992-2505 532 F
along@clark.edu
LONG, Antonio 404-756-4477 125 D
along@atlm.edu
LONG, Aubrey, E 386-481-2800 102 C
longa@cookman.edu
LONG, Bobbie 972-548-6866 483 H
blong@collin.edu
LONG, Brenda, J 252-222-6151 369 A
bjl@carteret.edu
LONG, Brittney 402-399-2454 297 C
blong@csm.edu
LONG, C. Adam 864-488-4583 459 B
along@limestone.edu
LONG, Carol, S 585-245-5531 353 C
long@geneseo.edu
LONG, Carolyn 304-442-3060 545 D
carolyn.long@mail.wvu.edu
LONG, Carrilyn 330-494-6170 402 B
clong@starkstate.edu
LONG, Catherine, E 607-255-2946 331 B
cel3@cornell.edu
LONG, Charla 615-966-2501 470 F
charla.long@lipscomb.edu

LORD, Patty, R .... 818-677-3776 ..... 35 F patty.lord@csun.edu
LORD, Resa .... 334-214-4843 .... 2 F resa.lord@cv.edu
LORDAN, John, J .... 718-817-3120 .... 334 C lordan@fordham.edu
LORDEN, Joan, F .... 704-687-5962 .... 379 A jflorden@uncc.edu
LORE, Peggy .... 303-352-3520 ..... 88 J peggy.lore@ucdenver.edu
LOREEN, Susan .... 425-640-1489 .... 533 I s.loreen@edcc.edu
LORENSON, James, A .... 906-932-4231 .... 251 C
LORENTZ, Gerald, F .... 518-783-6203 .... 355 G gerald.lorentz@esc.edu
LORENZ, Chuck .... 610-527-0200 .... 445 J clorenz@rosemont.edu
LORENZ, Georgia .... 310-434-4277 ..... 68 D lorenz_georgia@smc.edu
LORENZ, Gina .... 425-352-8880 .... 532 B glorenz@cascadia.edu
LORENZ, Heather .... 603-668-2211 .... 305 I h.lorenz@snhu.edu
LORENZ, Tracy .... 602-429-1198 ..... 19 B tracy.lorenz@west.edu
LORENZANA, Ruth, G .... 818-767-0888 ..... 79 H ruth.lorenzana@woodbury.edu
LORENZE, Gregory, F .... 303-256-9322 ..... 85 L glorenz@jwu.edu
LORENZEN, Zac .... 402-572-8500 .... 298 D zlorenzen@kaplan.edu
LORENZET, Steven, J .... 609-896-5152 .... 313 F slorenzet@rider.edu
LORENZETTI, Jennifer .... 937-294-0592 .... 401 H jennifer@saa.edu
LORENZO, Jerilyn .... 808-734-9899 .... 141 J jilorenz@hawaii.edu
LORENZO, JR., Joseph .... 303-797-5711 ..... 81 D joe.lorenzo@arapahoe.edu
LORENZO, Lorisa .... 727-864-7810 .... 105 E lorenzll@eckerd.edu
LORIA, Annette .... 909-594-5611 ..... 58 A aloria@mtsac.edu
LORIA, Sal .... 713-743-9092 .... 503 D sloria@uh.edu
LORIG, Beverly, T .... 540-458-8595 .... 530 D blorig@wlu.edu
LORIMER, David, W .... 606-693-5000 .... 203 F dlorimer@kmbc.edu
LORIMER, Linda, K .... 203-432-2321 ..... 96 A linda.lorimer@yale.edu
LORIMER, Stephen, A .... 606-693-5000 .... 203 F slorimer@kmbc.edu
LORIMER, Susan, L .... 916-568-3031 ..... 55 J lorimes@losrios.edu
LORIMER, Thomas, H .... 606-693-5000 .... 203 F tlorimer@kmbc.edu
LORING, Christopher .... 413-585-2902 .... 244 G cloring@smith.edu
LORINO, Anthony, P .... 504-862-8698 .... 215 C alorino@tulane.edu
LORION, Raymond .... 410-704-2571 .... 228 E rlorion@towson.edu
LORTON-ROWLAND, Julie 317-921-4715 .... 175 I jlorton@ivytech.edu
LORTZ, Peter .... 206-934-3746 .... 537 D peter.lortz@seattlecolleges.edu
LORUSSO, Dominick, P .... 610-989-1491 .... 450 F dlorusso@vfmac.edu
LOSCAR, Angelique .... 415-476-8039 ..... 75 A angelique.loscar@ucsf.edu
LOSCHEIDER, Paul, H .... 630-637-5678 .... 159 G phloscheider@noctrl.edu
LOSCHIAVO, Sharon .... 352-395-5763 .... 117 F sharon.loschiavo@sfcollege.edu
LOSEY, Teri, L .... 616-331-2100 .... 251 F loseyt@gvsu.edu
LOSHIN, David .... 954-262-1404 .... 114 B loshin@nsu.nova.edu
LOSINGER, Regina .... 607-778-5040 .... 324 G losingerr@sunybroome.edu
LOSS, Amy .... 618-842-3711 .... 152 G lossa@iecc.edu
LOSS, Jeffrey, W .... 570-577-1911 .... 423 E jeffrey.loss@bucknell.edu
LOSSING, David, E .... 810-766-6647 .... 259 C dalossin@umflint.edu
LOSTETTER, Ron .... 262-524-7200 .... 546 H rlosett@carrollu.edu
LOSTRACCO, Joe, M .... 512-223-7607 .... 481 B lostracc@austincc.edu
LOTFI, Vahid .... 810-762-3171 .... 259 C vahid@umflint.edu
LOTFI, Vahid .... 810-762-3164 .... 259 C vahid@umflint.edu
LOTH, Karen, M .... 616-331-6000 .... 251 F lothk@gvsu.edu
LOTHAMER, Mary Ellen .... 615-383-4848 .... 478 F mlothamer@watkins.edu
LOTHRINGER, Bobby .... 940-898-3036 .... 502 D rlothringer@twu.edu
LOTHRINGER, Rebecca .... 940-565-3793 .... 504 D rebecca.lothringer@unt.edu
LOTHROP, Mary .... 802-654-0524 .... 515 E mary.lothrop@ccv.edu
LOTITO, Tom .... 757-493-6000 ..... 99 G
LOTRIONTE, John, D .... 901-321-3550 .... 467 I jlotrion@cbu.edu
LOTT, Elizabeth, S .... 570-208-5991 .... 432 G eslott@kings.edu
LOTT, Lois .... 216-707-8130 .... 394 B llott@kent.edu
LOTT, Patricia, D .... 850-474-3419 .... 121 D plott@uwf.edu
LOTT, Vicki, V .... 512-505-3076 .... 488 D vvlott@htu.edu
LOTT, Wayne, J .... 801-422-4147 .... 509 H wayne_lott@byu.edu
LOTTER, Dorothea, J .... 417-268-1000 .... 278 H dlotter@agts.edu
LOTTI, Jemina, C .... 918-595-7866 .... 412 H jlotti@tulsacc.edu
LOTVEN, Ann, C .... 662-846-4010 .... 273 H alotven@deltastate.edu
LOU, Gary .... 808-853-1040 .... 141 C garyl@pacrim.edu
LOU, Kris .... 503-370-5328 .... 421 D klou@willamette.edu
LOUALLEN, Cheryl .... 937-382-6661 .... 405 I cheryl_louallen@wilmington.edu
LOUCHE, Suzee, S .... 321-674-8099 .... 108 H slouche@fit.edu
LOUCHOUARN, Patrick .... 409-740-4710 .... 497 F louchoup@tamug.edu
LOUCKS, Bill .... 573-592-5289 .... 293 B bill.loucks@westminster-mo.edu
LOUCKS, C. Melvin .... 626-448-0023 ..... 51 G president@itsla.edu
LOUCY, Brian, M .... 315-445-4174 .... 338 B loucyb@lemoyne.edu
LOUDEN, Sandy .... 731-352-4095 .... 467 E loudens@bethelu.edu
LOUDEN, William, F .... 812-488-2376 .... 180 E bl9@evansville.edu
LOUDEN-HANES, Marie, A .... 419-434-4504 .... 404 B louden-hanes@findlay.edu
LOUDENSLAGER, Anne .... 570-662-4809 .... 443 C aloudens@mansfield.edu
LOUDER, Corey .... 660-626-2203 .... 278 D clouder@atsu.edu
LOUDERBACK, Joseph .... 732-729-3822 .... 309 C jlouderback@devry.edu
LOUDIN, Rose Ellen .... 304-473-8600 .... 545 G loudin_r@wvwc.edu
LOUDON, Tina .... 360-650-3240 .... 539 F tina.loudon@wwu.edu
LOUGEE, Wendy, P .... 612-624-1807 .... 272 A wlougee@umn.edu
LOUGHERY, James, F .... 215-968-8041 .... 423 F loughery@bucks.edu
LOUGHLEY, Heather .... 614-433-0095 ..... 19 A heather.loughley@phoenix.edu
LOUGHLIN, Monica .... 504-520-7400 .... 217 A mloughli@xula.edu
LOUGHMAN, Ann .... 518-262-5435 .... 322 D loughma@mail.amc.edu
LOUGHRAN, Kristine .... 513-732-5218 .... 403 E loughrke@ucmail.uc.edu
LOUGHRAN, Sean .... 203-837-9330 ..... 91 A loughrans@wcsu.edu
LOUIE, Irwin, K .... 818-779-8423 ..... 53 B ilouie@kingsuniversity.edu
LOUIE, Larry .... 415-869-2900 .... 235 G larry.louie@hult.edu
LOUIE, Sharon .... 949-451-5226 ..... 70 E slouie@ivc.edu
LOUIS, Michael, A .... 314-505-7301 .... 280 D louism@csl.edu
LOUIS, Murielle .... 212-226-7300 .... 346 E mlouis@pbcny.edu
LOUMA, David, M .... 906-227-2355 .... 256 C daluoma@nmu.edu
LOUNSBERRY, Gary .... 973-803-5000 .... 315 D glounsberry@somerset.edu
LOUREIRO, Rita, D .... 561-237-7035 .... 113 D rloureiro@lynn.edu
LOURO, Jeffrey .... 508-999-8171 .... 237 A jlouro@umassd.edu
LOUSTAUNAU, Jeffrey .... 207-326-2251 .... 219 D j.loustaunau@mma.edu
LOUTH, Richard .... 212-998-2118 .... 344 B richard.louth@nyu.edu
LOUTHERBACK, George .... 254-295-4698 .... 504 C gloutherback@umhb.edu
LOUTTIT, Julianne, E .... 724-287-8711 .... 423 G julianne.louttit@bc3.edu
LOUWAGIE, Vincent .... 210-349-9928 .... 491 G vince.louwagie@ost.edu
LOVALLO, Charles, G .... 973-877-3400 .... 309 H lovallo@essex.edu
LOVATO, Barbara .... 505-925-8991 .... 321 G bllovato@unm.edu
LOVATO, Mildred, P .... 575-461-4413 .... 318 G mildredl@mesalands.edu
LOVE, Anne .... 718-420-4212 .... 360 A alove@wagner.edu
LOVE, Arlyn .... 541-962-3496 .... 418 C alove@eou.edu
LOVE, Charles .... 864-503-5577 .... 463 B clove@uscupstate.edu
LOVE, David .... 814-393-2334 .... 442 B dlove@clarion.edu
LOVE, Deborah, A .... 757-221-1306 .... 518 A dalove@wm.edu
LOVE, Deborah, E .... 504-862-8083 .... 215 C dlove1@tulane.edu
LOVE, Hannah .... 325-236-8277 .... 500 G hannah.love@tstc.edu
LOVE, Jamica .... 617-731-7195 .... 243 G jlove@pmc.edu
LOVE, Jan .... 404-727-6324 .... 129 D jlove3@emory.edu
LOVE, Jane .... 864-294-2248 .... 458 E jane.love@furman.edu
LOVE, Jeffrey, M .... 248-340-0600 .... 247 I love@baker.edu
LOVE, Julie, N .... 970-247-7503 ..... 84 K studenthousing@fortlewis.edu
LOVE, Kathryn .... 239-687-5430 .... 101 H klove@avemarialaw.edu
LOVE, Kathy, S .... 912-443-3024 .... 136 H klove@savannahtech.edu
LOVE, Kensey .... 740-753-7007 .... 391 H love_k@hocking.edu
LOVE, Louise .... 312-369-7495 .... 148 D llove@colum.edu
LOVE, Nyassa .... 510-885-2743 ..... 34 E nyassa.love@csueastbay.edu
LOVE, Patty .... 970-943-7052 ..... 89 E plove@western.edu
LOVE, Peter .... 860-701-5071 ..... 93 E love_p@mitchell.edu
LOVE, Robert .... 417-862-9533 .... 282 A rlove@globaluniversity.edu
LOVE, Ronald .... 662-254-3624 .... 276 B rlove@mvsu.edu
LOVE, Tommy .... 503-838-8281 .... 419 C lovet@wou.edu
LOVE, Tony .... 432-552-2633 .... 507 D love_t@utpb.edu
LOVEDAY, Joyce .... 253-589-4333 .... 532 G joyce.loveday@cptc.edu
LOVELACE, Betty, M .... 614-236-6611 .... 386 E blovelac@capital.edu
LOVELACE, Diane .... 215-641-6584 .... 436 G dlovelac@mc3.edu
LOVELACE, Everett .... 209-384-6192 ..... 57 C everett.lovelace@mccd.edu
LOVELACE, Rhonda .... 501-370-5297 ..... 23 B rlovelace@philander.edu
LOVELADY, III, Artis .... 832-252-4617 .... 483 C artis@cbshouston.edu
LOVELAND, David, A .... 607-746-4013 .... 355 F lovelada@delhi.edu
LOVELESS, Cecelia .... 360-596-5204 .... 538 E cloveless@spscc.ctc.edu
LOVELESS, Cindy .... 940-397-4241 .... 491 B cindy.loveless@mwsu.edu
LOVELESS, Elizabeth, B .... 563-333-6271 .... 188 F lovelesselizabethb@sau.edu
LOVELESS, Shelly .... 406-247-3000 .... 295 F sloveless@msubillings.edu
LOVELIDGE, Robert .... 979-830-4194 .... 482 C rlovelidge@blinn.edu
LOVELIS, Buffy .... 580-559-5651 .... 407 J blovelis@ecok.edu
LOVELL, Ava .... 505-277-5111 .... 321 C alovell@salud.unm.edu
LOVELL, Ellen .... 719-336-1541 ..... 86 B library@lamarcc.edu
LOVELL, Ellen, M .... 802-258-9245 .... 513 H emlovell@marlboro.edu
LOVELL, JR., Ernest, L .... 601-403-1183 .... 276 E elovell@prcc.edu
LOVELL, Michael, R .... 414-229-4331 .... 551 D mlovell@uwm.edu
LOVELL, Rebecca .... 225-359-9235 .... 209 J rlovell@catc.edu
LOVELL, Sharon .... 540-568-2705 .... 520 H lovellse@jmu.edu
LOVELL, Susan .... 706-562-1681 .... 127 G lovell_susan@columbusstate.edu
LOVELL, Susan .... 212-472-1500 .... 343 G slovell@nysid.edu
LOVELY, Christine, D .... 916-278-6078 ..... 36 A clovely@csus.edu
LOVELY-WATSON, Henryett .... 903-923-2429 .... 509 E hlovely-watson@wileyc.edu
LOVERIDGE, Robert .... 801-863-8161 .... 511 F loveriro@uvu.edu
LOVERING, James .... 802-387-6795 .... 513 G jlovering@landmark.edu
LOVETT, Christopher, M .... 814-886-6400 .... 437 B clovett@mtaloy.edu
LOVETT, David, L .... 717-477-1164 .... 443 E dllove@ship.edu
LOVETT, Leslie .... 304-367-4786 .... 543 B leslie.lovett@pierpont.edu
LOVETT, Michael .... 256-215-4247 .... 2 E mlovett@cacc.edu
LOVETT, Rod, M .... 217-351-2409 .... 161 C rlovett@parkland.edu
LOVICK, Reed .... 252-527-6223 .... 371 G rlovick@lenoircc.edu
LOVIG, Kristin .... 641-269-4974 .... 185 D lovigkk@grinnell.edu
LOVIK, Eric .... 252-335-0821 .... 369 G eric_lovik@albemarle.edu
LOVIN, Eddie .... 615-547-1231 .... 468 B elovin@cumberland.edu
LOVINCE, Thomas .... 504-671-5627 .... 210 F tlovin@dcc.edu
LOVING, Julie .... 434-832-7630 .... 526 E lovingj@cvcc.vccs.edu
LOVINGOOD, Deborah, F .. 630-466-7900 .... 168 B dlovingood@waubonsee.edu
LOVINGOOD, Linda .... 828-835-4242 .... 374 F llovingood@tricountycc.edu
LOVINS, Darrell .... 601-318-6610 .... 278 C dlovins@wmcarey.edu
LOVINS, Greg, M .... 828-262-2030 .... 377 D lovinsgm@appstate.edu
LOVINS, Sandy .... 813-974-8063 .... 121 A slovins@usf.edu
LOVITT, Carl, R .... 860-832-2228 ..... 90 G lovittcar@ccsu.edu
LOVSTUEN, Brenda, C .... 319-895-4292 .... 183 G blovstuen@cornellcollege.edu
LOVVORN, Judi .... 229-217-4163 .... 134 F jlovvorn@moultrietech.edu
LOW, Beverly .... 315-228-7368 .... 329 G balow@colgate.edu
LOW, Catherine Yu-Ling .... 808-371-5443 .... 141 B cfo@orientalmedicine.edu
LOW, Douglas .... 812-749-1298 .... 178 H dlow@oak.edu
LOW, Joanne .... 415-561-1850 ..... 40 C jlow@ccsf.edu
LOW, Kathryn, G .... 207-786-6066 .... 217 C klow@bates.edu
LOW, Ryan .... 207-623-3344 .... 219 I ryan.low@maine.edu
LOW, Wai Hoa .... 808-521-2288 .... 141 B whlow@orientalmedicine.edu
LOW-HOGAN, Nancy .... 973-761-9000 .... 315 B nancy.lowhogan@shu.edu
LOWBRIDGE, John .... 270-824-1835 .... 202 G john.lowbridge@kctcs.edu
LOWDEN, Paul .... 616-732-1194 .... 250 C plowden@davenport.edu
LOWDENBACK, Roy .... 502-863-8044 .... 201 A roy_lowdenback@georgetowncollege.edu
LOWDER, Diane, M .... 804-752-7218 .... 523 C dianelowder@rmc.edu
LOWDERMILK, Robert, S .. 336-342-4261 .... 373 E lowdermilkr@rockinghamcc.edu
LOWE, Adam .... 423-478-6206 .... 474 E alowe04@clevelandstatecc.edu
LOWE, Brenda .... 806-720-7307 .... 490 F brenda.lowe@lcu.edu
LOWE, Byron .... 662-254-3600 .... 276 B blowe@mvsu.edu
LOWE, Carmen .... 617-627-4239 .... 245 C carmen.lowe@tufts.edu
LOWE, Carrie, B .... 865-573-4517 .... 469 L cblowe@johnsonu.edu
LOWE, Charles .... 561-297-3500 .... 119 A clowe@fau.edu
LOWE, Ellen .... 760-591-3012 .... 122 J elowe@usa.edu
LOWE, JR., Eugene, Y .... 847-491-5255 .... 160 E eyljr@northwestern.edu
LOWE, Flora .... 563-242-4023 .... 182 C flora.lowe@ashford.edu
LOWE, JR., James .... 251-405-7130 .... 2 C jlowe@bishop.edu
LOWE, Janet, S .... 307-766-3307 .... 556 H jlowe@uwyo.edu
LOWE, John .... 912-525-4895 .... 136 F jlowe@scad.edu
LOWE, Judy .... 423-697-2686 .... 474 D
LOWE, Kathy .... 205-665-6100 .... 9 B lowek@montevallo.edu
LOWE, Kathy .... 707-638-5806 ..... 73 A kathy.lowe@tu.edu
LOWE, Kayarda .... 334-872-2533 .... 6 H
LOWE, Keri .... 616-988-1000 .... 249 F
LOWE, Mark, S .... 701-483-2328 .... 381 G mark.lowe@dickinsonstate.edu
LOWE, Melissa .... 502-585-9911 .... 206 D mlowe@spalding.edu
LOWE, Myra .... 304-293-0305 .... 545 A mlowe@mail.wvu.edu
LOWE, OFM, Philip, J .... 610-358-4241 .... 437 D lowep@neumann.edu
LOWE, Rick, D .... 910-630-7027 .... 367 B rlowe@methodist.edu
LOWE, Robt, S .... 630-844-5290 .... 145 F slowe@aurora.edu
LOWE, Sharon .... 772-462-7476 .... 111 B slowe@irsc.edu
LOWE, Stephen, H .... 864-427-3681 .... 463 A lowesh@mailbox.sc.edu
LOWE, Steve, D .... 864-379-8779 .... 458 A

LUGERING, Charlotte 800-523-1578 122 C
clugering@teu.edu
LUGG, Linda, L 603-513-5101 306 E
linda.lugg@law.unh.edu
LUGG, Thomas, W 610-359-5336 426 G
tlugg@dccc.edu
LUGO, Daniel, G 717-291-3953 429 F
daniel.lugo@fandm.edu
LUGO, Efrain 787-620-2040 560 D
elugo@aupr.edu
LUGO, Eric 646-660-6095 326 C
eric.lugo@baruch.cuny.edu
LUGO, Javier 787-600-2819 568 C
javier.lugo3@upr.edu
LUGO, Josue 787-600-4124 568 C
josue.lugo@upr.edu
LUGO, Lester 336-334-7595 378 A
llugo@ncat.edu
LUGO, Maria de los, A 787-766-1717 565 I
um_mlugo@suagm.edu
LUGO, Maria Ines 787-264-1912 564 B
milugo@sg.inter.edu
LUGO, Nazario 787-257-7373 565 G
nalugo@suagm.edu
LUGO, Ruth, E 212-343-1234 341 B
rlugo@mcny.edu
LUGO, Udeth 407-646-2573 116 D
ulugo@rollins.edu
LUGO, Victoria 805-654-6455 77 F
vlugo@vcccd.edu
LUGO-DEJESUS, Waleska 413-572-5272 238 F
cpickron@wsc.ma.edu
LUIKART, Nancy 563-288-6073 184 G
nluikart@eicc.edu
LUING, Kevin, L 973-278-5400 323 H
kevin@berkeleycollege.edu
LUING, Kevin, L 973-278-5400 307 F
kevin@berkeleycollege.edu
LUJAN, Annette 719-846-5679 88 F
annette.lujan@trinidadstate.edu
LUJAN, Linda 480-732-7010 15 E
linda.lujan@cgc.edu
LUJAN, Manuel 361-593-4060 498 D
manuel.lujan@tamuk.edu
LUJAN, Nereida 620-417-1104 196 F
nereida.lujan@sccc.edu
LUKAC, Dan 513-244-4617 388 E
dan_lukac@mail.msj.edu
LUKACEVICH, James 785-243-1435 192 A
jlukacevich@cloud.edu
LUKACSKO, Debbie 201-684-7535 313 C
dlukacsk@ramapo.edu
LUKAS, Veronica 718-631-6367 328 F
vlukas@qcc.cuny.edu
LUKASIEWICZ, Barbara 313-845-9606 252 B
bluka@hfcc.edu
LUKASIK, Douglas, S 607-778-5028 324 G
lukasikds@sunybroome.edu
LUKASKIEWICZ, Robert, P 802-773-5900 513 D
rob.lukaskiewicz@csj.edu
LUKASZEWSKI, Patricia, L 919-508-2220 380 E
pllukaszewski@peace.edu
LUKE, Josh 419-995-8847 399 B
luke.40@osu.edu
LUKE, Kristie 580-745-2176 412 C
kluke@se.edu
LUKE, Sarah 207-288-5015 217 H
sluke@coa.edu
LUKEHART, Debra 515-271-2169 184 D
debra.lukehart@drake.edu
LUKEN, James, O 843-349-2783 456 G
joluken@coastal.edu
LUKHAUP, Walter 724-480-3376 426 A
walter.lukhaup@ccbc.edu
LUKICH, Donna, J 304-336-8108 544 D
lukichda@westliberty.edu
LUKMAN, Roy 407-303-8520 100 G
roy.lukman@adu.edu
LUKOSHUS, Wes, K 219-989-2217 178 K
lukoshus@purduecal.edu
LULJAK, Thomas, L 414-229-4035 551 D
tluljak@uwm.edu
LULLI, Linda, S 401-232-6011 453 C
lslulli@bryant.edu
LUM-AKANA, Aileen 808-455-0606 142 D
aileenla@hawaii.edu
LUMETTA, Joanne 734-432-5689 254 D
jlumetta@madonna.edu
LUMM, John 734-487-2031 250 F
jlumm@emich.edu
LUMM, Werner 920-390-2820 548 D
werner.lumm@mbbc.edu
LUMMUS, John 864-646-1548 461 F
jlummus@tctc.edu
LUMPKIN, Ann 985-732-6640 211 A
LUMPKIN, Ilene 201-291-1111 307 F
igl@berkeleycollege.edu
LUMPKIN, James 318-257-4526 215 F
jlumpkin@latech.edu
LUMPKIN, Scott, R 303-871-2647 89 A
slumpkin@du.edu
LUMPKINS, Paris 216-771-1700 386 B
plumpkins@bryantstratton.edu

LUMPP, David, A 651-641-8217 263 A
lumpp@csp.edu
LUMPP, Marycate 303-458-4058 87 I
mlumpp@regis.edu
LUNA, Andrew, L 256-765-4221 9 C
alluna@una.edu
LUNA, Edna 931-363-9824 471 A
eluna@martinmethodist.edu
LUNA, Frank 602-285-7667 16 A
frank.luna@pcmail.maricopa.edu
LUNA, Gene 803-777-4283 462 A
genel@sc.edu
LUNA, J. Nikky 304-457-6203 540 E
lunajn@ab.edu
LUNA, Leslie 520-383-8401 18 I
lluna@tocc.cc.az.us
LUNA, Marlene 801-878-1062 303 D
mluna@roseman.edu
LUNA, Olga 787-766-1912 562 I
oluna@inter.edu
LUNA, Rita 608-822-2701 555 D
rluna@swtc.edu
LUNA, Shirley 936-468-2605 496 B
sluna@sfasu.edu
LUNAN, Kathy 314-529-9332 284 C
klunan@maryville.edu
LUNARDI, Joseph, M 610-660-1221 446 C
jlunardi@sju.edu
LUNBECK, Jo 870-972-3593 20 B
jlunbeck@asusystem.edu
LUNCEFORD, Casey 772-462-7693 111 B
cluncefo@irsc.edu
LUND, Bob 719-502-2040 87 B
bob.lund@ppcc.edu
LUND, Eric 507-786-3069 271 C
lund@stolaf.edu
LUND, Jon 563-387-1428 187 D
lundjon@luther.edu
LUND, Karla 406-874-6186 294 F
lundk@milescc.edu
LUND, Kristen 812-488-2241 180 E
kl147@evansville.edu
LUND, Lisa 989-328-1219 255 E
lisal@montcalm.edu
LUND, Stephen, R 608-263-5722 550 J
slund@ohr.wisc.edu
LUNDAHL, Deb 402-375-7209 299 G
delunda1@wsc.edu
LUNDAY, Herbert 417-255-7225 286 D
herblunday@missouristate.edu
LUNDBERG, Cliff 805-565-7188 79 A
clundber@westmont.edu
LUNDBERG, Erik 734-615-4445 259 A
lerikl@umich.edu
LUNDBERG, Peter 954-965-7272 107 H
plundberg@careercollege.edu
LUNDBERG, Shon, R 515-964-0601 185 A
lundbergs@faith.edu
LUNDBLAD, Larry, A 218-855-8053 265 J
llundblad@clcmn.edu
LUNDBLAD, Tracey 302-736-2372 97 A
luncbltr@wesley.edu
LUNDBURG, Wes 907-834-1610 11 B
plundburg@pwscc.edu
LUNDEEN, Bruce 810-766-4017 247 G
bruce.lundeen@baker.edu
LUNDEEN, Sally 414-229-4189 551 D
slundeen@uwm.edu
LUNDEN, Steve, M 509-313-5624 534 F
slunden@plant.gonzaga.edu
LUNDERMAN, Dedria 850-729-5361 114 A
lundermand@nwfsc.edu
LUNDQUIST, Daniel 518-244-2018 348 A
1lundqd@sage.edu
LUNDQUIST, Sara 714-564-6085 63 F
lundquist_sara@sac.edu
LUNDRIGAN, Kathleen 513-244-4330 388 E
kathleen_lundrigan@mail.msj.edu
LUNDSTREM, Karen 718-260-5140 328 D
klundstrem@citytech.cuny.edu
LUNDSTROM, Joel 785-587-2800 195 A
joellundstrom@matc.net
LUNDSTROM, Linda 781-595-6768 236 C
llundstrom@mariancourt.edu
LUNDY, Constance, L 484-365-7785 434 H
lundy@lincoln.edu
LUNDY, Elizabeth 503-594-3020 415 A
elizabethl@clackamas.edu
LUNDY, Jennifer 412-365-1145 425 C
jlundy@chatham.edu
LUNGSTRUM, Anthony 573-592-1638 293 D
anthony.lungstrum@williamwoods.edu
LUNIN, Jeanne 212-353-4107 331 A
lunin@cooper.edu
LUNN, D. Paul 919-513-6210 378 C
dplunn@ncsu.edu
LUNNERMON, JR.,
James, G 410-651-6434 227 E
jglunnermonii@umes.edu
LUNSFORD, Dale, A 903-233-3100 490 A
dalelunsford@letu.edu
LUNSFORD, Dan, G 828-689-1141 366 I
dlunsford@mhc.edu
LUNSFORD, Frances, M 336-599-1181 372 G
lunsfof@piedmontcc.edu

LUNSFORD, Larry 305-348-2797 119 C
larry.lunsford@fiu.edu
LUO, Lucy 516-364-0808 343 A
lluo@nycollege.edu
LUONG, Carmen 718-482-5511 328 B
carmenl@lagcc.cuny.edu
LUONG, Huan 972-860-8102 484 H
hluong@dcccd.edu
LUOTTO, John, A 304-326-1234 541 K
jluotto@salemu.edu
LUPIEN, Alfred 605-322-8090 464 G
alfred.lupien@mtmc.edu
LUPIN, Daniel 928-777-3762 14 C
lupind@erau.edu
LUPINETTI, Jude 985-867-2225 214 G
acdean@sjasc.edu
LUPO, Bernadette 413-662-5203 238 C
bernadette.lupo@mcla.edu
LUPO, Susan 734-462-4400 258 A
slupo@schoolcraft.edu
LUPOLE, Barbara, H 610-799-1510 434 D
blupole@lccc.edu
LUPTAK, Andrew, J 262-243-5700 547 C
andrew.luptak@cuw.edu
LUPTON, Deborah 410-337-6135 222 I
dlupton@goucher.edu
LUPTON, Mark 704-272-5406 374 A
mlupton@spcc.edu
LURIA, J 845-731-3700 362 A
yv@ksrnet.com
LUSBY, Mary Lee 402-354-7058 299 C
marylee.lusby@methodistcollege.edu
LUSH, Mary Jean 662-332-8500 275 D
mjlush@msdelta.edu
LUSH, Susan 617-369-3870 244 E
slush@mfa.org
LUSHBAUGH, Jeffery 609-777-3083 316 A
jlushbaugh@tesc.edu
LUSIGNAN, Susan, C 585-389-2147 342 D
slusign6@naz.edu
LUSK, D. Claude 806-291-3436 508 E
luskc@wbu.edu
LUSK, David 252-493-7260 372 H
dlusk@email.pittcc.edu
LUSK, Ju-Hsin 423-697-3338 474 D
LUSK, Kent 312-553-5628 147 C
klusk1@ccc.edu
LUSK, Kevin 304-243-2389 546 A
klusk@wju.edu
LUSK, Susan 310-954-4037 57 H
slusk@msmc.la.edu
LUSSIER, Dan 731-989-6672 469 B
dlussier@fhu.edu
LUSSIER, Michel 207-741-5519 219 A
mlussier@smccme.edu
LUSSKIN, Elizabeth 718-260-3392 346 C
elusskin@poly.edu
LUST, Kevin 217-789-1017 157 B
kevin.lust@llcc.edu
LUSTER, Pamela, T 619-388-2721 65 G
pluster@sdccd.edu
LUSTIG, Alice 732-235-5378 316 G
lustigac@umdnj.edu
LUSTIG, Kevin 928-541-7777 16 H
klustig@ncu.edu
LUTCHEN, Kenneth, R 617-353-2800 232 E
klutch@bu.edu
LUTER, Gary, S 813-253-3333 123 A
gluter@ut.edu
LUTES, Jean 610-519-6518 450 H
jean.lutes@villanova.edu
LUTES, Natalie 303-556-5726 86 F
lutesn@msudenver.edu
LUTGEN, Roxanne, M 715-365-4413 555 A
rlutgen@nicoletcollege.edu
LUTGRING, Ray 812-488-2589 180 E
rl5@evansville.edu
LUTHER, Judith 502-585-9911 206 D
jluther@spalding.edu
LUTHER, Nikol 208-792-5272 144 B
ncluther@lcsc.edu
LUTHER, Patricia 760-245-4271 77 H
pat.luther@vvc.edu
LUTOMSKI, Robert 212-229-5459 342 E
lutomskr@newschool.edu
LUTRICK, Candee 972-825-4612 495 F
clutrick@sagu.edu
LUTRICK, Donny 972-825-4824 495 F
dlutrick@sagu.edu
LUTTMAN, Paul 765-966-2656 176 H
pluttman@ivytech.edu
LUTTRELL, Curt 503-768-6036 416 G
luttrell@lclark.edu
LUTY, Carl 410-617-2697 223 I
cluty@loyola.edu
LUTY, Paul, J 503-943-7308 420 G
luty@up.edu
LUTZ, Cathleen, A 570-321-4069 435 D
lutz@lycoming.edu
LUTZ, Charles 419-448-3351 402 E
clutz@tiffin.edu
LUTZ, Dan 765-285-8984 169 G
dlutz@bsu.edu

LUTZ, Debra, K 989-686-9386 250 D
dklutz@delta.edu
LUTZ, Heather 434-961-5275 528 B
hlutz@pvcc.edu
LUTZ, J. Gary 610-758-3708 434 E
jgl3@lehigh.edu
LUTZ, Kim, L 810-766-4271 247 G
kim.lutz@baker.edu
LUTZ, Mitzi 660-562-1119 287 B
mitzi@nwmissouri.edu
LUTZ, Natalie 816-654-7032 283 F
nlutz@kcumb.edu
LUTZ, Nate, K 612-874-3780 265 C
nate_lutz@mcad.edu
LUTZ, Paula 406-994-4288 295 C
plutz@montana.edu
LUTZ, Susan 303-871-2118 89 A
susan.lutz@du.edu
LUTZKA, David, R 218-722-4000 263 E
davidl@dbumn.edu
LUU, Khien 563-876-3353 184 B
kluu@dwci.com
LUUKKONEN, John 212-594-4000 357 H
jluukkonen@tcicollege.edu
LUVERA, Michael 509-963-2959 532 C
luveram@cwu.edu
LUX, David 401-232-6433 453 C
dlux@bryant.edu
LUX, Kate 312-662-4033 144 H
klux@adler.edu
LUXNER, Catherine 570-961-4703 435 F
luxner@marywood.edu
LUXTON, Andrea, T 269-471-3404 247 D
aluxton@andrews.edu
LUY, Peggy, S 217-424-6330 158 G
pluy@millikin.edu
LUYK, Jim 616-957-6046 249 B
jluyk@calvinseminary.edu
LUYMES, Robyn 616-732-1157 250 C
rluymes3@davenport.edu
LUZADER, Timothy, B 765-494-3981 178 J
tluzader@purdue.edu
LUZAR, E. Jane 317-278-5082 174 D
ejluzar@iupui.edu
LUZURIAGA, Katherine 508-856-6282 237 C
katherine.luzuriaga@umassmed.edu
LY, Geisce 707-962-2661 42 C
geisce-ly@redwoods.edu
LY, Vi 323-265-8723 54 G
lyv@elac.edu
LYALL, James 303-556-3892 86 F
jlyall1@msudenver.edu
LYBYER, Debra 208-792-2313 144 B
dlybyer@lcsc.edu
LYDA-SAVICH, Kim 858-576-1287 19 A
kim.savich@phoenix.edu
LYDDON, Jerri, L 620-417-1151 196 F
jerrilynn.lyddon@sccc.edu
LYDDON, Susan 718-482-5169 328 B
slyddon@lagcc.cuny.edu
LYDEN, Michael, P 814-824-3652 436 C
mlyden@mercyhurst.edu
LYDER, Courtney 310-825-9621 74 C
clyder@sonnet.ucla.edu
LYDIC, R. Jeffrey 724-847-6581 429 H
jlydic@geneva.edu
LYDON, Carol Ann 828-694-1882 368 E
ca_lydon@blueridge.edu
LYDON, Christopher 508-565-1801 245 A
clydon@stonehill.edu
LYDON, John 504-394-7744 214 B
jlydon@olhcc.edu
LYDY, Kenneth, A 937-382-6661 405 I
kenneth_lydy@wilmington.edu
LYGHT, Bill 912-201-6104 137 D
blyght@southuniversity.edu
LYKE, Alan, D 719-884-5000 86 J
adlyke@nbc.edu
LYKINS, Elyce, M 570-385-6125 440 D
eml10@psu.edu
LYKINS, Jason 660-263-3900 279 F
jlykins@cccb.edu
LYKINS, Karen 931-372-3214 474 B
klykins@tntech.edu
LYKOUDIS, Michael, N 574-631-7473 180 G
lykoudis.1@nd.edu
LYLE, Aaron 310-314-6103 30 A
LYLE, Donald, L 724-458-2122 430 B
dllyle@gcc.edu
LYLE, J. Gary 410-777-2836 221 C
jglyle@aacc.edu
LYLE, Lisa 732-729-3868 309 C
llyle@devry.edu
LYLE, William 215-489-4987 426 H
william.lyle@delval.edu
LYLES, Carol, S 256-765-4201 9 C
cslyles@una.edu
LYMAN, Barbara, G 717-477-1371 443 E
bglyman@ship.edu
LYMPANY, John 859-985-3990 199 A
john_lympany@berea.edu
LYN, Janice 334-244-3620 1 G
jlyn@aum.edu

LYNCH, Bruce, G ... 336-334-4556 ... 379 B bglynch@uncg.edu

LYNCH, Christopher ... 251-460-7725 ... 9 D clynch@usouthal.edu

LYNCH, Cynthia ... 414-847-3340 ... 549 B cynthialynch@miad.edu

LYNCH, Cynthia, D ... 414-847-3340 ... 549 B cynthialynch@miad.edu

LYNCH, Darlene ... 219-980-6614 ... 174 B darlynch@iun.edu

LYNCH, Deborah ... 407-708-2144 ... 117 H lynchd@seminolestate.edu

LYNCH, Dianne ... 828-227-7100 ... 380 A dlynch@wcu.edu

LYNCH, Dianne ... 573-876-7210 ... 290 C dlynch@stephens.edu

LYNCH, James ... 315-792-5316 ... 341 E jlynch@mvcc.edu

LYNCH, Janet, D ... 815-288-5511 ... 164 B lynchj@svcc.edu

LYNCH, Jim Hughes ... 912-279-5713 ... 127 E jlynch@ccga.edu

LYNCH, Joe ... 717-337-6518 ... 429 I jlynch@gettysburg.edu

LYNCH, Julie ... 219-769-3321 ... 170 C jlynch@brownmackie.edu

LYNCH, Julie ... 512-499-4309 ... 505 B jlynch@utsystem.edu

LYNCH, Kathryn ... 781-283-3583 ... 245 E klynch@wellesley.edu

LYNCH, Kelly ... 781-239-6350 ... 230 E klynch@babson.edu

LYNCH, Kevin, P ... 315-268-6718 ... 329 B klynch@clarkson.edu

LYNCH, Kris ... 252-399-6329 ... 362 E klynch@barton.edu

LYNCH, Lisa ... 781-736-3883 ... 232 F lisalynch@brandeis.edu

LYNCH, Lisa, A ... 989-729-3422 ... 248 F lisa.lynch@baker.edu

LYNCH, Melinda ... 859-336-5082 ... 206 A melindalynch@sccky.edu

LYNCH, Michael ... 508-999-8845 ... 237 A mlynch4@umassd.edu

LYNCH, Michael ... 315-568-3052 ... 342 H mlynch@nycc.edu

LYNCH, Michael, F ... 703-993-3840 ... 519 E mlynch@gmu.edu

LYNCH, Michelle ... 502-863-8015 ... 201 A michelle_lynch@georgetowncollege.edu

LYNCH, Paul ... 703-284-1608 ... 521 D paul.lynch@marymount.edu

LYNCH, Paul, F ... 315-445-4551 ... 338 B lynchpf@lemoyne.edu

LYNCH, Richard, E ... 972-708-7340 ... 487 B dick_lynch@gial.edu

LYNCH, Robert ... 240-567-7306 ... 224 D bob.lynch@montgomerycollege.edu

LYNCH, Robert, P ... 407-888-8689 ... 108 B blynch@fcim.edu

LYNCH, Rose ... 908-835-2306 ... 317 C lynchr@warren.edu

LYNCH, Scott ... 970-207-4500 ... 89 D scottl@uscareerinstitute.edu

LYNCH, Stephen, J ... 401-865-2233 ... 453 H sjlynch@providence.edu

LYNCH, Susan, M ... 570-286-3058 ... 436 B smh@mccannschool.com

LYNCH, William, F ... 215-895-2167 ... 427 H wfl27@drexel.edu

LYNCH-CARIS, Terri ... 810-762-9859 ... 253 C tlynch@kettering.edu

LYNCH MAESTAS, Michael ... 785-864-2277 ... 197 B mvlm@ku.edu

LYND-BALTA, Eileen ... 585-385-8116 ... 348 F elynd-balta@sjfc.edu

LYNDGAARD, David ... 320-363-3350 ... 271 A dlyndgaard@csbsju.edu

LYNEMA, Dawn, A ... 616-988-3624 ... 253 F dlynema@kuyper.edu

LYNG, Heather ... 802-287-8231 ... 513 F gmc@bkstr.com

LYNG-GLIDDI, Diana, L ... 518-327-6314 ... 345 H dlyngglidi@paulsmiths.edu

LYNK, Angel ... 334-347-2623 ... 3 F alynk@escc.edu

LYNN, Angela ... 309-298-1891 ... 168 C an-lynn@wiu.edu

LYNN, Crystal ... 540-828-5356 ... 517 B clynn@bridgewater.edu

LYNN, Dahlia ... 207-780-4524 ... 220 G dlynn@usm.maine.edu

LYNN, Kathy ... 802-865-6485 ... 513 C lynn@champlain.edu

LYNN, Ken ... 281-998-6306 ... 493 G ken.lynn@sjcd.edu

LYNN, Kerrie ... 423-746-5206 ... 476 F klynn@twcnet.edu

LYNN, Laura ... 410-662-2797 ... 272 C laura.lynn@waldenu.edu

LYNN, Michael ... 219-785-5380 ... 179 A mlynn@pnc.edu

LYNN, Richard ... 251-809-1556 ... 5 B richard.lynn@jdcc.edu

LYNN, Richardson, R ... 404-872-3593 ... 125 F rlynn@johnmrshall.edu

LYNN, Terence ... 413-775-1440 ... 239 E lynnt@gcc.mass.edu

LYNN, Vicki ... 501-450-1494 ... 22 A lynn@hendrix.edu

LYNNE, Christopher ... 928-541-7777 ... 16 H clynne@ncu.edu

LYNOTT, Patricia ... 603-645-9596 ... 305 I p.lynott@snhu.edu

LYON, Bob ... 423-425-4717 ... 477 F bob-lyon@utc.edu

LYON, Doug ... 970-247-7010 ... 84 K lyon_d@fortlewis.edu

LYON, JR., James, C ... 773-442-4100 ... 160 A j-lyonjr@neiu.edu

LYON, Larry ... 254-710-3588 ... 482 A larry_lyon@baylor.edu

LYON, Larry ... 919-761-2372 ... 377 A llyon@sebts.edu

LYON, Lisa ... 808-974-7636 ... 141 F llyon@hawaii.edu

LYON, Mary Eilleen ... 616-331-2221 ... 251 F lyonme@gvsu.edu

LYON, Misty ... 309-341-5422 ... 146 D mlyon@sandburg.edu

LYON, Tammy ... 910-938-6247 ... 369 F lyont@coastalcarolina.edu

LYON, Wade ... 620-417-1064 ... 196 F wade.lyon@sccc.edu

LYONS, Anthony ... 620-227-9203 ... 192 E alyons@dc3.edu

LYONS, Becky ... 406-657-2240 ... 295 D blyons@msubillings.edu

LYONS, Cheryl, C ... 501-450-3140 ... 25 H clyons@uca.edu

LYONS, Cindy ... 239-590-7904 ... 119 B clyons@fgcu.edu

LYONS, Darrin ... 518-255-5227 ... 354 E lyonsd@cobleskill.edu

LYONS, Eilene ... 314-513-4401 ... 288 H elyons@stlcc.edu

LYONS, Frankie ... 336-249-8186 ... 370 B fwlyons@davidsonccc.edu

LYONS, Gary ... 405-425-1932 ... 409 E gary.lyons@oc.edu

LYONS, Ivory ... 330-823-2469 ... 404 C lyonsil@mountunion.edu

LYONS, James ... 503-943-8607 ... 420 G lyons@up.edu

LYONS, Joan ... 510-580-6719 ... 80 A jlyons@cci.edu

LYONS, Julie ... 417-865-2815 ... 281 G lyonsj@evangel.edu

LYONS, Kyra, A ... 202-319-5608 ... 97 E lyonsk@cua.edu

LYONS, Larry ... 304-865-6035 ... 541 J larry.lyons@ovu.edu

LYONS, Mary, E ... 619-260-4520 ... 76 D president@sandiego.edu

LYONS, Marybeth ... 315-792-7505 ... 356 B smbl@sunyit.edu

LYONS, Melinda ... 928-541-7777 ... 16 H mlyons@ncu.edu

LYONS, Michael ... 781-239-2443 ... 239 G mlyons@massbay.edu

LYONS, Nicholas, A ... 315-312-2222 ... 354 A nicholas.lyons@oswego.edu

LYONS, Patrick, G ... 973-761-9498 ... 315 B patrick.lyons@shu.edu

LYONS, Pattyanne ... 617-349-8178 ... 236 B plyons@lesley.edu

LYONS, Peter ... 404-413-2578 ... 131 G lyonsp@gsu.edu

LYONS, Phil ... 715-232-1683 ... 552 E lyonsp@uwstout.edu

LYONS, Richard, K ... 510-643-2027 ... 73 H lyons@haas.berkeley.edu

LYONS, Sharon, K ... 563-588-7829 ... 187 C sharon.lyons@loras.edu

LYONS, Shawn ... 859-238-5500 ... 199 G shawn.lyons@centre.edu

LYONS, Sheila ... 601-352-9666 ... 273 C bookstore@belhaven.edu

LYONS, Steve ... 218-723-6167 ... 262 G slyons@css.edu

LYONS, Steven, J ... 937-775-5745 ... 406 C steven.lyons@wright.edu

LYONS, Yolanda ... 719-389-6245 ... 82 D yolanda.lyons@coloradocollege.edu

LYSENG, Brenda ... 651-779-3447 ... 266 A brenda.lyseng@century.edu

LYSIONEK, Christine ... 610-902-8406 ... 424 B christine.lysionek@cabrini.edu

LYSIONEK, Peter ... 215-885-2360 ... 435 E plysionek@manor.edu

LYSLE, Jane, H ... 302-225-6274 ... 96 H lyslej@gbc.edu

LYSNE, Marit ... 507-222-4080 ... 261 G mlysne@carleton.edu

LYTCH, Carol, E ... 717-290-8701 ... 433 F president@lancasterseminary.edu

LYTER, Lloyd, L ... 570-348-6282 ... 435 F lyter@marywood.edu

LYTLE, Alexis ... 619-275-4700 ... 46 K alexis@fashioncareerscollege.com

LYTLE, Anne ... 212-772-4242 ... 327 E alytle@hunter.cuny.edu

LYTLE, Carol, J ... 712-749-2440 ... 183 C lytlec@bvu.edu

LYTLE, David ... 210-434-6711 ... 492 B dlytle@lake.ollusa.edu

LYTLE, James, R ... 570-586-2400 ... 422 G jlytle@bbc.edu

LYTLE, Rick, S ... 325-674-2503 ... 478 I lytler@acu.edu

LYTLE, Rodney ... 828-298-3325 ... 380 D rlytle@warren-wilson.edu

LYTTLE, Marsha, J ... 810-762-9660 ... 253 C mlyttle@kettering.edu

LYTTLE, Mary Jo ... 724-357-7942 ... 442 F mjlyttle@iup.edu

LYTTLE, Sonya ... 843-525-8248 ... 461 E slyttle@tcl.edu

LYTTON, Billy ... 704-922-6480 ... 370 G lytton.billy@gaston.edu

L'ALLIER, Kristi ... 218-235-2153 ... 269 F k.laillier@vcc.edu

L'ETOILE, Michelle ... 617-422-7210 ... 243 B mletoile@nesl.edu

L'HEUREUX, Robert, W ... 712-362-0421 ... 186 A rl'heureux@iowalakes.edu

M

MA, Dongxin ... 512-454-1188 ... 480 F info@aoma.edu

MA, Duc ... 520-626-1188 ... 18 L mad2@email.arizona.edu

MA, Jim ... 630-942-4034 ... 148 A maj127@cod.edu

MA, John ... 323-731-2383 ... 60 H johnma@psuca.edu

MA, Michelle ... 714-241-6186 ... 41 B mma@coastline.edu

MA, Qing ... 626-289-7719 ... 26 K

MA, Qingyun ... 213-740-2083 ... 76 F archdean@usc.edu

MA, Stephen ... 831-646-4040 ... 57 G sma@mpc.edu

MAAG, Traci ... 605-886-3450 ... 464 H tmaag@national.edu

MAANUM, Jeanne ... 612-659-6251 ... 267 B jeanne.maanum@minneapolis.edu

MAAS, Bruce ... 608-262-5381 ... 550 J bruce.mass@cio.wisc.edu

MAAS, Kathy ... 715-468-2815 ... 555 G kathy.maas@witc.edu

MAAS, Paula ... 212-229-8947 ... 342 E maasp@neschool.edu

MAASS, Julie ... 979-830-4141 ... 482 C jmaass@blinn.edu

MAATSCH, Darrell ... 210-567-2890 ... 507 A maatsch@uthscsa.edu

MABE, Mark ... 816-271-4261 ... 286 G mabe@missouriwestern.edu

MABERRY, Sue ... 310-665-6925 ... 60 B maberry@otis.edu

MABERY, Dan ... 870-230-5083 ... 21 I maberyd@hsu.edu

MABREY, Emilee ... 812-330-6293 ... 175 J emabrey@ivytech.edu

MABRY, Dawn ... 260-399-7700 ... 181 A dmabry@sf.edu

MABRY, James ... 480-461-7325 ... 15 I james.mabry@mcmail.maricopa.edu

MABRY, Rodney, H ... 903-566-7119 ... 506 E president@uttyler.edu

MABRY, Teresa, A ... 937-328-6014 ... 387 H mabryt@clarkstate.edu

MAC EWAN, Peter ... 216-987-4702 ... 389 B peter.macewan@tri-c.edu

MACADAM, Martha, P ... 717-872-3820 ... 443 D martha.macadam@millersville.edu

MACALUSO, Anthony ... 718-990-2452 ... 348 G macalusa@stjohns.edu

MACALUSO, Daniel ... 909-621-8335 ... 49 F dmacaluso@hmc.edu

MACAN, Drew ... 802-443-5261 ... 514 A cmacan@middlebury.edu

MACAPINLAC, Jonas, D ... 671-735-2944 ... 559 G jmacapinlac@uguam.uog.edu

MACARI, Emir, J ... 916-278-6366 ... 36 A emacari@ecs.csus.edu

MACARTHUR, John ... 661-362-2220 ... 56 G sstaats@masters.edu

MACAULAY, Barbara ... 617-732-2800 ... 241 C

MACCARTHY, Stephen, J ... 215-898-8721 ... 448 J

MACCHI, Thomas, J ... 215-572-2942 ... 422 C macchit@arcadia.edu

MACCORQUODALE, Patricia ... 520-621-2848 ... 18 L pmac@email.arizona.edu

MACCUISH, Spencer ... 805-581-1233 ... 45 J

MACCULLOCH, Heather ... 718-409-7331 ... 356 C hmacculloch@sunymaritime.edu

MACDONALD, Brian ... 802-654-2588 ... 514 D bmacdonald@smcvt.edu

MACDONALD, Christopher 912-478-5406 ... 131 E cmacdonald@georgiasouthern.edu

MACDONALD, David ... 419-772-2200 ... 398 H d-macdonald@onu.edu

MACDONALD, Dick ... 928-681-5562 ... 16 F dmacdonald@mohave.edu

MACDONALD, Dori ... 310-434-4416 ... 68 D macdonald_dori@smc.edu

MACDONALD, Duncan ... 607-431-4032 ... 335 A macdonaldd@hartwick.edu

MACDONALD, Elizabeth ... 636-949-4396 ... 283 J emacdonald@lindenwood.edu

MACDONALD, Eric ... 207-974-4685 ... 218 H emacdonald@emcc.edu

MACDONALD, Gordon ... 303-762-6890 ... 84 D gordon.macdonald@denverseminary.edu

MACDONALD, Gregory ... 610-330-5069 ... 433 B macdonag@lafayette.edu

MACDONALD, Gregory ... 540-868-7275 ... 527 C gmacdonald@lfcc.edu

MACDONALD, Ida ... 903-566-7064 ... 506 E ida_macdonald@uttyler.edu

MACDONALD, James ... 978-921-4242 ... 242 C james.macdonald@montserrat.edu

MACDONALD, Jean ... 716-926-8932 ... 335 E jmacdonald@hilbert.edu

MACDONALD, Keith ... 508-531-1296 ... 237 D kcmacdonald@bridgew.edu

MACDONALD, Nancy ... 518-454-2161 ... 330 C macdonan@strose.edu

MACDONALD, Randall, M . 863-680-4165 ... 109 E rmacdonald1@flsouthern.edu

MACDONALD, Richard, M . 301-295-3188 ... 558 D richard.macdonald@usuhs.edu

MACDONALD, Ronnie ... 631-244-3480 ... 332 C macdonar@dowling.edu

MACDONALD, William, L .. 740-366-9330 ... 399 E macdonald.24@osu.edu

MACDONALD-DENNIS, Chris, A ... 651-696-6210 ... 264 J cmacdona@macalester.edu

MACDONELL, Chuck, C ... 402-552-2693 ... 297 B macdonell@clarksoncollege.edu

MACDONNELL, Lisa ... 313-993-1229 ... 258 G macdonnl@udmercy.edu

MACDOUGALL, Bonnie ... 201-447-7100 ... 307 E bmacdougall@bergen.edu

MACDOUGALL, Judy ... 253-589-5570 ... 532 G

MACDOUGALL, Judy ... 253-589-5570 ... 532 G judy.macdougall@cptc.edu

MACDOWELL, Michael, A . 570-674-6215 ... 436 F mmacdowe@misericordia.edu

MACE, Michael, R ... 406-657-1015 ... 296 C macem@rocky.edu

MACE, Paul ... 410-334-2932 ... 229 E pmace@worwic.edu

MACEACHRAN, Joanne ... 352-588-8462 ... 116 G joanne.maceachran@saintleo.edu

MACEDO, Maria ... 425-739-8355 ... 535 H maria.macedo@lwtc.edu

MACELROY, Molly ... 518-388-6117 ... 358 G macelrom@union.edu

MACENCZAK, Kimberly, C 706-385-1442 ... 136 B kim.macenczak@point.edu

MACEO, Brenda, K ... 213-740-5371 ... 76 F maceo@usc.edu

MACEWAN, Bonnie ... 334-844-1714 ... 1 F macewbj@auburn.edu

MACFARLAND, Randolph, M ... 303-762-6900 ... 84 D randy.macfarland@denverseminary.edu

MACFARLANE, Jack, P ... 559-453-0123 ... 66 H jack.macfarlane@sjvc.edu

MACFARLANE, Lisa ... 603-862-3290 ... 306 C lisa.macfarlane@unh.edu

MACFERRAN, Dan ... 904-636-6646 ... 19 A dan.macferran@phoenix.edu

MACFIE, Thomas, E ... 931-598-1274 ... 472 L tmacfie@sewanee.edu

MACGILLIVRAY, Diane, N . 617-373-2520 ... 243 F

MACH, Stella ... 312-935-4180 ... 162 G smach@robertmorris.edu

MACHADO, Daisy, L ... 212-280-1558 ... 358 I dmachado@uts.columbia.edu

MACHADO, Diane ... 718-405-3262 ... 330 A diane.machado@mountsaintvincent.edu

MACHALA, Asharaine ... 360-331-0307 ... 536 A mfa@nila.edu

MACHALA, Janis ... 425-564-2732 ... 531 G janis.machala@bellevuecollege.edu

MACHALA, Suzanne ... 281-425-6360 ... 489 M smachala@lee.edu

MACHALSKI, Thomas ... 248-683-0311 ... 258 E tmachalski@sscms.edu

MACHAMER, A. Amber ... 510-885-4361 ... 34 E annmarie.machamer@csueastbay.edu

MACHARG, Janie ... 310-243-3818 ... 34 D jmacharg@csudh.edu

MACHELL, James ... 405-974-5701 ... 413 B jmachell@uco.edu

MACHEN, James, B ... 352-392-1311 ... 120 C president@ufl.edu

MACHEN, Paul ... 210-486-2157 ... 479 D pmachen@alamo.edu

MACHIA, Michael ... 580-628-6291 ... 409 B michael.machia@north-ok.edu
MACHIELSON, Allen, J ... 260-982-5052 ... 177 H ajmachielson@manchester.edu
MACHLIS, Gedelyah ... 718-232-7800 ... 361 D
MACHNIK, Michael, E ... 908-526-1200 ... 313 D mmachnik@raritanval.edu
MACHON, Margaret ... 708-974-5708 ... 159 B machon@morainevalley.edu
MACHT, Barbara, E ... 240-500-2000 ... 223 A machtb@hagerstowncc.edu
MACHTLEY, Ronald, K ... 401-232-6008 ... 453 C rmac@bryant.edu
MACHUCA, Melilssa ... 602-943-2311 ... 19 B melissa.machuca@west.edu
MACIAS, Edward, S ... 314-935-3000 ... 292 I macias@wustl.edu
MACIAS, Erica ... 509-865-0420 ... 535 A macias_e@heritage.edu
MACIAS, Isabel ... 408-288-3172 ... 67 D isabel.macias@sjcc.edu
MACIAS, Paige, L ... 949-824-5108 ... 74 B plmacias@uci.edu
MACIAS, Sandy ... 650-961-9300 ... 61 B smacias@paloaltou.edu
MACIAS, Tom ... 760-757-2121 ... 57 E tmacias@miracosta.edu
MACIAS, Trisha ... 719-549-2951 ... 83 H trisha.macias@colostate-pueblo.edu
MACIEJ-HINER, Marian, G 608-342-1314 ... 552 B maciejhm@uwplatt.edu
MACIEJEWSKI, Felice, E ... 708-524-6873 ... 150 C fmaciejewski@dom.edu
MACIEL, Anthony ... 714-241-6225 ... 41 B amaciel@coastline.edu
MACIEL, Rene ... 210-924-4338 ... 481 G rene.maciel@bua.edu
MACIK, Lillian ... 254-867-4893 ... 500 C lillian.macik@systems.tstc.edu
MACINNIS, Stewart, D ... 540-464-7207 ... 529 F macinnissd@vmi.edu
MACINTOSH, Kay, H ... 410-810-7408 ... 229 D kmacintosh2@washcoll.edu
MACINTYRE, Bennett ... 406-447-4374 ... 293 G bmacintyre@carroll.edu
MACIONUS, Joseph ... 203-576-5616 ... 94 C jmacionus@stvincentscollege.edu
MACIULAITIS, Mark ... 631-632-6090 ... 352 C mark.maciulaitis@stonybrook.edu
MACK, Carol ... 503-725-3419 ... 418 G mackc@pdx.edu
MACK, Carol ... 843-525-8250 ... 461 E cmack@tcl.edu
MACK, Chuck ... 513-727-3377 ... 396 G
MACK, Craig ... 781-239-3157 ... 239 G cmack@massbay.edu
MACK, Glenn ... 770-938-4711 ... 133 D
MACK, Jeffrey, A ... 813-974-2539 ... 121 A jmack@admin.usf.edu
MACK, Johnny ... 503-399-6243 ... 414 J johnny.mack@chemeketa.edu
MACK, Jon ... 610-917-1467 ... 450 E jmack@vfcc.edu
MACK, Joseph ... 607-431-4209 ... 335 A mackj@hartwick.edu
MACK, Joseph, J ... 570-674-6336 ... 436 F jmack@misericordia.edu
MACK, Kari ... 845-687-5214 ... 358 E mackk@sunyulster.edu
MACK, Kimberly, J ... 252-536-6399 ... 371 B mackk@halifaxcc.edu
MACK, Lauren ... 704-971-8500 ... 363 F
MACK, Lesley, A ... 414-955-8733 ... 548 G lmack@mcw.edu
MACK, Linda ... 336-517-2109 ... 362 G lmack@bennett.edu
MACK, Marva ... 973-877-3346 ... 309 H mack@essex.edu
MACK, Melvin ... 803-934-3401 ... 459 G mmack@morris.edu
MACK, Qing, L ... 860-253-3008 ... 91 B qmack@asnuntuck.edu
MACK, Teresa ... 803-793-5106 ... 457 F mackt@denmarktech.edu
MACK, Timothy, P ... 724-357-2244 ... 442 F tmack@iup.edu
MACK, Tom ... 803-641-3479 ... 462 B tomm@usca.edu
MACK-HISGEN, Maura ... 518-262-5033 ... 322 D mmack@mail.amc.edu
MACKAY, Danielle ... 845-398-4102 ... 349 H dmackay@stac.edu
MACKAY, Edward, R ... 603-862-0918 ... 306 B ed.mackay@usnh.edu
MACKAY, Jeff ... 503-883-2436 ... 416 H jmackay@linfield.edu
MACKAY, Tara ... 480-212-1704 ... 18 C
MACKAY, William, M ... 617-266-1400 ... 231 E
MACKE, Charles ... 931-372-3414 ... 474 B cmacke@tntech.edu
MACKE, Lisa ... 615-547-1353 ... 468 B lmacke@cumberland.edu
MACKEL, Carol ... 814-254-0400 ... 425 G cmackel@pa.gov
MACKEL, Thomas, J ... 678-839-6252 ... 139 A tmackel@westga.edu
MACKENZIE, Lorie ... 315-229-5600 ... 349 E lmackenzie@stlawu.edu
MACKERSIE, Chris ... 253-912-3655 ... 536 H cmackers@pierce.ctc.edu
MACKEY, Angela ... 305-949-9500 ... 106 B amackey@cci.edu
MACKEY, Craig ... 973-300-2344 ... 315 F cmackey@sussex.edu
MACKEY, JoAnn ... 508-270-4021 ... 239 G jmackey@massbay.edu
MACKEY, Peter, F ... 570-577-3260 ... 423 E pete.mackey@bucknell.edu
MACKEY, Roberta ... 850-872-3866 ... 110 H rmackey@gulfcoast.edu
MACKEY, Thomas ... 518-587-2100 ... 355 G thomas.mackey@esc.edu
MACKEY, Thomas, A ... 713-500-3267 ... 506 F thomas.a.mackey@uth.tmc.edu
MACKIE, Keith ... 828-327-7000 ... 369 B kmackie@cvcc.edu
MACKIE-MASON, Jeffrey, K ... 734-647-3576 ... 259 A jmm@umich.edu
MACKIN, Brian, W ... 205-975-8221 ... 8 F bmackin@uab.edu
MACKIN, Janet ... 212-614-6110 ... 346 A jmackin@chpnet.org
MACKIN, Jim ... 402-461-7482 ... 298 A jmackin@hastings.edu
MACKIN, OFM, Kevin ... 845-569-3202 ... 342 A kevin.mackin@msmc.edu
MACKIN, Mary Beth ... 262-472-1533 ... 553 A mackinm@uww.edu
MACKINNEY, Eleanor ... 847-214-7374 ... 150 F epmackinney@aol.com
MACKINNON, George ... 847-619-7290 ... 163 B gmackinnon@roosevelt.edu
MACKINNON, Thomas, S .. 414-288-8020 ... 548 F thomas.mackinnon@marquette.edu
MACKINTOSH, Carol ... 315-792-3228 ... 359 E cmackintosh@utica.edu
MACKLIN, James, F ... 518-629-7353 ... 336 C j.macklin@hvcc.edu
MACKLIN, Joe ... 434-848-6417 ... 524 B jmacklin@saintpauls.edu
MACKNIK, Heather ... 315-652-6500 ... 324 L hmmacknik@bryantstratton.edu
MACKSEY-ETHIER, Jennifer ... 413-662-5210 ... 238 C j.ethier@mcla.edu
MACLACHLAN, Scott ... 561-207-5325 ... 114 D maclachs@palmbeachstate.edu
MACLAREN, James ... 504-865-5225 ... 215 C maclaren@tulane.edu
MACLEAN, Richard ... 907-277-1000 ... 10 E richard.maclean@chartercollege.edu
MACLEAN, Roger ... 406-243-2900 ... 294 I roger.maclean@umontana.edu
MACLEISH, Padraic ... 760-872-2000 ... 43 K padraicm@deepsprings.edu
MACLELLAN, Shannon ... 734-995-4892 ... 249 G macles@cuaa.edu
MACLENNAN, Kevin, L ... 303-492-6694 ... 88 H kevin.maclennan@colorado.edu
MACLENNAN, Richard ... 301-387-3056 ... 222 H rick.maclennan@garrettcollege.edu
MACLEOD, Ann-Mary ... 505-925-8550 ... 321 G annmary@unm.edu
MACLEOD, Catherine ... 212-431-2833 ... 343 E cmacleod@nyls.edu
MACLEOD, David, J ... 563-588-8000 ... 184 I dmacleod@emmaus.edu
MACLEOD, Ian ... 508-830-5269 ... 238 D imacleod@maritime.edu
MACLEOD, Kelly ... 727-726-1153 ... 103 I kellymacleod@clearwater.edu
MACLEOD, Kimberly, M ... 607-746-4603 ... 355 F macleokm@delhi.edu
MACLEOD, Melissa, A ... 724-458-2050 ... 430 B mamacleod@gcc.edu
MACLEOD, Peter ... 510-883-2056 ... 45 B pmacleod@dspt.edu
MACLEOD, Robert ... 813-974-6015 ... 121 A rmacleod@usf.edu
MACLEOD, Stephen, C ... 978-867-4068 ... 235 A steve.macleod@gordon.edu
MACLIN, Sharonda ... 620-242-0501 ... 195 C maclins@mcpherson.edu
MACMAHON, James ... 435-797-2478 ... 511 E jim.macmahon@usu.edu
MACMASTER, Donald ... 989-358-7344 ... 247 C macmastd@alpenacc.edu
MACMILLAN, Cynthia ... 609-984-1130 ... 316 A cmacmillan@tesc.edu
MACMILLAN, David, F ... 415-422-2047 ... 76 E macmillan@usfca.edu
MACMORRIS, Anne ... 609-771-2674 ... 308 F macmorri@tcnj.edu
MACMUNN, Craig ... 207-221-8702 ... 218 C cmacmunn@kaplan.edu
MACNAMARA, Timothy ... 307-778-1256 ... 556 E tmacnama@lccc.wy.edu
MACNAUGHTON, Kevin, J 919-515-2732 ... 378 C kevin_macnaughton@ncsu.edu
MACNEIL, M. A. J. Lex ... 630-515-7275 ... 158 F lmacne@midwestern.edu
MACNEIL, Monty, R ... 860-679-2808 ... 95 A macneil@nso.uchc.edu
MACNEIL, Roderick, L ... 860-679-2808 ... 94 G macneil@nso.uchc.edu
MACNEILL, Andrew, J ... 619-388-2797 ... 65 G amacneil@sdccd.edu
MACNEW, James ... 215-637-7700 ... 431 A jmacnew@holyfamily.edu
MACONACHY, W. Vic ... 301-369-2800 ... 221 F wvmaconachy@capitol-college.edu
MACOPSON, Elmer, R ... 828-652-0603 ... 372 B elmerm@mcdowelltech.edu
MACOSKO, Ron ... 830-792-7421 ... 494 E rpmacosko@schreiner.edu
MACPHEE, Donna, H ... 212-851-7487 ... 330 F dhm18@columbia.edu
MACPHERSON, Andy ... 903-463-8777 ... 487 C macphersona@grayson.edu
MACPHERSON, Corey ... 617-745-3525 ... 234 A corey.s.macpherson@enc.edu
MACPHERSON, Heidi ... 608-785-8042 ... 551 C hmacpherson@uwlax.edu
MACREADY, Neil, A ... 909-748-8049 ... 76 C neil_macready@redlands.edu
MACRINA, Francis, L ... 804-827-2262 ... 526 B macrina@vcu.edu
MACRITCHIE, Andrea ... 508-854-4461 ... 240 F amacritchie@qcc.mass.edu
MACRO, Venessa ... 515-271-3133 ... 184 D venessa.macro@drake.edu
MACTAGGART, Julie ... 563-589-3619 ... 189 F jmactaggart@dbq.edu
MACUILA, Terry ... 606-242-0974 ... 203 D terry.macuila@kctcs.edu
MACUMBER, Linda, K ... 563-333-6336 ... 188 F macumberlindak@sau.edu
MACUR, Kenneth, M ... 785-227-3380 ... 191 B macurk@bethanylb.edu
MACVARISH, Greg ... 312-662-4141 ... 144 H gmacvarish@adler.edu
MACWILLIAMS, Erika ... 305-809-3277 ... 108 I erika.macwilliams@fkcc.edu
MADAIO-O'BRIEN, Melanie ... 617-353-2256 ... 232 E asmelmad@bu.edu
MADAMA, Patrick ... 732-906-2551 ... 311 D pmadama@middlesexcc.edu
MADANIPOUR, Manouche 617-928-7376 ... 242 E mmadanipour@mountida.edu
MADDALI, Ramesh ... 601-877-6146 ... 272 F rmaddali@alcorn.edu
MADDEN, Beverly ... 650-574-6538 ... 67 G maddenb@smccd.edu
MADDEN, Charles, E ... 478-387-4804 ... 131 A
MADDEN, Christopher ... 214-648-0702 ... 507 E christopher.madden@utsouthwestern.edu
MADDEN, Deanna ... 808-983-4152 ... 140 H dmadden@tokai.edu
MADDEN, Fred, H ... 856-415-2272 ... 310 D fmadden@gccnj.edu
MADDEN, Joe ... 936-639-1301 ... 480 D jmadden@angelina.edu
MADDEN, John ... 575-624-7111 ... 318 C john.madden@roswell.enmu.edu
MADDEN, Margaret, E ... 315-267-2108 ... 354 C maddenme@potsdam.edu
MADDEN, Mike ... 417-447-8170 ... 287 D maddenm@otc.edu
MADDEN, Paul ... 740-351-3421 ... 401 I pmadden@shawnee.edu
MADDEN, Richard ... 931-363-9844 ... 471 A rmadden@martinmethodist.edu
MADDEN, Susan ... 240-567-5274 ... 224 D susan.madden@montgomerycollege.edu
MADDEN, Warren, R ... 515-294-6162 ... 182 E wmadden@iastate.edu
MADDIGAN, Susan ... 508-362-2131 ... 239 D smaddigan@capecod.edu
MADDIN, Brent ... 212-228-1888 ... 347 C
MADDIRALA, James ... 601-979-2244 ... 274 G james.maddirala@jsums.edu
MADDOCKS, Peter ... 617-989-4328 ... 245 F maddocksp@wit.edu
MADDOX, Cole ... 404-364-8535 ... 135 E cmaddox@oglethorpe.edu
MADDOX, David ... 619-201-8700 ... 65 D
MADDOX, Dusty ... 407-226-6465 ... 104 K dmaddox@devry.edu
MADDOX, Gregory, H ... 713-313-7889 ... 500 B maddox_gh@tsu.edu
MADDOX, Janet, H ... 404-364-8462 ... 135 E jmaddox@oglethorpe.edu
MADDOX, Julie, A ... 219-464-5333 ... 181 C julie.maddox@valpo.edu
MADDOX, Kelley, L ... 770-534-6270 ... 126 E kmaddox@brenau.edu
MADDOX, Kenneth ... 256-372-4871 ... 1 A kenneth.maddox@aamu.edu
MADDOX, Lori, B ... 615-353-3305 ... 475 E lori.maddox@nscc.edu
MADDOX, Nedra ... 704-484-4103 ... 369 E maddox@clevelandcc.edu
MADDOX, Rebecca ... 706-295-6321 ... 130 E rmaddox@highlands.edu
MADDOX, Richard ... 402-643-7408 ... 297 D richard.maddox@cune.edu
MADDOX, Ronald, W ... 910-893-1686 ... 362 J maddox@campbell.edu
MADDOX, Tangella ... 312-341-3584 ... 163 B tmaddox@roosevelt.edu
MADDUX, Gary ... 256-824-2679 ... 8 G gary.maddux@us.army.mil
MADDY, Angela, M ... 620-792-9322 ... 190 H maddya@bartonccc.edu
MADDY, Faith, D ... 314-968-7457 ... 292 J faithmaddy41@webster.edu
MADELONE, Laura ... 607-436-2526 ... 353 E madelolm@oneonta.edu
MADELUNG, Donald, G ... 608-663-2000 ... 548 C dmadelung@mediainstitute.edu
MADER, Deanna ... 304-696-2682 ... 544 B maderd@marshall.edu
MADER, James ... 412-346-2100 ... 444 E jmader@pia.edu
MADER, Louis ... 212-772-4521 ... 327 E lmader@hunter.cuny.edu
MADER, Sharon, B ... 504-280-6556 ... 213 E smader@uno.edu
MADGES, William ... 610-660-1282 ... 446 C wmadges@sju.edu
MADHAVARAU, Leela ... 909-748-8285 ... 76 C leela_madhavarau@redlands.edu
MADIGAN, Kay ... 330-652-9919 ... 390 H kaymadigan@eticollege.edu
MADIN, Laurence, P ... 508-289-2515 ... 246 E lmadin@whoi.edu
MADISON, Anna ... 617-287-7232 ... 236 G anna.madison@umb.edu
MADISON, Jennifer ... 940-898-3103 ... 502 D jmadison@twu.edu
MADISON, Jennifer, L ... 716-372-7978 ... 345 C jmadison@obi.edu
MADISON, Katheryn ... 541-684-4644 ... 419 F kmadison@pioneerpacific.edu
MADISON, Olivia, M ... 515-294-1443 ... 182 E omadison@iastate.edu
MADISON, S. (Sean) ... 954-201-8800 ... 102 E smadison@broward.edu
MADISON, Sandra ... 305-899-4933 ... 101 M smadison@mail.barry.edu
MADLOCK, Calvin ... 661-722-6300 ... 28 K cmadlock@avc.edu
MADONNA, JR., Richard, A ... 212-280-7100 ... 358 I rmadonna@uts.columbia.edu
MADORE, Keith, L ... 207-768-9568 ... 220 F keith.madore@umpi.edu
MADORMA, James ... 708-342-3250 ... 150 B jmadorma@devry.edu
MADOSKI, Larry ... 714-542-8086 ... 31 C lmadoski@bristoluniversity.edu
MADRAY, Van ... 252-493-7750 ... 372 H vmadray@email.pittcc.edu
MADRID, Maria, E ... 787-728-1515 ... 568 D mmadrid@sagrado.edu
MADRID, Regina ... 505-454-2534 ... 318 F rmadrid@luna.edu
MADSEN, Alice ... 206-878-3710 ... 535 B amadsen@highline.edu
MADSEN, Gary, L ... 512-223-7087 ... 481 B gmadsen@austincc.edu
MADSEN, Jan, D ... 402-280-3386 ... 297 F janmadsen@creighton.edu
MADSEN, Patrick, O ... 336-334-5454 ... 379 B pomadsen@uncg.edu
MADSEN, Sandra, K ... 509-527-4571 ... 539 B sandra.madsen@wwcc.edu
MADSEN, Stephanie, D ... 410-382-4674 ... 224 C smadsen@mcdaniel.edu
MADSON, Greg ... 406-791-5359 ... 296 F gmadson01@ugf.edu
MADULI, Ed ... 408-741-2082 ... 78 E ed_maduli@wvm.edu
MAEA, Cheri ... 703-414-4056 ... 518 C cmaea@devry.edu
MAEDA, John ... 401-454-6764 ... 454 B president@risd.edu
MAEDA, Sandy ... 808-455-0462 ... 142 D smaeda@hawaii.edu
MAEL, Laura ... 608-663-2000 ... 548 C lmael@mediainstitute.edu
MAELSON, Diane, C ... 215-204-3745 ... 447 H diane.maleson@temple.edu
MAENE, Sara ... 304-876-5112 ... 544 C smaene@shepherd.edu
MAERTINS, Bryan ... 903-923-3442 ... 500 E bryan.maertins@tstc.edu
MAES, Sue, C ... 785-532-5644 ... 194 D scmaes@ksu.edu
MAESTAS, Belen ... 719-587-7321 ... 80 L bmaestas@adams.edu
MAESTAS, Joseph ... 970-945-8691 ... 82 G
MAESTAS, Ricardo ... 432-837-8032 ... 501 E rmaestas@sulross.edu

MAKI, Jackie 817-515-5379 496 C
jackie.maki@tccd.edu
MAKI, William, D 218-755-2012 265 I
wmaki@bemidjistate.edu
MAKIN, Linda 801-863-8457 511 F
linda.makin@uvu.edu
MAKKENA, Rani 309-649-6230 165 F
rani.makkena@src.edu
MAKOFSKE, Rose 215-619-7383 436 G
rmakofske@mc3.edu
MAKOSY, Stephen, G 716-625-6300 324 K
sgmakosy@bryantstratton.edu
MAKOSY, Steve 716-677-9500 325 A
sgmakosy@bryantstratton.edu
MAKOWSKI, Sharon 203-576-5478 94 C
smakowski@stvincentscollege.edu
MAKREZ, Heather 978-934-4809 237 B
heather_makrez@uml.edu
MAKSYMICZ, Kathy, E 330-287-1283 399 A
maksymicz.1@osu.edu
MALARA, Kathleen 718-817-4160 334 C
kmalara@fordham.edu
MALARET, Frank 916-558-2402 56 D
malarej@scc.losrios.edu
MALARTE-FELDMAN, Claire, L 603-862-2398 306 C
clmf@cisunix.unh.edu
MALASKA, Amy 330-490-7321 405 F
amalaska@walsh.edu
MALASKA, Amy, K 330-490-7321 405 F
amalaska@walsh.edu
MALASPINA, Margaret 860-906-5096 91 C
mmalaspina@ccc.commnet.edu
MALAT, Heide 651-690-6805 270 L
hlmalat@stkate.edu
MALATESTA, Addy 570-408-4020 452 A
adelene.malatesta@wilkes.edu
MALATESTA, Matthew, J 518-388-6112 358 G
malatesm@union.edu
MALAVE, Andres 954-262-1150 114 B
malave@nsu.nova.edu
MALAVE, Mara 787-480-2402 561 E
mamalave@sanjuancapital.com
MALAVE, Sarah 787-738-2161 567 D
sarah.malave@upr.edu
MALAVEZ, Jessica 718-260-5006 328 D
jmalavez@citytech.cuny.edu
MALBROUGH, Sara 912-525-5920 136 F
sedorsey@scad.edu
MALCHOW, Larry, P 920-748-8347 550 D
malchowl@ripon.edu
MALCOLM, Barbara 810-989-2118 248 G
barbara.malcolm@baker.edu
MALCOLM, III, Everett, J 904-620-2600 120 D
emalcolm@unf.edu
MALCOLM, John, M 413-597-4057 246 D
john.m.malcolm@williams.edu
MALCOLM, Joshua 910-521-6201 379 C
joshua.malcolm@uncp.edu
MALCOLM, Kathy 309-796-5038 145 H
malcolmk@bhc.edu
MALCOLM, Roy 256-726-8455 6 C
malcolm@oakwood.edu
MALCOLM, Ward 304-434-8000 542 I
wmalcolm@eastern.wvnet.edu
MALCOLM, Yvonnie 508-849-3427 230 C
ymalcolm@annamaria.edu
MALCONIAN, Sara 617-324-4538 241 D
MALDONADO, Cesar 956-364-4022 500 D
cesar.maldonado@tstc.edu
MALDONADO, Cesar 956-364-4020 500 C
cesar.maldonado@harlingen.tstc.edu
MALDONADO, Debi 909-931-7599 79 C
dmaldonado@westwood.edu
MALDONADO, Gilda 619-388-2817 65 G
gmaldona@sdccd.edu
MALDONADO, Ileana 787-725-8120 562 C
imaldonado@eap.edu
MALDONADO, Jo Ann 973-642-8578 315 C
joann.maldonado@shu.edu
MALDONADO, Juan 510-217-4736 29 H
jgmaldanado@argosy.edu
MALDONADO, Juan, L 956-721-5101 489 J
president@laredo.edu
MALDONADO, Kenneth 787-751-0178 565 F
kenmaldona@suagm.edu
MALDONADO, Lourdes 787-766-1717 565 I
lmaldonado@suagm.edu
MALDONADO, Magda 939-202-9953 568 C
magda.maldonado2@upr.edu
MALDONADO, Robert 585-389-2840 342 D
rmaldon0@naz.edu
MALDONADO, Rosemarie 212-237-8911 327 F
rmaldonado@jjay.cuny.edu
MALDONADO, Victor 787-878-5475 563 B
vmaldonado@arecibo.inter.edu
MALDONADO, Wanda 787-758-2525 567 G
wanda.maldonado1@upr.edu
MALDONADO-RUIZ, Alberto 787-257-7373 565 G
ue_amaldona@suagm.edu
MALECHA, Marvin, J 919-515-8302 378 C
marvin_malecha@ncsu.edu
MALECKE, Kenneth 313-927-1445 254 E
kmalecke@marygrove.edu

MALEK, Casey 620-227-9349 192 E
dcccgolf@dc3.edu
MALEK, Debby 620-227-9260 192 E
dmalek@dc3.edu
MALEKZADEH, Ali, R 785-532-7227 194 D
MALEN, Ann 970-491-5709 83 F
elizabeth.malen@colostate.edu
MALEWSKI, Erik 678-794-7575 133 A
emalewsk@kennesaw.edu
MALEY, Beth 859-344-3614 206 I
beth.maley@thomasmore.edu
MALEY, Brian 513-745-3315 406 E
maley@xavier.edu
MALEY, Daniel 269-488-4298 253 A
dmaley@kvcc.edu
MALEY, David, C 607-274-3480 336 G
maley@ithaca.edu
MALEY, Leasa, A 814-362-7539 449 B
maley@pitt.edu
MALEY, Robert 215-968-8116 423 F
maleyr@bucks.edu
MALEY, Sandra, J 609-497-7720 312 F
human.resources@ptsem.edu
MALFITANO, Gregory, J 561-237-7277 113 D
gmalfitano@lynn.edu
MALHAS, Faris, A 419-372-7581 385 E
fmalhas@bgsu.edu
MALHOTRA, Devinder 320-308-4909 269 A
dmmalhotra@stcloudstate.edu
MALHOTRA, Rajiv 617-732-2791 241 C
rajiv.malhotra@mcphs.edu
MALIEKAL, Jose 585-395-2394 352 F
jmalieka@brockport.edu
MALIG, Jannet 562-860-2451 39 A
jmalig@cerritos.edu
MALIK, Christopher, P 716-839-8332 331 F
cmalik@daemen.edu
MALIK, David, J 219-980-6966 174 B
dmalik@iun.edu
MALIK, Rick 312-225-6288 167 G
rmalik@vandercook.edu
MALIK, Tarun 980-598-1020 365 I
tarun.malik@jwu.edu
MALIK, Zafar, A 312-939-0111 150 D
zafar@eastwest.edu
MALIN, John 217-854-3231 146 A
jmali@blackburn.edu
MALINOWSKI, Sarah 201-761-6239 314 F
smalinowski@spc.edu
MALISCH, Susan, M 773-508-7750 157 C
smalisc@luc.edu
MALISOS, Gary 561-273-6500 118 A
gmalisos@southuniversity.edu
MALIWESKY, Martin 614-287-3669 389 A
mmaliwes@cscc.edu
MALKEMES, Janet 704-330-4806 369 D
janet.malkemes@cpcc.edu
MALKEWICZ, Lisa 574-257-3206 169 I
malkew@bethelcollege.edu
MALKIEWICZ, OFM, Stephen 414-425-8300 550 E
smalkiewicz@shst.edu
MALKOWSKI, Brenda 417-255-7966 286 D
brendamalkowski@missouristate.edu
MALKOWSKI, Keith 989-686-9449 250 D
MALL, Scot 502-423-0149 19 A
scot.mall@phoenix.edu
MALLACH, Sachi 610-526-6005 430 D
smallach@harcum.edu
MALLAMACE, Debra, L 732-750-1800 307 F
dlm@berkeleycollege.edu
MALLARD, Jessica 806-651-2777 499 A
jmallard@mail.wtamu.edu
MALLARD, Kina, S 865-471-3219 467 G
kmallard@cn.edu
MALLERY, Mike 503-352-2258 419 E
mallerym@pacificu.edu
MALLET, Chris 801-274-3280 512 F
cmallet@wgu.edu
MALLET, Colleen 845-437-5276 359 F
MALLETT, Justin 217-245-3271 152 D
justin.mallett@ic.edu
MALLETT, Kristi 918-343-7796 411 H
kmallett@rsu.edu
MALLETTE, Richard 847-735-5277 155 G
mallette@lakeforest.edu
MALLIA, Maria 201-559-6072 310 B
malliam@felician.edu
MALLO, Ted, A 330-972-6021 403 B
tamallo@uakron.edu
MALLORY, Brian 864-503-5796 463 B
mallory-brian@uscupstate.edu
MALLORY, Carolyn, R 361-570-4130 504 A
malloryc@uhv.edu
MALLORY, Dale, E 585-292-3040 341 H
dmallory@monroecc.edu
MALLORY, David, G 716-270-5348 333 C
mallory@ecc.edu
MALLORY, Katrina 404-237-7573 126 B
kmallory@bauder.edu
MALLORY, Kristen 909-621-8267 40 G
kristen.mallory@cmc.edu
MALLORY, Kristin 304-734-6605 542 H
kmallory@bridgemont.edu

MALLORY, Tim 714-459-1114 78 H
tmallory@wsulaw.edu
MALLOW, Richard 909-484-4311 46 F
MALLOY, Dorothy, A 610-519-7857 450 H
dorothy.malloy@villanova.edu
MALLOY, Jeffrey 812-535-5219 179 E
jmalloy@smwc.edu
MALLOY, Kathleen, A 724-925-4028 451 E
malloyka@wccc.edu
MALLOY, Leanne 317-955-6150 177 I
lmalloy@marian.edu
MALLOY, Michael, J 508-373-5611 241 C
michael.malloy@mcphs.edu
MALLOY, Patrick 212-243-5150 334 E
dean@gts.edu
MALLOY, SJ, Richard, G 570-941-6153 450 C
richard.malloy@scranton.edu
MALLOY, Thomas, K 610-499-4174 451 F
tkmalloy@widener.edu
MALLOZZI, Catherine 321-253-2929 106 G
cmallozz@cci.edu
MALM, Betsy 312-813-5140 162 G
bmalm@robertmorris.edu
MALM, James 719-549-2940 83 H
james.malm@colostate-pueblo.edu
MALMGREN, Betty, M 707-256-7112 58 F
bmalmgren@napavalley.edu
MALMGREN, Irene 626-914-8881 40 B
imalmgren@citruscollege.edu
MALMROSE, John 843-792-2721 459 D
malmrose@musc.edu
MALONE, Allison 870-574-4544 24 A
amalone@sautech.edu
MALONE, Anne, B 412-924-1379 444 H
amalone@pts.edu
MALONE, Brenda, R 919-962-1554 378 E
brenda_malone@unc.edu
MALONE, Brian 505-277-8900 321 C
bmalone@unm.edu
MALONE, Dan 214-333-6883 484 D
dan@dbu.edu
MALONE, Dean 630-515-7145 16 E
dmalon@midwestern.edu
MALONE, Dean, P 630-515-7145 158 F
dmalon@midwestern.edu
MALONE, Deborah 610-282-1100 427 A
debbie.malone@desales.edu
MALONE, Elbert, R 803-536-8213 460 G
malone@scsu.edu
MALONE, Jennifer 318-342-5397 216 E
jmalone@ulm.edu
MALONE, Jill 727-725-2688 106 F
mmalone@cci.edu
MALONE, John 651-962-6925 272 B
j9malone@stthomas.edu
MALONE, Judith, A 781-891-2016 231 D
jmalone@bentley.edu
MALONE, Kathy 219-980-6701 174 B
kalmalon@iun.edu
MALONE, Lora 817-272-2594 505 C
lmalone@uta.edu
MALONE, Marisa 317-554-8327 170 B
mamalone@brownmackie.edu
MALONE, Mary Frances 203-254-4000 92 H
malone@fairfield.edu
MALONE, Maureen 610-989-1453 450 F
mmalone@vfmac.edu
MALONE, Michael, F 413-545-5270 236 F
mmalone@umass.edu
MALONE, Michael, P 815-753-6065 160 B
mmalone@niu.edu
MALONE, Nina, R 310-233-4651 54 I
malonenr@lahc.edu
MALONE, Pamela 528-587-2100 355 G
pamela.malone@esc.edu
MALONE, Rachel 941-554-1522 101 A
rmalone@argosy.edu
MALONE, Ted, E 765-494-4600 178 J
temalone@purdue.edu
MALONE, Virginia, J 314-340-3339 282 F
malonev@hssu.edu
MALONE-FENNER, Shirley 617-879-2248 246 C
smalone-fenner@wheelock.edu
MALONEY, Barry, M 508-929-8020 238 G
bmaloney@worcester.edu
MALONEY, Cordelia 312-996-8586 167 B
cordelia@uic.edu
MALONEY, Dena 661-763-7710 72 E
dmaloney@taftcollege.edu
MALONEY, Gerald, J 404-894-0881 130 F
jerry.maloney@bks.gatech.edu
MALONEY, Kathryn, A 530-752-2396 73 I
kamaloney@ucdavis.edu
MALONEY, Krisellen 210-458-4889 506 D
krisellen.maloney@utsa.edu
MALONEY, Maureen, A 510-649-2464 48 J
maloney@gtu.edu
MALONEY, Maureen, L 203-358-0700 94 F
mmaureen@bridgeport.edu
MALONEY, Michael 212-280-1530 358 I
mmaloney@uts.columbia.edu
MALONEY, Michelle 610-917-1406 450 E
mmmaloney@vfcc.edu

MALONEY, Rebecca, S 504-866-7426 214 A
rmaloney@nds.edu
MALONEY, Shari 320-762-4466 265 F
sharim@alextech.edu
MALONEY, Vicky, G 803-778-6612 455 G
maloneyvg@cctech.edu
MALONEY, Vincent, U 802-626-6413 515 G
vincent.maloney@lyndonstate.edu
MALOOF, Lisa 770-868-4069 133 C
lmaloof@laniertech.edu
MALOSH, Ann 541-917-4923 416 I
malosha@linnbenton.edu
MALOTT, F. Stephen 573-341-4122 291 E
malott@mst.edu
MALOTT, Michelle, L 218-477-2574 267 F
michelle.malott@mnstate.edu
MALOTT, Pat 719-384-6841 87 A
pat.malott@ojc.edu
MALOVEY, Troy 412-200-3002 19 A
troy.malovey@phoenix.edu
MALOY, Frances, J 518-388-6739 358 G
MALOY, Michael, T 610-436-3309 444 A
mmaloy@wcupa.edu
MALOY, Stanley 619-594-5142 37 A
smaloy@sciences.sdsu.edu
MALOY, Vicky 319-368-6465 187 H
vmaloy@mtmercy.edu
MALPASS, Scott, C 574-631-8877 180 G
malpass.1@nd.edu
MALSHEIMER, Cheryl 305-809-3201 108 I
cheryl.malsheimer@fkcc.edu
MALSON, Don, G 573-875-7421 280 A
dgmalson@ccis.edu
MALTA, Anthony 318-342-3547 216 E
malta@ulm.edu
MALTBIE, Randy 256-840-4112 7 A
rmaltbie@snead.edu
MALTBY, Lee 773-878-3728 163 F
lmaltby@staugustine.edu
MALTBY, Marc 270-686-4544 203 B
marc.maltby@kctcs.edu
MALTESE, Vincent 734-384-4128 255 D
vmaltese@monroeccc.edu
MALTINO, Frank 973-408-3955 309 E
fmaltino@drew.edu
MALTZ, Mara 631-656-2131 334 B
mmaltz@ftc.edu
MALTZMAN, Forrest 202-994-6510 98 C
forrest@gwu.edu
MALUTICH, Stephen 832-201-3626 480 B
smalutich@houston.aiuniv.edu
MALVEAUX, Brent 251-343-8200 6 F
brent.malveaux@remingtoncollege.edu
MALVERS, Dennis 978-656-3116 240 B
malversd@middlesex.mass.edu
MALY, Lonn, D 651-641-8203 263 A
maly@csp.edu
MALZACHER, Valerie, I 715-425-3224 552 C
valerie.i.malzacher@uwrf.edu
MAMA, Robin 732-571-3543 311 E
rmama@monmouth.edu
MAMARCHEV, Helen 239-590-1022 119 B
hmamarchev@fgcu.edu
MAMARIL, Liz 858-653-6740 52 D
MAMI, Gwendolyn 303-352-7004 86 F
gmami@msudenver.edu
MAMON, Troy 404-527-4520 126 I
tmamon@carver.edu
MAMONIS, JR., Peter 619-275-4700 46 K
peter@fashioncareerscollege.com
MAN, Gordon 808-734-9124 141 J
goman@hawaii.edu
MANAHAN, Jamie 773-298-3329 163 I
manahan@sxu.edu
MANAHAN, Richard, A 423-439-5381 473 F
manahanr@etsu.edu
MANAHAN, Ronald, E 574-372-5100 171 H
manahare@grace.edu
MANARO, James, V 410-778-7204 229 D
jmanaro2@washcoll.edu
MANASERI, Christopher 808-455-0260 142 D
cmanaser@hawaii.edu
MANASSAH, Michele 815-836-5455 156 F
manassmi@lewisu.edu
MANAUTOU, Teresa 787-864-2222 563 F
tmantou@inter.edu
MANAZIR, Theodore 802-728-1275 516 A
tmanazir@vtc.vsc.edu
MANCE, Charles 724-938-1535 441 G
mance@calu.edu
MANCE, Jerry 757-455-3349 530 C
jmance@vwc.edu
MANCHESTER, Betsy 323-953-4000 54 H
manchepb@lacitycollege.edu
MANCHESTER-MOLAK, Ann 401-865-2406 453 H
ammolak@providence.edu
MANCHION, Jody 816-584-6272 287 E
jody.manchion@park.edu
MANCHUR, Fred, M 937-395-8775 394 D
fred.manchur@khnetwork.org
MANCINI, Donna 610-896-1230 430 G
dmancini@haverford.edu

MANZIONE, Lara ... 301-431-5450 ... 225 B
lmanzione@nlc.edu
MANZIONE, Louis ... 860-768-5015 ... 95 B
manzione@hartford.edu
MANZKE, Rob ... 715-346-3738 ... 552 D
rmanzke@uwsp.edu
MANZO, Pablo ... 916-856-3400 ... 55 J
manzop@losrios.edu
MAO, Ruixuan ... 847-214-7440 ... 150 F
rmao@elgin.edu
MAOLA, Chad ... 727-398-8454 ... 159 F
cmaola@nuhs.edu
MAPHUMULO, Peter ... 703-845-6222 ... 527 F
pmaphumulo@nvcc.edu
MAPLES, Cathy ... 956-364-4300 ... 500 D
cathy.maples@tstc.edu
MAPLES, Christopher ... 541-885-1100 ... 418 E
christopher.maples@oit.edu
MAPLES, Stephen ... 775-784-4700 ... 303 A
smaples@unr.edu
MAPLES-STERRY, Brenda ... 513-569-1555 ... 387 G
brenda.maples-sterry@cincinnatistate.edu
MAPLEY, Gordon ... 816-271-4100 ... 286 G
gmapley@missouriwestern.edu
MAR, Pansy ... 415-565-8902 ... 74 A
marp@uchastings.edu
MARA, Gerald ... 202-687-5974 ... 98 D
marag@georgetown.edu
MARA, Glenn, L ... 510-987-9405 ... 73 G
glenn.mara@ucop.edu
MARA, Mary ... 425-637-1010 ... 532 E
mmara@cityu.edu
MARA, Stacy, J ... 920-832-7486 ... 548 B
stacy.j.mara@lawrence.edu
MARABETI, Hilary, B ... 615-230-3355 ... 476 C
hilary.marabeti@volstate.edu
MARABLE, Shelia ... 205-929-6437 ... 5 E
smarable@lawsonstate.edu
MARAGAKIS, Emmanuel ... 775-784-6925 ... 303 A
maragaki@ce.unr.edu
MARAK, Randy ... 713-646-2912 ... 494 I
rmarak@stcl.edu
MARANDE, Robert, P ... 570-389-5333 ... 441 F
rmarande@bloomu.edu
MARANO, Jeanne ... 973-655-5333 ... 311 F
maranoj@mail.montclair.edu
MARANO, Nicole, C ... 443-334-2260 ... 226 E
nmarano@stevenson.edu
MARANTO-PHILLIPS, Tracy ... 318-869-5191 ... 208 H
tmphillips@centenary.edu
MARAVIGLIA, James, L ... 805-756-2311 ... 33 I
jmaravig@calpoly.edu
MARBACH, Joseph, R ... 215-951-1015 ... 432 I
marbach@lasalle.edu
MARBERRY, Thomas, L ... 405-912-9004 ... 408 D
tmarberry@hc.edu
MARBERT, Larry, D ... 305-284-5660 ... 122 I
lmarbert@miami.edu
MARBLE, Alan, D ... 417-455-5534 ... 280 H
amarble@crowder.edu
MARBLE, Amanda, F ... 208-467-8402 ... 144 E
afmarble@nnu.edu
MARBLE, Dexter ... 405-224-3140 ... 413 E
dmarble@usao.edu
MARBLE, Jan ... 507-389-5120 ... 267 E
janice.marble@mnsu.edu
MARBLE, Julie ... 318-678-6865 ... 19 A
julie.marble@phoenix.edu
MARBURGER, Ann, M ... 937-255-6565 ... 557 C
ann.marburger@afit.edu
MARBUT, Terry ... 256-782-5034 ... 4 L
tmarbut@jsu.edu
MARCANO, Dea ... 714-744-7045 ... 39 F
marcano@chapman.edu
MARCANO, Walbert ... 787-257-0000 ... 567 C
walbert.marcano@upr.edu
MARCANTONIO, James ... 573-681-5018 ... 283 I
marcantonioj@lincolnu.edu
MARCDANTE, Karen ... 414-955-8279 ... 548 G
kwendel@mcw.edu
MARCEL, Yorgun ... 712-749-1227 ... 183 C
marcely@bvu.edu
MARCEL, Yorgun ... 330-263-2262 ... 388 F
ymarcel@wooster.edu
MARCELLA, Pat ... 636-227-2100 ... 284 B
pat.marcella@logan.edu
MARCELLO, Kathleen, A ... 717-245-1554 ... 427 F
marcellk@dickinson.edu
MARCH, Ben ... 903-233-3810 ... 490 A
benmarch@letu.edu
MARCH, Ken ... 913-981-8702 ... 464 H
kmarch@national.edu
MARCHAL, Jerry ... 859-858-3511 ... 198 E
jmarchal@asbury.edu
MARCHAND, William ... 516-686-7904 ... 343 D
wmarchan@nyit.edu
MARCHANT, Jim ... 909-621-8241 ... 62 H
jim_marchant@pitzer.edu
MARCHANT, Karen ... 605-626-7781 ... 466 A
karen.marchang@northern.edu
MARCHANT, Lloyd ... 660-263-4110 ... 286 H
lloydm@macc.edu
MARCHANT, T. Eston ... 919-718-7246 ... 369 C
bmarchant@cccc.edu
MARCHASE, Richard, B ... 205-934-1294 ... 8 F
marchase@uab.edu
MARCHBANKS, Pete ... 979-845-8423 ... 497 E
pete-marchbanks@tamu.edu
MARCHELLETTA, Barbara ... 207-947-4591 ... 217 D
bmarchelletta@bealcollege.edu
MARCHELLO, Sara, L ... 757-221-2801 ... 518 A
sallie.marchello@wm.edu
MARCHESE, Cynthia, C ... 212-687-4303 ... 307 F
ccm@berkeleycollege.edu
MARCHESE, Cynthia, C ... 212-687-3730 ... 323 H
ccm@berkeleycollege.edu
MARCHESE, Paul ... 718-631-6690 ... 328 F
pmarchese@qcc.cuny.edu
MARCHILDON, Scott ... 207-221-4230 ... 221 A
smarchildon@une.edu
MARCHIONE, Susan, M ... 716-839-8447 ... 331 F
smarchio@daemen.edu
MARCHIONINI, Gary ... 919-962-8363 ... 378 E
gary@ils.unc.edu
MARCHIORI, Dennis, M ... 563-884-5500 ... 61 A
dennis.marchiori@palmer.edu
MARCHIORI, Dennis, M ... 563-884-5500 ... 188 E
dennis.marchiori@palmer.edu
MARCHIORI, Dennis, M ... 563-884-5500 ... 114 E
dennis.marchiori@palmer.edu
MARCHU, Gene ... 760-773-2567 ... 42 A
gmarchu@collegeofthedesert.edu
MARCI, Mark ... 412-281-2600 ... 447 A
mmarci@western-school.com
MARCIAL, Myriam ... 787-891-0925 ... 563 A
mmarcial@aguadilla.inter.edu
MARCIAL VEGA, Ivonne, M ... 787-945-7010 ... 562 C
rectoria@eap.edu
MARCIL, Alvina, O ... 680-488-2471 ... 560 C
alvinam@palau.edu
MARCILLE, Andrea, M ... 868-701-6393 ... 558 H
andrea.m.marcille@uscg.mil
MARCIN, Heidi, C ... 585-785-1609 ... 334 A
marcinhc@flcc.edu
MARCINEK, Myron ... 570-961-4786 ... 435 F
mmarcinek@marywood.edu
MARCO, Rachel ... 815-288-5511 ... 164 B
marcor@svcc.edu
MARCOCCIA, Louis, G ... 315-443-3037 ... 357 C
lmarcocc@syr.edu
MARCOE, Timothy ... 570-784-3123 ... 441 F
frtim@bloomu.edu
MARCOGLIESE, Marie ... 651-450-3546 ... 266 F
mmarcog@inverhills.edu
MARCOLINE, Beverly, J ... 315-792-3041 ... 359 E
bmarcoline@utica.edu
MARCONE, Luigi ... 203-837-9314 ... 91 A
marconel@wcsu.edu
MARCOTTE, Sharon ... 218-335-4253 ... 264 G
sharon.marcotte@lltc.edu
MARCUCCILLI, Christine, M ... 260-481-6106 ... 174 C
marcuccc@ipfw.edu
MARCUM, Judith, W ... 859-846-5834 ... 204 H
jmarcum@midway.edu
MARCUM, Marie ... 603-542-7744 ... 304 G
mmarcum@ccsnh.edu
MARCUM, Roger, L ... 859-336-5082 ... 206 A
rmarcum@sccky.edu
MARCUS, Jamie, E ... 207-778-7000 ... 220 C
MARCUS, John ... 508-541-1508 ... 233 G
jmarcus@dean.edu
MARCUS, Lynn ... 978-762-4000 ... 240 D
lmarcus@northshore.edu
MARCUS, Nancy ... 850-644-3500 ... 119 D
nmarcus@fsu.edu
MARCUS, Robert, J ... 317-940-9910 ... 170 F
rmarcus@butler.edu
MARCUS, William ... 406-243-4154 ... 294 I
william.marcus@umontana.edu
MARCUS BURGER, Sally ... 304-766-3131 ... 544 F
marcussc@wvstateu.edu
MARCUS-NEWHALL, Amy ... 909-607-2822 ... 69 A
amy.marcus-newhall@scrippscollege.edu
MARCUSE, Adrian, G ... 212-752-1530 ... 338 C
adrian.marcuse@limcollege.edu
MARCUSE, Elizabeth, S ... 212-752-1530 ... 338 C
elizabeth.marcuse@limcollege.edu
MARCUSSEN, Thomas ... 414-229-4537 ... 551 D
marcusse@uwm.edu
MARCY, Mary, B ... 415-485-3200 ... 45 C
president@dominican.edu
MARCZYNSKI, Jerry ... 775-784-4898 ... 303 A
marczyns@unr.edu
MARDEN, Rose ... 210-341-1366 ... 491 G
rmarden@ost.edu
MARDIROSIAN, Haig ... 813-253-6100 ... 123 A
hmardirosian@ut.edu
MARDIS, Michael ... 502-852-5787 ... 207 E
mike.mardis@louisville.edu
MAREK, Cynthia ... 507-457-1443 ... 271 B
cmarek@smumn.edu
MAREK, Diane ... 847-233-7700 ... 160 D
dmarek@nc.edu
MAREK, Robin ... 401-232-6804 ... 453 C
rmarek@bryant.edu
MAREK, Sandra ... 660-263-4110 ... 286 H
sandram@macc.edu
MARES, Maria ... 787-864-2222 ... 563 F
mmares@inter.edu
MARFELL, Julie ... 859-253-3637 ... 200 K
julie.marfell@frontier.edu
MARFISE, Larry, J ... 813-253-6240 ... 123 A
lmarfise@ut.edu
MARGERUM, Eric, W ... 812-888-5127 ... 181 D
emargerum@vinu.edu
MARGHEIM, Jeffrey ... 386-822-7020 ... 121 F
jmarghei@stetson.edu
MARGISON, Richard, L ... 205-934-5493 ... 8 F
margison@uab.edu
MARGLIOTTI, Garrett, D ... 412-578-6010 ... 424 I
gdmargliotti@carlow.edu
MARGOLIS, Liza ... 340-693-1053 ... 568 E
lmargol@live.uvi.edu
MARGON, Bruce ... 831-459-2425 ... 75 C
margon@ucsc.edu
MARGULES, Gary, S ... 954-262-7507 ... 114 B
margules@nsu.nova.edu
MARGULIES, Anne ... 617-495-9092 ... 235 D
anne_margulies@harvard.edu
MARGULIES, L ... 718-853-8500 ... 358 A
MARGULIES, Mordechai ... 718-854-2290 ... 323 I
MARHAVER, Brian ... 315-866-1550 ... 335 D
marhavebt@herkimer.edu
MARI, Mike ... 707-468-3165 ... 57 A
mari@mendocino.edu
MARIANI, Cynthia ... 860-231-5387 ... 95 D
cmariani@usj.edu
MARIANI, Elsa ... 787-257-7373 ... 565 G
emariani@suagm.edu
MARIANI, Michael, A ... 716-625-6300 ... 324 K
mamariani@bryantstratton.edu
MARIANI, William ... 716-829-8194 ... 332 E
marianiw@dyc.edu
MARIANO, Anthony, A ... 802-485-2230 ... 514 C
tmariano@norwich.edu
MARIANS, Kenneth, J ... 646-888-6639 ... 339 E
kmarians@sloankettering.edu
MARICHAL-LUGO, Carlos ... 787-993-8866 ... 567 B
carlos.marichal@upr.edu
MARICK, Gregory, J ... 714-830-0250 ... 30 B
gmarick@aii.edu
MARICS, Joseph, F ... 417-268-1000 ... 278 H
jmarics@agts.edu
MARIGLIANO, Tom ... 312-752-2262 ... 155 C
thomas.marigliano@kendall.edu
MARIN, Gerardo ... 415-422-2199 ... 76 E
marin@usfca.edu
MARIN, Noemi ... 561-297-3850 ... 119 A
nmarin@fau.edu
MARIN CRESPO, Reinaldo ... 787-896-2252 ... 562 B
rmarin@edpcollege.edu
MARIN-HILL, Angelica ... 214-648-3684 ... 507 E
angelica.marin-hill@utsouthwestern.edu
MARINACCIO, Jessica ... 212-854-1222 ... 330 F
jm996@columbia.edu
MARINACE, Betsy ... 973-684-6861 ... 312 E
bmarinace@pccc.edu
MARINELLI, Bryan, D ... 401-865-1822 ... 453 H
bmarinel@providence.edu
MARINETTI, Mike ... 920-465-2454 ... 551 B
marinetm@uwgb.edu
MARINI, Jacob ... 212-237-8449 ... 327 F
jmarini@jjay.cuny.edu
MARINI, Janice, K ... 215-955-2244 ... 448 C
janice.marini@jefferson.edu
MARINI, Mario ... 724-589-2022 ... 448 B
mmarini@thiel.edu
MARINI, Stephen, T ... 508-854-4872 ... 240 F
smarini@qcc.mass.edu
MARINIS, Jeremy ... 419-448-3301 ... 402 E
marinisjj@tiffin.edu
MARINO, Chris ... 864-646-1836 ... 461 F
cmarino@tctc.edu
MARINO, James ... 856-225-6046 ... 314 D
jmarino@camden.rutgers.edu
MARINO, Kathy ... 973-290-4089 ... 308 G
kmarino@cse.edu
MARINO, Lucille ... 785-864-7431 ... 197 B
lmarino@ku.edu
MARINO, Mary Ellen ... 505-438-8884 ... 320 G
maryellen@acupuncturecollege.edu
MARINO, Michael ... 717-295-1100 ... 452 J
michael.marino@yti.edu
MARINO, Michael ... 717-767-0303 ... 452 J
michael.marino@yti.edu
MARINO, Patricia ... 518-262-9550 ... 322 D
marinop@mail.amc.edu
MARINO, Robert ... 585-389-2604 ... 342 D
rmarino9@naz.edu
MARINO, Robert ... 802-860-2751 ... 513 C
MARINSHAW, Ruth ... 919-962-4314 ... 378 E
ruth_marinshaw@unc.edu
MARINUCCI, Dorothy ... 718-817-3000 ... 334 C
marinucci@fordham.edu
MARION, Anne ... 407-628-6264 ... 122 C
amarion@teu.edu
MARION, D. Keith ... 803-754-4100 ... 457 D
MARION, Joseph ... 504-286-5389 ... 214 J
jmarion@suno.edu
MARION, Lucy, N ... 706-721-3771 ... 130 D
lumarion@georgiahealth.edu
MARION, Michael ... 916-691-7738 ... 56 B
marionm@crc.losrios.edu
MARION, Paul ... 978-934-3107 ... 237 B
paul_marion@uml.edu
MARION, Paul ... 419-448-3413 ... 402 E
marionp@tiffin.edu
MARION, Phyllis, C ... 619-239-0391 ... 37 F
pmarion@cwsl.edu
MARIS, Melinda ... 309-677-3961 ... 146 C
mmaris@bradley.edu
MARIUCCI, Robert ... 805-546-3210 ... 43 I
rmariucc@cuesta.edu
MARIX, Amy ... 225-578-3103 ... 212 H
MARIZ, George ... 360-650-3446 ... 539 F
george.mariz@wwu.edu
MARK, ASC, JoAnn ... 316-942-4291 ... 195 F
markj@newmanu.edu
MARK, Joy ... 620-947-3121 ... 197 A
joym@tabor.edu
MARK JONES, John ... 903-468-8144 ... 498 B
john.jones@tamuc.edu
MARKELL, Dawn ... 517-338-3048 ... 249 D
dmarkell@cleary.edu
MARKER, John ... 831-582-4796 ... 35 E
jmarker@csumb.edu
MARKERT, Stephen ... 713-221-8946 ... 503 F
markerts@uhd.edu
MARKEY, John ... 210-341-1366 ... 491 G
eowens@ost.edu
MARKEY, Nanette ... 301-696-3620 ... 223 C
markey@hood.edu
MARKEY-GRABILL, Mindy ... 937-393-3431 ... 402 A
mmarkey@sscc.edu
MARKGRAF, Karl, F ... 715-836-4411 ... 551 A
markgraf@uwec.edu
MARKHAM, Ian, S ... 703-461-1701 ... 522 I
imarkham@vts.edu
MARKHAM, Joseph ... 770-962-7580 ... 132 D
jmarkham@gwinnetttech.edu
MARKIEWICZ, Renee, J ... 508-849-3291 ... 230 C
rmarkiewicz@annamaria.edu
MARKIN, Rodney ... 402-559-7687 ... 300 H
rmarkin@unmc.edu
MARKLE, Chris, A ... 570-372-4425 ... 447 E
marklec@susqu.edu
MARKLE, Elizabeth ... 775-831-1314 ... 303 E
emarkle@sierranevada.edu
MARKLE, Sue ... 412-346-2100 ... 444 E
smarkle@pia.edu
MARKLE, William, J ... 610-359-5113 ... 426 G
wmarkle@dccc.edu
MARKLEY, Bradley, A ... 717-766-2511 ... 436 D
bmarkley@messiah.edu
MARKLEY, Neil ... 707-664-4068 ... 37 D
neil.markley@sonoma.edu
MARKLEY, Rebecca ... 800-962-7682 ... 293 A
bmarkley@wma.ed
MARKMAN, Rebecca ... 888-974-3436 ... 46 M
rmarkman@fidm.edu
MARKOV, Kornelia ... 928-776-2087 ... 19 C
kornelia.markov@yc.edu
MARKOVICH, Matt ... 415-485-9591 ... 42 B
matt.markovich@marin.edu
MARKOVICH, Sue ... 330-499-9600 ... 393 I
smarkov@kent.edu
MARKOWITZ, Marianne ... 315-448-5040 ... 349 C
MARKOWITZ, Martin, S ... 848-445-3600 ... 314 C
markowitz@business.rutgers.edu
MARKOWITZ, Michael ... 215-637-7700 ... 431 A
mmarkowitz@holyfamily.edu
MARKOWSKI, Vincent ... 201-684-7432 ... 313 C
vmarkows@ramapo.edu
MARKS, Andrea, M ... 210-567-7020 ... 507 A
marksa@uthscsa.edu
MARKS, Debra, J ... 714-449-7463 ... 70 G
dmarks@scco.edu
MARKS, Ellen ... 906-487-2500 ... 255 B
ebmarks@mtu.edu
MARKS, Erica ... 718-260-3298 ... 346 C
emarks@poly.edu
MARKS, Ian, R ... 440-510-1112 ... 386 C
irmarks@bryantstratton.edu
MARKS, Janice, L ... 443-518-4617 ... 223 D
jmarks@howardcc.edu
MARKS, Leota ... 913-288-7200 ... 194 C
lmarks@kckcc.edu
MARKS, Lilly ... 303-724-5369 ... 88 J
lilly.marks@ucdenver.edu
MARKS, Lisa, M ... 618-453-1067 ... 165 B
marks04@siu.edu
MARKS, Mary ... 603-206-8151 ... 304 D
mmarks@ccsnh.edu
MARKS, Michelle ... 703-993-8705 ... 519 E
mmarks@gmu.edu
MARKS, Ronald ... 504-865-5314 ... 215 C
rmarks@tulane.edu
MARKS, Ruth Ann ... 952-888-4777 ... 270 C
rmarks@nwhealth.edu
MARKS, RuthAnn ... 952-888-4777 ... 270 C
rmarks@nwhealth.edu
MARKS, Sandra ... 562-860-2451 ... 39 A
smarks@cerritos.edu
MARKS, William ... 410-293-1521 ... 559 B
pao@usna.edu

MARTERER, Aaron, C .... 803-777-1006.... 462 A
marterer@sc.edu
MARTHALER, Kristin .... 952-563-1250.... 464 H
MARTHERS, Paul .... 518-276-6143.... 347 D
marthp@rpi.edu
MARTI, Dennis, N .... 216-221-8584.... 405 E
dmarti@vmcad.edu
MARTI, Eduardo .... 212-794-5676.... 326 B
eduardo.marti@mail.cuny.edu
MARTI, Marilyn .... 787-834-5151.... 565 D
mmarti@email.pucpr.edu
MARTI, Quinn, E .... 216-221-8584.... 405 E
qmarti@vmcad.edu
MARTI, Tammy, S .... 563-588-7142.... 187 C
tammy.marti@loras.edu
MARTI-VEITH, Virginia ...... 216-221-8584.... 405 E
vmv@vmcad.edu
MARTIN, Aaron .... 337-482-6397.... 216 D
aaronmartin@louisiana.edu
MARTIN, Adrienne .... 530-752-0860...... 73 I
almartin@ucdavis.edu
MARTIN, Alan .... 405-425-5371.... 409 E
alan.martin@oc.edu
MARTIN, Alan, B .... 304-293-7398.... 545 A
alan.martin@mail.wvu.edu
MARTIN, Andrea .... 713-348-4661.... 493 C
andrea@rice.edu
MARTIN, Angela .... 937-461-5174.... 396 C
angela.martin@staffmiamijacobs.edu
MARTIN, Angela .... 859-257-5701.... 207 D
angelam@uky.edu
MARTIN, Angela, A .... 515-574-1064.... 185 I
martin_a@iowacentral.edu
MARTIN, Ann .... 303-964-5718...... 87 I
amartin@regis.edu
MARTIN, Ann .... 660-562-1570.... 287 B
amartin@nwmissouri.edu
MARTIN, Ann .... 828-251-6512.... 378 D
amartin@unca.edu
MARTIN, Anna, B .... 757-221-2553.... 518 A
martin@wm.edu
MARTIN, Anthony .... 219-989-2220.... 178 K
anthony.martin@purduecal.edu
MARTIN, Anthony .... 281-649-3152.... 487 H
amartin@hbu.edu
MARTIN, April .... 251-343-7227...... 3 D
april.martin@vc.edu
MARTIN, Barbara .... 802-828-2800.... 515 E
martinb@ccv.edu
MARTIN, Barry .... 303-273-3900...... 83 B
bemartin@mines.edu
MARTIN, Bethany, A .... 315-386-7555.... 355 E
martinb@canton.edu
MARTIN, Bobby .... 405-491-6339.... 412 D
bgmartin@snu.edu
MARTIN, Bonnie .... 678-891-3394.... 131 C
bmartin@gpc.edu
MARTIN, Bonnie, G .... 607-746-4495.... 355 F
martinbg@delhi.edu
MARTIN, Bridgit .... 920-403-3963.... 550 F
bridgit.martin@snc.edu
MARTIN, Brock .... 219-785-5225.... 179 A
bmartin@pnc.edu
MARTIN, Bruce .... 575-439-3624.... 319 E
iconick@nmsua.nmsu.edu
MARTIN, JR., C. Vernon ... 305-626-3714.... 109 A
vmartin@fmuniv.edu
MARTIN, Cameron .... 717-560-8206.... 433 D
cmartin@lbc.edu
MARTIN, Cameron, K .... 801-321-7115.... 511 B
cmartin@utahsbr.edu
MARTIN, Carla .... 318-487-7750.... 209 F
cmartin@lacollege.edu
MARTIN, Carla .... 870-575-8577...... 25 B
martinc@uapb.edu
MARTIN, Carmella .... 904-470-8081.... 105 G
carmella.martin0906@ewc.edu
MARTIN, Carolyn, R .... 804-289-8088.... 525 E
cmartin@richmond.edu
MARTIN,
Carolyn (Biddy), A .... 413-542-2234.... 230 A
bmartin@amherst.edu
MARTIN, Cecelia .... 251-460-6591....... 9 D
cgmartin@usouthal.edu
MARTIN, Charles .... 340-693-1511.... 568 E
cmartin@live.uvi.edu
MARTIN, Charlie .... 727-376-6911.... 122 E
cmartin@trinitycollege.edu
MARTIN, Christa, S .... 931-540-2644.... 475 A
cmartin@columbiastate.edu
MARTIN, Christine, M .... 304-293-8020.... 545 A
chris.martin@mail.wvu.edu
MARTIN, Christopher, L .... 318-869-5149.... 208 H
cmartin@centenary.edu
MARTIN, Cindy .... 616-234-3673.... 251 E
cmartin@grcc.edu
MARTIN, Clarence "Gus" ... 310-243-3766...... 34 D
gmartin@csudh.edu
MARTIN, Cleo .... 843-525-8203.... 461 E
ctmartin@tcl.edu
MARTIN, Constance, M ..... 704-687-8842.... 379 A
comartin@uncc.edu
MARTIN, Curt .... 970-248-1396...... 82 F
cumartin@coloradomesa.edu
MARTIN, Curtis .... 256-372-8214....... 1 A
curtis.martin@aamu.edu
MARTIN, D. Michael .... 415-380-1504...... 48 E
michaelmartin@ggbts.edu
MARTIN, Dan, J .... 412-268-2349.... 424 J
djmartin@cmu.edu
MARTIN, Daniel .... 312-935-2016.... 162 G
dmartin@robertmorris.edu
MARTIN, Daniel, J .... 206-281-2114.... 537 H
dmartin@spu.edu
MARTIN, Dave .... 724-852-3463.... 451 B
dmartin@waynesburg.edu
MARTIN, David .... 323-469-3300...... 27 H
MARTIN, David .... 414-847-3213.... 549 B
davidmartin@miad.edu
MARTIN, David .... 212-787-5300.... 322 F
MARTIN, David .... 502-852-4653.... 207 E
dcmart02@louisville.edu
MARTIN, David .... 423-636-7319.... 477 A
dmartin@tusculum.edu
MARTIN, David .... 718-420-4341.... 360 A
dmartin@wagner.edu
MARTIN, David .... 910-893-1610.... 362 J
dmartin@campbell.edu
MARTIN, David .... 502-852-8220.... 207 E
dcmart02@louisville.edu
MARTIN, David .... 570-674-6294.... 436 F
dmartin@misericordia.edu
MARTIN, David, G .... 585-385-8079.... 348 F
dmartin@sjfc.edu
MARTIN, David, J .... 979-845-0532.... 497 E
david-j-martin@tamu.edu
MARTIN, David, W .... 605-394-2400.... 466 B
david.martin@sdsmt.edu
MARTIN, Debbie .... 973-290-4208.... 308 G
dmartin@cse.edu
MARTIN, Deborah .... 312-629-6800.... 164 C
dmartin@saic.edu
MARTIN, Deborah .... 717-477-1121.... 443 E
dkmart@ship.edu
MARTIN, Deidre .... 803-641-3448.... 462 B
deidrem@usca.edu
MARTIN, Desiree .... 718-409-7271.... 356 C
dmartin@sunymaritime.edu
MARTIN, Dewey .... 314-246-7560.... 292 J
deweymartin21@webster.edu
MARTIN, Diana .... 859-246-6344.... 201 H
diana.martin@kctcs.edu
MARTIN, Diane .... 704-463-3052.... 375 F
diane.martin@fsmail.pfeiffer.edu
MARTIN, Diane, C .... 202-994-0513...... 98 C
dmartin@gwu.edu
MARTIN, Donald, L .... 706-233-7203.... 137 A
dmartin@shorter.edu
MARTIN, Donald, L .... 262-554-2010.... 158 E
dlcdcphd@comcast.net
MARTIN, Donna, P .... 270-901-1116.... 201 I
donna.martin@kctcs.edu
MARTIN, Dorothy .... 207-768-2806.... 218 J
dmartin@nmcc.edu
MARTIN, Dorothy .... 229-430-4610.... 124 A
dorothy.martin@asurams.edu
MARTIN, Dorothy .... 718-429-6600.... 359 G
dorothy.martin@vaughn.edu
MARTIN, Dorothy, J .... 205-348-4894....... 8 E
dot@ua.edu
MARTIN, Earl, F .... 509-313-6289.... 534 F
martine@gonzaga.edu
MARTIN, III, Earl Joe .... 225-752-4230.... 209 C
jmartin@iticollege.edu
MARTIN, Edd .... 254-295-4524.... 504 C
emartin@umhb.edu
MARTIN, Edward .... 775-445-4272.... 303 B
marti691@wnc.edu
MARTIN, Edward .... 931-363-9832.... 471 A
emartin@martinmethodist.edu
MARTIN, Elaine, R .... 508-856-2399.... 237 C
elaine.martin@umassmed.edu
MARTIN, Elizabeth .... 906-487-7253.... 251 A
beth.martin@finlandia.edu
MARTIN, Emily .... 251-580-2101....... 5 A
emartin@faulknerstate.edu
MARTIN, Eric .... 212-752-1530.... 338 C
eric.martin@limcollege.edu
MARTIN, Erica .... 319-385-6214.... 186 E
erica.martin@iwc.edu
MARTIN, Etienne .... 614-287-2491.... 389 A
emarti10@cscc.edu
MARTIN, G. Steven .... 510-642-5716...... 73 H
gsm@berkeley.edu
MARTIN, Geoffrey .... 419-530-1242.... 404 F
geoffrey.martin@utoledo.edu
MARTIN, George, E .... 512-448-8411.... 493 E
georgem@stedwards.edu
MARTIN, George, M .... 716-888-8208.... 325 F
martin@canisius.edu
MARTIN, Gerardina .... 610-738-0496.... 444 A
gmartin@wcupa.edu
MARTIN, Greg .... 515-964-6368.... 183 H
gcmartin@dmacc.edu
MARTIN, Gregg, F .... 202-685-3924.... 557 I
gregg.martin@ndu.edu
MARTIN, Harold, L .... 336-334-7940.... 378 A
hmartin@ncat.edu
MARTIN, Ilia .... 954-492-5353.... 103 F
imartin@citycollege.edu
MARTIN, Irene .... 860-343-5740...... 91 G
imartin@mxcc.commnet.edu
MARTIN, Jack .... 815-967-7302.... 162 I
jmartin@rockfordcareercollege.edu
MARTIN, James .... 409-747-9055.... 507 C
j5martin@utmb.edu
MARTIN, James, J .... 501-882-8851...... 20 C
jjmartin@asub.edu
MARTIN, Jan .... 323-469-3300...... 27 H
MARTIN, Jan .... 212-787-5300.... 322 F
MARTIN, Jana .... 918-293-5339.... 410 E
jana.s.martin@okstate.edu
MARTIN, Jennifer .... 940-898-3415.... 502 D
jmartin@twu.edu
MARTIN, Jill .... 800-567-2344.... 547 A
jmartin@menominee.edu
MARTIN, Jim .... 248-340-0600.... 247 I
james.martin@baker.edu
MARTIN, Jim David .... 415-575-6165...... 32 G
jmartin@ciis.edu
MARTIN, Jimmy .... 832-813-6680.... 490 E
james.d.martin@lonestar.edu
MARTIN, Joel, W .... 413-545-6330.... 236 F
jmartin@provost.umass.edu
MARTIN, John .... 860-486-2709...... 94 G
jmartin@foundation.uconn.edu
MARTIN, John .... 916-631-8108...... 33 F
MARTIN, John .... 502-597-6242.... 203 G
john.martin@kysu.edu
MARTIN, John, A .... 585-594-6100.... 344 F
presidentsoffice@roberts.edu
MARTIN, John, A .... 585-594-6100.... 347 F
presidentsoffice@roberts.edu
MARTIN, John, O .... 413-545-0361.... 236 F
jomartin@admin.umass.edu
MARTIN, JR., John, R ...... 817-515-7765.... 496 C
john.martin@tccd.edu
MARTIN, John, U .... 941-487-4444.... 120 A
jmartin@ncf.edu
MARTIN, Jose .... 602-557-1013...... 19 A
jose.martin@phoenix.edu
MARTIN, Joshua .... 508-854-7513.... 240 F
jmartin@qcc.mass.edu
MARTIN, Joshua .... 612-343-4469.... 270 A
jdmartin@northcentral.edu
MARTIN, Juanita, K .... 330-972-7082.... 403 B
juanita@uakron.edu
MARTIN, Jules .... 212-998-1300.... 344 B
jules.martin@nyu.edu
MARTIN, Karen, O .... 912-279-5750.... 127 E
kmartin@ccga.edu
MARTIN, Katherine .... 319-273-2737.... 182 G
katherine.martin@uni.edu
MARTIN, Kathy .... 503-228-6528.... 414 E
MARTIN, Kathy .... 704-406-4636.... 364 E
kmartin@gardner-webb.edu
MARTIN, Kathy .... 712-274-5148.... 187 G
martink@morningside.edu
MARTIN, Kathy .... 208-792-2282.... 144 B
kmartin@lcsc.edu
MARTIN, Kathy .... 615-963-5254.... 474 A
kmartin@tnstate.edu
MARTIN, Keith .... 716-338-1261.... 337 E
keithmartin@mail.sunyjcc.edu
MARTIN, Keith .... 918-343-7631.... 411 H
kmartin@rsu.edu
MARTIN, Kelley .... 316-295-5568.... 193 B
kelley_martin@friends.edu
MARTIN, Kenneth .... 972-937-7612.... 491 C
kenneth.martin@navarrocollege.edu
MARTIN, Kenneth, M .... 717-815-1211.... 452 G
kmartin@ycp.edu
MARTIN, Kevin .... 302-225-6241...... 96 H
martink@gbc.edu
MARTIN, Kevin .... 618-650-2345.... 165 C
kemarti@siue.edu
MARTIN, Kyle, R .... 208-496-1010.... 143 A
martink@byui.edu
MARTIN, Lara .... 561-237-7459.... 113 D
lmartin@lynn.edu
MARTIN, Laura .... 404-471-6054.... 123 I
lmartin@agnesscott.edu
MARTIN, Leandra .... 408-298-2181...... 67 D
leandra.martin@sjcc.edu
MARTIN, Lee .... 419-448-2169.... 391 F
lmartin@heidelberg.edu
MARTIN, Leigh, S .... 770-720-5634.... 136 C
lsm@reinhardt.edu
MARTIN, Linda .... 609-586-4800.... 311 B
martinl@mccc.edu
MARTIN, Lisa .... 504-865-3428.... 213 F
lmartin@loyno.edu
MARTIN, Lisa .... 918-343-7614.... 411 H
lmartin@rsu.edu
MARTIN, Lizbeth, J .... 510-436-1040...... 50 H
martin@hnu.edu
MARTIN, Lois .... 612-977-5307.... 261 F
lois.martin@capella.edu
MARTIN, Lonnie .... 717-560-8254.... 433 D
lmartin@lbc.edu
MARTIN, Louisa .... 603-668-2211.... 305 I
l.martin@snhu.edu
MARTIN, Louisa, A .... 210-431-5005.... 493 F
lmartin@stmarytx.edu
MARTIN, Lynn .... 734-973-3507.... 259 F
lgmartin@wccnet.edu
MARTIN, Lynn .... 515-271-1681.... 184 A
lynn.martin@dmu.edu
MARTIN, Maggie .... 229-391-5135.... 123 H
mmartin@abac.edu
MARTIN, Marcus, L .... 434-243-2079.... 525 F
mlm8n@virginia.edu
MARTIN, Marie .... 651-604-4131.... 265 B
MARTIN, Marie .... 803-780-1229.... 463 C
martin@voorhees.edu
MARTIN, Mariel, L .... 518-580-8212.... 351 B
mariel@skidmore.edu
MARTIN, Mark, A .... 989-837-4497.... 256 E
martinm@northwood.edu
MARTIN, Michael .... 212-636-6875.... 334 C
mimartin@law.fordham.edu
MARTIN, Michael .... 408-541-0100...... 41 E
mmartin@cogswell.edu
MARTIN, Michael .... 918-647-1361.... 407 E
mmartin@carlalbert.edu
MARTIN, Michaeld .... 303-534-6290...... 83 E
MARTIN, Michele .... 802-586-7711.... 514 G
mmartin@sterlingcollege.edu
MARTIN, Michelle .... 765-459-0561.... 176 C
mmartin@ivytech.edu
MARTIN, Michelle .... 609-894-9311.... 308 B
mmartin@bcc.edu
MARTIN, Mirta, M .... 804-524-5166.... 529 H
mmartin@vsu.edu
MARTIN, Mona .... 310-434-4692...... 68 D
martin_mona@smc.edu
MARTIN, Pamela .... 641-673-1182.... 190 C
martinp@wmpenn.edu
MARTIN, Patricia .... 507-786-3009.... 271 C
martinp@stolaf.edu
MARTIN, Paul .... 518-276-8711.... 347 D
martip@rpi.edu
MARTIN, Paul .... 617-730-7155.... 243 D
paul.martin@newbury.edu
MARTIN, Paul .... 510-841-1905...... 27 J
pmartin@absw.edu
MARTIN, Peggy Murray ..... 305-626-3749.... 109 A
pmartin@fmuniv.edu
MARTIN, Peter, A .... 386-763-2651.... 114 E
peter.martin@palmer.edu
MARTIN, Quincy .... 708-456-0300.... 166 F
qmartin@triton.edu
MARTIN, Rafael .... 972-883-4824.... 506 A
rafael.martin@utdallas.edu
MARTIN, Randy .... 870-972-2093...... 20 D
rmartin@astate.edu
MARTIN, Ray .... 254-295-4590.... 504 C
rmartin@umhb.edu
MARTIN, Richard, D .... 706-776-0105.... 136 A
dmartin@piedmont.edu
MARTIN, Robert .... 810-766-8756.... 248 C
robert.martin@baker.edu
MARTIN, Robert .... 845-758-7419.... 323 D
martin@bard.edu
MARTIN, Robert .... 505-424-2302.... 318 D
rmartin@iaia.edu
MARTIN, Robert, E .... 303-233-4697...... 83 C
robt@schooloftrades.com
MARTIN, Robert, K .... 217-581-5983.... 150 E
rmartin@eiu.edu
MARTIN, Ron .... 618-262-8641.... 153 A
martinr@iecc.edu
MARTIN, Ron .... 417-690-3248.... 279 J
martin@cofo.edu
MARTIN, Ronald, C .... 814-732-2743.... 442 E
martinr@edinboro.edu
MARTIN, Roneida .... 847-543-2641.... 148 B
rmartin@clcillinois.edu
MARTIN, Rosalynn .... 256-782-5007....... 4 L
martin@jsu.edu
MARTIN, Roy, J .... 225-578-2284.... 212 H
rjmartin@lsu.edu
MARTIN, Ruth .... 619-201-8685...... 65 D
ruth.martin@sdcc.edu
MARTIN, Ryan .... 201-360-4024.... 310 E
rmartin@hccc.edu
MARTIN, Sally, L .... 920-498-6866.... 555 C
sally.martin@nwtc.edu
MARTIN, Scott .... 706-355-5037.... 125 C
smartin@athenstech.edu
MARTIN, Sean .... 602-557-7424...... 19 A
sean.martin@apollogrp.edu
MARTIN, Shane .... 310-338-7457...... 56 E
smartin@lmu.edu
MARTIN, Staci .... 903-983-8200.... 489 I
smartin@kilgore.edu
MARTIN, Susan .... 415-749-4533...... 65 I
smartin@sfai.edu
MARTIN, Susan .... 502-863-8407.... 201 A
susan_martin@georgetowncollege.edu
MARTIN, Susan .... 734-487-2211.... 250 F
sue.martin@emich.edu
MARTIN, Susan, D .... 865-974-2445.... 477 D
sdmartin@utk.edu
MARTIN, Susan, M .... 630-942-3324.... 148 A
martinsu@cod.edu

MARZUK, Peter, M .... 212-746-1203.... 360 C
pmmarzuk@med.cornell.edu
MAS, Desander .... 212-410-8086.... 343 B
dmas@nycpm.edu
MAS, Nestor .... 787-257-7373.... 565 G
ue_nestor@suagm.edu
MASCAL, Vince .... 831-647-4106...... 57 F
vince.mascal@miis.edu
MASCARIN, Mary Louise ... 609-894-9311.... 308 B
mmascari@bcc.edu
MASCARO, Juan .... 828-884-8108.... 362 H
mascarjc@brevard.edu
MASCARO, Maria, S .... 787-841-2000.... 565 B
exaluminos@pucpr.edu
MASCIANTONIO, John ...... 215-596-8531.... 450 B
j.mascia@usciences.edu
MASCOLO, Marc .... 912-344-2506.... 124 G
marc.mascolo@armstrong.edu
MASEK, Phyllis, J .... 573-592-5213.... 293 B
phyllis.masek@westminster-mo.edu
MASELLA, Joanne .... 561-803-2827.... 114 C
joanne_masella@pba.edu
MASENTHIN, Kim .... 262-243-5700.... 547 C
kim.masenthin@cuw.edu
MASER, Jill .... 302-736-2521...... 97 A
maserjil@wesley.edu
MASH, David .... 617-266-1400.... 231 E
MASH, David .... 864-388-8320.... 459 A
dmash@lander.edu
MASH, Ron .... 740-753-6079.... 391 H
mash_r@hocking.edu
MASHBURN, Scott .... 423-746-5203.... 476 F
smashburn@twcnet.edu
MASHECK, Kim .... 641-423-2530.... 186 J
kmasheck@kaplan.edu
MASHETT, Jayne .... 215-248-7020.... 425 D
mashettj@chc.edu
MASHLAN, Alexa .... 405-682-1611.... 409 F
amashlan@occc.edu
MASI, Jessica .... 207-216-4401.... 219 C
jmasi@yccc.edu
MASINI, Blase, E .... 773-442-4890.... 160 A
b-masini@neiu.edu
MASINI, Marco .... 630-829-6006.... 145 G
mmasini@ben.edu
MASIUK, Wendy .... 413-755-4211.... 241 B
wmasiuk@stcc.edu
MASKEY, Cynthia, L .... 217-786-2436.... 157 B
cynthia.maskey@llcc.edu
MASLAR, David, R .... 607-778-5033.... 324 G
maslardr@sunybroome.edu
MASLIN, Adrienne .... 860-343-5759...... 91 G
amaslin@mxcc.commnet.edu
MASLOWSKY, Craig .... 518-464-8500.... 333 E
cmaslowsky@excelsior.edu
MASLYN, Dave .... 401-874-4602.... 454 E
dcm@uri.edu
MASO, Marta, E .... 773-442-5210.... 160 A
m-maso@neiu.edu
MASO-FLEISHMAN,
Roberta .... 619-477-6310...... 73 D
rmaso-fleishman@usuniversity.edu
MASON, Allen .... 360-596-5283.... 538 E
amason@spscc.ctc.edu
MASON, Andrea .... 585-340-9632.... 329 F
amason@crcds.edu
MASON, April, C .... 785-532-6224.... 194 D
masona@ksu.edu
MASON, Benjamin .... 410-276-0306.... 226 D
bmason@host.sdc.edu
MASON, Beverly .... 701-627-4738.... 381 B
bmason@fbcc.bia.edu
MASON, Cameran .... 781-283-2223.... 245 E
cmason@wellesley.edu
MASON, Chip .... 601-968-8945.... 273 C
cmason@belhaven.edu
MASON, Dan, J .... 641-422-4281.... 188 A
masondan@niacc.edu
MASON, Deborah, P .... 513-529-2346.... 396 E
masonda@muohio.edu
MASON, Doug, R .... 208-496-3400.... 143 A
masond@byui.edu
MASON, Etta .... 615-297-7545.... 467 A
masone@aquinascollege.edu
MASON, Holly .... 740-366-9172.... 386 H
hmason@cotc.edu
MASON, J. Mike .... 208-732-6203.... 143 E
mmason@csi.edu
MASON, J. W .... 870-972-3081...... 20 D
jmason@astate.edu
MASON, James .... 505-424-2302.... 318 D
jmason@iaia.edu
MASON, Jeff .... 678-359-5573.... 132 A
jeffreym@gdn.edu
MASON, Jenifer, R .... 870-972-3964...... 20 D
jrmason@astate.edu
MASON, Jerry .... 509-527-2092.... 539 C
jerry.mason@wallawalla.edu
MASON, John, M .... 334-844-4784........ 1 F
jmm0027@auburn.edu
MASON, Linda .... 423-585-6809.... 476 D
linda.mason@ws.edu
MASON, Lisa .... 216-265-3151.... 386 D
lmmason@bryantstratton.edu
MASON, Mary Ellen .... 410-777-2707.... 221 C
memason@aacc.edu
MASON, Mary Jo .... 203-371-7955...... 94 B
masonm@sacredheart.edu
MASON, Matthew .... 717-560-8254.... 433 D
mmason@lbc.edu
MASON, Michael .... 636-949-4978.... 283 J
mmason@lindenwood.edu
MASON, Natasha .... 912-583-3291.... 126 F
nmason@bpc.edu
MASON, Natasha, W .... 478-289-2032.... 129 B
nwmason@ega.edu
MASON, Orenthia .... 903-593-8311.... 499 D
omason@texascollege.edu
MASON, Phil .... 912-279-5710.... 127 E
pmason@ccga.edu
MASON, Phyllis .... 740-245-7228.... 404 E
pmason@rio.edu
MASON, Rachel .... 562-860-2451...... 39 A
rmason@cerritos.edu
MASON, Rick .... 606-242-0138.... 203 D
rick.mason@kctcs.edu
MASON, Robert .... 941-487-4845.... 120 A
rmason@ncf.edu
MASON, Rochelle .... 719-389-6800...... 82 D
rmason@coloradocollege.edu
MASON, Ron .... 203-837-8736...... 91 A
masonr@wcsu.edu
MASON, Ronald .... 203-582-3950...... 93 H
ronaldv.p.mason@quinnipiac.edu
MASON, JR., Ronald, F .... 225-771-4680.... 214 H
ronald_mason@sus.edu
MASON, JR., Russell, D ... 701-627-4738.... 381 B
rmason@fbcc.bia.edu
MASON, Sally .... 319-335-3549.... 182 F
sally-mason@uiowa.edu
MASON, Stephen .... 502-597-6260.... 203 G
stephen.mason@kysu.edu
MASON, Stephen .... 803-793-5155.... 457 F
masons@denmarktech.edu
MASON, Stephen .... 918-594-8166.... 410 D
smason@osugiving.com
MASON, Steven, D .... 903-233-3230.... 490 A
stevenmason@letu.edu
MASON, Terry, W .... 515-294-0153.... 182 E
oriole@iastate.edu
MASON, Thelma .... 212-650-5816.... 326 G
tmason@ccny.cuny.edu
MASON, Tisa .... 785-628-4277.... 192 I
tmason@fhsu.edu
MASON JENNINGS,
Martha .... 269-749-7644.... 257 A
mjennings@olivetcollege.edu
MASON-KINSEY,
Natalie, L .... 718-951-4128.... 326 F
nmasonkinsey@brooklyn.cuny.edu
MASOUM, Nazi .... 949-794-9090...... 71 F
nazim@stanbridge.edu
MASS, Gregory .... 973-596-5745.... 312 C
mass@njit.edu
MASSA, Gary, R .... 513-745-3335.... 406 E
massag@xavier.edu
MASSA, Laurie .... 216-397-4661.... 392 L
lmassa@jcu.edu
MASSA, Margot .... 808-974-7348.... 141 F
margota@hawaii.edu
MASSA, Robert, J .... 610-330-5120.... 433 B
massar@lafayette.edu
MASSA, Tina .... 518-587-2100.... 355 G
tina.massa@esc.edu
MASSANO, Donna, R .... 508-999-8043.... 237 A
dmassano@umassd.edu
MASSARI, Lydia, I .... 787-751-0178.... 565 F
ac_lmassari@suagm.edu
MASSARI, Mark .... 805-893-3400...... 75 B
mark.massari@athletics.ucsb.edu
MASSARO, Chris John ...... 615-898-2450.... 473 G
chris.massaro@mtsu.edu
MASSARO, Patrick, W .... 724-287-8711.... 423 G
patrick.massaro@bc3.edu
MASSARO, SJ, Thomas ..... 510-549-5040...... 68 C
tmassaro@jstb.edu
MASSARO, Vincent .... 914-395-2314.... 350 C
vmassaro@sarahlawrence.edu
MASSARONI, Larry .... 914-606-7895.... 360 E
larry.massaroni@sunywcc.edu
MASSE, Carol .... 414-847-3270.... 549 B
carolmasse@miad.edu
MASSE, Michelle .... 225-578-4807.... 212 H
mmasse@lsu.edu
MASSE, Raymond .... 207-755-5258.... 218 G
rmasse@cmcc.edu
MASSE, Wendy .... 860-434-5232...... 93 D
wmasse@lymeacademy.edu
MASSELL, Laura .... 802-654-0532.... 515 E
laura.massell@mail.ccv.vsc.edu
MASSENA, Deborah .... 618-235-2700.... 165 D
deborah.massena@swic.edu
MASSENA, James, R .... 269-471-3307.... 247 D
massenaj@andrews.edu
MASSENBURG, Gerald .... 973-353-5541.... 314 E
geraldm@andromeda.rutgers.edu
MASSENGALE, Kathy .... 505-662-5919.... 321 E
kmasseng@unm.edu
MASSEY, Anne .... 812-855-2809.... 173 E
amassey@indiana.edu
MASSEY, April .... 202-274-5194.... 100 A
amassey@udc.edu
MASSEY, Bethany .... 615-966-6302.... 470 F
bethany.massey@lipscomb.edu
MASSEY, David .... 503-883-2259.... 416 H
dmassey@linfield.edu
MASSEY, Dennis .... 252-493-7220.... 372 H
dmassey@email.pittcc.edu
MASSEY, Diane .... 610-647-4400.... 431 C
dmassey@immaculata.edu
MASSEY, Edwin, R .... 772-462-4701.... 111 B
emassey@irsc.edu
MASSEY, Gary .... 573-875-7756.... 280 A
gamassey@ccis.edu
MASSEY, Janet .... 610-358-4260.... 437 D
jmassey@neumann.edu
MASSEY, Laura .... 971-722-7700.... 419 G
laura.massey@pcc.edu
MASSEY, Marge .... 972-279-6511.... 479 H
mmassey@amberton.edu
MASSEY, Michael .... 919-209-2087.... 371 F
mtmassey@johnstoncc.edu
MASSEY, Pamela, L .... 501-450-3237...... 25 H
pamm@uca.edu
MASSEY, Perry, A .... 910-672-1475.... 377 G
pmassey@uncfsu.edu
MASSEY, Rufus .... 706-368-6945.... 126 C
wmassey@berry.edu
MASSEY, Sandra .... 870-512-7841...... 20 F
sandra_massey@asun.edu
MASSEY, Therisa .... 281-873-0262.... 483 I
library@commonwealth.edu
MASSEY, Thomas, P .... 508-793-7408.... 233 B
tmassey@clarku.edu
MASSEY, Walter .... 312-899-5136.... 164 C
wmassey@saic.edu
MASSEY, Walter, T .... 404-413-3407.... 131 G
wmassey@gsu.edu
MASSI, Christopher, A .... 301-846-2479.... 222 G
cmassi@frederick.edu
MASSIE, Chase .... 580-581-2245.... 407 D
cmassie@cameron.edu
MASSIE, Maribeth .... 207-221-4519.... 221 A
bmassie@une.edu
MASSIE, Matt .... 937-512-2772.... 401 J
matt.massie@sinclair.edu
MASSIE, Patricia .... 606-759-7141.... 203 A
patee.massie@kctcs.edu
MASSIS, Bruce .... 614-287-2461.... 389 A
bmassis@cscc.edu
MASSMAN, Joseph .... 816-654-7105.... 283 F
jmassman@kcumb.edu
MASSOELS, William .... 219-866-6184.... 179 D
billm@saintjoe.edu
MASSON, Mary .... 802-654-2234.... 514 D
mmasson@smcvt.edu
MASSUCCO, Julie .... 802-241-2520.... 515 E
julie.massucco@vsc.edu
MAST, Amy, H .... 330-684-8982.... 403 C
amast1@uakron.edu
MAST, Gregg, A .... 732-247-5241.... 312 A
gmast@nbts.edu
MAST, Maura .... 617-287-6330.... 236 G
maura.mast@umb.edu
MAST, Russell, F .... 229-333-5941.... 139 C
rmast@valdosta.edu
MAST HEWITT, Marilyn ..... 630-620-2136.... 160 C
registrar@seminary.edu
MAST HEWITT, Marilyn, R 630-620-2196.... 160 C
registrar@seminary.edu
MASTANDUNO, Michael ... 603-646-3999.... 304 J
michael.mastanduno@dartmouth.edu
MASTELLER, John, Q .... 805-525-4417...... 72 I
jmasteller@thomasaquinas.edu
MASTERNAK, Donald .... 517-629-0350.... 247 A
dmasternak@albion.edu
MASTERS, Bradley .... 318-345-9239.... 210 H
bmasters@ladelta.edu
MASTERS, Carolyn, B .... 814-871-7605.... 429 G
masters004@gannon.edu
MASTERS, Deborah, C .... 415-338-1681...... 37 B
dmasters@sfsu.edu
MASTERS, Debra, G .... 405-466-2952.... 408 G
dgmasters@langston.edu
MASTERS, Janelle .... 701-224-5525.... 382 D
janelle.masters@bismarckstate.edu
MASTERS, Karen .... 617-296-8300.... 235 J
karen_masters@laboure.edu
MASTERS, Rebecca .... 803-323-2225.... 463 E
mastersr@winthrop.edu
MASTERSON, Ana .... 928-757-0860...... 16 F
amasterson@mohave.edu
MASTERSON, Christine ...... 425-602-3015.... 531 E
cmasters@bastyr.edu
MASTERSON, John, A .... 620-365-5116.... 190 D
masterson@allencc.edu
MASTERSON, Lisanne .... 828-694-1806.... 368 E
lisannem@blueridge.edu
MASTERSON, Robert .... 559-730-3862...... 42 D
bobm@cos.edu
MASTERSON, Thomas, J ... 989-774-1850.... 249 C
maste1tj@cmich.edu
MASTRANGELO, Joseph ..... 212-799-5000.... 337 H
MASTRE, Tom, M .... 831-656-1095.... 558 A
tmastre@nps.edu
MASTRO, Steve .... 707-654-1074...... 33 C
smastro@csum.edu
MASTROIANNI, Michael .... 815-921-2195.... 162 H
m.mastroianni@rockvalleycollege.edu
MASTROMONICO, Jeff ...... 803-641-2837.... 462 B
jeffm@usca.edu
MASUDA, Walter .... 530-741-6761...... 80 K
wmasuda@yccd.edu
MASULLO, Sharon .... 215-567-7080.... 422 D
smasullo@edmc.edu
MASUTANI, Carol .... 808-734-9528.... 141 J
masutani@hawaii.edu
MATA, Armando .... 773-907-4360.... 147 D
amata@ccc.edu
MATA, Cindy .... 956-364-4647.... 500 D
cindy.mata@tstc.edu
MATA, Margaret .... 325-942-2012.... 480 E
margaret.mata@angelo.edu
MATA, Sherri .... 817-531-6552.... 502 C
smata@txwes.edu
MATACHEK, John .... 651-523-2252.... 264 A
jmatachek@hamline.edu
MATCHETT, Jill .... 715-634-4790.... 547 J
jmatchett@lco-college.edu
MATE, Robert, L .... 765-494-5860.... 178 J
rmate@purdue.edu
MATEJKOVIC, Edward, M .. 610-436-3555.... 444 A
ematejkovic@wcupa.edu
MATEN, Lionel .... 662-915-7328.... 277 D
lmaten@olemiss.edu
MATERN, Cindy .... 253-879-3369.... 538 H
cmatern@pugetsound.edu
MATHENA, Cindy .... 904-826-0084.... 122 J
cmathena@usa.edu
MATHENEY, H. Scott .... 630-617-3025.... 150 H
hscottm@elmhurst.edu
MATHENY, Christopher ...... 920-735-2401.... 554 A
matheny@fvtc.edu
MATHENY, Kevin .... 503-493-6521.... 415 E
kmatheny@cu-portland.edu
MATHENY, Samuel .... 215-871-6170.... 444 C
samuelmat@pcom.edu
MATHENY, Stephen .... 828-395-1293.... 371 D
smatheny@isothermal.edu
MATHER, Bruce, J .... 630-617-3178.... 150 H
brucem@elmhurst.edu
MATHER, Jannah, H .... 801-581-6194.... 511 C
jmather@socwk.utah.edu
MATHER, Kim .... 978-867-4246.... 235 A
kim.mather@gordon.edu
MATHER, William .... 407-888-4000.... 113 A
wmather@orlando.chefs.edu
MATHERLY, Cheryl .... 918-631-3225.... 413 F
cheryl-matherly@utulsa.edu
MATHERS, Jill .... 402-474-5315.... 298 C
jmathers@kaplanuniversity.edu
MATHERSON, Akua, J .... 336-334-7631.... 378 A
amathers@ncat.edu
MATHES, Cassie, M .... 417-625-9365.... 286 B
mathes-c@mssu.edu
MATHES, James .... 850-644-1841.... 119 D
jmathes@admin.fsu.edu
MATHES, Leon .... 504-865-3148.... 213 F
mathes@loyno.edu
MATHESON, Marian, F .... 413-542-5187.... 230 A
mfmatheson@amherst.edu
MATHESON, Regina, M .... 563-333-5838.... 188 F
mathesonreginam@sau.edu
MATHEU, Federico, M .... 787-766-1717.... 565 I
um_fmatheu@suagm.edu
MATHEW, Bruce, E .... 608-785-9214.... 555 F
mathewb@westerntc.edu
MATHEW, Prakash, C .... 701-231-7701.... 382 B
prakash.mathew@ndsu.edu
MATHEW, Roy .... 915-747-5117.... 506 B
rmathew@utep.edu
MATHEW, Thomson .... 918-495-7016.... 411 C
tmathew@oru.edu
MATHEWS, Beth .... 912-688-6016.... 135 D
bmathews@ogeecheetech.edu
MATHEWS, Bill .... 334-683-5156........ 5 D
bmathews@judson.edu
MATHEWS, Carla, R .... 248-341-2188.... 256 F
crmathew@oaklandcc.edu
MATHEWS, Darren .... 970-247-7428...... 84 K
mathews_d@fortlewis.edu
MATHEWS, David .... 269-782-1270.... 258 C
president@swmich.edu
MATHEWS, Jeanne .... 706-236-2226.... 126 C
jmathews@berry.edu
MATHEWS, Jennifer .... 508-565-1915.... 245 A
jmathews@stonehill.edu
MATHEWS, Karen .... 937-376-6076.... 387 A
kmathews@centralstate.edu
MATHEWS, Marc .... 859-233-8100.... 207 A
mmathews@transy.edu
MATHEWS, Paul .... 410-234-4622.... 225 E
MATHEWS, Rebecca, B .... 618-537-6940.... 158 A
rbmathews@mckendree.edu
MATHIASEN, Rebecca .... 402-354-7034.... 299 C
rebecca.mathiasen@methodistcollege.edu

MAURANO, Steven, J .... 401-865-2775.... 453 H
smaurano@providence.edu
MAURER, Amybeth .... 847-214-7423.... 150 F
amaurer@elgin.edu
MAURER, Bobby Jo .... 309-341-7315.... 155 F
bmaurer@knox.edu
MAURER, Carmen, K .... 402-472-3906.... 300 E
cmaurer@nebraska.edu
MAURER, Charles .... 212-757-1190.... 322 H
cmaurer@funeraleducation.org
MAURER, Erin, C .... 864-622-6074.... 455 C
emaurer@andersonuniversity.edu
MAURER, Harold, M .... 402-559-4200.... 300 H
hmmaurer@unmc.edu
MAURER, John .... 401-841-2188.... 558 B
MAURER, Julie .... 740-964-7091.... 386 H
jmaurer@cotc.edu
MAURER, Linda .... 314-889-1423.... 281 I
lmaurer@fontbonne.edu
MAURER, Marcia, C .... 618-650-3956.... 165 C
mamaure@siue.edu
MAURER, Michael, S .... 217-581-7568.... 150 E
msmaurer@eiu.edu
MAURER, Paulette, A .... 708-709-3630.... 161 D
pmaurer@prairiestate.edu
MAURER, Roy, E .... 708-709-3580.... 161 D
rmaurer@prairiestate.edu
MAURER, Ryan, S .... 937-327-6114.... 406 B
rmaurer@wittenberg.edu
MAURIELLO, Thomas .... 718-862-7241.... 339 H
thomas.mauriello@manhattan.edu
MAURIN, Kay .... 985-549-2118.... 216 C
kmaurin@selu.edu
MAURO, Brian .... 201-443-8936.... 310 A
brian_mauro@fdu.edu
MAURO, Laurie .... 304-263-6262.... 541 F
lmauro@martinsburginstitute.edu
MAURO, Maria .... 954-499-9819.... 104 J
mmauro@devry.edu
MAUSSER, Richard, F .... 216-397-1630.... 392 L
rmausser@jcu.edu
MAUST, Scott .... 309-341-7892.... 155 F
smaust@knox.edu
MAVI, Pam .... 513-732-5229.... 403 E
pam.mavi@uc.edu
MAVOGIANNIS, Sophia .... 646-230-1360.... 355 G
sophia.mavogiannis@esc.edu
MAVRINAC, Mary Ann .... 585-275-4461.... 359 B
maryann.mavrinac@rochester.edu
MAVROS, Jeffrey .... 309-556-3024.... 153 F
jmavros@iwu.edu
MAVROUDHIS,
Athina-Eleni .... 617-850-1289.... 235 F
amavroudhis@hchc.edu
MAWE, Lynn .... 503-699-6309.... 416 J
lmawe@marylhurst.edu
MAX, Barbara .... 303-333-4224...... 81 G
bmax@aspen.edu
MAX, Sheryl .... 816-995-2842.... 287 H
sheryl.max@researchcollege.edu
MAXEINER, Amy .... 815-455-8717.... 157 H
amaxeiner@mchenry.edu
MAXEINER, Maddy .... 320-589-6386.... 271 G
maxeinme@morris.umn.edu
MAXEY, Charles .... 805-493-3360...... 33 B
maxey@clunet.edu
MAXEY, Larry .... 619-388-2699...... 65 G
lmaxey@sdccd.edu
MAXEY, Michael, C .... 540-375-2200.... 523 G
maxey@roanoke.edu
MAXEY, Steve .... 660-359-3948.... 287 A
smaxey@mail.ncmissouri.edu
MAXFIELD, Judith .... 620-227-9253.... 192 E
maxfield@dc3.edu
MAXFIELD, Michelle .... 313-425-3723.... 247 H
michelle.maxfield@baker.edu
MAXIE-ASHFORD,
Leslie, M .... 502-272-3101.... 198 H
lmaxie-ashford@bellarmine.edu
MAXIN, Leslie .... 724-503-1001.... 451 A
lmaxin@washjeff.edu
MAXON, John .... 256-824-6108...... 8 G
john.maxon@uah.edu
MAXON, Stacey .... 405-271-2300.... 413 D
stacey-maxon@ouhsc.edu
MAXSON, Carol .... 615-248-1258.... 476 G
cmaxson@trevecca.edu
MAXSON, Randy, R .... 574-267-5428.... 176 E
rmaxson@ivytech.edu
MAXSON, Robert .... 785-243-1435.... 192 A
bmaxson@cloud.edu
MAXSON, Susan .... 765-459-0561.... 176 C
smaxson@ivytech.edu
MAXWELL, Alice .... 850-201-6049.... 122 A
maxwella@tcc.fl.edu
MAXWELL, Barbara, A .... 509-527-5208.... 540 B
maxwelba@whitman.edu
MAXWELL, Bruce .... 509-682-6835.... 539 E
bmaxwell@wvc.edu
MAXWELL, Cathy .... 260-482-9171.... 176 F
cmaxwell28@ivytech.edu
MAXWELL, Chris .... 706-245-7226.... 129 C
cmaxwell@ec.edu
MAXWELL, Daniel .... 713-743-5390.... 503 D
dmmaxwell@central.uh.edu
MAXWELL, David, E .... 515-271-2191.... 184 D
david.maxwell@drake.edu
MAXWELL, Gloria .... 816-604-4290.... 285 E
gloria.maxwell@mcckc.edu
MAXWELL, Jack .... 785-242-5200.... 195 I
jack.maxwell@ottawa.edu
MAXWELL, James .... 972-524-3341.... 495 H
MAXWELL, III, James, D .. 515-964-0601.... 185 A
maxwellj@faith.edu
MAXWELL, Jewerl .... 937-766-3616.... 386 G
jmaxwell@cedarville.edu
MAXWELL, Jim .... 402-557-7786.... 296 H
jim.maxwell@bellevue.edu
MAXWELL, JR., John, B ... 205-348-1202...... 8 E
jmaxwell@cchs.ua.edu
MAXWELL, Kim .... 970-542-3169...... 86 G
kim.maxwell@morgancc.edu
MAXWELL, Lafayette .... 919-572-1625.... 362 C
lmaxwell@apexsot.edu
MAXWELL, Laura .... 678-407-5726.... 130 C
lmaxwell@ggc.edu
MAXWELL, Melvin .... 601-877-3000.... 272 F
mmaxwell@alcorn.edu
MAXWELL, Richard .... 662-254-3412.... 276 B
rmax@mvsu.edu
MAXWELL, Rick .... 972-860-4722.... 484 G
rmaxwell@dcccd.edu
MAXWELL, Simon .... 785-594-8341.... 190 F
simon.maxwell@bakeru.edu
MAXWELL, Valarie .... 940-397-4346.... 491 B
valarie.maxwell@mwsu.edu
MAXWELL, Veda .... 501-370-5284...... 23 B
vmaxwell@philander.edu
MAXWELL-DOHERTY,
Melissa .... 805-493-3330...... 33 B
revmmmd@clunet.edu
MAXWELL-DOHERTY,
Scott .... 805-493-3230...... 33 B
revsjmd@clunet.edu
MAY, Bobbie Jo, C .... 919-496-1567.... 374 G
may@vgcc.edu
MAY, Brian .... 325-942-2169.... 480 E
brian.may@angelo.edu
MAY, Brian, J .... 325-942-2165.... 480 E
brian.may@angelo.edu
MAY, Bruce .... 608-785-8095.... 551 C
bmay@uwlax.edu
MAY, Bryan .... 803-778-7841.... 455 G
maybw@cctech.edu
MAY, Carol .... 920-735-2542.... 554 A
mayc@fvtc.edu
MAY, Cecil .... 334-386-7154...... 3 G
cmay@faulkner.edu
MAY, Chad, L .... 215-637-7700.... 431 A
cmay@holyfamily.edu
MAY, Christopher, V .... 314-977-3185.... 289 C
cmay8@slu.edu
MAY, Daniel, J .... 419-434-4553.... 404 B
may@findlay.edu
MAY, David, J .... 603-862-2727.... 306 C
david.may@unh.edu
MAY, Gary, S .... 404-894-6825.... 130 F
gary.may@coe.gatech.edu
MAY, Gordon, F .... 248-942-3300.... 256 F
gfmay@oaklandcc.edu
MAY, Janet .... 520-206-4740...... 17 H
jmay3@pima.edu
MAY, Janet .... 712-279-5227.... 183 A
janet.may@briarcliff.edu
MAY, Janet, B .... 205-934-8132...... 8 F
jmay@uab.edu
MAY, Jefferson, J .... 864-388-8314.... 459 A
jmay@lander.edu
MAY, Jerry, A .... 734-647-6030.... 259 A
jamay@umich.edu
MAY, Joe .... 225-922-1643.... 209 G
jmay@lctcs.edu
MAY, Katharyn, A .... 608-263-9725.... 550 J
kamay@wisc.edu
MAY, Lori, K .... 901-345-1000.... 472 I
lori.may@remingtoncollege.edu
MAY, Mariani .... 310-577-3000...... 80 E
slmay@yosan.edu
MAY, Mary .... 817-810-0226.... 483 K
mary.may@concordia.edu
MAY, Mel, A .... 216-987-2204.... 389 B
mel.may@tri-c.edu
MAY, Michael .... 724-738-4573.... 443 F
michael.may@sru.edu
MAY, Michelle .... 605-455-6064.... 465 A
mmay@olc.edu
MAY, Nancy, S .... 617-373-2700.... 243 F
MAY, Nina .... 609-586-4800.... 311 B
mayn@mccc.edu
MAY, Paul, A .... 508-213-2377.... 243 E
paul.may@nichols.edu
MAY, Robert, E .... 276-739-2432.... 529 A
rmay@vhcc.edu
MAY, Ron .... 574-936-8898.... 169 D
ron.may@ancilla.edu
MAY, Ronald .... 253-964-6736.... 536 H
rmay@pierce.ctc.edu
MAY, Sarah, E .... 478-301-2413.... 134 A
may_se@mercer.edu
MAY, Susan, A .... 920-735-5731.... 554 A
may@fvtc.edu
MAY, Tobi .... 518-562-4170.... 329 C
tobi.may@clinton.edu
MAY, Vicki, L .... 602-749-4615...... 13 K
vmay@devry.edu
MAY, Walter, P .... 770-720-5540.... 136 C
wpm@reinhardt.edu
MAY, William, V .... 254-710-1221.... 482 A
william_may@baylor.edu
MAY-RICCIUTI, Heather ..... 304-829-7335.... 540 H
hricciuti@bethanywv.edu
MAYABB, Patricia .... 214-841-3634.... 485 F
pmayabb@dts.edu
MAYATT, Darlene .... 601-484-8724.... 275 A
dmayatt@meridiancc.edu
MAYBANK, Denise, B .... 517-355-7535.... 255 A
maybank@msu.edu
MAYBELL, Steven, A .... 206-281-2824.... 537 H
maybes@spu.edu
MAYBURY, Greg .... 616-395-7671.... 252 D
maybury@hope.edu
MAYDEN, Kimberly, A .... 618-537-6825.... 158 A
kamayden@mckendree.edu
MAYDEN, Sharrie .... 702-895-0970.... 302 I
sharrie.mayden@unlv.edu
MAYER, Brenna, S .... 914-654-5289.... 330 B
bmayer@cnr.edu
MAYER, Charles .... 336-249-8186.... 370 B
cmayer@davidsonccc.edu
MAYER, Connie .... 518-445-2393.... 322 C
amae@albanylaw.edu
MAYER, Ed .... 419-334-8400.... 402 D
emayer01@terra.edu
MAYER, Erin .... 713-221-8543.... 503 F
mayere@uhd.edu
MAYER, Louis, J .... 610-660-1321.... 446 C
lmayer@sju.edu
MAYER, Marni Saling .... 360-752-8325.... 531 H
msmayer@btc.ctc.edu
MAYERS, Darryl .... 617-287-5458.... 236 G
darryl.mayers@umb.edu
MAYES, Brent .... 770-229-3327.... 137 F
bmayes@sctech.edu
MAYES, David, M .... 501-882-4420...... 20 C
dmmayes@asub.edu
MAYES, Florence .... 803-738-7512.... 459 E
maysf@midlandstech.edu
MAYES, John, A .... 203-432-3503...... 96 A
john.mayes@yale.edu
MAYES, Lakeisha, E .... 757-823-8396.... 522 E
lemayes@nsu.edu
MAYES, Linda, F .... 651-631-5145.... 270 B
lfmayes@nwc.edu
MAYES, Michara, N .... 713-313-6815.... 500 B
mayesmn@tsu.edu
MAYES, Rick .... 479-936-5162...... 22 H
rmayes@nwacc.edu
MAYES, JR., Robert, G ...... 251-981-3771...... 2 G
robert@columbiasouthern.edu
MAYEWSKI, Raymond .... 585-275-4786.... 359 B
raymond_mayewski@urmc.rochester.edu
MAYFIELD, Amanda, B ...... 860-439-2088...... 92 G
amanda.mayfield@conncoll.edu
MAYFIELD, Andrea .... 662-476-5025.... 274 B
ascott@eastms.edu
MAYFIELD, Buddy .... 660-831-4176.... 286 F
mayfieldb@moval.edu
MAYFIELD, Connie .... 562-860-2451...... 39 A
cmayfield@cerritos.edu
MAYFIELD, Donny .... 423-746-5253.... 476 F
dmayfield@twcnet.edu
MAYFIELD, Gary .... 601-925-3849.... 275 C
mayfield@mc.edu
MAYFIELD, Mike, W .... 828-262-2070.... 377 D
mayfldmw@appstate.edu
MAYFIELD, Panny .... 662-621-4157.... 273 F
pmayfield@coahomacc.edu
MAYFIELD, Rachel .... 660-831-4139.... 286 F
mayfieldr@moval.edu
MAYHER, Michael, E .... 440-525-7255.... 394 F
mmayher@lakelandcc.edu
MAYHEW, Glen, R .... 540-985-8539.... 520 I
grmayhew@jchs.edu
MAYHEW, Kelly .... 619-388-3136...... 65 F
kmayhew@sdccd.edu
MAYHEW, Marty .... 520-206-6661...... 17 H
mmayhew@pima.edu
MAYHEW, Sally, A .... 618-537-6838.... 158 A
samayhew@mckendree.edu
MAYHEW, Sam .... 229-248-3946.... 126 A
sam.mayhew@bainbridge.edu
MAYHEW, Steven .... 620-231-7000.... 196 C
smayhew@pittstate.edu
MAYHEW, Susan, L .... 276-498-4190.... 516 C
MAYHORNE, John, F .... 443-412-2382.... 223 B
jmayhorne@harford.edu
MAYHUE, Richard, L .... 818-909-5517...... 56 G
rmayhue@tms.edu
MAYLE, Glenn .... 928-344-7500...... 12 A
glenn.mayle@azwestern.edu
MAYLER, Teresa .... 252-536-7207.... 371 B
maylert@halifaxcc.edu
MAYLONE, Theresa, M .... 718-990-2517.... 348 G
maylonet@stjohns.edu
MAYNARD, Barbara .... 314-256-8858.... 278 G
maynard@ai.edu
MAYNARD, C. Jack .... 812-237-2309.... 173 B
provost@indstate.edu
MAYNARD, Francyenne ...... 972-273-3109.... 485 C
fmaynard@dcccd.edu
MAYNARD, Kimberly, L ..... 304-896-7345.... 543 C
kimberly.maynard@southernwv.edu
MAYNARD, Nelly .... 773-821-2453.... 146 G
nmaynard@csu.edu
MAYNARD, Pamela .... 973-877-3115.... 309 H
maynard@essex.edu
MAYNARD, Rebecca, A ...... 207-768-2715.... 218 J
bmaynard@nmcc.edu
MAYNARD, Scott .... 662-325-3344.... 275 F
smaynard@career.msstate.edu
MAYNARD NELSON,
Jeanette .... 612-861-7554.... 260 G
jeanette@alfredadler.edu
MAYNARD-REID, Pedrito .. 509-527-2028.... 539 C
pedrito.maynard-reid@wallawalla.edu
MAYNE, Florence, P .... 512-499-4517.... 505 B
fmayne@utsystem.edu
MAYNE, Kevin .... 508-373-9410.... 231 B
kevin.mayne@becker.edu
MAYNE, Kevin .... 860-701-5002...... 93 E
mayne_k@mitchell.edu
MAYO, Bob .... 518-276-8300.... 347 D
mayor@rpi.edu
MAYO, Cindy .... 870-743-3000...... 22 G
cmayo@northark.edu
MAYO, Dan .... 252-493-7304.... 372 H
dmayo@email.pittcc.edu
MAYO, Donna .... 706-864-1840.... 134 G
dtmayo@northgeorgia.edu
MAYO, Douglas .... 507-389-6830.... 267 E
douglas.mayo@mnsu.edu
MAYO, Karen .... 859-246-6525.... 201 H
karen.mayo@kctcs.edu
MAYO, Lindsey .... 978-556-3621.... 240 E
lmayo@necc.mass.edu
MAYO, Michael .... 501-205-8826...... 21 C
mmayo@cbc.edu
MAYO, Sandra .... 951-571-6160...... 63 I
sandra.mayo@mvc.edu
MAYO, Sandra .... 951-571-6160...... 63 J
sandra.mayo@mvc.edu
MAYO, Sandra .... 512-245-2361.... 501 F
sm37@txstate.edu
MAYO, Sandra, L .... 818-947-2617...... 55 E
mayosl@lavc.edu
MAYO, Stephen, L .... 626-395-4951...... 32 H
steve@mayo.caltech.edu
MAYO, William, E .... 337-491-2684.... 212 E
william.mayo@sowela.edu
MAYOL, Myrna .... 787-250-0000.... 566 G
myrna.mayol@upr.edu
MAYORGA, Oscar, J .... 518-783-2330.... 350 I
MAYPOLE, Joanne .... 303-784-8045...... 85 M
jmaypole@jiu.edu
MAYRAND, Leslie .... 325-486-6247.... 480 E
leslie.mayrand@angelo.edu
MAYROSE, Julie .... 920-686-6125.... 550 H
julie.mayrose@sl.edu
MAYROSE, William .... 413-775-1212.... 239 E
mayroseb@gcc.mass.edu
MAYS, JR., Allen, R .... 217-245-3162.... 152 D
amays@ic.edu
MAYS, Anna .... 972-860-8261.... 484 H
amays@dcccd.edu
MAYS, Beth, A .... 410-777-2480.... 221 C
bamays@aacc.edu
MAYS, Jon .... 513-861-6400.... 402 I
jon.mays@myunion.edu
MAYS, Louis, E .... 937-393-3431.... 402 A
lmays@sscc.edu
MAYS, Marilyn .... 972-273-3501.... 485 C
mmays@dcccd.edu
MAYS, Nathaniel .... 617-349-8539.... 236 B
nmays@lesley.edu
MAYS, Pamela .... 972-273-3116.... 485 C
pmays@dcccd.edu
MAYS, Robert .... 706-737-1471.... 125 G
rmays@aug.edu
MAYS, Shirley, L .... 602-682-6800...... 17 F
smays@phoenixlaw.edu
MAYS, Susan .... 615-771-7821.... 478 H
susan.mays@williamsoncc.edu
MAYSAMI, Ramin .... 910-521-6466.... 379 C
ramin.maysami@uncp.edu
MAYSILLES, Michael, E ..... 973-618-3236.... 308 C
mmaysilles@caldwell.edu
MAYSON, Adrianna .... 845-434-5750.... 357 A
amayson@sullivan.suny.edu
MAZA-DUERTO, Aristides . 786-331-1000.... 113 J
MAZACHEK, Julliann .... 785-670-4483.... 197 F
jmazachek@wufoundation.org
MAZEL, David .... 719-587-7771...... 80 L
dbmazel@adams.edu
MAZER, Vickie .... 301-687-7053.... 228 C
vmmazer@frostburg.edu

MCCANDLESS, John 513-529-2223 396 E
mccandjm@muohio.edu
MCCANDLESS, N. Jane 678-839-5170 139 A
jmccandl@westga.edu
MCCANDLESS, Raymond 419-434-4565 404 B
mccandless@findlay.edu
MCCANE, Latitia 251-405-7013 2 C
lmccane@bishop.edu
MCCANN, Aimee, C 262-472-5955 553 A
mccanna@uww.edu
MCCANN, Bonnie 614-947-6017 391 B
mccannb@franklin.edu
MCCANN, Diane 410-532-5393 225 D
dmccann@ndm.edu
MCCANN, Heidi 978-632-6600 240 C
MCCANN, Jack 423-869-6298 470 E
jack.mccann@lmunet.edu
MCCANN, James, D 910-962-7410 379 D
mccannj@uncw.edu
MCCANN, Jean, A 636-584-6601 281 E
mccannja@eastcentral.edu
MCCANN, Jeff 336-725-8344 375 G
mccannrj@pbc.edu
MCCANN, John 512-863-1752 496 A
mccannj@southwestern.edu
MCCANN, Linda 215-968-8003 423 F
mccannl@bucks.edu
MCCANN, Ralph, J 770-484-1204 133 G
lru@lru.edu
MCCANNON, Mindy 706-295-6846 131 B
mmccannon@gntc.edu
MCCAPE, Margaret, S 603-513-5261 306 E
margaret.mccape@law.unh.edu
MCCARDELL, Aaron 630-353-7049 149 B
amccardell@devry.edu
MCCARDELL, JR.,
John, M 931-598-1101 472 L
jmmccard@sewanee.edu
MCCAREL, Lori 757-233-8786 530 C
lmccarel@vwc.edu
MCCARN, Sarah 912-525-5838 136 F
smccarn@scad.edu
MCCARRAHER, Charlotte 609-894-9311 308 B
cmccarra@bcc.edu
MCCARREN, Gerard, H 973-275-2111 310 F
gerard.mccarren@shu.edu
MCCARRICK, Richard, G 914-594-4503 343 F
richard_mccarrick@nymc.edu
MCCARROLL, Colleen 312-235-3531 164 F
c.mccarroll@shimer.edu
MCCARROLL, John, F 515-294-6137 182 E
jmccarol@iastate.edu
MCCARRON, Anne 414-382-6068 546 B
anne.mccarron@alverno.edu
MCCARRON, Thomas 818-677-2333 35 F
tom.mccarron@csun.edu
MCCARRON-BURNS,
Ann, K 716-673-3333 352 A
ann.burns@fredonia.edu
MCCARRY, Tim 325-670-1434 487 F
facilities@hsutx.edu
MCCARTER, Debbie, L 423-585-6844 476 D
debbie.mccarter@ws.edu
MCCARTER, Merdis, J 336-750-2400 380 B
mccarter@wssu.edu
MCCARTER, Rachel 610-902-8256 424 B
MCCARTHY, Anne 651-523-2335 264 A
MCCARTHY, Ashley 607-431-4990 335 A
mccarthya3@hartwick.edu
MCCARTHY, Barbara 914-773-3741 345 F
bmccarthy@pace.edu
MCCARTHY, Barbara 860-253-3102 91 B
bmccarthy@asnuntuck.edu
MCCARTHY, Brittny 818-677-2123 35 F
brittny.mccarthy@csun.edu
MCCARTHY, Carla, M 401-841-2220 558 B
MCCARTHY, Casey, J 218-755-3888 265 I
cmccarthy@bemidjistate.edu
MCCARTHY, Christian 508-767-7424 230 D
cmccarthy@assumption.edu
MCCARTHY, Claire, H 212-353-4266 331 A
mccart3@cooper.edu
MCCARTHY, Colby 610-861-1330 437 A
mectm01@moravian.edu
MCCARTHY, Daniel 985-549-2055 216 C
dmccarthy@selu.edu
MCCARTHY, David, B 402-461-7397 298 A
dmccarthy@hastings.edu
MCCARTHY, David, W 706-886-6831 138 D
dmcarthy@tfc.edu
MCCARTHY, Douglas 602-285-7245 16 A
douglas.mccarthy@pcmail.maricopa.edu
MCCARTHY, Elizabeth, K 508-678-2811 239 B
elizabeth.mccarthy@bristolcc.edu
MCCARTHY, Faith 530-221-4275 69 C
shastaonline@clearwire.net
MCCARTHY, Faith 530-221-4275 69 C
registrar@shasta.edu
MCCARTHY, Hannah, M 617-730-7035 243 D
hannah.mccarthy@newbury.edu
MCCARTHY, James 617-573-8000 245 B
jmccarthy@suffolk.edu
MCCARTHY, James 609-652-4335 313 E
james.mccarthy@stockton.edu

MCCARTHY, James 610-861-5506 437 H
jmccarthy@northampton.edu
MCCARTHY, Joan 402-461-7700 298 A
jmccarthy@hastings.edu
MCCARTHY, John, C 202-319-5259 97 E
mccartjc@cua.edu
MCCARTHY, John, H 617-373-2240 243 F
MCCARTHY, John, J 413-545-5220 236 F
jmccarthy@grad.umass.edu
MCCARTHY, Katherine 815-753-5600 160 B
kmccarthy1@niu.edu
MCCARTHY, Kelly 708-235-3966 151 E
kmccarthy@govst.edu
MCCARTHY, Kevin 315-568-3267 342 H
kmccarthy@nycc.edu
MCCARTHY, Kevin 518-255-5217 354 E
mccartk@cobleskill.edu
MCCARTHY, Kevin 704-330-6907 369 D
kevin.mccarthy@cpcc.edu
MCCARTHY, Kevin 704-355-2000 363 D
kevin.mccarthy@carolinashealthcare.org
MCCARTHY, Kevin 425-564-2191 531 G
kevin.mccarthy@bellevuecollege.edu
MCCARTHY, Kevin, E 630-637-5134 159 G
kemccarthy@nactrl.edu
MCCARTHY, Lisa 609-771-2082 308 F
mccarthy@tcnj.edu
MCCARTHY, Margo, M 203-576-5556 94 C
mmccarthy@stvincentscollege.edu
MCCARTHY, Mark, D 216-397-4213 392 L
mmccarthy@jcu.edu
MCCARTHY, Mary 607-778-5210 324 G
mccarthyma@sunybroome.edu
MCCARTHY, Maureen 770-499-3545 133 A
mmccar10@kennesaw.edu
MCCARTHY, SJ, Michael 408-554-4715 68 C
mcmccarthy@scu.edu
MCCARTHY, Michael, E 585-385-8025 348 F
mmccarthy@sjfc.edu
MCCARTHY, Monique 239-687-5423 101 H
mmccarthy@avemarialaw.edu
MCCARTHY, Pamela 413-585-2840 244 G
pmccarth@smith.edu
MCCARTHY, Patricia 724-357-2218 442 F
mccarthy@iup.edu
MCCARTHY, Paul, J 214-860-2010 485 A
pmccarthy@dcccd.edu
MCCARTHY, Peter, X 386-506-3107 104 F
mccartp@daytonastate.edu
MCCARTHY, Regina, K 603-641-4142 306 D
regina.mccarthy@unh.edu
MCCARTHY, Robert, L 860-486-2128 94 G
r.mccarthy@uconn.edu
MCCARTHY, Rosemary 412-536-1173 432 H
rosemary.mccarthy@laroche.edu
MCCARTHY, Sean 312-777-8726 153 B
smccarthy@aii.edu
MCCARTHY, Sherry 573-592-4368 293 D
smccarth@williamwoods.edu
MCCARTHY, Suzanne 908-852-1400 308 E
library@centenarycollege.edu
MCCARTHY, Thomas 718-862-7977 339 H
thomas.mccarthy@manhattan.edu
MCCARTIN, Sean 541-485-1780 417 E
seanmccartin@newhop.edu
MCCARTNEY, Kathleen 617-495-3401 235 D
hgsedean@gse.harvard.edu
MCCARTNEY, William, G 765-496-2270 178 J
mccart@purdue.edu
MCCARTNEY, JR.,
William, L 252-328-6050 377 E
mccartneyw@ecu.edu
MCCARTY, Alison 617-964-1100 230 B
amccarty@ants.edu
MCCARTY, II, Gerald 810-766-4206 248 C
gerald.mccartyii@baker.edu
MCCARTY, Josh 870-759-4143 26 B
jmccarty@wbcoll.edu
MCCARTY, Kyla 417-690-3292 279 J
mccarty@cofo.edu
MCCARTY, Richard, C 615-322-4219 478 A
richard.mccarty@vanderbilt.edu
MCCARTY, Susan 212-772-4850 327 E
susan.mccarty@hunter.cuny.edu
MCCARTY, Therese, A 518-388-6102 358 G
mccartyt@union.edu
MCCARTY, Thomas 415-276-8143 19 A
thomas.mccarty@phoenix.edu
MCCARTY-HARRIS,
Yulanda 330-941-3370 406 F
ymccartyharris@ysu.edu
MCCARVEL, Thomas, J 406-447-4409 293 G
tmccarve@carroll.edu
MCCASKEY, Michael, J 518-255-5427 354 E
mccaskmj@cobleskill.edu
MCCASKILL, Angela 202-651-5000 98 B
angela.mccaskill@gallaudet.edu
MCCASKILL, Rock 864-644-5538 461 B
rmccaskill@swu.edu
MCCASKILL, Sharrell 202-651-5642 98 B
sharrell.mccaskill@gallaudet.edu
MCCASKILL, Susan 828-339-4251 374 C
susanm@southwesterncc.edu
MCCASLIN, Blake 423-746-5332 476 F
mccaslin@twcnet.edu

MCCASLIN, John 931-553-0071 471 I
john.mccaslin@miller-motte.com
MCCASLIN, Julie 423-746-5214 476 F
jmccaslin@twcnet.edu
MCCASLIN, Randall 814-732-1346 442 E
rmccaslin@edinboro.edu
MCCASLIN, Sharon 314-889-4567 281 I
smccaslin@fontbonne.edu
MCCAUGHTRY, Samuel, L 814-456-7504 428 G
mccaughtrys@eriebc.edu
MCCAUL, Kevin, D 701-231-7411 382 B
kevin.mccaul@ndsu.edu
MCCAULEY, Brian 618-374-5180 161 E
brian.mccauley@principia.edu
MCCAULEY, Dennis 215-968-8394 423 F
mccauley@bucks.edu
MCCAULEY, Howard 816-271-4266 286 G
admissn@missouriwestern.edu
MCCAULEY, James, L 860-444-8280 558 H
james.l.mccauley@uscg.mil
MCCAULEY, Kevin, R 805-893-8182 75 B
kevin.mccauley@chancellor.ucsb.edu
MCCAULEY, Linda 404-727-7976 129 D
linda.mccauley@emory.edu
MCCAULEY, Pat 402-461-7419 298 A
pmccauley@hastings.edu
MCCAULEY, Terry, L 248-232-4550 256 F
tlmccaul@oaklandcc.edu
MCCAUSLAND, Bill 813-974-1868 121 A
mccausland@usf.edu
MCCAUSLAND, Randy 850-644-2591 119 D
rmccausland@admin.fsu.edu
MCCAUSLIN, Lauren 617-243-2139 236 A
lmccauslin@lasell.edu
MCCAW, Ian, J 254-710-1222 482 A
ian_mccaw@baylor.edu
MCCAW, Matt, S 312-939-0111 150 D
matt@eastwest.edu
MCCAWLEY, Loree, L 831-479-6234 31 I
lomccawl@cabrillo.edu
MCCAY, Bill 509-865-8520 535 A
mccay_b@heritage.edu
MCCAY, T. Dwayne 321-674-8889 108 H
tdmccay@fit.edu
MCCHESNEY, Rob 309-467-6396 151 B
rmcchesney@eureka.edu
MCCLAFFERTY, Joe 406-496-4301 296 B
jmcclafferty@mtech.edu
MCCLAIN, Beth 309-694-5323 152 C
bmcclain@icc.edu
MCCLAIN, Davina 318-357-4592 216 B
mcclaind@nsula.edu
MCCLAIN, Elman 206-934-5437 537 E
elman.mcclain@seattlecolleges.edu
MCCLAIN, James 626-914-8794 40 B
jmcclain@citruscollege.edu
MCCLAIN, James, W 870-838-2910 20 A
jmcclain@smail.anc.edu
MCCLAIN, Jason 304-829-7601 540 H
jmcclain@bethanywv.edu
MCCLAIN, Jeremy 662-846-4300 273 H
jmcclain@deltastate.edu
MCCLAIN, June 912-427-5847 124 C
jmcclain@altamahatech.edu
MCCLAIN, Lisa, L 504-520-7593 217 A
lmcclain@xula.edu
MCCLAIN, Mark 937-766-7933 386 G
mcclain@cedarville.edu
MCCLAIN, Paula, D 919-681-1560 364 C
pmmclain@duke.edu
MCCLAIN, Samantha, E 515-574-1080 185 I
mcclain@iowacentral.edu
MCCLAIN, Tim 360-486-8875 537 B
tmc@stmartin.edu
MCCLANAHAN, Ana, M 919-513-2311 374 H
ammcclanahan@waketech.edu
MCCLANAHAN, Keith 501-882-8811 20 C
mkmcclanahan@asub.edu
MCCLANAHAN,
Thomas, H 559-278-0840 35 A
thomas_mcclanahan@csufresno.edu
MCCLAY, Diana, D 423-439-5890 473 F
mccladyd@etsu.edu
MCCLAY, Kelly 609-343-4939 307 C
mcclay@atlantic.edu
MCCLEAN, Freda 212-220-8316 326 D
fmcclean@bmcc.edu
MCCLEAN, Jerry 209-954-5033 66 D
jmcclean@deltacollege.edu
MCCLEANON, Charles 312-850-7154 147 F
cmccleanon@ccc.edu
MCCLEARY, Kathryn, S 410-778-7470 229 D
kmccleary2@washcoll.edu
MCCLEARY, Keith 517-264-3981 246 H
MCCLEARY, Tim 406-638-3121 294 E
baaxpaa@lbhc.edu
MCCLEERY, Steve 575-392-5004 319 B
smccleery@nmjc.edu
MCCLEISH, Joan, M 515-643-6625 187 F
jmccleish@mercydesmoines.org
MCCLELLAN, Cissy 802-860-2711 513 C
mcclella@champlain.edu
MCCLELLAN, Craig 304-326-1465 541 K
cmcclellan@salemu.edu

MCCLELLAN, Debralee 301-846-2477 222 G
dmcclellan@frederick.edu
MCCLELLAN, Debralee 843-525-8210 461 E
dmcclellan@tcl.edu
MCCLELLAN, Edie 414-847-3233 549 B
ediemcclellan@miad.edu
MCCLELLAN, Fletcher 717-361-1555 428 F
mcclelef@etown.edu
MCCLELLAN, George, S 260-481-6844 174 C
mcclellg@ipfw.edu
MCCLELLAN, Jane 201-200-3196 312 B
jmcclellan@njcu.edu
MCCLELLAN, Jeffrey, C 618-536-3331 165 A
jmclell@siue.edu
MCCLELLAN, Laura 276-739-2425 529 A
lmcclellan@vhcc.edu
MCCLELLAN, Mack 405-585-4426 409 D
mark.mcclellan@okbu.edu
MCCLELLAN, Mia, C 619-482-6369 71 D
mmcclellan@swccd.edu
MCCLELLAN, Patricia 828-251-6001 378 D
pmcclell@unca.edu
MCCLELLAN, Steven, J 501-569-3202 24 E
sjmcclellan@ualr.edu
MCCLELLAND, Charles, F 713-313-7216 500 B
mcclellandcf@tsu.edu
MCCLELLAND, Lou 303-492-8631 88 H
lou.mcclelland@colorado.edu
MCCLELLAND, Scott 954-382-6575 122 F
smcclelland@tiu.edu
MCCLELLAND, II,
Thomas, H 337-475-5908 215 G
tmcclelland@mcneese.edu
MCCLELLON, Leslie 303-352-3786 84 A
leslie.mcclellon@ccd.edu
MCCLENAGAN, Cindy, M 806-291-1106 508 E
cindym@wbu.edu
MCCLENDON, Bev 479-788-7082 24 D
bev.mcclendon@uafs.edu
MCCLENDON, Mark 940-397-4567 491 B
mark.mcclendon@mwsu.edu
MCCLENDON, Mark 817-515-5203 496 C
mark.mcclendon@tccd.edu
MCCLENDON, Rick 540-665-5445 524 E
rmcclend@su.edu
MCCLENDON, Rodney, P 979-862-1065 497 E
rpm@tamu.edu
MCCLENDON, Vivienne 707-654-1283 33 C
vmcclendon@csum.edu
MCCLEON, Mitch 601-635-2111 274 A
mmcleon@eccc.edu
MCCLESKEY, Tom 770-426-2660 133 E
thomas.mccleskey@life.edu
MCCLINTOCK, Darlene 724-589-2027 448 B
dmcclintock@thiel.edu
MCCLINTOCK, Kate 707-527-4797 68 E
kmcclintock@santarosa.edu
MCCLINTOCK, Marta 724-938-4251 441 G
mcclintock@calu.edu
MCCLINTOCK, Melvin, A 240-895-4309 226 A
mamcclintock@smcm.edu
MCCLINTOCK, Patty 812-237-2305 173 B
patty.mcclintock@indstate.edu
MCCLINTON, JR.,
Flandus 225-771-5021 214 I
flandus_mcclinton@subr.edu
MCCLINTON, Marguerite 214-379-5518 492 F
mmcclinton@pqc.edu
MCCLISTER, Lisa 813-988-5131 108 A
mcclisterl@floridacollege.edu
MCCLOSKEY, Erin, E 814-472-3100 446 B
emccloskey@francis.edu
MCCLOSKEY, James 412-396-5286 428 D
mccloskey@duq.edu
MCCLOSKEY, James, M 302-356-6880 97 C
james.m.mccloskey@wilmu.edu
MCCLOSKEY, JR.,
John, R 610-796-3005 421 G
john.mccloskey@alvernia.edu
MCCLOUD, Alyssa 973-313-6146 315 B
alyssa.mccloud@shu.edu
MCCLOUD, Elizabeth, K 717-361-1404 428 F
mccloudek@etown.edu
MCCLOY, Alfred 561-391-1148 105 B
amccloy@dmac.edu
MCCLOY, Eric 215-572-8521 422 C
mccloy@arcadia.edu
MCCLUNEY, Alice 828-395-1495 371 D
amccluney@isothermal.edu
MCCLUNG, Alan 423-614-8410 470 C
amcclung@leeuniversity.edu
MCCLUNG, Denise 304-424-8230 545 C
denise.mcclung@mail.wvu.edu
MCCLUNG, Hugh 281-649-3308 487 H
hmcclung@hbu.edu
MCCLUNG, Mary 770-537-6065 139 F
mary.mcclung@westgatech.edu
MCCLUNG, Philip, L 336-734-7212 370 F
pmcclung@forsythtech.edu
MCCLURE, A. Glann 610-917-1453 450 E
agmcclure@vfcc.edu
MCCLURE, Alyssa 903-223-3060 498 F
amcclure@tamut.edu
MCCLURE, Amber 575-461-4413 318 G
amberm@mesalands.edu

MCCLURE, Amy .... 740-368-3562 .... 400 G aamcclur@owu.edu
MCCLURE, Carter, B .... 843-686-6503 .... 470 B cmcclure@lanecollege.edu
MCCLURE, Dan .... 503-821-8970 .... 419 D dan@pnca.edu
MCCLURE, David .... 254-526-1166 .... 482 H david.mcclure@ctcd.edu
MCCLURE, Erin .... 361-593-2795 .... 498 D erin.mcclure@tamuk.edu
MCCLURE, Guy .... 256-233-8296 .... 1 E guy.mcclure@athens.edu
MCCLURE, H. Lawrence .... 215-780-1331 .... 446 G larry@salus.edu
MCCLURE, Jennifer .... 847-214-7319 .... 150 F jmcclure@elgin.edu
MCCLURE, John .... 773-602-5000 .... 147 E
MCCLURE, Joy .... 770-394-8300 .... 125 A jmcclure@aii.edu
MCCLURE, Kelly .... 215-991-3573 .... 432 I mcclure@lasalle.edu
MCCLURE, Ken .... 417-836-5233 .... 286 C kmcclure@missuristate.edu
MCCLURE, Kitara .... 509-533-7378 .... 533 B kitata.mcclure@scc.spokane.edu
MCCLURE, Larry .... 215-780-1400 .... 446 G larry@salus.edu
MCCLURE, Mike .... 541-956-7237 .... 420 B mmclure@roguecc.edu
MCCLURE, Robert .... 845-446-1522 .... 559 A robert.mcclure@wpaog.org
MCCLURE, Tonya .... 478-757-3467 .... 127 A tmcclure@centralgatech.edu
MCCLURE, Wesley, C .... 731-426-7595 .... 470 B mcclure@lanecollege.edu
MCCLURE, William .... 718-997-5790 .... 328 E william.mcclure@qc.cuny.edu
MCCLURE, William .... 972-929-9324 .... 486 D wmcclure@devry.edu
MCCLURE, William, S .... 413-545-2111 .... 236 F billmcclure@contined.umass.edu
MCCLUSKEY, Denise .... 419-824-3509 .... 395 E dmccluskey@lourdes.edu
MCCLUSKEY, Eugene .... 207-768-2786 .... 218 J emccluskey@nmcc.edu
MCCLUSKEY, Jennifer .... 314-529-9561 .... 284 C jmccluskey@maryville.edu
MCCLUSKEY, Peter .... 860-255-3510 .... 92 F pmccluskey@txcc.commnet.edu
MCCLUSKEY-FAWCETT, Kathleen, A .... 785-864-2768 .... 197 B kamf@ku.edu
MCCLYMONT, Jay, W .... 717-766-2511 .... 436 D jmcclymont@messiah.edu
MCCOEY, Margaret .... 215-951-1222 .... 432 I mccoey@lasalle.edu
MCCOLGIN, Cathleen, C .... 315-498-2790 .... 345 D mccolgic@sunyocc.edu
MCCOLLETT, Sherry .... 207-621-3141 .... 220 B umafa@maine.edu
MCCOLLOCH, Mark .... 443-840-1021 .... 222 D mmocolloch@ccbcmd.edu
MCCOLLOUGH, Laura, L .... 907-474-1886 .... 10 I lcmccollough@alaska.edu
MCCOLLUM, Alonzo, L .... 516-876-3068 .... 353 D mccolluma@oldwestbury.edu
MCCOLLUM, Estella .... 785-864-2468 .... 197 B estellam@ku.edu
MCCOLLUM, James .... 717-871-5955 .... 443 D james.mccollum@millersville.edu
MCCOLLUM, Julie .... 816-584-6206 .... 287 E julie.mccollum@park.edu
MCCOLLUM, Kenneth .... 718-940-5952 .... 349 A kmcollum@sjcny.edu
MCCOLLUM, Kenneth .... 631-687-5150 .... 349 B kmccollum@sjcny.edu
MCCOLLUM, Rick, L .... 501-450-3132 .... 25 H rickm@uca.edu
MCCOLLUM, Scott .... 937-512-3068 .... 401 J scott.mccullum@sinclair.edu
MCCOLSKEY, Erin, S .... 561-868-3139 .... 114 D mccolske@palmbeachstate.edu
MCCOMAS, Richard .... 580-581-2524 .... 407 D richardm@cameron.edu
MCCOMB, Beverly, S .... 919-536-7220 .... 370 C mccombb@durhamtech.edu
MCCOMB, Brenda .... 541-737-4881 .... 418 F brenda.mccomb@oregonstate.edu
MCCOMBS, Ed .... 928-724-6635 .... 13 L emccombs@dinecollege.edu
MCCOMBS, Gillian, M .... 214-768-2400 .... 495 A gmccombs@smu.edu
MCCOMBS, John .... 412-731-8690 .... 445 F jmccombs@rpts.edu
MCCOMBS, Tyrone .... 856-756-5400 .... 314 A mccombs@rowan.edu
MCCONACHIE, Michael .... 972-377-1015 .... 483 H mmcconachie@collin.edu
MCCONAHAY, Mark .... 812-855-2654 .... 173 E mcconaha@indiana.edu
MCCONATHY, Jamie .... 870-862-8131 .... 23 G jmcconathy@southark.edu
MCCONATHY, Terry, M .... 318-257-4262 .... 215 F tmm@latech.edu
MCCONKEY, Lucilia .... 570-945-8253 .... 432 E lucilia.mcconkey@keystone.edu
MCCONNAUGHAY, Philip .... 814-863-1521 .... 438 G pjm30@psu.edu
MCCONNAUGHAY, Philip, J .... 814-863-1521 .... 439 D pjm30@psu.edu
MCCONNELL, Blake .... 618-658-8331 .... 156 B james.mcconnell@doc.illinois.gov
MCCONNELL, C. Douglas .. 626-584-5205 .... 48 B provost@fuller.edu
MCCONNELL, Charlessa, E 540-338-1776 .... 522 G
MCCONNELL, Cheryl, M .... 816-501-4087 .... 288 A cheryl.mcconnell@rockhurst.edu
MCCONNELL, Frank, J .... 706-864-1606 .... 134 G mmcconnell@northgeorgia.edu
MCCONNELL, Gaye .... 704-216-3600 .... 373 F gaye.mcconnell@rccc.edu
MCCONNELL, James .... 512-313-3000 .... 483 K james.mcconnell@concordia.edu
MCCONNELL, Jason .... 423-869-6333 .... 470 E jason.mcconnell@lmunet.edu
MCCONNELL, Joyce, E .... 304-293-3199 .... 545 A joyce.mcconnell@mail.wvu.edu
MCCONNELL, Judy, A .... 940-565-2741 .... 504 D judith.mcconnell@unt.edu
MCCONNELL, Kathy .... 619-849-2412 .... 62 L kathymcconnell@pointloma.edu
MCCONNELL, Marcia .... 706-232-5374 .... 126 C
MCCONNELL, Penny, J .... 217-443-8747 .... 148 G pmcconn@dacc.edu
MCCONNELL, Richard, W .. 260-359-4043 .... 173 A rmcconnell@huntington.edu
MCCONNELL, Robert .... 334-876-9270 .... 4 B rmcconnell@wccs.edu
MCCONNELL, Savannah .... 304-296-8282 .... 545 F smcconnell@wvjcmorgantown.edu
MCCONNELLOGUE, Ken .... 303-860-5600 .... 88 G ken.mcconnellogue@cu.edu
MCCONOUGHEY, Gina .... 309-694-5505 .... 152 C gmccono@icc.edu
MCCOO, Myron, S .... 603-646-0007 .... 304 J myron.s.mccoo@dartmouth.edu
MCCOOL, Bobby .... 606-886-3863 .... 201 G bobby.mccool@kctcs.edu
MCCOOL, Jeffery .... 575-492-4711 .... 319 B jmccool@nmjc.edu
MCCOOL, Joan, L .... 716-878-4436 .... 353 A mccoolj l@buffalostate.edu
MCCOOL, Tom .... 765-269-5670 .... 176 D tmccool@ivytech.edu
MCCORD, Carol .... 812-856-2291 .... 173 E camccord@indiana.edu
MCCORD, Christopher .... 815-753-1061 .... 160 B mccord@niu.edu
MCCORD, Elizabeth .... 415-451-2832 .... 66 B emccord@sfts.edu
MCCORD, Jeff, D .... 423-354-5207 .... 475 F jdmccord@northeaststate.edu
MCCORD, S. Alan .... 248-204-2400 .... 254 B amccord@ltu.edu
MCCORMACK, Amy .... 708-524-6770 .... 150 C amccormack@dom.edu
MCCORMACK, Bridey .... 806-457-4200 .... 486 I bmccormack@fpctx.edu
MCCORMACK, Corky .... 417-447-8172 .... 287 D mccormac@otc.edu
MCCORMACK, Erin .... 801-302-2800 .... 510 G erin.mccormack@neumont.edu
MCCORMACK, Gary .... 713-942-3400 .... 505 A mccormack@stthom.edu
MCCORMACK, John .... 708-596-2000 .... 164 H jmccormack@ssc.edu
MCCORMACK, Laurie .... 816-584-6210 .... 287 E laurie.mccormack@park.edu
MCCORMACK, Mike .... 205-726-2916 .... 6 G hmmccorm@samford.edu
MCCORMICK, Adrienne .... 716-673-3158 .... 352 A adrienne.mccormick@fredonia.edu
MCCORMICK, Al .... 800-962-7682 .... 293 A amccormick@wma.edu
MCCORMICK, Brad .... 618-985-8340 .... 154 G bradmccormick@jalc.edu
MCCORMICK, Charlie, T .... 830-792-7371 .... 494 E ctmccormick@schreiner.edu
MCCORMICK, Christine, B 413-545-2705 .... 236 F cmccormick@educ.umass.edu
MCCORMICK, David .... 312-567-4972 .... 153 C dmccormick@iitri.org
MCCORMICK, Deanna .... 563-588-6315 .... 183 E deanna.mccormick@clarke.edu
MCCORMICK, Heidi, A .... 330-263-2533 .... 388 F hmccormick@wooster.edu
MCCORMICK, Jim, S .... 303-963-3363 .... 82 C jimmccormick@ccu.edu
MCCORMICK, John .... 801-957-4024 .... 512 D john.mccormick@slcc.edu
MCCORMICK, Joseph, P .... 717-771-4052 .... 440 H jpm32@psu.edu
MCCORMICK, Kelly, L .... 303-765-3121 .... 85 D kmccormick@iliff.edu
MCCORMICK, Kevin, M .... 630-515-6053 .... 158 F kmccor@midwestern.edu
MCCORMICK, Kimberly .... 423-697-2647 .... 474 D
MCCORMICK, Mark .... 205-247-8831 .... 7 F mmccormick@stillman.edu
MCCORMICK, Mark .... 856-351-2670 .... 315 A mmccormick@salemcc.edu
MCCORMICK, Megan .... 310-377-5501 .... 56 F mmccormick@marymountpv.edu
MCCORMICK, Michael, R .. 315-386-7222 .... 355 E mccormic@canton.edu
MCCORMICK, Patricia .... 334-395-8800 .... 7 B mccormick@southuniversity.edu
MCCORMICK, Patrick, T .... 509-313-6715 .... 534 F mccormick@calvin.gonzaga.edu
MCCORMICK, Randy .... 501-225-9337 .... 19 A randy.mccormick@phoenix.edu
MCCORMICK, Reenie .... 410-334-2939 .... 229 E rmccormick@worwic.edu
MCCORMICK, Robert .... 312-362-6627 .... 149 A bmccormi@depaul.edu
MCCORMICK, Vicky .... 626-396-2456 .... 29 I vicky.mccormick@artcenter.edu
MCCORRY, Laurie, K .... 617-228-2465 .... 239 C lkmccorry@bhcc.mass.edu
MCCORRY-ANDALIS, Catherine, M .... 915-747-5648 .... 506 B cmandalis@utep.edu
MCCORVEY, Angela, E .... 850-474-7448 .... 121 D amccorv0@uwf.edu
MCCORY, Denise .... 216-987-5544 .... 389 B denise.mccory@tri-c.edu
MCCOULLUM, Valarie, S .... 215-898-6081 .... 448 J cade@pobox.upenn.edu
MCCOURT, Mary Frances .. 812-855-7618 .... 173 D mmmccour@indiana.edu
MCCOWAN, Carla .... 217-333-3701 .... 167 D cmccowan@illinois.edu
MCCOWAN, Thema .... 865-273-8851 .... 471 B thema.mccowan@maryvillecollege.edu
MCCOWN, William .... 318-342-1036 .... 216 E mccown@ulm.edu
MCCOY, Brian, T .... 508-213-2242 .... 243 E brian.mccoy@nichols.edu
MCCOY, Carole, A .... 315-786-2230 .... 337 F cmccoy@sunyjefferson.edu
MCCOY, Cindy, L .... 304-236-7637 .... 543 C cindy.mccoy@southernwv.edu
MCCOY, Dara .... 903-813-2335 .... 481 A dmccoy@austincollege.edu
MCCOY, David, M .... 804-289-8718 .... 525 E dmccoy2@richmond.edu
MCCOY, Donna .... 405-789-7661 .... 412 E donna.mccoy@swcu.edu
MCCOY, Elizabeth, W .... 801-581-5701 .... 511 C liz.mccoy@utah.edu
MCCOY, Holly, M .... 724-738-2650 .... 443 F holly.mccoy@sru.edu
MCCOY, Hugh .... 715-324-6900 .... 549 G hugh.mccoy@ni.edu
MCCOY, J. Kelly .... 229-931-2320 .... 131 F kellly.mccoy@gsw.edu
MCCOY, James .... 203-932-7306 .... 95 C jmccoy@newhaven.edu
MCCOY, Janee .... 914-964-4296 .... 329 D
MCCOY, John .... 510-436-1240 .... 50 H mccoy@hnu.edu
MCCOY, John .... 423-236-2444 .... 473 B jmccoy@southern.edu
MCCOY, Jolie, A .... 605-394-1924 .... 466 B jolie.mccoy@sdsmt.edu
MCCOY, Julie .... 803-938-3753 .... 462 G jmccoy@uscsumter.edu
MCCOY, Keith .... 773-838-7514 .... 147 H kmccoy@ccc.edu
MCCOY, Marilyn .... 847-491-4335 .... 160 E mmccoy@northwestern.edu
MCCOY, Mark .... 765-658-6732 .... 171 B markmccoy@depauw.edu
MCCOY, Mary .... 409-882-3080 .... 501 B mary.mccoy@lsco.edu
MCCOY, Mary .... 405-682-1611 .... 409 F mmccoy@occc.edu
MCCOY, Matthew, J .... 541-383-7210 .... 414 I mmccoy@cocc.edu
MCCOY, Mike .... 256-216-3300 .... 1 E mike.mccoy@athens.edu
MCCOY, Myron, F .... 816-483-9600 .... 289 E myron@spst.edu
MCCOY, Paddy .... 509-527-2343 .... 539 C paddy.mccoy@wallawalla.edu
MCCOY, Patrick, J .... 828-262-3187 .... 377 D mccoypj@appstate.edu
MCCOY, Peggy .... 406-496-4402 .... 296 A pmccoy@mtech.edu
MCCOY, Peggy, S .... 406-496-4404 .... 296 B pmccoy@mtech.edu
MCCOY, Robert .... 907-474-7500 .... 10 I rpmccoy@alaska.edu
MCCOY, Shelly .... 931-393-1600 .... 475 D smccoy@mscc.edu
MCCOY, Stephen, L .... 276-328-2677 .... 525 G slm4u@uvawise.edu
MCCOY, Sue .... 212-353-4167 .... 331 A mccoy@cooper.edu
MCCOY, Thomas .... 406-994-2891 .... 295 C tommccoy@montana.edu
MCCOY, William, K .... 570-577-1609 .... 423 E bill.mccoy@bucknell.edu
MCCOY GRISSOM, Shelly . 419-251-1203 .... 395 I mccoygrissom@mercycollege.edu
MCCRACKEN, Carolyn .... 423-354-2509 .... 475 F cgmccracken@northeaststate.edu
MCCRACKEN, Jeff, B .... 919-966-5730 .... 378 E jeff_mccracken@unc.edu
MCCRACKEN, Joann .... 610-989-1450 .... 450 F jbmiller@vfmac.edu
MCCRACKEN, Larry .... 503-517-1879 .... 421 C lmccracken@westernseminary.edu
MCCRACKEN, Mike .... 620-235-4624 .... 196 C mmccrack@pittstate.edu
MCCRAE, Byron .... 724-503-1001 .... 451 A bmccrae@washjeff.edu
MCCRANEY, Michelle .... 386-506-4110 .... 104 F mccranm@daytonastate.edu
MCCRANEY, Steven .... 601-925-3204 .... 275 C smccraney@mc.edu
MCCRARY, Betty, M .... 318-797-5364 .... 213 D betty.mccrary@lsus.edu
MCCRARY, Brian .... 678-839-6619 .... 139 A bmccrary@westga.edu
MCCRARY, Kevin .... 386-506-3475 .... 104 F mccrak@daytonastate.edu
MCCRARY, Sammi .... 405-912-9064 .... 408 D
MCCRATE, Mitchell, D .... 513-556-3483 .... 403 D mitchell.mccrate@uc.edu
MCCRAW, Bethany, J .... 254-710-1715 .... 482 A bethany_mccraw@baylor.edu
MCCRAW, Ed .... 903-785-7661 .... 492 D emccraw@parisjc.edu
MCCRAW, Patti, H .... 864-488-4571 .... 459 B pmccraw@limestone.edu
MCCRAY, JR., John, H .... 401-277-5489 .... 454 E drmccray@uri.edu
MCCRAY, Richard .... 304-214-8838 .... 543 D rmccray@wvncc.edu
MCCRAY, Suzanne .... 479-575-4883 .... 24 C smccray@uark.edu
MCCRAY-ROBERTS, Patty .. 360-417-6442 .... 536 G proberts@pencol.edu
MCCREADIE, Maureen .... 215-968-8004 .... 423 F mccreadi@bucks.edu
MCCREADY, Peggy, A .... 203-432-2038 .... 96 A peggy.mccready@yale.edu
MCCREADY, Randall .... 262-595-2004 .... 552 A randall.mccready@uwp.edu
MCCREARY, Lynn .... 940-565-2378 .... 504 D mccreary@unt.edu
MCCREDIE, Wendy .... 414-443-3608 .... 549 D mccrediw@mtmary.edu
MCCREE, Bernard, L .... 610-683-4032 .... 443 A mccree@kutztown.edu
MCCREE, Ray .... 410-837-6807 .... 229 A rmccree@ubalt.edu
MCCREE, Robin .... 704-991-0252 .... 374 D mmccree5540@stanly.edu
MCCREERY, Deborah, M .... 973-290-4455 .... 308 G dmccreery@cse.edu
MCCREERY, Shane .... 309-438-3383 .... 153 D msmcre@ilstu.edu
MCCRILLIS, Neal, R .... 706-565-4036 .... 127 G mccrillis_neal@columbusstate.edu
MCCRIMMON, Donald, A .. 315-655-7117 .... 325 H damccrimmon@cazenovia.edu
MCCROHAN, Betty, A .... 979-532-6304 .... 509 D bettym@wcjc.edu
MCCRORY, Cynthia .... 704-922-6406 .... 370 G mccrory.cynthia@gaston.edu
MCCRORY, Marianne .... 985-858-2978 .... 210 G marianne.mccrory@fletcher.edu
MCCRORY, Robert, L .... 585-275-4973 .... 359 B rmcc@lle.rochester.edu
MCCROW, Rich .... 661-720-2002 .... 52 L rmccrow@bakersfieldcollege.edu
MCCROY-HEINS, Michelle . 201-692-2190 .... 310 A michelle_mccroy@fdu.edu
MCCRYSTAL, Mary .... 216-373-5331 .... 397 F mmccrystal@ndc.edu
MCCUBBIN, Jeff .... 970-491-5841 .... 83 F jeff.mccubbin@colostate.edu
MCCUBBIN, Todd, A .... 573-882-6017 .... 291 B mccubbint@missouri.edu
MCCUE, Brian .... 773-907-4855 .... 147 D bmccue@ccc.edu
MCCUE, Cindy .... 631-420-2319 .... 356 A cynthia.mccue@farmingdale.edu
MCCUE, James .... 914-674-7880 .... 340 F jmccue@mercy.edu
MCCUE, Jeff .... 617-287-5152 .... 236 G jeff.mccue@umb.edu
MCCUE, Jennie .... 949-582-4320 .... 70 F jmccue@saddleback.edu
MCCUE, Mary, E .... 419-559-2204 .... 402 D mmccue@terra.edu
MCCUEN, Kathleen .... 630-652-8609 .... 149 C kmccuen@devry.edu
MCCUIEN-SMITH, Cassandra .... 501-450-3173 .... 25 H cmccuien@uca.edu
MCCUISTION, Dirk, S .... 303-530-2100 .... 81 I dmccuistion@bcmt.org

MCCULLAR, Ron ... 706-245-7226 ... 129 C
rmccullar@ec.edu
MCCULLEN, Ann, S ... 904-620-2100 ... 120 D
amccullen@unf.edu
MCCULLOCH, Dave ... 770-962-7580 ... 132 D
dmcculloch@gwinnetttech.edu
MCCULLOCH, Greg ... 618-252-5400 ... 164 I
greg.mcculloch@sic.edu
MCCULLOCH, Joseph ... 318-675-5000 ... 213 B
jmccul@lsuhsc.edu
MCCULLOCH, Krystal ... 417-873-7303 ... 281 D
kmcculloch@drury.edu
MCCULLOCH, Lisa ... 505-224-4688 ... 317 K
lmcculloch2@cnm.edu
MCCULLOCH, Sonja ... 912-260-4402 ... 137 B
sonja.mcculloch@sgc.edu
MCCULLOH, Edna ... 330-490-7191 ... 405 F
emcculloh@walsh.edu
MCCULLOH, Julie, A ... 509-313-6572 ... 534 F
mcculloh@gu.gonzaga.edu
MCCULLOH, Thayne, M ... 509-313-6102 ... 534 F
president@gonzaga.edu
MCCULLOH, Waylyn, C ... 563-333-6078 ... 188 F
mccullohwaylync@sau.edu
MCCULLOUGH, Barbara ... 360-538-4034 ... 534 G
bmccullo@ghc.edu
MCCULLOUGH, Barbara ... 423-614-8567 ... 470 C
mccullough@leeuniversity.edu
MCCULLOUGH, Catherine . 802-728-1247 ... 516 A
cmccull@vtc.vsc.edu
MCCULLOUGH, Cris ... 916-484-8209 ... 56 A
mccullc@arc.losrios.edu
MCCULLOUGH, Desiree, A 731-881-7014 ... 477 G
dmccull1@utm.edu
MCCULLOUGH, Doreen ... 802-773-5900 ... 513 D
dmccullough@csj.edu
MCCULLOUGH, James ... 918-293-5068 ... 410 E
james.mccullough@okstate.edu
MCCULLOUGH, John, P ... 304-336-8000 ... 544 D
mcculljp@westliberty.edu
MCCULLOUGH,
Jonathan, W ... 903-434-8115 ... 491 F
jmccullough@ntcc.edu
MCCULLOUGH, Larry, D ... 336-887-3000 ... 366 C
lmccullough@laureluniversity.edu
MCCULLOUGH, Laura, L ... 304-414-4445 ... 542 J
lmccullough@kvctc.edu
MCCULLOUGH, Lois, N ... 419-783-2317 ... 389 H
lmccullough@defiance.edu
MCCULLOUGH, Randy ... 419-559-2355 ... 402 D
rmccullough01@terra.edu
MCCULLOUGH,
Richard, D ... 412-268-1180 ... 424 J
rm5g@andrew.cmu.edu
MCCULLOUGH, Robert, R . 216-368-5445 ... 386 F
robert.mccullough@case.edu
MCCULLOUGH, Sherri ... 719-502-2061 ... 87 B
sherri.mccullough@ppcc.edu
MCCULLOUGH, Willie, G ... 606-326-2068 ... 201 F
willie.mccullough@kctcs.edu
MCCULLUM, B. J ... 309-854-1723 ... 145 H
mccullumb@bhc.edu
MCCULLY, Clare ... 617-730-7089 ... 243 D
clare.mccully@newbury.edu
MCCUNE, John ... 781-239-2527 ... 239 G
jmccune@massbay.edu
MCCUNE, John ... 716-673-3373 ... 352 A
thomas.mccune@fredonia.edu
MCCURDY, Clantha ... 617-727-9420 ... 236 D
cmccurdy@osfa.mass.edu
MCCURDY, Debra, L ... 419-995-8200 ... 392 K
mccurdy.d@rhodesstate.edu
MCCURDY, Eugene, M ... 608-796-3921 ... 553 C
emmccurdy@viterbo.edu
MCCURDY, Lauren ... 205-226-4625 ... 2 B
lmccurdy@bsc.edu
MCCURDY, Lyndon, C ... 937-327-7325 ... 406 B
lmccurdy@wittenberg.edu
MCCURLEY, Steve ... 918-540-6196 ... 408 J
smccurley@neo.edu
MCCURREN, Cynthia ... 616-331-3558 ... 251 F
mccurrec@gvsu.edu
MCCURRY, David ... 619-849-2370 ... 62 L
davidmccurry@pointloma.edu
MCCURRY, Faith ... 803-535-1424 ... 460 C
mccurryf@octech.edu
MCCURRY, Rickey, N ... 812-877-8211 ... 179 B
rickey.mccurry@rose-hulman.edu
MCCURTY, Kenyetta ... 334-387-3877 ... 1 D
kenyettamccurty@amridgeuniversity.edu
MCCUSKEY, Beth, M ... 765-494-1022 ... 178 J
bmccuske@purdue.edu
MCCUTCHAN, Molly, M ... 734-384-4245 ... 255 D
mmccutchan@monroeccc.edu
MCCUTCHEN, Michael, F ... 731-989-6901 ... 469 B
mmccutchen@fhu.edu
MCCUTCHEON, Bruce, E ... 610-330-5530 ... 433 B
mccutchb@lafayette.edu
MCCUTCHEON, Fran ... 508-588-9100 ... 240 A
MCCUTCHEON, John, F ... 413-545-9682 ... 236 F
jmccutch@admin.umass.edu
MCCUTCHEON, Kathleen ... 614-292-4164 ... 398 I
MCCUTCHEON, Robert, R .. 304-637-1216 ... 541 A
mccutcheonr@dewv.edu
MCCUTCHEON, Ron ... 541-885-1120 ... 418 E
ron.mccutcheon@oit.edu
MCDADE, Linda ... 570-348-6249 ... 435 F
lmcdade@marywood.edu
MCDADE, Lucinda ... 909-625-8767 ... 40 F
lucinda.mcdade@cgu.edu
MCDADE, William ... 773-834-3861 ... 166 G
wmcdade@bsd.uchicago.edu
MCDADE-CLAY,
W. Thomas ... 585-340-9648 ... 329 F
tmcdadeclay@crcds.edu
MCDAID, James ... 617-879-7960 ... 238 B
jmcdaid@massart.edu
MCDANIEL, Brenda ... 540-362-7439 ... 520 A
bmcdaniel@hollins.edu
MCDANIEL, C. Joan ... 846-846-5781 ... 204 H
jmcdaniel@midway.edu
MCDANIEL, Cindy ... 810-762-5620 ... 255 G
cindy.mcdanie@mcc.edu
MCDANIEL, Cliff ... 817-461-8741 ... 480 H
MCDANIEL, Craig ... 706-295-6928 ... 131 B
cmcdaniel@gntc.edu
MCDANIEL, Diane ... 765-677-2117 ... 175 B
diane.mcdaniel@indwes.edu
MCDANIEL, Donna, N ... 402-557-7184 ... 296 H
donna.mcdaniel@bellevue.edu
MCDANIEL, Garry ... 614-947-6126 ... 391 B
mcdanieg@franklin.edu
MCDANIEL, Gary, R ... 949-214-3055 ... 43 C
gary.mcdaniel@cui.edu
MCDANIEL, Jervaise ... 618-842-3711 ... 152 G
mcdanielj@iecc.edu
MCDANIEL, John ... 615-322-1741 ... 478 A
john.mcdaniel@vanderbilt.edu
MCDANIEL, Joy ... 580-371-2371 ... 408 I
jmcdaniel@mscok.edu
MCDANIEL, Juley ... 620-223-2700 ... 193 A
juleym@fortscott.edu
MCDANIEL, Julie ... 937-484-1337 ... 405 A
jmcdaniel@urbana.edu
MCDANIEL, Kay ... 225-359-9207 ... 209 J
kaymcdaniel@catc.edu
MCDANIEL, Kristina, D ... 573-840-9695 ... 290 F
mcdank@trcc.edu
MCDANIEL, Lance ... 304-384-5258 ... 543 G
mcdaniell26@mycu.concord.edu
MCDANIEL, Laura ... 701-231-8330 ... 382 B
laura.mcdaniel@ndsu.edu
MCDANIEL, Lucinda ... 870-933-7906 ... 20 B
lmcdaniel@asusystem.edu
MCDANIEL, Mary, W ... 864-388-8242 ... 459 A
mmcdaniel@lander.edu
MCDANIEL, Mary Lee ... 601-857-3395 ... 274 C
mlmcdaniel@hindscc.edu
MCDANIEL, Mick, R ... 607-844-8222 ... 357 I
mcdanim@tc3.edu
MCDANIEL, Natalie ... 614-221-7770 ... 396 B
MCDANIEL, Peter ... 864-250-7000 ... 99 G
MCDANIEL, Thomas ... 864-596-9015 ... 457 E
tom.mcdaniel@converse.edu
MCDANIEL, Thomas ... 610-921-7672 ... 421 E
tmcdaniel@alb.edu
MCDANIELS, Tammy ... 918-781-7263 ... 407 B
mcdanielsta@bacone.edu
MCDANNELL, Carol ... 419-448-3441 ... 402 E
cmcdannell@tiffin.edu
MCDAVID, Courtney ... 860-832-3003 ... 90 G
mcdavidc@ccsu.edu
MCDAVIS, Roderick, J ... 740-593-1804 ... 400 D
mcdavis@ohio.edu
MCDAVIS, Roderick, J ... 740-593-1804 ... 399 G
mcdavis@ohio.edu
MCDERMOTT, A. Keith ... 617-541-2454 ... 241 A
kmcderm@rcc.mass.edu
MCDERMOTT, Ann, B ... 508-793-2443 ... 233 C
amcdermo@holycross.edu
MCDERMOTT, Brian ... 308-398-7387 ... 297 A
bmcdermott@cccneb.edu
MCDERMOTT, Christine ... 315-568-3105 ... 342 H
cmcdermott@nycc.edu
MCDERMOTT, Christine ... 302-736-2491 ... 97 A
mcdermch@wesley.edu
MCDERMOTT, David ... 617-287-7128 ... 236 E
dmcdermott@umassp.edu
MCDERMOTT, Dennis ... 718-489-5362 ... 348 E
dmcdermott@sfc.edu
MCDERMOTT, Diane ... 312-226-6294 ... 156 G
busofc@lexingtoncolleg.edu
MCDERMOTT, Emily ... 617-287-6500 ... 236 G
emily.mcdermott@umb.edu
MCDERMOTT, Harry ... 520-621-7428 ... 18 L
mcdermott@health.arizona.edu
MCDERMOTT, Joan ... 303-556-8300 ... 86 F
mcdermoj@msudenver.edu
MCDERMOTT, John, R ... 563-588-7132 ... 187 C
john.mcdermott@loras.edu
MCDERMOTT, Marty ... 231-777-0462 ... 256 A
marty.mcdermott@muskegoncc.edu
MCDERMOTT, Patrice ... 410-455-3150 ... 227 D
mcdermot@umbc.edu
MCDERMOTT, Richard, L .. 713-500-4963 ... 506 F
richard.l.mcdermott@uth.tmc.edu
MCDERMOTT, Robert, B ... 610-785-6268 ... 446 A
rmcdermott@scs.edu
MCDERMOTT, Robin ... 440-375-7251 ... 394 E
rmcdermott@lec.edu
MCDEVITT, Brigid ... 206-934-6314 ... 537 E
brigid.mcdevitt@seattlecolleges.edu
MCDEVITT, Jenna ... 740-587-6655 ... 389 I
mcdevitts@denison.edu
MCDIARMID, Bill ... 919-966-1356 ... 378 E
bmcd@email.unc.edu
MCDILL, M. Augustus ... 843-661-1128 ... 458 D
mmcdill@fmarion.edu
MCDILL, Sandy ... 602-787-7352 ... 15 J
sandy.mcdill@paradisevalley.edu
MCDOLE, Rob ... 803-754-4100 ... 457 D
MCDONAGH, David ... 212-749-2802 ... 339 I
dmcdonagh@msmnyc.edu
MCDONALD, Anita, D ... 814-375-4705 ... 439 E
adm10@psu.edu
MCDONALD, Ann, M ... 978-632-6600 ... 240 C
a_mcdonald@mwcc.mass.edu
MCDONALD, Anna ... 805-898-4018 ... 47 C
amcdonald@fielding.edu
MCDONALD, Barbara ... 218-322-2402 ... 266 G
barbara.mcdonald@itascacc.edu
MCDONALD, Becky ... 937-298-3399 ... 394 D
becky.mcdonald@kcma.edu
MCDONALD, Carl ... 912-260-4203 ... 137 B
carl.mcdonald@sgc.edu
MCDONALD, Cathy ... 701-328-4111 ... 381 E
cathy.mcdonald@ndus.edu
MCDONALD, Chanchai ... 901-448-4930 ... 477 E
cmcdon12@uthsc.edu
MCDONALD, Christopher .. 949-582-4820 ... 70 F
cmcdonald@saddleback.edu
MCDONALD, Clay ... 281-487-1170 ... 499 B
cmcdonald@txchiro.edu
MCDONALD, Dana ... 301-846-2452 ... 222 G
dmcdonald@frederick.edu
MCDONALD, David ... 503-838-8211 ... 419 C
mcdonald@wou.edu
MCDONALD, David ... 608-757-7759 ... 553 G
dmcdonald@blackhawk.edu
MCDONALD, Debbie ... 626-966-4576 ... 28 F
info@agu.edu
MCDONALD, Deborah ... 845-938-5706 ... 559 A
addimssion@usma.edu
MCDONALD, Denise ... 434-544-8665 ... 521 B
mcdonald@lynchburg.edu
MCDONALD, Dennis ... 518-454-5170 ... 330 C
mcdonald@strose.edu
MCDONALD, Dotty ... 337-550-1313 ... 212 J
MCDONALD, Eric ... 864-587-4200 ... 461 D
mcdonalde@smcsc.edu
MCDONALD, Evelyn ... 901-321-3530 ... 467 I
emcdonal@cbu.edu
MCDONALD, Frank ... 212-346-1800 ... 345 F
fmcdonald@pace.edu
MCDONALD, Fritz ... 319-368-6473 ... 187 H
fmcdonald@mtmercy.edu
MCDONALD, Gary ... 415-422-2699 ... 76 E
mcdonald@usfca.edu
MCDONALD, Ginger ... 978-478-3400 ... 246 G
gmcdonald@zbc.edu
MCDONALD, J. David ... 316-978-3285 ... 198 A
david.mcdonald@wichita.edu
MCDONALD, Jack, J ... 203-582-8621 ... 93 H
jack.mcdonald@quinnipiac.edu
MCDONALD, James ... 435-586-7898 ... 511 D
mcdonaldj@suu.edu
MCDONALD, James, L ... 415-451-2810 ... 66 B
jmcdonald@sfts.edu
MCDONALD, Jan ... 864-977-7151 ... 460 A
jan.mcdonald@ngu.edu
MCDONALD, Jason ... 503-943-7147 ... 420 G
mcdonaja@up.edu
MCDONALD, Jennifer ... 714-241-6163 ... 41 B
jmcdonald@coastline.edu
MCDONALD, Jessyna ... 202-274-5533 ... 100 A
jmcdonald@udc.edu
MCDONALD, Joan, T ... 215-895-2902 ... 427 H
mcdonajt@drexel.edu
MCDONALD, Johnny ... 662-252-8000 ... 276 G
jbmcdonald@rustcollege.edu
MCDONALD, Joseph ... 518-631-9869 ... 358 H
mcdonalj@uniongraduatecollege.edu
MCDONALD, Joseph ... 256-761-6443 ... 7 G
jmcdonald@talladega.edu
MCDONALD, Joseph ... 239-590-1102 ... 119 B
jmcdonald@fgcu.edu
MCDONALD, Julia, J ... 270-745-5394 ... 208 A
julia.mcdonald@wku.edu
MCDONALD, Katie ... 603-228-1541 ... 306 E
kmcdonald@piercelaw.edu
MCDONALD, Kevin ... 585-475-6795 ... 347 G
kgmpro@rit.edu
MCDONALD, Krista ... 513-785-3100 ... 396 F
mcdonak@muohio.edu
MCDONALD, Kurt ... 417-690-3200 ... 279 J
purch@cofo.edu
MCDONALD, Latrice ... 601-928-6206 ... 275 E
latrice.mcdonald@mgccc.edu
MCDONALD, Leander ... 701-766-1133 ... 381 A
leander.mcdonald@littlehoop.edu
MCDONALD, Lori ... 949-214-3074 ... 43 C
lori.mcdonald@cui.edu
MCDONALD, Maggie ... 205-226-7737 ... 2 B
mmcdonal@bsc.edu
MCDONALD, Maria, E ... 724-430-4145 ... 439 G
MCDONALD, Martha ... 626-914-8602 ... 40 B
mmcdonald@citruscollege.edu
MCDONALD, Mary ... 910-277-5047 ... 376 C
mhm@sapc.edu
MCDONALD, Mary, E ... 706-542-9167 ... 138 G
marymcd@uga.edu
MCDONALD, Matt, C ... 507-786-3255 ... 271 C
mcdonamc@stolaf.edu
MCDONALD, Michael ... 567-661-7203 ... 400 I
michael_mcdonald6@owens.edu
MCDONALD, Michael, A ... 269-337-7162 ... 252 K
michael.mcdonald@kzoo.edu
MCDONALD, Patrick, S ... 716-880-2345 ... 340 D
patrick.s.mcdonald@medaille.edu
MCDONALD, Paul, R ... 626-966-4576 ... 28 F
paulmcdonald@agu.edu
MCDONALD, Pete ... 706-295-6960 ... 131 B
pmcdonald@gntc.edu
MCDONALD, Peter ... 559-278-2403 ... 35 A
pmcdonald@csufresno.edu
MCDONALD, Sallie ... 671-735-2233 ... 559 G
salliemcd@uguam.uog.edu
MCDONALD, Scott ... 979-458-0996 ... 497 E
smcdonald@tamu.edu
MCDONALD, Shireen, E ... 505-272-0878 ... 321 G
semcdonald@salud.unm.edu
MCDONALD, Steven ... 401-277-4955 ... 454 B
smcdonal@risd.edu
MCDONALD, Sue ... 818-932-3026 ... 45 A
smcdonald@devry.edu
MCDONALD, Susan, K ... 785-827-5541 ... 194 F
smcdonald@kwu.edu
MCDONALD, Tammy ... 361-698-2177 ... 485 G
tmcdonal1@delmar.edu
MCDONALD, Terrence, J ... 734-764-0322 ... 259 A
tmcd@umich.edu
MCDONALD, Tim ... 706-265-7515 ... 133 C
tmcdonal@laniertech.edu
MCDONALD, Tim ... 256-726-8399 ... 6 C
tmcdonald@oakwood.edu
MCDONALD, Timothy ... 816-501-4077 ... 288 A
timothy.mcdonald@rockhurst.edu
MCDONALD, Todd ... 231-348-6603 ... 256 B
tmcdonald@ncmich.edu
MCDONALD, Todd, M ... 602-942-4141 ... 14 D
tmcdonal@cci.edu
MCDONALD, Tom ... 212-229-5900 ... 342 E
mcdonalt@newschool.edu
MCDONALD, William ... 315-866-0300 ... 335 D
mcdonaldwh@herkimer.edu
MCDONALD, William ... 617-951-2350 ... 242 G
bill.mcdonald@necb.edu
MCDONALD, William, A ... 973-748-9000 ... 307 H
bill_mcdonald@bloomfield.edu
MCDONALD, William, M ... 706-542-7774 ... 138 G
bmcdonal@uga.edu
MCDONALD-RASH, Jean .. 848-932-7057 ... 314 B
jrash@rci.rutgers.edu
MCDONNEL, Wendy ... 605-221-3100 ... 464 D
wmcdonnel@kilian.edu
MCDONNELL, Betty ... 217-641-4549 ... 154 I
mcdonnell@jwcc.edu
MCDONNELL, Brian, A ... 401-341-2185 ... 454 D
mcdonneb@salve.edu
MCDONNELL,
Constance, F ... 570-941-7640 ... 450 C
constance.mcdonnell@scranton.edu
MCDONNELL, Heidi ... 908-852-1400 ... 308 E
0553txt@fheg.follett.com
MCDONNELL, John ... 773-481-8253 ... 147 I
jmcdonnell@ccc.edu
MCDONNELL, John ... 215-991-3778 ... 432 I
mcdonnell72@lasalle.edu
MCDONNELL, John ... 716-270-5612 ... 333 A
mcdonnellj@ecc.edu
MCDONNELL, John ... 801-581-5791 ... 511 C
john.mcdonnell@utah.edu
MCDONNELL, Joseph ... 207-780-4020 ... 220 G
jmcdonnell@usm.maine.edu
MCDONNELL, Teresa, H ... 603-513-1308 ... 306 F
tessa.mcdonnell@granite.edu
MCDONOUGH, Ann ... 702-774-4619 ... 302 I
ann.mcdonough@unlv.edu
MCDONOUGH, David ... 207-786-6231 ... 217 C
dmcdonou@bates.edu
MCDONOUGH, David ... 508-793-7258 ... 233 B
dmcdonough@clarku.edu
MCDONOUGH, Eileen ... 305-899-3085 ... 101 M
emcdonough@mail.barry.edu
MCDONOUGH,
Jennifer, N ... 330-569-5957 ... 391 G
mcdonoughjn@hiram.edu
MCDONOUGH, Kathleen ... 413-552-2261 ... 239 F
kmcdonough@hcc.edu
MCDONOUGH, Michael ... 802-447-4658 ... 514 F
mmcdonough@svc.edu
MCDONOUGH, Michael, J 585-292-2170 ... 341 H
mmcdonough@monroecc.edu
MCDONOUGH, Patrick ... 610-807-9221 ... 431 D
MCDONOUGH, Peter, G ... 609-258-2511 ... 312 G
pmcd@princeton.edu

MCGINTY, Evelyn, J .... 936-261-1725.... 496 G
ejmcginty@pvamu.edu
MCGINTY, Jack .... 412-809-5100.... 444 G
mcginty.john@pti.edu
MCGINTY, James, J .... 732-255-0400.... 312 D
jmcginty@ocean.edu
MCGINTY, Jill .... 312-935-4860.... 162 G
jmcginty@robertmorris.edu
MCGINTY, John .... 410-617-6811.... 223 I
jmcginty@loyola.edu
MCGINTY, John, W .... 410-617-6811.... 225 D
jmcginty@ndm.edu
MCGINTY, Louis .... 804-523-2280.... 527 A
mmcginty@ccwa.vccs.edu
MCGINTY, Mac, L .... 804-523-2280.... 527 B
mmcginty@ccwa.vccs.edu
MCGIRR, Kathleen .... 215-641-6603.... 436 G
kmcgirr@mc3.edu
MCGIRT, David .... 910-893-1265.... 362 J
mcgirt@campbell.edu
MCGIVNEY, R, J .... 860-768-4401...... 95 B
rmcgivney@hartford.edu
MCGIVNEY, Sean .... 719-549-2753...... 83 H
sean.mcgivney@colostate-pueblo.edu
MCGLADDERY, Nicole .... 805-581-1233...... 45 J
MCGLADE, Jacqueline .... 973-290-4122.... 308 G
jmcglade@cse.edu
MCGLAMERY, Matt .... 970-247-7065...... 84 K
mcglamery_m@fortlewis.edu
MCGLASSON, Robert .... 417-328-1535.... 290 A
bmcglasson@sbuniv.edu
MCGLEN, Nancy, E .... 716-286-8060.... 344 D
nmcglen@niagara.edu
MCGLONE, John, K .... 606-326-2400.... 201 F
john.mcglone@kctcs.edu
MCGLOTHIN, Kris .... 302-735-7696...... 97 A
bkwesley@bncollege.edu
MCGLOTHIN-ELLER,
Vince .... 847-866-3907.... 151 D
vince.mcglothin-eller@garrett.edu
MCGLOTHLAN, Mary .... 503-255-0332.... 417 C
mmcglothlan@multnomah.edu
MCGLOTHLIN, Michael, G 276-498-4190.... 516 C
MCGLOUGHLIN, Stephen .. 916-691-7589...... 56 B
mcglous@crc.losrios.edu
MCGLYNN, Ken .... 443-518-4802.... 223 D
kmcglynn@howardcc.edu
MCGOFF, Michael, F .... 607-777-2143.... 351 F
mmcgoff@binghamton.edu
MCGOLDRICK, Deirdre, E .. 253-535-7444.... 536 E
mcgoldde@plu.edu
MCGOLDRICK, John .... 215-951-1015.... 432 I
mcgoldri@lasalle.edu
MCGONIGAL, Terry, P .... 509-777-4345.... 540 C
tmcgonigal@whitworth.edu
MCGONIGLE, Gregory .... 440-775-5191.... 397 G
greg.mcgonigle@oberlin.edu
MCGONIGLE, Mary .... 610-519-4070.... 450 H
mary.mcgonigle@villanova.edu
MCGONIGLE, Robert, B ...... 570-208-5875.... 432 G
rbmcgoni@kings.edu
MCGONIGLE, Steve .... 215-951-1075.... 432 I
mcgonigle@lasalle.edu
MCGORDY, Sandra .... 817-515-7463.... 496 C
sandra.mcgordy@tccd.edu
MCGOUGH, David .... 802-635-1323.... 515 F
david.mcgough@jsc.edu
MCGOUGH, Lucy .... 276-935-4349.... 516 D
lmcgough@asl.edu
MCGOUGH, Marsha .... 425-602-3036.... 531 E
mmcgough@bastyr.edu
MCGOVERN, Bruce .... 713-646-2920.... 494 I
bmcgovern@stcl.edu
MCGOVERN, Daniel .... 516-686-7533.... 343 D
dmcgover@nyit.edu
MCGOVERN, Lorrie .... 352-588-7390.... 116 G
lorrie.mcgovern@saintleo.edu
MCGOVERN, Mark, S .... 401-865-2702.... 453 H
mmcgovrn@providence.edu
MCGOVERN, Martin, P ...... 508-565-1321.... 245 A
mmcgovern@stonehill.edu
MCGOVERN, Terry .... 615-230-3352.... 476 C
terry.mcgovern@volstate.edu
MCGOVERN, Thomas .... 617-236-8800.... 234 G
tmcgovern@fisher.edu
MCGOWAN, Bill .... 828-898-8776.... 366 D
mcgowanb@lmc.edu
MCGOWAN, Bruce, W .... 918-877-8101.... 408 G
bwmcgowan@langston.edu
MCGOWAN, Carl .... 904-398-4141.... 121 E
MCGOWAN, Charlotte .... 269-782-1347.... 258 C
cmcgowan@swmich.edu
MCGOWAN, Chris .... 573-651-2163.... 289 K
cwmcgowan@semo.edu
MCGOWAN, James .... 516-877-3162.... 322 A
mcgowan2@adelphi.edu
MCGOWAN, Jeanne .... 215-641-5571.... 430 C
mcgowan.j@gmc.edu
MCGOWAN, Joanna .... 610-892-1401.... 439 C
jxm1019@psu.edu
MCGOWAN, John .... 205-348-5610........ 8 E
john.mcgowan@ua.edu
MCGOWAN, John, P .... 256-824-2623........ 8 G
john.mcgowan@uah.edu
MCGOWAN, Joseph, J ...... 502-272-8234.... 198 H
jmcgowan@bellarmine.edu
MCGOWAN, Joumana .... 909-594-5611...... 58 A
jmcgowan@mtsac.edu
MCGOWAN, Kent .... 406-243-5373.... 294 I
kent.mcgowan@umontana.edu
MCGOWAN, Kevin .... 239-687-5335.... 101 H
kmcgowan@avemarialaw.edu
MCGOWAN, Lisa .... 717-846-5000.... 452 H
MCGOWAN, Paul .... 617-552-3055.... 232 B
paul.mcgowan.2@bc.edu
MCGOWAN, Richard .... 217-875-7200.... 162 F
rmcgowan@richland.edu
MCGOWAN, Sindi .... 770-537-5746.... 139 F
sindi.mcgowan@westgatech.edu
MCGOY, Jeff .... 618-634-3236.... 164 E
jeffm@shawneecc.edu
MCGRADY, Patricia .... 973-543-6528.... 307 B
treasurer@acs350.org
MCGRADY, Ronald, L .... 330-325-6799.... 397 D
rmcgrady@neomed.edu
MCGRAIL, Annmarie .... 914-773-3741.... 345 F
amcgrail@pace.edu
MCGRAIL, Frederick, J ...... 610-758-4487.... 434 E
fjm208@lehigh.edu
MCGRAIL, III, James, J .... 740-264-5591.... 390 F
jmcgrail@egcc.edu
MCGRAIL, Jennifer .... 580-581-2988.... 407 D
jbowen@cameron.edu
MCGRAIL, Margaret .... 914-674-3031.... 340 F
mmcgrail@mercy.edu
MCGRANAHAN, Mary, S ... 617-552-3300.... 232 B
mary.mcgranahan@bc.edu
MCGRANE, Jack, V .... 973-748-9000.... 307 H
jack_mcgrane@bloomfield.edu
MCGRANE, Wendy .... 417-625-9386.... 286 B
mcgrane-w@mssu.edu
MCGRANN, Loretta, A .... 718-940-5980.... 349 A
lmcgrann@sjcny.edu
MCGRANN, Loretta, A .... 631-687-5142.... 349 B
lmcgrann@sjcny.edu
MCGRATH, Abigail .... 312-567-3497.... 153 C
amcgrat1@iit.edu
MCGRATH, Andrew, S .... 608-757-7764.... 553 G
amcgrath@blackhawk.edu
MCGRATH, Breeda .... 312-467-2507.... 146 F
bmcgrath@thechicagoschool.edu
MCGRATH, Charlene .... 859-441-4500.... 202 B
charlene.mcgrath@kctcs.edu
MCGRATH, Cheryl .... 508-565-1111.... 245 A
cmcgrath1@stonehill.edu
MCGRATH, Deborah, F ...... 603-526-3609.... 303 G
dmcgrath@colby-sawyer.edu
MCGRATH, Debra .... 312-369-7151.... 148 D
dmcgrath@colum.edu
MCGRATH, Jamie .... 260-399-7700.... 181 A
jmcgrath@sf.edu
MCGRATH, Janet .... 716-827-2428.... 358 D
mcgrath@trocaire.edu
MCGRATH, John .... 212-594-4000.... 357 H
jmcgrath@tcicollege.edu
MCGRATH, Joseph, C .... 800-955-2527.... 282 D
jmcgrath@grantham.edu
MCGRATH, Laurie .... 503-552-1694.... 417 D
lmcgrath@ncnm.edu
MCGRATH, Mark .... 215-242-1501.... 425 D
mcgrathm@chc.edu
MCGRATH, Robert .... 404-407-7401.... 130 F
robert.mcgrath@gtri.gatech.edu
MCGRATH, Thomas .... 508-565-1086.... 245 A
tmcgrath@stonehill.edu
MCGRATH, Tim .... 619-388-2600...... 65 G
tmcgrath@sdccd.edu
MCGRATH, William .... 212-346-1200.... 345 F
wmcgrath@pace.edu
MCGRAW, Annette .... 716-375-2234.... 348 C
amcgraw@sbu.edu
MCGRAW, Darryl, D .... 919-866-5108.... 374 H
ddmcgraw@waketech.edu
MCGRAW, Jason .... 610-896-1228.... 430 G
jmcgraw@haverford.edu
MCGRAW, Matt .... 540-863-2866.... 526 F
mmcgraw@dslcc.edu
MCGRAW, Packy .... 518-694-7257.... 322 B
packy.mcgraw@acphs.edu
MCGREAL, Paul, E .... 937-229-3795.... 404 A
pmcgreal1@udayton.edu
MCGREEVEY, Michael .... 315-364-3275.... 360 D
mmcgreevey@wells.edu
MCGREEVY, Bill .... 303-914-6634...... 87 G
bill.mcgreevy@rrcc.edu
MCGREEVY, John, T .... 574-631-6642.... 180 G
mcgreevy.5@nd.edu
MCGREGOR, Patricia .... 860-297-2120...... 94 E
patricia.mcgregor@trincoll.edu
MCGREGOR, Tiffany .... 610-361-2487.... 437 D
mcgregot@neumann.edu
MCGREGOR, Wilson, E ...... 254-710-2663.... 482 A
bud_mcgregor@baylor.edu
MCGREGORY, Richard .... 262-472-4985.... 553 A
mcgregor@uww.edu
MCGREW, Kevin .... 218-723-6198.... 262 G
kmcgrew@css.edu
MCGREW, Mackenzie .... 843-525-8218.... 461 E
MCGREW, Paula, L .... 304-473-8461.... 545 G
mcgrew_p@wwc.edu
MCGREW, Shea .... 906-487-3443.... 255 B
smcgrew@mtu.edu
MCGRIFF, Ilona .... 336-517-2201.... 362 G
imcgriff@bennett.edu
MCGRIFF, Sheryl .... 313-993-1017.... 258 G
mcgrifsj@udmercy.edu
MCGRIFF-POWERS,
Kathleen .... 716-851-1017.... 333 A
mcgrifpowers@ecc.edu
MCGRISKEN, June .... 718-489-5352.... 348 E
jmcgrisken@sfc.edu
MCGUCKIN, Corrie, A .... 812-374-5173.... 176 A
cmcguckin@ivytech.edu
MCGUCKIN, Denis .... 516-686-7791.... 343 D
dmcgucki@nyit.edu
MCGUCKIN, Tammy .... 262-595-2571.... 552 A
mcguckin@uwp.edu
MCGUCKIN, Tammy, L ...... 850-474-2382.... 121 D
tmcguckin@uwf.edu
MCGUFFEY, Michael, J ...... 304-696-3648.... 544 B
mcguffey@marshall.edu
MCGUFFIN, Kurt .... 816-271-5623.... 286 G
kmcguffin@missouriwestern.edu
MCGUFFIN, Steven .... 740-699-2484.... 400 B
mcguffin@ohiou.edu
MCGUIGAN, Richard .... 937-769-1809.... 384 B
MCGUIGAN, Richard .... 937-769-1809.... 384 B
rmcguigan@antioch.edu
MCGUINESS, Ilona .... 410-617-5547.... 223 I
imcguiness@loyola.edu
MCGUINNESS, Maureen ..... 940-565-2648.... 504 D
moe@unt.edu
MCGUINNESS, Paul, M .... 219-785-5730.... 179 A
mcguinpm@pnc.edu
MCGUINNESS, Thomas, P 617-552-3310.... 232 B
thomas.mcguinness@bc.edu
MCGUIRE, Ann .... 216-421-8019.... 388 A
amcguire@cia.edu
MCGUIRE, Christine .... 617-353-4176.... 232 E
chmcguir@bu.edu
MCGUIRE, David .... 561-273-6500.... 118 A
ddmcguire@southuniversity.edu
MCGUIRE, David .... 561-697-9200.... 137 D
dmcguire@southuniversity.edu
MCGUIRE, David, T .... 435-586-7755.... 511 D
mcguire@suu.edu
MCGUIRE, Ellen .... 570-504-7000.... 425 F
MCGUIRE, Jamie .... 336-838-6482.... 375 C
jamie.mcguire@wilkescc.edu
MCGUIRE, Jane .... 615-230-3204.... 476 C
jane.mcguire@volstate.edu
MCGUIRE, Janelle .... 810-989-2356.... 248 G
janelle.mcguire@baker.edu
MCGUIRE, Katherine .... 404-471-6176.... 123 I
kmcguire@agnesscott.edu
MCGUIRE, Kathleen .... 508-541-1615.... 233 G
kmcguire@dean.edu
MCGUIRE, Mark, T .... 740-284-5249.... 391 A
mmcguire@franciscan.edu
MCGUIRE, Michael .... 303-871-3518...... 89 A
mmcguire@du.edu
MCGUIRE, Michael, D .... 202-687-3439...... 98 D
mcguirmd@georgetown.edu
MCGUIRE, Michael, J .... 785-670-1763.... 197 F
michael.mcguire@washburn.edu
MCGUIRE, Nancy .... 712-279-5455.... 183 A
nancy.mcguire@briarcliff.edu
MCGUIRE, Nona, S .... 614-236-6908.... 386 E
nmcguire@capital.edu
MCGUIRE, Patricia, A .... 202-884-9050...... 99 H
mcguirep@trinitydc.edu
MCGUIRE, Phyllis .... 415-239-3014...... 40 C
pmcguire@ccsf.edu
MCGUIRE, Rachel, L .... 641-422-4104.... 188 A
mcguirac@niacc.edu
MCGUIRE, Ruth, A .... 651-631-5343.... 270 B
ramcguire@nwc.edu
MCGUIRE, Tara .... 402-280-3973.... 297 F
taramcguire@creighton.edu
MCGUIRE-CLOSSON,
Margaret .... 610-861-4558.... 437 H
mclosson@northampton.edu
MCGUIRK, Dewey .... 813-880-8017.... 111 C
deweymcguirk@academy.edu
MCGUIRL-HADLEY, Joy ...... 508-999-8148.... 237 A
jhadley@umassd.edu
MCGUKIN, Wanda, R .... 678-839-6431.... 139 A
wmcgukin@westga.edu
MCGURGAN, Susan .... 513-231-2223.... 384 H
smcgurgan@athenaeum.edu
MCGURIK, Paul .... 972-660-5701.... 490 C
MCGURIMAN, Joseph .... 215-641-6605.... 436 G
jmcgurim@mc3.edu
MCGURIMAN, Timothy .... 312-915-7802.... 157 C
tmcguri@luc.edu
MCGURK, Mark, A .... 520-626-1677...... 18 L
mcgurkm@email.arizona.edu
MCGURL, George .... 802-468-1241.... 515 D
george.mcgurl@castleton.edu
MCGURN, Joseph, P .... 740-283-6278.... 391 A
jmcgurn@franciscan.edu
MCGURREN, Cynthia .... 978-542-7591.... 238 E
cmcgurren@salemstate.edu
MCGURTY, Thomas, S .... 617-627-3264.... 245 C
thomas.mcgurty@tufts.edu
MCGUTHRY, John, W .... 909-869-6442...... 33 J
jwmcguthry@csupomona.edu
MCHALE, Barbara .... 215-641-5521.... 430 C
mchale.b@gmc.edu
MCHARGUE, Jackie .... 828-250-2370.... 378 D
jmchargu@unca.edu
MCHARRIS, Michael .... 315-792-5489.... 341 E
mmcharris@mvcc.edu
MCHENRY, Bart .... 949-582-4907...... 70 F
bmchenry@saddleback.edu
MCHENRY, Renee .... 417-823-3448.... 289 I
rmchenry@forest.edu
MCHENRY, Stephanie .... 216-687-3673.... 388 D
s.y.mchenry@csuohio.edu
MCHONE, Michael, L .... 276-223-4798.... 529 C
mmchone@wcc.vccs.edu
MCHUGH, Carol, G .... 203-285-2061...... 91 D
cmchugh@gwcc.commnet.edu
MCHUGH, Elizabeth .... 360-867-6808.... 534 D
mchughe@evergreen.edu
MCHUGH, Eveline .... 330-337-6403.... 383 J
college@awc.edu
MCHUGH, John .... 704-748-1055.... 370 G
mchugh.john@gaston.edu
MCHUGH, Kevin .... 207-786-6341.... 217 C
kmchugh@bates.edu
MCHUGH, Mary .... 865-251-1800.... 473 A
library@southcollegetn.edu
MCHUGH, Shelley .... 402-465-2123.... 299 H
smchugh@nebrwesleyan.edu
MCHUGH, Tracy .... 630-889-6607.... 159 F
tmchugh@nuhs.edu
MCILLECE, Michelle .... 319-399-8844.... 183 F
mmcillec@coe.edu
MCILNAY, Sandy .... 816-604-4616.... 285 E
sandy.mcilnay@mcckc.edu
MCILVANE, Amy .... 770-426-2648.... 133 E
mcilvane@life.edu
MCINALLY, David, W .... 814-332-3782.... 421 F
dave.mcinally@allegheny.edu
MCINERNEY, Tammy .... 203-837-8290...... 91 A
hammershoyt@wcsu.edu
MCINNES, Robert .... 704-334-6882.... 367 H
rmcinnes@nlts.edu
MCINNIS, Dion .... 281-283-2021.... 503 E
mcinnis@uhcl.edu
MCINNIS, Robert, L .... 704-216-6400.... 366 G
rmcinnis@livingstone.edu
MCINNIS, W. Dale .... 910-410-1806.... 373 B
mcinnisd@richmondcc.edu
MCINTIRE, Dennis, K .... 770-720-9221.... 136 C
dkm@reinhardt.edu
MCINTIRE, Mary .... 713-348-2599.... 493 C
maryb@rice.edu
MCINTOSH, Becky, R .... 864-941-8358.... 460 D
mcintosh.b@ptc.edu
MCINTOSH, Bedford .... 909-621-8025...... 40 F
bedford.mcintosh@cgu.edu
MCINTOSH, Carl, R .... 803-938-3733.... 462 G
mcintocr@uscsumter.edu
MCINTOSH, Cecilia, A .... 423-439-4221.... 473 F
mcintosc@etsu.edu
MCINTOSH, Craig .... 518-276-3992.... 347 D
mcintc@rpi.edu
MCINTOSH, Gary .... 425-889-7790.... 536 C
gary.mcintosh@northwestu.edu
MCINTOSH, Gayle .... 253-879-3905.... 538 H
gmcintosh@pugetsound.edu
MCINTOSH, Glenn .... 248-370-3352.... 256 G
mcintosh@oakland.edu
MCINTOSH, Jennifer .... 304-293-5496.... 542 H
jennifer.mcintosh@mail.wvu.edu
MCINTOSH, Jennifer, A .... 304-293-5496.... 545 A
jennifer.mcintosh@mail.wvu.edu
MCINTOSH, Joe .... 817-515-5377.... 496 C
joe.mcintosh@tccd.edu
MCINTOSH, Joe, E .... 336-734-7297.... 370 F
jmcintosh@forsythtech.edu
MCINTOSH, John .... 256-331-5323........ 6 B
jmcintosh@nwscc.edu
MCINTOSH, John, L .... 574-520-4338.... 174 E
jmcintos@iusb.edu
MCINTOSH, Jonathan .... 208-882-1566.... 144 C
jmcintosh@nsa.edu
MCINTOSH, Julie .... 419-434-4062.... 404 B
mcintosh@findlay.edu
MCINTOSH, Keith .... 520-206-4809...... 17 H
kwmcintosh@pima.edu
MCINTOSH, Mathew .... 440-834-3728.... 393 G
mmcinto3@kent.edu
MCINTOSH, Nicole .... 701-349-3621.... 383 E
nicolemcintosh@trinitybiblecollege.edu
MCINTOSH, Sandra .... 800-818-2261.... 304 I
smcintosh@dwc.edu
MCINTOSH, Tanisha .... 734-432-5755.... 254 D
tmcintosh@madonna.edu
MCINTOSH, Tim .... 541-683-5141.... 416 A
tmcintosh@gutenberg.edu
MCINTOSH-DOTY, Mikail .. 512-313-3000.... 483 K
mikail.doty@concordia.edu

MCINTURF, Rob ... 910-962-2681 ... 379 D mcinturfr@uncw.edu
MCINTYRE, Faye, S ... 678-839-6467 ... 139 A fmcintyr@westga.edu
MCINTYRE, Jacqueline ... 516-364-0808 ... 343 A jmcintyre@nycollege.edu
MCINTYRE, James ... 513-244-8616 ... 387 E james.mcintyre@ccuniversity.edu
MCINTYRE, James, P ... 617-552-3246 ... 232 B james.mcintyre@bc.edu
MCINTYRE, Janet ... 503-491-7589 ... 417 B janet.mcintyre@mhcc.edu
MCINTYRE, Julie ... 518-244-2255 ... 348 A mcinitj@sage.edu
MCINTYRE, Karen ... 412-392-3976 ... 445 A kmcintyre@pointpark.edu
MCINTYRE, Kevin ... 806-743-7425 ... 502 B kevin.mcintyre@ttuhsc.edu
MCINTYRE, Kevin, M ... 610-527-0200 ... 445 J kmcintyre@rosemont.edu
MCINTYRE, Leonard, A ... 803-536-7173 ... 460 G lamcintyre@scsu.edu
MCINTYRE, Mary, F ... 412-396-6668 ... 428 D mcintyre@duq.edu
MCINTYRE, Michael ... 601-643-8404 ... 273 G mike.mcintyre@colin.edu
MCINTYRE, Pam ... 636-422-2240 ... 289 B pmcintyre@stlcc.edu
MCINTYRE, Richard ... 401-874-4126 ... 454 E mcintyre@uri.edu
MCINTYRE, Susan, H ... 252-222-6230 ... 369 A shm@carteret.edu
MCINTYRE, William, A ... 603-882-6923 ... 304 E bmcintyre@ccsnh.edu
MCINTYRE, Willie ... 910-672-1157 ... 377 G wmcintyre@uncfsu.edu
MCISAAC, Penny, J ... 561-868-3583 ... 114 D mcisaacp@palmbeachstate.edu
MCISAAC-TRACY, Jeannie . 406-657-2387 ... 295 D jmtracy@msubillings.edu
MCIVER, John ... 208-885-6651 ... 144 G jmciver@uidaho.edu
MCJUNKIN, Gayle ... 507-222-4335 ... 261 G gmcjunki@carleton.edu
MCKAIN, Joshua ... 617-236-8800 ... 234 G jmckain@fisher.edu
MCKAMEY, Sheldon ... 406-994-6342 ... 295 C smckamey@montana.edu
MCKANE, Heather, L ... 630-844-5448 ... 145 F hmckane@aurora.edu
MCKANN, Helen ... 804-594-1523 ... 527 B hmckann@jtcc.edu
MCKAY, Alan, B ... 540-665-1280 ... 524 E amckay@su.edu
MCKAY, Bill ... 509-542-5531 ... 532 H bmckay@columbiabasin.edu
MCKAY, David ... 617-266-1400 ... 231 E
MCKAY, Emily ... 701-224-2410 ... 382 D emily.mckay@bismarckstate.edu
MCKAY, Eugene ... 501-882-8956 ... 20 C emckay@asub.edu
MCKAY, Kerri ... 313-664-7441 ... 249 E kmckay@collegeforcreativestudies.edu
MCKAY, Kevin ... 425-640-1547 ... 533 I kevin.mckay@edcc.edu
MCKAY, Kimberly ... 956-872-2096 ... 494 H kjmckay@southtexascollege.edu
MCKAY, Marian, A ... 812-941-2340 ... 175 A mmckay@ius.edu
MCKAY, Michael, E ... 609-258-5491 ... 312 G mckay@princeton.edu
MCKAY, Richard ... 281-998-6150 ... 494 B richard.mckay@sjcd.edu
MCKAY, Sally ... 615-460-6456 ... 467 D sally.mckay@belmont.edu
MCKAY, Scott ... 870-235-4290 ... 23 I semckay@saumag.edu
MCKAY, Shaun, L ... 631-451-4736 ... 356 D mckays@sunysuffolk.edu
MCKAYLE-STOLZ, Camille . 340-693-1201 ... 568 E cmckayl@uvi.edu
MCKEAN, Debbie ... 602-943-2311 ... 19 B debbie.mckean@west.edu
MCKEAN, James ... 740-774-7200 ... 400 A mckean@ohio.edu
MCKEARNEY, James, L ... 650-325-5621 ... 64 G frjamesmck@gmail.com
MCKECHNIE, Janna ... 701-858-3373 ... 382 A janna.mckechnie@minotstateu.edu
MCKECHNIE, Sally ... 360-650-3340 ... 539 F sally.mckechnie@wwu.edu
MCKECHNIE, Susan, E ... 410-706-7776 ... 227 C smckechnie@af.umaryland.edu
MCKEE, Andrew ... 260-399-7700 ... 181 A amckee@sf.edu
MCKEE, Anne ... 865-981-8298 ... 471 B anne.mckee@maryvillecollege.edu
MCKEE, Bruce, G ... 641-422-4348 ... 188 A mckeebru@niacc.edu
MCKEE, Diann, E ... 812-237-2372 ... 173 B diann.mckee@indstate.edu
MCKEE, Eugenia ... 314-529-9509 ... 284 C gmckee@maryville.edu
MCKEE, J, P ... 803-323-2205 ... 463 E mckeej@winthrop.edu
MCKEE, John ... 212-650-7997 ... 326 G jmckee@ccny.cuny.edu
MCKEE, John, C ... 409-747-9080 ... 507 C jcmckee@utmb.edu
MCKEE, Jonathon ... 808-984-3213 ... 142 E jvmckee@hawaii.edu
MCKEE, Kasey ... 636-922-8472 ... 288 B kmckee@stchas.edu
MCKEE, Kathrine ... 937-327-7811 ... 406 B kmckee@wittenberg.edu
MCKEE, Lauren ... 408-274-7900 ... 67 C lauren.mckee@evc.edu
MCKEE, Lori ... 419-755-4828 ... 397 C lmckee@ncstatecollege.edu
MCKEE, Lori ... 575-646-2172 ... 319 D lomckee@nmsu.edu
MCKEE, Mike ... 386-752-1822 ... 108 G mike.mckee@fgc.edu
MCKEE, Sallye ... 312-341-3525 ... 163 B smckee01@roosevelt.edu
MCKEE, Suzanne ... 334-683-2347 ... 5 G smckee@marionmilitary.edu
MCKEE-LEONE, Virginia ... 951-222-8250 ... 64 A virginia.mckee-leone@rcc.edu
MCKEEGAN, John ... 503-883-2202 ... 416 H jmckeeg@linfield.edu
MCKEEN, Jerry ... 505-566-3322 ... 320 D mckeenj@sanjuancollege.edu
MCKEEVER, Diane, M ... 312-942-6830 ... 163 D diane_m_mckeever@rush.edu
MCKEEVER, Matt ... 303-797-5859 ... 81 D matt.mckeever@arapahoe.edu
MCKEEVER, Stephen, W ... 405-744-6501 ... 410 C stephen.mckeever@okstate.edu
MCKEEVER, William, P ... 716-829-7807 ... 332 E mckeever@dyc.edu
MCKELLIPS, Stephen ... 850-474-2233 ... 121 D smckellips@uwf.edu
MCKELLOGG, James, M ... 859-344-3302 ... 206 I jim.mckellogg@thomasmore.edu
MCKELVEY, C. Richard ... 512-863-1484 ... 496 A mckelver@southwestern.edu
MCKELVEY, Scott ... 970-204-8255 ... 85 A scott.mckelvey@frontrange.edu
MCKELVIE, OSF, Roberta .. 610-796-5509 ... 421 G roberta.mckelvie@alvernia.edu
MCKENDALL, Keith ... 504-816-4375 ... 209 A kmckendall@dillard.edu
MCKENDREE, Lynda ... 713-525-2151 ... 505 A mckendla@stthom.edu
MCKENNA, Catherine ... 718-405-3233 ... 330 A catherine.mckenna@mountsaintvincent.edu
MCKENNA, David ... 903-886-5753 ... 498 B david.mckenna@tamuc.edu
MCKENNA, Heidi ... 510-883-7160 ... 45 B hmckenna@dspt.edu
MCKENNA, Joann, C ... 781-891-2455 ... 231 D jmckenna@bentley.edu
MCKENNA, John ... 518-587-2100 ... 355 G john.mckenna@esc.edu
MCKENNA, John, E ... 213-385-2322 ... 79 I
MCKENNA, Kevin, M ... 508-793-7468 ... 233 B kmckenna@clarku.edu
MCKENNA, Megan ... 440-375-7508 ... 394 E mmckenna@lec.edu
MCKENNA, Michael ... 713-623-2040 ... 480 J mmckenna@aii.edu
MCKENNA, Patrick ... 404-894-6088 ... 130 F pat.mckenna@carnegie.gatech.edu
MCKENNA, Sheila ... 412-392-3450 ... 445 A smckenna@pointpark.edu
MCKENNA-FRAZIER, Lynn 260-399-7700 ... 181 A lfrazier@sf.edu
MCKENNA-GRANT, Patricia ... 860-768-5433 ... 95 B mckenna@hartford.edu
MCKENZIE, Andre, A ... 718-990-1892 ... 348 G mckenzia@stjohns.edu
MCKENZIE, Bobby ... 334-874-5700 ... 2 H bmckenzie@ccal.edu
MCKENZIE, Bruce ... 708-832-5095 ... 168 G bmckenzie@westwood.edu
MCKENZIE, Connie, L ... 757-446-6070 ... 518 G hedriccl@evms.edu
MCKENZIE, Elizabeth ... 617-573-8705 ... 245 B emckenzi@suffolk.edu
MCKENZIE, Fred, R ... 630-844-5420 ... 145 F mckenzie@aurora.edu
MCKENZIE, Joy ... 615-383-4848 ... 478 F jmckenzie@watkins.edu
MCKENZIE, Justin, D ... 336-750-3044 ... 380 B mckenziej@wssu.edu
MCKENZIE, Laura ... 208-282-2661 ... 143 H mckelaur@isu.edu
MCKENZIE, Lauren, J ... 310-233-4501 ... 54 I mckenzlj@lahc.edu
MCKENZIE, Lester ... 931-372-3073 ... 474 B lmckenzie@tetech.edu
MCKENZIE, Lisa ... 518-454-5114 ... 330 C mckenzil@strose.edu
MCKENZIE, Patricia, M ... 936-639-1301 ... 480 D mckenzie@angelina.edu
MCKENZIE, Peter, C ... 617-552-8740 ... 232 B peter.mckenzie@bc.edu
MCKENZIE, Pia ... 919-807-7100 ... 367 I mckenziep@nccommunitycolleges.edu
MCKENZIE, Scott ... 714-992-7052 ... 59 E smckenzie@fullcoll.edu
MCKENZIE, Sheri ... 415-703-9535 ... 32 C smckenzie@cca.edu
MCKENZIE, Steven, E ... 215-955-3900 ... 448 C steven.mckenzie@jefferson.edu
MCKENZIE, Terri ... 509-533-7015 ... 533 B terri.mckenzie@scc.spokane.edu
MCKEON, Judith, O ... 540-985-9083 ... 520 I jomckeon@jchs.edu
MCKEON, Meg ... 712-749-2123 ... 183 C mckeonm@bvu.edu
MCKEON, Michael ... 925-631-4552 ... 64 F mfm4@stmarys-ca.edu
MCKEON, Thomas, K ... 918-595-7868 ... 412 H tmckeon@tulsacc.edu
MCKEOWN, Patricia ... 360-752-8333 ... 531 H pmckeown@btc.ctc.edu
MCKERNAN, Steve ... 505-272-2071 ... 321 C smckernan@salud.unm.edu
MCKESSON, Leslie ... 828-448-3156 ... 375 B lmckesson@wpcc.edu
MCKETHAN, Lisa, H ... 254-710-1011 ... 482 A lisa_mckethan@baylor.edu
MCKEVER, Ted ... 928-692-3076 ... 16 F tmckever@mohave.edu
MCKEVITT, Sallie ... 301-369-2800 ... 221 F sjmckevitt@capitol-college.edu
MCKEY, Jim ... 765-983-1636 ... 171 E jimmckey@earlham.edu
MCKEY, Marites ... 808-687-7015 ... 140 G mckey@hpu.edu
MCKIBBENS, Donna ... 617-879-2242 ... 246 C dmckibbens@wheelock.edu
MCKIBBIN, Barbara ... 704-484-4116 ... 369 E mckibbin@clevelandcc.edu
MCKIE, Betty ... 970-542-3208 ... 86 G betty.mckie@morgancc.edu
MCKIEL, Allen ... 503-838-8886 ... 419 C mckiela@wou.edu
MCKIERNAN, Gavin ... 305-809-3281 ... 108 I gavin.mckiernan@fkcc.edu
MCKIM, Dana ... 704-463-3409 ... 375 F dana.mckim@fsmail.pfeiffer.edu
MCKIMMY, Kim ... 740-774-7200 ... 400 A kellyk@ohio.edu
MCKINEY, David ... 541-888-7229 ... 420 C dmckiney@socc.edu
MCKINION, Randall, L ... 800-672-3060 ... 376 G
MCKINLEY, Amy, L ... 419-372-0621 ... 385 F amckinl@bgsu.edu
MCKINLEY, Kathy ... 919-536-7244 ... 370 C mckinleyk@durhamtech.edu
MCKINLEY, Patricia ... 713-525-3575 ... 505 A mckinley@stthom.edu
MCKINLEY, Randy ... 574-251-3250 ... 172 M rmckinley@holycrossvillage.com
MCKINLEY, Ronald, B ... 409-772-2636 ... 507 C rbmckinl@utmb.edu
MCKINNEY, Bryan ... 870-245-5250 ... 22 I mckinneyb@obu.edu
MCKINNEY, Bryan ... 870-245-5513 ... 22 I mckinneyb@obu.edu
MCKINNEY, Cathy ... 301-937-8448 ... 226 H cmckinney@tesst.com
MCKINNEY, Charlie ... 603-880-8308 ... 306 A tmc@thomasmorecollege.edu
MCKINNEY, Chris ... 706-721-4062 ... 130 D chmckinney@georgiahealth.edu
MCKINNEY, David, C ... 828-398-7124 ... 368 B dmckinney@abtech.edu
MCKINNEY, Donald, W ... 252-334-2084 ... 367 C don.mckinney@macuniversity.edu
MCKINNEY, Frances, H ... 410-651-6668 ... 227 E fhmckinney@umes.edu
MCKINNEY, Joan, C ... 270-789-5214 ... 199 F jmckinney@campbellsville.edu
MCKINNEY, Larry, J ... 530-226-4130 ... 69 H lmckinney@simpsonu.edu
MCKINNEY, Marion ... 610-436-3307 ... 444 A mmckinney@wcupa.edu
MCKINNEY, Mary ... 407-823-2827 ... 120 B mary.mckinney@ucf.edu
MCKINNEY, Michael ... 724-589-2193 ... 448 B mmckinney@thiel.edu
MCKINNEY, Nancy ... 360-596-5268 ... 538 E nmckinney@spscc.ctc.edu
MCKINNEY, Paul ... 662-325-7428 ... 275 F kpm137@msstate.edu
MCKINNEY, Richard, L ... 785-864-3136 ... 197 B rlm@ku.edu
MCKINNEY, Robert ... 734-995-7328 ... 249 G mckinr@cuaa.edu
MCKINNEY, Scott ... 828-398-7111 ... 368 B smckinney@abtech.edu
MCKINNEY, Sheryl ... 678-872-8012 ... 130 E smckinne@highlands.edu
MCKINNEY, Shortie ... 978-934-4460 ... 237 B shortie_mckinney@uml.edu
MCKINNEY, Stephen ... 610-861-1442 ... 437 A mckinney@moravian.edu
MCKINNEY, Tim ... 507-288-4563 ... 263 B tmckinney@crossroadscollege.edu
MCKINNEY, Tim ... 304-442-3313 ... 545 D t.mckinney@mail.wvu.edu
MCKINNEY, Veronica ... 251-809-1532 ... 5 B veronica.mckinney@jdcc.edu
MCKINNEY, William ... 229-333-5952 ... 139 C wjmckinney@valdosta.edu
MCKINNEY, William, J ... 813-988-5131 ... 108 A bj@floridacollege.edu
MCKINNIES, Magi ... 617-349-8546 ... 236 B mmckinni@lesley.edu
MCKINNON, Brad ... 256-766-6610 ... 4 C bmckinnon@hcu.edu
MCKINNON, Brenda ... 740-389-4636 ... 395 H mckinnonb@mtc.edu
MCKINNON, Maureen ... 816-501-4831 ... 288 A maureen.mckinnon@rockhurst.edu
MCKINNON, Maurice ... 209-575-6362 ... 80 H mckinnonm@mjc.edu
MCKINNON, Robert, G ... 770-720-5516 ... 136 C rgm@reinhardt.edu
MCKINNON, Sarah ... 617-369-4054 ... 244 E smckinnon@smfa.edu
MCKINNON, Susan, J ... 850-474-3386 ... 121 D smckinnon@uwf.edu
MCKINNON, Ted, M ... 512-245-2396 ... 501 F tm02@txstate.edu
MCKINNON, Theresa ... 615-327-6185 ... 471 C tmckinnon@mmc.edu
MCKINNON, Will ... 801-863-8922 ... 511 F will.mckinnon@uvu.edu
MCKINZIE, Kathy, F ... 864-592-4808 ... 461 C mckinziek@sccsc.edu
MCKINZIE, Steve ... 704-637-4666 ... 363 E smckinzie@catawba.edu
MCKINZIE, Wes ... 405-425-5132 ... 409 E wes.mckinzie@oc.edu
MCKIRDY, Pamela, R ... 336-272-7102 ... 364 G mckirdyp@greensboro.edu
MCKIRNAN, Lori ... 614-236-6814 ... 386 E lmckirna@capital.edu
MCKISSICK, Milton, E ... 803-536-8938 ... 460 G mckissick@scsu.edu
MCKISSON, Kevin ... 281-476-1501 ... 493 H kevin.mckisson@sjcd.edu
MCKNIGHT, Avery ... 850-599-3591 ... 118 L avery.mcknight@famu.edu
MCKNIGHT, Carrie ... 650-508-3717 ... 59 H cmknight@ndnu.edu
MCKNIGHT, Cynthia ... 440-684-6102 ... 405 B cmcknigh@ursuline.edu
MCKNIGHT, Frank ... 330-490-7226 ... 405 F fmcknight@walsh.edu
MCKNIGHT, Irby ... 972-825-4662 ... 495 F imcknight@sagu.edu
MCKNIGHT, Janet ... 414-256-1202 ... 549 D mcknighj@mtmary.edu
MCKNIGHT, Lindy ... 415-239-3006 ... 40 C lmcknigh@ccsf.edu
MCKNIGHT, Sandra ... 216-987-4832 ... 389 B sandra.mcknight@tri-c.edu
MCKONE, Kevin ... 601-643-8369 ... 273 G kevin.mckone@colin.edu
MCKOWN, Charles ... 620-441-5264 ... 192 D mckown@cowley.edu
MCKOWN, Johnette ... 254-299-8649 ... 490 G jmckown@mclennan.edu
MCKOWN, Richard, A ... 919-536-7200 ... 370 C mckownr@durhamtech.edu
MCKOY, Dana ... 910-362-7029 ... 368 H dmckoy@cfcc.edu
MCKULA, Patrick, R ... 724-925-4085 ... 451 E mckulap@wccc.edu
MCKUSICK, James ... 406-243-2541 ... 294 I james.mckusick@umontana.edu
MCLACKEN, Susan ... 401-232-6881 ... 453 C smcdonal@bryant.edu
MCLAIN, Charles ... 215-368-7538 ... 424 C cmclain@cbs.edu
MCLAIN, Ed ... 970-786-4484 ... 10 H emclain@uaa.alaska.edu
MCLAIN, Katherine ... 916-691-7411 ... 56 B mclaink@crc.losrios.edu
MCLAIN, Mandy ... 715-324-6900 ... 549 G mandy.mclain@ni.edu
MCLAIN, Tony, L ... 906-635-2202 ... 253 H tmclain@lssu.edu
MCLANE, Anne, P ... 214-648-5617 ... 507 E anne.mclane@utsouthwestern.edu
MCLANE, Curren ... 202-639-1835 ... 98 A cmclane@corcoran.org
MCLARAN, Diane ... 503-316-3229 ... 414 J diane.mclaran@chemeketa.edu
MCLARIN, Jenny ... 484-664-3804 ... 437 C mclarin@muhlenberg.edu
MCLARTY, Bruce ... 501-279-4449 ... 21 H bible@harding.edu
MCLAUGHLIN, Al ... 412-642-9072 ... 427 E amclaughlin@devry.edu
MCLAUGHLIN, Anne, E ... 202-541-5219 ... 100 B mclaughlin@wtu.edu

MCLAUGHLIN, Carrie .... 716-286-8405.... 344 D
cmclaughlin@niagara.edu
MCLAUGHLIN, David .... 212-998-2415.... 344 B
david.mclaughlin@nyu.edu
MCLAUGHLIN, Deborah .... 508-999-8051.... 237 A
dmclaughlin@umassd.edu
MCLAUGHLIN, Doris, A .... 336-758-4814.... 380 C
mclaugda@wfu.edu
MCLAUGHLIN, Ed .... 716-286-8600.... 344 D
edm@niagara.edu
MCLAUGHLIN, Ed .... 541-684-4644.... 419 F
emclaughlin@pioneerpacific.edu
MCLAUGHLIN, Francis, X . 718-817-4300.... 334 C
mclaughlin@fordham.edu
MCLAUGHLIN,
Gerald (Jerry) .... 215-641-5550.... 430 C
mclaughlin.g@gmc.edu
MCLAUGHLIN, Henry, J .... 646-660-6000.... 326 C
henry.mclaughlin@baruch.cuny.edu
MCLAUGHLIN, James .... 518-388-6284.... 358 G
mclaughj@union.edu
MCLAUGHLIN, John .... 401-456-8235.... 454 A
jmclaughlin@ric.edu
MCLAUGHLIN, Joyce .... 978-934-4237.... 237 B
joyce_mclaughlin@uml.edu
MCLAUGHLIN, Kevin .... 401-863-9525.... 453 B
kevin_mclaughlin@brown.edu
MCLAUGHLIN, Kevin .... 415-503-6253...... 66 A
kmclaughlin@sfcm.edu
MCLAUGHLIN, Laine .... 847-628-1561.... 154 K
lmclaughlin@judsonu.edu
MCLAUGHLIN, Larry .... 617-552-3605.... 232 B
larry.mclaughlin@bc.edu
MCLAUGHLIN, Laura .... 636-227-2100.... 284 B
laura.mclaughlin@logan.edu
MCLAUGHLIN, Laurie .... 951-487-6410...... 58 B
lmclaugh@msjc.edu
MCLAUGHLIN, Laurie, L ... 612-626-1499.... 272 A
mclau001@umn.edu
MCLAUGHLIN, LaVerne ..... 229-430-4799.... 124 A
laverne.mclaughlin@asurams.edu
MCLAUGHLIN, Leah .... 918-647-1370.... 407 E
lmclaughlin@carlalbert.edu
MCLAUGHLIN, Margaret .... 386-752-1822.... 108 G
maggie.mclaughlin@fgc.edu
MCLAUGHLIN,
Margaret, K .... 412-578-6071.... 424 I
mclaughlinmk@carlow.edu
MCLAUGHLIN, Mark .... 513-745-3409.... 406 E
mclaughlin@xavier.edu
MCLAUGHLIN, Mark, W ..... 860-832-0065...... 90 G
mclaughlinm@ccsu.edu
MCLAUGHLIN, Mary .... 603-526-3755.... 303 G
mmclaughlin@colby-sawyer.edu
MCLAUGHLIN, Mary, R ...... 518-454-5170.... 330 C
mclaughr@strose.edu
MCLAUGHLIN, Mike .... 319-398-4947.... 187 B
mclaug@kirkwood.edu
MCLAUGHLIN, Neil .... 203-837-9308...... 91 A
mclaughlinn@wcsu.edu
MCLAUGHLIN, Nora .... 503-777-7774.... 420 A
nora.mclaughlin@reed.edu
MCLAUGHLIN, Patrick, A .. 260-481-6128.... 174 C
mclaughp@ipfw.edu
MCLAUGHLIN, Sabrina ...... 850-474-2433.... 121 D
smclaughlin2@uwf.edu
MCLAUGHLIN, Sandee ...... 805-591-6220...... 43 I
smclaugh@cuesta.edu
MCLAUGHLIN, Steven .... 404-385-3383.... 130 F
steven.mclaughlin@provost.gatech.edu
MCLAUGHLIN, Suzanne .... 816-483-9600.... 289 E
sue.mclaughlin@spst.edu
MCLAUGHLIN, Timothy, G 315-655-7244.... 325 H
tmclaughlin@cazenovia.edu
MCLAUGHLIN, Virginia, L . 757-221-2315.... 518 A
vamcla@wm.edu
MCLAURIN, Lisa, H .... 919-209-2178.... 371 F
lhmclaurin@johnstoncc.edu
MCLAWHORN, Toni, D ..... 540-375-2303.... 523 G
mclawhorn@roanoke.edu
MCLAY, Melody, H .... 607-871-2612.... 322 E
mclaym@alfred.edu
MCLEAN, Amber .... 906-635-2382.... 253 H
amclean@lssu.edu
MCLEAN, Anita .... 609-258-3285.... 312 G
amclean@princeton.edu
MCLEAN, Brandon .... 402-844-7102.... 299 I
brandon@northeast.edu
MCLEAN, Deborah .... 907-842-5109...... 10 I
dlmclean@alaska.edu
MCLEAN, Edward .... 910-672-1315.... 377 G
emclean@uncfsu.edu
MCLEAN, Jack .... 773-508-3912.... 157 C
jmclean@luc.edu
MCLEAN, James, E .... 205-348-6052........ 8 E
jmclean@bamaed.ua.edu
MCLEAN, Janna .... 815-939-5231.... 161 A
jmclean@olivet.edu
MCLEAN, Jennifer .... 909-447-2506...... 40 H
jmclean@cst.edu
MCLEAN, Jennifer .... 570-326-3761.... 440 L
jmclean@pct.edu
MCLEAN, Karen, P .... 515-271-1463.... 184 A
karen.mclean@dmu.edu

MCLEAN, Mary .... 773-838-7883.... 147 H
mmclean2@ccc.edu
MCLEAN, Michael, F .... 805-525-4417...... 72 I
mmclean@thomasaquinas.edu
MCLEAN, Natalie .... 336-273-4431.... 362 G
nmclean@bennett.edu
MCLEAN, Pat .... 417-690-3441.... 279 J
mclean@cofu.edu
MCLEAN, Roger .... 704-216-6025.... 366 G
rmclean@livingstone.edu
MCLEAN, Sandra .... 972-438-6932.... 492 E
smclean@parkercc.edu
MCLEAN, Steven .... 661-362-5933...... 41 I
steven.mclean@canyons.edu
MCLEAN, Valis .... 620-365-5116.... 190 D
mclean@allencc.edu
MCLEAN, William, H .... 847-491-7050.... 160 E
wmclean@northwestern.edu
MCLEANE, David .... 870-574-4458...... 24 A
dmcleane@sautech.edu
MCLELLAN, Carolyn .... 757-822-7124.... 528 G
cmclellan@tcc.edu
MCLELLAN, Holly, H .... 251-626-3303........ 8 C
hmclellan@ussa.edu
MCLELLAN, Mark, R .... 435-797-1180.... 511 E
mark.mclellan@usu.edu
MCLELLAND, Brandy .... 310-243-3569...... 34 D
bmclelland@csudh.edu
MCLEMORE, Maria, R .... 651-201-1745.... 265 E
maria.mclemore@so.mnscu.edu
MCLENDON, George, L ..... 713-348-4026.... 493 C
mclendon@rice.edu
MCLENDON, Ginny .... 252-823-5166.... 370 D
mclendong@edgecombe.edu
MCLENDON, Joan, S .... 919-209-2079.... 371 F
jsmclendon@johnstoncc.edu
MCLENDON, Paul .... 870-235-4013...... 23 I
paulmclendon@saumag.edu
MCLENNAN, Dale .... 978-232-2101.... 234 D
dmclenna@endicott.edu
MCLENNAN, William, L ..... 650-723-1762...... 71 G
mclennan@stanford.edu
MCLEOD, Allan .... 215-871-6652.... 444 C
allanm@pcom.edu
MCLEOD, Carol .... 504-278-6418.... 211 E
cmcleod@nunez.edu
MCLEOD, Gregory, K .... 904-808-7400.... 116 F
gregmcleod@sjrstate.edu
MCLEOD, Joetta .... 701-255-3285.... 383 G
jmcleod@uttc.edu
MCLEOD, Kimberly, R .... 713-313-1857.... 500 B
mcleodkr@tsu.edu
MCLEOD, Mark .... 404-727-7457.... 129 D
rmcleod@emory.edu
MCLEOD, Martha .... 860-253-3001...... 91 B
mmcleod@asnuntuck.edu
MCLEOD, Michael .... 863-784-7441.... 117 J
michael.mcleod@southflorida.edu
MCLEOD, Michael, J .... 516-877-3177.... 322 A
mcleod@adelphi.edu
MCLEOD, Pat .... 419-448-3353.... 402 E
mcleodp@tiffin.edu
MCLEOD, Steve .... 901-761-1353.... 469 C
smcleod@hst.edu
MCLEOD, Susan .... 910-576-6222.... 372 D
mcleods@montgomery.edu
MCLEOD, Terry .... 706-867-3230.... 134 G
tmcleod@northgeorgia.edu
MCLESKEY, Stephanie .... 828-689-1128.... 366 I
smcleskey@mhc.edu
MCLIN, SR., Kevin, J .... 334-727-4553........ 8 B
kjones2056@mytu.tuskegee.edu
MCLLWAIN, Daryl .... 207-780-5510.... 220 G
darylmc@usm.maine.edu
MCLOGAN, Matthew, E ...... 616-331-2190.... 251 F
mcloganm@gvsu.edu
MCLOUD, Debbie .... 479-575-2159...... 24 C
dmcloud@uark.edu
MCLOUGHLIN, John .... 516-299-3848.... 339 A
john.mcloughlin@liu.edu
MCLOUGHLIN, John .... 516-299-2824.... 339 A
john.mclouglin@liu.edu
MCLOUGHLIN, Paul, J ...... 610-330-5082.... 433 B
mcloughp@lafayette.edu
MCLOUGHLIN, Suzanne ..... 516-876-3109.... 353 D
mcloughlins@oldwestbury.edu
MCLURE, Amanda .... 954-783-7339.... 106 J
amclure@cci.edu
MCMAHAN, Carla .... 864-977-7090.... 460 A
carla.mcmahan@ngu.edu
MCMAHAN, David .... 423-636-7315.... 477 A
dmcmahan@tusculum.edu
MCMAHAN, Kerrin .... 323-265-8723...... 54 G
mcmahakm@elac.edu
MCMAHAN, Mendi, M .... 214-333-5119.... 484 D
mendi@dbu.edu
MCMAHAN, Oliver, L .... 423-478-7037.... 472 H
omcmahan@ptseminary.edu
MCMAHAN, Robert, K .... 810-762-9864.... 253 C
mcmahan@kettering.edu
MCMAHAN, Shari .... 657-278-7000...... 35 B
smcmahan@fullerton.edu
MCMAHAN, Terry .... 239-513-1122.... 111 A
tmcmahan@hodges.edu

MCMAHILL, Janet, M .... 515-271-3726.... 184 D
janet.mcmahill@drake.edu
MCMAHON, Bernadette, B . 312-369-7436.... 148 D
bmcmahon@colum.edu
MCMAHON, Charles, P ..... 504-988-8555.... 215 C
cpm@tulane.edu
MCMAHON, Cindy .... 212-962-0002.... 342 G
cmcmahon@nyci.edu
MCMAHON, Cyndi .... 978-867-4236.... 235 A
cyndi.mcmahon@gordon.edu
MCMAHON, David .... 413-748-3210.... 244 H
dmcmahon@springfieldcollege.edu
MCMAHON, Doug .... 727-864-8587.... 105 E
mcmahodh@eckerd.edu
MCMAHON, Ellen .... 847-574-5212.... 156 A
emcmahon@lfgsm.edu
MCMAHON, James, P .... 414-288-7208.... 548 F
james.mcmahon@marquette.edu
MCMAHON, Jessica .... 252-527-6223.... 371 G
jmcmahon@lenoircc.edu
MCMAHON, Kathleen, N .... 401-254-3161.... 454 C
kmcmahon@rwu.edu
MCMAHON, Kevin .... 213-613-2200...... 70 H
kevin_mcmahon@sciarc.edu
MCMAHON, M.J .... 928-523-6515...... 16 I
mj.mcmahon@nau.edu
MCMAHON, Marie .... 619-388-7497...... 65 H
mmcmahon@sdccd.edu
MCMAHON, Mary Pat .... 207-725-3225.... 217 E
mmcmahon@bowdoin.edu
MCMAHON, Melody, L .... 773-371-5460.... 146 E
mmcmahon@ctu.edu
MCMAHON, Natalie .... 601-276-3865.... 277 B
nmcmahon@smcc.edu
MCMAHON, Patricia .... 513-862-2743.... 391 E
MCMAHON, Rebecca .... 216-987-4865.... 389 B
rebecca.mcmahon@tri-c.edu
MCMAHON, Renee, M .... 406-447-5501.... 293 G
rmcmahon@carroll.edu
MCMAHON, Roberta .... 708-524-6790.... 150 C
rmcmahon@dom.edu
MCMAHON, Shelly, A .... 740-368-3201.... 400 G
samcmaho@owu.edu
MCMAHON, Stephen .... 802-654-2516.... 514 D
smcmahon@smcvt.edu
MCMAHON, Timothy, J .... 412-359-1000.... 448 F
tmcmahon@triangle-tech.edu
MCMAHON, Timothy, J .... 412-359-1000.... 448 G
tmcmahon@triangle-tech.edu
MCMAINS, Robert, E .... 765-494-8000.... 178 J
remcmains@purdue.edu
MCMAKIN, Sandy .... 210-805-3005.... 504 B
mcmakin@uiwtx.edu
MCMANIGLE, John .... 301-295-3016.... 558 D
john.mcmanigle@usuhs.edu
MCMANIS, Michael .... 660-626-2522.... 278 D
mcmanis@atsu.edu
MCMANNESS, Matthew .... 215-951-1050.... 432 I
mcmanness@lasalle.edu
MCMANUS, Amy .... 919-497-3330.... 366 H
amcmanus@louisburg.edu
MCMANUS, Bill .... 864-977-2094.... 460 A
bill.mcmanus@ngu.edu
MCMANUS, Cecil .... 919-546-8417.... 376 F
cmcmanus@shawu.edu
MCMANUS, D. Kim .... 804-758-6705.... 528 C
kmcmanus@rappahannock.edu
MCMANUS, Janet .... 816-501-3618.... 278 I
janet.mcmanus@avila.edu
MCMANUS, Jeffrey .... 239-348-4715.... 101 I
jeff.mcmanus@avemaria.edu
MCMANUS, Kathryn .... 602-978-7541...... 18 H
kathryn.mcmanus@thunderbird.edu
MCMANUS, Michael .... 303-797-5654...... 81 D
michael.mcmanus@arapahoe.edu
MCMANUS, Sandra .... 423-893-2000.... 478 D
sandra.mcmanus@vc.edu
MCMANUS, Teresa .... 718-289-5439.... 326 E
teresa.mcmanus@bcc.cuny.edu
MCMASTER, Dennis .... 724-503-1001.... 451 A
dmcmaster@washjeff.edu
MCMASTER, Jeff .... 617-217-9036.... 231 A
jmcmaster@baystate.edu
MCMASTER, Pam .... 402-481-8718.... 296 I
pam.mcmaster@bryanlgh.org
MCMASTER, Robert .... 612-625-9883.... 272 A
mcmaster@umn.edu
MCMASTERS, Mark .... 405-325-2252.... 413 C
mmcmasters@ou.edu
MCMATH, Robert .... 479-575-7678...... 24 C
rmcmath@uark.edu
MCMEANS, Orlando, F .... 304-766-4291.... 544 F
mcmeanso@wvstateu.edu
MCMENAMIN,
Margaret, M .... 908-709-7100.... 316 B
mcmenamin@ucc.edu
MCMICHAEL, Cyndi .... 248-204-4109.... 254 B
cmcmichael@ltu.edu
MCMICHAEL, Robert .... 717-560-8240.... 433 D
bmcmichael@lbc.edu
MCMICKLE, Marvin, A .... 585-340-9680.... 329 F
mmcmickle@crcds.edu
MCMILLAN, Caroline .... 912-486-7056.... 129 B
cmcmillan@ega.edu

MCMILLAN, Cindy .... 251-343-8200........ 6 F
cindy.mcmillan@remingtoncollege.edu
MCMILLAN, Doug .... 574-520-5511.... 174 E
dmcmillan@iusb.edu
MCMILLAN, Douglas .... 580-745-2206.... 412 C
dmcmillan@se.edu
MCMILLAN, Forrest .... 325-670-1250.... 487 F
fmcmill@hsutx.edu
MCMILLAN, Jacqueline ...... 937-775-4271.... 406 C
jacqueline.mcmillan@wright.edu
MCMILLAN, Jane .... 580-745-2604.... 412 C
jmcmillan@se.edu
MCMILLAN, Joseph .... 512-444-8082.... 499 E
jtmcmillan@texastcm.edu
MCMILLAN, Judy .... 210-486-4567.... 479 B
jmcmillan@alamo.edu
MCMILLAN, Judy .... 757-822-5121.... 528 G
jmcmillan@tcc.edu
MCMILLAN, Karon .... 601-925-3212.... 275 C
kmcmilla@mc.edu
MCMILLAN, Laura .... 770-794-7691.... 133 A
MCMILLAN, III, Lex, O ..... 610-921-7600.... 421 E
lmcmillan@alb.edu
MCMILLAN, Marilyn .... 212-998-2001.... 344 B
marilyn.mcmillan@nyu.edu
MCMILLAN, Mary .... 310-303-7302...... 56 F
mmcmillan@marymountpv.edu
MCMILLAN, Minnie .... 334-874-5700........ 2 H
mmcmillan@ccal.edu
MCMILLEN, Bonnie, K .... 814-362-0968.... 449 B
mcmillen@pitt.edu
MCMILLEN, Jeremy .... 903-675-6371.... 502 F
jmcmillen@tvcc.edu
MCMILLEN, Jeremy, P .... 903-463-8600.... 487 C
mcmillenj@grayson.edu
MCMILLEN, William .... 419-530-2739.... 404 F
william.mcmillen@utoledo.edu
MCMILLIAN, Carey .... 816-271-4582.... 286 G
mcmilli@missouriwestern.edu
MCMILLIN, David .... 417-626-1234.... 287 C
dmcmillin@occ.edu
MCMILLIN, Jennifer .... 417-626-1234.... 287 C
jmcmillin@occ.edu
MCMILLIN, Lisa .... 601-635-2111.... 274 A
lmcmillan@eccc.edu
MCMILLIN, Nicole .... 605-367-4821.... 466 D
nicole.mcmillin@southeasttech.edu
MCMILLIN, Renee .... 303-292-0015...... 84 C
r.mcmillin@denverschoolofnursing.edu
MCMILLION, David .... 706-776-0114.... 136 A
dmcmillion@piedmont.edu
MCMILLION, Eric, C .... 859-858-3511.... 198 E
eric.mcmillion@asbury.edu
MCMILLON, Avis .... 732-224-2967.... 308 A
amcmillon@brookdalecc.edu
MCMINIMY, Gisele .... 316-295-5377.... 193 B
mcminimy@friends.edu
MCMOORE-GRAY, Vicki .... 704-216-6222.... 366 G
vmcmoore@livingstone.edu
MCMOY, Johnny .... 256-352-8117...... 10 A
johnny.mcmoy@wallacestate.edu
MCMULLAN, James .... 601-679-3570.... 274 B
jmcmullan@eastms.edu
MCMULLEN, Eileen .... 215-567-7080.... 422 D
emcmullen@aii.edu
MCMULLEN, Judith .... 216-987-4836.... 389 B
judith.mcmullen@tri-c.edu
MCMULLEN, Kenneth, J .... 704-366-5066.... 376 B
kmcmullen@rts.edu
MCMULLEN, Linda, H .... 706-880-8021.... 133 B
lmcmullen@lagrange.edu
MCMULLEN, Michael .... 315-498-2566.... 345 D
mcmullem@sunyocc.edu
MCMULLEN, Michael, C .... 214-459-2208.... 480 G
mmcmullen@argosy.edu
MCMULLEN, Patricia .... 202-319-5403...... 97 E
mcmullep@cua.edu
MCMULLEN, Ruth .... 707-524-1721...... 68 E
rmcmullen@santarosa.edu
MCMULLEN, William .... 817-515-1268.... 496 C
william.mcmullen@tccd.edu
MCMULLIN, Angeline .... 423-614-8357.... 470 C
amcmullin@leeuniversity.edu
MCMULLIN, Sallie, D .... 434-395-2598.... 521 A
mcmullinsd@longwood.edu
MCMURDOCK, Linda .... 310-338-3756...... 56 E
lmcmurdock@lmu.edu
MCMURRAY, Aaron, P .... 509-777-3730.... 540 C
amcmurray@whitworth.edu
MCMURRAY, Brock .... 661-763-7811...... 72 E
bmcmurray@taftcollege.edu
MCMURRAY, Jeffrey .... 903-886-5852.... 498 B
jeffrey.mcmurray@tamuc.edu
MCMURRAY, Kelly .... 301-934-7624.... 222 C
kmcmurray@csmd.edu
MCMURRY, Alice .... 717-872-3820.... 443 D
alice.mcmurry@millersville.edu
MCMURRY, Marna, R .... 910-256-0255.... 367 F
mdavenport@moc.edu
MCNAB, Pat .... 513-727-3300.... 396 G
MCNABB, David .... 970-521-6655...... 86 K
david.mcnabb@njc.edu
MCNABB, Deana, M .... 406-338-5421.... 293 F
deana_mcnabb@bfcc.org

MEAD, Doug ... 567-661-7277 ... 400 I
douglas_mead@owens.edu
MEAD, JR., George, F ... 334-475-5785 ... 215 G
mead@mcneese.edu
MEAD, JR., George, F ... 337-475-5785 ... 215 G
mead@mcneese.edu
MEAD, K. Ann ... 270-745-2434 ... 208 A
ann.mead@wku.edu
MEAD, Stephen, W ... 630-752-5113 ... 168 H
stephen.mead@wheaton.edu
MEAD, Steven ... 860-255-3473 ... 92 F
smead@txcc.commnet.edu
MEAD, Susan ... 845-431-8036 ... 332 D
mead@sunydutchess.edu
MEAD-ROACH, Amanda ... 314-644-9100 ... 288 I
amead2@stlcc.edu
MEADE, Elizabeth ... 610-606-4637 ... 425 A
emeade@cedarcrest.edu
MEADE, Haley ... 212-431-2164 ... 343 E
hmeade@nyls.edu
MEADE, Linda, B ... 724-946-7339 ... 451 C
meadelb@westminster.edu
MEADE, Marianne ... 610-989-1240 ... 450 F
mmeade@vfmac.edu
MEADERS-BOOTH,
Jacqueline, D ... 314-984-7611 ... 289 A
jmeadersbooth@stlcc.edu
MEADOR, Diane ... 907-796-6457 ... 11 A
diane.meador@uas.alaska.edu
MEADOR, JR., John, M ... 607-777-2346 ... 351 F
jmeador@binghamton.edu
MEADOR, Mark ... 615-966-6223 ... 470 F
mark.meador@lipscomb.edu
MEADOR, Michele ... 775-673-7249 ... 302 H
mmeador@tmcc.edu
MEADOR, Roy ... 517-750-1200 ... 258 D
rmeador@arbor.edu
MEADOR, Ruby ... 870-762-3125 ... 20 A
rmeador@smail.anc.edu
MEADOR, Ryan ... 816-943-7316 ... 281 A
rmeador@devry.edu
MEADOR, Vernie ... 870-633-4480 ... 21 F
vmeador@eacc.edu
MEADORS, Mark ... 918-343-7860 ... 411 H
mmeadors@rsu.edu
MEADOWS, David, D ... 814-641-0714 ... 432 A
meadowd@juniata.edu
MEADOWS, David, J ... 804-524-5995 ... 529 H
pbullock@vsu.edu
MEADOWS, Dawn ... 863-638-7246 ... 123 D
dawn.meadows@warner.edu
MEADOWS, Dean ... 863-638-7255 ... 123 D
dean.meadows@warner.edu
MEADOWS, Dennis ... 304-696-2599 ... 544 B
meadowsd@marshall.edu
MEADOWS, Ed ... 850-484-1700 ... 115 B
emeadows@pensacolastate.edu
MEADOWS, Evelyn ... 928-724-6950 ... 13 L
emeadows@dinecollege.edu
MEADOWS, Mark ... 619-482-6494 ... 71 D
mmeadows@swccd.edu
MEADOWS, Robyn, L ... 717-541-3920 ... 97 B
rlmeadows@widener.edu
MEADOWS, Steve ... 304-384-5180 ... 543 G
meadows@concord.edu
MEADOWS, Wanda ... 334-244-3260 ... 1 G
wmeadow2@aum.edu
MEAGHER, Paula, G ... 915-831-4530 ... 486 G
pmeagher@epcc.edu
MEALER, Donna ... 731-286-3312 ... 475 B
mealer@dscc.edu
MEALY, Robert ... 212-799-5000 ... 337 H
MEANA, Marta ... 702-895-2267 ... 302 I
marta.meana@unlv.edu
MEANER, Christopher, M ... 412-578-6069 ... 424 I
meanercm@carlow.edu
MEANEY, Hank ... 516-561-0050 ... 325 E
MEANEY, Heather, L ... 518-381-1250 ... 350 E
meaneyhl@sunysccc.edu
MEANS, Ben ... 217-228-5432 ... 161 F
meansbe@quincy.edu
MEANS, Gary, A ... 724-925-4061 ... 451 E
meansg@wccc.edu
MEANS, John ... 918-335-6892 ... 411 B
jmeans@okwu.edu
MEANS, Margie ... 706-776-0123 ... 136 A
mmeans@piedmont.edu
MEANS, Steve ... 800-686-7022 ... 93 C
smeans@lincolncollegene.edu
MEANY, Birgit ... 907-852-3333 ... 10 F
birgit.meany@ilisagvik.edu
MEANY, David ... 509-359-6335 ... 533 H
dmeany@ewu.edu
MEANY, Mary, T ... 920-832-6561 ... 548 B
mary.t.meany@lawrence.edu
MEARA, Mark ... 609-894-9311 ... 308 B
mmeara@bcc.edu
MEARINI, Mary Ann ... 516-877-3265 ... 322 A
mearini@adelphi.edu
MEARNS, Geoffrey, S ... 859-572-5123 ... 205 H
mearns@nku.edu
MEARS, Bobby ... 757-789-1747 ... 526 H
bmears@es.vccs.edu
MEARS, Laura ... 301-846-2429 ... 222 G
lmears@frederick.edu
MEARS, Melena ... 814-332-4392 ... 421 F
mmears@allegheny.edu
MEARS, Michael, J ... 941-752-5267 ... 118 J
mearsm@scf.edu
MEARS, Philip, N ... 325-942-2191 ... 480 E
nolen.mears@angelo.edu
MEARS, Ted ... 320-252-1489 ... 269 A
husky@bkstr.com
MEASAMER, Ronnie ... 919-718-7409 ... 369 C
rmeasamer@cccc.edu
MEASE, Ervin, J ... 610-799-1112 ... 434 D
emease@lccc.edu
MEASE, Stephen ... 802-865-6432 ... 513 C
smease@champlain.edu
MECCA, Kim ... 570-504-0920 ... 433 A
meccak@lackawanna.edu
MECH, Terrence, F ... 570-208-5943 ... 432 G
tfmech@kings.edu
MECHAM, Melissa, E ... 425-637-1010 ... 532 E
mmecham@cityu.edu
MECHAM, Steven, J ... 435-797-1967 ... 511 E
steve.mecham@usu.edu
MECHE, Eddie, P ... 337-475-5501 ... 215 G
emeche@mcneese.edu
MECHE, Lance ... 972-825-4747 ... 495 F
lmeche@sagu.edu
MECHNIG, Virginia ... 630-353-7049 ... 149 B
vmechnig@devry.edu
MECK, Bill ... 319-208-5069 ... 189 D
bmeck@scciowa.edu
MECK, Heather, J ... 814-472-3264 ... 446 B
hmeck@francis.edu
MECKEL, David ... 415-703-9561 ... 32 C
dmeckel@cca.edu
MECKLEY, Philip, S ... 785-827-5541 ... 194 F
pmeckley@kwu.edu
MEDA, Pat ... 626-529-8261 ... 60 F
pmeda@pacificoaks.edu
MEDA-POLLACK, Andro ... 407-843-3984 ... 110 E
careers@fortiscollege.edu
MEDAGLIA, Frank ... 804-594-1414 ... 527 B
fmedaglia@jtcc.edu
MEDALEN, Brenda, L ... 605-336-6588 ... 465 D
bmedalen@sfseminary.edu
MEDBURY, Doug ... 425-235-2352 ... 537 A
dmedbury@rtc.edu
MEDCALF, Elizabeth ... 301-687-4161 ... 228 C
emedcalf@frostburg.edu
MEDDERS, Alan ... 706-507-8954 ... 127 G
medders_alan@columbusstate.edu
MEDDERS, Mike, W ... 903-566-7393 ... 506 E
mmedders@uttyler.edu
MEDDINGS, Nancy ... 805-922-6966 ... 26 L
nmeddings@hancockcollege.edu
MEDEARIS, Cheryl ... 605-856-5880 ... 465 C
cheryl.medearis@sintegleska.edu
MEDEARIS, Ellen ... 919-667-2500 ... 364 C
ellen.medearis@duke.edu
MEDEIROS, Brad ... 508-626-4911 ... 238 A
bmedeiros@framingham.edu
MEDEIROS, Dave ... 803-786-3007 ... 457 C
dave@columbiasc.edu
MEDEIROS, Denis, M ... 816-235-1301 ... 291 C
medeirosd@umkc.edu
MEDEMA, Pam ... 815-288-5511 ... 164 B
medemap@svcc.edu
MEDENBLIK, Jackie ... 708-239-4821 ... 166 C
jackie.medenblik@trnty.edu
MEDENBLIK, Julius, T ... 616-957-6024 ... 249 B
jmedenblik@calvinseminary.edu
MEDFORD, Adriane ... 215-567-7080 ... 422 D
amedford@aii.edu
MEDFORD, Mike ... 404-687-4576 ... 127 F
medfordm@ctsnet.edu
MEDINA, JR., Alfredo ... 518-782-6558 ... 350 I
amedina@siena.edu
MEDINA, Amber ... 402-461-7757 ... 298 A
amedina@hastings.edu
MEDINA, Celia ... 787-815-0000 ... 567 A
celia.medina@upr.edu
MEDINA, Cynthia ... 303-751-8700 ... 81 H
medina@bel-rea.com
MEDINA, Deborah, M ... 716-851-1828 ... 333 A
medina@ecc.edu
MEDINA, Kim ... 303-256-9785 ... 85 L
kmedina@jwu.edu
MEDINA, Mara ... 787-780-0070 ... 560 H
mmedina@caribbean.edu
MEDINA, Maria ... 973-684-5651 ... 312 E
mmedina@pccc.edu
MEDINA, Nancy ... 773-442-5240 ... 160 A
n-medina4@neiu.edu
MEDINA, Reinalda ... 718-997-4455 ... 328 E
reinalda.medina@qc.cuny.edu
MEDINA, Victor ... 203-285-2157 ... 91 D
vmedina@gwcc.commnet.edu
MEDINA, Widylia ... 787-890-2681 ... 566 H
widylia.medina@upr.edu
MEDINA-KEISER, Isabel ... 719-587-8226 ... 80 L
isabelmedinakeiser@adams.edu
MEDLEY, Brenda ... 504-520-7392 ... 217 A
bdmedley@xula.edu
MEDLEY, India ... 202-291-9020 ... 99 F
MEDLEY, Lara ... 303-273-3200 ... 83 B
lara.medley@is.mines.edu
MEDLEY, Mike ... 435-896-9714 ... 512 C
michael.medley@snow.edu
MEDLEY-WEEKS, Clarice ... 214-379-5565 ... 492 F
cweeks@pqc.edu
MEDLIN, Melissa, T ... 256-765-4276 ... 9 C
mtmedlin@una.edu
MEDLOCK, Vicky ... 540-665-4936 ... 524 E
vmedlock@su.edu
MEDRANO, Jennifer ... 801-832-2126 ... 512 G
jmedrano@westminstercollege.edu
MEDRO, Alfred ... 619-265-0107 ... 62 K
amedro@platt.edu
MEDWICK, Peter ... 215-972-2017 ... 440 J
pmedwick@pafa.edu
MEE, Christine, L ... 843-349-2091 ... 456 G
christin@coastal.edu
MEE, David ... 615-460-6785 ... 467 D
david.mee@belmont.edu
MEE, Gail, C ... 313-845-9650 ... 252 B
gmee@hfcc.edu
MEECE, Jill, N ... 606-679-8501 ... 203 C
jill.meece@kctcs.edu
MEEHAN, Edward, J ... 256-824-6533 ... 8 G
edward.meehan@uah.edu
MEEHAN, Gabriel, M ... 916-484-8354 ... 56 A
meehang@arc.losrios.edu
MEEHAN, Martin, T ... 978-934-4744 ... 237 B
marty_meehan@uml.edu
MEEHAN, Mary, J ... 414-382-6064 ... 546 B
mary.meehan@alverno.edu
MEEHAN, Nicole ... 312-915-7666 ... 157 C
nleduc@luc.edu
MEEHAN, Patricia ... 856-227-7200 ... 308 D
pmeehan@camdencc.edu
MEEHAN, Paula, T ... 616-632-2852 ... 247 E
meehapau@aquinas.edu
MEEHAN, William, A ... 256-782-5881 ... 4 L
pres@jsu.edu
MEEK, Laura ... 614-251-4642 ... 398 F
meekl@ohiodominican.edu
MEEK, Leslie ... 320-589-6200 ... 271 G
meekles@morris.umn.edu
MEEK, Scott ... 602-787-7902 ... 15 J
scott.meek@paradisevalley.edu
MEEKER, April, M ... 605-642-6092 ... 465 H
april.meeker@bhsu.edu
MEEKER, Steve, L ... 605-642-6385 ... 465 H
steve.meeker@bhsu.edu
MEEKER, William, C ... 408-944-6004 ... 61 A
bill.meeker@palmer.edu
MEEKMA, Glenn, A ... 269-471-3484 ... 247 D
meekma@andrews.edu
MEEKS, Andy ... 859-572-5575 ... 205 H
meeksa@nku.edu
MEEKS, Glenn ... 773-995-2042 ... 146 G
gmeeks@csu.edu
MEEKS, Harry, L ... 812-888-4511 ... 181 D
hmeeks@vinu.edu
MEEKS, J. Duane ... 561-803-2610 ... 114 C
duane_meeks@pba.edu
MEEKS, Joseph, D ... 770-423-6742 ... 133 A
jmeeks@kennesaw.edu
MEEKS, Kimela, A ... 812-888-4377 ... 181 D
kmeeks@vinu.edu
MEEKS, Laura, M ... 740-264-5591 ... 390 F
lmeeks@egcc.edu
MEEKS, Makeda ... 305-226-9999 ... 109 C
mmeeks@mm.fnc.edu
MEEKS, Makeda ... 305-821-3333 ... 109 B
mmeeks@mm.fnc.edu
MEEKS, Makeda ... 305-821-3333 ... 109 D
mmeeks@mm.fnc.edu
MEEKS, Mark ... 478-445-5851 ... 130 B
mark.meeks@gcsu.edu
MEEKS, Matthew ... 972-241-3371 ... 484 E
mmeeks@dallas.edu
MEEKS, Susan ... 478-387-4801 ... 131 A
MEEKS, Tom ... 216-373-5206 ... 397 F
tmeeks@ndc.edu
MEEKS, Toni ... 505-888-8898 ... 320 H
toni@acupuncturecollege.edu
MEEKS, Toni ... 505-888-8898 ... 320 G
toni@acupuncturecollege.edu
MEENAN, Robert, F ... 617-638-4640 ... 232 E
rmeenan@bu.edu
MEER, Jonathan, D ... 609-896-5167 ... 313 F
jmeer@rider.edu
MEERTS, John ... 860-685-3800 ... 95 E
jmeerts@wesleyan.edu
MEESE, JoAnna ... 724-439-4900 ... 434 A
jmeese@laurel.edu
MEESE, Paul ... 303-678-3707 ... 85 A
paul.meese@frontrange.edu
MEESKE, Susan ... 303-870-3601 ... 298 A
smeeske@hastings.edu
MEGAHED, Nivine ... 312-261-3232 ... 159 E
nivine.megahed@nl.edu
MEGALE, Nicole ... 517-264-3850 ... 246 H
MEGORDEN, Timothy, M ... 218-299-4161 ... 262 I
megorden@cord.edu
MEGREDY, Jill ... 785-227-3380 ... 191 B
megredyj@bethanylb.edu
MEHA, Arapata ... 808-675-3739 ... 140 D
mehaa@byuh.edu
MEHALIK, Susan ... 724-503-1001 ... 451 A
smehalik@washjeff.edu
MEHDIZADEH, Mojden ... 925-229-6849 ... 43 D
mmehdizadeh@4cd.edu
MEHL, Shelley ... 501-450-3127 ... 25 H
shelleym@uca.edu
MEHLENBACHER, Robert ... 407-569-1169 ... 107 I
bob.mehlenbacher@fcc.edu
MEHLER, Mark ... 609-771-2186 ... 308 F
mehler@tcnj.edu
MEHLHOFF, Monte ... 605-626-7781 ... 466 A
mehlhofm@northern.edu
MEHLIG, Lisa ... 815-921-4070 ... 162 H
l.mehlig@rockvalleycollege.edu
MEHNERT-MELAND,
Karen, B ... 218-477-2447 ... 267 F
meland@mnstate.edu
MEHOLIC, Christine ... 732-987-2327 ... 310 C
meholicc@georgian.edu
MEHRING, Teresa, A ... 620-341-5171 ... 192 G
tmehring@emporia.edu
MEHTA, Chander, S ... 713-313-1895 ... 500 B
mehta_cs@tsu.edu
MEHTA, Usha ... 775-850-0700 ... 302 C
umehta@morrison.neumont.edu
MEI, Jeffrey ... 617-731-7170 ... 243 G
meijeffery@pmc.edu
MEIER, Beth, A ... 919-760-8427 ... 367 A
meierb@meredith.edu
MEIER, Gayle ... 770-394-8300 ... 125 A
gmeier@aii.edu
MEIER, Harvey ... 402-486-2502 ... 300 C
hameier@ucollege.edu
MEIER, Jared ... 970-248-1698 ... 82 F
jmeier@coloradomesa.edu
MEIER, Jay ... 701-224-5666 ... 382 D
jay.meier@bismarckstate.edu
MEIER, Karen, F ... 757-683-5026 ... 522 F
kmeier@odu.edu
MEIER, Neal ... 513-487-1174 ... 402 I
neal.meier@myunion.edu
MEIER, Susan ... 812-535-5299 ... 179 E
smeier@smwc.edu
MEIER WELTZIEN, Lynn ... 406-683-7180 ... 294 J
l_weltzien1@umwestern.edu
MEIERGERD, Joseph ... 314-768-1730 ... 283 G
meiergerd@kenrick.edu
MEIERS, Chris ... 913-588-0146 ... 197 C
cmeiers@kumc.edu
MEIGHEN, Bethany ... 304-357-4716 ... 542 A
bethanymeighen@ucwv.edu
MEIGHEN, Mark, A ... 724-946-7191 ... 451 C
meighema@westminster.edu
MEIKLE, Paulette ... 662-846-4339 ... 273 H
pmeikleyaw@deltastate.edu
MEIKLEJOHN, Scott, A ... 207-725-3148 ... 217 E
smeiklej@bowdoin.edu
MEIKSINS, Peter ... 216-687-5559 ... 388 D
p.meiksins@csuohio.edu
MEILMAN, Philip, W ... 202-687-6985 ... 98 D
pwm9@georgetown.edu
MEINE, Laurel ... 712-279-5433 ... 183 A
laurel.meine@briarcliff.edu
MEINEKE, John ... 309-796-5053 ... 145 H
meinekej@bhc.edu
MEINEL, William, G ... 215-368-5000 ... 422 I
bmeinel@biblical.edu
MEINERTS, Marita, K ... 651-631-5168 ... 270 B
mkmeinerts@nwc.edu
MEINHARDT, Stephanie ... 972-881-5847 ... 483 H
smeinhardt@collin.edu
MEINTANIS, Maria ... 312-261-3092 ... 159 E
maria.meintanis@nl.edu
MEIR, Michael ... 212-594-4000 ... 357 H
mmeir@tcicollege.edu
MEIS, Aaron ... 513-745-2941 ... 406 E
meisa@xavier.edu
MEIS, Darrell ... 719-587-7912 ... 80 L
djmeis@adams.edu
MEISCHEID, Michelle ... 252-862-1252 ... 373 C
meischei@roanokechowan.edu
MEISEL, Joseph, S ... 401-863-9499 ... 453 B
joseph_meisel@brown.edu
MEISELES, Gary ... 502-597-6438 ... 203 G
gary.meiseles@kysu.edu
MEISELS, Samuel, J ... 312-893-7100 ... 151 A
smeisels@erikson.edu
MEISER, Michelle ... 717-728-2312 ... 425 B
michellemeiser@centralpenn.edu
MEISER, Patricia ... 860-768-4989 ... 95 B
pmeiser@hartford.edu
MEISLAHN, Nancy, H ... 860-685-2269 ... 95 E
nmeislahn@wesleyan.edu
MEISNER, Jane ... 515-244-4221 ... 181 F
meisnerj@aib.edu
MEISSNER, Ken ... 712-749-2111 ... 183 C
meissnerk@bvu.edu
MEISTER, Barbara ... 740-477-7858 ... 398 D
MEISTER, Tony ... 660-944-2899 ... 280 B
tmeister@conception.edu

MEISTERLING, Richard, E . 319-399-8555 .... 183 F
rmeister@coe.edu
MEITZ, Mark, G .... 434-223-6242 .... 519 G
mmeitz@hsc.edu
MEITZNER, June .... 507-285-7213 .... 268 I
june.meitzner@roch.edu
MEIXSEL-CORDERO, Terri 623-245-4600 .... 18 J
tmeixsell@uti.edu
MEJEUR, Sharon, K .... 260-399-7700 .... 181 A
smejeur@sf.edu
MEJIA, Gary .... 559-453-7103 .... 48 A
gary.mejia@fresno.edu
MEJIA, Jorge .... 415-282-7600 .... 28 B
jorgemejia@actcm.edu
MEJIA, Juan, E .... 956-872-8336 .... 494 H
jmejia@southtexascollege.edu
MEJIA, Natalia .... 305-949-9500 .... 106 B
nmejia@cci.edu
MEJIA KRUG, Miroslava ... 312-341-3583 .... 163 B
mmkrug@roosevelt.edu
MEJIAS, Ida, A .... 787-250-1912 .... 563 G
iamejias@metro.inter.edu
MEJIAS, Nelson .... 787-753-6335 .... 562 G
nmejias@icprjc.edu
MELANCON, Girard .... 225-216-8068 .... 209 H
melancong@mybrcc.edu
MELANSON, Chris .... 207-948-9141 .... 219 H
cmelanson@unity.edu
MELANSON, Leigh Anne ... 603-862-3290 .... 306 C
leigh-anne.melanson@unh.edu
MELARAGNI, Robert .... 617-670-4401 .... 234 G
rmelaragni@fisher.edu
MELARAGNO, Steven .... 401-254-3667 .... 454 C
smelaragno@rwu.edu
MELBY, Darlene .... 805-378-1550 .... 77 D
dmelby@vcccd.edu
MELBY, Diane .... 304-876-5176 .... 544 C
dmelby@shepherd.edu
MELBY, Laurie .... 714-241-6110 .... 41 B
lmelby@coastline.edu
MELCHER, Mike .... 806-291-3425 .... 508 E
melcherp@wbu.edu
MELCHER, Rick, W .... 610-921-7748 .... 421 E
rmelcher@alb.edu
MELCHERT, Russell, B .... 816-235-1607 .... 291 C
melchertr@umkc.edu
MELCHIOR, Vonda .... 813-253-7107 .... 110 M
vmelchior@hccfl.edu
MELDREM, Joyce, A .... 563-588-7164 .... 187 C
joyce.meldrem@loras.edu
MELDRUM, John .... 313-883-8512 .... 257 E
meldrum.john@shms.edu
MELECKI, Thomas, G .... 512-475-6203 .... 505 D
tom.melecki@austin.utexas.edu
MELEG, Mike .... 309-796-5002 .... 145 H
melegm@bhc.edu
MELEIS, Afaf, I .... 215-898-8281 .... 448 J
meleis@nursing.upenn.edu
MELEN, Pia .... 714-533-1495 .... 70 B
pmelen@southbaylo.edu
MELENDEZ, Briseida .... 787-265-3813 .... 567 F
registro@uprm.edu
MELENDEZ, Edwin .... 787-738-2161 .... 567 D
edwin.melendez3@upr.edu
MELENDEZ, John .... 201-200-3507 .... 312 B
jmelendez@njcu.edu
MELENDEZ, Leonardo .... 787-720-4476 .... 566 D
decanatoacademico@colmizpa.edu
MELENDEZ, Luis, F .... 203-285-2218 .... 91 D
lmelendez@gwcc.commnet.edu
MELENDEZ, Mercedes .... 212-343-1234 .... 341 B
mmelendez@mcny.edu
MELENDEZ, Nildalee .... 787-852-1430 .... 562 F
nmelendez@hccpr.edu
MELENDEZ, Nitza .... 787-725-8120 .... 562 C
nmelendez@eap.edu
MELENDEZ, Rosa .... 787-754-7597 .... 562 I
rmelendez@inter.edu
MELENDEZ, Ruben .... 908-709-7085 .... 316 B
ruben.melendez@ucc.edu
MELENDEZ, Yahaira .... 787-620-2040 .... 560 D
melendezy@aupr.edu
MELENDY, Brenda .... 361-593-4141 .... 498 D
brenda.melendy@tamuk.edu
MELENDY, Lisa, M .... 413-597-2477 .... 246 D
lisa.m.melendy@williams.edu
MELETIES, Panayiotis .... 718-262-2806 .... 329 A
meleties@york.cuny.edu
MELGAR, Sergio .... 859-323-0053 .... 207 D
smelgar@uky.edu
MELHART, Bonnie .... 817-257-7729 .... 499 C
b.melhart@tcu.edu
MELIKECHI, Noureddine .... 302-857-6656 .... 96 C
nmelikechi@desu.edu
MELILLO, SR., Thomas, V 216-707-8200 .... 394 B
tmelillo@kent.edu
MELINA, Livio .... 202-526-3799 .... 99 D
MELINE, Doug .... 530-242-7990 .... 69 D
dmeline@shastacollege.edu
MELINE, Randy .... 641-784-5213 .... 185 B
meline@graceland.edu
MELISI, Mary Ann .... 610-558-5611 .... 437 D
melisim@neumann.edu

MELIUS, Laura .... 859-622-1571 .... 200 J
laura.melius@eku.edu
MELKONIAN, Madeleine .... 718-405-3236 .... 330 A
madeleine.melkonian@mountsaintvincent.edu
MELKY, Huda, N .... 270-745-5121 .... 208 A
huda.melky@wku.edu
MELL, Doug .... 715-232-1198 .... 552 E
melld@uwstout.edu
MELLAND, Helen .... 406-657-3784 .... 295 C
helen.melland@montana.edu
MELLEGAARD, Corey .... 605-995-2648 .... 464 C
comelleg@dwu.edu
MELLEMA, Barbara, J .... 712-722-6020 .... 184 C
bmellema@dordt.edu
MELLENDORF, Gabrielle .... 606-546-1602 .... 207 B
gmellendorf@unionky.edu
MELLER, Julie .... 312-935-4473 .... 162 G
jmeller@robertmorris.edu
MELLICHAMP, James .... 706-776-0110 .... 136 A
jmellichamp@piedmont.edu
MELLICHAMP, James, F .... 706-776-0100 .... 136 A
president@piedmont.edu
MELLING, Alice .... 206-934-3693 .... 537 D
alice.melling@seattlecolleges.edu
MELLINGER, Laurie, A .... 717-866-7581 .... 429 A
lemllinger@evangelical.edu
MELLO, James, A .... 860-768-5365 .... 95 B
jmello@hartford.edu
MELLO, Jeffrey, A .... 518-783-2321 .... 350 I
jmello@siena.edu
MELLON, Edward, J .... 703-323-3083 .... 527 F
emellon@nvcc.edu
MELLON, Suzanne, K .... 603-641-7150 .... 305 G
skmellon@anselm.edu
MELLONI, Suzanne .... 508-999-9299 .... 237 A
smelloni@umassd.edu
MELLOTT, David, M .... 717-290-8723 .... 433 F
rgawn@lancasterseminary.edu
MELLOTT, Ramona, N .... 928-523-6534 .... 16 I
ramona.mellott@nau.edu
MELLOW, Gail, O .... 718-482-5050 .... 328 B
gmellow@lagcc.cuny.edu
MELMER, Rick .... 605-677-5612 .... 465 G
rick.melmer@usd.edu
MELNICK, Julie .... 402-844-7123 .... 299 I
juliem@northeast.edu
MELNICK, Marie .... 215-637-7700 .... 431 A
mmelnick@holyfamily.edu
MELNICZEK, Eric, J .... 336-841-4558 .... 365 C
emelnicz@highpoint.edu
MELNIK, JoAnn .... 724-964-8811 .... 437 E
jmelnik@ncstrades.edu
MELNYK, Bernadette .... 614-292-4844 .... 398 I
melnyk.15@osu.edu
MELO, Manuel .... 787-523-6000 .... 562 G
mmelo@icprjc.edu
MELOAN, Andrea .... 816-415-7831 .... 293 C
meloana@william.jewell.edu
MELOAN, Ross, B .... 270-809-3735 .... 205 A
rmeloan@murraystate.edu
MELOCHE, Kyle .... 410-857-2275 .... 224 C
kmeloche@mcdaniel.edu
MELOY, Joseph, P .... 414-277-7227 .... 549 C
meloy@msoe.edu
MELOY, William .... 850-484-1476 .... 115 B
wmeloy@pensacolastate.edu
MELTON, Chad .... 903-233-4421 .... 490 A
chadmelton@letu.edu
MELTON, David, V .... 617-364-3510 .... 232 A
dmelton@boston.edu
MELTON, Judi .... 206-264-9100 .... 531 D
judim@bgu.edu
MELTON, Lori .... 252-985-5404 .... 375 E
lmelton@ncwc.edu
MELTON, Marie, C .... 434-961-5209 .... 528 B
mmelton@pvcc.edu
MELTON, Mark, A .... 919-516-4029 .... 376 D
mamelton@st-aug.edu
MELTON, Matthew .... 423-614-8115 .... 470 C
mmelton@leeuniversity.edu
MELTON, Melissa .... 251-380-2271 .... 7 E
mmelton@shc.edu
MELTON, Michelle .... 336-917-5721 .... 376 E
michelle.melton@salem.edu
MELTON, Nancy .... 859-985-3313 .... 199 A
meltonn@berea.edu
MELTON, Randall .... 269-927-8139 .... 253 G
melton@lakemichigancollege.edu
MELTON, Rita, A .... 864-592-4836 .... 461 C
meltonr@sccsc.edu
MELTON, Steve .... 828-297-3811 .... 368 G
smelton@cccti.edu
MELTON PAGES, Joyce .... 817-598-6245 .... 508 F
jpages@wc.edu
MELUSKY, Marie, B .... 814-472-3126 .... 446 B
mmelusky@francis.edu
MELVIN, Cynthia .... 601-977-7716 .... 277 C
cmelvin@tougaloo.edu
MELVIN, Dana .... 412-304-0738 .... 429 B
damelvin@cci.edu
MELVIN, Marilee, A .... 630-752-5517 .... 168 H
marilee.melvin@wheaton.edu
MELVIN, Matt .... 785-864-4381 .... 197 B
mattmelvin@ku.edu

MEMBRINO, Charles .... 617-585-1239 .... 242 I
itshelp@necmusic.edu
MEMOLI, Phil .... 239-513-1122 .... 111 A
pmemoli@hodges.edu
MEN, Su-hua .... 941-752-5250 .... 118 J
mens@scf.edu
MENA, Robert .... 213-738-6716 .... 71 E
studentaffairs@swlaw.edu
MENA, Salvador, B .... 718-982-2335 .... 327 A
salvador.mena@csi.cuny.edu
MENA, Terry .... 561-297-3547 .... 119 A
tmena@fau.edu
MENADIER, Judy .... 352-854-2322 .... 103 K
menadiej@cf.edu
MENANTEAUX,
Kathleen, A .... 309-649-6222 .... 165 F
kathleen.menanteaux@src.edu
MENARD, Christopher, J ... 617-358-1171 .... 232 E
cjmenard@bu.edu
MENARD, Connie .... 940-898-3826 .... 502 D
cmenard@twu.edu
MENARD, Michael .... 860-570-9208 .... 94 G
michael.menard@uconn.edu
MENARD, Richard, R .... 401-841-7004 .... 558 B
richard.menard@usnwc.edu
MENASCHE, Kathleen, T .... 410-386-8108 .... 221 G
kmenasche@carrollcc.edu
MENCER, James .... 405-425-5260 .... 409 E
book.store@oc.edu
MENCHACA, Leticia .... 520-206-4973 .... 17 H
lmenchaca@pima.edu
MENCHINI, Patricia .... 802-728-1533 .... 516 A
pmenchini@vtc.edu
MENDEDO, Tilahun, M .... 334-874-5700 .... 2 H
tmendedo@ccal.edu
MENDEL, Maurice, I .... 901-678-5877 .... 474 C
mmendel@memphis.edu
MENDELL, Sean, M .... 513-751-1206 .... 384 E
sean@aic.arts.edu
MENDELSON, Eleonor .... 831-476-9424 .... 47 E
admissions@fivebranches.edu
MENDENHALL, Beverly, A . 817-202-6232 .... 495 E
bevm@swau.edu
MENDENHALL, Diane .... 402-472-2841 .... 300 G
dmendenhall@huskeralum.org
MENDENHALL, Leslie .... 816-995-2820 .... 287 H
leslie.mendenhall@researchcollege.edu
MENDENHALL, Robert, W . 801-274-3280 .... 512 F
rwm@wgu.edu
MENDENHALL, Thomas .... 407-330-7020 .... 100 H
MENDES, Godfrey .... 614-947-6027 .... 391 B
godfrey.mendes@frankli.edu
MENDES, Wendy .... 559-734-9000 .... 66 E
wendym@sjvc.edu
MENDEZ, Ana .... 312-935-4080 .... 162 G
amendez@robertmorris.edu
MENDEZ, Ariel .... 787-766-1717 .... 565 I
armendez@suagm.edu
MENDEZ, Celestino .... 605-626-2601 .... 466 A
tino.mendez@northern.edu
MENDEZ, Celia .... 787-276-0130 .... 567 C
celia.mendez@upr.edu
MENDEZ, José, F .... 787-766-1717 .... 565 I
ac_jmendez@suagm.edu
MENDEZ, Jose, F .... 787-751-2262 .... 565 F
ac_jmendez@suagm.edu
MENDEZ, JR., Jose, F .... 787-751-0178 .... 565 F
jmendez@suagm.edu
MENDEZ, Larry .... 903-510-2281 .... 503 A
lmen@tjc.edu
MENDEZ, Magaly .... 787-815-0000 .... 567 A
magaly.mendez@upr.edu
MENDEZ, Maria .... 562-860-2451 .... 39 A
mmendez@cerritos.edu
MENDEZ, Rolando, J .... 787-284-1912 .... 564 A
rmendez@ponce.inter.edu
MENDEZ, Sheyla .... 787-250-0000 .... 566 G
sheyla.mendez@upr.edu
MENDEZ FERREIRA, Julio 787-896-2252 .... 562 B
jmendez@edpcollege.edu
MENDEZ VARGAS,
Nydia, T .... 787-896-2252 .... 562 B
nmendez@edpcollege.edu
MENDIAS, Lauren .... 432-837-8140 .... 501 E
lmendias@sulross.edu
MENDICK, Kay .... 701-777-4300 .... 381 F
kay.mendick@und.edu
MENDIETA, Juan .... 305-237-7611 .... 113 H
jmendiet@mdc.edu
MENDIETTA, Dorianna .... 559-730-3821 .... 42 D
doriannam@cos.edu
MENDINI, Shauna .... 435-865-8185 .... 511 D
mendini_s@suu.edu
MENDIOLA, Emma .... 210-486-0367 .... 479 E
emendiola@alamo.edu
MENDIOLA, Francisco .... 691-320-2480 .... 559 D
mendiolaf@comfsm.fm
MENDIOLA, Mark, B .... 671-735-2957 .... 559 G
funduog@gmail.com
MENDOLA, Richard, A .... 404-727-7879 .... 129 D
rich.mendola@emory.edu
MENDONEZ RUSSELL,
Bernadette .... 561-862-4400 .... 114 D
russellb@palmbeachstate.edu

MENDOZA, Beth, A .... 920-929-2137 .... 554 G
bmendoza@morainepark.edu
MENDOZA, Eric .... 559-791-2460 .... 53 A
emendoza@portervillecollege.edu
MENDOZA, Graciano .... 831-479-6279 .... 31 I
grmendoz@cabrillo.edu
MENDOZA, Mark .... 615-872-0188 .... 19 A
marka.mendoza@phoenix.edu
MENDOZA, Robert .... 714-432-5045 .... 41 D
rmendoza@occ.cccd.edu
MENDOZA, Sandra .... 219-980-6954 .... 174 B
sleone@iun.edu
MENDOZA, Theresa .... 657-278-7030 .... 35 B
tmendoza@fullerton.edu
MENDOZA-WELCH,
Maxine .... 903-886-5851 .... 498 B
maxine.mmendo@tamu.edu
MENEAR, Anne, P .... 660-263-3900 .... 279 F
MENEAR, Anne, P .... 660-263-3900 .... 279 F
arm@cccb.edu
MENEFEE, Ron .... 620-665-3569 .... 193 H
menefeer@hutchcc.edu
MENEGHIN, Cindy, L .... 973-655-7917 .... 311 F
meneghinc@mail.montclair.edu
MENELEY, Theresa .... 713-221-8612 .... 503 F
meneleyt@uhd.edu
MENENDEZ, Jacqueline, R 305-284-5505 .... 122 I
jmenendez@miami.edu
MENENDEZ, Marco .... 510-464-3221 .... 62 D
mmenendez@peralta.edu
MENESES, Jilma .... 503-725-4432 .... 418 G
ljmeneses@pdx.edu
MENEZES, Edirle .... 408-273-2204 .... 58 G
emenezes@nhu.edu
MENG, William .... 718-940-5884 .... 349 A
wmeng@sjcny.edu
MENGHINI, Becci .... 608-262-8967 .... 550 J
menghini@chancellor.wisc.edu
MENGHINI, Charles, T .... 312-225-6288 .... 167 G
cmenghini@vandercook.edu
MENGINE, Tina .... 814-732-1732 .... 442 E
tmengine@edinboro.edu
MENGLER, Thomas, M .... 210-436-3722 .... 493 F
tmengler@stmarytx.edu
MENITOFF, Michael .... 310-824-1586 .... 26 D
MENJARES, Pete .... 562-777-4048 .... 31 A
pete.menjares@biola.edu
MENJARES, Pete, C .... 559-453-2010 .... 48 A
fpupres@fresno.edu
MENJARES, Pete, C .... 559-453-2010 .... 47 K
pete.menjares@fresno.edu
MENJIVAR, Claudia .... 718-357-0500 .... 349 F
cmenjivar@edaff.com
MENK, David, A .... 507-933-6539 .... 263 J
dmenk@gustavus.edu
MENKE, Laura .... 319-208-5193 .... 189 D
lmenke@scciowa.edu
MENKE, Pamela .... 305-237-3715 .... 113 H
pmenke@mdc.edu
MENKE, Scott .... 262-595-2155 .... 552 A
scott.menke@uwp.edu
MENKING, Cornell .... 575-646-3199 .... 319 D
MENLOVE, Ronda, R .... 435-797-3728 .... 511 E
ronda.menlove@usu.edu
MENN, Esther .... 773-256-0762 .... 157 D
emenn@lstc.edu
MENNE, Renee, A .... 563-588-7130 .... 187 C
renee.menne@loras.edu
MENNECHEY, Pamela .... 407-708-2380 .... 117 H
mennechey@seminolestate.edu
MENNEKE, Beth, R .... 314-505-7761 .... 280 D
mennekeb@csl.edu
MENNICKE, Sue .... 717-291-3911 .... 429 F
susan.mennicke@fandm.edu
MENNINGER, Gaynia .... 785-242-5200 .... 195 I
gaynia.menninger@ottawa.edu
MENNINGER, Jay, E .... 802-656-3290 .... 514 H
jay.menninger@uvm.edu
MENNS, Melvin .... 202-722-8111 .... 99 G
melvin.menns@strayer.edu
MENOGAN, Kelle .... 601-977-7828 .... 277 C
kmenogan@tougaloo.edu
MENON, Ajay .... 970-491-2398 .... 83 F
ajay.menon@colostate.edu
MENSAH, Michael, O .... 570-941-4049 .... 450 C
michael.mensah@scranton.edu
MENSAH, Vincent .... 304-424-8223 .... 545 C
vincent.mensah@mail.wvu.edu
MENSAH-DARTEY, Virgil .... 678-422-4100 .... 99 G
MENSCHING, Ron .... 630-889-6606 .... 159 F
rmensching@nuhs.edu
MENSHOUSE, Nancy, L .... 606-326-2199 .... 201 F
nancy.menshouse@kctcs.edu
MENTE, Patrick, J .... 607-436-2596 .... 353 E
mentepj@oneonta.edu
MENTZER, Cathy .... 717-264-4141 .... 452 C
cmentzer@wilson.edu
MENY, Eileen, M .... 617-912-9128 .... 232 C
emeny@bostonconservatory.edu
MENZ, Harald .... 304-829-7915 .... 540 H
hmenz@bethanywv.edu
MENZ, Leslie, E .... 309-655-2180 .... 163 G
leslie.menz@osfhealthcare.org

MENZANO, Silvestro .... 703-284-6861 .... 521 D
silvestro.menzano@marymount.edu
MENZEL, Carol, A .... 410-334-2946 .... 229 E
cmenzel@worwic.edu
MENZER, Paul .... 540-887-7058 .... 521 C
pmenzer@mbc.edu
MENZIES, Andre' .... 504-816-4570 .... 209 A
amenzies@dillard.edu
MENZIES, John, K .... 973-275-2516 .... 315 B
john.menzies@shu.edu
MEOLA, Christine .... 212-346-1095 .... 345 F
cmeola@pace.edu
MEONSKE, Kali .... 330-325-6492 .... 397 D
kmeonske@neomed.edu
MEOTTI, Michael, P .... 860-493-0230 .... 90 F
meottim@ct.edu
MERAT, Carl .... 434-592-7062 .... 520 K
cmerat@liberty.edu
MERCADANTE, Richard ..... 727-791-2527 .... 116 H
mercadante.richard@spcollege.edu
MERCADO, Caroline .... 570-372-4753 .... 447 E
mercado@susqu.edu
MERCADO, Christopher ..... 386-734-3303 .... 109 G
cmercado@ftccollege.edu
MERCADO, Elizabeth .... 856-351-2910 .... 315 A
emercado@salemcc.edu
MERCADO, Frank .... 201-360-4043 .... 310 E
fmercado@hccc.edu
MERCADO, Harry .... 787-740-3555 .... 566 C
harry.mercado@uccaribe.edu
MERCADO, Juan Carlos .... 212-925-6625 .... 326 G
jmercado@ccny.cuny.edu
MERCADO, Leo, A .... 843-953-3020 .... 456 C
leo.mercado@citadel.edu
MERCADO, Maritza E, M ... 212-247-3434 .... 339 G
mmercado@mandl.edu
MERCADO-OCASIO,
Iris, M .... 787-894-2828 .... 566 G
iris.mercado@upr.edu
MERCED, Randolph .... 215-717-6827 .... 448 I
rmerced@uarts.edu
MERCER, Amber .... 206-934-6794 .... 537 F
amber.mercer@seattlecolleges.edu
MERCER, Bobby .... 740-377-2520 .... 402 F
mercer.tsbc@gmail.com
MERCER, Brenda, D .... 919-735-5151 .... 375 A
bdmercer@waynecc.edu
MERCER, Brigid .... 206-268-4483 .... 530 I
bmercer@antioch.edu
MERCER, David, M .... 585-567-9322 .... 336 B
david.mercer@houghton.edu
MERCER, Ellen .... 920-923-8112 .... 548 E
emercer@marianuniversity.edu
MERCER, Frank .... 386-506-4461 .... 104 F
mercerf@daytonastate.edu
MERCER, JR., John .... 704-463-3352 .... 375 F
john.mercer@fsmail.pfeiffer.edu
MERCER, John, D .... 850-872-3807 .... 110 H
jmercer@gulfcoast.edu
MERCER, Karen .... 319-895-4342 .... 183 G
kmercer@cornellcollege.edu
MERCER, Laura .... 937-512-4571 .... 401 J
laura.mercer@sinclair.edu
MERCER, Leneil .... 313-487-7420 .... 209 F
mercer@lacollege.edu
MERCER, Leslie, K .... 651-201-1862 .... 265 E
leslie.mercer@so.mnscu.edu
MERCER, Molly .... 724-738-2179 .... 443 F
molly.mercer@sru.edu
MERCER, Paul .... 207-326-2337 .... 219 D
paul.mercer@mma.edu
MERCER, Peter, P .... 201-684-7607 .... 313 C
pmercer@ramapo.edu
MERCER, Sally, A .... 240-895-4309 .... 226 A
samercer@smcm.edu
MERCER, Tracy .... 605-773-3455 .... 465 F
tracym@sdbor.edu
MERCHANT, Betty .... 210-458-4370 .... 506 D
betty.merchant@utsa.edu
MERCHANT, Janie .... 575-646-6014 .... 319 D
jpence@nmsu.edu
MERCHANT, Joshua .... 517-629-0242 .... 247 A
jmerchant@albion.edu
MERCHANT, Joshua, D ..... 517-629-0321 .... 247 A
jdmerchant@albion.edu
MERCHANT, Walter, G ..... 540-563-8000 .... 524 F
wmerchant@skyline.edu
MERCHLEWITZ, Ann, E ..... 507-457-1587 .... 271 B
amerchle@smumn.edu
MERCIER, Casey .... 601-477-4223 .... 274 H
casey.mercier@jcjc.edu
MERCIER, Collette, R .... 801-627-8304 .... 510 H
mercierc@owatc.edu
MERCIER, William, C .... 812-237-7829 .... 173 B
william.mercier@indstate.edu
MERCINCAVAGE, Janet, E . 570-208-5878 .... 432 G
jemercin@kings.edu
MERCK, II, William, F .... 407-823-2351 .... 120 B
william.merck@ucf.edu
MERCOGLIANO, Amy .... 609-771-2495 .... 308 F
mercogli@tcnj.edu
MERCOMES, Brenda, W ..... 617-541-5383 .... 241 A
brendam@rcc.mass.edu
MERCURIO, Andrew, L ...... 828-298-3325 .... 380 D
almercurio@warren-wilson.edu

MERCURIO, Gloria .... 201-761-6125 .... 314 F
gmercurio@spc.edu
MERCURIO, Sherry .... 614-947-6581 .... 391 B
mercuris@franklin.edu
MERDINGER, Joan .... 408-924-2450 .... 37 C
joan.merdinger@sjsu.edu
MEREDITH, Brian .... 270-745-6169 .... 208 A
brian.meredith@wku.edu
MEREDITH, Cynthia, L ...... 731-661-5202 .... 477 B
cmeredit@uu.edu
MEREDITH, Daniel .... 864-941-8442 .... 460 D
meredith.d@ptc.edu
MEREDITH, Dave .... 504-280-7013 .... 213 E
MEREDITH, Don, L .... 901-761-1354 .... 469 C
hstlib@hst.edu
MEREDITH, Gloria .... 847-578-3270 .... 163 C
gloria.meredith@rosalindfranklin.edu
MEREDITH, John, R .... 517-750-1200 .... 258 D
randym@arbo.edu
MEREDITH, Joyce .... 740-587-6515 .... 389 I
meredithj@denison.edu
MEREDITH, Marc .... 310-665-6815 .... 60 B
marcm@otis.edu
MEREDITH, Patricia .... 813-463-7163 .... 29 F
pmeredith@argosy.edu
MEREDITH, Steven .... 573-681-5109 .... 283 I
meredith@lincolnu.edu
MERELLA, Bartholomew, J . 202-541-5264 .... 100 B
merella@wtu.edu
MERES, Cynthia, L .... 607-436-3388 .... 353 E
merescl@oneonta.edu
MERFALEN, Barbara, K ...... 670-234-5498 .... 560 B
barbaram@nmcnet.edu
MERFELD, Laura, L .... 641-422-4355 .... 188 A
merfelau@niacc.edu
MERGEN, Amy .... 419-824-3677 .... 395 E
amergen@lourdes.edu
MERGENTHAL, James .... 215-895-0476 .... 427 H
jem38@drexel.edu
MERGET, Kathleen .... 845-451-1776 .... 331 E
k_merget@culinary.edu
MERGIOTTI, James, J .... 215-670-9494 .... 438 E
president@peirce.edu
MERGL, Francine, R .... 716-888-8211 .... 325 F
merglf@canisius.edu
MERGLER, Nancy, L .... 405-325-3221 .... 413 C
nmergler@ou.edu
MERIANS, Linda .... 212-817-7130 .... 327 B
lmerians@gc.cuny.edu
MERICKEL, Mark .... 707-664-2394 .... 37 D
mark.merickel@sonoma.edu
MERICLE, Margaret, E .... 559-442-8210 .... 72 B
margaret.mericle@fresnocitycollege.edu
MERIDITH, Pamela .... 870-759-4139 .... 26 B
pmeridith@wbcoll.edu
MERIGOLD, Mary .... 716-896-0700 .... 359 H
merigoldm@villa.edu
MERILAT, Meliinda .... 832-252-0745 .... 483 C
melinda.merilat@cbshouston.edu
MERILLAT, Jason, C .... 610-566-1776 .... 452 B
jmerillat@williamson.edu
MERIMEE, Nancy, S .... 913-971-3427 .... 195 D
nsmerimee@mnu.edu
MERINAR, Whitney, A .... 570-321-4144 .... 435 D
merinar@lycoming.edu
MERINGOLO,
Salvatore, M .... 540-654-1372 .... 525 D
tmeringo@umw.edu
MERINO, Robert .... 281-998-6150 .... 493 G
robert.merino@sjcd.edu
MERIWETHER, Jan .... 434-947-8127 .... 523 B
jmeriwether@randolphcollege.edu
MERIWETHER, Jason .... 615-329-8854 .... 468 I
jmeriwether@fisk.edu
MERJIL, Mark .... 909-384-8990 .... 65 C
mmerjil@sbccd.cc.ca.us
MERKEL, Cynthia, F .... 906-635-2674 .... 253 H
cmerkel@lssu.edu
MERKEL, Denise .... 520-417-4148 .... 13 E
merkeld@cochise.edu
MERKEL, Diane .... 518-564-2195 .... 354 B
dmerk001@plattsburgh.edu
MERKEL, Luz, I .... 509-777-4225 .... 540 C
lmerkel@whitworth.edu
MERKEL-VEER, Chelly .... 701-766-1302 .... 381 A
chelly.merkel@littlehoop.edu
MERKIN, Yitzchok .... 301-962-5111 .... 229 F
ymerkin@yeshiva.edu
MERKLE, Barbara .... 940-397-4334 .... 491 B
barbara.merkle@mwsu.edu
MERKLE, Ben .... 208-882-1566 .... 144 C
bmerkle@nsa.edu
MERKLE, H. Bart .... 616-331-3585 .... 251 F
merkleb@gvsu.edu
MERKLE, Jean .... 563-425-5765 .... 189 G
merklej@uiu.edu
MERKLE, Joseph, F .... 717-815-1460 .... 452 G
jmerkle@ycp.edu
MERKLE, Karen, L .... 410-386-8107 .... 221 G
kmerkle@carrollcc.edu
MERKLE, Patricia .... 315-568-3277 .... 342 H
pmerkle@nycc.edu
MERKLEY, Brett .... 801-524-8132 .... 510 E
bmerkley@idsbc.edu

MERKT, Mary Lou .... 864-294-2140 .... 458 E
marylou.merkt@furman.edu
MERKX, Gilbert .... 919-684-5830 .... 364 C
gilbert.merkx@duke.edu
MERL, Jill .... 808-544-9364 .... 140 G
jmerl@hpu.edu
MERLI, Janet .... 201-559-6040 .... 310 B
merlij@felician.edu
MERLINO, Keith .... 412-809-5100 .... 444 G
merlino.keith@pti.edu
MERLO, Barbara .... 254-526-1223 .... 482 H
barbara.merlo@ctcd.edu
MERRELL, Donna .... 660-248-6214 .... 279 G
dmerrell@centralmethodist.edu
MERRELL, Linda .... 859-525-6510 .... 205 C
lkmerrell@national-college.edu
MERRELL, Melinda, M .... 425-235-5846 .... 537 A
mmerrell@rtc.edu
MERRELL, Sue .... 937-512-2917 .... 401 J
sue.merrell@sinclair.edu
MERRICK, Bernard, D .... 412-365-1231 .... 425 C
merrick@chatham.edu
MERRICK, Jocelyn .... 413-662-5193 .... 238 C
j.merrick@mcla.edu
MERRICK, Robyn .... 225-771-4200 .... 214 H
robyn_merrick@sus.edu
MERRICK, Robyn .... 225-771-4200 .... 214 I
robyn_merrick@sus.edu
MERRICK, Sara .... 601-984-2300 .... 277 E
smerrick@umc.edu
MERRICK, Vallyn .... 410-951-6300 .... 228 B
vmerrick@coppin.edu
MERRIFIELD, Mary .... 314-529-9510 .... 284 C
mmerrifield@maryville.edu
MERRIGAN, John .... 660-543-4161 .... 290 H
merrigan@ucmo.edu
MERRIHEW, Mark, W .... 620-417-1202 .... 196 F
mark.merrihew@sccc.edu
MERRILL, Chad .... 828-694-1901 .... 368 E
chadm@blueridge.edu
MERRILL, Dale .... 714-997-6849 .... 39 F
merrill@chapman.edu
MERRILL, H. Donald .... 704-233-8284 .... 380 F
dmerrill@wingate.edu
MERRILL, Joanne .... 603-897-8257 .... 305 F
jmerrill@rivier.edu
MERRILL, Kristin .... 513-244-8151 .... 387 E
kristin.merrill@ccuniversity.edu
MERRILL, Martha, C .... 860-439-2200 .... 92 G
mcmer@conncoll.edu
MERRILL, Melvin .... 229-391-4894 .... 123 H
mmerrill@abac.edu
MERRILL, Michael .... 212-647-7801 .... 355 G
michael.merrill@esc.edu
MERRILL, Paul .... 256-331-5223 .... 6 B
merrill@nwscc.edu
MERRILL, Robert .... 410-225-5274 .... 224 B
rmerrill@mica.edu
MERRILL, Scott, M .... 508-793-2438 .... 233 C
smerrill@holycross.edu
MERRILL, Steve .... 801-601-4917 .... 509 F
ssmerrill@argosy.edu
MERRILL, Timothy, W .... 804-752-7212 .... 523 C
timothymerrill@rmc.edu
MERRILL-DOSS, Jean .... 573-518-2262 .... 285 I
jeanmer@mineralarea.edu
MERRIMAN, William, J ...... 718-862-7374 .... 339 H
william.merriman@manhattan.edu
MERRIMAN, JR.,
William, R .... 620-229-6223 .... 196 G
dick.merriman@sckans.edu
MERRION, Margaret, M ..... 269-387-5811 .... 260 C
margaret.merrion@wmich.edu
MERRIS, Justin .... 312-935-4159 .... 162 G
jmerris@robertmorris.edu
MERRITT, Adam .... 910-392-4660 .... 367 D
adam.merritt@miller-motte.com
MERRITT, Bert .... 850-484-1140 .... 115 B
bmerritt@pensacolastate.edu
MERRITT, Christine, C .... 315-859-4111 .... 334 H
cmerritt@hamilton.edu
MERRITT, Deborah, J .... 804-745-2444 .... 517 C
djmerritt@bryantstratton.edu
MERRITT, Jaci, M .... 903-434-8103 .... 491 F
jmerritt@ntcc.edu
MERRITT, James, A .... 608-246-6330 .... 554 D
jamerritt1@madisoncollege.org
MERRITT, Judy, M .... 205-853-1200 .... 5 C
jmerritt@jeffstateonline.com
MERRITT, Scott .... 318-869-5708 .... 208 H
smerritt@centenary.edu
MERRITT, Stephen, R .... 610-519-7499 .... 450 H
stephen.merritt@villanova.edu
MERRITT, Susan, M .... 212-346-1810 .... 345 F
smerritt@pace.edu
MERRITT, Wayne .... 704-406-3939 .... 364 E
wmerritt@gardner-webb.edu
MERRITT MILLER, Beth .... 916-278-6231 .... 36 A
merrittmillerb@csus.edu
MERRYMAN, Ed .... 408-554-5076 .... 68 C
emerryman@scu.edu
MERRYMAN, Jason .... 423-236-2893 .... 473 B
jasonmerryman@southern.edu
MERRYMAN, Jon .... 870-245-5506 .... 22 I
merrymanj@obu.edu

MERRYMAN, Marjorie .... 212-749-2802 .... 339 I
mmerryman@msmnyc.edu
MERSETH, Juel, O .... 507-344-7854 .... 261 C
juel.merseth@blc.edu
MERSON, Michael, H .... 919-681-7760 .... 364 C
michael.merson@duke.edu
MERTEN, Elizabeth .... 712-749-2062 .... 183 C
mertenl@bvu.edu
MERTES, Scott .... 989-773-6622 .... 255 C
smertes@midmich.edu
MERTH, LeAnn .... 402-486-2535 .... 300 C
lemerth@ucollege.edu
MERTH, Paula, B .... 651-290-6376 .... 272 E
paula.merth@wmitchell.edu
MERTLER, Craig .... 561-237-7441 .... 113 D
cmertler@lynn.edu
MERTZ, Jennifer, L .... 610-758-3181 .... 434 E
jlm207@lehigh.edu
MERVINE, Ed .... 310-577-3000 .... 80 E
financialaid@yosan.edu
MERVYN, Frances .... 617-327-6777 .... 241 F
frances_mervyn@mspp.edu
MERYHEW, Barb .... 307-268-2249 .... 556 A
bmeryhew@caspercollege.edu
MERZ, Nancy .... 816-235-1154 .... 291 C
merzn@umkc.edu
MERZ, Soon, O .... 512-223-7035 .... 481 B
smerz@austincc.edu
MESA, Tina .... 210-486-3901 .... 479 C
tmesa@alamo.edu
MESAROS, Cyndi .... 805-922-6966 .... 26 L
cmesaros@hancockcollege.edu
MESCH, Barry .... 617-559-8613 .... 235 E
bmesch@hebrewcollege.edu
MESCHIEVITZ, Catherine ... 561-297-3282 .... 119 A
cmeschie@fau.edu
MESCON, Timothy, S .... 706-507-8950 .... 127 G
mescon_timothy@columbusstate.edu
MESEROLE, Brooke .... 910-362-7062 .... 368 H
bmeserole@cfcc.edu
MESERVE, Mary .... 207-786-6097 .... 217 C
mmeserve@bates.edu
MESERVEY, Patricia, M ..... 978-542-6134 .... 238 E
pmeservey@salemstate.edu
MESHKATY, Shahra .... 619-260-2298 .... 76 D
meshkaty@sandiego.edu
MESICS, Linda, L .... 610-799-1585 .... 434 D
lmesics@lccc.edu
MESINA, Irene .... 808-845-9195 .... 142 B
irene@hcc.hawaii.edu
MESLER, Cecelia .... 616-632-2868 .... 247 E
meslecec@aquinas.edu
MESMAN MICHAELIS,
Michelle .... 503-222-3225 .... 415 H
mmesman@cci.edu
MESNER, Lindsey .... 800-962-7682 .... 293 A
lmesner@wma.edu
MESONAS, Lenny .... 908-526-1200 .... 313 D
lmesonas@raritanval.edu
MESQUITA, Joseph .... 860-512-3215 .... 91 F
jmesquita@mcc.commnet.edu
MESSA, Emily .... 832-842-8184 .... 503 C
eamessa@uh.edu
MESSA, Emily .... 832-842-8184 .... 503 D
eamessa@uh.edu
MESSAROS, Jean .... 570-674-6320 .... 436 F
srjean@misericordia.edu
MESSER, Brian .... 913-451-1431 .... 178 I
MESSER, Brian .... 913-451-1431 .... 17 B
MESSER, Brian .... 913-451-1431 .... 195 I
brian.messer@ottawa.edu
MESSER, Brian .... 913-451-1431 .... 196 A
MESSER, Brian .... 913-451-1431 .... 549 H
MESSER, Emily, W .... 770-233-7312 .... 137 A
emesser@shorter.edu
MESSER, J, B .... 405-682-7812 .... 409 F
jmesser@occc.edu
MESSER, Kirk, D .... 414-410-4425 .... 546 G
kdmesser@stritch.edu
MESSER, Stanley, B .... 848-445-2000 .... 314 C
smesser@rci.rutgers.edu
MESSER, Thomas, C .... 904-596-2411 .... 122 D
tmesser@tbc.org
MESSER, Toni .... 972-883-2693 .... 506 A
tmesser@utdallas.edu
MESSER-ROY, Stephanie ... 228-897-3886 .... 275 E
stephanie.roy@mgccc.edu
MESSERE, Fritz .... 315-312-2285 .... 354 A
fritz.messere@oswego.edu
MESSICK, Fred .... 626-584-5367 .... 48 B
fmessick@fuller.edu
MESSICK, Gary, A .... 260-422-5561 .... 173 C
gamessick@indianatech.edu
MESSIER, David, H .... 508-831-5216 .... 246 F
dmessier@wpi.edu
MESSINA, Cliff .... 859-282-9999 .... 204 C
cmessina@lincolntech.com
MESSINA, John, A .... 330-972-7800 .... 403 B
jam125@uakron.edu
MESSINA, Kimberlee .... 650-949-7209 .... 47 H
messinakimberlee@foothill.edu
MESSINA, Marianne .... 812-877-8840 .... 179 B
messina@rose-hulman.edu

MICHAEL, Noreen, M .... 340-693-1003.... 568 E
nmichae@live.uvi.edu
MICHAEL, Pamela .... 315-312-2102.... 354 A
pamela.michael@oswego.edu
MICHAEL, Sandra .... 215-637-7700.... 431 A
smichael@holyfamily.edu
MICHAEL, Steve, O .... 215-572-2924.... 422 C
michaels@arcadia.edu
MICHAEL-PICKETT,
Stephanie .... 704-922-6215.... 370 G
michael.stephanie@gaston.edu
MICHAELIDES, Anthony ..... 661-362-3253...... 41 I
anthony.michaelides@canyons.edu
MICHAELIDES, Barbara ..... 318-342-5550.... 216 E
michaelides@ulm.edu
MICHAELIS, Jim .... 801-863-8996.... 511 F
michaeji@uvu.edu
MICHAELIS, Margaret .... 408-864-8857...... 47 G
michaelismargaret@deanza.edu
MICHAELIS, Randall, B ...... 509-777-4303.... 540 C
rmichaelis@whitworth.edu
MICHAELS, Alan, C .... 614-292-2631.... 398 I
michaels.23@osu.edu
MICHAELS, Andrea, P .... 508-793-7773.... 233 B
amichaels@clarku.edu
MICHAELS, Brent .... 910-678-8209.... 370 E
michaelb@faytechcc.edu
MICHAELS, Cathy .... 718-262-2238.... 329 A
ctsia@york.cuny.edu
MICHAELS, Daniel .... 217-228-5432.... 161 F
dmichaels@quincy.edu
MICHAELS, George, H .... 805-893-2378...... 75 B
george@id.ucsb.edu
MICHAELS, Jeff, A .... 717-477-1171.... 443 E
jamich@ship.edu
MICHAELS, Lynda .... 570-389-4061.... 441 F
lmichael@bloomu.edu
MICHAELS, Meredith .... 949-824-4923...... 74 B
m.michaels@uci.edu
MICHAELS, Sheri .... 319-385-6229.... 186 E
sheri.michaels@iwc.edu
MICHAELS, Sue .... 916-660-7272...... 69 F
smichaels@sierracollege.edu
MICHAELSEN, Kevin .... 919-760-8565.... 367 A
michaelsen@meredith.edu
MICHAELSON, Dorcas, M . 651-523-2210.... 264 A
dmichaelson01@hamline.edu
MICHAELSON, John .... 541-881-5590.... 420 E
jmichaelson@tvcc.cc
MICHAELSON FISHER,
Bonnie .... 410-778-7261.... 229 D
bfisher2@washcoll.edu
MICHAJLA, Patty .... 425-640-1516.... 533 I
pmichajl@edcc.edu
MICHAL, Barbara, M .... 706-419-1275.... 128 B
michal@covenant.edu
MICHALAK, Sarah .... 919-962-1301.... 378 E
smichala@email.unc.edu
MICHALENKO, John .... 412-397-4399.... 445 H
michalenko@rmu.edu
MICHALERYA, William, D . 610-758-5802.... 434 E
wdm1@lehigh.edu
MICHALSKI, Greg .... 904-632-3017.... 109 F
gmichals@fscj.edu
MICHALSKI, Monica .... 718-489-5274.... 348 E
mmichalski@sfc.edu
MICHALSKI, Tim .... 361-570-4820.... 504 A
michalskit@uhv.edu
MICHAUD, Paul .... 908-526-1200.... 313 D
pmichaud@raritanval.edu
MICHAUD, Paul .... 912-478-7765.... 131 E
pmichaud@georgiasouthern.edu
MICHEALS, Deborah .... 724-480-3515.... 426 A
deb.micheals@ccbc.edu
MICHEL, Mike .... 410-293-1901.... 559 B
michel@usna.edu
MICHELINI, Debra .... 847-543-2383.... 148 B
dmichelini@clcillinois.edu
MICHELINI, Rick, H .... 724-287-8711.... 423 G
rick.michelini@bc3.edu
MICHELL, Peter .... 925-631-4571...... 64 F
pmichell@stmarys-ca.edu
MICHELS, Therese .... 402-557-7115.... 296 H
therese.michels@bellevue.edu
MICHELSON, Peggy .... 314-529-6543.... 284 C
pmichelson@maryville.edu
MICIAK, Alan, R .... 412-396-1372.... 428 D
miciaka@duq.edu
MICKANIS, Judith, L .... 570-577-3171.... 423 E
mickanis@bucknell.edu
MICKELSEN, Scott, R .... 308-367-5253.... 301 B
smickelsen4@unl.edu
MICKELSON, Doug .... 414-256-1252.... 549 D
mickelsd@mtmary.edu
MICKENS, Charles .... 517-371-5140.... 258 F
mickensc@cooley.edu
MICKENS, George .... 623-245-4600...... 18 J
gmickens@uti.edu
MICKENS, Helen .... 517-371-5140.... 258 F
mickensh@cooley.edu
MICKENS, Kendrick .... 610-359-5340.... 426 G
kmickens@dccc.edu
MICKEY, James, C .... 210-458-4133.... 506 D
jim.mickey@utsa.edu
MICKEY, Marty .... 847-947-5580.... 159 E
mmickey@nl.edu
MICKEY-BOGGS, Shari ...... 513-745-3657.... 406 E
mickeyboggss@xavier.edu
MICKLES, Muriel, B .... 434-832-7656.... 526 E
micklesm@cvcc.vccs.edu
MICKOOL, Richard .... 937-525-3815.... 406 B
rmickool@wittenberg.edu
MIDANIK, Lorraine, T .... 510-642-5039...... 73 H
swdean@berkeley.edu
MIDCAP, Richard, D .... 410-827-5858.... 222 B
rmidcap@chesapeake.edu
MIDDEKER, Vicki .... 303-464-2308...... 87 H
vmiddeker@westwood.edu
MIDDENDORF, Sandra .... 651-641-3599.... 264 H
smiddendorf001@luthersem.edu
MIDDENDORF, Terry .... 651-523-2302.... 264 A
tmiddendorf@hamline.edu
MIDDLEBROOK, Sharon ... 254-659-7502.... 487 G
smiddlebrook@hillcollege.edu
MIDDLEMIST, George, M .. 303-556-5043...... 86 F
middlemi@msudenver.edu
MIDDLESWARTH, Jean, E . 336-575-3901.... 370 F
jmiddleswarth@forsythtech.edu
MIDDLETON, Antoinette .... 212-220-1267.... 326 D
amiddleton@bmcc.cuny.edu
MIDDLETON, Charles, R ... 312-341-3800.... 163 B
cmiddleton@roosevelt.edu
MIDDLETON, David .... 973-761-9080.... 315 B
david.middleton@shu.edu
MIDDLETON, Dawcett .... 405-733-7450.... 411 I
wzjones@rose.edu
MIDDLETON, Jacqueline ... 330-263-2580.... 388 F
jkmiddleton@wooster.edu
MIDDLETON, James, E ...... 541-383-7201.... 414 I
jmiddleton@cocc.edu
MIDDLETON, Joan .... 301-934-7568.... 222 C
joanm@csmd.edu
MIDDLETON, Joan .... 301-934-7853.... 222 C
joanm@csmd.edu
MIDDLETON, Joseph .... 718-960-8421.... 327 C
joseph.middleton@lehman.cuny.edu
MIDDLETON, Kenna .... 859-622-1515.... 200 J
kenna.middleton@eku.edu
MIDDLETON, Lowell .... 757-727-5640.... 519 H
lowell.middleton@hamptonu.edu
MIDDLETON, Lyle .... 501-205-8830...... 21 C
lmiddleton@cbc.edu
MIDDLETON, Melinda, L ... 812-877-8259.... 179 B
melinda.l.middleton@rose-hulman.edu
MIDDLETON, Michael, A ... 573-882-3394.... 291 B
middletonm@missouri.edu
MIDDLETON, Nigel, T .... 303-273-3327.... 83 B
nmiddlet@mines.edu
MIDDLETON, Norma, L ..... 336-316-2151.... 365 A
nmiddlet@guilford.edu
MIDDLETON, Renee, A ..... 740-593-4400.... 399 G
middletr@ohio.edu
MIDDLETON, Rich .... 859-622-2966.... 200 J
rich.middleton@eku.edu
MIDDLETON, Rodney, C ... 989-328-1202.... 255 E
rodm@montcalm.edu
MIDDLETON, Whittaker, V . 803-535-5347.... 456 D
wmiddleton@claflin.edu
MIDGETT, Pam .... 940-397-4182.... 491 B
pam.midgett@mwsu.edu
MIDGETTE, Juanita .... 252-335-3586.... 377 F
jmidgette@mail.ecsu.edu
MIDGLEY, Michael, T .... 512-223-7579.... 481 B
midgley@austincc.edu
MIDHA, Chand .... 330-972-7857.... 403 B
cmidha@uakron.edu
MIDKIFF, Lindsay .... 870-633-4480...... 21 F
lindsay.midkiff@eacc.edu
MIDKIFF, Lori, A .... 304-929-5472.... 543 A
lmidkiff@newriver.edu
MIDKIFF, Mike .... 903-923-2136.... 486 F
mmidkiff@etbu.edu
MIDKIFF, JR., Robert, M .. 570-577-1561.... 423 E
robert.midkiff@bucknell.edu
MIDKIFF, Sabrina .... 713-500-3015.... 506 F
sabrina.midkiff@uth.tmc.edu
MIDKIFF, Scott, F .... 540-231-4227.... 529 G
midkiff@vt.edu
MIDONECK, Shari, R .... 212-746-2088.... 360 C
srmidone@med.cornell.edu
MIDTHUN, Steve .... 414-277-7224.... 549 C
midthun@msoe.edu
MIEDEMA, Linda, L .... 321-433-7380.... 102 D
miedemal@brevardcc.edu
MIEKLE, Tom .... 909-594-5611...... 58 A
tmiekle@mtsac.edu
MIELE, Carol .... 201-493-3617.... 307 E
cmiele@bergen.edu
MIELKE, Dan .... 541-962-3399.... 418 C
dmielke@eou.edu
MIERS, Michael .... 508-849-3326.... 230 C
mmiers@annamaria.edu
MIERTSCHIN, Charla .... 507-457-5299.... 269 G
cmiertschin@winona.edu
MIES, Jay .... 620-672-5641.... 196 D
jaym@prattcc.edu
MIGLAW, Kari, L .... 831-656-2077.... 558 A
klmiglaw@nps.edu
MIGLER, Jerome .... 520-206-4999...... 17 H
jmigler@pima.edu
MIGNAULT, Richard .... 845-451-1369.... 331 E
r_mignau@culinary.edu
MIGNOGNA, Janice .... 215-780-1235.... 446 G
janice@salus.edu
MIGNOGNA, Janice .... 215-780-1400.... 446 G
janice@salus.edu
MIGUEL, George .... 520-383-8401...... 18 I
gmiguel@tocc.cc.az.us
MIGYANKO, Stephanie, M 724-439-4900.... 434 A
smigyanko@laurel.edu
MIHAL, Ruthie .... 704-355-5316.... 363 D
ruthie.mihal@carolinashealthcare.org
MIHALAKIS, Marina .... 401-454-6764.... 454 B
mmihalak@risd.edu
MIHALCIN, Patricia .... 724-287-8711.... 423 G
patricia.mihalcin@bc3.edu
MIHALEVICH, Rick .... 573-897-5000.... 284 A
MIHALIC, Angela .... 214-648-2168.... 507 E
angela.mihalic@utsouthwestern.edu
MIHALIK, Brian .... 803-777-4290.... 462 A
bmahalik@hrsm.sc.edu
MIHALY, Christine .... 734-973-3477.... 259 F
cmihaly@wccnet.edu
MIHALY, Marc .... 802-831-1237.... 515 B
mmmmihaly@vermontlaw.edu
MIHALYO, JR.,
Michael, P .... 304-637-1303.... 541 A
mihalyom@dewv.edu
MIHALYOV, David .... 585-395-2577.... 352 F
dmihalyo@brockport.edu
MIHARA, Darrell .... 425-388-9581.... 534 C
dmihara@everettcc.edu
MIHEL, George, J .... 815-288-5511.... 164 B
mihelg@svcc.edu
MIHELICH, Lucinda .... 719-549-3080...... 87 F
cindy.mihelich@pueblocc.edu
MIHLBACHLER, Dennis ...... 217-532-6961.... 156 B
dennis.mihlbachler@doc.illinois.gov
MIHM-HEROLD,
Wendy, A .... 563-562-3263.... 188 B
mihm-heroldw@portal.nicc.edu
MIHOPULOS, Sheryl, L ...... 516-877-3365.... 322 A
mihopulos@adelphi.edu
MIKALSON, Joan .... 518-608-8144.... 333 E
jmikalson@excelsior.edu
MIKE, James .... 717-477-1151.... 443 E
jhmike@ship.edu
MIKEL, Ed .... 206-268-4617.... 530 I
emikel@antioch.edu
MIKELL, Ashley .... 802-865-6428.... 513 C
mikell@champlain.edu
MIKESCH, Gregory .... 314-768-1603.... 283 G
mikesch@kenrick.edu
MIKESELL, Brian .... 413-528-7274.... 230 F
bmikesell@simons-rock.edu
MIKESELL, Leslie .... 530-283-0202...... 47 B
lmikesell@frc.edu
MIKESIC, Patrick .... 785-594-8447.... 190 F
patrick.mikesic@bakeru.edu
MIKEWORTH, Becky, L ...... 618-544-8657.... 152 H
mikeworthb@iecc.edu
MIKHAIL, Michael, B .... 312-413-3375.... 167 B
MIKHAIL, Osama, I .... 713-500-3047.... 506 F
osama.i.mikhail@uth.tmc.edu
MIKKELSEN, Andrea .... 507-457-5024.... 269 G
amikkelsen@winona.edu
MIKKELSEN, Carmelita .... 251-580-2213........ 5 A
cmikkelsen@faulknerstate.edu
MIKKELSEN, Morris, E .... 319-273-2611.... 182 G
morris.mikkelsen@uni.edu
MIKLUSAK, Courtney .... 619-239-0391...... 37 F
cmiklusak@cwsl.edu
MIKNAVICH, Marie .... 315-866-0300.... 335 D
miknavimt@herkimer.edu
MIKO, Matthew .... 202-408-2400...... 99 G
MIKOWSKI, Thomas .... 616-632-2853.... 247 E
mikowtho@aquinas.edu
MIKSA, Anthony .... 815-455-8673.... 157 H
tmiksa@mchenry.edu
MIKUS, Robert, L .... 717-867-6234.... 434 C
mikus@lvc.edu
MIKUSZEWSKI, Barbara .... 216-987-4497.... 389 B
barbara.mikuszewski@tri-c.edu
MILACCI, Fred .... 434-592-4043.... 520 K
fmilacci@liberty.edu
MILADIN, Judith, G .... 315-255-1743.... 325 G
miladin@cayuga-cc.edu
MILAM, B. Hofler .... 336-758-7415.... 380 C
MILAM, John, H .... 540-868-7249.... 527 C
jmilam@lfcc.edu
MILAM, Kathy, L .... 937-382-6661.... 405 I
kathy_milam@wilmington.edu
MILAM, Linda .... 918-781-7247.... 407 B
milaml@bacone.edu
MILANO, Joy .... 616-222-3000.... 253 F
jmilano@kuyper.edu
MILANO, Todd, A .... 717-728-2200.... 425 B
toddmilano@centralpenn.edu
MILARDOVICH, Julia .... 916-278-6322.... 36 A
juliam@csus.edu
MILASINOVIC, Milan .... 212-752-1530.... 338 C
milan.milasinovic@limcollege.edu
MILAVETZ, Barry .... 701-777-4278.... 381 F
barry.milavetz@und.edu
MILBOURNE, John, M .... 321-674-7160.... 108 H
jmilbour@fit.edu
MILBURN, Milo, C .... 740-283-3771.... 391 A
mmilburn@franciscan.edu
MILBURN, Tim, R .... 208-467-8644.... 144 E
trmilburn@nnu.edu
MILBY, Kevin, S .... 859-238-5534.... 199 G
kevin.milby@centre.edu
MILBY, Megan, H .... 859-238-5516.... 199 G
megan.milby@centre.edu
MILDON, Todd, B .... 206-616-6811.... 539 A
tmildon@uw.edu
MILEHAM, Mardi .... 503-883-2217.... 416 H
mmileham@linfield.edu
MILEM, Jill .... 936-468-2401.... 496 B
jmilem@sfasu.edu
MILENTIS, John .... 260-480-4156.... 176 F
jmilentis@ivytech.edu
MILES, Arletha .... 914-773-3856.... 345 F
lmiles@pace.edu
MILES, Belinda .... 216-987-4787.... 389 B
belinda.miles@tri-c.edu
MILES, Billie .... 802-654-2930.... 514 D
bmiles@smcvt.edu
MILES, Candice .... 202-274-5000.... 100 A
cmiles@udc.edu
MILES, Cindy .... 619-644-7569...... 49 A
cindy.miles@gcccd.edu
MILES, David, A .... 201-692-2227.... 310 A
dmiles@fdu.edu
MILES, Donald .... 814-472-3360.... 446 B
dmiles@francis.edu
MILES, Frank .... 334-244-3467........ 1 G
fmiles1@aum.edu
MILES, Herb, E .... 979-230-3474.... 482 D
herb.miles@brazosport.edu
MILES, Jason .... 425-889-7800.... 536 C
jason.miles@northwestu.edu
MILES, Jennifer .... 662-329-7129.... 276 A
jmiles@vpss.muw.edu
MILES, Kevin, J .... 610-799-1169.... 434 D
kmiles@lccc.edu
MILES, Kim .... 626-585-7400...... 61 F
kxmiles@pasadena.edu
MILES, Linda .... 252-398-6505.... 363 G
milesl@chowan.edu
MILES, Lora .... 618-650-2020.... 165 C
lflamm@siue.edu
MILES, Martin .... 757-727-5635.... 519 H
martin.miles@hamptonu.edu
MILES, Mary, E .... 502-852-6688.... 207 E
maryelizabeth.miles@louisville.edu
MILES, Ray .... 337-475-5192.... 215 G
rmiles@mcneese.edu
MILES, Richard .... 513-721-7944.... 391 D
rmiles@gbs.edu
MILES, Stephannie .... 704-461-6873.... 362 F
stephanniemiles@bac.edu
MILES, Stephen .... 941-487-4200.... 120 A
miles@ncf.edu
MILES, Suzanne, L .... 520-206-4747...... 17 H
smiles@pima.edu
MILES, Tom .... 478-445-4027.... 130 B
tom.miles@gcsu.edu
MILES, Vernon .... 870-230-5134...... 21 I
vmiles@hsu.edu
MILES, Veryl, V .... 202-319-5139...... 97 E
miles@cua.edu
MILES, Vickie .... 334-670-3732........ 8 A
vmiles@troy.edu
MILES, Vicky .... 303-446-4855...... 86 I
MILES, Wendy .... 508-373-9705.... 231 B
wendy.miles@becker.edu
MILETTI, Linnette .... 787-841-2000.... 565 B
lmiletti@pucpr.edu
MILEWICZ, Mark .... 910-521-6630.... 379 C
mark.milewicz@uncp.edu
MILEWSKI, Douglas, J ...... 973-275-2473.... 310 F
douglas.milewski@shu.edu
MILEY, Abigail .... 812-488-2272.... 180 E
am275@evansville.edu
MILFORD, William .... 516-299-2345.... 339 A
william.milford@liu.edu
MILHAM, Donna .... 616-451-3511.... 250 C
dmilham@davenport.edu
MILHAUSEN, Michael .... 503-399-6527.... 414 J
michael.milhausen@chemeketa.edu
MILHIZER, Eugene, R .... 239-687-5301.... 101 H
ermilhizer@avemarialaw.edu
MILHOLLAND, Tom, A ...... 325-674-2918.... 478 I
milholland@acu.edu
MILICH, Marianne .... 219-980-6618.... 174 B
mmilich@iun.edu
MILICI, Roger .... 212-636-6545.... 334 C
milici@fordham.edu
MILIONI, Mark, L .... 417-268-6008.... 278 J
mmilioni@gobbc.edu
MILIONIS, Daren .... 503-375-7012.... 415 F
dmilionis@corban.edu
MILJEVICH, Greg .... 715-365-4486.... 555 A
gmiljevidh@nicoletcollege.edu

MILLER, Karen, L .... 913-588-1665 .... 197 C
kmiller@kumc.edu
MILLER, Kate .... 605-995-2901 .... 464 C
kamiller1@dwu.edu
MILLER, Kate, C .... 979-845-3651 .... 497 E
kcmiller@tamu.edu
MILLER, Katen .... 216-987-3471 .... 389 B
karen.miller@tri-c.edu
MILLER, Kathleen .... 239-590-7600 .... 119 B
kmiller@fgcu.edu
MILLER, SSJ, Kathryn .... 215-248-7167 .... 425 D
kmiller@chc.edu
MILLER, Kathy .... 847-628-1088 .... 154 K
kmiller@judsonu.edu
MILLER, Kay .... 707-654-1135 ...... 33 C
kmiller@csum.edu
MILLER, Keith .... 864-250-8175 .... 458 G
keith.miller@gvltec.edu
MILLER, Keith, T .... 804-524-5070 .... 529 H
ktmiller@vsu.edu
MILLER, Kelly .... 317-788-3437 .... 180 F
kmiller@uindy.edu
MILLER, Ken .... 407-646-2999 .... 116 D
kmiller@rollins.edu
MILLER, Ken .... 502-456-6506 .... 206 H
kmiller@sullivan.edu
MILLER, Kenneth .... 740-857-1311 .... 401 F
kmiller@rosedale.edu
MILLER, Kenneth, P .... 814-898-6111 .... 439 F
kqm3@psu.edu
MILLER, Kent .... 573-288-6373 .... 280 I
kmiller@culver.edu
MILLER, Kevin .... 800-686-7022 ...... 93 C
kmiller@lincolncollegene.edu
MILLER, Kevin, D .... 973-408-3109 .... 309 E
theoadm@drew.edu
MILLER, Kieron .... 562-907-4236 ...... 79 F
kmiller@whittier.edu
MILLER, Kimberly, A .... 410-822-5400 .... 222 B
kmiller@chesapeake.edu
MILLER, Kimberly, D .... 812-877-8176 .... 179 B
kimberly.miller@rose-hulman.edu
MILLER, Kimela .... 575-835-5888 .... 319 A
kmiller@admin.nmt.edu
MILLER, Koby .... 270-247-8521 .... 204 G
kmiller@midcontinent.edu
MILLER, Kris .... 775-753-2135 .... 302 F
kris.miller@gbcnv.edu
MILLER, L. Christopher ..... 414-288-7206 .... 548 F
l.christopher.miller@marquette.edu
MILLER, Larry .... 228-896-2506 .... 275 E
larry.miller@mgccc.edu
MILLER, Larry, S .... 270-686-4502 .... 203 B
larry.miller@kctcs.edu
MILLER, Laura, M .... 717-766-2511 .... 436 D
lmiller@messiah.edu
MILLER, Lauren .... 312-935-6026 .... 162 G
lmiller@robertmorris.edu
MILLER, Lawrence, W .... 540-432-4133 .... 518 F
millerlw@emu.edu
MILLER, Leangela .... 559-737-6214 ...... 42 D
leangelam@cos.edu
MILLER, Lee .... 740-826-8171 .... 397 A
leem@muskingum.edu
MILLER, Lester .... 908-526-1200 .... 313 D
lmiller@raritanval.edu
MILLER, Lewis, R .... 317-940-9714 .... 170 F
lmiller@butler.edu
MILLER, Linda .... 618-395-1169 .... 152 I
millerli@iecc.edu
MILLER, Linda, G .... 270-809-2154 .... 205 A
lmiller@murraystate.edu
MILLER, Linda, J .... 262-691-5526 .... 555 E
lmiller@wctc.edu
MILLER, Lisa .... 708-210-5767 .... 164 H
lmiller@ssc.edu
MILLER, Lisa .... 563-244-7002 .... 184 F
lmiller@eicc.edu
MILLER, Lisa .... 620-672-5641 .... 196 D
lisam@prattcc.edu
MILLER, Lisa .... 805-378-1572 ...... 77 D
lisamiller@vcccd.edu
MILLER, Lisa .... 516-678-5000 .... 341 F
lmiller@molloy.edu
MILLER, Lisa, R .... 318-342-5431 .... 216 E
lmiller@ulm.edu
MILLER, Lori .... 412-261-2647 .... 432 D
lmiller@kaplan.edu
MILLER, Lucy, T .... 727-816-3448 .... 114 F
millerl@phcc.edu
MILLER, Lyn .... 765-983-1214 .... 171 E
milleli@earlham.edu
MILLER, M. Brad .... 407-851-2525 .... 106 K
brmiller@cci.edu
MILLER, Marc, D .... 706-737-1418 .... 125 G
mmiller@aug.edu
MILLER, Marcia .... 202-685-2650 .... 557 I
millerm@ndu.edu
MILLER, Marcia, K .... 316-284-5315 .... 191 C
mmiller@bethelks.edu
MILLER, Margaret, C .... 847-543-2101 .... 148 B
ecd185@clcillinois.edu
MILLER, Margaret, L .... 423-439-4300 .... 473 F
millerml@etsu.edu
MILLER, Margaret, M .... 609-258-5813 .... 312 G
mmmiller@princeton.edu
MILLER, Marie .... 620-341-5278 .... 192 G
mmiller@emporia.edu
MILLER, Marilynn .... 406-657-2244 .... 295 D
mmiller@msubillings.edu
MILLER, Mark .... 318-869-5117 .... 208 H
mmiller@centenary.edu
MILLER, Mark .... 304-929-1392 .... 541 H
mmiller@mountainstate.edu
MILLER, Mark, A .... 303-245-4775 ...... 86 H
markm@naropa.edu
MILLER, Mark, A .... 740-376-4741 .... 395 G
mark.miller@marietta.edu
MILLER, Marlene, R .... 702-968-2023 .... 303 D
mmiller@roseman.edu
MILLER, Martin .... 409-740-4504 .... 497 F
millerm@tamug.edu
MILLER, Marty, L .... 757-823-9539 .... 522 E
mlmiller@nsu.edu
MILLER, Martyn, J .... 215-204-7708 .... 447 H
martyn.miller@temple.edu
MILLER, Mary .... 203-432-2900 ...... 96 A
mary.miller@yale.edu
MILLER, Mary, E .... 209-228-4430 ...... 74 D
mmiller7@ucmerced.edu
MILLER, Mary, K .... 828-327-7000 .... 369 B
mkmiller@cvcc.edu
MILLER, MaryAnne .... 617-228-2102 .... 239 C
mmiller@bhcc.mass.edu
MILLER, Marylou .... 559-453-7104 ...... 48 A
marylou.miller@fresno.edu
MILLER, Matt .... 989-386-6600 .... 255 C
mmiller@midmich.edu
MILLER, Matthew .... 973-300-2338 .... 315 F
mmiller@sussex.edu
MILLER, Matthew .... 678-839-5500 .... 139 A
mmiller@westga.edu
MILLER, Megan .... 410-225-2420 .... 224 B
memiller@mica.edu
MILLER, Melinda, A .... 315-386-7085 .... 355 E
millerm@canton.edu
MILLER, Melissa .... 843-661-8104 .... 458 B
melissa.miller@fdtc.edu
MILLER, Melissa, A .... 585-785-1639 .... 334 A
millerma@flcc.edu
MILLER, Melissa, C .... 386-312-4106 .... 116 F
melissamiller@sjrstate.edu
MILLER, Melvin .... 802-485-2134 .... 514 C
miller@norwich.edu
MILLER, Merianne .... 828-251-6676 .... 378 D
mmiller@unca.edu
MILLER, Merrill .... 315-228-1000 .... 329 G
mmiller@colgate.edu
MILLER, Michael .... 406-683-7636 .... 294 J
m_miller@umwestern.edu
MILLER, Michael .... 805-893-2118 ...... 75 B
mike.miller@sa.ucsb.edu
MILLER, Michael .... 715-425-0629 .... 552 C
michael.miller@uwrf.edu
MILLER, Michael .... 715-682-1202 .... 549 F
mmiller@northland.edu
MILLER, Michael .... 715-425-0629 .... 552 C
michael.miller@uwrf.edu
MILLER, Michael, A .... 512-471-4110 .... 505 D
mike.miller@austin.utexas.edu
MILLER, Michael, C .... 704-463-3030 .... 375 F
mike.miller@fsmail.pfeiffer.edu
MILLER, Michael, D .... 805-756-2344 ...... 33 I
mdmiller@calpoly.edu
MILLER, Michael, H .... 410-293-1500 .... 559 B
millerm@usna.edu
MILLER, Michael, R .... 330-471-8205 .... 395 F
mimiller@malone.edu
MILLER, Michael, S .... 510-436-1360 ...... 50 H
mmiller@hnu.edu
MILLER, Michael Patrick .... 708-524-5921 .... 150 C
mmiller@dom.edu
MILLER, Michelle .... 802-860-2729 .... 513 C
miller@champlain.edu
MILLER, Michelle, R .... 757-727-5447 .... 519 H
MILLER, Mike .... 229-430-4646 .... 124 A
mike.miller@asurams.edu
MILLER, Mike, B .... 336-386-3235 .... 374 E
millerm@surry.edu
MILLER, Miryom, R .... 845-434-5240 .... 362 B
lehu5@aol.com
MILLER, Morris .... 253-589-5565 .... 532 G
morris.miller@cptc.edu
MILLER, Nancy .... 517-787-0800 .... 252 J
millernancya@jccmi.edu
MILLER, Nancy .... 530-938-5404 ...... 42 E
millern@siskiyous.edu
MILLER, Nancy, W .... 323-226-6301 ...... 55 G
MILLER, Nelson .... 616-301-6800 .... 258 F
millern@cooley.edu
MILLER, Nora, R .... 662-329-7145 .... 276 A
nmiller@vpfa.muw.edu
MILLER, Pam .... 985-380-2436 .... 211 I
pam.miller@ltc.edu
MILLER, Pamela .... 505-566-3217 .... 320 D
millerp@sanjuancollege.edu
MILLER, Pamela .... 402-241-6405 .... 299 I
pamm@northeast.edu
MILLER, Parks .... 706-776-0102 .... 136 A
parksmiller@piedmont.edu
MILLER, Patricia, A .... 816-322-0110 .... 279 D
pat.miller@calvary.edu
MILLER, Patrick .... 817-257-7825 .... 499 C
p.miller@tcu.edu
MILLER, Paul .... 662-243-1902 .... 274 B
pmiller@eastms.edu
MILLER, Paul .... 402-935-9400 .... 299 A
pmiller@nechristian.edu
MILLER, Paul .... 310-476-9777 ...... 28 G
pmiller@ajula.edu
MILLER, Peggy .... 806-742-2781 .... 502 A
peggy.miller@ttu.edu
MILLER, Peter .... 215-596-8542 .... 450 B
p.miller@usciences.edu
MILLER, Rachel, S .... 620-327-8213 .... 193 E
rachelsm@hesston.edu
MILLER, Randall, C .... 304-260-4380 .... 542 G
rmiller@blueridgectc.edu
MILLER, Randi .... 201-360-4073 .... 310 E
rmiller@hccc.edu
MILLER, Ray .... 402-363-5656 .... 301 E
lrmiller@york.edu
MILLER, Ray .... 402-449-2920 .... 297 H
rmiller6053@graceu.edu
MILLER, Remy .... 901-272-5107 .... 471 D
rmiller@mca.edu
MILLER, Richard, A .... 970-247-7426 ...... 84 K
miller_r@fortlewis.edu
MILLER, Richard, B .... 417-625-9565 .... 286 B
miller-r@mssu.edu
MILLER, Richard, C .... 270-745-5468 .... 208 A
richard.c.miller@wku.edu
MILLER, Richard, K .... 781-292-2301 .... 234 H
richard.miller@olin.edu
MILLER, Richard, L .... 713-500-3603 .... 506 F
richard.l.miller@uth.tmc.edu
MILLER, Rick .... 262-691-5323 .... 555 E
rmiller@wctc.edu
MILLER, Rob .... 913-758-6160 .... 197 D
millerr@stmary.edu
MILLER, Robert .... 352-392-1336 .... 120 C
rmiller@admin.ufl.edu
MILLER, Robert .... 908-852-1400 .... 308 E
millerr@centenarycollege.edu
MILLER, Robert .... 269-387-2073 .... 260 C
bob.miller@wmich.edu
MILLER, Robert, B .... 626-585-7170 ...... 61 F
rbmiller@pasadena.edu
MILLER, Robert, B .... 626-585-7178 ...... 61 F
rbmiller@pasadena.edu
MILLER, Robert, B .... 626-585-7170 ...... 61 F
rbmiller@pasadena.edu
MILLER, Robert, G .... 901-333-4368 .... 476 B
rgmiller1@southwest.tn.edu
MILLER, Robert, H .... 225-771-5170 .... 214 I
rhmillerjr@aol.com
MILLER, Robert, H .... 216-368-6269 .... 386 F
robert.miller@case.edu
MILLER, Robert, L .... 217-581-7249 .... 150 E
rlmiller@eiu.edu
MILLER, Robert, M .... 864-294-2111 .... 458 E
bob.miller@furman.edu
MILLER, Robert, R .... 540-828-5383 .... 517 B
rmiller@bridgewater.edu
MILLER, Rodney, E .... 316-978-3389 .... 198 A
rodney.miller@wichita.edu
MILLER, Rodney, E .... 706-419-1134 .... 128 B
miller@covenant.edu
MILLER, Roger .... 269-488-4257 .... 253 A
rmiller@kvcc.edu
MILLER, Roger, M .... 205-329-7909 .... 3 A
roger.miller@ecacolleges.com
MILLER, Roland, G .... 847-543-2551 .... 148 B
com624@clcillinois.edu
MILLER, Ross .... 973-642-3888 .... 307 F
rem@berkeleycollege.edu
MILLER, Ross .... 973-642-3888 .... 323 H
rem@berkeleycollege.edu
MILLER, Ruby .... 480-517-8152 ...... 16 B
ruby.miller@riosalado.edu
MILLER, Rush, G .... 412-648-7747 .... 449 A
rgmiller@mail.pitt.edu
MILLER, Ruth .... 650-306-3125 ...... 67 F
miller@smccd.edu
MILLER, Ruth .... 785-594-4530 .... 190 F
ruth.miller@bakeru.edu
MILLER, Ruth .... 319-895-5267 .... 183 G
rmiller@cornellcollege.edu
MILLER, Ryan .... 918-561-1109 .... 410 D
ryan.miller@okstate.edu
MILLER, Sally .... 707-664-4444 ...... 37 D
sally.miller@sonoma.edu
MILLER, Samira .... 323-822-9700 ...... 72 K
samira.miller@touro.edu
MILLER, Samuel, T .... 229-928-1387 .... 131 F
sam.miller@gsw.edu
MILLER, Sandra .... 973-720-2659 .... 317 D
millers@wpunj.edu
MILLER, Sandra .... 716-827-4348 .... 358 D
millers@trocaire.edu
MILLER, Scott, D .... 304-829-7111 .... 540 H
smiller@bethanywv.edu
MILLER, Shari, K .... 716-673-3438 .... 352 A
shari.miller@fredonia.edu
MILLER, Sharon .... 248-341-2000 .... 256 F
MILLER, Sharon .... 863-297-1093 .... 115 C
smiller@polk.edu
MILLER, Sharyne, A .... 845-341-4689 .... 345 E
sharyne.miller@sunyorange.edu
MILLER, Stacey, A .... 802-656-3434 .... 514 H
stacey.miller@uvm.edu
MILLER, Stan, W .... 574-535-7515 .... 171 G
stanreg@goshen.edu
MILLER, Stephanie .... 417-328-1797 .... 290 A
smiller@sbuniv.edu
MILLER, Stephanie .... 651-793-1278 .... 267 A
stephanie.miller@metrostate.edu
MILLER, Stephanie .... 405-878-2416 .... 409 D
stephanie.miller@okbu.edu
MILLER, Stephen .... 925-631-4970 ...... 64 F
scmiller@stmarys-ca.edu
MILLER, Stephen .... 240-684-2037 .... 227 F
smiller@umuc.edu
MILLER, Steve .... 912-871-1801 .... 135 D
smiller@ogeecheetech.edu
MILLER, Steve .... 206-934-6075 .... 537 D
steve.miller@seattlecolleges.edu
MILLER, Steve, S .... 419-995-8457 .... 392 K
miller.s@rhodesstate.edu
MILLER, Steve, T .... 573-629-3123 .... 282 E
smiller@hlg.edu
MILLER, Stuart, C .... 626-395-6393 ...... 32 H
scmiller@caltech.edu
MILLER, Sue .... 912-260-4427 .... 137 B
sue.miller@sgc.edu
MILLER, Susan .... 508-362-2131 .... 239 D
smiller@capecod.edu
MILLER, Susan, S .... 901-272-5152 .... 471 D
smiller@mca.edu
MILLER, Susan, T .... 219-785-5300 .... 179 A
smiller@pnc.edu
MILLER, Tamara, D .... 913-288-7136 .... 194 C
tmiller@kckcc.edu
MILLER, Tammi .... 406-247-3000 .... 295 F
tmiller@msubilings.edu
MILLER, Tammi .... 406-247-3010 .... 295 D
tmiller@msugillings.edu
MILLER, Tamsin .... 865-882-4730 .... 476 A
miller@roanestate.edu
MILLER, Tana, J .... 806-651-4911 .... 499 A
tmiller@mail.wtamu.edu
MILLER, Tara .... 641-648-4611 .... 186 C
tara.miller@iavalley.edu
MILLER, Tate .... 831-647-4656 ...... 57 F
tate.miller@miis.edu
MILLER, Terence .... 414-288-7289 .... 548 F
terence.miller@marquette.edu
MILLER, Terry .... 937-382-6661 .... 405 I
terry_miller@wilmington.edu
MILLER, Terry, W .... 253-535-7674 .... 536 E
millertw@plu.edu
MILLER, Thomas .... 541-956-7147 .... 420 B
tmiller@roguecc.edu
MILLER, Thomas, D .... 812-877-8210 .... 179 B
thomas.miller@rose-hulman.edu
MILLER, Thomas, K .... 919-513-5006 .... 378 C
tkm@ncsu.edu
MILLER, Thomas, P .... 520-626-0202 ...... 18 L
tpm@email.arizona.edu
MILLER, Tim, I .... 270-809-3978 .... 205 A
tmiller@murraystate.edu
MILLER, Tina .... 909-931-7599 ...... 79 C
tmiller2@westwood.edu
MILLER, Tina .... 906-248-3354 .... 248 H
tinamiller@bmcc.edu
MILLER, Todd .... 908-852-1400 .... 308 E
facilities@centenarycollege.edu
MILLER, Troy .... 516-686-7742 .... 343 D
tmille02@nyit.edu
MILLER, Troy .... 901-320-9700 .... 478 C
tmiller@victory.edu
MILLER, Tyrus .... 831-459-5079 ...... 75 C
tyrus@ucsc.edu
MILLER, Valerie .... 740-593-4141 .... 399 G
millerv@ohio.edu
MILLER, Van .... 254-298-8456 .... 496 D
van.miller@templejc.edu
MILLER, Vernease .... 704-945-7313 .... 375 F
vernease.miller@fsmail.pfeiffer.edu
MILLER, Vince .... 208-282-1045 .... 143 H
millvince@isu.edu
MILLER, Walter .... 877-248-6724 ...... 14 I
wmiller@hmu.edu
MILLER, Walter, C .... 505-277-2331 .... 321 C
wcmiller@unm.edu
MILLER, Wayne, C .... 614-947-6153 .... 391 B
millerw@franklin.edu
MILLER, Wendy .... 847-214-7308 .... 150 F
wmiller@elgin.edu
MILLER, William .... 561-297-3165 .... 119 A
miller@fau.edu
MILLER, William, D .... 419-434-4605 .... 404 B
miller@findlay.edu
MILLER, William, L .... 724-287-8711 .... 423 G
william.miller@bc3.edu

MILLER, Yvonne, R .... 334-395-8800 .... 7 B
ymiller@southuniversity.edu
MILLER-ARMBRISTER, Julane .... 973-972-7525 .... 316 C
millerjw@umdnj.edu
MILLER-BOREN, Joyce ...... 217-641-4528 .... 154 I
millerj@jwcc.edu
MILLER-HOGG, Jen .... 919-760-8581 .... 367 A
jmh@meredith.edu
MILLER HOLST, Sandra .... 602-787-7668 ...... 15 J
sandra.miller.holst@paradisevalley.edu
MILLER-KERMANI, Donn .. 321-674-7648 .... 108 H
dkermani@fit.edu
MILLER-MUTIA, Donnel .... 510-849-8257 ...... 60 G
dmiller-mutia@psr.edu
MILLER-PARKER, Donna ... 206-934-6827 .... 537 F
donna.miller-parker@seattlecolleges.edu
MILLER-REID, M. Susan ... 925-631-4352 ...... 64 F
msm9@stmarys-ca.edu
MILLER START, Roni .... 213-624-1200 ...... 46 L
rmiller@fidm.edu
MILLER-SUBER, Evelyn, V 516-463-6473 .... 335 G
evelyn.v.miller-suber@hofstra.edu
MILLER-YOW, Ronnie .... 501-370-5344 ...... 23 B
miller-yow@philander.edu
MILLERICK, Frank .... 774-354-0481 .... 231 B
frank.millerick@becker.edu
MILLERICK, Timothy, P ..... 903-813-2228 .... 481 A
tmillerick@austincollege.edu
MILLET, Michelle .... 216-397-3053 .... 392 L
mmillet@jcu.edu
MILLETTE, Paul .... 802-287-8224 .... 513 F
millettep@greenmtn.edu
MILLETTE, Paulette .... 207-216-4342 .... 219 C
pmillette@yccc.edu
MILLHORN, David, E .... 865-974-4048 .... 477 C
millhorn@tennessee.edu
MILLHORN, David, E .... 865-974-8913 .... 477 C
millhorn@tennessee.edu
MILLICAN, Valorie, L .... 816-654-7332 .... 283 F
vmillican@kcumb.edu
MILLIGAN, Ariel .... 863-686-1444 .... 106 E
amilligan@cci.edu
MILLIGAN, Laura .... 573-840-9607 .... 290 F
lmilligan@trcc.edu
MILLIGAN, Lee .... 503-297-5544 .... 417 G
lmilligan@ocac.edu
MILLIGAN, Margaret, J ...... 812-888-4277 .... 181 D
pmilligan@vinu.edu
MILLIGAN, Shaun .... 409-740-4830 .... 497 F
milligans@tamug.edu
MILLIGAN, Tom .... 970-491-6621 ...... 83 F
tom.milligan@colostate.edue.edu
MILLIGAN, Troy .... 405-422-1206 .... 411 G
milligant@redlandscc.edu
MILLIGAN, Yuri Rodgers ... 757-727-5253 .... 519 H
yuri.milligan@hamptonu.edu
MILLIKAN, Jessica .... 707-256-7205 ...... 58 F
jmillikan@napavalley.edu
MILLIKEN, Barbara .... 330-494-6170 .... 402 B
bmilliken@starkstate.edu
MILLIKEN, James, B .... 402-472-8636 .... 300 E
president@nebraska.edu
MILLIKEN, Richard .... 402-935-9400 .... 299 A
rmilliken@nechristian.edu
MILLIKEN, Ronald, P .... 207-778-7105 .... 220 C
milliken@maine.edu
MILLIKEN, Stephanie .... 270-534-3394 .... 203 E
stephanie.milliken@kctcs.edu
MILLIKIN, Mary .... 918-343-7615 .... 411 H
mmillikin@rsu.edu
MILLIMAN, Nick .... 269-467-9945 .... 251 B
nmilliman@glenoaks.edu
MILLINGTON, Anne .... 919-735-5151 .... 375 A
annemill@waynecc.edu
MILLION, Christina, C .... 404-413-1430 .... 131 G
cmillion@gsu.edu
MILLIRONS, Anna, S .... 540-985-8530 .... 520 I
asmillirons@jchs.edu
MILLIS, Jack .... 714-532-6049 ...... 39 F
millis@chapman.edu
MILLMAN, Sheila, U .... 310-233-4321 ...... 54 I
millmasu@lahc.edu
MILLNER, F. Ann .... 801-626-6001 .... 511 G
amillner@weber.edu
MILLNER, Timothy .... 410-225-4251 .... 224 B
tmillner@mica.edu
MILLNER, Vaughn, S .... 251-460-6283 .... 9 D
vmillner@usouthal.edu
MILLNITZ, Steve .... 308-398-7407 .... 297 A
smillnitz@cccneb.edu
MILLOY, Gretchen .... 651-255-6162 .... 271 D
gmilloy@unitedseminary.edu
MILLOY, Pamela, M .... 515-263-6023 .... 185 C
pmilloy@grandview.edu
MILLOY, Phyllis .... 757-822-1063 .... 528 G
pmilloy@tcc.edu
MILLS, Andrew .... 212-659-7200 .... 338 A
MILLS, Barry .... 207-725-3221 .... 217 E
bmills@bowdoin.edu
MILLS, Bernice .... 207-221-4314 .... 221 A
bmills@une.edu
MILLS, Brian .... 217-732-3168 .... 156 H
bmills@lincolnchristian.edu
MILLS, Chris .... 610-896-1039 .... 430 G
cmills@haverford.edu
MILLS, Crystal .... 717-290-8719 .... 433 F
cmills@lancasterseminary.edu
MILLS, Dan .... 616-222-1444 .... 250 A
dan.mills@cornerstone.edu
MILLS, Daniel .... 602-386-4151 ...... 11 G
dan.mills@arizonachristian.edu
MILLS, David .... 937-766-7986 .... 386 G
millsd@cedarville.edu
MILLS, Dora .... 207-221-4621 .... 221 A
dmills2@une.edu
MILLS, Douglas .... 202-462-2101 ...... 99 A
mills@iwp.edu
MILLS, Ed .... 785-890-3641 .... 195 H
emills@nwktc.edu
MILLS, Edward .... 916-278-6060 ...... 36 A
emills@csus.edu
MILLS, Edward, D .... 912-478-1193 .... 131 E
edmills@georgiasouthern.edu
MILLS, F. Joe .... 931-221-7444 .... 473 E
millsj@apsu.edu
MILLS, Geofrey .... 413-565-1000 .... 230 G
gmills@baypath.edu
MILLS, George, H .... 253-879-3211 .... 538 H
gmills@pugetsound.edu
MILLS, JR., Gordon, E ...... 251-460-6447 .... 9 D
gmills@usouthal.edu
MILLS, Janie, A .... 319-368-6461 .... 187 H
jmills@mtmercy.edu
MILLS, Jock, S .... 541-737-4514 .... 418 F
jock.mills@oregonstate.edu
MILLS, John .... 606-368-6121 .... 198 C
johnmills@alc.edu
MILLS, John .... 903-223-3049 .... 498 F
john.mills@tamut.edu
MILLS, John, W .... 518-327-6223 .... 345 H
jmills@paulsmiths.edu
MILLS, Jonathan .... 415-575-6283 ...... 32 G
jmills@ciis.edu
MILLS, Joyce, W .... 678-915-7306 .... 137 G
jmills0@spsu.edu
MILLS, Karen .... 602-371-1188 ...... 17 B
MILLS, Katherine .... 574-936-8898 .... 169 D
kathy.mills@ancilla.edu
MILLS, Kelly .... 863-638-7254 .... 123 D
kelly.mills@warner.edu
MILLS, Kim .... 307-754-6404 .... 556 G
kim.mills@northwestcollege.edu
MILLS, Kyra .... 660-562-1134 .... 287 B
kyra@nwmissouri.edu
MILLS, Linda .... 212-998-9712 .... 344 B
linda.mills@nyu.edu
MILLS, Martha .... 530-741-6757 ...... 80 K
mmills@yccd.edu
MILLS, Matthew .... 912-201-8018 .... 137 D
mmills@southuniversity.edu
MILLS, Michael .... 940-397-4428 .... 491 B
michael.mills@mwsu.edu
MILLS, Michael .... 918-631-2510 .... 413 F
michael-mills@utulsa.edu
MILLS, Michael, E .... 847-491-4477 .... 160 E
michael-mills@northwestern.edu
MILLS, Nancy .... 914-633-2625 .... 336 E
nmills@iona.edu
MILLS, Nancy .... 320-308-3976 .... 269 A
nfmills@stcloudstate.edu
MILLS, Ossie .... 918-495-7312 .... 411 C
omills@oru.edu
MILLS, Patti .... 201-692-2132 .... 310 A
patti_mills@fdu.edu
MILLS, Patty .... 513-244-1646 .... 388 E
patty_mills@mail.msj.edu
MILLS, Priscilla, L .... 928-523-7855 ...... 16 I
priscilla.mills@nau.edu
MILLS, R. Dean .... 573-882-6686 .... 291 B
millsr@missouri.edu
MILLS, Randy, W .... 336-750-2706 .... 380 B
millsrw@wssu.edu
MILLS, Ron .... 513-874-0432 .... 394 I
MILLS, Ronald .... 937-746-6633 .... 395 C
rmills@lincolntech.com
MILLS, Sandra, M .... 513-487-3206 .... 335 B
smills@huc.edu
MILLS, Sandy .... 262-646-6508 .... 549 E
smills@nashotah.edu
MILLS, William, R .... 617-552-8661 .... 232 B
william.mills@bc.edu
MILLS-JONES, Johnnie ...... 601-432-6234 .... 274 G
johnnie.mills.jones@jsums.edu
MILLS WOOLSEY, Linda ... 585-567-9315 .... 336 B
lindamills.woolsey@houghton.edu
MILLSAP, Byron .... 405-325-5161 .... 413 C
bmillsap@ou.edu
MILLSAPPS, Michael .... 970-339-6376 ...... 81 A
michael.millsapps@aims.edu
MILLSAPS, Brooke .... 828-298-3325 .... 380 D
bmillsaps@warren-wilson.edu
MILLSAPS, John .... 404-962-3053 .... 139 B
john.millsaps@usg.edu
MILLSON-MARTULA, Christopher, A .... 434-544-8204 .... 521 B
millsonmartula@lynchburg.edu
MILLSTONE, Linda, H .... 512-471-2437 .... 505 D
lindam@austin.utexas.edu
MILLUSH, Mary Ann .... 630-942-2269 .... 148 A
millush@cod.edu
MILLWOOD, Kent, A .... 864-231-2049 .... 455 C
kmillwood@andersonuniversity.edu
MILNARICH, Sarah .... 361-354-2741 .... 483 B
sarahm@coastalbend.edu
MILNE, Sheila .... 252-399-6326 .... 362 E
smilne@barton.edu
MILNER, Eric .... 401-341-2218 .... 454 D
eric.milner@salve.edu
MILNER, Jocelyn, L .... 608-263-5658 .... 550 J
jlmilner@wisc.edu
MILNER, Michael .... 617-732-2800 .... 241 C
michael.milner@mcphs.edu
MILNER, Susan, V .... 336-633-0174 .... 373 A
svmilner@randolph.edu
MILNES, Robert, W .... 940-565-4003 .... 504 D
milnes@unt.edu
MILONE-NUZZO, Paula, F 814-863-0245 .... 438 G
pxm36@psu.edu
MILOWICKI, Gene, V .... 904-317-3805 .... 109 F
gmilowic@fscj.edu
MILROY, James, B .... 585-245-5601 .... 353 C
milroy@geneseo.edu
MILSO, Lisa .... 978-762-4000 .... 240 D
lmilso@northshore.edu
MILSOM, Penny .... 443-840-5426 .... 222 D
mmilsom@ccbcmd.edu
MILSTEIN, Linda .... 732-224-2214 .... 308 A
lmilstein@brookdalecc.edu
MILSTEIN, Marc .... 212-960-5233 .... 361 M
mmilstei@yu.edu
MILSTONE, David, M .... 508-999-8640 .... 237 A
dmilstone@umassd.edu
MILTENBERGER, Susan ..... 410-225-2201 .... 224 B
smiltenb@mica.edu
MILTON, Alice .... 205-929-6306 .... 5 E
amilton@lawsonstate.edu
MILTON, Barbara, J .... 973-655-4349 .... 311 F
miltonb@mail.montclair.edu
MILTON, Michael .... 704-366-5066 .... 276 F
mmilton@rts.edu
MILTON, Michael, A .... 704-366-5066 .... 376 B
mmilton@rts.edu
MILTON, Michael, A .... 704-366-5066 .... 115 K
michaelmilton@rts.edu
MILTON, Mike .... 704-366-5066 .... 276 F
mmilton@rts.edu
MILTON, Sandy, B .... 770-720-5661 .... 136 C
sbm1@reinhardt.edu
MILTON, Shirlette, G .... 713-313-7551 .... 500 B
milton_sg@tsu.edu
MILZ, George .... 713-646-1864 .... 494 I
gmilz@stcl.edu
MIMMS, Jacqueline .... 661-654-2160 ...... 34 A
jmimms@csub.edu
MIMMS, Lee, S .... 818-779-8040 ...... 53 B
lmimms@kingsuniversity.edu
MIMS, Janet .... 843-863-8004 .... 456 B
jmims@csuniv.edu
MIMS, Jason .... 432-264-5008 .... 488 B
jmims@howardcollege.edu
MIMS, Lloyd .... 561-803-2400 .... 114 C
lloyd_mims@pba.edu
MIMS, Yolanda, L .... 504-286-5335 .... 214 J
ymims@suno.edu
MIN, Sangki .... 913-288-7686 .... 194 C
smin@kckcc.edu
MINAAI, Brian .... 808-956-7935 .... 141 E
bminaai@hawaii.edu
MINAR, Thomas .... 202-885-3424 ...... 97 D
tjm@american.edu
MINARDI, Judy .... 617-573-8415 .... 245 B
jminardi@suffolk.edu
MINARDI, Lonna, J .... 602-216-3165 ...... 11 F
lminardi@argosy.edu
MINATOYA, Lydia .... 206-934-3712 .... 537 D
lydia.minatoya@seattlecolleges.edu
MINCH, Kevin .... 660-785-5384 .... 290 G
kminch@truman.edu
MINCHEFF, Chris .... 303-753-6046 ...... 88 B
MINCHELLO, Brian .... 617-879-2205 .... 246 C
bminchello@wheelock.edu
MINCKLER, Tye .... 254-968-9877 .... 497 A
minckler@tarleton.edu
MINCKS, Kathy .... 907-564-8272 ...... 10 D
kmincks.akpacprop@gci.net
MINDEMAN, Tad .... 706-419-1434 .... 128 B
mindeman@covenant.edu
MINDERMAN, James, W ... 812-888-4227 .... 181 D
jwminderman@vinu.edu
MINE, Jodi .... 808-934-2742 .... 142 A
mine@hawaii.edu
MINEHAN, Cathy .... 617-521-3806 .... 244 F
cathy.minehan@simmons.edu
MINEO, Michael .... 718-817-4931 .... 334 C
mineo@fordham.edu
MINER, Judy, C .... 650-949-7200 ...... 47 H
minerjudy@fhda.edu
MINER, Madonne .... 801-626-6424 .... 511 G
madonneminer@weber.edu
MINER, Marlene, R .... 513-745-5660 .... 403 F
marlene.miner@uc.edu
MINERVINI, Ron .... 617-730-7222 .... 243 D
ron.minervini@newbury.edu
MINFORD, Joell .... 412-392-3422 .... 445 A
jminford@pointpark.edu
MING, Amanda .... 248-476-1122 .... 254 G
aming@mispp.edu
MINGEE, Sheila .... 217-709-0923 .... 156 C
smingee@lakeviewcol.edu
MINGENBACK, Mary .... 620-341-5413 .... 192 G
mmingenb@emporia.edu
MINGER, David .... 503-491-7316 .... 417 B
david.minger@mhcc.edu
MINGLE, James, J .... 607-255-3903 .... 331 B
jjm19@cornell.edu
MINGO, Rhonda .... 864-596-9016 .... 457 E
rhonda.mingo@converse.edu
MINGO, Susan .... 207-454-1032 .... 219 B
smingo@wccc.me.edu
MINHAS, Omer .... 419-772-2529 .... 398 H
o-minhas@onu.edu
MINI, Susan .... 815-753-0495 .... 160 B
smini@niu.edu
MINICK, Evelyn .... 610-660-1905 .... 446 C
minick@sju.edu
MINICK, Thomas .... 610-790-1901 .... 421 G
thomas.minick@alvernia.edu
MINICK, Thomas, R .... 239-280-2525 .... 101 I
thomas.minick@avemaria.edu
MINIEA, D. Scott .... 573-592-1633 .... 293 D
scott.miniea@williamwoods.edu
MINIS, Elizabeth .... 816-604-4114 .... 285 E
lisa.minis@mcckc.edu
MINK, Randy, L .... 412-397-4901 .... 445 H
mink@rmu.edu
MINK, Rose .... 901-751-8453 .... 471 F
rmink@mabts.edu
MINK-SALAS, Kandy .... 657-278-3211 ...... 35 B
kmink@fullerton.edu
MINKIEWICZ, Jennifer, V .. 216-221-8584 .... 405 E
jennifermink@vmcad.edu
MINKLER, James .... 509-533-3538 .... 533 C
jim.minkler@spokanefalls.edu
MINKLER, Jim .... 509-533-3764 .... 533 A
jimm@spokanefalls.edu
MINKLER, Steven .... 860-343-5706 ...... 91 G
sminkler@mxcc.commnet.edu
MINKOWITZ, Honey .... 201-761-7130 .... 314 F
hminkowitz@spc.edu
MINKS, Larry .... 580-745-2500 .... 412 C
lminks@se.edu
MINNE, Erin .... 309-438-7681 .... 153 D
eminne@ilstu.edu
MINNER, Sam, H .... 540-831-5404 .... 523 A
sminner@radford.edu
MINNICH, Bryan .... 785-827-5541 .... 194 F
bryan.minnich@kwu.edu
MINNICH, Donna .... 973-596-3603 .... 312 C
donna.minnich@njit.edu
MINNICH, Peggy .... 513-244-4531 .... 388 E
peggy_minnich@mail.msj.edu
MINNICH, Thomas .... 304-734-6699 .... 542 H
tminnich@bridgemont.edu
MINNICH, William .... 650-991-3525 ...... 44 E
wminnich@devry.edu
MINNICK, Ann, M .... 651-696-6036 .... 264 J
aminnick@macalester.edu
MINNICK, Charlie .... 563-242-4023 .... 182 C
charlie.minnick@ashford.edu
MINNICK, Shea .... 770-960-1298 .... 132 F
sminnick@ict-ils.edu
MINNICK, Susan .... 262-691-5392 .... 555 E
sminnick@wctc.edu
MINNICK, William, C .... 712-707-7226 .... 188 D
bminnick@nwciowa.edu
MINNIEFIELD, Angela, L ... 323-563-4897 ...... 39 G
angelaminniefield@cdrewu.edu
MINNIHAN, Jacki .... 815-921-4482 .... 162 H
j.minnihan@rockvalleycollege.edu
MINNIS, Phil .... 618-985-3741 .... 154 G
philminnis@jalc.edu
MINNIS, Sarah, L .... 919-536-7200 .... 370 C
minniss@durhamtech.edu
MINNIS, Stephen, D .... 913-360-7400 .... 191 A
sminnis@benedictine.edu
MINNITI, Lea .... 513-745-2872 .... 406 E
minnitil@xavier.edu
MINNIX, Roy .... 914-337-9300 .... 330 G
roy.minnix@concordia-ny.edu
MINOR, Diana, Y .... 909-869-3704 ...... 33 J
dyminor@csupomona.edu
MINOR, Diane .... 312-553-2500 .... 147 B
dminor1@ccc.edu
MINOR, DoVeanna, F .... 205-348-8462 .... 8 E
dfulton@as.ua.edu
MINOR, Frankie, D .... 573-882-7275 .... 291 B
minorf@missouri.edu
MINOR, JR., Hassan .... 202-806-2530 ...... 98 E
svp@howard.edu
MINOR, Leslie .... 541-383-7238 .... 414 I
lminor@cocc.edu
MINOR, Lottie .... 901-369-0835 ...... 99 G
lottie.minor@strayer.edu

MINOR, Scott 916-631-8108 33 F
MINOR, Tamra 518-956-8110 351 E tminor@uamail.albany.edu
MINOW, Martha 617-495-4601 235 D minow@law.harvard.edu
MINTER, Doug 309-268-8385 151 I doug.minter@heartland.edu
MINTER, Doug, O 507-933-7527 263 J dminter@gustavus.edu
MINTER, Michelle 609-258-6110 312 G mminter@princeton.edu
MINTER, Penny 731-426-7550 470 B pminter@lanecollege.edu
MINTERN, Janet 252-493-7286 372 H jmintern@email.pittcc.edu
MINTON, James 980-598-1800 365 I james.minton@jwu.edu
MINTON, Randy, F 912-583-3109 126 F rminton@bpc.edu
MINTZ, Alan, E 718-933-6700 341 G amintz@monroecollege.edu
MINTZ, Marcia, B 202-687-6400 98 D mbm23@georgetown.edu
MINUS, Daryl 252-638-7200 370 A minusd@cravencc.edu
MINUS, Molly, E 512-448-8581 493 E mollym@stedwards.edu
MIRABAL, Elizabeth 602-216-3163 11 F emirabal@argosy.edu
MIRABAL, Gloria 787-480-2355 561 E gmirabal@sanjuancapital.com
MIRABAL, Larry 505-424-2316 318 D lmirabal@iaia.edu
MIRABELL, Julie, L 440-964-4316 393 E jmirabell@kent.edu
MIRABELLA, Mike 888-974-3436 46 M mmirabella@fidm.edu
MIRABILE, Kathleen 800-231-3803 12 E
MIRABILE, Kathleen 602-212-0501 17 C kmirabile@theparalegalinstitute.edu
MIRABITO, Donna 248-689-8282 259 E dmirabit@walshcollege.edu
MIRABITO, Michael 570-348-6209 435 F mirabito@marywood.edu
MIRACKY, SJ, James, F 410-617-2327 223 I jjmiracky@loyola.edu
MIRACLE, William, D 540-828-5380 517 B wmiracle@bridgewater.edu
MIRANDA, Albert 714-484-7394 59 D amiranda@cypresscollege.edu
MIRANDA, Alex 805-969-3626 60 J amiranda@pacifica.edu
MIRANDA, Candida 312-567-3134 153 C miranda@iit.edu
MIRANDA, Deana 312-935-6657 162 G dmiranda@robertmorris.edu
MIRANDA, Edmund (Rick) 562-860-2451 39 A ermiranda@cerritos.edu
MIRANDA, Elizabeth 787-250-1912 563 G emiranda@metro.inter.edu
MIRANDA, Elizabeth 787-738-2161 567 D elizabeth.miranda@upr.edu
MIRANDA, Enid 787-841-2000 565 B emiranda@pucpr.edu
MIRANDA, Gloria 310-660-3735 45 E gmiranda@elcamino.edu
MIRANDA, Marie, L 734-764-2550 259 A mlmirand@umich.edu
MIRANDA, Mark 732-571-3593 311 E mmiranda@monmouth.edu
MIRANDA, Mirta 305-593-1223 102 H mmiranda@albizu.edu
MIRANDA, Paul 718-429-6600 359 G paul.miranda@vaughn.edu
MIRANDA, Rick 970-491-6614 83 F rick.miranda@colostate.edu
MIRANDA, Robert 714-992-7090 59 E bmiranda@fullcoll.edu
MIRANDA, Rowan, A 734-764-7270 259 A rowanm@umich.edu
MIRANDA, Steve 323-468-0404 50 L
MIRANDA-RODRÍGUEZ, Edna 787-993-8860 567 B edna.miranda1@upr.edu
MIRANTE, Aida 401-341-2140 454 D mirantea@salve.edu
MIRCH, Mary 818-240-1000 48 D mmirch@glendale.edu
MIRECKI, Julie 920-693-1193 554 C julie.mirecki@gotoltc.edu
MIRELES, Rod 936-261-1905 496 G rmireles@pvamu.edu
MIRENDA, Rosalie, M 610-558-5501 437 D rmirenda@neumann.edu
MIRES, Mike 208-769-7783 144 D
MIRIZZI, Ray 859-572-6421 205 H mirizzir1@nku.edu
MIRMIRAN, Amir 305-348-2522 119 C amir.mirmiran@fiu.edu
MIROCHA, Ken 563-441-4116 184 H kmirocha@eicc.edu
MIRON, Luis 504-865-3530 213 F lmiron@loyno.edu
MIRON, Nancy 323-343-3050 35 D nmiron@cslanet.calstatela.edu
MIROTZNIK, Jerrold 718-951-5024 326 F jerrym@brooklyn.cuny.edu
MIRRO, Roberta 631-249-3048 356 A sm711/bncollege@bncollege.com
MIRSHAB, Bahman 248-204-3050 254 B bmirshab@ltu.edu
MIRUS, Tarrah 229-391-5014 123 H tmirus@abac.edu
MIRZA, Zoaib 312-662-4233 144 H zmirza@adler.edu
MISAK, M. David 580-774-3275 412 F david.misak@swosu.edu
MISANTONE, Louis 781-762-1211 234 F drlou@fine-ne.com
MISCAVAGE, Denise 570-674-6248 436 F dmiscava@misericordia.edu
MISCH, Donald 303-492-0025 88 H donald.misch@colorado.edu
MISCHE, Terri 320-308-6675 269 A tamische@stcloudstate.edu
MISCHKE, Joel, P 414-443-8812 553 D joel.mischke@wlc.edu
MISCHKE, Trevor 402-972-4250 464 H
MISERENDINO, Peter 203-287-3026 93 F paier.admin@snet.net
MISGEN, Sherry 312-899-5216 164 C smisgen@saic.edu
MISHEK, Mark 651-213-4006 264 B mmishek@hazelden.edu
MISHLER, Jeremy 231-591-2345 250 H mishlerj@ferris.edu
MISHLER, Richard 814-886-6339 437 B rmishler@mtaloy.edu
MISHOE, Shelley, C 757-683-4960 522 F smishoe@odu.edu
MISHRA, Banamber 337-475-5010 215 G bmishra@mcneese.edu
MISHRA, Sharda, D 615-327-6156 471 C smishra@mmc.edu
MISHRA, Tara 479-788-7002 24 D tara.mishra@uafs.edu
MISIANO, Chris 434-592-3144 520 K cjmisiano@liberty.edu
MISICK, Jennifer 718-289-5906 326 E jennifer.misick@bcc.cuny.edu
MISKO, Elaine, J 412-578-6137 424 I miskoej@carlow.edu
MISKOVIC, Linda 714-628-4901 63 G miskovic_linda@sccollege.edu
MISKUS, Lynn 219-473-4310 170 G lmiskus@ccsj.edu
MISNER, John 706-778-8500 136 A jmisner@piedmont.edu
MISNER, John 706-776-0115 136 A jmisner@piedmont.edu
MISRA, Hara, P 540-231-4000 518 I
MISRA, Ravi, P 414-955-8778 548 G rmisra@mcw.edu
MISSAKIAN, Anais 401-454-6184 454 B amissaki@risd.edu
MISSEL, Chris 912-588-2580 124 C cmissel@altamahatech.edu
MISSELL, Katherine 619-260-4551 76 D kmissell@sandiego.edu
MISSURELLI, David 262-551-6200 546 I dmissurelli@carthage.edu
MISTICK, Barbara, K 717-262-2000 452 C barbara.mistick@wilson.edu
MISTO, RSM, Leona 401-341-2229 454 D mistol@salve.edu
MITCHAM, Aaron 412-396-5098 428 D mitchama@duq.edu
MITCHAM, Larry, G 678-359-5059 132 A larrym@gdn.edu
MITCHELL, Alan 256-331-5362 6 B mitchell@nwscc.edu
MITCHELL, Amanda 706-754-7724 135 A amitchell@northgatech.edu
MITCHELL, Andrea 954-783-7339 106 J amitchell@cci.edu
MITCHELL, Annette 706-295-6359 130 E 1208mgr@fheg.follett.com
MITCHELL, Asia 312-341-2107 163 B amitchell@roosevelt.edu
MITCHELL, Audrey 256-765-4124 9 C admitchell@una.edu
MITCHELL, Bede 912-478-5116 131 E wbmitch@georgiasouthern.edu
MITCHELL, Beth 828-765-7351 372 A bmitchell@mayland.edu
MITCHELL, Betsy 626-395-6148 32 H betsy.mitchell@caltech.edu
MITCHELL, Bonnie 508-626-4651 238 A bonniem@framingham.edu
MITCHELL, Bradley, J 937-382-6661 405 I brad_mitchell@wilmington.edu
MITCHELL, Brenda 479-788-7519 24 D brenda.mitchell@uafs.edu
MITCHELL, Brenda, S 301-322-0858 225 F bmitchell@pgcc.edu
MITCHELL, Brian 504-865-5261 215 C brian@tulane.edu
MITCHELL, Brian, S 504-314-2818 215 C brian@tulane.edu
MITCHELL, Carl 910-678-8373 370 E mitchelc@faytechcc.edu
MITCHELL, Cathryn 912-538-3101 137 E cmitchell@southeasterntech.edu
MITCHELL, Cathy 806-894-9611 494 G cmitchell@southplainscollege.edu
MITCHELL, Charles 607-735-1937 332 I cmitchell@elmira.edu
MITCHELL, Chase 435-283-7340 512 C chase.mitchell@snow.edu
MITCHELL, Chrisie 845-431-8976 332 D chrisie.mitchell@sunydutchess.edu
MITCHELL, Cindy 765-269-5380 176 D cmitchell@ivytech.edu
MITCHELL, Craig 206-517-4541 537 G cmitchell@siom.edu
MITCHELL, Daisy 773-481-8830 147 I dmitchell@ccc.edu
MITCHELL, David 415-503-6218 66 A dlmitchell@sfcm.edu
MITCHELL, David, B 301-405-5726 227 B chief@umpd.umd.edu
MITCHELL, David, C 360-475-7100 536 D dmitchell@olympic.edu
MITCHELL, Debbie 760-921-5408 61 C dmitchell@paloverde.edu
MITCHELL, Debbie 734-432-4076 254 D doffman@madonna.edu
MITCHELL, Debra 562-947-8755 71 A debramitchell@scuhs.edu
MITCHELL, Debra 562-902-3311 71 A debramitchell@scuhs.edu
MITCHELL, Don 602-386-4183 11 G don.mitchell@arizonachristian.edu
MITCHELL, Donald 217-206-6690 167 C mitchell.donald@uis.edu
MITCHELL, Donna 740-245-7302 404 E mitchell@rio.edu
MITCHELL, Douglas 951-827-5802 74 E douglas.mitchell@ucr.edu
MITCHELL, III, Earnest, L 731-426-7604 470 B ernest@lanecollege.edu
MITCHELL, IV, Enzley 312-567-7124 153 C emitche2@iit.edu
MITCHELL, Franklin, L 864-488-8239 459 B fmitchell@limestone.edu
MITCHELL, Gary 575-763-0535 508 E mitchellg@wbu.edu
MITCHELL, Geoffrey 601-984-1115 277 E gmitchell@umc.edu
MITCHELL, Gerald, A 919-866-5143 374 H gamitchell@waketech.edu
MITCHELL, Gregory 843-477-2032 458 H greg.mitchell@hgtc.edu
MITCHELL, Gregory 903-886-5719 498 B gregory.mitchell@tamuc.edu
MITCHELL, Horace 661-654-2241 34 A hmitchell@csub.edu
MITCHELL, James 212-678-4084 357 G jm331@tc.columbia.edu
MITCHELL, James, M 334-876-9231 4 B jmitchell@wccs.edu
MITCHELL, James, W 202-806-6565 98 E jwmitchell@howard.edu
MITCHELL, Jaynie 281-476-1501 493 H jaynie.mitchell@sjcd.edu
MITCHELL, Jeff 319-398-4983 187 B jmitche@kirkwood.edu
MITCHELL, Jennifer, E 757-455-8785 530 C jemitchell@vwc.edu
MITCHELL, Joan 801-274-3280 512 F jmitchell@wgu.edu
MITCHELL, Joann 215-898-6630 448 J joannm@pobox.upenn.edu
MITCHELL, John 912-344-2529 124 G john.mitchell@armstrong.edu
MITCHELL, Johnica 704-437-6808 125 H jmitchel@augustatech.edu
MITCHELL, Judy 815-280-6640 154 J jmitchel@jjc.edu
MITCHELL, Karen 615-230-3505 476 C karen.mitchell@volstate.edu
MITCHELL, Kathy, J 276-739-2440 529 A kmitchell@vhcc.edu
MITCHELL, Ken, H 919-209-2112 371 F khmitchell@johnstoncc.edu
MITCHELL, Kent, H 781-280-3571 240 B mitchellk@middlesex.mass.edu
MITCHELL, Kerrie 575-492-2114 321 H kmitchell@usw.edu
MITCHELL, Kim 502-456-6508 206 H kmitchell@sullivan.edu
MITCHELL, Larry, K 252-451-8224 372 E lkm@nash.cc.nc.us
MITCHELL, Laura 970-225-4860 82 A laura.mitchell@collegeamerica.edu
MITCHELL, Lawrence, E 216-368-3283 386 F lawrence.e.mitchell@case.edu
MITCHELL, Lorraine, C 252-862-1272 373 C lcmitchell@roanokechowan.edu
MITCHELL, Lynn 215-884-8942 452 D academicdean@woninstitute.edu
MITCHELL, M. Ellen 312-567-3362 153 C mitchelle@iit.edu
MITCHELL, Margaret 773-702-8221 166 G mmm17@uchicago.edu
MITCHELL, Maria 610-372-4721 445 C mmitchell@racc.edu
MITCHELL, Marionette 713-525-3120 505 A marion@stthom.edu
MITCHELL, Mark 540-338-1776 522 G
MITCHELL, Mary Lou 619-239-0391 37 F mmitchell@cwsl.edu
MITCHELL, Matt 573-592-5301 293 B matt.mitchell@westminster-mo.edu
MITCHELL, Melissa 308-432-6221 299 E mmitchell@csc.edu
MITCHELL, Monique 252-862-1262 373 C mitchellm@roanokechowan.edu
MITCHELL, Patrice, B 912-344-2590 124 G patrice.mitchell@armstrong.edu
MITCHELL, Patricia 301-860-3416 228 A pmitchell@bowiestate.edu
MITCHELL, Patricia 270-831-9652 202 D patty.mitchell@kctcs.edu
MITCHELL, Patricia 601-979-2282 274 G patricia.b.mitchell@jsums.edu
MITCHELL, Paula 915-831-4030 486 G pmitche8@epcc.edu
MITCHELL, Peg, P 302-356-6810 97 C peg.p.mitchell@wilmu.edu
MITCHELL, Permon 803-934-3175 459 G pmitchell@morris.edu
MITCHELL, Randolph 904-470-8150 105 G randolph.mitchell@ewc.edu
MITCHELL, Renee, D 773-995-2040 146 G rmitch26@csu.edu
MITCHELL, Richard, L 718-855-3661 336 D rmitchell@idc.edu
MITCHELL, Rick, L 330-287-1277 399 A mitchell.246@osu.edu
MITCHELL, Robert 504-398-2250 214 B rmitchell@olhcc.edu
MITCHELL, Robin 563-288-6103 184 G rmitchell@eicc.edu
MITCHELL, Ronald, S 417-625-9531 286 B mitchell-r@mssu.edu
MITCHELL, Rose 973-748-9000 307 H rose_mitchell@bloomfield.edu
MITCHELL, Rose 815-802-8110 155 A rmitchell@kcc.edu
MITCHELL, Rosemary, C 609-497-7750 312 F seminary.relations@ptsem.edu
MITCHELL, Sandra, L 303-964-5304 87 I smitchell@regis.edu
MITCHELL, Saralyn 256-233-8146 1 E saralyn.mitchell@athens.edu
MITCHELL, Shannon 502-968-7191 199 D shmitchell@brownmackie.edu
MITCHELL, Sharon, L 716-645-2720 351 G smitch@buffalo.edu
MITCHELL, Sheila 731-661-5953 477 B smitchell@uu.edu
MITCHELL, Stephen 845-434-5750 357 A smitchell@sullivan.suny.edu
MITCHELL, Stephen, R 202-687-3922 98 D mitchelr@georgetown.edu
MITCHELL, Steve 225-216-8404 209 H mitchells@mybrcc.edu
MITCHELL, Tedd 806-743-2900 502 B tedd.mitchell@ttuhsc.edu
MITCHELL, Thomas, J 352-392-5407 120 C tmitchell@uff.ufl.edu
MITCHELL, Thomas, J 716-827-2471 358 D mitchellt@trocaire.edu
MITCHELL, Thomas, R 956-326-2460 497 D tmitchell@tamiu.edu
MITCHELL, Todd 270-534-3256 203 E todd.mitchell@kctcs.edu
MITCHELL, Venita 573-592-4239 293 D vmitchel@williamwoods.edu
MITCHELL, William 413-545-2222 236 F wmitchell@cns.umass.edu
MITCHELL, William, A 508-999-9130 237 A wmitchell@umassd.edu
MITCHELL-CRUMP, Pamela 860-512-2605 91 F pmitchell-crump@mcc.commnet.edu
MITCHELL JACKSON, Susan 214-828-8266 497 C smitchelljackson@bcd.tamhsc.edu
MITCHELL-KERNAN, Claudia 310-825-4383 74 C cmkernan@gdnet.ucla.edu
MITCHELSON, Ron 252-328-9471 377 E mitchelsonr@ecu.edu
MITCHLEY, Jill 570-484-2526 443 B jmitchle@lhup.edu
MITCHUM, Lori, A 270-809-2596 205 A lori.mitchum@murraystate.edu
MITHANI, Alex 800-533-3378 138 F amithani@uofa.edu
MITHANI, Amynah 713-973-3136 486 C amithani@devry.edu
MITHANI, Nick 800-533-3378 138 F nmithani@uofa.edu

MITIKU, Abainesh ... 304-766-3096 ... 544 F mitiku@wvstateu.edu
MITJANS, Dolores ... 787-882-2065 ... 566 A compras@unitecpr.net
MITMAN, Gregg ... 608-262-1723 ... 550 J gmitman@med.wisc.edu
MITNICK, Eric ... 619-961-4303 ... 72 J emitnick@tjsl.edu
MITOVA, Katia ... 312-467-8607 ... 146 F kmitova@thechicagoschool.edu
MITRA, Brian ... 718-368-5115 ... 328 A bmitra@kbcc.cuny.edu
MITSUI, Mark ... 206-934-3601 ... 537 D mark.mitsui@seattlecolleges.edu
MITSUI, Mark ... 206-934-3601 ... 537 C mark.mitsui@seattlecolleges.edu
MITTA, Ave, M ... 540-985-4097 ... 520 I ammitta@jchs.edu
MITTELMEIER, Ashley, E ... 304-457-6323 ... 540 E mittelmeierae@ab.edu
MITTELSTAEDT, Robert, E . 480-965-2468 ... 11 J robert.mittelstaedt@asu.edu
MITTEN, Edeline ... 718-270-2422 ... 352 D emitten@downstate.edu
MITTERNDORFER, Sylvia .. 757-221-3595 ... 518 A smmitt@wm.edu
MITTLEMAN, Michael, H ... 215-780-1280 ... 446 G president@salus.edu
MITTLESTEAD, Eric ... 559-730-3908 ... 42 D ericm@cos.edu
MITTMAN, Paul, A ... 480-858-9100 ... 18 E p.mittman@scnm.edu
MITTON, Gregory, S ... 484-664-3175 ... 437 C mitton@muhlenberg.edu
MITTS, Kenneth ... 210-784-2000 ... 498 E kenneth.mitts@tamusa.tamus.edu
MITTUCH, Maggie, A ... 253-879-3673 ... 538 H mmittuch@pugetsound.edu
MITZE, Marne, D ... 310-506-4451 ... 61 H marne.mitze@pepperdine.edu
MITZEL, Thomas, M ... 512-448-8460 ... 493 E thomasmi@stedwards.edu
MIX, Kerry ... 281-998-6150 ... 494 B kerry.mix@sjcd.edu
MIXNER, Mark, P ... 610-436-2731 ... 444 A mmixner@wcupa.edu
MIXON, Bill ... 205-853-1200 ... 5 C bmixon@jeffstateonline.com
MIXON, Janine ... 415-442-7284 ... 48 F jmixon@ggu.edu
MIXON, Margie ... 318-345-9270 ... 210 H margiemixon@ladelta.edu
MIXON, Margie, F ... 318-397-6130 ... 210 J mmixon@myneltc.edu
MIXTER, John ... 401-341-2334 ... 454 D mixterj@salve.edu
MIYAMOTO, Michael, H ... 563-589-3270 ... 189 F mmiyamoto@dbq.edu
MIYAMOTO, Norma ... 760-744-1150 ... 61 D nmiyamoto@palomar.edu
MIYARES, Javier ... 301-985-7077 ... 227 F president-office@umuc.edu
MIYASAKI, Kevin, T ... 208-496-1155 ... 143 A miyasakik@byui.edu
MIYASHIRO, James ... 951-222-8586 ... 64 A james.miyashiro@rcc.edu
MIYASHIRO, Ross ... 562-938-4130 ... 54 E rmiyashiro@lbcc.edu
MIZAK, Pat ... 716-888-3202 ... 325 F mizakp@canisius.edu
MIZANIN, Lynn, M ... 216-834-1400 ... 396 D mizanin.lynn@acr.edu
MIZE, Charles ... 478-301-2951 ... 134 A mize_c@mercer.edu
MIZE, Chuck ... 918-456-5511 ... 409 A mize@nsuok.edu
MIZE, Kyle, C ... 325-649-8049 ... 488 C kmize@hputx.edu
MIZE, Lewis ... 620-227-9376 ... 192 E lmize@dc3.edu
MIZE, Matt ... 478-445-5771 ... 130 B matt.mize@gcsu.edu
MIZE, Nancy ... 252-328-6387 ... 377 E mizen@ecu.edu
MIZELL, Catherine, S ... 865-974-3245 ... 477 C cmizell@tennessee.edu
MIZERA, Peter, J ... 708-235-2210 ... 151 E pmizera@govst.edu
MIZUTOWICZ, Wanda ... 972-883-2603 ... 506 A wmizuto@utdallas.edu
MLADENOVIC, Jeanette ... 503-494-4460 ... 418 D provost@ohsu.edu
MLODZIK, Leigh, D ... 920-748-8704 ... 550 D mlodzikl@ripon.edu
MLYNARSKI, Miriam ... 856-227-7200 ... 308 D mmlynarski@camdencc.edu
MNCUBE-BARNES, Fatima 615-327-5770 ... 471 C fbarnes@mmc.edu
MO, Jayne ... 516-686-7584 ... 343 D owbooks@nyit.edu
MOAK, James ... 502-863-7970 ... 201 A james_moak@georgetowncollege.edu
MOATS, Nancy, I ... 405-224-3140 ... 413 E nmoats@usao.edu
MOATS, Scott ... 952-446-4210 ... 263 C moatss@crown.edu
MOBASSERI, Maria ... 217-403-4599 ... 161 C mmobasseri@parkland.edu
MOBERG, Bret ... 847-578-8308 ... 163 C bret.moberg@rosalindfranklin.edu
MOBERG, Kathleen ... 408-864-8292 ... 47 G mobergkathleen@deanza.edu
MOBLEY, Bob ... 863-638-7213 ... 123 D bob.mobley@warner.edu
MOBLEY, Cathryn ... 434-832-7635 ... 526 E mobleyc@cvcc.vccs.edu
MOBLEY, Cedric ... 410-225-2343 ... 224 B cmobley@mica.edu
MOBLEY, Cheryl ... 601-925-3310 ... 275 C cmobley@mc.edu
MOBLEY, Karen ... 912-871-1638 ... 135 D kmobley@ogeecheetech.edu
MOBLEY, Marilyn, S ... 216-368-8877 ... 386 F marilyn.mobley@case.edu
MOBLEY, Ralph ... 404-894-3754 ... 130 F ralph.mobley@success.gatech.edu
MOBLEY, Tracey, A ... 803-313-7152 ... 462 D tmobley@mailbox.sc.edu
MOBLEY, Wanda ... 336-517-2267 ... 362 G wmobley@bennett.edu
MOBLEY-BELK, Karen, A ... 706-729-2321 ... 125 G kmobley@aug.edu
MOBLEY-SMITH, Miriam ... 773-821-2589 ... 146 G msmith56@csu.edu
MOCABEE, Norma ... 626-815-4550 ... 30 G nmocabee@apu.edu
MOCARSKY, Michelle ... 215-248-7036 ... 425 D mocarskym@chc.edu
MOCCIA, Mario, L ... 618-453-7250 ... 165 B mmoccia@siu.edu
MOCHAN, Eugene ... 215-871-6444 ... 444 C genem@pcom.edu
MOCK, Ashley ... 229-391-5055 ... 123 H amock@abac.edu
MOCK, Diana ... 559-453-5505 ... 47 K dbmock@fresno.edu
MOCK, Diana ... 559-453-5505 ... 48 A dbmock@fresno.edu
MOCK, Gerald, L ... 772-462-7315 ... 111 B gmock@irsc.edu
MOCK, Keith ... 334-386-7876 ... 3 G kmock@faulkner.edu
MOCK, Kelly ... 314-529-9579 ... 284 C kmock@maryville.edu
MOCK, Raymond, F ... 513-529-6023 ... 396 E mockrf@muohio.edu
MOCK, JR., Robert, C ... 859-257-1911 ... 207 D robert.mock@uky.edu
MOCK, Robert, M ... 716-827-2431 ... 358 D mockr@trocaire.edu
MOCNIK, Joe ... 478-445-0980 ... 130 B joe.mocnik@gcsu.edu
MODELANE, Dan ... 508-541-1614 ... 233 G dmodelane@dean.edu
MODENE, Kathleen, R ... 314-991-6229 ... 279 H kmodene@chamberlain.edu
MODENSTEIN, Susan ... 212-592-2000 ... 350 F smodenstein@sva.edu
MODERSOHN, Ellen, E ... 563-387-1350 ... 187 D ellen.modersohn@luther.edu
MODESTOU, Jennifer, A ... 319-335-0705 ... 182 F jennifer-modestou@uiowa.edu
MODICA, Joseph, B ... 610-341-5826 ... 428 E jmodica@eastern.edu
MODICA-NAPOLITANO, Josephine ... 978-837-5115 ... 242 A josephine.modicanapolitano@merrimack.edu
MODIG, James, E ... 785-864-3431 ... 197 B jmodig@ku.edu
MODISETTE, Carol ... 405-271-2353 ... 413 D carol-modisette@ouhsc.edu
MODISHER, Christine, A ... 615-366-4437 ... 473 D christine.modisher@tbr.edu
MODLIN, Andrew ... 540-887-7260 ... 521 C amodlin@mbc.edu
MODLIN, Cynthia ... 252-789-0225 ... 371 H cmodlin@martincc.edu
MODLIN, Jason, E ... 919-497-3210 ... 366 H jmodlin@louisburg.edu
MODRCIN, Mary Anne ... 423-869-6319 ... 470 E maryanne.modrcin@lmunet.edu
MODRZAKOWSKI, Malcolm ... 304-647-6302 ... 544 E mmodrzakowski@osteo.wvsom.edu
MOE, Marie ... 701-483-2787 ... 381 G marie.moe@dickinsonstate.edu
MOE, Peggy ... 425-235-2285 ... 537 A pmoe@rtc.edu
MOE, Roxanna ... 907-564-8265 ... 10 D rmoe@alaskapacific.edu
MOE, Warren ... 503-654-8000 ... 419 F wmoe@pioneerpacific.edu
MOEDER, Lawrence, E ... 785-532-6420 ... 194 D larrym@ksu.edu
MOEDER, Lawrence, E ... 785-532-6250 ... 194 D larrym@ksu.edu
MOEGENBURG, Stacey ... 845-341-4286 ... 345 E stacey.moegenburg@sunyorange.edu
MOEGGENBERG, Richard .. 517-437-7341 ... 252 C richard.moeggenberg@hillsdale.edu
MOEGLIN, Maureen ... 402-457-2236 ... 298 G mmoeglin@mccneb.edu
MOELLER, Bret ... 617-228-2293 ... 239 C bmoeller@bhcc.mass.edu
MOEN, Matthew, C ... 605-677-5221 ... 465 G matthew.moen@usd.edu
MOEN, Stuart ... 281-873-0262 ... 483 I s.moen@commonwealth.edu
MOENKHAUS, Kevin, P ... 515-271-3902 ... 184 D kevin.moenkhaus@drake.edu
MOERSCHBAECHER, Joseph, M ... 504-568-4804 ... 213 A jmoers@lsuhsc.edu
MOEZ, Chrystal ... 262-619-6830 ... 554 B moezc@gtc.edu
MOFFAT, David ... 225-634-2636 ... 209 K moffatda@catc.edu
MOFFAT, Heather ... 812-888-4120 ... 181 D hmoffat@vinu.edu
MOFFATT, Tammy, L ... 603-646-2846 ... 304 J tammy.l.moffatt@dartmouth.edu
MOFFETT, Danielle ... 575-538-6675 ... 321 I moffettd@wnmu.edu
MOFFETT, Nelle ... 805-437-8979 ... 34 B nelle.moffett@csuci.edu
MOFFETT, Rafael ... 405-466-3444 ... 408 G rmoffett@langston.edu
MOFFETT, Randy ... 225-342-6950 ... 215 D randy.moffett@la.gov
MOFFETT, Raphael ... 210-999-8321 ... 502 E raphael.moffett@trinity.edu
MOFFETT, Thomas ... 518-562-4130 ... 329 C thomas.moffett@clinton.edu
MOFFITT, Clinton ... 559-278-3902 ... 35 A clinton_moffitt@csufresno.edu
MOFFITT, Jamie, H ... 541-346-3003 ... 419 B jmoffitt@uoregon.edu
MOFFITT, Lisa ... 615-327-3927 ... 469 K moffitt@guptoncollege.edu
MOFFITT, Michael ... 765-677-2201 ... 175 B michael.moffitt@indwes.edu
MOFFITT, Thomas, J ... 610-566-1776 ... 452 B tmoffitt@williamson.edu
MOGARD, Naomi ... 763-493-4500 ... 270 H naomi.mogard@rasmussen.edu
MOGCK, Steven, A ... 312-329-4131 ... 159 A steve.mogck@moody.edu
MOGHALU, Arthur ... 662-254-3364 ... 276 B arthur.moghalu@mvsu.edu
MOGREN, Brian ... 651-846-1384 ... 269 C brian.mogren@saintpaul.edu
MOHAMADIAN, Habib, P . 225-771-5290 ... 214 I mohamad@engr.subr.edu
MOHAMED, Carol, W ... 412-648-7861 ... 449 A pauca5@pitt.edu
MOHAMMADI, Aghajan ... 718-262-2333 ... 329 A aghajan@york.cuny.edu
MOHAMMADI, Amir ... 302-857-6200 ... 96 C amohammadi@desu.edu
MOHAMMADI, Rameen ... 315-312-2232 ... 354 A rameen.mohammadi@oswego.edu
MOHAMMED, Abdul, K ... 919-530-7082 ... 378 B amohammed@nccu.edu
MOHAN, David ... 440-834-3714 ... 393 G hmohan1@kent.edu
MOHDZAIN, Zaidy ... 870-235-4057 ... 23 I azmohdzain@saumag.edu
MOHIYEDDINI, Sohila ... 714-533-1495 ... 70 B soh@southbaylo.edu
MOHLER, JR., R. Albert ... 502-897-4121 ... 206 C mohler@sbts.edu
MOHLER-FARIA, Dana ... 508-531-1201 ... 237 D dmohlerfaria@bridgew.edu
MOHN, Kate ... 612-874-3737 ... 265 C kmohn@mcad.edu
MOHNEY, Len ... 661-362-3207 ... 41 I len.mohney@canyons.edu
MOHNING, David, D ... 615-322-3591 ... 478 A d.mohning@vanderbilt.edu
MOHR, James, R ... 724-946-7115 ... 451 C mohrjr@westminister.edu
MOHR, Jean Marie ... 845-398-4106 ... 349 H jmohr@stac.edu
MOHR, Joan, I ... 203-582-8959 ... 93 H joan.isaacmohr@quinnipiac.edu
MOHR, Karl, F ... 530-752-2063 ... 73 I kfmohr@ucdavis.edu
MOHR, Rick ... 937-529-2201 ... 403 A mohr@united.edu
MOHR, Sharon ... 763-488-2525 ... 266 D sharon.mohr@hennepintech.edu
MOHR, Thomas ... 303-373-2008 ... 88 C
MOHR, Wayne, C ... 570-389-4303 ... 441 F wmohr@bloomu.edu
MOHRBACHER, Bob ... 509-793-2055 ... 531 I bobm@bigbend.edu
MOHRBUTTER, Trent, L ... 252-451-8336 ... 372 E tlmohrbutter@nash.cc.nc.us
MOHS, Marlene ... 651-690-6932 ... 270 L mmohn@stkate.edu
MOHSEN, Bashir ... 201-216-9901 ... 309 F eicollege@verizon.net
MOHSINI, Virga ... 617-824-7858 ... 234 B virga_mohsini@emerson.edu
MOIANI, Thomas ... 215-596-7532 ... 450 B t.moiani@usciences.edu
MOINESTER, Eli ... 610-526-6197 ... 430 D emoinester@harcum.edu
MOIOLA, Tena ... 858-566-1200 ... 44 B tmoiola@disd.edu
MOIR, Chris ... 216-987-3492 ... 389 B chris.moir@tri-c.edu
MOIR, Margaret (Peg), A ... 419-755-4704 ... 397 C pmoir@ncstatecollege.edu
MOIST, Kirk, L ... 715-833-6224 ... 553 H kmoist@cvtc.edu
MOJICA, Agnes ... 787-892-4320 ... 564 B amojica@sg.inter.edu
MOJICA, Francis, J ... 787-723-4481 ... 561 B fmojica@ceaprc.edu
MOJICA, Jorge, E ... 787-852-1430 ... 562 F jmojica@hccpr.edu
MOJOCK, Charles, R ... 352-365-3523 ... 112 J mojockc@lscc.edu
MOK, Jacqueline ... 410-516-8068 ... 223 F jmok1@jhu.edu
MOK, Jacqueline, L ... 520-621-1856 ... 18 L jlmok@email.arizona.edu
MOK, May ... 510-666-8248 ... 26 H mmok@aimc.edu
MOKEL, Haroon ... 202-408-2400 ... 99 G haroon.mokel@strayer.edu
MOKOSSO, Henry, E ... 504-286-5250 ... 214 J hmokosso@suno.edu
MOKRZECKI, Elizabeth ... 413-572-8019 ... 238 F emokrzecki@wsc.ma.edu
MOKUAU, Noreen, K ... 808-956-6300 ... 141 G noreen@hawaii.edu
MOLALENGE, Teshome, H 540-828-5751 ... 517 B tmolalen@bridgewater.edu
MOLAND, Millie ... 970-248-1304 ... 82 F mmoland@coloradomesa.edu
MOLARO, Anthony ... 708-709-3551 ... 161 D amolaro@prairiestate.edu
MOLASSO, Billy ... 619-947-6787 ... 391 B molassob@franklin.edu
MOLCHANY, Jim ... 610-282-1100 ... 427 A jim.molchany@desales.edu
MOLD, Jean ... 435-722-6900 ... 510 N jean@ubatc.edu
MOLDAVAN, Carla ... 706-295-6306 ... 130 E cmoldava@highlands.edu
MOLDENHAUER, Susan ... 307-766-6620 ... 556 H amsm@uwyo.edu
MOLDER, Kandi ... 918-335-6237 ... 411 B kmolder@okwu.edu
MOLDER, Mark ... 918-335-6843 ... 411 B mmolder@okwu.edu
MOLDOVAN, Randi ... 614-947-6543 ... 391 B randi.moldovan@franklin.edu
MOLDSTAD, Donald, L ... 507-344-7312 ... 261 C donm@blc.edu
MOLDSTAD, Jonathan, L ... 507-344-7889 ... 261 C jmoldstad@blc.edu
MOLEN, Brent ... 801-426-8234 ... 511 A president@ucdh.edu
MOLEN, Kenneth ... 801-226-1081 ... 511 A director@ucdh.edu
MOLENAAR, James, H ... 320-222-5211 ... 268 G jim.molenaar@ridgewater.edu
MOLENKAMP, Kathy, L ... 616-538-2330 ... 251 D kmolenkamp@gbcol.edu
MOLER, Misty ... 704-216-3623 ... 373 F misty.moler@rccc.edu
MOLESWORTH, Mark, D ... 608-342-1567 ... 552 B moleswom@uwplatt.edu
MOLEY, Linda ... 620-252-7115 ... 192 B lmoley@coffeyville.edu
MOLIDOR, Christian ... 225-578-1351 ... 212 H molidor@lsu.edu
MOLIFE, Brenda ... 508-531-1201 ... 237 D bmolife@bridgew.edu
MOLIKEN, Laura ... 610-409-3606 ... 450 D lmoliken@ursinus.edu
MOLINA, Carlos ... 718-518-6658 ... 327 D cmolina@hostos.cuny.edu
MOLINA, Carlos ... 202-495-3876 ... 99 C cmolina@dhs.edu
MOLINA, Jose, A ... 787-738-2161 ... 567 D jose.molina3@upr.edu
MOLINA, Juan ... 787-664-0345 ... 568 C jc.molina@upr.edu
MOLINA, Michael ... 806-742-2116 ... 502 A michael.molina@ttu.edu
MOLINAR, Anthony ... 415-351-3556 ... 65 I amolinar@sfai.edu
MOLINARO, Brian ... 315-792-5545 ... 341 E bmolinaro@mvcc.edu
MOLITIERNO, Jason, J ... 203-396-8324 ... 94 B molitiernoj@sacredheart.edu
MOLIVER, Donald ... 732-571-3422 ... 311 E dmoliver@monmouth.edu
MOLL, Amy ... 208-426-5719 ... 142 I amoll@boisestate.edu
MOLL, John ... 480-654-7777 ... 15 I john.moll@mesacc.edu

MOLL, Jonathan 781-239-4022 230 E jmoll@babson.edu

MOLL, Monica, M 419-372-2346 385 E mmoll@bgsu.edu

MOLL, Stephen 305-919-5700 119 C molls@fiu.edu

MOLLA, Mike 410-225-2215 224 B mmolla@mica.edu

MOLLAHAN, David, J 334-683-2301 5 G dmollahan@marionmilitary.edu

MOLLBERG, Barbara, J 507-285-7111 268 I barb.mollberg@roch.edu

MOLLEN, Elizabeth 607-778-5008 324 G mollenes@sunybroome.edu

MOLLENKAMP, Brian 734-207-9581 255 F mmollenkamp@mts.edu

MOLLENKAMP, Brian, L 734-207-9581 255 F bmollenkamp@mts.edu

MOLLENKOPF, Robert 724-480-3387 426 A robert.mollenkopf@ccbc.edu

MOLLER, Amanda 312-752-2170 155 C amanda.moller@kendall.edu

MOLLER, Edward 617-928-4515 242 E enmoller@mountida.edu

MOLLER, Jerry, E 806-371-5297 479 G jemoller@actx.edu

MOLLER, Mark 740-587-6668 389 I moller@denison.edu

MOLLER, Steffen 503-594-3390 415 A steffenm@clackamas.edu

MOLLEUR, Sherri 802-322-1626 513 E sherri.molleur@goddard.edu

MOLLICONI, Mary 402-461-7320 298 A mmolliconi@hastings.edu

MOLLIS, Kristi, L 561-912-1211 107 B kmollis@evergladesuniversity.edu

MOLLO, Peter 508-541-1664 233 G pmollo@dean.edu

MOLLOY, Marcie, A 410-822-5400 222 B mamolloy@chesapeake.edu

MOLNAR, Imre 313-664-7890 249 E imolnar@collegeforcreativestudies.edu

MOLNAR, James 610-660-1295 446 C jmolnar@sju.edu

MOLNAR, Susan 617-254-2610 244 B

MOLOHON, Brian, J 651-631-5237 270 B bjmolohon@nwc.edu

MOLONEY, Jacqueline 978-934-2943 237 B jacqueline_moloney@uml.edu

MOLS, Frank 717-867-6118 434 C mols@lvc.edu

MOLTA, Phyllis 617-588-1347 231 C pmolta@bfit.edu

MOLYNEUX, Annette 215-895-1415 427 H ajm26@drexel.edu

MOLZ, Chris 215-222-4200 445 G cmolz@walnuthillcollege.edu

MOMAN, Frank 317-921-4396 175 K fmoman@ivytech.edu

MOMAN, Orthella, P 601-977-7778 277 C omoman@tougaloo.edu

MOMAN, Tim 602-432-8414 11 C

MOMANY, Christopher, P 517-265-5161 246 H cmomany@adrian.edu

MOMAYEZI, Betty 678-466-4143 127 D bettymomayezi@clayton.edu

MOMAYEZI, Nasser 678-466-4700 127 D nassermomayezi@clayton.edu

MOMBERG, Joel 813-974-1899 121 A jmomberg@usf.edu

MOMINEY, Michael 954-262-8252 114 B mominey@nsu.nova.edu

MONACO, A, G 225-578-8200 212 H amonaco@lsu.edu

MONACO, Anthony, P 617-627-3300 245 C anthony.monaco@tufts.edu

MONACO, Dennis 978-232-2357 234 D dmonaco@endicott.edu

MONACO, Pamela 316-684-5335 196 G pamela.monaco@sckans.edu

MONACO, Salvatore 415-738-8107 58 J smonaco@new.edu

MONAGAN, Paul, R 903-510-2130 503 A pmon@tjc.edu

MONAGHAN, Thomas, S 239-280-2522 101 I tmonaghan@avemaria.edu

MONAHAN, JR., Charles, F 617-732-2880 241 C charles.monahan@mcphs.edu

MONAHAN, Daniel 508-565-1373 245 A dmonahan@stonehill.edu

MONAHAN, Quin 704-461-6802 362 F quinmonahan@bac.edu

MONAN, SJ, J. Donald 617-552-2128 232 B j.donald.monan@bc.edu

MONASCH, Chris, P 718-990-6223 348 G monaschc@stjohns.edu

MONAST, Louise 401-847-6650 454 D louise.monast@salve.edu

MONCHEK, Lana 305-595-9500 100 F

MONCHUSIE, David 816-584-6434 287 E david.monchusie@park.edu

MONCK-MARCELLINO, Caitlin 718-780-0322 324 F caitlin.monck-marcellino@brooklaw.edu

MONCRIFFE, Pritchard 405-466-3215 408 G pmoncriffe@langston.edu

MONCURE, Betty 601-979-2227 274 G betty.j.moncure@jsums.edu

MONCURE, Thomas, M 703-993-2619 519 E tmoncure@gmu.edu

MONDAY, JR., Elden, R 206-239-2315 531 B emonday@aii.edu

MONDAY, Eric, N 225-578-4342 212 H emonday@lsu.edu

MONDAY, Kathryn, J 804-289-8771 525 E kmonday@richmond.edu

MONDEH, Sama 205-247-8151 7 F smondeh@stillman.edu

MONDEIK, Shelly 715-675-3331 555 B mondeik@ntc.edu

MONDELLI, Robert 973-684-6626 312 E rmondelli@pccc.edu

MONDOU, Sherry, B 253-879-3204 538 H smondou@pugetsound.edu

MONDROS, Jacqueline 212-452-7085 327 E jmondros@hunter.cuny.edu

MONDZIEL, Marlene 804-819-4902 526 C mmondziel@vccs.edu

MONE, Jennifer 516-463-7310 335 G jennifer.mone@hofstra.edu

MONET, Dawn 206-239-2302 531 B dmonet@aii.edu

MONETA, Larry 919-684-3737 364 C larry.moneta@duke.edu

MONEY, Barbara 972-599-3151 483 H bmoney@collin.edu

MONEY, Ken 601-366-8880 278 B kmoney@wbs.edu

MONEY, Royce 325-674-4974 478 I moneyr@acu.edu

MONEYHAM, Valerie, Z 850-474-2041 121 D vmoneyha@uwf.edu

MONFETTE, Francine 401-341-2231 454 D monfettf@salve.edu

MONGE, Eduardo 714-997-6847 39 F monge@chapman.edu

MONGELLI, Antoinette 310-983-3525 74 C mongelli@volunteer.ucla.edu

MONGEON, Mike 508-373-9458 231 B michael.mongeon@becker.edu

MONGER, Malika, S 608-243-4449 554 D mmonger@madisoncollege.org

MONGER, Todd 612-343-3513 270 A tjmonger@northcentral.edu

MONGILLO, Anne, M 516-463-6776 335 G anne.mongillo@hofstra.edu

MONHEIT, Alan, C 732-235-2865 317 A monheiac@umdnj.edu

MONHEIT, Yidel 718-853-2442 361 G

MONHOLLON, Michael 325-670-5870 487 F mmonholl@hsutx.edu

MONIACI, Steve, C 281-649-3096 487 H smoniaci@hbu.edu

MONIODIS, Paul 410-837-5270 229 A pmoniodis@ubalt.edu

MONIZ, Karyn 980-598-1108 365 I karyn.moniz@jwu.edu

MONIZ, Richard 980-598-1603 365 I richard.moniz@jwu.edu

MONK, David, H 814-865-2526 438 G dhm6@psu.edu

MONK, Earl 718-951-5137 326 F emonk@brooklyn.cuny.edu

MONK, Matthew 802-828-8556 515 A matthew.monk@vcfa.edu

MONK, Suzanne 662-476-5014 274 B smonk@eastms.edu

MONK, Tammy 304-384-5325 543 G tmonk@concord.edu

MONKS, Birgit 909-652-6876 39 E birgit.monks@chaffey.edu

MONKS, Laura 931-438-0028 475 D lmonks@mscc.edu

MONN, Linda, S 717-749-6191 440 B lsm4@psu.edu

MONNAT, Angela, B 585-385-8042 348 F amonnat@sjfc.edu

MONNES, Mark, J 419-755-4824 397 C mmonnes@ncstatecollege.edu

MONNIN, Martha 907-852-3333 10 F humanresources@ilisagvik.edu

MONNOT, Charles 405-208-5295 410 A cmonnot@okcu.edu

MONOD, Kelly 941-752-5491 118 J monodk@scf.edu

MONREAL, Ismare 305-892-7567 112 A ismare.monreal@jwu.edu

MONREAL, Raul 602-243-8040 16 D raul.monreal@smcmail.maricopa.edu

MONROE, Amannda 614-257-5009 390 B amonroe2@devry.edu

MONROE, Dennis 334-420-4266 7 H dmonroe@trenholmstate.edu

MONROE, J.P 541-346-2085 419 B jpmonroe@uoregon.edu

MONROE, Joseph, W 859-257-5770 207 D joe.monroe@uky.edu

MONROE, Judith 407-823-2351 120 B judith.monroe@ucf.edu

MONROE, Larry, D 606-474-3282 201 D lmonroe@kcu.edu

MONROE, Murphy 312-369-7133 148 D mmonroe@colum.edu

MONROE, Randall, L 570-326-3761 440 L rmonroe@pct.edu

MONROE, Taunya, N 336-517-2161 362 G tmonroe@bennett.edu

MONROE, W. Sam 409-984-6100 501 C sam.monroe@lamarpa.edu

MONROE, Walter 386-481-2497 102 C monroew@cookman.edu

MONROE, William 713-743-9007 503 D wmonroe@uh.edu

MONS, Marie 404-894-4582 130 F marie.mons@finaid.gatech.edu

MONSEES, Matthew 703-526-5869 516 E mamonsees@argosy.edu

MONSON, Amy 859-442-1149 202 B amy.monson@kctcs.edu

MONSON, Terry 906-487-7338 251 A terry.monson@finlandia.edu

MONTAG, Jerry 815-753-1747 160 B jerry.montag@niu.edu

MONTAGNINO, Chris 608-249-6611 547 G cmontagnino@msn.herzing.edu

MONTAGUE, Evan 517-483-1046 254 A montage@lcc.edu

MONTAGUE, Krista 406-247-5781 295 D kmontague@msubillings.edu

MONTAGUE, Marlena, O 671-735-5641 559 E marlena.montague@guamcc.edu

MONTAGUE, Orinthia 952-358-8283 268 A orinthia.montague@normandale.edu

MONTALBAN, Silvia 646-557-4409 327 F smontalban@jjay.cuny.edu

MONTALBANO, Ivonne 713-221-8060 503 F montalbanoi@uhd.edu

MONTALVO, Alfredo 787-725-8120 562 C amontalvo0035@eap.edu

MONTALVO, Carmen 787-878-5475 563 B cmontalv@arecibo.inter.edu

MONTALVO, Francisco, N 787-279-1912 563 D fmontalvo@bayamon.inter.edu

MONTALVO, Luis 617-262-5000 231 G luis.montalvo@the-bac.edu

MONTALVO, Provi 787-878-5475 563 B pmontalvo@arecibo.inter.edu

MONTALVO, Veronica 203-596-6164 93 G vmontalvo@post.edu

MONTANARI, James 815-836-5222 156 F montanja@lewisu.edu

MONTANEZ, John 212-220-8011 326 D jmontanez@bmcc.cuny.edu

MONTANEZ, Robert 916-691-7204 56 B montanr@crc.losrios.edu

MONTANEZ, Sabiana 386-734-3303 109 G smontanez@ftccollege.edu

MONTANEZ-LOPEZ, Nilda 787-740-3001 566 C nilda.montanez@uccaribe.edu

MONTANO, Elisa 310-531-9683 29 E emontano@argosy.edu

MONTANO, Marrybell 801-818-8900 510 I marrybell.montano@provocollege.edu

MONTANO-CORDOVA, Ruby, S 909-593-3511 75 E rmontano-cordova@laverne.edu

MONTEAU, Shannon 406-395-4313 296 E smonteau@stonechild.edu

MONTECALVO, Frank 814-472-3002 446 B fmontecalvo@francis.edu

MONTEFUSCO, Anthony 401-254-3023 454 C amontefusco@rwu.edu

MONTEIRO, F. Marconi 210-924-4338 481 G marconi.monteiro@bua.edu

MONTEIRO, Kenneth, P 415-338-1693 37 B monteiro@sfsu.edu

MONTEITH, Delos, D 828-339-4236 374 C delos@southwesterncc.edu

MONTEITH, Kellie 828-227-7147 380 A monteith@wcu.edu

MONTEITH, Monte 505-346-2340 321 B monte.monteith@bie.edu

MONTEL, Gary, E 260-982-5223 177 H gemontel@manchester.edu

MONTELEONE, Paul 318-473-6477 212 I pmonteleone@lsua.edu

MONTELONGO, Angie 713-525-3572 505 A montela@stthom.edu

MONTEMAGNO, Carlo, D 513-556-2933 403 D carlo.montemagno@uc.edu

MONTEMAYOR, Roland 415-452-5703 40 C rmontema@ccsf.edu

MONTEMURRO, Kimberly 914-633-2246 336 E kmontemurro@iona.edu

MONTERECY, Monty 206-934-3628 537 D orestes.monterecy@seattlecolleges.edu

MONTERO, Grecia 609-771-3132 308 F montero@tcnj.edu

MONTERO, Janina 310-825-1404 74 C jmontero@saonet.ucla.edu

MONTES, Bruce, A 773-508-7601 157 C bmontes@luc.edu

MONTES, Darlene 818-364-7792 55 A montesd@lamission.edu

MONTES, Porfirio 787-863-2390 563 E porfirio.montes@fajardo.inter.edu

MONTES, Susan, R 305-284-6021 122 I smontes@miami.edu

MONTES-BURGOS, Carmen 787-993-8952 567 B carmen.montes1@upr.edu

MONTES-MORALES, Maria 347-964-8600 324 C mmontes@boricuacollege.edu

MONTESI, Christy 662-846-4646 273 H cmontesi@deltastate.edu

MONTESINO, María del C 787-720-1022 560 F recaudaciones@atlanticcollege.edu

MONTEVIRGEN, Alexis, S 510-748-2288 62 C amontevirgen@peralta.edu

MONTEZON, Juice 612-343-4188 270 A jjmontez@northcentral.edu

MONTGOMERY, Adrienne 978-837-5196 242 A montgomerya@merrimack.edu

MONTGOMERY, Carol 312-362-5361 149 A cmontgo1@depaul.edu

MONTGOMERY, Cathy 912-427-6265 124 C cmontgomery@altamahatech.edu

MONTGOMERY, Cindy 229-226-1621 138 C cmontgomery@thomasu.edu

MONTGOMERY, Clyde 405-466-3423 408 G cmontgomery@langston.edu

MONTGOMERY, Dale 479-619-4234 22 H dmontgom@nwacc.edu

MONTGOMERY, Darrell 330-337-6403 383 J business@awc.edu

MONTGOMERY, Giles 325-235-7482 500 G giles.montgomery@tstc.edu

MONTGOMERY, Isalene 386-506-3961 104 F montgoi@daytonastate.edu

MONTGOMERY, Jacque 303-724-1528 88 J jacque.montgomery@ucdenver.edu

MONTGOMERY, Joe 509-544-4935 532 H jmontgomery@columbiabasin.edu

MONTGOMERY, John 951-343-4963 31 J jmontgomery@calbaptist.edu

MONTGOMERY, John 575-562-4002 318 B john.montgomery@enmu.edu

MONTGOMERY, Judith, R 207-725-3281 217 E jmontgom@bowdoin.edu

MONTGOMERY, Karen, L 817-531-6579 502 C kmontgomery@txwes.edu

MONTGOMERY, Keith 715-261-6223 553 B keith.montgomery@uwc.edu

MONTGOMERY, Kit, P 214-333-5242 484 D kit@dbu.edu

MONTGOMERY, Laura, M 630-752-5227 168 H laura.montgomery@wheaton.edu

MONTGOMERY, Lisa 312-567-3777 153 C montgomeryl@iit.edu

MONTGOMERY, Lisa 713-221-8100 503 F montgomeryl@uhd.edu

MONTGOMERY, Lisa, P 843-792-5050 459 D montgoml@musc.edu

MONTGOMERY, Lyman 937-708-5798 405 H lmontgomery@wilberforce.edu

MONTGOMERY, Martha 254-442-5114 482 I martha.montgomery@cisco.edu

MONTGOMERY, Nancy 562-860-2451 39 A nmontgomery@cerritos.edu

MONTGOMERY, Nancy 575-439-3798 319 E nancy@nmsua.nmsu.edu

MONTGOMERY, Roark 903-875-7487 491 C roark.montgomery@navarrocollege.edu

MONTGOMERY, Robert, J 248-232-4806 256 F rjmontgo@oaklandcc.edu

MONTGOMERY, Soncerey, L 336-750-2314 380 B montgomerysl@wssu.edu

MONTGOMERY, Susan 740-588-1446 400 E montgoms@ohio.edu

MONTGOMERY, Tammy 916-484-8101 56 A montgot2@arc.losrios.edu

MONTGOMERY, Toni-Marie 847-491-7552 160 E t-montgomery@northwestern.edu

MONTGOMERY, Tony 662-476-5062 274 B tmontgomery@eastms.edu

MONTGOMERY, Tonya 502-597-6434 203 G tonya.montgomery@kysu.edu

MONTGOMERY, Trent 256-372-5725 1 A trent.montgomery@aamu.edu

MONTGOMERY RICE, Valerie 404-752-1194 134 E vmontgomeryrice@msm.edu

MONTI, Joseph 407-644-1408 116 D jmonti@rollins.edu

MONTICINO, Michael 940-565-2497 504 D

MONTIJO, Minerva 716-896-0700 359 H montijom@villa.edu

MONTINI, Christine 330-494-1214 386 A cmontini@edmc.edu

MONTNEY, Kevin 920-206-2312 548 D kevin.montney@mbbc.edu

MONTOGMERY, Nash, D .. 757-823-8462 .... 522 E ndmontgomery@nsu.edu
MONTONE, Richard ... 413-644-4776 .... 230 F rmontone@simons-rock.edu
MONTOYA, Adrian ... 210-486-3135 .... 479 C amontoya@alamo.edu
MONTOYA, Bernadette ... 575-646-2447 .... 319 D bermonto@nmsu.edu
MONTOYA, Debra ... 818-401-1282 .... 42 F dmontoya@columbiacollege.edu
MONTOYA, Loretta ... 505-224-3457 .... 317 K lmontoya@cnm.edu
MONTOYA, Mitzi, M ... 480-727-1955 .... 11 J mitzi.montoya@asu.edu
MONTOYA, Rolando ... 305-237-3872 .... 113 H rmontoya@mdc.edu
MONTOYA, Sharon ... 928-428-8286 .... 14 B sharon.montoya@eac.edu
MONTOYA, Valerie ... 505-346-2330 .... 321 B valerie.montoya@bie.edu
MONTRALLO, Pamela ... 435-652-7522 .... 512 B montrallo@dixie.edu
MONTREAL, Steven ... 262-243-5700 .... 547 C steve.montreal@cuw.edu
MONTS, Lester, P ... 734-764-3982 .... 259 A lmonts@umich.edu
MONTS DE OCA, Clint ... 941-487-4801 .... 120 A cmontsdeoca@ncf.edu
MOO-YOUNG, Keith ... 302-343-4500 .... 35 D kmooyou@exchange.calstate.edu
MOODY, Barbara ... 207-941-7000 .... 218 A moodyb@husson.edu
MOODY, Bill ... 678-717-3630 .... 129 G bmoody@gsc.edu
MOODY, Brad ... 501-760-4213 .... 22 F bmoody@npcc.edu
MOODY, Charles ... 602-850-8000 .... 17 G cmoody@phoenixseminary.edu
MOODY, Christopher, M ... 302-855-1665 .... 96 E cmoody@dtcc.edu
MOODY, D. L ... 817-461-8741 .... 480 H dlmoody@abconline.org
MOODY, Donna ... 618-235-2700 .... 165 D donna.moody@swic.edu
MOODY, Jan ... 601-928-6207 .... 275 E janet.moody@mgccc.edu
MOODY, Jeff, T ... 219-942-1459 .... 170 I jmoody@ccr.edu
MOODY, Kay ... 219-942-1459 .... 170 I kay.moody@ccr.edu
MOODY, Linda ... 213-477-2560 .... 57 H lmoody@msmc.la.edu
MOODY, Marilyn ... 208-426-1234 .... 142 I marilynmoody@boisestate.edu
MOODY, Marilyn ... 503-725-3000 .... 418 G
MOODY, Marla ... 417-447-4842 .... 287 D moodym@otc.edu
MOODY, Michelle, L ... 757-594-8819 .... 517 L mlmoody@cnu.edu
MOODY, Monica ... 478-757-5224 .... 139 E mmoody@wesleyancollege.edu
MOODY, Nancy, B ... 423-636-7301 .... 477 A nmoody@tusculum.edu
MOODY, Tim ... 912-279-5762 .... 127 E tmoody@ccga.edu
MOODY-SHEPHERD, Eleanor ... 212-870-1215 .... 344 A emoody.shepherd@nyts.edu
MOOLENAR-WIRSY, Pamela ... 678-891-2433 .... 131 C pamela.moolenar-wirsy@gpc.edu
MOON, Agnes ... 410-225-2347 .... 224 B amoon@mica.edu
MOON, Beverly ... 662-846-4834 .... 273 H bmoon@deltastate.edu
MOON, David ... 719-255-3566 .... 88 I cmoon@uccs.edu
MOON, Deborah, J ... 412-268-6011 .... 424 J deborahm@andrew.cmu.edu
MOON, Don ... 434-592-3237 .... 520 K donmoon@liberty.edu
MOON, Freddie, P ... 256-766-6610 .... 4 C pmoon@hcu.edu
MOON, Gary, W ... 404-233-3949 .... 136 D gmoon@richmont.edu
MOON, Greg ... 503-517-1880 .... 421 C gmoon@westernseminary.edu
MOON, Greta ... 760-245-4271 .... 77 H greta.moon@vvc.edu
MOON, Hope ... 440-365-5222 .... 395 D
MOON, Hyon ... 949-480-4139 .... 69 J hmoon@soka.edu
MOON, Joshua ... 605-626-3336 .... 466 A joshua.moom@northern.edu
MOON, Kevin ... 847-317-7023 .... 166 E kmoon@tiu.edu
MOON, Lee, L ... 904-620-2833 .... 120 D l.moon@unf.edu
MOON, Lynn ... 757-823-8053 .... 522 E lymoon@nsu.edu
MOON, Mary ... 212-757-1190 .... 322 H mmoon@funeraleducation.org
MOON, Michael, J ... 503-370-6017 .... 421 D mmoon@willamette.edu
MOON, Pamela ... 270-926-4040 .... 200 F pmoon@daymarcollege.edu
MOON, Randy ... 251-460-6121 .... 9 D rmoon@usouthal.edu
MOON, Susan ... 573-288-6441 .... 280 I smoon@culver.edu
MOONEY, Carol Ann ... 574-284-4602 .... 179 F mooney@saintmarys.edu
MOONEY, Catherine ... 209-954-5642 .... 66 D cmooney@deltacollege.edu
MOONEY, Debra ... 513-745-3204 .... 406 E mooney@xavier.edu
MOONEY, Dee ... 575-492-2115 .... 321 H dmooney@usw.edu
MOONEY, Hank ... 918-465-1804 .... 408 A hmooney@eosc.edu
MOONEY, Kim ... 603-899-4284 .... 305 A mooneyk@franklinpierce.edu
MOONEY, Mary, K ... 806-371-5311 .... 479 G mkmooney@actx.edu
MOONEY, Sandra, N ... 281-649-3256 .... 487 H smooney@hbu.edu
MOONEY, Thelma ... 936-294-4047 .... 501 D tgm001@shsu.edu
MOONEYHAN, Allen ... 870-512-7864 .... 20 F allen_mooneyhan@asun.edu
MOONO, Steady ... 610-819-2070 .... 436 G smoono@mc3.edu
MOORADIAN, Ronald, G ... 562-903-4757 .... 31 A ron.mooradian@biola.edu
MOORE, Albert ... 408-741-2146 .... 78 E albert_moore@wvm.edu
MOORE, Alicia ... 541-383-7262 .... 414 I amoore@cocc.edu
MOORE, Allison, O ... 816-654-7204 .... 283 F aomoore@kcumb.edu
MOORE, Allyson, L ... 203-432-0800 .... 96 A allyson.moore@yale.edu
MOORE, Amanda ... 501-450-1303 .... 22 A moore@hendrix.edu
MOORE, Anita, W ... 662-252-8000 .... 276 G amoore@rustcollege.edu
MOORE, Ann ... 601-403-1250 .... 276 E amoore@prcc.edu
MOORE, Anne ... 845-398-4084 .... 349 H amoore@stac.edu
MOORE, Anne ... 413-236-1641 .... 239 A amoore@berkshirecc.edu
MOORE, Anne, C ... 618-453-2522 .... 165 B dcarlson@lib.siu.edu
MOORE, Anthony ... 270-384-8108 .... 204 D moorea@lindsey.edu
MOORE, Arthur, L ... 859-238-5575 .... 199 G art.moore@centre.edu
MOORE, Barbara ... 914-251-6018 .... 354 D barbara.moore@purchase.edu
MOORE, Barbara ... 662-329-7288 .... 276 A bmoore@edhs.muw.edu
MOORE, Barbara ... 585-340-9593 .... 329 F bmoore@crcds.edu
MOORE, Barbara ... 718-997-5421 .... 328 E barbara.moore@qc.cuny.edu
MOORE, Barbara, C ... 803-705-4604 .... 455 D mooreb@benedict.edu
MOORE, Barbe ... 724-357-4077 .... 442 F bmoore@iup.edu
MOORE, Barry, L ... 561-993-1134 .... 114 D mooreb@palmbeachstate.edu
MOORE, Becky ... 706-865-2134 .... 138 E bmoore@truett.edu
MOORE, III, Berrien ... 405-325-3095 .... 413 C berrien@ou.edu
MOORE, Bert, S ... 972-883-2355 .... 506 A bmoore@utdallas.edu
MOORE, Beverly ... 714-556-3610 .... 77 B beverly.moore@vanguard.edu
MOORE, Beverly ... 845-434-5750 .... 357 A bmoore@sullivan.suny.edu
MOORE, Billy ... 662-846-4200 .... 273 H bmoore@deltastate.edu
MOORE, Brad ... 505-224-4423 .... 317 K bmoore28@cnm.edu
MOORE, Brad, D ... 336-278-5490 .... 364 D bmoore6@elon.edu
MOORE, Brett, C ... 607-735-1724 .... 332 I bmoore@elmira.edu
MOORE, Brian ... 845-569-3275 .... 342 A brian.moore@msmc.edu
MOORE, Bridget ... 325-670-1482 .... 487 F bmoore@jsutx.edu
MOORE, Carl, C ... 251-460-6419 .... 9 D ccmoore@usouthal.edu
MOORE, Catherine ... 732-987-2602 .... 310 C moorec@georgian.edu
MOORE, Charlette ... 501-882-8876 .... 20 C camoore@asub.edu
MOORE, Chris ... 205-802-1594 .... 3 B chris.moore@vc.edu
MOORE, Christine ... 619-961-4323 .... 72 J cmoore@tjsl.edu
MOORE, Christopher, W ... 208-496-3526 .... 143 A moorec@byui.edu
MOORE, Claire, E ... 443-352-4306 .... 226 E cmoore@stevenson.edu
MOORE, Cynthia ... 310-434-4305 .... 68 D moore_cynthia@smc.edu
MOORE, Dan ... 580-745-2006 .... 412 C dmoore@se.edu
MOORE, Dana ... 215-635-7300 .... 430 A dmoore@gratz.edu
MOORE, Danny, B ... 252-398-6448 .... 363 G moored@chowan.edu
MOORE, Daryl, J ... 209-667-3959 .... 36 D dmoore@csustan.edu
MOORE, David ... 563-589-3351 .... 189 F dmoore@dbq.edu
MOORE, David, C ... 562-860-2451 .... 39 A dcmoore@cerritos.edu
MOORE, David, P ... 256-824-6285 .... 8 G david.moore@uah.edu
MOORE, David, T ... 585-292-2902 .... 341 H dmoore53@monroecc.edu
MOORE, Davis ... 314-644-9196 .... 288 I dfmoore@stlcc.edu
MOORE, Debbie ... 706-886-6831 .... 138 D dmoore@tfc.edu
MOORE, Deborah, D ... 785-670-1538 .... 197 F deborah.moore@washburn.edu
MOORE, Debra, J ... 601-362-9991 .... 273 B debra.moore@antonellicollege.edu
MOORE, Denise ... 913-469-8500 .... 194 B dmoore56@jccc.edu
MOORE, Denise ... 404-215-3486 .... 134 D dmoore@morehouse.edu
MOORE, Dennis, T ... 585-785-1294 .... 334 A mooredt@flcc.edu
MOORE, Dirk, S ... 276-944-6810 .... 519 A dsmoore@ehc.edu
MOORE, Donald ... 856-256-4199 .... 314 A moored@rowan.edu
MOORE, Edward ... 773-508-8928 .... 157 C emoore@luc.edu
MOORE, Edwin ... 707-965-7103 .... 60 I emoore@puc.edu
MOORE, Elinore ... 773-838-7528 .... 147 H emoore20@ccc.edu
MOORE, Ernest ... 404-880-6423 .... 127 C emoore@cau.edu
MOORE, Evelyn, J ... 319-399-8526 .... 183 F emoore@coe.edu
MOORE, Francis, X ... 434-395-2034 .... 521 A moorefx@longwood.edu
MOORE, Frederick, V ... 712-749-2103 .... 183 C mooref@bvu.edu
MOORE, Garret ... 740-587-6482 .... 389 I moore@denison.edu
MOORE, Gary ... 615-329-8663 .... 468 I gmoore@fisk.edu
MOORE, George, E ... 215-204-6542 .... 447 H george.moore@temple.edu
MOORE, Glen ... 601-928-6297 .... 275 E glen.moore@mgccc.edu
MOORE, Gordon ... 404-894-3959 .... 130 F gordon.moore@omed.gatech.edu
MOORE, Gregory ... 404-894-1420 .... 130 F gregory.moore@health.gatech.edu
MOORE, Gregory, R ... 859-323-5823 .... 207 D grmoor2@uky.edu
MOORE, Gwendolyn ... 912-443-5711 .... 136 H gmoore@savannahtech.edu
MOORE, Gwendolyn ... 334-874-5700 .... 2 H smoore@ccal.edu
MOORE, Hallie ... 216-791-5000 .... 388 C hallie.moore@case.edu
MOORE, Harry ... 215-751-8800 .... 426 B hmoore@ccp.edu
MOORE, Holly ... 206-934-6867 .... 537 F holly.moore@seattlecolleges.edu
MOORE, Honour ... 215-827-0567 .... 431 A hmoore@holyfamily.edu
MOORE, JR., Howard, J ... 334-874-5700 .... 2 H hmoore@ccal.edu
MOORE, Hsiao-Ping, H ... 248-204-3500 .... 254 B hmoore@ltu.edu
MOORE, Jacques ... 207-859-4732 .... 217 G jrmoore@colby.edu
MOORE, James ... 520-494-5406 .... 13 D james.moore7@centralaz.edu
MOORE, James, E ... 215-951-1017 .... 432 I mooreje@lasalle.edu
MOORE, James, H ... 520-621-1483 .... 18 L jim.moore@uafoundation.org
MOORE, James, K ... 814-866-6641 .... 433 C jkmoore@lecom.edu
MOORE, James, R ... 847-317-8036 .... 166 E jmoore@tiu.edu
MOORE, Jamillah ... 805-652-5502 .... 77 C jmoore@vcccd.edu
MOORE, Jana ... 928-317-6052 .... 12 A jana.moore@azwestern.edu
MOORE, Janice ... 717-728-2219 .... 425 B janicemoore@centralpenn.edu
MOORE, Jason ... 205-391-5809 .... 6 I jmoore@sheltonstate.edu
MOORE, Jay ... 805-654-6340 .... 77 F jmooret@vcccd.edu
MOORE, Jeanette ... 510-235-7800 .... 43 E jmoore@contracosta.edu
MOORE, Jeanie ... 704-216-3500 .... 373 F jeanie.moore@rccc.edu
MOORE, Jennie ... 617-670-4427 .... 234 G jmoore@fisher.edu
MOORE, Joe ... 812-265-2580 .... 177 A ljmoore@ivytech.edu
MOORE, John ... 585-475-2154 .... 347 G jfmfms@rit.edu
MOORE, John, F ... 540-231-8991 .... 529 G jmoore1@vt.edu
MOORE, Johnnie ... 434-582-2250 .... 520 K jrmoore@liberty.edu
MOORE, Johnny ... 870-762-3180 .... 20 A jmoore@smail.anc.edu
MOORE, Johnny, M ... 501-370-5275 .... 23 B jmoore@philander.edu
MOORE, Joseph ... 630-942-2371 .... 148 A moorej7718@cod.edu
MOORE, Joseph, B ... 617-349-8500 .... 236 B jbmoore@lesley.edu
MOORE, Josh ... 614-508-7221 .... 392 A jmoore@hondros.edu
MOORE, Joy, A ... 740-389-4636 .... 395 H moorej@mtc.edu
MOORE, Juanna, S ... 214-828-8907 .... 497 C jmoore@bcd.tamhsc.edu
MOORE, Judy ... 815-599-3457 .... 152 B judy.moore@highland.edu
MOORE, Judy, S ... 574-535-7522 .... 171 G judysm@goshen.edu
MOORE, Karen ... 816-604-5229 .... 285 B karen.moore@mcckc.edu
MOORE, Kathy, J ... 740-826-8114 .... 397 A moore@muskingum.edu
MOORE, Keirsten ... 614-236-6679 .... 386 E kmoore@capital.edu
MOORE, Keith, E ... 757-455-3354 .... 530 C kmoore@vwc.edu
MOORE, Kelly, T ... 630-743-0682 .... 168 E kmoore@westwood.edu
MOORE, Kenneth ... 937-512-3107 .... 401 J kenneth.moore@sinclair.edu
MOORE, Kimberly ... 434-295-0136 .... 521 I kmoore@ncbt.edu
MOORE, Kimberly, M ... 972-860-7100 .... 484 I kimberlymoore@dcccd.edu
MOORE, Kristen ... 913-266-8604 .... 196 A
MOORE, Kyle ... 806-651-2006 .... 499 A kmoore@mail.wtamu.edu
MOORE, Lara ... 541-962-3368 .... 418 C lmoore@eou.edu
MOORE, Laura ... 567-661-7410 .... 400 I laura_moore@owens.edu
MOORE, Lee ... 361-593-2153 .... 498 D lee.moore@tamuk.edu
MOORE, Lee ... 361-593-2303 .... 498 D lee.moore@tamuk.edu
MOORE, Lesa ... 251-442-2207 .... 9 A lmoore@umobile.edu
MOORE, Leslie ... 253-833-9111 .... 534 H lmoore@greenriver.edu
MOORE, Lew ... 501-279-4347 .... 21 H lmoore@harding.edu
MOORE, Lew Rita ... 513-861-6400 .... 402 I lewrita.moore@munion.edu
MOORE, Linda ... 309-671-2734 .... 158 C lmoore@methodistcol.edu
MOORE, Linda ... 617-824-8570 .... 234 B linda_moore@emerson.edu
MOORE, Linda, H ... 217-351-2551 .... 161 C lmoore@parkland.edu
MOORE, Lisa ... 925-631-4328 .... 64 F lmoore@stmarys-ca.edu
MOORE, Lisia ... 916-649-8168 .... 52 F lmoore@kaplan.edu
MOORE, Lorna, G ... 336-758-5301 .... 380 C moore@wfu.edu
MOORE, Lynn ... 541-440-4600 .... 420 F lynn.moore@umpqua.edu
MOORE, Lynn ... 603-752-1113 .... 304 H lmoore@ccsnh.edu
MOORE, Mal, M ... 205-348-3600 .... 8 E mmoore@ia.ua.edu
MOORE, Marcia, K ... 843-953-8200 .... 457 B moorem@cofc.edu
MOORE, Margie ... 405-262-2552 .... 411 G moorem@redlandscc.edu
MOORE, Marilyn ... 402-481-8781 .... 296 I marilyn.moore@bryanlgh.org
MOORE, Marilyn, A ... 814-871-7614 .... 429 G moore037@gannon.edu
MOORE, Mark ... 405-974-2499 .... 413 B mmoore@uco.edu
MOORE, Mark ... 402-363-5600 .... 301 E dmark.moore@gmail.com
MOORE, Mark ... 740-351-3207 .... 401 I mmoore@shawnee.edu
MOORE, Marlene ... 503-370-6285 .... 421 D moorem@willamette.edu
MOORE, Martha ... 734-372-4900 .... 258 F moorem@cooley.edu
MOORE, Mary ... 410-287-1053 .... 222 A mmoore@cecil.edu

MOORE, Mary, C .... 317-788-6150 .... 180 F
moore@uindy.edu

MOORE, Mary, E .... 617-353-3050 .... 232 E
mmoore@bu.edu

MOORE, Mary Pat .... 319-296-4255 .... 185 F
mary.moore@hawkeyecollege.edu

MOORE, Mary Rita .... 708-456-0300 .... 166 F
mpatrice@triton.edu

MOORE, Matt .... 504-280-6218 .... 213 E
msmoore2@uno.edu

MOORE, Matt .... 605-995-2187 .... 464 C
mamoore@dwu.edu

MOORE, Maureen .... 352-588-8121 .... 116 G
maureen.moore@saintleo.edu

MOORE, Mazie .... 314-889-1421 .... 281 I
mmoore@fontbonne.edu

MOORE, Melody, L .... 804-706-5122 .... 527 B
mmoore@jtcc.edu

MOORE, Michael .... 941-359-7674 .... 116 B
mmoore@ringling.edu

MOORE, Michael .... 989-729-3437 .... 248 F
michael.moore@baker.edu

MOORE, Michael .... 701-777-6772 .... 381 F
michael.moore@research.und.edu

MOORE, Michael, A .... 231-843-5900 .... 260 B
mamoore@westshore.edu

MOORE, Michael, P .... 509-865-8585 .... 535 A
moore_m@heritage.edu

MOORE, Michael, R .... 317-274-0622 .... 174 D
mmoore1@iupui.edu

MOORE, Mickey .... 423-614-8430 .... 470 C
mmoore@leeuniversity.edu

MOORE, Mike .... 949-480-4155 ...... 69 J
mmoore@soka.edu

MOORE, Mike, K .... 701-788-4706 .... 381 H
mike.moore@mayvillestate.edu

MOORE, Mitchell, L .... 540-665-1298 .... 524 E
mmoore7@su.edu

MOORE, Monika .... 909-607-9226 ...... 40 F
monika.moore@cgu.edu

MOORE, Nancy .... 908-526-1200 .... 313 D
nmoore@raritanval.edu

MOORE, Nicole .... 314-889-1496 .... 281 I
nmoore@fontbonne.edu

MOORE, Paige .... 803-758-2700 .... 455 B
pmoore@allenuniversity.edu

MOORE, Pamela .... 541-684-4644 .... 419 F
pmoore@pioneerpacific.edu

MOORE, Patrice .... 504-671-6535 .... 210 F
pmoore@dcc.edu

MOORE, Paul .... 229-732-5910 .... 124 E
paulmoore@andrewcollege.edu

MOORE, Paul, A .... 419-372-8556 .... 385 E
pmoore@bgsu.edu

MOORE, Philip, S .... 803-777-2814 .... 462 A
philmoore@sc.edu

MOORE, R. Bartley .... 202-687-0454 ...... 98 D
rbm9@georgetown.edu

MOORE, Ray .... 334-876-9248 .... 4 B
rmoore@wccs.edu

MOORE, Reggie .... 504-456-3141 .... 208 E
rmoore@dcc.edu

MOORE, Renee .... 210-805-5864 .... 504 B
reneem@uiwtx.edu

MOORE, Renee, R .... 865-639-6604 .... 475 G
rmoore@pstcc.edu

MOORE, Robert, G .... 719-389-6693 ...... 82 D
robert.moore@coloradocollege.edu

MOORE, Robert, M .... 207-859-1104 .... 219 G
moorer@thomas.edu

MOORE, Robin .... 402-761-8270 .... 300 B
rmoore@southeast.edu

MOORE, Robin .... 757-822-1724 .... 528 G
rmoore@tcc.edu

MOORE, Rochelle .... 337-521-8957 .... 211 J
rochelle.moore@southlouisiana.edu

MOORE, Roderick, B .... 276-964-7286 .... 528 E
rod.moore@sw.edu

MOORE, Roger .... 501-882-8906 ...... 20 C
rlmoore@asub.edu

MOORE, Roy .... 615-898-2813 .... 473 G
roy.moore@mtsu.edu

MOORE, Russell .... 303-492-2890 ...... 88 H
rmoore@colorado.edu

MOORE, Russell, D .... 502-897-4112 .... 206 C
rmoore@sbts.edu

MOORE, Russell, D .... 502-897-4897 .... 206 C
rmoore@sbts.edu

MOORE, Sandra .... 859-622-6587 .... 200 J
sandra.moore@eku.edu

MOORE, Sandy .... 757-388-2900 .... 524 D
smoore@snu.edu

MOORE, Sarah .... 253-879-3207 .... 538 H
smoore@pugetsound.edu

MOORE, Sean .... 603-862-3827 .... 306 C
sean.moore@unh.edu

MOORE, Shanee', S .... 214-860-2138 .... 485 A
ksmoore@dcccd.edu

MOORE, Sharamie, T .... 337-475-5493 .... 215 G
strahan@mcneese.edu

MOORE, Sharon .... 860-412-7273 ...... 92 D
smoore@qvcc.commnet.edu

MOORE, Sharyn .... 650-543-3798 ...... 57 B
smoore@menlo.edu

MOORE, Shirley .... 937-778-7861 .... 390 G
smoore@edisonohio.edu

MOORE, Stan .... 817-274-4284 .... 482 B

MOORE, Stephan .... 770-394-8300 .... 125 A
smoore@aii.edu

MOORE, Steve, B .... 979-458-6018 .... 496 F
steve.moore@tamus.edu

MOORE, Steven, C .... 239-590-1919 .... 119 B
cmoore@fgcu.edu

MOORE, Stuart .... 251-380-2240 .... 7 E
smoore@shc.edu

MOORE, Sylvia .... 406-444-0314 .... 294 H
smoore@montana.edu

MOORE, Teresa .... 806-291-3752 .... 508 E
teresam@wbu.edu

MOORE, Teri, D .... 540-674-3600 .... 527 E
tmoore@nr.edu

MOORE, Theresa .... 608-796-3172 .... 553 C
trmoore@viterbo.edu

MOORE, Thomas .... 510-659-6105 ...... 59 J
tmoore@ohlone.edu

MOORE, Thomas .... 870-972-3030 ...... 20 D
tmoore@astate.edu

MOORE, Thomas .... 864-503-5200 .... 463 B
tmoore@uscupstate.edu

MOORE, Thomas, J .... 989-774-3500 .... 249 C
thomas.j.moore@cmich.edu

MOORE, Tim .... 706-379-5166 .... 140 A
tsmoore@yhc.edu

MOORE, Timothy .... 617-353-0750 .... 232 E
mooretj@bu.edu

MOORE, Timothy .... 847-214-7651 .... 150 F
tmoore@elgin.edu

MOORE, Timothy .... 518-255-5323 .... 354 E
mooretw@cobleskill.edu

MOORE, Timothy, J .... 919-530-7420 .... 378 B
tmoore@nccu.edu

MOORE, Tina .... 217-234-5346 .... 156 B
tmoore@lakeland.cc.il.us

MOORE, Todd, H .... 316-284-5230 .... 191 C
tmoore@bethelks.edu

MOORE, JR., Tom, A .... 205-329-7871 .... 3 A
tom.moore@ecacolleges.com

MOORE, Tonja .... 305-348-2168 .... 119 C
tonja.moore@fiu.edu

MOORE, Tony .... 225-771-3201 .... 214 H
tony_moore@sus.edu

MOORE, Torin, Y .... 413-542-2161 .... 230 A
tmoore@amherst.edu

MOORE, Wayne .... 956-882-6567 .... 505 E
wayne.moore@utb.edu

MOORE, William .... 201-692-7200 .... 310 A
wmoore@fdu.edu

MOORE, William (Joe) .... 605-688-4678 .... 466 C
william.moore@sdstate.edu

MOORE, Winifred, B .... 843-953-7477 .... 456 C
bo.moore@citadel.edu

MOORE-ASSEM,
Carolyn, D .... 919-530-5294 .... 378 B
cmoore@nccu.edu

MOORE-JONES,
Yolanda, V .... 919-536-7201 .... 370 C
jonesym@durhamtech.edu

MOORE-LINN, Cathleen .... 671-735-2600 .... 559 G
cmoore@uguam.uog.edu

MOORE-PIZON, Thomas .... 813-621-0041 .... 106 C
tmoore@cci.edu

MOORE-RAMSEY, Donna .... 216-987-5339 .... 389 B
donna.moore-ramsey@tri-c.edu

MOORER, Glynda, M .... 517-355-2488 .... 255 A
moorerg@msu.edu

MOORES, Lisa .... 301-295-3185 .... 558 D
lisa.moores@usuhs.edu

MOORHEAD, Tracey, A .... 219-299-3654 .... 262 I
moorhead@cord.edu

MOORHOUSE, Dian .... 954-262-5393 .... 114 B
dian@nsu.nova.edu

MOORMAN, Annorrah .... 309-556-3052 .... 153 F
amoorman@iwu.edu

MOORMAN, Cathy .... 765-998-5123 .... 180 B
ctmoorman@taylor.edu

MOORMAN, Jack, W .... 919-515-3000 .... 378 C
jack_moorman@ncsu.edu

MOORMAN, Jeanne, M .... 419-995-8481 .... 399 B
moorman.35@osu.edu

MOORMAN, Thomas, D .... 817-735-2505 .... 504 E
thomas.moorman@unthsc.edu

MOORMANN, Kay .... 815-455-8783 .... 157 H
lmoormann@mchenry.edu

MOORS, Dean .... 402-462-4000 .... 297 A
dmoors@cccneb.edu

MOORWOOD, Woody .... 626-815-3855 ...... 30 G
wmoorwood@apu.edu

MOOS, Michael .... 317-917-3623 .... 178 A
mmoos@martin.edu

MOOS, William, H .... 509-335-0200 .... 539 D
bill.moos@wsu.edu

MOOSBRUGGER,
Daniel, P .... 706-865-2134 .... 138 E
dmoosbrugger@truett.edu

MOOSE, Richard, E .... 315-267-2377 .... 354 C
moosere@potsdam.edu

MOOSMANN, Gloria .... 216-987-4788 .... 389 B
gloria.moosmann@tri-c.edu

MOOT, Bradley .... 212-678-8035 .... 337 G
brmoot@jtsa.edu

MOOTHART, Kathy .... 319-385-6209 .... 186 E
kathy.moothart@iwc.edu

MOOTZ, Jay .... 916-739-7151 ...... 76 A
jmootz@pacific.edu

MOPPERT, Jan .... 610-499-4177 .... 451 F
jamoppert@widener.edu

MORA, Aracely .... 714-628-4880 ...... 63 G
mora_aracely@sccollege.edu

MORA, Francisco .... 503-845-3110 .... 417 A
francisco.mora@mtangel.edu

MORA, Michelle .... 818-240-1000 ...... 48 D
mmora@glendale.edu

MORA, Peter, L .... 609-343-4901 .... 307 C
mora@atlantic.edu

MORAH, Emeka, O .... 937-708-5705 .... 405 H
emorah@wilberforce.edu

MORAIN, Tom .... 641-784-5053 .... 185 B
tmorain@gracelend.edu

MORALE, Joseph, L .... 903-927-3232 .... 509 E
jmorale@wileyc.edu

MORALE, Mary .... 937-708-5782 .... 405 H
mmorale@wilberforce.edu

MORALE, Sonja .... 903-566-7059 .... 506 E
smorale@uttyler.edu

MORALES, Ada .... 787-882-2065 .... 566 A
colocaiones@unitecpr.net

MORALES, Adelina, C .... 325-942-2073 .... 480 E
adelina.morales@angelo.edu

MORALES, Angel .... 787-852-1430 .... 562 F
amorales@hccpr.edu

MORALES, Aurea .... 718-963-4112 .... 324 C
amorales@boricuacollege.edu

MORALES, David .... 713-221-8513 .... 503 F
moralesd@uhd.edu

MORALES, Edwin .... 787-265-3864 .... 567 F
edwin.morales3@upr.edu

MORALES, Edwin .... 787-786-3030 .... 560 G
emorales@ucb.edu.pr

MORALES, George .... 806-743-2952 .... 502 B
george.morales@ttuhsc.edu

MORALES, George .... 336-917-5405 .... 376 E
george.morales@salem.edu

MORALES, Ileana .... 787-878-5475 .... 563 B
imorales@arecibo.inter.edu

MORALES, Irma .... 787-863-2390 .... 563 E
irma.morales@fajardo.inter.edu

MORALES, James .... 435-797-1712 .... 511 E
james.morales@usu.edu

MORALES, Jossue .... 787-891-0925 .... 563 A
jomorales@aguadilla.inter.edu

MORALES, Karen, G .... 787-841-2000 .... 565 B
karen_morales@pucpr.edu

MORALES, Lorraine .... 520-206-6577 ...... 17 H
lomorales@pima.edu

MORALES, Milga .... 718-951-5352 .... 326 F
milga@brooklyn.cuny.edu

MORALES, Nora .... 361-354-2239 .... 483 B
moralesn@coastlbend.edu

MORALES, Ramona .... 305-593-1223 .... 102 H
rmorales@albizu.edu

MORALES, Robert .... 805-965-0581 ...... 68 B
moralesr@sbcc.edu

MORALES, Rosalia .... 787-864-2222 .... 563 F
rmorales@inter.edu

MORALES, Sandra .... 787-857-3600 .... 563 C
smorales@br.inter.edu

MORALES, Tomas .... 909-537-5002 ...... 36 B
tmorales@csusb.edu

MORALES-MARTINEZ,
Maria .... 787-264-1912 .... 564 B
marimo@sg.inter.edu

MORAMARCO, Jacques .... 310-453-8300 ...... 45 G
jacques@emperors.edu

MORAN, Alan .... 216-987-3484 .... 389 B
alan.moran@tri-c.edu

MORAN, Carmella .... 630-844-5132 .... 145 F
cmoran@aurora.edu

MORAN, Christyn .... 610-527-0200 .... 445 J
christyn@rosemont.edu

MORAN, Francis, J .... 540-234-9261 .... 526 D
moranf@brcc.edu

MORAN, III, James, D .... 717-720-4200 .... 441 E
jmoran@passhe.edu

MORAN, James, J .... 615-353-3249 .... 475 E
josh.moran@nscc.edu

MORAN, James, M .... 203-576-4735 ...... 94 F
jmoran@bridgeport.edu

MORAN, Kathryn, A .... 317-788-3367 .... 180 F
kmoran@uindy.edu

MORAN, Ken .... 502-456-6504 .... 206 H
kmoran@sullivan.edu

MORAN, Lauren, E .... 386-226-7024 .... 105 H
lauren.moran@erau.edu

MORAN, Maggie .... 662-562-3277 .... 276 D
mmoran@northwestms.edu

MORAN, Michael .... 413-565-1000 .... 230 G
mmoran@baypath.edu

MORAN, Nichole .... 610-436-2813 .... 444 A
nmoran@wcupa.edu

MORAN, Patricia .... 610-606-4609 .... 425 A
pmoran@cedarcrest.edu

MORAN, Patrick .... 307-766-4175 .... 556 H
therock@uwyo.edu

MORAN, Paul, J .... 570-208-5948 .... 432 G
pjmoran@kings.edu

MORAN, Sam, E .... 540-365-4250 .... 519 C
semoran@ferrum.edu

MORAN, Stephanie .... 303-404-5157 ...... 85 A
steph.moran@frontrange.edu

MORAN, Tracy .... 585-389-2030 .... 342 D
tmoran8@naz.edu

MORAN, Virginia .... 760-245-4271 ...... 77 H
virginia.moran@vvc.edu

MORAN, Wes .... 706-378-2903 .... 126 C
wmoran@berry.edu

MORAN, Yvette .... 602-274-1885 ...... 17 E
ymoran@pihma.edu

MORAN-BROWN, Carol .... 802-865-6426 .... 513 C
moran@champlain.edu

MORANO, Lori .... 518-464-8648 .... 333 E
lmorano@excelsior.edu

MORANSKI, Karen .... 217-206-7413 .... 167 C
moranski.karen@uis.edu

MORANT, Blake .... 336-758-5430 .... 380 C
morantbd@wfu.edu

MORAVEC, Todd, A .... 518-564-2072 .... 354 B
moraveta@plattsburgh.edu

MORAZ, Kristen, L .... 561-237-7602 .... 113 D
kmoraz@lynn.edu

MORBER, Timothy, T .... 330-471-8279 .... 395 F
tmorber@malone.edu

MORCIGLIO, Jean .... 517-483-1862 .... 254 A
morcigj@lcc.edu

MORDACH, John .... 312-942-5600 .... 163 D
john_mordach@rush.edu

MORDI, John .... 787-765-1915 .... 564 D
jmordi@inter.edu

MORDOSKY, Anthony, A .... 856-256-4402 .... 314 A
mordosky@rowan.edu

MORE, George .... 412-281-2600 .... 447 A
gmore@western-school.com

MOREA, Marilisa .... 312-467-8606 .... 146 F
mmorea@thechicagoschool.edu

MOREAU, Donald .... 603-641-7350 .... 305 G
dmoreau@anselm.edu

MOREAU, Joseph .... 650-949-6119 ...... 47 F
moreaujoe@fhda.edu

MOREAU, Matt .... 740-389-6786 .... 399 D
moreau.1@osu.edu

MOREDOCK, Gerald, M .... 615-248-7773 .... 476 G
gmoredock@trevecca.edu

MOREE, Chris .... 318-676-7811 .... 211 D
chris.moree@nwltc.edu

MOREFIELD, Bill, R .... 423-318-2735 .... 476 D
bill.morefield@ws.edu

MOREHEAD, Bobbi .... 314-921-9290 .... 292 A
bmorehead@ugst.edu

MOREHEAD, Jere, W .... 706-583-0506 .... 138 G
morehead@uga.edu

MOREHEAD, Kaleybra .... 870-543-5963 ...... 23 H
kmorehead@seark.edu

MOREHEAD, Kaleybra, M .... 870-543-5963 ...... 23 H
kmorehead@seark.edu

MOREHEAD, Michael, A .... 575-646-5858 .... 319 D
mmorehea@nmsu.edu

MOREHOUSE, JR.,
Percy, A .... 303-556-3022 ...... 86 F
morehoup@msudenver.edu

MOREIRA, Antonio, R .... 410-455-6576 .... 227 D
moreira@umbc.edu

MOREL, Derek .... 504-280-6102 .... 213 E

MORELAND, Jeremy .... 480-557-3231 ...... 19 A
jeremy.moreland@phoenix.edu

MORELAND, Mark .... 503-654-8000 .... 419 F
mmoreland@pioneerpacific.edu

MORELAND, Robert .... 260-665-4111 .... 180 D
morelandr@trine.edu

MORELL-MARRERO,
Idalia .... 787-993-8897 .... 567 B
idalia.morell1@upr.edu

MORELLI, Brad .... 405-974-3573 .... 413 B
bmorelli@uco.edu

MORELLI, Gilda .... 617-552-4094 .... 232 B
gilda.morelli@bc.edu

MORELLI, Michael .... 330-339-3391 .... 394 A
mmorrell2@kent.edu

MORELLO, Debra .... 607-778-5199 .... 324 G
morelloda@sunybroome.edu

MORELLO, John, T .... 540-654-1269 .... 525 D
jmorello@umw.edu

MORELLO, Joseph .... 650-738-4271 ...... 67 H
morelloj@smccd.edu

MORELOCK, Luann .... 309-655-7353 .... 163 G
luann.morelock@osfhealthcare.org

MORELOCK, Tommy .... 352-854-2322 .... 103 K
moreloct@cf.edu

MORENA, Pat .... 718-368-5069 .... 328 A
pmorena@kbcc.cuny.edu

MORENCY, Maurice .... 212-752-1530 .... 338 C
maurice.morency@limcollege.edu

MORENO, Amy, R .... 717-291-3989 .... 429 F
amy.moreno@fandm.edu

MORENO, Charlotte .... 831-459-2009 ...... 75 C
cmoreno@ucsc.edu

MORENO, Christian .... 831-443-1700 ...... 50 C
christian_moreno@heald.edu

MORENO, Gertrud .... 903-875-7315 .... 491 C
gettie.moreno@navarrocollege.edu

MORENO, Luis, S .... 815-288-5511 .... 164 B
morenol@svcc.edu

MORENO, Monica 818-364-7863 55 A morenomm@lamission.edu
MORENO, Patricia 281-873-0262 483 I p.moreno@commonwealth.edu
MORENO-RIANO, Gerson 757-352-4500 523 E gmorenoriano@regent.edu
MORENO-WEINERT, Inez 602-243-8134 16 D inez.moreno-weinert@smcmail.maricopa.edu
MORERA-GONZÁLEZ, Angel 787-993-8871 567 B angel.morera1@upr.edu
MORESCHI, Tracy, L 503-255-0332 417 C tmoreschi@multnomah.edu
MOREST, Vanessa 203-857-3368 92 C vmorest@ncc.commnet.edu
MORETTA, Amy 937-298-3399 394 D amy.moretta@kcma.edu
MORETTI, James 215-567-7080 422 D jmoretti@edmc.edu
MORETTI, JoAnn 561-297-0853 119 A jmoretti@fau.edu
MORETTI, Linda 716-829-7811 332 E moretti@dyc.edu
MOREY, Ann, N 818-677-2878 35 F ann.morey@csun.edu
MOREY, Diane 661-362-3214 41 I diane.morey@canyons.edu
MOREY, Megan 413-542-2985 230 A mmorey@amherst.edu
MORGAN, Alan 913-234-0713 191 J alan.morgan@cleveland.edu
MORGAN, Alikhan 914-606-6745 360 E alikhan.morgan@sunywcc.edu
MORGAN, Allen 865-471-3372 467 G amorgan@cn.edu
MORGAN, Andre 832-252-0722 483 C andre.morgan@cbshouston.edu
MORGAN, Ann 212-875-4403 323 C gradcourses@bankstreet.edu
MORGAN, Ann 661-395-4453 52 L amorgan@bakersfieldcollege.edu
MORGAN, Anna, B 731-661-5410 477 B amorgan@uu.edu
MORGAN, Annette 903-983-8217 489 I amorgan@kilgore.edu
MORGAN, Barbara 617-879-2118 246 C bmorgan@wheelock.edu
MORGAN, Betsy, S 269-467-9945 251 B bmorgan@glenoaks.edu
MORGAN, Bronwyn 870-762-3172 20 A bmorgan@anc.edu
MORGAN, Bruce 765-966-2656 176 H bmorgan4@ivytech.edu
MORGAN, Bruce 423-775-7233 467 F bruce.morgan@bryan.edu
MORGAN, Bryant 802-251-7690 513 H bmorgan@marlboro.edu
MORGAN, Camella 253-833-9111 534 H cmorgan@greenriver.edu
MORGAN, Candice 919-854-2121 19 A candice.morgan@phoenix.edu
MORGAN, Carlene, J 919-516-4098 376 D cjmorgan@st-aug.edu
MORGAN, Chris 908-737-0600 311 A cmorgan@kean.edu
MORGAN, Chris 951-343-4369 31 J cmorgan@calbaptist.edu
MORGAN, David 765-361-6382 181 E morgand@wabash.edu
MORGAN, Deborah 918-540-6312 408 J demorgan@neo.edu
MORGAN, Derek 303-273-3288 83 B dmorgan@mines.edu
MORGAN, Derrick 940-565-2834 504 D
MORGAN, Elizabeth 909-621-8101 40 G elizabeth.morgan@cmc.edu
MORGAN, Elizabeth, M 207-768-2700 218 J emorgan@nmcc.edu
MORGAN, Eloise, L 914-337-9300 330 G eloise.morgan@concordia-ny.edu
MORGAN, Gary 847-543-2499 148 B eng034@clcillinois.edu
MORGAN, Gilbert 443-885-3125 224 E gilbert.morgan@morgan.edu
MORGAN, Ginny 510-841-9230 79 J vmorgan@wi.edu
MORGAN, Greg 541-463-5516 416 E morgang@lanecc.edu
MORGAN, Heath 660-831-4087 286 F morganh@moval.edu
MORGAN, J. Reid 336-758-5122 380 C jrm@wfu.edu
MORGAN, Janice 408-855-5397 78 F janice.morgan@wvm.edu
MORGAN, Jason 713-576-3816 19 A jason.morgan@phoenix.edu
MORGAN, Jason 256-352-8225 10 A jason.morgan@wallacestate.edu
MORGAN, Jay 270-809-4274 205 A jmorgan@murraystate.edu
MORGAN, Jim 575-461-4413 318 G jimm@mesalands.edu
MORGAN, Joanne, L 919-658-8558 367 F jmorgan@moc.edu
MORGAN, John 973-684-5402 312 E jmorgan@pccc.edu
MORGAN, John 928-717-7721 19 C john.morgan@yc.edu
MORGAN, John, G 615-366-4403 473 D chancellor@tbr.edu
MORGAN, Joshua 575-492-2769 319 B jmorgan@nmjc.edu
MORGAN, Ken 478-825-6304 129 F morgank@fvsu.edu
MORGAN, LaRoyce 770-612-2170 99 G
MORGAN, Lela, M 401-825-2142 453 D lmorgan@ccri.edu
MORGAN, Lily 620-331-4100 193 I lmorgan@indycc.edu
MORGAN, Linda 276-466-7998 529 D lindamorgan@vic.edu
MORGAN, Lissa 901-572-2441 467 C lissa.morgan@bchs.edu
MORGAN, Marji 509-963-1858 532 C mmorgan@cwu.edu
MORGAN, Mark 407-708-2224 117 H morganm@seminolestate.edu
MORGAN, Melanie 979-830-4146 482 C melanie.morgan@blinn.edu
MORGAN, Melissa 215-574-9600 431 B mmorgan@hussianart.edu
MORGAN, Mia 781-595-6768 236 C mmorgan@mariancourt.edu
MORGAN, Michael, D 205-726-2727 6 G mmorgan@samford.edu
MORGAN, Michael, D 518-564-3066 354 B morganmd@plattsburgh.edu
MORGAN, Michael, L 608-262-4048 550 I mmorgan@uwsa.edu
MORGAN, Mike 510-666-8248 26 H mmorgan@aimc.edu
MORGAN, Nancy 386-506-4579 104 F morgann@daytonastate.edu
MORGAN, Ophelia 201-360-4198 310 E omorgan@hccc.edu
MORGAN, Pamela 940-397-4785 491 B pamela.morgan@mwsu.edu
MORGAN, Patricia 207-221-4273 221 A pmorgan1@une.edu
MORGAN, Patricia 707-256-7305 58 F pmorgan@napavalley.edu
MORGAN, Paul 970-943-3087 89 E pmorgan@western.edu
MORGAN, Peggy 303-914-6337 87 G peggy.morgan@rrcc.edu
MORGAN, R. Gregory 617-452-2082 241 D
MORGAN, Randy 559-791-2232 53 A rmorgan@portervillecollege.edu
MORGAN, Scott 360-867-6913 534 D sustainabilitydirector@evergreen.edu
MORGAN, Scott 509-533-7042 533 A scott.morgan@scc.spokane.edu
MORGAN, Scott 509-279-6040 533 A smorgan@iel.spokane.com
MORGAN, Scott 509-533-7042 533 B scott.morgan@scc.spokane.edu
MORGAN, Sharon, E 973-596-5560 312 C sharon.e.morgan@njit.edu
MORGAN, Stephen, R 801-832-2750 512 G smorgan@westminstercollege.edu
MORGAN, Steve 206-934-6424 537 F steve.morgan@seattlecolleges.edu
MORGAN, Steve 740-695-9500 385 B smorgan@belmontcollege.edu
MORGAN, Steven 304-424-8289 545 C steven.morgan@mail.wvu.edu
MORGAN, Susan, P 585-785-1454 334 A morgansp@flcc.edu
MORGAN, Thomas, F 612-330-1773 261 B morgan@augsburg.edu
MORGAN, Tyler, S 801-524-8161 510 E tmorgan@ldsbc.edu
MORGAN, Warren, H 413-542-2267 230 A whmorgan@amherst.edu
MORGAN-CLEMENT, Linda 330-263-2602 388 F lclement@wooster.edu
MORGAN FOSTER, Stacey 509-359-6015 533 H sfoster@ewu.edu
MORGAN RIGGS, Janet 717-337-6010 429 I jriggs@gettysburg.edu
MORGAN-RUSSELL, Simon, N 419-372-2340 385 E smorgan@bgsu.edu
MORGANLANDER, Beth 718-261-5800 324 D jobplacement@bramsonort.edu
MORGANO, Sam, V 330-569-5335 391 G morganosv@hiram.edu
MORGANS, Jaime 660-263-4110 286 H jaimem@macc.edu
MORGANSTEIN, Penny 212-472-1500 343 G pmorganstein@mysid.edu
MORGANTI, Danielle 856-415-2113 310 D dmorganti@gccnj.edu
MORGEN, Evelyn, B 860-679-3323 95 A emorgen@uchc.edu
MORGEN, Sandra 541-346-2800 419 B smorgen@uoregon.edu
MORGENSTERN, Patricia 269-467-9945 251 B pmorgenstern@glenoaks.edu
MORGENTHALER, Diane, S 203-392-6300 90 I morgenthald1@southernct.edu
MORI, Amy 518-437-1802 324 I amori@bryantstratton.edu
MORI, Darryl 626-396-4288 29 I darryl.mori@artcenter.edu
MORI, Priscilla 805-893-3285 75 B priscilla.mori@ombuds.ucsb.edu
MORIARTY, Christy, A 302-855-5927 96 E cmoriart@dtcc.edu
MORIARTY, Debra 410-704-2055 228 E dmoriarty@towson.edu
MORIARTY, Donna, E 914-594-4536 343 F donna_moriarty@nymc.edu
MORIARTY, John 305-899-3957 101 M jmoriarty@mail.barry.edu
MORIARTY, Joseph 812-357-6231 180 A jmoriarty@saintmeinrad.edu
MORIARTY, Karen 330-823-6045 404 C moriarkl@mountunion.edu
MORIARTY, Maureen 617-928-4071 242 E mmoriarty@mountida.edu
MORICONI, Jill 814-254-0557 425 G jmoriconi@pa.gov
MORICONI, Kimberly, A 816-604-6544 285 A kim.moriconi@mcckc.edu
MORIN, Christine 207-755-5215 218 G cmorin@cmcc.edu
MORIN, Erin 336-770-3294 379 E morine@uncsa.edu
MORIN, III, Frederick, C 802-656-2156 514 H frederick.morin@uvm.edu
MORIN, Jeff 715-346-4920 552 D jmorin@uwsp.edu
MORIN, Kevin, A 414-277-7129 549 C morin@msoe.edu
MORIN, Regina 660-785-7468 290 G rmorin@truman.edu
MORIN, Robert 775-445-4254 303 B rpmorin@wnc.edu
MORINEC, Maire 707-864-7000 70 A maire.morinec@solano.edu
MORISHITA, Leroy, M 510-885-3877 34 E leroy.morishita@csueastbay.edu
MORISTON, Shelley 303-292-0015 84 C s.moriston@denverschoolofnursing.edu
MORITZ, Patricia 303-724-1679 88 J pat.moritz@ucdenver.edu
MORIWAKI, Sharene 808-847-9843 142 B sharene@hcc.hawaii.edu
MORLEY, Del 660-562-1363 287 B dmorley@nwmissouri.edu
MORLEY, Elizabeth 607-431-4122 335 A morleye@hartwick.edu
MORLEY, John 312-850-7230 147 F jmorley@ccc.edu
MORLEY, Kathleen 254-710-2061 482 A kathleen_morley@baylor.edu
MORLEY, Mary 732-255-0400 312 D mmorley@ocean.edu
MORLEY, Mary, N 626-395-6354 32 H mmorley@caltech.edu
MORLEY, Richard, H 949-451-5472 70 E rmorley@ivc.edu
MORLEY, Sandy 517-264-7193 258 B smorley@sienaheights.edu
MORLEY, Steve 765-998-5841 180 B stmorley@taylor.edu
MORLEY, Yvonne, Y 859-238-5220 199 G yvonne.morley@centre.edu
MORLEY-MOWER, Cynthia 213-763-7072 55 D morleycn@lattc.edu
MORLIER, Margaret, M 770-720-5579 136 C mmm@reinhardt.edu
MORNINGSTAR, Ellen 585-271-3657 348 B registrar@stbernards.edu
MORNINGSTAR, Scott 406-586-3585 294 G scott.morningstar@montanabiblecollege.edu
MORO, Martin 734-995-7589 249 G morom@cuaa.edu
MORODOMI, Joyce, K 559-323-2100 66 C jmorodomi@sjcl.edu
MOROI, Katsumi 213-613-2200 70 H kmoroi@sciarc.edu
MORONEY, James 617-254-2610 244 B
MORONEY, Mary, F 401-232-6298 453 C mmoroney@bryant.edu
MOROONEY, Kevin, M 814-865-3540 438 G kxm@psu.edu
MOROSKO, Linda 330-494-6170 402 B lmorosko@starkstate.edu
MOROSOFF, Wendy 914-251-6370 354 D wendy.morosoff@purchase.edu
MOROTTI, Allan 907-474-6440 10 I aamorotti@alaska.edu
MOROUKIAN, Mike 603-513-1356 306 F mike.moroukian@granite.edu
MOROWSKI, James 701-788-4619 381 H james.morowski@mayvillestate.edu
MOROZOWICH, Mark 202-319-5683 97 E morozowich@cua.edu
MORPHEW, Jeanne 763-488-2503 266 D jeanne.morphew@hennepintech.edu
MORPHEW, Michael 317-613-4800 169 F
MORRAL, Melissa 585-340-9633 329 F morral@crcds.edu
MORRELL, Daniel 617-989-4076 245 F morrelld@wit.edu
MORRELL, Nancy 303-546-3513 86 H nancym@naropa.edu
MORRELL, Sarah 508-678-2811 239 B sarah.morrell@bristolcc.edu
MORRICE, Pelema, I 402-554-2200 301 A
MORRILL, Allen 724-589-2124 448 B amorrill@thiel.edu
MORRILL, Bill 575-492-2791 319 B bmorrill@nmjc.edu
MORRILL, Deborah, H 210-567-6395 507 A morrill@uthscsa.edu
MORRILL, Donald, D 813-258-7409 123 A dmorrill@ut.edu
MORRIS, Adam 562-903-4730 31 A adam.morris@biola.edu
MORRIS, Alice, H 713-646-1796 494 I amorris@stcl.edu
MORRIS, Andrew 585-389-2801 342 D amorris8@naz.edu
MORRIS, Angela 502-895-3411 204 F amorris@lpts.edu
MORRIS, Ann 903-693-2014 492 C amorris@panola.edu
MORRIS, Ann 704-216-3542 373 F ann.morris@rccc.edu
MORRIS, Ann 419-824-3694 395 E amorris@lourdes.edu
MORRIS, Anne 910-410-1811 373 B amorris@richmondcc.edu
MORRIS, Barbara 970-247-7314 84 K morris_b@fortlewis.edu
MORRIS, Barbara 410-532-5367 225 D bmorris@ndm.edu
MORRIS, Barry 601-318-6139 278 C bmorris@wmcarey.edu
MORRIS, Ben 252-940-6374 368 C benm@beaufortccc.edu
MORRIS, Bernadette 845-257-3101 352 B morrisb@newpaltz.edu
MORRIS, Beth 828-765-7351 372 A bmorris@mayland.edu
MORRIS, Bevan, H 641-472-8194 187 E president@mum.edu
MORRIS, Beverly 937-298-3399 394 D beverly.morris@khnetwork.org
MORRIS, Brenda 870-584-4471 25 C bmorris@cccua.edu
MORRIS, Brett 859-622-3840 200 J admissions@eku.edu
MORRIS, Carlton, E 334-724-4191 8 B cmorris@mytu.tuskegee.edu
MORRIS, Cheryl 405-631-3399 408 C
MORRIS, Clark 816-415-5997 293 C morrisc@william.jewell.edu
MORRIS, Clark, W 816-415-5997 293 C morrisc@william.jewell.edu
MORRIS, Corinne 402-844-7361 299 I corinne@northeast.edu
MORRIS, Craig 541-552-6319 419 A cmorris@sou.edu
MORRIS, Cricket 252-985-5145 375 E lmorris@ncwc.edu
MORRIS, Dan 702-651-5500 302 E dan.morris@csn.edu
MORRIS, Daryl 334-244-3295 1 G dmorris@aum.edu
MORRIS, David 602-243-8127 16 D david.morris@smcmail.maricopa.edu
MORRIS, Delesa 561-803-2022 114 C delesa_morris@pba.edu
MORRIS, Diana 800-567-2344 547 A dmorris@menominee.edu
MORRIS, Diane 202-639-1816 98 A dmorris@corcoran.org
MORRIS, Don 314-968-7450 292 J morrisdo@webster.edu
MORRIS, Dottie 603-358-2206 306 G dmorris@keene.edu
MORRIS, Duncan, D 860-253-3052 91 B dmorris@asnuntuck.edu
MORRIS, Emma, W 706-385-1058 136 B emma.morris@point.edu
MORRIS, Gary 315-312-2255 354 A gary.morris@oswego.edu
MORRIS, Genevieve 251-380-3020 7 E gmorris@shc.edu
MORRIS, Geri 419-227-3141 404 D geri@unoh.edu
MORRIS, Glenn 352-335-2332 100 D
MORRIS, Henry 507-389-1150 267 E henry.morris@mnsu.edu
MORRIS, Jacqueline 205-366-8950 7 F jmorris@stillman.edu
MORRIS, Jake 615-966-2000 470 F jake.morris@lipscomb.edu
MORRIS, Jay 740-699-2489 400 B morrisj@ohiou.edu

MORRIS, Jeff 620-251-7700 192 B
jeffm@coffeyville.edu
MORRIS, Jeffery, B 785-532-6415 194 D
jbmorris@ksu.edu
MORRIS, Jennifer, M 650-325-5621 64 G
jennifer.morris@stpatricksseminary.org
MORRIS, Jerry, R 606-474-3121 201 D
jmorris@kcu.edu
MORRIS, Jim 386-752-1822 108 G
jim.morris@fgc.edu
MORRIS, Joe 601-923-1700 276 F
jmorris@rts.edu
MORRIS, Joe, E 205-853-1200 5 C
jmorris@jeffstateonline.com
MORRIS, John 808-739-8555 140 E
jmorris@chaminade.edu
MORRIS, John, K 801-581-4466 511 C
john.morris@legal.utah.edu
MORRIS, Juanita 731-427-2550 470 B
jmorris@lanecollege.edu
MORRIS, Julia, M 304-457-6205 540 E
auviljm@ab.edu
MORRIS, Karen 803-641-3489 462 B
karenm@usca.edu
MORRIS, Katherine, W 937-775-2809 406 C
kathy.morris@wright.edu
MORRIS, Kathryn 317-940-9903 170 F
kmorris@butler.edu
MORRIS, Kenneth, W 319-895-4484 183 G
kmorris@cornellcollege.edu
MORRIS, Kevin 936-294-1753 501 D
upd_khm@shsu.edu
MORRIS, Kevin 281-922-3479 494 B
kevin.morris@sjcd.edu
MORRIS, Kimberly 770-412-4005 137 F
kmorris@sctech.edu
MORRIS, Kizzy 570-422-2820 442 D
kmorris@po-box.esu.edu
MORRIS, Kyle 307-755-2160 557 B
kmorris@wyotech.edu
MORRIS, LaSonia 318-670-9319 215 A
lmorris@susla.edu
MORRIS, Laura 832-813-6793 490 E
laura.k.morris@lonestar.edu
MORRIS, Laura, M 302-295-1179 97 C
laura.m.morris@wilmu.edu
MORRIS, Lawrence, J 202-319-5142 97 E
morrisl@cua.edu
MORRIS, Lela 817-598-6488 508 F
morris@wc.edu
MORRIS, Linda, M 570-327-4770 440 L
lmorris@pct.edu
MORRIS, Lonnie 301-860-3427 228 A
lmorris@bowiestate.edu
MORRIS, Loren, L 620-665-3523 193 H
morrisl@hutchcc.edu
MORRIS, M. Scott 404-894-2499 130 F
scott.morris@ohr.gatech.edu
MORRIS, Marie, S 765-641-4020 169 E
msmorris@anderson.edu
MORRIS, Mark 360-438-4394 537 B
mmorris@stmartin.edu
MORRIS, Mellasenah 410-234-4655 225 E
MORRIS, Michele, M 561-237-7788 113 D
mmorris@lynn.edu
MORRIS, Nancy 615-230-3272 476 C
nancy.morris@volstate.edu
MORRIS, Nerissa, E 305-284-4476 122 I
nmorris@miami.edu
MORRIS, Nora 763-433-1632 265 G
nora.morris@anokaramsey.edu
MORRIS, Pearl, A 505-863-7576 321 D
pmorris@gallup.unm.edu
MORRIS, Phil 803-822-3559 459 E
morrisp@midlandstech.edu
MORRIS, Princilla, E 615-329-8888 468 I
psmart@fisk.edu
MORRIS, Rachel 216-373-5320 397 F
rmorris@ndc.edu
MORRIS, Reggie 323-241-5200 55 C
morrisr@lasc.du
MORRIS, Renea 740-593-2563 399 G
morrisr@ohio.edu
MORRIS, Rick 864-977-7777 460 A
publicsafety@ngu.edu
MORRIS, Rita, R 740-351-3208 401 I
rmorris@shawnee.edu
MORRIS, III, Robert 520-459-1610 508 E
morrisb@wbu.edu
MORRIS, Robert, D 404-413-2502 131 G
robinmorris@gsu.edu
MORRIS, Robert, J 765-285-1300 169 G
rmorris@bsu.edu
MORRIS, Sandra, L 843-792-8720 459 D
morriss@musc.edu
MORRIS, Sarah, L 816-235-1023 291 C
morrissl@umkc.edu
MORRIS, Steve 270-789-5017 199 F
srmorris@campbellsville.edu
MORRIS, Steve 606-539-4209 207 C
steve.morris@ucumberlands.edu
MORRIS, Tammy, H 336-599-1181 372 G
morrist@piedmontcc.edu
MORRIS, Tiffany, D 336-342-4261 373 E
morrist@rockinghamcc.edu
MORRIS, Tom 570-586-2400 422 G
tmorris@bbc.edu
MORRIS, Tracy, L 815-224-0393 153 E
tracy_morris@ivcc.edu
MORRIS, Trevor 817-531-7587 502 C
tmorris@txwes.edu
MORRIS, Valerie, B 843-953-8222 457 B
morrisv@cofc.edu
MORRIS, Wanda 310-900-1600 45 F
morris_w@compton.edu
MORRIS, Wayne 618-262-8641 153 A
morrisw@iecc.edu
MORRIS, Wendi 478-296-6179 135 C
wmorris@oftc.edu
MORRIS, William 432-685-4641 491 A
wmorris@midland.edu
MORRIS, William, G 315-267-2579 354 C
morriswg@potsdam.edu
MORRIS, William, R 512-492-3060 480 F
wmorris@aoma.edu
MORRIS, Willie 630-753-9091 160 D
wmorris@nc.edu
MORRIS-POWELL, Donna 336-334-7593 378 A
demorris@ncat.edu
MORRIS WOOD, JR.,
Dossie 910-843-5304 367 G
MORRISETTE, Joanna 919-735-5151 375 A
jmmorrisette@waynecc.edu
MORRISON, Barry, F 401-232-6017 453 C
bmorriso@bryant.edu
MORRISON, Bennett 440-834-3726 393 G
bmorri11@kent.edu
MORRISON, Betty 630-829-6347 145 G
bmorrison@ben.edu
MORRISON, Brenda, M 443-412-2409 223 B
bmorrison@harford.edu
MORRISON, Caleb 803-313-7100 462 E
calebm@mailbox.sc.edu
MORRISON, Carberta, A 856-225-2949 314 D
cammor@camden.rutgers.edu
MORRISON, Carol 239-513-1122 111 A
cmorrison@hodges.edu
MORRISON, Darrell 479-788-7035 24 D
darrell.morrison@uafs.edu
MORRISON, David 770-534-6167 126 E
dmorrison@brenau.edu
MORRISON, David 270-534-3387 203 E
david.morrison@kctcs.edu
MORRISON, Don 641-628-5280 183 D
morrisond@central.edu
MORRISON, Edwina 406-444-6570 294 H
emorrison@montana.edu
MORRISON, Gail 651-450-3512 266 F
gmorris@inverhills.edu
MORRISON, Gale, M 805-893-4175 75 B
gale.morrison@graddiv.ucsb.edu
MORRISON, George, H 304-236-7640 543 C
george.morrison@southernwv.edu
MORRISON, Holly 478-757-2647 133 H
holly.morrison@maconstate.edu
MORRISON, James 617-746-1990 235 G
james.morrison@hult.edu
MORRISON, Jason 580-477-7767 414 C
jason.morrison@wosc.edu
MORRISON, Jean 617-353-2000 232 E
jmorrison@bu.edu
MORRISON, Jenni 419-783-2380 389 H
jmorrison@defiance.edu
MORRISON, Jennifer 800-523-1578 122 C
jmorrison@teu.edu
MORRISON, Jennifer, K 508-767-7007 230 D
jemorrison@assumption.edu
MORRISON, Julie 734-973-5010 259 F
jmorriso@wccnet.edu
MORRISON, Kelly, S 434-381-6337 524 K
morrison@sbc.edu
MORRISON, Kirk 858-513-9240 182 C
kirk.morrison@ashford.edu
MORRISON, Leonard 781-891-2575 231 D
lmorrison@bentley.edu
MORRISON, Marty, G 540-654-2287 525 D
mmorris3@umw.edu
MORRISON, Maureen, V 203-773-8542 90 C
morrison@albertus.edu
MORRISON, Michael 626-650-2306 48 H
MORRISON, Nancy 212-998-4924 344 B
nancy.morrison@nyu.edu
MORRISON, Rebecca, L 414-955-4949 548 G
rmorriso@mcw.edu
MORRISON, Regina 650-738-4350 67 H
morrison@smccd.edu
MORRISON, Rhonda 316-322-3124 191 G
rmorrison@butlercc.edu
MORRISON, Ricky 419-227-3141 404 D
rmorrison@unoh.edu
MORRISON, Rob 503-682-3903 419 F
rmorrison@pioneerpacific.edu
MORRISON, Rodney 856-225-6510 314 D
rodneymo@camden.rutgers.edu
MORRISON, Rodney 419-448-2391 391 F
rmorriso@heidelberg.edu
MORRISON, Scott, D 540-828-5376 517 B
smorriso@bridgewater.edu
MORRISON, Sharon 580-745-2702 412 C
smorrison@se.edu
MORRISON, Thomas 812-855-6992 173 D
morrison@indiana.edu
MORRISON, Tim 909-607-1113 40 E
tim_morrison@cuc.claremont.edu
MORRISON, Tom 812-855-6992 173 E
morrisot@indiana.edu
MORRISON-BEEDY,
Dianne 813-974-2191 121 A
dmbeedy@health.usf.edu
MORRISON-SHETLAR,
Alison 336-278-6490 364 D
amorrison4@elon.edu
MORRISS-OLSON,
Melissa 413-565-1000 230 G
mmolson@baypath.edu
MORRISSEY, Ann, M 401-874-4846 454 E
morrissey@uri.edu
MORRISSEY, Jeff, P 417-836-5770 286 C
jeffmorrissey@missouristate.edu
MORRISSEY, Marietta 973-655-4314 311 F
morrisseym@mail.montclair.edu
MORRISSEY, Morgan 518-445-3207 322 C
mmorr@albanylaw.edu
MORRISSEY, Sharron 919-807-7100 367 I
morrissey@nccommunitycolleges.edu
MORRO, Robert 610-519-4589 450 H
robert.morro@villanova.edu
MORROBEL-SOSA, Anny 718-960-8111 327 C
morrobel.sosa@lehman.cuny.edu
MORROBEL-SOSA, Anny 915-747-5536 506 B
amorrobel@utep.edu
MORRONE, Anastasia 317-274-3479 174 D
amorrone@iupui.edu
MORROS, Lucy, S 636-949-2000 283 J
lmorros@lindenwood.edu
MORROW, Barbara, A 314-340-5763 282 F
morrowb@hssu.edu
MORROW, David 215-222-4200 445 G
dmorrow@walnuthillcollege.edu
MORROW, David, M 518-736-3622 334 D
dmorrow@fmcc.suny.edu
MORROW, Dorothy 402-557-7296 296 H
dorothy.morrow@bellevue.edu
MORROW, Frances 330-490-7312 405 F
fmorrow@walsh.edu
MORROW, Jacqueline, R 717-720-4045 442 F
MORROW, Jean 617-585-1250 242 I
jean.morrow@necmusic.edu
MORROW, Jeffrey, S 330-665-1084 398 E
jmorrow@ocm.edu
MORROW, Jessica 918-335-6268 411 B
jmorrow@okwu.edu
MORROW, Joyce 319-273-2701 182 G
joyce.morrow@uni.edu
MORROW, Laurie 318-357-3162 211 B
lmorrow@ltc.edu
MORROW, Liz 573-681-5011 283 I
morrowl@lincolnu.edu
MORROW, Marjann 325-574-7608 508 I
mmorrow@wtc.edu
MORROW, S. Rex 219-785-5550 179 A
smorrow@pnc.edu
MORROW, Wanda 713-646-1825 494 I
wmorrow@stcl.edu
MORROW-JENSEN,
Amanda 408-453-9900 50 F
amorrow-jensen@henley-putnam.edu
MORSBERGER, Michael, J 202-994-6419 98 C
mjm@gwu.edu
MORSCHES, Michael 708-974-5310 159 B
morschesm@morainevalley.edu
MORSE, Charles, C 508-831-5540 246 F
cmorse@wpi.edu
MORSE, Katherine 206-934-7791 537 D
katherine.morse@seattlecolleges.edu
MORSE, Marc 702-651-3008 302 E
marc.morse@csn.edu
MORSE, Mark 212-349-4330 334 G
mmorse@globe.edu
MORSE, Robert 603-526-3698 303 G
rmorse@colby-sawyer.edu
MORSE, Sarah 410-626-2522 225 G
sarah.morse@sjca.edu
MORSE, William 253-879-2808 538 H
wmorse@pugetsound.edu
MORSETTE, Clarice 406-395-4313 296 E
camorsette@yahoo.com
MORSMAN, Elaine 607-587-4061 355 C
morsmaem@alfredstate.edu
MORSOVILLO, Michael 708-524-6793 150 C
morsomike@dom.edu
MORT, Dale 717-569-7071 433 D
dmort@lbc.edu
MORTALI, Jill, M 603-646-3007 304 J
jill.m.mortali@dartmouth.edu
MORTEN, George 805-437-8516 34 B
george.morten@csuci.edu
MORTENSEN, Alan 815-584-2806 156 B
alan.mortensen@doc.illinois.gov
MORTENSEN, Brad 801-626-6002 511 G
bmortensen@weber.edu
MORTENSEN, Dan 863-667-5006 118 F
dmortensen@seu.edu
MORTENSEN, John 435-797-1110 511 E
john.mortensen@usu.edu
MORTENSEN, Larry 719-587-7402 80 L
lsmorten@adams.edu
MORTENSON, Donald, W 206-281-2522 537 H
dmort@spu.edu
MORTENSON, Stacey 701-627-4738 381 B
smorte@fbcc.bia.edu
MORTHLAND, Betsey 309-796-5285 145 H
morthlandb@bhc.edu
MORTIMER, Ian 802-651-5911 513 C
mortimer@champlain.edu
MORTIMER, Lee, E 513-556-0364 403 D
lee.mortimer@uc.edu
MORTIMER, Theresa 617-287-6800 236 G
theresa.mortimer@umb.edu
MORTLAND, Stephen 765-998-5206 180 B
stmortlan@taylor.edu
MORTON, Allen 203-837-9600 91 A
mortona@wcsu.edu
MORTON, Amy, M 508-831-5874 246 F
ammorton@wpi.edu
MORTON, Brad 973-290-4477 308 G
bmorton@cse.edu
MORTON, Clarresa 540-665-4517 524 E
cmorton@su.edu
MORTON, Danny 704-484-4032 369 E
morton@clevelandcc.edu
MORTON, Darren, M 718-990-6707 348 G
mortond@stjohns.edu
MORTON, Diane 301-846-2442 222 G
dmorton@frederick.edu
MORTON, John 808-956-7038 141 E
jmorton@hawaii.edu
MORTON, John, F 808-956-7038 141 I
jmorton@hawaii.edu
MORTON, Leo, E 816-235-1101 291 C
mortonle@umkc.edu
MORTON, Lisa 414-276-5200 170 I
lmorton@ccr.edu
MORTON, Lynn 704-337-2574 376 A
mortonl@queens.edu
MORTON, Lynn 704-337-2506 376 A
mortonl@queens.edu
MORTON, Marcia 417-667-8181 280 E
mmorton@cottey.edu
MORTON, Margaret 212-353-4208 331 A
mortonnyc@cooper.edu
MORTON, Mary 518-587-2100 355 G
mary.morton@esc.edu
MORTON, Nina 304-357-4944 542 A
ninamorton@ucwv.edu
MORTON, Penny 218-726-6397 271 F
pmorton@d.umn.edu
MORTON, Reggie 404-799-4500 126 H
rmorton@brownmackie.edu
MORY, Scott, M 213-740-2383 76 F
mory@usc.edu
MOSBO, John 812-488-1178 180 E
jm545@evansville.edu
MOSBURG, Calleb, N 580-327-8540 409 C
cnmosburg@nwosu.edu
MOSBY, Christel 602-639-7500 14 H
MOSBY, David, C 301-322-0655 225 F
dmosby@pgcc.edu
MOSBY, Gail 304-766-3047 544 F
gmosby@wvstateu.edu
MOSBY, John 650-738-4484 67 H
mosbyj@smccd.edu
MOSBY, Katy 423-461-8735 471 J
kmosby@milligan.edu
MOSBY-WILSON,
Shatiqua, A 504-286-5030 214 J
swilson@suno.edu
MOSCA, David 301-445-2772 227 A
dmosca@usmd.edu
MOSCA, Joseph, L 330-941-3321 406 F
jmosca@ysu.edu
MOSCARIELLO, Dawn, M 610-359-5298 426 G
dmoscariello@dccc.edu
MOSCATO, Robin, A 609-258-3330 312 G
moscato@princeton.edu
MOSCATO, Timothy 503-228-6528 414 E
MOSCHELLA, Deborah 508-626-4930 238 A
dmoschella@framingham.edu
MOSCHELLA, Jayne 561-912-1211 107 B
jmoschella@evergladesuniversity.edu
MOSELEY, David 479-968-0300 20 G
dmoseley@atu.edu
MOSELEY, James, G 317-738-8010 171 F
jmoseley@franklincollege.edu
MOSELEY, Lynne 707-638-5223 73 A
lynne.moseley@tu.edu
MOSELEY-JONES, Vickie 252-638-7225 370 A
moseleyv@cravencc.edu
MOSER, Bobby, D 614-292-1889 398 I
moser.2@osu.edu
MOSER, Donald, J 336-758-3904 380 C
moserdj@wfu.edu
MOSER, Drew 765-998-5384 180 B
drmoser@taylor.edu

MUELLER, Edward, A .... 603-862-3220.... 306 C edward.mueller@unh.edu
MUELLER, Harry .... 765-289-2291.... 176 B hmueller@ivytech.edu
MUELLER, John, P .... 414-410-4059.... 546 G jpmueller@stritch.edu
MUELLER, Joseph .... 307-382-1647.... 557 A jmueller@wwcc.wy.edu
MUELLER, Julie .... 636-949-4901.... 283 J jmueller@lindenwood.edu
MUELLER, Kathyrn .... 714-432-5646...... 41 D kmueller@occ.cccd.edu
MUELLER, Lloyd .... 503-338-2412.... 415 B lmueller@clatsopcc.edu
MUELLER, Martin .... 212-229-5896.... 342 E muellerm@newschool.edu
MUELLER, Michael, R .... 817-735-5475.... 504 E michael.mueller@unthsc.edu
MUELLER, Michelle .... 734-477-8976.... 259 F mimueller@wccnet.edu
MUELLER, OSU, Pam .... 270-686-4319.... 199 B pam.mueller@brescia.edu
MUELLER, Ralph .... 860-768-4648...... 95 B rmueller@hartford.edu
MUELLER, Steven, D .... 937-229-3141.... 404 A smueller1@udayton.edu
MUELLER, Steven, P .... 949-214-3386...... 43 C steve.mueller@cui.edu
MUELLER, Tim .... 701-224-2437.... 381 E tim.mueller@ndus.edu
MUELLER, Vilma .... 973-618-3384.... 308 C vmueller@caldwell.edu
MUELLER, William, J .... 423-266-4574.... 136 D bmueller@richmont.edu
MUELLER-ROEBKE, Jenny 402-643-7374.... 297 D jenny.roebke@cune.edu
MUERTZ, Julie, A .... 618-235-2700.... 165 D julie.muertz@swic.edu
MUESELER, Christine .... 724-838-4232.... 447 C mueseler@setonhill.edu
MUETHER, John .... 407-366-9493.... 276 F jmuether@rts.edu
MUETHER, John, R .... 407-366-9493.... 115 K jmuether@rts.edu
MUFFETT, Andrew .... 765-269-5900.... 176 D amuffett@ivytech.edu
MUGDH, Mrinal .... 281-283-3020.... 503 E mugdh@uhcl.edu
MUGG, Heather .... 404-727-9326.... 129 D hmugg@emory.edu
MUGGEP, Louis .... 845-398-4174.... 349 H lmuggeo@stac.edu
MUGGLETON, Mary .... 585-271-3657.... 348 B mmuggleton@stbernards.edu
MUGLER, Dale, H .... 330-972-5365.... 403 B dmugler@uakron.edu
MUGRIDGE, Philip .... 610-341-1721.... 428 E pmugridg@eastern.edu
MUGWANYA, Edmond, M . 818-779-8448...... 53 B emugwanya@kingsuniversity.edu
MUHA, Beth .... 202-885-2591...... 97 D beth@american.edu
MUHA, David .... 973-408-3206.... 309 E dmuha@drew.edu
MUHA, Priscilla .... 925-631-4522...... 64 F pdm2@stmarys-ca.edu
MUHA, Susan .... 216-987-3110.... 389 B susan.muha@tri-c.edu
MUHAMMED, Robert .... 336-750-3299.... 380 B muhammedr@wssu.edu
MUHLFELDER, Leslie, F .... 610-330-5060.... 433 B muhlfell@lafayette.edu
MUIR, Bernard .... 302-831-4006...... 96 I bmm@udel.edu
MUIR, JR., Harry, P .... 262-521-5435.... 553 B harry.muir@uwc.edu
MUIR, Janette .... 703-993-8891.... 519 E jmuir@gmu.edu
MUIR, Julie .... 916-649-8168...... 52 F
MUIR, Karen .... 614-287-2512.... 389 A kmuir@cscc.edu
MUIR, Thorton .... 770-426-2624.... 133 E tmuir@life.edu
MUIR, Troy .... 330-337-6403.... 383 J business@awc.edu
MUITE, Paul .... 305-899-3076.... 101 M pmuite@mail.barry.edu
MUKASA, Samuel .... 603-862-1781.... 306 C sam.mukasa@unh.edu
MUKERJEA, Rabindra, N .... 765-494-9708.... 178 J rnmukerjea@purdue.edu
MUKHARJI, Indrani .... 847-491-3005.... 160 E indrani@northwestern.edu
MULADORE, James, G ...... 989-964-4045.... 257 G jgm@svsu.edu
MULARCZYK, Linda .... 508-767-7157.... 230 D lmularczyk@assumption.edu
MULCAHEY, William .... 319-363-8213.... 187 H mulcahey@mtmercy.edu
MULCAHY, Kevin, F .... 716-878-4698.... 353 A mulcahkf@buffalostate.edu
MULCAHY, Mary .... 814-362-0259.... 449 B mnp1@pitt.edu
MULCAHY, R. Timothy .... 612-624-5054.... 272 A mulcahy@umn.edu
MULCAHY, Sean .... 913-360-7500.... 191 A smulcahy@benedictine.edu
MULCRONE, Michael .... 847-214-7820.... 150 F mmulccrone@elgin.edu
MULDER, Craig, A .... 231-995-1061.... 256 D cmulder@nmc.edu
MULDER, Lori .... 616-395-7811.... 252 D mulderl@hope.edu
MULDERICK, Thomas, J .... 610-799-1941.... 434 D tmulderick@lccc.edu
MULERO, Daritza .... 787-258-1501.... 561 F dmulero@columbiaco.edu
MULERO, Minerva .... 787-864-2222.... 563 F mmulero@inter.edu
MULFORD, David, H .... 540-375-2290.... 523 G mulford@roanoke.edu
MULGREW, Frank .... 203-591-5040...... 93 G fmulgrew@post.edu
MULHALL, Lawrence, P .... 864-833-8301.... 460 E lmulhall@presby.edu
MULHERIN, April, C .... 207-778-7081.... 220 C april.mulherin@maine.edu
MULHERIN, Lynn .... 407-712-1466...... 19 A lynn.mulherin@phoenix.edu
MULHERN, Jean, K .... 937-382-6661.... 405 I jean_mulhern@wilmington.edu
MULHERN, Michelle .... 330-325-6263.... 397 D mmulhern@neomed.edu
MULHOLLAND, William .... 413-236-2122.... 239 A wmulholl@berkshirecc.edu
MULKERN, Denise .... 973-972-4339.... 316 C mulkernde@umdnj.edu
MULKEY, Amelia .... 850-973-1604.... 113 K mulkeya@nfcc.edu
MULKEY, Betty .... 859-572-5763.... 205 H mulkey@nku.edu
MULKEY, Stephen .... 207-948-9100.... 219 H smulkey@unity.edu
MULKEY, Tom .... 575-492-2144.... 321 H tmulkey@usw.edu
MULL, Brenda .... 570-372-4451.... 447 E mullb@susqu.edu
MULL, Ray .... 304-327-4062.... 543 F rmull@bluefieldstate.edu
MULLALY, Lisa .... 703-396-6608.... 518 E lmullaly@devry.edu
MULLANE, William, S .... 512-223-1024.... 481 B wmullane@austincc.edu
MULLANEY, Kathryn, L ...... 315-229-5896.... 349 E kmullaney@stlawu.edu
MULLANEY, Kristin .... 603-228-3000.... 306 F kristin.mullaney@granite.edu
MULLANEY, Kristin .... 406-657-1007.... 296 C kristin.mullaney@rocky.edu
MULLANEY, Siri .... 928-226-4211...... 13 F siri.mullaney@coconino.edu
MULLARKEY, Patrick .... 570-208-5928.... 432 G patrickmullarkey@kings.edu
MULLEN, Adrienne, A .... 323-265-8613...... 54 G mullenaa@elac.edu
MULLEN, Amber .... 540-831-5096.... 523 A amullen@radford.edu
MULLEN, Deborah, F .... 404-687-4520.... 127 F mullend@ctsnet.edu
MULLEN, Denise .... 503-297-5544.... 417 G dmullen@ocac.edu
MULLEN, Eric .... 616-234-4164.... 251 E emullen@grcc.edu
MULLEN, James, H .... 814-332-5380.... 421 F james.mullen@allegheny.edu
MULLEN, Jennifer .... 757-683-3580.... 522 F jmullen@odu.edu
MULLEN, Kate .... 518-327-6480.... 345 H kmullen@paulsmiths.edu
MULLEN, OFM, Kevin, J ... 518-783-2302.... 350 I kmullen@siena.edu
MULLEN, Kimberly .... 703-562-1691.... 127 G mullen_kimberly@columbusstate.edu
MULLEN, Michael .... 610-361-5222.... 437 D mullenm@neumann.edu
MULLEN, Michael, D .... 919-515-2446.... 378 C mike.mullen@ncsu.edu
MULLEN, Micheal, D .... 859-257-3027.... 207 D mike.mullen@uky.edu
MULLEN, Patty .... 415-955-2041...... 27 A pmullen@alliant.edu
MULLEN, Shirley, A .... 585-567-9310.... 336 B shirley.mullen@houghton.edu
MULLEN, Steve, L .... 716-851-1294.... 333 B mullens@ecc.edu
MULLEN, Steven, K .... 214-333-5170.... 484 D stevem@dbu.edu
MULLEN, William .... 612-874-3762.... 265 C william_mullen@mcad.edu
MULLEN, III, William, F ... 703-784-2105.... 557 H william.f.mullen@usmc.mil
MULLENS, Rob, A .... 541-346-8835.... 419 B athleticdirector@uoregon.edu
MULLER, Andrew .... 843-355-4150.... 463 D mullera@wiltech.edu
MULLER, Christine .... 303-762-6972...... 84 D christine.muller@denverseminary.edu
MULLER, Christopher .... 617-353-3261.... 232 E cmuller@bu.edu
MULLER, David .... 212-241-8716.... 342 B
MULLER, Eugene, W .... 973-748-9000.... 307 H eugene_muller@bloomfield.edu
MULLER, Janet .... 502-213-2179.... 202 F janet.muller@kctcs.edu
MULLER, Joe .... 405-974-2502.... 413 B jmuller2@uco.edu
MULLER, John, B .... 402-557-7001.... 296 H john.muller@bellevue.edu
MULLER, Joseph .... 860-253-3055...... 91 B jmuller@asnuntuck.edu
MULLER, Joyce, D .... 410-857-2292.... 224 C jmuller@mcdaniel.edu
MULLER, Katharine .... 310-434-3701...... 68 D muller_katherine@smc.edu
MULLER, Kathy .... 304-865-6127.... 541 J kathy.muller@ovu.edu
MULLER, Kim .... 806-651-2345.... 499 A kmuller@wtamu.edu
MULLER, Ralph, W .... 215-662-2203.... 448 J ralph.muller@uphs.upenn.edu
MULLER, Steve .... 802-387-1632.... 513 G smuller@landmark.edu
MULLER, Susan, M .... 270-809-3590.... 205 A smuller1@murraystate.edu
MULLERY, Colleen .... 707-826-5086...... 36 E cbm1@humboldt.edu
MULLIGAN, Brendan .... 617-369-3458.... 244 E bmulligan@mfa.org
MULLIGAN, Maura .... 617-989-4232.... 245 F mulliganm@wit.edu
MULLIGAN, Rob .... 916-608-6500...... 56 C
MULLIGAN, Susan, C .... 973-877-3071.... 309 H mulligan@essex.edu
MULLIGAN, Thomas, E .... 330-569-5940.... 391 G mulligante@hiram.edu
MULLIKEN, Taffy .... 719-502-3019...... 87 B taffy.mulliken@ppcc.edu
MULLIKIN, Demeri, C .... 651-757-4004.... 262 H dmullikin@cva.edu
MULLIKIN, Jane .... 419-473-2700.... 389 C jmullikin@daviscollege.edu
MULLIN, Carol .... 610-359-5318.... 426 G cmullin@dccc.edu
MULLIN, OSB, Douglas .... 320-363-2737.... 271 A dmullin@csbsju.edu
MULLIN, John .... 972-377-1575.... 483 H jmullin@collin.edu
MULLIN, Kathi .... 603-513-1318.... 306 F kathi.mullin@granite.edu
MULLIN, Mark, E .... 573-341-4175.... 291 E memullin@mst.edu
MULLINAX, Carl, F .... 814-866-8120.... 433 C cmullinax@lecom.edu
MULLINAX, Kenneth .... 334-229-4104...... 1 C kmullinax@alasu.edu
MULLINAX, Melissa .... 828-328-7244.... 366 E melissa.mullinax@lr.edu
MULLINS, Andrew, P .... 662-915-7111.... 277 D amullins@olemiss.edu
MULLINS, Ann, M .... 662-846-4670.... 273 H amullins@deltastate.edu
MULLINS, Brian .... 859-622-2821.... 200 J brian.mullins@eku.edu
MULLINS, JR., C. David .... 423-439-4343.... 473 F mullinsc@etsu.edu
MULLINS, Dixie .... 409-772-5302.... 507 C dimullin@utmb.edu
MULLINS, James, L .... 765-494-2900.... 178 J jmullins@purdue.edu
MULLINS, Judy .... 660-785-4150.... 290 G jmullins@truman.edu
MULLINS, Liza .... 904-256-7082.... 111 L lmullin1@ju.edu
MULLINS, Sharon .... 281-425-6388.... 489 M smullins@lee.edu
MULLINS, Steve .... 714-879-3901...... 50 I smullins@hiu.edu
MULLINS, William .... 740-826-8120.... 397 A wmullins@muskingum.edu
MULLIS, Jay .... 478-274-7879.... 135 C jmullis@oftc.edu
MULLIS, Joe, W .... 910-678-8217.... 370 E mullisj@faytechcc.edu
MULLIS, Terri .... 913-758-6114.... 197 D mullis15@stmary.edu
MULLIS, Tres .... 540-458-8165.... 530 D tmullis@wlu.edu
MULLOWNEY, William, J .. 407-582-3411.... 123 B bmullowney@valenciacollege.edu
MULLOY, Josetta .... 251-380-3470...... 7 E mulloy@shc.edu
MULQUEEN, Joann .... 914-831-0418.... 330 D jmulqueen@cw.edu
MULRENAN, Holly .... 203-576-5518...... 94 C hmulrenan@stvincentscollege.edu
MULROE, Michael .... 312-942-6214.... 163 D mike_mulroe@rush.edu
MULROONEY, Bill .... 310-660-3418...... 45 E bmulroon@elcamino.edu
MULROONEY, Debra .... 503-253-3443.... 417 H dmulrooney@ocom.edu
MULROY-BOWDEN, Linda, A .... 601-342-1845.... 552 B mulroy@uwplatt.edu
MULROY-DEGENHART, Carmella .... 814-865-7611.... 438 G qum11@psu.edu
MULRYAN, Michael .... 714-879-3901...... 50 I mdmulryan@hiu.edu
MULSHINE, James, L .... 312-942-3589.... 163 D james_l_mulshine@rush.edu
MULSO, Sara, K .... 651-641-8857.... 263 A smulso@csp.edu
MULSO, William .... 507-537-6267.... 269 E william.mulso@smsu.edu
MULTARI, James .... 516-678-5000.... 341 F jmultari@molloy.edu
MULTHAUF, Christopher .... 847-574-5270.... 156 A cmulthauf@lfgsm.edu
MULTOP, Kevin .... 541-383-7578.... 414 I kmultop@cocc.edu
MULVEY, Julie .... 508-588-9100.... 240 A
MULVEY, Kristin .... 815-280-2353.... 154 J kmulvey@jjc.edu
MULVEY, Lisa .... 516-299-2263.... 339 A lisa.mulvey@liu.edu
MULVIHILL, Rosemary .... 781-768-7029.... 244 A rosemary.mulvihill@regiscollege.edu
MULVILLE, Matthew, H .... 716-888-2220.... 325 F mulville@canisius.edu
MUMA, Richard, D .... 316-978-5761.... 198 A richard.muma@wichita.edu
MUMAW, Dennis .... 312-935-6821.... 162 G dmumaw@robertmorris.edu
MUMFORD, John, W .... 814-641-3452.... 432 A mumford@juniata.edu
MUMMERT, John .... 650-949-7070...... 47 H mummertjohn@foothill.edu
MUMMERT, Kelly .... 304-243-2226.... 546 A kmummert@wju.edu
MUMPER, Michael .... 719-587-7436...... 80 L mmumper@adams.edu
MUNA, Esther, A .... 671-735-5700.... 559 E gccpresident@guamcc.edu
MUNA, Joann, W .... 671-735-5539.... 559 E hr@guamcc.edu
MUNCASTER, Karen .... 617-262-5000.... 231 G karen.muncaster@the-bac.edu
MUNCHEL, Christopher, T . 765-285-5608.... 169 G cmunchel@bsu.edu
MUNCHEL, Jeff .... 410-532-5324.... 225 D jmunchel@ndm.edu
MUNCHY, Karl .... 706-737-1611.... 125 G kmunchy@aug.edu
MUND, Barb .... 701-671-2204.... 382 G barb.mund@ndscs.edu
MUNDAHL, Daniel, L .... 507-344-7739.... 261 C costello@blc.edu
MUNDAY, Andy .... 620-252-7046.... 192 B andym@coffeyville.edu
MUNDEY, Maryjo .... 740-389-6786.... 399 D mundey.2@osu.edu
MUNDT, Mary, H .... 517-355-6527.... 255 A mundtm@msu.edu
MUNDY, Amy .... 361-570-4354.... 504 A mundya@uhv.edu
MUNDY, II, Roy, W .... 859-846-5300.... 204 H rmundy@midway.edu
MUNDY, Susan, R .... 516-876-3033.... 353 D mundys@oldwestbury.edu
MUNDY, Tiina .... 910-879-5556.... 368 D tmundy@bladencc.edu
MUNERA, Marcela .... 305-573-1600.... 101 E mmunera@atienterprises.edu
MUNFORD, Michael .... 507-537-7858.... 269 E michael.munford@smsu.edu
MUNFORD, Teresa, L .... 757-221-1009.... 518 A tlmunf@wm.edu
MUNGAL, Godfrey .... 408-554-2375...... 68 C mgmungal@scu.edu
MUNGER, James .... 208-426-4010.... 142 I jmunger@boisestate.edu
MUNGER, Mary Lynn .... 816-604-3155.... 285 D marylynn.munger@mcckc.edu
MUNGO, T. Rein .... 843-349-2577.... 456 G tmungo@coastal.edu
MUNIER, Craig, D .... 402-472-2030.... 300 G cmunier1@unl.edu
MUNIN, Eugene .... 239-280-1516.... 101 I eugene.munin@avemaria.edu
MUNITZ, Barry .... 775-831-1314.... 303 E
MUNIZ, Amanda .... 361-593-3797.... 498 D kaam003@tamuk.edu
MUNIZ, Diana .... 602-286-8031...... 15 G diana.muniz@gwmail.maricopa.edu
MUNIZ, Herman .... 787-276-0270.... 567 C herman.muniz@upr.edu
MUNLEY, Anne .... 570-348-6231.... 435 F annemunley@marywood.edu
MUNN, Kathie, A .... 906-932-4231.... 251 C kathiem@gogebic.edu
MUNNERLYN, Rebecca, B . 803-786-3649.... 457 C rbmunnerlyn@columbiasc.edu
MUNNERLYN, Samuel .... 334-420-4216........ 7 H smunnerlyn@trenholmstate.edu

MUNNS, Craig 305-820-5003 118 D cmunns@sec.edu
MUNNS, Sarah 573-592-4296 293 D sarah.munns@williamwoods.edu
MUNOZ, Al 831-755-6914 49 E amunoz@hartnell.edu
MUNOZ, Candelario 805-546-3147 43 I cmunoz@cuesta.edu
MUNOZ, Carmen 818-401-1035 42 F cmunoz@columbiacollege.edu
MUNOZ, Chris 713-348-6271 493 C chris.munoz@rice.edu
MUNOZ, Ivette 787-725-8120 562 C imunoz@eap.edu
MUNOZ, Juan, S 806-742-7025 502 A juan.munoz@ttu.edu
MUNOZ, M. Angelica 269-471-3251 252 A munozm@andrews.edu
MUNOZ, Maria 787-284-1912 564 A mmunoz@ponce.inter.edu
MUNOZ, Marisol 787-766-1717 565 I ac_mmunoz@suagm.edu
MUNOZ, Rene 717-872-3820 443 D rene.munoz@millersville.edu
MUNRO, Alex 717-299-7776 448 A munro@stevenscollege.edu
MUNRO, Molly 561-297-2114 119 A mmunro@fau.edu
MUNRO, Stuart, J 508-767-7041 230 D smunro@assumption.edu
MUNROE, Anthony, E 312-850-7031 147 F amunroe@ccc.edu
MUNROE, Jane Ann 714-449-7446 70 G jmunroe@scco.edu
MUNROE, Jeffrey 616-392-8555 260 D jeff@westernsem.edu
MUNROE, Richard 229-226-1621 138 C rmunroe@thomasu.edu
MUNSICK, Trudy, R 307-674-6446 556 F tmunsick@sheridan.edu
MUNSIL, Len 602-489-5300 11 G
MUNSON, Amy 309-268-8633 151 I amy.munson@heartland.edu
MUNSON, David, C 734-647-7010 259 A munson@umich.edu
MUNSON, Leo, W 817-257-7104 499 C l.munson@tcu.edu
MUNSON, Nina 480-557-1712 19 A nina.munson@phoenix.edu
MUNSON, Shana 940-552-6291 507 F smunson@vernoncollege.edu
MUNSON, Wanda 281-998-6150 493 G wanda.munson@sjcd.edu
MUNSON, William 713-743-5470 503 D wfmunson@central.uh.edu
MUNSTER, Charles 718-636-3453 346 D cmunster@pratt.edu
MUNSTER, Mercedes 504-671-5213 210 F mmunst@dcc.edu
MUNT, Glada, C 512-863-1381 496 A muntg@southwestern.edu
MUNTZ, Bill 229-245-5147 139 C bmuntz@valdosta.edu
MUNTZ, Palmer 503-255-0332 417 C pmuntz@multnomah.edu
MURABITO, William, J 845-434-5750 357 A wmurabito@sullivan.suny.edu
MURACA, Paul 713-798-6617 481 H muraca@bcm.edu
MURALI, Viji 509-335-8017 539 D vijimurali@wsu.edu
MURASKO, Donna 215-895-1892 427 H dm37@drexel.edu
MURASSO, Thomas 914-323-5337 339 J thomas.murasso@mville.edu
MURATA, Susan 808-734-9267 141 J smurata@hawaii.edu
MURCHISON, Andrea 310-577-3000 80 E administrator@yosan.edu
MURDAUGH, Jim 850-201-8660 122 A murdaugj@tcc.fl.edu
MURDEN MCCLURE, Tori 502-585-9911 206 D tmcclure@spalding.edu
MURDEN-WALDU, Romell 773-481-8451 147 I rmurden@ccc.edu
MURDOCH, Colin 415-503-6230 66 A jmg@sfcm.edu
MURDOCH, Janice, W 864-656-3942 456 E janw@clemson.edu
MURDOCH, Jessica 978-665-3338 237 E jmurdoch@fitchburgstate.edu
MURDOCH, William, G 909-558-6604 54 D wmurdoch@llu.edu
MURDOCK, Alan, K 336-734-7757 370 F amurdock@forsythtech.edu
MURDOCK, Cristian 870-972-2060 20 D cmurdock@astate.edu
MURDOCK, Margaret 307-766-3152 556 H murdock@uwyo.edu
MURDOCK, Rebecca 605-575-2068 466 E rebecca.murdock@usiouxfalls.edu
MURDOCK, Susan 740-374-8716 405 G smurdock@wscc.edu
MURDOCK-TANGYE, Annette 501-569-3180 24 E amtangye@ualr.edu
MURDZAK, Karen 814-732-1020 442 E kmurdzak@edinboro.edu
MURGA, Mario 617-327-6777 241 F mario_murga@mspp.edu
MURGUIA, Kim 210-732-3000 482 F
MURGUIA, Stephanie 562-860-2451 39 A smurguia@cerritos.edu
MURIANA, Joseph, P 718-817-3020 334 C jmuriana@fordham.edu
MURIANKA, Luke 315-858-0940 336 A lmurianka@hts.edu
MURILLO, Alice 415-239-3321 40 C amurillo@ccsf.edu
MURILLO, Jennifer 832-813-6576 490 E jennifer.h.murillo@lonestar.edu
MURILLO, Kindred 530-541-4660 53 G murillo@ltcc.edu
MURLEY, James 954-762-5253 119 A jmurley@fau.edu
MURNANE, Ryan 757-352-4891 523 E ryanmur@regent.edu
MURO, Mary 303-923-4154 81 E mmuro@argosy.edu
MURPH, Shelia 603-577-6585 304 I smurph@dwc.edu
MURPH, Yvette, U 662-254-3636 276 B yvette.murph@mvsu.edu
MURPHEY, Connie 912-478-1263 131 E cmurphey@georgiasouthern.edu
MURPHEY, Diane 580-349-1446 410 B diane@opsu.edu
MURPHREE, Danny, W 806-291-3635 508 E murphree@wbu.edu
MURPHREE, David 806-291-3641 508 E dmurphree@wbu.edu
MURPHREE, Edith, C 404-727-2827 129 D edith.murphree@emory.edu
MURPHREY, Hiram Todd 252-638-7263 370 A murphret@cravencc.edu
MURPHY, Amy 508-793-3880 233 C amurphy@holycross.edu
MURPHY, Amy, L 806-742-5433 502 A amy.murphy@ttu.edu
MURPHY, Ann, B 303-556-3245 86 F murphann@msudenver.edu
MURPHY, Anne 312-942-6886 163 D anne_murphy@rush.edu
MURPHY, Barbara, E 802-635-1240 515 F jscpres@jsc.edu
MURPHY, Beth, M 804-745-2444 517 C bmmurphy@bryantstratton.edu
MURPHY, Bill 507-457-5014 269 G jmurphy@winona.edu
MURPHY, Bill 585-275-4124 359 B bill.murphy@rochester.edu
MURPHY, Bonnie, D 805-756-1131 33 I bdmurphy@calpoly.edu
MURPHY, Bret 775-753-2217 302 F bret.murphy@gbcnv.edu
MURPHY, Brian 718-997-5910 328 E brian.murphy@qc.cuny.edu
MURPHY, Brian 408-864-8705 47 G murphybrian@deanza.edu
MURPHY, Brian 936-468-2803 496 B murphybm1@sfasu.edu
MURPHY, Brian, F 912-525-5200 136 F bmurphy@scad.edu
MURPHY, Bruce, T 334-953-5613 557 D bruce.murphy@maxwell.af.mil
MURPHY, Carolyn 402-471-2505 299 D cmurphy@nscs.edu
MURPHY, Catherine 516-299-3981 338 E cathy.murphy@liu.edu
MURPHY, Catherine 202-651-5019 98 B catherine.murphy@gallaudet.edu
MURPHY, Catherine 615-460-6418 467 D catherine.murphy@belmont.edu
MURPHY, Chad 309-649-6266 165 F chad.murphy@src.edu
MURPHY, Charles, J 585-275-2815 359 B cj.murphy@rochester.edu
MURPHY, Charles, J 509-313-6139 534 F murphyc@gonzaga.edu
MURPHY, Christine 516-877-3056 322 A murphy2@adelphi.edu
MURPHY, Colleen, F 336-272-7102 364 G colleen.murphy@greensboro.edu
MURPHY, JR., Cornelius, B 315-470-6681 355 A cbmurphy@esf.edu
MURPHY, Dan 803-786-3701 457 C dan@columbiasc.edu
MURPHY, Daniel 315-733-2300 359 C dmurphy@uscny.edu
MURPHY, Darin 617-369-3650 244 E dmurphy@mfa.org
MURPHY, Darlene 802-654-0534 515 E darlene.murphy@ccv.edu
MURPHY, David, W 315-498-2213 345 D murphydw@sunyocc.edu
MURPHY, Denise 301-687-4457 228 C dmurphy@frostburg.edu
MURPHY, Dennis, J 610-361-2448 437 D murphydj@neumann.edu
MURPHY, Diane Lyden 315-443-3707 357 C dlmurphy@syr.edu
MURPHY, Donna, M 831-459-4750 75 C donnam@ucsc.edu
MURPHY, Douglas 501-686-5730 24 F dlmurphy@uams.edu
MURPHY, Gaye 480-731-8638 15 D gaye.murphy@domail.maricopa.edu
MURPHY, Gene 601-857-3330 274 C temurphy@hindscc.edu
MURPHY, Jack 773-481-8124 147 I jmurphy@ccc.edu
MURPHY, Jacqueline 802-654-3000 514 D admissions@smcvt.edu
MURPHY, III, James, E 704-894-2373 363 I jamurphy@davidson.edu
MURPHY, James, P 717-846-5000 452 H
MURPHY, Jan 309-438-7018 153 D jshane@ilstu.edu
MURPHY, Janice 410-334-2808 229 E jmurphy@worwic.edu
MURPHY, Jason, J 920-923-7178 548 E jjmurphy25@marianuniversity.edu
MURPHY, Jean, D 313-831-5200 250 G jdmurphy@etseminary.edu
MURPHY, Jim 973-748-9000 307 H jim_murphy@bloomfield.edu
MURPHY, John 518-956-8140 351 E jmurphy@uamail.albany.edu
MURPHY, John 203-837-8395 91 A murphyj@wcsu.edu
MURPHY, John 210-458-3090 506 D john.murphy@utsa.edu
MURPHY, John, D 207-834-7516 220 D jdmurphy@maine.edu
MURPHY, John, T 716-829-8147 332 E murphyj@dyc.edu
MURPHY, Joseph, M 740-427-5120 394 C murphyjm@kenyon.edu
MURPHY, Josephine 718-368-5144 328 A jmurphy@kbcc.cuny.edu
MURPHY, Joyce, A 508-856-4842 237 C joyce.murphy@umassmed.edu
MURPHY, Julliann 231-843-5913 260 B jmmurphy@westshore.edu
MURPHY, Justin 325-649-8701 488 C jmurphy@hputx.edu
MURPHY, Karen 318-257-4205 215 F kmurphy@latech.edu
MURPHY, Kathleen 717-262-2008 452 C kmurphy@wilson.edu
MURPHY, Kathleen 216-687-3613 388 D kathleen.murphy@csuohio.edu
MURPHY, Kathleen, M 508-767-7110 230 D kamurphy@assumption.edu
MURPHY, Keith 478-825-6454 129 F murphyk@fvsu.edu
MURPHY, Keith 718-409-7349 356 C kmurphy@sunymaritime.edu
MURPHY, Kenneth, R 903-510-2547 503 A kmur@tjc.edu
MURPHY, Kimberly 512-863-1286 496 A murphyk@southwestern.edu
MURPHY, Lamar, R 585-276-3262 359 B lamar.murphy@rochester.edu
MURPHY, Larry 515-244-4221 181 F murphyl@aib.edu
MURPHY, Laura 508-929-8649 238 G lmurphy@worcester.edu
MURPHY, Linda 978-837-5131 242 A murphyl@merrimack.edu
MURPHY, Lisa 480-860-2700 14 F lmurphy@taliesin.edu
MURPHY, Lisa 307-778-1110 556 E lmurphy@lccc.wy.edu
MURPHY, Lisa, B 863-638-7690 123 D lisa.murphy@warner.edu
MURPHY, M. Patrick 336-278-7640 364 D murphyp@elon.edu
MURPHY, Margaret, L 757-446-5828 518 G murphyml@evms.edu
MURPHY, Marie 508-531-1338 237 D
MURPHY, Marilyn, J 319-368-6465 187 H marilyn@mtmercy.edu
MURPHY, Mark 914-633-2458 336 E mmurphy@iona.edu
MURPHY, Mary 812-429-1406 177 C mmurpy@ivytech.edu
MURPHY, Mary, K 404-752-1942 134 E mmurphy@msm.edu
MURPHY, Mary, K 607-753-2303 353 B maryk.murphy@cortland.edu
MURPHY, Marybeth 212-217-3800 333 F marybeth_murphy@fitnyc.edu
MURPHY, Maryjan 831-459-2120 75 C mjmurphy@ucsc.edu
MURPHY, Maureen 617-824-8575 234 B maureen_murphy@emerson.edu
MURPHY, Maureen 732-224-2204 308 A mmurphy@brookdalecc.edu
MURPHY, Michael 845-398-4118 349 H mmurphy@stac.edu
MURPHY, Michael 925-631-4366 64 F mmurphy@stmarys-ca.edu
MURPHY, Michael, C 412-268-8251 424 J mm1v@andrew.cmu.edu
MURPHY, Mollie 202-685-3933 557 I murphym@ndu.edu
MURPHY, Nancy 850-729-5365 114 A murphyn@nwfsc.edu
MURPHY, Neal 912-287-6584 135 F nmurphy@okefenokeetech.edu
MURPHY, Pamela 724-938-4427 441 G murphy_p@calu.edu
MURPHY, Patricia, B 804-484-1581 525 E pmurphy@richmond.edu
MURPHY, Paul 570-674-6272 436 F pmurphy@misericordia.edu
MURPHY, Paul 413-542-5338 230 A prmurphy@amherst.edu
MURPHY, Paul 805-922-6966 26 L pmurphy@hancockcollege.edu
MURPHY, Paul, J 860-548-5392 94 A murphp2@rpi.edu
MURPHY, Paul, V 216-397-4953 392 L pvmurphy@jcu.edu
MURPHY, Paul, W 617-726-0422 242 B pwmurphy@mghihp.edu
MURPHY, Penny, A 870-230-5348 21 I murphyp@hsu.edu
MURPHY, Peter, F 270-809-7064 205 A pmurphy@murraystate.edu
MURPHY, Peter, T 413-597-4351 246 D peter.t.murphy@williams.edu
MURPHY, Pollie 757-727-5201 519 H pollie.muphy@hamptonu.edu
MURPHY, Pollie 757-727-5237 519 H pollie.murphy@hamptonu.edu
MURPHY, Robert 508-767-7225 230 D rtmurphy@assumption.edu
MURPHY, Robert 315-781-3622 335 F murphy@hws.edu
MURPHY, Robert 901-381-3939 478 E robert@visible.edu
MURPHY, Robert, P 716-829-8199 332 E murphyrp@dyc.edu
MURPHY, Sean 407-888-4000 113 A smurphy1@careered.com
MURPHY, Stephen, C 203-432-8090 96 A stephen.murphy@yale.edu
MURPHY, Steven, J 773-298-3310 163 I murphy@sxu.edu
MURPHY, Susan, H 607-255-7595 331 B shm1@cornell.edu
MURPHY, Susan, L 415-422-2620 76 E murphy@usfca.edu
MURPHY, Suzanne 212-678-3755 357 G smurphy@tc.columbia.edu
MURPHY, Suzanne, K 215-596-8888 450 B s.murphy@usciences.edu
MURPHY, Theresa 513-556-6381 403 D theresa.murphy@uc.edu
MURPHY, Thomas 516-876-3215 353 D murphyt@oldwestbury.edu
MURPHY, Todd 323-343-2500 35 D tmurphy@cslanet.calstatela.edu
MURPHY, Wayne 718-289-5245 326 E wayne.murphy@bcc.cuny.edu
MURPHY CHURCH, Linda 401-709-8408 454 B lchurch@risd.edu
MURPHY-FREEBOLIN, Lorie 563-588-6571 183 E lorie.murphy-freebolin@clarke.edu
MURPHY-STETZ, Katherine 312-567-3080 153 C murphy@iit.edu
MURR, Christopher 512-245-3975 501 F cm18@txstate.edu
MURRAH, Matt 214-333-6886 484 D matt@dbu.edu
MURRAY, Adam, L 270-809-5604 205 A amurray@murraystate.edu
MURRAY, Adrienne, M 704-894-2915 363 I admurray@davidson.edu
MURRAY, Ann 307-778-1113 556 E amurray@lccc.wy.edu
MURRAY, Ann Marie 315-866-0300 335 D murrayam@herkimer.edu
MURRAY, Barbara, M 909-748-8544 76 C barbara_murray@redlands.edu
MURRAY, Betty 254-968-9070 497 A murray@tarleton.edu
MURRAY, Brian 972-721-5008 503 B bmurray@udallas.edu
MURRAY, Charles 205-387-0511 2 A cmurray@bscc.edu
MURRAY, Cherry, A 617-495-5829 235 D camurray@seas.harvard.edu
MURRAY, Christopher, D 208-885-6154 144 G chrismurray@uidaho.edu
MURRAY, David 732-224-2449 308 A dmurray@brookdalecc.edu
MURRAY, Deborah 423-614-8175 470 C debmurray@leeuniversity.edu
MURRAY, Debra, H 717-361-1164 428 F murraydh@etown.edu

MURRAY, Dennis, J ... 845-575-3000 ... 340 B
dennis.murray@marist.edu
MURRAY, Don ... 402-486-2536 ... 300 C
domurray@ucollege.edu
MURRAY, Douglas, J ... 575-624-8020 ... 319 C
dmurray@nmmi.edu
MURRAY, Eric ... 425-352-8810 ... 532 B
emurray@cascadia.edu
MURRAY, Eric, H ... 404-816-4533 ... 132 E
ericm@atl.herzing.edu
MURRAY, Frank ... 509-542-4835 ... 532 H
fmurray@columbiabasin.edu
MURRAY, George, W ... 803-754-4100 ... 457 D
MURRAY, Gloria, J ... 812-941-2385 ... 175 A
glomurra@ius.edu
MURRAY, Harris ... 803-535-1255 ... 460 C
murrayh@octech.edu
MURRAY, Harris ... 803-535-1257 ... 460 C
murrayh@octech.edu
MURRAY, Helen ... 260-399-7700 ... 181 A
hmurray@sf.edu
MURRAY, Jay, E ... 203-596-4630 ... 93 G
jmurray@post.edu
MURRAY, Jill ... 570-504-1575 ... 433 A
murrayj@lackawanna.edu
MURRAY, Joanne, S ... 781-283-2492 ... 245 E
jmurray@wellesley.edu
MURRAY, John ... 312-332-0707 ... 166 B
MURRAY, John ... 812-237-2785 ... 173 B
john.murray@indstate.edu
MURRAY, Karen ... 254-968-9103 ... 497 A
kmurray@tarleton.edu
MURRAY, Kathleen, M ... 651-696-6160 ... 264 J
kmurray@macalester.edu
MURRAY, Lisa ... 212-229-5155 ... 342 E
murrayl@newschool.edu
MURRAY, Louise ... 973-290-4430 ... 308 G
lmurray@cse.edu
MURRAY, Lynne ... 202-651-5006 ... 98 B
lynne.murray@gallaudet.edu
MURRAY, Mark, J ... 904-264-2172 ... 116 C
mark.murray@iws.edu
MURRAY, Michael ... 626-584-2040 ... 48 B
mdmurray@fuller.edu
MURRAY, Michael ... 517-437-7341 ... 252 C
michael.murray@hillsdale.edu
MURRAY, Michele ... 206-296-6066 ... 538 B
mmurray@seattleu.edu
MURRAY, Nancy, K ... 219-464-5989 ... 181 C
nancy.murray@valpo.edu
MURRAY, Percy ... 903-923-2421 ... 509 E
pmurray@wileyc.edu
MURRAY, Peter ... 650-949-7259 ... 47 H
murraypeter@foothill.edu
MURRAY, Peter, J ... 410-706-2461 ... 227 C
pmurray@umaryland.edu
MURRAY, Renae ... 561-803-2155 ... 114 C
renae_murray@pba.edu
MURRAY, Robert ... 208-769-3474 ... 144 D
robert_murray@nic.edu
MURRAY, Robert ... 309-556-1000 ... 153 F
bmurray@iwu.edu
MURRAY, Robert ... 845-398-4125 ... 349 H
rmurray@stac.edu
MURRAY, Robert ... 860-444-8520 ... 558 H
robert.murray@uscga.edu
MURRAY, Robert, C ... 434-223-6020 ... 519 G
rcmurray@hsc.edu
MURRAY, Rose-Marie ... 305-949-9500 ... 106 B
rmurray@cci.edu
MURRAY, OFM, Russel ... 518-783-2418 ... 350 I
rmurray@siena.edu
MURRAY, Sharon ... 518-292-1753 ... 348 A
murras2@sage.edu
MURRAY, Steven ... 870-338-6474 ... 25 D
MURRAY, Steven ... 657-278-2614 ... 35 B
smurray@fullerton.edu
MURRAY, Susan ... 509-682-6435 ... 539 E
smurray@wvc.edu
MURRAY, Suzette ... 630-466-7900 ... 168 B
smurray@waubonsee.edu
MURRAY, Tamsen ... 714-879-3901 ... 50 I
tmurray@hiu.edu
MURRAY, Thomas ... 336-770-3277 ... 379 E
murrayt@uncsa.edu
MURRAY, Thomas, K ... 563-387-1862 ... 187 D
murrayto@luther.edu
MURRAY, Trish ... 704-894-2099 ... 363 I
trmurray@davidson.edu
MURRAY, William, G ... 516-671-2213 ... 360 B
bmurray@webb-institute.edu
MURRAY-JENSEN, Julie ... 541-880-2221 ... 416 D
jensen@klamathcc.edu
MURRAY-LAURY, Janice ... 908-737-7080 ... 311 A
jmurray@kean.edu
MURRAY-RUST, Catherine 404-894-8914 ... 130 F
catherine.rust@library.gatech.edu
MURRELL, James, T ... 931-363-9823 ... 471 A
jmurrell@martinmethodist.edu
MURRELL, Michele ... 321-433-7055 ... 102 D
murrellm@brevardcc.edu
MURRELL, Shana ... 508-531-1290 ... 237 D
shana.murrell@bridgew.edu
MURRELL, Terry ... 712-274-6400 ... 190 B
terry.murrell@witcc.edu
MURRIL, Antoinette ... 312-567-3012 ... 153 C
amurril@iit.edu
MURRIN, Michael ... 716-926-8900 ... 335 E
mmurrin@hilbert.edu
MURRY, LaKeisha ... 901-381-3939 ... 478 E
keisha@visible.edu
MURRY, Tracy ... 941-487-4504 ... 120 A
tmurry@ncf.edu
MURTAGH, Michael ... 309-467-6315 ... 151 B
mmurtagh@eureka.edu
MURTAGH GITTO, Ann ... 413-528-7297 ... 230 F
agitto@simons-rock.edu
MURTAUGH, Kelly ... 651-423-8319 ... 266 B
kelly.murtaugh@dctc.edu
MURTAUGH, Peter, T ... 314-286-4813 ... 287 G
ptmurtaugh@ranken.edu
MURTHA, Brenda ... 605-274-5217 ... 464 A
brenda.murtha@augie.edu
MURUAKO, Dominic ... 205-366-8854 ... 7 F
dmuruako@stillman.edu
MURVIN, David ... 561-391-1148 ... 105 B
dmurvin@dmac.edu
MURY, Hal ... 919-209-2000 ... 371 F
hemury@johnstoncc.edu
MUSAL, Edward ... 914-251-6923 ... 354 D
edward.musal@purchase.edu
MUSCARELLA, Joseph ... 516-572-0605 ... 342 C
joseph.muscarella@ncc.edu
MUSCENTE, Catherine ... 516-678-5000 ... 341 F
cmuscente@molloy.edu
MUSCIO, Fugen ... 270-809-3538 ... 205 A
fmuscio@murraystate.edu
MUSE, Bill ... 830-792-7355 ... 494 E
bmuse@schreiner.edu
MUSE, Clyde ... 601-857-3240 ... 274 C
vcmuse@hindscc.edu
MUSE, Douglas ... 870-612-2167 ... 25 E
douglas.muse@uaccb.edu
MUSE, Gail ... 662-472-2312 ... 274 D
gmuse@holmescc.edu
MUSE, Justin ... 540-365-4441 ... 519 C
jmuse@ferrum.edu
MUSEWICZ, Suellen ... 570-961-7824 ... 433 A
musewiczs@lackawanna.edu
MUSGRAVE, Dan ... 575-624-8214 ... 319 C
musgrave@nmmi.edu
MUSGROVE, Robert ... 320-629-5120 ... 268 E
musgrover@pinetech.edu
MUSHRUSH, Tiffany ... 440-646-8370 ... 405 B
tmushrush@ursuline.edu
MUSIAL, Angela ... 661-722-6300 ... 28 K
amusial1@avc.edu
MUSICH, Michelle ... 828-765-7351 ... 372 A
mmusich@mayland.edu
MUSICK, Chris ... 614-823-1370 ... 400 H
cmusick@otterbein.edu
MUSICK, Kelly ... 409-933-8496 ... 483 F
kmusick@com.edu
MUSIL, Becky ... 254-867-2033 ... 500 F
becky.musil@tstc.edu
MUSKAVITCH, John, W ... 909-389-3269 ... 65 B
jmuskavitch@craftonhills.edu
MUSKETT, Milford ... 319-398-4911 ... 187 B
mmusket@kirkwood.edu
MUSKRAT, Bruce ... 817-274-4284 ... 482 B
MUSMANN, Klaus ... 714-816-0366 ... 73 B
klaus.musmann@trident.edu
MUSOLF, David, E ... 608-262-3956 ... 550 J
musolf@secfac.wisc.edu
MUSOLF, Shelly, R ... 260-422-5561 ... 173 C
srmusolf@indianatech.edu
MUSSA-MULDOON, Carla, R ... 310-233-4450 ... 54 I
muldoonc@lahc.edu
MUSSANO, Frank, P ... 717-815-1365 ... 452 G
fmussano@ycp.edu
MUSSELMAN, Kathy, I ... 615-898-2929 ... 473 G
kathy.musselman@mtsu.edu
MUSSELWHITE, Laura ... 706-204-2368 ... 130 E
lmusselw@highlands.edu
MUSSELWHITE, Laura ... 706-295-6331 ... 130 E
lmusselw@highlands.edu
MUSSER, Jeff ... 616-331-2207 ... 251 F
musserj@gvsu.edu
MUSSER, Steve ... 717-560-8248 ... 433 D
smusser@lbc.edu
MUSSO, Daniele ... 913-360-7975 ... 191 A
dmusso@benedictine.edu
MUSTAFA, Mustafa ... 201-216-9901 ... 309 F
MUSTARD, Barbara ... 605-394-2228 ... 466 B
barbara.mustard@sdsmt.edu
MUSTER, Robert ... 612-659-6104 ... 267 B
robert.muster@minneapolis.edu
MUSTERMAN, Cynthia, A ... 314-421-0949 ... 290 D
musterman@siba.edu
MUTCHLER, Jane ... 219-989-3194 ... 178 K
jane.mutchler@purduecal.edu
MUTH, Richard ... 724-294-3309 ... 442 F
richard.muth@iup.edu
MUTONE, Paul ... 860-297-4224 ... 94 E
paul.mutone@trincoll.edu
MUTUA, Makau, W ... 716-645-2052 ... 351 G
mutua@buffalo.edu
MUYET, Javier, A ... 787-850-9318 ... 567 E
javier.muyet@upr.edu
MUYSKENS, James, L ... 718-997-5550 ... 328 E
james.muyskens@qc.cuny.edu
MUYSKENS, Judy, A ... 402-465-2110 ... 299 H
provost@nebrwesleyan.edu
MUZIA, Raymond ... 757-825-2900 ... 528 F
muziar@tncc.edu
MUZZY, Nikole ... 907-773-4040 ... 147 D
nmuzzy@ccc.edu
MUÑIZ, Maria ... 787-841-2000 ... 565 B
mmuniz@pucpr.edu
MUÑOZ-MUÑOZ, Miguel, A ... 787-250-0000 ... 566 G
miguel.munoz3@upr.edu
MWAURA, John ... 973-748-9000 ... 307 H
john_mwaura@bloomfield.edu
MWENJA, Dominic ... 858-653-3000 ... 33 D
dmwenja@calmu.edu
MYAZOE-DEBRUM, Diane, C ... 692-528-5033 ... 560 A
dcmyazoe@yahoo.com
MYAZOE-DEBRUM, Diane, C ... 692-625-3394 ... 560 A
dcmyazoe@cmi.edu
MYDLOWEC, Sally, P ... 215-885-2360 ... 435 E
smydlowec@manor.edu
MYER, Bonnie ... 360-736-9391 ... 532 D
bmyer@centralia.edu
MYER, Marci ... 206-934-3669 ... 537 D
marci.myer@seattlecolleges.edu
MYERS, Alvin, B ... 434-395-2300 ... 521 A
myersab@longwood.edu
MYERS, Amy, A ... 717-291-4082 ... 429 F
amy.myers@fandm.edu
MYERS, Barbara, S ... 912-358-3051 ... 136 G
myersb@savannahstate.edu
MYERS, Beth ... 843-863-7516 ... 456 B
myers@csuniv.edu
MYERS, Bradley, A ... 614-292-1556 ... 398 I
myers.7@osu.edu
MYERS, Camille ... 843-525-8359 ... 461 E
cmyers@tcl.edu
MYERS, Carol ... 706-355-5080 ... 125 C
cmeyers@athenstech.edu
MYERS, Charles ... 215-596-8791 ... 450 B
c.myers@usciences.edu
MYERS, Cheryl ... 706-649-1290 ... 128 A
cmyers@columbustech.edu
MYERS, Cheryl ... 504-571-1290 ... 210 F
cmyers@dcc.edu
MYERS, Dale ... 830-792-7235 ... 494 E
dtmyers@schreiner.edu
MYERS, Daniel, J ... 574-631-2799 ... 180 G
dmyers@nd.edu
MYERS, Donald ... 202-885-2709 ... 97 D
don@american.edu
MYERS, Donald, C ... 901-333-5259 ... 476 B
dmyers@southwest.tn.edu
MYERS, Eveadean ... 701-231-7703 ... 382 B
evie.myers@ndsu.edu
MYERS, Gary ... 709-379-3111 ... 140 A
glmyers@yhc.edu
MYERS, Gary, D ... 504-816-8003 ... 213 H
gmeyers@nobts.edu
MYERS, Greg ... 606-546-1520 ... 207 B
gmyers@unionky.edu
MYERS, Jaime ... 661-726-1911 ... 73 F
jaime.myers@uav.edu
MYERS, James ... 650-325-9122 ... 64 G
vat2ins@aol.com
MYERS, James ... 618-537-6828 ... 158 A
jamyers@mckendree.edu
MYERS, James ... 443-334-2910 ... 226 E
jmmyers@stevenson.edu
MYERS, James, L ... 803-536-8480 ... 460 G
myers@scsu.edu
MYERS, Jeannette ... 843-661-1291 ... 458 D
jmyers@fmarion.edu
MYERS, Jimmy ... 239-590-7406 ... 119 B
jimyers@fgcu.edu
MYERS, Joe ... 931-393-1553 ... 475 D
jmyers@mscc.edu
MYERS, Jolene ... 406-377-9410 ... 294 B
myers@dawson.edu
MYERS, Jonna ... 580-774-3233 ... 412 F
jonna.myers@swosu.edu
MYERS, Julie, K ... 845-758-7518 ... 323 D
myers@bard.edu
MYERS, Karen, S ... 330-287-1275 ... 399 A
myers.444@osu.edu
MYERS, Kelly ... 815-802-8260 ... 155 A
kmyers@kcc.edu
MYERS, Ken ... 864-644-5215 ... 461 B
kmyers@swu.edu
MYERS, Keri ... 316-323-6739 ... 191 G
kmyers7@butlercc.edu
MYERS, Kevin ... 361-570-4840 ... 504 A
myersk@uhv.edu
MYERS, Laura ... 740-593-2620 ... 399 G
myersl@ohio.edu
MYERS, Lynne, M ... 508-793-2265 ... 233 C
lmyers@holycross.edu
MYERS, Marci ... 620-223-2700 ... 193 A
marcim@fortscott.edu
MYERS, Margaret ... 701-777-2015 ... 381 F
margaret.myers@und.edu
MYERS, Mark ... 907-474-5837 ... 10 I
mdmyers@alaska.edu
MYERS, Mary ... 239-489-6768 ... 105 F
mmyers@edison.edu
MYERS, Mary, L ... 320-222-7534 ... 268 G
mary.myers@ridgewater.edu
MYERS, Mary Beth ... 317-274-1505 ... 174 D
mbmyers@iupui.edu
MYERS, Michael ... 847-982-2500 ... 152 A
myers@htc.edu
MYERS, Michelle ... 816-584-6727 ... 287 E
michelle.meyers@park.edu
MYERS, Nathan, D ... 419-289-5970 ... 384 G
nmyers@ashland.edu
MYERS, Patricia ... 518-587-2100 ... 355 G
patricia.myers@esc.edu
MYERS, Patricia, T ... 865-539-7242 ... 475 G
pmyers@pstcc.edu
MYERS, Paul ... 503-943-7134 ... 420 G
myers@up.edu
MYERS, Randy, E ... 620-665-3579 ... 193 H
myersr@hutchcc.edu
MYERS, Robert ... 310-434-4200 ... 68 D
myers_robert@smc.edu
MYERS, Robert ... 240-500-2000 ... 223 A
myersr@hagerstowncc.edu
MYERS, Robert ... 574-257-3524 ... 169 I
myersr@bethelcollege.edu
MYERS, Robert, M ... 706-886-6831 ... 138 D
rmyers@tfc.edu
MYERS, Robin ... 870-508-6101 ... 20 E
rmyers@asumh.edu
MYERS, Ronnie ... 212-305-5199 ... 330 F
rm36@columbia.edu
MYERS, Sara, J ... 386-312-4037 ... 116 F
sallymyers@sjrstate.edu
MYERS, Sherri ... 828-627-4544 ... 371 C
smyers@haywood.edu
MYERS, Sue Ann ... 703-591-7042 ... 529 E
MYERS, Thomas ... 314-505-7329 ... 280 D
myerst@csl.edu
MYERS, Tim ... 972-825-4723 ... 495 F
tmyers@sagu.edu
MYHRE, Terry ... 801-304-4224 ... 509 I
tmyhre@globeuniversity.edu
MYINT, Myo ... 408-855-5316 ... 78 F
myo.myint@wvm.edu
MYKRIS, Michael ... 505-428-1318 ... 320 E
michael.mykris@sfcc.edu
MYLES, Deborah ... 281-476-1501 ... 493 H
deborah.myles@sjcd.edu
MYLES, Mary ... 601-979-2321 ... 274 G
mary.b.myles@jsums.edu
MYLETT, Bradford ... 641-472-1110 ... 187 E
admissions@mum.edu
MYLREA, Brian ... 260-481-6923 ... 174 C
mylreab@ipfw.edu
MYO, Min ... 661-654-2172 ... 34 A
mmyo@csub.edu
MYRICK, Dean ... 336-342-4261 ... 373 E
myrickd@rockinghamcc.edu
MYRICK, Jessica ... 501-205-8870 ... 21 C
jmyrick@cbc.edu
MYROW, Steve ... 310-434-4871 ... 68 D
myrow_steve@smc.edu
MYRTAJ, Myftar ... 617-588-1321 ... 231 C
mmyrtaj@bfit.edu
MYRTLE, Jamie ... 913-971-3513 ... 195 D
jmyrtle@mnu.edu
MYSCOFSKI, Carole ... 309-556-3577 ... 153 F
myscofsk@iwu.edu
MYSLINSKI, Carienne ... 215-965-4035 ... 436 H
cmyslinski@moore.edu
MYSZKA, Kristine ... 217-544-6464 ... 163 H

N

NAATZ, Duey ... 715-232-5243 ... 552 E
naatzd@uwstout.edu
NABI, Lynn ... 903-586-2518 ... 489 B
lnabi@jacksonville-college.edu
NABOR, Steven, E ... 801-626-6603 ... 511 G
snabor@weber.edu
NABORS, Larry, J ... 662-720-7235 ... 276 C
ljnabors@nemcc.edu
NABORS, Melody, L ... 901-321-3236 ... 467 I
mnabors@cbu.edu
NABORS, Murray ... 816-271-4510 ... 286 G
mnabors@missouriwestern.edu
NACCARATO, Shawn ... 620-235-4128 ... 196 C
snaccarato@pittstate.edu
NACCO, Stephen ... 908-709-7005 ... 316 B
nacco@ucc.edu
NACE, Timothy ... 765-998-5125 ... 180 B
tmnace@taylor.edu
NACHLAS, Rachel ... 301-624-2836 ... 222 G
rnachlas@frederick.edu
NACHMAN, Ralph, L ... 212-746-7723 ... 360 C
rlnachm@med.cornell.edu

NAVARRO, JoAnn .... 607-777-3060 .... 351 F
navarro@binghamton.edu
NAVARRO, Renee .... 415-476-7700 .... 75 A
renee.navarro@ucsf.edu
NAVARRO, Victor .... 480-732-7020 .... 15 E
victor.navarro@cgc.edu
NAVARRO-JUSINO, Adam 830-372-8072 .... 499 F
anavarro-jusino@tlu.edu
NAVE, Felicia, M .... 926-261-2175 .... 496 G
fmnave@pvamu.edu
NAVE, Jeffery, W .... 504-282-4455 .... 213 H
jnave@nobts.edu
NAVETTA, Nancy .... 717-545-4747 .... 432 F
NAVIN, Tom .... 802-258-3173 .... 514 E
tom.navin@worldlearning.org
NAVRAN, Darius .... 216-432-8971 .... 387 B
navran@chancelloru.edu
NAWN, Ruth .... 603-513-1320 .... 306 F
ruth.nawn@granite.edu
NAYLER, Ronald .... 847-467-5810 .... 160 E
r-nayler@northwestern.edu
NAYLOR, Bob .... 435-722-6900 .... 510 N
bob@ubatc.edu
NAYLOR, Patricia .... 973-408-3103 .... 309 E
pnaylor@drew.edu
NAYLOR, Richard .... 508-373-9453 .... 231 B
richard.naylor@becker.edu
NAYLOR, Suzette .... 816-802-3519 .... 283 E
snaylor@kcai.edu
NAYLOR, Tere, E .... 816-932-6744 .... 289 D
tnaylor@saintlukescollege.edu
NAYLOR, Tracy .... 270-686-9550 .... 199 B
tracy.naylor@brescia.edu
NAYLOR-JOHNSON,
Darrell .... 912-525-8031 .... 136 F
dnaylorj@scad.edu
NAYLOR MOORE, Barbara 662-252-8000 .... 276 G
bmoore@rustcollege.edu
NAYOR, Gregory .... 215-717-6606 .... 448 I
gnayor@uarts.edu
NAZARENKO, Tatiana .... 805-565-6070 .... 79 A
tnazarenko@westmont.edu
NAZARIAN, Nick .... 909-652-6541 .... 39 E
nick.nazarian@chaffey.edu
NAZARIO-TORRES,
Juan, C .... 787-620-2040 .... 560 D
jcnazario@aupr.edu
NAZEMETZ, Alex, P .... 814-362-7555 .... 449 B
nazemetz@pitt.edu
NDIAYE, Momar .... 309-438-5365 .... 153 D
mndiaye@ilstu.edu
NEACE, Thomas .... 606-487-3204 .... 202 C
thomas.neace@kctcs.edu
NEAD, Margaret, A .... 585-271-3778 .... 329 F
mnead@crcds.edu
NEAL, Bill .... 704-484-4097 .... 369 E
nealb@clevelandcc.edu
NEAL, Brenda .... 304-260-4380 .... 542 G
bneal@blueridgectc.edu
NEAL, Brigette .... 313-664-7470 .... 249 E
bneal@collegeforcreativestudies.edu
NEAL, Charles, V .... 607-587-4019 .... 355 C
nealcv@alfredstate.edu
NEAL, Donna, V .... 252-493-7309 .... 372 H
dneal@email.pittcc.edu
NEAL, Gary, W .... 210-999-7411 .... 502 E
gneal@trinity.edu
NEAL, James, G .... 212-854-2247 .... 330 F
jneal@columbia.edu
NEAL, Jason .... 909-593-3511 .... 75 E
jneal@laverne.edu
NEAL, Kathleen, E .... 860-701-5380 .... 93 E
neal_k@mitchell.edu
NEAL, Kerry .... 626-529-8092 .... 60 F
kneal@pacificoaks.edu
NEAL, Kurtis, R .... 325-942-2168 .... 480 E
kurtis.neal@angelo.edu
NEAL, JR., L. Cameron .... 972-881-5891 .... 483 H
cneal@collin.edu
NEAL, La Vonne .... 815-753-9055 .... 160 B
lneal1@niu.edu
NEAL, Lyle .... 402-761-8224 .... 300 B
lneal@southeast.edu
NEAL, Mary, Y .... 804-752-7259 .... 523 C
mneal@rmc.edu
NEAL, Michael, A .... 661-654-2287 .... 34 A
mneal@csub.edu
NEAL, Nicole .... 740-351-3245 .... 401 I
nneal@shawnee.edu
NEAL, Phillip .... 270-901-1114 .... 201 I
phil.neal@kctcs.edu
NEAL, Robin .... 916-484-8172 .... 56 A
nealr@arc.losrios.edu
NEAL, Rodney .... 909-558-4543 .... 54 D
rneal@llu.edu
NEAL, Shandon .... 225-771-3590 .... 214 I
NEAL, Shannon .... 504-816-4228 .... 209 A
sneal@dillard.edu
NEAL, Stephanie, A .... 304-710-3141 .... 542 K
neal@mctc.edu
NEAL, Steven, M .... 330-287-1211 .... 399 A
neal.2@osu.edu
NEAL, Susan .... 918-631-3246 .... 413 F
susan-neal@utulsa.edu
NEAL, Thomas, G .... 409-984-6156 .... 501 C
tom.neal@lamarpa.edu
NEAL, Thomas, M .... 714-547-9625 .... 32 B
tneal@calcoast.edu
NEAL, Tom .... 503-838-8043 .... 419 C
nealt@wou.edu
NEAL, William, G .... 808-675-3457 .... 140 D
nealw@byuh.edu
NEAL, Willie .... 972-860-8225 .... 484 H
wneal@dcccd.edu
NEAL, Willie .... 214-860-8784 .... 485 B
wneal@dcccd.edu
NEAL, Willie, H .... 434-381-6144 .... 524 K
wneal@sbc.edu
NEAL, Zeal .... 501-279-4331 .... 21 H
zneal@harding.edu
NEALEIGH, Michael .... 405-224-3140 .... 413 E
mnealeigh@usao.edu
NEALEN, Mary Kaye .... 406-791-5378 .... 296 F
mnealen@ugf.edu
NEALON, Jacquelyn .... 516-686-7925 .... 343 D
jnealon@nyit.edu
NEALON, Marisol .... 415-575-6120 .... 32 G
mmendoza@ciis.edu
NEALON, Michael .... 517-483-1016 .... 254 A
nealonm@lcc.edu
NEALON-WOODS,
Michele .... 312-379-1683 .... 146 F
mnealon-woods@thechicagoschool.edu
NEANDER, Jessica .... 727-864-8148 .... 105 E
neandejs@eckerd.edu
NEAPOLITAN, Jane .... 410-704-2131 .... 228 E
jneapolitan@towson.edu
NEAR, Hollis .... 206-726-5040 .... 533 D
hnear@cornish.edu
NEARY, Michele, A .... 847-491-8466 .... 160 E
m-neary@northwestern.edu
NEARY, Robert .... 315-866-0300 .... 335 D
nearyrd@herkimer.edu
NEASE, Owen .... 504-282-4455 .... 213 H
financialaid@nobts.edu
NEAU, George .... 510-567-6174 .... 72 D
chancellor@sum.edu
NEAULT, Lynn .... 619-388-7800 .... 65 H
lneault@sdccd.edu
NEAULT, Lynn, C .... 619-388-6922 .... 65 E
lneault@sdccd.edu
NEAVE, Jessica .... 617-217-9204 .... 231 A
jneave@baystate.edu
NEAVES, Mitchell .... 340-693-1046 .... 568 E
mneaves@live.uvi.edu
NEBEKER-CHRISTENSEN,
Annie .... 801-581-7066 .... 511 C
anebeker@sa.utah.edu
NEBEL, Andreia .... 402-552-6178 .... 297 B
nebel@clarksoncollege.edu
NEBESKY, Michael .... 864-656-2390 .... 456 E
mnebeske@clemson.edu
NECESSARY, David .... 276-739-2448 .... 529 A
dnecessary@vhcc.edu
NECESSARY, Russell, D .... 276-328-0322 .... 525 G
rdn2f@uvawise.edu
NECHIPURENKO, Erin .... 508-626-4951 .... 238 A
enechipurenko@framingham.edu
NECULA, Cristina .... 718-960-2416 .... 327 C
cristina.necula@lehman.cuny.edu
NEDDERMAN, Robert, M .. 402-461-7410 .... 298 A
bnedderman@hastings.edu
NEDELL, Thomas .... 617-373-2240 .... 243 F
NEDERHOFF, Arlan .... 712-722-6010 .... 184 C
anederho@dordt.edu
NEDERHOOD, Al .... 323-319-9500 .... 73 C
NEDWEK, Brian .... 417-823-3447 .... 289 I
bnedwek@forest.edu
NEEB, Jennifer, K .... 610-799-1120 .... 434 D
jneeb@lccc.edu
NEEDHAM, Frankie .... 828-898-8763 .... 366 D
needham@lmc.edu
NEEDHAM, James .... 361-825-2778 .... 498 C
james.needham@tamucc.edu
NEEDHAM, Jodie .... 312-427-2737 .... 154 H
6needham@jmls.edu
NEEDHAM, Michele .... 630-466-7900 .... 168 B
mneedham@waubonsee.edu
NEEFE, Diane .... 608-785-9539 .... 555 F
neefed@westerntc.edu
NEEL, Buster .... 702-992-2302 .... 302 G
buster.neel@nsc.edu
NEEL, Ellen .... 623-845-3371 .... 15 H
e.neel@gcmail.maricopa.edu
NEEL, Joel .... 805-756-2193 .... 33 I
jneel@calpoly.edu
NEELY, Chrystal .... 404-752-1782 .... 134 E
cneely@msm.edu
NEELY, Dail .... 940-397-6273 .... 491 B
dail.neely@mwsu.edu
NEELY, Dorothy .... 530-251-8881 .... 53 H
dneely@lassencollege.edu
NEELY, Erin .... 740-695-9500 .... 385 B
eneely@belmontcollege.edu
NEELY, Jennifer .... 615-248-1237 .... 476 G
jneely@trevecca.edu
NEELY, Monty, K .... 503-838-8271 .... 419 C
neelyk@wou.edu
NEELY, Nicole .... 814-827-4430 .... 450 A
mailliar@pitt.edu
NEELY, Renee .... 575-562-2314 .... 318 B
renee.neely@enmu.edu
NEELY, Robert .... 940-898-3301 .... 502 D
rneely@twu.edu
NEELY-MORRIS, Felecia .... 903-510-2490 .... 503 A
fnee@tjc.edu
NEENAN, Benedict, T .... 660-944-2859 .... 280 B
benedict@conception.edu
NEENAN, SJ, William, B ... 617-552-1640 .... 232 B
william.neenan@bc.edu
NEER, Stephen .... 312-261-3031 .... 159 E
stephen.neer@nl.edu
NEESAM, Jaci, E .... 415-422-6762 .... 76 E
neesam@usfca.edu
NEESE, John, M .... 325-670-1273 .... 487 F
jneese@hsutx.edu
NEESE, Susan .... 253-680-7025 .... 531 F
sneese@bates.ctc.edu
NEESMITH, Debra .... 704-216-3640 .... 373 F
debra.neesmith@rccc.edu
NEEVE, Tasia, S .... 415-442-7833 .... 48 F
tneeve@ggu.edu
NEF, Dennis, L .... 559-278-4468 .... 35 A
dennisn@csufresno.edu
NEFF, Jon .... 319-398-7195 .... 187 B
jneff@kirkwood.edu
NEFF, Kathryn .... 573-518-2378 .... 285 I
kneff@mineralarea.edu
NEFF, Lori, A .... 609-497-7880 .... 312 F
lori.neff@ptsem.edu
NEFF, Scott .... 740-774-6300 .... 389 D
sneff@daymarcollege.edu
NEFF, Sherri, A .... 913-288-7201 .... 194 C
sneff@kckcc.edu
NEGBENEBOR, Anthony, I . 704-406-4622 .... 364 E
anegbenebor@gardner-webb.edu
NEGIP, Marilyn .... 617-243-2242 .... 236 A
mnegip@lasell.edu
NEGLIA, Frank, A .... 973-290-4344 .... 308 G
fneglia@cse.edu
NEGLIA, Michael, S .... 904-620-2923 .... 120 D
mneglia@unf.edu
NEGRÓN, Luis .... 787-850-9319 .... 567 E
luis.negron4@upr.edu
NEGRON, Ciara, M .... 203-576-4568 .... 94 F
cnegron@bridgeport.edu
NEGRON, Elizabeth .... 787-757-1520 .... 567 C
elizabeth.negron@upr.edu
NEGRON, Frankie .... 787-761-0640 .... 566 F
NEGRON, Gisela .... 787-257-7373 .... 565 G
gnegron@suagm.edu
NEGRON, Lillian .... 787-786-3030 .... 560 G
lnegron@ucb.edu.pr
NEGRON, Luz .... 787-743-4041 .... 561 F
lznegron@columbiaco.edu
NEGRON, Lymari .... 787-891-0825 .... 563 A
lynegron@aguadilla.inter.edu
NEGRON, Olga .... 787-832-6000 .... 562 G
mortiz@icprjc.edu
NEGRON, Pablo, E .... 518-629-7154 .... 336 C
p.negron@hvcc.edu
NEGRON-PORTILLO,
Luis, M .... 787-751-1912 .... 564 C
lmnegron@inter.edu
NEHER, Kenneth, R .... 618-650-2536 .... 165 C
kneher@siue.edu
NEHRBAS, Mark .... 740-284-5843 .... 391 A
mnehrbas@franciscan.edu
NEHRING, Matthew, S .... 719-587-7504 .... 80 L
msnehrin@adams.edu
NEHRING, Wendy, M .... 423-439-7051 .... 473 F
nehringw@etsu.edu
NEIDECK, Robert .... 765-998-5222 .... 180 B
rbneideck@taylor.edu
NEIDERBACH, Michael, A . 607-871-2329 .... 322 E
neiderbach@alfred.edu
NEIDORF, David .... 760-872-2000 .... 43 K
dneidorf@deepsprings.edu
NEIDY, Jon .... 309-677-2374 .... 146 C
neidy@bradley.edu
NEIFERT, Roger .... 316-322-3144 .... 191 G
rneifert@butlercc.edu
NEIGHBOR, Edward .... 407-823-5269 .... 120 B
james.neighbor@ucf.edu
NEIGHBORS, Janie .... 940-668-7333 .... 491 E
jneighbors@nctc.edu
NEIGLER, Peter .... 212-924-5900 .... 357 B
pneigler@swedishinstitute.edu
NEIHEISEL, Steve .... 208-885-5690 .... 144 G
steven@uidaho.edu
NEIHOF, JR., John, E .... 606-693-5000 .... 203 F
jneihof@kmbc.edu
NEIKIRK, Mark .... 859-572-1449 .... 205 H
neikirkm1@nku.edu
NEIL, Amy .... 631-244-3207 .... 332 C
neila@dowling.edu
NEIL, Jon .... 518-580-5490 .... 351 B
jneil@skidmore.edu
NEIL, Linda .... 773-481-8408 .... 147 I
lneil@ccc.edu
NEIL, Stephanie .... 206-876-6100 .... 538 A
sneil@theseattleschool.edu
NEILL, Christine .... 602-243-8185 .... 16 D
christine.neill@smcmail.maricopa.edu
NEILL, Sarah .... 617-521-2124 .... 244 F
sarah.neill@simmons.edu
NEILL, Sharon .... 212-772-4460 .... 327 E
sharon.neill@hunter.cuny.edu
NEILSEN, Ardis .... 805-922-6966 .... 26 L
aneilsen@hancockcollege.edu
NEILSON, Eric, G .... 312-503-0340 .... 160 E
egneilson@northwestern.edu
NEILSON, Leanne .... 805-493-3145 .... 33 B
neilson@clunet.edu
NEILSON, Richard, P .... 516-671-2215 .... 360 B
rneilson@webb-institute.edu
NEILSON, Steven .... 407-646-2185 .... 116 D
sneilson@rollins.edu
NEIMAN, Gershon .... 845-731-3700 .... 362 A
NEIMEYER, Nicole .... 419-227-3141 .... 404 D
nniemeye@unoh.edu
NEIN, Daniel, F .... 207-786-6207 .... 217 C
dnein@bates.edu
NEINER, Catherine .... 404-471-6425 .... 123 I
cneiner@agnesscott.edu
NEISES, Marlene .... 414-382-6017 .... 546 B
marlene.neises@alverno.edu
NEITZ, Stephen .... 717-815-1924 .... 452 G
sneitz@ycp.edu
NEITZEL, Alan .... 405-736-0315 .... 411 I
aneitzel@rose.edu
NEJAD, Hassan .... 201-684-7406 .... 313 C
hnejad@ramapo.edu
NELANT, Dan .... 317-805-1782 .... 541 K
dnelant@salemu.edu
NELANT, Sri .... 317-805-1791 .... 541 K
snelant@salemu.edu
NELKENBAUM,
Avrohom Yaakov .... 718-645-0536 .... 341 D
NELL, Sharon .... 512-448-8620 .... 493 E
sharonn@stedwards.edu
NELLENBACK, Marie, A .... 315-255-1743 .... 325 G
marie.nellenback@cayuga-cc.edu
NELLER, Irene .... 562-903-4727 .... 31 A
irene.neller@biola.edu
NELLESEN, Gary .... 909-594-5611 .... 58 A
gnellese@mtsac.edu
NELLIS, Ginny .... 802-258-3283 .... 514 E
ginny.nellis@worldlearning.org
NELLIS, M. Duane .... 208-885-6365 .... 144 G
dnellis@uidaho.edu
NELLIS, Virginia .... 802-258-9233 .... 513 H
gnellis@marlboro.edu
NELLSON, Tom .... 419-448-3346 .... 402 E
nellsont@tiffin.edu
NELMS, Chad .... 864-231-2025 .... 455 C
cnelms@andersonuniversity.edu
NELMS, Charlie .... 919-530-6104 .... 378 B
cnelms@nccu.edu
NELMS, Jim, A .... 936-261-1932 .... 496 G
janelms@pvamu.edu
NELMS, Kristi .... 217-854-3231 .... 146 A
kristi.nelms@blackburn.edu
NELSEN, Erin .... 717-299-7772 .... 448 A
nelsen@stevenscollege.edu
NELSEN, Jeff, A .... 515-574-1115 .... 185 I
nelsen@iowacentral.edu
NELSEN, Robert, S .... 956-665-2100 .... 506 C
president@utpa.edu
NELSON, Andrew .... 830-372-8011 .... 499 F
anelson@tlu.edu
NELSON, Andrew, J .... 715-836-5368 .... 551 A
nelsonan@uwec.edu
NELSON, Anthony .... 301-860-3590 .... 228 A
anelson@bowiestate.edu
NELSON, April .... 580-477-7896 .... 414 C
april.nelson@wosc.edu
NELSON, JR., Arthur .... 806-354-5463 .... 502 B
arthur.nelson@ttuhsc.edu
NELSON, Audrey .... 434-848-6442 .... 524 B
anelson@saintpauls.edu
NELSON, Barry, C .... 979-436-9200 .... 497 B
nelson@tamhsc.edu
NELSON, Bill .... 573-681-5555 .... 283 I
nelsonb@lincolnu.edu
NELSON, Bob .... 218-281-8547 .... 271 E
bnelson@umn.edu
NELSON, Brandi .... 701-662-1509 .... 382 F
brandi.nelson@lrsc.edu
NELSON, Brenda .... 718-405-3223 .... 330 A
brenda.nelson@mountsaintvincent.edu
NELSON, Brian .... 651-290-6357 .... 272 E
brian.nelson@wmitchell.edu
NELSON, Brian .... 832-813-6508 .... 490 E
brian.nelson@lonestar.edu
NELSON, Brian .... 334-649-5000 .... 557 E
NELSON, Bruce, F .... 336-278-7280 .... 364 D
bnelson@elon.edu
NELSON, Camile .... 617-573-8157 .... 245 B
cnelson@suffolk.edu
NELSON, Carla, P .... 432-552-2100 .... 507 D
nelson_c@utpb.edu
NELSON, Carol .... 218-751-8670 .... 270 D
carolnelson@oakhills.edu
NELSON, Carolyn .... 510-885-3942 .... 34 E
carolyn.nelson@csueastbay.edu

NELSON, Charles .... 334-386-7220....... 3 G cnelson@faulkner.edu
NELSON, Charles .... 425-249-4775.... 538 G chuck.nelson@tlc.edu
NELSON, Cherrie .... 801-626-7496.... 511 G cgnelson@weber.edu
NELSON, Christopher .... 757-388-2900.... 524 D
NELSON, Christopher, B .... 410-626-2510.... 225 G chris.nelson@sjca.edu
NELSON, Claire, N .... 207-778-7295.... 220 C claire@maine.edu
NELSON, Craig, V .... 801-524-8103.... 510 E cnelson@ldsbc.edu
NELSON, Daniel .... 651-638-6241.... 261 D dc-nelson@bethel.edu
NELSON, David, A .... 717-245-1830.... 427 F nelsond@dickinson.edu
NELSON, David, J .... 312-942-6256.... 163 D david_j_nelson@rush.edu
NELSON, David, P .... 336-770-3262.... 379 E nelsond@uncsa.edu
NELSON, Deborah, L .... 773-702-8051.... 166 G dnelson@uchicago.edu
NELSON, Denise .... 207-780-5644.... 220 G dnelson@usm.maine.edu
NELSON, Diane, L .... 415-422-2441...... 76 E dlnelson3@usfca.edu
NELSON, Dirk .... 806-651-2730.... 499 A jdnelson@mail.wtamu.edu
NELSON, Don .... 570-740-0750.... 435 C dnelson@luzerne.edu
NELSON, Dorothy, A .... 248-370-2552.... 256 G danelson@oakland.edu
NELSON, Douglas .... 860-231-5291...... 95 D dnelson@usj.edu
NELSON, Edwin, C .... 724-925-4003.... 451 E nelsone@wccc.edu
NELSON, Eldon .... 956-882-5000.... 505 E eldon.nelson@utb.edu
NELSON, Elizabeth, A .... 713-798-2500.... 481 H enelson@bcm.edu
NELSON, Eric .... 302-736-2571...... 97 A nelsoner@wesley.edu
NELSON, Eric .... 570-674-6725.... 436 F enelson@misericordia.edu
NELSON, Erik .... 215-572-2944.... 422 C nelson@arcadia.edu
NELSON, Evelyn, C .... 561-237-7816.... 113 D enelson@lynn.edu
NELSON, Fred .... 605-642-6848.... 465 H fred.nelson@bhsu.edu
NELSON, Garet, B .... 802-626-6446.... 515 G garet.nelson@lyndonstate.edu
NELSON, Gena, C .... 315-267-2330.... 354 C nelsongc@potsdam.edu
NELSON, Gersham .... 660-543-4750.... 290 H ganelson@ucmo.edu
NELSON, Greg .... 408-288-3723...... 67 D greg.nelson@sjcc.edu
NELSON, James .... 903-566-7002.... 506 E jnelson@uttyler.edu
NELSON, James, A .... 304-327-4103.... 543 F jnelson@bluefieldstate.edu
NELSON, James, E .... 617-573-8379.... 245 B jnelson@suffolk.edu
NELSON, James, H .... 606-693-5000.... 203 F jnelson@kmbc.edu
NELSON, Jane, A .... 612-330-1603.... 261 B nelsonj@augsburg.edu
NELSON, Janet, A .... 315-255-1743.... 325 G helsonj@cayuga-cc.edu
NELSON, Janice .... 949-214-3334...... 43 C janice.nelson@cui.edu
NELSON, Jeff .... 218-235-2193.... 269 F j.nelson@vcc.edu
NELSON, Jeffrey, D .... 419-372-2853.... 385 E nelsonj@bgsu.edu
NELSON, Jen .... 208-459-5121.... 143 D jnelson@collegeofidaho.edu
NELSON, Jennifer .... 770-975-4000.... 127 B
NELSON, Jesse .... 509-963-1515.... 532 C nelsonje@cwu.edu
NELSON, Jim .... 606-693-5000.... 203 F jnelson@kmbc.edu
NELSON, Joan .... 605-867-5856.... 465 A jnelson@olc.edu
NELSON, Joan .... 713-743-2603.... 503 D jmnelson2@uh.edu
NELSON, Joan, A .... 603-283-2396.... 303 F jnelson@antioch.edu
NELSON, Joan, M .... 713-743-2603.... 503 C jmnelson2@uh.edu
NELSON, Joanne, E .... 518-564-2090.... 354 B jnels003@plattsburgh.edu
NELSON, Joel .... 775-850-0700.... 302 C jnelson@morrison.neumont.edu
NELSON, John, R .... 513-732-5200.... 403 E
NELSON, Joseph .... 907-796-6057...... 11 A joseph.nelson@uas.alaska.edu
NELSON, Joseph .... 907-796-6057...... 11 A joe.nelson@uas.alaska.edu
NELSON, Joseph, G .... 740-427-5172.... 394 C nelson@kenyon.edu
NELSON, Joy .... 617-236-8800.... 234 G jnelson@fisher.edu
NELSON, Judith, L .... 561-237-7161.... 113 D jlnelson@lynn.edu
NELSON, Karen .... 760-419-1288.... 128 B karen.nelson@covenant.edu
NELSON, Karen .... 503-943-7485.... 420 G nelsonk@up.edu
NELSON, Karen, L .... 617-262-5000.... 231 G karen.nelson@the-bac.edu
NELSON, Karen, S .... 724-653-2190.... 427 G knelson@dec.edu
NELSON, Kathleen .... 973-300-6556.... 315 F knelson@sussex.edu
NELSON, Kathleen, J .... 651-638-6126.... 261 D k-nelson@bethel.edu
NELSON, Keith, R .... 989-463-7303.... 247 B nelsonkr@alma.edu
NELSON, Kelly .... 410-617-2341.... 223 I knelson@loyola.edu
NELSON, Kent, E .... 208-885-2272.... 144 G kentnelson@uidaho.edu
NELSON, Kevin .... 970-943-3045...... 89 E knelson@western.edu
NELSON, Kris .... 251-442-2945........ 9 A knelson@umobile.edu
NELSON, Kristine .... 714-484-7230...... 59 D knelson@cypresscollege.edu
NELSON, Layne Meredith .. 970-943-2885...... 89 E lnelson@western.edu
NELSON, Linda, J .... 404-413-2567.... 131 G lnelson@gsu.edu
NELSON, Linda, J .... 404-413-3300.... 131 G lnelson@gsu.edu
NELSON, Lisa .... 570-740-0732.... 435 C lnelson@luzerne.edu
NELSON, Lisa .... 360-992-2488.... 532 F lnelson@clark.edu
NELSON, Mark .... 205-348-4893........ 8 E mnelson@ua.edu
NELSON, Mark .... 205-348-8272........ 8 E mnelson@ua.edu
NELSON, Mark .... 419-372-6067.... 385 E nelsonm@bgsu.edu
NELSON, Martha .... 415-257-1310...... 45 C martha.nelson@dominican.edu
NELSON, Martha .... 414-256-1211.... 549 D nelsonm@mtmary.edu
NELSON, Mike .... 619-684-8771...... 59 B mnelson@newschoolarch.edu
NELSON, Mindy .... 509-527-4299.... 539 B mindy.nelson@wwcc.edu
NELSON, Murrey .... 415-503-6286...... 66 A mnelson@sfcm.edu
NELSON, Nadine .... 402-486-2504.... 300 C nanelson@ucollege.edu
NELSON, Nancy, N .... 915-831-6631.... 486 G nnelson2@epcc.edu
NELSON, Norris, J .... 952-944-0080.... 263 I nnelson@nti.edu
NELSON, Peggy, L .... 208-524-3000.... 143 G peggy.nelson@my.eitc.edu
NELSON, Peter, C .... 312-996-2400.... 167 B nelson@uic.edu
NELSON, Phil .... 909-469-5661...... 78 I pnelson@westernu.edu
NELSON, Rebecca .... 773-244-5759.... 159 H rnelson1@northpark.edu
NELSON, Rencelly .... 691-320-2480.... 559 D rencelly@comfsm.fm
NELSON, Richard .... 518-327-6247.... 345 H rnelson@paulsmiths.edu
NELSON, Richard .... 843-953-2232.... 456 C richard.nelson@citadel.edu
NELSON, Richard, D .... 812-288-8878.... 178 E macfs@mindspring.com
NELSON, Ross .... 970-247-7427...... 84 K nelson_r@fortlewis.edu
NELSON, Samantha .... 256-306-2441........ 2 D snelson@calhoun.edu
NELSON, Stephanie .... 432-837-8303.... 501 E
NELSON, Stephen .... 207-780-5242.... 220 G snelson@usm.maine.edu
NELSON, Steve .... 504-568-4009.... 213 A snelso1@lsuhsc.edu
NELSON, Steve .... 954-885-3500.... 112 D
NELSON, Steve .... 715-395-4619.... 552 F snelson@uwsuper.edu
NELSON, Steven, J .... 313-993-1524.... 258 G nelsonsj@udmercy.edu
NELSON, Sue .... 707-256-7150...... 58 F snelson@napavalley.edu
NELSON, Sunny .... 912-525-5225.... 136 F snelson@scad.edu
NELSON, Susan, E .... 973-972-9794.... 316 C nelsonsu@umdnj.edu
NELSON, Suzy .... 315-228-7425.... 329 G snelson@colgate.edu
NELSON, Tammy .... 207-768-2747.... 218 J tnelson@nmcc.edu
NELSON, Terence .... 949-582-4473...... 70 F tnelson14@saddleback.edu
NELSON, Thomas .... 678-915-7464.... 137 G tnelson@spsu.edu
NELSON, Tim .... 510-723-6648...... 39 C tnelson@chabotcollege.edu
NELSON, Tim .... 301-891-4045.... 229 B tnelson@wau.edu
NELSON, Timothy .... 419-267-1226.... 397 E tnelson@northweststate.edu
NELSON, Timothy, J .... 231-995-1010.... 256 D tnelson@nmc.edu
NELSON, Tommy .... 920-686-6281.... 550 H tommy.nelson@sl.edu
NELSON, Tonya .... 505-566-3220.... 320 D nelsont@sanjuancollege.edu
NELSON, Troy .... 417-626-1234.... 287 C occadmin@occ.edu
NELSON, Vincent, C .... 319-335-3294.... 182 F vincent-nelson@uiowa.edu
NELSON, Wilbert .... 602-285-7174...... 16 A wilbert.nelson@pcmail.maricopa.edu
NELSON, William, C .... 202-274-6168.... 100 A wnelson@udc.edu
NELSON, William, G .... 937-395-5616.... 394 D william.nelson@kcma.edu
NELSON, William, L .... 800-867-2243...... 60 C
NELSON-BAILEY, Robin .... 781-239-3171.... 239 G nelsonbailey@massbay.edu
NELSON-HENSLEY, Sheila 412-392-3498.... 445 A snelsonhensley@pointpark.edu
NELSON MOELLER, Rachel .... 610-330-5810.... 433 B moellerr@lafayette.edu
NELSON NASH, Denise .... 626-395-4638...... 32 H dnn@caltech.edu
NELSON-RUSSOM, Lynn, A .... 610-499-1183.... 451 F lanelsonrussom@widener.edu
NELSON WINGER, Elyse .. 309-556-3005.... 153 F enelsonw@iwu.edu
NEMCIK, Henry .... 505-277-1586.... 321 C hnemcik@unm.edu
NEMECEK, Barbara .... 516-877-4607.... 322 A bnemecek@adelphi.edu
NEMES, James .... 610-648-3200.... 439 H jan16@psu.eud
NEMETH, Kevin .... 209-667-3111...... 36 D knemeth@csustan.edu
NEMITZ, Carol .... 319-385-6217.... 186 E cnemitz@iwc.edu
NEMITZ, James, W .... 304-647-6368.... 544 E jnemitz@osteo.wvsom.edu
NEMITZ, Penny, L .... 419-372-0614.... 385 F pnemitz@bgsu.edu
NEMMERT, Jim .... 888-974-3436...... 46 M jnemmert@fidm.edu
NENON, Thomas, J .... 901-678-2156.... 474 C tnenon@memphis.edu
NEPHEW, Marvin .... 937-328-6125.... 387 H nephewm@clarkstate.edu
NEPOMUCENO, Tina .... 708-209-3545.... 148 E tina.nepomuceno@cuchicago.edu
NEPPER, Terry, S .... 806-651-2747.... 499 A tnepper@mail.wtamu.edu
NEPTUNE, Vivian .... 787-999-9531.... 568 B vneptune@law.upr.edu
NERGER, Janice, L .... 970-491-6974...... 83 F janice.nerger@colostate.edu
NERI, Elaine .... 813-880-8013.... 111 C eneri@academy.edu
NERIA, Angela .... 620-235-4603.... 196 C aneria@pittstate.edu
NERLAND, Douglas, R .... 813-988-5131.... 108 A development@floridacollege.edu
NERLAND, Douglas, R .... 813-988-5131.... 108 A nerlandd@floridacollege.edu
NERO, Lut .... 610-399-2069.... 442 A lnero@cheyney.edu
NERO, Patrick .... 202-994-6650...... 98 C
NERY, Annebelle .... 760-773-2519...... 42 A anery@collegeofthedesert.edu
NERY, Karen .... 910-893-1630.... 362 J nery@campbell.edu
NERZAK, J. Peter .... 865-694-6517.... 475 G pnerzak@pstcc.edu
NESBARY, Dale, K .... 231-777-0311.... 256 A dale.nesbary@muskegoncc.edu
NESBIT, Cortni .... 860-628-4751...... 93 C cnesbit@lincolncollegene.edu
NESBIT, Jim .... 937-298-3399.... 394 D jim.nesbit@kcma.edu
NESBIT, Ryan, A .... 706-542-2802.... 138 G rnesbit@uga.edu
NESBITT, Jacquelyn, H ...... 803-981-7195.... 463 H jnesbitt@yorktech.edu
NESBITT, Joan, M .... 573-341-4111.... 291 E nesbittj@mst.edu
NESBITT, Richard, L .... 413-597-2211.... 246 D richard.l.nesbitt@williams.edu
NESBITT, Shawna .... 214-648-2168.... 507 E shawna.nesbitt@utsouthwestern.edu
NESBITT, Thomas, W .... 315-267-2180.... 354 C nesbittw@potsdam.edu
NESCI, Anthony .... 716-851-1449.... 333 C nesci@ecc.edu
NESHEIM-KAUFFMAN, Rhonda, K .... 641-422-4500.... 188 A nesherho@niacc.edu
NESHIEM, Sheri .... 813-205-5166...... 29 F sneshiem@argosy.edu
NESIN, Jeffrey .... 212-592-2000.... 350 F jnesin@sva.edu
NESLER, Mitchell, S .... 518-587-2100.... 355 G mitchell.nesler@esc.edu
NESLER, Timothy, C .... 352-395-5160.... 117 F tim.nesler@sfcollege.edu
NESMITH, Dee .... 432-335-6429.... 492 A dnesmith@odessa.edu
NESMITH, Robert, M .... 859-238-5356.... 199 G bob.nesmith@centre.edu
NESMITH, Sylvia, L .... 843-953-6976.... 456 C sylvia.nesmith@citadel.edu
NESS, Claudia, L .... 509-527-5040.... 540 B nesscl@whitman.edu
NESS, Eric .... 570-389-4517.... 441 F eness@bloomu.edu
NESS, James .... 480-557-7430...... 19 A james.ness@phoenix.edu
NESS, Maurice, E .... 501-450-3138...... 25 H eness@uca.edu
NESS, Melvin, M .... 212-463-0400.... 358 B meln@touro.edu
NESS, Roberta, B .... 713-500-9052.... 506 F roberta.b.ness@uth.tmc.edu
NESS, Susan .... 701-858-3065.... 382 A susan.ness@minotstateu.edu
NESSAN, Craig, L .... 563-589-0207.... 190 A cnessan@wartburgseminary.edu
NESSEL, Lori, A .... 973-642-8700.... 315 C lori.nessel@shu.edu
NESSER, Ellen .... 724-873-2760.... 441 G nesser@calu.edu
NESTI, CSSP, Donald .... 713-942-5069.... 505 A nesti@stthom.edu
NESTLER, George .... 914-594-4470.... 343 F george_nestler@nymc.edu
NESTMAN, Lane .... 817-735-2688.... 504 E lane.nestman@unthsc.edu
NESTOR, David, A .... 802-656-3380.... 514 H david.nestor@uvm.edu
NESTOR, John .... 614-287-2525.... 389 A jnestor@cscc.edu
NESTOR, Mark .... 215-596-8910.... 450 B m.nestor@usciences.edu
NESTOR, Sally .... 970-542-3151...... 86 G sally.nestor@morgancc.edu
NETHERTON, James, S ..... 478-301-2710.... 134 A netherton_js@mercer.edu
NETHERTON, Shane .... 918-595-7895.... 412 H snetherton@tulsacc.edu
NETTELL, Katie .... 701-662-1517.... 382 F katie.nettell@lrsc.edu
NETTLES, Evelyn .... 615-963-7004.... 474 A enettles1@tnstate.edu
NETTLES, Ronald, E .... 601-643-8300.... 273 G ronnie.nettles@colin.edu
NETTLETON, Patricia, A .... 859-371-9393.... 198 G panettleton@beckfield.edu
NETTLETON, Peter .... 859-371-9393.... 198 G pnettleton@beckfield.edu
NETZHAMMER, Mel .... 360-546-9581.... 539 D mel.netzhammer@vancouver.wsu.edu
NEU, Frances .... 727-341-3319.... 116 H neu.frances@spcollege.edu
NEUBAUER, Judith .... 732-235-8961.... 316 C neubauer@umdnj.edu
NEUBAUER, Kirk .... 563-387-1434.... 187 D neubauki@luther.edu
NEUBAUER, Lane, B .... 215-951-5157.... 432 I neubauer@lasalle.edu
NEUBAUER, Trish .... 563-387-1567.... 187 D neubautr@luther.edu
NEUBERGER, Boruch .... 410-484-7200.... 225 C byn@nirc.edu
NEUBERGER, Paul, M .... 920-923-7613.... 548 E pmneuberger@marianuniversity.edu
NEUBERGER, Sheftel, M ... 410-484-7200.... 225 C sheftel@nirc.edu
NEUDIGATE, Marcia .... 859-341-5627.... 199 E mneudigate@brownmackie.edu
NEUENDORF, Karen .... 734-995-7439.... 249 G neuenke@cuaa.edu
NEUERBURG, Kent .... 985-549-2135.... 216 C kent.neuerburg@selu.edu
NEUFELD, Amy .... 913-621-8772.... 192 F aneufeld@donnelly.edu
NEUFELD, Don .... 626-812-3020...... 30 G dneufeld@apu.edu
NEUFELD, Iris .... 419-358-3322.... 385 D neufeldi@bluffton.edu
NEUFELD, Jane, F .... 773-508-3852.... 157 C jneufe@luc.edu
NEUFELD, Kenley .... 805-965-0581...... 68 B neufeld@sbcc.edu
NEUFELD, Philip .... 559-278-2227...... 35 A pneufeld@csufresno.edu
NEUFELDT, Ellen, J .... 757-683-3442.... 522 F eneufeld@odu.edu
NEUFIND, Nate .... 402-941-6009.... 298 I neufind@midlandu.edu
NEUFVILLE, Janette .... 301-576-0123.... 229 B jneufvil@wau.edu

NEUHARD, Ian .... 772-462-7898 .... 111 B
ineuhard@irsc.edu
NEUHAUSER, John, J .... 802-654-2212 .... 514 D
jneuhauser@smcvt.edu
NEUHOF, Jennifer .... 718-817-3727 .... 334 C
neuhof@fordham.edu
NEUHOFF, Martin, C .... 260-422-5561 .... 173 C
mcneuhoff@indianatech.edu
NEULS, Daniel .... 281-476-1501 .... 493 H
daniel.neuls@sjcd.edu
NEUMAN, Dawn .... 805-437-8441 .... 34 B
dawn.neuman@csuci.edu
NEUMAN, Yisroel .... 732-367-1060 .... 307 G
NEUMANN, Gregory .... 716-645-3131 .... 351 G
buffalo@bkstr.com
NEUMANN, Jessica .... 785-670-1727 .... 197 F
jessica.neumann1@washburn.edu
NEUMANN, Kathleen .... 309-298-1066 .... 168 C
k-neumann@wiu.edu
NEUMANN, Pamela, R .... 716-839-8325 .... 331 F
pneumann@daemen.edu
NEUMAYR, Mark .... 928-523-6517 .... 16 I
mark.neumayr@nau.edu
NEUN, Stephen .... 603-283-2150 .... 303 F
sneun@antioch.edu
NEUNER, Jerome, L .... 716-888-2120 .... 325 F
neuner@canisius.edu
NEUPAUER, Nicholas, C .... 724-287-8711 .... 423 G
nicholas.neupauer@bc3.edu
NEUTENS, James, J .... 865-305-9290 .... 477 E
jneutens@mc.utmck.edu
NEUVILLE, Jeff .... 828-327-7000 .... 369 B
jneuville@cvcc.edu
NEVAREZ, Gerard .... 575-646-3635 .... 319 D
gerardn@nmsu.edu
NEVATT, Aaron .... 415-338-1912 .... 37 B
anevatt@sfsu.edu
NEVE, Nancy .... 906-635-2080 .... 253 H
nneve@lssu.edu
NEVEAU, Judy .... 310-434-4303 .... 68 D
neveau_judy@smc.edu
NEVELS, Andrea .... 773-244-5565 .... 159 H
anevels@northpark.edu
NEVELS, JR., Harry, V .... 434-848-1825 .... 524 B
hnevels@saintpauls.edu
NEVELS, Lyle .... 510-642-4096 .... 73 H
lnevels@berkeley.edu
NEVEU, Debra .... 504-816-4546 .... 209 A
dneveu@dillard.edu
NEVILLE, David .... 858-642-8163 .... 58 I
dneville@nu.edu
NEVILLE, Frank .... 703-993-8703 .... 519 E
fnevill2@gmu.edu
NEVILLE, Nancy .... 216-421-7427 .... 388 A
nneville@cia.edu
NEVILLS, Landee .... 417-328-1826 .... 290 A
lnevills@sbuniv.edu
NEVIN, Amy .... 518-631-9844 .... 358 H
nevina@uniongraduatecollege.edu
NEVINS, Daniel .... 212-678-8067 .... 337 G
danevins@jtsa.edu
NEVOIS, Dana, A .... 636-481-3488 .... 283 D
dnevois@jeffco.edu
NEW, Lynn .... 903-923-2093 .... 486 F
lnew@etbu.edu
NEW, Michael, J .... 802-654-2635 .... 514 D
mnew@smcvt.edu
NEW, William, G .... 409-772-6015 .... 507 C
wgnew@utmb.edu
NEWBERG, Bella .... 760-750-4444 .... 36 C
newberg@csusm.edu
NEWBERN, Judson .... 615-322-2715 .... 478 A
judson.newbern@vanderbilt.edu
NEWBERRY, Anthony .... 502-213-2121 .... 202 F
tony.newberry@kctcs.edu
NEWBERRY, Beth .... 502-585-9911 .... 206 D
bnewberry@spalding.edu
NEWBERRY, Elizabeth .... 651-450-3654 .... 266 F
enewber@inverhills.edu
NEWBERRY, JR.,
James, H .... 502-863-8043 .... 201 A
jim_newberry@georgetowncollege.edu
NEWBERRY, Leanna, J .... 620-421-6700 .... 194 G
leannan@labette.edu
NEWBERRY, Robert .... 575-624-7180 .... 318 C
robert.newberry@roswell.enmu.edu
NEWBOLD, Pamela .... 330-823-6572 .... 404 C
newbolph@mountunion.edu
NEWBORN, Janis .... 256-726-7460 .... 6 C
jnewborn@oakwood.edu
NEWBOULD, Ian .... 540-654-1241 .... 525 D
inewboul@umw.edu
NEWBURN, Rita .... 501-244-5125 .... 19 D
rita.newburn@arkansasbaptist.edu
NEWBY, Belita .... 256-726-8245 .... 6 C
bfleming@oakwood.edu
NEWBY, Greg .... 907-450-8663 .... 10 I
gbnewby@alaska.edu
NEWBY, Gretchen .... 314-275-3548 .... 161 E
gretchen.newby@principia.edu
NEWBY, Jennifer .... 541-383-7238 .... 414 I
jnewby@cocc.edu
NEWBY, Stephen, M .... 206-281-2938 .... 537 H
newbys@spu.edu
NEWBY, Teresa .... 952-446-4484 .... 263 C
newbyt@crown.edu
NEWBY, Vanessa .... 708-534-4551 .... 151 E
vnewby@govst.edu
NEWCOMB, Ron .... 770-975-4000 .... 127 B
NEWCOMB, Sherri .... 718-631-6381 .... 328 F
snewcomb@qcc.cuny.edu
NEWCOMB, Terry .... 315-364-3370 .... 360 D
tnewcomb@wells.edu
NEWCOMBE, David, A .... 540-365-4463 .... 519 C
dnewcombe@ferrum.edu
NEWCOMBE, Pat .... 413-782-1201 .... 246 A
pnewcombe@law.wne.edu
NEWCOMBE, Rodd .... 321-674-7110 .... 108 H
newcombe@fit.edu
NEWCOME, Beth .... 304-367-4298 .... 543 B
beth.newcome@pierpont.edu
NEWCOMER, Jan, A .... 501-450-3130 .... 25 H
jann@uca.edu
NEWELL, AJ .... 540-654-1934 .... 525 D
anewell@umw.edu
NEWELL, Alton, E .... 724-503-1001 .... 451 A
anewell@washjeff.edu
NEWELL, Bridget .... 801-832-2822 .... 512 G
bnewell@westminstercollege.edu
NEWELL, Cindy .... 785-826-2638 .... 194 E
cnewell@salina.k-state.edu
NEWELL, Diane .... 251-380-9090 .... 3 G
dnewell@faulkner.edu
NEWELL, Glen, C .... 336-334-7731 .... 378 A
gcnewell@ncat.edu
NEWELL, James .... 718-270-2488 .... 352 D
james.newell@downstate.edu
NEWELL, James .... 856-256-4012 .... 314 A
newell@rowan.edu
NEWELL, Jennifer, M .... 585-343-0055 .... 334 F
jmnewell@genesee.edu
NEWELL, JR., John, H .... 843-953-7154 .... 457 B
newellj@cofc.edu
NEWELL, Keith .... 912-260-4377 .... 137 B
keith.newell@sgc.edu
NEWELL, Keith .... 912-260-4392 .... 137 B
keith.newell@sgc.edu
NEWELL, Keith .... 912-260-4377 .... 137 B
keith.newell@sgc.edu
NEWELL, Mallory .... 408-864-8777 .... 47 G
newellmallory@deanza.edu
NEWELL, Peggy .... 617-627-6550 .... 245 C
peggy.newell@tufts.edu
NEWELL, Rand, E .... 207-948-9201 .... 219 H
rnewell@unity.edu
NEWELL, Tamara, J .... 405-425-5475 .... 409 E
tammy.newell@oc.edu
NEWGARD, Debra .... 651-905-3400 .... 261 E
NEWGARD, Debra .... 612-977-5414 .... 261 F
debra.newgard@capella.edu
NEWGENT, Matt .... 405-262-2552 .... 411 G
newgentm@redlandscc.edu
NEWHALL, JR., Edward .... 401-454-6307 .... 454 B
enewhall@risd.edu
NEWHOFF, Marilyn .... 619-594-6516 .... 37 A
mnewhoff@mail.sdsu.edu
NEWHOUSE, Dollie .... 843-661-1362 .... 458 D
NEWHOUSE, Gary .... 847-635-1640 .... 160 F
garyn@oakton.edu
NEWHOUSE, Greg .... 619-388-7673 .... 65 H
gnewhous@sdccd.edu
NEWHOUSE, Greg .... 619-388-7673 .... 65 H
gnewhouse@sdccd.edu
NEWHOUSE, Valerie, K .... 712-362-0434 .... 186 A
vnewhouse@iowalakes.edu
NEWINS, Anne .... 209-384-6185 .... 57 C
newins.a@mccd.edu
NEWITZ, Laurie, H .... 718-780-7503 .... 324 F
laurie.newitz@brooklaw.edu
NEWKIRK, Charlene .... 412-469-6300 .... 425 H
cnewkirk@ccac.edu
NEWKIRK, Krista, L .... 704-687-5727 .... 379 A
krista.newkirk@uncc.edu
NEWKIRK, Vann .... 256-372-5104 .... 1 A
vann.newkirk@aamu.edu
NEWKIRK, Vann .... 256-372-5266 .... 1 A
vann.newkirk@aamu.edu
NEWKOFSKY, Stephen .... 315-268-6467 .... 329 B
steve.newkofsky@clarkson.edu
NEWKOME, George, R .... 330-972-6458 .... 403 B
newkome@uakron.edu
NEWLAND, Jamesetta .... 212-346-1600 .... 345 F
jnewland@pace.edu
NEWLIN, Toni .... 765-998-5211 .... 180 B
tnnewlin@taylor.edu
NEWMAN, Allison .... 518-276-6359 .... 347 D
newmaa3@rpi.edu
NEWMAN, Barry .... 516-364-0808 .... 343 A
bnewman@nycollege.edu
NEWMAN, Carolyn .... 631-656-3191 .... 334 B
cnewman@ftc.edu
NEWMAN, Carrie .... 814-824-3311 .... 436 C
cnewman@mercyhurst.edu
NEWMAN, David, E .... 607-274-3177 .... 336 G
dnewman@ithaca.edu
NEWMAN, Denise .... 989-328-1245 .... 255 E
denisen@montcalm.edu
NEWMAN, Elizabeth .... 781-239-4538 .... 230 E
enewman1@babson.edu
NEWMAN, Ethel .... 321-433-5151 .... 102 D
newmane@brevardcc.edu
NEWMAN, Gail .... 925-439-2181 .... 43 G
gnewman@losmedanos.edu
NEWMAN, James .... 201-216-8722 .... 315 E
jnewman@stevens.edu
NEWMAN, James .... 401-454-6394 .... 454 B
jnewman@risd.edu
NEWMAN, Janet .... 715-422-5476 .... 554 E
janet.newman@mstc.edu
NEWMAN, Janis, J .... 713-313-1183 .... 500 B
newmanjj@tsu.edu
NEWMAN, Jeanine .... 337-491-2030 .... 212 E
jeanine.newman@sowela.edu
NEWMAN, Jeffery, G .... 515-064-0601 .... 185 A
newmanj@faith.edu
NEWMAN, Kathleen .... 410-516-4065 .... 223 F
knewman@jhu.edu
NEWMAN, Kay, S .... 334-387-3877 .... 1 D
kaynewman@amridgeuniversity.edu
NEWMAN, Keith .... 765-677-2105 .... 175 B
keith.newman@indwes.edu
NEWMAN, Lester, C .... 903-730-4890 .... 489 C
lnewman@jarvis.edu
NEWMAN, Linda, L .... 734-764-7403 .... 259 A
newmanll@umich.edu
NEWMAN, Lori, L .... 563-884-5408 .... 188 E
lori.newman@palmer.edu
NEWMAN, Marc, A .... 919-516-4092 .... 376 D
manewman@st-aug.edu
NEWMAN, Michael .... 212-463-0400 .... 358 B
michael.newman@touro.edu
NEWMAN, Michelle .... 901-333-4217 .... 476 B
mnewman@southwest.tn.edu
NEWMAN, Nancy, J .... 402-465-2375 .... 299 H
njn@nebrwesleyan.edu
NEWMAN, Norm .... 260-480-4202 .... 176 F
nnewman@ivytech.edu
NEWMAN, Robert, D .... 801-581-8816 .... 511 C
robert.newman@hum.utah.edu
NEWMAN, Russ .... 858-635-4535 .... 27 A
rnewman@alliant.edu
NEWMAN, Russ .... 858-635-4535 .... 27 E
rnewman@alliant.edu
NEWMAN, Sandra .... 713-973-3028 .... 486 C
snewman@devry.edu
NEWMAN, Scott .... 801-524-8167 .... 510 E
snewman@ldsbc.edu
NEWMAN, Scott .... 918-293-4666 .... 410 E
scott.newman@okstate.edu
NEWMAN, Toni .... 703-709-5875 .... 522 H
NEWMAN, Vaughn .... 405-273-5331 .... 408 B
vnewman@familyoffaithcollege.edu
NEWMEN, Patricia, N .... 207-859-4460 .... 217 G
pnnewmen@colby.edu
NEWNHAM, David .... 916-608-6500 .... 56 C
NEWSCHWANDER, Gregg .... 334-244-3658 .... 1 G
gnewschw@aum.edu
NEWSCHWANDER, Gregg .... 334-844-5662 .... 1 F
gen0002@auburn.edu
NEWSOM, Deborah .... 515-271-3710 .... 184 D
deborah.newsom@drake.edu
NEWSOM, M. Nadine .... 765-459-0561 .... 176 C
mnewson@ivytech.edu
NEWSOM, Stephanie, R .... 319-352-8539 .... 189 J
stephanie.newsom@wartburg.edu
NEWSOM, Thomas, W .... 214-692-8080 .... 480 I
tnewsom@aii.edu
NEWSOME, Chevelle .... 916-278-6470 .... 36 A
cnewsome@csus.edu
NEWSOME, Gary .... 815-939-5120 .... 161 A
gnewsome@olivet.edu
NEWSOME, John, T .... 601-984-1738 .... 277 E
jtnewsome@umc.edu
NEWSOME, Mark .... 336-506-4121 .... 368 A
mark.newsome@alamancecc.edu
NEWSOME, Moses .... 718-270-6987 .... 328 C
mnewsome@mec.cuny.edu
NEWSOME, Pam .... 612-874-3798 .... 265 C
pam_newsome-prochniak@mcad.edu
NEWSOME, Sarah .... 850-973-9675 .... 113 K
newsomes@nfcc.edu
NEWTON, Andrea .... 541-463-5315 .... 416 E
newtona@lanecc.edu
NEWTON, Andrew .... 706-721-4018 .... 130 D
anewton@georgiahealth.edu
NEWTON, Billy .... 505-566-3775 .... 320 D
newtonb@sanjuancollege.edu
NEWTON, Bryan .... 803-593-9231 .... 455 A
newtonbd@atc.edu
NEWTON, Carolyn .... 330-263-2004 .... 388 F
cnewton@wooster.edu
NEWTON, Christopher .... 501-370-5204 .... 23 B
cnewton@philander.edu
NEWTON, Deborah .... 203-392-5900 .... 90 I
newtond2@southernct.edu
NEWTON, Diane, D .... 501-450-3184 .... 25 H
dnewton@uca.edu
NEWTON, Dorian .... 510-430-2262 .... 57 D
newton@mills.edu
NEWTON, Dusty .... 308-865-8702 .... 300 F
newtond@unk.edu
NEWTON, Eric, D .... 864-242-5100 .... 455 E
NEWTON, Fred .... 602-387-7000 .... 19 A
fred.newton@apollogrp.edu
NEWTON, H. Joseph .... 979-845-7361 .... 497 E
jnewton@tamu.edu
NEWTON, Jeff .... 419-530-4484 .... 404 F
jeff.newton2@utoledo.edu
NEWTON, Jeffrey, L .... 617-253-3952 .... 241 D
NEWTON, John .... 630-617-3020 .... 150 H
newtonj@elmhurst.edu
NEWTON, Joseph, A .... 229-333-5974 .... 139 C
jnewton@valdosta.edu
NEWTON, LaCresha .... 501-370-4001 .... 19 D
lacresha.newton@arkansasbaptist.edu
NEWTON, Lynette .... 402-826-8688 .... 297 G
lynette.newton@doane.edu
NEWTON, Martin .... 205-726-2131 .... 6 G
cnewton@samford.edu
NEWTON, Michael .... 559-438-4222 .... 49 I
michael_newton@heald.edu
NEWTON, Michael, L .... 270-384-8099 .... 204 D
newtonm@lindsey.edu
NEWTON, Nell, J .... 574-631-6789 .... 180 G
nell.newton@nd.edu
NEWTON, Sandra .... 252-492-2061 .... 374 G
newton@vgcc.edu
NEWTON, Steven, D .... 517-750-1200 .... 258 D
snewton@arbor.edu
NEWTON, Traci .... 910-892-3178 .... 365 B
tnewton@heritagebiblecollege.edu
NEWTON, Verne .... 845-575-3000 .... 340 B
verne.newton@marist.edu
NEWTON, Warren .... 207-262-7817 .... 220 B
wnewton@maine.edu
NEY, Cheryl, L .... 323-343-3808 .... 35 D
cney@cslanet.calstatela.edu
NEY, Geraldine .... 207-221-8722 .... 218 C
gney@kaplan.edu
NEYENS, Richard .... 303-282-3414 .... 88 D
NG, Bart .... 630-829-6187 .... 145 G
bng@ben.edu
NG, Charles .... 800-782-2422 .... 33 E
cng@mail.cnuas.edu
NG, Charlie .... 909-382-4091 .... 65 A
NG, Jacob .... 510-466-7365 .... 62 E
jacng@peralta.edu
NG, Peh Peh .... 320-589-6300 .... 271 G
pehng@morris.umn.edu
NGAI, Godwin .... 626-571-5110 .... 54 C
ngai@les.edu
NGIRALMAU, Hilda .... 680-488-3036 .... 560 C
hildan@palau.edu
NGIRAMENGIOR, Todd .... 680-488-2471 .... 560 C
toddn@palau.edu
NGIRMERIIL, Glendalynn .... 680-488-3036 .... 560 C
glendalynn@palau.edu
NGO, Pam .... 727-873-4264 .... 121 C
pngo@mail.usf.edu
NGOM, Mbare .... 443-885-3509 .... 224 E
mbare.ngom@morgan.edu
NGUYEN, Charles, C .... 202-319-5160 .... 97 E
nguyen@cua.edu
NGUYEN, Christine .... 714-241-6144 .... 41 B
cnguyen@coastline.edu
NGUYEN, Dana .... 954-783-7339 .... 106 J
dnguyen@cci.edu
NGUYEN, Danny .... 408-855-5417 .... 78 F
danny.nguyen@wvm.edu
NGUYEN, Hieu .... 808-739-8577 .... 140 E
hnguyen@chaminade.edu
NGUYEN, Hoa .... 225-768-1700 .... 214 C
hoa.nguyen@ololcollege.edu
NGUYEN, Hoa .... 219-866-6151 .... 179 D
NGUYEN, Joseph .... 909-384-8677 .... 65 C
nguyen@sbccd.cc.ca.us
NGUYEN, Kay .... 562-860-2451 .... 39 A
knguyen@cerritos.edu
NGUYEN, Lan .... 703-526-5861 .... 516 E
lknguyen@argosy.edu
NGUYEN, Luan, P .... 671-735-2639 .... 559 G
nguyen@uguam.uog.edu
NGUYEN, Tamie .... 323-343-5808 .... 35 D
tnguyen@cslanet.calstatela.edu
NGUYEN, Tuyen .... 714-628-4844 .... 63 G
nguyen_tuyen@sccollege.edu
NGUYEN, Vincent .... 903-510-2371 .... 503 A
vngu@tjc.edu
NGWABA, Maurice, C .... 410-651-6656 .... 227 E
mcngwaba@umes.edu
NI, Yi .... 603-526-3648 .... 303 G
yni@colby-sawyer.edu
NIANOURIS, Eric .... 704-637-4463 .... 363 E
enianour@catawba.edu
NIBLETT, Tonie, M .... 256-228-6001 .... 6 A
nibletttt@nacc.edu
NICA, Claude .... 310-665-6870 .... 60 B
cnica@otis.edu
NICASTRO, Alana .... 619-849-2709 .... 62 L
alananicastro@pointloma.edu
NICASTRO, Vincent, P .... 610-519-4110 .... 450 H
vincent.nicastro@villanova.edu
NICCHI, Frank, J .... 315-568-3100 .... 342 H
fnicchi@nycc.edu

NIETO, Linda, A ... 402-552-3039 ... 297 B nieto@clarksoncollege.edu
NIEUWEBOER, Mariyn ... 603-577-6511 ... 304 I nieuweboer@dwc.edu
NIEUWSMA, Randal, G ... 616-526-6334 ... 249 A nieuwr@calvin.edu
NIEVES, Alfredo ... 787-766-1717 ... 565 I alnieves@suagm.edu
NIEVES, Beatriz ... 787-766-1717 ... 565 ! um_bnieves@suagm.edu
NIEVES, Brenda ... 626-396-2204 ... 29 I brenda.nieves@artcenter.edu
NIEVES, Danily ... 787-882-2065 ... 566 A
NIEVES, Drusila, F ... 845-675-4564 ... 344 G drusila.nieves@nyack.edu
NIEVES, Gladys, T ... 787-765-3560 ... 562 A gnieves@edpcollege.edu
NIEVES, Idalia ... 787-664-0336 ... 568 C idalia.nieves@upr.edu
NIEVES, Ivette ... 787-279-1912 ... 563 D inieves@bayamon.inter.edu
NIEVES, Lamberto, C ... 201-761-6085 ... 314 F lnieves@spc.edu
NIEVES, Liliam ... 787-725-8120 ... 562 C programaextension@eap.edu
NIEVES, Lourdes ... 305-821-3333 ... 109 B lourdes@mm.fnc.edu
NIEVES, Lourdes ... 305-821-3333 ... 109 C lourdes@mm.fnc.edu
NIEVES, Lourdes ... 305-821-3333 ... 109 D lourdes@mm.fnc.edu
NIEVES, Lourdes, M ... 787-765-1915 ... 564 D lmnieves@inter.edu
NIEVES, Mayra ... 212-237-8918 ... 327 F mnieves@jjay.cuny.edu
NIEVES, Nancy ... 787-265-3858 ... 567 F placement@uprm.edu
NIEVES, Wilfredo ... 860-906-5101 ... 91 C wnieves@ccc.commnet.edu
NIEVES VAZQUEZ, Gladys 787-765-3560 ... 562 B nievglad@edpcollege.edu
NIEWENHOUS, Susan ... 208-792-2395 ... 144 B sniewenh@lcsc.edu
NIEWOONDER, Patricia ... 269-488-4434 ... 253 A pniewoonder@kvcc.edu
NIGAGLIONI, Guillermo ... 787-754-7120 ... 562 H
NIGGLI, Susan ... 585-275-7761 ... 359 B sniggli@admin.rochester.edu
NIGH, Theresa ... 317-738-8090 ... 171 F tnigh@franklincollege.edu
NIGHTINGALE, Charles ... 443-518-4615 ... 223 D cnightingale@howardcc.edu
NIGHTINGALE, Lisa ... 972-860-8051 ... 484 H lnightingale@dcccd.edu
NIGLIAZZO, Marc, A ... 245-519-5400 ... 498 A
NIGRO, Frank ... 530-242-7760 ... 69 D fnigro@shastacollege.edu
NIGRO, Mary ... 516-299-3605 ... 339 A mary.nigro@liu.edu
NIGRO, Nick ... 419-473-2700 ... 389 C nnigro@daviscollege.edu
NIGRO, Richard, A ... 215-951-1360 ... 432 I nigro@lasalle.edu
NIGRO, Stephen, M ... 413-542-2101 ... 230 A smnigro@amherst.edu
NIGUIDULA, Amanda ... 305-348-3532 ... 119 C amanda.niguidula@fiu.edu
NIKAS, Peter ... 262-554-2010 ... 549 A dr.peter_nikas@gmx.com
NIKIAS, C. L, M ... 213-740-2111 ... 76 F uscpresident@usc.edu
NIKOLAKIS, Michael ... 251-580-2121 ... 5 A mnikolakis@faulknerstate.edu
NILA, Ed ... 818-386-5605 ... 62 F enila@pgi.edu
NILAND, Eileen, A ... 716-888-2620 ... 325 F nilande@canisius.edu
NILAND, Joe ... 251-442-2288 ... 9 A jniland@umobile.edu
NILES, Jerry ... 540-231-3205 ... 529 G niles@vt.edu
NILES, Mark ... 206-296-4000 ... 538 B nilesm@seattleu.edu
NILES, Maryann ... 781-280-3703 ... 240 B nilesm@middlesex.mass.edu
NILL, Jack ... 417-862-9533 ... 282 A info@globaluniversity.edu
NILSEN, Kenneth ... 201-216-5206 ... 315 E knilsen@stevens.edu
NILSEN, Spencer ... 510-654-2934 ... 46 J snilsen@expression.edu
NILSSON, Andreas ... 719-542-3181 ... 85 I anilsson@intelliteccollege.edu
NILSSON, Elizabeth ... 603-668-6660 ... 305 B
NIMES, Johnny, C ... 478-825-6520 ... 129 F nimesj@fvsu.edu
NIMMER, Carole, E ... 660-543-4580 ... 290 H cnimmer@ucmo.edu
NIMMER, Raymond ... 713-743-2100 ... 503 D rnimmer@uh.edu
NIMMO, Steven ... 706-776-0113 ... 136 A snimmo@piedmont.edu
NIMOCKS DEN HERDER, Mittie ... 608-342-1261 ... 552 B nimocksm@uwplatt.edu
NIMON, Opie ... 312-949-7610 ... 152 E onimon@ico.edu
NIMPS, Roger, L ... 419-995-8369 ... 399 B nimps.1@osu.edu
NIMS, Vince ... 510-848-5232 ... 47 I vnims@fst.edu
NING, Bin ... 734-487-4924 ... 250 F bning@emich.edu
NINO-MORENO, Eduardo . 859-233-8777 ... 207 A enino@transy.edu
NINOS, Katherine ... 505-467-6819 ... 321 A
NIP, Kit ... 319-385-6250 ... 186 E knip@iwc.edu
NIPP, Amanda ... 402-844-7733 ... 299 I amandan@northeast.edu
NIPP, Tim, J ... 731-881-7601 ... 477 G timnipp@utm.edu
NIPPER, G. Edward ... 870-235-4031 ... 23 I genipper@saumag.edu
NIPPER, Susan, H ... 252-451-8221 ... 372 E snipper@nash.cc.nc.us
NIPPERT, Karen, F ... 901-333-4283 ... 476 B knippert@southwest.tn.edu
NIROOMAND, Farhang ... 361-570-4230 ... 504 A niroomandf@uhv.edu
NIROUMAND, Madjid ... 714-432-5991 ... 41 D mniroumand@occ.cccd.edu
NISBET, Jane, A ... 603-862-1948 ... 306 C jan.nisbet@unh.edu
NISENBOYM, Svetlana ... 718-261-5800 ... 324 D snisenboym@bramsonort.edu
NISH, Melinda ... 619-421-6700 ... 71 D
NISHIDA, Susan, S ... 808-454-4700 ... 141 H susansyn@hawaii.edu
NISHIGUCHI, Earl, K ... 808-245-8274 ... 142 C earln@hawaii.edu
NISHIME, Jeanie ... 310-660-3472 ... 45 E jnishime@elcamino.edu
NISHIMOTO, John, H ... 714-449-7409 ... 70 G jnishimoto@scco.edu
NISSEL, Chaim ... 646-685-0115 ... 361 M drnissel@yu.edu
NISSEN, Jill ... 314-367-8700 ... 288 F jill.nissen@stlcop.edu
NISSEN, John ... 802-387-7145 ... 513 G johnnissen@landmark.edu
NISSEN, Lindsey ... 319-296-4269 ... 185 F lindsey.nissen@hawkeyecollege.edu
NISSEN, Sarah, J ... 218-477-2549 ... 267 F nissen@mnstate.edu
NISSLEY, Nick ... 513-569-1601 ... 387 G nick.nissley@cincinnatistate.edu
NISWANDER, Frederick ... 252-328-6975 ... 377 E niswanderf@ecu.edu
NISWONGER, Joseph, R ... 414-410-4504 ... 546 G jrniswonger@stritch.edu
NITECKI, Danuta ... 215-895-2750 ... 427 H dan44@drexel.edu
NITSCH, Wanda ... 760-591-3012 ... 122 J wnitsch@usa.edu
NITTA, Gary ... 808-245-8230 ... 142 C gnitta@hawaii.edu
NIVELE, Joanne ... 303-581-9955 ... 320 G joanne@acupuncturecollege.edu
NIX, Julie ... 256-782-5815 ... 4 L jnix@jsu.edu
NIX, Orvie ... 806-651-2345 ... 499 A onix@wtamu.edu
NIX, Preston, L ... 504-282-4455 ... 213 H pnix@nobts.edu
NIX, Rachel ... 870-574-1521 ... 24 A rnix@sautech.edu
NIX, Sheila ... 210-431-2178 ... 493 F snix@stmarytx.edu
NIX, Stephan ... 361-593-2000 ... 498 D stephan.nix@tamuk.edu
NIXON, Andrea ... 507-222-4043 ... 261 G anixon@carleton.edu
NIXON, David, E ... 734-384-4166 ... 255 D dnixon@monroeccc.edu
NIXON, Gwen ... 314-513-4290 ... 288 H gnixon@stlcc.edu
NIXON, Jude ... 978-542-7267 ... 238 E jnixon@salemstate.edu
NIXON, LeAnne ... 601-477-4008 ... 274 H leanne.nixon@jcjc.edu
NIXON, Monica ... 206-296-6070 ... 538 B mnixon@seattleu.edu
NIXON, Philip ... 256-726-7398 ... 6 C pnixon@oakwood.edu
NIXON, Susan ... 318-487-7401 ... 209 F nixon@lacollege.edu
NIXON, Terry ... 325-793-4721 ... 490 H tnixon@mcm.edu
NIXON, Tina, S ... 334-833-4410 ... 4 E tnixon@huntingdon.edu
NIXON, Valerie, B ... 607-587-3985 ... 355 C nixonvb@alfredstate.edu
NJIE, Valerie ... 412-402-9779 ... 423 A vnjie@mcg-btc.org
NJOGU, Wamucii, E ... 773-442-5700 ... 160 A w-njogu@neiu.edu
NNADI, Eucharia, E ... 702-968-2038 ... 303 D ennadi@roseman.edu
NNAZOR, Reginald ... 937-376-6007 ... 387 A rnnazor@centralstate.edu
NNOROMELE, Patrick, C ... 859-622-2973 ... 200 J patrick.nnoromele@eku.edu
NOACK, Kelly ... 309-794-7477 ... 145 E kellynoack@augustana.edu
NOAH, Tara ... 660-359-3948 ... 287 A tnoah@mail.ncmissouri.edu
NOBILE, Bryan ... 601-643-8468 ... 273 G bryan.nobile@colin.edu
NOBLE, Ann ... 281-649-3304 ... 487 H aanoble@hbu.edu
NOBLE, Barbara ... 314-340-3621 ... 282 F nobleb@hssu.edu
NOBLE, Darren ... 563-425-5208 ... 189 G nobled@uiu.edu
NOBLE, Doug ... 540-654-1235 ... 525 D dnoble@umw.edu
NOBLE, Janice ... 925-424-1103 ... 39 D jnoble@laspositascollege.edu
NOBLE, John, H ... 413-597-2313 ... 246 D john.h.noble@williams.edu
NOBLE, Kate ... 402-474-5315 ... 298 C knoble@kaplanuniversity.edu
NOBLE, Ronald, J ... 209-667-3177 ... 36 D rnoble@csustan.edu
NOBLE, Seth ... 970-542-3248 ... 86 G seth.noble@morgancc.edu
NOBLE, Shlomo ... 585-473-2810 ... 357 D
NOBLE-GOODMAN, Stuart 909-748-8142 ... 76 C stuart_noblegoodman@redlands.edu
NOBLES, Daryle ... 910-678-8225 ... 370 E noblesd@faytechcc.edu
NOBLES, Rodney ... 262-691-5362 ... 555 E rnobles@wctc.edu
NOBLES, Susan, Q ... 252-493-7287 ... 372 H snobles@email.pittcc.edu
NOBLES, Tammy ... 573-681-5271 ... 283 I noblest@lincolnu.edu
NOBLETT, Jeffrey ... 719-389-6681 ... 82 D jnoblett@coloradocollege.edu
NOBLIN, Patricia ... 973-300-2754 ... 315 F pnoblin@sussex.edu
NOBLITT, Jeff ... 630-466-7900 ... 168 B jnoblitt@waubonsee.edu
NOBLITT, Mariea ... 610-740-3780 ... 425 A mtnoblitt@cedarcrest.edu
NOBLITT, William ... 620-341-5454 ... 192 G wnoblitt@emporia.edu
NOBUO, Adora ... 680-488-2471 ... 560 C adoraa@palau.edu
NOCE, Joe ... 215-780-1294 ... 446 G pcobookstore@mattmccoy.com
NOCELLA, Frank ... 973-300-2115 ... 315 F fnocella@sussex.edu
NOCKUNAS, Michael ... 413-572-5468 ... 238 F mnockunas@wsc.ma.edu
NODA, Keisuke ... 845-752-3000 ... 358 F dpknoda@aol.com
NODES, Jennifer ... 239-348-4710 ... 101 I jennifer.nodes@avemaria.edu
NODGE, Andrea ... 734-432-5737 ... 254 D anodge@madonna.edu
NODINE, Barbara, F ... 215-572-4009 ... 422 C nodineb@arcadia.edu
NODINE, Chad ... 276-328-0196 ... 525 G jcn5g@uvawise.edu
NODLAND, Rita ... 701-224-5692 ... 382 D rita.nodland@bismarckstate.edu
NODZENSKI, Peter ... 309-796-5374 ... 145 H nodzenskip@bhc.edu
NOE, Bryan, D ... 205-934-8227 ... 8 F bnoe@uab.edu
NOE, Danielle ... 904-680-7659 ... 107 J dnoe@fcsl.edu
NOE, Godfrey, F ... 404-237-7573 ... 126 B gnoe@bauder.edu
NOEHRE, Edwin, R ... 608-258-2401 ... 554 D enoehre@madisoncollege.org
NOEL, Amy ... 910-592-8084 ... 373 G anoel@sampsoncc.edu
NOEL, Bill ... 502-451-0815 ... 206 H bnoel@sullivan.edu
NOEL, Bill ... 502-451-0815 ... 206 G bnoel@sullivan.edu
NOEL, Cheryl, A ... 724-925-4058 ... 451 E noelc@wccc.edu
NOEL, Dan ... 719-638-6580 ... 84 I dnoel@cci.edu
NOEL, Erin ... 559-453-2000 ... 48 A erin.noel@fresno.edu
NOEL, JR., J. Andrew ... 607-255-8832 ... 331 B jan16@cornell.edu
NOEL, Joanne ... 973-803-5000 ... 315 D jnoel@somerset.edu
NOEL, John, D ... 563-562-3263 ... 188 B noelj@portal.nicc.edu
NOEL, Marie ... 973-290-4209 ... 308 G mnoel@cse.edu
NOEL, Michelle ... 775-673-7000 ... 302 H mnoel@tmcc.edu
NOEL, Norma ... 575-646-4986 ... 319 D nnoel@nmsu.edu
NOEL, Shawn ... 301-387-3052 ... 222 H shawn.noel@garrettcollege.edu
NOEL, Stuart ... 678-891-3986 ... 131 C stuart.noel@gpc.edu
NOEL, Terry ... 724-532-5095 ... 446 E terry.noel@email.stvincent.edu
NOEL-ELKINS, Amelia ... 309-438-3217 ... 153 D anoelel@ilstu.edu
NOELL, Sarah ... 860-768-4408 ... 95 B snoell@hartford.edu
NOFFINGER, Dave ... 702-369-9944 ... 301 F
NOFFSINGER, Lynda, D ... 336-888-6352 ... 365 C lnoffsin@highpoint.edu
NOFRI, Julia, E ... 203-365-4837 ... 94 B nofrij@sacredheart.edu
NOFTSINGER, Mark, P ... 540-375-2283 ... 523 G noftsinger@roanoke.edu
NOGLE, Ryan ... 716-851-1281 ... 333 B nogle@ecc.edu
NOHLGREN, Bethany ... 845-758-7099 ... 323 D nohlgren@bard.edu
NOHNER, OSB, Sharon ... 320-363-5285 ... 262 F snohner@csbsju.edu
NOHRE, Kathy ... 320-762-4591 ... 265 F kathyn@alextech.edu
NOHRIA, Nitin ... 617-495-6653 ... 235 D nnohria@hbs.harvard.edu
NOISETTE, Yvonne ... 843-574-6083 ... 461 G yvonne.noisette@tridenttech.edu
NOJAN, Mehran ... 315-312-2345 ... 354 A mehran.nojan@oswego.edu
NOLAN, Beth ... 202-994-6503 ... 98 C bnolan@gwu.edu
NOLAN, Brian ... 301-447-5223 ... 225 A nolan@msmary.edu
NOLAN, Brian, E ... 423-439-4211 ... 473 F president@etsu.edu
NOLAN, Cathy, M ... 301-784-5000 ... 221 B cnolan@allegany.edu
NOLAN, Charles, S ... 781-292-2201 ... 234 H charles.nolan@olin.edu
NOLAN, Christina ... 973-748-9000 ... 307 H christina_nolan@bloomfield.edu
NOLAN, Colleen ... 304-876-5106 ... 544 C cnolan@shepherd.edu
NOLAN, Deborah ... 410-704-2452 ... 228 E dnolan@towson.edu
NOLAN, Deborah, O ... 610-409-3586 ... 450 D dnolan@ursinus.edu
NOLAN, Ernest ... 734-432-5313 ... 254 D enolan@madonna.edu
NOLAN, Jennifer (Jaime) ... 605-688-6361 ... 466 C jennifer.nolan@sdstate.edu
NOLAN, Jim ... 505-467-6821 ... 321 A pres@swc.edu
NOLAN, Joel, B ... 315-733-2300 ... 359 C
NOLAN, John ... 239-513-1135 ... 123 F jnolan@wolford.edu
NOLAN, Judy ... 914-251-6067 ... 354 D judy.nolan@purchase.edu
NOLAN, Kelly ... 310-544-6419 ... 64 H kelly.nolan@usw.salvationarmy.org
NOLAN, Linda ... 510-885-4918 ... 34 E linda.nolan@csueastbay.edu
NOLAN, Lisa ... 515-294-9860 ... 182 E lknolan@iastate.edu
NOLAN, Nikol ... 785-460-5496 ... 192 C nikol.nolan@colbycc.edu
NOLAN-WEISS, Sharon, E . 716-645-2266 ... 351 G senolan@buffalo.edu
NOLAN YOUNG, Pamela .. 413-585-2141 ... 244 G pnolan@smith.edu
NOLAND, T. Raiford ... 205-652-3536 ... 9 E trnoland@uwa.edu
NOLDER, Deborah ... 606-759-7141 ... 203 A debbie.nolder@kctcs.edu
NOLDNER, Tracy ... 605-367-7487 ... 466 D tracy.noldner@southeasttech.edu
NOLDON, Denise ... 510-235-7800 ... 43 E dnoldon@contracosta.edu
NOLE, Laura ... 206-878-3710 ... 535 B lnole@highline.edu
NOLEN, Donald, R ... 919-530-5350 ... 378 B dnolen@nccu.edu
NOLES, Jody ... 334-291-4922 ... 2 F jody.noles@cv.edu
NOLES, Kimberly ... 478-274-7761 ... 135 C knoles@oftc.edu
NOLL, Eric ... 518-388-6108 ... 358 G nolle@union.edu
NOLLEY, Bob ... 804-527-7087 ... 99 G bob.nolley@strayer.edu
NOLLEY, Dennis ... 903-675-6343 ... 502 F dnolley@tvcc.edu
NOLOT, Terry, L ... 812-246-3301 ... 177 B tnolot@ivytech.edu
NOLSER, Michael ... 303-534-6290 ... 83 E michael.nosler@colostate.edu
NOLT, David ... 406-683-7201 ... 294 J d_nolt@umwestern.edu

NOVO, Frank .... 617-964-1111 .... 230 B
fnovo@ants.edu
NOVOBILSKI, Andrew .... 814-871-7401 .... 429 G
novobils001@gannon.edu
NOVOTNY, April .... 614-236-6565 .... 386 E
anovotny@capital.edu
NOVOTNY, Doreen .... 650-949-6210 .... 47 H
NOVOTNY, Dorene .... 650-949-6210 .... 47 F
novotnydorene@fhda.edu
NOVOTNY, Frank, J .... 719-587-7622 .... 80 L
fjnovotn@adams.edu
NOVOTNY, Jodi .... 425-235-2464 .... 537 A
jnovotny@rtc.edu
NOVOTNY, Matthew .... 330-941-3552 .... 406 F
mmnovotny@ysu.edu
NOVOTNY, Ranata .... 303-986-2320 .... 83 A
ranata@csha.net
NOVOTNY, Richard, J .... 440-525-7358 .... 394 F
rnovotny@lakelandcc.edu
NOWACZYK, Ronald .... 814-393-2223 .... 442 B
rnowaczyk@clarion.edu
NOWAK, Jack .... 541-880-2224 .... 416 D
nowak@klamathcc.edu
NOWAK, Janice .... 904-470-8192 .... 105 G
janice.nowak@ewc.edu
NOWAK, Karen .... 213-251-3636 .... 29 J
knowak@aii.edu
NOWAK, Linda, I .... 209-667-3288 .... 36 D
lnowak@csustan.edu
NOWAK, Meg .... 607-431-4501 .... 335 A
nowakm@hartwick.edu
NOWAK, Patricia .... 219-980-6501 .... 174 B
nowakpat@indiana.edu
NOWAK, Susan .... 585-389-2731 .... 342 D
snowak8@naz.edu
NOWAK, Thomas, S .... 845-848-4000 .... 332 B
thomas.nowak@dc.edu
NOWAK, Tom .... 574-936-8898 .... 169 D
tom.nowak@ancilla.edu
NOWAK, Tony, J .... 414-847-3240 .... 549 B
tonynowak@miad.edu
NOWAKOWSKI,
Bernadette .... 413-265-2214 .... 233 D
nowakowskib@elms.edu
NOWAKOWSKI, Rodney .... 205-934-3036 .... 8 F
rnowakow@uab.edu
NOWEL, OP, Mark, D .... 401-865-2649 .... 453 H
mnowel@providence.edu
NOWELL, Cheryl .... 305-348-2434 .... 119 C
nowell@fiu.edu
NOWICKI, Carol .... 510-885-3763 .... 34 E
carol.nowicki@csueastbay.edu
NOWICKI, Laura .... 740-593-1969 .... 399 G
nowicki@ohio.edu
NOWICKI, Maria .... 419-251-1583 .... 395 I
maria.nowicki@mercycollege.edu
NOWICKI, Stephen .... 919-668-2728 .... 364 C
snowicki@duke.edu
NOWLAN, Marilyn, L .... 860-727-6782 .... 92 I
mnowlan@goodwin.edu
NOWLIN, Brian .... 562-985-5537 .... 35 C
bnowlin@sculb.edu
NOWLIN, Steve .... 626-396-2397 .... 29 I
stephen.nowlin@artcenter.edu
NOWOGORSKI, Barbara .... 570-961-7835 .... 433 A
nowogorskib@lackawanna.edu
NOYA, Christine, A .... 443-352-4477 .... 226 E
cnoya@stevenson.edu
NOYA, Roberto .... 207-778-7050 .... 220 C
roberto.noya@maine.edu
NOYER, Rich .... 206-878-3710 .... 535 B
rnoyer@highline.edu
NOYES, Charlie .... 617-989-4407 .... 245 F
noyesc1@wit.edu
NOYES, Daniel .... 585-567-6260 .... 336 B
daniel.noyes@houghton.edu
NOYES, Doug .... 605-455-6076 .... 465 A
dnoyes@olc.edu
NOYES, Linda .... 516-299-3281 .... 338 E
linda.noyes@liu.edu
NRI, Monique, N .... 212-229-5592 .... 342 E
nrim@newschool.edu
NTI, Richard .... 423-775-6596 .... 472 G
rnti@ogs.edu
NTOKO, Alfred .... 718-262-2804 .... 329 A
antoko@york.cuny.edu
NUARA, Frank .... 212-875-4619 .... 323 C
fnuara@bankstreet.edu
NUBEL, Anna .... 402-280-2222 .... 297 F
annanubel@creighton.edu
NUCCI, John, A .... 617-973-1103 .... 245 B
jnucci@suffolk.edu
NUCCI, Lisa .... 813-342-3726 .... 19 A
lisa.nucci@phoenix.edu
NUCCIARONE, Mary, B .... 574-631-6436 .... 180 G
nucciarone.2@nd.edu
NUCCIO, Beth .... 616-777-5206 .... 247 G
beth.nuccio@baker.edu
NUCKOLS, Jack .... 304-734-6623 .... 542 H
jnuckols@bridgemont.edu
NUCKOLS, Melanie, L .... 336-734-7332 .... 370 F
mnuckols@forsythtech.edu
NUDELMAN, Felice .... 937-769-1351 .... 384 A
fnudelman@antioch.edu
NUESELL, Jerry, J .... 919-508-2314 .... 380 E
jnuesell@peace.edu
NUESELL, Lisa .... 919-381-6912 .... 367 F
lnuesell@moc.edu
NUFER, Ken .... 719-549-3220 .... 87 F
ken.nufer@pueblocc.edu
NUGEN, Deb .... 402-399-2442 .... 297 C
dnugen@csm.edu
NUGENT, Barli .... 212-799-5000 .... 337 H
NUGENT, Christine, R .... 828-298-3325 .... 380 D
cnugent@warren-wilson.edu
NUGENT, Joe .... 831-479-6140 .... 31 I
jonugent@cabrillo.edu
NUGENT, John, D .... 860-439-5266 .... 92 G
john.nugent@conncoll.edu
NUGENT, Kim .... 713-973-3100 .... 486 C
knugent@devry.edu
NUGENT, S. Georgia .... 740-427-5111 .... 394 C
nugent@kenyon.edu
NUGENT, Timothy, M .... 860-444-8598 .... 558 H
timothy.m.nugent@uscg.mil
NULL, David .... 608-265-1988 .... 550 J
dnull@library.wisc.edu
NULL, Greg .... 800-444-1440 .... 444 E
gnull@pia.edu
NULL, Wesley .... 254-710-6120 .... 482 A
wesley_null@baylor.edu
NULPH, Wendy .... 972-438-6932 .... 492 E
wnulph@parkercc.edu
NUMRICH, Camille .... 401-825-2237 .... 453 D
cnumrich@ccri.edu
NUNAMAKER, Gail .... 989-386-6692 .... 255 C
gnunamaker@midmich.edu
NUNAN, David .... 714-772-3330 .... 28 J
davidnunan@gmail.com
NUNES, Grafton, J .... 216-421-7410 .... 388 A
gnunes@cia.edu
NUNES, Victoria .... 650-306-3274 .... 67 F
nunes@smccd.edu
NUNEZ, Cheryl, L .... 513-745-3539 .... 406 E
nunezc@xavier.edu
NUNEZ, Elsa .... 860-465-5222 .... 90 F
nuneze@easternct.edu
NUNEZ, Elsa, M .... 860-465-5222 .... 90 H
nunez@easternct.edu
NUNEZ, Francisco .... 787-780-5134 .... 564 G
fnunez@nationalcollegepr.edu
NUNEZ, Frank .... 408-864-5437 .... 47 G
nunezfrank@fhda.edu
NUNEZ, Gabriel .... 305-593-1223 .... 102 H
gnunez@albizu.edu
NUNEZ, Ivon .... 973-596-3478 .... 312 C
nunez@njit.edu
NUNEZ, Jessica .... 830-591-7226 .... 495 D
jnunez@swtjc.cc.tx.us
NUNEZ, Jose .... 650-358-6836 .... 67 E
nunezj@smccd.edu
NUNEZ, Jose Ramon .... 562-938-4695 .... 54 E
jnunez@lbcc.edu
NUNEZ, Juan .... 617-287-4818 .... 236 G
juan.nunez@umb.edu
NUNEZ, Lois .... 617-928-4500 .... 242 E
lanunez@mountida.edu
NUNEZ, Rigo .... 503-552-1664 .... 417 D
rnunez@ncnm.edu
NUNEZ, Steve .... 815-288-5511 .... 164 B
nunezs@svcc.edu
NUNEZ, William .... 402-472-2116 .... 300 G
wnunez2@unl.edu
NUNEZ, William, J .... 402-472-2097 .... 300 G
wnunez2@unl.edu
NUNEZ, III, William, J .... 337-550-1201 .... 212 J
NUNEZ, Yancy .... 806-894-9611 .... 494 G
ynunez@southplainscollege.edu
NUNLEY, Beth .... 815-802-8142 .... 155 A
bnunley@kcc.edu
NUNLEY, Ernest, L .... 276-739-2510 .... 529 A
enunley@vhcc.edu
NUNLEY, Gayle, R .... 802-656-8513 .... 514 H
gayle.nunley@uvm.edu
NUNLEY, Jeff .... 813-988-5131 .... 108 A
bookstore@floridacollege.edu
NUNN, Dana .... 970-248-1868 .... 82 F
dnunn@coloradomesa.edu
NUNN, Diane, L .... 203-773-4474 .... 90 C
dlnunn@albertus.edu
NUNN, Erin .... 440-375-7080 .... 394 E
enunn@lec.edu
NUNN, Helen, S .... 570-372-4450 .... 447 E
nunn@susqu.edu
NUNN, Rod .... 314-539-5302 .... 288 G
rodnunn@stlcc.edu
NUNNA, Ramakrishna .... 559-278-2500 .... 35 A
rnunna@csufresno.edu
NUNNALLY, Gladys .... 804-524-6714 .... 529 H
nunnally@vsu.edu
NUNNELLY, Laura .... 505-473-6176 .... 320 F
laura.nunnelly@santafeuniversity.edu
NUNZIATIA, Ray .... 407-843-3984 .... 110 E
rnunziatia@fortiscollege.edu
NURNBERGER, Charles .... 757-825-2717 .... 528 F
nurnbergerc@tncc.edu
NUSBAUM, Nancy .... 512-245-2244 .... 501 F
nn01@txstate.edu
NUSENBAUM, Tatiana .... 212-349-4330 .... 334 G
tnusenbaum@globe.edu
NUSSBAUM, Daniel .... 860-231-5770 .... 95 D
dnussbaum@usj.edu
NUSSBAUM, Irwin .... 860-768-7904 .... 95 B
nussbaum@hartford.edu
NUSSBAUM, Renee .... 419-755-4772 .... 397 C
rnussbau@ncstatecollege.edu
NUSSBAUMER, John .... 248-751-7800 .... 258 F
nussbauj@cooley.edu
NUSSBUAM, Sara Gittie .... 303-629-8200 .... 90 B
NUSSEN, Jack .... 757-771-9978 .... 116 G
jack.nussen@saintleo.edu
NUSTAD, Grant .... 303-876-7100 .... 464 H
gnustad@national.edu
NUTEFALL, Jennifer .... 408-554-6829 .... 68 C
jnutefall@scu.edu
NUTI, Larry .... 925-631-4901 .... 64 F
lnuti@stmarys-ca.edu
NUTT, Jill .... 616-395-7765 .... 252 D
nutt@hope.edu
NUTT, Jill, M .... 616-234-4031 .... 251 E
jnutt@grcc.edu
NUTTALL, Neil .... 660-359-3948 .... 287 A
nnuttall@mail.ncmissouri.edu
NUTTER, Cheryl .... 419-251-1519 .... 395 I
cheryl.nutter@mercycollege.edu
NUTTER, Doug .... 301-860-3402 .... 228 A
dnutter@bowiestate.edu
NUTTER, Susan, K .... 919-515-7188 .... 378 C
susan_nutter@ncsu.edu
NUTTLE, Louise, C .... 423-439-6052 .... 473 F
nuttle@etsu.edu
NUTTY, David .... 207-780-4276 .... 220 G
dnutty@usm.maine.edu
NWAKEZE, Peter .... 718-933-6700 .... 341 G
pnwakeze@monroecollege.edu
NWANKWO, Charles .... 337-491-2442 .... 212 E
charles.nwankwo@sowela.edu
NWANNE, Andrew, I .... 260-422-5561 .... 173 C
ainwanne@indianatech.edu
NWAOHA, Ugo .... 909-941-9410 .... 62 J
unwaoha@plattcollege.edu
NWARIAKU, Fiemu, E .... 214-648-9968 .... 507 E
fiemu.nwariku@utsouthwestern.edu
NWOKEAFOR, Cosmos .... 301-860-3232 .... 228 A
cnwokeafor@bowiestate.edu
NWOSU, Peter .... 615-963-2515 .... 474 A
pnwosu@tnstate.edu
NYAMAPFENE, Kingston .... 713-313-4275 .... 500 B
nyamapfenek@tsu.edu
NYBERG, Christopher, L .... 315-684-6083 .... 354 F
nybergcl@morrisville.edu
NYBERG, Christopher, L .... 315-684-6056 .... 354 F
nybergcl@morrisville.edu
NYBERG, Connie .... 307-855-2207 .... 556 B
cnyberg@cwc.edu
NYBERG-COMINS, Laura .... 608-822-2352 .... 555 D
lnybergcomins@swtc.edu
NYBORG, Adam .... 760-872-2000 .... 43 K
anyborg@deepsprings.edu
NYCE, Douglas, J .... 540-432-4206 .... 518 F
douglas.nyce@emu.edu
NYCZ, Mandy .... 920-403-3181 .... 550 F
mandy.nycz@snc.edu
NYE, David, J .... 303-963-3197 .... 82 C
dnye@ccu.edu
NYE, Fumiko .... 954-783-7339 .... 106 J
fnye@cci.edu
NYE, Jamey .... 916-691-7226 .... 56 B
nyej@crc.losrios.edu
NYE, Linda, R .... 276-223-4869 .... 529 C
lnye@wcc.vccs.edu
NYE, Valerie .... 505-424-2392 .... 318 D
vnye@iaia.edu
NYGAARD, Steve .... 415-422-6824 .... 76 E
ssnygaard@usfca.edu
NYGARD, Gordon, A .... 206-281-2308 .... 537 H
gnygard@spu.edu
NYGREEN, Ted .... 914-606-6789 .... 360 E
ted.nygreen@sunywcc.edu
NYHAMMER, Diane, L .... 815-921-4007 .... 162 H
d.nyhammer@rockvalleycollege.edu
NYHART, Brant .... 602-386-4178 .... 11 G
brant.nyhart@arizonachristian.edu
NYHUS, Orrin .... 763-433-1346 .... 265 G
orrin.nyhus@anokaramsey.edu
NYIRENDA, Stanley, M .... 410-651-7531 .... 227 E
snyirenda@umes.edu
NYKIEL, Ronald .... 207-941-7111 .... 218 A
nykielr@husson.edu
NYLEN, Judith .... 718-636-3506 .... 346 D
jnylen@pratt.edu
NYMAN, Walter, D .... 570-326-3761 .... 440 L
wnyman@pct.edu
NYPAVER, David .... 330-972-6876 .... 403 B
nypaver@uakron.edu
NYQUIST, J. Paul .... 312-329-4112 .... 159 A
paul.nyquist@moody.edu
NYQUIST, Paul .... 734-207-9581 .... 255 F
pnyquist@mts.edu
NYRE, Joseph, E .... 914-633-2203 .... 336 E
jnyre@iona.edu
NYSTROM, David .... 562-903-4703 .... 31 A
david.nystrom@biola.edu
NYUL, Renata .... 617-373-7666 .... 243 F
NZAMUTUNA, Issmael .... 951-785-2006 .... 53 E
inzamutu@lasierra.edu
NZEOGWU, Okeleke .... 702-968-1659 .... 303 D
onzeogwu@roseman.edu

O

O BRIEN, John, P .... 315-445-4444 .... 338 B
obrienjp@lemoyne.edu
OAKES, Brian .... 410-617-2475 .... 223 I
boakes@loyola.edu
OAKES, Edward .... 540-831-7515 .... 523 A
eoakes@radford.edu
OAKES, Mary .... 312-369-6802 .... 148 D
moakes@colum.edu
OAKES, Ronald, L .... 660-263-3900 .... 279 F
president@cccb.edu
OAKLEY, Christina .... 561-912-1211 .... 107 B
coakley@evergladesuniversity.edu
OAKLEY, Danielle .... 608-262-8350 .... 550 J
droakley@uhs.wisc.edu
OAKLEY, Eloy .... 562-938-4122 .... 54 E
eoakley@lbcc.edu
OAKLEY, Leigh .... 859-846-5395 .... 204 H
loakley@midway.edu
OAKLEY OCKERT, Melissa .... 919-536-7200 .... 370 C
ockertm@durhamtech.edu
OAKMAN, Tommy .... 828-694-1725 .... 368 E
t_oakman@blueridge.edu
OAKS, Beth .... 605-642-6411 .... 465 H
beth.oaks@bhsu.edu
OAKS, Diane, G .... 949-451-5277 .... 70 E
doaks@ivc.edu
OAKS, Geneva .... 951-343-4738 .... 31 J
goaks@calbaptist.edu
OAKS, Kelly .... 808-933-0824 .... 141 F
koaks3@hawaii.edu
OANES, Laura .... 507-457-1489 .... 271 B
loanes@smumn.edu
OATES, Bruce .... 847-635-1705 .... 160 F
boates@oakton.edu
OATES, Bruce .... 847-635-1753 .... 160 F
boates@oakton.edu
OATES, Richard .... 706-864-1620 .... 134 G
roates@northgeorgia.edu
OATEY, Jennifer, S .... 218-299-3455 .... 262 I
joatey@cord.edu
OATMAN, Robert, R .... 860-701-6194 .... 558 H
robert.r.oatman@uscg.mil
OBARA, Daniel, J .... 724-925-4001 .... 451 E
obarad@wccc.edu
OBASANYA, Terryl .... 404-756-5727 .... 134 E
tobasanya@msm.edu
OBBINK, Kim .... 406-994-6550 .... 295 C
kobbink@montana.edu
OBERBILLIG, Lynn .... 413-585-2701 .... 244 G
loberbil@smith.edu
OBERFELDT, Kathleen .... 718-390-3158 .... 360 A
koberfel@wagner.edu
OBERGFELL, Ann .... 260-481-6100 .... 174 C
obergfea@ipfw.edu
OBERHELMAN, Don .... 805-756-1407 .... 33 I
obe@calpoly.edu
OBERHOLTZER, Brent .... 717-867-6111 .... 434 C
oberholt@lvc.edu
OBERLANDER, Cyril .... 585-245-5528 .... 353 C
oberland@geneseo.edu
OBERLANDER, Janell .... 605-394-4034 .... 466 F
janell.oberlander@wdt.edu
OBERLE, George .... 540-891-3013 .... 526 I
goberle@germanna.edu
OBERLIN, Craig .... 714-432-5952 .... 41 D
coberlin@occ.cccd.edu
OBERMAN, Anne .... 320-363-5999 .... 262 F
aoberman@csbsju.edu
OBERMEISTER, Tuvia, M .... 718-377-0777 .... 346 G
OBERMEYER, Carole .... 316-295-5779 .... 193 B
obermeyer@friends.edu
OBERMEYER, Larry .... 712-274-6400 .... 190 B
larry.obermeyer@witcc.edu
OBERQUELL, Christian .... 406-265-3761 .... 295 E
coberquell@msun.edu
OBERSCHLAKE, Timothy .... 330-490-7241 .... 405 F
toberschlake@walsh.edu
OBERSTEIN, Leonard .... 410-484-7200 .... 225 C
OBERTO, Janet .... 617-262-5000 .... 231 G
janet.oberto@the-bac.edu
OBILADE, Sandra, O .... 270-686-4209 .... 199 B
sandra.obilade@brescia.edu
OBLANDER, Douglas .... 843-208-8256 .... 462 C
oblander@uscb.edu
OBLOY, Leonard .... 248-683-0446 .... 258 E
lobloy@sscms.edu
OBRECHT, LeAnn .... 308-865-8248 .... 300 F
obrechtls@unk.edu
OBRECHT, LeAnn .... 308-865-8218 .... 300 F
obrechtls@unk.edu
OBRENTZ, Barbara .... 678-891-2684 .... 131 C
barbara.obrentz@gpc.edu
OBRESLEY, Amber .... 406-791-5248 .... 296 F
aobresley01@ugf.edu

OLER, Gregory, S .... 410-516-8000.... 223 F
goler@jhu.edu

OLESON, Elizabeth .... 563-589-3178.... 189 F
eoleson@dbq.edu

OLESON-BRIGGS, Susan .. 704-330-6022.... 369 D
susan.oleson@cpcc.edu

OLESZEWSKI, Susan .... 215-276-6070.... 446 G
sueo@salus.edu

OLGUIN, Albert .... 310-900-1600...... 45 F
olguin_a@compton.edu

OLGUIN, Javier, E .... 972-860-5306.... 484 I
javiereolguin@dcccd.edu

OLGUIN-RYAN, Elizabeth .. 915-831-6325.... 486 G
eolguin@epcc.edu

OLIAN, Judy, D .... 310-825-7982...... 74 C
judy.olian@anderson.ucla.edu

OLIARO, Paul, M .... 559-278-2541...... 35 A
poliaro@csufresno.edu

OLIN, Jen .... 207-948-9273.... 219 H
jolin@unity.edu

OLIN, Joanna .... 413-559-5521.... 235 C

OLIN, Robert, F .... 205-348-5972........ 8 E
olin@as.ua.edu

OLINER, Alex .... 212-349-4330.... 334 G
aoliner@globe.edu

OLINER, Martin .... 212-349-4330.... 334 G
moliner@globe.edu

OLING-SISAY, Mary .... 740-351-3251.... 401 I
moling-sisay@shawnee.edu

OLINGER, CSC, Gerard, J . 503-943-8532.... 420 G
olinger@up.edu

OLINGER, Richard, P .... 814-868-7767.... 433 C
rpolinger@mch1.org

OLINGER, Ronald, J .... 913-360-7413.... 191 A
rolinger@benedictine.edu

OLION, LaDelle .... 910-672-1074.... 377 G
lolion@uncfsu.edu

OLIPHANT, Uretz, S .... 217-333-5465.... 167 D
uretz.oliphant@carle.com

OLIVA, Giacomo .... 212-217-4040.... 333 F
giacomo_oliva@fitnyc.edu

OLIVA, Joseph, E .... 718-990-6421.... 348 G
olivaj@stjohns.edu

OLIVA, Robert .... 718-951-5696.... 326 F
boliva@brooklyn.cuny.edu

OLIVARES, Carlos .... 787-279-1912.... 563 D
colivares@bayamon.inter.edu

OLIVARES, Cecilia .... 309-268-8061.... 151 I
cecilia.olivares@heartland.edu

OLIVARES, Jose .... 201-360-4131.... 310 E
jolivares@hccc.edu

OLIVAREZ, Juan .... 616-632-2880.... 247 E
jro002@aquinas.edu

OLIVE, David, W .... 276-326-4466.... 516 L
dolive@bluefield.edu

OLIVE, Nancy .... 605-331-6770.... 466 E
nancy.olive@usiouxfalls.edu

OLIVE-TAYLOR, Becky .... 336-278-6500.... 364 D
oliveb@elon.edu

OLIVEIRA, Sandra, J .... 401-865-2602.... 453 H
solivei6@providence.edu

OLIVER, Alice .... 954-446-6172.... 100 I
aoliver@aiufl.edu

OLIVER, Astrid .... 970-247-7507...... 84 K
oliver_a@fortlewis.edu

OLIVER, Bob .... 435-283-7221.... 512 C
bob.oliver@snow.edu

OLIVER, Carolyne, B .... 713-313-7097.... 500 B
olivercb@tsu.edu

OLIVER, Cary .... 615-226-3990.... 472 A
coliver@nadcedu.com

OLIVER, Daniel, T .... 831-656-2511.... 558 A
dtoliver@nps.edu

OLIVER, Denita .... 256-215-4290........ 2 E
doliver@cacc.edu

OLIVER, Donna, H .... 662-254-3425.... 276 B
doliver@mvsu.edu

OLIVER, Erik .... 802-383-6662.... 513 C
eoliver@champlain.edu

OLIVER, James .... 229-430-4702.... 124 A
james.oliver@asurams.edu

OLIVER, Janet, W .... 231-995-1076.... 256 D
joliver@nmc.edu

OLIVER, Jeanette, J .... 713-313-7104.... 500 B
oliver_jj@tsu.edu

OLIVER, Jeanne .... 503-352-2740.... 419 E
jeanne1@pacificu.edu

OLIVER, Jeannie .... 901-369-0835...... 99 G

OLIVER, Jenea .... 816-235-6011.... 291 C
oliverj@umkc.edu

OLIVER, Joseph .... 303-280-7591...... 84 G
joliver@devry.edu

OLIVER, Kenneth, R .... 660-248-6223.... 279 G
koliver@centralmethodist.edu

OLIVER, Lillian, M .... 787-723-4481.... 561 B
loliver@ceaprc.edu

OLIVER, OSF, M. Marilyn . 260-399-7700.... 181 A
moliver@sf.edu

OLIVER, Melvin, L .... 805-893-8354...... 75 B
moliver@ltsc.ucsb.edu

OLIVER, Parker .... 931-598-1586.... 472 L
pwoliver@sewanee.edu

OLIVER, Patricia Belton ..... 713-743-2400.... 503 D
poliver@central.uh.edu

OLIVER, Richard, E .... 573-884-6705.... 291 B
oliverr@missouri.edu

OLIVER, Robert, C .... 605-274-4111.... 464 A
rob.oliver@augie.edu

OLIVER, Ruben, D .... 405-466-2996.... 408 G
rdoliver@langston.edu

OLIVER, Samuel W. "Dub" 903-923-2222.... 486 F
doliver@etbu.edu

OLIVER, Sandi .... 803-738-7699.... 459 E
olivers@midlandstech.edu

OLIVER, Sharon, J .... 919-530-5313.... 378 B
soliver@nccu.edu

OLIVER, Sharon, M .... 207-581-1561.... 220 A
smoliver@maine.edu

OLIVER, Shawn .... 609-497-7818.... 312 F
shawn.oliver@ptsem.edu

OLIVER, Sylvester, W .... 662-252-8000.... 276 G
syoliver@rustcollege.edu

OLIVER, Thomas .... 830-372-8050.... 499 F
toliver@tlu.edu

OLIVER, Zachary .... 808-791-5253.... 140 B
zoliver@argosy.edu

OLIVER PUTNAM,
Patricia, T .... 619-260-7430...... 76 D
poliver@sandiego.edu

OLIVER TORRES,
Marie, A .... 787-480-2351.... 561 E
mtorres@sanjuancapital.com

OLIVERA, Robert .... 510-261-8500...... 61 G
robert.olivera@patten.edu

OLIVERAS, Esteban .... 202-274-5248.... 100 A
eoliveras@udc.edu

OLIVERAS, Ivette .... 787-848-1589.... 564 I
ioliveras@popac.edu

OLIVERI, Carl .... 570-340-6016.... 435 F
coliveri@marywood.edu

OLIVERIA, Steve .... 707-468-3081...... 57 A
soliveria@mendocino.edu

OLIVERIO, Ashley .... 406-447-5415.... 293 G
aoliverio@carroll.edu

OLIVERO, Paula .... 724-738-2683.... 443 F
paula.olivero@sru.edu

OLIVEROS, Claire .... 971-722-5841.... 419 G
colivero@pcc.edu

OLIVERSON, Richard .... 316-942-4291.... 195 F
oliversonr@newmanu.edu

OLIVETTE, Michael .... 914-606-6912.... 360 E
michael.olivette@sunywcc.edu

OLIVIERI, Janies .... 787-250-1912.... 563 G
jolivieri@metro.inter.edu

OLIVIERI-LENAHAN,
Elizabeth .... 914-633-2547.... 336 E
eolivieri@iona.edu

OLIVO, Cynthia, D .... 626-585-7074...... 61 F
cdolivo@pasadena.edu

OLKHOVSKAYA, Elena ...... 510-436-1037...... 50 H
olkhovskaya@hnu.edu

OLLEY, Lorraine .... 847-566-6401.... 167 F
lolley@usml.edu

OLLIFF, Thomas .... 954-201-7693.... 102 E
toliff@broward.edu

OLLILA, Les .... 715-324-6900.... 549 G
les.ollila@ni.edu

OLLIVER, James .... 727-394-6111.... 116 H
olliver.james@spcollege.edu

OLLSON, Joanne .... 413-782-1343.... 246 A
jollson@wne.edu

OLMSTEAD, Audrey .... 248-689-8282.... 259 E
aolmstead@walshcollege.edu

OLMSTEAD, Karen, L .... 410-543-6489.... 228 D
klolmstead@salisbury.edu

OLMSTEAD, Steve .... 918-293-4744.... 410 E
steve.olmstead@okstate.edu

OLMSTEAD, Thomas .... 505-473-6027.... 320 F
thomas.olmstead@santafeuniversity.edu

OLMSTEAD, Wayne .... 775-753-2274.... 302 F
wayne.olmstead@gbcnv.edu

OLMSTED, Jane .... 270-745-5787.... 208 A
jane.olmsted@wku.edu

OLMSTED, Joanna .... 585-275-4827.... 359 B
joanna.olmsted@rochester.edu

OLNEY, Douglas, P .... 218-755-2764.... 265 I
dolney@bemidjistate.edu

OLSCHWANG, Alana .... 909-607-8135...... 40 F
alana.olschwang@cgu.edu

OLSEN, Anika .... 928-523-1428...... 16 I
anika.olsen@nau.edu

OLSEN, Ann, E .... 502-272-8133.... 198 H
aolsen@bellarmine.edu

OLSEN, Burke .... 540-261-8416.... 524 H
burke.olsen@svu.edu

OLSEN, Danny, R .... 801-422-5648.... 509 H
danny_olsen@byu.edu

OLSEN, Gary, R .... 610-519-4580.... 450 H
gary.olsen@villanova.edu

OLSEN, Jim .... 651-255-6164.... 271 D
jolsen@unitedseminary.edu

OLSEN, Jo .... 218-723-7040.... 262 G
jolsen@css.edu

OLSEN, John, S .... 901-843-3795.... 472 K
olsen@rhodes.edu

OLSEN, Julene .... 435-722-6900.... 510 N
julene@ubatc.edu

OLSEN, Julie, A .... 765-361-6206.... 181 E
olsenj@wabash.edu

OLSEN, Kenneth, E .... 732-255-0400.... 312 D
kolsen@ocean.edu

OLSEN, Kris .... 714-628-7303...... 39 F
kolsen@chapman.edu

OLSEN, Matthew .... 918-495-7707.... 411 C
maolsen@oru.edu

OLSEN, Michelle .... 701-224-2540.... 381 E
michelle.olsen@ndus.edu

OLSEN, Morgan, R .... 480-727-9920...... 11 J
morgan.r.olsen@asu.edu

OLSEN, Pete .... 831-645-1363...... 57 G
polsen@mpc.edu

OLSEN, Renee .... 208-792-2151.... 144 B
rmolsen@lcsc.edu

OLSEN, JR., Robert, C ...... 516-671-2277.... 360 B
rolsen@webb-institute.edu

OLSEN, Steve .... 515-244-4221.... 181 F
olsens@aib.edu

OLSEN, Steven, A .... 310-825-3444...... 74 C
solsen@conet.ucla.edu

OLSEN, Tannie .... 918-495-7975.... 411 C
tolsen@oru.edu

OLSEN, Teresa .... 315-228-7318.... 329 G
tolsen@colgate.edu

OLSEN KELLY, Jodi .... 206-296-5405.... 538 B
jkelly@seattleu.edu

OLSHINSKY, Martin .... 304-214-8800.... 543 D
molshinsky@wvncc.edu

OLSON, Bette .... 402-465-7518.... 299 H
bolson@nebrwesleyan.edu

OLSON, Cari .... 701-858-3323.... 382 A
cari.olson@minotstateu.edu

OLSON, Carolyn .... 320-308-5156.... 269 B
colson@sctcc.edu

OLSON, Chris .... 916-608-6500...... 56 C

OLSON, Christa .... 515-271-2084.... 184 D
christa.olson@drake.edu

OLSON, Craige, J .... 801-581-8951.... 511 C
dentaled@hsc.utah.edu

OLSON, Diane .... 701-349-3621.... 383 E
dianeolson@trinitybiblecollege.edu

OLSON, Don .... 218-723-6471.... 262 G
dolson@css.edu

OLSON, Doug, A .... 715-833-6237.... 553 H
dolson@cvtc.edu

OLSON, Douglas .... 708-456-0300.... 166 F
dolson@triton.edu

OLSON, Dustin .... 805-893-4151...... 75 B
dustin.olson@police.ucsb.edu

OLSON, Eric .... 215-895-2079.... 427 H
eric.j.olson@drexel.edu

OLSON, Gail, M .... 651-201-1750.... 265 E
gail.olson@so.mnscu.edu

OLSON, Heidi, L .... 320-222-5209.... 268 G
heidi.olson@ridgewater.edu

OLSON, Ian .... 907-474-5317...... 10 I
inolson@alaska.edu

OLSON, Jeffery, D .... 651-638-6241.... 261 D
jeff-olson@bethel.edu

OLSON, Jeffrey .... 605-455-6055.... 465 A
jolson@olc.edu

OLSON, Joan, G .... 612-874-3745.... 265 C
joan_olson@mcad.edu

OLSON, Joe .... 541-440-4600.... 420 F
joe.olson@umpqua.edu

OLSON, John .... 804-521-5999.... 521 F

OLSON, John .... 425-388-9407.... 534 C
jolson@everettcc.edu

OLSON, Judith .... 760-591-3012.... 122 J
jolson@usa.edu

OLSON, Kerry, J .... 409-882-3362.... 501 B
kerry.olson@lsco.edu

OLSON, Ksenia .... 218-723-6139.... 262 G
kolson@nebook.com

OLSON, Laura, A .... 605-331-6627.... 466 E
laura.olson@usiouxfalls.edu

OLSON, Linda .... 610-341-5930.... 428 E
lolson@eastern.edu

OLSON, Lois, A .... 612-330-1162.... 261 B
olson3@augsburg.edu

OLSON, Louise .... 401-454-6323.... 454 B
lolson@risd.edu

OLSON, Lynette .... 620-235-4113.... 196 C
lolson@pittstate.edu

OLSON, Lynn .... 207-893-7801.... 219 F
lolson@sjcme.edu

OLSON, Lynn, F .... 508-793-7294.... 233 B
lolson@clarku.edu

OLSON, Mark .... 773-244-5728.... 159 H
molson@northpark.edu

OLSON, Mark, J .... 703-812-4757.... 520 J
molson@leland.edu

OLSON, Marlene .... 860-343-5869...... 91 G
molson@mxcc.commnet.edu

OLSON, MaryEllen .... 325-674-2000.... 478 I
meo10b@acu.edu

OLSON, Matthew .... 781-280-3802.... 240 B
olsonm@middlesex.mass.edu

OLSON, Matthew .... 715-324-6900.... 549 G
matt.olson@ni.edu

OLSON, Megan .... 907-786-1764...... 10 H
anmo@uaa.alaska.edu

OLSON, Michael .... 504-864-7047.... 213 F
olson@loyno.edu

OLSON, Nancy .... 641-585-8147.... 189 I
olsonn@waldorf.edu

OLSON, Nancy .... 217-732-3168.... 156 H
nolson@lincolnchristian.edu

OLSON, Neil .... 573-882-3768.... 291 B
olsonne@missouri.edu

OLSON, Ray, A .... 614-235-4136.... 402 G
rolson@tlsohio.edu

OLSON, Robert, N .... 503-370-6104.... 421 D
bolson@willamette.edu

OLSON, Roberta, K .... 605-688-5178.... 466 C
roberta.olson@sdstate.edu

OLSON, Sandra .... 508-929-8025.... 238 G
solson@worcester.edu

OLSON, Sara, M .... 402-465-2185.... 299 H
solson@nebrwesleyan.edu

OLSON, Scott .... 906-635-2828.... 253 H
solson@lssu.edu

OLSON, Scott, R .... 507-457-5003.... 269 G
solson@winona.edu

OLSON, Shari, L .... 602-243-8150...... 16 D
shari.olson@smcmail.maricopa.edu

OLSON, Shelly, Y .... 715-833-6675.... 553 H
solson@cvtc.edu

OLSON, Sheryl .... 763-424-0882.... 268 B
solson@nhcc.edu

OLSON, Stanley, N .... 563-589-0200.... 190 A
solson@wartburgseminary.edu

OLSON, Stephen .... 765-998-5119.... 180 B
stolson@taylor.edu

OLSON, Steve, J .... 253-535-7177.... 536 E
olsonsj@plu.edu

OLSON, Teresa .... 510-883-2068...... 45 B
tolson@dspt.edu

OLSON, Terry .... 701-572-9275.... 383 A
tolson@wscfoundation.com

OLSON, Todd .... 202-687-4056...... 98 D
tao4@georgetown.edu

OLSON, Warren .... 785-227-3380.... 191 B
olsonw@bethanylb.edu

OLSON, Wendy, Z .... 509-777-4306.... 540 C
wolson@whitworth.edu

OLSON-LOY, Sandra .... 320-589-6013.... 271 G
olsonloy@morris.umn.edu

OLSSON, Jackie .... 763-424-0731.... 268 B
jolsson@nhcc.edu

OLSSON, Pam .... 252-222-6156.... 369 A
pro@carteret.edu

OLSSON, Roy .... 616-331-3358.... 251 F
olssonr@gvsu.edu

OLSTEIN, Binyamin .... 847-982-2500.... 152 A
olstein@htc.edu

OLSWANG, Steven .... 425-637-1010.... 532 E
solswang@cityu.edu

OLSZEWSKI, Gabriel, G ..... 203-432-2330...... 96 A
gabriel.olszewski@yale.edu

OLTMAN, Eva .... 502-213-4245.... 202 F
eva.oltman@kctcs.edu

OLTROGGE, Michael .... 402-494-2311.... 299 B
moltrogge@thenicc.edu

OLUIC, Steven .... 440-525-7079.... 394 F
soluic@lakelandcc.edu

OLUKA, Uzoma .... 219-981-1111.... 176 G
uoluka@ivytech.edu

OLZINSKI, Len .... 570-740-0370.... 435 C
lolzinski@luzerne.edu

OMACHONU, John .... 615-898-2329.... 473 G
john.omachonu@mtsu.edu

OMAN, Jim .... 816-483-9600.... 289 E
jim.oman@spst.edu

OMAN, Lauren .... 724-589-2000.... 448 B
loman@thiel.edu

OMAN, Nina .... 509-865-8500.... 535 A
oman_n@heritage.edu

OMATICK, Lori, A .... 724-430-4191.... 439 G
lao11@psu.edu

OMDAHL, Becky .... 651-793-1466.... 267 A
becky.omdahl@metrostate.edu

OMLOR, Jim .... 248-340-0600.... 247 I
james.omlor@baker.edu

OMUNDSON, J. Andrew .... 864-941-8376.... 460 D
omundson.a@ptc.edu

ONAIFO, Greg .... 212-410-8044.... 343 B
gonaifo@nycpm.edu

ONARAL, Banu .... 215-895-2247.... 427 H
banu.onaral@drexel.edu

ONASCH, Charles .... 419-372-7197.... 385 E
conasch@bgsu.edu

ONDREYKA, Terry .... 512-245-2550.... 501 F
to16@txstate.edu

ONDRUS, Sherri .... 480-731-8014...... 15 D
sherri.ondrus@domail.maricopa.edu

ONEAL, Gayle .... 804-524-5087.... 529 H
goneal@vsu.edu

ONEAL, Susan .... 918-595-7378.... 412 H
soneal@tulsacc.edu

ONEST, Trevor .... 304-829-7757.... 540 H
tonest@bethanywv.edu

ONEY, Veronica, E .... 302-855-1667...... 96 E
voney@dtcc.edu

ONGARO, Giulio .... 209-946-2417...... 76 A
gongaro@pacific.edu

ONION, David, S .... 512-232-6531.... 505 D
onion@austin.utexas.edu

ONION, Matthew ... 606-326-2113 ... 201 F
matthew.onion@kctcs.edu
ONION, Patricia ... 360-383-3070 ... 540 A
ponion@whatcom.ctc.edu
ONISHI, Joni ... 808-934-2514 ... 142 A
jonishi@hawaii.edu
ONLEY, Francesca ... 215-637-7700 ... 431 A
fonley@holyfamily.edu
ONO, Santa, J ... 513-556-2201 ... 403 D
santa.ono@uc.edu
ONODERA, Yasushi ... 479-964-0832 ... 20 G
yonodera@atu.edu
ONOFRIETTI, Joseph ... 617-735-9746 ... 234 C
onofrij@emmanuel.edu
ONORATO, Suzanne ... 404-471-6000 ... 123 I
sonorato@agnesscott.edu
ONORIO, Joe ... 216-328-8754 ... 390 E
jonorio@devry.edu
ONSAGER, Erin ... 303-937-4553 ... 82 E
eonsager@chu.edu
ONSAGER, Lawrence, W ... 269-471-3275 ... 247 D
lonsager@andrews.edu
ONTIVEROS, Mary, R ... 970-491-7197 ... 83 F
mary.ontiveros@colostate.edu
ONTIVEROS, Ramiro ... 916-649-2400 ... 31 F
ONTJES, Joe ... 316-677-9400 ... 197 G
jontjes@watc.edu
ONTL, Lynn ... 518-255-5225 ... 354 E
ontll@cobleskill.edu
ONUFER, David, S ... 704-847-5600 ... 377 B
bookstore@ses.edu
ONWILER, Thomas ... 408-270-6410 ... 67 B
thomas.onwiler@sjeccd.org
ONWUBUARIRI, Marie ... 510-841-1905 ... 27 J
marieo@absw.edu
ONWUEME, Inno ... 724-357-2209 ... 442 F
ionwueme@iup.edu
ONWUMECHILI, Chuka ... 202-806-7694 ... 98 E
conwumechili@howard.edu
ONWUNLI, Agatha ... 850-599-3115 ... 118 L
agatha.onwunli@famu.edu
ONYEAGHALA, Raphael ... 507-537-6218 ... 269 E
raphael.onyeaghala@smsu.edu
ONZICK, Joseph ... 630-844-5630 ... 145 F
jonzick@aurora.edu
OORDT, Stan ... 712-722-3771 ... 184 C
stano@dordt.edu
OOSTERHOUS, Karen ... 724-503-1001 ... 451 A
koosterhous@washjeff.edu
OPALKA, Susan ... 602-393-5900 ... 13 A
sopalka@carrington.edu
OPAR, Michael, E ... 563-333-6152 ... 188 F
oparmichaele@sau.edu
OPATZ, Joe ... 952-358-8150 ... 268 A
joe.opatz@normandale.edu
OPATZ, Patrick ... 651-779-3279 ... 266 A
patrick.opatz@century.edu
OPAVA, Susan, C ... 805-756-1508 ... 33 I
sopava@calpoly.edu
OPERO, Haydee ... 305-418-4220 ... 115 D
hopero@pupr.edu
OPGENORTH, Timothy ... 312-996-5563 ... 167 B
timothy1@uic.edu
OPHEIM, Cynthia, L ... 512-245-2205 ... 501 F
co01@txstate.edu
OPITZ, Brian, R ... 724-287-8711 ... 423 G
brian.opitz@bc3.edu
OPLER, Daniel ... 718-405-3235 ... 330 A
daniel.opler@mountsaintvincent.edu
OPLT, Toni, L ... 314-984-7529 ... 289 A
toplt@stlcc.edu
OPP, Mike ... 651-423-8232 ... 266 B
mike.opp@dctc.edu
OPP, Susan ... 510-885-3716 ... 34 E
susan.opp@csueastbay.edu
OPPEL, Amanda ... 918-879-8400 ... 464 H
OPPENHEIM, Liza ... 603-623-0313 ... 305 E
loppenheim@nhia.edu
OPPENHEIMER, Martin ... 617-627-3337 ... 245 C
martin.oppenheimer@tufts.edu
OPPENHEIMER, Phillip, R ... 209-946-2561 ... 76 A
poppenhe@pacific.edu
OPPERMAN, Mary George 607-255-3621 ... 331 B
mgo5@cornell.edu
OPPERMANN, James ... 414-382-6120 ... 546 B
jim.oppermann@alverno.edu
OPPMANN, Andrew ... 615-494-7800 ... 473 G
andrew.oppmann@mtsu.edu
OPREAN, Celeste, P ... 828-694-1773 ... 368 E
celesteo@blueridge.edu
OPRISKO, George, W ... 765-361-6480 ... 181 E
opriskow@wabash.edu
OQUENDO, Carmen ... 787-250-1912 ... 563 G
coquendo@metro.inter.edu
OQUENDO, Diane ... 646-660-6154 ... 326 C
diane.oquendo@baruch.cuny.edu
OQUENDO, Diane ... 718-951-5038 ... 326 F
diane@brooklyn.cuny.edu
OQUENDO, Migdalia ... 787-728-1515 ... 568 D
moquendo@sagrado.edu
OR, Scott ... 208-376-7731 ... 142 H
sor@boisebible.edu
ORACION, Donna ... 575-624-7403 ... 318 C
donna.oracion@roswell.enmu.edu
ORAHOOD, Mary Alyce ... 513-745-3895 ... 406 E
orahood@xavier.edu
ORAM, Leatrice ... 603-283-2128 ... 303 F
loram@antioch.edu
ORAM, MaryLou ... 570-622-7622 ... 436 A
marylou.oram@mccann.edu
ORAMALU, Lawrencina ... 651-290-6416 ... 272 E
lawrencina.oramalu@wmitchell.edu
ORANCHAK, Celeste, A ... 201-355-1301 ... 310 B
oranchakc@felician.edu
ORANGE, Janice ... 205-929-6396 ... 5 E
jorange@lawsonstate.edu
ORANGE, Kathleen ... 251-380-3499 ... 7 E
orange@shc.edu
ORANGE, Taur, D ... 212-217-4170 ... 333 F
taur_orange@fitnyc.edu
ORANTE, Newin, P ... 510-464-3413 ... 62 D
norante@peralta.edu
ORAVECZ, Joseph, A ... 308-865-8528 ... 300 F
oraveczja@unk.edu
ORAVETZ, Teresa ... 203-332-5014 ... 91 E
toravetz@hcc.commnet.edu
ORBAN, Joseph ... 318-670-9360 ... 215 A
jorban@susla.edu
ORBIK, Jay ... 815-753-6670 ... 160 B
jorbik@niu.edu
ORCHARD, James, P ... 651-641-8705 ... 263 A
orchard@csp.edu
ORCUTT, Jo-Ann ... 570-961-7873 ... 433 A
orcuttj@lackawanna.edu
ORD, Kent, J ... 406-683-7301 ... 294 J
k_ord@umwestern.edu
ORDOYNE, Charles, R ... 985-448-4420 ... 216 A
charles.ordoyne@nicholls.edu
ORDUNA, Aubray ... 402-552-3100 ... 297 B
ORDUNA, Aubray, D ... 402-552-6118 ... 297 B
orduna@clarksoncollege.edu
ORDWAY, Jennifer, N ... 989-964-4917 ... 257 G
jnordway@svsu.edu
ORE, Dwayne ... 407-438-6000 ... 118 H
OREIRO, David ... 360-676-2772 ... 535 K
doreiro@nwic.edu
ORELLANA, Darcy ... 978-656-3558 ... 240 B
orellanad@middlesex.mass.edu
ORELLANA, Victoria ... 201-360-4121 ... 310 E
vorellana@hccc.edu
ORENSTEIN, David ... 908-835-2339 ... 317 C
dorenstein@warren.edu
ORGAN, Regina ... 575-492-2761 ... 319 B
rorgan@nmjc.edu
ORGERA, Jeffrey, M ... 520-626-8745 ... 18 L
jorgera@email.arizona.edu
ORGERON, Elizabeth ... 518-255-5842 ... 354 E
orgeroed@cobleskill.edu
ORICK, Ron ... 479-788-7019 ... 24 D
ron.orick@uafs.edu
ORIDE, Leighton ... 808-245-8224 ... 142 C
loride@hawaii.edu
ORIOLO, Michael ... 315-866-0300 ... 335 D
orioloma@herkimer.edu
ORIS, James, T ... 513-529-3734 ... 396 E
orisjt@muohio.edu
ORITZ, Fernando ... 509-313-4054 ... 534 F
oritz2@gonzaga.edu
ORKIN, Michael ... 510-466-7300 ... 62 E
morkin@peralta.edu
ORLANDO, Donald, A ... 724-805-2010 ... 446 E
don.orlando@stvincent.edu
ORLANDO, Mary ... 508-457-1313 ... 242 F
morlando@ngs.edu
ORLANDO, Matthew ... 207-725-3804 ... 217 E
morlando@bowdoin.edu
ORLANDO, Michael ... 517-264-7171 ... 258 B
morlando@sienaheights.edu
ORLANDO, Stephen, F ... 352-392-0186 ... 120 C
sfo@ufl.edu
ORLANDO RIVERA, Jose ... 305-418-4220 ... 115 D
jorlando@pupr.edu
ORLAUSKI, Brian ... 951-487-3080 ... 58 B
sguarino@msjc.edu
ORLE TANTILLO, Astrida ... 312-413-7329 ... 167 B
tantillo@uic.edu
ORLOWSKI, Martin, A ... 248-522-3882 ... 256 F
maorlows@oaklandcc.edu
ORME, James ... 517-321-0242 ... 251 G
jorme@glcc.edu
ORME, Michael, R ... 801-422-3080 ... 143 A
mike_orme@byui.edu
ORME, Michael, R ... 801-422-3080 ... 509 H
michael_orme@byu.edu
ORME, Robyn ... 517-321-0242 ... 251 G
rorme@glcc.edu
ORMENO, Alex ... 212-924-5900 ... 357 B
aormeno@swedishinstitute.edu
ORMEROD, Michelle ... 617-879-2270 ... 246 C
mormerod@wheelock.edu
ORMISTON, Gayle, L ... 304-696-3716 ... 544 B
ormiston@marshall.edu
ORMOND, Janet ... 334-291-4964 ... 2 F
janet.ormond@cv.edu
ORMOND, Tom ... 478-445-6848 ... 130 B
tom.ormond@gcsu.edu
ORMSBEE, Christine ... 405-744-1000 ... 410 C
ormsbee@okstate.edu
ORMSBEE, David ... 937-766-4547 ... 386 G
ormsbeed@cedarville.edu
ORMSBY, Colin ... 509-359-4217 ... 533 H
cormsby@ewu.edu
ORNE, Tracy ... 217-641-4106 ... 154 I
torne@jwcc.edu
ORNELAS, Daniel ... 323-265-8751 ... 54 G
ornelad@elac.edu
ORNELAS, Nohemy ... 805-546-3143 ... 43 I
nohemy_ornelas@cuesta.edu
ORNER, Lita ... 240-500-2000 ... 223 A
ornerl@hagerstowncc.edu
ORNER, Robert, H ... 407-366-9493 ... 115 K
borner@rts.edu
ORNES, W. Harold ... 217-581-3328 ... 150 E
whornes@eiu.edu
ORNT, Daniel, B ... 585-475-4861 ... 347 G
dboihst@rit.edu
OROK, Michael ... 615-963-5139 ... 474 A
morok@tnstate.edu
ORONA, Edward ... 330-941-2377 ... 406 F
eorona@ysu.edu
ORONA, Frank ... 505-747-2161 ... 320 A
forona@nnmc.edu
OROSAN, Andronic ... 419-755-3913 ... 399 C
orosan.1@osu.edu
OROSZ, David ... 216-373-5322 ... 397 F
dorosz@ndc.edu
OROURKE, Steven, R ... 724-658-9066 ... 428 H
orourkes@eriebcs.com
OROZA, Lourdes ... 305-237-2154 ... 113 H
loroza1@mdc.edu
OROZCO, Samuel ... 520-383-8401 ... 18 I
sorozco@tocc.cc.az.us
OROZCO-MONROY, Rose ... 505-224-4700 ... 317 K
rorozco@cnm.edu
ORR, Charlotte ... 256-766-6610 ... 4 C
corr@hcu.edu
ORR, Collin ... 360-867-6450 ... 534 D
orrc@evergreen.edu
ORR, Debra ... 617-521-2180 ... 244 F
debra.orr@simmons.edu
ORR, Herb ... 785-242-5200 ... 195 I
herb.orr@ottawa.edu
ORR, Jaimie ... 419-448-3319 ... 402 E
orrrj@tiffin.edu
ORR, Jeff ... 678-915-7489 ... 137 G
jorr@spsu.edu
ORR, Mark, C ... 925-631-4399 ... 64 F
morr@stmarys-ca.edu
ORR, Michael ... 847-735-5021 ... 155 G
morr@lakeforest.edu
ORR, Pattie ... 254-710-3200 ... 482 A
pattie_orr@baylor.edu
ORR, Richard ... 860-486-5796 ... 94 G
richard.orr@uconn.edu
ORR, Robert ... 478-445-1196 ... 130 B
robert.orr@gcsu.edu
ORR, Sandra ... 304-766-3381 ... 544 F
sorr@wvstateu.edu
ORR, Shaun ... 208-496-9340 ... 143 A
orrs@byui.edu
ORR, Stephanie, W ... 850-263-3261 ... 101 L
sworr@baptistcollege.edu
ORR, Sylvia ... 623-935-8413 ... 15 F
sylvia.orr@estrellamountain.edu
ORR, II, Thomas ... 530-529-8980 ... 69 D
torr@shastacollege.edu
ORR, Trina ... 828-227-7290 ... 380 A
torr@wcu.edu
ORRELL, Eloise ... 650-940-7730 ... 47 H
orrelleloise@foothill.edu
ORRIS, Erika ... 630-353-7049 ... 149 B
eorris@devry.edu
ORRISON, Russell ... 423-236-2336 ... 473 B
rorrison@southern.edu
ORSAK, Geoffrey ... 918-631-3244 ... 413 F
geoffrey-orsak@utulsa.edu
ORSBORN, Ruthie, J ... 334-874-5700 ... 2 H
rorsborn@ccal.edu
ORSCHELN, Kathryn, B ... 734-487-3060 ... 250 F
kathy.orscheln@emich.edu
ORSCHELN, Paul ... 859-572-5825 ... 205 H
orschelnp1@nku.edu
ORSCHIEDT, Gretchen ... 860-297-4123 ... 94 E
gretchen.orschiedt@trincoll.edu
ORSER, Paul, N ... 336-758-5311 ... 380 C
orser@wfu.edu
ORSHANSKY, Mariya ... 510-628-8010 ... 54 B
morshansky@lincolnuca.edu
ORSI, Michael ... 239-687-5331 ... 101 H
frorsi@avemarialaw.edu
ORSINI, SPHR, Teri ... 704-337-2297 ... 376 A
orsinit@queens.edu
ORT, Shirley, A ... 919-962-2315 ... 378 E
sao@unc.edu
ORTA, Edna ... 787-743-7979 ... 565 H
ut_eorta@suagm.edu
ORTA, Jose ... 305-223-4561 ... 116 E
ORTALE, Lynn ... 215-248-7030 ... 425 D
ortalel@chc.edu
ORTALO-MAGNE', Francois ... 608-262-1234 ... 550 J
ORTBERG, Jennifer, L ... 714-895-8965 ... 41 C
jortberg@gwc.cccd.edu
ORTEGA, Ana, M ... 787-743-7979 ... 565 H
ut_aortega@suagm.edu
ORTEGA, Carmen ... 787-257-7373 ... 565 G
ue_cortega@suagm.edu
ORTEGA, Carolyn, M ... 973-655-7327 ... 311 F
ortegac@mail.montclair.edu
ORTEGA, David ... 210-486-1227 ... 479 E
dortega@alamo.edu
ORTEGA, David, F ... 541-485-1780 ... 417 E
davidortega@newhope.edu
ORTEGA, J. Martin ... 210-486-0721 ... 479 E
jortega@alamo.edu
ORTEGA, Janet ... 602-243-8287 ... 16 D
ORTEGA, Jeff ... 916-722-8200 ... 38 D
jortega@carrington.edu
ORTEGA, Luz, D ... 787-480-2407 ... 561 E
lortega@sanjuancapital.com
ORTEGA, Richard ... 510-436-1198 ... 50 H
rortega@hnu.edu
ORTEGA, Suzanne ... 919-962-4614 ... 377 C
stortega@northcarolina.edu
ORTEGON, Ricardo ... 212-986-4343 ... 307 F
ricardo@berkeleycollege.edu
ORTEGON, Ricardo ... 212-986-4343 ... 323 H
ricardo@berkeleycollege.edu
ORTELLI, Tracy, A ... 502-410-6200 ... 200 L
tortelli@galencollege.edu
ORTEN, Mark ... 740-587-8504 ... 389 I
ortenm@denison.edu
ORTH, Linda ... 423-425-4669 ... 477 F
linda-orth@utc.edu
ORTIZ, Ann ... 910-893-1669 ... 362 J
ortiz@campbell.edu
ORTIZ, Ariel ... 787-766-1717 ... 565 I
um_aortiz@suagm.edu
ORTIZ, Blanca ... 787-767-2040 ... 568 B
ORTIZ, Christine ... 617-253-4860 ... 241 D
ORTIZ, Daniel ... 617-287-5910 ... 236 G
daniel.ortiz@umb.edu
ORTIZ, Darnyd, W ... 787-265-3807 ... 567 F
decasac@uprm.edu
ORTIZ, Edna ... 787-786-3030 ... 560 G
eortiz@ucb.edu.pr
ORTIZ, Eduardo ... 787-250-1912 ... 563 G
ehortiz@metro.inter.edu
ORTIZ, Elizabeth ... 818-947-2361 ... 55 E
ortizme@lavc.edu
ORTIZ, Elizabeth, F ... 312-362-8588 ... 149 A
eortiz4@depaul.edu
ORTIZ, Emma, L ... 773-838-7530 ... 147 H
eortiz@ccc.edu
ORTIZ, Erika ... 954-322-4460 ... 112 C
ortize@jmvu.edu
ORTIZ, Eugene ... 505-661-4682 ... 321 E
eortiz3@unm.edu
ORTIZ, Francisco ... 787-761-0640 ... 566 F
oficinadelpresidente@utcpr.edu
ORTIZ, Hilda, L ... 787-863-2390 ... 563 E
hilda.ortiz@fajardo.inter.edu
ORTIZ, Hiram ... 787-850-9312 ... 567 E
hiram.ortiz@upr.edu
ORTIZ, Holly ... 661-835-1111 ... 67 J
ORTIZ, Holly ... 805-339-2999 ... 68 A
ORTIZ, Holly ... 661-835-1111 ... 67 K
ORTIZ, Holly ... 805-922-8256 ... 67 M
ORTIZ, Holly ... 805-967-9677 ... 67 L
ORTIZ, J. Michael ... 909-869-2290 ... 33 J
jmo@csupomona.edu
ORTIZ, Jeanne ... 562-907-4233 ... 79 F
jortiz@whittier.edu
ORTIZ, Jennifer ... 210-486-4208 ... 479 B
jortiz157@alamo.edu
ORTIZ, Johnathan ... 505-454-2596 ... 318 F
jortiz@luna.edu
ORTIZ, Jose, M ... 510-466-7202 ... 62 A
jortiz@peralta.edu
ORTIZ, Joseph, E ... 787-857-3600 ... 563 C
jeortiz@br.inter.edu
ORTIZ, Judy ... 503-352-7309 ... 419 E
ortiz@pacificu.edu
ORTIZ, Kendra ... 787-780-0070 ... 560 H
kortiz@caribbean.edu
ORTIZ, Kim ... 312-329-6673 ... 146 F
kortiz@thechicagoschool.edu
ORTIZ, Kristina ... 212-752-1530 ... 338 C
kristina.ortiz@limcollege.edu
ORTIZ, Laura ... 630-942-2971 ... 148 A
ortizl@cod.edu
ORTIZ, Lillian ... 203-575-8034 ... 92 A
lortiz@nvcc.commnet.edu
ORTIZ, Lourdes, Z ... 787-257-0000 ... 567 C
lourdes.ortiz2@upr.edu
ORTIZ, Luis, A ... 787-767-4300 ... 568 B
luortiz@onelinkpr.net
ORTIZ, Luz ... 787-864-2222 ... 563 F
luzortiz@inter.edu
ORTIZ, Luz, M ... 787-832-6000 ... 562 G
mortiz@icprjc.edu
ORTIZ, Luz, M ... 215-503-4094 ... 448 C
luz.ortiz@jefferson.edu
ORTIZ, Mario ... 219-785-5476 ... 179 A
mortiz@pnc.edu

ORTIZ, Migdalia 787-279-1912 563 D morti@bayamon.inter.edu
ORTIZ, Myrta 787-815-0000 567 A myrta.ortiz1@upr.edu
ORTIZ, Noe 210-486-4600 479 B nortiz@alamo.edu
ORTIZ, Noel 787-753-6335 562 G nortiz@icprjc.edu
ORTIZ, Norma 787-620-2040 560 D nortiz@aupr.edu
ORTIZ, Nuria 650-289-3336 64 G nuria.ortiz@stpatrickseminary.org
ORTIZ, Rafael 787-725-6500 561 A rortiz@albizu.edu
ORTIZ, Ralph 559-734-9000 66 E ralpho@sjvc.edu
ORTIZ, Rosa 787-738-2161 567 D rosa.ortiz1@upr.edu
ORTIZ, Samantha 303-556-3519 88 J samantha.ortiz@ucdenver.edu
ORTIZ, Vivian 781-239-3101 239 G vortiz@massbay.edu
ORTIZ, Zoraida 787-743-7979 565 H zortiz@suagm.edu
ORTIZ ALVAREZ, Lelis Antonio 954-322-4460 112 C lelisortiz@jmvu.edu
ORTIZ-CINTRÓN, Jesús 787-993-8878 567 B jesus.ortiz3@upr.edu
ORTIZ-CINTRÓN, Jesús 787-993-8869 567 B jesus.ortiz3@upr.edu
ORTIZ COLON, Yadira 787-725-8120 562 C yortiz@eap.edu
ORTIZ FLORES, Ileana 787-896-2252 562 B iortiz@edpcollege.edu
ORTIZ PARRA, Erika Jose 954-322-4460 112 C ortize@jmvu.edu
ORTIZ PARRA, Lelis 954-322-4460 112 C ortizlelis@jmvu.edu
ORTIZ-ZAYAS, Jose, E 787-857-3600 563 C jeortiz@br.inter.edu
ORTMAN, William, B 973-618-3259 308 C wortman@caldwell.edu
ORTMEIER, Shane 605-882-5284 464 E ortmeies@lakeareatech.edu
ORTMEYER, Rose Ann 573-681-5044 283 I ortmeyr@lincolnu.edu
ORTNER, Richard 617-912-9134 232 C rortner@bostonconservatory.edu
ORTON, Donna, J 641-422-4216 188 A ortondon@niacc.edu
ORTON, Mozelle 801-957-4561 512 D mozelle.orton@slcc.edu
ORTQUIST-AHRENS, Leslie 859-985-3670 199 A ortquistahrensl@berea.edu
ORTSTADT, Andrew, D 314-935-8604 292 I aortstadt@wustl.edu
ORUM-ALEXANDER, Gail 323-563-5851 39 G gailorum@cdrewu.edu
ORVIS, Arleen 563-387-1005 187 D orvisarl@luther.edu
ORWIG, Greg 509-777-4580 540 C gorwig@whitworth.edu
ORWIGHO, Godfrey 419-530-3955 404 F godfrey.ovwigho@utoledo.edu
ORZA, Deanna 770-781-6770 133 C dorza@laniertech.edu
ORZECHOWSKI, Laurie 419-824-3959 395 E lorzechowski@lourdes.edu
ORZECHOWSKI, Michael 212-280-1301 358 I morzechowski@uts.columbia.edu
ORZOLEK, Jeffrey, P 540-831-5376 523 A jorzolek@radford.edu
ORZOLEK, Mariah 419-783-2358 389 H morzolek@defiance.edu
OSAGIE, Linda 214-860-8604 485 B losagie@dcccd.edu
OSANTOWSKI, Kimberly 248-204-3940 254 B kosantows@ltu.edu
OSATHANUGRAH, Vim 510-666-8248 26 H vim@aimc.edu
OSAWA, Steve 510-659-6111 59 J sosawa@ohlone.edu
OSBAHR, Diane 712-325-3235 186 F dosbahr@iwcc.edu
OSBON, Cindy 301-846-2593 222 G cosbon@frederick.edu
OSBORN, Bill 928-757-0817 16 F bosborn@mohave.edu
OSBORN, Carolyn, S 830-792-7282 494 E cosborn@schreiner.edu
OSBORN, Dan 586-791-6610 248 B daniel.osborn@baker.edu
OSBORN, David, R 303-762-6918 84 D david.osborn@denverseminary.edu
OSBORN, Dawn 805-962-8179 29 A
OSBORN, Edward, H 860-465-5303 90 H osborne@easternct.edu
OSBORN, Jeffrey 609-771-2724 308 F josborn@tcnj.edu
OSBORN, Lou 714-704-2727 79 B losborn@westwood.edu
OSBORN, Matthew 419-267-1381 397 E mosborn@northweststate.edu
OSBORN, Micahel, A 614-885-5585 401 B mosborn@pcj.edu
OSBORN, Richard, E 423-439-8300 473 F osbornr@etsu.edu
OSBORN, Terry 941-359-4200 121 B
OSBORNE, Becky 217-353-2005 161 C bosborne@parkland.edu
OSBORNE, Curtis 510-649-2477 48 J cosborne@gtu.edu
OSBORNE, John 305-428-5700 113 I josborne@aii.edu
OSBORNE, John 405-425-5463 409 E john.osborne@oc.edu
OSBORNE, John, N 270-745-5747 208 A john.osborne@wku.edu
OSBORNE, Kari 410-837-4397 229 A kpsborne@ubalt.edu
OSBORNE, Kenneth, T 401-254-3166 454 C kosborne@rwu.edu
OSBORNE, Kevin 336-342-4261 373 E osbornek@rockinghamcc.edu
OSBORNE, Larry 808-735-4825 140 E losborne@chaminade.edu
OSBORNE, Lynn 336-838-6175 375 C lynn.osborne@wilkescc.edu
OSBORNE, Margaret, H 315-255-1743 325 G osbornem@cayuga-cc.edu
OSBORNE, Matthew, S 517-750-1200 258 D mosborne@arbor.edu
OSBORNE, Michelle 518-454-5141 330 C osbornem@strose.edu
OSBORNE, Shelley 704-991-0203 374 D sosborne7501@stanly.edu
OSBORNE, Steven, C 843-953-5574 457 B osbornes@cofc.edu
OSBORNE, Tom 402-472-3011 300 G tosborne2@unl.edu
OSBORNE, Travis, G 530-226-4978 69 H tosborne@simpsonu.edu
OSBORNE-ADAMS, Dawn 607-777-2388 351 F ombudsman@binghamton.edu
OSBORNE-ELLIOTT, Miriam 340-692-4187 568 E mosborn@live.uvi.edu
OSBOURN, John 541-956-7426 420 B josbourn@roguecc.edu
OSBOURNE, John 304-829-7395 540 H josbourne@bethanywv.edu
OSBURN, Monica 919-515-2423 378 C monica_osburn@ncsu.edu
OSBURN, Monica, Z 910-521-6202 379 C monica.osburn@uncp.edu
OSBURN, Toby, W 337-475-5607 215 G tosburn@mcneese.edu
OSBY, Rachel, V 256-824-6549 8 G rachel.osby@uah.edu
OSEBY, Todd 651-779-3276 266 A todd.oseby@century.edu
OSEEKEY, Leonard 716-829-7677 332 E oseekey@dyc.edu
OSEGUEDA, Roberto 915-747-5680 506 B osegueda@utep.edu
OSENGA, Annette 510-780-4500 53 J aosenga@lifewest.edu
OSGOOD, Dorothy 803-705-4623 455 D osgoodd@benedict.edu
OSGOOD, Ken 303-273-3596 83 B kosgood@mines.edu
OSHERSON, Julie 802-387-6732 513 G josherson@landmark.edu
OSHINSKI, Susan 815-226-4010 163 A soshinski@rockford.edu
OSHIRO, Cathie, R 620-792-9234 190 H oshiroc@bartonccc.edu
OSHIRO, James 503-554-2235 415 I joshiro@georgefox.edu
OSHIRO, Robyn 808-454-4700 141 H robyno@hawaii.edu
OSINGA, Mark, L 864-596-9041 457 E mark.osinga@converse.edu
OSIRIM, Mary 610-526-5074 423 D
OSIRIS, Charles 805-922-6966 26 L cosiris@hancockcollege.edu
OSKAMP, Shirley 802-287-8388 513 F oskamps@greenmtn.edu
OSMAN, Cathy 802-258-9293 513 H cosman@marlboro.edu
OSMANSON, Deb 402-449-2844 297 H dosmanson@graceu.edu
OSMER, Patrick, S 614-292-6031 398 I osmer.1@osu.edu
OSMUN, Molly, M 641-844-5706 186 D molly.osmun@iavalley.edu
OSORIO, Jennifer 718-357-0500 349 F josorio@edaff.com
OSSORIO, Devon 573-288-6571 280 I dossorio@culver.edu
OST, Sue 406-265-3525 295 E osts@msun.edu
OSTASH, Heather 760-384-6249 52 M hostash@cerrocoso.edu
OSTDIEK, Donald 713-348-4786 493 C dho@rice.edu
OSTEEN, Charles 760-384-6115 52 M charles.osteen@cerrocoso.edu
OSTENDARP, Timothy 443-352-4348 226 E tostendarp@stevenson.edu
OSTENDORF, Ellen 410-337-6431 222 I
OSTER, Ben Zion 323-937-3763 80 D boster@yoec.edu
OSTER, Cynthia 856-691-8600 309 B coster@cccnj.edu
OSTER, Joseph 410-704-2364 228 E joster@towson.edu
OSTERBIND, Kelly 256-782-5400 4 L kosterbi@jsu.edu
OSTERHOLT, James 505-984-6109 320 C josterholt@sjcsf.edu
OSTERHOUDT, Lori, B 607-746-4692 355 F osterhlb@delhi.edu
OSTERTHUN, Stu 402-323-3401 300 B sosterthun@southeast.edu
OSTIN, Daniel 732-235-4565 316 G ostindj@umdnj.edu
OSTLER, Jon 435-283-7361 512 C jon.ostler@snow.edu
OSTOJIC, Diane 708-596-2000 164 H dostojic@ssc.edu
OSTOLAZA, Magda, A 787-257-7373 565 G ue_mostolaza@suagm.edu
OSTRANDER, David 352-588-8250 116 G david.ostrander@saintleo.edu
OSTRANDER, Doris 202-298-2551 98 A dostrander@corcoran.org
OSTRANDER, Gary, K 808-956-7837 141 G gko@hawaii.edu
OSTRANDER, Jean, M 641-422-4177 188 A ostrajea@niacc.edu
OSTRANDER, Richard 616-222-1589 250 A rick.ostrander@cornerstone.edu
OSTRANDER, Tammy 218-723-6173 262 G tostrand@css.edu
OSTREICHER, Arica 312-939-0111 150 D arica@eastwest.edu
OSTROSKE, Georgette 516-918-3607 324 E gostroske@bcl.edu
OSTROW, James 617-243-2111 236 A jostrow@lasell.edu
OSTRYE, Mary, E 317-921-4313 175 I mostrye@ivytech.edu
OSTWINKLE, Christopher, M 563-556-5110 188 B ostwinkc@nicc.edu
OSUNDE, Samuel 662-254-9041 276 B sosunde@mvsu.edu
OSWALD, Gloria 305-626-3641 109 A goswald@fmuniv.edu
OSWALD, Mike, R 208-356-1320 143 A oswaldrm@byui.edu
OSWALD, P.J 503-517-1800 421 C pjoswald@westernseminary.edu
OSWALD, Peter 217-854-3231 146 A peter.oswald@blackburn.edu
OSWALD, Phil 920-403-3016 550 F phil.oswald@snc.edu
OSWALD, Sharon 662-325-2580 275 F soswald@cobilan.msstate.edu
OSWALT, Natalie 936-591-9075 492 C noswalt@panola.edu
OTAIGBE, Michael, I 703-878-2810 99 G mio@strayer.edu
OTERO, Emeterio, M 585-262-1610 341 H eotero@monroecc.edu
OTERO, Juan 787-766-1717 565 I juotero@suagm.edu
OTERO PABON, Evelyn Camille 787-725-8120 562 C cotero@eap.edu
OTHMAN, Saib 630-844-4229 145 F sothman@aurora.edu
OTIS, Linda 228-497-7649 275 E linda.otis@mgccc.edu
OTO, Rod, M 507-222-4190 261 G roto@carleton.edu
OTOUPAL, Vince 831-582-3534 35 E votoupal@csumb.edu
OTSUKA, Tami 714-532-6067 39 F otsuka@chapman.edu
OTT, Alexander 516-686-1037 343 D aott@nyit.edu
OTT, Deanna 501-205-8838 21 C dott@cbc.edu
OTT, Emlyn, A 614-235-4136 402 G eott@tlsohio.edu
OTT, Jay, W 719-884-5000 86 J jwott@nbc.edu
OTT, Luisa 520-494-5283 13 D luisa.ott@centralaz.edu
OTT, Martha 207-221-8745 218 C mott@kapan.edu
OTT, Randall 202-319-5188 97 E ott@cua.edu
OTT, Steven, H 704-687-7630 379 A shott@uncc.edu
OTT ROWLANDS, Sue 540-231-6779 529 G sottrowlands@vt.edu
OTTAWAY, Thomas 208-282-3585 143 H ottathom@isu.edu
OTTEMAN, Marcie 989-774-1042 249 C ottem1mm@cmich.edu
OTTEN, Robert 703-526-6927 521 D robert.otten@marymount.edu
OTTENHOFF, John 208-459-5334 143 D jottenhoff@collegeofidaho.edu
OTTERBACHER, Jon 920-593-8400 550 B jon.otterbacher@rasmussen.edu
OTTERNESS, Naomi 828-771-3783 380 D nottern@warren-wilson.edu
OTTERSON, Robert 605-688-4111 466 C robert.otterson@sdstate.edu
OTTERVIK, Jennifer 410-234-4594 225 E
OTTESON, Rick 218-855-8136 265 J rotteson@clcmn.edu
OTTEY, Jacqueline 201-447-7204 307 E jottey@bergen.edu
OTTINGER, Denise 785-670-2100 197 F denise.ottinger@washburn.edu
OTTINGER, Marie 334-386-7512 3 G mottinger@faulkner.edu
OTTINGER, Marybeth 636-481-3467 283 D mottinge@jeffco.edu
OTTINO, Julio, M 847-491-3195 160 E jm-ottino@northwestern.edu
OTTLEY, David 435-797-1266 511 E dave.ottley@usu.edu
OTTO, Eric, H 812-464-1765 181 B eotto@usi.edu
OTTO, Raimondi 732-224-2239 308 A craimondi@brookdalecc.edu
OTTO, Richard, H 312-461-0600 145 A ifitzgerald@aaart.edu
OTTO, Rick 479-979-1351 26 A rotto@ozarks.edu
OTTO, Robert 212-217-3637 333 F robert_otto@fitnyc.edu
OTTO, Sheryl 874-925-6342 151 G sotto@harpercollege.edu
OTTO, Theophil 509-359-2264 533 H totto@ewu.edu
OTTOBONI, John 408-554-5355 68 C jottoboni@scu.edu
OTTOSON, Robin 620-947-3121 197 A robino@tabor.edu
OTTOSSON, John 641-673-1015 190 C ottossonj@wmpenn.edu
OTTS, Tonya 803-793-5192 457 F tonyao@denmarktech.edu
OTTWELL, Dawn 314-837-6777 288 C dottwell@slcconline.edu
OTU, Emmanual 262-595-2345 552 A
OTUONYE, Francis, O 931-372-3374 474 B fotuonye@tntech.edu
OTWELL, Michelle 386-386-7380 3 G motwell@faulkner.edu
OTY, Karla 580-581-2899 407 D koty@cameron.edu
OUART, Michael, D 573-882-7477 291 B ouartm@missouri.edu
OUBRAHAM, Ourida 201-216-5411 315 E oobraha@stevens.edu
OUBRE, Linda 415-338-2670 37 B loubre@sfsu.edu
OUDENHOVEN, D. Arnie 847-635-1675 160 F aoudenho@oakton.edu
OUDENHOVEN, Elizabeth 303-360-4703 83 K betsy.oudenhoven@ccaurora.edu
OUELLETTE, Alicia 518-445-3305 322 C aouel@albanylaw.edu
OUELLETTE, James 802-831-1209 515 B jouellette@vermontlaw.edu
OUELLETTE, Michelle, M 518-564-3095 354 B ouel8653@plattsburgh.edu
OUIMET, Maurice 802-468-1352 515 D maurice.ouimet@castleton.edu
OUIMETTE, Nina 325-670-2357 487 F noiumette@hsutx.edu
OUIMETTE, Nina 325-671-2357 490 H nouimette@hsutx.edu
OULETTE, Helen 617-873-0689 233 A helen.oulette@cambridgecollege.edu
OURS, Alan 559-453-2269 48 A alan.ours@fresno.edu
OUSLEY, Chris 503-338-2326 415 B cousley@clatsopcc.edu
OUSLEY, Kim, P 770-671-1200 124 F kousley@argosy.edu
OUSLEY, Larry 517-750-1200 258 D lousley@arbor.edu
OUTEN, Jason 828-835-4229 374 F jouten@tricountycc.edu
OUTLEY, Patrice 318-274-2288 215 E outleyp@gram.edu
OUTON, Peggy, M 412-397-6001 445 H outon@rmu.edu
OUZOMGI, Samir 215-881-7552 438 H sxo2@psu.edu
OVADIA, Zak 904-620-2016 120 D zovadia@unf.edu
OVEDIA, Nicole, R 561-237-7237 113 D novedia@lynn.edu
OVEL, Steven, J 319-398-5466 187 B steve.ovel@kirkwood.edu

OVER, Lucinda 626-914-8538 40 B
lover@citruscollege.edu
OVER, Megan 314-529-9343 284 C
mover@maryville.edu
OVERBY, Dave 218-299-6521 267 D
dave.overby@minnesota.edu
OVERCASH, Shannon 508-541-1841 233 G
sovercash@dean.edu
OVEREND, Gregory 203-932-7430 95 C
goverend@newhaven.edu
OVEREND, Wendy 805-969-3626 60 J
woverend@pacifica.edu
OVERFIELD, Joan, T 203-254-4000 92 H
jtoverfield@fairfield.edu
OVERLAND, Wanda 320-308-3111 269 A
wioverland@stcloudstate.edu
OVERLEY, Kelly 806-742-1780 502 A
kelly.overley@ttu.edu
OVERLY, Kristie 610-917-1414 450 E
kaoverly@vfcc.edu
OVERMAN, Jan, G 336-342-4261 373 E
overmanj@rockinghamcc.edu
OVEROCKER, Josh 405-974-3636 413 B
joverocker@uco.edu
OVERSTROM, Eric 508-831-5222 246 F
ewo@wpi.edu
OVERTON, Chrystal 580-477-7831 414 C
chrystal.overton@wosc.edu
OVERTON, James 617-287-7799 236 G
james.overton@umb.edu
OVERTON, Lindi 573-876-7105 290 C
loverton@stephens.edu
OVERTON, Reginald 412-237-3127 425 H
roverton@ccac.edu
OVERTON, Richard 631-420-2700 356 A
foundation@farmingdale.edu
OVERTON, Robert, A 864-488-4543 459 B
roverton@limestone.edu
OVERTON, JR., Sam 815-921-4445 162 H
s.overton@rockvalleycollege.edu
OVERTON-ADKINS,
Betty, J 517-750-1200 258 D
boverton@arbor.edu
OVERTON-HEALY, Julia 607-871-2971 322 E
overton@alfred.edu
OVERTURF, Kellie 970-332-5755 86 G
kellie.overturf@morgancc.edu
OVERY, Lara 757-822-1422 528 G
lovery@tcc.edu
OVESON, Kip, R 320-222-6930 268 G
kip.oveson@ridgewater.edu
OW, Debora 510-559-5264 60 E
dow@plts.edu
OWAN, Edna 808-675-3474 140 D
edna.owan@byuh.edu
OWAN, Robert 808-675-3951 140 D
owanb@byuh.edu
OWCZARCZAK, Kathleen 716-625-6300 324 K
kowczarczak@bryantstratton.edu
OWCZARCZAK, Kathleen 716-884-9120 324 J
kowczarczak@bryantstratton.edu
OWCZARCZAK, Kathleen 716-677-9500 325 A
kowczarczak@bryantstratton.edu
OWCZAREK, Scott 608-262-3964 550 J
owczarek@em.wisc.edu
OWEN, Barbara 207-755-5233 218 G
bowen@cmcc.edu
OWEN, Bob 270-745-2243 208 A
bob.owen@wku.edu
OWEN, David, L 671-734-1812 559 F
dowen@piu.edu
OWEN, Harvey 717-872-3024 443 D
harvey.owen@millersville.edu
OWEN, James (Chris) 863-667-5146 118 F
jcowen@seu.edu
OWEN, Jane 940-397-4315 491 B
jane.owen@mwsu.edu
OWEN, Jane, S 724-852-3225 451 B
jowen@waynesburg.edu
OWEN, Janet, D 904-620-2500 120 D
jowen@unf.edu
OWEN, John 419-448-2073 391 F
jowen@heidelberg.edu
OWEN, Kay 601-709-0966 273 C
kowen@belhaven.edu
OWEN, Kelli 606-783-2700 204 I
k.owen@moreheadstate.edu
OWEN, Ken 765-658-4634 171 B
kowen@depauw.edu
OWEN, Kyle 940-397-4648 491 B
kyle.owen@mwsu.edu
OWEN, Michael, G 973-655-4498 311 F
owenm@mail.montclair.edu
OWEN, Pam, D 715-874-4655 553 H
powen@cvtc.edu
OWEN, Pamela 501-450-1358 22 A
owen@hendrix.edu
OWEN, Polly 614-287-2639 389 A
powen@cscc.edu
OWEN, Samantha 671-734-1812 559 F
sowen@piu.edu
OWEN, William 402-457-2715 298 G
bowen@mccneb.edu
OWENBY, Judy 828-835-4212 374 F
jowenby@tricountycc.edu

OWENS, Ann 918-465-1761 408 A
aowens@eosc.edu
OWENS, Anthony 615-329-8882 468 I
aowens@fisk.edu
OWENS, Antwane 214-379-5573 492 F
aowens@pqc.edu
OWENS, Bertha 501-370-5215 23 B
bowens@philander.edu
OWENS, Billy 501-244-6137 19 D
billy.owens@arkansasbaptist.edu
OWENS, Casey 417-455-5618 280 H
caseyowens@crowder.edu
OWENS, Claudia 740-374-8716 405 G
cowens1@wscc.edu
OWENS, Deborah, E 716-829-8198 332 E
owensde@dyc.edu
OWENS, Derek, V 718-990-2043 348 G
owensd@stjohns.edu
OWENS, Don 254-295-4691 504 C
dowens@umhb.edu
OWENS, Drake 318-357-4414 216 B
owensd@nsula.edu
OWENS, Estelle 806-291-1171 508 E
owensest@wbu.edu
OWENS, Ilona, T 336-272-7102 364 G
lowens@greensboro.edu
OWENS, Irene 919-530-6485 378 B
iowens@nccu.edu
OWENS, James 609-633-9658 316 A
jowens@tesc.edu
OWENS, James, R 859-858-3511 198 E
jim.owens@asbury.edu
OWENS, Jennifer 501-312-0007 23 D
jennifer.owens@remingtoncollege.edu
OWENS, Jeremy 800-818-2261 304 I
jowens@dwc.edu
OWENS, Jessie, A 530-754-8920 73 I
jaowens@ucdavis.edu
OWENS, Kate 570-945-8222 432 E
kate.owens@keystone.edu
OWENS, Kathleen, C 215-641-5548 430 C
owens.k@gmc.edu
OWENS, Kimberly 814-768-3430 443 B
kowens@lhup.edu
OWENS, Kimberly 610-740-3780 425 A
kowens@cedarcrest.edu
OWENS, Kristine 515-643-6659 187 F
kowens@mercydesmoines.org
OWENS, Lillian 205-853-1200 5 C
lowens@jeffstateonline.com
OWENS, O'dell 513-569-1515 387 G
odell.owens@cincinnatistate.edu
OWENS, Pamela 815-921-4503 162 H
p.owens@rockvalleycollege.edu
OWENS, Penny 816-415-5083 293 C
owensp@william.jewell.edu
OWENS, Petina 504-568-6130 213 A
powens@lsuhsc.edu
OWENS, Rick 252-493-7243 372 H
rowens@email.pittcc.edu
OWENS, Rita 617-552-4981 232 B
rita.long@bc.edu
OWENS, Robert 931-372-3392 474 B
rowens@tntech.edu
OWENS, Roger 949-451-5758 70 E
rowens@ivc.edu
OWENS, Sandra 920-339-6471 81 A
sandra.owens@aims.edu
OWENS, Sharon 404-270-5082 138 B
sowens5@spelman.edu
OWENS, Sheila 662-720-7246 276 C
sbowens@nemcc.edu
OWENS, Stephanie, R 706-233-7448 137 A
sowens@shorter.edu
OWENS, Steve 870-972-3362 20 B
sowens@asusystem.edu
OWENS, Susan 254-295-8686 504 C
sowens@umhb.edu
OWENS, Thomas 919-681-8263 364 C
thomas.owens@duke.edu
OWENS, Tiffany 606-368-6055 198 C
tiffanyowens@alc.edu
OWENS, Valerie 304-876-5465 544 C
vowens@shepherd.edu
OWENS, Victoria 502-597-5960 203 G
victoria.owens@kysu.edu
OWENS, Waylan 817-923-1921 495 G
wowens@swbts.edu
OWENS, William, R 203-329-7929 3 A
bill.owens@ecacolleges.com
OWENS, Wilma, G 760-744-1150 61 D
wowens@palomar.edu
OWENS-PELTON,
Lesley, C 315-655-7287 325 H
lcowenspelton@cazenovia.edu
OWENS-SOUTHHALL,
Mary, E 410-951-3090 228 B
mowens@coppin.edu
OWINGS, Colleen, H 916-484-8411 56 A
owingsc@arc.losrios.edu
OWL, Diane 828-835-4220 374 F
dowl@tricountycc.edu
OWSLEY, Diane 270-706-8406 202 A
diane.owsley@kctcs.edu

OWSLEY, Larry, L 502-852-5143 207 E
llowsl01@louisville.edu
OWSLEY, Laura 502-863-8007 201 A
laura_owsley@georgetowncollege.edu
OWSLEY, Stacy 520-383-8401 18 I
sowsley@tocc.cc.az.us
OWSTON, James 304-929-1356 541 H
jowston@mountainstate.edu
OWUSU-ADUEMIRI,
Kwadwo 850-412-7469 118 L
kwadwo.owusuaduemiri@famu.edu
OWUSU-ANSAH, Edward 570-422-3152 442 D
eowusu-ansah@po-box.esu.edu
OWUSU-SEKYERE,
Emmanuel 410-951-3862 228 B
manny@coppin.edu
OXENDINE, Christy 336-272-7102 364 G
christy.oxendine@greensboro.edu
OXENHANDLER, David 703-790-3200 525 B
OXENRIDER, Jack 517-607-4285 252 C
jack.oxenrider@hillsdale.edu
OXFORD-PICKERAL, Misti 352-335-2332 100 D
info@acupuncturist.edu
OXHOLM, III, Carl 215-572-2909 422 C
oxholm@arcadia.edu
OXLEY, Walter, R 614-885-5585 401 B
woxley@pcj.edu
OXMAN, Steven 602-943-2311 19 B
steven.oxman@west.edu
OXTOBY, David, W 909-621-8131 63 A
david.oxtoby@pomona.edu
OYAMA, Jannine 808-845-9116 142 B
jannine@hcc.hawaii.edu
OYEKAN, Adebayo, O 713-313-4341 500 B
oyekan_ao@tsu.edu
OYOLA, Elias 212-694-1000 324 C
eoyola@boricuacollege.edu
OZATALAY, Savas 610-499-4319 451 F
sozatalay@widener.edu
OZAYSIN, Gokhan 912-525-5808 136 F
gozaysin@scad.edu
OZECHOSKI, Mary-Alice 302-736-2443 97 A
ozechoskima@wesley.edu
OZEE, Nancy 815-802-8842 155 A
nozee@kcc.edu
OZGA, Bruce, M 305-892-7027 112 A
bruce.ozga@jwu.edu
OZMENT, Suzanne 205-665-6015 9 B
sozment@montevallo.edu
OZOLINS, Sondrea, S 317-940-9535 170 F
sozolins@butler.edu
OZOLS, Ruta 315-229-5908 349 E
rozols@stlawu.edu
OZUG, Steve 508-678-2811 239 B
steven.ozug@bristolcc.edu
OZUNA, Teofilo 956-665-3311 506 C
ozuna@utpa.edu
OZUROVICH, John 949-582-4865 70 F
jozurovich@saddleback.edu
O' DONNELL, Ricky 607-436-3573 353 E
odonnera@oneonta.edu
O'BANION, Rebecca 254-295-4603 504 C
robanion@umhb.edu
O'BANNER, Mary 305-626-3614 109 A
mary.obanner@fmuniv.edu
O'BANNER-JACKSON,
Marie 601-979-7092 274 G
marie.obanner-jackson@jsums.edu
O'BAR, Gary 210-485-0102 479 A
gobar@alamo.edu
O'BARR, Allen, H 919-966-3658 378 E
aobarr@email.unc.edu
O'BEIRNE, Kirsten 610-526-5041 423 D
kobeirne@brynmawr.edu
O'BEIRNE, OSF,
Marguerite 610-558-5511 437 D
mobeirne@neumann.edu
O'BERRY, V. Diane 803-780-1142 463 C
doberry@voorhees.edu
O'BRIEN, Alyssa 847-543-2409 148 B
aobrien@clcillinois.edu
O'BRIEN, Ann 509-452-5100 536 F
O'BRIEN, Brad, T 309-649-6294 165 F
brad.obrien@src.edu
O'BRIEN, Catherine 281-998-6150 493 G
catherine.obrien@sjcd.edu
O'BRIEN, Chris 319-398-5504 187 B
cobrien@kirkwood.edu
O'BRIEN, Colleen 386-481-2920 102 C
obrienc@cookman.edu
O'BRIEN, David, J 850-474-2626 121 D
dobrien@uwf.edu
O'BRIEN, David, M 671-735-2905 559 G
dobrien@uguam.uog.edu
O'BRIEN, Diane, E 570-408-4734 452 A
diane.obrien@wilkes.edu
O'BRIEN, Eddie 706-865-2134 138 E
eobrien@truett.edu
O'BRIEN, Eileen, M 978-542-7529 238 E
eobrien@salemstate.edu
O'BRIEN, Elizabeth 415-749-4581 65 I
eobrien@sfai.edu
O'BRIEN, Gwen 574-284-4595 179 F
gobrien@saintmarys.edu

O'BRIEN, Ian 701-349-3621 383 E
ianobrien@trinitybiblecollege.edu
O'BRIEN, Irene 973-353-5541 314 E
jobrien@andromeda.rutgers.edu
O'BRIEN, J. Patrick 806-651-2100 499 A
pobrien@mail.wtamu.edu
O'BRIEN, J. Randall 865-471-3200 467 G
robrien@cn.edu
O'BRIEN, Janet, L 912-478-5371 131 E
jlobrien@georgiasouthern.edu
O'BRIEN, Jennifer, E 610-758-4679 434 E
jeo211@lehigh.edu
O'BRIEN, Jim 480-965-9118 11 J
james.obrien@asu.edu
O'BRIEN, John 763-424-0820 268 B
jobrien@nhcc.edu
O'BRIEN, John, F 617-422-7221 243 B
O'BRIEN, Kathleen 414-382-6084 546 B
kathleen.obrien@alverno.edu
O'BRIEN, Kelly 860-297-2046 94 E
kelly.obrien@trincoll.edu
O'BRIEN, Kevin 865-573-4517 469 L
kobrien@johnsonu.edu
O'BRIEN, Margaret, A 605-256-5049 465 I
peg.o'brien@dsu.edu
O'BRIEN, Mary 707-546-4000 45 H
mobrien@empirecollege.com
O'BRIEN, Mary Eileen 845-848-7801 332 B
mary.eileen.obrien@dc.edu
O'BRIEN, Maureen 310-287-4379 55 F
obrienma@wlac.edu
O'BRIEN, Maureen 724-830-1075 447 C
obrien@setonhill.edu
O'BRIEN, Michael, E 419-530-4987 404 F
michael.obrien6@utoledo.edu
O'BRIEN, Michael, J 217-442-7232 148 G
mobrien@dacc.edu
O'BRIEN, Michael, J 573-882-4421 291 B
obrienm@missouri.edu
O'BRIEN, Michael, J 610-841-3333 441 D
mobrien@psb.edu
O'BRIEN, Paul, R 772-462-7376 111 B
pobrien@irsc.edu
O'BRIEN, Stacey 217-641-4241 154 I
obrien@jwcc.edu
O'BRIEN, Susan 256-824-6133 8 G
susan.obrien@uah.edu
O'BRIEN, Suzanne 810-989-5747 257 H
sobrien@sc4.edu
O'BRIEN, Wayne, R 434-395-2409 521 A
obrienwr@longwood.edu
O'BRIEN, William, T 724-287-8711 423 G
william.obrien@bc3.edu
O'BRIEN FRIEDERICHS,
Jane 781-239-2461 239 G
jobrienfriederichs@massbay.edu
O'BRYAN, Dan 775-831-1314 303 E
dobryan@sierranevada.edu
O'BRYANT, Theresa, M 413-662-5231 238 C
theresa.obryant@mcla.edu
O'BRYON, Laura 541-552-8106 419 A
obryon@sou.edu
O'CALLAGHAN, Cecelia 608-771-2201 308 F
ocallagh@tcnj.edu
O'CALLAGHAN, Cindy 617-735-9779 234 C
ocallac@emmanuel.edu
O'CALLAGHAN, Karen 516-463-6605 335 G
karen.ocallaghan@hofstra.edu
O'CALLAGHAN, Scott 802-447-6359 514 F
socall@svc.edu
O'CARROLL, Theresa 708-974-5248 159 B
ocarroll@morainevalley.edu
O'CINNSEALAIGH,
Benedict 513-231-2223 384 H
bocinnsealaigh@athenaeum.edu
O'CONNELL, Catharine 540-887-7030 521 C
coconnell@mbc.edu
O'CONNELL, Colleen 215-884-8942 452 D
planning@woninstitute.edu
O'CONNELL, Daniel 978-867-4246 235 A
daniel.oconnell@gordon.edu
O'CONNELL, Danny, J 330-941-3549 406 F
djoconnell@ysu.edu
O'CONNELL, David, J 563-333-6092 188 F
oconnelldavidj@sau.edu
O'CONNELL, Erin, E 206-281-2175 537 H
ocone@spu.edu
O'CONNELL, Heather, A 302-356-6814 97 C
heather.a.oconnell@wilmu.edu
O'CONNELL, John 260-481-6977 174 C
oconnelj@ipfw.edu
O'CONNELL, Margaret, M 315-498-2211 345 D
president@sunyocc.edu
O'CONNELL, Mark 269-965-3931 253 B
oconnellm@kellogg.edu
O'CONNELL, Melissa, E 386-312-4232 116 F
melissaoconnell@sjrstate.edu
O'CONNELL, Robert, G 617-333-2050 233 F
boconnel@curry.edu
O'CONNELL, Ryan 617-369-3617 244 E
roconnell@smfa.edu
O'CONNELL, Sean 203-773-8068 90 C
soconnell@albertus.edu
O'CONNER, Terrence 305-628-6516 117 A
toconner@stu.edu

O'CONNOR, Barbara .... 860-486-4806..... 94 G
barbara.o'connor@uconn.edu
O'CONNOR, OSFS,
Bernard, F .... 610-282-1100..... 427 A
boconnor@desales.edu
O'CONNOR, Bill .... 425-564-5454..... 531 G
bill.oconnor@bellevuecollege.edu
O'CONNOR, Brian .... 406-994-3211..... 295 C
boconnor@montana.edu
O'CONNOR, Charles, D ..... 402-472-9339.... 300 G
O'CONNOR, Christi .... 323-953-4000..... 54 H
oconnoca@lacitycollege.edu
O'CONNOR,
Christopher, K .... 617-254-2610..... 244 B
O'CONNOR, Claudia .... 703-284-6901..... 521 D
claudia.oconnor@marymount.edu
O'CONNOR, Colleen, M .... 973-720-2125..... 317 D
oconnorc1@wpunj.edu
O'CONNOR, Daniel .... 661-395-4231..... 52 L
doconnor@bakersfieldcollege.edu
O'CONNOR, Deirdre, M ..... 570-577-3141..... 423 E
deirdre.oconnor@bucknell.edu
O'CONNOR, Diane .... 215-641-6416..... 436 G
doconnor@mc3.edu
O'CONNOR, Edward, R ..... 203-582-5202..... 93 H
edward.oconnor@quinnipiac.edu
O'CONNOR, Ellen .... 617-287-5100..... 236 G
ellen.oconnor@umb.edu
O'CONNOR, Ellen, M .... 215-955-6835..... 448 C
ellen.oconnor@jefferson.edu
O'CONNOR, James .... 212-229-5300..... 342 E
oconnorj@newschool.edu
O'CONNOR, James .... 319-273-2761..... 182 G
james.oconnor@uni.edu
O'CONNOR, James .... 404-894-9044..... 130 F
james.oconnor@oit.gatech.edu
O'CONNOR, Jeremiah .... 508-793-2564..... 233 C
joconnor@holycross.edu
O'CONNOR, Jim .... 707-638-5997..... 73 A
jim.oconnor@tu.edu
O'CONNOR, Jody .... 415-575-6153..... 32 G
joconnor@ciis.edu
O'CONNOR, John .... 214-768-2011..... 495 A
joconnor@smu.edu
O'CONNOR, Joseph .... 607-778-5379..... 324 G
oconnorjt@sunybroome.edu
O'CONNOR, Joyce, E .... 773-371-5408..... 146 E
joyceoco@ctu.edu
O'CONNOR, Kathleen .... 617-243-2199..... 236 A
koconner@lasell.edu
O'CONNOR, Kathleen .... 608-663-6715..... 547 F
koconnor@edgewood.edu
O'CONNOR, Kevin .... 949-582-4788..... 70 F
koconnor@saddleback.edu
O'CONNOR, Kevin, J .... 559-456-2777..... 27 B
koconnor@alliant.edu
O'CONNOR, Marcia .... 423-473-2390..... 474 E
moconnor@clevelandstatecc.edu
O'CONNOR, Margaret .... 314-454-7557..... 282 B
maoconnor@bjc.org
O'CONNOR, Margaret, J .... 770-720-5921..... 136 C
poc@reinhardt.edu
O'CONNOR, Mark, F .... 617-552-3315..... 232 B
mark.oconnor@bc.edu
O'CONNOR, Martin .... 570-348-6211..... 435 F
oconnor@marywood.edu
O'CONNOR, Mary .... 480-731-8403..... 15 D
mary.oconnor@domail.maricopa.edu
O'CONNOR, Matthew, L ..... 203-582-8297..... 93 H
matthew.oconnor@quinnipiac.edu
O'CONNOR, Melissa .... 612-659-6097..... 267 B
melissa.oconnor@minneapolis.edu
O'CONNOR, Michael .... 815-802-8908..... 155 A
moconnor@kcc.edu
O'CONNOR, Mike, J .... 828-262-3190..... 377 D
oconnormj@appstate.edu
O'CONNOR, Patricia .... 714-459-1175..... 78 H
poconnor@wsulaw.edu
O'CONNOR, Patricia, G ..... 619-275-4700..... 46 K
patoatfcc@aol.com
O'CONNOR, Patrick .... 708-974-5555..... 159 B
oconnorp@morainevalley.edu
O'CONNOR, Robert .... 315-781-3535..... 335 F
oconnor@hws.edu
O'CONNOR, Sheila .... 402-457-2733..... 298 G
soconnor7@mccneb.edu
O'CONNOR, Thomas, J ...... 703-993-3256..... 519 E
toconno2@gmu.edu
O'CONNOR, William, R ...... 386-822-7500..... 121 F
woconnor@stetson.edu
O'CONNOR-BENSON, Pat 239-597-7101..... 119 B
poconnor@fgcu.edu
O'CONNOR-GOMEZ,
Doreen .... 562-907-4352..... 79 F
doconnor@whittier.edu
O'CONNOR-JOHNSTON,
Elizabeth .... 508-362-2131..... 239 D
eoconnorjohnston@capecod.edu
O'DANIEL, Carolyn .... 502-213-5333..... 202 F
O'DANIEL, Rosemary .... 309-341-5456..... 146 D
rodaniel@sandburg.edu
O'DAY, Gail, R .... 336-758-4315..... 380 C
odaygr@wfu.edu
O'DAY, Steven, P .... 717-291-3989..... 429 F
steven.oday@fandm.edu

O'DELL, Carol, S .... 912-583-3125..... 126 F
codell@bpc.edu
O'DELL, Cynthia .... 219-980-6509..... 174 B
codell@iun.edu
O'DELL, Jacqueline .... 417-781-5633..... 292 B
jacqueline.odell@vatterott.edu
O'DELL, James .... 617-912-9166..... 232 C
jodell@bostonconservatory.edu
O'DELL, Tim .... 843-661-8300..... 458 B
tim.odell@fdtc.edu
O'DELL MAINOUS,
Rosalie .... 937-775-3133..... 406 C
rosalie.mainous@wright.edu
O'DESKY, Ryan .... 608-249-6611..... 547 G
O'DONLEY, Rudy .... 918-465-1802..... 408 A
rodonley@eosc.edu
O'DONNELL, Anne .... 215-893-5272..... 426 E
anne.odonnell@curtis.edu
O'DONNELL, Bill .... 217-228-5432..... 161 F
odonnbi@quincy.edu
O'DONNELL, Bill, J .... 574-520-4218..... 174 E
odonnell@iusb.edu
O'DONNELL, Brennan .... 718-862-7301..... 339 H
brennan.odonnell@manhattan.edu
O'DONNELL, Eileen .... 617-327-6777..... 241 F
eileen_healy@mspp.edu
O'DONNELL, OP, Gabriel . 202-495-3832..... 99 C
dean@dhs.edu
O'DONNELL, James .... 402-375-7394..... 299 G
jaodonn1@wsc.edu
O'DONNELL, John .... 781-239-3101..... 239 G
jodonnell@massbay.edu
O'DONNELL, Karen .... 813-880-8011..... 111 C
kodonnell@academy.edu
O'DONNELL, Kevin .... 802-225-3356..... 514 B
kevin.odonnell@neci.edu
O'DONNELL, Lauren .... 814-641-3322..... 432 A
odonnel@juniata.edu
O'DONNELL, Matthew .... 206-543-1829..... 539 A
odonnel@uw.edu
O'DONNELL, Michael .... 512-499-4601..... 505 B
modonnell@utsystem.edu
O'DONNELL, Michael .... 520-319-3300..... 12 J
miodonnell@brownmackie.edu
O'DONNELL, Michael .... 262-741-8538..... 554 B
odonnellm@gtc.edu
O'DONNELL, SSJ, Patricia 215-248-7125..... 425 D
podonnel@chc.edu
O'DONNELL, Patrick .... 562-860-2451..... 39 A
podonnell@cerritos.edu
O'DONNELL, Ralph .... 660-944-2920..... 280 B
rodonnell@conception.edu
O'DONNELL, Timothy, T ... 540-636-2900..... 517 K
president@christendom.edu
O'DONOGHUE,
Patricia, P .... 312-362-8760..... 149 A
podonog1@depaul.edu
O'DONOVAN, Stephen .... 254-526-1934..... 482 H
stephen.o'donovan@ctcd.edu
O'DOWD, Kathleen .... 734-432-5300..... 254 D
kodowd@madonna.edu
O'DRISCOLL, Brian .... 503-352-2917..... 419 E
odriscob@pacificu.edu
O'DRISCOLL, Daniel .... 508-541-1641..... 233 G
dodriscoll@dean.edu
O'DRISCOLL, Dean .... 435-865-8054..... 511 D
odriscoll@suu.edu
O'DRISCOLL, Sue .... 540-545-7399..... 524 E
sodrisco09@su.edu
O'DWYER, Anne .... 413-528-7240..... 230 F
aodwyer@simons-rock.edu
O'DWYER, Timothy .... 503-768-7860..... 416 G
odwyer@lclark.edu
O'FARRELL, Kevin, D .... 727-376-6911..... 122 E
kofarrell@trinitycollege.edu
O'FARRELL, Mark, T .... 727-376-6911..... 122 E
mofarrell@trinitycollege.edu
O'FLAHERTY, Kevin .... 215-646-7300..... 430 C
oflaherty.k@gmc.edu
O'FLANNERY ANDERSON,
Jennifer .... 561-297-3015..... 119 A
joflanne@fau.edu
O'GORMAN, Deb .... 775-829-9000..... 302 H
dogorman@tmcc.edu
O'GORMAN, Jane .... 706-864-1918..... 134 G
jogorman@northgeorgia.edu
O'GORMAN, Ryan .... 845-848-7600..... 332 B
ryan.ogorman@dc.edu
O'GRADY, Elaine .... 845-569-3508..... 342 A
elaine.ogrady@msmc.edu
O'GRADY EISENMANN,
Sharon .... 610-660-1290..... 446 C
seisenma@sju.edu
O'GUIN, Julie .... 615-232-7384..... 469 F
joguin@iadtnashville.com
O'GUYNN, Valarie .... 310-900-1600..... 45 F
oguynn_v@elcamino.edu
O'HAGAN, Jill .... 860-412-7311..... 92 D
johagan@qvcc.commnet.edu
O'HAGAN, Patricia .... 808-734-9569..... 141 J
ohaganp@hawaii.edu
O'HAIR, Dan .... 859-257-7805..... 207 D
ohair@uky.edu
O'HAIR, Mary, J .... 859-257-2813..... 207 D
mjohair@uky.edu

O'HALLA, Kevin .... 616-234-3638..... 251 E
kohalla@grcc.edu
O'HALLORAN, Teresa .... 715-836-2387..... 551 A
ohallote@uwec.edu
O'HANIAN, Hunter .... 617-879-7045..... 238 B
hohanian@massart.edu
O'HANLON, James, P .... 402-472-3041..... 300 G
johanlon1@unl.edu
O'HARA, Christine, S .... 716-286-8776..... 344 D
cso@niagara.edu
O'HARA, Colleen .... 773-298-3780..... 163 I
ohara@sxu.edu
O'HARA, Edward .... 203-837-9109..... 91 A
oharae@wcsu.edu
O'HARA, James, P .... 609-896-5367..... 313 F
johara@rider.edu
O'HARA, Marcy .... 805-565-6114..... 79 A
mohara@westmont.edu
O'HARA, Noreen .... 914-323-5165..... 339 J
noreen.ohara@mville.edu
O'HARA, Patrick .... 715-732-3888..... 555 C
patrick.ohara@nwtc.edu
O'HARA, Sabine .... 202-274-7174..... 100 A
sabine.ohara@udc.edu
O'HARA, William, T .... 401-232-6477..... 453 C
wohara@bryant.edu
O'HARE, Katie .... 617-323-6662..... 241 F
katie_ohare@mspp.edu
O'HARE, Lyn .... 828-771-3012..... 380 D
lohare@warren-wilson.edu
O'HARE, Susan .... 610-861-1588..... 437 A
mesio01@moravian.edu
O'HEARN, Christopher .... 760-245-4271..... 77 H
christopher.o'hearn@vvc.edu
O'HERN, Susan .... 518-465-8500..... 333 E
sohern@excelsior.edu
O'HERRON, Virginia, S ..... 757-683-4141..... 522 F
voherron@odu.edu
O'KANE, Gail .... 612-659-6299..... 267 B
gail.okane@minneapolis.edu
O'KARMA, Theodore .... 818-345-8414..... 42 F
tokarma@columbiacollege.edu
O'KEEFE, Barbara, J .... 847-491-7023..... 160 E
b-okeefe@northwestern.edu
O'KEEFE, Louise .... 256-824-2445..... 8 G
louise.okeefe@uah.edu
O'KEEFE, Martha .... 540-891-3094..... 526 I
mokeefe@germanna.edu
O'KEEFE, Mildred .... 516-876-3247..... 353 D
okeefem@oldwestbury.edu
O'KEEFE, Paterick .... 716-829-7753..... 332 E
O'KEEFE, Paul .... 508-830-5063..... 238 D
pokeefe@maritime.edu
O'KEEFE, Paul .... 781-736-2120..... 232 F
pokeefe@brandeis.edu
O'KEEFE, Steve .... 618-985-3741..... 154 G
steveokeefe@jalc.edu
O'KEEFE, Susan .... 732-571-3521..... 311 E
okeefe@monmouth.edu
O'KEEFE, Tim .... 701-777-2611..... 381 F
timo@undfoundation.org
O'KEEFFE, Mary Ellen .... 206-934-3701..... 537 D
maryellen.okeeffe@seattlecolleges.edu
O'KEEFFE, Michael .... 727-341-3352..... 116 H
okeeffe.mike@spcollege.edu
O'KEEFFE, Phillip, D .... 765-494-0226..... 178 J
pokeeffe@purdue.edu
O'KELLY, Keiren .... 773-371-5442..... 146 E
kokelly@ctu.edu
O'KIEF, Kristy .... 605-995-2656..... 464 C
krokief@dwu.edu
O'KIEF, Mary .... 541-245-7596..... 420 B
mokief@roguecc.edu
O'LARE, Russell, D .... 412-268-1001..... 424 J
rdo@andrew.cmu.edu
O'LAUGHLIN, Jeanne .... 305-899-3010..... 101 M
jolaughlin@mail.barry.edu
O'LEARY, Allison .... 203-575-8276..... 92 A
aoleary@nvcc.commnet.edu
O'LEARY, David .... 610-361-2330..... 437 D
olearyd@neumann.edu
O'LEARY, Eileen, K .... 508-565-1347..... 245 A
eoleary@stonehill.edu
O'LEARY, Hazel, R .... 615-329-8555..... 468 I
srucker@fisk.edu
O'LEARY, Kara .... 574-284-4578..... 179 F
koleary@saintmarys.edu
O'LEARY, Michael .... 410-337-6501..... 222 I
michael.oleary@goucher.edu
O'LEARY, Mick .... 301-846-2585..... 222 G
moleary@frederick.edu
O'LEARY, Nicole .... 617-349-8888..... 236 B
noleary@lesley.edu
O'LEARY, Rita .... 610-647-4400..... 431 C
roleary@immaculata.edu
O'LEARY-ARCHER, Lynn ... 909-447-2565..... 40 H
olearyarcher@cst.edu
O'LINGER, Jennifer .... 256-551-3125..... 4 J
jennifer.o'linger@drakestate.edu
O'MALEY-LAMSON, Patty . 765-983-1424..... 171 E
pattyo@earlham.edu
O'MALLEY, Deborah, A ...... 617-879-5097..... 241 C
deborah.omalley@mcphs.edu

O'MALLEY, Mary .... 908-526-1200..... 313 D
momalley@raritanval.edu
O'MALLEY, Michelle .... 603-577-6583..... 304 I
omalley@dwc.edu
O'MALLEY, Richard .... 979-830-4054..... 482 C
richard.omalley@blinn.edu
O'MALLEY, Timothy, L .... 619-260-4770..... 76 D
tomalley@sandiego.edu
O'MARA, Charles, A .... 845-451-1285..... 331 E
c_omara@culinary.edu
O'MEARA, George .... 617-266-1400..... 231 E
O'MEARA, Kathy .... 802-468-1292..... 515 D
kathy.omeara@castleton.edu
O'MEARA, Ron .... 229-333-2111..... 139 I
ron.omeara@wiregrass.edu
O'MUIRCHEARTAIGH,
Colm .... 773-702-9693..... 166 G
colm@uchicago.edu
O'NEAL, Alan .... 773-821-2897..... 146 G
aoneal@csu.edu
O'NEAL, Bruce .... 936-294-1833..... 501 D
boneal@shsu.edu
O'NEAL, Christian .... 501-683-7208..... 24 E
cjoneal@ualr.edu
O'NEAL, Dennis .... 254-710-3871..... 482 A
dennis_oneal@baylor.edu
O'NEAL, Ginger, H .... 252-335-0821..... 369 G
goneal@albemarle.edu
O'NEAL, Michelle .... 856-351-2649..... 315 A
moneal@salemcc.edu
O'NEAL, Stephanie .... 404-760-1402..... 128 F
soneal@keller.edu
O'NEAL, Tom .... 407-882-1120..... 120 B
oneal@ucf.edu
O'NEAL MOSLEY, Toni ...... 404-215-2680..... 134 D
tmosley@morehouse.edu
O'NEIL, Alicia, M .... 202-994-2371..... 98 C
oneila@gwu.edu
O'NEIL, Christine .... 906-487-7328..... 251 A
christine.oneil@finlandia.edu
O'NEIL, Joyce .... 406-496-3730..... 296 A
joneil@mtech.edu
O'NEIL, Laura, L .... 607-777-2131..... 351 F
loneil@binghamton.edu
O'NEIL, Lisa .... 406-265-3748..... 295 E
loneil@msun.edu
O'NEIL, Michael .... 617-732-2885..... 241 C
michael.oneil@mcphs.edu
O'NEIL, Patricia, A .... 413-585-2550..... 244 G
toneil@smith.edu
O'NEIL, Tabitha .... 773-602-5125..... 147 E
toneil@ccc.edu
O'NEIL, Thomas, E .... 585-385-8013..... 348 F
toneil@sjfc.edu
O'NEIL, Tom .... 661-722-6300..... 28 K
loneil@avc.edu
O'NEIL-GARRETT, Mary ..... 360-417-6225..... 536 G
mogarrett@pencol.edu
O'NEILL, Bettyann .... 706-236-2261..... 126 C
boneill@berry.edu
O'NEILL, Dale, A .... 919-209-2106..... 371 F
daoneill@johnstoncc.edu
O'NEILL, Daniel .... 978-762-4000..... 240 D
daoneill@northshore.edu
O'NEILL, David .... 518-587-2100..... 355 G
david.o'neill@esc.edu
O'NEILL, Denise .... 609-652-4332..... 313 E
denise.oneill@stockton.edu
O'NEILL, Gerry, J .... 252-246-1337..... 375 D
goneill@wilsoncc.edu
O'NEILL, Jerry, F .... 412-731-8690..... 445 F
joneill@rpts.edu
O'NEILL, Jim .... 423-493-4224..... 476 E
oneillj@tntemple.edu
O'NEILL, Kate .... 575-737-6200..... 321 F
koneill@unm.edu
O'NEILL, Meggan .... 201-559-6018..... 310 B
oneillm@felician.edu
O'NEILL, Michael .... 610-519-7926..... 450 H
mike.oneill@villanova.edu
O'NEILL, Mollie .... 919-668-6330..... 364 C
molly.oneill@duke.edu
O'NEILL, Patrick .... 303-404-5400..... 85 A
patrick.o'neill@frontrange.edu
O'NEILL, Priscilla .... 262-595-2233..... 552 A
oneillp@uwp.edu
O'NEILL, Russ .... 330-966-5455..... 402 B
roneill@starkstate.edu
O'NEILL, Shannon .... 518-782-5830..... 350 I
soneill@siena.edu
O'NEILL, Shawn .... 201-216-8143..... 315 E
shawn.oneill@stevens.edu
O'NEILL, Stephen .... 507-786-3062..... 271 C
oneill@stolaf.edu
O'NEILL, Thomas .... 315-228-7418..... 329 G
toneill@colgate.edu
O'NEILL, Walter J, H .... 312-341-2090..... 163 B
woneill@roosevelt.edu
O'NEILL, William .... 402-559-1952..... 300 H
woneill@unmc.edu
O'NEILL, William, J .... 617-573-8300..... 245 B
woneill@suffolk.edu
O'NIELL, Claudia .... 720-890-8922..... 85 F
registrar@itea.edu

P

PAIKOWSKI, Gary .... 903-463-8707.... 487 C
paikowski@grayson.edu
PAINE, Clarke, C .... 717-291-3991.... 429 F
clarke.paine@fandm.edu
PAINE, Gage .... 512-471-1133.... 505 D
gage.paine@austin.utexas.edu
PAINE, James .... 636-227-2100.... 284 B
james.paine@logan.edu
PAINE, Paula .... 785-242-5200.... 196 A
PAINE, Paula .... 785-242-5200.... 195 I
paula.paine@ottawa.edu
PAINE, Paula .... 785-242-5200.... 17 B
PAINE, Paula .... 785-242-5200.... 178 I
PAINE, Paula .... 785-242-5200.... 549 H
PAINO, Troy, D .... 660-785-4100.... 290 G
tpaino@truman.edu
PAIR-CUNNINGHAM,
Stephanie, S .... 301-322-0649.... 225 F
pairss@pgcc.edu
PAISANT, Julie .... 408-924-2250...... 37 C
julie.paisant@sjsu.edu
PAIZ, Larry, P .... 214-350-9722.... 484 A
larry.paiz@cri.edu
PAJAK, Daniel, T .... 304-829-7217.... 540 H
dpajak@bethanywv.edu
PAJE-MANALO, Leila, L .... 603-862-3491.... 306 C
leila.paje-manalo@unh.edu
PAJEROWSKI, Patrick .... 973-684-5329.... 312 E
PAJIC, Natasa .... 859-233-8213.... 207 A
npajic@transy.edu
PAK, Scott .... 714-816-0366...... 73 B
scott.pak@trident.edu
PAKALA, James, C .... 314-434-4044.... 280 F
jim.pakala@covenantseminary.edu
PAKHMANOV, Laura .... 732-729-3837.... 309 C
lpakhmanov@devry.edu
PAKOWSKI, Lawrence .... 910-755-7324.... 368 F
pakowskil@brunswickcc.edu
PAKSTIS, John .... 978-934-4331.... 237 B
john_pakstis@uml.edu
PALACIO, Michelle .... 305-348-1757.... 119 C
michelle.palacio@fiu.edu
PALACIOS, Elizabeth .... 254-710-3653.... 482 A
liz_palacios@baylor.edu
PALACIOS, Luz, M .... 787-786-3030.... 560 G
lpalacios@ucb.edu.pr
PALAGONIA, Michael .... 802-635-1205.... 515 F
michael.palagonia@jsc.edu
PALAMIOTIS, Nikki .... 678-915-4276.... 137 G
npalamio@spsu.edu
PALAMOUNTAIN, Valerie .. 434-961-5333.... 528 B
vpalamountain@pvcc.edu
PALAN, Kay .... 269-387-5050.... 260 C
kay.palan@wmich.edu
PALANCIA SHIPP, Jen ...... 410-677-3160.... 228 D
jpalanciashipp@salisbury.edu
PALANGI, Anthony .... 518-743-2246.... 355 D
palangia@sunyacc.edu
PALANTZAS, Nicholas .... 781-821-2222.... 240 A
PALARDY, William, B .... 781-899-5500.... 231 F
rev.palardy@blessedjohnxxiii.edu
PALASOTA, Joanna, E .... 713-525-3151.... 505 A
palasota@stthom.edu
PALASOTA, John .... 713-525-6918.... 505 A
japalaso@stthom.edu
PALATELLA, Anna Marie .... 724-925-4091.... 451 E
palatellaa@wccc.edu
PALAZOLA, Cecelia .... 901-272-5142.... 471 D
cpalazola@mca.edu
PALCZEWSKI, Christine ..... 716-896-0700.... 359 H
cepalcz@villa.edu
PALCZEWSKI, Christine, E 716-896-0700.... 359 H
cepalcz@villa.edu
PALEFSKY, Lou .... 212-875-4679.... 323 C
finaid@bankstreet.edu
PALEN, Lisa .... 203-575-8100...... 92 A
lpalen@nvcc.commnet.edu
PALERMO, Lisa .... 651-730-5100.... 263 G
lpalermo@globeuniversity.edu
PALERMO, Marty .... 561-586-0121.... 110 I
PALERMO, Pam .... 231-995-1533.... 256 D
ppalermo@nmc.edu
PALERMO, Pamela, J .... 440-964-4274.... 393 E
ppalermo@kent.edu
PALERMO, Tina .... 561-586-0121.... 110 I
PALESE, Rick .... 312-225-6288.... 167 G
rpalese@vandercook.edu
PALEY, Noelle .... 607-753-2336.... 353 B
noelle.paley@cortland.edu
PALIK, Pelma .... 691-320-2481.... 559 D
pelmap@comfsm.fm
PALINKAS, Robert, D .... 217-333-2711.... 167 D
palinkas@illinois.edu
PALINSKY, David, W .... 661-336-5147...... 52 K
dpalinsk@kccd.edu
PALK, Laura .... 405-325-4124.... 413 C
lpalk@ou.edu
PALLA, Joe .... 707-527-1000...... 68 E
jpalla@santarosa.edu
PALLADINO, Mark .... 215-951-2700.... 444 D
palladinom@philau.edu
PALLADINO, Michael .... 732-571-3421.... 311 E
mpalladi@monmouth.edu
PALLADINO, Michael .... 212-752-1530.... 338 C
michael.palladino@limcollege.edu
PALLADINO, Michael, A .... 215-898-9386.... 448 J
mikep@isc.upenn.edu
PALLADINO, Richard .... 914-633-2351.... 336 E
rpalladino@iona.edu
PALLADINO, Robert .... 740-283-6405.... 391 A
rpalladino@franciscan.edu
PALLAVICINI, Maria, G .... 209-946-2551...... 76 A
mpallavicini@pacific.edu
PALLEJA, Sandra .... 212-237-8873.... 327 F
spalleja@jjay.cuny.edu
PALLONE, Donna, L .... 724-287-8711.... 423 G
donna.pallone@bc3.edu
PALM, Don .... 530-747-5220...... 56 D
palmd@scc.losrios.edu
PALM, Elizabeth, A .... 847-735-5107.... 155 G
palm@lakeforest.edu
PALM, Matt .... 419-448-2020.... 391 F
mpalm@heidelberg.edu
PALM, Risa, I .... 404-413-2574.... 131 G
risapalm@gsu.edu
PALM, Ryan .... 814-824-3320.... 436 C
rpalm@mercyhurst.edu
PALMA, Eugene .... 516-877-3505.... 322 A
palma@adelphi.edu
PALMA, Yazmin .... 305-273-4499.... 103 J
yazmin@cbt.edu
PALMATIER, Bob .... 205-940-7806........ 3 I
bpalmatier@edaff.com
PALMER, April, A .... 843-383-8214.... 457 A
apalmer@coker.edu
PALMER, Betty, G .... 404-627-2681.... 126 D
betty.palmer@beulah.org
PALMER, Bobbi .... 859-282-8989.... 132 F
bpalmer@ict-ils.edu
PALMER, Brian .... 904-256-7374.... 111 L
bpalmer@ju.edu
PALMER, Bruce, H .... 508-999-8634.... 237 A
bpalmer@umassd.edu
PALMER, C. Eddie .... 337-482-6965.... 216 D
palmer@louisiana.edu
PALMER, C. Patrick .... 517-264-7606.... 258 B
ppalmer@sienaheights.edu
PALMER, Charles .... 813-545-4527.... 458 C
charlespalmer@forrrestcollege.edu
PALMER, Colleen .... 617-585-1295.... 242 I
colleen.palmer@necmusic.edu
PALMER, Dale, J .... 404-413-3434.... 131 G
dpalmer@gsu.edu
PALMER, Daniel .... 605-773-3455.... 465 F
daniel.palmer2@sdbor.edu
PALMER, Daniel, E .... 330-675-8823.... 393 J
dpalmer1@kent.edu
PALMER, David .... 901-321-4321.... 467 I
david.palmer@cbu.edu
PALMER, Donald, F .... 330-672-2312.... 393 D
dpalmer@kent.edu
PALMER, Doreen, E .... 603-641-4164.... 306 D
doreen.palmer@unh.edu
PALMER, Douglas, J .... 979-862-6649.... 497 E
dpalmer@tamu.edu
PALMER, Eric .... 810-766-4237.... 247 G
ericpalmer@baker.edu
PALMER, Eric .... 810-766-4238.... 248 C
eric.palmer@baker.edu
PALMER, Eric, F .... 804-287-6591.... 525 E
epalmer@richmond.edu
PALMER, Gail .... 785-670-1151.... 197 F
gail.palmer@washburn.edu
PALMER, Gary .... 620-223-2700.... 193 A
garyp@fortscott.edu
PALMER, Gregory .... 914-323-5194.... 339 J
greg.palmer@mville.edu
PALMER, Harvey, J .... 585-475-2146.... 347 G
hjpeen@rit.edu
PALMER, Jack .... 318-342-1345.... 216 E
palmer@ulm.edu
PALMER, Jacqueline .... 202-408-2400...... 99 G
PALMER, Jan, E .... 304-293-6978.... 545 A
jpalmer@hsc.wvu.edu
PALMER, Janice .... 860-832-1791...... 90 G
palmerj@ccsu.edu
PALMER, Jed .... 907-834-1662...... 11 B
jbpalmer@pwscc.edu
PALMER, Jeffrey, L .... 302-831-3007...... 96 I
jpalmer@udel.edu
PALMER, Jim .... 325-574-7905.... 508 I
jpalmer@wtc.edu
PALMER, John .... 651-846-1482.... 269 C
john.palmer@saintpaul.edu
PALMER, John .... 320-308-3143.... 269 A
jwpalmer@stcloudstate.edu
PALMER, Jonathan .... 618-374-5148.... 161 E
president@principia.edu
PALMER, Joseph .... 315-792-5318.... 341 E
jpalmer@mvcc.edu
PALMER, Joy Jimena, J ..... 626-448-0023...... 51 G
academicdean@itsla.edu
PALMER, Joyce .... 315-792-5477.... 341 E
jpalmer@mvcc.edu
PALMER, Julio .... 787-841-2000.... 565 B
jpalmer@pucpr.edu
PALMER, Kevin .... 573-875-7329.... 280 A
kpalmer@ccis.edu
PALMER, Kris, R .... 660-284-4800.... 282 G
PALMER, Linda .... 801-422-3605.... 509 H
linda_palmer@byu.edu
PALMER, Lisa .... 706-771-4089.... 125 H
lpalmer@augustatech.edu
PALMER, Lisa .... 918-595-7831.... 412 H
lpalmer@tulsacc.edu
PALMER, Magali .... 787-279-1912.... 563 D
mpalmer@bayamon.inter.edu
PALMER, Marila, D .... 903-935-7963.... 486 F
mpalmer@etbu.edu
PALMER, Martha .... 660-284-4800.... 282 G
PALMER, Mel .... 706-548-8505.... 136 A
mpalmer@piedmont.edu
PALMER, Michael, D .... 757-352-4406.... 523 E
mpalmer@regent.edu
PALMER, Nikki .... 907-822-3201...... 10 B
info@akbible.edu
PALMER, Patricia .... 501-812-2210...... 23 C
ppalmer@pulaskitech.edu
PALMER, Rick .... 435-879-4287.... 512 B
palmer@dixie.edu
PALMER, Ron .... 304-637-1252.... 541 A
palmerr@dewv.edu
PALMER, Roxanne .... 772-466-4822.... 101 J
roxanne.palmer@aviator.edu
PALMER, Russell, A .... 516-877-3249.... 322 A
palmer@adelphi.edu
PALMER, Sallie .... 702-369-9944.... 301 F
spalmer@aii.edu
PALMER, Sandra .... 203-575-8046...... 92 A
spalmer@nvcc.commnet.edu
PALMER, Scott .... 952-888-4777.... 270 C
spalmer@nwhealth.edu
PALMER, Scott .... 541-684-7291.... 417 F
spalmer@nwcu.edu
PALMER, Susan, M .... 320-363-5298.... 262 F
spalmer@csbsju.edu
PALMER, Tom .... 706-864-1818.... 134 G
tpalmer@northgeorgia.edu
PALMER, Tom .... 706-864-1786.... 134 G
tpalmer@northgeorgia.edu
PALMER NOONE, Laura ... 202-686-0876...... 99 E
PALMER NOONE, Laura ... 703-709-5875.... 522 H
PALMERI, Marian, K .... 570-208-5900.... 432 G
mkpalmer@kings.edu
PALMIERI, Becky .... 518-587-2100.... 355 G
becky.palmieri@esc.edu
PALMIERI, Ernie .... 914-251-5985.... 354 D
ernie.palmieri@purchase.edu
PALMIERI, Ernie .... 914-251-6530.... 354 D
ernie.palmieri@purchase.edu
PALMIERI, Mark .... 315-279-5418.... 337 K
mpalmier@mail.keuka.edu
PALMIERI, Robert .... 315-866-0300.... 335 D
palmierrh@herkimer.edu
PALMIERI-MOUDED,
Kimberly, J .... 718-390-4345.... 348 G
palmierk@stjohns.edu
PALMINI, Bill .... 415-565-4611...... 74 A
palminib@uchastings.edu
PALMITER, Lia Richards .... 570-961-4799.... 435 F
lpalmiter@marywood.edu
PALMORE, Marcus .... 703-709-5875.... 522 H
mpalmore@potomac.edu
PALMOUR, Mack .... 678-717-3861.... 129 G
mpalmour@gsc.edu
PALO, Eric, E .... 425-235-2331.... 537 A
epalo@rtc.edu
PALOK, Debra .... 623-845-3536...... 15 H
debra.palok@gcmail.maricopa.edu
PALOMARIA, Sam .... 903-233-4171.... 490 A
sampalomaria@letu.edu
PALOMBI,
Peggy Shaddock .... 205-391-5830........ 6 I
pspalombi@sheltonstate.edu
PALOMBO, Tom, J .... 336-316-2290.... 365 A
tpalombo@guilford.edu
PALOMO, Giovanni .... 212-226-5500.... 323 A
gpalomo@aii.edu
PALOMO, William .... 671-735-2365.... 559 G
safety@uguam.uog.edu
PALONE, James, E .... 330-471-8255.... 395 F
jpalone@malone.edu
PALONSKY, Stuart, B .... 573-882-3893.... 291 B
palonskys@missouri.edu
PALOS, Jim .... 773-481-8175.... 147 I
jpalos4@ccc.edu
PALOV, Susan, K .... 814-269-2090.... 449 D
palov@pitt.edu
PALSA, Megan .... 972-860-8142.... 484 H
mpalsa@dcccd.edu
PALSAK, Angela .... 269-782-1310.... 258 C
apalsak@swmich.edu
PALSER, Philip, V .... 715-833-6364.... 553 H
ppalser@cvtc.edu
PALTER-GILL, Dianne .... 978-762-4000.... 240 D
dpalterg@northshore.edu
PALTY, Michelle .... 888-974-3436...... 46 M
mpalty@fidm.edu
PALUBNIAK, Dan .... 908-526-1200.... 313 D
dpalubu@raritanval.edu
PALUMBO, Andrew .... 518-292-1926.... 348 A
paluma@sage.edu
PALUMBO, Daniel .... 212-237-8299.... 327 F
dpalumbo@jjay.cuny.edu
PALUMBO, Katey .... 508-929-8835.... 238 G
kpalumbo2@worcester.edu
PALUMBO, Samuel, P .... 716-270-4608.... 333 C
palumbo@ecc.edu
PALZER, Jon, A .... 585-785-1224.... 334 A
palzerja@flcc.edu
PAMERLEAU, Gayle .... 724-836-9870.... 449 C
gaylep@pitt.edu
PAMINTUAN, Lisa .... 516-364-0808.... 343 A
pamintuan@nycollege.edu
PAN, Judy .... 847-679-3135.... 155 E
judy@ksi.edu
PAN, Shouan .... 480-461-7300...... 15 I
shouan.pan@mcmail.maricopa.edu
PANAIA, Sharon .... 724-335-5336.... 438 A
spanaia@oaa.edu
PANAYOTOVA, Evelina ...... 610-790-1905.... 421 G
evelina.panayotova@alvernia.edu
PANCHAL, Praveen .... 212-650-8223.... 326 G
ppanchal@ccny.cuny.edu
PANCHANATHEN,
Sethuraman .... 480-965-4831...... 11 J
panch@asu.edu
PANCHUCK, Paula .... 617-663-7054.... 236 A
ppanchuck@lasell.edu
PANCHUK, Victor .... 404-880-8016.... 127 C
vpanchuk@cau.edu
PANCIC-MEIER, Vanesa ..... 503-682-3903.... 419 F
vpancics-meier@pioneerpacific.edu
PANCIERA, Kathy .... 651-290-7522.... 272 E
kathy.panciera@wmitchell.edu
PANDE, Sameer .... 281-283-3008.... 503 E
pande@uhcl.edu
PANDELADIS, Leo .... 717-720-4030.... 441 E
lpandeladis@passhe.edu
PANDEY, Bhuban, R .... 512-448-8442.... 493 E
bhubanp@stedwards.edu
PANDEY, Bishun .... 740-389-6786.... 399 D
pandey.1@osu.edu
PANDIAN, R. Devadoss ..... 630-637-5354.... 159 G
rdpandian@noctrl.edu
PANDIT, Kavita, K .... 706-542-2202.... 138 G
pandit@uga.edu
PANDO, Paula .... 201-360-4021.... 310 E
ppando@hccc.edu
PANEBIANCO, Anthony, F . 315-792-7191.... 356 B
panebia@sunyit.edu
PANEBIANCO, Anthony, F . 315-684-6038.... 354 F
panebiaf@morrisville.edu
PANEITZ, Becky .... 479-619-4191...... 22 H
bpaneitz@nwacc.edu
PANELLA, Bill .... 920-750-5900.... 550 A
bill.panella@rasmussen.edu
PANESAR, Paul .... 858-499-0202...... 41 H
panesar@coleman.edu
PANESAR, Paul, S .... 858-499-0202...... 41 G
panesar@coleman.edu
PANETTA, Carol .... 617-277-3915.... 232 D
panettac@bgsp.edu
PANG, Alex .... 310-506-4561...... 61 H
alex.pang@pepperdine.edu
PANG, Eddie .... 808-735-4856.... 140 E
epang@chaminade.edu
PANG, Lily .... 310-506-4130...... 61 H
lily.pang@pepperdine.edu
PANGALLO, Karen .... 978-762-4000.... 240 D
kpangal@northshore.edu
PANGBORN, Joseph .... 401-841-6555.... 558 B
PANGBORN, Robert, N ...... 814-865-2505.... 438 G
rnp1@psu.edu
PANGBURN, William .... 212-237-8204.... 327 F
bpangburn@jjay.cuny.edu
PANGELINAN, Leo .... 670-234-5498.... 560 B
leop@nmcnet.edu
PANGONIS, Patricia .... 440-375-7000.... 394 E
tpangonis@lec.edu
PANHANS, Matthew, A ...... 414-277-7287.... 549 C
panhans@msoe.edu
PANI, Eric, A .... 318-342-1025.... 216 E
pani@ulm.edu
PANICCIA, Lindsey .... 812-332-1559.... 175 J
lpaniccia@ivytech.edu
PANKEY, Bruce .... 301-628-5427.... 225 B
bpankey@nlc.edu
PANKEY, Susan .... 802-860-2778.... 513 C
PANKIEVICH, Michael .... 617-989-4575.... 245 F
pankievichm@wit.edu
PANKRATZ, Chris .... 865-882-4560.... 476 A
pankratzcs@roanestate.edu
PANLILIO, Carmen .... 201-200-3234.... 312 B
cpanlilo@njcu.edu
PANNABECKER, Lois .... 574-257-7619.... 169 I
pannabl@bethelcollege.edu
PANNEGGIANTE, John ...... 201-559-6089.... 310 B
pane@felician.edu
PANNELL, Randall .... 864-977-7011.... 460 A
randall.pannell@ngu.edu
PANNELL, Vernese .... 212-410-8054.... 343 B
vpannel@nycpm.edu

PANNILL, W. Stephen ... 410-287-1025 ... 222 A spannill@cecil.edu
PANNKUK, Matthew ... 620-417-1161 ... 196 F matthew.pannkuk@sccc.edu
PANOFF, Virginia ... 231-348-6698 ... 256 B vpanoff@ncmich.edu
PANTALEO, Mark ... 251-981-3771 ... 2 G mark.pantaleo@columbiasouthern.edu
PANTANO, Laura ... 603-428-2241 ... 305 D lpantano@nec.edu
PANTIC, Zorica ... 617-989-4476 ... 245 F panticz@wit.edu
PANTOJA, Antonio, L ... 787-279-1912 ... 563 D apantoja@bayamon.inter.edu
PANTOJA, Veronica ... 818-785-2726 ... 38 K
PANTONE, Dirk ... 303-220-1200 ... 81 J dirk.pantone@cffp.edu
PANU, Al ... 678-717-3835 ... 129 G apanu@gsc.edu
PANZARELLA, Amy ... 304-724-3700 ... 540 F apanzarella@apus.edu
PANZECA, Linda ... 513-244-4393 ... 388 E linda_panzeca@mail.msj.edu
PANZER, Richard ... 845-752-3000 ... 358 F r.panzer@uts.edu
PANZICA, John ... 401-333-7121 ... 453 D jpanzica@ccri.edu
PAOLELLI, Arthur ... 518-381-1202 ... 350 E paolela@sunysccc.edu
PAOLINI, Francine ... 616-632-2131 ... 247 E paolifra@aquinas.edu
PAOLUCCI, Jeff ... 719-384-6833 ... 87 A jeff.paolucci@ojc.edu
PAONESSA, Lourdes ... 305-341-6600 ... 102 F lpaonessa@brownmackie.edu
PAPADIMITRIOU, Dimitri ... 914-758-7426 ... 230 F dpb@bard.edu
PAPADIMITRIOU, Dimitri, B ... 845-758-7426 ... 323 D dbp@levy.bard.edu
PAPADIMOS, Peter, J ... 419-530-8411 ... 404 F peter.papadimos@utoledo.edu
PAPADOPOULOS, Michael 518-783-2376 ... 350 I mpapadopoulos@siena.edu
PAPAFIL, Drucie, A ... 757-446-6143 ... 518 G papafida@evms.edu
PAPAGEORGE, Anne ... 215-898-7241 ... 448 J fresvp@upenn.edu
PAPAJOHN, Michelle ... 631-687-5151 ... 349 A mpapajohn@sjcny.edu
PAPAJOHN, Michelle ... 631-687-5151 ... 349 B mpapajohn@sjcny.edu
PAPALEO, Stefano ... 561-237-7831 ... 113 D spapaleo@lynn.edu
PAPALIA, Daria ... 845-451-1359 ... 331 E d_papalia@culinary.edu
PAPALIA, Jean, M ... 617-627-2306 ... 245 C jean.papalia@tufts.edu
PAPANDREA, Vincent ... 718-429-6600 ... 359 G vincent.papandrea@vaughn.edu
PAPANIKOLAOU, Constantia ... 617-994-6928 ... 236 D cpapanikolaou@bhe.mass.edu
PAPARO, Michael ... 315-781-3344 ... 335 F paparo@hws.edu
PAPATHOMAS, Thomas, V 848-445-6533 ... 314 C papathom@rci.rutgers.edu
PAPAZIAN, Mary, A ... 203-392-5250 ... 90 I papazianm1@southernct.edu
PAPAZIAN, Richard ... 617-873-0235 ... 233 A richard.papazian@cambridgecollege.edu
PAPE, Sabrina ... 845-437-5787 ... 359 F sapape@vassar.edu
PAPER, Teresa, A ... 563-441-4173 ... 184 H tapaper@eicc.edu
PAPESCH, Katherine ... 217-732-3155 ... 156 I kpapesch@lincolncollege.edu
PAPICH, Mark ... 210-829-6053 ... 504 B papich@uiwtx.edu
PAPIESE, Paul ... 509-542-4837 ... 532 H ppapiese@columbiabasin.edu
PAPILLO, Nicholas, J ... 203-254-4000 ... 92 H npapillo@fairfield.edu
PAPINCHAK, John, R ... 412-268-7404 ... 424 J jp7p@andrew.cmu.edu
PAPINI, Dennis ... 605-688-4723 ... 466 C dennis.papini@sdstate.edu
PAPLAUSKAS, Leonard, P . 860-679-3173 ... 95 A paplauskas@adp.uchc.edu
PAPMARCOS, Steven, D ... 757-823-8920 ... 522 E sdpapamarcos@nsu.edu
PAPP, Daniel, S ... 770-423-6033 ... 133 A dpapp@kennesaw.edu
PAPPALARDO, Faye ... 410-386-8188 ... 221 G fpappalardo@carrollcc.edu
PAPPALARDO, Thomas, J . 412-924-1778 ... 444 H tpappalardo@pts.edu
PAPPALY, Joe ... 510-490-6900 ... 80 A jpappaly@cci.edu
PAPPAS, Amy ... 703-284-1681 ... 521 D amy.pappas@marymount.edu
PAPPAS, Domenica, G ... 312-567-3035 ... 153 C pappas@iit.edu
PAPPAS, Gregory, J ... 718-817-4350 ... 334 C pappas@fordham.edu
PAPPAS, James, P ... 405-325-6361 ... 413 C jpappas@ou.edu
PAPPAS, Joanna ... 773-508-7429 ... 157 C jpappas@luc.edu
PAPPAS, John ... 918-628-3700 ... 407 C jpappas@brownmackie.edu
PAPPAS, Kathrine ... 413-782-1327 ... 246 A kpappas@wne.edu
PAPPAS, Richard, J ... 616-698-7111 ... 250 C rpappas@davenport.edu
PAPPAS, Tony, A ... 641-422-4350 ... 188 A pappaton@niacc.edu
PAPPATHAN, Matthew ... 802-828-8740 ... 402 I matt.pappathan@myunion.edu
PAPPIN, Diana, J ... 765-966-2656 ... 176 H dpappin@ivytech.edu
PAPROCKI, Ronald, J ... 585-275-2800 ... 359 B rpaprocki@admin.rochester.edu
PAPSON, Melissa ... 724-222-5330 ... 438 F mpapson@penncommercial.edu
PAQUET, Casey ... 727-864-7987 ... 105 E paquetcd@eckerd.edu
PAQUETTE, James ... 410-617-2283 ... 223 I jrpaquette1@loyola.edu
PAQUETTE, Kevin ... 207-893-7797 ... 219 F kpaquett@sjcme.edu
PAQUETTE, Patricia ... 206-934-4105 ... 537 C patricia.paquette@seattlecolleges.edu
PAQUIN, Delbert ... 928-724-6772 ... 13 L dpaquin@dinecollege.edu
PARA, Donald ... 562-985-4128 ... 35 C donald.para@csulb.edu
PARADIS, Rick ... 516-759-2040 ... 360 B rparadis@webb-institute.edu
PARADIS, Ronald, S ... 541-383-7599 ... 414 I rparadis@cocc.edu
PARADISE, Lou, V ... 504-280-6723 ... 213 E provost@uno.edu
PARADISE, Melanie ... 865-539-7130 ... 475 G mmparadise@pstcc.edu
PARADISE, Richard ... 321-433-7202 ... 102 D paradiser@brevardcc.edu
PARADKAR, Vishvas ... 719-389-6454 ... 82 D vishvas.paradkar@coloradocollege.edu
PARAMORE, Marcus ... 334-241-8622 ... 8 A marcus@troy.edu
PARAMORE, Mary ... 252-493-7216 ... 372 H mparamore@email.pittcc.edu
PARAS, Ernesto ... 312-332-0707 ... 166 B
PARASKA, William, F ... 404-413-4401 ... 131 G bparaska@gsu.edu
PARASKOS, John, A ... 508-856-2323 ... 237 C john.paraskos@umassmed.edu
PARCEL, Julie ... 636-922-8383 ... 288 B jparcel@stchas.edu
PARCELLS, Fred ... 215-785-0111 ... 440 I
PARCELLS, Rex ... 254-659-7821 ... 487 G rparcells@hillcollege.edu
PARCHMAN, Louis ... 870-762-3128 ... 20 A lparchman@smail.anc.edu
PARDALES, Michael, J ... 716-888-3294 ... 325 F pardalem@canisius.edu
PARDIE, Lynn ... 217-206-6600 ... 167 C pardie.lynn@uis.edu
PARDIECK, David, L ... 309-677-3086 ... 146 C dlp@bradley.edu
PARDINI, John ... 856-351-2914 ... 315 A jpardini@salemcc.edu
PARDINI, Ron ... 775-784-1660 ... 303 A ronp@cabnr.unr.edu
PARDO, Liane ... 407-628-5870 ... 106 H lpardo@cci.edu
PARDUE, Karen ... 207-221-4361 ... 221 A kpardue@une.edu
PARDUE, Stacy ... 919-760-8346 ... 367 A pardues@meredith.edu
PAREDES, Edith ... 954-322-4460 ... 112 C paredese@jmvu.edu
PAREKH, Purvi ... 201-684-7115 ... 313 C purvi@ramapo.edu
PARENT, Cyrille ... 719-502-2975 ... 87 B cyrille.parent@ppcc.edu
PARENT, Jason ... 207-768-2808 ... 218 J jparent@nmcc.edu
PARENT, Kim, R ... 805-893-3858 ... 75 B kim.parent@sa.ucsb.edu
PARENTE, JR., James, A .. 612-624-2535 ... 272 A paren001@umn.edu
PARFITT, Mark ... 518-743-2245 ... 355 D parfittm@sunyacc.edu
PARGE, Theodore, C ... 630-844-5262 ... 145 F tparge@aurora.edu
PARHAM, Dave ... 678-915-7333 ... 137 G dparham@spsu.edu
PARHAM, Loretta ... 404-978-2018 ... 138 B lparham@auctr.edu
PARHAM, Martha ... 714-438-4605 ... 41 A mparham@mail.cccd.edu
PARHAM, Patricia ... 805-652-5512 ... 77 C pparham@vcccd.edu
PARHAM, Sandra ... 310-243-3700 ... 34 D sparham@csudh.edu
PARHAM, Thomas, A ... 949-824-4804 ... 74 B taparham@uci.edu
PARHAM, Walter, H ... 803-777-7854 ... 462 A t.parham@sc.edu
PARIAN, Lolita ... 831-443-1700 ... 50 C lolita_parian@heald.edu
PARIANTE, Jody ... 212-431-2137 ... 343 E jody.pariante@nyls.edu
PARINI, Shelly ... 503-594-3015 ... 415 A shellyp@clackamas.edu
PARIS, Lisa ... 215-670-9127 ... 438 E lparis@peirce.edu
PARIS, Margaret, L ... 541-346-3813 ... 419 B mparis@uoregon.edu
PARIS, Mark, S ... 302-356-6829 ... 97 C mark.s.paris@wilmu.edu
PARIS, III, Oren ... 479-248-7236 ... 21 G oparis3@ecollege.edu
PARIS, Robin ... 615-383-4848 ... 478 F rparis@watkins.edu
PARIS, Susan ... 617-989-4589 ... 245 F pariss@wit.edu
PARIS, Wendell ... 305-626-3762 ... 109 A wparis@fmuniv.edu
PARISEAU, Anita ... 303-273-3296 ... 83 B anita.pariseau@is.mines.edu
PARISH, David ... 630-889-6512 ... 159 F dparish@nuhs.edu
PARISH, Janet ... 386-506-3075 ... 104 F parishj@daytonastate.edu
PARISH, Michael, C ... 906-248-8400 ... 248 H mparish@bmcc.edu
PARISH, Paula ... 210-434-6711 ... 492 B pparish@lake.ollusa.edu
PARISI, Dawn ... 352-588-8251 ... 116 G dawn.parisi@saintleo.edu
PARISI, Joseph ... 636-949-4812 ... 283 J jparisi@lindenwood.edu
PARISI, Michael ... 410-293-1104 ... 559 B parisi@usna.edu
PARISI, Rob ... 805-922-6966 ... 26 L rparisi@hancockcollege.edu
PARISI, Robert ... 805-922-6966 ... 26 L rparisi@hancockcollege.edu
PARISI, Valarie, M ... 313-577-1335 ... 260 A dv6552@wayne.edu
PARK, Chan, J ... 561-237-7186 ... 113 D cpark@lynn.edu
PARK, Choong Gi ... 562-926-1023 ... 63 B elpis@yahoo.com
PARK, Daniel, L ... 509-527-5999 ... 540 B park@whitman.edu
PARK, Daniel, W ... 858-822-1236 ... 74 F dwpark@ucsd.edu
PARK, David ... 714-533-3946 ... 37 E dpark@calums.edu
PARK, Debra, S ... 716-888-2790 ... 325 F parkd@canisius.edu
PARK, E.K. (Eun) ... 530-898-6880 ... 34 C ekpark@csuchico.edu
PARK, George ... 310-453-8300 ... 45 G george@emperors.edu
PARK, Heerei ... 408-260-0208 ... 47 D korean@fivebranches.edu
PARK, Hojin ... 215-884-8942 ... 452 D admissions@woninstitute.edu
PARK, Jack, C ... 210-567-2020 ... 507 A parkjc@uthscsa.edu
PARK, James, E ... 816-654-7108 ... 283 F jpark@kcumb.edu
PARK, James, S ... 540-464-7390 ... 529 F parkjs@vmi.edu
PARK, Jessica ... 213-252-5100 ... 26 C
PARK, John, B ... 213-385-2322 ... 79 I
PARK, Julia ... 213-487-0110 ... 45 D financialaid@dula.edu
PARK, Kathryn ... 409-933-8201 ... 483 F kpark@com.edu
PARK, Kevin ... 404-687-4533 ... 127 F parkk@ctsnet.edu
PARK, Linda ... 315-279-5208 ... 337 K lpark@mail.keuka.edu
PARK, Matthew ... 940-397-4501 ... 491 B matthew.park@mwsu.edu
PARK, Mi ... 562-926-1023 ... 63 B mhpark@ptsa.edu
PARK, Michelle ... 714-533-1495 ... 70 B isa@southbaylo.edu
PARK, Mimi ... 714-533-1495 ... 70 B mimi@southbaylo.edu
PARK, Myung ... 425-739-8287 ... 535 H myung.park@lwtc.edu
PARK, No Hee ... 310-206-6063 ... 74 C npark@dent.ucla.edu
PARK, Shelley, S ... 859-622-2361 ... 200 J shelley.park@eku.edu
PARK, Steve ... 972-860-7771 ... 484 F spark@dcccd.edu
PARK, Sunny ... 806-720-7507 ... 490 F sunny.park@lcu.edu
PARK, Yong Hee ... 714-533-1495 ... 70 B yhpark@southbaylo.edu
PARK, Yung Won ... 610-917-1457 ... 450 E ywpark@vfcc.edu
PARKE, Lydia ... 215-780-1417 ... 446 G lparke@salus.edu
PARKER, Aaron, L ... 601-426-6346 ... 277 A aparker@southeasternbaptist.edu
PARKER, Al ... 765-447-9550 ... 172 J al.parker@harrison.edu
PARKER, Anthony, O ... 229-430-3502 ... 124 B aparker@albanytech.edu
PARKER, Beverly ... 318-670-9571 ... 215 A bparker@susla.edu
PARKER, Brent ... 215-619-7416 ... 436 G bparker@mc3.edu
PARKER, Brian ... 212-659-3610 ... 338 A bparker@tkc.edu
PARKER, Bruce ... 212-243-5150 ... 334 E bparker@gts.edu
PARKER, Cassandra ... 202-274-5323 ... 100 A cparker@udc.edu
PARKER, Cathy ... 601-484-8799 ... 275 A cparker@meridiancc.edu
PARKER, Charles, R ... 850-263-3261 ... 101 L crparker@baptistcollege.edu
PARKER, Collier, B ... 570-340-6000 ... 435 F cbparker@marywood.edu
PARKER, Craig ... 502-897-4885 ... 206 C cparker@sbts.edu
PARKER, Cynthia ... 706-295-6346 ... 130 E cparker@highlands.edu
PARKER, Cynthia, L ... 401-598-1345 ... 453 E cparker@jwu.edu
PARKER, Dana, C ... 610-436-2627 ... 444 A dparker@wcupa.edu
PARKER, Danny, M ... 864-231-2145 ... 455 C dparker@andersonuniversity.edu
PARKER, Darnell ... 410-778-7457 ... 229 D dparker2@washcoll.edu
PARKER, Darrell ... 828-227-7401 ... 380 A dfparker@wcu.edu
PARKER, Darrell, F ... 864-503-5566 ... 463 B dparker@uscupstate.edu
PARKER, David ... 336-506-4301 ... 368 A parkerdw@alamancecc.edu
PARKER, Deborah ... 870-762-3151 ... 20 A dparker@smail.anc.edu
PARKER, Diane ... 617-243-2137 ... 236 A dparker@lasell.edu
PARKER, Donna ... 610-526-6004 ... 430 D dparker@harcum.edu
PARKER, Donna ... 610-399-2000 ... 442 A dparker@cheyney.edu
PARKER, Frank ... 619-298-1829 ... 71 C
PARKER, Frank ... 936-294-1786 ... 501 D fparker@shsu.edu
PARKER, Gail, C ... 318-342-1961 ... 216 E gparker@ulm.edu
PARKER, George ... 530-741-6700 ... 80 I
PARKER, Gilbert, A ... 607-729-1581 ... 331 G gparker@davisny.edu
PARKER, Gilda ... 713-221-8563 ... 503 F parkergil@uhd.edu
PARKER, Heidi ... 641-673-1031 ... 190 C parkerh@wmpenn.edu
PARKER, Jack ... 617-353-4639 ... 232 E jjparker@bu.edu
PARKER, James ... 570-662-4000 ... 443 C jparker@mansfield.edu
PARKER, James, T ... 801-581-6857 ... 511 C jparker@purchasing.utah.edu
PARKER, Janet ... 910-892-3178 ... 365 B jparker@heritagebiblecollege.edu
PARKER, Janice, C ... 312-658-5100 ... 165 G janice.parker@tbiil.edu
PARKER, Jeffrey ... 303-315-2750 ... 88 J jeff.parker@ucdenver.edu
PARKER, Jerome, S ... 610-359-5100 ... 426 G jparker@dccc.edu
PARKER, Jill ... 530-752-2599 ... 73 I jblack@ucdavis.edu
PARKER, Jim, O ... 504-816-8592 ... 213 H jparker@nobts.edu
PARKER, Jo Ellen ... 434-381-6210 ... 524 K jparker@sbc.edu
PARKER, John ... 813-463-7153 ... 101 B joparker@argosy.edu
PARKER, John ... 941-554-1549 ... 101 A johparker@argosy.edu
PARKER, Jonathan, K ... 951-343-4213 ... 31 J jparker@calbaptist.edu
PARKER, Joyce, E ... 310-233-4551 ... 54 I parkerje@lahc.edu
PARKER, Karen, L ... 434-582-2445 ... 520 K kparker@liberty.edu
PARKER, Kathleen ... 320-363-2121 ... 271 A kparker@csbsju.edu
PARKER, Kathleen ... 320-363-5195 ... 262 F kparker@csbsju.edu
PARKER, Keith ... 561-732-4424 ... 117 B kparker@svdp.edu
PARKER, Keith, S ... 310-794-6811 ... 74 C kparker@support.ucla.edu
PARKER, Kevin ... 845-758-7511 ... 323 D parker@bard.edu
PARKER, Kim ... 214-637-3530 ... 508 D kparker@wadecollege.edu
PARKER, Kim ... 713-646-1803 ... 494 I kparker@stcl.edu

PARKER, Linda .... 843-863-8054 .... 456 B
lparker@csuniv.edu
PARKER, Linda, M .... 518-388-6123 .... 358 G
parkerl@union.edu
PARKER, Maria .... 870-584-4471 ...... 25 C
mparker@cccua.edu
PARKER, Maria, D .... 205-665-6050 .... 9 B
parkermd@montevallo.edu
PARKER, Mark .... 405-208-5315 .... 410 A
mparker@okcu.edu
PARKER, Mary .... 310-393-0411 ...... 61 E
mfparker@rand.org
PARKER, Mary, G .... 801-581-3490 .... 511 C
mgparker@sa.utah.edu
PARKER, Mary Jo .... 713-221-8471 .... 503 F
parkerm@uhd.edu
PARKER, Melanie, L .... 617-715-5329 .... 241 D
PARKER, Micah .... 951-343-4318 ...... 31 J
miparker@calbaptist.edu
PARKER, Mike .... 731-352-4239 .... 467 E
parkerm@bethelu.edu
PARKER, Peggy .... 910-892-3178 .... 365 B
pparker@heritagebiblecollege.edu
PARKER, Pennie .... 407-646-2636 .... 116 D
pparker@rollins.edu
PARKER, Philip, L .... 812-464-1865 .... 181 B
plparker@usi.edu
PARKER, Pippin .... 212-229-5859 .... 342 E
parkerp@newschool.edu
PARKER, Randy .... 336-334-4822 .... 371 A
PARKER, Rebecca .... 510-549-4724 ...... 71 I
rparker@sksm.edu
PARKER, Robert .... 404-471-6236 .... 123 I
rparker@agnesscott.edu
PARKER, Robin, L .... 513-529-6734 .... 396 E
parkerrl@muohio.edu
PARKER, Rodney .... 410-617-2310 .... 223 I
rparker1@loyola.edu
PARKER, Ron .... 979-230-3480 .... 482 D
ron.parker@brazosport.edu
PARKER, Sandra .... 513-745-5736 .... 403 F
sandra.parker@uc.edu
PARKER, Savander .... 408-274-7900 ...... 67 C
savander.parker@evc.edu
PARKER, Sherry .... 407-277-0311 .... 107 B
sparker@evergladesuniversity.edu
PARKER, Sirena .... 662-329-7127 .... 276 A
sparker@ss.muw.edu
PARKER, Sonia .... 801-957-4446 .... 512 D
sonia.parker@slcc.edu
PARKER, Teresa .... 740-389-4636 .... 395 H
parkert@mtc.edu
PARKER, Terry .... 303-273-3399 ...... 83 B
tparker@mines.edu
PARKER, Thomas, H .... 413-542-2328 .... 230 A
admissions@amherst.edu
PARKER, Tim .... 205-879-5588 .... 3 G
tparker@faulkner.edu
PARKER, Zoann .... 302-328-7508 ...... 97 A
parker@wesle.edu
PARKER AMES, Gwen .... 845-675-4446 .... 344 G
gwen.ames@nyack.edu
PARKER-AYERS, Jennifer .. 256-372-4735 .... 1 A
martin.sherrill@aamu.edu
PARKER-BELL, Bernice ...... 904-470-8261 .... 105 G
bparkerbell@ewc.edu
PARKER-JEFFRIES, Terry .. 704-463-3057 .... 375 F
terry.jeffries@fsmail.pfeiffer.edu
PARKER-KELLY, Darlene .. 323-563-9340 ...... 39 G
darleneparkerkelly@cdrewu.edu
PARKES, Martin, J .... 717-867-6038 .... 434 C
parkes@ivc.edu
PARKHURST, Abbie .... 540-828-5782 .... 517 B
aparkhur@bridgewater.edu
PARKIN, Janice .... 312-341-4327 .... 163 B
jparkin01@roosevelt.edu
PARKINSON, Alan, R .... 801-422-4327 .... 509 H
alan_parkinson@byu.edu
PARKINSON, Ann .... 252-335-0821 .... 369 G
aparkinson@albemarle.edu
PARKINSON, David .... 435-797-1645 .... 511 E
david.parkinson@usu.edu
PARKINSON, III,
Henry, C .... 978-665-3160 .... 237 E
hparkinson@fitchburgstate.edu
PARKINSON, Michael .... 314-529-9553 .... 284 C
mparkinson@maryville.edu
PARKINSON, Tracy .... 843-383-8012 .... 457 A
tparkinson@coker.edu
PARKISON, Kathy .... 765-455-9205 .... 174 A
kparkiso@iuk.edu
PARKS, Adrian .... 803-535-5812 .... 456 D
adrian.parks@sodexo.com
PARKS, Amanda .... 276-326-4348 .... 516 L
aparks@bluefield.edu
PARKS, Amy .... 216-987-6130 .... 389 B
amy.parks@tri-c.edu
PARKS, Ann .... 660-263-4110 .... 286 H
annp@macc.edu
PARKS, Brenda .... 309-298-1944 .... 168 C
bs-parks@wiu.edu
PARKS, Carlton .... 626-284-2777 ...... 27 D
cparks@alliant.edu
PARKS, Charlotte, P .... 404-413-7064 .... 131 G
cparks@gsu.edu
PARKS, Cherri, S .... 303-963-3357 ...... 82 C
cparks@ccu.edu
PARKS, Colin .... 202-462-2101 ...... 99 A
parks@iwp.edu
PARKS, Cynthia .... 706-737-1431 .... 125 G
cparks@aug.edu
PARKS, Donald, K .... 850-201-8071 .... 107 C
dparks@flagler.edu
PARKS, Earl .... 202-651-5494 ...... 98 B
earl.parks@gallaudet.edu
PARKS, Jeffrey .... 281-476-1501 .... 493 H
jeffrey.parks@sjcd.edu
PARKS, Joseph .... 573-875-4842 .... 291 D
parksj@umsl.edu
PARKS, Julie .... 616-234-3714 .... 251 E
jparks@grcc.edu
PARKS, Marshall .... 970-351-1814 ...... 89 B
marshall.parks@unco.edu
PARKS, Maureen .... 217-333-2590 .... 167 A
mparks@uillinois.edu
PARKS, Michael .... 210-567-2791 .... 507 A
parksm@uthscsa.edu
PARKS, Patricia .... 714-816-0366 ...... 73 B
patricia.parks@trident.edu
PARKS, Sherrie .... 325-235-7402 .... 500 G
sherrie.parks@tstc.edu
PARKS, Susie, M .... 619-201-8670 ...... 65 D
susie.parks@sdcc.edu
PARKS, Thomas, N .... 801-581-7236 .... 511 C
tom.parks@utah.edu
PARKS, Tom .... 617-262-5000 .... 231 G
thomas.parks@the-bac.edu
PARKS, Valerie .... 915-779-8031 .... 483 J
vparks@computercareercenter.com
PARKS, Vanasia Conley ..... 423-425-4467 .... 477 F
vanasia-parks@utc.edu
PARKS POOLEY,
Barbara, D .... 319-368-6470 .... 187 H
bpooley@mtmercy.edu
PARKYN, David, L .... 773-244-5710 .... 159 H
dparkyn@northpark.edu
PARLE, Joseph, D .... 713-785-5995 .... 483 C
joe.parle@cbshouston.edu
PARLETT, Ray, M .... 585-567-9333 .... 336 B
ray.parlett@houghton.edu
PARLIER, Melanie .... 850-436-8444 .... 123 C
melanie.parlier@vc.edu
PARMANN, Maureen .... 810-767-4000 .... 248 C
maureen.parmann@baker.edu
PARMER, Janet .... 707-527-4679 ...... 68 E
jparmer@santarosa.edu
PARMER, Marsha .... 503-223-2245 .... 416 F
mparmer@westernculinary.com
PARMLEY, Ross .... 918-631-2421 .... 413 F
ross-parmley@utulsa.edu
PARNELL, Kathleen .... 410-617-2354 .... 223 I
kmparnell@loyola.edu
PARNELL, Lauren .... 912-583-3211 .... 126 F
lparnell@bpc.edu
PARNELL, Paul .... 951-372-7015 ...... 63 K
paul.parnell@norcocollege.edu
PARNELL, Philip .... 701-671-2669 .... 382 G
philip.parnell@ndscs.edu
PARNELL, Rob Roy .... 512-463-1808 .... 500 H
robroy.parnell@tsus.edu
PARNELL, Todd .... 417-873-7201 .... 281 D
tparnell@drury.edu
PARNES, Marvin, G .... 734-936-3933 .... 259 A
mgparnes@umich.edu
PARNHAM, Gary .... 617-236-8800 .... 234 G
gparnham@fisher.edu
PARNIA, Ezat .... 626-529-8008 ...... 60 F
eparnia@pacificoaks.edu
PARNUM CADBURY,
Sarah .... 218-951-5144 .... 432 I
cadbury@lasalle.edu
PAROLINI, Roger, K .... 630-844-5489 .... 145 F
rparolin@aurora.edu
PARPART, Amanda, L .... 605-256-5244 .... 465 I
amanda.parpart@dsu.edu
PARR, Loraine .... 904-731-4949 .... 106 D
lparr@cci.edu
PARR, Ronald, G .... 901-333-4737 .... 476 B
rgparr@southwest.tn.edu
PARR, Tracey .... 212-431-2854 .... 343 E
tracey.parr@nyls.edu
PARR, Vanna .... 940-898-3525 .... 502 D
vparr@twu.edu
PARR-BARRETT, Cindy, A . 217-443-8759 .... 148 G
cparrett@dacc.edu
PARR WALKER, Diane ...... 574-631-7790 .... 180 G
diane.parr.walker@nd.edu
PARRA, Carlos, P .... 423-236-2746 .... 473 B
cpaarra@southern.edu
PARRA, Claudia .... 954-322-4460 .... 112 C
parrac@jmvu.edu
PARRA DE ORTIZ,
Alicia, F .... 954-322-4460 .... 112 C
aliciafernandaparra@jmvu.edu
PARRAVICINI, Marcelo, S . 203-591-5042 ...... 93 G
mparravicini@post.edu
PARRENT, Condoa .... 817-515-6532 .... 496 C
condoa.parrent@tccd.edu
PARRENT, Jonathan, V ...... 270-824-8571 .... 202 G
jay.parrent@kctcs.edu
PARRENT, Rick .... 615-230-3321 .... 476 C
rick.parrent@volstate.edu
PARRENT, Robert, W .... 501-450-5074 ...... 25 H
rparrent@uca.edu
PARRETT, Brenda, J .... 601-643-8301 .... 273 G
brenda.parrett@colin.edu
PARRIERA, Keri .... 360-383-3330 .... 540 A
kparriera@whatcom.ctc.edu
PARRILL, Jacqueline .... 740-366-9407 .... 386 H
parrill.9@osu.edu
PARRILL, Jacqueline .... 740-366-9407 .... 399 E
parril.9l@osu.edu
PARRIOTT, Karen .... 307-532-8264 .... 556 C
karen.parriott@ewc.wy.edu
PARRIS, Gina .... 864-294-2322 .... 458 E
gina.parris@furman.edu
PARRISH, Austen, L .... 213-738-6710 ...... 71 E
deansoffice@swlaw.edu
PARRISH, Dave .... 770-531-6420 .... 133 C
dparrish@laniertech.edu
PARRISH, Debra, J .... 906-353-4600 .... 253 D
dparrish@kbocc.org
PARRISH, Gretchen .... 336-342-4261 .... 373 E
parrishg@rockinghamcc.edu
PARRISH, Holly, A .... 717-240-5247 .... 439 D
hap15@psu.edu
PARRISH, J. Michael .... 408-924-4800 ...... 37 C
mparrish@science.sjsu.edu
PARRISH, Jenni .... 415-565-4881 ...... 74 A
parrishj@uchastings.edu
PARRISH, John .... 336-342-4261 .... 373 E
parrishj@rockinghamcc.edu
PARRISH, Paula .... 858-566-1200 ...... 44 B
pparrish@disd.edu
PARROTT, Mike .... 843-208-8040 .... 462 C
rparrot@uscb.edu
PARROTT, Roger .... 601-968-5919 .... 273 C
president@belhaven.edu
PARROTT-ROBBINS,
Rebecca .... 606-242-0256 .... 203 D
rebecca.robbins@kctcs.edu
PARRY, John .... 970-491-3939 ...... 83 F
john.parry@colostate.edu
PARRY, John .... 216-687-4808 .... 388 D
john.parry@csuohio.edu
PARRY, Laura, S .... 518-783-8282 .... 350 I
lparry@siena.edu
PARRY, Susan .... 845-341-4251 .... 345 E
susan.parry@sunyorange.edu
PARSCAL, Tina .... 866-621-0124 ...... 89 C
tina.parscal@rockies.edu
PARSHALL, William .... 267-468-8022 .... 447 H
william.parshall@temple.edu
PARSLEY, Nancy, L .... 847-578-8401 .... 163 C
nancy.parsley@rosalindfranklin.edu
PARSNIK, Pamela .... 570-674-6310 .... 436 F
pparsnik@misericordia.edu
PARSON, Lisa .... 620-278-4264 .... 196 H
lparson@sterling.edu
PARSON, Mark .... 715-232-1151 .... 552 E
parsonm@uwstout.edu
PARSON, Nancy, P .... 309-298-1066 .... 168 C
np-parsons@wiu.edu
PARSONS, Amy .... 970-491-5257 ...... 83 F
amy.parsons@colostate.edu
PARSONS, Brigitte .... 715-365-4406 .... 555 A
bparsons@nicoletcollege.edu
PARSONS, Carole, H .... 603-526-3674 .... 303 G
cparsons@colby-sawyer.edu
PARSONS, Cynthia .... 804-765-5800 .... 524 I
PARSONS, Duncan, A .... 423-354-2588 .... 475 F
daparsons@northeaststate.edu
PARSONS, Edy .... 319-363-8213 .... 187 H
eparsons@mtmercy.edu
PARSONS, Eric .... 802-447-6324 .... 514 F
eparsons@svc.edu
PARSONS, Faye .... 772-546-5534 .... 110 N
fayeparsons@hsbc.edu
PARSONS, JR., Frank, R ... 334-833-4294 .... 4 E
fparsons@huntingdon.edu
PARSONS, Geoffrey, J ...... 843-349-2054 .... 456 G
parsons@coastal.edu
PARSONS, James .... 951-222-8856 ...... 64 A
jim.parsons@rcc.edu
PARSONS, James .... 207-859-1250 .... 219 G
maintenance@thomas.edu
PARSONS, Jessica .... 614-221-7770 .... 396 B
PARSONS, Larry, R .... 304-473-8042 .... 545 G
parsons@wvwc.edu
PARSONS, Marty .... 479-619-4217 ...... 22 H
mparsone1@nwacc.edu
PARSONS, Pamela .... 406-771-4314 .... 295 G
pparsons@msugf.edu
PARSONS, Patrick .... 309-694-5593 .... 152 C
patrick.parsons@icc.edu
PARSONS, Paul, F .... 336-278-5724 .... 364 D
pparsons@elon.edu
PARSONS, Priscilla .... 409-880-7691 .... 501 A
priscilla.parsons@lamar.edu
PARTAIN, Julie .... 229-931-2249 .... 137 C
jpartain@southgatech.edu
PARTAIN, Pam .... 706-272-2985 .... 128 C
ppartain@daltonstate.edu
PARTAIN, Suzanne .... 303-333-4224 ...... 81 G
spartain@aspen.edu
PARTARRIEU, Roberto .... 703-416-1441 .... 520 C
rpartarrieu@ipsciences.edu
PARTCH, Nancy .... 815-825-2086 .... 155 D
nancy.partch@kishwaukeecollge.edu
PARTCH, Nancy .... 815-825-2086 .... 155 D
nancy.partch@kishwaukeecollege.edu
PARTEE, Ben .... 805-965-0581 ...... 68 B
partee@sbcc.edu
PARTEN, Janice .... 559-278-2364 ...... 35 A
jparten@csufresno.edu
PARTLETT, David .... 404-712-8815 .... 129 D
david.partlett@emory.edu
PARTNEL, Paul .... 951-372-7015 ...... 63 I
paul.partnel@nc.edu
PARTON, Becky .... 217-786-2351 .... 157 B
becky.parton@llcc.edu
PARTON, Dwayne .... 918-781-3689 .... 407 B
partond@bacone.edu
PARTON, LeAnne .... 509-793-2004 .... 531 I
leannep@bigbend.edu
PARTON, Sabrena .... 706-233-7465 .... 137 A
sparton@shorter.edu
PARTON, William .... 479-968-0417 ...... 20 G
wparton@atu.edu
PARTRIDGE, Kristen .... 405-325-3163 .... 413 C
kpartridge@ou.edu
PARTRIDGE, Patrick .... 801-274-3280 .... 512 F
ppartridge@wgu.edu
PARVIZI, Nasrin .... 607-753-5582 .... 353 B
nasrin.parvizi@cortland.edu
PARZIALE, Anthony .... 561-868-3239 .... 114 D
parziala@palmbeachstate.edu
PARZY, Robert .... 847-925-6649 .... 151 G
rparzy@harpercollege.edu
PASCAL, Kenneth, C .... 713-623-2040 .... 480 J
kpascal@aii.edu
PASCAL, Sandra, E .... 617-989-4478 .... 245 F
pascals@wit.edu
PASCALE, Lynn .... 203-287-3031 ...... 93 F
paier.admission@snet.net
PASCARELLA, John .... 936-294-1401 .... 501 D
jbp014@shsu.edu
PASCARIELLO, Jacqueline . 631-632-6840 .... 352 C
jacqueline.pascariello@stonybrook.edu
PASCHAL, Linda, L .... 414-955-8208 .... 548 G
lpaschal@mcw.edu
PASCHALL, Bill .... 720-855-6014 ...... 85 B
billp@heritage-education.com
PASCHALL, Danny .... 562-903-4874 ...... 31 A
danny.paschall@biola.edu
PASCOE, Frank, H .... 815-740-3216 .... 167 E
fpascoe@stfrancis.edu
PASCOE, Tammie .... 903-983-8105 .... 489 I
tpascoe@kilgore.edu
PASCUA, Vance .... 916-577-2200 ...... 79 G
vpascua@jessup.edu
PASCUAL, Candice .... 727-725-2688 .... 106 F
cpascual@cci.edu
PASCUAL, Mytha .... 310-900-1600 ...... 45 F
pascual_m@compton.edu
PASCUCCI, Richard, A .... 215-871-6690 .... 444 C
richardp@pcom.edu
PASCUZZI, Maria .... 305-474-6814 .... 117 A
mpascuzzi@stu.edu
PASEK, Heidi .... 406-771-4397 .... 295 G
hpasek@msugf.edu
PASHA, Stephanie .... 508-831-6655 .... 246 F
spasha@wpi.edu
PASKER, Mark .... 563-876-3353 .... 184 B
mpasker@dwci.edu
PASKETT, Lindy .... 307-855-2120 .... 556 B
lpaskett@cwc.edu
PASKEY, Louise .... 262-551-5800 .... 546 I
lpaskey@carthage.edu
PASKOFF, Beth, M .... 225-578-1480 .... 212 H
bpaskoff@lsu.edu
PASKUS, John .... 413-236-2109 .... 239 A
jpaskus@berkshirecc.edu
PASOUR, Katherine .... 828-328-7126 .... 366 E
katherine.pasour@lr.edu
PASQUERELLA, Lynn .... 413-538-2500 .... 242 D
commish@mtholyoke.edu
PASQUINI, Angela .... 212-749-2802 .... 339 I
finaid@msmnyc.edu
PASS-STERN, Bernice .... 212-614-6176 .... 346 A
bstern@chpnet.org
PASSAFIUME, Marisa .... 718-862-7796 .... 339 H
marisa.passafiume@manhattan.
edumanhattan.edu
PASSALACQUA, Dominic ... 315-792-3393 .... 359 E
dpassalacqua@utica.edu
PASSARO, Joanne .... 262-524-7364 .... 546 H
jpassaro@carrollu.edu
PASSIN, Cathey .... 610-647-4400 .... 431 C
cpassin@immaculata.edu
PASSMORE, Joe .... 423-746-5333 .... 476 F
jpassmore@twcnet.edu
PASTERIS, Marc .... 309-467-6305 .... 151 B
mpasteris@eureka.edu
PASTERNAK, Reuven .... 631-444-2701 .... 352 C

PAUL, Sonia 256-726-7134 6 C
spaul@oakwood.edu

PAUL, Susan 440-365-5222 395 D

PAUL, Tina 870-612-2017 25 E
tina.paul@uaccb.edu

PAUL, Tonya 419-772-3106 398 H
t-paul@onu.edu

PAUL, William 225-248-1015 213 G

PAULDINE, David, J 630-515-4566 149 B
dpauldine@devry.edu

PAULE, Romeo 415-949-7308 47 H
pauleromeo@fhda.edu

PAULETTI, Daniel 610-436-2552 444 A
dpauletti@wcupa.edu

PAULEY, Amy, I 585-785-1541 334 A
pauleyai@flcc.edu

PAULEY, Ann 202-884-9725 99 H
pauleya@trinitydc.edu

PAULEY, Edward 817-923-1921 495 G
epauley@swbts.edu

PAULEY-HEARD, LeAnn 847-628-1565 154 K
lpauleyheard@judsonu.edu

PAULI, Mary Louise 781-891-2660 231 D
mpauli@bentley.edu

PAULI, Wayne, E 605-256-5800 465 I
wayne.pauli@dsu.edu

PAULIEN, Jon 909-558-4536 54 D
jpaulien@llu.edu

PAULIN, Christopher 860-512-2753 91 F
cpaulin@mcc.commnet.edu

PAULINE, Rose Lee 215-951-1014 432 I
pauline@lasalle.edu

PAULISON, Wayne 918-631-2616 413 F
wayne-paulison@utulsa.edu

PAULK, Carol 912-443-3025 136 H
cpaulk@savannahtech.edu

PAULK, Taylor 405-912-9018 408 D
books@hc.edu

PAULLI, OFM, Kenneth, P 518-783-4290 350 I
kpaulli@siena.edu

PAULNACK, Karl 617-912-9124 232 C
kpaulnack@bostonconservatory.edu

PAULO, Joseph 803-754-4100 457 D

PAULOS, Christine 651-748-2619 266 A
christine.paulos@century.edu

PAULOSKI, SP, Pam 773-371-5420 146 E
presoffice@ctu.edu

PAULS, Kenton 712-707-7111 188 D
kenton.pauls@nwciowa.edu

PAULS, Robin, H 618-985-3741 154 G
robinpauls@jalc.edu

PAULSEN, A. William 912-201-8000 137 D
bpaulsen@southuniversity.edu

PAULSEN, John, E 937-327-7317 406 B
jpaulsen@wittenberg.edu

PAULSON, Cheri 781-239-3845 230 E
cpaulson@babson.edu

PAULSON, Chuck 612-659-6102 267 B
chuck.paulson@minneapolis.edu

PAULSON, Dennis 623-572-3415 16 E
dpauls@midwestern.edu

PAULSON, Dennis, J 630-515-7352 158 F
dpauls@midwestern.edu

PAULSON, Don 208-282-2130 143 H
pauldona@isu.edu

PAULSON, Janet 503-594-3162 415 A
jpaulson@clackamas.edu

PAULSON, Lawrie 701-252-3467 381 C
paulson@jc.edu

PAULSON, Nancy 218-855-8054 265 J
npaulson@clcmn.edu

PAULSON, Nicole 612-798-3718 265 D
npaulson@msbcollege.edu

PAULSON, Robert 361-593-3106 498 D
robert.paulson@tamuk.edu

PAULSON, Stephen, M 423-775-7333 467 F
steve@bryan.edu

PAULSON, Susan 757-373-7370 116 G
susan.paulson@saintleo.edu

PAULSON, Veronica 605-626-2537 466 A
paulsonv@northern.edu

PAULUS, Jim 620-947-3121 197 A
jimp@tabor.edu

PAULUS, Michael 206-281-2414 537 H

PAULUS, Michael, L 419-372-2891 385 E
mpaulus@bgsu.edu

PAULY, John, J 414-288-7511 548 F
john.pauly@marquette.edu

PAULY, Susan, E 336-721-2603 376 E
susan.pauly@salem.edu

PAUR, Dave 435-613-5357 512 A
dave.paur@usu.edu

PAUSTIAN, Kevin, W 563-884-5721 188 E
kevin.paustian@palmer.edu

PAUSTIAN, Tony 515-633-2439 183 H
adpaustian@dmacc.edu

PAVAN, Ron 615-547-1348 468 B
rpavan@cumberland.edu

PAVAN, Tammi 615-547-1228 468 B
tpavan@cumberland.edu

PAVAO, Debbie 408-541-0100 41 E
dpavao@cogswell.edu

PAVE, Adam, D 909-607-0109 40 I
adam_pave@kgi.edu

PAVEGLIO, Kevin 757-671-7171 518 H
kpaveglio@ecpi.edu

PAVEK, Annette 320-762-4411 265 F
annettep@alextech.edu

PAVELCHAK, Mark 323-343-2730 35 D
mpavelc@calstatela.edu

PAVELOI, Chris 330-499-9600 393 I
cpaveloi@kent.edu

PAVER, Jonathan 541-917-4534 416 I
paverj@linnbenton.edu

PAVEY, Carl, E 517-750-1200 258 D
cpavey@arbor.edu

PAVEZA, Gregory 203-392-7036 90 I
pavezag1@southernct.edu

PAVIGLIANITI, Angela 773-371-5445 146 E
angelap@ctu.edu

PAVIN, Anna 805-437-8425 34 B
anna.pavin@csuci.edu

PAVLIK, Donna 773-298-3258 163 I
pavlik@sxu.edu

PAVLIK, Joni, P 919-718-7222 369 C
jpavlik@cccc.edu

PAVLOCK, Tamara 412-291-6310 422 E
tpavlock@aii.edu

PAVLOVICH, Mark, G 610-436-3303 444 A
mpavlovich@wcupa.edu

PAVON, Tracie 515-961-1630 189 C
tracie.pavon@simpson.edu

PAVONE, Cassandra 828-689-1196 366 I
cpavone@mhc.edu

PAVONE, Gerri Lynn 586-445-7242 254 C
pavoneg@macomb.edu

PAVONE, Joseph 401-825-2114 453 D
jpavone@ccri.edu

PAVONE, Peter, J 414-276-5200 546 F
pjpavone@bryantstratton.edu

PAVY, Edwin, C 270-789-5227 199 F
ecpavy@campbellsville.edu

PAWLAK, Katherine 863-680-3964 109 E
kpawlak@flsouthern.edu

PAWLAK, Therese 906-932-4231 251 C
theresep@gogebic.edu

PAWLAWSKI, Eddie 615-547-1225 468 B
epawlawski@cumberland.edu

PAWLICKI, Frederick, W 785-864-4790 197 B
fpawlick@ku.edu

PAWLOSKI, Chris, J 989-964-7122 257 G
cjpawlos@svsu.edu

PAWLOW, Thomas, A 618-744-0426 158 A
tapawlow@mckendree.edu

PAWLOWSKI, Ceceile 716-896-0700 359 H
pawlowskic@villa.edu

PAWLOWSKI, Eugene 212-998-2775 344 B
gene.pawlowski@nyu.edu

PAWLUK, Steve 951-785-2320 53 E
spawluk@lasierra.edu

PAWLYSHYN, Nancy 914-674-7315 340 F
npawlyshyn@mercy.edu

PAXSON, Christina, H 401-863-2234 453 B
president@brown.edu

PAXTON, Ellen 513-727-3463 396 G

PAXTON, Ellen 513-785-3291 396 F
paxtonec@muohio.edu

PAXTON, Helen, S 973-353-5262 314 E
hs.paxton@rutgers.edu

PAXTON, Mike 303-546-3543 86 H
mikep@naropa.edu

PAXTON, Pat 330-684-8920 403 C
ppaxton@uakron.edu

PAXTON, Patricia, A 330-287-1254 399 A
bxsosuati@bncollege.com

PAYBA, Shane 808-984-3496 142 E
payba@hawaii.edu

PAYDAR, Nasser, H 317-274-4500 174 D
paydar@iupui.edu

PAYLO, Keith 412-392-3862 445 A
kpaylo@pointpark.edu

PAYNE, Angela 601-481-1357 275 A
apayne@meridiancc.edu

PAYNE, Anna Beth 570-372-4238 447 E
paynea@susqu.edu

PAYNE, Betsy, P 828-262-6432 377 D
paynebp@appstate.edu

PAYNE, Brandi 406-994-2845 295 C
bpayne@montana.edu

PAYNE, Bryson 706-864-1915 134 G
bpayne@northgeorgia.edu

PAYNE, C. Michael 740-264-5591 390 F
mpayne@egcc.edu

PAYNE, Carol 404-894-5596 130 F
carol.payne@business.gatech.edu

PAYNE, Carolyn 606-546-1304 207 B
cpayne@unionky.edu

PAYNE, Cathy 276-326-4233 516 L
cpayne@bluefield.edu

PAYNE, Charles, R 765-285-5466 169 G
cpayne@bsu.edu

PAYNE, Dan 406-683-7142 294 J
d_payne@umwestern.edu

PAYNE, Darrell 318-487-7559 209 F
payne@lacollege.edu

PAYNE, Deborah 618-985-4928 154 G
deborahpayne@jalc.edu

PAYNE, Don 303-762-6943 84 D
don.payne@denverseminary.edu

PAYNE, Donna 314-529-9676 284 C
dpayne@maryville.edu

PAYNE, Donna, G 252-328-6940 377 E
payned@ecu.edu

PAYNE, Gail, D 434-381-6324 524 K
payne@sbc.edu

PAYNE, George, M 240-567-2582 224 D
george.payne@montgomerycollege.edu

PAYNE, Hal, D 716-878-5550 353 A
paynehd@buffalostate.edu

PAYNE, JR., Harry, E 813-988-5131 108 A
president@floridacollege.edu

PAYNE, Harvey 803-754-4100 457 D

PAYNE, Jack, M 352-392-1971 120 C
jackpayne@ifas.ufl.edu

PAYNE, James 318-274-2504 215 E
payneja@gram.edu

PAYNE, Jamie, A 405-744-7420 410 C
jamie.payne@okstate.edu

PAYNE, Jennifer 802-586-7711 514 G
jpayne@sterlingcollege.edu

PAYNE, John, F 671-735-5558 559 E
john.payne2@guamcc.edu

PAYNE, John, K 802-654-2629 514 D
jpayne@smcvt.edu

PAYNE, Judith 605-256-5693 465 I
judy.payne@dsu.edu

PAYNE, June, P 765-285-1264 169 G
jpayne@bsu.edu

PAYNE, Karen, W 570-326-3761 440 L
kpayne@pct.edu

PAYNE, Kathryn, E 215-951-1941 432 I
paynek@lasalle.edu

PAYNE, Kent 847-214-7552 150 F
kpayne@elgin.edu

PAYNE, Lisa 618-437-5321 162 D
payne@rlc.edu

PAYNE, Lisa 256-233-8274 1 E
lisa.payne@athens.edu

PAYNE, Maggie 530-898-4015 34 C
mpayne@csuchico.edu

PAYNE, Marc 903-463-8714 487 C
paynem@grayson.edu

PAYNE, Mary 515-271-1452 184 A
mary.payne@dmu.edu

PAYNE, Michael, J 215-951-1841 432 I
payne@lasalle.edu

PAYNE, Molly 617-732-2218 241 C
molly.payne@mcphs.edu

PAYNE, Natalie 215-965-4039 436 H
npayne@moore.edu

PAYNE, O, J 641-648-6101 186 C
orintheo.payne@iavalley.edu

PAYNE, Pat 617-349-8850 234 E
ppayne@lesley.edu

PAYNE, Patricia 617-349-8841 236 B
ppayne@lesley.edu

PAYNE, Ralph, C 304-256-0279 543 A
rpayne@newriver.edu

PAYNE, Shari, L 412-397-6235 445 H
payne@rmu.edu

PAYNE, Sharon 804-355-0671 525 A
spayne@upsem.edu

PAYNE, Sherri 702-651-2678 302 E
sherri.payne@csn.edu

PAYNE, Stephen, D 269-471-6534 247 D
stephen@andrews.edu

PAYNE, Stephen, D 269-405-2837 252 A
stephen@andrews.edu

PAYNE, Steven, W 772-462-7805 111 B
spayne@irsc.edu

PAYNE, Susan, B 919-334-1520 374 H
sbpayne@waketech.edu

PAYNE, Suzie 562-860-2451 39 A
rpayne@cerritos.edu

PAYNE, Sylvia, M 317-274-4417 174 D
payne@iupui.edu

PAYNE, Tena 270-534-3342 203 E
tena.payne@kctcs.edu

PAYNE, Terry 828-298-3325 380 D
tpayne@warren-wilson.edu

PAYNE, Thomas, L 573-882-3846 291 B
paynet@missouri.edu

PAYNE, Vernon 269-387-2136 260 C
vernon.payne@wmich.edu

PAYNE, Wesley, A 573-840-9689 290 F
wpayne@trcc.edu

PAYNE, William 218-726-7033 271 F
wpayne@d.umn.edu

PAYNTER, Ronald 212-817-7609 327 B
rpaynter@gc.cuny.edu

PAYTON, Alvin 229-333-2123 139 I
alvin.payton@wiregrass.edu

PAYTON, Annie 478-825-6343 129 F
paytona@fvsu.edu

PAYTON, Donald 407-708-2434 117 H
paytond@seminolestate.edu

PAYTON, Ian 386-481-2527 102 C
paytoni@cookman.edu

PAYTON, Kizzy 225-922-2391 209 G
kpayton@lctcs.edu

PAYTON, Shannon 304-214-8917 543 D
spayton@wvncc.edu

PAYTON, Tom 937-393-3431 402 A
tpayton@sscc.edu

PAZ, Harold, L 717-531-8323 438 G
hlp10@psu.edu

PAZ, Harold, L 717-531-8323 440 A
hlp10@psu.edu

PAZ, Marvin 575-527-7694 319 G
mpaz@nmsu.edu

PAZICH, Betty 805-965-0581 68 B
pazich@sbcc.edu

PAZZANI, Michael, J 951-827-5535 74 E
michael.pazzani@ucr.edu

PEABODY, Kimberley 518-629-8012 336 C
k.peabody@hvcc.edu

PEABODY, Rita 417-626-1234 287 C
rpeabody@occ.edu

PEACE, Derryle 903-886-5764 498 B
derryle.peace@tamuc.edu

PEACE, Marci, H 336-272-7102 364 G
mpeace@greensboro.edu

PEACH, Jennifer 415-380-1646 48 E
jenniferpeach@ggbts.edu

PEACH, John 330-672-3111 393 D
jpeach@kent.edu

PEACH, Kyle 618-262-8641 153 A
peachk@iecc.edu

PEACHES, John 662-252-8000 276 G
jpeaches@rustcollege.edu

PEACOCK, Ann 919-718-7542 369 C
apeacock@cccc.edu

PEACOCK, Clyde 785-830-2753 193 D
clyde.peacock@bie.edu

PEACOCK, Jenny, L 919-508-2022 380 E
jlpeacock@peace.edu

PEACOCK, Kenneth, E 828-262-2040 377 D
peacockke@appstate.edu

PEACOCK, Ross 440-775-6927 397 G
ross.peacock@oberlin.edu

PEACOCK, Steve 612-330-1583 261 B
peacock@augsburg.edu

PEACOCK, Steve 229-217-4234 134 F
speacock@moultrietech.edu

PEACOCK, Walter, H 229-333-5791 139 C
wpeacock@valdosta.edu

PEACOCK-LANDRUM,
Linda, G 920-465-2163 551 B
peacockl@uwgb.edu

PEAK, Douglas, C 817-515-3076 496 C
doug.peak@tccd.edu

PEAK, JR., James, F 804-204-1230 516 J
jpeak@btsr.edu

PEAK, Jamie 215-612-6600 432 C
jpeak@chicareers.com

PEAK, Scott, S 414-229-5576 551 D
speak@uwm.edu

PEAKE, Jaklin 503-493-6545 415 E
jpeake@cu-portland.edu

PEAL, Regina, A 614-287-5343 389 A
rpeal@cscc.edu

PEAL MORROW, Rebecca . 610-921-7641 421 E
rmorrow@alb.edu

PEAR, Douglas, R 410-455-3263 227 D
pear@umbc.edu

PEARCE, Jared 641-673-2107 190 C
pearcej@wmpenn.edu

PEARCE, Jeff 505-473-6470 320 F
jeff.pearce@santafeuniversity.edu

PEARCE, Jennifer 614-823-1600 400 H
jpearce@otterbein.edu

PEARCE, Katheryn, P 386-822-7459 121 F
kpearce@stetson.edu

PEARCE, Kenneth, D 910-362-7423 368 H
kpearce@cfcc.edu

PEARCE, Kim 612-977-5436 261 F
kim.pearce@capella.edu

PEARCE, Laurence, W 803-777-8161 462 A
lpearce@mailbox.sc.edu

PEARCE, Michael 813-974-1780 121 A
mpearce@usf.edu

PEARCE, Nathaniel 704-334-6882 367 H
npearce@nlts.edu

PEARCE, Richard, R 540-654-1246 525 D
rpearce@umw.edu

PEARCE, Rick 309-268-8100 151 I
rick.pearce@heartland.edu

PEARCEY, Lynne, G 336-334-5016 379 B
l_pearce@uncg.edu

PEARIGEN, Rob 601-974-1001 275 B
rob.pearigen@millsaps.edu

PEARL, Donald 240-567-5006 224 D
donald.pearl@montgomerycollege.edu

PEARL, Melany 434-592-4020 520 K
mapearl@liberty.edu

PEARLMUTTER,
Roberta, S 401-456-8043 454 A
rpearlmutter@ric.edu

PEARON, Jill, R 315-267-2108 354 C
pearonjr@potsdam.edu

PEARRING, Yu Yok 808-974-7501 141 F
yuyok@hawaii.edu

PEARSALL, Joel, K 208-467-8772 144 E
jkpearsall@nnu.edu

PEARSALL, Kim 405-945-3250 410 F

PEMBROOK, Randall, G ..... 785-670-1649.... 197 F
randy.pembrook@washburn.edu
PENA, Andrew ..... 915-747-7933.... 506 B
ampena@utep.edu
PENA, Augusto, E ..... 828-262-6252.... 377 D
penaae@appstate.edu
PENA, Damien ..... 805-437-3218..... 34 B
damien.pena@csuci.edu
PENA, Diana, A ..... 956-872-3558.... 494 H
dpena@southtexascollege.edu
PENA, Fred ..... 254-298-8321.... 496 D
fred.pena@templejc.edu
PENA, Fred ..... 956-364-4337.... 500 D
fred.pena@tstc.edu
PENA, Jesus ..... 610-683-4700.... 443 A
pena@kutztown.edu
PENA, JR., Jose, A ..... 956-721-5312.... 489 J
jpena@laredo.edu
PENA, Juanita ..... 719-846-5537..... 88 F
juanita.pena@trinidadstate.edu
PENA, Laura ..... 915-532-3737.... 508 H
lpena@westerntech.edu
PENA, Maria ..... 360-417-6340.... 536 G
mpena@pencol.edu
PENA, Michelle ..... 305-220-4120.... 115 F
cemdir@ptcmatt.com
PENA, Nova ..... 915-595-1935.... 489 E
PENA, Robert ..... 361-593-4783.... 498 D
robert.pena@tamuk.edu
PENA, Rosa ..... 787-797-1166.... 564 F
rpena@mechtech.edu
PENA, Sandra, V ..... 956-326-2365.... 497 D
sandra@tamiu.edu
PENA, Stan ..... 575-538-6470.... 321 I
stan.pena@wnmu.edu
PENA, Stephen ..... 480-245-7971..... 14 J
stephen.pena@ibconline.edu
PENA-WARFIELD,
Roseanna ..... 508-362-2131.... 239 D
rpenawar@capecod.edu
PENCE, Bill ..... 540-868-7061.... 527 C
bpence@lfcc.edu
PENCE, Heather ..... 404-297-9522.... 131 D
penceh@gptc.edu
PENCE, Lorence, L ..... 304-647-6295.... 544 E
lpence@osteo.wvsom.edu
PENCE, Nadine, S ..... 765-361-6434.... 181 E
pencen@wabash.edu
PENCIU, Christian ..... 972-929-9315.... 486 D
cpenciu@devry.edu
PENDAKUR,
Sumun (Sumi) ..... 909-607-3470..... 49 F
spendakur@hmc.edu
PENDERGAST,
Katherine, N ..... 617-373-2230.... 243 F
PENDERGAST, Linda ..... 309-672-5534.... 158 C
lpendergast@methodistcol.edu
PENDERGRAFT, Susan ..... 336-386-3380.... 374 E
pendergrafts@surry.edu
PENDERGRASS, Martha ..... 919-843-5048.... 378 E
mjpender@email.unc.edu
PENDERGRASS, Toni ..... 505-566-3209.... 320 D
pendergrasst@sancollege.edu
PENDERGRAST, Runan ..... 859-246-6305.... 201 H
runan.pendergrast@kctcs.edu
PENDERS, Brooke ..... 860-528-4111..... 92 I
bpenders@goodwin.edu
PENDLETON, Brandon ..... 312-553-5654.... 147 C
bpendleton2@ccc.edu
PENDLETON, Dennis, F ..... 530-757-8663..... 73 I
dfpendleton@ucdavis.edu
PENDLETON, Janis, S ..... 803-327-7402.... 456 F
jpendleton@clintonjuniorcollege.edu
PENDLETON, Kathy, J ..... 502-852-6585.... 207 E
kathy.pendleton@louisville.edu
PENDLETON, Laurence ..... 615-963-7923.... 474 A
laurence.pendleton@tnstate.edu
PENDLETON, Penny ..... 479-788-7121..... 24 D
penny.pendleton@uafs.edu
PENDSE, Ravi ..... 316-978-5053.... 198 A
ravi.pendse@wichita.edu
PENFIELD, Gary, M ..... 401-456-8123.... 454 A
gpenfield@ric.edu
PENGRA, Matt ..... 407-679-0100.... 110 F
mpengra@fullsail.com
PENISTEN, Douglas ..... 918-456-5511.... 409 A
penisten@nsuok.edu
PENITENTI, Kim ..... 510-261-8500..... 61 G
kim.penitenti@patten.edu
PENKALA, Robert ..... 586-445-7636.... 254 C
penkalar@macomb.edu
PENKE, Ann, K ..... 920-565-1242.... 548 A
penkea@lakeland.edu
PENKOVA, Snejanka ..... 787-764-0000.... 568 B
snejanka.penkova@upr.edu
PENLAND, Joni, M ..... 502-410-6200.... 200 L
jpenland@galencollege.edu
PENLAND, Lynn, R ..... 812-488-2360.... 180 E
lp22@evansville.edu
PENLAND, Nathan ..... 417-328-1828.... 290 A
npenland@sbuniv.edu
PENLER, Karen ..... 216-373-6364.... 397 F
kpenler@ndc.edu
PENLEY, Julie ..... 915-831-7001.... 486 G
jpenley@epcc.edu
PENLEY, Larry, E ..... 602-978-7873..... 18 H
larry.penley@thunderbird.edu
PENMAN, Jane ..... 570-484-2204.... 443 B
jpenman@lhup.edu
PENN, Ann, E ..... 919-966-3576.... 378 E
ann_penn@unc.edu
PENN, Cris ..... 614-688-4940.... 398 I
penn.4@osu.edu
PENN, David ..... 407-447-7300.... 110 A
dpenn@ftccollege.edu
PENN, Deborah ..... 620-947-3121.... 197 A
deborahp@tabor.edu
PENN, Mark, A ..... 801-878-1058.... 303 D
mpenn@roseman.edu
PENN, Ray ..... 423-869-6312.... 470 E
rpenn@lmunet.edu
PENNA, Anthony ..... 617-552-3475.... 232 B
anthony.penna@bc.edu
PENNA, Nancy ..... 612-977-5522.... 261 F
nancy.penna@capella.edu
PENNARTZ, Kathy ..... 940-397-4214.... 491 B
kathy.pennartz@mwsu.edu
PENNER, Julie ..... 815-836-5667.... 156 F
pennerju@lewisu.edu
PENNETTI, Dianna ..... 212-854-3362.... 323 E
dpennetti@barnard.edu
PENNEY, R. William ..... 386-822-7045.... 121 F
bpenney@stetson.edu
PENNIECOOK, Tricia, Y ..... 909-558-4578..... 54 D
tpenniecook@llu.edu
PENNINGS, Rhonda, R ..... 712-324-5061.... 188 C
rpennings@nwicc.edu
PENNINGTON, David ..... 740-420-5906.... 398 D
dpennington@ohiochristian.edu
PENNINGTON, Karen, L ..... 973-655-4311.... 311 F
penningtonk@mail.montclair.edu
PENNINGTON, Laurie ..... 928-428-8231..... 14 B
laurie.pennington@eac.edu
PENNINGTON, Paul ..... 513-244-8181.... 387 E
paul.pennington@ccuniversity.edu
PENNINGTON, Rebecca, A 814-375-4766.... 439 E
rxs163@psu.edu
PENNINGTON, Ronald ..... 636-922-8271.... 288 B
rpennington@stchas.edu
PENNINGTON, Sabrina ..... 765-966-2656.... 176 H
spenning@ivytech.edu
PENNINGTON, Sandra ..... 801-375-5125.... 510 J
spennington@rmuohp.edu
PENNINGTON, Sherry, R .. 417-667-8181.... 280 E
spennington@cottey.edu
PENNINI, Susan, W ..... 617-333-2165.... 233 F
spennini@curry.edu
PENNIPEDE, Barbara, S ..... 914-923-2699.... 345 F
bpennipede@pace.edu
PENNIPIECE, Deirdre ..... 718-960-8675.... 327 C
deirdre.pettipiece@lehman.cuny.edu
PENNISON, Bret ..... 504-865-2290.... 213 F
bmpennis@loyno.edu
PENNISTON, Mary Ann ..... 660-541-5127.... 287 B
mpenn@nwmissouri.edu
PENNIX, James ..... 540-831-5460.... 523 A
jpennix@radford.edu
PENNIX, James ..... 540-831-5371.... 523 A
jpennix@radford.edu
PENNOCK, Margaret ..... 605-367-7667.... 466 D
margaret.pennock@southeasttech.edu
PENNOYER, Douglas ..... 562-903-4844..... 31 A
doug.pennoyer@biola.edu
PENNY, Helen ..... 229-333-5366.... 139 I
helen.penny@wiregrass.edu
PENNY, Rick ..... 440-525-7320.... 394 F
rpenny@lakelandcc.edu
PENNY, Robert ..... 601-923-1600.... 276 F
bpenny@rts.edu
PENNYWELL, Judith ..... 219-989-1104.... 178 K
judith.pennywell@purduecal.edu
PENROD, Curtis ..... 318-357-5960.... 216 B
penrodc@nsula.edu
PENROD, Donald ..... 562-985-5091..... 35 C
dpenrod@csulb.edu
PENROSE, Betsy, S ..... 315-786-2249.... 337 F
bpenrose@sunyjefferson.edu
PENROSE, John ..... 513-875-3344.... 387 C
john.penrose@chatfield.edu
PENRY, Jason, C ..... 325-942-2116.... 480 E
jason.penry@angelo.edu
PENSE, Christine ..... 610-861-5312.... 437 H
cpense@northampton.edu
PENSIS, Claude ..... 602-639-7500..... 14 H
PENSKAR, Donald ..... 269-387-8804.... 260 C
donald.penskar@wmich.edu
PENSON, Amy, M ..... 828-395-1296.... 371 D
apenson@isothermal.edu
PENTICUFF, Joy ..... 512-313-3000.... 483 K
joy.penticuff@concordia.edu
PENYACK, Megan ..... 781-595-6768.... 236 C
mpenyack@mariancourt.edu
PENZENSTADLER, SSND,
Joan ..... 414-256-1226.... 549 D
penzenj@mtmary.edu
PENZIUL, Carl ..... 607-844-8222.... 357 I
penziuc@tc3.edu
PEOPLE, Yasha ..... 732-247-5241.... 312 A
ypeople@nbts.edu
PEOPLES, Gregory, A ..... 734-487-0074.... 250 F
gregory.peoples@emich.edu
PEOPLES, Peg ..... 845-758-7432.... 323 D
peoples@bard.edu
PEOPLES, Verjanis ..... 225-771-2290.... 214 I
verjanis_peoples@subr.edu
PEPALL, Lynne ..... 617-627-3106.... 245 C
lynne.pepall@tufts.edu
PEPE, Alicia ..... 518-292-1915.... 348 A
pepea@sage.edu
PEPE, Joseph ..... 239-513-1122.... 111 A
jpepe@hodges.edu
PEPICELLO, William ..... 602-387-7000..... 19 A
bill.pepicello@phoenix.edu
PEPIN, James ..... 334-649-5000.... 557 E
PEPIN, Phyllis, A ..... 409-944-1222.... 486 K
ppepin@gc.edu
PEPION, Kenneth ..... 970-247-7334..... 84 K
pepion_k@fortlewis.edu
PEPITO, Bobby ..... 714-542-8086..... 31 C
bpepito@kensington.edu
PEPITONE, Dianne ..... 914-831-0367.... 330 D
dpepitone@cw.edu
PEPLINSKI, Michael ..... 724-938-4950.... 441 G
peplinski@calu.edu
PEPLOW, Nena ..... 309-677-3223.... 146 C
nena@bradley.edu
PEPOY, Joseph ..... 586-791-6610.... 248 B
joe.pepoy@baker.edu
PEPPARD, Paul ..... 407-569-1366.... 107 I
paul.peppard@fcc.edu
PEPPARD, Sandra ..... 407-569-1331.... 107 I
sandi.peppard@fcc.edu
PEPPARD, Timothy ..... 216-397-4444.... 392 L
tpeppard@jcu.edu
PEPPERS, Larry, C ..... 540-458-8602.... 530 D
peppersl@wlu.edu
PEPPIN, Patricia ..... 480-461-7456..... 15 I
pat.peppin@mcmail.maricopa.edu
PERAGALLO, Nilda, P ..... 305-284-2107.... 122 I
nperagallo@miami.edu
PERALES, Jose ..... 585-385-8067.... 348 F
jperales@sjfc.edu
PERALTA, Tracy ..... 505-925-8800.... 321 G
tlperalt@unm.edu
PERANTONI, Ed ..... 636-949-4705.... 283 J
aperantoni@lindenwood.edu
PERANTONI, Janet, L ..... 908-526-1200.... 313 D
jperanto@raritanval.edu
PERCHINSKY, Tessa, A ..... 715-833-6256.... 553 H
tperchinsky@cvtc.edu
PERCIANTE, Linda, K ..... 303-963-3237..... 82 C
lperciante@ccu.edu
PERCIVAL, Nicole ..... 620-331-4100.... 193 I
npercival@indycc.edu
PERCUOCO, Robert, E ..... 563-884-5460.... 114 E
robert.percuoco@palmer.edu
PERCUOCO, Robert, E ..... 563-884-5460.... 188 E
robert.percuoco@palmer.edu
PERCUOCO, Robert, E ..... 563-884-5460..... 61 A
robert.percuoco@palmer.edu
PERCY, Paul, M ..... 423-652-4811.... 470 A
PERCY, Stephen ..... 216-687-3786.... 388 D
s.percy@csuohio.edu
PERCY, Steve ..... 410-837-5359.... 229 A
spercy@ubalt.edu
PERDIKIS, Galen ..... 904-953-7035.... 262 E
perdikis.galen@mayo.edu
PERDOMO, Jose, A ..... 425-235-2352.... 537 A
jperdomo@rtc.edu
PERDOMO, Lisa ..... 513-487-1261.... 402 I
lisa.perdomo@myunion.edu
PERDUE, K. Alan ..... 304-876-5009.... 544 C
aperdue@shepherd.edu
PERDUE, Mark ..... 859-858-3511.... 198 E
mark.perdue@asbury.edu
PERDUE, Robin, A ..... 843-383-8025.... 457 A
rperdue@coker.edu
PERDUE, Tina, K ..... 740-376-4730.... 395 G
tina.perdue@marietta.edu
PERDUE, Wendy, C ..... 804-289-1779.... 525 E
wperdue@richmond.edu
PEREBOOM, Maarten, L ..... 410-543-6450.... 228 D
mlpereboom@salisbury.edu
PERECHI, Reuben ..... 904-470-8078.... 105 G
rperechi@ewc.edu
PERECMAN, Dov ..... 845-434-5240.... 362 B
dperecman@fallsburgyeshiva.com
PEREGOY, Robert ..... 406-275-4976.... 296 D
bob_peregoy@skc.edu
PEREGRINE, Rebecca ..... 801-840-4800.... 510 A
rperegrine@cci.edu
PEREIRA, Freyja ..... 707-527-4512..... 68 E
fpereira@santarosa.edu
PEREIRA, Kim ..... 309-438-2559.... 153 D
kpereira@ilstu.edu
PEREIRA, Malin ..... 704-687-7198.... 379 A
mpereira@uncc.edu
PEREIRA, Sandra ..... 508-849-3363.... 230 C
spereira@annamaria.edu
PERERA, Curtis ..... 360-752-8330.... 531 H
cperera@btc.ctc.edu
PERERA-BRIDGES, Sonali . 310-434-3493..... 68 D
perera_sonali@smc.edu
PERES, Phyllis ..... 202-885-2125..... 97 D
academicaffairs@american.edu
PERESS, Kenneth ..... 906-635-2634.... 253 H
kperess@lssu.edu
PERETZ, Marc ..... 989-964-7013.... 257 G
mhp@svsu.edu
PERETZ, Marc, H ..... 989-964-4387.... 257 G
mhp@svsu.edu
PEREY, James ..... 928-649-6513..... 19 C
james.perey@yc.edu
PEREZ, Andrew ..... 518-438-3111.... 340 A
andyp@mariacollege.edu
PEREZ, Angel ..... 909-621-8129..... 62 H
angel_perez@pitzer.edu
PEREZ, Angeles ..... 787-725-6500.... 561 A
aperez@albizu.edu
PEREZ, Antonio ..... 212-220-1234.... 326 D
aperez@bmcc.cuny.edu
PEREZ, Awilda ..... 787-766-1717.... 565 I
um_aperez@suagm.edu
PEREZ, Barbara ..... 310-900-1600..... 45 F
bperez@elcamino.edu
PEREZ, Brigette ..... 914-674-7323.... 340 F
bperez@mercy.edu
PEREZ, Carlos ..... 787-754-8000.... 566 E
cperez@pupr.edu
PEREZ, Carlos ..... 787-622-8000.... 566 E
cperez@pupr.edu
PEREZ, Carlos ..... 956-364-4236.... 500 D
charlie.perez@tstc.edu
PEREZ, Carmen, I ..... 787-279-1912.... 563 D
cperez@bayamon.inter.edu
PEREZ, Cheryle ..... 787-852-1430.... 562 F
cperez@hccpr.edu
PEREZ, Daisy ..... 787-264-1912.... 564 B
daisy.perez@sg.inter.edu
PEREZ, Denise, G ..... 504-280-7446.... 213 E
dgperez@uno.edu
PEREZ, Diana ..... 805-922-6966..... 26 L
dperez@hancockcollege.edu
PEREZ, Donna ..... 225-359-9294.... 209 J
dperez@catc.edu
PEREZ, Doris ..... 787-891-0925.... 563 A
dperez@aguadilla.inter.edu
PEREZ, Doris, U ..... 671-735-5517.... 559 E
planninganddevelopment@guamcc.edu
PEREZ, Enrique ..... 714-480-7460..... 63 E
perez_enrique@rsccd.edu
PEREZ, Ernesto ..... 305-644-1171.... 104 D
ernesto@dademedical.edu
PEREZ, Gay ..... 434-243-3605.... 525 F
bgd2j@virginia.edu
PEREZ, Glenda ..... 787-746-1400.... 562 E
gperez@huertas.edu
PEREZ, Heather, K ..... 816-604-3007.... 285 D
heatherk.perez@mcckc.edu
PEREZ, Irving, H ..... 303-923-4155..... 81 E
ihperez@argosy.edu
PEREZ, Ivelisse ..... 787-834-9595.... 566 B
iperez@uaa.edu
PEREZ, Jesus ..... 718-951-5908.... 326 F
jperez@brooklyn.cuny.edu
PEREZ, Joel ..... 503-554-2305.... 415 I
jperez@georgefox.edu
PEREZ, Jose ..... 787-738-2161.... 567 D
jose.perez@upr.edu
PEREZ, Joseph, L ..... 860-444-8352.... 558 H
joseph.l.perez@uscg.mil
PEREZ, Juan ..... 787-880-6577.... 567 A
juan.perez@upr.edu
PEREZ, Juan ..... 406-275-4978.... 296 D
juan_perez@skc.edu
PEREZ, L. Jeffrey ..... 843-953-6965.... 456 C
jeff.perez@citadel.edu
PEREZ, Lance, C ..... 402-472-3751.... 300 G
lperez1@unl.edu
PEREZ, Leonor ..... 619-644-7000..... 49 C
leonor.perez@gcccd.edu
PEREZ, Lydia ..... 212-742-8770.... 358 B
lydia.perez@touro.edu
PEREZ, Lynn ..... 620-672-5641.... 196 D
lynnp@prattcc.edu
PEREZ, Lynwood, C ..... 407-366-9493.... 115 K
lperez@rts.edu
PEREZ, Lynwood, C ..... 407-366-9493.... 276 F
lperez@rts.edu
PEREZ, Manuel ..... 916-484-8851..... 56 A
perezm@arc.losrios.edu
PEREZ, Manuel ..... 562-985-4151..... 35 C
mperez@csulb.edu
PEREZ, Margarita ..... 251-380-3025....... 7 E
mperez@shc.edu
PEREZ, Maria ..... 787-891-0925.... 563 A
mperez@aguadilla.inter.edu
PEREZ, Maria del C ..... 787-284-1912.... 564 A
mcperezr@ponce.inter.edu
PEREZ, Michael, G ..... 801-581-6510.... 511 C
mike.perez@fm.utah.edu
PEREZ, Michelle ..... 717-871-8943.... 443 D
michelle.perez@millersville.edu
PEREZ, Miguel, E ..... 787-752-4575.... 567 C
miguel.perez8@upr.edu
PEREZ, Miralys ..... 787-600-0979.... 568 C
miralys.perez@upr.edu

PEREZ, Monte, E ... 818-364-7796 ... 55 A
perezme@lamission.edu

PEREZ, Myrna ... 787-786-3030 ... 560 G
mperez@ucb.edu.pr

PEREZ, Ocar ... 305-821-3333 ... 109 D
operez@mm.fnc.edu

PEREZ, Omar ... 787-740-1611 ... 566 C
omar.perez@uccaribe.edu

PEREZ, Oscar ... 305-821-3333 ... 109 B
operez@mm.fnc.edu

PEREZ, Oscar ... 305-821-3333 ... 109 C
operez@mm.fnc.edu

PEREZ, Pedro-Rabel ... 787-250-1912 ... 563 G
prabell@metrolinter.edu

PEREZ, Raymond ... 702-968-1975 ... 303 D
rperez@roseman.edu

PEREZ, Ricardo ... 818-240-1000 ... 48 D
perez@glendale.edu

PEREZ, Ron ... 760-744-1150 ... 61 D
rperez@palomar.edu

PEREZ, Rowena Ellen ... 671-735-5640 ... 559 E
rowenaellen.perez@guamcc.edu

PEREZ, Rueben ... 785-864-4351 ... 197 B
rperez@ku.edu

PEREZ, Ruperto ... 404-894-2575 ... 130 F
ruperto.perez@vpss.gatech.edu

PEREZ, Scott, L ... 818-677-2901 ... 35 F
scott.perez@csun.edu

PEREZ, Sonny, P ... 671-735-2372 ... 559 G
sonnypz@uguam.uog.edu

PEREZ, Suleyma ... 773-442-5400 ... 160 A
s-perez6@neiu.edu

PEREZ, Tony ... 940-553-4403 ... 507 F
tperez@vernoncollege.edu

PEREZ, Wanda ... 787-878-5475 ... 563 B
wperez@arecibo.inter.edu

PEREZ, William ... 787-780-0070 ... 560 H
wperez@caribbean.edu

PEREZ-FRANCO, Mayte ... 619-260-2395 ... 76 D
mpf@sandiego.edu

PEREZ GARCIA, Cesar ... 208-732-6250 ... 143 E
cperez@csi.edu

PEREZ-LOPEZ, Myrna, E ... 787-763-6700 ... 562 D
meperez@se-pr.edu

PEREZ-SILVA, Glaisma ... 860-906-5042 ... 91 C
gperez-silva@ccc.commnet.edu

PEREZ-TORO, Angeles ... 787-725-6500 ... 561 A
aperez@albizu.edu

PEREZCASTANEDA, Tana .. 603-668-6660 ... 305 B

PERFECTO, Gerardo ... 787-768-2934 ... 567 C
gerardo.perfecto@upr.edu

PERFETTI, Anthony ... 516-678-5000 ... 341 F
aperfetti@molly.edu

PERFETTI, Heather ... 845-341-4768 ... 345 E
heather.perfetti@sunyorange.edu

PERFETTI, Lisa, R ... 509-527-5187 ... 540 B
perfetlr@whitman.edu

PERFETTI, Margi, L ... 301-387-3042 ... 222 H
margi.perfetti@garrettcollege.edu

PERGI, Brenan ... 740-283-6445 ... 391 A
bpergi@franciscan.edu

PERGL, Denise ... 254-526-1291 ... 482 H
denise.pergl@ctcd.edu

PERGOLA-RIVERA,
Maribelle ... 787-993-8951 ... 567 B
maribelle.pergola@upr.edu

PERGOLIS, Robert ... 631-687-1417 ... 349 B
rpergolis@sjcny.edu

PERGOLIS, Robert ... 718-940-5419 ... 349 A
rpergolis@sjcny.edu

PERGOLIZZI, Frank ... 304-442-3121 ... 545 D
frank.pergolizzi@mail.wvu.edu

PERGOLIZZI, Vanessa ... 860-913-2160 ... 92 I
vpergolizzi@goodwin.edu

PERHAM, Andrea ... 802-635-1341 ... 515 F
andrea.perham@jsc.edu

PERI, Jonathan ... 610-358-4585 ... 437 D
perij@neumann.edu

PERIGARD, Julie ... 360-779-9993 ... 535 J
jperigard@ncad.edu

PERILLO, Brian, R ... 848-932-7490 ... 314 B
bperillo@alumni.rutgers.edu

PERILLO, Cheryl ... 312-980-9250 ... 154 B
cperillo@iadtchicago.edu

PERILLO, Patricia, A ... 540-231-6272 ... 529 G
pperillo@vt.edu

PERIN, Thomas ... 567-661-7880 ... 400 I
thomas_perin@owlens.edu

PERINO, Donna, B ... 814-456-7504 ... 428 G
perinod@eriebc.edu

PERKINS, Abby ... 937-224-0061 ... 395 B
aperkins@swcollege.net

PERKINS, JR., Andrew, M 336-285-4551 ... 378 A
perkins@ncat.edu

PERKINS, Anika, M ... 662-329-7119 ... 276 A
aperkins@pa.muw.edu

PERKINS, Bethany ... 603-645-9611 ... 305 I
b.perkins@snhu.edu

PERKINS, Bruce ... 405-878-2033 ... 409 D
bruce.perkins@okbu.edu

PERKINS, Carolyn ... 717-262-2006 ... 452 C
cperkins@wilson.edu

PERKINS, Caron ... 432-552-2747 ... 507 D
perkins_c@utpb.edu

PERKINS, Charles ... 620-792-9245 ... 190 H
perkinsc@bartonccc.edu

PERKINS, Claude, G ... 804-257-5835 ... 530 A
cgperkins@vuu.edu

PERKINS, Crasha ... 540-831-5765 ... 523 A

PERKINS, D. Clay ... 252-334-2004 ... 367 C
clay.perkins@macuniversity.edu

PERKINS, David, G ... 913-684-5621 ... 558 F

PERKINS, Edward ... 781-736-4505 ... 232 F
perkins@brandeis.edu

PERKINS, OP, Ignatius ... 615-297-7545 ... 467 A
perkinsi@aquinascollege.edu

PERKINS, Jeffrey ... 617-682-1502 ... 234 E
jperkins@eds.edu

PERKINS, Jeri Parris ... 864-833-7000 ... 460 E
jpperkins@presby.edu

PERKINS, Jim ... 601-979-2024 ... 274 G
james.perkins@jsums.edu

PERKINS, Joseph, E ... 919-572-1689 ... 362 C
jperkins@apexsot.edu

PERKINS, Joshua, L ... 330-471-8270 ... 395 F
jperkins@malone.edu

PERKINS, Kathy ... 417-447-8114 ... 287 D

PERKINS, Keith ... 757-727-6988 ... 519 H
keith.perkins@hamptonu.edu

PERKINS, Keith ... 937-376-6640 ... 387 A
kperkins@centralstate.edu

PERKINS, Kenneth, B ... 434-395-2010 ... 521 A
perkinskb@longwood.edu

PERKINS, JR., Louis ... 202-238-2332 ... 98 E
louis.perkins@howard.edu

PERKINS, Lynn ... 815-921-4268 ... 162 H
g.perkins@rockvalleycollege.edu

PERKINS, Mary ... 847-214-7414 ... 150 F
mperkins@elgin.edu

PERKINS, Michele ... 561-297-3735 ... 119 A
mperkins@fau.edu

PERKINS, Michele, D ... 603-428-2222 ... 305 D
mperkins@nec.edu

PERKINS, Myrna, L ... 620-792-9270 ... 190 H
perkinsm@bartonccc.edu

PERKINS, Pamela, M ... 620-417-1011 ... 196 F
pam.perkins@sccc.edu

PERKINS, Peter ... 315-792-7273 ... 356 B
peter.perkins@sunyit.edu

PERKINS, Priscilla, L ... 413-782-1531 ... 246 A
pperkins@wne.edu

PERKINS, Robert, J ... 570-945-8276 ... 432 E
robert.perkins@keystone.edu

PERKINS, Russell ... 800-955-2527 ... 282 D
rperkins@grantham.edu

PERKINS, Sarah ... 650-738-4321 ... 67 H
perkinss@smccd.edu

PERKINS, Susan, K ... 732-906-2505 ... 311 D
sperkins@middlesexcc.edu

PERKINS, Tracey, G ... 603-526-3702 ... 303 G
tperkins@colby-sawyer.edu

PERKINS, Will ... 573-341-4212 ... 291 E
asksdp@mst.edu

PERKINS, Will ... 503-352-2212 ... 419 E
wperkins@pacificu.edu

PERKINS BROWN, Jayne . 912-478-5218 ... 131 E
jperkins@georgiasouthern.edu

PERKINSON, A, P ... 276-944-6806 ... 519 A
bperkinson@ehc.edu

PERKINSON, James ... 757-822-5150 ... 528 G
jperkinson@tcc.edu

PERKINSON, Stephen ... 330-867-1996 ... 397 B

PERKNER, Stanislav ... 209-478-0800 ... 50 K
sperkner@humphreys.edu

PERKO, Janet, A ... 330-471-8340 ... 395 F
jperko@malone.edu

PERKOWSKI, C, L ... 718-259-2525 ... 324 A

PERKOWSKI, Henry ... 212-678-3016 ... 357 G
hp2125@tc.columbia.edu

PERKOWSKI, Linda ... 989-774-7860 ... 249 C
perko1lc@cmich.edu

PERKOWSKI, Peter ... 330-494-1214 ... 386 A
pperkowski@brownmackie.edu

PERL, Emily ... 410-337-6122 ... 222 I
eperl@goucher.edu

PERLAS, Char ... 408-855-5041 ... 78 F
char.perlas@wvm.edu

PERLICK, Nick ... 615-898-2502 ... 473 G
nick.perlick@mtsu.edu

PERLIN, Jeremy ... 513-487-3215 ... 335 B
jperlin@huc.edu

PERLMAN, Harvey ... 402-472-2116 ... 300 G
hperlman1@unl.edu

PERLMAN, Lynn ... 617-277-3915 ... 232 D
perlmanl@bgsp.edu

PERLOFF, Carey ... 415-439-2422 ... 28 C
cep@act-sf.org

PERLOW, Yaakov ... 718-438-2727 ... 361 O

PERLSTROM, Christine, L .. 847-574-5208 ... 156 A
cperlstrom@lfgsm.edu

PERMAN, Jay, A ... 410-706-7002 ... 227 C
jperman@umaryland.edu

PERMENTER, Andrew, H ... 863-667-5078 ... 118 F
ahpermenter@seu.edu

PERNA, Michael ... 201-200-3542 ... 312 B
mperna@njcu.edu

PERNAL, Michael, E ... 860-465-5215 ... 90 H
pernal@easternct.edu

PERNELL, Leroy ... 407-254-3268 ... 118 L
leroy.pernell@famu.edu

PERNETTI, Tim, R ... 732-445-8610 ... 314 B
ad@scarletknights.com

PERNICIARO, Richard ... 609-343-5670 ... 307 C
rpernici@atlantic.edu

PERNICK HUBER,
Maureen ... 716-827-2444 ... 358 D
huberm@trocaire.edu

PERNOT, Laurent ... 312-553-2500 ... 147 B
lpernot@ccc.edu

PERNSTEINER, George, P . 541-346-5794 ... 418 B
george_pernsteiner@ous.edu

PERONE, Julie ... 610-436-2301 ... 444 A
jperone@wcupa.edu

PERONI-CALLAHAN,
Kathy ... 617-521-2150 ... 244 F
kathleen.peroni-callahan@simmons.edu

PEROO, Rama ... 620-441-5587 ... 192 D
peroo@cowley.edu

PEROZZI, Brett ... 801-626-6361 ... 511 G
brettperozzi@weber.edu

PERR, Yechiel, I ... 718-327-7600 ... 360 I
yfr1@verizon.net

PERRA, Thomas, J ... 860-768-4636 ... 95 B
perra@hartford.edu

PERREAULT, Melanie, L ... 410-548-4085 ... 228 D
mlperreault@salisbury.edu

PERREN, Ray ... 229-333-2119 ... 139 I
ray.perren@wiregrass.edu

PERRENOD, William, L ... 914-337-9300 ... 330 G
william.perrenod@concordia-ny.edu

PERRES, Irving ... 718-232-7800 ... 361 D

PERRET, Geraldine ... 973-618-3536 ... 308 C
gperret@caldwell.edu

PERRETTI, Richel ... 814-863-5538 ... 438 G
rap126@psu.edu

PERRI, Christine ... 619-216-6668 ... 71 D
cperri@swccd.edu

PERRI, Geraldine, M ... 626-914-8821 ... 40 B
gperri@citruscollege.edu

PERRI, Mary Lynn ... 440-646-8329 ... 405 B
mperri@ursuline.edu

PERRI, Michael ... 352-273-6214 ... 120 C
mperri@phhp.ufl.edu

PERRI, Ralph ... 361-593-2174 ... 498 D
ralph.perri@tamuk.edu

PERRIN, Amy ... 847-214-7217 ... 150 F
aperrin@elgin.edu

PERRIN, Annette ... 585-266-0430 ... 333 D
aperrin@cci.edu

PERRIN, David, H ... 336-334-5494 ... 379 B
dhperrin@uncg.edu

PERRIN, Dawn ... 513-569-1706 ... 387 G
dawn.perrin@cincinnatistate.edu

PERRIN, Jean ... 574-289-7001 ... 176 E
jperrin@ivytech.edu

PERRIN, L. Timothy ... 806-720-7125 ... 490 F
tim.perrin@lcu.edu

PERRIN, Nicholas ... 630-752-5227 ... 168 H
nicholas.perrin@wheaton.edu

PERRIN, Ralph ... 530-242-7730 ... 69 D
rperrin@shastacollege.edu

PERRINE, Mary, A ... 315-786-2485 ... 337 F
mperrine@sunyjefferson.edu

PERRINE, Paul ... 828-298-3325 ... 380 D
pperrine@warren-wilson.edu

PERRINE, Richard ... 603-897-8206 ... 305 F
rperrine@rivier.edu

PERRING, Sally, A ... 559-323-2100 ... 66 C
sperring@sjcl.edu

PERRITON, Caleb ... 307-755-2114 ... 557 B
cperriton@wyotechstaff.edu

PERRON, Evelyn, R ... 603-206-8121 ... 304 D
eperron@ccsnh.edu

PERRONE, Dona, J ... 203-371-7897 ... 94 B
registrar@sacredheart.edu

PERRONE, Kim ... 518-631-9852 ... 358 H
perronek@uniongraduatecollege.edu

PERRONE, Mary ... 315-792-7333 ... 356 B
mary.perrone@sunyit.edu

PERROTTA, Steve ... 603-513-1341 ... 306 F
steve.perrotta@granite.edu

PERROTTI, James ... 860-297-2054 ... 94 E
james.perrotti@trincoll.edu

PERRUCI,
Gamaliel (Gama) ... 740-376-4741 ... 395 G
gama.perruci@marietta.edu

PERRUCI,
Gamaliel (Gama) ... 740-376-4760 ... 395 G
gama.perruci@marietta.edu

PERRY, Angela, G ... 919-536-7250 ... 370 C
perrya@durhamtech.edu

PERRY, Anne ... 708-342-3747 ... 150 B
aperry3@devry.edu

PERRY, Beth ... 304-929-1338 ... 541 H
bperry@mountainstate.edu

PERRY, Candace ... 404-756-4004 ... 125 D
cperry@atlm.edu

PERRY, Candace ... 218-322-2340 ... 266 G
candace.perry@itascacc.edu

PERRY, Carol, A ... 304-710-3141 ... 542 K
perry@mctc.edu

PERRY, Carolyn, J ... 573-592-5212 ... 293 B
carolyn.perry@westminster-mo.edu

PERRY, Chad, L ... 505-925-8547 ... 321 G
cperry@unm.edu

PERRY, Christine, M ... 617-573-8470 ... 245 B
cperry@suffolk.edu

PERRY, Claudia ... 314-644-9745 ... 288 I
cperry@stlcc.edu

PERRY, Cynthia, R ... 757-594-7003 ... 517 L
cperry@cnu.edu

PERRY, David, L ... 850-644-1240 ... 119 D
dlperry@admin.fsu.edu

PERRY, Derrick ... 702-579-3530 ... 302 A
dperry@kaplan.edu

PERRY, Dexter ... 919-572-1625 ... 362 C
dperry@apexsot.edu

PERRY, Don ... 214-378-1732 ... 484 F
don.perry@dcccd.edu

PERRY, Douglas, E ... 815-939-5240 ... 161 A
dperry@olivet.edu

PERRY, Douglas, G ... 260-422-5561 ... 173 C
dgperry@indianatech.edu

PERRY, Eddie, L ... 540-654-1025 ... 525 D
eperry@umw.edu

PERRY, Erma ... 334-687-3543 ... 4 A
eperry@wallace.edu

PERRY, Frank, E ... 412-397-6233 ... 445 H
perry@rmu.edu

PERRY, Gary ... 561-297-3288 ... 119 A
perryg@fau.edu

PERRY, George ... 210-458-4450 ... 506 D
george.perry@utsa.edu

PERRY, George ... 304-260-4380 ... 542 G
gperry@blueridgectc.edu

PERRY, Gretchen ... 845-758-7276 ... 323 D
gperry@bard.edu

PERRY, Gwendolyn ... 919-546-8564 ... 376 F
gperry@shawu.edu

PERRY, James ... 903-813-2277 ... 481 A
jperry@austincollege.edu

PERRY, Janet ... 970-207-4500 ... 89 D
janetp@uscareerinstitute.edu

PERRY, Janet ... 405-682-1611 ... 409 F
jcperry@occc.edu

PERRY, Jason ... 801-581-8514 ... 511 C
jason.perry@utah.edu

PERRY, Jeff ... 800-962-7682 ... 293 A
jperry@wma.edu

PERRY, Jerry ... 303-724-2133 ... 88 J
jerry.perry@ucdenver.edu

PERRY, Jessica, M ... 787-743-7979 ... 565 H
ut_jperry@suagm.edu

PERRY, Johanna, L ... 914-337-9300 ... 330 G
johanna.perry@concordia-ny.edu

PERRY, John ... 815-802-8552 ... 155 A
jperry@kcc.edu

PERRY, John, F ... 864-503-5242 ... 463 B
jperry@uscupstate.edu

PERRY, Jonathan, C ... 479-575-5276 ... 24 C
jperry@uark.edu

PERRY, Judy, A ... 432-837-8058 ... 501 E
jperry@sulross.edu

PERRY, Katherine ... 315-498-2602 ... 345 D
perryka@sunyocc.edu

PERRY, Kimberly ... 530-895-2484 ... 31 H
perryki@butte.edu

PERRY, Kristine ... 973-300-2772 ... 315 F
kperry@sussex.edu

PERRY, Laura ... 315-268-6760 ... 329 B
lperry@clarkson.edu

PERRY, Mansco ... 651-696-6735 ... 264 J
mperry@macalester.edu

PERRY, Margaret ... 202-495-3828 ... 99 C
advance@dhs.edu

PERRY, Maria ... 215-884-8942 ... 452 D
cfo@woninstitute.edu

PERRY, Marilynn ... 732-571-3489 ... 311 E
mperry@monmouth.edu

PERRY, Mark ... 417-862-9533 ... 282 A
mperry@globaluniversity.edu

PERRY, Mark ... 559-734-9000 ... 66 E
president@sjvc.edu

PERRY, Mark ... 559-734-9000 ... 67 A
president@sjvc.edu

PERRY, Mark ... 559-734-9000 ... 66 H
markp@sjvc.edu

PERRY, Mark ... 559-734-9000 ... 66 K
president@sjvc.edu

PERRY, Mark, A ... 559-734-9000 ... 66 G
president@sjvc.edu

PERRY, Marva ... 781-239-3151 ... 239 G
mperry@massbay.edu

PERRY, Mary Elaine ... 610-660-1045 ... 446 C
mperry01@sju.edu

PERRY, Maryann, B ... 508-565-1105 ... 245 A
mperry@stonehill.edu

PERRY, Melissa ... 386-312-4058 ... 116 F
melissaperry@sjrstate.edu

PERRY, Meredith ... 423-425-4431 ... 477 F
meredith-perry@utc.edu

PERRY, Michael ... 559-734-9000 ... 66 E
mikep@sjvc.edu

PERRY, Michael ... 321-674-7127 ... 108 H
perrymj@fit.edu

PERRY, Michael, J ... 315-386-7315 ... 355 E
perrymj@canton.edu

PERRY, Nancy 410-386-8231 221 G nperry@carrollcc.edu
PERRY, Nauleen, A 302-857-1080 96 G nperry@dtcc.edu
PERRY, Pat, B 252-246-1327 375 D pperry@wilsoncc.edu
PERRY, Paul 231-995-1114 256 D pperry@nmc.edu
PERRY, Ralph, F 256-824-6880 8 G foster.perry@uah.edu
PERRY, Renee 602-285-7433 16 A renee.perry@pcmail.maricopa.edu
PERRY, Robert, K 423-746-5209 476 F rkperry@twcnet.edu
PERRY, Roberta 610-526-2967 445 J rperry@rosemont.edu
PERRY, Robin 704-637-4384 363 E raperry@catawba.edu
PERRY, Roslyn 606-783-2571 204 I ro.perry@moreheadstate.edu
PERRY, Sam, J 773-508-3598 157 C sperry@luc.edu
PERRY, Scott 312-777-8664 153 B smperry@aii.edu
PERRY, Stephanie, D 276-328-0240 525 G sdh9y@uvawise.edu
PERRY, Steve 864-294-2458 458 E steve.perry@furman.edu
PERRY, Steven 201-684-7363 313 C sperry@ramapo.edu
PERRY, Steven 325-738-3341 500 G steven.perry@tstc.edu
PERRY, Steven, R 607-436-2513 353 E perrysr@oneonta.edu
PERRY, Stuart 320-363-5047 262 F sperry@csbsju.edu
PERRY, Stuart 320-363-5047 271 A sperry@csbsju.edu
PERRY, Sue, A 856-691-8600 309 B sperry@cccnj.edu
PERRY, Thomas, D 740-376-4408 395 G tom.perry@marietta.edu
PERRY, Tom 479-524-7122 22 C tperry@jbu.edu
PERRY, Walter 215-596-8890 450 B w.perry@usciences.edu
PERRY, Wayne 334-387-3877 1 D wayneperry@amridgeuniversity.edu
PERRY, William, L 217-581-2011 150 E wlperry@eiu.edu
PERRY-JOHNSON, Arlethia 770-423-6350 133 A aperryjo@kennesaw.edu
PERRY-NAUSE, Sharon 419-448-3504 402 E perrynauses@tiffin.edu
PERRY-SPEARS, Megan 218-723-6029 262 G mperryspears@css.edu
PERRY-THOMPSON, Laura 814-269-7070 449 D lpt@pitt.edu
PERRYMAN, Larry 707-468-3069 57 A lperryman@mendocino.edu
PERRYMAN, Linda 864-225-7653 458 C lindaperryman@forrestcollege.edu
PERRYMAN, Nancy, S 309-655-4119 163 G nancy.s.perryman@osfhealthcare.org
PERSAUD, Damindra 718-261-5800 324 D dpersaud@bramsonort.edu
PERSAUD, June 973-877-3407 309 H persaud@essex.edu
PERSAUD, Roxanne 718-489-5379 348 E rpersaud@sfc.edu
PERSHING, David, W 801-581-5701 511 C david.pershing@utah.edu
PERSICHITTE, Kay, A 307-766-3145 556 H kpersi@uwyo.edu
PERSICO, Frank, G 202-319-5100 97 E persico@cua.edu
PERSICO, Sebastian, T 212-817-7600 327 B spersico@gc.cuny.edu
PERSINGER, Bill 931-221-6309 473 E persingerb@apsu.edu
PERSKY, Ira 718-982-2240 327 A ira.persky@csi.cuny.edu
PERSON, Andy 914-330-1450 340 F aperson@mercy.edu
PERSON, Gretchen 615-322-2457 478 A religiouslife@vanderbilt.edu
PERSON, Mark 601-979-2021 274 G mark.s.person@jsums.edu
PERSON, Ruth, J 810-762-5725 259 C rjperson@umflint.edu
PERSON, Undrell 505-424-2330 318 D uperson@iaia.edu
PERSON, Walter 202-686-0876 99 E walter.person@potomac.edu
PERSONS, William 334-229-4276 1 C wpersons@alasu.edu
PERSSON, Carol 413-572-5365 238 F cpersson@wsc.ma.edu
PERSSON, Katherine 281-312-1640 490 E katherine.persson@lonestar.edu
PERTL, Brian, G 920-832-6614 548 B brian.g.pertl@lawrence.edu
PERUGGI, Regina, S 718-368-5109 328 A president@kbcc.cuny.edu
PERUSO, Dominick, F 814-472-3005 446 B dperuso@francis.edu
PERUSSE, Charles, E 919-962-1000 377 C ceperusse@northcarolina.edu
PERVI, Susan, D 202-319-5714 97 E pervi@cua.edu
PERVIER, Curt 432-685-4677 491 A cpervier@midland.edu
PERZESKI, Donna, M 216-916-7506 394 B dmp@kent.edu
PESARCHICK, Robert, A 610-785-6204 446 A rpesarchick@scs.edu
PESCARMONA, Denee 661-362-5042 41 I denee.pescarmona@canyons.edu
PESCOVITZ, Ora, H 734-647-9351 259 A opescovi@umich.edu
PESEK, James, G 814-393-2600 442 B jpesek@clarion.edu
PESHEK, Mary 712-274-5274 187 G peshek@morningside.edu
PESKA, Don 817-735-2149 504 E don.peska@unthsc.edu
PESOLD, Dan 314-968-7130 292 J pesoldd@webster.edu
PESOTSKI, Chris 215-717-6170 448 I cpesotski@uarts.edu
PESSINK, Martin 903-983-8650 489 I mpessink@kilgore.edu
PESTA, Donna 518-255-5624 354 E pestadh@cobleskill.edu
PESTA, John 570-408-4641 452 A john.pesta@wilkes.edu
PESTANA, John 508-565-1315 245 A jpestana@stonehill.edu
PESTELLO, Fred, P 315-445-4120 338 B president@lemoyne.edu
PESTRUE, Wendy 419-783-2463 389 H wpestrue@defiance.edu
PETA, Jamie 303-546-5283 86 H jamiep@naropa.edu
PETAK, Katty 402-399-2411 297 C vpetak@csm.edu
PETCHER, Douglas 312-362-7595 149 A dpetcher@depaul.edu
PETE, Mary, C 907-543-4502 10 I mpete@alaska.edu
PETER, Beth, C 651-641-8795 263 A peter@csp.edu
PETER, David 812-888-4166 181 D dpeter@vinu.edu
PETER, Florence, L 692-625-3394 560 A flpeter@cmi.edu
PETER, Joakim 691-330-2620 559 D jojo@comfsm.fm
PETER, Lori 660-263-3900 279 F lbp@cccb.edu
PETERKA, Cynthia, J 443-518-4809 223 D cpeterka@howardcc.edu
PETERMAN, Francine 718-997-5220 328 E francine.peterman@qc.cuny.edu
PETERMAN, Francine 973-655-7030 311 F petermanf@mail.montclair.edu
PETERS, Anna 212-659-3610 338 A
PETERS, Bob 360-736-9391 532 D bpeters@centralia.edu
PETERS, Brett 414-229-4126 551 D
PETERS, Brian, S 847-491-8420 160 E b-peters2@northwestern.edu
PETERS, C. Ellen 253-879-3104 538 H epeters@pugetsound.edu
PETERS, Chad 864-644-5325 461 B cpeters@swu.edu
PETERS, Cherise 334-229-6771 1 C cpeters@alasu.edu
PETERS, Clark 814-732-2921 442 E cpeters@edinboro.edu
PETERS, Craig 605-367-5462 466 D craig.peters@southeasttech.edu
PETERS, Daniel, J 402-461-7303 298 A dpeters@hastings.edu
PETERS, David 407-569-1320 107 I david.peters@fcc.edu
PETERS, David, R 304-473-8540 545 G
PETERS, Deborah 406-896-5832 295 D deborah.peters@msubillings.edu
PETERS, Doug, D 218-477-2306 267 F petersd@mnstate.edu
PETERS, Earic 323-953-4000 54 H peterseb@lacitycollege.edu
PETERS, Eva 909-621-8471 62 H eva_peters@pitzer.edu
PETERS, Fred, M 903-510-2627 503 A fpet@tjc.edu
PETERS, Gordon, C 801-818-8900 510 I gordonp@provocollege.edu
PETERS, Hermina, P 202-274-6256 100 A hpeters@udc.edu
PETERS, J. Lee 860-768-4165 95 B lpeters@hartford.edu
PETERS, James 616-538-2330 251 D jpeters@gbcol.edu
PETERS, Jana 661-763-7809 72 E jpeters@taftcollege.edu
PETERS, Jerry 760-252-2411 30 H jpeters@barstow.edu
PETERS, Jessica 620-365-5116 190 D peters@allencc.edu
PETERS, John, E 270-824-8593 202 G john.peters@kctcs.edu
PETERS, John, G 815-753-9500 160 B jpeters@niu.edu
PETERS, Joseph, R 502-410-6200 200 L jpeters@galencollege.edu
PETERS, Joyce 662-685-4771 273 E jpeters@bmc.edu
PETERS, Kirk 860-255-3561 92 F kpeters@txcc.commnet.edu
PETERS, Larry 580-349-1560 410 B lpeters@opsu.edu
PETERS, Lee 617-262-5000 231 G lee.peters@the-bac.edu
PETERS, Leonard 203-432-3262 96 A leonard.peters@yale.edu
PETERS, Libby 606-436-5721 202 C libby.peters@kctcs.edu
PETERS, RET., MaryAnn 401-841-7004 558 B
PETERS, MaryAnne 610-341-5834 428 E mpeters@eastern.edu
PETERS, Matthew 570-702-8914 431 L mpeters@johnson.edu
PETERS, Melissa 386-481-2580 102 C petersm@cookman.edu
PETERS, Michael, P 505-984-6098 320 C president@sjcsf.edu
PETERS, Michele 716-827-4333 358 D petersm@trocaire.edu
PETERS, Monica 936-633-5250 480 D mpeters@angelina.edu
PETERS, Nikki 620-431-2820 195 E npeters@neosho.edu
PETERS, Pamela, J 607-746-4635 355 F peterspj@delhi.edu
PETERS, Randall 770-228-7365 137 F rpeters@sctech.edu
PETERS, Robert 715-232-1168 552 E petersb@uwstout.edu
PETERS, Ronald, E 404-527-7702 132 G rpeters@itc.edu
PETERS, Sarah 503-961-6200 418 A speters@pioneerpacific.edu
PETERS, Scott 573-897-5000 284 A
PETERS, Sheila 615-329-8575 468 I speters@fisk.edu
PETERS, Steve 316-295-5567 193 B steve_peters@friends.edu
PETERS, Sue 925-631-4842 64 F speters@stmarys-ca.edu
PETERS, Suzanne 413-545-0356 236 F sepeters@finaid.umass.edu
PETERS, Terry 515-244-4221 181 F peterst@aib.edu
PETERS, Thomas, A 417-836-4525 286 C
PETERS, Timothy, C 949-214-3363 43 C tim.peters@cui.edu
PETERS, Tom, D 308-398-7365 297 A tpeters@cccneb.edu
PETERS, Vincent 651-638-6124 261 D v-peters@bethel.edu
PETERS-NGUYEN, Diane 808-735-4772 140 E dpeters@chaminade.edu
PETERSDORFF, Joe 478-988-6800 134 C jpetersdorff@middlegatech.edu
PETERSEN, Aaron 517-437-7341 252 C aaron.petersen@hillsdale.edu
PETERSEN, Barbara 814-254-0471 425 G bpetersen@pa.gov
PETERSEN, Calvin 402-280-2796 297 F creighton@bkstr.com
PETERSEN, Carol 319-273-2333 182 G carol.petersen@uni.edu
PETERSEN, Dana 207-216-4454 219 C dpetersen@yccc.edu
PETERSEN, Debra 260-459-4545 175 C dpetersen@ibcfortwayne.edu
PETERSEN, Donna 813-974-6603 121 A dpeters@hsc.usf.edu
PETERSEN, Dorene 503-244-0726 414 D dorenepetersen@achs.edu
PETERSEN, George 805-493-3419 33 B gjpeters@clunet.edu
PETERSEN, Glenn 507-457-5031 269 G gpetersen@winona.edu
PETERSEN, Karl 314-768-7800 286 A kpetersen@missouricollege.com
PETERSEN, Kristin 402-471-2505 299 D kpetersen@nscs.edu
PETERSEN, Linda 785-243-1435 192 A lpetersen@cloud.edu
PETERSEN, Mark, A 336-758-6053 380 C map@wfu.edu
PETERSEN, Mark, T 540-378-5125 523 G petersen@roanoke.edu
PETERSEN, Marty 425-602-3027 531 E mpetersen@bastyr.edu
PETERSEN, Mary, S 206-296-2043 538 B marypete@seattleu.edu
PETERSEN, Melinda 503-725-8212 418 G melinda.petersen@pdx.edu
PETERSEN, Page 507-433-0650 268 H ppeterse@riverland.edu
PETERSEN, Stephen 847-925-6255 151 G speterse@harpercollege.edu
PETERSEN, Stephen, H 901-678-5426 474 C shptrsen@memphis.edu
PETERSEN, Ted 815-802-8602 155 A tpetersen@kcc.edu
PETERSEN, Tina 916-577-2200 79 G tpetersen@jessup.edu
PETERSON, Al, L 661-824-2977 58 H
PETERSON, Andrew 215-596-8877 450 B a.peterson@usciences.edu
PETERSON, Andrew, J 704-366-4853 276 F apeterson@rts.edu
PETERSON, Arlene 718-482-5088 328 B apeterson@lagcc.cuny.edu
PETERSON, Arthur 626-571-8811 77 A arthurp@uwest.edu
PETERSON, Arthur 626-571-8811 77 A apeterson@uwest.edu
PETERSON, Barbara 732-224-2643 308 A bpeterson@brookdalecc.edu
PETERSON, Bill 706-233-7469 137 A bpeterson@shorter.edu
PETERSON, Bruce, A 320-308-6639 269 B bpeterson@sctcc.edu
PETERSON, Bruce, E 740-376-4736 395 G bruce.peterson@marietta.edu
PETERSON, Carolyn 919-546-3750 376 F cpeterson@shawu.edu
PETERSON, Cathleen 816-941-7470 281 A cpeterson@devry.edu
PETERSON, Chad 612-436-7520 265 D cpeterson@msbcollege.edu
PETERSON, JR., Charles 804-523-5821 527 A cpeterson@reynolds.edu
PETERSON, Charles, D 701-231-7456 382 B charles.peterson@ndsu.edu
PETERSON, Charles, I 773-244-5615 159 H cpeterson@northpark.edu
PETERSON, Chris 501-569-3167 24 E tlcampbell@ualr.edu
PETERSON, Chris 405-491-6333 412 D cpeterso@snu.edu
PETERSON, Christine 443-423-1467 224 B cpetersn@mica.edu
PETERSON, Cindy 913-971-3533 195 D cpeterso@mnu.edu
PETERSON, Cynthia 903-923-2257 486 F cpeterson@etbu.edu
PETERSON, Cynthia, L 706-778-8500 136 A cpeterson@piedmont.edu
PETERSON, David 309-672-5916 158 C dpeterson@methodistcol.edu
PETERSON, David 651-675-4700 264 F dpeterson@msp.chefs.edu
PETERSON, Deborah, A 952-885-5412 270 C dpeterson@nwhealth.edu
PETERSON, Dennis, R 563-884-5442 188 E dennis.peterson@palmer.edu
PETERSON, Derek 605-688-4163 466 C derek.peterson@sdstate.edu
PETERSON, Dolores 610-372-4721 445 C dpeterson@racc.edu
PETERSON, Don 209-384-6182 57 C peterson.d@mccd.edu
PETERSON, Frances 606-759-7141 203 A frances.peterson@kctcs.edu
PETERSON, Freddie 318-274-2222 215 E petersonf@gram.edu
PETERSON, G. P. (Bud) 404-894-5051 130 F president@gatech.edu
PETERSON, Gail 414-326-2303 547 B gpeterso@ccon.edu
PETERSON, Graham 870-862-8131 23 G gpeterson@southark.edu
PETERSON, Greg 562-938-4140 54 E gpeterson@lbcc.edu
PETERSON, Greg 507-457-2800 269 G gpeterson@winona.edu
PETERSON, Heather 609-343-5008 307 C hpeterso@atlantic.edu
PETERSON, Jacqueline, D 508-793-2414 233 C jpeterso@holycross.edu
PETERSON, James 510-540-7747 54 B jamespeterson@lincolnuca.edu
PETERSON, James 616-234-4017 251 E jpeter@grcc.edu
PETERSON, James, R 509-527-4686 539 B
PETERSON, Jill 916-278-6940 36 A jill.peteson@csus.edu
PETERSON, JoAnn 712-279-1633 183 A joann.peterson@briarcliff.edu
PETERSON, Joanne 309-341-7793 155 F jpeterso@knox.edu
PETERSON, Joe 435-613-5220 512 A joe.peterson@usu.edu
PETERSON, John, A 671-735-2170 559 G jpeterson@uguam.uog.edu

PETERSON, John, A ... 671-735-0219 ... 559 G jpeterson@uguam.uog.edu
PETERSON, Joyce, C ... 218-722-4000 ... 263 E joycep@dbumn.edu
PETERSON, Julie ... 773-702-0689 ... 166 G juliep@uchicago.edu
PETERSON, Kate, M ... 541-737-0759 ... 418 F kate.peterson@oregonstate.edu
PETERSON, Kathy ... 269-782-1492 ... 258 C kpeterson@swmich.edu
PETERSON, Kent, A ... 414-277-7176 ... 549 C peterson@msoe.edu
PETERSON, Kirk ... 937-484-1242 ... 405 A kpeterson@urbana.edu
PETERSON, Klay ... 864-503-5254 ... 463 B kpeterson@uscupstate.edu
PETERSON, Kurtis, M ... 860-882-1690 ... 94 D
PETERSON, Larry, E ... 618-634-3221 ... 164 E larryp@shawneecc.edu
PETERSON, Laura ... 940-397-4919 ... 491 B laura.peterson@mwsu.edu
PETERSON, Laura, K ... 614-235-4136 ... 402 G lpeterson@tlsohio.edu
PETERSON, Leland ... 802-586-7711 ... 514 G lpeterson@sterlingcollege.edu
PETERSON, Linda ... 305-899-3020 ... 101 M lpeterson@mail.barry.edu
PETERSON, Linda ... 813-974-6061 ... 121 A lpeterso@admin.usf.edu
PETERSON, Linda ... 215-885-2360 ... 435 E lpeterson@manor.edu
PETERSON, Linda, C ... 865-694-6404 ... 475 G lcpeterson@pstcc.edu
PETERSON, Linda, M ... 563-556-5110 ... 188 B petersol@nicc.edu
PETERSON, Lori ... 612-330-1637 ... 261 B petersol@augsburg.edu
PETERSON, Lori ... 406-447-5432 ... 293 G lpeterson@carroll.edu
PETERSON, Maggie ... 406-496-4316 ... 296 B mpeterson@mtech.edu
PETERSON, Marc ... 214-768-3417 ... 495 A mpeterso@smu.edu
PETERSON, Margaret ... 406-496-4316 ... 296 A mpeterson@mtech.edu
PETERSON, Margrette ... 510-869-6512 ... 64 J mpeterson@samuelmerritt.edu
PETERSON, Marie ... 206-296-6241 ... 538 B mpeters@seattleu.edu
PETERSON, Mark ... 651-450-3373 ... 266 F mpeters@inverhills.edu
PETERSON, Melissa, E ... 716-851-1775 ... 333 C petersonm@ecc.edu
PETERSON, Michael ... 215-248-7141 ... 425 D petersonm@chc.edu
PETERSON, Michael, E ... 260-422-5561 ... 173 C mepterson@indianatech.edu
PETERSON, Michael, W ... 512-448-8788 ... 493 E michaelp@stedwards.edu
PETERSON, Michele ... 970-247-7435 ... 84 K peterson_m@fortlewis.edu
PETERSON, Michele ... 505-566-3363 ... 320 D petersonm@sanjuancollege.edu
PETERSON, Michelle ... 507-285-7180 ... 268 I michelle.peterson@roch.edu
PETERSON, Nedra ... 818-767-0888 ... 79 H nedra.peterson@woodbury.edu
PETERSON, Nicole ... 931-221-7979 ... 473 E petersonn@apsu.edu
PETERSON, Norman ... 406-994-7150 ... 295 C normp@montana.edu
PETERSON, Pamela ... 831-459-5380 ... 75 C pgpeters@ucsc.edu
PETERSON, Pamela ... 561-912-2166 ... 107 B ppeterson@evergladesuniversity.edu
PETERSON, Paul ... 218-683-8800 ... 268 C paul.peterson@northlandcollege.edu
PETERSON, Penelope, L ... 847-491-3828 ... 160 E p-peterson@northwestern.edu
PETERSON, Phyllis, M ... 815-740-3848 ... 167 E ppeterson@stfrancis.edu
PETERSON, Polly, J ... 701-252-3467 ... 381 C ppeterso@jc.edu
PETERSON, Randolph, L ... 479-979-1431 ... 26 A rpeterson@ozarks.edu
PETERSON, Rebecca ... 802-865-6425 ... 513 C peterson@champlain.edu
PETERSON, Robert ... 801-840-4800 ... 510 A rpeterson@cci.edu
PETERSON, Robert, P ... 508-856-4296 ... 237 C robert.peterson@umassmed.edu
PETERSON, Rod ... 330-823-2683 ... 404 C petersro@mountunion.edu
PETERSON, Roy ... 262-243-5700 ... 547 C roy.peterson@cuw.edu
PETERSON, Samantha ... 918-335-6223 ... 411 B speterson@okwu.edu
PETERSON, Scott ... 740-392-6868 ... 396 I scott.peterson@mvnu.edu
PETERSON, Stella ... 770-426-2930 ... 133 E peterson@life.edu
PETERSON, Steven ... 313-425-3700 ... 247 H steven.peterson@baker.edu
PETERSON, Susan, K ... 785-532-6221 ... 194 D skp@ksu.edu
PETERSON, Thomas ... 732-906-2512 ... 311 D tpeterson@middlesexcc.edu
PETERSON, Timothy ... 763-279-2475 ... 261 E tpeterson@browncollege.edu
PETERSON, Trayce ... 765-983-1501 ... 171 E petertr@earlham.edu
PETERSON, Tyler ... 334-244-3615 ... 1 G tpeters7@aum.edu
PETERSON, Tyler ... 334-244-3266 ... 1 G tpeters7@aum.edu
PETERSON, Val, L ... 801-863-8424 ... 511 F petersva@uvu.edu
PETERSON, Vance, T ... 818-677-4400 ... 35 F vance.peterson@csun.edu
PETERSON, Wendy ... 509-335-5586 ... 539 D wendyp@wsu.edu
PETERSON, Wilbur (Pete) .. 615-547-1275 ... 468 B ppeterson@cumberland.edu
PETERSON-SENIUK, Peggy ... 419-473-2700 ... 389 C pseniuk@daviscollege.edu
PETERSON-VEATCH, Ross . 574-535-7508 ... 171 G rosspv@goshen.edu
PETHE-COOK, Marlyn ... 813-253-6231 ... 123 A mpethe@ut.edu
PETHICK, Michael ... 231-591-3900 ... 250 H pethicj@ferris.edu
PETILLO, John, J ... 203-371-7900 ... 94 B petilloj@sacredheart.edu
PETINAK, Craig ... 909-384-8978 ... 65 C cpetinak@sbccd.cc.ca.us
PETIPRIN, Gary ... 502-272-8480 ... 198 H gpetiprin@bellarmine.edu
PETISCE, Virginia, C ... 508-457-1313 ... 242 F vpetisce@ngs.edu
PETIT, Charles, P ... 617-912-9113 ... 232 C cpetit@bostonconservatory.edu
PETIT, Jeanne, D ... 616-395-7447 ... 252 D petit@hope.edu
PETITT, Charles, W ... 336-725-8344 ... 375 G petittc@pbc.edu
PETITT, Pamela ... 206-268-4022 ... 530 I ppetitt@antioch.edu
PETITTI, Mario ... 440-525-7328 ... 394 F mpetitti@lakelandcc.edu
PETKASH, John ... 607-778-5011 ... 324 G petkashjc@sunybroome.edu
PETKE, Debra ... 860-434-5232 ... 93 D dpetke@lymeacademy.edu
PETKO, Karen ... 330-823-7288 ... 404 C petkokl@mountunion.edu
PETLEY, Kathleen ... 518-629-4574 ... 336 C k.petley@hvcc.edu
PETR, Carrie ... 402-826-8271 ... 297 G carrie.petr@doane.edu
PETRAGNANI, Joseph, F ... 610-660-1528 ... 446 C petragna@sju.edu
PETRANOVICH, Ron ... 505-863-7596 ... 321 D ronp@gallup.unm.edu
PETRAS, Donna ... 586-263-6266 ... 254 C petrasd@macomb.edu
PETREE, Daniel ... 585-395-2623 ... 352 F dpetree@brockport.edu
PETRELLA, Yvonne ... 315-312-2270 ... 354 A yvonne.petrella@oswego.edu
PETRI, Basia ... 503-682-1862 ... 419 F bpetri@pioneerpacific.edu
PETRI, Elizabeth ... 413-662-5219 ... 238 C e.petri@mcla.edu
PETRICCA, Joe ... 323-856-7721 ... 28 E jpetricca@afi.com
PETRICHENKO, Kathleen, J ... 410-822-5400 ... 222 B kpetrichenko@chesapeake.edu
PETRICK, Joseph ... 802-287-8377 ... 513 F petrickj@greenmtn.edu
PETRICK, Laurie ... 920-832-6525 ... 548 B laurie.a.petrick@lawrence.edu
PETRIDIS, Heather ... 626-815-4570 ... 30 G hpetridis@apu.edu
PETRIE, Bruce ... 303-632-2300 ... 83 I bpetrie@coloradotech.edu
PETRIE, Mark, J ... 716-878-3641 ... 353 A petriemj@buffalostate.edu
PETRIE, Nancy ... 914-337-9300 ... 330 G nancy.petrie@concordia-ny.edu
PETRIETES, Cindy ... 414-229-5064 ... 551 D
PETRIKAT, Douglas ... 714-547-9625 ... 32 B dpetrikat@calcoast.edu
PETRILLO, Emilia, K ... 410-328-8404 ... 227 C epetr001@umaryland.edu
PETRILLO, Tracee ... 781-239-5695 ... 230 E tpetrillo@babson.edu
PETRITUS, Paul ... 585-720-0660 ... 325 B ppetritus@bryantstratton.edu
PETRIZZO, Louis, S ... 631-451-4235 ... 356 D petrizl@sunysuffolk.edu
PETRO, John, G ... 412-321-7550 ... 424 A
PETRO, Patrice, S ... 414-229-4523 ... 551 D ppetro@uwm.edu
PETRO, Tony ... 239-687-5443 ... 101 H tpetro@avemarialaw.edu
PETROCCIA, Anthony, M ... 315-568-3256 ... 342 H apetrocc@nycc.edu
PETROCCO-NAPULI, Kristina, L ... 315-568-3886 ... 342 H kpetrocco@nycc.edu
PETROFF, Les ... 317-738-8108 ... 171 F lpetroff@franklincollege.edu
PETROKA, Louise, A ... 203-285-2393 ... 91 D lpetroka@gwcc.commnet.edu
PETROSIAN, Anahid ... 956-872-6790 ... 494 H anahid@southtexascollege.edu
PETROSKI, Paul, S ... 410-706-8338 ... 227 C ppetrosk@umaryland.edu
PETROSKY, Elaine ... 330-675-8864 ... 393 J epetrosk@kent.edu
PETROSKY, Joseph ... 586-498-4181 ... 254 C petroskyj@macomb.edu
PETROVICH, Jason, G ... 765-658-4218 ... 171 B jpetrovich@depauw.edu
PETROVICH, Tamberly ... 831-582-4137 ... 35 E tpetrovich@csumb.edu
PETRUCCI, Michele ... 724-357-2295 ... 442 F michelep@iup.edu
PETRUCCIO, Diane ... 440-646-8390 ... 405 B dpetruc@ursuline.edu
PETRUS, John ... 412-536-1033 ... 432 H john.petrus@laroche.edu
PETRUS, Robin ... 607-778-5201 ... 324 G petrusre@sunybroome.edu
PETRUSCH, Suzanne, M ... 210-436-3995 ... 493 F spetrusch@stmarytx.edu
PETRUSO, Karl ... 817-272-7215 ... 505 C petruso@uta.edu
PETRUZZELLI, Barbara, W . 845-569-3601 ... 342 A barbara.petruzzelli@msmc.edu
PETRUZZELLI, Dominic, A 973-655-6500 ... 311 F petruzzellid@mail.montclair.edu
PETRY, Laura ... 312-332-0707 ... 166 B
PETRY, Ric ... 614-222-3227 ... 388 G rpetry@ccad.edu
PETRYSHAK, Bruce ... 615-898-5570 ... 473 G bruce.petryshak@mtsu.edu
PETRYSHYN, Laryssa ... 716-829-8119 ... 332 E petryshl@dyc.edu
PETSCH, Verl, E ... 307-532-8248 ... 556 C verl.petsch@ewc.wy.edu
PETSCHE, Carolyn ... 815-599-3577 ... 152 B carolyn.petsche@highland.edu
PETSCHE, Daniel ... 660-944-2875 ... 280 B daniel@conception.edu
PETTAY, Robert ... 213-834-4259 ... 146 F rpettay@thechicagoschool.edu
PETTAZZONI, Jodi, E ... 336-334-5531 ... 379 B jepettaz@uncg.edu
PETTEGREW, Larry ... 800-672-3060 ... 376 G
PETTEWAY, Venetia, S ... 810-762-7899 ... 253 C vpettewa@kettering.edu
PETTIBONE, John, C ... 770-720-5939 ... 136 C jcp@reinhardt.edu
PETTIFORD, Anthony ... 937-376-6223 ... 387 A apettiford@centralstate.edu
PETTIGRASS, Valerie ... 518-437-1802 ... 324 I vpettigrass@bryantstratton.edu
PETTIGREW, Frank, E ... 419-289-5051 ... 384 G fpettigr@ashland.edu
PETTIGREW, Jason ... 605-229-8350 ... 465 B jason.pettigrew@presentation.edu
PETTINARI, Gayle ... 719-549-3329 ... 87 F gayle.pettinari@pueblocc.edu
PETTINGER, Connie ... 708-209-3045 ... 148 E constance.pettinger@cuchicago.edu
PETTINICO, JR., Nicholas . 860-832-1766 ... 90 G pettinico@ccsu.edu
PETTIS, Curtis ... 937-376-6349 ... 387 A cpettis@centralstate.edu
PETTIS, Stephanie ... 251-575-8265 ... 1 B spettis@ascc.edu
PETTIS-WALDEN, Karen, M ... 804-523-5029 ... 527 A kpettis-walden@reynolds.edu
PETTIT, Charlene, M ... 920-924-3112 ... 554 G cpettit@morainepark.edu
PETTIT, Cyndi ... 214-333-5235 ... 484 D cyndi@dbu.edu
PETTIT, Frederick ... 570-208-5881 ... 432 G frederickpettit@kings.edu
PETTIT, Gretchen, A ... 636-584-6535 ... 281 E gmpettet@eastcentral.edu
PETTIT, Patricia, A ... 217-424-6488 ... 158 G ppettit@millikin.edu
PETTIT, Paul, E ... 214-841-3705 ... 485 F ppettit@dts.edu
PETTITT, Maureen ... 360-416-7919 ... 538 D maureen.pettitt@skagit.edu
PETTUS, Algray, L ... 936-261-1387 ... 496 G alpettus@pvamu.edu
PETTUS, James ... 410-287-6060 ... 222 A pett0916@cecil.edu
PETTY, Daniel, W ... 813-988-5131 ... 108 A pettyd@floridacollege.edu
PETTY, Jamie ... 706-295-7733 ... 130 E jpetty@highlands.edu
PETTY, JoBeth ... 601-968-8901 ... 273 C jbpetty@belhaven.edu
PETTY, Jonathan ... 806-291-3588 ... 508 E pettyj@wbu.edu
PETTY, Jovan ... 703-812-4757 ... 520 J jpetty@leland.edu
PETTY, Leslie ... 734-462-4400 ... 258 A lpetty@schoolcraft.edu
PETTY, Leslie ... 708-802-6213 ... 163 I petty@sxu.edu
PETTY, Marcia, L ... 504-865-3030 ... 213 F mlpetty@loyno.edu
PETTY, Mark ... 319-385-6231 ... 186 E mpetty@iwc.edu
PETTY, Michael, E ... 812-429-1411 ... 177 C mpetty@ivytech.edu
PETTY, Mikel, D ... 256-824-4368 ... 8 G mikel.petty@uah.edu
PETTY, Nina ... 817-515-5433 ... 496 C nina.petty@tccd.edu
PETTY, Tricia, L ... 304-293-8500 ... 545 A tricia.petty@mail.wvu.edu
PETTY, Yolanda ... 478-471-5364 ... 133 H yolanda.petty@maconstate.edu
PETTY-WARD, Paula, J ... 931-540-2572 ... 475 A ppettyward@columbiastate.edu
PETTYJOHN, Susan, H ... 828-262-2090 ... 377 D pettyjohnsh@appstate.edu
PETULA, Eileen, E ... 610-328-8399 ... 447 F epetula1@swarthmore.edu
PETZ, Dan ... 620-672-5641 ... 196 D danp@prattcc.edu
PETZNICK, Michelle, L ... 641-422-4205 ... 188 A petznmic@niacc.edu
PEUGH-WADE, Martha, A . 415-422-2444 ... 76 E peugh@usfca.edu
PEWE, Richard, P ... 517-607-2518 ... 252 C rich.pewe@hillsdale.edu
PEYSER, Roma ... 503-297-5544 ... 417 G rpeyser@ocac.edu
PEYTON, James ... 206-878-3710 ... 535 B jpeyton@highline.edu
PEYTON, Janice ... 936-270-7392 ... 490 E janice.peyton@lonestar.edu
PEYTON, Marcia ... 706-754-7789 ... 135 A mpeyton@northgatech.edu
PEYTON, Virginia ... 501-812-2206 ... 23 C vpeyton@pulaskitech.edu
PEZOLD, Frank ... 361-825-2349 ... 498 C frank.pezold@tamucc.edu
PEZZAROSSI, Alba ... 773-481-8872 ... 147 I apezzarossi@ccc.edu
PEZZELLE, Patrick ... 406-293-2721 ... 294 C ppezzell@fvcc.edu
PEZZI, Eileen ... 315-464-7853 ... 352 E pezzie@upstate.edu
PEZZOLI, Jean ... 808-984-3234 ... 142 E pezzoli@hawaii.edu
PEZZUTO, John ... 808-933-2909 ... 141 F pezzuto@hawaii.edu
PFAFF, Jason ... 410-423-3618 ... 19 A jason.pfaff@phoenix.edu
PFANG, Raymond ... 817-923-8459 ... 483 G raymond.pfang@fishermore.edu
PFANNENSTIEHL, Craig ... 617-217-9050 ... 231 A cfp@baystate.edu
PFAUTZ, Chris ... 804-594-1556 ... 527 B cpfautz@jtcc.edu
PFEFER, Mark, T ... 913-234-0796 ... 191 J mark.pfefer@cleveland.edu
PFEFFER, Carole ... 502-272-8184 ... 198 H cpfeffer@bellarmine.edu
PFEFFER, Miriam ... 718-782-2200 ... 324 C mpfeffer@boricuacollege.edu
PFEFFER, Richard ... 732-224-2262 ... 308 A rpfeffer@brookdalecc.edu
PFEFFER, Richard, J ... 732-224-2262 ... 308 A rpfeffer@brookdalecc.edu
PFEIFER, Alan, D ... 815-288-5511 ... 164 B pfeifer@svcc.edu
PFEIFER, Brette ... 785-460-5509 ... 192 C brette.pfeifer@colbycc.edu
PFEIFER, Donald ... 413-236-2131 ... 239 A dpfeifer@berkshirecc.edu
PFEIFER, Joseph ... 503-251-5775 ... 421 A jpfeifer@uws.edu
PFEIFER, Tad ... 308-535-3684 ... 298 H pfeifert@mpcc.edu
PFEIFFER, Charlotte, D ... 574-520-5536 ... 174 E cpfeifer@iusb.edu
PFEIFFER, Francine ... 202-220-1336 ... 314 B francine@rutgers.edu
PFEIFFER, Jay ... 717-262-2006 ... 452 C jay.pfeiffer@wilson.edu
PFEIFFER, Kelley ... 636-922-8544 ... 288 B kpfeiffer@stchas.edu
PFEIFFER, Marcia, F ... 314-513-4208 ... 288 H mpfeiffer@stlcc.edu
PFEIFFER, Mary ... 716-829-7808 ... 332 E pfeiffer@dyc.edu
PFEIFFER, Patricia, D ... 772-462-7301 ... 111 B ppfeiffe@irsc.edu
PFEIFFER, Pattie ... 919-735-5151 ... 375 A ppfeiffer@waynecc.edu
PFEIL, Robert ... 716-286-8689 ... 344 D fpfeil@niagara.edu

PFLEIGER, Kelly .... 215-368-5000.... 422 I
kpfleiger@biblical.edu
PFLUKE, Deanna .... 585-266-0430.... 333 D
dpfluke@cci.edu
PFURSICH, Fred .... 562-907-4236...... 79 F
fpfursich@whittier.edu
PFUTZENREUTER,
Richard, H .... 612-625-4517.... 272 A
pfutz001@umn.edu
PHAIAH, Peter .... 218-281-8505.... 271 E
phaiah@umn.edu
PHAIRE-WASHINGTON,
Linda .... 334-229-8343........ 1 C
lphaire@alasu.edu
PHAKITTHONG, Rachelle .. 715-675-3331.... 555 B
phakitth@ntc.edu
PHALIN, Teri .... 715-365-4464.... 555 A
tphalin@nicoletcollege.edu
PHAM, Hue .... 714-432-5764...... 41 D
hpham@occ.cccd.edu
PHAM, Michael .... 206-934-4193.... 537 E
michael.pham@seattlecolleges.edu
PHAM, Tom .... 972-438-6932.... 492 E
tpham@parkercc.edu
PHAM, Tom, C .... 617-984-1699.... 243 H
tpham@quincycollege.edu
PHAN, Luyen .... 507-222-4451.... 261 G
phan@carleton.edu
PHAN, Minh .... 504-866-7426.... 214 A
frphan@nds.edu
PHAN, Nga .... 619-684-8815...... 59 B
nphan@newschoolarch.edu
PHARO, SCN, Diane .... 812-357-6598.... 180 A
dpharo@saintmeinrad.edu
PHARR, Christine .... 402-399-2419.... 297 C
msellers@csm.edu
PHARR, Dianne .... 254-442-5151.... 482 I
dianne.pharr@cisco.edu
PHARR, Maria .... 252-493-7224.... 372 H
mpharr@email.pittcc.edu
PHEASANT, Clayton, N ...... 570-348-6285.... 435 F
pheasant@marywood.edu
PHEASANT, Joel, C .... 814-641-5334.... 432 A
pheasaj@juniata.edu
PHELAN, Carol .... 617-585-1139.... 242 I
carol.phelan@necmusic.edu
PHELAN, Carol .... 516-877-3154.... 322 A
phelan@adelphi.edu
PHELAN, Daniel, J .... 517-787-0800.... 252 J
phelandanielj@jccmi.edu
PHELAN, Kelley .... 619-275-4700...... 46 K
kelley@fashioncareerscollege.com
PHELAN JOHNSON,
Marcia .... 860-297-2041...... 94 E
marcia.johnson@trincoll.edu
PHELAN-NINH, Jennifer .... 315-792-7500.... 356 B
jennifer.phelan@sunyit.edu
PHELON, Elmer .... 212-237-8541.... 327 F
ephelon@jjay.cuny.edu
PHELPS, Bill .... 870-245-5567...... 22 I
phelpswr@obu.edu
PHELPS, Camille .... 580-745-2080.... 412 C
cphelps@se.edu
PHELPS, Craig .... 660-626-2391.... 278 D
cphelps@atsu.edu
PHELPS, Cynthia .... 212-960-5836.... 361 M
cphelps@yu.edu
PHELPS, Dani, J .... 610-841-3333.... 441 D
dphelps@psb.edu
PHELPS, Debbie .... 620-331-4100.... 193 I
dphelps@indycc.edu
PHELPS, Dennis, L .... 504-282-4455.... 213 H
dphelps@nobts.edu
PHELPS, Devon, N .... 419-995-8389.... 399 B
phelps.2@osu.edu
PHELPS, Esther .... 330-337-6403.... 383 J
depemp@raex.com
PHELPS, Gary, L .... 330-471-8127.... 395 F
gphelps@malone.edu
PHELPS, Gina, S .... 601-977-0960.... 278 A
gina.phelps@vc.edu
PHELPS, Hilary .... 860-343-5856...... 91 G
hphelps@mxcc.commnet.edu
PHELPS, Janet .... 603-206-8115.... 304 D
jphelps@ccsnh.edu
PHELPS, Jean .... 718-262-2285.... 329 A
phelps@york.cuny.edu
PHELPS, Joel .... 802-447-6306.... 514 F
jphelps@svc.edu
PHELPS, Martha .... 270-824-8591.... 202 G
martha.phelps@kctcs.edu
PHELPS, Sherri .... 870-245-5410...... 22 I
phelpss@obu.edu
PHELPS, Susan, Q .... 336-734-7236.... 370 F
sphelps@forsythtech.edu
PHELPS-ELLERKER, Lena .. 863-784-7303.... 117 J
lena.phelps@southflorida.edu
PHENICIE, Christopher, N . 864-488-4549.... 459 B
cphenicie@limestone.edu
PHENIX, Amy .... 612-626-1616.... 272 A
pheni001@umn.edu
PHHIPPS, Heidi .... 602-943-2311...... 19 B
heidi.phipps@west.edu
PHIFER, James, R .... 319-399-8686.... 183 F
jphifer@coe.edu

PHILBECK, Daniel, L .... 864-587-4223.... 461 D
philbed@smcsc.edu
PHILBERT, Martin, A .... 734-763-5454.... 259 A
philbert@umich.edu
PHILBIN, Catherine .... 617-296-8300.... 235 J
catherine_philbin@laboure.edu
PHILBIN, Kathleen .... 585-389-2451.... 342 D
kphilbi8@naz.edu
PHILIE, Lauren .... 802-635-1657.... 515 F
lauren.philie@jsc.edu
PHILIP, Chuck .... 574-289-7001.... 176 E
cphilip@ivytech.edu
PHILIP, George, M .... 518-956-8010.... 351 E
presmail@uamail.albany.edu
PHILIPKOSKY, Thomas, G 843-953-6907.... 456 C
tom.philipkosky@citadel.edu
PHILIPP, Diane .... 517-437-7341.... 252 C
diane.philipp@hillsdale.edu
PHILIPP, Shirin .... 617-349-9600.... 236 B
philipp@lesley.edu
PHILIPPA, Laine, M .... 414-410-4187.... 546 G
lmphilippa@stritch.edu
PHILIPPON, Roger .... 207-755-5357.... 218 G
rphilippon@cmcc.edu
PHILIPS, JR., Billy, U .... 806-743-1388.... 502 B
billy.philips@ttuhsc.edu
PHILLEY, Tim .... 918-495-6970.... 411 C
tphilley@oru.edu
PHILLIP, Thomas, G .... 262-243-5700.... 547 C
thomas.phillip@cuw.edu
PHILLIPS, Adrian .... 313-496-2820.... 259 G
aphilli1@wcccd.edu
PHILLIPS, Adrienne .... 662-252-8000.... 276 G
aphillips@rustcollege.edu
PHILLIPS, Alice .... 502-447-1000.... 206 F
aphillips@spencerian.edu
PHILLIPS, Allison .... 336-838-6491.... 375 C
allison.phillips@wilkescc.edu
PHILLIPS, Amanda .... 724-653-2195.... 427 G
aphillips@dec.edu
PHILLIPS, Andrew, T .... 410-293-1583.... 559 B
aphillip@usna.edu
PHILLIPS, Brad, C .... 607-733-7177.... 332 H
bphillips@ebi-college.com
PHILLIPS, Brian .... 562-903-4897...... 31 A
brian.phillips@biola.edu
PHILLIPS, Bridget .... 217-479-7031.... 157 F
bridget.phillips@mac.edu
PHILLIPS, Carol .... 910-938-6343.... 369 F
phillipsc@coastalcarolina.edu
PHILLIPS, Christopher, G .. 410-706-2261.... 227 C
cphillip@umaryland.edu
PHILLIPS, Cinda, K .... 812-749-1271.... 178 H
cphillip@oak.edu
PHILLIPS, Cindy .... 417-477-8212.... 287 D
phillipc@otc.edu
PHILLIPS, Clay .... 866-331-4153.... 467 E
phillipsc@bethelu.edu
PHILLIPS, Cliff .... 407-831-9816.... 103 E
cphillips@citycollege.edu
PHILLIPS, Cynthia .... 610-841-3333.... 441 D
cphillips@psb.edu
PHILLIPS, Dave .... 870-777-5722...... 25 F
dave.phillips@uacch.edu
PHILLIPS, Dave .... 615-248-1683.... 476 G
dphillips@trevecca.edu
PHILLIPS, David .... 410-516-8341.... 223 F
dphillips@jhu.edu
PHILLIPS, Dedric .... 720-859-7900...... 81 C
PHILLIPS, Denise .... 972-721-5168.... 503 B
dphilli@udallas.edu
PHILLIPS, Dianna .... 732-224-2265.... 308 A
PHILLIPS, Dianne .... 225-768-1736.... 214 C
marilyn.phillips@ololcollege.edu
PHILLIPS, Dorothy, E .... 606-679-8501.... 203 C
dorothy.phillips@kctcs.edu
PHILLIPS, Douglas .... 585-275-3311.... 359 B
dphillips@admin.rochester.edu
PHILLIPS, E. Clorisa .... 276-466-7910.... 529 D
PHILLIPS, Earnest .... 702-895-2388.... 302 I
earnest.phillips@unlv.edu
PHILLIPS, Edward .... 504-520-6787.... 217 A
ephillips@xula.edu
PHILLIPS, Elaine, W .... 405-273-5331.... 408 B
ephillips@familyoffaithcollege.edu
PHILLIPS, Eli, H .... 205-226-4600........ 2 B
ephillip@bsc.edu
PHILLIPS, Faith .... 740-366-9492.... 399 E
phillips.495@osu.edu
PHILLIPS, Faith .... 740-366-9492.... 386 H
phillips.495@osu.edu
PHILLIPS, Gail, G .... 615-353-3703.... 475 E
gail.phillips@nscc.edu
PHILLIPS, Gary, A .... 765-361-6224.... 181 E
phillipg@wabash.edu
PHILLIPS, Gina .... 817-531-6548.... 502 C
gphillips@txwes.edu
PHILLIPS, Glen .... 478-387-4731.... 131 A
PHILLIPS, Heather .... 218-477-4363.... 267 F
phillipshe@mnstate.edu
PHILLIPS, Hugh, H .... 334-833-4581........ 4 E
bphillips@huntingdon.edu
PHILLIPS, Idelia, P .... 941-752-5218.... 118 J
phillii@scf.edu

PHILLIPS, J. Lynn .... 757-569-6701.... 528 A
ledwards@pdc.edu
PHILLIPS, Jacqueline .... 860-885-2309...... 92 E
PHILLIPS, James, J .... 847-491-8880.... 160 E
j-phillips@northwestern.edu
PHILLIPS, James, K .... 910-630-7149.... 367 B
jphillips@methodist.edu
PHILLIPS, James, L .... 713-798-6598.... 481 H
phillips@bcm.edu
PHILLIPS, Janet, E .... 540-224-6973.... 520 I
jephillips@jchs.edu
PHILLIPS, Jeffrey, J .... 404-880-8480.... 127 C
jphillips@cau.edu
PHILLIPS, Jennifer .... 915-779-8031.... 483 J
jphillips@computercareercenter.com
PHILLIPS, Jennifer .... 212-592-2000.... 350 F
jphillips2@sva.edu
PHILLIPS, Jennifer .... 315-859-4243.... 334 H
jlphillips@hamilton.edu
PHILLIPS, Jerrett .... 918-456-5511.... 409 A
phillijd@nsuok.edu
PHILLIPS, Jo, C .... 870-759-4101...... 26 B
jphillips@wbcoll.edu
PHILLIPS, Joanne .... 423-775-6596.... 472 G
jphillips@ogs.edu
PHILLIPS, John, A .... 619-260-4523...... 76 D
jphillips@sandiego.edu
PHILLIPS, John, C .... 216-373-5308.... 397 F
jphillips@ndc.edu
PHILLIPS, Joseph, M .... 206-296-5700.... 538 B
phillipsj@seattleu.edu
PHILLIPS, June .... 318-670-6365.... 215 A
jphillips@susla.edu
PHILLIPS, Karen .... 413-775-1305.... 239 E
phillips@gcc.mass.edu
PHILLIPS, Kevin, J .... 203-932-7318...... 95 C
kphillips@newhaven.edu
PHILLIPS, Kimberley, L ...... 718-951-3136.... 326 F
kphillips@brooklyn.cuny.edu
PHILLIPS, Kristen .... 315-364-3475.... 360 D
PHILLIPS, Larry, M .... 936-639-1301.... 480 D
phillips@angelina.edu
PHILLIPS, Laurel, E .... 814-362-7531.... 449 B
leb2@pitt.edu
PHILLIPS, Linda .... 580-581-2238.... 407 D
lindap@cameron.edu
PHILLIPS, Lynette .... 516-299-2461.... 338 E
lynette.phillips@liu.edu
PHILLIPS, Margaret, R .... 304-293-2545.... 545 A
margaret.phillips@mail.wvu.edu
PHILLIPS, Mari Anne .... 417-667-8181.... 280 E
mphillips@cottey.edu
PHILLIPS, Marie .... 413-265-2365.... 233 D
phillipsmarie@elms.edu
PHILLIPS, Mary, T .... 678-915-7230.... 137 G
phillips@spsu.edu
PHILLIPS, Matthew .... 815-394-5003.... 163 A
mphillips@rockford.edu
PHILLIPS, Melissa, C .... 828-733-5883.... 372 A
mphillips@mayland.edu
PHILLIPS, Michael, C .... 843-953-4942.... 457 B
phillipsm@cofc.edu
PHILLIPS, Mike .... 309-796-5012.... 145 H
phillipsm@bhc.edu
PHILLIPS, Monika .... 870-512-7703...... 20 F
monika_phillips@asun.edu
PHILLIPS, Morgan .... 910-642-7141.... 374 B
mphillips@sccnc.edu
PHILLIPS, Myra .... 804-524-5352.... 529 H
mhphilli@vsu.edu
PHILLIPS, Nyambura, M ...... 609-894-9311.... 308 B
nphillip@bcc.edu
PHILLIPS, Pamela .... 920-498-5418.... 555 C
pamela.phillips@nwtc.edu
PHILLIPS, Patricia .... 401-454-6563.... 454 B
pphillip02@risd.edu
PHILLIPS, Patricia, L .... 757-789-1723.... 526 H
phillips@es.vccs.edu
PHILLIPS, Phil, E .... 310-506-7227...... 61 H
phil.phillips@pepperdine.edu
PHILLIPS, Rachel .... 215-965-4025.... 436 H
rphillips@moore.edu
PHILLIPS, Ralph .... 480-860-2700...... 14 F
rphillips@taliesin.edu
PHILLIPS, Ralph, N .... 724-847-6766.... 429 H
rphillip@geneva.edu
PHILLIPS, Raymond, B .... 207-859-4209.... 217 G
ray.phillips@colby.ed
PHILLIPS, Rebecca, J .... 724-847-6843.... 429 H
rjphilli@geneva.edu
PHILLIPS, Richard .... 276-523-7467.... 527 D
rphillips@me.vccs.edu
PHILLIPS, Richard, W .... 901-722-3220.... 473 C
rphillips@sco.edu
PHILLIPS, Rita, M .... 515-294-0231.... 182 E
rphillip@iastate.edu
PHILLIPS, Sandy .... 724-222-5330.... 438 F
sphillips@penncommercial.edu
PHILLIPS, Shannon .... 843-863-7035.... 456 B
sphillip@csuniv.edu
PHILLIPS, Sheri .... 417-865-2811.... 281 G
phillipss@evangel.edu
PHILLIPS, Stephen, S .... 443-412-2286.... 223 B
sphillips@harford.edu

PHILLIPS, Steve .... 845-675-4741.... 344 G
steve.phillips@nyack.edu
PHILLIPS, Sue .... 570-702-8916.... 431 L
sphillips@johnson.edu
PHILLIPS, Susan, D .... 518-956-8030.... 351 E
provost@uamail.albany.edu
PHILLIPS, Susanne, D .... 610-399-2217.... 442 A
sphillips@cheyney.edu
PHILLIPS, Teddy .... 479-619-3107...... 22 H
tphillips6@nwacc.edu
PHILLIPS, Teddy .... 815-226-3387.... 163 A
tphillips@rockford.edu
PHILLIPS, Teri, P .... 253-535-7187.... 536 E
phillitp@plu.edu
PHILLIPS, Terri .... 406-243-2665.... 294 I
terri.phillips@umontana.edu
PHILLIPS, Terry .... 219-980-7718.... 176 G
tphillips74@ivytech.edu
PHILLIPS, Terry Don .... 864-656-1935.... 456 E
pterry@clemson.edu
PHILLIPS, Timothy .... 563-333-6259.... 188 F
phillipstimothy@sau.edu
PHILLIPS, Tina, A .... 610-499-1161.... 451 F
taphillips@widener.edu
PHILLIPS, Tom .... 570-389-4775.... 441 F
tphilli2@bloomu.edu
PHILLIPS, Valerie .... 619-596-2766...... 26 J
valerie@advancedtraining.edu
PHILLIPS, Vickie .... 229-430-4766.... 124 A
vickie.phillips@asurams.edu
PHILLIPS, Virginia .... 619-684-8869...... 59 B
vphillips@newschoolarch.edu
PHILLIPS, Wendy, S .... 724-838-7399.... 424 I
phillipsws@carlow.edu
PHILLIPS, William .... 859-622-3515.... 200 J
william.phillips@eku.edu
PHILLIPS, William .... 401-232-6045.... 453 C
wphillip@bryant.edu
PHILLIPS, Wilma, D .... 334-386-7274........ 3 G
wphillips@faulkner.edu
PHILLIPS, Winfred, M .... 352-392-9122.... 120 C
wphil@ufl.edu
PHILLIPS, Yancy .... 812-237-2100.... 173 B
yancy.phillips@indstate.edu
PHILLIPS-CALHOUN, Fran 404-215-2645.... 134 D
fpcalhoun@morehouse.edu
PHILLIPS-HAUSER, Robin . 336-838-6122.... 375 C
robin.phillips@wilkescc.edu
PHILLIPS-LOWE, Angela ... 614-234-5717.... 396 H
aphillips-lowe@mccn.edu
PHILLIPS-MADSON,
Robyn .... 509-452-5100.... 536 F
PHILPOT, Richard .... 510-780-4500...... 53 J
rphilpot@lifewest.edu
PHILPOTT, Cecil .... 252-331-4881.... 369 G
caphilpott@albemarle.edu
PHILPOTT, Jeffrey, L .... 212-938-5500.... 355 B
jphilpott@sunyopt.edu
PHILYAW, Michael .... 828-726-2303.... 368 G
mphilyaw@cccti.edu
PHINAZEE, Karen, B .... 919-532-5663.... 374 H
kbphinazee@waketech.edu
PHINNEY, D. Nathan .... 330-471-8194.... 395 F
nphinney@malone.edu
PHINNEY, James .... 419-755-4720.... 397 C
jphinney@ncstatecollege.edu
PHINNEY, Nancy, L .... 805-565-6055...... 79 A
nphinney@westmont.edu
PHINNEY, Raymond, R .... 207-834-7562.... 220 D
rphinney@maine.edu
PHIPPS, Adam .... 301-784-5000.... 221 B
aphipps@allegany.edu
PHIPPS, Angela .... 606-368-6134.... 198 C
angelaphipps@alc.edu
PHIPPS, Gayle .... 704-216-3580.... 373 F
gayle.phipps@rccc.edu
PHIPPS, Kim, S .... 717-796-5085.... 436 D
kphipps@messiah.edu
PHIPPS, Kylene .... 406-874-6292.... 294 F
phippsk@milescc.edu
PHIPPS, Sid .... 410-626-2545.... 225 G
sid.phipps@sjca.edu
PHIPPS, Terry .... 972-825-4802.... 495 F
tphipps@sagu.edu
PHIPPS, Wayne .... 706-233-7358.... 137 A
wphipps@shorter.edu
PHIPPS-BOGER, Jayne ...... 336-372-5061.... 375 C
jayne.boger@wilkescc.edu
PHLEGAR, Charles, D .... 607-255-5142.... 331 B
cdp25@cornell.edu
PHOENIX, Dru .... 505-471-5756.... 321 A
admissions@swc.edu
PHUNG, Minh, N .... 202-885-3541...... 97 D
mphung@american.edu
PIAGET, Nicole .... 207-780-4071.... 220 G
npiaget@usm.maine.edu
PIANEZZOLA, Cristina .... 801-863-8204.... 511 F
cristina.pianezzola@uvu.edu
PIANKA, Stephanie .... 212-998-2910.... 344 B
stephanie.pianka@nyu.edu
PIANTA, Robert, C .... 434-243-5483.... 525 F
rcp4p@virginia.edu
PIAR, Daniel .... 704-971-8500.... 363 F

PINA, Elsa 915-351-8100 480 C
PINA, Jason 508-531-1276 237 D
PINA, Jason, B 401-874-2101 454 E
jbpina@uri.edu
PINA HOUDE, Ana Maria 915-351-8100 480 C
PINCHBACK, Keith 501-882-8855 20 C
gkpinchback@asub.edu
PINCHBACK, Rebekah 248-218-2096 257 D
rpinchback@rc.edu
PINCHOT, III, Gifford 206-780-6203 531 C
gifford.pinchot@bgi.edu
PINCKNEY, Al 414-297-6279 554 F
pincknea@matc.edu
PINCKNEY, Jloundia 843-574-6120 461 G
jloundia.pinckney@tridenttech.edu
PINDAR, Kassy 702-579-3556 302 A
kpindar@kaplan.edu
PINDER, Elaine 202-462-2101 99 A
pinder@iwp.edu
PINDER, Kymberly 505-277-2112 321 C
kpinder@unm.edu
PINDER, Walt 912-427-5778 124 C
wpinder@altamahatech.edu
PINE, Gary 626-815-5081 30 G
PINE, Karey 585-475-6230 347 G
ktprla@rit.edu
PINEDA, Gladys 212-423-2768 335 C
gladys.pineda@helenefuld.edu
PINEDA, Marika 541-463-5824 416 E
pinedam@lanecc.edu
PINEDO, Ciriaco 909-652-6160 39 E
cid.pinedo@chaffey.edu
PINEIRO, Mildred 787-728-1515 568 D
mpineiro@sagrado.edu
PINEIRO, Pedro 718-997-4446 328 E
pedro.pineiro@qc.cuny.edu
PINER, Brandy 803-981-7391 463 H
bpiner@yorktech.edu
PINERO, Luis, A 608-263-2378 550 J
lapinero@vc.wisc.edu
PINES, Darryll, J 301-405-3869 227 B
pines@umd.edu
PINES, Shlomo 908-354-6057 317 H
PINESCHI, David 916-348-4689 45 I
dpineschi@epic.edu
PINET, Celine 831-646-4033 57 G
cpinet@mpc.edu
PINI, John 781-891-2228 231 D
jpini@bentley.edu
PINI, John, A 781-891-2228 231 D
jpini@bentley.edu
PINION, Liz 406-791-5290 296 F
lpinion01@ugf.edu
PINIZZOTTO, Russell 617-989-4485 245 F
pinizzottor@wit.edu
PINK, Bill 405-945-3240 410 F
PINK, Kathleen 641-844-5739 186 B
kathy.pink@iavalley.edu
PINK, Kathy 641-844-5539 186 D
kathy.pink@iavalley.edu
PINK, Kevin 641-683-5128 185 G
kpink@indianhills.edu
PINK, Rodney 718-488-6012 338 G
rodney.pink@liu.edu
PINK, Thomas, A 906-635-2315 253 H
tpink@lssu.edu
PINKALL, Rita 620-672-5641 196 D
ritap@prattcc.edu
PINKARD, Elfred, A 704-378-1000 366 A
epinkard@jcsu.edu
PINKE, Taylor, A 813-258-7401 123 A
tpinke@ut.edu
PINKERMAN, Loren, L 706-880-8234 133 B
lpinkerman@lagrange.edu
PINKERTON, Mary 262-472-1712 553 A
pinkertm@uww.edu
PINKHAM, JoEllen 585-389-2060 342 D
jpinkha0@naz.edu
PINKHAM, Wesley, M 818-779-8413 53 B
wpinkham@kingsuniversity.edu
PINKNEY, Adrell, L 504-286-5229 214 J
apinkney@suno.edu
PINKNEY, Dwayne 919-962-1091 378 E
dpinkney@email.unc.edu
PINKOWSKI, JR.,
Richard, J 716-926-8820 335 E
rickp@hilbert.edu
PINKSTON, Glen, P 580-581-2225 407 D
glenp@cameron.edu
PINKSTON, Paul 920-465-2373 551 B
pinkstop@uwgb.edu
PINKSTON, Scott 870-368-7371 23 A
spinkston@ozarka.edu
PINKSTON, Terri, B 405-325-3021 413 C
terri@ou.edu
PINKSTON-MCKEE, Ria 773-291-6251 147 G
rmckee@ccc.edu
PINN, Carolyn 518-381-1176 350 E
taylorc@sunysccc.edu
PINNELL, Julie 402-826-8565 297 G
julie.pinnell@doane.edu
PINNER, Ray 256-824-6350 8 G
ray.pinner@uah.edu
PINNEY, Denise, M 973-642-8871 315 C
denise.pinney@shu.edu
PINNICK, Denise 812-749-1267 178 H
dpinnick@oak.edu
PINNICK, Maureen 317-738-8028 171 F
mpinnick@franklincollege.edu
PINO, Diana 713-718-5115 487 I
diana.pino@hccs.edu
PINO, Lori 510-780-4500 53 J
lpino@lifewest.edu
PINOCCI, Tina, M 856-256-4604 314 A
pinocci@rowan.edu
PINOTTI, Gerald 708-209-3032 148 E
jerry.pinotti@cuchicago.edu
PINS, Jacqueline, J 608-757-7772 553 G
jpins@blackhawk.edu
PINSKY, Linda 973-278-5400 307 F
lsp@berkeleycollege.edu
PINSKY, Linda 212-986-4343 323 H
lsp@berkeleycollege.edu
PINSON, J. Matthew 615-383-1340 469 A
president@fwbbc.edu
PINTAK, Lawrence, E 509-335-8535 539 D
lpintak@wsu.edu
PINTER-LUCKE, Claudia, L 909-869-3328 33 J
clpinterluck@csupomona.edu
PINTO, John 712-274-5158 187 G
pinto@morningside.edu
PINTO, Neville 502-852-6281 207 E
ngpint01@louisville.edu
PINTO, Savio 773-291-6501 147 G
spinto3@ccc.edu
PIONG, Chee 561-912-1211 107 B
cpiong@evergladesuniversity.edu
PIOTRKOWSKI, Joann 440-646-8327 405 B
jpiotrkowski@ursuline.edu
PIOTROWSKI, Shari 404-413-2273 131 G
spiotrowski@gsu.edu
PIPER, Everett, G 918-335-6234 411 B
epiper@okwu.edu
PIPER, Judy 336-334-4703 379 B
jrpiper@uncg.edu
PIPER, Renee 985-446-8111 216 A
renee.piper@nicholls.edu
PIPER, Richard 913-627-4126 194 C
rpiper@kckcc.edu
PIPER, Terry 305-899-3649 101 M
tpiper@mail.barry.edu
PIPER, Wendy, L 740-368-3177 400 G
wlpiper@owu.edu
PIPERATA, Diana 215-637-7700 431 A
dpiperata@holyfamily.edu
PIPES, Dianne, L 210-431-4373 493 F
dpipes@stmarytx.edu
PIPES, Elizabeth, M 617-726-8003 242 B
epipes@mghihp.edu
PIPES, III, J. Kelly 336-838-6424 375 C
kelly.pipes@wilkescc.edu
PIPINSKI, Ann, L 570-702-8901 431 L
apipinski@johnson.edu
PIPITONE, Linda 314-889-1493 281 I
lpipitone@fontbonne.edu
PIPKIN, Lisa, W 252-334-2020 367 C
lisa.pipkin@macuniversity.edu
PIPPIN, Jeff 310-506-7500 61 H
jeff.pippin@pepperdine.edu
PIPPIN, Jill 315-786-2238 337 F
jpippin@sunyjefferson.edu
PIRIUS, Landon 763-424-0712 268 B
lpirius@nhcc.edu
PIRKLE, Bill 803-641-3395 462 B
billp@usca.edu
PIRKLE, Martha 706-880-8245 133 B
mpirkle@lagrange.edu
PIRKUL, Hasan 972-883-6813 506 A
hpirkul@utdallas.edu
PIRRELLO, Joe 212-226-5500 323 A
jpirrello@aii.edu
PIRRMAN, Martin, E 706-880-8232 133 B
mpirrman@lagrange.edu
PIRRONG, Cary 405-208-5463 410 A
cpirrong@okcu.edu
PIRSCH, Lori 402-557-7467 296 H
lori.pirsch@bellevue.edu
PIRSCHEL, C. Sue 419-434-5333 404 B
pirschel@findlay.edu
PIRTLE, Gina 219-473-4379 170 G
gpirtle@ccsj.edu
PIRTLE, Pamela 847-491-7458 160 E
p-pirtle@northwestern.edu
PIRTLE, Ron 601-968-8990 273 C
rpirtle@belhaven.edu
PISA, Michael 315-312-3572 354 A
michael.pisa@oswego.edu
PISA, Michael, C 315-312-3572 354 A
michael.pisa@oswego.edu
PISANI, Carol 973-290-4491 308 G
cpisani@cse.edu
PISANI, Carol 973-290-4364 308 G
cpisani@cse.edu
PISANO, Douglas, J 617-732-2874 241 C
douglas.pisano@mcphs.edu
PISANO, Etta, D 843-792-2842 459 D
pisanoe@musc.edu
PISANO, Lou 860-832-1760 90 G
lpisano@ccsu.edu
PISANO, Rebecca, L 410-704-2451 228 E
rpisano@towson.edu
PISCHKE, Kevin 916-577-2200 79 G
kpischke@jessup.edu
PISCOPO, Carmine, R 401-865-2727 453 H
cpiscopo@providence.edu
PISHKIN, Richard, J 617-228-2427 239 C
rpishkin@bhcc.mass.edu
PISKADLO, Kevin 508-565-1306 245 A
kpiskadlo@stonehill.edu
PISORS, Jesse 918-495-6610 411 C
jpisors@oru.edu
PISTILLI, Fran 860-738-6325 92 B
fpistilli@nwcc.commnet.edu
PISTILLO, Jason 602-383-8228 18 K
jay@uat.edu
PISTORINO, Thomas, G 781-768-7075 244 A
t.pistorino@regiscollege.edu
PISZKER, James 814-824-2429 436 C
jpiszker@mercyhurst.edu
PITARO, Teresa 781-239-4452 230 E
tpitaro@babson.edu
PITCHER, Brian 509-358-7551 539 D
bpitcher@wsu.edu
PITCHER, Carole, D 302-295-1133 97 C
carole.d.pitcher@wilmu.edu
PITCHER, Christopher, G 302-295-1152 97 C
christopher.g.pitcher@wilmu.edu
PITCHER, Darren 509-533-3514 533 C
darren.pitcher@spokanefalls.edu
PITCHER, Darrin 509-533-3514 533 A
darrin.pitcher@spokanefalls.edu
PITCHER, John, K 856-691-8600 309 B
jpitcher@cccnj.edu
PITCHER, Mark 918-293-5412 410 E
mark.pitcher@okstate.edu
PITCHER, Paula 609-343-5015 307 C
ppitcher@atlantic.edu
PITCHER, Scott 641-585-8112 189 I
pitchers@waldorf.edu
PITCHFORD, Jeffery, L 501-450-3185 25 H
jeffp@uca.edu
PITCHFORD, Nicola 415-480-1880 45 C
nicola.pitchford@dominican.edu
PITCHFORD, Steven, L 662-254-3327 276 B
steven.pitchford@mvsu.edu
PITCOCK, Beth 559-323-2100 66 C
bpitcock@sjcl.edu
PITEGOFF, Peter 207-780-4344 220 G
pitegoff@usm.maine.edu
PITHIS, Nancy 617-236-8800 234 G
npithis@fisher.edu
PITMAN, Bruce 716-645-2711 351 G
cas-dean@buffalo.edu
PITMAN, Bruce, M 208-885-6757 144 G
bpitman@uidaho.edu
PITNEY, Pat 907-474-7907 10 I
kppitney@alaska.edu
PITONAK, Audrey 304-357-4745 542 A
audreypitonak@ucwv.edu
PITONZO, Beth 336-334-4822 371 A
bpitonzo@gtcc.edu
PITRE, Donna 985-447-0924 211 G
donna.pitre@ltc.edu
PITRE, Donna 985-632-5177 211 G
donna.pitre@ltc.edu
PITRE, Jude 318-276-2401 210 B
PITRE, Milagros 787-815-0000 567 A
milagros.pitre@upr.edu
PITRUZZELLO, Carl 203-932-7047 95 C
cpitruzzello@newhaven.edu
PITSCHMANN, Louis, A 205-348-7561 8 E
lpitschm@bama.ua.edu
PITSIRI, Lisa 405-736-0315 411 I
lpitsiri@rose.edu
PITT, Ronald, E 401-456-8003 454 A
rpitt@ric.edu
PITTENGER, David 304-696-2350 544 B
pittengerd@marshall.edu
PITTENGER, Mike 858-635-4475 27 E
mpittenger@alliant.edu
PITTENGER, Susan, D 315-568-3069 342 H
spittenger@nycc.edu
PITTER, Yeruchem 516-225-4700 346 K
PITTMAN, Alexander 419-586-0360 406 D
alex.pittman@wright.edu
PITTMAN, Crystal 864-941-8328 460 D
pittman.cg@ptc.edu
PITTMAN, Dale 626-585-7077 61 F
depittman@pasadena.edu
PITTMAN, David 903-586-2518 489 B
dpittman@jacksonville-college.edu
PITTMAN, Don, A 918-610-8303 411 D
don.pittman@ptstulsa.edu
PITTMAN, Edward, L 845-437-5426 359 F
edpittman@vassar.edu
PITTMAN, James 541-885-1800 418 E
james.pittman@oit.edu
PITTMAN, Jane, D 540-665-3489 524 E
jpittman@su.edu
PITTMAN, Jeannette 406-683-7215 294 J
j_stewart@umwestern.edu
PITTMAN, Julia 410-462-8380 221 E
jpittman@bccc.edu
PITTMAN, Karan 229-732-5944 124 E
karanpittman@andrewcollege.edu
PITTMAN, Kathy, L 985-549-2150 216 C
kpittman@selu.edu
PITTMAN, L. Monique 269-471-3297 247 D
pittman@andrews.edu
PITTMAN, Nancy 918-610-8303 411 D
nancy.pittman@ptstulsa.edu
PITTMAN, Patrick 910-362-7043 368 H
ppittman@cfcc.edu
PITTMAN, Shannon 325-649-8052 488 C
spittman@hputx.edu
PITTMAN, Stanley, G 260-982-5270 177 H
sgpittman@manchester.edu
PITTMAN, Stephanie, M 262-554-2010 549 A
pittmanmwc@aol.com
PITTMAN, Sue 715-232-1151 552 E
pittmans@uwstout.edu
PITTMAN, Suzanne 478-445-6283 130 B
suzanne.pittman@gcsu.edu
PITTMAN, W. Randall 205-726-2331 6 G
rpittman@samford.edu
PITTMAN, Wayne 205-726-2020 6 G
rwpittma@samford.edu
PITTMAN-SCHULZ,
Kimberley 707-826-3132 36 E
kimberleyps@humboldt.edu
PITTS, Bessie 513-569-1596 387 G
bessie.pitts@cincinnatistate.edu
PITTS, Carl 770-531-6305 133 C
cpitts@laniertech.edu
PITTS, Chuck 713-942-9505 488 A
capitts@hgst.edu
PITTS, Eleanor 205-929-6389 5 E
epitts@lawsonstate.edu
PITTS, Gail, S 248-341-2151 256 F
gspitts@oaklandcc.edu
PITTS, Gary 229-227-2414 138 A
gpitts@southwestgatech.edu
PITTS, James, E 850-644-0538 119 D
jpitts@admin.fsu.edu
PITTS, Karen, H 315-684-6068 354 F
pittskh@morrisville.edu
PITTS, Mark 619-849-2548 62 L
markpitts@pointloma.edu
PITTS, Mike 417-328-1412 290 A
mpitts@sbuniv.edu
PITTS, Otis 828-328-7179 366 E
otis.pitts@lr.edu
PITTS, Paul 618-650-2333 165 C
ppitts@siue.edu
PITTS-TAYLOR, Victoria 212-817-8895 327 B
womstu@gc.cuny.edu
PITZER, Timothy, G 330-471-8434 395 F
tpitzer@malone.edu
PITZNER, Alex, C 717-901-5124 430 F
apitzner@harrisburgu.edu
PIUMETTI FARLAND, Lisa 310-338-7896 56 E
lpiumett@lmu.edu
PIUROWSKI, Robert, C 914-337-9300 330 G
robert.piurowski@concordia-ny.edu
PIVERAL, Joyce 660-562-1671 287 B
piveral@nwmissouri.edu
PIXLEY, Alan 479-788-7093 24 D
alan.pixley@uafs.edu
PIXLEY, Sue 641-683-5106 185 G
spixley@indianhills.edu
PIXLEY, Susan 320-629-5161 268 E
pixleys@pinetech.edu
PIXLEY, Susan 651-846-1471 269 C
susan.pixley@saintpaul.edu
PIXLEY, Zaide, E 269-337-5755 252 K
zaide.pixley@kzoo.edu
PIZAM, Abraham 407-903-8010 120 B
abraham.pizam@ucf.edu
PIZARRO, Isel, A 610-527-2912 445 J
rosemont_store@fheg.follett.com
PIZER, Lori 518-292-7785 348 A
inst_res@sage.edu
PIZIO, Jennifer 419-251-1710 395 I
jennifer.pizio@mercycollege.edu
PIZZANO, Patti 704-461-6573 362 F
pattipizzano@bac.edu
PIZZO, Lauren 276-944-6940 519 A
lpizzo@ehc.edu
PIZZUTI, Linda, J 309-677-3153 146 C
lindap@bradley.edu
PIZZUTO, William, J 203-236-9818 94 G
william.j.pizzuto@uconn.edu
PJATAK, Jennifer 203-932-7082 95 C
jpjatak@newhaven.edu
PLACCO, Christopher 401-598-2900 453 E
cplacco@jwu.edu
PLACE, Linna, F 816-235-6230 291 C
placel@umkc.edu
PLACE, Ted, P 816-654-7286 283 F
tplace@kcumb.edu
PLACENCIO-ABREU, Lidia 956-380-8183 493 D
psecretary@riogrande.edu
PLACERES, Sonia 787-738-2161 567 D
sonia.placeres@upr.edu
PLACEY, David 650-543-3910 57 B
dplacey@menlo.edu

PLACIDI, Kathleen 434-381-6596 524 K kplacidi@sbc.edu
PLACIDO, Rob 940-898-3980 502 D rplacido@twu.edu
PLAEHN, Kristin, H 253-535-7615 536 E plaehnkh@plu.edu
PLAGENS, Leslie, F 325-649-8705 488 C lplagens@hputx.edu
PLAGGEMEYER, Ted 775-674-7552 302 H tplaggemeyer@tmcc.edu
PLAKE, John 417-865-2811 281 G plakej@evangel.edu
PLANCHOCK, Norann 318-677-3100 216 B planchockn@nsula.edu
PLANELL, Lilia 787-728-1515 568 D lplanell@sagrado.edu
PLANETA, Michael 815-740-3496 167 E mplaneta@stfrancis.edu
PLANK, Donna 254-295-4591 504 C dplank@umhb.edu
PLANK, Kirke, E 608-757-7727 553 G kplank@blackhawk.edu
PLANT, David 419-783-2306 389 H dplant@defiance.edu
PLANT, Fred, W 219-464-5436 181 C fred.plant@valpo.edu
PLANT, Jonathan 361-593-2599 498 D jonathan.plant@tamuk.edu
PLANT, Ken 801-418-1450 510 L stevenprovo@aol.com
PLANT, Maureen, C 301-443-5362 225 A mplant@msmary.edu
PLANTE, Dawn, M 440-525-7327 394 F dplante@lakelandcc.edu
PLANTE, John, J 412-396-4937 428 D plantej@duq.edu
PLANTEFABER, Lisa 413-572-5733 238 F lplantefaber@wsc.ma.edu
PLAPLER, Dina 860-679-4593 95 A dplapler@foundation.uconn.edu
PLASSE, Robert 413-572-8131 238 F rplasse@wsc.ma.edu
PLATA, Ernest, J 903-923-2476 509 E eplata@wileyc.edu
PLATE, William 561-297-3025 119 A wplate@fau.edu
PLATER-ZYBERK, Elizabeth, M 305-284-5000 122 I epz@miami.edu
PLATH, Shannon 415-749-4530 65 I splath@sfai.edu
PLATI, Heather 207-893-7898 219 F hplati@sjcme.edu
PLATOVSKY, Jonathan 718-268-4700 347 A
PLATSOUCAS, Christopher 757-683-3274 522 F cplatsoucas@odu.edu
PLATT, Jeffrey 716-829-7766 332 E plattjh@dyc.edu
PLATT, Mary 714-997-6607 39 F platt@chapman.edu
PLATT, Rich 240-895-4922 226 A rdplatt@smcm.edu
PLATT, Sharon 412-536-1120 432 H sharon.platt@laroche.edu
PLATT, Steve 541-278-5904 414 G splatt@bluecc.edu
PLATTER, Michael 202-419-0400 99 G
PLATUKUS, Graceann 570-740-0355 435 C gplatukus@luzerne.edu
PLAYER, Kathy 602-639-7500 14 H
PLAZA, Gloria 312-935-6625 162 G gplaza@robertmorris.edu
PLAZA, Laurie 610-526-6038 430 D lplaza@harcum.edu
PLEAS, Dorothy, J 630-637-5156 159 G djpleas@noctrl.edu
PLEAS-BAILEY, Dawn, E 620-229-6336 196 G dawn.pleas-bailey@sckans.edu
PLEASANT, Klint 248-218-2058 257 D kpleasant@rc.edu
PLEASANT, Lori 850-973-9469 113 K pleasantl@nfcc.edu
PLEASANT, Robert 740-533-4600 400 D pleasanr@ohio.edu
PLEASANTS, David, J 608-796-3913 553 C djpleasants@viterbo.edu
PLECENIK, Jeanne 914-455-2650 340 F jplecenik@mercy.edu
PLEGER, Kimberly 253-680-7102 531 F kpleger@bates.ctc.edu
PLEGER, Tom 608-356-8351 553 B thomas.pleger@uwc.edu
PLEMMONS, Donna 501-450-1351 22 A plemmons@hendrix.edu
PLEMMONS, Kim 704-403-1751 362 I kim.plemmons@carolinashealthcare.org
PLEMONS, Debbie 312-578-3884 168 D dplemons@westwood.edu
PLESEK, Joseph 219-981-4951 176 G jplesek@ivytech.edu
PLESSNER, Von, R 419-267-1350 397 E vplessner@northweststate.edu
PLETCHER, Ann, M 864-596-9086 457 E ann.pletcher@converse.edu
PLETCHER, Barbara 561-297-2145 119 A pletcher@fau.edu
PLETCHER, Jill, M 316-978-3435 198 A jill.pletcher@wichita.edu
PLETCHER, Kathy 920-465-2383 551 B pletchek@uwgb.edu
PLETSCHER, Anthony, W 215-368-5000 422 I tpletscher@biblical.edu
PLEUSS, Carol, J 330-684-8928 403 C cjpleus@uakron.edu
PLEWE, Stanley, J 435-652-7504 512 B splewe@dixie.edu
PLINSKE, Kathleen, A 407-582-4100 123 B kplinske@valenciacollege.edu
PLINSKI, Christie 503-491-7197 417 B christie.plinski@mhcc.edu
PLISKA, John 415-338-2037 37 B jpliska@sfsu.edu
PLOEGER, SM, Bernard 808-735-4741 140 E bploeger@chaminade.edu
PLOESSL, Jodie 407-712-1404 19 A jodie.ploessl@phoenix.edu
PLONSKY, Christine, A 512-471-4780 505 D chris.plonsky@athletics.utexas.edu
PLOTKIN, David 503-699-6316 416 J dplotkin@marylhurst.edu
PLOTKIN, Helen, S 501-450-1225 22 A plotkin@hendrix.edu
PLOTKOWSKI, Paul 616-331-6260 251 F plotkowp@gvsu.edu
PLOTNICK, Tamra 212-346-1244 345 F tplotnick@pace.edu
PLOTT, Richard, K 972-860-8325 484 I richardplott@dcccd.edu
PLOTTS, Debra 334-214-4866 2 F debra.plotts@cv.edu
PLOTTS, Donald, L 419-755-4811 397 C dplotts@ncstatecollege.edu
PLOTTS, Douglas, J 610-861-1560 437 A plottsd@moravian.edu
PLOTTS, John 972-721-5266 503 B jplotts@udallas.edu
PLOTTS, John, E 415-476-4148 75 A john.plotts@ucsf.edu
PLOUF, Joe 425-602-3043 531 E
PLOWFIELD, Lisa Ann 717-771-4121 440 H lap33@psu.edu
PLOWMAN, Donde 402-472-9500 300 G dplowman2@unl.edu
PLUCHUTA, Alexander 610-359-5057 426 G apluchut@dccc.edu
PLUEMER, Julie 608-822-2369 555 D jpluemer@swtc.edu
PLUG, Dawn 330-339-3391 394 A dplug@kent.edu
PLUHTA, Elizabeth, A 206-934-5141 537 F elizabeth.pluhta@seattlecolleges.edu
PLUMB, Anne, M 901-572-2842 467 C anne.plumb@bchs.edu
PLUMB, Richard 310-338-2834 56 E rplumb@lmu.edu
PLUMLY, Wayne, L 229-245-3825 139 C lwplumly@valdosta.edu
PLUMMER, Dale, H 610-566-1776 452 B dplummer@williamson.edu
PLUMMER, Deborah, L 508-856-2179 237 C deborah.plummer@umassmed.edu
PLUMMER, Dianne 617-989-4036 245 F plummerd@wit.edu
PLUMMER, James, D 650-723-3938 71 G plummer@ee.stanford.edu
PLUMMER, James, D 513-556-1299 403 D james.plummer@uc.edu
PLUMMER, Lisa 610-902-8549 424 B lisa.m.plummer@cabrini.edu
PLUMMER, Meredith 760-366-5284 43 H mplummer@cmccd.edu
PLUMMER, Robert, M 423-439-4218 473 F plummerb@etsu.edu
PLUMMER, Troy, A 515-263-6050 185 C tplummer@grandview.edu
PLUMMER, Vince 701-671-2319 382 G vince.plummer@ndscs.edu
PLUNKETT, Cathy 205-802-1200 3 B cathy.plunkett@vc.edu
PLUNKETT, Christine, A 802-862-9616 513 B cplunkett@burlington.edu
PLUNKETT, Jackie 314-529-9398 284 C jplunkett@maryville.edu
PLUNKETT, James, C 215-951-1500 432 I plunkett@lasalle.edu
PLUNKETT, Nancy 916-638-1616 50 A nancy_plunkett@heald.edu
PLUSCH, Kimberly 302-225-6256 96 H pluschk@gbc.edu
PLUTCHAK, Scott 205-934-5460 8 F tscott@uab.edu
PLUTCHOK, Yisroel 718-438-5476 360 G
PLUTE, David 307-754-6025 556 G david.plute@northwestcollege.edu
PLUTINO-CALABRESE, Stella 585-389-2465 342 D splutin2@naz.edu
PLUZDRAK, Nancy 203-523-4712 19 A nancy.pluzdrak@phoenix.edu
PLYLER, Chris, P 803-777-7695 462 A plyler.chris@sc.edu
PLYMALE, Chad 585-567-9480 336 B chad.plymale@houghton.edu
PLYMPTON, Margaret, F 610-758-3178 434 E mfp3@lehigh.edu
PNACEK, Kevin, M 517-780-4579 248 D kevin.pnacek@baker.edu
POARCH, Mark 828-726-2214 368 G mpoarch@cccti.edu
POAT, Erica 618-634-3375 164 E ericap@shawneecc.edu
POATS, Lillian, B 713-313-7978 500 B poats_lb@tsu.edu
POBAT, Peter 718-368-5109 328 A ppobat@kbcc.cuny.edu
POBLENZ, Scott, B 978-468-7111 235 B spoblenz@gcts.edu
POBLETE, Juan 831-459-4792 75 C jpoblete@ucsc.edu
POCHARD, Brad 864-294-3406 458 E brad.pochard@furman.edu
POCHE, Paulette, M 985-549-5638 216 C ppoche@selu.edu
POCOCK, Beth 828-884-8287 362 H pocockba@brevard.edu
PODELL, David 212-517-0520 340 C dpodell@mmm.edu
PODEMSKI, Richard, S 850-474-7713 121 D rpodemski@uwf.edu
PODESTÁ, Guido 608-262-9833 550 J gpodesta@wisc.edu
PODIS, JoAnne 440-646-8107 405 B jpodis@ursuline.edu
PODOBNIK, Lois 402-471-2505 299 D lpodobnik@nscs.edu
PODOLEFSKY, Aaron, M 716-878-4101 353 A podoleam@buffalostate.edu
PODOLSKY, Daniel, K 214-648-2508 507 E priscilla.alderman@utsouthwestern.edu
POE, JR., Donald 704-463-3041 375 F don.poe@fsmail.pfeiffer.edu
POE, Donnis 318-335-3944 210 D dpoe@ltc.edu
POE, Elmer 252-328-9066 377 E poee@ecu.edu
POEHLER, M, J 816-802-3393 283 E mpoehler@kcai.edu
POEHLERT, Edward 760-757-2121 57 E epoehlert@miracosta.edu
POEHLS, Alice 202-885-2210 97 D apoehls@american.edu
POELKER, Scott 843-574-6197 461 G scott.poelker@tridenttech.edu
POELKING, Karen, L 216-373-5234 397 F kpoelking@ndc.edu
POELVOORDE, Tracy, L 309-779-7708 166 D poelvoordet@trinityqc.com
POERTNER, Gary 949-582-4840 70 D gpoertner@socccd.edu
POETTKER, Tricia 617-537-6843 158 A tapoettker@mckendree.edu
POETZL, Steven 541-485-1780 417 E stevepoetzl@newhope.edu
POFF, Elaine, G 954-262-7261 114 B poff@nsu.nova.edu
POFF, Robert, C 812-246-3301 177 B rpoff@ivytech.edu
POGGENDORF, Brenda, P 540-375-2270 523 G poggendorf@roanoke.edu
POGLIANO, Mark 734-462-4400 258 A mpogliano@schoolcraft.edu
POGUE, Brian, W 603-646-2106 304 J brian.w.pogue@dartmouth.edu
POGUE, Frank, G 318-247-3811 215 E
POGUE, Gregory 609-771-3078 308 F pogueg@tcnj.edu
POGUE, Roslynn 318-342-5327 216 E pogue@ulm.edu
POHAS, Joanie 310-338-3068 56 E jpohas@lmu.edu
POHERO, Mary Jane 973-596-3106 312 C mary.j.pohero@njit.edu
POHL, Charles, A 215-503-6988 448 C charles.pohl@jefferson.edu
POHL, Don 314-286-3653 287 G dpohl@ranken.edu
POHL, Henry, S 518-262-5919 322 D pohlh@mail.amc.edu
POHL, Laurie 617-353-9814 232 E lpohl@bu.edu
POHL, Sara 815-825-2086 155 D sarapohl@kishwaukeecollege.edu
POHLIG, Holly 407-646-2161 116 D hpohlig@rollins.edu
POHLMAN, Nancy, A 815-740-3496 167 E npohlman@stfrancis.edu
POHLSON, Scott 605-677-5434 465 G scott.pohlson@usd.edu
POINDEXTER, Freddy, D 816-654-7910 283 F fpoindexter@kcumb.edu
POINDEXTER, Jeanne 757-382-9900 99 G
POINTDEXTER, Michael, C 916-558-2142 56 D poindem@scc.losrios.edu
POINTER, Shandretta 813-621-0041 106 C spointer@cci.edu
POINTS, Dan 405-733-7359 411 I dpoints@rose.edu
POINTS, David 731-426-7625 470 B dpoints@lanecollege.edu
POIRIER, Clare 508-999-8002 237 A cpoirier@umassd.edu
POIRIER, J. Nicolas 315-568-3197 342 H npoirier@nycc.edu
POIRIER, Janet, L 603-641-7010 305 G jpoirier@anselm.edu
POIRRIER, Gail, P 337-482-6808 216 D poirrier@louisiana.edu
POISEL, Mark Allen 212-346-1200 345 F mpoisel@pace.edu
POITER, Emilia 410-532-5184 225 D epoiter@ndm.edu
POKORA, Thomas 810-766-4103 248 C tom.pokora@baker.edu
POKORNY, Anita, R 330-325-6476 397 D app@neomed.edu
POKOSH, Tricia 740-392-6868 396 I tricia.pokosh@mvnu.edu
POKOT, Elena 262-472-1001 553 A pokote@uww.edu
POKRAS, Martha 617-627-3389 245 C martha.pokras@tufts.edu
POL, Lou 402-554-2303 301 A lpol@unomaha.edu
POLACK, Joseph 330-499-9600 393 I jpolack@kent.edu
POLAK, Joseph (Chip) 603-645-9604 305 I j.polak@snhu.edu
POLANCO, Alison 305-666-9242 103 H apolanco@citycollege.edu
POLAND, Jennifer 724-222-5330 438 F jpoland@penncommercial.edu
POLAND, Russell 615-327-6171 471 C rpoland@mmc.edu
POLANIECKI, Andrew 574-239-8315 172 M apolaniecki@hcc-nd.edu
POLATAJKO, Mark, M 937-775-2002 406 C mark.polatajko@wright.edu
POLAZZI, Eileen, M 973-748-9000 307 H eileen_polazzi@bloomfield.edu
POLCYN, Laura, J 253-535-8225 536 E polcyn@plu.edu
POLCZYNSKI, Mimi 618-545-3363 155 B mpolczynski@kaskaskia.edu
POLD, Rein, A 814-393-2166 442 B rpold@clarion.edu
POLDEN, Donald, J 408-554-4362 68 C dpolden@scu.edu
POLDING, Carl, E 320-222-5218 268 G carl.polding@ridgewater.edu
POLDING, John 973-720-2887 317 D poldingj@wpunj.edu
POLE, Rhonda 605-995-2902 464 C rhpole@dwu.edu
POLEMENI, Anthony 212-463-0400 358 B apolemeni@touro.edu
POLESHEK, Jeffrey, A 941-359-7635 116 B jpoleshe@ringling.edu
POLETTI, Ed 215-972-2053 440 J epoletti@pafa.edu
POLGAR, Rebecca 410-234-4900 225 E
POLICANO, Andrew, J 949-824-8470 74 B policano@uci.edu
POLICASTRO, Mike 422-472-7141 474 E mpolicastro@clevelandstatecc.edu
POLIN, Michael 941-782-5927 433 C mpolin@lecom.edu
POLINAK, Peter 315-781-3337 335 F polinak@hws.edu
POLING, Jana 503-255-0332 417 C jpoling@multnomah.edu
POLING-BOLLAS, Betty 513-241-4338 384 C betty.bollas@antonellicollege.edu
POLIRSTOK, Susan 908-737-3750 311 A polirsts@kean.edu
POLIS, Kathi 704-330-6976 369 D kathy.polis@cpcc.edu
POLISENO, Nick 212-226-7300 346 E nickpoliseno@pbcny.edu
POLISI, Joseph, W 212-799-5000 337 H
POLIZZI, Dianne 617-243-2133 236 A dpolizzi@lasell.edu
POLK, Ali 831-476-9424 47 E marketing@fivebranches.edu
POLK, Alisa, L 540-636-2900 517 K finaid@christendom.edu
POLK, Anjanetta 765-459-0561 176 C apolk5@ivytech.edu
POLK, Fred 213-637-1360 79 D fpolk@westwood.edu
POLK, Laura 301-934-7506 222 C laurap@csmd.edu
POLK-BRIDGES, Dawn 214-692-8080 480 I dpolkbridges@aii.edu

POLKOWSKI, James, R ..... 734-462-4400.... 258 A
jpolkows@schoolcraft.edu
POLL, Michael .... 724-552-4372.... 447 C
mpoll@setonhill.edu
POLLACK, Ann, M .... 310-794-0387...... 74 C
apollack@resadmin.ucla.edu
POLLACK, Dianne .... 802-241-2520.... 515 C
dianne.pollak@vsc.edu
POLLACK, Gary .... 509-335-4750.... 539 D
gary.pollack@wsu.edu
POLLACK, Glenn .... 914-251-5976.... 354 D
glenn.pollack@purchase.edu
POLLACK, Martha, E .... 734-763-1282.... 259 A
pollackm@umich.edu
POLLACK, Meyer .... 323-731-2383...... 60 H
pollack@psuca.edu
POLLACK, Pamela .... 718-951-3118.... 326 F
pamela@brooklyn.cuny.edu
POLLACK, Tessa, M .... 210-434-6711.... 492 B
tmpollack@lake.ollusa.edu
POLLAK, Georgia, B .... 212-960-5285.... 361 M
gpollak@yu.edu
POLLARD, Al .... 254-299-8669.... 490 G
apollard@mclennan.edu
POLLARD, III, Alton, B ...... 202-806-0500...... 98 E
abpollard@howard.edu
POLLARD, Charles .... 479-524-7200...... 22 C
cpollard@jbu.edu
POLLARD, Cindy .... 503-517-1026.... 421 B
cpollard@warnerpacific.edu
POLLARD, DeRionne, P ..... 240-567-5264.... 224 D
president@montgomerycollege.edu
POLLARD, Jamie, B .... 515-294-0123.... 182 E
jbp@iastate.edu
POLLARD, Janet, L .... 361-593-2439.... 498 D
janet.pollard@tamuk.edu
POLLARD, Jennie .... 972-860-8201.... 484 H
jpollard@dcccd.edu
POLLARD, Jennifer, A .... 716-645-2450.... 351 G
pollardj@buffalo.edu
POLLARD, Leslie .... 256-726-7000........ 6 C
lpollard@oakwood.edu
POLLARD, Mary Lee .... 518-464-8500.... 333 E
mpollard@excelsior.edu
POLLARD, Natalie, M .... 609-896-5340.... 313 F
pollardn@rider.edu
POLLARD, Pamela .... 914-606-6851.... 360 E
pamela.pollard@sunywcc.edu
POLLARD, Richard .... 657-278-2714...... 35 B
rpollard@fullerton.edu
POLLARD, Sherry .... 573-882-8420.... 291 B
pollards@missouri.edu
POLLARD, Thomas, D .... 203-432-3565...... 96 A
thomas.pollard@yale.edu
POLLARD, William, L .... 718-270-5000.... 328 C
wlpollard@mec.cuny.edu
POLLCHIK, Allan .... 740-774-7200.... 400 A
pollchic@ohio.edu
POLLENZ, Hal .... 212-678-8000.... 337 G
hapollenz@jtsa.edu
POLLERT, Tim .... 708-596-2000.... 164 H
tpollert@ssc.edu
POLLEY, Debra Lee .... 518-454-2066.... 330 C
polleyd@strose.edu
POLLICINO MURPHY,
Elizabeth .... 631-687-2629.... 349 B
epollicinomurphy@sjcny.edu
POLLION, Sean .... 231-348-6621.... 256 B
spollion@ncmich.edu
POLLITZ, John, H .... 715-836-3715.... 551 A
pollitjh@uwec.edu
POLLMAN, Janeen .... 701-228-5458.... 382 E
bookcell@dakotacollege.edu
POLLOCK, Charles, R .... 413-782-1233.... 246 A
cpollock@wne.edu
POLLOCK, Holly .... 606-783-2000.... 204 I
h.pollock@moreheadstate.edu
POLLOCK, Jill .... 303-860-5600...... 88 G
jill.pollock@cu.edu
POLLOCK, Kevin, A .... 810-989-5545.... 257 H
kapollock@sc4.edu
POLLOCK, Matthew .... 570-586-2400.... 422 G
mpollock@bbc.edu
POLLOCK, Shannon .... 770-975-4000.... 127 B
POLO, Jose, R .... 787-738-2161.... 567 D
rechumanos@upr.edu
POLONSKY, Kenneth .... 773-702-9306.... 166 G
polonsky@bsd.uchicago.edu
POLSBY, Daniel, D .... 703-993-8087.... 519 E
polsby@gmu.edu
POLSDOFER, Duane .... 641-585-8121.... 189 I
polsdofed@waldorf.edu
POLSELLI, Larry .... 616-554-5827.... 250 C
lpolselli@davenport.edu
POLSKY, John .... 212-686-9244.... 322 G
POLSON, Mary, E .... 717-245-1835.... 427 F
polsonm@dickinson.edu
POLSON, William Jerry ...... 580-745-2212.... 412 C
jpolson@se.edu
POLTERSDORF, Todd .... 973-300-2253.... 315 F
tpoltersdorf@sussex.edu
POLVERINI, Peter, J .... 734-763-3311.... 259 A
neovas@umich.edu

POLYCHRONIS, Paul, D .... 660-543-4060.... 290 H
ppolychr@ucmo.edu
POLYOT, Susan .... 207-947-4591.... 217 D
spolyot@bealcollege.edu
POLZ, Sue .... 312-935-4563.... 162 G
spolz@robertmorris.edu
POMAJZL, Jacque .... 402-826-8294.... 297 G
jacque.pomajzl@doane.edu
POMAKOY, Keith .... 864-592-4634.... 461 C
pomakoyk@sccsc.edu
POMALES, Eleuterio .... 787-758-2525.... 567 G
eleuterio.pomales@upr.edu
POMALES, Reinaldo .... 787-758-2525.... 567 G
reinaldo.pomales@upr.edu
POMERENK, Julia .... 509-335-5511.... 539 D
pomerenk@wsu.edu
POMEROY, Claire .... 916-734-3578...... 73 I
claire.pomeroy@ucdmc.ucdavis.edu
POMEROY, Colin, J .... 920-433-6621.... 546 D
colin.pomeroy@bellincollege.edu
POMFREY, Elaine .... 641-472-7000.... 187 E
epomfrey@mum.edu
POMMERER, Ron .... 701-845-7700.... 382 C
ron.pommerer@vcsu.edu
POMPEI, Eric .... 310-314-6160...... 30 A
POMPER, Gwen, E .... 303-492-8223...... 88 H
gwen.pomper@colorado.edu
POMPEY, JR., Robert .... 336-334-7587.... 378 A
rpompey@ncat.edu
POMPLUN, Joann .... 605-626-2283.... 466 A
jpomplun@northern.edu
POMYKALSKI, James .... 570-372-4529.... 447 E
pomykalski@susqu.edu
PONCE, Chris, B .... 909-621-8192...... 63 A
chris.ponce@pomona.edu
PONCE, Christy .... 915-831-6614.... 486 G
cponce29@epcc.edu
PONCE, Omar .... 787-766-1717.... 565 I
um_oponce@suagm.edu
PONCE DE LEON, Monica 734-764-1315.... 259 A
mpdl@umich.edu
PONCELET, Jolene .... 507-453-2662.... 267 C
jponcelet@southeastmn.edu
POND, Eugene, W .... 214-841-3725.... 485 F
epond@dts.edu
POND, Lallon .... 540-887-7274.... 521 C
lpond@mbc.edu
PONDER, Anne .... 828-251-6500.... 378 D
chanoffi@unca.edu
PONDER, Betty, J .... 828-251-6100.... 378 D
bponder@unca.edu
PONDER, Denis .... 928-314-9515...... 12 A
denis.ponder@azwesteren.edu
PONDER, E. Cheryl .... 601-877-6380.... 272 F
ecponder@alcorn.edu
PONDER, Leslee .... 940-397-4350.... 491 B
leslee.ponder@mwsu.edu
PONDER, Nathan .... 318-473-6591.... 212 I
nponder@lsua.edu
PONESSE, Matthew .... 614-251-4500.... 398 F
ponessem@ohiodominican.edu
PONOROFF, Lawrence .... 520-621-1498...... 18 L
lponoroff@law.arizona.edu
PONREMY, Sue .... 708-524-6965.... 150 C
sponremy@dom.edu
PONS, Jose, L .... 787-844-8181.... 568 A
jose.pons@upr.edu
PONSETTO, Jean .... 773-325-7504.... 149 A
jlentipo@depaul.edu
PONTEP, Tanya .... 818-654-1721...... 62 F
tpontep@pgi.edu
PONTI, Marilyn, K .... 509-527-5986.... 540 B
pontimk@whitman.edu
PONTICELLI, Jan .... 530-741-6795...... 80 K
jpontice@yccd.edu
PONTINEN, Jodi .... 218-749-7753.... 266 I
j.pontinen@mr.mnscu.edu
PONTIUS, JR., John, M .... 518-608-8384.... 333 E
jpontius@excelsior.edu
PONTO, Patricia, A .... 269-337-7191.... 252 K
pat.ponto@kzoo.edu
PONTON, Cynthia, L .... 434-381-6136.... 524 K
cponton@sbc.edu
PONTON, Dennis, K .... 716-878-5903.... 353 A
pontondk@buffalostate.edu
PONTURO, Joseph .... 973-328-5500.... 309 A
jponturo@ccm.edu
POOL, David .... 513-772-9888.... 398 G
david.pool@omw.edu
POOL, Deborah, A .... 845-938-6947.... 559 A
8drm@usma.edu
POOL, Madonna .... 301-387-3743.... 222 H
madonna.pool@garrettcollege.edu
POOLE, Bill .... 817-272-3571.... 505 C
bpoole@uta.edu
POOLE, Cary .... 817-531-4872.... 502 C
cpoole@txwes.edu
POOLE, Clifford .... 678-717-3724.... 129 G
cpoole@gsc.edu
POOLE, David .... 951-343-4409...... 31 J
dpoole@calbaptist.edu
POOLE, Dorothy .... 408-924-1177...... 37 C
dorothy.poole@sjsu.edu

POOLE, John .... 434-832-7615.... 526 E
poolej@cvcc.vccs.edu
POOLE, Lana .... 573-875-7237.... 280 A
llpoole@ccis.ede
POOLE, Mary Ellen .... 415-503-6251...... 66 A
abeckett@sfcm.edu
POOLE, Myra .... 252-862-1267.... 373 C
poolem@roanokechowan.edu
POOLE, Paula .... 717-560-8257.... 433 D
ppoole@lbc.edu
POOLE, Penny .... 806-291-3414.... 508 E
poolep@wbu.edu
POOLE, Philip .... 205-726-2823........ 6 G
ppoole@samford.edu
POOLE, Robert, S .... 615-327-6273.... 471 C
rpoole@mmc.edu
POOLE, Russell .... 303-724-0425...... 88 J
russell.poole@ucdenver.edu
POOLE, Scott .... 865-974-5267.... 477 D
scott.poole@utk.edu
POOLE, Sherilyn .... 708-235-7594.... 151 E
spoole@govst.edu
POOLE, Stan .... 870-245-5196...... 22 I
pooles@obu.edu
POOLE, Thomas, G .... 814-865-2507.... 438 G
tgp1@psu.edu
POOLE, Warren, E .... 252-335-3670.... 377 F
wepoole@mail.ecsu.edu
POOLER, Traci, M .... 270-384-8100.... 204 D
poolert@lindsey.edu
POOLER, III, Willis .... 270-384-8070.... 204 D
poolerw@lindsey.edu
POOLEY, Allison .... 602-429-1198...... 19 B
allison.pooley@west.edu
POOLMAN, Leslie, J .... 717-245-1269.... 427 F
poolman@dickinson.edu
POON, Christine, A .... 614-292-2666.... 398 I
poon.36@osu.edu
POON, Percy .... 702-895-3017.... 302 I
percy.poon@unlv.edu
POON, Tom .... 909-621-8736...... 62 H
thomas_poon@pitzer.edu
POOR, H. Vincent .... 609-258-1816.... 312 G
poor@princeton.edu
POOR, Joan .... 660-785-4105.... 290 G
pjpoor@truman.edu
POORANDI, Masood .... 386-481-2340.... 102 C
poorandm@cookman.edu
POORE, Alanna .... 312-850-7037.... 147 F
apoore@ccc.edu
POORE, Sharon .... 859-442-1175.... 202 B
sharon.poore@kctcs.edu
POORMAN, Brad .... 325-793-4910.... 490 H
bpoorman@mcm.edu
POORMAN, Joshua .... 325-793-4608.... 490 H
poorman.joshua@mcm.edu
POORMAN, Julie .... 617-266-1400.... 231 E
POORMAN, Julie .... 252-328-6373.... 377 E
poormanj@ecu.edu
POORMAN, CSC, Mark, L . 503-943-7207.... 420 G
poorman@up.edu
POOS, Lawrence, R .... 202-319-5115...... 97 E
poos@cua.edu
POOVEY, Gena, E .... 864-488-4509.... 459 B
gpoovey@limestone.edu
POOVEY, Sara .... 256-439-6833........ 3 J
sbrenizer@gadsdenstate.edu
POPA, Hope .... 312-662-4011.... 144 H
hpopa@adler.edu
POPE, Alexis .... 931-372-3888.... 474 B
apope@tntech.edu
POPE, Bonnie, G .... 336-734-7412.... 370 F
bpope@forsythtech.edu
POPE, Christina .... 315-464-4582.... 352 E
popec@upstate.edu
POPE, Eric .... 248-204-2210.... 254 B
epope@ltu.edu
POPE, Iris .... 760-872-2000...... 43 K
buck@deepsprings.edu
POPE, Jasmine .... 479-619-2673...... 22 H
jpope5@nwacc.edu
POPE, John .... 770-412-4034.... 137 F
jpope@sctech.edu
POPE, Kiesha, L .... 804-523-5137.... 527 A
kpope@reynolds.edu
POPE, Myron .... 405-974-5370.... 413 B
mpope5@uco.edu
POPE, Sharon .... 570-372-4108.... 447 E
popes@susqu.edu
POPE, Tom .... 606-589-3023.... 203 D
tom.pope@kctcs.edu
POPE-DAVIS, Donald, B .... 574-631-8052.... 180 G
pope-davis.1@nd.edu
POPENFOOSE, G. Stephen 574-372-5100.... 171 H
popenfgs@grace.edu
POPHAM, Heidi .... 706-295-6598.... 131 B
hpopham@gntc.edu
POPIELSKI, Kathy .... 716-827-4343.... 358 D
popielskik@trocaire.edu
POPIELSKI, Michael .... 574-289-7001.... 176 E
mpopielski@ivytech.edu
POPIOLEK, Marcus .... 313-664-7665.... 249 E
mpopiolek@collegeforcreativestudies.edu

POPKIN, Eric .... 719-389-6657...... 82 D
epopkin@coloradocollege.edu
POPKO, John, P .... 206-296-6222.... 538 B
jpopko@seattleu.edu
POPKO, Susan .... 408-554-6940...... 68 C
spopko@scu.edu
POPLAWSKI, Lisa .... 509-359-4555.... 533 H
lpoplawski@ewu.edu
POPOLI, John, N .... 847-574-5210.... 156 A
jpopoli@lfgsm.edu
POPOLOSKI, Tanya .... 603-623-0313.... 305 E
tpopoloski@nhia.edu
POPOOLA, Joseph, K .... 803-934-3290.... 459 G
jpopoola@morris.edu
POPOVICH, Donna, B .... 813-253-6237.... 123 A
dpopovich@ut.edu
POPOVICH, Joseph .... 443-885-3372.... 224 E
joseph.popovich@morgan.edu
POPOVICS, Alexander, J .... 518-629-7307.... 336 C
a.popovics@hvcc.edu
POPP, Connie .... 414-382-6352.... 546 B
connie.popp@alverno.edu
POPP, Jodi .... 920-686-6127.... 550 H
jodi.popp@sl.edu
POPP, Melissa, D .... 636-584-6703.... 281 E
garrism@eastcentral.edu
POPP, Nathaniel .... 570-561-1818.... 446 D
POPP, Randall .... 918-594-8031.... 410 D
randall.popp@okstate.edu
POPP, William, C .... 770-720-5568.... 136 C
wcp@reinhardt.edu
POPPE, Jan, R .... 989-964-2058.... 257 G
jrpoppe@svsu.edu
POPPE, Kenneth .... 860-832-1633...... 90 G
poppe@ccsu.edu
POPPO, Kristin .... 617-873-0232.... 233 A
kristin.poppo@cambridgecollege.edu
POPPRE, Beth .... 480-219-6026.... 278 D
bpoppre@atsu.edu
PORADA, Kenneth .... 740-245-7214.... 404 E
kporada@rio.edu
PORAT, Moshe .... 215-204-1836.... 447 H
moshe.porat@temple.edu
PORATH, Wiona .... 517-264-7613.... 258 B
wporath@sienaheights.edu
PORCARELLO, Irene .... 713-718-7071.... 487 I
irene.porcarello@hccs.edu
PORCH, Linda .... 215-965-4037.... 436 H
lporch@moore.edu
PORCHE, Demetrius .... 504-568-4106.... 213 A
dporch@lsuhsc.edu
PORCHE, JR., Francis .... 337-491-2445.... 212 E
francis.porche@sowela.edu
PORCHIA, Christine .... 910-678-8583.... 370 E
porchiac@faytechcc.edu
PORETTE, Joanne .... 845-848-7813.... 332 B
joanne.porette@dc.edu
PORFIDO, Nancy .... 609-343-5095.... 307 C
porfido@atlantic.edu
PORNKITTICHOTCHAROEN,
Gib .... 617-541-5399.... 241 A
gibp@rcc.mass.edu
PORPIGLIA, Karen, R .... 716-673-3109.... 352 A
karen.porpiglia@fredonia.edu
PORT, Jeffrey, L .... 651-638-6439.... 261 D
jport@bethel.edu
PORTE, Meaghen .... 503-297-5544.... 417 G
mporte@ocac.edu
PORTELA, Stanley .... 787-752-4540.... 567 C
stanley.portela@upr.edu
PORTELA IRIGOYEN,
Celso, E .... 787-725-8120.... 562 C
cportela@centro.eap.edu
PORTELLEZ, Humberto .... 207-834-8646.... 220 D
humberto.portellez@maine.edu
PORTER, Aaron, K .... 423-775-7574.... 467 F
aaron.porter@bryan.edu
PORTER, Andrew, C .... 215-898-7014.... 448 J
andyp@gse.upenn.edu
PORTER, Ava, G .... 540-985-8531.... 520 I
agporter@jchs.edu
PORTER, Barbara, A .... 540-831-5408.... 523 A
bporter@radford.edu
PORTER, Barbara, A .... 202-994-3121...... 98 C
porter@gwu.edu
PORTER, Bonisha .... 229-430-4741.... 124 A
bonisha.porter@asurams.edu
PORTER, Brandi .... 540-365-4428.... 519 C
bporter@ferrum.edu
PORTER, Brenda, I .... 607-871-2186.... 322 E
porterbi@alfred.edu
PORTER, Brian .... 818-932-3036...... 45 A
bporter@devry.edu
PORTER, Charles .... 251-405-7118........ 2 C
cporter@bishop.edu
PORTER, Charles .... 206-296-4490.... 538 B
porterc@seattleu.edu
PORTER, Christine, M .... 540-654-1058.... 525 D
cjporter@umw.edu
PORTER, Clifford .... 229-430-4660.... 124 A
clifford.porter@asurams.edu
PORTER, Clyde .... 972-860-7760.... 484 F
cporter@dcccd.edu
PORTER, Curtis, R .... 505-277-2611.... 321 C
cporter@unm.edu

POWAZEK, Jack, J .... 310-825-2411...... 74 C
powazek@ucla.edu
POWE, David, L .... 601-984-1018.... 277 E
dpowe@umc.edu
POWEL, Wayne .... 814-472-3004.... 446 B
wpowel@francis.edu
POWELL, Aaron .... 360-867-6238.... 534 D
powella@evergreen.edu
POWELL, April .... 559-453-2027...... 48 A
agp@fresno.edu
POWELL, Betty .... 713-221-8072.... 503 F
powellb@uhd.edu
POWELL, Brett .... 870-245-5410...... 22 I
powellb@obu.edu
POWELL, Carl .... 734-487-4591.... 250 F
crpowell@emich.edu
POWELL, Charles .... 203-432-7458...... 96 A
charles.powell@yale.edu
POWELL, Chuck .... 631-632-9085.... 352 C
chuck.powell@stonybrook.edu
POWELL, Curtis, N .... 518-276-6359.... 347 D
powelc2@rpi.edu
POWELL, Darrin .... 859-336-1746.... 202 A
darrin.powell@kctcs.edu
POWELL, Dave .... 269-964-6653.... 260 C
dave.powell@wmich.edu
POWELL, DeAnna .... 254-968-9431.... 497 A
powell@tarleton.edu
POWELL, Deborah .... 301-447-5840.... 225 A
dpowell@msmary.edu
POWELL, Deborah, L .... 434-381-6179.... 524 K
dpowell@sbc.edu
POWELL, Debra .... 303-937-4200...... 82 E
dpowell@chu.edu
POWELL, Denise .... 912-538-3162.... 137 E
dpowell@southeasterntech.edu
POWELL, Edna .... 310-506-6464...... 61 H
edna.powell@pepperdine.edu
POWELL, Glenn .... 706-721-1896.... 130 D
gpowell@georgiahealth.edu
POWELL, Gregory, S .... 903-693-2022.... 492 C
gpowell@panola.edu
POWELL, Hiram .... 386-481-2956.... 102 C
powellh@cookman.edu
POWELL, Jack .... 317-955-6312.... 177 I
jpowell@marian.edu
POWELL, Jack, P .... 317-955-6312.... 177 I
jpowell@marian.edu
POWELL, Jane .... 213-738-6836...... 71 E
jpowell@swlaw.edu
POWELL, Jason .... 540-365-4376.... 519 C
jpowell@ferrum.edu
POWELL, Jason, B .... 860-832-2398...... 90 G
powell@ccsu.edu
POWELL, Jay .... 205-970-9215........ 7 C
jpowell@sebc.edu
POWELL, Jennifer .... 601-477-5454.... 274 H
jennifer.powell@jcjc.edu
POWELL, Jill .... 704-355-8894.... 363 D
jill.powell@carolinashealthcare.org
POWELL, John .... 502-897-4617.... 206 C
jpowell@sbts.edu
POWELL, John .... 304-734-6689.... 542 H
jpowell@bridgemont.edu
POWELL, John .... 304-766-5727.... 542 J
jpowell@kvctc.edu
POWELL, JR., John, W ..... 843-953-5200.... 456 C
john.powell@citadel.edu
POWELL, Karan, H .... 304-724-3700.... 540 F
kpowell@apus.edu
POWELL, Karen .... 650-378-7359...... 67 G
powellk@smccd.edu
POWELL, Katherine .... 706-236-1707.... 126 C
kpowell@berry.edu
POWELL, Kathleen, I .... 740-587-6521.... 389 I
powellk@denison.edu
POWELL, Kevin .... 804-524-5691.... 529 H
manager525@nebook.com
POWELL, Linda .... 503-883-2627.... 416 H
lpowell@linfield.edu
POWELL, Lyn .... 352-854-2322.... 103 K
powelll@cf.edu
POWELL, Marjorie, L .... 410-706-3950.... 227 C
mlpowell@af.umaryland.edu
POWELL, Nancy, L .... 606-679-8501.... 203 C
nancy.powell@kctcs.edu
POWELL, Necole .... 314-367-8700.... 288 F
necole.powell@stlcop.edu
POWELL, Patricia .... 334-222-6591...... 5 F
ppowell@lbwcc.edu
POWELL, Patsy .... 912-871-1603.... 135 D
ppowell@ogeecheetech.edu
POWELL, Patty, T .... 615-230-3441.... 476 C
patty.powell@volstate.edu
POWELL, Peter .... 615-445-3456.... 468 G
ppowell@devry.edu
POWELL, Phillip .... 919-530-6392.... 378 B
ppowell@nccu.edu
POWELL, R. Tony, A .... 270-809-2664.... 205 A
rpowell@murraystate.edu
POWELL, Randall .... 903-566-7101.... 506 E
rpowell@uttyler.edu
POWELL, Richard, S .... 904-620-2015.... 120 D
rsp@unf.edu
POWELL, Roger .... 909-384-8910...... 65 C
rpowell@sbccd.cc.ca.us
POWELL, Shalisa .... 219-769-3321.... 170 C
sdpowell@brownmackie.edu
POWELL, Skeet .... 254-298-8692.... 496 D
skeetpowell@templejc.edu
POWELL, Stephanie, E .... 850-263-3261.... 101 L
POWELL, Sue .... 601-936-5555.... 274 C
cspowell@hindscc.edu
POWELL, Theresa, A .... 215-204-6556.... 447 H
theresa.powell@temple.edu
POWELL, Thomas .... 252-789-0293.... 371 H
tpowell@martincc.edu
POWELL, Thomas, H .... 301-447-5600.... 225 A
powell@msmary.edu
POWELL, Tim .... 559-445-5565...... 32 A
registrar@calchristiancollege.edu
POWELL, Todd .... 785-628-4233.... 192 I
tpowell@fhsu.edu
POWELL, Todd .... 803-799-9082.... 461 A
jtpowell@southuniversity.edu
POWELL, III, Tommie .... 504-278-6423.... 211 E
tpowell@nunez.edu
POWELL, Torence .... 916-691-7170...... 56 B
powellt@crc.losrios.edu
POWELL, Wayne .... 828-328-7334.... 366 E
powellw@lr.edu
POWELL, William, W .... 601-266-4964.... 277 F
william.powell@usm.edu
POWELL-COHEN, Sheila ... 305-626-3657.... 109 A
shelia.powellcohen@fmuniv.edu
POWER, Christopher .... 513-745-5700.... 403 F
christopher.power@uc.edu
POWER, Colleen .... 510-883-7153...... 45 B
cpower@dspt.edu
POWER-BARNES,
Marie, R .... 609-984-4839.... 316 A
mpowerbarnes@tesc.edu
POWER ROBISON,
Elizabeth .... 562-907-4219...... 79 F
eprobison@whittier.edu
POWERS, Amber .... 215-576-0800.... 445 D
apowers@rrc.edu
POWERS, Andrew .... 740-593-1911.... 399 G
powersa@ohio.edu
POWERS, Barbara .... 989-686-9032.... 250 D
bjpowers@delta.edu
POWERS, Cindy .... 304-896-7382.... 543 C
cindy.powers@southernwv.edu
POWERS, Danielle .... 856-227-7200.... 308 D
dpowers@camdencc.edu
POWERS, David .... 206-296-5300.... 538 B
powersda@seattleu.edu
POWERS, Elizabeth, A .... 401-232-6085.... 453 C
bpowers@bryant.edu
POWERS, Frank .... 509-533-3429.... 533 C
frankp@spokanefalls.edu
POWERS, John .... 650-926-0250...... 71 G
jfpowers@stanford.edu
POWERS, Jon, R .... 740-368-3082.... 400 G
jrpowers@owu.edu
POWERS, Joshua .... 812-237-8378.... 173 B
joshua.powers@indstate.edu
POWERS, Keri .... 508-531-1324.... 237 D
keri.powers@bridgew.edu
POWERS, Lisa, M .... 814-865-7517.... 438 G
lmr8@psu.edu
POWERS, Lynn .... 407-708-2138.... 117 H
powers@seminolestate.edu
POWERS, Mark, R .... 508-626-4545.... 238 A
mpowers@framingham.edu
POWERS, Mikal .... 956-607-1056...... 19 A
mikal.powers@phoenix.edu
POWERS, Patrick .... 407-646-2115.... 116 D
ppowers@rollins.edu
POWERS, Peter, K .... 717-766-2511.... 436 D
ppowers@messiah.edu
POWERS, Phillippa .... 585-475-6938.... 347 G
pxpcrp@rit.edu
POWERS, Richard .... 512-313-3000.... 483 K
richard.powers@concordia.edu
POWERS, Sherry .... 859-858-3511.... 198 E
sherry.powers@asbury.edu
POWERS, Susan .... 802-865-5490.... 513 C
spowers@champlain.edu
POWERS, Suzanne .... 417-328-1689.... 290 A
spowers@sbuniv.edu
POWERS, Tim .... 949-794-9090...... 71 F
tpowers@stanbridge.edu
POWERS, Tracy, J .... 812-237-5000.... 173 B
tracy.powers@indstate.edu
POWERS, Tyrone .... 410-777-7496.... 221 C
tpowers@aacc.edu
POWERS, William, B .... 312-987-1435.... 154 H
6powers@jmls.edu
POWERS, JR., William, C . 512-471-1232.... 505 D
president@po.utexas.edu
POWERS-LEE, Susan, G .... 617-373-2842.... 243 F
POWERS-SCHAUB, Gail .... 231-777-5331.... 248 E
gail.powersschaub@baker.edu
POWLESS, David .... 205-970-9225........ 7 C
dpowless@sebc.edu
POWLEY, Mary, R .... 585-385-8057.... 348 F
mpowley@sjfc.edu
POYNTER, Barry .... 859-622-5012.... 200 J
barry.poynter@eku.edu
POYTHRESS, James, W ..... 540-857-6004.... 529 B
jpoythress@virginiawestern.edu
POZNANSKI, Brad, F .... 603-656-6023.... 305 G
bfpoznanski@anselm.edu
POZZI, Dave .... 626-568-8850...... 53 D
PRABHU, Vilas, A .... 717-872-3596.... 443 D
vilas.prabhu@millersville.edu
PRACHER, Mark .... 310-287-4467...... 55 F
prachem@wlac.edu
PRADO, Lenore .... 305-628-6514.... 117 A
lprado@stu.edu
PRADO, Marivi .... 305-474-6880.... 117 A
mprado@stu.edu
PRAET, Diane, M .... 313-993-3313.... 258 G
praetdm@udmercy.edu
PRAETORIUS, Elizabeth ..... 718-409-7204.... 356 C
lpraetorius@sunymaritime.edu
PRAETZEL, Gary, D .... 716-286-8270.... 344 D
gdp@niagara.edu
PRALL, J. Andrew .... 260-399-7700.... 181 A
jprall@sf.edu
PRANGE, Raphaella .... 217-424-6395.... 158 G
rpalmer@millikin.edu
PRANGER, Henriette, M ..... 860-727-6740...... 92 I
hpranger@goodwin.edu
PRANGLIN, Roxie .... 806-651-2037.... 499 A
rpranglin@wtamu.edu
PRASAD, Lorraine .... 718-997-5760.... 328 E
lorraine.prasad@qc.cuny.edu
PRASAD, Rashmi .... 907-786-4126...... 10 H
afrp2@uaa.alaska.edu
PRASIFKA, Matthew .... 713-525-3512.... 505 A
prasifm@stthom.edu
PRASKI, Pat .... 989-729-3457.... 248 F
pat.praski@baker.edu
PRASLOVA, Ludmilla .... 714-556-3610...... 77 B
lpraslova@vanguard.edu
PRASSE, David, P .... 312-915-6992.... 157 C
dprasse@luc.edu
PRASTACOS, Gregory .... 201-216-8366.... 315 E
gregory.prastacos@stevens.edu
PRASTER, Donald, O .... 570-326-3761.... 440 L
dpraster@pct.edu
PRATER, Bob .... 913-469-8500.... 194 B
bprater@jccc.edu
PRATER, Margaret .... 731-286-3585.... 475 B
prater@nwtnworks.org
PRATER, Michael .... 574-520-4319.... 174 E
maprater@iusb.edu
PRATER, Steve .... 580-477-7894.... 414 C
steve.prater@wosc.edu
PRATER, Susan .... 405-974-2300.... 413 B
sprater4@uco.edu
PRATER, Todd .... 706-880-8924.... 133 B
tprater@lagrange.edu
PRATHER, Alphonse .... 931-552-7600.... 468 C
aprather@daymarinstitute.edu
PRATHER, Kerry, N .... 317-738-8121.... 171 F
kprather@franklincollege.edu
PRATHER, Ruth, L .... 407-582-2216.... 123 B
rprather@valenciacollege.edu
PRATHER, Sean .... 925-424-1690...... 39 D
sprather@laspositascollege.edu
PRATHER, Tammy .... 662-329-7131.... 276 A
tprather@registrar.muw.edu
PRATT, Andrew, L .... 816-415-7557.... 293 C
pratta@william.jewell.edu
PRATT, Anne .... 802-251-7607.... 513 H
apratt@marlboro.edu
PRATT, Barbara .... 908-835-2355.... 317 C
pratt@warren.edu
PRATT, Bernard .... 207-778-7009.... 220 C
ben.pratt@maine.edu
PRATT, Charles .... 201-200-2141.... 312 B
cpratt@njcu.edu
PRATT, Dan .... 913-288-7150.... 194 C
dpratt1@kckcc.edu
PRATT, Edward .... 225-771-4545.... 214 I
edward_pratt@subr.edu
PRATT, Edward, E .... 561-297-0567.... 119 A
epratt2@fau.edu
PRATT, Eric .... 601-925-7652.... 275 C
epratt@mc.edu
PRATT, Estina .... 310-900-1600...... 45 F
pratt_e@compton.edu
PRATT, G. Michael .... 513-529-1809.... 396 E
prattgm@muohio.edu
PRATT, G. Michael .... 513-785-3200.... 396 F
prattgm@muohio.edu
PRATT, Harold, W .... 417-836-4252.... 286 C
wpratt@missouristate.edu
PRATT, James .... 812-749-1215.... 178 H
jpratt@oak.edu
PRATT, James .... 509-372-7258.... 539 D
jrpratt@wsu.edu
PRATT, Janice .... 520-494-6602...... 13 D
janice.pratt@centralaz.edu
PRATT, Jonathan, R .... 763-417-8250.... 262 A
PRATT, Judy .... 513-244-8674.... 387 E
judy.pratt@ccuniversity.edu
PRATT, Kris .... 812-749-1408.... 178 H
kpratt@oak.edu
PRATT, Linda, R .... 402-472-5242.... 300 E
lpratt@nebraska.edu
PRATT, Lisa .... 218-726-8829.... 271 F
lpratt@d.umn.edu
PRATT, Michael .... 252-985-5146.... 375 E
mpratt@ncwc.edu
PRATT, Michael .... 205-652-3565........ 9 E
mpratt@uwa.edu
PRATT, Robert, C .... 517-750-1200.... 258 D
bpratt@arbor.edu
PRATT, Sarah .... 213-740-8867...... 76 F
pratt@usc.edu
PRATT, JR., Theodore, W .. 360-650-3450.... 539 F
ted.pratt@cc.wwu.edu
PRATT, Zane .... 502-897-4043.... 206 C
zpratt@sbts.edu
PRATT-CLARKE, Menah ..... 217-333-4238.... 167 D
menahpc@illinois.edu
PRATT-CLARKE, Menah ..... 217-333-0885.... 167 D
menahpc@illinois.edu
PRATTE, John .... 870-972-3079...... 20 D
jpratte@astate.edu
PRATTELLA, Todd .... 914-674-7844.... 340 F
tprattella@mercy.edu
PRATTS, Luis, N .... 787-780-0070.... 560 H
lpratts@caribbean.edu
PRAY, G. Jon .... 414-288-7532.... 548 F
jon.pray@marquette.edu
PRAYOR, Sharon .... 773-291-6210.... 147 G
sprayor@ccc.edu
PREA, Karri .... 602-274-4300...... 12 K
PREAS, Derek .... 903-468-3148.... 498 B
derek.preas@tamuc.edu
PREATHER, Gary .... 817-515-6742.... 496 C
gary.preather@tccd.edu
PREBLE, Edwin, G .... 575-624-8070.... 319 C
preble@nmmi.edu
PREBLE, Holly .... 909-621-8130...... 62 H
holly_preble@pitzer.edu
PREBLE, Mark .... 774-455-7537.... 236 E
mpreble@umassp.edu
PRECHTER, Patricia .... 504-398-2213.... 214 B
pprechter@olhcc.edu
PRECHTL, Gregory, D .... 716-673-3101.... 352 A
gregory.prechtl@fredonia.edu
PRECIADO, Danielle .... 510-723-6608...... 39 C
dpreciado@chabotcollege.edu
PRECISE, Leigh .... 816-483-9600.... 289 E
leighp@spst.edu
PRECZEWSKI, Stanley .... 678-407-5231.... 130 C
spreczewski@ggc.edu
PREDIC, Beba .... 303-937-4202...... 82 E
bpredic@chu.edu
PREECE, Barbara .... 760-750-4350...... 36 C
bpreece@csusm.edu
PREECE, Jennifer, J .... 301-405-2033.... 227 B
preece@umd.edu
PREGEANT, Gene, E .... 985-549-5888.... 216 C
gpregeant@selu.edu
PREGITZER, Kurt .... 208-885-6442.... 144 G
kpregitzer@uidaho.edu
PREHN, Kevin .... 858-279-4500...... 52 H
kprehn@kaplan.edu
PREISINGER, George, T ..... 248-370-2127.... 256 G
preising@oakland.edu
PREISLER, Karen .... 979-532-6381.... 509 D
karenp@wcjc.edu
PRELLWITZ, Andrew .... 920-748-8175.... 550 D
prellwitz@ripon.edu
PRELOCK, Patricia, A .... 802-656-2216.... 514 H
patricia.prelock@uvm.edu
PREMNATH, Devadasan, N 585-271-3657.... 348 B
dnprem@stbernards.edu
PREMO, Brenda .... 909-469-5385...... 78 I
bpremo@westernu.edu
PREMO, Greg, V .... 253-535-8787.... 536 E
premogv@plu.edu
PRENATT, Ann, B .... 314-935-7746.... 292 I
aprenatt@wustl.edu
PRENDERGAST, Colleen .... 319-368-6463.... 187 H
cprendergast@mtmercy.edu
PRENDERGAST, Debra, L .. 708-709-3689.... 161 D
dprendergast@prairiestate.edu
PRENDERGAST, Jocelyn .... 781-762-1211.... 234 F
drlyn@fine-ne.com
PRENDERGAST, Nancy .... 847-635-1661.... 160 F
nprender@oakton.edu
PRENDERGAST,
Thomas, M .... 419-755-4712.... 397 C
tprendergast@ncstatecollege.edu
PRENGAMAN, Diane .... 410-225-2285.... 224 B
dprengam@mica.edu
PRENOVOST, Jason .... 206-878-3710.... 535 B
jprenovo@highline.edu
PRENTICE, Ernest, D .... 402-559-6045.... 300 H
edprenti@unmc.edu
PRENTICE, Marilyn .... 847-214-7992.... 150 F
mprentice@elgin.edu
PRENTISS, Kay .... 508-849-3228.... 230 C
kprentiss@annamaria.edu
PREOCANIN, Shelley .... 812-866-7097.... 172 A
preocanins@hanover.edu
PREPEJCHAL, Mary .... 956-364-4041.... 500 D
mary.prepejchal@tstc.edu

PRESCOD-CAESAR, Pamela .... 610-328-8397 .... 447 F
ppresco1@swarthmore.edu
PRESCOTT, Dennis .... 575-646-1613 .... 319 D
dprescot@nmsu.edu
PRESCOTT, Herman .... 202-274-5072 .... 100 A
tprescott@udc.edu
PRESCOTT, Jay, B .... 515-263-2890 .... 185 C
jprescott@grandview.edu
PRESCOTT, Loren, D .... 570-408-4000 .... 452 A
loren.prescott@wilkes.edu
PRESCOTT, Michael, L .... 985-549-2222 .... 216 C
michael.prescott@selu.edu
PRESCOTT, Patricia, M .... 516-671-0439 .... 360 B
pprescot@webb-institute.edu
PRESENT, Melissa .... 212-678-8820 .... 337 G
mepresent@jtsa.edu
PRESENT, Wendy .... 716-338-1070 .... 337 E
wendypresent@mail.sunyjcc.edu
PRESLEY, Brian .... 276-935-4349 .... 516 D
bpresley@asl.edu
PRESLEY, Cheryl .... 765-983-1311 .... 171 E
preslch@earlham.edu
PRESLEY, Doretha .... 601-977-4461 .... 277 C
dpresley@tougaloo.edu
PRESLEY, Ethel, R .... 601-979-2241 .... 274 G
ethel.r.presley@jsums.edu
PRESLEY, Leandrew .... 662-621-4207 .... 273 F
lpresley@coahomacc.edu
PRESLEY, Shawn .... 740-427-5158 .... 394 C
presleys@kenyon.edu
PRESLEY, Vivian, M .... 662-621-4130 .... 273 F
vpresley@coahomacc.edu
PRESNELL, Anita .... 910-576-6222 .... 372 D
presnella@montgomery.edu
PRESNELL, Sam .... 828-765-7351 .... 372 A
spresnell@mayland.edu
PRESS, Jim .... 231-995-1327 .... 256 D
jpress@nmc.edu
PRESSER, Art .... 800-290-4226 .... 469 E
apresser@hchs.edu
PRESSEY, Natalie .... 212-229-5660 .... 342 E
presseyn@newschool.edu
PRESSIMONE, J. Michael .. 610-796-8259 .... 421 G
mike.pressimone@alvernia.edu
PRESSLEY, Becky .... 864-379-8832 .... 458 A
pressley@erskine.edu
PRESSLEY, Dan .... 706-754-7791 .... 135 A
dpressley@northgatech.edu
PRESSLEY, Johnny .... 513-244-8620 .... 387 E
johnny.pressley@ccuniversity.edu
PRESSLEY, Pamela .... 903-927-3202 .... 509 E
ppressley@wileyc.edu
PRESSMAN, Avraham .... 570-346-1747 .... 452 F
PRESSON, Mark, A .... 563-588-8000 .... 184 I
mpresson@emmaus.edu
PRESSON, Paul .... 801-832-2424 .... 512 G
pkpresson@westminstercollege.edu
PRESSWOOD, Kristy .... 386-506-3822 .... 104 F
presswk@daytonastate.edu
PRESSWOOD, Theresa .... 281-283-2015 .... 503 E
presswood@uhcl.edu
PREST, Stacy .... 509-527-4294 .... 539 B
stacy.prest@wwcc.edu
PRESTA, James .... 847-970-4869 .... 167 F
jpresta@usml.edu
PRESTA, Paul .... 859-336-5082 .... 206 A
ppresta@sccky.edu
PRESTAGE, Karen .... 334-229-4243 .... 1 C
kprestage@alasu.edu
PRESTENBACH, Celeste .... 205-329-7926 .... 3 A
celeste.prestenbach@ecacolleges.com
PRESTFELDT, Carl, F .... 270-809-3472 .... 205 A
cprestfeldt@murraystate.edu
PRESTI, Coral .... 203-857-7123 .... 92 C
cpresti@ncc.commnet.edu
PRESTIACOMO, Angela, M 518-381-1381 .... 350 E
prestiam@sunysccc.edu
PRESTON, Alda .... 913-288-7167 .... 194 C
apreston@kckcc.edu
PRESTON, April .... 615-366-4404 .... 473 D
april.preston@tbr.edu
PRESTON, Betty, E .... 419-755-4756 .... 397 C
bpreston@ncstatecollege.edu
PRESTON, Cynthea .... 530-541-4660 .... 53 G
preston@ltcc.edu
PRESTON, Daniel .... 503-883-2294 .... 416 H
dpreston@linfield.edu
PRESTON, David .... 979-230-3256 .... 482 D
david.preston@brazosport.edu
PRESTON, Elizabeth .... 413-572-5213 .... 238 F
lpreston@wsc.ma.edu
PRESTON, Harold, R .... 325-670-1497 .... 487 F
hpreston@hsutx.edu
PRESTON, James .... 559-925-3146 .... 78 D
jamespreston@whccd.edu
PRESTON, James .... 312-329-4140 .... 159 A
james.preston@moody.edu
PRESTON, Jeffrey, H .... 912-279-5751 .... 127 E
jpreston@ccga.edu
PRESTON, Joanne .... 305-809-3538 .... 108 I
joanne.preston@fkcc.edu
PRESTON, Joanne .... 508-678-2811 .... 239 B
joanne.preston@bristolcc.edu
PRESTON, Karen .... 503-725-5460 .... 418 G
prestonk@pdx.edu
PRESTON, Kenneth, G .... 330-972-8254 .... 403 B
kpreston@uakron.edu
PRESTON, Kenneth, G .... 330-972-7845 .... 403 B
kpreston@uakron.edu
PRESTON, Laura, C .... 443-412-2438 .... 223 B
lpreston@harford.edu
PRESTON, Lauri .... 301-891-4089 .... 229 B
laurip@wau.edu
PRESTON, Quiana .... 815-921-4187 .... 162 H
q.preston@rockvalleycollege.edu
PRESTON, Robert .... 240-567-5327 .... 224 D
robert.preston@montgomerycollege.edu
PRESTON, Thomas .... 302-857-7749 .... 96 C
tpreston@desu.edu
PRESTON, Travis .... 661-255-1050 .... 32 F
tpreston@calarts.edu
PRESTWICH, Aaron .... 308-432-6231 .... 299 E
aprestwich@csc.edu
PRESTWICH, Kimberly .... 208-732-6293 .... 143 E
kprestwich@csi.edu
PRESTWICH, Paul .... 307-754-6200 .... 556 G
paul.prestwich@northwestcollege.edu
PRETS, Richard .... 281-998-6150 .... 493 G
richard.prets@sjcd.edu
PRETTI, Janet .... 541-469-5017 .... 420 C
jpretti@socc.edu
PRETTO, Felix .... 212-594-4000 .... 357 H
fpretto@tcicollege.edu
PRETTO, Ninah .... 973-748-9000 .... 307 H
ninah_pretto@bloomfield.edu
PRETTY, Keith, A .... 989-837-4203 .... 256 E
pretty@northwood.edu
PRETTYMAN, James .... 435-613-5612 .... 512 A
james.prettyman@usu.edu
PRETTYMAN, Ronald .... 812-237-4089 .... 173 B
ron.prettyman@indstate.edu
PREUSZ, Mike .... 864-644-5048 .... 461 B
mpreusz@swu.edu
PREVAUX, Steven, D .... 813-974-1669 .... 121 A
prevaux@usf.edu
PREVOST, Blair .... 903-923-2326 .... 486 F
bprevost@etbu.edu
PREVOST, JR., Hugh, L .... 423-425-4735 .... 477 F
hugh-prevost@utc.edu
PREWETT, Nick .... 573-882-6200 .... 291 B
prewettn@missouri.edu
PREWITT, Michael .... 304-696-3765 .... 544 B
prewitta@marshall.edu
PREWITT, Steve .... 615-966-5804 .... 470 F
steve.prewitt@lipscomb.edu
PREZANT, Robert, S .... 973-655-5108 .... 311 F
prezantr@mail.montclair.edu
PRIBBENOW, Dean .... 608-663-2200 .... 547 F
dpribbenow@edgewood.edu
PRIBBENOW, Paul, C .... 612-330-1212 .... 261 B
president@augsburg.edu
PRIBBLE, Ronald, L .... 320-222-5204 .... 268 G
ronald.pribble@ridgewater.edu
PRIBULSKY, Christopher ... 814-262-3824 .... 441 A
cpribulsky@pennhighlands.edu
PRIBUSH, Bonnie, L .... 317-738-8251 .... 171 F
bpribush@franklincollege.edu
PRICCI, Erica .... 570-504-8111 .... 433 A
pricci@lackawanna.edu
PRICE, Adrian .... 501-370-5383 .... 23 B
aprice@philander.edu
PRICE, Adrienne .... 909-594-5611 .... 58 A
aprice@mtsac.edu
PRICE, Alan Paul .... 262-335-5203 .... 553 B
paul.price@uwc.edu
PRICE, Bill .... 540-231-4000 .... 518 I
PRICE, Bryan .... 757-455-3401 .... 530 C
bprice@vwc.edu
PRICE, Byron .... 718-270-5110 .... 328 C
bprice@mec.cuny.edu
PRICE, Cecil, D .... 336-758-5218 .... 380 C
price@wfu.edu
PRICE, Chad, P .... 208-496-2338 .... 143 A
pricec@byui.edu
PRICE, Cynthia .... 614-257-4640 .... 390 B
cprice@devry.edu
PRICE, Cynthia, J .... 206-281-2179 .... 537 H
cprice@spu.edu
PRICE, Danny .... 706-368-5644 .... 126 C
dprice@berry.edu
PRICE, David, E .... 706-778-8500 .... 136 A
dprice2@piedmont.edu
PRICE, Dawne .... 402-494-2311 .... 299 B
dprice@thenicc.edu
PRICE, Debbie, M .... 318-435-2163 .... 210 L
dprice@ltc.edu
PRICE, Donald .... 423-775-6597 .... 472 G
PRICE, Donna .... 931-221-7907 .... 473 E
priced@apsu.edu
PRICE, Ernie .... 858-774-8798 .... 19 A
ernie.price@phoenix.edu
PRICE, Fred .... 718-270-5190 .... 328 C
fredprice@mec.cuny.edu
PRICE, Gary .... 541-259-5808 .... 416 I
priceg@linnbenton.edu
PRICE, Gordon .... 541-383-7592 .... 414 I
gprice@cocc.edu
PRICE, Greg .... 334-670-3507 .... 8 A
wgprice@troy.edu
PRICE, Irene, L .... 517-750-1200 .... 258 D
iprice@arbor.edu
PRICE, James .... 706-771-4096 .... 125 H
jprice@augustatech.edu
PRICE, James, B .... 610-436-3063 .... 444 A
jprice@wcupa.edu
PRICE, Jason .... 806-457-4200 .... 486 I
jprice@fpctx.edu
PRICE, Jennifer .... 518-262-5679 .... 322 D
pricej@mail.amc.edu
PRICE, Jennifer, M .... 301-322-0864 .... 225 F
pricejx@pgcc.edu
PRICE, Jerry .... 714-997-6721 .... 39 F
jprice@chapman.edu
PRICE, Jewel, A .... 818-240-1000 .... 48 D
jprice@glendale.edu
PRICE, Jill .... 715-365-4531 .... 555 A
jmrjenovich@nicoletcollege.edu
PRICE, Jo Ann .... 270-444-9676 .... 200 G
jprice@daymarcollege.edu
PRICE, Kayli .... 417-624-7070 .... 284 D
kprice@messengercollege.edu
PRICE, Kendrick .... 252-493-7627 .... 372 H
kprice@email.pittcc.edu
PRICE, Kevin, L .... 208-496-1705 .... 143 A
priceke@byui.edu
PRICE, Linda, A .... 301-784-5000 .... 221 B
lprice@allegany.edu
PRICE, Linda, L .... 812-877-8165 .... 179 B
price@rose-hulman.edu
PRICE, Lisa .... 618-437-5321 .... 162 D
price@rlc.edu
PRICE, Lori .... 214-379-5485 .... 492 F
lprice@pqc.edu
PRICE, Major .... 419-755-4387 .... 399 C
price.157@osu.edu
PRICE, Marjorie .... 805-986-5804 .... 77 E
mprice@vcccd.edu
PRICE, Marla .... 717-755-2300 .... 422 F
maprice@aii.edu
PRICE, Marquetta .... 404-627-2681 .... 126 D
marquetta.price@beulah.org
PRICE, Megan .... 864-388-8019 .... 459 A
mprice@lander.edu
PRICE, Michael .... 218-935-0417 .... 272 D
michael.price@wetcc.edu
PRICE, Mike .... 952-446-4141 .... 263 C
pricem@crown.edu
PRICE, Natalie .... 304-734-6607 .... 542 H
nprice@bridgemont.edu
PRICE, Nathan, R .... 304-457-6322 .... 540 E
pricenr@ab.edu
PRICE, Nikol .... 623-935-8087 .... 15 F
nikol.price@estrellamountain.edu
PRICE, Paula .... 312-777-8594 .... 153 B
pprice@aii.edu
PRICE, Phillip .... 252-940-6213 .... 368 C
phillipp@beaufortccc.edu
PRICE, Robert .... 602-243-8030 .... 16 D
robert.price@smcmail.maricopa.edu
PRICE, Robin .... 304-637-1243 .... 541 A
pricer@dewv.edu
PRICE, Roger, W .... 608-243-4742 .... 554 D
rwprice@madisoncollege.org
PRICE, Ron .... 757-221-3115 .... 518 A
PRICE, JR., Ron .... 801-863-8740 .... 511 F
rprice@uvu.edu
PRICE, Ronald, N .... 708-126-9949 .... 157 C
rprice@lumc.edu
PRICE, Sarah .... 270-686-4501 .... 203 B
sarah.price@kctcs.edu
PRICE, Vincent .... 215-898-7227 .... 448 J
provost@pobox.upenn.edu
PRICE, Virginia .... 717-334-6286 .... 435 A
vprice@ltsg.edu
PRICE, Viviane .... 303-220-1200 .... 81 J
viviane.price@cffp.edu
PRICE, W. Craig .... 504-282-4455 .... 213 H
cprice@nobts.edu
PRICE, Walter .... 972-524-3341 .... 495 H
PRICE BLOUNT, Grady .... 903-886-5781 .... 498 B
grady.blount@tamuc.edu
PRICE CURTIS, William .... 405-466-3210 .... 408 G
wpcurtis@langston.edu
PRICE-PERRY, Cassandra, F .... 901-334-5821 .... 471 E
cfperry@memphisseminary.edu
PRICHARD, Donna .... 218-235-2177 .... 269 F
d.prichard@vcc.edu
PRICHARD, Marion, L .... 580-774-3249 .... 412 F
marion.prichard@swosu.edu
PRICHARD, Patricia, A .... 503-517-1806 .... 421 C
paprichard@westernseminary.edu
PRICKEL, Timothy, J .... 812-877-8438 .... 179 B
timothy.j.prickel@rose-hulman.edu
PRICKETT, Juanita (Nita), M .... 785-539-3571 .... 195 B
nprickett@mccks.edu
PRIDAL, Cathryn .... 417-667-8181 .... 280 E
cpridal@cottey.edu
PRIDE, Miriam, R .... 217-854-3231 .... 146 A
mprid@blackburn.edu
PRIDE, Nicole .... 336-256-0863 .... 378 A
npride@ncat.edu
PRIDEAUX, Debra, K .... 785-628-4430 .... 192 I
dprideau@fhsu.edu
PRIDEAUX-BRUNE, Diana, E .... 413-597-2303 .... 246 D
diana.e.prideaux-brune@williams.edu
PRIDGIN, Reba .... 479-979-1413 .... 26 A
rpridgin@ozarks.edu
PRIDMORE, Paige .... 317-738-8100 .... 171 F
ppridmore@franklincollege.edu
PRIEMER, Sue Ann .... 724-437-4600 .... 441 B
spriemer@piht.edu
PRIES, Lynn, L .... 630-637-5104 .... 159 G
llpries@noctrl.edu
PRIEST, Barry .... 910-879-5579 .... 368 D
bpriest@bladencc.edu
PRIEST, Catherine .... 856-351-2624 .... 315 A
cpriest@salemcc.edu
PRIEST, Jeffrey, M .... 803-641-3269 .... 462 B
jeffp@usca.edu
PRIEST, Kevin .... 715-324-6900 .... 549 G
kevin.priest@ni.edu
PRIEST, Margaret .... 313-831-5200 .... 250 G
mpriest@etseminary.edu
PRIEST, Rebecca .... 330-494-6170 .... 402 B
rpriest@starkstate.edu
PRIESTLEY, Keith .... 731-352-4000 .... 467 E
priestleyk@bethelu.edu
PRIETO, Adanid .... 787-766-1717 .... 565 I
a_prieto@suagm.edu
PRIETO, Armando .... 202-274-5025 .... 100 A
apreito@udc.edu
PRIETO, Celia .... 516-686-7406 .... 343 D
cprieto@nyit.edu
PRIETO, Diana .... 970-491-5836 .... 83 F
diana.prieto@colostate.edu
PRIETO, Eduardo .... 386-226-6000 .... 105 H
eduardo.prieto@erau.edu
PRIETO, Eduardo .... 800-522-6787 .... 105 I
eduardo.prieto@erau.edu
PRIETO, Lisa .... 956-665-2100 .... 506 C
president@utpa.edu
PRIGAL, Helena .... 212-431-2318 .... 343 E
hprigal@nyls.edu
PRIGGE, Bill .... 678-915-7778 .... 137 G
bprigge@spsu.edu
PRIGGIE, Richard, W .... 309-794-7213 .... 145 E
richardpriggie@augustana.edu
PRIHODA, Susan, L .... 281-283-2626 .... 503 E
prihoda@uhcl.edu
PRILLELTENSKY, Isaac .... 305-284-3505 .... 122 I
isaacp@miami.edu
PRIMAVERA, Louis, H .... 631-665-1600 .... 358 B
louis.primavera@touro.edu
PRIMIANO, Leonard .... 610-902-8330 .... 424 B
leonard.primiano@cabrini.edu
PRIMO, John .... 405-733-7356 .... 411 I
jprimo@rose.edu
PRIMOFF, Mark .... 845-758-7412 .... 323 D
primoff@bard.edu
PRIMOZICH, Tracy .... 800-287-8822 .... 169 H
primotr@bethanyseminary.edu
PRIMROSE, Bruce .... 909-599-5433 .... 54 A
bprimrose@lifepacific.edu
PRIMUS, Joanna .... 719-590-6708 .... 83 J
PRIMUS, Lester .... 860-906-5050 .... 91 C
lprimus@ccc.commnet.edu
PRINCE, Bobby, A .... 901-678-4376 .... 474 C
baprince@memphis.edu
PRINCE, James, E .... 269-337-7225 .... 252 K
james.prince@kzoo.edu
PRINCE, Jeff .... 510-642-9494 .... 73 H
jprince@berkeley.edu
PRINCE, Judith .... 864-552-4243 .... 463 B
jprince@uscupstate.edu
PRINCE, Ken .... 812-866-7051 .... 172 A
princek@hanover.edu
PRINCINSKY, Julianne, T .. 810-766-4036 .... 248 C
julianne.princinsky@baker.edu
PRINDIVILLE, Barbara, A .. 262-691-5435 .... 555 E
bprindiville@wctc.edu
PRINGLE, Cindi .... 909-537-3521 .... 36 B
cpringle@csusb.edu
PRINGLE, Ernest .... 803-641-3345 .... 462 B
epringle@usca.edu
PRINGLE, Karen .... 541-888-7211 .... 420 C
karen.pringle@socc.edu
PRINGLE, Nancy, E .... 607-274-3836 .... 336 G
npringle@ithaca.edu
PRINGLE, Randy .... 903-923-2233 .... 486 F
rpringle@etbu.edu
PRINTUP, Roger .... 212-998-4251 .... 344 B
roger.printup@nyu.edu
PRIOLEAU, Darwin .... 585-395-5806 .... 352 F
dpriolea@brockport.edu
PRIOLEAU, Rachelle, P .... 814-393-2225 .... 442 B
rprioleau@clarion.edu
PRIOLEAU-TAYLOR, Erica . 803-536-7061 .... 460 G
esprioleau@scsu.edu
PRIOR, Roberta .... 203-285-2209 .... 91 D
rprior@gwcc.commnet.edu
PRISCO, Anne .... 201-559-6022 .... 310 B
priscoa@felician.edu

PRISELAC, Thomas ... 310-423-5711 ... 38 M
PRISLIN, Radmilla ... 619-594-4163 ... 37 A
rprislin@sunstroke.sdsu.edu
PRISLOVSKY, Andrew ... 901-321-3278 ... 467 I
aprislov@cbu.edu
PRITCHARD, Brett ... 256-215-4254 ... 2 E
bpritchard@cacc.edu
PRITCHARD, Lamar ... 713-743-1253 ... 503 D
flpritchard@uh.edu
PRITCHARD, Mandie ... 541-440-4600 ... 420 F
mandie.pritchard@umpqua.edu
PRITCHARD, Michael, H ... 301-846-2417 ... 222 G
mpritchard@frederick.edu
PRITCHARD, Rod ... 319-399-8605 ... 183 F
rpritcha@coe.edu
PRITCHARD, Sarah ... 515-271-4069 ... 184 D
sarah.pritchard@drake.edu
PRITCHARD, Sarah, M ... 847-491-7640 ... 160 E
spritchard@northwestern.edu
PRITCHARD, Tom ... 425-564-2206 ... 531 G
thomas.pritchard@bellevuecollege.edu
PRITCHETT, Alondrea, J ... 334-229-4737 ... 1 C
apritchett@alasu.edu
PRITCHETT, Beth ... 304-327-4139 ... 543 F
bpritchett@bluefieldstate.edu
PRITCHETT, Carolyn, H ... 205-940-7800 ... 3 I
cpritchett@edaff.com
PRITCHETT, H. Franklin ... 678-839-6582 ... 139 A
fpritche@westga.edu
PRITCHETT, Merrill, R ... 410-837-6207 ... 229 A
mpritchett@ubalt.edu
PRITCHETT, Nikki ... 850-644-2003 ... 119 D
npritchett@admin.fsu.edu
PRITCHETT, Wendell, E ... 856-225-6095 ... 314 D
chancellor@camden.rutgers.edu
PRITTS, Barry, R ... 304-473-8040 ... 545 G
pritts@wvwc.edu
PRITZ, Stephen, J ... 352-392-1374 ... 120 C
spritz@ufl.edu
PRITZKER, Barry ... 518-580-5654 ... 351 B
bpritzke@skidmore.edu
PRIVETT, James, E ... 803-938-3758 ... 462 G
jamesp@uscsumter.edu
PRIVETT, SJ, Stephen, A ... 415-422-6762 ... 76 E
privett@usfca.edu
PROBST, Mark ... 804-523-5790 ... 527 A
mprobst@reynolds.edu
PROBST, Robert ... 513-556-9808 ... 403 D
robert.probst@uc.edu
PROBSTFELD, Carol, F ... 941-752-5326 ... 118 J
probstc@scf.edu
PROBY, James ... 719-638-6580 ... 84 I
jproby@cci.edu
PROCARIO-FOLEY, Carl ... 914-633-2632 ... 336 E
cprocariofoley@iona.edu
PROCHNOW, Allen, J ... 262-243-5700 ... 547 C
allen.prochnow@cuw.edu
PROCK, Jim ... 870-972-2656 ... 20 D
jprock@astate.edu
PROCTER, Everett ... 949-794-9090 ... 71 F
eprocter@stanbridge.edu
PROCTER, Ken ... 478-445-4441 ... 130 B
ken.procter@gcsu.edu
PROCTER, Sharon ... 313-664-7889 ... 249 E
sprocter@collegeforcreativestudies.edu
PROCTOR, Catherine ... 732-247-5241 ... 312 A
cproctor@nbts.edu
PROCTOR, Christina ... 530-541-4660 ... 53 G
proctor@ltcc.edu
PROCTOR, Matt ... 417-626-1234 ... 287 C
pres@occ.edu
PROCTOR, Michael, A ... 520-626-5531 ... 18 L
mproctor@arizona.edu
PROCTOR, Patricia ... 501-374-0804 ... 19 D
patricia.proctor@arkansasbaptist.edu
PROCTOR, R. Leland ... 336-599-1181 ... 372 G
proctol@piedmontcc.edu
PROCTOR, William, L ... 904-819-6210 ... 107 C
proctorw@flagler.edu
PROEFROCK, Steve ... 269-467-9945 ... 251 B
sproefrock@glenoaks.edu
PROENZA, Luis, M ... 330-972-7074 ... 403 B
proenza@uakron.edu
PROFETA, Glen ... 714-432-5861 ... 41 D
gprofeta@occ.cccd.edu
PROFETA, Patricia, C ... 772-462-7590 ... 111 B
pprofeta@irsc.edu
PROFETA, Philip, S ... 585-275-5811 ... 359 B
philip_profeta@urmc.rochester.edu
PROFFITT, David ... 757-352-4876 ... 523 E
jdowney@regent.edu
PROFFITT, Randall, K ... 813-374-5343 ... 176 A
rproffit@ivytech.edu
PROFFITT, Roger ... 620-227-9422 ... 192 E
rproffitt@dc3.edu
PROFFITT, Ron ... 276-739-2421 ... 529 A
rproffitt@vhcc.edu
PROFIT, Loretta ... 225-634-2636 ... 209 K
lprofit@catc.edu
PROFITT, Adam ... 513-721-7944 ... 391 D
adamprofitt@gbs.edu
PROGAR, Patrick, R ... 973-618-3212 ... 308 C
progar@caldwell.edu

PROHASKA, Jonathan ... 603-577-6414 ... 304 I
prohaska_jonathan@dwc.edu
PROHASKA, Thomas, R ... 703-993-1918 ... 519 E
tprohask@gmu.edu
PROITE, Rosanne ... 512-245-2931 ... 501 F
rp45@txstate.edu
PROKOVICH, Jeffrey, D ... 724-458-3846 ... 430 B
jdprokovich@gcc.edu
PROKUSKI, Meredith ... 863-680-4110 ... 109 E
mprokuski@flsouthern.edu
PROMADES, Frederick, C ... 401-341-2117 ... 454 D
promadef@salve.edu
PRONKO, Nick, G ... 814-871-7471 ... 429 G
pronko001@gannon.edu
PROPER, Amy ... 703-329-9100 ... 99 G
PROPER, Sheryle, A ... 814-332-2701 ... 421 F
sheryle.proper@allegheny.edu
PROPHET, Mary Webb ... 740-587-6215 ... 389 I
prophet@denison.edu
PROPP, Timothy ... 602-978-7593 ... 18 H
tim.propp@thunderbird.edu
PROPST, Jennifer ... 828-448-6051 ... 375 B
jpropst@wpcc.edu
PROPST, Joan, L ... 304-457-6251 ... 540 E
propstjl@ab.edu
PROPST, Kent ... 660-248-6238 ... 279 G
kpropst@centralmethodist.edu
PROPST, Marlene ... 541-917-4784 ... 416 I
propstm@linnbenton.edu
PROPST, William, S ... 310-794-6027 ... 74 C
wpropst@finance.ucla.edu
PROSPER, Yamilette ... 787-891-0925 ... 563 A
yprosper@aguadilla.inter.edu
PROSSER, Deborah ... 678-717-3587 ... 129 G
dprosser@gsc.edu
PROSSER, Robert, D ... 731-352-4240 ... 467 E
prosserb@bethelu.edu
PROSSER, Sally ... 620-672-5641 ... 196 D
sallyp@prattcc.edu
PROSSER, Steve ... 731-352-4000 ... 467 E
prossers@bethelu.edu
PROSTANO, Laura ... 914-323-7124 ... 339 J
laura.prostano@mville.edu
PROTAS, Elizabeth, J ... 409-772-3001 ... 507 C
eprotas@utmb.edu
PROTHERO, Charles, L ... 570-945-8015 ... 432 E
charlie.prothero@keystone.edu
PROTO, Angelo, B ... 516-877-3680 ... 322 A
proto@adelphi.edu
PROTSKY, Julia ... 440-449-1700 ... 384 I
julia.protsky@atsinstitute.edu
PROUDFIT, Ann ... 216-987-5892 ... 389 B
ann.proudfit@tri-c.edu
PROUDFOOT, Donald, W ... 903-510-2975 ... 503 A
dpro@tjc.edu
PROUDFOOT, Tony ... 765-285-1560 ... 169 G
tproudfoot@bsu.edu
PROUGH, Donald, S ... 409-772-4793 ... 507 C
dsprough@utmb.edu
PROUGH, Gene ... 850-718-2288 ... 103 D
proughg@chipola.edu
PROULX, David, R ... 717-291-3993 ... 429 F
dave.proulx@fandm.edu
PROULX, Dennis ... 802-468-1249 ... 515 D
dennis.proulx@castleton.edu
PROULX, Diane ... 402-399-2456 ... 297 C
dproulx@csm.edu
PROULX-CURRY, Pamela ... 207-974-4603 ... 218 H
pproulx-curry@emcc.edu
PROUSE, Margaret, R ... 302-857-1065 ... 96 G
mprouse@dtcc.edu
PROUT, Deborah ... 775-831-1314 ... 303 E
dprout@sierranevada.edu
PROUT, Wilson ... 716-926-8910 ... 335 E
wprout@hilbert.edu
PROUTY, Steve ... 941-752-5204 ... 118 J
proutys@scf.edu
PROVAN, Amy ... 410-532-5379 ... 225 D
aprovan@ndm.edu
PROVENCHER, Susan ... 603-668-6660 ... 305 B
PROVENCIO-VASQUEZ,
Elias ... 915-747-8217 ... 506 B
eprovenciovasquez@utep.edu
PROVENZA, Joseph, S ... 904-819-6359 ... 107 C
jprovenza@flagler.edu
PROVINCE, Anne ... 512-492-3051 ... 480 F
aprovince@aoma.edu
PROVINE, Rick, E ... 765-658-4435 ... 171 B
provine@depauw.edu
PROVOST, David, J ... 802-865-6400 ... 513 C
djprovost@champlain.edu
PRUCE, Dora ... 216-397-4565 ... 392 L
dpruce@jcu.edu
PRUCHNICKI, Jennifer ... 580-581-2209 ... 407 D
jpruchni@cameron.edu
PRUCNAL, James, R ... 256-549-8242 ... 3 J
jprucnal@gadsdenstate.edu
PRUDEN, Elizabeth ... 513-487-1232 ... 402 I
elizabeth.pruden@myunion.edu
PRUDHOMME, Harvey, J ... 503-370-6348 ... 421 D
hprudhom@willamette.edu
PRUE, Stephen ... 785-832-6644 ... 193 D
stephen.prue@bie.edu

PRUETT, Diana ... 662-243-2675 ... 274 B
dpruett@eastms.edu
PRUETT, Karen ... 910-521-6270 ... 379 C
karen.pruitt@uncp.edu
PRUETT, Kristine ... 570-408-4676 ... 452 A
kristine.pruett@wilkes.edu
PRUETT, Robert, R ... 919-658-7760 ... 367 F
rpruett@moc.edu
PRUETT, Tim ... 740-245-7358 ... 404 E
tpruett@rio.edu
PRUIT, John ... 214-860-8613 ... 485 B
jpruit@dcccd.edu
PRUITT, Aaron ... 541-684-7217 ... 417 F
aaronp@nwcu.edu
PRUITT, Chris ... 402-449-2917 ... 297 H
cpruitt@graceu.edu
PRUITT, Dennis, A ... 803-777-4172 ... 462 A
dpruitt@sc.edu
PRUITT, George, A ... 609-984-1105 ... 316 A
gpruitt@tesc.edu
PRUITT, John ... 408-848-4732 ... 48 C
jpruitt@gavilan.edu
PRUITT, Karl ... 205-929-6348 ... 5 E
kpruitt@lawsonstate.edu
PRUITT, Leah, L ... 864-587-4225 ... 461 D
pruittl@smcsc.edu
PRUITT, Nancy ... 315-228-7220 ... 329 G
npruitt@colgate.edu
PRUITT, Samory, T ... 205-348-8376 ... 8 E
samory.pruitt@ua.edu
PRUITT, Steven ... 561-237-7834 ... 113 D
spruitt@lynn.edu
PRUITT, Valerie ... 713-777-4433 ... 509 C
vpruitt@westwood.edu
PRULL, Richard, W ... 401-456-8437 ... 454 A
rprull@ric.edu
PRUNENCA, Mary Ellen ... 602-978-7200 ... 18 H
maryellen.prunenca@thunderbird.edu
PRUNTY, Bonnie, S ... 607-274-3141 ... 336 G
bprunty@ithaca.edu
PRUNTY, Kathleen, A ... 909-869-3380 ... 33 J
kaprunty@csupomona.edu
PRUNTY, Patricia ... 845-431-8402 ... 332 D
prunty@sunydutchess.edu
PRUNTY, Rose ... 715-365-4525 ... 555 A
rprunty@nicoletcollege.edu
PRUNTY, Rose ... 715-365-4481 ... 555 A
rprunty@nicoletcollege.edu
PRUS, Mark ... 607-753-2207 ... 353 B
mark.prus@cortland.edu
PRUSHA, Todd ... 319-398-5565 ... 187 B
tprusha@kirkwood.edu
PRUSKOWSKI, Nancy ... 215-968-8514 ... 423 F
pruskows@bucks.edu
PRUSS, Linda ... 513-244-4408 ... 388 E
linda_pruss@mail.msj.edu
PRUSSIN, Shari ... 212-217-4000 ... 333 F
shari_prussin@fitnyc.edu
PRUTOW, Dennis, J ... 412-731-8690 ... 445 F
dprutow@rpts.edu
PRY, George ... 412-809-5100 ... 444 G
pry.georgel@pti.edu
PRYCE-SHEEHAN, Linda ... 559-453-2263 ... 47 K
linda.pryce-sheehan@fresno.edu
PRYCE-SHEEHAN, Linda ... 559-453-2038 ... 48 A
linda.pryce-sheehan@fresno.edu
PRYJMAK, Myron ... 718-409-7311 ... 356 C
mpryjmak@sunypurchase.edu
PRYLES, Kathyrn ... 508-588-9100 ... 240 A
PRYOR, Charles ... 212-752-1530 ... 338 C
charles.pryor@limcollege.edu
PRYOR, Douglas ... 305-809-3184 ... 108 I
douglas.pryor@fkcc.edu
PRYOR, Glen, E ... 435-586-7737 ... 511 D
pryor@suu.edu
PRYOR, Kim, A ... 336-342-4261 ... 373 E
pryork@rockinghamcc.edu
PRYOR, Raymond, G ... 570-208-5828 ... 432 G
rgpryor@kings.edu
PRYOR, Sara ... 812-855-9973 ... 173 E
spryor@indiana.edu
PRZEKURAT, Paris ... 405-422-1442 ... 411 G
przekuratp@redlandscc.edu
PRZBYLSKI, Jeannene ... 661-255-1050 ... 32 F
jeannene@calarts.edu
PRZYGOCKI, Ginny ... 989-686-9276 ... 250 D
vlprzygo@delta.edu
PRZYGODA, Melitha, R ... 203-576-4588 ... 94 F
mprzygod@bridgeport.edu
PRZYWARA, Richard, T ... 610-430-4156 ... 444 A
rprzywara@wcufoundation.org
PSAILA, Marisa ... 585-475-4932 ... 347 G
mxpdar@rit.edu
PSARRIS, Kleanthis ... 718-951-3170 ... 326 F
lpsarris@brooklyn.cuny.edu
PTAK, David, H ... 402-844-7046 ... 299 I
davep@northeast.edu
PTAK, Jeffrey ... 703-414-4070 ... 518 C
jptak@devry.edu
PUCCI, Tom ... 724-938-4351 ... 441 G
pucci@calu.edu
PUCCIARELLI, Matthew, G ... 718-990-7614 ... 348 G
pucciarm@stjohns.edu

PUCINE, Richard ... 315-792-5309 ... 341 E
rpucine@mvcc.edu
PUCKETT, Benjamin ... 727-726-1153 ... 103 I
benpuckett@clearwater.edu
PUCKETT, Christopher ... 303-315-6619 ... 88 J
chris.puckett@ucdenver.edu
PUCKETT, Jack ... 252-492-2061 ... 374 G
puckett@vgcc.edu
PUCKETT, Jackie, A ... 864-488-4585 ... 459 B
jpuckett@limestone.edu
PUCKETT, Jeff ... 608-363-2651 ... 546 E
puckettj@beloit.edu
PUCKETT, Wendy ... 270-247-8521 ... 204 G
wpuckett@midcontinent.edu
PUCKETT-BOLER, Laura ... 864-503-5194 ... 463 B
lpuckett-boler@uscupstate.edu
PUDDESTER, Frederick, W ... 413-597-4421 ... 246 D
frederick.w.puddester@williams.edu
PUDNEY, JR., Terry ... 315-652-6500 ... 324 L
tmpudneyjr@bryantstratton.edu
PUENTE, Miguel ... 509-865-8508 ... 535 A
puente_m@heritage.edu
PUENTE, Miguel ... 509-865-8697 ... 535 A
puente_m@heritage.edu
PUEPPKE, Steven, G ... 517-355-0123 ... 255 A
pueppke@msu.edu
PUETT, Debbie ... 828-395-1481 ... 371 D
dpuett@isothermal.edu
PUFFER, Anna, L ... 606-436-5721 ... 202 C
lois.puffer@kctcs.edu
PUGH, Benjamin, W ... 318-670-9302 ... 215 A
bpugh@susla.edu
PUGH, Chad ... 405-789-7661 ... 412 E
chad.pugh@swcu.edu
PUGH, Daniel ... 479-575-5004 ... 24 C
djpugh@uark.edu
PUGH, David ... 912-525-6980 ... 136 F
dpugh@scad.edu
PUGH, Don ... 573-334-6825 ... 289 J
dpugh@sehosp.org
PUGH, Jason ... 601-928-6233 ... 275 E
jason.pugh@mgccc.edu
PUGH, Jeremy ... 801-832-2685 ... 512 G
jpugh@westminstercollege.edu
PUGH, John ... 907-796-6568 ... 11 A
john.pugh@uas.alaska.edu
PUGH, Maureen, N ... 570-372-4157 ... 447 E
pugh@susqu.edu
PUGH, Nathaniel ... 631-451-4129 ... 356 D
pughn@sunysuffolk.edu
PUGH, Paul, F ... 610-519-4200 ... 450 H
paul.pugh@villanova.edu
PUGH, Viki ... 561-803-2012 ... 114 C
viki_pugh@pba.edu
PUGH, W. Russ ... 330-684-8916 ... 403 C
wrp@uakron.edu
PUGH-SEEMSTER, Nora ... 405-682-7831 ... 409 F
npseemster@occc.edu
PUGLIESE, Gloria ... 215-951-1882 ... 432 I
pugliese@lasalle.edu
PUGLIESE, Mike, A ... 918-663-9000 ... 411 E
mikep@plattcollege.org
PUGLIESE, Stephen ... 610-647-4400 ... 431 C
spugliese@immaculata.edu
PUGLIESI, Karen, L ... 928-523-1580 ... 16 I
karen.pugliesi@nau.edu
PUGLISI, Michael, J ... 276-944-6662 ... 519 A
mpuglisi@ehc.edu
PUGNAIRE, Michele, P ... 508-856-4250 ... 237 C
michele.pugnaire@umassmed.edu
PUHALA, Kimberly ... 617-984-1727 ... 243 H
kpuhala@quincycollege.edu
PUHL, Diane ... 313-927-1443 ... 254 E
dpuhl@marygrove.edu
PUICH, Sam ... 801-302-2800 ... 510 G
sam.puich@neumont.edu
PUIG, Ivan, O ... 787-257-7373 ... 565 G
ivpuig@suagm.edu
PUKYS, Gail ... 330-499-9600 ... 393 I
gpukys@kent.edu
PULAKOS, Joan ... 208-885-6716 ... 144 G
pulakos@uidaho.edu
PULASKI, Edward ... 315-792-3087 ... 359 E
PULAVARTI, Srinivas ... 804-289-6010 ... 525 E
spulavar@richmond.edu
PULEIO, Samuel, T ... 814-393-2280 ... 442 B
spuleio@clarion.edu
PULIAFICO, Venus ... 216-368-4530 ... 386 F
venus.puliafico@case.edu
PULIAFITO, Carmen, A ... 323-442-1900 ... 76 F
deanksom@usc.edu
PULICE, Jon ... 814-732-1763 ... 442 E
jpulice@edinboro.edu
PULIDO, Susie ... 602-286-8224 ... 15 G
susie.pulido@gwmail.maricopa.edu
PULLEN, Roderick, C ... 340-693-1536 ... 568 E
rpullen@live.uvi.edu
PULLER, Beverly, J ... 219-785-5337 ... 179 A
bpuller@pnc.edu
PULLEY, Brett ... 757-727-5000 ... 519 H
brett.pulley@hamptonu.edu
PULLEY, Eric ... 618-985-3741 ... 154 G
ericpulley@jalc.edu

Q

QUINCY, Barbara, I ... 724-946-7928 ... 451 C
quincybi@westminster.edu
QUINDT, Willie ... 308-635-6083 ... 301 D
wquindt@wncc.edu
QUINER, Michael, W ... 509-527-4975 ... 540 B
quinerm@whitman.edu
QUINLAN, Brian ... 508-213-2112 ... 243 E
brian.quinlan@nichols.edu
QUINLAN, Carolyn ... 517-265-5161 ... 246 H
QUINLAN, Catherine ... 213-821-2344 ... 76 F
cquinlan@usc.edu
QUINLAN, Joseph ... 201-761-7302 ... 314 F
jquinlan@spc.edu
QUINLAN, Maureen ... 619-684-8779 ... 59 B
mquinlan@newschoolarch.edu
QUINLAN BRAME, Julie ... 414-382-6371 ... 546 B
julie.quinlan@alverno.edu
QUINLEY, Linda ... 913-758-6102 ... 197 D
quinleyl@stmary.edu
QUINLEY, Melissa ... 828-398-7633 ... 368 B
mquinley@abtech.edu
QUINLIVAN, Gary ... 724-537-4597 ... 446 E
gary.quinlivan@email.stvincent.edu
QUINN, Aaron ... 740-245-7234 ... 404 E
aquinn@rio.edu
QUINN, Anita ... 906-487-2281 ... 255 B
aquin@mtu.edu
QUINN, Anthony ... 734-384-4279 ... 255 D
aquinn@monroeccc.edu
QUINN, Arthur ... 561-732-4424 ... 117 B
aquinn@svdp.edu
QUINN, Belinda ... 419-473-2700 ... 389 C
bquinn@daviscollege.edu
QUINN, Bill ... 281-487-1170 ... 499 B
bquinn@txchiro.edu
QUINN, Bonnie ... 781-768-7184 ... 244 A
bonnie.quinn@regiscollege.edu
QUINN, Brian ... 657-278-3058 ... 35 B
bquinn@fullerton.edu
QUINN, Bridget ... 212-787-5300 ... 322 F
info@amda.edu
QUINN, Brigid ... 402-878-2380 ... 298 E
bquinn@littlepriest.edu
QUINN, Catherine ... 215-248-7137 ... 425 D
quinnc@chc.edu
QUINN, Charles, C ... 512-223-8119 ... 481 B
cquinn@austincc.edu
QUINN, Christine, J ... 312-261-3315 ... 159 E
christine.quinn@nl.edu
QUINN, Christopher ... 207-221-8761 ... 218 C
cquinn@kaplan.edu
QUINN, Edward, M ... 202-687-4134 ... 98 D
quinne@georgetown.edu
QUINN, Erin ... 802-443-5253 ... 514 A
quinn@middlebury.edu
QUINN, Evelyn ... 732-987-2314 ... 310 C
quinne@georgian.edu
QUINN, Frank ... 619-849-2338 ... 62 L
frankquinn@pointloma.edu
QUINN, Gianna ... 215-641-5554 ... 430 C
quinn.g@gmc.edu
QUINN, Jack, F ... 716-851-1200 ... 333 C
jquinn@ecc.edu
QUINN, Jack, F ... 716-851-1200 ... 333 A
jquinn@ecc.edu
QUINN, Jack, F ... 716-851-1200 ... 333 B
jquinn@ecc.edu
QUINN, John ... 605-394-4800 ... 464 H
jquinn@national.edu
QUINN, JR., John, F ... 401-341-2206 ... 454 D
quinnj@salve.edu
QUINN, Joseph, G ... 718-817-3013 ... 334 C
jgquinn@fordham.edu
QUINN, Kathy ... 314-529-9476 ... 284 C
kquinn@maryville.edu
QUINN, Kevin ... 920-403-3051 ... 550 F
kevin.quinn@snc.edu
QUINN, Kevin, C ... 315-443-8338 ... 357 C
kcquinn@syr.edu
QUINN, SJ, Kevin, P ... 570-941-7500 ... 450 C
presidentquinn@scranton.edu
QUINN, Kimbra ... 806-894-9611 ... 494 G
kquinn@southplainscollege.edu
QUINN, Laurie ... 603-822-5417 ... 306 F
laurie.quinn@granite.edu
QUINN, Leslie ... 913-469-8500 ... 194 B
lquinn2@jccc.edu
QUINN, Linda ... 402-941-6280 ... 298 I
quinn@midlandu.edu
QUINN, Marisa, A ... 401-863-2453 ... 453 B
marisa_quinn@brown.edu
QUINN, Michael ... 206-296-5500 ... 538 B
quinnm@seattleu.edu
QUINN, Michael, G ... 585-292-2151 ... 341 H
mquinn@monroecc.edu
QUINN, Michael, J ... 434-947-8100 ... 523 B
mjquinn@randolphcollege.edu
QUINN, Michael, P ... 401-598-2945 ... 453 E
mquinn@jwu.edu
QUINN, Michelle ... 970-351-2773 ... 89 B
michelle.quinn@unco.edu
QUINN, Patrick ... 714-997-6947 ... 39 F
pjquinn@chapman.edu
QUINN, Patrick, A ... 315-792-3006 ... 359 E
pquinn@utica.edu
QUINN, Penny ... 620-792-9303 ... 190 H
quinnp@bartonccc.edu
QUINN, Robert, E ... 563-588-7736 ... 187 C
bob.quinn@loras.edu
QUINN, Sarah, F ... 610-660-1230 ... 446 C
squinn@sju.edu
QUINN, Shaman ... 307-754-6232 ... 556 G
shaman.quinn@northwestcollege.edu
QUINN, Sharon ... 410-455-2540 ... 227 D
squinn@umbc.edu
QUINN, Stephen ... 973-618-3320 ... 308 C
squinn@caldwell.edu
QUINN, Susan ... 707-524-1598 ... 68 E
squinn@santarosa.edu
QUINN, Tania ... 914-654-5257 ... 330 B
tquinn@cnr.edu
QUINN, Teresa ... 845-437-5370 ... 359 F
QUINN, Thomas ... 989-275-5000 ... 253 E
tom.quinn@kirtland.edu
QUINN, Wade ... 252-493-7279 ... 372 H
wquinn@email.pittcc.edu
QUINN, William, P ... 302-356-6775 ... 97 C
william.p.quinn@wilmu.edu
QUINNETT, Jim ... 325-793-4611 ... 490 H
jquinnett@mcm.edu
QUINONES, Carlos, A ... 787-753-0039 ... 564 E
QUINONES, Irma ... 787-758-2525 ... 567 G
irma.quinones1@upr.edu
QUINONES, Jose ... 787-257-0000 ... 567 C
jose.quinones@upr.edu
QUINONES, Rosa ... 787-257-0000 ... 567 C
rosa.quinones1@upr.edu
QUINONEZ, Virginia ... 312-329-6623 ... 146 F
vquinonez@thechicagoschool.edu
QUINT, Doug ... 620-242-0586 ... 195 C
quintd@mcpherson.edu
QUINT, Julie ... 314-256-8808 ... 278 G
quint@ai.edu
QUINTAL, Jorge ... 336-334-5536 ... 379 B
j_quinta@uncg.edu
QUINTAL, Rollande ... 508-849-3340 ... 230 C
rquintal@annamaria.edu
QUINTANA, Elena ... 312-662-4021 ... 144 H
lkunard@adler.edu
QUINTANA, Javier ... 787-279-1912 ... 563 D
jquintana@bayamon.inter.edu
QUINTANA, Karla ... 505-428-1203 ... 320 E
karla.quintana@sfcc.edu
QUINTANA, Lawrence ... 505-454-2502 ... 318 F
lquintana@luna.edu
QUINTANA, Rosaura ... 787-815-0000 ... 567 A
rosaura.quintana@upr.edu
QUINTANA HERNANDEZ,
Carmen ... 787-896-2252 ... 562 B
cquintana@edpcollege.edu
QUINTANILLA, Hector ... 817-531-4840 ... 502 C
hquintanilla@txwes.edu
QUINTANILLA, Kelly ... 361-825-2659 ... 498 C
kelly.quintanilla@tamucc.edu
QUINTANS, Joel ... 817-272-2025 ... 505 C
quintas@uta.edu
QUINTERO-DEVLAEMINCK,
Monica ... 503-682-1862 ... 419 F
monicaqd@pioneerpacific.edu
QUINTERO-JIMENEZ,
Noel ... 787-725-6500 ... 561 A
nquintero@albizu.edu
QUINTONG, Joel, R ... 203-416-3417 ... 94 B
quintongj@sacredheart.edu
QUINTYNE, Renee ... 845-398-4207 ... 349 H
rquintyn@stac.edu
QUINZE, Tiffany ... 217-228-5432 ... 161 F
quinzti@quincy.edu
QUIREY, Debbie ... 405-744-2212 ... 409 B
dquirey@okstate.edu
QUIRK, Donna ... 312-915-8723 ... 157 C
dquirk@luc.edu
QUIRK, Joe ... 360-442-2207 ... 535 I
jquirk@lowercolumbia.edu
QUIRK, Patrick ... 239-687-5303 ... 101 H
pquirk@avemarialaw.edu
QUIRK-BAILEY, Sheila ... 847-925-6668 ... 151 G
squirk@harpercollege.edu
QUIROGA, Mercedes, A ... 954-201-6511 ... 102 E
mquiroga@broward.edu
QUIROS, Kristi ... 830-372-8060 ... 499 F
kquiros@tlu.edu
QUIROZ, Gloria ... 773-878-3256 ... 163 F
gquiroz@staugustine.edu
QUISENBERRY, JR.,
Henry, L ... 334-347-2623 ... 3 F
cquisenberry@escc.edu
QUISENBERRY,
Sharron, S ... 515-294-6344 ... 182 E
sharronq@iastate.edu
QUIST, Arlene ... 605-455-6011 ... 465 A
aquist@olc.edu
QUISTGARD, Fred ... 207-216-4406 ... 219 C
fquistgard@yccc.edu
QURESHI, Aamir ... 202-872-4700 ... 99 B
aamir@medtech.edu

R

RAAB, Amy ... 614-257-5015 ... 390 B
araab@devry.edu
RAAB, David ... 212-463-0400 ... 358 B
david.raab@touro.edu
RAAB, Jennifer, J ... 212-772-4242 ... 327 E
jennifer.raab@hunter.cuny.edu
RAAB, Lettie, M ... 936-261-5900 ... 496 G
lmraab@pvamu.edu
RAAB, Maryrose ... 315-792-7215 ... 356 B
maryrose.raab@sunyit.edu
RAADA, Hank ... 602-639-7500 ... 14 H
RAATTAMA, Kristina ... 305-348-2103 ... 119 C
maija.raattama@fiu.edu
RABALAIS, Nicole ... 615-248-1237 ... 476 G
nrabalais@trevecca.edu
RABB, Harriet ... 212-327-8070 ... 347 H
harriet.rabb@rockefeller.edu
RABBITT, Kara, M ... 973-720-2180 ... 317 D
rabbittk@wpunj.edu
RABBITT, Rhonda, M ... 608-796-3384 ... 553 C
rmrabbitt@viterbo.edu
RABENOLD, Scott ... 865-974-9557 ... 477 D
srabenol@utk.edu
RABENSTEIN, Dallas ... 951-827-5034 ... 74 E
dallas.rabenstein@ucr.edu
RABER, II, Donald, R ... 864-833-8189 ... 460 E
draber@presby.edu
RABIDEAU, Melissa ... 314-837-6777 ... 288 C
mrabideau@slcconline.edu
RABIDEAU, Shelly, S ... 317-940-8423 ... 170 F
srabidea@butler.edu
RABIL, Alison ... 919-684-3501 ... 364 C
alison.rabil@duke.edu
RABINEAU, Kevin ... 269-965-3931 ... 253 B
rabineauk@kellogg.edu
RABINOVICH, Oleg ... 718-818-6470 ... 349 G
RABINOVICH, Sheryl ... 213-624-1200 ... 46 L
srabinovich@fidm.edu
RABINOWITCH, Janet ... 812-855-4773 ... 173 E
jrabinow@indiana.edu
RABINOWITZ, Celia, E ... 240-895-4267 ... 226 A
cerabinowitz@smcm.edu
RABINOWITZ, Eli ... 718-377-0777 ... 346 G
RABINOWITZ, Stuart ... 516-463-6800 ... 335 G
president@hofstra.edu
RABINOWITZ, Vita ... 212-772-4150 ... 327 E
vita.rabinowitz@hunter.cuny.edu
RABITOY, Eric ... 626-914-8788 ... 40 B
erabitoy@citruscollege.edu
RABLE, Michelle, A ... 419-824-3816 ... 395 E
mrable@lourdes.edu
RABY, Susan ... 315-312-2260 ... 354 A
susan.raby@oswego.edu
RACCANELLO, Paul ... 415-485-3223 ... 45 C
raccanello@dominican.edu
RACE, Debbie ... 828-251-6417 ... 378 D
drace@unca.edu
RACE, John ... 614-251-4303 ... 398 F
racej@ohiodominican.edu
RACE, Mary Jo ... 412-624-4200 ... 449 A
mar6@pitt.edu
RACER, Jennifer ... 419-755-4040 ... 397 C
racer.5@osu.edu
RACETTE, Patrick ... 906-353-4600 ... 253 D
pracette@kbocc.org
RACHAL, Michael ... 504-865-2486 ... 213 F
rachal@loyno.edu
RACHAVONG, Darrelene ... 972-883-6236 ... 506 A
dar@utdallas.edu
RACHFORD, Jennifer ... 909-607-2201 ... 63 A
jennifer.rachford@pomona.edu
RACHITA, David, A ... 281-283-2568 ... 503 E
rachita@uhcl.edu
RACINA, Kris ... 907-474-2600 ... 10 I
khracina@alaska.edu
RACINE, Anne ... 406-338-5411 ... 293 F
anne_racine@bfcc.org
RACINE, Gail, M ... 508-767-7283 ... 230 D
gracine@assumption.edu
RACINE, Leo ... 508-678-2811 ... 239 B
leo.racine@bristolcc.edu
RACINE, Rudy ... 603-668-6660 ... 305 B
RACIOPPI, Gerald ... 817-515-1254 ... 496 C
gerald.racioppi@tccd.edu
RACKETT, Peter ... 516-773-5564 ... 558 I
rackettp@usmma.edu
RACKLEY, Denise, Q ... 910-592-8084 ... 373 G
drackley@sampsoncc.edu
RACKLEY, J. Mike ... 662-325-9311 ... 275 F
mike.rackley@msstate.edu
RACKLEY, Richard, W ... 865-688-9422 ... 468 K
info@fountainheadcollege.com
RACKLEY, Steven, P ... 419-434-4651 ... 404 B
rackley@findlay.edu
RACKLIFFE, Jerry, J ... 404-413-3000 ... 131 G
jracklif@gsu.edu
RACZYNSKI, Patricia, A ... 205-934-5121 ... 8 F
trish@uab.edu
RADAKOVICH, Dan ... 404-894-5411 ... 130 F
drad@athletics.gatech.edu
RADANT, Tia ... 651-450-3397 ... 266 F
tradant@inverhills.edu
RADCLIFFE, Denise ... 651-730-5100 ... 263 G
dradcliffe@globeuniversity.edu
RADCLIFFE, Shelby ... 323-259-2961 ... 59 I
radcliffe@oxy.edu
RADCLIFFE, Steve ... 513-244-4381 ... 388 E
steve_radcliffe@mail.msj.edu
RADDATZ, Susan ... 651-423-8205 ... 266 B
susan.raddatz@dctc.edu
RADECKE, Mark Wm ... 570-372-4220 ... 447 E
radecke@susqu.edu
RADECKI, Pete ... 417-873-7899 ... 281 D
pradecki@drury.edu
RADEL, Marie ... 765-455-9468 ... 174 A
meradel@iuk.edu
RADEL, Nicholas, F ... 864-294-2795 ... 458 E
nick.radel@furman.edu
RADEMACHER, Eric ... 513-556-3304 ... 403 D
eric.rademacher@uc.edu
RADER, Brian ... 503-399-8074 ... 414 J
brian.rader@chemeketa.edu
RADER, Claude, K ... 410-951-3858 ... 228 B
drader@coppin.edu
RADER, Rachel ... 931-372-3016 ... 474 B
rrader@tntech.edu
RADERSTORF, D. Michael ... 404-413-0776 ... 131 G
mraderstorf@gsu.edu
RADFORD, Amy, J ... 901-843-3870 ... 472 K
radford@rhodes.edu
RADFORD, Laurie ... 503-552-1617 ... 417 D
lradford@ncnm.edu
RADFORD, Marilyn ... 270-384-8022 ... 204 D
radfordm@lindsey.edu
RADFORD, Ron ... 256-395-2211 ... 7 D
rradford@suscc.edu
RADFORD-HILL, Sheila ... 563-387-1486 ... 187 D
radfsh01@luther.edu
RADFORD-WEDEMEYER,
Margaret-Ann ... 410-337-6183 ... 222 I
margaret-ann.radford-wedemeyer@goucher.edu
RADIONOFF, Kathleen, A ... 608-258-2309 ... 554 D
kradionoff@madisoncollege.org
RADISH, Ross ... 215-596-7573 ... 450 B
r.radish@usciences.edu
RADKE, Cheryl ... 623-245-4600 ... 18 J
cradke@uticuti.edu
RADKE, William ... 405-974-3371 ... 413 B
wradke@uco.edu
RADLIFF, Mary ... 518-255-5211 ... 354 E
radliffmd@cobleskill.edu
RADLO, Dolores ... 508-373-9705 ... 231 B
dolores.radlo@becker.edu
RADLOWSKI, Mark, E ... 315-792-5467 ... 341 E
mradlowski@mvcc.edu
RADNEY, Ron ... 661-654-3271 ... 34 A
rradney@csub.edu
RADOVANIC, Joyce, A ... 814-269-7114 ... 449 D
joyceara@pitt.edu
RADSON, Darrell ... 906-487-3555 ... 255 B
dradson@mtu.edu
RADSON, Darrell, J ... 309-677-2255 ... 146 C
radson@bradley.edu
RADT, Jennifer ... 513-732-5327 ... 403 E
jennifer.radt@uc.edu
RADTKE, Elizabeth, L ... 651-523-2201 ... 264 A
bradtke@hamline.edu
RADTKE, Eric, C ... 708-709-3638 ... 161 D
eradtke@prairiestate.edu
RADULESCU, Eugen ... 713-348-6725 ... 493 C
eugen@rice.edu
RADVANSKY, Sandy, M ... 740-284-5357 ... 391 A
sradvansky@franciscan.edu
RADWAN, Ann, B ... 320-308-4287 ... 269 A
abradwan@stcloudstate.edu
RADYCKI, Diane, C ... 610-861-1680 ... 437 A
medjr01@moravian.edu
RAE, Lisa ... 802-258-3149 ... 514 E
lisa.rae@worldlearning.org
RAE, Sherri ... 814-269-2060 ... 449 D
srae@pitt.edu
RAEFORD, James, E ... 540-828-5408 ... 517 B
jraeford@bridgewater.edu
RAEHPOUR, Julia, E ... 715-833-6669 ... 553 H
jraehpour@cvtc.edu
RAEKER-REBEK, Mary ... 763-433-1317 ... 265 G
mary.raeker-rebek@anokaramsey.edu
RAEL, Lois ... 505-984-6141 ... 320 C
lois.rael@sjcsf.edu
RAEL, Rolando ... 719-589-7032 ... 88 F
rolando.rael@trinidadstate.edu
RAEMISCH, Richard, F ... 608-246-6037 ... 554 D
rraemisch@madisoncollege.org
RAFATTI, Colleen ... 863-784-7411 ... 117 J
colleen.rafatti@southflorida.edu
RAFERT, J. Bruce ... 701-231-7131 ... 382 B
bruce.rafert@ndsu.edu
RAFES, Richard ... 315-792-3738 ... 359 E
rsrafes@utica.edu
RAFFAELLE, Ryne ... 585-475-2055 ... 347 G
ryne.raffaelle@rit.edu
RAFFAELLI, Bethany, M ... 920-924-6431 ... 554 G
braffaelli@morainepark.edu
RAFFENSPERGER,
Thomas ... 413-572-5233 ... 238 F
traffensperger@westfield.ma.edu

RAFFERTY, Bobbie .... 502-585-9911.... 206 D brafferty@spalding.edu
RAFFETTO, William .... 281-998-6150.... 493 G william.raffetto@sjcd.edu
RAFFTERY, Cher, A .... 651-641-8235.... 263 A rafftery@csp.edu
RAFIEE, Farnoosh .... 606-326-2069.... 201 F farnoosh.rafiee@kctcs.edu
RAFIEYMEHR, Ali .... 603-641-4107.... 306 D ali.rafieymehr@unh.edu
RAFIEYMEHR, Ali .... 603-641-4107.... 306 C ali.rafieymehr@unh.edu
RAFINSKI, Karen, E .... 937-328-6001.... 387 H rafinskik@clarkstate.edu
RAFN, H. Jeffrey .... 920-498-5411.... 555 C jeff.rafn@nwtc.edu
RAFOOL, Dawn, M .... 863-638-3818.... 123 D dawn.rafool@warner.edu
RAFOTH, Mary Ann .... 412-397-6020.... 445 H rafoth@rmu.edu
RAFTERY, Francis .... 973-290-4475.... 308 G president@cse.edu
RAGAN, Jody .... 515-961-1517.... 189 C jody.ragan@simpson.edu
RAGAN, Kathleen, E .... 973-655-3450.... 311 F ragank@mail.montclair.edu
RAGAN, Kay .... 760-921-5428...... 61 C kay.ragan@paloverde.edu
RAGAN, Nola .... 605-698-3966.... 465 E nragan@swc.tc
RAGAN, Ronald, E .... 336-841-9193.... 365 C rragan@highpoint.edu
RAGAN, Stephen, W .... 913-971-3393.... 195 D sragan@mnu.edu
RAGAR, Mel .... 785-670-2312.... 197 F mel.ragar@washburn.edu
RAGENOVICH, Cassie .... 509-527-2815.... 539 C cassie.ragenovich@wallawalla.edu
RAGER, Janie .... 615-361-7555.... 468 E jrager@daymarinstitute.edu
RAGER, Keith .... 814-254-0591.... 425 G rorager@pa.gov
RAGER, Mary Jo .... 352-365-3550.... 112 J ragermj@lscc.edu
RAGIO, Patricia, L .... 513-244-4871.... 388 E patricia_ragio@mail.msj.edu
RAGLAND, Heather .... 901-272-5126.... 471 D hragland@mca.edu
RAGLAND, Janet .... 903-233-3815.... 490 A janetragland@letu.edu
RAGLAND, Jasmine .... 706-233-7236.... 137 A 1150mgr@fheg.follett.com
RAGLAND, Mary .... 276-935-4349.... 516 D mragland@asl.edu
RAGLAND, Matthew .... 334-244-3138........ 1 G mragland@aum.edu
RAGLAND, Ruth, A .... 956-882-4322.... 505 E ruthann.ragland@utb.edu
RAGNO, John .... 718-489-5364.... 348 E jragno@sfc.edu
RAGO, Gregory .... 410-225-2351.... 224 B grago@mica.edu
RAGOSTA, Linda .... 508-541-1898.... 233 G lragosta@dean.edu
RAGSDALE, Chad .... 417-626-1234.... 287 C ragsdale.chad@occ.edu
RAGSDALE, Jennifer .... 201-761-6062.... 314 F jragsdale@spc.edu
RAGSDALE, Jill .... 507-284-9024.... 262 D deborah.rains@victoriacollege.edu
RAGSDALE, Katherine, H ... 617-682-1520.... 234 E kragsdale@eds.edu
RAGSDALE, Keisha .... 336-517-2220.... 362 G kragsdale@bennett.edu
RAGSDALE, Lisa, B .... 704-233-8710.... 380 F lisa.ragsdale@wingate.edu
RAGSDALE, Lyn .... 713-348-4824.... 493 C lyn.ragsdale@rice.edu
RAGSDALE, JR., Roy Lee . 704-233-8118.... 380 F lragsdale@wingate.edu
RAGUCCI, Al .... 212-962-0002.... 342 G aragucci@nyci.edu
RAHEIM, Salome .... 860-570-9141...... 94 G salome.raheim@uconn.edu
RAHM, Carmen .... 509-963-2925.... 532 C rahmc@cwu.edu
RAHM, Clare .... 216-687-3673.... 388 D c.rahm@csuohio.edu
RAHMAN, Malik .... 209-946-2011...... 76 A mrahman@pacific.edu
RAHMAN, Pervez .... 773-907-4452.... 147 D prahman@ccc.edu
RAHMANI, Loretta .... 909-593-3511...... 75 E lrahmani@laverne.edu
RAHN, Daniel .... 501-686-5680...... 24 F drahn@uams.edu
RAHN, Diane .... 419-251-1726.... 395 I diane.rahn@mercycollege.edu
RAHN, Jason, M .... 651-641-8706.... 263 A rahn@csp.edu
RAHNAMAY-AZAR, Amir .. 404-894-7444.... 130 F a.azar@gatech.edu
RAHR, JR., Carl, H .... 607-587-3535.... 355 C rahrch@alfredstate.edu
RAI, Sanjay .... 240-567-7711.... 224 D sanjay.rai@montgomerycollege.edu
RAIBLEY, Jon .... 503-517-1899.... 421 C jraibley@westernseminary.edu
RAICH, Mike .... 218-262-6702.... 266 E michaelraich@hibbing.edu
RAICHE, Brian .... 651-730-5100.... 263 G braiche@globeuniversity.edu
RAICHE, Carol .... 978-232-2068.... 234 D craiche@endicott.edu
RAICHE, Cheryl .... 617-217-9224.... 231 A craiche@baystate.edu
RAICHIK, Shimon .... 323-937-2079...... 80 D
RAICHLE, Christopher .... 617-262-5000.... 231 G christopher.raichle@the-bac.edu
RAIKES-COLBERT, Deborah .... 973-408-3515.... 309 E draikesc@drew.edu
RAILEY, III, Clayton .... 610-359-5230.... 426 G crailey@dccc.edu
RAILEY, JR., George, A ..... 510-723-6626...... 39 C grailey@chabotcollege.edu
RAILEY, Kevin, J .... 716-878-5601.... 353 A raileykj@buffalostate.edu
RAILEY III, Clayton, A ...... 610-359-5359.... 426 G crailey@dccc.edu
RAILSBACK, Brian .... 828-227-7383.... 380 A brailsba@wcu.edu
RAILSBACK, Travis .... 205-348-5848........ 8 E trailsback@sa.ua.edu
RAIMER, Ben, G .... 409-772-5033.... 507 C bgraimer@utmb.edu
RAIMO, James .... 845-569-3227.... 342 A james.raimo@msmc.edu
RAINE, Meredith .... 713-500-3050.... 506 F meredith.raine@uth.tmc.edu
RAINE, Micheal .... 925-969-3353...... 52 C mraine@jfku.edu
RAINER, Don .... 205-652-3576........ 9 E drainer@uwa.edu
RAINES, C. Fay .... 256-824-6345........ 8 G fay.raines@uah.edu
RAINES, Christy .... 479-968-0302...... 20 G themphill@atu.edu
RAINES, Deborah .... 703-284-1530.... 521 D debbie.raines@marymount.edu
RAINES, Jess, N .... 740-374-8716.... 405 G jraines@wscc.edu
RAINES, Patrick .... 615-460-6000.... 467 D pat.raines@belmont.edu
RAINES, Scott .... 432-264-5190.... 488 B sraines@howardcollege.edu
RAINES, Shirley, C .... 901-678-2234.... 474 C sraines@memphis.edu
RAINEY, David, L .... 860-548-2404...... 94 A
RAINEY, Jack, T .... 973-618-3230.... 308 C jrainey@caldwell.edu
RAINEY, John .... 229-226-1621.... 138 C jrainey@thomasu.edu
RAINEY, Kelli .... 704-378-3572.... 366 A krainey@jcsu.edu
RAINEY, Millicent .... 336-517-2154.... 362 G mrainey@bennett.edu
RAINONE, John, J .... 207-216-4465.... 219 C jrainone@yccc.edu
RAINS, Ben .... 501-812-2268...... 23 C brains@pulaskitech.edu
RAINS, Debbie .... 361-582-2560.... 508 B
RAINS, TJ .... 414-410-4535.... 546 G tjrains@stritch.edu
RAINVILLE, Lynn .... 434-295-7210.... 524 K lrainville@sbc.edu
RAINWATER, Robert .... 276-466-7924.... 529 D robertrainwater@vic.edu
RAIOLA, Jill .... 203-285-2007...... 91 D jraiola@gwcc.commnet.edu
RAISANEN, Gregg .... 320-762-4618.... 265 F greggr@alextech.edu
RAISIAN, John .... 650-723-1198...... 71 G raisian@hoover.stanford.edu
RAISL, Gary .... 858-646-3126...... 67 I graisl@sandfordburnham.org
RAISOVICH, Andy .... 304-367-4682.... 543 H andy.raisovich@fairmontstate.edu
RAISOVICH, Joanie .... 304-367-4131.... 543 H joanie.raisovich@fairmontstate.edu
RAJA, Jay .... 704-687-5737.... 379 A jraja@uncc.edu
RAJA, Tasleem .... 312-939-0113.... 150 D tasleem@eastwest.edu
RAJA, Tasleem .... 312-939-0111.... 150 D tasleem@eastwest.edu
RAJABALLEY, Michael .... 787-751-0160.... 561 H mrajaballey@cmpr.pr.gov
RAJABZADEH, Mehdi .... 415-955-2031...... 27 A mrajabzadeh@alliant.edu
RAJALA, Sarah, A .... 662-325-2270.... 275 F rajala@bagley.msstate.edu
RAJALA, Thomas .... 928-777-6692...... 14 C thomas.rajala@erau.edu
RAJAN, Paul, G .... 212-563-6647.... 358 F p.rajan@uts.edu
RAJAN, Ravi .... 914-251-6750.... 354 D ravi.rajan@purchase.edu
RAKER, Russell .... 702-992-2356.... 302 G russell.raker@nsc.edu
RAKERS, Jason, T .... 330-941-3035.... 406 F jtrakers@ysu.edu
RAKES, Thomas, A .... 731-881-7500.... 477 G trakes@utm.edu
RAKES, Thomas, D .... 910-962-3174.... 379 D rakest@uncw.edu
RAKESTRAW, Jennie .... 803-323-2151.... 463 E rakestrawj@winthrop.edu
RAKIN, Aluka .... 692-625-3394.... 560 A
RAKOCZY, Dana .... 562-907-4974...... 79 F drakoczy@whittier.edu
RAKOCZY, Laura, A .... 585-785-1274.... 334 A lakoczla@flcc.edu
RAKOFF, Jill .... 860-701-5131...... 93 E rakoff_j@mitchell.edu
RAKOFF, Steve .... 817-515-3584.... 496 C steve.rakoff@tccd.edu
RALEIGH, Betsy .... 206-268-4008.... 530 I eraleigh@antioch.edu
RALEIGH, Edith .... 734-432-5457.... 254 D eraleigh@madonna.edu
RALEIGH, Mary-Jeanne ...... 240-895-4289.... 226 A mjraleigh@smcm.edu
RALEY, Karen, C .... 240-895-3219.... 226 A kcraley@smcm.edu
RALEY, Leonard, R .... 301-445-1941.... 227 A lraley@usmd.edu
RALL, John, P .... 270-809-3399.... 205 A jrall@murraystate.edu
RALLO, Joseph .... 806-742-0012.... 502 A joseph.rallo@ttu.edu
RALLO, Joseph, C .... 325-942-2073.... 480 E president@angelo.edu
RALLS, Diana .... 209-228-4306...... 74 D dralls@ucmerced.edu
RALLS, R. Scott .... 919-807-6950.... 367 I ralls@nccommunitycolleges.edu
RALPH, Brian .... 704-337-2445.... 376 A ralphb@queens.edu
RALPH, Ken .... 719-389-6945...... 82 D ken.ralph@coloradocollege.edu
RALPH, Michael .... 504-286-5329.... 214 J mralph@suno.edu
RALPH, Nicole, M .... 217-786-2342.... 157 B nicole.ralph@llcc.edu
RALPH, Scott .... 317-955-6789.... 177 I sralph@marian.edu
RALPH, Susan .... 229-248-2585.... 126 A sralph@bainbridge.edu
RALSTON, Craig .... 727-726-1153.... 103 I craigralston@clearwater.edu
RALSTON, Debra, J .... 716-372-7978.... 345 C dralston@obi.edu
RALSTON, Nancy, M .... 402-552-2557.... 297 B ralston@clarksoncollege.edu
RALSTON, Pamela .... 805-546-3123...... 43 I pamela_ralston@cuesta.edu
RALSTON, Ramona, M .... 315-267-2154.... 354 C ralstorm@potsdam.edu
RALSTON, Tracy .... 203-596-4564...... 93 G tralston@post.edu
RAMADAN, Neddie .... 973-278-5400.... 323 H nnr@berkeleycollege.edu
RAMAGE, Angela, R .... 706-886-6831.... 138 D arramage@tfc.edu
RAMAGE, Emily .... 217-234-5404.... 156 B eramagel@lakeland.cc.il.us
RAMAGE, Sally .... 559-278-2741...... 35 A sally_ramage@csufresno.edu
RAMAGE, Thomas, R .... 217-351-2231.... 161 C ramage@parkland.edu
RAMAGOS, Caroline .... 601-477-4249.... 274 H caroline.ramagos@jcjc.edu
RAMAKER, Dawn .... 641-585-8197.... 189 I ramakerd@waldorf.edu
RAMAKER, Jason .... 641-585-8160.... 189 I ramakerj@waldorf.edu
RAMAKRISHNAN, Jolly .... 610-399-2032.... 442 A jramakrishnan@cheyney.edu
RAMALHO, Erika, A .... 814-871-5584.... 429 G ramalho001@gannon.edu
RAMAN, Saravana .... 714-300-0300...... 70 I sraman@scitech.edu
RAMASWAMY, Nandini ..... 317-940-9032.... 170 F nramaswa@butler.edu
RAMASWAMY, Sunder .... 831-647-4102...... 57 F sunder.ramaswamy@miis.edu
RAMASWAMY, Sunder ...... 802-443-5908.... 514 A ramaswam@middlebury.edu
RAMBISH, Medea .... 630-466-7900.... 168 B mrambish@waubonsee.edu
RAMBO, Tom .... 570-372-4136.... 447 E rambo@susqu.edu
RAMCHAND, Latha .... 713-743-4604.... 503 D ramchand@uh.edu
RAMCHARAN, Harold .... 919-546-8521.... 376 F hramcharan@shawu.edu
RAMDATH, Danielle, D ...... 413-585-3017.... 244 G gradstdy@smith.edu
RAMDATH, Danielle, D ...... 413-585-3017.... 244 G dramdath@smith.edu
RAMDATH, Sanjay .... 336-334-4822.... 371 A shramdath@gtcc.edu
RAMER, Rod .... 509-434-5325.... 533 C rramer@ccs.spokane.edu
RAMER, Rod .... 509-434-5325.... 533 A rramer@ccs.spokane.edu
RAMER, Rodney .... 509-434-5325.... 533 B rod.ramer@ccs.spokane.edu
RAMES, Marysz .... 605-688-4493.... 466 C marysz.rames@sdstate.edu
RAMESH, S, K .... 818-677-4501...... 35 F s.ramesh@csun.edu
RAMET, Carlos .... 989-964-4042.... 257 G ramet@svsu.edu
RAMEY, Alfred .... 201-200-3156.... 312 B aramey@njcu.edu
RAMEY, Alice .... 417-447-2631.... 287 D rameya@otc.edu
RAMEY, Diana, M .... 254-710-2005.... 482 A diana_ramey@baylor.edu
RAMEY, Iris .... 336-517-1761.... 362 G iris.ramey@bennett.edu
RAMEY, Kenneth, H .... 859-572-5125.... 205 H ramey@nku.edu
RAMEY, Lane .... 816-501-4633.... 288 A lane.ramey@rockhurst.edu
RAMEY, Susan .... 814-641-0440.... 428 B
RAMEY, Teresa .... 843-661-1182.... 458 D tramey@fmarion.edu
RAMEZANE, Marsha .... 650-574-6161...... 67 G ramezane@smccd.edu
RAMI, Janet .... 225-771-2360.... 214 I janet_rami@subr.edu
RAMICONE, Arthur, G .... 412-624-6576.... 449 A aramicone@cfo.pitt.edu
RAMIREZ, Alberto .... 301-624-2636.... 222 G aramirez@frederick.edu
RAMIREZ, Alfred .... 818-240-1000...... 48 D aramirez@glendale.edu
RAMIREZ, Arthur .... 831-459-2158...... 75 C apr@soe.ucsc.edu
RAMIREZ, Aurelio .... 617-879-7847.... 238 B aramirez@massart.edu
RAMIREZ, Cecilia .... 757-825-3525.... 528 F ramirezc@tncc.edu
RAMIREZ, Cliff .... 909-607-4124...... 40 F cliff.ramirez@cgu.edu
RAMIREZ, Daniel .... 956-872-6411.... 494 H dramirez@southtexascollege.edu
RAMIREZ, David .... 909-652-6630...... 39 E david.ramirez@chaffey.edu
RAMIREZ, David .... 610-328-8175.... 447 F dramire1@swarthmore.edu
RAMIREZ, Glenda .... 281-487-1170.... 499 B gramirez@txchiro.edu
RAMIREZ, Irving .... 347-964-8600.... 324 C iramirez@boricuacollege.edu
RAMIREZ, Joe .... 818-364-7853...... 55 A ramirejs@lamission.edu
RAMIREZ, John, S .... 562-463-7593...... 63 H jsramirez@riohondo.edu
RAMIREZ, Jose .... 787-620-2040.... 560 D jramirez@aupr.edu
RAMIREZ, Jose, L .... 915-831-2634.... 486 G jramir20@epcc.edu
RAMIREZ, Juan .... 909-469-5622...... 78 I jramirez@westernu.edu
RAMIREZ, Kathy .... 406-447-5185.... 293 G kramirez@carroll.edu
RAMIREZ, Laura, M .... 323-265-8973...... 54 G ramirelm@elac.edu
RAMIREZ, Loida, R .... 787-744-8519.... 561 J lramirez@ediccollege.com
RAMIREZ, Maria Luisa ...... 956-721-5394.... 489 J mlramirez@laredo.edu
RAMIREZ, Mayra, I .... 787-723-4481.... 561 B mramirez@ceaprc.edu
RAMIREZ, Minita .... 956-326-2278.... 497 D minita@tamiu.edu
RAMIREZ, Richard, M .... 805-756-2091...... 33 I rramirez@calpoly.edu
RAMIREZ, Roberto .... 361-593-3312.... 498 D roberto.ramirez@tamuk.edu
RAMIREZ, Sam .... 361-825-5826.... 498 C samuel.ramirez@tamucc.edu
RAMIREZ, Sam .... 440-826-2908.... 384 K sramirez@bw.edu
RAMIREZ, Val .... 361-593-5500.... 498 D val.ramirez@tamuk.edu
RAMIREZ, Yvonne .... 718-430-2541.... 361 M yramire1@aecom.yu.edu
RAMIREZ- RIVERA, Rafael 787-878-5475.... 563 B rramirez@arecibo.inter.edu
RAMIREZ HERNANDEZ, Edith .... 787-896-2252.... 562 B eramirez@edpcollege.edu
RAMIREZ-JASSO, Diana .... 617-262-5000.... 231 G diane.ramirez-jasso@the-bac.edu
RAMIREZ-MENDEZ, Pablo, A .... 787-890-2681.... 566 H pablo.ramirez@upr.edu
RAMIREZ SILVA, Juan ...... 787-815-0000.... 567 A upra_rect@upr.clu.edu

RAMIREZ-SOTO, Ismael .... 508-999-8006 .... 237 A iramirezsoto@umassd.edu

RAMM, Jennifer .... 254-295-5527 .... 504 C jramm@umhb.edu

RAMMING, Ron .... 918-463-2931 .... 407 H rronald@connorsstate.edu

RAMON, Luciano .... 956-794-4002 .... 489 J lramon@laredo.edu

RAMON, Maria .... 787-744-1060 .... 564 F mramon@mechtech.edu

RAMON, Ralph .... 325-574-7625 .... 508 I rramon@wtc.edu

RAMON, Scott .... 312-629-6100 .... 164 C sramon@saic.edu

RAMONES, Eric .... 408-848-4753 .... 48 C eramones@gavilan.edu

RAMOS, Ana-Maria .... 214-860-1416 .... 485 A amramos@dcccd.edu

RAMOS, Anthony .... 210-805-1201 .... 504 B aramos@uiwtx.edu

RAMOS, Antonio .... 787-284-1912 .... 564 A aramos@ponce.inter.edu

RAMOS, Charlene .... 248-204-2334 .... 254 B cramos@ltu.edu

RAMOS, Daisy .... 787-738-2161 .... 567 D daisy.ramos@upr.edu

RAMOS, Daniel .... 909-941-9410 .... 62 J dramos@plattcollege.edu

RAMOS, Edith .... 787-878-6000 .... 562 G eramos@icprjc.edu

RAMOS, Gladys .... 787-738-2161 .... 567 D gladys.ramos@upr.edu

RAMOS, Harry .... 714-830-0203 .... 30 B hramos@aii.edu

RAMOS, Irma .... 951-487-3156 .... 58 B iramos@msjc.edu

RAMOS, Jorge .... 787-765-3560 .... 562 A

RAMOS, Josue .... 787-878-5475 .... 563 B jramos@arecibo.inter.edu

RAMOS, Julio .... 787-720-4476 .... 566 D biblioteca@colmizpa.edu

RAMOS, Kianna .... 651-675-4700 .... 264 F kramos@msp.chefs.edu

RAMOS, Maria .... 903-886-5091 .... 498 B maria.ramos@tamuc.edu

RAMOS, Maria, A .... 787-863-2390 .... 563 E maria.ramos@fajardo.inter.edu

RAMOS, Nancy, L .... 401-254-3455 .... 454 C nramos@rwu.edu

RAMOS, Patricia .... 212-343-1234 .... 341 B pramos@mcny.edu

RAMOS, Patricia .... 310-434-3311 .... 68 D ramos_patricia@smc.edu

RAMOS, Rebecca .... 401-865-2345 .... 453 H rramos@providence.edu

RAMOS, Richard, O .... 515-961-1536 .... 189 C rich.ramos@simpson.edu

RAMOS, Rudy .... 310-900-1600 .... 45 F ramos_r@compton.edu

RAMOS, Theresa .... 505-277-5251 .... 321 C tramos@unm.edu

RAMOS, Wilberto .... 256-761-8757 .... 7 G wramos@talladega.edu

RAMOS, Yolanda .... 432-685-4733 .... 491 A yramos@midland.edu

RAMOS-ROMAN, Constancia .... 787-725-6500 .... 561 A cramos@albizu.edu

RAMPAUL, Andre .... 212-757-1190 .... 322 H arampaul@funeraleducation.org

RAMPENTHAL, Janet .... 619-849-2209 .... 62 L janetrampenthal@pointloma.edu

RAMPERSAD, Dave .... 334-386-7105 .... 3 G drampersad@faulkner.edu

RAMPINO, Tatiana .... 203-576-5990 .... 94 C trampino@stvincentscollege.edu

RAMPP, Carrie, E .... 570-577-1557 .... 423 E carrie.rampp@bucknell.edu

RAMPY, Bill .... 512-245-6761 .... 501 F wr15@txstate.edu

RAMS, Kimberly .... 949-824-4521 .... 74 B k.rams@uci.edu

RAMS, Richard .... 714-484-7374 .... 59 D rrams@cypresscollege.edu

RAMSAMMY, Jillian .... 352-854-2322 .... 103 K jillian.ramsammy@cf.edu

RAMSAY, John .... 434-223-7154 .... 519 G jramsay@hsc.edu

RAMSAY, John, G .... 484-664-3134 .... 437 C ramsay@muhlenberg.edu

RAMSBOTTOM, Mary, M .. 317-940-9516 .... 170 F mramsbot@butler.edu

RAMSDELL, Twyla .... 651-213-4180 .... 264 B tramsdell@hazelden.edu

RAMSDEN-MEIER, Joanna 319-226-2004 .... 182 A ramsdejl@ihs.org

RAMSETH, Mark, R .... 614-235-4136 .... 402 G mramseth@tlsohio.edu

RAMSEY, Berkley, C .... 434-797-8400 .... 526 G bramsey@dcc.vccs.edu

RAMSEY, Betty Jo .... 910-642-7141 .... 374 B bjramsey@sccnc.edu

RAMSEY, David .... 813-253-6227 .... 123 A dramsey@ut.edu

RAMSEY, Dawn .... 678-915-4287 .... 137 G dramsey@spsu.edu

RAMSEY, Derrick .... 410-951-3748 .... 228 B dramsey@coppin.edu

RAMSEY, Gerald .... 619-388-7810 .... 65 H gramsey@sdccde.du

RAMSEY, Heather .... 215-567-7080 .... 422 D hramsey@edmc.edu

RAMSEY, James, R .... 502-852-5417 .... 207 E jrrams02@louisville.edu

RAMSEY, Jason .... 719-590-6766 .... 83 J jramsey@coloradotech.edu

RAMSEY, Joel .... 620-223-2700 .... 193 A joelr@fortscott.edu

RAMSEY, Julie, L .... 717-337-6921 .... 429 I ramsey@gettysburg.edu

RAMSEY, Marleen .... 509-527-4289 .... 539 B marleen.ramsey@wwcc.edu

RAMSEY, Marty .... 828-227-7335 .... 380 A mramsey@wcu.edu

RAMSEY, Nancy .... 931-540-2553 .... 475 A nramsey@columbiastate.edu

RAMSEY, Natasha .... 217-228-5432 .... 161 F ramsera@quincy.edu

RAMSEY, Paul, G .... 206-543-7718 .... 539 A pramsey@uw.edu

RAMSEY, Sandy .... 828-898-8748 .... 366 D ramseys@lmc.edu

RAMSEY, Tom .... 425-249-4748 .... 538 G tom.ramsey@tlc.edu

RAMSEY, Vickie .... 530-251-8852 .... 53 H vramsey@lassencollege.edu

RAMSEY-HAMACHER, Paige .... 352-588-8489 .... 116 G paige.ramsey.hamacher@saintleo.edu

RAMSEYER, Chuck .... 479-936-5188 .... 22 H cramseyer@nwacc.edu

RAMSEYER, Larry, E .... 989-686-9234 .... 250 D leramsey@delta.edu

RAMSOWER, Reagan .... 254-710-3554 .... 482 A reagan_ramsower@baylor.edu

RAMTALLIE, Melodi .... 561-273-6500 .... 118 A mramtallie@southuniversity.edu

RAMÍREZ-SILVA, Juan .... 787-815-0000 .... 566 G rectoria@upra.edu

RANABARGAR, Kerry, D ... 620-431-2820 .... 195 E kranabargar@neosho.edu

RANALDI, Diane .... 413-565-1000 .... 230 G dranaldi@baypath.edu

RANALLI, Carlee, K .... 814-641-3103 .... 432 A ranallc@juniata.edu

RANALLI, George .... 212-650-7118 .... 326 G gr1@ccny.cuny.edu

RANCE, DeLonn, L .... 417-268-1000 .... 278 H drance@agts.edu

RANCOURT, Ann .... 603-358-2118 .... 306 G arancour@keene.edu

RAND, Amy .... 417-455-5740 .... 280 H arand@crowder.edu

RAND, Kathryn .... 701-777-2104 .... 381 F rand@law.und.edu

RAND, Steven .... 207-780-5107 .... 220 G srand@usm.maine.edu

RAND, Valarie .... 312-280-3500 .... 153 B vrand@aii.edu

RANDALL, Archie .... 307-433-8363 .... 556 D arandall@ibmc.edu

RANDALL, Charles .... 650-493-4430 .... 69 I crandall@itp.edu

RANDALL, Christina, E .... 517-750-1200 .... 258 D crandall@arbor.edu

RANDALL, David .... 617-253-4861 .... 241 D

RANDALL, Donna, M .... 517-629-0210 .... 247 A drandall@albion.edu

RANDALL, Greg .... 256-840-4166 .... 7 A grandall@snead.edu

RANDALL, Greg .... 509-682-6465 .... 539 E grandall@wvc.edu

RANDALL, John .... 949-214-3358 .... 43 C john.randall@cui.edu

RANDALL, Kathleen .... 315-792-3164 .... 359 E krandall@utica.edu

RANDALL, Kenneth, C .... 205-348-5117 .... 8 E kcrandal@law.ua.edu

RANDALL, Meridith .... 530-242-7500 .... 69 D mrandall@shastacollege.edu

RANDALL, Monica .... 410-951-3596 .... 228 B mrandall@coppin.edu

RANDALL, Monica, E .... 410-951-3845 .... 228 B mrandall@coppin.edu

RANDALL, Robin .... 508-286-8232 .... 246 B rrandall@wheatonma.edu

RANDALL, Ruth .... 913-469-8500 .... 194 B ruthrandall@jccc.edu

RANDALL, Stacey .... 630-466-7900 .... 168 B srandall@waubonsee.edu

RANDALL, Taylor .... 801-587-3869 .... 511 C taylor.randall@utah.edu

RANDAZZA, Paula .... 603-897-8303 .... 305 F prandazza@rivier.edu

RANDAZZO, Jennifer, L .... 563-884-5888 .... 188 E jennifer.randazzo@palmer.edu

RANDAZZO, Mary .... 248-204-2309 .... 254 B mrandazzo@ltu.edu

RANDAZZO, Nino .... 312-935-4000 .... 162 G nrandazzo@robertmorris.edu

RANDEL, Jess .... 785-460-5481 .... 192 C jess.randel@colbycc.edu

RANDELS, George .... 209-946-2011 .... 76 A grandels@pacific.edu

RANDERS, Mary .... 650-543-3925 .... 57 B mary.randers@menlo.edu

RANDERSON, Mike .... 573-875-7661 .... 280 A dmranderson@ccis.edu

RANDHAWA, Sabah, U .... 541-737-2111 .... 418 F osu.provost@oregonstate.edu

RANDLE, Benjamin .... 716-829-7836 .... 332 E randleb@dyc.edu

RANDLE, Dawn .... 850-644-1085 .... 119 D drandle@admin.fsu.edu

RANDLE, John .... 231-591-2892 .... 250 H randlej@ferris.edu

RANDLE, William, M .... 336-334-7979 .... 378 A wrandle@ncat.edu

RANDLES, Christopher, M . 217-351-2513 .... 161 C crandles@parkland.edu

RANDLES, Jill, A .... 559-323-2100 .... 66 C jrandles@sjcl.edu

RANDO, Robert, A .... 937-775-3409 .... 406 C robert.rando@wright.edu

RANDOLPH, A.J .... 817-735-2336 .... 504 E a.j.randolph@unthsc.edu

RANDOLPH, Robert, M .... 617-258-5484 .... 241 D

RANDOLPH, Susan .... 816-501-2450 .... 278 I susan.randolph@avila.edu

RANDORF, Lori .... 330-672-5368 .... 393 D lrandorf@kent.edu

RANDY GREEN, Jonathan . 937-327-6406 .... 406 B jgreen@wittenberg.edu

RANE-SZOSTAK, Donna .... 949-582-4324 .... 70 F draneszostak@saddleback.edu

RANELLI, F. Edward .... 850-474-2348 .... 121 D eranelli@uwf.edu

RANES, Rodney .... 618-395-7777 .... 152 I ranesr@iecc.edu

RANES, Zachary, T .... 727-376-6911 .... 122 E zranes@trinitycollege.edu

RANEY, Curt .... 240-895-4395 .... 226 A ccraney@smcm.edu

RANEY, Jonna, G .... 405-878-2178 .... 409 D jonna.raney@okbu.edu

RANEY, Kristen, A .... 715-833-6491 .... 553 H kraney@cvtc.edu

RANGE, Ronald .... 205-391-2644 .... 6 I rrange@sheltonstate.edu

RANGEL, Andrea .... 806-894-9611 .... 494 G arangel@southplainscollege.edu

RANGEL, Juan, M .... 816-604-1503 .... 284 H juan.rangel@mcckc.edu

RANGUETTE, Renea, L .... 608-757-7700 .... 553 G rranguette@blackhawk.edu

RANHEIM, John .... 314-434-4044 .... 280 F john.ranheim@covenantseminary.edu

RANIERI, Ann, E .... 610-526-6084 .... 430 D aranieri@harcum.edu

RANIERI, Steve .... 513-875-3344 .... 387 C steve.ranieri@chatfield.edu

RANIERI, Tracey, M .... 607-436-2446 .... 353 E ranieritm@oneonta.edu

RANJEL, Mary .... 210-924-4338 .... 481 G mary.ranjel@bua.edu

RANK, Carin .... 413-559-5385 .... 235 C

RANK, Kathy .... 303-458-4922 .... 87 I krank@regis.edu

RANK, Mark .... 717-815-1218 .... 452 G mrank@ycp.edu

RANKIN, Arthur .... 318-473-6581 .... 212 I arankin@lsua.edu

RANKIN, David, F .... 870-235-4001 .... 23 I dfrankin@saumag.edu

RANKIN, Diana .... 614-456-4600 .... 393 B drankin@kaplan.edu

RANKIN, Donna .... 479-968-0394 .... 20 G drankin@atu.edu

RANKIN, Emily .... 909-621-8054 .... 69 A emily.rankin@scrippscollege.edu

RANKIN, James, M .... 479-575-5900 .... 24 C rankinj@uark.edu

RANKIN, Jason, A .... 501-450-5015 .... 25 H jrankin@uca.edu

RANKIN, Jeffrey, D .... 309-457-2314 .... 158 H jeffr@monmouthcollege.edu

RANKIN, Mona, G .... 516-876-3160 .... 353 D rankinm@oldwestbury.edu

RANKIN, Stephanie, A .... 717-361-1569 .... 428 F rankins@etown.edu

RANKIN, Stephen .... 214-768-4502 .... 495 A rankins@smu.edu

RANKIN, Walter .... 202-687-8700 .... 98 D rankinw@georgetown.edu

RANKIS, Ray .... 646-312-5046 .... 326 C ray.rankis@baruch.cuny.edu

RANSDELL, Gary, A .... 270-745-4346 .... 208 A gary.ransdell@wku.edu

RANSDELL, Junell, A .... 217-786-4506 .... 157 B junell.ransdell@llcc.edu

RANSOM, Scott, B .... 817-735-2509 .... 504 E scott.ransom@unthsc.edu

RANSOME, Sheri .... 706-291-5339 .... 137 A sransome@shorter.edu

RANTA, Richard, R .... 901-678-2350 .... 474 C rranta@memphis.edu

RANTZ, Kristen .... 406-791-5291 .... 296 F krantz01@ugf.edu

RANTZ, Rick .... 805-735-3366 .... 26 L rrantz@hancockcollege.edu

RAO, Julie, M .... 585-245-5553 .... 353 C rao@geneseo.edu

RAO, Michael .... 804-828-1200 .... 526 B president@vcu.edu

RAPACCIOLI, Donna .... 718-817-4100 .... 334 C rapaccioli@fordham.edu

RAPANOS, John .... 212-986-4343 .... 323 H jmr@berkeleycollege.edu

RAPANOS, John .... 212-986-4343 .... 307 F jmr@berkeleycollege.edu

RAPAPORT, Ross, J .... 989-774-3381 .... 249 C rapap1rj@cmich.edu

RAPAPPORT, Laury .... 408-260-0208 .... 47 D mindbody@fivebranches.edu

RAPE, Bruce, M .... 217-443-8786 .... 148 G brape@dacc.edu

RAPELYE, Janet, L .... 609-258-6150 .... 312 G jrapelye@princeton.edu

RAPER, Neely .... 706-291-5337 .... 137 A nraper@shorter.edu

RAPESS, Paul .... 516-299-2214 .... 339 A paul.rapess@liu.edu

RAPIER, Brenda .... 706-419-1126 .... 128 B rapier@covenant.edu

RAPIER, Debbie, A .... 859-344-3513 .... 206 I debbie.rapier@thomasmore.edu

RAPOPORT, Nancy .... 702-895-5831 .... 302 I nancy.rapoport@unlv.edu

RAPOSA, Donna .... 781-239-2500 .... 239 G draposa@massbay.edu

RAPOSA, Kristina .... 781-292-2264 .... 234 H kristina.raposa@olin.edu

RAPOZA, Mark, F .... 401-865-2064 .... 453 H mrapoza@providence.edu

RAPP, Cynthia, K .... 620-417-1012 .... 196 F cynthia.rapp@sccc.edu

RAPP, Gary .... 316-295-5838 .... 193 B rappg@friends.edu

RAPP, John .... 713-798-4517 .... 481 H jrapp@bcm.edu

RAPP, Karen .... 323-260-8108 .... 54 G rappk@elac.edu

RAPP, Norman .... 615-329-8848 .... 468 I nrapp@fisk.edu

RAPP, Peter .... 503-494-8744 .... 418 D hutching@ohsu.edu

RAPP, Timothy .... 301-295-4231 .... 558 D timothy.rapp@usuhs.edu

RAPP, Virginia .... 310-660-3773 .... 45 E vrapp@elcamino.edu

RAPPLEY, Marsha, D .... 517-353-1730 .... 255 A rappley@msu.edu

RAPTOSH, Joseph .... 412-321-8383 .... 424 A

RARIG, Jenny, M .... 610-359-5148 .... 426 G jrarig@dccc.edu

RARIG, Kris .... 757-825-2801 .... 528 F rarigk@tncc.edu

RASBAND, James, R .... 801-422-6383 .... 509 H james_rasband@byu.edu

RASBERRY, Charles, J .... 914-395-2522 .... 350 C crasberry@sarahlawrence.edu

RASBERRY, Sandra .... 601-968-8703 .... 273 C srasberry@belhaven.edu

RASCATI, Ralph, J .... 770-499-3550 .... 133 A rrascati@kennesaw.edu

RASCH, Carla .... 785-670-1074 .... 197 F carla.rasch@washburn.edu

RASCH, J. Lee .... 608-785-9210 .... 555 F raschl@westerntc.edu

RASCO, Glenn .... 770-975-4000 .... 127 B

RASCOE, Monica .... 716-851-1102 .... 333 C rascoe@ecc.edu

RASHED, D. Omar .... 864-622-6031 .... 455 C orashed@andersonuniversity.edu

RASHED, Jamal, A .... 906-227-2947 .... 256 C jrashed@nmu.edu

RASHID, Jerry, T .... 570-321-4137 .... 435 D rashid@lycoming.edu

RASK, Brenda .... 303-718-5907 .... 81 A brenda.rask@aims.edu

RASK, Brenda .... 970-339-6332 .... 81 A brenda.rask@aims.edu

RASK, Kevin .... 719-389-6446 .... 82 D kevin.rask@coloradocollege.edu

RASKIND, Wayne .... 313-577-2519 .... 260 A raskind@wayne.edu

RASKOB, Gary, E .... 405-271-2232 .... 413 D gary-raskob@ouhsc.edu

RASMUSSEN, Bob .... 417-626-1234 .... 287 C rasmussen.bob@occ.edu

RASMUSSEN, Bob .... 801-863-8491 .... 511 F bob.rasmussen@uvu.edu

RASMUSSEN, Brock .... 612-874-3749 .... 265 C brock_rasmussen@mcad.edu

RASMUSSEN, Bruce, D .... 402-280-2720 .... 297 F bdrass@creighton.edu

RASMUSSEN, Cheryl 785-442-6021 193 F crasmussen@highlandcc.edu
RASMUSSEN, Clyde 509-793-2053 531 I clyder@bigbend.edu
RASMUSSEN, Connie, A 308-432-6366 299 E crasmussen@csc.edu
RASMUSSEN, David, W 850-644-5488 119 D dwrasmussen@admin.fsu.edu
RASMUSSEN, Dillon 312-578-3898 168 D drasmussen@westwood.edu
RASMUSSEN, Don 303-546-5284 86 H donald@naropa.edu
RASMUSSEN, George, A 361-593-3712 498 D allen.rasmussen@tamuk.edu
RASMUSSEN, Jack, L 801-626-6273 511 G jrasmussen@weber.edu
RASMUSSEN, Karla, R 757-455-3290 530 C krasmussen@vwc.edu
RASMUSSEN, Linda 601-266-4050 277 F linda.rasmussen@usm.edu
RASMUSSEN, Lowell, C 320-589-6100 271 G rasmuslc@morris.umn.edu
RASMUSSEN, Mabel 407-277-0311 107 B mrasmussen@evergladesuniversity.edu
RASMUSSEN, Michele, A 610-526-5375 423 D mrasmuss@brynmawr.edu
RASMUSSEN, Phil 425-889-5271 536 C phil.rasmussen@northwestu.edu
RASMUSSEN, Rob 815-479-7599 157 H rrasmuss@mchenry.edu
RASMUSSEN, Robert, H 225-578-2154 212 G rrasmus@lsu.edu
RASMUSSEN, Robert, K 213-740-6473 76 F rrasmussen@law.usc.edu
RASMUSSEN, Scott 208-282-2507 143 H rasmscot@isu.edu
RASMUSSON, Beth 605-626-2655 466 A rasmussb@northern.edu
RASNAKE, Martha, L 276-964-7389 528 E martha.rasnake@sw.edu
RASNICK, JR., William, B 423-439-7900 473 F rasnick@etsu.edu
RASOR, Mark 918-540-6213 408 J mrasor@neo.edu
RASPE, Kristina, E 213-821-3070 76 F kraspe@re.usc.edu
RASPILLER, Ted 979-209-7210 482 C ted.raspiller@blinn.edu
RASS, Heike 215-972-2031 440 J hrass@pafa.org
RASSOUL, Hamid 321-674-7260 108 H rassoul@fit.edu
RAST, Lawrence, R 260-452-2101 170 J lawrence.rast@ctsfw.edu
RASUL, David 916-558-2376 56 D rasuld@scc.losrios.edu
RASZEWSKI, Thomas 410-864-3621 226 B traszewski@stmarys.edu
RATCHFORD, Jerome 770-423-6310 133 A jratchfo@kennesaw.edu
RATCLIFF, Chris 870-460-1058 25 A ratcliff@uamont.edu
RATCLIFF, Christine, L 662-252-8000 276 G cratcliff@rustcollege.edu
RATCLIFF, Terry, D 509-777-3499 540 C tratcliff@whitworth.edu
RATCLIFFE, Jackson 415-485-3225 45 C jratcliffe@dominican.edu
RATCLIFFE, R. Samuel 540-464-7560 529 F ratcliffers@vmi.edu
RATERS, Michael, P 765-361-6289 181 E ratersm@wabash.edu
RATH, Phillip, S 812-888-5101 181 D prath@vinu.edu
RATHBONE, Thomas, M 607-436-3224 353 E rathbotm@oneonta.edu
RATHBUN, Robert, D 570-577-3200 423 E bob.rathbun@bucknell.edu
RATHBURN, III, Carlisle, B 903-223-3001 498 F carlisle.rathburn@tamut.edu
RATHE, Dean 303-914-6303 87 G dean.rathe@rrcc.edu
RATHEAL, Juli 432-552-2530 507 D ratheal_j@utpb.edu
RATHJE, James, A 507-354-8221 264 K rathjeja@mlc-wels.edu
RATHJEN, Arthur, H 920-424-1020 551 E rathjena@uwosh.edu
RATHKE, Debra 567-661-7247 400 I debra_rathke@owens.edu
RATHKE, Sheila, W 412-624-4248 449 A rathke@pitt.edu
RATHMELL, Daniel 607-729-1581 331 G danrathmell@davisny.edu
RATIGAN, Jim 702-895-2380 302 I james.ratigan@unlv.edu
RATLIFF, Ceci 509-542-4811 532 H cratliff@columbiabasin.edu
RATLIFF, Gerald, L 315-267-2108 354 C ratlifgl@potsdam.edu
RATLIFF, Jill 606-783-9555 204 I ji.ratliff@moreheadstate.edu
RATLIFF, John 704-272-5375 374 A jratliff@spcc.edu
RATLIFF, Kelly, M 530-754-6170 73 I kmratliff@ucdavis.edu
RATLIFF, Kerry 606-368-6064 198 C kerryratliff@alc.edu
RATLIFF, Kevin 540-453-2264 526 D ratliffk@brcc.edu
RATLIFF, Rosanna 214-828-8247 497 C rratliff@bcd.tamhsc.edu
RATLIFF, Thomas 765-677-2116 175 B thomas.ratliff@indwes.edu
RATLIFF, Thomas, R 304-462-4112 544 A thomas.ratliff@glenville.edu
RATLIFF, Vickie 276-523-7462 527 D vratliff@me.vccs.edu
RATLIFFE, Celina 503-699-6315 416 J cratliffe@marylhurst.edu
RATNER, Hilary, H 313-577-5600 260 A aa3411@wayne.edu
RATNER, Neil 845-352-3431 361 K shaareitorah@optonline.net
RATTIGAN, Paulette 401-232-6320 453 C prattiga@bryant.edu
RATTY, Michael 617-732-2130 241 C michael.ratty@mcphs.edu
RAUB, Tammara 607-871-2128 322 E raubt@alfred.edu
RAUBENHEIMER, Dianne 919-760-8913 367 A raubenhe@meredith.edu
RAUCH, Dena 319-398-5476 187 B dena.rauch@kirkwood.edu
RAUCH, Kenneth, E 260-422-5561 173 C kerauch@indianatech.edu
RAUCKHORST, Ashlee 740-774-7200 400 A rauckhor@ohio.edu
RAUDENBUSH, Joan, M 215-881-7386 438 H jmr28@psu.edu
RAUDENBUSH, Reid, C 410-778-7855 229 D rraudenbush2@washcoll.edu
RAULT, Pamela, V 504-280-7083 213 E pkvrana@uno.edu
RAULUK, Ruth 412-392-3996 445 A rrauluk@pointpark.edu
RAUP, Glenn 303-369-5151 87 D glenn.raup@plattcolorado.edu
RAUP, Kristin, A 412-578-6534 424 I raupka@carlow.edu
RAUSCH, Diane 805-986-5826 77 E drausch@vcccd.edu
RAUSCHENBACH, Timothy 317-573-8930 541 K trauschenbach@salemu.edu
RAUSCHER, Victor, E 518-445-2302 322 C vraus@albanylaw.edu
RAUTZHAN, Peter 610-282-1100 427 A peter.rautzhan@desales.edu
RAVALIN, Tamara 559-737-3879 42 D tamarar@cos.edu
RAVE, Carole 360-676-2772 535 K crave@nwic.edu
RAVELLI, James, B 503-943-7540 420 G ravelli@up.edu
RAVENELL, Alma 903-927-3275 509 E arravenell@wileyc.edu
RAVENELL, Johnnie 704-337-2330 376 A ravenelj@queens.edu
RAVENELLE, Robert, G 508-767-7325 230 D rravenel@assumption.edu
RAVER, C. Cybele 212-998-5555 344 B cybele.raver@nyu.edu
RAVERT WARD, Nancy 302-477-2191 97 B nmravertward@widener.edu
RAVINDRAN, Tharanee, M 256-824-6036 8 G tharanee.ravindran@uah.edu
RAVISHANKER, Ganesan 781-283-2095 245 E gravisha@wellesley.edu
RAWICZ, Diane 707-654-1039 33 C drawicz@csum.edu
RAWITCH, Allen, B 913-588-1258 197 C arawitch@kumc.edu
RAWITCH, Cynthia, Z 818-677-2957 35 F cynthia.rawitch@csun.edu
RAWITSCH, Mark 707-468-3082 57 A mrawitsc@mendocino.edu
RAWL, Carolyn, D 334-244-3934 1 G crawl@aum.edu
RAWLEIGH, Camilla, B 717-815-6521 452 G crawleig@ycp.edu
RAWLES, Scott 318-869-5106 208 H srawles@centenary.edu
RAWLEY, Albert 434-791-5654 516 G brawley@averett.edu
RAWLINGS, Becky 360-383-3404 540 A brawling@whatcom.ctc.edu
RAWLINGS, Douglas, H 207-778-7292 220 C rawling@maine.edu
RAWLINGS, Gilbert 410-276-0306 226 D grawlings@host.sdc.edu
RAWLINGS, Lynnette 330-385-7463 393 F lrawling@kent.edu
RAWLINGS, Michelle 859-233-8116 207 A registrar@transy.edu
RAWLINS, Benjamin 615-327-6141 471 C brawlins@mmc.edu
RAWLINS, Brad 870-972-2468 20 D brawlins@astate.edu
RAWLINS, V. Lane 940-565-2026 504 D president@unt.edu
RAWLINSON, Eddy 214-860-2392 485 A ebrawlinson@dcccd.edu
RAWLINSON, Ina, R 919-735-5151 375 A irrawlinson@waynecc.edu
RAWLS, Casey 601-403-1197 276 E crawls@prcc.edu
RAWLS, Terry 415-808-1430 49 G terry_rawls@heald.edu
RAWN, Mary, K 973-275-2891 315 B mary.rawn@shu.edu
RAWSKI, Jim 706-379-3111 140 A jkrawski@yhc.edu
RAWSON, Ken 903-586-2518 489 B deanofstudents@jacksonville-college.edu
RAWSON, Shawn 269-782-1474 258 C srawson01@swmich.edu
RAXTER, Jen 508-999-8034 237 A jraxter@umassd.edu
RAY, Aisha 312-893-7137 151 A aray@erikson.edu
RAY, Anita 706-245-7226 129 C aray@ec.edu
RAY, Barry, D 864-231-2015 455 C bray@andersonuniversity.edu
RAY, Bernard 615-327-6294 471 C bray@mmc.edu
RAY, Brandon 360-442-2254 535 I bray@lowercolumbia.edu
RAY, Cara 678-717-3622 129 G cray@gsc.edu
RAY, Chad 704-330-6909 369 D chad.ray@cpcc.edu
RAY, JR., Charles, A 504-816-8010 213 H cray@nobts.edu
RAY, Darby, K 207-786-8241 217 C dray3@bates.edu
RAY, David 502-410-6200 200 L dray@galencollege.edu
RAY, David, H 405-325-6426 413 C dray@ou.edu
RAY, Douglas 305-623-2445 117 A dray@stu.edu
RAY, Edward, J 541-737-4133 418 F pres.office@oregonstate.edu
RAY, Gary 940-898-3010 502 D gray@twu.edu
RAY, James 423-893-2000 478 D james.ray@vc.edu
RAY, Janell 713-942-9505 488 A jray@hgst.edu
RAY, Jeffrey 678-915-7234 137 G jray@spsu.edu
RAY, Jerry 912-583-3115 126 F jray@bpc.edu
RAY, Jess, D 309-438-2264 153 D jdray@ilstu.edu
RAY, Joe, F 662-246-6308 275 D jray@msdelta.edu
RAY, John, C 979-230-3202 482 D john.ray@brazosport.edu
RAY, Johnnie 865-974-9767 477 C jray@utfi.org
RAY, Judy, K 336-841-9201 365 C jray@highpoint.edu
RAY, Kate 904-953-2919 262 E kray@mayo.edu
RAY, Katerina, R 419-372-8575 385 E krray@bgsu.edu
RAY, Kathlin, D 775-784-6500 303 A kray@unr.edu
RAY, Keith, H 217-732-3168 156 H pres@lincolnchristian.edu
RAY, Ken 813-253-7054 110 M kray6@hccfl.edu
RAY, Lee Ann 979-436-9105 497 B ray@tamhsc.edu
RAY, Lorena 918-872-7706 412 E lorena.ray@swcu.edu
RAY, Marsha, M 215-751-8042 426 B mray@ccp.edu
RAY, Monica 256-372-5555 1 A monica.ray@aamu.edu
RAY, Nicholas, T 812-941-2411 175 A nicray@ius.edu
RAY, Patricia 859-223-9608 206 E pray@spencerian.edu
RAY, JR., R. Richard 616-395-7785 252 D ray@hope.edu
RAY, Rhonda 503-760-3131 414 F rhonda@birthingway.edu
RAY, Roxie, L 203-576-4290 94 F roxieray@bridgeport.edu
RAY, S. Alan 630-617-3100 150 H president@elmhurst.edu
RAY, Sally 270-659-6933 208 A sally.ray@wku.edu
RAY, Sarah 802-443-5000 514 A ray@middlebury.edu
RAY, Scott 903-923-2148 486 F sray@etbu.edu
RAY, Shawn 305-892-7015 112 A shawn.ray@jwu.edu
RAY, Valerie 765-966-2656 176 H vray@ivytech.edu
RAY, William 503-352-2786 419 E raywb@pacificu.edu
RAYBUCK, Diane, R 330-972-6427 403 B drr9@uakron.edu
RAYBURN, John 713-500-3079 506 F john.rayburn@uth.tmc.edu
RAYBURN, Judy, M 731-881-7020 477 G jrayburn@utm.edu
RAYBURN, T. Monroe 202-319-5765 97 E rayburn@cua.edu
RAYCHOUDHURY, Samir, S 803-705-4648 455 D raychoudhurys@benedict.edu
RAYE, Brenda 330-494-1214 386 A braye@brownmackie.edu
RAYER, Susan, S 859-233-8193 207 A careerdevelopment@transy.edu
RAYMAN, Jack, R 814-865-2377 438 G jxr1@psu.edu
RAYMOND, Alice 256-551-3148 4 J alice.raymond@drakestate.edu
RAYMOND, Annette 973-748-9000 307 H annette_raymond@bloomfield.edu
RAYMOND, Bruce 719-549-2142 83 H bruce.raymond@colostate-pueblo.edu
RAYMOND, Chris 413-572-5243 238 F craymond@wsc.ma.edu
RAYMOND, Diane 603-428-2223 305 D draymond@nec.edu
RAYMOND, SR., John, R 414-955-8225 548 G jraymond@mcw.edu
RAYMOND, Margaret 608-262-1234 550 J mraymond2@wisc.edu
RAYMOND, Mary 909-621-8144 63 A mary.raymond@pomona.edu
RAYMOND, Monica 805-339-6370 67 J
RAYMOND, Monica 805-339-6370 68 A
RAYMOND, Monica 805-339-6370 67 K
RAYMOND, Monica 805-339-6370 67 M
RAYMOND, Patricia 860-343-5772 91 G praymond@mxcc.commnet.edu
RAYMOND, Sarah 406-496-4384 296 B sraymond@mtech.edu
RAYMOND, Thomas 605-455-6012 465 A traymond@olc.edu
RAYMUNDO, Laurie 671-735-2184 559 G lraymundo@gmail.com
RAYNER, Jill 706-864-1688 134 G jprayner@northgeorgia.edu
RAYNOR, Bill 781-239-2665 239 G braynor@massbay.edu
RAYNOR, Nathan 706-865-2134 138 E nraynor@truett.edu
RAZIANO, Deborah, A 985-448-4110 216 A deborah.raziano@nicholls.edu
RAZO, Bridget 661-722-6300 28 K brazo@avc.edu
RAZO, Gabriel 312-553-5901 147 C grazo@ccc.edu
RAZZAGHI, Farzaneh 956-665-2755 506 C farzaneh@utpa.edu
RE, Doug 415-239-3759 40 C dre@ccsf.edu
RE, John 864-225-7653 458 C johnre@forrestcollege.edu
RE, Robin 740-774-6300 389 D rre@daymarcollege.edu
RE, Robin 740-687-6126 389 F rre@daymarcollege.edu
REA, Ann, W 207-947-4591 217 D librarian@bealcollege.edu
REA, Gail 314-454-8848 282 B grea@bjc.org
REABACK, Roslyn 203-932-7263 95 C rreaback@newhaven.edu
READ, Allison 860-297-2013 94 E allison.read@trincoll.edu
READ, Deborah 805-756-1445 33 I dawread@calpoly.edu
READ, Jen 704-357-8020 362 D jread@aii.edu
READ, Marsha 775-327-2363 303 A read@unr.edu
READ, Melissa, P 508-541-1652 233 G mread@dean.edu
READEY, Mary, L 614-292-0257 398 I readey.3@osu.edu
READING, Sarah 781-239-2782 239 G sreading@massbay.edu
READY, Deana 573-592-4236 293 D deana.ready@williamwoods.edu
REAGAN, Cheryl 518-562-4110 329 C cheryl.reagan@clinton.edu
REAGAN, Daniel, W 603-641-4131 306 D dan.reagan@unh.edu
REAGAN, Kate, M 423-869-6389 470 E kate.reagan@lmunet.edu
REAGAN, Margy 202-884-9707 99 H reaganm@trinitydc.edu
REAGAN, Melinda 972-279-6511 479 H mreagan@amberton.edu

REAGINS-LILLY, Soncia, R 512-471-5017 505 D soncia.r.lilly@austin.utexas.edu
REAGLE, Mike 859-622-3855 200 J mike.reagle@eku.edu
REAGLES, Patricia, J 507-344-7306 261 C patti.reagles@blc.edu
REAL, Yannick 562-860-2451 39 A yreal@cerritos.edu
REALE, Todd, D 502-272-8242 198 H treale@bellarmine.edu
REALIVASQUEZ, Yvonne 432-837-8032 501 E yrealivasquez@sulross.edu
REAM, Daniel, L 804-862-6208 523 F dream@rbc.edu
REAM, Debbie 213-477-2505 57 H dream@msmc.la.edu
REAP, Mary 413-265-2293 233 D reapm@elms.edu
REARDON, Colleen 708-524-6643 150 C creardon@dom.edu
REARDON, Maureen 508-457-1313 242 F mreardon@ngs.edu
REARDON, Pat 256-824-2561 8 G reardonp@uah.edu
REARDON, Penny 304-434-8000 542 I reardon@eastern.wvnet.edu
REARDON, Thomas, J 662-915-5056 277 D sparky@olemiss.edu
REARDON, Timothy 440-646-8312 405 B treardon@ursuline.edu
REARIC, Sue 619-644-7576 49 A sue.rearic@gcccd.edu
REAS, Rae-Ellen 425-640-1401 533 I raeellen.reas@edcc.edu
REASH, Brenda 252-222-6000 369 A
REASONER, Carroll 319-335-2841 182 F carroll-reasoner@uiowa.edu
REASONER, Elliott 630-743-0689 168 E sreasoner@westwood.edu
REASSO, Robert 207-973-1069 218 A reassor@husson.edu
REAUME, Vicki 734-487-2410 250 F vreaume@emich.edu
REAVES, Donald, J 336-750-2041 380 B chancellorsoffice@wssu.edu
REAVES, Ken 678-872-4201 130 E kreaves@highlands.edu
REAVES, Kenneth, M 863-680-3007 109 E kreaves@flsouthern.edu
REAVES, Leonard 419-448-3271 402 E reavesl@tiffin.edu
REAVES, Nicole 724-925-4212 451 E reavesn@wccc.edu
REAVES, Nicole 724-925-6952 451 E reavesn@wccc.edu
REAVIS, Bob 785-654-2416 190 D breavis@allencc.edu
REAVIS, Ralph 434-528-5276 530 B reavis@vul.edu
REBA, Kathleen 516-678-5000 341 F kreba@molloy.edu
REBER, Christopher, M 814-676-6591 442 B creber@clarion.edu
REBER, Christopher, M 814-676-6591 442 C creber@clarion.edu
REBHOLZ, Catherine, R 414-276-5200 546 F krrebholz@bryantstratton.edu
REBIMBUS, Michael 803-705-4357 455 D rebimbus@benedict.edu
REBORI, Christine 636-949-4477 283 J crebori@lindenwood.edu
REBRO, Jan 425-637-1010 532 E jrebro@cityu.eu
REBULL, Patrick 305-237-0564 113 H prebull@mdc.edu
RECA, Michael, F 609-896-5080 313 F reca@rider.edu
RECA ZIPP, Marcella 815-479-7515 157 H mrecazipp@mchenry.edu
RECCHIA, Karen 318-678-6000 209 I krecchia@bpcc.edu
RECH, Tara 510-594-3670 32 C trech@cca.edu
RECHEIUNGEL, Winfred 680-488-3036 560 C winfredr@palau.edu
RECHLIN, Mike 304-358-2000 541 C mike@future.edu
RECHTSCHAFFEN, Joyce, A 202-220-1364 312 G jrechtsc@princeton.edu
RECINOS, Diane 973-278-5400 307 F dr@berkeleycollege.edu
RECINOS, Diane 973-278-5000 323 H dr@berkeleycollege.edu
RECK, Una Mae 574-520-4220 174 E maereck@iusb.edu
RECKER, OSB, Ralph 503-845-3320 417 A ralph.recker@mtangel.edu
RECKER, Sandy, M 563-588-7362 187 C sandy.recker@loras.edu
RECKNER, Angela, T 215-489-2203 426 H angela.reckner@delval.edu
RECKTENWALD, Kay 561-297-0026 119 A kreckten@fau.edu
RECLER, Edward, R 419-434-4791 404 B reckere1@findlay.edu
RECOD, Pamela 910-323-5614 363 A
RECORD, Ann 731-668-7240 478 G ann.record@wtbc.edu
RECORD, Kim 336-334-5952 379 B ksrecord@uncg.edu
RECTOR, Billy, C 713-313-6898 500 B rectorbc@tsu.edu
RECTOR, Brenda 865-882-4526 476 A rectorbw@roanestate.edu
RECTOR, Dave 360-596-5305 538 E drector@spscc.stc.edu
RECTOR, David 660-785-7607 290 G daverec@truman.edu
RECTOR, Dawn 480-858-9100 18 E d.rector@scnm.edu
RECTOR, Jeff 423-493-4224 476 E rectorj@tntemple.edu
RECTOR, Lallene, J 847-866-3904 151 D ljr@garrett.edu
RECTOR, Larry 865-573-4517 469 L lrector@johnsonu.edu
RECTOR, Patricia 918-465-1769 408 A prector@eosc.edu
RECTOR, Rob 417-447-4852 287 D rectorr@otc.edu
RECZNIK, Joel, S 740-284-5236 391 A jrecznik@franciscan.edu
RECZNIK, John 740-283-6497 391 A jlrecznik@franciscan.edu
RECZNIK, Mark, E 740-284-5845 391 A mrecznik@franciscan.edu
REDD, Annie 386-481-2520 102 C redda@cookman.edu
REDD, Cliff 713-743-4921 503 D rbredd@central.uh.edu
REDD, Randy 901-751-8453 471 F rredd@mabts.edu
REDD, Rea 724-852-3254 451 B rredd@waynesburg.edu
REDD, Scott 703-448-3393 276 F sredd@rts.edu
REDD, Scott 703-448-3393 523 D sredd@rts.edu
REDD, Theresa, M 202-806-0870 98 E tredd@howard.edu
REDDA, Kinfe, K 850-412-5102 118 L kinfe.redda@famu.edu
REDDAY, Darlene 605-698-3966 465 E dredday@swc.tc
REDDER, Kelly 585-475-7412 347 G karrar@rit.edu
REDDER, Vince 605-995-2631 464 C viredder@dwu.edu
REDDERSON, Jeff, P 864-294-3262 458 E jeff.redderson@furman.edu
REDDI, Lakshmi 305-348-2455 119 C lakshmi.reddi@fiu.edu
REDDICK, Amanda 678-891-2782 131 C amanda.reddick@gpc.edu
REDDICK, Michael 317-788-3372 180 F mreddick@uindy.edu
REDDICK, Niles 229-391-4782 123 H nreddick@abac.edu
REDDING, Lee 313-593-5000 259 B lredding@umd.umich.edu
REDDING, Melanie 865-471-3229 467 G mredding@cn.edu
REDDING, Michael, W 541-346-5022 419 B mredding@uoregon.edu
REDDING, Russell 215-345-1500 426 H russell.redding@delval.edu
REDDINGTON, Kathleen 575-527-7604 319 G kredding@nmsu.edu
REDDY, Chandra 615-963-7561 474 A creddy@tnstate.edu
REDDY, Indra, K 361-593-4271 497 B ireddy@pharmacy.tamhsc.edu
REDDY, John, M 724-337-1000 424 G jreddy@careerta.edu
REDDY, Michael, S 205-934-4720 8 F mreddy@uab.edu
REDDY, Narem 678-466-4100 127 D naremreddy@clayton.edu
REDDY, JR., Robert, A 440-775-8142 397 G rob.reddy@oberlin.edu
REDDY, Venkateshwar 719-255-3408 88 I vreddy@uccs.edu
REDEKER, Michael 314-505-7000 280 D redekerm@csl.edu
REDEKER, Wade 620-341-5264 192 G wredekeri@emporia.edu
REDES, Cliff 231-876-3105 248 A cliff.redes@baker.edu
REDFERN, Mylan 432-552-2220 507 D redfern_m@utpb.edu
REDFERN, Paul, W 717-337-6829 429 I predfern@gettysburg.edu
REDFERN, Vance 575-538-6310 321 I redfernw@wnmu.edu
REDFIELD, David 916-484-8408 56 A redfied@arc.losrios.edu
REDHEAD, Catherine 406-683-7450 294 J c_redhead@umwestern.edu
REDHORN-CHAMBERLAIN, Sharon 402-878-2380 298 E sredhorn@littlepriest.edu
REDING, Cheryl 913-360-7384 191 A creding@benedictine.edu
REDING, Nichole 503-760-3131 414 F nichole@birthingway.edu
REDING, Terrence 585-345-6850 334 F tareding@genesee.edu
REDINGER, Larry, L 909-594-5611 58 A lredinge@mtsac.edu
REDINGTON, Joseph 570-674-6756 436 F jredingt@misericordia.edu
REDLER, Susan 212-431-2121 343 E sredler@nyls.edu
REDLICH, Philip, N 414-805-5726 548 G predlich@mcw.edu
REDLIN, Greg 662-846-4004 273 H gredlin@deltastate.edu
REDLINGER, Lawrence, J 972-883-6188 506 A redling@utdallas.edu
REDMAN, Barbara, K 313-577-4070 260 A ae9080@wayne.edu
REDMAN, Chris 785-749-8497 193 D president@haskell.edu
REDMAN, Donald, L 717-334-6286 435 A dredman@ltsg.edu
REDMAN, Robert, R 503-255-0332 417 C rredman@multnomah.edu
REDMAN, Thomas, J 978-232-2005 234 D tredman@endicott.edu
REDMOND, Angie 641-844-5712 186 D angie.redmond@iavalley.edu
REDMOND, Carmen 650-949-6166 47 H redmondcarmen@foothill.edu
REDMOND, Carmen 650-949-6166 47 G redmondcarmen@fhda.edu
REDMOND, John 845-752-3000 358 F j.redmond@uts.edu
REDMOND, Katrina 845-848-4034 332 B katrina.redmond@dc.edu
REDMOND, Michael, J 303-458-4944 87 I mredmond@regis.edu
REDMOND, Minor (Will) 717-871-5344 443 D minor.redmond@millersville.edu
REDMOND, Thomas, E 202-274-5935 100 A tredmond@udc.edu
REDO, Keith 516-678-5000 341 F kredo@molloy.edu
REDONNETT, Rosa 207-973-3231 219 I rosar@maine.edu
REDTOMAHAWK, James 701-255-3285 383 G jredtomahawk@uttc.edu
REDWINE, Jamie 540-458-8184 530 D jredwine@wlu.edu
REDWINE, Marian 405-491-6336 412 D maredwin@snu.edu
REDWINE, Mike 405-491-6335 412 D mredwine@snu.edu
REDWINE, William 606-783-2680 204 I b.redwine@moreheadstate.edu
REECE, Bryan 562-860-2451 39 A breece@cerritos.edu
REECE, David 910-695-3831 373 H reeced@sandhills.edu
REECE, E. Albert 410-706-7410 227 C deanmed@som.umaryland.edu
REECE, Jeremy 870-733-6786 22 E jreece@midsouthcc.edu
REECE, Marilyn 256-228-6001 6 A reecem@nacc.edu
REECE, Ronda 405-945-8631 410 F
REECE, Sheila 903-785-7661 492 D sreece@parisjc.edu
REECE, Terry 805-546-3283 43 I treece@cuesta.edu
REECK-IRBY, Joanne 612-330-1111 261 B reeck@augsburg.edu
REED, Alexis 304-876-5157 544 C apalladi@shepherd.edu
REED, Amanda, E 814-269-7081 449 D acampbel@pitt.edu
REED, Ann 304-462-4117 544 A ann.reed@glenville.edu
REED, Anne, E 207-941-7176 219 E reeda@nescom.edu
REED, Annie, G 818-947-2320 55 E reedag@lavc.edu
REED, Barrett 870-584-4471 25 C breed@cccua.edu
REED, Beverly 630-942-4218 148 A reedbe@cod.edu
REED, Beverly, S 301-322-0495 225 F reedbs@pgcc.edu
REED, Brian, V 802-656-0903 514 H brian.reed@uvm.edu
REED, Bruce 956-665-2292 506 C bjreed@utpa.edu
REED, Burton, J 402-554-2262 301 A breed@unomaha.edu
REED, Charlene, K 330-672-2121 393 D creed2@kent.edu
REED, Charles, B 562-951-4700 33 H creed@calstate.edu
REED, Christine 805-922-6966 26 L creed@hancockcollege.edu
REED, Christopher, S 603-526-3797 303 G chreed@colby-sawyer.edu
REED, Claudia 310-954-4371 57 H creed@msmc.la.edu
REED, Cristina 810-762-9584 253 C creed@kettering.edu
REED, Dallas, F 212-986-4343 323 H dfr@berkeleycollege.edu
REED, Dan 530-898-6451 34 C dmreed@csuchico.edu
REED, David, D 906-487-3043 255 B ddreed@mtu.edu
REED, Dee 812-535-5212 179 E dreed@smwc.edu
REED, Dennis, J 818-947-2625 55 E reeddj@lavc.edu
REED, Diane 757-594-7202 517 L dreed@cnu.edu
REED, Donna 971-722-4497 419 G donna.reed@pcc.edu
REED, Doug 870-245-5167 22 I reedd@obu.edu
REED, Elizabeth 305-899-4013 101 M ereed@mail.barry.edu
REED, Eloise 903-923-3222 500 E eloise.reed@tstc.edu
REED, Francesca 703-284-5901 521 D francesca.reed@marymount.edu
REED, Gary 214-645-0137 507 E gary.reed@utsouthwestern.edu
REED, Harry 713-646-1852 494 I hreed@stcl.edu
REED, Hazell 919-530-6893 378 B hreed@nccu.edu
REED, Helen 970-351-2601 89 B helen.reed@unco.edu
REED, James, D 806-651-2055 499 A jreed@mail.wtamu.edu
REED, Jeff 515-292-9694 182 B
REED, Jeffrey, G 920-923-8760 548 E jreed@marianuniversity.edu
REED, Jerry 570-389-4040 441 F jreed@bloomu.edu
REED, John 425-249-4800 538 G john.reed@tlc.edu
REED, John 617-253-6700 241 D
REED, Jonathan 909-593-3511 75 E jreed@laverne.edu
REED, Karen, A 419-755-4538 397 C kreed@ncstatecollege.edu
REED, Kate 847-317-4064 166 E kreed@tiu.edu
REED, Kathleen, O 717-334-6286 435 A kreed@ltsg.edu
REED, Kathy 310-338-4404 56 E kathy.reed@lmu.edu
REED, Kathy, S 217-581-3227 150 E ksreed@eiu.edu
REED, Kendall 515-271-1515 184 A kendall.reed@dmu.edu
REED, Kenneth 575-492-2132 321 H kreed@usw.edu
REED, Kevin 310-206-1355 74 C kreed@conet.ucla.edu
REED, Kimberly 270-745-2434 208 A kim.reed@wku.edu
REED, Kristen 217-245-3054 152 D kristen.reed@ic.edu
REED, LaTonya 870-574-4504 24 A lreed@sautech.edu
REED, Leah 719-384-6890 87 A leah.reed@ojc.edu
REED, Lee 202-687-2435 98 D athletics@georgetown.edu
REED, Leslie 410-209-6006 221 E lreed@bccc.edu
REED, Linda 901-572-2640 467 C linda.reed@bchs.edu
REED, Lisa 740-774-6300 389 D lreed@daymarcollege.edu
REED, Lori 507-457-5005 269 G lreed@winona.edu
REED, Mamie 205-652-3447 9 E mlr@uwa.edu
REED, Mark, C 203-254-4000 92 H mcreed@fairfield.edu
REED, Mark, F 610-861-1360 437 A mreed@moravian.edu
REED, Mark, H 603-650-1488 304 J mark.h.reed@dartmouth.edu
REED, Mark, V 607-777-6112 351 F mreed@binghamton.edu
REED, Maryanne 304-293-5746 545 A maryanne.reed@mail.wvu.edu
REED, Matthew 413-552-2227 239 F mreed@hcc.edu
REED, Meredith 504-398-2236 214 B mreed@olhcc.edu
REED, Michael, E 413-597-4376 246 D michael.e.reed@williams.edu

REID, Linda, S ... 207-581-1288 ... 220 A
linda@maine.edu
REID, Mark ... 206-281-2624 ... 537 H
mreid@spu.edu
REID, Melissa ... 606-546-1610 ... 207 B
REID, Michael ... 325-942-2017 ... 480 E
michael.reid@angelo.edu
REID, Michelle ... 701-231-8887 ... 382 B
michelle.reid@ndsu.edu
REID, Michelle ... 330-499-9600 ... 393 I
mreid6@kent.edu
REID, Pam ... 601-643-8442 ... 273 G
pam.reid@colin.edu
REID, Pamela, T ... 860-231-5221 ... 95 D
preid@usj.edu
REID, Patricia ... 216-987-4659 ... 389 B
patricia.reid@tri-c.edu
REID, Richard, H ... 337-475-5588 ... 215 G
rreid@mcneese.edu
REID, Shannon ... 603-271-2722 ... 304 A
REID, Stanley, G ... 512-476-2772 ... 481 C
president@austingrad.edu
REID, JR., Thomas, G ... 412-731-8690 ... 445 F
treid@rpts.edu
REID, Tina, S ... 864-592-4683 ... 461 C
reidt@sccsc.edu
REID, Victoria ... 612-338-7224 ... 272 C
victoria.reid@waldenu.edu
REID-CHASSIAKOS, Linda ... 818-677-3689 ... 35 F
linda.reid.chassiakos@csun.edu
REID-HART, De Reese ... 773-602-5118 ... 147 E
REID-MARTINEZ, Kathaleen ... 405-691-3800 ... 408 H
kreidmartinez@macu.edu
REIDELL, Mary Frances ... 412-578-6174 ... 424 I
reidellmf@carlow.edu
REIDENBERG, Marcus, M ... 212-746-6227 ... 360 C
mmreid@med.cornell.edu
REIDHEAD, Christine ... 505-786-4186 ... 318 I
creidhead@navajotech.edu
REIDHEAD, Van, A ... 570-422-3539 ... 442 D
vreidhead@po-box.esu.edu
REIDY, Fran ... 352-588-8246 ... 116 G
fran.reidy@saintleo.edu
REIDY, Joseph, P ... 202-806-2550 ... 98 E
jreidy@howard.edu
REIDY, Robert, C ... 650-723-6324 ... 71 G
rcr@stanford.edu
REIDY, Stephanie ... 410-462-8245 ... 221 E
sreidy@bccc.edu
REIF, L. Rafael ... 617-253-0148 ... 241 D
REIF, Steven, J ... 248-246-2511 ... 256 F
sjreif@oaklandcc.edu
REIFENHEISER, Paul ... 845-434-5750 ... 357 A
preifenh@sullivan.suny.edu
REIFF, Henry, B ... 410-857-2512 ... 224 C
hreiff@mcdaniel.edu
REIFF, Marianne ... 802-322-1719 ... 513 E
marianne.reiff@goddard.edu
REIFLER, Sylvia ... 617-217-9237 ... 231 A
sreifler@baystate.edu
REIFSCHNEIDER, Carol ... 406-265-3768 ... 295 E
reifschneider@msun.edu
REIGELMAN, Milton, M ... 859-238-5287 ... 199 G
milton.reigelman@centre.edu
REIGH, Darryel ... 405-224-3140 ... 413 E
dreigh@usao.edu
REIGHARD, Erica ... 814-262-6440 ... 441 A
ereighard@pennhighlands.edu
REIGHLEY, Twila ... 517-355-5040 ... 255 A
reighley@msu.edu
REIGOSA, Teresa ... 305-237-3536 ... 113 H
treigosa@mdc.edu
REIHER, William ... 692-625-8424 ... 560 A
REILENDER, Catherine, L ... 859-846-5315 ... 204 H
creilender@midway.edu
REILLY, Elizabeth, H ... 330-972-7331 ... 403 B
reilly@uakron.edu
REILLY, James ... 312-553-2500 ... 147 B
jreilly1@ccc.edu
REILLY, John, H ... 518-956-8050 ... 351 E
jreilly@uamail.albany.edu
REILLY, Joseph, R ... 973-313-6233 ... 315 B
joseph.reilly@shu.edu
REILLY, Joseph, R ... 973-761-9016 ... 310 F
joseph.reilly@shu.edu
REILLY, Karen ... 301-624-2862 ... 222 G
kreilly@frederick.edu
REILLY, Karen ... 301-624-2849 ... 222 G
kreilly@frederick.edu
REILLY, Karen ... 701-671-2189 ... 382 G
karen.reilly@ndscs.edu
REILLY, Kevin ... 540-365-4407 ... 519 C
kreilly@ferrum.edu
REILLY, Kevin, P ... 608-262-2321 ... 550 I
kreilly@uwsa.edu
REILLY, Kristie ... 908-737-3460 ... 311 A
kreilly@kean.edu
REILLY, Marie, T ... 814-863-7033 ... 439 D
mtr12@psu.edu
REILLY, MaryBeth ... 718-982-2426 ... 327 A
marybeth.reilly@csi.cuny.edu
REILLY, Maureen ... 518-743-2306 ... 355 D
reillym@sunyacc.edu
REILLY, Patricia ... 617-627-2000 ... 245 C
patricia.reilly@tufts.edu
REILLY, Paul, J ... 215-951-1100 ... 432 I
reilly@lasalle.edu
REILLY, Seamus ... 217-353-2170 ... 161 C
sereilly@parkland.edu
REILLY-KELLY, Tracy ... 360-992-2163 ... 532 F
tkelly@clark.edu
REILLY-MYKLEBUST, Alice ... 715-425-9884 ... 552 C
alice.m.reilly-myklebust@uwrf.edu
REIMAN, Dennis, M ... 904-997-2940 ... 109 F
dennis.reiman@fscj.edu
REIMANN, Jan ... 573-334-9181 ... 284 E
jan@metrobusinesscollege.edu
REIMANN, Rick ... 518-587-2100 ... 355 G
rick.reimann@esc.edu
REIMER, Carol ... 907-822-3201 ... 10 B
registrar@akbible.edu
REIMER, Dawn ... 763-488-2518 ... 266 D
dawn.reimer@hennepintech.edu
REIMER, Denise, M ... 608-243-4484 ... 554 D
dmreimer@madisoncollege.org
REIMER, Kevin ... 559-453-5556 ... 48 A
kevin.reimer@fresno.edu
REIMER, Linda ... 212-229-5350 ... 342 E
reimerl@newschool.edu
REIMER, Martin ... 712-274-6400 ... 190 B
martin.reimer@witcc.edu
REIMER, Michael ... 201-360-4156 ... 310 E
mreimer@hccc.edu
REIMER, Mike ... 620-241-0723 ... 191 I
mike.reimer@centralchristian.edu
REIMONDO, Sue ... 859-985-3212 ... 199 A
sue_reimondo@berea.edu
REIN, Jennifer, L ... 785-827-5541 ... 194 F
jennifer.rein@kwu.edu
REIN, Kim ... 303-914-6260 ... 87 G
kim.rein@rrcc.edu
REINA, Juana ... 212-650-5426 ... 326 G
jreina@ccny.cuny.edu
REINBOLD, Sue ... 607-729-8915 ... 332 H
sreinbold@ebi-college.com
REINCKE, Nancy ... 515-271-2161 ... 184 D
nancy.reincke@drake.edu
REINDL, Kay ... 209-478-0800 ... 50 K
kreindl@humphreys.edu
REINEMUND, Steven ... 336-758-5110 ... 380 C
steve@wfu.edu
REINER, Christian ... 435-586-7783 ... 511 D
christianreiner@suu.edu
REINERT, Duane ... 660-944-2852 ... 280 B
dreinert@conception.edu
REINERT, Stephen, L ... 848-932-7787 ... 314 C
sreinert@rci.rutgers.edu
REING, Linda ... 212-875-4605 ... 323 C
alumrel@bankstreet.edu
REINHARD, Brian ... 618-664-6801 ... 151 F
brian.reinhard@greenville.edu
REINHARDT, Alan, J ... 508-213-2201 ... 243 E
alan.reinhardt@nichols.edu
REINHARDT, John, W ... 402-472-1344 ... 300 H
jreinhardt@unmc.edu
REINHARDT, Rosemary ... 208-426-1422 ... 142 I
rosemaryreinhardt@boisestate.edu
REINHARDT, Sharon ... 209-384-6188 ... 57 C
reinhardt.s@mccd.edu
REINHART, Charles, W ... 812-888-4480 ... 181 D
creinhart@vinu.edu
REINHART, Kellee, C ... 205-348-5938 ... 8 D
kreinhar@uasystem.ua.edu
REINHART, Rose ... 419-995-8310 ... 392 K
reinhart.r@rhodesstate.edu
REINHARTSEN, Steven, C ... 336-506-4146 ... 368 A
reinhart@alamancecc.edu
REINHOLD, David ... 269-387-4564 ... 260 C
david.reinhold@wmich.edu
REINKE, Brenda ... 405-682-7510 ... 409 F
breinke@occc.edu
REINKE, Jane ... 763-424-0819 ... 268 B
jreinke@nhcc.edu
REINLAND, Jeffrey, E ... 509-527-4312 ... 539 B
jeffrey.reinland@wwcc.edu
REINLIE, Carla ... 850-729-5357 ... 114 A
reinliec@nwfsc.edu
REINSCH FRIESE, Ellen ... 937-775-2709 ... 406 C
ellen.friese@wright.edu
REINSCHMIDT, Sheryl ... 323-856-7698 ... 28 E
sreinschmidt@afi.com
REINSCHMIEDT, Lynn ... 662-325-2663 ... 275 F
rein@provost.msstate.edu
REINTS, Cindi, P ... 319-895-4216 ... 183 G
creints@cornellcollege.edu
REIS, Elizabeth ... 708-974-5283 ... 159 B
reis@morainevalley.edu
REIS, Paul ... 203-837-9805 ... 91 A
reisp@wcsu.edu
REIS, Raul ... 305-348-2000 ... 119 C
REIS, Sally ... 860-486-4037 ... 94 G
sally.reis@uncon.edu
REISBERG, Jeff ... 727-873-4552 ... 121 C
reisberg@mail.usf.edu
REISCHE, Jim ... 641-269-3400 ... 185 D
reischej@grinnell.edu
REISECK, Carol, J ... 708-209-3262 ... 148 E
carol.reiseck@cuchicago.edu
REISETTER, Mary ... 641-585-8681 ... 189 I
reisettem@waldorf.edu
REISETTER-HART, Judith ... 414-382-6431 ... 546 B
judith.reisetter@alverno.edu
REISH, Brenda, J ... 800-287-8822 ... 169 H
reishbr@bethanyseminary.edu
REISH, Joseph, G ... 269-387-5202 ... 260 C
joe.reish@wmich.edu
REISIG, Jerry ... 212-870-1213 ... 344 A
jreisig@nyts.edu
REISINGER, Amanda, B ... 740-588-1275 ... 407 A
amreisinger@zanestate.edu
REISINGER, Scot, H ... 319-368-6472 ... 187 H
sreisinger@mtmercy.edu
REISINGER, Tracy ... 503-699-6253 ... 416 J
treisinger@marylhurst.edu
REISKE, Matthew ... 573-882-6574 ... 291 B
reiskem@missouri.edu
REISMAN, Lonn ... 254-968-9178 ... 497 A
reisman@tarleton.edu
REISS, Michael, A ... 718-377-0777 ... 346 G
REISS, Mitchell, B ... 410-778-7201 ... 229 D
mreiss2@washcoll.edu
REISS, Richard ... 201-692-7003 ... 310 A
reissr@fdu.edu
REISS, Yona ... 212-960-5347 ... 361 M
yreiss@yu.edu
REISSENWEBER, Beth, W ... 630-844-5490 ... 145 F
breissen@aurora.edu
REISSER, Linda ... 971-722-5292 ... 419 G
lreisser@pcc.edu
REIST, David ... 785-442-6010 ... 193 F
dreist@highlandcc.edu
REITCHEL, Meghan ... 207-859-1105 ... 219 G
registrar@thomas.edu
REITER, Emily ... 213-613-2200 ... 70 H
emily_reiter@sciarc.edu
REITER, Laurie ... 800-567-2344 ... 547 A
lreiter@menominee.edu
REITER, Sharon, L ... 909-869-3016 ... 33 J
slreiter@csupomona.edu
REITMAN, Bruce ... 617-627-3158 ... 245 C
bruce.reitman@tufts.edu
REITMAN, Tzipora ... 845-574-4595 ... 347 I
zreitman@sunyrockland.edu
REITNOUR, Brian ... 585-567-9622 ... 336 B
brian.reitnour@houghton.edu
REITTER, Kim ... 314-977-2828 ... 289 C
reitterk@slu.edu
REITZ, Chris ... 801-524-8109 ... 510 E
creitz@ldsbc.edu
REITZ, Nancy ... 916-484-8215 ... 56 A
reitzn@arc.losrios.edu
REKE, Daniel, R ... 937-778-7878 ... 390 G
dreke@edisonohio.edu
REKOWSKI, Lois, T ... 740-264-5591 ... 390 F
lrekowski@egcc.edu
REL, Ricardo ... 575-646-5909 ... 319 D
rrel@nmsu.edu
RELAY, Lyn ... 718-368-5034 ... 328 A
lrelay@kbcc.cuny.edu
RELEFORD, Michele ... 336-750-2171 ... 380 B
relefordmi@wssu.edu
RELIHAN, Constance, C ... 334-844-4900 ... 1 F
relihco@auburn.edu
RELL, Amy ... 303-556-3850 ... 84 A
amy.rell@ccd.edu
RELLINGER, Brian, A ... 740-368-3131 ... 400 G
barellin@owu.edu
RELYEA, Steven, W ... 858-534-3390 ... 74 F
srelyea@ucsd.edu
REMBACZ, Mark ... 307-382-1646 ... 557 A
mrembacz@wwcc.wy.edu
REMBERT, Johnny ... 904-470-8277 ... 105 G
jlrembert@ewc.edu
REMCHO, Vince ... 541-737-8181 ... 418 F
vincent.remcho@oregonstate.edu
REMELTS, Glenn, A ... 616-526-6299 ... 249 A
remelt@calvin.edu
REMENDER, Kathleen, A ... 810-762-9794 ... 253 C
kremende@kettering.edu
REMIAS, Roberta ... 586-498-4170 ... 254 C
remiasr@macomb.edu
REMIERES-MORIN, Pamela ... 207-755-5224 ... 218 G
premieres@cmcc.edu
REMILLARD, Theresa ... 413-755-4336 ... 241 B
remillard@stcc.edu
REMINGTON, Judith, V ... 847-491-8413 ... 160 E
j-remington@northwestern.edu
REMLEY, Daniel, C ... 570-577-1195 ... 423 E
dan.remley@bucknell.edu
REMLIN, Brittany ... 813-935-5700 ... 116 A
brittanyremlin@remingtoncollege.edu
REMMENGA, Kurt ... 641-784-5190 ... 185 B
remmenga@graceland.edu
REMMERS, Dawn ... 817-272-0777 ... 505 C
dremmers@uta.edu
REMPEL, Valerie ... 559-453-2319 ... 47 K
valerie.rempel@fresno.edu
REMSBURG, Barbara ... 801-587-0851 ... 511 C
bremsburg@housing.utah.edu
REMSBURG, Katherine, M ... 317-738-8135 ... 171 F
kremsburg@franklincollege.edu
REMULLA, Regan ... 323-259-2970 ... 59 I
rremulla@oxy.edu
REN, Linda ... 510-592-9688 ... 59 G
linda@npu.edu
RENACIA, Victorina M, Y ... 671-735-2978 ... 559 G
vrenacia@uguam.uog.edu
RENAGHAN, Dorothy ... 617-287-5450 ... 236 G
dorothy.renaghan@umb.edu
RENAGHAN, Maureen ... 626-857-4147 ... 40 B
mestrada@citruscollege.edu
RENARD, Jessica ... 561-273-6500 ... 118 A
jrenard@southuniversity.edu
RENAUD, Angela ... 401-598-1400 ... 453 E
arenaud@jwu.edu
RENAUD, Robert, E ... 717-245-1072 ... 427 F
renaudr@dickinson.edu
RENAUD, Steve ... 512-444-8082 ... 499 E
info@texastcm.edu
RENAULT, Heather, M ... 518-783-2423 ... 350 I
hrenault@siena.edu
RENBARGER, Bridgette ... 402-399-2646 ... 297 C
brenbarger@csm.edu
RENCIS, Joseph ... 931-372-3172 ... 474 B
jrencis@tntech.edu
RENDEL, Barbara ... 513-244-8124 ... 387 E
barbara.rendel@ccuniversity.edu
RENDER, Philip ... 843-477-2171 ... 458 H
philip.render@hgtc.edu
RENDON, Michael ... 361-825-2414 ... 498 C
michael.rendon@tamucc.edu
RENDON, Mindy, P ... 785-670-1065 ... 197 F
mindy.rendon@washburn.edu
RENDON, Rudolph, L ... 512-448-8445 ... 493 E
rudolphr@stedwards.edu
RENEAR, Allen, H ... 217-333-3280 ... 167 D
renear@illinois.edu
RENEAU, Daniel, D ... 318-257-3785 ... 215 F
reneau@latech.edu
RENER, Christine ... 616-331-3498 ... 251 F
renerc@gvsu.edu
RENEW, Steve ... 760-773-2551 ... 42 A
srenew@collegeofthedesert.edu
RENEY, Richard ... 978-762-4000 ... 240 D
rreney@northshore.edu
RENFREW, Michelle ... 907-474-5337 ... 10 I
mmrenfrew@alaska.edu
RENFRO, Bryan ... 319-296-4427 ... 185 F
bryan.renfro@hawkeyecollege.edu
RENFRO, Chrissy ... 307-778-1310 ... 556 E
crenfro@lccc.wy.edu
RENFRO, Glen, G ... 423-652-6368 ... 470 A
gerenfro@king.edu
RENFRO, Linda ... 541-245-7517 ... 420 B
lrenfro@roguecc.edu
RENFRO, Roy, E ... 903-463-8717 ... 487 C
renfror@grayson.edu
RENGIIL, Yoichi, K ... 671-735-2249 ... 559 G
yoichi@uguam.uog.edu
RENICK, James ... 601-979-2323 ... 274 G
james.c.renick@jsums.edu
RENICK, Timothy, M ... 404-413-2580 ... 131 G
trenick@gsu.edu
RENIFF, William, M ... 440-826-2212 ... 384 K
breniff@bw.edu
RENK, Mike ... 701-671-2217 ... 382 G
mike.renk@ndscs.edu
RENKEN, Tracy ... 202-884-9095 ... 99 H
renkent@trinitydc.edu
RENN, Joanne, M ... 757-455-3303 ... 530 C
jrenn@vwc.edu
RENNA, Matt ... 914-773-3813 ... 345 F
mrenna@pace.edu
RENNELL, Charles ... 518-327-6021 ... 345 H
crennell@paulsmiths.edu
RENNELL, Valerie, D ... 814-641-3141 ... 432 A
rennelv@juniata.edu
RENNER, Cathy ... 812-488-2519 ... 180 E
cr4@evansville.edu
RENNER, Daniel ... 303-446-4854 ... 86 I
renner@dcpa.org
RENNER, Tom, L ... 616-395-7860 ... 252 D
trenner@hope.edu
RENNERT, Mordechai ... 718-438-5476 ... 360 G
RENNIE, Christopher ... 810-989-5642 ... 257 H
ccrennie@sc4.edu
RENNIE, Robert, J ... 904-997-2901 ... 109 F
rrennie@fscj.edu
RENNIGER, Phyllis, R ... 904-632-3327 ... 109 F
prenning@fscj.edu
RENNINGER, Laura ... 304-876-5461 ... 544 C
lrenning@shepherd.edu
RENNIX, Louise ... 843-525-8318 ... 461 E
lrennix@tcl.edu
RENO, Adam ... 301-846-2560 ... 222 G
areno@frederick.edu
RENO, Eric ... 210-486-5484 ... 479 A
ereno@alamo.edu
RENO-MUNRO, Jane ... 843-953-6378 ... 457 B
munroj@cofc.edu
RENOLA, Elaine ... 409-944-1387 ... 486 K
erenola@gc.edu

RENSBERGER, Jeffrey, L ... 713-646-1853.... 494 I
jrensberger@stcl.edu
RENTENBACH, Amy .... 404-364-8303.... 135 E
arentenbach@oglethorpe.edu
RENTMEESTER, Matt, G ..... 920-433-6657.... 546 D
matt.rentmeester@bellincollege.edu
RENTNER, Terry .... 419-372-2079.... 385 E
trentne@bgsu.edu
RENTON, Steve .... 559-730-3902...... 42 D
stever@cos.edu
RENTON, Steve .... 559-737-6216...... 42 D
stever@cos.edu
RENTSCH, Janet, D .... 989-964-7120.... 257 G
jrentsch@svsu.edu
RENTSCHLER, Gina .... 417-865-2811.... 281 G
rentschlerg@evangel.edu
RENTTO, Jessica .... 619-594-6018...... 37 A
jrentto@mail.sdsu.edu
RENTZ, Bruce .... 616-451-3511.... 250 C
brentz@davenport.edu
RENTZ, Gretchen .... 419-586-0336.... 406 D
gretchen.rentz@wright.edu
RENTZ, Linda, T .... 517-586-3010.... 249 D
lrentz@cleary.edu
RENTZ, Shirley, A .... 618-537-6533.... 158 A
sarentz@mckendree.edu
RENVILLE, Allen .... 530-895-2239...... 31 H
renvilleal@butte.edu
RENWICK, Michael, D .... 860-297-2055...... 94 E
michael.renwick@trincoll.edu
RENY, Denise .... 207-741-5568.... 219 A
dreny@smccme.edu
RENY, James .... 207-741-5888.... 219 A
jreny@smccme.edu
RENZ, Amy Button .... 785-532-5050.... 194 D
arenz@ksu.edu
RENZ, Christopher, M .... 510-883-2084...... 45 B
crenz@dspt.edu
RENZI, Paul, F .... 540-458-8596.... 530 D
prenzi@wlu.edu
RENZULLI, Virgil, N .... 480-965-4980...... 11 J
renzulli@asu.edu
REOHR, Janet .... 716-896-0700.... 359 H
reohrj@villa.edu
REOME, Darryl .... 860-343-5897...... 91 G
dreome@mxcc.commnet.edu
REPAC, Richard, A .... 301-687-4331.... 228 C
rrepac@frostburg.edu
REPENNING, Thomas .... 301-934-7630.... 222 C
tomr@csmd.edu
REPETSKI, Michael .... 330-941-1457.... 406 F
michael.repetski@cis.ysu.edu
REPHANN, Lola .... 212-752-1530.... 338 C
lola.rephann@limcollege.edu
REPMAN, Denise .... 504-671-5330.... 210 F
drepma@dcc.edu
REPP, A. Drew .... 260-399-7700.... 181 A
arepp@sf.edu
REPP, Lolita .... 316-684-5335.... 196 G
lolita.repp@sckans.edu
REPP, Philip, C .... 765-285-1034.... 169 G
prepp@bsu.edu
REPPERT, David .... 610-796-8463.... 421 G
david.reppert@alvernia.edu
REQUA, Cynthia .... 253-589-5535.... 532 G
cynthia.requa@cptc.edu
RERKO, Renee, L .... 651-603-6318.... 263 A
rerko@csp.edu
RERRICK, Charlotte .... 212-757-1190.... 322 H
crerrick@funeraleducation.org
RESCH, Richard .... 703-709-5875.... 522 H
RESEBURG, Rhoda .... 503-493-6509.... 415 E
rreseburg@cu-portland.edu
RESETAR, Patricia .... 216-475-7520.... 401 E
RESH-KAMP, Jamie .... 301-387-3742.... 222 H
jamie.reshkamp@garrettcollege.edu
RESIDES, Diane, L .... 443-412-2142.... 223 B
dresides@harford.edu
RESNICK, Coleen .... 508-541-1655.... 233 G
cresnick@dean.edu
RESNICK, Donald .... 631-244-3416.... 332 C
resnickd@dowling.edu
RESNIK, Kim .... 770-394-8300.... 125 A
kresnik@aii.edu
RESSEL, Dawn .... 406-243-5661.... 294 I
dawn.ressel@umontana.edu
RESSLER, Koreen .... 701-854-8001.... 383 D
koreenr@sbci.edu
RESTINE, Nan .... 940-898-2202.... 502 D
lrestine@twu.edu
RESTO-OLIVO, Josephine .. 787-620-2040.... 560 D
jolivo@aupr.edu
RESTO TORRES, Juan .... 787-765-4210.... 561 C
jresto@cempr.edu
RESTUM, John .... 734-207-9581.... 255 F
jrestum@mts.edu
RETCHIN, Sheldon, M .... 804-828-9771.... 526 B
retchin@mcvh-vcu.edu
RETCHLESS, Lindsay .... 814-362-5273.... 449 B
lhr2@pitt.edu
RETELLE, Mary Louise .... 508-849-3242.... 230 C
mretelle@annamaria.edu
RETHANS, Arno .... 530-898-6101...... 34 C
arethans@csuchico.edu
RETIF, Earl .... 504-865-5731.... 215 C
eretif@tulane.edu
RETKA, James .... 218-683-8643.... 268 C
james.retka@northlandcollege.edu
RETTERER, Oscar .... 717-291-4169.... 429 F
oscar.retterer@fandm.edu
RETTIG, James .... 410-293-6900.... 559 B
rettig@usna.edu
RETTIG, Perry, R .... 920-424-1410.... 551 E
rettig@uwosh.edu
RETTLER, Peter, J .... 262-335-5706.... 554 G
prettler@morainepark.edu
RETZAK, Lynn .... 920-693-1282.... 554 C
lynn.retzak@gotoltc.edu
REUSS, Patricia, B .... 406-657-2168.... 295 D
preuss@msubillings.edu
REUTER, Sara .... 541-885-1628.... 418 E
sara.reuter@oit.edu
REUTER, Sarah .... 860-768-5101...... 95 B
reuter@hartford.edu
REUTER, William, D .... 716-851-1700.... 333 A
reuter@ecc.edu
REUTTER, John .... 256-551-3119........ 4 J
john.reutter@drakestate.edu
REVELEY, III, W. Taylor .... 757-221-1693.... 518 A
taylor@wm.edu
REVELL, Leana .... 863-784-7120.... 117 J
leana.revell@southflorida.edu
REVELS, Judith, A .... 910-272-3347.... 373 D
jrevels@robeson.edu
REVELS, Tim, D .... 864-578-8770.... 460 F
trevels@sherman.edu
REVELT, Joseph, E .... 717-871-2390.... 443 D
joseph.revelt@millersville.edu
REVENAUGH, Ken .... 314-392-2356.... 285 J
revenaug@mobap.edu
REVENIS, Anthony .... 301-295-3068.... 558 D
anthony.revenis@usuhs.edu
REVILLA, Elva .... 517-483-1413.... 254 A
revillae@lcc.edu
REX, Barbara .... 805-493-3175...... 33 B
rex@clunet.edu
REX, Lisa Youngkin .... 610-330-5060.... 433 B
rexl@lafayette.edu
REXILIUS-TUTHILL, Reiko . 518-327-6319.... 345 H
rtuthill@paulsmiths.edu
REXROAT, Dee, A .... 319-895-4241.... 183 G
drexroat@cornellcollege.edu
REXRODE, Richard, R .... 660-263-3900.... 279 F
rrr@cccb.edu
REY, Jennifer .... 307-855-2113.... 556 B
jrey@cwc.edu
REY, Michael .... 970-225-4860...... 82 A
michael.rey@collegeamerica.edu
REYER, Otto .... 909-469-5350...... 78 I
oreyer@westernu.edu
REYES, Alicia .... 773-702-8666.... 166 G
areyes1@uchicago.edu
REYES, Angel .... 718-782-2200.... 324 C
areyes@boricuacollege.edu
REYES, April .... 805-966-3888...... 31 D
areyes2@brooks.edu
REYES, Arturo .... 707-864-7000...... 70 A
arturo.reyes@solano.edu
REYES, Carlos .... 916-484-8428...... 56 A
reyesc@arc.losrios.edu
REYES, George, R .... 512-223-8007.... 481 B
rey@austincc.edu
REYES, Ginger .... 805-437-8521...... 34 B
ginger.reyes@csuci.edu
REYES, Jennifer .... 201-447-7456.... 307 E
jreyes@bergen.edu
REYES, Jimmy .... 319-398-5630.... 187 B
jreyes@kirkwood.edu
REYES, Joseph .... 831-755-6950...... 49 E
jreyes@hartnell.edu
REYES, Livette .... 939-292-2481.... 568 C
livette.reyes@upr.edu
REYES, Lolita, C .... 671-735-5611.... 559 E
lolita.reyes@guamcc.edu
REYES, Mario, S .... 208-885-7146.... 144 G
mreyes@uidaho.edu
REYES, Maritza .... 787-850-0000.... 567 E
maritza.reyes@upr.edu
REYES, Monica, B .... 989-964-7489.... 257 G
mbreyes@svsu.edu
REYES, Pedro .... 512-322-3789.... 505 B
preyes@utsystem.edu
REYES, Ray .... 619-660-4206...... 49 B
ray.reyes@gcccd.edu
REYES, Raymond .... 509-313-3667.... 534 F
reyes@gu.gonzaga.edu
REYES, Robert, G .... 214-860-2090.... 485 A
rreyes@dcccd.edu
REYES, Rosana .... 570-740-0336.... 435 C
rreyes@luzerne.edu
REYES, Saul .... 863-297-5282.... 115 C
sreyes@polk.edu
REYES GONZÁLEZ, Edwin 787-250-0000.... 566 G
edwin.reyes4@upr.edu
REYES-ROSELLO, Rosana .. 845-341-4537.... 345 E
rosana.reyesrosello@sunyorange.edu
REYMANN, Linda .... 443-352-4203.... 226 E
lreymann@stevenson.edu
REYNA, Cynthia .... 870-862-8131...... 23 G
creyna@southark.edu
REYNA, Deirdre .... 956-721-5140.... 489 J
dreyna@laredo.edu
REYNA, Dorotea .... 415-575-6135...... 32 G
dreyna@ciis.edu
REYNA, Marilu, A .... 210-784-1101.... 498 E
mreyna@tamusa.tamus.edu
REYNA, Mario .... 956-872-6116.... 494 H
reyna@southtexascollege.edu
REYNA, Oscar, E .... 956-326-2468.... 497 D
oreyna@tamiu.edu
REYNA, Tony .... 713-942-5920.... 505 A
reynat@stthom.edu
REYNA, Yolanda .... 210-486-3333.... 479 C
yreyna@alamo.edu
REYNARD, Betty .... 409-839-2048.... 500 I
bjreynard@lit.edu
REYNDERS, John, C .... 712-274-5100.... 187 G
reynders@morningside.edu
REYNOLDS, Angela .... 479-968-0396...... 20 G
areynolds@atu.edu
REYNOLDS, Anne .... 478-445-5331.... 130 B
anne.reynolds@gcsu.edu
REYNOLDS, Brad .... 706-865-2134.... 138 E
breynolds@truett.edu
REYNOLDS, Carolyn, H ..... 276-523-2400.... 527 D
creynolds@me.vccs.edu
REYNOLDS, Colleen .... 309-268-8188.... 151 I
colleen.reynolds@heartland.edu
REYNOLDS, Curtis .... 352-392-1336.... 120 C
curtrey@ufl.edu
REYNOLDS, Cynthia .... 847-233-7700.... 160 D
careynolds@nc.edu
REYNOLDS, Debra .... 860-738-6309...... 92 B
dreynolds@nwcc.commnet.edu
REYNOLDS, Diane, L .... 804-828-3430.... 526 B
dlreynol@vcu.edu
REYNOLDS, Don .... 334-386-7240........ 3 G
dreynolds2@faulkner.edu
REYNOLDS, Eleanor, L ...... 248-370-3364.... 256 G
reynolds@oakland.edu
REYNOLDS, Elizabeth, P .... 304-293-4245.... 545 A
liz.reynolds@mail.wvu.edu
REYNOLDS, Ellen .... 914-395-2329.... 350 C
REYNOLDS, Gail .... 740-374-8716.... 405 G
greynolds@wscc.edu
REYNOLDS, Gary .... 719-255-3505...... 88 I
greynold@uccs.edu
REYNOLDS, Glenn .... 757-826-1883.... 516 K
REYNOLDS, Holly .... 770-718-5314.... 126 E
hreynolds@brenau.edu
REYNOLDS, Jack .... 706-272-4456.... 128 C
jreynolds@daltonstate.edu
REYNOLDS, James .... 708-456-0300.... 166 F
jreyno11@triton.edu
REYNOLDS, James, M .... 937-382-6661.... 405 I
jim_reynolds@wilmington.edu
REYNOLDS, Jami .... 301-387-3035.... 222 H
jami.reynolds@garrettcollege.edu
REYNOLDS, Jeff .... 970-339-6484...... 81 A
jeff.reynolds@aims.edu
REYNOLDS, John, C .... 626-815-3887...... 30 G
jreynolds@apu.edu
REYNOLDS, John Mark ...... 281-649-3232.... 487 H
jmnreynolds@hbu.edu
REYNOLDS, Judith, L .... 617-573-8302.... 245 B
jreynolds@suffolk.edu
REYNOLDS, Karen .... 802-773-5900.... 513 D
karen.reynolds@csj.edu
REYNOLDS, Kathryn .... 440-525-7729.... 394 F
kreynolds@lakelandcc.edu
REYNOLDS, Kay .... 978-665-3140.... 237 E
kay.reynolds@fitchburgstate.edu
REYNOLDS, Kevin .... 503-725-5087.... 418 G
reynoldk@pdx.edu
REYNOLDS, Kevin .... 503-725-5993.... 418 G
reynoldsk@pdx.edu
REYNOLDS, Kevin, W .... 330-941-2742.... 406 F
kwreynolds@ysu.edu
REYNOLDS, Kimberly .... 785-243-1435.... 192 A
kreynolds@cloud.edu
REYNOLDS, Lana .... 405-382-9218.... 412 B
l.reynolds@sscok.edu
REYNOLDS, Linda .... 859-572-5208.... 205 H
reynoldsl@nku.edu
REYNOLDS, Liz .... 914-594-4229.... 343 F
nymc@bkstr.com
REYNOLDS, Lois, G .... 865-694-6693.... 475 G
lreynolds@pstcc.edu
REYNOLDS, Mary .... 630-753-9087.... 160 D
mreynolds@nc.edu
REYNOLDS, Michael, C ...... 334-844-4367........ 1 F
reynom2@auburn.edu
REYNOLDS, Nancy, W .... 270-686-4244.... 199 B
nancy.reynolds@brescia.edu
REYNOLDS, Norman .... 812-749-1272.... 178 H
nreynolds@oak.edu
REYNOLDS, Patrick, D .... 315-859-4607.... 334 H
preynold@hamilton.edu
REYNOLDS, Randall .... 615-460-6443.... 467 D
randall.reynolds@belmont.edu
REYNOLDS, JR.,
Raymond .... 404-727-5786.... 129 D
raymond.reynolds@emory.edu
REYNOLDS, Richard .... 617-627-3334.... 245 C
dick.reynolds@tufts.edu
REYNOLDS, Robert .... 269-965-3931.... 253 B
reynoldsr@kellogg.edu
REYNOLDS, Scott .... 615-226-3990.... 472 A
sreynolds@nadcedu.com
REYNOLDS, Sean, B .... 847-491-3741.... 160 E
sean.reynolds@northwestern.edu
REYNOLDS, Sharon, P .... 336-633-0234.... 373 A
spreynolds@randolph.edu
REYNOLDS, Stephanie, C .. 315-792-5456.... 341 E
sreynolds@mvcc.edu
REYNOLDS, JR., Steven .... 440-375-7350.... 394 E
sreynolds@lec.edu
REYNOLDS, Thomas, E ...... 303-458-4087...... 87 I
treynold@regis.edu
REYNOLDS, Thomas, L ...... 704-687-7248.... 379 A
tlreynol@uncc.edu
REYNOLDS, Virginia .... 916-691-7359...... 56 B
mcreyng@crc.losrios.edu
REYNOLDS, Wally .... 815-455-8547.... 157 H
wreynold@mchenry.edu
REYNOLDS, William, D ...... 616-395-7748.... 252 D
reynolds@hope.edu
REYNOLDS, William, F ...... 973-596-3004.... 312 C
william.reynolds@njit.edu
REYNOLDS, William, G ..... 202-687-2461...... 98 D
wgr2@georgetown.edu
REYNOLDS-CASPER,
ReGina .... 620-792-9362.... 190 H
casperr@bartonccc.edu
REYNOLDS-SUNDET,
Rosemary .... 903-510-2547.... 503 A
REYNVAAN, Debbie .... 360-538-4101.... 534 G
dreynvaa@ghc.edu
REZAC, Barb .... 605-668-1292.... 464 G
barbara.rezac@mtmc.edu
REZAC, Ken .... 402-461-2503.... 297 A
krezac@cccneb.edu
REZAI, Saeed .... 801-832-2527.... 512 G
srezai@westminstercollege.edu
REZENDES, George .... 860-892-5774...... 92 E
grezendes@trcc.commnet.edu
REZNIK, Inna .... 516-572-7637.... 342 C
inna.reznik@ncc.edu
RHAMES, Ronald .... 803-822-3261.... 459 E
rhamesr@midlandstech.edu
RHEA, Jessica .... 239-590-7016.... 119 B
jrhea@fgcu.edu
RHEA, Kristy, K .... 540-828-5433.... 517 B
thouff@bridgewater.edu
RHEA, Mitchell .... 423-478-6231.... 474 E
mrhea01@clevelandstatecc.edu
RHEA, Teresa, C .... 256-549-8230........ 3 J
trhea@gadsdenstate.edu
RHEAD, Lori .... 608-363-2630.... 546 E
rheadl@beloit.edu
RHEAULT, Wendy .... 847-578-8805.... 163 C
wendy.rheault@rosalindfranklin.edu
RHEAUME, Steve .... 603-535-2266.... 307 A
srheaume@plymouth.edu
RHEE, Anthony .... 334-241-9597........ 8 A
arhee@troy.edu
RHEE, Edmund .... 626-448-0023...... 51 G
RHEIN, John .... 610-430-4163.... 444 A
jrhein@wcupa.edu
RHEINSCHMIDT,
Richard, E .... 319-399-8643.... 183 F
rrheinsc@coe.edu
RHEW, Steven, W .... 336-334-5806.... 379 B
steve_rhew@uncg.edu
RHI-KLEINERT, Susan .... 818-364-7778...... 55 A
rhiks@lamission.edu
RHIM, Choonhee, L .... 323-265-8625...... 54 G
rhimcl@elac.edu
RHIMES, Ilee .... 213-740-7197...... 76 F
irhimes@usc.edu
RHINE, Lisa .... 859-572-6447.... 205 H
rhinel1@nku.edu
RHINE, Marjorie .... 262-472-1268.... 553 A
rhinem@uww.edu
RHINE, Randy .... 308-432-6201.... 299 E
rrhine@csc.edu
RHINEHARDT, Kimrey .... 919-843-0381.... 377 C
kwr@northcarolina.edu
RHINEHART, Leslie, L .... 814-362-7658.... 449 B
llr5@pitt.edu
RHINEHART, Marilyn .... 913-469-8500.... 194 B
marilynr@jccc.edu
RHINESMITH, Betsy .... 630-829-6018.... 145 G
brhinesmith@ben.edu
RHOADES, Dianne .... 252-536-7239.... 371 B
rhoadesd@halifaxcc.edu
RHOADES, IV, Mack, B ...... 713-743-9370.... 503 D
mrhoades@uh.edu
RHOADES, Margot .... 301-447-5215.... 225 A
margot_rhoades@msmary.edu
RHOADES, Richard, G .... 256-824-6343........ 8 G
richard.rhoades@uah.edu
RHOADES, Samuel, T .... 804-257-5811.... 530 A
strhoades@aol.com

RHOADES, Valerie 719-346-9300 86 G valerie.rhoades@morgancc.edu
RHOADES WILLIAMS, Castine 706-821-8311 135 G crhoades@paine.edu
RHOADS, Bill 620-768-2909 193 A billr@fortscott.edu
RHOADS, George 732-235-9700 317 A rhoads@umdnj.edu
RHOADS, Judith, L 270-824-8562 202 G judithl.rhoads@kctcs.edu
RHOADS, Kay, M 803-934-3255 459 G krhoads@morris.edu
RHOADS, Linden 206-543-0905 539 A lrhoads@uw.edu
RHOADS, Michael 802-839-8317 514 B michael.rhoads@neci.edu
RHODA, Christopher 207-859-1124 219 G chris@thomas.edu
RHODARMER, Melanie 828-251-6700 378 D mrhodarm@unca.edu
RHODE, Carolyn 336-506-4128 368 A carolyn.rhode@alamancecc.edu
RHODE, Charles, G 404-894-4114 130 F chuck.rhode@facilities.gatech.edu
RHODEN, Brenda 256-761-6204 7 G brhoden@talladega.edu
RHODEN, Deborah 256-840-4137 7 A drhoden@snead.edu
RHODEN, Joyce 334-727-8011 8 B jrhoden@tuskegee.edu
RHODEN, Laura 336-744-0900 363 B laura@carolina.edu
RHODEN, Richard, R 337-475-5887 215 G rrhoden@mcneese.edu
RHODES, Anthony, P 212-592-2000 350 F arhodes@sva.edu
RHODES, Ashley 713-777-4433 509 C arhodes@westwood.edu
RHODES, Benjamin, J 309-556-3710 153 F brhodes@iwu.edu
RHODES, Carla 706-880-8240 133 B crhodes@lagrange.edu
RHODES, Carol, C 302-739-4060 96 D crhodes1@dtcc.edu
RHODES, Chuck 707-664-4033 37 D chuck.rhodes@sonoma.edu
RHODES, David 318-371-3035 211 C drhodes@ltc.edu
RHODES, David, J 251-578-1313 6 E jrhodes@rstc.edu
RHODES, David, J 212-592-2000 350 F drhodes@sva.edu
RHODES, David, J 740-376-4503 395 G david.rhodes@marietta.edu
RHODES, Dawn, M 317-274-4511 174 D dawnrhod@iupui.edu
RHODES, Edward 703-993-4180 519 E edrhodes@gmu.edu
RHODES, Fred, W 502-272-8150 198 H frhodes@bellarmine.edu
RHODES, Gale 502-852-5727 207 E gale.rhodes@louisville.edu
RHODES, Gary, L 804-523-5200 527 A grhodes@reynolds.edu
RHODES, Jack, W 843-953-3708 456 C jack.rhodes@citadel.edu
RHODES, Jeff 956-665-2209 506 C rhodesjh@utpa.edu
RHODES, Jo Ann 803-754-4100 457 D
RHODES, John 410-225-2201 224 B jrhodes@mica.edu
RHODES, Kaia 916-789-8600 50 B kaia_rhodes@heald.edu
RHODES, Kathleen, S 256-824-6775 8 G kathleen.rhodes@uah.edu
RHODES, Kathy 360-596-5240 538 E krhodes@spscc.ctc.edu
RHODES, Kay 806-742-5170 502 A kay.rhodes@ttu.edu
RHODES, Lawrence 212-799-5000 337 H
RHODES, Lisa, D 404-270-5728 138 B lrhodes@spelman.edu
RHODES, Marlene 314-644-9245 288 I mrhodes@stlcc.edu
RHODES, Michelle 616-331-3234 251 F rhodesmi@gvsu.edu
RHODES, Phil 281-649-3417 487 H prhodes@hbu.edu
RHODES, Randall 301-687-4212 228 C rrhodes@frostburg.edu
RHODES, Rebecca 509-533-7075 533 A rebecca.rhodes@scc.spokane.edu
RHODES, Richard, M 512-223-7598 481 B rrhodes@austincc.edu
RHODES, Robert 325-674-2024 478 I rlr12a@acu.edu
RHODES, Robert 575-492-2640 319 B rrhodes@nmjc.edu
RHODES, Ruth 312-225-6288 167 G rrhodes@vandercook.edu
RHODES, Sandra 513-421-3212 395 A srhodes@swcollege.net
RHODES, Simon 317-274-7211 174 D srhodes@iupui.edu
RHODES, Tammy 479-968-0272 20 G trhodes@atu.edu
RHODES, Tara 570-702-8950 431 L trhodes@johnson.edu
RHODES, Vincent, A 757-446-7070 518 G rhodesva@evms.edu
RHOLES, Julia 662-915-7092 277 D jrholes1@olemiss.edu
RHONE, Henry, G 804-828-1244 526 B hgrhone@vcu.edu
RHOTEN, Darrell 305-386-9900 106 A drhoten@cci.edu
RHOTON, James, M 843-863-7050 456 B jrhoton@csuniv.edu
RHOTON, Patrick 740-392-6868 396 I patrick.rhoton@mvnu.edu
RHUE, Monika 704-371-6741 366 A mrhue@jcsu.edu
RHUEMS, Ken 417-455-5596 280 H krhuems@crowder.edu
RHYNE, Sandra 803-754-4100 457 D
RHYNE, Teresa, L 757-455-3345 530 C trhyne@vwc.edu
RHYNER, Jennifer 262-554-2010 158 E midwestcollegefa@aol.com
RHYNS, Ukeyco 773-602-5016 147 E urhyns@ccc.edu
RHYS WIETECHA, Raji, A 520-626-5502 18 L rhys@email.arizona.edu
RIAL, Scott 847-543-2652 148 B srial@clcillinois.edu
RIAS, Curtis 212-650-7073 326 G curtis@ccny.cuny.edu
RIBAKOW, Larry 410-484-7200 225 C
RIBAR, Robert 304-829-7744 540 H rribar@bethanywv.edu
RIBAR, Tom 724-852-3302 451 B tribar@waynesburg.edu
RIBARICH, Marie 914-654-5320 330 B mribarich@cnr.edu
RIBEAU, Sidney 202-806-2500 98 E sidney.ribeau@howard.edu
RIBERDY, Michelle 413-552-2547 239 F mriberdy@hcc.edu
RIBICH, Fred, D 319-352-8320 189 J fred.ribich@wartburg.edu
RIBNIK, Emily 330-499-9600 393 I eribnik@kent.edu
RIBORDY, J. Clark 785-242-5200 195 I clark.ribordy@ottawa.edu
RIBORDY, J. Clark 785-242-5200 196 A
RIBORDY, J. Clark 785-242-5200 17 B
RIBORDY, J. Clark 785-242-5200 178 I
RIBORDY, J. Clark 785-242-5200 549 H
RICARDI, Jennifer 916-638-1616 50 A jennifer_ricardi@heald.edu
RICATTO, Pascal, J 201-493-3572 307 E pjricatto@bergen.edu
RICCA, Beth 201-684-7455 313 C bricca@ramapo.edu
RICCARDI, JR., Louis, D 415-442-7224 48 F lriccardi@ggu.edu
RICCARDI, Richard 203-392-5232 90 I riccardir1@southernct.edu
RICCI, Jose, L 787-727-7727 568 D jricci@sagrado.edu
RICCI, Jose, L 787-728-1515 568 D jricci@sagrado.edu
RICCIARDI, Julie, E 919-508-2362 380 E jricciardi@peace.edu
RICCIO, JudyAnn 203-365-4899 94 B riccioj@sacredheart.edu
RICCIO, Richard, A 201-692-7050 310 A riccio@fdu.edu
RICE, Adrian 212-824-2220 335 B arice@huc.edu
RICE, Ann 803-584-3446 462 E annerice@mailbox.sc.edu
RICE, Ann, M 916-734-0751 73 I ann.rice@ucdmc.ucdavis.edu
RICE, Camellia, N 910-362-7065 368 H crice@cfcc.edu
RICE, Charles, L 301-295-3013 558 D charles.rice@usuhs.edu
RICE, Cheryl 330-494-6170 402 B crice@starkstate.edu
RICE, Cheryl, A 678-836-6280 139 A crice@westga.edu
RICE, Clementine 810-766-4192 248 C clementine.rice@baker.edu
RICE, Cynthia, E 410-706-3171 227 C crice@umaryland.edu
RICE, Daniel, B 785-628-4260 192 I drice@fhsu.edu
RICE, Debi 253-752-2020 534 E financialaid@faithseminary.edu
RICE, Denise 434-848-6447 524 B drice@saintpauls.edu
RICE, Dennis 925-631-4794 64 F drice@stmarys-ca.edu
RICE, Donnie 256-352-8041 10 A donnie.rice@wallacestate.edu
RICE, Edward 662-246-6442 275 D erice@msdelta.edu
RICE, Elaine, K 610-785-6216 446 A krice@scs.edu
RICE, Eric, L 253-752-2020 534 E deanofstudents@faithseminary.edu
RICE, Fran 605-229-8468 465 B fran.rice@presentation.edu
RICE, Gary 907-786-1544 10 H angar@uaa.alaska.edu
RICE, Gary 323-464-2777 27 I grice@ca.aada.org
RICE, Hannah 314-918-2519 281 F hrice@eden.edu
RICE, Heather 256-228-6001 6 A riceh@nacc.edu
RICE, Howard, T 270-809-2535 205 A hrice@murraystate.edu
RICE, James, P 570-577-3655 423 E rice@bucknell.edu
RICE, James, W 320-222-7474 268 G jim.rice@ridgewater.edu
RICE, Jodie 213-381-3333 53 C jrice@lac.edu
RICE, John 775-753-2260 302 F john.rice@gbcnv.edu
RICE, Jonah 618-252-5400 164 I jonah.rice@sic.edu
RICE, Larry 305-892-5366 112 A larry.rice@jwu.edu
RICE, Larry, D 918-343-7612 411 H lrice@rsu.edu
RICE, Leo 617-349-8598 236 B lrice@lesley.edu
RICE, Linda 757-822-5201 528 G lrice@tcc.edu
RICE, Malcolm 256-824-6347 8 G malcom.rice@uah.edu
RICE, Margaret 718-960-4992 327 C margaret.rice@lehman.cuny.edu
RICE, Margaret, H 361-570-4145 504 A ricem@uhv.edu
RICE, Mark, P 218-477-2062 267 F ricem@mnstate.edu
RICE, Michele 814-262-6447 441 A mrice@pennhighlands.edu
RICE, Nathan 806-743-3238 502 B nathan.rice@ttuhsc.edu
RICE, Patrick 305-809-3228 108 I patrick.rice@fkcc.edu
RICE, Peggy 815-836-5350 156 F ricepe@lewisu.edu
RICE, Peter 201-684-7601 313 C price@ramapo.edu
RICE, Priscilla 215-968-8450 423 F ricep@bucks.edu
RICE, Rachel 207-768-9447 220 F rachel.rice@umpi.edu
RICE, Sabra, L 336-386-3276 374 E rices@surry.edu
RICE, Scott 217-333-0560 167 D serice@uillinois.edu
RICE, Sharyn 978-632-6600 240 C s_rice@mwcc.mass.edu
RICE, Sherwin 910-879-5646 368 D srice@bladencc.edu
RICE, Stephen, C 301-295-3896 558 D stephen.rice@usuhs.edu
RICE, Stuart, A 773-834-2493 166 A sarice@ttic.edu
RICE, Susan, I 336-633-0282 373 A sirice@randolph.edu
RICE, Tammy 949-582-4701 70 F trice@saddleback.edu
RICE, Teresa 337-269-0620 208 D theresar@bluecliffcollege.com
RICE, Thomas 310-206-9345 74 C trice@conet.ucla.edu
RICE, Thomas, M 712-274-5222 187 G rice@morningside.edu
RICE, Tom, W 319-335-0256 182 F tom-rice@uiowa.edu
RICE-CLAYBORN, Kathy 501-450-3134 25 H kathyc@uca.edu
RICE-EVANS, Marla, D 910-962-7055 379 D riceevansm@uncw.edu
RICE MCADAMS, Beverly 864-231-2075 455 C bmcadams@andersonuniversity.edu
RICH, Arthur 402-457-2681 298 G aarich@mccneb.edu
RICH, Jack, W 325-674-2013 478 I richj@acu.edu
RICH, Jeffrey 651-523-2963 264 A jrich02@hamline.edu
RICH, John 620-341-5274 192 G jrich@emporia.edu
RICH, Kathy 781-280-3501 240 B richk@middlesex.mass.edu
RICH, Laura 910-893-4364 362 J richl@campbell.edu
RICH, Martha 315-279-5368 337 K mrich@mail.keuka.edu
RICH, Mary, L 203-576-5756 94 C mrich@stvincentscollege.edu
RICH, Melanie, M 315-464-6548 352 E richm@upstate.edu
RICH, Scott 620-278-4294 196 H srich@sterling.edu
RICH, Scott 620-278-2173 196 H
RICH, Steven 617-236-8800 234 G srich@fisher.edu
RICH, Steven, W 217-581-6616 150 E swrich@eiu.edu
RICH, Tammy 570-484-2128 443 B trich@lhup.edu
RICH, Timothy, A 651-631-5489 270 B tarich@nwc.edu
RICH-COATES, Robin 757-789-1748 526 H rrich-coates@es.vccs.edu
RICHARD, Brett 337-491-2006 212 E brett.richard@sowela.edu
RICHARD, Christine, G 201-291-1111 307 F cgr@berkeleycollege.edu
RICHARD, Christine, G 201-291-1111 323 H cgr@berkeleycollege.edu
RICHARD, David 407-646-2232 116 D dcrichard@rollins.edu
RICHARD, Delores 662-621-4205 273 F drichard@coahomacc.edu
RICHARD, Ellen 415-439-2309 28 C erichard@act-sf.org
RICHARD, Francis, D 904-620-2700 120 D drichard@unf.edu
RICHARD, George 440-826-2325 384 K grichard@bw.edu
RICHARD, Mark 256-840-4110 7 A mrichard@snead.edu
RICHARD, Mark 814-871-7763 429 G richard004@gannon.edu
RICHARD, Robert 337-482-6923 216 D bookstore@louisiana.edu
RICHARD, Roseann 707-654-1175 33 C rrichard@csum.edu
RICHARD, Ryan 318-255-7950 215 F ryan@latechalumni.org
RICHARD, Thomas 603-358-2326 306 G trichard@keene.edu
RICHARD, Thomas, J 207-768-2795 218 J trichard@nmcc.edu
RICHARD, Valerie 704-403-3507 362 I valerie.richard@carolinashealthcare.org
RICHARDELLO, Denise 413-662-5201 238 C denise.richardello@mcla.edu
RICHARDS, Calvin, R 214-860-2232 485 A crichards@dcccd.edu
RICHARDS, Char 262-524-6891 546 H crichard@carrollu.edu
RICHARDS, Charlie 262-646-6528 549 E crichards@nashotah.edu
RICHARDS, Connie, L 229-333-5699 139 C clrichards@valdosta.edu
RICHARDS, David 626-584-5458 48 B richards@fuller.edu
RICHARDS, David, J 517-321-0242 251 G drichards@glcc.edu
RICHARDS, Debra, L 304-424-8201 545 C debbie.richards@mail.wvu.edu
RICHARDS, Doug 573-651-5923 289 K drichards@semo.edu
RICHARDS, Faith 605-455-6029 465 A frichards@olc.edu
RICHARDS, Freddie, L 936-261-5100 496 G flrichards@pvamu.edu
RICHARDS, Gwyn 812-855-2435 173 E grichar@indiana.edu
RICHARDS, Harry, J 603-862-3000 306 C harry.richards@unh.edu
RICHARDS, Heather 703-821-8570 524 J hrichards@stratford.edu
RICHARDS, Heraldo 615-963-5160 474 A hrichards@tnstate.edu
RICHARDS, James, E 314-516-4570 291 D jamesrichards@umsl.edu
RICHARDS, Josh 816-932-6748 289 D jmrichards@saintlukescollege.edu
RICHARDS, Katharine 630-466-7900 168 B krichards@waubonsee.edu
RICHARDS, Kathi, S 937-778-7843 390 G krichards@edisonohio.edu
RICHARDS, Kathy, A 906-227-1237 256 C kathrich@nmu.edu
RICHARDS, Kent 218-733-5969 266 H k.richards@lsc.edu
RICHARDS, Kevin 503-961-6200 418 A krichards@pioneerpacific.edu
RICHARDS, Larry, J 801-524-8101 510 E pres@ldsbc.edu
RICHARDS, Lawrence 610-399-2405 442 A police@cheyney.edu
RICHARDS, Lawrence, D 765-973-8201 173 F laudrich@iue.edu
RICHARDS, Lee, P 602-850-8000 17 G lrichards@phoenixseminary.edu
RICHARDS, Leon 808-734-9565 141 J lr24@hawaii.edu
RICHARDS, Mark 510-642-5872 73 H mark_richards@berkeley.edu

RICHARDS, Maryanne ... 508-830-5039 ... 238 D
mrichards@maritime.edu
RICHARDS, Matthew ... 207-741-5927 ... 219 A
mrichards@smccme.edu
RICHARDS, Melissa ... 414-847-3336 ... 549 B
melissarichards@miad.edu
RICHARDS, Michael, D ... 702-651-5600 ... 302 E
mike.richards@csn.edu
RICHARDS, Randy ... 561-803-2543 ... 114 C
randy_richards@pba.edu
RICHARDS, Renae, L ... 801-524-8144 ... 510 E
renae@ldsbc.edu
RICHARDS, Robin ... 650-306-3234 ... 67 F
richardsr@smccd.edu
RICHARDS, Roger, C ... 850-263-3261 ... 101 L
rcrichards@baptistcollege.edu
RICHARDS, Sandra, K ... 850-263-3261 ... 101 L
skrichards@baptistcollege.edu
RICHARDS, Sandra, K ... 800-328-2660 ... 101 L
skrichards@baptistcollege.edu
RICHARDS, Scott ... 413-236-3015 ... 239 A
srichards@berkshirecc.edu
RICHARDS, Steve ... 320-762-4692 ... 265 F
stever@alextech.edu
RICHARDS, Steve ... 574-237-0774 ... 170 E
jrichards@brownmackie.edu
RICHARDS, Susan ... 307-754-6243 ... 556 G
susan.richards@northwestcollege.edu
RICHARDS, Terry ... 513-745-2984 ... 406 E
richardst1@xavier.edu
RICHARDS, Thomas ... 573-882-2011 ... 291 A
richardstf@umsystem.edu
RICHARDS, Tracey ... 215-619-7330 ... 436 G
trichards@mc3.edu
RICHARDS, William ... 845-341-4701 ... 345 E
president@sunyorange.edu
RICHARDSON, Andrea ... 419-772-2028 ... 398 H
a-richardson.3@onu.edu
RICHARDSON, Becky ... 229-391-2624 ... 134 F
brichardson@moultrietech.edu
RICHARDSON, Bernard, L . 202-806-7280 ... 98 E
brichardson@howard.edu
RICHARDSON, Beverly ... 501-370-5280 ... 23 B
bevrich@philander.edu
RICHARDSON, Beverly, A . 609-894-9311 ... 308 B
brichard@bcc.edu
RICHARDSON, Bonita, L ... 412-237-4413 ... 425 H
brichardson@ccac.edu
RICHARDSON, Brent ... 847-628-2540 ... 154 K
brichardson@judsonu.edu
RICHARDSON, Brittney ... 215-885-2360 ... 435 E
brichardson@manor.edu
RICHARDSON, Bruce ... 520-515-3602 ... 13 E
richardsonb@cochise.edu
RICHARDSON, Camille ... 252-940-6236 ... 368 C
camiller@beaufortccc.edu
RICHARDSON, Carole ... 518-891-2915 ... 344 E
carol.richardson@nccc.edu
RICHARDSON, Charles, J . 518-381-1210 ... 350 E
richarcj@sunysccc.edu
RICHARDSON, Christine ... 315-655-7147 ... 325 H
cwrichardson@cazenovia.edu
RICHARDSON,
Christopher ... 540-261-4234 ... 524 H
christopher.richardson@svu.edu
RICHARDSON, Cinzia ... 973-720-2976 ... 317 D
richardsonc@wpunj.edu
RICHARDSON, Cliff ... 303-556-2413 ... 84 A
cliff.richardson@ccd.edu
RICHARDSON, D. Scott ... 616-331-2215 ... 251 F
richarsc@gvsu.edu
RICHARDSON, Donna ... 214-645-5485 ... 507 E
donna.richardson@utsouthwestern.edu
RICHARDSON, Emily ... 386-822-7518 ... 121 F
ecrichar@stetson.edu
RICHARDSON, Gail ... 918-335-6285 ... 411 B
grichardson@okwu.edu
RICHARDSON, Greer ... 215-951-1806 ... 432 I
richards@lasalle.edu
RICHARDSON, Greg, C ... 606-474-3250 ... 201 D
greg@kcu.edu
RICHARDSON, Guy, L ... 601-923-1650 ... 276 F
grichardson@rts.edu
RICHARDSON, Hannah ... 302-292-6100 ... 99 G
RICHARDSON, Irene ... 513-244-4432 ... 388 E
irene_richardson@mail.msj.edu
RICHARDSON, James ... 509-682-6400 ... 539 E
jrichardson@wvc.edu
RICHARDSON, James, A ... 225-578-6745 ... 212 H
parich@lsu.edu
RICHARDSON, Jennifer ... 518-454-2023 ... 330 C
richardj@strose.edu
RICHARDSON, John ... 706-771-4111 ... 125 H
jrichard@augustatech.edu
RICHARDSON, John ... 303-837-0825 ... 81 F
jrichardson@aii.edu
RICHARDSON, John, F ... 502-852-6293 ... 207 E
john.richardson@louisville.edu
RICHARDSON, CM,
John, T ... 312-362-8711 ... 149 A
jrichard@depaul.edu
RICHARDSON, Julie ... 413-559-5471 ... 235 C
admissions@hampshire.edu
RICHARDSON, Karry, D ... 573-629-3016 ... 282 E
krichardson@hlg.edu
RICHARDSON, Kevin ... 405-789-7661 ... 412 E
kevin.richardson@swcu.edu
RICHARDSON, Kim ... 502-456-6504 ... 206 H
kdrichardson@sullivan.edu
RICHARDSON, Krista ... 419-995-8312 ... 392 K
richardson.k@rhodesstate.edu
RICHARDSON, Linda, C ... 972-860-7105 ... 484 I
lrichardson@dcccd.edu
RICHARDSON, Linda, L ... 518-783-2307 ... 350 I
richardson@siena.edu
RICHARDSON, Luns, C ... 803-934-3211 ... 459 G
lcrichardson@morris.edu
RICHARDSON, Lynne, D ... 540-654-1561 ... 525 D
lrichar2@umw.edu
RICHARDSON, Mark ... 503-494-8220 ... 418 D
somdeansoffice@ohsu.edu
RICHARDSON, Mary ... 229-430-3588 ... 124 B
mrichardson@albanytech.edu
RICHARDSON, Melanie ... 360-438-4367 ... 537 B
mrichardson@stmartin.edu
RICHARDSON, Michael ... 417-667-8181 ... 280 E
mrichardson@cottey.edu
RICHARDSON,
Michael, W ... 406-496-4213 ... 296 A
mrichardson@mtech.edu
RICHARDSON,
Michael, W ... 406-496-4213 ... 296 B
mrichardson@mtech.edu
RICHARDSON, Michele ... 802-860-2756 ... 513 C
richards@champlain.edu
RICHARDSON, Nancy ... 603-645-9631 ... 305 I
n.richardson@snhu.edu
RICHARDSON, Pamela ... 717-396-7833 ... 440 K
prichardson@pcad.edu
RICHARDSON, Perry ... 513-785-3221 ... 396 F
richarp3@muohio.edu
RICHARDSON, Ralph, C ... 785-532-5660 ... 194 D
vetdean@ksu.edu
RICHARDSON, Rebecca, L 205-358-8543 ... 9 B
richardr@montevallo.edu
RICHARDSON, Rick ... 302-736-2461 ... 97 A
workcontrol@wesley.edu
RICHARDSON, Rick ... 254-968-9890 ... 497 A
rrichardson@tarleton.edu
RICHARDSON, Roger ... 607-274-1623 ... 336 G
rrichard@ithaca.edu
RICHARDSON, Rusty ... 615-547-4401 ... 468 B
rrichardson@cumberland.edu
RICHARDSON, Sarah ... 402-280-2703 ... 297 F
sarahrichardson@creighton.edu
RICHARDSON, Saundra ... 910-410-1722 ... 373 B
sarichardson@richmondcc.edu
RICHARDSON, Scott ... 570-674-6247 ... 436 F
srichard@misericordia.edu
RICHARDSON, Silvana, F .. 608-796-3670 ... 553 C
sfrichardson@viterbo.edu
RICHARDSON, Steven ... 562-860-2451 ... 39 A
srichardson@cerritos.edu
RICHARDSON, Terry ... 404-297-9522 ... 131 D
richardt@gptc.edu
RICHARDSON, Terry ... 276-944-6231 ... 519 A
trichard@ehc.edu
RICHARDSON, Thomas, C 662-329-7386 ... 276 A
trichardson@as.muw.edu
RICHARDSON, Thomas, J . 717-872-3162 ... 443 D
tom.richardson@millersville.edu
RICHARDSON, Tracy ... 812-535-5154 ... 179 E
trichard@smwc.edu
RICHARDSON, Valerie ... 256-549-8228 ... 3 J
vrichardson@gadsdenstate.edu
RICHARDSON, Virginia ... 304-327-4402 ... 543 F
jrichardson@bluefieldstate.edu
RICHARDSON, W. Mark ... 510-204-0733 ... 40 A
RICHARDSON, Wayne, M . 201-692-7071 ... 310 A
wrichard@fdu.edu
RICHARDSON, William ... 802-651-5924 ... 513 C
RICHELSON, Linda ... 617-873-0471 ... 233 A
linda.richelson@cambridgecollege.edu
RICHEMOND, Donna, L ... 978-762-4000 ... 240 D
drichemo@northshore.edu
RICHES, Jonathan, S ... 610-292-9852 ... 445 E
jonathan.riches@reseminary.edu
RICHESON, Caren ... 812-749-1225 ... 178 H
cricheso@oak.edu
RICHEY, Anthony ... 334-244-3570 ... 1 G
arichey@aum.edu
RICHEY, D, M ... 859-257-3912 ... 207 D
mrichey@email.uky.edu
RICHEY, James, H ... 321-433-7000 ... 102 D
richeyj@brevardcc.edu
RICHEY, Lizabeth, R ... 580-327-8593 ... 409 C
lrrichey@nwosu.edu
RICHEY, Matthew ... 507-786-3418 ... 271 C
richeym@stolaf.edu
RICHEY, Melody, H ... 901-843-3730 ... 472 K
richey@rhodes.edu
RICHEY, Patrick, E ... 716-888-2480 ... 325 F
richeyp@canisius.edu
RICHEY, Suzanne ... 423-636-7303 ... 477 A
srichey@tusculum.edu
RICHEY, Thomas ... 562-860-2451 ... 39 A
trichey@cerritos.edu
RICHEY, Warren, A ... 901-843-3845 ... 472 K
richeyw@rhodes.edu
RICHIE, Darren, A ... 303-963-3187 ... 82 C
drichie@ccu.edu
RICHIE, Patricia, V ... 561-868-3540 ... 114 D
richiep@palmbeachstate.edu
RICHIEZ, Anthony ... 305-342-5272 ... 107 G
arichiez@careercollege.edu
RICHMAN, Jack, M ... 919-962-6462 ... 378 E
jrichman@email.unc.edu
RICHMAN, John ... 701-671-2221 ... 382 G
john.richman@ndscs.edu
RICHMAN, Melissa, G ... 212-517-0562 ... 340 C
mrichman@mmm.edu
RICHMAN, Robert ... 561-297-3166 ... 119 A
rrichman@fau.edu
RICHMAN, Steve ... 660-359-3948 ... 287 A
srichman@mail.ncmissouri.edu
RICHMOND, Jayne, E ... 401-874-5505 ... 454 E
richmond@uri.edu
RICHMOND, Jennifer ... 304-776-6290 ... 541 B
jrichmond@cci.edu
RICHMOND, Lisa, T ... 630-752-5101 ... 168 H
lisa.richmond@wheaton.edu
RICHMOND, Margaret ... 603-358-2276 ... 306 G
mrichmon@keene.edu
RICHMOND, Nicola ... 520-206-4886 ... 17 H
ncrichmond@pima.edu
RICHMOND, Rollin, C ... 707-826-3311 ... 36 E
rollinr@humboldt.edu
RICHMOND, Steve ... 606-783-5236 ... 204 I
s.richmond@moreheadstate.edu
RICHMOND, Vicki ... 757-825-3519 ... 528 F
richmondvc@tncc.edu
RICHMOND, Vicki ... 757-825-3810 ... 528 F
richmondvc@tncc.edu
RICHTER, Brian ... 785-227-3380 ... 191 B
richterb@bethanylb.edu
RICHTER, Darlene ... 336-725-8344 ... 375 G
richterd@pbc.edu
RICHTER, Deborah ... 563-244-7030 ... 184 F
drichter@eicc.edu
RICHTER, Erich ... 336-725-8344 ... 375 G
richtere@pbc.edu
RICHTER, Mark, H ... 260-422-5561 ... 173 C
mhrichter@indianatech.edu
RICHTER, Sara ... 580-349-1472 ... 410 B
saraj@opsu.edu
RICHTER, Sheila, W ... 814-824-2287 ... 436 C
srichter@mercyhurst.edu
RICHTER, Suzanna, L ... 717-358-5843 ... 429 F
suzanna.richter@fandm.edu
RICHTERS, Stephen, P ... 318-342-1025 ... 216 E
richters@ulm.edu
RICHTMAN, Margaret ... 507-457-1618 ... 271 B
mrichtma@smumn.edu
RICHWALSKY, Michael ... 216-397-3022 ... 392 L
mrichwalsky@jcu.edu
RICIOPPO, Eric ... 631-370-3300 ... 350 D
ericioppo@sbmelville.edu
RICK, Mary, A ... 517-750-1200 ... 258 D
mrick@arbor.edu
RICKARD, Emma Lee ... 803-774-3354 ... 455 G
rickardel@cctech.edu
RICKARD, Jennifer, J ... 610-526-5154 ... 423 D
jrickard@brynmawr.edu
RICKARD, Lawrence, R ... 414-288-7320 ... 548 F
larry.rickard@marquette.edu
RICKARD, Scott ... 406-657-1763 ... 295 D
srickard@msubillings.edu
RICKARD, Vickie ... 615-547-1247 ... 468 B
vrickard@cumberland.edu
RICKARD, Walter ... 518-828-4181 ... 330 E
walter.rickard@sunycgcc.edu
RICKARDS, Laura ... 732-255-0400 ... 312 D
lrickards@ocean.edu
RICKENBAKER, Michael ... 478-445-4467 ... 130 B
michael.rickenbaker@gcsu.edu
RICKER, Curtis ... 912-478-0779 ... 131 E
cricker@georgiasouthern.edu
RICKER, Deborah, D ... 717-815-1510 ... 452 G
dricker@ycp.edu
RICKER, Don ... 419-227-3141 ... 404 D
dricker@unoh.edu
RICKER, Virginia, A ... 803-786-3310 ... 457 C
gricker@columbiasc.edu
RICKERT, Gail Ann ... 717-337-6579 ... 429 I
grickert@gettysburg.edu
RICKETT, Melanie ... 540-863-2807 ... 526 F
mrickett@dslcc.edu
RICKETTS, Carole ... 325-793-3819 ... 490 H
cricketts@mcm.edu
RICKETTS, Lloyd ... 609-771-2186 ... 308 F
ricketts@tcnj.edu
RICKETTS, Mike ... 423-697-4433 ... 474 D
RICKETTS, Traci ... 907-277-1000 ... 10 E
contact@chartercollege.edu
RICKEY, Jeffrey ... 315-229-5226 ... 349 E
jrickey@stlawu.edu
RICKEY, Mary, C ... 718-261-5800 ... 324 D
mrickey@ortopsusa.org
RICKNER, Donald ... 949-582-4968 ... 70 F
drickner@saddleback.edu
RICKS, Suzy ... 208-524-3000 ... 143 G
suzanne.ricks@my.eitc.edu
RICKS, Venus ... 717-867-6165 ... 434 C
ricks@lvc.edu
RICO, Antonio ... 915-779-8031 ... 483 J
ccctrain@aol.com
RICO, Oscar ... 661-654-2394 ... 34 A
orico@csub.edu
RICO-GUTIERREZ, Luis, C 515-294-7427 ... 182 E
lrico@iastate.edu
RICORDATI, Timothy ... 630-617-3089 ... 150 H
timothy.ricordati@elmhurst.edu
RIDD-YOUNG, Kristi ... 866-680-2756 ... 510 F
president@midwifery.edu
RIDDELL, Jeffrey, R ... 206-726-5020 ... 533 D
jriddell@cornish.edu
RIDDELL, Richard ... 919-684-2641 ... 364 C
richard.riddell@duke.edu
RIDDELL, Terrence ... 217-228-5432 ... 161 F
riddete@quincy.edu
RIDDER, Kari ... 402-941-6523 ... 298 I
ridder@midlandu.edu
RIDDER, Steven, G ... 386-323-5025 ... 105 H
ridders@erau.edu
RIDDICK, Vera, E ... 757-683-3689 ... 522 F
vriddick@odu.edu
RIDDLE, Catherine ... 518-262-3593 ... 322 D
riddlec@mail.amc.edu
RIDDLE, Joyce, E ... 304-462-4107 ... 544 A
joyce.riddle@glenville.edu
RIDDLE, Marianne ... 502-863-8020 ... 201 A
marianne_riddle@georgetowncollege.edu
RIDDLE, Mark ... 310-578-1080 ... 28 L
mriddle@antioch.edu
RIDEL, Robert ... 480-557-9112 ... 19 A
robert.ridel@phoenix.edu
RIDENOUR, Nancy, A ... 505-272-6284 ... 321 C
nridenour@salud.unm.edu
RIDENS, Sheryl, L ... 858-499-0202 ... 41 G
sridens@coleman.edu
RIDEOUT, Dane ... 845-938-2022 ... 559 A
8gc@usma.edu
RIDEOUT, Kathy ... 585-275-8902 ... 359 B
kathy_rideout@urmc.rochester.edu
RIDER, Elizabeth, A ... 717-361-1333 ... 428 F
riderea@etown.edu
RIDER, Jeff ... 870-759-4194 ... 26 B
jrider@wbcoll.edu
RIDER, Jonathan ... 703-812-4757 ... 520 J
jrider@leland.edu
RIDER, Robert ... 865-974-2201 ... 477 D
brider@utk.edu
RIDGE, Ruth, A ... 513-861-6400 ... 402 I
ruth.ridge@myunion.edu
RIDGE, Sean ... 865-573-4517 ... 469 L
sridge@johnsonu.edu
RIDGEDELL, Ken, W ... 985-549-2121 ... 216 C
kridgedell@selu.edu
RIDGELL, Reilly, A ... 671-735-5530 ... 559 E
deansoffice@guamcc.edu
RIDGELY, Barbara, S ... 302-739-4622 ... 96 D
bridgely@dtcc.edu
RIDGELY, Glenda ... 864-388-8305 ... 459 A
gridgely@lander.edu
RIDGEWAY, Duff ... 319-368-6468 ... 187 H
dridgeway@mtmercy.edu
RIDGWAY, Dan ... 216-649-8900 ... 394 B
dridgway@kent.edu
RIDGWAY, Susan, M ... 989-837-4219 ... 256 E
ridgway@northwood.edu
RIDINGS, Maureen ... 508-541-1656 ... 233 G
mridings@dean.edu
RIDINGTON, M. Thomas ... 610-341-4377 ... 428 E
tridingt@eastern.edu
RIDLEY, Carolyn, L ... 859-858-3511 ... 198 E
carolyn.ridley@asbury.edu
RIDLEY, Emmett, L ... 804-524-5068 ... 529 H
eridley@vsu.edu
RIDLEY, Scott ... 806-742-1988 ... 502 A
scott.ridley@ttu.edu
RIDLEY, JR., Wadell ... 610-660-1223 ... 446 C
wridley@sju.edu
RIDLON, Walter ... 207-755-5409 ... 218 G
wridlon@cmcc.edu
RIDOUT, Thomas, M ... 563-562-3263 ... 188 B
ridoutt@nicc.edu
RIDPATH, Amy ... 540-374-4300 ... 99 G
RIEBENACK, Kristen, R ... 260-399-7700 ... 181 A
kriebenack@sf.edu
RIECK, Ray ... 217-234-5224 ... 156 B
rrieck@lakeland.cc.il.us
RIEDEL, Eric ... 612-312-2393 ... 272 C
eric.riedel@waldenu.edu
RIEDEL, Eric, R ... 330-569-5240 ... 391 G
riedeler@hiram.edu
RIEDEL, Herbert, H ... 334-222-6591 ... 5 F
hriedel@lbwcc.edu
RIEDEL CARNEY,
Elizabeth ... 651-690-6836 ... 270 L
eacarney@stkate.edu
RIEDER, Richard ... 217-420-6029 ... 158 G
rrieder@millikin.edu
RIEDER, JR., Robert, W ... 256-824-6633 ... 8 G
riederr@uah.edu
RIEDINGER, Jeffrey, M ... 517-355-2352 ... 255 A
ispdean@msu.edu

RIEDINGER, Lee 865-974-8701 477 D
lrieding@utk.edu

RIEDY, Joshua 701-777-4237 381 F
joshua.riedy@und.edu

RIEFKOHL, Jorge 787-780-0070 560 H
jriefkohl@caribbean.edu

RIEGELNEGG, F. Dennis 219-866-6157 179 D
fdr@saintjoe.edu

RIEGER, Mark 302-831-2501 96 I
mrieger@udel.edu

RIEGLE, Stephanie, L 734-936-2254 259 A
sbrugler@umich.edu

RIEHL, Gretchen, K 972-860-7140 484 I
griehl@dcccd.edu

RIEHL, Shelle 360-438-4463 537 B
rshahanriehl@stmartin.edu

RIEHL, Shelle 503-517-1814 421 C
sriehl@westernseminary.edu

RIEHS, Steven 630-515-7702 149 B
sriehs@devry.edu

RIEKEMAN, Guy, F 770-426-2601 133 E
riekeman@life.edu

RIEKER, Michael 856-566-6993 316 I
riekermg@umdnj.edu

RIEL, Paul 904-620-4663 120 D
priel@unf.edu

RIELLO, Heidi, A 413-662-5331 238 C
heidi.riello@mcla.edu

RIEMAN, Barbara, M 716-851-1421 333 B
rieman@ecc.edu

RIENZI, Beth 661-654-6324 34 A
brienzi@csub.edu

RIEPMA, Edward 949-794-9090 71 F
eriepma@stanbridge.edu

RIES, Barry 507-389-1242 267 E
barry.ries@mnsu.edu

RIES, Cheryl 906-487-7317 251 A
cheryl.ries@finlandia.edu

RIES, Heidi, R 937-255-3633 557 C
heidi.ries@afit.edu

RIES, Karen 641-423-2530 186 J
revans@kaplan.edu

RIES, Kenneth 320-629-5195 268 E
riesk@pinetech.edu

RIES, Thomas Karl 651-641-8211 263 A
ries@csp.edu

RIESENBERG, Carol 509-533-7075 533 B
carol.riesenberg@scc.spokane.edu

RIESGO, Andrea 760-366-5285 43 H
ariesgo@cmccd.edu

RIESSLAND, Larry 308-865-8524 300 F
riesslandl@unk.edu

RIESTER, Jon 812-866-7021 172 A
riester@hanover.edu

RIESTER, Leslie 971-722-8288 419 G
lriester@pcc.edu

RIESTRA, Miguel 787-622-8000 115 D
mriestra@pupr.edu

RIESTRA, Miguel, A 787-622-8000 566 E
mriestra@pupr.edu

RIFE, Ron 972-241-3371 484 E
rrife@dallas.edu

RIFFE, Cindy 918-335-6842 411 B
criffe@okwu.edu

RIFFE, Denver 304-487-3845 541 I
driffe@educorp.edu

RIFFE, Keith 509-452-5100 536 F

RIFFEE, William, H 352-273-6309 120 C
riffee@cop.ufl.edu

RIFFEL, Beth 620-947-3121 197 A
bethr@tabor.edu

RIFFEY, Candy 701-323-8623 381 D
criffey@mohs.org

RIFKIN, Benjamin 609-771-2277 308 F
rifkin@tcnj.edu

RIGALI, Mary 203-596-4504 93 G
mrigali@post.edu

RIGBY, Heather 248-476-1122 254 G
hrigby@mispp.edu

RIGBY, Marguerite, S 313-577-2300 260 A
aa3492@wayne.edu

RIGBY, Ullin, K 804-257-5608 530 A
ukrigby@vuu.edu

RIGEL, Bill 863-638-7243 123 D
bill.rigel@warner.edu

RIGG, Jenny 307-778-4326 556 E
jrigg@lccc.wy.edu

RIGGERT, Mark 402-557-7070 296 H
bubookstore@fheg.follett.com

RIGGINS, David, W 828-689-1219 366 I
driggins@mhc.edu

RIGGINS, Shawn 816-364-5399 292 F
shawn.riggins@vatterott-college.edu

RIGGLE, Elise 419-755-4313 397 C
riggle.17@osu.edu

RIGGLE, Elise 419-755-4313 399 C
riggle.17@osu.edu

RIGGLE, Steve, E 818-779-8040 53 B
mclemens@kingsuniversity.edu

RIGGLEMAN, John, S 517-750-1200 258 D
sriggleman@arbor.edu

RIGGLEMAN, Tim 304-434-8000 542 I
torigglem@eastern.wvnet.edu

RIGGS, Allen 435-283-7125 512 C
allen.riggs@snow.edu

RIGGS, Becky 870-862-8131 23 G
briggs@southark.edu

RIGGS, Bonnie 423-697-4465 474 D

RIGGS, Channing 612-624-6868 272 A
riggs035@umn.edu

RIGGS, David 765-677-2808 175 B
david.riggs@indwes.edu

RIGGS, Dennis 502-895-3411 204 F
driggs@lpts.edu

RIGGS, Jesse, A 816-322-0110 279 D
jesse.riggs@calvary.edu

RIGGS, Jim 417-455-5466 280 H
jriggs@crowder.edu

RIGGS, Jim 818-240-1000 48 D
jriggs@glendale.edu

RIGGS, Joyce 270-824-8581 202 G
joyce.riggs@kctcs.edu

RIGGS, M. Peggy 516-299-4206 338 E
peggy.riggs@liu.edu

RIGGS, Robert, F 214-841-3617 485 F
rriggs@dts.edu

RIGHI, Paul, A 617-228-3474 239 C
prighi@bhcc.mass.edu

RIGNEY, Doug 205-934-5493 8 F
drigney@uab.edu

RIGNEY, Jack 330-941-1909 406 F
jprigney@ysu.edu

RIGNEY, Margaret 918-463-2931 407 H
mrigney@connorsstate.edu

RIGNEY, Steve 505-348-3750 464 H

RIGSBEE, Craig 530-895-2521 31 H
rigsbeecr@butte.edu

RIGSBEE, David 217-641-4533 154 I
drigsbee@jwcc.edu

RIGSBY, Dave 503-370-6217 421 D
drigsby@willamette.edu

RIGSBY, Ellen, M 309-467-6311 151 B
eraid@eureka.edu

RIHA, James 618-235-2700 165 D
james.riha@swic.edu

RIHACEK, Robin 708-210-5754 164 H
rrihacek@ssc.edu

RIHL-LEWINSKY, Elizabeth 215-572-2956 422 C
rihll@arcadia.edu

RIIS, Janet 406-447-5423 293 G
jriis@carroll.edu

RIKEL, Randy 903-223-3005 498 F
randy.rikel@tamut.edu

RILEY, Anthony, G 806-894-9611 494 G
triley@southplainscollege.edu

RILEY, Bruce 608-785-8218 551 C
briley@uwlax.edu

RILEY, Carla 320-589-6066 271 G
rileycj@morris.umn.edu

RILEY, Christine 828-251-6500 378 D
criley@unca.edu

RILEY, Doreen, K 216-397-4345 392 L
driley@jcu.edu

RILEY, Edward 617-254-2610 244 B

RILEY, Eileen 412-809-5100 444 G
riley.eileen@pti.edu

RILEY, Elaine 254-526-1106 482 H
elaine.riley@ctcd.edu

RILEY, Francis, D 617-495-1780 235 D
francis_riley@harvard.edu

RILEY, George, F 610-519-7715 450 H
george.riley@villanova.edu

RILEY, Herb 860-231-5311 95 D
hriley@usj.edu

RILEY, Jamie, R 434-395-2394 521 A
rileyjr@longwood.edu

RILEY, Jan 334-222-6591 5 F
lriley@lbwcc.edu

RILEY, Jeannette 508-999-8268 237 A
j1riley@umassd.edu

RILEY, Ken 432-685-4569 491 A
kriley@midland.edu

RILEY, Kimberly 816-604-4523 285 E
kim.riley@mcckc.edu

RILEY, Marsha 406-247-3009 295 D
marsha.riley@msubillings.edu

RILEY, Marsha 406-247-3000 295 F
marsha.riley@msubillings.edu

RILEY, P. Thomas 703-654-1040 525 D
priley@umw.edu

RILEY, Patrick 440-684-6022 405 B
priley@ursuline.edu

RILEY, Robert, A 717-867-6202 434 C
riley@lvc.edu

RILEY, Robert, K 253-535-7119 536 E
rileyrk@plu.edu

RILEY, Sabrina 402-486-2514 300 C
sariley@ucollege.edu

RILEY, Sarah 900-652-6176 39 E
sarah.riley@chaffey.edu

RILEY, Scott, T 218-285-2205 268 F
sriley@rrcc.mnscu.edu

RILEY, Stacy 262-564-3108 554 B
rileys@gtc.edu

RILEY, Susan 513-732-5324 403 E
rileysu@email.uc.edu

RILEY, Tammy 606-478-7200 205 F
tmriley@national-college.edu

RILEY, Teri 330-941-4628 406 F
triley@ysu.edu

RILEY, Terisa 361-593-2410 498 D
terisa.riley@tamuk.edu

RILEY, Terisa, C 361-593-3612 498 D
terisa.riley@tamuk.edu

RILEY, Tisa, R 717-221-1300 430 E
trriley@hacc.edu

RILEY, Vicki 304-214-8857 543 D
vriley@wvncc.edu

RILEY, Wayne, J 615-327-6904 471 C
wjriley@mmc.edu

RILEY HAUSER, Ellen 715-682-4591 555 G
ellen.hauser@witc.edu

RILING, Dean 918-836-6886 412 G
driling@mail.spartan.edu

RILLING, David, S 864-488-4573 459 B
drilling@limestone.edu

RILLORTA, Rhoda 704-355-3243 363 D
rhoda.rillorta@carolinashealthcare.org

RIMA, Kyle 801-832-2008 512 G
krima@westminstercollege.edu

RIMAI, Monica 503-725-5878 418 G
monica.rimai@pdx.edu

RIMANDO-CHAREUNSAP, Rosie 206-934-6763 537 F
rosie.rimando-chareunsap@seattlecolleges.edu

RIMER, Barbara, K 919-966-3215 378 E
brimer@unc.edu

RIMER, Michelle 828-328-7473 366 E
michelle.rimer@lr.edu

RIMIRCH, Bruce 680-488-2471 560 C
brucer@palau.edu

RIMMER, Jessica 405-691-3800 408 H
jrimmer@macu.edu

RIMMER, Kelly, R 717-240-5217 439 D
kog2@psu.edu

RIMPAU, Jim 406-994-2828 295 C
rimpau@montana.edu

RINALDI, Marylyn 858-784-8469 69 B
mrinaldi@scripps.edu

RINARD, Pat 727-341-3064 116 H
rinard.pat@spcollege.edu

RINAS, Craig 972-825-4612 495 F
crinas@sagu.edu

RINCK, Jared 816-604-6740 285 A
jared.rinck@mcckc.edu

RINCON, Frank, L 909-537-5185 36 B
frincon@csusb.edu

RINCON, Mary Beth 219-989-2251 178 K
mbrincon@purduecal.edu

RINCONES, Liza 210-308-8584 489 G

RINCONES-GÓMEZ, Rigoberto 954-201-6500 102 E

RINDE, Carla, M 610-409-3599 450 D
crinde@ursinus.edu

RINDE, Pat, J 701-252-3467 381 C
rinde@jc.edu

RINDERKNECHT, Bethany 319-368-6467 187 H
brinderknecht@mtmercy.edu

RINDERKNECHT, Deborah 814-269-2989 449 D
drinderk@pitt.edu

RINDO, Michael, J 715-836-4742 551 A
rindomj@uwec.edu

RINDO, Michael, J 715-836-4741 551 A
rindomj@uwec.edu

RINE, Veronica 740-755-7600 386 H
vrine@cotc.edu

RINEHART, Gerald, D 612-624-3560 272 A
g-rine@umn.edu

RINEHART, James 334-670-3399 8 A
rinehart@troy.edu

RINEHART, Jenna 319-352-8220 189 J
jenna.rinehart@wartburg.edu

RINEHART, Kenton, W 845-575-3000 340 B
kent.rinehart@marist.edu

RINEHART, Richard, J 570-577-3213 423 E
r.rinehart@bucknell.edu

RINEHART, Shelley 281-998-6150 494 B
shelley.rinehart@sjcd.edu

RINER, William, F 803-313-7104 462 D
wriner@mailbox.sc.edu

RINEY, OSU, Judith, N 270-686-4288 199 B
judith.riney@brescia.edu

RING, David 631-244-3054 332 C
ringd@dowling.edu

RING, Jeff 503-491-7286 417 B
jeff.ring@mhcc.edu

RING, Joshua 828-328-7927 366 E
joshua.ring@lr.edu

RING, Neal 864-242-5100 455 E

RING, Patricia 508-793-3459 233 C
pring@holycross.edu

RING, Ray 212-817-7390 327 B
rring@gc.cuny.edu

RING, Timothy 513-585-2402 387 D
timothy.ring@thechristcollege.edu

RINGA, Melanie 914-961-8313 349 I
finance@svots.edu

RINGENBERG, Ron 574-296-6212 169 C
rringenb@ambs.edu

RINGER-FISHER, Denise 412-261-2647 432 D
dringer-fisher@kaplan.edu

RINGGER, Nick 907-822-3201 10 B
nringger@akbible.edu

RINGHOFF, Paul 404-364-8364 135 E
pringhoff@oglethorpe.edu

RINGKAMP, Patricia, M 570-577-3167 423 E
pat.ringkamp@bucknell.edu

RINGLE, John 217-206-6190 167 C
ringle.john@uis.edu

RINGLE, Martin, D 503-777-7254 420 A
martin.ringle@reed.edu

RINGLE, Suzanne 602-286-8110 15 G
suzanne.ringle@gwmail.maricopa.edu

RINGLEN, Ringlen, P 691-320-2480 559 D
rringlen@comfsm.fm

RINGLER, Neil, H 315-470-6606 355 A
neilringler@esf.edu

RINGO, Teresa, T 936-294-1061 501 D
reg_tat@shsu.edu

RINGOLD, Debra 503-370-6440 421 D
dringold@willamette.edu

RINGOLD, Gordon 831-459-4229 75 C
ringold@ucsc.edu

RINGSTAD, Ann 907-474-5922 10 I
atringstad@alaska.edu

RINGWOOD, Karen, K 203-597-9036 94 F
klozada@bridgeport.edu

RINI, Anthony 617-373-4774 243 F

RINI, Lisa 212-686-9040 360 F
lrini@woodtobecoburn.edu

RINK, Darrel, C 479-788-7390 24 D
chris.rink@uafs.edu

RINKE, Patricia, A 515-263-2912 185 C
prinke@grandview.edu

RINKENBAUGH, Bill 316-322-3297 191 G
brinkenb@butlercc.edu

RINKER, Jonathan, A 304-877-6428 540 G
jon.rinker@abc.edu

RINKER, Linda 616-554-5183 250 C
lrinker@davenport.edu

RINN, Martha 830-372-8110 499 F
mrinn@tlu.edu

RINNE, Henry 479-788-7431 24 D
henry.rinne@uafs.edu

RINNE, Jason 660-831-4088 286 F
rinnej@moval.edu

RINNERT, Jennifer 904-819-6376 107 C
jrinnert@flagler.edu

RIO, Deborah 661-362-3298 41 I
debbie.rio@canyons.edu

RIORDAN, Catherine, A 360-650-3480 539 F
catherine.riordan@wwu.edu

RIORDAN, Charles 302-831-1073 96 I
riordan@udel.edu

RIORDAN, Christine 303-871-4324 89 A
christine.riordan@du.edu

RIORDAN, Jean 773-298-3135 163 I
riordan@sxu.edu

RIORDAN, Jennifer 717-564-4112 432 B
jriordan@kaplan.edu

RIORDAN, Kevin 708-596-2000 164 H
kriordan@ssc.edu

RIORDAN, Marsha 641-673-1045 190 C
riordanm@wmpenn.edu

RIORDAN, Phil 561-237-7749 113 D
priordan@lynn.edu

RIORDAN, Rob 619-398-4902 50 G

RIOS, Adlin 787-728-1545 568 D
adlinrios@sagrado.edu

RIOS, Alfonso 323-357-6209 54 G
riosa@elac.edu

RIOS, Charlene 509-793-2020 531 I
charlener@bigbend.edu

RIOS, Ed 718-982-2460 327 A
eduardo.rios@csi.cuny.edu

RIOS, Eddie 801-274-3280 512 F
erios@wgu.edu

RIOS, Francisca 956-665-2551 506 C
frios@utpa.edu

RIOS, Francisco 360-650-3319 539 F
francisco.rios@wwu.edu

RIOS, Ilka, C 787-758-2525 567 G
ilka.rios@upr.edu

RIOS, Irene 203-777-7100 90 C
irios@albertus.edu

RIOS, Juan Carlos 305-223-4561 116 E

RIOS, Laura 787-279-1912 563 D
lriosr@bayamon.inter.edu

RIOS, Lourdes 787-884-6000 562 G
lrios@icprjc.edu

RIOS, Thomas, R 262-472-1172 553 A
riost@uww.edu

RIOS, William 787-738-2161 567 D
william.rios3@upr.edu

RIOS, Zilka 787-798-4050 566 C
zilka.rios@uccaribe.edu

RIOS-HUSAIN, Silvia Patricia 704-922-6217 370 G
husain.silvia@gaston.edu

RIOS-KRAVITZ, Rhonda 916-558-2254 56 D
rioskrr@scc.losrios.edu

RIOTTO, Karen, M 585-395-5484 352 F
kriotto@brockport.edu

RIPEPI, Maria ... 412-536-1527 ... 432 H maria.ripepi@laroche.edu
RIPICH, Danielle ... 207-602-2306 ... 221 A dripich@une.edu
RIPLEY, Anneliese ... 406-683-7537 ... 294 J a_ripley@umwestern.edu
RIPLEY, Dave ... 701-477-7862 ... 383 F dripley@tm.edu
RIPLEY, Melissa ... 423-636-7300 ... 477 A mripley@tusculum.edu
RIPLEY, Ronald, L ... 414-288-1656 ... 548 F ronald.ripley@marquette.edu
RIPOSA, Gerry ... 562-985-5381 ... 35 C griposa@csulb.edu
RIPPEN, Kelly ... 308-345-8107 ... 298 H rippenk@mpcc.edu
RIPPERDA, Jan ... 618-545-3041 ... 155 B jripperda@kaskaskia.edu
RIPPETOE, Mark, L ... 530-226-4833 ... 69 H mrippetoe@simpsonu.edu
RIPPEY, Sharon, T ... 315-859-4672 ... 334 H srippey@hamilton.edu
RIPPINGER, Timothy ... 414-288-4771 ... 548 F timothy.rippinger@marquette.edu
RIPPKE, Greg ... 419-473-2700 ... 389 C grippke@daviscollege.edu
RIPPLE, David ... 313-577-2275 ... 260 A bb2607@wayne.edu
RIPPLE, Scott ... 765-658-4555 ... 171 B sripple@depauw.edu
RIPTON, Elizabeth, R ... 585-292-2243 ... 341 H eripton@monroecc.edu
RIQUEZ, Elizabeth ... 973-720-2202 ... 317 D riqueze@wpunj.edu
RISACHER, Sheila ... 507-537-6221 ... 269 E sheila.risacher@smsu.edu
RISBUD, Subhash, H ... 530-752-6659 ... 73 I shrisbud@ucdavis.edu
RISCHBIETER, Natalie ... 678-359-5073 ... 132 A natalier@gdn.edu
RISELING, Susan ... 608-262-4527 ... 550 J riseling@wisc.edu
RISEMAN, Stacy ... 401-454-6340 ... 454 B sriseman@risd.edu
RISING, Evelyn ... 575-492-2119 ... 321 H erising@usw.edu
RISNER, Sam ... 606-337-1457 ... 199 H srisner@ccbbc.edu
RISSE, Duane ... 303-352-3356 ... 84 A duane.risse@ccd.edu
RISSER, Barbara, G ... 585-785-1201 ... 334 A risserbg@flcc.edu
RISSLER, Jennifer ... 415-749-4586 ... 65 I jrissler@sfai.edu
RISSMEYER, Patricia ... 617-735-9722 ... 234 C rissmeye@emmanuel.edu
RISTAINO, John ... 401-341-2159 ... 454 D john.ristaino@salve.edu
RISTE, Brian ... 920-832-7694 ... 548 B brian.riste@lawrence.edu
RISTINE, Jennifer ... 401-949-2820 ... 453 F jristine@inteducators.org
RITACCO, Judith ... 508-531-1244 ... 237 D judith.ritacco@bridgew.edu
RITACCO, Kevin ... 508-854-4200 ... 240 F kevinr@qcc.mass.edu
RITCH, Donna ... 920-465-2274 ... 551 B ritchd@uwgb.edu
RITCH, Wendy, A ... 973-972-0645 ... 316 H ritchwe@umdnj.edu
RITCHEY, Fred, L ... 903-233-4210 ... 490 A fredritchey@letu.edu
RITCHEY, Mary, K ... 706-886-6831 ... 138 D mritchey@tfc.edu
RITCHEY, William, V ... 757-594-7047 ... 517 L bill.ritchey@cnu.edu
RITCHIE, Anne ... 505-473-6655 ... 320 F anne.ritchie@santafeuniversity.edu
RITCHIE, David ... 765-998-5397 ... 180 B dvritchie@taylor.edu
RITCHIE, Derek ... 610-341-1955 ... 428 E dritchie@eastern.edu
RITCHIE, Gloria ... 412-809-5100 ... 444 G ritchie.gloria@pti.edu
RITCHIE, Jay ... 707-638-5802 ... 73 A jay.ritchie@tu.edu
RITENBAUGH, Robert, C ... 334-844-4190 ... 1 F ritenrc@auburn.edu
RITER, Jayme, S ... 716-878-3041 ... 353 A riterjs@buffalostate.edu
RITER, Steve ... 915-747-7890 ... 506 B sriter@utep.edu
RITO, Edward ... 513-671-1920 ... 385 A
RITSCHDORFF, John ... 845-575-3000 ... 340 B john.ritschdorff@marist.edu
RITTENBERG, Stephen, A ... 212-854-2254 ... 330 F sar3@columbia.edu
RITTENBERGER, Alexis ... 724-503-1001 ... 451 A arittenberger@washjeff.edu
RITTER, Gretchen ... 512-232-3312 ... 505 D ritterg@mail.utexas.edu
RITTER, James ... 330-675-8935 ... 393 J jritter@kent.edu
RITTER, Joe ... 618-374-5176 ... 161 E joe.ritter@principia.edu
RITTER, Karen, R ... 336-633-0206 ... 373 A krritter@randolph.edu
RITTER, Kathy ... 904-620-2730 ... 120 D k.ritter@unf.edu
RITTER, Mark ... 864-503-5939 ... 463 B mritter@uscupstate.edu
RITTER, Melvin ... 910-695-3811 ... 373 H ritterm@sandhills.edu
RITTER, Michael ... 618-664-7122 ... 151 F michael.ritter@greenville.edu
RITTER, Monica ... 412-365-1280 ... 425 C mritter@chatham.edu
RITTER, Nancy ... 575-527-7650 ... 319 G naritter@nmsu.edu
RITTERBROWN, Michael ... 818-240-1000 ... 48 D michaelr@glendale.edu
RITTLE, Dennis ... 785-825-5422 ... 191 E drittle@brownmackie.edu
RITTLE, Dennis ... 870-368-7371 ... 23 A drittle@ozarka.edu
RITTLING, Mary, E ... 336-249-8186 ... 370 B merittli@davidsonccc.edu
RITTS, Bonnie, B ... 585-785-1278 ... 334 A rittsbb@flcc.edu
RITZ, Cathy ... 661-362-3639 ... 41 I cathy.ritz@canyons.edu
RITZ, Darlene ... 619-275-4700 ... 46 K darlene@fashioncareerscollege.com
RITZ, Robert, L ... 434-592-4800 ... 520 K rlritz@liberty.edu
RITZ, Steven ... 831-459-2635 ... 75 C sritz@scipp.ucsc.edu
RITZE, Nancy ... 718-289-5156 ... 326 E nancy.ritze@bcc.cuny.edu
RITZMAN, Elizabeth ... 708-524-6520 ... 150 C eritzman@dom.edu
RITZMAN, Richard ... 901-678-2832 ... 474 C rritzman@memphis.edu
RIUTTA, Janice ... 262-564-3072 ... 554 B riuttaj@gtc.edu
RIVALEAU, Susan, A ... 843-953-4973 ... 457 B rivaleaus@cofc.edu
RIVARD, Timothy ... 781-239-2631 ... 239 G trivard@massbay.edu
RIVAS, Jess ... 626-396-2263 ... 29 I jesus.rivas@artcenter.edu
RIVELAND, Bruce ... 360-475-7500 ... 536 D briveland@olympic.edu
RIVERA, Abigail ... 787-863-2390 ... 563 E abigail.rivera@fajardo.inter.edu
RIVERA, Al ... 520-383-8401 ... 18 I arivera@tocc.cc.az.us
RIVERA, Alba ... 787-743-7979 ... 565 H albrivera@suagm.edu
RIVERA, Angel ... 787-765-3560 ... 562 A arivera@edpcollege.edu
RIVERA, Angel ... 787-738-2161 ... 567 D angel.rivera42@upr.edu
RIVERA, Angel ... 718-368-5026 ... 328 A arivera@kbcc.cuny.edu
RIVERA, Angel, A ... 787-720-4476 ... 566 D presidente@colmizpa.edu
RIVERA, Annelis ... 787-480-2452 ... 561 E armarques@sanjuancapital.com
RIVERA, Arcilia ... 787-864-2222 ... 563 F ariverag@inter.edu
RIVERA, Beatriz ... 787-250-1912 ... 563 G brivera@metro.inter.edu
RIVERA, Beatriz ... 787-751-0500 ... 568 B beatriz.rivera6@upr.edu
RIVERA, Carlos, E ... 787-725-8120 ... 562 C planificacion@eap.edu
RIVERA, Carmen ... 787-250-1912 ... 563 G crivera@metro.inter.edu
RIVERA, Carmen ... 773-878-3606 ... 163 F crivera@staugustine.edu
RIVERA, Carmen, G ... 787-864-2222 ... 563 F cgrivera@inter.edu
RIVERA, Carmen, J ... 787-743-7979 ... 565 H ut_crivera@suagm.edu
RIVERA, Carmen, M ... 787-258-1501 ... 561 F crivera@columbiaco.edu
RIVERA, Caroline ... 757-822-1191 ... 528 G crivera@tcc.edu
RIVERA, Daliana ... 787-780-5134 ... 564 H drivera@nuc.edu
RIVERA, Damaris ... 312-935-4144 ... 162 G drivera@robertmorris.edu
RIVERA, Diana ... 787-284-1912 ... 564 A drivera@ponce.inter.edu
RIVERA, Dianne ... 787-864-2222 ... 563 F drivera@inter.edu
RIVERA, Edfel ... 787-738-2161 ... 567 D edfel.rivera@upr.edu
RIVERA, Edith ... 212-817-7410 ... 327 B erivera@gc.cuny.edu
RIVERA, Edwin ... 787-279-1912 ... 563 D edrivera@bayamon.inter.edu
RIVERA, Eileen ... 787-864-2222 ... 563 F eirivera@inter.edu
RIVERA, Elaine ... 956-665-5372 ... 506 C erivera11@utpa.edu
RIVERA, Eric ... 619-594-5211 ... 37 A erivera@mail.sdsu.edu
RIVERA, Eric ... 215-702-4241 ... 444 B erivera@pbu.edu
RIVERA, Francisco ... 787-765-1915 ... 564 D frivera@inter.edu
RIVERA, Gerardo ... 787-841-0003 ... 564 A grivera@ponce.inter.edu
RIVERA, Gilbert ... 505-454-3311 ... 318 J vpacademicaffairs@nmhu.edu
RIVERA, Gilbert ... 973-684-6107 ... 312 E grivera@pccc.edu
RIVERA, Hortensia ... 760-921-5502 ... 61 C hdeleon@paloverde.edu
RIVERA, Janely ... 312-935-2004 ... 162 G jrivera@robertmorris.edu
RIVERA, Janet ... 787-264-1912 ... 564 B janriver@sg.inter.edu
RIVERA, Janice ... 787-789-4251 ... 560 F jrivera@atlanticcollege.edu
RIVERA, Jason ... 909-607-7283 ... 62 H jason_rivera@pitzer.edu
RIVERA, Jessica ... 305-222-2812 ... 107 G jrivera@careercollege.edu
RIVERA, Jesus, M ... 787-258-1501 ... 561 F jrivera@columbiaco.edu
RIVERA, Johana ... 718-270-6016 ... 328 C jrivera@mec.cuny.edu
RIVERA, Jose, A ... 787-751-1912 ... 564 C jorivera@inter.edu
RIVERA, Jose, A ... 787-264-1912 ... 564 B joseanibalrivera@sg.inter.edu
RIVERA, Jose, J ... 787-727-7033 ... 568 D jjrivera@sagrado.edu
RIVERA, Juan, L ... 787-620-2040 ... 560 D jrivera@aupr.edu
RIVERA, Julio, C ... 262-551-5850 ... 546 I jrivera@carthage.edu
RIVERA, Laura ... 832-813-6564 ... 490 E laura.rivera@lonestar.edu
RIVERA, Lisette ... 787-250-1912 ... 563 G lriverao@metro.inter.edu
RIVERA, Liza ... 347-964-8600 ... 324 C lrivera@boricuacollege.edu
RIVERA, Luis ... 787-765-3560 ... 562 A lrivera@edpcollege.edu
RIVERA, Luis, R ... 773-947-6306 ... 157 G lrivera@mccormick.edu
RIVERA, Marcelino ... 787-743-7979 ... 565 H ut_mrivera@suagm.edu
RIVERA, Margarita ... 787-765-4210 ... 561 C
RIVERA, Mari Lillian ... 787-763-6700 ... 562 D registro@se-pr.edu
RIVERA, Maria de los, M ... 787-753-6000 ... 562 G mrivera@icprjc.edu
RIVERA, Maria de Lourdes 787-751-1912 ... 564 C maridela@inter.edu
RIVERA, Mary Ann ... 757-388-2900 ... 524 D
RIVERA, Maximina ... 908-737-6800 ... 311 A mrivera@kean.edu
RIVERA, Mayra ... 787-765-3560 ... 562 A mrivera@edpcollege.edu
RIVERA, Mayra ... 708-456-0300 ... 166 F
RIVERA, Michael ... 309-796-5049 ... 145 H riveram@bhc.edu
RIVERA, Milagros ... 787-621-2835 ... 560 D mrivera@aupr.edu
RIVERA, Milagros, M ... 787-786-3030 ... 560 G mrivera@ucb.edu.pr
RIVERA, Mildred ... 787-798-3001 ... 566 C mildred.rivera@uccaribe.edu
RIVERA, Nelson ... 787-758-2525 ... 567 G nelson.rivera13@upr.edu
RIVERA, Nelson ... 215-248-6376 ... 435 B nrivera@ltsp.edu
RIVERA, Olga ... 787-753-6335 ... 562 G orivera@icprjc.edu
RIVERA, Ramon ... 787-480-2421 ... 561 E rrivera@sanjuancapital.com
RIVERA, Rosa, M ... 856-225-6836 ... 314 D rosarive@camden.rutgers.edu
RIVERA, Rosita, A ... 787-764-0000 ... 568 B rosa.rivera.rivera@upr.edu
RIVERA, Ruben, L ... 207-859-4127 ... 217 G rlrivera@colby.edu
RIVERA, Sandra ... 787-480-2396 ... 561 E srivera@sanjuancapital.com
RIVERA, Schvalla ... 812-888-4204 ... 181 D srivera@vinu.edu
RIVERA, Serafin ... 787-279-1912 ... 563 D sriverat@bayamon.inter.edu
RIVERA, Sergio ... 210-486-3888 ... 479 C srivera@alamo.edu
RIVERA, Teresita ... 787-882-2065 ... 566 A admisiones@unitecpr.net
RIVERA, Tina ... 916-789-8600 ... 50 B tina_rivera@heald.edu
RIVERA, Tresban ... 970-225-4860 ... 82 A tresban.rivera@collegeamerica.edu
RIVERA, Victor ... 787-480-2396 ... 561 E vrivera@sanjuancapital.com
RIVERA, Victoria ... 806-743-4570 ... 502 B victoria.rivera@ttuhsc.edu
RIVERA, Virna ... 787-786-3030 ... 560 G virivera@ucb.edu.pr
RIVERA, Wayne ... 719-846-5592 ... 88 F wayne.rivera@trinidadstate.edu
RIVERA, Yolanda ... 787-758-2525 ... 567 G yolanda.rivera3@rcm.upr.edu
RIVERA BAEZ, Angel, F ... 787-896-2252 ... 562 B afrivera@edpcollege.edu
RIVERA CRESPO, Luz, E ... 787-896-2252 ... 562 B lrivera2@edpcollege.edu
RIVERA DELGADO, Melba 787-896-2137 ... 562 B mgrivera@edpcollege.edu
RIVERA-DREYER, Ivette ... 860-512-3382 ... 91 F irivera-dreyer@mcc.commnet.edu
RIVERA GONZALEZ, Sonia ... 787-890-2681 ... 566 H sonia.rivera13@upr.edu
RIVERA MOLINA, Veronica ... 787-896-2252 ... 562 B vrivera@edpcollege.edu
RIVERA MORALES, Lizbeth, J ... 787-832-6772 ... 567 F asesorialegal@uprm.edu
RIVERA NEGRON, Adrian, O ... 787-725-8120 ... 562 C actividadesculturales@eap.edu
RIVERA SANTIAGO, Blanca ... 787-744-1060 ... 564 F brivera@mechtech.edu
RIVERA SANTOS, Jorge ... 787-265-3878 ... 567 F rector.uprm@upr.edu
RIVERA-SANTOS, Jorge ... 787-832-4040 ... 566 G rector.uprm@upr.edu
RIVERA-TORRES, Carmen, A ... 787-993-8872 ... 567 B carmen.rivera35@upr.edu
RIVERA-VERA, Nydia, N ... 787-896-2252 ... 562 B nrivera@edpcollege.edu
RIVERMAN, Becky ... 425-235-2352 ... 537 A briverman@rtc.edu
RIVERO, Brenda ... 601-928-6380 ... 275 E brenda.rivero@mgccc.edu
RIVERO, Dania ... 305-348-3875 ... 119 C dania.rivero@fiu.edu
RIVERO, David, A ... 305-284-1650 ... 122 I darivero@miami.edu
RIVERO, Estela ... 518-442-5800 ... 351 E erivero@uamail.albany.edu
RIVERO, Orlando ... 305-593-1223 ... 102 H orivero@albizu.edu
RIVERO, William, T ... 601-318-6122 ... 278 C ovid@wmcarey.edu
RIVERO, Yaidany ... 305-474-6965 ... 117 A yrivero@stu.edu
RIVERS, Andrew ... 202-806-2500 ... 98 E andrew.rivers@howard.edu
RIVERS, Denise, Z ... 716-286-8761 ... 344 D dzr@niagara.edu
RIVERS, John, D ... 330-471-8133 ... 395 F jrivers@malone.edu
RIVERS, Larry, E ... 478-825-6315 ... 129 F riversl@fvsu.edu
RIVERS, Nancy, A ... 434-982-2662 ... 525 F nan9k@virginia.edu
RIVERS, Verna ... 340-693-1087 ... 568 E vrivers@live.uvi.edu
RIVES, Dan ... 812-855-2239 ... 173 E drives@indiana.edu
RIVES, Dan ... 812-855-3027 ... 173 D drives@indiana.edu
RIVES, Joseph ... 309-762-8090 ... 168 C j-rives@wiu.edu
RIVET, Elizabeth ... 413-565-1000 ... 230 G erivete@baypath.edu
RIVETT, Donna ... 772-462-7656 ... 111 B drivett@irsc.edu
RIXEN, Mary ... 580-371-2371 ... 408 I mrixen@mscok.edu
RIZA, Robert ... 254-659-7791 ... 487 G rriza@hillcollege.edu
RIZK, Michelle ... 907-450-8191 ... 10 G michelle.rizk@alaska.edu
RIZOR, Brenda ... 419-995-8431 ... 392 K rizor.b@rhodesstate.edu
RIZVI, S. Abu ... 802-656-9102 ... 514 H abu.rizvi@uvm.edu
RIZVI, Syed ... 714-628-4967 ... 63 G rizvi_syed@sccollege.edu
RIZVI, Teresa, J ... 937-229-3241 ... 404 A trizvi1@udayton.edu
RIZZA, James ... 508-767-7419 ... 230 D j.rizza@assumption.edu
RIZZA, Robert, A ... 507-538-5027 ... 262 B rizza.robert@mayo.edu
RIZZI, Gino ... 518-828-4181 ... 330 E rizzi@sunycgcc.edu
RIZZO, Bryan ... 734-432-5604 ... 254 D brizzo@madonna.edu
RIZZO, Christine ... 315-786-2291 ... 337 F crizzo@sunyjefferson.edu
RIZZO, Christopher ... 724-773-3957 ... 439 A clr4@psu.edu
RIZZO, Frank ... 703-284-1650 ... 521 D frank.rizzo@marymount.edu

RIZZO, Matt .... 802-831-1206 .... 515 B
mrizzo@vermontlaw.edu
RIZZO, Pete .... 402-844-7151 .... 299 I
pete@northeast.edu
RIZZUTO, James, T .... 719-384-6821 .... 87 A
jim.rizzuto@ojc.edu
ROA, Irma .... 323-464-2777 .... 27 I
iroa@ca.aada.org
ROACH, Bill .... 864-587-4396 .... 461 D
roachb@smcsc.edu
ROACH, Colleen .... 617-228-2177 .... 239 C
croach@bhcc.mass.edu
ROACH, David .... 315-228-7611 .... 329 G
droach@colgate.edu
ROACH, J. Terrance .... 301-405-4942 .... 227 B
troach@umd.edu
ROACH, Jack .... 843-661-8121 .... 458 B
jack.roach@fdtc.edu
ROACH, Kenneth .... 704-334-6882 .... 367 H
kroach@nlts.edu
ROACH, Virginia .... 212-875-4668 .... 323 C
vroach@bankstreet.edu
ROACHE, Marjorie .... 708-596-2000 .... 164 H
mroache@ssc.edu
ROADCUP, David .... 513-244-8184 .... 387 E
david.roadcup@ccuniversity.edu
ROADES, Nicole .... 937-393-3431 .... 402 A
nroades@sscc.edu
ROADRUCK, Nancy, L .... 330-972-7425 .... 403 B
nancy5@uakron.edu
ROAN, Kimberly .... 763-576-4813 .... 265 H
kroan@anokatech.edu
ROAN, Lisa, A .... 607-733-7177 .... 332 H
lroan@ebi-college.com
ROAN, Tina .... 440-684-6085 .... 405 B
troan@ursuline.edu
ROANE, Kevin .... 732-571-3452 .... 311 E
kroane@monmouth.edu
ROARK, Deborah .... 817-531-4498 .... 502 C
droark@txwes.edu
ROARK, Donna .... 606-487-3128 .... 202 C
donna.roark@kctcs.edu
ROARK, Harold .... 503-352-3060 .... 419 E
roark@pacificu.edu
ROARK, Ian .... 432-335-6685 .... 492 A
iroark@odessa.edu
ROARK, Jack .... 406-756-3872 .... 294 C
jroark@fvcc.edu
ROARK, John, A .... 270-809-3536 .... 205 A
jroark3@murraystate.edu
ROARK, Tony .... 208-426-2030 .... 142 I
troark@boisestate.edu
ROATCH, Gay .... 910-576-6222 .... 372 D
roatchg@montgomery.edu
ROBACK, Joseph, M .... 570-941-4385 .... 450 C
joseph.roback@scranton.edu
ROBAIN LACAILLE,
Jemma .... 718-482-5077 .... 328 B
jlacaille@lagcc.cuny.edu
ROBAR, Stephen, F .... 814-362-7586 .... 449 B
robar@pitt.edu
ROBARDS, Paul .... 478-934-3149 .... 134 B
probards@mgc.edu
ROBB, Annette, D .... 937-255-6800 .... 557 C
annette.robb@afit.edu
ROBB, James .... 517-371-5140 .... 258 F
robbj@cooley.edu
ROBB, Jim .... 870-743-3000 .... 22 G
jrobb@northark.edu
ROBB, Mercy .... 630-829-6095 .... 145 G
mrobb@ben.edu
ROBB, Sarah .... 620-431-2820 .... 195 E
srobb@neosho.edu
ROBB, Susan, E .... 804-828-6772 .... 526 B
sarobb@vcu.edu
ROBB SHIMKO, Molly .... 724-830-4620 .... 447 C
shimko@setonhill.edu
ROBBEN, Richard, W .... 734-764-3400 .... 259 A
rrobben@umich.edu
ROBBERT, Sharon .... 708-239-4771 .... 166 C
sharon.robbert@trnty.edu
ROBBIE, Kimberly .... 510-659-6165 .... 59 J
krobbie@ohlone.edu
ROBBINS, Canty .... 901-678-3855 .... 474 C
crobbns1@memphis.edu
ROBBINS, Charles .... 707-527-4498 .... 68 E
crobbins@santarosa.edu
ROBBINS, Dennis .... 626-815-3004 .... 30 G
drobbins@apu.edu
ROBBINS, Gayle, M .... 706-542-2273 .... 138 G
grobbins@uga.edu
ROBBINS, George .... 518-276-6216 .... 347 D
robbig@rpi.edu
ROBBINS, Ginger .... 601-925-3210 .... 275 C
grobbins@mc.edu
ROBBINS, Kelly .... 509-574-4775 .... 540 D
krobbins@yvcc.edu
ROBBINS, Kristi .... 614-823-1232 .... 400 H
krobbins@otterbein.edu
ROBBINS, Mark .... 315-443-2255 .... 357 C
robbinsm@syr.edu
ROBBINS, Mark .... 260-399-7700 .... 181 A
mrobbins@sf.edu
ROBBINS, Marty .... 512-472-2471 .... 494 F
marty.robbins@ssw.edu
ROBBINS, Mary .... 936-294-2771 .... 501 D
robbins@shsu.edu
ROBBINS, Nickey, L .... 870-508-6108 .... 20 E
nrobbins@asumh.edu
ROBBINS, Patricia, A .... 903-923-3262 .... 500 E
parobbins@tstc.edu
ROBBINS, Richard .... 260-399-7700 .... 181 A
rrobbins@sf.edu
ROBBINS, Robert .... 954-201-7554 .... 102 E
rrobbins@broward.edu
ROBBINS, Ruth .... 215-965-4038 .... 436 H
rrobbins@moore.edu
ROBBINS, Sandra .... 617-735-9715 .... 234 C
robbins@emmanuel.edu
ROBBINS, Scott, D .... 731-881-7775 .... 477 G
sdrobbins@utm.edu
ROBBINS, Shawna, L .... 760-252-2411 .... 30 H
srobbins@barstow.edu
ROBBINS, Stacey .... 773-291-6413 .... 147 G
ssrobbins@ccc.edu
ROBBINS, Thomas .... 802-241-2520 .... 515 C
thomas.robbins@vsc.edu
ROBBINS, Thomas, G .... 617-353-5533 .... 232 E
tqresq@bu.edu
ROBBINS SMITH, Patricia 562-860-2451 .... 39 A
probbinssmith@cerritos.edu
ROBECK, Judy .... 507-433-0511 .... 268 H
jrobeck@riverland.edu
ROBEL, Lauren .... 812-855-9011 .... 173 E
lrobel@indiana.edu
ROBEL, Lauren .... 812-855-5752 .... 173 D
provost@indiana.edu
ROBELOTTO, Vince .... 706-379-3111 .... 140 A
vrobelotto@yhc.edu
ROBERDS, Lauren .... 314-644-9673 .... 288 G
lroberds@stlcc.edu
ROBERS, Pam .... 262-551-5778 .... 546 I
probers@carthage.edu
ROBERSON, Angela, M .... 309-677-1000 .... 146 C
nickie@bradley.edu
ROBERSON, Carrie .... 870-230-5518 .... 21 I
robersc@hsu.edu
ROBERSON, Dennis .... 312-567-3032 .... 153 C
robersond@itt.edu
ROBERSON, Gail .... 318-869-5701 .... 208 H
groberson@centenary.edu
ROBERSON, James, A .... 919-335-1020 .... 374 H
jaroberson@waketech.edu
ROBERSON, James, L .... 904-620-1360 .... 120 D
len.roberson@unf.edu
ROBERSON, Janet .... 434-791-5891 .... 516 G
roberson@averett.edu
ROBERSON, John .... 910-893-1221 .... 362 J
robersonj@campbell.edu
ROBERSON, Katie .... 561-912-1211 .... 107 B
kroberson@evergladesuniversity.edu
ROBERSON, Larry .... 912-443-5828 .... 136 H
lroberson@savannahtech.edu
ROBERSON, Mark, A .... 951-552-8652 .... 31 J
maroberson@calbaptist.edu
ROBERSON, Marla .... 864-646-1753 .... 461 F
mrobers1@tctc.edu
ROBERSON, Miriam, C .... 904-819-6204 .... 107 C
robersonm@flagler.edu
ROBERSON, Richard, E .... 717-766-2511 .... 436 D
rroberso@messiah.edu
ROBERSON, Rita, G .... 304-236-7648 .... 543 C
rita.roberson@southernwv.edu
ROBERSON, Rose .... 415-452-5257 .... 40 C
rroberso@ccsf.edu
ROBERSON, Steve .... 336-334-5393 .... 379 B
shrobers@uncg.edu
ROBERSON, Valerie .... 815-280-2246 .... 154 J
vroberso@jjc.edu
ROBERSTSON, Sandra, L .... 501-569-3204 .... 24 E
slrobertson@ualr.edu
ROBERT, Bernadette .... 310-954-4099 .... 57 H
brobert@msmc.la.edu
ROBERT, Charlyn, A .... 508-213-2368 .... 243 E
charlie.robert@nichols.edu
ROBERT, Jean .... 908-852-1400 .... 308 E
robertj@centenarycollege.edu
ROBERT, Kleinschmidt .... 732-255-0400 .... 312 D
rkleinschmidt@ocean.edu
ROBERTON, Margaret, R .... 919-866-5838 .... 374 H
mrroberton@waketech.edu
ROBERTS, Aaron .... 402-643-7233 .... 297 D
aaron.roberts@cune.edu
ROBERTS, Al .... 434-736-2005 .... 528 D
al.roberts@southside.edu
ROBERTS, Alan, L .... 772-462-7235 .... 111 B
aroberts@irsc.edu
ROBERTS, Amanda .... 573-876-7101 .... 290 C
aroberts@stephens.edu
ROBERTS, Amanda, T .... 919-866-5933 .... 374 H
atroberts@waketech.edu
ROBERTS, Amber .... 616-331-3266 .... 251 F
roberamb@gvsu.edu
ROBERTS, Amy .... 412-281-2600 .... 447 A
aroberts@western-school.com
ROBERTS, Antonia .... 803-793-5197 .... 457 F
robertsa@denmarktech.edu
ROBERTS, Barbara .... 360-676-2772 .... 535 K
broberts@nwic.edu
ROBERTS, Betsy .... 707-527-4811 .... 68 E
eroberts@santarosa.edu
ROBERTS, Betty .... 601-877-6151 .... 272 F
broberts@alcorn.edu
ROBERTS, Bianca .... 661-255-1050 .... 32 F
broberts@calarts.edu
ROBERTS, Bob, E .... 304-293-3136 .... 545 A
bob.roberts@mail.wvu.edu
ROBERTS, Brent .... 406-657-2320 .... 295 D
broberts@msubillings.edu
ROBERTS, Carolyn .... 313-927-1474 .... 254 E
croberts@marygrove.edu
ROBERTS, Catherine, C .... 480-342-4850 .... 262 E
roberts.catherine@mayo.edu
ROBERTS, Charlie, W .... 225-578-3814 .... 212 H
croberts@lsualumni.org
ROBERTS, Cheryl .... 503-399-6591 .... 414 J
cheryl.roberts@chemeketa.edu
ROBERTS, Cheryl, A .... 340-692-4192 .... 568 E
crobert@live.uvi.edu
ROBERTS, Christine, B .... 919-209-2116 .... 371 F
cbroberts@johnstoncc.edu
ROBERTS, Christopher, B .... 334-844-2308 .... 1 F
robercr@auburn.edu
ROBERTS, Colleen, T .... 540-831-5500 .... 523 A
ctroberts@radford.edu
ROBERTS, Craig, W .... 573-651-2513 .... 289 K
croberts@semo.edu
ROBERTS, Creighton .... 912-358-3004 .... 136 G
robertsc@savannahstate.edu
ROBERTS, Cynthia .... 219-785-5219 .... 179 A
croberts@pnc.edu
ROBERTS, Cynthia, A .... 412-624-8076 .... 449 A
croberts@cfo.pitt.edu
ROBERTS, Dave .... 775-674-7616 .... 302 H
droberts@tmcc.edu
ROBERTS, David .... 203-932-7435 .... 95 C
droberts@newhaven.edu
ROBERTS, David .... 860-465-5395 .... 90 H
robertsda@easternct.edu
ROBERTS, David, M .... 213-740-6811 .... 76 F
dave.roberts@usc.edu
ROBERTS, Dawn .... 515-244-4221 .... 181 F
robertsd@aib.edu
ROBERTS, Dennis .... 530-938-5313 .... 42 E
robertsd@siskiyous.edu
ROBERTS, Doug .... 707-527-1709 .... 68 E
droberts@santarosa.edu
ROBERTS, Ed .... 432-264-5055 .... 488 B
eroberts@howardcollege.edu
ROBERTS, Ernst, E .... 915-831-6517 .... 486 G
erobert9@epcc.edu
ROBERTS, III,
Francis (Tri), A .... 859-246-6556 .... 201 H
tri.roberts@kctcs.edu
ROBERTS, Franklin, D .... 207-778-7215 .... 220 C
froberts@maine.edu
ROBERTS, Gail .... 229-225-5206 .... 138 A
groberts@southwestgatech.edu
ROBERTS, Gail .... 419-448-2013 .... 391 F
groberts@heidelberg.edu
ROBERTS, Gary .... 617-627-3313 .... 245 C
gary.roberts@tufts.edu
ROBERTS, Gary, A .... 501-450-3416 .... 25 H
garyr@uca.edu
ROBERTS, Gary, O .... 607-871-2715 .... 322 E
roberts@alfred.edu
ROBERTS, Gary, R .... 317-274-2581 .... 174 D
robertsg@iupui.edu
ROBERTS, Gayla .... 903-675-6212 .... 502 F
groberts@tvcc.edu
ROBERTS, Glenda, V .... 607-746-4545 .... 355 F
robertgv@delhi.edu
ROBERTS, Glenn .... 978-632-6600 .... 240 C
g_roberts@mwcc.mass.edu
ROBERTS, Gregory, W .... 434-982-3200 .... 525 F
groberts@virginia.edu
ROBERTS, Gregory, W .... 425-739-8251 .... 535 H
greg.roberts@lwtc.edu
ROBERTS, Heather .... 916-660-7900 .... 69 F
hroberts@sierracollege.edu
ROBERTS, James .... 843-863-8083 .... 456 B
jroberts@csuniv.edu
ROBERTS, James .... 570-674-6758 .... 436 F
jroberts@misericordia.edu
ROBERTS, James, S .... 919-684-3501 .... 364 C
james.roberts@duke.edu
ROBERTS, Janet .... 248-341-2020 .... 256 F
jerobert@oaklandcc.edu
ROBERTS, Jayne .... 850-718-2209 .... 103 D
robertsj@chipola.edu
ROBERTS, Jean .... 231-777-0519 .... 256 A
jean.roberts@muskegoncc.edu
ROBERTS, Jeanette, C .... 608-262-1414 .... 550 J
jroberts@pharmacy.wisc.edu
ROBERTS, Jeanne, M .... 813-253-6203 .... 123 A
jroberts@ut.edu
ROBERTS, Jeffrey, T .... 765-494-1730 .... 178 J
jtrob@purdue.edu
ROBERTS, Jennifer .... 740-364-9644 .... 399 E
roberts.862@osu.edu
ROBERTS, Jeri .... 207-948-9261 .... 219 H
jroberts@unity.edu
ROBERTS, Jim, O .... 910-893-1240 .... 362 J
roberts@campbell.edu
ROBERTS, Jimmy .... 254-298-8340 .... 496 D
jdr@templejc.edu
ROBERTS, John .... 903-593-8311 .... 499 D
jroberts@texascollege.edu
ROBERTS, John .... 713-743-2992 .... 503 D
jwroberts@central.uh.edu
ROBERTS, Jon .... 501-279-4257 .... 21 H
jroberts@harding.edu
ROBERTS, Jonathan .... 912-344-2910 .... 124 G
jonathan.roberts@armstrong.edu
ROBERTS, Juanita .... 334-727-8894 .... 8 B
jroberts@tuskegee.edu
ROBERTS, Karen .... 559-737-6257 .... 42 D
karenr@cos.edu
ROBERTS, Kay Lynn .... 580-745-2977 .... 412 C
kroberts@se.edu
ROBERTS, Kelley .... 706-867-3280 .... 134 G
karoberts@northgeorgia.edu
ROBERTS, Kevin, J .... 325-674-2675 .... 478 I
robertsk@acu.edu
ROBERTS, Kevin, W .... 518-564-5022 .... 354 B
robertkw@plattsburgh.edu
ROBERTS, II, Laurence, W 315-792-3340 .... 359 E
lroberts@utica.edu
ROBERTS, Leonard .... 973-748-9000 .... 307 H
leonard_roberts@bloomfield.edu
ROBERTS, Lila .... 678-466-4357 .... 127 D
lilaroberts@clayton.edu
ROBERTS, Linsday .... 614-221-7770 .... 396 B
ROBERTS, Lisa .... 618-374-5068 .... 161 E
lisa.roberts@principia.edu
ROBERTS, Lonnie, V .... 912-427-5816 .... 124 C
lroberts@altamahatech.edu
ROBERTS, Mark .... 276-466-7869 .... 529 D
markroberts@vic.edu
ROBERTS, Mark .... 740-284-5345 .... 391 A
mroberts@franciscan.edu
ROBERTS, Mark, A .... 407-823-2771 .... 120 B
roberts@ucf.edu
ROBERTS, Mary .... 478-445-5384 .... 130 B
mary.roberts@gcsu.edu
ROBERTS, Mary .... 831-582-3609 .... 35 E
mroberts@csumb.edu
ROBERTS, Mary Margaret .... 662-329-7295 .... 276 A
mmroberts@alumni.muw.edu
ROBERTS, Melvin .... 856-227-7200 .... 308 D
mroberts@camdencc.edu
ROBERTS, Michael .... 907-773-4462 .... 147 D
mroberts39@ccc.edu
ROBERTS, Michael, H .... 843-349-2282 .... 456 G
mroberts@coastal.edu
ROBERTS, Michelle, A .... 662-846-4000 .... 273 H
mroberts@deltastate.edu
ROBERTS, Mike .... 319-398-7797 .... 187 B
mrobert@kirkwood.edu
ROBERTS, Nancy .... 610-606-4640 .... 425 A
nroberts@cedarcrest.edu
ROBERTS, Patrick, S .... 330-569-5278 .... 391 G
robertsps@hiram.edu
ROBERTS, Patty, J .... 318-869-5747 .... 208 H
pjrobert@centenary.edu
ROBERTS, Paul .... 229-225-4098 .... 138 A
proberts@southwestgatech.edu
ROBERTS, Paul .... 205-970-9221 .... 7 C
proberts@sebc.edu
ROBERTS, Paul, G .... 773-508-8901 .... 157 C
prober2@luc.edu
ROBERTS, Pauline .... 225-923-2524 .... 208 C
ROBERTS, Phyllis, A .... 276-964-7588 .... 528 E
phyllis.roberts@sw.edu
ROBERTS, Randal, R .... 503-517-1860 .... 421 C
rroberts@westernseminary.edu
ROBERTS, Randall .... 606-886-3863 .... 201 G
randall.roberts@kctcs.edu
ROBERTS, Richard .... 201-684-7616 .... 313 C
rroberts@ramapo.edu
ROBERTS, Rick .... 904-620-2955 .... 120 D
rtrobert@unf.edu
ROBERTS, Rick .... 210-999-7328 .... 502 E
rick.roberts@trinity.edu
ROBERTS, Robin .... 479-575-4804 .... 24 C
ROBERTS, Robin .... 317-738-8759 .... 171 F
rroberts@franklincollege.edu
ROBERTS, Robin .... 302-857-6120 .... 96 C
rroberts@desu.edu
ROBERTS, Ruth .... 972-825-4656 .... 495 F
rroberts@sagu.edu
ROBERTS, Sallyann .... 815-226-4083 .... 163 A
sroberts@rockford.edu
ROBERTS, Sarah .... 405-491-6312 .... 412 D
saroberts@snu.edu
ROBERTS, Scott .... 702-895-2816 .... 302 I
scott.roberts@unlv.edu
ROBERTS, Shandel .... 415-433-9200 .... 68 F
sroberts@saybrook.edu
ROBERTS, Shannon .... 215-248-7111 .... 425 D
roberts@chc.edu
ROBERTS, Stephen, W .... 248-370-2445 .... 256 G
swrobert@oakland.edu
ROBERTS, Steve .... 817-531-4403 .... 502 C
sroberts@txwes.edu
ROBERTS, Susan .... 262-564-3224 .... 554 B
robertss@gtc.edu

ROBERTS, Terri, L ... 317-738-8119 ... 171 F troberts@franklincollege.edu
ROBERTS, Tracy ... 270-809-3759 ... 205 A troberts@murraystate.edu
ROBERTS, Tucson ... 334-774-5113 ... 3 F troberts@escc.edu
ROBERTS, Vanessa ... 325-793-4681 ... 490 H vroberts@mcm.edu
ROBERTS, Vonnie, W ... 405-466-2999 ... 408 G vwroberts@langston.edu
ROBERTS, Wayne ... 601-643-8351 ... 273 G wayne.roberts@colin.edu
ROBERTS, William ... 201-692-2629 ... 310 A william_roberts@fdu.edu
ROBERTS, William, C ... 240-895-4387 ... 226 A wcroberts@smcm.edu
ROBERTS, William, R ... 906-487-2622 ... 255 B wrrobert@mtu.edu
ROBERTS-CORB, Carol ... 562-985-4187 ... 35 C crcorb@csulb.edu
ROBERTS-DEUTSCH, Marcia ... 808-845-9110 ... 142 B robertsd@hawaii.edu
ROBERTS KRIEGER, Robin ... 405-945-3228 ... 410 F
ROBERTSON, Alan, D ... 708-709-3568 ... 161 D arobertson@prairiestate.edu
ROBERTSON, Ali ... 269-956-3931 ... 253 B robertsona@kellogg.edu
ROBERTSON, April ... 706-355-5114 ... 125 C arobertson@athenstech.edu
ROBERTSON, Beverly ... 828-689-1244 ... 366 I brobertson@mhc.edu
ROBERTSON, Blake ... 501-337-5000 ... 21 D brobertson@coto.edu
ROBERTSON, Carole ... 312-488-6006 ... 146 F crobertson@thechicagoschool.edu
ROBERTSON, Charlotta ... 619-388-2801 ... 65 G crobertson@sdccd.edu
ROBERTSON, Christopher . 205-929-1655 ... 5 H admissions@miles.edu
ROBERTSON, Courtney ... 941-907-2262 ... 107 B crobertson@evergladesuniversity.edu
ROBERTSON, Craig, L ... 618-537-6856 ... 158 A clrobertson@mckendree.edu
ROBERTSON, Darlene ... 937-769-1820 ... 384 B drobertson@antioch.edu
ROBERTSON, Debbie ... 405-382-9248 ... 412 B d.robertson@sscok.edu
ROBERTSON, Debora ... 712-279-1771 ... 183 A debora.robertson@briarcliff.edu
ROBERTSON, Diana ... 785-864-7224 ... 197 B drobertson@ku.edu
ROBERTSON, Don ... 507-537-6018 ... 269 E don.robertson@smsu.edu
ROBERTSON, Don, E ... 270-809-6831 ... 205 A drobertson@murraystate.edu
ROBERTSON, Doug ... 504-456-3141 ... 208 E dougr@bluecliffcollege.com
ROBERTSON, Douglas ... 305-348-3681 ... 119 C douglas.robertson@fiu.edu
ROBERTSON, Gloria ... 269-660-8021 ... 257 C robertsong@millercollege.edu
ROBERTSON, Ian ... 828-298-3325 ... 380 D irobert@warren-wilson.edu
ROBERTSON, J. D ... 435-652-7576 ... 512 B jrobertson@dixie.edu
ROBERTSON, James ... 361-698-1561 ... 485 G jrobert@delmar.edu
ROBERTSON, Jennifer ... 903-675-6215 ... 502 F jrobertson@tvcc.edu
ROBERTSON, Jill ... 303-273-3207 ... 83 B jill.robertson@is.mines.edu
ROBERTSON, John ... 402-844-7011 ... 299 I johnr@northeast.edu
ROBERTSON, Jon, H ... 561-237-7701 ... 113 D jrobertson@lynn.edu
ROBERTSON, Joseph, E ... 503-494-8252 ... 418 D president@ohsu.edu
ROBERTSON, Leonard, A .. 972-721-5236 ... 503 B lrobertson@udallas.edu
ROBERTSON, Martha ... 785-827-5541 ... 194 F martha.robertson@kwu.edu
ROBERTSON, Mary ... 870-512-7812 ... 20 F mary_robertson@asun.edu
ROBERTSON, Michael, N .. 901-722-3226 ... 473 C mike.robertson@sco.edu
ROBERTSON, Patricia ... 843-574-6057 ... 461 G patricia.robertson@tridenttech.edu
ROBERTSON, Paul ... 402-878-2380 ... 298 E probertson@littlepriest.edu
ROBERTSON, Randall, A ... 336-734-7334 ... 370 F rrobertson@forsythtech.edu
ROBERTSON, Richard, J ... 760-757-2121 ... 57 E drobertson@miracosta.edu
ROBERTSON, Roby, D ... 501-569-8572 ... 24 E rdrobertson@ualr.edu
ROBERTSON, Russell ... 847-578-3000 ... 163 C russell.robertson@rosalindfranklin.edu
ROBERTSON, Sandra, L ... 501-569-8736 ... 24 E slrobertson@ualr.edu
ROBERTSON, Sharon, N ... 703-323-3198 ... 527 F srobertson@nvcc.edu
ROBERTSON, Stacey ... 309-677-2380 ... 146 C smr@bradley.edu
ROBERTSON, Stacey, M ... 309-677-3538 ... 146 C smr@bradley.edu
ROBERTSON, Summer ... 704-406-3271 ... 364 E srobertson@gardner-webb.edu
ROBERTSON, Teresa ... 303-963-3283 ... 82 C trobertson@ccu.edu
ROBERTSON, Thomas, S ... 215-898-4715 ... 448 J robertson@wharton.upenn.edu
ROBERTSON, William, J ... 717-866-5775 ... 429 A wrobertson@evangelical.edu
ROBESKY, Jim ... 217-228-5432 ... 161 F robesja@quincy.edu
ROBESON, Dan ... 518-292-8657 ... 348 A robesd@sage.edu
ROBICHAUD, Betin ... 508-213-2292 ... 243 E betin.robichaud@nichols.edu
ROBICHAUD, Karen ... 615-966-5602 ... 470 F karen.robichaud@lipscomb.edu
ROBICHAUD, Rob ... 208-321-8800 ... 143 B rrobichaud@brownmackie.edu
ROBICHAUX, Renee ... 337-550-1233 ... 212 J
ROBIE, Curt, D ... 413-572-5280 ... 238 F crobie@wsc.ma.edu
ROBILLARD, Jean, E ... 319-335-8064 ... 182 F jean-robillard@uiowa.edu
ROBILLARD, Marc ... 617-353-3502 ... 232 E robillrd@bu.edu
ROBIN, Brandon ... 318-487-7498 ... 209 F brandonrobin@lacollege.edu
ROBIN, Tracy ... 212-229-1671 ... 342 E robint@newschool.edu
ROBINETTE, Jennifer ... 304-255-0793 ... 543 G robinettej@concord.edu
ROBINETTE, Stephen, H ... 417-836-4127 ... 286 C steverobinette@missouristate.edu
ROBINS, Linda ... 580-371-2371 ... 408 I lrobins@mscok.edu
ROBINS, Luke ... 360-417-6200 ... 536 G lrobins@pencol.edu
ROBINS, Mary ... 650-543-3735 ... 57 B mrobins@menlo.edu
ROBINSON, Albert ... 410-951-3803 ... 228 B arobinson@coppin.edu
ROBINSON, Alfred, L ... 573-681-6156 ... 283 I robinsona@lincolnu.edu
ROBINSON, Alteia, L ... 202-231-3302 ... 557 J alteia.robinson@dodiis.mil
ROBINSON, Andrew ... 603-358-2108 ... 306 G arobinso@keene.edu
ROBINSON, Angela ... 817-515-5242 ... 496 C angela.robinson@tccd.edu
ROBINSON, Audrey ... 540-665-4928 ... 524 E arobinso2@su.edu
ROBINSON, Beatriz, G ... 305-474-6846 ... 117 A brobinson@stu.edu
ROBINSON, Bev ... 208-459-5680 ... 143 D brobinson@collegeofidaho.edu
ROBINSON, Beverly ... 972-825-4798 ... 495 F brobinson@sagu.edu
ROBINSON, Beverly ... 615-329-8657 ... 468 I brobinson@fisk.edu
ROBINSON, Brent ... 440-375-7111 ... 394 E brobinson@lec.edu
ROBINSON, Calvin ... 859-341-5800 ... 206 I calvin.robinson@thomasmore.edu
ROBINSON, Carrie ... 318-670-9663 ... 215 A crobinson@susla.edu
ROBINSON, Cassandra, M 301-860-4000 ... 228 A crobinson@bowiestate.edu
ROBINSON, Chad ... 970-943-3123 ... 89 E crobinson@western.edu
ROBINSON, Charles ... 479-575-7955 ... 24 C cfrobins@uark.edu
ROBINSON, Charles, F ... 510-987-9800 ... 73 G charles.robinson@ucop.edu
ROBINSON, Chase, F ... 212-817-7200 ... 327 B crobinson@gc.cuny.edu
ROBINSON, Cheryl ... 407-582-6883 ... 123 B crobinson@valenciacollege.edu
ROBINSON, Christine, M .. 414-410-4183 ... 546 G cmrobinson@stritch.edu
ROBINSON, Christopher, D ... 336-246-3900 ... 375 C chris.robinson@wilkescc.edu
ROBINSON, Constance, V . 315-267-2573 ... 354 C harpercv@potsdam.edu
ROBINSON, Daniel ... 909-469-5561 ... 78 I drobinson@westernu.edu
ROBINSON, David ... 405-945-3241 ... 410 F
ROBINSON, David, W ... 503-494-4460 ... 418 D provost@ohsu.edu
ROBINSON, Deborah ... 540-831-6008 ... 523 A drobinson7@radford.edu
ROBINSON, Deborah, M ... 330-588-2586 ... 395 F drobinson@malone.edu
ROBINSON, Deborah, P ... 850-201-6109 ... 122 A robinsd@tcc.fl.edu
ROBINSON, Debra A, G ... 573-341-6154 ... 291 E debrar@mst.edu
ROBINSON, OSB, Denis ... 812-357-6522 ... 180 A drobinson@saintmeinrad.edu
ROBINSON, Denise ... 859-572-5688 ... 205 H robinson@nku.edu
ROBINSON, Dindy ... 817-257-5019 ... 499 C d.robinson@tcu.edu
ROBINSON, Dorothy, K ... 203-432-4949 ... 96 A dorothy.robinson@yale.edu
ROBINSON, Doug ... 318-798-4107 ... 213 D doug.robinson@lsus.edu
ROBINSON, Douglas, W ... 562-985-5587 ... 35 C drobinso@csulb.edu
ROBINSON, Duan ... 731-426-7525 ... 470 B drobinson@lanecollege.edu
ROBINSON, Edward ... 202-686-0876 ... 99 E library@potomac.edu
ROBINSON, Edward, G ... 608-757-7713 ... 553 G erobinson@blackhawk.edu
ROBINSON, Elaine ... 816-483-9600 ... 289 E elaine.robinson@spst.edu
ROBINSON, Elwood ... 617-868-1000 ... 233 A elwood.robinson@cambridgecollege.edu
ROBINSON, Gail, D ... 901-334-5826 ... 471 E grobinson@memphisseminary.edu
ROBINSON, Gary ... 859-336-5082 ... 206 A grobinson@sccky.edu
ROBINSON, Gary ... 607-431-4420 ... 335 A robinsong@hartwick.edu
ROBINSON, Gina ... 910-755-7343 ... 368 F robinsong@brunswickcc.edu
ROBINSON, Gregory ... 407-823-5348 ... 120 B greg.robinson@ucf.edu
ROBINSON, Gregory ... 773-291-6211 ... 147 G grobinson@ccc.edu
ROBINSON, Irene, M ... 281-756-3501 ... 479 F irobinson@alvincollege.edu
ROBINSON, J. Edward ... 718-960-8245 ... 327 C je.robinson@lehman.cuny.edu
ROBINSON, Jane, L ... 614-947-6001 ... 391 B robinsoj@franklin.edu
ROBINSON, Janet, H ... 419-824-3809 ... 395 E jrobinson@lourdes.edu
ROBINSON, Janice, S ... 212-678-3732 ... 357 G jsr167@tc.columbia.edu
ROBINSON, Jeannette ... 973-877-3084 ... 309 H robinson@essex.edu
ROBINSON, Jennifer ... 617-951-2350 ... 242 G jennifer.robinson@necb.edu
ROBINSON, Jill ... 714-556-3610 ... 77 B jill.robinson@vanguard.edu
ROBINSON, Jo-Ann ... 937-708-5772 ... 405 H jrobinson@wilberforce.edu
ROBINSON, JoAnne ... 706-771-5730 ... 125 H jrobinso@augustatech.edu
ROBINSON, Joanne, P ... 856-225-2776 ... 314 D jprobins@camden.rutgers.edu
ROBINSON, Judith, G ... 757-446-5841 ... 518 G robinsjg@evms.edu
ROBINSON, Karen ... 415-380-1616 ... 48 E karenrobinson@ggbts.edu
ROBINSON, Kasi ... 404-681-6500 ... 134 D krobinso@morehouse.edu
ROBINSON, Kelley ... 518-244-2201 ... 348 A robink3@sage.edu
ROBINSON, Kenneth, I ... 714-808-4830 ... 59 C krobinson@nocccd.edu
ROBINSON, Kent ... 502-213-2118 ... 202 F kent.robinson@kctcs.edu
ROBINSON, Kevin ... 559-734-9000 ... 66 E kevinr@sjvc.edu
ROBINSON, Kevin, W ... 610-660-1357 ... 446 C krobinso@sju.edu
ROBINSON, LaNita ... 218-733-7616 ... 266 H l.robinson@lsc.edu
ROBINSON, Larry ... 973-761-9655 ... 315 B larry.robinson@shu.edu
ROBINSON, Larry ... 850-599-3276 ... 118 L larry.robinson@famu.edu
ROBINSON, Larry, J ... 701-845-7217 ... 382 C larry.robinson@vcsu.edu
ROBINSON, LeAnne ... 912-871-1608 ... 135 D lrobinson@ogeecheetech.edu
ROBINSON, Lorene, K ... 302-857-6050 ... 96 C lrobinso@desu.edu
ROBINSON, Lorne, T ... 651-696-6358 ... 264 J robinson@macalester.edu
ROBINSON, Louester ... 843-722-5556 ... 461 G lou.robinson@tridenttech.edu
ROBINSON, Lynne, P ... 301-447-5296 ... 225 A lrobinso@msmary.edu
ROBINSON, Margaret, A ... 620-229-6232 ... 196 G margaret.robinson@sckans.edu
ROBINSON, Marjorie ... 951-785-2167 ... 53 E mrobinso@lasierra.edu
ROBINSON, Mary ... 410-276-0306 ... 226 D mrobinson@host.sdc.edu
ROBINSON, Mary ... 716-896-0700 ... 359 H robinsonm@villa.edu
ROBINSON, Mary Kate ... 713-623-2040 ... 480 J mkrobinson@aii.edu
ROBINSON, Meri ... 706-507-8433 ... 127 G robinson_meri@columbusstate.edu
ROBINSON, Michael ... 405-744-6528 ... 410 C michael.robinson@okstate.edu
ROBINSON, Michele' ... 847-925-6221 ... 151 G mrobinso@harpercollege.edu
ROBINSON, Mick ... 406-444-6570 ... 294 H mirobinson@montana.edu
ROBINSON, Mike ... 205-226-4935 ... 2 B mrobinso@bsc.edu
ROBINSON, Mitch ... 931-221-7883 ... 473 E robinsonm@apsu.edu
ROBINSON, Monica ... 251-578-1313 ... 6 E mrobinson@rstc.edu
ROBINSON, Morris ... 318-678-6005 ... 209 I mrobinson@bpcc.edu
ROBINSON, Myra ... 703-729-8800 ... 99 G
ROBINSON, Neal ... 802-654-2512 ... 514 D nrobinson@smcvt.edu
ROBINSON, Nechelle ... 800-533-3378 ... 138 F nrobinson@uofa.edu
ROBINSON, Nell ... 334-244-3424 ... 1 G nrobins3@aum.edu
ROBINSON, Norm ... 615-248-1296 ... 476 G nrobinson@trevecca.edu
ROBINSON, Oscar ... 937-769-1823 ... 384 B orobinson@antioch.edu
ROBINSON, Pam ... 405-878-2243 ... 409 D pam.robinson@okbu.edu
ROBINSON, Patricia ... 661-362-3992 ... 41 I patty.robinson@canyons.edu
ROBINSON, Patricia ... 920-993-5133 ... 554 A robinsop@fvtc.edu
ROBINSON, Paul, A ... 734-647-3502 ... 259 A probins@umich.edu
ROBINSON, Perry, H ... 740-587-6624 ... 389 I robinson@denison.edu
ROBINSON, Peter, J ... 585-275-4036 ... 359 B peter_robinson@urmc.rochester.edu
ROBINSON, Ralph ... 302-857-7381 ... 96 C rrobinson@desu.edu
ROBINSON, Regina ... 318-670-9617 ... 215 A rrobinson@susla.edu
ROBINSON, Robbie ... 225-342-6950 ... 215 D robbie.robinson@la.gov
ROBINSON, Robert ... 678-717-3749 ... 129 G rrobinson@gsc.edu
ROBINSON, Robert ... 909-621-8136 ... 63 A robert.robinson@pomona.edu
ROBINSON, Robert ... 802-654-2524 ... 514 D rrobinson@smcvt.edu
ROBINSON, Robert, L ... 717-815-1553 ... 452 G rrobinso@ycp.edu
ROBINSON, Robin ... 508-626-4688 ... 238 A rrobinson@framingham.edu
ROBINSON, Ronald, R ... 864-597-4051 ... 463 G robinsonrr1@wofford.edu
ROBINSON, Rosemary ... 256-824-6203 ... 8 G rosemary.robinson@uah.edu
ROBINSON, Roy ... 253-879-3653 ... 538 H rrobinson@pugetsound.edu
ROBINSON, Rufus ... 843-746-5100 ... 99 G
ROBINSON, Sandra, L ... 407-823-5529 ... 120 B sandra.robinson@ucf.edu
ROBINSON, Sandra, T ... 313-922-3311 ... 259 G srobins1@wcccd.edu
ROBINSON, Sandy ... 216-987-4867 ... 389 B sandy.robinson@tri-c.edu
ROBINSON, Scott ... 901-320-9740 ... 478 C srobinson@victory.edu
ROBINSON, Shana ... 323-822-9700 ... 72 K shana.robinson@touro.edu
ROBINSON, Sharon ... 704-233-8249 ... 380 F s.robinson@wingate.edu
ROBINSON, Sharon ... 518-244-2466 ... 348 A robins@sage.edu
ROBINSON, Sharon ... 580-745-2364 ... 412 C srobinson@se.edu
ROBINSON, Shawn ... 813-253-7755 ... 110 M srobinson37@hccfl.edu
ROBINSON, Sid ... 909-537-5007 ... 36 B sidr@csusb.edu
ROBINSON, Stephanie, R .. 559-442-4600 ... 72 B stephanie.robinson@fresnocitycollege.edu
ROBINSON, Steve, E ... 304-293-0169 ... 545 A steve.robinsonr@mail.wvu.edu
ROBINSON, Sunnie ... 860-444-8508 ... 558 H sunnie.robinson@uscg.mil
ROBINSON, T. Joan ... 443-885-3350 ... 224 E joan.robinson@morgan.edu
ROBINSON, Theotis ... 865-974-0518 ... 477 C trobins4@tennessee.edu
ROBINSON, Timothy ... 904-620-2657 ... 120 D trobinso@unf.edu
ROBINSON, Tom ... 308-635-6182 ... 301 D robinson@wncc.edu
ROBINSON, Tony ... 828-669-8012 ... 367 E trobinson@montreat.edu
ROBINSON, Tray ... 530-898-4764 ... 34 C trobinson@csuchico.edu
ROBINSON, Vickie, S ... 919-658-7757 ... 367 F vrobinson@moc.edu
ROBINSON, Wade ... 316-978-3021 ... 198 A wade.robinson@wichita.edu
ROBINSON, Wade, A ... 316-978-3021 ... 198 A wade.robinson@wichita.edu
ROBINSON, Walter, A ... 530-752-2971 ... 73 I warobinson@ucdavis.edu
ROBINSON, Warren ... 803-705-4662 ... 455 D robinson@benedict.edu
ROBINSON, Wayne ... 718-473-8960 ... 328 D wrobinson@citytech.cuny.edu

ROBINSON, Wayne .... 718-260-4900.... 328 D wrobinson@citytech.cuny.edu
ROBINSON, Wayne .... 307-855-2104.... 556 B wrobinson@cwc.edu
ROBINSON, Wayne, G .... 919-718-7214.... 369 C wrobinson@cccc.edu
ROBINSON, Wendi .... 614-947-6768.... 391 B robinsow@franklin.edu
ROBINSON, Wendy .... 212-616-7299.... 335 C wendy.robinson@helenefuld.edu
ROBINSON, Wendy .... 515-964-6222.... 183 H wsrobinson@dmacc.edu
ROBINSON, William .... 410-621-2355.... 227 E wrobinson3@umes.edu
ROBINSON-ARMSTRONG, Abbie .... 310-338-7598...... 56 E arobinso@lmu.edu
ROBINSON-GARDNER, Dorris, R .... 601-979-2455.... 274 G dorris.r.gardner@jsums.edu
ROBINSON KLOOS, Jennifer .... 651-690-8831.... 270 L jrkloos@stkate.edu
ROBINSON-LEWIS, Denise .... 973-720-2885.... 317 D lewisd@wpunj.edu
ROBINSON-PAUL, Ann ..... 701-231-8325.... 382 B anne.robinson-paul@ndsu.edu
ROBINSON PIPPINS, Shirley .... 901-320-9710.... 478 C
ROBISON, Dan .... 312-280-3500.... 153 B drobison@aii.edu
ROBISON, Daniel, J .... 304-293-2395.... 545 A djrobison@mail.wvu.edu
ROBISON, Jeff .... 540-261-8410.... 524 H jeff.robison@svu.edu
ROBISON, Linda, K .... 504-280-6207.... 213 E lrobison@uno.edu
ROBISON, Lori .... 419-267-1342.... 397 E lrobison@northweststate.edu
ROBISON, Margaret .... 910-362-7101.... 368 H mrobison@cfcc.edu
ROBISON, Mike .... 662-562-3438.... 276 D jmrobison@northwestms.edu
ROBISON, Mike .... 559-438-4222...... 49 I mike_robison@heald.edu
ROBISON, Richard .... 707-654-1093...... 33 C rrobison@csum.edu
ROBISON, Ruth, E .... 808-974-7313.... 141 F rrobison@hawaii.edu
ROBITAILLE, Marilyn .... 254-968-9632.... 497 A robitaille@tarleton.edu
ROBLES, Elizabeth .... 213-477-2769...... 57 H erobles@msmc.la.edu
ROBLES, Laura .... 310-243-2547...... 34 D lrobles@csudh.edu
ROBLES, Pedro .... 787-786-3030.... 560 G probles@ucb.edu.pr
ROBLES, Ray .... 787-864-2222.... 563 F rayroble@inter.edu
ROBLES, Ruben .... 909-748-8289...... 76 C ruben_robles@redlands.edu
ROBNETT, Regi .... 207-221-4102.... 221 A rrobnett@une.edu
ROBOLE, Donna .... 715-425-3502.... 552 C donna.robole@uwrf.edu
ROBOMAN, Lourdes .... 691-350-2296.... 559 D comfsmyap@comfsm.fm
ROBOTHAM, Donald .... 212-817-8013.... 327 B drobotham@gc.cuny.edu
ROBOTHAM, Tena .... 847-628-2002.... 154 K trobotham@judsonu.edu
ROBUCK, Chris .... 503-594-3090.... 415 A chrisr@clackamas.edu
ROBUSTELLI, Carlo .... 309-556-3902.... 153 F crobuste@iwu.edu
ROBY, Mary .... 704-406-4293.... 364 E
ROBY, Peter, P .... 617-373-2672.... 243 F
ROCA, Carmen .... 305-593-1223.... 102 H croca@albizu.edu
ROCA, Carmen .... 305-592-1223.... 561 A croca@albizu.edu
ROCA, Joan .... 507-389-5953.... 267 E joan.roca@mnsu.edu
ROCAP, Donna .... 845-431-8066.... 332 D rocap@sunydutchess.edu
ROCCHETTI, Lisa .... 310-453-8300...... 45 G lisa@emperors.edu
ROCCIA, Miriam, I .... 314-516-5291.... 291 D roccia@umsl.edu
ROCCO, Denine, M .... 330-972-2672.... 403 B drocco@uakron.edu
ROCCO, Frederick .... 916-564-1525.... 402 I frederick.rocco@myunion.edu
ROCCO, Karen, S .... 412-362-8500.... 444 F pims5808@aol.com
ROCHA, Collette, G .... 323-343-3075...... 35 D crocha@cslanet.calstate.edu
ROCHA, Daniel .... 210-486-3200.... 479 C drocha@alamo.edu
ROCHA, Mark, W .... 626-585-7201...... 61 F mwrocha@pasadena.edu
ROCHAT, Angela .... 970-247-7695...... 84 K rochat_a@fortlewis.edu
ROCHE, Amarilis .... 787-848-1589.... 564 I aroche@popac.edu
ROCHE, Daniel .... 973-655-4158.... 311 F roched@mail.montclair.edu
ROCHE, Denise, A .... 716-829-7673.... 332 E roche@dyc.edu
ROCHE, Isabel .... 802-440-4406.... 513 A iroche@bennington.edu
ROCHE, James .... 413-545-6330.... 236 F jroche@provost.umass.edu
ROCHE, Jason .... 313-993-1092.... 258 G rochejj@udmercy.edu
ROCHE, Mary Beth .... 570-504-1589.... 433 A rochem@lackawanna.edu
ROCHE, Sibyl .... 651-757-4051.... 262 H sjroche@cva.edu
ROCHE, Stephen, H .... 407-303-8016.... 100 G stephen.roche@adu.edu
ROCHEFORT, Mary .... 218-723-6505.... 262 G mrochefo@css.edu
ROCHELEAU, James .... 916-485-3276.... 402 I james.rocheleau@myunion.edu
ROCHELEAU, Richard .... 310-338-6534...... 56 E rrochele@lmu.edu
ROCHLITZ, Mendel .... 718-853-8500.... 358 A
ROCHON, Gilbert, L .... 334-727-8501........ 8 B rochon@tuskegee.edu
ROCHON, Ronald, S .... 812-465-1617.... 181 B rochon@usi.edu
ROCHON, Sandra .... 978-762-4000.... 240 D srochon@northshore.edu
ROCHON, Thomas, R .... 607-274-3111.... 336 G president@ithaca.edu
ROCK, Arlene, M .... 413-782-1538.... 246 A arock@wne.edu
ROCK, David .... 662-915-7063.... 277 D rock@olemiss.edu
ROCK, David .... 727-784-0003.... 103 B drock@cfi.edu
ROCK, Harry .... 413-748-3914.... 244 H hrock@springfieldcollege.edu
ROCK, Jennifer .... 215-489-2917.... 426 H jennifer.rock@delval.edu
ROCK, John .... 504-568-8448.... 213 A jrock@lsuhsc.edu
ROCK, John .... 305-348-0570.... 119 C john.rock@fiu.edu
ROCK, Megan .... 203-396-8086...... 94 B rockm@sacredheart.edu
ROCK, Susan .... 516-299-3057.... 339 A susan.rock@liu.edu
ROCK, Thomas .... 212-678-3083.... 357 G tpr4@tc.columbia.edu
ROCKE, Mike .... 562-947-8755...... 71 A mikerocke@scuhs.edu
ROCKECHARLIE, Barbara ... 704-372-0266.... 366 B brockecharlie@kingscollegecharlotte.edu
ROCKETT, Beth Ann .... 612-343-4741.... 270 A barocket@northcentral.edu
ROCKETT, Jeri, M .... 651-962-6780.... 272 B gmrockett@stthomas.edu
ROCKETT, Kathryn, S .... 516-299-2523.... 338 E kathryn.rockett@liu.edu
ROCKETT, Sandra .... 731-286-3238.... 475 B rockett@dscc.edu
ROCKEY, Marci .... 217-786-2320.... 157 B marci.rockey@llcc.edu
ROCKEY, Robin .... 570-484-2544.... 443 B rrockey@lhup.edu
ROCKEY, Tim .... 210-486-0926.... 479 E trockey@alamo.edu
ROCKHILL, Linda .... 718-779-1430.... 346 B info@plazacollege.edu
ROCKHILL, Wendy .... 206-934-6921.... 537 E wendy.rockhill@seattlecolleges.edu
ROCKHOLD, Robin .... 601-984-2810.... 277 E rrockhold@umc.edu
ROCKLAND-MILLER, Harry, S .... 413-545-2337.... 236 F rockmill@uhs.umass.edu
ROCKLIN, Thomas, R .... 319-335-3557.... 182 F thomas-rocklin@uiowa.edu
ROCKMAN, Adam .... 718-997-5500.... 328 E adam.rockman@qc.cuny.edu
ROCKS, JR., Thomas, E ..... 412-261-2647.... 432 D trocks@kaplan.edu
ROCKWELL-HOPKINS, Melissa .... 713-743-8750.... 503 D mrockwel@central.uh.edu
ROCQUE, Jenna .... 207-795-2270.... 217 F rocqueje@cmhc.org
ROCQUE, Marc .... 215-527-2961.... 422 C rocquem@arcadia.edu
ROCQUEMORE, Ronda .... 773-481-8103.... 147 I rrocquemore@ccc.edu
RODARTE, Isabel .... 505-747-2241.... 320 A irodarte@nnmc.edu
RODARTE, Susana .... 915-831-2018.... 486 G srodart7@epcc.edu
RODAS, Daniel, J .... 516-299-2049.... 338 E daniel.rodas@liu.edu
RODAS, Mary .... 516-364-0808.... 343 A mrodas@nycollege.edu
RODDEN, Greg, A .... 863-638-7215.... 123 D greg.rodden@warner.edu
RODDINI, Martin .... 516-572-7331.... 342 C martin.roddini@ncc.edu
RODDY, Chris .... 269-927-8620.... 253 G croddy@lakemichigancollege.edu
RODDY, Jackie .... 615-217-9347.... 468 D jroddy@daymarinstitute.edu
RODDY, Lowell .... 931-221-7213.... 473 E roddyl@apsu.edu
RODDY, Shirley .... 405-691-3800.... 408 H sroddy@macu.edu
RODE, Joe .... 817-515-7741.... 496 C joe.rode@tccd.edu
RODECKER, Daniel .... 518-580-5860.... 351 B drodecke@skidmore.edu
RODEMANN, Jaclyn .... 732-255-0400.... 312 D jrodemann@ocean.edu
RODENFELS, Clint, R .... 512-223-4721.... 481 B crodenfe@austincc.edu
RODERICK, Gerald, K .... 410-778-7810.... 229 D jroderick2@washcoll.edu
RODESILER, Carrie .... 386-752-1822.... 108 G carrie.rodesiler@fgc.edu
RODGER, Doug .... 712-324-5061.... 188 C drodger@nwicc.edu
RODGERS, Ardie .... 405-733-7434.... 411 I arodgers@rose.edu
RODGERS, Beverly .... 218-335-4262.... 264 G beverly.rodgers@lltc.edu
RODGERS, JR., Bob .... 404-233-3949.... 136 D brodgers@richmont.edu
RODGERS, Carol .... 301-431-5440.... 225 B crodgers@nlc.edu
RODGERS, Christie .... 636-949-4697.... 283 J crodgers@lindenwood.edu
RODGERS, Christopher ...... 718-817-4755.... 334 C chrodgers@fordham.edu
RODGERS, Denise, V .... 973-972-3645.... 316 C rodgerdv@umdnj.edu
RODGERS, Fredrick .... 716-896-0700.... 359 H rodgersf@villa.edu
RODGERS, Harold .... 574-257-3320.... 169 I rodgerh@bethelcollege.edu
RODGERS, Kenneth, G ...... 919-530-5079.... 378 B krodgers@nccu.edu
RODGERS, Larry .... 541-737-4582.... 418 F larry.rodgers@oregonstate.edu
RODGERS, Laurie, A .... 314-719-3661.... 281 I lrodgers@fontbonne.edu
RODGERS, Mark, E .... 570-340-6001.... 435 F mrodgers@marywood.edu
RODGERS, Mary, P .... 662-246-6263.... 275 D mrodgers@msdelta.edu
RODGERS, Mike .... 214-818-1369.... 484 B mrodgers@criswell.edu
RODGERS, Norma, L .... 918-595-7868.... 412 H nrodgers@tulsacc.edu
RODGERS, Phillip .... 503-725-5442.... 418 G prodgers@pdx.edu
RODGERS, Ronald, F .... 603-862-0960.... 306 B ron.rodgers@usnh.edu
RODGERS, Ronald, F .... 603-862-0960.... 306 C ron.rogers@unh.edu
RODGERS, Ruby .... 270-534-3184.... 203 E ruby.rodgers@kctcs.edu
RODGERS, Ruth .... 317-955-6321.... 177 I rrodgers@marian.edu
RODGERS, Teresa, P .... 334-670-3221........ 8 A trodgers@troy.edu
RODGERS, Terreta .... 404-225-4604.... 125 E trodgers@atlantatech.edu
RODGERS, Thomas, C .... 585-385-8184.... 348 F trodgers@sjfc.edu
RODGERS, Victor .... 671-735-5640.... 559 E victor.rodgers@guamcc.edu
RODIC, Melissa .... 248-340-0600.... 247 I melissa.rodic@baker.edu
RODIER, Elizabeth, A .... 302-855-1690...... 96 E brodier@dtcc.edu
RODIN, Merrill .... 213-477-2861...... 57 H mrodin@msmc.la.edu
RODKIN, Carolyn .... 510-848-5232...... 47 I crodkin@fst.edu
RODKIN, Dan .... 352-395-4171.... 117 F dan.rodkin@sfcollege.edu
RODLER, Trina .... 323-856-7699...... 28 E trodler@afi.com
RODNE, Anne .... 561-912-1211.... 107 B arodne@evergladesuniversity.edu
RODNEY, Mae, L .... 336-750-2440.... 380 B rodneyml@wssu.edu
RODNING, Janet, M .... 770-720-5954.... 136 C jmr@reinhardt.edu
RODOCKER, Jason, L .... 540-458-8753.... 530 D jrodocker@wlu.edu
RODOLF, Mark .... 405-974-3611.... 413 B mrodolf@uco.edu
RODOLFA, Emil, R .... 530-752-0871...... 73 I errodolfa@ucdavis.edu
RODRICK-SCHNAATH, Heidi .... 215-248-6312.... 435 B hrodrick-schnaath@ltsp.edu
RODRIGUE, Kelly, J .... 985-448-4154.... 216 A kelly.rodrigue@nicholls.edu
RODRIGUE, Morris .... 530-242-7525...... 69 D mrodrigue@shastacollege.edu
RODRIGUES, Leon .... 651-638-6810.... 261 D l-rodrigues@bethel.edu
RODRIGUEZ, Abel .... 787-834-9595.... 566 B arodriguez@uaa.edu
RODRIGUEZ, Adrian .... 817-515-1007.... 496 C adrian.rodiguez@tccd.edu
RODRIGUEZ, Aida, E .... 787-852-1430.... 562 F arodriguez@hccpr.edu
RODRIGUEZ, Alex .... 386-734-3303.... 109 G arodriguez@ftccollege.edu
RODRIGUEZ, Alfred .... 210-999-7206.... 502 E alfred.rodriguez@trinity.edu
RODRIGUEZ, Alma .... 805-654-6360...... 77 F arodriguez@vcccd.edu
RODRIGUEZ, Andy .... 970-248-1337...... 82 F arodrigu@coloradomesa.edu
RODRIGUEZ, Angel .... 787-834-9595.... 566 B arodriguez@uaa.edu
RODRIGUEZ, Anita .... 402-449-2821.... 297 H arodriguez@graceu.edu
RODRIGUEZ, Aristalia .... 212-772-4804.... 327 E aristalia.rodriguez@hunter.cuny.edu
RODRIGUEZ, Arlene .... 413-755-4218.... 241 B arodriguez@stcc.edu
RODRIGUEZ, Armando .... 787-279-1912.... 563 D arodriguez@bayamon.inter.edu
RODRIGUEZ, Armando .... 787-841-2000.... 565 B armando_rodriguez@pucpr.edu
RODRIGUEZ, Barbara .... 305-821-3333.... 109 C bjrodriguez@mm.fnc.edu
RODRIGUEZ, Barbara .... 305-821-3333.... 109 B bjrodriguez@mm.fnc.edu
RODRIGUEZ, Barbara .... 305-821-3333.... 109 C bjrodriguez@mm.fnc.edu
RODRIGUEZ, Barbara .... 305-821-3333.... 109 D bjrodriguez@mm.fnc.edu
RODRIGUEZ, Carlos .... 787-765-4210.... 561 C
RODRIGUEZ, Carmen .... 787-878-5475.... 563 B clrodri@arecibo.inter.edu
RODRIGUEZ, Carmen, J ...... 787-480-2411.... 561 E crodriguez03@sanjuancapital.com
RODRIGUEZ, Charles .... 210-784-1170.... 498 E charles.rodriguez@tamusa.tamus.edu
RODRIGUEZ, Clanbette ...... 787-857-3600.... 563 C crodriguez@br.inter.edu
RODRIGUEZ, Claribel .... 787-621-2835.... 560 D crodriguez@aupr.edu
RODRIGUEZ, Claribette ...... 787-257-7373.... 565 G clrodriguez@suagm.edu
RODRIGUEZ, Daisy .... 787-766-1717.... 565 I drodriguez@mail.suagm.edu
RODRIGUEZ, Damaris .... 787-780-5134.... 564 H drodriguez@nuc.edu
RODRIGUEZ, Daniel, B .... 312-503-3466.... 160 E daniel.rodriguez@law.northwestern.edu
RODRIGUEZ, Daron .... 312-279-3997...... 29 F darodriguez@argosy.edu
RODRIGUEZ, Diana .... 925-424-1405...... 39 D drodriguez@laspositascollege.edu
RODRIGUEZ, Diana .... 787-852-1430.... 562 F drodriguez@hccpr.edu
RODRIGUEZ, Ed .... 816-802-3436.... 283 E erodriguez@kcai.edu
RODRIGUEZ, Edgar .... 787-841-2000.... 565 B edrodrios@pucpr.edu
RODRIGUEZ, Edgar, D .... 787-257-7373.... 565 G ue_erodrigue@suagm.edu
RODRIGUEZ, Edwin .... 787-744-1060.... 564 F erodriguez@mechtech.edu
RODRIGUEZ, Elisamuel .... 787-720-4476.... 566 D decanatofinanzas@colmizpa.edu
RODRIGUEZ, Elizabeth .... 573-882-8279.... 291 A rodriguezea@umsystem.edu
RODRIGUEZ, Elsa .... 787-765-3560.... 562 A errivera@edpcollege.edu
RODRIGUEZ, Fernando, A . 787-844-8959.... 568 A fernando.rodriguez5@upr.edu
RODRIGUEZ, Francisco .... 787-250-8581.... 568 B arquitecto.pr@gmail.com
RODRIGUEZ, Francisco .... 760-757-2121...... 57 E frodriguez@miracosta.edu
RODRIGUEZ, Fred .... 785-864-4904.... 197 B fredrod@ku.edu
RODRIGUEZ, JR., Gerardo .... 956-872-3746.... 494 H gerry@southtexascollege.edu
RODRIGUEZ, Glorimar .... 787-780-5134.... 564 H glrodriguez@nuc.edu
RODRIGUEZ, Havidan .... 956-665-2011.... 506 C havidan@utpa.edu
RODRIGUEZ, Heather .... 210-805-1242.... 504 B hrodrig1@uiwtx.edu
RODRIGUEZ, Irma, I .... 787-841-2000.... 565 B irodriguez@pucpr.edu
RODRIGUEZ, Israel .... 787-780-0070.... 560 H irodriguez@caribbean.edu
RODRIGUEZ, Jalibeth .... 787-841-2000.... 565 B jalibeth_rodriguez@pucpr.edu
RODRIGUEZ, James .... 787-834-5225.... 564 F jrodriguez@mechtech.edu
RODRIGUEZ, Jennifer .... 214-647-6305...... 19 A jennifer.rodriguez@phoenix.edu
RODRIGUEZ, John .... 505-473-6659.... 320 F john.rodriguez@santafeuniversity.edu

RODRIGUEZ, Jorge ... 303-282-3422 ... 88 D

RODRIGUEZ, Jorge ... 787-257-7373 ... 565 G
ac_jrodrigue@suagm.edu

RODRIGUEZ, Jorge, L ... 718-990-1485 ... 348 G
rodriguj@stjohns.edu

RODRIGUEZ, Jose ... 518-694-7200 ... 322 B
jose.rodriguez@acphs.edu

RODRIGUEZ, Jose ... 787-279-1912 ... 563 D
jarodriguez@bayamon.inter.edu

RODRIGUEZ, Jose Ginel ... 787-269-4510 ... 566 C
jose.ginel@uccaribe.edu

RODRIGUEZ, Jose Ginel ... 787-798-6904 ... 566 C
jose.ginel@uccaribe.edu

RODRIGUEZ, Josifina ... 787-257-0000 ... 567 C
josifina.rodriguez@upr.edu

RODRIGUEZ, Juan ... 954-446-6144 ... 100 I
jrodriguez@aiufl.edu

RODRIGUEZ, Juanita ... 787-754-2744 ... 568 B
juana.rodriguez4@upr.edu

RODRIGUEZ, Judith ... 212-226-7300 ... 346 E
judithrodriguez@pbcny.edu

RODRIGUEZ, Julio ... 787-766-1717 ... 565 I
um_jurodrigu@suagm.edu

RODRIGUEZ, Katrina ... 970-351-2796 ... 89 B
katrina.rodriguez@unco.edu

RODRIGUEZ, L. J ... 305-237-3240 ... 113 H
ljrodriguez@mdc.edu

RODRIGUEZ, Leslie ... 847-233-7700 ... 160 D
lrodriguez@nc.edu

RODRIGUEZ, Lisa, R ... 909-593-3511 ... 75 E
lrodriguez@laverne.edu

RODRIGUEZ, Luis ... 908-737-4600 ... 311 A
lurodrig@kean.edu

RODRIGUEZ, Maria ... 305-223-4561 ... 116 E
rodriguez@sjvcs.edu

RODRIGUEZ, Maria ... 787-738-2161 ... 567 D
maria.rodriguez46@upr.edu

RODRIGUEZ, Maria-Judith 413-542-2372 ... 230 A
hr@amherst.edu

RODRIGUEZ, Marisol ... 787-257-0000 ... 567 C
marisol.rodriguez@upr.edu

RODRIGUEZ, Mary, J ... 419-755-4767 ... 397 C
mrodriguez@ncstatecollege.edu

RODRIGUEZ, Mary Ann ... 310-243-3750 ... 34 D
marodriguez@csudh.edu

RODRIGUEZ, Mayra ... 787-743-7979 ... 565 H
ut_mrodriguez@suagm.edu

RODRIGUEZ, Melba ... 773-442-4200 ... 160 A
m-rodriguez44@neiu.edu

RODRIGUEZ, Meredith ... 386-481-2991 ... 102 C
rodriguezm@cookman.edu

RODRIGUEZ, Miguel ... 939-292-8915 ... 568 C
miguel.rodriguez10@upr.edu

RODRIGUEZ, Milagros ... 787-765-1915 ... 564 D
mrodrigo@inter.edu

RODRIGUEZ, Moises ... 210-924-4338 ... 481 G
moises.rodriguez@bua.edu

RODRIGUEZ, Narce ... 971-722-7249 ... 419 G
nrodrigu@pcc.edu

RODRIGUEZ, Nilda ... 787-284-1912 ... 564 A
nilrodri@ponce.inter.edu

RODRIGUEZ, Nilda ... 914-422-4213 ... 345 F
nrodriguez@pace.edu

RODRIGUEZ, Nilda, E ... 787-852-1430 ... 562 F
nrodriguez@hccpr.edu

RODRIGUEZ, Norma ... 562-860-2451 ... 39 A
nrodriguez@cerritos.edu

RODRIGUEZ, Obed ... 787-834-9595 ... 566 B
obedr@uaa.edu

RODRIGUEZ, Oscar ... 910-592-8084 ... 373 G
orodriguez@sampsoncc.edu

RODRIGUEZ, Pablo ... 773-878-7950 ... 163 F
prodriguez@staugustine.edu

RODRIGUEZ, Raquel ... 559-934-2218 ... 78 C
raquelrodriguez@whccd.edu

RODRIGUEZ, Raul ... 714-480-7450 ... 63 E
rodriguez_raul@rsccd.edu

RODRIGUEZ, Raymond ... 312-589-7471 ... 150 G
rrodriguez@ellis.edu

RODRIGUEZ, Reuban, B ... 804-828-8940 ... 526 B
rbrodriguez@vcu.edu

RODRIGUEZ, Ricardo, S ... 972-860-7241 ... 484 I
ricardorodriguez@dcccd.edu

RODRIGUEZ, Ronald ... 504-762-3021 ... 210 F
rrodri@dcc.edu

RODRIGUEZ, Rosa ... 860-832-1652 ... 90 G
rosa.rodriguez@ccsu.edu

RODRIGUEZ, Rosa ... 787-621-2835 ... 560 D
rrodriguez@aupr.edu

RODRIGUEZ, Rosalie, M ... 814-641-3125 ... 432 A
rodrigr@juniata.edu

RODRIGUEZ, Seph ... 626-529-8469 ... 60 F
srodriguez@pacificoaks.edu

RODRIGUEZ, Shari, M ... 574-284-4581 ... 179 F
srodriguez@saintmarys.edu

RODRIGUEZ, Sherri ... 818-947-2726 ... 55 E
rodrigsa@lavc.edu

RODRIGUEZ, Silvio ... 305-237-7445 ... 113 H
srodrig2@mdc.edu

RODRIGUEZ, Sonya, F ... 575-624-8066 ... 319 C
sonya@nmmi.edu

RODRIGUEZ, Stephanie ... 310-660-3601 ... 45 E
srodriguez@elcamino.edu

RODRIGUEZ, Steven ... 949-214-3003 ... 43 C
steven.rodriguez@cui.edu

RODRIGUEZ, Sylvia ... 305-474-6871 ... 117 A
srodriguez@stu.edu

RODRIGUEZ, Teresita ... 310-434-4774 ... 68 D
rodriguez_teresita@smc.edu

RODRIGUEZ, Vanessa ... 305-273-4499 ... 103 J
vanessa.rodriguez@cbt.edu

RODRIGUEZ, Velia ... 559-737-3775 ... 42 D
veliar@cos.edu

RODRIGUEZ, Victor ... 361-593-5781 ... 498 D
tamukcso@tamuk.edu

RODRIGUEZ, Victoria ... 512-475-8620 ... 505 D
v.rodriguez@mail.utexas.edu

RODRIGUEZ, Vince ... 714-241-6195 ... 41 B
vrodriguez@coastline.edu

RODRIGUEZ, Wanda ... 787-257-0000 ... 567 C
wanda.rodriguez@upr.edu

RODRIGUEZ, Zulyn ... 787-764-0000 ... 568 B
zulyn.rodriguez@upr.edu

RODRIGUEZ-CANCEL, Jaime, L ... 787-723-4481 ... 561 B
jarodriguez@ceaprc.edu

RODRIGUEZ-CHARDAVOYNE, Esther ... 718-518-4308 ... 327 D
erodriguez@hostos.cuny.edu

RODRIGUEZ DE ARZOLA, Olga ... 787-840-2575 ... 565 A

RODRIGUEZ-DORESTANT, Simone ... 718-804-8805 ... 328 C
simone@mec.cuny.edu

RODRIGUEZ-GARCIA, Ileana ... 787-725-6500 ... 561 A
irodriguez@sju.albizu.edu

RODRIGUEZ-GARCIA, Ileana ... 305-593-1223 ... 102 H
cvazquez@albizu.edu

RODRIGUEZ-GUILLEN, Linda ... 956-364-4427 ... 500 D
lindarodriguez-guillen@tstc.edu

RODRIGUEZ-IRIZARRY, Carlos ... 787-725-6500 ... 561 A
crodriguez@albizu.edu

RODRIGUEZ-LOPEZ, Miguel, A ... 787-723-4481 ... 561 B
centro@ceaprc.edu

RODRIGUEZ-MENENDEZ, Gerardo ... 805-898-2909 ... 47 C
grodriguez@fielding.edu

RODRIGUEZ-MERCADO, Rafael ... 787-758-2525 ... 567 G
rafael.rodriguez18@upr.edu

RODRIGUEZ-MONTALVO, Astrid, J ... 787-834-5151 ... 565 D
armontalvo@email.pucpr.edu

RODRIGUEZ-PAZ, Maria ... 787-620-2040 ... 560 D
mrodriguez_paz@aupr.edu

RODRIGUEZ-QUINONES, Jose ... 787-725-6500 ... 561 A
jrodriguezq@albizu.edu

RODRIQUES, Linda ... 201-360-4651 ... 310 E
lrodriques@hccc.edu

RODRIQUEZ, Jason ... 503-883-2574 ... 416 H
jrodriqu@linfield.edu

RODRIQUEZ, Mike ... 505-984-6058 ... 320 C

RODRIQUEZ, Nicky, M ... 219-942-1459 ... 170 I
nrodriquez@ccr.edu

RODRIQUEZ, Steve ... 918-293-4888 ... 410 E
stephen.r.rodriquez@okstate.edu

RODRIQUEZ, Sylvia ... 925-424-1542 ... 39 D
srodriquez@laspositascollege.edu

RODRIQUEZ, Vincent ... 210-283-5096 ... 504 B
vincent@uiwtx.edu

RODRÍGUEZ, Glenda ... 787-765-3560 ... 562 A
glenda@edpcollege.edu

RODRÍGUEZ, Ibis ... 787-766-1717 ... 565 I
ibrodriguez@suagm.edu

RODRÍGUEZ, Luis ... 787-850-9305 ... 567 E
luis.rodriguez39@upr.edu

RODRÍGUEZ-MERCADO, Rafael ... 787-758-2525 ... 566 G
rafael.rodriguez18@upr.edu

RODRÍGUEZ-RODRÍGUEZ, Fernando ... 787-844-8181 ... 566 G
fernando.rodriguez5@upr.edu

RODSKI, Pete ... 502-213-7227 ... 202 F
peter.rodski@kctcs.edu

RODSTROM, Kim ... 330-823-2292 ... 404 C
rodstrkt@mountunion.edu

ROE, David, L ... 973-972-1412 ... 316 F
roeda@umdnj.edu

ROE, Dean ... 734-995-7309 ... 249 G
roed@cuaa.edu

ROE, Herb ... 605-221-3134 ... 464 D
hroe@kilian.edu

ROE, Michael ... 845-431-8018 ... 332 D
michael.roe@sunydutchess.edu

ROE, Michael ... 845-341-4205 ... 345 E
michael.roe@sunyorange.edu

ROE, Michael, D ... 206-281-2252 ... 537 H
mroe@spu.edu

ROE, Robert ... 989-463-7326 ... 247 B
roe@alma.edu

ROEBUCK, Randy ... 316-677-9535 ... 197 G
rroebuck@watc.edu

ROECKER, Pamela ... 617-735-9985 ... 234 C
roeckerp@emmanuel.edu

ROECKLE, Charles, A ... 512-471-1232 ... 505 D
c.roeckle@mail.utexas.edu

ROECKS, Jan ... 650-306-3201 ... 67 F
jroecks@smccd.edu

ROEDEL, Glenn ... 215-780-1296 ... 446 G
groedel@salus.edu

ROEDER, Barclay ... 907-564-8333 ... 10 D
broeder@alaskapacific.edu

ROEDER, Lynn, M ... 252-328-9297 ... 377 E
roederl@ecu.edu

ROEHL, Bob ... 206-546-4514 ... 538 C
broehl@shoreline.edu

ROELFS, Melinda, A ... 620-235-4226 ... 196 C
maroelfs@pittstate.edu

ROELFS, Pamela, J ... 860-486-4240 ... 94 G
pamela.roelfs@uconn.edu

ROELFSEMA, Cheryl, E ... 815-224-0419 ... 153 E
cheryl_roelfsema@ivcc.edu

ROELKE, Scott ... 651-423-8297 ... 266 B
scott.roelke@dctc.edu

ROELL, William ... 609-896-5009 ... 313 F
wroell@rider.edu

ROELLKE, Christopher ... 845-437-5600 ... 359 F
chroellke@vassar.edu

ROELOFS, Lyle, D ... 859-985-3522 ... 199 A
roelofsl@berea.edu

ROENIGK, Ashley ... 410-532-5395 ... 225 D
aroenigk@ndm.edu

ROER, Robert, D ... 910-962-4117 ... 379 D
roer@uncw.edu

ROERIG, Sandra, C ... 318-675-5000 ... 213 B
sroeri@lsuhsc.edu

ROESSLER, Billy ... 940-668-7731 ... 491 E
broessler@nctc.edu

ROETHEMEYER, Robert, V . 260-452-2146 ... 170 J
robert.roethemeyer@ctsfw.edu

ROETHER, Diane ... 940-668-4283 ... 491 E
droether@nctc.edu

ROETHLER, Don ... 701-224-5485 ... 382 D
donald.roethler@bismarckstate.edu

ROETHLISBERGER, Michael, J ... 989-774-2317 ... 249 C
roeth1mj@cmich.edu

ROETTGER, Walter ... 312-261-3073 ... 159 E
walter.roettger@nl.edu

ROETZEL, Mary ... 617-369-4292 ... 244 E
mroetzel@mfa.org

ROFF, Lucinda, L ... 205-348-3924 ... 8 E
lroff@sw.ua.edu

ROGALSKI, Joseph, T ... 941-355-9080 ... 105 D
jrogalski@ewcollege.org

ROGALSKY, Amy ... 405-974-5376 ... 413 B
arogalsky@uco.edu

ROGAN, Doreen ... 207-216-4320 ... 219 C
drogan@yccc.edu

ROGAN, Fred, R ... 205-726-2837 ... 6 G
cfrogan@samford.edu

ROGAN, Margaret ... 617-824-8590 ... 234 B
margaret_rogan@emerson.edu

ROGAN, Mary, T ... 718-289-5151 ... 326 E
mary.rogan@bcc.cuny.edu

ROGAN, Patricia, M ... 317-274-6862 ... 174 D
progan@iupui.edu

ROGAN, William, D ... 615-230-3595 ... 476 C
william.rogan@volstate.edu

ROGELSTAD, Todd ... 701-845-7209 ... 382 C
todd.rogelstad@vcsu.edu

ROGENTINE, Linda ... 218-723-6022 ... 262 G
lrogenti@css.edu

ROGER-GORDON, A. Patrick ... 212-346-1295 ... 345 F
arogergordon@pace.edu

ROGERS, Adam ... 212-592-2000 ... 350 F
arogers@sva.edu

ROGERS, Angela, K ... 561-237-7297 ... 113 D
arogers@lynn.edu

ROGERS, Beth ... 513-244-8134 ... 387 E
beth.rogers@ccuniversity.edu

ROGERS, Brian ... 503-494-8362 ... 418 D
cdrcadmin@ohsu.edu

ROGERS, Brian, D ... 907-474-7112 ... 10 I
uaf.chancellor@alaska.edu

ROGERS, Cheryl, L ... 903-510-3217 ... 503 A
crog@tjc.edu

ROGERS, Christopher ... 610-647-4400 ... 431 C
crogers@immaculata.edu

ROGERS, Cindy, A ... 972-860-8186 ... 484 H
car3810@dcccd.edu

ROGERS, Craig, L ... 270-789-5057 ... 199 F
crogers@campbellsville.edu

ROGERS, Dana ... 409-882-3372 ... 501 B
dana.rogers@lsco.edu

ROGERS, Dana, N ... 409-882-3397 ... 501 B
dana.rogers@lsco.edu

ROGERS, David, E ... 315-684-6054 ... 354 F
rogersde@morrisville.edu

ROGERS, Deborah ... 215-641-6506 ... 436 G
drogers@mc3.edu

ROGERS, Donna ... 252-789-0290 ... 371 H
drogers@martincc.edu

ROGERS, Dwayne ... 318-487-7216 ... 209 F
rogers@lacollege.edu

ROGERS, Elizabeth ... 931-372-3317 ... 474 B
erogers@tntech.edu

ROGERS, Elizabeth, A ... 336-278-6350 ... 364 D
rogers@elon.edu

ROGERS, Fred, A ... 507-222-5411 ... 261 G
frogers@carleton.edu

ROGERS, Gail ... 423-746-5202 ... 476 F
grogers@twcnet.edu

ROGERS, Gannon ... 707-668-5663 ... 44 A

ROGERS, Glen ... 414-382-6269 ... 546 B
glen.rogers@alverno.edu

ROGERS, Greg ... 623-845-4526 ... 15 H
greg.rogers@gcmail.maricopa.edu

ROGERS, Greg ... 412-392-3924 ... 445 A
grogers@pointpark.edu

ROGERS, Harry, C ... 215-898-7091 ... 448 J
library@pobox.upenn.edu

ROGERS, Hudson ... 239-590-7329 ... 119 B
hrogers@fgcu.edu

ROGERS, J. Orion ... 540-831-5958 ... 523 A
jorogers@radford.edu

ROGERS, Jack, T ... 541-737-3010 ... 418 F
jack.rogers@oregonstate.edu

ROGERS, James ... 212-327-8506 ... 347 H
jrogers@mail.rockefeller.edu

ROGERS, James ... 212-517-0435 ... 340 C
jrogers@mmm.edu

ROGERS, Janet ... 614-287-2727 ... 389 A
jrogers@cscc.edu

ROGERS, Jason ... 615-460-6441 ... 467 D
jason.rogers@belmont.edu

ROGERS, Jeanette ... 205-853-1200 ... 5 C
jrogers@jeffstateonline.com

ROGERS, Jenica, P ... 315-267-2482 ... 354 C
rogersjp@potsdam.edu

ROGERS, Jesse ... 858-598-1200 ... 30 D
jerogers@aii.edu

ROGERS, Jesse, W ... 940-397-4211 ... 491 B
jesse.rogers@mwsu.edu

ROGERS, Jessica ... 941-487-4900 ... 120 A
ncalum@ncf.edu

ROGERS, Jevita ... 719-255-3460 ... 88 I
jrogers3@uccs.edu

ROGERS, Johnell ... 803-934-3256 ... 459 G
jrogers@morris.edu

ROGERS, Jolayne ... 816-322-0110 ... 279 D
jolayne.rogers@calvary.edu

ROGERS, Jolene, R ... 712-362-0491 ... 186 A
jrogers@iowalakes.edu

ROGERS, Jolynn ... 509-359-2383 ... 533 H
jrogers@ewu.edu

ROGERS, Joseph ... 320-363-5230 ... 271 A
jrogers@csbsju.edu

ROGERS, Joseph, T ... 610-527-0200 ... 445 J
jtrogers@rosemont.edu

ROGERS, Joyce ... 317-916-7850 ... 175 I
jrogers@ivytech.edu

ROGERS, Judith ... 340-692-4132 ... 568 E
jrogers@live.uvi.edu

ROGERS, Judy, R ... 417-667-8181 ... 280 E
jrogers@cottey.edu

ROGERS, Kathleen, R ... 617-521-2276 ... 244 F
kathleen.rogers@simmons.edu

ROGERS, Katrina ... 805-898-2924 ... 47 C
krogers@fielding.edu

ROGERS, Keri ... 832-813-6597 ... 490 E
keri.rogers@lonestar.edu

ROGERS, Kiri ... 267-502-4890 ... 423 C
kiri.rogers@brynathyn.edu

ROGERS, Lalita ... 903-927-3304 ... 509 E
lestes@wileyc.edu

ROGERS, Leslie, D ... 252-493-7322 ... 372 H
lrogers@email.pittcc.edu

ROGERS, Lisa, C ... 615-898-5345 ... 473 G
lisa.rogers@mtsu.edu

ROGERS, Mary ... 619-388-6591 ... 65 E
mrogers@sdccd.edu

ROGERS, Meryl ... 631-851-6296 ... 356 G
rogersm@sunysuffolk.edu

ROGERS, Michael, B ... 607-735-1891 ... 332 I
mrogers@elmira.edu

ROGERS, Michael, F ... 843-953-7696 ... 456 C
mike.rogers@citadel.edu

ROGERS, Mike ... 209-946-2569 ... 76 A
mrogers@pacific.edu

ROGERS, Mike ... 270-686-4481 ... 203 B
mike.rogers@kctcs.edu

ROGERS, Nancy, B ... 812-237-7900 ... 173 B
nancy.rogers@indstate.edu

ROGERS, Patricia, A ... 781-891-2622 ... 231 D
progers@bentley.edu

ROGERS, Patricia, L ... 218-755-2965 ... 265 I
progers@bemidjistate.edu

ROGERS, Phil ... 208-459-5282 ... 143 D
progers@collegeofidaho.edu

ROGERS, Philip ... 252-328-6105 ... 377 E
rogersp@ecu.edu

ROGERS, Phyllis ... 254-295-4501 ... 504 C
progers@umhb.edu

ROGERS, Phyllis ... 864-592-4816 ... 461 C
rogersp@sccsc.edu

ROGERS, Ralph ... 510-780-4500 ... 53 J
rrogers@lifewest.edu

ROGERS, Ralph, V .... 219-989-2446.... 178 K
rvrogers@purduecal.edu
ROGERS, Randy .... 317-921-4737.... 175 K
rrogers@ivytech.edu
ROGERS, Randy .... 336-386-3466.... 374 E
rogersr@surry.edu
ROGERS, Ray .... 407-646-2195.... 116 D
rrogers@rollins.edu
ROGERS, Richard, L .... 313-664-7474.... 249 E
rrogers@collegeforcreativestudies.edu
ROGERS, Richard, R .... 909-593-3511...... 75 E
rrogers2@laverne.edu
ROGERS, Rita .... 252-862-1232.... 373 C
rogersri@roanokechowan.edu
ROGERS, Rob .... 352-638-9762.... 102 B
rrogers@beaconcollege.edu
ROGERS, Rodney, K .... 419-372-2915.... 385 E
rrogers@bgsu.edu
ROGERS, Russell .... 201-216-5688.... 315 E
rrogers@stevens.edu
ROGERS, Sandra .... 801-422-1801.... 509 H
sandra_rogers@byu.edu
ROGERS, Scott .... 828-726-2488.... 368 G
srogers@cccti.edu
ROGERS, Scott .... 509-542-4834.... 532 H
srogers@columbiabasin.edu
ROGERS, Scott, S .... 330-385-1070.... 400 F
srogers@ovct.edu
ROGERS, Shannon .... 479-394-7622...... 23 E
srogers@rmcc.edu
ROGERS, Sharon .... 609-894-9311.... 308 B
srogers@bcc.edu
ROGERS, Stacy .... 859-344-3309.... 206 I
stacy.rogers@thomasmore.edu
ROGERS, Stephanie .... 318-678-6000.... 209 I
srogers@bpcc.edu
ROGERS, Stephen, K .... 405-744-8052.... 410 C
steve.rogers@okstate.edu
ROGERS, Susan .... 706-379-3111.... 140 A
srogers@yhc.edu
ROGERS, Susan .... 972-883-4325.... 506 A
susan.rogers@utdallas.edu
ROGERS, Tamara, E .... 617-496-3069.... 235 D
tamara_rogers@harvard.edu
ROGERS, Tammy .... 706-880-8344.... 133 B
trogers@lagrange.edu
ROGERS, Tammy .... 202-319-5232...... 97 E
rogerst@cua.edu
ROGERS, Tamy .... 214-333-5158.... 484 D
tamy@dbu.edu
ROGERS, Theresa .... 925-969-3449...... 52 C
trogers@jfku.edu
ROGERS, Thomas .... 502-213-7310.... 202 F
thomas.rogers@kctcs.edu
ROGERS, Tracy .... 719-587-7990...... 80 L
tracy_rogers@adams.edu
ROGERS, Vivian, D .... 757-499-7900.... 517 D
vdrogers@bryantstratton.edu
ROGERS, W. Timothy .... 865-974-6593.... 477 D
timrogers@utk.edu
ROGERS-ADKINSON,
Diana .... 573-651-2408.... 289 K
drogersadkinson@semo.edu
ROGERSON, Andrew .... 707-664-2028...... 37 D
andrew.rogerson@sonoma.edu
ROGERSON, Joanie .... 360-736-9391.... 532 D
jrogerson@centralia.edu
ROGG, Cathie .... 616-698-7111.... 250 C
crogg@davenport.edu
ROGGE, Ann .... 302-736-2445...... 97 A
roggean@wesley.edu
ROGNSTAD, Lynn, B .... 605-677-6497.... 465 G
lynn.rognstad@usd.edu
ROGOFF, Mai-Lan, A .... 508-856-5652.... 237 C
mai-lan.rogoff@umassmed.edu
ROGOW, Robert .... 859-622-1409.... 200 J
robert.rogow@eku.edu
ROGSTAD, Mark .... 509-574-4671.... 540 D
mrogstad@yvcc.edu
ROHALY, Julie .... 615-217-9347.... 468 D
jrohaly@daymarinstitute.edu
ROHAN, James, P .... 920-465-2075.... 551 B
rohanj@uwgb.edu
ROHANNA, Susan .... 610-902-8602.... 424 B
susan.rohanna@cabrini.edu
ROHDE, Leslie .... 612-861-7554.... 260 G
leslie@alfredadler.edu
ROHDE, Scott, W .... 608-785-8711.... 551 C
srohde@uwlax.edu
ROHDE-BROWN, Juliet ..... 805-962-8179...... 29 A
ROHDER, Kelly .... 815-280-2915.... 154 J
krohder@jjc.edu
ROHLEDER, Ann .... 812-357-6610.... 180 A
arohleder@saintmeinrad.edu
ROHLEDER, John .... 651-779-3496.... 266 A
john.rohleder@century.edu
ROHLENA, Robbie .... 712-274-5426.... 187 G
rohlena@morningside.edu
ROHLER, James .... 740-363-1146.... 396 A
jrohler@mtso.edu
ROHLFS, Steven .... 301-447-5295.... 225 A
rohlfs@msmary.edu
ROHLOF, Jason .... 612-624-9022.... 272 A
rohloff@umn.edu
ROHM, Robert, K .... 937-766-7603.... 386 G
rohmr@cedarville.edu
ROHNER, Christy .... 270-686-4243.... 199 B
christy.rohner@brescia.edu
ROHNER, Tom .... 630-889-6661.... 159 F
trohner@nuhs.edu
ROHR, Ann .... 970-207-4500...... 89 D
annr@uscareerinstitute.edu
ROHR, Ann .... 970-207-4550...... 86 D
ROHRBACH, Anne, L .... 814-865-5471.... 438 G
alr3@psu.edu
ROHRBACH, Daniel, W ..... 937-255-6565.... 557 C
daniel.rohrbach@afit.edu
ROHRBACK, Jane, T .... 248-204-3160.... 254 B
jrohrback@ltu.edu
ROHRBAUGH, Suzanne ..... 252-335-0821.... 369 G
suzanne_rohrbaugh@albemarle.edu
ROHRER, Douglas .... 270-901-3490.... 208 A
douglas.rohrer@wku.edu
ROHRER, Katherine .... 609-258-7800.... 312 G
krohrer@princeton.edu
ROHRER, Mary .... 507-457-2602.... 269 G
mrohrer@winona.edu
ROHRS, Dawn, M .... 816-654-7012.... 283 F
drohrs@kcumb.edu
ROHWER, Keith .... 402-941-6332.... 298 I
rohwer@midlandu.edu
ROIDT, Joseph, M .... 304-637-1277.... 541 A
roidtj@dewv.edu
ROIG, Lizzette, A .... 787-844-9231.... 568 A
lizzette.roig@upr.edu
ROJAS, Carmen, I .... 787-743-4041.... 561 F
crojas@columbiaco.edu
ROJAS, Jason .... 860-297-4166...... 94 E
jason.rojas@trincoll.edu
ROJAS, Lydia .... 787-744-1060.... 564 F
lrojas@mechtech.edu
ROJAS, Rodney .... 213-613-2200...... 70 H
rodney_rojas@sciarc.edu
ROJCEWICZ, Peter, M ...... 206-268-4108.... 530 I
projcewicz@antioch.edu
ROJO, Richard .... 209-946-2311...... 76 A
rrojo@pacific.edu
ROKAS, Tracy .... 615-460-5405.... 467 D
tracy.rokas@belmont.edu
ROKOS, Jean, M .... 231-995-1248.... 256 D
jrokos@nmc.edu
ROKOS, Nicole .... 561-297-3880.... 119 A
nrokos@fau.edu
ROKOWSKY, Eli .... 845-425-1370.... 345 B
ROKOWSKY, Israel .... 845-425-1370.... 345 B
ROKSANDIC, Stevo .... 614-234-1644.... 396 H
sroksandic@mchs.com
ROKUSEK, Jim .... 605-367-6109.... 466 D
jim.rokusek@southeasttech.edu
ROLAND, Cheryl .... 269-387-8412.... 260 C
cheryl.roland@wmich.edu
ROLAND, Christy .... 515-244-4221.... 181 F
rolandc@aib.edu
ROLAND, David, E .... 706-233-7329.... 137 A
droland@shorter.edu
ROLAND, Harriet, A .... 803-533-3790.... 460 G
rolandha@scsu.edu
ROLAND, Kirc, J .... 360-442-2471.... 535 I
kroland@lowercolumbia.edu
ROLAND, Mark .... 515-244-4221.... 181 F
rolandm@aib.edu
ROLAND, Meg .... 503-699-3336.... 416 J
mroland@marylhurst.edu
ROLAND, Suzie .... 434-239-5222.... 521 H
ROLD, Gary, F .... 630-617-3078.... 150 H
garyr@elmhurst.edu
ROLDAN, Marggi .... 864-578-8770.... 460 F
mroldan@sherman.edu
ROLEN, Chris .... 408-741-2092...... 78 E
chris_rolen@wvm.edu
ROLEN, Scott .... 541-917-4420.... 416 I
rolens@linnbenton.edu
ROLEY, V. Vance .... 808-956-8377.... 141 G
vroley@hawaii.edu
ROLFE, Cynthia .... 405-974-2688.... 413 B
crolfe@uco.edu
ROLFE, Rial, D .... 806-743-2905.... 502 B
rial.rolfe@ttuhsc.edu
ROLFE, Stanley, T .... 785-864-3881.... 197 B
srolfe@ku.edu
ROLFES, Katherine .... 337-521-8906.... 211 J
krolfes@southlouisiana.edu
ROLFS, Trevor .... 620-792-9378.... 190 H
rolfst@bartonccc.edu
ROLFSON, Eric, F .... 207-581-1151.... 220 A
eric.rolfson@maine.edu
ROLHEISER, Ronald .... 210-341-1366.... 491 G
rrolheiser@ost.edu
ROLL, Debbie .... 907-564-8220...... 10 D
droll@alaskapacific.edu
ROLLANS, Mary Ann .... 479-968-0234...... 20 G
mrollans@atu.edu
ROLLE, Kevin, A .... 256-372-5230........ 1 A
kevin.rolle@aamu.edu
ROLLENE, Jerry .... 479-524-7212...... 22 C
jrollene@jbu.edu
ROLLER, Laura .... 612-330-1720.... 261 B
roller@augsburg.edu
ROLLER, Steven, A .... 617-228-2394.... 239 C
sroller@bhcc.mass.edu
ROLLESTON, George .... 440-826-2081.... 384 K
grollest@bw.edu
ROLLEY, LuAnn, K .... 802-656-7892.... 514 H
luann.rolley@uvm.edu
ROLLING, OSB, Brendan .. 913-360-7655.... 191 A
brolling@benedictine.edu
ROLLINGS, Dave .... 775-445-4223.... 303 B
dcr@wnc.edu
ROLLINS, Andrea .... 619-594-6416...... 37 A
arollins@mail.sdsu.edu
ROLLINS, Cheryl .... 443-885-4429.... 224 E
cheryl.rollins@morgan.edu
ROLLINS, Karen .... 860-509-9511...... 93 A
krollins@hartsem.edu
ROLLINS, Pam .... 334-420-4253........ 7 H
prollins@trenholmstate.edu
ROLLINS, Stephen, J .... 907-786-1825...... 10 H
srollins@uaa.alaska.edu
ROLLISON, Jeffrey, D .... 610-647-4400.... 431 C
jrollison@immaculata.edu
ROLLMAN, Catherine, A .... 804-752-7270.... 523 C
crollman@rmc.edu
ROLLO, Ann .... 315-364-3235.... 360 D
arollo@wells.edu
ROLLO, J. Michael .... 239-590-7910.... 119 B
jmrollo@fgcu.edu
ROLLOCK, Alysa, C .... 765-494-5830.... 178 J
acrollock@purdue.edu
ROLLS, Dickie .... 620-252-7575.... 192 B
dickier@coffeyville.edu
ROLON, Maricruz .... 787-743-7979.... 565 H
mrolon@suagm.edu
ROLON, Reynaldo .... 787-279-1912.... 563 D
rrolon@bayamon.inter.edu
ROLPH, Chris .... 865-573-4517.... 469 L
crolph@johnsonu.edu
ROM, Cristine .... 216-421-7440.... 388 A
crom@cia.edu
ROM, Kjetil .... 541-881-5746.... 420 E
krom@tvcc.cc
ROMA, Lawrence, J .... 607-777-2224.... 351 F
lroma@binghamton.edu
ROMAGNI, Joanne .... 312-362-4560.... 149 A
jromagni@depaul.edu
ROMAGNOLI, Janice .... 615-655-7274.... 325 H
jaromagnoli@cazenovia.edu
ROMAIN, Pete .... 212-517-0414.... 340 C
promain@mmm.edu
ROMALI, Reagan, F .... 773-907-4451.... 147 D
rromali@ccc.edu
ROMAN, Albert, J .... 619-482-6328...... 71 D
aroman@swccd.edu
ROMAN, Brunilda .... 787-480-2410.... 561 E
broman@sanjuancapital.com
ROMAN, Catalin .... 505-277-5521.... 321 C
gcroman@unm.edu
ROMAN, Cathy .... 717-291-4197.... 429 F
cathy.roman@fandm.edu
ROMAN, Cynthia .... 248-942-3334.... 256 F
caroman@oaklandcc.edu
ROMAN, Elba, I .... 787-890-2681.... 566 H
elba.roman@upr.edu
ROMAN, Ivan, F .... 787-882-2065.... 566 A
director_ejecutivo@unitecpr.net
ROMAN, Jose Luis .... 787-480-2461.... 561 E
jroman@sanjuancapital.com
ROMAN, Juan, E .... 787-841-2000.... 565 B
jroman@pucpr.edu
ROMAN, Kristen .... 312-850-7186.... 147 F
1118mgr@fheg.follett.com
ROMAN, Marcia .... 407-708-4722.... 117 H
romanm@seminolestate.edu
ROMAN, Maria .... 559-791-2364...... 53 A
mroman@portervillecollege.edu
ROMAN, Nilsa, M .... 787-891-0925.... 563 A
nroman@aguadilla.inter.edu
ROMAN, Paul .... 724-838-4215.... 447 C
roman@setonhill.edu
ROMAN, Susan .... 708-524-6986.... 150 C
sroman@dom.edu
ROMAN, Vladimir .... 787-763-6425.... 562 I
vroman@inter.edu
ROMAN-LAGUNAS,
Victoria, A .... 773-442-5420.... 160 A
v-roman-lagunas@neiu.edu
ROMAN-VARGAS,
Madeline .... 773-489-8910.... 147 I
mroman-vargas@ccc.edu
ROMANELLO, Mary .... 202-884-9000...... 99 H
romanellom@trinitydc.edu
ROMANO, C. Renee .... 217-333-1300.... 167 D
romano3@illinois.edu
ROMANO, Carol, A .... 301-295-1180.... 558 D
carol.romano@usuhs.edu
ROMANO, Christopher ...... 201-684-7309.... 313 C
cromano@ramapo.edu
ROMANO, Daniel, A .... 309-298-2517.... 168 C
da-romano@wiu.edu
ROMANO, Denise .... 973-972-5399.... 316 C
romano@umdnj.edu
ROMANO, Fred, D .... 630-515-6388.... 158 F
froman@midwestern.edu
ROMANO, Joseph .... 718-420-4599.... 360 A
joe.romano@wagner.edu
ROMANO, Joyce, C .... 407-582-3401.... 123 B
jromano@valenciacollege.edu
ROMANO, Judith, J .... 864-294-3470.... 458 E
judith.romano@furman.edu
ROMANO, Michael .... 623-245-4600...... 18 J
mromano@uti.edu
ROMANO, Nicole .... 302-356-6846...... 97 C
nicole.romano@wilmu.edu
ROMANO, Pam .... 910-272-3531.... 373 D
promano@robeson.edu
ROMANO, Sandra .... 340-693-1238.... 568 E
sromano@live.uvi.edu
ROMANO, Susan, M .... 585-785-1275.... 334 A
romanosm@flcc.edu
ROMANO, Wendy .... 215-871-6300.... 444 C
wendyr@pcom.edu
ROMANO, Xavier .... 559-456-2777...... 27 B
xromano@alliant.edu
ROMANOVITCH, Theresa .. 508-678-2811.... 239 B
theresa.romanovitch@bristolcc.edu
ROMANTIC, Thomas, W .... 607-255-8574.... 331 B
twr2@cornell.edu
ROMAY, Carlos .... 407-253-5354.... 103 A
ROMBALSKI, Patrick, H ..... 617-552-2052.... 232 B
patrick.rombalski@bc.edu
ROMBOUTS, Stephen, R .... 814-472-3009.... 446 B
srombouts@francis.edu
ROME, Alan, K .... 440-943-7600.... 401 G
cpl@dioceseofcleveland.org
ROME, Alyson .... 785-826-2605.... 194 E
arome@k-state.edu
ROME, Dennis .... 262-595-2364.... 552 A
dennis.rome@uwp.edu
ROME, JoAnne .... 413-552-2183.... 239 F
jrome@hcc.edu
ROME, Kevin, D .... 919-530-6342.... 378 B
krome@nccu.edu
ROMELDA, Simmons .... 478-825-6219.... 129 F
simmonsr@fvsu.edu
ROMEO, Alexa .... 213-251-3636...... 29 J
aromeo@aii.edu
ROMEO, Lynn .... 732-571-7518.... 311 E
lromeo@monmouth.edu
ROMEO, Monica .... 716-286-8536.... 344 D
mromeo@niagara.edu
ROMER, Christine, E .... 636-922-8362.... 288 B
cromer@stchas.edu
ROMERO, Aldemaro .... 618-650-5047.... 165 C
aromero@siue.edu
ROMERO, Alison .... 808-942-1000.... 141 D
careers.hnl.ea@remingtoncollege.edu
ROMERO, Angel, F .... 787-765-1915.... 564 D
aromero@inter.edu
ROMERO, Charles .... 913-588-8011.... 197 C
cromero@kumc.edu
ROMERO, Christina .... 714-564-6091...... 63 F
romero_christina@sac.edu
ROMERO, Connie .... 505-747-2227.... 320 A
cvromero@nnmc.edu
ROMERO, David .... 575-624-8250.... 319 C
romero@nmmi.edu
ROMERO, Georg .... 831-479-5771...... 31 I
geromero@cabrillo.edu
ROMERO, Herminio .... 787-622-8000.... 566 E
hromero@pupr.edu
ROMERO, Hilario .... 505-747-2204.... 320 A
hilario@nnmc.edu
ROMERO, Narda .... 914-674-7841.... 340 F
nromero@mercy.edu
ROMERO, Peter .... 505-473-6328.... 320 F
peter.romero@santafeuniversity.edu
ROMERO, Reyna .... 713-221-8231.... 503 F
romeror@uhd.edu
ROMERO, Sally .... 970-943-2150...... 89 E
sromero@western.edu
ROMERO, Van, D .... 575-835-5646.... 319 A
vromero@nmt.edu
ROMERO, Victoria .... 909-621-8149...... 69 A
victoria.romero@scrippscollege.edu
ROMERO-LEGGOTT,
Valerie .... 505-272-2728.... 321 C
vromero@salud.unm.edu
ROMESBURG, Kerry, D ..... 904-256-7016.... 111 L
kromesb@ju.edu
ROMESBURG, Rosemarie .. 304-367-4284.... 543 B
rosemarie.romesburg@pierpont.edu
ROMICH, Barbara .... 704-484-5332.... 369 E
romich@clevelandcc.edu
ROMIG, Kenneth, J .... 724-946-7141.... 451 C
romigkj@westminster.edu
ROMIG, Thomas, J .... 785-670-1662.... 197 F
thomas.romig@washburn.edu
ROMINE, Connie .... 740-593-4300.... 399 G
romine@ohio.edu
ROMINGER, Anna .... 219-980-6636.... 174 B
arominge@iun.edu
ROMKEMA, Priscilla .... 605-642-6341.... 465 H
priscilla.romkema@bhsu.edu
ROMO, Michael .... 650-508-3453...... 59 H
mromo@ndnu.edu
ROMO, Ricardo .... 210-458-4101.... 506 D
president@utsa.edu

ROSEN-BRAND, Amy .... 716-878-4500.... 353 A
rosenba@buffalostate.edu
ROSEN SINGLETON, Suzanne .... 202-448-7213...... 98 B
suzanne.singleton@gallaudet.edu
ROSENBALM, Whitney .... 972-238-6023.... 485 D
wrosenbalm@dcccd.edu
ROSENBAUM, Carol .... 212-463-0400.... 358 B
carolr@touro.edu
ROSENBAUM, David, R ..... 864-941-8377.... 460 D
rosenbaum.d@ptc.edu
ROSENBAUM, Irving .... 954-262-1507.... 114 B
irv@nsu.nova.edu
ROSENBAUM, Thomas, F .. 773-702-8810.... 166 G
provost@uchicago.edu
ROSENBERG, Alannah .... 949-582-4854...... 70 F
aorrison@saddleback.edu
ROSENBERG, Brian, C .... 651-696-6207.... 264 J
rosenbergb@macalester.edu
ROSENBERG, Chaim .... 718-854-2290.... 323 I
ROSENBERG, Eric .... 973-720-2303.... 317 D
rosenbergel@wpunj.edu
ROSENBERG, Harry .... 702-968-2020.... 303 D
jseip@roseman.edu
ROSENBERG, Jane .... 626-529-8033...... 60 F
jrosenberg@pacificoaks.edu
ROSENBERG, John .... 801-422-2779.... 509 H
john_rosenberg@byu.edu
ROSENBERG, Kris .... 503-251-2821.... 421 A
krosenberg@uws.edu
ROSENBERG, Lea .... 414-258-4810.... 549 D
rosenbel@mtmary.edu
ROSENBERG, Mark .... 305-348-2111.... 119 C
mark.rosenberg@fiu.edu
ROSENBERG, Michael .... 845-257-2800.... 352 B
rosenbem@newpaltz.edu
ROSENBERG, Naomi .... 617-636-2143.... 245 C
naomi.rosenberg@tufts.edu
ROSENBERG, Richard, M .. 717-337-6396.... 429 I
rrosenbe@gettysburg.edu
ROSENBERG, Samuel .... 201-684-7624.... 313 C
sjrosenb@ramapo.edu
ROSENBERG, Samuel .... 312-341-3697.... 163 B
srosenbe@roosevelt.edu
ROSENBERGER, Benjamin . 610-372-4721.... 445 C
brosenberger@racc.edu
ROSENBERGER, Jeanne .... 408-554-4583...... 68 C
jrosenberger@scu.edu
ROSENBERGER, Steven, H 614-823-1150.... 400 H
srosenberger@otterbein.edu
ROSENBLATT, Jim .... 601-925-7104.... 275 C
jim.rosenblatt@mc.edu
ROSENBLOOM, Stuart .... 312-461-0600.... 145 A
srosenbloom@aaart.edu
ROSENBLUM, Donald .... 954-262-8402.... 114 B
donr@nsu.nova.edu
ROSENBLUM, Yosef .... 718-854-2290.... 323 I
ROSENBOOM, David .... 661-255-1050...... 32 F
drosenbo@calarts.edu
ROSENDAHL, Matthew ...... 715-246-6561.... 555 G
matt.rosendahl@witc.edu
ROSENFELD, Lynn, R .... 661-255-1050...... 32 F
lynn@calarts.edu
ROSENFELD, Renee .... 215-637-7700.... 431 A
rlrosenfeld@holyfamily.edu
ROSENFELD, Sholom .... 718-774-5050.... 357 F
ROSENFELDT, Mary .... 513-745-3022.... 406 E
rosenfeldt@xavier.edu
ROSENGART, Sharon .... 973-720-3019.... 317 D
rosengarts@wpunj.edu
ROSENGARTEN, Jayne ...... 212-237-8624.... 327 F
jrosengarten@jjay.cuny.edu
ROSENGARTEN, Jeffrey ..... 212-960-5239.... 361 M
rosengar@yu.edu
ROSENGARTEN, Lewis ...... 607-753-4808.... 353 B
lewis.rosengarten@cortland.edu
ROSENHECK, Sari .... 845-434-5750.... 357 A
sarir@sullivan.suny.edu
ROSENHEIN, Jon .... 212-799-5000.... 337 H
ROSENKRANS, Jane .... 949-582-4340...... 70 F
jrosenkrans@saddleback.edu
ROSENRAUCH, Yair .... 718-259-5300.... 324 D
yrosen@bramsonort.edu
ROSENSAFT, Jean, B .... 212-824-2209.... 335 B
jrosensaft@huc.edu
ROSENSTEIN, Arthur .... 858-566-1200...... 44 B
arthur@disd.edu
ROSENSTEIN, Gloria .... 858-566-1200...... 44 B
gloria@disd.edu
ROSENSTEIN, Ilena .... 860-768-4418...... 95 B
rosenstei@hartford.edu
ROSENSTEIN, Ilene .... 213-740-7711...... 76 F
irosenst@usc.edu
ROSENSTEIN, Paul .... 617-559-8600.... 235 E
prosenstein@hebrewcollege.edu
ROSENSTOCK, Esther .... 443-334-2653.... 226 E
erosenstock@stevenson.edu
ROSENSTOCK, Linda .... 310-825-6381.... 74 C
lindarosenstock@ph.ucla.edu
ROSENSTONE, Steven, J .... 651-201-1696.... 265 E
steven.rosenstone@so.mnscu.edu
ROSENTHAL, Amy .... 817-202-6211.... 495 E
arosenthal@swau.edu
ROSENTHAL, Cheryl .... 671-824-8595.... 234 B
cheryl_rosenthal@emerson.edu
ROSENTHAL, David, S .... 617-495-2010.... 235 D
drose@uhs.harvard.edu
ROSENTHAL, Eric .... 847-925-6677.... 151 G
erosenth@harpercollege.edu
ROSENTHAL, Jeffrey, E ...... 315-255-1743.... 325 G
rosenthal@cayuga-cc.edu
ROSENTHAL, Jonathan, M 309-438-2920.... 153 D
jmrosen@ilstu.edu
ROSENTHAL, Josh .... 310-289-5123...... 77 I
ROSENTHAL, Rachel .... 916-608-6500...... 56 C
ROSENTHAL, Rich .... 704-330-6316.... 369 D
rich.rosenthal@cpcc.edu
ROSENTHAL, Robert .... 860-685-2010...... 95 E
rrosenthal@wesleyan.edu
ROSENTHALL, John .... 803-536-4744.... 460 G
jroseenth@scsu.edu
ROSENWALD, Nancy .... 803-321-5229.... 459 H
nancy.rosenwald@newberry.edu
ROSETH, Lisa .... 218-723-6016.... 262 G
lroseth@css.edu
ROSEVEAR, Scott, G .... 570-577-3200.... 423 E
scott.rosevear@bucknell.edu
ROSEVEARE, Mark .... 864-592-4763.... 461 C
rosevearem@sccsc.edu
ROSIENE, Tracy .... 860-885-2603...... 92 E
trosiene@trcc.commnet.edu
ROSIER, Therese .... 706-737-1400.... 125 G
trosier@aug.edu
ROSINE, Greg, J .... 269-387-2072.... 260 C
greg.rosine@wmich.edu
ROSINSKI, Shonda .... 337-521-8934.... 211 J
srosinski@southlouisiana.edu
ROSKOWSKI, Ed .... 520-515-3688...... 13 E
roskoe@cochise.edu
ROSKOWSKI, Pamela .... 415-476-5455...... 75 A
proskowski@police.ucsf.edu
ROSKY, Bruce .... 818-610-6543...... 55 B
roskybr@piercecollege.edu
ROSMUS, Julie .... 802-773-5900.... 513 D
julie.rosmus@csj.edu
ROSNER, Christine .... 215-637-7700.... 431 A
crosner@holyfamily.edu
ROSNER-LENGELE, Julie, A .... 215-572-2815.... 422 C
rosner@arcadia.edu
ROSNER-SALAZAR, Ari Senghor .... 303-556-4724...... 84 A
ari.rosner@ccd.edu
ROSNIK, Peter .... 413-775-1441.... 239 E
rosnick@gcc.mass.edu
ROSOFF, Nancy .... 215-572-2900.... 422 C
ROSOFF, Nancy, G .... 856-225-6486.... 314 D
nrosoff@camden.rutgers.edu
ROSONET, Kay .... 228-497-7629.... 275 E
kay.rosonet@mgccc.edu
ROSOWSKY, David .... 518-276-6298.... 347 D
rosowd@rpi.edu
ROSPOND, Raylene .... 515-271-2982.... 184 D
raylene.rospond@drake.edu
ROSPOND, Raylene .... 515-271-1814.... 184 D
raylene.rospond@drake.edu
ROSS, Anthony .... 610-917-1418.... 450 E
amross@vfcc.edu
ROSS, Anthony, J .... 651-641-8815.... 263 A
ross@csp.edu
ROSS, Anthony, R .... 323-343-3100...... 35 D
tross@cslanet.calstatela.edu
ROSS, Arthur, J .... 304-293-6607.... 545 A
ajross@hsc.wvu.edu
ROSS, Beverly .... 334-420-4332........ 7 H
bross@trenholmstate.edu
ROSS, Bob .... 386-226-6198...... 14 C
robert.ross@erau.edu
ROSS, Carla .... 510-869-6618...... 64 J
cross@samuelmerritt.edu
ROSS, Carmin, E .... 217-875-7200.... 162 F
cross@richland.edu
ROSS, Cheryl, A .... 212-854-2268.... 330 F
cheryl.ross@columbia.edu
ROSS, Christine, C .... 434-223-6056.... 519 G
cross@hsc.edu
ROSS, Christopher .... 425-637-1010.... 532 E
c.ross@cityu.edu
ROSS, Clark, G .... 704-894-2204.... 363 I
clross@davidson.edu
ROSS, Corey .... 903-233-4460.... 490 A
coreyross@letu.edu
ROSS, Cynthia, S .... 580-581-2201.... 407 D
cross@cameron.edu
ROSS, David .... 501-279-4930...... 21 H
dross@harding.edu
ROSS, David .... 270-247-8521.... 204 G
dross@midcontinent.edu
ROSS, David, A .... 972-708-7340.... 487 B
david_ross@gial.edu
ROSS, David, L .... 804-828-6610.... 526 B
dlross@vcu.edu
ROSS, Deanna .... 208-459-5222.... 143 D
dross@collegeofidaho.edu
ROSS, Denise .... 704-991-0264.... 374 D
dross7926@stanly.edu
ROSS, Donald, E .... 561-237-7782.... 113 D
dross@lynn.edu
ROSS, Duffy .... 301-447-5366.... 225 A
ross@msmary.edu
ROSS, Elizabeth .... 617-735-9701.... 234 C
ross@emmanuel.edu
ROSS, Elizabeth .... 212-229-8947.... 342 E
rosse@newschool.edu
ROSS, Eric .... 660-263-4110.... 286 H
ericr@macc.edu
ROSS, JR., Ervin .... 386-481-2561.... 102 C
rosse@cookman.edu
ROSS, Frank, E .... 773-442-4600.... 160 A
f-ross@neiu.edu
ROSS, Gary .... 706-233-7326.... 137 A
gross@shorter.edu
ROSS, Gary, L .... 315-228-7401.... 329 G
gross@colgate.edu
ROSS, George, E .... 989-774-3131.... 249 C
president@cmich.edu
ROSS, Gerald .... 410-225-2399.... 224 B
gross@mica.edu
ROSS, James, A .... 734-384-4259.... 255 D
jross@monroeccc.edu
ROSS, James, H .... 573-884-8738.... 291 A
rossjh@health.missouri.edu
ROSS, Jason .... 864-977-7026.... 460 A
jason.ross@ngu.edu
ROSS, Jennifer, A .... 260-422-5561.... 173 C
jaross@indianatech.edu
ROSS, Jerrold .... 718-990-1305.... 348 G
rossj@stjohns.edu
ROSS, JoAnn .... 304-929-1595.... 541 H
jross@mountainstate.edu
ROSS, Joe .... 570-504-9639.... 425 F
ROSS, John .... 903-589-4014.... 490 D
jross@lonmorris.edu
ROSS, John, A .... 785-628-4431.... 192 I
jross@fhsu.edu
ROSS, Julie, S .... 617-627-3360.... 245 C
j.ross@tufts.edu
ROSS, Karen .... 734-432-5529.... 254 D
kross@madonna.edu
ROSS, Kathleen .... 650-574-6532...... 67 G
rossk@smccd.edu
ROSS, Keith .... 314-392-2301.... 285 J
rossk@mobap.edu
ROSS, Ken .... 816-941-0430.... 281 A
kross@devry.edu
ROSS, Ken .... 863-297-1096.... 115 C
kross@polk.edu
ROSS, Kevin, M .... 561-237-7823.... 113 D
kross@lynn.edu
ROSS, Larry, W .... 610-799-1128.... 434 D
lross@lccc.edu
ROSS, Laura .... 407-708-2058.... 117 H
rossl@seminolestate.edu
ROSS, Lauren .... 937-512-2625.... 401 J
lauren.ross@sinclair.edu
ROSS, Luana .... 406-275-4959.... 296 D
luana_ross@skc.edu
ROSS, Lucy .... 763-576-4797.... 265 H
lross@anokatech.edu
ROSS, Meg .... 662-562-3204.... 276 D
mross@northwestms.edu
ROSS, Mettha, M .... 312-939-0111.... 150 D
mettha@eastwest.edu
ROSS, Michael, D .... 614-885-5585.... 401 B
mross@pcj.edu
ROSS, Mindy .... 845-341-4541.... 345 E
mindy.ross@sunyorange.edu
ROSS, Nancy, J .... 207-795-7596.... 217 F
rossnj@cmhc.org
ROSS, Pam .... 706-385-1487.... 136 B
pam.ross@point.edu
ROSS, Pam .... 864-231-2032.... 455 C
pbryant@andersonuniversity.edu
ROSS, Patricia, A .... 937-778-7887.... 390 G
pross@edisonohio.edu
ROSS, Paul .... 307-382-1696.... 557 A
pross@wwcc.wy.edu
ROSS, Peter, G .... 989-774-4456.... 249 C
ross1pg@cmich.edu
ROSS, III, Phillip .... 410-704-4053.... 228 E
pross@towson.edu
ROSS, Ramsey .... 850-729-5229.... 114 A
ramseyr@nwfsc.edu
ROSS, Rebecca .... 610-436-2501.... 444 A
rross2@wcupa.edu
ROSS, Richard, S .... 860-297-2258...... 94 E
richard.ross@trincoll.edu
ROSS, Rick .... 360-417-6533.... 536 G
rross@pencol.edu
ROSS, Robert .... 404-527-4537.... 126 I
rross@carver.edu
ROSS, Ronald .... 973-877-3078.... 309 H
ross@essex.edu
ROSS, Ryan .... 303-556-3926...... 84 A
ryan.ross@ccd.edu
ROSS, Sadie .... 518-587-2100.... 355 G
sadie.ross@esc.edu
ROSS, Sal .... 210-690-9000.... 487 E
sross@hallmarkcollege.edu
ROSS, Sandy .... 406-243-2572.... 294 I
sandy.ross@umontana.edu
ROSS, Scott, T .... 304-877-6428.... 540 G
admissions@abc.edu
ROSS, Sonia .... 210-690-9000.... 487 D
sross@hallmarkcollege.edu
ROSS, Sonia .... 210-690-9000.... 487 E
sross@hallmarkcollege.edu
ROSS, Stephen .... 541-552-6258.... 419 A
rosss@sou.edu
ROSS, Stephen, C .... 724-847-6541.... 429 H
scross@geneva.edu
ROSS, Terryl, J .... 541-737-4381.... 418 F
terryl.ross@oregonstate.edu
ROSS, Thelma .... 484-365-7583.... 434 H
tross@lincoln.edu
ROSS, Thelma, L .... 800-561-2606.... 434 H
tross@lincoln.edu
ROSS, Thomas, W .... 919-962-4622.... 377 C
tomross@northcarolina.edu
ROSS, Todd .... 626-815-6000...... 30 G
tross@apu.edu
ROSS, Tricia .... 212-799-5000.... 337 H
ROSS, Vikki, F .... 210-562-6200.... 507 A
rossv@uthscsa.edu
ROSS-JONES, Marvel, E .... 716-884-9120.... 324 J
merossjones@bryantstratton.edu
ROSS-LEE, Barbara .... 516-686-3996.... 343 D
brosslee@nyit.edu
ROSSANO, Michael .... 215-596-1116.... 450 B
m.rossano@usciences.edu
ROSSBACHER, Lisa, A .... 678-915-7230.... 137 G
rossbach@spsu.edu
ROSSELLI, Hilda .... 503-838-8471.... 419 C
rossellh@wou.edu
ROSSELLI, Robert .... 509-542-4688.... 532 H
rrosselli@columbiabasin.edu
ROSSER, James, M .... 323-343-3030...... 35 D
jrosser@cslanet.calstatela.edu
ROSSER, Sue, V .... 415-338-1141...... 37 B
srosser@sfsu.edu
ROSSER, William .... 805-493-3553...... 33 B
rosser@clunet.edu
ROSSETTI, Elspeth .... 408-554-4861...... 68 C
erossetti@scu.edu
ROSSI, Jason .... 773-697-2215.... 149 D
jrossi@devry.edu
ROSSI, Joanne .... 650-508-3613...... 59 H
jrossi@ndnu.edu
ROSSI, John, J .... 626-256-4673...... 40 D
jrossi@coh.org
ROSSI, Michael, J .... 978-837-5244.... 242 A
michael.rossi@merrimack.edu
ROSSI, SJ, Philip, J .... 414-288-7230.... 548 F
philip.rossi@marquette.edu
ROSSI, Ralph .... 518-433-8277.... 351 D
ralph.rossi@suny.edu
ROSSI, Richard .... 650-508-3585...... 59 H
rrossi@ndnu.edu
ROSSI, Richard, E .... 402-280-2775.... 297 F
rrossi@creighton.edu
ROSSI, Susan .... 330-382-7417.... 393 F
srossi3@kent.edu
ROSSI, Vincent .... 413-565-1000.... 230 G
vrossi@baypath.edu
ROSSI-LE, Laura .... 978-232-2055.... 234 D
lrossile@endicott.edu
ROSSIGNOL, Paul .... 505-888-8898.... 320 G
paul@acupuncturecollege.edu
ROSSINI, Sarah .... 704-637-4111.... 363 E
srossini@catawba.edu
ROSSINI, Tania .... 718-390-3187.... 360 A
trossini@wagner.edu
ROSSITER, Andrew .... 808-923-9741.... 141 G
andrewro@hawaii.edu
ROSSKNECHT, Jenny .... 541-956-7017.... 420 B
jrossknecht@roguecc.edu
ROSSMAN, Carl, A .... 724-836-9903.... 449 C
crossman@pitt.edu
ROSSMAN, Marty .... 630-637-5601.... 159 G
mprossman@noctrl.edu
ROSSMAN, Randy, S .... 517-750-1200.... 258 D
rrossman@arbor.edu
ROSSMAN, Rodger .... 252-335-0821.... 369 G
rodger_rossman@albemarle.edu
ROSSMANN, Brian .... 406-994-5298.... 295 C
brossmann@montana.edu
ROSSMANN, Kathleen .... 205-226-4660........ 2 B
krossman@bsc.edu
ROSSMEIER, Joseph, G ...... 301-322-0987.... 225 F
jrossmeier@pgcc.edu
ROSSMILLER, Lindsay .... 406-657-1051.... 296 C
lindsay.rosmiller@rocky.edu
ROSSO, Corey .... 703-892-5100...... 99 G
ROSSON, Barry .... 561-297-0268.... 119 A
rosson@fau.edu
ROSSON, Barry, T .... 561-297-1211.... 119 A
rosson@fau.edu
ROSSON, Michael .... 718-368-5144.... 328 A
mrosson@kbcc.cuny.edu
ROST, Dawn .... 920-832-7685.... 548 B
dawn.m.rost@lawrence.edu
ROST, Gregory, S .... 215-573-9163.... 448 J
gregrost@pobox.upenn.edu

ROY, Pallabi 410-337-6062 222 I pallabi.roy@goucher.edu
ROY, Paul 650-493-4430 69 I proy@itp.edu
ROY, Rina 916-484-8108 56 A royr@arc.losrios.edu
ROY, Tracey 218-322-2409 266 I troy@itascacc.edu
ROY, Tracey 218-322-2409 266 E troy@itascacc.edu
ROY, Tracey 218-322-2409 269 F t.roy@itascacc.edu
ROYAL, Angela 636-949-4983 283 J aroyal@lindenwood.edu
ROYAL, Bryan, K 804-257-5630 530 A bkroyal@vuu.edu
ROYAL, Carmen 609-343-5087 307 C croyal@atlantic.edu
ROYAL, Christina 216-987-4577 389 B tina.royal@tri-c.edu
ROYAL, Robert 540-338-2700 517 G rroyal@cdu.edu
ROYALL, Ann 617-262-5000 231 G ann.royall@the-bac.edu
ROYBAL, Katy 405-425-1876 409 E katy.roybal@oc.edu
ROYBAL, Walter 719-587-8281 80 L wsroybal@adams.edu
ROYCE, Lee, G 601-925-3200 275 C lroyce@mc.edu
ROYE, Shauna 202-495-3837 99 C sroye@dhs.edu
ROYER, Anna 405-945-8611 410 F
ROYER, Drew 603-623-0313 305 E droyer@nhia.edu
ROYER, Joseph, M 765-641-4000 169 E jmroyer@anderson.edu
ROYER, Roma 602-850-8000 17 G rroyer@phoenixseminary.edu
ROYOS, Andre 915-779-8031 483 J aroyos@computercareercenter.com
ROYS, Cindy 631-730-2028 324 E croys@bcl.edu
ROYSTER, Jacqueline, J 404-894-1728 130 F jacqueline.royster@iac.gatech.edu
ROYSTER, James 216-485-0900 393 A
ROYSTER, Robynne 415-703-9532 32 C rroyster@cca.edu
ROYSTON, Rosemary, R 706-379-3111 140 A rosemary@yhc.edu
ROYUK, Brent 402-643-7304 297 D brent.royuk@cune.edu
ROZ, Mugur 617-850-1545 235 F mroz@hchc.edu
ROZADA, Mayra 787-891-0925 563 A mrozada@aguadilla.inter.edu
ROZAK, Edward 508-830-5030 238 D erozak@maritime.edu
ROZANSKA, M. Paul 215-637-7700 431 A smprozanska@holyfamily.edu
ROZANSKI, Kathy 856-256-5400 314 A rozanski@rowan.edu
ROZANSKI, Mordechai 609-896-5001 313 F mrozanski@rider.edu
ROZANSKY, Kristen, B 717-531-1315 440 A kbr2@psu.edu
ROZEBOOM, Dave 512-428-8515 493 E daver@stedwards.edu
ROZEK, Charles, E 216-368-4390 386 F cer2@case.edu
ROZELL, Laura 518-327-6291 345 H lrozell@paulsmiths.edu
ROZEMA, Burton, J 708-239-4760 166 C burt.rozema@trnty.edu
ROZEMBAJGIER, John 614-885-5585 401 B jrozembajgier@pcj.edu
ROZEWSKI, Mark 812-464-1849 181 B mrozewski@usi.edu
ROZIER, Dekhasta, B 919-516-4022 376 D dbrozier@st-aug.edu
ROZIN, Miriam 503-399-8486 414 J miriam.rozin@chemeketa.edu
ROZIN, Vladmir 212-463-0400 358 B vladmirr@touro.edu
ROZNER, Frances 714-992-7832 70 G frozner@scco.edu
ROZOWSKI, Casey 612-343-4430 270 A cmrozows@northcentral.edu
RUANO, Norman 773-878-3894 163 F nruano@iwe.staugustine.edu
RUBACK, Ginger 954-492-5353 103 F gruback@citycollege.edu
RUBACK, Sally, A 920-929-2126 554 G sruback@morainepark.edu
RUBBELKE, Thomas, J 651-641-8700 263 A rubbelke@csp.edu
RUBECK, Dustin, D 972-241-3371 484 E drubeck@dallas.edu
RUBEK, Cindy 719-590-6851 83 J crubek@coloradotech.edu
RUBEL, Carol 617-587-5650 242 H rubelc@neco.edu
RUBEL, Robert, J 401-841-3339 558 B
RUBEL, Tom 641-683-5252 185 G trubel@indianhills.edu
RUBEL, Tom 641-683-5111 185 G trubel@indianhills.edu
RUBEMEYER, Susan 636-922-8360 288 B srubemeyer@stchas.edu
RUBENSTEIN, David 856-256-4222 314 A rubenstein@rowan.edu
RUBENSTEIN, David 202-687-1972 98 D dr94@georgetown.edu
RUBENSTEIN, Nancy 419-448-2106 391 F nrubenst@heidelberg.edu
RUBENZAHL, Ira, H 413-755-4906 241 B irubenzahl@stcc.edu
RUBERO, Maria, D 787-250-1912 563 G mdrubero@metro.inter.edu
RUBES, Larry 804-706-5041 527 B lrubes@jtcc.edu
RUBEY, Charles 812-298-2329 177 D crubey@ivytech.edu
RUBIN, Gary, N 410-704-2358 228 E grubin@towson.edu
RUBIN, Henry 617-984-1643 243 H hrubin@quincycollege.edu
RUBIN, James 602-787-6546 15 J james.rubin@paradisevalley.edu
RUBIN, Joshua 718-436-2122 357 E
RUBIN, Lisa 770-426-2725 133 E lrubin@life.edu
RUBIN, Marge 920-720-6811 554 A rubin@fvtc.edu
RUBIN, Mark, E 804-828-1235 526 B merubin@vcu.edu
RUBIN, Moshe 516-239-9002 350 H
RUBIN, Rachel 860-486-2337 94 G rachel.rubin@uconn.edu
RUBIN, Steve 719-219-9636 82 B steverubindvm@att.net
RUBINO, Cynthia 914-694-1122 323 H cnr@berkeleycollege.edu
RUBINO, John 207-941-7109 218 A rubinoj@husson.edu
RUBINO, Joseph 410-293-1549 559 B rubino@usna.edu
RUBINO, Karen, M 401-456-8849 454 A krubino@ric.edu
RUBINO, Michael, H 508-767-7156 230 D rubino@assumption.edu
RUBINSTEIN, Mark 603-862-2053 306 C mark.rubinstein@unh.edu
RUBIO, Christian 318-342-1539 216 E rubio@ulm.edu
RUBIO, Christopher 310-689-3200 42 H crubio@kaplan.edu
RUBIO, Olga, D 956-721-5296 489 J drubio@laredo.edu
RUBIO, Paty 518-580-5705 351 B prubio@skidmore.edu
RUBIO, Peter 305-593-1223 102 H prubio@albizu.edu
RUBLE, Celeste 507-433-0666 268 H celeste.ruble@riverland.edu
RUBLE, Jim 785-227-3380 191 B rublej@bethanylb.edu
RUBLE, Joel 559-925-3127 78 D joelruble@whccd.edu
RUBLE, Justin 304-260-4380 542 G jruble@blueridgectc.edu
RUBLE, Michelle 301-934-4711 222 C micheller@csmd.edu
RUBLE, Robert, W 607-735-1802 332 I rruble@elmira.edu
RUBRITZ, Gerald 814-886-6460 437 B grubritz@mtaloy.edu
RUBY, Carl, A 937-766-7871 386 G rubyc@cedarville.edu
RUCABADO, Angel 787-993-8958 567 B angel.rucabado@upr.edu
RUCCIUS, Frederick, E 215-955-8733 448 C frederick.ruccius@jefferson.edu
RUCH, Cathleen 701-671-2687 381 E cathleen.ruch@ndus.edu
RUCH, Doug 678-891-3269 131 C druch@gpc.edu
RUCH, J. Chuck 309-677-3100 146 C cruch@bradley.edu
RUCH, Lisa 815-965-7314 162 I lruch@rockfordcareercollege.edu
RUCH, Nate, P 612-343-4747 270 A npruch@northcentral.edu
RUCHALA, Patsy, L 775-784-6841 303 A pruchala@unr.edu
RUCKENSTEIN, Andrei, E 617-353-4791 232 E andreir@bu.edu
RUCKER, Alena Jewel 304-981-6247 542 H
RUCKER, Cedric, B 540-654-1655 525 D crucker@umw.edu
RUCKER, Jewel 304-981-6247 545 D jewel.rucker@mail.wvu.edu
RUCKER, Marty, K 423-585-6983 476 D marty.rucker@ws.edu
RUCKER, Patricia, A 215-670-9282 438 E parucker@peirce.edu
RUCKER, Paul 206-685-9223 539 A uwalumni@uw.edu
RUCKER, Richard 937-433-3410 390 I rrucker@edaff.com
RUCKER, Robert, E 662-685-4771 273 E erucker@bmc.edu
RUCKER, Robin 937-376-6692 387 A rrucker@centralstate.edu
RUCKER, Sherri, B 615-329-8555 468 I srucker@fisk.edu
RUCKER-FRANKLIN, Yvonne 870-633-4480 21 F yrucker@eacc.edu
RUCKER-SHAMU, Marian 301-860-3849 228 A mshamu@bowiestate.edu
RUD, A.G 509-335-4853 539 D ag.rud@wsu.edu
RUDA, Ryan 620-276-9597 193 C ryan.ruda@gcccks.edu
RUDASILL, Susann 850-644-1571 119 D srudasill@fsu.edu
RUDATSIKIRA, Emmanuel 269-471-6648 247 D rudatsikira@andrews.edu
RUDAWITZ, Linda 503-517-1397 421 B lrudawitz@warnerpacific.edu
RUDD, M. David 801-581-8620 511 C david.rudd@csbs.utah.edu
RUDD, Martin 920-832-2610 553 B martin.rudd@uwc.edu
RUDD, Theda 517-884-6784 255 A ruddt@msu.edu
RUDD WEITZEL, Jann 636-949-4846 283 J jweitzel@lindenwood.edu
RUDDEN, David 847-214-7925 150 F drudden@elgin.edu
RUDDICK, Steve, L 913-588-7281 197 C sruddick@ku.edu
RUDDY, Margaret, E 561-237-7822 113 D mruddy@lynn.edu
RUDE, John 323-267-3724 54 G rudejc@elac.edu
RUDEAU, William 609-771-2187 308 F rudeau@tcnj.edu
RUDECOFF, Christine, A 315-684-6055 354 F rudecoc@morrisville.edu
RUDEEN, P. Kevin 405-271-2288 413 D kevin-rudeen@ouhsc.edu
RUDENGA, Elizabeth 708-239-4739 166 C liz.rudenga@trnty.edu
RUDER, Ann 620-672-5641 196 D annr@prattcc.edu
RUDGERS, Lisa, M 734-763-3526 259 A rudgers@umich.edu
RUDIG, Lynn 608-785-9892 555 F rudigl@westerntc.edu
RUDIGER, Brenda 906-487-2400 255 B brudiger@mtu.edu
RUDIGER, Jennifer 715-232-1151 552 E rudigerj@uwstout.edu
RUDIN, Brent 765-998-5113 180 B brent_rudin@tayloru.edu
RUDLEY, John, M 713-313-7044 500 B rudleyjm@tsu.edu
RUDLOFF, William, J 724-738-2465 443 F william.rudloff@sru.edu
RUDNEY, Gwen 320-589-6411 271 G rudneygl@morris.umn.edu
RUDNICK, Joseph 310-825-1042 74 C jrudnick@college.ucla.edu
RUDNICKI, Rosemary 512-448-8540 493 E rosemars@stedwards.edu
RUDNIK, Jeffrey, A 270-686-4324 199 B jeffrey.rudnik@brescia.edu
RUDNITSKI, Rose 201-559-3551 310 B rudnitskir@felician.edu
RUDOLPH, Brian, A 636-584-6732 281 E barudolp@eastcentral.edu
RUDOLPH, Marva 865-974-2498 477 D mrudolp1@utk.edu
RUDOLPH, Mary Kay 707-524-1516 68 E mrudolph@santarosa.edu
RUDY, Donna 240-500-2000 223 A rudyd@hagerstowncc.edu
RUE, Melissa 502-895-3411 204 F mrue@lpts.edu
RUE, Penny, E 858-534-4370 74 F prue@ucsd.edu
RUEB, Shirley 316-942-4291 195 F ruebs@newmanu.edu
RUEBEL, James, S 765-285-1024 169 G jruebel@bsu.edu
RUEBNER, Ralph 312-987-2384 154 H ruebner@jmls.edu
RUEFLE, Colleen 412-536-1069 432 H colleen.ruefle@laroche.edu
RUEGER, Nancy 718-409-5985 356 C nrueger@sunymaritime.edu
RUEGER, Tom 847-628-2017 154 K trueger@judsonu.edu
RUEGER, William 718-409-7323 356 C wrueger@sunymaritime.edu
RUEGG, Texas 903-813-2371 481 A truegg@austincollege.edu
RUEL, Martha 619-594-5332 37 A mruel@mail.sdsu.edu
RUEL, Martha 619-594-0807 37 A mruel@mail.sdsu.edu
RUELL, John 435-283-7250 512 C john.ruell@snow.edu
RUELLE, Joan 336-278-6572 364 D jruelle@elon.edu
RUESCH, Sherry 435-652-7551 512 B ruesch@dixie.edu
RUESCHMANN, Eva 413-559-5378 235 C
RUETER, Kenneth, J 870-307-7326 22 D ken.rueter@lyon.edu
RUETTEN, Amy 417-667-8181 280 E aruetten@cottey.edu
RUFENER, Patrick, S 330-684-8906 403 C psr8@uakron.edu
RUFF, Corey 325-674-2665 478 I clr06a@acu.edu
RUFF, Debbie 214-828-8195 497 C druff@bcd.tamhsc.edu
RUFF, Joy, C 305-237-2090 113 H jruff@mdc.edu
RUFF, Kathleen, C 330-325-6259 397 D kcruff@neomed.edu
RUFF, Margaret 903-785-7661 492 D mruff@parisjc.edu
RUFF, Rosemary, H 479-575-3845 24 C rruff@uark.edu
RUFFER, Carla 901-272-5160 471 D cruffer@mca.edu
RUFFIN, Beverly, W 713-313-1376 500 B ruffinbw@tsu.edu
RUFFIN, Cynthia 919-572-1625 362 C cruffin@apexsot.edu
RUFFIN, Juretta 919-572-1625 362 C registrar@apexsot.edu
RUFFIN, Kathi 610-896-1249 430 G kruffin@haverford.edu
RUFFIN, Kimberly, N 312-341-2281 163 B kruffin@roosevelt.edu
RUFFIN, Lea Nora 302-477-2027 97 B ljruffin@widener.edu
RUFFIN, Shanda 803-780-1360 463 C sruffin@voorhees.edu
RUFFING, Rebecca 315-866-0300 335 D ruffingrj@herkimer.edu
RUFFINO, John, J 703-323-3023 527 F jruffino@nvcc.edu
RUFFNER, Candi 313-425-3700 247 H candi.ruffner@baker.edu
RUFFOLO, Linda, L 260-481-6659 174 C ruffolo@ipfw.edu
RUFFRAGE, Jo 315-792-7172 356 B ruffraj@sunyit.edu
RUFFULO, Anna 773-834-2500 166 A
RUFINO, Paul 856-415-2173 310 D prufino@gccnj.edu
RUFO, Joseph 315-470-6622 355 A jlrufo@esf.edu
RUFTY, Rebeca, C 919-515-1989 378 C rcrufty@ncsu.edu
RUGEN, Richard 570-389-4115 441 F rrugen@bloomu.edu
RUGGIERI, David 407-447-7300 110 A druggieri@ftccollege.edu
RUGGIERO, Bruno 985-448-4262 216 A bruno.ruggiero@nicholls.edu
RUGGLES, Jennifer 216-368-1723 386 F jor15@case.edu
RUHGE, Christina 402-474-5315 298 C cruhge@kaplanuniversity.edu
RUHL, Chris 317-921-4474 175 I cruhl@ivytech.edu
RUHL, Taylor 760-355-6351 51 A taylor.ruhl@imperial.edu
RUHLAND, Sheila 920-929-2127 554 G sruhland@morainepark.edu
RUIBAL, Pilar 787-751-0160 561 H pruibal@cmpr.pr.gov
RUIZ, Alberto 361-593-2837 498 D alberto.ruiz@tamuk.edu
RUIZ, Alfredo 269-471-6979 247 D jaruiz@andrews.edu
RUIZ, Andrew 806-894-9611 494 G aruiz@southplainscollege.edu
RUIZ, Carol 973-748-9000 307 H carol_ruiz@bloomfield.edu
RUIZ, Eddy, A 208-885-7716 144 G ruiz@uidaho.edu
RUIZ, Encarnacion 209-228-4240 74 D eruiz@ucmerced.edu
RUIZ, Eric, A 815-740-5037 167 E eruiz@stfrancis.edu
RUIZ, Israel 617-253-1882 241 D
RUIZ, Joaquin 520-621-4090 18 L jruiz@email.arizona.edu
RUIZ, OP, John Martin 202-495-3821 99 C jruiz@dhs.edu
RUIZ, Jose 787-863-2390 563 E jose.ruiz@fajardo.inter.edu
RUIZ, Kathleen 310-377-5501 56 F kruiz@marymountpv.edu
RUIZ, Kris 936-294-3492 501 D kjk001@shsu.edu

RUST, Kathleen .... 630-617-3419.... 150 H
kathyrst@elmhurst.edu
RUST, Mark, M .... 410-857-2503.... 224 C
mrust@mcdaniel.edu
RUST, Melissa .... 501-686-2532...... 24 B
mrust@uasys.edu
RUST, Tom .... 406-247-5785.... 295 D
trust@msubillings.edu
RUSTON, Lauren .... 407-478-0500.... 110 L
laurenr@orl.herzing.edu
RUSTOWICZ, Mary Louis .. 716-896-0700.... 359 H
rustowim@villa.edu
RUTBERG, Barbara .... 617-824-8275.... 234 B
barbara_rutberg@emerson.edu
RUTE, Warren .... 908-526-1200.... 313 D
wrute@raritanval.edu
RUTENBECK, Jeffrey .... 202-885-2019...... 97 D
jeff@american.edu
RUTH, David, A .... 215-895-2501.... 427 H
ruthda@drexel.edu
RUTH, Rick .... 717-477-1835.... 443 E
reruth@ship.edu
RUTH, Tommy .... 606-546-1226.... 207 B
truth@unionky.edu
RUTHENBECK, Julie, J ...... 325-942-2255.... 480 E
julie.ruthenbeck@angelo.edu
RUTHER, Aisha .... 312-850-7176.... 147 F
aruther@ccc.edu
RUTHERFORD, Ann, O ...... 406-874-6196.... 294 F
rutherforda@milescc.edu
RUTHERFORD, Cynthia ..... 215-572-4091.... 422 C
rutherfc@arcadia.edu
RUTHERFORD, Gina .... 850-973-9414.... 113 K
rutherfordg@nfcc.edu
RUTHERFORD, Greg, F ..... 803-327-8050.... 463 H
grutherford@yorktech.edu
RUTHERFORD, Jeff .... 916-638-7582...... 66 K
RUTHERFORD, Joan, M .... 419-251-1301.... 395 I
joan.rutherford@mercycollege.edu
RUTHERFORD, John, D ..... 214-648-0400.... 507 E
john.rutherford@utsouthwestern.edu
RUTHERFORD, Karen, W ... 803-705-4671.... 455 D
rutherk@benedict.edu
RUTHERFORD, Laurie, G ... 713-500-2101.... 506 F
laurie.g.rutherford@uth.tmc.edu
RUTHERFORD, Lisa, H ...... 608-263-7400.... 550 J
lrutherford@vc.wisc.edu
RUTHERFORD, Marylyn ..... 973-877-3408.... 309 H
rutherford@essex.edu
RUTHERFORD, Paul .... 304-327-4403.... 543 F
prutherford@bluefieldstate.edu
RUTHERFORD, Van .... 937-327-7891.... 406 B
vrutherford@wittenberg.edu
RUTHERMAN, Kathy .... 270-852-3142.... 204 A
krutherman@kwc.edu
RUTIGLIANO, Serafina ...... 212-772-4451.... 327 E
serafina.rutigliano@hunter.cuny.edu
RUTKOWSKI, Edmund .... 718-636-3784.... 346 D
ekow@pratt.edu
RUTKOWSKI, Sandra .... 419-824-3762.... 395 E
srutkowski@lourdes.edu
RUTLAND, Mark .... 918-495-6888.... 411 C
mrutland@oru.edu
RUTLEDGE, Brian .... 601-984-1010.... 277 E
brutledge@umc.edu
RUTLEDGE, Catherine .... 484-365-8087.... 434 H
crutledge@lincoln.edu
RUTLEDGE, James .... 662-846-4021.... 273 H
jrutledge@deltastate.edu
RUTLEDGE, Janet .... 410-455-1781.... 227 D
jrutledge@umbc.edu
RUTLEDGE, John, E .... 803-313-7156.... 462 D
rutledj@mailbox.sc.edu
RUTLEDGE, Melissa, B ...... 540-378-5120.... 523 G
rutledge@roanoke.edu
RUTLEDGE, Susan .... 314-392-2355.... 285 J
rutledges@mobap.edu
RUTLEDGE, Todd .... 417-269-3873.... 280 G
trutle@coxcollege.edu
RUTT, Charles, D .... 660-543-4370.... 290 H
rutt@ucmo.edu
RUTT, Jack, H .... 540-432-4478.... 518 F
ruttj@emu.edu
RUTT, Richard .... 503-352-7377.... 419 E
ruttra@pacificu.edu
RUTTEN, Erich .... 651-962-6561.... 272 B
erutten@stthomas.edu
RUTTER, Robert .... 920-403-3964.... 550 F
bob.rutter@snc.edu
RUUD, William, N .... 717-477-1301.... 443 E
wnruud@ship.edu
RUX, Shirley, K .... 701-788-4754.... 381 H
shirley.rux@mayvillestate.edu
RUYLE, Dianna .... 217-854-3231.... 146 A
druyl@blackburn.edu
RUYS, Jasmine .... 661-362-3466...... 41 I
jasmine.ruys@canyons.edu
RUZICH, Steve .... 708-596-2000.... 164 H
sruzich@ssc.edu
RUZICKA, James .... 402-461-7337.... 298 A
jruzicka@hastings.edu
RYALL, Patrick .... 503-768-7294.... 416 G
ryall@lclark.edu
RYALS, Reginald .... 540-423-9055.... 526 I
rryals@germanna.edu
RYAN, Aaron .... 304-876-5527.... 544 C
aryan@shepherd.edu
RYAN, Adam .... 660-944-2827.... 280 B
adam@conception.edu
RYAN, Andrew .... 718-862-8000.... 339 H
andrew.ryan@manhattan.edu
RYAN, Anne .... 207-221-8723.... 218 C
aryan@kaplan.edu
RYAN, Barry, T .... 949-783-4800...... 78 A
barry.ryan@westcoastuniversity.edu
RYAN, Bruce .... 607-844-8222.... 357 I
ryanb@tc3.edu
RYAN, Bryan, K .... 919-866-5146.... 374 H
bkryan@waketech.edu
RYAN, Carroll .... 714-882-7800...... 33 G
cryan@calsouthern.edu
RYAN, Catherine .... 413-572-5218.... 238 F
cryan@wsc.ma.edu
RYAN, Chenise .... 205-934-4076........ 8 F
cryan@uab.edu
RYAN, Christopher .... 508-830-5003.... 238 D
cryan@maritime.edu
RYAN, Curtis, W .... 801-832-2148.... 512 G
cryan@westminstercollege.edu
RYAN, Dan .... 800-962-7682.... 293 A
dryan@wma.edu
RYAN, Duane .... 575-562-2112.... 318 B
duane.ryan@enmu.edu
RYAN, G. Jeremiah .... 225-922-2800.... 209 G
RYAN, Gail, L .... 313-577-6595.... 260 A
gailryan@wayne.edu
RYAN, Greg .... 714-992-7092...... 59 E
gryan@fullcoll.edu
RYAN, Heather .... 574-237-0774.... 170 E
hryan@brownmackie.edu
RYAN, Helen, G .... 502-272-8426.... 198 H
hryan@bellarmine.edu
RYAN, James .... 617-262-5000.... 231 G
james.ryan@the-bac.edu
RYAN, James .... 734-462-4400.... 258 A
jryan@schoolcraft.edu
RYAN, James, G .... 336-217-5128.... 378 A
jgryan@ncat.edu
RYAN, Jerry .... 318-345-9262.... 210 H
jryan@ladelta.edu
RYAN, CSC, John .... 570-208-5899.... 432 G
jjryan@kings.edu
RYAN, John, F .... 802-656-4418.... 514 H
jfryan@uvm.edu
RYAN, Judith, S .... 207-581-1581.... 220 A
judyryan@maine.edu
RYAN, Karen .... 386-822-7515.... 121 F
kryan@stetson.edu
RYAN, Kathleen .... 508-541-1515.... 233 G
kryan@dean.edu
RYAN, Kathleen .... 617-732-5042.... 241 C
kathleen.ryan@mcphs.edu
RYAN, Kent .... 386-246-4801.... 104 F
ryank@daytonastate.edu
RYAN, Kevin .... 305-428-5700.... 113 I
kryan@aii.edu
RYAN, Kyle .... 781-899-5500.... 231 F
kryan@blessedjohnxxiii.edu
RYAN, Larry .... 505-277-2847.... 321 C
larry@unm.edu
RYAN, Lawrence .... 310-577-3000...... 80 E
lryan@yosan.edu
RYAN, Leslie .... 619-684-8811...... 59 B
lryan@newschoolarch.edu
RYAN, Linda, S .... 515-271-2147.... 184 D
linda.ryan@drake.edu
RYAN, Lori .... 602-331-7500...... 12 B
lryan@aii.edu
RYAN, Loyd .... 501-450-1348...... 22 A
ryan@hendrix.edu
RYAN, Mark, R .... 573-882-0314.... 291 B
ryanmr@missouri.edu
RYAN, Martin, B .... 973-353-5713.... 314 E
mbryan@andromeda.rutgers.edu
RYAN, Mary .... 501-686-6730...... 24 F
ryanmaryl@uams.edu
RYAN, Mary .... 419-473-2700.... 389 C
mryan@daviscollege.edu
RYAN, Mary, A .... 651-962-6133.... 272 B
maryan@stthomas.edu
RYAN, Melissa .... 904-725-0525.... 104 A
mryan@concorde.edu
RYAN, Michael .... 617-585-1187.... 242 I
michael.ryan@necmusic.edu
RYAN, Molly .... 661-255-1050...... 32 F
mryan@calarts.edu
RYAN, Patricia .... 540-674-3613.... 527 E
pryan@nr.edu
RYAN, Patricia, C .... 573-651-2249.... 289 K
pryan@semo.edu
RYAN, Peter .... 662-325-3742.... 275 F
ryan@cvm.msstate.edu
RYAN, SJ, Peter .... 314-768-1685.... 283 G
ryan@kenrick.edu
RYAN, Philip .... 508-362-2131.... 239 D
pryan@capecod.edu
RYAN, Robert .... 800-782-2422...... 33 E
rryan851@earthlink.net
RYAN, Ron .... 954-262-8856.... 114 B
ronr@nsu.nova.edu
RYAN, Rosaleen .... 831-646-4035...... 57 G
rryan@mpc.edu
RYAN, Scott .... 817-272-3181.... 505 C
sdryan@uta.edu
RYAN, Sean .... 334-683-2333........ 5 G
sryan@marionmilitary.edu
RYAN, Sean, J .... 502-272-8376.... 198 H
sryan@bellarmine.edu
RYAN, Sharon .... 213-624-1200...... 46 L
sryan@fidm.edu
RYAN, Spencer .... 405-878-5177.... 412 A
shryan@stgregorys.edu
RYAN, Susan .... 386-822-7181.... 121 F
sryan@stetson.edu
RYAN, Suzanne .... 812-856-5572.... 173 E
sryan@indiana.edu
RYAN, Thomas, J .... 718-862-7356.... 339 H
thomas.ryan@manhattan.edu
RYAN, Tiffiney .... 618-634-3242.... 164 E
tiffineyr@shawneecc.edu
RYAN, Tim .... 845-451-1352...... 43 J
t_ryan@culinary.edu
RYAN, Tim .... 574-520-4261.... 174 E
timryan@iusb.edu
RYAN, Tim .... 845-452-9600.... 331 E
t_ryan@culinary.edu
RYAN, Timothy, M .... 207-725-3247.... 217 E
tryan@bowdoin.edu
RYAN, Valerie .... 858-642-8513...... 58 I
vryan@nu.edu
RYAN, Vicky .... 419-473-2700.... 389 C
vryan@daviscollege.edu
RYAN, Victoria .... 239-687-5351.... 101 H
vryan@avemarialaw.edu
RYAN, Walter, F .... 812-941-2210.... 175 A
wryan@ius.edu
RYAN-HOFFMAN,
Maureen .... 732-987-2218.... 310 C
ryan-hoffman@georgian.edu
RYANT, Marion .... 229-430-4609.... 124 A
marion.ryant@asurams.edu
RYBA, Carla .... 412-367-4000.... 424 H
director3@careerta.edu
RYCHLEC, Tim .... 713-313-1810.... 500 B
rychlect@tsu.edu
RYCHLEWSKI, Judith, A .... 816-415-5938.... 293 C
rychlewskij@william.jewell.edu
RYCHLY, Carol, J .... 706-737-1422.... 125 G
crychly@aug.edu
RYCZKOWSKI, Sandy .... 920-498-6829.... 555 C
sandra.ryczkowski@nwtc.edu
RYDEN, Tod .... 325-235-7366.... 500 G
tod.ryden@tstc.edu
RYDER, Ellen .... 508-793-2419.... 233 C
eryder@holycross.edu
RYDER, Laura .... 717-755-2300.... 422 F
lryder@aii.edu
RYDER-FOX, Jennifer .... 530-898-5844...... 34 C
jrfox@csuchico.edu
RYDL, Chareny, L .... 979-845-3158.... 497 E
chareny@tamu.edu
RYE, Colleen .... 906-635-2626.... 253 H
crye@lssu.edu
RYEA, Alan, E .... 802-656-2010.... 514 H
alan.ryea@uvm.edu
RYERSON, James .... 703-284-5926.... 521 D
james.ryerson@marymount.edu
RYERSON, Lisa Marsh .... 315-364-3265.... 360 D
president@wells.edu
RYKEN, Philip, G .... 630-752-5002.... 168 H
philip.ryken@wheaton.edu
RYLE, Jerry .... 203-365-7651...... 94 B
rylef@sacredheart.edu
RYLES, Ruby .... 718-368-5000.... 328 A
rryles@kbcc.cuny.edu
RYMAN, Denny, G .... 318-342-1622.... 216 E
ryman@ulm.edu
RYMER, Angie .... 318-676-7811.... 211 D
arymer@nwltc.edu
RYON, Diane .... 704-372-0266.... 366 B
dryon@kingscollegecharlotte.edu
RYS, Stanley, C .... 847-566-6401.... 167 F
srys@usml.edu
RYSLINGE, Birgitte .... 971-722-7555.... 419 G
birgitte.ryslinge@pcc.edu
RYSTROM, Andrea .... 651-779-3953.... 266 A
andrea.rystrom@century.edu
RYTHER, Richard, H .... 585-292-2122.... 341 H
rryther@monroecc.edu
RZONCA, Chet .... 319-335-2527.... 182 F
chet-rzonca@uiowa.edu
RZONCA, Chet, S .... 319-335-2527.... 182 F
chet-rzonca@uiowa.edu
RZONCA, Stephen .... 910-892-3178.... 365 B
srzonca@heritagebiblecollege.edu

S

SÁEZ-HERNÁNDEZ,
Samuel .... 787-993-8896.... 567 B
samuel.saez@upr.edu
S.A. LEON GUERRERO,
Ann S, A .... 671-735-2941.... 559 G
annsalg@uguam.uog.edu
SAACKE, David .... 540-458-8400.... 530 D
dsaacke@wlu.edu
SAADL, Christine .... 610-796-8356.... 421 G
christine.saadl@alvernia.edu
SAAED, Jan .... 801-832-2232.... 512 G
jsaaed@westminstercollege.edu
SAARIAHO, Ginger, K .... 617-552-9168.... 232 B
ginger.saariaho@bc.edu
SAATKAMP, JR.,
Herman, J .... 609-652-4521.... 313 E
president@stockton.edu
SAAVEDRA, Adrianna .... 520-494-5287...... 13 D
adriana.saavedra@centralaz.edu
SAAVEDRA, Marc .... 505-277-1670.... 321 C
msaav@unm.edu
SAAVEDRA, Michael .... 505-454-3053.... 318 J
SAAVEDRA, Rebecca .... 409-772-1901.... 507 C
rsaavedr@utmb.edu
SABA, Farrokh .... 413-565-1000.... 230 G
fsaba@baypath.edu
SABATINE, Stephanie .... 906-635-6664.... 253 H
ssabatine@lssu.edu
SABATINI, JR., John, A .... 410-843-8278.... 272 C
john.sabatini@laureate.net
SABATINO, Charles, A .... 330-941-3589.... 406 F
casabatino@ysu.edu
SABATINO, Patricia .... 718-678-8817.... 340 F
psabatino@mercy.edu
SABATKA, Hauli .... 402-461-7433.... 298 A
hsabatka@hastings.edu
SABATTINI, Mark .... 904-680-7621.... 107 J
msabattini@fcsl.edu
SABATTIS, Robert, G .... 973-642-4586.... 312 C
robert.g.sabattis@njit.edu
SABBAGH, Thomas .... 603-228-1355.... 305 A
SABBAR, Carol .... 262-551-5950.... 546 I
csabbar@carthage.edu
SABBIA, Richard .... 518-828-4181.... 330 E
richard.sabbia@sunycgcc.edu
SABELLA, Marc .... 530-541-4660...... 53 G
sabella@ltcc.edu
SABETY, Pari .... 937-769-1374.... 384 A
psabety@antioch.edu
SABEY, Brenda .... 435-652-7841.... 512 B
sabey@dixie.edu
SABIN, Christopher, P .... 910-938-6321.... 369 F
sabinc@coastalcarolina.edu
SABIN, Lance .... 612-375-1900.... 264 D
lsabin@ipr.edu
SABIN, Melody .... 864-578-8770.... 460 F
msabin@sherman.edu
SABIN, Nancy .... 603-228-3000.... 306 F
nancy.sabin@granite.edu
SABINE, Neil .... 765-973-8389.... 173 F
nsabine@iue.edu
SABINO, Lyn .... 330-363-4227.... 384 J
lsabino@aultman.com
SABINSON, Allen .... 215-895-1621.... 427 H
allen.c.sabinson@drexel.edu
SABITSANA, Andrea .... 312-915-8722.... 157 C
asabits@luc.edu
SABLAN, Becky .... 670-234-5498.... 560 B
beckys@nmcnet.edu
SABLE, Marjorie .... 573-882-0914.... 291 B
sablem@missouri.edu
SABLE, Ray .... 229-333-5875.... 139 C
rasable@valdosta.edu
SABLO, Kahan .... 814-732-2313.... 442 E
ksablo@edinboro.edu
SABO, Arlene .... 518-564-2022.... 354 B
sabocaa@plattsburgh.edu
SABO, Rebekah .... 412-261-2647.... 432 D
rsabo@kaplan.edu
SABO, Sylvia .... 814-254-0569.... 425 G
ssabo@pa.gov
SABOE, Mike .... 843-820-5090.... 461 G
mike.saboe@tridenttech.edu
SABOL, Pamela, J .... 814-269-7030.... 449 D
pjsabol@pitt.edu
SABOLD, Steven .... 412-346-2122.... 444 E
ssabold@pia.edu
SABOLO, Martin .... 217-479-7130.... 157 F
martin.sabolo@mac.edu
SABOTA, Fred .... 727-864-8895.... 105 E
sabotafr@eckerd.edu
SABOU, Michelle, L .... 864-977-7004.... 460 A
michelle.sabou@ngu.edu
SABOUNI, Ikhlas .... 936-261-9800.... 496 G
isabouni@pvamu.edu
SACCENTI, Thomas, M ...... 740-376-4611.... 395 G
tom.saccenti@marietta.edu
SACCO, Albert .... 806-742-3451.... 502 A
al.sacco-jr@ttu.edu
SACCO, Denise .... 904-680-7706.... 107 J
dsacco@fcsl.edu
SACCO, John .... 617-296-8300.... 235 J
john_sacco@laboure.edu
SACCOCCIO, Louis, J .... 401-874-4486.... 454 E
ljslaw@uri.edu
SACCUCCI, Bonnie, A .... 401-874-9500.... 454 E
saccucci@uri.edu

SACHER, Lesley .... 850-644-8869 .... 119 D
lsacher@admin.fsu.edu
SACHNOFF, Neil .... 732-906-2601 .... 311 D
nsachnoff@middlesexcc.edu
SACHS, Benjamin, P .... 504-988-7800 .... 215 C
bsachs@tulane.edu
SACHS, Michael .... 212-752-1530 .... 338 C
michael.sachs@limcollege.edu
SACHS, Steven, G .... 703-323-3387 .... 527 F
ssachs@nvcc.edu
SACK, Bob .... 616-222-1421 .... 250 A
bob.sack@cornerstone.edu
SACK, Chuck .... 610-558-5627 .... 437 D
sackc@neumann.edu
SACKETT, Christopher .... 585-345-6878 .... 334 F
cmsackett@genesee.edu
SACKETT, Geoffrey, M .... 703-448-3393 .... 523 D
admissions.washington@rts.edu
SACKETT, Mike .... 562-947-8755 .... 71 A
mikesackett@scuhs.edu
SACKS, Arlene .... 305-653-6713 .... 402 I
arlene.sacks@myunion.edu
SACKS, Martha .... 305-892-7046 .... 112 A
martha.sacks@jwu.edu
SACOPULOS, Eugenia .... 219-981-4432 .... 176 G
esacopul@ivytech.edu
SACOPULOS, Melony, A .... 812-237-4141 .... 173 B
melony.sacopulos@indstate.edu
SACZAWA, Eric .... 508-373-9454 .... 231 B
eric.saczawa@becker.edu
SADAN, Avishai .... 213-740-3124 .... 76 F
dentdean@usc.edu
SADAO, Amy .... 215-898-5911 .... 448 J
info@icaphila.org
SADD, Tracy .... 717-361-1260 .... 428 F
saddt@etown.edu
SADDLEMIRE, John .... 860-486-2265 .... 94 G
john.saddlemire@uconn.edu
SADDLEMIRE, Melissa, A .... 570-961-4733 .... 435 F
saddlemire@marywood.edu
SADDLER, Sterling .... 309-298-1690 .... 168 C
s-saddler2@wiu.edu
SADDORIS-TRAUGHBER, Janiece, L .... 217-424-6318 .... 158 G
jtraughber@millikin.edu
SADEGHIPOUR, Keya .... 215-204-5285 .... 447 H
keya.sadeghipour@temple.edu
SADID, Hossein .... 804-289-8150 .... 525 E
hsadid@richmond.edu
SADLEK, Gregory, M .... 216-687-3660 .... 388 D
g.sadlek@csuohio.edu
SADLEK, Lance, A .... 563-333-6252 .... 188 F
sadleklancea@sau.edu
SADLER, David, L .... 925-969-3372 .... 52 C
dsadler@jfku.edu
SADLER, Martin .... 404-687-4512 .... 127 F
sadlerm@ctsnet.edu
SADLER, Paul, L .... 806-291-1163 .... 508 E
sadlerp@wbu.edu
SADLER, Tommy .... 731-661-5218 .... 477 B
tsadler@uu.edu
SADOWSKI, Brigette .... 419-824-3726 .... 395 E
bsadowski@lourdes.edu
SADOWSKI, David .... 401-874-4807 .... 454 E
dsadowski@uri.edu
SADOWSKI, Sherri .... 717-262-2006 .... 452 C
sherri.sadowski@wilson.edu
SADWICK, Rick, F .... 585-262-1695 .... 341 H
rsadwick@monroecc.edu
SAECHAO, Jenny .... 559-438-4222 .... 49 I
jenny_saechao@heald.edu
SAEED, Najam .... 651-846-1324 .... 269 C
najam.saeed@saintpaul.edu
SAENZ, Miguel .... 320-308-5570 .... 269 A
msaenz@stcloudstate.edu
SAENZ, Rogelio .... 210-458-2715 .... 506 D
rogelio.saenz@utsa.edu
SAENZ, Ruben .... 956-488-5808 .... 494 H
rsaenz@southtexascollege.edu
SAES, Jose .... 510-783-2100 .... 49 J
jose_saes@heald.edu
SAETRE, David .... 715-682-1253 .... 549 F
dsaetre@northland.edu
SAEVIG, Daniel, J .... 419-530-4008 .... 404 F
daniel.saevig@utoledo.edu
SAFADY, Randa, S .... 512-499-4777 .... 505 B
rsafady@utsystem.edu
SAFARZADEH, Mohammad .... 714-533-3946 .... 37 E
msafar@calums.edu
SAFFOLD, J.E.(Penny) .... 415-338-2032 .... 37 B
psaffold@sfsu.edu
SAFFORD, Mary, C .... 828-448-3539 .... 375 B
msafford@wpcc.edu
SAFINICK, Nancy .... 310-506-4136 .... 61 H
nancy.safinick@pepperdine.edu
SAFLEY, Ellen .... 972-883-2916 .... 506 A
safley@utdallas.edu
SAFLEY, Mallory .... 770-531-6330 .... 133 C
msafley@laniertech.edu
SAFLEY, Michael, W .... 910-630-7157 .... 367 B
msafley@methodist.edu
SAFRAN, Robert, L .... 717-764-9550 .... 426 D
rsafran@csb.edu
SAFRAN, Robert, L .... 717-764-9550 .... 426 C
rsafran@csb.edu
SAFYER, Andrew .... 516-877-4354 .... 322 A
asafyer@adelphi.edu
SAGANSKI, Gary .... 313-845-9670 .... 252 B
saganski@hfcc.edu
SAGARDIA OLIVERAS, Paula .... 787-863-2390 .... 563 E
paula.sagardia@fajardo.inter.edu
SAGE, James .... 715-346-4446 .... 552 D
jsage@uwsp.edu
SAGE, James, L .... 330-972-6542 .... 403 B
jsage@uakron.edu
SAGE, Roger .... 952-356-3602 .... 464 H
rsage@national.edu
SAGE, William, M .... 512-232-7806 .... 505 D
bsage@law.utexas.edu
SAGER, Scott .... 615-966-5156 .... 470 F
scott.sager@lipscomb.edu
SAGER BOROWICZ, Laurie .... 715-675-3331 .... 555 B
sager@ntc.edu
SAGER GENTRY, Jennifer .... 804-819-4961 .... 526 C
jgentry@vccs.edu
SAGERS, Keith .... 404-297-9522 .... 131 D
sagersr@gptc.edu
SAGERT, Patty .... 763-795-4720 .... 270 F
patty.sagert@rasmussen.edu
SAGESTER, Fred .... 606-539-4059 .... 207 C
fred.sagester@ucumberlands.edu
SAGGIO, Joseph, J .... 602-944-3335 .... 11 D
jsaggio@aicag.edu
SAGHAFI, Shirin .... 703-330-8400 .... 99 G
shirin.saghafi@strayer.edu
SAH, Cynthia .... 312-987-1407 .... 154 H
6sah@jmls.edu
SAHLBERG, Bert .... 208-792-2200 .... 144 B
bhsahlberg@lcsc.edu
SAHLHOFF, Kathleen, A .... 715-836-3373 .... 551 A
sahlhoka@uwec.edu
SAHLI, Daniel .... 330-941-3700 .... 406 F
desahli@ysu.edu
SAHNI, Ashish .... 831-459-4380 .... 75 C
ashish@ucsc.edu
SAHS, Scott .... 507-281-7787 .... 268 I
scott.sahn@roch.edu
SAIA, Sue .... 620-441-5274 .... 192 D
saias@cowley.edu
SAIFF, Edward .... 201-684-7723 .... 313 C
esaiff@ramapo.edu
SAIGAL, Sunil .... 973-596-6506 .... 312 C
sunil.saigal@njit.edu
SAIKIA, Paul .... 717-815-1245 .... 452 G
psaikia@ycp.edu
SAILS, JR., Verties .... 901-333-4143 .... 476 B
vsails@southwest.tn.edu
SAIMON, Joseph .... 691-320-2480 .... 559 D
jsaimon@comfsm.fm
SAIN, Becky .... 704-484-4093 .... 369 E
sain@clevelandcc.edu
SAIN, Nathan .... 479-979-1331 .... 26 A
nsain@ozarks.edu
ST. AMAND, Gerard, A .... 859-572-5129 .... 205 H
stamand@nku.edu
ST. AMAND, Judith, A .... 508-929-8089 .... 238 G
jstamand@worcester.edu
ST. ANDRE, Joe .... 318-678-6000 .... 209 I
st@bpcc.edu
ST. ANGELO, Paul .... 317-916-7826 .... 175 K
pstangelo@ivytech.edu
ST. ANTOINE, Tom .... 561-803-2279 .... 114 C
tom_stantoine@pba.edu
ST. ARNAULD, Cheri .... 602-639-7500 .... 14 H
ST. CLAIR, Ann, F .... 406-496-4284 .... 296 B
astclair@mtech.edu
ST. CLAIR, Don, E .... 818-767-0888 .... 79 H
don.stclair@woodbury.edu
ST. CLAIR, Gloriana .... 412-268-2447 .... 424 J
gstclair@andrew.cmu.edu
ST. CLAIR, Karen .... 307-674-6446 .... 556 F
kstclair@sheridan.edu
ST. COLUMBIA, Rhonda .... 870-338-6474 .... 25 D
ST. CROIX, Jerome, S .... 585-292-2278 .... 341 H
jstcroix@monroecc.edu
ST. DENNIS, Grady, I .... 507-933-7661 .... 263 J
stdennis@gustavus.edu
ST. JACQUES, Yvette .... 631-632-6335 .... 352 C
yvette.stjacques@stonybrook.edu
ST. JAMES, Tim .... 860-253-3087 .... 91 B
tstjames@asnuntuck.edu
ST. JEAN, Robert .... 603-899-4022 .... 305 A
stjean@franklinpierce.edu
ST. JOHN, Caron .... 256-824-6736 .... 8 G
caron.stjohn@uah.edu
ST. JOHN, Cynthia .... 920-686-6350 .... 550 H
cynthia.st.john@sl.edu
ST. JOHN, Meredith .... 617-558-1788 .... 243 C
mstjohn@nesa.edu
ST. JOHN, Ronald .... 718-262-5114 .... 329 A
stjohn@york.cuny.edu
ST. LOUIS, Daniel, C .... 828-327-7000 .... 369 B
dstlouis@cvcc.edu
ST. LOUIS, Moise .... 802-654-2663 .... 514 D
mstlouis@smcvt.edu
ST. MARKS, Wanda .... 406-395-4313 .... 296 E
wstmarks@stonecild.edu
ST. MAURO, Anne .... 609-258-3403 .... 312 G
stmauro@princeton.edu
ST. MICHEL, Peter .... 207-621-3119 .... 220 B
stmichel@maine.edu
ST. ONER, Indira .... 954-783-7339 .... 106 J
istoner@cci.edu
ST. ONGE, Steven .... 518-562-4120 .... 329 C
steve.stonge@clinton.edu
ST. ONGE, Susan .... 321-674-6400 .... 108 H
sstonge@fit.edu
ST. OURS, Paulette .... 207-602-2400 .... 221 A
pstours@une.edu
ST. PETER, David, L .... 207-768-9577 .... 220 F
david.stpeter@umpi.edu
ST. PETER, Heidi .... 802-654-2674 .... 514 D
hstpeter2@smcvt.edu
ST. PIERRE, Traci .... 207-780-4771 .... 220 G
stspierre@usm.maine.edu
ST. PIERRE-SLEBODA, Cheryl .... 617-928-4516 .... 242 E
csleboda@mountida.edu
ST. PREUX, Morisset .... 617-427-0060 .... 241 A
mpreux@rcc.mass.edu
ST. ROMAIN, Claudette, L .... 973-642-8498 .... 315 C
claudette.stromain@shu.edu
SAINTJONES, Jerome .... 256-372-5654 .... 1 A
jerome.saintjones@aamu.edu
SAINTVIL, Yamiley .... 718-409-7220 .... 356 C
ysaintvil@sunymaritime.edu
SAIRS, Reuben .... 740-857-1311 .... 401 F
rsairs@rosedale.edu
SAJDAK, Jeff .... 616-957-6016 .... 249 B
jsajdak@calvinseminary.edu
SAJKO, Helena .... 860-768-7834 .... 95 B
sajko@hartford.edu
SAJOR, Mike .... 602-557-7575 .... 19 A
michael.sajor@apollogrp.edu
SAKAGUCHI, Gary .... 559-638-3641 .... 72 C
gary.sakaguchi@reedleycollege.edu
SAKAI, Eric .... 802-828-2800 .... 515 E
sakaie@ccv.edu
SAKAI, Eric .... 425-739-8100 .... 535 H
eric.sakai@lwtc.edu
SAKAI, Hiro .... 949-480-4008 .... 69 J
sakai@soka.edu
SAKAI, Marcia .... 808-974-7750 .... 141 F
marcias@hawaii.edu
SAKAI, Marcia .... 808-974-7400 .... 141 F
marcias@hawaii.edu
SAKAKI, Judy, K .... 510-987-0158 .... 73 G
judy.sakaki@ucop.edu
SAKALLA, Khaled .... 206-575-1865 .... 535 D
SAKAMOTO, Clyde .... 808-984-3636 .... 142 E
clydes@hawaii.edu
SAKIMOTO, Tak .... 323-462-1384 .... 58 E
taks@mi.edu
SAKO, Kathleen, E .... 716-851-1658 .... 333 C
sako@ecc.edu
SAKO, Wanda .... 808-983-4109 .... 140 H
wsako@tokai.edu
SAKOFS, Mitch .... 860-832-2102 .... 90 G
sakofsm@ccsu.edu
SAKS, Deborah .... 916-558-2582 .... 56 D
saksd@scc.losrios.edu
SAKS, Greg .... 310-243-3787 .... 34 D
gsaks@csudh.edu
SAKS, Ron .... 614-222-4019 .... 388 G
rsaks@ccad.edu
SALA, Anca .... 810-766-4111 .... 248 C
anca.sala@baker.edu
SALA, Andrea .... 310-243-2182 .... 34 D
asala@csudh.edu
SALADIN, Lisa .... 843-792-3328 .... 459 D
saladinl@musc.edu
SALAHUDDIN, Mecca .... 210-486-2897 .... 479 D
msalahuddin1@alamo.edu
SALAMY, James .... 315-866-0300 .... 335 D
salamyjr@herkimer.edu
SALANE, Linda, B .... 803-786-3748 .... 457 C
lsalane@columbiasc.edu
SALANI, Chris .... 906-487-7378 .... 251 A
chris.salani@finlandia.edu
SALARI, Gholamereza .... 717-394-6211 .... 426 C
rsalari@csb.edu
SALAS, Charles, G .... 860-685-2002 .... 95 E
csalas@wesleyan.edu
SALAS, Ezra .... 209-416-3700 .... 49 L
SALAS-BELTRAN, Rocio .... 714-533-1495 .... 70 B
rsbeltran@southbaylo.edu
SALATINO, Michael .... 630-829-6667 .... 145 G
msalatino@ben.edu
SALAVITABAR, Hadi .... 845-257-2930 .... 352 B
salavith@newpaltz.edu
SALAWAY, Kevin, J .... 570-450-3015 .... 439 K
kjs27@psu.edu
SALAY, Lawrence .... 203-285-2046 .... 91 D
lsalay@gwcc.commnet.edu
SALAZ, Eduardo .... 925-631-4212 .... 64 F
els3@stmarys-ca.edu
SALAZ, Mark .... 520-494-5250 .... 13 D
mark.salaz@centralaz.edu
SALAZAR, Alma .... 909-931-7599 .... 79 C
asalazar@westwood.edu
SALAZAR, David .... 562-985-4131 .... 35 C
salazar@csulb.edu
SALAZAR, Ed .... 928-541-7777 .... 16 H
esalazar@ncu.edu
SALAZAR, Marilu .... 361-593-2861 .... 498 D
marilu.salazar@tamuk.edu
SALAZAR, Michael .... 562-860-2451 .... 39 A
msalazar@cerritos.edu
SALAZAR-VALENTINE, Marcia .... 419-372-8183 .... 385 E
marcias@bgsu.edu
SALBU, Steven, C .... 404-894-2600 .... 130 F
steven.salbu@mgt.gatech.edu
SALCHENBERGER, Linda, M .... 414-288-7141 .... 548 F
linda.salchenberger@marquette.edu
SALCIDO, Kevin, J .... 480-965-6608 .... 11 J
kevin.j.salcido@asu.edu
SALDANA, Irma .... 773-291-6775 .... 147 G
isaldana@ccc.edu
SALDANA, Pedro .... 409-984-6200 .... 501 C
saldanap@lamarpa.edu
SALDANA-TALLEY, Jane .... 707-778-3931 .... 68 E
lsaldana-talley@santarosa.edu
SALDIVOR, Rhonda .... 903-593-8311 .... 499 D
rsaldivor@texascollege.edu
SALE, Gene .... 561-803-2352 .... 114 C
gene_sale@pba.edu
SALE, Rachel .... 573-681-5442 .... 283 I
saler@lincolnu.edu
SALEH, Bahaa .... 407-882-3326 .... 120 B
besaleh@creol.ucf.edu
SALEH, Donald, A .... 315-443-5559 .... 357 C
dasaleh@syr.edu
SALEM, Susan .... 310-954-4112 .... 57 H
ssalem@msmc.la.edu
SALEM, Susan .... 801-957-4447 .... 512 D
susan.salem@slcc.edu
SALEMME, Brenda .... 716-488-3023 .... 337 D
brendasalemme@jamestownbusinesscollege.edu
SALEMME, Kevin .... 978-837-5377 .... 242 A
kevin.salemme@merrimack.edu
SALERNO, Dena .... 570-372-4302 .... 447 E
salerno@susqu.edu
SALES, Vince .... 916-278-7043 .... 36 A
vsales@csus.edu
SALESTROM, Charles .... 308-535-3681 .... 298 H
salestromc@mpcc.edu
SALFI, Maureen .... 716-286-8686 .... 344 D
mes@niagara.edu
SALGUERO, Jossie .... 787-766-1912 .... 562 I
jsalguer@inter.edu
SALIBA, Elizabeth .... 602-285-7748 .... 16 A
e.saliba@pcmail.maricopa.edu
SALIBA, Joseph, E .... 937-229-2245 .... 404 A
jsaliba1@udayton.edu
SALIBA, Tony, E .... 937-229-2306 .... 404 A
tsaliba1@udayton.edu
SALIBA, Yvette, C .... 407-303-6413 .... 100 G
yvette.saliba@adu.edu
SALICHS, Eduardo .... 787-765-1915 .... 564 D
esalichs@inter.edu
SALII, Uroi, N .... 680-488-2471 .... 560 C
usalii@palau.edu
SALIM, Ellis, P .... 810-766-4276 .... 247 G
ellis.salim@baker.edu
SALIMAN, Merna, S .... 816-604-3044 .... 285 D
merna.saliman@mcckc.edu
SALIMAN, Todd .... 303-860-5600 .... 88 G
todd.saliman@cu.edu
SALIMBENE, Franklyn, P .... 781-891-2462 .... 231 D
fsalimbene@bentley.edu
SALINAS, Alberto .... 956-721-5357 .... 489 J
albert.salinas@laredo.edu
SALINAS, Antonio .... 575-439-3601 .... 319 E
antsalin@nmsua.nmsu.edu
SALINAS, Felix .... 210-486-4788 .... 479 B
fsalinas26@alamo.edu
SALINAS, Gilberto .... 956-326-2760 .... 497 D
gsalinas@tamiu.edu
SALINAS, Jessica .... 956-665-3361 .... 506 C
lopezj@utpa.edu
SALINAS, Lelia .... 956-872-7209 .... 494 H
lelias1@southtexascollege.edu
SALINAS, Sallie .... 714-241-4901 .... 41 B
ssalinas@coastline.edu
SALINAS, Stacy .... 973-748-9000 .... 307 H
stacy_salinas@bloomfield.edu
SALINE, Terrie .... 309-341-7436 .... 155 F
tsaline@knox.edu
SALINGER, Sharon, V .... 949-824-7761 .... 74 B
sharon.salinger@uci.edu
SALISBURY, Kathleen .... 603-862-0938 .... 306 B
kathleen.salisbury@usnh.edu
SALISBURY, Mark .... 309-794-7504 .... 145 E
marksalisbury@augustana.edu
SALIVA, Sara .... 787-264-1912 .... 564 B
smsaliva@sg.inter.edu
SALKIN, Patricia .... 631-761-7100 .... 358 B
patricia.salkin@touro.edu
SALKIN, Patricia, E .... 518-445-2351 .... 322 C
psalk@albanylaw.edu

SALLAN, Veena 270-686-4639 203 B
veena.sallan@kctcs.edu

SALLEE, David, L 816-415-5026 293 C
salleed@william.jewell.edu

SALLEE, L. James 219-785-5667 179 A
jsallee@pnc.edu

SALLEH-BARONE, Normah 708-974-5209 159 B
salleh-barone@morainevalley.edu

SALLENBACH, Paul 562-427-0861 44 H
psallenbach@devry.edu

SALLER, Richard, P 650-723-9784 71 G
rsaller@stanford.edu

SALLEY, Dug 610-282-1100 427 A
dug.salley@desales.edu

SALLIN, Dennis 573-897-5000 284 A

SALLY, Dana 828-227-7307 380 A
dsally@wcu.edu

SALMEIER, Michael 909-599-5433 54 A

SALMERI, Patrice 612-330-1166 261 B
salmeri@augsburg.edu

SALMI, SJ, Richard, P 251-380-3866 7 E
raslmi@shc.edu

SALMO, James, G 401-456-8105 454 A
jsalmo@ric.edu

SALMON, Edward, L 262-646-6508 549 E
esalmon@nashotah.edu

SALMON, Mark 334-670-3342 8 A
msalmon@troy.edu

SALMON, Marla 206-543-8736 539 A
msalmon@uw.edu

SALMON, Robert, O 801-281-7630 510 M
robert.salmon@stevenshenager.edu

SALMON, Sheri 205-226-4692 2 B
ssalmon@bsc.edu

SALMONA, Riccardo 212-799-5000 337 H

SALMOND, Susan, W 973-972-4322 316 H
salmonsu@umdnj.edu

SALOMANSON, Kristen 231-591-3801 250 H
kristen_salomonson@ferris.edu

SALOME, Joann 575-835-5206 319 A
jsalome@admin.nmt.edu

SALOMON, Carol 212-353-4187 331 A
salomo@cooper.edu

SALOMON, Mattisyahu 732-367-1060 307 G

SALOMON, Rachel 629-625-5979 560 A
rsalomon@cmi.edu

SALOMON-FERNÁNDEZ, Yves 781-239-3159 239 G
ysalomonfernandez@massbay.edu

SALOMONE, Joseph, J 215-895-4948 427 H
salomojj@drexel.edu

SALOMONSON, Kristen 231-591-3801 250 H
kristen_salomonson@ferris.edu

SALONEN, Neil Albert 203-576-4665 94 F
nas@bridgeport.edu

SALONER, Garth 650-723-1940 71 G
saloner@stanford.edu

SALOUN, Pamela 414-256-1207 549 D
salounp@mtmary.edu

SALOVEY, Peter 203-432-4444 96 A
peter.salovey@yale.edu

SALOWITZ, Stewart, I 309-556-3206 153 F
salowitz@iwu.edu

SALOWITZ, Susan 860-343-5724 91 G
ssalowitz@mxcc.commnet.edu

SALTALAMACHIA, Joseph 207-948-9205 219 H
jsalty@unity.edu

SALTER, Anne 404-364-8514 135 E
asalter@oglethorpe.edu

SALTER, Brooke 912-538-3129 137 E
bsalter@southeasterntech.edu

SALTER, James 415-457-4440 45 C

SALTER, Ruth 229-430-3986 124 A
ruth.salter@asurams.edu

SALTER-SMITH, Cassandra, L 716-839-8237 331 F
csalters@daemen.edu

SALTIEL, Henry 718-482-6120 328 B
hsaltiel@lagcc.cuny.edu

SALTONSTALL, Thomas, L 617-228-3311 239 C
tlsaltonstall@bhcc.mass.edu

SALTZ, Ira, S 724-983-2825 440 E

SALTZMAN, Robert 516-463-4134 335 G
robert.saltzman@hofstra.edu

SALVA, William, M 914-337-9300 330 G
william.salva@concordia-ny.edu

SALVADOR, Cinnamon, A 337-475-5711 215 G
csalvador@mcneese.edu

SALVADOR, Susan, M 585-292-2121 341 H
ssalvador@monroecc.edu

SALVAGGIO, Brian 508-531-1267 237 D

SALVAIL, Leslie, H 410-777-2709 221 C
lhsalvail@aacc.edu

SALVATO, Alfred 215-503-7570 448 C
alfred.salvato@jefferson.edu

SALVATO, Alfred, C 215-503-7570 448 C
alfred.salvato@jefferson.edu

SALVATO, Scott 516-678-5000 341 F
ssalvato@molloy.edu

SALVESEN, Guy 858-646-3114 67 I
gsalvesen@sandfordburnham.org

SALVIDIO, Nanci 413-572-8123 238 F
nsalvidio@wsc.ma.edu

SALVO, Robyn 732-571-3470 311 E
rsalvo@monmouth.edu

SALVUCCI, James 443-334-2215 226 E
jsalvucci@stevenson.edu

SALYERS, Catherine, A 219-866-6187 179 D
cathys@saintjoe.edu

SALZMAN, Christine 201-714-2198 310 E
csalzman@hccc.edu

SALZMANN, Nick 847-628-2492 154 K
nsalzmann@judsonu.edu

SAM, David 847-214-7374 150 F
dsam@elgin.edu

SAM, David, A 540-423-9039 526 I
dsam@germanna.edu

SAM, Mary 218-855-8159 265 J
msam@clcmn.edu

SAMA, Eduardo 305-553-6065 107 G
esama@careercollege.edu

SAMAHA, Ahmed 803-641-3411 462 B
ahmeds@usca.edu

SAMALOT-RIVERA, OP, Yamil, A 787-786-4508 561 I
ysamalot@cedoc.edu

SAMANGO, Melissa 610-526-6196 430 D
msamango@harcum.edu

SAMANT, Ajay 904-620-2590 120 D
ajay.samant@unf.edu

SAMANTA, Shivajl 434-961-5229 528 B
ssamanta@pvcc.edu

SAMBERG, Carol 212-875-4680 323 C
csamberg@bankstreet.edu

SAMBERG, Wendy 203-285-2108 91 D
wsamberg@gwcc.commnet.edu

SAMDAHL, JR., Donald, H 540-464-7228 529 F
samdahldh@vmi.edu

SAMDPERIL, Debra 617-369-3116 244 E
dsamdperil@smfa.edu

SAMEK, Linda 503-554-2871 415 I
lsamek@georgefox.edu

SAMEK, Tom 503-375-7031 415 F
tsamek@corban.edu

SAMENFINK, William, H 978-232-2402 234 D
bsamenfi@endicott.edu

SAMENTO, Courtney 515-244-4221 181 F
samentoc@aib.edu

SAMET, Jan 301-696-3934 223 C
jsamet@hood.edu

SAMHAN, Tisha, L 318-795-4215 213 D
tisha.samhan@lsus.edu

SAMHAT, Nayef 740-427-5114 394 C
samhatn@kenyon.edu

SAMIA, Cris 425-564-2973 531 G
cris.samia@bellevuecollege.edu

SAMIIAN, Vida 559-278-3056 35 A
vida_samiian@csufresno.edu

SAMITORE, Wendy 509-527-4300 539 B
wendy.samitore@wwcc.edu

SAMMAKIA, Bahgat 607-777-4818 351 F
bahgat@binghamton.edu

SAMMARCO, Ed 800-955-2527 282 D

SAMMARCO, Erica, C 716-888-2100 325 F
sammarce@canisius.edu

SAMMARTINO, Hallie, G 718-990-2781 348 G
sammarth@stjohns.edu

SAMMIS, Robert 626-914-8550 40 B
rsammis@citruscollege.edu

SAMMONS, Dallas 606-783-2060 204 I
d.sammons@moreheadstate.edu

SAMMONS, Gregory, S 607-587-3992 355 C
sammongs@alfredstate.edu

SAMMONS, Gregory, S 607-587-3911 355 C
sammongs@alfredstate.edu

SAMMONS, Kenneth, R 509-313-6951 534 F
ksammons@plant.gonzaga.edu

SAMMONS, Morgan 415-955-2066 27 A
msammons@alliant.edu

SAMOLEWICZ, Mark 201-216-5218 315 E
msamolew@stevens.edu

SAMOLEWSKI, Patrick, C 989-964-4221 257 G
pcs@svsu.edu

SAMONS, Jenni 517-780-4553 248 D
jenni.samons@baker.edu

SAMORA, Tracy 719-549-2850 83 H
tracy.samora@colostate-pueblo.edu

SAMP, Mike 307-766-5188 556 H
bowhntr@uwyo.edu

SAMPERTON, Amy 910-678-8236 370 E
samperta@faytechcc.edu

SAMPH, Thomas 203-596-4652 93 G
tsamph@post.edu

SAMPITE, Chris 318-869-5018 208 H
csampite@centenary.edu

SAMPLE, Bradford, W 423-775-7232 467 F
bradford.sample@bryan.edu

SAMPLE, Mark 704-991-0247 374 D
jsample7479@stanly.edu

SAMPLE, Michael 812-855-0850 173 D
mmsample@indiana.edu

SAMPLE, Mike 812-855-0850 173 E
mmsample@indiana.edu

SAMPLE, Rick, A 301-369-2800 221 F
rsample@capitol-college.edu

SAMPLE, Steven, B 213-740-5400 76 F

SAMPLE-PURTLEBAUGH, Charlene 765-288-8681 172 K
charlene.purtlebaugh@harrison.edu

SAMPLER, Georgianna, W 818-947-2770 55 E
samplegw@lavc.edu

SAMPLER, Jason 337-550-1302 212 J
jsampler@lsue.edu

SAMPLES, Janet 859-442-4121 202 B
janet.samples@kctcs.edu

SAMPLES, Jim 562-903-4751 31 A
jim.samples@biola.edu

SAMPLES, Robert, D 314-516-5665 291 D
bob@umsl.edu

SAMPLEY, Curtis 334-387-3877 1 D
curtissampley@amridgeuniversity.edu

SAMPSON, Ann 660-359-3948 287 A
asampson@mail.ncmissouri.edu

SAMPSON, Betty, J 509-865-8600 535 A
sampson_b@heritage.edu

SAMPSON, Christina 304-829-7401 540 H
csampson@bethanywv.edu

SAMPSON, Christopher 920-465-2527 551 B
sampsonc@uwgb.edu

SAMPSON, Connie, B 404-413-3230 131 G
csampson@gsu.edu

SAMPSON, David, G 518-381-1370 350 E
sampsodg@sunysccc.edu

SAMPSON, Diana 206-546-4512 538 C
dsampson@shoreline.edu

SAMPSON, Laura 845-434-5750 357 A
lsampson@sullivan.suny.edu

SAMPSON, Marsha 406-657-2085 295 D
msampson@msubillings.edu

SAMPSON, Michael 928-523-2611 16 I

SAMPSON, Robert 401-841-1323 558 B

SAMPSON, Sharon 412-731-8690 445 F
bookstore@rpts.edu

SAMPSON, Sonya 207-755-5246 218 G
ssampson@cmcc.edu

SAMPSON, Therese 609-343-5116 307 C
sampson@atlantic.edu

SAMPSON, Zora, J 608-342-1688 552 B
sampsonz@uwplatt.edu

SAMRA, Rajinder 925-424-1027 39 D
rsamra@laspositascollege.edu

SAMS, Catherine, T 864-656-4233 456 E
willsam@clemson.edu

SAMS, Susan 714-997-6829 39 F
sams@chapman.edu

SAMS, Timothy, E 518-276-6201 347 D
samst@rpi.edu

SAMSON, Agniel 256-726-7357 6 C
samson@oakwood.edu

SAMSON, Keri 563-589-3775 189 F
ksamson@dbq.edu

SAMSON, Kim, M 218-477-2133 267 F
samson@mnstate.edu

SAMUEL, Bryan 423-425-5670 477 F
bryan-samuel@utc.edu

SAMUEL, Jacinta 692-625-6724 560 A
jsamuel@cmi.edu

SAMUEL LOFTUS, Barbara 570-674-6195 436 F
bloftus@misericordia.edu

SAMUELS, A. Dexter 615-963-5646 474 A
asamuels01@tnstate.edu

SAMUELS, Darlette, C 731-426-7595 470 B
dsamuels@lanecollege.edu

SAMUELS, Deby, K 615-966-7133 470 F
deby.samuels@lipscomb.edu

SAMUELS, Diana 410-276-0306 226 D
dsamuels@host.sdc.edu

SAMUELS, Elena 212-220-8061 326 D
esamuels@bmcc.cuny.edu

SAMUELS, Milton 617-427-0060 241 A
msamuels@rcc.mass.edu

SAMUELS, Robert 401-874-2288 454 E
rsamuels@mail.uri.edu

SAMUELS, Sandra 973-353-5231 314 E
szsamuls@newark.rutgers.edu

SAMUELS, Scott 248-218-2057 257 D
ssamuels@rc.edu

SAMUELS-JONES, Michelle 240-684-2290 227 F
student-services@umuc.edu

SAMUELSON, Cecil, O 801-422-2521 509 H
cecil_samuelson@byu.edu

SAMUELSON, Erik 425-249-4759 538 G
erik.samuelson@tlc.edu

SAMUELSON, Pamela 570-372-4272 447 E
samuelson@susqu.edu

SAMUELSON, Scott 847-317-4194 166 E
ssamuels@tiu.edu

SAN JOSE, Rodney 309-677-3131 146 C
rodney@bradley.edu

SAN NICOLAS, Heidi, E 671-735-2481 559 G
heidisan@ite.net

SAN NICOLAS, Jennifer 760-384-6367 52 M
jsannico@cerrocoso.edu

SANABRIA, Roberto, A 773-442-5416 160 A
r-sanabria1@neiu.edu

SANAGUSTIN, Mary 760-744-1150 61 D
msanagustin@palomar.edu

SANAI, Fardin 518-956-8062 351 E
fsanai@uamail.albany.edu

SANANES, Amram 718-339-1090 361 H
amramsananes@verizon.net

SANANES, Josh 718-339-1090 361 H
rjsananes@mikdashmelech.org

SANBERG, Paul 813-974-3154 121 A
psanberg@usf.edu

SANBORN, Brett 303-220-1200 81 J
brett.sanborn@cffp.edu

SANBORN, Esther 773-298-3419 163 I
sanborn@sxu.edu

SANBORN, Jennifer 413-538-2500 242 D
jsanborn@mtholyoke.edu

SANBORN, Karen 734-432-5843 254 D
ksanborn@madonna.edu

SANBORN, Merlene 207-974-4871 218 H
msanborn@emcc.edu

SANCHEZ, Andrew, E 505-925-8508 321 G
aesanchz@unm.edu

SANCHEZ, Angel, A 209-667-3646 36 D
aasanchez@csustan.edu

SANCHEZ, Ann 914-961-8313 349 I
aks@svots.edu

SANCHEZ, Anna 505-224-4687 317 K
asanchez420@cnm.edu

SANCHEZ, Bonifacio 692-625-3394 560 A
pecatflo@yahoo.com

SANCHEZ, Caridad 305-821-3333 109 D
csanchez@mm.fnc.edu

SANCHEZ, Caridad 305-821-3333 109 B
csanchez@mm.fnc.edu

SANCHEZ, Caridad 305-821-3333 109 C
csanchez@mm.fnc.edu

SANCHEZ, Cheryl 719-336-1516 86 B
cheryl.sanchez@lamarcc.edu

SANCHEZ, Diane 210-829-5866 504 B
castaned@uiwtx.edu

SANCHEZ, Domingo 505-747-2143 320 A
domingo_sanchez@nnmc.edu

SANCHEZ, Elda, E 361-593-3805 498 D
elda.sanchez@tamuk.edu

SANCHEZ, Frank 212-794-5775 326 B
frank.sanchez@mail.cuny.edu

SANCHEZ, Gregory 619-388-3354 65 F
gsanchez@sdccd.edu

SANCHEZ, Hector Ruben 787-751-1912 564 C
rsanchez@inter.edu

SANCHEZ, Ines 787-850-9348 567 E
ines.sanchez@upr.edu

SANCHEZ, John 210-434-6711 492 B
jdsanchez@lake.ollusa.edu

SANCHEZ, Jorge, R 714-241-6338 41 B
jsanchez@coastline.edu

SANCHEZ, Jose 787-878-5475 563 B
jsanchez@arecibo.inter.edu

SANCHEZ, Joseph 817-735-2522 504 E
joseph.sanchez@unthsc.edu

SANCHEZ, Juan, M 512-471-2877 505 D
jsanchez@mail.utexas.edu

SANCHEZ, Judy 623-845-3481 15 H
judy.sanchez@gcmail.maricopa.edu

SANCHEZ, Julian 919-684-6756 364 C
julian.sanchez@duke.edu

SANCHEZ, Leopoldo, A 314-863-2772 280 D
sanchezl@csl.edu

SANCHEZ, Librada 973-720-2586 317 D
sanchezl@wpunj.edu

SANCHEZ, Lisa 323-343-3694 35 D
lsanchez@cslanet.calstate.edu

SANCHEZ, Luis 520-494-5266 13 D
luis.sanchez@centralaz.edu

SANCHEZ, Luiz, P 805-922-6966 26 L
lsanchez@hancockcollege.edu

SANCHEZ, Mark 559-442-8226 72 B
mark.sanchez@fresnocitycollege.edu

SANCHEZ, Nancy 801-957-4041 512 D
nancy.sanchez@slcc.edu

SANCHEZ, Nicolas 928-855-7812 16 F
nsanchez@mohave.edu

SANCHEZ, Omar 305-821-3333 109 C
omarsnc@mm.fnc.edu

SANCHEZ, Omar 305-821-3333 109 B
omarsnc@mm.fnc.edu

SANCHEZ, Omar 305-821-3333 109 D
omarsnc@mm.fnc.edu

SANCHEZ, Ramiro 805-654-6464 77 F
rsanchez@vcccd.edu

SANCHEZ, Rebecca 951-343-4236 31 J
rsanchez@calbaptist.edu

SANCHEZ, Richard, M 903-875-7308 491 C
richard.sanchez@navarrocollege.edu

SANCHEZ, Roxanne 210-434-6711 492 B
rlsanchez@lake.ollusa.edu

SANCHEZ, Samuel 787-751-1912 564 C
ssamuel@inter.edu

SANCHEZ, Sandra 310-233-4041 54 I
sanches@lahc.edu

SANCHEZ, Steven 314-977-2611 289 C
ssanche6@slu.edu

SANCHEZ, William 605-575-2038 466 E
william.sanchez@usiouxfalls.edu

SANCHEZ, Willie 402-363-5620 301 E
willie.sanchez@york.edu

SANCHEZ, Xiomara 787-743-4041 561 F
xsanchez@columbiaco.edu

SANTIVASCI, Joseph .... 610-436-3085.... 444 A
jsantivasci@wcupa.edu
SANTIZO, Roberto .... 847-628-2532.... 154 K
rsantizo@judsonu.edu
SANTOMAURO, Kristine, M .... 302-225-6233...... 96 H
santomk@gbc.edu
SANTORA, Anthony .... 908-737-6000.... 311 A
afs@kean.edu
SANTORE, JR., Chuck .... 724-439-4900.... 434 A
csantore@laurel.edu
SANTOS, Adele Naude .... 617-253-4401.... 241 D
SANTOS, Allison .... 312-280-3500.... 153 B
asantos@aii.edu
SANTOS, Ana, L .... 973-642-8392.... 315 C
ana.santos@shu.edu
SANTOS, Carlo .... 408-288-3761...... 67 B
SANTOS, Carmen, K .... 671-735-5548.... 559 E
carmen.kweksantos@guamcc.edu
SANTOS, Carol .... 508-999-8388.... 237 A
csantos1@umassd.edu
SANTOS, Catherine .... 315-312-2500.... 354 A
catherine.santos@oswego.edu
SANTOS, Claudio .... 787-844-8621.... 568 A
claudio.santos@upr.edu
SANTOS, Cynthia .... 713-221-8136.... 503 F
santosc@uhd.edu
SANTOS, Helena .... 617-243-2127.... 236 A
hsantos@lasell.edu
SANTOS, Kennia .... 787-480-2453.... 561 E
kisantos@sanjuancapital.com
SANTOS, Leslie .... 209-228-2977...... 74 D
lsantos@ucmerced.edu
SANTOS, Mae .... 323-343-3555...... 35 D
msantos@cslanet.calstatela.edu
SANTOS, Maria .... 561-273-6500.... 118 A
msantos@southuniversity.edu
SANTOS, Maria del, C .... 787-743-7979.... 565 H
ut_masantos@suagm.edu
SANTOS, Maricarmen .... 787-743-7979.... 565 H
m_santos@suagm.edu
SANTOS, Maritza .... 787-878-5475.... 563 B
msantos@arecibo.inter.edu
SANTOS, Matthew .... 610-683-4113.... 443 A
santos@kutztown.edu
SANTOS, Paul .... 704-330-6689.... 369 D
paul.santos@cpcc.edu
SANTOS, Ramon .... 305-223-4561.... 116 E
santos@sjvcs.edu
SANTOS, Robert .... 212-650-8830.... 326 G
rdsantos@ccny.cuny.edu
SANTOS, Sandra .... 787-758-2525.... 567 G
sandra.santos@upr.edu
SANTOS DE BARONA, Maryann .... 765-494-2336.... 178 J
msdb@purdue.edu
SANTOS-GEORGE, Arlene . 847-543-2310.... 148 B
asgeorge@clcillinois.edu
SANTOSTEFANO, Donald .. 717-867-6341.... 434 C
facilities-services@lvc.edu
SANTUCCI, George .... 412-281-2600.... 447 A
gsantucci@western-school.com
SANTUCCI, Wayne .... 212-517-0544.... 340 C
wsantucci@mmm.edu
SANYAL, Rajib, N .... 765-285-8192.... 169 G
rnsanyal@bsu.edu
SAO, Ry-Yon .... 425-637-1010.... 532 E
rgsao@cityu.edu
SAPARILAS, John, W .... 919-866-5450.... 374 H
jwsaparilas@waketech.edu
SAPATA, Tony .... 708-237-5050.... 160 D
tsapata@nc.edu
SAPERSTEIN, Shari .... 954-262-7202.... 114 B
ssaperst@nsu.nova.edu
SAPERSTONE, Barbara, L .. 703-323-3222.... 527 F
bsaperstone@nvcc.edu
SAPHIRE, Diane, G .... 210-999-8483.... 502 E
dsaphire@trinity.edu
SAPIENZA, Matthew .... 646-746-4275.... 326 B
matthew.sapienza@mail.cuny.edu
SAPIENZA, Michael, C .... 423-775-7224.... 467 F
misapienza@bryan.edu
SAPIENZA, Neil .... 330-684-8940.... 403 C
nbs@uakron.edu
SAPIENZA, Neil, B .... 330-972-8940.... 403 B
nbst@uakron.edu
SAPIRO, Virginia .... 617-353-2401.... 232 E
vsapiro@bu.edu
SAPONARA, Manuel .... 787-878-9218.... 567 A
manuel.saponara@upr.edu
SAPP, Aimee .... 573-592-4391.... 293 D
asapp@williamwoods.edu
SAPP, Buddy .... 912-871-1634.... 135 D
bsapp@ogeecheetech.edu
SAPP, Fred .... 910-672-1204.... 377 G
fsapp@uncfsu.edu
SAPP, Geneva .... 509-865-8631.... 535 A
sapp_g@heritage.edu
SAPP, Jeremy, B .... 512-279-2850.... 508 C
jeremy.sapp@vc.edu
SAPP, Judy .... 606-877-1421.... 203 C
judy.sapp@kctcs.edu
SAPP, Lauren .... 850-599-3370.... 118 L
lauren.sapp@famu.edu
SAPP, Marge .... 843-525-8276.... 461 E
msapp@tcl.edu
SAPP, Mary, M .... 305-284-3856.... 122 I
msapp@miami.edu
SAPP, Sarah .... 662-562-3274.... 276 D
ssapp@northwestms.edu
SAPP, Tracie, W .... 706-425-3183.... 138 G
sapp@uga.edu
SAPPENFIELD, Elizabeth .... 317-738-8075.... 171 F
esappenfield@franklincollege.edu
SAPPENFIELD, George, O . 336-386-3280.... 374 E
sappeng@surry.edu
SAPPINGTON, Eric .... 660-831-4168.... 286 F
sappingtone@moval.edu
SAPPINGTON, Lee Ann ..... 970-339-6223...... 81 A
leeann.sappington@aims.edu
SAPYTA, Lynn .... 630-942-2219.... 148 A
sapytal@cod.edu
SARA, Ligaya .... 680-488-2471.... 560 C
ligayas@palau.edu
SARA, Tejnder .... 334-727-8704........ 8 B
tsara@tuskegee.edu
SARAC, Isa .... 703-591-7042.... 529 E
SARACCO, Melanie .... 714-867-5009...... 70 C
SARACENO, William .... 509-542-4408.... 532 H
bsaraceno@columbiabasin.edu
SARAJIAN, Charles .... 973-655-7480.... 311 F
sarajianc@mail.montclair.edu
SARAKA, Mike .... 570-422-3691.... 442 D
msaraka@esufoundation.org
SARANTAKOS, Paul .... 217-351-2385.... 161 C
psarantakos@parkland.edu
SARBER, Sarah .... 765-455-9204.... 174 A
shawkins@iuk.edu
SARGE, Billy .... 859-344-3402.... 206 I
billy.sarge@thomasmore.edu
SARGEANT, Kari .... 815-802-8256.... 155 A
ksargeant@kcc.edu
SARGENT, Anneila, I .... 626-395-6100...... 32 H
afs@caltech.edu
SARGENT, Ed .... 425-739-8100.... 535 H
ed.sargent@lwtc.edu
SARGENT, Frank .... 401-598-1033.... 453 E
fsargent@jwu.edu
SARGENT, Gary .... 254-295-4242.... 504 C
gsargent@umhb.edu
SARGENT, Jeffrey .... 708-456-0300.... 166 F
jsargent@triton.edu
SARGENT, Jenell .... 404-270-5447.... 138 B
jsargent@spelman.edu
SARGENT, Joe, E .... 423-585-6836.... 476 D
joe.sargent@ws.edu
SARGENT, Judy, L .... 701-777-4251.... 381 F
judy.sargent@und.edu
SARGENT, Madeline .... 215-568-9215.... 436 E
msargent@phmc.org
SARGENT, Marilyn .... 858-642-8308...... 58 I
msargent@nu.edu
SARGENT, Mark, L .... 805-565-6007...... 79 A
msargent@westmont.edu
SARGENT, Peter, E .... 314-968-7006.... 292 J
sargenpe@webster.edu
SARHAN, Mostafa .... 912-358-4190.... 136 G
vpaa@savannahstate.edu
SARIAN, Richard .... 216-421-7432.... 388 A
rsarian@cia.edu
SARIDAKIS, Dianne .... 215-965-4048.... 436 H
dsaridakis@moore.edu
SARIKAS, Bridget .... 202-806-2411...... 98 E
bridget.sarikas@howard.edu
SARIN, Sanjiv .... 336-334-7920.... 378 A
sarin@ncat.edu
SARIN, Sanjiv .... 336-334-7810.... 378 A
sarin@ncat.edu
SARKAR, Amin .... 256-372-5092........ 1 A
amin.sarkar@aamu.edu
SARKAR, Ratna .... 713-348-4293.... 493 C
rgs1@rice.edu
SARLES, Harry .... 913-684-3097.... 558 F
harry.sarles@us.army.mil
SARMIENTO, Reine .... 718-482-5414.... 328 B
rsarmiento@lagcc.cuny.edu
SARNA, Ruth .... 785-594-8409.... 190 F
ruth.sarna@bakeru.edu
SARNESO, Bernard, J .... 814-269-7900.... 449 D
sarneso@pitt.edu
SARNOVSKY, Joseph .... 407-708-2430.... 117 H
sarnovsj@seminolestate.edu
SARRA, Amanda .... 561-912-1211.... 107 B
asarra@evergladesuniversity.edu
SARRAFIAN, Armen .... 312-553-5911.... 147 C
asarrafian@ccc.edu
SARRATORE, Steve, T .... 260-481-6536.... 174 C
sarrator@ipfw.edu
SARRATORE, Steven, T ...... 260-481-6116.... 174 C
sarrator@ipfw.edu
SARRATORI, Peter .... 315-781-3647.... 335 F
sarratori@hws.edu
SARRETT, David, C .... 804-828-7235.... 526 B
dcsarrett@vcu.edu
SARRETT, Michele .... 304-929-1352.... 541 H
msarrett@mountainstate.edu
SARSAR, Saliba .... 732-571-4474.... 311 E
sarsar@monmouth.edu
SARTAIN, S, L .... 816-559-5612.... 287 E
sartain@park.edu
SARTARELLI, Jose, V .... 304-293-7800.... 545 A
jose.sartarelli@mail.wvu.edu
SARTIN, Mici .... 405-691-3800.... 408 H
msartin@macu.edu
SARTIN MANTANO, Katrina .... 503-517-1018.... 421 B
ksartinmantano@warnerpacific.edu
SARTINI, Chad .... 540-857-8922.... 529 B
csartini@virginiawestern.edu
SARTOR, Curtis .... 847-628-1017.... 154 K
csartor@judsonu.edu
SARVELA, Paul .... 618-536-3465.... 165 A
psarvela@siu.edu
SARVER, Angel, M .... 417-268-6010.... 278 J
asarver@gobbc.edu
SARVEY, Sharon .... 252-399-6401.... 362 E
sisarvey@barton.edu
SARVIS, Randall, F .... 937-382-6661.... 405 I
randy_sarvis@wilmington.edu
SASAKI, Charles .... 808-734-9517.... 141 J
sasakich@hawaii.edu
SASAKI, Edwin .... 661-654-2554...... 34 A
esasaki@csub.edu
SASS, Michael .... 518-694-7367.... 322 B
michael.sass@acphs.edu
SASS, Sharon, A .... 561-868-3147.... 114 D
sasss@palmbeachstate.edu
SASS, Terricita, E .... 757-823-8679.... 522 E
tesass@nsu.edu
SASSAMAN, Margo, J .... 717-872-3312.... 443 D
margo.sassaman@millersville.edu
SASSE, Benjamin, E .... 402-941-6000.... 298 I
president@midlandu.edu
SASSER, Dell .... 606-436-5721.... 202 C
dell.sasser@kctcs.edu
SASSER, Jackson, N .... 352-395-5164.... 117 F
j.sasser@sfcollege.edu
SASSER, Jennifer .... 503-675-3964.... 416 J
jsasser@marylhurst.edu
SASSER, Rachelle .... 310-900-1600...... 45 F
sasser_r@compton.edu
SASSER, Susan, M .... 919-735-5151.... 375 A
msm@waynecc.edu
SASSMAN, Jen, L .... 319-352-8262.... 189 J
jennifer.sassman@wartburg.edu
SASSO, Gary, M .... 610-758-3221.... 434 E
gms208@lehigh.edu
SASTRY, S. Shankar .... 510-642-5771...... 73 H
sastry@coe.berkeley.edu
SATCHWELL, Carol .... 315-655-7144.... 325 H
csatchwell@cazenovia.edu
SATELE, Arleen .... 619-660-4654...... 49 B
arleen.satele@gcccd.edu
SATEY, Linda, S .... 828-448-3531.... 375 B
lsatey@wpcc.edu
SATHER, Steven, M .... 609-258-6479.... 312 G
sather@princeton.edu
SATKOWIAK, Ann, E .... 865-539-7153.... 475 G
asatkowiak@pstcc.edu
SATKOWSKI, John .... 567-661-7204.... 400 I
john_satkowski@owens.edu
SATO, Kay .... 516-299-2584.... 339 A
kay.sato@liu.edu
SATO, Sara .... 808-544-0238.... 140 G
ssato@hpu.edu
SATO, Tami, A .... 714-449-7447...... 70 G
tsato@scco.edu
SATRIANA, Dan .... 970-351-2399...... 89 B
dan.satriana@unco.edu
SATTAR, Mo .... 413-565-1000.... 230 G
msattar@baypath.edu
SATTERFIELD, Billy .... 281-283-2480.... 503 E
satterfield@uhcl.edu
SATTERFIELD, Derick .... 336-342-4261.... 373 E
satterfieldd@rockinghamcc.edu
SATTERFIELD, Jay .... 731-989-6058.... 469 B
jsatterfield@fhu.edu
SATTERLEE, Kevin .... 208-426-1203.... 142 I
ksatterl@boisestate.edu
SATTERLEE, Richard .... 718-862-7352.... 339 H
richard.satterlee@manhattan.edu
SATTERLY, Amy .... 812-749-1392.... 178 H
asatterly@oak.edu
SATTERLY, Eric .... 502-272-8098.... 198 H
esatterly@bellarmine.edu
SATTERTHWAITE, Shad ..... 405-325-3546.... 413 D
shad@ou.edu
SATTERTHWAITE, Shad, B 405-325-3546.... 413 C
shad@ou.edu
SATTERWHITE, Robin .... 806-743-3223.... 502 B
robin.satterwhite@ttuhsc.edu
SATTLER, Brian .... 409-880-8396.... 501 A
brian.sattler@lamar.edu
SATTLER, Joan, L .... 309-677-3180.... 146 C
jls@bradley.edu
SATTLER, Michael .... 315-472-6603.... 325 D
msattler@bryantstratton.edu
SAUBERT, IV, Carl, W .... 636-227-2100.... 284 B
carl.saubert@logan.edu
SAUCEDA, Marshall .... 310-338-5808...... 56 E
msauceda@lmu.edu
SAUCEMAN, Fred, W .... 423-439-4317.... 473 F
sauceman@etsu.edu
SAUCIER, Claudia .... 504-671-5602.... 210 F
csauci@dcc.edu
SAUCIER, Ruth, M .... 360-475-7250.... 536 D
rsaucier@olympic.edu
SAUCIER, Todd .... 207-581-1138.... 220 A
todd.saucier@umit.maine.edu
SAUDER, Ron .... 404-727-4499.... 129 D
ron.sauder@emory.edu
SAUDER, Vinita, R .... 423-236-2580.... 473 B
sauder@southern.edu
SAUDERS, Charlette, R ...... 574-372-5100.... 171 H
saudercr@grace.edu
SAUER, Alan, R .... 860-297-2043...... 94 E
alan.sauer@trincoll.edu
SAUER, James .... 610-341-5957.... 438 D
jsauer@eastern.edu
SAUER, James, L .... 610-341-5957.... 428 E
jsauer@eastern.edu
SAUER, Jenni .... 610-647-4400.... 431 C
jsauer@immaculata.edu
SAUER, Marty, R .... 630-637-5801.... 159 G
mrsauer@noctrl.edu
SAUER, Mike .... 702-895-1073.... 302 I
sauer@unlv.edu
SAUER, Peter .... 340-693-1102.... 568 E
psauer@live.uvi.edu
SAUERESSIG, Sarah .... 785-587-2800.... 195 A
sarahsaueressig@matc.net
SAUERS, Darlene .... 724-838-4210.... 447 C
sauers@setonhill.edu
SAUERS, Diane .... 256-233-8260........ 1 E
diane.sauers@athens.edu
SAUERWEIN, David, A ...... 603-526-3758.... 303 G
dsauerwein@colby-sawyer.edu
SAUERWEIN, Rachel .... 802-831-1237.... 515 B
cwiegand@vermontlaw.edu
SAUK, John, J .... 502-852-5295.... 207 E
john.sauk@louisville.edu
SAUL, Amy .... 610-861-1509.... 437 A
awsaul@moravian.edu
SAUL, J. Beau .... 607-844-8222.... 357 I
saulj@tc3.edu
SAULE, Mara, R .... 802-656-2020.... 514 H
mara.saule@uvm.edu
SAULNIER, Richard .... 212-237-8118.... 327 F
rsaulnier@jjay.cuny.edu
SAULS, Con .... 276-466-7935.... 529 D
consauls@vic.edu
SAULS, Jina, M .... 276-935-4349.... 516 D
jsauls@asl.edu
SAULS, Steve .... 305-348-3505.... 119 C
steve.sauls@fiu.edu
SAULSBERRY, Keith .... 334-556-2470........ 4 A
ksaulsberry@wallace.edu
SAUM, Rob .... 386-506-3484.... 104 F
saumr@daytonastate.edu
SAUNDERS, Amber .... 318-676-7811.... 211 D
asaunders@nwltc.edu
SAUNDERS, Benjie .... 540-831-7109.... 523 A
bookstor@radford.edu
SAUNDERS, Brian .... 310-544-6487...... 64 H
brian.saunders@usw.salvationarmy.org
SAUNDERS, C. Tom .... 912-279-5757.... 127 E
tsaunders@ccga.edu
SAUNDERS, Gary .... 910-576-6222.... 372 D
saundersg@montgomery.edu
SAUNDERS, Gayle, M .... 217-875-7200.... 162 F
gsaunder@richland.edu
SAUNDERS, Jerry .... 617-731-7143.... 243 G
jsaunders@pmc.edu
SAUNDERS, Joseph .... 304-766-3353.... 544 F
saundejs@wvstateu.edu
SAUNDERS, Julie .... 713-646-1815.... 494 I
jsaunders@stcl.edu
SAUNDERS, Kari .... 314-744-5301.... 285 J
saundersk@mobap.edu
SAUNDERS, Kathy .... 716-614-6201.... 344 C
saundersk@niagaracc.suny.edu
SAUNDERS, Keith .... 319-335-0553.... 182 F
keith-saunders@uiowa.edu
SAUNDERS, Kenneth, K ..... 516-572-7664.... 342 C
kenneth.saunders@ncc.edu
SAUNDERS, Kevin .... 831-582-3397...... 35 E
kesaunders@csumb.edu
SAUNDERS, Laura .... 912-871-1600.... 135 D
lsaunders@ogeecheetech.edu
SAUNDERS, Laura .... 425-564-2301.... 531 G
laura.saunders@bellevuecollege.edu
SAUNDERS, Laverna, M .... 412-396-6136.... 428 D
lsaunders@duq.edu
SAUNDERS, Lenore .... 323-953-4000...... 54 H
saundele@lacitycollege.edu
SAUNDERS, Mark .... 405-878-5402.... 412 A
msaunders@stgregorys.edu
SAUNDERS, Mary, M .... 434-395-2063.... 521 A
saundersmm@longwood.edu
SAUNDERS, Mary Jane ..... 561-297-3450.... 119 A
president@fau.edu
SAUNDERS, Melinda, D .... 304-896-7364.... 543 C
melinda.saunders@southernwv.edu
SAUNDERS, Robert .... 334-983-6556........ 8 A
rsaunders@troy.edu
SAUNDERS, Scott .... 310-314-6063...... 30 A

SCHAFFER, James, P .... 610-330-5000.... 433 B
schaffej@lafayette.edu
SCHAFFER, Joe .... 307-778-1102.... 556 E
jschaffer@lccc.wy.edu
SCHAFFER, Kerry .... 812-877-8172.... 179 B
schaffer@rose-hulman.edu
SCHAFFER, Mindy, M .... 410-822-5400.... 222 B
mschaffer@chesapeake.edu
SCHAFFER, Sandy .... 931-393-1536.... 475 D
sschaffer@mscc.edu
SCHAFFHAUSER, Anthony . 218-736-1528.... 267 D
anthony.schaffhauserl@minnesota.edu
SCHAFFNER, Barbara, H .... 614-823-1735.... 400 H
bschaffner@otterbein.edu
SCHAFFNER, Bradley .... 507-222-4267.... 261 G
bschaffner@carleton.edu
SCHAFRICK, James, A .... 203-773-8507...... 90 C
jschafrick@albertus.edu
SCHAKE, Kurt .... 916-376-8888...... 80 C
kschake@wyotech.edu
SCHALK, Lawrence, E .... 269-471-3484.... 247 D
schalk@andrews.edu
SCHALL, Jeffrey .... 603-752-1113.... 304 H
jschall@ccsnh.edu
SCHALL, Lawrence, M .... 404-364-8320.... 135 E
lschall@oglethorpe.edu
SCHALLENKAMP, Kay .... 605-642-6111.... 465 H
kay.schallenkamp@bhsu.edu
SCHALLOCK, Heather .... 715-365-4518.... 555 A
hschallock@nicoletcollege.edu
SCHALO, Pamela, A .... 530-226-4702...... 69 H
pschalo@simpsonu.edu
SCHAMANN, Matthew .... 716-926-8925.... 335 E
mschamann@hilbert.edu
SCHAMP, Rosemary .... 856-374-4941.... 308 D
rschamp@camdencc.edu
SCHANCK, Donald, S .... 401-863-9570.... 453 B
donald_schanck@brown.edu
SCHANDORFF, M. Gene ..... 208-467-8665.... 144 E
meschandorff@nnu.edu
SCHANIEL, William .... 678-839-4780.... 139 A
wschanie@westga.edu
SCHANTZ, Janet, D .... 317-738-8009.... 171 F
jschantz@franklincollege.edu
SCHANTZ, Mark .... 205-226-4650........ 2 B
mschantz@bsc.edu
SCHANTZ, Peter, K .... 740-368-3404.... 400 G
pkschant@owu.edu
SCHANZ, Jeff .... 518-276-6205.... 347 D
schanj@rpi.edu
SCHAPER, Nikki .... 760-757-2121...... 57 E
nschaper@miracosta.edu
SCHAPER, Sue .... 208-459-5837.... 143 D
sschaper@collegeofidaho.edu
SCHAPERKOTTER, Nancy .. 715-422-5526.... 554 E
nancy.schaperkotter@mstc.edu
SCHAPIRA, Ruth .... 215-635-7300.... 430 A
rschapira@gratz.edu
SCHAPIRO, Chaim .... 973-455-9031.... 313 B
chaimschap@aol.com
SCHAPIRO, Mendel .... 323-937-3763...... 80 D
SCHAPIRO, Morton, O .... 847-491-7456.... 160 E
nu-president@northwestern.edu
SCHAPP, Rebecca, M .... 408-554-4528...... 68 C
rschapp@scu.edu
SCHAPPERT, David .... 610-861-1540.... 437 A
dschappert@moravian.edu
SCHARBACH, Bruce .... 480-857-5560...... 15 E
b.scharbach@cgc.edu
SCHARER, Gregory .... 937-775-2620.... 406 C
greg.scharer@wright.edu
SCHARER, Lloyd, S .... 517-321-0242.... 251 G
lscharer@glcc.edu
SCHARFENBERGER,
James .... 315-312-3214.... 354 A
james.scharfenberger@oswego.edu
SCHARLE, Joyce .... 215-646-7300.... 430 C
scharle.j@gmc.edu
SCHARMAN, Janet, S .... 801-422-2387.... 509 H
jan_scharman@byu.edu
SCHARMER, Judy .... 575-624-8076.... 319 C
scharmer@nmmi.edu
SCHARPER, Alice .... 805-965-0581...... 68 B
scharper@sbcc.edu
SCHARTMAN, Laura, A ...... 248-370-2387.... 256 G
schartma@oakland.edu
SCHATTEN, Steve, A .... 610-758-3375.... 434 E
sas308@lehigh.edu
SCHATTMAN, Lisa .... 858-566-1200...... 44 B
lschattman@disd.edu
SCHATZ, Erica .... 252-946-6194.... 368 C
ericas@beaufortccc.edu
SCHATZ, Julianne .... 336-272-7102.... 364 G
julies@greensboro.edu
SCHATZEL, Kim .... 734-487-3200.... 250 F
kschatze@emich.edu
SCHAUB, J. Michael .... 202-687-3493...... 98 D
jms46@georgetown.edu
SCHAUB, Linda .... 517-750-1200.... 258 D
lindas@arbor.edu
SCHAUB, Mark .... 616-331-3898.... 251 F
schaubm@gvsu.edu
SCHAUBACH, Bryan .... 540-857-7273.... 529 B
bschaubach@virginiawestern.edu

SCHAUER, Ariane .... 310-377-5501...... 56 F
aschauer@marymountpv.edu
SCHAUER, Rhonda .... 701-224-2497.... 381 E
rhonda.schauer@ndus.edu
SCHAUMANN, Neils .... 619-239-0391...... 37 F
nschaumann@cwsl.edu
SCHAUS, Deborah .... 256-233-8136........ 1 E
deborah.schaus@athens.edu
SCHAUS, Jim .... 740-593-0982.... 399 G
schaus@ohio.edu
SCHAWEL, Cary .... 847-635-1745.... 160 F
carys@oakton.edu
SCHEARS, Ben .... 620-441-5245.... 192 D
schears@cowley.edu
SCHEBLER, Meg .... 563-242-4023.... 182 C
meg.schebler@ashford.edu
SCHEBLO, David .... 765-459-0561.... 176 C
dscheblo@ivytech.edu
SCHECHTER, Aaron, M ...... 718-377-0777.... 346 G
SCHECHTER, Mendel .... 718-377-0777.... 346 G
SCHECHTER, Steven .... 718-951-5391.... 326 F
sschechter@brooklyn.cuny.edu
SCHECK, Stephen .... 503-838-8226.... 419 C
schecks@wou.edu
SCHEER, Brenda, C .... 801-581-8254.... 511 C
scheer@arch.utah.edu
SCHEERER, Jerry .... 214-860-8735.... 485 B
jscheerer@dcccd.edu
SCHEERER, Teresa .... 215-785-0111.... 440 I
SCHEETT, Rod .... 701-355-8181.... 383 H
scheett@umary.edu
SCHEETZ, Anita, A .... 406-768-6341.... 294 D
ascheetz@fpcc.edu
SCHEFF, Deborah, M .... 314-977-2802.... 289 C
scheff@slu.edu
SCHEFFEL, Kent .... 618-468-5000.... 156 E
kscheffe@lc.edu
SCHEFFKE, Joan .... 435-797-7191.... 511 E
joan.scheffke@usu.edu
SCHEFFLER, Jonathan, C ... 310-243-2139...... 34 D
jscheffler@csudh.edu
SCHEFFLER, Keith .... 281-425-6489.... 489 M
kscheffl@lee.edu
SCHEHR, Terra .... 410-617-2271.... 223 I
tschehr@loyola.edu
SCHEIB, Roger .... 620-417-1240.... 196 F
roger.scheib@sccc.edu
SCHEIBMEIR, Monica, S ... 785-670-1526.... 197 F
monica.scheibmeir@washburn.edu
SCHEID, Cheryl, R .... 901-448-4930.... 477 E
cscheid@uthsc.edu
SCHEIDT, Douglas .... 585-395-2510.... 352 F
dscheidt@brockport.edu
SCHEINBERG, Mark, E ...... 860-727-6757...... 92 I
mscheinberg@goodwin.edu
SCHEINER, Steve .... 660-596-7208.... 290 B
sscheiner@sfccmo.edu
SCHEINMAN, Steven, J ..... 315-464-9720.... 352 E
scheinms@upstate.edu
SCHELCHER, Cindy .... 408-741-2165...... 78 G
cindy.schelcher@wvm.edu
SCHELCHER, Cindy .... 408-741-2165...... 78 G
cindy.schelcher@westvalley.edu
SCHELCHER, Cynthia .... 408-741-2165...... 78 E
cindy_schelcher@wvm.edu
SCHELL, Courtney .... 307-755-2122.... 557 B
cschell@wyotechstaff.edu
SCHELL, John .... 407-823-5711.... 120 B
rick.schell@ucf.edu
SCHELL, Karen .... 518-292-1719.... 348 A
schelk@sage.edu
SCHELL, Michael, J .... 541-885-1452.... 418 E
michael.schell@oit.edu
SCHELLACK, Emil, F .... 913-971-3299.... 195 D
cpolice@mnu.edu
SCHELLENBERGER,
Lauren .... 573-288-6429.... 280 I
lschellenberger@culver.edu
SCHELLHORN, Henry .... 909-621-8080...... 40 F
henry.schellhorn@cgu.edu
SCHEMENT, Jorge, R .... 732-932-7500.... 314 C
comminfo.dean@rutgers.edu
SCHEMMEL, Evelyn, A .... 808-955-1500.... 141 A
evelyn_schemmel@heald.edu
SCHEMPER, Lugene, L .... 616-526-6121.... 249 B
lschempe@calvin.edu
SCHENA, Donna .... 240-567-3085.... 224 D
donna.schena@montgomerycollege.edu
SCHENCK, Ken .... 765-677-2258.... 175 B
ken.schenck@indwes.edu
SCHENCK, Robert, B .... 252-335-0821.... 369 G
rschenck@albemarle.edu
SCHENEWERK, Randal .... 573-875-7256.... 280 A
raschenewerk@ccis.edu
SCHENK, Christy .... 623-572-3325...... 16 E
cschen@midwestern.edu
SCHENK, Daniel, L .... 812-429-1389.... 177 C
dschenk@ivytech.edu
SCHENK, Dina .... 312-467-2114.... 146 F
dschenk@tcsedsystem.edu
SCHENK, Evelyn .... 989-275-5000.... 253 E
evelyn.schenk@kirtland.edu
SCHENK, Glenn .... 310-287-4275...... 55 F
schenkga@wlac.edu

SCHENK, Kim .... 925-685-1230...... 43 F
kschenk@dvc.edu
SCHENK, Margie .... 812-429-1423.... 177 C
mschenk@ivytech.edu
SCHENK, Matthew, R .... 757-446-6043.... 518 G
schenkmr@evms.edu
SCHENK, Rebecca, J .... 716-878-4312.... 353 A
schenkrj@buffalostate.edu
SCHENK, Stacy, L .... 814-886-6357.... 437 B
sschenk@mtaloy.edu
SCHENKEL, Beverly, S .... 660-562-1149.... 287 B
bevs@nwmissouri.edu
SCHENKEL, Donald .... 260-399-7700.... 181 A
dschenkel@sf.edu
SCHENKER, Beth .... 312-922-9012.... 165 E
bschenker@spertus.edu
SCHEPEL, Bill .... 708-239-4805.... 166 C
bill.schepel@trnty.edu
SCHEPENS, Bennett .... 845-675-4543.... 344 G
bennett.schepens@nyack.edu
SCHEPENS, Dona, P .... 845-675-4618.... 344 G
dona.schepens@nyack.edu
SCHEPLER, Richard, A .... 630-617-3456.... 150 H
dscheplr@elmhurst.edu
SCHEPP, Robina, C .... 212-346-1281.... 345 F
rschepp@pace.edu
SCHEPPARD, Carol, A .... 540-828-5608.... 517 B
cscheppa@bridgewater.edu
SCHEPS, Steve .... 215-780-1251.... 446 G
sscheps@salus.edu
SCHER, Anne .... 510-869-6130...... 64 J
ascher@samuelmerritt.edu
SCHERER, Andrew, E .... 973-596-5695.... 312 C
andrew.e.scherer@njit.edu
SCHERER, Jayson, R .... 262-691-5226.... 555 E
jscherer9@wctc.edu
SCHERER, Melanie .... 847-543-2627.... 148 B
mscherer@clcillinois.edu
SCHERER, Nancy, J .... 423-439-7457.... 473 F
scherern@etsu.edu
SCHERER, Robert .... 972-721-5000.... 503 B
SCHERER, Tim .... 989-275-5000.... 253 E
tim.scherer@kirtland.edu
SCHERER, Urte .... 671-734-1812.... 559 F
uscherer@piu.edu
SCHERGER, Celinda .... 419-448-3313.... 402 E
schergercm@tiffin.edu
SCHERLING, Sarah .... 303-524-5198...... 82 C
sscherling@ccu.edu
SCHERMAN, Cathie .... 815-455-8781.... 157 H
cscherman@mchenry.edu
SCHERMERHORN, Donald 251-343-8200........ 6 F
donald.schermerhorn@remingtoncollege.edu
SCHERMERHORN, Robert . 574-239-8335.... 172 M
rschermerhorn@hcc-nd.edu
SCHERR, Albert .... 603-513-5144.... 306 E
albert.scherr@law.unh.edu
SCHERRENS, Maurice, W .. 703-993-8750.... 519 E
mscherre@gmu.edu
SCHERRENS, Maurice, W .. 803-321-5102.... 459 H
mscherrens@newberry.edu
SCHERRENS, Sandra, J ..... 703-993-8760.... 519 E
sscherre@gmu.edu
SCHERSTEN, Mark .... 517-264-7667.... 258 B
mschersten@sienaheights.edu
SCHERTZ, Mary, H .... 574-296-6218.... 169 C
mschertz@ambs.edu
SCHERTZ, Ronald, L .... 401-825-2179.... 453 D
rschertz@ccri.edu
SCHERWITZ, Shelli .... 254-867-3375.... 500 F
shelli.sherwitz@tstc.edu
SCHERWITZ, Shelli .... 325-235-7425.... 500 G
shelli.scherwitz@tstc.edu
SCHERZER, Erin .... 973-642-8242.... 315 C
erin.scherzer@shu.edu
SCHETTLER, Martha, A ...... 330-569-5205.... 391 G
shettlerma@hiram.edu
SCHEUBER, Arthur, F .... 414-288-1463.... 548 F
arthur.scheuber@marquette.edu
SCHEUERMANN, Angela ..... 336-838-6558.... 375 C
angela.scheuermann@wilkescc.edu
SCHEUERMANN, Laurie .... 530-749-3851...... 80 K
lscheuer@yccd.edu
SCHEUERMANN, Michael .. 215-895-0244.... 427 H
mes27@drexel.edu
SCHEUERMANN,
Thomas, A .... 541-737-4771.... 418 F
tom.scheuermann@oregonstate.edu
SCHEULEN, Kathy .... 573-897-5000.... 284 A
SCHEURER, Timothy, E ...... 740-351-3550.... 401 I
tscheurer@shawnee.edu
SCHEWE, Sharon, R .... 651-641-8228.... 263 A
schewe@csp.edu
SCHEXNAYDER, Ken .... 239-590-1083.... 119 B
kschexnayder@fgcu.edu
SCHEXNIDER-FIELDS,
Ingenue, S .... 504-520-6209.... 217 A
itschexn@xula.edu
SCHEXSNAYDER, Harold ... 337-948-0384.... 212 C
SCHEYETTE, Anna, M .... 803-777-7886.... 462 A
anna.scheyette@sc.edu
SCHIAVELLI, Mel, D .... 703-323-4291.... 527 F
mschiavelli@nvcc.edu

SCHIAVO, Antoinette .... 215-637-7700.... 431 A
schiavo@holyfamily.edu
SCHIAVONE, Claudia .... 203-773-8514...... 90 C
cschiavone@albertus.edu
SCHIAVONE, Robert, W ..... 414-425-8300.... 550 E
rschiavone@shst.edu
SCHIAVONI, Robert .... 603-646-9758.... 305 I
r.schiavoni@snuh.edu
SCHIAZZA, Douglas, J ...... 413-597-3696.... 246 D
douglas.schiazza@williams.edu
SCHICK, Beth Ann .... 814-871-7659.... 429 G
shick001@gannon.edu
SCHICK, Marilyn .... 815-455-8591.... 157 H
mschick@mchenry.edu
SCHICK, Marvin .... 732-985-6533.... 313 A
SCHICK, Peggy .... 207-780-4771.... 220 G
mschick@usm.maine.edu
SCHICK, Wendell .... 419-227-3141.... 404 D
wschick@unoh.edu
SCHICKLING, William .... 716-614-5931.... 344 C
bschickling@niagaracc.suny.edu
SCHIDLOW, Daniel .... 215-895-2000.... 427 H
daniel.schidlow@drexelmed.edu
SCHIEBER, Amy, K .... 660-944-2847.... 280 B
aschieber@conception.edu
SCHIEBER, Craig .... 425-637-1010.... 532 E
cschieber@city.edu
SCHIEBER, Gary, W .... 816-604-1320.... 284 H
gary.schieber@mcckc.edu
SCHIEBER, Jeanette .... 660-944-2839.... 280 B
jschieber@conception.edu
SCHIEFELBEIN, Dan, C ...... 515-574-1156.... 185 I
schiefelbein@iowacentral.edu
SCHIEFEN, Kate, M .... 585-262-1616.... 341 H
kschiefen@monroecc.edu
SCHIELE, Ann, E .... 614-234-5032.... 396 H
aschiele@mccn.edu
SCHIELE, Evelyn, R .... 847-543-2622.... 148 B
eschiele@clcillinois.edu
SCHIELE, Jerome, H .... 301-860-3705.... 228 A
jschiele@bowiestate.edu
SCHIERLING, Jessica, L ..... 785-227-3380.... 191 B
schierlingj@bethanylb.edu
SCHIERLMAN, Dixie .... 785-826-2643.... 194 E
dixies@k-state.edu
SCHIFANO, John, C .... 585-720-0660.... 325 B
jcschifano@bryantstratton.edu
SCHIFF, Ed .... 561-297-3080.... 119 A
schiff@fau.edu
SCHIFF, Sidney .... 845-356-1980.... 346 H
SCHIFFER, James .... 845-257-3520.... 352 B
schiffej@newpaltz.edu
SCHIFFER, Peter, E .... 217-333-0034.... 167 D
pschiffe@illinois.edu
SCHIFFGENS, Hope .... 412-536-1266.... 432 H
hope.schiffgens@laroche.edu
SCHIFILLITI, Roy .... 617-879-2419.... 246 C
rschifilliti@wheelock.edu
SCHIFINO, Charlie .... 401-874-2611.... 454 E
schifino@uri.edu
SCHILBERG, Ruth, E .... 972-708-7379.... 487 B
dean-students@gial.edu
SCHILDT, Brenda .... 785-749-8445.... 193 D
bschildt@haskell.edu
SCHILL, Michael, C .... 530-226-4179...... 69 H
mschill@simpsonu.edu
SCHILL, Michael, H .... 773-702-9495.... 166 G
mschill@uchicago.edu
SCHILLER, Elizabeth, N ...... 207-859-4622.... 217 G
enschill@colby.edu
SCHILLER, Teri .... 845-352-3431.... 361 K
shaareitorah@optonline.net
SCHILLIG, Stephen .... 330-339-3391.... 394 A
sschil10@kent.edu
SCHILLING, Denise .... 909-469-5294...... 78 I
dschilling@westernu.edu
SCHILLING, Eileen .... 732-255-0400.... 312 D
eshilling@ocean.edu
SCHILLING, Jennifer .... 503-682-1862.... 419 F
jschilling@pioneerpacific.edu
SCHILLING, Jerry .... 850-201-8590.... 122 A
schillig@tcc.fl.edu
SCHILLING, JoAnna .... 562-860-2451...... 39 A
jschilling@cerritos.edu
SCHILLING, Mary, E .... 757-221-3228.... 518 A
meschi@wm.edu
SCHILLING, Michael .... 530-898-6212...... 34 C
mlschilling@csuchico.edu
SCHILLING, Peter .... 781-595-6768.... 236 C
pschilling@mariancourt.edu
SCHILLING, Susan .... 315-472-6603.... 325 D
smschilling@bryantstratton.edu
SCHILLO, Stephen, A .... 412-396-6063.... 428 D
schillo@duq.edu
SCHILT, Louis, J .... 480-212-1704...... 18 C
SCHILZ, Nancy .... 402-465-2237.... 299 H
nschilz@nebrwesleyan.edu
SCHILZ, Thomas .... 619-388-7500...... 65 H
tschilz@sdccd.edu
SCHIMELFINIG, Marianne . 610-660-3140.... 446 C
mschimel@sju.edu
SCHIMER, Maria, R .... 330-325-6357.... 397 D
maria@neomed.edu

SCHIMETZ, Colette 701-228-5444 382 E colette.schimetz@dakotacollege.edu
SCHIMPF, Martin 208-426-1202 142 I mschimpf@boisestate.edu
SCHINABECK, Karen, M 434-395-2077 521 A schinabeckkm@longwood.edu
SCHINDLER, Christian 443-627-7331 272 C christian.schindler@waldenu.edu
SCHINDLER, Kerry 254-965-8875 492 G kschindler@rangercollege.edu
SCHINDLER, Lindsay 417-328-1806 290 A lschindler@sbuniv.edu
SCHION, Donna 409-984-6101 501 C donna.schion@lamarpa.edu
SCHIPPER, Chris 505-566-3449 320 D schipperc@sanjuancollege.edu
SCHIPPER, OSB, William 320-363-2791 271 A wschipper@csbsju.edu
SCHIPPOREIT, Kim 308-865-8527 300 F schipporeitk@unk.edu
SCHIRER-SUTER, Myron 978-867-4419 235 A myron.schirersuter@gordon.edu
SCHIRMER, Barbara 419-783-2402 389 H
SCHIRMER-SMITH, Sally, J 413-565-1000 230 G salsmith@baypath.edu
SCHISSLER, John 330-490-7263 405 F jschissler@walsh.edu
SCHISSLER, Kathy 303-914-6214 87 G kathy.schissler@rrcc.edu
SCHIZER, David, M 212-854-2675 330 F dschiz@law.columbia.edu
SCHLABACH, June 603-535-2338 307 A jlschlabach@plymouth.edu
SCHLACHTER, Stephany, S 815-836-5639 156 F schlacst@lewisu.edu
SCHLACK, Marilyn, J 269-488-4200 253 A mschlack@kvcc.edu
SCHLAF, John 309-341-7255 155 F jschlaf@knox.edu
SCHLAG, Kevin 808-675-3653 140 D kevin@byuh.edu
SCHLAK, Tim 712-707-7238 188 D tim.schlak@nwciowa.edu
SCHLAPP, Andrew 316-978-3001 198 A andy.schlapp@witchita.edu
SCHLATHER, Mary Margaret 540-338-2700 517 G srschlather@cdu.edu
SCHLECHTE, Dawn 217-234-5210 156 B dschlechte@lakeland.cc.il.us
SCHLECT, Brenda 208-882-1566 144 C bschlect@nsa.edu
SCHLEETER, Kathy 913-588-4874 197 C kschleeter@kumc.edu
SCHLEGEL, Alice 509-542-4823 532 H aschlegel@columbiabasin.edu
SCHLEGEL, Len 518-262-9331 322 D schlegell@mail.amc.edu
SCHLEICH, David, J 503-552-1702 417 D president@ncnm.edu
SCHLEICHER, Julie 781-239-3053 239 G jschleicher@massbay.edu
SCHLEICHER, Susan 210-434-6711 492 B sschleicher@lake.ollusa.edu
SCHLEICHER, Susan, A 210-434-6711 492 B saschleicher@lake.ollusa.edu
SCHLEIFER, H. William 603-897-8630 305 F bschleifer@rivier.edu
SCHLENBECKER, Darlene 847-925-6008 151 G dschlenb@harpercollege.edu
SCHLENDER, Keith 419-517-8920 395 E kschlender@lourdes.edu
SCHLENKER, Steven 215-702-4340 444 B sschlenker@pbu.edu
SCHLEPP, Blair 602-944-3335 11 D bschlepp@aicag.edu
SCHLEPPENBACH, Barbara 217-228-5432 161 F bschlepp@quincy.edu
SCHLESINGER, Kenneth 718-960-8000 327 C kenneth.schlesinger@lehman.cuny.edu
SCHLESINGER, Leonard, A 781-239-4263 230 E lschlesinger@babson.edu
SCHLESINGER, Patrick 510-642-2866 73 H pschlesinger@berkeley.edu
SCHLESSINGER, Shirley 601-815-5235 277 E sschlessinger@umc.edu
SCHLEY, Alisa, S 715-833-6266 553 H ahoepner1@cvtc.edu
SCHLICHT, Terri 913-469-8500 194 B tschlich@jccc.edu
SCHLICHTING, Linda, G 804-257-5727 530 A lgschlichting@vuu.edu
SCHLICKEISER, Gary, G 503-777-7570 420 A gary.schlickeiser@reed.edu
SCHLICKMANN, Paul 860-832-3038 90 G paulschlickmann@ccsu.edu
SCHLICTMAN, Tom 803-822-3034 459 E schlictmant@midlandstech.edu
SCHLIMGEN, Matt 317-931-2382 170 H mschlimgen@cts.edu
SCHLIMMER, Jim 901-321-3275 467 I jschlimm@cbu.edu
SCHLIMPERT, Charles, E 503-280-8509 415 E cschlimpert@cu-portland.edu
SCHLINGMANN, Dirk 864-503-5663 463 B dschlingmann@uscupstate.edu
SCHLISSEL, Mark, S 401-863-2706 453 B mark_schlissel@brown.edu
SCHLOER, Wolfgang 217-333-6104 167 D wfschlor@illinois.edu
SCHLOSSER, David 507-222-4150 261 G dschloss@carleton.edu
SCHLOSSER, Dennis, J 631-423-0483 350 G dschlosser@icseminary.edu
SCHLOSSER-BACON, Angela 616-632-2860 247 E schloang@aquinas.edu
SCHLOSSMAN, Paul 818-240-1000 48 D pschloss@glendale.edu
SCHLOTTER, Pat 303-457-2757 84 J
SCHLOTTERHAUSEN, Lisa 651-779-3934 266 A lisa.schlotterhausen@century.edu
SCHLUETER, Carol, J 504-865-5722 215 C cjs@tulane.edu
SCHLUETER, Lita 978-468-7111 235 B litas@gcts.edu
SCHLUTT, Fred 907-474-7246 10 I efschluttjr@alaska.edu
SCHMAEF, Robert 800-290-4226 469 E rschmaef@hchs.edu
SCHMAILZL, Randy 402-457-2415 298 G rschmailzl@mccneb.edu
SCHMAL, Daniel 414-443-8875 553 D dan.schmal@wlc.edu
SCHMALENBERG, Kate 218-793-2401 268 C kate.schmalenberg@northlandcollege.edu
SCHMALL, Steve 507-285-7214 268 I steve.schmall@roch.edu
SCHMALTZ, John 860-768-7987 95 B schmaltz@hartford.edu
SCHMALTZ, Kim 503-682-1862 419 F kschmaltz@pioneerpacific.edu
SCHMALZ, Glen, J 701-845-7201 382 C glen.schmalz@vcsu.edu
SCHMEIDEL, Stacey 704-894-2798 363 I
SCHMELCZER, Moshe 773-463-7738 165 H mschmelczer@aol.com
SCHMELKIN, Liora, P 516-463-5408 335 G liora.p.schmelkin@hofstra.edu
SCHMELZ, Kimberly, G 608-342-1024 552 B schmelzk@uwplatt.edu
SCHMELZER, Ginger 608-249-6611 547 G ginger@msn.herzing.edu
SCHMEUSSER, Meghan, R 302-356-6809 97 C meghan.r.schmeusser@wilmu.edu
SCHMID, Gary 414-443-8821 553 D gary.schmid@wlc.edu
SCHMID, Karen, L 219-785-5750 179 A kschmid@pnc.edu
SCHMID, Mark 937-512-3020 401 J mark.schmid@sinclair.edu
SCHMID, Mark, A 312-595-1006 166 G mschmid@inv.uchicago.edu
SCHMID, Patti, A 856-691-8600 309 B paschmid@cccnj.edu
SCHMIDLI, Troy 517-265-5161 246 H
SCHMIDT, Adeny 951-785-2210 53 E aschmidt@lasierra.edu
SCHMIDT, Amy 608-785-9139 555 F schmidta@westerntc.edu
SCHMIDT, Ann, C 334-271-1670 6 D aschmidt@princeinstitute.edu
SCHMIDT, Betsy 317-738-8054 171 F bschmidt@franklincollege.edu
SCHMIDT, Brian 503-375-7199 415 F bschmidt@corban.edu
SCHMIDT, Carol 419-995-8218 392 K schmidt.c@rhodesstate.edu
SCHMIDT, Chris 515-244-4221 181 F schmidtc@aib.edu
SCHMIDT, Chris, R 419-995-8342 392 K schmidt.cr@rhodesstate.edu
SCHMIDT, Christina 585-271-3657 348 B admissions@stbernards.edu
SCHMIDT, Christopher 270-384-8136 204 D schmidtc@lindsey.edu
SCHMIDT, Chuck 509-542-4747 532 H cschmidt@columbiabasin.edu
SCHMIDT, Clayton, F 334-387-3877 1 D claytonschmidt@amridgeuniversity.edu
SCHMIDT, Curt 612-659-6902 267 B curt.schmidt@minneapolis.edu
SCHMIDT, Dan 701-224-5735 382 D daniel.j.schmidt@bismarckstate.edu
SCHMIDT, Danielle 515-244-4221 181 F schmidtd@aib.edu
SCHMIDT, David, E 785-628-4487 192 I dschmidt@fhsu.edu
SCHMIDT, David, O 701-777-4151 381 F david.schmidt@research.und.edu
SCHMIDT, Denise 973-328-5245 309 A dschmidt@ccm.edu
SCHMIDT, Eric, R 608-796-3017 553 C erschmidt@viterbo.edu
SCHMIDT, Ernest 515-964-0601 185 A schmidte@faith.edu
SCHMIDT, Gene 989-386-6604 255 C gschmidt@midmich.edu
SCHMIDT, Harry, R 847-259-1840 147 A hschmidt@christianlifecollege.edu
SCHMIDT, James 507-457-5020 269 G jschmidt@winona.edu
SCHMIDT, James, W 312-996-2695 167 B jschmidt@uic.edu
SCHMIDT, Jaqueline, L 620-341-5221 192 G jschmidt@emporia.edu
SCHMIDT, Jaqueline, L 620-341-5223 192 G jschmidt@emporia.edu
SCHMIDT, Jeffrey 410-704-3414 228 E jschmidt@towson.edu
SCHMIDT, John 334-670-3201 8 A jschmidt@troy.edu
SCHMIDT, Jolene 515-271-3957 184 D jolene.schmidt@drake.edu
SCHMIDT, Jona, M 605-256-5857 465 I jona.schmidt@dsu.edu
SCHMIDT, Julie 402-826-8200 297 G julie.schmidt@doane.edu
SCHMIDT, Karen 309-556-3172 153 F kschmidt@iwu.edu
SCHMIDT, Keith, E 712-749-2230 183 C schmidt@bvu.edu
SCHMIDT, Kristopher 563-242-4023 182 C kris.schmidt@ashford.edu
SCHMIDT, Martin, A 617-253-7817 241 D
SCHMIDT, Mellis 505-747-2213 320 A mschmidt@nnmc.edu
SCHMIDT, Michael, E 402-554-2336 301 A mschmidt@unomaha.edu
SCHMIDT, Patricia 631-656-2176 334 B pschmidt@ftc.edu
SCHMIDT, Patty 309-649-6272 165 F patty.schmidt@src.edu
SCHMIDT, Phil 801-274-3280 512 F pschmidt@wgu.edu
SCHMIDT, Rachel 216-687-5594 388 D r.m.schmidt@csuohio.edu
SCHMIDT, Rachelle, M 651-846-1348 269 C rachelle.schmidt@saintpaul.edu
SCHMIDT, Shana 715-833-6410 553 H sschmidt42@cvtc.edu
SCHMIDT, Soren 906-487-7239 251 A soren.schmidt@finlandia.edu
SCHMIDT, Steven, P 208-426-1614 142 I sschmid2@boisestate.edu
SCHMIDT, Susan 712-324-5061 188 C sschmidt@nwicc.edu
SCHMIDT, Tabitha 816-802-3445 283 E tschmidt@kcai.edu
SCHMIDT, Wayne 765-677-2245 175 B wayne.schmidt@indwes.edu
SCHMIDT-NORRIS, Jenae 607-778-5001 324 G norrisjs@sunybroome.edu
SCHMIEDEL, Mary, E 202-687-3911 98 D schmiedm@georgetown.edu
SCHMIEDL, Joe 808-544-1105 140 G jschmiedl@hpu.edu
SCHMIEG, Rose, A 540-665-5534 524 E rschmieg@su.edu
SCHMIESING, David, A 740-284-6513 391 A dschmiesing@franciscan.edu
SCHMILL, Stuart 617-258-5514 241 D
SCHMINKE, Elyse 303-477-7240 85 B elyses@heritage-education.com
SCHMIT, Clayton, J 803-461-3211 459 C clayton.schmit@lr.edu
SCHMIT, Matt 563-441-4125 184 H
SCHMIT, Michele 920-498-7106 555 C michele.schmit@nwtc.edu
SCHMIT, Shelly, M 641-422-4211 188 A schmishe@niacc.edu
SCHMITH, Sue, C 404-876-1227 126 G sue.schmith@bccr.edu
SCHMITT, Barbara 570-662-4854 443 C bschmitt@mansfield.edu
SCHMITT, Deborah, F 716-851-1270 333 B schmitt@ecc.edu
SCHMITT, Karen 815-825-2086 155 D karen.schmitt@kishwaukeecollege.edu
SCHMITT, Karen, R 907-786-6494 10 H apkrs@uaa.alaska.edu
SCHMITT, Linda 908-821-9701 315 D lschmitt@somerset.edu
SCHMITT, Patrick 408-741-2011 78 E
SCHMITT, Sue, A 206-296-5760 538 B sschmitt@seattleu.edu
SCHMITTLEIN, David, C 617-253-2804 241 D
SCHMITTMANN, Beate 515-294-3220 182 E schmittb@iastate.edu
SCHMITZ, Cody 612-343-4410 270 A cschmitz@northcentral.edu
SCHMITZ, Diane 503-399-6031 414 J diane.schmitz@chemeketa.edu
SCHMITZ, Donna 701-252-3467 381 C dschmitz@jc.edu
SCHMITZ, Polly, C 509-527-5168 540 B schmitpc@whitman.edu
SCHMITZ, Stevie 406-657-1134 296 C schmitzs@rocky.edu
SCHMOKE, Kurt, L 202-806-2650 98 E kurt.schmoke@howard.edu
SCHMOLL, Beverly, J 419-530-5451 404 F beverly.schmoll@utoledo.edu
SCHMOLL, Bob 788-227-3380 191 B schmollb@bethanylb.edu
SCHMONSKY, Judy 518-694-7222 322 B judith.schmonsky@acphs.edu
SCHMOOCK, Allen 208-792-2215 144 B atschmoock@lcsc.edu
SCHMOTTER, James, W 203-837-8300 91 A schmotterj@wcsu.edu
SCHMOTZER, Mark 516-299-3547 338 E mark.schmotzer@liu.edu
SCHMOYER, Andrea 312-379-1617 146 F aschmoyer@thechicagoschool.edu
SCHMUCKER, James, I 308-635-6123 301 D schmucke@wncc.edu
SCHMUTTE, Gregory, T 413-205-3364 229 G gregory.schmutte@aic.edu
SCHMUTTE, Jerry 402-461-7455 298 A
SCHMUTZ, Betsy 314-968-6960 292 J schmutz@webster.edu
SCHNABEL, Bobby 812-856-1079 173 E schnabel@indiana.edu
SCHNABL, JC 413-545-5542 236 F schnabl@admin.umass.edu
SCHNACKENBERG, Scott 212-678-3706 357 G sps19@tc.columbia.edu
SCHNAIDMAN, Yaakov 570-346-1747 452 F
SCHNALL, David 212-340-7705 361 M dschnall@yu.edu
SCHNAPP, Derek 217-206-6716 167 C schnapp.derek@uis.edu
SCHNARR, Carmin, A 812-888-4332 181 D cschnarr@vinu.edu
SCHNEBERGER, Scott 618-374-5155 161 E scott.schneberger@principia.edu
SCHNECK, Ken 802-258-9238 513 H kschneck@marlboro.edu
SCHNEIDER, Ali 814-871-7490 429 G schneider@gannon.edu
SCHNEIDER, Alvin 281-425-6489 489 M aschneider@lee.edu
SCHNEIDER, Amye 620-792-9302 190 H schneidera@bartonccc.edu
SCHNEIDER, Audrey 215-204-4607 447 H audrey.schneider@temple.edu
SCHNEIDER, Carrie 651-423-8244 266 B carrie.schneider@dctc.edu
SCHNEIDER, Chad 740-389-4636 395 H schneiderc@mtc.edu
SCHNEIDER, Colleen 316-448-5400 464 H
SCHNEIDER, Debbie 314-531-7925 289 C bksustlouis@bncollege.com
SCHNEIDER, Edward, D 530-226-4156 69 H eschneider@simpsonu.edu
SCHNEIDER, JR., Elmer, E 979-845-8058 497 E eschneider@tamu.edu
SCHNEIDER, Greg 913-288-7155 194 C gschneid@kckcc.edu
SCHNEIDER, Helen 410-617-2995 223 I hschneider@loyola.edu
SCHNEIDER, Howard 631-632-6265 352 C howard.schneider@stonybrook.edu
SCHNEIDER, Jed, S 315-445-4500 338 B schneij@lemoyne.edu
SCHNEIDER, Jeffrey, A 814-332-3355 421 F jschneider@allegheny.edu
SCHNEIDER, Joan 660-562-1250 287 B jschneider@nwmissouri.edu
SCHNEIDER, Joanne 315-228-7362 329 G jschneider@colgate.edu
SCHNEIDER, Judy 704-922-6226 370 G schneider.judy@gaston.edu
SCHNEIDER, Julia 816-271-4369 286 G schneide@missouriwestern.edu
SCHNEIDER, Karen 510-436-1160 50 H schneider@hnu.edu
SCHNEIDER, Kenneth, J 507-266-7095 262 B schneider.kenneth@mayo.edu
SCHNEIDER, Marc 770-426-2700 133 E marcs@life.edu
SCHNEIDER, Mark 641-269-3018 185 D schneidm@grinnell.edu
SCHNEIDER, Matthew 608-249-6611 547 G mschneider@msn.herzing.edu
SCHNEIDER, Michael, P 620-242-0405 195 C schneidm@mcpherson.edu
SCHNEIDER, Pamela 732-987-2234 310 C schneiderp@georgian.edu
SCHNEIDER, Richard, W 802-485-2065 514 C pres@norwich.edu
SCHNEIDER, Scott 563-588-6354 183 E scott.schneider@clarke.edu
SCHNEIDER, Sharyn 510-594-3706 32 C sschneider@cca.edu
SCHNEIDER, Steve 402-872-2393 299 F sschneider@peru.edu
SCHNEIDER, Tammi 909-607-3217 40 F tammi.schneider@cgu.edu
SCHNEIDER, Tina 419-995-8326 399 B schneider.290@osu.edu

SCHNEIDER, Tina 419-995-8326 392 K
tschneider@lima.ohio-state.edu

SCHNEIDER, Todd 970-542-3218 86 G
todd.schneider@morgancc.edu

SCHNEIDER, Tom 727-864-8409 105 E
schneite@eckerd.edu

SCHNEIDER, Wayne, R 785-827-5541 194 F
kwaynes@kwu.edu

SCHNEIDERMAN, Edward, S 718-933-6700 341 G
eschneid@monroecollege.edu

SCHNEIKART-LUEBBE, Christine 316-978-3149 198 A
christine.luebbe@wichita.edu

SCHNEITER, Ellen 207-621-3300 220 B
ellen.schneiter@maine.edu

SCHNEITER, R. Wane 540-464-7212 529 F
schneiterrw@vmi.edu

SCHNELL, Ann, B 585-785-1532 334 A
schnelab@flcc.edu

SCHNELL, Bill 610-353-7630 425 E
wschnell@kaplan.edu

SCHNELL, Carolyn, A 701-231-7189 382 B
carolyn.schnell@ndsu.edu

SCHNELL, Judy 308-635-6106 301 D
jschnell@wncc.edu

SCHNELL, Tamara 217-786-2353 157 B
tammy.schnell@llcc.edu

SCHNELLER, Barbara 610-436-2513 444 A
bschneller@wcupa.edu

SCHNELLER, Beverly 410-837-6205 229 A
bscneller@ubalt.edu

SCHNEPF, Chester, H 203-285-2151 91 D
cschnepf@gwcc.commnet.edu

SCHNICK, Robert, M 814-866-8165 433 C
rschnick@lecom.edu

SCHNITKEY, Dawn, I 517-750-1200 258 D
danderso@arbor.edu

SCHNITZER, Carol, N 518-580-5849 351 B
cschnitz@skidmore.edu

SCHNOOR, Chuck 520-494-5303 13 D
chuck.schnoor@centralaz.edu

SCHNOOR, Neal, H 308-865-8208 300 F
schnoorn@unk.edu

SCHNORBUS, Richard 228-392-2994 277 G
richard.schnorbus@vc.edu

SCHNUPP, Chris 718-357-0500 349 F
cschnupp@edaff.com

SCHNUR, Fred 212-678-8008 337 G
frschnur@jtsa.edu

SCHNURR, Dean, D 419-372-0613 385 F
dschnur@bgsu.edu

SCHOBER, Michael 212-229-5777 342 E
schober@newschool.edu

SCHOCHET, Ezra, B 323-937-3763 80 D
eschochet@yoec.edu

SCHOCK, Pam 559-453-7715 47 K
pschock@fresno.edu

SCHODOWSKI, Francis 717-872-3820 443 D
francis.schodowski@millersville.edu

SCHODZINSKI, E.J 740-699-2503 400 B
schodzin@ohio.edu

SCHODZINSKI, E.J 740-699-2356 400 B
schodzin@ohio.edu

SCHOEFFLER, Susan 775-445-3249 303 B
schoeffs@wnc.edu

SCHOELER, Mary 715-394-8266 552 F
mschoele@uwsuper.edu

SCHOELLES, SSJ, Patricia, A 585-271-3657 348 B
pschoelles@stbernards.edu

SCHOEN, David 716-286-8001 344 D
schoen@niagara.edu

SCHOEN, Linda 614-251-4715 398 F
schoenl@ohiodominican.edu

SCHOEN, Linda, M 503-223-2245 416 F
lschoen@westernculinary.com

SCHOENBACHLER, Denise 815-753-1755 160 B
denises@niu.edu

SCHOENECKE, Marvin 417-690-2204 279 J
schoenecke@cofo.edu

SCHOENECKER, Craig, V 651-201-1864 265 E
craig.schoenecker@so.mnscu.edu

SCHOENECKER, Mark 719-587-7696 80 L
mwschoen@adams.edu

SCHOENEFELD, Dale, A 918-631-2881 413 F
schoend@utulsa.edu

SCHOENER, Lois 607-735-1890 332 I
lschoener@elmira.edu

SCHOENFELD, Diane 617-573-8454 245 B
dschoenf@suffolk.edu

SCHOENFELD, Michael 802-443-3177 514 A
schoenfe@middlebury.edu

SCHOENFELD, Michael, J 919-681-3788 364 C
michael.schoenfeld@duke.edu

SCHOENFELDER, Louis 605-995-2191 464 C
loschoen@dwu.edu

SCHOENGOOD, Matthew, G 212-817-7400 327 B
mschoengood@gc.cuny.edu

SCHOENHERR, Holly 320-308-3203 269 A
hjschoenherr@stcloudstate.edu

SCHOENLE, JR., Gerald, W 716-645-2230 351 G
gws3@buffalo.edu

SCHOENWETTER, Beth 414-256-0169 549 D
schoenwb@mtmary.edu

SCHOENWILL, Chad 719-389-6941 82 D
cschoenwill@coloradocollege.edu

SCHOEPHOERSTER, Richard, T 915-747-6444 506 B
schoephoerster@utep.edu

SCHOETTLE, William 517-371-5140 258 F
schoettw@cooley.edu

SCHOFE, Kathy, D 706-737-1444 125 G
kschofe@aug.edu

SCHOFFMAN, Garth, D 330-684-8938 403 C
gds@uakron.edu

SCHOFIELD, Anna, M 614-222-3274 388 G
aschofield@ccad.edu

SCHOFIELD, Audrey 561-803-2145 114 C
audrey_schofield@pba.edu

SCHOFIELD, Krystal, R 813-253-6239 123 A
kschofield@ut.edu

SCHOFIELD, Sherri 906-248-8424 248 H
sschofield@bmcc.edu

SCHOFIELD, Wil 559-244-5920 72 A
wil.schofield@scccd.edu

SCHOH, Eric 507-457-5210 269 G
eschoh@winona.edu

SCHOKKER, Andrea 218-726-7103 271 F
aschokke@d.umn.edu

SCHOKNECHT, Pat 407-646-2700 116 D
pschoknecht@rollins.edu

SCHOLBE, Karen 314-529-9392 284 C
kscholbe@maryville.edu

SCHOLES, J. Scott 208-732-6250 143 E
sscholes@csi.edu

SCHOLL, Bill 765-285-5131 169 G
wgscholl@bsu.edu

SCHOLL, Heather 847-214-7177 150 F
hscholl@elgin.edu

SCHOLL, Timothy 402-474-5315 298 C
tscholl@kaplanuniversity.edu

SCHOLL-FIEDLER, Anne 410-455-2216 227 D
afielder@umbc.edu

SCHOLL-FIEDLER, Anne, E 443-394-9257 226 E
ascholl-fiedler@stevenson.edu

SCHOLLA, James 320-308-5028 269 B
jscholla@sctcc.edu

SCHOLLE, Peter, A 575-835-5302 319 A
bureau@gis.nmt.edu

SCHOLLES, Holly 503-760-3131 414 F
holly@birthingway.edu

SCHOLLMEIER, John 507-457-1436 271 B
jschollm@smumn.edu

SCHOLTE, Hugh 509-793-2291 531 I

SCHOLTEN, Brian 607-274-3075 336 G
bscholten@ithaca.edu

SCHOLZ, Ben 201-761-7109 314 F
bscholz@spc.edu

SCHOLZ, Daniel, J 414-410-4010 546 G
djscholz@stritch.edu

SCHOLZ, Greg 603-428-2470 305 D
gscholz@nec.edu

SCHOLZ, Joan, M 262-243-5700 547 C
joan.scholz@cuw.edu

SCHOLZE, Roberta 217-351-2383 161 C
rscholze@parkland.edu

SCHONBERGER, Beth 215-635-7300 430 A
bschonberger@gratz.edu

SCHONE, Jeffrey, L 507-354-8221 264 K
schonejl@mlc-wels.edu

SCHONEBOOM, Donna, L 712-749-2103 183 C
schoneboom@bvu.edu

SCHONGALLA-BOWMAN, Nancy, L 609-497-7890 312 F
nancy.schongalla@ptsem.edu

SCHOOF, Aaron, D 773-244-5564 159 H
aschoof@northpark.edu

SCHOOK, Lawrence 217-265-5440 167 A
schook@uillinois.edu

SCHOOLCRAFT, Tracy, A 717-477-1148 443 E
tascho@ship.edu

SCHOOLFIELD, David 417-269-8423 280 G
david.schoolfield@coxcollege.edu

SCHOOLMASTER, Andrew 817-257-7160 499 C
a.schoolmaster@tcu.edu

SCHOOLNIK, Rita, W 860-628-4751 93 C
rschoolnik@lincolncollegene.edu

SCHOON, Kristin, M 651-641-8839 263 A
schoon@csp.edu

SCHOONMAKER, Linda 253-589-5555 532 G
linda.schoonmaker@cptc.edu

SCHOONMAKER, Lori, A 304-367-4841 543 H
lori.schoonmaker@fairmontstate.edu

SCHOONMAKER, Nancy 616-222-1415 250 A
nancy.schoonmaker@cornerstone.edu

SCHOONMAKER, Stephen 501-337-5000 21 D
sschoonmaker@coto.edu

SCHOONOVER, Sandra 406-243-2611 294 I
sandra.schoonover@umontana.edu

SCHOONVELD, Tim 616-395-7698 252 D
schoonveld@hope.edu

SCHOOP, Michael 216-987-4045 389 B
michael.schoop@tri-c.edu

SCHOOR, Alan 212-463-0400 358 B
alan.schoor@touro.edu

SCHOPP, Mary, C 414-847-3215 549 B
maryschopp@miad.edu

SCHOPP, Mary, E 312-942-5959 163 D
me_schopp@rush.edu

SCHORE, Robin 609-586-4800 311 B
schorer@mccc.edu

SCHORIN, Gerald, A 914-395-2218 350 C
gschorin@sarahlawrence.edu

SCHORLE, Thomas 413-565-1000 230 G
tschorle@baypath.edu

SCHORMAN, Rob 513-727-3294 396 F
schormr@muohio.edu

SCHORMAN, Rob 513-727-3211 396 G

SCHORNACK, Julie, A 714-449-7418 70 G
jschornack@scco.edu

SCHORNACK, Kent, A 515-263-2986 185 C
kschornack@grandview.edu

SCHORR, Neil 973-972-0169 316 C
schorrne@umdnj.edu

SCHORR, Timothy, B 608-796-3774 553 C
tbschorr@viterbo.edu

SCHORSKE, Nanda 415-883-2211 42 B
nanda.schorske@marin.edu

SCHOTT, Brett, T 314-367-8700 288 F
brett.schott@stlcop.edu

SCHOTT, Charles 212-998-1398 344 B
charles.schott@nyu.edu

SCHOTT, Doug, W 423-775-2041 467 F
doschott@bryan.edu

SCHOTT, Linda, K 207-768-9525 220 F
linda.schott@umpi.edu

SCHOTT, Marshall 832-842-4664 503 C
mschott@uh.edu

SCHOTT, Marshall 713-743-0749 503 D
mschott@central.uh.edu

SCHOTT, Richard, G 716-851-1610 333 C
schott@ecc.edu

SCHOTTLAENDER, Brian E, C 858-534-3060 74 F
becs@ucsd.edu

SCHOTTLER, David, A 585-292-2814 341 H
dschottler@monroecc.edu

SCHOU, Larry 605-677-5481 465 G
larry.schou@usd.edu

SCHOUWE, Cecilia 657-278-3128 35 B
cschowe@fullerton.edu

SCHOVANEC, Lawrence 806-742-2566 502 A
lawrence.schovanec@ttu.edu

SCHOWE, Dorothy, A 636-584-6507 281 E
schoweda@eastcentral.edu

SCHRADER, Cheryl, B 573-341-4116 291 E
schrader@mst.edu

SCHRADER, Claudia 718-270-5010 328 C
cschrader@mec.cuny.edu

SCHRADER, Claudia 973-720-3093 317 D
schraderc@wpunj.edu

SCHRADER, Ed, L 770-534-6110 126 E
eschrader@brenau.edu

SCHRADER, Kathleen 805-654-6400 77 F
kschrader@vcccd.edu

SCHRADER, Marcus 317-789-8240 171 A
mschrader@crossroads.edu

SCHRADER, Thomas 630-942-3890 148 A
schrader@cod.edu

SCHRAG, Betty 574-535-7501 171 G
bettyls@goshen.edu

SCHRAG, Dale 316-284-5356 191 C
dschrag@bethelks.edu

SCHRAGE, Charles 217-206-7395 167 C
schrage.charles@uis.edu

SCHRAGE, Doug 907-474-7681 10 I
drschrage@alaska.edu

SCHRAGE, Jim 661-362-3222 41 I
jim.schrage@canyons.edu

SCHRAM, Kandis 865-981-8290 471 B
kandis.schram@maryvillecollege.edu

SCHRAMM, Aubrey, A 920-433-6635 546 D
aubrey.schramm@bellincollege.edu

SCHRAMM, Christine, M 937-229-2229 404 A
cschramm1@udayton.edu

SCHRAMM, Peter, W 419-289-5414 384 G
pschramm@ashland.edu

SCHRAMMEL, Debra, S 215-670-9270 438 E
dsschrammel@peirce.edu

SCHRANZ, Michael 719-632-8116 85 H
mschranz@intelliteccollege.edu

SCHRANZ, Michael, V 719-632-8116 85 I
mschranz@intellitec.edu

SCHRANZ, William 402-643-7246 297 D
bill.schranz@cune.edu

SCHRECK, Christopher, J 614-885-5585 401 B
cschreck@pcj.edu

SCHRECK, Jayne, A 309-457-2129 158 H
jayne@monmouthcollege.edu

SCHRECK, Peter 484-384-2973 438 D
pshreck@eastern.edu

SCHREFFLER, Paul 304-367-4920 543 B
paul.schreffler@pierpont.edu

SCHREIBER, Bradley, C 585-395-5161 352 F
bschreib@brockport.edu

SCHREIBER, Carl, W 540-338-1776 522 G

SCHREIBER, David 310-314-6113 30 A

SCHREIBER, Jim 785-628-4279 192 I
jschreib@fhsu.edu

SCHREIBMAN, Andi 925-424-1585 39 D
aschreibman@laspositascollege.edu

SCHREIBMAN, Marla, H 718-951-5065 326 F
marlag@brooklyn.cuny.edu

SCHREIER, Chad 406-657-1746 295 D
chad.schreier@msubillings.edu

SCHREINER, Rebecca 618-537-6514 158 A
rlschreiner@mckendree.edu

SCHREINER, Scott 701-777-2681 381 F
scott.schreiner@und.edu

SCHREINER, Steven 609-771-2529 308 F
schreine@tcnj.edu

SCHREMMER, Johnna, M 620-235-4761 196 C
jschremm@pittstate.edu

SCHRIEFER, John 304-647-6205 544 E
jschriefer@osteo.wvsom.edu

SCHRIER, Hugh 301-387-3098 222 H
hugh.schrier@garrettcollege.edu

SCHRINER, Brian 305-348-3181 119 C
brian.schriner@fiu.edu

SCHROAT, David 313-593-5430 259 B
dschroat@umd.umich.edu

SCHROCK, Jason 562-761-7593 42 G
jasonradnwc@verizon.net

SCHROCK, Lynford 740-857-1311 401 F
lschrock@rosedale.edu

SCHROCK, Missy, K 574-296-6223 169 C
mkschrock@ambs.edu

SCHRODER, Arlie 405-422-1287 411 G
schrodera@redlandscc.edu

SCHRODER, Beth 410-617-2295 223 I
enschroder@loyola.edu

SCHRODER, Michael 760-750-8727 36 C
mschrode@csusm.edu

SCHROEDER, Betzi 973-803-5000 315 D
bschroeder@somerset.edu

SCHROEDER, Brock 740-392-6868 396 I
brock.shroeder@mvnu.edu

SCHROEDER, Creighton 770-938-4711 133 D

SCHROEDER, David, E 973-803-5000 315 D
dschroeder@somerset.edu

SCHROEDER, Debbie 308-865-8950 300 F
schroederd@unk.edu

SCHROEDER, Debra 218-723-6595 262 G
dschroed@css.edu

SCHROEDER, Dennis, J 818-364-7650 55 A
schroedj@lamission.edu

SCHROEDER, Douglas, R 651-631-5160 270 B
drschroeder@nwc.edu

SCHROEDER, Francie 512-863-1454 496 A
schroedf@southwestern.edu

SCHROEDER, Fritz 410-516-6328 223 F
fschroed@jhu.edu

SCHROEDER, Gail, M 440-964-4321 393 E
gschroe1@kent.edu

SCHROEDER, Henning 612-625-2809 272 A
schro601@umn.edu

SCHROEDER, Jennifer 785-243-1435 192 A
jschroeder@cloud.edu

SCHROEDER, John 480-988-8821 15 E
john.schroeder@cgc.edu

SCHROEDER, Lisa 409-880-2137 500 I
lwschroeder@lit.edu

SCHROEDER, Michael 912-358-3202 136 G
schroedm@savannahstate.edu

SCHROEDER, Patricia 414-382-6284 546 B
patricia.schroeder@alverno.edu

SCHROEDER, Philip 719-587-7306 80 L
philip_schroeder@adams.edu

SCHROEDER, Phillip 320-308-5580 269 B
pschroeder@sctcc.edu

SCHROEDER, Ross 979-830-4118 482 C
ross.schroeder@blinn.edu

SCHROEDER, Sally 515-964-6291 183 H
ssschroeder@dmacc.edu

SCHROEDER, Sandra 620-343-4600 192 H
sschroeder@fhtc.edu

SCHROEDER, Stephanie 320-629-5126 268 E
schroeders@pinetech.edu

SCHROEDER, Stephen, C 727-816-3403 114 F
schroes@phcc.edu

SCHROEDER, Steven 414-443-8601 553 D
steve.schroeder@wlc.edu

SCHROEDER, Tracy 617-353-2780 232 E
tas@bu.edu

SCHROEDER-BIEK, Julie 574-284-4333 179 F
jsbiek@saintmarys.edu

SCHROEDERS, Jacqueline 973-972-4624 316 D
schroejm@umdnj.edu

SCHROER, Tara 785-460-5487 192 C
tara.schroer@colbycc.edu

SCHROER, Timothy 507-786-3615 271 C
schroert@stolaf.edu

SCHROTH, Katie 715-346-3930 552 D
kschroth@uwsp.edu

SCHROTT, Jason 602-387-7000 19 A
jason.schrott@phoenix.edu

SCHROYER, Carol 301-696-3411 223 C
schroyerl@hood.edu

SCHRUM, Jake, B 512-863-1454 496 A
schrum@southwestern.edu

SCHRYNEMAKERS, Gladys 718-488-3404 338 G
gladys.schrynemakers@liu.edu

SCHUBERT, Donna 334-670-5830 8 A
schubert@troy.edu

SCHWARZ, May, L ... 614-235-4136 ... 402 G
mschwarz@tlsohio.edu

SCHWARZ, Steven ... 718-997-5903 ... 328 E
steven.schwarz@qc.cuny.edu

SCHWARZ, Thomas ... 386-822-7405 ... 121 F
tschwarz@stetson.edu

SCHWARZ, Thomas, J ... 914-251-6010 ... 354 D
thomas.schwarz@purchase.edu

SCHWARZER, Chris ... 770-394-8300 ... 125 A
cschwarzer@aii.edu

SCHWARZMILLER, Paul ... 412-237-3034 ... 425 H
pschwarzmiller@ccac.edu

SCHWEBEL, Lisa ... 718-951-4114 ... 326 F
lisas@brooklyn.cuny.edu

SCHWEDER, Wendy ... 803-641-3689 ... 462 B
wendys@usca.edu

SCHWEER, Harlan, M ... 630-942-3821 ... 148 A
schweer@cod.edu

SCHWEHN, Mark, R ... 219-464-5310 ... 181 C
mark.schwehn@valpo.edu

SCHWEIGER, Theresa ... 941-756-0690 ... 433 C
tschweiger@lecom.edu

SCHWEIGERT, Rich ... 303-534-6290 ... 83 E
rich.schweigert@colostate.edu

SCHWEITZER, Carrie ... 972-860-4848 ... 484 G
cschweitzer@dcccd.edu

SCHWEITZER, Cathie ... 413-748-3333 ... 244 H
cschweitzer@springfieldcollege.edu

SCHWEITZER, Connie, J ... 989-964-4160 ... 257 G
schw@svsu.edu

SCHWEITZER, Glenna, L ... 734-763-9954 ... 259 A
glenna@umich.edu

SCHWEITZER, Laura ... 518-631-9841 ... 358 H
schweitzerl@uniongraduatecollege.edu

SCHWEITZER, Mike ... 210-999-8409 ... 502 E
mschweit@trinity.edu

SCHWEITZER, Steven, J ... 800-287-8822 ... 169 H
schwest@bethanyseminary.edu

SCHWENK, Terry ... 978-232-2066 ... 234 D
terrys@endicott.edu

SCHWENK, Thomas, L ... 775-784-6001 ... 303 A
tschwenk@medicine.nevada.edu

SCHWENN, John, O ... 706-272-4438 ... 128 C
jschwenn@daltonstate.edu

SCHWERDT, Mark ... 603-880-8308 ... 306 A
tmc@thomasmorecollege.edu

SCHWERTNER, Melanie ... 325-574-6503 ... 508 I
mschwertner@wtc.edu

SCHWIEBERT, Ryan ... 828-339-4600 ... 374 C
ryans@southwesterncc.edu

SCHWIETERMAN, Jerry ... 219-473-4239 ... 170 G
jschwieterman@ccsj.edu

SCHWIETZ, Michele ... 970-351-2161 ... 89 B
michele.schwietz@unco.edu

SCHWINDEL, Justine, R ... 864-833-8637 ... 460 E
jschwinde@presby.edu

SCHWINER, Mary ... 920-923-8937 ... 548 E
mschwiner@marianuniversity.edu

SCHWINGENDORF,
Keith, E ... 219-785-5449 ... 179 A
kschwingendorf@pnc.edu

SCHWINKE, Victoria ... 573-897-5000 ... 284 A

SCIAME, Joseph, A ... 718-990-1941 ... 348 G
sciamej@stjohns.edu

SCIAME-GIESECKE, Sue ... 765-455-9227 ... 174 A
sgieseck@iuk.edu

SCIANNA, Dominic ... 718-990-6185 ... 348 G
sciannad@stjohns.edu

SCIANNAMEO, Louise, C ... 412-578-2090 ... 424 I
sciannameolc@carlow.edu

SCIGLITANO, JR.,
Anthony, C ... 973-275-5847 ... 315 B
anthony.sciglitano@shu.edu

SCIMECA, Joel ... 970-225-4860 ... 82 A
joel.scimeca@collegeamerica.edu

SCIOLA, Michael, A ... 860-685-3377 ... 95 E
msciola@wesleyan.edu

SCIOTTO, Page, C ... 401-598-2145 ... 453 E
psciotto@jwu.edu

SCIPIO, Julius ... 478-825-6330 ... 129 F
scipioj@fvsu.edu

SCIPLE, Judith, A ... 302-739-4068 ... 96 D
sciple@dtcc.edu

SCIPLE, Melinda ... 662-476-5040 ... 274 B
msciple@eastms.edu

SCISM, Bruce ... 615-230-3555 ... 476 C
bruce.scism@volstate.edu

SCISM, Darby ... 773-508-2876 ... 157 C
dscism@luc.edu

SCIUTO, Jim ... 925-631-8043 ... 64 F
jsciuto@stmarys-ca.edu

SCIVALLY, Louis ... 501-882-4434 ... 20 C
lfscivally@asub.edu

SCLAFANI, Joseph, D ... 813-253-6262 ... 123 A
jsclafani@ut.edu

SCLAFANI, Michael ... 718-399-4211 ... 346 D
msclafan@pratt.edu

SCLAFANI, Sandra ... 212-875-4675 ... 323 C
ssclafani@bankstreet.edu

SCOBEE, Georgia ... 225-216-8608 ... 209 H
scobeeg@mybrcc.edu

SCOBEY, David ... 212-229-5613 ... 342 E
scobeyd@newschool.edu

SCOBY, Jerry, L ... 231-591-2164 ... 250 H
scobyj@ferris.edu

SCOFIELD, Elizabeth, A ... 215-951-1040 ... 432 I
scofield@lasalle.edu

SCOFIELD, Jeff ... 808-974-7324 ... 141 F
jscofiel@hawaii.edu

SCOGGINS, Amy ... 229-227-2687 ... 138 A
ascoggins@southwestgatech.edu

SCOGGINS, M, W ... 303-273-3280 ... 83 B
presoffice@mines.edu

SCOGIN, James ... 903-223-3110 ... 498 F
james.scogin@tamut.edu

SCOLERI, Marc ... 212-226-5500 ... 323 A
mscoleri@aii.edu

SCOLFORO, David ... 610-917-3952 ... 450 E
dmscolforo@vfcc.edu

SCOMA, Sam ... 309-796-5650 ... 145 H
scomas@bhc.edu

SCOPA, Pat ... 606-589-3042 ... 203 D
pat.scopa@kctcs.edu

SCOPAS, Constantine ... 212-686-9244 ... 322 G

SCOPELLITI, Theresa ... 570-961-7840 ... 433 A
scopellitit@lackawanna.edu

SCORDINO, Anthony ... 914-606-6521 ... 360 E
anthony.scordino@sunywcc.edu

SCORSE, Bill ... 417-873-7200 ... 281 D
bscorse@drury.edu

SCORZELLO, Joseph ... 617-254-2610 ... 244 B

SCOTKA, Mary, F ... 210-434-6711 ... 492 B
mscotka@lake.ollusa.edu

SCOTT, A. Nicole ... 260-422-5561 ... 173 C
anscott@indianatech.edu

SCOTT, Adrian ... 717-564-4112 ... 432 B
ascott@kaplan.edu

SCOTT, Adrienne ... 610-353-7630 ... 425 E
ascott@kaplan.edu

SCOTT, Alexander ... 718-488-1290 ... 338 G
alexander.scott@liu.edu

SCOTT, Alicia ... 404-756-4054 ... 125 D
ascott@atlm.edu

SCOTT, Angela ... 305-899-3666 ... 101 M
ascott@mail.barry.edu

SCOTT, Anne ... 940-898-2586 ... 502 D
ascott2@twu.edu

SCOTT, Annie ... 860-343-5767 ... 91 G
ascott@mxcc.commnet.edu

SCOTT, Bette, J ... 405-325-1974 ... 413 C
bscott@ou.edu

SCOTT, Bill ... 260-399-7700 ... 181 A
bscott@sf.edu

SCOTT, Billy ... 662-254-3319 ... 276 B
bscott@mvsu.edu

SCOTT, Bob ... 580-349-1597 ... 410 B
bobs@opsu.edu

SCOTT, Candice ... 830-792-7318 ... 494 E
cscott@schreiner.edu

SCOTT, Catherine, R ... 509-533-3567 ... 533 A
cscott@ccs.spokane.edu

SCOTT, Cathy ... 509-533-7082 ... 533 B
cathy.scott@scc.spokane.edu

SCOTT, Charles ... 423-425-4463 ... 477 F
charles-scott@utc.edu

SCOTT, Christopher, D ... 815-772-7218 ... 159 C
cdscott@morrisontech.edu

SCOTT, Clifford ... 617-266-2030 ... 242 H
scottc@neco.edu

SCOTT, Connie, L ... 314-434-2212 ... 282 I

SCOTT, Constance, E ... 260-422-5561 ... 173 C
cescott@indianatech.edu

SCOTT, Danny ... 254-298-8524 ... 496 D
danny.scott@templejc.edu

SCOTT, Dave ... 360-416-7751 ... 538 D
dave.scott@skagit.edu

SCOTT, David ... 410-651-7933 ... 227 E
dlscott@umes.edu

SCOTT, David ... 740-774-7200 ... 400 A
scottd1@ohio.edu

SCOTT, David, L ... 850-474-2587 ... 121 D
dscott@uwf.edu

SCOTT, Dawn, M ... 262-524-7297 ... 546 H
dscott@carrollu.edu

SCOTT, Deborah, C ... 508-831-6075 ... 246 F
dscott@wpi.edu

SCOTT, Deloria ... 270-707-3823 ... 202 E
deloria.scott@kctcs.edu

SCOTT, Donna ... 512-404-4807 ... 481 D
dscott@austinseminary.edu

SCOTT, Dwayne ... 870-733-6770 ... 22 E
djscott@midsouthcc.edu

SCOTT, Eileen ... 856-256-4139 ... 314 A
scotte@rowan.edu

SCOTT, Elijah ... 706-295-6318 ... 130 E
escott@highlands.edu

SCOTT, Fred ... 979-230-3213 ... 482 D
fred.scott@brazosport.edu

SCOTT, Gayanne ... 719-255-3388 ... 88 I
gscott@uccs.edu

SCOTT, Gaye Lynn ... 512-223-3770 ... 481 B
gls@austincc.edu

SCOTT, George ... 386-752-1822 ... 108 G
george.scott@fgc.edu

SCOTT, Heidi ... 618-468-5110 ... 156 E
hscott@lc.edu

SCOTT, Henrietta ... 803-774-3339 ... 455 G
scotth@cctech.edu

SCOTT, Jamal ... 708-342-3300 ... 150 B
jscott@devry.edu

SCOTT, James ... 305-899-3950 ... 101 M
jscott@mail.barry.edu

SCOTT, James ... 602-978-7784 ... 18 H
james.scott@thunderbird.edu

SCOTT, James ... 307-766-6226 ... 556 H
jscott@uwyo.edu

SCOTT, James, C ... 940-565-2791 ... 504 D
james.scott@unt.edu

SCOTT, James, K ... 573-882-6008 ... 291 B
scottj@missouri.edu

SCOTT, Janice, L ... 727-816-3424 ... 114 F
cessnaj@phcc.edu

SCOTT, Jeff ... 765-289-2291 ... 176 B
jscott@ivytech.edu

SCOTT, Jeffrey ... 740-392-6868 ... 396 I
jeffrey.scott@mvnu.edu

SCOTT, Jeffrey, F ... 212-854-6639 ... 330 F
jscott@columbia.edu

SCOTT, Jo Ann ... 662-252-8000 ... 276 G
jscott2@rustcollege.edu

SCOTT, John ... 808-942-1000 ... 141 D
john.scott@remingtoncollege.edu

SCOTT, John, H ... 276-632-5621 ... 522 C

SCOTT, Kai ... 970-225-4860 ... 82 A
kai.scott@collegeamerica.edu

SCOTT, Kathleen ... 805-654-6468 ... 77 F
kscott@vcccd.edu

SCOTT, Kathleen ... 973-300-2295 ... 315 F
kscott@sussex.edu

SCOTT, Kathleen, E ... 937-255-3636 ... 557 C
kathleen.scott@afit.edu

SCOTT, Kathleen, J ... 410-543-6070 ... 228 D
kjscott@salisbury.edu

SCOTT, Kenneth ... 518-458-5359 ... 330 C
scottk@strose.edu

SCOTT, Lana ... 580-477-7719 ... 414 C
lana.scott@wosc.edu

SCOTT, Laura ... 707-864-7000 ... 70 A
laura.scott@solano.edu

SCOTT, Leon, L ... 919-516-4127 ... 376 D
llscott@st-aug.edu

SCOTT, Linda ... 706-776-0116 ... 136 A
lscott@piedmont.edu

SCOTT, Linda ... 804-524-5304 ... 529 H
lscott@vsu.edu

SCOTT, Lisa, M ... 570-372-4415 ... 447 E
scottl@susqu.edu

SCOTT, Lloyd, M ... 828-262-2120 ... 377 D
scottlm@appstate.edu

SCOTT, Louis, B ... 404-413-2400 ... 131 G
lscott01@gsu.edu

SCOTT, Louise ... 563-425-5214 ... 189 G
scottl@uiu.edu

SCOTT, Lynnette, F ... 484-365-8051 ... 434 H
lscott@lincoln.edu

SCOTT, Madeleine ... 740-593-1808 ... 399 G
scottm@ohio.edu

SCOTT, Marcia ... 805-546-3119 ... 43 I
mscott@cuesta.edu

SCOTT, CSA, Marie ... 920-923-7624 ... 548 E
mscott@marianuniversity.edu

SCOTT, Mark ... 412-809-5100 ... 444 G
scott.mark@pti.edu

SCOTT, Mark ... 731-989-6002 ... 469 B
mscott@fhu.edu

SCOTT, Mark, J ... 901-321-4126 ... 467 I
mscott5@cbu.edu

SCOTT, Martha Lou ... 254-710-1761 ... 482 A
martha_lou_scott@baylor.edu

SCOTT, Mary ... 617-984-1768 ... 243 H
mscott@quincycollege.edu

SCOTT, Mary, K ... 949-214-3201 ... 43 C
mary.scott@cui.edu

SCOTT, Megan ... 309-341-7948 ... 155 F
mscott@knox.edu

SCOTT, Melissa ... 800-962-7682 ... 293 A
mscott@wma.edu

SCOTT, Michael ... 540-863-2850 ... 526 F
mscott@dslcc.edu

SCOTT, Michael, H ... 817-257-7858 ... 499 C
m.scott@tcu.edu

SCOTT, Michael, R ... 540-863-2850 ... 526 F
mscott@dslcc.edu

SCOTT, Michelle, T ... 240-567-5276 ... 224 D
michelle.scott@montgomerycollege.edu

SCOTT, Neil ... 334-386-7200 ... 3 G
nscott@faulkner.edu

SCOTT, Patricia, A ... 410-706-7347 ... 227 C
pscott@umaryland.edu

SCOTT, Patty ... 541-888-7401 ... 420 C
pscott@socc.edu

SCOTT, Paula ... 219-877-3100 ... 170 D
pmscott@brownmackie.edu

SCOTT, Phyllis ... 305-899-3900 ... 101 M
pscott@mail.barry.edu

SCOTT, Rejeanor ... 252-823-5166 ... 370 D
scottr@edgecombe.edu

SCOTT, Renay ... 567-661-7005 ... 400 I
renay_scott@owens.edu

SCOTT, Rhonda, J ... 423-236-2932 ... 473 B
rjscott@southern.edu

SCOTT, Richard ... 269-965-3931 ... 253 B
scottr@kellogg.edu

SCOTT, Richard ... 801-957-3263 ... 512 D
richard.scott@slcc.edu

SCOTT, Richard, I ... 501-450-3198 ... 25 H
ricks@uca.edu

SCOTT, Richard, L ... 269-471-3284 ... 247 D
scott@andrews.edu

SCOTT, Richard, M ... 352-365-3525 ... 112 J
scottr@lscc.edu

SCOTT, Robert, A ... 516-877-3838 ... 322 A
ras@adelphi.edu

SCOTT, Robert, F ... 785-628-5866 ... 192 I
rfscott@fhsu.edu

SCOTT, Ronald, B ... 513-529-0143 ... 396 E
scottrb@muohio.edu

SCOTT, Ronald, G ... 803-327-8031 ... 463 H
rscott@yorktech.edu

SCOTT, Ruth, A ... 724-287-8711 ... 423 G
ruth.scott@bc3.edu

SCOTT, Sally ... 703-654-1266 ... 525 D
sscott2@umw.edu

SCOTT, Sean ... 901-272-5139 ... 471 D
sscott@mca.edu

SCOTT, Sharion ... 516-678-5000 ... 341 F
sscott@molloy.edu

SCOTT, Sharon ... 802-635-1208 ... 515 F
sharon.scott@jsc.edu

SCOTT, Sharron, R ... 802-635-1208 ... 515 F
sharron.scott@jsc.edu

SCOTT, Sherrill, B ... 731-426-7522 ... 470 B
sbscott@lanecollege.edu

SCOTT, Shirley ... 256-726-7346 ... 6 C
shirleyps@oakwood.edu

SCOTT, Stephen, C ... 919-866-5141 ... 374 H
scscott@waketech.edu

SCOTT, Steven, A ... 620-235-4100 ... 196 C
sascott@pittstate.edu

SCOTT, Susan ... 740-364-9513 ... 399 E
scott.37@osu.edu

SCOTT, Susan ... 740-366-9513 ... 386 H
scott.37@osu.edu

SCOTT, Tawana ... 864-877-1598 ... 460 A
tawana.scott@ngu.edu

SCOTT, Teresa, M ... 209-575-6530 ... 80 F
scottt@yosemite.edu

SCOTT, Thomas, R ... 864-656-3311 ... 456 E

SCOTT, Tina, M ... 302-356-6940 ... 97 C
tina.m.scott@wilmu.edu

SCOTT, Todd ... 734-462-4400 ... 258 A
tscott@schoolcraft.edu

SCOTT, Vann ... 256-840-4188 ... 7 A
vscott@snead.edu

SCOTT, Wayne ... 731-989-6790 ... 469 B
wscott@fhu.edu

SCOTT, Will ... 727-725-2688 ... 106 F
wscott@cci.edu

SCOTT, Winston ... 321-674-8472 ... 108 H
wscott@fit.edu

SCOTT DIXON, Shartoyea ... 301-937-8448 ... 226 H
sscottdixon@tesst.com

SCOTT-DUEX, Sandra ... 715-425-4444 ... 552 C
sandra.scott-duex@uwrf.edu

SCOTT-ELIOTT, Ardrina ... 340-693-1043 ... 568 E
aelliot@live.uvi.edu

SCOTT-KINNEY, Wanda, A ... 803-705-4680 ... 455 D
scottkinney@benedict.edu

SCOTT-SCURRY, Darlene ... 434-924-3200 ... 525 F
ds7sb@virginia.edu

SCOTT-SMITH,
Christine, K ... 671-735-2332 ... 559 G
csctsmith@uguam.uog.edu

SCOTT SOUFAS, Teresa ... 215-204-7747 ... 447 H

SCOTT SOUFAS, Teresa ... 215-204-7747 ... 447 H
teresa.scott.soufas@temple.edu

SCOTT-TRAMMELL,
Suzanne ... 205-934-4470 ... 8 F
sstrammell@uab.edu

SCOTT-WILLIAMS, Alison ... 212-799-5000 ... 337 H

SCOTTI, Frank ... 714-879-3901 ... 50 I
fscotti@hiu.edu

SCOTTO, TOR, Dominic ... 740-283-6276 ... 391 A
dscotto@franciscan.edu

SCOTTO, Kathleen, W ... 973-972-5333 ... 316 E
scottoka@umdnj.edu

SCOTTO, Kathleen, W ... 973-972-5455 ... 316 C
scottoka@umdnj.edu

SCOUBES, Jim ... 530-283-0202 ... 47 B
jscoubes@frc.edu

SCOUFOS, Lucretia ... 580-745-2278 ... 412 C
lscoufos@se.edu

SCOUTEN, Margaret, A ... 434-381-6109 ... 524 K
jyf@sbc.edu

SCOVELL, Gail, A ... 212-772-4220 ... 327 E
gail.scovell@hunter.cuny.edu

SCOVENS, Tarsha ... 215-751-8164 ... 426 B
tscovens@ccp.edu

SCOZZARI, Ron ... 704-216-0760 ... 373 F
ron.scozzari@rccc.edu

SCRAGG, Raymond ... 216-421-7312 ... 388 A
rscragg@cia.edu

SCRANAGE, Kimberly ... 304-876-5009 ... 544 C
kscranag@shepherd.edu

SCRANTON, Alec ... 319-335-5672 ... 182 F

SEIBLE, Frieder ... 858-534-6237 ... 74 F
fseible@ucsd.edu
SEIBOLD, Kathy ... 208-459-5882 ... 143 D
kseibold@collegeofidaho.edu
SEIBOLD, Kathy ... 716-896-0700 ... 359 H
seiboldke@villa.edu
SEIBRING, Scott ... 309-556-3096 ... 153 F
iwufaid@iwu.edu
SEIBRING, Steve, D ... 309-556-3135 ... 153 F
sseibrin@iwu.edu
SEICHRIST, Pipa ... 305-538-3193 ... 113 G
SEIDEL, Andrew, B ... 214-841-3514 ... 485 F
aseidel@dts.edu
SEIDEL, Angela ... 814-536-5168 ... 424 E
aseidel@crbc.net
SEIDEL, Angela ... 814-536-5168 ... 424 D
aseidel@crbc.net
SEIDEL, Ethan, A ... 410-857-2200 ... 224 C
eseidel@mcdaniel.edu
SEIDELMAN, James, E ... 801-832-2581 ... 512 G
cseidelman@westminstercollege.edu
SEIDEMANN, Jonathan ... 410-484-7200 ... 225 C
SEIDEN, Dena ... 813-879-6000 ... 107 A
dseiden@cci.edu
SEIDEN, Peggy ... 610-328-8489 ... 447 F
pseiden1@swarthmore.edu
SEIDENSTICKER, Duane, P ... 414-847-3274 ... 549 B
duaneseidensticker@miad.edu
SEIDL, Daniel, J ... 920-498-5712 ... 555 C
daniel.seidl@nwtc.edu
SEIDLER, Nick ... 414-277-6922 ... 549 C
seidler@msoe.edu
SEIDMAN, Robin ... 603-577-6381 ... 304 I
rseidman@dwc.edu
SEIDMAN, Stephen, B ... 512-245-2119 ... 501 F
ss76@txstate.edu
SEIF, Gershon ... 874-982-2500 ... 152 A
seif@htc.edu
SEIFERT, Alice ... 914-923-2616 ... 345 F
aseifert@pace.edu
SEIFRIED, Brent ... 970-267-3202 ... 19 A
brent.seifried@phoenix.edu
SEIGART, Denise ... 443-334-2821 ... 226 E
dseigart@stevenson.edu
SEIGEL, Denise ... 516-299-3392 ... 339 A
denise.seigel@liu.edu
SEIGLE, Mark ... 310-243-3771 ... 34 D
mseigle@csudh.edu
SEIJO, Haydee ... 787-764-0000 ... 568 B
hseijo@degi.uprrp.edu
SEILER, Susan ... 414-256-1230 ... 549 D
mktg@mtmary.edu
SEINFELD, Lynn ... 847-635-2186 ... 160 F
lynns@oakton.edu
SEIPEL, Joseph, H ... 804-828-2787 ... 526 B
jseipel@vcu.edu
SEIPP, Dale ... 503-517-1024 ... 421 B
dseipp@warnerpacific.edu
SEISERT, Christina ... 631-273-5112 ... 338 F
christina.seisert@liu.edu
SEITHEL, William, W ... 312-362-7552 ... 149 A
wseithel@depaul.edu
SEITZ, Carl ... 586-498-4066 ... 254 C
seitzc@macomb.edu
SEITZ, Gina ... 801-281-7630 ... 510 M
gina.seitz@stevenshenager.edu
SEITZ, Kathy ... 828-726-2269 ... 368 G
kseitz@cccti.edu
SEITZ, Rebecca ... 573-592-4222 ... 293 D
rebecca.seitz@williamwoods.edu
SEITZ, William ... 409-740-4748 ... 497 F
seitzw@tamug.edu
SEITZER, Joan, M ... 410-827-5808 ... 222 B
jseitzer@chesapeake.edu
SEIVERS, Lana ... 615-898-2874 ... 473 G
lana.seivers@mtsu.edu
SEIVWRIGHT, Hazel ... 718-488-1223 ... 338 G
hazel.seivwright@liu.edu
SEIXAS, Karyn ... 626-395-6161 ... 32 H
karyn@caltech.edu
SEJDINAJ, John, A ... 574-631-4130 ... 180 G
sejdinaj.1@nd.edu
SEK, Mary, S ... 610-861-1567 ... 437 A
memss01@moravian.edu
SEKELSKY, Mary Jo, S ... 810-762-3434 ... 259 C
maryjoss@umflint.edu
SEKUL, Michelle ... 601-928-6267 ... 275 E
michelle.sekul@mgccc.edu
SEKULA, Jennifer ... 763-231-3155 ... 264 C
jsekula@herzing.edu
SEKULICH, Brad ... 704-687-7747 ... 379 A
sekulich@uncc.edu
SELANDER, Ralph ... 843-349-5296 ... 458 H
ralph.selander@hgtc.edu
SELBE, James, E ... 270-707-3705 ... 202 E
james.selbe@kctcs.edu
SELBE, James, H ... 240-684-2303 ... 227 F
jselbe@umuc.edu
SELBERT, Daphne ... 435-652-7711 ... 512 B
selbert@dixie.edu
SELBY, Rosemary ... 478-553-2055 ... 135 B
rselby@oftc.edu
SELBY, Sara ... 912-449-7580 ... 139 D
sselby@waycross.edu
SELBY, Sara, E ... 912-449-7600 ... 139 D
sselby@waycross.edu
SELBY, Sara, E ... 912-449-7580 ... 139 D
sselby@waycross.edu
SELBY, Steve ... 714-992-7081 ... 59 E
sselby@fullcoll.edu
SELBY, Terri, P ... 802-654-2462 ... 514 D
tselby@smcvt.edu
SELDEN, Richard ... 410-234-4525 ... 225 E
SELDERS, Ronald, J ... 304-637-1268 ... 541 A
seldersr@dewv.edu
SELF, George ... 520-515-5385 ... 13 E
selfg@cochise.edu
SELF, Michael ... 615-329-8697 ... 468 I
mself@fisk.edu
SELF, Phyllis ... 309-298-2762 ... 168 C
p-self@wiu.edu
SELF, Sheila ... 918-456-5511 ... 409 A
selfsj@nsuok.edu
SELF-DAVIS, LeAnn ... 731-989-6931 ... 469 B
ldavis@fhu.edu
SELGO, Tim ... 616-331-8800 ... 251 F
selgot@gvsu.edu
SELIG, C. Wood ... 757-683-3369 ... 522 F
wselig@odu.edu
SELIGMAN, Joel ... 585-275-8356 ... 359 B
seligman@rochester.edu
SELIGMAN, Richard, P ... 626-395-6073 ... 32 H
richard.seligman@caltech.edu
SELIGMANN, Wendy ... 828-298-3325 ... 380 D
wseligmann@warren-wilson.edu
SELIGSOHN, Andrew, J ... 856-225-6754 ... 314 D
ajs@camden.rutgers.edu
SELIMO, Tony ... 973-300-2229 ... 315 F
tselimo@sussex.edu
SELKIRK, Sara, E ... 816-654-7214 ... 283 F
sselkirk@kcumb.edu
SELL, JR., Edgar, S ... 410-857-2711 ... 224 C
esell@mcdaniel.edu
SELL, James, H ... 215-781-3939 ... 423 F
sellj@bucks.edu
SELL, Justin ... 605-688-5625 ... 466 C
justin.sell@sdstate.edu
SELL, Randall, L ... 402-554-3408 ... 301 A
rsell@unomaha.edu
SELL, Sean ... 619-298-1829 ... 71 C
SELLARS, John ... 641-784-5111 ... 185 B
jsellars@graceland.edu
SELLARS, John, D ... 816-833-0524 ... 282 C
jsellars@graceland.edu
SELLARS, Mary Ann ... 731-286-3320 ... 475 B
sellars@dscc.edu
SELLARS, Telly ... 502-213-2181 ... 202 F
telly.sellars@kctcs.edu
SELLECK, Mike ... 806-720-7775 ... 490 F
SELLEN, Mary ... 757-594-7130 ... 517 L
mary.sellen@cnu.edu
SELLER, Marc ... 620-241-0723 ... 191 I
marc.seller@centralchristian.edu
SELLERGREN, Ellen ... 773-907-4409 ... 147 D
esellergren@ccc.edu
SELLERS, Calvin ... 662-915-7234 ... 277 D
csellers@olemiss.edu
SELLERS, JR., Cleveland, L ... 803-780-1019 ... 463 C
csellers@voorhees.edu
SELLERS, Cynthia ... 334-727-4746 ... 8 B
sellersc@mytu.tuskegee.edu
SELLERS, James, E ... 216-368-5872 ... 386 F
jes3@case.edu
SELLERS, Jeffrey ... 513-861-6400 ... 402 I
jeff.sellers@myunion.edu
SELLERS, Jennifer ... 802-287-8072 ... 513 F
sellersj@greenmtn.edu
SELLERS, Kevin, M ... 336-841-9148 ... 365 C
ksellers@highpoint.edu
SELLERS, Patrick, J ... 704-894-2078 ... 363 I
pasellers@davidson.edu
SELLERS, Patti ... 602-850-8000 ... 17 G
psellers@phoenixseminary.edu
SELLERS, Randy ... 806-720-7161 ... 490 F
randy.sellers@lcu.edu
SELLERS, Sandra ... 601-979-2015 ... 274 G
sandra.sellers@jsums.edu
SELLERS, Terrie, O ... 912-408-3024 ... 136 H
toliver@savannahtech.edu
SELLERS, Timothy ... 315-279-5685 ... 337 K
tsellers@keuka.edu
SELLERS, William, W ... 800-962-7682 ... 293 A
bsellers@wma.edu
SELLICK, Megan ... 570-208-5900 ... 432 G
megansellick@kings.edu
SELLMANN, James, D ... 671-735-2805 ... 559 G
jsellman@uguam.uog.edu
SELLNAN, Ron ... 507-453-2738 ... 267 C
rsellnan@southeastmn.edu
SELLNER, Hildegard ... 907-796-6226 ... 11 A
hildegard.sellner@uas.alaska.edu
SELLS, Ben ... 765-998-5389 ... 180 B
bnsells@taylor.edu
SELLS, Debra, K ... 615-898-5342 ... 473 G
debra.sells@mtsu.edu
SELLS, Vicki, G ... 931-598-3220 ... 472 L
vsells@sewanee.edu
SELMAN, Brenda, V ... 573-884-9153 ... 291 B
selmanb@missouri.edu
SELMER, Paula ... 518-244-2093 ... 348 A
selmep@sage.edu
SELMO, Barbara, J ... 781-239-6147 ... 230 E
bselmo@babson.edu
SELMON, John ... 231-777-0265 ... 256 A
SELMON, Michael, L ... 989-463-7176 ... 247 B
selmon@alma.edu
SELSOR, Melinda, K ... 636-481-3329 ... 283 D
mselsor@jeffco.edu
SELTZ, Paul ... 651-641-8225 ... 263 A
seltz@csp.edu
SELTZER, Robert ... 561-297-4747 ... 119 A
seltzerr@fau.edu
SELVIN, Molly ... 213-738-6624 ... 71 E
interdisciplinary@swlaw.edu
SELZER, Michael, M ... 605-394-2436 ... 466 B
michael.selzer@sdsmt.edu
SEMAH, Charles ... 732-431-1600 ... 315 G
SEMANIK, Janet ... 217-786-2217 ... 157 B
janet.semanik@llcc.edu
SEMANIK, Joyce ... 949-582-4342 ... 70 F
jsemanik@saddleback.edu
SEMENCHUCK, Amy ... 815-967-7326 ... 162 I
asemenchuck@rockfordcareercollege.edu
SEMENOFF, Michael ... 310-377-5501 ... 56 F
msemenoff@marymountpv.edu
SEMENZA, Michael, L ... 401-341-2465 ... 454 D
semenzam@salve.edu
SEMIEN, Karen, L ... 818-386-1769 ... 62 F
kjackson@pgi.edu
SEMMEL, Abraham ... 718-268-4700 ... 347 A
SEMMEL, Ralph ... 443-778-6278 ... 223 F
ralph.semmel@jhuapl.edu
SEMMEL, Stacey ... 561-297-2748 ... 119 A
ssemmel@fau.edu
SEMMER, Margaret ... 219-981-2351 ... 176 G
msimmer1@ivytech.edu
SEMMES, Laurel ... 386-752-1822 ... 108 G
laurel.semmes@fgc.edu
SEMMES, Paul ... 931-372-3118 ... 474 B
psemmes@tntech.edu
SEMPLE, John ... 708-596-2000 ... 164 H
jsemple@ssc.edu
SEMPLE, Lloyd ... 313-596-0200 ... 258 G
semplell@udmercy.edu
SEMPREBON, Gina ... 413-565-1000 ... 230 G
gsempreb@baypath.edu
SEMRAU, Marv ... 701-858-3000 ... 382 A
marv.semrau@minotstateu.edu
SEMTNER, Anita ... 405-878-5295 ... 412 A
amsemtner@stgregorys.edu
SEMTNER, Pat ... 706-419-1138 ... 128 B
pat.semtner@covenant.edu
SEN, Arup ... 716-829-7658 ... 332 E
SENA, Anthony ... 505-747-2291 ... 320 A
asena@nnmc.edu
SENA, Donato ... 505-454-3369 ... 318 J
dfsena@nmhu.edu
SENCER, Stephen, D ... 404-727-6123 ... 129 D
SENECA, Eric ... 225-768-0804 ... 214 C
eric.seneca@ololcollege.edu
SENEGAL, Pamela ... 919-718-7254 ... 369 C
psenegal@cccc.edu
SENEGAL, Pamela, G ... 919-536-7200 ... 370 C
senegalp@durhamtech.edu
SENEQUE, Guy ... 516-877-3650 ... 322 A
seneque@adelphi.edu
SENESE, Jeffrey ... 401-598-4739 ... 453 E
jsenese@jwu.edu
SENFT, James ... 847-543-2975 ... 148 B
jsenft@clcillinois.edu
SENG, Chris ... 970-491-4860 ... 83 F
christopher.seng@colostate.edu
SENG, Victoria, S ... 731-881-7855 ... 477 G
vseng@utm.edu
SENGENBERGER, Jennifer ... 719-502-3198 ... 87 B
jennifer.sengenberger@ppcc.edu
SENGER, Susan ... 651-846-1490 ... 269 C
susan.senger@saintpaul.edu
SENGUPTA, Shivaji ... 212-694-1000 ... 324 C
ssengupta@boricuacollege.edu
SENICH, Greg ... 303-986-2320 ... 83 A
greg@csha.net
SENIOR, Ann Marie ... 609-984-1151 ... 316 A
amsenior@tesc.edu
SENIOR, CP, Donald, P ... 773-371-5420 ... 146 E
president@ctu.edu
SENIOR, Sandra ... 212-616-7271 ... 335 C
sandra.senior@helenefuld.edu
SENIOR, Timothy, C ... 610-785-6200 ... 446 A
rectorscs@adphila.org
SENKBEIL, Peter ... 949-214-3202 ... 43 C
peter.senkbeil@cui.edu
SENKER, Richard ... 813-253-7017 ... 110 M
rsenker@hccfl.edu
SENKFOR, Sherrie ... 618-650-2190 ... 165 C
ssenkfo@siue.edu
SENKO, John ... 313-927-1519 ... 254 E
jsenko@marygrove.edu
SENN, Gary ... 803-641-3558 ... 462 B
garys@usca.edu
SENNYEY, Pongracz ... 512-448-8470 ... 493 E
pongracz@stedwards.edu
SENSER, Randie ... 212-247-3434 ... 339 G
SENSI, Patricia ... 732-224-2232 ... 308 A
psensi@brookdalecc.edu
SENTE, Marjory ... 928-350-4509 ... 17 K
msente@prescott.edu
SENTELL, Julie ... 325-574-7650 ... 508 I
jsentell@wtc.edu
SENTER, Jerry ... 662-862-8016 ... 274 E
tjsenter@iccms.edu
SENTER, Timothy, C ... 662-862-8460 ... 274 E
tcsenter@iccms.edu
SENTERS, Margaret ... 606-546-1213 ... 207 B
msenters@unionky.edu
SEO, Hoon ... 213-487-0110 ... 45 D
drubook@hotmail.com
SEO, Un Kyo ... 213-487-0110 ... 45 D
info@dula.edu
SEPA, Lisa ... 808-984-3577 ... 142 E
sepa@hawaii.edu
SEPANIC, Michael, J ... 856-225-6026 ... 314 D
msepanic@camden.rutgers.edu
SEPE, Matt ... 781-280-3523 ... 240 B
sepem@middlesex.mass.edu
SEPICH, Kim, W ... 336-249-8186 ... 370 B
kwsepich@davidsoncc.edu
SEPION, Dan ... 605-394-2348 ... 466 B
SEPKO, Cathy ... 864-977-7068 ... 460 A
cathy.sepko@ngu.edu
SEPPELT, Troy ... 970-248-1536 ... 82 F
tseppelt@coloradomesa.edu
SEPPER, Dennis, G ... 253-535-7467 ... 536 E
sepperdg@plu.edu
SEPPY, Donna ... 692-625-3394 ... 560 A
SEPT, Megann ... 415-351-3509 ... 65 I
msept@sfai.edu
SEPULVEDA, Ciro ... 256-726-7223 ... 6 C
csepulveda@oakwood.edu
SEPULVEDA, Marco ... 312-850-7075 ... 147 F
msepulveda@ccc.edu
SEPÚLVEDA, Carmen ... 787-850-9383 ... 567 E
carmen.sepulveda1@upr.edu
SERAFIN, Renata ... 210-486-4689 ... 479 B
rserafin@alamo.edu
SERAICHICK, Laura ... 603-358-2526 ... 306 G
lseraich@keene.edu
SERAPHIN, Micheal, K ... 503-370-6055 ... 421 D
mseraphi@willamette.edu
SERBALIK, James ... 518-783-2314 ... 350 I
serbalik@siena.edu
SERBALIK, Sandy ... 518-783-2596 ... 350 I
sserbalik@siena.edu
SERBAN, Andreea ... 714-438-4698 ... 41 A
aserban@mail.cccd.edu
SERBEIN, John ... 909-748-8011 ... 76 C
john_serbein@redlands.edu
SERCK, Steve ... 336-334-3067 ... 379 B
slserck@uncg.edu
SERDYUK, Yana, V ... 708-209-3053 ... 148 E
yana.serdyuk@cuchicago.edu
SERETTA, Bill ... 413-205-3448 ... 229 G
bill.seretta@aic.edu
SERIANNI, Catherine, E ... 716-286-8571 ... 344 D
cs@niagara.edu
SERIO, Vincent ... 208-426-1459 ... 142 I
vinceserio@boisestate.edu
SERLING, Deborah ... 614-337-8370 ... 398 F
serlingd@ohiodominican.edu
SERMERSHEIM, Katherine, L ... 618-453-7524 ... 165 B
sermersh@siu.edu
SERMONS, Debra ... 913-667-5700 ... 191 H
dsermons@cbts.edu
SERMONS, Penny ... 252-940-6243 ... 368 C
pennys@beaufortccc.edu
SERNA, Denise ... 505-663-3416 ... 321 E
dmserna@unm.edu
SERNA, Frank ... 619-849-2783 ... 62 L
frankserna@pointloma.edu
SERNA, Ricky ... 505-747-2116 ... 320 A
raserna@nnmc.edu
SERNAU, Scott ... 574-520-4429 ... 174 E
ssernau@iusb.edu
SERNELL, J. Jeffrey ... 814-269-7020 ... 449 D
sernell@pitt.edu
SEROTA COTE, Pamela ... 603-526-3750 ... 303 G
pamela.serotacote@colby-sawyer.edu
SEROTKIN, Patricia ... 814-472-3222 ... 446 B
pserotkin@francis.edu
SEROTKIN, Rita, S ... 336-316-2211 ... 365 A
sserotkinrs@guilford.edu
SEROTKIN, Rita, S ... 336-316-2211 ... 365 A
serotkinrs@guilford.edu
SEROVICH, Julianne ... 813-974-7196 ... 121 A
jserovich@usf.edu
SERPLISS, Ron ... 563-244-7021 ... 184 F
rserpliss@eicc.edu
SERR, Jim ... 815-280-6641 ... 154 J
jim.serr@jjc.edu
SERR, Roger, L ... 717-477-1308 ... 443 E
rlserr@ship.edu

SHAILOR, Barbara ... 203-432-8187 ... 96 A barbara.shailor@yale.edu
SHAIN, Sue ... 978-556-3710 ... 240 E sshain@necc.mass.edu
SHAIN, Yeruchim ... 732-431-1600 ... 315 G
SHAINDLIN, Andrew ... 412-268-6286 ... 424 J shaindlin@andrew.cmu.edu
SHAINK, Dick ... 810-762-0453 ... 255 G dick.shaink@mcc.edu
SHAKE, Miranda ... 217-554-6846 ... 156 C mshake@lakeviewcol.edu
SHAKER, Lucy, G ... 773-244-5526 ... 159 H lshaker@northpark.edu
SHAKLEE, Ronald ... 330-941-4740 ... 406 F rshaklee@ysu.edu
SHALALA, Donna, E ... 305-284-5155 ... 122 I dshalala@miami.edu
SHALAMOV, Marina ... 718-261-5800 ... 324 D mshalamov@bramsonort.edu
SHALITA, Mindi ... 609-984-1114 ... 316 A mshalita@tesc.edu
SHALLA, Annie ... 970-521-6702 ... 86 K annie.shalla@njc.edu
SHALLBERG, Mary Ann, H 281-283-2004 ... 503 E shallberg@uhcl.edu
SHALLCROSS, Dorothy ... 303-797-5647 ... 81 D dorothy.shallcross@arapahoe.edu
SHALLENBERGER, Grant, W ... 409-740-4943 ... 497 F shalleng@tamug.edu
SHALLEY, Heather ... 610-989-1200 ... 450 F hshalley@vfmac.edu
SHALLO, Michael, J ... 914-594-4574 ... 343 F michael_shallo@nymc.edu
SHALVA, Sara ... 617-559-8610 ... 235 E sshalva@hebrewcollege.edu
SHAMASH, Yacov ... 631-632-8380 ... 352 C yacov.shamash@stonybrook.edu
SHAMBACH, Teresa ... 330-369-3200 ... 402 H tbcmail@tbc-trumbullbusiness.com
SHAMBAUGH, Jeannine ... 330-363-5420 ... 384 J jshambaugh@aultman.com
SHAMGOCHIAN, Maureen 508-929-8938 ... 238 G mshamgochian@worcester.edu
SHAMIM, Jina ... 415-476-8850 ... 75 A jinashamim@ucsf.edu
SHAMPENY, Renelle ... 518-587-2100 ... 355 G renelle.shampeny@esc.edu
SHAMS, Arian ... 714-300-0300 ... 70 I ashams@scitech.edu
SHAMS, Nazila ... 714-300-0300 ... 70 I nshams@scitech.edu
SHAMS, Parviz ... 714-300-0300 ... 70 I pshams@scitech.edu
SHAMSUDDIN, Hakeemah 773-291-6313 ... 147 G hshamsuddin1@ccc.edu
SHANAFELT, Rebecca, S ... 727-816-3288 ... 114 F shanafr@phcc.edu
SHANAHAN, Judy ... 636-949-4900 ... 283 J jshanahan@lindenwood.edu
SHANAHAN, Megan ... 906-353-4600 ... 253 D megan@kbocc.org
SHANBLATT, Stephanie ... 517-483-1156 ... 254 A shanbls@lcc.edu
SHANCHEZ, Dwight ... 202-274-6430 ... 100 A dshanchez@udc.edu
SHANDLEY, Thomas, C ... 704-894-2225 ... 363 I toshandley@davidson.edu
SHANE, J. Michael ... 716-372-2155 ... 348 C jmshane@eznet.net
SHANEBERGER, Roy ... 314-539-5207 ... 288 G rshaneberger@stlcc.edu
SHANER, Carl, L ... 570-326-3761 ... 440 L cshaner@pct.edu
SHANER, Cecilia ... 808-544-1189 ... 140 G cshaner@hpu.edu
SHANK, Barbara, W ... 651-962-5801 ... 272 B bwshank@stthomas.edu
SHANK, Harold ... 304-865-6003 ... 541 J harold.shank@ovu.edu
SHANK, Larry ... 740-826-6109 ... 397 A lshank@muskingum.edu
SHANK, Leanne, M ... 540-458-8940 ... 530 D lshank@wlu.edu
SHANK, Matthew, D ... 703-284-1598 ... 521 D matthew.shank@marymount.edu
SHANK, Scott ... 434-381-6100 ... 524 K sshank@sbc.edu
SHANK, Theresa ... 240-500-2000 ... 223 A tmshank@hagerstowncc.edu
SHANKAR, Jai ... 831-647-3537 ... 57 F jshankar@miis.edu
SHANKAR, Jille ... 509-793-2031 ... 531 I jilles@bigbend.edu
SHANKEL, James, V ... 724-741-1028 ... 424 I shankeljv@carlow.edu
SHANKLE, Nancy ... 325-674-2402 ... 478 I shanklen@acu.edu
SHANKLIN, Bart ... 309-298-1544 ... 168 C b-shanklin@wiu.edu
SHANKLIN, Carol ... 785-532-7927 ... 194 D shanklin@ksu.edu
SHANKLIN, Iris ... 404-756-4916 ... 125 D ishanklin@atlm.edu
SHANKMAN, Kimberly, C . 913-360-7413 ... 191 A kshankman@benedictine.edu
SHANKS, Alane, K ... 617-731-7101 ... 243 G ashanks@pmc.edu
SHANKS, Carol ... 314-918-2501 ... 281 F cshanks@eden.edu
SHANKS, Martha ... 828-398-7112 ... 368 B mshanks@abtech.edu
SHANKWEILER, Jean ... 310-660-3350 ... 45 E jshankweiler@elcamino.edu
SHANLEY, OP, Brian, J ... 401-865-2153 ... 453 H bshanley@providence.edu
SHANLEY, Deborah, A ... 718-951-5214 ... 326 F dshanley@brooklyn.cuny.edu
SHANLEY, Mark, G ... 540-831-5433 ... 523 A mshanley@radford.edu
SHANLEY, Michael, V ... 978-665-3178 ... 237 E mshanley@fitchburgstate.edu
SHANMUGARATNAM, Carol ... 781-283-2308 ... 245 E cshanmug@wellesley.edu
SHANNON, Beth ... 301-431-5413 ... 225 B bshannon@nlc.edu
SHANNON, Cheryl ... 203-285-2321 ... 91 D cshannon@gwcc.commnet.edu
SHANNON, David ... 405-878-2381 ... 409 D david.shannon@okbu.edu
SHANNON, Henry, D ... 909-652-6100 ... 39 E henry.shannon@chaffey.edu
SHANNON, Jeff ... 479-575-2702 ... 24 C jshannon@uark.edu
SHANNON, Jim ... 901-321-3305 ... 467 I jshannon@cbu.edu
SHANNON, Joe ... 903-693-2028 ... 492 C jshannon@panola.edu
SHANNON, John ... 260-665-4224 ... 180 D shannonj@trine.edu
SHANNON, John, T ... 973-655-4214 ... 311 F shannonj@mail.montclair.edu
SHANNON, Kelly ... 312-915-6159 ... 157 C kshann2@luc.edu
SHANNON, Linda, A ... 718-990-6578 ... 348 G shannonl@stjohns.edu
SHANNON, Mike ... 956-872-3535 ... 494 H mshannon@southtexascollege.edu
SHANNON, Pat ... 208-426-1125 ... 142 I pshannon@boisestate.edu
SHANNON, Scott, S ... 315-470-6537 ... 355 A sshannon@esf.edu
SHANNON, Susan, K ... 717-766-2511 ... 436 D sshannon@messiah.edu
SHANTZ, Dale ... 989-275-5000 ... 253 E dale.shantz@kirkland.edu
SHAO, Alan, T ... 843-953-6651 ... 457 B shaoa@cofc.edu
SHAO, Dawei ... 505-888-8898 ... 320 G drshao@acupuncturecollege.edu
SHAPE, Ronald ... 605-721-5220 ... 464 H rshape@national.edu
SHAPIRO, Adam ... 760-750-4195 ... 36 C ashapiro@csusm.edu
SHAPIRO, Adrian ... 713-973-3123 ... 486 C ashapiro@devry.edu
SHAPIRO, Anne ... 607-255-3581 ... 331 B as57@cornell.edu
SHAPIRO, Claire, R ... 901-843-3750 ... 472 K shapiro@rhodes.edu
SHAPIRO, Deborah ... 213-765-2121 ... 335 B dshapiro@huc.edu
SHAPIRO, E. Gary ... 989-774-3931 ... 249 C shapi1eg@cmich.edu
SHAPIRO, Helen ... 831-459-5852 ... 75 C hshapiro@ucsc.edu
SHAPIRO, Herbert ... 561-297-2146 ... 119 A hshapir3@fau.edu
SHAPIRO, Howard, N ... 313-577-2024 ... 260 A ay1511@wayne.edu
SHAPIRO, Jeff ... 973-877-3142 ... 309 H shapiro@essex.edu
SHAPIRO, Jeffrey ... 513-618-1923 ... 387 F jshapiro@ccms.edu
SHAPIRO, Joe ... 619-594-5822 ... 37 A jshapiro@mail.sdsu.edu
SHAPIRO, Jon, A ... 920-924-3363 ... 554 G jshapiro@morainepark.edu
SHAPIRO, Joseph, I ... 304-691-1700 ... 544 B shapiroj@marshall.edu
SHAPIRO, Larry, J ... 314-362-6827 ... 292 I shapirol@wustl.edu
SHAPIRO, Norman ... 201-447-7107 ... 307 E nshapiro@bergen.edu
SHAPIRO, Philip ... 781-239-5698 ... 230 E pshapiro@babson.edu
SHAPIRO, Sandra ... 216-791-5000 ... 388 C sxs131@case.edu
SHAPIRO, Tracie ... 502-863-8149 ... 201 A tracie_shapiro@georgetowncollege.edu
SHAPIRO, Yonason ... 718-941-8000 ... 341 A
SHAPLEIGH, Shari ... 607-844-8222 ... 357 I shaples@tc3.edu
SHAPLEY, Steven ... 651-675-4700 ... 264 F sshapley@msp.chefs.edu
SHAPOVAL, Sandy ... 918-610-8303 ... 411 D sandy.shapoval@ptstulsa.edu
SHARAR, Bill ... 510-659-6524 ... 59 J bsharar@ohlone.edu
SHARBAUGH, Catherine ... 610-896-1089 ... 430 G csharbau@haverford.edu
SHARBAUGH, Sheila, M ... 302-356-3917 ... 97 C sheila.m.sharbaugh@wilmu.edu
SHARBAUGH, Tim ... 724-357-3145 ... 442 F timshar@iup.edu
SHARDLOW, Mark ... 607-871-2144 ... 322 E shardlow@alfred.edu
SHARER, C. Gregory ... 607-753-4721 ... 353 B greg.sharer@cortland.edu
SHARER, Jack ... 502-895-3411 ... 204 F jsharer@lpts.edu
SHARFMAN, Glenn, R ... 260-982-5051 ... 177 H grsharfman@manchester.edu
SHARIAT, Vahid ... 714-816-0366 ... 73 B vahid.shariat@trident.edu
SHARIF, Yasmin ... 740-245-7215 ... 404 E ysharif@rio.edu
SHARIF, Zaki ... 740-245-7407 ... 404 E zsharif@rio.edu
SHARIK, Terry ... 906-487-2454 ... 255 B
SHARKEY, Jeffrey ... 410-234-4700 ... 225 E
SHARKEY, Jeffrey ... 410-234-4700 ... 223 F jsharkey@jhu.edu
SHARKEY, Melissa ... 641-628-5180 ... 183 D sharkeym@central.edu
SHARKIN, Bruce ... 610-683-4072 ... 443 A sharkin@kutztown.edu
SHARLAND, David ... 703-284-1607 ... 521 D david.sharland@marymount.edu
SHARMA, Anand, D ... 787-265-3809 ... 567 F egraduados.uprm@upr.edu
SHARMA, Madhav, P ... 570-389-4973 ... 441 F msharma@bloomu.edu
SHARMA, Micky, M ... 815-753-1209 ... 160 B msharma@niu.edu
SHARMA, Nimala ... 714-816-0366 ... 73 B nimala.sharma@trident.edu
SHARMA, Ravindra ... 732-571-3450 ... 311 E rsharma@monmouth.edu
SHARMA, Sanjay ... 802-656-3175 ... 514 H sanjay.sharma@uvm.edu
SHARMA, Venkat ... 205-652-3414 ... 9 E vsharma@uwa.edu
SHARMAN, III, W. Robert 609-497-7756 ... 312 F alumni@ptsem.edu
SHARON, Daniel ... 914-632-5400 ... 341 G dsharon@monroecollege.edu
SHARP, Andrew ... 601-477-4025 ... 274 H andrew.sharp@jcjc.edu
SHARP, Bobby, H ... 828-262-4090 ... 377 D sharpbh@appstate.edu
SHARP, Carol ... 856-256-4750 ... 314 A sharp@rowan.edu
SHARP, Connie ... 602-337-3044 ... 12 I cdsharp@brownmackie.edu
SHARP, Corey ... 765-289-2291 ... 176 B csharp@ivytech.edu
SHARP, David ... 870-245-5181 ... 22 I sharpd@obu.edu
SHARP, Debbie ... 940-668-4213 ... 491 E dsharp@nctc.edu
SHARP, Janet, M ... 812-374-5183 ... 176 A jsharp19@ivytech.edu
SHARP, Jennifer ... 630-743-0699 ... 168 E jsharp@westwood.edu
SHARP, Jessica ... 304-929-1425 ... 541 H jsharp@mountainstate.edu
SHARP, Joe ... 561-803-2102 ... 114 C joe_sharp@pba.edu
SHARP, John ... 979-458-6000 ... 496 F chancellor@tamus.edu
SHARP, John, M ... 304-877-6428 ... 540 G john.sharp@abc.edu
SHARP, Jordon ... 435-652-7513 ... 512 B jsharp@dixie.edu
SHARP, Kelvin, W ... 806-894-9611 ... 494 G ksharp@southplainscollege.edu
SHARP, Larry ... 909-537-5004 ... 36 B lsharp@csusb.edu
SHARP, Linda ... 870-680-8717 ... 20 F linda_sharp@asun.edu
SHARP, Linda ... 573-876-7277 ... 290 C lsharp@stephens.edu
SHARP, Louise ... 325-649-8008 ... 488 C lsharp@hputx.edu
SHARP, Melody, F ... 540-224-4694 ... 520 I mfsharp@jchs.edu
SHARP, Monica, A ... 405-325-3337 ... 413 C msharp@ou.edu
SHARP, Nick ... 417-690-2224 ... 279 J sharp@cofo.edu
SHARP, Randy ... 323-343-3440 ... 35 D rsharp@cslanet.calstatela.edu
SHARP, Shayna ... 208-524-3000 ... 143 G shayna.sharp@my.eitc.edu
SHARP, Stacy, M ... 859-846-5347 ... 204 H smsharp@midway.edu
SHARP, Steven ... 435-797-0174 ... 511 E steve.sharp@usu.edu
SHARP, Suzanne ... 573-876-7207 ... 290 C ssharp@stephens.edu
SHARP, Tina ... 256-465-4317 ... 9 C ksvick@una.edu
SHARPE, Allan ... 915-532-3737 ... 508 H asharpe@westerntech.edu
SHARPE, Aubrey, D ... 903-510-2900 ... 503 A asha@tjc.edu
SHARPE, Carol ... 217-641-4521 ... 154 I csharpe@jwcc.edu
SHARPE, Clarence ... 218-723-6044 ... 262 G csharpe@css.edu
SHARPE, Jessica, G ... 336-272-7102 ... 364 G jessica.sharpe@greensboro.edu
SHARPE, Jon ... 916-568-3058 ... 55 J sharpej@losrios.edu
SHARPE, Martha, S ... 757-683-4046 ... 522 F msharpe@odu.edu
SHARPE, Paul ... 219-981-4218 ... 174 B pwsharpe@iun.edu
SHARPE, Shane ... 205-348-5500 ... 8 E ssharpe@ua.edu
SHARPLES, Russell ... 704-463-3401 ... 375 F russ.sharples@fsmail.pfeiffer.edu
SHARPS, Alonia, C ... 301-322-0170 ... 225 F asharps@pgcc.edu
SHARRAR, Jack ... 415-439-2412 ... 28 C jsharrar@act-sf.org
SHARROCK, Christopher ... 215-717-6121 ... 448 I csharrock@uarts.edu
SHATTUCK, Larry ... 410-532-5551 ... 225 D lshattuck@ndm.edu
SHATTUCK, R. Cooper ... 205-348-8345 ... 8 D cshattuck@uasystem.ua.edu
SHATTUCK, Wendy ... 626-396-2403 ... 29 I wendy.shattuck@artcenter.edu
SHAUGHNESSY, Anne ... 617-824-8525 ... 234 B anne_shaughnessy@emerson.edu
SHAUGHNESSY, Joseph ... 781-768-7133 ... 244 A joseph.shaughnessy@regiscollege.edu
SHAUGHNESSY, Joseph ... 254-659-7821 ... 487 G jxs@hillcollege.edu
SHAUGHNESSY, Josette ... 915-831-6330 ... 486 G jshaugh2@epcc.edu
SHAUL, Lesa ... 205-652-3460 ... 9 E lcc@uwa.edu
SHAUNAK, Raj ... 662-243-1911 ... 274 B rshaunak@eastms.edu
SHAUNAK, Sudershan ... 760-757-2121 ... 57 E sshaunak@miracosta.edu
SHAUT, William ... 607-753-2211 ... 353 B william.shaut@cortland.edu
SHAVER, Debra, D ... 413-585-2523 ... 244 G dshaver@smith.edu
SHAVER, Joan, L ... 520-626-6154 ... 18 L jshaver@nursing.arizona.edu
SHAVER, Joseph ... 304-326-1481 ... 541 K jshaver@salemu.edu
SHAVER, Judson, R ... 212-517-0560 ... 340 C jshaver@mmm.edu
SHAVER, Wren ... 513-772-9888 ... 398 G wren.shaver@omw.edu
SHAVERS, Frances, L ... 574-631-9159 ... 180 G shavers.1@nd.edu
SHAVKIN, April ... 770-394-8300 ... 125 A jpetty@aii.edu
SHAW, Anne, C ... 910-938-6322 ... 369 F shawa@coastalcarolina.edu
SHAW, Barbara, L ... 209-946-2424 ... 76 A bshaw@pacific.edu
SHAW, Becky ... 413-585-4940 ... 244 G rshaw@smith.edu
SHAW, Brad ... 618-664-7021 ... 151 F brad.shaw@greenville.edu
SHAW, Brian, R ... 202-231-8698 ... 557 J brian.shaw@dodiis.mil
SHAW, Chip ... 806-743-1500 ... 502 B chip.shaw@ttuhsc.edu
SHAW, Dale ... 985-858-5760 ... 210 G dale.shaw@fletcher.edu
SHAW, Darlene, L ... 843-792-2228 ... 459 D shawd@musc.edu
SHAW, David ... 662-325-3570 ... 275 F dshaw@research.msstate.edu
SHAW, David ... 979-230-3234 ... 482 D david.shaw@brazosport.edu
SHAW, Debora ... 812-855-3261 ... 173 E shawd@indiana.edu
SHAW, Deborah, L ... 334-844-1134 ... 1 F shawdeb@auburn.edu
SHAW, Heidi ... 413-265-2340 ... 233 D shawh@elms.edu
SHAW, Howard ... 256-726-7312 ... 6 C hshaw@oakwood.edu
SHAW, James, A ... 606-783-2599 ... 204 I j.shaw@moreheadstate.edu
SHAW, Jen, D ... 352-392-1261 ... 120 C jends@dso.ufl.edu
SHAW, Jerone ... 662-621-4085 ... 273 F jshaw@coahomacc.edu
SHAW, Karen ... 828-232-5109 ... 378 D kshaw@unca.edu
SHAW, Katie, R ... 407-303-5548 ... 100 G katie.shaw@adu.edu
SHAW, Kevin ... 909-469-5401 ... 78 I kshaw@westernu.edu

SHAW, Linda 480-732-7307 15 E linda.shaw@cgc.edu
SHAW, Lori 620-331-2480 193 I lshaw@indycc.edu
SHAW, Marc 212-794-5404 326 B marc.shaw@mail.cuny.edu
SHAW, Mary, V 815-740-3403 167 E mshaw@stfrancis.edu
SHAW, Nadine 973-877-3275 309 H shaw@essex.edu
SHAW, Nancy 802-241-2520 515 C nancy.shaw@vsc.edu
SHAW, Penelope 707-826-3942 36 E pjs25@humboldt.edu
SHAW, Peta-Gaye 706-821-8251 135 G pshaw@paine.edu
SHAW, Raymond 978-837-3507 242 A raymond.shaw@merrimack.edu
SHAW, Richard 770-426-1776 133 E richard.shaw@life.edu
SHAW, Richard 806-291-1162 508 E shawr@wbu.edu
SHAW, Robert, A 801-832-2474 512 G rshaw@westminstercollege.edu
SHAW, Robert, S 570-348-6245 435 F rsshaw@marywood.edu
SHAW, Ron 304-829-7349 540 H rshaw@bethanywv.edu
SHAW, Russell 601-857-3961 274 C rdshaw@hindscc.edu
SHAW, Teresa 909-602-2505 63 A teresa.shaw@pomona.edu
SHAW, Tom 269-965-3931 253 B tshaw@kellogg.edu
SHAW, Tom, A 312-329-4261 159 A tshaw@moody.edu
SHAW, Wade, H 478-301-2459 134 A shaw_wh@mercer.edu
SHAW-BURNETT, Margaret, A 716-878-5907 353 A shawma@buffalostate.edu
SHAW HORTON, Sheilah 410-617-2842 223 I sshorton@loyola.edu
SHAWANOKASIC, Norman 800-567-2344 547 A nshawanokasic@menominee.edu
SHAWN, Donna, S 913-627-4171 194 C dshawn@kckcc.edu
SHAWNEY, Lisa 603-513-1335 306 F lisa.shawney@granite.edu
SHAWVER, William, G 513-529-9203 396 E shawvewg@muohio.edu
SHAY, Carla, E 231-843-5942 260 B ceshay@westshore.edu
SHAY, Kristine, M 585-245-5571 353 C shay@geneseo.edu
SHAY, Pamela 614-947-6135 391 B shayp@franklin.edu
SHAY, Robert 573-882-2606 291 B shayr@missouri.edu
SHAYNAK, Tracy, E 570-577-1375 423 E tracy.shaynak@bucknell.edu
SHCHEGOL, Alex 718-522-9073 323 B ashchegol@asa.edu
SHEA, Donald, A 904-620-2500 120 D d.shea.138994@unf.edu
SHEA, Donna 617-353-5124 232 E dshea@bu.edu
SHEA, James, P 701-355-8100 383 H president@umary.edu
SHEA, Jane 508-854-4358 240 F jshea@qcc.mass.edu
SHEA, Kevin, J 617-552-3250 232 B k.shea@bc.edu
SHEA, Kim 203-285-2013 91 D kshea@gwcc.commnet.edu
SHEA, Lori, L 906-786-5802 248 I sheal@baycollege.edu
SHEA, Rich, J 814-886-6474 437 B rshea@mtaloy.edu
SHEA, JR., Robert 401-825-1000 453 D rshea@ccri.edu
SHEA, Timothy, P 978-542-6517 238 E tshea@salemstate.edu
SHEA-BYRNES, Pamela, G 718-990-6479 348 G sheabyrp@stjohns.edu
SHEAFFER, Ellen 301-387-3003 222 H ellen.sheaffer@garrettcollege.edu
SHEAFFER, Karen, M 570-321-4311 435 D sheaffer@lycoming.edu
SHEAFFER, Susan 315-733-2300 359 C ssheaffer@uscny.edu
SHEAHAN, John 217-351-2555 161 C jsheahan@parkland.edu
SHEAHAN, Mary 479-394-7622 23 E msheahan@rmcc.edu
SHEAR, Kris 707-524-1579 68 E kshear@santarosa.edu
SHEAR, Skip 660-944-2853 280 B sshear@conception.edu
SHEARD, Reed 805-565-7171 79 A rsheard@westmont.edu
SHEARED, Vanessa 916-278-6639 36 A vsheared@saclink.csus.edu
SHEARER, George 661-833-7120 44 C gshearer@devry.edu
SHEARER, Nancy, B 607-587-3959 355 C shearenb@alfredstate.edu
SHEARER, Richard 320-308-2244 269 A rsshearer@stcloudstate.edu
SHEARIN, Lisa 252-246-1310 375 D lshearin@wilsoncc.edu
SHEARIN, Wally, M 336-506-4279 368 A shearin@alamancecc.edu
SHEARON, Randall 919-735-5151 375 A shearon@waynecc.edu
SHEARRILL, Charmagne 661-255-1050 32 F hrdirector@calarts.edu
SHEASGREEN, William 607-274-3306 336 G wsheasgreen@ithacalondon.co.uk
SHEBAR, Susan 516-299-3835 338 E susan.shebar@liu.edu
SHEBRON, Brandon 314-264-1802 478 B brandon.shebron@vatterott-college.edu
SHECKELLS, Sara 617-730-7072 243 D sara.sheckells@newbury.edu
SHECTERLE, Ross, A 414-425-8300 550 E rshecterle@shst.edu
SHEDD, Jean, E 847-491-8546 160 E j-shedd@northwestern.edu
SHEDD, Sally 757-455-3283 530 C sshedd@vwc.edu
SHEDRICK, Karen, R 601-877-6111 272 F karen@alcorn.edu
SHEDRON, Brandon 314-264-1802 168 A brandon.shedron@vatterott-college.edu
SHEDRON, Brandon 314-264-1802 414 B brandon.shedron@vatterott-college.edu
SHEDRON, Brandon 314-264-1802 414 A brandon.shedron@vatterott-college.edu
SHEDRON, Brandon 314-264-1802 292 H brandon.shedron@vatterott-college.edu
SHEDRON, Brandon 314-264-1902 292 B brandon.shedron@vatterott.edu
SHEDRON, Brandon 314-264-1802 292 G brandon.shedron@vatterott-college.edu
SHEDRON, Brandon 314-264-1802 292 F brandon.shedron@vatterott-college.edu
SHEDRON, Brandon 314-264-1802 301 C brandon.shedron@vatterott-college.edu
SHEDRON, Brandon 314-264-1802 405 D brandon.shedron@vatterott-college.edu
SHEEHAN, Diep 781-768-7078 244 A diep.sheehan@regiscollege.edu
SHEEHAN, Eugene 970-351-2817 89 B eugene.sheehan@unco.edu
SHEEHAN, Heather 701-224-5465 382 D heather.sheehan@bismarckstate.edu
SHEEHAN, James, P 413-545-1581 236 F sheehan@admin.umass.edu
SHEEHAN, Maria, C 775-673-7025 302 H msheehan@tmcc.edu
SHEEHAN, Martha 617-349-8267 236 B msheeha4@lesley.edu
SHEEHAN, Phil 360-992-2118 532 F psheehan@clark.edu
SHEEHAN, Rhonda 518-631-9835 358 H sheehanr@uniongraduatecollege.edu
SHEEHAN, Robert, J 410-546-4127 228 D rjsheehan@salisbury.edu
SHEEHAN, Robert, J 843-349-2089 456 G sheehan@coastal.edu
SHEEHAN, Tim 801-957-5090 512 D tim.sheehan@slcc.edu
SHEEHAN, Timothy 651-213-4166 264 B tsheehan@hazelden.edu
SHEEHAN MASSARO, Maureen 937-327-7517 406 B mmassaro@wittenberg.edu
SHEEHEY, John, D 802-654-2571 514 D jsheehey@smcvt.edu
SHEEHY, Colette 434-924-3349 525 F cc@virginia.edu
SHEEHY, Harry 603-646-2465 304 J harry.sheehy@dartmouth.edu
SHEEHY, Molly, H 978-656-3105 240 B sheehym@middlesex.mass.edu
SHEEKS, Gina 706-507-8730 127 G sheeks_gina@columbusstate.edu
SHEELEY, Brian 859-344-3572 206 I brian.sheeley@thomasmore.edu
SHEELEY, Robert, G 203-392-6050 90 I sheeleyr1@southernct.edu
SHEERAN, Robert, M 513-745-3151 406 E sheeran@xavier.edu
SHEERER, Marilyn 252-328-5419 377 E sheererm@ecu.edu
SHEETS, Christine 740-593-4094 399 G sheetsch@ohio.edu
SHEETS, Heather 312-467-2381 146 F heathersheets@thechicagoschool.edu
SHEETS, Helene 419-824-3965 395 E hsheets@lourdes.edu
SHEETS, Julie 573-518-2206 285 I jsheets@mineralarea.edu
SHEETS, Sarah 304-326-1243 541 K ssheets@salemu.edu
SHEFFER, Ilene 574-520-4344 174 E isheffer@iusb.edu
SHEFFER, Mary 603-513-5175 306 E mary.sheffer@law.unh.edu
SHEFFIELD, Ann, D 814-332-2357 421 F ann.sheffield@allegheny.edu
SHEFFIELD, Betty 251-580-2134 5 A bsheffield@faulknerstate.edu
SHEFFIELD, Cindy 630-753-9091 160 D csheffield@nc.edu
SHEFFIELD, Linda 434-736-2002 528 D linda.sheffield@southside.edu
SHEFFIELD, Ric, S 740-427-5117 394 C sheffier@kenyon.edu
SHEFFLETTE, Nancy, A 501-882-4581 20 C nashefflette@asub.edu
SHEFTIC, Alissa 269-927-6749 253 G asheftic@lakemichigancollege.edu
SHEGAN, Christine 570-662-4900 443 C cshegan@mansfield.edu
SHEHEANE, Dene 404-894-1238 130 F dene.sheheane@dev.gatech.edu
SHEHEE, Amy 859-985-3002 199 A sheheea@berea.edu
SHEIBLEY, Thomas, J 610-660-1030 446 C tsheible@sju.edu
SHEIDLER, Ann 419-473-2700 389 C asheidler@daviscollege.edu
SHEIN, David 845-758-7454 323 D shein@bard.edu
SHEKLETON, James, F 605-773-3455 465 F jims@sdbor.edu
SHELB, Jane 937-775-5515 406 C jane.schelb@wright.edu
SHELBY, Barbara 740-588-1315 407 A bshelby@zanestate.edu
SHELBY, Liz 541-552-7672 419 A shelbyl@sou.edu
SHELBY, Michael 727-784-0003 103 B mshelby@cfi.edu
SHELBY, R. Dennis 312-935-4244 154 A rdshelby@icsw.edu
SHELBY, Valerie, J 601-979-1240 274 G valerie.j.shelby@jsums.edu
SHELDON, Frederick, H 225-578-2887 212 H fsheld@lsu.edu
SHELDON, Jane 308-865-8525 300 F sheldonj@unk.edu
SHELDON, Marianne 510-430-3221 57 D mshel@mills.edu
SHELDON, Michael 207-221-4591 221 A msheldon@une.edu
SHELDON, Todd 402-363-5601 301 E tlsheldon@york.edu
SHELEY, Joseph 209-667-3201 36 D president@csustan.edu
SHELL, Cathy 828-898-8740 366 D shell@lmc.edu
SHELL, Christina 734-487-2382 250 F chris.shell@emich.edu
SHELL, Larry 405-744-5370 410 C larry.shell@okstate.edu
SHELL, Martin 650-723-4186 71 G mshell@stanford.edu
SHELLEDY, David 312-942-7120 163 D david_shelledy@rush.edu
SHELLENBARGER, Lauren 602-243-8084 16 D
SHELLEY, Chris 815-288-5511 164 B shellec@svcc.edu
SHELLEY, Daniel 585-475-6736 347 G drsadm@rit.edu
SHELLEY, Ena, M 317-940-9752 170 F eshelley@butler.edu
SHELLEY, Jeff 205-929-3416 5 E jshelley@lawsonstate.edu
SHELLEY, MargE 913-469-8500 194 B mshelley@jccc.edu
SHELLEY, Michael 773-256-0721 157 D mshelley@lstc.edu
SHELLEY, Stephen 940-397-4110 491 B stephen.shelley@mwsu.edu
SHELLY, Heather 715-682-1254 549 F hshelly@northland.edu
SHELLY, Peggy 215-780-1284 446 G pshelly@salus.edu
SHELLY, Thomas, R 248-218-2011 257 D rshelly@rc.edu
SHELMAN, Gary 210-486-3920 479 C jshelman@alamo.edu
SHELNUT, Lindsey 662-241-7494 276 A lshelnut@sa.muw.edu
SHELOW, Stephen, G 814-865-1864 438 G sps8@psu.edu
SHELPMAN, David 740-286-1554 389 E dshelpman@daymarcollege.edu
SHELTON, Alice 317-955-6022 177 I ashelton@marian.edu
SHELTON, Amy 615-794-4254 472 F ashelton@omorecollege.edu
SHELTON, Beth 903-785-7661 492 D bshelton@parisjc.edu
SHELTON, Charlita 877-442-0505 89 C charlita.shelton@rockies.edu
SHELTON, Donna 276-523-7478 527 D dshelton@me.vccs.edu
SHELTON, Garry, M 540-857-7282 529 B mshelton@virginiawestern.edu
SHELTON, Joyce, A 847-317-7172 166 E
SHELTON, M. Dwight 540-231-8775 529 G mdsjr@vt.edu
SHELTON, Myles 409-944-1200 486 K mshelton@gc.edu
SHELTON, Nancy, B 434-395-2129 521 A sheltonnb@longwood.edu
SHELTON, Rachel 617-682-1507 234 E rshelton@eds.edu
SHELTON, Robby, C 931-363-9890 471 A rshelton@martinmethodist.edu
SHELTON, Scott 252-328-6964 377 E sheltonj@ecu.edu
SHELTON, Sharron 940-552-6291 507 F sshelton@vernoncollege.edu
SHELTON, Tanya, L 304-457-6310 540 E sheltontl@ab.edu
SHELTON, Terri, L 336-256-0426 379 B shelton@uncg.edu
SHELTON, Treva 812-866-7056 172 A shelton@hanover.edu
SHELTON, Vickie 806-371-5017 479 G vlshelton@actx.edu
SHELTON, W. Brian 706-886-6831 138 D bshelton@tfc.edu
SHELTON-CLARK, Anne 662-621-4220 273 F ashelton-clark@coahomacc.edu
SHEMMER, Rosalie 914-323-5484 339 J rosalie.shemmer@mville.edu
SHEMTOV, Kasriel 248-414-6900 254 F rabbi@theshul.net
SHEMWELL, James 870-762-3134 20 A jshemwell@smail.anc.edu
SHEMWELL, Latasha 270-926-4040 200 F lshemwell@daymarcollege.edu
SHEN, Shiji 908-737-3470 311 A sshen@kean.edu
SHEN, Sunny 516-739-1545 343 C academic_dean@nyctcm.edu
SHENETTE, John 413-585-2400 244 G jshenett@smith.edu
SHENK, Sara, W 574-295-3726 169 C swshenk@ambs.edu
SHENNAN, Andrew 781-283-3583 245 E ashennan@wellesley.edu
SHENOSKY, Joseph, T 610-785-6520 446 A jshenosky@scs.edu
SHENOY, Kallya 661-654-2115 34 A kshenoy@csub.edu
SHENOY, Kallya 661-654-3425 34 A kshenoy@csub.edu
SHENTON, Helen 617-495-3650 235 D helen_shenton@harvard.edu
SHEPARD, Bruce 360-650-3480 539 F president@wwu.edu
SHEPARD, II, Charles 419-434-4628 404 B shepard@findlay.edu
SHEPARD, Dave 757-221-2255 518 A dbshep@wm.edu
SHEPARD, James, P 334-844-1007 1 F jshepard@auburn.edu
SHEPARD, Joseph 575-538-6238 321 I shepardj@wnmu.edu
SHEPARD, Kathy, J 717-728-2261 425 B kathyshepard@centralpenn.edu
SHEPARD, Loretta 303-492-6937 88 H lorrie.shepard@colorado.edu
SHEPARD, Nancy 530-938-5331 42 E shepard@siskiyous.edu
SHEPARD, Richard, K 303-477-7240 85 B rshepard@heritage-education.com
SHEPARD, Robert, S 919-684-3363 364 C robert.shepard@duke.edu
SHEPARD, Robin 209-381-6470 57 C shepard.r@mccd.edu
SHEPARD-SMITH, Andrew 931-221-7881 473 E shepardsmitha@apsu.edu
SHEPARDSON, Andrew, J 781-891-2161 231 D ashepardson@bentley.edu
SHEPARDSON, J. Andrew 781-891-2161 231 D ashepardson@bentley.edu
SHEPARDSON, Timothy, M 715-738-3852 553 H tshepardson@cvtc.edu
SHEPELSKY, Ernie 718-429-6600 359 G ernie.shepelsky@vaughn.edu
SHEPHARD, Debra 605-882-5284 464 E shephard@lakeareatech.edu
SHEPHERD, Candace, H 334-271-1670 6 D cshepherd@princeinstitute.edu
SHEPHERD, Chad 314-367-8700 288 F chad.shepherd@stlcop.edu
SHEPHERD, Danielle 610-328-8009 447 F dshephe1@swarthmore.edu
SHEPHERD, Gay 931-372-3234 474 B gshepherd@tntech.edu
SHEPHERD, Gregory, J 305-284-3420 122 I shepherd@miami.edu
SHEPHERD, Janet 563-425-5788 189 G shepherdj@uiu.edu
SHEPHERD, Joseph, E 626-395-5802 32 H joseph.e.shepherd@caltech.edu
SHEPHERD, Judy 434-949-1049 528 D judy.shepherd@southside.edu
SHEPHERD, Karla, M 410-837-4760 229 A kshepherd@ubalt.edu

SHEPHERD, Lewis ... 870-230-5089 ... 21 I
shephel@hsu.edu

SHEPHERD, Margaret, A ... 206-543-7604 ... 539 A
mshep@uw.edu

SHEPHERD, Nancy ... 505-566-3264 ... 320 D
shepherdn@sanjuancollege.edu

SHEPHERD, Paul ... 715-425-4444 ... 552 C
paul.shepherd@uwrf.edu

SHEPHERD, Susan, B ... 330-363-4349 ... 384 J
sshepherd@aultman.com

SHEPHERD, Tamara, A ... 703-461-1723 ... 522 I
tshepherd@vts.edu

SHEPHERD, Teanca ... 724-503-1001 ... 451 A
tshepherd@washjeff.edu

SHEPHERD-GREGG, Debbie ... 740-392-6868 ... 396 I
dshepher@mvnu.edu

SHEPPARD, Beth ... 847-866-3877 ... 164 D
beth.sheppard@seabury.edu

SHEPPARD, Charles ... 714-459-1152 ... 78 H
csheppard@wsulaw.edu

SHEPPARD, Elizabeth ... 478-387-4882 ... 131 A

SHEPPARD, Ellen ... 704-355-5316 ... 363 D
ellen.sheppard@carolinascollege.edu

SHEPPARD, Eric, J ... 757-727-6970 ... 519 H
eric.sheppard@hamptonu.edu

SHEPPARD, James, A ... 620-229-6227 ... 196 G
james.sheppard@sckans.edu

SHEPPARD, Lyle ... 910-630-7225 ... 367 B
lsheppard@methodist.edu

SHEPPARD, Matt ... 218-299-6519 ... 267 D
matt.sheppard@minnesota.edu

SHEPPARD, Nancy ... 412-809-5100 ... 444 G
sheppard.nancy@pti.edu

SHEPPARD, Phillip ... 508-588-9100 ... 240 A

SHEPPARD, Rebecca ... 856-691-8600 ... 309 B
bsheppard@cccnj.edu

SHEPPARD, Tina, F ... 573-341-4218 ... 291 E
tinas@mst.edu

SHEPPARD, Vicki ... 336-917-5090 ... 376 E
vicki.sheppard@salem.edu

SHEPPERD, Rhonda ... 304-929-1404 ... 541 H
shepperd@mountainstate.edu

SHEPPERSON, Dale ... 317-632-5553 ... 177 G
dshepperson@lincolntech.com

SHEPROW, Lauren ... 631-632-4896 ... 352 C
lauren.sheprow@stonybrook.edu

SHEPTAK, Dale ... 440-375-7131 ... 394 E
dsheptak@lec.edu

SHER, Daniel, P ... 303-492-7505 ... 88 H
daniel.sher@colorado.edu

SHER, Ephraim, Y ... 845-434-5240 ... 362 B
esher@fallsburgyeshiva.com

SHERADIN, Pamela ... 315-364-3221 ... 360 D
psheridan@wells.edu

SHEREMAN, Sandra ... 562-985-5537 ... 35 C
ssherem@csulb.edu

SHEREN, Deborah ... 216-373-5347 ... 397 F
dsheren@ndc.edu

SHERER, Michael ... 574-535-7406 ... 171 G
msherer@goshen.edu

SHERER, Tyler ... 619-594-2522 ... 37 A
tsherer@mail.sdsu.edu

SHERIDAN, Catherine ... 614-222-3205 ... 388 G
csheridan@ccad.edu

SHERIDAN, Chris ... 216-368-2774 ... 386 F
chris.sheridan@case.edu

SHERIDAN, Debra ... 305-348-6457 ... 119 C
debra.sheridan@fiu.edu

SHERIDAN, Eileen ... 617-730-7010 ... 243 D
eileen.sheridan@newbury.edu

SHERIDAN, John ... 620-341-5208 ... 192 G
jsherida@emporia.edu

SHERIDAN, Kathleen ... 312-261-3149 ... 159 E
kathleen.sheridan@nl.edu

SHERIDAN, Maureen, E ... 570-208-5865 ... 432 G
mesherid@kings.edu

SHERIDAN, Neil, G ... 810-762-9728 ... 253 C
nsherida@kettering.edu

SHERIDAN, Nora ... 978-556-3616 ... 240 E
nsheridan@necc.mass.edu

SHERIDAN, Pamela ... 610-436-3383 ... 444 A
psheridan@wcupa.edu

SHERIDON, Paul ... 541-485-1780 ... 417 E
paulsheridon@newhope.edu

SHERIFF, Robyn ... 435-613-5233 ... 512 A
robyn.sheriff@usu.edu

SHERIFF-TAYLOR, Patricia 601-979-2127 ... 274 G
patricia.sherriff-taylor@jsums.edu

SHERLIN, Joe, H ... 423-439-4210 ... 473 F
sherlin@etsu.edu

SHERLOCK, Jean ... 818-733-2600 ... 59 A

SHERLOCK, Julia, B ... 989-774-3068 ... 249 C
julia.b.sherlock@cmich.edu

SHERMAN, Ann ... 617-243-2162 ... 236 A
asherman@lasell.edu

SHERMAN, Ann, M ... 906-227-2330 ... 256 C
asherman@nmu.edu

SHERMAN, Catherine ... 724-503-1001 ... 451 A
csherman@washjeff.edu

SHERMAN, Curt ... 402-643-7369 ... 297 D
curt.sherman@cune.edu

SHERMAN, Debra ... 985-732-6640 ... 211 A

SHERMAN, JR., Douglas .. 401-739-5000 ... 453 G
dsherman@neit.edu

SHERMAN, Gary ... 860-231-5360 ... 95 D
gsherman@usj.edu

SHERMAN, George ... 718-631-6273 ... 328 F
gsherman@qcc.cuny.edu

SHERMAN, George, M ... 978-232-2009 ... 234 D
gsherman@endicott.edu

SHERMAN, Glen ... 973-720-2761 ... 317 D
shermang@wpunj.edu

SHERMAN, Hugh ... 740-593-2000 ... 399 G
shermanh@ohio.edu

SHERMAN, III, James ... 605-856-5880 ... 465 C
james.sherman@sintegleska.edu

SHERMAN, Jennifer ... 719-549-3322 ... 87 F
jennifer.sherman@pueblocc.edu

SHERMAN, Jill ... 502-456-6509 ... 206 G
jsherman@sctd.edu

SHERMAN, Julee ... 660-248-6203 ... 279 G
jsherman@centralmethodist.edu

SHERMAN, Kristen ... 617-670-4419 ... 234 G
ksherman01@fisher.edu

SHERMAN, Malcolm ... 781-736-2000 ... 232 F
msherman@brandeis.edu

SHERMAN, Michael ... 708-763-6505 ... 162 E
michael.sherman@resu.edu

SHERMAN, Mike ... 330-972-7593 ... 403 B
provost@uakron.edu

SHERMAN, Robert, A ... 631-656-2117 ... 334 B
rsherman@ftc.edu

SHERMAN, Roger, H ... 631-656-2189 ... 334 B
rhsherman@ftc.edu

SHERMAN, Ruby ... 240-567-1720 ... 224 D
ruby.sherman@montgomerycollege.edu

SHERMAN, Ruth, D ... 617-333-2364 ... 233 F
rsherman@curry.edu

SHERMAN, Sharon ... 609-896-5120 ... 313 F
sherman@rider.edu

SHERMAN, Todd ... 907-474-7231 ... 10 I
tlsherman@alaska.edu

SHERMIS, Mark, D ... 330-972-7680 ... 403 B
shermis@uakron.edu

SHERRARD, Catherine, E ... 812-246-3301 ... 177 B
csherrard@ivytech.edu

SHERRELL, J. Michael ... 865-974-2178 ... 477 D
jsherrel@utk.edu

SHERRELL, Jeff ... 205-226-4939 ... 2 B
jsherrel@bsc.edu

SHERRICK, Rebecca, L ... 630-844-5476 ... 145 F
sherrick@aurora.edu

SHERRILL, Audrey ... 704-922-6223 ... 370 G
sherrill.audrey@gaston.edu

SHERRILL, Christy ... 501-812-2214 ... 23 C
csherrill@pulaskitech.edu

SHERRILL, Jan-Mitchell ... 412-392-8026 ... 445 A
jsherrill@pointpark.edu

SHERRILL, Linda, G ... 517-750-1200 ... 258 D
lsherrill@arbor.edu

SHERROD, Vicki ... 478-289-2105 ... 129 B
vsherrod@ega.edu

SHERRON, Catherine ... 859-344-3387 ... 206 I
catherine.sherron@thomasmore.edu

SHERROUSE, Laura ... 706-721-2301 ... 130 D
lsherrouse@georgiahealth.edu

SHERRY, J.P ... 916-568-3042 ... 55 J
sherryj@losrios.edu

SHERRY, Michael ... 716-652-8900 ... 325 J
msherry@cks.edu

SHERRY, Richard, J ... 651-638-6287 ... 261 D
r-sherry@bethel.edu

SHERSTAD, Brian, P ... 616-538-2330 ... 251 D
bsherstad@gbcol.edu

SHERWEN, Laurie ... 215-596-8501 ... 450 B
l.sherwen@usciences.edu

SHERWIN, Paul ... 415-338-1541 ... 37 B
psherwin@sfsu.edu

SHERWOOD, David, G ... 262-646-6534 ... 549 E
dsherwood@nashotah.edu

SHERWOOD, Dennis ... 262-564-3218 ... 554 B
sherwoodd@gtc.edu

SHERWOOD, James ... 631-451-4330 ... 356 E
sherwoj@sunysuffolk.edu

SHERWOOD, Marian, D ... 814-332-2983 ... 421 F
marian.sherwood@allegheny.edu

SHERWOOD, Mary ... 361-825-2621 ... 498 C
mary.sherwood@tamucc.edu

SHERWOOD, Mary Frances ... 337-491-2657 ... 212 E
mary.sherwood@sowela.edu

SHERWOOD, Regina ... 617-521-2082 ... 244 F
regina.sherwood@simmons.edu

SHERWOOD, Robbie ... 510-780-4500 ... 53 J
rsherwood@lifewest.edu

SHERWOOD COOPER, Kristi ... 713-798-7552 ... 481 H
kgc@bcm.edu

SHESKI, Harry ... 505-287-6641 ... 319 H
hsheski@nmsu.edu

SHETLER, Clay, E ... 574-535-7351 ... 171 G
clayes@goshen.edu

SHETTY, Devdas ... 202-274-5027 ... 100 A
dshetty@udc.edu

SHEUCRAFT, Derrek, G ... 615-353-3272 ... 475 E
derrek.sheucraft@nscc.edu

SHEVACH, Shirley ... 718-518-6650 ... 327 D
sshevach@hostos.cuny.edu

SHEW, Mike ... 913-385-7700 ... 198 B
mshew@wrightcc.edu

SHEW, Rick ... 828-726-2704 ... 368 G
rshew@cccti.edu

SHEWMAKER, Julie ... 317-931-2313 ... 170 H
jshewmaker@cts.edu

SHEWMAKER, Stephen ... 325-674-2710 ... 478 I
sbs02a@acu.edu

SHEWMAKER, Stephen, M 706-542-0006 ... 138 G
sshew@uga.edu

SHI, Yuwei ... 831-647-4155 ... 57 F
yuwei.shi@miis.edu

SHIAO, Jerry ... 408-435-8989 ... 69 G
jshiao@svuca.edu

SHIBA, Margaret ... 808-933-0829 ... 141 F
mshiba@hawaii.edu

SHIBATA, Martin, C ... 805-756-2501 ... 33 I
mshibata@calpoly.edu

SHIBAZAKI, Kozue ... 210-567-2648 ... 507 A
shibazaki@uthscsa.edu

SHIBLEY, Deborah ... 254-526-1347 ... 482 H
deborah.shibley@ctcd.edu

SHIBLEY, Lisa, R ... 717-871-2390 ... 443 D
lisa.shibley@millersville.edu

SHIBLEY, Robert ... 716-829-3981 ... 351 G
rshibley@buffalo.edu

SHIBUYA, Hisatake ... 323-462-1384 ... 58 E

SHICKLE, SR., Richard, C . 540-665-4533 ... 524 E
rshickle@su.edu

SHIDELER, Janet, L ... 518-783-2320 ... 350 I
jshideler@siena.edu

SHIDELER, Lorri, P ... 814-641-3605 ... 432 A
shidell@juniata.edu

SHIDELER, Margo ... 318-869-5073 ... 208 H
mshideler@centenary.edu

SHIEH, Charles ... 863-638-2975 ... 123 E
shiehc@webber.edu

SHIELDS, Brenda ... 610-399-2080 ... 442 A
bshields@cheyney.edu

SHIELDS, Brian ... 301-552-1400 ... 229 C
bshields@bible.edu

SHIELDS, Carmen ... 763-424-0902 ... 268 B
cshields@nhcc.edu

SHIELDS, Carolyn, C ... 313-577-1620 ... 260 A

SHIELDS, Chris ... 248-218-2114 ... 257 D
cshields@rc.edu

SHIELDS, Daniel ... 845-848-7818 ... 332 B
daniel.shields@dc.edu

SHIELDS, David ... 248-689-8282 ... 259 E
david.shields@walshcollege.edu

SHIELDS, JR., David, P ... 256-765-4223 ... 9 C
dpshields@una.edu

SHIELDS, Deanna, J ... 304-367-4775 ... 543 H
deanna.shields@fairmontstate.edu

SHIELDS, Dennis, J ... 608-342-1234 ... 552 B
shieldsd@uwplatt.edu

SHIELDS, Francis ... 860-439-2570 ... 92 G
fjshi@conncoll.edu

SHIELDS, George, C ... 570-577-3292 ... 423 E
george.shields@bucknell.edu

SHIELDS, Gregory, J ... 803-799-9082 ... 461 A
gshields@southuniversity.edu

SHIELDS, Jerri ... 575-392-5018 ... 319 B
jshields@nmjc.edu

SHIELDS, Jonathan ... 402-486-2897 ... 300 C
joshield@ucollege.edu

SHIELDS, Joseph ... 740-593-0371 ... 399 G
shieldj1@ohio.edu

SHIELDS, Lauren ... 410-386-8442 ... 221 G
lshields@carrollcc.edu

SHIELDS, Melany ... 716-896-0700 ... 359 H
shieldsm@villa.edu

SHIELDS, Michelle ... 517-780-4550 ... 248 D
michelle.shields@baker.edu

SHIELDS, Peter, C ... 781-736-4520 ... 232 F
pshields@brandeis.edu

SHIELDS, Portia, H ... 615-963-7401 ... 474 A
president@tnstate.edu

SHIELDS, Ronald ... 402-363-5661 ... 301 E
ron.shields@york.edu

SHIELDS, Sally ... 309-649-6250 ... 165 F
sally.shields@src.edu

SHIELDS, Theodosia, T ... 919-530-5233 ... 378 B
tshields@nccu.edu

SHIELDS, Todd ... 479-575-5900 ... 24 C
tshild@uark.edu

SHIELDS, Vickie ... 509-359-6081 ... 533 H
vshields@ewu.edu

SHIELL, Steve ... 907-834-1622 ... 11 B
sshiell@pwscc.edu

SHIELS, Michael ... 262-691-7823 ... 555 E
mshiels@wctc.edu

SHIFFERT, John ... 678-466-4460 ... 127 D
johnshiffert@clayton.edu

SHIFFLER, Ronald ... 704-337-2234 ... 376 A
shifflerr@queens.edu

SHIFFLETT, Lee, A ... 540-568-7926 ... 520 H
shiffla@jmu.edu

SHIFFLETT, Pamela, D ... 540-423-9039 ... 526 I
pshifflett@germanna.edu

SHIFFMAN, Paul ... 518-464-8803 ... 333 E
pshiffman@excelsior.edu

SHIFFRAR, Margaret, M ... 973-353-5834 ... 314 E
mag@psychology.rutgers.edu

SHIGEHARA, Deborah ... 808-934-2516 ... 142 A
deborahs@hawaii.edu

SHILK, Peggy ... 814-371-2090 ... 448 D
pshilk@triangle-tech.edu

SHILL, Deb ... 641-269-3230 ... 185 D
shilldeb@grinnell.edu

SHILLER, Barry ... 530-752-6888 ... 73 I
bhshiller@ucdavis.edu

SHILLET, Gary ... 212-592-2000 ... 350 F
gshillet@sva.edu

SHILS, Nancy ... 215-895-1106 ... 450 B
n.shils@usciences.edu

SHIMABUKURO, Julie ... 314-935-4893 ... 292 I
jshimabukuro@wustl.edu

SHIMEK, Dennis, W ... 209-667-3351 ... 36 D
dshimek@csustan.edu

SHIMEK, Gary, S ... 414-277-7181 ... 549 C
shimek@msoe.edu

SHIMIZU, Jeffery ... 310-434-4317 ... 68 D
shimizu_jeffery@smc.edu

SHIMIZU, Stacey ... 309-556-3190 ... 153 F
abroad@iwu.edu

SHIMMEL, Debra, L ... 717-815-1232 ... 452 G
dshimmel@ycp.edu

SHIMMEL, Kurt ... 724-738-2008 ... 443 F
kurt.shimmel@sru.edu

SHIN, David, H ... 714-527-0691 ... 46 A
info@evangelia.edu

SHIN, Jason ... 714-533-3946 ... 37 E
jshin@calums.edu

SHIN, Jason ... 714-533-1495 ... 70 B
jshin@southbaylo.edu

SHINAGEL, Michael ... 617-495-2930 ... 235 D
michael_shinagel@harvard.edu

SHINBERGER, Darcie, R ... 309-298-1993 ... 168 C
dr-shinberger@wiu.edu

SHINDLER, Kenda E, G ... 573-592-4216 ... 293 D
kshindle@williamwoods.edu

SHINE, Kenneth, I ... 512-499-4224 ... 505 B
kshine@utsystem.edu

SHINER, Mark ... 315-228-7680 ... 329 G
mshiner@colgate.edu

SHINGLE, Barbara ... 814-472-3170 ... 446 B
bshingle@francis.edu

SHINGLE, Betty ... 724-222-5330 ... 438 F
bshingle@penncommercial.edu

SHINGLES, Stan, L ... 989-774-3686 ... 249 C
shing1sl@cmich.edu

SHINN, David ... 217-641-4514 ... 154 I
dshinn@jwcc.edu

SHINTAKU, Rich ... 530-752-8787 ... 73 I
rshintaku@ucdavis.edu

SHINVILLE, Padriac ... 309-268-8000 ... 151 I
padriac.shinville@heartland.edu

SHIPES, Bertie ... 912-427-5800 ... 124 C
bshipes@altamahatech.edu

SHIPLEY, Aletha ... 614-287-2640 ... 389 A
ashipley@cscc.edu

SHIPLEY, David ... 205-726-2064 ... 6 G
dsshiple@samford.edu

SHIPLEY, John, R ... 305-284-6297 ... 122 I
jshipley@miami.edu

SHIPLEY, Robert ... 918-631-3092 ... 413 F
robert-shipley@utulsa.edu

SHIPLEY, Sheryl ... 765-269-5700 ... 176 D
sshipley13@ivytech.edu

SHIPLEY, Suzanne ... 304-876-5107 ... 544 C
sshipley@shepherd.edu

SHIPMAN, Doug ... 618-395-7777 ... 152 I
shipmand@iecc.edu

SHIPMAN, Jean, P ... 801-581-8771 ... 511 C
jean.shipman@utah.edu

SHIPMAN, Richard ... 517-353-5940 ... 255 A
shipmanr@msu.edu

SHIPP, Daniel ... 402-554-2779 ... 301 A

SHIPP, Judith ... 217-206-7122 ... 167 C
shipp.judy@uis.edu

SHIPP, Kevin ... 325-235-7337 ... 500 G
kevin.shipp@tstc.edu

SHIPP, Melvin, D ... 614-292-3246 ... 398 I
shipp.25@osu.edu

SHIPP, Steve ... 940-397-4539 ... 491 B
steve.shipp@mwsu.edu

SHIPP, Tina ... 251-981-3771 ... 2 G
tina.shipp@columbiasouthern.edu

SHIPPEE, Ellen ... 603-535-2255 ... 307 A
eshippee@plymouth.edu

SHIPPEN, Tyler ... 312-777-7635 ... 145 C
tshippen@argosy.edu

SHIPPER, Jody ... 213-740-5086 ... 76 F
jshipper@usc.edu

SHIPPEY, JR., Robert, C ... 276-326-4202 ... 516 L
rshippey@bluefield.edu

SHIPPS, Mark, H ... 740-368-3310 ... 400 G
mhshipps@owu.edu

SHIPSHOCK, Amy ... 651-675-4700 ... 264 F
ashipshock@msp.chefs.edu

SHIPULA, Anthony, J ... 570-675-9107 ... 440 F
ajs39@psu.edu

SHIPWAY, Ann, M ... 304-260-4380 ... 542 G
ashipway@blueridgectc.edu

SHULTZ, John, C 419-289-5160 384 G
jshultz@ashland.edu
SHULTZ, Kari 423-236-2484 473 B
kshultz@southern.edu
SHULTZ, Walter, J 570-326-3761 440 L
wshultz@pct.edu
SHULUK, William 239-489-9356 105 F
wshuluk@edison.edu
SHUMAKE, Connie, C 502-852-3551 207 E
ccshum01@louisville.edu
SHUMAKER, Beth 276-466-7912 529 D
bshumaker@vic.edu
SHUMAKER, Deb 989-275-5000 253 E
deb.shumaker@kirtland.edu
SHUMAKER, Nancy 507-285-7461 268 I
nancy.shumaker@roch.edu
SHUMAKER, Steve, A 570-586-2400 422 G
sshumaker@bbc.edu
SHUMAN, Jenny 478-296-6117 135 C
jshuman@oftc.edu
SHUMAN, Kelli, R 605-394-1203 466 B
kelli.shuman@sdsmt.edu
SHUMAN, Michaeline, M 814-332-2381 421 F
michaeline.shuman@allegheny.edu
SHUMAN, Ruth 617-243-2140 236 A
rshuman@lasell.edu
SHUMAN, Shari, A 904-620-2002 120 D
sshuman@unf.edu
SHUMAN, Victoria 304-793-6898 544 E
vshuman@osteo.wvsom.edu
SHUMANTE, Walter 903-927-3249 509 E
wshumate@wileyc.edu
SHUMPERT, Glenn 803-641-3444 462 B
glenns@usca.edu
SHUMWAY, Nicolas 713-348-4810 493 C
shumway@rice.edu
SHUPALA, Christine 361-825-2643 498 C
christine.shupala@tamucc.edu
SHUPE, Della 952-885-5417 270 C
dshupe@nwhealth.edu
SHUPE, Elizabeth 540-887-7216 521 C
eshupe@mbc.edu
SHUPE, Gary 217-641-4505 154 I
gshupe@jwcc.edu
SHUPE, John 845-257-3335 352 B
shupej@newpaltz.edu
SHUPP, Edward, K 610-758-4200 434 E
eks0@lehigh.edu
SHUPP, Matthew, R 610-892-1289 439 C
mrs32@psu.edu
SHUPP, Michael, D 515-263-6136 185 C
mshupp@grandview.edu
SHUPPY, Brian, L 801-626-6114 511 G
bshuppy@weber.edu
SHUR, Barry 303-724-2911 88 J
barry.shur@ucdenver.edu
SHURAN, Melanie 847-578-3403 163 C
melanie.shuran@rosalindfranklin.edu
SHURES, Aaron, G 217-206-6003 167 C
shures.aaron@uis.edu
SHURTZ, Mary Ann 703-734-5325 524 J
mshurtz@stratford.edu
SHURTZ, II, Richard, R 703-821-8570 524 J
rshurtz@stratford.edu
SHUSTER, Arthur 828-298-3325 380 D
ashuster@warren-wilson.edu
SHUSTER, Patricia 603-641-7150 305 G
pshuster@anselm.edu
SHUTE, Marcus, W 404-880-6990 127 C
mwshute@cau.edu
SHUTE, William 202-955-9091 505 B
wshute@utsystem.edu
SHUTLER, Troy 419-755-4896 397 C
tshutler@ncstatecollege.edu
SHUTT, Allison 501-450-3897 22 A
shutt@hendrix.edu
SHUTT, Barbara, C 207-859-5415 217 G
bcshutt@colby.edu
SHUTT, Gary 405-744-4800 410 C
gary.shutt@okstate.edu
SHUTTER, Jamie, L 512-475-8445 505 D
j.shutter@uhs.utexas.edu
SHUTTER, Susan, S 412-578-6351 424 I
shutterss@carlow.edu
SHYDIAN, Joanne 706-750-4954 36 C
jshydian@csusm.edu
SHYTLE, Louise 606-326-2077 201 F
louise.shytle@kctcs.edu
SIAHMAKOUN, Azad 812-877-8400 179 B
azad.siahmakoun@rose-hulman.edu
SIAMUNDELE, Andre 315-364-3215 360 D
asiamundele@wells.edu
SIAS, Mary, E 502-597-6260 203 G
mary.sias@kysu.edu
SIBAL, Thomas 574-936-8898 169 D
tom.sibal@ancilla.edu
SIBENALLER-WOODALL,
Beth 712-324-5061 188 C
beths@nwicc.edu
SIBERT, Alan 706-864-1940 134 G
aksibert@northgeorgia.edu
SIBERT, Kimberley 740-366-9233 386 H
ksibert@cotc.edu
SIBERT, Sonja 775-753-2181 302 F
sonja.sibert@gbcnv.edu
SIBLEY, Debra, H 504-568-6107 213 A
dsible@lsuhsc.edu
SICARD, OP, Kenneth, R 401-865-2055 453 H
ksicard@providence.edu
SICARD, Rex, E 785-243-1435 192 A
rsicard@cloud.edu
SICHTERMAN, David 313-927-1391 254 E
dsichterman@marygrove.edu
SICIENSKY, Emily 931-540-2704 475 A
esiciensky@columbiastate.edu
SICILIANO, Julie 413-782-1553 246 A
jsicilia@wne.edu
SICILIANO, Stephen, N 231-995-1373 256 D
ssiciliano@nmc.edu
SICKBERT, Alan, A 651-523-2421 264 A
asickbert01@hamline.edu
SICKLER, Jan 641-472-7000 187 E
jsickler@mum.edu
SICKLES, Susan 513-772-9888 398 G
susan.sickles@omw.edu
SICONOLFI, Steven 815-226-4065 163 A
ssiconolfi@rockford.edu
SIDBURY, Carmen 404-270-5705 138 B
csidbury@spelman.edu
SIDDARAJU, Raj 309-649-6387 165 F
raj.siddaraju@src.edu
SIDDENS, Nancy 217-732-3168 156 H
nsiddens@lincolnchristian.edu
SIDDIQI, Melanie 909-652-6780 39 E
melanie.siddiqi@chaffey.edu
SIDDIQI, Muhammad 708-656-8000 159 D
muhammad.siddiqi@morton.edu
SIDDIQUI, Martuza 651-793-1910 267 A
SIDEBOTTOM, Daniel 607-753-2501 353 B
daniel.sidebottom@cortland.edu
SIDEBOTTOM, Sara, L 859-572-5588 205 H
sidebottoms@nku.edu
SIDERAKIS, John 212-650-7226 326 G
jsiderakis@ccny.cuny.edu
SIDERAS, John, F 216-368-4340 386 F
john.sideras@case.edu
SIDERS, Janet 229-931-2000 131 F
janet.siders@gsw.edu
SIDES, Diane, O 573-651-2256 289 K
dosides@semo.edu
SIDES, Karen 210-486-2339 479 D
ksides@alamo.edu
SIDHU, Elda 702-895-5185 302 I
elda.sidhu@unlv.edu
SIDLE, Meg 606-218-5290 207 F
margaretsidle@upike.edu
SIDNEY, Cheri 773-995-3534 146 G
csidney@csu.edu
SIDOCK, Andrew 217-479-7066 157 F
andrew.sidock@mac.edu
SIDOR, Stanley, M 704-272-5352 374 A
ssidor@spcc.edu
SIDORKIN, Alexander 401-456-8110 454 A
asidorkin@ric.edu
SIDOTI, Dennis 860-412-7351 92 D
dsidoti@qvcc.commnet.edu
SIDWELL, Scott, A 415-422-2923 76 E
sasidwell@usfca.edu
SIDY, Victor 480-860-2700 14 F
vsidy@earthlink.net
SIEBECKER, Carl 703-821-8570 524 J
csiebecker@stratford.edu
SIEBENECK, Paula, J 419-995-8458 392 K
siebeneck.p@rhodesstate.edu
SIEBENMORGEN, Tom 501-450-1333 22 A
SIEBENS, Libby 509-682-6436 539 E
lsiebens@wvc.edu
SIEBER, Frederick, C 610-519-7730 450 H
frederick.sieber@villanova.edu
SIEBER, Yvonne 620-327-8112 193 E
yvonnes@hesston.edu
SIEBERT, David, J 847-735-5040 155 G
siebert@lakeforest.edu
SIEBERT, Eleanor 310-954-4015 57 H
esiebert@msmc.la.edu
SIEBERT, Laurie 248-689-8282 259 E
lsiebert@walshcollege.edu
SIEBERT, Mary Anne 501-450-1372 22 A
siebert@hendrix.edu
SIEBERT, Scotti 417-873-7434 281 D
ssiebert@drury.edu
SIECKE, Elizabeth 201-684-7318 313 C
esiecke@ramapo.edu
SIEDE, Cristy 612-977-5220 261 F
cristy.siede@capella.edu
SIEDOW, James, N 919-681-6438 364 C
jim.siedow@duke.edu
SIEDZIK, Richard 401-232-6505 453 C
rsiedzik@bryant.edu
SIEFERT, Ruth 507-285-7472 268 I
ruth.siefert@roch.edu
SIEFFERMAN, Larry, D 706-213-2139 125 C
lsiefferman@athenstech.edu
SIEGEL, Donald, S 518-442-4910 351 E
dsiegel@uamail.albany.edu
SIEGEL, Fred 909-621-8965 40 F
fred.siegel@cgu.edu
SIEGEL, Gale, J 215-881-7600 438 H
gxs1@psu.edu
SIEGEL, James 845-574-4729 347 I
jsiegel3@sunyrockland.edu
SIEGEL, Larry 978-934-2107 237 B
larry_siegel@uml.edu
SIEGEL, Lawrence, J 212-430-4204 361 M
lsiegel@aecom.yu.edu
SIEGEL, Martha 310-689-3200 42 H
msiegel@kaplan.edu
SIEGEL, Peter, M 530-752-4998 73 I
pmsiegel@ucdavis.edu
SIEGER, Eric 507-222-4183 261 G
esieger@carleton.edu
SIEGERT, Gerald, A 513-556-5006 403 D
gerald.siegert@uc.edu
SIEGERT, Kara, O 410-543-6023 228 D
kosiegert@salisbury.edu
SIEGFRIED, Jessica 435-283-7169 512 C
jessica.siegfried@snow.edu
SIEGFRIED, Kathy 610-861-5460 437 H
ksiegfried@northampton.edu
SIEGGREEN, Stephanie 989-964-7028 257 G
smsieggr@svsu.edu
SIEGMANN, Starla, C 414-443-8862 553 D
starla.siegmann@wlc.edu
SIEKER, Tina 636-922-8314 288 B
tsieker@stchas.edu
SIEMER, Richard 410-951-3594 228 B
rsiemer@coppin.edu
SIEMERING, John 920-498-5488 555 C
john.siemering@nwtc.edu
SIEMERS, Barbara 830-792-7368 494 E
jbsiemers@schreiner.edu
SIEMINSKI, Daniel, W 814-865-6574 438 G
dws8@psu.edu
SIEMINSKI, Randy, B 315-386-7300 355 E
sieminski@canton.edu
SIEMINSKI, Randy, B 315-386-7335 355 E
sieminski@canton.edu
SIEMSEN, Deanna 719-336-6646 86 B
deanna.siemsen@lamarcc.edu
SIEMSEN, Jack, E 402-465-2337 299 H
jes@nebrwesleyan.edu
SIENER, Estelle, M 716-888-2450 325 F
siener@canisius.edu
SIEREN, Kristin 515-244-4221 181 F
sierenk@aib.edu
SIERRA CONCEPCION,
Yadexy 787-744-1060 564 F
ysierra@mechtech.edu
SIERRA-CORTES,
Frank Jimmy 787-834-5151 565 D
fjsierra@email.pucpr.edu
SIEVERS, Cara 901-272-5111 471 D
csievers@mca.edu
SIEVERS, Debbie 708-974-5330 159 B
sievers@morainevalley.edu
SIFFERLEN, Ned, J 937-512-2510 401 J
ned.sifferlen@sinclair.edu
SIFFRING, Ed 402-643-7230 297 D
ed.siffring@cune.edu
SIFUENTES, Alma 831-459-3755 75 C
alma@ucsc.edu
SIFUENTES, Lucas, J 410-532-5390 225 D
lsifuentes@ndm.edu
SIFUENTES, Miguel 915-747-5544 506 B
msifuentes@utep.edu
SIGAUKE, Erica 417-667-8181 280 E
esigauke@cottey.edu
SIGG, John 607-274-3237 336 G
sigg@ithaca.edu
SIGGINS, Jack, A 202-994-6455 98 C
siggins@gwu.edu
SIGGINS, Judy, U 607-778-5182 324 G
sigginsj@sunybroome.edu
SIGISMOND, William, D 585-292-3220 341 H
wsigismond@monroecc.edu
SIGLER, Beth 804-281-3908 19 A
beth.sigler@phoenix.edu
SIGLER, Jeffrey 718-270-4979 328 C
jeffrey@mec.cuny.edu
SIGLER, Julius, A 434-544-8232 521 B
sigler.ja@lynchburg.edu
SIGLER, Katie 405-491-6365 412 D
ksigler@snu.edu
SIGLER, Kenneth 419-755-4011 399 C
sigler.1@osu.edu
SIGLER, Todd, D 618-453-3771 165 B
todds@dps.siu.edu
SIGLER, Wayne 703-993-2391 519 E
wsigler@gmu.edu
SIGMAN, Stuart 310-476-9777 28 G
ssigman@ajula.edu
SIGMON, Judy 336-917-5471 376 E
judy.sigmon@salem.edu
SIGMON, Patty 540-365-4449 519 C
psigmon@ferrum.edu
SIGNOR, Mary 212-998-2352 344 B
mary.signor@nyu.edu
SIGNORELLO, John 973-761-9615 315 B
john.signorello@shu.edu
SIGNORELLO, Rose 713-525-3162 505 A
signorr@stthom.edu
SIGUAW, Judy 252-328-1098 377 E
siguawj@ecu.edu
SIGURDSON, Chris, W 765-496-2644 178 J
sig@purdue.edu
SIGWORTH, Steve 713-798-4951 481 H
sigworth@bcm.edu
SIHOTA HE'BERT,
Gurdeep 559-244-5990 72 A
gurdeep.sihota@sccd.edu
SIKES, Pamela, J 619-260-4595 76 D
psikes@sandiego.edu
SIKES, Steddon, L 402-363-5668 301 E
slsikes@york.edu
SIKO, Kari 843-863-7765 456 B
ksiko@csuniv.edu
SIKORA, James 406-791-5362 296 F
jsikora@ugf.edu
SIKORA, Patty 253-833-9111 534 H
psikora@greenriver.edu
SIKORSKI, Henry 631-420-2142 356 A
henry.sikorski@farmingdale.edu
SIKORSKY, LC, Charles 703-416-1441 520 C
csikorsky@ipsciences.edu
SIKOSKI, Aco 219-464-4715 176 G
asikoski@ivytech.edu
SILAFAU, Emey 684-699-9155 559 C
e.silafau@amsamoa.edu
SILAK, Cathy 503-955-1001 415 E
csilak@cu-portland.edu
SILANDER, Liisa 401-454-6349 454 B
lsilande@risd.edu
SILANSKIS, Theresa 410-837-6838 229 A
tsilanskis@ubalt.edu
SILBER, Daniel, K 573-288-6325 280 I
dsilber@culver.edu
SILBER, Irene 612-977-4132 261 F
irene.silber@capella.edu
SILBER, Jeffrey, A 607-255-2016 331 B
jas9@cornell.edu
SILBER, Michael, H 507-284-3293 262 E
silber.michael@mayo.edu
SILBERBERGER, Cindy 760-757-2121 57 E
csilberberger@miracosta.edu
SILBERLING, Rosanne 818-299-5500 78 A
rsilberling@westcoastuniversity.edu
SILBERMAN, Gerald, L 610-683-4106 443 A
silberma@kutztown.edu
SILBERQUIT, Paul 203-285-2368 91 D
psilberquit@gwcc.commnet.edu
SILBERSTEIN, Dara, J 607-777-2815 351 F
lael@binghamton.edu
SILCOX, Greg 602-787-6622 15 J
greg.silcox@paradisevalley.edu
SILER, Ginni 706-802-5136 130 E
gsiler@highlands.edu
SILER, Linda, K 616-538-2330 251 D
lsiler@gbcol.edu
SILES, Marcelo, E 757-683-4419 522 F
msiles@odu.edu
SILICIANO, John, A 607-255-3062 331 B
jas83@cornell.edu
SILK, Eleana 914-961-8313 349 I
es@svots.edu
SILK, Elizabeth 708-524-6481 150 C
esilk@dom.edu
SILK, Mary, L 692-625-4410 560 A
mlsilk@hotmail.com
SILK, Melody 701-854-8020 383 D
melodys@sbci.edu
SILK, Robert 781-736-4050 232 F
rsilk@brandeis.edu
SILLCOX, James 718-260-3148 346 C
jsillcox@poly.edu
SILLEN, Andrew 718-951-5074 326 F
asillen@brooklyn.cuny.edu
SILLIMAN, Robert 502-213-4294 202 F
bob.silliman@kctcs.edu
SILLIMAN, Steve 509-313-3522 534 F
silliman@gonzaga.edu
SILLS, CreSaundra, Y 410-617-2232 223 I
csills@loyola.edu
SILLS, Karen 404-297-9522 131 D
sillsk@gptc.edu
SILMAN, Linda, C 314-516-5406 291 D
lindas@umsl.edu
SILMAN, Shawn 281-998-6150 494 A
shawn.silman@sjcd.edu
SILTANEN, Susan 601-266-4373 277 F
susan.siltanen@usm.edu
SILVA, Adelina 210-485-0153 479 A
asilva@alamo.edu
SILVA, Alan 651-690-6500 270 L
ajsilva@stkate.edu
SILVA, Billee 239-489-9362 105 F
bsilva@edison.edu
SILVA, Dashia 718-261-5800 324 D
dsilva@bramsonort.edu
SILVA, Denise 615-871-2260 99 G
SILVA, Efrain 760-355-6249 51 A
efrain.silva@imperial.edu
SILVA, Hilda 956-882-5133 505 E
hilda.silva@utb.edu
SILVA, Jack 401-454-6480 454 B
jsilva@risd.edu
SILVA, Jessica, L 401-456-8047 454 A
jsilva@ric.edu

SIMPSON, Gregory 309-438-5669 153 D gsimpso@ilstu.edu
SIMPSON, Jack 423-461-8955 471 J jasimpson@milligan.edu
SIMPSON, Jacklyn, A 704-687-7501 379 A jasimpso@uncc.edu
SIMPSON, III, James, D 904-632-5049 109 F jsimpson@fscj.edu
SIMPSON, James, E 434-395-2093 521 A simpsonje@longwood.edu
SIMPSON, Jane 678-839-5306 139 A jsimpson@westga.edu
SIMPSON, Juliene 973-290-4207 308 G jsimpson@cse.edu
SIMPSON, Kurt 815-599-3501 152 B kurt.simpson@highland.edu
SIMPSON, Larry 662-562-3219 276 D jlsimpson@northwestms.edu
SIMPSON, Lawrence, J 617-266-1400 231 E
SIMPSON, Mallory, M 815-753-9506 160 B mmsimpson@niu.edu
SIMPSON, Mallory, M 313-593-5130 259 B
SIMPSON, Mark 801-626-6047 511 G marksimpson1@weber.edu
SIMPSON, Matthew 252-335-3532 377 F mdsimpson@mail.escu.edu
SIMPSON, Megan 706-368-7739 130 E msimpson@highlands.edu
SIMPSON, Micah 205-970-9243 7 C msimpson@sebc.edu
SIMPSON, Michael, A 304-788-6886 545 B masimpson@mail.wvu.edu
SIMPSON, Michael, E 518-564-2155 354 B simpsome@plattsburgh.edu
SIMPSON, Michael, J 415-338-2218 37 B msimpson@sfsu.edu
SIMPSON, Nancy, P 864-231-2029 455 C nsimpson@andersonuniversity.edu
SIMPSON, Patricia 605-642-6551 465 H patricia.simpson@bhsu.edu
SIMPSON, Philip 321-433-5078 102 D simpsonp@brevardcc.edu
SIMPSON, Phyllis 225-768-1713 214 C psimpson@ololcollege.edu
SIMPSON, Ralph 484-365-7528 434 H rsimpson@lincoln.edu
SIMPSON, Rebecca 502-852-6397 207 E becky.simpson@louisville.edu
SIMPSON, Renee, K 407-582-1506 123 B rsimpson@valenciacollege.edu
SIMPSON, Richard 614-236-6383 386 E rsimpson@law.capital.edu
SIMPSON, Robert 248-222-1503 250 A robert.simpson@cornerstone.edu
SIMPSON, Robert 731-661-5219 477 B rsimpson@uu.edu
SIMPSON, Robert, G 714-484-7308 59 D rsimpson@cypresscollege.edu
SIMPSON, Robert, L 810-762-7949 253 C rsimpson@kettering.edu
SIMPSON, Sarah 803-780-1263 463 C simpson@voorhees.edu
SIMPSON, Stacey 541-278-5933 414 G ssimpson@bluecc.edu
SIMPSON, Stephen, J 301-687-4211 228 C ssimpson@frostburg.edu
SIMPSON, Susan 217-786-9629 157 B susan.simpson@llcc.edu
SIMPSON, Suzanne 662-846-4050 273 H ssimpson@deltastate.edu
SIMPSON, Ted 410-225-2531 224 B tsimpson@mica.edu
SIMPSON, Teresa 409-880-8879 501 A teresa.simpson@lamar.edu
SIMPSON, Thomas, W 864-429-7732 463 A twsimpso@mailbox.sc.edu
SIMPSON, Todd 402-872-2304 299 F tsimpson@peru.edu
SIMPSON, Tony 909-537-5166 36 B tsimpson@csusb.edu
SIMPSON, Traci 305-899-3150 101 M tsimpson@mail.barry.edu
SIMS, Alan 215-596-8813 450 B a.sims@usciences.edu
SIMS, Bradford (Brad) 812-237-3166 173 B bradford.sims@indstate.edu
SIMS, Charles, E 206-934-4136 537 C charles.sims@seattlecolleges.edu
SIMS, Dale 615-366-3921 473 D dale.sims@tbr.edu
SIMS, Damon 814-865-0909 438 G drs37@psu.edu
SIMS, David 478-471-2780 133 H david.sims@maconstate.edu
SIMS, Donald, R 662-254-3551 276 B d-ray@mvsu.edu
SIMS, Dora 281-756-3524 479 F dsims@alvincollege.edu
SIMS, Frank 641-673-1703 190 C simsf@wmpenn.edu
SIMS, Gayle 919-536-7250 370 C simso@durhamtech.edu
SIMS, George, E 251-380-2262 7 E gsims@shc.edu
SIMS, Glenn 910-410-1684 373 B glenns@richmondcc.edu
SIMS, Jack 814-871-7464 429 G sims003@gannon.edu
SIMS, Jane 402-354-7073 299 C jane.sims@methodistcollege.edu
SIMS, Jeanette 704-687-5827 379 A aoster@uncc.edu
SIMS, John 973-720-2397 317 D simsj@wpunj.edu
SIMS, Kathy, L 310-206-7774 74 C ksims@career.ucla.edu
SIMS, Lesley 510-436-1405 50 H sims@hnu.edu
SIMS, Leslie 304-424-8221 545 C leslie.sims@mail.wvu.edu
SIMS, Marcella 251-405-7133 2 C msims@bishop.edu
SIMS, Mary, J 831-656-3658 558 A mjsims@nps.edu
SIMS, Mary, L 803-536-8198 460 G msims@scsu.edu
SIMS, Patricia 256-551-1717 4 J patricia.sims@drakestate.edu
SIMS, Phil, W 903-875-7543 491 C phil.sims@navarrocollege.edu
SIMS, Roberta, L 570-577-3310 423 E roberta.sims@bucknell.edu
SIMS, Sue, A 803-938-3729 462 G sues@uscsumter.edu
SIMS, Suzanne 256-216-3314 1 E suzanne.sims@athens.edu
SIMS-TUCKER, Bernita, M 410-651-3553 227 E bsimstucker@umes.edu
SIMSHEUSER, Carrie, L 816-654-7072 283 F csimsheuser@kcumb.edu
SIMSON, Earl, L 401-456-8106 454 A esimson@ric.edu
SIMSON, Gary, J 478-301-2602 134 A simson_g@mercer.edu
SINATRA, Ann 610-989-1327 450 F asinatra@vfmac.edu
SINCAVAGE, Joseph 610-436-3535 444 A jsincavage@wcupa.edu
SINCLAIR, Joyce 512-313-3000 483 K joyce.sinclair@concordia.edu
SINCLAIR, Kelli 630-466-7900 168 B ksinclair@waubonsee.edu
SINCLAIR, Nancy 270-384-8001 204 D sinclairn@lindsey.edu
SINCLAIR, Rick 509-467-1727 535 C rsinclai@interface.edu
SINDER, Janet 718-780-7975 324 F janet.sinder@brooklaw.edu
SINDLE, Patricia 870-574-4492 24 A psindle@sautech.edu
SINDLINGER, Susan 312-369-7984 148 D ssindlinger@colum.edu
SINDT, Christopher 925-631-4088 64 F csindt@stmarys-ca.edu
SINE, Josh 435-652-7591 512 B jsine@dixie.edu
SINES, Robert, G 330-675-8821 393 J rsines@kent.edu
SINEWAY, Carla 989-775-4123 257 F sineway.carla@sagchip.edu
SINEX, Nancy 765-983-1600 171 E nancys@earlham.edu
SINGARELLA, Thomas, A 901-448-5694 477 E tsingare@uthsc.edu
SINGEL, David 406-994-4371 295 C dsingel@montana.edu
SINGELL, Larry 812-855-1646 173 E
SINGER, David 518-445-3211 322 C dsing@albanylaw.edu
SINGER, Ethan, A 619-594-5166 37 A singer@mail.sdsu.edu
SINGER, John 561-297-2279 119 A singer@fau.edu
SINGER, Judith 617-495-1961 235 D judith_singer@harvard.edu
SINGER, Lynn, T 216-368-4389 386 F lts5@case.edu
SINGER, Mark 201-684-7550 313 C msinger@ramapo.edu
SINGER, Mark 914-493-1909 343 F mark_singer@nymc.edu
SINGER, Nancy 314-516-5517 291 D singerna@umsl.edu
SINGER, Nancy 801-957-4186 512 D nancy.singer@slcc.edu
SINGER, Patricia 561-297-3693 119 A patty@fau.edu
SINGER, Tara 812-237-8764 173 B tara.singer@indstate.edu
SINGER, Terry, L 502-852-6402 207 E terry.singer@louisville.edu
SINGER, Timothy 315-498-2485 345 D singert@sunyocc.edu
SINGER, Yossi 718-268-4700 347 A
SINGH, Amit 216-987-5556 389 B amit.singh@tri-c.edu
SINGH, Avena 541-888-1583 420 C asingh@socc.edu
SINGH, Hamwant (Neil) 718-429-6600 359 G neil.singh@vaughn.edu
SINGH, Harinder 510-981-2881 62 B hsingh@peralta.edu
SINGH, Holly 219-464-5333 181 C holly.singh@valpo.edu
SINGH, Inder 845-451-1361 331 E i_singh@culinary.edu
SINGH, Kanwal 914-395-2303 350 C ksingh@slc.edu
SINGH, Nancy 559-251-5025 32 A library@calchristiancollege.edu
SINGH, Sarjit 920-748-8169 550 D singhs@ripon.edu
SINGH, Shailindar 315-267-2335 354 C singhs@potsdam.edu
SINGH, Surya, P 918-877-8151 408 G ssingh@langston.edu
SINGH, Tanuja 210-436-3706 493 F tsingh@stmarytx.edu
SINGH, Vijai, P 412-624-4555 449 A singh@pitt.edu
SINGH CHAUHAN, Indrajeet 212-423-2769 335 C indrajeet.singh@helenefuld.edu
SINGH MOONILALL, Seeta 561-912-1211 107 B seetas@evergladesuniversity.edu
SINGHA, Suman 860-486-3619 94 G suman.singha@uconn.edu
SINGHAL, Meena 562-938-4311 54 E msinghal@lbcc.edu
SINGLETARY, Chip 850-201-8535 122 A singlech@tcc.fl.edu
SINGLETARY, James, M 740-392-6868 396 I jim.singletary@mvnu.edu
SINGLETARY, Michael 360-383-3035 540 A msingletary@whatcom.ctc.edu
SINGLETARY, Shelia 985-732-6640 211 A
SINGLETON, Alma (Nickie) 904-680-7601 107 J nsingleton@fcsl.edu
SINGLETON, Brian 313-496-2778 259 G bsingle1@wcccd.edu
SINGLETON, David 302-831-1110 96 I dsing@udel.edu
SINGLETON, Gena, L 713-646-1778 494 I gsingleton@stcl.edu
SINGLETON, Ginny 601-426-6346 277 A gsingleton@southeasternbaptist.edu
SINGLETON, Gregory 931-221-7005 473 E singletong@apsu.edu
SINGLETON, H. Wells 954-262-8731 114 B singlew@nsu.nova.edu
SINGLETON, J. Ron 864-488-8274 459 B rsingleton@limestone.edu
SINGLETON, Janet 404-880-8286 127 C jsingleton@cau.edu
SINGLETON, John, L 817-257-7871 499 C j.singleton@tcu.edu
SINGLETON, LaMonica 336-750-3240 380 B singletonls@wssu.edu
SINGLETON, Loy 205-348-4787 8 E loy.singleton@ua.edu
SINGLETON, Maxine, B 757-569-6713 528 A msingleton@pdc.edu
SINGLETON, Robin 870-762-3161 20 A rsingleton@smail.anc.edu
SINGLETON, Shawn, T 859-233-8154 207 A ssingleton@transy.edu
SINGLETON, Stanley 317-917-3309 178 A ssingleton@martin.edu
SINGLETON-YOUNG, Patricia 843-349-2304 456 G psyoung@coastal.edu
SINHA, Monica 510-592-9688 59 G monica@npu.edu
SINIARD, Michelle 478-988-6840 134 C msiniard@middlegatech.edu
SINIARI, Jayne 215-728-4700 438 B jayne.siniari@jevs.org
SINISI, Daniel, F 814-472-3332 446 B dsinisi@francis.edu
SINK, Christopher 413-528-7229 230 F csink@simons-rock.edu
SINK, Joyce, A 540-375-2201 523 G sink@roanoke.edu
SINK, Susanna, C 724-357-2202 442 F scsink@iup.edu
SINK, Tom 567-661-7221 400 I thomas_sink@owens.edu
SINKOW, Alexis 610-558-5625 437 D sinkowa@neumann.edu
SINN, Brad 320-363-5211 262 F bsinn@csbsju.edu
SINNAMON, Carol 864-644-5133 461 B csinnamon@swu.edu
SINNAMON, Walt 864-644-5221 461 B wsinnamon@swu.edu
SINNOTT, Anneliese 313-831-5200 250 G asinnott@etseminary.edu
SINNOTT, Cindy Ann 636-573-9300 286 E csinnott@motech.edu
SINON, Victoria 312-777-8657 153 B vsinon@aii.edu
SINSABAUGH, Emily, F 716-375-2334 348 C esinsaba@sbu.edu
SINTEF, Paul, R 512-448-8773 493 E paulrs@stedwards.edu
SINUTKO, John 805-378-1454 77 D jsinutko@vcccd.edu
SIPE, Brian 912-279-5819 127 E bsipe@ccga.edu
SIPLE, Samuel, D 724-589-2842 448 B ssiple@thiel.edu
SIPP, Richard, G 419-372-2276 385 E rsipp@bgsu.edu
SIPPEL, Len 320-308-2286 269 A lcsippel@stcloudstate.edu
SIPPIN, Ana, M 305-348-2421 119 C sippina@fiu.edu
SIRACH, Gina 618-252-5400 164 I gina.sirach@sic.edu
SIRANGELO-ELBADAWY, Catherine 201-360-4261 310 E csirangelo@hccc.edu
SIRBAUGH, William, A 540-868-7093 527 C bsirbaugh@lfsbdc.org
SIRBU, Jerald, B 303-369-5151 87 D jbs@plattcolorado.edu
SIRENO, Peter, J 229-317-6705 128 D peter.sireno@darton.edu
SIRIANNI, Frank 212-636-6265 334 C sirianni@fordham.edu
SIRIANNI, John, F 515-961-1620 189 C john.sirianni@simpson.edu
SIRIMANGKALA, Pawena 305-899-3453 101 M psirimangkala@mail.barry.edu
SIRJU-JOHNSON, Nicole 607-777-4472 351 F njohnson@binghamton.edu
SIRMON, John 850-973-9495 113 K sirmonj@nfcc.edu
SIRNEY, Marie 626-966-4576 28 F mariesirney@agu.edu
SIROTA, Robert 212-749-2802 339 I rsirota@msmnyc.edu
SIRRINE, Erica 863-638-7678 123 D erica.sirrine@warner.edu
SISCO, Rodney, K 630-752-5028 168 H rodney.sisco@wheaton.edu
SISCO, Teri 951-487-3110 58 B tsisco@msjc.edu
SISCOE, Denita 813-974-8462 121 A dsiscoe@usf.edu
SISE, Jack, R 518-783-2315 350 I jsise@siena.edu
SISK, Beth 402-399-2415 297 C bsisk@csm.edu
SISK, Kathy 706-864-1604 134 G ksisk@northgeorgia.edu
SISK, Ronald, D 605-336-6588 465 D rsisk@sfseminary.edu
SISKAR, John, F 716-878-3787 353 A siskarjf@buffalostate.edu
SISLER, Mark 740-389-6786 399 D sisler.2@osu.edu
SISNEROS, Caroline 818-386-5642 62 F csisneros@pgi.edu
SISNEROS, Kathy 970-491-6384 83 F kathy.sisneros@colostate.edu
SISNEROS, Lori 303-937-4577 82 E lsisneros@chu.edu
SISNEROS, Patrick 425-388-9026 534 C psisnero@everettcc.edu
SISOIAN, Katherine 210-436-3331 493 F ksisoian@stmarytx.edu
SISON, Christine, B 671-735-5565 559 E christine.sison@guamcc.edu
SISSION, Amanda 843-863-7991 456 B asission@csuniv.edu
SISSON, Cindy, N 574-372-5100 171 H sissoncn@grace.edu
SISSON, Jeanne, M 518-580-5664 351 B jsisson@skidmore.edu
SISSON, Karen 909-621-8132 63 A karen.sisson@pomona.edu
SISSON, Laura 205-226-4861 2 B lsisson@bsc.edu
SISSON, Linda, G 248-370-3266 256 G lgsisson@oakland.edu
SISSON, Paul, D 318-797-5374 213 D paul.sisson@lsus.edu
SISSON, Philip 978-322-8488 240 B sissonp@middlesex.mass.edu
SISSON, Russell 606-546-1321 207 B rsisson@unionky.edu
SISSONS, Nancy 516-299-4249 338 E nancy.sissons@liu.edu
SISTARE, Janet 704-991-0189 374 D jsistare6776@stanly.edu
SISTARENIK, Daniel 845-257-3250 352 B sistared@newpaltz.edu
SITARSKI, Karen 856-415-2110 310 D ksitarski@gccnj.edu
SITES, John 954-776-4456 112 E jsites@keiseruniversity.edu
SITHARAMAN, Sri 706-507-8963 127 G sri@columbusstate.edu
SITKO, Dan, J 336-334-4822 371 A djsitko@gtcc.edu

SLOAN, Candice, Y ... 864-587-4282 ... 461 D
sloanc@smcsc.edu
SLOAN, Damon, N ... 815-740-3398 ... 167 E
dsloan@stfrancis.edu
SLOAN, Jeff ... 405-912-9455 ... 408 D
jsloan@hc.edu
SLOAN, Lee ... 361-698-1259 ... 485 G
lsloan@delmar.edu
SLOAN, Michael ... 309-694-5512 ... 152 C
msloan@icc.edu
SLOAN, Robert, B ... 281-649-3153 ... 487 H
rsloan@hbu.edu
SLOAN, Ron ... 765-289-2291 ... 176 B
rsloan9@ivytech.edu
SLOAN, Susan ... 310-243-3639 ... 34 D
ssloan@csudh.edu
SLOAN, Susan ... 315-364-3264 ... 360 D
ssloan@wells.edu
SLOAN, Susan ... 503-253-3443 ... 417 H
ssloan@ocom.edu
SLOANE, Tomecca ... 919-760-8633 ... 367 A
sloaneto@meredith.edu
SLOAS, Ike ... 901-843-3880 ... 472 K
SLOBERT, Yantee ... 585-385-8423 ... 348 F
yslobert@sjfc.edu
SLOCUM, Cameron, W ... 409-772-3448 ... 507 C
cwslocum@utmb.edu
SLOCUM, Jeff ... 315-655-7290 ... 325 H
jslocum@cazenovia.edu
SLOCUM, Stacy, S ... 585-385-8388 ... 348 F
sslocum@sjfc.edu
SLOCUMB, Douglas ... 423-478-7036 ... 472 H
dslocumb@ptseminary.edu
SLOKA, Sandra, L ... 815-740-5026 ... 167 E
ssloka@stfrancis.edu
SLOMBIA, Sonia ... 937-376-6574 ... 387 A
sslombia@centralstate.edu
SLOMOVITS, Mendel ... 732-414-2834 ... 317 F
SLOMOVITS, Yosef ... 732-367-1060 ... 307 G
SLON, Dennis ... 310-338-5127 ... 56 E
dslon@lmu.edu
SLONAC, Kevin ... 262-551-5727 ... 546 I
kslonac@carthage.edu
SLONE, Jason ... 419-448-5851 ... 402 E
slonej@tiffin.edu
SLONE, Tammy, L ... 937-766-7987 ... 386 G
slonet@cedarville.edu
SLOSS, Robert, E ... 401-232-6046 ... 453 C
rsloss@bryant.edu
SLOTKIN, Jacquelyn, H ... 619-239-0391 ... 37 F
jslotkin@cwsl.edu
SLOTTOW, Timothy, P ... 734-764-7272 ... 259 A
tslottow@umich.edu
SLOUGH, Rebecca ... 574-296-6228 ... 169 C
rslough@ambs.edu
SLOVAK, Jeffrey ... 708-534-4981 ... 151 E
jslovak@govst.edu
SLOVER, Kimberly, S ... 603-526-3647 ... 303 G
kslover@colby-sawyer.edu
SLOWENSKY, Joseph ... 714-744-7882 ... 39 F
slowensky@chapman.edu
SLUDER, Richard, D ... 660-543-4811 ... 290 H
sluder@ucmo.edu
SLUDER, Robin ... 423-478-7727 ... 472 H
rsluder@ptseminary.edu
SLUIS, Kimberly ... 630-637-5152 ... 159 G
kasluis@noctrl.edu
SLUSARCZYK, Richard ... 212-226-7300 ... 346 E
rslusar@pbcny.edu
SLUSHER, Cindy ... 503-222-3225 ... 415 H
cslusher@cci.edu
SLUSHER, Jennifer, J ... 540-985-8502 ... 520 I
jjslusher@jchs.edu
SLUSHER, Max ... 609-894-9311 ... 308 B
gslusher@bcc.edu
SLUSSER, Karen, L ... 570-389-4055 ... 441 F
kslusse2@bloomu.edu
SLUTSKY, Madeleine ... 630-353-9027 ... 149 B
mslutsky@devry.edu
SLY, Doug ... 509-793-2003 ... 531 I
dougs@bigbend.edu
SMAIL, Audra ... 502-456-6504 ... 206 H
asmail@sullivan.edu
SMAIL, John ... 704-687-5630 ... 379 A
jsmail@uncc.edu
SMALES, Sandra ... 617-984-1723 ... 243 H
ssmales@quincycollege.edu
SMALL, Angus ... 901-435-1627 ... 470 D
angus_small@loc.edu
SMALL, Barbara ... 847-925-6682 ... 151 G
bsmall@harpercollege.edu
SMALL, Brenda, L ... 423-585-6772 ... 476 D
brenda.small@ws.edu
SMALL, Brent ... 575-562-2194 ... 318 B
brent.small@enmu.edu
SMALL, Cindy ... 406-265-3787 ... 295 E
csmall@msun.edu
SMALL, Daniel, E ... 202-994-6620 ... 98 C
dsmall@gwu.edu
SMALL, Daphne ... 650-949-7046 ... 47 H
smalldaphne@foothill.edu
SMALL, Darlene ... 843-383-8039 ... 457 A
dsmall@coker.edu
SMALL, David ... 406-638-3110 ... 294 E
smalld@lbhc.edu
SMALL, Gillian ... 212-794-5417 ... 326 B
gillian.small@mail.cuny.edu
SMALL, Hank ... 843-863-7080 ... 456 B
hsmall@csuniv.edu
SMALL, Jacquelyn ... 863-667-5157 ... 118 F
jrsmall@seu.edu
SMALL, Joe, A ... 509-526-6432 ... 539 B
joe.small@wwcc.edu
SMALL, John, J ... 630-637-5701 ... 159 G
jjsmall@noctrl.edu
SMALL, Jonathan ... 617-951-2350 ... 242 G
jonathan.small@necb.edu
SMALL, Jonathan, A ... 317-940-9249 ... 170 F
jasmall@butler.edu
SMALL, Mario ... 773-702-8798 ... 166 G
mariosmall@uchicago.edu
SMALL, Natissia ... 314-516-5128 ... 291 D
smalln@umsl.edu
SMALL, Virginia ... 718-246-6456 ... 338 G
virginia.small@liu.edu
SMALLEN, David, L ... 315-859-4169 ... 334 H
dsmallen@hamilton.edu
SMALLEY, David ... 217-732-3155 ... 156 I
dsmalley@lincolncollege.edu
SMALLEY, James ... 507-223-7252 ... 267 G
james.smalley@mnwest.edu
SMALLEY, Michelle ... 414-258-4810 ... 549 D
smalleym@mtmary.edu
SMALLEY, Reid ... 860-343-5736 ... 91 G
rsmalley@mxcc.commnet.edu
SMALLEY, Robin ... 727-864-7756 ... 105 E
smallerm@eckerd.edu
SMALLS, Eppechal, T ... 937-708-5710 ... 405 H
esmalls@wilberforce.edu
SMALLS, Gerald ... 803-705-4694 ... 455 D
smallsg@benedict.edu
SMALLS, Mary, L ... 803-536-8638 ... 460 G
smallsml@scsu.edu
SMALLWOOD, Pamela ... 417-865-2811 ... 281 G
smallwoodp@evangel.edu
SMALLWOOD, Will ... 405-878-2703 ... 409 D
will.smallwood@okbu.edu
SMARKEL, Jim ... 419-434-4203 ... 406 A
business@winebrenner.edu
SMARRELLI, JR., John ... 901-321-3250 ... 467 I
jsmarrel@cbu.edu
SMARRITO, Fiona ... 845-758-7245 ... 323 D
smarrito@bard.edu
SMART, III, Clifton, M ... 417-836-8500 ... 286 C
president@missouristate.edu
SMART, Denise, T ... 512-245-2311 ... 501 F
ds37@txstate.edu
SMART, James, G ... 305-284-4505 ... 122 I
jsmart@miami.edu
SMART, Lucille ... 315-781-3449 ... 335 F
smart@hws.edu
SMART, Robert ... 509-865-8652 ... 535 A
smart_r@heritage.edu
SMART, Scott ... 575-562-2611 ... 318 B
scott.smart@enmu.edu
SMART, William ... 615-297-7545 ... 467 A
smartb@aquinascollege.edu
SMARZIK, Linda, S ... 512-223-9214 ... 481 B
lsmarzik@austincc.edu
SMATRESK, Neal ... 702-895-3201 ... 302 I
president@unlv.edu
SMAY, Kevin ... 412-237-3094 ... 425 H
ksmay@ccac.edu
SMEATON, John, W ... 610-758-3890 ... 434 E
jws2@lehigh.edu
SMEDINGHOFF, Susan ... 708-456-0300 ... 166 F
ssmeding@triton.edu
SMEDLEY, Patricia ... 615-460-6403 ... 467 D
patricia.smedley@belmont.edu
SMEDLEY, Susan ... 361-354-2399 ... 483 B
smedleys@coastalbend.edu
SMEE, Sheryl ... 619-849-2509 ... 62 L
sherylsmee@pointloma.edu
SMEED, Shane ... 913-266-8620 ... 178 I
SMEED, Shane ... 913-266-8620 ... 17 B
SMEED, Shane ... 913-266-8620 ... 196 A
SMEED, Shane ... 913-266-8620 ... 195 I
shane.smeed@ottawa.edu
SMEED, Shane ... 913-266-8620 ... 549 H
SMELSER, Dick ... 865-694-6565 ... 475 G
rwsmelser@pstcc.edu
SMELTZ, Emily ... 724-357-5555 ... 442 F
emily.smeltz@iup.edu
SMELTZER, Brian, K ... 717-815-1293 ... 452 G
bksmeltzer@ycp.edu
SMELTZER, Jill, M ... 276-944-6923 ... 519 A
jsmeltzer@ehc.edu
SMETAK, Robert ... 312-280-3500 ... 153 B
rsmetak@aii.edu
SMETANKA, John ... 724-805-2227 ... 446 E
john.smetanka@email.stvincent.edu
SMETANKA, Julia ... 248-457-2731 ... 252 E
SMIALEK, Tami ... 706-419-1169 ... 128 B
tami.smialek@covenant.edu
SMIALEK, William ... 903-730-4890 ... 489 C
william.smialek@jarvis.edu
SMICK-ATTISANO,
Regina, A ... 603-862-1025 ... 306 C
regina.smick-attisano@unh.edu
SMID, Terry ... 563-425-5359 ... 189 G
smidt@uiu.edu
SMIELL, John, R ... 202-885-2840 ... 97 D
jsmiell@american.edu
SMIERCIAK, Marc ... 773-489-8989 ... 147 I
msmierciak@ccc.edu
SMILEY, Brad ... 903-675-6218 ... 502 F
bsmiley@tvcc.edu
SMILEY, Ellen ... 318-274-3228 ... 215 E
smileye@gram.edu
SMILEY, Joseph ... 727-712-5851 ... 116 H
smiley.joseph@spcollege.edu
SMILEY, Scott ... 432-552-2605 ... 507 D
smiley_s@utpb.edu
SMILLIE, Catherine ... 734-973-3624 ... 259 F
csmillie@wccnet.edu
SMIRNOFF, Joel ... 216-791-5000 ... 388 C
avt6@case.edu
SMIT, Cori ... 318-342-5329 ... 216 E
scroggins@ulm.edu
SMITH, A. J. Stewart ... 609-258-5590 ... 312 G
smithajs@princeton.edu
SMITH, Adrienne ... 413-755-4561 ... 241 B
asmith@stcc.edu
SMITH, Alan ... 714-997-6652 ... 39 F
smith@chapman.edu
SMITH, Alastair ... 415-338-1759 ... 37 B
aksmith@sfsu.edu
SMITH, Alex G, H ... 570-372-4109 ... 447 E
smithal@susqu.edu
SMITH, Alexa ... 870-612-2165 ... 25 E
alexa.smith@uaccb.edu
SMITH, Alfred ... 334-229-4231 ... 1 C
asmith@alasu.edu
SMITH, Alfred, S ... 334-229-4232 ... 1 C
asmith@alasu.edu
SMITH, Allison ... 360-475-7100 ... 536 D
asmith@olympic.edu
SMITH, Amy ... 310-578-1080 ... 28 L
amysmith@antioch.edu
SMITH, Amy, E ... 716-926-8877 ... 335 E
asmith@hilbert.edu
SMITH, Amy, L ... 269-337-7156 ... 252 K
amy.smith@kzoo.edu
SMITH, Andrea ... 503-552-1692 ... 417 D
acsmith@ncnm.edu
SMITH, Andrew, D ... 803-461-3277 ... 459 C
andy.smith@lr.edu
SMITH, Angela ... 720-890-8922 ... 85 F
finance@itea.edu
SMITH, Ann ... 334-229-4406 ... 1 C
annsmith@alasu.edu
SMITH, Ann, T ... 859-238-5459 ... 199 G
ann.smith@centre.edu
SMITH, Anson ... 203-332-5229 ... 91 E
asmith@hcc.commnet.edu
SMITH, Art ... 870-236-6901 ... 21 E
artsmith@crc.edu
SMITH, Ashley ... 260-359-4171 ... 173 A
asmith@huntington.edu
SMITH, Ashley ... 252-493-7229 ... 372 H
adsmith@email.pittcc.edu
SMITH, Audrey ... 215-780-1364 ... 446 G
audrey@salus.edu
SMITH, Audrey, Y ... 413-585-4900 ... 244 G
aysmith@smith.edu
SMITH, Barbara ... 205-366-8816 ... 7 F
bsmith@stillman.edu
SMITH, Barbara ... 404-756-4098 ... 125 D
bsmith@atlm.edu
SMITH, Barry, C ... 570-586-2400 ... 422 G
bsmith@bbc.edu
SMITH, Barry, V ... 731-989-6009 ... 469 B
bvsmith@fhu.edu
SMITH, Bea, W ... 864-503-5235 ... 463 B
bwsmith@uscupstate.edu
SMITH, Becky ... 770-531-6347 ... 133 C
bsmith@laniertech.edu
SMITH, Belinda ... 252-862-1220 ... 373 C
smithb@roanokechowan.edu
SMITH, Benjamin, J ... 620-431-2820 ... 195 E
bsmith@neosho.edu
SMITH, Benny, R ... 828-398-7482 ... 368 B
brsmith@abtech.edu
SMITH, Beth ... 910-576-6222 ... 372 D
smithb@montgomery.edu
SMITH, Beth ... 870-972-2586 ... 20 D
smitty@astate.edu
SMITH, Betsy, R ... 251-626-3303 ... 8 C
bsmith2@ussa.edu
SMITH, Betty ... 610-917-1426 ... 450 E
blsmith@vfcc.edu
SMITH, Betty, J ... 910-678-8250 ... 370 E
smithbj@faytechcc.edu
SMITH, Bettye Parker ... 601-977-7737 ... 277 C
bpsmith@tougaloo.edu
SMITH, Beverly ... 214-379-5412 ... 492 F
bsmith@pqc.edu
SMITH, Beverly, H ... 405-466-3204 ... 408 G
bhsmith@langston.edu
SMITH, Bill ... 401-232-6078 ... 453 C
bsmith8@bryant.edu
SMITH, Bill ... 928-314-9472 ... 12 A
bill.smith@azwestern.edu
SMITH, Bill ... 213-763-3612 ... 55 D
smithb@lattc.edu
SMITH, Billy, R ... 731-989-6623 ... 469 B
bsmith@fhu.edu
SMITH, Blair ... 480-557-1241 ... 19 A
blair.smith@phoenix.edu
SMITH, Bob ... 904-819-6332 ... 107 C
bsmith@flagler.edu
SMITH, Bob ... 806-742-2184 ... 502 A
bob.smith@ttu.edu
SMITH, Bobby ... 254-442-5111 ... 482 I
bobby.smith@cisco.edu
SMITH, Bobby ... 731-424-3520 ... 475 C
bsmith@jscc.edu
SMITH, Brad ... 719-384-6869 ... 87 A
brad.smith@ojc.edu
SMITH, Brad ... 206-264-9100 ... 531 D
brads@bgu.edu
SMITH, Brad, D ... 937-766-7872 ... 386 G
smthb@cedarville.edu
SMITH, Bradley ... 574-257-3363 ... 169 I
smithb@bethelcollege.edu
SMITH, Bradley, A ... 610-921-7529 ... 421 E
bsmith@alb.edu
SMITH, Bradley, R ... 308-432-6345 ... 299 E
bsmith@csc.edu
SMITH, Brenda ... 601-643-8318 ... 273 G
brenda.smith@colin.edu
SMITH, Brenda, A ... 585-292-2365 ... 341 H
bsmith2@monroecc.edu
SMITH, Brenda, C ... 785-227-3380 ... 191 B
bsmith@bethanylb.edu
SMITH, Brian ... 260-399-7700 ... 181 A
bsmith@sf.edu
SMITH, Brian ... 407-569-1337 ... 107 I
brian.smith@fcc.edu
SMITH, Brian ... 301-552-1400 ... 229 C
bsmith@bible.edu
SMITH, Brian ... 517-321-0242 ... 251 G
bsmith@glcc.edu
SMITH, Brian, D ... 518-255-5623 ... 354 E
smithbd@cobleskill.edu
SMITH, Brian, K ... 401-454-6207 ... 454 B
bsmith@risd.edu
SMITH, Brian, L ... 334-833-4575 ... 4 E
bsmith@huntingdon.edu
SMITH, Brian, P ... 301-552-1400 ... 229 C
bsmith@bible.edu
SMITH, Brien, N ... 812-237-2000 ... 173 B
brien.smith@indstate.edu
SMITH, Britt ... 432-264-5040 ... 488 B
bsmith@howardcollege.edu
SMITH, Bruce ... 503-777-7527 ... 420 A
smithb@reed.edu
SMITH, Bruce ... 217-244-8446 ... 167 D
smithb@law.uiuc.edu
SMITH, Bruce ... 310-434-4209 ... 68 D
smith_bruce@smc.edu
SMITH, Bruce ... 701-777-2791 ... 381 F
bsmith@aero.und.edu
SMITH, Bryan ... 270-706-8616 ... 202 A
bryan.smith@kctcs.edu
SMITH, Bryan ... 757-789-1732 ... 526 H
bsmith@es.vccs.edu
SMITH, Bryan ... 757-789-1727 ... 526 H
bsmith@es.vccs.edu
SMITH, Byron ... 315-312-3642 ... 354 A
byron.smith@oswego.edu
SMITH, Calvin ... 314-968-7138 ... 292 J
smithca@webster.edu
SMITH, Candace, E ... 202-994-3566 ... 98 C
cesmith@gwu.edu
SMITH, Carl ... 760-245-4271 ... 77 H
carl.smith@vvc.edu
SMITH, Carol ... 970-247-7265 ... 84 K
smith_c@fortlewis.edu
SMITH, Carol ... 973-278-5400 ... 307 F
crs@berkeleycollege.edu
SMITH, Carol ... 973-405-2111 ... 323 H
crs@berkeleycollege.edu
SMITH, Carol, L ... 765-658-4580 ... 171 B
clsmith@depauw.edu
SMITH, Carola ... 805-965-0581 ... 68 B
smithc@sbcc.edu
SMITH, Carolyn ... 305-273-4499 ... 103 J
carolyn@cbt.edu
SMITH, Carolyn ... 307-766-2376 ... 556 H
csmith@uwyo.edu
SMITH, Carolyn, A ... 304-697-7550 ... 541 D
csmith@huntingtonjuniorcollege.edu
SMITH, Carolyn, S ... 414-288-7184 ... 548 F
SMITH, Cary ... 715-324-6900 ... 549 G
cary.smith@ni.edu
SMITH, Catherine, E ... 585-292-2341 ... 341 H
ksmith@monroecc.edu
SMITH, Cathy, A ... 801-524-8106 ... 510 E
csmith@ldsbc.edu
SMITH, Caye ... 619-849-2313 ... 62 L
cayesmith@pointloma.edu
SMITH, Charles, M ... 770-454-9270 ... 99 G
SMITH, Charles Roger ... 202-462-2101 ... 99 A
smith@iwp.edu

SMITH, John, W 401-454-6501 454 B jsmith@risd.edu
SMITH, Johnny 828-395-1435 371 D jsmith@isothermal.edu
SMITH, Joianne 847-635-1739 160 F joismith@oakton.edu
SMITH, Jonathan, E 216-397-4605 392 L jsmith@jcu.edu
SMITH, Joseph, T 410-706-7302 227 C jtsmith@af.umaryland.edu
SMITH, Josephine 412-809-5100 444 G smith.josephine@pti.edu
SMITH, Joy, S 864-656-0471 456 E joy@clemson.edu
SMITH, Joyce 256-726-7356 6 C jsmith@oakwood.edu
SMITH, Joyya 912-478-8746 131 E jsmith@georgiasouthern.edu
SMITH, JP 513-771-2424 385 I jpsmith@brownmackie.edu
SMITH, Judith, L 310-206-3961 74 C judis@college.ucla.edu
SMITH, Judy 814-824-3650 436 C jsmith@mercyhurst.edu
SMITH, Juli 661-654-2066 34 A jsmith101@csub.edu
SMITH, June 402-481-3967 296 I june.smith@bryanlgh.org
SMITH, Justin 910-642-7141 374 B jsmith@sccnc.edu
SMITH, Kara 337-475-5148 215 G ksmith2@mcneese.edu
SMITH, Karen, J 251-981-3771 2 G karen.smith@columbiasouthern.edu
SMITH, Karen, J 914-831-0343 330 D ksmith@cw.edu
SMITH, Karina 541-888-7316 420 C ksmith@socc.edu
SMITH, Katherine 702-968-2010 303 D ksmith@roseman.edu
SMITH, Kathleen, E 562-902-3367 71 A kathleensmith@scuhs.edu
SMITH, Kathleen, M 502-852-5419 207 E kathleen@louisville.edu
SMITH, Kathryn 503-517-7462 420 A smithk@reed.edu
SMITH, Kathy 760-630-1555 52 J ksmith@kaplan.edu
SMITH, Kathy 614-234-2230 396 H ksmith@mccn.edu
SMITH, Kathy 614-292-2991 398 I
SMITH, Kathy, S 336-888-6391 365 C ksmith@highpoint.edu
SMITH, Katie, J 651-631-5222 270 B kjsmith@nwc.edu
SMITH, Katrina 806-291-3540 508 E smithk@wbu.edu
SMITH, Kay 515-244-4221 181 F smithk@aib.edu
SMITH, Kay 843-953-7402 457 B smithkh@cofc.edu
SMITH, Keisha 954-499-9661 104 J ksmith@devry.edu
SMITH, Keith 252-451-8264 372 E ksmith@nash.cc.nc.us
SMITH, Keith 973-328-5400 309 A ksmith@ccm.edu
SMITH, Keith 731-989-6053 469 B ksmith@fhu.edu
SMITH, Kelly 231-876-3107 248 A kelly.smith@baker.edu
SMITH, Kelly 907-564-8289 10 D kelsmith@alaskapacific.edu
SMITH, Kelly, A 804-523-5449 527 A kasmith@reynolds.edu
SMITH, Kenneth 508-929-8121 238 G kenneth.smith@worcester.edu
SMITH, Kenneth, A 724-847-6610 429 H kasmith@geneva.edu
SMITH, JR., Kent, J 405-466-3201 408 G kjsmith@langston.edu
SMITH, Kevin 419-995-8294 399 B smith.178@osu.edu
SMITH, Kevin, B 409-880-8400 501 A kevin.smith@lamar.edu
SMITH, Kevin, J 773-508-7605 157 C ksmit23@luc.edu
SMITH, Khrystal 864-503-5125 463 B ksmith@uscupstate.edu
SMITH, Kimberly 860-701-6540 558 H kimberly.r.smith@uscg.mil
SMITH, Kris 808-544-0840 140 G ksmith@hpu.edu
SMITH, Kris, M 703-993-8841 519 E ksmitr@gmu.edu
SMITH, Krista 229-928-1331 131 F krista.smith@gsw.edu
SMITH, Kristal 907-277-1000 10 E contact@chartercollege.edu
SMITH, Kristen 516-686-7751 343 D
SMITH, Krystal 304-462-4101 544 A krystal.smith@glenville.edu
SMITH, Kyle 325-574-7952 508 I ksmith@wtc.edu
SMITH, Kyle 325-235-7415 500 G kyle.smith@tstc.edu
SMITH, Lane, M 205-726-2905 6 G
SMITH, Larry 310-954-4018 57 H lsmith@msmc.la.edu
SMITH, LaTisha, T 314-340-3662 282 F smithl@hssu.edu
SMITH, Latoya 812-488-2413 180 E ls103@evansville.edu
SMITH, Laura 502-213-2136 202 F laura.smith@kctcs.edu
SMITH, Laura, L 361-570-4801 504 A smithl@uhv.edu
SMITH, Laura, M 252-536-7237 371 B smithl@halifaxcc.edu
SMITH, Laurens, H 435-797-2373 511 E lhsmith@cc.usu.edu
SMITH, Lawrence 516-463-7202 335 G lawrence.smith@hofstra.edu
SMITH, Lawrence, J 304-766-3011 544 F lsmith@wvstateu.edu
SMITH, Leanne 901-572-2444 467 C leanne.smith@bchs.edu
SMITH, Lee 928-541-7777 16 H lsmith@ncu.edu
SMITH, Leila 606-436-5721 202 C leila.smith@kctcs.edu
SMITH, Les 801-375-5125 510 J lsmith@rmuohp.edu
SMITH, Leslie 415-452-5132 40 C lsmith@ccsf.edu
SMITH, Leslie 601-643-8340 273 G leslie.smith@colin.edu
SMITH, Lewis 312-503-0501 160 E ljsmith@northwestern.edu
SMITH, Linda 724-836-7188 449 C ljs20@pitt.edu
SMITH, Linda 662-846-4740 273 H lindasmith@deltastate.edu
SMITH, Linda 402-572-8500 298 D lsmith@kaplan.edu
SMITH, Linda 340-693-4023 568 E lsmith@live.uvi.edu
SMITH, Linda, P 856-351-2644 315 A lsmith@salemcc.edu
SMITH, Lisa 931-363-9805 471 A lsmith@martinmethodist.edu
SMITH, Lori, A 602-216-3110 11 F losmith@argosy.edu
SMITH, Lorraine 716-375-7873 348 C lsmith@sbu.edu
SMITH, LuAnn 801-863-8472 511 F smithlu@uvu.edu
SMITH, Lura 978-656-3110 240 B smithlm@middlesex.mass.edu
SMITH, Lynn 606-546-1206 207 B tlsmith@unionky.edu
SMITH, M. Scott 859-257-4772 207 D mssmith@uky.edu
SMITH, Mable, H 702-968-2075 303 D msmith@roseman.edu
SMITH, Mackenzie 530-752-2110 73 I macsmith@ucdavis.edu
SMITH, Malia 808-543-8068 140 G msmith@hpu.edu
SMITH, Marcie 334-844-5588 1 F smithmc@auburn.edu
SMITH, Margaret 607-778-5180 324 G smithma@sunybroome.edu
SMITH, Margaret, D 931-540-2517 475 A margaret.smith@columbiastate.edu
SMITH, Marian 270-384-7351 204 D smithm@lindsey.edu
SMITH, Marian 410-225-2237 224 B mariansmith@mica.edu
SMITH, Marianne 626-914-8701 40 B msmith@citruscollege.edu
SMITH, Marianne 610-896-1298 430 G msmith@haverford.edu
SMITH, Maribel 305-628-6704 117 A maribel.smith@stu.edu
SMITH, Marilyn 303-914-6301 87 G marilyn.smith@rrcc.edu
SMITH, Marilyn 763-433-1306 265 G marilyn.smith@anokaramsey.edu
SMITH, Marilyn, T 617-253-3292 241 D
SMITH, Marjorie 304-929-1320 541 H msmith@mountainstate.edu
SMITH, Mark 607-871-2494 322 E msmith@alfred.edu
SMITH, Mark 518-276-6266 347 D smithm@rpi.edu
SMITH, Mark 904-256-7067 111 L mark@jaxbcm.com
SMITH, Mark 219-785-5211 179 A msmith@pnc.edu
SMITH, Mark, A 713-743-2619 503 D marksmith@uh.edu
SMITH, Mark, A 254-298-8344 496 D mark.a.smith@templejc.edu
SMITH, Mark, A 740-477-7713 398 D mark.smith@ohiochristian.edu
SMITH, Mark, J 765-494-2604 178 J mjts@purdue.edu
SMITH, Mark, W 314-935-6489 292 I msmith@wustl.edu
SMITH, Marla 605-995-7157 464 F marla.smith@mitchelltech.edu
SMITH, Marlaine 561-297-3207 119 A
SMITH, Marshall, W 804-594-1571 527 B msmith@jtcc.edu
SMITH, Martha, J 757-352-4070 523 E martsmi@regent.edu
SMITH, Martha, J 260-359-4040 173 A msmith@huntington.edu
SMITH, Martha, L 601-403-1269 276 E mbyrd@prcc.edu
SMITH, Martin, W 309-556-3710 153 F mwsmith@iwu.edu
SMITH, Marvin 563-288-6162 184 G msmith@eicc.edu
SMITH, Mary, A 713-500-9236 506 F mary.a.smith@uth.tmc.edu
SMITH, Mary, C 478-289-2165 129 B mcsmith@ega.edu
SMITH, Mary, E 401-841-7367 558 B
SMITH, Mary, J 701-323-6271 381 D msmith@mohs.org
SMITH, Matt 931-372-3124 474 B mrsmith@tntech.edu
SMITH, Matthew 269-399-7700 181 A msmith@sf.edu
SMITH, Matthew 717-815-6579 452 G cmsmith@ycp.edu
SMITH, Matthew, J 253-535-7545 536 E smithmf@plu.edu
SMITH, Maureen, A 617-296-8300 235 J maureen_smith@laboure.edu
SMITH, Megan 312-935-4141 162 G msmith@robertmorris.edu
SMITH, Melissa 415-439-2413 28 C mysmith@act-sf.org
SMITH, Micah 731-989-6005 469 B msmith@fhu.edu
SMITH, Michael 434-223-6219 519 G msmith@hsc.edu
SMITH, Michael 912-478-2527 131 E msmith@georgiasouthern.edu
SMITH, Michael 770-426-1193 133 E michael.smith@life.edu
SMITH, Michael 225-236-3200 214 D mike.smith@remingtoncollege.edu
SMITH, Michael 919-966-4107 378 E msmith@sog.unc.edu
SMITH, Michael 513-585-0361 387 D michael.smith@thechristcollege.edu
SMITH, Michael 806-720-7521 490 F michael.smith@lcu.edu
SMITH, Michael, D 617-495-1566 235 D mike_smith@harvard.edu
SMITH, Michael, J 401-874-4977 454 E msmith@foundation.uri.edu
SMITH, Michael, J 419-824-3723 395 E msmith@lourdes.edu
SMITH, Michael, P 704-403-3218 362 I michael.p.smith@carolinashealthcare.org
SMITH, Michael, T 314-984-7652 289 A mtsmith@stlcc.edu
SMITH, Michael, W 202-687-4798 98 D smithm4@georgetown.edu
SMITH, Michelle 225-615-3056 19 A michelle.smith2@phoenix.edu
SMITH, Mike 803-584-3446 462 E pmsmith@mailbox.sc.edu
SMITH, Mike 903-586-2518 489 B msmith@jacksonville-college.edu
SMITH, Misty 918-343-7707 411 H msmith@rsu.edu
SMITH, Morgan 252-222-6240 369 A mbs@carteret.edu
SMITH, Morgan 603-428-2477 305 D msmith@nec.edu
SMITH, Myra, D 413-755-4414 241 B msmith@stcc.edu
SMITH, JR., Myron, J 423-636-7320 477 A jsmith@tusculum.edu
SMITH, N. Daniel 864-242-5100 455 E
SMITH, Nan, L 610-359-7355 426 G nsmith@dccc.edu
SMITH, Nancy 719-255-4411 88 I nsmith2@uccs.edu
SMITH, Nancy, L 607-746-4665 355 F smithnl@delhi.edu
SMITH, Nichloas, A 508-767-7416 230 D na.smith@assumption.edu
SMITH, Nicola 425-640-1554 533 I nsmith@edcc.edu
SMITH, Noreen 212-343-1234 341 B nsmith@mcny.edu
SMITH, Norene, R 318-283-0836 210 I
SMITH, Norene, R 318-368-3179 210 K nsmith@ltc.edu
SMITH, Norma 972-599-3159 483 H nsmith@collin.edu
SMITH, Norma, M 207-768-2788 218 J nsmith@nmcc.edu
SMITH, Norman 727-864-7676 105 E smithnr@eckerd.edu
SMITH, Norman 256-228-6001 6 A smithn@nacc.edu
SMITH, Ole, M 801-422-5500 509 H ole_smith@byu.edu
SMITH, Orson 907-786-1910 10 H opsmith@uaa.alaska.edu
SMITH, Paige 936-294-3981 501 D paigesmith@shsu.edu
SMITH, Pam 303-937-4225 82 E psmith@chu.edu
SMITH, Pam 727-341-3080 116 H smith.pam@spcollege.edu
SMITH, Pamela 518-694-7268 322 B pamela.smith@acphs.edu
SMITH, Pamela, A 918-631-2329 413 F pamela-smith@utulsa.edu
SMITH, Pamela, J 215-368-5000 422 I psmith@biblical.edu
SMITH, Pat, A 559-323-2100 66 C psmith@sjcl.edu
SMITH, Patricia 909-537-5040 36 B psmith@csusb.edu
SMITH, Patricia 931-372-3331 474 B plsmith@tntech.edu
SMITH, Patricia, A 516-876-3092 353 D smithp@oldwestbury.edu
SMITH, Paul 360-867-6115 534 D smithpa@evergreen.edu
SMITH, Paul, M 616-392-8555 260 D pauls@westernsem.edu
SMITH, Paula 270-789-5211 199 F pjsmith@campbellsville.edu
SMITH, Paula, M 617-984-1654 243 H psmith@quincycollege.edu
SMITH, Paula, V 641-269-3100 185 D smithp@grinnell.edu
SMITH, Peggy 843-349-5269 458 H peggy.smith@hgtc.edu
SMITH, Peggy 340-693-1446 568 E psmith@live.uvi.edu
SMITH, Penny, L 814-871-7748 429 G smith006@gannon.edu
SMITH, Peter, L 563-589-3668 189 F plsmith@dbq.edu
SMITH, Peyton 608-262-8214 550 J plsmith@bascom.wisc.edu
SMITH, Philip 678-891-2445 131 C philip.smith@gpc.edu
SMITH, Pierre 312-935-4232 154 A psmith@icsw.edu
SMITH, Rachel, E 814-865-7641 438 G rem4@psu.edu
SMITH, Rae Marie 336-334-4822 371 A rmsmith@gtcc.edu
SMITH, Raechell 816-802-3574 283 E raechell@earthlink.net
SMITH, Ralph 605-331-6689 466 E ralph.smith@usiouxfalls.edu
SMITH, Rand 847-735-5124 155 G rsmith@lakeforest.edu
SMITH, Randall, R 626-584-5363 48 B rsmith@fuller.edu
SMITH, Randy 912-427-5829 124 C rsmith@altamahatech.edu
SMITH, Randy 920-498-5505 555 C randall.smith@nwtc.edu
SMITH, Randy, L 405-585-5810 409 D randy.smith@okbu.edu
SMITH, Rashad 270-852-3126 204 A rsmith@kwc.edu
SMITH, Rayma 513-569-1616 387 G rayma.smith@cincinnatistate.edu
SMITH, Rebecca, F 614-823-1400 400 H rsmith@otterbein.edu
SMITH, Regina 310-660-3670 45 E rsmith@elcamino.edu
SMITH, Regina 310-660-3444 45 E rsmith@elcamino.edu
SMITH, Regina 212-757-1190 322 H rtsmith@funeraleducation.org
SMITH, Rene 843-349-7835 458 H rene.smith@hgtc.edu
SMITH, Richard 770-787-8530 131 D smithr@gptc.edu
SMITH, Richard 336-272-7102 364 G richard.smith@greensboro.edu
SMITH, Richard 701-788-4697 381 H richard.e.smith@mayvillestate.edu
SMITH, Richard, A 540-375-2203 523 G rsmith@roanoke.edu
SMITH, Richard, J 314-935-4848 292 I rjsmith@wustl.edu
SMITH, Richard, L 512-223-7792 481 B rlsmith@austincc.edu
SMITH, Richard, M 972-708-7340 487 B richard_smith@gial.edu
SMITH, Richard, S 718-409-7350 356 C rsmith@sunymaritime.edu
SMITH, Rick 715-682-1597 549 F rsmith@northland.edu
SMITH, Rick, H 910-695-3716 373 H smithr@sandhills.edu
SMITH, Rilda 405-878-2416 409 D rilda.smith@okbu.edu

SMRHA, Judith .... 785-594-8337 .... 190 F
judy.smrha@bakeru.edu
SMUCKER, Amy .... 330-966-5456 .... 402 B
asmucker@starkstate.edu
SMULSON, Erik .... 202-687-0100 ...... 98 D
ems62@georgetown.edu
SMUNT, Timothy, L .... 414-229-6256 .... 551 D
tsmunt@uwm.edu
SMURDON, Melissa, J ...... 317-940-8200 .... 170 F
msmurdon@butler.edu
SMUTZ, Wayne, D .... 814-863-6726 .... 438 G
wds4@psu.edu
SMYER, Michael, A .... 570-577-1561 .... 423 E
smyer@bucknell.edu
SMYKIL, Paula .... 603-899-4341 .... 305 A
smykilp@franklinpierce.edu
SMYLE, Faye .... 707-256-7156 ...... 58 F
fsmyle@napavalley.edu
SMYRE, Russell .... 704-216-6130 .... 366 G
rsmyre@livingstone.edu
SMYRE HINES, Beverly ...... 706-771-4156 .... 125 H
bsmyre@augustatech.edu
SMYRL, Kevin, A .... 404-364-8333 .... 135 E
ksmyrl@oglethorpe.edu
SMYTH, Curt .... 207-602-2562 .... 221 A
csmyth@une.edu
SMYTH, Nancy, J .... 716-645-1267 .... 351 G
sw-dean@buffalo.edu
SMYTH-MCGAHA, Bonnie . 501-882-8826 ...... 20 C
bmsmyth@asub.edu
SMYTHE, Jennifer .... 503-352-2770 .... 419 E
smythej@pacificu.edu
SNAPP, Diana .... 207-326-2243 .... 219 D
diana.snapp@mma.edu
SNAPP, John .... 325-670-1507 .... 487 F
john.snapp@hsutx.edu
SNARE, Charles .... 308-432-6203 .... 299 E
csnare@csc.edu
SNAVELY, Deanne .... 724-357-2609 .... 442 F
deanne.snavely@iup.edu
SNEAD, III, L. Rucker ...... 434-223-6106 .... 519 G
rsnead@hsc.edu
SNEDDEN, Kelly .... 316-942-4291 .... 195 F
sneddenk@newmanu.edu
SNEDDON, Jay, N .... 208-732-6247 .... 143 E
jsneddon@csi.edu
SNEED, Bronwyn, C .... 870-235-4023 ...... 23 I
bcsneed@saumag.edu
SNEED, Carlos .... 651-523-2423 .... 264 A
csneed@hamline.edu
SNEED, Donna .... 314-984-7513 .... 289 A
dsneed20@stlcc.edu
SNEED, Janice .... 318-670-9471 .... 215 A
jsneed@susla.edu
SNEED, Mike .... 501-812-2238 ...... 23 C
msneed@pulaskitech.edu
SNEERINGER, Megan .... 215-641-6535 .... 436 G
msneerin@mc3.edu
SNELL, Carolyn, R .... 803-535-5338 .... 456 D
csnell@claflin.edu
SNELL, Cudore, L .... 202-806-7300 ...... 98 E
csnell@howard.edu
SNELL, Kim .... 937-298-3399 .... 394 D
kim.snell@kcma.edu
SNELL, Laurence, I .... 904-632-3294 .... 109 F
lsnell@fscj.edu
SNELLGROVE, Michael, R . 256-824-2560 ...... 8 G
michael.snellgrove@uah.edu
SNELLING, John .... 602-787-6840 ...... 15 J
john.snelling@paradisevalley.edu
SNELSON, Pamela .... 717-291-3843 .... 429 F
pam.snelson@fandm.edu
SNIDER, Ann .... 614-253-3537 .... 398 F
snidera@ohiodominican.edu
SNIDER, Darlene .... 509-527-3689 .... 539 B
darlene.snider@wwcc.edu
SNIDER, Dean, C .... 509-527-5288 .... 540 B
sniderdc@whitman.edu
SNIDER, Donnie .... 325-674-2946 .... 478 I
donnie.snider@acu.edu
SNIDER, Dwayne .... 254-968-9103 .... 497 A
snider@tarleton.edu
SNIDER, Glen .... 928-428-8217 ...... 14 B
glen.snider@eac.edu
SNIDER, Katharine, J .... 717-291-3989 .... 429 F
kate.snider@fandm.edu
SNIDER, Kevin, J .... 724-334-6051 .... 440 C
kjs33@psu.edu
SNIDER, Lisa .... 318-371-3035 .... 211 C
lsnider@ltc.edu
SNIDER, Lora .... 859-622-2246 .... 200 J
lora.snider@eku.edu
SNIDER, Neil .... 205-652-3614 .... 9 E
nsnider@uwa.edu
SNIP, Bob .... 502-897-4703 .... 206 C
besnip@sbts.edu
SNIPES, Lloyd .... 803-327-7402 .... 456 F
SNITKER, Connie .... 319-363-8213 .... 187 H
csnitker@mtmercy.edu
SNODDY, Catherine, E ...... 304-697-7550 .... 541 D
csnoddy@huntingtonjuniorcollege.edu
SNODDY, Rebeckah .... 765-973-8585 .... 173 F
rrieder@iue.edu
SNODGRASS, Burnie, L ...... 417-836-4040 .... 286 C
bsnodgrass@missouristate.edu
SNODGRASS, Gregory ...... 512-245-2208 .... 501 F
gs03@txstate.edu
SNODGRASS, Madelyn ...... 512-472-4133 .... 494 F
madelyn.snodgrass@ssw.edu
SNODGRASS, Mark, T ...... 815-740-3432 .... 167 E
msnodgrass@stfrancis.edu
SNODGRASS, Wendell ...... 563-425-5202 .... 189 G
snodgrassw@uiu.edu
SNOE, Terri .... 412-392-4207 .... 445 A
tsnoe@pointpark.edu
SNOOK, Dawn .... 704-637-4416 .... 363 E
dsnook@catawba.edu
SNOREK, Karen .... 507-332-5890 .... 269 D
karen.snorek@southcentral.edu
SNOVER, Lydia, S .... 617-253-5838 .... 241 D
SNOW, Barbara .... 607-962-9223 .... 331 C
snow@corning-cc.edu
SNOW, Brent .... 210-784-1200 .... 498 E
brent.snow@tamusa.tamus.edu
SNOW, Cathy, C .... 478-757-5173 .... 139 E
csnow@wesleyancollege.edu
SNOW, Gregory, J .... 408-944-6008 ...... 61 A
greg.snow@palmer.edu
SNOW, Joe .... 918-781-7245 .... 407 B
snowj@bacone.edu
SNOW, Kathryn .... 815-288-5511 .... 164 B
snowk@svcc.edu
SNOW, Laura .... 816-483-9600 .... 289 E
laura.snow@spst.edu
SNOW, Laura .... 801-581-5113 .... 511 C
laura.snow@utah.edu
SNOW, Marie .... 904-470-8124 .... 105 G
marie.snow@ewc.edu
SNOW, Natalie .... 610-683-4153 .... 443 A
snow@kutztown.edu
SNOW, Nicholas .... 973-761-9018 .... 315 B
nicholas.snow@shu.edu
SNOW-FLAMER, Keith ...... 707-476-4177 ...... 42 C
keith-snowflamer@redwoods.edu
SNOW FLESHER, LeAnn ... 510-841-1905 ...... 27 J
lflesher@absw.edu
SNOWDEN, Bradley, C ...... 540-665-5455 .... 524 E
bsnowden@su.edu
SNOWDEN, Kent .... 334-241-9783 .... 8 A
kesnowden@troy.edu
SNOWDEN, Michael, T ...... 337-475-5426 .... 215 G
msnowden@mcneese.edu
SNOWDEN, Monique, L .... 805-898-4154 ...... 47 C
msnowden@fielding.edu
SNOWDEN, Scott .... 908-737-5170 .... 311 A
snowdens@kean.edu
SNOWHILL, Lucia .... 805-893-5383 ...... 75 B
snowhill@library.ucsb.edu
SNUFFIN, Gary .... 901-722-3260 .... 473 C
gsnuffin@sco.edu
SNUGGS, Kristi, L .... 252-823-5166 .... 370 D
snuggsk@edgecombe.edu
SNYDER, Alan, J .... 610-758-6964 .... 434 E
ajs410@lehigh.edu
SNYDER, Alan, R .... 301-687-4242 .... 228 C
arsnyder@frostburg.edu
SNYDER, Andrea .... 717-545-4747 .... 432 F
SNYDER, Angie, P .... 479-248-7236 ...... 21 G
angie@ecollege.edu
SNYDER, Arthur, E .... 260-422-5561 .... 173 C
aesnyder@indianatech.edu
SNYDER, Barbara, H .... 801-581-7793 .... 511 C
bsnyder@sa.utah.edu
SNYDER, Barbara, R .... 216-368-4344 .... 386 F
barbara.snyder@case.edu
SNYDER, C. Vernon .... 419-530-4249 .... 404 F
vernon.snyder@utoledo.edu
SNYDER, Chris .... 724-830-1895 .... 447 C
csnyder@setonhill.edu
SNYDER, Christopher .... 662-325-2522 .... 275 F
cas741@msstate.edu
SNYDER, Cindy, L .... 540-654-2062 .... 525 D
csnyder@umw.edu
SNYDER, Connie .... 229-248-2504 .... 126 A
csnyder@bainbridge.edu
SNYDER, Daniel, C .... 303-975-5010 ...... 89 H
dsnyder@westwood.edu
SNYDER, David .... 415-485-9506 ...... 42 B
david.snyder@marin.edu
SNYDER, David, W .... 717-545-4747 .... 432 F
SNYDER, Deborah .... 202-408-2400 ...... 99 G
SNYDER, Dee Dee .... 330-287-1223 .... 399 A
snyder.426@osu.edu
SNYDER, Diane, E .... 210-485-0010 .... 479 A
dsnyder12@alamo.edu
SNYDER, Dianne, O .... 704-403-1521 .... 362 I
dianne.snyder@carolinashealthcare.org
SNYDER, Donald .... 702-895-3308 .... 302 I
donald.snyder@unlv.edu
SNYDER, Donald, W .... 610-799-1121 .... 434 D
dsnyder@lccc.edu
SNYDER, Edward, A .... 203-432-6035 ...... 96 A
edward.snyder@yale.edu
SNYDER, Gerry .... 505-473-6292 .... 320 F
gerry.snyder@santafeuniversity.edu
SNYDER, Grant, S .... 610-359-5060 .... 426 G
gsnyder@dccc.edu
SNYDER, Gregory, J .... 810-762-3488 .... 259 C
gsnyders@umflint.edu
SNYDER, Jackie .... 315-866-0300 .... 335 D
snyderje@herkimer.edu
SNYDER, Jan, E .... 712-324-5061 .... 188 C
jsnyder@nwicc.edu
SNYDER, Jane .... 617-232-8026 .... 232 D
snyderj@bgsp.edu
SNYDER, Jason .... 205-970-9235 .... 7 C
jsnyder@sebc.edu
SNYDER, Jeff, B .... 651-631-5142 .... 270 B
jbsnyder@nwc.edu
SNYDER, Jenefer .... 757-822-2430 .... 528 G
jsnyder@tcc.edu
SNYDER, Jim .... 859-336-5082 .... 206 A
jsnyder@sccky.edu
SNYDER, John, F .... 724-738-2028 .... 443 F
john.snyder@sru.edu
SNYDER, John, R .... 419-995-8300 .... 399 B
snyder.4@osu.edu
SNYDER, Jon, D .... 212-875-4466 .... 323 C
jsnyder@bankstreet.edu
SNYDER, Julie, A .... 419-372-9623 .... 385 E
jmaiuri@bgsu.edu
SNYDER, Katherine .... 301-687-4105 .... 228 C
ksnyder@frostburg.edu
SNYDER, Keith .... 423-236-2929 .... 473 B
kasnyder@southern.edu
SNYDER, Kenneth .... 517-629-0213 .... 247 A
ksnyder@albion.edu
SNYDER, Ky, L .... 619-260-2930 ...... 76 D
kysnyder@sandiego.edu
SNYDER, Linda, L .... 603-646-2485 .... 304 J
linda.l.snyder@dartmouth.edu
SNYDER, Lisa .... 864-977-7669 .... 460 A
lisa.snyder@ngu.edu
SNYDER, Lisa, M .... 260-356-4070 .... 173 A
lsnyder@huntington.edu
SNYDER, Lorraine, G .... 312-915-6411 .... 157 C
lsnyde2@luc.edu
SNYDER, Marcella .... 304-336-8345 .... 544 D
msnyder@westliberty.edu
SNYDER, Marian, L .... 610-799-1734 .... 434 D
msnyder@lccc.edu
SNYDER, Mary .... 719-255-4119 ...... 88 I
mary.snyder@uccs.edu
SNYDER, Mary Beth .... 248-370-4200 .... 256 G
mbsnyder@oakland.edu
SNYDER, Matthew .... 315-792-5331 .... 341 E
msnyder2@mvcc.edu
SNYDER, Ned .... 910-392-4660 .... 367 D
SNYDER, Paul .... 239-590-7050 .... 119 B
psnyder@fgcu.edu
SNYDER, Peggy .... 602-235-4179 .... 196 C
psnyder@pittstate.edu
SNYDER, Randolph .... 614-947-6024 .... 391 B
randy.snyder@franklin.edu
SNYDER, Reonna .... 515-244-4221 .... 181 F
snyderr@aib.edu
SNYDER, Rob, A .... 724-287-8711 .... 423 G
rob.snyder@bc3.edu
SNYDER, Robert, A .... 707-826-3722 ...... 36 E
ras1@humboldt.edu
SNYDER, Robert, J .... 610-282-1100 .... 427 A
robert.snyder@desales.edu
SNYDER, Ryan .... 716-270-5119 .... 333 C
ascsnyderr@ecc.edu
SNYDER, Sandra .... 503-552-1514 .... 417 D
ssnyder@ncnm.edu
SNYDER, Sheri .... 580-628-6208 .... 409 B
sheri.snyder@north-ok.edu
SNYDER, Stephen, E .... 229-931-2037 .... 131 F
stephen.snyder@gsw.edu
SNYDER, Steven, C .... 540-636-2900 .... 517 K
ssnyder@christendom.edu
SNYDER, Susan, M .... 716-829-3316 .... 351 G
student-health@buffalo.edu
SNYDER, Terry .... 610-896-1272 .... 430 G
tsnyder@haverford.edu
SNYDER, Thomas, J .... 317-921-4265 .... 175 I
tsnyder@ivytech.edu
SNYDER, Timothy, L .... 410-617-2495 .... 223 I
tlsnyder@loyola.edu
SNYDER, Vicki .... 740-392-6868 .... 396 I
vsnyder@mvnu.edu
SNYDER, Walter, W .... 816-654-7122 .... 283 F
wsnyder@kcumb.edu
SOARDS, Kathy .... 419-267-1314 .... 397 E
ksoards@northweststate.edu
SOBA, Steven .... 603-645-9611 .... 305 I
s.soba@snhu.edu
SOBANET, Jennifer .... 303-404-5560 ...... 85 A
jennifer.sobanet@frontrange.edu
SOBCZYK, Jim .... 415-502-5256 ...... 75 A
jsobczyk@ucsf.edu
SOBEK, Christine, J .... 630-466-7900 .... 168 B
csobek@waubonsee.edu
SOBH, Tarek, M .... 203-576-4111 ...... 94 F
sobh@bridgeport.edu
SOBIESUO, Andrew .... 843-953-5537 .... 457 B
sobiesuoa@cofc.edu
SOBINA, Debra .... 814-676-6591 .... 442 C
dsobina@clarion.edu
SOBISCH, Andreas .... 216-397-4183 .... 392 L
sobisch@jcu.edu
SOBKY-SHAFFER, Yvette ... 310-665-6819 ...... 60 B
ysobky@otis.edu
SOBLEY, Susan .... 662-329-7210 .... 276 A
ssobley@comptroller.muw.edu
SOBOLESKE, Mark .... 303-986-2320 ...... 83 A
marks@csha.net
SOBOTOR, William, J .... 901-572-2772 .... 467 C
bill.sobotor@bchs.edu
SOBOTTA, Sharon .... 925-631-4193 ...... 64 F
ssobotta@stmarys-ca.edu
SOCCI, Patrick, J .... 516-463-5676 .... 335 G
patrick.socci@hofstra.edu
SOCHA, Maureen .... 413-755-4460 .... 241 B
mesocha@stcc.edu
SOCKWELL, Patricia .... 301-431-5415 .... 225 B
psockwell@nlc.edu
SOCORRO, Julio .... 954-965-7272 .... 107 D
SODEN, Richard .... 212-938-4030 .... 355 B
rsoden@sunyopt.edu
SODERBERG, Lynn .... 707-826-5555 ...... 36 E
lls47@humboldt.edu
SODERQUIST, Rich .... 815-802-8173 .... 155 A
rsoderquist@kcc.edu
SOEFFING, William .... 605-331-6759 .... 466 E
william.soeffing@usiouxfalls.edu
SOEFFKER-CULICERTO,
Heike, I .... 304-929-6731 .... 543 A
hsoeffker@newriver.edu
SOFFA, Kari .... 661-362-5417 ...... 41 I
kari.soffa@canyons.edu
SOFISH, Marion .... 408-283-7500 ...... 37 C
marion.sofish@sjsu.edu
SOFO, Dianna .... 973-290-4478 .... 308 G
dsofo@cse.edu
SOFRANKO, Greg .... 724-938-4274 .... 441 G
sofranko@calu.edu
SOFTLEIGH, George .... 718-270-6095 .... 328 C
george@mec.cuny.edu
SOHAN, Donna .... 860-412-7261 ...... 92 D
dsohan@qvcc.commnet.edu
SOHL, Amanda .... 614-236-6574 .... 386 E
asteiner@capital.edu
SOHM, Michael .... 952-446-4161 .... 263 C
sohmm@crown.edu
SOHN, Christopher .... 937-766-2789 .... 386 G
chrissohn@cedarville.edu
SOHN, Eugene .... 718-518-4284 .... 327 D
esohn@hostos.cuny.edu
SOHOLT, Pam, B .... 701-788-4823 .... 381 H
pam.soholt@mayvillestate.edu
SOIFER, Aviam .... 808-956-6363 .... 141 G
soifer@hawaii.edu
SOIFER, B, T .... 626-395-4241 ...... 32 H
pmachair@caltech.edu
SOIFER, Yitzchok .... 845-362-3053 .... 323 F
SOIFFER, Stephen .... 718-260-5400 .... 328 D
ssoiffer@citytech.cuny.edu
SOIKA, Brian .... 713-348-4726 .... 493 C
brian.soika@rice.edu
SOILEAU, Deidre .... 410-209-6045 .... 221 E
dsoileau@bccc.edu
SOILEAU, M, J .... 407-823-5538 .... 120 B
mj@ucf.edu
SOJKA, Gregory, S .... 513-732-5209 .... 403 E
sojkagy@email.uc.edu
SOJO, Norma, I .... 787-265-3810 .... 567 F
library@uprm.edu
SOKANY, Stephen, G .... 330-672-2222 .... 393 D
ssokany@kent.edu
SOKENU, Julius .... 805-378-1448 ...... 77 D
jsokenu@vcccd.edu
SOKOL, Karen, A .... 973-642-8738 .... 315 C
karen.sokol@shu.edu
SOKOL, Moshe, Z .... 718-820-4800 .... 358 B
sokolm@touro.edu
SOKOLS, Patricia, L .... 864-488-8255 .... 459 B
psokols@limestone.edu
SOKOLSKY, Pierre, V .... 801-581-6958 .... 511 C
ps@physics.utah.edu
SOLA, Peter, L .... 651-631-5349 .... 270 B
plsola@nwc.edu
SOLAN, George .... 252-399-6399 .... 362 E
gsolan@barton.edu
SOLANA, Tony .... 305-821-3333 .... 109 B
tsolana@mm.fnc.edu
SOLANA, Tony .... 305-821-3333 .... 109 C
tsolana@mm.fnc.edu
SOLAND, Nathan .... 507-786-3310 .... 271 C
solandn@stolaf.edu
SOLANDER, Sondra, K .... 620-431-2820 .... 195 E
ssolander@neosho.edu
SOLANO, Hugo .... 787-725-6500 .... 561 A
nsolano@sju.albizu.edu
SOLANO, Laura .... 719-549-3221 ...... 87 F
laura.solano@pueblocc.edu
SOLARI, Joe, P .... 317-788-3425 .... 180 F
jsolari@uindy.edu
SOLBACH, Robin .... 732-987-2681 .... 310 C
solbach@georgian.edu
SOLBERG, Bennett .... 703-821-8570 .... 524 J
bsolberg@stratford.edu

SOLBERG, Eric, J ... 563-588-7969 ... 187 C
eric.solberg@loras.edu
SOLBERG, Larry ... 715-425-3774 ... 552 C
larry.c.solberg@uwrf.edu
SOLBERG, Lori ... 605-995-2805 ... 464 C
losolber@dwu.edu
SOLBERG, Susan, R ... 708-709-3758 ... 161 D
ssolberg@prairiestate.edu
SOLBRIG, Ronald ... 208-282-2330 ... 143 H
solbrona@isu.edu
SOLDWISCH, Sandie ... 708-763-1598 ... 162 E
sandie.soldwisch@resu.edu
SOLEMSAAS, Rachel ... 775-673-7013 ... 302 H
rsolemsaas@tmcc.edu
SOLES, David ... 212-998-8259 ... 344 B
david.soles@nyu.edu
SOLES, Jason ... 903-923-2011 ... 486 F
jsoles@etbu.edu
SOLHEIM, Derek, N ... 319-352-8330 ... 189 J
derek.solheim@wartburg.edu
SOLHEIM, Joan, C ... 704-847-5600 ... 377 B
jsolheim@ses.edu
SOLINGA, Elaine, F ... 860-439-2058 ... 92 G
efsol@conncoll.edu
SOLINGER, Diane, P ... 218-477-2322 ... 267 F
solinger@mnstate.edu
SOLIS, Enrique ... 512-223-7612 ... 481 B
enrique.solis@austincc.edu
SOLIS, JR., Federico ... 956-764-5866 ... 489 J
fsolis@laredo.edu
SOLIS, Rafael ... 787-758-2525 ... 567 G
rafael.solis@upr.edu
SOLIS, Robert ... 774-455-7711 ... 236 E
rsolis@umassp.edu
SOLIS, Vincent, R ... 956-764-5950 ... 489 J
vincent.solis@laredo.edu
SOLITRO, Patricia, A ... 508-854-4203 ... 240 F
pats@qcc.mass.edu
SOLIZ, Sandra ... 713-525-3103 ... 505 A
solizs@stthom.edu
SOLL, Andrew ... 978-542-6120 ... 238 E
asoll@salemstate.edu
SOLLARS, David ... 785-670-2045 ... 197 F
david.sollars@washburn.edu
SOLLENBERGER, Donna, K ... 409-772-6116 ... 507 C
dksoll@utmb.edu
SOLLER, Dan ... 301-447-7407 ... 225 A
soller@msmary.edu
SOLLER, Kerry ... 614-251-4718 ... 398 F
sollerk@ohiodominican.edu
SOLLEY, Anna ... 602-285-7433 ... 16 A
anna.solley@pcmail.maricopa.edu
SOLLOSI, Nancy, B ... 336-334-4822 ... 371 A
nbsollosi@gtcc.edu
SOLMS, Daniel ... 765-677-2138 ... 175 B
daniel.solms@indwes.edu
SOLNICK, Steven, L ... 828-298-3325 ... 380 D
president@warren-wilson.edu
SOLODUCHA, Kathy, J ... 816-501-4250 ... 288 A
kathy.soloducha@rockhurst.edu
SOLOFF, Laura ... 310-314-6021 ... 30 A
SOLOMON, Aron ... 718-854-2290 ... 323 I
rabbisolomon@bhsy.org
SOLOMON, Brenda ... 310-303-7293 ... 56 F
bsolomom@marymountpv.edu
SOLOMON, Daniel, L ... 919-515-7277 ... 378 C
solomon@ncsu.edu
SOLOMON, Debbie ... 425-235-2352 ... 537 A
dsolomon@rtc.edu
SOLOMON, Eric, S ... 214-828-8408 ... 497 C
esolomon@bcd.tamhsc.edu
SOLOMON, Ira ... 504-865-5422 ... 215 C
isolomon@tulane.edu
SOLOMON, Jeffrey, S ... 508-831-5288 ... 246 F
solomon@wpi.edu
SOLOMON, Jeremy ... 781-239-3122 ... 239 G
jsolomon@massbay.edu
SOLOMON, Jill ... 617-277-3915 ... 232 D
jsolomon@bgsp.edu
SOLOMON, Laura ... 212-217-3650 ... 333 F
laura_solomon@fitnyc.edu
SOLOMON, Mark, R ... 248-689-8282 ... 259 E
msolomon@walshcollege.edu
SOLOMON, Mary Ellen ... 412-392-6190 ... 445 A
mesolomon@pointpark.edu
SOLOMON, Mendel ... 973-267-9404 ... 313 B
rabbisolo@aol.com
SOLOMON, Michelle ... 256-726-7508 ... 6 C
msolomon@oakwood.edu
SOLOMON, Rayman, L ... 856-225-6191 ... 314 D
raysol@camlaw.rutgers.edu
SOLOMON, Robert ... 912-754-2879 ... 136 H
rsolomon@savannahtech.edu
SOLOMON, Samuel, B ... 617-373-2597 ... 243 F
SOLOMON, Shoshana ... 973-267-9404 ... 313 B
rca069@aol.com
SOLOMON, Sigrid, B ... 937-382-6661 ... 405 I
sigrid_solomon@wilmington.edu
SOLOMON, William, G ... 478-301-2771 ... 134 A
solomon_wg@mercer.edu
SOLOMONS, Mary, L ... 518-580-5619 ... 351 B
msolomon@skidmore.edu
SOLOMONSON, Heidi ... 651-213-4126 ... 264 B
SOLORZANO, Fernando ... 562-985-4101 ... 35 C
fsolorza@csulb.edu
SOLT, Karen ... 630-942-2292 ... 148 A
soltka@cod.edu
SOLT, Michael ... 562-985-5306 ... 35 C
msolt@csulb.edu
SOLTAN, Joanna ... 617-369-3655 ... 244 E
jsoltan@smfa.edu
SOLTIS, Corinne ... 907-796-6255 ... 11 A
corinne.soltic@uas.alaska.edu
SOLTIS, Karen ... 412-291-6322 ... 422 E
ksoltis@aii.edu
SOLTIS, Kay, W ... 253-535-8725 ... 536 E
soltiskw@plu.edu
SOLTMAN, Mary ... 360-596-5210 ... 538 E
msoltman@spscc.ctc.edu
SOLTYS, Jonathan ... 630-889-6620 ... 159 F
jsoltys@nuhs.edu
SOLTZ, David, L ... 570-389-4526 ... 441 F
dsoltz@bloomu.edu
SOLVERSON, Natalie ... 608-785-8006 ... 551 C
nsolverson@uwlax.edu
SOM, Andrew ... 415-338-3145 ... 37 B
asom@sfsu.edu
SOMAN, Rajiv, S ... 513-732-5212 ... 403 E
somanrs@ucmail.uc.edu
SOMAN, Sherril ... 616-331-3327 ... 251 F
somans@gvsu.edu
SOMER, Marcia ... 925-685-1230 ... 43 F
msomer@dvc.edu
SOMERA, R. Ray, D ... 671-735-5528 ... 559 E
reneray.somera@guamcc.edu
SOMERO, Marty ... 970-351-2502 ... 89 B
marty.somero@unco.edu
SOMERS, Christine ... 570-674-6314 ... 436 F
csomers@misericordia.edu
SOMERS, Cindy ... 303-797-5972 ... 81 D
cindy.somers@arapahoe.edu
SOMERS, Kevin ... 870-743-3000 ... 22 G
ksomers@northark.edu
SOMERS, Michael ... 508-531-1256 ... 237 D
msomers@bridgew.edu
SOMERS, Micki ... 870-743-3000 ... 22 G
msomers@northark.edu
SOMERS, Robert, J ... 410-455-2695 ... 227 D
somers@umbc.edu
SOMERS, Vickie, L ... 336-278-5584 ... 364 D
somersv@elon.edu
SOMERSON, Rosanne ... 401-277-4945 ... 454 B
rsomerso@risd.edu
SOMERVELL, Ronald ... 703-284-6941 ... 521 D
ronald.somervell@marymount.edu
SOMERVILLE, Charles ... 304-696-2424 ... 544 B
somervil@marshall.edu
SOMERVILLE, Dionne, D ... 570-389-4062 ... 441 F
dsomervi@bloomu.edu
SOMERVILLE, Mary ... 303-556-4587 ... 88 J
mary.somerville@ucdenver.edu
SOMERVILLE, Tim ... 951-719-2994 ... 63 C
doc@golfcollege.edu
SOMERVILLE, Tom ... 216-987-4883 ... 389 B
tom.somerville@tri-c.edu
SOMICH, Michael, L ... 919-613-7611 ... 364 C
msomich@duke.edu
SOMMA, Ann Marie ... 518-327-6201 ... 345 H
asomma@paulsmiths.edu
SOMMA, Lauren ... 951-781-2727 ... 64 C
lsomma@sagecollege.edu
SOMMA, Victor ... 508-425-1216 ... 240 F
vsomma@qcc.mass.edu
SOMMER, John ... 201-360-4042 ... 310 E
jsommer@hccc.edu
SOMMER, Maralyn, T ... 870-230-5320 ... 21 I
sommerm@hsu.edu
SOMMER, Sally, W ... 419-358-3317 ... 385 D
sommers@bluffton.edu
SOMMER, Toni ... 805-546-3120 ... 43 I
tsommer@cuesta.edu
SOMMER-KRESSE, Sue ... 843-953-6684 ... 457 B
sommerkresses@cofc.edu
SOMMERFELD, Curtis ... 541-956-7238 ... 420 B
curt@roguecc.edu
SOMMERFELD, Curtis ... 541-956-7016 ... 420 B
curt@roguecc.edu
SOMMERFELDT, Scott, D ... 801-422-2674 ... 509 H
scott_sommerfeldt@byu.edu
SOMMERS, Bill ... 970-945-8691 ... 82 G
SOMMERS, Janet, B ... 651-631-5201 ... 270 B
jbsommers@nwc.edu
SOMMERS, Mary ... 308-865-8520 ... 300 F
sommersm@unk.edu
SOMMERS, Mary, C ... 713-942-5048 ... 505 A
sommers@stthom.edu
SOMMERS, Rhoda, C ... 330-471-8538 ... 395 F
rsommers@malone.edu
SOMMERVILLE, Jan ... 616-632-2881 ... 247 E
sommejan@aquinas.edu
SOMMERVILLE, Sandi ... 407-905-2200 ... 115 E
SOMMERVILLE, Tim ... 407-905-2200 ... 115 E
SOMPOLSKI, Robert ... 847-635-1690 ... 160 F
somplski@oakton.edu
SOMVICHIAN, Kamol ... 323-731-2383 ... 60 H
ksomvichian@psuca.edu
SON, Brian ... 312-752-2504 ... 155 C
brian.son@kendall.edu
SONDER, Henk, E ... 401-456-9577 ... 454 A
hsonder@ric.edu
SONDEY, Joann ... 914-831-0288 ... 330 D
jsondey@cw.edu
SONDEY, Stephen ... 201-684-7496 ... 313 C
ssondey@ramapo.edu
SONENBERG, Dave ... 402-437-2619 ... 300 B
dsonenbe@southeast.edu
SONES, Amerian ... 214-828-8478 ... 497 C
sones@bcd.tamhsc.edu
SONES, Rodney ... 740-477-7786 ... 398 D
rsones@ohiochristian.edu
SONEY, Ralph, G ... 252-862-1308 ... 373 C
soneyr@roanokechowan.edu
SONG, A. Li ... 516-364-0808 ... 343 A
asong@nycollege.edu
SONG, Connie ... 513-231-2223 ... 384 H
csong@athenaeum.edu
SONG, Hee Sook ... 770-279-0507 ... 130 A
academic@gcuniv.edu
SONG, Hee Sook ... 770-279-0507 ... 130 A
financial.aid@gcuniv.edu
SONG, John, M ... 213-385-2322 ... 79 I
SONG, Shin-Min (Simon) ... 330-672-2644 ... 393 D
ssong3@kent.edu
SONGER, Dan ... 814-362-7506 ... 449 B
songer@pitt.edu
SONGSTER, Nora ... 707-546-4000 ... 45 H
nsongster@empirecollege.com
SONI, P. Sarita ... 812-855-3931 ... 173 E
sonip@indiana.edu
SONI, Varun ... 213-740-6110 ... 76 F
vasoni@usc.edu
SONJA, Daniels ... 310-243-3784 ... 34 D
sdaniels@csudh.edu
SONNEMA, Roy ... 719-549-2865 ... 83 H
roy.sonnema@colostate-pueblo.edu
SONNENBERG, Jeff ... 602-557-1740 ... 19 A
jeff.sonnenberg@phoenix.edu
SONNENBERG, Judith ... 512-863-1252 ... 496 A
sonnenbj@southwestern.edu
SONNENBERGER, David ... 630-829-6538 ... 145 G
dsonnenberger@ben.edu
SONNENBLICK, Carol ... 718-552-1170 ... 328 D
csonnenblick@citytech.cuny.edu
SONNENFELD, Gerald ... 864-656-7701 ... 456 E
sonneng@clemson.edu
SONNENSTEIN, Mark ... 718-933-6700 ... 341 G
ssonnenstein@monroecollege.edu
SONNENSTRAHL, Samuel ... 202-651-5060 ... 98 B
samuel.sonnenstrahl@gallaudet.edu
SONNER, Mary ... 423-636-7345 ... 477 A
msonner@tusculum.edu
SONNLEITNER, Thomas, G ... 920-424-3030 ... 551 E
sonnleit@uwosh.edu
SONNTAG, Dave ... 509-313-6192 ... 534 F
sonntagd@gonzaga.edu
SONNTAG, Gabriela ... 909-748-8096 ... 76 C
gabriela_sonntag@redlands.edu
SONNTAG, Michael, E ... 207-768-9520 ... 220 F
michael.sonntag@umpi.edu
SONOBE, Blake, I ... 580-774-3771 ... 412 F
blake.sonobe@swosu.edu
SONODA, Kazuhiro ... 509-865-8581 ... 535 A
sonoda_k@heritage.edu
SONQUIST, Eric, J ... 805-893-8585 ... 75 B
eric.sonquist@ia.ucsb.edu
SONSTEBY, Jill ... 651-638-6254 ... 261 D
jks44888@bethel.edu
SOOHOO, Liane ... 206-239-2222 ... 531 B
lsoohoo@aii.edu
SOONS, Peter, D ... 802-654-2374 ... 514 D
psoons@smcvt.edu
SOOS, Lori ... 716-286-8390 ... 344 D
lsoos@niagara.edu
SOOY, Lindsay ... 419-448-2340 ... 391 F
lsooy@heidelberg.edu
SOPCICH, Joseph, M ... 913-469-8500 ... 194 B
jsopcich@jccc.edu
SOPCZYK, Debbie ... 518-464-8728 ... 333 E
dsopczyk@excelsior.edu
SOPER, Elaine ... 304-647-6260 ... 544 E
esoper@osteo.wvsom.edu
SOPER, Sarah ... 765-973-8231 ... 173 F
saeaton@iue.edu
SOPKO, Bryn ... 503-943-7331 ... 420 G
sopko@up.edu
SOPP, Linda ... 413-577-4016 ... 236 F
lsopp@admin.umass.edu
SORA, Gail ... 603-623-0313 ... 305 E
gsora@nhia.edu
SORACI, Ross ... 617-739-1700 ... 243 A
rsoraci@aii.edu
SORBER, Ken ... 801-274-3280 ... 512 F
ksorber@wgu.edu
SORBER, Todd ... 973-684-5656 ... 312 E
tsorber@pccc.edu
SORCE, Tanya ... 973-290-4465 ... 308 G
tsorce@cse.edu
SORDELET, Teresa ... 260-399-7700 ... 181 A
tsordelet@sf.edu
SORELLE, Patrick ... 920-465-2323 ... 551 B
sorellep@uwgb.edu
SOREM, James ... 918-631-2288 ... 413 F
james-sorem@utulsa.edu
SORENSEN, Carl, K ... 804-289-8166 ... 525 E
csorense@richmond.edu
SORENSEN, Charles, W ... 715-232-2441 ... 552 E
sorensenc@uwstout.edu
SORENSEN, Cheri ... 602-387-5814 ... 19 A
cheri.sorensen@phoenix.edu
SORENSEN, Dennis ... 815-802-8360 ... 155 A
dsorensen@kcc.edu
SORENSEN, Gary ... 928-428-8247 ... 14 B
gary.sorensen@eac.edu
SORENSEN, Niles, F ... 704-687-7201 ... 379 A
nfsorens@uncc.edu
SORENSEN, Rachel ... 515-244-4221 ... 181 F
sorensenr@aib.edu
SORENSEN, Richard, E ... 540-231-6601 ... 529 G
sorensen@vt.edu
SORENSEN, Robin ... 704-378-1048 ... 366 A
rsorensen@jcsu.edu
SORENSEN, Roseann, T ... 718-390-4536 ... 348 G
sorenser@stjohns.edu
SORENSEN, Sarah ... 801-524-8149 ... 510 E
ssorenson@ldsbc.edu
SORENSEN, Zak ... 616-538-2330 ... 251 D
zsorensen@gbcol.edu
SORENSON, Nancy ... 651-523-2103 ... 264 A
nsorenson01@hamline.edu
SORENSON, Shad ... 801-863-7072 ... 511 F
shad.sorenson@uvu.edu
SOREY, Kellie ... 757-822-1122 ... 528 G
ksorey@tcc.edu
SOREY, Kellie ... 757-822-1065 ... 528 G
ksorey@tcc.edu
SORG, Charlotte ... 419-267-1317 ... 397 E
csorg@northweststate.edu
SORIA, Deborah ... 559-925-3316 ... 78 D
deborahsoria@whccd.edu
SORIA, Laura ... 773-777-4220 ... 160 D
lsoria@nc.edu
SORIA, Rick ... 219-879-9137 ... 176 G
rsoria@ivytech.edu
SORIANO, Brenda ... 212-962-0002 ... 342 G
bsoriano@nyci.edu
SORIANO, Esteban ... 831-755-6822 ... 49 E
esoriano@hartnell.edu
SORIERO, Julie ... 617-253-4499 ... 241 D
SORK, Victoria ... 310-825-7755 ... 74 C
vlsork@ucla.edu
SORLEY, Julie ... 740-477-7801 ... 398 D
SOROCHTY, Roger, W ... 918-631-2895 ... 413 F
roger-sorochty@utulsa.edu
SOROKA, Leonard, G ... 215-637-7700 ... 431 A
lsoroka@holyfamily.edu
SOROKES, Lawrence ... 716-375-2304 ... 348 C
lsorokes@sbu.edu
SORRELL, Carson ... 315-684-6065 ... 354 F
sorrelc@morrisville.edu
SORRELL, Carson ... 315-792-7456 ... 356 B
sorrelc@sunyit.edu
SORRELL, Clyde, H ... 240-567-5271 ... 224 D
rocky.sorrell@montgomerycollege.edu
SORRELL, Garry ... 660-596-7301 ... 290 B
gsorrell@sfccmo.edu
SORRELL, Michael, J ... 214-379-5550 ... 492 F
president@pqc.edu
SORRELLS, Glenn ... 972-279-6511 ... 479 H
gsorrells@amberton.edu
SORRELS, Paul ... 830-279-3013 ... 501 E
psorrels@sulross.edu
SORRENTINO, Donna Marie ... 603-862-2930 ... 306 C
dms@unh.edu
SORRENTINO, Sebastian ... 860-768-4034 ... 95 B
sorrentin@hartford.edu
SORRENTO, Anthony ... 973-300-2769 ... 315 F
asorrento@sussex.edu
SORROW, Russ, L ... 770-484-1204 ... 133 G
rsorrow@lru.edu
SORTOR, Janet, M ... 207-741-5504 ... 219 A
jsortor@smccme.edu
SORTOR, Marci, J ... 507-786-3004 ... 271 C
sortor@stolaf.edu
SORVAAG, Scott ... 507-457-6612 ... 271 B
ssorvaag@smumn.edu
SOSA, Dona ... 212-343-1234 ... 341 B
dsosa@mcny.edu
SOSA, Horacio ... 856-256-4129 ... 314 A
sosa@rowan.edu
SOSA, Ismael ... 830-591-7281 ... 495 D
ismael.sosa@swtjc.cc.tx.us
SOSA, Leticia ... 787-761-0640 ... 566 F
biblioteca@cbp.edu
SOSA, Victor ... 603-862-2001 ... 306 C
victor.sosa@unh.edu
SOSA-HEGARTY, Dina, M ... 972-860-7205 ... 484 I
dinasosa-hegarty@dcccd.edu
SOSNOFF, J.D ... 314-421-0949 ... 290 D
sosnoff@siba.edu
SOSSEN, Nina ... 413-545-4741 ... 236 F
nsossen@admin.umass.edu

SOSTER, Jennifer, C 765-658-4198 171 B jsoster@depauw.edu

SOTHERDEN, James, J 717-691-6012 436 D jsotherd@messiah.edu

SOTHERLAND, Paul, R 269-337-7012 252 K paul.sotherland@kzoo.edu

SOTHMANN, Mark, S 843-792-3031 459 D sothmann@musc.edu

SOTIROS, James 707-638-5460 73 A james.sotiros@tu.edu

SOTO, Amilcar 787-878-5475 563 B asoto@arecibo.inter.edu

SOTO, Arlene 541-756-6445 420 C asoto@socc.edu

SOTO, Bobby 214-333-5360 484 D bobby@dbu.edu

SOTO, Carlos 813-253-7860 110 M csoto@hccfl.edu

SOTO, Edgar 520-206-3260 17 H esoto@pima.edu

SOTO, Emilia 787-740-6631 566 C emilia.soto@uccaribe.edu

SOTO, Emilia 787-269-4510 566 C emilia.soto@uccaribe.edu

SOTO, Grisselle 787-725-8120 562 C gsoto0056@eap.edu

SOTO, Heriberto 787-751-1912 564 C herisoto@inter.edu

SOTO, Jose 402-323-3412 300 B jsoto@southeast.edu

SOTO, Limaris 787-725-8120 562 C lisotoa@eap.edu

SOTO, Luis, A 787-864-2222 563 F luissoto@inter.edu

SOTO, Monica 305-899-3057 101 M msoto@mail.barry.edu

SOTO-CRUZ, Nilsa 787-834-5151 565 D nsoto@email.pucpr.edu

SOTO-GREENE, Maria, L 973-972-9151 316 F sotogrml@umdnj.edu

SOTO MENDEZ, Aracelia 787-896-2252 562 B asoto@edpcollege.edu

SOTONA, Shirley 404-876-1227 126 G shirley.sotona@bccr.edu

SOTTER, Trudy 724-964-8811 437 E tsotterfa@aol.com

SOTTILE, Christian 912-525-5000 136 F

SOUBA, JR., Wiley, W 603-650-1200 304 J wiley.w.souba.jr@dartmouth.edu

SOUCIE, James 207-326-2241 219 D jim.soucie@mma.edu

SOUCY, Erin 207-834-7830 220 D esoucy@maine.edu

SOUCY, Ken, R 937-229-2641 404 A ksoucy1@udayton.edu

SOUCY, Matthew, R 906-786-5802 248 I soucym@baycollege.edu

SOUHRADA, Rick 209-384-6135 57 C souhrada.r@mccd.edu

SOULES, Robert, C 518-388-6176 358 G soulesr@union.edu

SOULLIERE, Robert 260-399-7700 181 A rsoulliere@sf.edu

SOULSBY, Eric 928-344-7609 12 A eric.soulsby@azwestern.edu

SOURBEER, Dan 760-744-1150 61 D dsourbeer@palomar.edu

SOURS, Richard 304-929-1560 541 H rsours@mountainstate.edu

SOUSA, Deborah 201-612-5278 307 E dsousa@bergen.edu

SOUSA, Marsha 907-796-6531 11 A mcsousa@uas.alaska.edu

SOUSA, Marsha 907-796-6518 11 A marsha.sousa@uas.alaska.edu

SOUSA, Sheryl, A 781-736-3630 232 F sousa@brandeis.edu

SOUSA-PEOPLES, Kim 336-334-5231 379 B ksp@uncg.edu

SOUTER, Sharon 254-295-4667 504 C ssouter@umhb.edu

SOUTH, Anne 410-225-2516 224 B asouth@mica.edu

SOUTH, Ashley 614-456-4600 393 B asouth@kaplan.edu

SOUTH, Gregory 530-938-5375 42 E gsouth@siskiyous.edu

SOUTH, James, D 580-774-7152 412 F james.south@swosu.edu

SOUTH, III, John, T 912-201-8101 137 D jsouthiii@southuniversity.edu

SOUTH, Shannon 970-564-6212 87 F shannon.south@pueblocc.edu

SOUTH, Stephen, A 828-398-2500 376 H ssouth@southcollegetn.edu

SOUTH, Stephen, A 865-251-1800 473 A ssouth@southcollegetn.edu

SOUTHALL, Ann 870-862-8131 23 G asouthall@southark.edu

SOUTHARAD, John 212-431-2825 343 E jsouthard@nyls.edu

SOUTHARD, Anne 850-729-6040 114 A southara@nwfsc.edu

SOUTHARD, Sonya 270-686-4526 203 B sonya.southard@kctcs.edu

SOUTHARDS, Mary, S 330-499-9600 393 I msouthar@kent.edu

SOUTHER, Donna 970-339-6453 81 A donna.souther@aims.edu

SOUTHERLAND, Janet, H 615-327-6207 471 C jsoutherland@mmc.edu

SOUTHERLAND, Johnnie 919-530-5321 378 B jsoutherland@nccu.edu

SOUTHERLAND, Ronald 330-339-3391 394 A rsoutherland@kent.edu

SOUTHERN, Debbie 309-341-7225 155 F dsouther@knox.edu

SOUTHERN, Lori 254-299-8686 490 G lsouthern@mclennan.edu

SOUTHWELL, Michael 570-422-2871 442 D msouthwell@po-box.esu.edu

SOUTHWOOD, John 706-802-5457 130 E jsouthwo@highlands.edu

SOUTHWOOD, Lori 859-572-6383 205 H southwoodl1@nku.edu

SOUTHWORTH, Linda 978-934-2373 237 B linda_southworth@uml.edu

SOUTULLO, Stephen, C 713-743-9103 503 D scsoutullo@uh.edu

SOUZA, Diana 231-348-6837 256 B dsouza@ncmich.edu

SOUZA, Nicole, L 212-346-1232 345 F nsouza@pace.edu

SOUZA, Thomas, A 408-944-6050 61 A thomas.souza@palmer.edu

SOVA, Devin, A 336-633-0212 373 A dasova@randolph.edu

SOVINE, Kim 304-414-4446 542 J ksovine@kvctc.edu

SOVYANHADI, Marta 256-726-7229 6 C msovyanhadi@oakwood.edu

SOWARD, Brunetta 414-297-8726 554 F sowardb@matc.edu

SOWELL, Debra 918-495-6703 411 C dsowell@oru.edu

SOWELL, Frank 662-254-3531 276 B frank.u.sowell@mvsu.edu

SOWELL, John, T 404-995-8484 276 F jsowell@rts.edu

SOWELL, Kathy 615-230-3476 476 C kathy.sowell@volstate.edu

SOWELL, Madison, U 540-261-4083 524 H madison.sowell@svu.edu

SOWELL, Richard, L 770-423-6565 133 A rsowell@kennesaw.edu

SOWER, Michelle 530-541-4660 53 G sower@ltcc.edu

SOWERS, Donna, S 301-846-2466 222 G dsowers@frederick.edu

SOWERS, Karen 865-974-3176 477 D kmsowers@utk.edu

SOWINSKI, Tomasz 212-472-1500 343 G tsowinski@nysid.edu

SOYARS, Tim 214-860-8587 485 B tsoyars@dcccd.edu

SOYRING, Mary 218-879-0811 266 C msoyring@fdltcc.edu

SOYSTER, Allen 617-373-2152 243 F

SOZANSKY, JR., Basil, W 218-726-8102 271 F bsozansk@d.umn.edu

SOZZO, Anthony, M 914-594-4491 343 F tony_sozzo@nymc.edu

SPACH, Robert, C 704-894-2420 363 I rospach@davidson.edu

SPADARO, Joseph 610-896-1045 430 G jspadaro@haverford.edu

SPADE, Douglas, R 713-798-7391 481 H dspade@bcm.edu

SPADEMAN, Robert 216-687-7284 388 D r.spademan@csuohio.edu

SPAETH, Jason 320-629-5100 268 E spaethj@pinetech.edu

SPAETH, Nick, A 950-565-1007 548 A spaethna@lakeland.edu

SPAETH, Paul, J 716-375-2323 348 C pspaeth@sbu.edu

SPAETH-BAUM, Barbara 701-671-2483 382 G barbara.baum@ndscs.edu

SPAGNA, Michael, E 818-677-2590 35 F michael.spagna@csun.edu

SPAGNOLO, Jean Paul 260-399-7700 181 A jspagnolo@sf.edu

SPAHR, Steven 301-687-4112 228 C sspahr@frostburg.edu

SPAID, Darla 814-732-1364 442 E dspaid@edinboro.edu

SPAIGHT, Lynn 828-251-6501 378 D lspaight@unca.edu

SPAIN, Ashley 309-692-4092 158 D arspain@midstate.edu

SPAIN, Diara 415-257-1343 45 C diara.spain@dominican.edu

SPAIN, James 573-882-5995 291 B spainj@missouri.edu

SPAIN, Jeff 217-228-5432 161 F spainje@quincy.edu

SPAIN, Judy 859-622-1842 200 J judy.spain@eku.edu

SPAIN, Lee 956-721-5138 489 J lee.spain@laredo.edu

SPAIN, William, R 401-841-3499 558 B

SPAK, Gale, T 973-596-8540 312 C gale.spak@njit.edu

SPAKES, Patricia 253-692-5646 539 A pspakes@uw.edu

SPALDING, Carol 704-216-3450 373 F carol.spalding@rccc.edu

SPALDING, David, P 603-646-2715 304 J david.p.spalding@dartmouth.edu

SPALDING, Kristina 626-914-8597 40 B kspaulding@citruscollege.edu

SPALDING, Richard, E 413-597-2483 246 D richard.e.spalding@williams.edu

SPALDING, Wendy 513-244-8492 387 E wendy.spalding@ccuniversity.edu

SPALLA, Tara 614-234-5950 396 H tspalla@mccn.edu

SPALTER, Mendel 323-937-3763 80 D mspalter@yoec.edu

SPALTER, Sholom 973-960-6670 313 B shspalter1@aol.com

SPALTER, Sholom 973-267-9404 313 B shspalter1@aol.com

SPANCAKE, Richard 229-391-4890 123 H rspancake@abac.edu

SPANEL, Megan 513-727-3200 396 G

SPANG, David 609-894-9311 308 B dspang@bcc.edu

SPANG, Zane 406-477-6215 294 A zspang@cdkc.edu

SPANGENBERG, Eric 509-335-3596 539 D ers@wsu.edu

SPANGENBERG, Laurie 906-786-5802 248 I laurie.spangenberg@baycollege.edu

SPANGLER, John, R 717-334-6286 435 A jspangler@ltsg.edu

SPANGLER, Lee 406-994-4399 295 C spangler@montana.edu

SPANGLER, Mary, S 713-718-5059 487 I mary.spangler@hccs.edu

SPANGLER, Michael 702-651-4959 302 E michael.spangler@csn.edu

SPANGLER, Stephanie 203-432-4446 96 A stephanie.spangler@yale.edu

SPANGLER, Todd 315-655-7121 325 H tspangler@cazenovia.edu

SPANIOL, Lee 217-234-5263 156 B lspaniol@lakeland.cc.il.us

SPANIOLO, James, D 817-272-2101 505 C jds@uta.edu

SPANJER, Pat 509-359-6358 533 H pspanjer@ewu.edu

SPANN, B. Steven 615-327-3927 469 K spann@guptoncollege.edu

SPANNER, Benjamin, J 312-332-0707 166 B

SPANO, Anthony 405-767-2206 407 I aspano@devry.edu

SPANO, David, B 704-687-0311 379 A dspano@uncc.edu

SPAR, Debora, L 212-854-2021 323 E dspar@barnard.edu

SPARANGES, Judith, M 508-849-3345 230 C jsparanges@annamaria.edu

SPARGEN, Dan 402-399-2600 297 C dspargen@csm.edu

SPARKES, Mike 281-425-6327 489 M msparkes@lee.edu

SPARKIA MOORE, Alisa 909-389-3333 65 B asmoore@sbccd.edu

SPARKMAN, Calvin 951-343-4356 31 J csparkman@calbaptist.edu

SPARKMAN, Margo 606-368-6039 198 C margosparkman@alc.edu

SPARKMAN, Susan 205-652-3587 9 E sgt@uwa.edu

SPARKS, Brad 618-235-2700 165 D bradley.sparks@swic.edu

SPARKS, Brian 918-540-6231 408 J bsparks@neo.edu

SPARKS, Cheryl, T 432-264-5030 488 B csparks@howardcollege.edu

SPARKS, Daniel 618-262-8641 153 A sparksd@iecc.edu

SPARKS, George, E 540-568-7073 520 H sparksge@jmu.edu

SPARKS, Jay 706-565-3669 127 G sparks_jay@columbusstate.edu

SPARKS, John, A 724-458-2056 430 B jasparks@gcc.edu

SPARKS, Jonathan, D 580-774-7081 412 F jon.sparks@swosu.edu

SPARKS, Kenton 610-341-5929 428 E ksparks@eastern.edu

SPARKS, Kevin 865-251-1800 473 A ksparks@southcollegetn.edu

SPARKS, Larry, D 662-915-7200 277 D lsparks@olemiss.edu

SPARKS, Mark 410-455-2872 227 D

SPARKS, Matt 606-783-2822 204 I m.sparks@moreheadstate.edu

SPARKS, Melanie 505-277-7464 321 C msparks@unm.edu

SPARKS, Preston 803-641-3569 462 B prestons@usca.edu

SPARKS, Roland 980-598-3105 365 I roland.sparks@jwu.edu

SPARKS, Sherry 412-924-1382 444 H sparks@pts.edu

SPARKS, Sonny 662-472-2312 274 D ssparks@holmescc.edu

SPARKS, Steve 919-497-3250 366 H ssparks@louisburg.edu

SPARKS, Tiffany 402-494-2311 299 B tsparks@thenicc.edu

SPARROW, Meghan 304-357-4741 542 A meghansparrow@ucwv.edu

SPARROW, Rebecca, M 607-255-2723 331 B rms18@cornell.edu

SPARROW, Suzanne 610-409-3600 450 D ssparrow@ursinus.edu

SPARY, Wayne 402-826-8228 297 G wayne.spary@doane.edu

SPATAFORE, Marisa 408-864-8672 47 G spataforemarisa@deanza.edu

SPATARO, Charles 270-706-8476 202 A charles.spataro@kctcs.edu

SPATARO, Keith 650-543-3853 57 B kspataro@menlo.edu

SPATARO, Nancy, C 717-815-1368 452 G nspataro@ycp.edu

SPATARO-WILSON, Jennifer, A 540-665-5412 524 E jspataro@su.edu

SPATES, Gerald 336-334-7800 378 A gspates@ncat.edu

SPATH, Christine 303-784-8637 85 M cspath@jiu.edu

SPATZ, Dan 541-506-6110 415 C dspatz@cgcc.cc.or.us

SPATZ, Ronald 907-786-1086 10 H afrms1@uaa.alaska.edu

SPAULDING, Angela 806-651-2730 499 A aspaulding@mail.wtamu.edu

SPAULDING, David, L 931-598-1325 472 L dspauldi@sewnee.edu

SPAULDING, II, Henry, W 740-392-6868 396 I henry.spaulding@mvnu.edu

SPAULDING, II, Henry, W 740-392-6868 396 I hspauldi@mvnu.edu

SPAULDING, James 563-588-6307 183 E james.spaulding@clarke.edu

SPAULDING, Thad 303-556-3591 84 A thad.spaulding@ccd.edu

SPAULDING, Tonia 912-583-3222 126 F tspaulding@bpc.edu

SPAUR, Rita 209-228-7865 74 D rspaur@ucmerced.edu

SPAVENTA, Jon 805-893-3702 75 B jon.spaventa@parec.ucsb.edu

SPAVENTA, Marilynn 805-965-0581 68 B spaventa@sbcc.edu

SPAYD, Alexandra 717-361-1123 428 F spaydal@etown.edu

SPAYER, Roger 847-925-6360 151 G rspayer@harpercollege.edu

SPAZIANI, Gina 978-656-3145 240 B spazianig@middlesex.mass.edu

SPEAKE, Dianne 850-644-6846 119 D dspeake@nursing.fsu.edu

SPEAKER, Cindy 315-364-3474 360 D cspeaker@wells.edu

SPEAKMAN, Thomas 717-477-1231 443 E twspea@ship.edu

SPEAKS, Michael, A 859-257-7619 207 D michael.speaks@uky.edu

SPEAKS, Tiffany 202-885-3651 97 D tspeaks@american.edu

SPEAR, Diana 618-262-8641 153 A speard@iecc.edu

SPEAR, Jeffrey, B 740-392-6868 396 I jspear@mvnu.edu

SPEAR, Margaret, E 814-865-6555 438 G mes10@psu.edu

SPEAR, Robert 208-885-0243 144 G rspear@uidaho.edu

SPEARMAN, Tim 619-961-4221 72 J tspearman@tjsl.edu

SPEARS, Barbara, A 334-420-4479 7 H bspears@trenholmstate.edu

SPEARS, Douglas 513-244-8428 387 E doug.spears@ccuniversity.edu

SPEARS, Gary Lee 662-562-3227 276 D glspears@northwestms.edu

SPEARS, Jacqueline, A 409-882-3018 501 B jackie.spears@lsco.edu

SPEARS, James 304-462-4125 544 A james.spears@glenville.edu

SPEARS, Lanny 859-858-2298 198 D

SPEARS, Linda, C 615-963-5281 474 A lspears@tnstate.edu

SPEARS, Marty 501-279-4789 21 H mspears@harding.edu

SPEARS, Ron 806-894-9611 494 G rspears@southplainscollege.edu

SPONSELLER, Eric .... 401-254-3192.... 454 C
esponsellers@rwu.edu
SPONSLER, Emily .... 901-381-3939.... 478 E
emily@visible.edu
SPOONER, David .... 518-276-6890.... 347 D
spoond@rpi.edu
SPOONER, John .... 616-538-2330.... 251 D
jspooner@gbcol.edu
SPOONER, Judith .... 330-869-3600.... 385 H
jspooner@brownmackie.edu
SPOONER, Matt .... 310-476-9777...... 28 G
mspooner@ajula.edu
SPOONER, Natalie, M .... 315-786-2268.... 337 F
nspooner@sunyjefferson.edu
SPOOR, Suzanne, J .... 410-777-2448.... 221 C
sjspoor@aacc.edu
SPOR, Arvid .... 626-914-8534...... 40 B
aspor@citruscollege.edu
SPORE, MaryBeth .... 724-537-4567.... 446 E
marybeth.spore@email.stvincent.edu
SPORE, Robert, B .... 540-464-7322.... 529 F
sporerb@vmi.edu
SPORES, Jon .... 360-383-3440.... 540 A
jspores@whatcom.ctc.edu
SPORLEDER, Brian, R .... 414-276-5200.... 546 F
brsporleder@bryantstratton.edu
SPORS, Jonathon, L .... 217-443-8577.... 148 G
jspors@dacc.edu
SPORTES, Christine .... 202-319-5050...... 97 E
sportes@cua.edu
SPORTSMAN, Joseph, S ... 513-244-4389.... 388 E
scott_sportsman@mail.msj.edu
SPOSILI, Michael .... 518-580-5610.... 351 B
msposili@skidmore.edu
SPOTO, Mary .... 352-588-8463.... 116 G
mary.spoto@saintleo.edu
SPOTZ, Jason .... 440-375-7000.... 394 E
jspotz@lec.edu
SPRADLEY, Minou .... 619-388-3520...... 65 F
mspradl@sdccd.edu
SPRADLIN, Michael, R .... 901-751-8453.... 471 F
mspradlin@mabts.edu
SPRADLING, Jane .... 337-550-1216.... 212 J
SPRADLING, John .... 903-785-7661.... 492 D
jspradling@parisjc.edu
SPRADLING, Steve .... 330-494-6170.... 402 B
sspradling@starkstate.edu
SPRAGG, Anna .... 203-582-5257...... 93 H
anna.spragg@quinnipiac.edu
SPRAGGINS, Lynn .... 256-378-2022........ 2 E
lspraggins@cacc.edu
SPRAGGINS, Timothy .... 334-244-3220........ 1 G
tspraggins@aum.edu
SPRAGUE, Brinton .... 425-739-8127.... 535 H
brinton.sprague@lwtc.edu
SPRAGUE, Carol .... 413-545-0698.... 236 F
sprague@research.umass.edu
SPRAGUE, Jennifer .... 505-984-6041.... 320 C
jsprague@sjcsf.edu
SPRAGUE, Jennifer .... 303-477-7240...... 85 B
jennifers@heritage-education.com
SPRAGUE, Jon, E .... 419-772-2276.... 398 H
j-sprague@onu.edu
SPRAGUE, Karen, U .... 541-346-1246.... 419 B
kus@uoregon.edu
SPRAGUE, Kendra .... 360-442-2121.... 535 I
ksprague@lowercolumbia.edu
SPRAGUE, Robert, L .... 310-287-4398...... 55 F
spragurl@wlac.edu
SPRAGUE, Todd .... 360-867-6042.... 534 D
spraguet@evergreen.edu
SPRAGUE, Viola .... 810-762-9668.... 253 C
vsprague@kettering.edu
SPRAKE, Timothy .... 425-637-1010.... 532 E
tsprake@cityu.edu
SPRAKER, Matt .... 615-248-1245.... 476 G
mspraker@trevecca.edu
SPRANGERS, Lynn .... 414-256-4810.... 549 D
sprangel@mtmary.edu
SPRANZA, John .... 706-295-6363.... 130 E
jspranza@highlands.edu
SPRATLIN, Jim .... 334-386-7265........ 3 G
jspratlin@faulkner.edu
SPRATLIN, Steve .... 256-395-2211........ 7 D
sspratlin@suscc.edu
SPRATT, Bruce, R .... 404-413-3071.... 131 G
bspratt@gsu.edu
SPRATT, Sharon .... 270-706-8478.... 202 A
sharon.spratt@kctcs.edu
SPRATT, Wanda .... 530-339-3610...... 69 D
wspratt@shastacollege.edu
SPRAW, Deanna .... 419-434-4589.... 404 B
spraw@findlay.edu
SPREHE, Tara .... 503-594-3370.... 415 A
taras@clackamas.edu
SPRENGEL, Archie .... 573-651-2217.... 289 K
awsprengel@semo.edu
SPRENGER, Cathy, J .... 717-477-1381.... 443 E
cjspre@ship.edu
SPRICK, David, W .... 715-836-2222.... 551 A
sprickdw@uwec.edu
SPRIGGS, Barry, L .... 610-799-1634.... 434 D
bspriggs@lccc.edu
SPRIGGS, Denise .... 704-971-8500.... 363 F
SPRIGGS, Edward, J .... 858-534-3475...... 74 F
espriggs@ucsd.edu
SPRIGGS, Janet .... 704-219-7165.... 373 F
janet.spriggs@rccc.edu
SPRIGGS, Jocelyn .... 501-244-5104...... 19 D
jocelyn.spriggs@arkansasbaptist.edu
SPRING, Corinne .... 201-559-3515.... 310 B
springc@felician.edu
SPRING, SCC, Joseph .... 973-543-6528.... 307 B
president@acs350.org
SPRING, Ted .... 910-362-7555.... 368 H
tspring@cfcc.edu
SPRING, Ted, D .... 304-929-5472.... 543 A
tspring@newriver.edu
SPRINGALL, Robert, G ...... 570-577-1101.... 423 E
r.springhall@bucknell.edu
SPRINGER, Colleen .... 641-844-5523.... 186 B
colleen.springer@iavalley.edu
SPRINGER, Colleen .... 641-844-7106.... 186 D
colleen.springer@iavalley.edu
SPRINGER, D. Bruce .... 410-777-2346.... 221 C
bdspringer@aacc.edu
SPRINGER, David .... 503-725-3997.... 418 G
david.springer@pdx.edu
SPRINGER, Karen .... 505-583-1074.... 244 C
SPRINGER, Laureen .... 405-491-6325.... 412 D
springer@snu.edu
SPRINGER, Mark .... 320-308-3093.... 269 A
mspringer@stcloudstate.edu
SPRINGER, Patrick .... 951-487-3590...... 58 B
pspringer@msjc.edu
SPRINGER, Rachelle .... 701-349-3621.... 383 E
rspringer@trinitybiblecollege.edu
SPRINGER, Robert, I .... 336-278-6644.... 364 D
springer@elon.edu
SPRINGER, Tracy .... 765-455-9356.... 174 A
tracylb@iuk.edu
SPRINGER-BALDWIN,
Nancy .... 512-472-4133.... 494 F
nancy.springer-baldwin@ssw.edu
SPRINGHORN, Polly .... 415-749-4504...... 65 I
pspringhorn@sfai.edu
SPRINKEL, Beth .... 916-608-6500...... 56 C
SPRINKLE, Dean, E .... 336-838-6128.... 375 C
dean.sprinkle@wilkescc.edu
SPRINKLE, Stephen, D ...... 619-260-4655...... 76 D
sdsprinkle@sandiego.edu
SPROLE, JoLynn, F .... 817-515-4563.... 496 C
jolynn.sprole@tccd.edu
SPROLES, Karyn, Z .... 412-578-2043.... 424 I
kzsproles@carlow.edu
SPROTT, Kendell, R .... 973-972-1818.... 316 F
sprottkr@umdnj.edu
SPROULS, David .... 212-472-1500.... 343 G
dsprouls@nysid.edu
SPROUSE, Judy .... 434-381-6323.... 524 K
jsprouse@sbc.edu
SPROUSE, Keith .... 435-722-6900.... 510 N
keiths@ubatc.edu
SPROUSE, Marlene .... 641-683-5104.... 185 G
msprouse@indianhills.edu
SPROWL, Don .... 765-677-1002.... 175 B
don.sprowl@indwes.edu
SPRUIELL, Clemit, W .... 205-652-3533........ 9 E
cspruiell@uwa.edu
SPRUIELL, Vicki, P .... 205-652-3627........ 9 E
vspruiell@uwa.edu
SPRUILL, Crhistina .... 806-291-3406.... 508 E
spruillc@wbu.edu
SPRUILL, Rose .... 210-486-2420.... 479 D
rspruill1@alamo.edu
SPRUILL, Wayne .... 615-383-1340.... 469 A
wspruill@fwbbc.edu
SPRUNGER, Philip, W .... 570-321-4038.... 435 D
sprunger@lycoming.edu
SPRY, Larry .... 816-322-0110.... 279 D
larry.spry@calvary.edu
SPRY, Susan .... 570-740-0407.... 435 C
sspry@luzerne.edu
SPUAZO, Mario .... 575-737-6200.... 321 F
mspuazo@unm.edu
SPUCK, Dennis, W .... 281-283-3500.... 503 E
spuck@uhcl.edu
SPURLING, Steven .... 415-239-3743...... 40 C
sspurlin@ccsf.edu
SPURLOCK, Chad .... 918-293-4622.... 410 E
chad.spurlock@okstate.edu
SPURLOCK, Jennifer .... 513-562-8771.... 384 D
jspurlock@artacademy.edu
SPURLOCK, Rhonda .... 918-343-7612.... 411 H
rspurlock@rsu.edu
SPURLOCK-EVANS, Karla .. 860-297-4234...... 94 E
karla.spurlockevans@trincoll.edu
SPURRIER, Robert, L .... 405-744-6796.... 410 C
robert.spurrier@okstate.edu
SPYBEY, Joseph .... 614-222-3246.... 388 G
jspybey@ccad.edu
SQUARE, Marilyn, C .... 713-313-7859.... 500 B
squaremc@tsu.edu
SQUIER, Steven .... 815-825-2086.... 155 D
steven.squier@kishwaukeecollege.edu
SQUIRE, Frances .... 559-934-2134...... 78 B
francessquire@whccd.edu
SQUIRE, Michael, E .... 630-637-5559.... 159 G
mesquire@noctrl.edu
SQUIRE, Roland .... 435-797-8380.... 511 E
roland.squire@usu.edu
SQUIRES, Nancy .... 631-632-6976.... 352 C
nancy.squires@stonybrook.edu
SQUIRES, Nicole .... 218-235-2171.... 269 F
n.squires@vcc.edu
SQUIRES, R. Duwane .... 304-473-8311.... 545 G
squires@wvwc.edu
SQUIRES, Roy .... 727-726-1153.... 103 I
roysquires@clearwater.edu
SQUIRES, Toni .... 651-641-8232.... 263 A
squires@csp.edu
SQUIREWELL, Robert .... 803-705-4698.... 455 D
squirewellr@benedict.edu
SREBRO, Michele, M .... 570-702-8953.... 431 L
msrebro@johnson.edu
SREBRO, Nathan .... 773-834-2500.... 166 A
SREENIVASAN, Katepalli ... 718-260-3761.... 346 C
krs3@nyu.edu
SREENIVASAN, Katepalli ... 212-992-7914.... 344 B
krs3@nyu.edu
SRIHARI, Hari .... 607-777-2871.... 351 F
srihari@binghamton.edu
SRIKANTH, Rajini .... 617-287-5520.... 236 G
rajini.srikanth@umb.edu
SRINIVASAN, Ganesan ...... 707-527-4880...... 68 E
gsrinivasan@santarosa.edu
SRODA, Kim .... 415-433-9200...... 68 F
ksroda@saybrook.edu
SROF, Brenda, S .... 574-535-7375.... 171 G
brendajs@goshen.edu
SROKA, Sandra .... 201-612-5233.... 307 E
ssroka@bergen.edu
STAAB, Eric, P .... 269-337-7172.... 252 K
eric.staab@kzoo.edu
STAATS, Mark .... 801-304-4224.... 509 I
mstaats@broadviewuniversity.edu
STAATS, Raymond, W .... 256-549-8221........ 3 J
rstaats@gadsdenstate.edu
STABEN, Charles, A .... 605-677-6497.... 465 G
chuck.staben@usd.edu
STABER, Karl, D .... 678-915-6481.... 137 G
kstaber@spsu.edu
STABILE, Margaret .... 708-456-0300.... 166 F
mstabile@triton.edu
STABILE, Randy .... 617-349-8388.... 236 B
rstabile@lesley.edu
STABILE, Steve .... 212-229-3500.... 342 E
stabiles@newschool.edu
STABOLEPSZY, Judy .... 570-577-2000.... 423 E
judy.stabolepszy@bucknell.edu
STACCHI, Heather .... 978-837-5095.... 242 A
stacchih@merrimack.edu
STACE, Peter, A .... 718-817-3200.... 334 C
stace@fordham.edu
STACEY, John .... 910-695-3822.... 373 H
stacyj@sandhills.edu
STACEY, Robert .... 206-543-2100.... 539 A
STACEY, Robert .... 281-649-3630.... 487 H
rstacey@hbu.edu
STACEY, Robert, D .... 281-649-3630.... 487 H
rstacey@hbu.edu
STACEY, Simon .... 410-455-2164.... 227 D
spstacey@umbc.edu
STACEY-CLEMONS, June .... 253-589-5546.... 532 G
june.stacey-clemons@cptc.edu
STACHACZ, John .... 570-408-4254.... 452 A
john.stachaz@wilkes.edu
STACHOWIAK, Kris .... 610-359-5310.... 426 G
kstachowiak@dccc.edu
STACHOWSKI,
Mary Albertine .... 716-896-0700.... 359 H
smalbertine@villa.edu
STACHURA, Hubert .... 212-752-1530.... 338 C
hubert.stachura@limcollege.edu
STACK, Barbara, J .... 920-832-6546.... 548 B
barbara.j.stack@lawrence.edu
STACK, Connie .... 336-506-4135.... 368 A
stackc@alamancecc.edu
STACK, Dana .... 619-388-7579...... 65 H
dandras@sdccd.edu
STACK, David, M .... 414-229-3713.... 551 D
david@uwm.edu
STACK, Dennis .... 585-567-9220.... 336 B
dennis.stack@houghton.edu
STACK, OSA, John, P .... 610-519-4550.... 450 H
john.stack@villanova.edu
STACK, Lisa, J .... 617-984-1652.... 243 H
lstack@quincycollege.edu
STACK, Lynne .... 508-286-8251.... 246 B
lstack@wheatoncollege.edu
STACK, Patrick .... 314-968-6921.... 292 J
stackpa@webster.edu
STACK, Richard .... 617-353-9344.... 232 E
rmstack@bu.edu
STACK, Shane .... 304-336-8365.... 544 D
sstack@westliberty.edu
STACKHOUSE, Paul .... 859-253-3637.... 200 K
paul.stackhouse@frontier.edu
STACKHOUSE TAETZCH,
Cindra .... 630-752-5049.... 168 H
cindra.taetzsch@wheaton.edu
STACKPOLE, Ronnie .... 813-988-5131.... 108 A
businessoffice@floridacollege.edu
STACKPOOLE, Kenneth ...... 321-674-8971.... 108 H
kenstackpoole@fit.edu
STACKPOOLE, Roger, W .... 315-445-4174.... 338 B
stackprw@lemoyne.edu
STACKS, Pamela .... 408-924-2427...... 37 C
pamela.stacks@jupiter.sjsu.edu
STACY, Charlene .... 765-644-7514.... 172 B
charlene.stacy@harrison.edu
STACY, Charlene .... 260-471-7667.... 172 F
charlene.stacy@harrison.edu
STACY, Jeanne .... 225-216-8591.... 209 H
stacyj@mybrcc.edu
STACY, Karin .... 847-214-7957.... 150 F
kstacy@elgin.edu
STACY, Mark, W .... 585-395-5149.... 352 F
mstacy@brockport.edu
STACY, Roger .... 580-371-2371.... 408 I
rstacy@mscok.edu
STADDEN, Mary .... 717-396-7833.... 440 K
mstadden@pcad.edu
STADING, Gary, L .... 713-221-2775.... 503 F
stadingg@uhd.edu
STADLER, Albert (Al) .... 417-625-9807.... 286 B
stadler-a@mssu.edu
STADLER, Holly .... 312-853-4780.... 163 B
hstadler@roosevelt.edu
STADLER, Ueli .... 503-777-7287.... 420 A
ueli.stadler@reed.edu
STADTFELD, Kathleen, A .... 734-973-3487.... 259 F
kstadtfeld@wccnet.edu
STAFFEL, Peter, L .... 304-336-8193.... 544 D
staffelp@westliberty.edu
STAFFIER, Carol .... 781-239-2703.... 239 G
cstaffier@massbay.edu
STAFFORD, Alan .... 325-670-1486.... 487 F
stafford@hsutx.edu
STAFFORD, Ben .... 409-984-6390.... 501 C
staffordbk@lamarpa.edu
STAFFORD, Cecilia .... 505-287-6639.... 319 H
stafford@nmsu.edu
STAFFORD, Charles, A ...... 845-938-3419.... 559 A
8sgs@usma.edu
STAFFORD, Ingrid, S .... 847-491-7350.... 160 E
i-stafford@northwestern.edu
STAFFORD, Jake .... 510-849-8239...... 48 J
jstafford@psr.edu
STAFFORD, James .... 254-295-4607.... 504 C
jstafford@umhb.edu
STAFFORD, Joanne .... 405-733-7373.... 411 I
jmcmillen@rose.edu
STAFFORD, Kathryn .... 734-477-8581.... 259 F
stafford@wccnet.edu
STAFFORD, Kenneth .... 785-532-6520.... 194 D
kens@ksu.edu
STAFFORD, Kyle .... 580-745-2236.... 412 C
kstafford@se.edu
STAFFORD, Mary .... 503-251-5707.... 421 A
mstafford@uws.edu
STAFFORD, Michael .... 281-290-5276.... 490 E
michael.d.stafford@lonestar.edu
STAFFORD, Pam .... 606-759-7141.... 203 A
pam.stafford@kctcs.edu
STAFFORD, Patricia, L .... 423-392-8000.... 473 F
staffordp@etsu.edu
STAFFORD, Thomas .... 212-237-8100.... 327 F
tstafford@jjay.cuny.edu
STAFFORD, Tomas, L .... 608-263-6105.... 550 I
tstafford@uwsa.edu
STAFFORD, William, S ...... 931-598-1288.... 472 L
theology@sewanee.edu
STAGER, Helen, H .... 570-941-4330.... 450 C
helen.stager@scranton.edu
STAGER, Karl .... 281-756-3509.... 479 F
kstager@alvincollege.edu
STAGGERS, Leroy .... 803-934-3274.... 459 G
lstaggers@morris.edu
STAGGS, Emily .... 864-587-4298.... 461 D
staggse@smcsc.edu
STAGNARO, Leta .... 510-742-2301...... 59 J
lstagnaro@ohlone.edu
STAGNI, Joshua .... 260-399-7700.... 181 A
jstagni@sf.edu
STAGNO, Phylis .... 212-247-3434.... 339 G
pstagno@mandl.edu
STAHL, Jason .... 989-686-9559.... 250 D
jfstahl@delta.edu
STAHL, Katy .... 206-268-4004.... 530 I
kstahl@antioch.edu
STAHL, Lauri .... 304-243-2000.... 546 A
STAHL, Norman, S .... 808-933-3115.... 141 F
nstahl@hawaii.edu
STAHL, Ritarose .... 920-686-6134.... 550 H
ritarose.stahl@sl.edu
STAHL, Sharon .... 314-935-5040.... 292 I
sstahl@wustl.edu
STAHL, Stephen, D .... 304-243-2321.... 546 A
sstahl@wju.edu
STAHL, Timothy, W .... 724-925-4073.... 451 E
stahlt@wccc.edu
STAHLE, Noel .... 641-673-1010.... 190 C
stahlen@wmpenn.edu

STARMER, Jamie 530-898-5253 34 C
jstarmer@csuchico.edu
STARNER, Wendy, S 717-766-2511 436 D
wstarner@messiah.edu
STARNES, Gina 318-795-4239 213 D
gina.starnes@lsus.edu
STARNES, Richard 828-227-7646 380 A
starnes@wcu.edu
STARNES, Scott 434-592-4191 520 K
sastarnes@liberty.edu
STARNES, Shane 704-461-6200 362 F
shanestarnes@bac.edu
STAROS, James, V 413-545-6223 236 F
jstaros@provost.umass.edu
STARR, Bettie, C 270-384-8030 204 D
starrb@lindsey.edu
STARR, Brian 806-720-7405 490 F
brian.starr@lcu.edu
STARR, Clara, H 415-241-2249 40 C
cstarr@ccsf.edu
STARR, Claudia 573-642-2251 293 D
claudia.starr@williamwoods.edu
STARR, Dolores 904-256-7016 111 L
dstarr@ju.edu
STARR, J. Barton 561-803-2250 114 C
barton_starr@pba.edu
STARR, Kenneth, W 254-710-3555 482 A
ken_starr@baylor.edu
STARR, Margaret, J 309-692-4092 158 D
mstarr@midstate.edu
STARR, Peter 202-885-2446 97 D
pstarr@american.edu
STARR, Sharon 704-922-6366 370 G
starr.sharon@gaston.edu
STARR, Terry 913-621-8718 192 F
tstarr@donnelly.edu
STARR, Valorie 620-278-4463 196 H
vstarr@sterling.edu
STARR-COHEN, Debra 305-597-9599 108 E
miami@fanh.com
STARR FIEDLER, Heather 412-392-3409 445 A
hstarr@pointpark.edu
STARRATT, Christopher 305-899-4757 101 M
cstarratt@mail.barry.edu
STARRATT, Joseph 509-335-4558 539 D
jstarratt@wsu.edu
STARRETT, David 573-986-7477 289 K
dstarrett@semo.edu
STARTUP, Allison 770-720-5542 136 C
afs@reinhardt.edu
STARTUP, Kenneth, M 870-759-4128 26 B
kstartup@wbcoll.edu
STASA, Joan 419-530-2814 404 F
joan.stasa@utoledo.edu
STASCHAK, John, J 716-250-7500 324 H
jjstaschak@bryantstratton.edu
STASHER, Jesse 702-968-2004 303 D
jstasher@roseman.edu
STASIAK, Joan, C 773-508-3143 157 C
jstasia@luc.edu
STASOLLA, Debbie 609-896-5228 313 F
dstasolla@rider.edu
STASSEN, Anne, K 215-972-2039 440 J
astassen@pafa.edu
STASSEN, Jodi 218-793-2539 268 C
jodistassen@northlandcollege.edu
STASSEN, Martha, L 413-545-5146 236 F
mstassen@acad.umass.edu
STASSIS, Bassel 973-684-6500 312 E
bstassis@pccd.edu
STATE, Timothy 847-735-6022 155 G
state@lakeforest.edu
STATEN, Michael 270-384-8106 204 D
statenm@lindsey.edu
STATEN, Shannon, D 502-852-6636 207 E
sdstat01@louisville.edu
STATES, Hollyce 508-588-9100 240 A
STATMORE, Kelly 203-910-7258 93 G
kstatmore@post.edu
STATMORE, Michael 203-591-5056 93 G
mstatmore@post.edu
STATON, Ann 940-898-3326 502 D
astaton@twu.edu
STATON, Trina, J 551-574-1312 185 I
staton@iowacentral.edu
STATON, Wendell 478-445-6341 130 B
wendell.staton@gcsu.edu
STATTON, Thomas, M 301-766-3653 223 G
tstatton@kaplan.edu
STATZELL, Donna, S 952-995-1447 266 D
dstatzell@hennepintech.edu
STAUB, Robert, H 318-342-5360 216 E
staub@ulm.edu
STAUDERMAN, Elizabeth 203-432-1345 96 A
elizabeth.stauderman@yale.edu
STAUDINGER, Scott 701-483-2984 381 G
scott.staudinger@dickinsonstate.edu
STAUDT, Denise 210-829-2761 504 B
staudt@uiwtx.edu
STAUDT, Loretta 202-319-5744 97 E
staudt@cua.edu
STAUFFENBERG, Serol 307-855-2272 556 B
serol@cwc.edu

STAUFFER, Denise 314-918-2620 281 F
dstauffer@eden.edu
STAUFFER, Donald, C 757-455-3384 530 C
dstauffer@vwc.edu
STAUFFER, George, B 848-932-5224 314 C
stauffer@masongross.rutgers.edu
STAUFFER, Glen 610-328-8654 447 F
gstauff1@swarthmore.edu
STAUFFER, Gregory 801-321-7104 511 B
gstaufferr@utahsbr.edu
STAUFFER, Larry 208-885-6470 144 G
stauffer@uidaho.edu
STAUFFER, Lynn 707-664-2171 37 D
lynn.stauffer@sonoma.edu
STAUFFER, Patricia 978-478-3400 246 G
pstauffer@zbc.edu
STAUFFER, II, Ronald, E 570-577-3305 423 E
ron.stauffer@bucknell.edu
STAUGLER, Elizabeth, J 419-586-0365 406 D
elizabeth.staugler@wright.edu
STAUNTON, Annette 419-448-3410 402 E
astaunto@tiffin.edu
STAUSS, Michelle 973-618-3555 308 C
mstauss@caldwell.edu
STAUTZ, Shay, D 520-621-3108 18 L
stautzs@email.arizona.edu
STAV, Eli 443-518-4769 223 D
estav@howardcc.edu
STAVENGA, Mink 619-482-6442 71 D
mstavenga@swccd.edu
STAVER, Mathew, D 434-592-5300 520 K
mstaver@liberty.edu
STAVITSKY, Alan 775-784-6656 303 A
ags@unr.edu
ST.CHARLES, Kenneth 504-520-7575 217 A
kstcharl@xula.edu
ST CLAIR, Ann 406-496-4284 296 A
astclair@mtech.edu
STEADMAN, Charles 972-721-5305 503 B
cstead@udallas.edu
STEADMAN, Jacqui 423-461-8686 471 J
jrsteadman@milligan.edu
STEADMAN, Jennifer, C 318-797-5108 213 D
jennifer.steadman@lsus.edu
STEADMAN, Jessica 937-695-0307 402 A
jsteadman@sscc.edu
STEADMAN, John 251-460-6140 9 D
jsteadman@usouthal.edu
STEADMAN, Mimi, H 716-839-8567 331 F
msteadma@daemen.edu
STEADMAN, Rick 310-689-3200 42 H
rsteadman@kaplan.edu
STEADMAN, Sheryl 801-832-2168 512 G
ssteadman@westminstercollege.edu
STEADMAN, II,
William, A 914-594-4607 343 F
gus_steadman@nymc.edu
STEAGALL, Jeffrey 801-626-6063 511 G
jeffsteagall@weber.edu
STEANE, Joanne, E 307-766-2130 556 H
jesteane@uwyo.edu
STEARNEY, Michael 920-465-2236 551 B
stearnem@uwgb.edu
STEARNS, Gail 714-628-7289 39 F
stearns@chapman.edu
STEARNS, J. David 251-460-6494 9 D
dstearns@usouthal.edu
STEARNS, Jill 209-575-6067 80 H
stearnsj@mjc.edu
STEARNS, Joan 352-873-5808 103 K
stearnsj@cf.edu
STEARNS, Keith 559-934-2234 78 B
keithstearns@whccd.edu
STEARNS, Marc 215-503-0155 448 C
marc.stearns@jefferson.edu
STEARNS, Mary, F 513-732-5278 403 E
mary.stearns@uc.edu
STEARNS, Peter, N 703-993-8776 519 E
pstearns@gmu.edu
STEARNS, Roger 956-665-2727 506 C
stearns@utpa.edu
STEARNS, Sandra 262-691-5368 555 E
sstearns@wctc.edu
STEARNS, Susan, M 515-263-2955 185 C
sstearns@grandview.edu
STEARNS, Thaine 707-664-2146 37 D
stearnst@sonoma.edu
STEARNS MOORE, Kai 714-808-4831 59 C
kstearns@nocccd.edu
STEARNS-SIMS, Elizabeth 406-447-6903 295 A
STEBACK, Thomas, G 410-857-2205 224 C
tsteback@mcdaniel.edu
STEBBINS, Barbara 207-228-8598 220 G
stebbins@usm.maine.edu
STEBBINS, Carla 515-271-1497 184 A
carla.stebbins@dmu.edu
STEBBINS, Charles 304-357-4372 542 A
charlesstebbins@ucwv.edu
STEBBINS, Gerald 304-829-7640 540 H
gstebbins@bethanywv.edu
STEBBINS, Todd, H 608-246-6976 554 D
stebbins@madisoncollege.org
STEC, Melissa, A 312-939-0111 150 D
melissa@eastwest.edu

STEC, Paul, T 518-783-2314 350 I
pstec@siena.edu
STECHSCHULTE,
Donald, W 570-577-1401 423 E
don.stechschulte@bucknell.edu
STECKER, Ann Page 603-526-3644 303 G
astecker@colby-sawyer.edu
STECKMANN, Chris 217-732-3155 156 I
csteckmann@lincolncollege.edu
STEED, Martha 903-233-3803 490 A
marthasteed@letu.edu
STEEDLEY, Dwight 251-442-2314 9 A
dsteedley@umobile.edu
STEEDLEY, Lorrie 863-638-7202 123 D
lorrie.steedley@warner.edu
STEEGE, Craig 815-316-4800 162 B
craig.steege@rasmussen.edu
STEEGE, David 262-551-5847 546 I
steege@carthage.edu
STEEGE, Judi 417-667-8181 280 E
jsteege@cottey.edu
STEEHLER, Jack, K 540-375-2540 523 G
jsteehler@roanoke.edu
STEEL, Ann, E 717-866-5775 429 A
asteel@evangelical.edu
STEEL, Diane, M 559-323-2100 66 C
dsteel@sjcl.edu
STEEL, John 620-654-2416 190 D
jsteel@allencc.edu
STEEL, Virginia 831-459-2076 75 C
vsteel@ucsc.edu
STEELE, Anne, C 740-826-8115 397 A
asteele@muskingum.edu
STEELE, Athornia 954-262-6100 114 B
asteele@nsu.nova.edu
STEELE, Cherie 253-589-6010 532 G
cherie.steele@cptc.edu
STEELE, Cheryl, L 434-381-6134 524 K
csteele@sbc.edu
STEELE, Claude 650-725-9090 71 G
STEELE, Clint 253-566-5207 538 F
csteele@tacomacc.edu
STEELE, Clover 212-247-3434 339 G
csteele@mandl.edu
STEELE, David 863-297-1000 115 C
dsteele@polk.edu
STEELE, David 408-924-3400 37 C
david.m.steele@sjsu.edu
STEELE, Diane 913-758-6102 197 D
quinleyl@stmary.edu
STEELE, Donna, M 731-989-6001 469 B
dsteele@fhu.edu
STEELE, Douglas 406-994-3293 295 C
dsteele@montana.edu
STEELE, E. Springs 610-660-1879 446 C
ssteele@sju.edu
STEELE, Emily 859-371-9393 198 G
esteele@beckfield.edu
STEELE, Everette 304-929-1655 541 H
esteele@mountainstate.edu
STEELE, Jessica 207-948-9293 219 H
jsteele@unity.edu
STEELE, Joanne 914-633-2691 336 E
jsteele@iona.edu
STEELE, Karen, B 718-631-6604 328 F
ksteele@qcc.cuny.edu
STEELE, Kemper 434-961-6585 528 B
ksteele@pvcc.edu
STEELE, Kevin, L 913-971-3278 195 D
klsteele@mnu.edu
STEELE, Larry, W 540-283-6647 522 D
lsteele@national-college.edu
STEELE, Laura, L 714-879-3901 50 I
llsteele@hiu.edu
STEELE, Leslie 615-547-1268 468 B
lsteele@cumberland.edu
STEELE, Linda, M 614-947-6583 391 B
steelel@franklin.edu
STEELE, Lynda, A 662-246-6301 275 D
lsteele@msdelta.edu
STEELE, Mitzi, B 540-375-2249 523 G
steele@roanoke.edu
STEELE, Patricia, A 301-405-9127 227 B
pasteele@umd.edu
STEELE, Patrick, W 701-788-4794 381 H
patrick.steele@mayvillestate.edu
STEELE, Renee 910-521-6533 379 C
renee.steele@uncp.edu
STEELE, Richard 404-894-2803 130 F
rich.steele@gatech.edu
STEELE, Sarah 203-582-8905 93 H
sarah.steele@quinnipiac.edu
STEELE, Scott 859-985-3416 199 A
steeles@berea.edu
STEELE, Steven 970-223-2669 85 E
ssteele@ibmc.edu
STEELE, Todd, J 810-762-9502 253 C
tsteele@kettering.edu
STEELE, Valerie 212-217-4530 333 F
valerie_steele@fitnyc.edu
STEELE-MIDDLETON,
Amanda 919-760-8424 367 A
registrar@meredith.edu
STEELMAN, Gary 513-785-1816 396 F
steelmge@muohio.edu

STEELY, Jeffrey 254-710-2464 482 A
jeff_steely@baylor.edu
STEELY, Wayne 860-231-5257 95 D
wsteely@usj.edu
STEEN, Franklin 212-772-4946 327 E
franklin.steen@hunter.cuny.edu
STEEN, James 281-649-3208 487 H
jsteen@hbu.edu
STEEN, Kenneth, L 540-654-1159 525 D
ksteen@umw.edu
STEEN, Sara Jayne 603-535-2210 307 A
sjsteen@plymouth.edu
STEEN, Traci 941-752-5220 118 J
steent@scf.edu
STEENHOEK, David 515-643-6680 187 F
dsteenhoek@mercydesmoines.org
STEENIS, Paul, R 309-341-7145 155 F
psteenis@knox.edu
STEENKEN, Betsy 304-327-4176 543 F
bsteenken@bluefieldstate.edu
STEENSLAND, Blaine, E 610-396-6066 439 B
bes2@psu.edu
STEENSON, Greg 651-690-8825 270 L
gpsteenson@stkate.edu
STEENWYK, Thomas, L 616-526-6549 249 A
steeto@calvin.edu
STEERE-SALAZAR, Carrie 415-502-8296 75 A
carrie.steere-salazar@ucsf.edu
STEEVES, Myron, R 714-836-7500 166 E
msteeves@tiu.edu
STEFANCO, Carolyn, J 404-471-6361 123 I
cstefanco@agnesscott.edu
STEFANI COMERFORD,
Sandra 650-574-6337 67 G
comerford@smccd.edu
STEFANICK, Susan, A 609-896-5065 313 F
stefanic@rider.edu
STEFANOWICZ, Michael 860-512-2663 91 F
mstefanowicz@mcc.commnet.edu
STEFANSKI, Kimberly 303-404-5481 85 A
kimberly.stefanski@frontrange.edu
STEFANSKY, Chaim 718-259-2525 324 A
STEFANSSON, Pamela 480-860-2700 14 F
nikita@taliesin.edu
STEFFAN, Dee 802-654-0505 515 E
steffand@ccv.edu
STEFFEE, David, J 616-632-2895 247 E
steffdav@aquinas.edu
STEFFEN, Lloyd, H 610-758-3877 434 E
lhs1@lehigh.edu
STEFFEN, Sally 909-621-8000 69 A
sally.steffen@scrippscollege.edu
STEFFEN, Susan, S 630-617-3172 150 H
susanss@elmhurst.edu
STEFFEN, Wayne 559-453-2215 48 A
wsteffen@fresno.edu
STEFFENS, Kate 410-245-2198 272 C
kate.steffens@waldenu.edu
STEFFENS, Kathy 217-732-3155 156 I
ksteffens@lincolncollege.edu
STEFFES, Gary 660-263-4110 286 H
garys@macc.edu
STEFFES, Jeanne, S 413-782-1282 246 A
jsteffes@wne.edu
STEFFES, Thomas 765-983-1366 171 E
steffto@earlham.edu
STEFFEY, Kara 402-431-6100 298 D
ksteffey@kaplan.edu
STEFLIK, Robert 940-397-4324 491 B
robert.steflik@mwsu.edu
STEGALL, Corre, A 318-255-7950 215 F
corre@latechalumni.org
STEGER, Alicia 516-572-9634 342 C
alicia.steger@ncc.edu
STEGER, Charles, W 540-231-6231 529 G
president@vt.edu
STEGER, Michael 561-803-2200 114 C
national@pba.edu
STEGMAN, Lindsay 765-658-4668 171 B
lindsaystegman@depauw.edu
STEGMAN, Stephen, J 518-629-7158 336 C
s.stegman@hvcc.edu
STEGMAYER, William, J 845-848-7822 332 B
william.stegmayer@dc.edu
STEGMEIER, Randy 360-650-3555 539 F
randy.stegmeier@wwu.edu
STEHLE, Allen, T 207-947-4591 217 D
astehle@bealcollege.edu
STEHNEY, Ann 301-628-5625 225 B
astehney@nlc.edu
STEHOUWER, Kristin 989-837-4224 256 E
stehouwer@northwood.edu
STEIB, Larissa, L 504-762-3188 210 F
lsteib@dcc.edu
STEIBE-PASALICH, Susan 574-631-7336 180 G
steibe-pasalich.1@nd.edu
STEIDEL, Michael 412-268-2082 424 J
ms44@andrew.cmu.edu
STEIDL, Douglas 330-672-2917 393 D
dsteidl@kent.edu
STEIL, Lora 563-387-1134 187 D
steilo02@luther.edu
STEIMEL, Rasalee, M 785-827-5541 194 F
rose@kwu.edu

STEIN, A, R 732-364-1220 307 D
STEIN, Beki 610-796-8202 421 G
beki.stein@alvernia.edu
STEIN, Bob 207-621-3447 220 B
rstein@maine.edu
STEIN, Carla 303-678-3755 85 A
carla.stein@frontrange.edu
STEIN, Charles, K 631-451-4236 356 D
steinc@sunysuffolk.edu
STEIN, Cliff 503-517-1878 421 C
cstein@westernseminary.edu
STEIN, Dov 248-414-6900 254 F
dstein@mji.edu
STEIN, Jeff 336-278-7304 364 D
jstein@elon.edu
STEIN, Jennifer 415-551-9313 32 C
jstein@cca.edu
STEIN, Jerrold 631-632-7320 352 C
jerrold.stein@stonybrook.edu
STEIN, John 914-594-4696 343 F
john_stein@nymc.edu
STEIN, John 404-894-6367 130 F
john.stein@vpss.gatech.edu
STEIN, Karen P, Z 585-785-1298 334 A
steinkp@flcc.edu
STEIN, Kathy 432-837-8770 501 E
kstein@sulross.edu
STEIN, Linda 610-917-1416 450 E
llstein@vfcc.edu
STEIN, Maria, K 617-373-2430 243 F
STEIN, Mark, A 507-354-8221 264 K
steinma@mlc-wels.edu
STEIN, Melanie 860-297-5244 94 E
melanie.stein@trincoll.edu
STEIN, N 732-364-1220 307 D
STEIN, Scott 802-447-6349 514 F
sstein@svc.edu
STEIN, Sue 503-352-7285 419 E
steins@pacificu.edu
STEIN, Thomas, J 724-847-6590 429 H
tjstein@geneva.edu
STEIN, Tom 423-636-7300 477 A
STEIN-SMITH, Kathy 201-692-2653 310 A
stein@fdu.edu
STEIN-STOVER, Barbara 858-635-4624 27 D
bstein-stover@alliant.edu
STEIN-WEBBER, Brian 510-559-2711 60 E
STEINACKER, Kathy 815-939-5359 161 A
ksteinac@olivet.edu
STEINBACH, Sandra 269-387-2365 260 C
sandra.steinbach@wmich.edu
STEINBACK, Robin 619-660-4226 49 B
robin.steinback@gcccd.edu
STEINBERG, Aaron 718-868-2300 323 G
STEINBERG, Bettie 516-562-1159 332 G
bsteinbe@lij.edu
STEINBERG, Bryan, E 302-356-6858 97 C
bryan.e.steinberg@wilmu.edu
STEINBERG, David, J 516-299-2501 338 E
president@liu.edu
STEINBERG, Igor, R 608-246-6112 554 D
isteinberg@madisoncollege.org
STEINBERG, James, B 315-443-5450 357 C
jbstein@syr.edu
STEINBERG, Joseph 973-642-8686 315 C
joseph.steinberg@shu.edu
STEINBERG, Kurt 617-879-7269 238 B
ksteinberg@massart.edu
STEINBERG, Laura, J 315-443-4341 357 C
ljs@syr.edu
STEINBERG, Leslie, R 213-738-6731 71 E
publicaffairs@swlaw.edu
STEINBERG, Sarah 410-516-8382 223 F
steinberg@jhu.edu
STEINBERG, Stacey 414-847-3255 549 B
staceysteinberg@miad.edu
STEINBERG, Stephanie 718-488-3311 338 G
stephanie.steinberg@liu.edu
STEINBOCK, Daniel 419-530-5099 404 F
daniel.steinbock@utoledo.edu
STEINBOCK, Valerie 928-541-7777 16 H
vsteinbock@ncu.edu
STEINE, Tracy 802-485-2015 514 C
nufinaide@norwich.edu
STEINER, Ann 717-291-3986 429 F
ann.steiner@fandm.edu
STEINER, David 440-646-8302 405 B
dsteiner@ursuline.edu
STEINER, David 212-772-4000 327 E
david.steiner@hunter.cuny.edu
STEINER, Deirdre 405-422-1467 411 G
deirdre.steiner@redlandscc.edu
STEINER, Fred 313-845-9621 252 B
fred@hfcc.edu
STEINER, Frederick, R 512-471-1922 505 D
fsteiner@austin.utexas.edu
STEINER, Glen, D 708-209-3328 148 E
glen.steiner@cuchicago.edu
STEINER, James, D 563-589-3210 189 F
jsteiner@dbq.edu
STEINER, Joseph, F 307-766-6556 556 H
jspharmd@uwyo.edu
STEINER, Kat 937-484-1282 405 A
ksteiner@urbana.edu
STEINER, Rita, L 410-617-2504 223 I
rsteiner@loyola.edu
STEINER, Rochelle 213-740-6264 76 F
rochelle.steiner@usc.edu
STEINER, Terry 406-657-1078 296 C
steinert@rocky.edu
STEINER, William, W 808-974-7393 141 F
steiner@hawaii.edu
STEINER-LANG, Kathy 314-935-5910 292 I
ksteiner@wustl.edu
STEINERT, Brandon 620-792-9307 190 H
steinertb@bartonccc.edu
STEINFELD, Peter, K 712-749-2205 183 C
steinfeld@bvu.edu
STEINFELD, Trudy 212-998-4735 344 B
trudy.steinfeld@nyu.edu
STEINHAGEN, Robert 206-316-2458 531 D
roberts@bgu.edu
STEINHOFF, Cynthia, K 410-777-2483 221 C
cksteinhoff@aacc.edu
STEINKAMP, Janet 320-308-5933 269 B
jsteinkamp@sctcc.edu
STEINKE, Deana, B 304-877-6428 540 G
financialaid@abc.edu
STEINKE, Pam 312-922-1884 157 E
psteinke@maccormac.edu
STEINKE, Robin, J 717-334-6286 435 A
rsteinke@ltsg.edu
STEINKEOWAY, Louise, A 407-851-2525 106 H
lsteinke@cci.edu
STEINKIRCHNER,
Linda, M 585-385-5242 348 F
lsteinkirchner@sjfc.edu
STEINMAN, Alan 616-331-3749 251 F
steinmaa@gvsu.edu
STEINMETZ, Amanda 307-674-6446 556 F
asteinmetz@sheridan.edu
STEINMETZ, Edward, J 570-941-4289 450 C
edward.steinmetz@scranton.edu
STEINMETZ, Joseph, E 614-292-1677 398 I
steinmetz.53@osu.edu
STEINMETZ, Michael 859-253-3637 200 K
michael.steinmetz@frontier.edu
STEINMETZ, Paul 203-837-8771 91 A
steinmetzp@wcsu.edu
STEINMETZ, Paul, M 203-837-9805 91 A
steinmetzp@wcsu.edu
STEINMETZ, Rob, R 717-221-1798 430 E
rrsteinm@hacc.edu
STEINNERD, Sarah 573-651-2588 289 K
ssteinnerd@semo.edu
STEINOUR, David 703-726-3602 98 C
steinour@gwu.edu
STEINROCK, Timothy, J 610-921-7654 421 E
tsteinrock@alb.edu
STEINRUCK, Jessica, M 202-231-3344 557 J
jessica.steinruck@dodiis.mil
STEINWAY, Harry, R 845-569-3544 342 A
harry.steinway@msmc.edu
STEINWEDEL, Cheryl 419-227-3141 404 D
csteinwedel@unoh.edu
STEITZ, John, A 740-284-5177 391 A
jsteitz@franciscan.edu
STEJSKAL, Patricia 815-479-7530 157 H
pstejskal@mchenry.edu
STEKETEE, Gail 617-353-3760 232 E
steketee@bu.edu
STELLA, Mark 304-384-5356 543 G
markstella@hotmail.com
STELLA, Steven 518-454-5139 330 C
stellas@strose.edu
STELLAR, James 718-997-5900 328 E
james.stellar@qc.cuny.edu
STELTER, Caroline, W 804-758-6728 528 C
cstelter@rappahannock.edu
STELZER, Stuart, P 479-979-1381 26 A
sstelzer@ozarks.edu
STEM, Elaine 252-492-2061 374 G
stem@vgcc.edu
STEMBRIDGE, Allen, F 269-471-3622 247 D
stem@andrews.edu
STEMBRIDGE,
Catherine, L 847-491-8056 160 E
c-stembridge@northwestern.edu
STEMKOSKI, Stephen 315-859-4301 334 H
sstemkos@hamilton.edu
STEMM, Wallis 480-610-3961 13 I
wstemm@devry.edu
STEMMER, John, K 502-272-8140 198 H
jstemmer@bellarmine.edu
STEMPER, Diane, L 614-292-3600 398 I
stemper.1@osu.edu
STEN, Andrea 503-493-6529 415 E
asten@cu-portland.edu
STENBECK, Amber, L 919-508-2037 380 E
astenbeck@peace.edu
STENBERG, Richard, W 937-327-7460 406 B
rstenberg@wittenberg.edu
STENBERG, Steve 503-517-1238 421 B
sstenberg@warnerpacific.edu
STENDARDI, Deborah, M 585-475-5040 347 G
dmsgrl@rit.edu
STENDER, Julie 435-652-7703 512 B
stender@dixie.edu
STENEHJEM, Keith, A 701-788-4755 381 H
keith.stenehjem@mayvillestate.edu
STENGEL, Mark 805-546-3159 43 I
mark_stengel@cuesta.edu
STENGER, JR., Harvey, G 607-777-2131 351 F
president@binghamton.edu
STENGER, Karen 440-826-2726 384 K
kstenger@bw.edu
STENKO, Michael 860-465-4509 90 H
stenkom@easternct.edu
STENNES-SPIDAHL,
Naomi, R 608-796-3481 553 C
nrstennesspidahl@viterbo.edu
STENNETT, Debbie 806-291-3500 508 E
stennettd@wbu.edu
STENNETTE, Jan 434-544-8381 521 B
stennette@lynchburg.edu
STENSON, Charlene 701-845-7105 382 C
charlene.stenson@vcsu.edu
STENSON, Charlene 701-845-7105 382 C
c.stenson@vcsu.edu
STENSON, Linnea 612-659-6103 267 B
linnea.stenson@minneapolis.edu
STENSRUD, Scott 808-544-0278 140 G
sstensrud@hpu.edu
STEORTS, Ken 901-381-3939 478 E
ken@visible.edu
STEPANOVICH, Michael 661-395-4840 52 L
mstepano@bakersfieldcollge.edu
STEPHAN, Andrew 330-494-6170 402 B
astephan@starkstate.edu
STEPHAN, Larry 928-777-3770 14 C
larry.stephan@erau.edu
STEPHAN, Lisa, M 920-565-1255 548 A
stephanlm@lakeland.edu
STEPHAN, Scott 517-629-0960 247 A
sstephan@alpha.albion.edu
STEPHAN, Sharon, R 402-472-7554 300 E
sstephan@nebraska.edu
STEPHAN, W. Karl 989-837-4211 256 E
stephan@northwood.edu
STEPHAN, William, B 317-231-2114 173 E
wstephan@indiana.edu
STEPHAN, William, B 812-855-0850 173 D
wstephan@indiana.edu
STEPHAN HAINS,
Theresa, R 716-878-6711 353 A
stephatr@buffalostate.edu
STEPHEN, Carolyn 530-895-2311 31 H
stephenca@butte.edu
STEPHEN, Cathleen 610-607-6205 445 C
cstephen@racc.edu
STEPHEN BURT,
M. Rachel 317-940-9867 170 F
rstephen@butler.edu
STEPHEN-SELBY,
Heather, M 425-235-2352 537 A
heatherstephen-selby@rtc.edu
STEPHENOFF, Gail, C 614-292-5648 398 I
stephenoff.1@osu.edu
STEPHENS, Amy, M 503-255-0332 417 C
astephens@multnomah.edu
STEPHENS, Arthur 828-227-7203 380 A
stephena@wcu.edu
STEPHENS, Barry 270-686-4516 203 B
barry.stephens@kctcs.edu
STEPHENS, Brian 575-234-9205 319 F
brstephe@nmsu.edu
STEPHENS, Cathy 217-641-4515 154 I
cstephens@jwcc.edu
STEPHENS, Charlene 302-736-2505 97 A
stephech@wesley.edu
STEPHENS, Christina 207-326-2441 219 D
christina.stephens@mma.edu
STEPHENS, Crystal 661-726-1911 73 F
crystal.stephens@uav.edu
STEPHENS, David 877-442-0505 89 C
david.stephens@rockies.edu
STEPHENS, David, J 931-363-9865 471 A
dstephens@martinmethodist.edu
STEPHENS, Diane, S 818-677-5929 35 F
diane.stephens@csun.edu
STEPHENS, Elisa 415-274-2200 26 E
STEPHENS, Fred, W 407-303-5752 100 G
fred.stephens@adu.edu
STEPHENS, Janice 256-378-2003 2 E
jstephens@cacc.edu
STEPHENS, Jay 541-552-8557 419 A
stephenj1@sou.edu
STEPHENS, Jerry, W 205-934-6360 8 F
jerryws@uab.edu
STEPHENS, Josh 806-720-7502 490 F
josh.stephens@lcu.edu
STEPHENS, Kevin, N 309-655-2291 163 G
kevin.n.stephens@osfhealthcare.org
STEPHENS, Mark 931-372-3224 474 B
mstephens@tntech.edu
STEPHENS, Mary 213-624-1200 46 L
mstephens@fidm.edu
STEPHENS, Mary, E 562-985-1658 35 C
mestephe@csulb.edu
STEPHENS, Mary Ann 330-672-2121 393 D
STEPHENS, Michael 323-259-2651 59 I
mstephens@oxy.edu
STEPHENS, JR.,
Norman, L 863-784-7110 117 J
norman.stephens@southflorida.edu
STEPHENS, Ralph 361-593-3814 498 D
ralph.stephens@tamuk.edu
STEPHENS, Richard 704-637-4466 363 E
rstephens@catawba.edu
STEPHENS, Robert 404-756-5223 134 E
rstephens@msm.edu
STEPHENS, Robert, E 816-654-7533 283 F
rstephens@kcumb.edu
STEPHENS, Ronald 270-769-1614 208 A
ron.stephens@wku.edu
STEPHENS, Rusty 252-246-1223 375 D
rstephens@wilsoncc.edu
STEPHENS, Sandra, S 901-722-3220 473 C
sandra@sco.edu
STEPHENS, Scott 205-665-6663 9 B
stephens@montevallo.edu
STEPHENS, Sharon 215-968-8468 423 F
stephens@bucks.edu
STEPHENS, Sonya 812-855-8783 173 E
sonsteph@indiana.edu
STEPHENS, Valerie 865-471-4727 467 G
vstephens@cn.edu
STEPHENS, Vincent, L 570-577-1095 423 E
vincent.stephens@bucknell.edu
STEPHENS, Virginia, L 203-396-8302 94 B
stephensv@sacredheart.edu
STEPHENSON, Alan, H 828-694-1821 368 E
ah_stephenson@blueridge.edu
STEPHENSON, Cathy 828-694-1807 368 E
ck_stephenson@blueridge.edu
STEPHENSON, Devin 573-840-9698 290 F
dstephenson@trcc.edu
STEPHENSON, Diane 217-732-3155 156 I
dstephenson@lincolncollege.edu
STEPHENSON, E. Frank 252-398-6278 363 G
stephf@chowan.edu
STEPHENSON, Errol 954-973-4760 101 D
estephenson@atienterprises.edu
STEPHENSON, Jeffrey 916-484-8376 56 A
stephej@arc.losrios.edu
STEPHENSON, Melissa, K 603-924-2481 305 D
mstephenson@nec.edu
STEPHENSON, Norman, J 308-635-6121 301 D
stephens@wncc.edu
STEPHENSON, Rod 206-878-3710 535 B
rstephen@highline.edu
STEPHENSON, Sally 716-851-1698 333 C
stephenson@ecc.edu
STEPHENSON, Susan, E 850-474-2487 121 D
sstephenson@uwf.edu
STEPHENSON, Thomas 610-328-8319 447 F
tstephe1@swarthmore.edu
STEPHERSON, Kenneth 814-824-2273 436 C
kstepherson@mercyhurst.edu
STEPHNEY, Jessie 601-877-6471 272 F
jstephney@alcorn.edu
STEPLETON, Jon 719-502-2017 87 B
jon.stepleton@ppcc.edu
STEPNER, Michael 619-684-8789 59 B
mstepner@newschoolarch.edu
STEPNIAK, Michael, J 540-665-4600 524 E
mstepnia@su.edu
STEPP, James, D 207-768-9560 220 F
james.stepp@umpi.edu
STEPP, Jim 606-368-6454 198 C
jamesstepp@alc.edu
STEPP, Joe, A 606-368-6027 198 C
joestepp@alc.edu
STEPPE, Stephen 412-536-1275 432 H
stephen.steppe@laroche.edu
STEPTOE, David 478-289-2049 129 B
dsteptoe@ega.edu
STERK, Claire, E 404-727-0785 129 D
claire.sterk@emory.edu
STERK, Jim 619-594-6357 37 A
adsdsu@mail.sdsu.edu
STERKOWITZ, Robert 708-974-5250 159 B
sterkowitz@morainevalley.edu
STERLING, Alan 972-721-5347 503 B
asterling@udallas.edu
STERLING, Althea 718-951-5916 326 F
asterling@brooklyn.cuny.edu
STERLING, Greg, E 574-631-8052 180 G
sterling.1@nd.edu
STERLING, Gregory, E 203-432-5304 96 A
gregory.sterling@yale.edu
STERLING, Marcia 505-566-3588 320 D
sterlingm@sanjuancollege.edu
STERLING, Michael 740-695-9500 385 B
msterling@belmontcollege.edu
STERLING, Monique 610-992-1700 99 G
STERLING, Rita, M 501-569-3302 24 E
rmsterling@ualr.edu
STERLING, Shauna 479-619-3136 22 H
ssterling1@nwacc.edu
STERLING, Walter, J 505-984-6070 320 C
dean@sjcsf.edu
STERN, Dana 419-473-2700 389 C
dstern@daviscolleg.edu
STERN, David 901-448-5529 477 E
dstern@uthsc.edu

STERN, David ... 901-448-5293 ... 477 E dstern@uthsc.edu
STERN, Deborah ... 215-576-0800 ... 445 D dstern@rrc.edu
STERN, Dennis ... 802-831-1155 ... 515 B dstern@vermontlaw.edu
STERN, Donna ... 203-371-7929 ... 94 B sternd@sacredheart.edu
STERN, Elliott ... 425-388-9142 ... 534 C estern@everett.edu
STERN, Gail ... 413-205-3549 ... 229 G gail.stern@aic.edu
STERN, Hal, S ... 949-824-7405 ... 74 B icsdean@uci.edu
STERN, Holly, C ... 973-596-6379 ... 312 C holly.stern@njit.edu
STERN, Howard, A ... 412-578-8828 ... 424 I hastern@carlow.edu
STERN, Jonathan, S ... 765-361-6152 ... 181 E sternj@wabash.edu
STERN, Joshua ... 215-572-2934 ... 422 C sternj@arcadia.edu
STERN, Joyce ... 641-269-3702 ... 185 D sternjm@grinnell.edu
STERN, Kevin, D ... 214-841-3426 ... 485 F kstern@dts.edu
STERN, Robert A, M ... 203-432-2279 ... 96 A robert.stern@yale.edu
STERN, Shannyn ... 928-541-7777 ... 16 H sstern@ncu.edu
STERN, Sharon ... 254-710-1010 ... 482 A sharon_stern@baylor.edu
STERN, Steve ... 608-263-1841 ... 550 J sjstern@wisc.edu
STERN, Susan ... 262-695-3451 ... 555 E sstern1@wctc.edu
STERN LANIAK, Lorna ... 215-572-2145 ... 422 C sternl@arcadia.edu
STERNBERG, Robert ... 405-744-5627 ... 410 C provost@okstate.edu
STERNER, Dennis, W ... 509-777-4411 ... 540 C dsterner@whitworth.edu
STERNER, Sheri ... 714-432-5081 ... 41 D ssterner@occ.cccd.edu
STERNS, Teresa, G ... 304-462-4110 ... 544 A teresa.sterns@glenville.edu
STERRETT, Joseph, D ... 610-758-4320 ... 434 E jds7@lehigh.edu
STERRETT, Myra ... 352-395-5150 ... 117 F myra.sterrett@sfcollege.edu
STERRITT, Patricia ... 252-335-0821 ... 369 G psterritt@albemarle.edu
STERRY, Barbara ... 954-262-5365 ... 114 B sterry@nsu.nova.edu
STETLER, P. Daniel ... 772-546-5534 ... 110 N danstetler@hsbc.edu
STETLER, Paul ... 772-546-5534 ... 110 N paulstetler@hsbc.edu
STETTER, Mark ... 970-491-7051 ... 83 F mark.stetter@colostate.edu
STEUER, Axel, D ... 217-245-3001 ... 152 D asteuer@ic.edu
STEUERWALD, Brian ... 317-917-3260 ... 178 A bsteu@martin.edu
STEURBAUT, Margo ... 213-740-2561 ... 76 F steurbau@usc.edu
STEVANUS, Linda ... 301-387-3011 ... 222 H linda.stevanus@garrettcollege.edu
STEVEN, Donald, A ... 609-896-5010 ... 313 F dsteven@rider.edu
STEVENS, Adrian ... 909-607-8684 ... 62 H adrian_stevens@pitzer.edu
STEVENS, Alison ... 206-934-4547 ... 537 D alison.stevens@seattlecolleges.edu
STEVENS, Andrea, N ... 662-329-7431 ... 276 A astevens@dev.muw.edu
STEVENS, Andrew ... 303-914-6201 ... 87 G andrew.stevens@rrcc.edu
STEVENS, Anne, A ... 704-461-6718 ... 362 F annestevens@bac.edu
STEVENS, Arshele ... 312-553-2500 ... 147 B astevens11@ccc.edu
STEVENS, Audrey ... 937-484-1319 ... 405 A astevens@urbana.edu
STEVENS, Blaine, K ... 413-205-3264 ... 229 G blaine.stevens@aic.edu
STEVENS, Bren ... 304-357-4911 ... 542 A brenstevens@ucwv.edu
STEVENS, Brenda, D ... 330-471-8328 ... 395 F bstevens@malone.edu
STEVENS, Carol ... 845-431-8974 ... 332 D cstevens@sunydutchess.edu
STEVENS, Cathleen, M ... 585-389-2001 ... 342 D csteven9@naz.edu
STEVENS, Cheryl, L ... 270-745-4448 ... 208 A cheryl.stevens@wku.edu
STEVENS, Darryl ... 281-756-3594 ... 479 F dstevens@alvincollege.edu
STEVENS, Debbie ... 641-673-2173 ... 190 C stevensd@wmpenn.edu
STEVENS, Dennis, G ... 434-223-6112 ... 519 G dstevens@hsc.edu
STEVENS, Donald ... 248-457-2760 ... 252 E
STEVENS, Doug ... 715-232-2488 ... 552 E stevensd@uwstout.edu
STEVENS, Elizabeth ... 651-690-8600 ... 270 L ejstevens@stkate.edu
STEVENS, Gladstone, H ... 650-289-3344 ... 64 G gladstone.stevens@stpatricksseminary.org
STEVENS, Greg ... 509-434-5037 ... 533 B greg.stevens@ccs.spokane.edu
STEVENS, Greg ... 509-434-5037 ... 533 C gstevens@ccs.spokane.edu
STEVENS, Greg, L ... 509-434-5037 ... 533 A gstevens@ccs.spokane.edu
STEVENS, Ian ... 704-216-7138 ... 373 F ian.stevens@rccc.edu
STEVENS, Irene, E ... 317-940-9470 ... 170 F istevens@butler.edu
STEVENS, Jameson ... 813-880-8056 ... 111 C jstevens@academy.edu
STEVENS, Jim ... 651-290-6328 ... 272 E jim.stevens@wmitchell.edu
STEVENS, John, V ... 540-665-4925 ... 524 E jstevens@su.edu
STEVENS, Karl P, B ... 740-427-5223 ... 394 C stevensk@kenyon.edu
STEVENS, Kasey ... 937-327-7800 ... 406 B kstevens@wittenberg.edu
STEVENS, Kat ... 304-367-4792 ... 543 H kat.stevens@fairmontstate.edu
STEVENS, Ken ... 312-279-3804 ... 29 F kcstevens@argosy.edu
STEVENS, Leslie ... 402-935-9400 ... 299 A lstevens@nechristian.edu
STEVENS, Mark ... 818-677-4069 ... 35 F mark.stevens@csun.edu
STEVENS, Mark, W ... 920-206-2314 ... 548 D mstevens@mbbc.edu
STEVENS, Marty ... 717-334-6286 ... 435 A mstevens@ltsg.edu
STEVENS, RSM, Maryanne ... 402-399-2435 ... 297 C mstevens@csm.edu
STEVENS, Maxwell ... 908-526-1200 ... 313 D mstevens@raritanval.edu
STEVENS, Michael ... 616-222-1430 ... 250 A michael.stevens@cornerstone.edu
STEVENS, Michele ... 806-457-4200 ... 486 I mstevens@fpctx.edu
STEVENS, Moira ... 207-775-3052 ... 218 E mstevens@meca.edu
STEVENS, Nick ... 906-487-7231 ... 251 A nick.stevens@finlandia.edu
STEVENS, Okarita ... 718-488-1043 ... 338 G okarita.stevens@liu.edu
STEVENS, Phil ... 207-775-3052 ... 218 E pstevens@meca.edu
STEVENS, Randy ... 909-558-4558 ... 54 D rstevens@llu.edu
STEVENS, Roger, K ... 847-259-1840 ... 147 A rstevens@christianlifecollege.edu
STEVENS, Ronald ... 845-434-5750 ... 357 A rstevens@sullivan.suny.edu
STEVENS, Roxanne ... 503-682-3903 ... 419 F rstevens@pioneerpacific.edu
STEVENS, Ruth ... 609-258-8108 ... 312 G stevens@princeton.edu
STEVENS, Shaun ... 586-790-2850 ... 248 B shaun.stevens@baker.edu
STEVENS, Sheri, R ... 207-621-3110 ... 220 B sheri@maine.edu
STEVENS, Timothy ... 207-228-8183 ... 220 G tstevens@usm.maine.edu
STEVENS, Timothy, S ... 847-491-7256 ... 160 E tstevens@northwestern.edu
STEVENS, Turney ... 615-966-7657 ... 470 F turney.stevens@lipscomb.edu
STEVENS, Vivian, M ... 918-561-8205 ... 410 D vivian.stevens@okstate.edu
STEVENS, Wayne ... 570-586-2400 ... 422 G wstevens@bbc.edu
STEVENS HAYNES, Gale ... 718-488-1001 ... 338 G gale.haynes@liu.edu
STEVENS-RICHMAN, Jana ... 718-260-3164 ... 346 C jrichman@poly.edu
STEVENS-TAYLOR, Calley ... 610-372-4721 ... 445 C cstevenstaylor@racc.edu
STEVENSON, Adalynn, J ... 660-543-4195 ... 290 H stevenson@ucmo.edu
STEVENSON, Bill ... 479-524-7119 ... 22 C wstevens@jbu.edu
STEVENSON, Daryl, H ... 585-567-9456 ... 336 B daryl.stevenson@houghton.edu
STEVENSON, Deirdra, M ... 405-466-3216 ... 408 G dmstevenson@langston.edu
STEVENSON, Duncan ... 253-964-6612 ... 536 H dstevenson@pierce.ctc.edu
STEVENSON, Elizabeth ... 508-830-6683 ... 238 D estevenson@maritime.edu
STEVENSON, Gwendolyn, A ... 937-778-7949 ... 390 G gstevenson@edisonohio.edu
STEVENSON, James, E ... 904-632-3191 ... 109 F james.stevenson@fscj.edu
STEVENSON, Jeffry, J ... 850-872-3805 ... 110 H jstevenson@gulfcoast.edu
STEVENSON, John ... 954-545-4500 ... 117 I
STEVENSON, John, A ... 303-492-2890 ... 88 H john.stevenson@colorado.edu
STEVENSON, Karen, L ... 615-353-3430 ... 475 E karen.stevenson@nscc.edu
STEVENSON, Laura ... 904-819-6205 ... 107 C lstevenson@flagler.edu
STEVENSON, Leslie, W ... 804-289-8141 ... 525 E lsteven2@richmond.edu
STEVENSON, Mark ... 724-266-3838 ... 448 H mstevenson@tsm.edu
STEVENSON, Martha ... 570-674-6224 ... 436 F mstevens@misericordia.edu
STEVENSON, Martha, A ... 205-226-4648 ... 2 B mstevens@bsc.edu
STEVENSON, Melissa ... 270-707-3811 ... 202 E melissa.stevenson@kctcs.edu
STEVENSON, Michael ... 207-780-4485 ... 220 G mstevenson@usm.maine.edu
STEVENSON, Michael ... 406-994-2513 ... 295 C michael@montana.edu
STEVENSON, Paula ... 954-545-4500 ... 117 I library@sfbc.edu
STEVENSON, Roberta ... 973-748-9000 ... 307 H
STEVENSON, Rosalie ... 864-941-8529 ... 460 D stevenson.r@ptc.edu
STEVENSON, Sarah ... 718-405-3723 ... 330 A sarah.stevenson@mountsaintvincent.edu
STEVENSON, Sharyn ... 870-762-3168 ... 20 A sstevenson@smail.anc.edu
STEVENSON, Susan, A ... 864-596-9031 ... 457 E susan.stevenson@converse.edu
STEVENSON, Susan, G ... 334-683-2303 ... 5 G sstevenson@marionmilitary.edu
STEVENSON, Tara ... 904-826-8508 ... 107 C tstevenson@flagler.edu
STEVENSON, Terree, L ... 740-368-3151 ... 400 G tlsteven@owu.edu
STEVENSON, JR., Tommy ... 662-325-2493 ... 275 F tstevenson@pres.msstate.edu
STEVENSON, Tricia ... 704-461-5094 ... 362 F triciastevenson@bac.edu
STEVENSON, Valerie, O ... 904-620-2920 ... 120 D vstevens@unf.edu
STEVENSON-MARSHALL, Brenda ... 609-652-4870 ... 313 E brenda.stevenson-marshall@stockton.edu
STEVENSON-RATLIFF, Peggy ... 803-535-5233 ... 456 D pratliff@claflin.edu
STEVER, Matthew ... 518-694-7221 ... 322 B matthew.stever@acphs.edu
STEVERSON, Les ... 228-897-7137 ... 278 C les.steverson@wmcarey.edu
STEVICK, David ... 585-567-9607 ... 336 B david.stevick@houghton.edu
STEVICK, Thomas ... 734-481-2303 ... 250 F tstevick@emich.edu
STEWARD, Agnes ... 253-840-8403 ... 536 H asteward@pierce.ctc.edu
STEWARD, Deborah ... 315-781-3500 ... 335 F stewart@hws.edu
STEWARD, Derrick ... 803-793-5147 ... 457 F stewardd@denmarktech.edu
STEWARD, Donald ... 937-376-6425 ... 387 A dsteward@centralstate.edu
STEWARD, Irene ... 217-709-0926 ... 156 C isteward@lakeviewcol.edu
STEWARD, Jerry ... 405-682-7879 ... 409 F jsteward@occc.edu
STEWARD, Kent, L ... 785-628-4206 ... 192 I ksteward@fhsu.edu
STEWARD, Kyle ... 662-325-3221 ... 275 F ksteward@pres.msstate.edu
STEWARD-BRIDGES, Stephanie ... 574-284-4721 ... 179 F sbridges@saintmarys.edu
STEWART, Avis ... 765-983-1393 ... 171 E aviss@earlham.edu
STEWART, Barbara ... 937-484-1395 ... 405 A bstewart@urbana.edu
STEWART, Barbara, A ... 408-554-4396 ... 68 C bstewart@scu.edu
STEWART, Barbara, E ... 608-785-5092 ... 551 C bstewart@uwlax.edu
STEWART, Beth ... 828-398-7650 ... 368 B bethstewart@abtech.edu
STEWART, Betsy ... 610-526-5632 ... 423 D estewart@brynmawr.edu
STEWART, Betty ... 940-397-4226 ... 491 B betty.stewart@mwsu.edu
STEWART, Billy, W ... 601-635-6200 ... 274 A bstewart@eccc.edu
STEWART, Brad, J ... 240-567-1312 ... 224 D brad.stewart@montgomerycollege.edu
STEWART, Brent, A ... 843-953-1618 ... 456 C brent.stewart@citadel.edu
STEWART, Brian ... 479-899-6644 ... 21 B
STEWART, Bryan ... 817-515-1011 ... 496 C bryan.stewart@tccd.edu
STEWART, Carolyn, G ... 803-327-8014 ... 463 H cstewart@yorktech.edu
STEWART, Carrie ... 310-665-6981 ... 60 B cstewart@otis.edu
STEWART, Colin ... 309-556-3850 ... 153 F
STEWART, Colin ... 540-338-1776 ... 522 G
STEWART, Concetta ... 914-674-7500 ... 340 F cstewart@mercy.edu
STEWART, Connie ... 989-328-1249 ... 255 E connies@montcalm.edu
STEWART, Constance ... 410-572-5640 ... 226 D cstewart@host.sdc.edu
STEWART, Craig ... 812-855-4240 ... 173 E stewart@iu.edu
STEWART, Dan ... 512-499-4616 ... 505 B dstewart@utsystem.edu
STEWART, Daniel, P ... 904-818-6238 ... 107 C stewartd@flagler.edu
STEWART, David ... 304-865-6089 ... 541 J david.stewart@ovu.edu
STEWART, David, C ... 304-293-5811 ... 545 A david.stewart@mail.wvu.edu
STEWART, David, R ... 651-638-6225 ... 261 D d-stewart@bethel.edu
STEWART, Dawn ... 614-823-3529 ... 400 H dstewart@otterbein.edu
STEWART, Dean ... 920-498-6995 ... 555 C dean.stewart@nwtc.edu
STEWART, Deborah ... 802-885-8370 ... 515 E stewartd@ccv.edu
STEWART, DeShaunta ... 773-907-4044 ... 147 D dstewart75@ccc.edu
STEWART, Diane ... 661-362-3503 ... 41 I diane.stewart@canyons.edu
STEWART, Dianne ... 912-688-6097 ... 135 D dstewart@ogeecheetech.edu
STEWART, Donette ... 864-503-5280 ... 463 B dstewart@uscupstate.edu
STEWART, Donna, H ... 630-942-3978 ... 148 A stewartdo@cod.edu
STEWART, Dorothy ... 313-993-1028 ... 258 G stewardm@udmercy.edu
STEWART, Doug ... 970-945-8691 ... 82 G
STEWART, Douglas, J ... 585-385-8427 ... 348 F dstewart@sjfc.edu
STEWART, Elizabeth, J ... 585-292-2536 ... 341 H estewart@monroecc.edu
STEWART, Emily ... 765-983-1393 ... 171 E stewaem@earlham.edu
STEWART, Evelyn ... 713-348-4927 ... 493 C estewrt@rice.edu
STEWART, Gloria ... 830-792-7265 ... 494 E gpstewart@schreiner.edu
STEWART, Gloria ... 740-376-4458 ... 395 G gloria.stewart@marietta.edu
STEWART, Graham, G ... 479-575-2801 ... 24 C stewartg@uark.edu
STEWART, Gregory ... 513-562-8744 ... 384 D gstewart@artacademy.edu
STEWART, Henry ... 334-670-3266 ... 8 A hstewart@troy.edu
STEWART, J. Andrew ... 573-341-4011 ... 291 E astewart@mst.edu
STEWART, Jacqueline ... 606-368-6059 ... 198 C jacquelinestewart@alc.edu
STEWART, James ... 410-951-2639 ... 228 B jstewart@coppin.edu
STEWART, James ... 731-352-4093 ... 467 E stewartj@bethelu.edu
STEWART, James ... 503-517-1898 ... 421 C jstewart@westernseminary.edu
STEWART, Janeen, K ... 319-352-8331 ... 189 J janeen.stewart@wartburg.edu
STEWART, Janice ... 973-618-3626 ... 308 C jstewart@caldwell.edu
STEWART, Janie ... 810-766-4209 ... 248 C janie.stewart@baker.edu
STEWART, Jeb ... 540-231-2134 ... 529 G jebs@vt.edu
STEWART, III, Jeffrey, V ... 478-757-6630 ... 133 H jeff.stewart@maconstate.edu
STEWART, Jerry, D ... 515-294-6762 ... 182 E jdstewa@iastate.edu
STEWART, Jo Moore ... 404-270-5061 ... 138 B jstewart@spelman.edu
STEWART, Joan, E ... 918-561-8208 ... 410 D joan.stewart@okstate.edu
STEWART, Joan, H ... 315-859-4105 ... 334 H jstewart@hamilton.edu
STEWART, John, R ... 563-589-3642 ... 189 F jstewart@dbq.edu
STEWART, III, John, W ... 205-665-6001 ... 9 B presidentsoffice@montevallo.edu
STEWART, Joseph, W ... 716-851-1977 ... 333 C stewart@ecc.edu
STEWART, Juarine ... 256-372-5750 ... 1 A juarine.stewart@aamu.edu
STEWART, Karen ... 630-466-7900 ... 168 B kstewart@waubonsee.edu
STEWART, Kate ... 850-201-6200 ... 122 A stewartk@tcc.fl.edu
STEWART, Kathryn ... 781-283-2214 ... 245 E kstewart@wellesley.edu
STEWART, Kevin ... 404-527-7711 ... 132 G kdstewart@itc.edu
STEWART, Larry ... 248-218-2023 ... 257 D lstewart@rc.edu
STEWART, Lea, P ... 732-445-4088 ... 314 C lstewart@rci.rutgers.edu

STOKES, Ellen, E ... 410-704-3255 ... 228 E
estokes@towson.edu
STOKES, Garnett, S ... 850-644-1765 ... 119 D
gstokes@fsu.edu
STOKES, H. Bruce ... 951-343-4487 ... 31 J
hbstokes@calbaptist.edu
STOKES, Judi ... 845-431-8405 ... 332 D
judi.stokes@sunydutchess.edu
STOKES, Larry ... 912-358-4190 ... 136 G
stokesl@savannahstate.edu
STOKES, Leroy ... 336-334-4822 ... 371 A
lstokes@gtcc.edu
STOKES, Madeline ... 251-405-4457 ... 2 C
mstokes@bishop.edu
STOKES, Mark ... 423-636-7316 ... 477 A
STOKES, Maureen, O ... 760-252-2411 ... 30 H
mstokes@barstow.edu
STOKES, Michael ... 423-478-6218 ... 474 E
mstokes@clevelandstatecc.edu
STOKES, Mickey, E ... 662-476-5068 ... 274 B
mstokes@eastms.edu
STOKES, Robert, D ... 610-519-4311 ... 450 H
robert.stokes@villanova.edu
STOKES, Scott, M ... 712-362-7913 ... 186 A
sstokes@iowalakes.edu
STOKES, Timothy ... 253-566-5022 ... 538 F
tstokes@tacomacc.edu
STOKES-WILSON, Lynette . 312-850-7301 ... 147 F
lstokes@ccc.edu
STOLAR, Steven, M ... 856-691-8600 ... 309 B
sstolar@cccnj.edu
STOLEE, Jessica ... 515-294-7612 ... 182 E
jstolee@iastate.edu
STOLL, James, G ... 978-542-6401 ... 238 E
jstoll@salemstate.edu
STOLL, Laura, K ... 573-341-6292 ... 291 E
lstoll@mst.edu
STOLL, Michael ... 585-345-6975 ... 334 F
msstoll@genesee.edu
STOLL, Nancy, C ... 617-573-8239 ... 245 B
nstoll@suffolk.edu
STOLL, Sherideen, S ... 419-372-8262 ... 385 E
sstoll@bgsu.edu
STOLL, William, S ... 314-935-7574 ... 292 I
stoll@wustl.edu
STOLLER, Brett ... 309-649-6211 ... 165 F
brett.stoller@src.edu
STOLLERY, Chris ... 206-726-5052 ... 533 D
cstollery@cornish.edu
STOLLSTEIMER, Terry ... 248-370-2160 ... 256 G
stollste@oakland.edu
STOLPER, Edward, M ... 626-395-6336 ... 32 H
ems@caltech.edu
STOLPER, Lauren, B ... 626-395-6361 ... 32 H
lstolper@caltech.edu
STOLT, Wilbur ... 701-777-2617 ... 381 F
wilbur.stolt@und.edu
STOLTE, Scott ... 702-968-5944 ... 303 D
sstolte@roseman.edu
STOLTZ, Jacklyn, C ... 860-701-5040 ... 93 E
stoltz_j@mitchell.edu
STOLTZ, Marlene ... 406-756-3846 ... 294 C
mstoltz@fvcc.edu
STOLTZ-LOIKE, Marion ... 212-287-3510 ... 358 B
mstoltz-loike@touro.edu
STOLWORTHY, Charity ... 970-675-3203 ... 82 H
charity.stolworthy@cncc.edu
STOLZ, Rebecca ... 323-259-2691 ... 59 I
rstolz@oxy.edu
STOLZER, Donna ... 908-526-1200 ... 313 D
dstolzer@raritanval.edu
STOMBER, Richard ... 973-720-2277 ... 317 D
stomberr@wpunj.edu
STOMPER, Jeffrey, A ... 847-543-2531 ... 148 B
stomper@clcillinois.edu
STONE, Adam ... 212-484-1303 ... 327 F
astone@jjay.cuny.edu
STONE, Amy, E ... 803-777-3106 ... 462 A
astone@sc.edu
STONE, Amy, E ... 803-777-4113 ... 462 A
astone@sc.edu
STONE, Barbara ... 312-235-3507 ... 164 F
b.stone@shimer.edu
STONE, Brad ... 310-338-5807 ... 56 E
bstone@lmu.edu
STONE, Carolyn ... 561-803-2567 ... 114 C
carolyn_stone@pba.edu
STONE, David ... 815-753-9282 ... 160 B
dastone@niu.edu
STONE, David ... 708-534-4515 ... 151 E
dstone@govst.edu
STONE, David, M ... 212-854-9962 ... 330 F
dms2148@columbia.edu
STONE, Denise ... 503-255-0332 ... 417 C
dstone@multnomah.edu
STONE, Dennis ... 704-971-8500 ... 363 F
STONE, Doreen ... 218-935-0417 ... 272 D
dstone@wetcc.edu
STONE, Eddie ... 931-393-1593 ... 475 D
estone@mscc.edu
STONE, Emily ... 925-685-1230 ... 43 F
estone@dvc.edu
STONE, Gaylund, K ... 262-243-5700 ... 547 C
gaylund.stone@cuw.edu

STONE, Glenice ... 662-720-7237 ... 276 C
gstone@nemcc.edu
STONE, Jan ... 602-371-1188 ... 195 I
jan.stone@ottawa.edu
STONE, Janice ... 806-720-7270 ... 490 F
janice.stone@lcu.edu
STONE, Jenna ... 315-268-3790 ... 329 B
jestone@clarkson.edu
STONE, John ... 661-362-2271 ... 56 G
jstone@masters.edu
STONE, John ... 262-472-1006 ... 553 A
stonej@uww.edu
STONE, Kai ... 303-477-7240 ... 85 B
kais@heritage-education.com
STONE, Karen, J ... 904-620-2828 ... 120 D
kstone@unf.edu
STONE, Karin ... 216-791-5000 ... 388 C
kls160@case.edu
STONE, Katie ... 503-223-2245 ... 416 F
kstone@westernculinary.com
STONE, Keith, H ... 530-221-4275 ... 69 C
pkstone@shasta.edu
STONE, Ken ... 773-896-2400 ... 146 H
kstone@ctschicago.edu
STONE, Kim ... 612-330-1173 ... 261 B
stonek@augsburg.edu
STONE, Marion ... 816-235-5758 ... 291 C
stonema@umkc.edu
STONE, Melissa ... 302-831-8189 ... 96 I
mstone@udel.edu
STONE, Michael, C ... 512-448-8605 ... 493 E
mikecs@stedwards.edu
STONE, Paul ... 817-599-8324 ... 508 F
stone@wc.edu
STONE, Pauline, M ... 704-366-5066 ... 376 B
pstone@rts.edu
STONE, Polly ... 601-923-1630 ... 276 F
pstone@rts.edu
STONE, Ralinda ... 817-598-6276 ... 508 F
rstone@wc.edu
STONE, Sandra ... 706-272-4420 ... 128 C
sstone@daltonstate.edu
STONE, Scott ... 410-225-2398 ... 224 B
sstone@mica.edu
STONE, Shelly, T ... 336-694-5707 ... 372 G
stones@piedmontcc.edu
STONE, Stanley, H ... 407-582-8088 ... 123 B
sstone@valenciacollege.edu
STONE, Sue ... 229-226-1621 ... 138 C
sstone@thomasu.edu
STONE, Susan ... 859-253-3637 ... 200 K
sstone@frontier.edu
STONE, Ty ... 937-512-2512 ... 401 J
ty.stone@sinclair.edu
STONE, Tyanne, S ... 205-652-3852 ... 9 E
tstone@uwa.edu
STONE, William ... 207-621-3501 ... 220 B
whstone@maine.edu
STONECIPHER,
Amanda, G ... 812-941-2674 ... 175 A
agstonec@ius.edu
STONEKING, Carole, B ... 336-841-9168 ... 365 C
stoneki@highpoint.edu
STONEKING, Eric ... 412-809-5100 ... 444 G
stoneking.eric@pti.edu
STONEMAN, Marcia, L ... 828-694-1804 ... 368 E
marcias@blueridge.edu
STONER, Jennifer, E ... 708-709-3949 ... 161 D
jstoner@prairiestate.edu
STONER, Keith ... 419-755-4810 ... 397 C
kstoner@ncstatecollege.edu
STONER, Ken ... 865-974-2571 ... 477 D
kstoner@utk.edu
STONER, Melinda ... 402-354-7230 ... 299 C
melinda.stoner@methodistcollege.edu
STONES, David, H ... 512-863-1951 ... 496 A
stonesd@southwestern.edu
STONESIFER, Cyndi ... 815-921-4158 ... 162 H
c.stonesifer@rockvalleycollege.edu
ST ONGE, Stephen ... 802-862-9616 ... 513 B
sstonge@burlington.edu
STOOKS, George, F ... 585-245-5663 ... 353 C
stooks@geneseo.edu
STOOKSBERRY, Robert ... 210-436-3301 ... 493 F
tstooksberry@stmarytx.edu
STOOPS, Angela ... 240-500-2000 ... 223 A
stoopsa@hagerstowncc.edu
STOOPS, Melinda, K ... 508-626-4596 ... 238 A
mstoops@framingham.edu
STOOPS, T.J ... 219-980-6832 ... 174 B
tkstoops@iun.edu
STOOS, Barbara ... 419-251-1702 ... 395 I
barbara.stoos@mercycollege.edu
STOPPENBRINK, Ken ... 559-934-2160 ... 78 B
kenstoppenbrink@whccd.edu
STOPPENBRINK,
Norman, V ... 818-779-8271 ... 53 B
nstoppenbrink@kingsuniversity.edu
STOPPER, Suzanne, T ... 570-326-3761 ... 440 L
rfisher@pct.edu
STOPPS, Charles ... 708-366-3288 ... 150 C
cstoops@dom.edu
STORCK, Carl ... 813-889-3427 ... 111 C
cstorck@academy.edu

STORCK, Christine, M ... 410-777-2219 ... 221 C
cmstorck@aacc.edu
STORCK, Dennis ... 850-872-3842 ... 110 H
dstorck@gulfcoast.edu
STORCK, Eileen ... 772-462-7361 ... 111 B
estorck@irsc.edu
STORER, Gail ... 614-222-3225 ... 388 G
gstorer@ccad.edu
STOREY, Bruce ... 309-796-5129 ... 145 H
storeyb@bhc.edu
STOREY, G. Paul ... 909-869-2951 ... 33 J
gpstorey@csupomona.edu
STOREY, Karen ... 906-635-2418 ... 253 H
kstorey@lssu.edu
STOREY, Linn ... 706-649-1935 ... 128 A
lstorey@columbustech.edu
STOREY, Richard, D ... 406-683-7151 ... 294 J
r_storey@umwestern.edu
STOREY GROVES,
Margaret ... 802-443-5196 ... 514 A
mgroves@middlebury.edu
STOREY-JOHNSON, Carol 212-746-1050 ... 360 C
cjohnso@med.cornell.edu
STORFA, Kristin ... 503-352-2883 ... 419 E
kstorfa@pacificu.edu
STORIE, Cheryl ... 240-582-2682 ... 227 F
financial-affairs@umuc.edu
STORIE, Leslie ... 606-759-7141 ... 203 A
leslie.mccord@kctcs.edu
STORIE, Monique, C ... 671-735-2162 ... 559 G
mstorie@uguam.uog.edu
STORIN, Matthew, V ... 574-631-6798 ... 180 G
storin.2@nd.edu
STORK, Gilbert, H ... 805-546-3118 ... 43 I
gstork@cuesta.edu
STORLAZZI, Caesar, T ... 203-432-0371 ... 96 A
caesar.storlazzi@yale.edu
STORM, Kathleen, H ... 509-777-4535 ... 540 C
kstorm@whitworth.edu
STORMER, P. Ronald ... 573-288-6485 ... 280 I
rstormer@culver.edu
STORMS, Joyce, A ... 616-538-2330 ... 251 D
jstorms@gbcol.edu
STORMS, Melanie ... 612-338-7224 ... 272 C
melanie.storms@waldenu.edu
STORR, Robert ... 203-432-2606 ... 96 A
robert.storr@yale.edu
STORRS, Regina, M ... 313-593-5020 ... 259 B
rstorrs@umd.umich.edu
STORY, Debra, D ... 518-629-4507 ... 336 C
d.story@hvcc.edu
STORY, Ed ... 606-759-7141 ... 203 A
ed.story@kctcs.edu
STORY, JR., John, H ... 315-733-4764 ... 359 C
jstory@uscny.edu
STORY, Lisa, L ... 712-324-5061 ... 188 C
lstory@nwicc.edu
STORY, Nancy ... 303-556-3801 ... 84 A
nancy.story@ccd.edu
STORY-HUFFMAN, Ru ... 229-931-2259 ... 131 F
ru.story-huffman@gsw.edu
STOSBERG, Tobey ... 816-276-4740 ... 287 H
tobey.stosberg@researchcollege.edu
STOSKOPF, Janna, M ... 701-231-6537 ... 382 B
janna.stoskopf@ndsu.edu
STOSZ, Sandra, L ... 860-444-8285 ... 558 H
sandra.l.stosz@uscg.mil
STOTLER, Doug ... 636-481-3386 ... 283 D
dstotler@jeffco.edu
STOTO, Robert ... 609-896-5140 ... 313 F
stoto@rider.edu
STOTTLEMEYER, Rebecca .. 304-876-5287 ... 544 C
bstottle@shepherd.edu
STOTTS, Bob ... 270-789-5017 ... 199 F
restotts@campbellsville.edu
STOTTS, James ... 404-215-2638 ... 134 D
jstotts@morehouse.edu
STOTTS, Keith ... 304-865-6003 ... 541 J
STOTTS, Melissa ... 701-662-1538 ... 382 F
melissa.stotts@lrsc.edu
STOUGH, Roger, R ... 703-993-2268 ... 519 E
rstough@gmu.edu
STOUGHTON, Charlotte ... 716-372-7978 ... 345 C
cstoughton@obi.edu
STOUP, Gregory ... 650-306-3145 ... 67 F
stoupg@smccd.edu
STOUT, Brandon ... 402-878-2380 ... 298 E
bstout@littlepriest.edu
STOUT, Chris ... 248-689-8282 ... 259 E
cstout@walshcollege.edu
STOUT, David, L ... 515-964-0601 ... 185 A
stoutd@faith.edu
STOUT, Karen, A ... 215-641-6500 ... 436 G
kstout@mc3.edu
STOUT, Michael ... 423-878-4440 ... 472 B
STOUT, Rebecca, Y ... 404-413-1500 ... 131 G
rebeccastout@gsu.edu
STOUT-STEWART,
Sherry, L ... 336-599-1181 ... 372 G
stewars@piedmontcc.edu
STOUTENBOROUGH,
Donna ... 540-986-1800 ... 205 D
dstoutenborough@national-college.edu
STOVALL, Alfred, J ... 662-252-8000 ... 276 G
ajstovall@rustcollege.edu

STOVALL, Barbara ... 256-726-7421 ... 6 C
bstovall@oakwood.edu
STOVALL, Bill ... 201-684-7506 ... 313 C
bstovall@ramapo.edu
STOVALL, George, A ... 434-924-6431 ... 525 F
gas5a@virginia.edu
STOVALL, Jerry ... 229-931-2562 ... 137 C
jstovall@southgatech.edu
STOVALL, Randall, H ... 352-518-1301 ... 114 F
stovalr@phcc.edu
STOVALL, Terri ... 817-923-1921 ... 495 G
tstovall@swbts.edu
STOVALL, Tina ... 217-234-5250 ... 156 B
tstovall@lakeland.cc.il.us
STOVALL, Tyler ... 510-642-5640 ... 73 H
tstovall@berkeley.edu
STOVALL, Vincent ... 703-284-1612 ... 521 D
vincent.stovall@marymount.edu
STOVER, Cherlyn ... 425-602-3093 ... 531 E
cstover@bastyr.edu
STOVER, Dennis, L ... 941-359-4200 ... 121 B
STOVER, Kathleen, J ... 847-214-7374 ... 150 F
kstover@elgin.edu
STOVER, Kathy, J ... 402-844-7268 ... 299 I
kathy@northeast.edu
STOVER, Keith ... 507-389-7207 ... 269 D
keith.stover@southcentral.edu
STOVER, Lois, T ... 240-895-2187 ... 226 A
ltstover@smcm.edu
STOVER, Mark ... 818-677-2271 ... 35 F
mark.stover@csun.edu
STOVER, Mary ... 207-255-1223 ... 220 E
mstover@maine.edu
STOVER, Paul, A ... 714-449-7461 ... 70 G
pstover@scco.edu
STOVER, Ronalda, S ... 803-778-6688 ... 455 G
stoverrs@cctech.edu
STOVER, Teri ... 903-223-3088 ... 498 F
teri.stover@tamut.edu
STOVERINK, Al ... 870-972-2066 ... 20 D
astoverink@astate.edu
STOWASSER, Melissa ... 843-574-6111 ... 461 G
melissa.stowasser@tridenttech.edu
STOWE, June ... 202-885-8678 ... 100 C
jstowe@wesleyseminary.edu
STOWE, Lentz ... 252-940-6306 ... 368 C
lentzs@beaufortccc.edu
STOWE, Patricia ... 405-682-1611 ... 409 F
pstowe@occc.edu
STOWE, Ron, M ... 336-316-2907 ... 365 A
stowerm@guilford.edu
STOWE, Susan ... 412-392-3931 ... 445 A
sstowe@pointpark.edu
STOWELL, Joseph, M ... 616-222-1428 ... 250 A
joe.stowell@cornerstone.edu
STOWELL, Mike ... 616-538-2330 ... 251 D
mstowell@gbcol.edu
STOWELL, Timothy ... 310-825-4321 ... 74 C
tstowell@college.ucla.edu
STOWERS, Deborah ... 256-824-6686 ... 8 G
debbie.stowers@uah.edu
STOWERS, Marian ... 269-337-7192 ... 252 K
marian.stowers@kzoo.edu
STOWERS, Rebecca ... 937-766-7872 ... 386 G
stowersr@cedarville.edu
STOWIK, Stanley ... 401-232-6240 ... 453 C
STOY, Michael ... 478-934-3011 ... 134 B
mstoy@mgc.edu
STRACHER, Janet ... 478-289-2109 ... 129 B
jstrach@ega.edu
STRADA, Richard ... 732-255-0400 ... 312 D
rstrada@ocean.edu
STRADA, Samuel, J ... 251-460-7189 ... 9 D
sstrada@usouthal.edu
STRADER, Bob, A ... 325-674-2932 ... 478 I
straderb@acu.edu
STRADER, Mark ... 315-786-2325 ... 337 F
mstrader@sunyjefferson.edu
STRADER, Scott, C ... 727-864-8248 ... 105 E
stradesc@eckerd.edu
STRADLEY, Bill ... 931-526-3660 ... 468 J
STRADLEY, Christina ... 254-968-9007 ... 497 A
stradley@tarleton.edu
STRAIGHT, Kendall ... 772-546-5534 ... 110 N
kendallstraight@hsbc.edu
STRAIN, David, M ... 479-979-1349 ... 26 A
dstrain@ozarks.edu
STRAIT, LuAnn ... 605-882-5284 ... 464 E
straitl@lakeareatech.edu
STRAIT, Tia ... 417-625-9328 ... 286 B
strait-t@mssu.edu
STRAIT, Willie ... 301-423-3600 ... 99 G
willie.strait@strayer.edu
STRAKA, Richard ... 507-389-6621 ... 267 E
richard.straka@mnsu.edu
STRAKA, Ronald ... 952-446-4127 ... 263 C
strakar@crown.edu
STRAMPEL, William, D ... 517-355-9616 ... 255 A
strampe3@msu.edu
STRAND, Mary ... 612-332-3361 ... 261 A
mstrand@aii.edu
STRAND, Naomi, M ... 785-227-3311 ... 191 B
strandn@bethanylb.edu

STRANEY, Donald, O 808-974-7444 141 F dstraney@hawaii.edu
STRANG, Bryce 503-943-8009 420 G strang@up.edu
STRANG, Fred, F 423-652-4708 470 A ffstrang@king.edu
STRANG, Steven 314-246-8025 292 J stevenstrang87@webster.edu
STRANGE, Alan 219-864-2400 178 F astrange@midamerica.edu
STRANGE, Thomas 423-585-2668 476 D thomas.strange@ws.edu
STRANIAK, Kimberly 330-369-3200 402 H tbcmail@tbc-trumbullbusiness.com
STRANO, Diana 603-897-8211 305 F dstrano@rivier.edu
STRANO, Kimberly 845-257-3215 352 B lavoiek@newpaltz.edu
STRANSKY, Timothy 615-383-3230 467 A stranskyt@dominicancampus.org
STRASENBURGH, David, R 585-395-2385 352 F dstrasen@brockport.edu
STRASS, Troy 503-352-2882 419 E troy.strass@pacificu.edu
STRASSER, Nora 316-295-5818 193 B strasser@friends.edu
STRATFORD, Denis, G 617-724-6340 242 B dgstratford@mghihp.edu
STRATFORD, James 620-672-5641 196 D jims@prattcc.edu
STRATFORD-YOUNCE, Carolyn 410-225-2263 224 B cstratford@mica.edu
STRATMAN, Debbie 931-553-0071 471 I debbie.stratman@miller-motte.com
STRATMAN, Jason, L 308-635-6740 301 D stratman@wncc.edu
STRATMAN, Victoria, D 626-395-5940 32 H victoria.stratman@caltech.edu
STRATMANN, Charles, M 904-632-3299 109 F cstratma@fscj.edu
STRATTON, Andrew, B 270-247-8521 204 G astratton@midcontinent.edu
STRATTON, Charles 808-942-1000 141 D
STRATTON, James 208-524-3000 143 G james.stratton@my.eitc.edu
STRATTON, Jonathan 772-546-5534 110 N jonstratton@hsbc.edu
STRATTON, Michael 518-454-5456 330 C strattom@mail.strose.edu
STRATTON, Nathan 701-328-4114 381 E nathan.stratton@ndus.edu
STRATTON, Nathan 701-255-3285 383 G nstratton@uttc.edu
STRAUB, Bernie 843-574-6994 461 G bernie.straub@tridenttech.edu
STRAUB, Dahnja 707-546-4000 45 H dstraub@empirecollege.com
STRAUB, Steve 920-735-5717 554 A straub@fvtc.edu
STRAUCH, Pierre 203-287-3018 93 F paier.admin@snet.net
STRAUCHLER, Orin 845-569-3547 342 A orin.strauchler@msmc.edu
STRAUGHAN, Rusty 573-518-2361 285 I rstraugh@mineralarea.edu
STRAUGHN, Greg 325-674-2850 478 I gbs00a@acu.edu
STRAUS, Susan 301-934-7567 222 C susans@csmd.edu
STRAUSBAUGH, Greg 541-684-7357 417 F gstrausbaugh@nwcu.edu
STRAUSBAUGH, Lisa 440-375-7379 394 E lstrausbaugh@lec.edu
STRAUSBAUGH, William, G 717-796-5375 436 D strausba@messiah.edu
STRAUSS, David, J 313-577-1010 260 A ak3096@wayne.edu
STRAUSS, Douglas 608-785-9235 555 F straussd@westerntc.edu
STRAUSS, Jason 510-841-9230 79 J jstrauss@wi.edu
STRAUSS, Jerome, F 804-828-9788 526 B jfstrauss@vcu.edu
STRAUSS, Jon, C 914-323-5230 339 J jon.strauss@mville.edu
STRAUSS, Ronald 919-962-4510 378 E ron_strauss@unc.edu
STRAUT COLLARD, Susan 718-940-5689 349 A sstrautcollard@sjcny.edu
STRAUTZ-SPRINGBORN, Shelly 989-328-1243 255 E shellys@montcalm.edu
STRAVERS, Meredith 269-965-3931 253 B straversm@kellogg.edu
STRAWBRIDGE, Richard 603-623-0313 305 E rickstrawbridge@nhia.edu
STRAWLEY, George 252-473-2264 369 G gstrawley@albemarle.edu
STRAWN, Roxanna 920-686-6150 550 H roxanna.strawn@sl.edu
STRAWN, Scott 405-491-6306 412 D sstrawn@snu.edu
STRAWSER, Jerry 979-845-4711 497 E jstrawser@tamu.edu
STRAWSER, Joyce, A 973-761-9225 315 B joyce.strawser@shu.edu
STRAYER, Colleen 419-530-2516 404 F colleen.strayer@utoledo.edu
STRAYER, James, E 308-398-7355 297 A jstrayer@cccneb.edu
STRAZDAS, Peter, J 269-387-8584 260 C peter.strazdas@wmich.edu
STREAR, Jay 310-476-9777 28 G jstrear@ajula.edu
STREBE, Chet, A 715-675-3331 555 B strebe@ntc.edu
STRECKENBEIN, Mark 609-343-5127 307 C strecken@atlantic.edu
STRECKER, Bill 636-922-8607 288 B bstrecker@stchas.edu
STRECKER, Deborah 610-896-1129 430 G dstrecke@haverford.edu
STREET, Aaron, J 870-235-5011 23 I ajstreet@saumag.edu
STREET, Helen 662-252-8000 276 G hstreet@rustcollege.edu
STREET, Kathleen, A 909-869-2572 33 J kastreet@csupomona.edu
STREET, Kenneth 936-639-1301 480 D kstreet@angelina.edu
STREET, Margaret, F 573-629-3006 282 E mstreet@hlg.edu
STREET, Scott, V 617-266-1400 231 E
STREET, Sheila 336-506-4186 368 A streets@alamancecc.edu
STREETER, Carrie 979-230-3215 482 D carrie.streeter@brazosport.edu
STREETER, Holly 319-425-5340 189 G streeterh@uiu.edu
STREETER, Karen 901-755-9399 233 A karen.streeter@cambridgecollege.edu
STREETER, Kelley 860-231-5228 95 D kstreeter@usj.edu
STREETER, Lucy 808-739-4686 140 E lstreete@chaminade.edu
STREETER, Montrose 315-781-3900 335 F streeter@hws.edu
STREFF, Frederick, M 540-674-3637 527 E fstreff@nr.edu
STREFF, Kevin, F 605-256-5077 465 I kevin.streff@dsu.edu
STREGE, Ron 715-346-3574 552 D rstrege@uwsp.edu
STREHLOW, Betty, J 320-222-5203 268 G betty.strehlow@ridgewater.edu
STREID, David 641-472-1130 187 E dstreid@mum.edu
STREIFFER, Rick 205-348-1288 8 E rhstreiffer@cchs.ua.edu
STREIM, Nancy 212-678-7407 357 G streim@tc.edu
STREIT, Gary, W 719-884-5000 86 J gwstreit@nbc.edu
STREIT, Linda, A 678-547-6799 134 A streit_la@mercer.edu
STRENGTH, Carli 817-591-1081 101 D cstrength@atienterprises.edu
STRETCHER, Gary, D 409-984-6209 501 C gary.stretcher@lamarpa.edu
STREUBERT, Helen, J 210-434-6711 492 B hjstreubert@lake.ollusa.edu
STREUFERT, Billie 605-331-6602 466 E billie.streufert@usiouxfalls.edu
STREY, Charles 641-628-5621 183 D streyc@central.edu
STREY, Mary, M 641-628-5188 183 D streym@central.edu
STRIBLING, Lance 404-270-2898 128 E lstribling@devry.edu
STRICHERZ, Shanda, L 605-336-6588 465 D shandas@sfseminary.edu
STRICKER, Edward, M 412-624-6880 449 A edstrick@pitt.edu
STRICKLAND, Brian 251-580-2214 5 A bstrickland@faulknerstate.edu
STRICKLAND, Brooke 334-556-2418 4 A bstrickland@wallace.edu
STRICKLAND, Carolyn, R 570-326-3761 440 L cstrickl@pct.edu
STRICKLAND, Charles 252-862-1256 373 C stricklandc@roanokechowan.edu
STRICKLAND, Claire, I 207-581-1593 220 A cpratt@maine.edu
STRICKLAND, Earnestine, J 512-505-3082 488 D eestrickland@htu.edu
STRICKLAND, Fatisha 215-567-7080 422 D fstrickland@aii.edu
STRICKLAND, Gary 912-279-5835 127 E gstrickland@ccga.edu
STRICKLAND, Gary, E 605-336-6588 465 D gstrickland@sfseminary.edu
STRICKLAND, Haywood, L 903-927-3200 509 E hstrickland@wileyc.edu
STRICKLAND, Joy 303-963-3012 82 C jstrickland@ccu.edu
STRICKLAND, Julie, M 912-486-7611 135 D jmstrickland@ogeecheetech.edu
STRICKLAND, Ken 229-217-4188 134 F kstrickland@moultrietech.edu
STRICKLAND, Les 480-423-6510 16 C les.strickland@scottsdalecc.edu
STRICKLAND, Liz, F 870-575-8471 25 B stricklandl@uapb.edu
STRICKLAND, Mark 727-341-3408 116 H strickland.mark@spcollege.edu
STRICKLAND, Michael, D 615-460-6420 467 D mike.strickland@belmont.edu
STRICKLAND, Michele 478-553-2097 135 B mstrickland@oftc.edu
STRICKLAND, Ora 304-348-0231 119 C ora.strickland@fiu.edu.edu
STRICKLAND, Pamela 732-235-9721 317 A ohmanpa@umdnj.edu
STRICKLAND, Randy 502-585-7101 206 D rstrickland@spalding.edu
STRICKLAND, Samuel 919-866-5826 374 H sstrickland@waketech.edu
STRICKLAND, Sandra, W 252-335-0821 369 G sstrickland@albemarle.edu
STRICKLAND, Sherry 254-559-7707 500 G sherry.strickland@tstc.edu
STRICKLAND, Sidney 215-327-8084 347 H strickland@rockefeller.edu
STRICKLAND, Tim, H 252-246-1375 375 D tstrickland@wilsoncc.edu
STRICKLAND, Tina 229-217-4141 134 F tstrickland@moultrietech.edu
STRICKLAND, Tonya 229-248-2515 126 A tstrickland@bainbridge.edu
STRICKLAND, Valerie 770-962-7580 132 D vstrickland@gwinnetttech.edu
STRICKLAND, Wayne, G 503-255-0332 417 C udub@multnomah.edu
STRICKLER, Michael, M 540-464-7102 529 F stricklermm@vmi.edu
STRICKLER, Tammy 505-224-4325 317 K tammys@cnm.edu
STRICKLIN, Jan 503-352-2890 419 E jstricklin@pacificu.edu
STRICKLIN, Linda 208-792-2439 144 B lsstricklin@lcsc.edu
STRICKLIN, Scott 662-325-8082 275 F sas24@msstate.edu
STRIEF, Kristi, L 563-556-5110 188 B striefk@nicc.edu
STRIEGEL, Nicole 417-455-5636 280 H nstriege@crowder.edu
STRIKWERDA, Carl, J 717-361-1193 428 F strikwerdac@etown.edu
STRIMKOVSKY, Lauri 215-248-7168 425 D strimkovsky@chc.edu
STRIMPLE, Karen 620-252-7555 192 B karens@coffeyville.edu
STRINGER, Christopher 609-984-1110 316 A cstringer@tesc.edu
STRINGER, Cindy 254-647-3120 492 G
STRINGER, Janet 650-306-3291 67 F stringerj@smccd.net
STRINGER, Martin 714-628-4816 63 G stringer_martin@sccollege.edu
STRINGER, Sarah 334-727-8254 8 B ssstringer@tuskegee.edu
STRINGER, Tommy 903-875-7380 491 C tommy.stringer@navarrocollege.edu
STRINGFELLOW, Alan 405-682-7522 409 F astringfellow@occc.edu
STRINGFELLOW, Catherine 256-395-2211 7 D cstringfellow@suscc.edu
STRIPE-PORTILLO, Jennifer 213-615-7264 146 F jstripe@thechicagoschool.edu
STRIPLING, Rosanne 903-223-3003 498 F rosanne.stripling@tamut.edu
STRIPLING, William, R 870-972-2048 20 D ricks@astate.edu
STRITIKUS, Tom 206-543-2100 539 A tstrit@uw.edu
STRMISKA, Kenneth, D 920-565-1478 548 A strmiskakd@lakeland.edu
STROBECK, Carol 973-290-4418 308 G cstrobeck@cse.edu
STROBEL, Corbin 620-665-3537 193 H strobelc@hutchcc.edu
STROBEL, Judy 406-874-6207 294 F strobelj@milescc.edu
STROBEL, Nathan 414-443-8825 553 D nathan.strobel@wlc.edu
STROBLE, Elizabeth, J 314-968-6996 292 J stroble@webster.edu
STROCKBINE, Richard 972-721-5207 503 B dick@udallas.edu
STRODEMIER, Tammy 360-736-9391 532 D tstrodmeier@centralia.edu
STROEH, Mark 713-692-0077 484 C
STROH, Melinda 617-353-3635 232 E strohm@bu.edu
STROHM, Bobbie, A 858-499-0202 41 G bstrohm@coleman.edu
STROHM, Leslie, C 919-962-1219 378 E strohm@email.unc.edu
STROHM, Shelly 203-332-5179 91 E sstrohm@hcc.commnet.edu
STROHMETZ, David 732-263-5121 311 E dstrohme@monmouth.edu
STROHMEYER, George 814-871-7436 429 G strohmeyer@gannon.edu
STROJNY, Duane 517-371-5140 258 F strojnyd@cooley.edu
STROKER, Robert 215-204-8301 447 H robert.stroker@temple.edu
STROLLO, Ronald, A 330-941-2385 406 F rastrollo@ysu.edu
STROLLO HOLBROOK, Toni 407-646-2355 116 D tsholbrook@rollins.edu
STROM, Donald 314-935-5514 292 I don_strom@wustl.edu
STROM, Laura, A 618-650-3330 165 C lstrom@siue.edu
STROM, Siri, J 509-865-8613 535 A strom_s@heritage.edu
STROM, Steven 845-451-1552 331 E s_strom@culinary.edu
STROMAN, Gerry, G 765-455-9316 174 A gstroman@iuk.edu
STROMAN, Jay 706-379-3111 140 A jtstroman@yhc.edu
STROMAN, Kent 585-567-9340 336 B kent.stroman@houghton.edu
STROMAN, Kozman 305-430-1168 109 A kozman.stroman@fmuniv.edu
STROMAN, Lauren 713-718-8091 487 I lauren.stroman@hccs.edu
STROMBERG, Lori, S 308-635-6703 301 D stromber@wncc.edu
STROMMEN, Kim 215-204-7000 447 H strommen@temple.edu
STROMPF, Richard 203-596-4588 93 G rstrompf@post.edu
STROMQUIST, Eric 503-961-6200 418 A estromquist@pioneerpacific.edu
STROMQUIST, Eric 888-624-2433 419 F estromquist@pioneerpacific.edu
STRONACH, Bruce 215-204-7000 447 H bruce.stronach@temple.edu
STRONG, Charles 318-371-3035 211 D cstrong@nwltc.edu
STRONG, Charles, T 318-371-3035 211 C cstrong@ltc.edu
STRONG, Charmaine, R 724-838-4242 447 C strong@setonhill.edu
STRONG, Chuck 662-562-3494 276 D cwstrong@northwestms.edu
STRONG, Douglas, M 206-281-2473 537 H dstrong@spu.edu
STRONG, Gary 402-941-6128 298 I strong@midlandu.edu
STRONG, Gary, E 310-825-1201 74 C gstrong@library.ucla.edu
STRONG, James, T 209-667-3203 36 D jtstrong@csustan.edu
STRONG, Karen 702-895-4074 302 I karen.strong@unlv.edu
STRONG, Kira 641-673-1014 190 C strongk@wmpenn.edu
STRONG, Kirk 801-422-5000 509 H kirk_strong@byu.edu
STRONG, III, L. Thomas 504-282-4455 213 H tstrong@nobts.edu
STRONG, Mike 909-389-3383 65 B mstrong@craftonhills.edu
STRONG, Robert, A 540-458-8418 530 D strongr@wlu.edu
STRONG, Shirley 415-575-6171 32 G sstrong@ciis.edu
STRONG, Walter, L 504-816-4359 209 A wstrong@dillard.edu
STROTHER, Jennielle 512-472-4133 494 F jennielle.strother@ssw.edu
STROTHER, Jennifer 425-564-4250 531 G jennifer.strother@bellevuecollege.edu
STROTHER, William 318-670-6472 215 A wstrother@susla.edu
STROTHMAN, Gary 815-825-2086 155 D gary.strothman@kishwaukeecollege.edu
STROUD, Annie 608-663-3317 547 F astroud@edgewood.edu
STROUD, Clarke 405-325-3161 413 C cstroud@ou.edu
STROUD, Clarke 405-271-4000 413 D clarke-stroud@ouhsc.edu
STROUD, Cynthia 904-680-7799 107 J cstroud@fcsl.edu
STROUD, George 610-902-8417 424 B george.stroud@cabrini.edu
STROUD, Jonathan 765-983-1600 171 E stroujo@earlham.edu
STROUD, Lewis 910-277-5149 376 C stroudl@sapc.edu
STROUD, Nancy 478-471-2728 133 H nancy.stroud@maconstate.edu
STROUD, Ron 915-831-2614 486 G jstroud2@epcc.edu

STROUP-BENHAM, Christine ..... 303-315-2835 ..... 88 J christine.stroup-benham@ucdenver.edu
STROUSE, Nancy ..... 702-895-2811 ..... 302 I nancy.strouse@unlv.edu
STROUSE, Robert, K ..... 714-850-4800 ..... 90 A strouse@taftu.edu
STROUSE, Robert, K ..... 714-850-4800 ..... 72 F strouse@taftu.edu
STROUTH, Crystal ..... 507-372-3451 ..... 267 G crystal.strouth@mnwest.edu
STROUTS, Paul ..... 404-894-1822 ..... 130 F paul.strouts@gatech.edu
STRUBEL, Eric ..... 215-574-9600 ..... 431 B estrubel@hussianart.edu
STRUBEL, John ..... 843-863-8044 ..... 456 B jstrubel@csuniv.edu
STRUBLE, Dan ..... 828-669-8012 ..... 367 E dstruble@montreat.edu
STRUBLE, Robert ..... 716-896-0700 ..... 359 H restruble@villa.edu
STRUBLER, David ..... 802-865-5725 ..... 513 C strubler@champlain.edu
STRUBY, Hazel ..... 478-445-2301 ..... 127 A hstruby@centralgatech.edu
STRUBY, Shannon ..... 402-354-7104 ..... 299 C shannon.struby@methodistcollege.edu
STRUCHTEMEYER, Derek, L ..... 770-720-5549 ..... 136 C dls@reinhardt.edu
STRUCK, Kathy ..... 605-367-4625 ..... 466 D kathy.struck@southeasttech.edu
STRUCKMEYER, Jacqueline ..... 931-221-7466 ..... 473 E struckmeyerj@apsu.edu
STRUDWICK, Daniel ..... 217-228-5432 ..... 161 F strudda@quincy.edu
STRUEBEL, Phil, J ..... 716-884-9120 ..... 324 J pjstruebel@bryantstratton.edu
STRUGAR-FRITSCH, Chris 517-483-1813 ..... 254 A strugarj@lcc.edu
STRULOEFF, Mark ..... 503-699-6252 ..... 416 J mstruloeff@marylhurst.edu
STRUNK, Jeffrey ..... 859-572-6448 ..... 205 H strunk@nku.edu
STRUNK, Mary, C ..... 518-783-2314 ..... 350 I strunk@siena.edu
STRUNK, Paul, J ..... 570-961-4760 ..... 435 F pjstrunk@marywood.edu
STRUNK, Vicki ..... 502-447-7634 ..... 205 E
STRUPP, Kerry ..... 920-923-7666 ..... 548 E kstrupp@marianuniversity.edu
STRUPPA, Daniele, C ..... 714-997-6826 ..... 39 F struppa@chapman.edu
STRYBOS, John ..... 210-485-0701 ..... 479 A jstrybos@alamo.edu
STRYDOM, Peet ..... 901-381-3939 ..... 478 E peet@visible.edu
STRYDOM, Sue ..... 901-381-3939 ..... 478 E sue@visible.edu
STRYKER, H. Ford ..... 814-865-4402 ..... 438 G hfs2@psu.edu
STRYKER, Joann ..... 570-422-3211 ..... 442 D jstryker@po-box.esu.edu
STRYKER, Joanne ..... 401-454-6177 ..... 454 B jstryker@risd.edu
STRYKER, Marcy ..... 518-464-8527 ..... 333 E mstryker@excelsior.edu
STRYSICK, Michael, P ..... 859-238-5710 ..... 199 G michael.strysick@centre.edu
STUARD, Avis ..... 504-520-7583 ..... 217 A astuard@xula.edu
STUART, Alesia, K ..... 251-578-1313 ..... 6 E akstuart@rstc.edu
STUART, Ann ..... 940-898-3201 ..... 502 D astuart@twu.edu
STUART, Beverly ..... 206-268-4507 ..... 530 I bstuart@antioch.edu
STUART, Carol, M ..... 252-334-2010 ..... 367 C carol.stuart@macuniversity.edu
STUART, Cledis, D ..... 870-235-4046 ..... 23 I cdstuart@sauniag.edu
STUART, Dana, S ..... 765-641-4114 ..... 169 E dsstuart@anderson.edu
STUART, D'Anne ..... 575-646-2431 ..... 319 D dstuart@nmsu.edu
STUART, Forrest, M ..... 864-294-2204 ..... 458 E forrest.stuart@furman.edu
STUART, Gail, W ..... 843-792-3941 ..... 459 D stuartg@musc.edu
STUART, Jay, L ..... 630-829-6431 ..... 145 G jstuart@ben.edu
STUART, John ..... 972-929-6777 ..... 486 D jstuart@devry.edu
STUART, Kathryn ..... 440-775-8540 ..... 397 G kathryn.stuart@oberlin.edu
STUART, Lofton, K ..... 865-974-2508 ..... 477 C jstuart@tennessee.edu
STUART, Maggie ..... 360-442-2531 ..... 535 I mstuart@lowercolumbia.edu
STUART, Martha Wynne ..... 434-924-3728 ..... 525 F mws4s@virginia.edu
STUART, Nancy, M ..... 860-768-5135 ..... 95 B nstuart@hartford.edu
STUART, Roberta, P ..... 413-559-5724 ..... 235 C
STUART, Susan ..... 913-288-7265 ..... 194 C sstuart@kckcc.edu
STUBAUS, Karen, R ..... 848-932-4889 ..... 314 B stubaus@oldqueens.rutgers.edu
STUBAUS, Karen, R ..... 848-932-4889 ..... 314 B diversity@rutgers.edu
STUBBE, Alethea, F ..... 712-324-5061 ..... 188 C aletheas@nwicc.edu
STUBBEMAN, Nancy ..... 513-569-1501 ..... 387 G nancy.stubbeman@cincinnatistate.edu
STUBBLEFIELD, Claire ..... 580-745-3090 ..... 412 C cstubblefield@se.edu
STUBBLEFIELD, Jay ..... 252-985-5136 ..... 375 E jstubblefield@ncwc.edu
STUBBLEFIELD, Michael ..... 225-771-3890 ..... 214 I michael_stubblefield@subr.edu
STUBBS, Gail ..... 617-287-5500 ..... 236 G gail.stubbs@umb.edu
STUBBS, Michelle ..... 912-486-7865 ..... 135 D mstubbs@ogeecheetech.edu
STUBBS, Sidney, J ..... 334-833-4236 ..... 4 E provost@huntingdon.edu
STUBBS, OSB, Simon ..... 985-892-1800 ..... 214 G brsimon@sjasc.edu
STUBER, Heidi ..... 206-934-3706 ..... 537 D heidi.stuber@seattlecolleges.edu
STUCHELL, Tina ..... 330-823-8584 ..... 404 C stuchetm@mountunion.edu
STUCK, Helen ..... 315-568-3133 ..... 342 H hstuck@nycc.edu
STUCK, Shelly ..... 315-568-3111 ..... 342 H sstuck@nycc.edu
STUCKEY, Jon, C ..... 717-766-2511 ..... 436 D jstuckey@messiah.edu
STUCKEY, Julie ..... 210-434-6711 ..... 492 B jstuckey@lake.ollusa.edu
STUCKEY, Larry ..... 816-802-3437 ..... 283 E lstuckey@kcai.edu
STUCKEY, Mike ..... 816-501-2414 ..... 278 I mike.stuckey@avila.edu
STUCKEY, Randall, M ..... 507-933-7514 ..... 263 J rstuckey@gustavus.edu
STUCKEY, Sheila ..... 502-597-6852 ..... 203 G sheila.stuckey@kysu.edu
STUCKEY, Thomas, L ..... 419-267-1310 ..... 397 E tstuckey@northweststate.edu
STUCKEY, Vicki ..... 618-395-7777 ..... 152 I stuckeyv@iecc.edu
STUCKLY, JR., Elton, E ..... 254-867-4800 ..... 500 F elton.stuckly@tstc.edu
STUCKLY, JR., Elton, E ..... 254-867-4824 ..... 500 C elton.stuckly@tstc.edu
STUCKWISCH, Barbara ..... 317-955-6210 ..... 177 I alumni@marian.edu
STUCKY, Duane ..... 618-536-3475 ..... 165 A dustucky@siu.edu
STUCKY, Gail ..... 316-284-5363 ..... 191 C gstucky@bethelks.edu
STUCKY, Kent, D ..... 260-665-4311 ..... 180 D stuckyk@trine.edu
STUDAWAY, Tina ..... 901-333-5049 ..... 476 B tstudaway@southwest.tn.edu
STUDDARD, Phil ..... 256-352-8060 ..... 10 A phil.studdard@wallacestate.edu
STUDDS, Susan, M ..... 202-231-3322 ..... 557 J susan.studds@dodiis.mil
STUDEBAKER, Brian ..... 574-239-8407 ..... 172 M bstudebaker@hcc-nd.edu
STUDENC, Bill ..... 828-227-7122 ..... 380 A bstudenc@wcu.edu
STUDENKA, Christopher ..... 480-423-6299 ..... 16 C christopher.studenka@scottsdalecc.edu
STUDER, Mary Ann ..... 419-783-2553 ..... 389 H mstuder@defiance.edu
STUDER, Nancy ..... 219-866-6150 ..... 179 D nancys@saintjoe.edu
STUDHAM, Scott ..... 612-625-8855 ..... 272 A studham@umn.edu
STUDINGER, Bob ..... 303-975-5020 ..... 89 H bstudinger@westwood.edu
STUDWELL, II, Raymond, W ..... 540-828-5660 ..... 517 B cstudwel@bridgewater.edu
STUDWELL, Roberta ..... 239-687-5501 ..... 101 H rstudwell@avemarialaw.edu
STUEBER, Ross ..... 734-995-7393 ..... 249 G stuebr@cuaa.edu
STUEBER, Ross ..... 262-243-5700 ..... 547 C ross.stueber@cuw.edu
STUGELMAYER, Lesley, A ..... 608-796-3808 ..... 553 C lastugelmayer@viterbo.edu
STUGELMEYER, Dennis ..... 605-698-3966 ..... 465 E dstugelmeyer@swc.tc
STUHL, Mordechai ..... 718-236-1171 ..... 346 J
STUHLER, Eric ..... 636-949-4617 ..... 283 J estuhler@lindenwood.edu
STUHR, Eloise, D ..... 713-743-8872 ..... 503 D edstuhr@central.uh.edu
STUHR, Eloise, D ..... 713-743-8165 ..... 503 C edstuhr@central.uh.edu
STUHR, Patricia, L ..... 715-389-6538 ..... 553 B patricia.stuhr@uwc.edu
STUIFBERGEN, Alexa, M ..... 512-471-4100 ..... 505 D astuifbergen@mail.utexas.edu
STULL, David, H ..... 440-775-8200 ..... 397 G david.stull@oberlin.edu
STULL, Elizabeth, K ..... 240-500-2000 ..... 223 A stullb@hagerstowncc.edu
STULL, Richard, E ..... 864-938-3901 ..... 460 E rstull@presby.edu
STULL, Robert, W ..... 915-747-5347 ..... 506 B rstull@utep.edu
STULTS, Karen ..... 410-225-2438 ..... 224 B kstults@mica.edu
STULTZ, James, L ..... 304-336-8029 ..... 544 D jstultz@westliberty.edu
STUMB, Paul ..... 615-547-1210 ..... 468 B pstumb@cumberland.edu
STUMBO, Christine ..... 606-368-6125 ..... 198 C christinestumbo@alc.edu
STUMME, Becky ..... 641-585-8138 ..... 189 I stummeb@waldorf.edu
STUMNE, James ..... 320-629-5114 ..... 268 E stumnej@pinetech.edu
STUMO, Karl, A ..... 253-535-7151 ..... 536 E stumo@plu.edu
STUMP, Colleen, C ..... 301-687-4161 ..... 228 C cstump@frostburg.edu
STUMP, Linda, J ..... 352-392-5445 ..... 120 C
STUMP, Shelley ..... 503-253-3443 ..... 417 H sstump@ocom.edu
STUMP, Tom ..... 406-994-2661 ..... 295 C stump@montana.edu
STUMPF, Christian, J ..... 814-269-1907 ..... 449 D stumpf@pitt.edu
STUMPF, Fran ..... 573-897-5000 ..... 284 A
STUMPF, Jessica ..... 763-576-4828 ..... 265 H jstumpf@anokatech.edu
STUMPF, Jessica ..... 763-433-1543 ..... 265 G jessica.stumpf@anokaramsey.edu
STUMPF, Michelle ..... 814-262-6436 ..... 441 A mstumpf@pennhighlands.edu
STUPAK, Elayne ..... 740-695-9500 ..... 385 B estupak@belmontcollege.edu
STUPAR, Eric, H ..... 202-231-2767 ..... 557 J eric.stupar@dodiis.mil
STUPPLE, Paul ..... 845-752-3000 ..... 358 F p.stupple@uts.edu
STUPPY, Charles ..... 216-397-4976 ..... 392 L cstuppy@jcu.edu
STURCH, Patty Jo ..... 740-264-5591 ..... 390 F psturch@egcc.edu
STURDEVANT, Nancee ..... 605-367-7464 ..... 466 D nancee.sturdevant@southeasttech.edu
STURDEVANT, Peggy ..... 641-784-5125 ..... 185 B peggys@graceland.edu
STURDEVANT, Ruthie ..... 573-681-5178 ..... 283 I sturdevr@lincolnu.edu
STURDIVANT, Alvin ..... 206-296-6066 ..... 538 B sturdial@seattleu.edu
STURDIVANT, Brian, C ..... 410-706-1678 ..... 227 C bsturdivant@umaryland.edu
STURDIVANT, Toni ..... 678-422-4100 ..... 99 G toni.sturdivant@strayer.edu
STURDON, Andrew ..... 614-837-4088 ..... 405 C
STURDY, Ryan ..... 785-460-5548 ..... 192 C ryan.sturdy@colbycc.edu
STURE, Linda ..... 907-563-7575 ..... 10 C
STURE, Stein ..... 303-492-5537 ..... 88 H stein.sture@colorado.edu
STURGEN, Sara ..... 304-357-4802 ..... 542 A uc_bkstr@fheg.follett.com
STURGEON, David ..... 231-777-5200 ..... 248 E david.sturgeon@baker.edu
STURGEON, Kathy, R ..... 217-443-8805 ..... 148 G ksturgeon@dacc.edu
STURGEON, Kimberley ..... 843-574-6195 ..... 461 G kim.sturgeon@tridenttech.edu
STURGEON, Paul ..... 270-706-8639 ..... 202 A paul.sturgeon@kctcs.edu
STURGEON, Timothy, A ..... 502-272-8131 ..... 198 H tsturgeon@bellarmine.edu
STURGILL, Stephen ..... 606-573-3228 ..... 203 D stephen.sturgill@kctcs.edu
STURGIS, Leah ..... 803-323-2189 ..... 463 E sturgisl@winthrop.edu
STURGIS, Thomas, C ..... 601-877-6138 ..... 272 F tsturgis@alcorn.edu
STURM, James, P ..... 716-926-8935 ..... 335 E jsturm@hilbert.edu
STURM, Joel ..... 212-410-8047 ..... 343 B jsturm@nycpm.edu
STURM, Joey ..... 337-482-6449 ..... 216 D joey.sturm@louisiana.edu
STURM, Neal, M ..... 973-443-8689 ..... 310 A sturm@fdu.edu
STURM-SMITH, Melissa ..... 515-271-2835 ..... 184 D melissa.sturm-smith@drake.edu
STURRUP, Daniel, H ..... 207-581-4707 ..... 220 A dsturrup@maine.edu
STURRUS, Teresa ..... 231-777-0251 ..... 256 A teresa.sturrus@muskegoncc.edu
STURTZ, Alan, J ..... 860-913-2034 ..... 92 I asturtz@goodwin.edu
STURZENBECKER, Diane ..... 716-488-3021 ..... 337 D financialaid@jamestownbusinesscollege.edu
STUTES, Ann, B ..... 806-291-1066 ..... 508 E stutesa@wbu.edu
STUTEVILLE, Rebekkah ..... 816-559-5634 ..... 287 E rebekkah.stuteville@park.edu
STUTTS, Rosie ..... 805-654-6313 ..... 77 F rstutts@vcccd.edu
STUTZ, Trevor ..... 937-778-7969 ..... 390 G tstutz@edisonohio.edu
STUTZMAN, Dallas ..... 620-327-8110 ..... 193 E dallass@hesston.edu
STUTZMAN, Timothy ..... 540-432-4197 ..... 518 F timothy.stutzman@emu.edu
STYER, Bryan ..... 312-939-4975 ..... 151 H bstyer@harrington.edu
STYFFE, Sharon ..... 216-987-2260 ..... 389 B sharon.styffe@tri-c.edu
STYLES, Elise ..... 864-977-7018 ..... 460 A elise.styles@ngu.edu
STYLES, Kathleen ..... 410-462-8365 ..... 221 E kstyles@bccc.edu
STYRON, Kelli ..... 254-968-9141 ..... 497 A styron@tarleton.edu
STYRON, Ken ..... 251-981-3771 ..... 2 G ken.styron@columbiasouthern.edu
SU, Nancy ..... 212-217-3640 ..... 333 F nancy_su@fitnyc.edu
SU, Renjeng ..... 503-725-2820 ..... 418 G renjengs@cecs.pdx.edu
SUAREZ, Angelica ..... 619-482-6315 ..... 71 D asuarez@swccd.edu
SUAREZ, Anthony ..... 602-386-4122 ..... 11 G anthony.suarez@arizonachristian.edu
SUAREZ, Carmen, A ..... 208-885-4285 ..... 144 G csuarez@uidaho.edu
SUAREZ, Jeri, L ..... 540-362-6000 ..... 520 A jsuarez@hollins.edu
SUAREZ, John ..... 718-488-1030 ..... 338 G john.suarez@liu.edu
SUAREZ, Keri ..... 269-471-3348 ..... 247 D ksuarez@andrews.edu
SUAREZ, Michelle ..... 618-453-5855 ..... 165 B msuarez@siu.edu
SUAREZ-HERRERO, Ismael ..... 787-863-2390 ..... 563 E ismael.suarez@fajardo.inter.edu
SUBBASWAMY, Kumble, R ..... 413-545-2211 ..... 236 F chancellor@umass.edu
SUBBIONDO, Joseph, L ..... 415-575-6105 ..... 32 G jsubbiondo@ciis.edu
SUBER, Jennifer ..... 601-477-4040 ..... 274 H jennifer.suber@jcjc.edu
SUBLETT, Roger, H ..... 513-861-6400 ..... 402 I roger.sublett@myunion.edu
SUBOCZ, Sue ..... 301-934-7539 ..... 222 C ssubocz@csmd.edu
SUBOCZ, Sue ..... 301-934-7846 ..... 222 C ssubocz@csmd.edu
SUBOTNICK, Stuart ..... 718-625-2200 ..... 324 F
SUBRAMANI, Suresh ..... 858-534-2230 ..... 74 F
SUBRAMANIAN, Ashok ..... 712-749-2422 ..... 183 C subramaniana@bvu.edu
SUBRAMANIAN, Chitra ..... 314-644-9167 ..... 288 I csubramanian@stlcc.edu
SUBRAMANIAN, Sandhya . 440-775-8401 ..... 397 G sandhya.subramanian@oberlin.edu
SUCHANIC, Angela, C ..... 302-356-6924 ..... 97 C angela.c.suchanic@wilmu.edu
SUCHAR, Charles, S ..... 773-325-7305 ..... 149 A csuchar@depaul.edu
SUCHON, Donnetta ..... 281-425-6400 ..... 489 M dsuchon@lee.edu
SUCHORSKI, Joan, M ..... 352-395-5200 ..... 117 F joan.suchorski@sfcollege.edu
SUDAK, Sarah ..... 615-898-5342 ..... 473 G sarah.sudak@mtsu.edu
SUDBECK, Amy ..... 651-846-3392 ..... 260 I asudbeck@argosy.edu
SUDDICK, Lori ..... 920-498-5401 ..... 555 C lori.suddick@nwtc.edu
SUDDITH, Judith, J ..... 540-843-0722 ..... 527 C jsuddith@lfcc.edu
SUDEALL, Monica ..... 256-551-1711 ..... 4 J monica.sudeall@drakestate.edu
SUDEIKIS, Barbara ..... 269-965-3931 ..... 253 B sudeikisb@kellogg.edu
SUDERMAN, Bonnie ..... 661-395-4610 ..... 52 L bsuderma@bakersfieldcollege.edu
SUDHAKAR, Rama ..... 203-254-4000 ..... 92 H rsudhakar@fairfield.edu
SUDHAKAR, Samuel ..... 309-341-5297 ..... 146 D ssudhakar@sandburg.edu
SUDKAMP, Thomas, A ..... 937-775-2097 ..... 406 C thomas.sudkamp@wright.edu
SUDKAMP, Thomas, A ..... 937-775-3035 ..... 406 C thomas.sudkamp@wright.edu
SUDOL, Mary ..... 845-434-5750 ..... 357 A msudol@sullivan.suny.edu
SUDOL, Ronald, A ..... 248-370-2140 ..... 256 G sudol@oakland.edu
SUESS, Jack, J ..... 410-455-2582 ..... 227 D jack@umbc.edu
SUESSER, John, P ..... 724-346-2073 ..... 423 G john.suesser@bc3.edu
SUFFEL, Charles ..... 201-216-8031 ..... 315 E csuffel@stevens.edu

SUNBURY, Mary Ann .... 704-463-3203.... 375 F
maryann.sunbury@fsmail.pfeiffer.edu
SUND, Andrew, C .... 773-878-7502.... 163 F
asund@staugustine.edu
SUND, Reyna .... 619-849-2446...... 62 L
reynasund@pointloma.edu
SUNDBERG, Lori, H .... 847-735-5030.... 155 G
lsundberg@lakeforest.edu
SUNDBERG, Lori, L .... 309-341-5214.... 146 D
lsundberg@sandburg.edu
SUNDBERG, Paul .... 313-577-2017.... 260 A
ez6182@wayne.edu
SUNDBORG, SJ,
Stephen, V .... 206-296-1891.... 538 B
sundborg@seattleu.edu
SUNDBY, Oliver .... 307-532-8304.... 556 C
oliver.sundby@ewc.wy.edu
SUNDEEN, Joseph, T .... 626-529-8234...... 60 F
tsundeen@pacificoaks.edu
SUNDERLAND, Jon, D ...... 509-313-6115.... 534 F
sunderland@gonzaga.edu
SUNDERMAN, Rick .... 614-947-6605.... 391 B
sundermr@franklin.edu
SUNDERMANN, Brigitte .... 970-255-2600...... 82 F
bsunderm@coloradomesa.edu
SUNDGREN, Donald, E ..... 434-982-5834.... 525 F
des5j@virginia.edu
SUNDQUIST, Mike .... 209-575-6081...... 80 H
sundquistm@yosemite.cc.ca.us
SUNDSEDT, Casey .... 847-628-1561.... 154 K
csundsedt@judsonu.edu
SUNDSMO, Alecia, D .... 717-245-1485.... 427 F
sundsmoa@dickinson.edu
SUNDSTEDT, Bernard .... 815-226-3371.... 163 A
bsunstedt@rockford.edu
SUNDSTROM, Sandra .... 507-786-3357.... 271 C
sundstro@stolaf.edu
SUNDY, Carolyn .... 606-589-3052.... 203 D
carolyn.sundy@kctcs.edu
SUNG, Mankyung .... 562-926-1023...... 63 B
psung@ptsa.edu
SUNI, Ellen, Y .... 816-235-1007.... 291 C
sunie@umkc.edu
SUNLEAF, Arthur, W .... 563-588-7137.... 187 C
arthur.sunleaf@loras.edu
SUNQUIST, Scott, W .... 626-584-5265...... 48 B
sunquist@fuller.edu
SUNSER, James .... 585-345-6812.... 334 F
jmsunser@genesee.edu
SUNSHINE, Eugene, S .... 847-491-5534.... 160 E
e-sunshine@northwestern.edu
SUNSHINE, Lisbet .... 415-338-1120...... 37 B
lisbet@sfsu.edu
SUNSHINE, Phyllis .... 410-337-6046.... 222 I
psunshine@goucher.edu
SUOREZ, Paula .... 760-384-6298...... 52 M
pasouroez@cerrocoso.edu
SUPALLA, Don, D .... 507-285-7215.... 268 I
donald.supalla@roch.edu
SUPENSKY, Jacqueline ...... 713-221-8493.... 503 F
supenskyj@uhd.edu
SUPERNAW, Robert, B ...... 704-233-8015.... 380 F
supernaw@wingate.edu
SUPOWITZ, Paul, A .... 412-624-2901.... 449 A
psupowit@pitt.edu
SUPPLEE, JR., Jack .... 859-257-8288.... 207 D
supplee@uky.edu
SUPPLEE, Janice .... 937-766-8319.... 386 G
suppleej@cedarville.edu
SUPURGECI, Jonna .... 605-668-1515.... 464 G
jsupurgeci@mtmc.edu
SURATY-CLARKE,
Mercedes .... 713-743-1185.... 503 D
msclarke@uh.edu
SURBAUGH, Joyce .... 304-734-6603.... 542 H
jsurbaugh@bridgemont.edu
SURBECK, III, Carlton, E .. 410-337-6100.... 222 I
csurbeck@goucher.edu
SURBROOK, Will .... 619-388-6589...... 65 E
wsurbroo@sdccd.edu
SURBROOK, Will .... 619-388-6589...... 65 H
wsurbroo@sdccd.edu
SURETHING, Nicole, A ...... 540-654-1053.... 525 D
nsurethi@umw.edu
SURGALA, David, J .... 570-577-3811.... 423 E
dsurgala@bucknell.edu
SURGE, Eric .... 231-777-5242.... 248 E
eric.surge@baker.edu
SURH, Tina .... 212-998-2371.... 344 B
tina.surh@nyu.edu
SURIEL, Wanda .... 781-768-7061.... 244 A
wanda.suriel@regiscollege.edu
SUROWIEC, Barbara .... 203-332-5049...... 91 E
bsurowiec@hcc.commnet.edu
SURPRENANT, Neil .... 518-327-6313.... 345 H
nsurprenant@paulsmiths.edu
SURRATT, David, A .... 610-527-0200.... 445 J
dsurratt@rosemont.edu
SURRELL, Matt .... 662-472-2312.... 274 D
msurrell@holmescc.edu
SURRIDGE, Jack, F .... 773-244-5676.... 159 H
jsurridge@northpark.edu
SURRIDGE, Margot .... 847-578-8594.... 163 C
margot.surridge@rosalindfranklin.edu
SURRIDGE, Mary, M .... 773-244-5710.... 159 H
msurridge@northpark.edu
SUSANKA, Thomas, J .... 805-525-4417...... 72 I
tsusanka@thomasaquinas.edu
SUSHINSKY, David, M .... 240-895-4282.... 226 A
dmsushinksy@smcm.edu
SUSICK, Timothy .... 724-938-4056.... 441 G
susick@calu.edu
SUSKI, Katharine, J .... 618-453-2987.... 165 B
ksuski@siu.edu
SUSMAN, Catherine, D ...... 541-346-1255.... 419 B
susman@uoregon.edu
SUSMAN, Jeffrey, L .... 330-325-6254.... 397 D
jsusman@neomed.edu
SUSMANN, Phillip .... 802-485-2213.... 514 C
susmann@norwich.edu
SUSPITSIN, Dmitry .... 216-325-9079.... 387 B
dsuspitsin@chancelloru.edu
SUSS, Stuart .... 718-368-5661.... 328 A
ssuss@kbcc.cuny.edu
SUSSENBACH, Michelle .... 618-664-7025.... 151 F
michelle.sussenbach@greenville.edu
SUSSKIND, Gary .... 718-953-5889.... 357 F
SUSSWEIN, Gary, J .... 512-471-4945.... 505 D
susswein@austin.utexas.edu
SUSTICH, Andrew .... 870-972-2025...... 20 D
sustich@astate.edu
SUSTICH, Andrew .... 870-972-2694...... 20 D
sustich@astate.edu
SUSTICH, Andrew .... 870-972-3029...... 20 D
sustich@astate.edu
SUSTICH, Andrew .... 870-972-2308...... 20 D
sustich@astate.edu
SUSZKO, Robert, K .... 973-761-9552.... 310 F
robert.suszko@shu.edu
SUTER, Cindy .... 419-448-2090.... 391 F
csuter@heidelberg.edu
SUTER, Rebecca .... 304-232-0361.... 542 E
rsuter@wvbc.edu
SUTER, Vicki .... 503-699-6339.... 416 J
vsuter@marylhurst.edu
SUTERA, Janice .... 703-993-2364.... 519 E
jsutera@gmu.edu
SUTERA, Natalie .... 860-548-2412...... 94 A
SUTERA, Paul, J .... 914-637-2710.... 336 E
psutera@iona.edu
SUTHERLAND, Cindy .... 620-252-7180.... 192 B
cindys@coffeyville.edu
SUTHERLAND, David .... 501-450-1254...... 22 A
sutherlandd@hendrix.edu
SUTHERLAND, David .... 218-879-0816.... 266 C
dsutherland@fdltcc.edu
SUTHERLAND, Deana .... 757-499-7900.... 517 D
dsuthlerland@bryantstratton.du
SUTHERLAND, Duncan .... 802-831-1359.... 515 B
dsutherland@vermontlaw.edu
SUTHERLAND, Gloria .... 479-575-4140...... 24 C
gsuther@uark.edu
SUTHERLAND, Jim .... 678-839-6410.... 139 A
sutherla@westga.edu
SUTHERLAND, Richard ...... 989-358-7368.... 247 C
sutherlr@alpenacc.edu
SUTHERLAND, Ronald .... 765-998-5118.... 180 B
rnsutherl@taylor.edu
SUTHERLAND, Sarah, R .... 931-598-5241.... 472 L
ssutherl@sewanee.edu
SUTHERLAND, Timothy ..... 219-980-6946.... 174 B
sutherla@iun.edu
SUTHERLAND, Todd .... 409-740-4598.... 497 F
sutherlt@tamug.tamu.edu
SUTHERLAND, Tricia .... 712-274-6400.... 190 B
tricia.sutherland@witcc.edu
SUTINEN, Paul .... 503-699-6242.... 416 J
psutinen@marylhurst.edu
SUTKOWSKI, Ernest, H ..... 914-831-0343.... 330 D
SUTKUS, Janel .... 412-268-8729.... 424 J
jsutkus@cmu.edu
SUTLIFF, Michael .... 714-432-0202...... 41 D
msutliff@occ.cccd.edu
SUTLIFF, Michael .... 714-432-5638...... 41 D
msutliff@occ.cccd.edu
SUTLIFF, Michael, A .... 323-241-5329...... 55 C
sutlifma@lasc.edu
SUTPHEN, David, B .... 641-628-5192.... 183 D
sutphend@central.edu
SUTPHEN, Debra .... 916-660-7502...... 69 F
dsutphen@sierracollege.edu
SUTTER, Frankie, K .... 910-592-8081.... 373 G
fsutter@sampsoncc.edu
SUTTER, Thaddeus .... 309-556-3059.... 153 F
tsutter@iwu.edu
SUTTERFIELD, Joellen .... 408-934-4900...... 49 K
joellen_sutterfield@heald.edu
SUTTERFIELD, Shirley .... 251-442-2414........ 9 A
ssutterfield@umobile.edu
SUTTHOFF, Maggi .... 425-235-2352.... 537 A
msutthoff@rtc.edu
SUTTLE, J. Lloyd .... 203-432-4453...... 96 A
j.suttle@yale.edu
SUTTLE, Mary .... 281-487-1170.... 499 B
msuttle@txchiro.edu
SUTTON, Ann .... 706-776-0100.... 136 A
asutton@piedmont.edu
SUTTON, Barbara .... 773-298-3504.... 163 I
sutton@sxu.edu
SUTTON, Barbara, B .... 252-335-3224.... 377 F
bbsutton@mail.ecsu.edu
SUTTON, Catherine .... 502-272-8062.... 198 H
csutton@bellarmine.edu
SUTTON, Deborah .... 252-527-6223.... 371 G
dsutton@lenoircc.edu
SUTTON, Deborah, S .... 252-527-6223.... 371 G
dsutton@lenoircc.edu
SUTTON, Ellen .... 630-942-2659.... 148 A
suttone@cod.edu
SUTTON, Janice .... 903-675-6229.... 502 F
jsutton@tvcc.edu
SUTTON, Jerry .... 816-414-3700.... 285 H
academicdean@mbts.edu
SUTTON, Judith .... 304-485-5487.... 541 G
jsutton@msc.edu
SUTTON, Kay .... 309-690-6886.... 152 C
ksutton@icc.edu
SUTTON, Kenneth, W .... 410-778-7269.... 229 D
ksutton2@washcoll.edu
SUTTON, Linda .... 913-288-7652.... 194 C
lsutton@kckcc.edu
SUTTON, Lynn .... 336-758-5480.... 380 C
suttonls@wfu.edu
SUTTON, Michael .... 909-607-3562...... 40 G
mike.sutton@cms.claremont.edu
SUTTON, Nancy .... 217-351-2402.... 161 C
nsutton@parkland.edu
SUTTON, Richard, C .... 270-745-2886.... 208 A
richard.sutton@wku.edu
SUTTON, Robert, E .... 509-452-5100.... 536 F
SUTTON, Shirley .... 425-640-1246.... 533 I
ssutton@edcc.edu
SUTTON, Stephanie .... 440-365-5222.... 395 D
SUTTON, Steve .... 660-562-1248.... 287 B
alumni@nwmissouri.edu
SUTTON, Whitney .... 970-248-1078...... 82 F
wsutton@coloradomesa.edu
SUTTON, William .... 423-425-2256.... 477 F
william-sutton@utc.edu
SUTTON-HAYWOOD,
Marilyn .... 919-546-8330.... 376 F
mhaywood@shawu.edu
SUTTON-JACKSON,
Vicky, L .... 803-934-3168.... 459 G
vsutton-jackson@morris.edu
SUTTON-SMITH, Leslie ..... 646-312-1190.... 326 C
leslie.sutton-smith@baruch.cuny.edu
SUTZKO, Christopher .... 570-208-5874.... 432 G
christophersutzko@kings.edu
SUVAK, Daniel, S .... 330-490-7183.... 405 F
dsuvak@walsh.edu
SUWAREH, BernaDette, W . 320-363-5455.... 262 F
bwsuwareh@csbsju.edu
SUYAMA, Barbara .... 262-695-7842.... 555 E
bsuyama@wctc.edu
SUZEWITS, Jeff .... 660-626-2701.... 278 D
jsuzewits@atsu.edu
SUZO, Michael .... 419-783-2361.... 389 H
msuzo@defiance.edu
SUZOR, Michael, J .... 413-755-4044.... 241 B
msuzor@stcc.edu
SUZOW, Bo .... 213-738-6762...... 71 E
mis@swlaw.edu
SUZUKI, Hayato .... 973-618-3419.... 308 C
hsuzuki@caldwell.edu
SUZUKI, Joyce .... 707-664-4470...... 37 D
joyce.suzuki@sonoma.edu
SUZUKI, Takeo .... 479-788-7166...... 24 D
takeo.suzuki@uafs.edu
SVAJDA, Deborah .... 254-298-8609.... 496 D
debbie.svajda@templejc.edu
SVALDI, David, P .... 719-587-7341...... 80 L
dpsvaldi@adams.edu
SVATOS, Liz, A .... 402-552-3038.... 297 B
svatos@clarksoncollege.edu
SVEC, Andrew .... 218-281-8438.... 271 E
asvec@umn.edu
SVEDBERG, Mary Kay .... 703-462-6590.... 530 F
msvedberg@westwood.edu
SVEDLOW, Andrew .... 970-351-2515.... 89 B
adrew.svedlow@unco.edu
SVEI, Yehuda .... 215-477-1000.... 447 G
talmudicalyeshiva@yahoo.com
SVENDSEN, Carol .... 303-721-1313...... 86 F
svendsec@msudenver.edu
SVENSON, Nancy .... 909-748-8739...... 76 C
nancy_svenson@redlands.edu
SVENSSON, Craig, K .... 765-494-1368.... 178 J
svensson@purdue.edu
SVENSSON, Nancy .... 510-841-1905...... 27 J
nsvensson@absw.edu
SVETE, Lee, J .... 574-631-5200.... 180 G
svete.1@nd.edu
SVOBODA, Angela, M .... 512-448-8622.... 493 E
asvoboda@stedwards.edu
SVOBODA, Debbie .... 301-654-7267.... 226 C
SVONAVEC, Stephen .... 478-274-7804.... 134 B
ssvonavec@mgc.edu
SWADDLE, John .... 757-221-2467.... 518 A
jpswad@wm.edu
SWAFFORD, Jeanna, C .... 731-881-7629.... 477 G
jswafford@utm.edu
SWAGER, Sarah, L .... 509-963-1515.... 532 C
swagers@cwu.edu
SWAGERS, Christin .... 918-781-7281.... 407 B
swagersc@bacone.edu
SWAGGER, Russell .... 701-255-3285.... 383 G
rswagger@uttc.edu
SWAHN, Monica, H .... 404-413-3505.... 131 G
mswahn@gsu.edu
SWAID, Samar .... 501-370-5334...... 23 B
sswaid@philander.edu
SWAIM, Kevin, C .... 765-361-6252.... 181 E
swaimk@wabash.edu
SWAIN, Carole .... 925-631-4695...... 64 F
cswain@stmarys-ca.edu
SWAIN, Corliss .... 507-786-3277.... 271 C
swain@stolaf.edu
SWAIN, Cristal .... 970-351-1142...... 89 B
cristal.wain@unco.edu
SWAIN, Emily .... 330-823-2674.... 404 C
swainej@mountunion.edu
SWAIN, Emily, L .... 304-367-4015.... 543 H
emily.swain@fairmontstate.edu
SWAIN, Erika .... 518-891-2915.... 344 E
eswain@nccc.edu
SWAIN, Heather, C .... 517-355-2262.... 255 A
SWAIN, Jackie .... 406-275-4755.... 296 D
jackie_swain@skc.edu
SWAIN, Jeffrey .... 305-626-3663.... 109 A
jeffrey.swain@fmuniv.edu
SWAIN, Laurie .... 757-789-1797.... 526 H
lswain@es.vccs.edu
SWAIN, Lee .... 415-282-7600...... 28 B
leeswain@actcm.edu
SWAIN, Richard .... 610-436-2747.... 444 A
rswain@wcupa.edu
SWAIN, Rodney .... 414-229-5895.... 551 D
rswain@uwm.edu
SWAIN, Ronald, L .... 512-863-1940.... 496 A
swainr@southwestern.edu
SWAIN, Scott, R .... 407-366-9493.... 115 K
sswain@rts.edu
SWAIN, Stuart, G .... 207-255-1224.... 220 E
sswain@maine.edu
SWALGA, Dan .... 412-392-3911.... 445 A
dswalga@pointpark.edu
SWALLOW, John, R .... 931-598-1101.... 472 L
jrswallo@sewanee.edu
SWALWELL, Joe .... 405-682-1611.... 409 F
jswalwell@occc.edu
SWAM, Vickie, E .... 254-968-9464.... 497 A
swam@tarleton.edu
SWAN, Beth Ann .... 215-503-8057.... 448 C
bethann.swan@jefferson.edu
SWAN, Bobi .... 503-493-6526.... 415 E
bswan@cu-portland.edu
SWAN, Deba .... 254-526-1237.... 482 H
deborah.swan@ctcd.edu
SWAN, III, George, W .... 313-496-2344.... 259 G
gswan1@wcccd.edu
SWAN, Kirsten .... 207-778-7347.... 220 C
kswan@maine.edu
SWAN, Marjorie .... 313-845-9601.... 252 B
mswan@hfcc.edu
SWAN, S. Tomeka .... 410-287-6060.... 222 A
tswan@cecil.edu
SWAN, Sharon, K .... 314-984-7623.... 289 A
sswan16@stlcc.edu
SWAN, Steve .... 360-650-3482.... 539 F
steve.swan@wwu.edu
SWAN, Terry, W .... 270-384-8148.... 204 D
swant@lindsey.edu
SWAN, William .... 718-636-3518.... 346 D
wswan@pratt.edu
SWANAGAN, Diana .... 706-233-7301.... 137 A
dswanagan@shorter.edu
SWANBERG, Jeff .... 815-967-7321.... 162 I
jswanberg@rockfordcareercollege.edu
SWANGER, Dustin .... 518-736-3622.... 334 D
dustin.swanger@fmcc.suny.edu
SWANGER, Rachel .... 310-393-0411...... 61 E
rswanger@rand.org
SWANGER, Stefanie .... 478-757-5218.... 139 E
sswanger@wesleyancollege.edu
SWANGER, Stefanie .... 478-757-5257.... 139 E
sswanger@wesleyancollege.edu
SWANGER, Thomas .... 760-750-4813...... 36 C
tswanger@csusm.edu
SWANK, Dennis, W .... 570-577-1505.... 423 E
dennis.swank@bucknell.edu
SWANK, Jamie, R .... 724-450-4045.... 430 B
jrswank@gcc.edu
SWANK, Larry, A .... 812-298-2266.... 177 D
lswank@ivytech.edu
SWANKE, Gail .... 800-567-2344.... 547 A
gswanke@menominee.edu
SWANN, John .... 315-792-7113.... 356 B
swannj@sunyit.edu
SWANN, Mildred .... 757-727-5425.... 519 H
alumni@hamptonu.edu
SWANN, Patricia .... 315-792-3060.... 359 E
SWANN, Richard .... 662-325-7404.... 275 F
rswann@spa.msstate.edu

SWANNACK, Patricia .... 732-571-3546.... 311 E
pswannac@monmouth.edu
SWANQUIST, Leah .... 847-635-1780.... 160 F
lswanqui@oakton.edu
SWANSON, Alison .... 515-961-1696.... 189 C
alison.swanson@simpson.edu
SWANSON, Barry, K .... 785-864-5978.... 197 B
bswanson@ku.edu
SWANSON, Brenda .... 781-762-1211.... 234 F
SWANSON, Brian, R .... 909-869-2261...... 33 J
bswanson@csupomona.edu
SWANSON, Chris .... 541-683-5141.... 416 A
cswanson@gutenberg.edu
SWANSON, Darren .... 320-363-5810.... 262 F
dswanson@csbsju.edu
SWANSON, Eleanor .... 732-571-7529.... 311 E
eswanson@monmouth.edu
SWANSON, Gary, L .... 724-946-7188.... 451 C
gswanson@westminster.edu
SWANSON, Greg .... 262-472-6703.... 553 A
swansong@uww.edu
SWANSON, Guy .... 816-501-4862.... 288 A
guy.swanson@rockhurst.edu
SWANSON, Heather .... 312-332-0707.... 166 B
SWANSON, Hope .... 802-241-2520.... 515 C
hope.swanson@vsc.edu
SWANSON, James, E .... 574-372-5700.... 171 H
swansoje@grace.edu
SWANSON, Jeanne .... 760-795-6840...... 57 E
jswanson@miracosta.edu
SWANSON, Jim, M .... 719-389-6651...... 82 D
jswanson@coloradocollege.edu
SWANSON, JR., Joe .... 404-752-1542.... 134 E
jswanson@msm.edu
SWANSON, Kathrine .... 215-641-6510.... 436 G
kswanson@mc3.edu
SWANSON, Kristen, M ...... 919-966-3731.... 378 E
swansok@email.unc.edu
SWANSON, Lou .... 970-491-2785...... 83 F
louis.swanson@colostate.edu
SWANSON, Margaret, A .... 309-694-8584.... 152 C
mswanson@icc.edu
SWANSON, Paul, P .... 740-392-6868.... 396 I
paul.swanson@mvnu.edu
SWANSON, R. Gregory ...... 859-858-3511.... 198 E
greg.swanson@asbury.edu
SWANSON, Richard .... 510-261-8500...... 61 G
richard.swanson@patten.edu
SWANSON, Rick .... 478-274-7871.... 135 C
rswanson@oftc.edu
SWANSON, Robert .... 419-448-2125.... 391 F
rswanso1@heidelberg.edu
SWANSON, Robert, P .... 716-286-8538.... 344 D
rps@niagara.edu
SWANSON, Ronald .... 770-407-1001...... 29 F
raswanson@argosy.edu
SWANSON, Ronald .... 770-407-1001.... 124 F
raswanson@argosy.edu
SWANSON, Steven .... 415-575-6178...... 32 G
sswanson@ciis.edu
SWANSON-MADDEN,
Pamela .... 618-395-7777.... 152 F
swansonp@iecc.edu
SWANSON-ORR, Tamara ... 503-845-3549.... 417 A
tamara.swanson@mtangel.edu
SWANSTROM, Eugene .... 847-317-8038.... 166 E
gswanstr@tiu.edu
SWANT, Steven .... 404-894-4615.... 130 F
steve.swant@carnegie.gatech.edu
SWANTON, Deborah .... 978-232-2430.... 234 D
dswanton@endicott.edu
SWANZEY, Thomas .... 201-692-2749.... 310 A
thomas_swanzey@fdu.edu
SWARBRICK,
John "Jack", B .... 574-631-7546.... 180 G
swarbrick.1@nd.edu
SWARNES, Neal, R .... 417-667-8181.... 280 E
nswarnes@cottey.edu
SWARR, Amy .... 630-617-5370.... 150 H
amys@elmhurst.edu
SWARTHOUT, Jeanne .... 928-524-7420...... 17 A
jeanne.swarthout@npc.edu
SWARTWOOD, Ron .... 719-549-3026...... 87 F
ron.swartwood@pueblocc.edu
SWARTWOUT, Donna, L .... 978-837-5503.... 242 A
donna.swartwout@merrimack.edu
SWARTZ, Brian, L .... 480-966-5394...... 19 A
brian.swartz@apollogrp.edu
SWARTZ, David, L .... 202-885-2612...... 97 D
dswartz@american.edu
SWARTZ, James, E .... 641-269-4892.... 185 D
swartz@grinnell.edu
SWARTZ, Mark .... 212-410-8457.... 343 B
mswartz@nycpm.edu
SWARTZ, Mary, K .... 757-683-3623.... 522 F
mswartz@odu.edu
SWARTZBAUGH, Keith ...... 956-380-8140.... 493 D
kswartzbaugh@riogrande.edu
SWARTZBECK, Susan .... 724-589-2150.... 448 B
swartzbeck@thiel.edu
SWARTZENDRUBER,
Loren, E .... 540-432-4100.... 518 F
lorens@emu.edu
SWARTZENTRUBER,
Dale, E .... 740-368-3811.... 400 G
deswartz@owu.edu
SWARTZLANDER, Barbara . 207-602-2363.... 221 A
bswartzlander@une.edu
SWARTZWELDER,
Roger, L .... 205-329-7903........ 3 A
roger.swartzwelder@ecacolleges.com
SWATCHICK, Abby .... 610-568-1474.... 421 G
abby.swatchick@alvernia.edu
SWATCHICK, Matthew, J .... 570-385-6114.... 440 D
mjs48@psu.edu
SWATFAGER-HANEY,
Patricia .... 410-532-5308.... 225 D
pswatfagerhaney@ndm.edu
SWEANY, Lisa .... 912-344-2730.... 124 G
lisa.sweany@armstrong.edu
SWEARENGIN, Paul .... 412-237-3050.... 425 H
pswearengin@ccac.edu
SWEARER, Randy .... 215-951-2705.... 444 D
swearerr@philau.edu
SWEARINGEN, Jodie .... 651-423-8216.... 266 B
jodie.swearingen@dctc.edu
SWEARINGIN, Bubba .... 940-325-2591.... 508 F
bswearingin@wc.edu
SWEAT, Carl .... 757-925-6342.... 528 A
csweat@pdc.edu
SWEATMAN, Robert, A ...... 217-245-3289.... 152 D
rsweatma@ic.edu
SWEDE, Marci .... 860-343-5779...... 91 G
mswede@mxcc.commnet.edu
SWEEDEN, Debi .... 270-926-4040.... 200 F
dsweeden@daymarcollege.edu
SWEEDLER, Alan, R .... 619-594-1354...... 37 A
asweedler@sciences.sdsu.edu
SWEEK, Cristina .... 541-278-5753.... 414 G
csweek@bluecc.edu
SWEELEY, Rebecca .... 209-228-4667...... 74 D
rsweeley@ucmerced.edu
SWEEN, Barbara .... 859-572-5650.... 205 H
sweenb@nku.edu
SWEENER, Kathleen .... 518-629-7320.... 336 C
k.sweener@hvcc.edu
SWEENEY, Beth .... 859-572-6371.... 205 H
sweeneyb@nku.edu
SWEENEY, Donnie .... 256-331-5438........ 6 B
dsweeney@nwscc.edu
SWEENEY, Jeff .... 503-699-6269.... 416 J
jsweeney@marylhurst.edu
SWEENEY, John, M .... 401-865-2281.... 453 H
john.sweeney@providence.edu
SWEENEY, Katherine .... 706-737-1405.... 125 G
ksweeney@aug.edu
SWEENEY, Kathleen, J .... 978-656-3046.... 240 B
sweeneyk@middlesex.mass.edu
SWEENEY, Laurie Beth ...... 614-222-3268.... 388 G
lsweeney@ccad.edu
SWEENEY, Marc .... 937-766-7480.... 386 G
msweeney@cedarville.edu
SWEENEY, Michael .... 510-883-2083...... 45 B
msweeney@dspt.edu
SWEENEY, Michael, E .... 513-231-2223.... 384 H
msweeney@athenaeum.edu
SWEENEY, Michael, L .... 423-461-1511.... 468 H
msweeney@ecs.edu
SWEENEY, Richard, T .... 973-596-3208.... 312 C
richard.sweeney@njit.edu
SWEENEY, Rick .... 978-867-4036.... 235 A
rick.sweeney@gordon.edu
SWEENEY, Robert, D .... 434-924-1008.... 525 F
rds2j@virginia.edu
SWEENEY, Robert, J .... 937-775-3346.... 406 C
robert.sweeney@wright.edu
SWEENEY, Timothy .... 252-335-0821.... 369 G
timothy_sweeney@albemarle.edu
SWEENEY, Trina, D .... 304-204-4340.... 544 F
sweeneyt@wvstateu.edu
SWEENEY, Victoria .... 630-889-6572.... 159 F
vsweeney@nuhs.edu
SWEENEY, Vince .... 608-265-2822.... 550 J
vsweeney@wisc.edu
SWEENEY, Yvette, M .... 636-922-8238.... 288 B
ysweeney@stchas.edu
SWEET, Brett .... 615-343-6735.... 478 A
brett.sweet@vanderbilt.edu
SWEET, Chris .... 503-699-6268.... 416 J
csweet@marylhurst.edu
SWEET, Darryl .... 415-565-4604...... 74 A
sweetd@uchastings.edu
SWEET, David .... 972-721-5288.... 503 B
dsweet@udallas.edu
SWEET, David, M .... 315-279-5249.... 337 K
dsweet@mail.keuka.edu
SWEET, Don .... 252-328-9103.... 377 E
sweetd@ecu.edu
SWEET, Doris Ann .... 508-767-7272.... 230 D
dasweet@assumption.edu
SWEET, Fred .... 616-222-1329.... 250 A
fred.sweet@cornerstone.edu
SWEET, Jodie, L .... 574-239-8374.... 172 M
jsweet@hcc-nd.edu
SWEET, Lu .... 307-382-1639.... 557 A
lsweet@wwcc.wy.edu
SWEET, Paul, R .... 616-538-2330.... 251 D
psweet@gbcol.edu
SWEET, Stephanie .... 631-244-3047.... 332 C
sweets@dowling.edu
SWEET, Stephen, A .... 919-658-7493.... 367 F
ssweet@moc.edu
SWEET, Susan, W .... 570-662-4849.... 443 C
ssweet@mansfield.edu
SWEET, Tracy .... 802-241-2520.... 515 C
tracy.sweet@vsc.edu
SWEETANA, Michael .... 610-282-1100.... 427 A
michael.sweetana@desales.edu
SWEETEN, Katie .... 918-540-6211.... 408 J
katiebs@neo.edu
SWEETENBURG-LEE,
Penni .... 804-257-5656.... 530 A
pbsweetenburg@vuu.edu
SWEETING, Don .... 407-366-9943.... 276 F
dsweeting@rts.edu
SWEETING, Donald, W ...... 407-366-9493.... 115 K
dsweeting@rts.edu
SWEETLAND, Dennis .... 603-641-7052.... 305 G
dsweetla@anselm.edu
SWEETLAND, Jane .... 805-437-8918...... 34 B
jane.sweetland@csuci.edu
SWEEZEY, Gail, M .... 717-337-6100.... 429 I
gsweezey@gettysburg.edu
SWEGAN, Gary, D .... 419-372-7799.... 385 E
gswegan@bgsu.edu
SWEITZER, JR., Frank, X .. 716-839-8222.... 331 F
fsweitze@daemen.edu
SWEITZER, Frederick .... 860-768-4504...... 95 B
sweitzer@hartford.edu
SWEITZER-RILEY, Beth, E . 260-982-5052.... 177 H
besweitzer-riley@manchester.edu
SWEIZER, Jim .... 703-330-5398.... 540 F
jsweizer@apus.edu
SWENDER, Herbert .... 620-276-9602.... 193 C
herbert.swender@gcccks.edu
SWENGLER, Eleni .... 410-386-8157.... 221 G
eswengler@carrollcc.edu
SWENSON, Andrew .... 402-643-7220.... 297 D
andrew.swenson@cune.edu
SWENSON, Beth, I .... 701-788-4750.... 381 H
beth.swenson@mayvillestate.edu
SWENSON, Cherie .... 262-524-7240.... 546 H
cswenson@carrollu.edu
SWENSON, Craig, D .... 312-899-9900...... 29 F
cswenson@argosy.edu
SWENSON, Jeff .... 651-846-3408.... 260 I
jswenson@argosy.edu
SWENSON, Jeffrey .... 651-846-3408.... 509 F
jswenson@argosy.edu
SWENSON, Jeffrey, F .... 612-330-1241.... 261 B
swensonj@augsburg.edu
SWENSON, Jenni .... 218-733-7600.... 266 H
jswenson@lsc.edu
SWENSON, Michael .... 507-457-2773.... 269 G
mswenson@winona.edu
SWENSON, III, Ralph, M .. 802-656-2699.... 514 H
ralph.swenson@uvm.edu
SWENSON, Randy, L .... 630-889-6544.... 159 F
rswenson@nuhs.edu
SWENSON, Tammy .... 423-697-4418.... 474 D
SWENSON, Terry .... 909-558-8348...... 54 D
tswenson@llu.edu
SWENTON, Gina, D .... 860-628-4751...... 93 C
gswenton@lincolncollegene.edu
SWERBINSKY, Megan .... 216-791-5000.... 388 C
megan.swerbinsky@case.edu
SWERDLOW, Nadia .... 818-364-7842...... 55 A
swerdln@lamission.edu
SWETICH, Mary .... 775-289-3589.... 302 F
mary.swetich@gbcnv.edu
SWETS, Paul .... 325-942-2024.... 480 E
paul.swets@angelo.edu
SWETT, Denise .... 650-949-7524...... 47 H
swettdenise@foothill.edu
SWICK, Dean .... 901-722-3202.... 473 C
dswick@sco.edu
SWICKARD, Allison .... 719-502-2666...... 87 B
allison.swickard@ppcc.edu
SWIECH, Carol, A .... 603-641-4148.... 306 D
carol.swiech@unh.edu
SWIECINSKI, Deborah, L .... 757-683-3127.... 522 F
dswiecin@odu.edu
SWIFT, Carole .... 563-441-2467.... 186 I
cswift@kucampus.edu
SWIFT, Catherine .... 406-444-0328.... 294 H
cswift@montana.edu
SWIFT, CM, James .... 314-768-7123.... 283 G
swift@kenrick.edu
SWIFT, Rick .... 803-754-4100.... 457 D
SWIFT, Sheila .... 318-670-9646.... 215 A
sswift@susla.edu
SWIFT, Vikki .... 208-792-2269.... 144 B
vswift@lcsc.edu
SWIFT, William .... 978-632-6600.... 240 C
w_swift@mwcc.mass.edu
SWIGART, Scott, A .... 585-385-8430.... 348 F
sswigart@sjfc.edu
SWIGER, John .... 559-448-8282...... 66 G
johns@sjvc.edu
SWIHART, Karin .... 620-278-4276.... 196 H
kswihart@sterling.edu
SWINDAL, James .... 412-396-6388.... 428 D
swindalj@duq.edu
SWINDALL, Linda .... 727-864-8217.... 105 E
swindal@eckerd.edu
SWINDELL, Hal .... 252-940-6444.... 368 C
halgs@beaufortccc.edu
SWINDELL, Jim .... 256-306-2539........ 2 D
jes@calhoun.edu
SWINDLE, Jackquline .... 713-718-5206.... 487 I
jackquline.swindle@hccs.edu
SWINDLE, Richard, V .... 678-547-6456.... 134 A
swindle_rv@mercer.edu
SWINDOLL, George .... 843-349-5238.... 458 H
george.swindoll@hgtc.edu
SWINEY, John .... 509-963-3130.... 532 C
swineyj@cwu.edu
SWINEY, Karen .... 910-521-6222.... 379 C
karen.swiney@uncp.edu
SWINEY, R. Preston .... 910-521-6228.... 379 C
preston.swiney@uncp.edu
SWINFORD, Bill .... 859-257-1705.... 207 D
wswin2@uky.edu
SWINFORD, Jessica, L .... 260-399-7700.... 181 A
SWINK, Doug .... 816-235-1213.... 291 C
swinkd@umkc.edu
SWINKLER, Mary .... 724-357-2555.... 442 F
mary.swinkler@iup.edu
SWINNEY, Victoria .... 405-208-5071.... 410 A
vswinney@okcu.edu
SWINSON, Phyllis .... 570-422-2820.... 442 D
pswinson@po-box.esu.edu
SWINTON, Brent, E .... 202-238-2444...... 98 E
bswinton@howard.edu
SWINTON, David, H .... 803-705-4681.... 455 D
swintond@benedict.edu
SWINTON, Kelly .... 515-244-4221.... 181 F
swintonk@aib.edu
SWIRSKI, Thomas .... 219-981-4213.... 174 B
tswirski@iun.edu
SWISHER, Gary .... 614-251-4734.... 398 F
swisherg@ohiodominican.edu
SWISHER, Susan .... 773-298-3070.... 163 I
swisher@sxu.edu
SWISHER, Wayne .... 701-777-2786.... 381 F
wayne.swisher@und.edu
SWISHER, William, K .... 859-344-3600.... 206 I
bill.swisher@thomasmore.edu
SWISS, Jane, M .... 260-399-7700.... 181 A
jswiss@sf.edu
SWITZER, Aimee .... 304-776-6290.... 541 B
aswitzer@cci.edu
SWITZER, Devon .... 718-409-7260.... 356 C
dswitzer@sunymaritime.edu
SWITZER, Gloria .... 714-459-1107...... 78 H
gswitzer@wsulaw.edu
SWITZER, Ray .... 864-592-4770.... 461 C
switzerr@sccsc.edu
SWITZER, Teri .... 719-255-3115...... 88 I
tswitzer@uccs.edu
SWOMLEY, Brian .... 610-917-3939.... 450 E
blswomley@vfcc.edu
SWORDS, Jason .... 229-317-6449.... 128 D
jason.swords@darton.edu
SYBEL, Lauri .... 802-728-1320.... 516 A
lsybel@vtc.vsc.edu
SYBROWSKY, Paul, K .... 540-261-8430.... 524 H
paul.sybrowsky@svu.edu
SYDNOR, Kim .... 443-885-4012.... 224 E
kim.sydnor@morgan.edu
SYDOW, Debbie, L .... 804-862-6220.... 523 F
dsydow@rbc.edu
SYED, Naim .... 603-206-8081.... 304 D
nsyed@ccsnh.edu
SYGIELSKI, John, J .... 717-221-1300.... 430 E
ski@hacc.edu
SYKES, Andrew .... 651-846-3388.... 260 I
asykes@argosy.edu
SYKES, Arthur .... 972-860-7688.... 484 I
artsykes@dcccd.edu
SYKES, David .... 860-343-5704...... 91 G
dsykes@mxcc.commnet.edu
SYKES, Dorothy .... 910-695-3724.... 373 H
sykesd@sandhills.edu
SYKES, Eric .... 617-824-8268.... 234 B
eric_sykes@emerson.edu
SYKES, JR., John, D .... 434-949-1019.... 528 D
john.sykes@southside.edu
SYKES, Margaret, D .... 937-778-7855.... 390 G
mmyers@edisonohio.edu
SYKES, Reginald .... 251-575-8223........ 1 B
rlsykes@ascc.edu
SYKES, Ted .... 518-437-1802.... 324 I
tcsykes@bryantstratton.edu
SYKORA, Sarah .... 781-239-6278.... 230 E
ssykora@babson.edu
SYKORA, Terrance .... 563-876-3353.... 184 B
SYKTICH, Jackie, D .... 814-371-6920.... 428 A
mainc@dbcollege.com
SYLER-JONES, Tracy .... 817-257-7811.... 499 C
t.syler-jones@tcu.edu
SYLVA, Alyson .... 954-262-5258.... 114 B
asilva@nsu.nova.edu
SYLVAIN, Anne .... 617-236-8800.... 234 G
asylvain@fisher.edu

SYLVESTER, Barbara 732-750-1800 307 F bms@berkeleycollege.edu
SYLVESTER, Barbara, N 903-813-2457 481 A bsylvester@austincollege.edu
SYLVESTER, Danielle 954-201-7395 102 E dsylves1@broward.edu
SYLVESTER, Douglas 480-965-6188 11 J douglas.sylvester@asu.edu
SYLVESTER, James 860-444-2683 558 H jsylvester@cgaalumni.org
SYLVESTER, Lori 918-495-7708 411 C lsylvester@oru.edu
SYLWESTER, Donald 402-643-7446 297 D don.sylwester@cune.edu
SYMANCYK, Daniel, F 410-777-2587 221 C dfsymancyk@aacc.edu
SYMANK, Kathryn, B 979-862-4572 497 E k-symank@tamu.edu
SYMONS, Gretchen, A 814-332-2159 421 F gretchen.symons@allegheny.edu
SYNAR, Eric 918-463-2931 407 H esynar@connorsstate.edu
SYNDER, Brittany 305-809-3233 108 I brittany.snyder@fkcc.edu
SYNDER, Jake 978-921-4242 242 C jake.synder@montserrat.edu
SYNDER, Jane 617-277-3915 232 D synderj@bgsp.edu
SYNDER, Ned 937-461-5174 396 C ned.synder@staffmiamijacobs.edu
SYNDER, Tamara 352-787-7660 102 B tsnyder@beaconcollege.edu
SYNODI, George, S 203-832-7273 95 C gsynodi@newhaven.edu
SYPHER, Beverly, D 765-494-9709 178 J bdsypher@purdue.edu
SYREK, Richard 845-574-4465 347 I rsyrek@sunyrockland.edu
SYRONEY, Mark 216-916-8074 394 B msyroney@kent.edu
SYVERTSON, Debra 701-228-5454 382 E deb.syvertson@dakotacollege.edu
SYVERUD, Kent, D 314-935-6420 292 I kdsyverud@wustl.edu
SZABADOS, Anna 801-957-3334 512 D anna.szabados@slcc.edu
SZABO, Julia 419-358-3245 385 D szaboj@bluffton.edu
SZABO, Mihaela, A 304-336-8270 544 D mszabo@westliberty.edu
SZAFRAN, Zvi 678-915-7238 137 G zszafran@spsu.edu
SZAKAS, Joe, S 207-621-3198 220 B szakas@maine.edu
SZALANKIEWICZ, Linda 413-552-2155 239 F lszalankiewicz@hcc.edu
SZALKIEWICZ, Joe 858-653-6740 52 D
SZANI, Phyllis 201-200-3350 312 B pszani@njcu.edu
SZANTO, Edit 208-732-6863 143 E eszanto@csi.edu
SZAREK, Michael 201-559-6047 310 B szarekm@felician.edu
SZASZ-PALMER, Suzy 434-395-2431 521 A palmerss@longwood.edu
SZATMARY, David, P 206-685-6306 539 A dszatmar@uw.edu
SZCZERBACKI, David 518-454-5120 330 C szczerbd@strose.edu
SZEJKO, Thomas 724-503-1001 451 A tszejko@washjeff.edu
SZEKERES, Shirley 585-389-2773 342 D sszeker3@naz.edu
SZELEST, Bruce 518-437-4928 351 E bszelest@uamail.albany.edu
SZELISTOWSKI, Warren 410-532-5110 225 D wszelistowski@ndm.edu
SZENTMIKLOSI, Jillian, M 407-582-4142 123 B jszentmiklosi@valenciacollege.edu
SZEP, Chris Ann 410-287-8327 222 A caszep@cecil.edu
SZERI, Andrew, J 510-642-5472 73 H graddean@berkeley.edu
SZESZYCKI, Donald, J 319-335-3565 182 F donald-szeszycki@uiowa.edu
SZIGETI, Elvira 315-464-4276 352 E szigetie@upstate.edu
SZKODZINSKI, Michael, W 920-832-7348 548 B michael.w.szkodzinski@lawrence.edu
SZMYD, John, S 847-566-6401 167 F jszmyd@usml.edu
SZOPINSKI, Leonard 918-343-7818 411 H lszopinski@rsu.edu
SZOTT, Thomas, G 217-443-8878 148 G tszott@dacc.edu
SZPYRKA, Susan 719-255-3678 88 I sszpyrka@uccs.edu
SZTAINBERG, Marcelo, O 773-442-6012 160 A m-sztainberg@neiu.edu
SZUCH, Paul 409-880-8185 500 I pjszuch@lit.edu
SZUCS, Joseph 409-740-4463 497 F szucsj@tamug.edu
SZUCS, Liane 513-244-4711 388 E liane_szucs@mail.msj.edu
SZUDY, Lois, F 614-823-1414 400 H lszudy@otterbein.edu
SZUR, Katalin 212-237-8041 327 F kszur@jjay.cuny.edu
SZUREK, Barbara 651-757-4044 262 H bszurek@cva.edu
SZYMANSKI, Ashley 623-245-4600 18 J aszymanski@uti.edu
SZYMANSKI, David, M 513-556-7001 403 D david.szymanski@uc.edu
SZYMANSKI, Edna, M 218-477-2243 267 F szymanski@mnstate.edu
SZYMANSKI, Lynda 651-690-6500 270 L laszymanski@stkate.edu
SZYMONIAK, Steve 956-364-4826 500 D steve.szymoniak@stc.edu
SZYMURSKI, Patricia 610-558-5530 437 D szymurst@neumann.edu

T

TA, Minh-Hoa 415-239-3363 40 C mhta@ccsf.edu
TABACHNICK, Sharon, E 901-722-3237 473 C stabachnick@sco.edu
TABACK, Peter 212-229-5667 342 E tabackp@newschool.edu
TABARELLA-REED, Cheryl 319-363-8213 187 H credd@mtmercy.edu
TABB, Myrtis 662-846-4023 273 H mtabb@deltastate.edu
TABB, Winston, G 410-516-8330 223 F wtabb@jhu.edu
TABBACK, George 201-684-6842 313 C gtabback@ramapo.edu
TABBUTT, Ken 360-867-6558 534 D tabbuttk@evergreen.edu
TABER, Michael, S 240-895-4900 226 A mstaber@smcm.edu
TABER, Ralph 717-291-4390 429 F ralph.taber@fandm.edu
TABER, Robert, L 919-684-3628 364 C taber002@mc.duke.edu
TABERNER, Ian 617-262-5000 231 G ian.taberner@the-bac.edu
TABERSKI, Carol, J 231-995-1058 256 D ctaberski@nmc.edu
TABERSKI, Michael 301-447-5848 225 A taberski@msmary.edu
TABLE, Charles 631-632-7035 352 C charles.taber@stonybrook.edu
TABOADA, Luz, E 915-831-7796 486 G ltaboad2@epcc.edu
TABOL, Tim 614-234-2682 396 H ttabol@mccn.edu
TABOR, Geoff 413-236-1610 239 A gtabor@berkshirecc.edu
TABOR, Pam 615-256-6896 466 H ptaborabc@gmail.com
TABOR, Robert 715-346-2606 552 D btabor@uwsp.edu
TABOR, Tammy 620-227-9217 192 E tamtabor@dc3.edu
TABOR, William 803-327-7402 456 F wtabor@clintonjuniorcollege.edu
TABRON, Judith, L 516-463-6316 335 G judith.t.tabron@hofstra.edu
TACCONE, Al 760-757-2121 57 E ataccone@miracosta.edu
TACHA, Deanell 310-506-4611 61 H deanelle.tacha@pepperdine.edu
TACKE, Diane, L 563-387-1507 187 D tackedia@luther.edu
TACKE, Paula 605-668-1545 464 G paula.tacke@mtmc.edu
TACKET, Karen 805-546-3100 43 I ktacket@cuesta.edu
TACKETT, Larry 304-510-8760 543 D ltackett@wvncc.edu
TADAMY, Everett, L 412-268-1018 424 J et19@andrew.cmu.edu
TADDEO, Justine 718-405-3376 330 A justine.taddeo@mountsaintvincent.edu
TADDIE, Daniel, L 479-979-1431 26 A dtaddie@ozarks.edu
TADDONIO, Anita Marie 734-432-5419 254 D sranita@madonna.edu
TADEMY, Everett, L 412-268-1018 424 J et19@andrew.cmu.edu
TADEO, Joseph 352-588-8244 116 G joseph.tadeo@saintleo.edu
TADEPALLI, Raghu 336-278-6000 364 D rtadepalli@elon.edu
TADLOCK, Katherine 740-597-2577 399 G tadlockk@ohio.edu
TADLOCK, Martin 218-755-2015 265 I mtadlock@bemidjistate.edu
TADLOCK, Patty 601-925-3200 275 C tadlock@mc.edu
TAETZSCH, Blixy, K 607-844-8222 357 I taetzsb@tc3.edu
TAFARO, John, P 513-875-3344 387 C john.tafaro@chatfield.edu
TAFAWA, Weusi, A 617-228-2115 239 C wtafawa@bhcc.mass.edu
TAFOYA, Yvette 562-860-2451 39 A ytafoya@cerritos.edu
TAFT, David 718-488-1004 338 G david.taft@liu.edu
TAFT, Samara 252-527-6223 371 G staft@lenoircc.edu
TAGGART, Bruce, M 610-758-3025 434 E bmt2@lehigh.edu
TAGGART, James 205-247-8031 7 F jtaggart@stillman.edu
TAGGART, James 801-627-8306 510 H taggartj@owatc.edu
TAGGART, Julie 614-222-4025 388 G jtaggart@ccad.edu
TAGGART, Kathleen, J 402-280-2360 297 F ktaggart@creighton.edu
TAGGART, Thomas 904-256-1234 107 J ttaggart@fcsl.edu
TAGLIARENI, James 910-272-3560 373 D jtagliareni@robeson.edu
TAGLIATELA, Gayle, S 203-932-7455 95 C gtagliatela@newhaven.edu
TAGOMORI, Alvin 808-984-3515 142 E atag@hawaii.edu
TAGYE, Jim 515-643-6678 187 F jtagye@mercydesmoines.org
TAHA, Dianne 516-773-5545 558 I tahad@usmma.edu
TAHTINEN, Dale, R 906-487-2318 255 B drtahtin@mtu.edu
TAILFEATHERS, Robert 406-338-5421 293 F rtailfeathers@bfcc.org
TAIT, Lane, H 830-792-7462 494 E ltait@schreiner.edu
TAIT, Melissa 847-214-7365 150 F mtait@elgin.edu
TAIT, Raymond 314-977-4817 289 C taitrc@slu.edu
TAKACS, Audrey 586-445-7314 254 C takacsa@macomb.edu
TAKACS, Sarolta 518-292-1704 348 A takacs@sage.edu
TAKAHASHI, Esme 805-482-2755 64 E registrar-sjs@stjohnsem.edu
TAKAHASHI, Tomoko 949-480-4047 69 J ttakahashi@soka.edu
TAKAMI, Andrew, B 812-246-3301 177 B atakami@ivytech.edu
TAKAMURA, Jeanette, C 212-851-2288 330 F jct8@columbia.edu
TAKASH, Joe 312-935-6600 162 G jtakash@robertmorris.edu
TAKAYAMA, Thomas 815-455-8561 157 H ttakayam@mchenry.edu
TAKEDA, Kenneth, B 310-287-4368 55 F takedakb@wlac.edu
TAKEDA-TINKER, Becky 720-279-0159 83 G
TAKEMOTO, Mary Ann 562-985-5587 35 C mtakemot@csulb.edu
TAKES, Faith, A 518-786-0855 341 C faith.takes@mildred-elley.edu
TAKIGUCHI, Amy 808-735-4707 140 E ahigashi@chaminade.edu
TAKIGUCHI, Mark 503-821-8960 419 D mtakiguchi@pnca.edu
TAKSAR, Stephen 603-535-2550 307 A sjtaksar@plymouth.edu
TALABER, Matthew 845-938-3415 559 A matthew.talaber@usma.edu
TALAVERA, Karla 661-255-1050 32 F talavera@calarts.edu
TALBERT, Donald 950-446-4352 263 C talbertd@crown.edu
TALBOOM, Scott 928-226-4374 13 F scott.talboom@coconino.edu
TALBOT, A. Scott 435-652-7601 512 B talbot@dixie.edu
TALBOT, Jeff, D 828-262-3190 377 D talbotjd@appstate.edu
TALBOT, Laura 956-872-5051 494 H ltalbot@southtexascollege.edu
TALBOT, Laura 610-328-8358 447 F ltalbot1@swarthmore.edu
TALBOT, Laura 901-448-6135 477 E ltalbot@uthsc.edu
TALBOT, Miranda 626-568-8850 53 D
TALBOT, William 212-594-4000 357 H btalbot@tcicollege.edu
TALBOTT, Jeffrey 909-748-8888 76 C jeffrey_talbott@redlands.edu
TALBOTT, John, E 805-893-2622 75 B john.talbott@ap.ucsb.edu
TALBOTT, Richard 251-380-2785 9 D rtalbott@usouthal.edu
TALBOTT, Robert 650-543-3714 57 B rtalbott@menlo.edu
TALBOTT, Sherry 540-828-5369 517 B stalbott@bridgewater.edu
TALDO, Chad 913-266-8637 196 A
TALDO, Tom 785-242-5200 195 I tom.taldo@ottawa.edu
TALENTINO, Andrea 802-485-2410 514 C atalenti@norwich.edu
TALENTINO, Karen, A 802-654-2216 514 D ktalentino@smcvt.edu
TALESH, Rameen, A 949-824-5590 74 B rtalesh@uci.edu
TALIAFERRO, Donna 314-362-9180 282 B dtaliaferro@bjc.org
TALIAFERRO, Kevin, C 202-231-8681 557 J kevin.taliaferro@dodiis.mil
TALIENTO, Tamela, K 931-431-9700 472 D ttaliento@nci.edu
TALKEN, Rebecca, G 816-654-7702 283 F btalken@kcumb.edu
TALL, Gregory 312-935-6706 162 G gtall@robertmorris.edu
TALLANT, Pat, L 903-434-8102 491 F ptallant@ntcc.edu
TALLANT, Steven, H 361-593-3207 498 D steven.tallant@tamuk.edu
TALLARIDA, Ronald, J 856-256-5413 314 A tallarida@rowan.edu
TALLENT, Edward 617-333-2935 233 F etallent0811@curry.edu
TALLERICO, Betty, L 724-458-3790 430 B bltallerico@gcc.edu
TALLEY, Brent 870-777-5722 25 F brent.talley@uacch.edu
TALLEY, Cybil 770-938-4711 133 D
TALLEY, Frederico, J 301-846-2442 222 G ftalley@frederick.edu
TALLEY, Randy 405-224-3140 413 E rtalley@usao.edu
TALLMAN, Doug 402-486-2534 300 C dotallma@ucollege.edu
TALLMAN, Jonathan 276-466-7959 529 D jtallman@vic.edu
TALLMAN, Joseph Ray 415-371-0002 60 A
TALLON, William 920-424-1444 551 E tallon@uwosh.edu
TALLY, Joseph 415-955-2157 27 F jtally@alliant.edu
TALLY, Joseph 415-955-2120 27 F jtally@alliant.edu
TALMADGE, Barbara 206-268-4300 530 I btalmadge@antioch.edu
TALMADGE, Rosemary 718-482-5059 328 B rtalmadge@lagcc.cuny.edu
TALMO, Richard 760-744-1150 61 D rtalmo@palomar.edu
TALUSAN, Liza 508-565-1323 245 A ltalusan@stonehill.edu
TAM, William, M 210-436-3335 493 F btam@stmarytx.edu
TAMADA, Michael, D 323-259-2966 59 I tamada@oxy.edu
TAMADA, Mike 503-778-6613 420 A tamadam@reed.edu
TAMANAHA, David 808-984-3253 142 E davidt@hawaii.edu
TAMASCO, Mary 973-353-5541 314 E tamasc@newark.rutgers.edu
TAMAYO, Carlo 956-882-3814 505 E carlo.tamayo@utb.edu
TAMAYO, Daniel 559-934-2432 78 C danieltamayo@whccd.edu
TAMBLING, Joan, M 603-862-0927 306 B joan.tambling@usnh.edu
TAMBOUE, Helene 803-705-4573 455 D tamboueh@benedict.edu
TAMBURRINO, Janet 315-866-0300 335 D tamburrjl@herkimer.edu
TAMEO, John 401-254-3859 454 C jtameo@rwu.edu
TAMERIUS, Travis 573-592-4241 293 D travis.tamerius@williamwoods.edu
TAMIR, Roy 765-455-9378 174 A roytamir@iuk.edu
TAMM, David, A 304-367-4131 543 H david.tamm@fairmontstate.edu
TAMMARO, Susan 781-768-7390 244 A susan.tammaro@regiscollege.edu
TAMMES, Eric 312-341-6960 163 B etammes@roosevelt.edu
TAMMEUS, Lisen 816-235-5613 291 C tammeusli@umkc.edu
TAMMONE, William 309-694-8584 152 C william.tammone@icc.edu
TAMTE-HORAN, Deborah 484-664-3190 437 C tamte-horan@muhlenberg.edu
TAN, Lay Tuan 657-278-5845 35 B lttan@fullerton.edu
TAN, Lin-Ying 512-444-8082 499 E
TAN, Nestor 310-233-4053 54 I tanng@lahc.edu
TAN, Norbert, N 805-654-6461 77 F ntan@vcccd.edu
TAN, Teng-Kee 816-235-2204 291 C tant@umkc.edu
TANAKA, Elizabeth 254-295-4949 504 C etanaka@umhb.edu
TANAKA, Kenneth 408-855-5438 78 F kenneth.tanaka@wvm.edu

TANAKA, Paul, N 515-294-5352 182 E
ptanaka@iastate.edu
TANAKA, Winona, M 918-631-3054 413 F
winona-tanaka@utulsa.edu
TANAKA, Yasuo 510-666-8248 26 H
ytanaka@aimc.edu
TANAKEYOWMA, Lilia 714-564-6971 63 F
tanakeyowma_lilia@sac.edu
TANBARA, Sabrina 212-799-5000 337 H
TANCK, Buddy Jo 913-294-4178 193 A
buddyt@fortscott.edu
TANDE, Korinne 402-471-2505 299 D
ktande@nscs.edu
TANDIA, Mary 410-337-3355 222 I
mary.tandia@goucher.edu
TANDY, Martha, A 817-598-6252 508 F
tandy@wc.edu
TANEDO, Martha 740-774-7200 400 A
tanedo@ohio.edu
TANG, Meiling 707-638-5880 73 A
meiling.tang@tu.edu
TANG, Michael 510-592-9688 59 G
michael@npu.edu
TANG, Philip 410-516-6087 223 F
ptang@jhu.edu
TANGEMAN, Bruce 402-323-3408 300 B
btangeman@southeast.edu
TANIGAWA, Shane 415-380-1388 48 E
shanetanigawa@ggbts.edu
TANJI, Lorelei, A 949-824-5212 74 B
ltanji@uci.edu
TANKING, Tony 913-360-7485 191 A
ttanking@benedictine.edu
TANKLEFSKY, Paul 617-573-8483 245 B
ptanklef@suffolk.edu
TANKSLEY, Wallace 614-222-6165 388 G
wtanksley@ccad.edu
TANNEHILL, Darcy, B 412-397-6301 445 H
tannehilld@rmu.edu
TANNEHILL, Steven 661-362-9375 41 I
steven.tannehill@canyons.edu
TANNENBAUM, Ilene 718-951-5580 326 F
ilenet@brooklyn.cuny.edu
TANNENBAUM, Michael 607-431-4405 335 A
tannenbaumm@hartwick.edu
TANNER, Audrey 661-255-1050 32 F
atanner@calarts.edu
TANNER, Beth, L 732-247-5241 312 A
btanner@nbts.edu
TANNER, Chris, A 503-494-7445 418 D
sondeansoffice@ohsu.edu
TANNER, Cindy 912-287-5829 135 F
ctanner@okefenokeetech.edu
TANNER, Cynthia, A 248-341-2137 256 F
catanner@oaklandcc.edu
TANNER, David 617-732-2908 241 C
david.tanner@mcphs.edu
TANNER, David, F 435-865-8735 511 D
tanner@suu.edu
TANNER, Douglas, R 229-333-5935 139 C
dtanner@valdosta.edu
TANNER, Elizabeth 210-486-3915 479 C
etanner@alamo.edu
TANNER, Kevin 734-995-7502 249 G
tannek@cuaa.edu
TANNER, Kim 765-983-1631 171 E
tanneki@earlham.edu
TANNER, Mary 423-425-4249 477 F
mary-tanner@utc.edu
TANNER, Mary 423-425-4633 477 F
mary-tanner@utc.edu
TANNER, Michael 601-643-8302 273 G
michael.tanner@colin.edu
TANNER, Norma, J 251-460-6141 9 D
ntanner@usouthal.edu
TANNER, Pamela 262-472-5227 553 A
tannerp@uww.edu
TANNER, Paula 254-295-8671 504 C
ptanner@umhb.edu
TANNER, Starla, H 919-530-5402 378 B
starla.tanner@nccu.edu
TANNER, Tara 406-791-5294 296 F
ttanner01@ugf.edu
TANNER, William, P 785-827-5541 194 F
buck.tanner@kwu.edu
TANNIRU, Mohan, R 248-370-3286 256 G
tanniru@oakland.edu
TANON, Alma 408-270-6432 67 C
alma.tanon@evc.edu
TANOUYE, Allyson, M 808-956-7927 141 G
atanouye@hawaii.edu
TANSEY, Barbara 252-940-6201 368 C
barbarat@beaufortccc.edu
TANSLEY, Robert 203-596-4502 93 G
btansley@post.edu
TANTILLO, Richard, C 315-859-4412 334 H
rtantill@hamilton.edu
TANTSITS, SCC, Gerardine 973-543-6528 307 B
deanregistrar@acs350.org
TANZER, Ken 415-703-9592 32 C
ktanzer@cca.edu
TANZER, Kim 434-924-7019 525 F
kmt8t@virginia.edu
TAPEDO, Burgess 785-830-2774 193 D
btapedo@bie.edu
TAPIA, Damaris 773-442-4205 160 A
d-tapia1@neiu.edu
TAPIA, Erren 219-473-4257 170 G
etapia@ccsj.edu
TAPIA URZUA, Andres 412-291-6423 422 E
atapia-urzua@aii.edu
TAPLEY, Robyn 321-674-8050 108 H
rtapley@fit.edu
TAPP, Paul 903-923-2042 486 F
ptapp@etbu.edu
TAPP, Rita 903-785-7661 492 D
rtapp@parisjc.edu
TAPPAN, Charlene 860-512-2912 91 F
ctappan@mcc.commnet.edu
TAPPER, Janet 503-251-5757 421 A
jtapper@uws.edu
TAPSCOTT, Michael, R 202-994-1463 98 C
tapscott@gwu.edu
TARANTELLI, Thomas, L 518-276-6234 347 D
tarant@rpi.edu
TARANTO, John, A 816-501-3630 278 I
john.taranto@avila.edu
TARAS, Marilyn 636-422-2240 289 B
mtaras@stlcc.edu
TARBELL, Levi 641-673-1024 190 C
tarbelll@wmpenn.edu
TARBELL, Mary 413-755-4855 241 B
tarbell@stcc.edu
TARBETT, Matthew 740-695-9500 385 B
mtarbett@belmontcollege.edu
TARBOX, James 619-594-4379 37 A
jtarbox@mail.sdsu.edu
TARBOX, Norm 801-626-6003 511 G
ntarbox@weber.edu
TARBOX, Sandra 717-477-1131 443 E
sltarbox@ship.edu
TARBY, Jay 216-397-1703 392 L
tarby@jcu.edu
TARDIF, Mark 207-948-9292 219 H
mtardif@unity.edu
TARENCE, Elaine, P 334-387-3877 1 D
elainetarence@amridgeuniversity.edu
TARGETT, Nancy, M 302-831-2841 96 I
ntargett@udel.edu
TARGONSKI, Conrad, A 608-796-3804 553 C
catargonski@viterbo.edu
TARGONSKI, Dave 704-461-6735 362 F
davetargonski@bac.edu
TARGONSKI, David 704-461-6248 362 F
davidtargonski@bac.edu
TARNOWSKI, Jeffrey 678-891-2520 131 C
jeffrey.tarnowski@gpc.edu
TARNOWSKI, Susan 612-332-3361 261 A
starnowski@aii.edu
TARO, Thomas 680-488-2746 560 C
tarothomas@yahoo.com
TAROLA, Robert 202-806-2411 98 E
robert.tarola@howard.edu
TARPEY, Andrea 413-755-4847 241 B
tarpey@stcc.edu
TARPEY, Gerard 914-923-2804 345 F
gtarpey@pace.edu
TARPLEE, Marc 803-327-8017 463 H
mtarplee@yorktech.edu
TARPLEY, Sue 706-236-2292 126 C
starpley@berry.edu
TARQUINO, Beth, A 716-250-7500 324 H
batarquino@bryantstratton.edu
TARR, Barbara, L 818-779-8240 53 B
btarr@kingsuniversity.edu
TARR, Steven 610-526-1425 422 A
steven.tarr@theamericancollege.edu
TARRANCE, Tina 407-847-8966 107 I
tina.tarrance@fcc.edu
TARRANT, David 952-446-4120 263 C
tarrantd@crown.edu
TARRANT, David, S 208-467-8520 144 E
dtarrant@nnu.edu
TARRANT, Kaneesha 562-938-4268 54 E
ktarrant@lbcc.edu
TARRER, Jerry 414-229-3262 551 D
jtarrer@uwm.edu
TARSIA, Robert 805-893-4080 75 B
robert.tarsia@audit.ucsb.edu
TART, Judy 202-884-9704 99 H
tartj@trinitydc.edu
TART, Judye 910-592-8081 373 G
jtart@sampsoncc.edu
TART, Kathryn 361-570-4376 504 A
tartk@uhv.edu
TART, Marla, L 919-866-5901 374 H
mltart@waketech.edu
TARTAGLIA, Joseph, F 973-596-5279 312 C
tartaglia@njit.edu
TARTT, Tom 205-652-5467 9 E
ttartt@uwa.edu
TARVER, Beverly 706-721-2821 130 D
btarver@georgiahealth.edu
TARVER, Jerome, S 301-736-3631 224 A
jerome.tarver@msbbcs.edu
TARVER, Micheal 479-968-0274 20 G
mtarver@atu.edu
TARVER, Stephanie, B 337-562-4249 215 G
starver@mcneese.edu
TARVER, III, Walter, L 609-652-4804 313 E
walter.tarver@stockton.edu
TARVER-ROSS, Cassandra 256-372-5835 1 A
cassandra.ross@aamu.edu
TARVIN, Patricia 412-809-5100 444 G
tarvin.pat@pti.edu
TASA, Ken 979-230-3320 482 D
ken.tasa@brazosport.edu
TASHIMA, Jaye 760-245-4271 77 H
jaye.tashima@vvc.edu
TASHMAN, Jodi, L 215-699-5700 433 G
jtashman@lsb.edu
TASKER, Janet 770-479-9538 136 C
jkt@reinhardt.edu
TASSIN, Shannon 318-487-7151 209 F
tassin@lacollege.edu
TASSON, Dana 503-725-5312 418 G
tassond@pdx.edu
TASSONI, John, P 513-529-7135 396 E
tassonjp@muohio.edu
TASTAD, Renee 303-404-5332 85 A
renee.tastad@frontrange.edu
TATARKA, Donna 973-290-4700 308 G
dtatarka@cse.edu
TATE, Allen 717-391-7285 448 A
tate@stevenscollege.edu
TATE, David 307-382-1882 557 A
dtate@wwcc.wy.edu
TATE, Don 864-587-4227 461 D
tated@smcsc.edu
TATE, Horace 973-408-3246 309 E
htate@drew.edu
TATE, Louella, H 512-223-0045 481 B
ltate@austincc.edu
TATE, Mike 254-968-9107 497 A
tate@tarleton.edu
TATE, Nancy, A 785-670-1648 197 F
nancy.tate@washburn.edu
TATE, Nancy, A 785-670-2111 197 F
nancy.tate@washburn.edu
TATE, Pam 417-255-7230 286 D
pamtate@missouristate.edu
TATE, Randall 870-972-2056 20 D
rtate@astate.edu
TATE, Robert, H 863-680-4347 109 E
rtate@flsouthern.edu
TATE, Susan, E 614-236-6813 386 E
state@capital.edu
TATE, Thomas, L 334-683-2321 5 G
ttate@marionmilitary.edu
TATE, Verlanda 205-929-1440 5 H
vtate@miles.edu
TATE, William, A 417-833-2551 279 E
wtate@cbcag.edu
TATGE, Kellie 320-762-4489 265 F
kelliet@alextech.edu
TATLOCK, Mark 661-362-2222 56 G
mtatlock@masters.edu
TATLOCK, Mark 661-362-2220 56 G
mtatlock@masters.edu
TATNALL, Amber 207-216-4392 219 C
atatnall@yccc.edu
TATOM, Lisa 936-294-1750 501 D
ljt002@shsu.edu
TATRO, Clayton 620-223-2700 193 A
claytont@fortscott.edu
TATRO, Donna, E 609-258-2845 312 G
tatro@princeton.edu
TATRO, Fred 617-364-3510 232 A
ftatro@boston.edu
TATSUI, Kiyoko 310-689-3200 42 H
ktatsui@kaplan.edu
TATUM, Ashley 940-668-7323 491 E
atatum@nctc.edu
TATUM, Beverly Daniel 404-270-5001 138 B
presidentsoffice@spelman.edu
TATUM, C. Ray 478-301-2653 134 A
tatum_cr@mercer.edu
TATUM, Judy, B 313-577-3291 260 A
jtatum@wayne.edu
TATUM, Lance 334-670-3617 8 A
ltatum@troy.edu
TATUM, Leila 770-426-2917 133 E
leila.tatum@life.edu
TATUM, Tanya 850-599-3777 118 L
tanya.tatum@famu.edu
TATUM, Terry 361-825-2693 498 C
terry.tatum@tamucc.edu
TATUM, Veronda 870-862-8131 23 G
vtatum@southark.edu
TAUB, Carol 503-253-3443 417 H
ctaub@ocom.edu
TAUBER, Hendy 323-937-3763 80 D
htauber@yoec.edu
TAUBMAN, Mark, B 585-275-0017 359 B
mark_taubman@urmc.rochester.edu
TAUER, Ritamarie 281-649-3702 487 H
rtauer@hbu.edu
TAUPIER, Andrea, S 413-748-3609 244 H
ataupier@springfieldcollege.edu
TAURIELLO, Claire 301-447-5202 225 A
tauriello@msmary.edu
TAUSSIG, Martha 870-512-7824 20 F
martha_taussig@asun.edu
TAUSZ, Jerrad 816-204-2109 19 A
jerrad.tausz@phoenix.edu
TAUZIN, Kristie, R 985-448-4509 216 A
kristie.tauzin@nicholls.edu
TAVADA, Dwight, L 810-762-9825 253 C
dtavada@kettering.edu
TAVAKOLI, Assad 910-672-1527 377 G
atavakoli@uncfsu.edu
TAVAKOLI, Roozbeh 716-829-7515 332 E
tavakoli@dyc.edu
TAVAKOLI, Sue 623-935-8020 15 F
sue.tavakoli@estrellamountain.edu
TAVARES, Shirley, A 787-725-8120 562 C
investigacion@eap.edu
TAVAREZ, Luis, A 856-256-4276 314 A
tavarez@rowan.edu
TAVELLI, Nancy, J 509-527-5297 540 B
tavelln@whitman.edu
TAVES, Bennett, C 206-934-6819 537 F
ben.taves@seattlecolleges.edu
TAVES, Michael, E 607-274-3061 336 G
taves@ithaca.edu
TAVES, Michael, E 607-274-3867 336 G
taves@ithaca.edu
TAYAR, Adina 610-892-1511 441 C
atayar@pit.edu
TAYEBI, Kandi 936-294-1971 501 D
kanditayebi@shsu.edu
TAYEH, Raja 402-826-6776 297 G
raja.tayeh@doane.edu
TAYLOE, John 252-398-1232 363 G
tayloj@chowan.edu
TAYLOR, Alicia 256-306-2621 2 D
ataylor@calhoun.edu
TAYLOR, Amy 410-704-4931 228 E
altaylor@towson.edu
TAYLOR, Andrea 562-985-5197 35 C
ataylor@csulb.edu
TAYLOR, Angela 757-388-2900 524 D
TAYLOR, Angie 859-441-4500 202 B
angie.taylor@kctcs.edu
TAYLOR, Anna 770-233-5560 137 F
ataylor@sctech.edu
TAYLOR, Anne Marie 925-969-3491 52 C
amtaylor@jfku.edu
TAYLOR, Barbara 540-423-9032 526 I
btaylor@germanna.edu
TAYLOR, Barry 305-348-3662 119 C
barry.taylor@fiu.edu
TAYLOR, Beck, A 509-777-3200 540 C
btaylor@whitworth.edu
TAYLOR, Bill 408-741-2642 78 G
bill.taylor@westvalley.edu
TAYLOR, Bill 641-782-1406 189 E
taylor@swcciowa.edu
TAYLOR, Blair 276-326-4282 516 L
btaylor@bluefield.edu
TAYLOR, Bradley 910-879-5661 368 D
btaylor@bladencc.edu
TAYLOR, Brandon 334-683-2378 5 G
btaylor@marionmilitary.edu
TAYLOR, Brandy 912-871-1616 135 D
btaylor@ogeecheetech.edu
TAYLOR, Brian 808-956-6182 141 G
taylorb@hawaii.edu
TAYLOR, Brian 402-935-9400 299 A
btaylor@nechristian.edu
TAYLOR, Carol, A 714-556-3610 77 B
officeofthepresident@vanguard.edu
TAYLOR, Cathy 615-460-6916 467 D
cathy.taylor@belmont.edu
TAYLOR, Celeste 706-355-5081 125 C
ctaylor@athenstech.edu
TAYLOR, Charles 256-331-5462 6 B
taylor@nwscc.edu
TAYLOR, Charles 417-873-7391 281 D
ctaylor@drury.edu
TAYLOR, Charles 330-325-6461 397 D
ctaylor@neomed.edu
TAYLOR, Charles, A 404-237-7573 126 B
ctaylor@bauder.edu
TAYLOR, Chelsa 276-739-2423 529 A
ctaylor@vhcc.edu
TAYLOR, Cherilyn, Y 803-536-7245 460 G
ctaylor@scsu.edu
TAYLOR, Cheryl 225-771-2151 214 I
cheryl_taylor@suson.subr.edu
TAYLOR, Cheryl, A 417-268-1000 278 H
ctaylor@agts.edu
TAYLOR, Chris 801-863-8484 511 F
taylorch@uvu.edu
TAYLOR, Craig 541-463-5364 416 E
taylorc@lanecc.edu
TAYLOR, Craig, B 503-554-2911 415 I
ctaylor@georgefox.edu
TAYLOR, Curtis, J 712-722-6006 184 C
curtis@dordt.edu
TAYLOR, Cynthia, S 972-860-7191 484 I
cynthiastaylor@dcccd.edu
TAYLOR, Cyrus, C 216-368-4437 386 F
casdean@case.edu

TAYLOR, Daniel .... 216-432-8945 .... 387 B
dataylor@chancelloru.edu

TAYLOR, Daniel .... 304-358-2000 .... 541 C

TAYLOR, Danny .... 615-966-7650 .... 470 F
danny.taylor@lipscomb.edu

TAYLOR, Darrell .... 304-896-7432 .... 543 C
darrell.taylor@southernwv.edu

TAYLOR, David .... 713-500-4535 .... 506 F
david.taylor@uth.tmc.edu

TAYLOR, David .... 276-326-4206 .... 516 L
dtaylor@bluefield.edu

TAYLOR, David .... 276-326-4257 .... 516 L
dtaylor@bluefield.edu

TAYLOR, David, E .... 202-885-2121 .... 97 D
taylor@american.edu

TAYLOR, David, M .... 205-652-3531 .... 9 E
dmt@uwa.edu

TAYLOR, Deb, A .... 864-622-6063 .... 455 C
dtaylor@andersonuniversity.edu

TAYLOR, Debora, W .... 512-448-8450 .... 493 E
deboraw@stedwards.edu

TAYLOR, Deborah .... 562-777-4069 .... 31 A
deborah.taylor@biola.edu

TAYLOR, Deborah, A .... 603-526-3760 .... 303 G
dtaylor@colby-sawyer.edu

TAYLOR, Deborah, D .... 336-734-7178 .... 370 F
ddtaylor@forsythtech.edu

TAYLOR, Delores, T .... 804-827-8730 .... 526 B
dttaylor@vcu.edu

TAYLOR, Denise .... 760-921-5429 .... 61 C
dtaylor@paloverde.edu

TAYLOR, Dennis .... 318-869-5360 .... 208 H
dtaylor@centenary.edu

TAYLOR, Dennis, D .... 740-392-6868 .... 396 I
denny.taylor@mvnu.edu

TAYLOR, Desiree .... 334-874-5700 .... 2 H
dtaylor@ccal.edu

TAYLOR, Dickerson, E .... 706-233-7240 .... 137 A
dtaylor@shorter.edu

TAYLOR, Dinny, S .... 413-597-3072 .... 246 D
dinny.s.taylor@williams.edu

TAYLOR, Don .... 949-582-4541 .... 70 F
dtaylor@saddleback.edu

TAYLOR, Don .... 415-338-3326 .... 37 B
dtaylor@sfsu.edu

TAYLOR, Donald .... 630-829-6240 .... 145 G
dtaylor@ben.edu

TAYLOR, Donald, R .... 870-307-7230 .... 22 D
donald.taylor@lyon.edu

TAYLOR, Donald, R .... 870-307-7203 .... 22 D
donald.taylor@lyon.edu

TAYLOR, Doug .... 404-687-4568 .... 127 F
taylord@ctsnet.edu

TAYLOR, Ed .... 206-616-7175 .... 539 A
edtaylor@uw.edu

TAYLOR, Edward .... 608-663-2333 .... 547 F
edtaylor@edgewood.edu

TAYLOR, Ella .... 503-838-8757 .... 419 C
taylore@wou.edu

TAYLOR, Ellen .... 540-831-5771 .... 523 A
eltaylor@radford.edu

TAYLOR, Erica .... 901-320-9730 .... 478 C
etaylor@victory.edu

TAYLOR, Francis, H .... 334-833-4556 .... 4 E
ftaylor@huntingdon.edu

TAYLOR, G. Christine .... 765-494-6969 .... 178 J
taylorgc@purdue.edu

TAYLOR, Gary .... 406-243-6131 .... 294 I
gary.taylor@umontana.edu

TAYLOR, Gary .... 865-251-1800 .... 473 A
gtaylor@southcollegetn.edu

TAYLOR, Gene, F .... 701-231-5614 .... 382 B
gene.taylor@ndsu.edu

TAYLOR, Geraldine, S .... 781-891-2222 .... 231 D
gtaylor@bentley.edu

TAYLOR, Gia .... 480-423-6300 .... 16 C
gia.taylor@scottsdalecc.edu

TAYLOR, Greg .... 307-755-2135 .... 557 B
gtaylor@wyotechstaff.edu

TAYLOR, Gregory .... 559-244-5909 .... 72 A
gregory.taylor@scccd.edu

TAYLOR, Gregory .... 314-719-3609 .... 281 I
gtaylor@fontbonne.edu

TAYLOR, Gregory .... 914-251-6831 .... 354 D
gregory.taylor@purchase.edu

TAYLOR, Gwen .... 706-771-4180 .... 125 H
gtaylor@augustatech.edu

TAYLOR, Howard, E .... 330-471-8235 .... 395 F
htaylor@malone.edu

TAYLOR, Hunter .... 252-536-7228 .... 371 B
huntert@halifaxcc.edu

TAYLOR, Ian, L .... 718-270-3171 .... 352 D
itaylor@downstate.edu

TAYLOR, Jackie .... 731-661-5302 .... 477 B
jtaylor@uu.edu

TAYLOR, Jacqueline .... 773-325-7585 .... 149 A
jtaylor@depaul.edu

TAYLOR, Jaime .... 931-221-7971 .... 473 E
taylorjr@apsu.edu

TAYLOR, James .... 502-456-6504 .... 206 H
jtaylor@sullivan.edu

TAYLOR, James .... 801-626-6055 .... 511 G
jamestaylor8@weber.edu

TAYLOR, James, H .... 606-539-4201 .... 207 C
presoff@ucumberlands.edu

TAYLOR, James, W .... 269-488-4208 .... 253 A
jwtaylor@kvcc.edu

TAYLOR, Jan .... 304-558-4128 .... 543 E
jan.taylor@wvresearch.org

TAYLOR, Janet, M .... 419-434-4615 .... 404 B
jantaylor@findlay.edu

TAYLOR, Janice .... 617-521-2360 .... 244 F
janice.taylor@simmons.edu

TAYLOR, Janie .... 817-461-8741 .... 480 H
jhall@abconline.org

TAYLOR, Jasmine, P .... 601-984-1340 .... 277 E
jptaylor@umc.edu

TAYLOR, Jason .... 609-586-4800 .... 311 B
taylorj@mccc.edu

TAYLOR, Jay, P .... 417-268-1000 .... 278 H
jtaylor@agts.edu

TAYLOR, Jeffrey, D .... 315-268-6477 .... 329 B
jdtaylor@clarkson.edu

TAYLOR, Jeffrey, S .... 814-871-7213 .... 429 G
taylor030@gannon.edu

TAYLOR, Jennifer .... 805-565-6085 .... 79 A
jmtaylor@westmont.edu

TAYLOR, Jim .... 253-964-6589 .... 536 H
jtaylor@pierce.ctc.edu

TAYLOR, Joe .... 970-248-1020 .... 82 F
jtaylor@coloradomesa.edu

TAYLOR, John .... 315-255-1743 .... 325 G
john.taylor@cayuga-cc.edu

TAYLOR, Joseph, R .... 801-581-3325 .... 511 C
jtaylor@utah.edu

TAYLOR, Joyce .... 501-812-2221 .... 23 C
jtaylor@pulaskitech.edu

TAYLOR, June .... 602-386-4104 .... 11 G
june.taylor@arizonachristian.edu

TAYLOR, K.D .... 801-863-8949 .... 511 F
taylorkd@uvu.edu

TAYLOR, Karen .... 585-785-1624 .... 334 A
taylorkm@flcc.edu

TAYLOR, Katherine, A .... 217-245-3035 .... 152 D
kataylor@ic.edu

TAYLOR, Kathy .... 773-291-6289 .... 147 G
ktaylor01@ccc.edu

TAYLOR, Kathy .... 870-230-5103 .... 21 I
taylork@hsu.edu

TAYLOR, Kathy, J .... 603-526-3766 .... 303 G
ktaylor@colby-sawyer.edu

TAYLOR, Keith .... 814-871-7609 .... 429 G
ktaylor@gannon.edu

TAYLOR, Kelley, G .... 334-844-4794 .... 1 F
taylokg@auburn.edu

TAYLOR, Kenneth .... 870-230-5214 .... 21 I
taylork@hsu.edu

TAYLOR, Kent .... 575-624-8235 .... 319 C
kent@nmmi.edu

TAYLOR, Kenya, S .... 308-865-8843 .... 300 F
taylorks@unk.edu

TAYLOR, Kerri .... 217-732-3155 .... 156 I
ktaylor@lincolncollege.edu

TAYLOR, Kristi .... 817-531-4403 .... 502 C
ktaylor@txwes.edu

TAYLOR, Ladd .... 601-928-6224 .... 275 E
ladd.taylor@mgccc.edu

TAYLOR, Lance .... 904-620-2820 .... 120 D
ltaylor@unf.edu

TAYLOR, LaTonya .... 630-752-5015 .... 168 H
media.relations@wheaton.edu

TAYLOR, Lauren, M .... 205-726-2956 .... 6 G
lmtaylor@samford.edu

TAYLOR, Leah, A .... 304-929-6701 .... 543 A
ltaylor@newriver.edu

TAYLOR, Lealon .... 405-682-7591 .... 409 F
ltaylor@occc.edu

TAYLOR, Lee, L .... 251-575-8225 .... 1 B
ltaylor@ascc.edu

TAYLOR, Leslie .... 740-363-1146 .... 396 A
ltaylor@mtso.edu

TAYLOR, Leslie .... 406-994-4570 .... 295 C
lesliet@montana.edu

TAYLOR, Linda .... 270-686-4595 .... 203 B
linda.taylor@kctcs.edu

TAYLOR, Linda .... 800-567-2344 .... 547 A
ltaylor@menominee.edu

TAYLOR, Linda .... 610-499-1039 .... 451 F
lmtaylor@widener.edu

TAYLOR, Loralyn .... 518-327-6231 .... 345 H
ltaylor@paulsmiths.edu

TAYLOR, Lori .... 740-245-7204 .... 404 E
ltaylor@rio.edu

TAYLOR, Marcie, J .... 765-641-4495 .... 169 E
mjtaylor@anderson.edu

TAYLOR, Margaret .... 870-575-8733 .... 25 B
taylorm@uapb.edu

TAYLOR, Margaret .... 814-898-6383 .... 439 F
mut100@psu.edu

TAYLOR, Margaret, G .... 540-674-3603 .... 527 E
ptaylor@nr.edu

TAYLOR, Marianne .... 508-678-2811 .... 239 B
marianne.taylor@bristolcc.edu

TAYLOR, Marilyn .... 520-621-3876 .... 18 L
taylorm@email.arizona.edu

TAYLOR, Marilyn, J .... 215-898-3425 .... 448 J
mjtaylor@design.upenn.edu

TAYLOR, Mark .... 601-477-4030 .... 274 H
mark.taylor@jcjc.edu

TAYLOR, Mark .... 562-938-4206 .... 54 E
mtaylor@lbcc.edu

TAYLOR, Mark .... 740-420-5919 .... 398 D
mtaylor@ohiochristian.edu

TAYLOR, Maurice .... 443-885-4075 .... 224 E
maurice.taylor@morgan.edu

TAYLOR, Melanie .... 562-903-4800 .... 31 A
melanie.taylor@biola.edu

TAYLOR, Mervin, V .... 340-693-1560 .... 568 E
mtaylor2@live.uvi.edu

TAYLOR, Mia .... 617-348-6220 .... 245 D
taylor@urbancollege.edu

TAYLOR, Michael .... 253-589-6085 .... 532 G
michael.taylor@cptc.edu

TAYLOR, Michael, A .... 812-877-8145 .... 179 B
michael.a.taylor@rose-hulman.edu

TAYLOR, Michele .... 610-841-3333 .... 441 D
mtaylor@psb.edu

TAYLOR, Michelle .... 801-863-8806 .... 511 F
taylormo@uvu.edu

TAYLOR, Michelle .... 918-495-6581 .... 411 C
mtaylor@oru.edu

TAYLOR, Michelle .... 610-902-8420 .... 424 B
michelle.rose.taylor@cabrini.edu

TAYLOR, Monica, M .... 302-831-7138 .... 96 I
mmtaylor@udel.edu

TAYLOR, Nancy, K .... 716-375-2317 .... 348 C
nktaylor@sbu.edu

TAYLOR, Orlando .... 202-706-5050 .... 146 F
otaylor@thechicagoschool.edu

TAYLOR, Pam .... 618-664-6513 .... 151 F
pam.taylor@greenville.edu

TAYLOR, Pat .... 417-328-1500 .... 290 A
ptaylor@sbuniv.edu

TAYLOR, Patricia .... 734-677-5003 .... 259 F
ptaylor@wccnet.edu

TAYLOR, Patricia .... 757-825-2898 .... 528 F
taylorp@tncc.edu

TAYLOR, Patty, A .... 530-226-4140 .... 69 H
ptaylor@simpsonu.edu

TAYLOR, Patty, L .... 920-565-1298 .... 548 A
taylorpl@lakeland.edu

TAYLOR, OSB, Paul .... 724-805-2527 .... 446 E
paut.taylor@email.stvincent.edu

TAYLOR, Peter, J .... 510-987-0111 .... 73 G
peter.taylor@ucop.edu

TAYLOR, Phillip .... 518-327-6272 .... 345 H
ptaylor@paulsmiths.edu

TAYLOR, Rad, W .... 518-783-2573 .... 350 I
rtaylor@siena.edu

TAYLOR, Reade .... 336-334-5200 .... 379 B
reade_taylor@uncg.edu

TAYLOR, Reina .... 440-834-3711 .... 393 G
rtaylor9@kent.edu

TAYLOR, Rich .... 405-325-7370 .... 413 C
rich.taylor@ou.edu

TAYLOR, Richard .... 814-393-2361 .... 442 B
rtaylor@clarion.edu

TAYLOR, Richard, A .... 214-841-3654 .... 485 F
rtaylor@dts.edu

TAYLOR, Rick .... 417-447-4802 .... 287 D
taylorrd@otc.edu

TAYLOR, Robbin, M .... 270-745-5858 .... 208 A
robbin.taylor@wku.edu

TAYLOR, Robert .... 712-722-6077 .... 184 C
rtaylor@dordt.edu

TAYLOR, Ron .... 209-384-6101 .... 57 C
ron.taylor@mccd.edu

TAYLOR, Russell .... 828-898-8770 .... 366 D
taylorrg@lmc.edu

TAYLOR, Sandi .... 909-748-8428 .... 76 C
sandi_taylor@redlands.edu

TAYLOR, Sharon .... 562-985-4162 .... 35 C
staylor@csulb.edu

TAYLOR, Sharon .... 412-924-1350 .... 444 H
staylor@pts.edu

TAYLOR, Sharon .... 360-438-4370 .... 537 B
staylor@stmartin.edu

TAYLOR, Sherri .... 229-732-5950 .... 124 E
sherritaylor@andrewcollege.edu

TAYLOR, Sherry .... 641-673-1048 .... 190 C
taylors@wmpenn.edu

TAYLOR, Sherry .... 417-447-8801 .... 287 D
taylorst@otc.edu

TAYLOR, Sheryl, S .... 712-722-6047 .... 184 C
staylor@dordt.edu

TAYLOR, Sonja .... 386-226-6326 .... 105 H
sonja.taylor@erau.edu

TAYLOR, Spence .... 864-455-7992 .... 462 F
staylor@bju.edu

TAYLOR, Stacey .... 617-732-2790 .... 241 C
stacey.taylor@mcphs.edu

TAYLOR, Stan .... 214-648-7518 .... 507 E
stan.taylor@utsouthwestern.edu

TAYLOR, Stephanie .... 423-614-8600 .... 470 C
staylor@leeuniversity.edu

TAYLOR, Stephanie .... 704-637-4470 .... 363 E
sataylor@catawba.edu

TAYLOR, Stephanie .... 317-921-4473 .... 175 K
staylor@ivytech.edu

TAYLOR, Stephanie .... 412-291-6200 .... 422 E
staylor@aii.edu

TAYLOR, Steve .... 662-325-0939 .... 275 F
steve.taylor@msstate.edu

TAYLOR, Steve, M .... 308-432-6210 .... 299 E
staylor@csc.edu

TAYLOR, Steve, P .... 262-243-5700 .... 547 C
steve.taylor@cuw.edu

TAYLOR, Steven, T .... 303-963-3138 .... 82 C
staylor@ccu.edu

TAYLOR, Sue .... 972-883-4694 .... 506 A
setaylor@utdallas.edu

TAYLOR, T. A .... 214-638-0484 .... 489 H
tataylor@kdstudio.com

TAYLOR, Tammy .... 903-927-3300 .... 509 E
ttaylor@wileyc.edu

TAYLOR, Tamra .... 801-524-8140 .... 510 E
ttaylor@ldsbc.edu

TAYLOR, Thomas .... 205-391-2617 .... 6 I
ttaylor@sheltonstate.edu

TAYLOR, Thomas .... 978-934-3933 .... 237 B
thomas_taylor@uml.edu

TAYLOR, Thomas, T .... 937-327-7012 .... 406 B
ttaylor@wittenberg.edu

TAYLOR, Tim .... 618-842-3711 .... 152 G
taylort@iecc.edu

TAYLOR, Timothy .... 803-376-5766 .... 455 B

TAYLOR, Tom .... 765-285-1444 .... 169 G
taylor@bsu.edu

TAYLOR, Toni .... 334-808-6305 .... 8 A
tltaylor@troy.edu

TAYLOR, Toni .... 509-359-6529 .... 533 H
ttaylor@ewu.edu

TAYLOR, Trace .... 785-227-3380 .... 191 B
traylort@bethanylb.edu

TAYLOR, Tyra .... 217-786-4509 .... 157 B
tyra.taylor@llcc.edu

TAYLOR, Valerie, A .... 570-941-6592 .... 450 C
valerie.taylor@scranton.edu

TAYLOR, Vernon .... 540-442-0395 .... 58 I
vtaylor@nu.edu

TAYLOR, Vicki .... 870-230-5148 .... 21 I
taylorv@hsu.edu

TAYLOR, Virginia .... 585-345-6886 .... 334 F
vmtaylor@genesee.edu

TAYLOR, Virginia, L .... 330-569-5214 .... 391 G
taylorvl@hiram.edu

TAYLOR, Vorley .... 740-366-9443 .... 386 H
taylor.1051@osu.edu

TAYLOR, Vorley .... 740-366-9443 .... 399 E
taylor.1051@osu.edu

TAYLOR, III, W.S. (Stu) .... 606-326-2409 .... 201 F
stu.taylor@kctcs.edu

TAYLOR, JR., Walter, F .... 614-235-4136 .... 402 G
wtaylor@tlsohio.edu

TAYLOR, Wes .... 507-389-7213 .... 269 D
wes.taylor@southcentral.edu

TAYLOR, William, F .... 804-706-5016 .... 527 B
ftaylor@jtcc.edu

TAYLOR, William, R .... 626-395-3727 .... 32 H
bill.taylor@cco.caltech.edu

TAYLOR, Yolanda, D .... 918-631-2327 .... 413 F
yolanda-taylor@utulsa.edu

TAYLOR-ALLEYNE, Dian .... 215-572-2932 .... 422 C
taylor-alleyne@arcadia.edu

TAYLOR-ARCHER,
Mordean .... 502-852-6153 .... 207 E
motayl01@louisville.edu

TAYLOR-BURCH, Linda, J .... 856-225-6039 .... 314 D
ltburch@camden.rutgers.edu

TAYLOR-DUPREE, Lesa .... 318-678-6000 .... 209 I
ltaylordupre@bpcc.edu

TAYLOR-KING, Sheila .... 603-513-1336 .... 306 F
sheila.taylor-king@granite.edu

TAYLOR-RODRIGUEZ,
Amanda .... 404-297-9522 .... 131 D
taylora@gptc.edu

TAYLOR-SAWYER, Sandra .... 575-769-4138 .... 318 A
sandra.sawyer@clovis.edu

TAYLOR-WEBB, Traki .... 301-860-3230 .... 228 A
ttaylorwebb@bowiestate.edu

TCHEOU, Pang .... 717-872-3350 .... 443 D
fathertcheou@gmail.com

TCHOUNWOU, Paul, B .... 601-979-2153 .... 274 G
paul.b.tchounwou@jsums.edu

TEACHEY, Colette, B .... 910-938-6234 .... 369 F
teacheyc@coastalcarolina.edu

TEACHMAN, Debra .... 575-439-3622 .... 319 E
teachman@nmsua.nmsu.edu

TEAFF, Richard, R .... 540-863-2827 .... 526 F
rteaff@dslcc.edu

TEAGUE, Barbara .... 606-546-4151 .... 207 B
bteague@unionky.edu

TEAGUE, Brad .... 501-450-3150 .... 25 H
bteague@uca.edu

TEAGUE, Clay .... 478-757-3544 .... 127 A
cteague@centralgatech.edu

TEAGUE, Dion .... 253-680-7023 .... 531 F
dteague@bates.ctc.edu

TEAGUE, Donna, O .... 812-488-2212 .... 180 E
dt52@evansville.edu

TEAGUE, Ellen .... 703-812-4757 .... 520 J
eteague@leland.edu

TEAGUE, Norwood .... 612-625-0775 .... 272 A
norwood@umn.edu

TEAGUE, Peggy, S .... 919-735-5151 .... 375 A
psteague@waynecc.edu

TEAGUE, Peter, W .... 717-560-8278.... 433 D
pteague@lbc.edu
TEAGUE, Rebecca .... 951-487-3072...... 58 B
rteague@msjc.edu
TEAGUE, Sharyn, J .... 910-221-2224.... 364 F
TEAGUE, Tracie .... 805-969-3626...... 60 J
tteague@pacifica.edu
TEAGUE, Willard .... 417-862-9533.... 282 A
wteague@globaluniversity.edu
TEAHEN, Rebecca, M .... 231-995-1855.... 256 D
rteahen@nmc.edu
TEAHEN, Roberta .... 231-591-3532.... 250 H
teahenr@ferris.edu
TEAL, Holly .... 970-248-1898...... 82 F
hteal@coloradomesa.edu
TEAL, Lysa .... 860-486-2434...... 94 G
lysa.teal@uconn.edu
TEAL, P, J .... 919-515-2191.... 378 C
pj_teal@ncsu.edu
TEAL, Rick .... 864-592-4618.... 461 C
tealr@sccsc.edu
TEAL, Rita, J .... 803-516-4586.... 460 G
rfjteal@scsu.edu
TEAT, Jonathan .... 214-333-5128.... 484 D
jonathan@dbu.edu
TEBBE, Robert .... 618-235-2700.... 165 D
robert.tebbe@swic.edu
TEBES, Mary, L .... 561-237-7902.... 113 D
mtebes@lynn.edu
TECLE, Barbara .... 310-665-6946...... 60 B
btecle@otis.edu
TEDESCHI, Lisa, F .... 603-526-3451.... 303 G
ltedeschi@colby-sawyer.edu
TEDESCO, Joanne .... 573-875-7207.... 280 A
jtedesco@ccis.edu
TEDESCO, Joseph, W .... 713-743-4207.... 503 D
jtedesco@uh.edu
TEDESCO, Lisa, A .... 404-727-2669.... 129 D
lisa.tedesco@emory.edu
TEDJESKE, David .... 610-519-6979.... 450 H
david.tedjeske@villanova.edu
TEDROW, Allen .... 724-836-9909.... 449 C
awt@pitt.edu
TEDUITS, Doug .... 713-222-5318.... 503 F
teduitsd@uhd.edu
TEED, Debbie .... 360-596-5451.... 538 E
dteed@spscc.ctc.edu
TEEGEN, Hildy .... 803-777-3176.... 462 A
teegen@moore.sc.edu
TEEHAN, Dyan .... 617-928-4780.... 242 E
dteehan@mountida.edu
TEEHAN, Kathleen .... 617-287-6020.... 236 G
kathleen.teehan@umb.edu
TEEL, Eunice .... 231-348-6615.... 256 B
eteel@ncmich.edu
TEEL, Lisa .... 405-682-1611.... 409 F
lteel@occc.edu
TEEL, Maria .... 662-685-4771.... 273 E
mteel@bmc.edu
TEEL, Nancy, A .... 617-427-0060.... 241 A
nteel@rcc.mass.edu
TEEMS, Larry .... 404-297-9522.... 131 D
teemsl@gptc.edu
TEEPLE, Cynthia .... 714-547-9625...... 32 B
cteeple@calcoast.edu
TEERINK, Susan, M .... 414-288-1583.... 548 F
susan.teerink@marquette.edu
TEETER, Deborah, J .... 785-864-4412.... 197 B
irdjt@ku.edu
TEETS, Andrew .... 814-871-5856.... 429 G
teets001@gannon.edu
TEETSEL, Craig .... 260-399-7700.... 181 A
cteetsel@sf.edu
TEEUWISSEN, John .... 304-766-3147.... 544 F
johntee@wvstateu.edu
TEGART, Doris, A .... 502-272-8208.... 198 H
dtegart@bellarmine.edu
TEGEGNE, Yahana .... 312-589-7442.... 150 G
ytegegne@ellis.edu
TEGERSTRAND, Julene, M 208-467-8338.... 144 E
jtegerstrand@nnu.edu
TEICHERT, Scott .... 801-626-7670.... 511 G
scottteichert@weber.edu
TEICHMAN, Carl, F .... 309-556-3429.... 153 F
cteich@iwu.edu
TEICHMAN, Shlomo .... 516-225-4700.... 346 K
teichman@mlb.edu
TEICHMILLER, Cheryl, A ... 920-923-7618.... 548 E
cteichmiller@marianuniversity.edu
TEIG, Trisha .... 801-832-2235.... 512 G
tteig@westminstercollege.edu
TEIS, Lawrence, B .... 512-245-2114.... 501 F
lt10@txstate.edu
TEITELBAUM, Aharon .... 845-783-0994.... 359 D
TEITELBAUM, Jeremy .... 860-486-2713...... 94 G
jeremy.teitelbaum@uconn.edu
TEITELBAUM, Kenneth .... 910-962-7671.... 379 D
teitelbaumk@uncw.edu
TEITLBAUM, Zalman .... 718-963-9770.... 359 A
ee@utsb.org
TEJADA, Carlos .... 716-286-8769.... 344 D
ctejada@niagara.edu
TEJADA, Lavinia .... 803-376-5700.... 455 B
ltejada@allenuniversity.edu
TEKIELE, Todd .... 517-629-0318.... 247 A
ttekiele@albion.edu
TEKIPPE, Stephanie, S .... 319-352-8628.... 189 J
stephanie.tekippe@wartburg.edu
TEKLEGIORGIS, Kidesti ..... 610-558-5615.... 437 D
teklegik@neumann.edu
TELFER, Richard, J .... 262-472-1918.... 553 A
telferr@uww.edu
TELFORD, Rebecca, P .... 937-778-7809.... 390 G
btelford@edisonohio.edu
TELL, Barbara .... 310-954-4348...... 57 H
btell@msmc.la.edu
TELLEEN, Jane, A .... 651-523-2202.... 264 A
jtelleen@hamline.edu
TELLEI, Patrick, U .... 680-488-1669.... 560 C
tellei@palau.edu
TELLER, Ryan .... 402-486-2538.... 300 C
ryteller@ucollege.edu
TELLES, Cathy .... 602-749-4660...... 13 K
ctelles@devry.edu
TELLES-IRVIN, Patricia ...... 847-491-5360.... 160 E
tellesirvin@northwestern.edu
TELLEZ, J. Carlos .... 574-372-5100.... 171 H
tellezjc@grace.edu
TELLI, Suzette .... 615-297-7545.... 467 A
tellis@aquinascollege.edu
TELLO, Steven .... 978-934-4240.... 237 B
steven_tello@uml.edu
TEMAAT, Beverly .... 620-227-9119.... 192 E
bgtemaat@dc3.edu
TEMPEL, Eugene, R .... 812-855-6679.... 173 E
etempel@indiana.edu
TEMPEL, Gene .... 812-855-4613.... 173 D
etempel@indiana.edu
TEMPERA, Jeffrey, L .... 631-451-4506.... 356 D
temperj@sunysuffolk.edu
TEMPKIN, Aron .... 802-485-2624.... 514 C
TEMPLE, Austin .... 318-357-6699.... 216 B
temple@nsula.edu
TEMPLE, Caleb .... 202-231-8015.... 557 J
caleb.temple@dodiis.mil
TEMPLE, David, W .... 315-464-5476.... 352 E
templed@upstate.edu
TEMPLE, Gary, M .... 817-202-6755.... 495 E
gtemple@swau.edu
TEMPLE, Glena, G .... 608-796-3392.... 553 C
ggtemple@viterbo.edu
TEMPLE, Jack .... 334-387-3877........ 1 D
jacktemple@amridgeuniversity.edu
TEMPLE, Jim .... 661-362-3535...... 41 I
james.temple@canyons.edu
TEMPLE, Lori .... 702-895-3628.... 302 I
lorit@unlv.edu
TEMPLE, Michael, P .... 252-398-6226.... 363 G
templm@chowan.edu
TEMPLE, Steve .... 480-212-1600...... 12 L
stemple@carrington.edu
TEMPLE, Susan .... 281-998-6150.... 493 G
susan.temple@sjcd.edu
TEMPLE, Tisha .... 512-863-1857.... 496 A
woodyj@southwestern.edu
TEMPLE, Vickie .... 318-678-6025.... 209 I
vtemple@bpcc.edu
TEMPLER, Lisa .... 409-933-8262.... 483 F
ltempler@com.edu
TEMPLETON, Debra, R .... 540-831-6030.... 523 A
drtemplet@radford.edu
TEMPLETON, Etheldra .... 215-871-6486.... 444 C
etheldrat@pcom.edu
TEMPLETON, Heidi .... 660-785-4016.... 290 G
heidi@truman.edu
TEMPLETON, Linda, B .... 219-980-6767.... 174 B
litemple@iun.edu
TEMPLETON, Rosalyn .... 406-265-3726.... 295 E
rosalyn.templeton@msun.edu
TEMPLETON, William .... 907-786-4005...... 10 H
anwgt@uaa.alaska.edu
TEMPLETON-CORNELL,
Vicki, L .... 315-267-2190.... 354 C
templevl@postdam.edu
TEMPLIN, Carl, R .... 435-586-5401.... 511 D
templin@suu.edu
TEMPLIN, JR., Robert, G .. 703-323-3101.... 527 F
rtemplin@nvcc.edu
TEMTE, Anne, T .... 218-683-8610.... 268 C
anne.temte@northlandcollege.edu
TENA, Lydia .... 915-831-8818.... 486 G
lpere121@epcc.edu
TENCHER, Donald, E .... 401-456-8007.... 454 A
dtencher@ric.edu
TENCZAR, JR., Robert, C .. 773-298-3326.... 163 I
tenczar@sxu.edu
TENDALL, Michael, W .... 309-794-7357.... 145 E
adsmt@augustana.edu
TENDALL, Stephen .... 563-333-6423.... 188 F
tendallstephen@sau.edu
TENENBAUM, Elchonon ..... 707-638-5507...... 73 A
rabbi@tu.edu
TENGERES, Laura, N .... 954-308-2224.... 101 C
tengeresl@aii.edu
TENGLIN, Ingrid, K .... 773-244-5601.... 159 H
itenglin@northpark.edu
TENIENTE-MATSON,
Cynthia .... 559-278-2083...... 35 A
cmatson@csufresno.edu
TENNANT, Otto .... 270-789-5034.... 199 F
otennant@campbellsville.edu
TENNASSEE, Paul, N .... 202-274-6277.... 100 A
ptennassee@udc.edu
TENNENT, Lee .... 864-646-1777.... 461 F
ltennent@tctc.edu
TENNENT, Timothy, C .... 859-858-2202.... 198 D
TENNER, Jack, D .... 409-880-1783.... 501 A
jack.tenner@lamar.edu
TENNESON, Richard, J ...... 563-387-1010.... 187 D
tennesri@luther.edu
TENNEY, David .... 713-348-8036.... 493 C
dtenney@rice.edu
TENNEY, Peter .... 509-532-8888.... 532 A
ptenney@carrington.edu
TENNEY, Randall .... 304-473-8099.... 545 G
tenney_r@wvwc.edu
TENNILL, William .... 217-245-3338.... 152 D
bill.tennill@ic.edu
TENNY, Elissa .... 312-899-5100.... 164 C
etenny@saic.edu
TENNYSON, Pat .... 423-869-6286.... 470 E
ptennyson@lmunet.edu
TENNYSON, Tenis .... 406-791-5305.... 296 F
ttennyson@ugf.edu
TENUTA, Robert .... 312-322-1733.... 165 E
rtenuta@spertus.edu
TEODORESCU, Daniel .... 404-727-5278.... 129 D
dteodor@emory.edu
TEOH, Celia .... 812-488-2602.... 180 E
ct81@evansville.edu
TEPATTI, Eileen, G .... 217-786-2885.... 157 B
eileen.tepatti@llcc.edu
TEPE, Chabha .... 636-227-2100.... 284 B
chabha.tepe@logan.edu
TEPE, Rodger, E .... 636-227-2100.... 284 B
rodger.tepe@logan.edu
TEPROVICH, Amy .... 239-489-9027.... 105 F
TEPROVICH, Amy .... 239-489-9316.... 105 F
ateprovich@edison.edu
TEPSA, Kristin .... 906-353-4602.... 253 D
ktepsa@kbocc.org
TERAQAWACHI, Lori .... 808-984-3406.... 142 E
loritera@hawaii.edu
TERAVEST, Daniel, J .... 707-259-6041...... 58 F
dteravest@napavalley.edu
TERCHEK, Daniel .... 212-472-1500.... 343 G
dterchek@nysid.edu
TEREBESSY, Hilarie .... 312-942-7100.... 163 D
hilarie_terebessy@rush.edu
TERENZIO, Marion .... 973-748-9000.... 307 H
marion_terenzio@bloomfield.edu
TERESA, Daniel .... 831-755-6840...... 49 E
dteresa@hartnell.edu
TERESHINSKI, Robert .... 605-668-1584.... 464 G
rtereshinski@mtmc.edu
TERESI, Mark .... 847-566-6401.... 167 F
mteresi@usml.edu
TERHAAR, Jody, L .... 320-363-5601.... 262 F
jterhaar@csbsju.edu
TERHORST, Dan .... 760-480-8474...... 78 J
dterhorst@wscal.edu
TERHUNE, James, S .... 207-859-4780.... 217 G
jterhune@colby.edu
TERKLA, Dawn, G .... 617-627-3274.... 245 C
dawn.terkla@tufts.edu
TERMOTT, Kenneth .... 732-247-5241.... 312 A
ktermott@nbts.edu
TERNES, Roger .... 715-425-3246.... 552 C
roger.ternes@uwrf.edu
TERP, Douglas, C .... 207-859-4770.... 217 G
dcterp@colby.edu
TERP, Jeff .... 317-921-4225.... 175 I
jterp@ivytech.edu
TERPACK, Sallie, A .... 814-732-1024.... 442 E
terpack@edinboro.edu
TERPENNING, Marlene, K . 740-284-5179.... 391 A
mterpenning@franciscan.edu
TERPSTRA, Duane .... 616-451-3511.... 250 C
dterpstra@davenport.edu
TERPSTRA, Joylita .... 423-478-7707.... 472 H
jterpstra@ptseminary.edu
TERRACINA, Lorraine .... 718-270-2187.... 352 D
lterracina@downstate.edu
TERRANOVA, Paul .... 913-588-7068.... 197 C
pterranova@kumc.edu
TERREGINO, Carol .... 732-235-4576.... 316 G
terregca@umdnj.edu
TERREGINO, Carol, A .... 732-235-4576.... 316 G
terregca@umdnj.edu
TERREL, Beth .... 812-535-5172.... 179 E
bterrel@smwc.edu
TERRELL, Bill .... 915-532-3737.... 508 H
bterrell@westerntech.edu
TERRELL, Billie, P .... 815-740-3399.... 167 E
bterrell@stfrancis.edu
TERRELL, C. Jeffrey .... 404-233-3949.... 136 D
jterrell@richmont.edu
TERRELL, Charles .... 304-434-8001.... 542 I
cterrell@eastern.wvnet.edu
TERRELL, Gaither, M .... 336-316-2143.... 365 A
gterrell@guilford.edu
TERRELL, Jan (Denny) .... 717-477-1375.... 443 E
dterrell@ship.edu
TERRELL, Janice .... 704-355-4305.... 363 D
janice.terrell@carolinascollege.edu
TERRELL, Mark .... 814-866-6641.... 433 C
mterrell@lecom.edu
TERRELL, Patricia .... 208-282-2315.... 143 H
terrpatr@isu.edu
TERRELL, Peg, J .... 765-966-2656.... 176 H
pterrell@ivytech.edu
TERRELL, Sherri, I .... 915-747-5302.... 506 B
siterrell@utep.edu
TERRELL, Tracy .... 509-963-3001.... 532 C
terrell@cwu.edu
TERRELL-BAMIRO, Caryl ... 480-732-7134...... 15 E
caryl.terrell-bamiro@cgc.edu
TERRELL-BROOKS,
Tabatha .... 601-979-4208.... 274 G
tabatha.terrell-brooks@jsums.edu
TERRELL-POWELL,
Yvonne, L .... 206-546-4509.... 538 C
yterrell@shoreline.edu
TERRIO, Dan, M .... 509-527-4981.... 540 B
terrio@whitman.edu
TERRIO, Paul, L .... 612-330-1049.... 261 B
terriop@augsburg.edu
TERRONEZ, Randy .... 515-244-4221.... 181 F
terronezr@aib.edu
TERRY, Alicia .... 760-757-2121...... 57 E
aterry@miracosta.edu
TERRY, Andy .... 205-853-1200........ 5 C
atterry@jeffstateonline.com
TERRY, Bill .... 845-758-7495.... 323 D
wterry@bard.edu
TERRY, Brooks .... 904-680-7700.... 107 J
bterry@fcsl.edu
TERRY, Bryan, J .... 973-655-4153.... 311 F
terryb@mail.montclair.edu
TERRY, Carol .... 707-826-5728...... 36 E
ct7002@humboldt.edu
TERRY, Carol, S .... 401-454-6278.... 454 B
cterry@risd.edu
TERRY, Denise .... 574-372-5100.... 171 H
denise.terry@grace.edu
TERRY, Ditamichelle .... 804-745-2444.... 517 C
ddterry@bryantstratton.edu
TERRY, Edward .... 828-726-2202.... 368 G
eterry@cccti.edu
TERRY, Esther .... 336-517-2225.... 362 G
eterry@bennett.edu
TERRY, Heidi .... 816-654-7152.... 283 F
hterry@kcumb.edu
TERRY, Homer .... 606-436-5721.... 202 C
homer.terry@kctcs.edu
TERRY, James, E .... 304-696-2486.... 544 B
terry@marshall.edu
TERRY, Jan, M .... 217-245-1097.... 157 B
jan.terry@llcc.edu
TERRY, John .... 605-718-6551.... 464 H
jterry@national.edu
TERRY, Justyn .... 724-266-3838.... 448 H
jterry@tsm.edu
TERRY, Karen .... 305-573-1600.... 101 E
kterry@atienterprises.edu
TERRY, Laura, C .... 423-439-4210.... 473 F
terryl@etsu.edu
TERRY, Martin, L .... 419-434-4521.... 404 B
terry@findlay.edu
TERRY, Missy, D .... 503-554-2101.... 415 I
terrym@georgefox.edu
TERRY, Neil, W .... 806-651-2530.... 499 A
nterry@mail.wtamu.edu
TERRY, Penelope .... 718-951-5924.... 326 F
pterry@brooklyn.cuny.edu
TERRY, Rondale .... 510-567-6174...... 72 D
rterry@sum.edu
TERRY, Sara Beth .... 334-833-4062........ 4 E
sbterry@huntingdon.edu
TERRY, Scott .... 304-929-1332.... 541 H
sterry@mountainstate.edu
TERRY, Stephen, B .... 843-383-8035.... 457 A
sterry@coker.edu
TERRY, Susan .... 206-543-0535.... 539 A
nahe@uw.edu
TERRY, Terri .... 205-348-0609........ 8 E
teri.terry@ua.edu
TERRY, Tina .... 606-886-3863.... 201 G
tterry0025@kctcs.edu
TERRY, Troy, M .... 864-294-2213.... 458 E
troy.terry@furman.edu
TERVALA, Debra .... 612-338-7224.... 272 C
debra.tervala@waldenu.edu
TESAR, Daniel .... 714-992-7048...... 59 E
dtesar@fullcoll.edu
TESFAGIORGIS, Gebre, H .. 515-294-1181.... 182 E
gebretes@iastate.edu
TESFAMARIAM, Biniam ..... 574-520-4104.... 174 E
biktesfa@iusb.edu
TESH, J. Michael .... 210-567-2590.... 507 A
tesh@uthscsa.edu
TESKE, Paul .... 303-315-2805...... 88 J
paul.teske@ucdenver.edu
TESKE, Yolanda .... 252-334-2012.... 367 C
yolanda.teske@macuniversity.edu
TESKEY, Michael .... 503-777-7593.... 420 A
michael.teskey@reed.edu

TESORIERE, Joseph, P ... 518-564-4601 ... 354 B
tesorijp@plattsburgh.edu
TESS, Dan, E ... 570-484-2238 ... 443 B
dtess@lhup.edu
TESS, Paul, A ... 507-354-8221 ... 264 K
tesspa@mlc-wels.edu
TESSIER, Michael, A ... 812-488-2956 ... 180 E
mt28@evansville.edu
TESSIER, Nanci ... 804-287-6425 ... 525 E
ntessier@richmond.edu
TESSIER-LAVIGNE, Marc ... 212-327-8080 ... 347 H
marctl@rockefeller.edu
TESSLER, Mark, A ... 734-763-0395 ... 259 A
tessler@umich.edu
TESSMANN, Cary, A ... 262-691-5214 ... 555 E
ctessmann@wctc.edu
TESTA, Henry ... 315-866-0300 ... 335 D
testahp@herkimer.edu
TESTA, Noelle ... 785-242-5200 ... 178 I
TESTA, Noelle ... 785-242-5200 ... 195 I
noelle.testa@ottawa.edu
TESTA, Noelle ... 785-242-5200 ... 196 A
TESTA, Noelle ... 785-242-5200 ... 17 B
TESTA, Noelle ... 785-242-5200 ... 549 H
TESTANI, Joseph, A ... 804-828-0100 ... 526 B
jatestani@vcu.edu
TESTI, Andrea ... 541-881-5761 ... 420 E
atesti@tvcc.cc
TESTINI, Ann ... 906-487-7361 ... 251 A
ann.testini@finlandia.edu
TESTY, Kellye, Y ... 206-543-2586 ... 539 A
lawdean@uw.edu
TETEN, Dixie ... 402-872-2226 ... 299 F
dteten@peru.edu
TETENS, Kristan ... 517-483-1116 ... 254 A
tetensk@lcc.edu
TETLOW, Kimberly ... 434-848-6413 ... 524 B
ktetlow@saintpauls.edu
TETLOW, Wendolyn, E ... 906-786-5802 ... 248 I
tetloww@baycollege.edu
TETRAULT, Martha, R ... 413-597-2681 ... 246 D
martha.r.tetrault@williams.edu
TETREAU, Jerry, C ... 480-245-7969 ... 14 J
jerry.tetreau@ibconline.edu
TETREAULT, Jules ... 603-899-4178 ... 305 A
tetreaj@franklinpierce.edu
TETREAULT, Robert, G ... 401-456-8216 ... 454 A
rtetreault@ric.edu
TETRICK, Angel ... 225-922-1643 ... 209 G
atetrick@lctcs.edu
TETSTILL, John ... 636-422-2040 ... 289 B
jhtetstill@stlcc.edu
TETTEH, Edem ... 706-821-8259 ... 135 G
etteh@paine.edu
TETTER, Stephanie ... 831-646-4082 ... 57 G
stetter@mpc.edu
TETZLAFF-BELHASEN, Chris, M ... 361-698-1308 ... 485 G
chris@delmar.edu
TETZLOFF, Jason ... 320-308-5377 ... 269 B
jtetzloff@sctcc.edu
TETZLOFF, Lisa ... 920-465-2200 ... 551 B
tetzlofl@uwgb.edu
TEUBER, Jonathan, P ... 773-442-4670 ... 160 A
j-teuber@neiu.edu
TEUFEL, Kyla ... 513-771-2424 ... 385 I
kteufel@brownmackie.edu
TEVEPAUGH, Dawn ... 336-334-4822 ... 371 A
adtevepaugh@gtcc.edu
TEVIS, Glenna, J ... 712-274-5269 ... 187 G
tevis@morningside.edu
TEW, Glade ... 808-675-3590 ... 140 D
glade.tew@byuh.edu
TEW, JR., John ... 816-584-6410 ... 287 E
john.tew@park.edu
TEW, Mark ... 325-649-8002 ... 488 C
mtew@hputx.edu
TEW, Rebecca ... 706-568-2039 ... 127 G
tew_rebecca@columbusstate.edu
TEWS, Anne ... 269-927-8117 ... 253 G
tews@lakemichigancollege.edu
TEXIDOR, Migdalia ... 787-250-1912 ... 563 G
mtexidor@metro.inter.edu
TEYMOURTASH, Janet, L ... 415-422-6636 ... 76 E
janet@usfca.edu
TEZENO, Albert ... 318-274-6190 ... 215 E
tezenoa@gram.edu
THACKER, Allison ... 713-348-4818 ... 493 C
invest@rice.edu
THACKER, Judy ... 619-275-4700 ... 46 K
judy@fashioncareerscollege.com
THACKER, Karen, S ... 610-796-8306 ... 421 G
karen.thacker@alvernia.edu
THACKER, Linda ... 314-529-6573 ... 284 C
lthacker@maryville.edu
THACKER, Lisa ... 334-285-5177 ... 4 K
lisa.thacker@istc.edu
THADEN, Mark ... 540-654-2160 ... 525 D
mthad2zw@umw.edu
THAI, Khi ... 954-762-5650 ... 119 A
thai@fau.edu
THAMES, Brenda ... 209-575-6060 ... 80 H
thamesb@mjc.edu
THAMES, James, H ... 214-841-3678 ... 485 F
jthames@dts.edu
THAMES, Jamie ... 478-757-4024 ... 139 E
jthames@wesleyancollege.edu
THAMES, Judith ... 317-813-2301 ... 175 D
jthames@ibcindianapolis.edu
THAMES, Kathleen, A ... 337-482-6397 ... 216 D
kat@louisiana.edu
THANNICKAL, Steve ... 918-495-6620 ... 411 C
sthannical@oru.edu
THAO-SCHUCK, May ... 651-905-3420 ... 261 E
mthao-schuk@browncollege.edu
THARAKAN, Ana ... 312-499-1813 ... 149 E
atharakan@devry.edu
THARP, Brent ... 912-478-5444 ... 131 E
btharp@georgiasouthern.edu
THARP, Carla ... 201-761-7360 ... 314 F
ctharp@spc.edu
THARP, Glen ... 602-254-3099 ... 14 E
ghtarp@edaff.edu
THARP, Jack, A ... 765-455-9214 ... 174 A
jtharp@iuk.edu
THARP, Jim ... 602-243-8062 ... 16 D
jim.tharp@smcmail.maricopa.edu
THARP, Karen ... 931-598-1270 ... 472 L
kmtharp@sewanee.edu
THARPE, Barbara ... 615-327-6827 ... 471 C
btharpe@mmc.edu
THARPE, Debbie ... 864-941-8319 ... 460 D
tharpe.d@ptc.edu
THARRINGTON, Sally ... 434-949-1061 ... 528 D
sally.tharrington@southside.edu
THATCHER, Deb ... 518-255-5523 ... 354 E
thatchdh@cobleskill.edu
THATCHER, Derek ... 740-366-9453 ... 386 H
dthatche@cotc.edu
THATCHER, Patricia ... 215-951-2730 ... 444 D
thatcherp@philau.edu
THATCHER, Paula ... 503-352-1556 ... 419 E
thatchep@pacificu.edu
THAXTON, Deron ... 318-473-6574 ... 212 I
dthaxton@lsua.edu
THAXTON, Gail ... 706-754-7701 ... 135 A
gthaxton@northgatech.edu
THAXTON, Glenn ... 214-234-4850 ... 486 H
gthaxton@cci.edu
THAXTON, Janlyn ... 325-670-1264 ... 487 F
jthaxton@hsutx.edu
THAYER, OP, Gerard ... 202-495-3834 ... 99 C
gthayer@dhs.edu
THAYER, Janelle, R ... 509-777-4216 ... 540 C
jthayer@whitworth.edu
THAYER, Jennifer ... 608-329-8202 ... 553 G
jthayer@blackhawk.edu
THAYER, Mary Ann ... 810-766-2057 ... 248 C
maryann.thayer@baker.edu
THAYER, Maureen ... 508-588-9100 ... 240 A
THAYER, Michael ... 248-457-2700 ... 252 E
THAYER, Scott ... 304-829-7138 ... 540 H
sthayer@bethanywv.edu
THAYER, Scott, W ... 626-585-7798 ... 61 F
swthayer@pasadena.edu
THAYNE, Lewis, E ... 717-867-6211 ... 434 C
thayne@lvc.edu
THE, James ... 817-202-6719 ... 495 E
jthe@swau.edu
THEEUWES, Jim ... 251-580-2154 ... 5 A
jtheeuwes@faulknerstate.edu
THEIS, Lori, C ... 318-257-2238 ... 215 F
ltheis@latech.edu
THEIS, Terry ... 330-339-3391 ... 394 A
ttheis1@kent.edu
THEISEN, Darlene, A ... 814-871-7609 ... 429 G
theisen001@gannon.edu
THEISEN, Jason ... 320-308-6012 ... 269 B
jtheisen@sctcc.edu
THEISS, Tom ... 217-773-4441 ... 156 B
tom.theiss@doc.illinois.gov
THELEN, Cindy ... 715-675-3331 ... 555 B
thelen@ntc.edu
THELLMAN, Wendy ... 678-717-3845 ... 129 G
wthellman@gsc.edu
THEOBALD, Brent ... 714-556-3610 ... 77 B
brent.theobald@vanguard.edu
THEOBALD, Michael, J ... 816-501-4061 ... 288 A
mike.theobald@rockhurst.edu
THEOBALD, Neil ... 812-855-7114 ... 173 E
theobald@indiana.edu
THEOBALD, Neil ... 812-855-3565 ... 173 D
theobald@indiana.edu
THEOBALD, Paul ... 712-749-2277 ... 183 C
theobaldp@bvu.edu
THEODORE, Steve ... 254-295-4500 ... 504 C
stheodore@umhb.edu
THEODOROPOULOS, Christine ... 805-756-1414 ... 33 I
ctheodor@calpoly.edu
THEODOSIOU, Constantine ... 718-862-7948 ... 339 H
constantine.theodosiou@manhattan.edu
THEODOULOU, Stella, Z ... 818-677-3317 ... 35 F
stella.theodoulou@csun.edu
THEOKAS, Mary ... 864-503-5392 ... 463 B
mtheokas@uscupstate.edu
THEONUGRAHA, Felix ... 847-317-4061 ... 166 E
ftheonu@tiu.edu
THEORET, Julie ... 802-635-1333 ... 515 F
julie.theoret@jsc.edu
THERIAULT, Monique ... 206-726-5013 ... 533 D
mtheriault@cornish.edu
THERIOT, Leo ... 417-833-2551 ... 279 E
ltheriot@cbcag.edu
THERIOT, Lisa, M ... 214-860-2247 ... 485 A
ltheriot@dcccd.edu
THERMER, Clifford ... 860-913-2058 ... 92 I
cthermer@goodwin.edu
THEROUX, Robert, R ... 401-739-5000 ... 453 G
rtheroux@neit.edu
THERRIEN, Michael ... 603-271-2474 ... 304 F
mtherrien@ccsnh.edu
THERRIEN, Michel ... 724-805-2324 ... 446 F
michel.therrien@email.stvincent.edu
THESENVITZ, Michael, D ... 918-631-2583 ... 413 F
michael-thesenvitz@utulsa.edu
THEULE, Ryan ... 661-362-5930 ... 41 I
ryan.theule@canyons.edu
THEULEN, Michael ... 413-782-1377 ... 246 A
mtheulen@wne.edu
THIBEAULT, Alan ... 207-602-2253 ... 221 A
athibeault@une.edu
THIBEAULT, Dennis ... 617-333-2158 ... 233 F
dthibeau@curry.edu
THIBEAULT, Nancy ... 937-512-2926 ... 401 J
nancy.thibeault@sinclair.edu
THIBODEAU, Heather ... 603-899-4340 ... 305 A
thibodeauh@franklinpierce.edu
THIBODEAU, John ... 262-564-3050 ... 554 B
thibodeauj@gtc.edu
THIBODEAU, Wayne, J ... 248-370-4240 ... 256 G
thibodea@oakland.edu
THIBODEAUX, Amy ... 337-491-2678 ... 212 E
amy.thibodeaux@sowela.edu
THIBODEAUX, Chad ... 337-475-5524 ... 215 G
cthibodeaux@mcneese.edu
THIBOUTOT, Paul ... 507-222-4190 ... 261 G
pthibout@carleton.edu
THIE, Susan ... 605-331-6592 ... 466 E
susan.thie@usiouxfalls.edu
THIEBAUX, Brian ... 760-921-5501 ... 61 C
bthiebaux@paloverde.edu
THIEHOFF, Jack, O ... 972-860-8365 ... 484 I
jthiehoff@dcccd.edu
THIEL, Chuck ... 810-762-5003 ... 255 G
chuck.thiel@mcc.edu
THIEL, OFM, Janet ... 610-358-4219 ... 437 D
thielj@neumann.edu
THIEL, John, E ... 203-254-4000 ... 92 H
jthiel@fairfield.edu
THIELE, Dianna ... 206-878-3710 ... 535 B
dthiele@highline.edu
THIELE, Dwain, L ... 214-648-8711 ... 507 E
dwain.thiele@utsouthwestern.edu
THIELE, Nicholas ... 573-276-4577 ... 289 K
nsthiele@semo.edu
THIELEMANN, Heather ... 936-294-1345 ... 501 D
thielemann@shsu.edu
THIEMANN, James, A ... 410-778-7710 ... 229 D
dthiemann2@washcoll.edu
THIEMENS, Mark, H ... 858-534-6882 ... 74 F
mthiemens@ucsd.edu
THIERFELDER, William, K ... 704-461-6726 ... 362 F
billthierfelder@bac.edu
THIERSTEIN, Joel ... 502-597-6442 ... 203 G
joel.thierstein@kysu.edu
THIES, Jeannie ... 636-949-4689 ... 283 J
jthies@lindenwood.edu
THIESEN, Lynn ... 707-476-4187 ... 42 C
lynn-thiesen@redwoods.edu
THIESFELDT, Steven, R ... 507-354-8221 ... 264 K
thiesfsr@mlc-wels.edu
THIESSEN, Alicia ... 816-584-6382 ... 287 E
alicia.thiessen@park.edu
THIESSEN, Ron ... 727-816-3236 ... 114 F
thiessr@phcc.edu
THIGPEN, Kenneth, A ... 610-285-5000 ... 439 L
kat2@psu.edu
THIGPEN, Paula ... 212-659-3605 ... 338 A
THIGPEN, Paula, M ... 410-864-3605 ... 226 B
pthigpen@stmarys.edu
THILL, Robert ... 212-353-4348 ... 331 A
thill@cooper.edu
THILLMAN, Peter ... 920-693-1119 ... 554 C
peter.thillman@gotoltc.edu
THIMMEL, Lori ... 973-642-8712 ... 315 C
lori.thimmel@shu.edu
THIMMESCH, Timothy ... 616-331-3845 ... 251 F
thimmest@gvsu.edu
THIMONS, Dennis ... 724-532-5084 ... 446 E
dennis.thimons@email.stvincent.edu
THING, Thomas ... 626-571-8811 ... 77 A
tthing@uwest.edu
THIONGO, Ken ... 239-687-5440 ... 101 H
kthiongo@avemarialaw.edu
THIRION, Jaimee ... 574-807-7381 ... 169 I
jaimee.thirion@bethelcollege.edu
THIRSK, William, T ... 845-575-3000 ... 340 B
william.thirsk@marist.edu
THISS, Ramona, H ... 540-985-9828 ... 520 I
rhthiss@jchs.edu
THISSEN, Sally, L ... 863-680-4127 ... 109 E
sthissen@flsouthern.edu
THISTLE, Dawn, M ... 508-767-7095 ... 230 D
dthistle@assumption.edu
THISTLETHWAITE, Polly ... 212-817-7060 ... 327 B
pthistlethwaite@gc.cuny.edu
THOBABEN, James ... 859-858-2369 ... 198 D
THODE, Arnold ... 563-441-4131 ... 184 H
athode@eicc.edu
THODY, Jennifer ... 603-448-2445 ... 305 C
jthody@lebanoncollege.edu
THOM, Greg ... 612-977-5470 ... 261 F
greg.thom@capella.edu
THOM, Michelle ... 952-358-8271 ... 268 A
michelle.thom@normandale.edu
THOMA, James ... 330-823-4772 ... 404 C
thomaje@mountunion.edu
THOMAN, Richard, C ... 651-628-3411 ... 270 B
rcthoman@nwc.edu
THOMAS, Adam ... 334-214-4880 ... 2 F
adam.thomas@cv.edu
THOMAS, Alexander ... 607-436-2520 ... 353 E
thomasa@oneonta.edu
THOMAS, Alice ... 410-276-0306 ... 226 D
athomas@host.sdc.edu
THOMAS, Alta, M ... 434-848-1805 ... 524 B
athomas@saintpauls.edu
THOMAS, Alvetta, P ... 404-225-4601 ... 125 E
athomas@atlantatech.edu
THOMAS, Alvina ... 318-345-9145 ... 210 H
athomas@ladelta.edu
THOMAS, Amy, A ... 440-964-4237 ... 393 E
aaiello@kent.edu
THOMAS, Andrew, P ... 973-972-4444 ... 316 E
andrew.thomas@umdnj.edu
THOMAS, Anisa ... 941-907-2262 ... 107 B
anithomas@evergladesuniversity.edu
THOMAS, Anita ... 410-837-4533 ... 229 A
athomas@ubalt.edu
THOMAS, Anne, C ... 317-788-3543 ... 180 F
athomas@uindy.edu
THOMAS, Annette ... 417-864-7220 ... 281 H
athomas@cci.edu
THOMAS, Auden ... 518-580-5590 ... 351 B
athomas@skidmore.edu
THOMAS, B. Elaine ... 413-559-5482 ... 235 C
THOMAS, Barbara ... 619-680-4430 ... 32 D
barbara.thomas@collegeamerica.edu
THOMAS, Barbara ... 903-785-7661 ... 492 D
bthomas@parisjc.edu
THOMAS, Barbara, J ... 415-422-6352 ... 76 E
thomasb@admin.usfca.edu
THOMAS, Barry ... 443-394-3377 ... 99 G
barry.thomas@strayer.edu
THOMAS, Becky ... 949-451-5484 ... 70 E
bthomas@ivc.edu
THOMAS, Bethel ... 615-460-6434 ... 467 D
bethel.thomas@belmont.edu
THOMAS, Brenda, R ... 501-569-3245 ... 24 E
brthomas2@ualr.edu
THOMAS, Brice ... 937-529-2201 ... 403 A
bthomas@united.edu
THOMAS, Bridgett ... 217-732-3155 ... 156 I
bthomas@lincolncollege.edu
THOMAS, Carl ... 541-885-1151 ... 418 E
carl.thomas@oit.edu
THOMAS, Carlos ... 225-771-6247 ... 214 I
carlos_thomas@subr.edu
THOMAS, Carol ... 916-608-6500 ... 56 C
THOMAS, Carol ... 614-508-7233 ... 392 A
cthomas@hondros.edu
THOMAS, Carolyn ... 989-358-7211 ... 247 C
thomasc@alpenacc.edu
THOMAS, Carolyn, D ... 504-520-7364 ... 217 A
cthomas@xula.edu
THOMAS, Carrie ... 603-526-3686 ... 303 G
cathomas@colby-sawyer.edu
THOMAS, Catherine ... 909-868-4034 ... 44 K
cthomas@devry.edu
THOMAS, Cecil ... 312-662-4222 ... 144 H
cthomas@adler.edu
THOMAS, Cheryl, M ... 334-727-8540 ... 8 B
cmthomas@mytu.tuskegee.edu
THOMAS, Christiana, J ... 504-280-6021 ... 213 E
cjthoma2@uno.edu
THOMAS, Christine ... 916-691-7333 ... 56 B
thomasc@crc.losrios.edu
THOMAS, Christine, L ... 715-346-4617 ... 552 D
cthomas@uwsp.edu
THOMAS, Claudine, R ... 215-965-4061 ... 436 H
cthomas@moore.edu
THOMAS, Clay ... 620-278-4240 ... 196 H
cthomas@sterling.edu
THOMAS, Clyde, G ... 503-554-2013 ... 415 I
cthomas@georgefox.edu
THOMAS, Corlisse ... 646-312-4574 ... 326 C
corlisse.thomas@baruch.cuny.edu
THOMAS, Dale ... 407-345-2819 ... 104 K
dthomas2@devry.edu
THOMAS, Dana, L ... 907-450-8018 ... 10 G
dlthomas@alaska.edu

THOMAS, Daphne, J 901-435-1539 470 D daphne_thomas@loc.edu
THOMAS, David 202-685-3140 557 I thomasd@ndu.edu
THOMAS, David 509-527-2194 539 C dave.thomas@wallawalla.edu
THOMAS, David, A 202-687-3883 98 D dat42@georgetown.edu
THOMAS, David, E 215-751-8000 426 B dthomas@ccp.edu
THOMAS, Debbie 919-530-6230 378 B dgthomas@nccu.edu
THOMAS, Deborah 402-559-5245 300 H thomasd@unmc.edu
THOMAS, Dene Kay 970-247-7100 84 K thomas_d@fortlewis.edu
THOMAS, Denee 361-570-4149 504 A thomasd@uhv.edu
THOMAS, Denita 601-635-2111 274 A dthomas@eccc.edu
THOMAS, Dianne 269-749-6638 257 A dthomas@olivetcollege.edu
THOMAS, Domani 718-368-5696 328 A dthomas@kbcc.cuny.edu
THOMAS, Downing 319-335-0370 182 F downing-thomas@uiowa.edu
THOMAS, Eddie, B 205-366-8848 7 F ethomas@stillman.edu
THOMAS, Fitzroy 301-891-4115 229 B fthomas@wau.edu
THOMAS, Flecia 815-479-7620 157 H fthomas@mchenry.edu
THOMAS, JR., Garth, E 304-981-6248 545 D garth.thomas@mail.wvu.edu
THOMAS, Giovannie 248-457-2752 252 E
THOMAS, Glennis 208-376-7731 142 H gthomas@boisebible.edu
THOMAS, Gregory, A 708-709-3501 161 D gthomas@prairiestate.edu
THOMAS, Helen 912-538-3126 137 E hthomas@southeasterntech.edu
THOMAS, Howard 248-689-8282 259 E hthomas@walshcollege.edu
THOMAS, Huw, F 617-636-6636 245 C huw.thomas@tufts.edu
THOMAS, SR., Ira 504-286-5432 214 J ithomas@suno.edu
THOMAS, J. Matthew 770-534-6174 126 E mthomas@brenau.edu
THOMAS, Jack 309-298-1824 168 C j-thomas2@wiu.edu
THOMAS, James 269-387-8785 260 C jim.thomas@wmich.edu
THOMAS, James 910-296-1974 371 E jthomas@jamessprunt.edu
THOMAS, Janell, D 701-323-6270 381 D jthomas@mohs.org
THOMAS, Janette, B 607-587-4122 355 C thomasj@alfredstate.edu
THOMAS, Jeremy 936-633-5213 480 D jthomas@angelina.edu
THOMAS, Jerry 319-385-6212 186 E jerry.thomas@iwc.edu
THOMAS, Jerry, P 614-236-6900 386 E jthomas@capital.edu
THOMAS, Jerry, R 940-565-2231 504 D jerry.thomas@unt.edu
THOMAS, Joan 413-755-4817 241 B jthomas@stcc.edu
THOMAS, Joan 715-232-1181 552 E thomasj@uwstout.edu
THOMAS, Joe 541-888-7399 420 C jthomas@socc.edu
THOMAS, Joe, R 318-257-2769 215 F jthomas@latech.edu
THOMAS, John 312-939-0111 150 D john@eastwest.edu
THOMAS, John 951-785-2064 53 E jthomas@lasierra.edu
THOMAS, John 918-610-8303 411 D john.thomas@ptstulsa.edu
THOMAS, Joseph 803-536-7033 460 G jthomas@scsu.edu
THOMAS, Joseph, M 610-921-7556 421 E jthomas@alb.edu
THOMAS, Joyce 417-447-6973 287 D thomasj@otc.edu
THOMAS, Julia, M 585-385-8015 348 F jthomas@sjfc.edu
THOMAS, Julie 830-591-4180 495 D jethomas@swtjc.edu
THOMAS, K. B 318-487-7389 209 F kbthomas@lacollege.edu
THOMAS, Kanet 310-506-4264 61 H kanet.thomas@pepperdine.edu
THOMAS, Karen 229-430-3525 124 B kthomas@albanytech.edu
THOMAS, Karla 773-298-3937 163 I kthomas@sxu.edu
THOMAS, Kathryn, S 706-355-5116 125 C kthomas@athenstech.edu
THOMAS, Katie 207-859-1295 219 G bookstore@thomas.edu
THOMAS, Kay 601-484-8689 275 A kthomas@meridiancc.edu
THOMAS, Keith 979-830-4151 482 C keith.thomas@blinn.edu
THOMAS, Kenneth 972-438-6932 492 E kthomas@parkercc.edu
THOMAS, Kevin, P 270-745-5065 208 A kevin.thomas@wku.edu
THOMAS, Lauree 409-772-1442 507 C lauthoma@utmb.edu
THOMAS, Laurita, E 734-647-5574 259 A laurita@umich.edu
THOMAS, Leigh 601-366-8880 278 B lthomas@wbs.edu
THOMAS, Letrell 912-871-1624 135 D lthomas@ogeecheetech.edu
THOMAS, Linda 309-772-2177 146 D lthomas@sadnburg.edu
THOMAS, Linda 340-693-1324 568 E lthomas2@live.uvi.edu
THOMAS, Lisa 651-905-3490 261 E lthomas@browncollege.edu
THOMAS, Marcia, M 913-234-0809 191 J marcia.thomas@cleveland.edu
THOMAS, Marcia, R 312-460-0600 145 A mthomas@aaart.edu
THOMAS, Maria 601-977-7769 277 C mthomas@tougaloo.edu
THOMAS, Mark 863-638-2345 123 D mark.thomas@warner.edu
THOMAS, Marlin, U 937-255-3025 557 C marlin.thomas@afit.edu
THOMAS, Mary Beth 617-735-9766 234 C thomasmb@emmanuel.edu
THOMAS, Matthew, D 507-933-7510 263 J mthomas@gustavus.edu
THOMAS, Maurice 856-351-2697 315 A mthomas@salemcc.edu
THOMAS, Maxcie 870-575-8101 25 B thomasm@uapb.edu
THOMAS, May 540-362-6519 520 A mthomas@hollins.edu
THOMAS, Melissa 503-554-2214 415 I mthomas@georgefox.edu
THOMAS, Michael 618-985-3741 152 F thomasm@iecc.edu
THOMAS, Michael 601-979-3060 274 G michael.thomas@jsums.edu
THOMAS, Michael, J 217-333-3631 167 D mthomas@illinois.edu
THOMAS, Mike, R 618-235-2700 165 D michael.thomas@swic.edu
THOMAS, Miriam 765-459-0561 176 C mthomas@ivytech.edu
THOMAS, Nancy 248-204-3203 254 B nthomas@ltu.edu
THOMAS, Nathan 309-677-3221 146 C nthomas@bradley.edu
THOMAS, Ned 713-348-4009 493 C elt@rice.edu
THOMAS, Nichole 828-689-1103 366 I nthomas@mhc.edu
THOMAS, Otis 443-885-3160 224 E otis.thomas@morgan.edu
THOMAS, Pam 630-889-6661 159 F pthomas@nuhs.edu
THOMAS, Patricia, A 202-274-6314 100 A pthomas@udc.edu
THOMAS, Paul 443-627-7322 272 C paul.thomas@waldenu.edu
THOMAS, Paul 901-333-5760 476 B pthomas@southwest.tn.edu
THOMAS, Pauline 870-575-8970 25 B thomasp@uapb.edu
THOMAS, Peter, A 508-831-6074 246 F pthomas@wpi.edu
THOMAS, Peter, I 419-530-4229 404 F peter.thomas@utoledo.edu
THOMAS, Phil 319-208-5053 189 D pthomas@scciowa.edu
THOMAS, Phil 608-822-3262 555 D
THOMAS, Randi Malcolm 513-529-4151 396 E randi.thomas@muohio.edu
THOMAS, Renard 661-362-3327 41 I renard.thomas@canyons.edu
THOMAS, Rhonda 662-329-7138 276 A rthomas@acadsupp.muw.edu
THOMAS, Richard 253-943-3158 533 F rthomas@devry.edu
THOMAS, Richard, R 847-491-2325 160 E r-thomas2@northwestern.edu
THOMAS, Rikki 757-727-5250 519 H rikki.thomas@hamptonu.edu
THOMAS, Robert, J 570-941-6486 450 C robert.thomas@scranton.edu
THOMAS, Ron 651-423-8213 266 B ron.thomas@dctc.edu
THOMAS, Ronald, C 718-262-2332 329 A rthomas@york.cuny.edu
THOMAS, Ronald, R 253-879-3201 538 H president@pugetsound.edu
THOMAS, Rosemary, M 239-590-1067 119 B rothomas@fgcu.edu
THOMAS, Ryan 801-626-7931 511 G ryanthomas2@weber.edu
THOMAS, Sam 662-915-7690 277 D sethomas@olemiss.edu
THOMAS, Sandra 760-252-2411 30 H sthomas@barstow.edu
THOMAS, Sandra 217-641-4344 154 I thomas@jwcc.edu
THOMAS, Sandra 405-974-2690 413 B sthomas@uco.edu
THOMAS, Scott 909-621-8075 40 F scott.thomas@cgu.edu
THOMAS, Shawn 229-391-4910 123 H sthomas@abac.edu
THOMAS, Stacey 765-455-9391 174 A stathoma@iuk.edu
THOMAS, Stephen, J 212-746-2999 360 C sjthoma@med.cornell.edu
THOMAS, Stephen, W 252-328-4400 377 E thomass@ecu.edu
THOMAS, Steve 432-685-4521 491 A steve@midland.edu
THOMAS, Stuart 970-339-6232 81 A stuart.thomas@aims.edu
THOMAS, Susan, L 618-650-3674 165 C suthoma@siue.edu
THOMAS, Suzanne, W 330-471-8239 395 F sthomas@malone.edu
THOMAS, Sylvia 951-222-8620 64 A sylvia.thomas@rcc.edu
THOMAS, Teresa 412-268-3580 424 J ts2h@andrew.cmu.edu
THOMAS, Teresa 615-898-2600 473 G teresa.thomas@mtsu.edu
THOMAS, Terri 502-456-6505 206 H tthomas@sullivan.edu
THOMAS, Terry 919-572-1625 362 C
THOMAS, Todd 423-652-6045 470 A tthomas@king.edu
THOMAS, Todd, S 518-464-8526 333 E tthomas@excelsior.edu
THOMAS, Tracy 205-226-4902 2 B tthomas@bsc.edu
THOMAS, Troy 405-842-8007 19 A troy.thomas@phoenix.edu
THOMAS, Tyrone 843-355-4152 463 D thomast@wiltech.edu
THOMAS, Valerie, A 410-455-3142 227 D valerie.thomas@umbc.edu
THOMAS, Vanrea 718-270-4885 328 C vanrea@mec.cuny.edu
THOMAS, Verian 850-599-3505 118 L verian.thomas@famu.edu
THOMAS, W, E 252-335-3292 377 F wethomas@mail.ecsu.edu
THOMAS, Wade, L 607-436-3458 353 E thomaswl@oneonta.edu
THOMAS, Wanda 330-675-8821 393 D wthomas4@kent.edu
THOMAS, Wilbert, L 757-727-5356 519 H bill.thomas@hamptonu.edu
THOMAS, William, A 713-313-6816 500 B thomaswa@tsu.edu
THOMAS, Willie, G 302-855-1689 96 E wthomas6@dtcc.edu
THOMAS FRATICELLI, Cynthia 787-265-3883 567 F cynthia.thomas@upr.edu
THOMAS-GLOVER, Linda 757-789-1775 526 H lglover@es.vccs.edu
THOMAS-GOLDEN, Tammalyn, M 919-516-4533 376 D tgolden@st-aug.edu
THOMAS-MADDOX, Candice 740-654-6711 400 C thomas@ohio.edu
THOMAS-MOBLEY, Linda 619-684-8843 59 B lthomas@newschoolarch.edu
THOMAS-PARROTT, Sharon 630-515-4577 149 B stparrott@devry.edu
THOMAS-SMITH, E. Joahanne 936-261-2175 496 G ejthomas-smith@pvamu.edu
THOMAS TROUPE, Jennifer 978-921-4242 242 C jennifer.troupe@montserrat.edu
THOMAS-WILLIAMS, Regina 912-443-5708 136 H rthomas@savannahtech.edu
THOMASI, SR., Edward, J 203-773-8506 90 C ethomasi@albertus.edu
THOMASON, Chris 870-777-5722 25 F chris.thomason@uacch.edu
THOMASON, Don 901-448-5500 477 E dthomaso@uthsc.edu
THOMASON, Don, A 513-244-8162 387 E don.thomason@ccuniversity.edu
THOMASON, Jerry 870-743-3000 22 G jthomaso@northark.edu
THOMASON, Mary 870-574-4719 24 A mthomaso@sautech.edu
THOMASON, Scotty 530-938-5220 42 E sthomason1@siskiyous.edu
THOMASON, Tommy, N 713-221-8100 503 F thomasont@uhd.edu
THOMASSON, Kim 859-253-0621 205 D kthomasson@national-college.edu
THOMASSON, Susan 704-355-3921 363 D susan.thomasson@carolinas.org
THOMES, Christopher, P 850-747-3250 110 H cthomes@gulfcoast.edu
THOMFORDE, Christopher, M 610-861-1364 437 A thomforde@moravian.edu
THOMLINSON, Gene 417-865-2811 281 G thomlinsong@evangel.edu
THOMPSOM, Cathy 423-614-8200 470 C cthompson@leeuniversity.edu
THOMPSON, Adelia, P 757-594-8759 517 L adelia.thompson@cnu.edu
THOMPSON, Al 509-359-2466 533 H athompson@ewu.edu
THOMPSON, Al 715-346-2481 552 D al.thompson@uwsp.edu
THOMPSON, Alan 406-447-6941 295 A thompsona@umhelena.edu
THOMPSON, Allison, L 318-342-6917 216 E althompson@ulm.edu
THOMPSON, Alton 302-857-6100 96 C athompson@desu.edu
THOMPSON, Amber 719-336-1592 86 B amber.thompson@lamarcc.edu
THOMPSON, Amber 828-395-1443 371 D athompson@isothermal.edu
THOMPSON, Amy 718-940-5713 349 A althompson@sjcny.edu
THOMPSON, Amy 631-687-2611 349 B althompson@sjcny.edu
THOMPSON, Amy 229-732-5938 124 E amythompson@andrewcollege.edu
THOMPSON, Amy 620-278-4228 196 H athompson@sterling.edu
THOMPSON, Amy, S 440-964-4224 393 E asthomps@kent.edu
THOMPSON, Ann 270-706-8444 202 A ann.thompson@kctcs.edu
THOMPSON, Ann, E 508-849-3342 230 C athompson@annamaria.edu
THOMPSON, Annette 210-283-5091 504 B athompson@uiwtx.edu
THOMPSON, Anthony 804-257-5837 530 A athompson@vuu.edu
THOMPSON, Antonio 520-888-5885 13 B athompson@carrington.edu
THOMPSON, April 607-777-2804 351 F athompso@binghamton.edu
THOMPSON, Barbara 334-556-2629 4 A bthompson@wallace.edu
THOMPSON, Barbara, A 260-359-4049 173 A bthompson@huntington.edu
THOMPSON, Beth 903-434-8106 491 F bthompson@ntcc.edu
THOMPSON, Bianca 973-972-8514 316 H thompsbm@umdnj.edu
THOMPSON, Bianca 973-972-8551 317 B thompsbm@umdnj.edu
THOMPSON, Bill, T 919-735-5151 375 A billt@waynecc.edu
THOMPSON, Bob 405-912-9453 408 D bthompson@hc.edu
THOMPSON, Bobby, W 540-365-4233 519 C bthompson@ferrum.edu
THOMPSON, Bradley 901-751-8453 471 F bthompson@mabts.edu
THOMPSON, Brenda 512-863-1290 496 A
THOMPSON, Brenda, L 812-888-4125 181 D bthompson@vinu.edu
THOMPSON, Brenda, S 304-293-3837 545 A brenda.thompson@mail.wvu.edu
THOMPSON, Brian, L 904-819-6249 107 C bthompson@flagler.edu
THOMPSON, C. Marty 405-271-2673 413 D marty-thompson@ouhsc.edu
THOMPSON, Carey 901-843-3000 472 K
THOMPSON, Carlene, M 317-274-7617 174 D hra@iupui.edu
THOMPSON, Carly 863-686-1444 106 E cthompso@cci.edu
THOMPSON, Carlyle 718-270-4987 328 C carlyle@mec.cuny.edu
THOMPSON, Carmela 716-878-4017 353 A thompsc@buffalostate.edu
THOMPSON, Caro 802-322-1644 513 E caro.thompson@goddard.edu
THOMPSON, Carolyn, J 505-277-2626 321 C cjtc@unm.edu
THOMPSON, Carrie 615-966-5250 470 F carrie.thompson@lipscomb.edu
THOMPSON, Cesarina 413-205-3056 229 G cesarina.thompson@aic.edu
THOMPSON, Charles 404-270-2918 128 I cthompson1@devry.edu
THOMPSON, Charles, G 413-542-2221 230 A cgthompson@amherst.edu
THOMPSON, Charles, S 423-652-4742 470 A csthomps@king.edu

THOMPSON, Cheryl .... 402-559-2792.... 300 H
cbthompson@unmc.edu
THOMPSON,
Christopher, J .... 651-962-5771.... 272 B
cjthompson@stthomas.edu
THOMPSON, Cindy .... 651-675-4700.... 264 F
cthompson@msp.chefs.edu
THOMPSON, Claudette ...... 305-386-9900.... 106 A
cthompson@cci.edu
THOMPSON, Cole, P .... 970-207-4500..... 89 D
THOMPSON, Corinne, B .... 802-656-7898.... 514 H
corinne.thompson@uvm.edu
THOMPSON, Cory .... 404-297-9522.... 131 D
thompsonc@gptc.edu
THOMPSON, Craig .... 646-888-6639.... 339 E
cthompson@mskcc.org
THOMPSON, Cynthia .... 217-206-7715.... 167 C
thompson.cynthia@uis.edu
THOMPSON, D. D .... 423-442-2001.... 469 D
thompson@hiwassee.edu
THOMPSON, Daniel, J .... 651-290-6362.... 272 E
dan.thompson@wmitchell.edu
THOMPSON, Darci .... 405-425-5065.... 409 E
darci.thompson@oc.edu
THOMPSON, Darlene .... 334-214-4807........ 2 F
darlene.thompson@cv.edu
THOMPSON, Dave .... 714-546-7600..... 41 B
dthompson@coastline.edu
THOMPSON, Dave .... 417-777-5062.... 279 A
dthompson@texascountytech.edu
THOMPSON, David .... 304-424-8303.... 545 C
dave.thompson@mail.wvu.edu
THOMPSON, David .... 434-961-5447.... 528 B
dthompson@pvcc.edu
THOMPSON, Dawn .... 503-777-7500.... 420 A
dthomp@reed.edu
THOMPSON, Dawn, M ...... 302-831-8939..... 96 I
dawnt@udel.edu
THOMPSON, Debbi, N .... 864-597-4208.... 463 G
thompsondn@wofford.edu
THOMPSON, Deborah .... 864-833-8278.... 460 E
dthompson@presby.edu
THOMPSON, Deborah, L .... 269-337-7318.... 252 K
debbie.roberts@kzoo.edu
THOMPSON, Debra .... 480-731-8510..... 15 D
debra.thompson@domail.maricopa.edu
THOMPSON, Delores .... 575-492-2519.... 319 B
dthompson@nmjc.edu
THOMPSON, Dennis, F ..... 580-774-3764.... 412 F
dennis.thompson@swosu.edu
THOMPSON, Desiree .... 207-454-1020.... 219 B
dthompsoa@wccc.me.edu
THOMPSON, Destiny, S .... 512-505-3037.... 488 D
dsthompson@htu.edu
THOMPSON, Diane .... 518-587-2100.... 355 G
diane.thompson@esc.edu
THOMPSON, Dick .... 207-973-3224.... 219 I
dick.thompson@maine.edu
THOMPSON, Donovan .... 718-289-5796.... 326 E
donovan.thompson@bcc.cuny.edu
THOMPSON, Dwayne, E .... 714-895-8727..... 41 C
dthompson@gwc.cccd.edu
THOMPSON, E. Maria .... 607-436-2517.... 353 E
thompsem@oneonta.edu
THOMPSON, Edward, J ..... 516-678-5000.... 341 F
ethompson@molloy.edu
THOMPSON, Eichelle .... 414-256-1210.... 549 D
thompsoe@mtmary.edu
THOMPSON, Eileen .... 617-879-2413.... 246 C
ethompson@wheelock.edu
THOMPSON, Emily .... 816-604-3022.... 285 D
emily.thompson@mcckc.edu
THOMPSON, Eric .... 617-369-3486.... 244 E
ethompson@smfa.edu
THOMPSON, Fannie, G ..... 301-736-3631.... 224 A
fannie.thompson@msbbcs.edu
THOMPSON, Fred .... 615-460-6670.... 467 D
fred.thompson@belmont.edu
THOMPSON, Gary .... 701-845-7197.... 382 C
gary.thompson@vcsu.edu
THOMPSON, Gary, B .... 518-783-2550.... 350 I
thompson@siena.edu
THOMPSON, III,
George, R .... 803-938-3839.... 462 G
bobt@uscsumter.edu
THOMPSON, Greg .... 843-349-5247.... 458 H
greg.thompson@hgtc.edu
THOMPSON, Greg .... 407-366-9493.... 115 K
gthompson@rts.edu
THOMPSON, Greg .... 513-861-6400.... 402 I
greg.thompson@myunion.edu
THOMPSON, Gregory .... 850-644-5260.... 119 D
gwthompson@fsu.edu
THOMPSON, III,
H. Lawrence .... 724-266-3838.... 448 H
lthompson@tsm.edu
THOMPSON, Haley .... 580-477-2000.... 414 C
haley.thompson@wosc.edu
THOMPSON, Helen .... 330-287-1231.... 399 A
thompson.959@osu.edu
THOMPSON, Herbert .... 386-481-2661.... 102 C
thompsoh@cookman.edu
THOMPSON, Howard .... 563-425-5307.... 189 G
thompsonh@uiu.edu
THOMPSON, J. Michael .... 209-228-4482...... 74 D
jthompson@ucmerced.edu
THOMPSON, Jack .... 479-619-4140...... 22 H
jthompson19@nwacc.edu
THOMPSON, James .... 301-736-3631.... 224 A
james.thompson@msbbcs.edu
THOMPSON, James, E ...... 573-882-4378.... 291 B
thompsonje@missouri.edu
THOMPSON, James, P ...... 865-974-7262.... 477 D
jthompson@utk.edu
THOMPSON, James, V ...... 916-563-3276...... 56 A
thompsj@arc.losrios.edu
THOMPSON, Jane, W .... 412-624-6576.... 449 A
jthompson@cfo.pitt.edu
THOMPSON, Janet .... 908-526-1200.... 313 D
jthompso@raritanval.edu
THOMPSON, Jean-Noel ..... 325-674-6802.... 478 I
jnthompson@acu.edu
THOMPSON, Jeanne, E ..... 715-394-8598.... 552 F
jthomp51@uwsuper.edu
THOMPSON, Jeff, S .... 256-824-2605........ 8 G
jeff.thompson@uah.edu
THOMPSON, Jeffrey, M ..... 909-537-5315...... 36 B
jthompso@csusb.edu
THOMPSON, Jeffrey, S ...... 775-784-4591.... 303 A
thompson@physics.unr.edu
THOMPSON, Jennifer .... 212-280-1317.... 358 I
jthompson@uts.columbia.edu
THOMPSON, Jennifer .... 815-921-4272.... 162 H
j.thompson@rockvalleycollege.edu
THOMPSON, Jeremy .... 718-951-5882.... 326 F
jeremythompson@brooklyn.cuny.edu
THOMPSON, Jerry .... 252-536-7265.... 371 B
thompsonj@halifaxcc.edu
THOMPSON, Jerry .... 407-851-2525.... 106 K
gthompson@cci.edu
THOMPSON, Jerry, L .... 501-882-4523...... 20 C
jthompson@asub.edu
THOMPSON, Jesse, M ...... 617-228-2208.... 239 C
jthompson@bhcc.mass.edu
THOMPSON, Jill .... 336-841-9044.... 365 C
jthompso@highpoint.edu
THOMPSON, Jim .... 585-275-2158.... 359 B
jathompson@admin.rochester.edu
THOMPSON, Joan .... 781-595-6768.... 236 C
jthompson@mariancourt.edu
THOMPSON, Joan .... 478-757-3429.... 127 A
jthompson@centralgatech.edu
THOMPSON, Joanna .... 304-327-4050.... 543 F
jthompson@bluefieldstate.edu
THOMPSON, Joe, H .... 563-387-1575.... 187 D
thompsjo@luther.edu
THOMPSON, John .... 252-985-5218.... 375 E
jthompson@ncwc.edu
THOMPSON, John .... 817-257-7860.... 499 C
j.thompson@tcu.edu
THOMPSON, John .... 562-938-4102...... 54 E
jthompson@lbcc.edu
THOMPSON, John .... 484-365-8061.... 434 H
jhthompson@lincoln.edu
THOMPSON, Jonathan .... 270-706-8456.... 202 A
jonathan.thompson@kctcs.edu
THOMPSON, Joseph, F ..... 973-596-5642.... 312 C
thompson@njit.edu
THOMPSON, Julie, G .... 828-694-1752.... 368 E
juliet@blueridge.edu
THOMPSON, Karen, S .... 252-328-6212.... 377 E
thompsonkar@ecu.edu
THOMPSON, Karla, K .... 575-234-9265.... 319 F
kthompso@nmsu.edu
THOMPSON, Kathryn, T .... 706-667-7979.... 125 G
kthompson@aug.edu
THOMPSON, Kelly, M .... 252-399-6314.... 362 E
kthompson@barton.edu
THOMPSON, Kelsel .... 214-379-5532.... 492 F
kthompson@pqc.edu
THOMPSON, Kevin, A .... 270-384-8400.... 204 D
thompsonk@lindsey.edu
THOMPSON, Kevin, J .... 701-483-2004.... 381 G
thompson@dsufamily.com
THOMPSON, Kristy .... 801-818-8900.... 510 I
kristyt@provocollege.edu
THOMPSON, Larry, R .... 941-359-7601.... 116 B
lthompson@ringling.edu
THOMPSON, Laurie, L .... 214-648-2626.... 507 E
laurie.thompson@utsouthwestern.edu
THOMPSON, Lenora, H ..... 757-683-4401.... 522 F
lthompso@odu.edu
THOMPSON, Leroy .... 918-360-9694.... 407 B
thompsol@bacone.edu
THOMPSON, Lisa .... 425-640-1148.... 533 I
lthompson@edcc.edu
THOMPSON, Lonnie .... 386-506-3824.... 104 F
thompsl@daytonastate.edu
THOMPSON, Lucy .... 309-457-2318.... 158 H
lucyt@monmouthcollege.edu
THOMPSON, Lynda .... 508-588-9100.... 240 A
THOMPSON, Lynda, N .... 540-863-2837.... 526 F
lthompson@dslcc.edu
THOMPSON, Lynn .... 386-481-2216.... 102 C
thompsol@cookman.edu
THOMPSON, Marcy .... 847-214-7486.... 150 F
mthompson@elgin.edu
THOMPSON, Mark .... 315-228-7385.... 329 G
mdthompson@colgate.edu
THOMPSON, Mark .... 732-906-4252.... 311 D
mthompson@middlesexcc.edu
THOMPSON, Mark, A .... 203-582-8914...... 93 H
mark.thompson@quinnipiac.edu
THOMPSON, Matt .... 641-782-1413.... 189 E
thompson@swcciowa.edu
THOMPSON, Matthew, R .... 863-680-4108.... 109 E
mthompson@flsouthern.edu
THOMPSON, Maxine .... 315-464-5234.... 352 E
thompsms@upstate.edu
THOMPSON, Maynard .... 812-855-2074.... 173 E
thompson@indiana.edu
THOMPSON, Melanie .... 815-753-9734.... 160 B
mthompson3@niu.edu
THOMPSON, Michael .... 850-599-3301.... 118 L
michael.thompson@famu.edu
THOMPSON, Michael .... 309-556-3760.... 153 F
mthomps4@iwu.edu
THOMPSON, Michael .... 404-687-4530.... 127 F
thompsonm@ctsnet.edu
THOMPSON, Michael .... 601-484-8700.... 275 A
mthompso@meridiancc.edu
THOMPSON, Michael .... 920-693-1265.... 554 C
michael.thompson@gotoltc.edu
THOMPSON, Nancy .... 620-343-4600.... 192 H
nthompson@fhtc.edu
THOMPSON, Nancy, R .... 315-859-4020.... 334 H
nthompso@hamilton.edu
THOMPSON, Natalie .... 607-778-5477.... 324 G
thompsonm@sunybroome.edu
THOMPSON, Nina .... 503-760-3131.... 414 F
nina@birthingway.edu
THOMPSON, Oletha .... 330-972-7274.... 403 B
othomps@uakron.edu
THOMPSON, Pat .... 972-825-4670.... 495 F
pthompson@sagu.edu
THOMPSON, Patricia, A .... 607-735-1730.... 332 I
pthompson@elmira.edu
THOMPSON, Paul .... 443-885-3300.... 224 E
paul.thompson@morgan.edu
THOMPSON, Paula, C .... 757-823-2291.... 522 E
pcthompson@nsu.edu
THOMPSON, Phyllis .... 423-439-4125.... 473 F
thompsop@etsu.edu
THOMPSON, Phyllis .... 803-705-4720.... 455 D
thompsonp@benedict.edu
THOMPSON, Priscilla, C .... 301-322-0462.... 225 F
thompspc@pgcc.edu
THOMPSON, Rebecca .... 808-245-8384.... 142 C
ret@hawaii.edu
THOMPSON, Richard, H ..... 914-654-5421.... 330 B
rthompson@cnr.edu
THOMPSON, Richard, P ..... 989-964-4294.... 257 G
thompson@svsu.edu
THOMPSON, Robert .... 920-206-2377.... 548 D
rthompson@mbbc.edu
THOMPSON, Robert, H ...... 415-485-9451...... 42 B
bob.thompson@marin.edu
THOMPSON, Robert, J .... 301-295-3013.... 558 D
robert.thompson@usuhs.edu
THOMPSON, Robin .... 541-885-1132.... 418 E
robin.thompson@oit.edu
THOMPSON, Roger, J .... 541-346-2542.... 419 B
rjt@uoregon.edu
THOMPSON, Ronald, C ..... 864-294-2092.... 458 E
ron.thompson@furman.edu
THOMPSON, Ronda .... 573-897-5000.... 284 A
THOMPSON, Roneile .... 605-274-4921.... 464 A
ronelle.thompson@augie.edu
THOMPSON, Sabrina .... 404-656-2202.... 139 B
sabrina.thompson@usg.edu
THOMPSON, Samantha ...... 605-721-5200.... 464 H
THOMPSON, Sandra .... 305-623-4210.... 109 A
sandra.thompson@fmuniv.edu
THOMPSON, Sara .... 605-995-2896.... 464 C
sathomps@dwu.edu
THOMPSON, Sara, M .... 202-319-5256...... 97 E
thompson@cua.edu
THOMPSON, Scott .... 530-242-7512...... 69 D
sthompson@shastacollege.edu
THOMPSON, Seth .... 607-844-8222.... 357 I
thompss@tc3.edu
THOMPSON, Sharon .... 704-216-6080.... 366 G
smthompson@livingstone.edu
THOMPSON, Sharon .... 910-755-7474.... 368 F
thompsons@brunswickcc.edu
THOMPSON, Sharon .... 215-751-8450.... 426 B
sthompson@ccp.edu
THOMPSON, Sharyl .... 317-829-9384.... 169 B
THOMPSON, Sheila .... 303-556-3022...... 86 F
sthomp83@msudenver.edu
THOMPSON, Sheila .... 517-586-3013.... 249 D
sthompson@cleary.edu
THOMPSON, Susan .... 843-349-7818.... 458 H
susan.thompson@hgtc.edu
THOMPSON, Suzanne .... 301-369-2800.... 221 F
sthompson@capitol-college.edu
THOMPSON, Teresa .... 912-478-1863.... 131 E
thompson@georgiasouthern.edu
THOMPSON, Teresa .... 734-432-5465.... 254 D
tthompson@madonna.edu
THOMPSON, Teri .... 765-494-2082.... 178 J
tlthompson@purdue.edu
THOMPSON, Terry, E .... 509-527-5777.... 540 B
thompste@whitman.edu
THOMPSON, Thomas .... 928-428-8376...... 14 B
thomas.thompson@eac.edu
THOMPSON, Thomas, E .... 803-536-8266.... 460 G
tthompson@scsu.edu
THOMPSON, Tisha, L .... 864-488-4618.... 459 B
tthompson@limestone.edu
THOMPSON, Tola .... 850-599-3225.... 118 L
tola.thompson@famu.edu
THOMPSON, Tracey .... 603-283-2165.... 303 F
tthompson4@antioch.edu
THOMPSON, Travis .... 501-279-4464...... 21 H
thompson@harding.edu
THOMPSON, Troy, J .... 336-841-9404.... 365 C
tthompso@highpoint.edu
THOMPSON, Vinton .... 212-343-1234.... 341 B
vthompson@mcny.edu
THOMPSON, Virginia .... 918-781-7275.... 407 B
thompsonv@bacone.edu
THOMPSON, Walter, J .... 603-880-8308.... 306 A
wthompson@thomasmorecollege.edu
THOMPSON, Wayne .... 570-504-9693.... 425 F
THOMPSON, William .... 856-374-4931.... 308 D
wthompson@camdencc.edu
THOMPSON, William .... 859-572-5768.... 205 H
thompsonw4@nku.edu
THOMPSON, William, R .... 717-299-7793.... 448 A
thompson@stevenscollege.edu
THOMPSON-BRADSHAW,
Adriane .... 419-772-2433.... 398 H
athompson@onu.edu
THOMPSON BROWN,
Kim .... 912-478-5224.... 131 E
kimthomp@georgiasouthern.edu
THOMPSON-MCCALL,
Andrea .... 207-228-8284.... 220 G
atmccall@usm.maine.edu
THOMPSON-SELLERS,
Ingrid .... 678-891-2773.... 131 C
ingrid.thompson-sellers@gpc.edu
THOMPSON-STACY,
Cheryl .... 540-868-7101.... 527 C
cstacy@lfcc.edu
THOMPSON-TWEEDY,
Sara .... 845-434-5750.... 357 A
stweedy@sullivan.suny.edu
THOMPSON-WELLS,
Amy, C .... 270-384-8065.... 204 D
thompsoa@lindsey.edu
THOMSEN, Cristina, M ...... 817-202-6732.... 495 E
thomsenc@swau.edu
THOMSEN, Marilyn .... 951-785-2000...... 53 E
mthomsen@lasierra.edu
THOMSEN, Pamela .... 218-855-8129.... 265 J
pthoms@clcmn.edu
THOMSEN, Sandy .... 818-364-7750...... 55 A
thomsens@lamission.edu
THOMSON, David, T .... 870-230-5129...... 21 I
thomsond@hsu.edu
THOMSON, Kendra .... 405-491-6312.... 412 D
kthomson@snu.edu
THOMSON, Lisa .... 407-646-2010.... 116 D
lthomson@rollins.edu
THOMSON, Margaret .... 859-442-1172.... 202 B
margaret.thomson@kctcs.edu
THOMSON, Michael, J .... 216-987-3944.... 389 B
j.michael.thomson@tri-c.edu
THOMSON, Thomas, J .... 864-488-4500.... 459 B
tthomson@limestone.edu
THOMSON, Tony .... 989-964-4891.... 257 G
THON, Forrest .... 219-981-4828.... 176 G
fthon@ivytech.edu
THOR, James, A .... 716-878-4312.... 353 A
thorja@buffalostate.edu
THOR, Linda, M .... 650-949-6100...... 47 F
thorlinda@fhda.edu
THOR, Nadine, L .... 810-762-7904.... 253 C
nthor@kettering.edu
THORDARSON, Karen .... 310-377-5501...... 56 F
kthodarson@marymountpv.edu
THORESON, Jay, H .... 218-299-3020.... 262 I
career@cord.edu
THORESON, Nick .... 602-942-4141...... 14 D
THORIN, Suzanne, E .... 315-443-2573.... 357 C
sethorin@syr.edu
THORIUS, James, D .... 515-961-1532.... 189 C
jim.thorius@simpson.edu
THORN, George .... 908-737-5050.... 311 A
gthorn@kean.edu
THORN, Jack .... 304-865-6022.... 541 J
jack.thorn@ovu.edu
THORN, Lawrence, B .... 318-342-5170.... 216 E
thorn@ulm.edu
THORN, Robert .... 724-938-4432.... 441 G
thorn@calu.edu
THORN, Sharon .... 610-399-2550.... 442 A
sthorn@cheyney.edu
THORN, Trevor .... 936-294-1584.... 501 D
trevor@shsu.edu
THORNBRUGH, Jean .... 918-610-8888.... 412 A
jtthornbrugh@stgregorys.edu

TIMMONS, Joseph, F .... 918-631-2710.... 413 F
joseph-timmons@utulsa.edu
TIMMONS, Keona .... 843-746-5100...... 99 G
TIMMONS, Lora .... 815-685-6779.... 162 G
ltimmons@robertmorris.edu
TIMMONS, Ray .... 803-593-9231.... 455 A
timmons@atc.edu
TIMMONS, Susan .... 864-941-8307.... 460 D
timmons.s@ptc.edu
TIMMONS, Tim .... 708-239-4787.... 166 C
tim.timmons@trnty.edu
TIMMONS, Tom .... 847-969-2820.... 154 C
TIMMS, Lindsay .... 478-757-5233.... 139 E
ltimms@wesleyancollege.edu
TIMPANO, Anne .... 540-654-1013.... 525 D
atimpano@umw.edu
TIMPSON, Brigham, J .... 312-341-2322.... 163 B
btimpson@roosevelt.edu
TIMS, Deana .... 870-512-7811...... 20 F
deana_tims@asun.edu
TIMS, Ray, L .... 919-532-5523.... 374 H
rltims@waketech.edu
TINAJERO, Josefina, V ...... 915-747-5572.... 506 B
tinajero@utep.edu
TINANT, Jason .... 605-455-6001.... 465 A
jtinant@olc.edu
TINCHER, Sandy .... 304-929-1636.... 541 H
stincher@mountainstate.edu
TINCHER, Steven .... 765-966-2656.... 176 H
stincher@ivytech.edu
TINDALL, Amanda .... 502-212-2255.... 202 F
amanda.tindall@kctcs.edu
TINDALL, David, W .... 206-281-2982.... 537 H
dtindall@spu.edu
TINDALL, Michelle .... 804-706-5228.... 527 B
mtindall@jtcc.edu
TINDELL, Tyrone .... 703-729-8800...... 99 G
TINEBRA, Karen .... 973-877-3053.... 309 H
tinebra@essex.edu
TINEBRA, Vincent .... 502-447-7634.... 205 E
TINERELLA, Vincent .... 501-977-2033...... 25 G
tinerella@uaccm.edu
TING, John .... 978-934-2576.... 237 B
john_ting@uml.edu
TINGEY, Jeff .... 208-282-4064.... 143 H
tingjeff@isu.edu
TINGEY, Kent, M .... 208-282-3198.... 143 H
tingkent@isu.edu
TINGLE, Caroline, D .... 386-312-4270.... 116 F
carolinetingle@sjrstate.edu
TINGLEFF, Brian, P .... 515-643-6663.... 187 F
btingleff@mercydesmoines.org
TINGSON-GATUZ, Connie . 734-432-5883.... 254 D
ctingson-gatuz@madonna.edu
TINKER, Nancy .... 860-465-5348...... 90 H
tinkern@easternct.edu
TINKEY, Danya .... 412-536-1029.... 432 H
dayna.tinkey@laroche.edu
TINKEY, Jim .... 412-536-1011.... 432 H
jim.tinkey@laroche.edu
TINKHAM, Brenda, S .... 252-398-6304.... 363 G
tinkhb@chowan.edu
TINLING, Walter .... 301-295-6013.... 558 D
walter.tinling@usuhs.edu
TINSLEY, Cheryl, K .... 828-884-8264.... 362 H
tinsleck@brevard.edu
TINSLEY, Harold .... 410-337-6170.... 222 I
htinsley@goucher.edu
TINSLEY, Joseph .... 706-821-8320.... 135 G
jtinsley@paine.edu
TINSLEY, Marie .... 718-473-8700.... 328 D
mtinsley@citytech.cuny.edu
TINTERA, Judi, E .... 321-674-6303.... 108 H
jtintera@fit.edu
TIO, Adrian .... 508-999-9295.... 237 A
atio@umassd.edu
TIONGSON, Lenie .... 703-821-8570.... 524 J
ltiongson@stratford.edu
TIPMORE, Barbara .... 270-686-4530.... 203 B
barbara.tipmore@kctcs.edu
TIPMORE, David .... 334-302-1013........ 5 G
dtipmore@marionmilitary.edu
TIPPENS, Darryl .... 310-506-4261...... 61 H
darryl.tippens@pepperdine.edu
TIPPETT, Bryan .... 623-935-8030...... 15 F
bryan.tippett@estrellamountain.edu
TIPPIN, Peggy .... 270-444-9676.... 200 G
ptippin@daymarcolleg.edu
TIPPIN, Rick .... 270-534-3216.... 203 E
rick.tippin@kctcs.edu
TIPPING, Sarah .... 913-266-8619.... 195 I
sarah.tipping@ottawa.edu
TIPPING, Sarah .... 913-266-8619.... 196 A
TIPPINS, Kira .... 559-442-4600...... 72 B
kira.tippins@fresnocitycollege.edu
TIPPS, Donna, F .... 256-765-4231........ 9 C
dftipps@una.edu
TIPPS, Jane .... 615-898-2670.... 473 G
jane.tipps@mtsu.edu
TIPS, Jean .... 817-735-5031.... 504 E
jean.tips@unthsc.edu
TIPTON, Alzada .... 630-617-3063.... 150 H
tiptona@elmhurst.edu
TIPTON, Joellen, N .... 936-294-1810.... 501 D
joellen@shsu.edu
TIPTON, Melanie, K .... 918-610-8303.... 411 D
melanie.tipton@ptstulsa.edu
TIPTON, Ryan .... 575-492-2137.... 321 H
rtipton@usw.edu
TIPTON-ROGERS, Donna ... 828-835-4204.... 374 F
dtipton@tricounty.edu
TIRADO, Betty, M .... 607-436-2081.... 353 E
tiradoem@oneonta.edu
TIRONE, Shannon .... 330-941-3732.... 406 F
stirone@ysu.edu
TIRPAK, Anne, M .... 773-371-5417.... 146 E
atirpak@ctu.edu
TIRSCH, Alerie .... 516-299-2816.... 339 A
alerie.tirsch@liu.edu
TISDALE, Bradley .... 601-923-1600.... 276 F
btisdale@rts.edu
TISDALE, Christy .... 207-786-6199.... 217 C
ctisdale@bates.edu
TISDALE, Elaine .... 904-632-3254.... 109 F
etisdale@fscj.edu
TISDALE, Henry, N .... 803-535-5412.... 456 D
tisdale@claflin.edu
TISDALE, James .... 843-208-8050.... 462 C
jtisdale@mailbox.sc.edu
TISDALE, Travis .... 276-656-0311.... 527 G
ttisdale@patrickhenry.edu
TISDALE, Verlie, A .... 803-535-5433.... 456 D
vtisdale@claflin.edu
TISNADO, Carmen .... 717-291-3985.... 429 F
carmen.tisnado@fandm.edu
TISON, Alan .... 407-569-1388.... 107 I
alan.tison@fcc.edu
TITCOMB, Cassidy .... 612-330-1098.... 261 B
titcomb@augsburg.edu
TITLER, R. Barry .... 301-447-5357.... 225 A
titler@msmary.edu
TITSWORTH, Scott .... 740-593-4828.... 399 G
titswort@ohio.edu
TITSWORTH, Tobie .... 918-343-7579.... 411 H
ttitsworth@rsu.edu
TITTLE, Matthew, D .... 801-524-8146.... 510 E
mtittle@ldsbc.edu
TITTMANN, Frederick, R .... 703-323-3060.... 527 F
ftittmann@nvcc.edu
TITUS, Charlie .... 617-287-7895.... 236 G
charlie.titus@umb.edu
TITUS, Elizabeth .... 575-646-1508.... 319 D
etitus@nmsu.edu
TITUS, Garrett .... 701-627-4738.... 381 B
gtitus@fbcc.bia.edu
TITUS, Iyana .... 212-220-1236.... 326 D
ititus@bmcc.cuny.edu
TITUS, Sherry .... 760-744-1150...... 61 D
stitus@palomar.edu
TITUS, Steve .... 507-457-7877.... 271 B
stitus@smumn.edu
TITUS, Varkey, K .... 478-471-2724.... 133 H
varkey.titus@maconstate.edu
TITUS, Winston .... 701-349-3621.... 383 E
wtitus@trinitybiblecollege.edu
TITZER, Mark .... 312-362-8053.... 149 A
mtitzer@depaul.edu
TIVEY, Margaret, K .... 508-289-3362.... 246 E
TIWARI, Suresh .... 651-779-3493.... 266 A
suresh.tiwari@century.edu
TIZOL, Iris .... 787-258-1502.... 561 F
itizol@columbiaco.edu
TJADEN, Scott .... 651-846-3407.... 260 I
stjaden@argosy.edu
TJADEN, Scott .... 651-846-2882...... 29 F
stjaden@argosy.edu
TO, Dai, L .... 925-631-4362...... 64 F
dlt4@stmarys-ca.edu
TO, Karen .... 719-389-6144...... 82 D
kto@coloradocollege.edu
TOBEK, Alexandra, C .... 626-395-6594...... 32 H
atobeck@caltech.edu
TOBEN, Bradley J, B .... 254-710-1911.... 482 A
brad_toben@baylor.edu
TOBIA, Rajia, C .... 210-567-2400.... 507 A
tobia@uthscsa.edu
TOBIAS, Barbara .... 330-325-6726.... 397 D
btobias@neomed.edu
TOBIAS-JOHNSON, Jaynn 847-628-1525.... 154 K
jtobias-johnson@judsonu.edu
TOBIN, Doreen .... 570-422-3463.... 442 D
dtobin@po-box.esu.edu
TOBIN, Elizabeth, H .... 217-245-3010.... 152 D
etobin@ic.edu
TOBIN, Gabrielle .... 516-299-3641.... 338 E
gabrielle.tobin@liu.edu
TOBIN, Gerry, A .... 814-824-2468.... 436 C
gtobin@mercyhurst.edu
TOBIN, Gregory, G .... 973-378-9835.... 315 B
gregory.tobin@shu.edu
TOBIN, John, M .... 617-373-7666.... 243 F
TOBIN, Kimberly .... 413-572-8030.... 238 F
ktobin@wsc.man.edu
TOBIN, Mary Ann .... 708-456-0300.... 166 F
mtobin@triton.edu
TOBIN, Ronald, W .... 805-893-2419...... 75 B
tobin@oap.ucsb.edu
TOBIN, JR., Walt .... 803-535-1202.... 460 C
tobinw@octech.edu
TOBIN, William, M .... 765-658-4156.... 171 B
wtobin@depauw.edu
TOBROCKE, Toby .... 518-587-2100.... 355 G
toby.tobrocke@esc.edu
TOBUREN, Amy .... 608-262-0925.... 550 J
atoburen@wisc.edu
TODA, Frank .... 541-506-6103.... 415 C
ftoda@cgcc.cc.or.us
TODARO, Julie, B .... 512-223-3071.... 481 B
jtodaro@austincc.edu
TODARO, Robert .... 510-885-3938...... 34 E
robert.todaro@csueastbay.edu
TODD, Barbara, J .... 303-492-2459...... 88 H
barbara.todd@colorado.edu
TODD, JR., Billy, R .... 214-841-3775.... 485 F
btodd@dts.edu
TODD, Christine .... 212-799-5000.... 337 H
TODD, Christine .... 440-934-3101.... 398 C
ctodd@ohiobusinesscollege.edu
TODD, Darrylinn .... 312-850-7048.... 147 F
dtodd4@ccc.edu
TODD, David .... 802-656-4900.... 514 H
david.todd@uvm.edu
TODD, Dwayne .... 614-222-4015.... 388 G
dtodd@ccad.edu
TODD, Jimmie, L .... 806-291-1045.... 508 E
toddj@wbu.edu
TODD, Jodi, L .... 215-702-4335.... 444 B
jtodd@pbu.edu
TODD, Jon .... 212-592-2000.... 350 F
jtodd@sva.edu
TODD, Keith .... 503-777-7510.... 420 A
ktodd@reed.edu
TODD, Lisa .... 937-766-4125.... 386 G
toddl@cedarville.edu
TODD, Marissa .... 573-442-2211.... 290 C
mtodd@stephens.edu
TODD, Patricia, A .... 315-386-7333.... 355 E
toddpa@canton.edu
TODD, Sarah, E .... 315-379-3975.... 355 E
todds@canton.edu
TODD, Sharon, O .... 850-872-3891.... 110 H
stodd@gulfcoast.edu
TODD, Timothy, S .... 270-809-4181.... 205 A
ttodd@murraystate.edu
TODESCHI, Kevin .... 757-631-8101.... 516 F
ktodeschi@atlanticuniv.edu
TODHUNTER, Jody .... 903-886-5072.... 498 B
jody.todhunter@tamuc.edu
TODINI, Vivian .... 212-237-8628.... 327 F
vtodini@jjay.cuny.edu
TODISH, Marian .... 616-632-2959.... 247 E
todismar@aquinas.edu
TODMAN, Lynn .... 312-662-4011.... 144 H
ltodman@adler.edu
TODO, Howard .... 808-956-8903.... 141 E
htodo@hawaii.edu
TODOKI, Gayle .... 808-947-4788.... 142 G
wmi@worldmedicineinstitute.com
TODT, David .... 641-472-7000.... 187 E
dtodt@mum.edu
TODT, David .... 740-351-3472.... 401 I
dtodt@shawnee.edu
TOEBBEN, Martha, A .... 636-922-8243.... 288 B
mtoebben@stchas.edu
TOENISKOETTER, Richard . 812-464-1899.... 181 B
rtoeniskoe@usi.edu
TOENNISSON, Jan .... 513-727-3379.... 396 G
TOERING, Rose .... 605-221-3211.... 464 D
rtoering@kilian.edu
TOEWS, Brian, G .... 215-702-4227.... 444 B
provost@pbu.edu
TOFT, Carl .... 401-825-2150.... 453 D
cetoft@ccri.edu
TOGLIA, Joan .... 914-674-7813.... 340 F
jtoglia@mercy.edu
TOGO, Clifford .... 808-235-7403.... 142 F
togo@hawaii.edu
TOKAR, Bradley, P .... 724-946-7100.... 451 C
tokarbp@westminster.edu
TOKARSKY, Andra, M .... 412-578-8897.... 424 I
tokarskyam@carlow.edu
TOKPAH, Christopher .... 610-359-5106.... 426 G
TOLA, Mary, A .... 301-687-4309.... 228 C
mtola@frostburg.edu
TOLA, Ron .... 610-896-1100.... 430 G
rtola@haverford.edu
TOLAND, Claude, W .... 954-308-2101.... 101 C
ctoland@aii.edu
TOLAND, Jane .... 617-262-5000.... 231 G
jane.toland@the-bac.edu
TOLANO-LEVEQUE,
Maryann .... 909-594-5611...... 58 A
mtolano@mtsac.edu
TOLBERT, Arnold .... 305-623-1440.... 109 A
arnold.tolbert@fmuniv.edu
TOLBERT, Dawn, C .... 706-233-7215.... 137 A
dtolbert@shorter.edu
TOLBERT, Herb .... 530-226-4773...... 69 H
htolbert@simpsonu.edu
TOLBERT, Leslie, P .... 520-621-3513...... 18 L
tolbert@email.arizona.edu
TOLBERT, Stephanie, B .... 919-497-3233.... 366 H
stolbert@louisburg.edu
TOLCHER, Edward, A .... 989-774-1441.... 249 C
tolch1e@cmich.edu
TOLEDO, Angelica .... 323-267-3746...... 54 G
toledoa@elac.edu
TOLEDO, Christian .... 787-257-0000.... 567 C
christian.toledo@upr.edu
TOLEDO, Diana .... 360-596-5206.... 538 E
dtoledo@spscc.ctc.edu
TOLEDO, Rich .... 209-946-2211...... 76 A
rtoledo@pacific.edu
TOLEDO, Rosa Enid .... 787-743-7979.... 565 H
ut_retoledo@suagm.edu
TOLER, Terry .... 405-491-6314.... 412 D
ttoler@snu.edu
TOLG, OSB, Killian .... 985-867-2228.... 214 G
frkillian@sjasc.edu
TOLIA, Sam .... 708-456-0300.... 166 F
stolia@triton.edu
TOLIVER, Felicia .... 270-706-8438.... 202 A
felicia.toliver@kctcs.edu
TOLIVER, Frank .... 704-971-8500.... 363 F
TOLIVER, Michael .... 510-217-4728...... 29 H
mgtoliver@argosy.edu
TOLIVER, Michael .... 510-217-4728.... 531 A
mgtoliver@argosy.edu
TOLIVER, Sherry .... 210-486-2212.... 479 D
stoliver@alamo.edu
TOLIVER-ROBERTS,
Rita, J .... 215-670-9265.... 438 E
rjtoliver@peirce.edu
TOLL, David, J .... 215-895-4982.... 427 H
dtoll@drexel.edu
TOLL, Ronald, B .... 239-590-7035.... 119 B
rtoll@fgcu.edu
TOLL, Ronda .... 757-499-7900.... 517 D
rftoll@bryantstratton.edu
TOLL, William .... 765-998-4931.... 180 B
btoll@cse.taylor.edu
TOLLE, Andrew .... 309-341-5325.... 146 D
atolle@sandburg.edu
TOLLE, Melissa .... 937-512-2259.... 401 J
melissa.tolle@sinclair.edu
TOLLE, Susan .... 805-493-3185...... 33 B
tolle@clunet.edu
TOLLEFSON, Deborah .... 336-334-5702.... 379 B
deborah_tollefson@uncc.edu
TOLLER, John .... 252-328-6352.... 377 E
tollerj@ecu.edu
TOLLESON, Joanne, P .... 770-781-6950.... 133 C
jtolleso@laniertech.edu
TOLLEY, Warren, D .... 406-756-3841.... 294 C
wtolley@fvcc.edu
TOLLISON, Scott .... 662-329-7152.... 276 A
stollison@bu.muw.edu
TOLLIVER, Joseph .... 315-229-5311.... 349 E
jtolliver@stlawu.edu
TOLLIVER, Ona .... 903-565-5645.... 506 E
otolliver@uttyler.edu
TOLMAN, David .... 208-426-1540.... 142 I
dtolman@boisestate.edu
TOLMASOFF, Bill .... 714-449-7823...... 70 G
btolmasoff@scco.edu
TOLSMA, Robert .... 303-315-3701...... 88 J
robert.tolsma@ucdenver.edu
TOLSON, Chris .... 270-789-5013.... 199 F
cytolson@campbellsville.edu
TOLSON, Janice .... 252-823-5166.... 370 D
tolsonj@edgecombe.edu
TOLSON, Kedra .... 314-513-4221.... 288 H
ktolson@stlcc.edu
TOLSON, Renae .... 850-201-6074.... 122 A
tolsonr@tcc.fl.edu
TOLSON, Stephanie .... 636-922-8512.... 288 B
stolson@stchas.edu
TOMA, Abe .... 808-544-0209.... 140 G
atoma@hpu.edu
TOMAN, Janelle .... 605-773-3455.... 465 F
janellet@sdbor.edu
TOMAN, Sherry .... 562-908-2500...... 46 C
stoman@cci.edu
TOMANEK, Debra, J .... 520-621-7380...... 18 L
dtomanek@email.arizona.edu
TOMANEK, Jody .... 308-535-3724.... 298 H
tomanekj@mpcc.edu
TOMANY, Maria-Claudia ... 507-389-1333.... 267 E
maria-claudia.tomany@mnsu.edu
TOMAS, Don .... 828-339-4242.... 374 C
d_tomas@southwesterncc.edu
TOMASEK, James, J .... 405-271-2085.... 413 D
TOMASIK, Paula, J .... 304-336-8340.... 544 D
ptomasik@westliberty.edu
TOMASZKIEWICZ, Ed .... 636-481-3501.... 283 D
etomaszk@jeffco.edu
TOMASZKIEWICZ, Teri .... 630-844-5511.... 145 F
ttomaszk@aurora.edu
TOMBERLIN, Lisa .... 229-468-2078.... 139 I
lisa.tomberlin@wiregrass.edu
TOMBLIN, Joanne, J .... 304-896-7439.... 543 C
joanne.tomblin@southernwv.edu
TOMBLIN-BYRD, Terri, L .. 304-710-3141.... 542 K
tomblin@mctc.edu

TORTI, Frank ..... 860-679-2594 ..... 94 G
frank.torti@uchc.edu
TORTI, Frank, M ..... 860-679-2594 ..... 95 A
ftorti@uchc.edu
TORTI, Sylvia ..... 801-581-7339 ..... 511 C
sylvia.torti@utah.edu
TORTORICI, Marianne ..... 209-384-6105 ..... 57 C
marianne.tortorici@mccd.edu
TORTURELLI, Joseph ..... 201-360-4693 ..... 310 E
jtorturelli@hccc.edu
TORULAGHA, Priye ..... 305-430-1185 ..... 109 A
priye.torulagha@fmuniv.edu
TORVESTAD, Pat ..... 501-686-8999 ..... 24 F
ptorvestad@uams.edu
TORVIK, Stan ..... 307-778-1174 ..... 556 E
storvik@lccc.wy.edu
TOSCANO, James, P ..... 757-822-1015 ..... 528 G
jtoscano@tcc.edu
TOSCHKOFF, Marisa, L ..... 989-837-4337 ..... 256 E
toschkof@northwood.edu
TOSH, Carol ..... 901-333-5025 ..... 476 B
catosh@southwest.tn.edu
TOSO, Mary ..... 605-274-5530 ..... 464 A
mary.toso@augie.edu
TOSTEN, Lori ..... 717-262-2017 ..... 452 C
ltosten@wilson.edu
TOSTEN, Rod ..... 717-337-6601 ..... 429 I
rtosten@gettysburg.edu
TOSTENSON, Wendi ..... 229-217-4142 ..... 134 F
wtostenson@moultrietech.edu
TOSTI-LANE, Dave ..... 206-726-5136 ..... 533 D
dtostilane@cornish.edu
TOSTON, Margaret, Y ..... 731-881-7710 ..... 477 G
mtoston@utm.edu
TOTH, Joseph ..... 732-255-0400 ..... 312 D
jtoth@ocean.edu
TOTINO, Nancy ..... 718-405-3252 ..... 330 A
nancy.totino@mountsaintvincent.edu
TOTINO, Robert ..... 617-989-4325 ..... 245 F
totinor@wit.edu
TOTTEN, Herman, L ..... 940-565-2445 ..... 504 D
totten@unt.edu
TOTTEN, Julie ..... 402-554-2322 ..... 301 A
jtotten@unomaha.edu
TOTTEN, Rita ..... 714-952-9066 ..... 28 A
TOTTEN, Willette ..... 870-575-4713 ..... 25 B
tottenw@uapb.edu
TOTTERMAN, Henrik ..... 617-746-1990 ..... 235 G
henrik.totterman@hult.edu
TOTTY, Angie, D ..... 501-882-4432 ..... 20 C
adtotty@asub.edu
TOU, Phillip ..... 510-763-7787 ..... 26 F
ktou@acchs.edu
TOUCHETTE, Lindsey ..... 239-590-1016 ..... 119 B
ltouchet@fgcu.edu
TOUGAS, Tim ..... 320-762-4402 ..... 265 F
timt@alextech.edu
TOUHY, Jack ..... 773-298-3541 ..... 163 I
TOULIATOS-MILES,
Diane, H ..... 314-516-5904 ..... 291 D
touliatosd@umsl.edu
TOUMA, Elizabeth ..... 415-503-6261 ..... 66 A
eat@sfcm.edu
TOUPS, David, L ..... 561-732-4424 ..... 117 B
dtoups@svdp.edu
TOURE, Kathleen ..... 252-862-1329 ..... 373 C
ktoure@roanokechowan.edu
TOURNQUIST, Wade ..... 734-487-0354 ..... 250 F
wtornquis@emich.edu
TOUS, Frances ..... 954-499-9749 ..... 104 J
ftous@devry.edu
TOUSSAINT, Edward ..... 651-290-6394 ..... 272 E
edward.toussaint@wmitchell.edu
TOUSSAINT, Jess ..... 630-466-7900 ..... 168 B
jtoussaint@waubonsee.edu
TOUTAIN, Henry, P ..... 740-427-5137 ..... 394 C
toutainh@kenyon.edu
TOUTGES, Greg, A ..... 218-477-2131 ..... 267 F
toutges@mnstate.edu
TOUZEAU, Karen, E ..... 573-882-4256 ..... 291 B
touzeauk@missouri.edu
TOUZEAU, Leigh, A ..... 865-539-7013 ..... 475 G
latouzeau@pstcc.edu
TOVAR, Cindy ..... 312-225-6288 ..... 167 G
ctovar@vandercook.edu
TOVAR, Jessica ..... 831-755-6720 ..... 49 E
jtovar@hartnell.edu
TOVAR, Rina ..... 386-822-7773 ..... 121 F
rtovar@stetson.edu
TOVARES, Carlos ..... 951-571-6162 ..... 63 J
carlos.tovares@mvc.edu
TOVES, Louise, M ..... 671-735-2995 ..... 559 G
lmtoves@uguam.uog.edu
TOVEY, David ..... 419-755-4222 ..... 399 C
tovey.2@osu.edu
TOWAI, Gibson ..... 680-488-2471 ..... 560 C
gibs2y@yahoo.com
TOWAL, Patricia ..... 340-692-4187 ..... 568 E
ptowal@live.uvi.edu
TOWERS, George ..... 304-384-5334 ..... 543 G
towers@concord.edu
TOWERS, George ..... 304-384-6303 ..... 543 G
towers@concord.edu

TOWERS, Joel ..... 212-229-8950 ..... 342 E
towersj@newschool.edu
TOWEY, James ..... 239-280-2511 ..... 101 I
jim.towey@avemaria.edu
TOWLE, David, C ..... 319-273-2676 ..... 182 G
david.towle@uni.edu
TOWLE, Roger, K ..... 724-458-3355 ..... 430 B
rktowle@gcc.edu
TOWLE, Thomas ..... 603-271-7755 ..... 304 F
ttowle@ccsnh.edu
TOWNE, Becky, L ..... 713-942-9505 ..... 488 A
btowne@hgst.edu
TOWNER, Mark ..... 978-232-2255 ..... 234 D
mtowner@endicott.edu
TOWNLEY, Rod ..... 704-216-3850 ..... 373 F
rod.townley@rccc.edu
TOWNS, Elmer ..... 434-592-4140 ..... 520 K
eltowns@liberty.edu
TOWNS, Elmer, L ..... 434-582-2169 ..... 520 K
eltowns@liberty.edu
TOWNS, Gail ..... 732-987-2266 ..... 310 C
townsg@georgian.edu
TOWNSEND, Bill ..... 601-925-3257 ..... 275 C
btownsen@mc.edu
TOWNSEND, Candace, V ... 337-475-5635 ..... 215 G
ctownsend@mcneese.edu
TOWNSEND, Debra ..... 315-228-7417 ..... 329 G
dtownsend@colgate.edu
TOWNSEND, Elizabeth, R .. 336-599-1181 ..... 372 G
townsee@piedmontcc.edu
TOWNSEND, George ..... 913-667-5700 ..... 191 H
gtownsend@cbts.edu
TOWNSEND, Heidi ..... 360-475-7160 ..... 536 D
htownsend@olympic.edu
TOWNSEND, James, R ..... 574-535-7368 ..... 171 G
james.townsend@goshen.edu
TOWNSEND, Janis ..... 972-721-4142 ..... 503 B
jtownsend@udallas.edu
TOWNSEND, Joshua, W ..... 410-334-2958 ..... 229 E
jtownsend@worwic.edu
TOWNSEND, Joyce ..... 636-949-4971 ..... 283 J
jtownsend@lindenwood.edu
TOWNSEND, Karen ..... 617-879-7065 ..... 238 B
ktownsend@massart.edu
TOWNSEND, Lani ..... 818-774-0550 ..... 46 G
TOWNSEND, Lani ..... 323-668-7555 ..... 27 K
TOWNSEND, Pam ..... 256-331-5233 ..... 6 B
townsend@nwscc.edu
TOWNSEND, Ralph ..... 507-457-5017 ..... 269 G
rtownsend@winona.edu
TOWNSEND, Sonia ..... 281-998-6150 ..... 494 B
sonia.townsend@sjcd.edu
TOWNSEND-GAMBLE,
Jennifer ..... 803-533-3750 ..... 460 G
jgamble2@scsu.edu
TOWNSHEND, John, R ..... 301-405-1691 ..... 227 B
jtownshe@umd.edu
TOWNSLEY, Debra, M ..... 919-508-2220 ..... 380 E
dmtownsley@peace.edu
TOWNSLEY, Michael ..... 801-565-5110 ..... 509 J
mtownsley@devry.edu
TOWNSLEY, R. Mike ..... 260-422-5561 ..... 173 C
rmtownsley@indianatech.edu
TOWNSLEY, Stacy ..... 620-229-6208 ..... 196 G
stacy.townsley@sckans.edu
TOWSLEY, Scott ..... 507-574-4929 ..... 540 D
stowsley@yvcc.edu
TOY, Charles ..... 517-371-5140 ..... 258 F
toyc@cooley.edu
TOY, Sharon, S ..... 405-744-5984 ..... 410 C
sharon.toy@okstate.edu
TOY-HALE, Bernadette ..... 270-686-4506 ..... 203 B
bernie.hale@kctcs.edu
TOYAMA, Gordon, K ..... 503-370-6265 ..... 421 D
gtoyama@willamette.edu
TOZER, Rich ..... 928-314-9565 ..... 12 A
rich.tozer@azwestern.edu
TRACEY, SC, Kathleen ..... 718-405-3775 ..... 330 A
kathleen.tracey@mountsaintvincent.edu
TRACEY, Kevin, J ..... 516-562-3467 ..... 332 G
TRACEY, Patrick ..... 401-739-5000 ..... 453 G
ptracey@neit.edu
TRACHIAN, Barkev ..... 336-725-8344 ..... 375 G
trachianb@pbc.edu
TRACHIER, Steven ..... 817-531-4874 ..... 502 C
strachier@txwes.edu
TRACHTA, Yvonne ..... 361-593-4338 ..... 498 D
yvonne.trachta@tamuk.edu
TRACHTE, Kent, C ..... 717-291-4000 ..... 429 F
kent.trachte@fandm.edu
TRACIA, Michele ..... 617-739-1700 ..... 243 A
mtracia@aii.edu
TRACY, Carla, B ..... 309-794-7266 ..... 145 E
carlatracy@augustana.edu
TRACY, David ..... 508-588-9100 ..... 240 A
TRACY, II, Edward ..... 313-993-1554 ..... 258 G
tracyeg@udmercy.edu
TRACY, Geofrey, L ..... 419-372-8262 ..... 385 E
gtracy@bgsu.edu
TRACY, Gloria ..... 941-752-5323 ..... 118 J
tracyg@scf.edu
TRACY, Heidi, L ..... 614-823-1400 ..... 400 H
htracy@otterbein.edu

TRACY, James, W ..... 859-257-5294 ..... 207 D
tracy@uky.edu
TRACY, Jerry, W ..... 818-767-0888 ..... 79 H
jerry.tracy@woodbury.edu
TRACY, Kim ..... 773-442-4190 ..... 160 A
k-tracy@neiu.edu
TRACY, Lindsay ..... 303-256-9452 ..... 85 L
lindsay.morgantracy@jwu.edu
TRACY, Morgan, A ..... 859-858-3511 ..... 198 E
morgan.tracy@asbury.edu
TRACY, Rhonda ..... 304-424-8242 ..... 545 C
rhonda.tracy@mail.wvu.edu
TRACY, Roy ..... 505-786-4111 ..... 318 I
rtracy@navajotech.edu
TRACY, Sandra, G ..... 901-843-3800 ..... 472 K
tracy@rhodes.edu
TRACY, Tim ..... 859-323-7601 ..... 207 D
tim.tracy@uky.edu
TRACY, Timothy, S ..... 859-257-2911 ..... 207 D
tim.tracy@uky.edu
TRACZYK, Joyce ..... 763-433-1243 ..... 265 G
joyce.traczyk@anokaramsey.edu
TRADO, Donna ..... 828-327-7000 ..... 369 B
dtrado@cvcc.edu
TRAFFIE, Tim ..... 651-523-2015 ..... 264 A
ttraffie@hamline.edu
TRAFFORD, Beth ..... 501-812-2232 ..... 23 C
btrafford@pulaskitech.edu
TRAFLET, Dianne, M ..... 973-761-9353 ..... 310 F
dianne.traflet@shu.edu
TRAHAN, Michael ..... 409-984-6378 ..... 501 C
michael.trahan@lamarpa.edu
TRAIGER, Jeff ..... 816-235-5660 ..... 291 C
traigerj@umkc.edu
TRAIL, Mary Ann ..... 609-652-4555 ..... 313 E
maryann.trail@stockton.edu
TRAINA, Lou ..... 239-280-1695 ..... 101 I
lou.traina@avemaria.edu
TRAINA, Samuel ..... 209-228-7964 ..... 74 D
straina@ucmerced.edu
TRAINA, Samuel ..... 209-228-2857 ..... 74 D
straina@ucmerced.edu
TRAINER, James, F ..... 610-519-7578 ..... 450 H
james.trainer@villanova.edu
TRAINER, Jason ..... 218-793-2437 ..... 268 C
jason.trainer@northlandcollege.edu
TRAINER, Jill ..... 916-278-4655 ..... 36 A
jill.trainer@csus.edu
TRAINER, Karin ..... 609-258-3170 ..... 312 G
ktrainer@princeton.edu
TRAINO, Joe ..... 928-226-4285 ..... 13 F
joe.traino@coconino.edu
TRAINOR, David, P ..... 515-294-6458 ..... 182 E
dtrainor@iastate.edu
TRAINOR, Joseph, G ..... 215-596-8862 ..... 450 B
j.traino@usciences.edu
TRAINOR, Judith, L ..... 508-831-5423 ..... 246 F
jtrainor@wpi.edu
TRAINOR, Timothy ..... 845-938-2000 ..... 559 A
8dean@usma.edu
TRAINOR, Tom ..... 651-638-6259 ..... 261 D
t-trainor@bethel.edu
TRAISTER, Jerry ..... 607-729-1581 ..... 331 G
jtraister@davisny.edu
TRAKINAT, Mary Beth ..... 309-268-8172 ..... 151 I
marybeth.trakinat@heartland.edu
TRAMDACK, Philip, J ..... 724-738-2630 ..... 443 F
philip.tramdack@sru.edu
TRAMEL, Caitlin ..... 212-353-4139 ..... 331 A
ctramel@cooper.edu
TRAMELLI, Marianne ..... 212-678-3148 ..... 357 G
mt772@tc.columbia.edu
TRAMMEL, Sheila ..... 318-257-2235 ..... 215 F
strammel@latech.edu
TRAMMELL, C. David ..... 859-858-3511 ..... 198 E
david.trammell@asbury.edu
TRAMMELL, Genie ..... 918-293-5210 ..... 410 E
genie.trammell@okstate.edu
TRAMMELL, Janice ..... 409-880-8419 ..... 501 A
janice.trammell@lamar.edu
TRAMMELL, NaTonia ..... 508-831-5796 ..... 246 F
ntrammell@wpi.edu
TRAMMELL, Phil ..... 940-898-3863 ..... 502 D
ptrammell@twu.edu
TRAMMELL, Webster, B ..... 732-224-2282 ..... 308 A
wtrammell@brookdalecc.edu
TRAMONTANO,
William, A ..... 718-951-5864 ..... 326 F
tramontano@brooklyn.cuny.edu
TRAMONTE, Michael ..... 713-500-3158 ..... 506 F
michael.tramonte@uth.tmc.edu
TRAMPF, Judith, M ..... 262-472-4672 ..... 553 A
trampfj@uww.edu
TRAMUTA, Daniel, M ..... 716-673-3253 ..... 352 A
daniel.tramuta@fredonia.edu
TRAMUTA, Daniel, M ..... 716-673-3181 ..... 352 A
daniel.tramuta@fredonia.edu
TRAN, Deborah ..... 415-565-4740 ..... 74 A
trand@uchastings.edu
TRAN, Dzung ..... 602-243-8128 ..... 16 D
dzung.tran@smcmail.maricopa.edu
TRAN, Hanh ..... 818-364-7608 ..... 55 A
tranh@lamission.edu
TRAN, Hieu ..... 502-456-6504 ..... 206 H
htran@sullivan.edu

TRAN, My Linh ..... 773-907-6814 ..... 147 D
mtran@ccc.edu
TRAN, Vu ..... 310-825-3101 ..... 74 C
vtran@saonet.ucla.edu
TRANDAHL, Pamela ..... 651-675-4700 ..... 264 F
ptrandahl@msp.chefs.edu
TRANEL, Mark ..... 314-516-5273 ..... 291 D
mtranel@umsl.edu
TRANQUADA, Jim ..... 323-259-2990 ..... 59 I
jtranqua@oxy.edu
TRANQUILLI, Andrew, A ..... 203-582-8774 ..... 93 H
andy.tranquilli@quinnipiac.edu
TRANSUE, Mary ..... 678-717-3410 ..... 129 G
mtransue@gsc.edu
TRANSUE, Pamela ..... 253-566-5100 ..... 538 F
ptransue@tacomacc.edu
TRANT, John, M ..... 956-665-2404 ..... 506 C
trantjm@utpa.edu
TRANT, Meg ..... 617-217-9018 ..... 231 A
mtrant@baystate.edu
TRAPANICK, Benjamin, J .. 508-626-4505 ..... 238 A
btrapanick@framingham.edu
TRAPASSO, Kristen, P ..... 315-445-4265 ..... 338 B
trapaskp@lemoyne.edu
TRAPP, Chris ..... 740-389-6786 ..... 399 D
trapp.22@osu.edu
TRAPP, Daniel ..... 313-883-8540 ..... 257 E
trapp.daniel@shms.edu
TRAPP, Erin ..... 303-556-5126 ..... 86 F
etrapp@msudenver.edu
TRAPP, Harry ..... 301-369-2800 ..... 221 F
htrapp@capitol-college.edu
TRAPP, Lori ..... 734-973-3529 ..... 259 F
lori@wccnet.edu
TRASK, Anna ..... 617-731-7109 ..... 243 G
atrask@pmc.edu
TRASK, Mark ..... 239-489-9099 ..... 105 F
mark.trask@edison.edu
TRASK, III, Tallman ..... 919-684-6600 ..... 364 C
t3@duke.edu
TRATHEN, Edwin ..... 518-891-2915 ..... 344 E
etrathen@nccc.edu
TRAUB, Gilbert ..... 718-409-7385 ..... 356 C
gtraub@sunymaritime.edu
TRAUBE, Eve ..... 212-410-8006 ..... 343 B
etraube@nycpm.edu
TRAUGH, Cecelia ..... 718-488-1088 ..... 338 G
cecelia.traugh@liu.edu
TRAUPMAN-CARR, Carol .. 610-861-1348 ..... 437 A
caroltcarr@moravian.edu
TRAUTH, Denise, M ..... 512-245-2121 ..... 501 F
president@txstate.edu
TRAUTMAN, Stewart ..... 352-854-2322 ..... 103 K
trautmas@cf.edu
TRAUTMANN, Roger ..... 503-255-0332 ..... 417 C
rtrautmann@multnomah.edu
TRAVENICK, Ron ..... 510-659-6107 ..... 59 J
rtravenick@ohlone.edu
TRAVER, Virginia ..... 239-687-5343 ..... 101 H
vtraver@avemarialaw.edu
TRAVER, William ..... 518-458-5337 ..... 330 C
traverw@strose.edu
TRAVERS, Michael, E ..... 919-761-2127 ..... 377 A
mtravers@sebts.edu
TRAVERS, Nan ..... 518-587-2100 ..... 355 G
nan.travers@esc.edu
TRAVERSI, Diane ..... 707-527-4508 ..... 68 E
dtraversi@santarosa.edu
TRAVERSO, Celeste ..... 787-620-2040 ..... 560 D
ctraverso@aupr.edu
TRAVERSO, Susan ..... 717-361-1416 ..... 428 F
traversos@etown.edu
TRAVIESO, Charlotte ..... 504-865-5616 ..... 215 C
ctraviel@tulane.edu
TRAVIS, Annie ..... 662-252-8094 ..... 276 G
atravis@rustcollege.edu
TRAVIS, Antonio, W ..... 404-756-4023 ..... 125 D
atravis@atlm.edu
TRAVIS, Artie, L ..... 301-860-3391 ..... 228 A
atravis@bowiestate.edu
TRAVIS, Brantly, D ..... 270-809-2155 ..... 205 A
btravis@murraystate.edu
TRAVIS, David ..... 530-242-7799 ..... 69 D
dtravis@shastacollege.edu
TRAVIS, Deborah, J ..... 916-691-7321 ..... 56 B
travisd@crc.losrios.edu
TRAVIS, Douglas, B ..... 512-472-4133 ..... 494 F
doug.travis@ssw.edu
TRAVIS, Frederick ..... 641-472-7000 ..... 187 E
ftravis@mum.edu
TRAVIS, Heather ..... 515-961-1579 ..... 189 C
heather.travis@simpson.edu
TRAVIS, Jeremy ..... 212-237-8600 ..... 327 F
jtravis@jjay.cuny.edu
TRAVIS, Kay ..... 270-534-3084 ..... 203 E
kay.travis@kctcs.edu
TRAVIS, Patricia, J ..... 914-594-4575 ..... 343 F
pat_travis@nymc.edu
TRAVIS, Scott ..... 616-395-7251 ..... 252 D
remenschneider@hope.edu
TRAVIS, Shawn ..... 985-858-5713 ..... 210 G
shawn.travis@fletcher.edu
TRAVIS, Terry, K ..... 215-951-1540 ..... 432 I
travis@lasalle.edu

TRAVIS, Thomas 631-687-1275 349 B
ttravis@sjcny.edu
TRAVIS, Thomas, G 718-940-5723 349 A
ttravis@sjcny.edu
TRAVIS, William 757-253-4297 528 F
travisw@tncc.edu
TRAWEEK, Vicki 817-598-6218 508 F
vtraweek@wc.edu
TRAWICK, Rebecca 909-652-6493 39 E
rebecca.trawick@chaffey.edu
TRAWICK, Thomas 404-880-8812 127 C
ttrawick@cau.edu
TRAXLER, Matt 651-450-3885 266 F
mtraxle@inverhills.edu
TRAXLER, Sue 507-222-5608 261 G
straxler@carleton.edu
TRAYLOR, Delores 256-761-6246 7 G
ddtraylor@talladega.edu
TRAYLOR, Judy, G 903-434-8242 491 F
jtraylor@ntcc.edu
TRAYLOR, Lauren 732-987-2478 310 C
traylorl@georgian.edu
TRAYNOR, Kathy 715-682-1227 549 F
ktraynor@northland.edu
TRAYNUM, Elise 415-565-4715 74 A
traynume@uchastings.edu
TRAYSTMAN, Richard 303-724-8155 88 J
richard.traystman@ucdenver.edu
TREACLE, James 330-494-6170 402 B
jtreacle@starkstate.edu
TREACY, SJ, Jack, R 408-554-4372 68 C
jtreacy@scu.edu
TREADAWAY, Glenda, J 828-262-6311 377 D
treadawaygj@appstate.edu
TREADWELL, Andrew 772-462-4804 111 B
atreadwe@irsc.edu
TREADWELL, Jane, B 217-206-6597 167 C
treadwell.jane@uis.edu
TREADWELL, Larry 305-474-6860 117 A
ltreadwell@stu.edu
TREADWELL, Melinda 603-358-2105 306 G
mtreadwe@keene.edu
TREAKLE-MOORE, Evelyn 202-806-7540 98 E
etreakle-moore@howard.edu
TREANOR, Laura 586-790-9683 248 B
laura.treanor@baker.edu
TREANOR, Shirley 650-949-7364 47 H
barkershirley@foothill.edu
TREANOR, William, M 202-662-9031 98 D
wtreanor@georgetown.edu
TREAT, Bruce, J 585-785-1216 334 A
treatbo@flcc.edu
TREAT, Tod 217-875-7200 162 F
ttreat@richland.edu
TREBAR, Robert 440-375-7115 394 E
rtrebar@lec.edu
TREBER, Karen, A 301-687-4102 228 C
ktreber@frostburg.edu
TREBOW, Elizabeth 818-654-1707 62 F
etrebow@pgi.edu
TRECARTIN, Ralph, R 585-395-2119 352 F
rtrecart@brockport.edu
TRECKER, Stan 617-585-6651 236 B
strecker@lesley.edu
TREDUP, Fred 702-895-3201 302 I
fred.tredup@unlv.edu
TREECE, T. Gerald 713-646-1776 494 I
gtreece@stcl.edu
TREESE WILSON, Jennifer 415-355-2000 27 A
jtreese@alliant.edu
TREFF, Shaya 732-370-3360 317 G
TREFF, Yisroel Meir 732-370-3360 317 G
TREFFILETTI, Elaine 914-674-7540 340 F
eegliskis@mercy.edu
TREFT, Paul 712-274-5221 187 G
treft@morningside.edu
TREGRE, Calvin, S 504-520-7539 217 A
ctregre@xula.edu
TREIZENBERG, Steven, J 616-234-5708 259 D
TRELA, D, J 810-762-3234 259 C
djtrela@umflint.edu
TRELISKY, Nina 973-720-2305 317 D
treliskyn@wpunj.edu
TRELLA, Joseph 610-282-1100 427 A
joseph.trella@desales.edu
TRELOW, Cheryl, D 660-543-4255 290 H
trelow@ucmo.edu
TREMBLAY,
Christopher, W 313-593-5300 259 B
cwtrem@umd.umich.edu
TREMBLAY, Pamela 706-880-8313 133 B
ptremblay@lagrange.edu
TREMBLAY, Rocky 203-285-2185 91 D
rtremblay@gwcc.commnet.edu
TREMBLE, Gayle 912-443-5724 136 H
gtremble@savannahtech.edu
TREMPE, James, P 419-530-2844 404 F
james.trempe@utoledo.edu
TRENDE, Richard 715-425-3133 552 C
richard.trende@uwrf.edu
TRENDT, Diana, J 608-342-1183 552 B
trendtd@uwplatt.edu
TRENIS, Neva, S 540-654-1688 525 D
ntrenis@umw.edu

TRENKELBACH, Henry 330-382-7420 393 F
htrenkel@kent.edu
TRENKELBACH, Henry 330-337-4206 393 H
htrenkel@kent.edu
TRENKLE, Lizza 254-659-7823 487 G
ltrenkle@hillcollege.edu
TRENSCH, Kit 678-915-7307 137 G
ktrensch@spsu.edu
TRENT, Coe Ann 336-342-4261 373 E
trentc@rockinghamcc.edu
TREPAL, Michael, J 212-410-8067 343 B
mtrepal@nycpm.edu
TREPKOWSKI, Patti 616-234-4226 251 E
ptrepkow@grcc.edu
TREPKOWSKI, Ronald, E 989-964-4285 257 G
ret@svsu.edu
TRESER-OSGOOD,
Nancy, J 909-621-8110 63 A
nancy.treser-osgood@pomona.edu
TRESNER, Erin, C 432-685-4526 491 A
TRESOLINI, Carol 919-962-3907 378 E
carol_tresolini@med.unc.edu
TRESS, Samuel, D 410-837-5529 229 A
stress@ubalt.edu
TRESSEL, James, P 330-972-5524 403 B
jtressel@uakron.edu
TRESSEL, Ryan 336-841-4519 365 C
rtressel@highpoint.edu
TRESSLER, Dan 575-538-6000 321 I
tresslerd@wumu.edu
TREUTHART, Jean, M 717-718-0328 430 E
jmtreuth@hacc.edu
TREVAN, Timothy, J 818-677-2160 35 F
timothy.j.trevan@csun.edu
TREVATHAN, Ed 314-977-8188 289 C
etravath@slu.edu
TREVATHAN, Michael, R 318-342-5242 216 E
trevathan@ulm.edu
TREVINIO, Jesus 605-677-5011 465 G
jesus.trevinio@usd.edu
TREVINO, Crispin 361-593-4036 498 D
crispin.trevino@tamuk.edu
TREVINO, JR., Esteban 956-721-5140 489 J
stevet@laredo.edu
TREVINO, Mary, T 956-326-2275 497 D
maryt@tamiu.edu
TREVINO, Melba 956-872-3113 494 H
melbat@southtexascollege.edu
TREVINO, Miguel, A 956-326-2283 497 D
mtrevino@tamiu.edu
TREVINO, Monica 405-224-3140 413 E
mtrevino@usao.edu
TREVINO, Rick 805-654-6400 77 F
rtrevino@vcccd.edu
TREVINO BAUER, Blanca 956-882-7081 505 E
blanca.bauer@utb.edu
TREVIS, Michael 310-660-3101 45 E
mtrevis@elcamino.edu
TREVISAN, Maurizio 212-650-5275 326 G
mtrevisan@ccny.cuny.edu
TREVISAN, Sandi 619-388-7752 65 H
strevisa@sdccd.edu
TREVOR, Mary 928-350-1101 17 K
mtrevor@prescott.edu
TREVOR, Tyler 406-444-0311 294 H
ttrevor@montana.edu
TREW, Marcy 330-494-1214 386 A
mtrew@brownmackie.edu
TREWERN, Jay 972-825-4606 495 F
jtrewern@sagu.edu
TREWYN, Ronald, W 785-532-6195 194 D
trewyn@ksu.edu
TREXLER, William, H 814-886-6421 437 B
wtrexler@mtaloy.edu
TREZISE, Rene, M 304-788-6872 545 B
rmtrezise@mail.wvu.edu
TRIANTAFILOU,
Nicholas, C 617-850-1280 235 F
pres_office@hchc.edu
TRIBBLE, Judy 812-535-5255 179 E
jtribble@smwc.edu
TRIBBLE, Sherman 919-572-1625 362 C
TRIBBLE-SPENCER, Kelly 410-276-0306 226 D
kspencer@host.sdc.edu
TRIBLE, Paul, S 757-594-7001 517 L
ptrible@cnu.edu
TRIBLEY, Walt 509-682-6605 539 E
wtribley@wvc.edu
TRICARICO, Kerri 212-998-2913 344 B
kerri.tricarico@nyu.edu
TRICE, Gwinetta, L 229-430-4739 124 A
gwinetta.trice@asurams.edu
TRICE, Matt 229-430-6618 124 B
mtrice@albanytech.edu
TRICE, Sarah 803-822-3321 459 E
trices@midlandstech.edu
TRICE, Thomas 805-756-2724 33 I
ttricei@calpoly.edu
TRICHE, Casie 985-448-4077 216 A
casie.triche@nicholls.edu
TRICHE, III, Charles, W 337-482-6396 216 D
ctriche@louisiana.edu
TRICKETT, David G, H 303-765-3102 85 D
dgtrickett@iliff.edu

TRICKEY, JR., Rafe, E 605-698-3966 465 E
etrickey@swc.tc
TRICKEY, JR.,
Rafe Edward 692-625-3994 560 A
TRICOLI, Robin, J 423-442-2001 469 D
president@hiwassee.edu
TRIDENTE, Teresa 201-216-5176 315 E
ttrident@stevens.edu
TRIERWEILER, Charles, S 205-329-7907 3 A
chuck.trierweiler@ecacolleges.com
TRIETLEY, JR., Richard, C 716-375-2513 348 C
rtrietley@sbu.edu
TRIEZENBERG, Glenn, E 616-526-6485 249 A
gtriezen@calvin.edu
TRIGALO, Ophir 312-567-3290 153 C
trigalo@iit.edu
TRIGG, Debra 510-659-7376 59 J
dtrigg@ohlone.edu
TRIGGS, Patricia 360-475-7480 536 D
ptriggs@olympic.edu
TRILLER, Mark, V 608-757-7701 553 G
mtriller@blackhawk.edu
TRILLI, Victor 316-942-4291 195 F
trilliv@newmanu.edu
TRIMARCHI, Valarie 703-302-1380 530 G
vtrimarchi@westwood.edu
TRIMBLE, Ferris, E 323-241-5467 55 C
trimblfe@lasc.edu
TRIMBLE, Joe 615-966-5672 470 F
joe.trimble@lipscomb.edu
TRIMBLE, Karen 530-741-6700 80 I
TRIMBLE, LaDonna 661-722-6300 28 K
ltrimble@avc.edu
TRIMBLE, Lisa 307-778-1603 556 E
lisatrimble@lcccfoundation.edu
TRIMBLE, Marshall 480-423-6314 16 C
marshall.trimble@scottsdalecc.edu
TRIMBLE, Michael, D 203-365-7557 94 B
trimblem@sacredheart.edu
TRIMBOLI, James 716-614-6202 344 C
trimboli@niagaracc.suny.edu
TRIMBOLI, Thomas, A 843-953-5528 457 B
trimbolit@cofc.edu
TRINCHESE, Rebecca 724-738-4340 443 F
rebecca.trinchese@sru.edu
TRINIDAD, Vanessa 787-884-6000 562 G
vtrinidad@icprjc.edu
TRINIDAD, Ysabel 805-437-8877 34 B
ysabel.trinidad@csuci.edu
TRINKLEIN, Andrea 404-727-4144 129 D
ajtrink@emory.edu
TRINKO, Lynn, A 419-995-8412 399 B
trinko.1@osu.edu
TRIONFI, Thomas, P 989-774-3166 249 C
trion1tp@cmich.edu
TRIPATHI, Satish, K 716-645-2901 351 G
president@buffalo.edu
TRIPLET, Jeff 971-722-4406 419 G
jtriplet@pcc.edu
TRIPLETT, Anastasia 540-868-7133 527 C
atriplett@lfcc.edu
TRIPLETT, Beth 563-588-6468 183 E
beth.triplett@clarke.edu
TRIPLETT, Clark 314-392-2221 285 J
triplett@mobap.edu
TRIPLETT, Jill 404-270-5677 138 B
jtriple1@spelman.ed
TRIPLETT, Lynn 781-768-7315 244 A
lynn.triplett@regiscollege.edu
TRIPLETT, Neal 919-668-9995 364 C
neal.triplett@duke.edu
TRIPLETT, R. Gilbert 214-828-8101 497 C
gtriplett@bcd.tamhsc.edu
TRIPLITT, Tom, A 864-294-3464 458 E
tom.triplitt@furman.edu
TRIPODI, Michael 908-737-7020 311 A
mtripodi@kean.edu
TRIPONEY, Vicky 609-771-2201 308 F
taponey@tcnj.edu
TRIPP, Harry, E 814-393-2351 442 B
htripp@clarion.edu
TRIPP, Susan 315-866-0300 335 D
trippsk@herkimer.edu
TRIPPETT, William 608-263-7727 553 B
william.trippett@uwc.edu
TRIPURANENI, Vinaya, L 909-593-3511 75 E
vtripuraneni@laverne.edu
TRISCIUZZI, Andrea 410-234-4670 225 E
TRISCORNIA, Star, L 620-417-1106 196 F
star.triscornia@sccc.edu
TRITAK, Ann 201-761-6272 314 F
atritak@spc.edu
TRITLE, Madonna 219-785-5244 179 A
mtritle@pnc.edu
TRIVEDI, Tushar 201-761-6264 314 F
ttrivedi@spc.edu
TRIVETT, Ali 276-466-7162 529 D
alitrivett@vic.edu
TRIVUNOVICH, Nick 813-974-4903 121 A
ntrivuno@usf.edu
TRIZZINO-PECOR, June 212-965-8340 322 A
trizzino@adelphi.edu
TRNCAK, Stephen 281-998-6348 493 G
stephen.trncak@sjcd.edu

TROASTLE, Greta, J 304-637-1331 541 A
troastleg@dewv.edu
TROCHIM, Shawn 254-299-8811 490 G
strochim@mclennan.edu
TROCHUCK, Mike 708-239-4836 166 C
mike.trochuck@trnty.edu
TROCINO, Sherry, M 607-735-1770 332 I
strocino@elmira.edu
TROELL, Luther 585-475-2411 347 G
ljtics@rit.edu
TROELSTRA, Kate 678-466-4300 127 D
katetroelstra@clayton.edu
TROHA, James 419-448-2383 391 F
jtroha@heidelberg.edu
TROIANO, Peter, F 203-392-5200 90 I
troianop2@southernct.edu
TROIANO, Peter, F 203-392-5556 90 I
troianop2@southernct.edu
TROILO, David 212-938-5658 355 B
dtroilo@sunyopt.edu
TROJAN, John 908-526-1200 313 D
jtrojan@raritanval.edu
TROLLINGER, Richard, W 859-238-5209 199 G
richard.trollinger@centre.edu
TROMANHAUSER,
David, C 423-775-7308 467 F
david.tromanhauser@bryan.edu
TROMBELLA, Jerry 201-559-6185 310 B
trombellaj@felician.edu
TROMBLEY, Jane, E 212-817-7179 327 B
jtrombley@gc.cuny.edu
TROMBLEY OAKES,
Martha 802-728-1732 516 A
moakes@vtc.edu
TRONGALE, Nicholas 630-889-6599 159 F
ntrongale@nuhs.edu
TRONTO, Stacie 252-328-9025 377 E
trontos@ecu.edu
TROPP, Judybeth 619-961-4319 72 J
jtropp@tjsl.edu
TROSSET, Carol 413-559-5890 235 C
TROST, Patricia, G 708-709-3637 161 D
ptrost@prairiestate.edu
TROSVIG, Kelli 206-616-0114 539 A
kelli@uw.edu
TROTMAN, Joylyn 256-726-8436 6 C
jtrotman@oakwood.edu
TROTTA, Neil 617-236-8867 234 G
ntrotta@fisher.edu
TROTTER, Cheryl 704-461-6714 362 F
cheryltrotter@bac.edu
TROTTER, Dennis, C 402-461-7326 298 A
dennis_trotter@hastings.edu
TROTTER, Johnny 706-295-6974 131 B
jtrotter@gntc.edu
TROTTER, Sheila, R 608-342-1836 552 B
trotter@uwplatt.edu
TROTTER, Steve 360-867-6185 534 D
trotters@evergreen.edu
TROTTIER, Sheila 701-477-7862 383 F
strottier@tm.edu
TROTTY, Willie, F 936-261-1550 496 G
wftrotty@pvamu.edu
TROTTY, Willie, F 936-261-3500 496 G
wftrotty@pvamu.edu
TROUP, James 203-575-8220 92 A
jtroup@nvcc.commnet.edu
TROUP, Pat 251-981-3771 2 G
pat.troup@columbiasouthern.edu
TROUPE, Bonnie, L 508-565-1069 245 A
btroupe@stonehill.edu
TROUT, Curtis, C 309-556-3195 153 F
ctrout@iwu.edu
TROUT, Darice 847-925-6070 151 G
dtrout@harpercollege.edu
TROUT, Margaret 503-370-6971 421 D
mtrout@willamette.edu
TROUT, Ryan 847-628-2521 154 K
ryan.trout@judsonu.edu
TROUTEN, Stefanie, K 304-336-8900 544 D
strouten@westliberty.edu
TROUTMAN, Dara, L 402-472-7143 300 E
dtroutman@nebraska.edu
TROUTMAN, Donald 570-321-4064 435 D
troutman@lycoming.edu
TROUTMAN, Marcus 312-922-1884 157 E
mtroutman@maccormac.edu
TROUTT, Amy 618-545-3048 155 B
atroutt@kaskaskia.edu
TROUTT, William, E 901-843-3730 472 K
trouttw@rhodes.edu
TROVALL, Carl 512-313-3000 483 K
carl.trovall@concordia.edu
TROVER, Clay 706-721-4854 130 D
ctrover@georgiahealth.edu
TROWBRIDGE,
Christian, A 302-295-1151 97 C
christian.a.trowbridge@wilmu.edu
TROWBRIDGE, Corey, D 316-322-0110 279 D
cory.trowbridge@calvary.edu
TROWBRIDGE, Cory, D 816-322-0110 279 D
security@calvary.edu
TROWBRIDGE, Larry 217-479-7079 157 F
larry.trowbridge@mac.edu

TROWBRIDGE, Raymond ... 518-828-4181 .... 330 E
trowbridge@sunycgcc.edu

TROXEL, Steve ... 620-365-5116 .... 190 D
troxel@allencc.edu

TROXLER, Debra, J ... 302-571-5380 .... 96 F
dtroxler@dtcc.edu

TROY, Randy ... 260-399-7700 .... 181 A
rtroy@sf.edu

TROY, Robert, C ... 718-960-7825 .... 327 C
robert.troy@lehman.cuny.edu

TROY, Shawn ... 989-386-6616 .... 255 C
stroy@midmich.edu

TROYER, Carol, A ... 717-334-6286 .... 435 A
ctroyer@ltsg.edu

TROYER, Cindy ... 903-566-7461 .... 506 E
ctroyer@uttyler.edu

TROYER, Mark, J ... 859-858-3511 .... 198 E
mark.troyer@asbury.edu

TROYER, Stephen ... 330-337-6403 .... 383 J
college@awc.edu

TRUBACZ, Joseph ... 303-273-3240 .... 83 B
jtrubacz@mines.edu

TRUCKENMILLER, Greg ... 518-736-3622 .... 334 D
gtrucken@fmcc.suny.edu

TRUDEAU, Dave ... 252-492-2061 .... 374 G
trudeau@vgcc.edu

TRUDEAU, Sara, L ... 202-526-3799 .... 99 D

TRUDEAU, Scott ... 248-204-3850 .... 254 B
strudeau@ltu.edu

TRUDEAU, Skip ... 765-998-5368 .... 180 B
sktrudeau@taylor.edu

TRUDEL, Jeannie ... 864-644-5486 .... 461 B
jtrudel@swu.edu

TRUDELL, Kyle ... 573-288-6450 .... 280 I
ktrudell@culver.edu

TRUE, Don ... 803-593-9231 .... 455 A
trued@atc.edu

TRUE, Douglas, K ... 319-335-3552 .... 182 F
douglas-true@uiowa.edu

TRUE, Elizabeth ... 617-928-4042 .... 242 E
eatrue@mountida.edu

TRUE, Jeanette ... 605-882-5284 .... 464 E
truej@lakeareatech.edu

TRUE, Reiko ... 415-955-2100 .... 27 F
rtrue@alliant.edu

TRUELOVE, Elaine ... 478-757-3414 .... 127 A
truelove@centralgatech.edu

TRUEMAN, Amy ... 607-844-8222 .... 357 I
truemaa@tc3.edu

TRUESDALE, Karen ... 678-891-2542 .... 131 C
ktruesda@gpc.edu

TRUESDELL, Cheryl, B ... 260-481-6506 .... 174 C
truesdel@ipfw.edu

TRUESDELL, Joanne ... 503-594-3000 .... 415 A
joannet@clackamas.edu

TRUESDELL, Nancy, D ... 920-832-6596 .... 548 B
nancy.d.truesdell@lawrence.edu

TRUETT, William, M ... 704-272-5363 .... 374 A
wtruett@spcc.edu

TRUFANT, Nicole ... 207-602-2157 .... 221 A
ntrufant@une.edu

TRUILLO, Lawrence, T ... 607-778-5207 .... 324 G
truillolt@sunybroome.edu

TRUITT, Bettie ... 309-796-5048 .... 145 H
truittb@bhc.edu

TRUITT, Jennifer ... 217-228-5432 .... 161 F
truitje@quincy.edu

TRUITT, Roy ... 510-567-6174 .... 72 D
rtruitt@sum.edu

TRUITT, Terry, C ... 765-641-4354 .... 169 E
tctruitt@anderson.edu

TRUITTT, Roy ... 510-567-6174 .... 72 D
rtruitt@sum.edu

TRUJILLO, Daniel, A ... 718-990-6774 .... 348 G
trujilld@stjohns.edu

TRUJILLO, Fidel, J ... 505-454-3020 .... 318 J
fidel@nmhu.edu

TRUJILLO, George ... 301-985-7283 .... 227 F
gtrujillo@umuc.edu

TRUJILLO, Tamara ... 707-638-5317 .... 73 A
tamara.trujillo@tu.edu

TRULOVE, Milyon ... 651-523-2207 .... 264 A
mtrulove01@hamline.edu

TRUMAN, Grace, H ... 561-868-3122 .... 114 D
trumang@palmbeachstate.edu

TRUMAN, Kevin, Z ... 816-235-2399 .... 291 C
trumank@umkc.edu

TRUMBLE, Elaine ... 207-893-7804 .... 219 F
etrumble@sjcme.edu

TRUMBLE, William ... 207-948-9151 .... 219 H
wtrumble@unity.edu

TRUMBOWER, Jeffrey, A ... 802-654-2492 .... 514 D
jtrumbower@smcvt.edu

TRUMPICK, Susan, A ... 518-743-2248 .... 355 D
trumpics@sunyacc.edu

TRUMPOWER, Peter ... 330-494-6170 .... 402 B
ptrumpower@starkstate.edu

TRUMPS, Thomas, H ... 540-464-7313 .... 529 F
trumpsth@vmi.edu

TRUONG, Chris ... 714-564-6043 .... 63 F
truong_chris@sac.edu

TRUONG, Tina ... 575-439-3703 .... 319 E
ttruong@nmsua.nmsu.edu

TRUONG, Tina ... 575-439-3703 .... 319 E
ttruong@nmsu.edu

TRUPP, Kim, L ... 334-844-4580 .... 1 F
truppki@auburn.edu

TRUSCHKE, Michael, E ... 310-506-4392 .... 61 H
michael.truschke@pepperdine.edu

TRUSHEIM, Dale, W ... 410-778-7709 .... 229 D
dtrusheim2@washcoll.edu

TRUSKOWSKI, Marilyn, C . 413-662-5598 .... 238 C
marilyn.truskowski@mcla.edu

TRUSS, B. Donta ... 478-827-7594 .... 129 F
trussd@fvsu.edu

TRUSSELL, Jay ... 828-884-8340 .... 362 H
trussellj@brevard.edu

TRUSTY, Denise ... 606-886-3863 .... 201 G
denise.trusty@kctcs.edu

TRUSTY, LeRoy, A ... 443-412-2145 .... 223 B
letrusty@harford.edu

TRUSZ, Robert, J ... 740-351-3610 .... 401 I
btrusz@shawnee.edu

TRUTNA, Kevin ... 530-741-6766 .... 80 K
ktrutna@yccd.edu

TRUTNA, Kevin ... 530-283-0202 .... 47 B
ktrutna@frc.edu

TRUXILLO, Betty, D ... 225-923-2524 .... 208 C
director@brsc.edu

TRYON, Sandy ... 515-964-6408 .... 183 H
sbtryon@dmacc.edu

TRZASKA, Ken, J ... 906-932-4231 .... 251 C
kent@gogebic.edu

TRZEBIATOWSKI, Brian ... 773-481-8287 .... 147 I
btrzebiatowski@ccc.edu

TRZECIAK, Jeffrey, G ... 314-935-5415 .... 292 I
jeffrey.trzeciak@wustl.edu

TRZEPACZ, Angie ... 270-809-6861 .... 205 A
atrzepacz@murraystate.edu

TRZOP, Chasity ... 502-968-7191 .... 199 D
ctrzop@brownmackie.edu

TSAFFARAS, Peter, H ... 617-984-1776 .... 243 H
ptsaffaras@quincycollege.edu

TSAI, Patty ... 866-323-0233 .... 63 D

TSANG, Chui, L ... 310-434-4200 .... 68 D
tsang_chui@smc.edu

TSARK, Gregory ... 321-674-7584 .... 108 H
gtsark@fit.edu

TSATSOULIS, Costas ... 940-565-4300 .... 504 D
costas.tsatsoulis@unt.edu

TSCHERTER, Andrea, G ... 812-888-5794 .... 181 D
atscherter@vinu.edu

TSCHETTER, Wesley ... 605-688-4128 .... 466 C
wesley.tschetter@sdstate.edu

TSCHETTER, Wesley, G ... 605-688-4920 .... 466 C
wesley.tschetter@sdstate.edu

TSCHUY, Eric ... 503-491-7469 .... 417 B
eric.tschuy@mhcc.edu

TSEGAI, Adiam ... 716-884-9120 .... 324 J
aktsegai@bryantstratton.edu

TSETSEKOS, George ... 215-895-2110 .... 427 H
tsetsekos@drexel.edu

TSO, Jaway ... 212-757-1190 .... 322 H
jtso@funeraleducation.org

TSO, Jay ... 212-757-1190 .... 322 H
jtso@funeraleducation.org

TSOUMAS, Linda, J ... 508-373-5709 .... 241 C
linda.tsoumas@mcphs.edu

TSUCHIYAMA, Ray ... 808-984-3471 .... 142 E
ray.tsuchiyama@gmail.com

TSUI, Christine ... 309-438-8606 .... 153 D
cktsui@ilstu.edu

TSUQUIASHI-DADDESIO,
Eva ... 724-738-4863 .... 443 F
eva.tsuquiashi@sru.edu

TSUTSUI, William, M ... 214-768-3212 .... 495 A
btsutsui@smu.edu

TUBB, Joe ... 806-894-9611 .... 494 G
jtubb@southplainscollege.edu

TUBBS, Carol ... 310-243-3389 .... 34 D

TUBBS, Jeffrey, L ... 704-406-4427 .... 364 E
jtubbs@gardner-webb.edu

TUBBS, Marcus ... 615-256-1463 .... 466 H
mtubbs@abcnash.edu

TUBBS, Richard, E ... 941-351-4742 .... 116 B
rtubbs@ringling.edu

TUBBS, Teresa ... 910-272-3662 .... 373 D
ttubbs@robeson.edu

TUBBS, Trenton ... 417-864-7220 .... 281 H
ttubbs@cci.edu

TUBMAN, Jonathan, G ... 202-885-3753 .... 97 D
jtubman@american.edu

TUBMAN, Lynn ... 215-248-7046 .... 425 D
tubmanl@chc.edu

TUCCI, Barbara ... 505-428-1264 .... 320 E
barbara.tucci@sfcc.edu

TUCCI, Jack, E ... 334-386-7100 .... 3 G
jtucci@faulkner.edu

TUCCI, Karen, L ... 740-264-5591 .... 390 F
ktucci@egcc.edu

TUCCI, LaVonne, R ... 218-722-4000 .... 263 E
lavonnet@dbumn.edu

TUCCI, Paul ... 518-587-2100 .... 355 G
paul.tucci@esc.edu

TUCHMAN, Nancy ... 773-508-2475 .... 157 C
ntuchma@luc.edu

TUCHMAN, Richard, J ... 203-932-7268 .... 95 C
rtuchman@newhaven.edu

TUCK, Amy ... 662-325-3221 .... 275 F
at25@msstate.edu

TUCK, Inez ... 336-334-7751 .... 378 A
ituck@ncat.edu

TUCK, Martin ... 740-774-7200 .... 399 G
tuck@ohio.edu

TUCK, Martin ... 740-774-7200 .... 400 A
tuck@ohio.edu

TUCKER, Ann, W ... 856-566-6434 .... 317 B
tuckeraw@umdnj.edu

TUCKER, Anne ... 509-434-5109 .... 533 C
atucker@ccs.spokane.edu

TUCKER, Anne ... 509-434-5108 .... 533 B
anne.tucker@ccs.spokane.edu

TUCKER, Anne, M ... 509-434-5109 .... 533 A
atucker@ccs.spokane.edu

TUCKER, Anthony ... 706-419-1663 .... 128 B
anthony.tucker@covenant.edu

TUCKER, Archie ... 256-372-8344 .... 1 A
archie.tucker@aamu.edu

TUCKER, Arlene, C ... 337-550-1288 .... 212 J

TUCKER, Barbara ... 608-822-2456 .... 555 D
btucker@swtc.edu

TUCKER, Bill ... 601-276-3726 .... 277 B
wtucker@smcc.edu

TUCKER, Carol, M ... 713-221-8269 .... 503 F
tuckerca@uhd.edu

TUCKER, Cecelia, T ... 757-683-5210 .... 522 F
ctucker@odu.edu

TUCKER, Cheryl ... 707-476-4293 .... 42 C
cheryl-tucker@redwoods.edu

TUCKER, David, C ... 812-888-4266 .... 181 D
dtucker@vinu.edu

TUCKER, Dawn ... 919-718-7437 .... 369 C
dmtucker@cccc.edu

TUCKER, Diane, P ... 617-353-2000 .... 232 E

TUCKER, Donald, L ... 330-471-8119 .... 395 F
dtucker@malone.edu

TUCKER, Eileen ... 610-660-1346 .... 446 C
tucker@sju.edu

TUCKER, G.L ... 218-846-3765 .... 267 D
gl.tucker@minnesota.edu

TUCKER, Geraldine ... 512-223-7572 .... 481 B
gtucker@austincc.edu

TUCKER, Herman, V ... 254-299-8660 .... 490 G
htucker@mclennan.edu

TUCKER, Irene ... 775-445-4234 .... 303 B
itucker@wnc.edu

TUCKER, James ... 518-327-6286 .... 345 H
jtucker@paulsmiths.edu

TUCKER, James, R ... 215-895-2800 .... 427 H
jrt55@drexel.edu

TUCKER, Jim ... 785-749-8460 .... 193 D
jtucker@haskell.edu

TUCKER, John ... 314-264-1802 .... 189 H
john.tucker@vatterott-college.edu

TUCKER, John ... 314-264-1802 .... 292 C
john.tucker@vatterott-college.edu

TUCKER, John, D ... 619-298-1829 .... 71 C

TUCKER, Jon ... 503-838-8063 .... 419 C
tuckerj@wou.edu

TUCKER, Karen ... 630-752-5060 .... 168 H
karen.tucker@wheaton.edu

TUCKER, Karin, T ... 323-856-7609 .... 28 E
ktucker@afi.com

TUCKER, Keith ... 210-829-3125 .... 504 B
tucker@uiwtx.edu

TUCKER, Ken ... 205-652-3471 .... 9 E
ktucker@uwa.edu

TUCKER, Kim ... 970-675-3335 .... 82 H
kim.tucker@cncc.edu

TUCKER, Laura ... 954-486-7728 .... 122 H

TUCKER, Mark ... 336-386-3217 .... 374 E
tuckerm@surry.edu

TUCKER, Mary, E ... 520-621-9438 .... 18 L
mtucker@email.arizona.edu

TUCKER, Michael, A ... 765-641-4295 .... 169 E
matucker@anderson.edu

TUCKER, NaDene ... 252-246-1425 .... 375 D
ntucker@wilsoncc.edu

TUCKER, Nate ... 423-473-1190 .... 470 C
ntucker@leeuniversity.edu

TUCKER, Ned ... 402-826-8601 .... 297 G
ned.tucker@doane.edu

TUCKER, Patrick ... 860-832-1786 .... 90 G
ptucker@ccsu.edu

TUCKER, Raymond, A ... 785-827-5541 .... 194 F
rtucker@kwu.edu

TUCKER, Raymond, T ... 304-367-4861 .... 543 H
raymond.tucker@fairmontstate.edu

TUCKER, Robert ... 325-649-8600 .... 488 C
rtucker@hputx.edu

TUCKER, Sandra ... 318-670-9641 .... 215 A
stucker@susla.edu

TUCKER, Sharon "Nyota" ... 229-430-2799 .... 124 A
nyota.tucker@asurams.edu

TUCKER, Sheryl ... 573-882-9576 .... 291 B
tuckers@missouri.edu

TUCKER, Sheryl ... 405-744-6368 .... 410 C
sheryl.tucker@okstate.edu

TUCKER, Stacy ... 913-288-7239 .... 194 C
stucker@kckcc.edu

TUCKER, Terry, W ... 607-587-3621 .... 355 C
tuckertw@alfredstate.edu

TUCKER, Thomas ... 770-407-1085 .... 124 F
tatucker@argosy.edu

TUCKER, Thomas, A ... 770-407-1085 .... 467 B
tatucker@argosy.edu

TUCKER, Todd ... 605-626-2530 .... 466 A
todd.tucker@northern.edu

TUCKER, Tommy ... 870-307-7324 .... 22 D
thomas.tucker@lyon.edu

TUCKER, Vicki ... 229-430-3536 .... 124 B
vtucker@albanytech.edu

TUCKER, Vicky ... 815-838-0500 .... 156 F
tuckervi@lewisu.edu

TUCKER, W. Steven ... 205-348-8396 .... 8 E
uadps01@bama.ua.edu

TUCKER-LOEWE,
Cheryle, L ... 618-650-3701 .... 165 C
chtucke@siue.edu

TUCKER-MCCLOUD,
Janice ... 740-826-8134 .... 397 A
jtucker@muskingum.edu

TUDELA, Virginia, C ... 671-735-5590 .... 559 E
deansoffice@guamcc.edu

TUDOR, Donna, K ... 615-248-7703 .... 476 G
dtudor@trevecca.edu

TUDOR, Gail ... 207-941-7039 .... 218 A
tudorg@husson.edu

TUDOR, Lisa ... 239-489-9350 .... 105 F
ltudor@edison.edu

TUEDIO, James, A ... 209-667-3531 .... 36 D
tuedio@csustan.edu

TUEL, Alexander ... 301-387-3028 .... 222 H
alexander.tuel@garrettcollege.edu

TUELLER, Steven ... 808-675-3935 .... 140 D
steve.tueller@byuh.edu

TUFANO, Joseph, J ... 718-990-5800 .... 348 G
tufanoj@stjohns.edu

TUFAU-AFRIYIE, Michelle . 508-854-7568 .... 240 F
mtufau@qcc.mass.edu

TUFFLI, Theresa ... 503-594-0630 .... 415 A
theresat@clackamas.edu

TUGGLE, Robert, L ... 940-898-3503 .... 502 D
rtuggle@twu.edu

TUGGLE, Van ... 601-477-5406 .... 274 H
joseph.tuggle@jcjc.edu

TUIA, Jennifer ... 360-596-5369 .... 538 E
jtuia@spscc.ctc.edu

TUITASI, Michael ... 310-434-4389 .... 68 D
tuitasi_michael@smc.edu

TUITASI, Sifagatogo ... 684-699-9155 .... 559 C
s.tuitasi@amsamoa.edu

TUITE, Jayme ... 724-222-5330 .... 438 F
jtuite@penncommercial.edu

TUITE, Kathleen ... 973-618-3534 .... 308 C
ktuite@caldwell.edu

TUITT, Frank ... 303-871-2591 .... 89 A
ftuitt@du.edu

TUKEY, Joan ... 207-947-4591 .... 217 D
jtukey@bealcollege.edu

TULAFONO, Grace ... 684-699-9155 .... 559 C
g.tulafono@amsamoa.edu

TULAK, William, H ... 985-858-5856 .... 210 G
william.tulak@fletcher.edu

TULL, Ashley ... 254-968-9080 .... 497 A
tull@tarleton.edu

TULLBANE, Joseph, D ... 920-403-3378 .... 550 F
joe.tullbane@snc.edu

TULLER, RN, Jodi ... 413-528-7253 .... 230 F
jtuller@simons-rock.edu

TULLIO, Ann ... 718-631-6215 .... 328 F
atullio@qcc.cuny.edu

TULLMAN, Howard, A ... 312-332-0707 .... 166 B

TULLOCH, Helen (Meg) ... 202-685-3948 .... 557 I
tullochh@ndu.edu

TULLY, Bettie, L ... 214-860-2105 .... 485 A
btully@dcccd.edu

TULLY, Greg, J ... 815-772-7218 .... 159 C
jprombo@morrisontech.edu

TULLY, Marci ... 561-912-1211 .... 107 B
mtully@evergladesuniversity.edu

TULLY, Patricia ... 860-685-2887 .... 95 E
ptully@wesleyan.edu

TULLY, Richard, B ... 317-921-4949 .... 175 I
dtully@ivytech.edu

TULLY-DARTEZ, Stephanie 870-862-8131 .... 23 G
stully-dartez@southark.edu

TUMA, Alicia ... 305-220-4120 .... 115 F
phadir@ptcmatt.com

TUMBLIN, Tom ... 859-858-2301 .... 198 D

TUMELTY, Susanne, M ... 718-960-1190 .... 327 C
susanne.tumelty@lehman.cuny.edu

TUMEO, Mark, A ... 904-620-1350 .... 120 D
m.tumeo@unf.edu

TUMER, Lisa, L ... 540-568-7820 .... 520 H
tumerll@jmu.edu

TUMEY, Terrance, J ... 530-752-4557 .... 73 I
tjtumey@ucdavis.edu

TUMMINO, Pauline ... 718-990-6106 .... 348 G
tumminop@stjohns.edu

TUMMOLO, Paul ... 212-353-4100 .... 331 A
pault@cooper.edu

TUNCAP, Michael ... 253-833-9111 .... 534 H
mtuncap@greenriver.edu

TUNCAY, Atilla 219-980-6745 174 B
atuncay@iun.edu
TUNE, Anders, S 937-327-7411 406 B
atune@wittenberg.edu
TUNE, Kathie 434-791-7106 516 G
ktune@averett.edu
TUNEBURG, Chris 216-361-2743 387 B
ctuneberg@chancelloru.edu
TUNG, Lisa 617-879-7335 238 B
ltung@massart.edu
TUNG, Yuming 315-470-4904 355 A
ytung@esf.edu
TUNGSETH, Margaret 641-628-5276 183 D
tungsethm@central.edu
TUNSIL, Debberin 386-752-1822 108 G
debbie.tunsil@fgc.edu
TUNSTALL, Denise, S 804-523-5029 527 A
dtunstall@reynolds.edu
TUNSTALL, Ken 432-335-6413 492 A
ktunstall@odessa.edu
TUNSTALL, Vincent 201-692-2823 310 A
vincent39_tunstall@fdu.edu
TUNSTILL, Hilda 931-393-1573 475 D
htunstill@mscc.edu
TUNSTILL, Jerry 931-393-1688 475 D
jtunstill@mscc.edu
TUNUGUNTLA, Rama 318-274-3234 215 E
tunuguntla@gram.edu
TUOMEY, Lianne, M 802-656-2027 514 H
lianne.tuomey@uvm.edu
TUPALA, Kay 920-498-5482 555 C
kay.tupala@nwtc.edu
TURAK, Ronald, A 716-338-1065 337 E
ronturak@mail.sunyjcc.edu
TURANO, Rosemary 617-964-1100 230 B
rturano@ants.edu
TURANSKY, June, S 302-857-1126 96 G
june.turansky@dtcc.edu
TURANSKY, June, S 302-739-3737 96 D
TURBEVILLE, Donna 910-642-7141 374 B
dturbeville@sccnc.edu
TURBEVILLE, John 315-470-6660 355 A
jturbev@esf.edu
TURBIDE, Gerard 607-274-3124 336 G
gturbide@ithaca.edu
TURBYFILL, Laurel 256-331-5368 6 B
lturbyfill@nwscc.edu
TURCIOS, Rita 212-312-4396 332 A
rturcios@devry.edu
TURCO, John, H 603-650-1423 304 J
john.h.turco@dartmouth.edu
TURCOTT, Scott 617-745-3000 234 A
scott.turcott@enc.edu
TURCOTTE, Jim 601-925-3809 275 C
turcotte@mc.edu
TURCOTTE, Lisa 361-593-2219 498 D
lisa.turcotte@tamuk.edu
TURCOTTE, Louis, H 812-877-8192 179 B
louis.turcotte@rose-hulman.edu
TURDICI, James 252-335-0821 369 G
jturdici@albemarle.edu
TUREC, Lori 800-955-2527 282 D
lturec@grantham.edu
TUREK, John, G 714-879-3901 50 I
jgturek@hiu.edu
TUREK, Joseph 434-544-8417 521 B
turek@lynchburg.edu
TURELL, Susan, C 814-393-2223 442 B
sturell@clarion.edu
TUREN, Christopher 310-965-0888 79 E
TURGEON, Paul 714-556-3610 77 B
paul.turgeon@vanguard.edu
TURGEON, Pennie 508-421-3813 233 B
pturgeon@clarku.edu
TURICO, Michael 602-538-9396 11 C
TURK, David, F 845-675-4422 344 G
david.turk@nyack.edu
TURKENKOPF, Iris 845-569-3203 342 A
iris.turkenkopf@msmc.edu
TURKETT, Tammy 803-754-4100 457 D
TURKKAN, Jaylan 415-405-3995 37 B
jturkkan@sfsu.edu
TURKOWSKI, Addie 320-308-2151 269 A
aturkowski@stcloudstate.edu
TURKS, Stacie 209-946-2225 76 A
sturks@pacific.edu
TURLETES, Christopher 907-786-1110 10 H
ancmt2@uaa.alaska.edu
TURLEY, Alicestyne 859-985-3783 199 A
turlleya@berea.edu
TURLEY, Cricket 620-276-9574 193 C
cricket.turley@gcccks.edu
TURLEY, Jason, J 740-376-4600 395 G
jason.turley@marietta.edu
TURLEY, Richard, T 636-481-3120 283 D
rturley@jeffco.edu
TURLEY-AMES, Kandi 208-282-3204 143 H
turlkand@isu.edu
TURLINGTON, Lisa 910-592-8081 373 G
lturlington@sampsoncc.edu
TURMAN, Paul 605-773-3455 465 F
paul.turman@sdbor.edu
TURMON, Janie 864-225-7653 458 C
janieturmon@forrestcollege.edu
TURNAGE, Kissie 559-251-4215 32 A
TURNAU, Michelle 651-255-6117 271 D
mturnau@unitedseminary.edu
TURNBO, Doreen, B 302-295-1192 97 C
doreen.b.turnbo@wilmu.edu
TURNBOUGH, Dale 205-934-9518 8 F
dalet@uab.edu
TURNBULL, Sara 641-423-2530 186 J
sturnbull@kaplan.edu
TURNER, A. Kay 870-575-8735 25 B
turnera@uapb.edu
TURNER, Adiran 318-397-6152 210 J
aturner@ltc.edu
TURNER, Andrea 612-330-1691 261 B
turner2@augsburg.edu
TURNER, Angela 614-456-4600 393 B
aturner@kaplan.edu
TURNER, B, P 334-387-3877 1 D
businessoffice@amridgeuniversity.edu
TURNER, Barbara 856-415-2297 310 D
bturner@gccnj.edu
TURNER, Barbara, J 870-759-4112 26 B
bturner@wbcoll.edu
TURNER, Barry 912-688-6958 135 D
bturner@ogeecheetech.edu
TURNER, Beth 315-781-3315 335 F
turner@hws.edu
TURNER, Brad 315-279-5604 337 K
bturner@mail.keuka.edu
TURNER, Bradley, G 800-342-7342 110 G
brad.turner@golfacademy.edu
TURNER, Brenda 334-386-7501 3 G
bturner@faulkner.edu
TURNER, Brent 407-646-2624 116 D
bturner@rollins.edu
TURNER, Carolyn 870-946-3506 25 D
TURNER, Carolyn 513-861-6400 402 I
carolyn.turner@myunion.edu
TURNER, Catherine, P 540-224-4644 520 I
cpturner@jchs.edu
TURNER, Christine 503-699-3381 416 J
cturner@marylhurst.edu
TURNER, Craig 270-852-3104 204 A
cturner@kwc.edu
TURNER, Curtis 719-336-1519 86 B
curtis.turner@lamarcc.edu
TURNER, Darron 817-257-5566 499 C
d.turner@tcu.edu
TURNER, Debra 304-384-5338 543 G
turner@concord.edu
TURNER, Donna 828-398-7160 368 B
dturner@abtech.edu
TURNER, Donna, A 252-246-1240 375 D
daturner@wilsoncc.edu
TURNER, Eddie, C 806-291-3615 508 E
turnere@wbu.edu
TURNER, Emily 212-312-4414 332 A
eturner@devry.edu
TURNER, Eric, A 870-759-4110 26 B
eturner@wbcoll.edu
TURNER, Fran 205-391-2663 6 I
ftruner@sheltonstate.edu
TURNER, Franklin, R 714-539-6561 71 H
TURNER, Gary 615-844-5276 469 A
gturner@fwbbc.edu
TURNER, J. Leigh 979-845-7725 497 E
jl-turner@tamu.edu
TURNER, James 607-844-8222 357 I
turnerj@tc3.edu
TURNER, James, C 434-924-2670 525 F
jct4w@virginia.edu
TURNER, Jana, D 901-572-2455 467 C
jana.turner@bchs.edu
TURNER, Janet 503-943-7311 420 G
turnerj@up.edu
TURNER, Jere 603-206-8165 304 D
jturner@ccsnh.edu
TURNER, Jim 419-755-4735 397 C
jturner@ncstatecollege.edu
TURNER, Joe 239-513-1122 111 A
jturner@hodges.edu
TURNER, John, H 541-278-5950 414 G
jturner@bluecc.edu
TURNER, John, T 910-695-3704 373 H
turnerj@sandhills.edu
TURNER, Joseph 704-378-1238 366 A
jturner@jcsu.edu
TURNER, Joseph, T 252-473-5936 369 G
joseph_turner@albemarle.edu
TURNER, June 760-921-5558 61 C
june.turner@paloverde.edu
TURNER, Kara 443-885-3350 224 E
kara.turner@morgan.edu
TURNER, Larry 704-355-7577 363 D
larry.turner@carolinashealthcare.org
TURNER, Lathan, E 252-328-6495 377 E
turnerla@ecu.edu
TURNER, Lauren 978-934-1804 237 B
lauren_turner@uml.edu
TURNER, Laurie, L 253-535-7361 536 E
turnerll@plu.edu
TURNER, Leslie 561-803-2473 114 C
leslie_turner@pba.edu
TURNER, Linda, E 617-541-5301 241 A
leturners@rcc.mass.edu
TURNER, Lois "Casey" 215-895-6711 427 H
lat59@drexel.edu
TURNER, Lori 507-457-1709 271 B
lturner@smumn.edu
TURNER, Louise 406-586-3585 294 G
louise.turner@montanabiblecollege.edu
TURNER, Margaret, W 410-951-3700 228 B
mturner@coppin.edu
TURNER, Marietta 217-351-2505 161 C
mturner@parkland.edu
TURNER, Mary 305-809-3544 108 I
mary.turner@fkcc.edu
TURNER, Mary 916-558-2226 56 D
turnerm@scc.losrios.edu
TURNER, Matt 304-696-6713 544 B
turner6@marshall.edu
TURNER, Michael 858-279-4500 52 H
mturner@kaplan.edu
TURNER, Michael 661-722-6300 28 K
sturner29@avc.edu
TURNER, Michael 218-723-6387 262 G
mturner@css.edu
TURNER, Michael, C 334-387-3877 1 D
mcturner@amridgeuniversity.edu
TURNER, Mitzi 270-247-8521 204 G
mturner@midcontinent.edu
TURNER, Nancy, L 608-342-1789 552 B
turnern@uwplatt.edu
TURNER, Pat, A 530-752-6068 73 I
paturner@ucdavis.edu
TURNER, Patrick 318-397-6166 210 J
patrick.turner@myneltc.edu
TURNER, Paul 859-246-6717 201 H
paul.turner@kctcs.edu
TURNER, Paul, S 561-237-7245 113 D
pturner@lynn.edu
TURNER, Peter 315-268-6544 329 B
pturner@clarkson.edu
TURNER, R. Gerald 214-768-3300 495 A
mjj@smu.edu
TURNER, Rachel 305-626-3605 109 A
rachel.turner@fmuniv.edu
TURNER, Ralph 850-599-3430 118 L
ralph.turner@famu.edu
TURNER, Rebecca 415-955-2139 27 F
rturner@alliant.edu
TURNER, Rebecca, B 812-941-2243 175 A
rebeturn@ius.edu
TURNER, Rebecca, E 256-782-5485 4 L
bturner@jsu.edu
TURNER, Rebecca, O 256-782-5540 4 L
rturner@jsu.edu
TURNER, Richard 417-447-8202 287 D
turnerr@otc.edu
TURNER, Robert 910-296-2416 371 E
rturner@jamessprunt.edu
TURNER, Ron 740-389-6786 399 D
turner.27@osu.edu
TURNER, Sally, J 716-673-3424 352 A
sally.turner@fredonia.edu
TURNER, Sandra 212-242-5499 358 C
sandra.turner@tsca.edu
TURNER, Sarah 319-296-4432 185 F
sarah.turner@hawkeyecollege.edu
TURNER, Sarah 304-384-5348 543 G
slturner@concord.edu
TURNER, Scott 208-282-3470 143 H
turnscot@isu.edu
TURNER, Sharon, P 859-323-5786 207 D
spturn2@uky.edu
TURNER, Shawna, C 270-745-6463 208 A
shawna.turner@wku.edu
TURNER, Stephen, R 219-785-5401 179 A
sturner@pnc.edu
TURNER, Steve 918-456-5511 409 A
turner@nsuok.edu
TURNER, Sue, Z 912-443-5485 136 H
sturner@savannahtech.edu
TURNER, Sylvia, C 714-564-5600 63 F
turner_sylvia@sac.edu
TURNER, Tara 410-951-3812 228 B
tturner@coppin.edu
TURNER, Teresa 804-745-2444 517 C
tlturner@bryantstratton.edu
TURNER, Terrance, A 903-233-4441 490 A
terryturner@letu.edu
TURNER, Thomas, H 540-375-2311 523 G
turner@roanoke.edu
TURNER, Tony 478-757-3432 127 A
tturner@centralgatech.edu
TURNER, Vickie 662-243-1940 274 B
vturner@eastms.edu
TURNER, Walter 404-627-2681 126 D
walter.turner@beulah.org
TURNER, Wilson 812-298-2320 177 D
wturner15@ivytech.edu
TURNER, Zoa Ann 972-524-3341 495 H
TURNER-MURRAY,
Sonya, M 740-587-6647 389 I
turner@denison.edu
TURNER-SAMPLE,
Margaret 480-517-4556 16 B
margaret.turner-sample@riosalado.edu
TURNER-WATTS, Sheryl 864-503-5490 463 B
sturner-watts@uscupstate.edu
TURNEY, Keith 303-273-3333 83 B
keith.turney@is.mines.edu
TURNIS, Jane 719-389-6138 82 D
jturnis@coloradocollege.edu
TURNOCK, Madeline 503-493-8550 415 E
mturnock@cu-portland.edu
TURNQUIST, David, C 303-724-1100 88 J
david.turnquist@ucdenver.edu
TURNQUIST, James 906-487-2313 255 B
jaturnqu@mtu.edu
TURNQUIST, Sandra 906-487-7240 251 A
sandra.turnquist@finlandia.edu
TUROS, Jessica 419-372-2356 385 E
jmturos@bgsu.edu
TURPEN, James 402-559-4388 300 H
jterpen@unmc.edu
TURPIN, Barbara 732-932-3625 314 C
turpin@envsci.rutgers.edu
TURPIN, Craig 502-213-2110 202 F
craig.turpin@kctcs.edu
TURPIN, Jennifer, E 415-422-6136 76 E
turpinj@usfca.edu
TURPIN, John, C 336-841-9000 365 C
jturpin@highpoint.edu
TURRENTINE, Cathryn 603-358-2117 306 G
cturrentine@keene.edu
TURTELTAUB, Rhea 310-794-5567 74 C
rheat@support.ucla.edu
TURZAI, Eric, C 717-361-1157 428 F
turzaiec@etown.edu
TURZANSKI, Edward, A 215-951-1391 432 I
turzansk@lasalle.edu
TUSACK, Donna 619-594-7500 37 A
donna.tusack@sdsu.edu
TUSCHAK, Mark 830-792-7215 494 E
mctuschak@schreiner.edu
TUSKI, Donald 207-775-5098 218 E
dtuski@meca.edu
TUTEN, Jane 803-641-3460 462 B
janet@usca.edu
TUTHILL, George, F 603-535-2286 307 A
gftuthilli@plymouth.edu
TUTHILL, John 775-673-7090 302 H
jtuthill@tmcc.edu
TUTHILL-RANGER, Nina 503-961-6200 418 A
ntuthill@pioneerpacific.edu
TUTSOCK, Robert, J 989-964-4082 257 G
tutsock@svsu.edu
TUTT, Betty, R 573-592-4354 293 D
btutt@williamwoods.edu
TUTT, Larry 270-831-9783 202 D
larry.tutt@kctcs.edu
TUTTER, Catherine 617-369-3602 244 E
ctutter@smfa.edu
TUTTLE, David, M 210-999-8843 502 E
dtuttle@trinity.edu
TUTTLE, Gail 315-792-3016 359 E
gtuttle@utica.edu
TUTTLE, Gail, C 336-841-9120 365 C
gtuttle@highpoint.edu
TUTTLE, Heather 517-327-6253 345 H
htuttle@paulsmiths.edu
TUTTLE, Isaac 573-442-2211 290 C
ituttle@stephens.edu
TUTTLE, James 253-589-5533 532 G
jim.tuttle@cptc.edu
TUTTLE, Katherine 570-465-2344 433 A
tuttlek@lackawanna.edu
TUTTLE, Nick 580-349-1353 410 B
nick.tuttle@opsu.edu
TUTTLE, Ronald 914-968-6200 349 D
ronald.tuttle@archny.org
TUTTLE, Stephen 212-217-4030 333 F
TUXHORN, Rick 620-242-0468 195 C
tuxhornr@mcpherson.edu
TUYTSCHAEVERS, Mary 575-492-2873 319 B
mtuytschaevers@nmjc.edu
TVARKUNAS, Michael 662-476-5059 274 B
mtvar@eastms.edu
TVRDY, Peggy 402-826-8260 297 G
peggy.tvrdy@doane.edu
TWADDELL, Gerald, E 859-344-3307 206 I
gerald.twaddell@thomasmore.edu
TWEED, Emily, J 952-888-4777 270 C
etweed@nwhealth.edu
TWEED, James 617-243-2225 236 A
jtweed@lasell.edu
TWEEDELL, Cynthia 270-247-8521 204 G
ctweedell@midcontinent.edu
TWEEDIE, Frank 401-598-2503 453 E
ftweedie@jwu.edu
TWENTER, Marcia 573-592-5226 293 B
marcia.twenter@westminster-mo.edu
TWIGGS, Sarah 706-764-3523 131 B
stwiggs@gntc.edu
TWILL, Sarah 937-775-3162 406 C
sarah.twill@wright.edu
TWILLEY, Robert 337-482-6541 216 D
rtwilley@louisiana.edu
TWILLEY, Shirley 918-463-6358 407 H
shirley.twilley@connorsstate.edu
TWISS, Camilie 603-594-2567 305 H

TWIST, Tony .... 317-299-0333.... 180 C
TWITTY, Brian .... 951-487-3103...... 58 B
btwitty@msjc.edu
TWO BULLS, Wayne .... 406-768-6312.... 294 D
wtwobulls@fpcc.edu
TWOHEY, Lisa .... 502-410-6200.... 200 L
ltwohey@galencollege.edu
TWOHIG, James .... 936-639-1301.... 480 D
jtwohig@angelina.edu
TWYMAN, Edward .... 262-595-2039.... 552 A
twyman@uwp.edu
TYBURSKI, Marcelle .... 315-228-7431.... 329 G
mtyburski@colgate.edu
TYBURSKI, Robert, L .... 315-228-7445.... 329 G
rtyburski@colgate.edu
TYDINGS, Flora, W .... 706-355-5110.... 125 C
ftydings@athenstech.edu
TYE, Ann .... 559-451-0334...... 19 A
ann.tye@phoenix.edu
TYKOCINSKI, Mark, L .... 215-955-1628.... 448 C
mark.tykocinski@jefferson.edu
TYKSINSKI, Deborah .... 315-792-7151.... 356 B
deborah.tyksinski@sunyit.edu
TYKWINSKI, Joseph .... 701-845-7332.... 382 C
joe.tykwinski@vcsu.edu
TYLER, Alan .... 360-438-4495.... 537 B
atyler@stmartin.edu
TYLER, Arthur, Q .... 713-718-8464.... 487 I
art.tyler@hccs.edu
TYLER, Carol .... 304-829-7567.... 540 H
ctyler@bethanywv.edu
TYLER, Greg .... 251-626-3303........ 8 C
gtyler@ussa.edu
TYLER, Gwendolyn, J .... 609-896-5058.... 313 F
tyler@rider.edu
TYLER, Harold .... 310-660-3504...... 45 E
htyler@elcamino.edu
TYLER, Jaimee .... 517-578-7178.... 244 D
jtyler@sbboston.com
TYLER, Jeanie .... 619-388-3924...... 65 F
jtyler@sdccd.edu
TYLER, Julie .... 901-320-9700.... 478 C
juliet@victory.edu
TYLER, Karlene, M .... 620-242-0441.... 195 C
tylerk@mcpherson.edu
TYLER, Ken, D .... 540-654-1876.... 525 D
ktyler2@umw.edu
TYLER, Kim .... 312-850-7013.... 147 F
TYLER, Melvin, C .... 816-235-1141.... 291 C
tylerm@umkc.edu
TYLER, Nathan .... 256-306-2817........ 2 D
ntyler@calhoun.edu
TYLER, Ralph .... 203-332-5081...... 91 E
rtyler@hcc.commnet.edu
TYLER, Rico .... 773-325-4680.... 149 A
rtyler@depaul.edu
TYLER, Victoria .... 914-455-3515.... 340 F
vtyler@mercy.edu
TYLER, Wanda .... 203-932-7427...... 95 C
wtyler@newhaven.edu
TYMANN, Daniel .... 978-867-4260.... 235 A
dan.tymann@gordon.edu
TYMAS-JONES, Raymond .. 801-581-3887.... 511 C
r.tymasjones@finearts.utah.edu
TYMKOW, Tony, A .... 708-534-4108.... 151 E
ttymkow@govst.edu
TYMOCZKO, Michelle .... 303-477-7240...... 85 B
michellet@heritage-education.com
TYMUS, Peter .... 516-299-3370.... 338 E
peter.tymus@liu.edu
TYNDALL, Brad .... 970-945-8691...... 82 G
TYNER, Dennis, J .... 785-242-5200.... 195 I
dennis.tyner@ottawa.edu
TYNER, JR., Gary .... 214-638-0484.... 489 H
tynerjr1@yahoo.com
TYNER, Kathy .... 214-638-0484.... 489 H
ktyner@kdstudio.com
TYNER, Kathy .... 619-482-6337...... 71 D
ktyner@swccd.edu
TYNER, Lee .... 662-915-7792.... 277 D
ltyner@olemiss.edu
TYNES, Craig .... 601-403-1155.... 276 E
ctynes@prcc.edu
TYNES, James .... 212-220-1377.... 326 D
jtynes@bmcc.cuny.edu
TYNES, Sheryl, R .... 210-999-8201.... 502 E
stynes@trinity.edu
TYNON, Kathy .... 402-872-2365.... 299 F
ktynon@peru.edu
TYNSKY, Troy .... 507-284-3293.... 262 E
tynsky.troy@mayo.edu
TYO, Keith, D .... 518-564-3930.... 354 B
tyokd@plattsburgh.edu
TYPOLT, Jeanie .... 406-586-3585.... 294 G
jeanie.typolt@montanabiblecollege.edu
TYPOLT, Ty .... 406-586-3585.... 294 G
typoltj@hotmail.com
TYRE, Yulanda .... 334-244-3553........ 1 G
ytyre@aum.edu
TYREE, Jonathan .... 434-947-8112.... 523 B
jtyree@randolphcollege.edu
TYRELL, Steve, J .... 518-891-2915.... 344 E
president@nccc.edu
TYRRELL, Elizabeth .... 408-270-6453...... 67 C
elizabeth.tyrrell@evc.edu
TYRRELL, Wil .... 914-323-7178.... 339 J
wil.tyrrell@mville.edu
TYSON, James, B .... 804-524-5569.... 529 H
jtyson@vsu.edu
TYSON, James, E .... 512-505-3149.... 488 D
jetyson@htu.edu
TYSON, Linda .... 252-399-6330.... 362 E
ltyson@barton.edu
TYSON, Thomas, N .... 410-334-2913.... 229 E
ttyson@worwic.edu
TYSON, William, R .... 919-893-9101.... 369 C
btyson@cccc.edu
TYSZLER, Ira .... 212-463-0400.... 358 B
tysz@touro.edu
TYUS, Bing .... 863-297-1004.... 115 C
btyus@polk.edu
TZENG, Julia .... 415-371-0002...... 60 A
TZENG, Walker .... 415-371-0002...... 60 A

U

UBAGO, Maria .... 323-343-2586...... 35 D
mubago@cslanet.calstatela.edu
UBARRI-DE LEÓN, Lydia .. 787-993-8858.... 567 B
lydia.ubarri@upr.edu
UBELL, Robert, N .... 718-260-3407.... 346 C
rubell@poly.edu
UCCI, Anthony .... 508-678-2811.... 239 B
anthony.ucci@bristolcc.edu
UCCI, Martha .... 508-565-1033.... 245 A
mucci@stonehill.edu
UCHIN, Robert, A .... 954-262-7311.... 114 B
ruchin@nsu.nova.edu
UDA, Jon .... 208-426-1304.... 142 I
jonuda@boisestate.edu
UDALL, David .... 928-428-8295...... 14 B
david.udall@eac.edu
UDD, Kris, J .... 402-449-2811.... 297 H
registrar@graceu.edu
UDDIN, Rita .... 718-260-5610.... 328 D
ruddin@citytech.cuny.edu
UDE, Georgia .... 931-363-9863.... 471 A
gude@martinmethodist.edu
UDE, Wayne .... 360-331-0307.... 536 A
UDEH, Igwe, E .... 504-286-5331.... 214 J
iudeh@suno.edu
UDELHOFEN, Angela, M ... 608-342-1125.... 552 B
rulea@uwplatt.edu
UDEN, Michael .... 262-243-5700.... 547 C
michael.uden@cuw.edu
UDEOGALANYA, Anthony . 718-270-6213.... 328 C
anthonyu@mec.cuny.edu
UDIS-KESSLER, Amanda ... 719-227-8177...... 82 D
audiskessler@coloradocollege.edu
UDKOW, David .... 516-686-7902.... 343 D
dudkow@nyit.edu
UDOH, Emmanuel .... 502-456-6504.... 206 H
eudoh@sullivan.edu
UDOM, Udoh .... 615-871-2260...... 99 G
UDOVIC, Edward, R .... 312-362-8042.... 149 A
eudovic@depaul.edu
UDOVIC, CM, Edward, R ... 312-362-8042.... 149 A
eudovic@depaul.edu
UDPA, Satish, S .... 517-355-5113.... 255 A
udpa@msu.edu
UECKER, Grant .... 605-995-7138.... 464 F
grant.uecker@mitchelltech.edu
UECKER, Milton, V .... 803-754-4100.... 457 D
UEDA, Rikklyn, S .... 619-239-0391...... 37 F
rueda@cwsl.edu
UEHARA, Edwina .... 206-685-2480.... 539 A
eddi@uw.edu
UEKI, Omdasu, T .... 680-488-2471.... 560 C
oueki@palau.edu
UERLING, Laura, J .... 508-565-1378.... 245 A
luerling@stonehill.edu
UFERT FAIRLESS,
Nancy, J .... 618-650-3187.... 165 C
nufert@siue.edu
UFFORD, Brian, K .... 207-778-7334.... 220 C
brian.ufford@maine.edu
UFOMATA, Titilayo .... 315-781-3304.... 335 F
ufomata@hws.edu
UGALDE, Aileen, M .... 305-284-2700.... 122 I
augalde@miami.edu
UGLIANO, Don .... 352-854-2322.... 103 K
uglianod@cf.edu
UGLUM, Abby .... 540-831-6667.... 523 A
aeeckhart@radford.edu
UGORJI, Lauren, D .... 609-258-5732.... 312 G
lauren@princeton.edu
UGRAS, Joseph, Y .... 215-951-5124.... 432 I
ugras@lasalle.edu
UHAL, Len .... 563-876-3353.... 184 B
svdalum@aol.com
UHAZY, Les .... 661-722-6300...... 28 K
luhazy@avc.edu
UHER, Bill .... 505-277-5598.... 321 C
wuher@salud.unm.edu
UHLIG, Ronald .... 858-642-8439...... 58 I
ruhlig@nu.edu
UHLINGER, Eleanor, S ...... 831-656-2342.... 558 A
euhlinger@nps.edu
UHLIR, James .... 715-232-2188.... 552 E
uhlirj@uwstout.edu
UJLAKI, Stephen, G .... 310-338-5800...... 56 E
stephen.ujlaki@lmu.edu
UKPOLO, Victor .... 504-286-5311.... 214 J
vukpolo@suno.edu
ULASZEK, David .... 312-567-3366.... 153 C
dulaszek@iit.edu
ULATE, David .... 650-738-7069...... 67 H
ulated@smccd.edu
ULBRICH, Casandra .... 586-445-7244.... 254 C
ulbrichc@macomb.edu
ULBRICHT, Walt .... 937-769-1854.... 384 B
wulbricht@antioch.edu
ULBRIGHT, Heather .... 503-375-7035.... 415 F
hulbright@corban.edu
ULIBARRI, Debbie .... 719-846-5533...... 88 F
debbie.ulibarri@trinidadstate.edu
ULIBARRI, Katherine .... 505-224-4413.... 317 K
kulibarri8@cnm.edu
ULIBARRI, Michael .... 831-647-4604...... 57 F
michael.ulibarri@miis.edu
ULLMAN, Christopher, C ... 847-259-1840.... 147 A
cullman@christianlifecollege.edu
ULLMAN, David, F .... 973-596-2915.... 312 C
david.ullman@njit.edu
ULLMAN, Julia .... 414-382-6053.... 546 B
julie.ullman@alverno.edu
ULLMANN, Brian .... 301-314-6650.... 227 B
ullmann@umd.edu
ULLOA, Alicia .... 361-354-2245.... 483 B
ulloaa@coastalbend.edu
ULLOA-HEATH, Julie .... 671-735-2290.... 559 G
julieuh@uguam.uog.edu
ULLOM, Craig, E .... 740-368-3135.... 400 G
ceullom@owu.edu
ULLRICH, Johannes .... 301-654-7267.... 226 C
ULLRICK, Sue .... 608-757-7716.... 553 G
sullrick@blackhawk.edu
ULMAN, Brenda .... 301-552-1400.... 229 C
bulman@bible.edu
ULMEN, Dan .... 406-265-3755.... 295 E
dulman@msun.edu
ULMER, Darlene .... 312-980-4838.... 154 B
dulmer@iadtchicago.edu
ULMER, Deborah .... 804-622-8700.... 527 B
dulmer@jtcc.edu
ULMER, Laverne .... 601-477-4238.... 274 H
laverne.ulmer@jcjc.edu
ULMER, Laverne .... 601-477-4022.... 274 H
laverne.ulmer@jcjc.edu
ULMSCHNEIDER, John, E . 804-828-1105.... 526 B
jeulmsch@vcu.edu
ULRICH, Dennis .... 513-569-1414.... 387 G
dennis.ulrich@cincinnatistate.edu
ULRICH, Gail, L .... 814-641-3194.... 432 A
ulrichg@juniata.edu
ULRICH, James .... 312-235-3523.... 164 F
j.ulrich@shimer.edu
ULRICH, Jana .... 704-991-0328.... 374 D
ulrich7442@stanly.edu
ULRICH, Karl .... 406-683-7115.... 294 J
k_ulrich@umwestern.edu
ULRICH, Paul .... 262-551-2112.... 546 I
pulrich@carthage.edu
ULRICH, Rae .... 312-499-4219.... 164 C
rulrich@saic.edu
ULRICH, Sigrid .... 718-270-1995.... 352 D
sigrid.ulrich@downstate.edu
ULRICH, Suzan .... 859-253-3637.... 200 K
suzan.ulrich@frontier.edu
ULRICH, Tina, J .... 231-995-1063.... 256 D
tulrich@nmc.edu
ULRICH, Trey, P .... 215-951-1671.... 432 I
ulrich@lasalle.edu
ULRICHSON, Borre .... 510-885-2920...... 34 E
borre.ulrichson@csueastbay.edu
ULSETH, Julie, A .... 810-762-9844.... 253 C
julseth@kettering.edu
ULSHAFER, Kevin, L .... 478-757-5125.... 139 E
kulshafer@wesleyancollege.edu
ULZ, Jennifer, A .... 252-222-6190.... 369 A
jau@carteret.edu
ULZ, Mary Ann .... 847-566-6401.... 167 F
mulz@usml.edu
UMANSKY, Lauri .... 870-972-3973...... 20 D
lumansky@astate.edu
UMBAUGH, Rob .... 970-339-6237...... 81 A
rob.umbaugh@aims.edu
UMBERGER, Stanley, F ...... 540-375-2293.... 523 G
umberger@roanoke.edu
UMBLE, Diane .... 717-872-3024.... 443 D
diane.umble@millersville.edu
UMEHIRA, Ron .... 808-455-0321.... 142 D
umehira@hawaii.edu
UMFRESS, Jason .... 843-383-8036.... 457 A
jumfress@coker.edu
UMHOEFER, Gary, A .... 920-403-3210.... 550 F
gary.umhoefer@snc.edu
UMMER, Christopher, T ..... 802-626-6477.... 515 G
christopher.ummer@lyndonstate.edu
UMSTATTD, Rustin .... 816-414-3700.... 285 H
rumstattd@mbts.edu
UMSTOT, David .... 619-388-6546...... 65 E
dumstot@sdccd.edu
UNBEHAGEN, Leonard .... 504-278-6438.... 211 E
lunbehagen@nunez.edu
UNDEM, Obert .... 406-657-1142.... 296 C
undemo@rocky.edu
UNDERBAKKE, Rick .... 509-682-6705.... 539 E
runderbakke@wvc.edu
UNDERCOFFER, Anita .... 909-652-6032...... 39 E
anita.undercoffer@chaffey.edu
UNDERWOOD, Alex .... 312-850-7125.... 147 F
aunderwood3@ccc.edu
UNDERWOOD, Allen .... 419-893-1986.... 391 F
aunderwo@heidelberg.edu
UNDERWOOD, Anita .... 845-675-4476.... 344 G
anita.underwood@nyack.edu
UNDERWOOD, Ann .... 806-651-2121.... 499 A
aunderwood@wtamu.edu
UNDERWOOD, Anthony .... 304-424-8209.... 545 C
anthony.underwood@mail.wvu.edu
UNDERWOOD, Chloris .... 954-486-7728.... 122 H
UNDERWOOD, Craig .... 610-861-1500.... 437 A
cunderwood@moravian.edu
UNDERWOOD, David .... 479-964-0540...... 20 G
dunderwood@atu.edu
UNDERWOOD, Dawn .... 812-237-3088.... 173 B
dawn.underwood@indstate.edu
UNDERWOOD, Elizabeth ... 479-788-7026...... 24 D
elizabeth.underwood@uafs.edu
UNDERWOOD, Glenda .... 617-587-5662.... 242 H
underwoodg@neco.edu
UNDERWOOD, James, C .. 618-545-3010.... 155 B
junderwood@kaskaskia.edu
UNDERWOOD, Julie, K ...... 608-262-1763.... 550 J
junderwood@wisc.edu
UNDERWOOD, Kathy, A .... 702-895-0283.... 302 I
kathyunderwood@unlv.edu
UNDERWOOD, Kelly, R ..... 540-831-5752.... 523 A
kunderwood@radford.edu
UNDERWOOD, Ken .... 865-573-4517.... 469 L
kunderwood@johnsonu.edu
UNDERWOOD, Richard ..... 615-248-1213.... 476 G
runderwood@trevecca.edu
UNDERWOOD, Robert, A .. 671-735-2990.... 559 G
raunderwood@uguam.uog.edu
UNDERWOOD, Von, E ...... 580-581-2491.... 407 D
vonu@cameron.edu
UNDERWOOD, William, D 478-301-2500.... 134 A
underwood_wd@mercer.edu
UNEBASAMI, Michael, T ... 808-956-6280.... 141 I
mune@hawaii.edu
UNELL, Murry .... 303-797-5901...... 81 D
murry.unell@arapahoe.edu
UNFERTH, Vickie, L .... 608-796-3841.... 553 C
vlunferth@viterbo.edu
UNGAR, Jacob .... 845-362-3053.... 323 F
UNGAR, Samuel, D .... 718-384-5460.... 361 I
UNGAR, Sanford, J .... 410-337-6040.... 222 I
sungar@goucher.edu
UNGAR, Shaya .... 732-370-3360.... 317 G
UNGARO, John .... 843-574-6891.... 461 G
john.ungaro@tridenttech.edu
UNGER, Karen .... 845-758-7490.... 323 D
kunger@bard.edu
UNGER, Maggie .... 952-446-4323.... 263 C
ungerm@crown.edu
UNGER, Myrna .... 701-662-1542.... 382 F
myrna.unger@lrsc.edu
UNGER, Robert, A .... 619-482-6330...... 71 D
runger@swccd.edu
UNGER, Sue .... 630-889-6565.... 159 F
sunger@nuhs.edu
UNIS, Corry, D .... 607-871-2115.... 322 E
unis@alfred.edu
UNKE, James, M .... 507-354-8221.... 264 K
unkejm@mlc-wels.edu
UNKLE, David, W .... 973-972-9659.... 316 H
unkleda@umdnj.edu
UNNIKRISHNAN, Raman .. 657-278-3362...... 35 B
runnikrishnan@fullerton.edu
UNRUH, David .... 310-825-1083...... 74 C
dunruh@summer.ucla.edu
UNRUH, David .... 215-926-2500.... 447 H
david.unruh@temple.edu
UNRUH, Nancy .... 620-276-9571.... 193 C
nancy.unruh@gcccks.edu
UNSWORTH, John .... 781-736-4540.... 232 F
unsworth@brandeis.edu
UNTERMAN, Ira .... 657-278-7295...... 35 B
iunterman@fullerton.edu
UNTERREINER, Coleen ...... 406-756-3962.... 294 C
cunterre@fvcc.edu
UNVER, Amira .... 973-290-4233.... 308 G
aunver@cse.edu
UPCHURCH, Jim .... 815-928-5429.... 161 A
jupchurch@olivet.edu
UPCHURCH, Rhodene .... 765-285-1532.... 169 G
rupchurch@bsu.edu
UPCHURCH, Sharon, K ..... 573-288-6478.... 280 I
supchurch@culver.edu
UPHAM, Daren .... 619-563-7201...... 58 I
dupham@nu.edu

VAN BAAREN, Valerie, L .. 973-655-5225 .... 311 F vanbaarenv@mail.montclair.edu
VAN BERGEN, Mildred ..... 516-876-4076 .... 355 G mildred.vanbergen@esc.edu
VAN BERKOM, Debbie ...... 701-224-5431 .... 382 D debbie.vanberkom@bismarckstate.edu
VAN BLARCOM, Ronald .... 949-214-3135 ...... 43 C ron.vanblarcom@cui.edu
VAN BROEKHOVEN, Rollin .... 704-243-0737 .... 472 G rvanbroekhoven@futurelead.org
VAN BRUNT, Brian .... 270-745-2701 .... 208 A brian.vanbrunt@wku.edu
VAN BRUNT, Troy, G .... 956-721-5326 .... 489 J troyvb@laredo.edu
VAN BUREN, David, P ...... 608-342-1262 .... 552 B vanburen@uwplatt.edu
VAN BUREN, Mary .... 386-226-6525 .... 105 H vanburem@erau.edu
VAN BUSKIRK, Christina, P .... 717-245-1640 .... 427 F vanbuski@dickinson.edu
VAN CANNEYT, Donna, S . 901-678-2810 .... 474 C dvncnnyt@memphis.edu
VAN CLEAVE, Martha .... 503-883-2308 .... 416 H mvcleave@linfield.edu
VAN CLEAVE, Martha .... 503-883-2449 .... 416 H mvcleave@linfield.edu
VAN CLEAVE, Rachel .... 415-442-6601 ...... 48 F rvancleave@ggu.edu
VAN CLEAVE, Robb .... 541-506-6150 .... 415 C rvancleave@cgcc.cc.or.us
VAN CLEAVE, Samuel, J ... 480-423-6003 ...... 16 C samuel.vancleave@scottsdalecc.edu
VAN CLEAVE, William .... 504-865-5767 .... 215 C wvanclea@tulane.edu
VAN CLEEF, Sarah, E .... 903-510-2033 .... 503 A svan@tjc.edu
VAN DAM, Dale .... 530-642-5644 ...... 56 C
VAN DE BOOGAARD, Eric .... 719-587-7951 ...... 80 L evdb@adams.edu
VAN DE CAR, Katharyn ..... 702-651-4516 .... 302 E kathy.vandecar@csn.edu
VAN DE LOO, John .... 715-365-4553 .... 555 A vandeloo@nicoletcollege.edu
VAN DE MOORTELL, Raymond .... 617-254-2610 .... 244 B
VAN DE PUTTE, Andre ..... 312-629-6100 .... 164 C avande2@saic.edu
VAN DEKKER, Angela .... 718-817-3800 .... 334 C avandekker@fordham.edu
VAN DEN ABBEELE, Georges .... 617-373-5173 .... 243 F
VAN DEN BERG, Rex .... 805-922-6966 ...... 26 L rvandenberg@hancockcollege.edu
VAN DEN BERGHE, Bruce .... 651-962-6060 .... 272 B b9vandenberg@stthomas.edu
VAN DEN HEEVER, Nicolaas .... 949-783-4800 ...... 78 A nvandenheever@westcoastuniversity.edu
VAN DEN HEUVEL, Nicole .... 713-348-4055 .... 493 C nvdh@rice.edu
VAN DEN HUL, Richard, D .... 360-650-3182 .... 539 F rich.vandenhul@wwu.edu
VAN DENEND, Michael, J 616-526-6142 .... 249 A vanden@calvin.edu
VAN DER BURG, Anna ..... 860-685-2810 ...... 95 E avanderburg@wesleyan.edu
VAN DER GIESSEN, Hans 203-576-4668 ...... 94 F hvdg@bridgeport.edu
VAN DER KAAY, Chris ..... 863-784-7204 .... 117 J christopher.vanderkaay@southflorida.edu
VAN DER KARR, Carol ..... 607-753-2206 .... 353 B carol.vanderkarr@cortland.edu
VAN DER KLEY, Jan .... 269-387-2365 .... 260 C jan.vanderkley@wmich.edu
VAN DER LEEUW, Sander 480-965-6214 ...... 11 J vanderle@asu.edu
VAN DER MEID, J. Scott . 781-736-3483 .... 232 F svanderm@brandeis.edu
VAN DER POL, Willem ..... 657-278-2065 ...... 35 B wvanderpol@fullerton.edu
VAN DER VEER, Mary Caroline .... 518-587-2100 .... 355 G marycaroline.powers@esc.edu
VAN DERVEER, Rachael, E .... 724-847-6596 .... 429 H revander@geneva.edu
VAN DEVEN, Randy .... 903-468-8181 .... 498 B randy.vandeven@tamuc.edu
VAN DIJK, Angela .... 212-772-4582 .... 327 E
VAN DINE, Kathryn, L ...... 563-588-8000 .... 184 I registrar@emmaus.edu
VAN DONSELAAR, Brian .. 712-722-6299 .... 184 C brianvd@dordt.edu
VAN DUSEN, Michael .... 561-912-2166 .... 107 B mvandusen@evergladesuniversity.edu
VAN DUSER, Kathy .... 773-371-5450 .... 146 E admissions@ctu.edu
VAN DUYNE, Patrick .... 815-280-6696 .... 154 J pvanduyn@jjc.edu
VAN DUZER, Jeffrey, B ..... 206-281-2087 .... 537 H vandj@spu.edu
VAN DYCK, Judy .... 503-725-4878 .... 418 G vandyckj@pdx.edu
VAN DYK, Leanne .... 616-392-8555 .... 260 D leanne.vandyk@westernsem.edu
VAN DYKE, James .... 920-923-8083 .... 548 E jvandyke@marianuniversity.edu
VAN DYKE, Jon .... 217-234-5378 .... 156 B jvandyke@lakeland.cc.il.us
VAN DYKE, Patricia .... 716-829-7802 .... 332 E vandykep@dyc.edu
VAN DYKEN, Douglas .... 616-395-7810 .... 252 D vandyken@hope.edu
VAN ECK, Thomas, A .... 616-526-8553 .... 249 A tveck@calvin.edu
VAN ELLIS, Wayne .... 562-907-4241 ...... 79 F wvanellis@law.whittier.edu
VAN ESS, Jami .... 928-226-4209 ...... 13 F jami.vaness@coconino.edu
VAN-ESS, Michelle .... 212-217-4132 .... 333 F michelle_vaness@fitnyc.edu
VAN ESSEN, Quentin .... 712-722-6080 .... 184 C quentin@dordt.edu
VAN FOSSEN, Brian, F ...... 570-340-6024 .... 435 F bvanfossen@marywood.edu
VAN FOSSEN, Dell Jean ... 951-785-2088 ...... 53 E dvanfoss@lasierra.edu
VAN FOSSEN, Drew .... 920-403-4427 .... 550 F drew.vanfossen@snc.edu
VAN GALEN, Dean, A .... 715-425-3201 .... 552 C dean.vangalen@uwrf.edu
VAN GIESON, Christine, N .... 805-893-3641 ...... 75 B christine.vangieson@sa.ucsb.edu
VAN GIESON, Cindy .... 517-780-4554 .... 248 D cindy.vangieson@baker.edu
VAN GILDER, Holly .... 330-490-7144 .... 405 F hvangilder@walsh.edu
VAN GINHOVEN, Lee, H .. 269-927-8611 .... 253 G vanginhoven@lakemichigancollege.edu
VAN GORDON, Beth .... 219-980-7202 .... 174 B vgordon@iun.edu
VAN GORDON, Elizabeth .. 574-520-4463 .... 174 E vgordon@iusb.edu
VAN GRONINGEN, Willis . 708-239-4880 .... 166 C bill.vangroningen@trnty.edu
VAN GRUENSVEN, Sheryl 920-465-2326 .... 551 B vangrues@uwgb.edu
VAN GUNDY, Doug .... 304-473-8243 .... 545 G vangundy@wvwc.edu
VAN HAMERSVELD, Pete .. 310-243-3825 ...... 34 D pvanhamersveld@csudh.edu
VAN HARPEN, Robin .... 414-229-2629 .... 551 D rvanharp@uwm.edu
VAN HEMERT, Ann .... 641-628-7645 .... 183 D vanhemerta@central.edu
VAN HEMERT, John, L ..... 540-674-3660 .... 527 E jvanhemert@nr.edu
VAN HOLLAND, Phyllis, L 360-417-6291 .... 536 G pvanholland@pencol.edu
VAN HOOK, Dianne, G ..... 661-362-3400 ...... 41 I dianne.vanhook@canyons.edu
VAN HOOK, Jayson .... 423-614-8695 .... 470 C jvanhook@leeuniversity.edu
VAN HORN, Brian, W .... 270-809-4159 .... 205 A bvanhorn@murraystate.edu
VAN HORN, Donald, L ...... 304-696-6433 .... 544 B vanhorn@marshall.edu
VAN HORN, Drew .... 828-328-7108 .... 366 E drew.vanhorn@lr.edu
VAN HORN, Fred .... 478-387-4778 .... 131 A
VAN HORN, Guy .... 843-863-7102 .... 456 B gvanhorn@csuniv.edu
VAN HORN, Keith, F .... 419-267-1303 .... 397 E kvanhorn@northweststate.edu
VAN HORN, Stu .... 916-608-6500 ...... 56 C
VAN HORN, Wayne .... 601-925-3297 .... 275 C wvanhorn@mc.edu
VAN HOUT, Vicky .... 920-735-5731 .... 554 A
VAN HOUTEN, Michael ..... 517-629-0567 .... 247 A mvanhouten@albion.edu
VAN KERCKVOORDE, Colette .... 413-528-7232 .... 230 F colette@simons-rock.edu
VAN KEUREN, Karen, A .... 585-785-1206 .... 334 A vankeuka@flcc.edu
VAN KIRK, Shannon .... 541-278-5916 .... 414 G svankirk@bluecc.edu
VAN KLEY, Eric .... 641-628-5310 .... 183 D vankleye@central.edu
VAN KLEY, Sandy .... 712-707-7145 .... 188 D svankley@nwciowa.edu
VAN LANINGHAM, Kathy, M .... 479-575-5910 ...... 24 C kvl@uark.edu
VAN LEAR, Michael, C ...... 808-955-1500 .... 141 A michael_vanlear@heald.edu
VAN LEIDEN, Melissa .... 785-594-8306 .... 190 F melissa.vanleiden@bakeru.edu
VAN LOO, Scott, D .... 419-289-5088 .... 384 G svanloo@ashland.edu
VAN MARTER, Dianne .... 313-831-5200 .... 250 G dvanmarter@etseminary.edu
VAN NAME, Carol .... 805-922-6966 ...... 26 L cvanname@hancockcollege.edu
VAN NATTA, Gretchen .... 312-341-2479 .... 163 B gvannatta@roosevelt.edu
VAN NESS, Forrest, L .... 314-516-6680 .... 291 D vannessf@umsl.edu
VAN NIEKERK, Andre .... 818-767-0888 ...... 79 H andre.vanniekerk@woodbury.edu
VAN NORMAN, Karen .... 973-761-9076 .... 315 B karen.vannorman@shu.edu
VAN OMMEREN, Ryan ...... 805-493-3211 ...... 33 B rvommere@clunet.edu
VAN OORT, Harlan .... 712-707-7190 .... 188 D hvanoort@nwciowa.edu
VAN ORMAN, Kit .... 315-364-3317 .... 360 D kit@wells.edu
VAN ORMAN, Sarah, A ..... 608-262-1885 .... 550 J svanorman@uhs.wisc.edu
VAN ORNAM, Donald, C .. 423-236-2750 .... 473 B vanornam@southern.edu
VAN ORSDEL, Lee .... 616-331-2621 .... 251 F vanorsdl@gvsu.edu
VAN ORT, Jennifer .... 518-381-1322 .... 350 E vanortjl@sunysccc.edu
VAN PELT, Cynthia .... 734-487-0455 .... 250 F cvanpelt@emich.edu
VAN REENEN, Johann .... 505-277-6128 .... 321 C jreenen@unm.edu
VAN RIPER, Lisa .... 804-289-8778 .... 525 E lvanripe@richmond.edu
VAN SCHARREL, Mark, H . 773-256-0676 .... 157 D mvanscha@lstc.edu
VAN SCHYNDEL, C. Richard .... 208-467-8445 .... 144 E crvanschyndel@nnu.edu
VAN SICKLE, Frederick, M 212-851-7929 .... 330 F fmv2001@columbia.edu
VAN SICKLE, Lee .... 773-298-3410 .... 163 I vansickle@sxu.edu
VAN SLYCK, Abigail, A ..... 860-439-2731 ...... 92 G abigail.van-slyck@conncoll.edu
VAN SLYKE, Craig .... 928-523-7941 ...... 16 I craig.vanslyke@nau.edu
VAN SOELEN, Timothy ...... 712-722-6228 .... 184 C timothyv@dcrdt.edu
VAN SOMEREN, Charles ... 202-462-2101 ...... 99 A vansomeren@iwp.edu
VAN STRATEN, Amy .... 920-831-4355 .... 554 A vanstrat@fvtc.edu
VAN TASSEL, Kristin .... 785-227-3380 .... 191 B vantasselk@bethanylb.edu
VAN THUYNE, Michael, E . 215-637-7700 .... 431 A mvanthuyne@holyfamily.edu
VAN TIL, Seth, J .... 724-458-3887 .... 430 B sjvantil@gcc.edu
VAN TRAN, Lac .... 312-942-3400 .... 163 D lac_tran@rush.edu
VAN UUM, Elizabeth .... 314-516-5774 .... 291 D vanuum@umsl.edu
VAN VACTOR, Myra .... 425-564-2255 .... 531 G myra.vanvactor@bellevuecollege.edu
VAN VALEN, Gretchen .... 607-274-3846 .... 336 G gvanvalen@ithaca.edu
VAN VECHTEN, Daniel .... 513-244-4466 .... 388 E daniel_van_vechten@mail.msj.edu
VAN VLECK, Thomas .... 660-626-2138 .... 278 D tvanvleck@atsu.edu
VAN VOLKENBURGH, Linda, C .... 513-861-6400 .... 402 I linda.van@myunion.edu
VAN VOORHIS, Sue, N ..... 612-625-8098 .... 272 A vanvo002@umn.edu
VAN WAGNER, Molly .... 715-425-3195 .... 552 C molly.van-wagner@uwrf.edu
VAN WAGNER, Thomas .... 202-231-4193 .... 557 J thomas.vanwagner@dodiis.mil
VAN WAGONER, Randall, J .... 315-792-5333 .... 341 E rvanwagoner@mvcc.edu
VAN WEELDEN, Kathy .... 603-428-2235 .... 305 D kvanweelden@nec.edu
VAN WIE, Lisa .... 518-629-8143 .... 336 C l.vanwie@hvcc.edu
VAN WINGERDEN, Thomas, J .... 616-526-6378 .... 249 A tjv6@calvin.edu
VAN WINKLE, Robynne ..... 541-440-4600 .... 420 F robynne.vanwinkle@umpqua.edu
VAN WYK, Natalie .... 610-361-5418 .... 437 D vanwykn@neumann.edu
VAN WYK, Sharon .... 304-724-3700 .... 540 F svanwyk@apus.edu
VAN ZANDT, David .... 212-229-5656 .... 342 E vanzandt@newschool.edu
VAN ZANDT, Patricia, R ... 423-439-4337 .... 473 F
VAN ZINDEREN, Gary .... 701-252-3467 .... 381 C gvanzind@jc.edu
VAN ZWOL, R. William ..... 520-318-2700 ...... 12 C rvanzwol@aii.edu
VAN ZYL, Henry .... 609-292-4000 .... 316 A phvanzyl@tesc.edu
VANACKER, Jason .... 414-443-8944 .... 553 D jason.vanacker@wlc.edu
VANARSDALL, Cathy .... 765-361-6421 .... 181 E vanarsdc@wabash.edu
VANASSE, Dennis .... 508-849-3372 .... 230 C dvanasse@annamaria.edu
VANAUSDLE, Steven, L ..... 509-527-4274 .... 539 B steven.vanausdle@wwcc.edu
VANBERGEIJK, Ernst .... 631-348-3117 .... 343 D evanberg@nyit.edu
VANCE, Carl .... 503-768-7801 .... 416 G cvance@lclark.edu
VANCE, Debra .... 812-330-6111 .... 175 J dvance@ivytech.edu
VANCE, Elaine .... 202-651-5288 ...... 98 B janet.vance@gallaudet.edu
VANCE, Linda, B .... 407-582-2586 .... 123 B lvance@valenciacollege.edu
VANCE, Maria .... 707-965-7000 ...... 60 I mvance@puc.edu
VANCE, Mickey .... 601-635-6208 .... 274 A mvance@eccc.edu
VANCE, Richard, N .... 765-658-4233 .... 171 B richardvance@depauw.edu
VANCE, Robert .... 414-577-2658 .... 159 E rvance@nl.edu
VANCE, ESQ., Sheilah ...... 610-399-2000 .... 442 A svance@cheyney.edu
VANCE, Susan .... 423-636-7331 .... 477 A svance@tusculum.edu
VANCE, W.C .... 419-289-4142 .... 384 G wvance@ashland.edu
VANCKO, Candace .... 518-255-5111 .... 354 E vanckocs@cobleskill.edu
VANCKO, Candace, S .... 607-746-4090 .... 355 F vanckocs@delhi.edu
VANCLEAVE, Donna .... 804-819-4695 .... 526 C dvancleave@vccs.edu
VANCOTT, Mary Grooms .... 707-826-3236 ...... 36 E vancott@humboldt.edu
VANDALL, Christopher, P .. 608-258-2448 .... 554 D cvandall@madisoncollege.org
VANDE YACHT, Dan .... 715-425-3342 .... 552 C daniel.vandeyacht@uwrf.edu
VANDE ZANDE, Carleen .... 920-424-3190 .... 551 E vandezac@uwosh.edu
VANDEGRIFT, OP, Raymond .... 202-495-3856 ...... 99 C rvandegrift@dhs.edu
VANDELINDER, David .... 313-993-1639 .... 258 G vandelda@udmercy.edu
VANDELL, Deborah, L .... 949-824-8026 ...... 74 B dvandell@uci.edu
VANDEMAN, Nancy .... 740-753-7009 .... 391 H vandeman_n@hocking.edu
VANDEN BOOM, Leonard, A .... 414-277-7154 .... 549 C vandenbo@msoe.edu
VANDENAKKER, John .... 313-883-8750 .... 257 E vandenakker.john@shms.edu
VANDENAVOND, Steve ...... 920-465-2641 .... 551 B vandenas@uwgb.edu
VANDENBERG, Patricia ..... 413-538-2899 .... 242 D pvandenb@mtholyoke.edu
VANDENBERGHE, Claire .... 585-395-5415 .... 352 F cvandenb@brockport.edu
VANDENBOSCH, Kathryn .. 608-262-4930 .... 550 J kvandenbosch@cals.wisc.edu
VANDER FEEN, Aimee ...... 605-331-6602 .... 466 E aimee.vanderfeen@usiouxfalls.edu
VANDER HOEK, Nancy ...... 605-229-8545 .... 465 B nancy.vanderhoek@presentation.edu
VANDER HOOVEN, James 520-383-8401 ...... 18 I
VANDER HORN, Alexis, A 563-884-5102 ...... 61 A alexis.vanderhorn@palmer.edu
VANDER HORN, Alexis, A 563-884-5102 .... 188 E alexis.vanderhorn@palmer.edu
VANDER PLOEG, Scott ..... 270-824-8684 .... 202 G scott.vanderploeg@kctcs.edu
VANDER SANDEN, Karen . 651-290-7526 .... 272 E karen.vandersanden@wmitchell.edu
VANDER STOEP, Scott, D . 616-395-7903 .... 252 D vanderstoep@hope.edu
VANDER VELDE, George ... 708-239-4792 .... 166 C george.vandervelde@trnty.edu
VANDER WEELE, Dennis .. 845-368-7200 .... 350 A dennis.vanderweele@use.salvationarmy.org
VANDER WERF, Dave .... 712-722-6020 .... 184 C davevw@dordt.edu
VANDER ZWAAG, Lora ..... 712-274-6400 .... 190 B lora.vanderzwaag@witcc.edu
VANDERBILT, Michelle ...... 253-943-2800 .... 533 F mvanderbilt@devry.edu
VANDERBILT, William .... 616-395-7850 .... 252 D vanderbilt@hope.edu
VANDERBOUT, Jennifer, L 660-543-8000 .... 290 H vanderbout@ucmo.edu
VANDERBURG, Judy, J ..... 503-838-8490 .... 419 C vanderj@wou.edu
VANDERBURGH, Paul, M . 937-229-2390 .... 404 A pvanderburgh1@udayton.edu
VANDERFORD, Brenda ..... 304-766-5107 .... 544 F bvanderf@wvstateu.edu
VANDERGRIFT, Peggy, L .. 205-853-1200 .... 5 C pvandy@jeffstateonline.com
VANDERHART, Mark .... 219-864-2400 .... 178 F mvanderhart@midamerica.edu
VANDERHILL, Dan .... 517-750-1200 .... 258 D danv@arbor.edu

VAUGHN, Deborah, S .... 662-915-1687 .... 277 D
dvaughn@olemiss.edu

VAUGHN, Denise .... 919-278-2673 .... 376 F
dvaughn@shawu.edu

VAUGHN, Edward, L .... 601-877-6227 .... 272 F
elvaughn@alcorn.edu

VAUGHN, Jason .... 417-328-1714 .... 290 A
jvaughn@sbuniv.edu

VAUGHN, Jennifer .... 270-852-3118 .... 204 A
jvaughn@kwc.edu

VAUGHN, Joseph .... 660-543-4621 .... 290 H
vaughn@ucmo.edu

VAUGHN, Joyce .... 870-575-8969 .... 25 B
vaughnj@uapb.edu

VAUGHN, Katherine .... 870-743-3000 .... 22 G
kvaughn@northark.edu

VAUGHN, Kellie .... 270-789-5001 .... 199 F
kpvaughn@campbellsville.edu

VAUGHN, La'Mont .... 847-578-3204 .... 163 C
lamont.vaughn@rosalindfranklin.edu

VAUGHN, Linda .... 904-743-1122 .... 112 B
lvaughn@jones.edu

VAUGHN, Lori .... 413-565-1000 .... 230 G
lvaughn@baypath.edu

VAUGHN, Michele .... 847-543-2153 .... 148 B
mvaughn@clcillinois.edu

VAUGHN, Patrick .... 636-422-2240 .... 289 B
pvaughn20@stlcc.edu

VAUGHN, Patti .... 617-262-5000 .... 231 G
patti.vaughn@the-bac.edu

VAUGHN, Renata .... 870-972-2054 .... 20 D
rvaughn@astate.edu

VAUGHN, Robert .... 323-856-7661 .... 28 E
rvaughn@afi.com

VAUGHN, Robert .... 610-372-4721 .... 445 C
rvaughn@racc.edu

VAUGHN, Ronald, L .... 813-253-6201 .... 123 A
president@ut.edu

VAUGHN, Sandra .... 662-252-8000 .... 276 G
svaughn@rustcollege.edu

VAUGHN, Suzanne, A .... 661-395-4301 .... 52 L
svaughn@bakersfieldcollege.edu

VAUGHN, Tarva .... 256-549-8671 .... 3 J
tvaughn@gadsdenstate.edu

VAUGHN, Troy .... 817-515-5034 .... 496 C
troy.vaughn@tccd.edu

VAUGHT, Wayne .... 816-235-2815 .... 291 C
vaughtw@umkc.edu

VAUPEL, Chris .... 516-877-3258 .... 322 A
cpvaupel@adelphi.edu

VAUPEL, Richard, D .... 423-493-4215 .... 476 E
vaupelr@tntemple.edu

VAVASOUR, JoEllen, L .... 914-654-5541 .... 330 B
jvavasour@cnr.edu

VAVOLIZZA, Ann .... 845-848-4001 .... 332 B
ann.vavolizza@dc.edu

VAVRICKA, Janda .... 414-277-2234 .... 549 C
vavricka@msoe.edu

VAWTER, Cheryl, D .... 509-777-4518 .... 540 C
cvawter@whitworth.edu

VAYDA, Melissa, M .... 717-728-2248 .... 425 B
melissavayda@centralpenn.edu

VAYDA, Michael, E .... 479-575-2034 .... 24 C
mvayda@uark.edu

VAZ, Maria, J .... 248-204-2400 .... 254 B
provost@ltu.edu

VAZQUEZ, Airlyn .... 787-882-2065 .... 566 A
biblioteca@unitecpr.net

VAZQUEZ, Carmen .... 718-289-5151 .... 326 E
carmen.vazquez@bcc.cuny.edu

VAZQUEZ, Carmen .... 305-593-1223 .... 102 H
cvazquez@albizu.edu

VAZQUEZ, Carmen, M .... 619-260-4588 .... 76 D
carmenvazquez@sandiego.edu

VAZQUEZ, David .... 239-590-1123 .... 119 B
dvazquez@fgcu.edu

VAZQUEZ, Frank .... 888-384-0849 .... 27 G
frankv@allied.edu

VAZQUEZ, Jaime .... 787-780-0070 .... 560 H
jvazquez@caribbean.edu

VAZQUEZ, Juan, A .... 714-628-4930 .... 63 G
vazquez_juan@sccollege.edu

VAZQUEZ, Magda .... 787-878-5475 .... 563 B
mavazquez@arecibo.inter.edu

VAZQUEZ, Maria .... 787-725-8120 .... 562 C
mvazquez0060@eap.edu

VAZQUEZ, Maria .... 787-864-2222 .... 563 F
mavazrom@inter.edu

VAZQUEZ, Marie .... 402-457-2430 .... 298 G
mvazquez@mccneb.edu

VAZQUEZ, Ramon .... 787-840-2955 .... 560 H
rvazquez@ponce.caribbean.edu

VAZQUEZ, Silvio .... 805-565-6200 .... 79 A
svazquez@westmont.edu

VAZQUEZ, Trina .... 828-398-2513 .... 376 H
tvazquez@southcollegenc.edu

VAZQUEZ, Vilmaris .... 787-878-5475 .... 563 B
vvazquez@arecibo.inter.edu

VAZQUEZ, Yanaira .... 939-292-8924 .... 568 C
yanaira.vazquez@upr.edu

VAZQUEZ-BARQUET, Ernesto .... 787-754-8000 .... 566 E
evazquez@pupr.edu

VAZQUEZ-BARQUET, Ernesto .... 787-622-8000 .... 115 D
evazquez@pupr.edu

VAZQUEZ-GARCIA, Heidi .. 802-287-4318 .... 513 F
vazquezgarciah@greenmtn.edu

VAZQUEZ-SKILLINGS, Rebecca, D .... 614-823-1354 .... 400 H
rvazquez-skillings@otterbein.edu

VAZQUEZTELL, Hernán .... 787-250-0000 .... 566 G
hernan.vazqueztell@upr.edu

VEACH, Grace .... 863-667-5061 .... 118 F
gveach@seu.edu

VEACH, Leslie .... 252-985-5369 .... 375 E
lveach@ncwc.edu

VEAL, Sharon .... 478-553-2056 .... 135 B
sveal@oftc.edu

VEAZEY, Barbara .... 270-534-3082 .... 203 E
barbara.veazey@kctcs.edu

VECCHIO, John .... 716-827-4344 .... 358 D
vecchioj@trocaire.edu

VECCHIO, Maria .... 201-559-6017 .... 310 B
vecchiom@felician.edu

VECCHIO, Paul .... 607-871-2193 .... 322 E
vecchio@alfred.edu

VECCHIONE, Tom .... 336-278-6538 .... 364 D
tvecchione@elon.edu

VECHINI, Jose, A .... 787-864-2222 .... 563 F
javechi@inter.edu

VEDDER, Lori .... 810-762-3444 .... 259 C
lvedder@umflint.edu

VEDIA, Roxanne .... 956-721-5437 .... 489 J
rvedia@laredo.edu

VEDVICK, Kathryn, A .... 206-934-6415 .... 537 F
kathy.vedvick@seattlecolleges.edu

VEDVIK, Ruth, A .... 920-748-8185 .... 550 D
vedvikr@ripon.edu

VEECH, Guthrie .... 314-837-6777 .... 288 C
gveech@slcconline.edu

VEEDER, Samantha .... 585-389-2310 .... 342 D
sveeder0@naz.edu

VEEN, Leslie .... 415-451-2834 .... 66 B
lveen@sfts.edu

VEENSTRA, Derick, A .... 301-369-2800 .... 221 F
rveenstra@capitol-college.edu

VEENSTRA, Dianne, M .... 301-369-2800 .... 221 F
dveenstra@capitol-college.edu

VEENSTRA, Myron .... 701-777-2127 .... 381 F
myron.veenstra@und.edu

VEENSTRA, Tim .... 517-586-3014 .... 249 D
tveenstra@cleary.edu

VEESER, Margaret, I .... 901-321-3324 .... 467 I
pveeser@cbu.edu

VEGA, Aixa .... 787-834-9595 .... 566 B
avega@uaa.edu

VEGA, Annette .... 787-878-5475 .... 563 B
avega@arecibo.inter.edu

VEGA, Barbara .... 432-837-8810 .... 501 E
bvega@sulross.edu

VEGA, Elsa .... 305-593-1223 .... 102 H
evega@albizu.edu

VEGA, Erlinda .... 787-264-1912 .... 564 B
yaremi@sg.inter.edu

VEGA, Eva .... 787-746-1400 .... 562 E
evega@huertas.edu

VEGA, Fredrick .... 787-250-1912 .... 563 G
fredrickvega@metro.inter.edu

VEGA, Javier .... 212-592-2000 .... 350 F
jvega@sva.edu

VEGA, Juan .... 787-844-8181 .... 568 A
juan.vegavega@upr.edu

VEGA, Lourdes .... 787-738-2161 .... 567 D
lourdes.vega@upr.edu

VEGA, Manfredo .... 787-620-2040 .... 560 D
mvega@aupr.edu

VEGA, Zaida .... 787-766-1717 .... 565 I
zvega@suagm.edu

VEHR, Gregory, J .... 513-556-3028 .... 403 D
greg.vehr@uc.edu

VEHRKENS, Kenneth, T .... 201-692-2671 .... 310 A
vehrkens@fdu.edu

VEILLEUX, John .... 817-531-4269 .... 502 C
jveilleux@txwes.edu

VEIT, Kenneth, J .... 215-871-6770 .... 444 C
kenv@pcom.edu

VEITCH, Jonathan .... 323-259-2691 .... 59 I
VEITH, Gene, E .... 540-338-1776 .... 522 G
VEJSICKY, Janet .... 740-826-8139 .... 397 A
janv@muskingum.edu

VELÁZQUEZ, Julio .... 787-850-9367 .... 567 E
VELA, JR., Cesar, E .... 956-721-5370 .... 489 J
cvela@laredo.edu

VELA, Robert, H .... 210-486-0930 .... 479 E
rvela63@alamo.edu

VELA, SM, Rudy .... 210-431-8094 .... 493 F
rvela3@stmarytx.edu

VELARDE, Jose .... 847-543-2602 .... 148 B
jvelarde@clcillinois.edu

VELARDE, Katie .... 719-549-2199 .... 83 H
katie.velarde@colostate-pueblo.edu

VELARDE, Mark .... 602-286-8327 .... 15 G
mark.velarde@gwmail.maricopa.edu

VELARDI, Lisa Marie .... 866-967-8822 .... 109 H
lvelardi@flatech.edu

VELASCO, Jessica .... 425-889-5212 .... 536 C
jessica.velasco@northwestu.edu

VELASCO, Steven, C .... 805-893-2434 .... 75 B
steve.velasco@bap.ucsb.edu

VELASQUEZ, Jaime .... 312-996-2969 .... 167 B
jaimev@uic.edu

VELASQUEZ, Lorrie .... 719-846-5534 .... 88 F
lorrie.velasquez@trinidadstate.edu

VELASQUEZ, Melissa .... 575-581-4145 .... 320 A
mvelasqu@nnmc.edu

VELAUTHAPILLAI, Ravi .... 910-362-7074 .... 368 H
rvelauthapillai@cfcc.edu

VELAZQUEZ, Acmin .... 787-844-8181 .... 568 A
acmin.velazquez@upr.edu

VELAZQUEZ, Carmen, G .... 787-253-7373 .... 565 G
ue_evelazquez@suagm.edu

VELAZQUEZ, Hilda .... 787-863-2390 .... 563 E
hilda.velazquez@fajardo.inter.edu

VELAZQUEZ, Isander .... 787-753-6335 .... 562 G
ivelazquez@icprjc.edu

VELAZQUEZ, Mei-Ling .... 787-834-5151 .... 565 B
mvelazquez@pucpr.edu

VELAZQUEZ, Veronica .... 787-863-2390 .... 563 E
veronica.velazquez@fajardo.inter.edu

VELAZQUEZ, Zoraida .... 787-841-2000 .... 565 B
zvelazquez@pucpr.edu

VELAZQUEZ-SEPULVEDA, Mei-Ling .... 787-834-5151 .... 565 D
mvelazquez@email.pucpr.edu

VELCO, Jim .... 312-427-2737 .... 154 H
6velco@jmls.edu

VELDERMAN, Joe .... 708-239-4837 .... 166 C
joe.velderman@trnty.edu

VELDHAUS, Nicki .... 513-244-4298 .... 388 E
nicki_veldhaus@mail.msj.edu

VELEK, Thomas .... 662-241-6850 .... 276 A
tvelek@as.muw.edu

VELEZ, Angel .... 787-250-1912 .... 563 G
avelez@metro.inter.edu

VELEZ, Ashley .... 787-841-2000 .... 565 B
VELEZ, Ginny .... 787-840-8108 .... 568 A
ginny.velez@upr.edu

VELEZ, Hector .... 787-890-2681 .... 566 H
hector.velez6@upr.edu

VELEZ, Marcos .... 787-761-0640 .... 566 F
VELEZ, María, C .... 787-753-6000 .... 562 G
mvelez@icprjc.edu

VELEZ, Roland .... 718-518-4406 .... 327 D
rvelez@hostos.cuny.edu

VELEZ, Rosa .... 787-758-2525 .... 567 G
rosa.velez2@upr.edu

VELEZ, Vivian .... 787-664-0331 .... 568 C
vivan.velez1@upr.edu

VELEZ, Wanda .... 845-675-4792 .... 344 G
wanda.velez@nyack.edu

VELEZ AROCHO, Jorge, I .... 787-841-2000 .... 565 B
jivelezarocho@pucpr.edu

VELEZ LUCE, Melissa .... 773-244-5273 .... 159 H
mvelezluce@northpark.edu

VELEZ-YELIN, Johanna .... 856-256-5440 .... 314 A
velez-yelin@rowan.edu

VELGUTH, Peter .... 989-386-6622 .... 255 C
pvelguth@midmich.edu

VELI, Ravil .... 802-485-2170 .... 514 C
rveli1@norwich.edu

VELKOFF, Townsend .... 570-321-4258 .... 435 D
velkoff@lycoming.edu

VELLACCIO, Frank .... 508-793-3010 .... 233 C
fvellacc@holycross.edu

VELLENGA, Barbara .... 605-331-6671 .... 466 E
barbara.vellenga@usiouxfalls.edu

VELLUCCI, Sherry .... 603-862-1506 .... 306 C
sherry.vellucci@unh.edu

VELO, Jason .... 209-946-2233 .... 76 A
jvelo@pacific.edu

VELORIA, Ruth .... 602-557-1544 .... 19 A
ruth.veloria@phoenix.edu

VELOSO, Antonio .... 860-412-7218 .... 92 D
aveloso@qvcc.commnet.edu

VELTRI, Sandra .... 303-404-5497 .... 85 A
sandy.veltri@frontrange.edu

VELTRI, Stephen, C .... 419-772-2205 .... 398 H
s-veltri@onu.edu

VELTRI, Valerie, L .... 412-531-4433 .... 426 F
info@deantech.edu

VELUPILLAI, Lakshman .... 225-578-6963 .... 212 H
lvelupillai@agcenter.lsu.edu

VELVEL, Lawrence, R .... 978-681-0800 .... 241 E
velvel@mslaw.edu

VENABLE, James, E .... 901-722-3260 .... 473 C
jvenable@sco.edu

VENABLE, Margaret .... 706-310-6219 .... 129 G
mvenable@gsc.edu

VENABLE, Rhonda .... 615-322-2571 .... 478 A
rhonda.r.venable@vanderbilt.edu

VENDITTI, Ferdinand .... 518-262-5376 .... 322 D
venditf@mail.amc.edu

VENDITTI, Leona .... 515-289-9200 .... 185 H
lvenditti@inste.edu

VENDITTI, Nicholas .... 515-289-9200 .... 185 H
nvenditti@inste.edu

VENEGAS, Valerie, A .... 714-895-5117 .... 41 C
vvenegas@gwc.cccd.edu

VENEKLASE, Dave .... 616-732-1095 .... 250 C
dveneklase@davenport.edu

VENEMA, Cornelius .... 219-864-2400 .... 178 F
cvenema@midamerica.edu

VENEMA, Kathryn .... 419-448-2028 .... 391 F
kvenema@heidelberg.edu

VENIE, Evan .... 312-567-3202 .... 153 C
venie@iit.edu

VENKAT, Rama .... 702-895-1094 .... 302 I
rama.venkat@unlv.edu

VENKER, Teri, H .... 608-263-5061 .... 553 B
teri.venker@uwex.uwc.edu

VENN, Martha, L .... 478-471-2730 .... 133 H
martha.venn@maconstate.edu

VENNEMAN, Martin .... 918-456-5511 .... 409 A
venneman@nsuok.edu

VENNER, Thomas .... 734-487-4344 .... 250 F
tom.venner@emich.edu

VENNERI, Richard .... 773-298-3946 .... 163 I
venneri@sxu.edu

VENSON, John .... 510-869-8726 .... 64 J
jvenson@samuelmerritt.edu

VENTA, Henry .... 409-880-8603 .... 501 A
henry.venta@lamar.edu

VENTER, Ryan .... 518-694-7357 .... 322 B
ryan.venter@acphs.edu

VENTERS, Monoka .... 850-245-0466 .... 118 K
monoka.venters@flbog.edu

VENTIMIGLIA, Laura .... 978-762-4000 .... 240 D
lventimi@northshore.edu

VENTIMIGLIA, Thomas .... 516-796-5923 .... 342 H
tventimig@nycc.edu

VENTO, Robert, D .... 318-257-2176 .... 215 F
bvento@latech.edu

VENTO-CIFELLI, Lauren .... 732-571-3456 .... 311 E
lvento@monmouth.edu

VENTOLINI, Gary .... 432-335-5113 .... 502 B
gary.ventolini@ttuhsc.edu

VENTURA, Frank, J .... 330-569-5974 .... 391 G
venturafj@hiram.edu

VENTURA, Jamey .... 802-635-1285 .... 515 F
jamey.ventura@jsc.edu

VENTURA, Nilo .... 650-543-3717 .... 57 B
nventura@menlo.edu

VENTURA, Paul .... 503-534-4008 .... 416 J
pventura@marylhurst.edu

VENTURA, Vincent .... 516-678-5000 .... 341 F
vventura@molloy.edu

VENTURELLA, Gordon, D .... 217-732-3168 .... 156 H
gdventurella@lincolnchristian.edu

VENTURINI, Vincent .... 662-254-3365 .... 276 B
vincent@mvsu.edu

VENUGOPAL, Junias, V .... 312-329-4113 .... 159 A
junias.venugopal@moody.edu

VENUGOPALAN, Devarajan .... 414-229-5561 .... 551 D
dv@uwm.edu

VENUTI, Andrea .... 315-498-2183 .... 345 D
venutia@sunyocc.edu

VENUTI, John, A .... 804-828-1210 .... 526 B
javenuti@vcu.edu

VER BERKMOES, John .... 616-945-5300 .... 250 A
john.verberkmoes@cornerstone.edu

VER STEEGH, Nancy, M .... 651-290-6342 .... 272 E
nancy.versteegh@wmitchell.edu

VERA, Fonda, L .... 972-238-6992 .... 485 D
fondav@dcccd.edu

VERA, Hernan .... 787-841-2000 .... 565 B
hvera@pucpr.edu

VERA, Sheila .... 787-480-2363 .... 561 E
shvera@sanjuancapital.com

VERACKA, Peter, G .... 614-885-5585 .... 401 B
pveracka@pcj.edu

VERAY, Jaime .... 787-725-6500 .... 561 A
jveray@albizu.edu

VERAY, Jaime .... 787-725-6500 .... 561 A
jveray@sju.albizu.edu

VERCAUTEREN, Tammy .... 303-404-5243 .... 85 A
tammy.vercauteren@frontrange.edu

VERDELL, Tommy .... 662-254-3580 .... 276 B
tverdell@mvsu.edu

VERDERBER, Carl .... 845-752-3000 .... 358 F
carlv@uts.edu

VERDEROSA, Patricia, K .... 717-337-6225 .... 429 I
pverdero@gettysburg.edu

VERDI, Ed .... 212-229-5323 .... 342 E
verdie@newschool.edu

VERDICCHIO, James .... 718-289-5923 .... 326 E
james.verdicchio@bcc.cuny.edu

VERDILE, Vincent, P .... 518-262-6008 .... 322 D
verdilv@mail.amc.edu

VERDUCE, Cynthia, P .... 260-422-5561 .... 173 C
cpverduce@indianatech.edu

VERDUGO, Hector .... 503-228-6528 .... 414 E
VERDUGO, Paula, E .... 909-593-3511 .... 75 E
pverdugo@laverne.edu

VEREBELY, James, S .... 402-557-7200 .... 296 H
jim.verebely@bellevue.edu

VEREEN, Karen .... 478-289-2271 .... 137 E
kvereen@southeasterntech.edu

VEREEN, Richard .... 678-359-5104 .... 132 A
richard_v@gdn.edu

VERES, III, John, G .... 334-244-3602 .... 1 G
jveres@aum.edu

VILLEGAS, Kevin, J .... 717-766-2511 .... 436 D
kvillega@messiah.edu
VILLEGAS-VIDAL, Ludi ...... 818-364-7643 ...... 55 A
villegl@lamission.edu
VILLELLA, Theresa .... 814-732-1297 .... 442 E
tvillella@edinboro.edu
VILLENEUVE, Martha .... 603-897-8260 .... 305 F
mvilleneuve@rivier.edu
VILLERS, Koreen .... 304-457-6455 .... 540 E
villerskr@ab.edu
VILLINES, Trish .... 870-743-3000 ...... 22 G
tvillines@northark.edu
VILLOLDO, Sergio .... 305-418-4220 .... 115 D
svilloldo@pupr.edu
VILLOLDO, Sergio .... 787-754-8000 .... 566 E
svilloldo@pupr.edu
VINARSKI, Cynthia, A .... 412-396-6596 .... 428 D
vinarski@duq.edu
VINCENT, Andrew .... 502-897-4785 .... 206 C
avincent@sbts.edu
VINCENT, Danny .... 740-826-8155 .... 397 A
dvincent@muskingum.edu
VINCENT, Elaine .... 312-235-3505 .... 164 F
e.vincent@shimer.edu
VINCENT, Endas .... 225-771-3670 .... 214 I
endas_vincent@subr.edu
VINCENT, Endas .... 225-771-3670 .... 214 H
endas_vincent@sus.edu
VINCENT, Eugenia .... 951-571-6384 ...... 63 J
eugenia.vincent@mvc.edu
VINCENT, Eugenia .... 951-571-6384 ...... 64 A
eugenia.vincent@rcc.edu
VINCENT, Gregory, J .... 512-471-3212 .... 505 D
gvincent@mail.utexas.edu
VINCENT, Herb .... 225-578-3861 .... 212 H
vincent@lsu.edu
VINCENT, Michael .... 928-523-5011 ...... 16 I
michael.vincent@nau.edu
VINCENT, Pat .... 270-399-1578 .... 200 E
pvincent@daymarcollege.edu
VINCENT, Sara .... 860-512-2909 ...... 91 F
svincent@mcc.commnet.edu
VINCENT, Shawn .... 706-721-8096 .... 130 D
svincent2@georgiahealth.edu
VINCENT, Stephanie .... 617-739-1700 .... 243 A
svincent@aii.edu
VINCENT, William, B .... 215-572-3802 .... 451 D
bvincent@wts.edu
VINCENT, William, K .... 951-639-5201 ...... 58 B
bvincent@msjc.edu
VINCENT, William, K .... 951-487-3420 ...... 58 B
bvincent@msjc.edu
VINCIGUERRA, Michael, J 815-740-3369 .... 167 E
mvinciguerra@stfrancis.edu
VINCZE, John .... 203-285-2310 ...... 91 D
jvincze@gwcc.commnet.edu
VINES, Erin .... 707-864-7256 ...... 70 A
erin.vines@solano.edu
VINES, Precious .... 252-536-7206 .... 371 B
vinesp@halifaxcc.edu
VINES, Robert .... 239-590-7044 .... 119 B
rvines@fgcu.edu
VINEYARD, Ed .... 580-548-2207 .... 409 B
edwin.vineyard@north-ok.edu
VINEYARD, George .... 618-536-2384 .... 165 B
gmv1@siu.edu
VINEYARD, John, P .... 931-598-1890 .... 472 L
jpvineya@sewanee.edu
VINEYARD, Judy .... 618-985-3741 .... 154 G
judyvineyard@jalc.edu
VINGER, Christopher, J ..... 973-642-3888 .... 307 F
cjv@berkeleycollege.edu
VINGER, Christopher, J ..... 973-642-3888 .... 323 H
cjv@berkeleycollege.edu
VINIAR, Barbara, A .... 410-827-5802 .... 222 B
bviniar@chesapeake.edu
VINING, Isaac .... 404-225-4750 .... 125 E
ivining@atlantatech.edu
VINK, Cher .... 715-468-2815 .... 555 G
cher.vink@witc.edu
VINOVRSKI, Bernie .... 559-278-2061 ...... 35 A
bernard_vinovrski@csufresno.edu
VINSKI, Jerome .... 908-526-1200 .... 313 D
jvinski@raritanval.edu
VINSON, Bonita .... 214-932-1111 .... 490 A
bonitavinson@letu.edu
VINSON, Larry, J .... 402-552-6108 .... 297 B
vinson@clarksoncollege.edu
VINSON, Richard .... 336-721-2619 .... 376 E
richard.vinson@salem.edu
VINSON, Valerie .... 404-880-8773 .... 127 C
vvinson@cau.edu
VINSON, Wendy .... 706-245-7226 .... 129 C
wvinson@ec.edu
VINT, Patricia .... 734-432-5595 .... 254 D
pvint@madonna.edu
VINZANT, Jeffrey, P .... 334-244-3576 .... 1 G
jvinzant@aum.edu
VIOLA, Jennifer .... 615-217-9347 .... 468 D
jviola@daymarinstitute.edu
VIOLA, Joe .... 541-383-7776 .... 414 I
jviola@cocc.edu
VIOLANTE, Marc, N .... 847-543-2580 .... 148 B
mviolante@clcillinois.edu
VIOLETTE, Glenn .... 650-949-7394 ...... 47 H
violettglenn@foothill.edu
VIOLLT, Kathleen .... 312-935-4155 .... 162 G
kviollt@robertmorris.edu
VIOLLT, Michael, P .... 312-935-6600 .... 162 G
mviollt@robertmorris.edu
VIOTTI, Karen .... 901-321-3254 .... 467 I
kviotti@cbu.edu
VIRASAWMI, Errol .... 516-364-0808 .... 343 A
errol@nycollege.edu
VIRELLO, Mark .... 617-296-8300 .... 235 J
mark_virello@laboure.edu
VIRES, Charles .... 731-989-6171 .... 469 B
cvires@fhu.edu
VIRES, Tina, E .... 864-488-8245 .... 459 B
tvires@limestone.edu
VIRGINT, Jacqueline .... 505-428-1409 .... 320 E
jacqueline.virgint@sfcc.edu
VIRIJEVICH, Diana .... 219-989-2056 .... 178 K
dvirijev@purduecal.edu
VIRK, Sunny .... 718-960-8261 .... 327 C
sunny.virk@lehman.cuny.edu
VIRKLER, Lyndon .... 802-225-3326 .... 514 B
lyndon.virkler@neci.edu
VIRTS, Paul, H .... 651-631-5096 .... 270 B
phvirts@nwc.edu
VIRTUCCI, Tom .... 954-262-7304 .... 114 B
tomv@nsu.nova.edu
VISCI, Chip .... 805-756-7008 ...... 33 I
vcisci@calpoly.edu
VISCOMI, Susan .... 716-926-8800 .... 335 E
sviscomi@hilbert.edu
VISCONAGE, Elizabeth, L .. 410-864-4261 .... 226 B
bvisconage@stmarys.edu
VISCUSI, Raymond .... 610-359-5070 .... 426 G
rviscusi@dccc.edu
VISENTIN, Peter .... 203-837-8680 ...... 91 A
narduccid@wcsu.edu
VISHWANATHA,
Jamboor, K .... 817-735-2560 .... 504 E
jamboor.vishwanatha@unthsc.edu
VISKER, Thomas .... 574-257-3417 .... 169 I
viskert@bethelcollege.edu
VISKOZKI, Lynette .... 318-869-5137 .... 208 H
lviskozki@centenary.edu
VISOT, Cynthia, S .... 813-974-1678 .... 121 A
cvisot@usf.edu
VISSCHER, Caitlin .... 508-373-9527 .... 231 B
caitlin.visscher@becker.edu
VISSCHER, Petra .... 410-225-4255 .... 224 B
pvisscher@mica.edu
VISTOCCO, Valerie .... 315-781-3309 .... 335 F
vistocco@hws.edu
VISUANO, Denise .... 503-838-8349 .... 419 C
visuanod@wou.edu
VITA, Claudine .... 610-526-6012 .... 430 D
cvita@harcum.edu
VITA, Paul .... 314-977-2500 .... 289 C
vitap@slu.edu
VITAGLIANO, James, V ..... 617-726-3136 .... 242 B
jvitagliano@mghihp.edu
VITALE, Bob .... 319-385-6270 .... 186 E
bob.vitale@iwc.edu
VITALE, Eve .... 810-762-9525 .... 253 C
evitale@kettering.edu
VITALE, Fran .... 480-423-6133 ...... 16 C
fran.vitale@scottsdalecc.edu
VITALE, Frank .... 410-888-9048 .... 226 F
fvitale@tai.edu
VITALE, James, M .... 215-670-9306 .... 438 E
jmvitale@peirce.edu
VITALE, Joseph .... 973-328-5060 .... 309 A
jvitale@ccm.edu
VITALE, Lori .... 816-995-2806 .... 287 H
lori.vitale@researchcollege.edu
VITALE, Michael .... 386-506-3079 .... 104 F
vitalem@daytonastate.edu
VITALE, Teeni .... 319-385-6478 .... 186 E
iwcbookstore@iwc.edu
VITALOS, Mark .... 610-606-4642 .... 425 A
mavitalo@cedarcrest.edu
VITANGELI, Kory, M .... 317-788-3485 .... 180 F
kvitangeli@uindy.edu
VITATOE, David, A .... 216-397-1984 .... 392 L
dvitatoe@jcu.edu
VITATOE, Steven, P .... 216-397-4277 .... 392 L
svitatoe@jcu.edu
VITELLI, Chris .... 209-588-5142 ...... 80 G
vitellic@yosemite.edu
VITELLI, Mary .... 407-628-6303 .... 116 D
mvitelli@rollins.edu
VITELLI, Michele .... 215-646-7300 .... 430 C
vitelli.m@gmc.edu
VITI, Elizabeth .... 717-337-6823 .... 429 I
eviti@gettysburg.edu
VITO, Melissa .... 520-621-0963 ...... 18 L
mmvito@email.arizona.edu
VITO, Ron .... 951-222-8490 ...... 64 A
ron.vito@rcc.edu
VITOLA, Anthony .... 203-332-5034 ...... 91 E
avitola@hcc.commnet.edu
VITOLINS, Constance, M ... 570-326-3761 .... 440 L
cvitolin@pct.edu
VITTER, Jeffrey, S .... 785-864-4904 .... 197 B
jsv@ku.edu
VITTES, Elliot .... 407-823-2373 .... 120 B
elliot@ucf.edu
VITTETOE, Stanley .... 727-791-2475 .... 116 H
vittetoe.stan@spcollege.edu
VITTO, Cindy .... 856-256-3553 .... 314 A
vitto@rowan.edu
VITTONE, Jason .... 573-592-4387 .... 293 D
jason.vittone@williamwoods.edu
VIVEIROS, Derek .... 508-678-2811 .... 239 B
derek.viveiros@bristolcc.edu
VIVEIROS, Nelia .... 215-204-3745 .... 447 H
nelia.viveiros@temple.edu
VIVERETTE, Maggie, J .... 229-333-5463 .... 139 C
mviveret@valdosta.edu
VIVERITO, Diane .... 708-974-5334 .... 159 B
viverito@morainevalley.edu
VIVIAN, Daniel .... 716-645-4540 .... 351 G
dtvivian@buffalo.edu
VIVIANO, Paul .... 619-543-6654 ...... 74 F
pviviano@ucsd.edu
VIVILECCHIA, Joe .... 603-623-0313 .... 305 E
jvivilecchia@nhia.edu
VIVONA, Joseph, F .... 301-445-1923 .... 227 A
jvivona@usmd.edu
VIZCARRONDO, Roberto ... 787-750-4405 .... 567 C
roberto.vizcarrondo@upr.edu
VIZZINI, Anthony, J .... 269-276-3253 .... 260 C
tony.vizzini@wmich.edu
VLACH, Erin .... 614-222-4000 .... 388 G
evlach@ccad.edu
VLAHAKIS, Stacy .... 312-752-2232 .... 155 C
stacy.vlahakis@kendall.edu
VLAHAKIS, Valerie .... 217-641-4561 .... 154 I
vlahakis@jwcc.edu
VLAHOS, Christopher, J .... 216-368-6280 .... 386 F
christopher.vlahos@case.edu
VLAHOV, David .... 415-476-1805 ...... 75 A
david.vlahov@nursing.ucsf.edu
VLIET, Rodney, M .... 562-903-4834 ...... 31 A
rod.vliet@biola.edu
VO, Thoa Hoang .... 972-860-4604 .... 484 G
tvo@dcccd.edu
VOELKER, Diana .... 718-488-1043 .... 338 G
diana.voelker@liu.edu
VOELKER, Joseph .... 860-768-4103 ...... 95 B
voelker@hartford.edu
VOELZ, Zach, r .... 920-565-1287 .... 548 A
voelzzr@lakeland.edu
VOELZKE, Max .... 692-625-4035 .... 560 A
mvoelzke@cmi.edu
VOGEL, Allan .... 605-626-2544 .... 466 A
vogel@northern.edu
VOGEL, Barry .... 305-892-7042 .... 112 A
barry.vogel@jwu.edu
VOGEL, Brenda, J .... 812-374-5118 .... 176 A
bvogel6@ivytech.edu
VOGEL, Carol, L .... 785-670-1509 .... 197 F
carol.vogel@washburn.edu
VOGEL, Christine .... 773-947-6316 .... 157 G
cvogel@mccormick.edu
VOGEL, Joanne .... 407-646-2194 .... 116 D
jvogel@rollins.edu
VOGEL, Kim .... 541-684-4644 .... 419 F
kvogel@pioneerpacific.edu
VOGEL, Kristin, D .... 920-403-3290 .... 550 F
kristin.vogel@snc.edu
VOGEL, Petra .... 802-586-7711 .... 514 G
pvogel@sterlingcollege.edu
VOGEL, Rich .... 352-588-8361 .... 116 G
rich.vogel@saintleo.edu
VOGEL, Richard .... 631-420-2189 .... 356 A
richard.vogel@farmingdale.edu
VOGEL, Robert .... 412-536-1032 .... 432 H
bob.vogel@laroche.edu
VOGEL, Robert, L .... 859-846-5310 .... 204 H
rvogel@midway.edu
VOGEL, Terri .... 660-562-1151 .... 287 B
tvogel@nwmissouri.edu
VOGEL, Wade .... 701-224-5597 .... 382 D
wade.vogel@bismarckstate.edu
VOGELE, William .... 617-731-7114 .... 243 G
vogelewi@pmc.edu
VOGELGESANG, Bruce ...... 314-539-5245 .... 288 G
bvogelgesang@stlcc.edu
VOGELMANN, Thomas, C . 802-656-0137 .... 514 H
thomas.vogelmann@uvm.edu
VOGELZANG HOOGSTRA,
Shirley .... 616-526-6453 .... 249 A
shoogstr@calvin.edu
VOGHEL-OCHS, Sydney .... 203-575-8297 ...... 92 A
svoghel-ochs@nvcc.commnet.edu
VOGL, Joseph, A .... 989-964-4051 .... 257 G
javogl@svsu.edu
VOGT, Gail .... 619-574-6909 ...... 60 D
gvogt@pacificcollege.edu
VOGT, Judy, W .... 843-349-2037 .... 456 G
jvogt@coastal.edu
VOGT, Kara .... 308-432-6224 .... 299 E
kvogt@csc.edu
VOGT, Mark, A .... 502-410-6200 .... 200 L
mvogt@galencollege.edu
VOGT, Randy .... 559-244-5940 ...... 72 A
randy.vogt@scccd.edu
VOGT, Tracy .... 734-384-4230 .... 255 D
tvogt@monroeccc.edu
VOHRA, Promod .... 815-753-2256 .... 160 B
pvohra@niu.edu
VOIGT, Darry .... 307-268-2596 .... 556 A
dvoigt@caspercollege.edu
VOIGT, Francis .... 802-225-3207 .... 514 B
francis.voigt@neci.edu
VOIGT, Lydia .... 504-865-2573 .... 213 F
voigt@loyno.edu
VOIGTS, Adam, J .... 515-263-2821 .... 185 C
avoigts@grandview.edu
VOIGTS, Sheryl .... 859-858-2208 .... 198 D
VOISIN, Tony, A .... 989-774-3346 .... 249 C
voisi1a@cmich.edu
VOISIN, Tony, A .... 989-774-3016 .... 249 C
voisi1a@cmich.edu
VOISINE, Scott, A .... 207-834-8644 .... 220 D
voisine@maine.edu
VOKES, Bill .... 724-838-4282 .... 447 C
vokes@setonhill.edu
VOLAK, Renee .... 973-408-3637 .... 309 E
finaid@drew.edu
VOLAND, Gerard .... 810-762-3177 .... 259 C
gvoland@umflint.edu
VOLANT, Adam, C .... 540-464-7221 .... 529 F
volantac@vmiaa.org
VOLDEN, Lora .... 907-786-6190 ...... 10 H
llvolden@uaa.alaska.edu
VOLES, Lorraine, A .... 202-994-8810 ...... 98 C
lvoles@gwu.edu
VOLIBER, Delores .... 501-244-5124 ...... 19 D
delores.voliber@arkansasbaptist.edu
VOLK, Gregory, A .... 503-768-7901 .... 416 G
gvolk@lclark.edu
VOLK, Mark .... 570-961-7850 .... 433 A
volkm@lackawanna.edu
VOLK, Michael, S .... 616-554-5695 .... 250 C
mvolk@davenport.edu
VOLKER, Janice .... 402-872-2228 .... 299 F
jvolker@peru.edu
VOLKER, Jeanette .... 402-437-2554 .... 300 B
jvolker@southeast.edu
VOLKERS, Erica .... 505-224-3699 .... 317 K
evolkers@cnm.edu
VOLKERT, Jo .... 415-338-7264 ...... 37 B
jvolkert@sfsu.edu
VOLL, William .... 914-923-2772 .... 345 F
wvoll@pace.edu
VOLLENDORF, Lisa .... 408-924-4300 ...... 37 C
lisa.vollendorf@sjsu.edu
VOLLMER, Raymond .... 443-885-3144 .... 224 E
raymond.vollmer@morgan.edu
VOLLMERT, Brian .... 815-753-5791 .... 160 B
bvollmert@niu.edu
VOLLRATH, David, A .... 574-520-4260 .... 174 E
vollrath@iusb.edu
VOLNICK, Stacy .... 561-297-0143 .... 119 A
svolnick@fau.edu
VOLP, Patricia, M .... 757-221-2510 .... 518 A
pmvolp@wm.edu
VOLPE, David .... 814-262-6464 .... 441 A
dvolpe@pennhighlands.edu
VOLPE, Ronald, J .... 301-696-3855 .... 223 C
volpe@hood.edu
VOLPE-CASALINO,
Kimberly .... 516-299-2621 .... 338 E
kimberly.volpe-casalino@liu.edu
VOLPI, Robert, P .... 413-597-2121 .... 246 D
robert.p.volpi@williams.edu
VOLTAS, Catherine .... 401-454-6629 .... 454 B
cvoltas@risd.edu
VOLTURO, Tom .... 918-343-7861 .... 411 H
tvolturo@rsu.edu
VOLTZ, Deborah, L .... 205-934-8320 .... 8 F
voltz@uab.edu
VOLTZ, Larry, E .... 202-274-6195 .... 100 A
lvoltz@udc.edu
VOMACHKA, Archie, J .... 215-572-2199 .... 422 C
vomachka@arcadia.edu
VON ARX, SJ, Jeffrey, P .. 203-254-4000 ...... 92 H
president@fairfield.edu
VON BEHREN, Linda .... 217-234-5211 .... 156 B
lvonbehr@lakeland.cc.il.us
VON DAUM THOLL,
Susan .... 617-264-7656 .... 234 C
tholl@emmanuel.edu
VON DER MEHDEN, Kass 707-546-4000 ...... 45 H
kvondermehden@empirecollege.com
VON EBERS, Marie .... 708-524-6950 .... 150 C
vonebers@dom.edu
VON ECKARDT, Barbara .... 401-454-6580 .... 454 B
bvonecka@risd.edu
VON EYE, Rochelle .... 605-995-2625 .... 464 C
rovoneye@dwu.edu
VON HASSELN, Bill .... 253-964-6715 .... 536 H
VON HERRMANN, Denise 404-364-8318 .... 135 E
dvonherrmann@oglethorpe.edu
VON MUNKWITZ-SMITH,
Jeffrey .... 617-353-8353 .... 232 E
jvon@bu.edu
VON PFAHL, Stephen .... 231-843-5985 .... 260 B
smvonpfahl@westshore.edu
VON SCHLIEDER, Lynn ..... 202-546-4734 .... 538 C
lvonschl@shoreline.edu
VON TRAPP, Jane .... 203-837-8419 ...... 91 A
vontrappj@wcsu.edu

WAGNER, Nancy .... 907-377-4398 .... 508 E
wagnern@wbu.edu
WAGNER, Nancy, B .... 860-832-2050 ...... 90 G
wagnernab@ccsu.edu
WAGNER, Owen, W .... 724-946-7335 .... 451 C
owagner@westminster.edu
WAGNER, Patrick .... 920-403-3017 .... 550 F
pat.wagner@snc.edu
WAGNER, Patsy .... 509-527-2635 .... 539 C
patsy.wagner@wallawalla.edu
WAGNER, Rich .... 612-374-5800 .... 263 F
rwagner@dunwoody.edu
WAGNER, Richard, A .... 413-796-2306 .... 246 A
rwagner@wne.edu
WAGNER, Richard, T .... 240-895-3421 .... 226 A
rtwagner@smcm.edu
WAGNER, Robin .... 717-337-7000 .... 429 I
rowagner@gettysburg.edu
WAGNER, Roger .... 760-366-5289 ...... 43 H
rwagner@cmccd.edu
WAGNER, Steve .... 218-733-5934 .... 266 H
s.wagner@lsc.edu
WAGNER, Susan .... 603-577-6559 .... 304 I
wagner@dwc.edu
WAGNER, Susan .... 520-795-0787 ...... 11 I
registrar@asaom.edu
WAGNER, Teresa, J .... 315-464-4252 .... 352 E
wagnert@upstate.edu
WAGNER, Timothy .... 614-287-2408 .... 389 A
twagner@cscc.edu
WAGNER, Tracy, A .... 941-359-7511 .... 116 B
twagner@ringling.edu
WAGNER, Tricia .... 417-269-8316 .... 280 G
twagner@coxcollege.edu
WAGNER, Virginia .... 414-382-6115 .... 546 B
virginia.wagner@alverno.edu
WAGNER, William .... 415-371-0002 ...... 60 A
WAGNER-FOSSEN, Dena ... 406-771-4312 .... 295 G
dfossen@msugf.edu
WAGNER-LIND, Wendy ..... 954-308-2620 .... 101 C
wwagner@aii.edu
WAGNER WEICK, Cynthia 209-946-2650 ...... 76 A
cweick@pacific.edu
WAGNITZ, Jeff .... 206-878-3710 .... 535 B
jwagnitz@highline.edu
WAGNON, Bill .... 205-226-4901 .... 2 B
bwagnon@bsc.edu
WAGONER, Dale .... 510-723-7202 ...... 39 C
dwagoner@chabotcollege.edu
WAGONER, Dale .... 510-723-6618 ...... 39 C
dwagoner@chabotcollege.edu
WAGOR, Walter .... 330-499-9600 .... 393 I
WAGSTAFF, Grayson .... 202-319-5417 ...... 97 E
wagstaff@cua.edu
WAGSTAFF, John .... 310-660-3262 ...... 45 E
jwagstaff@elcamino.edu
WAGSTAFF, Robert .... 617-951-2350 .... 242 G
robert.wagstaff@necb.edu
WAGUESPACK, Cathy .... 504-398-2111 .... 214 B
cwaguespack@olhcc.edu
WAGUESPACK, F. Poche ... 251-981-3771 .... 2 G
poche@columbiasouthern.edu
WAHL, Chris .... 201-360-4030 .... 310 E
cwahl@hccc.edu
WAHL, Doug, J .... 715-232-2501 .... 552 E
wahld@uwstout.edu
WAHL, John .... 435-722-6900 .... 510 N
john@ubatc.edu
WAHL, Lynette .... 651-523-3000 .... 264 A
lwahl@hamline.edu
WAHL, Robert .... 860-255-3472 ...... 92 F
rwahl@txcc.commnet.edu
WAHLBECK, Mary .... 630-428-9548 .... 149 J
mwahlbeck@devry.edu
WAHLBERG, David, C .... 218-477-2175 .... 267 F
david.wahlberg@mnstate.edu
WAHLER, Rick .... 661-362-2267 ...... 56 G
rwahler@masters.edu
WAHLERS, Mark, E .... 503-280-8578 .... 415 E
mwahlers@cu-portland.edu
WAHLERT, Christine, A ..... 816-654-7285 .... 283 F
cwahlert@kcumb.edu
WAHLFELDT, Tracy, D .... 217-443-8772 .... 148 G
twahlfeldt@dacc.edu
WAHLSTROM, David, A .... 617-989-4552 .... 245 F
wahlstromd@wit.edu
WAHR, David .... 567-661-7401 .... 400 I
david_wahr@owens.edu
WAHR, Linda .... 312-329-2213 .... 159 A
lwahr@moody.edu
WAI HLA, Maung .... 408-260-0208 ...... 47 D
doctoral@fivebranches.edu
WAID, Monica, K .... 941-359-7511 .... 116 B
mwaid@ringling.edu
WAID, Patti, W .... 209-228-4483 ...... 74 D
pwaid@ucmerced.edu
WAIDE, Linda .... 256-331-5321 .... 6 B
lwaide@nwscc.edu
WAINDLE, Kaylene .... 207-741-5571 .... 219 A
kwaindle@smccme.edu
WAINES, Bridgette .... 904-680-7780 .... 107 J
bwaines@fcsl.edu
WAINSCOTT, Denise .... 606-546-1218 .... 207 B
wainscot@unionky.edu
WAINWRIGHT, Lisa .... 312-629-1236 .... 164 C
lwainwright@saic.edu
WAINWRIGHT, William, S 985-732-6640 .... 211 A
WAIS, Marc .... 212-998-4401 .... 344 B
marc.wais@nyu.edu
WAIT, Mark .... 615-322-7660 .... 478 A
mark.wait@vanderbilt.edu
WAITE, Boyd, A .... 410-293-1582 .... 559 B
waite@usna.edu
WAITE, Dan .... 949-214-3472 ...... 43 C
dan.waite@cui.edu
WAITE, David .... 541-885-1075 .... 418 E
david.waite@oit.edu
WAITE, George .... 616-234-3818 .... 251 E
gwaite@grcc.edu
WAITE, Joann .... 509-313-5870 .... 534 F
waite@gonzaga.edu
WAITE, Michelle .... 402-472-2116 .... 300 G
mwaite1@unl.edu
WAITE, William .... 973-300-2100 .... 315 F
wwaite@sussex.edu
WAITE, Zauyah .... 412-365-2794 .... 425 C
zwaite@chatham.edu
WAITE-FRANZEN, Ellen, J 603-646-2643 .... 304 J
ellen.waite-franzen@dartmouth.edu
WAITERS, Ernest .... 301-860-4040 .... 228 A
ewaiters@bowiestate.edu
WAITES, Alan .... 785-460-5402 .... 192 C
alan.waites@colbycc.edu
WAITES, Cheryl .... 313-577-4401 .... 260 A
dv7029@wayne.edu
WAITMAN, Russ .... 913-945-7087 .... 197 C
rwaitman@kumc.edu
WAITZ, Ian, A .... 617-253-0218 .... 241 D
WAJDA, Phillip, J .... 518-388-8394 .... 358 G
wajdap@union.edu
WAJERT, Susan, C .... 309-779-7710 .... 166 D
wajertsc@ihs.org
WAJLER, Nancy .... 847-925-6910 .... 151 G
nwajler@harpercollege.edu
WAKE, Sue .... 606-539-4201 .... 207 C
sue.wake@ucumberlands.edu
WAKEFIELD, Jill .... 206-934-3872 .... 537 C
jill.wakefield@seattlecolleges.edu
WAKEFIELD, Larry .... 229-430-4609 .... 124 A
larry.wakefield@asurams.edu
WAKELEE, Dan .... 805-437-8542 ...... 34 B
dan.wakelee@csuci.edu
WAKELING, William, M ..... 617-373-5001 .... 243 F
WAKEMAN, Joe .... 740-753-6098 .... 391 H
wakeman_j@hocking.edu
WAKEMAN, Wendy .... 626-584-5423 ...... 48 B
wwakeman@fuller.edu
WAKSDAHL, Robert, B ...... 715-394-8383 .... 552 F
rwaksdah@uwsuper.edu
WALBERT, BJ .... 301-552-1400 .... 229 C
bwalbert@bible.edu
WALBERT, Janet, E .... 215-572-2088 .... 422 C
walbertj@arcadia.edu
WALBERT, Mark .... 309-438-7306 .... 153 D
mswalber@ilstu.edu
WALBERT, Tim .... 501-812-2366 ...... 23 C
twalbert@pulaskitech.edu
WALBORN, Ronald .... 845-770-5716 .... 344 G
ronald.walborn@nyack.edu
WALBORN, Wanda, F .... 845-675-4457 .... 344 G
wanda.walborn@nyack.edu
WALCH, Darlene, M .... 906-227-2117 .... 256 C
dwalch@umu.edu
WALCHESKI, Michael .... 651-603-6184 .... 263 A
walcheski@csp.edu
WALCHONSKY, OSBM,
Marie Francis .... 215-885-2360 .... 435 E
sfrancis@manor.edu
WALCK, Barbara .... 716-614-5902 .... 344 C
bwalck@niagaracc.suny.edu
WALCK, Brad .... 405-382-9231 .... 412 B
b.walck@sscok.edu
WALCROFT, Marie, B .... 215-699-5700 .... 433 G
mwalcroft@lsb.edu
WALCZAK, David .... 954-308-2370 .... 101 C
dwalczak@aii.edu
WALD, Jonathan, D .... 941-355-9080 .... 105 D
jwald@ewcollege.org
WALDECK, Steve .... 661-362-2767 ...... 56 G
swaldeck@masters.edu
WALDEN, Daniel .... 323-242-5511 ...... 55 C
waldendw@lasc.edu
WALDEN, Tom .... 270-247-8521 .... 204 G
twalden@midcontinent.edu
WALDEN, Valerie .... 361-570-4815 .... 504 A
waldenv@uhv.edu
WALDMANN, Robert, G .... 718-429-6600 .... 359 G
robert.waldmann@vaughn.edu
WALDNER, George, W .... 717-815-1221 .... 452 G
gwaldner@ycp.edu
WALDNER, Joanne, L .... 978-232-2013 .... 234 D
jwaldner@endicott.edu
WALDNER, Louann .... 559-737-4838 ...... 42 D
louannw@cos.edu
WALDO, Susan .... 575-646-1631 .... 319 D
swaldo@nmsu.edu
WALDO, Susan .... 575-646-1722 .... 319 D
swaldo@nmsu.edu
WALDREN,
Henry "Tre", M .... 419-995-8081 .... 392 K
waldren.t@rhodesstate.edu
WALDREP, Dwain .... 205-970-9231 .... 7 C
dwaldrep@sebc.edu
WALDRIP, Brenda .... 601-318-6188 .... 278 C
brenda.waldrip@wmcarey.edu
WALDRON, Cathy .... 561-586-0121 .... 110 I
WALDRON, David, E .... 512-448-8453 .... 493 E
dwaldron@stedwards.edu
WALDRON, Gregory, T .... 860-439-2408 ...... 92 G
gregory.waldron@conncoll.edu
WALDRON, Janet, E .... 207-581-1554 .... 220 A
jwaldron@maine.edu
WALDRON, Kathleen .... 973-720-2222 .... 317 D
waldronk@wpunj.edu
WALDRON, Sara .... 973-408-3390 .... 309 E
swaldron@drew.edu
WALDROP, Heath .... 870-862-8131 ...... 23 G
hwaldrop@southark.edu
WALDROP, Nadine .... 602-944-3335 ...... 11 D
nwaldrop@aicag.net
WALDROP, Tony, G .... 407-823-2303 .... 120 B
twaldrop@ucf.edu
WALDROUP, Linda, L .... 812-888-4333 .... 181 D
lwaldroup@vinu.edu
WALDRUP, Bobby, E .... 904-620-2700 .... 120 D
bwaldrup@unf.edu
WALDRUP, J. Charles .... 336-334-7592 .... 378 A
cwaldrup@ncat.edu
WALDSTEIN, Edith, J .... 319-352-8272 .... 189 J
edith.waldstein@wartburg.edu
WALDVOGEL, Marlene .... 517-264-7190 .... 258 B
mwaldvogel@sienaheights.edu
WALE, Rebecca .... 503-883-2602 .... 416 H
rwale@linfield.edu
WALEHWA, Joshua .... 314-977-2484 .... 289 C
jwalehwa@slu.edu
WALEK, Chuck .... 972-708-7574 .... 487 B
chuck_walek@gial.edu
WALENGA, Gail, A .... 513-529-7506 .... 396 E
walengga@muohio.edu
WALENTA, Michael .... 616-331-6737 .... 251 F
walentam@gvsu.edu
WALERIUS, Kenneth .... 419-434-4601 .... 404 B
walerius@findlay.edu
WALESBY, Anthony, J .... 734-763-0325 .... 259 A
walesby@umich.edu
WALETZKO, Chuck .... 952-358-8146 .... 268 A
chuck.waletzko@normandale.edu
WALFORD, Ron .... 502-213-5101 .... 202 F
ronald.walford@kctcs.edu
WALHOUT, Matthew .... 616-526-6566 .... 249 A
mwalhout@calvin.edu
WALK, Kerry .... 310-665-6979 ...... 60 B
kwalk@otis.edu
WALKE, Lindsey .... 843-863-8047 .... 456 B
lwalke@csuniv.edu
WALKER, Adam .... 262-243-5700 .... 547 C
adam.walker@cuw.edu
WALKER, Alan, G .... 563-425-5201 .... 189 G
walkera@uiu.edu
WALKER, Albert .... 314-340-3380 .... 282 F
walkera@hssu.edu
WALKER, Alonzo, P .... 414-955-8656 .... 548 G
awalker@mcw.edu
WALKER, Anne, E .... 713-348-8025 .... 493 C
anne.e.walker@rice.edu
WALKER, Anthony, H .... 757-823-2199 .... 522 E
ahwalker@nsu.edu
WALKER, Barbara .... 713-798-3437 .... 481 H
blw@bcm.edu
WALKER, Beth .... 313-664-7641 .... 249 E
bwalker@collegeforcreativestudies.edu
WALKER, Bev .... 419-755-4786 .... 397 C
bwalker@ncstatecollege.edu
WALKER, Bill, M .... 501-569-3186 ...... 24 E
wxwalker@ualr.edu
WALKER, Blaine .... 918-836-6886 .... 412 G
bwalker@mail.spartan.edu
WALKER, Brenda, S .... 803-705-4730 .... 455 D
walkerb@benedict.edu
WALKER, Bruce, R .... 304-558-0695 .... 543 E
walkerb@hepc.wvnet.edu
WALKER, Carol .... 352-273-4000 .... 120 C
cjw@ufl.edu
WALKER, Carol .... 352-588-8308 .... 116 G
carol.walker@saintleo.edu
WALKER, Charlene .... 859-246-6438 .... 201 H
charlene.walker@kctcs.edu
WALKER, Cherilee .... 913-288-7134 .... 194 C
cwalker@kckcc.edu
WALKER, Cheryl .... 713-677-7440 .... 497 B
cwalker@ibt.tamhsc.edu
WALKER, Christopher .... 405-224-3140 .... 413 E
cwalker@usao.edu
WALKER, Cindy .... 334-386-7305 .... 3 G
cwalker@faulkner.edu
WALKER, Claire .... 727-942-0069 .... 115 H
claire.walker@rasmussen.edu
WALKER, Dalbert, N .... 772-546-5534 .... 110 N
dalbertwalker@hsbc.edu
WALKER, David .... 864-833-8310 .... 460 E
dwalker@presby.edu
WALKER, David, S .... 717-796-5237 .... 436 D
dwalker@messiah.edu
WALKER, Debbie .... 803-822-3269 .... 459 E
walkerd@midlandstech.edu
WALKER, Debi .... 510-649-2400 ...... 48 J
dwalker@gtu.edu
WALKER, Deborah .... 510-849-8290 ...... 60 G
dwalker@psr.edu
WALKER, Deborah .... 845-675-4430 .... 344 G
deborah.walker@nyack.edu
WALKER, Demetra .... 843-355-4131 .... 463 D
walkerd@wiltech.edu
WALKER, Diana .... 312-410-8979 .... 146 F
dwalker@thechicagoschool.edu
WALKER, Diane .... 330-499-9600 .... 393 I
dcwalker@kent.edu
WALKER, Donna .... 972-238-6880 .... 485 D
dwalker1@dcccd.edu
WALKER, Douglas .... 845-675-4595 .... 344 G
douglas.walker@nyack.edu
WALKER, Dwayne .... 215-489-2372 .... 426 H
dwayne.walker@delval.edu
WALKER, Eddie .... 318-869-5116 .... 208 H
ewalker@centenary.edu
WALKER, Elaine .... 909-447-2510 ...... 40 H
ewalker@cst.edu
WALKER, Elizabeth .... 215-893-5265 .... 426 E
elizabeth.walker@curtis.edu
WALKER, Ellen, L .... 330-569-5250 .... 391 G
walkerel@hiram.edu
WALKER, Eric .... 501-370-5274 ...... 23 B
ewalker@philander.edu
WALKER, Eunice, E .... 870-235-5113 ...... 23 I
eewalker@saumag.edu
WALKER, Gail, D .... 208-467-8844 .... 144 E
gwalker@nnu.edu
WALKER, George .... 216-687-3583 .... 388 D
george.walker@csuohio.edu
WALKER, Gerry .... 816-584-6256 .... 287 E
gerry.walker@park.edu
WALKER, Graham .... 540-338-1776 .... 522 G
WALKER, Gwendolyn, M ... 716-839-8244 .... 331 F
gwalker@daemen.edu
WALKER, H. Fred .... 585-475-5955 .... 347 G
hfwast@rit.edu
WALKER, Ivan .... 910-672-1811 .... 377 G
iwalker@uncfsu.edu
WALKER, Jack .... 865-882-4567 .... 476 A
walkerjd@roanestate.edu
WALKER, Janice, B .... 513-745-3101 .... 406 E
walkerj@xavier.edu
WALKER, Jeannie .... 714-744-7078 ...... 39 F
walker@chapman.edu
WALKER, Jeff, W .... 404-413-1521 .... 131 G
jeffwalker@gsu.edu
WALKER, Jefferson .... 256-322-3103 .... 7 G
jwalker@talladega.edu
WALKER, Jen, C .... 859-622-1303 .... 200 J
jen.walker@eku.edu
WALKER, Jeremy .... 847-851-5468 ...... 83 J
WALKER, Jewell .... 870-575-7099 ...... 25 B
walkerj@uapb.edu
WALKER, Jim .... 806-894-9611 .... 494 G
jwalker@southplainscollege.edu
WALKER, Joe .... 828-227-7441 .... 380 A
jwalker@wcu.edu
WALKER, John .... 949-794-9090 ...... 71 F
jwalker@stanbridge.edu
WALKER, John .... 575-528-7220 .... 319 G
jwalker@nmsu.edu
WALKER, Joshua .... 805-581-1233 ...... 45 J
WALKER, Josie .... 985-549-5920 .... 216 C
jwalker@selu.edu
WALKER, Judith, D .... 402-559-6409 .... 300 H
jdwalker@unmc.edu
WALKER, Judy .... 734-929-9092 .... 249 D
jwalker@cleary.edu
WALKER, Karen .... 573-651-2253 .... 289 K
kmwalker@semo.edu
WALKER, Kate .... 651-696-6562 .... 264 J
kwalker@macalester.edu
WALKER, Katherine .... 941-752-5320 .... 118 J
walkerk@scf.edu
WALKER, Ken .... 859-256-3100 .... 201 E
ken.walker@kctcs.edu
WALKER, Kenneth .... 205-652-3665 .... 9 E
kwalker@uwa.edu
WALKER, Kevin .... 615-343-6601 .... 478 A
kevin.walker@vanderbilt.edu
WALKER, Kimberly, G .... 314-935-6976 .... 292 I
kimberly.walker@wustl.edu
WALKER, Kristin .... 972-937-7612 .... 491 C
kristin.walker@navarrocollege.edu
WALKER, Kyle .... 817-923-1921 .... 495 G
admissions@swbts.edu
WALKER, L. David .... 864-833-8310 .... 460 E
dwalker@presby.edu
WALKER, Larry .... 831-646-4290 ...... 57 G
lwalker@mpc.edu
WALKER, Larry .... 405-878-2009 .... 409 D
larry.walker@okbu.edu
WALKER, Larry .... 425-388-9328 .... 534 C
lwalker@everettcc.edu

WALLS-UPCHURCH, L. Ida .... 901-448-4444 .... 477 E
iupchurch@uthsc.edu
WALLY, William .... 680-488-6223 .... 560 C
willyw@palau.edu
WALN, Ursula .... 402-872-2341 .... 299 F
uwaln@peru.edu
WALNOHA, Melinda .... 760-921-5404 ...... 61 C
mwalnoha@paloverde.edu
WALPOLE, Arch .... 757-499-7900 .... 517 D
afwalpole@bryantstratton.edu
WALPOLE, Tommy, A .... 318-342-5419 .... 216 E
walpole@ulm.edu
WALRATH, Ron .... 803-461-3237 .... 459 C
ronald.walrath@lr.edu
WALSER, Ardie, D .... 212-650-8022 .... 326 G
walser@ccny.cuny.edu
WALSH, Ann .... 516-299-3874 .... 339 A
ann.walsh@liu.edu
WALSH, Clifton .... 915-747-6636 .... 506 B
cwalsh@utep.edu
WALSH, Cynthia .... 817-257-7855 .... 499 C
c.walsh@tcu.edu
WALSH, Denise .... 559-438-4222 ...... 49 I
denise_walsh@heald.edu
WALSH, Erin .... 718-405-3345 .... 330 A
erin.walsh@mountsaintvincent.edu
WALSH, Jack .... 724-266-3838 .... 448 H
jwalsh@tsm.edu
WALSH, James .... 312-410-8996 .... 146 F
jwalsh@thechicagoschool.edu
WALSH, James, A .... 904-276-6839 .... 116 F
tonywalsh@sjrstate.edu
WALSH, Janet .... 314-984-7387 .... 289 A
jwalsh@stlcc.edu
WALSH, Jeff .... 352-588-7337 .... 116 G
jeffrey.walsh@saintleo.edu
WALSH, Jodi .... 508-849-3266 .... 230 C
jwalsh@annamaria.edu
WALSH, John .... 978-632-6600 .... 240 C
j_walsh@mwcc.mass.edu
WALSH, John .... 406-657-2363 .... 295 D
jwalsh@msubillings.edu
WALSH, John .... 406-896-5872 .... 295 D
jwalsh@msubillings.edu
WALSH, John .... 775-682-7190 .... 303 A
walshj@unr.edu
WALSH, John, T .... 909-748-8368 ...... 76 C
john_walsh@redlands.edu
WALSH, Joseph, T .... 847-491-3485 .... 160 E
vp-research@northwestern.edu
WALSH, Julianne .... 617-879-7073 .... 238 B
jwalsh@massart.edu
WALSH, Kathleen .... 312-261-3828 .... 159 E
kathleen.walsh@nl.edu
WALSH, Kimberly, A .... 563-588-7417 .... 187 C
kimberly.walsh@loras.edu
WALSH, Lawrence .... 610-436-3564 .... 444 A
lwalsh@wcupa.edu
WALSH, Lindy .... 802-862-9616 .... 513 B
lwalsh@burlington.edu
WALSH, Margaret .... 614-251-4605 .... 398 F
walshm@ohiodominican.edu
WALSH, Margurete .... 215-951-1013 .... 432 I
walshm@lasalle.edu
WALSH, Mark .... 813-974-2660 .... 121 A
mwalsh@usf.edu
WALSH, Mark, C .... 630-844-5111 .... 145 F
mwalsh@aurora.edu
WALSH, Mary, T .... 504-314-2537 .... 215 C
mary@tulane.edu
WALSH, Mary Beth .... 914-597-2163 .... 360 C
mwalsh@burke.org
WALSH, Mary Lee .... 434-961-6540 .... 528 B
mwalsh@pvcc.edu
WALSH, Melissa .... 215-965-4042 .... 436 H
mwalsh@moore.edu
WALSH, Michael .... 414-297-6246 .... 554 F
walshm@matc.edu
WALSH, Michael .... 503-943-7205 .... 420 G
walsh@up.edu
WALSH, Michael, D .... 540-568-5681 .... 520 H
walshmd@jmu.edu
WALSH, Michael, J .... 518-564-2100 .... 354 B
walshmj@plattsburgh.edu
WALSH, Michela .... 314-513-4218 .... 288 H
mwalsh@stlcc.edu
WALSH, Michele, M .... 781-891-2070 .... 231 D
mwalsh1@bentley.edu
WALSH, Patricia, J .... 417-255-7904 .... 286 D
pwalsh@missouristate.edu
WALSH, Philip .... 207-786-6240 .... 217 C
pwalsh@bates.edu
WALSH, Richard .... 541-552-6258 .... 419 A
walshr@sou.edu
WALSH, Rosalie, K .... 406-447-5440 .... 293 G
rwalsh@carroll.edu
WALSH, Susan .... 541-552-6114 .... 419 A
walsh@sou.edu
WALSH, Susan .... 209-384-6082 ...... 57 C
walsh.s@mccd.edu
WALSH, Tammy .... 941-359-7505 .... 116 B
twalsh@ringling.edu
WALSH, Thomas, J .... 315-443-2881 .... 357 C
twalsh@syr.edu
WALSH, Timothy .... 919-684-5055 .... 364 C
tim.walsh@duke.edu
WALSH, Timothy, J .... 716-878-4201 .... 353 A
walshtj@buffalostate.edu
WALSH, Timothy, L .... 662-915-7375 .... 277 D
tim@olemiss.edu
WALSH-KANE, Erin .... 610-358-4262 .... 437 D
kanee@neumann.edu
WALSHOK, Mary, L .... 858-534-3411 ...... 74 F
mwalshok@ucsd.edu
WALSKI, Don .... 507-457-5555 .... 269 G
dwalski@winona.edu
WALSTEAD, Brenda .... 360-992-2474 .... 532 F
bwalstead@clark.edu
WALSTRUM, John, W .... 253-589-5500 .... 532 G
john.walstrum@cptc.edu
WALTER, Almar .... 419-434-6967 .... 404 B
waltera@findlay.edu
WALTER, B. Oliver .... 307-766-4106 .... 556 H
owalter@uwyo.edu
WALTER, Blake .... 630-620-2105 .... 160 C
bwalter@seminary.edu
WALTER, George, J .... 610-519-6456 .... 450 H
george.walter@villanova.edu
WALTER, James .... 623-572-3340 ...... 16 E
jwalte@midwestern.edu
WALTER, Jim .... 706-355-5120 .... 125 C
jwalter@athenstech.edu
WALTER, John, M .... 661-362-2239 ...... 56 G
jwalter@masters.edu
WALTER, Kelly .... 617-353-2300 .... 232 E
kwalter@bu.edu
WALTER, Kristy .... 617-243-2147 .... 236 A
kwalter@lasell.edu
WALTER, Lisa, A .... 715-232-2266 .... 552 E
walterl@uwstout.edu
WALTER, Robyn, C .... 636-584-6617 .... 281 E
walterr@eastcentral.edu
WALTER, Ruth .... 412-809-5100 .... 444 G
walter.ruth@pti.edu
WALTER, Shulem .... 718-855-4092 .... 346 L
WALTER, Susan .... 530-541-4660 ...... 53 G
walter@ltcc.edu
WALTER, Tom, G .... 678-717-3553 .... 129 G
twalter@gsc.edu
WALTER, Willis .... 386-481-2087 .... 102 C
walterw@cookman.edu
WALTER-MACK, Kathy .... 816-604-1587 .... 284 H
kathy.walter-mack@mcckc.edu
WALTER-SCHUMACHER, Joan .... 414-382-6064 .... 546 B
joan.walter@alverno.edu
WALTERREIT, Jay .... 989-358-7215 .... 247 C
walterrj@alpenacc.edu
WALTERS, Alice .... 845-569-3259 .... 342 A
alice.walters@msmc.edu
WALTERS, Carmen .... 504-762-3015 .... 210 F
cwalte@dcc.edu
WALTERS, Dale .... 423-236-2860 .... 473 B
dwalters@southern.edu
WALTERS, Dave .... 270-789-5007 .... 199 F
dlwalters@campbellsville.edu
WALTERS, Evon, W .... 631-548-2565 .... 356 F
waltere@sunysuffolk.edu
WALTERS, Gary, D .... 609-258-3535 .... 312 G
walters@princeton.edu
WALTERS, Irene, A .... 260-481-6104 .... 174 C
walters@ipfw.edu
WALTERS, Isaac .... 267-256-0200 ...... 99 G
WALTERS, Jennifer, L .... 413-585-2797 .... 244 G
jwalters@smith.edu
WALTERS, Jim .... 951-343-4323 ...... 31 J
jmwalters@calbaptist.edu
WALTERS, Joanna .... 785-242-5200 .... 178 I
WALTERS, Joanna .... 785-242-5200 .... 196 A
WALTERS, Joanna .... 785-242-5200 ...... 17 B
WALTERS, Joanna .... 785-242-5200 .... 549 H
WALTERS, Joanna, L .... 785-242-5200 .... 195 I
joanna.walters@ottawa.edu
WALTERS, Joe .... 303-963-3376 ...... 82 C
jwalters@ccu.edu
WALTERS, June .... 870-762-3102 ...... 20 A
jwalters@smail.anc.edu
WALTERS, Kathie .... 319-226-2003 .... 182 A
waltersks@ihs.org
WALTERS, Kelly .... 661-834-0126 ...... 66 F
kelly.walters@sjvc.edu
WALTERS, Kent, L .... 904-264-2172 .... 116 C
kwalters@iws.edu
WALTERS, Leigh Anne .... 973-290-4219 .... 308 G
lwalters@cse.edu
WALTERS, Linda .... 212-686-9040 .... 360 F
lwalters@woodtobecoburn.edu
WALTERS, Linda .... 570-740-0462 .... 435 C
lwalters@luzerne.edu
WALTERS, Maria .... 623-245-4600 ...... 18 J
mwalters@uti.edu
WALTERS, Mark .... 608-262-3666 .... 550 J
mwalters@ohr.wisc.edu
WALTERS, Meridee .... 505-428-1232 .... 320 E
meridee.walters@sfcc.edu
WALTERS, Michael .... 309-341-5290 .... 146 D
mwalters@sandburg.edu
WALTERS, Michael, R .... 606-783-2053 .... 204 I
m.walters@moreheadstate.edu
WALTERS, Richard .... 314-918-2561 .... 281 F
rwalters@eden.edu
WALTERS, Richard, P .... 423-775-6597 .... 472 G
WALTERS, Rick .... 803-313-7464 .... 462 D
walterc3@mailbox.sc.edu
WALTERS, Ricki .... 507-433-0534 .... 268 H
rwalters@riverland.edu
WALTERS, Robby .... 828-395-1602 .... 371 D
rwalters@isothermal.edu
WALTERS, Robert .... 310-665-6916 ...... 60 B
rwalters@otis.edu
WALTERS, Robert .... 540-231-6077 .... 529 G
rwalters@vt.edu
WALTERS, Roland .... 540-365-4267 .... 519 C
rwalters@ferrum.edu
WALTERS, Tamyra .... 269-749-7197 .... 257 A
twalters@olivetcollege.edu
WALTERS, Tanaya .... 980-598-1835 .... 365 I
tanaya.walters@jwu.edu
WALTERS, Timothy, L .... 509-359-2777 .... 533 H
twalters@ewu.edu
WALTERS, Tyler .... 540-231-5595 .... 529 G
tyler.walters@vt.edu
WALTERS, William .... 650-543-3827 ...... 57 B
wwalters@menlo.edu
WALTERS, William, D .... 336-334-5824 .... 379 B
bill_walters@uncg.edu
WALTERSCHEID, Dianne .... 940-668-4274 .... 491 E
dwalterscheid@nctc.edu
WALTHER, Barb .... 734-995-7499 .... 249 G
walthb@cuaa.edu
WALTHER-THOMAS, Christine, S .... 804-828-3382 .... 526 B
cswalthertho@vcu.edu
WALTHERS, Bruce .... 970-204-8100 ...... 85 A
bruce.walthers@frontrange.edu
WALTHERS, Kevin, G .... 925-424-1001 ...... 39 D
kwalthers@laspositascollege.edu
WALTHOUR, Scott, N .... 419-772-3100 .... 398 H
s-walthour@onu.edu
WALTON, Ali .... 303-871-2287 ...... 89 A
alison.walton@du.edu
WALTON, Anita, B .... 919-530-7517 .... 378 B
awalton@nccu.edu
WALTON, Connie .... 318-247-3811 .... 215 E
WALTON, Dean .... 617-236-8800 .... 234 G
dwalton@fisher.edu
WALTON, Ed .... 417-328-1622 .... 290 A
ewalton@sbuniv.edu
WALTON, Edward .... 513-861-6400 .... 402 I
ed.walton@myunion.edu
WALTON, Edward, I .... 803-777-7000 .... 462 A
ed.walton@sc.edu
WALTON, Elaine, L .... 262-551-5702 .... 546 I
ewalton@carthage.edu
WALTON, F. Carl .... 484-365-7222 .... 434 H
fwalton@lincoln.edu
WALTON, James, M .... 360-736-9391 .... 532 D
jwalton@centralia.edu
WALTON, James, W .... 972-708-7340 .... 487 B
jim_walton@gial.edu
WALTON, Jason, L .... 561-237-7787 .... 113 D
jwalton@lynn.edu
WALTON, Jeffrey, T .... 518-327-6236 .... 345 H
jwalton@paulsmiths.edu
WALTON, Jinx, P .... 412-624-6100 .... 449 A
jpw@pitt.edu
WALTON, Karen .... 610-282-1100 .... 427 A
karen.walton@desales.edu
WALTON, Kathy, M .... 512-223-7213 .... 481 B
kwalton@austincc.edu
WALTON, Kathy, S .... 310-287-4396 ...... 55 F
waltonks@wlac.edu
WALTON, Lindsay .... 910-755-7330 .... 368 F
waltonl@brunswickcc.edu
WALTON, Mary Ann .... 941-637-5644 .... 105 F
mwalton@edison.edu
WALTON, Robert .... 909-621-8026 ...... 40 E
rwalton@cuc.claremont.edu
WALTON, Robin .... 609-777-5654 .... 316 A
rwalton@tesc.edu
WALTON, Sheila .... 425-739-8314 .... 535 H
sheila.walton@lwtc.edu
WALTON, Susan .... 701-777-2731 .... 381 F
susan.walton@und.edu
WALTON, Trudy, J .... 323-241-5279 ...... 55 C
waltontj@lasc.edu
WALTZ, John .... 304-473-8510 .... 545 G
waltz@wvwc.edu
WALTZ, Stephen .... 603-577-6000 .... 304 I
swaltz@dwc.edu
WALTZ, JR., Thomas, A .... 717-872-3282 .... 443 D
thomas.waltz@millersville.edu
WALWORTH, Maurice .... 906-635-2211 .... 253 H
mwalworth@lssu.edu
WALYUCHOW, Ashley .... 361-570-4343 .... 504 A
walyuchowa@uhv.edu
WALZEL, JR., Robert, L .... 785-864-3421 .... 197 B
robert.walzel@ku.edu
WAMBAUGH, Genie, M .... 859-344-3684 .... 206 I
genie.wambaugh@thomasmore.edu
WAMBSGANS, Cynthia .... 408-254-6900 ...... 58 G
cwabmsgans@nhu.edu
WAMBUGU-COBB, Angela .... 718-482-5028 .... 328 B
awcobb@lagcc.cuny.edu
WAMPLER, Fredrick, H .... 215-898-5859 .... 448 J
fhoopes@ben.dev.upenn.edu
WAMPLER, Jim .... 423-236-2782 .... 473 B
jwampler@southern.edu
WAMSLEY, Allan, A .... 636-481-3342 .... 283 D
awamsley@jeffco.edu
WAMSLEY, Michelle, E .... 804-287-6615 .... 525 E
mwamsley@richmond.edu
WAN, Laura .... 562-938-4302 ...... 54 E
lwan@lbcc.edu
WANDOLOWSKI, John .... 630-942-2972 .... 148 A
wandol@cod.edu
WANG, Alvin .... 407-823-3449 .... 120 B
alvin.wang@ucf.edu
WANG, Amy .... 323-343-3170 ...... 35 D
awang@cslanet.calstatela.edu
WANG, Ching-Hua .... 415-482-1888 ...... 45 C
ching-hua.wang@dominican.edu
WANG, David .... 212-226-7300 .... 346 E
dwang@pbcny.edu
WANG, Howard .... 657-278-2800 ...... 35 B
hwang@fullerton.edu
WANG, Jenny .... 860-906-5106 ...... 91 C
jwang@ccc.commnet.edu
WANG, Jianping .... 914-606-6963 .... 360 E
jianping.wang@sunywcc.edu
WANG, Jin .... 801-832-2601 .... 512 G
jwang@westminstercollege.edu
WANG, Jing .... 916-278-6566 ...... 36 A
jwang@csus.edu
WANG, Jinhao .... 956-872-3508 .... 494 H
jwang@southtexascollege.edu
WANG, Lan .... 731-426-7654 .... 470 B
lwang@lanecollege.edu
WANG, Lei .... 210-434-6711 .... 492 B
lwang@lake.ollusa.edu
WANG, Lei .... 850-201-9775 .... 122 A
wangl@tcc.fl.edu
WANG, Minghui .... 609-431-4997 .... 335 A
wangm@hartwick.edu
WANG, Ray .... 909-869-3088 ...... 33 J
jwang@csupomona.edu
WANG, Sara .... 415-355-1601 ...... 28 B
sarawang@actcm.edu
WANG, Tracy .... 310-577-3000 ...... 80 E
swang@yosan.edu
WANG, Willis, G .... 617-353-2000 .... 232 E
wgwang@bu.edu
WANG, Xiaoping .... 423-354-2552 .... 475 F
xpwang@northeaststate.edu
WANG, Xinying .... 501-450-1226 ...... 22 A
wang@hendrix.edu
WANG, Xuemao .... 513-556-1515 .... 403 D
xuemao.wang@uc.edu
WANG, Ying Qiu .... 408-733-1878 ...... 75 D
yingwang@uewm.edu
WANG, Yingchen .... 575-234-9237 .... 319 F
ycwang@nmsu.edu
WANG, Yumin .... 203-576-4395 ...... 94 F
yuminw@bridgeport.edu
WANG, Yungzeng .... 951-827-4237 ...... 74 E
yunzeng.wang@ucr.edu
WANG-WELDON, Louise .... 810-989-2120 .... 248 G
louise.wangweldon@baker.edu
WANKE, Tom, S .... 414-277-7191 .... 549 C
wanke@msoe.edu
WANKEL, Laura, A .... 617-373-4384 .... 243 F
WANLESS, Terry .... 916-278-6348 ...... 36 A
twanless@csus.edu
WANNER, Samuel, L .... 616-526-6689 .... 249 A
slw3@calvin.edu
WANOUS, Mike .... 605-274-4712 .... 464 A
mike.wanous@augie.edu
WANSICK, Janet .... 918-302-3617 .... 408 A
jwansick@eosc.edu
WANT, JuAn .... 618-536-6682 .... 165 B
towens@siu.edu
WANTZ, Steven .... 410-386-8154 .... 221 G
swantz@carrollcc.edu
WANZA, Mary .... 410-951-3400 .... 228 B
mwanza@coppin.edu
WAPPES, Loran .... 218-879-0839 .... 266 C
loran@fdltcc.edu
WARBURG, Jason .... 831-647-3516 ...... 57 F
jason.warburg@miis.edu
WARCH, David, P .... 651-696-6475 .... 264 J
dwarch@macalester.edu
WARD, Annette, P .... 740-245-7431 .... 404 E
award@rio.edu
WARD, Audrey .... 336-517-1502 .... 362 G
award@bennett.edu
WARD, Avery, W .... 443-412-2361 .... 223 B
award@harford.edu
WARD, Barry .... 310-303-7311 ...... 56 F
bward@marymountpv.edu
WARD, Beth, I .... 413-559-5838 .... 235 C
WARD, Bill .... 520-206-2610 ...... 17 H
wward@pima.edu
WARD, Bill .... 843-863-7514 .... 456 B
wward@csuniv.edu

WASHBURN, Joyce 785-460-5403 192 C joyce.washburn@colbycc.edu
WASHBURN, Kevin 505-277-4700 321 C washburn@law.unm.edu
WASHBURN, Lois, M 904-470-8266 105 G lois.washburn@ewc.edu
WASHBURN, Terri 248-689-8282 259 E twashburn@walshcollege.edu
WASHBURNE, Cynthia 860-512-3353 91 F cwashburne@mcc.commnet.edu
WASHINGTON, A. Eugene 310-825-5687 74 C ewashington@mednet.ucla.edu
WASHINGTON, Al 314-264-1000 292 D alfred.washington@vatterott.edu
WASHINGTON, Andre 859-442-4176 202 B andre.washington@kctcs.edu
WASHINGTON, Aubrey 340-692-4151 568 E awashin@live.uvi.edu
WASHINGTON, August 615-322-8333 478 A august.j.washington@vanderbilt.edu
WASHINGTON, Cheryl 334-874-5700 2 H cwashington@ccal.edu
WASHINGTON, Christopher, L 614-947-6129 391 B washingc@franklin.edu
WASHINGTON, Crystal 773-838-7535 147 H cwashington59@ccc.edu
WASHINGTON, Dana 815-802-8962 155 A dwashington@kcc.edu
WASHINGTON, DeSandra 910-678-0037 370 E washingd@faytechcc.edu
WASHINGTON, Earlie 269-387-2638 260 C earlie.washington@wmich.edu
WASHINGTON, Eric 718-960-8181 327 C eric.washington@lehman.cuny.edu
WASHINGTON, Fred, E 936-261-9100 496 G fewashington@pvamu.edu
WASHINGTON, Fred, E 936-261-2140 496 G fewashington@pvamu.edu
WASHINGTON, Gregory 847-851-5309 145 B
WASHINGTON, Gregory 949-824-6002 74 B gregory.washington@uci.edu
WASHINGTON, Harold 816-483-9600 289 E haroldw@spst.edu
WASHINGTON, Harry 484-365-8064 434 H hwashington@lincoln.edu
WASHINGTON, Ingrid 859-442-1148 202 B ingrid.washington@kctcs.edu
WASHINGTON, J. Leon 610-758-3100 434 E jnw207@lehigh.edu
WASHINGTON, James Bernard 252-536-7220 371 B washingtonj@halifaxcc.edu
WASHINGTON, Jennifer 860-515-3820 90 E jwashington@charteroak.edu
WASHINGTON, Kaye 318-670-9450 215 A kwashington@susla.edu
WASHINGTON, Kelvin 803-533-3736 460 G kwashington@scsu.edu
WASHINGTON, Kheysia, H 318-670-9417 215 A kwashington@susla.edu
WASHINGTON, L. Marshall 717-358-2975 430 E lmwashin@hacc.edu
WASHINGTON, Leila 410-951-3660 228 B lwashington@coppin.edu
WASHINGTON, Mary 229-317-6761 128 D mary.washington@darton.edu
WASHINGTON, Maurice 404-653-7857 134 D mwashington@morehouse.edu
WASHINGTON, Michael 813-227-4161 111 D mwashington@online.academy.edu
WASHINGTON, Michael 901-435-1601 470 D michael_washington@loc.edu
WASHINGTON, Pamela 405-974-5537 413 B pwashington@uco.edu
WASHINGTON, Tanisha 602-331-7500 12 B tawashington@aii.edu
WASHINGTON, Ted, M 615-353-3228 475 E ted.washington@nscc.edu
WASHINGTON, William, O 847-317-7091 166 E wwashington@tiu.edu
WASHINGTON, Willie 803-705-4734 455 D washingtonw@benedict.edu
WASHINGTON-LACEY, Bonita 765-983-1515 171 E washibo@earlham.edu
WASHINGTON-WOODS, Paula 870-235-4145 23 I pwwoods@saumag.edu
WASHKEVICH, Stephen 978-632-6600 240 C s_washkevich@mwcc.mass.edu
WASHKO, Chris 907-834-1631 11 B cwashko@pwscc.edu
WASHKO, Mary Jo 804-523-5345 527 A mwashko@reynolds.edu
WASHOUSKY, Richard, C 716-851-1500 333 B washousky@ecc.edu
WASICSKO, Mark 859-572-5229 205 H wasicskom1@nku.edu
WASIELEWSKI, Laura 603-656-6051 305 G lwasielewski@anselm.edu
WASIK, David, G 330-972-7926 403 B wasik@uakron.edu

WASILENKO, William, J 757-446-8480 518 G wasilewj@evms.edu
WASILOWSKI, Stuart 704-290-5240 374 A swasilowski@spcc.edu
WASIOLEK, Sue 919-684-6313 364 C dean.sue@duke.edu
WASKIE, Kenneth, G 607-777-2184 351 F kwaskie@binghamton.edu
WASKOSKY, Julia 815-802-8510 155 A jwaskosky@kcc.edu
WASKOW, Iris 310-476-9777 28 G iwaskow@ajula.edu
WASLEY, Patrick 415-338-3068 37 B pwasley@sfsu.edu
WASSBERG, Catherine 651-523-2616 264 A cwassberg01@hamline.edu
WASSEL, Robert 314-977-2041 289 C rwassel@slu.edu
WASSENAAR, Dave 714-484-7345 59 D dwassenaar@cypresscollege.edu
WASSENAAR, JR., James, R 305-348-4190 119 C wassenaa@fiu.edu
WASSENBERG, Pinky, S 217-206-6523 167 C wassenberg.pinky@uis.edu
WASSERMAN, Ahron 303-629-8200 90 B
WASSERMAN, Ed 510-642-3383 73 H
WASSERMAN, Harriet 206-934-4344 537 E harriet.wasserman@seattlecolleges.edu
WASSERMAN, Joy 847-328-1124 335 B jwasserman@huc.edu
WASSERMAN, Scott 775-784-4901 302 D scott_wasserman@nshe.nevada.edu
WASSON, Dale 817-272-5401 505 C wasson@uta.edu
WASSON, George 314-984-7763 289 A gwasson@stlcc.edu
WASSON, Leslie 928-532-6148 17 A leslie.wasson@npc.edu
WASSON, Tanlee, T 812-941-2293 175 A tawasson@ius.edu
WASSON, Thomas 601-857-3367 274 C thwasson@hindscc.edu
WASSUM, Elizabeth 276-944-6763 519 A ewassum@ehc.edu
WASTAWY, Sohair 309-438-3481 153 D sfwasta@ilstu.edu
WASTLER, Cyndi, L 703-339-2516 99 G clw@strayer.edu
WASUKANIS, John, T 561-868-3480 114 D wasukanj@palmbeachstate.edu
WATANABE, Mie 808-956-6423 141 E mie@hawaii.edu
WATERFIELD, James, R 757-683-4631 522 F rwater@odu.edu
WATERMAN, Christopher 310-206-6469 74 C cwater@arts.ucla.edu
WATERMAN, Wyatt 630-752-5325 168 H wyatt.waterman@wheaton.edu
WATERS, Barry, D 989-774-7493 249 C water1b@cmich.edu
WATERS, Christine 810-424-5294 259 C cwaters@umflint.edu
WATERS, Christopher, C 336-278-5055 364 D cwaters@elon.edu
WATERS, Gary 706-236-2251 126 C gwaters@berry.edu
WATERS, Gloria, S 617-353-2704 232 E gwaters@bu.edu
WATERS, Gloriana 212-794-5353 326 B gloriana.waters@mail.cuny.edu
WATERS, Gregory, L 973-655-7374 311 F watersg@mail.montclair.edu
WATERS, Jeff 417-328-1632 290 A jwaters@sbuniv.edu
WATERS, Jennifer 312-369-7831 148 D jwaters@colum.edu
WATERS, Joan 334-291-4951 2 F joan.waters@cv.edu
WATERS, John, B 512-472-4133 494 F john.waters@ssw.edu
WATERS, Jonathan, S 757-594-8895 517 L jwaters@cnu.edu
WATERS, Lynne, T 808-956-8109 141 E lynnew@hawaii.edu
WATERS, Marlo 707-965-6676 60 I mwaters@puc.edu
WATERS, Melissa 770-426-2901 133 E melissa.waters@life.edu
WATERS, Michelle 252-335-0821 369 G michelle_waters@albemarle.edu
WATERS, Myra 410-837-5159 229 A mwaters@ubalt.edu
WATERS, Ron 707-476-4331 42 C ron-waters@redwoods.edu
WATERS, Roy, S 318-257-2893 215 F roy@latech.edu
WATERS, Sarah 419-372-2011 385 E waterss@bgsu.edu
WATERS, Shari 714-997-6726 39 F swaters@chapman.edu
WATERS, Sharon 570-326-3761 440 L swaters@pct.edu

WATERS, Taylor 410-626-2512 225 G taylor.waters@sjca.edu
WATFORD, John 229-931-2004 137 C jwatford@southgatech.edu
WATFORD, Lettie 229-931-2145 131 F lettie.watford@gsw.edu
WATHEN, Cory 916-691-7418 56 B wathenc@crc.losrios.edu
WATKIN, Anna Maria, S 217-351-2596 161 C amwatkin@parkland.edu
WATKIN, Steve 661-654-3277 34 A swatkin@csub.edu
WATKINS, Alison, L 941-359-6111 116 B awatkins@ringling.edu
WATKINS, Brenda, F 864-488-4544 459 B bwatkins@limestone.edu
WATKINS, Bryan 773-244-5770 159 H bjwatkins@northpark.edu
WATKINS, Dan 215-612-6600 432 C dwatkins@chicareers.com
WATKINS, Daniel 601-979-2433 274 G daniel.watkins@jsums.edu
WATKINS, Dorla 816-584-6231 287 E dorla.watkins@park.edu
WATKINS, Faye 757-727-5371 519 H faye.watkins@hamptonu.edu
WATKINS, Frank 772-462-7475 111 B fwatkins@irsc.edu
WATKINS, Jameson 913-588-7387 197 C jwatkins@kumc.edu
WATKINS, Jennifer 918-463-2931 407 H jennifer.watkins@connorsstate.edu
WATKINS, Joe 619-849-2650 62 L jwatkins@pointloma.edu
WATKINS, John 724-938-1569 441 G watkins@calu.edu
WATKINS, Judi 707-967-2901 58 F jwatkins@napavalley.edu
WATKINS, Kristin 971-722-4696 419 G kwatkins@pcc.edu
WATKINS, Laurie 307-382-1647 557 A lwatkins@wwcc.wy.edu
WATKINS, Lee 610-896-1023 430 G lwatkins@haverford.edu
WATKINS, Marie 585-389-2304 342 D mwatkin2@naz.edu
WATKINS, Marilyn 765-973-8211 173 F mwatkins@iue.edu
WATKINS, Mark 620-421-6700 194 G markw@labette.edu
WATKINS, Nancy 704-355-5043 363 D nancy.watkins@carolinashealthcare.org
WATKINS, Pamela, L 337-475-5883 215 G pwatkins@mcneese.edu
WATKINS, Pat, E 727-864-8854 105 E watkinpe@eckerd.edu
WATKINS, Rebecca, R 828-398-7151 368 B bwatkins@abtech.edu
WATKINS, Robert, S 678-839-6580 139 A bwatkins@westga.edu
WATKINS, Ruth 217-333-1350 167 D rwatkins@illinois.edu
WATKINS, Susan, J 617-745-3855 234 A susan.j.watkins@enc.edu
WATKINS, Wayne, H 330-972-8124 403 B wwatkins@uakron.edu
WATKINS, William 818-677-2391 35 F william.watkins@csun.edu
WATKINS-WENDELL, Katie 330-972-6764 403 B kwatkin@uakron.edu
WATMAN, Mark 603-428-2908 305 D mwatman@nec.edu
WATMAN, Mark 603-428-2383 305 D mwatman@nec.edu
WATNICK, Beryl 305-653-7141 402 I beryl.watnick@munion.edu
WATRET, John 386-226-6970 105 I john.watret@erau.edu
WATRING, Jack, W 573-882-3518 291 B watringj@missouri.edu
WATROUS, Robert 610-683-1320 443 A watrous@kutztown.edu
WATROUS, Robert, T 610-683-1320 443 A watrous@kutztown.edu
WATSON, Angela 270-831-9671 202 D angie.watson@kctcs.edu
WATSON, Angela, R 405-466-3259 408 G akwatson@langston.edu
WATSON, Aretha 732-906-4243 311 D awatson@middlesexcc.edu
WATSON, Benjamin, O 803-780-1039 463 C bowatson@voorhees.edu
WATSON, Beverly 540-535-3592 524 E brecny@su.edu
WATSON, Billy 864-977-7123 460 A jw.watson@ngu.edu
WATSON, Bobby 214-698-0461 485 A ecc5100@dcccd.edu
WATSON, Christopher 847-491-4100 160 E christopher-watson@northwestern.edu
WATSON, Craig, T 404-727-6115 129 D craig.watson@emory.edu
WATSON, Dana 254-526-1733 482 H dana.watson@ctcd.edu

WATSON, Danelle, L 717-766-2511 436 D dwatson@messiah.edu
WATSON, Daryl 301-736-3631 224 A daryl.watson@msbbcs.edu
WATSON, David 937-529-2201 403 A dwatson@united.edu
WATSON, David 803-778-7882 455 G watsonds@cctech.edu
WATSON, Debraha 313-943-4500 259 G dwatson1@wcccd.edu
WATSON, Doug 402-941-6519 298 I watson@midlandu.edu
WATSON, Dwight, C 319-273-2717 182 G dwight.watson@uni.edu
WATSON, Ellen 718-270-1176 352 D ewatson@downstate.edu
WATSON, Ellen 901-678-8324 474 C eiwatson@memphis.edu
WATSON, Ernest 219-866-6128 179 D ernestw@saintjoe.edu
WATSON, Ernestine 973-972-6288 316 C ewatson@umdnj.edu
WATSON, George, H 302-831-2793 96 I ghw@udel.edu
WATSON, James, D 516-367-8311 329 E
WATSON, James, W 304-336-8200 544 D watsonjw@westliberty.edu
WATSON, Jeff 903-729-0256 502 F jwatson@tvcc.edu
WATSON, Jennifer 618-453-6689 165 B jlwatson@siu.edu
WATSON, Jill 562-903-4808 31 A jill.watson@biola.edu
WATSON, John 479-968-0319 20 G jwwatson@atu.edu
WATSON, John 972-273-3353 485 C jwatson@dcccd.edu
WATSON, Johnnie, B 901-435-1676 470 D johnnie_watson@loc.edu
WATSON, Jonelle 701-858-3577 382 A jonelle.watson@minotstateu.edu
WATSON, Joseph 518-828-4181 330 E watson@sunycgcc.edu
WATSON, Justin 574-239-8367 172 M jwatson@hcc-nd.edu
WATSON, Karan, L 979-845-4016 497 E provost@tamu.edu
WATSON, Kathryn, J 727-864-7673 105 E watsonkj@eckerd.edu
WATSON, Kathye 918-781-7294 407 B watsonk@bacone.edu
WATSON, Keith 509-452-5100 536 F
WATSON, Kimberly 419-251-1852 395 I kimberly.watson@mercycollege.edu
WATSON, Kimberly 314-529-9505 284 C kwatson@maryville.edu
WATSON, Kirk 309-854-1810 145 H watsonk@bhc.edu
WATSON, Larry, J 936-261-3800 496 G ljwatson@pvamu.edu
WATSON, Lemuel 803-777-3828 462 A watsonlw@mailbox.sc.edu
WATSON, Lisa 225-644-6277 211 F lwatson@rpcc.edu
WATSON, Lisa 406-874-6181 294 F watsonl@milescc.edu
WATSON, Lori 313-664-7431 249 E lwatson@collegeforcreativestudies.edu
WATSON, Lynda 903-434-8204 491 F lwatson@ntcc.edu
WATSON, Malcolm, W 781-736-3249 232 F watson@brandeis.edu
WATSON, Marsha 312-261-3048 159 E marsha.watson@nl.edu
WATSON, Marva 907-786-1800 10 H anmw@uaa.alaska.edu
WATSON, Mary 205-853-1200 5 C mwatson@jeffstateonline.com
WATSON, Mary 509-682-6614 539 E mwatson@wvc.edu
WATSON, Melissa 870-512-7805 20 F melissa_watson@asun.edu
WATSON, Michael, E 989-964-7310 257 G mewatson@svsu.edu
WATSON, Michael, W 920-424-2184 551 E watson@uwosh.edu
WATSON, Nancy 712-279-5416 183 A nancy.watson@briarcliff.edu
WATSON, Pamela, G 409-772-1510 507 C pgwatson@utmb.edu
WATSON, Patricia, A 607-254-1350 331 B paw37@cornell.edu
WATSON, Paul 715-346-4771 552 D pwatson@uwsp.edu
WATSON, Peggy 817-257-7125 499 C p.watson@tcu.edu
WATSON, Phil 816-235-5776 291 C watsonp@umkc.edu
WATSON, Phyllis 850-599-3474 118 L phyllis.watson@famu.edu
WATSON, Rebecca 205-934-3555 8 F bwatson@uab.edu
WATSON, Renee' 502-597-6346 203 G renee.watson@kysu.edu

WEBB, Lindsie, B ... 330-684-8941 ... 403 C
llamb@uakron.edu
WEBB, Lisa ... 214-768-4564 ... 495 A
lisawebb@smu.edu
WEBB, Maria ... 973-443-8533 ... 310 A
mwebb@fdu.edu
WEBB, Mark, F ... 931-598-1284 ... 472 L
mwebb@sewanee.edu
WEBB, Melessia, D ... 423-354-5106 ... 475 F
mdwebb@northeaststate.edu
WEBB, Michael ... 815-921-2151 ... 162 H
m.webb@rockvalleycollege.edu
WEBB, Michelle ... 207-453-5020 ... 218 I
mwebb@kvcc.me.edu
WEBB, Mona ... 904-743-1122 ... 112 B
mwebb@jones.edu
WEBB, R. Brian ... 254-710-8797 ... 482 A
brian_webb@baylor.edu
WEBB, Randall, J ... 318-357-6441 ... 216 B
webb@nsula.edu
WEBB, Randy ... 870-733-6750 ... 22 E
rwebb@midsouthcc.edu
WEBB, Reggie ... 863-669-2305 ... 115 C
rwebb@polk.edu
WEBB, Reggie ... 540-828-8014 ... 517 B
rwebb@bridgewater.edu
WEBB, Reginald ... 863-669-2305 ... 115 C
rwebb@polk.edu
WEBB, Richard, E ... 610-896-1290 ... 430 G
rwebb@haverford.edu
WEBB, Robert, L ... 781-891-2283 ... 231 D
rwebb@bentley.edu
WEBB, Steffani ... 913-588-1400 ... 197 C
swebb@kumc.edu
WEBB, Susan ... 785-242-5200 ... 195 I
susan.webb@ottawa.edu
WEBB, Terrance, S ... 608-246-6270 ... 554 D
tswebb@madisoncollege.org
WEBB, Terry ... 607-777-4787 ... 351 F
twebb@binghamton.edu
WEBB, Truly ... 651-793-1272 ... 267 A
truly.webb@metrostate.edu
WEBB, Vicki ... 870-307-7227 ... 22 D
vicki.webb@lyon.edu
WEBB, Vincent ... 936-294-1632 ... 501 D
vjw002@shsu.edu
WEBB, Virginia, E ... 610-526-1308 ... 422 A
virginia.webb@theamericancollege.edu
WEBB, Walter, W ... 815-939-5333 ... 161 A
wwebb@olivet.edu
WEBB, JR., William, C ... 810-762-3324 ... 259 C
bwebb@umflint.edu
WEBB SHARPE, Lisa ... 517-483-1106 ... 254 A
sharpel@lcc.edu
WEBBER, Chris ... 618-395-7777 ... 152 I
webberc@iecc.edu
WEBBER, Eleanor ... 802-635-1309 ... 515 F
eleanor.webber@jsc.edu
WEBBER, Henry, S ... 314-935-7877 ... 292 I
hwebber@wustl.edu
WEBBER, Karen, B ... 303-458-3561 ... 87 I
kwebber@regis.edu
WEBBER, Ken, P ... 641-422-4275 ... 188 A
webbeken@niacc.edu
WEBBER, Leah ... 617-928-4513 ... 242 E
lwebber@mountida.edu
WEBBER, Louise ... 909-621-8265 ... 40 F
louise.webber@cgu.edu
WEBBER, Mike ... 415-422-2508 ... 76 E
webberm@usfca.edu
WEBBER, Tracy, E ... 828-765-7351 ... 372 A
twebber@mayland.edu
WEBBER-COLBERT, Wilma, F ... 662-915-7735 ... 277 D
wcolbert@olemiss.edu
WEBER, Allison ... 920-693-1631 ... 554 C
allison.weber@gotoltc.edu
WEBER, Brad ... 620-252-7076 ... 192 B
bradw@coffeyville.edu
WEBER, Brian ... 570-945-8130 ... 432 E
brian.weber@keystone.edu
WEBER, Bruce, W ... 302-831-1211 ... 96 I
bweber@udel.edu
WEBER, Charlotte ... 304-696-4812 ... 544 B
cweber@rcbi.org
WEBER, Cheryl ... 617-585-1157 ... 242 I
cheryl.weber@necmusic.edu
WEBER, Chris ... 231-995-1039 ... 256 D
cweber@nmc.edu
WEBER, Daniel, R ... 773-442-4000 ... 160 A
d-weber3@neiu.edu
WEBER, Dave ... 507-285-7217 ... 268 I
dave.weber@roch.edu
WEBER, Dave, N ... 507-285-7217 ... 268 I
dave.weber@roch.edu
WEBER, Dawn ... 419-289-4142 ... 384 G
dweber1@ashland.edu
WEBER, Donna, J ... 715-836-3871 ... 551 A
weberdj@uwec.edu
WEBER, Eric ... 801-957-4136 ... 512 D
eric.weber@slcc.edu
WEBER, Ernest ... 718-270-2431 ... 352 D
ernest.weber@downstate.edu
WEBER, Girard, W ... 847-543-2201 ... 148 B
jweber@clcillinois.edu
WEBER, J. Christopher ... 570-577-1795 ... 423 E
weber@bucknell.edu
WEBER, Jacqueline, J ... 573-592-5307 ... 293 B
jackie.weber@westminster-mo.edu
WEBER, Janet ... 419-473-2700 ... 389 C
jweber@daviscollege.edu
WEBER, Jeff ... 414-443-8819 ... 553 D
jeff.weber@wlc.edu
WEBER, Joan ... 509-574-4984 ... 540 D
jweber@yvcc.edu
WEBER, Jodi ... 903-434-8114 ... 491 F
jweber@ntcc.edu
WEBER, Joe ... 931-221-7618 ... 473 E
weberj@apsu.edu
WEBER, Joe ... 440-375-7000 ... 394 E
jweber@lec.edu
WEBER, John ... 219-785-5273 ... 179 A
jweber@pnc.edu
WEBER, Jolanta, A ... 509-313-6504 ... 534 F
weberj@gonzaga.edu
WEBER, Joseph, F ... 979-845-4728 ... 497 E
vpsa@tamu.edu
WEBER, Julie ... 575-646-3202 ... 319 D
jeweber@nmsu.edu
WEBER, Keith, A ... 513-244-4350 ... 388 E
keith_weber@mail.msj.edu
WEBER, Kevin ... 502-585-9911 ... 206 D
kweber@spalding.edu
WEBER, Leann ... 701-228-5426 ... 382 E
leann.weber@dakotacollege.edu
WEBER, Lou Anne ... 864-503-5197 ... 463 B
lweber@uscupstate.edu
WEBER, Margaret ... 740-284-5244 ... 391 A
mweber@franciscan.edu
WEBER, Margaret, J ... 310-568-5615 ... 61 H
margaret.weber@pepperdine.edu
WEBER, Mark ... 920-498-5663 ... 555 C
mark.weber@nwtc.edu
WEBER, Marsha, L ... 218-477-2076 ... 267 F
marsha.weber@mnstate.edu
WEBER, Mary ... 831-646-4048 ... 57 G
mweber@mpc.edu
WEBER, Melissa ... 320-589-6414 ... 271 G
weberm@morris.umn.edu
WEBER, Melissa, A ... 570-577-1201 ... 423 E
melissa.weber@bucknell.edu
WEBER, Merlin, D ... 530-226-4501 ... 69 H
mweber@simpsonu.edu
WEBER, Nancy ... 843-525-8226 ... 461 E
nweber@tcl.edu
WEBER, Peter, M ... 401-863-7799 ... 453 B
peter_weber@brown.edu
WEBER, Phil ... 740-857-1311 ... 401 F
pweber@rosedale.edu
WEBER, Randy ... 719-502-3563 ... 87 B
randy.weber@ppcc.edu
WEBER, Scott ... 716-645-6029 ... 351 G
sweber@buffalo.edu
WEBER, OP, Sharon, R ... 517-264-7102 ... 258 B
srweber@sienaheights.edu
WEBER, Stephen ... 405-224-3140 ... 413 E
sweber@usao.edu
WEBER, Susan ... 212-501-3050 ... 323 D
weber@bgc.bard.edu
WEBER, Susan ... 847-628-2465 ... 154 K
sweber@judsonu.edu
WEBER, Teresa ... 914-323-5304 ... 339 J
teresa.weber@mville.edu
WEBER, Wayne, C ... 608-342-1547 ... 552 B
weberwa@uwplatt.edu
WEBER, William, V ... 217-581-2921 ... 150 E
wvweber@eiu.edu
WEBLEY, Radha ... 707-826-4502 ... 36 E
rw76@humboldt.edu
WEBSTER, Alex ... 425-637-1010 ... 532 E
alexwebster@cityu.edu
WEBSTER, Carita ... 281-476-1501 ... 493 H
carita.webster@sjcd.edu
WEBSTER, Frank, R ... 404-816-4533 ... 132 E
fwebster@atl.herzing.edu
WEBSTER, Gary ... 510-580-5521 ... 80 A
gwebster@cci.edu
WEBSTER, Jack ... 703-414-4013 ... 518 C
jwebster@devry.edu
WEBSTER, Jeremy ... 740-593-2723 ... 399 G
webstej1@ohio.edu
WEBSTER, Jerome ... 419-559-2326 ... 402 D
jwebster@terra.edu
WEBSTER, John, W ... 951-785-2041 ... 53 E
jwebster@lasierra.edu
WEBSTER, Kacy ... 515-727-2100 ... 187 A
kwebster@hamiltonia.edu
WEBSTER, LaTika ... 317-738-8080 ... 171 F
lwebster@franklincollege.edu
WEBSTER, Linda ... 573-592-5288 ... 293 B
linda.webster@westminster-mo.edu
WEBSTER, Lynn ... 208-459-5325 ... 143 D
lwebster@collegeofidaho.edu
WEBSTER, Margo ... 510-204-0753 ... 40 A
mwebster@cdsp.edu
WEBSTER, Mary, L ... 626-395-6304 ... 32 H
mwebster@caltech.edu
WEBSTER, Matthew, H ... 859-344-3306 ... 206 I
matthew.webster@thomasmore.edu
WEBSTER, Michael ... 610-361-2222 ... 437 D
websterm@neumann.edu
WEBSTER, Michael, N ... 410-857-2202 ... 224 C
mwebster@mcdaniel.edu
WEBSTER, Nancy, J ... 228-392-2994 ... 277 G
nancy.webster@vc.edu
WEBSTER, Ondes ... 865-471-3352 ... 467 G
owebster@cn.edu
WEBSTER, Reede, O ... 612-659-6312 ... 267 B
reede.webster@minneapolis.edu
WEBSTER, Richard, C ... 410-334-2896 ... 229 E
rwebster@worwic.edu
WEBSTER, Robert, O ... 518-437-4550 ... 351 E
rwebster@uamail.albany.edu
WEBSTER, Scott ... 508-999-8202 ... 237 A
swebster@umassd.edu
WEBSTER, Tom ... 903-923-2157 ... 486 F
twebster@etbu.edu
WEBSTER, Valerie ... 229-293-6135 ... 137 B
valerie.webster@sgc.edu
WEBSTER, Wayne, P ... 920-748-8351 ... 550 D
websterw@ripon.edu
WEBSTER, William, C ... 212-243-5150 ... 334 E
webster@gts.edu
WECHSLER, Barton, J ... 573-882-3304 ... 291 B
wechslerb@missouri.edu
WECKMAN, Judith ... 859-985-3791 ... 199 A
judith_weckman@berea.edu
WEDDELL, Leslie ... 719-389-6038 ... 82 D
leslie.weddell@coloradocollege.edu
WEDDERBURN, Anette ... 301-860-3939 ... 228 A
awedderburn@bowiestate.edu
WEDDINGTON, Brenda ... 773-907-4755 ... 147 D
bweddington@ccc.edu
WEDDINGTON, Hank ... 828-328-7035 ... 366 E
hank.weddington@lr.edu
WEDDLE-WEST, Karen, D ... 901-678-2531 ... 474 C
kweddle@memphis.edu
WEDEL, Allen ... 316-284-5242 ... 191 C
awedel@bethelks.edu
WEDES, Lloyd ... 713-973-3137 ... 486 C
lwedes@devry.edu
WEDGE, Luann ... 616-234-4170 ... 251 E
lwedge@grcc.edu
WEDIG, Tyler ... 319-895-4378 ... 183 G
twedig@cornellcollege.edu
WEDLER, Andrea ... 518-445-2388 ... 322 C
awedl@albanylaw.edu
WEDLER-JOHNSON, Darlene ... 941-752-5247 ... 118 J
wedlerd@scf.edu
WEDLOCK, Monica ... 404-687-4516 ... 127 F
wedlockm@ctsnet.edu
WEDMAN, John ... 573-882-4546 ... 291 B
wedmanj@missouri.edu
WEE, Liang, C ... 563-562-3263 ... 188 B
weel@portal.nicc.edu
WEEAKS, Cindy ... 325-942-2043 ... 480 E
cindy.weeaks@angelo.edu
WEECH, Darwin ... 928-428-8473 ... 14 B
darwin.weech@eac.edu
WEED, Anne ... 315-279-5202 ... 337 K
aweed@mail.keuka.edu
WEEDE, Thomas, D ... 317-940-8408 ... 170 F
tweede@butler.edu
WEEDEN, Jared ... 315-781-3700 ... 335 F
weeden@hws.edu
WEEDMAN, Gary, E ... 865-573-4517 ... 469 L
gweedman@johnsonu.edu
WEEKES, Eric, B ... 386-226-6499 ... 105 H
eric.weekes@erau.edu
WEEKLEY, Matt ... 402-375-7318 ... 299 G
maweekl1@wsc.edu
WEEKS, David ... 626-815-6000 ... 30 G
dweeks@apu.edu
WEEKS, Donald ... 603-752-1113 ... 304 H
dweeks@ccsnh.edu
WEEKS, Donna ... 601-968-5922 ... 273 C
dweeks@belhaven.edu
WEEKS, Honya ... 202-495-3820 ... 99 C
assistant@dhs.edu
WEEKS, Larry, D ... 904-819-6350 ... 107 C
lweeks@flagler.edu
WEEKS, Patricia ... 609-652-4826 ... 313 E
patty.weeks@stockton.edu
WEEKS, Randy ... 303-893-4000 ... 86 I
ntc@dcpa.org
WEEMS, Heather ... 320-308-3102 ... 269 A
hlweems@stcloudstate.edu
WEEMS, Howard ... 256-726-7047 ... 6 C
hweems@oakwood.edu
WEEMS, Jeff ... 918-465-1750 ... 408 A
jweems@eosc.edu
WEEMS, Linda ... 575-562-2147 ... 318 B
linda.weems@enmu.edu
WEEMS, Lorne ... 201-684-7543 ... 313 C
lweems@ramapo.edu
WEEMS, Renita ... 615-687-6973 ... 466 H
abcofficeacademicaffairs@gmail.com
WEEMS, Rick ... 541-552-6554 ... 419 A
weemsr@sou.edu
WEEMS, William, A ... 713-500-5224 ... 506 F
william.a.weems@uth.tmc.edu
WEERASURIYA, Yasith ... 949-794-9090 ... 71 F
yasithw@stanbridge.edu
WEERHEIM, Revalee ... 307-755-2150 ... 557 B
rweerheim@wyotechstaff.edu
WEERS, Terry ... 830-372-8009 ... 499 F
tweers@tlu.edu
WEESE, JR., Narvel, G ... 304-293-2545 ... 545 A
narvel.weese@mail.wvu.edu
WEETER, Mark ... 918-335-6803 ... 411 B
mweeter@okwu.edu
WEFFER, Rafaela ... 312-362-6477 ... 149 A
rweffer@depaul.edu
WEGENER, David ... 414-256-1248 ... 549 D
wegenerd@mtmary.edu
WEGER, Brandon ... 618-544-8657 ... 152 F
wegerb@iecc.edu
WEGER, Cora ... 618-544-8657 ... 152 F
wegerc@iecc.edu
WEGLARZ, Joseph, R ... 845-575-3000 ... 340 B
joseph.weglarz@marist.edu
WEGLARZ, Reinhard ... 816-604-1176 ... 284 H
reinhard.weglarz@mcckc.edu
WEGLEIN, Jessica ... 410-225-2503 ... 224 B
jweglein@mica.edu
WEGMAN, Barbara, A ... 260-452-2153 ... 170 J
barb.wegman@ctsfw.edu
WEGMAN, Patie ... 707-527-4906 ... 68 E
pwegman@santarosa.edu
WEGNER, Janis ... 320-629-5123 ... 268 E
wegnerj@pinetech.edu
WEGNER, Mary Kay ... 425-235-2352 ... 537 A
mwegner@rtc.edu
WEGNER, Paige ... 715-833-6245 ... 553 H
pwegner3@cvtc.edu
WEGRZYN, David, C ... 401-865-1160 ... 453 H
dwegrzyn@providence.edu
WEHLBURG, Catherine ... 817-257-7156 ... 499 C
c.wehlburg@tcu.edu
WEHLE, Arlean ... 504-398-2181 ... 214 B
awehle@olhcc.edu
WEHMEIER, Teresa ... 620-417-1603 ... 196 F
teresa.wehmeier@sccc.edu
WEHNER, David, J ... 805-756-2161 ... 33 I
dwehner@calpoly.edu
WEHNER, STD, James, A ... 504-866-7426 ... 214 A
rector@nds.edu
WEHR, Joseph ... 215-635-7300 ... 430 A
jwehr@gratz.edu
WEHRBEIN, Nancy ... 402-465-2488 ... 299 H
nwehrbei@nebrwesleyan.edu
WEHRENBERG, Fritz ... 515-961-1684 ... 189 C
fritz.wehrenberg@simpson.edu
WEHRLE-EINHORN, Juanita, L ... 937-775-3207 ... 406 C
juanita.wehrle-einhorn@wright.edu
WEHRLEY, James, B ... 336-841-4560 ... 365 C
jwehrley@highpoint.edu
WEHRLI, Dana ... 636-949-4806 ... 283 J
dwehrli@lindenwood.edu
WEHRUNG, Melodye ... 717-477-1161 ... 443 E
mwwehr@ship.edu
WEHRY, Peter ... 715-324-6900 ... 549 G
peter.wehry@ni.edu
WEI, Belle ... 530-898-6101 ... 34 C
bellewei@csuchico.edu
WEI, Belle ... 408-924-3800 ... 37 C
belle.wei@sjsu.edu
WEI, Cheng-I ... 301-405-2072 ... 227 B
wei@umd.edu
WEI, Timothy ... 402-472-3181 ... 300 G
twei3@unl.edu
WEIAND, Steven ... 847-578-8349 ... 163 C
steven.weiand@rosalindfranklin.edu
WEIBLE, Frederick ... 717-846-5000 ... 452 H
WEIBLE, JR., Raymond ... 814-262-3816 ... 441 A
rweible@pennhighlands.edu
WEICH, Ronald ... 410-837-5518 ... 229 A
rweich@ubalt.edu
WEICHOLD, Mark, H ... 979-845-2217 ... 497 E
mark.weichold@qatar.tamu.edu
WEIDA, Michael ... 845-431-8054 ... 332 D
weida@sunydutchess.edu
WEIDEL, Susan ... 307-766-4123 ... 556 H
weidel@uwyo.edu
WEIDEMANN, Craig, D ... 814-865-7581 ... 438 G
cdw12@psu.edu
WEIDEMANN, Gregory ... 860-486-2917 ... 94 G
gregory.weidemann@uconn.edu
WEIDENSAUL, Rebecca, L ... 215-895-2501 ... 427 H
rebecca@drexel.edu
WEIDER, Susan ... 425-602-3014 ... 531 E
sweider@bastyr.edu
WEIDNER, Donald ... 850-644-3071 ... 119 D
dweidner@law.fsu.edu
WEIDNER, Karen, K ... 402-844-7330 ... 299 I
karenkw@northeast.edu
WEIDNER, Laura, E ... 410-777-2371 ... 221 C
leweidner@aacc.edu
WEIDNER, Ted ... 402-472-3131 ... 300 G
tweidner2@unl.edu
WEIER, Gary, M ... 864-242-5100 ... 455 E
WEIGAND, Donald ... 914-606-6709 ... 360 E
donald.weigand@sunywcc.edu
WEIGAND, Mark, T ... 317-788-3350 ... 180 F
weigand@uindy.edu

WELDON, Leslie .... 406-657-2188.... 295 D
leslie.weldon@msubillings.edu
WELDON, Leslie .... 618-634-3337.... 164 E
lesliew@shawneecc.edu
WELDON, Rich .... 803-593-9231.... 455 A
weldonr@atc.edu
WELDON, Stephanie, J ...... 603-206-8111.... 304 D
sjweldon@ccsnh.edu
WELGE, Vicky, L .... 217-443-8702.... 148 G
voliver@dacc.edu
WELKER, Dan .... 928-428-8300...... 14 B
dan.welker@eac.edu
WELKER, Joan, C .... 570-484-2181.... 443 B
jwelker@lhup.edu
WELKER, Josh .... 217-641-4110.... 154 I
jwelker@jwcc.edu
WELKER, Kristen .... 605-668-1577.... 464 G
kristen.welker@mtmc.edu
WELKER, Mark .... 336-758-3898.... 380 C
welker@wfu.edu
WELKEY, Sharon .... 210-832-2115.... 504 B
welkey@uiwtx.edu
WELLBORN, Linda .... 417-865-2811.... 281 G
wellbornl@evangel.edu
WELLER, Lisa .... 610-225-5007.... 428 E
lweller2@eastern.edu
WELLER, Steve .... 972-438-6932.... 492 E
sweller@parkercc.edu
WELLER, Vicki .... 410-617-2201.... 223 I
vweller@loyola.edu
WELLER-DENGEL, Pamela . 507-389-6061.... 267 E
pamela.weller-dengel@mnsu.edu
WELLHAM, Ann .... 301-387-3045.... 222 H
ann.wellham@garrettcollege.edu
WELLHAUSEN, Chad .... 712-542-5117.... 186 F
cwellhausen@iwcc.edu
WELLINGTON, Eric, R .... 610-359-5127.... 426 G
ewellington@dccc.edu
WELLIVER, Suzy, L .... 610-799-1946.... 434 D
swelliver@lccc.edu
WELLMAN, Barbara .... 217-228-5432.... 161 F
wellmba@quincy.edu
WELLMAN, Christopher ..... 660-543-4331.... 290 H
cwellman@ucmo.edu
WELLMAN, Debra .... 407-646-2280.... 116 D
dwellman@rollins.edu
WELLMAN, Ronald, D .... 336-758-5616.... 380 C
wellmanr@wfu.edu
WELLNER, Justin .... 831-582-3044...... 35 E
jwellner@csumb.edu
WELLS, Ann .... 229-248-2516.... 126 A
ann.wells@bainbridge.edu
WELLS, Barbara .... 865-981-8278.... 471 B
barbara.wells@maryvillecollege.edu
WELLS, Barbara .... 901-333-4259.... 476 B
bwells@southwest.tn.edu
WELLS, Beth .... 503-845-3243.... 417 A
beth.wells@mtangel.edu
WELLS, Bill .... 912-478-2622.... 131 E
wwells@georgiasouthern.edu
WELLS, Billy .... 706-864-1630.... 134 G
bewells@northgeorgia.edu
WELLS, Bonnie .... 860-439-5001...... 92 G
bonnie.wells@conncoll.edu
WELLS, Brad .... 510-885-3803...... 34 E
brad.wells@csueastbay.edu
WELLS, Brent .... 281-283-2180.... 503 E
wellsb@uhcl.edu
WELLS, Brian, J .... 502-776-1443.... 206 B
WELLS, C. Gene .... 812-488-2664.... 180 E
gw5@evansville.edu
WELLS, Carole .... 610-683-4212.... 443 A
wells@kutztown.edu
WELLS, Cathy .... 253-833-9111.... 534 H
cwells@greenriver.edu
WELLS, Christina .... 217-479-7030.... 157 F
christina.wells@mac.edu
WELLS, Christopher, J .... 765-658-4060.... 171 B
christopherwells@depauw.edu
WELLS, Christopher, J .... 765-658-4226.... 171 B
christopherwells@depauw.edu
WELLS, Dan .... 812-877-8205.... 179 B
dan.wells@rose-hulman.edu
WELLS, David, A .... 817-515-5250.... 496 C
david.wells@tccd.edu
WELLS, David, J .... 315-386-7411.... 355 E
wellsd@canton.edu
WELLS, Debra .... 724-335-5336.... 438 A
dwells@oaa.edu
WELLS, Douglas .... 605-394-1763.... 466 B
douglas.wells@sdsmt.edu
WELLS, Elaine .... 212-938-5690.... 355 B
ewells@sunyopt.edu
WELLS, Gail, V .... 716-878-4631.... 353 A
wellsgv@buffalostate.edu
WELLS, Gail, W .... 859-572-5788.... 205 H
wells@nku.edu
WELLS, JR., Henry, D .... 919-572-1625.... 362 C
hdwells@apexsot.edu
WELLS, Jayne, E .... 608-785-9141.... 555 F
wellsj@westerntc.edu
WELLS, Jeremy .... 515-727-2100.... 187 A
jeremywells@hamiltonia.edu
WELLS, Jeremy .... 515-727-2100.... 186 H
WELLS, Johann .... 334-291-4954........ 2 F
johann.wells@cv.edu
WELLS, John, M .... 252-335-0821.... 369 G
jmwells@albemarle.edu
WELLS, John, T .... 804-684-7103.... 518 A
wells@vims.edu
WELLS, John, W .... 828-689-1250.... 366 I
jwells@mhc.edu
WELLS, Jovita .... 202-274-6260.... 100 A
jwells@udc.edu
WELLS, Keith, P .... 303-762-6963...... 84 D
keith.wells@denverseminary.edu
WELLS, La Shawn .... 925-609-6650...... 38 F
lbwells@carrington.edu
WELLS, Linda, S .... 617-353-2852.... 232 E
lwells@bu.edu
WELLS, Lisa .... 540-887-7330.... 521 C
lwells@mbc.edu
WELLS, Marilyn .... 570-422-3536.... 442 D
mwells@po-box.esu.edu
WELLS, Nancy, L .... 716-645-4666.... 351 G
nwells@buffalo.edu
WELLS, Nick .... 785-460-4684.... 192 C
nick.wells@colbycc.edu
WELLS, Pamela, Y .... 856-225-6140.... 314 D
pmcwells@camden.rutgers.edu
WELLS, Paul, S .... 740-374-8716.... 405 G
pwells1@wscc.edu
WELLS, R. Hal .... 612-874-3634.... 265 C
hal_wells@mcad.edu
WELLS, Rebecca .... 270-831-9682.... 202 D
rebecca.wells@kctcs.edu
WELLS, Regina, A .... 302-454-3941...... 96 F
rwells@dtcc.edu
WELLS, Richard, H .... 920-424-0200.... 551 E
wellsr@uwosh.edu
WELLS, JR., Robert, J .... 864-656-0244.... 456 E
rjwells@clemson.edu
WELLS, Samuel, E .... 919-866-5170.... 374 H
sewells@waketech.edu
WELLS, Sherry .... 913-758-6123.... 197 D
wellss@stmary.edu
WELLS, Sherry .... 409-880-8968.... 501 A
sherry.wells@lamar.edu
WELLS, Tanesha .... 909-472-0640...... 29 D
twells@argosy.du
WELLS, Teri .... 304-896-7443.... 543 C
teri.wells@southernwv.edu
WELLS, Twyla, C .... 919-209-2119.... 371 F
tcwells@johnstoncc.edu
WELLS, Virginia, D .... 757-221-4386.... 518 A
vdwell@wm.edu
WELLS, Warren .... 660-785-4121.... 290 G
wwells@truman.edu
WELLS, William .... 207-780-4995.... 220 G
wells@maine.edu
WELLS, William, C .... 419-995-8213.... 392 K
wells.w@rhodesstate.edu
WELLS, William, T .... 336-758-5154.... 380 C
wellswt@wfu.edu
WELLS-BOOTH, Shawna .... 352-638-9733.... 102 B
swellsbooth@beaconcollege.edu
WELP, Cindy .... 712-274-5114.... 187 G
welp@morningside.edu
WELSCH, Cheryl .... 845-434-5750.... 357 A
cwelsch@sullivan.suny.edu
WELSCH, Colleen .... 269-782-1204.... 258 C
cwelsch@swmich.edu
WELSCH, Gabriel .... 814-641-3131.... 432 A
welschg@juniata.edu
WELSH, Connie .... 406-444-0614.... 294 H
cwelsh@montana.edu
WELSH, David .... 860-255-3513...... 92 F
dwelsh@txcc.commnet.edu
WELSH, Johnelle .... 254-526-1298.... 482 H
johnelle.welsh@ctcd.edu
WELSH, Judith .... 540-338-2700.... 517 G
jwelsh@cdu.edu
WELSH, Marcia, G .... 570-422-3546.... 442 D
mwelsh@po-box.esu.edu
WELSH, Patrick, J .... 610-785-6265.... 446 A
pwelsh@scs.edu
WELSH, Sarah .... 617-264-7756.... 234 C
swelsh@emmanuel.edu
WELSH, Susan, T .... 478-757-5155.... 139 E
swelsh@wesleyancollege.edu
WELSH, Suzanne, P .... 610-328-8316.... 447 F
swelsh1@swarthmore.edu
WELSH, Tasha, D .... 636-481-3157.... 283 D
twelsh@jeffco.edu
WELSH, Tracy .... 605-688-4121.... 466 C
tracy.welsh@sdstate.edu
WELSH, William, J .... 570-941-6300.... 450 C
william.welsh@scranton.edu
WELTER, Linda Allaire .... 617-879-2233.... 246 C
lwelter@wheelock.edu
WELTER, Stephen .... 619-594-2978...... 37 A
swelter@mail.sdsu.edu
WELTJEN, Scott .... 716-270-5239.... 333 C
weltjen@ecc.edu
WELTON, Ronald, J .... 516-876-3135.... 353 D
weltonr@oldwestbury.edu
WELTY, John, D .... 559-278-2324...... 35 A
john_welty@csufresno.edu
WELZ, Linda .... 626-914-8811...... 40 B
lwelz@citruscollege.edu
WEN, H. Joseph .... 310-243-3745...... 34 D
jwen@csudh.edu
WEN, Hui-Men .... 941-487-4601.... 120 A
hwen@ncf.edu
WENBERG, Carrie .... 314-889-1403.... 281 I
cwenberg@fontbonne.edu
WENCK, Lisa, M .... 607-436-2518.... 353 E
wencklm@oneonta.edu
WENDALL, Alan, B .... 215-951-1916.... 432 I
wendall@lasalle.edu
WENDEL, Shirley, A .... 913-288-7626.... 194 C
swendel@kckcc.edu
WENDELN, Sheila .... 803-321-5140.... 459 H
sheila.wendeln@newberry.edu
WENDEROFF, Karen .... 212-650-7125.... 326 G
kwenderoff@ccny.cuny.edu
WENDEROTH, Christine .... 773-753-0735.... 157 G
cwendero@lstc.edu
WENDEROTH, Christine .... 773-256-0735.... 157 D
cwenderoth@jkmlibrary.org
WENDLER, David, O .... 507-354-8221.... 264 K
wendledo@mlc-wels.edu
WENDOVER, Wendy .... 303-963-3268...... 82 C
wwendover@ccu.edu
WENDT, Donna .... 706-771-4150.... 125 H
dwendt@augustatech.edu
WENDT, Hunter .... 586-498-4090.... 254 C
wendth@macomb.edu
WENDT, Tim .... 217-353-3673.... 161 C
twendt@parkland.edu
WENDZEL, Anita .... 941-907-2262.... 107 B
awendzel@evergladesuniversity.edu
WENER, Kara .... 507-457-6632.... 271 B
kwener@smumn.edu
WENGER, Andrea, S .... 540-432-4208.... 518 F
wengeras@emu.edu
WENNER, Annamaria .... 617-989-4410.... 245 F
wennera@wit.edu
WENNER, Cheryl .... 610-606-4612.... 425 A
cwenner@cedarcrest.edu
WENNER, Shawn .... 407-851-2525.... 106 K
swenner@cci.edu
WENNERGREN, Mindy ...... 801-832-2186.... 512 G
mwennergren@westminstercollege.edu
WENNERSTROM, Zandy ...... 303-762-6887...... 84 D
zandy.wennerstrom@denverseminary.edu
WENRICK, Jason .... 707-664-3155...... 37 D
jason.wenrick@sonoma.edu
WENSEL, Tara .... 208-459-5016.... 143 D
twensel@collegeofidaho.edu
WENSLEY, Roy .... 925-631-4409...... 64 F
rwensley@stmarys-ca.edu
WENSOWITCH, Andrea ...... 419-448-2261.... 391 F
awensowi@heidelberg.edu
WENTHE, Andrew .... 563-425-5260.... 189 G
wenthea@uiu.edu
WENTHE, Phyllis, J .... 563-333-6276.... 188 F
wenthephyllisj@sau.edu
WENTLAND, Briana .... 320-363-5512.... 262 F
bwentland@csbsju.edu
WENTWORTH, Craig, R ...... 229-225-5069.... 138 A
cwentworth@southwestgatech.edu
WENTWORTH, Jackie .... 605-995-2151.... 464 C
jawentwo@dwu.edu
WENTWORTH, Kristen .... 207-326-2280.... 219 D
kristen.wentworth@mma.edu
WENTWORTH, Monica ...... 615-966-6296.... 470 F
monica.wentworth@lipscomb.edu
WENTWORTH, Renae .... 864-242-5100.... 455 E
WENTZ, James .... 601-984-1010.... 277 E
jwentz@umc.edu
WENTZ, Meridith .... 715-232-5312.... 552 E
wentzm@uwstout.edu
WENYIKA, Reggies .... 405-789-7661.... 412 E
reggies.wenyika@swcu.edu
WENZ, Donald, A .... 718-951-5511.... 326 F
donald@brooklyn.cuny.edu
WENZEL, Claudia .... 216-397-4248.... 392 L
cwenzel@jcu.edu
WENZEL, Loren, A .... 304-336-8152.... 544 D
lwenzel@westliberty.edu
WEPNER, Shelley .... 914-323-5192.... 339 J
shelley.wepner@mville.edu
WERA, Chris .... 303-871-7785...... 89 A
cjwera@du.edu
WERBEL DASHEFSKY,
Linda .... 718-489-5370.... 348 E
lwerbel@sfc.edu
WERBER, Frank .... 646-312-1112.... 326 C
frank.werber@baruch.cuny.edu
WERBY, Elisabeth, A .... 617-373-2101.... 243 F
WERDANN, Frank .... 607-431-4340.... 335 A
werdannf@hartwick.edu
WERGIN, Arlene, V .... 410-455-2624.... 227 D
wergin@umbc.edu
WERLE, Kathy .... 949-451-5565...... 70 E
kwerle@ivc.edu
WERLING, Karen, J .... 229-931-2902.... 137 C
kwerling@southgatech.edu
WERMAN, Steve .... 970-248-1881...... 82 F
swerman@coloradomesa.edu
WERMUTH, Thomas, S ...... 845-575-3000.... 340 B
thomas.wermuth@marist.edu
WERNE, Stanley, J .... 812-888-4361.... 181 D
swerne@vinu.edu
WERNER, Adria .... 314-513-4208.... 288 H
awerner@stlcc.edu
WERNER, Elizabether .... 727-726-1153.... 103 I
elizabethwerner@clearwater.edu
WERNER, Kathleen .... 301-369-2800.... 221 F
kwerner@capitol-college.edu
WERNER, Larry .... 651-846-3387.... 260 I
lwerner@argosy.edu
WERNER, Paul, F .... 316-978-3030.... 198 A
paul.werner@wichita.edu
WERNER, Shraga .... 718-941-8000.... 341 A
WERNIG, Stephanie .... 402-280-1164.... 297 F
wernig@creighton.edu
WERNON, Michael .... 813-621-0041.... 106 C
mwernon@cci.edu
WEROSH, Keith .... 630-889-6547.... 159 F
kwerosh@nuhs.edu
WERT, Joseph, L .... 812-941-2391.... 175 A
jwert@ius.edu
WERTHEIMER, Howard ...... 404-385-7604.... 130 F
howard.wertheimer@spaceplan.gatech.edu
WERTHEIMER, Molly .... 570-450-3051.... 440 G
mmw9@psu.edu
WERTHMANN, David .... 314-256-8806.... 278 G
werthmann@ai.edu
WERTIME, Richard, A .... 215-572-2963.... 422 C
wertime@arcadia.edu
WERTMAN, Devin .... 406-477-6215.... 294 A
dwertman@cdkc.edu
WERTMAN, William .... 406-477-6215.... 294 A
bwertman@cdkc.edu
WERTS, Shelley .... 323-242-5536...... 55 C
wertss@lasc.edu
WERTSCH, James, V .... 314-935-0915.... 292 I
jwertsch@wustl.edu
WESCOTT, Jon .... 814-269-7112.... 449 D
wescott@pitt.edu
WESELOH, Robert, W .... 913-588-1443.... 197 C
rweseloh@kumc.edu
WESENER, Kelly .... 815-753-6102.... 160 B
kwesener@niu.edu
WESENER MICHAEL,
Kelly .... 815-753-6103.... 160 B
kwesener@niu.edu
WESLEY, Derek, M .... 607-587-3930.... 355 C
wesleydm@alfredstate.edu
WESLEY, III, Homer, A ...... 719-255-3582...... 88 I
hwesley@uccs.edu
WESLEY, Jeanne .... 540-891-3095.... 526 I
jwesley@germanna.edu
WESLEY, Kevin, P .... 585-276-3575.... 359 B
kwesley@alumni.rochester.edu
WESLEY, Olan, L .... 334-229-4317........ 1 C
owesley@alasu.edu
WESLEY, Vernon, L .... 617-745-3717.... 234 A
vernon.l.wesley@enc.edu
WESLEY, Vinetta .... 256-306-2828........ 2 D
vlw@calhoun.edu
WESLOW, Suzanne .... 414-229-4463.... 551 D
sweslow@uwm.edu
WESNER, Katrin .... 910-962-4126.... 379 D
wesnerk@uncw.edu
WESNER, Samantha .... 610-921-7531.... 421 E
swesner@alb.edu
WESOLEK, Christina .... 718-405-3334.... 330 A
christina.wesolek@mountsaintvincent.edu
WESOLOWSKI, James .... 716-677-9500.... 325 A
jawesolowski@bryantstratton.edu
WESS, Linda .... 814-536-5168.... 424 E
lwess@crbc.net
WESS, Linda .... 814-536-5168.... 424 D
lwess@crbc.net
WESSE, David .... 318-473-6408.... 212 I
dwesse@lsua.edu
WESSEL, Walter, G .... 217-424-6217.... 158 G
wwessell@millikin.edu
WESSELLS, Christopher, W 619-260-6886...... 76 D
chris@sandiego.edu
WESSELS, Andrew .... 800-766-6067.... 541 H
awessels@mountainstate.edu
WESSELS, Gus .... 979-532-6505.... 509 D
gusw@wcjc.edu
WESSMAN, Kathleen .... 240-567-7971.... 224 D
kathleen.wessman@montgomerycollege.edu
WEST, Allen .... 903-693-1171.... 492 C
awest@panola.edu
WEST, Amy .... 731-425-2621.... 475 C
awest12@jscc.edu
WEST, Andrew .... 512-472-4133.... 494 F
andrew.west@ssw.edu
WEST, Bernadette .... 732-235-4535.... 317 A
westbm@umdnj.edu
WEST, Caroline, S .... 310-206-8264...... 74 C
cwest@ponet.ucla.edu
WEST, Cathy .... 361-698-1265.... 485 G
cwest@delmar.edu
WEST, Charlene, C .... 919-536-7235.... 370 C
westc@durhamtech.edu
WEST, Cheryl .... 508-270-4108.... 239 G
cwest@massbay.edu

WHEELER, Cassandra, L .... 956-326-4473.... 497 D
cwheeler@tamiu.edu
WHEELER, Cecilia, B .... 919-528-4737.... 374 G
wheelerc@vgcc.edu
WHEELER, Darrell, P .... 312-915-7024.... 157 C
dwheeler@luc.edu
WHEELER, Ed, R .... 678-359-5018.... 132 A
edw@gdn.edu
WHEELER, Erin .... 518-631-9850.... 358 H
wheelere@uniongraduatecollege.edu
WHEELER, Frank, E .... 402-363-5646.... 301 E
fwheeler@york.edu
WHEELER, Gary .... 269-467-9945.... 251 B
gwheeler@glenoaks.edu
WHEELER, H. William .... 434-592-3003.... 520 K
hwwheeler@liberty.edu
WHEELER, Ike .... 870-512-7865...... 20 F
ike_wheeler@asun.edu
WHEELER, John, D .... 216-368-5555.... 386 F
john.wheeler@case.edu
WHEELER, Jolene .... 928-724-6694...... 13 L
jwheeler@dinecollege.edu
WHEELER, Karen, J .... 501-569-3204...... 24 E
kjwheeler@ualr.edu
WHEELER, Laurie .... 707-965-7200...... 60 I
lwheeler@puc.edu
WHEELER, Linda .... 706-272-4547.... 128 C
lwheeler@daltonstate.edu
WHEELER, Lisa .... 318-678-6000.... 209 I
lwheeler@bpcc.edu
WHEELER, Lisa .... 952-358-8286.... 268 A
lisa.wheeler@normandale.edu
WHEELER, Margaret .... 314-991-6200.... 279 H
mwheeler@devry.com
WHEELER, Mark .... 208-426-1140.... 142 I
mwheeler@boisestate.edu
WHEELER, Mary .... 254-526-1200.... 482 H
mary.wheeler@ctcd.edu
WHEELER, Mary Anne .... 850-973-1605.... 113 K
wheelerm@nfcc.edu
WHEELER, Michelle .... 907-564-8210...... 10 D
mwheeler@alaskapacific.edu
WHEELER, Michelle .... 248-476-1122.... 254 G
mwheeler@mispp.edu
WHEELER, Nolan .... 360-442-2201.... 535 I
nwheeler@lowercolumbia.edu
WHEELER, Pamela .... 503-413-7165.... 416 H
pwheele@linfield.edu
WHEELER, Susan .... 309-694-8855.... 152 C
swheeler@icc.edu
WHEELER, Susan, L .... 540-568-3727.... 520 H
wheel2sl@jmu.edu
WHEELER, Terry .... 561-803-2500.... 114 C
terry_wheeler@pba.edu
WHEELER, Thomas .... 816-604-5240.... 285 B
thomas.wheeler@mcckc.edu
WHEELER, Tim .... 425-739-8252.... 535 H
tim.wheeler@lwtc.edu
WHEELER-DUNNER,
Audrea .... 251-405-7168........ 2 C
awheeler@bishop.edu
WHEELESS, Jim .... 912-443-5858.... 136 H
jwheeless@savannahtech.edu
WHEELESS, Kent .... 252-399-6338.... 362 E
kwheeles@barton.edu
WHEELIS, Tina .... 870-368-2008...... 23 A
twheelis@ozarka.edu
WHEELOCK, Pam .... 612-624-3557.... 272 A
WHEELOCK, William .... 330-941-3165.... 406 F
wwheelock@ysu.edu
WHEELWRIGHT,
Steven, C .... 808-675-3700.... 140 D
wheelwrights@byuh.edu
WHEETLEY, John .... 209-473-5200...... 50 E
john_wheetley@heald.edu
WHELAN, JR., Donald, J .. 817-257-7785.... 499 C
d.whelan@tcu.edu
WHELAN, Janet .... 410-837-4779.... 229 A
jwhelan@ubalt.edu
WHELAN, John .... 254-710-8562.... 482 A
john_whelan@baylor.edu
WHELAN, Matthew .... 631-632-6857.... 352 C
matthew.whelan@stonybrook.edu
WHELAN, Michaele .... 781-736-2106.... 232 F
mwhelan@brandeis.edu
WHELAN, Robert .... 718-289-5162.... 326 E
robert.whelan@bcc.cuny.edu
WHELIHAN, Tom .... 218-846-3778.... 267 D
tom.whelihan@minnesota.edu
WHERRY, Cassandra, J ..... 641-269-3424.... 185 D
wherry@grinnell.edu
WHETSTANE, Matt .... 231-876-3104.... 248 A
matt.whetstane@baker.edu
WHETSTON, Michael .... 207-326-2256.... 219 D
michael.whetston@mma.edu
WHETSTONE, Colleen .... 803-793-5172.... 457 F
whetstonec@denmarktech.edu
WHETTEN, Judd .... 808-675-3400.... 140 D
whettenj@byuh.edu
WHICKER, Paul, R .... 603-283-2391.... 303 F
pwhicker@antioch.edu
WHIDDON, Tifini .... 936-633-4555.... 480 D
twhiddon@angelina.edu
WHIFFEN, Sarah, E .... 585-785-1263.... 334 A
whiffes@flcc.edu

WHIKEHART, John, R .... 812-330-6001.... 175 J
jwhikeha@ivytech.edu
WHILLOCK, David .... 817-257-5918.... 499 C
d.whillock@tcu.edu
WHIPPLE, P. Michael .... 504-861-5543.... 213 F
pmwhipple@loyno.edu
WHIPPY, Helen J, D .... 671-735-2994.... 559 G
hwhippy@uguam.uog.edu
WHISENAND, Gary, D .... 509-777-4313.... 540 C
gwhisenand@whitworth.edu
WHISENANT, Mary Alice ... 540-365-4235.... 519 C
mwhisenant@ferrum.edu
WHISENHUNT, Denise ...... 619-388-3498...... 65 F
dwhisenh@sdccd.edu
WHISENHUNT, Denise ...... 619-388-2678...... 65 G
dwhisenh@sdccd.edu
WHISENHUNT, Susan, S .. 828-398-2562.... 376 H
swhisenhunt@southcollegenc.edu
WHISENNAND, Jack .... 405-382-9950.... 412 B
j.whisennand@sscok.edu
WHISETON-COMER, Freda 708-534-4518.... 151 E
fcomer@govst.edu
WHISLER, Janice .... 219-785-5283.... 179 A
jwhisler@pnc.edu
WHISLER, Ruth .... 928-344-7505...... 12 A
ruth.whisler@azwestern.edu
WHISLER, Ryan .... 740-477-7721.... 398 D
rwhisler@ohiochristman
WHISMAN, Kathryn, E .... 520-621-3324...... 18 L
kwhisman@email.arizona.edu
WHISMAN, Linda, A .... 213-738-6729...... 71 E
library@swlaw.edu
WHISNANT, David, M .... 864-597-4294.... 463 G
whistnantdm@wofford.edu
WHISNANT, Rebecca, S .... 937-229-3421.... 404 A
rwhisnant1@udayton.edu
WHITACRE, Aaron .... 540-868-7073.... 527 C
lwhitacre@lfcc.edu
WHITACRE, Caroline .... 614-292-1582.... 398 I
whitacre.3@osu.edu
WHITACRE, Norma .... 360-475-7360.... 536 D
nwhitacre@olympic.edu
WHITAKER, A. Dale .... 765-494-0615.... 178 J
dwhittake@purdue.edu
WHITAKER, Bret .... 740-366-9410.... 399 E
whitaker.77@osu.edu
WHITAKER, Cindy .... 505-254-7575...... 18 G
cwhitaker@theartcenter.edu
WHITAKER, Dan .... 603-448-2445.... 305 C
WHITAKER, Debbie .... 951-222-8434...... 64 A
debbie.whitaker@rcc.edu
WHITAKER, Evans, P .... 864-231-2100.... 455 C
ewhitaker@andersonuniversity.edu
WHITAKER, Gwen, D .... 336-734-7471.... 370 F
gwhitaker@forsythtech.edu
WHITAKER, Helene, M ...... 610-861-5460.... 437 H
hwhitaker@northampton.edu
WHITAKER, Herman .... 818-299-5500...... 78 A
hwhitaker@westcoastuniversity.edu
WHITAKER, Janice .... 972-825-4759.... 495 F
jwhitaker@sagu.edu
WHITAKER, Jason .... 859-233-8289.... 207 A
jwhitaker@transy.edu
WHITAKER, Keila .... 405-945-3252.... 410 F
WHITAKER, Keisha .... 407-843-3984.... 110 E
kwhitaker@fortiscollege.edu
WHITAKER, Lon .... 541-962-3773.... 418 C
lwhitake@eou.edu
WHITAKER, Michelle .... 910-672-1958.... 377 G
mwhitaker@uncfsu.edu
WHITAKER, Nashanta .... 336-315-7800...... 99 G
WHITAKER, Rob .... 706-802-5105.... 130 E
rwhitake@highlands.edu
WHITAKER, JR.,
Russell, E .... 804-862-6200.... 523 F
rwhitaker@rbc.edu
WHITAKER, Scott .... 505-428-1268.... 320 E
scott.whitaker@sfcc.edu
WHITAKER, Shari .... 315-655-7332.... 325 H
sswhitaker@cazenovia.edu
WHITAKER, Whit .... 706-236-2227.... 126 C
awhitaker@berry.edu
WHITAKER-LEA, Laura ...... 828-689-1212.... 366 I
lwhitaker-lea@mhc.edu
WHITBY, Holly .... 615-248-1320.... 476 G
hwhitby@trevecca.edu
WHITCOMB, Connie, F ...... 716-375-2351.... 348 C
cwhitcomb@sbu.edu
WHITCOMB, Michael, E .... 860-685-5340...... 95 E
mwhitcomb@wesleyan.edu
WHITCUP, Cary .... 703-414-4032.... 518 C
cwhitcup@devry.edu
WHITE, A. Jay .... 812-941-2362.... 175 A
jwhite04@ius.edu
WHITE, Aaron .... 901-272-5136.... 471 D
finaid@mca.edu
WHITE, Adam, J .... 434-381-6113.... 524 K
ajwhite@sbc.edu
WHITE, Alan, R .... 252-328-6249.... 377 E
whiteal@ecu.edu
WHITE, Alisa .... 903-566-7104.... 506 E
awhite@uttyler.edu
WHITE, Alison Boord .... 302-225-6343...... 96 H
whitea@gbc.edu

WHITE, Andrew .... 631-632-7100.... 352 C
andrew.white@stonybrook.edu
WHITE, Andrew, W .... 207-786-6491.... 217 C
awhite@bates.edu
WHITE, Ann, H .... 812-465-1173.... 181 B
awhite@usi.edu
WHITE, Anne .... 253-964-6623.... 536 H
awhite@pierce.ctc.edu
WHITE, Anthony .... 410-225-2311.... 224 B
awhite03@mica.edu
WHITE, Barbara, L .... 972-860-8348.... 484 I
bwhite@dcccd.edu
WHITE, Belva .... 404-727-2584.... 129 D
belva.white@ctrl.emory.edu
WHITE, Betsy .... 810-989-2117.... 248 G
betsy.white@baker.edu
WHITE, Bradley .... 615-963-5817.... 474 A
bwhite2@tnstate.edu
WHITE, Brian .... 503-768-7307.... 416 G
bdwhite@lclark.edu
WHITE, Brian .... 419-755-4227.... 399 C
white.808@osu.edu
WHITE, Byron .... 216-523-7292.... 388 D
byron.white@csuohio.edu
WHITE, Caleb .... 608-822-2446.... 555 D
cwhite@swtc.edu
WHITE, Carol, C .... 919-866-5925.... 374 H
ccwhite@waketech.edu
WHITE, Carolee .... 315-228-7488.... 329 G
cwhite@colgate.edu
WHITE, Charles, B .... 210-999-7345.... 502 E
cwhite@trinity.edu
WHITE, Charlie .... 276-223-4848.... 529 C
cwhite@wcc.vccs.edu
WHITE, Christina, C .... 770-534-6299.... 126 E
cwhite@brenau.edu
WHITE, Courtney .... 864-646-1484.... 461 F
cwhite12@tctc.edu
WHITE, Craig .... 217-424-6344.... 158 G
ccwhite@millikin.edu
WHITE, Curtis .... 706-821-8239.... 135 G
cwhite@paine.edu
WHITE, Curtis .... 419-289-5777.... 384 G
cwhite@ashland.edu
WHITE, Cynthia, L .... 972-758-3871.... 483 H
clwhite@collin.edu
WHITE, Daniel .... 907-474-6222...... 10 I
dmwhite@alaska.edu
WHITE, Danny .... 716-645-3454.... 351 G
ub-athleticdirector@buffalo.edu
WHITE, David .... 252-328-1552.... 377 E
whited@ecu.edu
WHITE, David .... 334-448-5112........ 8 A
whited@troy.edu
WHITE, David .... 336-887-3000.... 366 C
dwhite@laureluniversity.edu
WHITE, David .... 304-424-8225.... 545 C
dave.white@mail.wvu.edu
WHITE, David, B .... 828-398-7175.... 368 B
dwhite@abtech.edu
WHITE, Dawn, H .... 937-327-7800.... 406 B
dwhite@wittenberg.edu
WHITE, Deborah .... 330-972-8259.... 403 B
dwhite1@uakron.edu
WHITE, Deborah .... 978-934-2173.... 237 B
deborah_white@uml.edu
WHITE, Deborah .... 810-762-3200.... 259 C
debwhite@umflint.edu
WHITE, Dewayne .... 212-678-3315.... 357 G
white@exchange.tc.columbia.edu
WHITE, Diane .... 703-284-1610.... 521 D
diane.white@marymount.edu
WHITE, Donald, T .... 540-464-7251.... 529 F
whitedt@vmi.edu
WHITE, Donna .... 304-829-7622.... 540 H
dwhite@bethanywv.edu
WHITE, Douglas .... 856-691-8600.... 309 B
dwhite@cccnj.edu
WHITE, Dwayne .... 601-877-6500.... 272 F
dwhite1@alcorn.edu
WHITE, Eddie .... 615-248-1242.... 476 G
ewhite@trevecca.edu
WHITE, Ernie .... 919-735-5151.... 375 A
ewhite@waynecc.edu
WHITE, Evelyn, M .... 256-761-6216........ 7 G
ewhite@talladega.edu
WHITE, Fred .... 817-212-4100.... 502 C
fwhite@law.txwes.edu
WHITE, Gary .... 215-953-5999...... 99 G
gary.white@strayer.edu
WHITE, Gary .... 615-226-3990.... 472 A
gwhite@nadcedu.com
WHITE, Gary, R .... 805-893-2182...... 75 B
gary.white@sa.ucsb.edu
WHITE, Hayne .... 704-272-5343.... 374 A
hwhite@spcc.edu
WHITE, J, H .... 334-387-3877........ 1 D
johnwhite@amridgeuniversity.edu
WHITE, Jackie .... 478-757-3400.... 127 A
jwhite@centralgatech.edu
WHITE, Jacqueline, M .... 401-865-2811.... 453 H
jwhite@providence.edu
WHITE, James .... 509-313-4049.... 534 F
whitej@gonzaga.edu

WHITE, James, M .... 410-651-8440.... 227 E
jmwhite@umes.edu
WHITE, Janet, C .... 608-757-7705.... 553 G
jwhite@blackhawk.edu
WHITE, Jennifer .... 909-777-3300...... 46 H
WHITE, Jerre .... 714-556-3610...... 77 B
jwhite@vanguard.edu
WHITE, Jerry, L .... 517-750-1200.... 258 D
jwhite@arbor.edu
WHITE, Jessie .... 254-659-7841.... 487 G
jwhite@hillcollege.edu
WHITE, Jim .... 231-995-1939.... 256 D
jwhite@nmc.edu
WHITE, Joan .... 928-226-4217...... 13 F
joan.white@coconino.edu
WHITE, Joel .... 541-917-4840.... 416 I
whitej@linnbenton.edu
WHITE, John .... 503-352-7355.... 419 E
whiteja@pacificu.edu
WHITE, John .... 404-687-4522.... 127 F
whitej@ctsnet.edu
WHITE, John .... 239-513-1122.... 111 A
jwhite@hodges.edu
WHITE, John, A .... 413-748-3408.... 244 H
jawhite@springfieldcollege.edu
WHITE, John, V .... 702-895-3301.... 302 I
john.white@unlv.edu
WHITE, Joshua .... 617-262-5000.... 231 G
joshua.white@the-bac.edu
WHITE, Judi .... 918-647-1474.... 407 E
jpwhite@carlalbert.edu
WHITE, Julie .... 773-481-8920.... 147 I
jwhite@ccc.edu
WHITE, Julie, R .... 315-464-4816.... 352 E
whitejul@upstate.edu
WHITE, Karen .... 207-453-5117.... 218 I
kwhite@kvcc.me.edu
WHITE, Karen, K .... 727-341-4656.... 116 H
white.karenkaufman@spcollege.edu
WHITE, Karen, L .... 574-520-4477.... 174 E
kwhite@iusb.edu
WHITE, Kelly, L .... 361-698-1641.... 485 G
kwhite@delmar.edu
WHITE, Kevin .... 919-684-2431.... 364 C
kwhite@duaa.duke.edu
WHITE, Kristie, L .... 804-342-5219.... 530 A
klwhite@vuu.edu
WHITE, Kyle .... 918-335-6289.... 411 B
kwhite@okwu.edu
WHITE, Ladylease .... 973-877-3494.... 309 H
white@essex.edu
WHITE, Laura, M .... 863-784-7154.... 117 J
laura.white@southflorida.edu
WHITE, Lauri .... 309-341-5461.... 146 D
lwhite@sandburg.edu
WHITE, Laurie .... 386-506-4499.... 104 F
whitela@daytonastate.edu
WHITE, Lawrence .... 302-831-7361...... 96 I
lawwhite@udel.edu
WHITE, Linda .... 901-435-1601.... 470 D
linda_white@loc.edu
WHITE, Lisa .... 417-626-1234.... 287 C
white.lisa@occ.edu
WHITE, Lisa, C .... 319-895-4361.... 183 G
lwhite@cornellcollege.edu
WHITE, Lori .... 213-381-3333...... 53 C
lwhite@lac.edu
WHITE, Lori, S .... 214-768-2821.... 495 A
lswhite@smu.edu
WHITE, Lynn .... 812-888-4241.... 181 D
lwhite@vinu.edu
WHITE, M. Chrisopher .... 252-398-6221.... 363 G
whitec@chowan.edu
WHITE, Mark .... 402-552-6067.... 297 B
whitemark@clarksoncollege.edu
WHITE, Marsha .... 800-422-2418.... 102 A
mwhite@baymedical.org
WHITE, Marsha, S .... 770-720-5512.... 136 C
msw@reinhardt.edu
WHITE, JR.,
Marshall Sonny .... 803-738-7600.... 459 E
whites@midlandstech.edu
WHITE, Mary Jean .... 334-745-6437........ 7 D
mjwhite@suscc.edu
WHITE, Mary Jo .... 303-492-8908...... 88 H
joey.white@colorado.edu
WHITE, Mary Jo .... 206-934-5378.... 537 F
maryjo.white@seattlecolleges.edu
WHITE, Maureen .... 860-701-5047...... 93 E
white_m@mitchell.edu
WHITE, Michael .... 229-317-6726.... 128 D
michael.white@darton.edu
WHITE, Michael .... 559-638-3641...... 72 C
michael.white@reedleycollege.edu
WHITE, Michael .... 559-638-3641...... 72 C
WHITE, Michael .... 304-442-3033.... 545 D
michael.white@mail.wvu.edu
WHITE, Michael, L .... 319-399-8643.... 183 F
mwhite@coe.edu
WHITE, Michele, M .... 540-568-6281.... 520 H
whitemm@jmu.edu
WHITE, Michelle .... 918-647-1399.... 407 E
mwhite@carlalbert.edu

WHITE, Missy 803-799-9082 461 A mwhite@southuniversity.edu
WHITE, Monica, J 716-673-3271 352 A monica.white@fredonia.edu
WHITE, Nolan (Bill), W 812-246-3301 177 B nwhite61@ivytech.edu
WHITE, Norman 863-638-7264 123 D norman.white@warner.edu
WHITE, O. Ivan 903-927-3384 509 E oiwhite@wileyc.edu
WHITE, Olivia, G 301-696-3573 223 C owhite@hood.edu
WHITE, P. Phillip 518-629-7149 336 C p.white@hvcc.edu
WHITE, Pamela 413-755-4452 241 B pjwhite@stcc.edu
WHITE, Pamela 515-294-5380 182 E pjwhite@iastate.edu
WHITE, Patricia 305-284-2394 122 I pwhite@miami.edu
WHITE, Patrick, E 765-361-6221 181 E whitep@wabash.edu
WHITE, Patty 406-447-4454 293 G pwhite@carroll.edu
WHITE, Perry, D 316-284-5241 191 C pwhite@bethelks.edu
WHITE, Peter 619-388-3464 65 F pwhite@sdccd.edu
WHITE, R. Barry 315-792-3011 359 E rwhite@utica.edu
WHITE, Randy 260-665-4171 180 D whiter@trine.edu
WHITE, Randy 407-774-6200 541 H rwhite@mountainstate.edu
WHITE, Ray 334-241-9538 8 A grwhite@troy.edu
WHITE, Ray 425-564-2446 531 G ray.white@bellevuecollege.edu
WHITE, Rebecca 229-209-5145 124 E rebeccawhite@andrewcollege.edu
WHITE, Rebecca, H 706-542-7140 138 G rhwhite@uga.edu
WHITE, Renee 617-521-2079 244 F renee.white@simmons.edu
WHITE, Rex 713-221-8505 503 F whiter@uhd.edu
WHITE, Rhonda 336-517-2183 362 G rjwhite@bennett.edu
WHITE, Richard E, T 206-726-5127 533 D retwhite@cornish.edu
WHITE, Robert 870-574-4463 24 A rwhite@sautech.edu
WHITE, Robert, L 937-327-7411 406 B rwhite@wittenberg.edu
WHITE, Robert, W 931-598-1210 472 L police@sewanee.edu
WHITE, Ronald, G 803-786-3091 457 C rwhite@columbiasc.edu
WHITE, Ronald, J 605-394-2493 466 B ronald.white@sdsmt.edu
WHITE, Roslyn 248-457-2734 252 E
WHITE, Sabrina 706-771-4037 125 H swhite@augustatech.edu
WHITE, Samantha 573-875-7352 280 A sjwhite@ccis.edu
WHITE, Samuel, L 601-877-6142 272 F slwhite@alcorn.edu
WHITE, Samuel, L 601-877-6388 272 F slwhite@alcorn.edu
WHITE, Shae 254-442-5127 482 I shae.white@cisco.edu
WHITE, Sharon 203-251-8406 94 G sharon.white@uconn.edu
WHITE, Shawn, A 304-788-6879 545 B sawhite@mail.wvu.edu
WHITE, Shelley 828-398-7937 368 B swhite@abtech.edu
WHITE, Stephanie, M 804-257-5745 530 A swhite@vuu.edu
WHITE, Stephen 718-862-7548 339 H stephen.white@manhattan.edu
WHITE, Stephen 615-898-5454 473 G stephen.white@mtsu.edu
WHITE, Stephen, E 401-254-3681 454 C swhite@rwu.edu
WHITE, Steven 316-978-3782 198 A steven.white@wichita.edu
WHITE, Sue 602-274-4300 12 K
WHITE, Susan 740-753-7203 391 H whites@hocking.edu
WHITE, Susan, E 912-583-3169 126 F swhite@bpc.edu
WHITE, Susan, K 913-627-4125 194 C swhite@kckcc.edu
WHITE, Tamisia 212-870-1229 344 A finaid@nyts.edu
WHITE, Tammy, S 205-652-3651 9 E thw@uwa.edu
WHITE, Terry, A 615-460-6617 467 D terry.white@belmont.edu
WHITE, Thelma 270-706-8409 202 A thelma.white@kctcs.edu
WHITE, Thomas 207-602-2939 221 A twhite5@une.edu
WHITE, Thomas 817-923-1921 495 G twhite@swbts.edu
WHITE, Timothy, L 352-846-0850 120 C tlwhite@ufl.edu
WHITE, Timothy, P 951-827-5201 74 E tim.white@ucr.edu
WHITE, Tracy 715-234-8176 553 B tracy.white@uwc.edu
WHITE, W. Scott 704-406-4259 364 E swhite@gardner-webb.edu
WHITE, Wayman 252-335-0821 369 G waywhite@albemarle.edu
WHITE, Wendy, S 215-746-5200 448 J generalcounsel@ogc.upenn.edu
WHITE, William 304-929-1658 541 H wwhite@mountainstate.edu
WHITE, William, A 407-582-1185 123 B bwhite@valenciacollege.edu
WHITE, William, H 508-929-8811 238 G wwhite@worcester.edu
WHITE, Woodie 504-286-5117 214 J wwhite@suno.edu
WHITE CASTENADA, April 626-395-8167 32 H april@caltech.edu
WHITECAVAGE, Michele 714-449-7404 70 G mwhitecavage@scco.edu
WHITED, Frances, P 330-287-1216 399 A whited.16@osu.edu
WHITEFIELD, Philip, D 573-341-7887 291 E pwhite@mst.edu
WHITEFORD, Aaron 503-768-7944 416 G ahw@lclark.edu
WHITEHAIR, Bruce 814-332-2451 421 F bwhitehair@allegheny.edu
WHITEHEAD, Carolyn 303-492-5366 88 H carolyn.whitehead@cufund.org
WHITEHEAD, Charles, L 618-931-0600 165 D chuck.whitehead@swic.edu
WHITEHEAD, Doug 435-652-7500 512 B dkw@dixie.edu
WHITEHEAD, George 435-652-7906 512 B whiteheg@dixie.edu
WHITEHEAD, Gwen 740-654-6711 400 C whitehea@ohio.edu
WHITEHEAD, Jeff 740-654-6711 400 C whitehej@ohio.edu
WHITEHEAD, Joe 601-266-4884 277 F joe.whitehead@usm.edu
WHITEHEAD, Johnny 713-348-6000 493 C johnny.whitehead@rice.edu
WHITEHEAD, Joyce, E 630-889-6610 159 F jwhitehead@nuhs.edu
WHITEHEAD, Pam 606-589-3155 203 D pamela.whitehead@kctcs.edu
WHITEHEAD, Richard, G 540-261-4347 524 H richard.whitehead@svu.edu
WHITEHEAD, Sharon, F 606-679-8501 203 C sharon.whitehead@kctcs.edu
WHITEHEAD, Teresa 575-769-4066 318 A teresa.whitehead@clovis.edu
WHITEHEAD, Tyree 561-912-2166 107 B twhitehead@evergladesuniversity.edu
WHITEHEAD, Wesley 229-248-2560 126 A wesley.whitehead@bainbridge.edu
WHITEHORN, Michael, A 325-670-1250 487 F mwhite@hsutx.edu
WHITEHOUSE, Deborah 859-622-1523 200 J deborah.whitehouse@eku.edu
WHITEHOUSE, Eric 239-477-2100 115 G eric.whitehouse@rasmussen.edu
WHITEHOUSE COBB, John 303-546-3517 86 H president@naropa.edu
WHITEHURST, Alan 540-261-4318 524 H alan.whitehurst@svu.edu
WHITEHURST, Alan 540-261-4318 524 H alalan.whitehurst@svu.edu
WHITELAW, Lydia 610-896-1177 430 G lwhitela@haverford.edu
WHITELEY, Herbert, E 217-333-2760 167 D hwhiteley@illinois.edu
WHITELEY, Janell 360-475-7504 536 D jwhiteley@olympic.edu
WHITELY, Patricia, A 305-284-4922 122 I pwhitely@miami.edu
WHITEMAN, Betty 386-822-8869 121 F bwhiteman@stetson.edu
WHITEMAN, Charles, H 814-863-0448 438 G chw17@psu.edu
WHITEMAN, Ray 574-807-7139 169 I ray.whiteman@bethelcollege.edu
WHITEMORE, Alan, T 617-989-4307 245 F whitemorea@wit.edu
WHITENECK, Peter 715-634-4790 547 J pwhiteneck@lco-college.edu
WHITESIDE, Christopher 559-442-4600 72 B christopher.whiteside@fresnocitycollege.edu
WHITESIDE, Detroit 619-321-3000 29 G dewhiteside@argosy.edu
WHITESIDE, Harold 615-898-2900 473 G harold.whiteside@mtsu.edu
WHITESIDE, Nadia 312-662-4036 144 H nwhiteside@adler.edu
WHITESIDE, Niki 281-998-6150 493 G niki.whiteside@sjcd.edu
WHITEY, Jeff 541-888-7634 420 C jwhitey@socc.edu
WHITFIELD, Gary 209-588-5112 80 G whitfieldg@yosemite.edu
WHITFIELD, Keith 919-660-0330 364 C keith.whitfield@duke.edu
WHITFIELD, Rick, N 910-962-3383 379 D whitfieldr@uncw.edu
WHITFIELD, Walter, V 252-789-0232 371 H wwhitfield@martincc.edu
WHITFILL, Jill 731-352-4083 467 E whitfillj@bethelu.edu
WHITFORD, Betty Lou 334-844-4448 1 F blw0017@auburn.edu
WHITFORD, Erin 325-942-2122 480 E erin.whitford@angelo.edu
WHITFORD, Jewel, L 406-395-4313 296 E jewelwhitford@hotmail.com
WHITHAM, Bruce 856-256-4981 314 A whitham@rowan.edu
WHITHAUS, Becky 573-897-5000 284 A
WHITING, Mary 870-460-1026 25 A whitingm@uamont.edu
WHITING, Raymond, A 706-729-2040 125 G rwhiting@aug.edu
WHITING, Sarah, M 713-348-4044 493 C sarah.whiting@rice.edu
WHITING, Scott 334-874-5700 2 H swhiting@ccal.edu
WHITING, Shari, K 315-859-4313 334 H swhiting@hamilton.edu
WHITING, Svea 970-943-7057 89 E swhiting@western.edu
WHITING, Todd 704-366-4853 376 B twhiting@rts.edu
WHITIS, Andrew 419-783-2490 389 H awhitis@defiance.edu
WHITIS, Andrew 419-434-4767 404 B whitis@findlay.edu
WHITIS, Matt 815-939-5350 161 A mwhitis@olivet.edu
WHITIS, Sarah 530-842-1245 42 E swhitis@siskiyous.edu
WHITLATCH, Frank 707-826-5101 36 E frank@humboldt.edu
WHITLATCH, Michael, D 712-749-2172 183 C whitlatch@bvu.edu
WHITLEDGE, Terry 907-474-7229 10 I terry@ims.uaf.edu
WHITLEY, Darrell, S 252-985-5105 375 E dwhitley@ncwc.edu
WHITLEY, Kay, E 432-837-8226 501 E kwhitley@sulross.edu
WHITLEY, Rebecca 575-492-2112 321 H rwhitley@usw.edu
WHITLING, Jacqueline 570-484-3045 443 B jwhitlin@lhup.edu
WHITLOCK, David, W 405-585-5801 409 D david.whitlock@okbu.edu
WHITLOCK, Doug 859-622-2977 200 J doug.whitlock@eku.edu
WHITLOCK, John, L 727-816-3325 114 F whitloj@phcc.edu
WHITLOCK, Luder 954-771-0376 112 I
WHITLOCK, Marshall 414-475-4846 189 G whitlockm@uiu.edu
WHITLOCK, Mary 661-836-6300 52 E mwhitlock@kaplan.edu
WHITLOCK, Roger 601-635-2111 274 A rwhitlock@eccc.edu
WHITLOCK, Sharon, K 765-494-9708 178 J whitlock@purdue.edu
WHITLOCK, Stephen 678-839-6426 139 A swhitlock@westga.edu
WHITLOCK, Veronica 212-472-1500 343 G vwhitlock@nysid.edu
WHITMAN, Carl, E 209-667-3343 36 D cwhitman@csustan.edu
WHITMAN, Chris 734-764-0747 259 A cwhitman@umich.edu
WHITMAN, David 651-604-4118 265 B
WHITMAN, Deirdre 914-674-7316 340 F dwhitman@mercy.edu
WHITMAN, John 510-885-3674 34 E john.whitman@csueastbay.edu
WHITMAN, Joshua 608-785-8616 551 C jwhitman@uwlax.edu
WHITMAN, Rebecca, R 616-234-4010 251 E rwhitman@grcc.edu
WHITMAN, William, D 989-386-6696 255 C wwhitman@midmich.edu
WHITMER, Ann 517-629-0440 247 A awhitmer@albion.edu
WHITMIRE, Teresa 479-619-4175 22 H twhitmire@nwacc.edu
WHITMORE, Joe 256-782-5777 4 L whitmore@jsu.edu
WHITMORE, Karen 973-328-5671 309 A kwhitmore@ccm.edu
WHITMORE, Kimberly, N 515-574-1138 185 I whitmore@iowacentral.edu
WHITMORE, Michele 802-635-1452 515 F michele.whitmore@jsc.edu
WHITMORE-HANSEN, Anne 518-564-2090 354 B hansenaw@plattsburgh.edu
WHITNABLE, Michael, D 740-374-8716 405 G mwhitnable@wscc.edu
WHITNEY, Candice 408-848-4754 48 C cwhitney@gavilan.edu
WHITNEY, Cynthia 732-987-2244 310 C whitneyc@georgian.edu
WHITNEY, Gleaves 616-331-3298 251 F whitneyg@gvsu.edu
WHITNEY, Glenda 573-897-5000 284 A
WHITNEY, Heidi 802-468-6072 515 D heidi.whitney@castleton.edu
WHITNEY, Holly 941-554-1580 101 A hwhitney@argosy.edu
WHITNEY, Jarrid 626-395-6341 32 H
WHITNEY, Joan, G 610-519-4050 450 H joan.whitney@villanova.edu
WHITNEY, Karen 602-557-1037 19 A karen.whitney@phoenix.edu
WHITNEY, Karen, M 814-393-2220 442 B president@clarion.edu
WHITNEY, Marian, D 315-684-6066 354 F whitnemd@morisville.edu
WHITNEY, Patricia, C 207-859-5002 217 G pcwhitne@colby.edu
WHITNEY, Patrick, F 312-595-4900 153 C whitney@id.iit.edu
WHITNEY, Paul 401-874-5224 454 E pwhitney@uri.edu
WHITNEY, Phyllis 319-385-6206 186 E phyllis.whitney@iwc.edu
WHITNEY, Richard 805-962-8179 29 A rwhitney@antioch.edu
WHITNEY, Richard, A 907-786-4754 10 H rich.whitney@uaa.alaska.edu
WHITSON, Brian 757-221-7876 518 A bwwhit@wm.edu
WHITSON, Janet 512-313-3000 483 K janet.whitson@concordia.edu
WHITSON, Jennifer, N 317-738-8021 171 F jwhitson@franklincollege.edu
WHITSON, Robert, E 405-744-2474 410 C bob.whitson@okstate.edu
WHITSON, Tony 901-435-1733 470 D tony_whitson@loc.edu
WHITT, Alton 205-934-0850 8 F awhitt@uab.edu
WHITT, Cynthia, L 423-869-6394 470 E cindy.whitt@lmunet.edu
WHITT, David, T 205-726-2386 6 G dtwhitt@samford.edu
WHITT, Edith, L 828-689-1151 366 I ewhitt@mhc.edu
WHITT, Elizabeth 314-977-3951 289 C ewhitt@slu.edu
WHITT, Larry 276-964-7648 528 E larry.whitt@sw.edu
WHITT, Marc 859-622-2301 200 J marc.whitt@eku.edu
WHITT, Susan 910-521-6212 379 C susan.whitt@uncp.edu
WHITTAKER, Debra, B 727-816-3405 114 F whittad@phcc.edu
WHITTAKER, Denise 760-921-5499 61 C denise.whittaker@paloverde.edu
WHITTAKER, Mark 904-819-6290 107 C mark@flagler.edu
WHITTAKER, Robert, E 802-626-6427 515 G robert.whittaker@lyndonstate.edu
WHITTAKER-DAVIS, Sharon 205-366-8838 7 F swhittaker@stillman.edu
WHITTEMORE, Nancy 661-255-1050 32 F nwhittem@calarts.edu
WHITTEN, Deborah 864-656-8128 456 E dbw@clemson.edu
WHITTEN, Kim 870-612-2016 25 E kim.whitten@uaccb.edu
WHITTEN, Pamela 517-355-3410 255 A pwhitten@msu.edu
WHITTEN, Patrice 850-484-1561 115 B pwhitten@pensacolastate.edu
WHITTEN, Virgina "Ginni" 281-425-6302 489 M vwhitten@lee.edu
WHITTENBURG, Nashia 912-344-2514 124 G nashia.whittenburg@armstrong.edu
WHITTENBURG, Scott, L 504-280-6321 213 E swhitten@uno.edu
WHITTEY, Chris 216-421-7455 388 A cwhittey@cia.edu
WHITTINGHAM, Michelle 831-459-1453 75 C michelle@ucsc.edu
WHITTINGHAM, Rachel 501-205-8876 21 C rwhittingham@cbc.edu
WHITTINGTON, Christine, A 336-272-7102 364 G cwhittington@greensboro.edu
WHITTINGTON, Connie 318-869-5101 208 H cwhitt@centenary.edu
WHITTINGTON, Donna 225-675-8270 211 F dwhittington@rpcc.edu
WHITTINGTON, Gerald, O 336-278-5434 364 D whitting@elon.edu

WHITTINGTON, Lee .... 828-765-7351.... 372 A
lwhittington@mayland.edu
WHITTINGTON, Ray .... 312-362-6781.... 149 A
rwhittin@depaul.edu
WHITTLESEY, Valerie, D .... 770-423-6023.... 133 A
vwhittle@kennesaw.edu
WHITTON, Mary Lou .... 913-768-1900.... 191 D
mwhitton@brownmackie.edu
WHITTUM, Terry, E .... 904-256-7099.... 111 L
twhittu@ju.edu
WHITTY, Jennifer .... 707-654-1720...... 33 C
jwhitty@csum.edu
WHITWELL, Jeff .... 615-898-2700.... 473 G
jeff.whitwell@mtsu.edu
WHITWORTH, Bruce .... 559-278-2795...... 35 A
bwhitwor@csufresno.edu
WHITWORTH, Ling, Y .... 434-395-2319.... 521 A
whitworthly@longwood.edu
WHORLEY, Frank .... 410-951-2600.... 228 B
fwhorley@coppin.edu
WHYNOTT, Anne .... 262-564-2758.... 554 B
whynotta@gtc.edu
WHYTE, Novia, P .... 516-463-6928.... 335 G
novia.p.whyte@hofstra.edu
WHYTE, William .... 262-564-3228.... 554 B
whytew@gtc.edu
WIAFE, Ronald .... 216-373-5274.... 397 F
rwiafe@ndc.edu
WIATER, Patrick .... 518-255-5423.... 354 E
wiaterpa@cobleskill.edu
WIBBELL, Lee .... 217-641-4314.... 154 I
lwibbel@jwcc.edu
WIBBENMEYER, Kana .... 773-508-3489.... 157 C
kwibben@luc.edu
WICHERN, Adam .... 718-405-3776.... 330 A
adam.wichern@mountsaintvincent.edu
WICHERT, Jerome, L .... 580-774-3786.... 412 F
jerome.wichert@swosu.edu
WICHROSKI, Pamela, J .... 207-786-6207.... 217 C
pwichros@bates.edu
WICHSER, John .... 301-696-3545.... 223 C
wichser@hood.edu
WICK, Martha .... 641-683-5259.... 185 G
martha.wich@indianhills.edu
WICK, Michael, R .... 715-836-2033.... 551 A
wickmr@uwec.edu
WICKEHAM, Daniel .... 414-955-8826.... 548 G
dwickeha@mcw.edu
WICKER-MCCREE,
Ingrid, L .... 919-530-7057.... 378 B
iwicker@nccu.edu
WICKERT, Jonathan, A .... 515-294-0070.... 182 E
wickert@iastate.edu
WICKIZER, Della, H .... 434-395-2074.... 521 A
wickizerdh@longwood.edu
WICKLAND, Mary .... 409-984-6115.... 501 C
mary.wickland@lamarpa.edu
WICKLESS, Megan .... 402-552-6119.... 297 B
wicklessmegan@clarksoncollege.edu
WICKLIFFE, Cari, S .... 314-977-2350.... 289 C
wicklics@slu.edu
WICKLUND, Greg, A .... 817-202-6743.... 495 E
wicklund@swau.edu
WICKLUND, Joe .... 218-723-6479.... 262 G
jwicklun@css.edu
WICKMAN, Larry .... 575-461-4413.... 318 G
larryw@mesalands.edu
WICKS, Donna .... 810-762-7853.... 253 C
dwicks@kettering.edu
WICKS, Michelle, D .... 304-204-4093.... 542 J
mwicks@kvctc.edu
WICKS, Natalie .... 313-993-1000.... 258 G
wicksnk@udmercy.edu
WIDDERS, Pat .... 479-788-7390...... 24 D
pat.widders@uafs.edu
WIDDIG, Bernd .... 617-552-3827.... 232 B
bernd.widdig@bc.edu
WIDENHOFER, Stephen, B 217-424-6300.... 158 G
swidenhofer@millikin.edu
WIDENHORN, Mirko .... 570-408-4135.... 452 A
mirko.widenhorn@wilkes.edu
WIDGER, Mari Jo .... 308-535-3773.... 298 H
widgerm@mpcc.edu
WIDING, II, Robert, E .... 216-368-1156.... 386 F
WIDMER, Robert, D .... 309-268-8100.... 151 I
rob.widmer@heartland.edu
WIDNER, Bobby .... 229-430-2837.... 124 B
bwidner@albanytech.edu
WIDNER, Roger, H .... 615-525-2814.... 467 B
rwidmer@argosy.edu
WIDNEY, Kaye, C .... 304-293-2831.... 545 A
kaye.widney@mail.wvu.edu
WIEBE, Harold, D .... 740-368-3656.... 400 G
hdwiebe@owu.edu
WIEBE, Henry, A .... 573-341-4579.... 291 E
wiebe@mst.edu
WIECHOWSKI, Linda .... 248-689-8282.... 259 E
lwiechow@walshcollege.edu
WIECKI, Lisa .... 864-388-8035.... 459 A
lwiecki@lander.edu
WIECKOWSKI, Ellen, G .... 412-397-6901.... 445 H
wieckowski@rmu.edu
WIED, Christine .... 979-830-4224.... 482 C
cwied@blinn.edu

WIEDA, Karen, S .... 636-584-6551.... 281 E
wiedaks@eastcentral.edu
WIEDENHOEFT, Jason .... 773-907-4830.... 147 D
jwiedenhoeft@ccc.edu
WIEDOWER, CSC,
Veronique .... 574-284-4886.... 179 F
vwiedowe@saintmarys.edu
WIEGAND, Stephanie .... 425-640-1423.... 533 I
stephanie.wiegand@edcc.edu
WIEGANDT, Scott, P .... 502-272-8496.... 198 H
swiegandt@bellarmine.edu
WIEGEL, Lisa .... 563-288-6003.... 184 G
lwiegel@eicc.edu
WIEGENSTEIN, Steve, C .... 573-875-8700.... 280 A
scwiegenstein@ccis.edu
WIEGERS, Lynn .... 818-677-2325...... 35 F
lynn.wiegers@csun.edu
WIEGERT, Tim .... 517-750-1200.... 258 D
twiegert@arbor.edu
WIEGMANN, Dawn, R .... 319-352-8437.... 189 J
dawn.wiegmann@wartburg.edu
WIEHE, Wallace .... 678-891-3016.... 131 C
wallace.wiehe@gpc.edu
WIELAND, John .... 502-213-3653.... 202 F
john.wieland@kctcs.edu
WIELENGA, Jay .... 712-707-7111.... 188 D
jayw@nwciowa.edu
WIELHORSKI, Karen .... 281-283-3930.... 503 E
wielhorski@uhcl.edu
WIELINSKI, Peter .... 218-631-7810.... 267 D
peter.wielinski@minnesota.edu
WIELK, Larry, J .... 203-371-7916...... 94 B
wielkl@sacredheart.edu
WIEMERS, Eugene, L .... 207-786-6261.... 217 C
ewiemers@bates.edu
WIEMEYER, Steve, R .... 402-449-2820.... 297 H
swiemeyer@graceu.edu
WIENCEK, John, M .... 813-974-3780.... 121 A
jwiencek@eng.usf.edu
WIENER, Evelyn .... 215-662-2869.... 448 J
wiener@pobox.upenn.edu
WIENER, Madeleine .... 858-635-4428...... 27 E
mwiener@alliant.edu
WIENER, Stuart, A .... 702-968-2008.... 303 D
swiener@roseman.edu
WIENER, William, R .... 336-334-5375.... 379 B
wrwiener@uncg.edu
WIENS, Ann .... 312-499-4214.... 164 C
awiens@saic.edu
WIENS, Chris .... 620-242-0436.... 195 C
wiensc@mcpherson.edu
WIER, Judyth .... 417-667-8181.... 280 E
jwier@cottey.edu
WIER, Karry .... 219-877-3100.... 170 D
kwier@brownmackie.edu
WIERDA, Bruce .... 231-777-0657.... 256 A
bruce.wierda@muskegoncc.edu
WIERGACZ, Nora .... 219-464-5335.... 181 C
nora.wiergacz@valpo.edu
WIERS, Alison .... 336-334-4822.... 371 A
ajwiers@gtcc.edu
WIERTEL, Anthony .... 716-926-8818.... 335 E
twiertel@hilbert.edu
WIERZBICKI, Andrzej .... 251-460-6280...... 9 D
awierzbi@jaguar1.usouthal.edu
WIESCAMP, Cheryl .... 970-247-7364...... 84 K
wiescamp_c@fortlewis.edu
WIESCHOWSKI, Marilyn .... 269-467-9945.... 251 B
mwieschowski@glenoaks.edu
WIESE, Barry .... 281-487-1170.... 499 B
bwiese@txchiro.edu
WIESE, Karen .... 641-269-4939.... 185 D
wiese@grinnell.edu
WIESE, Vicki .... 605-995-3023.... 464 F
vicki.wiese@mitchelltech.edu
WIESEHAN, Terry .... 765-973-8221.... 173 F
twieseha@iue.edu
WIESEMANN, Lois .... 801-957-4255.... 512 D
lois.wiesemann@slcc.edu
WIESEN, Elizabeth .... 207-893-6630.... 219 F
lwiesen@sjcme.edu
WIESENBURG, Denis .... 601-266-5116.... 277 F
denis.wiesenburg@usm.edu
WIESENTHAL, Steve .... 773-834-3529.... 166 G
swiesenthal@uchicago.edu
WIESNER, Bob .... 803-641-3522.... 462 B
bobw@usca.edu
WIESNER, Don .... 316-942-4291.... 195 F
wiesnerd@newmanu.edu
WIETZ, Ophelia .... 305-220-4120.... 115 F
libdir@ptcmatt.com
WIEWEL, Wim .... 503-725-4411.... 418 G
president@pdx.edu
WIEZBICKI-STEVENS,
Kathy .... 413-565-1000.... 230 G
kwiezbic@baypath.edu
WIG, Jeff .... 218-894-5172.... 265 J
jwig@clcmn.edu
WIGAND, Debra .... 920-686-6121.... 550 H
debra.wigand@sl.edu
WIGENT, Rodney .... 215-596-7545.... 450 B
r.wigent@usciences.edu
WIGER, Shannon .... 320-308-5980.... 269 B
swiger@sctcc.edu

WIGFALL, Arthur .... 212-463-0400.... 358 B
arthur.wigfall@touro.edu
WIGGAM, Marilyn .... 614-257-5034.... 390 B
mwiggam@devry.edu
WIGGINS, Amy, F .... 252-862-1200.... 373 C
wigginsa@roanokechowan.edu
WIGGINS, Annette .... 715-634-4790.... 547 J
awiggins@lco-college.edu
WIGGINS, Charles .... 828-395-1306.... 371 D
cpwiggins@isothermal.edu
WIGGINS, David .... 405-789-7661.... 412 E
david.wiggins@swcu.edu
WIGGINS, Devon .... 903-510-2385.... 503 A
dwig@tjc.edu
WIGGINS, Glenn .... 617-989-4470.... 245 F
wigginsg@wit.edu
WIGGINS, Jack .... 409-839-2014.... 500 I
jowiggins@lit.edu
WIGGINS, Jana .... 229-217-4139.... 134 F
jwiggins@moultrietech.edu
WIGGINS, Jill .... 417-873-6980.... 281 D
jillwiggins@drury.edu
WIGGINS, Lavaugn .... 334-874-5700.......... 2 H
lwiggins@ccal.edu
WIGGINS, Milton .... 937-708-5707.... 405 H
mwiggins@wilberforce.edu
WIGGINS, Robert, W .... 503-517-1820.... 421 C
rwiggins@westernseminary.edu
WIGGINS, Sandra .... 541-684-4644.... 419 F
swiggins@pioneerpacific.edu
WIGGINS, Timothy .... 630-515-3136.... 149 B
twiggins@devry.edu
WIGGINTON, Van .... 281-542-2050.... 493 H
van.wigginton@sjcd.edu
WIGHT, Chuck .... 801-581-8796.... 511 C
chuck.wight@utah.edu
WIGHT, Laura .... 406-771-4318.... 295 G
laura.wight@msugf.edu
WIGHT, Randall .... 870-245-5107...... 22 I
wight@obu.edu
WIGHTMAN, Beth, A .... 818-677-2969...... 35 F
beth.wightman@csun.edu
WIGHTMAN, Maurice, C .... 315-475-5142.... 351 A
mcwightman20@aol.com
WIGHTMAN, Todd .... 208-524-3000.... 143 G
todd.wightman@my.eitc.edu
WIGINTON, Chad .... 580-477-7918.... 414 C
chad.wiginton@wosc.edu
WIGINTON, Melissa .... 512-404-4862.... 481 D
mwiginton@austinseminary.edu
WIGLE, Stanley .... 219-981-4278.... 174 B
swigle@iun.edu
WIGLEY, Mark, A .... 212-854-3473.... 330 F
maw152@columbia.edu
WIGNALL, Eric .... 574-936-8898.... 169 D
eric.wignall@ancilla.edu
WIGNALL, Scott .... 309-467-6302.... 151 B
swignall@eureka.edu
WIGNER, Dee .... 620-276-9577.... 193 C
dee.wigner@gcccks.edu
WIGNES, David, R .... 608-785-9140.... 555 F
wignesd@westerntc.edu
WIGREN, Katrina .... 912-201-8035.... 137 D
kwigren@southuniversity.edu
WIHBEY, Jean .... 561-207-5400.... 114 D
wihbeyj@palmbeachstate.edu
WIHL, Gary, S .... 314-935-6820.... 292 I
wihl@wustl.edu
WIKE, Lauren, C .... 910-630-7167.... 367 B
lwike@methodist.edu
WIKE, Wayne, D .... 704-233-8319.... 380 F
wike@wingate.edu
WILBANKS, Cynthia, H .... 734-763-5554.... 259 A
wilbanks@umich.edu
WILBANKS, Jennifer .... 660-596-7229.... 290 B
jwilbanks@sfccmo.edu
WILBANKS, Jennifer .... 803-276-9000.... 460 D
wilbanks.j@ptc.edu
WILBANKS, Laura .... 734-484-1322.... 250 F
laura.wilbanks@emich.edu
WILBER, Renita .... 800-567-2344.... 547 A
rwilber@menominee.edu
WILBON, Matisa .... 502-272-8172.... 198 H
mwilbon@bellarmine.edu
WILBORN, Colin .... 254-295-8642.... 504 C
cwilborn@umhb.edu
WILBORN, Keeta, P .... 770-534-6260.... 126 E
kwilborn@brenau.edu
WILBORN, Willie .... 954-499-9864.... 104 J
wwilborn@devry.edu
WILBOUR, Jim .... 407-673-7406.... 113 C
jwilbour@lincolntech.com
WILBRATTE, Barry .... 713-525-2100.... 505 A
wilbratt@stthom.edu
WILBUR, Denise .... 210-567-2004.... 507 A
wilburd@uthscsa.edu
WILBUR, Kathleen, M .... 989-774-3871.... 249 C
wilbu1km@cmich.edu
WILBUR, Peter .... 401-254-3365.... 454 C
pwilbur@rwu.edu
WILBURN, Brenda .... 606-783-2024.... 204 I
b.wilburn@moreheadstate.edu
WILBURN, Eric .... 903-923-2099.... 486 F
ewilburn@etbu.edu

WILBURN, Howard, L .... 336-725-8344.... 375 G
wilburnh@pbc.edu
WILBURN, James, R .... 310-506-7490...... 61 H
james.wilburn@pepperdine.edu
WILBURN, Jim .... 410-287-1017.... 222 A
jwilburn@cecil.edu
WILBURN, Sherryl, E .... 601-974-1200.... 275 B
wilbuse@millsaps.edu
WILCH, Peter, J .... 415-422-6606...... 76 E
pwilch@usfca.edu
WILCOCKSON, Mark .... 773-442-5100.... 160 A
m-wilcockson@neiu.edu
WILCOTS, Barbara .... 303-871-2706...... 89 A
bwilcots@du.edu
WILCOX, Bonnie .... 843-383-8010.... 457 A
bwilcox@coker.edu
WILCOX, Dean .... 336-770-3399.... 379 E
wilcoxd@uncsa.edu
WILCOX, Denise .... 909-469-5393...... 78 I
dwilcox@westernu.edu
WILCOX, Denise .... 918-781-7215.... 407 B
wilcoxd@bacone.edu
WILCOX, Eva .... 585-266-0430.... 333 D
ewilcox@cci.edu
WILCOX, Heather .... 303-797-5674...... 81 D
heather.wilcox@arapahoe.edu
WILCOX, Jerry .... 203-837-8242...... 91 A
wilcoxj@wcsu.edu
WILCOX, Kathleen, J .... 937-328-6060.... 387 H
wilcoxk@clarkstate.edu
WILCOX, Kevin .... 518-956-8120.... 351 E
kwilcox@uamail.albany.edu
WILCOX, Kim .... 970-351-2496...... 89 B
kim.wilcox@unco.edu
WILCOX, Kim, A .... 517-355-1524.... 255 A
kwilcox@msu.edu
WILCOX, Ralph .... 813-974-5543.... 121 A
rcwilcox@usf.edu
WILCOX, Randy .... 229-226-1621.... 138 C
rwilcox@thomasu.edu
WILCOX, Robbin .... 419-267-1460.... 397 E
rwilcox@northweststate.edu
WILCOX, Robert, M .... 803-777-6112.... 462 A
wilcox.robert@sc.edu
WILCOX, Sharon .... 414-382-6127.... 546 B
sharon.wilcox@alverno.edu
WILCOXON, Sharisue .... 712-279-1628.... 183 A
sharisue.wilcoxon@briarcliff.edu
WILCOXSON, Douglas, A .. 859-858-3511.... 198 E
doug.wilcoxson@asbury.edu
WILCOXSON, Elizabeth .... 314-644-9274.... 288 I
ewilcoxson@stlcc.edu
WILCZENSKI, Felicia .... 617-287-7592.... 236 G
felicia.wilczenski@umb.edu
WILD, Bradford .... 617-989-4361.... 245 F
wildb@wit.edu
WILD, David .... 970-225-4860...... 82 A
david.wild@collegeamerica.edu
WILD, Larry .... 847-628-2036.... 154 K
lwild@judsonu.edu
WILD, Linda .... 402-557-7154.... 296 H
linda.wild@bellevue.edu
WILD, Lorie .... 206-281-2608.... 537 H
wildl@spu.edu
WILD, Lynn, A .... 585-475-6543.... 347 G
lynn.wild@rit.edu
WILD, Robert, M .... 314-935-5127.... 292 I
rob.wild@wustl.edu
WILD, Terry, D .... 727-726-1153.... 103 I
terrywild@clearwater.edu
WILDE, Harold, R .... 630-637-5454.... 159 G
hrwilde@noctrl.edu
WILDECK, Steven, C .... 608-265-3040.... 553 B
steven.wildeck@uwc.edu
WILDENBORG, Paul, J .... 507-457-1442.... 271 B
pwildenb@smumn.edu
WILDENTHAL, B. Hobson . 972-883-2271.... 506 A
wildenbh@utdallas.edu
WILDER, Aliza .... 860-486-4038...... 94 G
aliza.wilder@uconn.edu
WILDER, Carmen, C .... 704-216-6009.... 366 G
cwilder@livingstone.edu
WILDER, Diane .... 610-896-1209.... 430 G
dwilder@haverford.edu
WILDER, Jennifer, A .... 919-530-7582.... 378 B
jwilder@nccu.edu
WILDER, Jim .... 419-434-4220.... 406 A
jwilder@winebrenner.edu
WILDER, Judy .... 207-755-5250.... 218 G
jwilder@cmcc.edu
WILDER, Keith .... 508-999-8220.... 237 A
kwilder@umassd.edu
WILDER, Martin, A .... 540-654-1301.... 525 D
mwilder@umw.edu
WILDER, Mary Gail .... 270-831-9737.... 202 D
mary.wilder@kctcs.edu
WILDER, Michael .... 630-752-5818.... 168 H
michael.wilder@wheaton.edu
WILDER, Richard, D .... 352-392-1271.... 120 C
rwilder@ufl.edu
WILDER, Stanley, J .... 704-687-3110.... 379 A
swilder2@uncc.edu
WILDER, Sterly .... 919-684-2782.... 364 C
sterly.wilder@daa.duke.edu

WILLIAMS, Chad ... 336-633-0183 ... 373 A gcwilliams@randolph.edu
WILLIAMS, Charles ... 630-829-6025 ... 145 G cwilliams@ben.edu
WILLIAMS, Charles, F ... 704-637-4550 ... 363 E cwilliam@catawba.edu
WILLIAMS, Charlie ... 908-737-3330 ... 311 A chwillia@kean.edu
WILLIAMS, Charlotte ... 828-328-7214 ... 366 E charlotte.williams@lr.edu
WILLIAMS, Charlotte Treby ... 609-258-7097 ... 312 G trebyw@princeton.edu
WILLIAMS, Chris ... 864-644-5303 ... 461 B cwilliams@swu.edu
WILLIAMS, Chris, C ... 417-268-6026 ... 278 J cwilliams@gobbc.edu
WILLIAMS, Chris, J ... 765-641-4235 ... 169 E cjwilliams@anderson.edu
WILLIAMS, Christal, D ... 816-802-3558 ... 283 E cdwilliams@kcai.edu
WILLIAMS, Christine ... 906-786-5802 ... 248 I williamc@baycollege.edu
WILLIAMS, Christine ... 515-273-1805 ... 19 A christine.williams@phoenix.edu
WILLIAMS, Christopher ... 516-299-3834 ... 338 E christopher.williams@liu.edu
WILLIAMS, Christopher ... 507-288-4563 ... 263 B cwilliams@crossroadscollege.edu
WILLIAMS, Christy ... 828-232-5116 ... 378 D cwilliam@unca.edu
WILLIAMS, Chuck, R ... 317-940-8491 ... 170 F crwillia@butler.edu
WILLIAMS, Clara, A ... 615-687-6895 ... 466 H cawilliams@abcnash.edu
WILLIAMS, Clark ... 541-278-5796 ... 414 G clwilliams@bluecc.edu
WILLIAMS, Clark ... 325-793-4765 ... 490 H williams.clark@mcm.edu
WILLIAMS, Clifford, S ... 860-515-3760 ... 90 E cwilliams@charteroak.edu
WILLIAMS, Connie ... 803-793-5129 ... 457 F williamsco@denmarktech.edu
WILLIAMS, Connie ... 513-556-6998 ... 403 D connie.williams@uc.edu
WILLIAMS, Corey ... 708-456-0300 ... 166 F cwillia1@triton.edu
WILLIAMS, Corrie ... 734-929-9104 ... 249 D cwilliams@cleary.edu
WILLIAMS, Crystal ... 503-771-1112 ... 420 A williamsc@reed.edu
WILLIAMS, Crystal, G ... 919-516-4362 ... 376 D cgwilliams@st-aug.edu
WILLIAMS, Cynthia ... 662-621-4126 ... 273 F cwilliams@coahomacc.edu
WILLIAMS, D. Newell ... 817-257-7231 ... 482 E n.williams@tcu.edu
WILLIAMS, Damon ... 608-265-5228 ... 550 J damon.williams@provost.wisc.edu
WILLIAMS, Dan ... 940-397-4239 ... 491 B dan.williams@mwsu.edu
WILLIAMS, III, Daniel, A ... 202-806-6763 ... 98 E dwilliams@howard.edu
WILLIAMS, Darlene ... 318-357-6100 ... 216 B darlene@nsula.edu
WILLIAMS, Darlene ... 510-261-8500 ... 61 G darlene.williams@patten.edu
WILLIAMS, Darrell, W ... 479-979-1208 ... 26 A dwwillia@ozarks.edu
WILLIAMS, David ... 270-247-8521 ... 204 G dwilliams@midcontinent.edu
WILLIAMS, David ... 916-608-6500 ... 56 C
WILLIAMS, David ... 325-793-4694 ... 490 H dwilliams@mcm.edu
WILLIAMS, David ... 615-322-8333 ... 478 A david.williams@vanderbilt.edu
WILLIAMS, David, B ... 614-292-6446 ... 398 I
WILLIAMS, David, S ... 706-542-3240 ... 138 G dwilliam@uga.edu
WILLIAMS, Dawn ... 504-816-4914 ... 209 A dwilliams@dillard.edu
WILLIAMS, Deborah, H ... 864-941-8367 ... 460 D williams.d@ptc.edu
WILLIAMS, Debra, J ... 724-925-4200 ... 451 E williamsd@wccc.edu
WILLIAMS, Denise ... 217-641-4231 ... 154 I williams@jwcc.edu
WILLIAMS, Dennis ... 405-789-6400 ... 412 D dwilliam@snu.edu
WILLIAMS, DeWayne ... 706-233-7357 ... 137 A dwilliams@shorter.edu
WILLIAMS, Diann, W ... 870-543-5929 ... 23 H dwilliams@seark.edu
WILLIAMS, Donald ... 410-276-0306 ... 226 D dwilliams@host.sdc.edu
WILLIAMS, Donald ... 570-674-6315 ... 436 F frdon@misericordia.edu
WILLIAMS, Donald, E ... 407-303-5671 ... 100 G don.williams@adu.edu
WILLIAMS, Donald, J ... 540-231-5991 ... 529 G dowilli3@vt.edu
WILLIAMS, Donald, S ... 906-487-2538 ... 255 B dswillia@mtu.edu
WILLIAMS, Donna, M ... 610-799-1107 ... 434 D dwilliams@lccc.edu
WILLIAMS, Doug ... 515-965-7024 ... 183 H dcwilliams@dmacc.edu
WILLIAMS, Drew, H ... 214-841-3636 ... 485 F dwilliams@dts.edu
WILLIAMS, E. Keith ... 404-756-4003 ... 125 D kwilliams@atlm.edu
WILLIAMS, Eddie, R ... 815-753-6009 ... 160 B ewilliam@niu.edu
WILLIAMS, Edward ... 336-506-4178 ... 368 A edward.williams@alamancecc.edu
WILLIAMS, Elizabeth ... 803-778-7873 ... 455 G williamsel@cctech.edu
WILLIAMS, Elizabeth, N ... 240-895-4467 ... 226 A enwilliams@smcm.edu
WILLIAMS, Emily, A ... 706-821-8224 ... 135 G ewilliams@paine.edu
WILLIAMS, Emmit ... 310-243-3799 ... 34 D ewilliams@csudh.edu
WILLIAMS, Eric ... 616-234-3720 ... 251 E ewilliam@grcc.edu
WILLIAMS, Erik, W ... 540-857-8914 ... 529 B ewilliams@virginiawestern.edu
WILLIAMS, Erika, T ... 817-515-3049 ... 496 C erika.williams@tccd.edu
WILLIAMS, Eunice ... 315-498-2565 ... 345 D williame@sunyocc.edu
WILLIAMS, F. Clark ... 615-343-2100 ... 478 A f.clark.williams@vanderbilt.edu
WILLIAMS, Falecia, D ... 407-582-1235 ... 123 B fawilliams@valenciacollege.edu
WILLIAMS, Fathia ... 985-858-5728 ... 210 G fathia.williams@fletcher.edu
WILLIAMS, Felica ... 304-327-4212 ... 543 F fblanks@bluefieldstate.edu
WILLIAMS, Frances ... 716-851-1198 ... 333 A williams@ecc.edu
WILLIAMS, Frank ... 716-839-8225 ... 331 F fwilliam@daemen.edu
WILLIAMS, Frank ... 580-559-5256 ... 407 J fwilliams@ecok.edu
WILLIAMS, Frank, G ... 217-245-3003 ... 152 D fwilliam@ic.edu
WILLIAMS, Fred ... 714-808-4746 ... 59 C fwilliams@nocccd.edu
WILLIAMS, JR., Freddie ... 334-229-4291 ... 1 C fwilliams@alasu.edu
WILLIAMS, G. Keith ... 404-880-6389 ... 127 C gkwilliams@cau.edu
WILLIAMS, Gail, C ... 757-446-5869 ... 518 G williamsgc@evms.edu
WILLIAMS, Gary ... 740-374-8716 ... 405 G gwilliams@wscc.edu
WILLIAMS, Gary ... 201-234-3114 ... 19 A gary.williams@phoenix.edu
WILLIAMS, Gary ... 956-384-2866 ... 493 D gwilliams@riogrande.edu
WILLIAMS, George ... 615-327-6815 ... 471 C gwilliams@mmc.edu
WILLIAMS, George, D ... 919-516-4236 ... 376 D gdwilliams@st-aug.edu
WILLIAMS, Georgia, E ... 252-398-6439 ... 363 G willig@chowan.edu
WILLIAMS, Gerald ... 256-761-6128 ... 7 G gwilliams@talladega.edu
WILLIAMS, Gerhild, S ... 314-935-5106 ... 292 I gerhildwilliams@wustl.edu
WILLIAMS, Gerry ... 303-333-4224 ... 81 G
WILLIAMS, Glenn ... 314-275-3524 ... 161 E glenn.williams@principia.edu
WILLIAMS, Glorya, E ... 229-430-4654 ... 124 A glorya.williams@asurams.edu
WILLIAMS, Gregory, D ... 432-335-6410 ... 492 A gwilliams@odessa.edu
WILLIAMS, Gregory, G ... 713-313-1962 ... 500 B williamsg@tsu.edu
WILLIAMS, H. James ... 616-331-7100 ... 251 F williahj@gvsu.edu
WILLIAMS, Harry, L ... 302-857-6001 ... 96 C hwilliams@desu.edu
WILLIAMS, Heidi ... 724-938-5700 ... 441 G williams_h@calu.edu
WILLIAMS, Hila ... 937-708-5252 ... 405 H hwilliams@wilberforce.edu
WILLIAMS, Irma ... 201-761-6052 ... 314 F iwilliams@spc.edu
WILLIAMS, Jack ... 615-383-1340 ... 469 A jack@fwbbc.edu
WILLIAMS, Jacqueline ... 718-951-5352 ... 326 F williams@brooklyn.cuny.edu
WILLIAMS, Jacqueline, H ... 410-951-6481 ... 228 B jwilliams@coppin.edu
WILLIAMS, James ... 303-871-2203 ... 89 A james.herbert@du.edu
WILLIAMS, James ... 417-865-2811 ... 281 G williamsj@evangel.edu
WILLIAMS, James ... 414-297-6492 ... 554 F williaje@matc.edu
WILLIAMS, James, C ... 317-738-8213 ... 171 F jwilliams@franklincollege.edu
WILLIAMS, James, E ... 620-341-5267 ... 192 G jwilliam@emporia.edu
WILLIAMS, James, F ... 303-492-7511 ... 88 H james.williams@colorado.edu
WILLIAMS, James, L ... 800-553-3378 ... 138 F jwilliams@uofa.edu
WILLIAMS, JR., James, L ... 540-464-7119 ... 529 F williamsjl@vmi.edu
WILLIAMS, James, V ... 904-256-7025 ... 111 L jwillia3@ju.edu
WILLIAMS, Jan ... 410-617-2928 ... 223 I jwilliams@loyola.edu
WILLIAMS, Jan, R ... 865-974-5061 ... 477 D jwillil3@utk.edu
WILLIAMS, Jane ... 401-456-8013 ... 454 A jwilliams@ric.edu
WILLIAMS, Jane Ann ... 501-450-3445 ... 25 H
WILLIAMS, Janelle, D ... 817-202-6510 ... 495 E janellew@swau.edu
WILLIAMS, Janet ... 601-318-6147 ... 278 C jwilliams@wmcarey.edu
WILLIAMS, Janice ... 205-929-6383 ... 5 E jwilliams@lawsonstate.edu
WILLIAMS, Jefferson, D ... 217-443-8871 ... 148 G jeff@dacc.edu
WILLIAMS, Jennifer, L ... 800-287-8822 ... 169 H willije1@bethanyseminary.edu
WILLIAMS, Jerome ... 401-254-3536 ... 454 C jwilliams@rwu.edu
WILLIAMS, Joan ... 319-208-5049 ... 189 D jwilliams@scciowa.edu
WILLIAMS, Joan ... 336-370-8639 ... 362 G jwilliams@bennett.edu
WILLIAMS, Joan, P ... 716-827-4341 ... 358 D williamsjo@trocaire.edu
WILLIAMS, Joanne ... 269-749-6630 ... 257 A jwilliams@olivetcollege.edu
WILLIAMS, John ... 607-587-4611 ... 355 C williajc@alfredstate.edu
WILLIAMS, John ... 212-817-7464 ... 327 B jwilliams3@gc.cuny.edu
WILLIAMS, John ... 504-280-6954 ... 213 E john.a.williams@uno.edu
WILLIAMS, John, D ... 903-813-2220 ... 481 A jwilliams@austincollege.edu
WILLIAMS, John, E ... 404-215-2618 ... 134 D jwilliam@morehouse.edu
WILLIAMS, John, F ... 718-270-2611 ... 352 D john.williams@downstate.edu
WILLIAMS, John, N ... 317-274-5403 ... 174 D jnwill01@iupui.edu
WILLIAMS, Jonathan ... 404-756-8919 ... 134 E jowilliams@msm.edu
WILLIAMS, Joni ... 404-225-4602 ... 125 E jwilliam@atlantatech.edu
WILLIAMS, Josh ... 310-578-1080 ... 28 L jwilliams10@antioch.edu
WILLIAMS, Joyce ... 626-815-4702 ... 30 G jwilliams@apu.edu
WILLIAMS, Judy ... 207-948-9165 ... 219 H jwilliams@unity.edu
WILLIAMS, Judy, G ... 501-569-3194 ... 24 E jwilliams1@ualr.edu
WILLIAMS, Julia ... 303-477-7240 ... 85 B juliaw@heritage-education.com
WILLIAMS, Julia, M ... 812-877-8186 ... 179 B julia.williams@rose-hulman.edu
WILLIAMS, Julian ... 732-571-7577 ... 311 E jwilliam@monmouth.edu
WILLIAMS, Julie ... 989-463-7176 ... 247 B williamsjm@alma.edu
WILLIAMS, Julie, E ... 603-862-1997 ... 306 C julie.williams@unh.edu
WILLIAMS, Julie, R ... 712-362-7912 ... 186 A jrwilliams@iowalakes.edu
WILLIAMS, Justin ... 254-968-9002 ... 497 A jwwilliams@tarleton.edu
WILLIAMS, Karen ... 770-229-3162 ... 137 F kwilliams@sctech.edu
WILLIAMS, Karen, L ... 219-981-4454 ... 176 G kwilliams@ivytech.edu
WILLIAMS, Kate ... 770-229-3155 ... 137 F kewilliams@sctech.edu
WILLIAMS, Kathleen ... 603-358-2101 ... 306 G kwilliams7@keene.edu
WILLIAMS, Kathleen ... 603-428-2390 ... 305 D kwilliams@nec.edu
WILLIAMS, Kathleen, L ... 717-337-6616 ... 429 I kawillia@gettysburg.edu
WILLIAMS, Kathy ... 406-496-4266 ... 296 A kwilliams@mtech.edu
WILLIAMS, Kathy ... 406-496-4266 ... 296 B kwilliams@mtech.edu
WILLIAMS, Keith, P ... 802-656-2045 ... 514 H keith.williams@uvm.edu
WILLIAMS, Kelley ... 316-295-5864 ... 193 B kwilliams@friends.edu
WILLIAMS, Kelly ... 601-409-3698 ... 450 D kwilliams@ursinus.edu
WILLIAMS, Kelwin ... 225-771-3920 ... 214 I kelwin_williams@subr.edu
WILLIAMS, Kent ... 316-322-3103 ... 191 G kwilliams@butlercc.edu
WILLIAMS, Kevin ... 518-956-8030 ... 351 E graduate@uamail.albany.edu
WILLIAMS, Kevin, L ... 989-774-3968 ... 249 C willi1kl@cmich.edu
WILLIAMS, Kevin, L ... 404-653-7806 ... 134 D kwilliams@morehouse.edu
WILLIAMS, Kim ... 248-218-2059 ... 257 D kwiliams@rc.edu
WILLIAMS, Kimberly ... 718-488-1602 ... 338 G kim.williams@liu.edu
WILLIAMS, Kimberly ... 708-239-4528 ... 166 C kim.williams@trnty.edu
WILLIAMS, Kris ... 270-831-9626 ... 202 D kris.williams@kctcs.edu
WILLIAMS, Kristi ... 304-204-4097 ... 542 J kwilliams@kvctc.edu
WILLIAMS, Kristin ... 202-994-5136 ... 98 C ksw@gwu.edu
WILLIAMS, Kyle ... 405-945-9152 ... 410 F
WILLIAMS, LaMoyne ... 225-359-9465 ... 209 J lawilliams@catc.edu
WILLIAMS, LaNeeca ... 719-549-2092 ... 83 H laneeca.williams@colostate-pueblo.edu
WILLIAMS, Larion ... 404-756-4666 ... 125 D lwilliams@atlm.edu
WILLIAMS, Larry ... 318-473-6540 ... 212 I lwilliams@lsua.edu
WILLIAMS, Larry ... 316-942-4291 ... 195 F williamsl@newmanu.edu
WILLIAMS, Larry, N ... 870-512-7851 ... 20 F larry_williams@asun.edu
WILLIAMS, LaTosha ... 406-791-5224 ... 296 F lwilliams01@ugf.edu
WILLIAMS, Laura, M ... 217-443-8776 ... 148 G lwms@dacc.edu
WILLIAMS, Lawrence ... 414-288-6303 ... 548 F lawrence.williams@marquette.edu
WILLIAMS, Lawrence, R ... 210-458-5191 ... 506 D lawrence.williams@utsa.edu
WILLIAMS, Lee, B ... 508-286-8218 ... 246 B williams_lee@wheatonma.edu
WILLIAMS, Leon, T ... 336-278-7248 ... 364 D lwilliams25@elon.edu
WILLIAMS, Leslie, K ... 319-273-2332 ... 182 G leslie.williams@uni.edu
WILLIAMS, Linda ... 916-660-7311 ... 69 F lwilliams@sierracollege.edu
WILLIAMS, Linda, C ... 540-985-8481 ... 520 I lcwilliams@jchs.edu
WILLIAMS, Linda, M ... 510-642-7516 ... 73 H lwilliams@berkeley.edu
WILLIAMS, Lisa ... 858-653-6740 ... 52 D
WILLIAMS, Lisa ... 615-383-4848 ... 478 F lwilliams@watkins.edu
WILLIAMS, Lisa ... 419-559-2395 ... 402 D lwilliams01@terra.edu
WILLIAMS, Lisa ... 419-448-3444 ... 402 E lwilliam@tiffin.edu
WILLIAMS, Lisa, L ... 325-793-3821 ... 490 H lwilliams@mcm.edu
WILLIAMS, Lois, H ... 704-637-4402 ... 363 E lhwillia@catawba.edu
WILLIAMS, Lonnie ... 870-972-3025 ... 20 D lonniew@astate.edu
WILLIAMS, Lonnie, R ... 870-972-3355 ... 20 D lonniew@astate.edu
WILLIAMS, Loretta ... 870-248-4000 ... 21 A loretta@blackrivertech.edu
WILLIAMS, Lucille, W ... 803-934-3258 ... 459 G lwilliams@morris.edu
WILLIAMS, Luther, S ... 334-727-8164 ... 8 B lswilliams@mytu.tuskegee.edu
WILLIAMS, Lyn ... 610-606-4666 ... 425 A lcwillia@cedarcrest.edu
WILLIAMS, Lynn ... 803-641-3352 ... 462 B lynnw@usca.edu
WILLIAMS, Lynne, M ... 715-394-8213 ... 552 F lwilli29@uwsuper.edu
WILLIAMS, Lyrae ... 719-389-6699 ... 82 D lyrae.willilams@coloradocollege.edu
WILLIAMS, Lyrae ... 719-389-6699 ... 82 D lyrae.williams@coloradocollege.edu
WILLIAMS, Madelyn ... 607-274-3529 ... 336 G mwilliams@ithaca.edu
WILLIAMS, Marcellette ... 617-287-7050 ... 236 E mwilliams@umassp.edu
WILLIAMS, Marchetta, L ... 803-938-3721 ... 462 G mlwillia@uscsumter.edu
WILLIAMS, Margaret ... 313-577-4501 ... 260 A eh4292@wayne.edu
WILLIAMS, Marilyn ... 415-949-7264 ... 47 H williamsmarilyn@fhda.edu
WILLIAMS, Mark ... 616-526-6293 ... 249 A wilm@calvin.edu
WILLIAMS, Martha ... 601-484-8614 ... 275 A mwilliam@meridiancc.edu
WILLIAMS, Martha, W ... 407-582-8090 ... 123 B mwilliams@valenciacollege.edu
WILLIAMS, Mary, B ... 814-641-3353 ... 432 A williabe@juniata.edu
WILLIAMS, Mary, K ... 334-229-4156 ... 1 C kwilliams@alasu.edu
WILLIAMS, Matt ... 252-492-2061 ... 374 G williamsm@vgcc.edu
WILLIAMS, Max, E ... 423-585-6861 ... 476 D max.williams@ws.edu

WILLIAMS, Melba .... 703-330-8400...... 99 G
WILLIAMS, Melinda .... 803-799-9082.... 461 A
mmwilliams@southuniversity.edu
WILLIAMS, Melisa, L .... 716-880-2448.... 340 D
melisa.l.williams@medaille.edu
WILLIAMS, Melva .... 504-520-7449.... 217 A
mewillia@xula.edu
WILLIAMS, Melvenia .... 803-535-5412.... 456 D
mwilliams@claflin.edu
WILLIAMS, Melvin .... 386-481-2900.... 102 C
wiliamsm@cookman.edu
WILLIAMS, Meredith .... 417-626-1234.... 287 C
mwilliams@occ.edu
WILLIAMS, Michael, C .... 205-329-7870........ 3 A
mike.williams@ecacolleges.com
WILLIAMS, Michelle .... 570-961-7833.... 433 A
williamsm@lackawanna.edu
WILLIAMS, Michelle, L ...... 314-286-4863.... 287 G
mlwilliams@ranken.edu
WILLIAMS, Molly .... 307-532-8325.... 556 C
molly.williams@ewc.wy.edu
WILLIAMS, Monette .... 252-335-3400.... 377 F
mdwilliams2@mail.escu.edu
WILLIAMS, Monica .... 313-993-1028.... 258 G
leonarmj@udmercy.edu
WILLIAMS, Monica .... 815-967-7306.... 162 I
mwilliams@rockfordcareercollege.edu
WILLIAMS, Murray, J .... 404-225-4620.... 125 E
mwilliams@atlantatech.edu
WILLIAMS, Myles .... 803-778-6643.... 455 G
williamsmh@cctech.edu
WILLIAMS, Nancy .... 515-244-4221.... 181 F
nancyw@aib.edu
WILLIAMS, Nancy .... 314-529-9471.... 284 C
nwilliams@maryville.edu
WILLIAMS, Natalie .... 303-650-5050...... 89 G
WILLIAMS, Nate .... 254-295-4696.... 504 C
nwilliams@umhb.edu
WILLIAMS, Nicole .... 910-755-7391.... 368 F
williamsn@brunswickcc.edu
WILLIAMS, Noel .... 606-759-7141.... 203 A
noel.williams@kctcs.edu
WILLIAMS, Orin .... 951-222-8201...... 64 A
orin.williams@rcc.edu
WILLIAMS, Owen .... 218-281-8395.... 271 E
owilliam@umn.edu
WILLIAMS, Patricia, M ...... 410-857-2234.... 224 C
pwilliams@mcdaniel.edu
WILLIAMS, Patricia, R .... 585-292-3026.... 341 H
pwilliams@monroecc.edu
WILLIAMS, Patrick, S .... 713-221-8982.... 503 F
williamsp@uhd.edu
WILLIAMS, Paul .... 760-245-4271...... 77 H
paul.williams@vvc.edu
WILLIAMS, Peter, E .... 317-955-6054.... 177 I
pewilliams@marian.edu
WILLIAMS, Petrina .... 814-824-2369.... 436 C
pwilliams@mercyhurst.edu
WILLIAMS, Philip, C .... 337-475-5556.... 215 G
pwilliams@mcneese.edu
WILLIAMS, Philip, M .... 315-733-2300.... 359 C
pwilliams@uscny.edu
WILLIAMS, Phillip, L .... 706-542-0939.... 138 G
pwilliam@uga.edu
WILLIAMS, Portia .... 212-678-3126.... 357 G
pgw2102@columbia.edu
WILLIAMS, R. Owen .... 859-233-8111.... 207 A
rowilliams@transy.edu
WILLIAMS, Rachel .... 256-726-8406........ 6 C
rwilliams@oakwood.edu
WILLIAMS, Raisa .... 610-896-1293.... 430 G
rwilliam@haverford.edu
WILLIAMS, Ramona, A ...... 423-439-4219.... 473 F
ramona@etsu.edu
WILLIAMS, Randy .... 252-985-5228.... 375 E
rwilliams@ncwc.edu
WILLIAMS, Ray .... 631-632-8950.... 352 C
ray.williams@stonybrook.edu
WILLIAMS, Rayanne .... 619-594-1686...... 37 A
william7@mail.sdsu.edu
WILLIAMS, Richard .... 229-430-4754.... 124 A
richard.williams@asurams.edu
WILLIAMS, Richard .... 312-915-7290.... 157 C
rwilli8@luc.edu
WILLIAMS, Richard (Biff) .. 812-237-2471.... 173 B
biff.williams@indstate.edu
WILLIAMS, Rick .... 870-743-3000...... 22 G
rickw@northark.edu
WILLIAMS, Rick, E .... 909-558-4510...... 54 D
rwilliams@llu.edu
WILLIAMS, Ritchie .... 662-720-7299.... 276 C
rwilliams@nemcc.edu
WILLIAMS, Robert .... 310-825-8011...... 74 C
bwilliams@asucla.ucla.edu
WILLIAMS, Robert .... 432-264-5095.... 488 B
rwilliams@howardcollege.edu
WILLIAMS, Robert, F .... 757-446-5099.... 518 G
williarf@evms.edu
WILLIAMS, Roger .... 603-623-0313.... 305 E
rwilliams@nhia.edu
WILLIAMS, Roger, L .... 814-865-6516.... 438 G
rlw1@psu.edu
WILLIAMS, Ron .... 915-747-7390.... 506 B
rwilliams@utep.edu
WILLIAMS, Ron .... 478-471-2490.... 133 H
ron.williams@maconstate.edu
WILLIAMS, Ronald .... 309-298-1066.... 168 C
rc-williams@wiu.edu
WILLIAMS, Ronnie, D .... 501-450-3416...... 25 H
ronniew@uca.edu
WILLIAMS, Rosemary .... 718-270-5104.... 328 C
rosemary@mec.cuny.edu
WILLIAMS, Ryan .... 631-423-0483.... 350 G
rwilliams@icseminary.edu
WILLIAMS, Ryan .... 845-569-3105.... 342 A
ryan.williams@msmc.edu
WILLIAMS, Sam .... 409-839-2014.... 500 I
slwilliams@lit.edu
WILLIAMS, Samuel .... 610-896-1032.... 430 G
sawillia@haverford.edu
WILLIAMS, Sandra .... 912-427-5818.... 124 C
swilliams@altamahatech.edu
WILLIAMS, Sara .... 570-702-8912.... 431 L
swilliams@johnson.edu
WILLIAMS, Sara .... 402-399-2467.... 297 C
swilliams@csm.edu
WILLIAMS, Sarah .... 614-508-7235.... 392 A
swilliams@hondros.edu
WILLIAMS, Saundra .... 919-807-7100.... 367 I
swilliams@nccommunitycolleges.edu
WILLIAMS, Scott .... 507-379-3335.... 268 H
scott.williams@riverland.edu
WILLIAMS, Scott .... 270-686-4503.... 203 B
scott.williams@kctcs.edu
WILLIAMS, Scott, K .... 315-733-2300.... 359 C
swilliams@uscny.edu
WILLIAMS, Scott, T .... 706-542-3375.... 138 G
scottw@uga.edu
WILLIAMS, Selase, W .... 617-349-8518.... 236 B
williams@lesley.edu
WILLIAMS, Shanae .... 951-639-5240...... 58 B
swilliams@msjc.edu
WILLIAMS, Shane .... 601-484-8620.... 275 A
swilliam@meridiancc.edu
WILLIAMS, Shaun .... 817-515-5154.... 496 C
shaun.williams@tccd.edu
WILLIAMS, Shawn, A .... 423-585-6849.... 476 D
shawn.williams@ws.edu
WILLIAMS, Shelitha, W ...... 585-292-3010.... 341 H
sdickerson@monroecc.edu
WILLIAMS, Sheree .... 502-213-2156.... 202 F
sheree.williams@kctcs.edu
WILLIAMS, Sherri .... 407-851-2525.... 106 K
sherriw@cci.edu
WILLIAMS, Shirley, J .... 610-796-8340.... 421 G
shirley.williams@alvernia.edu
WILLIAMS, Stacie .... 803-641-3321.... 462 B
staciew@usca.edu
WILLIAMS, Stelfanie .... 252-492-2061.... 374 G
swilliams@vgcc.edu
WILLIAMS, Stephen .... 270-247-8521.... 204 G
swilliams@midcontinent.edu
WILLIAMS, Stephen .... 414-277-7114.... 549 C
williams@msoe.edu
WILLIAMS, Stephen, R .... 419-755-4811.... 397 C
swilliam@ncstatecollege.edu
WILLIAMS, Steve .... 479-788-7807...... 24 D
steve.williams@uafs.edu
WILLIAMS, Steve .... 256-840-4174........ 7 A
swilliams@snead.edu
WILLIAMS, Steve .... 903-693-2023.... 492 C
swilliams@panola.edu
WILLIAMS, Steve .... 814-362-0917.... 449 B
swillie@pitt.edu
WILLIAMS, Steven .... 909-941-9410...... 62 J
swilliams@plattcollege.edu
WILLIAMS, Sue .... 715-841-8000.... 550 C
sue.williams@rasmussen.edu
WILLIAMS, Sue .... 360-992-2619.... 532 F
swilliams@clark.edu
WILLIAMS, Susan .... 828-448-3178.... 375 B
swilliams@wpcc.edu
WILLIAMS, Susan, D .... 828-694-1824.... 368 E
susanw@blueridge.edu
WILLIAMS, Susan, D .... 203-576-4651...... 94 F
swilliams@bridgeport.edu
WILLIAMS, Susanna .... 425-235-2356.... 537 A
swilliams@rtc.edu
WILLIAMS, Susie, S .... 916-568-3041...... 55 J
willias@losrios.edu
WILLIAMS, Suzanne .... 336-917-5588.... 376 E
suzanne.williams@salem.edu
WILLIAMS, T. H. Lee .... 405-325-6670.... 413 C
lwilliams@ou.edu
WILLIAMS, Tamara .... 567-661-7198.... 400 I
tamara_williams5@owens.edu
WILLIAMS, Tamara, R .... 253-531-7203.... 536 E
williatr@plu.edu
WILLIAMS, Tasha .... 312-850-7492.... 147 F
rwilliams44@ccc.edu
WILLIAMS, Ted .... 813-974-0537.... 121 A
williamst@admin.usf.edu
WILLIAMS, Teresa .... 815-599-3445.... 152 B
teresa.williams@highland.edu
WILLIAMS, Teresa .... 217-228-5432.... 161 F
willite@quincy.edu
WILLIAMS, Teresa .... 615-966-7076.... 470 F
teresa.williams@lipscomb.edu
WILLIAMS, Teresa, G .... 704-233-8210.... 380 F
tgwilliams@wingate.edu
WILLIAMS, Terri .... 404-364-8320.... 135 E
twilliams1@oglethorpe.edu
WILLIAMS, Terri, B .... 724-847-6892.... 429 H
twilliam@geneva.edu
WILLIAMS, Terria, C .... 803-535-5720.... 456 D
twilliams@claflin.edu
WILLIAMS, Terry .... 601-484-8615.... 275 A
twilliam@meridiancc.edu
WILLIAMS, Theodore, D .... 304-829-7465.... 540 H
twilliams@bethanywv.edu
WILLIAMS, Thomas .... 218-281-8583.... 271 E
will3140@umn.edu
WILLIAMS, Tiffaney .... 706-821-8282.... 135 G
tiwilliams@paine.edu
WILLIAMS, Tiffany, S .... 816-235-5599.... 291 C
williamsti@umkc.edu
WILLIAMS, Tim .... 502-895-3411.... 204 F
twilliams@lpts.edu
WILLIAMS, Todd .... 901-320-9700.... 478 C
twilliams@victory.edu
WILLIAMS, Todd, J .... 215-702-4861.... 444 B
president@pbu.edu
WILLIAMS, Todd Allyn ...... 888-316-9377.... 387 B
WILLIAMS, Tom .... 318-678-6000.... 209 I
twilliams@bpcc.edu
WILLIAMS, Toni, J .... 803-983-3722.... 462 G
toniw@uscsumter.edu
WILLIAMS, Tonjua, L .... 727-341-3344.... 116 H
williams.tonjua@spcollege.edu
WILLIAMS, Tracey, Y .... 270-707-3825.... 202 E
twilliams0139@kctcs.edu
WILLIAMS, Traci, N .... 423-746-5213.... 476 F
twilliams@twcnet.edu
WILLIAMS, Tracy .... 801-524-1923.... 510 E
williamstl@ldsbc.edu
WILLIAMS, Trudy .... 412-392-8085.... 445 A
twilliams@pointpark.edu
WILLIAMS, Trysta .... 785-587-2800.... 195 A
trystawilliams@matc.net
WILLIAMS, Tyler, R .... 208-496-1331.... 143 A
williamst@byui.edu
WILLIAMS, Valerie .... 229-430-3867.... 124 B
vwilliams@albanytech.edu
WILLIAMS, Valerie .... 405-271-2688.... 413 D
valerie-williams@ouhsc.edu
WILLIAMS, Valerie, A .... 305-626-3622.... 109 A
vwilliam@fmuniv.edu
WILLIAMS, Vaughn, A .... 770-423-6284.... 133 A
vwilliam@kennesaw.edu
WILLIAMS, Velma, J .... 804-828-1347.... 526 B
vjwillia@vcu.edu
WILLIAMS, Vera, A .... 985-549-2241.... 216 C
vera.williams@selu.edu
WILLIAMS, Vicki .... 501-492-0570...... 19 D
vicki.williams@arkansasbaptist.edu
WILLIAMS, Vicki .... 662-846-4011.... 273 H
vwilliams@deltastate.edu
WILLIAMS, Vickie .... 334-214-4803........ 2 F
vickie.williams@cv.edu
WILLIAMS, Walter .... 205-929-6317........ 5 E
wwilliams@lawsonstate.edu
WILLIAMS, Wanda, K .... 713-500-3864.... 506 F
wanda.k.williams@uth.tmc.edu
WILLIAMS, Wendy, E .... 843-953-5506.... 457 B
williamsw@cofc.edu
WILLIAMS, William, F .... 724-738-2001.... 443 F
william.williams@sru.edu
WILLIAMS, William, T .... 303-458-4122...... 87 I
wwilliam@regis.edu
WILLIAMS, Willie .... 478-825-6473.... 129 F
williamsw@fvsu.edu
WILLIAMS, Willie .... 713-718-8570.... 487 I
willie.williams@hccs.edu
WILLIAMS, Wilma, L .... 870-235-4097...... 23 I
wlwilliams@saumag.edu
WILLIAMS, Wright .... 847-543-2210.... 148 B
wwilliams@clcillinois.edu
WILLIAMS, Yolanda .... 813-879-6000.... 107 A
ywilliams@cci.edu
WILLIAMS, Yolanda .... 407-708-2069.... 117 H
williamy@seminolestate.edu
WILLIAMS, Zena .... 773-380-6850.... 168 F
zwilliams@westwood.edu
WILLIAMS-BETHEA,
Melanie .... 212-678-3702.... 357 G
mwilliams@tc.edu
WILLIAMS-COTE, Anna ...... 617-984-1626.... 243 H
awilliams@quincycollege.edu
WILLIAMS-GAUDIOSO,
Amy .... 610-359-5341.... 426 G
awilliam@dccc.edu
WILLIAMS-GOLDSTEIN,
Brittany .... 201-684-7609.... 313 C
bwillia1@ramapo.edu
WILLIAMS-HARMON,
Arlitha .... 559-791-2374...... 53 A
arlitha.williams@portervillecollege.edu
WILLIAMS-KIRKSEY,
Shirley .... 404-880-6774.... 127 C
skirksey@cau.edu
WILLIAMS KNIGHT,
Emily .... 312-752-2104.... 155 C
helena.vasilopoulos@kendall.edu
WILLIAMS LOSTON,
Adena .... 210-486-2900.... 479 A
aloston@alamo.edu
WILLIAMS LOSTON,
Adena .... 210-486-2900.... 479 D
aloston@alamo.edu
WILLIAMS MALLETT,
Denise .... 313-993-1496.... 258 G
williamd@udmercy.edu
WILLIAMS-PEREZ, Kendra 319-226-2040.... 182 A
williakb@ihs.org
WILLIAMS RUSHIN,
Palisa .... 859-246-6522.... 201 H
palisa.rushin@kctcs.edu
WILLIAMSON, Angela .... 417-690-2208.... 279 J
awilliamson@cofo.edu
WILLIAMSON, Bob .... 360-992-2123.... 532 F
bwilliamson@clark.edu
WILLIAMSON, Carla .... 919-658-7749.... 367 F
cwilliamson@moc.edu
WILLIAMSON, Carol .... 641-628-7667.... 183 D
williamsonc@central.edu
WILLIAMSON, Celia .... 940-565-4961.... 504 D
celia@unt.edu
WILLIAMSON, Colin, W ..... 570-326-3761.... 440 L
cwilliam@pct.edu
WILLIAMSON, Dean .... 936-261-2188.... 496 G
cdwilliamson@pvamu.edu
WILLIAMSON, Debbie .... 843-863-7050.... 456 B
dwilliam@csuniv.edu
WILLIAMSON, Donna .... 717-544-4786.... 433 E
dfwillia@lancastergeneralcollege.edu
WILLIAMSON, George .... 619-849-2610...... 62 L
georgewilliamson@pointloma.edu
WILLIAMSON, Gerald .... 706-886-6831.... 138 D
jerryw@tfc.edu
WILLIAMSON, Handy .... 573-882-9061.... 291 B
williamsonha@missouri.edu
WILLIAMSON, Harold, A ... 573-882-5606.... 291 A
williamsonh@health.missouri.edu
WILLIAMSON, JR.,
Harold, A .... 573-882-5606.... 291 B
williamsonh@health.missouri.edu
WILLIAMSON, Heather ...... 254-442-5001.... 482 I
heather.williamson@cisco.edu
WILLIAMSON, James, E ..... 706-542-5813.... 138 G
jwilliamson@police.uga.edu
WILLIAMSON, James, R ..... 858-784-8469...... 69 B
gradprgm@scripps.edu
WILLIAMSON, Jeff .... 507-372-3408.... 267 G
jeff.williamson@mnwest.edu
WILLIAMSON, Joann .... 803-641-3668.... 462 B
joannw@usca.edu
WILLIAMSON, Katherine .... 252-492-2061.... 374 G
williamsonk@vgcc.edu
WILLIAMSON, Keith, M ..... 804-524-5285.... 529 H
kwilliamson@vsu.edu
WILLIAMSON, Kimberly .... 252-493-7217.... 372 H
kwilliamson@email.pittcc.edu
WILLIAMSON, Kimberly .... 773-481-8186.... 147 I
kwilliamson13@ccc.edu
WILLIAMSON, Laurel .... 281-998-6184.... 493 G
laurel.williamson@sjcd.edu
WILLIAMSON, Laurel .... 281-484-1900.... 494 B
laurel.williamson@sjcd.edu
WILLIAMSON, Laurel .... 281-476-1501.... 493 H
laurel.williamson@sjcd.edu
WILLIAMSON, Marty .... 661-654-2111...... 34 A
mwilliamson@csub.edu
WILLIAMSON, Marvel .... 405-208-5900.... 410 A
mwilliamson@okcu.edu
WILLIAMSON, Michael ...... 843-383-8300.... 457 A
mwilliamson@coker.edu
WILLIAMSON, Nancy .... 301-985-7080.... 227 F
legal-affairs@umuc.edu
WILLIAMSON, Nancy .... 516-572-7406.... 342 C
nancy.williamson@ncc.edu
WILLIAMSON, Pamela .... 757-823-2037.... 522 E
pwilliamson@nsu.edu
WILLIAMSON, Patricia, A .. 815-224-0440.... 153 E
patty_williamson@ivcc.edu
WILLIAMSON, Pauline ...... 410-532-3164.... 225 D
pwilliamson@ndm.edu
WILLIAMSON, Rhea .... 707-826-4189...... 36 E
rhea.williamson@humboldt.edu
WILLIAMSON, Sean .... 706-245-7226.... 129 C
swilliamson@ec.edu
WILLIAMSON, Shane .... 636-949-4728.... 283 J
swilliamson@lindenwood.edu
WILLIAMSON, Sharon .... 603-526-3756.... 303 G
sewillia@colby-sawyer.edu
WILLIAMSON, Sharon .... 806-742-4250.... 502 A
sharon.williamson@ttu.edu
WILLIAMSON, Sheila, D .... 336-599-1181.... 372 G
willias1@piedmontcc.edu
WILLIAMSON, Stan .... 205-652-3652........ 9 E
swilliamson@uwa.edu
WILLIAMSON, Stephanie ... 801-281-7630.... 510 M
stephanie.williamson@stevenshenager.edu
WILLIAMSON, Sue .... 306-416-7679.... 538 D
sue.williamson@skagit.edu
WILLIAMSON, Tari .... 704-366-5066.... 376 B
twilliamson@rts.edu
WILLIAMSON, Tom .... 651-450-3680.... 266 F
twillia@inverhills.edu

WILLIAMSON, Tommy ...... 336-721-2824.... 376 E
tommy.williamson@salem.edu
WILLIAR, Marc, G .... 904-819-6220.... 107 C
mwilliar@flagler.edu
WILLIARD, Stacey .... 724-266-3838.... 448 H
swilliard@tsm.edu
WILLIE, John .... 318-487-7194.... 209 F
willie@lacollege.edu
WILLIFORD, A. Michael .... 740-593-1059.... 399 G
willifor@ohio.edu
WILLIFORD, Andrea, G ...... 478-757-5170.... 139 E
awilliford@wesleyancollege.edu
WILLIFORD, Craig .... 847-317-8001.... 166 E
president@tiu.edu
WILLIFORD, Darryl .... 301-860-4186.... 228 A
dwilliford@bowiestate.edu
WILLIFORD, David .... 615-383-1340.... 469 A
dwilliford@fwbbc.edu
WILLIFORD, Don .... 325-670-1491.... 487 F
willifrd@hsutx.edu
WILLIFORD, G. Craig ...... 954-382-6400.... 122 F
WILLIFORD, Joey .... 662-720-7564.... 276 C
jewilliford@nemcc.edu
WILLIFORD, Lynn, E ...... 919-962-1339.... 378 E
lynn_williford@unc.edu
WILLIFORD, Pamela, K .... 325-670-1347.... 487 F
pwillifo@hsutx.edu
WILLIHNGANZ, Shirley, C 502-852-6153.... 207 E
scwill01@louisville.edu
WILLINGER, Katie .... 920-693-1247.... 554 C
katie.willinger@gotoltc.edu
WILLINGHAM, Paul .... 281-283-2222.... 503 E
willingham@uhcl.edu
WILLINGHAM, Ralph .... 817-598-6248.... 508 F
rwillingham@wc.edu
WILLINGHAM, Ricky .... 256-551-5219........ 4 J
ricky.willingham@drakestate.edu
WILLINGHAM-HINTON,
Shelley, M .... 919-516-4190.... 376 D
swhinton@st-aug.edu
WILLIS, Bob .... 334-983-6556........ 8 A
rwillis@troy.edu
WILLIS, Brandon .... 904-596-2476.... 122 D
bwillis@tbc.edu
WILLIS, Brian .... 828-398-7929.... 368 B
bwillis@abtech.edu
WILLIS, Christine .... 617-369-3581.... 244 E
cwillis@smfa.edu
WILLIS, Christopher .... 412-536-1194.... 432 H
christopher.willis@laroche.edu
WILLIS, Cliff, K .... 814-332-2860.... 421 F
cliff.willis@allegheny.edu
WILLIS, Connie .... 510-464-3232...... 62 D
cwillis@peralta.edu
WILLIS, Darley .... 716-851-1118.... 333 A
willis@ecc.edu
WILLIS, Dave .... 541-463-5566.... 416 E
willisd@lanecc.edu
WILLIS, Doug .... 318-257-3267.... 215 F
doug@latech.edu
WILLIS, Douglas .... 972-377-1793.... 483 H
dwillis@collin.edu
WILLIS, Edward, M .... 757-823-8141.... 522 E
emwillis@nsu.edu
WILLIS, Eric, R .... 319-352-8470.... 189 J
rick.willis@wartburg.edu
WILLIS, Gary .... 800-962-7682.... 293 A
gwillis@wma.edu
WILLIS, Gerry .... 401-341-2200.... 454 D
willisg@salve.edu
WILLIS, Harvey .... 973-328-5232.... 309 A
hwillis@ccm.edu
WILLIS, James, A .... 585-395-2129.... 352 F
jwillis@brockport.edu
WILLIS, Jason .... 859-572-5746.... 205 H
willisj2@nku.edu
WILLIS, Jeff .... 270-384-8097.... 204 D
willisj@lindsey.edu
WILLIS, Joy .... 601-857-3224.... 274 C
joy.willis@hindscc.edu
WILLIS, Kathy .... 618-468-5700.... 156 E
kwillis@lc.edu
WILLIS, Kim .... 309-677-4118.... 146 C
goblue@bradley.edu
WILLIS, Kimberley, D .... 585-292-2197.... 341 H
kwillis@monroecc.edu
WILLIS, Lesia .... 718-522-9073.... 323 B
lwillis@asa.edu
WILLIS, Lisa .... 312-850-7066.... 147 F
lwillis04@ccc.edu
WILLIS, Lori, A .... 541-383-7572.... 414 I
lwillis@cocc.edu
WILLIS, Mark, D .... 804-828-0138.... 526 B
mdwillis@vcu.edu
WILLIS, Michaela .... 402-872-2221.... 299 F
mwillis@peru.edu
WILLIS, Paul .... 229-391-5052.... 123 H
pwillis@abac.edu
WILLIS, Sharon .... 301-295-3578.... 558 D
sharon.willis@usuhs.edu
WILLIS, Steven .... 336-517-2302.... 362 G
swillis@bennett.edu
WILLIS, Tamie, L .... 405-425-5320.... 409 E
tamie.willis@oc.edu

WILLIS, Wanda, J .... 904-470-8251.... 105 G
wanda.willi098@ewc.edu
WILLIS-RIVERA, Jennifer ... 715-425-3531.... 552 C
jennifer.willis-rivera@uwrf.edu
WILLISON, Brian .... 608-249-6611.... 547 G
bwillison@msn.herzing.edu
WILLITS, Jenny .... 719-255-3820...... 88 I
jwillits@uccs.edu
WILLITS, Lynn .... 314-529-9333.... 284 C
lwillits@maryville.edu
WILLITS, Mary Lou .... 802-287-8316.... 513 F
willitsml@greenmtn.edu
WILLKIE, Dan .... 619-388-7527...... 65 H
dwillkie@sdccd.edu
WILLMAN, Katharine .... 248-645-3360.... 250 B
kwillman@cranbrook.edu
WILLMANN, Ellie .... 207-326-2232.... 219 D
ellie.willmann@mma.edu
WILLMARTH, Ephraim .... 315-858-0945.... 336 A
ejwillmarth@hts.edu
WILLMON, Nixon .... 256-228-6001........ 6 A
willmonn@nacc.edu
WILLMORE, Sharman .... 513-732-5296.... 403 E
sharman.willmore@uc.edu
WILLOME, Donna .... 585-389-2501.... 342 D
dwillom0@naz.edu
WILLOUGHBY, Dan .... 714-992-7036...... 59 E
dwilloughby@fullcoll.edu
WILLOUGHBY, Gordon, C 724-287-8711.... 423 G
gordon.willoughby@bc3.edu
WILLOUGHBY, J. Michael 512-245-2581.... 501 F
jw02@txstate.edu
WILLOUGHBY, Karen, P ... 412-536-1201.... 432 H
karen.willoughby@laroche.edu
WILLOUGHBY, Thomas ..... 303-871-3383...... 89 A
twilloug@du.edu
WILLRICH, Penny, L .... 602-682-6800...... 17 F
pwillrich@phoenixlaw.edu
WILLS, Deleen .... 503-375-7003.... 415 F
dwills@corban.edu
WILLS, Deri .... 803-641-3787.... 462 B
deriw@usca.edu
WILLS, G. Benjamin .... 702-968-1611.... 303 D
bwills@roseman.edu
WILLS, Joe .... 530-898-4143...... 34 C
jwills@csuchico.edu
WILLS, Mike .... 417-836-7635.... 286 C
mikewills@missouristate.edu
WILLS, Mike .... 573-592-1191.... 293 D
mike.wills@williamwoods.edu
WILLS, Penelope .... 928-776-2022...... 19 C
penny.wills@yc.edu
WILLS, Scott, D .... 419-772-2705.... 398 H
s-wills@onu.edu
WILLS, Yvonne .... 636-922-8315.... 288 B
ywills@stchas.edu
WILLSON, Robert, W .... 692-625-3031.... 560 A
rwwillson@cmi.edu
WILLY, Randy .... 312-589-7473.... 150 G
rwilly@ellis.edu
WILMER, Elizabeth .... 540-857-7313.... 529 B
ewilmer@virginiawestern.edu
WILMER, Elizabeth .... 540-857-7385.... 529 B
ewilmer@virginiawestern.edu
WILMER, Susan .... 215-895-1970.... 427 H
wilmers@drexel.edu
WILMER, Wesley .... 402-449-2945.... 297 H
wwilmer232@graceu.edu
WILMES, Douglas, R .... 304-788-6865.... 545 B
drwilmes@mail.wvu.edu
WILMES, Gerald .... 660-562-1350.... 287 B
gwilmes@nwmissouri.edu
WILMES, Regina .... 856-566-6726.... 316 I
wilmesrr@umdnj.edu
WILMESHERR, Jon .... 828-765-7351.... 372 A
jwilmesherr@mayland.edu
WILMOTH, Dirk, E .... 276-944-6814.... 519 A
dwilmoth@ehc.edu
WILMOTH, Jamie .... 865-882-4270.... 476 A
wilmoth@roanestate.edu
WILMOTH, Jay .... 407-851-2525.... 106 K
jwilmoth@cci.edu
WILMOTH, Karen, L .... 304-637-1374.... 541 A
wilmothk@dewv.edu
WILMOTH, Margaret, C ..... 404-413-1082.... 131 G
mwilmoth@gsu.edu
WILMOTH, Nikki .... 254-659-7771.... 487 G
nwilmoth@hillcollege.edu
WILMOTH, Wendy .... 620-223-2700.... 193 A
wendyw@fortscott.edu
WILMOWSKY, Joseph .... 718-774-3430.... 325 I
WILSEY, Mary, M .... 585-785-1360.... 334 A
wilseym@flcc.edu
WILSON, Alan, G .... 660-263-3900.... 279 F
awilson@cccb.edu
WILSON, Alla .... 570-422-3589.... 442 D
awilson@po-box.esu.edu
WILSON, Amy .... 206-876-6100.... 538 A
awilson@theseattleschool.edu
WILSON, Andrea .... 510-885-3639...... 34 E
andrea.wilson@csueastbay.edu
WILSON, Andrew, G .... 412-578-2095.... 424 I
wilsonag@carlow.edu

WILSON, Angela .... 618-252-5400.... 164 I
angela.wilson@sic.edu
WILSON, Angulus .... 559-453-2000...... 48 A
angulus.wilson@fresno.edu
WILSON, Anne .... 213-738-6845...... 71 E
awilson@swlaw.edu
WILSON, Annette .... 972-860-4689.... 484 G
arwlson@dcccd.edu
WILSON, Anthony .... 727-726-1153.... 103 I
anthonywilson@clearwater.edu
WILSON, Arthur, L .... 260-359-4031.... 173 A
awilson@huntington.edu
WILSON, Barbara .... 217-333-6677.... 167 D
bjwilson@illinois.edu
WILSON, Barbara .... 719-389-6791...... 82 D
bwilson@coloradocollege.edu
WILSON, Barbara .... 770-534-6203.... 126 E
bwilson@brenau.edu
WILSON, Barbara, A .... 262-243-5700.... 547 C
barbara.wilson@cuw.edu
WILSON, Barbara-Jan .... 860-685-2547...... 95 E
bjwilson@wesleyan.edu
WILSON, Becky .... 806-742-3681.... 502 A
becky.wilson@ttu.edu
WILSON, Belyn .... 831-443-1700...... 50 C
belyn_wilson@heald.edu
WILSON, Beth .... 214-768-3601.... 495 A
bethw@smu.edu
WILSON, Bob .... 909-537-3139...... 36 B
bwilson@csusb.edu
WILSON, Bob .... 714-556-3610...... 77 B
bwilson@vanguard.edu
WILSON, Braden .... 270-843-6750.... 200 B
bwilson@daymarcollege.edu
WILSON, Bradley .... 724-738-2379.... 443 F
bradley.wilson@sru.edu
WILSON, Bruce .... 904-680-7720.... 107 J
bwilson@fcsl.edu
WILSON, Bryan, W .... 828-652-0635.... 372 B
bryanwi@mcdowelltech.edu
WILSON, Carlton, E .... 919-530-6794.... 378 B
cwilson@nccu.edu
WILSON, Carmen .... 608-758-6565.... 553 B
carmen.wilson@uwc.edu
WILSON, Carol, J .... 815-740-3840.... 167 E
cwilson@stfrancis.edu
WILSON, Carolyn .... 615-966-5837.... 470 F
carolyn.wilson@lipscomb.edu
WILSON, Catherine .... 707-527-4763...... 68 E
cwilson@santarosa.edu
WILSON, Cathy .... 616-234-3971.... 251 E
cwilson@grcc.edu
WILSON, Cecil, B .... 304-293-2021.... 545 A
cbwilson@mail.wvu.edu
WILSON, Charlene .... 909-558-4040...... 54 D
cwilson@llu.edu
WILSON, Charles .... 913-288-7674.... 194 C
drchuck@kckcc.edu
WILSON, Charles .... 704-922-6428.... 370 G
wilson.charles@gaston.edu
WILSON, JR., Charles, E .. 757-683-3925.... 522 F
cwilson@odu.edu
WILSON, Charles (Gary) .... 731-881-7340.... 477 G
cwilson@utm.edu
WILSON, Charleston, D .... 262-646-6517.... 549 E
cwilson@nashotah.edu
WILSON, Cheryl, L .... 817-257-7834.... 499 C
c.l.wilson@tcu.edu
WILSON, Chris .... 518-454-5436.... 330 C
wilsonc@strose.edu
WILSON, Chris .... 701-231-7215.... 382 B
chris.wilson@ndsu.edu
WILSON, Christina .... 325-793-4607.... 490 H
wilson.christina@mcm.edu
WILSON, Christine .... 785-243-1435.... 192 A
cwilson@cloud.edu
WILSON, Christopher, K .... 216-687-5009.... 388 D
c.wilson46@csuohio.edu
WILSON, Chuck, A .... 301-314-8249.... 227 B
chuckw@umd.edu
WILSON, Cindy .... 360-538-4262.... 534 G
cwilson@ghc.edu
WILSON, Cleveland .... 803-535-1419.... 460 C
wilsonc@octech.edu
WILSON, Clive .... 937-298-3399.... 394 D
clive.wilson@kcma.edu
WILSON, Cynthia .... 251-928-8133........ 9 D
cwilson@usouthal.edu
WILSON, Cynthia, A .... 847-866-3936.... 151 D
cynthia.wilson@garrett.edu
WILSON, Cynthia, L .... 713-348-5048.... 493 C
clwilson@rice.edu
WILSON, Daniel .... 252-940-6233.... 368 C
danielw@beaufortccc.edu
WILSON, Daniel, B .... 740-826-8164.... 397 A
dwilson@muskingum.edu
WILSON, Darin .... 678-407-5000.... 130 C
WILSON, Dave .... 509-467-1727.... 535 C
dwilson@interface.edu
WILSON, David .... 443-885-3200.... 224 E
david.wilson@morgan.edu
WILSON, David .... 432-837-0107.... 501 E
dwilson@sulross.edu

WILSON, David, C .... 314-968-7488.... 292 J
wilson@webster.edu
WILSON, David, E .... 215-895-6038.... 427 H
david.e.wilson@drexel.edu
WILSON, David, P .... 814-472-3211.... 446 B
dwilson@francis.edu
WILSON, Deborah .... 860-512-3613...... 91 F
dwilson@mcc.commnet.edu
WILSON, Debra, J .... 208-732-6245.... 143 E
dwilson@csi.edu
WILSON, Debra, J .... 906-248-8442.... 248 H
dwilson@bmcc.edu
WILSON, Delwin, C .... 207-725-3706.... 217 E
dwilson@bowdoin.edu
WILSON, Denise .... 704-290-5247.... 374 A
d-wilson@spcc.edu
WILSON, Derek, J .... 303-273-3986...... 83 B
dwilson@mines.edu
WILSON, JR., Donald, D .. 770-720-5953.... 136 C
ddw@reinhardt.edu
WILSON, Donna .... 570-484-2121.... 443 B
dwilson@lhup.edu
WILSON, Doug .... 251-442-2406........ 9 A
dwilson@umobile.edu
WILSON, Douglas .... 205-726-4266........ 6 G
dwilson@samford.edu
WILSON, Dwayne, H .... 731-989-6094.... 469 B
dwilson@fhu.edu
WILSON, D'Andre, H .... 757-873-3100...... 99 G
WILSON, Edward .... 913-588-1696.... 197 C
ewilson2@kumc.edu
WILSON, Elaine .... 606-679-8501.... 203 C
elaine.wilson@kctcs.edu
WILSON, Elizabeth .... 229-931-2090.... 131 F
liz.wilson@gsw.edu
WILSON, Elizabeth, K .... 404-471-6000.... 123 I
ewilson@agnesscott.edu
WILSON, III, Ernest, J ...... 213-740-9891...... 76 F
ernestw@usc.edu
WILSON, Floarine .... 502-597-6271.... 203 G
floarine.wilson@kysu.edu
WILSON, Fran .... 817-274-4284.... 482 B
WILSON, Gary .... 816-604-4125.... 285 E
gary.wilson@mcckc.edu
WILSON, Geri .... 419-627-8345.... 398 B
gwilson@ohiobusinesscollege.edu
WILSON, Gordon, N .... 801-581-3079.... 511 C
gordon.wilson@aux.utah.edu
WILSON, Greg .... 864-644-5329.... 461 B
gwilson@swu.edu
WILSON, H. David .... 316-293-2602.... 197 C
dwilson@kumc.edu
WILSON, Huie, G .... 850-263-3261.... 101 L
hgwilson@baptistcollege.edu
WILSON, Ian .... 801-863-8951.... 511 F
ian.wilson@uvu.edu
WILSON, J. David .... 270-809-2310.... 205 A
david.wilson@murraystate.edu
WILSON, Jack, T .... 270-686-4291.... 199 B
jack.wilson@brescia.edu
WILSON, Jacqueline .... 334-683-2309........ 5 G
jwilson@marionmilitary.edu
WILSON, James .... 334-285-5177........ 4 K
james.wilson@istc.edu
WILSON, James .... 860-628-4751...... 93 C
jwilson@lincolncollegene.edu
WILSON, James .... 336-316-2132.... 365 A
jwilson@guilford.edu
WILSON, JR., James, D .... 302-295-1194...... 97 C
jim.d.wilson@wilmu.edu
WILSON, JR., James, J .... 936-261-2175.... 496 G
jjwilson@pvamu.edu
WILSON, JR., James, J .... 936-261-5256.... 496 G
jjwilson@pvamu.edu
WILSON, James, R .... 740-826-8113.... 397 A
jrwilson@muskingum.edu
WILSON, Jan .... 316-295-5824.... 193 B
jan_wilson@friends.edu
WILSON, Janice, E .... 706-865-2134.... 138 E
jwilson@truett.edu
WILSON, Jean .... 405-325-6723.... 413 D
jean-wilson@ouhsc.edu
WILSON, Jeff .... 615-966-7617.... 470 F
jeff.wilson@lipscomb.edu
WILSON, Jennifer .... 858-635-4526...... 27 E
jwilson@alliant.edu
WILSON, Jerre, W .... 703-784-6917.... 557 H
jerre.wilson@usmc.mil
WILSON, Jerry .... 719-255-3594...... 88 I
jwilson@uccs.edu
WILSON, Jim .... 641-844-5550.... 186 B
jim.wilson@iavalley.edu
WILSON, Jo .... 480-654-7700...... 15 I
jo.anne.wilson@mcmail.maricopa.edu
WILSON, Joan, B .... 323-731-2383...... 60 H
jbwilson@psuca.edu
WILSON, Joanne .... 608-342-1854.... 552 B
wilsonj@uwplatt.edu
WILSON, Jocelyn, M .... 516-671-2213.... 360 B
jwilson@webb-institute.edu
WILSON, JoEllen, B .... 770-720-5545.... 136 C
jew@reinhardt.edu
WILSON, John .... 928-757-0878...... 16 F
jwilson@mohave.edu

WILSON, John .... 413-748-3249 .... 244 H
jwilson@springfieldcollege.edu
WILSON, John .... 212-217-4200 .... 333 F
john_wilsonn@fitnyc.edu
WILSON, John, R .... 804-355-0671 .... 525 A
jwilson@upsem.edu
WILSON, Josh .... 706-272-2473 .... 128 C
jwilson@daltonstate.edu
WILSON, Judge .... 859-985-3131 .... 199 A
judge_wilson@berea.edu
WILSON, Kathryn .... 585-395-2137 .... 352 F
kwilson@brockport.edu
WILSON, Kathryn .... 330-672-6317 .... 393 D
kwilson3@kent.edu
WILSON, Kathy .... 865-981-8211 .... 471 B
kathy.wilson@maryvillecollege.edu
WILSON, Kathy .... 864-578-8770 .... 460 F
kwilson@sherman.edu
WILSON, Kathy, A .... 863-638-2930 .... 123 E
wilsonka@webber.edu
WILSON, Keisha .... 704-330-1455 .... 366 A
kwilson@jcsu.edu
WILSON, Kelly .... 417-625-9363 .... 286 B
wilson-k@mssu.edu
WILSON, Kelly .... 740-264-5591 .... 390 F
kwilson@egcc.edu
WILSON, Kenneth, B .... 252-335-3283 .... 377 F
kbwilson@mail.ecsu.edu
WILSON, Kenny .... 636-481-3356 .... 283 D
kwilso20@jeffco.edu
WILSON, Kevin .... 570-945-8376 .... 432 E
kevin.wilson@keystone.edu
WILSON, Kevin, H .... 304-637-1337 .... 541 A
wilsonk@dewv.edu
WILSON, Kevin, O .... 706-396-7591 .... 135 G
kwilson@paine.edu
WILSON, Kim, L .... 402-472-9212 .... 300 G
kwilson4@unl.edu
WILSON, Kimberly, R .... 859-257-9555 .... 207 D
kwilson@uky.edu
WILSON, Kym .... 202-806-1277 .... 98 E
ka_wilson@howard.edu
WILSON, Larry, L .... 972-860-7613 .... 484 I
larrywilson@dcccd.edu
WILSON, Laura .... 619-684-8781 .... 59 B
lwilson@newschoolarch.edu
WILSON, Laura, J .... 410-778-7849 .... 229 D
lwilson3@washcoll.edu
WILSON, Laura, L .... 650-723-9633 .... 71 G
laura.wilson@stanford.edu
WILSON, Leon, C .... 334-229-5176 .... 1 C
lwilson@alasu.edu
WILSON, Linda .... 336-334-7880 .... 378 A
wilsonl@ncat.edu
WILSON, Lisa .... 770-531-2558 .... 133 C
lwilson@laniertech.edu
WILSON, Lisa .... 415-354-9194 .... 32 E
lwilson@baychef.com
WILSON, Lisa .... 505-566-3447 .... 320 D
wilsonl@sanjuancollege.edu
WILSON, Lizabeth, A .... 206-543-1760 .... 539 A
betsyw@uw.edu
WILSON, Lloyd .... 334-649-5000 .... 557 E
lloyd.wilson@maxwell.af.mil
WILSON, Lloyd, L .... 334-953-4827 .... 557 D
lloyd.wilson@maxwell.af.mil
WILSON, Lonny, L .... 641-673-1118 .... 190 C
wilsonl@wmpenn.edu
WILSON, Lori, J .... 570-577-3334 .... 423 E
lwilson@bucknell.edu
WILSON, Lorraine .... 707-524-1506 .... 68 E
lwilson@santarosa.edu
WILSON, Louise, B .... 315-255-1743 .... 325 G
wilsonl@cayuga-cc.edu
WILSON, Lucy, P .... 478-301-2460 .... 134 A
wilson_l@mercer.edu
WILSON, Lynn .... 715-836-5521 .... 551 A
wilsonly@uwec.edu
WILSON, Marcus .... 806-743-3025 .... 502 B
marcus.wilson@ttuhsc.edu
WILSON, Margaret .... 660-626-2354 .... 278 D
mwilson@atsu.edu
WILSON, Mark .... 605-718-2401 .... 466 F
mark.wilson@wdt.edu
WILSON, Mark .... 423-472-7141 .... 474 E
mwilson@clevelandstatecc.edu
WILSON, Mark .... 931-372-3961 .... 474 B
mwilson@tntech.edu
WILSON, Mark .... 215-887-5511 .... 451 D
mwilson@wts.edu
WILSON, Martha .... 207-221-4985 .... 221 A
mwilson13@une.edu
WILSON, Mary .... 931-598-1381 .... 472 L
mewilson@sewanee.edu
WILSON, Mary Ellen .... 912-449-7500 .... 139 D
mwilson@waycross.edu
WILSON, Matthew .... 734-462-4400 .... 258 A
mwilson@schoolcraft.edu
WILSON, Melinda .... 575-234-9212 .... 319 F
memarine@nmsu.edu
WILSON, Meltida .... 337-373-0172 .... 211 J
meltida.wilson@southlouisiana.edu
WILSON, Michael, D .... 714-556-3610 .... 77 B
mdwilson@vanguard.edu
WILSON, Michael, P .... 610-861-1365 .... 437 A
wilson@moravian.edu
WILSON, Michelle .... 870-633-4480 .... 21 F
rwilson@eacc.edu
WILSON, Monica .... 603-646-2215 .... 304 J
monica.wilson@dartmouth.edu
WILSON, Myra .... 740-389-6786 .... 399 D
wilson.2025@osu.edu
WILSON, Nancy .... 617-627-4179 .... 245 C
nancy.wilson@tufts.edu
WILSON, Natalie, L .... 412-578-6171 .... 424 I
wilsonnl@carlow.edu
WILSON, Neyle .... 843-349-5201 .... 458 H
neyle.wilson@hgtc.edu
WILSON, Pamala, P .... 270-831-9658 .... 202 D
pamala.wilson@kctcs.edu
WILSON, Pamela, M .... 803-376-5701 .... 455 B
pwilson@allenuniversity.edu
WILSON, Patricia .... 205-366-8151 .... 7 F
mpwilson@stillman.edu
WILSON, Patricia .... 302-831-2078 .... 96 I
wilsonp@udel.edu
WILSON, Paul .... 734-207-9581 .... 255 F
pwilson@mts.edu
WILSON, Paul, T .... 765-658-6776 .... 171 B
ptwilson@depauw.edu
WILSON, Peggy, M .... 865-694-6403 .... 475 G
pwilson@pstcc.edu
WILSON, Perry, T .... 843-661-1486 .... 458 D
WILSON, Phillip .... 479-394-7622 .... 23 E
pwilson@rmcc.edu
WILSON, Randi .... 314-889-1410 .... 281 I
rwilson@fontbonne.edu
WILSON, Randy .... 270-707-3718 .... 202 E
randy.wilson@kctcs.edu
WILSON, Renee .... 770-938-4711 .... 133 D
WILSON, Richard, F .... 309-556-3151 .... 153 F
president@iwu.edu
WILSON, Rickie, W .... 270-901-1004 .... 201 I
rickw.wilson@kctcs.edu
WILSON, Roger .... 425-889-5336 .... 536 C
roger.wilson@northwestu.edu
WILSON, Rosemary .... 734-973-3724 .... 259 F
wilbur@wccnet.edu
WILSON, S. Dale .... 864-941-8331 .... 460 D
wilson.d@ptc.edu
WILSON, Sarudzayi .... 954-382-6413 .... 122 F
swilson@tiu.edu
WILSON, Shannon .... 317-917-5731 .... 175 K
swilson@ivytech.edu
WILSON, Sharon .... 847-214-7485 .... 150 F
swilson@elgin.edu
WILSON, Shawn .... 785-784-5225 .... 189 G
wilsons@uiu.edu
WILSON, Shawn .... 989-964-7147 .... 257 G
swilson@svsu.edu
WILSON, Sherry .... 601-979-2010 .... 274 G
sherry.l.wilson@jsums.edu
WILSON, Sherry .... 828-726-2306 .... 368 G
swilson@cccti.edu
WILSON, Sherwood, G .... 540-231-4416 .... 529 G
sgwilson@vt.edu
WILSON, Shirley .... 213-624-1200 .... 46 L
swilson@fidm.edu
WILSON, Sonali, B .... 216-687-3543 .... 388 D
s.b.wilson@csuohio.edu
WILSON, Stephan, M .... 405-744-9805 .... 410 C
stephan.m.wilson@okstate.edu
WILSON, Stephanie .... 540-828-5749 .... 517 B
swilson@bridgewater.edu
WILSON, Stephenie, F .... 215-572-4819 .... 422 C
wilsons@arcadia.edu
WILSON, Steve .... 513-556-6703 .... 403 D
steve.wilson@uc.edu
WILSON, Susan .... 219-785-5236 .... 179 A
swilson@pnc.edu
WILSON, Susan, A .... 802-322-1641 .... 513 E
susan.wilson@goddard.edu
WILSON, Susanne .... 270-831-9804 .... 202 D
susanne.wilson@kctcs.edu
WILSON, Suzanne .... 617-585-1100 .... 242 I
suzanne.wilson@necmusic.edu
WILSON, Ted, H .... 270-707-3865 .... 202 E
ted.wilson@kctcs.edu
WILSON, Terrance .... 305-626-3713 .... 109 A
terrance.wilson@fmuniv.edu
WILSON, Terry .... 515-244-4221 .... 181 F
wilsont@aib.edu
WILSON, Timothy, B .... 805-565-6038 .... 79 A
twilson@westmont.edu
WILSON, Todd, A .... 812-464-1755 .... 181 B
tawilson3@usi.edu
WILSON, Tommy .... 706-649-1894 .... 128 A
twilson@columbustech.edu
WILSON, Torrez .... 706-821-8634 .... 135 G
tmwilson@paine.edu
WILSON, Tracy .... 601-928-6230 .... 275 E
tracy.wilson@mgccc.edu
WILSON, Tressey, D .... 936-361-1700 .... 496 G
tdwilson@pvamu.edu
WILSON, Valerie .... 870-574-4514 .... 24 A
vwilson@sautech.edu
WILSON, Valvia .... 601-977-7844 .... 277 C
vwilson@tougaloo.edu
WILSON, Vicki .... 859-246-6316 .... 201 H
vicki.wilson@kctcs.edu
WILSON, Vicki .... 724-852-3375 .... 451 B
vwilson@waynesburg.edu
WILSON, Victor, K .... 843-953-5522 .... 457 B
wilsonw@cofc.edu
WILSON, Warren .... 605-642-6930 .... 465 H
warren.wilson@bhsu.edu
WILSON, Wendy .... 229-430-4658 .... 124 A
wendy.wilson@asurams.edu
WILSON, William .... 423-354-2541 .... 475 F
wrwilson@northeaststate.edu
WILSON, William .... 715-682-1865 .... 549 F
bwilson@northland.edu
WILSON, William, P .... 207-859-4692 .... 217 G
wpwilson@colby.edu
WILSON, Yolanda, S .... 336-734-7251 .... 370 F
ywilson@forsythtech.edu
WILSON, Yvette .... 212-280-1396 .... 358 I
ywilson@uts.columbia.edu
WILSON-ANSTEY,
Elizabeth, A .... 212-746-1057 .... 360 C
eaanstey@med.cornell.edu
WILSON-BARKER, Sharon 207-992-1934 .... 218 A
wilsonbarkers@husson.edu
WILSON-FENNELL, Nicole 734-462-4400 .... 258 A
nwilson@schoolcraft.edu
WILSON-OYELARAN,
Eileen, B .... 269-337-7220 .... 252 K
wilsonoy@kzoo.edu
WILSON-PARKER,
Sharnita, L .... 252-335-3747 .... 377 F
slwilson@mail.ecsu.edu
WILSON-PORTER, Cyndi ... 210-829-2706 .... 504 B
porter@uiwtx.edu
WILSON-STALLINGS,
Samaria .... 617-682-1508 .... 234 E
swilson@eds.edu
WILSON-TAYLOR, Sharon . 312-369-7221 .... 148 D
swilson-taylor@colum.edu
WILT, Jason .... 269-782-2702 .... 258 C
jwilt@swmich.edu
WILT, Jeff .... 816-604-6704 .... 285 A
jeff.wilt@mcckc.edu
WILT, Larry, M .... 410-455-2356 .... 227 D
wilt@umbc.edu
WILT, Richard, W .... 610-799-1186 .... 434 D
rwilt@lccc.edu
WILTBANK, J. Kelley .... 207-973-3229 .... 219 I
university.counsel@maine.edu
WILTENBURG, Robert, E ... 314-935-4806 .... 292 I
rewilten@wustl.edu
WILTENMUTH, III,
John, P .... 540-654-1047 .... 525 D
jwiltenm@umw.edu
WILTGEN, JR., James, N .. 501-450-1223 .... 22 A
wiltgen@hendrix.edu
WILTGEN, Jim .... 501-450-1222 .... 22 A
wiltgen@hendrix.edu
WILTON, Courtney .... 503-594-3010 .... 415 A
courtneyw@clackamas.edu
WILTON, John .... 510-642-3100 .... 73 H
vcaf@berkeley.edu
WILTSCHEK, Walt .... 260-982-5243 .... 177 H
wjwiltschek@manchester.edu
WILTSE, Mary Alane .... 518-828-4181 .... 330 E
wiltse@sunycgcc.edu
WILTSE, Mike .... 989-686-9110 .... 250 D
michaelwiltse@delta.edu
WILTZIUS, Pierre .... 805-893-5024 .... 75 B
mlpsdean@ltsc.ucsb.edu
WIMBERLEY,
Bernadette, H .... 302-225-6312 .... 96 H
wimberlb@gbc.edu
WIMBISH, Gary .... 301-891-4112 .... 229 B
chaplain@wau.edu
WIMBISH, Jennifer, L .... 972-860-8251 .... 484 H
jwimbish@dcccd.edu
WIMBUSH, James .... 812-855-2739 .... 173 E
jwimbush@indiana.edu
WIMER, Valinda .... 386-822-8850 .... 121 F
vwimer@stetson.edu
WIMES, Edward, D .... 402-472-7161 .... 300 E
ewimes@nebraska.edu
WIMMER, Edward, E .... 419-372-0709 .... 385 F
ewimmer@bgsu.edu
WIMS, Daniel, K .... 256-372-5275 .... 1 A
daniel.wims@aamu.edu
WIMS, Lois, A .... 401-825-2124 .... 453 D
lawims@ccri.edu
WIN, Judith .... 413-528-7350 .... 230 F
jwin@simons-rock.edu
WIN, U. Ba .... 413-528-7392 .... 230 F
bawin@simons-rock.edu
WINANT, Richard, M .... 718-270-7411 .... 352 D
rwinant@downstate.edu
WINCH, Eric, D .... 973-642-8289 .... 315 C
eric.winch@shu.edu
WINCHELL, Barbra .... 845-569-3298 .... 342 A
barbara.winchell@msmc.edu
WINCHESTER, Andrea .... 731-425-2644 .... 475 C
awinchester@jscc.edu
WINCHESTER, Elizabeth, A 314-977-2354 .... 289 C
wincheea@slu.edu
WINCHESTER, Gina, S .... 270-809-5086 .... 205 A
gwinchester@murraystate.edu
WINCHESTER, Paul .... 316-295-5836 .... 193 B
winchp@friends.edu
WINCHESTER, Samuel .... 800-672-3060 .... 376 G
WINCHESTER, Sara .... 732-255-0400 .... 312 D
swinchester@ocean.edu
WIND, Joseph, E .... 859-572-5916 .... 205 H
wind@nku.edu
WINDER, Katie .... 541-917-4547 .... 416 I
winderk@linnbenton.edu
WINDERL, James .... 845-434-5750 .... 357 A
jwinderl@sullivan.suny.edu
WINDERS, Tim .... 806-894-9611 .... 494 G
twinders@southplainscollege.edu
WINDHAM, Ana, M .... 210-999-7306 .... 502 E
awindham@trinity.edu
WINDHAM, Don .... 772-462-7357 .... 111 B
dwindham@irsc.edu
WINDHAM, Greg .... 662-720-7210 .... 276 C
gwindham@nemcc.edu
WINDHAM, Jameka .... 216-373-5287 .... 397 F
jwindham@ndc.edu
WINDHAM, James, R .... 662-915-7448 .... 277 D
jwindham@olemiss.edu
WINDHOLZ, Kevin .... 405-208-5600 .... 410 A
kwindholz@okcu.edu
WINDLE, Frank, H .... 215-871-6750 .... 444 C
frankwi@pcom.edu
WINDLE, Lawrence, B .... 956-380-8100 .... 493 D
rgbipresident@riogrande.edu
WINDROW, Vincent .... 615-898-5812 .... 473 G
vincent.windrow@mtsu.edu
WINDSOR, Lang .... 281-756-3639 .... 479 F
lwindsor@alvincollege.edu
WINDY BOY, Helen .... 406-395-4313 .... 296 E
hwindyboy@stonechild.edu
WINE, Stony .... 252-527-6223 .... 371 G
swine@lenoircc.edu
WINEBARGER, Conley, F .. 336-734-7182 .... 370 F
cwinebarger@forsythtech.edu
WINEBRAKE, James, J .... 585-475-2447 .... 347 G
jjwgpt@rit.edu
WINEGAR, Lucien, T .... 610-409-3720 .... 450 D
twinegar@ursinus.edu
WINEGARD, Kathryn .... 660-248-6208 .... 279 G
kwinegar@centralmethodist.edu
WINEGARDEN, Alan, D .... 651-641-8258 .... 263 A
winegarden@csp.edu
WINER, Toby, R .... 212-346-1200 .... 345 F
twiner@pace.edu
WINES, Ed .... 952-358-8159 .... 268 A
ed.wines@normandale.edu
WINES, Margaret .... 212-616-7250 .... 335 C
margaret.wines@helenefuld.edu
WINFIELD, Robert, A .... 734-763-6880 .... 259 A
rwinf@umich.edu
WINFREE, Kemp, W .... 304-746-1991 .... 544 B
kwinfree@marshall.edu
WINFREE, Terri, L .... 708-709-3953 .... 161 D
twinfree@prairiestate.edu
WINFREY, Marion .... 617-287-7500 .... 236 G
marion.winfrey@umb.edu
WINFREY, Steve .... 606-759-7141 .... 203 A
steve.winfrey@kctcs.edu
WINFREY GRIFFIN, Polly . 609-258-6191 .... 312 G
polly@princeton.edu
WING, Derek .... 425-602-3107 .... 531 E
media@bastyr.edu
WING, Edward .... 401-863-3330 .... 453 B
edward_wing_md@brown.edu
WING, Kattie .... 479-575-3806 .... 24 C
kattie@uark.edu
WINGARD, Alan, B .... 706-233-7248 .... 137 A
awingard@shorter.edu
WINGARD, Larry, R .... 724-847-6733 .... 429 H
lwingard@geneva.edu
WINGATE, C. Keith .... 415-565-4682 .... 74 A
wingatek@uchastings.edu
WINGATE, Margaret .... 850-201-8366 .... 122 A
wingatem@tcc.fl.edu
WINGATE, Susan, F .... 903-923-3231 .... 500 E
susan.wingate@tstc.edu
WINGE, Jennifer, D .... 330-263-2116 .... 388 F
jwinge@wooster.edu
WINGER, Philip, E .... 570-372-4135 .... 447 E
winger@susqu.edu
WINGER, Philip, G .... 716-375-2622 .... 348 C
pwinger@sbu.edu
WINGET, Paul .... 515-244-4221 .... 181 F
wingetp@aib.edu
WINGFIELD, Albert, B .... 260-452-2106 .... 170 J
al.wingfield@ctsfw.edu
WINGFIELD, Rob .... 912-449-7598 .... 139 D
rwing@waycross.edu
WINGFIELD, Tim .... 865-573-4517 .... 469 L
twingfield@johnsonu.edu
WINGLER, Mike .... 336-838-6178 .... 375 C
michael.wingler@wilkescc.edu
WINGO, Nancie .... 505-984-6103 .... 320 C
alumni@sjcsf.edu
WINGROVE, Betty .... 765-289-2291 .... 176 B
bwingrov@ivytech.edu

WINGS, Aaron .... 319-398-5403.... 187 B
aaron.wings@kirkwood.edu
WINICKI, John .... 215-885-2360.... 435 E
jwinicki@manor.edu
WINIGER, Brent .... 603-897-8215.... 305 F
bwiniger@rivier.edu
WINIGER, Brent .... 701-355-8303.... 383 H
bwiniger@umary.edu
WININGS, Kathy .... 845-752-3000.... 358 F
academics@uts.edu
WINISTORFER, Paul, M .... 540-231-5481.... 529 G
pwinisto@vt.edu
WINKELBAUER, Brian .... 303-273-3140...... 83 B
bwinkelb@mines.edu
WINKELMAN, Bryce .... 360-596-5333.... 538 E
bwinkelman@spscc.ctc.edu
WINKELMANN, John, F .... 608-363-2350.... 546 E
winkelj@beloit.edu
WINKLEMAN, Mark .... 512-651-4750.... 464 H
WINKLER, Carol, J .... 314-286-3651.... 287 G
cjwinkler@ranken.edu
WINKLER, Chris .... 512-313-3000.... 483 K
chris.winkler@concordia.edu
WINKLER, David .... 502-456-6509.... 206 G
dwinkler@sctd.edu
WINKLER, Janet .... 678-466-5050.... 127 D
janetwinkler@clayton.edu
WINKLER, Linda .... 570-408-4600.... 452 A
WINKLER, Roy .... 765-289-2291.... 176 B
rwinkler@ivytech.edu
WINKLEY, Robert .... 617-585-1280.... 242 I
robert.winkley@necmusic.edu
WINN, Emmett .... 334-844-5771........ 1 F
winne@auburn.edu
WINN, James .... 603-645-9700.... 305 I
j.winn@snhu.edu
WINN, Jewell .... 615-963-7401.... 474 A
jwinn@tnstate.edu
WINN, Regina .... 318-670-9411.... 215 A
rwinn@susla.edu
WINNEY, Maureen .... 518-587-2100.... 355 G
maureen.winney@esc.edu
WINNEY, Sonia .... 979-209-7336.... 482 C
sonia.winney@blinn.edu
WINNIFORD, Janet .... 801-626-6008.... 511 G
jwinniford@weber.edu
WINNINGHAM, Laura .... 909-389-3323...... 65 B
lwinningham@craftonhills.edu
WINOGRAD, Katharine, W 505-224-4412.... 317 K
winograd@cnm.edu
WINQUIST, Melissa .... 480-858-9100...... 18 E
m.winquist@scnm.edu
WINRICH, J. Steven .... 859-238-5317.... 199 G
steve.winrich@centre.edu
WINSHIP, Nancy, K .... 781-736-4002.... 232 F
winship@brandeis.edu
WINSLOW, Bridgette .... 517-265-5161.... 246 H
WINSLOW, Christopher ..... 775-674-7500.... 302 H
cwinslow@tmcc.edu
WINSLOW, Kathy .... 252-985-5134.... 375 E
kwinslow@ncwc.edu
WINSLOW, Mark .... 405-789-6400.... 412 D
mwinslow@snu.edu
WINSLOW, Nadine, J .... 775-673-7025.... 302 H
nwinslow@tmcc.edu
WINSLOW, Valerie .... 908-737-7100.... 311 A
vwinslow@kean.edu
WINSLOW-SCHABER,
Deborah, J .... 716-888-2240.... 325 F
winslowd@canisius.edu
WINSOME, Thais .... 408-855-5217...... 78 F
thais.winsome@wvm.edu
WINSOR, Susan, A .... 803-593-9231.... 455 A
winsors@atc.edu
WINSTEL, Susan, M .... 412-578-6330.... 424 I
winstelsm@carlow.edu
WINSTON, Bruce, E .... 757-352-4306.... 523 E
brucwin@regent.edu
WINSTON, David .... 870-512-7829...... 20 F
david_winston@asun.edu
WINSTON, Eric .... 312-369-7418.... 148 D
ewinston@colum.edu
WINSTON, Jeannie .... 501-569-3345...... 24 E
eewinston@ualr.edu
WINSTON, Kathleen .... 951-639-5560...... 58 B
kwinston@msjc.edu
WINSTON, Mark, D .... 973-353-5222.... 314 E
winstonm@andromeda.rutgers.edu
WINSTON, JR.,
Matthew, M .... 706-542-0054.... 138 G
mwinston@uga.edu
WINSTON, Robert, P .... 717-245-1363.... 427 F
winston@dickinson.edu
WINSTON, Robin .... 678-891-3417.... 131 C
robin.winston@gpc.edu
WINSTON, Van Buren .... 212-217-3400.... 333 F
vanburen_winston@fitnyc.edu
WINSTON-MUIR, Jeanni .... 301-846-2489.... 222 G
jwinston-muir@frederick.edu
WINTEMUTE, Mike .... 512-463-1808.... 500 H
mike.wintemute@tsus.edu
WINTER, Barbara, J .... 620-235-4152.... 196 C
bwinter@pittstate.edu
WINTER, Karla, R .... 563-562-3263.... 188 B
winterk@nicc.edu
WINTER, Roy .... 213-252-5100...... 26 C
WINTER, Stacey, O .... 701-231-8954.... 382 B
stacey.winter@ndsu.edu
WINTER, Tara .... 518-255-5418.... 354 E
wintert@cobleskill.edu
WINTER, Valerie .... 609-894-9311.... 308 B
vwinter@bcc.edu
WINTER, Walt .... 850-484-1903.... 115 B
wwinter@pensacolastate.edu
WINTER, JR., William, F ... 618-650-5380.... 165 C
wwinter@siue.edu
WINTERBAUER, Nancy, S . 848-932-7832.... 314 B
winterbauer@oldqueens.rutgers.edu
WINTEREGG, Steven .... 937-766-3235.... 386 G
winteregg@cedarville.edu
WINTERER, James, C .... 651-962-6404.... 272 B
jcwinterer@stthomas.edu
WINTERFIELD, Catherine ... 973-300-2119.... 315 F
cwinterfield@sussex.edu
WINTERHALTER, Teresa .... 912-344-3135.... 124 G
teresa.winterhalter@armstrong.edu
WINTERMEYER,
Stephen, F .... 317-274-8214.... 174 D
swinter@iupui.edu
WINTERS, Amy .... 845-687-5124.... 358 E
wintersa@sunyulster.edu
WINTERS, Chet .... 610-372-4721.... 445 C
cwinters@racc.edu
WINTERS, Curt, D .... 215-702-4206.... 444 B
cwinters@pbu.edu
WINTERS, Hyla .... 702-651-4554.... 302 E
hyla.winters@csn.edu
WINTERS, James, W .... 630-617-6447.... 150 H
jwinters@elmhurst.edu
WINTERS, Jill .... 414-961-3897.... 549 D
jwinters@ccon.edu
WINTERS, Jill, M .... 414-326-2301.... 547 B
jwinters@ccon.edu
WINTERS-DUNN, Teresa ... 413-265-2210.... 233 D
wintersdunnt@elms.edu
WINTERS-PALACIO, CM .... 312-850-7247.... 147 F
cwinterspalacio@ccc.edu
WINTERSTEEN, Wendy ...... 515-294-2518.... 182 E
wwinters@iastate.edu
WINTERSTEIN, James, F .... 630-889-6604.... 159 F
jwinterstein@nuhs.edu
WINTERWOOD, Fawn .... 614-947-6235.... 391 B
fawn.winterwood@franklin.edu
WINWARD, Cindy .... 866-680-2756.... 510 F
office@midwifery.edu
WIORA, Margaret, A .... 630-637-5454.... 159 G
mawiora@noctrl.edu
WIORKOWSKI, John .... 972-883-2274.... 506 A
wiorkow@utdallas.edu
WIPPERMAN, Gary, L .... 319-352-8353.... 189 J
gary.wipperman@wartburg.edu
WIPPMAN, David .... 612-625-4841.... 272 A
dwippman@umn.edu
WIRPEL, Justin .... 214-376-1000.... 492 F
jwirpel@pqc.edu
WIRT, Gary, L .... 302-225-6260...... 96 H
wirtgl@gbc.edu
WIRT, Susan .... 706-507-8463.... 127 G
wirt_susan@columbusstate.edu
WIRTH, Diane .... 209-575-6507...... 80 F
wirthd@yosemite.edu
WIRTH, Karen .... 612-874-3665.... 265 C
kwirth@mcad.edu
WIRTH, Michael .... 865-974-3031.... 477 D
mwirth@utk.edu
WIRTH, Ross .... 614-947-6128.... 391 B
wirthr@franklin.edu
WIRTH, Sandy .... 860-913-2063...... 92 I
swirth@goodwin.edu
WIRTZ, James, J .... 831-656-3781.... 558 A
jwirtz@nps.edu
WIRTZ, Kelly, J .... 515-574-2823.... 185 I
wirtz@iowacentral.edu
WISBEY, Randal, R .... 951-785-2020...... 53 E
rwisbey@lasierra.edu
WISBEY, Tom .... 434-949-1038.... 528 D
tom.wisbey@southside.edu
WISCH, Richard .... 201-692-7271.... 310 A
wisch@fdu.edu
WISCHNOWSKI, Michael .. 585-385-7316.... 348 F
mwischnowski@sjfc.edu
WISCOTT, Richard .... 303-256-9300...... 85 L
rwiscott@jwu.edu
WISE, Adam, K .... 617-353-5282.... 232 E
awise@bu.edu
WISE, Cheri, L .... 419-995-8475.... 399 B
wise.179@osu.edu
WISE, Eliezer .... 215-635-7300.... 430 A
ewise@gratz.edu
WISE, Janet .... 505-428-1217.... 320 E
janet.wise@sfcc.edu
WISE, Jessica .... 740-333-5115.... 402 A
jwise@sscc.edu
WISE, Jody .... 626-914-8656...... 40 B
jwise@citruscollege.edu
WISE, L. Anthony .... 865-694-6616.... 475 G
lawise@pstcc.edu
WISE, Maria .... 480-732-7274...... 15 E
maria.wise@cgc.edu
WISE, Mary, B .... 336-278-6642.... 364 D
wisemary@elon.edu
WISE, Mary, K .... 402-457-2250.... 298 G
mwise@mccneb.edu
WISE, Phyllis .... 217-333-6290.... 167 A
pmwise@illinois.edu
WISE, Phyllis, M .... 217-333-6290.... 167 D
pmwise@illinois.edu
WISE, Sandra .... 941-554-1600.... 101 A
slwise@argosy.edu
WISE, Sandra .... 615-525-2832...... 29 F
slwise@argosy.edu
WISE, Steve .... 304-818-2009.... 543 A
swise@newriver.edu
WISE, Teresa .... 205-348-5256........ 8 E
WISE, Tim .... 601-974-1243.... 275 B
wiseta@millsaps.edu
WISE, Timothy .... 352-873-5828.... 103 K
wiset@cf.edu
WISEL, Lee Marie .... 301-891-4222.... 229 B
lwisel@wau.edu
WISEMAN, Ana Maria .... 864-597-4510.... 463 G
wisemana@wofford.edu
WISEMAN, Bob .... 859-257-5929.... 207 D
rdwise2@uky.edu
WISEMAN, Chris .... 504-861-5499.... 213 F
cwiseman@loyno.edu
WISEMAN, Christine, M .... 773-298-3309.... 163 I
president@sxu.edu
WISEMAN, Donna .... 301-405-2336.... 227 B
dlwise@umd.edu
WISEMAN, Frederick .... 802-635-1348.... 515 F
frederick.wiseman@jsc.edu
WISEMAN, James, V .... 262-524-7221.... 546 H
jwiseman@carrollu.edu
WISEMAN, Jeff .... 229-931-2394.... 137 C
jwiseman@southgatech.edu
WISEMAN, Tina .... 573-288-6307.... 280 I
twiseman@culver.edu
WISER, Bob, H .... 801-524-8107.... 510 E
bwiser@ldsbc.edu
WISER, Elizabeth, A .... 802-656-3370.... 514 H
elizabeth.wiser@uvm.edu
WISER, Hayes .... 843-525-8333.... 461 E
hwiser@tcl.edu
WISHING, III, Lee, S .... 724-458-3332.... 430 B
lswishing@gcc.edu
WISHON, Angela .... 214-648-0455.... 507 E
angela.wishon@utsouthwestern.edu
WISHON, Gordon, D .... 480-965-9334...... 11 J
gordon.wishon@asu.edu
WISHON, Phillip, M .... 540-568-6572.... 520 H
wishonpm@jmu.edu
WISLER, Jacki .... 704-357-8020.... 362 D
jwisler@aii.edu
WISLOCK, Robert .... 570-389-4529.... 441 F
rwislock@bloomu.edu
WISNER, Arthur, S .... 410-857-2218.... 224 C
awisner@mcdaniel.edu
WISNER, David .... 716-896-0700.... 359 H
dmwisner@villa.edu
WISNER, Jay .... 802-485-2075.... 514 C
jwisner@norwich.edu
WISNER, Marie .... 651-638-6543.... 261 D
m-wisner@bethel.edu
WISNER, Paul .... 714-892-7711...... 41 C
pwisner@gwc.cccd.edu
WISNESKI, Thomas, E .... 610-566-1776.... 452 B
twisneski@williamson.edu
WISNEWSKI, Michael .... 401-341-2275.... 454 D
michael.wisnewski@salve.edu
WISNIEWSKA, Sophia, T ... 610-892-1231.... 439 C
stw1@psu.edu
WISNIEWSKI, Allison, A ... 856-225-6422.... 314 D
aemery@camden.rutgers.edu
WISNIEWSKI, Michael .... 215-951-1070.... 432 I
wisniews@lasalle.edu
WISNIOWICZ, Lisa .... 630-844-6852.... 145 F
lwisni@aurora.edu
WISOFSKY, Tami .... 979-230-3308.... 482 D
tami.wisofsky@brazosport.edu
WISSINGER, Kristin .... 724-222-5330.... 438 F
kwissinger@penncommercial.edu
WISSMAN, Wayne .... 202-541-5236.... 100 B
wwissman@wtu.edu
WISSMILLER, Andrew .... 310-206-6771...... 74 C
awissmiller@ais.ucla.edu
WISSMILLER, Kia .... 713-525-3117.... 505 A
kritick@stthom.edu
WISSWELL, Keith, R .... 858-499-0202...... 41 G
kwisswell@coleman.edu
WIST, Gregory .... 212-220-1299.... 326 D
gwist@bmcc.cuny.edu
WISTRCILL, Tom .... 330-972-7080.... 403 B
krex@uakron.edu
WISTROM, Carl, H .... 773-244-4961.... 159 H
cwistrom@northpark.edu
WISWALL, Derry .... 660-248-6296.... 279 G
dwiswall@centralmethodist.edu
WISWALL, Irv .... 503-883-2575.... 416 H
irvw@linfield.edu
WISZMANN, Joann .... 253-964-6506.... 536 H
jwiszmann@pierce.ctc.edu
WITBRODT, William, H ...... 314-935-5765.... 292 I
bill_witbrodt@wustl.edu
WITCHNER, Anne .... 412-268-4886.... 424 J
awow@andrew.cmu.edu
WITH, Elizabeth .... 940-565-4909.... 504 D
elizabeth.with@unt.edu
WITHEM, Ron .... 402-472-7132.... 300 E
rwithem@nebraska.edu
WITHERELL, Meghan .... 530-938-5500...... 42 E
witherellm@siskiyous.edu
WITHERELL, Michael, S .... 805-893-8270...... 75 B
witherell@research.ucsb.edu
WITHERELL, Paula .... 716-926-8792.... 335 E
witherell@hilbert.edu
WITHERITE, Richard, L ...... 606-337-1015.... 199 H
rwitherite@ccbbc.edu
WITHERS, Allen, B .... 304-929-5011.... 543 A
awithers@newriver.edu
WITHERS, Dale .... 707-965-7150...... 60 I
dwithers@puc.edu
WITHERS, Gail .... 620-672-5641.... 196 D
gailw@prattcc.edu
WITHERS, Gary .... 503-493-6207.... 415 E
gwithers@cu-portland.edu
WITHERS, Stacie .... 816-995-2832.... 287 H
stacie.withers@researchcollege.edu
WITHERSPOON,
Everette, L .... 336-750-2131.... 380 B
witherspoone@wssu.edu
WITHERSPOON, Karen .... 212-650-6400.... 326 G
kwitherspoon@ccny.cuny.edu
WITHERSPOON, Patricia ... 915-747-7018.... 506 B
withersp@utep.edu
WITHROW, Amy, S .... 717-780-2437.... 430 E
aswithro@hacc.edu
WITKOVSKY, Lowell, D ..... 814-641-3360.... 432 A
witkovl@juniata.edu
WITKOWSKI, Barbara .... 609-894-9311.... 308 B
bwitkows@bcc.edu
WITKOWSKI, Tammy, T ..... 717-221-1300.... 430 E
ttwitkow@hacc.edu
WITMER, Kenneth, D .... 610-436-2321.... 444 A
kwitmer@wcupa.edu
WITMER, Timothy, Z .... 215-572-3831.... 451 D
twitmer@wts.edu
WITRAK, Marty .... 218-723-6021.... 262 G
mwitrak@css.edu
WITRYK, Ted .... 269-337-7391.... 252 K
ted.witryk@kzoo.edu
WITSCHEN, Peter, J .... 954-262-8832.... 114 B
witschen@nova.edu
WITSON, Mike .... 740-588-1304.... 407 A
mwitson@zanestate.edu
WITT, JR., Al .... 704-334-6882.... 367 H
awitt@nlts.edu
WITT, Allen .... 813-259-6151.... 110 M
awitt3@hccfl.edu
WITT, Anne .... 704-334-6882.... 367 H
abwitt@nlts.edu
WITT, Betsy, A .... 864-488-4619.... 459 B
bwitt@limestone.edu
WITT, Don .... 859-257-3458.... 207 D
dwitt@uky.edu
WITT, Jack .... 567-661-7314.... 400 I
fjwitt@owens.edu
WITT, Karen .... 202-639-1763...... 98 A
kwitt@corcoran.org
WITT, Marie, D .... 215-898-9155.... 448 J
witt@pobox.upenn.edu
WITT, Robert, E .... 205-348-5861........ 8 D
rwitt@uasystem.ua.edu
WITT, Sherra .... 423-472-7141.... 474 E
switt@clevelandatatecc.edu
WITT, Tiffanie .... 270-824-8575.... 202 G
tiffanie.witt@kctcs.edu
WITTE, Bob .... 417-626-1234.... 287 C
witte.bob@occ.edu
WITTE, Dennis, E .... 708-209-3205.... 148 E
dennis.witte@cuchicago.edu
WITTE, John .... 616-526-6547.... 249 A
jwitte@calvin.edu
WITTE, Lisa .... 417-626-1234.... 287 C
witte.lisa@occ.edu
WITTE, Lois, J .... 417-667-8181.... 280 E
lwitte@cottey.edu
WITTE, Peter, T .... 816-235-2731.... 291 C
wittep@umkc.edu
WITTE, Sarah .... 541-962-3594.... 418 C
switte@eou.edu
WITTEMAN, Mike .... 760-630-1555...... 52 J
mwitteman@kaplan.edu
WITTENBERG, Diane .... 626-396-2326...... 29 I
diane.wittenberg@artcenter.edu
WITTENBORG, Karin .... 434-924-3026.... 525 F
kw7g@virginia.edu
WITTENMYER, Kathryn ...... 415-503-6223...... 66 A
klw@sfcm.edu
WITTER, Kevin, G .... 540-857-7341.... 529 B
kwitter@virginiawestern.edu
WITTHOFT, Andrea .... 618-437-5321.... 162 D
witthoft@rlc.edu
WITTIG, William .... 313-993-1532.... 258 G
wittigw@udmercy.edu

WOOD, Cathy, R .... 202-319-5606...... 97 E
woodcr@cua.edu

WOOD, Charlene .... 828-479-9256.... 374 F
cwaldroup@tricountycc.edu

WOOD, Charles .... 850-201-6428.... 122 A
woodc@tcc.fl.edu

WOOD, Chris .... 302-736-2316...... 97 A
chriswood@wesley.edu

WOOD, Chris .... 903-923-2062.... 486 F
cwood@etbu.edu

WOOD, Cliff, L .... 845-574-4214.... 347 I
cwood@sunyrockland.edu

WOOD, Cristel .... 671-734-1812.... 559 F
cwood@piu.edu

WOOD, Darrow .... 718-260-5497.... 328 D
dwood@citytech.cuny.edu

WOOD, David .... 713-973-3010.... 486 C
dbwood@devry.edu

WOOD, David .... 206-665-4600.... 180 D
woodd@trine.edu

WOOD, David .... 713-973-3000.... 149 B
dwood4@devry.edu

WOOD, David, H .... 906-227-2112.... 256 C
dwood@nmu.edu

WOOD, David, S .... 864-597-4020.... 463 G
woodds@wofford.edu

WOOD, Debra .... 704-216-6079.... 366 G
dwood@livingstone.edu

WOOD, Donald .... 432-335-6340.... 492 A
dwood@odessa.edu

WOOD, Donna, G .... 918-595-7841.... 412 H
dwood@tulsacc.edu

WOOD, Douglas, M .... 717-766-2511.... 436 D
dwood@messiah.edu

WOOD, Elaine .... 704-357-8020.... 362 D
ewood@aii.edu

WOOD, Elizabeth, A .... 607-778-5319.... 324 G
woodea@sunybroome.edu

WOOD, Elizabeth, B .... 609-258-3354.... 312 G
lizwood@princeton.edu

WOOD, Erin .... 701-662-1598.... 382 F
erin.wood@lrsc.edu

WOOD, Evelyn .... 606-487-3141.... 202 C
evelyn.wood@kctcs.edu

WOOD, Faye .... 843-863-7502.... 456 B
fwood@csuniv.edu

WOOD, Fred .... 218-281-8343.... 271 E
fewood@crk.umn.edu

WOOD, Fred .... 423-478-6229.... 474 E
fwood@clevelandstatecc.edu

WOOD, Gail .... 607-753-2221.... 353 B
gail.wood@cortland.edu

WOOD, Gary, M .... 262-595-2430.... 552 A
gary.wood@uwp.edu

WOOD, Gaye .... 704-991-0221.... 374 D
gwood7693@stanly.edu

WOOD, Gayle, E .... 865-539-7160.... 475 G
gwood@pstcc.edu

WOOD, Jack .... 989-686-9822.... 250 D
jackwood@delta.edu

WOOD, Jan .... 251-442-2456...... 9 A
jwood@umobile.edu

WOOD, Jane .... 816-584-6483.... 287 E
jane.wood@park.edu

WOOD, Janice, R .... 707-965-6315...... 60 I
jwood@puc.edu

WOOD, Jason .... 307-855-2111.... 556 B
jswood@cwc.edu

WOOD, Jeff .... 509-574-4691.... 540 D
jwood@yvcc.edu

WOOD, Jeffrey, A .... 309-438-7602.... 153 D
jwood@ilstu.edu

WOOD, Jerry .... 402-826-8258.... 297 G
jerry.wood@doane.edu

WOOD, Jocelyn .... 215-222-4200.... 445 G
jmwood@walnuthillcollege.edu

WOOD, John .... 314-286-4855.... 287 G
jewood@ranken.edu

WOOD, John .... 307-855-2162.... 556 B
jwood@cwc.edu

WOOD, Joseph, S .... 410-837-5244.... 229 A
jwood@ubalt.edu

WOOD, Joyce .... 765-998-5117.... 180 B
jywood@taylor.edu

WOOD, Julia, H .... 865-694-6530.... 475 G
jwood@pstcc.edu

WOOD, Kathryn .... 909-748-8069...... 76 C
kathryn_wood@redlands.edu

WOOD, Kathryn .... 671-735-2658.... 559 G
kwood@uguam.uog.edu

WOOD, Kelley .... 325-670-1251.... 487 F
kwood@hsutx.edu

WOOD, Kim .... 865-251-1800.... 473 A
kwood@southcollegetn.edu

WOOD, Kris .... 270-706-8412.... 202 A
kris.wood@kctcs.edu

WOOD, Kurt, W .... 563-884-5127.... 188 E
kurt.wood@palmer.edu

WOOD, Kurt, W .... 563-884-5127...... 61 A
kurt.wood@palmer.edu

WOOD, Kurt, W .... 563-884-5127.... 114 E
kurt.wood@palmer.edu

WOOD, Larry, E .... 931-598-1374.... 472 L
lwood@sewanee.edu

WOOD, Laura .... 617-627-3345.... 245 C
laura.wood@tufts.edu

WOOD, Laura .... 903-923-8207.... 492 C
lwood@panola.edu

WOOD, Lisa .... 202-319-6794...... 97 E
woodlm@cua.edu

WOOD, Lynn .... 617-873-0154.... 233 A
lynn.wood@cambridgecollege.edu

WOOD, Lynne, O .... 520-621-3175...... 18 L
lowood@email.arizona.edu

WOOD, Lynsey .... 207-221-8752.... 218 C

WOOD, M. Ann .... 517-371-5140.... 258 F
woodann@cooley.edu

WOOD, Mark .... 909-621-8146...... 63 A
mark.wood@pomona.edu

WOOD, Mark, D .... 310-233-4426...... 54 I
woodmd@lahc.edu

WOOD, Mark, U .... 530-226-4603...... 69 H
mwood@simpsonu.edu

WOOD, Martin .... 719-255-3438...... 88 I
mwood@uccs.edu

WOOD, Michael .... 952-446-4100.... 263 C
woodm@crown.edu

WOOD, Michael .... 609-652-4294.... 313 E
michael.wood@stockton.edu

WOOD, Michael .... 570-408-4300.... 452 A
michael.wood@wilkes.edu

WOOD, Michael, A .... 316-978-3575.... 198 A
mike.wood@wichita.edu

WOOD, Michael, T .... 301-369-2800.... 221 F
president@capitol-college.edu

WOOD, Murray .... 661-362-3433...... 41 I
murray.wood@canyons.edu

WOOD, Pamela, R .... 919-658-7753.... 367 F
pwood@moc.edu

WOOD, Richard, C .... 806-743-2200.... 502 B
richard.wood@ttuhsc.ttu.edu

WOOD, Richard, J .... 251-460-7021........ 9 D
rwood@usouthal.edu

WOOD, Robert .... 904-620-4200.... 120 D
robert.wood@unf.edu

WOOD, Robert .... 610-989-1257.... 450 F
rwood@vfmac.edu

WOOD, Robert, A .... 740-368-3945.... 400 G
rawood@owu.edu

WOOD, Robert, H .... 315-268-6474.... 329 B
rwood@clarkson.edu

WOOD, Robert, S .... 901-334-5830.... 471 E
rswood@memphisseminary.edu

WOOD, Ronald, A .... 507-537-6272.... 269 E
ron.wood@smsu.edu

WOOD, Shelia .... 504-286-5368.... 214 J
swood@suno.edu

WOOD, Sherri, L .... 573-882-0683.... 291 B
woods@missouri.edu

WOOD, Steve .... 828-835-4254.... 374 F
swood@tricountycc.edu

WOOD, Susan .... 804-819-4972.... 526 C
swood@vccs.edu

WOOD, Therese .... 269-749-7623.... 257 A
twood@olivetcollege.edu

WOOD, Tiffany .... 706-385-1019.... 136 B
tiffany.wood@point.edu

WOOD, Tim .... 616-331-2240.... 251 F
woodt@gvsu.edu

WOOD, Tom .... 615-966-6174.... 470 F
tom.wood@lipscombs.edu

WOOD, Vicky .... 740-389-4636.... 395 H
woodv@mtc.edu

WOOD, W. Keith .... 252-334-2034.... 367 C
keith.wood@macuniversity.edu

WOOD, Wayne .... 508-678-2811.... 239 B
wayne.wood@bristolcc.edu

WOOD, Wende .... 843-377-2156.... 456 A
wwood@charlestonlaw.edu

WOOD, William, W .... 610-921-7749.... 421 E
wwood@alb.edu

WOOD, Wm. Michael .... 989-686-9216.... 250 D
williamwood@delta.edu

WOOD, Yolanda .... 716-829-7602.... 332 E
woodyo@dyc.edu

WOODALL, Betty, C .... 919-209-2019.... 371 F
bcwoodall@johnstoncc.edu

WOODALL, David, M .... 425-739-8200.... 535 H
david.woodall@lwtc.edu

WOODALL, Stephen .... 404-756-4635.... 125 D
swoodall@atlm.edu

WOODALL, Stephen .... 812-464-1845.... 181 B
sgwoodall@usi.edu

WOODARD, Brandyn .... 641-628-5134.... 183 D
woodardb@central.edu

WOODARD, Brett .... 610-660-3101.... 446 C
bwoodard@sju.edu

WOODARD, Chrystal .... 318-357-5961.... 216 B
woodardc@nsula.edu

WOODARD, Donna .... 252-398-6280.... 363 G
woodad@chowan.edu

WOODARD, Greg .... 206-239-2275.... 531 B
gwoodard@aii.edu

WOODARD, Howard .... 478-327-7376.... 130 B
howard.woodard@gcsu.edu

WOODARD, Joanne, G .... 919-515-4559.... 378 C
joanne_woodard@ncsu.edu

WOODARD, Johnnie, D .... 704-499-9200...... 99 G

WOODARD, Kimberly .... 334-727-8076........ 8 B

WOODARD, Lance, L .... 615-353-3367.... 475 E
lance.woodard@nscc.edu

WOODARD, Laura, J .... 318-342-5447.... 216 E
woodard@ulm.edu

WOODARD, Patricia .... 850-599-3225.... 118 L
patricia.woodard@famu.edu

WOODARD, Timothy, E .... 919-658-7793.... 367 F
twoodard@moc.edu

WOODBERRY, Peter, N .... 401-825-2147.... 453 D
pwoodberry@ccri.edu

WOODBROOKS, Catherine, M .... 508-767-7325.... 230 D
cwoodbroo@assumption.edu

WOODBURN, Don, A .... 620-227-9378.... 192 E
donwoodburn@dc3.edu

WOODBURN, Steve, M .... 303-963-3233...... 82 C
swoodburn@ccu.edu

WOODBURN, Steven .... 252-335-0821.... 369 G
steven_woodburn@albemarle.edu

WOODCOCK, Jonathan .... 603-623-0313.... 305 E
jwoodcock@nhia.edu

WOODCOCK, Tony .... 617-585-1200.... 242 I
tony.woodcock@necmusic.edu

WOODDELL, Kathleen .... 540-338-2700.... 517 G
kwooddell@cdu.edu

WOODEN, Mark .... 602-639-7500...... 14 H

WOODEN, Michael .... 802-728-1378.... 516 A
mwooden@vtc.vsc.edu

WOODEN, Ontario, S .... 919-530-5235.... 378 B
owooden@nccu.edu

WOODERSON, Linda .... 417-328-1715.... 290 A
lwooderson@sbuniv.edu

WOODFIELD, Richard .... 419-995-8222.... 392 K
woodfield.r@rhodesstate.edu

WOODFIN, Paul .... 254-867-4802.... 500 F
paul.woodfin@tstc.edu

WOODFORD, Steve .... 865-251-1800.... 473 A
swoodford@southcollegetn.edu

WOODHEAD, Jennifer .... 910-755-7359.... 368 F
woodheadj@brunswickcc.edu

WOODHOUSE, Bryan, M .... 608-246-6516.... 554 D
woodhouse@madisoncollege.org

WOODHOUSE, Francine .... 702-651-5600.... 302 E
francine.woodhouse@csn.edu

WOODHOUSE, Michelle .... 757-822-7242.... 528 G
mwoodhouse@tcc.edu

WOODLAND, Calvin .... 202-274-6203.... 100 A
calvin.woodland@udc.edu

WOODLE, Tom .... 843-349-2357.... 456 G
twoodle@coastal.edu

WOODLEE, Barbara, W .... 207-453-5129.... 218 I
bwoodlee@kvcc.me.edu

WOODLEE, Stephanie, A .... 325-674-2412.... 478 I
stephanie.woodlee@acu.edu

WOODLEY, Charlie .... 706-396-8145.... 135 G
cwoodley@paine.edu

WOODLEY, Michael, P .... 701-252-3467.... 381 C
woodley@jc.edu

WOODLEY, Sandra, K .... 512-499-4798.... 505 B
swoodley@utsystem.edu

WOODLEY, Xeturah .... 303-360-4729...... 83 K
xeturah.woodley@ccaurora.edu

WOODMAN, Keith .... 925-288-5800...... 49 H
keith_woodman@heald.edu

WOODMANSEE, Holly, M .... 206-546-6955.... 538 C
hwoodmansee@shoreline.edu

WOODMANSEE, Ken .... 901-843-3874.... 472 K
woodmanseek@rhodes.edu

WOODRICK, Rebecca .... 601-266-6618.... 277 F
rebecca.woodrick@usm.edu

WOODRING, N. Susan .... 814-949-5631.... 438 I
swd1@psu.edu

WOODROW, Adam .... 413-782-1583.... 246 A
awoodrow@wne.edu

WOODRUFF, Aaron .... 309-438-8631.... 153 D
apwoodr@ilstu.edu

WOODRUFF, Hollie, E .... 252-399-6368.... 362 E
hewoodruff@barton.edu

WOODRUFF, John .... 413-565-1000.... 230 G
jwoodruff@baypath.edu

WOODRUFF, Kenneth, A .... 843-953-6859.... 456 C
ken.woodruff@citadel.edu

WOODRUFF, Kevin .... 423-493-4250.... 476 E
cierpke@prodigy.net

WOODRUFF, Kristin .... 785-442-6016.... 193 F
kwoodruff@highlandcc.edu

WOODRUFF, Martha .... 903-983-8287.... 489 I
mwoodruff@kilgore.edu

WOODRUFF, Nellie .... 850-599-3611.... 118 L
nellie.woodruff@famu.edu

WOODRUFF, Paul, B .... 512-475-7000.... 505 D
pbw@mail.utexas.edu

WOODRUFF, Steven, W .... 336-342-4261.... 373 E
woodruffs@rockinghamcc.edu

WOODRUFF, Tina .... 215-871-6870.... 444 C
tinawo@pcom.edu

WOODRUFFE, Danielle .... 201-216-5139.... 315 E
dwoodruf@stevens.edu

WOODS, Amy .... 520-325-0123...... 18 G
amw@theartcenter.edu

WOODS, Amy, K .... 845-575-3000.... 340 B
amy.k.coppola@marist.edu

WOODS, Anya .... 617-349-8624.... 236 B
awoods@lesley.edu

WOODS, JR., Arnold, A .... 641-269-3250.... 185 D
woods@grinnell.edu

WOODS, Benjamin, E .... 575-646-1727.... 319 D
bwoods@nmsu.edu

WOODS, Brandy .... 618-634-3417.... 164 E
brandyw@shawneecc.edu

WOODS, Brett .... 828-227-7124.... 380 A
bwoods@wcu.edu

WOODS, Carolyn .... 251-368-7603........ 5 B
carolyn.woods@jdcc.edu

WOODS, Dannie .... 601-925-3830.... 275 C
drwoods@mc.edu

WOODS, Deborah .... 330-382-7452.... 393 F
dwoods1@kent.edu

WOODS, Debra .... 714-449-7434...... 70 G
danderson@scco.edu

WOODS, Debra, D .... 724-925-4083.... 451 E
woodsde@wccc.edu

WOODS, Deirdre .... 913-621-8720.... 192 F
dwoods@donnelly.edu

WOODS, Dianne, M .... 219-464-5368.... 181 C
dianne.woods@valpo.edu

WOODS, Gilda, Q .... 540-365-4290.... 519 C
gwoods@ferrum.edu

WOODS, James, M .... 630-515-6173.... 158 F
jwoods@midwestern.edu

WOODS, Jami .... 336-386-3266.... 374 E
woodsj@surry.edu

WOODS, Jann .... 928-757-0803...... 16 F
jwoods@mohave.edu

WOODS, Jason .... 563-242-4023.... 182 C
jason.woods@ashford.edu

WOODS, John, J .... 601-857-3387.... 274 C
jjwoods@hindscc.edu

WOODS, Joshua, L .... 256-765-4225........ 9 C
jlwoods@una.edu

WOODS, Kristin, J .... 804-289-8026.... 525 E
kwoods@richmond.edu

WOODS, Kristy, F .... 202-865-7470...... 98 E
kristy.woods@howard.edu

WOODS, Larry .... 484-365-7211.... 434 H
lwoods@lincoln.edu

WOODS, Linda .... 619-388-7434...... 65 H
lwoods@sdccd.edu

WOODS, Marilyn .... 586-791-6610.... 248 B
marilyn.woods@baker.edu

WOODS, Marilyn, J .... 956-882-7147.... 505 E
marilyn.woods@utb.edu

WOODS, Mary .... 830-792-7375.... 494 E
zmwoods@schreiner.edu

WOODS, Mary Lou .... 909-621-8000...... 63 A
marylou.woods@pomona.edu

WOODS, Maura, A .... 718-990-1985.... 348 G
woodsm@stjohns.edu

WOODS, Norma .... 478-289-2002.... 129 B
nwoods@ega.edu

WOODS, Pamela .... 304-214-8911.... 543 D
pwoods@wvncc.edu

WOODS, Patrick .... 312-341-6360.... 163 B
pwoods@roosevelt.edu

WOODS, R. Dean .... 864-231-2068.... 455 C
dwoods@andersonuniversity.edu

WOODS, Rebekah .... 517-787-0800.... 252 J
woodsrebekahs@jccmi.edu

WOODS, Richard, G .... 765-361-6188.... 181 E
woodsr@wabash.edu

WOODS, Rick .... 508-213-2111.... 243 E
rick.woods@nichols.edu

WOODS, Robert .... 334-386-7313........ 3 G
rwoods@faulkner.edu

WOODS, Roderick .... 803-327-7402.... 456 F
rwoods@clintonjuniorcollege.edu

WOODS, Sandra, L .... 970-491-3366...... 83 F
sandra.wood@colostate.edu

WOODS, Scott .... 731-425-2638.... 475 C
swoods@jscc.edu

WOODS, Sharmon .... 520-325-0123...... 18 G

WOODS, Sharon, R .... 260-359-4014.... 173 A
swoods@huntington.edu

WOODS, Susan .... 781-280-3200.... 240 B
woodss@middlesex.mass.edu

WOODS, Timothy .... 559-442-8222...... 72 B
tim.woods@fresnocitycollege.edu

WOODS, Tracie, J .... 225-771-4680.... 214 H
tracie_woods@sus.edu

WOODS, Tracy .... 478-289-2035.... 129 B
twoods@ega.edu

WOODS, Victor .... 918-465-1811.... 408 A
vwoods@eosc.edu

WOODSIDE, Christina, S .... 704-847-5600.... 377 B
cwoodside@ses.edu

WOODSON, Corliss, B .... 804-523-5877.... 527 A
cwoodson@reynolds.edu

WOODSON, Heather .... 704-922-6310.... 370 G
woodson.heather@gaston.edu

WOODSON, Kendra, B .... 864-231-2120.... 455 C
kwoodson@andersonuniversity.edu

WOODSON, Lenee .... 973-290-4227.... 308 G
lwoodson@cse.edu

WOODSON, Lovisa .... 215-635-7300.... 430 A
lwoodson@gratz.edu

WRIGHT, Gary .... 404-215-2636.... 134 D
gwright@morehouse.edu
WRIGHT, Gayla .... 509-359-6824.... 533 H
gwright@ewu.edu
WRIGHT, George, C .... 936-261-2111.... 496 G
gcwright@pvamu.edu
WRIGHT, Gregory, R .... 610-292-9852.... 445 E
greg.wright@reseminary.edu
WRIGHT, Irvin .... 570-389-4492.... 441 F
iwright@bloomu.edu
WRIGHT, James .... 510-659-6220...... 59 J
jwright@ohlone.edu
WRIGHT, JR., James, A .... 864-231-2061.... 455 C
jwright@andersonuniversity.edu
WRIGHT, Jason .... 315-568-3268.... 342 H
jwright@nycc.edu
WRIGHT, Jeff .... 360-650-6400.... 539 F
jeff.wright@wwu.edu
WRIGHT, Jeffrey .... 207-326-2215.... 219 D
jeff.wright@mma.edu
WRIGHT, Jeffrey .... 802-287-8395.... 513 F
jwright@greenmtn.edu
WRIGHT, Jeffrey, E .... 765-641-4544.... 169 E
jewright@anderson.edu
WRIGHT, Jerry .... 517-265-5161.... 246 H
WRIGHT, Jill .... 309-694-5361.... 152 C
jwright@icc.edu
WRIGHT, Jimmy .... 606-886-3863.... 201 G
jimmy.wright@kctcs.edu
WRIGHT, Joann .... 708-974-5358.... 159 B
wright@morainevalley.edu
WRIGHT, John .... 845-569-3592.... 342 A
john.wright@msmc.edu
WRIGHT, John, E .... 304-336-8180.... 544 D
jewright@westliberty.edu
WRIGHT, John, W .... 352-392-0466.... 120 C
jwright@jou.ufl.edu
WRIGHT, Jonas .... 415-503-6297...... 66 A
jwright@sfcm.edu
WRIGHT, Julie .... 573-288-6640.... 280 I
jwright@culver.edu
WRIGHT, Karen, F .... 270-384-7313.... 204 D
wrightk@lindsey.edu
WRIGHT, Karen, M .... 606-679-8501.... 203 C
karen.wright@kctcs.edu
WRIGHT, Kay .... 979-230-3377.... 482 D
kay.wright@brazosport.edu
WRIGHT, Keith .... 703-414-4129.... 518 C
kwright@devry.edu
WRIGHT, Kristine, A .... 612-626-0302.... 272 A
wrigh084@umn.edu
WRIGHT, Laura .... 616-538-2330.... 251 D
lwright@gbcol.edu
WRIGHT, LeAnne .... 903-223-3078.... 498 F
leanne.wright@tamut.edu
WRIGHT, Leroy .... 231-591-2686.... 250 H
wrightl@ferris.edu
WRIGHT, Linda .... 717-901-5112.... 430 F
lwright@harrisburgu.net
WRIGHT, Logan, S .... 816-483-9600.... 289 E
lswright@spst.edu
WRIGHT, Lori .... 216-791-5000.... 388 C
lxw21@case.edu
WRIGHT, Lynn, C .... 304-724-3700.... 540 F
lwright@apus.edu
WRIGHT, Matt .... 706-419-1557.... 128 B
matt.wright@covenant.edu
WRIGHT, Matthew .... 615-322-2451.... 478 A
matthew.wright@vanderbilt.edu
WRIGHT, May, F .... 270-824-8649.... 202 G
may.wright@kctcs.edu
WRIGHT, Meghan .... 828-898-8729.... 366 D
wrightm@lmc.edu
WRIGHT, Michael .... 229-931-2351.... 137 C
mwright@southgatech.edu
WRIGHT, Michael, D .... 660-543-4272.... 290 H
mwright@ucmo.edu
WRIGHT, Michael, G .... 313-577-8155.... 260 A
dx2558@wayne.edu
WRIGHT, Mike .... 717-757-1100.... 452 J
mike.wright@yti.edu
WRIGHT, Milton .... 773-838-7606.... 147 H
mwright@ccc.edu
WRIGHT, Nathan .... 218-322-2323.... 266 G
nathan.wright@itascacc.edu
WRIGHT, Norman .... 801-863-8239.... 511 F
norman.wright@uvu.edu
WRIGHT, Nova .... 540-863-2868.... 526 F
nwright@dslcc.edu
WRIGHT, Paul .... 610-902-8562.... 424 B
paul.r.wright@cabrini.edu
WRIGHT, Paul, G .... 727-816-3466.... 114 F
wrightp@phcc.edu
WRIGHT, Peter .... 603-513-5163.... 306 E
peter.wright@law.unh.edu
WRIGHT, Peter .... 920-206-2395.... 548 D
peter.wright@mbbc.edu
WRIGHT, Phil .... 503-584-7261.... 414 J
phil.wright@chemeketa.edu
WRIGHT, Randy .... 314-968-6918.... 292 J
wrightra@webster.edu
WRIGHT, Raymond, M ...... 401-874-2186.... 454 E
wrightr@egr.uri.edu
WRIGHT, Renee .... 814-838-7673.... 429 C
rwright@fortisinstitute.edu
WRIGHT, Rick, L .... 785-539-3571.... 195 B
rwright@mcck.edu
WRIGHT, Robert .... 304-624-7695.... 542 D
rwright@wvbc.edu
WRIGHT, Robert, E .... 570-504-7000.... 425 F
WRIGHT, Robin .... 859-441-4500.... 202 B
robin.wright@kctcs.edu
WRIGHT, Rodner, B .... 850-599-3244.... 118 L
rodner.wright@famu.edu
WRIGHT, Russell .... 206-393-3557.... 531 A
rwwright@argosy.edu
WRIGHT, Shelly, A .... 845-257-3291.... 352 B
wrights@newpaltz.edu
WRIGHT, Sheri .... 760-757-2121...... 57 E
swright@miracosta.edu
WRIGHT, Sherry .... 870-230-5352...... 21 I
wrights@hsu.edu
WRIGHT, Sonia .... 530-938-5373...... 42 E
swright5@siskiyous.edu
WRIGHT, Stan .... 318-357-5716.... 216 B
ralphw@nsula.edu
WRIGHT, Stephanie .... 336-334-4822.... 371 A
swweeks@gtcc.edu
WRIGHT, Stephen .... 928-523-6533...... 16 I
stephen.wright@nau.edu
WRIGHT, Susan, F .... 716-878-4301.... 353 A
orrsf@buffalostate.edu
WRIGHT, Thomas .... 423-473-2750.... 474 E
twright@clevelandstatecc.edu
WRIGHT, Tim .... 307-268-2706.... 556 A
twright@caspercollege.edu
WRIGHT, Timothy, S .... 863-680-4297.... 109 E
twright@flsouthern.edu
WRIGHT, Voncille, T .... 512-223-3128.... 481 B
vwright@austincc.edu
WRIGHT, Willard .... 661-722-6300...... 28 K
wwright9@avc.edu
WRIGHT, William, A .... 805-565-7262...... 79 A
wright@westmont.edu
WRIGHT, Willie .... 314-984-7740.... 289 A
wwright@stlcc.edu
WRIGHT-DUBOSE, Alexis . 843-355-4165.... 463 D
wrighta@wiltech.edu
WRIGHT-HENDERSON,
Jacquita, L .... 302-657-5112...... 96 F
jwright@dtcc.edu
WRIGHT-HOWARD, Debra 619-388-3513...... 65 F
dewright@sdccd.edu
WRIGHT-MOORE, Karyn ... 516-686-7958.... 343 D
kwrightm@nyit.edu
WRIGHT-PETERSON,
Virginia .... 507-284-3293.... 262 E
wrightpeterson.virginia@mayo.edu
WRIGHT-SANDERS,
Barbara .... 775-673-7123.... 302 H
bsanders@tmcc.edu
WRIGHT-SWADEL,
William .... 919-660-1050.... 364 C
william.wright-swadel@duke.edu
WRIGHTEN, Karen .... 843-899-8049.... 461 G
karen.wrighten@tridenttech.edu
WRIGHTMAN, Diane .... 775-727-2017.... 302 F
diane.wrightman@gbcnv.edu
WRIGHTON, Mark, S .... 314-935-5100.... 292 I
wrighton@wustl.edu
WRIGHTSON,
Madeleine, V .... 610-526-6008.... 430 D
mwrightson@harcum.edu
WRIGHTSON, Sam .... 610-647-4400.... 431 C
swrightson@immaculata.edu
WRIGLEY, Dawn .... 518-828-4181.... 330 E
wrigley@sunycgcc.edu
WRIGLEY, Steve .... 404-962-3240.... 139 B
steve.wrigley@usg.edu
WRIGLEY, Telaina .... 931-221-6353.... 473 E
wrigleyt@apsu.edu
WRIGLEY, Vicki, A .... 217-362-6485.... 158 G
vwrigley@millikin.edu
WRINN, Stephen .... 859-257-8432.... 207 D
smwrin2@uky.edu
WRISTON, Mandy .... 304-929-1434.... 541 H
mwriston@mountainstate.edu
WRISTON, Welton .... 423-478-7993.... 472 H
wwriston@ptseminary.edu
WROBBEL, Karen .... 847-317-7178.... 166 E
kwrobbel@tiu.edu
WROBEL, Deborah, R .... 443-412-2240.... 223 B
dwrobel@harford.edu
WROBLEWSKI, Carol .... 317-940-9904.... 170 F
cwroble1@butler.edu
WROBLEWSKI, Kathleen .... 413-565-1000.... 230 G
kwroblew@baypath.edu
WROBLEWSKI, Ray .... 724-339-7542.... 437 F
director@nbi.edu
WRUBEL, Rob .... 602-387-7000...... 19 A
rob.wrubel@apollogrp.edu
WRUCK, Craig .... 320-308-5370.... 269 A
ccwruck@stcloudstate.edu
WRY, Joan, R .... 802-654-2466.... 514 D
jwry@smcvt.edu
WU, Bill .... 510-592-9688...... 59 G
wjw@npu.edu
WU, Chin Shun .... 626-571-8811...... 77 A
president@uwest.edu
WU, Diana .... 510-642-4181...... 73 H
dwu@unex.berkeley.edu
WU, Felix .... 518-442-3535.... 351 E
wuf@csc.albany.edu
WU, Frank, H .... 415-565-4700...... 74 A
wuf@uchastings.edu
WU, Helen .... 262-554-3278.... 549 A
helen_wu@yahoo.com
WU, Jin .... 516-364-0808.... 343 A
jwu@nycollege.edu
WU, John .... 640-466-7900.... 168 B
jwu@waubonsee.edu
WU, Jonathan .... 626-289-9004...... 26 K
WU, Katherine .... 212-986-4343.... 323 H
knw@berkeleycollege.edu
WU, Qianzhi .... 512-454-1188.... 480 F
WU, S. David .... 610-758-5308.... 434 E
sdw1@lehigh.edu
WU, Sonia .... 941-487-5000.... 120 A
swu@ncf.edu
WU, Wen-Shuo .... 562-947-8755...... 71 A
wen-shuowu@scuhs.edu
WU, Yenbo .... 415-338-1293...... 37 B
ywu@sfsu.edu
WUBAH, Daniel, A .... 540-231-4167.... 529 G
wubah@vt.edu
WUBBEN, Kris .... 608-822-2706.... 555 D
kwubben@swtc.edu
WUBBENA, Dan .... 712-274-6400.... 190 B
dan.wubbena@witcc.edu
WUCHENICH,
Christopher, L .... 803-777-8400.... 462 A
clw@mailbox.sc.edu
WUENSCHEL, Carol, M ..... 301-696-3556.... 223 C
wuenschel@hood.edu
WUERTZ, John, A .... 319-352-8318.... 189 J
john.wuertz@wartburg.edu
WUERZEBERGER, Ken ...... 913-758-6307.... 197 D
wuerzeberger53@stmary.edu
WUEST, Kelly .... 702-651-5928.... 302 E
kelly.wuest@csn.edu
WUESTENBERG, Pam, J .... 512-245-7952.... 501 F
pw05@txstate.edu
WULF, Lincoln .... 719-502-3178...... 87 B
lincoln.wulf@ppcc.edu
WULFEMEYER, Lori .... 619-961-4315...... 72 J
loriw@tjsl.edu
WULFERT, Edelgard .... 518-442-4654.... 351 E
ewulfert@uamail.albany.edu
WULFF, Deborah .... 805-546-3125...... 43 I
deborah_wulff@cuesta.edu
WULFF, Debra .... 973-290-4445.... 308 G
dwulff@cse.edu
WULFF, Susan .... 816-501-3767.... 278 I
susan.wulff@avila.edu
WULLERT, Christine .... 610-375-1212.... 438 C
cwullert@paceinstitute.com
WUNDER, Francine .... 313-577-8155.... 260 A
fwunder@wayne.edu
WUNDERLICH, Dustin .... 208-459-5820.... 143 D
dwunderlich@collegeofidaho.edu
WUNDERLICH, Kathryn ..... 607-844-8222.... 357 I
wunderk@tc3.edu
WUNDERLICH, Mark, E ..... 518-388-8031.... 358 G
wunderlm@union.edu
WUNDERLICH, Tom .... 757-683-4388.... 522 F
twunderl@odu.edu
WUNDERLICH, Warren, P . 507-933-7507.... 263 J
wwunderl@gustavus.edu
WUNDERLY, Nancy .... 610-683-4060.... 443 A
wunderly@kutztown.edu
WUNKER, Charles .... 863-638-2916.... 123 E
wunkerc@webber.edu
WUNSCHL, Lyn .... 630-652-8318.... 149 C
lwunschl@devry.edu
WUORI, Misti, L .... 701-788-4631.... 381 H
misti.wuori@mayvillestate.edu
WURM, Sharon .... 775-673-7074.... 302 H
swurm@tmcc.edu
WURMFELD, Claire .... 321-674-8057.... 108 H
cwurmfeld@fit.edu
WURST, Karin, A .... 517-355-4597.... 255 A
wurst@msu.edu
WURTZ, Joseph .... 913-360-7500.... 191 A
jwurtz@benedictine.edu
WURTZ, Keith .... 909-389-3206...... 65 B
kwurtz@craftonhills.edu
WURTZEL, Julie, A .... 563-562-3263.... 188 B
wurtzelj@nicc.edu
WURZER, Christine .... 916-608-6500...... 56 C
WUSTMAN, Brent .... 803-641-3293.... 462 B
wustman-brent@aramark.com
WUTHO, Rita .... 301-860-4170.... 228 A
rwutoh@bowiestate.edu
WUTHRICH, Philip .... 979-532-6305.... 509 D
philipw@wcjc.edu
WUTOH, Anthony .... 202-806-6530...... 98 E
awutoh@howard.edu
WYACCO, Suzette .... 505-863-7623.... 321 D
swyacco@gallup.unm.edu
WYACO, Suzette .... 505-863-7623.... 321 D
swyaco@unm.edu
WYAND, Diane, A .... 518-564-2130.... 354 B
wyandda@plattsburgh.edu
WYANDOTTE, Annette, M .. 812-941-2208.... 175 A
awyandot@ius.edu
WYANT, Robert .... 814-827-4457.... 450 A
wyant@pitt.edu
WYATT, Adrienne, L .... 404-752-1591.... 134 E
ahammonds@msm.edu
WYATT, Alicia .... 325-793-4748.... 490 H
awyatt@mcm.edu
WYATT, Ben .... 859-280-1246.... 204 B
bwyatt@lextheo.edu
WYATT, Brad .... 615-966-7600.... 470 F
brad.wyatt@lipscomb.edu
WYATT, Bruce .... 503-883-2217.... 416 H
bwyatt@linfield.edu
WYATT, Carl, V .... 512-245-9650.... 501 F
cw23@txstate.edu
WYATT, Clarence, R .... 859-238-5243.... 199 G
clarence.wyatt@centre.edu
WYATT, Harry .... 740-593-2911.... 399 G
wyatth@ohio.edu
WYATT, Jan .... 603-668-6660.... 305 B
WYATT, Jimmy .... 865-471-7164.... 467 G
jwyatt@cn.edu
WYATT, Joy, D .... 440-826-2180.... 384 K
jwyatt@bw.edu
WYATT, Linda, L .... 913-288-7243.... 194 C
lwyatt@kckcc.edu
WYATT, Lisa .... 707-664-2153...... 37 D
lisa.wyatt@sonoma.edu
WYATT, Mark, A .... 951-343-4474...... 31 J
mwyatt@calbaptist.edu
WYATT, Rick .... 620-241-0723.... 191 I
rick.wyatt@centralchristian.edu
WYATT, Robert, L .... 843-383-8010.... 457 A
rwyatt@coker.edu
WYATT, Scott, L .... 435-283-7010.... 512 C
scott.wyatt@snow.edu
WYATT, Shay .... 801-832-2344.... 512 G
swyatt@westminstercollege.edu
WYATT, Stephen, W .... 859-257-5678.... 207 D
swwyat2@uky.edu
WYATT, Terri .... 804-257-5726.... 530 A
vuu@bkstr.com
WYATT, Tracey, L .... 402-363-5675.... 301 E
tlwyatt@york.edu
WYBLE, Shannon .... 410-778-7200.... 229 D
swyble2@washcoll.edu
WYBORNY, Jeff .... 206-726-5024.... 533 D
jwyborny@cornish.edu
WYBOURNE, Martin, N ...... 603-646-2404.... 304 J
martin.n.wybourne@dartmouth.edu
WYCHE, Anita .... 757-499-7900.... 517 D
abwyche@bryantstratton.edu
WYCHE, Barbara .... 434-848-6429.... 524 B
bwyche@saintpauls.edu
WYCHE, Sandy .... 972-860-4282.... 484 G
swyche@dcccd.edu
WYCKOFF, Blaine, M .... 330-325-6191.... 397 D
bwyckoff@neomed.edu
WYCKOFF, Harold .... 910-678-8287.... 370 E
wyckoffh@faytechcc.edu
WYCKOFF, Steven .... 718-960-8720.... 327 C
steven.wyckoff@lehman.cuny.edu
WYCOFF, Jennifer .... 205-929-1456........ 5 H
jwycoff@miles.edu
WYCOFF, Joseph .... 914-633-2000.... 336 E
jwycoff@iona.edu
WYCOFF-HORN, Marcie .... 608-785-8127.... 551 C
mwycoff-horn@uwlax.edu
WYDEN, Leon .... 419-448-3272.... 402 E
wydenl@tiffin.edu
WYDER, Bruce .... 330-494-6170.... 402 B
bwyder@starkstate.edu
WYKE, Rebecca .... 207-973-3343.... 219 I
wyke@maine.edu
WYKERT, Todd .... 307-268-2555.... 556 A
twykert@caspercollege.edu
WYKES, Paul .... 508-793-7385.... 233 B
pwykes@clarku.edu
WYKOFF, Randolph, F ...... 423-439-4243.... 473 F
wykoff@etsu.edu
WYKOFF, Tom .... 330-684-8910.... 403 C
twykoff@uakron.edu
WYLD, Jean, A .... 413-748-3959.... 244 H
jwyld@springfieldcollege.edu
WYLDMON, Constance, V . 601-266-4119.... 277 F
connie.wyldmon@usm.edu
WYLIE, Ann, G .... 301-405-1603.... 227 B
awylie@umd.edu
WYLIE, Brian .... 978-232-2440.... 234 D
bwylie@endicott.edu
WYLIE, Kelly .... 512-463-1808.... 500 H
kelly.wylie@tsus.edu
WYLIE, Michael .... 513-569-1492.... 387 G
michael.wylie@cincinnatistate.edu
WYLIE, Richard, E .... 978-232-2001.... 234 D
rwylie@endicott.edu
WYLIE, Ruth .... 304-929-1523.... 541 H
rwylie@mountainstate.edu
WYLIE, Thomas .... 419-267-1203.... 397 E
twylie@northweststate.edu

X

Y

YEE, Atom 408-554-4455 68 C ayee@scu.edu
YEE, David 415-239-3669 40 C dyee@ccsf.edu
YEE, Robert 617-989-4590 245 F yeer@wit.edu
YEE, Sandra, G 313-577-4020 260 A aj0533@wayne.edu
YEH, Frank 662-252-8000 276 G fyeh@rustcollege.edu
YEH, Li-An 919-530-7001 378 B lyeh@nccu.edu
YEHL, Robert, F 870-230-5014 21 I yehlb@hsu.edu
YEHUDAH, Shoshana 212-463-0400 358 B shulys@touro.edu
YEIGH, Bjong, W 315-684-6044 354 F president@morrisville.edu
YEIGH, Bjong, W 315-792-7400 356 B wolf.yeigh@sunyit.edu
YEKOVICH, Robert 713-348-4837 493 C yekovr@rice.edu
YELIN, Louise 914-251-6550 354 D louise.yelin@purchase.edu
YELLE, Dave 413-565-1000 230 G dyelle@baypath.edu
YELLE, Richard, W 203-576-4222 94 F ryelle@bridgeport.edu
YELLEN, David, N 312-915-7120 157 C dyellen@luc.edu
YELNOSKY, Robert, E 814-641-3707 432 A yelnosr@juniata.edu
YELVINGTON, Philip, R 901-321-3396 467 I pyelving@cbu.edu
YELVINGTON, Sherry 901-272-5125 471 D syelvington@mca.edu
YEN, Charlie 310-434-3002 68 D yen_charlie@smc.edu
YEN, Flora, B 916-568-3132 55 J yenf@losrios.edu
YEN, Johanna, C 954-763-9840 101 G atom@atom.edu
YEN, S.C. Max 260-481-6839 174 C yens@ipfw.edu
YENA, John, A 401-598-1100 453 E jyena@jwu.edu
YENCHA, Tom 304-424-8309 545 C tom.yencha@mail.wvu.edu
YENSAN, Lester, K 401-874-5371 454 E yensan@mail.uri.edu
YENSON, Evelyn 206-934-3227 537 C evelyn.yenson@seattlecolleges.edu
YENTCH, Richard 562-938-4869 54 E ryentch@lbcc.edu
YENTES, Matt 863-638-2963 123 E yentesms@webber.edu
YEO, Frances 850-484-1795 115 B fyeo@pensacolastate.edu
YEO, Frederick, L 920-424-3322 551 E yeof@uwosh.edu
YEOMANS, Jennifer 603-888-1311 305 F jyeomans@rivier.edu
YEONOPOLUS, Jim 254-526-1781 482 H jim.yeonopolus@ctcd.edu
YEP, Katie 651-846-1372 269 C katie.yep@saintpaul.edu
YEPES, Maria, E 323-265-8957 54 G yepesme@elac.edu
YEPES, Maria Elena 323-265-8957 54 G yepesme@elac.edu
YERGEN, Norman 951-785-2307 53 E nyergen@lasierra.edu
YERGER, Linda 360-475-7300 536 D lyerger@olympic.edu
YERGER, Mark 570-577-1795 423 E mark.yerger@bucknell.edu
YERICH, Nicolette 660-248-6255 279 G nyerich@centralmethodist.edu
YERK, Melanie 239-939-4766 118 I myerk@swfc.edu
YERKES, Kate 603-513-1373 306 F kate.yerkes@granite.edu
YESKEVICZ, Bevin 205-802-1200 3 B kevin.yeskevicz@vc.edu
YESTRAMSKI, Joanne 978-934-2206 237 B joanne_yestramski@uml.edu
YETMAN, Barbara, H 215-968-8045 423 F yetmanb@bucks.edu
YETMAR, Theresa 785-594-8316 190 F theresa.yetmar@bakeru.edu
YEVIN, G. Bernard 336-734-7224 370 F gyevin@forsythtech.edu
YEW, Phillip 213-487-0110 45 D chinese@dula.edu
YIANOUKOS, Steven, J 315-268-6622 329 B stevey@clarkson.edu
YIGZAW, Erika 503-244-0726 414 D erikayigzaw@achs.edu
YIH, T, C 562-985-5314 35 C yih@csulb.edu
YIH, T. C 239-590-7021 119 B tcyih@fgcu.edu
YILIBUW, Dolores 859-280-1224 204 B dyilibuw@lextheo.edu
YIN, Kong 713-221-8975 503 F yink@uhd.edu
YINGLING, Julie, R 419-434-4550 404 B yinglingj@findlay.edu
YINGLING, Kevin, W 304-696-3170 544 B yingling@marshall.edu
YIRKA, Carl, A 802-831-1443 515 B cyirka@vermontlaw.edu
YLINEN, Jeff 612-374-5800 263 F jylinen@dunwoody.edu
YOACHIM, Maureen 610-740-3725 425 A bookstore@cedarcrest.edu
YOAKUM, Katrina, M 785-864-3261 197 B kyoakum@ku.edu
YOANNONE, Carol 412-237-4421 425 H cyoannone@ccac.edu
YOCHUM, Denise 253-964-6776 536 H dyochum@pierce.ctc.edu
YOCHUM, Gilbert, R 757-683-3521 522 F gyochum@odu.edu
YOCKEY, Glenn 830-372-8040 499 F gyockey@tlu.edu
YOCOM, Jim 574-520-4806 174 E jyocom@iusb.edu
YOCUM, Amanda 330-325-6758 397 D ayocum1@neomed.edu
YOCUM, Stephanie 559-730-3988 42 D stephaniey@cos.edu
YODER, Alfred 740-857-1311 401 F ayoder@rosedale.edu
YODER, Anita, R 574-535-7114 171 G anitay@goshen.edu
YODER, Brad, L 260-422-5561 173 C blyoder@indianatech.edu
YODER, Brent 620-327-8231 193 E brenty@hesston.edu
YODER, Dan 541-440-4600 420 F dan.yoder@umpqua.edu
YODER, Donna, K 814-886-6368 437 B dyoder@mtaloy.edu
YODER, Ernest 989-774-7570 249 C yoder1el@cmich.edu
YODER, James, A 508-289-2252 246 E jyoder@whoi.edu
YODER, Judy 276-944-6867 519 A jyoder@ehc.edu
YODER, Julie 301-387-3101 222 H julie.yoder@garrettcollege.edu
YODER, Mari 419-267-1268 397 E myoder@northweststate.edu
YODER, Norris 828-328-7145 366 E norris.yoder@lr.edu
YODER, Robert, E 574-535-7244 171 G robertey@goshen.edu
YODER, Twila, K 540-432-4100 518 F yodertk@emu.edu
YOHANNES, Edna 323-563-5985 39 G ednayohannes@cdrewu.edu
YOHE, Roger 480-461-7151 15 I roger.yohe@mcmail.maricopa.edu
YOHNK, Dean 262-595-2188 552 A yohnk@uwp.edu
YOHO, Robert 515-271-1464 184 A robert.yoho@dmu.edu
YOHO, Steven, K 912-201-8105 137 D syoho@southuniversity.edu
YOIA, Dominic 203-582-5224 93 H dominic.yoia@quinnipiac.edu
YOK, Larry 206-878-3710 535 B lyok@highline.edu
YOKOTOBI, Fusako 760-245-4271 77 H fusako.yokotobi@vvc.edu
YOKOYAMA, Janis, K 213-738-6714 71 E deansoffice@swlaw.edu
YOLITZ, Brian, D 651-201-1777 265 E brian.yolitz@so.mnscu.edu
YONAN, Jonathan 610-225-5704 428 E jyonan@eastern.edu
YONEMITSU, Lori 206-546-4552 538 C lyonemitsu@shoreline.edu
YONG, Henry, C 408-270-6471 67 C henry.yong@evc.edu
YONG, Yan Yan 540-834-1048 526 I yyong@germanna.edu
YONGUE, Marelle 337-482-6826 216 D darlene@louisiana.edu
YONKERS, Molly, L 507-933-7588 263 J myunkers@gustavus.edu
YONUTAS, Dave 352-395-5379 117 F dave.yonutas@sfcollege.edu
YOON, Michelle 562-926-1023 63 B mhyoon@ptsa.edu
YOON, Youngjune 213-381-2221 64 I koreandean@samra.edu
YOPP, Jan 919-962-4364 378 E jan_yopp@unc.edu
YOPP, John 859-257-2756 207 D jyopp@uky.edu
YORDAN, Carlos 973-408-3365 309 E cyordan@drew.edu
YORDY, Jonathan 816-271-5647 286 G jyordy@missouriwestern.edu
YORK, Aaron 903-875-7328 491 C aaron.york@navarrocollege.edu
YORK, Allison 319-398-4998 187 B ayork@kirkwood.edu
YORK, Brenda 406-994-2824 295 C byork@montana.edu
YORK, Corey 914-251-6080 354 D corey.york@purchase.edu
YORK, David 512-492-3032 480 F dyork@aoma.edu
YORK-LEMELIN, Lisa 207-453-5128 218 I lyork@kvcc.me.edu
YORKER, Beatrice 323-343-4600 35 D byorker@calstatela.edu
YORTSOS, Yannis, C 213-740-0617 76 F yortsos@usc.edu
YOSHIDA, James 808-934-2508 142 A jamesyos@hawaii.edu
YOSHIKAWA, Naoto 808-983-4105 140 H yoshinao@tokai.edu
YOSHIMURA, Marlys 408-453-9900 50 F myoshimura@henley-putnam.edu
YOSHIMURA, Nancy 949-480-4045 69 J nyoshimura@soka.edu
YOSHINA, Eileen 360-596-5383 538 E eyoshina@spscc.ctc.edu
YOSHINO, Lori 909-621-8856 62 H lori_yoshino@pitzer.edu
YOST, Devon 970-225-4860 82 A devon.yost@collegeamerica.edu
YOST, Robert, A 704-334-6882 367 H ryost@nlts.edu
YOUATT, June, P 517-432-1075 255 A youatt@msu.edu
YOUHOUSE, John 610-558-5518 437 D youhousej@neumann.edu
YOUKEY, Jerry, R 864-455-7880 462 A youkey@mailbox.sc.edu
YOUKEY, Jerry, R 864-455-7992 462 F
YOUMANS, Art 201-761-7403 314 F ayoumans@spc.edu
YOUNESSI, Houman 860-548-7880 94 A youneh@rpi.edu
YOUNG, Al 205-929-3424 5 E ayoung@lawsonstate.edu
YOUNG, Alissa 270-707-3717 202 E alissa.young@kctcs.edu
YOUNG, Amanda 864-644-5558 461 B ayoung@swu.edu
YOUNG, Amber 256-824-6604 8 G amber.young@uah.edu
YOUNG, Amy 973-278-5400 307 F amy@berkeleycollege.edu
YOUNG, Andrew 812-888-4323 181 D ayoung@vinu.edu
YOUNG, Ann, S 859-238-5480 199 G ann.young@centre.edu
YOUNG, Barbara 662-562-3202 276 D ba_young@northwestms.edu
YOUNG, Benjamin 317-916-7918 175 I byoung@ivytech.edu
YOUNG, Beth 815-825-2086 155 D beth.young@kishwaukeecollege.edu
YOUNG, Betty 478-553-2090 135 B byoung@oftc.edu
YOUNG, Betty, K 713-718-7628 487 I betty.young@hccs.edu
YOUNG, Bradley, J 310-233-4066 54 I youngbj@lahc.edu
YOUNG, Brandon 815-288-5561 156 B brandon.young@doc.illinois.gov
YOUNG, Brian, A 402-280-2121 297 F bay@creighton.edu
YOUNG, Cathy 617-912-9139 232 C cyoung@bostonconservatory.edu
YOUNG, Charlotte 321-674-7400 108 H cyoung@fit.edu
YOUNG, Cheryl, D 513-529-8600 396 E youngcd@muohio.edu
YOUNG, Clifford 909-537-5717 36 B cyoung@csusb.edu
YOUNG, Colletta 541-956-7296 420 B cyoung@roguecc.edu
YOUNG, Connie 217-709-0931 156 C cyoung@lakeviewcol.edu
YOUNG, Corey, D 601-877-4063 272 F cyoung1@alcorn.edu
YOUNG, Dale 478-445-5497 130 B dale.young@gcsu.edu
YOUNG, Dan 336-316-2898 365 A youngfd@guilford.edu
YOUNG, Dana 541-881-5580 420 E dyoung@tvcc.cc
YOUNG, Danielle 440-775-8692 397 G danielle.young@oberlin.edu
YOUNG, Darlene, P 812-941-2306 175 A dyoung01@ius.edu
YOUNG, David 270-237-3577 200 H dayoung@daymarcollege.edu
YOUNG, David, L 434-582-2071 520 K dlyoung@liberty.edu
YOUNG, Deborah 606-589-3323 203 D deborah.young@kctcs.edu
YOUNG, Deborah 718-270-6059 328 C young@mec.cuny.edu
YOUNG, Denise 706-867-3281 134 G dyoung@northgeorgia.edu
YOUNG, Dennis 513-244-4727 388 E dennis_young@mail.msj.edu
YOUNG, Djuana 832-842-9058 503 D dyoun2@central.uh.edu
YOUNG, Donald, B 808-956-7703 141 G young@hawaii.edu
YOUNG, Donald, R 336-744-0900 363 B don@carolina.edu
YOUNG, Donna 480-423-6300 16 C donna.young@scottsdalecc.edu
YOUNG, Doug 937-484-1308 405 A dyoung@urbana.edu
YOUNG, Edward 704-337-2464 376 A younge@queens.edu
YOUNG, Eldon 714-484-7177 59 D eyoung@cypresscollege.edu
YOUNG, Evelyn 661-654-2241 34 A eyoung3@csub.edu
YOUNG, F. Rick 662-476-8442 274 B ryoung@eastms.edu
YOUNG, F. Russell 601-928-6205 275 E russell.young@mgccc.edu
YOUNG, Garland 423-461-8720 471 J rgyoung@milligan.edu
YOUNG, Gene 936-294-1477 501 D young@shsu.edu
YOUNG, Gerald 507-222-4057 261 G gyoung@carleton.edu
YOUNG, Gwyn 601-643-8318 273 G gwyn.young@colin.edu
YOUNG, Harry, A 215-204-3317 447 H harry.young@temple.edu
YOUNG, Heather, M 916-734-4745 73 I heather.young@ucdmc.ucdavis.edu
YOUNG, Hester 843-863-8020 456 B hyoung@csuniv.edu
YOUNG, J.R 412-536-1100 432 H jr.young@laroche.edu
YOUNG, Jackie 502-585-7130 206 D jyoung04@spalding.edu
YOUNG, James 708-656-8000 159 D james.young@morton.edu
YOUNG, James, B 847-491-8542 160 E jbyoung@northwestern.edu
YOUNG, Jan 435-613-5205 512 A jan.young@usu.edu
YOUNG, Janet 209-228-4419 74 D jyoung@ucmerced.edu
YOUNG, Jay 614-251-4715 398 F youngj@ohiodominican.edu
YOUNG, Jeff 931-372-3311 474 B jyoung@tntech.edu
YOUNG, Joanna 603-862-3530 306 C joanna.young@unh.edu
YOUNG, Joanna, C 603-862-3530 306 C joanna.young@unh.edu
YOUNG, John 973-328-5026 309 A jyoung@ccm.edu
YOUNG, John 315-781-3748 335 F jyoung@hws.edu
YOUNG, John 937-327-7800 406 B jyoung@wittenberg.edu
YOUNG, John 303-360-4707 83 K john.young@ccaurora.edu
YOUNG, John, O 203-392-6275 90 I youngj1@southernct.edu
YOUNG, John, O 989-837-4423 256 E young@northwood.edu
YOUNG, John, W 770-720-5522 136 C jyw@reinhardt.edu
YOUNG, Johnny 757-683-6702 522 F
YOUNG, Jon 910-672-1460 377 G jyoung@uncfsu.edu
YOUNG, Jonathan 804-524-5987 529 H jyoung@vsu.edu
YOUNG, Jordan, M 802-862-9616 513 B jyoung@burlington.edu
YOUNG, Joseph 619-388-7672 65 H jyoung@sdccd.edu
YOUNG, Julian, M 843-661-1228 458 D jyoung@fmarion.edu
YOUNG, K. Richard 801-422-3695 509 H richard_young@byu.edu
YOUNG, JR., Karl, J 985-380-2436 211 I karl.young@ltc.edu
YOUNG, Kay 817-598-6303 508 F kyoung@wc.edu
YOUNG, Kay, F 508-213-2114 243 E kay.young@nichols.edu
YOUNG, Kelly 325-674-2795 478 I kelly.young@acu.edu
YOUNG, Ken 516-678-8000 341 F kyoung@molloy.edu
YOUNG, Keri 618-453-2391 165 B keri.young@siu.edu
YOUNG, Kerry, A 315-786-2279 337 F kyoung@sunyjefferson.edu
YOUNG, Kimberly 760-252-2411 30 H kyoung@barstow.edu
YOUNG, Kristen 702-895-0143 302 I kristen.young@unlv.edu

ZAKEL, Lori 937-512-2881 401 J
lori.zakel@sinclair.edu
ZAKERY, Fatemeh 314-256-8163 282 F
zakeryf@hssu.edu
ZAKOWSKI, Paul 630-942-2895 148 A
zakows@cod.edu
ZAKRI, Kathleen, M 315-652-6500 324 L
kzakri@bryantstratton.edu
ZAKRZEWSKI, Mary 215-885-2360 435 E
mzak@manor.edu
ZALABAK, Robert 630-657-7020 19 A
robert.zalabak@phoenix.edu
ZALACCA, James, A 315-267-2314 354 C
zalaccja@potsdam.edu
ZALAPI, Diane 248-476-1122 254 G
dzalapi@mispp.edu
ZALESKY, Maria 951-343-4358 31 J
mzalesky@calbaptist.edu
ZALETEL, Cora 719-549-2576 83 H
cora.zaletel@colostate-pueblo.edu
ZALOOM, Victor 409-880-8229 501 A
victor.zaloom@lamar.edu
ZALOT, Marcella, K 207-859-4904 217 G
mkzalot@colby.edu
ZAMBARDI, Victor, A 248-370-3112 256 G
zambardi@oakland.edu
ZAMBELLA, BethAnn 717-361-1428 428 F
zambellab@etown.edu
ZAMBELLI, William, W 914-337-9300 330 G
william.zambelli@concordia-ny.edu
ZAMBITO, Angela, R 304-336-8490 544 D
azambito@westliberty.edu
ZAMBLE, Anthony 773-244-5568 159 H
azamble@northpark.edu
ZAMBONI, Garnett 785-825-5422 191 E
kzamboni@brownmackie.edu
ZAMBONINO, Maria 773-878-3813 163 F
mzambonino@staugustine.edu
ZAMBRANA, Maritza 787-279-1912 563 D
mzambrana@bayamon.inter.edu
ZAMBRANO, Thomas 732-987-2613 310 C
zambrano@georgian.edu
ZAMBRUN, Christina 260-665-4242 180 D
zambrunc@trine.edu
ZAMOJSKI, David 617-353-4380 232 E
zamojski@bu.edu
ZAMORA, Felix, A 214-860-8700 485 B
fzamora@dcccd.edu
ZAMORA, Juan 305-628-6593 117 A
jzamora@stu.edu
ZAMORA, Teri 956-364-4400 500 D
teri.zamora@tstc.edu
ZAMORA-AGUILAR, Beatrice 619-482-6379 71 D
bzamora@swccd.edu
ZAMPANO, Gary, S 570-941-4273 450 C
gary.zampano1@scranton.edu
ZAMUDIO, Cynthia 210-486-4601 479 B
czamudio1@alamo.edu
ZANDBERGEN, Dianne, V 616-222-3000 253 F
diannez@kuyper.edu
ZANDER, Douglas 717-872-3371 443 D
doug.zander@millersville.edu
ZANDER, Kirk 406-756-3806 294 C
kzander@fvcc.edu
ZANDERS, Ann 225-216-8723 209 H
zandersa@mybrcc.edu
ZANDERS, Joan, A 703-323-3014 527 F
jzanders@nvcc.edu
ZANE, Cynthia, A 716-926-8923 335 E
czane@hilbert.edu
ZANE, Gary 207-948-9241 219 H
gzane@unity.edu
ZANE, Ken 860-628-4751 93 C
kzane@lincolncollegene.edu
ZANELLA-LITKE, Joanne 508-999-8942 237 A
jzanella@umassd.edu
ZANETTI, Erika, P 713-348-2939 493 C
epz@rice.edu
ZANETTI, Mary, L 508-856-6009 237 C
mary.zanetti@umassmed.edu
ZANFINI-PARKER, Christine 508-767-7329 230 D
chparker@assumption.edu
ZANG, Connie 740-366-9246 386 H
czang@cotc.edu
ZANG, Frank 208-426-5391 142 I
frankzang@boisestate.edu
ZANG, Paul 810-766-4112 248 C
paul.zang@baker.edu
ZANGAGLIA, Eric 814-269-7005 449 D
zangagli@pitt.edu
ZANGER, Kate 563-588-6313 183 E
kate.zanger@clarke.edu
ZANGHI, Palma 716-896-0700 359 H
zanghi@villa.edu
ZANGHI, Palma, M 716-896-0700 359 H
zanghi@villa.edu
ZANGO-HALEY, Linda 718-262-2495 329 A
lzangohaley@york.cuny.edu
ZANIOS, Jamie, T 641-422-4162 188 A
zaniojam@niacc.edu
ZANJANI, Mellissia 609-586-4800 311 B
zanjanim@mccc.edu

ZANK, Gary 256-824-6575 8 G
gary.zank@uah.edu
ZANKICH, Mark, A 310-233-4171 54 I
zankicma@lahc.edu
ZANKO, Michael 973-655-5457 311 F
zankom@mail.montclair.edu
ZANON, Lewis 847-855-2649 149 I
lzanon@keller.edu
ZANSITIS, Richard, A 713-348-5237 493 C
zansitis@rice.edu
ZANT, Don 662-325-2231 275 F
dzant@budgetplan.msstate.edu
ZAPALSKA, Alina, M 860-444-8334 558 H
alina.m.zapalska@uscg.mil
ZAPATA, Fred 210-999-7401 502 E
fred.zapata@trinity.edu
ZAPATA, Jesse, T 210-458-2700 506 D
jesse.zapata@utsa.edu
ZAPATA, Rafael, A 401-865-2878 453 H
rzapata@providence.edu
ZAPATA, Sergio 915-351-8100 480 C
ZAPOLSKI, Mike 309-794-7223 145 E
mikezapolski@augustana.edu
ZAPPALA, Henry, W 617-824-8281 234 B
hank_zappala@emerson.edu
ZAPPALORTI, Robert, E 203-287-3028 93 F
paier.admin@snet.net
ZAPPE, Christopher 717-337-6820 429 I
czappe@gettysburg.edu
ZAPPI, Mark, E 337-482-6685 216 D
zappi@louisiana.edu
ZAPPIA, Gerard 585-389-2570 342 D
gzappia4@naz.edu
ZAPPONE, Michael 412-291-6248 422 E
mzappone@aii.edu
ZAPROROZHETZ, Laurene, E 937-255-5894 557 C
laurene.zaporozhetz@afit.edu
ZARAGOZA, Federico 210-485-0015 479 A
fzaragoza@alamo.edu
ZARCHI, Shloime 718-434-0784 325 I
ZAREMBA, Terah 269-965-3931 253 B
zarembat@kellogg.edu
ZARET, David 812-855-5021 173 D
zaret@iu.edu
ZARET, David 812-855-5021 173 E
zaret@indiana.edu
ZAREVA, John 503-255-0332 417 C
jzareva@multnomah.edu
ZARIAROW, Esmail 954-783-7339 106 J
ezariarow@cci.edu
ZARING, Gayle 618-544-8657 152 H
zaringg@iecc.edu
ZARKOWSKI, Pamela 313-993-1585 258 G
zarkowp1@udmercy.edu
ZARLING, Mark, G 507-354-8221 264 K
zarlinmg@mlc-wels.edu
ZARNDT, Jason 502-495-1040 200 C
jzarndt@daymarcollege.edu
ZAROD, Joan 212-686-0620 322 G
ZAROS, Alexander 732-235-9738 317 A
zarosaj@umdnj.edu
ZARR, Joel 719-549-3062 87 F
joel.zarr@pueblocc.edu
ZARRAS, Ginny 313-593-5666 259 B
gzarras@umd.umich.edu
ZARRILLO, Deirdre 518-292-1704 348 A
zarrid@sage.edu
ZARRINNAM, Ali, R 608-246-6446 554 D
azarrinnam@madisoncollege.edu
ZARTERN, Ken 432-335-6606 492 A
kzartner@odessa.edu
ZARUBA, Charlie 863-686-1444 106 E
czaruba@cci.edu
ZASTE, Kathe 701-477-7862 383 F
kzaste@tm.edu
ZASTOUPIL, Brenda 701-355-8244 383 H
brendaz@umary.edu
ZATAR, Wael 304-696-6043 544 B
zatar@marshall.edu
ZAUFT, Richard 617-824-8912 234 B
richard_zauft@emerson.edu
ZAVADA, Michael, S 973-761-9022 315 B
michael.zavada@shu.edu
ZAVADA, Paul 262-551-2158 546 I
pzavada@carthage.edu
ZAVADA, Robert 570-674-8018 436 F
rzavada@misericordia.edu
ZAVAGNO, James 510-885-4149 34 E
jim.zavagno@csueastbay.edu
ZAVALA, Joseph 858-642-8024 58 I
jzavala@nu.edu
ZAVALA-COLÓN, Maria de los Angeles 787-993-8877 567 B
maria.zavala1@upr.edu
ZAVALA-QUIÑONES, Javier 787-993-8854 567 B
javier.zavala@upr.edu
ZAVORSKY, Gerald, S 570-340-6059 435 F
zavorsky@marywood.edu
ZAWACKI, Rosemary 810-766-4028 247 G
rosemary.zawacki@baker.edu
ZAWACKI, Rosemary 810-766-4028 248 C
rosemary.zawacki@baker.edu

ZAWALICH, Barbara 508-849-3401 230 C
bzawalich@annamaria.edu
ZAWIA, Nasser, H 401-874-5909 454 E
nzawia@uri.edu
ZAWISLAK, Susan, E 302-453-3721 96 F
zawislak@dtcc.edu
ZAWISTOWSKI, Lee 845-569-3229 342 A
lee.zawistowski@msmc.edu
ZAWODNY, Laurel, E 419-372-2211 385 E
lzawodn@bgsu.edu
ZAYAITZ, Anne, E 610-683-4305 443 A
zayaitz@kutztown.edu
ZAYAN, Margaret, H 203-576-4956 94 F
mzayan@bridgeport.edu
ZAYAS, Brendaliz 787-258-1501 561 F
bzayas@columbiaco.edu
ZAYAS, Haydee 787-480-2440 561 E
hzayas@sanjuancapital.com
ZAYAS, Luis, H 512-471-1937 505 D
lzayas@austin.utexas.edu
ZAYAS, Myriam 787-841-2000 565 B
mzayas@pucpr.edu
ZAYAS, Nelson 727-784-0003 103 B
nzayas@cfi.edu
ZAYAS, Niza 787-786-3030 560 G
nzayas@ucb.edu.pr
ZAYTOUN, Kelli 937-775-4818 406 C
kelli.zaytoun@wright.edu
ZAZUETA, Fedro, S 352-392-0365 120 C
fsz@ufl.edu
ZAZZALI, Robert 856-256-4110 314 A
zazzali@rowan.edu
ZBOCK, Jason 607-778-5024 324 G
zbockjp@sunybroome.edu
ZDANCEWICZ, Heather 703-461-1716 522 I
hzdancewicz@vts.edu
ZDEBLICK, Mick 312-942-7881 163 D
mick_zdeblick@rush.edu
ZDZIARSKI, II, Eugene, L 540-375-2592 523 G
zdziarski@roanoke.edu
ZEALAND, Matthew, J 434-582-2000 520 K
mjzealan@liberty.edu
ZEBEDIS, Frank, J 803-323-3333 463 E
zebedisf@winthrop.edu
ZEBROWSKI, Michael, J 414-288-7172 548 F
michael.zebrowski@marquette.edu
ZECCA, Frank 956-665-5078 506 C
zecca@utpa.edu
ZECCA, Marie 267-341-3650 431 A
mzecca@holyfamily.edu
ZECH, Susan 323-464-2777 27 I
ZECH, Susan 212-686-9244 322 G
ZECKOVICH, Kim 906-932-4231 251 C
kimz@gogebic.edu
ZEEK, Raymond 203-285-2210 91 D
rzeek@gwcc.commnet.edu
ZEFF, Ira, A 402-465-2360 299 H
izeff@nebrwesleyan.edu
ZEFF, Jane 973-720-2379 317 D
zeffj@wpunj.edu
ZEGARSKI, Len 619-684-8788 59 B
lzegarski@newschoolarch.edu
ZEGER, Brian 212-799-5000 337 H
ZEGER, Scott, L 410-516-8770 223 F
scott.zeger@jhu.edu
ZEGESTOWSKY, Jane, R 215-885-2360 435 E
jzegestowsky@manor.edu
ZEGLEN, Marie 352-392-0456 120 C
zeglenm@ufl.edu
ZEHR, David 603-535-2235 307 A
zehr@plymouth.edu
ZEHREN, Carolyn, F 218-477-2085 267 F
zehren@mnstate.edu
ZEICH, Heidi, E 202-319-5615 97 E
zeich@cua.edu
ZEIDENSTEIN, Darrow 713-348-6090 493 C
darrowz@rice.edu
ZEIFANG, Kathleen 703-284-1543 521 D
kathleen.zeifang@marymount.edu
ZEIGER, Britt 641-472-1126 187 E
housing@mum.edu
ZEIGER, Spencer 706-272-2480 128 C
szeiger@daltonstate.edu
ZEIGLER, Michael 803-535-5340 456 D
mike.zeigler@claflin.edu
ZEIGLER, Michael, C 717-867-6060 434 C
zeigler@lvc.edu
ZEIGLER, Robert 210-486-0961 479 A
rzeigler@alamo.edu
ZEIGLER, Robert, E 210-486-0959 479 E
rzeigler@alamo.edu
ZEIGLER, Sara 859-622-2222 200 J
sara.zeigler@eku.edu
ZEILE, Carol 989-463-7227 247 B
zeile@alma.edu
ZEILENGA, Jeffrey 573-882-5397 291 B
zeilingaj@missouri.edu
ZEILER, Tennille 562-997-5491 44 H
tzeiler@devry.edu
ZEILMAN, JR., Charles 318-473-6486 212 I
czeilman@lsua.edu
ZEIMET, Dan, L 563-333-6202 188 F
zeimetdaniell@sau.edu

ZEIS, TOR, Gabriel 814-472-3001 446 B
gzeis@francis.edu
ZEISER, Richard, A 860-768-4181 95 B
zeiser@hartford.edu
ZEISS, P. Anthony 704-330-6566 369 D
tony.zeiss@cpcc.edu
ZEISS, Timothy 732-224-2887 308 A
tzeiss@brookdalecc.edu
ZEITHAML, Carl, P 434-924-3176 525 F
cpz6n@virginia.edu
ZEITLOW, Terry 574-257-3310 169 I
zeitlt@bethelcollege.edu
ZEITZER, Glen 973-278-5400 307 F
gz@berkeleycollege.edu
ZEITZER, Glen 212-986-4343 323 H
gz@berkeleycollege.edu
ZELECHOWSKI, Deborah 773-697-2200 149 D
dzelechowski@devry.edu
ZELENAK, Christine 609-896-5395 313 F
czelenak@rider.edu
ZELENSKI, Paul 517-371-5140 258 F
zelensp@cooley.edu
ZELENZ, Margot 218-723-6460 262 G
mzelenz@css.edu
ZELESKY, Jason 508-793-7423 233 B
jzelesky@clarku.edu
ZELESNIK, Kelly 440-365-5222 395 D
ZELEZA, SJ, Paul, T 310-338-2716 56 E
paul.zeleza@lmu.edu
ZELEZNY, Lynnette 559-278-2636 35 A
lynnette@csufresno.edu
ZELEZNY, Lynnette 559-278-0333 35 A
lynnette@csufresno.edu
ZELLER, Florence, D 215-871-6120 444 C
florencez@pcom.edu
ZELLER, John, H 215-898-5169 448 J
jzeller@ben.dev.upenn.edu
ZELLER, Lisa, L 303-963-3210 82 C
lzeller@ccu.edu
ZELLERS, Andrew 270-831-9627 202 D
andrew.zellers@kctcs.edu
ZELLERS, Jeff, W 740-826-8139 397 A
jzellers@muskingum.edu
ZELLMER, Aaron 952-562-4200 464 H
ZELLMER, Jill, A 617-627-3298 245 C
jill.zellmer@tufts.edu
ZELLO, Gary 317-613-4800 169 F
ZELTWANGER, Todd 574-936-8898 169 D
todd.zeltwanger@ancilla.edu
ZEMAN, Janet 845-569-3159 342 A
janet.zeman@msmc.edu
ZEMAN, Mary 860-509-9502 93 A
mzeman@hartsem.edu
ZEMAN, Mary Beth 973-720-2971 317 D
zemanm@wpunj.edu
ZEMBLE, Stephen 602-387-7000 19 A
stephen.zemble@phoenix.edu
ZEMBRODT, Belle 859-572-5634 205 H
zembrodt@nku.edu
ZEMEK, Anne 832-813-6538 490 E
anne.zemek@lonestar.edu
ZEMKE, Mary Ann 541-885-1105 418 E
maryann.zemke@oit.edu
ZENCHECK, Jack 718-430-8889 361 M
zencheck@yu.edu
ZENELIS, John, G 703-993-2223 519 E
jzenelis@gmu.edu
ZENG, Zheng 512-454-1188 480 F
info@aoma.edu
ZENGER, Sheahon 785-864-3143 197 B
kuathletics@ku.edu
ZENNER, Art 405-733-7343 411 I
azenner@rose.edu
ZENO, Mark 419-448-2058 391 F
mzeno@heidelberg.edu
ZENO, Sonnybel 787-763-3393 562 I
szeno@inter.edu
ZENSEN, Sanford 423-775-7255 467 F
zensensa@bryan.edu
ZENTMEYER, James, R 248-370-3570 256 G
zentmeye@oakland.edu
ZENZ, Cathy 808-974-7326 141 F
zenz@hawaii.edu
ZENZ, David, M 517-437-7341 252 C
david.zenz@hillsdale.edu
ZEONE, Alicia 217-479-7059 157 F
alicia.zeone@mac.edu
ZEPEDA, Andrea 918-335-6833 411 B
azepeda@okwu.edu
ZEPH, Lucille, A 207-581-3113 220 A
lzeph@maine.edu
ZEPPOS, Nicholas 615-322-1813 478 A
nick.zeppos@vanderbilt.edu
ZERA, Richard 978-934-2654 237 B
richard_zera@uml.edu
ZERAH, Carol 516-299-3952 339 A
carol.zerah@liu.edu
ZERBE, Jack 336-316-2351 365 A
jzerbe@guilford.edu
ZERBE, Linda 610-282-1100 427 A
linda.zerbe@desales.edu
ZERBONIA, Lisa 563-441-2454 186 I
lzerbonia@kucampus.edu

ZORIC, Joseph .... 740-284-5801.... 391 A
jzoric@franciscan.edu
ZORN, David, C .... 303-837-0825...... 81 F
zornd@aii.edu
ZORN, Diane .... 941-955-8862.... 116 B
ZORN, Jenny .... 909-537-5024...... 36 B
jzorn@csusb.edu
ZORN, Linda .... 530-879-9069...... 31 H
zornli@butte.edu
ZOU, Bingzeng .... 415-282-7600...... 28 B
bingzou@actem.edu
ZOUMADAKIS, Bill .... 801-957-4042.... 512 D
bill.zoumadakis@slcc.edu
ZOZAYA, Pat .... 702-651-5078.... 302 E
pat.zozaya@csn.edu
ZRALY, Sharon .... 845-452-1614.... 331 E
s_zraly@culinary.edu
ZRIMSEK, Becky .... 507-222-4160.... 261 G
rzrimsek@carleton.edu
ZUBERBUELER, OP,
Mary Anne .... 615-297-7545.... 467 A
srmanne@aquinascollege.edu
ZUBIZARRETA, John .... 803-786-3014.... 457 C
jzubizarreta@columbiasc.edu
ZUCALLA, Fred, P .... 315-733-2300.... 359 C
fzucalla@uscny.edu
ZUCCARELLI, Anthony, J ... 909-558-4528...... 54 D
azuccarelli@llu.edu
ZUCCARELLO, Patricia .... 708-709-2947.... 161 D
pzuccarello@prairiestate.edu
ZUCCHETTO, Vincent .... 718-960-8242.... 327 C
vincent.zucchetto@lehman.cuny.edu
ZUCCONI, Michael, J .... 540-432-4211.... 518 F
michael.zucconi@emu.edu
ZUCKER, Avraham .... 718-382-8702.... 361 C
ZUCKER, Lauren .... 610-543-2500...... 99 G
ZUCKER, Nicole, M .... 215-572-2103.... 422 C
zuckern@arcadia.edu
ZUCKERMAN-AVILES,
Stephanie, B .... 716-878-5811.... 353 A
zuckersb@buffalostate.edu
ZUDEKOFF, Rosanne .... 203-773-8502...... 90 C
zudekoff@albertus.edu
ZUEHLKE, Karen, A .... 920-924-6320.... 554 G
zkuehlke@morainepark.edu
ZUELKE, Bill .... 503-534-4073.... 416 J
bzuelke@marylhurst.edu
ZUG, Mary Ann .... 515-271-1440.... 184 A
maryann.zug@dmu.edu
ZUHLKE, James .... 610-436-3316.... 444 A
jzuhlke@wcupa.edu
ZUICHES, Carol .... 773-702-8604.... 166 G
czuiches@uchicago.edu
ZUIDEMA, Leah .... 712-722-6328.... 184 C
lzuidema@dordt.edu
ZUKER, Fred .... 281-487-1170.... 499 B
fzuker@txchiro.edu
ZUKOR, Tevya .... 412-648-7930.... 449 A
tez5@pitt.edu
ZUKOSKI, Charles, F .... 716-645-2992.... 351 G
provost@buffalo.edu
ZUKOWSKI, Joanne .... 803-325-2873.... 463 H
jzukowski@yorktech.edu
ZULUAGA, Hoober .... 516-918-3679.... 324 E
hzuluaga@bcl.edu
ZUMBACH, Deborah, J ...... 319-335-3815.... 182 F
deborah-zumbach@uiowa.edu
ZUMWALT, Debra, L .... 650-723-6397...... 71 G
zumwalt@stanford.edu
ZUMWINKEL, Donna .... 314-984-7590.... 289 A
dzumwinkel@stlcc.edu
ZUNIGA, Donna, P .... 936-291-0452.... 489 M
dzuniga@lee.edu
ZUNIGA, Kelly .... 713-718-8596.... 487 I
kelly.zuniga@hccs.edu
ZUNIGA, Leo .... 210-485-0035.... 479 A
lzuniga@alamo.edu
ZUPAN, Mark .... 585-275-3316.... 359 B
mark.zupan@simon.rochester.edu
ZUPANCICH, Patti .... 218-235-2166.... 269 F
p.zupancich@vcc.edu
ZURAW, Peter .... 781-283-2474.... 245 E
pzuraw@wellesley.edu
ZURAWSKA, Izabela .... 708-456-0300.... 166 F
izurawsk@triton.edu
ZURAWSKY, Walter .... 718-260-3725.... 346 C
zurawsky@poly.edu
ZUREK, Ronald, M .... 775-784-4031.... 303 A
zurek@unr.edu
ZURZOLO, Debbie .... 575-769-4030.... 318 A
debbie.zurzolo@clovis.edu
ZUSCHIN, Andrea, P .... 540-365-4456.... 519 C
azuschin@ferrum.edu
ZUZACK, Judith, A .... 724-287-8711.... 423 G
judith.zuzack@bc3.edu
ZUZEVICH, Theresa .... 661-362-3644...... 41 I
theresa.zuzevich@canyons.edu
ZUZOLO, Renee .... 330-652-9919.... 390 H
reneezuzolo@eticollege.edu
ZVACEK, Susan, M .... 785-864-2600.... 197 B
szvacek@ku.edu
ZVARITCH, Jeanne .... 330-337-6403.... 383 J
college@awc.edu
ZVOSEC, Almut .... 216-421-7447.... 388 A
azvosec@cia.edu
ZWEIG, Yitzchak .... 305-534-7050.... 122 B
yzweig@talmudicu.edu
ZWEIG, Yochanan .... 305-534-7050.... 122 B
rosh@talmudicu.edu
ZWICK, Ann, O .... 606-679-8501.... 203 C
ann.zwick@kctcs.edu
ZWICKEY, Heather .... 503-552-1742.... 417 D
hzwickey@ncnm.edu
ZWIER, Robert .... 585-594-6659.... 347 F
zwier_robert@roberts.edu
ZWINGER, Sarah, E .... 724-458-2183.... 430 B
sezwinger@gcc.edu
ZWIREN, Martin .... 718-960-1117.... 327 C
martin.zwiren@lehman.cuny.edu
ZWISLER, Stasia .... 847-574-5222.... 156 A
szwisler@lfgsm.edu
ZYLSTRA, Art .... 206-264-9100.... 531 D
artz@bgu.edu
ZYLSTRA, Brian .... 641-628-5641.... 183 D
zylstrab@central.edu
ZYLSTRA, James .... 608-266-1739.... 553 F
james.zylstra@wtcsystem.edu
ZYMARIS, Joyce .... 508-588-9100.... 240 A

Accreditation Index of Institutions by Regional, National, Professional and Specialized Agencies

Degree levels are shown by the following symbols: (C) diploma/certificate; (A) associate; (B) baccalaureate; (M) master's; (S) beyond master's but less than doctorate; (FP) first professional; (D) doctorate.

AA: Commission on Accreditation of Allied Health Education Programs: anesthesiologist assistant (M)

AAB: Aviation Accreditation Board International: aviation (A,B,M)

AAFCS: American Association of Family and Consumer Sciences: family and consumer science (B)

ABHES: Accrediting Bureau of Health Education Schools: allied health (C,A,B)

ACAE: Accreditation Commission for Audiology Education: audiology (D)

ACBSP: Accreditation Council for Business Schools and Programs: business administration, management, accounting and related business fields (A,B,M,D)

ACCSC: Accrediting Commission of Career Schools and Colleges: occupational, trade, and technical education (C,A,B,M)

ACFEI: American Culinary Federation, Inc.: culinary arts and culinary management (C,A,B)

Art Institute of Colorado, The ... CO ... 81
Pikes Peak Community College ... CO ... 87
Pueblo Community College ... CO ... 87
Manchester Community College ... CT ... 91
Delaware Technical Community College, Stanton-Wilmington Campus ... DE ... 96
Delaware Technical Community College, Terry Campus ... DE ... 96
Art Institute of California, A College of Argosy University - San Diego, Th ... CA ... 30
Art Institute of Fort Lauderdale, The ... FL ... 101
Florida State College at Jacksonville ... FL ... 109
Gulf Coast State College ... FL ... 110
Hillsborough Community College ... FL ... 110
Keiser University ... FL ... 112
Le Cordon Bleu College of Culinary Arts in Miami ... FL ... 112
Le Cordon Bleu College of Culinary Arts in Orlando ... FL ... 113
Lincoln College of Technology ... FL ... 113
Pensacola State College ... FL ... 115
Art Institute of Atlanta, The ... GA ... 125
Chattahoochee Technical College ... GA ... 127
College of Coastal Georgia ... GA ... 127
Gwinnett Technical College ... GA ... 132
Le Cordon Bleu College of Culinary Arts in Atlanta ... GA ... 133
North Georgia Technical College ... GA ... 135
Savannah Technical College ... GA ... 136
Kapiolani Community College ... HI ... 141
University of Hawaii Hawaii Community College ... HI ... 142
University of Hawaii Kauai Community College ... HI ... 142
University of Hawaii Leeward Community College ... HI ... 142
University of Hawaii Maui College ... HI ... 142
Boise State University ... ID ... 142
Idaho State University ... ID ... 143
College of DuPage ... IL ... 148
Illinois Institute of Art, The ... IL ... 153
Joliet Junior College ... IL ... 154
Kendall College ... IL ... 155
Le Cordon Bleu College of Culinary Arts in Chicago ... IL ... 156
Southwestern Illinois College ... IL ... 165
Harrison College - Indianapolis Downtown Campus ... IN ... 172
Ivy Tech Community College-Central Indiana IN ... 175
Ivy Tech Community College of Indiana-Bloomington ... IN ... 175
Ivy Tech Community College of Indiana-East Central ... IN ... 176
Ivy Tech Community College of Indiana-North Central ... IN ... 176
Ivy Tech Community College of Indiana-Northeast ... IN ... 176
Ivy Tech Community College of Indiana-Northwest ... IN ... 176
Des Moines Area Community College ... IA ... 183
Indian Hills Community College ... IA ... 185
Iowa Western Community College ... IA ... 186
Kirkwood Community College ... IA ... 187
Johnson County Community College ... KS ... 194
Bowling Green Technical College ... KY ... 201
Jefferson Community and Technical College KY ... 202
Sullivan University ... KY ... 206
West Kentucky Community and Technical College ... KY ... 203
Bossier Parish Community College ... LA ... 209
Capital Area Technical College Baton Rouge Campus ... LA ... 209
Delgado Community College ... LA ... 210
South Louisiana Community College Ardoin Campus ... LA ... 211
Southern Maine Community College ... ME ... 219
Anne Arundel Community College ... MD ... 221
Wor-Wic Community College ... MD ... 229
Holyoke Community College ... MA ... 239
Salter College ... MA ... 244
Art Institute of Michigan, The ... MI ... 247
Baker College of Muskegon ... MI ... 248
Grand Rapids Community College ... MI ... 251
Henry Ford Community College ... MI ... 252
Macomb Community College ... MI ... 254
Northwestern Michigan College ... MI ... 256
Oakland Community College ... MI ... 256
Schoolcraft College ... MI ... 258
Washtenaw Community College ... MI ... 259
Art Institutes International Minnesota, The ... MN ... 261
Hennepin Technical College ... MN ... 266
Le Cordon Bleu College of Culinary Arts in Minneapolis/St Paul ... MN ... 264
Saint Paul College-A Community & Technical College ... MN ... 269
East Central College ... MO ... 281
Hickey College ... MO ... 282
L'Ecole Culinaire ... MO ... 283
Ozarks Technical Community College ... MO ... 287
Saint Louis Community College at Forest Park ... MO ... 288
University of Montana - College of Technology, The ... MT ... 295
Metropolitan Community College ... NE ... 298
Southeast Community College ... NE ... 300
Art Institute of Las Vegas, The ... NV ... 301
College of Southern Nevada ... NV ... 302
Le Cordon Bleu College of Culinary Arts in Las Vegas ... NV ... 302
Truckee Meadows Community College ... NV ... 302
Southern New Hampshire University ... NH ... 305
Atlantic Cape Community College ... NJ ... 307
Hudson County Community College ... NJ ... 310
Central New Mexico Community College ... NM ... 317
Navajo Technical College ... NM ... 318
Monroe College ... NY ... 341
Paul Smith's College ... NY ... 345
Schenectady County Community College ... NY ... 350
State University of New York College of Agriculture and Technology at Coble skill .. NY ... 354
State University of New York College of Technology at Delhi ... NY ... 355
Alamance Community College ... NC ... 368
Art Institute of Charlotte, The ... NC ... 362
Asheville - Buncombe Technical Community College ... NC ... 368
Central Piedmont Community College ... NC ... 369
Guilford Technical Community College ... NC ... 371
Lenoir Community College ... NC ... 371
Wake Technical Community College ... NC ... 374
Art Institute of Ohio-Cincinnati, The ... OH ... 384
Cincinnati State Technical and Community College ... OH ... 387
Columbus State Community College ... OH ... 389
Cuyahoga Community College ... OH ... 389
Hocking College ... OH ... 391
Sinclair Community College ... OH ... 401
Zane State College ... OH ... 407
Platt College ... OK ... 411
Platt College-OKC Central ... OK ... 411
Lane Community College ... OR ... 416
Le Cordon Bleu College of Culinary Arts in Portland ... OR ... 416
Southwestern Oregon Community College ... OR ... 420
Art Institute of Philadelphia ... PA ... 422
Art Institute of Pittsburgh ... PA ... 422
Harrisburg Area Community College ... PA ... 430
Indiana University of Pennsylvania ... PA ... 442
Pennsylvania College of Technology ... PA ... 440
Westmoreland County Community College .. PA ... 451
YTI Career Institute ... PA ... 452
Universidad del Este ... PR ... 565
Greenville Technical College ... SC ... 458
Horry-Georgetown Technical College ... SC ... 458
Spartanburg Community College ... SC ... 461
Trident Technical College ... SC ... 461
Nashville State Community College ... TN ... 475
Walters State Community College ... TN ... 476
Art Institute of Dallas ... TX ... 480
Art Institute of Houston, The ... TX ... 480
Austin Community College District ... TX ... 481
Culinary Institute LeNotre ... TX ... 484
Del Mar College ... TX ... 485
El Centro College ... TX ... 485
Lamar University ... TX ... 501
Le Cordon Bleu College of Culinary Arts in Austin ... TX ... 489
St. Philip's College ... TX ... 479
San Jacinto College North ... TX ... 494
Salt Lake Community College ... UT ... 512
Dabney S. Lancaster Community College ... VA ... 526
ECPI College of Technology ... VA ... 518
J. Sargeant Reynolds Community College ... VA ... 527
Stratford University ... VA ... 524
Tidewater Community College ... VA ... 528
Art Institute of Seattle, The ... WA ... 531
Bellingham Technical College ... WA ... 531
Lake Washington Institute of Technology ... WA ... 535
Olympic College ... WA ... 536
Renton Technical College ... WA ... 537
Seattle Central Community College ... WA ... 537
Skagit Valley College ... WA ... 538
South Puget Sound Community College ... WA ... 538
Spokane Community College ... WA ... 533
Walla Walla University ... WA ... 539
Mountain State University ... WV ... 541
Pierpont Community & Technical College ... WV ... 543
West Virginia Northern Community College .. WV ... 543
Blackhawk Technical College ... WI ... 553
Fox Valley Technical College ... WI ... 554
Madison Area Technical College ... WI ... 554
Milwaukee Area Technical College ... WI ... 554
Waukesha County Technical College ... WI ... 555

ACICS: Accrediting Council for Independent Colleges and Schools: business and business related programs (C,A,B,M)

Fortis Institute ... AL ... 3
ITT Technical Institute ... AL ... 4
Prince Institute - Southeast ... AL ... 6
Virginia College ... AL ... 3
Charter College ... AK ... 10
Anthem College ... AZ ... 11
Art Institute of Phoenix, The ... AZ ... 12
Art Institute of Tucson, The ... AZ ... 12
Brookline College ... AZ ... 12
Brown Mackie College-Phoenix ... AZ ... 12
Brown Mackie College-Tucson ... AZ ... 12
Bryman School, The ... AZ ... 12
Carrington College - Mesa ... AZ ... 12
Carrington College - Phoenix ... AZ ... 13
Carrington College - Tucson ... AZ ... 13
Carrington College - Westside ... AZ ... 13
Golf Academy of America ... AZ ... 14
ITT Technical Institute ... AZ ... 14
Lamson College ... AZ ... 15
Le Cordon Bleu College of Culinary Arts in Scottsdale ... AZ ... 15
Sanford-Brown College ... AZ ... 18
Bryan College ... AR ... 21
ITT Technical Institute ... AR ... 22
Academy of Couture Art ... CA ... 26
American University of Health Sciences ... CA ... 28
Bergin University of Canine Studies ... CA ... 30
Bristol University ... CA ... 31
Brooks Institute ... CA ... 31
Bryan College ... CA ... 31
California Culinary Academy ... CA ... 32
California International Business University .. CA ... 33
California Miramar University ... CA ... 33
California University of Management and Sciences ... CA ... 37
Cambridge Junior College ... CA ... 38
Charter College-Oxnard ... CA ... 39
Coleman University ... CA ... 41
Design Institute of San Diego ... CA ... 44
Empire College School of Business ... CA ... 45
Everest College-Ontario Metro ... CA ... 46
Everest College-San Bernardino ... CA ... 46
Fashion Careers College ... CA ... 46
Golf Academy of America ... CA ... 48
International Academy of Design and Technology ... CA ... 51
ITT Technical Institute ... CA ... 51
ITT Technical Institute ... CA ... 52
Kaplan College ... CA ... 52
LA College International ... CA ... 53
Le Cordon Bleu College of Culinary Arts in Los Angeles ... CA ... 53
Lincoln University ... CA ... 54
NewSchool of Architecture and Design ... CA ... 59
Northwestern Polytechnic University ... CA ... 59
Pacific States University ... CA ... 60
Professional Golfers Career College ... CA ... 63
Sage College ... CA ... 64
Santa Barbara Business College ... CA ... 67
Santa Barbara Business College ... CA ... 68
Silicon Valley University ... CA ... 69
South Coast College ... CA ... 70
Southern States University ... CA ... 71
University of Antelope Valley ... CA ... 73
West Coast University ... CA ... 78
Westwood College-Anaheim ... CA ... 79
Westwood College-Inland Empire ... CA ... 79
Westwood College - Los Angeles Campus .. CA ... 79
Westwood College-South Bay ... CA ... 79
Anthem College ... CO ... 81
Colorado Heights University ... CO ... 82
Everest College ... CO ... 84
Institute of Business and Medical Careers ... CO ... 85
ITT Technical Institute ... CO ... 85
Prince Institute-Rocky Mountains ... CO ... 87
Redstone College ... CO ... 87
Remington College-Colorado Springs ... CO ... 88
Westwood College-Denver North ... CO ... 89
Westwood College-Denver South ... CO ... 89
Sanford-Brown College-Farmington ... CT ... 94
Radians College ... DC ... 99
Art Institute of Fort Lauderdale, The ... FL ... 101
Brown Mackie College-Miami ... FL ... 102
City College ... FL ... 103
College of Business and Technology ... FL ... 103
Digital Media Arts College ... FL ... 105
Everest Institute ... FL ... 105
Everest Institute ... FL ... 106
Everest University-Brandon Campus ... FL ... 106
Everest University-Jacksonville Campus ... FL ... 106
Everest University-Lakeland Campus ... FL ... 106
Everest University-Largo ... FL ... 106
Everest University-Melbourne Campus ... FL ... 106
Everest University-North Orlando Campus ... FL ... 106
Everest University-Orange Park ... FL ... 106
Everest University-Pompano Beach Campus FL ... 106
Everest University-South Orlando Campus ... FL ... 106
Everest University-Tampa Campus ... FL ... 107
Florida Career College ... FL ... 107
Florida Technical College ... FL ... 109
Florida Technical College ... FL ... 110
Fortis College ... FL ... 110
Golf Academy of America ... FL ... 110
International Academy of Design and Technology ... FL ... 111
International Academy of Design and Technology-Online ... FL ... 111
ITT Technical Institute ... FL ... 111
Jones College ... FL ... 112
Jose Maria Vargas University ... FL ... 112
Kaplan College ... FL ... 112
Key College ... FL ... 112
Le Cordon Bleu College of Culinary Arts in Miami ... FL ... 112
Le Cordon Bleu College of Culinary Arts in Orlando ... FL ... 113
Lincoln College of Technology ... FL ... 113
Millennia Atlantic University ... FL ... 113
Professional Golfers Career College ... FL ... 115
Professional Training Center ... FL ... 115
Sanford-Brown Institute ... FL ... 117
Schiller International University ... FL ... 117
Southern Career College ... FL ... 118
Southern Technical College ... FL ... 118
Southwest Florida College ... FL ... 118
Stenotype Institute of Jacksonville ... FL ... 121
Virginia College ... FL ... 123
Brown Mackie College-Atlanta ... GA ... 126
Gwinnett College ... GA ... 132
ITT Technical Institute ... GA ... 132
Le Cordon Bleu College of Culinary Arts in Atlanta ... GA ... 133
Lincoln College of Technology ... GA ... 133
Sanford-Brown College ... GA ... 136
Westwood College-Atlanta Midtown ... GA ... 139
Westwood College-Atlanta Northlake ... GA ... 139
Brown Mackie College-Boise ... ID ... 143
Carrington College - Boise ... ID ... 143
ITT Technical Institute ... ID ... 144
College of Office Technology, The ... IL ... 148
International Academy of Design and Technology ... IL ... 154
International Academy of Design and Technology-Schaumburg ... IL ... 154
ITT Technical Institute ... IL ... 154
Rockford Career College ... IL ... 162
Sanford-Brown College ... IL ... 164
SOLEX College ... IL ... 164
Taylor Business Institute ... IL ... 165
Tribeca Flashpoint Media Arts Academy ... IL ... 166
Westwood College-Chicago Loop ... IL ... 168
Westwood College-DuPage ... IL ... 168
Westwood College-O'Hare Airport ... IL ... 168
Westwood College-River Oaks ... IL ... 168
Art Institute of Indianapolis, The ... IN ... 169
Brown Mackie College-Fort Wayne ... IN ... 170
Brown Mackie College-Indianapolis ... IN ... 170
Brown Mackie College-Merrillville ... IN ... 170
Brown Mackie College-Michigan City ... IN ... 170
Brown Mackie College-South Bend ... IN ... 170
College of Court Reporting, Inc. ... IN ... 170
Harrison College - Anderson Campus ... IN ... 172
Harrison College - Columbus Indiana Campus ... IN ... 172
Harrison College - Elkhart Campus ... IN ... 172
Harrison College - Evansville Campus ... IN ... 172
Harrison College - Fort Wayne Campus ... IN ... 172
Harrison College - Indianapolis Downtown Campus ... IN ... 172
Harrison College - Indianapolis East Campus ... IN ... 172
Harrison College - Indianapolis Northwest Campus ... IN ... 172
Harrison College - Lafayette Campus ... IN ... 172
Harrison College - Muncie Campus ... IN ... 172
Harrison College - Terre Haute Campus ... IN ... 172
International Business College ... IN ... 175
ITT Technical Institute ... IN ... 175
Kaplan College ... IN ... 177
MedTech College ... IN ... 178
National College ... IN ... 178
Brown Mackie College-Quad Cities ... IA ... 183
ITT Technical Institute ... IA ... 186
Art Institutes International - Kansas City, The ... KS ... 190
Bryan College ... KS ... 191
ITT Technical Institute ... KS ... 194
Pinnacle Career Institute ... KS ... 196
Wright Career College ... KS ... 198
Beckfield College ... KY ... 198
Brown Mackie College-Hopkinsville ... KY ... 199
Brown Mackie College-Louisville ... KY ... 199
Brown Mackie College-Northern Kentucky ... KY ... 199
Daymar College-Bellevue ... KY ... 200
Daymar College-Bowling Green ... KY ... 200
Daymar College-Louisville ... KY ... 200
Daymar College-Louisville East ... KY ... 200
Daymar College-Madisonville ... KY ... 200
Daymar College-Owensboro ... KY ... 200
Daymar College-Paducah ... KY ... 200
Daymar College-Scottsville ... KY ... 200
ITT Technical Institute ... KY ... 201
Lincoln College of Technology ... KY ... 204
National College ... KY ... 205
Spencerian College ... KY ... 206
Sullivan College of Technology and Design . KY ... 206
Career Technical College ... LA ... 208
Delta School of Business & Technology, DBA Delta Tech ... LA ... 208
ITT Technical Institute ... LA ... 209
Beal College ... ME ... 217
ITT Technical Institute ... MD ... 223
ITT Technical Institute ... MA ... 235
Salter College ... MA ... 244
Sanford-Brown College of Boston, Inc. ... MA ... 244
International Academy of Design and Technology ... MI ... 252
ITT Technical Institute ... MI ... 252
Michigan Jewish Institute ... MI ... 254
Academy College ... MN ... 260
Art Institutes International Minnesota, The ... MN ... 261
Brown College ... MN ... 261
Duluth Business University, Inc. ... MN ... 263
Globe University ... MN ... 263
Globe University/Minnesota School of Business ... MN ... 263
ITT Technical Institute ... MN ... 264
Le Cordon Bleu College of Culinary Arts in Minneapolis/St Paul ... MN ... 264
Minneapolis Business College ... MN ... 265
Minnesota School of Business ... MN ... 265
ITT Technical Institute ... MS ... 274

Institution	State	Page
Virginia College	MS	277
Virginia College	MS	278
Bolivar Technical College	MO	279
Brown Mackie College-St. Louis	MO	279
Bryan College	MO	279
Everest College	MO	281
Hickey College	MO	282
ITT Technical Institute	MO	282
ITT Technical Institute	MO	283
Metro Business College	MO	284
Missouri College	MO	286
Pinnacle Career Institute	MO	287
Sanford-Brown College	MO	289
Stevens Institute of Business & Arts	MO	290
Texas County Technical College	MO	290
ITT Technical Institute	NE	298
Art Institute of Las Vegas, The	NV	301
Everest College	NV	301
ITT Technical Institute	NV	301
Le Cordon Bleu College of Culinary Arts in Las Vegas	NV	302
Morrison University	NV	302
Lebanon College	NH	305
Eastwick College	NJ	309
Brookline College	NM	317
Carrington College - Albuquerque	NM	317
ITT Technical Institute	NM	318
Art Institute of New York City, The	NY	323
Elmira Business Institute	NY	332
Everest Institute	NY	333
ITT Technical Institute	NY	337
Long Island Business Institute	NY	338
Mildred Elley	NY	341
Olean Business Institute	NY	345
Professional Business College	NY	346
SBI Campus-An Affiliate of Sanford-Brown	NY	350
Art Institute of Charlotte, The	NC	362
ITT Technical Institute	NC	365
King's College	NC	366
Living Arts College @ School of Communication Arts	NC	366
Miller-Motte Technical College	NC	367
South College	NC	376
ATS Institute of Technology	OH	384
Beckfield College	OH	385
Bradford School	OH	385
Brown Mackie College-Akron	OH	385
Brown Mackie College-Cincinnati	OH	385
Brown Mackie College-Findlay	OH	385
Brown Mackie College-North Canton	OH	386
Daymar College-Chillicothe	OH	389
Daymar College-Jackson	OH	389
Daymar College-Lancaster	OH	389
Daymar College-New Boston	OH	389
Fortis College	OH	390
Gallipolis Career College	OH	391
Hondros College	OH	392
ITT Technical Institute	OH	392
Lincoln College	OH	394
Lincoln College of Technology	OH	395
Miami-Jacobs Career College	OH	396
Ohio Business College	OH	398
Ohio Business College, Lorain Branch	OH	398
Ohio Valley College of Technology	OH	400
Stautzenberger College	OH	402
Trumbull Business College	OH	402
Brown Mackie College-Tulsa	OK	407
Clary Sage College	OK	407
Community Care College	OK	407
ITT Technical Institute	OK	408
Oklahoma Technical College	OK	411
Carrington College - Portland	OR	414
Everest College	OR	415
ITT Technical Institute	OR	416
Le Cordon Bleu College of Culinary Arts in Portland	OR	416
Oregon Culinary Institute	OR	418
Pioneer Pacific College	OR	419
Art Institute of Philadelphia	PA	422
Art Institute of York - Pennsylvania, The	PA	422
Bradford School	PA	423
Cambria-Rowe Business College	PA	424
Consolidated School of Business	PA	426
Douglas Education Center	PA	427
DuBois Business College	PA	428
Erie Business Center South	PA	428
Erie Business Center, Main	PA	428
Everest Institute	PA	429
Fortis Institute	PA	429
ITT Technical Institute	PA	431
Kaplan Career Institute	PA	432
Kaplan Career Institute - ICM Campus	PA	432
Lansdale School of Business	PA	433
Laurel Business Institute	PA	434
Laurel Technical Institute	PA	434
McCann School of Business & Technology	PA	435
McCann School of Business & Technology	PA	436
Newport Business Institute	PA	437
Pace Institute	PA	438
Penn Commercial Business/Technical School	PA	438
Pennsylvania Institute of Health and Technology	PA	441
Sanford-Brown Institute-Pittsburgh	PA	447
Sanford-Brown Institute-Wilkins Township	PA	447
South Hills School of Business and Technology	PA	447
Yorktowne Business Institute	PA	452
Atlantic University College	PR	560
EDIC College	PR	561
Humacao Community College	PR	562
Instituto de Banca y Comercio	PR	562
John Dewey College	PR	564
National University College	PR	564
Brown Mackie College-Greenville	SC	455
Forrest College	SC	458
Golf Academy of America	SC	458
ITT Technical Institute	SC	458
Miller-Motte Technical College	SC	459
Daymar Institute	TN	468
International Academy of Design and Technology	TN	469
ITT Technical Institute	TN	469
Miller-Motte Technical College	TN	471
National College of Business and Technology	TN	472
Virginia College School of Business and Health	TN	478
West Tennessee Business College	TN	478
Anamarc College	TX	480
Career Point College	TX	482
Court Reporting Institute of Dallas	TX	484
Everest College	TX	486
Franklin College	TX	486
International Academy of Design and Technology	TX	488
ITT Technical Institute	TX	488
ITT Technical Institute	TX	489
Le Cordon Bleu College of Culinary Arts in Austin	TX	489
Le Cordon Bleu College of Culinary Arts in Dallas	TX	489
Lighthouse College	TX	490
North American College	TX	491
Sanford-Brown College	TX	494
Sanford-Brown College-Houston	TX	494
Texas School of Business	TX	499
Texas School of Business-Friendswood	TX	500
Vet Tech Institute of Houston	TX	508
Virginia College at Austin	TX	508
Westwood College-Dallas	TX	509
Westwood College-Fort Worth	TX	509
Westwood College-Houston South	TX	509
Art Institute of Salt Lake City, The	UT	509
Broadview University	UT	509
Eagle Gate College	UT	509
Everest College	UT	510
ITT Technical Institute	UT	510
Neumont University	UT	510
Provo College	UT	510
Bon Secours Memorial College of Nursing	VA	517
California University of Management and Sciences Virginia	VA	517
Everest College	VA	519
Fortis College	VA	519
Global Health College	VA	519
iGlobal University	VA	520
ITT Technical Institute	VA	520
Miller-Motte Technical College	VA	521
National College	VA	521
National College	VA	522
Sanford-Brown College-Tysons Corner	VA	524
Sentara College of Health Sciences	VA	524
Stratford University	VA	524
Virginia International University	VA	529
Westwood College-Annandale	VA	530
Westwood College-Arlington Ballston	VA	530
Bainbridge Graduate Institute	WA	531
Carrington College - Spokane	WA	532
Everest College	WA	534
International Academy of Design and Technology	WA	535
ITT Technical Institute	WA	535
ITT Technical Institute	WV	541
Mountain State College	WV	541
National College	WV	541
Valley College - Martinsburg Campus	WV	542
West Virginia Business College	WV	542
West Virginia Junior College	WV	545
ITT Technical Institute	WI	547
Sanford-Brown College-Milwaukee	WI	550
Institute of Business and Medical Careers	WY	556

ACUP: Accreditation Commission for Acupuncture and Oriental Medicine: acupuncture (C,M,D)

Institution	State	Page
Arizona School of Acupuncture and Oriental Medicine	AZ	11
#Asian Institute of Medical Studies	AZ	12
Phoenix Institute of Herbal Medicine and Acupuncture	AZ	17
Academy of Chinese Culture and Health Sciences	CA	26
Acupuncture and Integrative Medicine College-Berkeley	CA	26
@Alhambra Medical University	CA	26
American College of Traditional Chinese Medicine	CA	28
Dongguk University	CA	45
Emperor's College of Traditional Oriental Medicine	CA	45
Five Branches University, Graduate School of Traditional Chinese Medicine	CA	47
Five Branches University: Graduate School of Traditional Chinese Medicine	CA	47
Pacific College of Oriental Medicine	CA	60
Samra University of Oriental Medicine	CA	64
South Baylo University	CA	70
Southern California University of Health Sciences	CA	71
Southern California University School of Oriental Medicine and Acupuncture	CA	71
@Stanton University	CA	71
University of East-West Medicine	CA	75
Yo San University of Traditional Chinese Medicine	CA	80
Colorado School of Traditional Chinese Medicine	CO	83
Institute of Taoist Education and Acupuncture	CO	85
Southwest Acupuncture College	CO	88
University of Bridgeport	CT	94
Academy for Five Element Acupuncture	FL	100
Acupuncture & Massage College	FL	100
Atlantic Institute of Oriental Medicine	FL	101
Dragon Rises College of Oriental Medicine	FL	105
East West College of Natural Medicine	FL	105
Florida College of Integrative Medicine	FL	108
Hawaii College of Oriental Medicine	HI	140
Institute of Clinical Acupuncture and Oriental Medicine	HI	141
World Medicine Institute	HI	142
Midwest College of Oriental Medicine	IL	158
National University of Health Sciences	IL	159
Pacific College of Oriental Medicine	IL	161
Tai Sophia Institute	MD	226
New England School of Acupuncture	MA	243
American Academy of Acupuncture and Oriental Medicine	MN	260
Northwestern Health Sciences University	MN	270
Southwest Acupuncture College	NM	320
Southwest Acupuncture College-Albuquerque	NM	320
New York Chiropractic College	NY	342
New York College of Health Professions	NY	343
New York College of Traditional Chinese Medicine	NY	343
Pacific College of Oriental Medicine	NY	345
Swedish Institute--College of Health Sciences	NY	357
Tri-State College of Acupuncture	NY	358
Daoist Traditions College of Chinese Medical Arts	NC	363
American Institute of Alternative Medicine	OH	383
National College of Natural Medicine	OR	417
Oregon College of Oriental Medicine	OR	417
Won Institute of Graduate Studies	PA	452
American College of Acupuncture and Oriental Medicine	TX	480
AOMA Graduate School of Integrative Medicine	TX	480
Texas College of Traditional Chinese Medicine	TX	499
Bastyr University	WA	531
Seattle Institute of Oriental Medicine	WA	537
Midwest College of Oriental Medicine	WI	549

ADNUR: National League for Nursing: nursing (A)

Institution	State	Page
Alabama Southern Community College	AL	1
Bevill State Community College	AL	2
Bishop State Community College	AL	2
Calhoun Community College	AL	2
Central Alabama Community College	AL	2
Gadsden State Community College	AL	3
George C. Wallace Community College - Dothan	AL	4
George Corley Wallace State Community College - Selma	AL	4
James H. Faulkner State Community College	AL	5
Jefferson Davis Community College	AL	5
Jefferson State Community College	AL	5
Lawson State Community College	AL	5
Lurleen B. Wallace Community College	AL	5
Northeast Alabama Community College	AL	6
Northwest - Shoals Community College	AL	6
Shelton State Community College	AL	6
Snead State Community College	AL	7
Southern Union State Community College	AL	7
Troy University	AL	8
University of Mobile	AL	9
University of West Alabama, The	AL	9
Wallace State Community College - Hanceville	AL	10
University of Alaska Anchorage	AK	10
Arizona Western College	AZ	12
Carrington College - Phoenix	AZ	13
Central Arizona College	AZ	13
Chandler-Gilbert Community College	AZ	15
Cochise College	AZ	13
Estrella Mountain Community College	AZ	15
Gateway Community College	AZ	15
Glendale Community College	AZ	15
Mesa Community College	AZ	15
Mohave Community College	AZ	16
Northland Pioneer College	AZ	17
Paradise Valley Community College	AZ	15
Phoenix College	AZ	16
Pima County Community College District	AZ	17
Scottsdale Community College	AZ	16
Yavapai College	AZ	19
Arkansas Northeastern College	AR	20
Arkansas State University-Jonesboro	AR	20
East Arkansas Community College	AR	21
National Park Community College	AR	22
North Arkansas College	AR	22
Phillips Community College of the University of Arkansas	AR	25
Southeast Arkansas College	AR	23
Southern Arkansas University	AR	23
University of Arkansas at Fort Smith	AR	24
University of Arkansas at Little Rock	AR	24
University of Arkansas Community College at Batesville	AR	25
Cerritos College	CA	39
Chaffey College	CA	39
College of Marin	CA	42
College of the Canyons	CA	41
Cypress College	CA	59
El Camino College	CA	45
Evergreen Valley College	CA	67
Golden West College	CA	41
Grossmont College	CA	49
Long Beach City College	CA	54
Los Angeles Harbor College	CA	54
Los Angeles Pierce College	CA	55
Los Angeles Valley College	CA	55
Monterey Peninsula College	CA	57
Moorpark College	CA	77
Ohlone College	CA	59
Pacific Union College	CA	60
Palomar College	CA	61
Riverside City College	CA	64
Saddleback College	CA	70
San Bernardino Valley College	CA	65
San Diego City College	CA	65
San Joaquin Delta College	CA	66
Santa Ana College	CA	63
Santa Barbara City College	CA	68
Santa Monica College	CA	68
Southwestern College	CA	71
Aims Community College	CO	81
Arapahoe Community College	CO	81
Colorado Mountain College	CO	82
Colorado Northwestern Community College	CO	82
Denver School of Nursing	CO	84
Front Range Community College	CO	85
Lamar Community College	CO	86
Morgan Community College	CO	86
Northeastern Junior College	CO	86
Otero Junior College	CO	87
Pikes Peak Community College	CO	87
Pueblo Community College	CO	87
Capital Community College	CT	91
Gateway Community College	CT	91
Goodwin College	CT	92
Naugatuck Valley Community College	CT	92
Norwalk Community College	CT	92
St. Vincent's College	CT	94
Three Rivers Community College	CT	92
Delaware Technical Community College, Owens Campus	DE	96
Delaware Technical Community College, Stanton-Wilmington Campus	DE	96
Delaware Technical Community College, Terry Campus	DE	96
University of the District of Columbia	DC	100
Adventist University of Health Sciences	FL	100
Broward College	FL	102
College of Central Florida	FL	103
Daytona State College	FL	104
Edison State College	FL	105
Florida Gateway College	FL	108
Florida State College at Jacksonville	FL	109
Gulf Coast State College	FL	110
Hillsborough Community College	FL	110
Indian River State College	FL	111
Keiser University	FL	112
Lake-Sumter Community College	FL	112
Miami Dade College	FL	113
Palm Beach State College	FL	114
Pasco-Hernando Community College	FL	114
Pensacola State College	FL	115
Polk State College	FL	115
St. Petersburg College	FL	116
Santa Fe College	FL	117
Seminole State College of Florida	FL	117
State College of Florida, Manatee-Sarasota	FL	118
Valencia College	FL	123
Abraham Baldwin Agricultural College	GA	123
Athens Technical College	GA	125
Bainbridge College	GA	126
College of Coastal Georgia	GA	127
Columbus Technical College	GA	128
Dalton State College	GA	128
Darton College	GA	128
Georgia Highlands College	GA	130
Georgia Northwestern Technical College	GA	131
Georgia Perimeter College	GA	131
Gordon State College	GA	132
Gwinnett Technical College	GA	132
Macon State College	GA	133
Middle Georgia College	GA	134
North Georgia College & State University	GA	134
South Georgia College	GA	137
Southwest Georgia Technical College	GA	138
West Georgia Technical College	GA	139
Kapiolani Community College	HI	141
University of Hawaii Hawaii Community College	HI	142

ANEST: Council on Accreditation of Nurse Anesthesia Educational Programs: nurse anesthesia (C,M,D)

ARCPA: Accreditation Review Commission on Education for the Physician Assistant: physician assisting programs (C,A,B,M)

Pacific University ... OR ... 419
Arcadia University ... PA ... 422
#Chatham University ... PA ... 425
DeSales University ... PA ... 427
Drexel University ... PA ... 427
Duquesne University ... PA ... 428
Gannon University ... PA ... 429
King's College ... PA ... 432
Lock Haven University ... PA ... 443
Marywood University ... PA ... 435
#Misericordia University ... PA ... 436
Pennsylvania College of Technology ... PA ... 440
Philadelphia College of Osteopathic Medicine ... PA ... 444
Philadelphia University ... PA ... 444
Saint Francis University ... PA ... 446
Salus University ... PA ... 446
Seton Hill University ... PA ... 447
University of Pittsburgh ... PA ... 449
Medical University of South Carolina ... SC ... 459
University of South Dakota, The ... SD ... 465
#Bethel University ... TN ... 467
#Christian Brothers University ... TN ... 467
Lincoln Memorial University ... TN ... 470
South College ... TN ... 473
Trevecca Nazarene University ... TN ... 476
Baylor College of Medicine ... TX ... 481
Texas Tech University ... TX ... 502
University of North Texas Health Science Center at Fort Worth ... TX ... 504
University of Texas Health Science Center at San Antonio ... TX ... 507
University of Texas Medical Branch, The ... TX ... 507
University of Texas - Pan American ... TX ... 506
University of Texas Southwestern Medical Center ... TX ... 507
University of Utah, The ... UT ... 511
Eastern Virginia Medical School ... VA ... 518
James Madison University ... VA ... 520
Jefferson College of Health Sciences ... VA ... 520
Shenandoah University ... VA ... 524
University of Washington ... WA ... 539
#Alderson Broaddus College ... WV ... 540
Mountain State University ... WV ... 541
#West Liberty University ... WV ... 544
#Carroll University ... WI ... 546
Marquette University ... WI ... 548
University of Wisconsin-La Crosse ... WI ... 551
University of Wisconsin-Madison ... WI ... 550

ART: National Association of Schools of Art and Design: art and design (C,A,B,M,D)

Auburn University ... AL ... 1
Jacksonville State University ... AL ... 4
University of Alabama at Birmingham ... AL ... 8
University of Alabama in Huntsville ... AL ... 8
University of Alabama, The ... AL ... 8
University of Montevallo ... AL ... 9
University of North Alabama ... AL ... 9
University of Alaska Anchorage ... AK ... 10
Arizona State University ... AZ ... 11
University of Arizona ... AZ ... 18
Arkansas State University-Jonesboro ... AR ... 20
University of Arkansas at Little Rock ... AR ... 24
University of Arkansas at Pine Bluff ... AR ... 25
University of Central Arkansas ... AR ... 25
Academy of Art University ... CA ... 26
American Film Institute Conservatory ... CA ... 28
Art Center College of Design ... CA ... 29
Azusa Pacific University ... CA ... 30
Biola University ... CA ... 31
California College of the Arts ... CA ... 32
California Institute of the Arts ... CA ... 32
California Polytechnic State University-San Luis Obispo ... CA ... 33
California State Polytechnic University-Pomona ... CA ... 33
California State University-Chico ... CA ... 34
California State University-Fullerton ... CA ... 35
California State University-Long Beach ... CA ... 35
California State University-Los Angeles ... CA ... 35
California State University-Northridge ... CA ... 35
California State University-Sacramento ... CA ... 36
California State University-San Bernardino ... CA ... 36
California State University-Stanislaus ... CA ... 36
Columbia College Hollywood ... CA ... 42
Fashion Institute of Design and Merchandising-Los Angeles ... CA ... 46
Fashion Institute of Design and Merchandising-Orange County ... CA ... 46
Fashion Institute of Design and Merchandising-San Diego ... CA ... 46
Fashion Institute of Design and Merchandising-San Francisco ... CA ... 47
Humboldt State University ... CA ... 36
Laguna College of Art & Design ... CA ... 53
Loyola Marymount University ... CA ... 56
New York Film Academy, Los Angeles ... CA ... 59
Otis College of Art and Design ... CA ... 60
San Diego State University ... CA ... 37
San Francisco Art Institute ... CA ... 65
San Francisco State University ... CA ... 37
San Jose State University ... CA ... 37
Sonoma State University ... CA ... 37
University of the Pacific ... CA ... 76
Woodbury University ... CA ... 79
Metropolitan State University of Denver ... CO ... 86
Rocky Mountain College of Art & Design ... CO ... 88
University of Denver ... CO ... 89
University of Northern Colorado ... CO ... 89
Lyme Academy College of Fine Arts ... CT ... 93
University of Bridgeport ... CT ... 94
University of Connecticut ... CT ... 94
University of Hartford ... CT ... 95
Delaware College of Art and Design ... DE ... 96
Corcoran College of Art and Design ... DC ... 98
Howard University ... DC ... 98
Florida International University ... FL ... 119
Florida State University ... FL ... 119
Miami Dade College ... FL ... 113
Ringling College of Art and Design ... FL ... 116
University of Florida ... FL ... 120
University of South Florida ... FL ... 121
Augusta State University ... GA ... 125
Columbus State University ... GA ... 127
Georgia Institute of Technology ... GA ... 130
Georgia Southern University ... GA ... 131
Georgia State University ... GA ... 131
Kennesaw State University ... GA ... 133
University of Georgia ... GA ... 138
University of West Georgia ... GA ... 139
Valdosta State University ... GA ... 139
Boise State University ... ID ... 142
University of Idaho ... ID ... 144
Bradley University ... IL ... 146
College of DuPage ... IL ... 148
Eastern Illinois University ... IL ... 150
Illinois State University ... IL ... 153
Northeastern Illinois University ... IL ... 160
Northern Illinois University ... IL ... 160
School of the Art Institute of Chicago ... IL ... 164
Southern Illinois University Carbondale ... IL ... 165
University of Illinois at Chicago ... IL ... 167
University of Illinois at Urbana-Champaign ... IL ... 167
Western Illinois University ... IL ... 168
Ball State University ... IN ... 169
Indiana State University ... IN ... 173
Indiana University Bloomington ... IN ... 173
Indiana University-Purdue University Indianapolis ... IN ... 174
Ivy Tech Community College of Indiana-Columbus ... IN ... 176
Ivy Tech Community College of Indiana-North Central ... IN ... 176
Ivy Tech Community College of Indiana-Southwest ... IN ... 177
Purdue University Main Campus ... IN ... 178
Saint Mary's College ... IN ... 179
University of Indianapolis ... IN ... 180
University of Notre Dame ... IN ... 180
University of Saint Francis ... IN ... 181
University of Southern Indiana ... IN ... 181
Vincennes University ... IN ... 181
Drake University ... IA ... 184
Emporia State University ... KS ... 192
Kansas State University ... KS ... 194
University of Kansas Main Campus ... KS ... 197
Washburn University ... KS ... 197
Wichita State University ... KS ... 198
Murray State University ... KY ... 205
University of Kentucky ... KY ... 207
Western Kentucky University ... KY ... 208
Louisiana State University and Agricultural and Mechanical College ... LA ... 212
Louisiana Tech University ... LA ... 215
McNeese State University ... LA ... 215
Nicholls State University ... LA ... 216
Northwestern State University ... LA ... 216
Southeastern Louisiana University ... LA ... 216
Southern University and A&M College ... LA ... 214
University of Louisiana at Lafayette ... LA ... 216
University of New Orleans ... LA ... 213
Maine College of Art ... ME ... 218
University of Southern Maine ... ME ... 220
Maryland Institute College of Art ... MD ... 224
Bridgewater State University ... MA ... 237
Lesley University ... MA ... 236
Massachusetts College of Art and Design ... MA ... 238
Montserrat College of Art ... MA ... 242
Mount Ida College ... MA ... 242
Salem State University ... MA ... 238
School of the Museum of Fine Arts-Boston ... MA ... 244
Suffolk University ... MA ... 245
University of Massachusetts Dartmouth ... MA ... 237
University of Massachusetts Lowell ... MA ... 237
Wentworth Institute of Technology ... MA ... 245
Central Michigan University ... MI ... 249
College for Creative Studies ... MI ... 249
Cranbrook Academy of Art ... MI ... 250
Ferris State University ... MI ... 250
Grand Rapids Community College ... MI ... 251
Grand Valley State University ... MI ... 251
Hope College ... MI ... 252
Lawrence Technological University ... MI ... 254
Siena Heights University ... MI ... 258
University of Michigan-Ann Arbor ... MI ... 259
Western Michigan University ... MI ... 260
College of Visual Arts ... MN ... 262
Minneapolis College of Art Design ... MN ... 265
Minnesota State University Moorhead ... MN ... 267
Minnesota State University, Mankato ... MN ... 267
Normandale Community College ... MN ... 268
St. Cloud State University ... MN ... 269
Belhaven University ... MS ... 273
Delta State University ... MS ... 273
Jackson State University ... MS ... 274
Mississippi State University ... MS ... 275
Mississippi University for Women ... MS ... 276
Mississippi Valley State University ... MS ... 276
University of Mississippi ... MS ... 277
University of Southern Mississippi ... MS ... 277
Kansas City Art Institute ... MO ... 283
Maryville University of Saint Louis ... MO ... 284
Saint Louis Community College at Florissant Valley ... MO ... 288
Saint Louis Community College at Meramec ... MO ... 289
Saint Louis University ... MO ... 289
University of Central Missouri ... MO ... 290
Washington University in St. Louis ... MO ... 292
Montana State University ... MT ... 295
Montana State University - Billings ... MT ... 295
University of Montana - Missoula, The ... MT ... 294
University of Nebraska at Omaha ... NE ... 301
University of Nebraska - Lincoln ... NE ... 300
Wayne State College ... NE ... 299
University of Nevada, Las Vegas ... NV ... 302
New Hampshire Institute of Art ... NH ... 305
Kean University ... NJ ... 311
Montclair State University ... NJ ... 311
New Jersey City University ... NJ ... 312
Rowan University ... NJ ... 314
William Paterson University of New Jersey ... NJ ... 317
Institute of American Indian Arts ... NM ... 318
Alfred University ... NY ... 322
College of Saint Rose, The ... NY ... 330
Cooper Union ... NY ... 331
Fashion Institute of Technology ... NY ... 333
Hartwick College ... NY ... 335
Mercy College ... NY ... 340
New School, The ... NY ... 342
New York School of Interior Design ... NY ... 343
Pratt Institute ... NY ... 346
Purchase College, State University of New York ... NY ... 354
Roberts Wesleyan College ... NY ... 347
Rochester Institute of Technology ... NY ... 347
Sage Colleges, The ... NY ... 348
St. John's University ... NY ... 348
School of Visual Arts ... NY ... 350
Skidmore College ... NY ... 351
Sotheby's Institute of Art ... NY ... 351
State University of New York at New Paltz ... NY ... 352
State University of New York College at Buffalo ... NY ... 353
State University of New York College at Oswego ... NY ... 354
Syracuse University Main Campus ... NY ... 357
Appalachian State University ... NC ... 377
East Carolina University ... NC ... 377
North Carolina State University ... NC ... 378
University of North Carolina at Pembroke ... NC ... 379
Western Carolina University ... NC ... 380
North Dakota State University Main Campus ... ND ... 382
University of North Dakota Main Campus ... ND ... 381
Art Academy of Cincinnati ... OH ... 384
Bowling Green State University ... OH ... 385
Central State University ... OH ... 387
Cleveland Institute of Art ... OH ... 388
Columbus College of Art & Design ... OH ... 388
Kent State University Main Campus ... OH ... 393
Lorain County Community College ... OH ... 395
Miami University ... OH ... 396
Ohio State University Main Campus, The ... OH ... 398
Ohio University Main Campus ... OH ... 399
Sinclair Community College ... OH ... 401
University of Akron, Main Campus, The ... OH ... 403
University of Cincinnati Main Campus ... OH ... 403
University of Cincinnati-Raymond Walters College ... OH ... 403
University of Dayton ... OH ... 404
University of Toledo ... OH ... 404
Youngstown State University ... OH ... 406
Oregon College of Art and Craft ... OR ... 417
Pacific Northwest College of Art ... OR ... 419
University of Oregon ... OR ... 419
Arcadia University ... PA ... 422
Bloomsburg University of Pennsylvania ... PA ... 441
Bucks County Community College ... PA ... 423
California University of Pennsylvania ... PA ... 441
Clarion University of Pennsylvania ... PA ... 442
Drexel University ... PA ... 427
Edinboro University of Pennsylvania ... PA ... 442
Indiana University of Pennsylvania ... PA ... 442
Kutztown University of Pennsylvania ... PA ... 443
La Roche College ... PA ... 432
Marywood University ... PA ... 435
Messiah College ... PA ... 436
Millersville University of Pennsylvania ... PA ... 443
Moore College of Art and Design ... PA ... 436
Penn State University Park ... PA ... 438
Pennsylvania Academy of the Fine Arts ... PA ... 440
Pennsylvania College of Art & Design ... PA ... 440
Philadelphia University ... PA ... 444
Slippery Rock University of Pennsylvania ... PA ... 443
Temple University ... PA ... 447
University of the Arts, The ... PA ... 448
West Chester University of Pennsylvania ... PA ... 444
Escuela de Artes Plasticas de Puerto Rico ... PR ... 562
Rhode Island College ... RI ... 454
Rhode Island School of Design ... RI ... 454
Salve Regina University ... RI ... 454
Anderson University ... SC ... 455
Benedict College ... SC ... 455
Clemson University ... SC ... 456
Coastal Carolina University ... SC ... 456
Columbia College ... SC ... 457
Converse College ... SC ... 457
Francis Marion University ... SC ... 458
Lander University ... SC ... 459
South Carolina State University ... SC ... 460
University of South Carolina Columbia ... SC ... 462
University of South Carolina Upstate ... SC ... 463
Winthrop University ... SC ... 463
University of South Dakota, The ... SD ... 465
Austin Peay State University ... TN ... 473
Belmont University ... TN ... 467
Carson-Newman College ... TN ... 467
East Tennessee State University ... TN ... 473
Memphis College of Art ... TN ... 471
Middle Tennessee State University ... TN ... 473
Tennessee State University ... TN ... 474
Tennessee Technological University ... TN ... 474
Union University ... TN ... 477
University of Memphis, The ... TN ... 474
University of Tennessee at Chattanooga ... TN ... 477
University of Tennessee, Knoxville ... TN ... 477
Watkins College of Art, Design & Film ... TN ... 478
Del Mar College ... TX ... 485
Midwestern State University ... TX ... 491
Southern Methodist University ... TX ... 495
Stephen F. Austin State University ... TX ... 496
Texas A & M University - Commerce ... TX ... 498
Texas Christian University ... TX ... 499
Texas Tech University ... TX ... 502
University of North Texas ... TX ... 504
University of Texas at Arlington, The ... TX ... 505
University of Texas at Austin ... TX ... 505
University of Texas at San Antonio ... TX ... 506
University of Texas of the Permian Basin ... TX ... 507
Brigham Young University ... UT ... 509
Southern Utah University ... UT ... 511
Weber State University ... UT ... 511
George Mason University ... VA ... 519
James Madison University ... VA ... 520
Old Dominion University ... VA ... 522
Virginia Commonwealth University ... VA ... 526
Virginia Polytechnic Institute and State University ... VA ... 529
Virginia State University ... VA ... 529
Cornish College of the Arts ... WA ... 533
Western Washington University ... WA ... 539
West Virginia University ... WV ... 545
Milwaukee Institute of Art & Design ... WI ... 549
University of Wisconsin-Madison ... WI ... 550
University of Wisconsin-Stevens Point ... WI ... 552
University of Wisconsin-Stout ... WI ... 552
University of Wisconsin-Whitewater ... WI ... 553
Casper College ... WY ... 556

AUD: American Speech-Language-Hearing Association: audiology (D)

Auburn University ... AL ... 1
University of South Alabama ... AL ... 9
Arizona State University ... AZ ... 11
University of Arizona ... AZ ... 18
University of Arkansas at Little Rock ... AR ... 24
San Diego State University ... CA ... 37
University of California-San Diego ... CA ... 74
University of Colorado Boulder ... CO ... 88
University of Northern Colorado ... CO ... 89
University of Connecticut ... CT ... 94
Gallaudet University ... DC ... 98
Nova Southeastern University ... FL ... 114
University of Florida ... FL ... 120
University of South Florida ... FL ... 121
Idaho State University ... ID ... 143
Illinois State University ... IL ... 153
Northern Illinois University ... IL ... 160
Northwestern University ... IL ... 160
Rush University ... IL ... 163
University of Illinois at Urbana-Champaign ... IL ... 167
Ball State University ... IN ... 169
Indiana University Bloomington ... IN ... 173
Purdue University Main Campus ... IN ... 178
University of Iowa ... IA ... 182
University of Kansas Main Campus ... KS ... 197
Wichita State University ... KS ... 198
University of Louisville ... KY ... 207
Louisiana State University Health Sciences Center-New Orleans ... LA ... 213
Louisiana Tech University ... LA ... 215
Towson University ... MD ... 228
University of Maryland College Park ... MD ... 227
Northeastern University ... MA ... 243
University of Massachusetts ... MA ... 236
Central Michigan University ... MI ... 249
Wayne State University ... MI ... 260
Western Michigan University ... MI ... 260
University of Minnesota-Twin Cities ... MN ... 272
University of Southern Mississippi ... MS ... 277
Missouri State University ... MO ... 286
Washington University in St. Louis ... MO ... 292
University of Nebraska - Lincoln ... NE ... 300
Montclair State University ... NJ ... 311
Adelphi University ... NY ... 322
City University of New York Brooklyn College ... NY ... 326
City University of New York Hunter College ... NY ... 327
Hofstra University ... NY ... 335
St. John's University ... NY ... 348

Syracuse University Main Campus ... NY ... 357
University at Buffalo-SUNY ... NY ... 351
East Carolina University ... NC ... 377
University of North Carolina at Chapel Hill ... NC ... 378
Kent State University Main Campus ... OH ... 393
Ohio State University Main Campus, The ... OH ... 398
Ohio University Main Campus ... OH ... 399
University of Akron, Main Campus, The ... OH ... 403
University of Cincinnati Main Campus ... OH ... 403
University of Oklahoma Health Sciences Center ... OK ... 413
@Pacific University ... OR ... 419
Bloomsburg University of Pennsylvania ... PA ... 441
Salus University ... PA ... 446
University of Pittsburgh ... PA ... 449
University of Puerto Rico-Medical Sciences Campus ... PR ... 567
University of South Dakota, The ... SD ... 465
East Tennessee State University ... TN ... 473
University of Memphis, The ... TN ... 474
University of Tennessee, Knoxville ... TN ... 477
Vanderbilt University ... TN ... 478
Lamar University ... TX ... 501
Texas Tech University Health Sciences Center ... TX ... 502
University of North Texas ... TX ... 504
University of Texas at Austin ... TX ... 505
University of Texas at Dallas, The ... TX ... 506
University of Utah, The ... UT ... 511
Utah State University ... UT ... 511
James Madison University ... VA ... 520
University of Washington ... WA ... 539
West Virginia University ... WV ... 545
University of Wisconsin-Madison ... WI ... 550
University of Wisconsin-Stevens Point ... WI ... 552

BBT: Commission on Accreditation of Allied Health Education Programs: blood bank technology (C,M)

Rush University ... IL ... 163
Johns Hopkins University ... MD ... 223
University of Cincinnati Main Campus ... OH ... 403
University of Texas Health Science Center at San Antonio ... TX ... 507
University of Texas Medical Branch, The ... TX ... 507
University of Texas Southwestern Medical Center ... TX ... 507

BI: Association for Biblical Higher Education: bible college education (C,A,B,M,FP,D)

Heritage Christian University ... AL ... 4
Huntsville Bible College ... AL ... 4
Selma University ... AL ... 6
Southeastern Bible College ... AL ... 7
Alaska Bible College ... AK ... 10
Ecclesia College ... AR ... 21
@American Evangelical University ... CA ... 28
Bethesda University of California ... CA ... 30
@Eternity Bible College ... CA ... 45
@Grace Mission University ... CA ... 48
Hope International University ... CA ... 50
@Horizon College of San Diego ... CA ... 50
King's University, The ... CA ... 53
Life Pacific College ... CA ... 54
Olivet University ... CA ... 60
Presbyterian Theological Seminary in America ... CA ... 63
SUM Bible College and Theological Seminary ... CA ... 72
William Jessup University ... CA ... 79
World Mission University ... CA ... 79
Nazarene Bible College ... CO ... 86
#Florida Christian College ... FL ... 107
Hobe Sound Bible College ... FL ... 110
Robert E. Webber Institute for Worship Studies, The ... FL ... 116
@South Florida Bible College ... FL ... 117
Trinity College of Florida ... FL ... 122
Beulah Heights University ... GA ... 126
Carver College ... GA ... 126
Toccoa Falls College ... GA ... 138
@New Hope Christian College-Hawaii ... HI ... 141
Boise Bible College ... ID ... 142
Lincoln Christian University ... IL ... 156
Moody Bible Institute ... IL ... 159
Crossroads Bible College ... IN ... 171
Emmaus Bible College ... IA ... 184
Faith Baptist Bible College and Seminary ... IA ... 185
Barclay College ... KS ... 190
Manhattan Christian College ... KS ... 195
Clear Creek Baptist Bible College ... KY ... 199
Kentucky Mountain Bible College ... KY ... 203
@Louisville Bible College ... KY ... 204
@Simmons College of Kentucky ... KY ... 206
#Washington Bible College/Capital Bible Seminary ... MD ... 229
Zion Bible College ... MA ... 246
Grace Bible College ... MI ... 251
Great Lakes Christian College ... MI ... 251
Kuyper College ... MI ... 253
@Puritan Reformed Theological Seminary ... MI ... 257
Crossroads College ... MN ... 263
Oak Hills Christian College ... MN ... 270
Southeastern Baptist College ... MS ... 277
Baptist Bible College ... MO ... 278
Calvary Bible College and Theological Seminary ... MO ... 279
Central Bible College ... MO ... 279
Central Christian College of the Bible ... MO ... 279
@Heartland Christian College ... MO ... 282
Ozark Christian College ... MO ... 287
Saint Louis Christian College ... MO ... 288
Montana Bible College ... MT ... 294
Grace University ... NE ... 297
Nebraska Christian College ... NE ... 299
Somerset Christian College ... NJ ... 315
Davis College ... NY ... 331
@Carolina Bible College ... NC ... 363
Carolina Christian College ... NC ... 363
Grace College of Divinity ... NC ... 364
Laurel University ... NC ... 366
@Native American Bible College ... NC ... 367
#Trinity Bible College ... ND ... 383
Allegheny Wesleyan College ... OH ... 383
Cincinnati Christian University ... OH ... 387
God's Bible School and College ... OH ... 391
Ohio Christian University ... OH ... 398
Rosedale Bible College ... OH ... 401
Tri-State Bible College ... OH ... 402
@Valor Christian College ... OH ... 405
Family of Faith College ... OK ... 408
Multnomah University ... OR ... 417
New Hope Christian College ... OR ... 417
Baptist Bible College and Seminary ... PA ... 422
Lancaster Bible College ... PA ... 433
Philadelphia Biblical University ... PA ... 444
Universidad Pentecostal Mizpa ... PR ... 566
Universidad Teologica Del Caribe ... PR ... 566
Columbia International University ... SC ... 457
#W.L. Bonner College ... SC ... 463
@All Saints Bible College ... TN ... 466
American Baptist College ... TN ... 466
Free Will Baptist Bible College ... TN ... 469
Johnson University ... TN ... 469
@Mid-South Christian College ... TN ... 471
Williamson Christian College ... TN ... 478
Arlington Baptist College ... TX ... 480
Baptist University of the Americas ... TX ... 481
B.H. Carroll Theological Institute ... TX ... 482
College of Biblical Studies-Houston ... TX ... 483
Dallas Christian College ... TX ... 484
Rio Grande Bible Institute ... TX ... 493
@Bethel College ... VA ... 516
@Washington Baptist University ... VA ... 530
Appalachian Bible College ... WV ... 540

BUS: AACSB-The Association to Advance Collegiate Schools of Business: business and management (B,M,D)

Auburn University ... AL ... 1
Auburn University at Montgomery ... AL ... 1
Jacksonville State University ... AL ... 4
Samford University ... AL ... 6
Tuskegee University ... AL ... 8
University of Alabama at Birmingham ... AL ... 8
University of Alabama in Huntsville ... AL ... 8
University of Alabama, The ... AL ... 8
University of Montevallo ... AL ... 9
University of South Alabama ... AL ... 9
University of Alaska Anchorage ... AK ... 10
University of Alaska Fairbanks ... AK ... 10
Arizona State University ... AZ ... 11
Northern Arizona University ... AZ ... 16
Thunderbird School of Global Management ... AZ ... 18
University of Arizona ... AZ ... 18
Arkansas State University-Jonesboro ... AR ... 20
Arkansas Tech University ... AR ... 20
Henderson State University ... AR ... 21
Ouachita Baptist University ... AR ... 22
Southern Arkansas University ... AR ... 23
University of Arkansas at Little Rock ... AR ... 24
University of Arkansas Main Campus ... AR ... 24
University of Central Arkansas ... AR ... 25
California Polytechnic State University-San Luis Obispo ... CA ... 33
California State Polytechnic University-Pomona ... CA ... 33
California State University-Bakersfield ... CA ... 34
California State University-Chico ... CA ... 34
California State University-East Bay ... CA ... 34
California State University-Fresno ... CA ... 35
California State University-Fullerton ... CA ... 35
California State University-Long Beach ... CA ... 35
California State University-Los Angeles ... CA ... 35
California State University-Northridge ... CA ... 35
California State University-Sacramento ... CA ... 36
California State University-San Bernardino ... CA ... 36
California State University-Stanislaus ... CA ... 36
Chapman University ... CA ... 39
Claremont Graduate University ... CA ... 40
Loyola Marymount University ... CA ... 56
Monterey Institute of International Studies ... CA ... 57
Naval Postgraduate School ... CA ... 558
Pepperdine University ... CA ... 61
San Diego State University ... CA ... 37
San Francisco State University ... CA ... 37
San Jose State University ... CA ... 37
Santa Clara University ... CA ... 68
Sonoma State University ... CA ... 37
Stanford University ... CA ... 71
University of California-Berkeley ... CA ... 73
University of California-Davis ... CA ... 73
University of California-Irvine ... CA ... 74
University of California-Los Angeles ... CA ... 74
University of California-Riverside ... CA ... 74
University of California-San Diego ... CA ... 74
University of San Diego ... CA ... 76
University of San Francisco ... CA ... 76
University of Southern California ... CA ... 76
University of the Pacific ... CA ... 76
Colorado State University ... CO ... 83
Colorado State University-Pueblo ... CO ... 83
Fort Lewis College ... CO ... 84
United States Air Force Academy ... CO ... 558
University of Colorado Boulder ... CO ... 88
University of Colorado Colorado Springs ... CO ... 88
University of Colorado DenverlAnschutz Medical Campus ... CO ... 88
University of Denver ... CO ... 89
University of Northern Colorado ... CO ... 89
Fairfield University ... CT ... 92
Quinnipiac University ... CT ... 93
Sacred Heart University ... CT ... 94
United States Coast Guard Academy ... CT ... 558
University of Connecticut ... CT ... 94
University of Hartford ... CT ... 95
Yale University ... CT ... 96
Delaware State University ... DE ... 96
University of Delaware ... DE ... 96
American University ... DC ... 97
George Washington University ... DC ... 98
Georgetown University ... DC ... 98
Howard University ... DC ... 98
Barry University ... FL ... 101
Florida Atlantic University ... FL ... 119
Florida Gulf Coast University ... FL ... 119
Florida International University ... FL ... 119
Florida State University ... FL ... 119
Jacksonville University ... FL ... 111
Rollins College ... FL ... 116
Stetson University ... FL ... 121
University of Central Florida ... FL ... 120
University of Florida ... FL ... 120
University of Miami ... FL ... 122
University of North Florida ... FL ... 120
University of South Florida ... FL ... 121
University of South Florida St. Petersburg ... FL ... 121
University of Tampa ... FL ... 123
University of West Florida ... FL ... 121
Augusta State University ... GA ... 125
Berry College ... GA ... 126
Clark Atlanta University ... GA ... 127
Clayton State University ... GA ... 127
Columbus State University ... GA ... 127
Dalton State College ... GA ... 128
Emory University ... GA ... 129
Georgia College & State University ... GA ... 130
Georgia Institute of Technology ... GA ... 130
Georgia Southern University ... GA ... 131
Georgia Southwestern State University ... GA ... 131
Georgia State University ... GA ... 131
Kennesaw State University ... GA ... 133
Mercer University ... GA ... 134
Morehouse College ... GA ... 134
North Georgia College & State University ... GA ... 134
Savannah State University ... GA ... 136
University of Georgia ... GA ... 138
University of West Georgia ... GA ... 139
Valdosta State University ... GA ... 139
University of Hawaii at Hilo ... HI ... 141
University of Hawaii at Manoa ... HI ... 141
Boise State University ... ID ... 142
Idaho State University ... ID ... 143
University of Idaho ... ID ... 144
Bradley University ... IL ... 146
DePaul University ... IL ... 149
Eastern Illinois University ... IL ... 150
Illinois Institute of Technology ... IL ... 153
Illinois State University ... IL ... 153
Loyola University Chicago ... IL ... 157
Northern Illinois University ... IL ... 160
Northwestern University ... IL ... 160
Southern Illinois University Carbondale ... IL ... 165
Southern Illinois University Edwardsville ... IL ... 165
University of Chicago ... IL ... 166
University of Illinois at Chicago ... IL ... 167
University of Illinois at Springfield ... IL ... 167
University of Illinois at Urbana-Champaign ... IL ... 167
Western Illinois University ... IL ... 168
Ball State University ... IN ... 169
Butler University ... IN ... 170
Indiana State University ... IN ... 173
Indiana University Bloomington ... IN ... 173
Indiana University Kokomo ... IN ... 174
Indiana University Northwest ... IN ... 174
Indiana University-Purdue University Fort Wayne ... IN ... 174
Indiana University South Bend ... IN ... 174
Indiana University Southeast ... IN ... 175
Purdue University Main Campus ... IN ... 178
University of Evansville ... IN ... 180
University of Notre Dame ... IN ... 180
University of Southern Indiana ... IN ... 181
Valparaiso University ... IN ... 181
Drake University ... IA ... 184
Iowa State University ... IA ... 182
University of Iowa ... IA ... 182
University of Northern Iowa ... IA ... 182
Emporia State University ... KS ... 192
Kansas State University ... KS ... 194
Pittsburg State University ... KS ... 196
University of Kansas Main Campus ... KS ... 197
Washburn University ... KS ... 197
Wichita State University ... KS ... 198
Bellarmine University ... KY ... 198
Eastern Kentucky University ... KY ... 200
Morehead State University ... KY ... 204
Murray State University ... KY ... 205
Northern Kentucky University ... KY ... 205
University of Kentucky ... KY ... 207
University of Louisville ... KY ... 207
Western Kentucky University ... KY ... 208
Grambling State University ... LA ... 215
Louisiana State University and Agricultural and Mechanical College ... LA ... 212
Louisiana State University in Shreveport ... LA ... 213
Louisiana Tech University ... LA ... 215
Loyola University New Orleans ... LA ... 213
McNeese State University ... LA ... 215
Nicholls State University ... LA ... 216
Northwestern State University ... LA ... 216
Southeastern Louisiana University ... LA ... 216
Southern University and A&M College ... LA ... 214
Tulane University ... LA ... 215
University of Louisiana at Lafayette ... LA ... 216
University of Louisiana at Monroe ... LA ... 216
University of New Orleans ... LA ... 213
University of Maine ... ME ... 220
University of Southern Maine ... ME ... 220
Frostburg State University ... MD ... 228
Loyola University Maryland ... MD ... 223
Morgan State University ... MD ... 224
Salisbury University ... MD ... 228
Towson University ... MD ... 228
University of Baltimore ... MD ... 229
University of Maryland College Park ... MD ... 227
University of Maryland Eastern Shore ... MD ... 227
Babson College ... MA ... 230
Bentley University ... MA ... 231
Boston College ... MA ... 232
Boston University ... MA ... 232
Brandeis University ... MA ... 232
Clark University ... MA ... 233
Harvard University ... MA ... 235
Massachusetts Institute of Technology ... MA ... 241
Northeastern University ... MA ... 243
Simmons College ... MA ... 244
Stonehill College ... MA ... 245
Suffolk University ... MA ... 245
University of Massachusetts ... MA ... 236
University of Massachusetts Boston ... MA ... 236
University of Massachusetts Dartmouth ... MA ... 237
University of Massachusetts Lowell ... MA ... 237
Western New England University ... MA ... 246
Worcester Polytechnic Institute ... MA ... 246
Central Michigan University ... MI ... 249
Eastern Michigan University ... MI ... 250
Grand Valley State University ... MI ... 251
Michigan State University ... MI ... 255
Michigan Technological University ... MI ... 255
Northern Michigan University ... MI ... 256
Oakland University ... MI ... 256
Saginaw Valley State University ... MI ... 257
University of Detroit Mercy ... MI ... 258
University of Michigan-Ann Arbor ... MI ... 259
University of Michigan-Dearborn ... MI ... 259
University of Michigan-Flint ... MI ... 259
Wayne State University ... MI ... 260
Western Michigan University ... MI ... 260
Minnesota State University Moorhead ... MN ... 267
Minnesota State University, Mankato ... MN ... 267
St. Cloud State University ... MN ... 269
University of Minnesota Duluth ... MN ... 271
University of Minnesota-Twin Cities ... MN ... 272
University of Saint Thomas ... MN ... 272
Winona State University ... MN ... 269
Jackson State University ... MS ... 274
Millsaps College ... MS ... 275
Mississippi State University ... MS ... 275
University of Mississippi ... MS ... 277
University of Southern Mississippi ... MS ... 277
Drury University ... MO ... 281
Missouri State University ... MO ... 286
Missouri Western State University ... MO ... 286
Rockhurst University ... MO ... 288
Saint Louis University ... MO ... 289
Southeast Missouri State University ... MO ... 289
Truman State University ... MO ... 290
University of Central Missouri ... MO ... 290
University of Missouri - Columbia ... MO ... 291
University of Missouri - Kansas City ... MO ... 291
University of Missouri - Saint Louis ... MO ... 291
Washington University in St. Louis ... MO ... 292
Montana State University ... MT ... 295
Montana State University - Billings ... MT ... 295
University of Montana - Missoula, The ... MT ... 294
Creighton University ... NE ... 297
University of Nebraska at Kearney ... NE ... 300
University of Nebraska at Omaha ... NE ... 301
University of Nebraska - Lincoln ... NE ... 300
University of Nevada, Las Vegas ... NV ... 302
University of Nevada, Reno ... NV ... 303
Dartmouth College ... NH ... 304
University of New Hampshire ... NH ... 306
College of New Jersey, The ... NJ ... 308
Fairleigh Dickinson University ... NJ ... 310
Monmouth University ... NJ ... 311

Montclair State University ... NJ ... 311
New Jersey Institute of Technology ... NJ ... 312
Ramapo College of New Jersey ... NJ ... 313
Rider University ... NJ ... 313
Rowan University ... NJ ... 314
Rutgers the State University of New Jersey Camden Campus ... NJ ... 314
Rutgers the State University of New Jersey Newark Campus ... NJ ... 314
Seton Hall University ... NJ ... 315
William Paterson University of New Jersey .. NJ ... 317
New Mexico State University Main Campus . NM ... 319
University of New Mexico Main Campus ... NM ... 321
Adelphi University ... NY ... 322
Alfred University ... NY ... 322
Baruch College/City University of New York . NY ... 326
Canisius College ... NY ... 325
Clarkson University ... NY ... 329
Columbia University in the City of New York NY ... 330
Cornell University ... NY ... 331
Fordham University ... NY ... 334
Hofstra University ... NY ... 335
Iona College ... NY ... 336
Ithaca College ... NY ... 336
Le Moyne College ... NY ... 338
Long Island University C.W. Post Campus ... NY ... 339
Manhattan College ... NY ... 339
Marist College ... NY ... 340
New York University ... NY ... 344
Niagara University ... NY ... 344
Pace University ... NY ... 345
Rensselaer Polytechnic Institute ... NY ... 347
Rochester Institute of Technology ... NY ... 347
St. Bonaventure University ... NY ... 348
St. John Fisher College ... NY ... 348
St. John's University ... NY ... 348
Siena College ... NY ... 350
State University of New York at Binghamton NY ... 351
State University of New York College at Geneseo ... NY ... 353
State University of New York College at Oneonta ... NY ... 353
State University of New York College at Oswego ... NY ... 354
State University of New York College at Plattsburgh ... NY ... 354
State University of New York Institute of Technology at Utica-Rome ... NY ... 356
State University of New York, The College at Brockport ... NY ... 352
Syracuse University Main Campus ... NY ... 357
Union Graduate College ... NY ... 358
University at Albany, SUNY ... NY ... 351
University at Buffalo-SUNY ... NY ... 351
University of Rochester ... NY ... 359
Appalachian State University ... NC ... 377
Duke University ... NC ... 364
East Carolina University ... NC ... 377
Elizabeth City State University ... NC ... 377
Elon University ... NC ... 364
Fayetteville State University ... NC ... 377
Meredith College ... NC ... 367
North Carolina Agricultural and Technical State University ... NC ... 378
North Carolina Central University ... NC ... 378
North Carolina State University ... NC ... 378
Queens University of Charlotte ... NC ... 376
University of North Carolina at Asheville ... NC ... 378
University of North Carolina at Chapel Hill ... NC ... 378
University of North Carolina at Charlotte ... NC ... 379
University of North Carolina at Greensboro .. NC ... 379
University of North Carolina Wilmington ... NC ... 379
Wake Forest University ... NC ... 380
Western Carolina University ... NC ... 380
Winston-Salem State University ... NC ... 380
North Dakota State University Main Campus. ND ... 382
University of North Dakota Main Campus ... ND ... 381
Bowling Green State University ... OH ... 385
Case Western Reserve University ... OH ... 386
Cleveland State University ... OH ... 388
John Carroll University ... OH ... 392
Kent State University Main Campus ... OH ... 393
Miami University ... OH ... 396
Ohio Northern University ... OH ... 398
Ohio State University Main Campus, The ... OH ... 398
Ohio University Main Campus ... OH ... 399
University of Akron, Main Campus, The ... OH ... 403
University of Cincinnati Main Campus ... OH ... 403
University of Dayton ... OH ... 404
University of Toledo ... OH ... 404
Wright State University Main Campus ... OH ... 406
Xavier University ... OH ... 406
Youngstown State University ... OH ... 406
Oklahoma State University ... OK ... 410
Southeastern Oklahoma State University ... OK ... 412
University of Oklahoma Norman Campus ... OK ... 413
University of Tulsa ... OK ... 413
Oregon State University ... OR ... 418
Portland State University ... OR ... 418
University of Oregon ... OR ... 419
University of Portland ... OR ... 420
Willamette University ... OR ... 421
Bloomsburg University of Pennsylvania ... PA ... 441
Carnegie Mellon University ... PA ... 424
Clarion University of Pennsylvania ... PA ... 442
Drexel University ... PA ... 427
Duquesne University ... PA ... 428
Indiana University of Pennsylvania ... PA ... 442
King's College ... PA ... 432
La Salle University ... PA ... 432
Lehigh University ... PA ... 434
Penn State Erie, The Behrend College ... PA ... 439
Penn State Great Valley School of Graduate Professional Studies ... PA ... 439
Penn State Harrisburg ... PA ... 439
Penn State University Park ... PA ... 438
Robert Morris University ... PA ... 445
Saint Joseph's University ... PA ... 446
Shippensburg University of Pennsylvania ... PA ... 443
Susquehanna University ... PA ... 447
Temple University ... PA ... 447
University of Pennsylvania ... PA ... 448
University of Pittsburgh ... PA ... 449
University of Scranton, The ... PA ... 450
Villanova University ... PA ... 450
West Chester University of Pennsylvania ... PA ... 444
Widener University ... PA ... 451
Universidad Del Turabo ... PR ... 565
Bryant University ... RI ... 453
Providence College ... RI ... 453
Roger Williams University ... RI ... 454
University of Rhode Island ... RI ... 454
Citadel, The Military College of South Carolina, The ... SC ... 456
Clemson University ... SC ... 456
Coastal Carolina University ... SC ... 456
College of Charleston ... SC ... 457
Francis Marion University ... SC ... 458
Lander University ... SC ... 459
South Carolina State University ... SC ... 460
University of South Carolina Aiken ... SC ... 462
University of South Carolina Columbia ... SC ... 462
University of South Carolina Upstate ... SC ... 463
Winthrop University ... SC ... 463
University of South Dakota, The ... SD ... 465
Belmont University ... TN ... 467
East Tennessee State University ... TN ... 473
Middle Tennessee State University ... TN ... 473
Tennessee State University ... TN ... 474
Tennessee Technological University ... TN ... 474
University of Memphis, The ... TN ... 474
University of Tennessee at Chattanooga ... TN ... 477
University of Tennessee at Martin ... TN ... 477
University of Tennessee, Knoxville ... TN ... 477
Vanderbilt University ... TN ... 478
Abilene Christian University ... TX ... 478
Baylor University ... TX ... 482
Lamar University ... TX ... 501
Midwestern State University ... TX ... 491
Prairie View A & M University ... TX ... 496
Rice University ... TX ... 493
St. Mary's University ... TX ... 493
Sam Houston State University ... TX ... 501
Southern Methodist University ... TX ... 495
Stephen F. Austin State University ... TX ... 496
Texas A & M International University ... TX ... 497
Texas A & M University ... TX ... 497
Texas A & M University - Commerce ... TX ... 498
Texas A & M University - Corpus Christi ... TX ... 498
Texas Christian University ... TX ... 499
Texas Southern University ... TX ... 500
Texas State University-San Marcos ... TX ... 501
Texas Tech University ... TX ... 502
Trinity University ... TX ... 502
University of Houston ... TX ... 503
University of Houston - Clear Lake ... TX ... 503
University of Houston - Downtown ... TX ... 503
University of Houston - Victoria ... TX ... 504
University of North Texas ... TX ... 504
University of St. Thomas ... TX ... 505
University of Texas at Arlington, The ... TX ... 505
University of Texas at Austin ... TX ... 505
University of Texas at Brownsville and Texas Southmost College, The ... TX ... 505
University of Texas at Dallas, The ... TX ... 506
University of Texas at El Paso ... TX ... 506
University of Texas at San Antonio ... TX ... 506
University of Texas at Tyler ... TX ... 506
University of Texas of the Permian Basin ... TX ... 507
University of Texas - Pan American ... TX ... 506
West Texas A & M University ... TX ... 499
Brigham Young University ... UT ... 509
Southern Utah University ... UT ... 511
University of Utah, The ... UT ... 511
Utah State University ... UT ... 511
Utah Valley University ... UT ... 511
Weber State University ... UT ... 511
University of Vermont ... VT ... 514
Christopher Newport University ... VA ... 517
College of William & Mary ... VA ... 518
George Mason University ... VA ... 519
James Madison University ... VA ... 520
Longwood University ... VA ... 521
Norfolk State University ... VA ... 522
Old Dominion University ... VA ... 522
Radford University ... VA ... 523
Shenandoah University ... VA ... 524
University of Richmond ... VA ... 525
University of Virginia ... VA ... 525
Virginia Commonwealth University ... VA ... 526
Virginia Military Institute ... VA ... 529
Virginia Polytechnic Institute and State University ... VA ... 529
Virginia State University ... VA ... 529
Washington and Lee University ... VA ... 530
Central Washington University ... WA ... 532
Eastern Washington University ... WA ... 533
Gonzaga University ... WA ... 534
Pacific Lutheran University ... WA ... 536
Seattle Pacific University ... WA ... 537
Seattle University ... WA ... 538
University of Washington ... WA ... 539
Washington State University ... WA ... 539
Western Washington University ... WA ... 539
Marshall University ... WV ... 544
West Virginia University ... WV ... 545
Marquette University ... WI ... 548
University of Wisconsin-Eau Claire ... WI ... 551
University of Wisconsin-La Crosse ... WI ... 551
University of Wisconsin-Madison ... WI ... 550
University of Wisconsin-Milwaukee ... WI ... 551
University of Wisconsin-Oshkosh ... WI ... 551
University of Wisconsin-Parkside ... WI ... 552
University of Wisconsin-River Falls ... WI ... 552
University of Wisconsin-Whitewater ... WI ... 553
University of Wyoming ... WY ... 556

BUSA: AACSB-The Association to Advance Collegiate Schools of Business: accounting (B,M,D)

Auburn University ... AL ... 1
Auburn University at Montgomery ... AL ... 1
University of Alabama at Birmingham ... AL ... 8
University of Alabama, The ... AL ... 8
University of Alaska Fairbanks ... AK ... 10
Arizona State University ... AZ ... 11
University of Arizona ... AZ ... 18
University of Arkansas Main Campus ... AR ... 24
California State University-Fullerton ... CA ... 35
San Diego State University ... CA ... 37
Santa Clara University ... CA ... 68
University of San Diego ... CA ... 76
University of Southern California ... CA ... 76
University of Colorado Denver|Anschutz Medical Campus ... CO ... 88
University of Denver ... CO ... 89
University of Northern Colorado ... CO ... 89
University of Connecticut ... CT ... 94
University of Delaware ... DE ... 96
George Washington University ... DC ... 98
Howard University ... DC ... 98
Florida International University ... FL ... 119
Florida State University ... FL ... 119
Stetson University ... FL ... 121
University of Central Florida ... FL ... 120
University of Florida ... FL ... 120
University of Miami ... FL ... 122
University of North Florida ... FL ... 120
University of South Florida ... FL ... 121
University of South Florida St. Petersburg ... FL ... 121
Georgia Southern University ... GA ... 131
Georgia State University ... GA ... 131
Kennesaw State University ... GA ... 133
University of Georgia ... GA ... 138
University of West Georgia ... GA ... 139
Boise State University ... ID ... 142
Idaho State University ... ID ... 143
University of Idaho ... ID ... 144
Bradley University ... IL ... 146
DePaul University ... IL ... 149
Eastern Illinois University ... IL ... 150
Illinois State University ... IL ... 153
Loyola University Chicago ... IL ... 157
Northern Illinois University ... IL ... 160
Southern Illinois University Carbondale ... IL ... 165
Southern Illinois University Edwardsville ... IL ... 165
University of Illinois at Chicago ... IL ... 167
University of Illinois at Urbana-Champaign ... IL ... 167
Western Illinois University ... IL ... 168
Ball State University ... IN ... 169
Indiana University Bloomington ... IN ... 173
University of Notre Dame ... IN ... 180
University of Southern Indiana ... IN ... 181
Drake University ... IA ... 184
Iowa State University ... IA ... 182
University of Iowa ... IA ... 182
Kansas State University ... KS ... 194
University of Kansas Main Campus ... KS ... 197
Wichita State University ... KS ... 198
University of Kentucky ... KY ... 207
University of Louisville ... KY ... 207
Western Kentucky University ... KY ... 208
Louisiana Tech University ... LA ... 215
Nicholls State University ... LA ... 216
Southeastern Louisiana University ... LA ... 216
University of Louisiana at Lafayette ... LA ... 216
University of Louisiana at Monroe ... LA ... 216
University of New Orleans ... LA ... 213
Loyola University Maryland ... MD ... 223
Morgan State University ... MD ... 224
Towson University ... MD ... 228
Bentley University ... MA ... 231
Suffolk University ... MA ... 245
University of Massachusetts ... MA ... 236
Central Michigan University ... MI ... 249
Grand Valley State University ... MI ... 251
Michigan State University ... MI ... 255
Oakland University ... MI ... 256
Western Michigan University ... MI ... 260
Mississippi State University ... MS ... 275
University of Mississippi ... MS ... 277
University of Southern Mississippi ... MS ... 277
Missouri State University ... MO ... 286
Truman State University ... MO ... 290
University of Central Missouri ... MO ... 290
University of Missouri - Columbia ... MO ... 291
University of Missouri - Saint Louis ... MO ... 291
University of Montana - Missoula, The ... MT ... 294
Creighton University ... NE ... 297
University of Nebraska - Lincoln ... NE ... 300
University of Nevada, Las Vegas ... NV ... 302
University of Nevada, Reno ... NV ... 303
Rider University ... NJ ... 313
Seton Hall University ... NJ ... 315
New Mexico State University Main Campus . NM ... 319
University of New Mexico Main Campus ... NM ... 321
Baruch College/City University of New York . NY ... 326
Hofstra University ... NY ... 335
Pace University ... NY ... 345
St. John's University ... NY ... 348
University at Albany, SUNY ... NY ... 351
University at Buffalo-SUNY ... NY ... 351
North Carolina Agricultural and Technical State University ... NC ... 378
North Carolina State University ... NC ... 378
University of North Carolina at Charlotte ... NC ... 379
University of North Carolina at Greensboro .. NC ... 379
Wake Forest University ... NC ... 380
Bowling Green State University ... OH ... 385
Case Western Reserve University ... OH ... 386
Cleveland State University ... OH ... 388
John Carroll University ... OH ... 392
Kent State University Main Campus ... OH ... 393
Miami University ... OH ... 396
Ohio State University Main Campus, The ... OH ... 398
Ohio University Main Campus ... OH ... 399
University of Akron, Main Campus, The ... OH ... 403
University of Dayton ... OH ... 404
Wright State University Main Campus ... OH ... 406
Oklahoma State University ... OK ... 410
University of Oklahoma Norman Campus ... OK ... 413
Oregon State University ... OR ... 418
Portland State University ... OR ... 418
University of Oregon ... OR ... 419
Lehigh University ... PA ... 434
Saint Joseph's University ... PA ... 446
Villanova University ... PA ... 450
University of Rhode Island ... RI ... 454
Clemson University ... SC ... 456
College of Charleston ... SC ... 457
University of South Carolina Columbia ... SC ... 462
Belmont University ... TN ... 467
East Tennessee State University ... TN ... 473
Middle Tennessee State University ... TN ... 473
Tennessee Technological University ... TN ... 474
University of Memphis, The ... TN ... 474
University of Tennessee at Chattanooga ... TN ... 477
University of Tennessee, Knoxville ... TN ... 477
Baylor University ... TX ... 482
Texas A & M University ... TX ... 497
Texas A & M University - Corpus Christi ... TX ... 498
Texas Christian University ... TX ... 499
Texas Tech University ... TX ... 502
University of Houston ... TX ... 503
University of Houston - Clear Lake ... TX ... 503
University of North Texas ... TX ... 504
University of Texas at Arlington, The ... TX ... 505
University of Texas at Austin ... TX ... 505
University of Texas at Dallas, The ... TX ... 506
University of Texas at El Paso ... TX ... 506
University of Texas at San Antonio ... TX ... 506
Brigham Young University ... UT ... 509
University of Utah, The ... UT ... 511
Utah State University ... UT ... 511
Weber State University ... UT ... 511
College of William & Mary ... VA ... 518
George Mason University ... VA ... 519
James Madison University ... VA ... 520
Old Dominion University ... VA ... 522
University of Richmond ... VA ... 525
University of Virginia ... VA ... 525
Virginia Commonwealth University ... VA ... 526
Virginia Polytechnic Institute and State University ... VA ... 529
Gonzaga University ... WA ... 534
University of Washington ... WA ... 539
Washington State University ... WA ... 539
Marshall University ... WV ... 544
West Virginia University ... WV ... 545
Marquette University ... WI ... 548
University of Wisconsin-Madison ... WI ... 550

CACREP: Council for Accreditation of Counseling & Related Educational Programs: addiction counseling, career counseling, marriage, couple and family counseling, mental health counseling, school counseling, student affairs and college counseling (M) and counselor education and supervision (D)

Auburn University ... AL ... 1
Auburn University at Montgomery ... AL ... 1
Jacksonville State University ... AL ... 4
Troy University ... AL ... 8
University of Alabama at Birmingham ... AL ... 8
University of Alabama, The ... AL ... 8
University of Montevallo ... AL ... 9
University of North Alabama ... AL ... 9

CEA: Commission on English Language Program Accreditation: english language (C)

CHIRO: Council on Chiropractic Education: chiropractic education (FP,D)

CIDA: Council for Interior Design Accreditation: interior design (B,M)

Purdue University Main Campus ... IN ... 178
Iowa State University ... IA ... 182
Kansas State University ... KS ... 194
University of Kentucky ... KY ... 207
University of Louisville ... KY ... 207
Louisiana State University and Agricultural and Mechanical College ... LA ... 212
Louisiana Tech University ... LA ... 215
University of Louisiana at Lafayette ... LA ... 216
Boston Architectural College ... MA ... 231
Endicott College ... MA ... 234
Mount Ida College ... MA ... 242
Newbury College ... MA ... 243
Suffolk University ... MA ... 245
Wentworth Institute of Technology ... MA ... 245
Central Michigan University ... MI ... 249
College for Creative Studies ... MI ... 249
Eastern Michigan University ... MI ... 250
Ferris State University ... MI ... 250
International Academy of Design and Technology ... MI ... 252
Lawrence Technological University ... MI ... 254
Michigan State University ... MI ... 255
Western Michigan University ... MI ... 260
University of Minnesota-Twin Cities ... MN ... 272
Mississippi College ... MS ... 275
Mississippi State University ... MS ... 275
University of Southern Mississippi ... MS ... 277
Maryville University of Saint Louis ... MO ... 284
University of Missouri - Columbia ... MO ... 291
University of Nebraska at Kearney ... NE ... 300
University of Nebraska - Lincoln ... NE ... 300
Art Institute of Las Vegas, The ... NV ... 301
University of Nevada, Las Vegas ... NV ... 302
Kean University ... NJ ... 311
Southwest University of Visual Arts ... NM ... 320
Cornell University ... NY ... 331
Fashion Institute of Technology ... NY ... 333
New York Institute of Technology ... NY ... 343
New York School of Interior Design ... NY ... 343
Pratt Institute ... NY ... 346
Rochester Institute of Technology ... NY ... 347
School of Visual Arts ... NY ... 350
State University of New York College at Buffalo ... NY ... 353
Syracuse University Main Campus ... NY ... 357
Villa Maria College of Buffalo ... NY ... 359
Appalachian State University ... NC ... 377
East Carolina University ... NC ... 377
High Point University ... NC ... 365
Meredith College ... NC ... 367
University of North Carolina at Greensboro ... NC ... 379
Western Carolina University ... NC ... 380
North Dakota State University Main Campus ... ND ... 382
Columbus College of Art & Design ... OH ... 388
Kent State University Main Campus ... OH ... 393
Miami University ... OH ... 396
Ohio State University Main Campus, The ... OH ... 398
Ohio University Main Campus ... OH ... 399
University of Akron, Main Campus, The ... OH ... 403
University of Cincinnati Main Campus ... OH ... 403
Oklahoma Christian University ... OK ... 409
Oklahoma State University ... OK ... 410
University of Central Oklahoma ... OK ... 413
University of Oklahoma Norman Campus ... OK ... 413
Art Institute of Portland, The ... OR ... 414
Marylhurst University ... OR ... 416
University of Oregon ... OR ... 419
Art Institute of Philadelphia ... PA ... 422
Art Institute of Pittsburgh ... PA ... 422
Chatham University ... PA ... 425
Drexel University ... PA ... 427
La Roche College ... PA ... 432
Moore College of Art and Design ... PA ... 436
Philadelphia University ... PA ... 444
Converse College ... SC ... 457
Winthrop University ... SC ... 463
South Dakota State University ... SD ... 466
Middle Tennessee State University ... TN ... 473
O'More College of Design ... TN ... 472
University of Memphis, The ... TN ... 474
University of Tennessee at Chattanooga ... TN ... 477
University of Tennessee, Knoxville ... TN ... 477
Watkins College of Art, Design & Film ... TN ... 478
Abilene Christian University ... TX ... 478
Art Institute of Dallas ... TX ... 480
Art Institute of Houston, The ... TX ... 480
Baylor University ... TX ... 482
Sam Houston State University ... TX ... 501
Stephen F. Austin State University ... TX ... 496
Texas Christian University ... TX ... 499
Texas State University-San Marcos ... TX ... 501
Texas Tech University ... TX ... 502
University of North Texas ... TX ... 504
University of Texas at Arlington, The ... TX ... 505
University of Texas at Austin ... TX ... 505
University of Texas at San Antonio ... TX ... 506
University of the Incarnate Word ... TX ... 504
Utah State University ... UT ... 511
Weber State University ... UT ... 511
James Madison University ... VA ... 520
Marymount University ... VA ... 521
Radford University ... VA ... 523
Virginia Commonwealth University ... VA ... 526
Virginia Polytechnic Institute and State University ... VA ... 529
Art Institute of Seattle, The ... WA ... 531
Bellevue College ... WA ... 531
Washington State University ... WA ... 539
West Virginia University ... WV ... 545
Mount Mary College ... WI ... 549
University of Wisconsin-Madison ... WI ... 550
University of Wisconsin-Stevens Point ... WI ... 552
University of Wisconsin-Stout ... WI ... 552

CLPSY: American Psychological Association: clinical psychology (D)

Auburn University ... AL ... 1
University of Alabama at Birmingham ... AL ... 8
University of Alabama, The ... AL ... 8
University of Alaska Fairbanks ... AK ... 10
Argosy University, Phoenix ... AZ ... 11
Arizona State University ... AZ ... 11
Midwestern University ... AZ ... 16
University of Arizona ... AZ ... 18
University of Arkansas Main Campus ... AR ... 24
Alliant International University-Fresno & Sacramento ... CA ... 27
Alliant International University-Los Angeles ... CA ... 27
Alliant International University-San Diego ... CA ... 27
Alliant International University-San Francisco ... CA ... 27
Argosy University, Orange County ... CA ... 29
#Argosy University, San Francisco Bay Area ... CA ... 29
Azusa Pacific University ... CA ... 30
Biola University ... CA ... 31
#Fielding Graduate University ... CA ... 47
Fuller Theological Seminary ... CA ... 48
#John F. Kennedy University ... CA ... 52
Loma Linda University ... CA ... 54
Palo Alto University ... CA ... 61
Pepperdine University ... CA ... 61
San Diego State University ... CA ... 37
University of California-Berkeley ... CA ... 73
University of California-Los Angeles ... CA ... 74
University of California-San Diego ... CA ... 74
University of LaVerne ... CA ... 75
University of Southern California ... CA ... 76
Wright Institute, The ... CA ... 79
University of Colorado Boulder ... CO ... 88
University of Colorado Colorado Springs ... CO ... 88
University of Denver ... CO ... 89
University of Connecticut ... CT ... 94
University of Hartford ... CT ... 95
Yale University ... CT ... 96
University of Delaware ... DE ... 96
American University ... DC ... 97
Catholic University of America, The ... DC ... 97
Gallaudet University ... DC ... 98
George Washington University ... DC ... 98
Howard University ... DC ... 98
Argosy University, Tampa ... FL ... 101
Carlos Albizu University Miami Campus ... FL ... 102
Florida Institute of Technology ... FL ... 108
Florida State University ... FL ... 119
Nova Southeastern University ... FL ... 114
University of Central Florida ... FL ... 120
University of Florida ... FL ... 120
University of Miami ... FL ... 122
University of South Florida ... FL ... 121
Argosy University, Atlanta ... GA ... 124
Emory University ... GA ... 129
Georgia State University ... GA ... 131
University of Georgia ... GA ... 138
Argosy University, Hawaii ... HI ... 140
University of Hawaii at Manoa ... HI ... 141
Idaho State University ... ID ... 143
Adler School of Professional Psychology ... IL ... 144
Argosy University, Chicago ... IL ... 145
Argosy University, Schaumburg ... IL ... 145
Chicago School of Professional Psychology ... IL ... 146
DePaul University ... IL ... 149
Illinois Institute of Technology ... IL ... 153
Loyola University Chicago ... IL ... 157
Northern Illinois University ... IL ... 160
Northwestern University ... IL ... 160
Roosevelt University ... IL ... 163
Rosalind Franklin University of Medicine & Science ... IL ... 163
Southern Illinois University Carbondale ... IL ... 165
University of Illinois at Chicago ... IL ... 167
University of Illinois at Urbana-Champaign ... IL ... 167
Wheaton College ... IL ... 168
Indiana State University ... IN ... 173
Indiana University Bloomington ... IN ... 173
Indiana University-Purdue University Indianapolis ... IN ... 174
Purdue University Main Campus ... IN ... 178
University of Indianapolis ... IN ... 180
University of Iowa ... IA ... 182
University of Kansas Main Campus ... KS ... 197
Wichita State University ... KS ... 198
Spalding University ... KY ... 206
University of Kentucky ... KY ... 207
University of Louisville ... KY ... 207
Louisiana State University and Agricultural and Mechanical College ... LA ... 212
University of Maine ... ME ... 220
Loyola University Maryland ... MD ... 223
Uniformed Services University of the Health Sciences ... MD ... 558
University of Maryland Baltimore County ... MD ... 227
University of Maryland College Park ... MD ... 227
Boston University ... MA ... 232
Clark University ... MA ... 233
Harvard University ... MA ... 235
Massachusetts School of Professional Psychology ... MA ... 241
Suffolk University ... MA ... 245
University of Massachusetts ... MA ... 236
University of Massachusetts Boston ... MA ... 236
Central Michigan University ... MI ... 249
Eastern Michigan University ... MI ... 250
Michigan State University ... MI ... 255
University of Detroit Mercy ... MI ... 258
University of Michigan-Ann Arbor ... MI ... 259
Wayne State University ... MI ... 260
Western Michigan University ... MI ... 260
Argosy University, Twin Cities ... MN ... 260
University of Minnesota-Twin Cities ... MN ... 272
Jackson State University ... MS ... 274
University of Mississippi ... MS ... 277
University of Southern Mississippi ... MS ... 277
Saint Louis University ... MO ... 289
#School of Professional Psychology at Forest Institute, The ... MO ... 289
University of Missouri - Columbia ... MO ... 291
University of Missouri - Kansas City ... MO ... 291
University of Missouri - Saint Louis ... MO ... 291
Washington University in St. Louis ... MO ... 292
University of Montana - Missoula, The ... MT ... 294
University of Nebraska - Lincoln ... NE ... 300
University of Nevada, Las Vegas ... NV ... 302
University of Nevada, Reno ... NV ... 303
Antioch University New England ... NH ... 303
Fairleigh Dickinson University ... NJ ... 310
Rutgers the State University of New Jersey New Brunswick Campus ... NJ ... 314
University of New Mexico Main Campus ... NM ... 321
Adelphi University ... NY ... 322
#City University of New York The City College ... NY ... 326
Fordham University ... NY ... 334
Hofstra University ... NY ... 335
Long Island University Brooklyn Campus ... NY ... 338
Long Island University C.W. Post Campus ... NY ... 339
New School, The ... NY ... 342
St. John's University ... NY ... 348
State University of New York at Binghamton ... NY ... 351
State University of New York at Stony Brook ... NY ... 352
Syracuse University Main Campus ... NY ... 357
Teachers College, Columbia University ... NY ... 357
University at Albany, SUNY ... NY ... 351
University at Buffalo-SUNY ... NY ... 351
University of Rochester ... NY ... 359
Yeshiva University ... NY ... 361
Duke University ... NC ... 364
East Carolina University ... NC ... 377
University of North Carolina at Chapel Hill ... NC ... 378
University of North Carolina at Greensboro ... NC ... 379
University of North Dakota Main Campus ... ND ... 381
Bowling Green State University ... OH ... 385
Case Western Reserve University ... OH ... 386
Kent State University Main Campus ... OH ... 393
Miami University ... OH ... 396
Ohio State University Main Campus, The ... OH ... 398
Ohio University Main Campus ... OH ... 399
University of Cincinnati Main Campus ... OH ... 403
University of Toledo ... OH ... 404
Wright State University Main Campus ... OH ... 406
Xavier University ... OH ... 406
Oklahoma State University ... OK ... 410
University of Tulsa ... OK ... 413
George Fox University ... OR ... 415
Pacific University ... OR ... 419
University of Oregon ... OR ... 419
Chestnut Hill College ... PA ... 425
Drexel University ... PA ... 427
Duquesne University ... PA ... 428
Immaculata University ... PA ... 431
Indiana University of Pennsylvania ... PA ... 442
La Salle University ... PA ... 432
Marywood University ... PA ... 435
Penn State University Park ... PA ... 438
Philadelphia College of Osteopathic Medicine ... PA ... 444
Temple University ... PA ... 447
University of Pittsburgh ... PA ... 449
Widener University ... PA ... 451
Carlos Albizu University ... PR ... 561
Ponce School of Medicine & Health Sciences ... PR ... 565
University of Rhode Island ... RI ... 454
University of South Carolina Columbia ... SC ... 462
University of South Dakota, The ... SD ... 465
University of Memphis, The ... TN ... 474
University of Tennessee, Knoxville ... TN ... 477
Vanderbilt University ... TN ... 478
Baylor University ... TX ... 482
Sam Houston State University ... TX ... 501
Southern Methodist University ... TX ... 495
Texas A & M University ... TX ... 497
Texas Tech University ... TX ... 502
University of Houston ... TX ... 503
University of North Texas ... TX ... 504
University of Texas at Austin ... TX ... 505
University of Texas Southwestern Medical Center ... TX ... 507
Brigham Young University ... UT ... 509
University of Utah, The ... UT ... 511
University of Vermont ... VT ... 514
Argosy University, Washington DC ... VA ... 516
Eastern Virginia Medical School ... VA ... 518
George Mason University ... VA ... 519
Norfolk State University ... VA ... 522
Old Dominion University ... VA ... 522
Regent University ... VA ... 523
University of Virginia ... VA ... 525
Virginia Commonwealth University ... VA ... 526
Virginia Polytechnic Institute and State University ... VA ... 529
Seattle Pacific University ... WA ... 537
University of Washington ... WA ... 539
Washington State University ... WA ... 539
Marshall University ... WV ... 544
West Virginia University ... WV ... 545
Marquette University ... WI ... 548
University of Wisconsin-Madison ... WI ... 550
University of Wisconsin-Milwaukee ... WI ... 551
Wisconsin School of Professional Psychology ... WI ... 553
University of Wyoming ... WY ... 556

CNCE: Accrediting Council for Continuing Education and Training: continuing education (C,A)

Southwest Institute of Healing Arts ... AZ ... 18
CBD College ... CA ... 38
Los Angeles ORT College ... CA ... 55
United Education Institute ... CA ... 73
Zarem/Golde ORT Technical Institute ... IL ... 169
Baton Rouge College ... LA ... 208
National Institute of Massotherapy ... OH ... 397
Mech-Tech College ... PR ... 564
Interface College ... WA ... 535
Valley College - Beckley Campus ... WV ... 542

COE: Council on Occupational Education: occupational, trade, and technical education (C,A)

J.F. Drake State Technical College ... AL ... 4
J.F. Ingram State Technical College ... AL ... 4
Reid State Technical College ... AL ... 6
Trenholm State Technical College ... AL ... 7
National Park Community College ... AR ... 22
University of Arkansas at Monticello ... AR ... 25
Advanced College ... CA ... 26
Advanced Training Associates ... CA ... 26
Hands-on Medical Massage School ... CA ... 49
#Infotech Career College ... CA ... 51
Colorado Academy of Veterinary Technology ... CO ... 82
Medtech College ... DC ... 99
Academy for Practical Nursing and Health Occupations ... FL ... 100
Florida Career College ... FL ... 107
Fortis College ... FL ... 110
Miami Ad School ... FL ... 113
Altamaha Technical College ... GA ... 124
Atlanta Technical College ... GA ... 125
Brown College of Court Reporting ... GA ... 126
Georgia Northwestern Technical College ... GA ... 131
Interactive College of Technology ... GA ... 132
Lanier Technical College ... GA ... 133
Moultrie Technical College ... GA ... 134
Oconee Fall Line Technical College-North Campus ... GA ... 135
Oconee Fall Line Technical College-South Campus ... GA ... 135
Ogeechee Technical College ... GA ... 135
South Georgia Technical College ... GA ... 137
Morrison Institute of Technology ... IL ... 159
Highland Community College-Technical Center ... KS ... 193
Galen College of Nursing ... KY ... 200
Cameron College ... LA ... 208
Capital Area Technical College Baton Rouge Campus ... LA ... 209
Capital Area Technical College Folkes Campus ... LA ... 209
Capital Area Technical College Jumonville Campus ... LA ... 210
Career Technical College ... LA ... 208
Central Louisiana Technical College Avoyelles Campus ... LA ... 210
Central Louisiana Technical College Huey P. Long Campus ... LA ... 210
Central Louisiana Technical College Oakdale Campus ... LA ... 210
Central Louisiana Technical Community College ... LA ... 210
L.E. Fletcher Technical Community College ... LA ... 210
Louisiana Culinary Institute ... LA ... 212
Northeast Louisiana Technical College Bastrop Campus ... LA ... 210
Northeast Louisiana Technical College Delta-Ouachita Campus ... LA ... 210
Northeast Louisiana Technical College Farmerville Campus ... LA ... 210
Northeast Louisiana Technical College Northeast Campus ... LA ... 210
Northeast Louisiana Technical College Ruston Campus ... LA ... 210
Northshore Technical Community College ... LA ... 211
Northwest Louisiana Technical College Natchitoches Campus ... LA ... 211
Northwest Louisiana Technical College Northwest Campus ... LA ... 211
Northwest Louisiana Technical College Shreveport Campus ... LA ... 211

South Central Louisiana Technical College Lafourche Campus ... LA ... 211
South Central Louisiana Technical College River Parishes Campus ... LA ... 211
South Central Louisiana Technical College Young Memorial Campus ... LA ... 211
South Louisiana Community College Ardoin Campus ... LA ... 211
South Louisiana Community College Charles B Coreil Campus ... LA ... 212
South Louisiana Community College Gulf Area Campus ... LA ... 212
South Louisiana Community College Teche Area Campus ... LA ... 212
South Louisiana Community College T.H. Harris Campus ... LA ... 212
Sowela Technical Community College ... LA ... 212
Concorde Career College ... TN ... 468
Fortis Institute ... TN ... 468
Kaplan Career Institute ... TN ... 469
North Central Institute ... TN ... 472
Center for Advanced Legal Studies ... TX ... 482
Computer Career Center ... TX ... 483
Kaplan College ... TX ... 489
Ogden-Weber Applied Technology College .. UT ... 510
Uintah Basin Applied Technology College ... UT ... 510
Career Training Solutions ... VA ... 517
Columbia College ... VA ... 518
Medtech College ... VA ... 521
RSHT ... VA ... 524
Southeast Culinary and Hospitality College .. VA ... 524

COMTA: Commission on Massage Therapy Accreditation: massage therapy, bodywork, aesthetics/esthetics and skin care (C,A)

Florida College of Natural Health ... FL ... 108
Elgin Community College ... IL ... 150
Kishwaukee College ... IL ... 155
Moraine Valley Community College ... IL ... 159
National University of Health Sciences ... IL ... 159
SOLEX College ... IL ... 164
Allegany College of Maryland ... MD ... 221
Community College of Baltimore County, The ... MD ... 222
Bristol Community College ... MA ... 239
#Salter College ... MA ... 244
Springfield Technical Community College ... MA ... 241
Lansing Community College ... MI ... 254
Northwestern Health Sciences University ... MN ... 270
Community College of Rhode Island ... RI ... 453
Technical College of the Lowcountry ... SC ... 461
Roane State Community College ... TN ... 476
Parker University ... TX ... 492

CONST: American Council for Construction Education: construction education (A,B)

Auburn University ... AL ... 1
Jefferson State Community College ... AL ... 5
Arizona State University ... AZ ... 11
Northern Arizona University ... AZ ... 16
John Brown University ... AR ... 22
University of Arkansas at Little Rock ... AR ... 24
California Polytechnic State University-San Luis Obispo ... CA ... 33
California State University-Chico ... CA ... 34
California State University-Fresno ... CA ... 35
California State University-Northridge ... CA ... 35
California State University-Sacramento ... CA ... 36
Colorado State University ... CO ... 83
Central Connecticut State University ... CT ... 90
Florida International University ... FL ... 119
Santa Fe College ... FL ... 117
University of Florida ... FL ... 120
University of North Florida ... FL ... 120
Georgia Institute of Technology ... GA ... 130
Georgia Southern University ... GA ... 131
Southern Polytechnic State University ... GA ... 137
Boise State University ... ID ... 142
Bradley University ... IL ... 146
Illinois State University ... IL ... 153
John A. Logan College ... IL ... 154
Southern Illinois University Edwardsville ... IL ... 165
Indiana State University ... IN ... 173
Purdue University Main Campus ... IN ... 178
Kansas State University ... KS ... 194
Eastern Kentucky University ... KY ... 200
Northern Kentucky University ... KY ... 205
Louisiana State University and Agricultural and Mechanical College ... LA ... 212
University of Louisiana at Monroe ... LA ... 216
University of Maryland Eastern Shore ... MD ... 227
Wentworth Institute of Technology ... MA ... 245
Eastern Michigan University ... MI ... 250
Ferris State University ... MI ... 250
Michigan State University ... MI ... 255
Minnesota State University Moorhead ... MN ... 267
Minnesota State University, Mankato ... MN ... 267
University of Southern Mississippi ... MS ... 277
Missouri State University ... MO ... 286
State Fair Community College ... MO ... 290
University of Central Missouri ... MO ... 290
University of Nebraska - Lincoln ... NE ... 300
University of Nevada, Las Vegas ... NV ... 302
Central New Mexico Community College ... NM ... 317
University of New Mexico Main Campus ... NM ... 321
Alfred State College ... NY ... 355
State University of New York College of Technology at Delhi ... NY ... 355
East Carolina University ... NC ... 377
North Carolina Agricultural and Technical State University ... NC ... 378
Western Carolina University ... NC ... 380
North Dakota State University Main Campus. ND ... 382
Bowling Green State University ... OH ... 385
Cincinnati State Technical and Community College ... OH ... 387
Columbus State Community College ... OH ... 389
University of Cincinnati Main Campus ... OH ... 403
University of Oklahoma Norman Campus ... OK ... 413
Oregon State University ... OR ... 418
Drexel University ... PA ... 427
Pennsylvania College of Technology ... PA ... 440
Roger Williams University ... RI ... 454
Clemson University ... SC ... 456
South Dakota State University ... SD ... 466
North Lake College ... TX ... 485
Texas A & M University ... TX ... 497
University of Houston ... TX ... 503
Brigham Young University ... UT ... 509
Weber State University ... UT ... 511
Virginia Polytechnic Institute and State University ... VA ... 529
Central Washington University ... WA ... 532
Edmonds Community College ... WA ... 533
University of Washington ... WA ... 539
Washington State University ... WA ... 539
Milwaukee School of Engineering ... WI ... 549
University of Wisconsin-Stout ... WI ... 552

COPSY: American Psychological Association: counseling psychology (D)

Auburn University ... AL ... 1
Arizona State University ... AZ ... 11
Colorado State University ... CO ... 83
University of Denver ... CO ... 89
University of Northern Colorado ... CO ... 89
#Howard University ... DC ... 98
University of Florida ... FL ... 120
University of Miami ... FL ... 122
Georgia State University ... GA ... 131
University of Georgia ... GA ... 138
Loyola University Chicago ... IL ... 157
Southern Illinois University Carbondale ... IL ... 165
University of Illinois at Urbana-Champaign ... IL ... 167
Ball State University ... IN ... 169
Indiana State University ... IN ... 173
Indiana University Bloomington ... IN ... 173
Purdue University Main Campus ... IN ... 178
University of Notre Dame ... IN ... 180
Iowa State University ... IA ... 182
University of Iowa ... IA ... 182
University of Kansas Main Campus ... KS ... 197
University of Kentucky ... KY ... 207
University of Louisville ... KY ... 207
Louisiana Tech University ... LA ... 215
University of Maryland College Park ... MD ... 227
Boston College ... MA ... 232
Western Michigan University ... MI ... 260
University of Minnesota-Twin Cities ... MN ... 272
University of Saint Thomas ... MN ... 272
University of Southern Mississippi ... MS ... 277
University of Missouri - Columbia ... MO ... 291
University of Missouri - Kansas City ... MO ... 291
University of Nebraska - Lincoln ... NE ... 300
Seton Hall University ... NJ ... 315
New Mexico State University Main Campus . NM ... 319
Fordham University ... NY ... 334
New York University ... NY ... 344
Teachers College, Columbia University ... NY ... 357
University at Albany, SUNY ... NY ... 351
University of North Dakota Main Campus ... ND ... 381
Cleveland State University ... OH ... 388
University of Akron, Main Campus, The ... OH ... 403
Oklahoma State University ... OK ... 410
University of Oklahoma Norman Campus ... OK ... 413
University of Oregon ... OR ... 419
Carlow University ... PA ... 424
Lehigh University ... PA ... 434
Penn State University Park ... PA ... 438
Tennessee State University ... TN ... 474
University of Memphis, The ... TN ... 474
University of Tennessee, Knoxville ... TN ... 477
Our Lady of the Lake University ... TX ... 492
Texas A & M University ... TX ... 497
Texas Tech University ... TX ... 502
Texas Woman's University ... TX ... 502
University of Houston ... TX ... 503
University of North Texas ... TX ... 504
University of Texas at Austin ... TX ... 505
Brigham Young University ... UT ... 509
University of Utah, The ... UT ... 511
Virginia Commonwealth University ... VA ... 526
Washington State University ... WA ... 539
West Virginia University ... WV ... 545
Marquette University ... WI ... 548
University of Wisconsin-Madison ... WI ... 550
University of Wisconsin-Milwaukee ... WI ... 551

CORE: Council of Rehabilitation Education: rehabilitation counseling (M)

Alabama Agricultural and Mechanical University ... AL ... 1
Alabama State University ... AL ... 1
Auburn University ... AL ... 1
Troy University ... AL ... 8
University of Alabama at Birmingham ... AL ... 8
University of Alabama, The ... AL ... 8
University of Arizona ... AZ ... 18
Arkansas State University-Jonesboro ... AR ... 20
University of Arkansas at Little Rock ... AR ... 24
University of Arkansas Main Campus ... AR ... 24
California State University-Fresno ... CA ... 35
California State University-Los Angeles ... CA ... 35
California State University-Sacramento ... CA ... 36
California State University-San Bernardino ... CA ... 36
San Diego State University ... CA ... 37
San Francisco State University ... CA ... 37
University of Northern Colorado ... CO ... 89
Central Connecticut State University ... CT ... 90
George Washington University ... DC ... 98
Florida Atlantic University ... FL ... 119
Florida State University ... FL ... 119
University of South Florida ... FL ... 121
#Fort Valley State University ... GA ... 129
Georgia State University ... GA ... 131
Thomas University ... GA ... 138
University of Hawaii at Manoa ... HI ... 141
University of Idaho ... ID ... 144
Adler School of Professional Psychology ... IL ... 144
Illinois Institute of Technology ... IL ... 153
Northeastern Illinois University ... IL ... 160
Northern Illinois University ... IL ... 160
Southern Illinois University Carbondale ... IL ... 165
University of Illinois at Urbana-Champaign ... IL ... 167
Ball State University ... IN ... 169
Drake University ... IA ... 184
University of Iowa ... IA ... 182
Emporia State University ... KS ... 192
University of Kentucky ... KY ... 207
Louisiana State University Health Sciences Center-New Orleans ... LA ... 213
Southern University and A&M College ... LA ... 214
University of Southern Maine ... ME ... 220
Coppin State University ... MD ... 228
University of Maryland Eastern Shore ... MD ... 227
Assumption College ... MA ... 230
Springfield College ... MA ... 244
University of Massachusetts Boston ... MA ... 236
Michigan State University ... MI ... 255
Wayne State University ... MI ... 260
Western Michigan University ... MI ... 260
Minnesota State University, Mankato ... MN ... 267
St. Cloud State University ... MN ... 269
Jackson State University ... MS ... 274
Mississippi State University ... MS ... 275
Maryville University of Saint Louis ... MO ... 284
Montana State University - Billings ... MT ... 295
UMDNJ-School of Health Related Professions ... NJ ... 317
@New Mexico Highlands University ... NM ... 318
City University of New York Hunter College . NY ... 327
Hofstra University ... NY ... 335
University at Buffalo-SUNY ... NY ... 351
East Carolina University ... NC ... 377
@North Carolina Agricultural and Technical State University ... NC ... 378
University of North Carolina at Chapel Hill ... NC ... 378
Winston-Salem State University ... NC ... 380
Bowling Green State University ... OH ... 385
Kent State University Main Campus ... OH ... 393
Ohio University Main Campus ... OH ... 399
Wilberforce University ... OH ... 405
Wright State University Main Campus ... OH ... 406
East Central University ... OK ... 407
Langston University ... OK ... 408
Portland State University ... OR ... 418
Western Oregon University ... OR ... 419
Edinboro University of Pennsylvania ... PA ... 442
Penn State University Park ... PA ... 438
University of Pittsburgh ... PA ... 449
University of Scranton, The ... PA ... 450
Bayamon Central University ... PR ... 560
Pontifical Catholic University of Puerto Rico, The ... PR ... 565
University of Puerto Rico-Rio Piedras Campus ... PR ... 568
Salve Regina University ... RI ... 454
South Carolina State University ... SC ... 460
University of South Carolina Columbia ... SC ... 462
@South Dakota State University ... SD ... 466
University of Memphis, The ... TN ... 474
University of Tennessee, Knoxville ... TN ... 477
Stephen F. Austin State University ... TX ... 496
Texas Tech University Health Sciences Center ... TX ... 502
University of North Texas ... TX ... 504
University of Texas at Austin ... TX ... 505
University of Texas at El Paso ... TX ... 506
University of Texas - Pan American ... TX ... 506
University of Texas Southwestern Medical Center ... TX ... 507
Utah State University ... UT ... 511
Virginia Commonwealth University ... VA ... 526
Western Washington University ... WA ... 539
West Virginia University ... WV ... 545
University of Wisconsin-Madison ... WI ... 550
University of Wisconsin-Stout ... WI ... 552

CS: ABET, Inc.: computer science (B)

Alabama Agricultural and Mechanical University ... AL ... 1
Auburn University ... AL ... 1
Jacksonville State University ... AL ... 4
University of Alabama at Birmingham ... AL ... 8
University of Alabama in Huntsville ... AL ... 8
University of Alabama, The ... AL ... 8
University of North Alabama ... AL ... 9
University of South Alabama ... AL ... 9
University of Alaska Fairbanks ... AK ... 10
Arizona State University ... AZ ... 11
Northern Arizona University ... AZ ... 16
Arkansas Tech University ... AR ... 20
University of Arkansas at Little Rock ... AR ... 24
University of Arkansas Main Campus ... AR ... 24
University of Central Arkansas ... AR ... 25
California Polytechnic State University-San Luis Obispo ... CA ... 33
California State Polytechnic University-Pomona ... CA ... 33
California State University-Chico ... CA ... 34
California State University-Dominguez Hills .. CA ... 34
California State University-Fullerton ... CA ... 35
California State University-Long Beach ... CA ... 35
California State University-Los Angeles ... CA ... 35
California State University-Northridge ... CA ... 35
California State University-Sacramento ... CA ... 36
California State University-San Bernardino ... CA ... 36
San Francisco State University ... CA ... 37
San Jose State University ... CA ... 37
Santa Clara University ... CA ... 68
University of California-Berkeley ... CA ... 73
University of California-Davis ... CA ... 73
University of California-Los Angeles ... CA ... 74
University of California-Riverside ... CA ... 74
University of California-Santa Barbara ... CA ... 75
University of Southern California ... CA ... 76
University of the Pacific ... CA ... 76
Metropolitan State University of Denver ... CO ... 86
Regis University ... CO ... 87
United States Air Force Academy ... CO ... 558
University of Colorado Boulder ... CO ... 88
University of Colorado Colorado Springs ... CO ... 88
University of Colorado Denver|Anschutz Medical Campus ... CO ... 88
Central Connecticut State University ... CT ... 90
Quinnipiac University ... CT ... 93
Southern Connecticut State University ... CT ... 90
University of Connecticut ... CT ... 94
University of New Haven ... CT ... 95
George Washington University ... DC ... 98
Howard University ... DC ... 98
University of the District of Columbia ... DC ... 100
Florida Agricultural and Mechanical University ... FL ... 118
Florida Atlantic University ... FL ... 119
Florida Institute of Technology ... FL ... 108
Florida International University ... FL ... 119
Florida Memorial University ... FL ... 109
Florida State University ... FL ... 119
University of Central Florida ... FL ... 120
University of North Florida ... FL ... 120
University of South Florida ... FL ... 121
Armstrong Atlantic State University ... GA ... 124
Georgia Institute of Technology ... GA ... 130
Georgia Southern University ... GA ... 131
Kennesaw State University ... GA ... 133
Macon State College ... GA ... 133
Mercer University ... GA ... 134
Southern Polytechnic State University ... GA ... 137
University of West Georgia ... GA ... 139
Boise State University ... ID ... 142
Idaho State University ... ID ... 143
University of Idaho ... ID ... 144
Illinois Institute of Technology ... IL ... 153
Illinois State University ... IL ... 153
Southern Illinois University Carbondale ... IL ... 165
Southern Illinois University Edwardsville ... IL ... 165
University of Illinois at Chicago ... IL ... 167
University of Illinois at Urbana-Champaign ... IL ... 167
Indiana University-Purdue University Fort Wayne ... IN ... 174
Indiana University-Purdue University Indianapolis ... IN ... 174
Purdue University Main Campus ... IN ... 178
Rose-Hulman Institute of Technology ... IN ... 179
University of Evansville ... IN ... 180
University of Notre Dame ... IN ... 180
Iowa State University ... IA ... 182
Kansas State University ... KS ... 194
University of Kansas Main Campus ... KS ... 197
Eastern Kentucky University ... KY ... 200
University of Kentucky ... KY ... 207
University of Louisville ... KY ... 207
Grambling State University ... LA ... 215
Louisiana State University and Agricultural and Mechanical College ... LA ... 212
Louisiana State University in Shreveport ... LA ... 213
Louisiana Tech University ... LA ... 215
McNeese State University ... LA ... 215
Southeastern Louisiana University ... LA ... 216
Southern University and A&M College ... LA ... 214
University of Louisiana at Lafayette ... LA ... 216
University of Louisiana at Monroe ... LA ... 216

CVT: Commission on Accreditation of Allied Health Education Programs: cardiovascular technology (C,A,B)

CYTO: Commission on Accreditation of Allied Health Education Programs: cytotechnology (C,B,M)

DA: American Dental Association: dental assisting (C,A)

DANCE: National Association of Schools of Dance: dance (C,A,B,M,D)

DENT: American Dental Association: dentistry (FP,D)

DETC: Distance Education and Training Council: home study schools (A,B,M,D)

DH: American Dental Association: dental hygiene (C,A,B,M)

DIETC: Academy of Nutrition and Dietetics: coordinated dietetics programs (B,M)

DIETD: Academy of Nutrition and Dietetics: didactic dietetics programs (B,M)

Northwest Missouri State University ... MO ... 287
Saint Louis University ... MO ... 289
Southeast Missouri State University ... MO ... 289
University of Central Missouri ... MO ... 290
Montana State University ... MT ... 295
University of Nebraska - Lincoln ... NE ... 300
University of Nevada, Las Vegas ... NV ... 302
University of Nevada, Reno ... NV ... 303
Keene State College ... NH ... 306
University of New Hampshire ... NH ... 306
College of Saint Elizabeth ... NJ ... 308
Montclair State University ... NJ ... 311
Rutgers the State University of New Jersey New Brunswick Campus ... NJ ... 314
New Mexico State University Main Campus . NM ... 319
University of New Mexico Main Campus ... NM ... 321
City University of New York Brooklyn College ... NY ... 326
City University of New York Herbert H. Lehman College ... NY ... 327
City University of New York Hunter College . NY ... 327
City University of New York Queens College NY ... 328
Cornell University ... NY ... 331
Long Island University C.W. Post Campus ... NY ... 339
New York University ... NY ... 344
Rochester Institute of Technology ... NY ... 347
Sage Colleges, The ... NY ... 348
State University of New York College at Buffalo ... NY ... 353
State University of New York College at Oneonta ... NY ... 353
State University of New York College at Plattsburgh ... NY ... 354
Syracuse University Main Campus ... NY ... 357
Appalachian State University ... NC ... 377
East Carolina University ... NC ... 377
Meredith College ... NC ... 367
North Carolina Agricultural and Technical State University ... NC ... 378
North Carolina Central University ... NC ... 378
University of North Carolina at Greensboro .. NC ... 379
Western Carolina University ... NC ... 380
North Dakota State University Main Campus. ND ... 382
@Ashland University ... OH ... 384
Bluffton University ... OH ... 385
Bowling Green State University ... OH ... 385
Case Western Reserve University ... OH ... 386
Kent State University Main Campus ... OH ... 393
Miami University ... OH ... 396
Ohio State University Main Campus, The ... OH ... 398
Ohio University Main Campus ... OH ... 399
University of Akron, Main Campus, The ... OH ... 403
University of Cincinnati Main Campus ... OH ... 403
University of Dayton ... OH ... 404
Youngstown State University ... OH ... 406
Langston University ... OK ... 408
Northeastern State University ... OK ... 409
Oklahoma State University ... OK ... 410
University of Central Oklahoma ... OK ... 413
University of Oklahoma Health Sciences Center ... OK ... 413
Oregon State University ... OR ... 418
Cedar Crest College ... PA ... 425
Drexel University ... PA ... 427
Immaculata University ... PA ... 431
Indiana University of Pennsylvania ... PA ... 442
La Salle University ... PA ... 432
Mansfield University of Pennsylvania ... PA ... 443
Marywood University ... PA ... 435
Messiah College ... PA ... 436
Penn State University Park ... PA ... 438
University of Pittsburgh ... PA ... 449
West Chester University of Pennsylvania ... PA ... 444
University of Puerto Rico-Rio Piedras Campus ... PR ... 568
Johnson & Wales University ... RI ... 453
University of Rhode Island ... RI ... 454
Clemson University ... SC ... 456
South Carolina State University ... SC ... 460
Winthrop University ... SC ... 463
South Dakota State University ... SD ... 466
Carson-Newman College ... TN ... 467
East Tennessee State University ... TN ... 473
Lipscomb University ... TN ... 470
Middle Tennessee State University ... TN ... 473
Tennessee State University ... TN ... 474
Tennessee Technological University ... TN ... 474
University of Memphis, The ... TN ... 474
University of Tennessee at Chattanooga ... TN ... 477
#University of Tennessee at Martin ... TN ... 477
University of Tennessee, Knoxville ... TN ... 477
Abilene Christian University ... TX ... 478
Baylor University ... TX ... 482
Lamar University ... TX ... 501
Prairie View A & M University ... TX ... 496
Sam Houston State University ... TX ... 501
Stephen F. Austin State University ... TX ... 496
Texas A & M University ... TX ... 497
Texas A & M University - Kingsville ... TX ... 498
Texas Christian University ... TX ... 499
#Texas Southern University ... TX ... 500
Texas State University-San Marcos ... TX ... 501
Texas Tech University ... TX ... 502
Texas Woman's University ... TX ... 502
University of Houston ... TX ... 503
University of Texas at Austin ... TX ... 505
University of the Incarnate Word ... TX ... 504
Brigham Young University ... UT ... 509
Utah State University ... UT ... 511
University of Vermont ... VT ... 514
James Madison University ... VA ... 520
Norfolk State University ... VA ... 522
Radford University ... VA ... 523
Virginia Polytechnic Institute and State University ... VA ... 529
Virginia State University ... VA ... 529
Bastyr University ... WA ... 531
Central Washington University ... WA ... 532
Seattle Pacific University ... WA ... 537
Marshall University ... WV ... 544
West Virginia University ... WV ... 545
University of Wisconsin-Green Bay ... WI ... 551
University of Wisconsin-Madison ... WI ... 550
University of Wisconsin-Stevens Point ... WI ... 552
University of Wisconsin-Stout ... WI ... 552
University of Wyoming ... WY ... 556

DIETI: Academy of Nutrition and Dietetics: dietetic post-baccalaureate internships

Oakwood University ... AL ... 6
University of Alabama at Birmingham ... AL ... 8
University of Alaska Anchorage ... AK ... 10
Arizona State University ... AZ ... 11
University of Arizona ... AZ ... 18
University of Arkansas for Medical Sciences AR ... 24
University of Central Arkansas ... AR ... 25
California Polytechnic State University-San Luis Obispo ... CA ... 33
California State Polytechnic University-Pomona ... CA ... 33
California State University-Chico ... CA ... 34
California State University-Fresno ... CA ... 35
California State University-Long Beach ... CA ... 35
California State University-Northridge ... CA ... 35
California State University-Sacramento ... CA ... 36
San Francisco State University ... CA ... 37
San Jose State University ... CA ... 37
University of California-Davis ... CA ... 73
University of California-Los Angeles ... CA ... 74
@University of California-San Diego ... CA ... 74
University of California-San Francisco ... CA ... 75
University of Southern California ... CA ... 76
University of Northern Colorado ... CO ... 89
University of Connecticut ... CT ... 94
University of Saint Joseph ... CT ... 95
University of Delaware ... DE ... 96
Florida State University ... FL ... 119
University of Florida ... FL ... 120
University of North Florida ... FL ... 120
Emory University ... GA ... 129
Life University ... GA ... 133
University of Georgia ... GA ... 138
Idaho State University ... ID ... 143
Benedictine University ... IL ... 145
@Bradley University ... IL ... 146
Eastern Illinois University ... IL ... 150
Illinois State University ... IL ... 153
Loyola University Chicago ... IL ... 157
Northern Illinois University ... IL ... 160
Rush University ... IL ... 163
Southern Illinois University Carbondale ... IL ... 165
University of Illinois at Urbana-Champaign ... IL ... 167
Ball State University ... IN ... 169
Indiana University-Purdue University Indianapolis ... IN ... 174
Iowa State University ... IA ... 182
University of Iowa ... IA ... 182
University of Kansas Medical Center ... KS ... 197
Eastern Kentucky University ... KY ... 200
Murray State University ... KY ... 205
University of Kentucky ... KY ... 207
@Western Kentucky University ... KY ... 208
Louisiana Tech University ... LA ... 215
McNeese State University ... LA ... 215
Southern University and A&M College ... LA ... 214
Tulane University ... LA ... 215
University of Louisiana at Lafayette ... LA ... 216
University of Maine ... ME ... 220
Johns Hopkins University ... MD ... 223
University of Maryland Baltimore ... MD ... 227
University of Maryland College Park ... MD ... 227
University of Maryland Eastern Shore ... MD ... 227
Boston University ... MA ... 232
Simmons College ... MA ... 244
Tufts University ... MA ... 245
University of Massachusetts ... MA ... 236
Andrews University ... MI ... 247
Central Michigan University ... MI ... 249
Michigan State University ... MI ... 255
University of Michigan-Ann Arbor ... MI ... 259
Western Michigan University ... MI ... 260
Concordia College ... MN ... 262
Mayo School of Health Sciences ... MN ... 262
University of Minnesota-Twin Cities ... MN ... 272
Mississippi State University ... MS ... 275
University of Southern Mississippi ... MS ... 277
Cox College ... MO ... 280
@Missouri State University ... MO ... 286
Saint Louis University ... MO ... 289
Southeast Missouri State University ... MO ... 289
@Montana State University ... MT ... 295
University of Nebraska - Lincoln ... NE ... 300
University of Nebraska Medical Center ... NE ... 300
University of Nevada, Las Vegas ... NV ... 302
University of Nevada, Reno ... NV ... 303
Keene State College ... NH ... 306
University of New Hampshire ... NH ... 306
College of Saint Elizabeth ... NJ ... 308
Montclair State University ... NJ ... 311
UMDNJ-School of Health Related Professions ... NJ ... 317
@New Mexico State University Main Campus . NM ... 319
University of New Mexico Main Campus ... NM ... 321
City University of New York Brooklyn College ... NY ... 326
City University of New York Herbert H. Lehman College ... NY ... 327
City University of New York Hunter College . NY ... 327
City University of New York Queens College NY ... 328
Cornell University ... NY ... 331
Long Island University C.W. Post Campus ... NY ... 339
New York University ... NY ... 344
Sage Colleges, The ... NY ... 348
State University of New York at Stony Brook NY ... 352
State University of New York College at Oneonta ... NY ... 353
Syracuse University Main Campus ... NY ... 357
Teachers College, Columbia University ... NY ... 357
University at Buffalo-SUNY ... NY ... 351
Appalachian State University ... NC ... 377
East Carolina University ... NC ... 377
@Lenoir-Rhyne University ... NC ... 366
Meredith College ... NC ... 367
North Carolina Central University ... NC ... 378
University of North Carolina at Greensboro .. NC ... 379
Western Carolina University ... NC ... 380
Bowling Green State University ... OH ... 385
Case Western Reserve University ... OH ... 386
Kent State University Main Campus ... OH ... 393
Ohio State University Main Campus, The ... OH ... 398
Oklahoma State University ... OK ... 410
University of Central Oklahoma ... OK ... 413
University of Oklahoma Health Sciences Center ... OK ... 413
Oregon Health & Science University ... OR ... 418
Oregon State University ... OR ... 418
@Cedar Crest College ... PA ... 425
Immaculata University ... PA ... 431
Indiana University of Pennsylvania ... PA ... 442
Marywood University ... PA ... 435
Penn State University Park ... PA ... 438
University of Puerto Rico-Medical Sciences Campus ... PR ... 567
University of Rhode Island ... RI ... 454
Medical University of South Carolina ... SC ... 459
Winthrop University ... SC ... 463
University of South Dakota, The ... SD ... 465
East Tennessee State University ... TN ... 473
Lipscomb University ... TN ... 470
University of Memphis, The ... TN ... 474
#University of Tennessee at Martin ... TN ... 477
University of Tennessee, Knoxville ... TN ... 477
Vanderbilt University ... TN ... 478
Baylor College of Medicine ... TX ... 481
Lamar University ... TX ... 501
Prairie View A & M University ... TX ... 496
Sam Houston State University ... TX ... 501
Stephen F. Austin State University ... TX ... 496
Texas A & M University ... TX ... 497
Texas A & M University - Kingsville ... TX ... 498
Texas State University-San Marcos ... TX ... 501
Texas Tech University ... TX ... 502
Texas Woman's University ... TX ... 502
University of Houston ... TX ... 503
University of Texas Health Science Center at Houston (UTHealth), The ... TX ... 506
University of the Incarnate Word ... TX ... 504
Brigham Young University ... UT ... 509
Utah State University ... UT ... 511
University of Virginia ... VA ... 525
Virginia Commonwealth University ... VA ... 526
Virginia Polytechnic Institute and State University ... VA ... 529
Virginia State University ... VA ... 529
Bastyr University ... WA ... 531
Central Washington University ... WA ... 532
Marshall University ... WV ... 544
West Virginia University ... WV ... 545
Mount Mary College ... WI ... 549
University of Wisconsin-Green Bay ... WI ... 551
University of Wisconsin-Madison ... WI ... 550
University of Wisconsin-Stout ... WI ... 552
Viterbo University ... WI ... 553

DIETT: Academy of Nutrition and Dietetics: dietetic technician (A)

Central Arizona College ... AZ ... 13
Chandler-Gilbert Community College ... AZ ... 15
Paradise Valley Community College ... AZ ... 15
Black River Technical College ... AR ... 21
Los Angeles City College ... CA ... 54
Merritt College ... CA ... 62
Orange Coast College ... CA ... 41
@Santa Rosa Junior College ... CA ... 68
Gateway Community College ... CT ... 91
Lincoln College of New England ... CT ... 93
Florida State College at Jacksonville ... FL ... 109
@Hillsborough Community College ... FL ... 110
Harper College ... IL ... 151
@Parkland College ... IL ... 161
Delgado Community College ... LA ... 210
Southern Maine Community College ... ME ... 219
Baltimore City Community College ... MD ... 221
Laboure College ... MA ... 235
Wayne County Community College District .. MI ... 259
Normandale Community College ... MN ... 268
Saint Louis Community College at Florissant Valley ... MO ... 288
@Great Falls College Montana State University ... MT ... 295
Southeast Community College ... NE ... 300
Truckee Meadows Community College ... NV ... 302
University of New Hampshire ... NH ... 306
Camden County College ... NJ ... 308
Middlesex County College ... NJ ... 311
Erie Community College North Campus ... NY ... 333
La Guardia Community College/City University of New York ... NY ... 328
State University of New York College of Agriculture and Technology at Morri sville . NY ... 354
Suffolk County Community College Eastern Campus ... NY ... 356
Trocaire College ... NY ... 358
Westchester Community College ... NY ... 360
Gaston College ... NC ... 370
Cincinnati State Technical and Community College ... OH ... 387
Columbus State Community College ... OH ... 389
Cuyahoga Community College ... OH ... 389
Owens Community College ... OH ... 400
Sinclair Community College ... OH ... 401
Youngstown State University ... OH ... 406
@Oklahoma State University - Oklahoma City OK ... 410
Community College of Allegheny County ... PA ... 425
Southwest Tennessee Community College .. TN ... 476
Tarrant County College District ... TX ... 496
Milwaukee Area Technical College ... WI ... 554

DMOLS: National Accrediting Agency for Clinical Laboratory Sciences: diagnostic molecular scientist (C,B,M)

University of Connecticut ... CT ... 94
University of Kansas Medical Center ... KS ... 197
Michigan State University ... MI ... 255
Northern Michigan University ... MI ... 256
State University of New York Upstate Medical University ... NY ... 352
University of North Carolina at Chapel Hill ... NC ... 378
Texas Tech University Health Sciences Center ... TX ... 502
University of Texas M.D. Anderson Cancer Center, The ... TX ... 507

DMS: Commission on Accreditation of Allied Health Education Programs: diagnostic medical sonography (C,A,B,M)

Lurleen B. Wallace Community College ... AL ... 5
Trenholm State Technical College ... AL ... 7
Virginia College ... AL ... 3
Wallace State Community College - Hanceville ... AL ... 10
Gateway Community College ... AZ ... 15
Arkansas State University-Jonesboro ... AR ... 20
University of Arkansas at Fort Smith ... AR ... 24
University of Arkansas for Medical Sciences AR ... 24
Charles R. Drew University of Medicine & Science ... CA ... 39
Cypress College ... CA ... 59
Foothill College ... CA ... 47
Loma Linda University ... CA ... 54
Merced College ... CA ... 57
Orange Coast College ... CA ... 41
Platt College ... CA ... 62
Santa Barbara City College ... CA ... 68
University of California-San Diego ... CA ... 74
University of Colorado DenverlAnschutz Medical Campus ... CO ... 88
Delaware Technical Community College, Owens Campus ... DE ... 96
Delaware Technical Community College, Stanton-Wilmington Campus ... DE ... 96
George Washington University ... DC ... 98
Adventist University of Health Sciences ... FL ... 100
Broward College ... FL ... 102
Cambridge Institute of Allied Health & Technology ... FL ... 102
Central Florida Institute ... FL ... 103
Hillsborough Community College ... FL ... 110
Keiser University ... FL ... 112
Miami Dade College ... FL ... 113
Nova Southeastern University ... FL ... 114
Palm Beach State College ... FL ... 114
Polk State College ... FL ... 115
Sanford-Brown Institute ... FL ... 117
Santa Fe College ... FL ... 117
Valencia College ... FL ... 123
Athens Technical College ... GA ... 125
Georgia Health Sciences University ... GA ... 130
Georgia Northwestern Technical College ... GA ... 131
Ogeechee Technical College ... GA ... 135
Sanford-Brown College ... GA ... 136
Boise State University ... ID ... 142
College of DuPage ... IL ... 148
Harper College ... IL ... 151
John A. Logan College ... IL ... 154
Rush University ... IL ... 163
Southern Illinois University Carbondale ... IL ... 165

DNUR: National League for Nursing: nursing (C)

DT: American Dental Association: dental laboratory technology (C,A)

EH: New England Association of Schools and Colleges, Commission on Institutions of Higher Education

EMT: Commission on Accreditation of Allied Health Education Programs: emergency medical technician-paramedic (C,A,B)

Institution	State	Page
Northwest - Shoals Community College	AL	6
Southern Union State Community College	AL	7
Trenholm State Technical College	AL	7
University of South Alabama	AL	9
Wallace State Community College - Hanceville	AL	10
University of Alaska Fairbanks	AK	10
Mohave Community College	AZ	16
Pima County Community College District	AZ	17
Yavapai College	AZ	19
#Arkansas Northeastern College	AR	20
Arkansas State University-Beebe	AR	20
Arkansas State University-Mountain Home	AR	20
Arkansas Tech University	AR	20
Black River Technical College	AR	21
East Arkansas Community College	AR	21
National Park Community College	AR	22
North Arkansas College	AR	22
NorthWest Arkansas Community College	AR	22
South Arkansas Community College	AR	23
Southeast Arkansas College	AR	23
University of Arkansas at Monticello	AR	25
University of Arkansas Community College at Batesville	AR	25
University of Arkansas Community College at Hope	AR	25
University of Arkansas for Medical Sciences	AR	24
American River College	CA	56
Bakersfield College	CA	52
Butte College	CA	31
California State University-Sacramento	CA	36
City College of San Francisco	CA	40
Crafton Hills College	CA	65
Cuesta College	CA	43
Foothill College	CA	47
Fresno City College	CA	72
Imperial Valley College	CA	51
#Mendocino College	CA	57
Moreno Valley College	CA	63
Mt. San Antonio College	CA	58
Napa Valley College	CA	58
Palomar College	CA	61
Point Loma Nazarene University	CA	62
Saddleback College	CA	70
Santa Rosa Junior College	CA	68
Southwestern College	CA	71
University of Antelope Valley	CA	73
University of California-Los Angeles	CA	74
Ventura College	CA	77
Victor Valley College	CA	77
Aims Community College	CO	81
Arapahoe Community College	CO	81
Colorado Mesa University	CO	82
Colorado Mountain College	CO	82
Community College of Aurora	CO	83
Pikes Peak Community College	CO	87
Pueblo Community College	CO	87
Capital Community College	CT	91
Delaware Technical Community College, Terry Campus	DE	96
Brevard Community College	FL	102
Broward College	FL	102
City College	FL	103
College of Central Florida	FL	103
Daytona State College	FL	104
Edison State College	FL	105
Florida Gateway College	FL	108
Florida State College at Jacksonville	FL	109
Gulf Coast State College	FL	110
Hillsborough Community College	FL	110
Indian River State College	FL	111
Miami Dade College	FL	113
Palm Beach State College	FL	114
Pasco-Hernando Community College	FL	114
Pensacola State College	FL	115
Polk State College	FL	115
St. Petersburg College	FL	116
Santa Fe College	FL	117
Seminole State College of Florida	FL	117
Tallahassee Community College	FL	122
Valencia College	FL	123
Georgia Northwestern Technical College	GA	131
Gwinnett Technical College	GA	132
Lanier Technical College	GA	133
Southeastern Technical College	GA	137
Brigham Young University-Idaho	ID	143
College of Southern Idaho	ID	143
Idaho State University	ID	143
Loyola University Chicago	IL	157
Indiana University-Purdue University Indianapolis	IN	174
Ivy Tech Community College of Indiana-Bloomington	IN	175
Ivy Tech Community College of Indiana-Columbus	IN	176
Ivy Tech Community College of Indiana-Kokomo	IN	176
Ivy Tech Community College of Indiana-North Central	IN	176
Ivy Tech Community College of Indiana-Northeast	IN	176
Ivy Tech Community College of Indiana-Southwest	IN	177
Ivy Tech Community College of Indiana-Wabash Valley	IN	177
Vincennes University	IN	181
Indian Hills Community College	IA	185
Kirkwood Community College	IA	187
Mercy College of Health Sciences	IA	187
Southeastern Community College	IA	189
University of Iowa	IA	182
Western Iowa Tech Community College	IA	190
Barton County Community College	KS	190
Coffeyville Community College	KS	192
Cowley County Community College	KS	192
Flint Hills Technical College	KS	192
Garden City Community College	KS	193
Hutchinson Community College and Area Vocational School	KS	193
Johnson County Community College	KS	194
Kansas City Kansas Community College	KS	194
Eastern Kentucky University	KY	200
Bossier Parish Community College	LA	209
Delgado Community College	LA	210
Louisiana State University and Agricultural and Mechanical College	LA	212
South Louisiana Community College	LA	211
Anne Arundel Community College	MD	221
Community College of Baltimore County, The	MD	222
Hagerstown Community College	MD	223
Howard Community College	MD	223
University of Maryland Baltimore County	MD	227
Kalamazoo Valley Community College	MI	253
Lansing Community College	MI	254
Century College	MN	266
Inver Hills Community College	MN	266
Mesabi Range Community & Technical College	MN	266
Northland Community and Technical College	MN	268
Ridgewater College	MN	268
Rochester Community and Technical College	MN	268
Saint Cloud Technical and Community College	MN	269
South Central College	MN	269
East Central Community College	MS	274
East Mississippi Community College	MS	274
Hinds Community College	MS	274
Holmes Community College	MS	274
Itawamba Community College	MS	274
Jones County Junior College	MS	274
Mississippi Gulf Coast Community College	MS	275
Northwest Mississippi Community College	MS	276
IHM Academy of EMS	MO	282
Ozarks Technical Community College	MO	287
Great Falls College Montana State University	MT	295
Montana State University - Billings	MT	295
Central Community College	NE	297
Creighton University	NE	297
Metropolitan Community College	NE	298
Northeast Community College	NE	299
College of Southern Nevada	NV	302
NHTI-Concord's Community College	NH	304
Central New Mexico Community College	NM	317
Eastern New Mexico University-Roswell	NM	318
New Mexico State University Dona Ana Community College	NM	319
Santa Fe Community College	NM	320
University of New Mexico Main Campus	NM	321
City University of New York Borough of Manhattan Community College	NY	326
Dutchess Community College	NY	332
Herkimer County Community College	NY	335
Hudson Valley Community College	NY	336
Monroe Community College	NY	341
St. John's University	NY	348
State University of New York College of Agriculture and Technology at Coble skill	NY	354
Blue Ridge Community College	NC	368
Catawba Valley Community College	NC	369
Piedmont Community College	NC	372
Southwestern Community College	NC	374
Western Carolina University	NC	380
Bismarck State College	ND	382
North Dakota State College of Science	ND	382
Columbus State Community College	OH	389
Fortis College	OH	390
Owens Community College	OH	400
University of Cincinnati-Raymond Walters College	OH	403
Youngstown State University	OH	406
Oklahoma City Community College	OK	409
Rogers State University	OK	411
Chemeketa Community College	OR	414
Lane Community College	OR	416
Oregon Health & Science University	OR	418
Portland Community College	OR	419
Harrisburg Area Community College	PA	430
Pennsylvania College of Technology	PA	440
Greenville Technical College	SC	458
Horry-Georgetown Technical College	SC	458
Trident Technical College	SC	461
Lake Area Technical Institute	SD	464
Chattanooga State Community College	TN	474
Columbia State Community College	TN	475
Jackson State Community College	TN	475
Northeast State Community College	TN	475
Roane State Community College	TN	476
Southwest Tennessee Community College	TN	476
Tennessee Technological University	TN	474
Volunteer State Community College	TN	476
Walters State Community College	TN	476
Austin Community College District	TX	481
Blinn College	TX	482
Brazosport College	TX	482
Brookhaven College	TX	484
Central Texas College	TX	482
College of the Mainland	TX	483
Collin County Community College District	TX	483
Galveston College	TX	486
Grayson County College	TX	487
Houston Community College	TX	487
Lone Star College System	TX	490
Paris Junior College	TX	492
San Antonio College	TX	479
San Jacinto College Central	TX	493
San Jacinto College North	TX	494
South Plains College	TX	494
Tarrant County College District	TX	496
Temple College	TX	496
Texas State Technical College West Texas	TX	500
University of Texas at Brownsville and Texas Southmost College, The	TX	505
University of Texas Health Science Center at San Antonio	TX	507
University of Texas Southwestern Medical Center	TX	507
Weatherford College	TX	508
#Wharton County Junior College	TX	509
Dixie State College of Utah	UT	512
University of Utah, The	UT	511
Utah Valley University	UT	511
Weber State University	UT	511
Central Virginia Community College	VA	526
J. Sargeant Reynolds Community College	VA	527
Jefferson College of Health Sciences	VA	520
National College	VA	522
Northern Virginia Community College	VA	527
Piedmont Virginia Community College	VA	528
Southside Virginia Community College	VA	528
Southwest Virginia Community College	VA	528
Tidewater Community College	VA	528
Virginia Commonwealth University	VA	526
Central Washington University	WA	532
Columbia Basin College	WA	532
Tacoma Community College	WA	538
University of Washington	WA	539
Blue Ridge Community and Technical College	WV	542
Lakeshore Technical College	WI	554
Northcentral Technical College	WI	555
Waukesha County Technical College	WI	555
Casper College	WY	556
Laramie County Community College	WY	556

ENG: ABET, Inc.: engineering (B,M)

Institution	State	Page
Alabama Agricultural and Mechanical University	AL	1
Auburn University	AL	1
Tuskegee University	AL	8
University of Alabama at Birmingham	AL	8
University of Alabama in Huntsville	AL	8
University of Alabama, The	AL	8
University of South Alabama	AL	9
University of Alaska Anchorage	AK	10
University of Alaska Fairbanks	AK	10
Arizona State University	AZ	11
Embry-Riddle Aeronautical University-Prescott Campus	AZ	14
Northern Arizona University	AZ	16
University of Arizona	AZ	18
Arkansas State University-Jonesboro	AR	20
Arkansas Tech University	AR	20
Harding University Main Campus	AR	21
John Brown University	AR	22
University of Arkansas at Little Rock	AR	24
University of Arkansas Main Campus	AR	24
California Institute of Technology	CA	32
California Maritime Academy	CA	33
California Polytechnic State University-San Luis Obispo	CA	33
California State Polytechnic University-Pomona	CA	33
California State University-Chico	CA	34
California State University-East Bay	CA	34
California State University-Fresno	CA	35
California State University-Fullerton	CA	35
California State University-Long Beach	CA	35
California State University-Los Angeles	CA	35
California State University-Northridge	CA	35
California State University-Sacramento	CA	36
Harvey Mudd College	CA	49
Humboldt State University	CA	36
Loyola Marymount University	CA	56
National Test Pilot Institute	CA	58
Naval Postgraduate School	CA	558
San Diego State University	CA	37
San Francisco State University	CA	37
San Jose State University	CA	37
Santa Clara University	CA	68
Stanford University	CA	71
University of California-Berkeley	CA	73
University of California-Davis	CA	73
University of California-Irvine	CA	74
University of California-Los Angeles	CA	74
University of California-Riverside	CA	74
University of California-San Diego	CA	74
University of California-Santa Barbara	CA	75
University of California-Santa Cruz	CA	75
University of San Diego	CA	76
University of Southern California	CA	76
University of the Pacific	CA	76
Colorado School of Mines	CO	83
Colorado State University	CO	83
Colorado State University-Pueblo	CO	83
Colorado Technical University	CO	83
Fort Lewis College	CO	84
United States Air Force Academy	CO	558
University of Colorado Boulder	CO	88
University of Colorado Colorado Springs	CO	88
University of Colorado DenverlAnschutz Medical Campus	CO	88
University of Denver	CO	89
Central Connecticut State University	CT	90
Fairfield University	CT	92
Trinity College	CT	94
United States Coast Guard Academy	CT	558
University of Bridgeport	CT	94
University of Connecticut	CT	94
University of Hartford	CT	95
University of New Haven	CT	95
Yale University	CT	96
University of Delaware	DE	96
Catholic University of America, The	DC	97
George Washington University	DC	98
Howard University	DC	98
University of the District of Columbia	DC	100
Embry-Riddle Aeronautical University	FL	105
Florida Agricultural and Mechanical University	FL	118
Florida Atlantic University	FL	119
Florida Gulf Coast University	FL	119
Florida Institute of Technology	FL	108
Florida International University	FL	119
Florida State University	FL	119
University of Central Florida	FL	120
University of Florida	FL	120
University of Miami	FL	122
University of North Florida	FL	120
University of South Florida	FL	121
University of West Florida	FL	121
Georgia Institute of Technology	GA	130
Mercer University	GA	134
Southern Polytechnic State University	GA	137
University of Georgia	GA	138
University of Hawaii at Manoa	HI	141
Boise State University	ID	142
Brigham Young University-Idaho	ID	143
Idaho State University	ID	143
University of Idaho	ID	144
Bradley University	IL	146
Illinois Institute of Technology	IL	153
Northern Illinois University	IL	160
Northwestern University	IL	160
Olivet Nazarene University	IL	161
Southern Illinois University Carbondale	IL	165
Southern Illinois University Edwardsville	IL	165
University of Illinois at Chicago	IL	167
University of Illinois at Urbana-Champaign	IL	167
Indiana Tech	IN	173
Indiana University-Purdue University Fort Wayne	IN	174
Indiana University-Purdue University Indianapolis	IN	174
Purdue University Calumet	IN	178
Purdue University Main Campus	IN	178
Rose-Hulman Institute of Technology	IN	179
Taylor University	IN	180
Trine University	IN	180
University of Evansville	IN	180
University of Notre Dame	IN	180
University of Southern Indiana	IN	181
Valparaiso University	IN	181
Dordt College	IA	184
Iowa State University	IA	182
St. Ambrose University	IA	188
University of Iowa	IA	182
Kansas State University	KS	194
University of Kansas Main Campus	KS	197
Wichita State University	KS	198
Murray State University	KY	205
University of Kentucky	KY	207
University of Louisville	KY	207
Western Kentucky University	KY	208
Louisiana State University and Agricultural and Mechanical College	LA	212
Louisiana Tech University	LA	215
McNeese State University	LA	215
Southern University and A&M College	LA	214
Tulane University	LA	215
University of Louisiana at Lafayette	LA	216
University of New Orleans	LA	213
Maine Maritime Academy	ME	219
University of Maine	ME	220
University of Southern Maine	ME	220
Capitol College	MD	221
Johns Hopkins University	MD	223
Loyola University Maryland	MD	223
Morgan State University	MD	224
United States Naval Academy	MD	559
University of Maryland Baltimore County	MD	227
University of Maryland College Park	MD	227
Boston University	MA	232
Franklin W. Olin College of Engineering	MA	234
Harvard University	MA	235
Massachusetts Institute of Technology	MA	241
Merrimack College	MA	242
Northeastern University	MA	243
Smith College	MA	244
Suffolk University	MA	245

Tufts University ... MA ... 245
University of Massachusetts ... MA ... 236
University of Massachusetts Dartmouth ... MA ... 237
University of Massachusetts Lowell ... MA ... 237
Wentworth Institute of Technology ... MA ... 245
Western New England University ... MA ... 246
Worcester Polytechnic Institute ... MA ... 246
Andrews University ... MI ... 247
Baker College of Flint ... MI ... 248
Calvin College ... MI ... 249
Central Michigan University ... MI ... 249
Ferris State University ... MI ... 250
Grand Valley State University ... MI ... 251
Hope College ... MI ... 252
Kettering University ... MI ... 253
Lake Superior State University ... MI ... 253
Lawrence Technological University ... MI ... 254
Michigan State University ... MI ... 255
Michigan Technological University ... MI ... 255
Oakland University ... MI ... 256
Saginaw Valley State University ... MI ... 257
University of Detroit Mercy ... MI ... 258
University of Michigan-Ann Arbor ... MI ... 259
University of Michigan-Dearborn ... MI ... 259
Wayne State University ... MI ... 260
Western Michigan University ... MI ... 260
Minnesota State University, Mankato ... MN ... 267
St. Cloud State University ... MN ... 269
University of Minnesota Duluth ... MN ... 271
University of Minnesota-Twin Cities ... MN ... 272
University of Saint Thomas ... MN ... 272
Winona State University ... MN ... 269
Jackson State University ... MS ... 274
Mississippi State University ... MS ... 275
University of Mississippi ... MS ... 277
Missouri University of Science & Technology MO ... 291
Saint Louis University ... MO ... 289
Southeast Missouri State University ... MO ... 289
University of Missouri - Columbia ... MO ... 291
University of Missouri - Kansas City ... MO ... 291
University of Missouri - Saint Louis ... MO ... 291
Washington University in St. Louis ... MO ... 292
Carroll College ... MT ... 293
Montana State University ... MT ... 295
Montana Tech of The University of Montana MT ... 296
University of Nebraska - Lincoln ... NE ... 300
University of Nevada, Las Vegas ... NV ... 302
University of Nevada, Reno ... NV ... 303
Daniel Webster College ... NH ... 304
Dartmouth College ... NH ... 304
University of New Hampshire ... NH ... 306
College of New Jersey, The ... NJ ... 308
Fairleigh Dickinson University ... NJ ... 310
Monmouth University ... NJ ... 311
New Jersey Institute of Technology ... NJ ... 312
Princeton University ... NJ ... 312
Rowan University ... NJ ... 314
Rutgers the State University of New Jersey New Brunswick Campus ... NJ ... 314
Stevens Institute of Technology ... NJ ... 315
New Mexico Institute of Mining and Technology ... NM ... 319
New Mexico State University Main Campus . NM ... 319
University of New Mexico Main Campus ... NM ... 321
Alfred University ... NY ... 322
City University of New York College of Staten Island ... NY ... 327
City University of New York The City College ... NY ... 326
Clarkson University ... NY ... 329
Columbia University in the City of New York NY ... 330
Cooper Union ... NY ... 331
Cornell University ... NY ... 331
Hofstra University ... NY ... 335
Manhattan College ... NY ... 339
New York Institute of Technology ... NY ... 343
Polytechnic Institute of New York University NY ... 346
Rensselaer Polytechnic Institute ... NY ... 347
Rochester Institute of Technology ... NY ... 347
State University of New York at Binghamton NY ... 351
State University of New York at New Paltz .. NY ... 352
State University of New York at Stony Brook NY ... 352
State University of New York College of Environmental Science and Forestry ... NY ... 355
State University of New York Maritime College ... NY ... 356
Syracuse University Main Campus ... NY ... 357
Union College ... NY ... 358
United States Merchant Marine Academy ... NY ... 558
United States Military Academy ... NY ... 559
University at Buffalo-SUNY ... NY ... 351
University of Rochester ... NY ... 359
Webb Institute ... NY ... 360
Duke University ... NC ... 364
East Carolina University ... NC ... 377
North Carolina Agricultural and Technical State University ... NC ... 378
North Carolina State University ... NC ... 378
University of North Carolina at Asheville ... NC ... 378
University of North Carolina at Charlotte ... NC ... 379
Western Carolina University ... NC ... 380
North Dakota State University Main Campus. ND ... 382
University of North Dakota Main Campus ... ND ... 381
Air Force Institute of Technology ... OH ... 557
Case Western Reserve University ... OH ... 386
Cedarville University ... OH ... 386
Central State University ... OH ... 387
Cleveland State University ... OH ... 388
Marietta College ... OH ... 395
Miami University ... OH ... 396
Ohio Northern University ... OH ... 398
Ohio State University Main Campus, The ... OH ... 398
Ohio University Main Campus ... OH ... 399
University of Akron, Main Campus, The ... OH ... 403
University of Cincinnati Main Campus ... OH ... 403
University of Dayton ... OH ... 404
University of Toledo ... OH ... 404
Wright State University Main Campus ... OH ... 406
Youngstown State University ... OH ... 406
Oklahoma Christian University ... OK ... 409
Oklahoma State University ... OK ... 410
Oral Roberts University ... OK ... 411
University of Central Oklahoma ... OK ... 413
University of Oklahoma Norman Campus ... OK ... 413
University of Tulsa ... OK ... 413
George Fox University ... OR ... 415
Oregon Institute of Technology ... OR ... 418
Oregon State University ... OR ... 418
Portland State University ... OR ... 418
University of Portland ... OR ... 420
Bucknell University ... PA ... 423
Carnegie Mellon University ... PA ... 424
Drexel University ... PA ... 427
Elizabethtown College ... PA ... 428
Gannon University ... PA ... 429
Geneva College ... PA ... 429
Grove City College ... PA ... 430
Lafayette College ... PA ... 433
Lehigh University ... PA ... 434
Messiah College ... PA ... 436
Penn State Erie, The Behrend College ... PA ... 439
Penn State Harrisburg ... PA ... 439
Penn State University Park ... PA ... 438
Penn State Wilkes-Barre ... PA ... 440
Philadelphia University ... PA ... 444
Robert Morris University ... PA ... 445
Swarthmore College ... PA ... 447
Temple University ... PA ... 447
University of Pennsylvania ... PA ... 448
University of Pittsburgh ... PA ... 449
Villanova University ... PA ... 450
Widener University ... PA ... 451
Wilkes University ... PA ... 452
York College of Pennsylvania ... PA ... 452
Inter American University of Puerto Rico Bayamon Campus ... PR ... 563
Universidad Del Turabo ... PR ... 565
Universidad Politecnica De Puerto Rico ... PR ... 566
University of Puerto Rico-Mayaguez Campus PR ... 567
Brown University ... RI ... 453
Roger Williams University ... RI ... 454
University of Rhode Island ... RI ... 454
Citadel, The Military College of South Carolina, The ... SC ... 456
Clemson University ... SC ... 456
South Carolina State University ... SC ... 460
University of South Carolina Columbia ... SC ... 462
South Dakota School of Mines and Technology ... SD ... 466
South Dakota State University ... SD ... 466
Christian Brothers University ... TN ... 467
Lipscomb University ... TN ... 470
Tennessee State University ... TN ... 474
Tennessee Technological University ... TN ... 474
Union University ... TN ... 477
University of Memphis, The ... TN ... 474
University of Tennessee at Chattanooga ... TN ... 477
University of Tennessee at Martin ... TN ... 477
University of Tennessee, Knoxville ... TN ... 477
Vanderbilt University ... TN ... 478
Baylor University ... TX ... 482
Lamar University ... TX ... 501
LeTourneau University ... TX ... 490
Midwestern State University ... TX ... 491
Prairie View A & M University ... TX ... 496
Rice University ... TX ... 493
St. Mary's University ... TX ... 493
Southern Methodist University ... TX ... 495
Tarleton State University ... TX ... 497
Texas A & M University ... TX ... 497
Texas A & M University at Galveston ... TX ... 497
Texas A & M University - Commerce ... TX ... 498
Texas A & M University - Kingsville ... TX ... 498
Texas Christian University ... TX ... 499
Texas State University-San Marcos ... TX ... 501
Texas Tech University ... TX ... 502
Trinity University ... TX ... 502
University of Houston ... TX ... 503
University of Houston - Clear Lake ... TX ... 503
University of North Texas ... TX ... 504
University of Texas at Arlington, The ... TX ... 505
University of Texas at Austin ... TX ... 505
University of Texas at Brownsville and Texas Southmost College, The ... TX ... 505
University of Texas at Dallas, The ... TX ... 506
University of Texas at El Paso ... TX ... 506
University of Texas at San Antonio ... TX ... 506
University of Texas at Tyler ... TX ... 506
University of Texas - Pan American ... TX ... 506
West Texas A & M University ... TX ... 499
Brigham Young University ... UT ... 509
Southern Utah University ... UT ... 511
University of Utah, The ... UT ... 511
Utah State University ... UT ... 511
Norwich University ... VT ... 514
University of Vermont ... VT ... 514
Christopher Newport University ... VA ... 517
George Mason University ... VA ... 519
Hampton University ... VA ... 519
Norfolk State University ... VA ... 522
Old Dominion University ... VA ... 522
Sweet Briar College ... VA ... 524
University of Virginia ... VA ... 525
University of Virginia's College at Wise, The VA ... 525
Virginia Commonwealth University ... VA ... 526
Virginia Military Institute ... VA ... 529
Virginia Polytechnic Institute and State University ... VA ... 529
Virginia State University ... VA ... 529
Eastern Washington University ... WA ... 533
Gonzaga University ... WA ... 534
Pacific Lutheran University ... WA ... 536
Saint Martin's University ... WA ... 537
Seattle Pacific University ... WA ... 537
Seattle University ... WA ... 538
University of Washington ... WA ... 539
Walla Walla University ... WA ... 539
Washington State University ... WA ... 539
Marshall University ... WV ... 544
West Virginia University ... WV ... 545
West Virginia University Institute of Technology ... WV ... 545
Marquette University ... WI ... 548
Milwaukee School of Engineering ... WI ... 549
University of Wisconsin-Madison ... WI ... 550
University of Wisconsin-Milwaukee ... WI ... 551
University of Wisconsin-Platteville ... WI ... 552
University of Wisconsin-Stevens Point ... WI ... 552
University of Wisconsin-Stout ... WI ... 552
University of Wyoming ... WY ... 556

ENGR: ABET, Inc.: applied science (A, B,M)

Troy University ... AL ... 8
University of North Alabama ... AL ... 9
University of Alaska Anchorage ... AK ... 10
University of California-Los Angeles ... CA ... 74
Colorado State University ... CO ... 83
Trinidad State Junior College ... CO ... 88
University of Florida ... FL ... 120
University of South Florida ... FL ... 121
Southern Polytechnic State University ... GA ... 137
Idaho State University ... ID ... 143
University of Illinois at Chicago ... IL ... 167
Purdue University Main Campus ... IN ... 178
University of Iowa ... IA ... 182
Murray State University ... KY ... 205
Nicholls State University ... LA ... 216
Southeastern Louisiana University ... LA ... 216
Tulane University ... LA ... 215
Johns Hopkins University ... MD ... 223
Uniformed Services University of the Health Sciences ... MD ... 558
University of Massachusetts Lowell ... MA ... 237
Oakland University ... MI ... 256
University of Michigan-Ann Arbor ... MI ... 259
Wayne State University ... MI ... 260
St. Cloud State University ... MN ... 269
University of Minnesota-Twin Cities ... MN ... 272
University of Central Missouri ... MO ... 290
Montana Tech of The University of Montana MT ... 296
University of Nevada, Las Vegas ... NV ... 302
City University of New York Hunter College . NY ... 327
Rochester Institute of Technology ... NY ... 347
Ohio University Main Campus ... OH ... 399
University of Akron, Main Campus, The ... OH ... 403
University of Cincinnati Main Campus ... OH ... 403
University of Findlay, The ... OH ... 404
University of Toledo ... OH ... 404
University of Oklahoma Health Sciences Center ... OK ... 413
Oregon Institute of Technology ... OR ... 418
Oregon State University ... OR ... 418
Bloomsburg University of Pennsylvania ... PA ... 441
Indiana University of Pennsylvania ... PA ... 442
Millersville University of Pennsylvania ... PA ... 443
Universidad Politecnica De Puerto Rico ... PR ... 566
Clemson University ... SC ... 456
East Tennessee State University ... TN ... 473
Texas A & M University - Corpus Christi ... TX ... 498
University of Houston - Clear Lake ... TX ... 503
University of Texas Health Science Center at Houston (UTHealth), The ... TX ... 506
University of Utah, The ... UT ... 511
Utah State University ... UT ... 511
James Madison University ... VA ... 520
Fairmont State University ... WV ... 543
Marshall University ... WV ... 544
West Virginia University ... WV ... 545

ENGT: ABET, Inc.: engineering technology (A,B)

Alabama Agricultural and Mechanical University ... AL ... 1
Arizona State University ... AZ ... 11
DeVry University - Phoenix Campus ... AZ ... 13
University of Arkansas at Little Rock ... AR ... 24
California Maritime Academy ... CA ... 33
California State Polytechnic University-Pomona ... CA ... 33
DeVry University - Fremont Campus ... CA ... 44
DeVry University - Long Beach Campus ... CA ... 44
DeVry University - Pomona Campus ... CA ... 44
DeVry University - Sacramento ... CA ... 44
DeVry University - Sherman Oaks Campus . CA ... 45
Colorado State University-Pueblo ... CO ... 83
DeVry University - Westminster Campus ... CO ... 84
Metropolitan State University of Denver ... CO ... 86
Central Connecticut State University ... CT ... 90
Naugatuck Valley Community College ... CT ... 92
Three Rivers Community College ... CT ... 92
University of Hartford ... CT ... 95
Delaware Technical Community College, Owens Campus ... DE ... 96
Delaware Technical Community College, Stanton-Wilmington Campus ... DE ... 96
University of Delaware ... DE ... 96
DeVry University - Miramar Campus ... FL ... 104
DeVry University - Orlando Campus ... FL ... 104
Florida Agricultural and Mechanical University ... FL ... 118
Augusta Technical College ... GA ... 125
DeVry University - Alpharetta Campus ... GA ... 128
DeVry University - Decatur Campus ... GA ... 128
Fort Valley State University ... GA ... 129
Georgia Piedmont Technical College ... GA ... 131
Georgia Southern University ... GA ... 131
Savannah State University ... GA ... 136
Savannah Technical College ... GA ... 136
Southern Polytechnic State University ... GA ... 137
Brigham Young University-Idaho ... ID ... 143
Idaho State University ... ID ... 143
Bradley University ... IL ... 146
DeVry University - Addison Campus ... IL ... 149
DeVry University - Chicago Campus ... IL ... 149
Morrison Institute of Technology ... IL ... 159
Northern Illinois University ... IL ... 160
Southern Illinois University Carbondale ... IL ... 165
Ball State University ... IN ... 169
Indiana State University ... IN ... 173
Indiana University-Purdue University Fort Wayne ... IN ... 174
Indiana University-Purdue University Indianapolis ... IN ... 174
Purdue University Calumet ... IN ... 178
Purdue University Main Campus ... IN ... 178
Purdue University North Central Campus ... IN ... 179
University of Northern Iowa ... IA ... 182
Butler Community College ... KS ... 191
Kansas State University-Salina, College of Technology and Aviation ... KS ... 194
Pittsburg State University ... KS ... 196
Murray State University ... KY ... 205
Northern Kentucky University ... KY ... 205
Delgado Community College ... LA ... 210
Grambling State University ... LA ... 215
Louisiana Tech University ... LA ... 215
McNeese State University ... LA ... 215
Nicholls State University ... LA ... 216
Northwestern State University ... LA ... 216
Southern University and A&M College ... LA ... 214
Central Maine Community College ... ME ... 218
Maine Maritime Academy ... ME ... 219
University of Maine ... ME ... 220
Capitol College ... MD ... 221
Northeastern University ... MA ... 243
Springfield Technical Community College ... MA ... 241
University of Massachusetts Lowell ... MA ... 237
Wentworth Institute of Technology ... MA ... 245
Baker College of Flint ... MI ... 248
Ferris State University ... MI ... 250
Lake Superior State University ... MI ... 253
Michigan Technological University ... MI ... 255
Northern Michigan University ... MI ... 256
Wayne State University ... MI ... 260
Western Michigan University ... MI ... 260
Minnesota State University, Mankato ... MN ... 267
University of Southern Mississippi ... MS ... 277
DeVry University - Kansas City Campus ... MO ... 281
Linn State Technical College ... MO ... 284
Missouri Southern State University ... MO ... 286
Missouri Western State University ... MO ... 286
Saint Louis Community College at Florissant Valley ... MO ... 288
Southeast Missouri State University ... MO ... 289
Montana State University ... MT ... 295
Montana State University - Northern ... MT ... 295
College of Southern Nevada ... NV ... 302
Nashua Community College ... NH ... 304
NHTI-Concord's Community College ... NH ... 304
University of New Hampshire ... NH ... 306
Burlington County College ... NJ ... 308
County College of Morris ... NJ ... 309
DeVry University - North Brunswick Campus. NJ ... 309
Essex County College ... NJ ... 309
Fairleigh Dickinson University ... NJ ... 310
Middlesex County College ... NJ ... 311
New Jersey Institute of Technology ... NJ ... 312
Passaic County Community College ... NJ ... 312
New Mexico State University Main Campus . NM ... 319
Alfred State College ... NY ... 355
Broome Community College ... NY ... 324
City University of New York Bronx Community College ... NY ... 326
City University of New York College of Staten Island ... NY ... 327
City University of New York Queensborough Community College ... NY ... 328
DeVry College of New York ... NY ... 332
Erie Community College North Campus ... NY ... 333
Excelsior College ... NY ... 333

Farmingdale State College ... NY ... 356
Hudson Valley Community College ... NY ... 336
Mohawk Valley Community College ... NY ... 341
Monroe Community College ... NY ... 341
Nassau Community College ... NY ... 342
New York City College of Technology/City University of New York ... NY ... 328
New York Institute of Technology ... NY ... 343
Onondaga Community College ... NY ... 345
Paul Smith's College ... NY ... 345
Rochester Institute of Technology ... NY ... 347
State University of New York College at Buffalo ... NY ... 353
State University of New York College of Agriculture and Technology at Morri sville . NY ... 354
State University of New York College of Environmental Science and Forestry ... NY ... 355
State University of New York Institute of Technology at Utica-Rome ... NY ... 356
SUNY Canton-College of Technology ... NY ... 355
Technical Career Institutes ... NY ... 357
Vaughn College of Aeronautics and Technology ... NY ... 359
Central Piedmont Community College ... NC ... 369
Forsyth Technical Community College ... NC ... 370
Gaston College ... NC ... 370
University of North Carolina at Charlotte ... NC ... 379
Western Carolina University ... NC ... 380
Bismarck State College ... ND ... 382
Cincinnati State Technical and Community College ... OH ... 387
Cleveland State University ... OH ... 388
Columbus State Community College ... OH ... 389
Cuyahoga Community College ... OH ... 389
DeVry University - Columbus Campus ... OH ... 390
James A. Rhodes State College ... OH ... 392
Kent State University Tuscarawas Campus .. OH ... 394
Lakeland Community College ... OH ... 394
Lorain County Community College ... OH ... 395
Miami University ... OH ... 396
Sinclair Community College ... OH ... 401
Stark State College ... OH ... 402
University of Akron, Main Campus, The ... OH ... 403
University of Cincinnati Main Campus ... OH ... 403
University of Dayton ... OH ... 404
University of Toledo ... OH ... 404
Youngstown State University ... OH ... 406
Zane State College ... OH ... 407
Oklahoma City Community College ... OK ... 409
Oklahoma State University ... OK ... 410
Southwestern Oklahoma State University ... OK ... 412
Oregon Institute of Technology ... OR ... 418
Bloomsburg University of Pennsylvania ... PA ... 441
California University of Pennsylvania ... PA ... 441
DeVry University - Fort Washington Campus PA ... 427
Drexel University ... PA ... 427
Penn State Altoona ... PA ... 438
Penn State Berks ... PA ... 439
Penn State DuBois ... PA ... 439
Penn State Erie, The Behrend College ... PA ... 439
Penn State Fayette, The Eberly Campus ... PA ... 439
Penn State Harrisburg ... PA ... 439
Penn State Hazleton ... PA ... 439
Penn State New Kensington ... PA ... 440
Penn State Shenango ... PA ... 440
Penn State Wilkes-Barre ... PA ... 440
Penn State Worthington-Scranton ... PA ... 440
Penn State York ... PA ... 440
Pennsylvania College of Technology ... PA ... 440
Point Park University ... PA ... 445
Temple University ... PA ... 447
University of Pittsburgh at Johnstown ... PA ... 449
University of Puerto Rico at Bayamon ... PR ... 567
University of Puerto Rico-Humacao ... PR ... 567
New England Institute of Technology ... RI ... 453
Denmark Technical College ... SC ... 457
Greenville Technical College ... SC ... 458
Horry-Georgetown Technical College ... SC ... 458
Midlands Technical College ... SC ... 459
Orangeburg-Calhoun Technical College ... SC ... 460
Piedmont Technical College ... SC ... 460
South Carolina State University ... SC ... 460
Spartanburg Community College ... SC ... 461
University of South Carolina Upstate ... SC ... 463
York Technical College ... SC ... 463
South Dakota State University ... SD ... 466
Austin Peay State University ... TN ... 473
Belmont University ... TN ... 467
Chattanooga State Community College ... TN ... 474
East Tennessee State University ... TN ... 473
Middle Tennessee State University ... TN ... 473
Southwest Tennessee Community College .. TN ... 476
University of Memphis, The ... TN ... 474
DeVry University - Houston Campus ... TX ... 486
DeVry University - Irving Campus ... TX ... 486
Houston Community College ... TX ... 487
LeTourneau University ... TX ... 490
Midwestern State University ... TX ... 491
Prairie View A & M University ... TX ... 496
Texas A & M University ... TX ... 497
Texas A & M University at Galveston ... TX ... 497
Texas A & M University - Corpus Christi ... TX ... 498
Texas Southern University ... TX ... 500
Texas Tech University ... TX ... 502
University of Houston ... TX ... 503
University of Houston - Downtown ... TX ... 503
University of North Texas ... TX ... 504
Brigham Young University ... UT ... 509
Weber State University ... UT ... 511
Vermont Technical College ... VT ... 516
DeVry University - Arlington Campus ... VA ... 518
Old Dominion University ... VA ... 522
Virginia State University ... VA ... 529
Central Washington University ... WA ... 532
DeVry University - Federal Way Campus ... WA ... 533
Eastern Washington University ... WA ... 533
Western Washington University ... WA ... 539
Bluefield State College ... WV ... 543
Bridgemont Community and Technical College ... WV ... 542
Fairmont State University ... WV ... 543
West Virginia University Institute of Technology ... WV ... 545
Milwaukee School of Engineering ... WI ... 549
Northeast Wisconsin Technical College ... WI ... 555
Waukesha County Technical College ... WI ... 555

EXSC: Commission on Accreditation of Allied Health Education Programs: exercise science (B,M)

Metropolitan State University of Denver ... CO ... 86
Central Connecticut State University ... CT ... 90
Southern Connecticut State University ... CT ... 90
Georgia State University ... GA ... 131
University of Indianapolis ... IN ... 180
University of Louisville ... KY ... 207
University of Louisiana at Monroe ... LA ... 216
University of Southern Maine ... ME ... 220
Salisbury University ... MD ... 228
Lasell College ... MA ... 236
Springfield College ... MA ... 244
Westfield State University ... MA ... 238
St. Catherine University ... MN ... 270
Missouri Baptist University ... MO ... 285
University of North Carolina at Charlotte ... NC ... 379
North Dakota State University Main Campus. ND ... 382
University of Mary ... ND ... 383
Kent State University Main Campus ... OH ... 393
Ohio Northern University ... OH ... 398
University of Central Oklahoma ... OK ... 413
Bloomsburg University of Pennsylvania ... PA ... 441
East Stroudsburg University of Pennsylvania PA ... 442
Eastern University ... PA ... 428
Indiana University of Pennsylvania ... PA ... 442
Slippery Rock University of Pennsylvania ... PA ... 443
West Chester University of Pennsylvania ... PA ... 444
South Dakota State University ... SD ... 466
Lyndon State College ... VT ... 515
Liberty University ... VA ... 520
Lynchburg College ... VA ... 521
Old Dominion University ... VA ... 522

FOR: Society of American Foresters: forestry (B,M)

Alabama Agricultural and Mechanical University ... AL ... 1
Auburn University ... AL ... 1
University of Alaska Fairbanks ... AK ... 10
Northern Arizona University ... AZ ... 16
University of Arkansas at Monticello ... AR ... 25
California Polytechnic State University-San Luis Obispo ... CA ... 33
Humboldt State University ... CA ... 36
University of California-Berkeley ... CA ... 73
Colorado State University ... CO ... 83
Yale University ... CT ... 96
University of Florida ... FL ... 120
University of Georgia ... GA ... 138
University of Idaho ... ID ... 144
Southern Illinois University Carbondale ... IL ... 165
University of Illinois at Urbana-Champaign ... IL ... 167
Purdue University Main Campus ... IN ... 178
Iowa State University ... IA ... 182
University of Kentucky ... KY ... 207
Louisiana State University and Agricultural and Mechanical College ... LA ... 212
Louisiana Tech University ... LA ... 215
University of Maine ... ME ... 220
University of Massachusetts ... MA ... 236
Michigan State University ... MI ... 255
Michigan Technological University ... MI ... 255
University of Minnesota-Twin Cities ... MN ... 272
Mississippi State University ... MS ... 275
University of Missouri - Columbia ... MO ... 291
University of Montana - Missoula, The ... MT ... 294
University of New Hampshire ... NH ... 306
Paul Smith's College ... NY ... 345
State University of New York College of Environmental Science and Forestry ... NY ... 355
#Duke University ... NC ... 364
North Carolina State University ... NC ... 378
Ohio State University Main Campus, The ... OH ... 398
Oklahoma State University ... OK ... 410
Oregon State University ... OR ... 418
Penn State University Park ... PA ... 438
Clemson University ... SC ... 456
University of Tennessee, Knoxville ... TN ... 477
Stephen F. Austin State University ... TX ... 496
Texas A & M University ... TX ... 497
Utah State University ... UT ... 511
Virginia Polytechnic Institute and State University ... VA ... 529
University of Washington ... WA ... 539
Washington State University ... WA ... 539
West Virginia University ... WV ... 545
University of Wisconsin-Madison ... WI ... 550
University of Wisconsin-Stevens Point ... WI ... 552

FUSER: American Board of Funeral Service Education: funeral service education (C,A,B)

Bishop State Community College ... AL ... 2
Jefferson State Community College ... AL ... 5
Mesa Community College ... AZ ... 15
Arkansas State University-Mountain Home ... AR ... 20
University of Arkansas Community College at Hope ... AR ... 25
American River College ... CA ... 56
Cypress College ... CA ... 59
Arapahoe Community College ... CO ... 81
Lincoln College of New England ... CT ... 93
University of the District of Columbia ... DC ... 100
Florida State College at Jacksonville ... FL ... 109
Miami Dade College ... FL ... 113
St. Petersburg College ... FL ... 116
Gupton Jones College of Funeral Service ... GA ... 132
Ogeechee Technical College ... GA ... 135
Carl Sandburg College ... IL ... 146
City Colleges of Chicago Malcolm X College IL ... 147
Southern Illinois University Carbondale ... IL ... 165
Worsham College of Mortuary Science ... IL ... 168
Ivy Tech Community College-Central Indiana IN ... 175
Ivy Tech Community College of Indiana-Northwest ... IN ... 176
Mid-America College of Funeral Service ... IN ... 178
Vincennes University ... IN ... 181
Des Moines Area Community College ... IA ... 183
Kansas City Kansas Community College ... KS ... 194
Delgado Community College ... LA ... 210
Community College of Baltimore County, The ... MD ... 222
FINE Mortuary College ... MA ... 234
Mount Ida College ... MA ... 242
#Wayne State University ... MI ... 260
University of Minnesota-Twin Cities ... MN ... 272
East Mississippi Community College ... MS ... 274
Holmes Community College ... MS ... 274
Mississippi Gulf Coast Community College .. MS ... 275
#Northwest Mississippi Community College ... MS ... 276
Saint Louis Community College at Forest Park ... MO ... 288
Mercer County Community College ... NJ ... 311
American Academy McAllister Institute of Funeral Service ... NY ... 322
Hudson Valley Community College ... NY ... 336
Nassau Community College ... NY ... 342
Simmons Institute of Funeral Service, Inc. ... NY ... 351
Fayetteville Technical Community College ... NC ... 370
Cincinnati College of Mortuary Science ... OH ... 387
University of Central Oklahoma ... OK ... 413
Mt. Hood Community College ... OR ... 417
Northampton Community College ... PA ... 437
Pittsburgh Institute of Mortuary Science ... PA ... 444
Piedmont Technical College ... SC ... 460
John A. Gupton College ... TN ... 469
Amarillo College ... TX ... 479
Commonwealth Institute of Funeral Service . TX ... 483
Dallas Institute of Funeral Service ... TX ... 485
San Antonio College ... TX ... 479
John Tyler Community College ... VA ... 527
Tidewater Community College ... VA ... 528
Lake Washington Institute of Technology ... WA ... 535
Milwaukee Area Technical College ... WI ... 554

HSA: Commission on Accreditation of Healthcare Management Education: healthcare management (M)

University of Alabama at Birmingham ... AL ... 8
Arizona State University ... AZ ... 11
University of Arkansas for Medical Sciences AR ... 24
California State University-Long Beach ... CA ... 35
San Diego State University ... CA ... 37
University of California-Los Angeles ... CA ... 74
University of Southern California ... CA ... 76
University of Colorado Denver|Anschutz Medical Campus ... CO ... 88
George Washington University ... DC ... 98
Georgetown University ... DC ... 98
University of Central Florida ... FL ... 120
University of Florida ... FL ... 120
University of Miami ... FL ... 122
University of North Florida ... FL ... 120
Armstrong Atlantic State University ... GA ... 124
Georgia State University ... GA ... 131
Governors State University ... IL ... 151
Northwestern University ... IL ... 160
Rush University ... IL ... 163
Indiana University-Purdue University Indianapolis ... IN ... 174
University of Iowa ... IA ... 182
University of Kansas Main Campus ... KS ... 197
University of Kentucky ... KY ... 207
Tulane University ... LA ... 215
University of Southern Maine ... ME ... 220
Johns Hopkins University ... MD ... 223
Boston University ... MA ... 232
Simmons College ... MA ... 244
University of Michigan-Ann Arbor ... MI ... 259
University of Minnesota-Twin Cities ... MN ... 272
University of Saint Thomas ... MN ... 272
Saint Louis University ... MO ... 289
University of Missouri - Columbia ... MO ... 291
Baruch College/City University of New York . NY ... 326
Columbia University in the City of New York NY ... 330
Cornell University ... NY ... 331
New York University ... NY ... 344
Union Graduate College ... NY ... 358
University of North Carolina at Chapel Hill ... NC ... 378
University of North Carolina at Charlotte ... NC ... 379
Ohio State University Main Campus, The ... OH ... 398
Xavier University ... OH ... 406
University of Oklahoma Health Sciences Center ... OK ... 413
Penn State University Park ... PA ... 438
Temple University ... PA ... 447
University of Pittsburgh ... PA ... 449
University of Scranton, The ... PA ... 450
Widener University ... PA ... 451
University of Puerto Rico-Medical Sciences Campus ... PR ... 567
Medical University of South Carolina ... SC ... 459
University of South Carolina Columbia ... SC ... 462
University of Memphis, The ... TN ... 474
Baylor University ... TX ... 482
Texas A & M University ... TX ... 497
Texas State University-San Marcos ... TX ... 501
Texas Tech University ... TX ... 502
Texas Woman's University ... TX ... 502
Trinity University ... TX ... 502
University of Houston - Clear Lake ... TX ... 503
George Mason University ... VA ... 519
Marymount University ... VA ... 521
Virginia Commonwealth University ... VA ... 526
University of Washington ... WA ... 539
Washington State University ... WA ... 539

HT: National Accrediting Agency for Clinical Laboratory Sciences: histologic technology (C,A,B)

Phoenix College ... AZ ... 16
California State University-Sacramento ... CA ... 36
Mt. San Antonio College ... CA ... 58
Goodwin College ... CT ... 92
Delaware Technical Community College, Stanton-Wilmington Campus ... DE ... 96
Barry University ... FL ... 101
Florida State College at Jacksonville ... FL ... 109
Miami Dade College ... FL ... 113
Darton College ... GA ... 128
Elgin Community College ... IL ... 150
Indiana University-Purdue University Indianapolis ... IN ... 174
Harford Community College ... MD ... 223
Lansing Community College ... MI ... 254
Argosy University, Twin Cities ... MN ... 260
Mayo School of Health Sciences ... MN ... 262
North Hennepin Community College ... MN ... 268
State University of New York College of Agriculture and Technology at Coble skill .. NY ... 354
Davidson County Community College ... NC ... 370
University of North Dakota Main Campus ... ND ... 381
Lakeland Community College ... OH ... 394
Youngstown State University ... OH ... 406
Drexel University ... PA ... 427
Harcum College ... PA ... 430
University of Pittsburgh ... PA ... 449
Community College of Rhode Island ... RI ... 453
Medical University of South Carolina ... SC ... 459
University of Tennessee Health Science Center ... TN ... 477
Houston Community College ... TX ... 487
St. Philip's College ... TX ... 479
Tarleton State University ... TX ... 497
University of Texas Health Science Center at San Antonio ... TX ... 507
University of Texas M.D. Anderson Cancer Center, The ... TX ... 507
Old Dominion University ... VA ... 522
Clover Park Technical College ... WA ... 532

IACBE: International Assembly for Collegiate Business Education: business programs in institutions that grant bachelor/graduate degrees (A,B,M,D)

Stillman College ... AL ... 7
John Brown University ... AR ... 22
University of the Ozarks ... AR ... 26
Azusa Pacific University ... CA ... 30
California Maritime Academy ... CA ... 33
John F. Kennedy University ... CA ... 52
National University ... CA ... 58
Pacific Union College ... CA ... 60
Albertus Magnus College ... CT ... 90
Goldey-Beacom College ... DE ... 96
Wilmington University ... DE ... 97
Edward Waters College ... FL ... 105
Hodges University ... FL ... 111
Lynn University ... FL ... 113
Nova Southeastern University ... FL ... 114
Palm Beach Atlantic University ... FL ... 114
Saint Leo University ... FL ... 116
Southeastern University ... FL ... 118
Webber International University ... FL ... 123
University of Guam ... GU ... 559
Lewis-Clark State College ... ID ... 144

IFSAC: International Fire Service Accreditation Congress Degree Assembly: fire and emergency related degree (A,B)

IPSY: American Psychological Association: pre-doctoral internships in professional psychology

JOUR: Accrediting Council on Education for Journalism and Mass Communications: journalism and mass communications (B,M)

Institution	State	Page
University of Oklahoma Norman Campus	OK	413
University of Oregon	OR	419
Penn State University Park	PA	438
Temple University	PA	447
University of Puerto Rico-Rio Piedras Campus	PR	568
University of South Carolina Columbia	SC	462
Winthrop University	SC	463
South Dakota State University	SD	466
University of South Dakota, The	SD	465
East Tennessee State University	TN	473
Middle Tennessee State University	TN	473
University of Memphis, The	TN	474
University of Tennessee at Chattanooga	TN	477
University of Tennessee at Martin	TN	477
University of Tennessee, Knoxville	TN	477
Abilene Christian University	TX	478
Baylor University	TX	482
Texas Christian University	TX	499
Texas State University-San Marcos	TX	501
University of North Texas	TX	504
University of Texas at Austin	TX	505
Brigham Young University	UT	509
Hampton University	VA	519
#Norfolk State University	VA	522
Virginia Commonwealth University	VA	526
Washington and Lee University	VA	530
University of Washington	WA	539
Marshall University	WV	544
West Virginia University	WV	545
Marquette University	WI	548
University of Wisconsin-Eau Claire	WI	551
University of Wisconsin-Oshkosh	WI	551

KIN: Commission on Accreditation of Allied Health Education Programs: kinesiotherapy (B)

Institution	State	Page
California State University-Long Beach	CA	35
San Diego State University	CA	37
University of Southern Mississippi	MS	277
Shaw University	NC	376
Norfolk State University	VA	522

LAW: American Bar Association: law (FP,D)

Institution	State	Page
Faulkner University	AL	3
Samford University	AL	6
University of Alabama, The	AL	8
Arizona State University	AZ	11
Phoenix School of Law	AZ	17
University of Arizona	AZ	18
University of Arkansas at Little Rock	AR	24
University of Arkansas Main Campus	AR	24
California Western School of Law	CA	37
Chapman University	CA	39
Golden Gate University	CA	48
Loyola Marymount University	CA	56
Pepperdine University	CA	61
Santa Clara University	CA	68
Southwestern Law School	CA	71
Stanford University	CA	71
Thomas Jefferson School of Law	CA	72
University of California-Berkeley	CA	73
University of California-Davis	CA	73
University of California-Hastings College of the Law	CA	74
#University of California-Irvine	CA	74
University of California-Los Angeles	CA	74
#University of LaVerne	CA	75
University of San Diego	CA	76
University of San Francisco	CA	76
University of Southern California	CA	76
University of the Pacific	CA	76
Western State University College of Law	CA	78
Whittier College	CA	79
University of Colorado Boulder	CO	88
University of Denver	CO	89
Quinnipiac University	CT	93
University of Connecticut	CT	94
Yale University	CT	96
Widener University School of Law	DE	97
American University	DC	97
Catholic University of America, The	DC	97
George Washington University	DC	98
Georgetown University	DC	98
Howard University	DC	98
University of the District of Columbia	DC	100
Ave Maria School of Law	FL	101
Barry University	FL	101
Florida Agricultural and Mechanical University	FL	118
Florida Coastal School of Law	FL	107
Florida International University	FL	119
Florida State University	FL	119
Nova Southeastern University	FL	114
St. Thomas University	FL	117
Stetson University	FL	121
University of Florida	FL	120
University of Miami	FL	122
Atlanta's John Marshall Law School	GA	125
Emory University	GA	129
Georgia State University	GA	131
Mercer University	GA	134
University of Georgia	GA	138
University of Hawaii at Manoa	HI	141
University of Idaho	ID	144
DePaul University	IL	149
Illinois Institute of Technology	IL	153
John Marshall Law School	IL	154
Loyola University Chicago	IL	157
Northern Illinois University	IL	160
Northwestern University	IL	160
Southern Illinois University Carbondale	IL	165
University of Chicago	IL	166
University of Illinois at Urbana-Champaign	IL	167
Indiana University Bloomington	IN	173
Indiana University-Purdue University Indianapolis	IN	174
University of Notre Dame	IN	180
Valparaiso University	IN	181
Drake University	IA	184
University of Iowa	IA	182
University of Kansas Main Campus	KS	197
Washburn University	KS	197
Northern Kentucky University	KY	205
University of Kentucky	KY	207
University of Louisville	KY	207
Louisiana State University Paul M. Hebert Law Center	LA	213
Loyola University New Orleans	LA	213
Southern University and A&M College	LA	214
Tulane University	LA	215
University of Southern Maine	ME	220
University of Baltimore	MD	229
University of Maryland Baltimore	MD	227
Boston College	MA	232
Boston University	MA	232
Harvard University	MA	235
New England Law I Boston	MA	243
Northeastern University	MA	243
Suffolk University	MA	245
#University of Massachusetts Dartmouth	MA	237
Western New England University	MA	246
Michigan State University	MI	255
Thomas M. Cooley Law School	MI	258
University of Detroit Mercy	MI	258
University of Michigan-Ann Arbor	MI	259
Wayne State University	MI	260
Hamline University	MN	264
University of Minnesota-Twin Cities	MN	272
University of Saint Thomas	MN	272
William Mitchell College of Law	MN	272
Mississippi College	MS	275
University of Mississippi	MS	277
Saint Louis University	MO	289
University of Missouri - Columbia	MO	291
University of Missouri - Kansas City	MO	291
Washington University in St. Louis	MO	292
University of Montana - Missoula, The	MT	294
Creighton University	NE	297
University of Nebraska - Lincoln	NE	300
University of Nevada, Las Vegas	NV	302
University of New Hampshire School of Law	NH	306
Rutgers the State University of New Jersey Camden Campus	NJ	314
Rutgers the State University of New Jersey Newark Campus	NJ	314
Seton Hall University School of Law	NJ	315
University of New Mexico Main Campus	NM	321
Albany Law School	NY	322
Brooklyn Law School	NY	324
City University of New York Queens College	NY	328
Columbia University in the City of New York	NY	330
Cornell University	NY	331
Fordham University	NY	334
Hofstra University	NY	335
New York Law School	NY	343
New York University	NY	344
Pace University	NY	345
St. John's University	NY	348
Syracuse University Main Campus	NY	357
Touro College	NY	358
University at Buffalo-SUNY	NY	351
Yeshiva University	NY	361
Campbell University	NC	362
Charlotte School of Law	NC	363
Duke University	NC	364
Elon University	NC	364
North Carolina Central University	NC	378
University of North Carolina at Chapel Hill	NC	378
Wake Forest University	NC	380
University of North Dakota Main Campus	ND	381
Capital University	OH	386
Case Western Reserve University	OH	386
Cleveland State University	OH	388
Ohio Northern University	OH	398
Ohio State University Main Campus, The	OH	398
University of Akron, Main Campus, The	OH	403
University of Cincinnati Main Campus	OH	403
University of Dayton	OH	404
University of Toledo	OH	404
Oklahoma City University	OK	410
University of Oklahoma Norman Campus	OK	413
University of Tulsa	OK	413
Lewis and Clark College	OR	416
University of Oregon	OR	419
Willamette University	OR	421
Drexel University	PA	427
Duquesne University	PA	428
Penn State Dickinson School of Law, The	PA	439
Temple University	PA	447
University of Pennsylvania	PA	448
University of Pittsburgh	PA	449
Villanova University	PA	450
Widener University	PA	451
Inter American University of Puerto Rico School of Law	PR	564
Pontifical Catholic University of Puerto Rico, The	PR	565
University of Puerto Rico-Rio Piedras Campus	PR	568
Roger Williams University	RI	454
Charleston School of Law	SC	456
University of South Carolina Columbia	SC	462
University of South Dakota, The	SD	465
University of Memphis, The	TN	474
University of Tennessee, Knoxville	TN	477
Vanderbilt University	TN	478
Baylor University	TX	482
St. Mary's University	TX	493
South Texas College of Law	TX	494
Southern Methodist University	TX	495
Texas Southern University	TX	500
Texas Tech University	TX	502
Texas Wesleyan University	TX	502
University of Houston	TX	503
University of Texas at Austin	TX	505
Brigham Young University	UT	509
University of Utah, The	UT	511
Vermont Law School	VT	515
Appalachian School of Law	VA	516
College of William & Mary	VA	518
George Mason University	VA	519
Judge Advocate General's Legal Center & School, The	VA	557
Liberty University	VA	520
Regent University	VA	523
University of Richmond	VA	525
University of Virginia	VA	525
Washington and Lee University	VA	530
Gonzaga University	WA	534
Seattle University	WA	538
University of Washington	WA	539
West Virginia University	WV	545
Marquette University	WI	548
University of Wisconsin-Madison	WI	550
University of Wyoming	WY	556

LIB: American Library Association: librarianship (M)

Institution	State	Page
University of Alabama, The	AL	8
University of Arizona	AZ	18
San Jose State University	CA	37
University of California-Los Angeles	CA	74
University of Denver	CO	89
#Southern Connecticut State University	CT	90
Catholic University of America, The	DC	97
Florida State University	FL	119
University of South Florida	FL	121
#Valdosta State University	GA	139
University of Hawaii at Manoa	HI	141
Dominican University	IL	150
University of Illinois at Urbana-Champaign	IL	167
Indiana University Bloomington	IN	173
University of Iowa	IA	182
Emporia State University	KS	192
University of Kentucky	KY	207
Louisiana State University and Agricultural and Mechanical College	LA	212
University of Maryland College Park	MD	227
Simmons College	MA	244
University of Michigan-Ann Arbor	MI	259
Wayne State University	MI	260
St. Catherine University	MN	270
University of Southern Mississippi	MS	277
#University of Missouri - Columbia	MO	291
Rutgers the State University of New Jersey New Brunswick Campus	NJ	314
#City University of New York Queens College	NY	328
Long Island University C.W. Post Campus	NY	339
Pratt Institute	NY	346
St. John's University	NY	348
Syracuse University Main Campus	NY	357
University at Albany, SUNY	NY	351
#University at Buffalo-SUNY	NY	351
North Carolina Central University	NC	378
University of North Carolina at Chapel Hill	NC	378
University of North Carolina at Greensboro	NC	379
Kent State University Main Campus	OH	393
University of Oklahoma Norman Campus	OK	413
Clarion University of Pennsylvania	PA	442
Drexel University	PA	427
University of Pittsburgh	PA	449
University of Puerto Rico-Rio Piedras Campus	PR	568
University of Rhode Island	RI	454
University of South Carolina Columbia	SC	462
University of Tennessee, Knoxville	TN	477
Texas Woman's University	TX	502
University of North Texas	TX	504
University of Texas at Austin	TX	505
University of Washington	WA	539
University of Wisconsin-Madison	WI	550
University of Wisconsin-Milwaukee	WI	551

LSAR: American Society of Landscape Architects: landscape architecture (B,M)

Institution	State	Page
Auburn University	AL	1
Arizona State University	AZ	11
University of Arizona	AZ	18
University of Arkansas Main Campus	AR	24
California Polytechnic State University-San Luis Obispo	CA	33
California State Polytechnic University-Pomona	CA	33
University of California-Berkeley	CA	73
University of California-Davis	CA	73
University of Southern California	CA	76
#Colorado State University	CO	83
University of Colorado DenverlAnschutz Medical Campus	CO	88
University of Connecticut	CT	94
Florida Agricultural and Mechanical University	FL	118
Florida International University	FL	119
University of Florida	FL	120
University of Georgia	GA	138
University of Idaho	ID	144
Illinois Institute of Technology	IL	153
University of Illinois at Urbana-Champaign	IL	167
Ball State University	IN	169
Purdue University Main Campus	IN	178
Iowa State University	IA	182
Kansas State University	KS	194
University of Kentucky	KY	207
Louisiana State University and Agricultural and Mechanical College	LA	212
Morgan State University	MD	224
University of Maryland College Park	MD	227
Boston Architectural College	MA	231
Harvard University	MA	235
University of Massachusetts	MA	236
Michigan State University	MI	255
University of Michigan-Ann Arbor	MI	259
University of Minnesota-Twin Cities	MN	272
Mississippi State University	MS	275
University of Nevada, Las Vegas	NV	302
Rutgers the State University of New Jersey New Brunswick Campus	NJ	314
University of New Mexico Main Campus	NM	321
City University of New York The City College	NY	326
Cornell University	NY	331
State University of New York College of Environmental Science and Forestry	NY	355
North Carolina Agricultural and Technical State University	NC	378
North Carolina State University	NC	378
#North Dakota State University Main Campus	ND	382
Ohio State University Main Campus, The	OH	398
Oklahoma State University	OK	410
University of Oklahoma Norman Campus	OK	413
University of Oregon	OR	419
Chatham University	PA	425
Penn State University Park	PA	438
Philadelphia University	PA	444
Temple University	PA	447
University of Pennsylvania	PA	448
Universidad Politecnica De Puerto Rico	PR	566
Rhode Island School of Design	RI	454
University of Rhode Island	RI	454
Clemson University	SC	456
Texas A & M University	TX	497
Texas Tech University	TX	502
University of Texas at Arlington, The	TX	505
University of Texas at Austin	TX	505
Utah State University	UT	511
University of Virginia	VA	525
Virginia Polytechnic Institute and State University	VA	529
University of Washington	WA	539
#Washington State University	WA	539
West Virginia University	WV	545
University of Wisconsin-Madison	WI	550

M: Middle States Association of Colleges and Schools, Commission on Higher Education

Institution	State	Page
&American Academy of Dramatic Arts, Los Angeles Campus	CA	27
&Culinary Institute of America at Greystone, The	CA	43
&Rensselaer at Hartford	CT	94
Delaware College of Art and Design	DE	96
Delaware State University	DE	96
Delaware Technical Community College, Owens Campus	DE	96
Delaware Technical Community College, Stanton-Wilmington Campus	DE	96
Delaware Technical Community College, Terry Campus	DE	96
Goldey-Beacom College	DE	96
University of Delaware	DE	96
Wesley College	DE	97
Wilmington University	DE	97
American University	DC	97
Catholic University of America, The	DC	97
Corcoran College of Art and Design	DC	98
Gallaudet University	DC	98
George Washington University	DC	98
Georgetown University	DC	98
Howard University	DC	98
Institute of World Politics, The	DC	99
National Defense University	DC	557
National Intelligence University	DC	557
Pontifical Faculty of the Immaculate Conception at the Dominican House of Studies	DC	99

MAAB: Accrediting Bureau of Health Education Schools: medical assisting (C,A)

MAC: Commission on Accreditation of Allied Health Education Programs: medical assisting (C,A)

MACTE: Montessori Accreditation Council for Teacher Education: Montessori teacher education (C)

MEAC: Midwifery Education Accreditation Council: midwifery education (C,A,B,M,D)

MED: Liaison Committee on Medical Education: medicine (FP,D)

- Tufts University ... MA ... 245
- University of Massachusetts Medical School ... MA ... 237
- #Central Michigan University ... MI ... 249
- Michigan State University ... MI ... 255
- #Oakland University ... MI ... 256
- University of Michigan-Ann Arbor ... MI ... 259
- Wayne State University ... MI ... 260
- Mayo Medical School ... MN ... 262
- University of Minnesota-Twin Cities ... MN ... 272
- University of Mississippi Medical Center ... MS ... 277
- Saint Louis University ... MO ... 289
- University of Missouri - Columbia ... MO ... 291
- University of Missouri - Kansas City ... MO ... 291
- Washington University in St. Louis ... MO ... 292
- Creighton University ... NE ... 297
- University of Nebraska Medical Center ... NE ... 300
- University of Nevada, Reno ... NV ... 303
- Dartmouth College ... NH ... 304
- #Rowan University ... NJ ... 314
- UMDNJ-New Jersey Medical School ... NJ ... 316
- UMDNJ-Robert Wood Johnson Medical School ... NJ ... 316
- University of New Mexico Main Campus ... NM ... 321
- Albany Medical College ... NY ... 322
- Columbia University in the City of New York ... NY ... 330
- #Hofstra University ... NY ... 335
- Mount Sinai School of Medicine ... NY ... 342
- New York Medical College ... NY ... 343
- New York University ... NY ... 344
- State University of New York at Stony Brook ... NY ... 352
- State University of New York Health Science Center at Brooklyn ... NY ... 352
- #State University of New York Upstate Medical University ... NY ... 352
- University at Buffalo-SUNY ... NY ... 351
- University of Rochester ... NY ... 359
- Weill Cornell Medical College ... NY ... 360
- Yeshiva University ... NY ... 361
- Duke University ... NC ... 364
- East Carolina University ... NC ... 377
- University of North Carolina at Chapel Hill ... NC ... 378
- Wake Forest University ... NC ... 380
- University of North Dakota Main Campus ... ND ... 381
- Case Western Reserve University ... OH ... 386
- Northeast Ohio Medical University ... OH ... 397
- Ohio State University Main Campus, The ... OH ... 398
- University of Cincinnati Main Campus ... OH ... 403
- University of Toledo ... OH ... 404
- Wright State University Main Campus ... OH ... 406
- University of Oklahoma Health Sciences Center ... OK ... 413
- Oregon Health & Science University ... OR ... 418
- #Commonwealth Medical College, The ... PA ... 425
- Drexel University ... PA ... 427
- Penn State Milton S. Hershey Medical Center College of Medicine ... PA ... 440
- Temple University ... PA ... 447
- Thomas Jefferson University ... PA ... 448
- University of Pennsylvania ... PA ... 448
- University of Pittsburgh ... PA ... 449
- Ponce School of Medicine & Health Sciences ... PR ... 565
- #San Juan Bautista School of Medicine ... PR ... 565
- Universidad Central Del Caribe ... PR ... 566
- University of Puerto Rico-Medical Sciences Campus ... PR ... 567
- Brown University ... RI ... 453
- Medical University of South Carolina ... SC ... 459
- University of South Carolina Columbia ... SC ... 462
- #University of South Carolina School of Medicine-Greenville ... SC ... 462
- University of South Dakota, The ... SD ... 465
- East Tennessee State University ... TN ... 473
- Meharry Medical College ... TN ... 471
- University of Tennessee Health Science Center ... TN ... 477
- Vanderbilt University ... TN ... 478
- Baylor College of Medicine ... TX ... 481
- Texas A & M University ... TX ... 497
- Texas Tech University ... TX ... 502
- Texas Tech University Health Sciences Center ... TX ... 502
- University of Texas Health Science Center at Houston (UTHealth), The ... TX ... 506
- #University of Texas Health Science Center at San Antonio ... TX ... 507
- University of Texas Medical Branch, The ... TX ... 507
- University of Texas Southwestern Medical Center ... TX ... 507
- University of Utah, The ... UT ... 511
- University of Vermont ... VT ... 514
- Eastern Virginia Medical School ... VA ... 518
- University of Virginia ... VA ... 525
- Virginia Commonwealth University ... VA ... 526
- University of Washington ... WA ... 539
- Marshall University ... WV ... 544
- West Virginia University ... WV ... 545
- Medical College of Wisconsin ... WI ... 548
- University of Wisconsin-Madison ... WI ... 550

MFCD: American Association for Marriage and Family Therapy: marriage and family therapy (M,D)

- Auburn University ... AL ... 1
- Alliant International University-Fresno & Sacramento ... CA ... 27
- Alliant International University-Irvine ... CA ... 27
- Alliant International University-Los Angeles ... CA ... 27
- Alliant International University-San Diego ... CA ... 27
- Chapman University ... CA ... 39
- Hope International University ... CA ... 50
- Loma Linda University ... CA ... 54
- San Diego State University ... CA ... 37
- University of San Diego ... CA ... 76
- Colorado State University ... CO ... 83
- Central Connecticut State University ... CT ... 90
- Fairfield University ... CT ... 92
- Southern Connecticut State University ... CT ... 90
- University of Connecticut ... CT ... 94
- University of Saint Joseph ... CT ... 95
- Florida State University ... FL ... 119
- Nova Southeastern University ... FL ... 114
- Mercer University ... GA ... 134
- University of Georgia ... GA ... 138
- Valdosta State University ... GA ... 139
- Northern Illinois University ... IL ... 160
- Northwestern University ... IL ... 160
- Christian Theological Seminary ... IN ... 170
- Purdue University Calumet ... IN ... 178
- Purdue University Main Campus ... IN ... 178
- #Iowa State University ... IA ... 182
- Friends University ... KS ... 193
- Kansas State University ... KS ... 194
- Louisville Presbyterian Theological Seminary ... KY ... 204
- University of Kentucky ... KY ... 207
- University of Louisville ... KY ... 207
- University of Louisiana at Monroe ... LA ... 216
- University of Maryland College Park ... MD ... 227
- University of Massachusetts Boston ... MA ... 236
- Michigan State University ... MI ... 255
- Argosy University, Twin Cities ... MN ... 260
- Bethel University ... MN ... 261
- St. Cloud State University ... MN ... 269
- Saint Mary's University of Minnesota ... MN ... 271
- University of Minnesota-Twin Cities ... MN ... 272
- Reformed Theological Seminary ... MS ... 276
- University of Southern Mississippi ... MS ... 277
- Saint Louis University ... MO ... 289
- School of Professional Psychology at Forest Institute, The ... MO ... 289
- University of Nebraska - Lincoln ... NE ... 300
- University of Nevada, Las Vegas ... NV ... 302
- Antioch University New England ... NH ... 303
- University of New Hampshire ... NH ... 306
- Seton Hall University ... NJ ... 315
- Iona College ... NY ... 336
- Syracuse University Main Campus ... NY ... 357
- University of Rochester ... NY ... 359
- Appalachian State University ... NC ... 377
- East Carolina University ... NC ... 377
- Pfeiffer University ... NC ... 375
- North Dakota State University Main Campus ... ND ... 382
- Ohio State University Main Campus, The ... OH ... 398
- University of Akron, Main Campus, The ... OH ... 403
- Oklahoma State University ... OK ... 410
- Lewis and Clark College ... OR ... 416
- University of Oregon ... OR ... 419
- Drexel University ... PA ... 427
- La Salle University ... PA ... 432
- Seton Hill University ... PA ... 447
- University of Rhode Island ... RI ... 454
- Converse College ... SC ... 457
- Abilene Christian University ... TX ... 478
- St. Mary's University ... TX ... 493
- Texas Tech University ... TX ... 502
- #University of Houston - Clear Lake ... TX ... 503
- Brigham Young University ... UT ... 509
- Utah State University ... UT ... 511
- Virginia Polytechnic Institute and State University ... VA ... 529
- Antioch University Seattle ... WA ... 530
- Pacific Lutheran University ... WA ... 536
- Seattle Pacific University ... WA ... 537
- Edgewood College ... WI ... 547
- University of Wisconsin-Stout ... WI ... 552

MIDWF: Accreditation Commission for Midwifery Education: nurse midwifery (C,M,D)

- California State University-Fullerton ... CA ... 35
- San Diego State University ... CA ... 37
- University of California-San Francisco ... CA ... 75
- University of Colorado DenverlAnschutz Medical Campus ... CO ... 88
- Yale University ... CT ... 96
- Georgetown University ... DC ... 98
- University of Florida ... FL ... 120
- University of Miami ... FL ... 122
- Emory University ... GA ... 129
- University of Illinois at Chicago ... IL ... 167
- University of Indianapolis ... IN ... 180
- University of Kansas Medical Center ... KS ... 197
- Frontier Nursing University ... KY ... 200
- University of Michigan-Ann Arbor ... MI ... 259
- Wayne State University ... MI ... 260
- University of Minnesota-Twin Cities ... MN ... 272
- UMDNJ-School of Health Related Professions ... NJ ... 317
- UMDNJ-School of Nursing ... NJ ... 316
- University of New Mexico Main Campus ... NM ... 321
- Columbia University in the City of New York ... NY ... 330
- New York University ... NY ... 344
- State University of New York at Stony Brook ... NY ... 352
- State University of New York Health Science Center at Brooklyn ... NY ... 352
- East Carolina University ... NC ... 377
- Case Western Reserve University ... OH ... 386
- Ohio State University Main Campus, The ... OH ... 398
- University of Cincinnati Main Campus ... OH ... 403
- Oregon Health & Science University ... OR ... 418
- Philadelphia University ... PA ... 444
- University of Pennsylvania ... PA ... 448
- University of Puerto Rico-Medical Sciences Campus ... PR ... 567
- Vanderbilt University ... TN ... 478
- Baylor University ... TX ... 482
- @Texas Tech University ... TX ... 502
- University of Utah, The ... UT ... 511
- Shenandoah University ... VA ... 524
- @Seattle University ... WA ... 538
- University of Washington ... WA ... 539
- Marquette University ... WI ... 548

MIL: Commission on Accreditation of Allied Health Education Programs: medical illustrator (M)

- Georgia Health Sciences University ... GA ... 130
- University of Illinois at Chicago ... IL ... 167
- Johns Hopkins University ... MD ... 223
- University of Texas Southwestern Medical Center ... TX ... 507

MLTAB: Accrediting Bureau of Health Education Schools: medical laboratory technician (C,A)

- Spencerian College ... KY ... 206
- Southwestern Oklahoma State University ... OK ... 412

MLTAD: National Accrediting Agency for Clinical Laboratory Sciences: medical laboratory technician (A)

- Calhoun Community College ... AL ... 2
- Gadsden State Community College ... AL ... 3
- Jefferson State Community College ... AL ... 5
- Wallace State Community College - Hanceville ... AL ... 10
- Phoenix College ... AZ ... 16
- Pima County Community College District ... AZ ... 17
- Arkansas State University-Beebe ... AR ... 20
- Arkansas State University-Jonesboro ... AR ... 20
- National Park Community College ... AR ... 22
- North Arkansas College ... AR ... 22
- Phillips Community College of the University of Arkansas ... AR ... 25
- De Anza College ... CA ... 47
- Southwestern College ... CA ... 71
- Arapahoe Community College ... CO ... 81
- Delaware Technical Community College, Owens Campus ... DE ... 96
- Brevard Community College ... FL ... 102
- Florida State College at Jacksonville ... FL ... 109
- Indian River State College ... FL ... 111
- Keiser University ... FL ... 112
- MedVance Institute of Fort Lauderdale ... FL ... 113
- Miami Dade College ... FL ... 113
- St. Petersburg College ... FL ... 116
- Central Georgia Technical College ... GA ... 127
- College of Coastal Georgia ... GA ... 127
- Dalton State College ... GA ... 128
- Darton College ... GA ... 128
- Georgia Piedmont Technical College ... GA ... 131
- Lanier Technical College ... GA ... 133
- North Georgia Technical College ... GA ... 135
- Okefenokee Technical College ... GA ... 135
- Southeastern Technical College ... GA ... 137
- Southwest Georgia Technical College ... GA ... 138
- West Georgia Technical College ... GA ... 139
- Wiregrass Georgia Technical College ... GA ... 139
- Kapiolani Community College ... HI ... 141
- Elgin Community College ... IL ... 150
- Illinois Central College ... IL ... 152
- John A. Logan College ... IL ... 154
- Kankakee Community College ... IL ... 155
- Kaskaskia College ... IL ... 155
- Oakton Community College ... IL ... 160
- Rend Lake College ... IL ... 162
- Shawnee Community College ... IL ... 164
- Southeastern Illinois College ... IL ... 164
- Southern Illinois University Carbondale ... IL ... 165
- Southern Illinois University Edwardsville ... IL ... 165
- Southwestern Illinois College ... IL ... 165
- Harrison College - Indianapolis East Campus ... IN ... 172
- Ivy Tech Community College of Indiana-North Central ... IN ... 176
- Ivy Tech Community College of Indiana-Southern Indiana ... IN ... 177
- Ivy Tech Community College of Indiana-Wabash Valley ... IN ... 177
- MedTech College ... IN ... 178
- Des Moines Area Community College ... IA ... 183
- Hawkeye Community College ... IA ... 185
- Indian Hills Community College ... IA ... 185
- Iowa Central Community College ... IA ... 185
- Barton County Community College ... KS ... 190
- Seward County Community College/Area Technical School ... KS ... 196
- Eastern Kentucky University ... KY ... 200
- Henderson Community College ... KY ... 202
- Madisonville Community College ... KY ... 202
- Somerset Community College ... KY ... 203
- Southeast Kentucky Community and Technical College ... KY ... 203
- Delgado Community College ... LA ... 210
- Louisiana State University at Alexandria ... LA ... 212
- MedVance Institute-Baton Rouge ... LA ... 213
- South Louisiana Community College Ardoin Campus ... LA ... 211
- Southern University at Shreveport-Louisiana ... LA ... 215
- University of Maine at Augusta ... ME ... 220
- University of Maine at Presque Isle ... ME ... 220
- Allegany College of Maryland ... MD ... 221
- Anne Arundel Community College ... MD ... 221
- Community College of Baltimore County, The ... MD ... 222
- Bristol Community College ... MA ... 239
- Bunker Hill Community College ... MA ... 239
- Mount Wachusett Community College ... MA ... 240
- Quincy College ... MA ... 243
- Springfield Technical Community College ... MA ... 241
- Baker College of Allen Park ... MI ... 247
- Baker College of Jackson ... MI ... 248
- Baker College of Owosso ... MI ... 248
- Baker College of Port Huron ... MI ... 248
- Ferris State University ... MI ... 250
- Kellogg Community College ... MI ... 253
- Macomb Community College ... MI ... 254
- Northern Michigan University ... MI ... 256
- Alexandria Technical & Community College ... MN ... 265
- Argosy University, Twin Cities ... MN ... 260
- Hibbing Community College, A Technical and Community College ... MN ... 266
- Lake Superior College ... MN ... 266
- Minnesota State Community and Technical College ... MN ... 267
- Minnesota West Community and Technical College ... MN ... 267
- North Hennepin Community College ... MN ... 268
- Rasmussen College - Mankato ... MN ... 270
- Rasmussen College - St. Cloud ... MN ... 270
- Saint Paul College-A Community & Technical College ... MN ... 269
- South Central College ... MN ... 269
- Copiah-Lincoln Community College ... MS ... 273
- Hinds Community College ... MS ... 274
- Meridian Community College ... MS ... 275
- Mississippi Delta Community College ... MS ... 275
- Mississippi Gulf Coast Community College ... MS ... 275
- Northeast Mississippi Community College ... MS ... 276
- Pearl River Community College ... MS ... 276
- Moberly Area Community College ... MO ... 286
- Ozarks Technical Community College ... MO ... 287
- Saint Louis Community College at Forest Park ... MO ... 288
- Three Rivers Community College ... MO ... 290
- Central Community College ... NE ... 297
- Mid-Plains Community College ... NE ... 298
- Southeast Community College ... NE ... 300
- College of Southern Nevada ... NV ... 302
- River Valley Community College ... NH ... 304
- Brookdale Community College ... NJ ... 308
- Camden County College ... NJ ... 308
- Mercer County Community College ... NJ ... 311
- Middlesex County College ... NJ ... 311
- Central New Mexico Community College ... NM ... 317
- San Juan College ... NM ... 320
- University of New Mexico-Gallup ... NM ... 321
- Broome Community College ... NY ... 324
- Dutchess Community College ... NY ... 332
- Erie Community College North Campus ... NY ... 333
- Farmingdale State College ... NY ... 356
- Nassau Community College ... NY ... 342
- Orange County Community College ... NY ... 345
- Alamance Community College ... NC ... 368
- Asheville - Buncombe Technical Community College ... NC ... 368
- Beaufort County Community College ... NC ... 368
- Central Piedmont Community College ... NC ... 369
- Coastal Carolina Community College ... NC ... 369
- College of the Albemarle ... NC ... 369
- Davidson County Community College ... NC ... 370
- Halifax Community College ... NC ... 371
- Sandhills Community College ... NC ... 373
- Southeastern Community College ... NC ... 374
- Southwestern Community College ... NC ... 374
- Stanly Community College ... NC ... 374
- Wake Technical Community College ... NC ... 374
- Western Piedmont Community College ... NC ... 375
- Bismarck State College ... ND ... 382
- Rasmussen College - Bismarck ... ND ... 383
- Cincinnati State Technical and Community College ... OH ... 387
- Clark State Community College ... OH ... 387
- Columbus State Community College ... OH ... 389
- Cuyahoga Community College ... OH ... 389
- Eastern Gateway Community College - Jefferson County Campus ... OH ... 390
- Edison State Community College ... OH ... 390
- Lakeland Community College ... OH ... 394
- Lorain County Community College ... OH ... 395
- Marion Technical College ... OH ... 395
- Shawnee State University ... OH ... 401
- Stark State College ... OH ... 402
- Washington State Community College ... OH ... 405
- Youngstown State University ... OH ... 406
- Zane State College ... OH ... 407

MT: National Accrediting Agency for Clinical Laboratory Sciences: medical technology (C,B)

MUS: National Association of Schools of Music: music (C,A,B,M,D)

University of Wisconsin-Green Bay ... WI ... 551
University of Wisconsin-La Crosse ... WI ... 551
University of Wisconsin-Madison ... WI ... 550
University of Wisconsin-Milwaukee ... WI ... 551
University of Wisconsin-Oshkosh ... WI ... 551
University of Wisconsin-Platteville ... WI ... 552
University of Wisconsin-River Falls ... WI ... 552
University of Wisconsin-Stevens Point ... WI ... 552
University of Wisconsin-Superior ... WI ... 552
University of Wisconsin-Whitewater ... WI ... 553
Viterbo University ... WI ... 553
Casper College ... WY ... 556
Northwest College ... WY ... 556
University of Wyoming ... WY ... 556

NAIT: The Association of Technology, Management, and Applied Engineering: technology, applied technology, engineering technology and technology-related programs (A,B,M)

Jacksonville State University ... AL ... 4
University of Arkansas at Fort Smith ... AR ... 24
University of Arkansas at Pine Bluff ... AR ... 25
California Polytechnic State University-San Luis Obispo ... CA ... 33
California State University-Chico ... CA ... 34
College of the Redwoods Community College District ... CA ... 42
San Jose State University ... CA ... 37
Central Connecticut State University ... CT ... 90
Idaho State University ... ID ... 143
Eastern Illinois University ... IL ... 150
Illinois State University ... IL ... 153
Northern Illinois University ... IL ... 160
Southern Illinois University Carbondale ... IL ... 165
Western Illinois University ... IL ... 168
Indiana State University ... IN ... 173
Ivy Tech Community College-Central Indiana IN ... 175
Ivy Tech Community College of Indiana-Bloomington ... IN ... 175
Ivy Tech Community College of Indiana-Columbus ... IN ... 176
Ivy Tech Community College of Indiana-East Central ... IN ... 176
Ivy Tech Community College of Indiana-Kokomo ... IN ... 176
Ivy Tech Community College of Indiana-Lafayette ... IN ... 176
Ivy Tech Community College of Indiana-North Central ... IN ... 176
Ivy Tech Community College of Indiana-Northeast ... IN ... 176
Ivy Tech Community College of Indiana-Northwest ... IN ... 176
Ivy Tech Community College of Indiana-Richmond ... IN ... 176
Ivy Tech Community College of Indiana-Southern Indiana ... IN ... 177
Ivy Tech Community College of Indiana-Southwest ... IN ... 177
Ivy Tech Community College of Indiana-Wabash Valley ... IN ... 177
Purdue University Main Campus ... IN ... 178
Iowa State University ... IA ... 182
University of Northern Iowa ... IA ... 182
Eastern Kentucky University ... KY ... 200
Morehead State University ... KY ... 204
Western Kentucky University ... KY ... 208
Baton Rouge Community College ... LA ... 209
Bossier Parish Community College ... LA ... 209
Capital Area Technical College Baton Rouge Campus ... LA ... 209
Delgado Community College ... LA ... 210
L.E. Fletcher Technical Community College . LA ... 210
Nicholls State University ... LA ... 216
Northeast Louisiana Technical College Delta-Ouachita Campus ... LA ... 210
Nunez Community College ... LA ... 211
River Parishes Community College ... LA ... 211
South Central Louisiana Technical College River Parishes Campus ... LA ... 211
South Louisiana Community College ... LA ... 211
South Louisiana Community College Ardoin Campus ... LA ... 211
Southeastern Louisiana University ... LA ... 216
Southern University at Shreveport-Louisiana LA ... 215
Sowela Technical Community College ... LA ... 212
University of Louisiana at Lafayette ... LA ... 216
University of Southern Maine ... ME ... 220
Central Michigan University ... MI ... 249
Bemidji State University ... MN ... 265
Minnesota State University Moorhead ... MN ... 267
St. Cloud State University ... MN ... 269
Alcorn State University ... MS ... 272
Holmes Community College ... MS ... 274
Jackson State University ... MS ... 274
East Central College ... MO ... 281
Linn State Technical College ... MO ... 284
Southeast Missouri State University ... MO ... 289
University of Central Missouri ... MO ... 290
University of Nebraska at Kearney ... NE ... 300
Farmingdale State College ... NY ... 356
State University of New York College at Buffalo ... NY ... 353
East Carolina University ... NC ... 377
Elizabeth City State University ... NC ... 377
North Carolina Agricultural and Technical State University ... NC ... 378
University of North Dakota Main Campus ... ND ... 381
Bowling Green State University ... OH ... 385
Kent State University Main Campus ... OH ... 393
Ohio Northern University ... OH ... 398
Ohio University Main Campus ... OH ... 399
Owens Community College ... OH ... 400
Southwestern Oklahoma State University ... OK ... 412
California University of Pennsylvania ... PA ... 441
Clarion University-Venango Campus ... PA ... 442
Millersville University of Pennsylvania ... PA ... 443
Pennsylvania College of Technology ... PA ... 440
Cleveland State Community College ... TN ... 474
Jackson State Community College ... TN ... 475
Middle Tennessee State University ... TN ... 473
Nashville State Community College ... TN ... 475
Northeast State Community College ... TN ... 475
Tennessee State University ... TN ... 474
Tennessee Technological University ... TN ... 474
Walters State Community College ... TN ... 476
Texas A & M University - Kingsville ... TX ... 498
Texas Southern University ... TX ... 500
University of Texas at Tyler ... TX ... 506
Norfolk State University ... VA ... 522
Virginia State University ... VA ... 529
Pierpont Community & Technical College ... WV ... 543
University of Wisconsin-Platteville ... WI ... 552

NATUR: Council on Naturopathic Medical Education: naturopathic medical education (FP,D)

Southwest College of Naturopathic Medicine & Health Sciences ... AZ ... 18
University of Bridgeport ... CT ... 94
@National University of Health Sciences ... IL ... 159
National College of Natural Medicine ... OR ... 417
Bastyr University ... WA ... 531

NDT: Commission on Accreditation of Allied Health Education Programs: neurodiagnostic technology (C,A)

Gateway Community College ... AZ ... 15
Orange Coast College ... CA ... 41
St. John's College ... IL ... 163
Indiana University-Purdue University Indianapolis ... IN ... 174
Kirkwood Community College ... IA ... 187
Scott Community College ... IA ... 184
Laboure College ... MA ... 235
Mayo School of Health Sciences ... MN ... 262
Minneapolis Community and Technical College ... MN ... 267
DeVry University - North Brunswick Campus. NJ ... 309
Catawba Valley Community College ... NC ... 369
Pamlico Community College ... NC ... 372
Cuyahoga Community College ... OH ... 389
Harcum College ... PA ... 430
Southeast Technical Institute ... SD ... 466
Alvin Community College ... TX ... 479
McLennan Community College ... TX ... 490
Bellevue College ... WA ... 531

NH: Higher Learning Commission, North Central Association

&Herzing University ... AL ... 4
American Indian College of the Assemblies of God ... AZ ... 11
Arizona Christian University (formerly Southwestern College) ... AZ ... 11
Arizona State University ... AZ ... 11
Arizona Western College ... AZ ... 12
Central Arizona College ... AZ ... 13
Chandler-Gilbert Community College ... AZ ... 15
Cochise College ... AZ ... 13
Coconino Community College ... AZ ... 13
&DeVry University - Mesa Center ... AZ ... 13
&DeVry University - Northeast Phoenix Center AZ ... 13
&DeVry University - Phoenix Campus ... AZ ... 13
Diné College ... AZ ... 13
Eastern Arizona College ... AZ ... 14
Estrella Mountain Community College ... AZ ... 15
Everest College Phoenix ... AZ ... 14
Frank Lloyd Wright School of Architecture ... AZ ... 14
Gateway Community College ... AZ ... 15
Glendale Community College ... AZ ... 15
Grand Canyon University ... AZ ... 14
Mesa Community College ... AZ ... 15
&Midwestern University ... AZ ... 16
Mohave Community College ... AZ ... 16
Northcentral University ... AZ ... 16
Northern Arizona University ... AZ ... 16
Northland Pioneer College ... AZ ... 17
&Ottawa University Arizona ... AZ ... 17
Paradise Valley Community College ... AZ ... 15
Phoenix College ... AZ ... 16
@Phoenix Seminary ... AZ ... 17
Pima County Community College District ... AZ ... 17
Prescott College ... AZ ... 17
Rio Salado College ... AZ ... 16
Scottsdale Community College ... AZ ... 16
South Mountain Community College ... AZ ... 16
Southwest College of Naturopathic Medicine & Health Sciences ... AZ ... 18
Southwest University of Visual Arts ... AZ ... 18
Thunderbird School of Global Management . AZ ... 18
Tohono O'odham Community College ... AZ ... 18
University of Advancing Technology ... AZ ... 18
University of Arizona ... AZ ... 18
University of Phoenix ... AZ ... 19
Western International University ... AZ ... 19
Yavapai College ... AZ ... 19
Arkansas Baptist College ... AR ... 19
Arkansas Northeastern College ... AR ... 20
Arkansas State University-Beebe ... AR ... 20
Arkansas State University-Jonesboro ... AR ... 20
Arkansas State University-Mountain Home ... AR ... 20
Arkansas State University-Newport ... AR ... 20
Arkansas Tech University ... AR ... 20
Black River Technical College ... AR ... 21
Central Baptist College ... AR ... 21
College of the Ouachitas ... AR ... 21
Cossatot Community College of the University of Arkansas ... AR ... 25
Crowley's Ridge College ... AR ... 21
East Arkansas Community College ... AR ... 21
Harding University Main Campus ... AR ... 21
Henderson State University ... AR ... 21
Hendrix College ... AR ... 22
John Brown University ... AR ... 22
Lyon College ... AR ... 22
Mid-South Community College ... AR ... 22
National Park Community College ... AR ... 22
North Arkansas College ... AR ... 22
NorthWest Arkansas Community College ... AR ... 22
Ouachita Baptist University ... AR ... 22
Ozarka College ... AR ... 23
Philander Smith College ... AR ... 23
Phillips Community College of the University of Arkansas ... AR ... 25
Pulaski Technical College ... AR ... 23
Rich Mountain Community College ... AR ... 23
South Arkansas Community College ... AR ... 23
Southeast Arkansas College ... AR ... 23
Southern Arkansas University ... AR ... 23
Southern Arkansas University Tech ... AR ... 24
University of Arkansas at Fort Smith ... AR ... 24
University of Arkansas at Little Rock ... AR ... 24
University of Arkansas at Monticello ... AR ... 25
University of Arkansas at Pine Bluff ... AR ... 25
University of Arkansas Community College at Batesville ... AR ... 25
University of Arkansas Community College at Hope ... AR ... 25
University of Arkansas Community College at Morrilton ... AR ... 25
University of Arkansas for Medical Sciences AR ... 24
University of Arkansas Main Campus ... AR ... 24
University of Central Arkansas ... AR ... 25
University of the Ozarks ... AR ... 26
Williams Baptist College ... AR ... 26
&Antioch University Los Angeles ... CA ... 28
&Antioch University Santa Barbara ... CA ... 29
&Concord Law School of Kaplan University ... CA ... 42
&DeVry University - Bakersfield ... CA ... 44
&DeVry University - Colton ... CA ... 44
&DeVry University - Daly City ... CA ... 44
&DeVry University - Fremont Campus ... CA ... 44
&DeVry University - Fresno ... CA ... 44
&DeVry University - Long Beach Campus ... CA ... 44
&DeVry University - Oakland Center ... CA ... 44
&DeVry University - Palmdale ... CA ... 44
&DeVry University - Pomona Campus ... CA ... 44
&DeVry University - Sacramento ... CA ... 44
&DeVry University - San Diego Campus ... CA ... 44
&DeVry University - San Jose ... CA ... 44
&DeVry University - Sherman Oaks Campus . CA ... 45
&Palmer College of Chiropractic, West Campus ... CA ... 61
Adams State University ... CO ... 80
Aims Community College ... CO ... 81
Arapahoe Community College ... CO ... 81
Art Institute of Colorado, The ... CO ... 81
College for Financial Planning ... CO ... 81
Colorado Christian University ... CO ... 82
Colorado College ... CO ... 82
Colorado Mesa University ... CO ... 82
Colorado Mountain College ... CO ... 82
Colorado Northwestern Community College . CO ... 82
Colorado School of Mines ... CO ... 83
Colorado State University ... CO ... 83
Colorado State University-Global Campus ... CO ... 83
Colorado State University-Pueblo ... CO ... 83
&Colorado Technical University ... CO ... 83
Colorado Technical University ... CO ... 83
Community College of Aurora ... CO ... 83
Community College of Denver ... CO ... 84
@Denver School of Nursing ... CO ... 84
Denver Seminary ... CO ... 84
&DeVry University - Colorado Springs Center CO ... 84
&DeVry University - Denver South Center ... CO ... 84
&DeVry University - Westminster Campus ... CO ... 84
Fort Lewis College ... CO ... 84
Front Range Community College ... CO ... 85
Iliff School of Theology ... CO ... 85
Jones International University ... CO ... 85
Lamar Community College ... CO ... 86
Metropolitan State University of Denver ... CO ... 86
Morgan Community College ... CO ... 86
Naropa University ... CO ... 86
National Theatre Conservatory ... CO ... 86
Nazarene Bible College ... CO ... 86
Northeastern Junior College ... CO ... 86
Otero Junior College ... CO ... 87
Pikes Peak Community College ... CO ... 87
Pueblo Community College ... CO ... 87
Red Rocks Community College ... CO ... 87
Regis University ... CO ... 87
Rocky Mountain College of Art & Design ... CO ... 88
@Rocky Vista University ... CO ... 88
Trinidad State Junior College ... CO ... 88
United States Air Force Academy ... CO ... 558
University of Colorado Boulder ... CO ... 88
University of Colorado Colorado Springs ... CO ... 88
University of Colorado Denver|Anschutz Medical Campus ... CO ... 88
University of Denver ... CO ... 89
University of Northern Colorado ... CO ... 89
University of the Rockies ... CO ... 89
Western State Colorado University ... CO ... 89
&American InterContinental University ... FL ... 100
&DeVry University - Fort Lauderdale ... FL ... 104
&DeVry University - Jacksonville ... FL ... 104
&DeVry University - Miami Center ... FL ... 104
&DeVry University - Miramar Campus ... FL ... 104
&DeVry University - Orlando Campus ... FL ... 104
&DeVry University - Orlando North Center ... FL ... 104
&DeVry University - Tampa Bay Campus ... FL ... 104
&DeVry University - Tampa East ... FL ... 105
&Herzing University ... FL ... 110
&Palmer College of Chiropractic, Florida Campus ... FL ... 114
&Rasmussen College - Fort Myers ... FL ... 115
&Rasmussen College - New Port Richey ... FL ... 115
&Rasmussen College - Ocala ... FL ... 115
&Rasmussen College - Tampa/Brandon ... FL ... 115
&Trinity International University, Florida Regional Center ... FL ... 122
&American InterContinental University ... GA ... 124
&DeVry University - Alpharetta Campus ... GA ... 128
&DeVry University - Atlanta Buckhead Center GA ... 128
&DeVry University - Atlanta Cobb/Galleria Center ... GA ... 128
&DeVry University - Atlanta/Perimeter Center . GA ... 128
&DeVry University - Decatur Campus ... GA ... 128
&DeVry University - Gwinnett Center ... GA ... 128
&DeVry University - Henry County ... GA ... 129
&Herzing University ... GA ... 132
Adler School of Professional Psychology ... IL ... 144
American Academy of Art ... IL ... 145
American InterContinental University ... IL ... 145
Augustana College ... IL ... 145
Aurora University ... IL ... 145
Benedictine University ... IL ... 145
Black Hawk College ... IL ... 145
Blackburn College ... IL ... 146
Blessing-Rieman College of Nursing ... IL ... 146
Bradley University ... IL ... 146
Carl Sandburg College ... IL ... 146
Chicago School of Professional Psychology . IL ... 146
Chicago State University ... IL ... 146
Chicago Theological Seminary ... IL ... 146
City Colleges of Chicago Harold Washington College ... IL ... 147
City Colleges of Chicago Harry S Truman College ... IL ... 147
City Colleges of Chicago Kennedy-King College ... IL ... 147
City Colleges of Chicago Malcolm X College IL ... 147
City Colleges of Chicago Olive-Harvey College ... IL ... 147
City Colleges of Chicago Richard J. Daley College ... IL ... 147
City Colleges of Chicago Wilbur Wright College ... IL ... 147
College of DuPage ... IL ... 148
College of Lake County ... IL ... 148
Columbia College Chicago ... IL ... 148
Concordia University Chicago ... IL ... 148
Danville Area Community College ... IL ... 148
DePaul University ... IL ... 149
&DeVry University - Addison Campus ... IL ... 149
&DeVry University - Chicago Campus ... IL ... 149
&DeVry University - Chicago Loop Center ... IL ... 149
&DeVry University - Chicago O'Hare Center .. IL ... 149
&DeVry University - Downers Grove ... IL ... 149
&DeVry University - Elgin Center ... IL ... 149
&DeVry University - Gurnee ... IL ... 149
&DeVry University - Naperville Center ... IL ... 149
&DeVry University - Schaumburg Center ... IL ... 150
&DeVry University - Tinley Park Campus ... IL ... 150
Dominican University ... IL ... 150
East-West University ... IL ... 150
Eastern Illinois University ... IL ... 150
Elgin Community College ... IL ... 150
Elmhurst College ... IL ... 150
Erikson Institute ... IL ... 151
Eureka College ... IL ... 151
Fox College ... IL ... 151
Garrett-Evangelical Theological Seminary ... IL ... 151
Governors State University ... IL ... 151
Greenville College ... IL ... 151
Harper College ... IL ... 151
Harrington College of Design ... IL ... 151
Heartland Community College ... IL ... 151
Hebrew Theological College ... IL ... 152
Highland Community College ... IL ... 152
Illinois Central College ... IL ... 152
Illinois College ... IL ... 152
Illinois College of Optometry ... IL ... 152

Institution	State	Page
Saint Mary Seminary and Graduate School of Theology	OH	401
Shawnee State University	OH	401
Sinclair Community College	OH	401
Southern State Community College	OH	402
Stark State College	OH	402
Terra State Community College	OH	402
Tiffin University	OH	402
Trinity Lutheran Seminary	OH	402
Union Institute & University	OH	402
United Theological Seminary	OH	403
University of Akron-Wayne College, The	OH	403
University of Cincinnati-Clermont College	OH	403
University of Cincinnati Main Campus	OH	403
University of Cincinnati-Raymond Walters College	OH	403
University of Dayton	OH	404
University of Findlay, The	OH	404
University of Mount Union	OH	404
University of Northwestern Ohio	OH	404
University of Rio Grande	OH	404
University of Toledo	OH	404
Urbana University	OH	405
Ursuline College	OH	405
Walsh University	OH	405
Washington State Community College	OH	405
Wilberforce University	OH	405
Wilmington College	OH	405
Winebrenner Theological Seminary	OH	406
Wittenberg University	OH	406
&Wright State University Lake Campus	OH	406
Wright State University Main Campus	OH	406
Xavier University	OH	406
Youngstown State University	OH	406
Zane State College	OH	407
Bacone College	OK	407
Cameron University	OK	407
Carl Albert State College	OK	407
Connors State College	OK	407
&DeVry University - Oklahoma City	OK	407
East Central University	OK	407
Eastern Oklahoma State College	OK	408
Langston University	OK	408
Mid-America Christian University	OK	408
Murray State College	OK	408
Northeastern Oklahoma Agricultural and Mechanical College	OK	408
Northeastern State University	OK	409
Northern Oklahoma College	OK	409
Northwestern Oklahoma State University	OK	409
Oklahoma Baptist University	OK	409
Oklahoma Christian University	OK	409
Oklahoma City Community College	OK	409
Oklahoma City University	OK	410
Oklahoma Panhandle State University	OK	410
Oklahoma State University	OK	410
&Oklahoma State University Center for Health Sciences College of Osteopathic Medicine	OK	410
Oklahoma State University Institute of Technology-Okmulgee	OK	410
Oklahoma State University - Oklahoma City	OK	410
&Oklahoma State University - Tulsa	OK	410
Oklahoma Wesleyan University	OK	411
Oral Roberts University	OK	411
Phillips Theological Seminary	OK	411
Redlands Community College	OK	411
Rogers State University	OK	411
Rose State College	OK	411
St. Gregory's University	OK	412
Seminole State College	OK	412
Southeastern Oklahoma State University	OK	412
Southern Nazarene University	OK	412
Southwestern Christian University	OK	412
Southwestern Oklahoma State University	OK	412
Tulsa Community College	OK	412
University of Central Oklahoma	OK	413
&University of Oklahoma Health Sciences Center	OK	413
University of Oklahoma Norman Campus	OK	413
University of Science and Arts of Oklahoma	OK	413
University of Tulsa	OK	413
Western Oklahoma State College	OK	414
&DeVry University - Portland	OR	415
&DeVry University - Fort Washington Campus	PA	427
&DeVry University - King of Prussia	PA	427
&DeVry University - Philadelphia	PA	427
&DeVry University - Pittsburgh	PA	427
Augustana College	SD	464
Black Hills State University	SD	465
&Colorado Technical University	SD	464
Dakota State University	SD	465
Dakota Wesleyan University	SD	464
Kilian Community College	SD	464
Lake Area Technical Institute	SD	464
Mitchell Technical Institute	SD	464
Mount Marty College	SD	464
National American University	SD	464
Northern State University	SD	466
Oglala Lakota College	SD	465
Presentation College	SD	465
Sinte Gleska University	SD	465
Sioux Falls Seminary	SD	465
Sisseton-Wahpeton College	SD	465
South Dakota School of Mines and Technology	SD	466
South Dakota State University	SD	466
Southeast Technical Institute	SD	466
University of Sioux Falls	SD	466
University of South Dakota, The	SD	465
Western Dakota Technical Institute	SD	466
&DeVry University - Memphis	TN	468
&DeVry University - Nashville	TN	468
&Harding School of Theology	TN	469
&American InterContinental University-Houston Campus	TX	480
&DeVry University - Austin	TX	486
&DeVry University - Fort Worth	TX	486
&DeVry University - Houston Campus	TX	486
&DeVry University - Irving Campus	TX	486
&DeVry University - Richardson	TX	486
&DeVry University - Sandy	UT	509
&DeVry University - Arlington Campus	VA	518
&DeVry University - Chesapeake	VA	518
&DeVry University - Manassas	VA	518
&Antioch University Seattle	WA	530
&DeVry University - Bellevue Center	WA	533
&DeVry University - Federal Way Campus	WA	533
Alderson Broaddus College	WV	540
American Public University System	WV	540
Appalachian Bible College	WV	540
Bethany College	WV	540
Blue Ridge Community and Technical College	WV	542
Bluefield State College	WV	543
Bridgemont Community and Technical College	WV	542
Concord University	WV	543
Davis & Elkins College	WV	541
Eastern West Virginia Community and Technical College	WV	542
Fairmont State University	WV	543
Future Generations Graduate School	WV	541
Glenville State College	WV	544
Huntington Junior College	WV	541
Kanawha Valley Community & Technical College	WV	542
Marshall University	WV	544
Mountain State University	WV	541
Mountwest Community and Technical College	WV	542
New River Community and Technical College	WV	543
Ohio Valley University	WV	541
Pierpont Community & Technical College	WV	543
&Potomac State College of West Virginia University	WV	545
Salem International University	WV	541
Shepherd University	WV	544
Southern West Virginia Community and Technical College	WV	543
University of Charleston	WV	542
West Liberty University	WV	544
West Virginia Northern Community College	WV	543
West Virginia State University	WV	544
West Virginia University	WV	545
West Virginia University at Parkersburg	WV	545
&West Virginia University Institute of Technology	WV	545
West Virginia Wesleyan College	WV	545
Wheeling Jesuit University	WV	546
Alverno College	WI	546
Bellin College, Inc.	WI	546
Beloit College	WI	546
Blackhawk Technical College	WI	553
Cardinal Stritch University	WI	546
Carroll University	WI	546
Carthage College	WI	546
Chippewa Valley Technical College	WI	553
College of Menominee Nation	WI	547
Columbia College of Nursing	WI	547
Concordia University Wisconsin	WI	547
&DeVry University - Milwaukee Center	WI	547
&DeVry University - Waukesha Center	WI	547
Edgewood College	WI	547
Fox Valley Technical College	WI	554
Gateway Technical College	WI	554
Herzing University	WI	547
Lac Courte Oreilles Ojibwa Community College	WI	547
Lakeland College	WI	548
Lakeshore Technical College	WI	554
Lawrence University	WI	548
Madison Area Technical College	WI	554
Maranatha Baptist Bible College & Seminary	WI	548
Marian University	WI	548
Marquette University	WI	548
Medical College of Wisconsin	WI	548
Mid-State Technical College	WI	554
Milwaukee Area Technical College	WI	554
Milwaukee Institute of Art & Design	WI	549
Milwaukee School of Engineering	WI	549
Moraine Park Technical College	WI	554
Mount Mary College	WI	549
Nicolet Area Technical College	WI	555
Northcentral Technical College	WI	555
Northeast Wisconsin Technical College	WI	555
Northland College	WI	549
&Ottawa University Wisconsin	WI	549
&Rasmussen College - Appleton	WI	550
&Rasmussen College - Green Bay	WI	550
&Rasmussen College - Wausau	WI	550
Ripon College	WI	550
Sacred Heart School of Theology	WI	550
Saint Norbert College	WI	550
Silver Lake College of the Holy Family	WI	550
Southwest Wisconsin Technical College	WI	555
University of Wisconsin Colleges	WI	553
University of Wisconsin-Eau Claire	WI	551
University of Wisconsin-Green Bay	WI	551
University of Wisconsin-La Crosse	WI	551
University of Wisconsin-Madison	WI	550
University of Wisconsin-Milwaukee	WI	551
University of Wisconsin-Oshkosh	WI	551
University of Wisconsin-Parkside	WI	552
University of Wisconsin-Platteville	WI	552
University of Wisconsin-River Falls	WI	552
University of Wisconsin-Stevens Point	WI	552
University of Wisconsin-Stout	WI	552
University of Wisconsin-Superior	WI	552
University of Wisconsin-Whitewater	WI	553
Viterbo University	WI	553
Waukesha County Technical College	WI	555
Western Technical College	WI	555
Wisconsin Indianhead Technical College	WI	555
Wisconsin Lutheran College	WI	553
Wisconsin School of Professional Psychology	WI	553
Casper College	WY	556
Central Wyoming College	WY	556
Eastern Wyoming College	WY	556
Laramie County Community College	WY	556
Northern Wyoming Community College District	WY	556
Northwest College	WY	556
University of Wyoming	WY	556
Western Wyoming Community College	WY	557

NMT: Joint Review Committee on Education Programs in Nuclear Medicine Technology: nuclear medicine technology (C,A,B)

Institution	State	Page
University of Alabama at Birmingham	AL	8
Gateway Community College	AZ	15
University of Arkansas for Medical Sciences	AR	24
#University of California-Los Angeles	CA	74
Gateway Community College	CT	91
Lincoln College of New England	CT	93
Delaware Technical Community College, Stanton-Wilmington Campus	DE	96
Adventist University of Health Sciences	FL	100
Cambridge Institute of Allied Health & Technology	FL	102
Hillsborough Community College	FL	110
Santa Fe College	FL	117
Armstrong Atlantic State University	GA	124
Georgia Health Sciences University	GA	130
College of DuPage	IL	148
Triton College	IL	166
Indiana University-Purdue University Indianapolis	IN	174
Allen College	IA	182
Mercy College of Health Sciences	IA	187
University of Iowa	IA	182
University of Kansas Medical Center	KS	197
Bluegrass Community and Technical College	KY	201
Jefferson Community and Technical College	KY	202
Delgado Community College	LA	210
Central Maine Medical Center College of Nursing and Health Professions	ME	217
Frederick Community College	MD	222
Johns Hopkins University	MD	223
Prince George's Community College	MD	225
Massachusetts College of Pharmacy and Health Sciences	MA	241
Regis College	MA	244
Salem State University	MA	238
Springfield Technical Community College	MA	241
University of Massachusetts Medical School	MA	237
Worcester State University	MA	238
Ferris State University	MI	250
Macomb Community College	MI	254
Mayo School of Health Sciences	MN	262
Saint Mary's University of Minnesota	MN	271
University of Mississippi Medical Center	MS	277
Saint Louis University	MO	289
University of Missouri - Columbia	MO	291
University of Nebraska Medical Center	NE	300
University of Nevada, Las Vegas	NV	302
Gloucester County College	NJ	310
UMDNJ-School of Health Related Professions	NJ	317
City University of New York Bronx Community College	NY	326
Molloy College	NY	341
University at Buffalo-SUNY	NY	351
Caldwell Community College and Technical Institute	NC	368
Forsyth Technical Community College	NC	370
University of North Carolina at Chapel Hill	NC	378
Cuyahoga Community College	OH	389
Kent State University Salem Campus	OH	393
Ohio State University Main Campus, The	OH	398
University of Cincinnati Main Campus	OH	403
University of Findlay, The	OH	404
University of Oklahoma Health Sciences Center	OK	413
Cedar Crest College	PA	425
Community College of Allegheny County	PA	425
Lancaster General College of Nursing and Health Sciences	PA	433
Misericordia University	PA	436
Robert Morris University	PA	445
Thomas Jefferson University	PA	448
University of Puerto Rico-Medical Sciences Campus	PR	567
Midlands Technical College	SC	459
Southeast Technical Institute	SD	466
Baptist Memorial College of Health Sciences	TN	467
Chattanooga State Community College	TN	474
South College	TN	473
Vanderbilt University	TN	478
Amarillo College	TX	479
Baylor University	TX	482
Del Mar College	TX	485
Galveston College	TX	486
Houston Community College	TX	487
University of the Incarnate Word	TX	504
University of Utah, The	UT	511
University of Vermont	VT	514
Old Dominion University	VA	522
Virginia Commonwealth University	VA	526
Bellevue College	WA	531
Kanawha Valley Community & Technical College	WV	542
West Virginia University	WV	545
Wheeling Jesuit University	WV	546

NRPA: National Recreation and Park Association: recreation, park resources, and leisure studies (B)

Institution	State	Page
Arizona State University	AZ	11
Northern Arizona University	AZ	16
Arkansas Tech University	AR	20
California Polytechnic State University-San Luis Obispo	CA	33
California State University-Chico	CA	34
California State University-Fresno	CA	35
California State University-Long Beach	CA	35
California State University-Sacramento	CA	36
San Francisco State University	CA	37
San Jose State University	CA	37
Metropolitan State University of Denver	CO	86
Georgia Southern University	GA	131
University of Georgia	GA	138
University of Idaho	ID	144
Chicago State University	IL	146
Eastern Illinois University	IL	150
Illinois State University	IL	153
University of Illinois at Urbana-Champaign	IL	167
University of St. Francis	IL	167
Western Illinois University	IL	168
Indiana State University	IN	173
Indiana University Bloomington	IN	173
University of Northern Iowa	IA	182
Kansas State University	KS	194
Pittsburg State University	KS	196
Eastern Kentucky University	KY	200
Western Kentucky University	KY	208
Grambling State University	LA	215
University of Maine at Machias	ME	220
Frostburg State University	MD	228
Springfield College	MA	244
Central Michigan University	MI	249
Ferris State University	MI	250
Minnesota State University, Mankato	MN	267
University of Mississippi	MS	277
University of Southern Mississippi	MS	277
Missouri State University	MO	286
Northwest Missouri State University	MO	287
Southeast Missouri State University	MO	289
University of Missouri - Columbia	MO	291
University of New Hampshire	NH	306
Ithaca College	NY	336
Saint Joseph's College, New York - Suffolk Campus	NY	349
State University of New York College at Cortland	NY	353
State University of New York, The College at Brockport	NY	352
Appalachian State University	NC	377
East Carolina University	NC	377
North Carolina Central University	NC	378
North Carolina State University	NC	378
University of North Carolina at Greensboro	NC	379
University of North Carolina Wilmington	NC	379
Winston-Salem State University	NC	380
Bowling Green State University	OH	385
Kent State University Main Campus	OH	393
Ohio University Main Campus	OH	399
University of Toledo	OH	404
Oklahoma State University	OK	410
California University of Pennsylvania	PA	441
East Stroudsburg University of Pennsylvania	PA	442
Lock Haven University	PA	443
Slippery Rock University of Pennsylvania	PA	443
Temple University	PA	447
York College of Pennsylvania	PA	452
Benedict College	SC	455
Clemson University	SC	456
Middle Tennessee State University	TN	473
University of Tennessee, Knoxville	TN	477
Texas A & M University	TX	497
Texas State University-San Marcos	TX	501
University of North Texas	TX	504
Brigham Young University	UT	509
University of Utah, The	UT	511
Utah State University	UT	511
George Mason University	VA	519
Longwood University	VA	521

Old Dominion University VA 522
Radford University VA 523
Virginia Wesleyan College VA 530
Eastern Washington University WA 533
Western Washington University WA 539
University of Wisconsin-La Crosse WI 551

NUR: National League for Nursing: nursing (B,M,D)

Oakwood University AL 6
Troy University AL 8
Tuskegee University AL 8
University of Alaska Anchorage AK 10
Arkansas State University-Jonesboro AR 20
Arkansas Tech University AR 20
Harding University Main Campus AR 21
Southern Arkansas University AR 23
University of Arkansas at Fort Smith AR 24
University of Arkansas at Little Rock AR 24
University of Arkansas at Monticello AR 25
University of Arkansas at Pine Bluff AR 25
Charles R. Drew University of Medicine & Science CA 39
Pacific Union College CA 60
Sonoma State University CA 37
Colorado State University-Pueblo CO 83
Denver School of Nursing CO 84
Metropolitan State University of Denver CO 86
Platt College CO 87
Quinnipiac University CT 93
Delaware State University DE 96
Wesley College DE 97
University of the District of Columbia DC 100
Adventist University of Health Sciences FL 100
Bethune Cookman University FL 102
Broward College FL 102
Edison State College FL 105
Florida Agricultural and Mechanical University FL 118
Florida State College at Jacksonville FL 109
Indian River State College FL 111
Miami Dade College FL 113
State College of Florida, Manatee-Sarasota FL 118
University of Tampa FL 123
Albany State University GA 124
Augusta State University GA 125
College of Coastal Georgia GA 127
Georgia College & State University GA 130
Georgia Southwestern State University GA 131
Gordon State College GA 132
LaGrange College GA 133
Macon State College GA 133
North Georgia College & State University GA 134
Piedmont College GA 136
Thomas University GA 138
University of Guam GU 559
Hawaii Pacific University HI 140
University of Hawaii at Hilo HI 141
Boise State University ID 142
Brigham Young University-Idaho ID 143
Bradley University IL 146
Chicago State University IL 146
Governors State University IL 151
Methodist College IL 158
Rockford College IL 163
Saint Francis Medical Center College of Nursing IL 163
St. John's College IL 163
Bethel College IN 169
Indiana State University IN 173
Indiana University East IN 173
Indiana University Northwest IN 174
Indiana University-Purdue University Fort Wayne IN 174
Indiana University-Purdue University Indianapolis IN 174
Purdue University Calumet IN 178
Purdue University North Central Campus IN 179
Saint Mary's College IN 179
University of Evansville IN 180
Vincennes University IN 181
Allen College IA 182
Iowa Wesleyan College IA 186
Emporia State University KS 192
Kansas Wesleyan University KS 194
Frontier Nursing University KY 200
Kentucky State University KY 203
Midway College KY 204
Northern Kentucky University KY 205
Thomas More College KY 206
Dillard University LA 209
Grambling State University LA 215
Louisiana State University at Alexandria LA 212
Loyola University New Orleans LA 213
Our Lady of Holy Cross College LA 214
Our Lady of the Lake College LA 214
University of New England ME 221
Bowie State University MD 228
Coppin State University MD 228
Notre Dame of Maryland University MD 225
Stevenson University MD 226
Washington Adventist University MD 229
Anna Maria College MA 230
Endicott College MA 234
Regis College MA 244
University of Massachusetts Dartmouth MA 237
Andrews University MI 247
Davenport University MI 250
Ferris State University MI 250
Lake Superior State University MI 253
St. Catherine University MN 270
Alcorn State University MS 272
Lincoln University MO 283
Missouri Southern State University MO 286
Southwest Baptist University MO 290
Webster University MO 292
Montana State University - Northern MT 295
Salish Kootenai College MT 296
Bryan LGH College of Health Sciences NE 296
Clarkson College NE 297
College of Saint Mary NE 297
Midland University NE 298
Nebraska Wesleyan University NE 299
Great Basin College NV 302
Roseman University of Health Sciences NV 303
Franklin Pierce University NH 305
Rivier College NH 305
College of Saint Elizabeth NJ 308
Kean University NJ 311
New Jersey City University NJ 312
Ramapo College of New Jersey NJ 313
Thomas Edison State College NJ 316
Eastern New Mexico University Main Campus NM 318
City University of New York College of Staten Island NY 327
City University of New York Medgar Evers College NY 328
City University of New York York College NY 329
Daemen College NY 331
Elmira College NY 332
Excelsior College NY 333
Farmingdale State College NY 356
New York City College of Technology/City University of New York NY 328
Saint Joseph's College, New York NY 349
State University of New York College of Technology at Delhi NY 355
Wagner College NY 360
Barton College NC 362
Gardner-Webb University NC 364
North Carolina Agricultural and Technical State University NC 378
North Carolina Central University NC 378
University of North Carolina at Chapel Hill NC 378
University of North Carolina at Greensboro NC 379
Dickinson State University ND 381
Jamestown College ND 381
Minot State University ND 382
Case Western Reserve University OH 386
Franciscan University of Steubenville OH 391
Kettering College of Medical Arts OH 394
Mercy College of Ohio OH 395
Miami University OH 396
Otterbein University OH 400
Shawnee State University OH 401
University of Rio Grande OH 404
Walsh University OH 405
Youngstown State University OH 406
Bacone College OK 407
East Central University OK 407
Langston University OK 408
Northeastern State University OK 409
Northwestern Oklahoma State University OK 409
Oklahoma Baptist University OK 409
Oklahoma City University OK 410
Oklahoma Panhandle State University OK 410
Rogers State University OK 411
Southwestern Oklahoma State University OK 412
University of Central Oklahoma OK 413
University of Oklahoma Health Sciences Center OK 413
University of Tulsa OK 413
Cedar Crest College PA 425
Clarion University of Pennsylvania PA 442
Clarion University-Venango Campus PA 442
DeSales University PA 427
East Stroudsburg University of Pennsylvania PA 442
Edinboro University of Pennsylvania PA 442
Gwynedd-Mercy College PA 430
Kutztown University of Pennsylvania PA 443
La Roche College PA 432
Mansfield University of Pennsylvania PA 443
Marywood University PA 435
Millersville University of Pennsylvania PA 443
Mount Aloysius College PA 437
Neumann University PA 437
Penn State University Park PA 438
Pennsylvania College of Technology PA 440
Slippery Rock University of Pennsylvania PA 443
University of Pittsburgh at Bradford PA 449
Inter American University of Puerto Rico Aguadilla Campus PR 563
Inter American University of Puerto Rico Arecibo Campus PR 563
Inter American University of Puerto Rico Metropolitan Campus PR 563
Pontifical Catholic University of Puerto Rico, The PR 565
Universidad Adventista de las Antillas PR 566
Universidad Metropolitana PR 565
University of Puerto Rico at Arecibo PR 567
University of Puerto Rico-Humacao PR 567
University of Puerto Rico-Mayaguez Campus PR 567
University of the Sacred Heart PR 568
Salve Regina University RI 454
Charleston Southern University SC 456
Coastal Carolina University SC 456
Francis Marion University SC 458
University of South Carolina Aiken SC 462
Presentation College SD 465
Aquinas College TN 467
Austin Peay State University TN 473
Cumberland University TN 468
Lincoln Memorial University TN 470
Lipscomb University TN 470
South College TN 473
Southern Adventist University TN 473
Tennessee State University TN 474
University of Tennessee at Martin TN 477
Vanderbilt University TN 478
Angelo State University TX 480
Houston Baptist University TX 487
Lamar University TX 501
Lubbock Christian University TX 490
Prairie View A & M University TX 496
Stephen F. Austin State University TX 496
Texas A & M International University TX 497
University of Texas at Brownsville and Texas Southmost College, The TX 505
Wayland Baptist University TX 508
Dixie State College of Utah UT 512
Utah Valley University UT 511
Weber State University UT 511
Southern Vermont College VT 514
University of the Virgin Islands VI 568
ECPI College of Technology VA 518
Norfolk State University VA 522
Virginia Commonwealth University VA 526
Alderson Broaddus College WV 540
Marshall University WV 544
Mountain State University WV 541
University of Charleston WV 542
West Virginia Wesleyan College WV 545
Cardinal Stritch University WI 546

NURSE: Commission on Collegiate Nursing Education: nursing (B,M,D)

Auburn University AL 1
Auburn University at Montgomery AL 1
Jacksonville State University AL 4
Samford University AL 6
South University AL 7
Spring Hill College AL 7
Stillman College AL 7
University of Alabama at Birmingham AL 8
University of Alabama in Huntsville AL 8
University of Alabama, The AL 8
University of Mobile AL 9
University of North Alabama AL 9
University of South Alabama AL 9
Arizona State University AZ 11
Grand Canyon University AZ 14
Northern Arizona University AZ 16
University of Arizona AZ 18
University of Phoenix AZ 19
Henderson State University AR 21
University of Arkansas at Little Rock AR 24
University of Arkansas for Medical Sciences AR 24
University of Arkansas Main Campus AR 24
University of Central Arkansas AR 25
American University of Health Sciences CA 28
Azusa Pacific University CA 30
Biola University CA 31
Brandman University CA 31
California Baptist University CA 31
California State University-Bakersfield CA 34
California State University-Channel Islands CA 34
California State University-Chico CA 34
California State University-Dominguez Hills CA 34
California State University-East Bay CA 34
California State University-Fresno CA 35
California State University-Fullerton CA 35
California State University-Long Beach CA 35
California State University-Los Angeles CA 35
California State University-Northridge CA 35
California State University-Sacramento CA 36
California State University-San Bernardino CA 36
California State University-San Marcos CA 36
California State University-Stanislaus CA 36
Concordia University CA 43
Dominican University of California CA 45
Fresno Pacific University CA 48
Holy Names University CA 50
Humboldt State University CA 36
Loma Linda University CA 54
Mount St. Mary's College CA 57
National University CA 58
Point Loma Nazarene University CA 62
Samuel Merritt University CA 64
San Diego State University CA 37
San Francisco State University CA 37
San Jose State University CA 37
University of California-Davis CA 73
University of California-Irvine CA 74
University of California-Los Angeles CA 74
University of California-San Francisco CA 75
University of San Diego CA 76
University of San Francisco CA 76
Vanguard University of Southern California CA 77
West Coast University CA 78
Western University of Health Sciences CA 78
Adams State University CO 80
American Sentinel University CO 81
Aspen University CO 81
Colorado Christian University CO 82
Colorado Mesa University CO 82
Regis University CO 87
University of Colorado Colorado Springs CO 88
University of Colorado Denver|Anschutz Medical Campus CO 88
University of Northern Colorado CO 89
Central Connecticut State University CT 90
Fairfield University CT 92
Sacred Heart University CT 94
Southern Connecticut State University CT 90
University of Connecticut CT 94
University of Hartford CT 95
University of Saint Joseph CT 95
Western Connecticut State University CT 91
Yale University CT 96
University of Delaware DE 96
Wilmington University DE 97
Catholic University of America, The DC 97
George Washington University DC 98
Georgetown University DC 98
Howard University DC 98
Trinity Washington University DC 99
Barry University FL 101
Florida Atlantic University FL 119
Florida Gulf Coast University FL 119
Florida International University FL 119
Florida Southern College FL 109
Florida State University FL 119
Jacksonville University FL 111
Keiser University FL 112
Northwest Florida State College FL 114
Nova Southeastern University FL 114
Palm Beach Atlantic University FL 114
Remington College-Tampa Campus FL 116
St. Petersburg College FL 116
South University FL 118
University of Central Florida FL 120
University of Florida FL 120
University of Miami FL 122
University of North Florida FL 120
University of South Florida FL 121
University of West Florida FL 121
Armstrong Atlantic State University GA 124
Brenau University GA 126
Clayton State University GA 127
Columbus State University GA 127
Emory University GA 129
Georgia Health Sciences University GA 130
Georgia Southern University GA 131
Georgia State University GA 131
Kennesaw State University GA 133
Mercer University GA 134
Shorter University GA 137
South University GA 137
University of West Georgia GA 139
Valdosta State University GA 139
Hawaii Pacific University HI 140
University of Hawaii at Manoa HI 141
Idaho State University ID 143
Lewis-Clark State College ID 144
Northwest Nazarene University ID 144
Aurora University IL 145
Benedictine University IL 145
Blessing-Rieman College of Nursing IL 146
DePaul University IL 149
Eastern Illinois University IL 150
Elmhurst College IL 150
Illinois State University IL 153
Illinois Wesleyan University IL 153
Lakeview College of Nursing IL 156
Lewis University IL 156
Loyola University Chicago IL 157
MacMurray College IL 157
McKendree University IL 158
Methodist College IL 158
Millikin University IL 158
North Park University IL 159
Northern Illinois University IL 160
Olivet Nazarene University IL 161
Resurrection University IL 162
Rush University IL 163
St. Anthony College of Nursing IL 163
Saint Xavier University IL 163
Southern Illinois University Edwardsville IL 165
Trinity Christian College IL 166
Trinity College of Nursing & Health Sciences IL 166
University of Illinois at Chicago IL 167
University of St. Francis IL 167
Western Illinois University IL 168
Anderson University IN 169
Ball State University IN 169
Goshen College IN 171
Huntington University IN 173
Indiana University Kokomo IN 174
Indiana University Northwest IN 174
Indiana University-Purdue University Indianapolis IN 174
Indiana University South Bend IN 174
Indiana University Southeast IN 175
Indiana Wesleyan University IN 175
Marian University IN 177
Purdue University Main Campus IN 178
University of Indianapolis IN 180
University of Saint Francis IN 181
University of Southern Indiana IN 181
Valparaiso University IN 181

Institution	State	Page
Columbia College of Nursing	WI	547
Concordia University Wisconsin	WI	547
Edgewood College	WI	547
Marian University	WI	548
Marquette University	WI	548
Milwaukee School of Engineering	WI	549
Silver Lake College of the Holy Family	WI	550
University of Wisconsin-Eau Claire	WI	551
University of Wisconsin-Green Bay	WI	551
University of Wisconsin-Madison	WI	550
University of Wisconsin-Milwaukee	WI	551
University of Wisconsin-Oshkosh	WI	551
Viterbo University	WI	553
Wisconsin Lutheran College	WI	553
University of Wyoming	WY	556

NW: Northwest Association of Schools and Colleges, Commission on Colleges

Institution	State	Page
Alaska Pacific University	AK	10
Ilisagvik College	AK	10
Prince William Sound Community College	AK	11
University of Alaska Anchorage	AK	10
University of Alaska Fairbanks	AK	10
University of Alaska Southeast	AK	11
Boise State University	ID	142
Brigham Young University-Idaho	ID	143
College of Idaho, The	ID	143
College of Southern Idaho	ID	143
@College of Western Idaho	ID	143
Eastern Idaho Technical College	ID	143
Idaho State University	ID	143
Lewis-Clark State College	ID	144
North Idaho College	ID	144
Northwest Nazarene University	ID	144
University of Idaho	ID	144
Aaniiih Nakoda College	MT	293
Blackfeet Community College	MT	293
Carroll College	MT	293
Chief Dull Knife College	MT	294
&City College at Montana State University Billings	MT	295
Dawson Community College	MT	294
Flathead Valley Community College	MT	294
Fort Peck Community College	MT	294
Great Falls College Montana State University	MT	295
&Highlands College of Montana Tech	MT	296
Little Big Horn College	MT	294
Miles Community College	MT	294
Montana State University	MT	295
Montana State University - Billings	MT	295
Montana State University - Northern	MT	295
Montana Tech of The University of Montana	MT	296
Rocky Mountain College	MT	296
Salish Kootenai College	MT	296
Stone Child College	MT	296
University of Great Falls	MT	296
&University of Montana - College of Technology, The	MT	295
University of Montana - Helena College of Technology, The	MT	295
University of Montana - Missoula, The	MT	294
University of Montana Western, The	MT	294
College of Southern Nevada	NV	302
Great Basin College	NV	302
Nevada State College	NV	302
Roseman University of Health Sciences	NV	303
Sierra Nevada College	NV	303
Truckee Meadows Community College	NV	302
University of Nevada, Las Vegas	NV	302
University of Nevada, Reno	NV	303
Western Nevada College	NV	303
Art Institute of Portland, The	OR	414
Blue Mountain Community College	OR	414
Central Oregon Community College	OR	414
Chemeketa Community College	OR	414
Clackamas Community College	OR	415
Clatsop Community College	OR	415
@Columbia Gorge Community College	OR	415
Concordia University	OR	415
Corban University	OR	415
Eastern Oregon University	OR	418
George Fox University	OR	415
Klamath Community College	OR	416
Lane Community College	OR	416
Lewis and Clark College	OR	416
Linfield College	OR	416
Linn-Benton Community College	OR	416
Marylhurst University	OR	416
Mount Angel Seminary	OR	417
Mt. Hood Community College	OR	417
Multnomah University	OR	417
National College of Natural Medicine	OR	417
Northwest Christian University	OR	417
Oregon College of Art and Craft	OR	417
@Oregon College of Oriental Medicine	OR	417
Oregon Health & Science University	OR	418
Oregon Institute of Technology	OR	418
Oregon State University	OR	418
Pacific Northwest College of Art	OR	419
Pacific University	OR	419
Portland Community College	OR	419
Portland State University	OR	418
Reed College	OR	420
Rogue Community College	OR	420
Southern Oregon University	OR	419
Southwestern Oregon Community College	OR	420
@Tillamook Bay Community College	OR	420
Treasure Valley Community College	OR	420
Umpqua Community College	OR	420
University of Oregon	OR	419
University of Portland	OR	420
University of Western States	OR	421
Warner Pacific College	OR	421
Western Oregon University	OR	419
Western Seminary	OR	421
Willamette University	OR	421
Brigham Young University	UT	509
Dixie State College of Utah	UT	512
LDS Business College	UT	510
Rocky Mountain University of Health Professions	UT	510
Salt Lake Community College	UT	512
Snow College	UT	512
Southern Utah University	UT	511
University of Utah, The	UT	511
Utah State University	UT	511
&Utah State University-College of Eastern Utah	UT	512
Utah Valley University	UT	511
Weber State University	UT	511
Western Governors University	UT	512
Westminster College	UT	512
Art Institute of Seattle, The	WA	531
Bastyr University	WA	531
Bates Technical College	WA	531
Bellevue College	WA	531
Bellingham Technical College	WA	531
Big Bend Community College	WA	531
Cascadia Community College	WA	532
Central Washington University	WA	532
Centralia College	WA	532
City University of Seattle	WA	532
Clark College	WA	532
Clover Park Technical College	WA	532
Columbia Basin College	WA	532
Cornish College of the Arts	WA	533
Eastern Washington University	WA	533
Edmonds Community College	WA	533
Everett Community College	WA	534
Evergreen State College, The	WA	534
Gonzaga University	WA	534
Grays Harbor College	WA	534
Green River Community College	WA	534
Heritage University	WA	535
Highline Community College	WA	535
Lake Washington Institute of Technology	WA	535
Lower Columbia College	WA	535
North Seattle Community College	WA	537
Northwest Indian College	WA	535
Northwest University	WA	536
Olympic College	WA	536
Pacific Lutheran University	WA	536
Peninsula College	WA	536
Pierce College District	WA	536
Renton Technical College	WA	537
Saint Martin's University	WA	537
Seattle Central Community College	WA	537
Seattle Pacific University	WA	537
Seattle University	WA	538
Shoreline Community College	WA	538
Skagit Valley College	WA	538
South Puget Sound Community College	WA	538
South Seattle Community College	WA	537
Spokane Community College	WA	533
Spokane Falls Community College	WA	533
Tacoma Community College	WA	538
Trinity Lutheran College	WA	538
University of Puget Sound	WA	538
University of Washington	WA	539
Walla Walla Community College	WA	539
Walla Walla University	WA	539
Washington State University	WA	539
Wenatchee Valley College	WA	539
Western Washington University	WA	539
Whatcom Community College	WA	540
Whitman College	WA	540
Whitworth University	WA	540
Yakima Valley Community College	WA	540

NY: New York State Board of Regents

Institution	State	Page
American Academy of Dramatic Arts	NY	322
Bramson O R T College	NY	324
Christie's Education, Inc.	NY	326
Cold Spring Harbor Laboratory/Watson School of Biological Sciences	NY	329
Elmezzi Graduate School of Molecular Medicine, The	NY	332
Globe Institute of Technology	NY	334
Holy Trinity Orthodox Seminary	NY	336
Institute of Design and Construction	NY	336
Louis V. Gerstner Jr. Graduate School of Biomedical Sciences at Memorial Sl oan-Kettering Cancer Ctr	NY	339
Memorial Hospital School of Nursing	NY	340
New York Academy of Art	NY	342
New York Career Institute	NY	342
New York College of Health Professions	NY	343
Northeastern Seminary	NY	344
Phillips Beth Israel School of Nursing	NY	346
Rabbi Isaac Elchanan Theological Seminary	NY	346
Richard Gilder Graduate School at the American Museum of Natural History	NY	347
Rockefeller University	NY	347
Salvation Army School for Officer Training	NY	350
Samaritan Hospital School of Nursing	NY	350
Technical Career Institutes	NY	357
Union Graduate College	NY	358
USC The Business College	NY	359
Wood Tobé-Coburn School	NY	360

OPD: Commission on Opticianry Accreditation: opticianry (A)

Institution	State	Page
Middlesex Community College	CT	91
Hillsborough Community College	FL	110
Miami Dade College	FL	113
Ogeechee Technical College	GA	135
Indiana University Bloomington	IN	173
Baker College of Jackson	MI	248
College of Southern Nevada	NV	302
Camden County College	NJ	308
Essex County College	NJ	309
Raritan Valley Community College	NJ	313
Southwestern Indian Polytechnic Institute	NM	321
Erie Community College North Campus	NY	333
New York City College of Technology/City University of New York	NY	328
Technical Career Institutes	NY	357
Durham Technical Community College	NC	370
Roane State Community College	TN	476
Tyler Junior College	TX	503
J. Sargeant Reynolds Community College	VA	527
Seattle Central Community College	WA	537

OPE: Commission on Accreditation of Allied Health Education Programs: orthotics and prosthetics (C,B,M)

Institution	State	Page
California State University-Dominguez Hills	CA	34
University of Hartford	CT	95
St. Petersburg College	FL	116
Georgia Institute of Technology	GA	130
Northwestern University	IL	160
Eastern Michigan University	MI	250
Century College	MN	266
University of Pittsburgh	PA	449
University of Texas Southwestern Medical Center	TX	507
University of Washington	WA	539

OPLT: Commission on Opticianry Accreditation: opthalmic laboratory technician (C)

Institution	State	Page
Southwestern Indian Polytechnic Institute	NM	321

OPT: American Optometric Association: optometry (FP,D)

Institution	State	Page
University of Alabama at Birmingham	AL	8
@Midwestern University	AZ	16
Southern California College of Optometry	CA	70
University of California-Berkeley	CA	73
@Western University of Health Sciences	CA	78
Nova Southeastern University	FL	114
Illinois College of Optometry	IL	152
Indiana University Bloomington	IN	173
@Massachusetts College of Pharmacy and Health Sciences	MA	241
New England College of Optometry, The	MA	242
Ferris State University	MI	250
University of Missouri - Saint Louis	MO	291
State University of New York College of Optometry	NY	355
Ohio State University Main Campus, The	OH	398
Northeastern State University	OK	409
Pacific University	OR	419
Salus University	PA	446
Inter American University of Puerto Rico School of Optometry	PR	564
Southern College of Optometry	TN	473
University of Houston	TX	503
@University of the Incarnate Word	TX	504

OPTR: American Optometric Association: optometric residency programs

Institution	State	Page
University of Alabama at Birmingham	AL	8
Southern California College of Optometry	CA	70
University of California-Berkeley	CA	73
Nova Southeastern University	FL	114
Illinois College of Optometry	IL	152
Indiana University Bloomington	IN	173
New England College of Optometry, The	MA	242
Ferris State University	MI	250
University of Missouri - Saint Louis	MO	291
State University of New York College of Optometry	NY	355
Ohio State University Main Campus, The	OH	398
Northeastern State University	OK	409
Pacific University	OR	419
Salus University	PA	446
Inter American University of Puerto Rico Bayamon Campus	PR	563
Southern College of Optometry	TN	473
University of Houston	TX	503

OPTT: American Optometric Association: optometric technician (A)

Institution	State	Page
Indiana University Bloomington	IN	173
Madison Area Technical College	WI	554

OSTEO: American Osteopathic Association, Office of Osteopathic Education: osteopathic medicine (FP,D)

Institution	State	Page
Midwestern University	AZ	16
Touro University-California	CA	73
Western University of Health Sciences	CA	78
@Rocky Vista University	CO	88
Nova Southeastern University	FL	114
Midwestern University	IL	158
@Marian University	IN	177
Des Moines University	IA	184
University of Pikeville	KY	207
University of New England	ME	221
Michigan State University	MI	255
@William Carey University	MS	278
A. T. Still University of Health Sciences	MO	278
Kansas City University of Medicine & Biosciences	MO	283
UMDNJ-School of Osteopathic Medicine	NJ	316
New York Institute of Technology	NY	343
Touro College	NY	358
@Campbell University	NC	362
Ohio University Main Campus	OH	399
Oklahoma State University Center for Health Sciences College of Osteopathic Medicine	OK	410
Lake Erie College of Osteopathic Medicine	PA	433
Philadelphia College of Osteopathic Medicine	PA	444
Lincoln Memorial University	TN	470
University of North Texas Health Science Center at Fort Worth	TX	504
Edward Via College of Osteopathic Medicine	VA	518
@Pacific Northwest University of Health Sciences	WA	536
West Virginia School of Osteopathic Medicine	WV	544

OT: American Occupational Therapy Association: occupational therapy (M,D)

Institution	State	Page
Alabama State University	AL	1
#Tuskegee University	AL	8
University of Alabama at Birmingham	AL	8
University of South Alabama	AL	9
Midwestern University	AZ	16
University of Central Arkansas	AR	25
California State University-Dominguez Hills	CA	34
Dominican University of California	CA	45
Loma Linda University	CA	54
Samuel Merritt University	CA	64
San Jose State University	CA	37
University of Southern California	CA	76
Colorado State University	CO	83
Quinnipiac University	CT	93
Sacred Heart University	CT	94
Howard University	DC	98
Barry University	FL	101
#Florida Agricultural and Mechanical University	FL	118
Florida Gulf Coast University	FL	119
Florida International University	FL	119
Nova Southeastern University	FL	114
University of Florida	FL	120
University of St. Augustine for Health Sciences	FL	122
Brenau University	GA	126
Georgia Health Sciences University	GA	130
Idaho State University	ID	143
Chicago State University	IL	146
Governors State University	IL	151
Midwestern University	IL	158
Rush University	IL	163
University of Illinois at Chicago	IL	167
Indiana University-Purdue University Indianapolis	IN	174
University of Indianapolis	IN	180
University of Southern Indiana	IN	181
St. Ambrose University	IA	188
University of Kansas Medical Center	KS	197
Eastern Kentucky University	KY	200
Spalding University	KY	206
Louisiana State University Health Sciences Center at Shreveport	LA	213
Louisiana State University Health Sciences Center-New Orleans	LA	213
Husson University	ME	218
University of New England	ME	221
University of Southern Maine	ME	220
Towson University	MD	228
American International College	MA	229
Bay Path College	MA	230
Boston University	MA	232
Salem State University	MA	238
Springfield College	MA	244
Tufts University	MA	245
Worcester State University	MA	238
Baker College of Flint	MI	248
Eastern Michigan University	MI	250
Grand Valley State University	MI	251
Saginaw Valley State University	MI	257
Wayne State University	MI	260
Western Michigan University	MI	260
College of Saint Scholastica, The	MN	262
St. Catherine University	MN	270
University of Minnesota-Twin Cities	MN	272
University of Mississippi Medical Center	MS	277
Maryville University of Saint Louis	MO	284

Rockhurst University ... MO ... 288
Saint Louis University ... MO ... 289
University of Missouri - Columbia ... MO ... 291
Washington University in St. Louis ... MO ... 292
College of Saint Mary ... NE ... 297
Creighton University ... NE ... 297
University of New Hampshire ... NH ... 306
Kean University ... NJ ... 311
Richard Stockton College of New Jersey, The ... NJ ... 313
Seton Hall University ... NJ ... 315
University of New Mexico Main Campus ... NM ... 321
Western New Mexico University ... NM ... 321
#City University of New York York College ... NY ... 329
Columbia University in the City of New York ... NY ... 330
Dominican College of Blauvelt ... NY ... 332
D'Youville College ... NY ... 332
Ithaca College ... NY ... 336
Keuka College ... NY ... 337
Long Island University Brooklyn Campus ... NY ... 338
Mercy College ... NY ... 340
New York Institute of Technology ... NY ... 343
New York University ... NY ... 344
Sage Colleges, The ... NY ... 348
State University of New York at Stony Brook ... NY ... 352
State University of New York Health Science Center at Brooklyn ... NY ... 352
Touro College ... NY ... 358
University at Buffalo-SUNY ... NY ... 351
Utica College ... NY ... 359
East Carolina University ... NC ... 377
Lenoir-Rhyne University ... NC ... 366
University of North Carolina at Chapel Hill ... NC ... 378
Winston-Salem State University ... NC ... 380
University of Mary ... ND ... 383
University of North Dakota Main Campus ... ND ... 381
Cleveland State University ... OH ... 388
Ohio State University Main Campus, The ... OH ... 398
Shawnee State University ... OH ... 401
University of Findlay, The ... OH ... 404
University of Toledo ... OH ... 404
Xavier University ... OH ... 406
University of Oklahoma Health Sciences Center ... OK ... 413
Pacific University ... OR ... 419
Alvernia University ... PA ... 421
Chatham University ... PA ... 425
Duquesne University ... PA ... 428
Elizabethtown College ... PA ... 428
Gannon University ... PA ... 429
Misericordia University ... PA ... 436
Philadelphia University ... PA ... 444
Saint Francis University ... PA ... 446
Temple University ... PA ... 447
Thomas Jefferson University ... PA ... 448
University of Pittsburgh ... PA ... 449
University of Scranton, The ... PA ... 450
University of the Sciences in Philadelphia ... PA ... 450
University of Puerto Rico-Medical Sciences Campus ... PR ... 567
New England Institute of Technology ... RI ... 453
Medical University of South Carolina ... SC ... 459
University of South Dakota, The ... SD ... 465
Belmont University ... TN ... 467
Milligan College ... TN ... 471
Tennessee State University ... TN ... 474
University of Tennessee Health Science Center ... TN ... 477
Texas Tech University Health Sciences Center ... TX ... 502
Texas Woman's University ... TX ... 502
University of Texas at El Paso ... TX ... 506
University of Texas Health Science Center at San Antonio ... TX ... 507
University of Texas Medical Branch, The ... TX ... 507
University of Texas - Pan American ... TX ... 506
University of Utah, The ... UT ... 511
James Madison University ... VA ... 520
Jefferson College of Health Sciences ... VA ... 520
Radford University ... VA ... 523
Shenandoah University ... VA ... 524
Virginia Commonwealth University ... VA ... 526
Eastern Washington University ... WA ... 533
University of Puget Sound ... WA ... 538
University of Washington ... WA ... 539
West Virginia University ... WV ... 545
Concordia University Wisconsin ... WI ... 547
Mount Mary College ... WI ... 549
University of Wisconsin-La Crosse ... WI ... 551
University of Wisconsin-Madison ... WI ... 550
University of Wisconsin-Milwaukee ... WI ... 551

OTA: American Occupational Therapy Association: occupational therapy assistant (C,A)

Wallace State Community College - Hanceville ... AL ... 10
Brown Mackie College-Phoenix ... AZ ... 12
Brown Mackie College-Tucson ... AZ ... 12
Pima Medical Institute-Mesa ... AZ ... 17
Pima Medical Institute-Tucson ... AZ ... 17
Pulaski Technical College ... AR ... 23
South Arkansas Community College ... AR ... 23
Grossmont College ... CA ... 49
Sacramento City College ... CA ... 56
Santa Ana College ... CA ... 63
Stanbridge College ... CA ... 71
Pima Medical Institute-Denver ... CO ... 87
Pueblo Community College ... CO ... 87
Goodwin College ... CT ... 92
Housatonic Community College ... CT ... 91
Lincoln College of New England ... CT ... 93
Manchester Community College ... CT ... 91
Delaware Technical Community College, Owens Campus ... DE ... 96
Delaware Technical Community College, Stanton-Wilmington Campus ... DE ... 96
Adventist University of Health Sciences ... FL ... 100
Daytona State College ... FL ... 104
Florida State College at Jacksonville ... FL ... 109
Keiser University ... FL ... 112
Polk State College ... FL ... 115
State College of Florida, Manatee-Sarasota ... FL ... 118
Augusta Technical College ... GA ... 125
Brown Mackie College-Atlanta ... GA ... 126
Darton College ... GA ... 128
Georgia Northwestern Technical College ... GA ... 131
Middle Georgia College ... GA ... 134
Kapiolani Community College ... HI ... 141
Brown Mackie College-Boise ... ID ... 143
City Colleges of Chicago Wilbur Wright College ... IL ... 147
Illinois Central College ... IL ... 152
John A. Logan College ... IL ... 154
Kaskaskia College ... IL ... 155
Lewis and Clark Community College ... IL ... 156
Lincoln Land Community College ... IL ... 157
Parkland College ... IL ... 161
Rend Lake College ... IL ... 162
Shawnee Community College ... IL ... 164
South Suburban College of Cook County ... IL ... 164
Southeastern Illinois College ... IL ... 164
Brown Mackie College-Fort Wayne ... IN ... 170
Brown Mackie College-Indianapolis ... IN ... 170
Brown Mackie College-Merrillville ... IN ... 170
Brown Mackie College-South Bend ... IN ... 170
University of Southern Indiana ... IN ... 181
Indian Hills Community College ... IA ... 185
Kirkwood Community College ... IA ... 187
Brown Mackie College-Kansas City ... KS ... 191
Brown Mackie College-Salina ... KS ... 191
Newman University ... KS ... 195
Washburn University ... KS ... 197
Brown Mackie College-Hopkinsville ... KY ... 199
Brown Mackie College-Louisville ... KY ... 199
Brown Mackie College-Northern Kentucky ... KY ... 199
Jefferson Community and Technical College ... KY ... 202
Madisonville Community College ... KY ... 202
Bossier Parish Community College ... LA ... 209
Delgado Community College ... LA ... 210
University of Louisiana at Monroe ... LA ... 216
Kennebec Valley Community College ... ME ... 218
Allegany College of Maryland ... MD ... 221
Community College of Baltimore County, The ... MD ... 222
Bristol Community College ... MA ... 239
North Shore Community College ... MA ... 240
Quinsigamond Community College ... MA ... 240
Springfield Technical Community College ... MA ... 241
Baker College of Allen Park ... MI ... 247
Baker College of Muskegon ... MI ... 248
Grand Rapids Community College ... MI ... 251
Macomb Community College ... MI ... 254
Mott Community College ... MI ... 255
Anoka Technical College ... MN ... 265
Herzing University ... MN ... 264
Northland Community and Technical College ... MN ... 268
St. Catherine University ... MN ... 270
Holmes Community College ... MS ... 274
Itawamba Community College ... MS ... 274
Pearl River Community College ... MS ... 276
Brown Mackie College-St. Louis ... MO ... 279
East Central College ... MO ... 281
Metropolitan Community College - Penn Valley ... MO ... 285
Moberly Area Community College ... MO ... 286
North Central Missouri College ... MO ... 287
Ozarks Technical Community College ... MO ... 287
St. Charles Community College ... MO ... 288
Saint Louis College of Health Careers-Fenton Campus ... MO ... 288
Saint Louis Community College at Meramec ... MO ... 289
Sanford-Brown College ... MO ... 289
State Fair Community College ... MO ... 290
Three Rivers Community College ... MO ... 290
University of Missouri - Kansas City ... MO ... 291
Central Community College ... NE ... 297
#College of Southern Nevada ... NV ... 302
River Valley Community College ... NH ... 304
Eastern New Mexico University-Roswell ... NM ... 318
Western New Mexico University ... NM ... 321
Erie Community College North Campus ... NY ... 333
Jamestown Community College ... NY ... 337
La Guardia Community College/City University of New York ... NY ... 328
Maria College of Albany ... NY ... 340
Mercy College ... NY ... 340
Orange County Community College ... NY ... 345
Rockland Community College ... NY ... 347
Suffolk County Community College Grant Campus ... NY ... 356
#Touro College ... NY ... 358
Cabarrus College of Health Sciences ... NC ... 362
Cape Fear Community College ... NC ... 368
Durham Technical Community College ... NC ... 370
Pitt Community College ... NC ... 372
North Dakota State College of Science ... ND ... 382
Brown Mackie College-Akron ... OH ... 385
Brown Mackie College-Findlay ... OH ... 385
Cincinnati State Technical and Community College ... OH ... 387
Cuyahoga Community College ... OH ... 389
James A. Rhodes State College ... OH ... 392
Kent State University at Ashtabula ... OH ... 393
Kent State University East Liverpool Campus ... OH ... 393
Lorain County Community College ... OH ... 395
Marion Technical College ... OH ... 395
North Central State College ... OH ... 397
Owens Community College ... OH ... 400
Shawnee State University ... OH ... 401
Sinclair Community College ... OH ... 401
Stark State College ... OH ... 402
Zane State College ... OH ... 407
Brown Mackie College-Tulsa ... OK ... 407
Murray State College ... OK ... 408
Oklahoma City Community College ... OK ... 409
Southwestern Oklahoma State University ... OK ... 412
Tulsa Community College ... OK ... 412
Linn-Benton Community College ... OR ... 416
Community College of Allegheny County ... PA ... 425
Harcum College ... PA ... 430
Kaplan Career Institute - ICM Campus ... PA ... 432
Lehigh Carbon Community College ... PA ... 434
Mercyhurst University ... PA ... 436
Penn State Berks ... PA ... 439
Penn State DuBois ... PA ... 439
Penn State Mont Alto ... PA ... 440
Pennsylvania College of Technology ... PA ... 440
Philadelphia University ... PA ... 444
#University of Puerto Rico-Humacao ... PR ... 567
Community College of Rhode Island ... RI ... 453
New England Institute of Technology ... RI ... 453
Brown Mackie College-Greenville ... SC ... 455
Greenville Technical College ... SC ... 458
#Trident Technical College ... SC ... 461
Lake Area Technical Institute ... SD ... 464
Nashville State Community College ... TN ... 475
Roane State Community College ... TN ... 476
Amarillo College ... TX ... 479
Anamarc College ... TX ... 480
Austin Community College District ... TX ... 481
Del Mar College ... TX ... 485
Houston Community College ... TX ... 487
Laredo Community College ... TX ... 489
Lone Star College System ... TX ... 490
Navarro College ... TX ... 491
Panola College ... TX ... 492
St. Philip's College ... TX ... 479
South Texas College ... TX ... 494
Salt Lake Community College ... UT ... 512
Jefferson College of Health Sciences ... VA ... 520
Southwest Virginia Community College ... VA ... 528
Tidewater Community College ... VA ... 528
Virginia Highlands Community College ... VA ... 529
Bates Technical College ... WA ... 531
Green River Community College ... WA ... 534
Lake Washington Institute of Technology ... WA ... 535
Pima Medical Institute-Seattle ... WA ... 536
Mountain State University ... WV ... 541
Fox Valley Technical College ... WI ... 554
Madison Area Technical College ... WI ... 554
Milwaukee Area Technical College ... WI ... 554
Western Technical College ... WI ... 555
Wisconsin Indianhead Technical College ... WI ... 555
Casper College ... WY ... 556

PA: National Accrediting Agency for Clinical Laboratory Sciences: pathologist's assistant (C,A,B,M)

Quinnipiac University ... CT ... 93
Rosalind Franklin University of Medicine & Science ... IL ... 163
Indiana University-Purdue University Indianapolis ... IN ... 174
University of Maryland Baltimore ... MD ... 227
Wayne State University ... MI ... 260
Duke University ... NC ... 364
Drexel University ... PA ... 427
West Virginia University ... WV ... 545

PDPSY: American Psychological Association: post-doctoral residency in professional psychology

University of California-Davis ... CA ... 73
University of California-Los Angeles ... CA ... 74
University of Southern California ... CA ... 76
University of Massachusetts Medical School ... MA ... 237
University of Michigan-Ann Arbor ... MI ... 259
Mayo School of Health Sciences ... MN ... 262
University of Rochester ... NY ... 359
University of Oklahoma Health Sciences Center ... OK ... 413
Brown University ... RI ... 453
University of Washington ... WA ... 539
Medical College of Wisconsin ... WI ... 548

PERF: Commission on Accreditation of Allied Health Education Programs: perfusionist (C,B,M)

Midwestern University ... AZ ... 16
University of Arizona ... AZ ... 18
Quinnipiac University ... CT ... 93
Barry University ... FL ... 101
Rush University ... IL ... 163
University of Iowa ... IA ... 182
University of Nebraska Medical Center ... NE ... 300
Long Island University C.W. Post Campus ... NY ... 339
State University of New York Upstate Medical University ... NY ... 352
University of Pittsburgh ... PA ... 449
Medical University of South Carolina ... SC ... 459
Vanderbilt University ... TN ... 478
Milwaukee School of Engineering ... WI ... 549

PH: Council on Education for Public Health: public health (B,M,D)

University of Alabama at Birmingham ... AL ... 8
University of Alaska Anchorage ... AK ... 10
University of Arizona ... AZ ... 18
University of Arkansas for Medical Sciences ... AR ... 24
#California State University-Fresno ... CA ... 35
California State University-Fullerton ... CA ... 35
California State University-Long Beach ... CA ... 35
California State University-Northridge ... CA ... 35
Charles R. Drew University of Medicine & Science ... CA ... 39
Claremont Graduate University ... CA ... 40
Loma Linda University ... CA ... 54
San Diego State University ... CA ... 37
San Francisco State University ... CA ... 37
San Jose State University ... CA ... 37
Touro University-California ... CA ... 73
University of California-Berkeley ... CA ... 73
University of California-Davis ... CA ... 73
University of California-Los Angeles ... CA ... 74
University of Southern California ... CA ... 76
Colorado State University ... CO ... 83
University of Colorado Denver|Anschutz Medical Campus ... CO ... 88
University of Northern Colorado ... CO ... 89
Southern Connecticut State University ... CT ... 90
University of Connecticut Health Center ... CT ... 95
Yale University ... CT ... 96
George Washington University ... DC ... 98
Florida Agricultural and Mechanical University ... FL ... 118
#Florida International University ... FL ... 119
Nova Southeastern University ... FL ... 114
University of Florida ... FL ... 120
University of Miami ... FL ... 122
University of North Florida ... FL ... 120
University of South Florida ... FL ... 121
University of West Florida ... FL ... 121
Armstrong Atlantic State University ... GA ... 124
Emory University ... GA ... 129
Georgia Health Sciences University ... GA ... 130
Georgia Southern University ... GA ... 131
Georgia State University ... GA ... 131
Mercer University ... GA ... 134
Morehouse School of Medicine ... GA ... 134
University of Georgia ... GA ... 138
University of Hawaii at Manoa ... HI ... 141
Idaho State University ... ID ... 143
Northern Illinois University ... IL ... 160
Northwestern University ... IL ... 160
Southern Illinois University Carbondale ... IL ... 165
University of Illinois at Chicago ... IL ... 167
Indiana University Bloomington ... IN ... 173
Indiana University-Purdue University Indianapolis ... IN ... 174
Des Moines University ... IA ... 184
University of Iowa ... IA ... 182
University of Kansas Main Campus ... KS ... 197
Eastern Kentucky University ... KY ... 200
University of Kentucky ... KY ... 207
University of Louisville ... KY ... 207
Western Kentucky University ... KY ... 208
Tulane University ... LA ... 215
University of New England ... ME ... 221
Johns Hopkins University ... MD ... 223
Morgan State University ... MD ... 224
Uniformed Services University of the Health Sciences ... MD ... 558
University of Maryland Baltimore ... MD ... 227
University of Maryland College Park ... MD ... 227
Boston University ... MA ... 232
Harvard University ... MA ... 235
Northeastern University ... MA ... 243
Tufts University ... MA ... 245
University of Massachusetts ... MA ... 236
University of Michigan-Ann Arbor ... MI ... 259
Wayne State University ... MI ... 260
University of Minnesota-Twin Cities ... MN ... 272
Jackson State University ... MS ... 274
University of Southern Mississippi ... MS ... 277
Saint Louis University ... MO ... 289
University of Missouri - Columbia ... MO ... 291
Washington University in St. Louis ... MO ... 292
University of Montana - Missoula, The ... MT ... 294
University of Nebraska Medical Center ... NE ... 300
University of Nevada, Reno ... NV ... 303
Dartmouth College ... NH ... 304

University of New Hampshire ... NH ... 306
New Jersey Institute of Technology ... NJ ... 312
Rutgers the State University of New Jersey New Brunswick Campus ... NJ ... 314
UMDNJ-School of Public Health ... NJ ... 317
New Mexico State University Main Campus . NM ... 319
University of New Mexico Main Campus ... NM ... 321
City University of New York Brooklyn College ... NY ... 326
City University of New York Graduate Center ... NY ... 327
City University of New York Herbert H. Lehman College ... NY ... 327
City University of New York Hunter College . NY ... 327
Columbia University in the City of New York NY ... 330
Mount Sinai School of Medicine ... NY ... 342
New York Medical College ... NY ... 343
New York University ... NY ... 344
State University of New York at Stony Brook NY ... 352
State University of New York Health Science Center at Brooklyn ... NY ... 352
University at Albany, SUNY ... NY ... 351
University at Buffalo-SUNY ... NY ... 351
University of Rochester ... NY ... 359
East Carolina University ... NC ... 377
University of North Carolina at Chapel Hill ... NC ... 378
University of North Carolina at Charlotte ... NC ... 379
University of North Carolina at Greensboro .. NC ... 379
Bowling Green State University ... OH ... 385
Case Western Reserve University ... OH ... 386
Cleveland State University ... OH ... 388
Northeast Ohio Medical University ... OH ... 397
Ohio State University Main Campus, The ... OH ... 398
Ohio University Main Campus ... OH ... 399
University of Akron, Main Campus, The ... OH ... 403
University of Toledo ... OH ... 404
Wright State University Main Campus ... OH ... 406
Youngstown State University ... OH ... 406
University of Oklahoma Health Sciences Center ... OK ... 413
Oregon Health & Science University ... OR ... 418
Oregon State University ... OR ... 418
Portland State University ... OR ... 418
Drexel University ... PA ... 427
East Stroudsburg University of Pennsylvania PA ... 442
Temple University ... PA ... 447
Thomas Jefferson University ... PA ... 448
University of Pennsylvania ... PA ... 448
University of Pittsburgh ... PA ... 449
West Chester University of Pennsylvania ... PA ... 444
University of Puerto Rico-Medical Sciences Campus ... PR ... 567
Brown University ... RI ... 453
University of South Carolina Columbia ... SC ... 462
East Tennessee State University ... TN ... 473
Meharry Medical College ... TN ... 471
University of Tennessee, Knoxville ... TN ... 477
Vanderbilt University ... TN ... 478
Texas A & M University ... TX ... 497
University of North Texas Health Science Center at Fort Worth ... TX ... 504
University of Texas Health Science Center at Houston (UTHealth), The ... TX ... 506
University of Texas Medical Branch, The ... TX ... 507
Brigham Young University ... UT ... 509
University of Utah, The ... UT ... 511
Westminster College ... UT ... 512
Eastern Virginia Medical School ... VA ... 518
Old Dominion University ... VA ... 522
University of Virginia ... VA ... 525
Virginia Commonwealth University ... VA ... 526
University of Washington ... WA ... 539
West Virginia University ... WV ... 545
Medical College of Wisconsin ... WI ... 548
University of Wisconsin-La Crosse ... WI ... 551
University of Wisconsin-Madison ... WI ... 550

PHAR: Accreditation Council for Pharmaceutical Education: pharmacy (FP,D)

Auburn University ... AL ... 1
Samford University ... AL ... 6
Midwestern University ... AZ ... 16
University of Arizona ... AZ ... 18
Harding University Main Campus ... AR ... 21
University of Arkansas for Medical Sciences AR ... 24
@California Northstate College of Pharmacy ... CA ... 33
Loma Linda University ... CA ... 54
Touro University-California ... CA ... 73
University of California-San Diego ... CA ... 74
University of California-San Francisco ... CA ... 75
University of Southern California ... CA ... 76
University of the Pacific ... CA ... 76
Western University of Health Sciences ... CA ... 78
@Regis University ... CO ... 87
University of Colorado Denver|Anschutz Medical Campus ... CO ... 88
University of Connecticut ... CT ... 94
@University of Saint Joseph ... CT ... 95
Howard University ... DC ... 98
Florida Agricultural and Mechanical University ... FL ... 118
Nova Southeastern University ... FL ... 114
Palm Beach Atlantic University ... FL ... 114
University of Florida ... FL ... 120
@University of South Florida ... FL ... 121
Mercer University ... GA ... 134
South University ... GA ... 137
University of Georgia ... GA ... 138
University of Hawaii at Hilo ... HI ... 141
Idaho State University ... ID ... 143
Chicago State University ... IL ... 146
Midwestern University ... IL ... 158
@Roosevelt University ... IL ... 163
@Rosalind Franklin University of Medicine & Science ... IL ... 163
Southern Illinois University Edwardsville ... IL ... 165
University of Illinois at Chicago ... IL ... 167
Butler University ... IN ... 170
@Manchester University ... IN ... 177
Purdue University Main Campus ... IN ... 178
Drake University ... IA ... 184
University of Iowa ... IA ... 182
University of Kansas Main Campus ... KS ... 197
Sullivan University ... KY ... 206
University of Kentucky ... KY ... 207
University of Louisiana at Monroe ... LA ... 216
Xavier University of Louisiana ... LA ... 217
@Husson University ... ME ... 218
@University of New England ... ME ... 221
@Notre Dame of Maryland University ... MD ... 225
University of Maryland Baltimore ... MD ... 227
@University of Maryland Eastern Shore ... MD ... 227
Massachusetts College of Pharmacy and Health Sciences ... MA ... 241
Northeastern University ... MA ... 243
@Western New England University ... MA ... 246
Ferris State University ... MI ... 250
University of Michigan-Ann Arbor ... MI ... 259
Wayne State University ... MI ... 260
University of Minnesota-Twin Cities ... MN ... 272
University of Mississippi ... MS ... 277
St. Louis College of Pharmacy ... MO ... 288
University of Missouri - Kansas City ... MO ... 291
University of Montana - Missoula, The ... MT ... 294
Creighton University ... NE ... 297
University of Nebraska Medical Center ... NE ... 300
Roseman University of Health Sciences ... NV ... 303
@Fairleigh Dickinson University ... NJ ... 310
Rutgers the State University of New Jersey New Brunswick Campus ... NJ ... 314
University of New Mexico Main Campus ... NM ... 321
Albany College of Pharmacy and Health Sciences ... NY ... 322
@D'Youville College ... NY ... 332
Long Island University Brooklyn Campus ... NY ... 338
St. John Fisher College ... NY ... 348
St. John's University ... NY ... 348
Touro College ... NY ... 358
University at Buffalo-SUNY ... NY ... 351
Campbell University ... NC ... 362
University of North Carolina at Chapel Hill ... NC ... 378
Wingate University ... NC ... 380
North Dakota State University Main Campus. ND ... 382
@Cedarville University ... OH ... 386
Northeast Ohio Medical University ... OH ... 397
Ohio Northern University ... OH ... 398
Ohio State University Main Campus, The ... OH ... 398
University of Cincinnati Main Campus ... OH ... 403
University of Findlay, The ... OH ... 404
University of Toledo ... OH ... 404
Southwestern Oklahoma State University ... OK ... 412
University of Oklahoma Health Sciences Center ... OK ... 413
Oregon State University ... OR ... 418
Pacific University ... OR ... 419
Duquesne University ... PA ... 428
Lake Erie College of Osteopathic Medicine .. PA ... 433
Temple University ... PA ... 447
Thomas Jefferson University ... PA ... 448
University of Pittsburgh ... PA ... 449
University of the Sciences in Philadelphia ... PA ... 450
Wilkes University ... PA ... 452
University of Puerto Rico-Medical Sciences Campus ... PR ... 567
University of Rhode Island ... RI ... 454
@Presbyterian College ... SC ... 460
South Dakota State University ... SD ... 466
Belmont University ... TN ... 467
East Tennessee State University ... TN ... 473
Lipscomb University ... TN ... 470
@South College ... TN ... 473
Union University ... TN ... 477
University of Tennessee Health Science Center ... TN ... 477
Texas A & M University - Kingsville ... TX ... 498
Texas Southern University ... TX ... 500
Texas Tech University Health Sciences Center ... TX ... 502
University of Houston ... TX ... 503
University of Texas at Austin ... TX ... 505
University of the Incarnate Word ... TX ... 504
University of Utah, The ... UT ... 511
Appalachian College of Pharmacy ... VA ... 516
Hampton University ... VA ... 519
Shenandoah University ... VA ... 524
Virginia Commonwealth University ... VA ... 526
University of Washington ... WA ... 539
Washington State University ... WA ... 539
@Marshall University ... WV ... 544
University of Charleston ... WV ... 542
West Virginia University ... WV ... 545
@Concordia University Wisconsin ... WI ... 547
University of Wisconsin-Madison ... WI ... 550
University of Wyoming ... WY ... 556

PLNG: Planning Accreditation Board: certified planning (B,M)

Alabama Agricultural and Mechanical University ... AL ... 1
Auburn University ... AL ... 1
Arizona State University ... AZ ... 11
University of Arizona ... AZ ... 18
California Polytechnic State University-San Luis Obispo ... CA ... 33
California State Polytechnic University-Pomona ... CA ... 33
San Jose State University ... CA ... 37
University of California-Berkeley ... CA ... 73
University of California-Irvine ... CA ... 74
University of California-Los Angeles ... CA ... 74
University of Southern California ... CA ... 76
University of Colorado Denver|Anschutz Medical Campus ... CO ... 88
Florida Atlantic University ... FL ... 119
Florida State University ... FL ... 119
University of Florida ... FL ... 120
Georgia Institute of Technology ... GA ... 130
University of Hawaii at Manoa ... HI ... 141
University of Illinois at Chicago ... IL ... 167
University of Illinois at Urbana-Champaign ... IL ... 167
Ball State University ... IN ... 169
Iowa State University ... IA ... 182
University of Iowa ... IA ... 182
Kansas State University ... KS ... 194
University of Kansas Main Campus ... KS ... 197
University of Louisville ... KY ... 207
University of New Orleans ... LA ... 213
Morgan State University ... MD ... 224
University of Maryland College Park ... MD ... 227
Harvard University ... MA ... 235
Massachusetts Institute of Technology ... MA ... 241
Tufts University ... MA ... 245
#University of Massachusetts ... MA ... 236
Eastern Michigan University ... MI ... 250
#Michigan State University ... MI ... 255
University of Michigan-Ann Arbor ... MI ... 259
Wayne State University ... MI ... 260
University of Minnesota-Twin Cities ... MN ... 272
Jackson State University ... MS ... 274
Missouri State University ... MO ... 286
University of Nebraska - Lincoln ... NE ... 300
Rutgers the State University of New Jersey New Brunswick Campus ... NJ ... 314
University of New Mexico Main Campus ... NM ... 321
City University of New York Hunter College . NY ... 327
Columbia University in the City of New York NY ... 330
Cornell University ... NY ... 331
New York University ... NY ... 344
Pratt Institute ... NY ... 346
University at Albany, SUNY ... NY ... 351
University at Buffalo-SUNY ... NY ... 351
East Carolina University ... NC ... 377
University of North Carolina at Chapel Hill ... NC ... 378
Cleveland State University ... OH ... 388
Ohio State University Main Campus, The ... OH ... 398
University of Cincinnati Main Campus ... OH ... 403
University of Oklahoma Norman Campus ... OK ... 413
Portland State University ... OR ... 418
University of Oregon ... OR ... 419
Indiana University of Pennsylvania ... PA ... 442
Temple University ... PA ... 447
University of Puerto Rico-Rio Piedras Campus ... PR ... 568
Clemson University ... SC ... 456
University of Memphis, The ... TN ... 474
Texas A & M University ... TX ... 497
Texas Southern University ... TX ... 500
University of Texas at Arlington, The ... TX ... 505
University of Texas at Austin ... TX ... 505
University of Utah, The ... UT ... 511
University of Virginia ... VA ... 525
Virginia Commonwealth University ... VA ... 526
Virginia Polytechnic Institute and State University ... VA ... 529
Eastern Washington University ... WA ... 533
University of Washington ... WA ... 539
University of Wisconsin-Madison ... WI ... 550
University of Wisconsin-Milwaukee ... WI ... 551

PNUR: National League for Nursing: practical nursing (C)

Bevill State Community College ... AL ... 2
Bishop State Community College ... AL ... 2
Calhoun Community College ... AL ... 2
Gadsden State Community College ... AL ... 3
George C. Wallace Community College - Dothan ... AL ... 4
George Corley Wallace State Community College - Selma ... AL ... 4
James H. Faulkner State Community College ... AL ... 5
Jefferson State Community College ... AL ... 5
Lawson State Community College ... AL ... 5
Northeast Alabama Community College ... AL ... 6
Shelton State Community College ... AL ... 6
Trenholm State Technical College ... AL ... 7
Front Range Community College ... CO ... 85
Northeastern Junior College ... CO ... 86
Pueblo Community College ... CO ... 87
Delaware Technical Community College, Terry Campus ... DE ... 96
College of Central Florida ... FL ... 103
Santa Fe College ... FL ... 117
Augusta Technical College ... GA ... 125
Columbus Technical College ... GA ... 128
Savannah Technical College ... GA ... 136
Carrington College - Boise ... ID ... 143
Carl Sandburg College ... IL ... 146
College of DuPage ... IL ... 148
Lake Land College ... IL ... 156
South Suburban College of Cook County ... IL ... 164
Ivy Tech Community College-Central Indiana IN ... 175
Ivy Tech Community College of Indiana-Bloomington ... IN ... 175
Ivy Tech Community College of Indiana-Columbus ... IN ... 176
Ivy Tech Community College of Indiana-East Central ... IN ... 176
Ivy Tech Community College of Indiana-Kokomo ... IN ... 176
Ivy Tech Community College of Indiana-Lafayette ... IN ... 176
Ivy Tech Community College of Indiana-North Central ... IN ... 176
Ivy Tech Community College of Indiana-Northeast ... IN ... 176
Ivy Tech Community College of Indiana-Northwest ... IN ... 176
Ivy Tech Community College of Indiana-Richmond ... IN ... 176
Ivy Tech Community College of Indiana-Southeast ... IN ... 177
Ivy Tech Community College of Indiana-Southern Indiana ... IN ... 177
Ivy Tech Community College of Indiana-Southwest ... IN ... 177
Ivy Tech Community College of Indiana-Wabash Valley ... IN ... 177
MedTech College ... IN ... 178
Vincennes University ... IN ... 181
Western Iowa Tech Community College ... IA ... 190
Dodge City Community College ... KS ... 192
Hutchinson Community College and Area Vocational School ... KS ... 193
Wichita Area Technical College ... KS ... 197
Southeast Kentucky Community and Technical College ... KY ... 203
L.E. Fletcher Technical Community College . LA ... 210
College of Southern Maryland ... MD ... 222
Howard Community College ... MD ... 223
Mount Wachusett Community College ... MA ... 240
Northern Essex Community College ... MA ... 240
Quincy College ... MA ... 243
Quinsigamond Community College ... MA ... 240
Davenport University ... MI ... 250
Grand Rapids Community College ... MI ... 251
Minneapolis Community and Technical College ... MN ... 267
Rochester Community and Technical College ... MN ... 268
Saint Paul College-A Community & Technical College ... MN ... 269
Meridian Community College ... MS ... 275
Mississippi Delta Community College ... MS ... 275
Mississippi Gulf Coast Community College .. MS ... 275
Metropolitan Community College - Penn Valley ... MO ... 285
Southeast Community College ... NE ... 300
Western Nebraska Community College ... NE ... 301
College of Southern Nevada ... NV ... 302
Kaplan College ... NV ... 302
NHTI-Concord's Community College ... NH ... 304
St. Joseph School of Nursing ... NH ... 305
Salem Community College ... NJ ... 315
Union County College ... NJ ... 316
Central New Mexico Community College ... NM ... 317
Farmingdale State College ... NY ... 356
Suffolk County Community College Ammerman Campus ... NY ... 356
Trocaire College ... NY ... 358
Durham Technical Community College ... NC ... 370
Gaston College ... NC ... 370
Rowan-Cabarrus Community College ... NC ... 373
Wayne Community College ... NC ... 375
Dickinson State University ... ND ... 381
North Dakota State College of Science ... ND ... 382
United Tribes Technical College ... ND ... 383
Cincinnati State Technical and Community College ... OH ... 387
Hocking College ... OH ... 391
Lorain County Community College ... OH ... 395
Carrington College - Portland ... OR ... 414
Harrisburg Area Community College ... PA ... 430
Lehigh Carbon Community College ... PA ... 434
Northampton Community College ... PA ... 437
Pennsylvania College of Technology ... PA ... 440
Reading Area Community College ... PA ... 445
Community College of Rhode Island ... RI ... 453
Central Carolina Technical College ... SC ... 455
Greenville Technical College ... SC ... 458
Horry-Georgetown Technical College ... SC ... 458
Midlands Technical College ... SC ... 459
Orangeburg-Calhoun Technical College ... SC ... 460
Technical College of the Lowcountry ... SC ... 461
Tri-County Technical College ... SC ... 461
Trident Technical College ... SC ... 461
University of South Carolina Lancaster ... SC ... 462
York Technical College ... SC ... 463
Lake Area Technical Institute ... SD ... 464

Austin Community College District ... TX ... 481
Cisco College ... TX ... 482
El Centro College ... TX ... 485
Ogden-Weber Applied Technology College .. UT ... 510
Snow College ... UT ... 512
Uintah Basin Applied Technology College ... UT ... 510
Utah State University-College of Eastern Utah ... UT ... 512
Vermont Technical College ... VT ... 516
Chippewa Valley Technical College ... WI ... 553
Milwaukee Area Technical College ... WI ... 554

POD: American Podiatric Medical Association: podiatry (FP,D)

Midwestern University ... AZ ... 16
Samuel Merritt University ... CA ... 64
@Western University of Health Sciences ... CA ... 78
Barry University ... FL ... 101
Rosalind Franklin University of Medicine & Science ... IL ... 163
Des Moines University ... IA ... 184
New York College of Podiatric Medicine ... NY ... 343
Kent State University College of Podiatric Medicine ... OH ... 394
Kent State University Main Campus ... OH ... 393
Temple University ... PA ... 447

POLYT: Commission on Accreditation of Allied Health Education Programs: polysomnographic technologist education (C,A)

Wallace State Community College - Hanceville ... AL ... 10
Gateway Community College ... AZ ... 15
Orange Coast College ... CA ... 41
Pueblo Community College ... CO ... 87
Central Florida Institute ... FL ... 103
Moraine Valley Community College ... IL ... 159
Mercy College of Health Sciences ... IA ... 187
Johnson County Community College ... KS ... 194
Bluegrass Community and Technical College KY ... 201
Bowling Green Technical College ... KY ... 201
West Kentucky Community and Technical College ... KY ... 203
Community College of Baltimore County, The ... MD ... 222
Montgomery College ... MD ... 224
Northern Essex Community College ... MA ... 240
Baker College of Flint ... MI ... 248
Minneapolis Community and Technical College ... MN ... 267
Coahoma Community College ... MS ... 273
Sanford-Brown College ... MO ... 289
Southeast Community College ... NE ... 300
Thomas Edison State College ... NJ ... 316
Genesee Community College ... NY ... 334
State University of New York at Stony Brook NY ... 352
Catawba Valley Community College ... NC ... 369
Central Carolina Community College ... NC ... 369
Lenoir Community College ... NC ... 371
Pitt Community College ... NC ... 372
Sandhills Community College ... NC ... 373
Cuyahoga Community College ... OH ... 389
Mercy College of Ohio ... OH ... 395
Linn-Benton Community College ... OR ... 416
Oregon Institute of Technology ... OR ... 418
East Tennessee State University ... TN ... 473
Miller-Motte Technical College ... TN ... 471
Roane State Community College ... TN ... 476
Volunteer State Community College ... TN ... 476
Alvin Community College ... TX ... 479
J. Sargeant Reynolds Community College ... VA ... 527
Highline Community College ... WA ... 535

PSPSY: American Psychological Association: combined professional-scientific psychology (D)

University of California-Santa Barbara ... CA ... 75
Florida State University ... FL ... 119
Northeastern University ... MA ... 243
Pace University ... NY ... 345
University at Buffalo-SUNY ... NY ... 351
Yeshiva University ... NY ... 361
Utah State University ... UT ... 511
James Madison University ... VA ... 520

PTA: American Physical Therapy Association: physical therapy (M,D)

Alabama State University ... AL ... 1
University of Alabama at Birmingham ... AL ... 8
University of South Alabama ... AL ... 9
@Midwestern University ... AZ ... 16
Northern Arizona University ... AZ ... 16
Arkansas State University-Jonesboro ... AR ... 20
@Harding University Main Campus ... AR ... 21
University of Central Arkansas ... AR ... 25
Azusa Pacific University ... CA ... 30
California State University-Fresno ... CA ... 35
California State University-Long Beach ... CA ... 35
California State University-Northridge ... CA ... 35
California State University-Sacramento ... CA ... 36
Chapman University ... CA ... 39
Loma Linda University ... CA ... 54
Mount St. Mary's College ... CA ... 57
Samuel Merritt University ... CA ... 64
@San Diego State University ... CA ... 37
San Francisco State University ... CA ... 37
University of California-San Francisco ... CA ... 75
University of Southern California ... CA ... 76
University of the Pacific ... CA ... 76
Western University of Health Sciences ... CA ... 78
Regis University ... CO ... 87
University of Colorado DenverlAnschutz Medical Campus ... CO ... 88
Quinnipiac University ... CT ... 93
Sacred Heart University ... CT ... 94
University of Connecticut ... CT ... 94
University of Hartford ... CT ... 95
University of Delaware ... DE ... 96
George Washington University ... DC ... 98
Howard University ... DC ... 98
Florida Agricultural and Mechanical University ... FL ... 118
Florida Gulf Coast University ... FL ... 119
Florida International University ... FL ... 119
Nova Southeastern University ... FL ... 114
University of Central Florida ... FL ... 120
University of Florida ... FL ... 120
University of Miami ... FL ... 122
University of North Florida ... FL ... 120
University of St. Augustine for Health Sciences ... FL ... 122
University of South Florida ... FL ... 121
Armstrong Atlantic State University ... GA ... 124
Emory University ... GA ... 129
Georgia Health Sciences University ... GA ... 130
Georgia State University ... GA ... 131
@Mercer University ... GA ... 134
North Georgia College & State University ... GA ... 134
Idaho State University ... ID ... 143
Bradley University ... IL ... 146
Governors State University ... IL ... 151
Midwestern University ... IL ... 158
Northern Illinois University ... IL ... 160
Northwestern University ... IL ... 160
Rosalind Franklin University of Medicine & Science ... IL ... 163
University of Illinois at Chicago ... IL ... 167
Indiana University-Purdue University Indianapolis ... IN ... 174
University of Evansville ... IN ... 180
University of Indianapolis ... IN ... 180
Clarke University ... IA ... 183
Des Moines University ... IA ... 184
St. Ambrose University ... IA ... 188
University of Iowa ... IA ... 182
University of Kansas Medical Center ... KS ... 197
@University of Saint Mary ... KS ... 197
Wichita State University ... KS ... 198
Bellarmine University ... KY ... 198
University of Kentucky ... KY ... 207
Louisiana State University Health Sciences Center at Shreveport ... LA ... 213
Louisiana State University Health Sciences Center-New Orleans ... LA ... 213
Husson University ... ME ... 218
University of New England ... ME ... 221
University of Maryland Baltimore ... MD ... 227
University of Maryland Eastern Shore ... MD ... 227
American International College ... MA ... 229
Boston University ... MA ... 232
@Massachusetts College of Pharmacy and Health Sciences ... MA ... 241
MGH Institute of Health Professions ... MA ... 242
Northeastern University ... MA ... 243
#Simmons College ... MA ... 244
Springfield College ... MA ... 244
University of Massachusetts Lowell ... MA ... 237
Andrews University ... MI ... 247
Central Michigan University ... MI ... 249
Grand Valley State University ... MI ... 251
Oakland University ... MI ... 256
University of Michigan-Flint ... MI ... 259
Wayne State University ... MI ... 260
College of Saint Scholastica, The ... MN ... 262
Mayo School of Health Sciences ... MN ... 262
St. Catherine University ... MN ... 270
University of Minnesota-Twin Cities ... MN ... 272
University of Mississippi Medical Center ... MS ... 277
Maryville University of Saint Louis ... MO ... 284
Missouri State University ... MO ... 286
Rockhurst University ... MO ... 288
Saint Louis University ... MO ... 289
Southwest Baptist University ... MO ... 290
University of Missouri - Columbia ... MO ... 291
Washington University in St. Louis ... MO ... 292
University of Montana - Missoula, The ... MT ... 294
Creighton University ... NE ... 297
University of Nebraska Medical Center ... NE ... 300
University of Nevada, Las Vegas ... NV ... 302
Franklin Pierce University ... NH ... 305
Richard Stockton College of New Jersey, The ... NJ ... 313
Rutgers the State University of New Jersey Camden Campus ... NJ ... 314
Seton Hall University ... NJ ... 315
UMDNJ-School of Health Related Professions ... NJ ... 317
University of New Mexico Main Campus ... NM ... 321
City University of New York College of Staten Island ... NY ... 327
City University of New York Hunter College . NY ... 327
Clarkson University ... NY ... 329
Columbia University in the City of New York NY ... 330
Daemen College ... NY ... 331
Dominican College of Blauvelt ... NY ... 332
D'Youville College ... NY ... 332
Ithaca College ... NY ... 336
Long Island University Brooklyn Campus ... NY ... 338
Mercy College ... NY ... 340
Nazareth College of Rochester ... NY ... 342
New York Institute of Technology ... NY ... 343
New York Medical College ... NY ... 343
New York University ... NY ... 344
Sage Colleges, The ... NY ... 348
State University of New York at Stony Brook NY ... 352
State University of New York Health Science Center at Brooklyn ... NY ... 352
State University of New York Upstate Medical University ... NY ... 352
Touro College ... NY ... 358
University at Buffalo-SUNY ... NY ... 351
Utica College ... NY ... 359
Duke University ... NC ... 364
East Carolina University ... NC ... 377
Elon University ... NC ... 364
University of North Carolina at Chapel Hill ... NC ... 378
Western Carolina University ... NC ... 380
Winston-Salem State University ... NC ... 380
University of Mary ... ND ... 383
University of North Dakota Main Campus ... ND ... 381
Cleveland State University ... OH ... 388
College of Mount St. Joseph ... OH ... 388
Ohio State University Main Campus, The ... OH ... 398
Ohio University Main Campus ... OH ... 399
University of Cincinnati Main Campus ... OH ... 403
University of Dayton ... OH ... 404
University of Findlay, The ... OH ... 404
University of Toledo ... OH ... 404
Walsh University ... OH ... 405
Youngstown State University ... OH ... 406
Langston University ... OK ... 408
University of Oklahoma Health Sciences Center ... OK ... 413
@George Fox University ... OR ... 415
Pacific University ... OR ... 419
Arcadia University ... PA ... 422
Chatham University ... PA ... 425
Drexel University ... PA ... 427
Duquesne University ... PA ... 428
Gannon University ... PA ... 429
Lebanon Valley College ... PA ... 434
Misericordia University ... PA ... 436
Neumann University ... PA ... 437
Saint Francis University ... PA ... 446
Slippery Rock University of Pennsylvania ... PA ... 443
Temple University ... PA ... 447
Thomas Jefferson University ... PA ... 448
University of Pittsburgh ... PA ... 449
University of Scranton, The ... PA ... 450
University of the Sciences in Philadelphia ... PA ... 450
Widener University ... PA ... 451
University of Puerto Rico-Medical Sciences Campus ... PR ... 567
University of Rhode Island ... RI ... 454
Medical University of South Carolina ... SC ... 459
University of South Carolina Columbia ... SC ... 462
University of South Dakota, The ... SD ... 465
Belmont University ... TN ... 467
East Tennessee State University ... TN ... 473
Tennessee State University ... TN ... 474
University of Tennessee at Chattanooga ... TN ... 477
University of Tennessee Health Science Center ... TN ... 477
Angelo State University ... TX ... 480
Baylor University ... TX ... 482
Hardin-Simmons University ... TX ... 487
Texas State University-San Marcos ... TX ... 501
Texas Tech University Health Sciences Center ... TX ... 502
Texas Woman's University ... TX ... 502
@University of North Texas Health Science Center at Fort Worth ... TX ... 504
University of Texas at El Paso ... TX ... 506
University of Texas Health Science Center at San Antonio ... TX ... 507
University of Texas Medical Branch, The ... TX ... 507
University of Texas Southwestern Medical Center ... TX ... 507
@University of the Incarnate Word ... TX ... 504
@Rocky Mountain University of Health Professions ... UT ... 510
University of Utah, The ... UT ... 511
University of Vermont ... VT ... 514
Hampton University ... VA ... 519
@Lynchburg College ... VA ... 521
Marymount University ... VA ... 521
Old Dominion University ... VA ... 522
@Radford University ... VA ... 523
Shenandoah University ... VA ... 524
Virginia Commonwealth University ... VA ... 526
Eastern Washington University ... WA ... 533
University of Puget Sound ... WA ... 538
University of Washington ... WA ... 539
@Marshall University ... WV ... 544
West Virginia University ... WV ... 545
Wheeling Jesuit University ... WV ... 546
Carroll University ... WI ... 546
Concordia University Wisconsin ... WI ... 547
Marquette University ... WI ... 548
University of Wisconsin-La Crosse ... WI ... 551
University of Wisconsin-Madison ... WI ... 550
University of Wisconsin-Milwaukee ... WI ... 551

PTAA: American Physical Therapy Association: physical therapy assistant (A)

Bishop State Community College ... AL ... 2
Calhoun Community College ... AL ... 2
Community College of the Air Force ... AL ... 557
George C. Wallace Community College - Dothan ... AL ... 4
Jefferson State Community College ... AL ... 5
South University ... AL ... 7
Wallace State Community College - Hanceville ... AL ... 10
@Brookline College ... AZ ... 12
Carrington College - Mesa ... AZ ... 12
Gateway Community College ... AZ ... 15
Mohave Community College ... AZ ... 16
Pima Medical Institute-Mesa ... AZ ... 17
Pima Medical Institute-Tucson ... AZ ... 17
Arkansas State University-Jonesboro ... AR ... 20
Arkansas Tech University ... AR ... 20
NorthWest Arkansas Community College ... AR ... 22
South Arkansas Community College ... AR ... 23
Carrington College California - Pleasant Hill CA ... 38
@Casa Loma College-Van Nuys ... CA ... 38
Cerritos College ... CA ... 39
College of the Sequoias ... CA ... 42
Concorde Career College ... CA ... 42
@Concorde Career College ... CA ... 42
@Concorde Career College ... CA ... 43
Loma Linda University ... CA ... 54
Ohlone College ... CA ... 59
Sacramento City College ... CA ... 56
San Diego Mesa College ... CA ... 65
@Stanbridge College ... CA ... 71
Arapahoe Community College ... CO ... 81
@Concorde Career College ... CO ... 84
Morgan Community College ... CO ... 86
Pima Medical Institute-Denver ... CO ... 87
Pueblo Community College ... CO ... 87
Capital Community College ... CT ... 91
Housatonic Community College ... CT ... 91
Manchester Community College ... CT ... 91
Naugatuck Valley Community College ... CT ... 92
Northwestern Connecticut Community-Technical College ... CT ... 92
Norwalk Community College ... CT ... 92
Tunxis Community College ... CT ... 92
Delaware Technical Community College, Owens Campus ... DE ... 96
Delaware Technical Community College, Stanton-Wilmington Campus ... DE ... 96
Broward College ... FL ... 102
College of Central Florida ... FL ... 103
@Concorde Career Institute ... FL ... 104
Daytona State College ... FL ... 104
#Florida Gateway College ... FL ... 108
Florida State College at Jacksonville ... FL ... 109
Gulf Coast State College ... FL ... 110
Herzing University ... FL ... 110
@Hodges University ... FL ... 111
Indian River State College ... FL ... 111
Keiser University ... FL ... 112
Miami Dade College ... FL ... 113
Pensacola State College ... FL ... 115
Polk State College ... FL ... 115
St. Petersburg College ... FL ... 116
Seminole State College of Florida ... FL ... 117
South University ... FL ... 118
State College of Florida, Manatee-Sarasota . FL ... 118
Athens Technical College ... GA ... 125
@Atlanta Technical College ... GA ... 125
Chattahoochee Technical College ... GA ... 127
Darton College ... GA ... 128
South University ... GA ... 137
Kapiolani Community College ... HI ... 141
Carrington College - Boise ... ID ... 143
Idaho State University ... ID ... 143
Black Hawk College ... IL ... 145
College of DuPage ... IL ... 148
Elgin Community College ... IL ... 150
Fox College ... IL ... 151
Illinois Central College ... IL ... 152
Kankakee Community College ... IL ... 155
Kaskaskia College ... IL ... 155
Lake Land College ... IL ... 156
Morton College ... IL ... 159
Oakton Community College ... IL ... 160
Southern Illinois University Carbondale ... IL ... 165
Southwestern Illinois College ... IL ... 165
Brown Mackie College-Fort Wayne ... IN ... 170
Brown Mackie College-South Bend ... IN ... 170
Ivy Tech Community College of Indiana-East Central ... IN ... 176
Ivy Tech Community College of Indiana-Northwest ... IN ... 176
@Ivy Tech Community College of Indiana-Southern Indiana ... IN ... 177
University of Evansville ... IN ... 180
University of Indianapolis ... IN ... 180
University of Saint Francis ... IN ... 181
Vincennes University ... IN ... 181
@Hawkeye Community College ... IA ... 185
Indian Hills Community College ... IA ... 185

RABN: Association of Advanced Rabbinical and Talmudic Schools: rabbinical and Talmudic education (B, M,D)

RAD: Joint Review Committee on Education in Radiologic Technology: radiography (C,A,B)

RADDOS: Joint Review Committee on Education in Radiologic Technology: medical dosimetry (C,B,M)

RADMAG: Joint Review Committee on Education in Radiologic Technology: magnetic resonance (C,B)

RTT: Joint Review Committee on Education in Radiologic Technology: radiation therapist/technologist (C,A,B)

SC: Southern Association of Colleges and Schools, Commission on Colleges

SCPSY: American Psychological Association: school psychology (D)

SP: American Speech-Language-Hearing Association: speech-language pathology (M,D)

SPAA: National Association of Schools of Public Affairs and Administration: public affairs and administration (M)

California State University-Chico ... CA ... 34
California State University-Dominguez Hills .. CA ... 34
California State University-Fresno ... CA ... 35
California State University-Fullerton ... CA ... 35
California State University-Long Beach ... CA ... 35
California State University-Los Angeles ... CA ... 35
California State University-San Bernardino ... CA ... 36
California State University-Stanislaus ... CA ... 36
Naval Postgraduate School ... CA ... 558
San Diego State University ... CA ... 37
San Francisco State University ... CA ... 37
San Jose State University ... CA ... 37
University of LaVerne ... CA ... 75
University of Southern California ... CA ... 76
University of Colorado DenverlAnschutz Medical Campus ... CO ... 88
University of Connecticut ... CT ... 94
University of Delaware ... DE ... 96
American University ... DC ... 97
George Washington University ... DC ... 98
Florida Atlantic University ... FL ... 119
Florida Gulf Coast University ... FL ... 119
Florida International University ... FL ... 119
Florida State University ... FL ... 119
University of Central Florida ... FL ... 120
University of North Florida ... FL ... 120
University of South Florida ... FL ... 121
Albany State University ... GA ... 124
Augusta State University ... GA ... 125
Clark Atlanta University ... GA ... 127
Georgia College & State University ... GA ... 130
Georgia Southern University ... GA ... 131
Georgia State University ... GA ... 131
Kennesaw State University ... GA ... 133
Savannah State University ... GA ... 136
University of Georgia ... GA ... 138
University of West Georgia ... GA ... 139
Valdosta State University ... GA ... 139
Boise State University ... ID ... 142
DePaul University ... IL ... 149
Governors State University ... IL ... 151
Northern Illinois University ... IL ... 160
Southern Illinois University Carbondale ... IL ... 165
Southern Illinois University Edwardsville ... IL ... 165
University of Illinois at Chicago ... IL ... 167
University of Illinois at Springfield ... IL ... 167
Indiana University Bloomington ... IN ... 173
Indiana University Northwest ... IN ... 174
Indiana University-Purdue University Fort Wayne ... IN ... 174
Indiana University-Purdue University Indianapolis ... IN ... 174
Indiana University South Bend ... IN ... 174
Iowa State University ... IA ... 182
Kansas State University ... KS ... 194
University of Kansas Main Campus ... KS ... 197
Wichita State University ... KS ... 198
Eastern Kentucky University ... KY ... 200
Kentucky State University ... KY ... 203
Northern Kentucky University ... KY ... 205
University of Kentucky ... KY ... 207
University of Louisville ... KY ... 207
Western Kentucky University ... KY ... 208
Grambling State University ... LA ... 215
Louisiana State University and Agricultural and Mechanical College ... LA ... 212
Southern University and A&M College ... LA ... 214
University of Maine ... ME ... 220
University of Baltimore ... MD ... 229
University of Maryland Baltimore County ... MD ... 227
University of Maryland College Park ... MD ... 227
Bridgewater State University ... MA ... 237
Harvard University ... MA ... 235
Northeastern University ... MA ... 243
Suffolk University ... MA ... 245
Central Michigan University ... MI ... 249
Eastern Michigan University ... MI ... 250
Grand Valley State University ... MI ... 251
Oakland University ... MI ... 256
Wayne State University ... MI ... 260
Western Michigan University ... MI ... 260
University of Minnesota-Twin Cities ... MN ... 272
Jackson State University ... MS ... 274
Mississippi State University ... MS ... 275
Missouri State University ... MO ... 286
Saint Louis University ... MO ... 289
University of Missouri - Columbia ... MO ... 291
University of Missouri - Kansas City ... MO ... 291
University of Missouri - Saint Louis ... MO ... 291
University of Nebraska at Omaha ... NE ... 301
University of Nevada, Las Vegas ... NV ... 302
Kean University ... NJ ... 311
Rutgers the State University of New Jersey Camden Campus ... NJ ... 314
Rutgers the State University of New Jersey New Brunswick Campus ... NJ ... 314
Rutgers the State University of New Jersey Newark Campus ... NJ ... 314
Seton Hall University ... NJ ... 315
New Mexico State University Main Campus . NM ... 319
University of New Mexico Main Campus ... NM ... 321
Baruch College/City University of New York . NY ... 326
City University of New York John Jay College of Criminal Justice ... NY ... 327
Long Island University Brooklyn Campus ... NY ... 338
Long Island University C.W. Post Campus ... NY ... 339
New School, The ... NY ... 342
New York University ... NY ... 344
State University of New York at Binghamton NY ... 351
State University of New York, The College at Brockport ... NY ... 352
Syracuse University Main Campus ... NY ... 357
University at Albany, SUNY ... NY ... 351
Appalachian State University ... NC ... 377
East Carolina University ... NC ... 377
North Carolina State University ... NC ... 378
University of North Carolina at Chapel Hill ... NC ... 378
University of North Carolina at Charlotte ... NC ... 379
University of North Carolina at Greensboro .. NC ... 379
University of North Carolina Wilmington ... NC ... 379
University of North Dakota Main Campus ... ND ... 381
Cleveland State University ... OH ... 388
Kent State University Main Campus ... OH ... 393
Ohio State University Main Campus, The ... OH ... 398
University of Akron, Main Campus, The ... OH ... 403
University of Dayton ... OH ... 404
University of Toledo ... OH ... 404
Wright State University Main Campus ... OH ... 406
Portland State University ... OR ... 418
University of Oregon ... OR ... 419
Willamette University ... OR ... 421
Carnegie Mellon University ... PA ... 424
Penn State Harrisburg ... PA ... 439
University of Pittsburgh ... PA ... 449
Villanova University ... PA ... 450
University of Puerto Rico-Rio Piedras Campus ... PR ... 568
College of Charleston ... SC ... 457
University of South Carolina Columbia ... SC ... 462
University of South Dakota, The ... SD ... 465
Tennessee State University ... TN ... 474
University of Memphis, The ... TN ... 474
University of Tennessee at Chattanooga ... TN ... 477
Texas A & M University ... TX ... 497
Texas Southern University ... TX ... 500
Texas State University-San Marcos ... TX ... 501
Texas Tech University ... TX ... 502
University of North Texas ... TX ... 504
University of Texas at Arlington, The ... TX ... 505
University of Texas at Austin ... TX ... 505
University of Texas at Dallas, The ... TX ... 506
University of Texas at El Paso ... TX ... 506
University of Texas at San Antonio ... TX ... 506
Brigham Young University ... UT ... 509
University of Utah, The ... UT ... 511
George Mason University ... VA ... 519
Old Dominion University ... VA ... 522
Virginia Commonwealth University ... VA ... 526
Virginia Polytechnic Institute and State University ... VA ... 529
Seattle University ... WA ... 538
University of Washington ... WA ... 539
West Virginia University ... WV ... 545

SURGA: Commission on Accreditation of Allied Health Education Programs: surgical assistant (C,A)

Gulf Coast State College ... FL ... 110
College of Southern Idaho ... ID ... 143
Madisonville Community College ... KY ... 202
Wayne County Community College District .. MI ... 259
University of Cincinnati Main Campus ... OH ... 403
Eastern Virginia Medical School ... VA ... 518

SURGT: Commission on Accreditation of Allied Health Education Programs: surgical technology (C,A)

Bevill State Community College ... AL ... 2
Calhoun Community College ... AL ... 2
James H. Faulkner State Community College ... AL ... 5
Lurleen B. Wallace Community College ... AL ... 5
Southern Union State Community College ... AL ... 7
Virginia College ... AL ... 3
Gateway Community College ... AZ ... 15
Mohave Community College ... AZ ... 16
Pima County Community College District ... AZ ... 17
North Arkansas College ... AR ... 22
South Arkansas Community College ... AR ... 23
Southeast Arkansas College ... AR ... 23
University of Arkansas at Fort Smith ... AR ... 24
University of Arkansas for Medical Sciences AR ... 24
American Career College-Los Angeles ... CA ... 27
American Career College-Orange County ... CA ... 28
Carrington College California - Citrus Heights ... CA ... 38
Carrington College California - San Jose ... CA ... 38
Concorde Career College ... CA ... 42
Concorde Career College ... CA ... 43
Everest College-Reseda ... CA ... 46
Fresno City College ... CA ... 72
Las Positas College ... CA ... 39
MiraCosta Community College District ... CA ... 57
North-West College ... CA ... 59
San Joaquin Valley College-Bakersfield ... CA ... 66
San Joaquin Valley College-Fresno ... CA ... 66
Skyline College ... CA ... 67
Southwestern College ... CA ... 71
Aims Community College ... CO ... 81
Concorde Career College ... CO ... 84
#Everest College ... CO ... 84
Manchester Community College ... CT ... 91
Brevard Community College ... FL ... 102
Central Florida Institute ... FL ... 103
College of Central Florida ... FL ... 103
Concorde Career Institute ... FL ... 104
Daytona State College ... FL ... 104
Everest Institute ... FL ... 105
Everest Institute ... FL ... 106
Florida State College at Jacksonville ... FL ... 109
Fortis College ... FL ... 110
Gulf Coast State College ... FL ... 110
Indian River State College ... FL ... 111
Keiser University ... FL ... 112
MedVance Institute of Fort Lauderdale ... FL ... 113
Palm Beach State College ... FL ... 114
Pensacola State College ... FL ... 115
Santa Fe College ... FL ... 117
Southeastern College ... FL ... 118
Virginia College ... FL ... 123
Albany Technical College ... GA ... 124
Athens Technical College ... GA ... 125
Augusta Technical College ... GA ... 125
Central Georgia Technical College ... GA ... 127
Columbus Technical College ... GA ... 128
Everest Institute ... GA ... 129
Georgia Northwestern Technical College ... GA ... 131
Gwinnett Technical College ... GA ... 132
Lanier Technical College ... GA ... 133
Middle Georgia Technical College ... GA ... 134
Moultrie Technical College ... GA ... 134
Ogeechee Technical College ... GA ... 135
Okefenokee Technical College ... GA ... 135
Savannah Technical College ... GA ... 136
Southeastern Technical College ... GA ... 137
Southern Crescent Technical College ... GA ... 137
Southwest Georgia Technical College ... GA ... 138
West Georgia Technical College ... GA ... 139
Wiregrass Georgia Technical College ... GA ... 139
Kapiolani Community College ... HI ... 141
Brown Mackie College-Boise ... ID ... 143
College of Southern Idaho ... ID ... 143
Eastern Idaho Technical College ... ID ... 143
Argosy University, Schaumburg ... IL ... 145
City Colleges of Chicago Malcolm X College IL ... 147
College of DuPage ... IL ... 148
College of Lake County ... IL ... 148
Elgin Community College ... IL ... 150
Illinois Central College ... IL ... 152
John Wood Community College ... IL ... 154
Parkland College ... IL ... 161
Prairie State College ... IL ... 161
Richland Community College ... IL ... 162
Robert Morris University ... IL ... 162
Rock Valley College ... IL ... 162
Triton College ... IL ... 166
Waubonsee Community College ... IL ... 168
Brown Mackie College-Fort Wayne ... IN ... 170
Brown Mackie College-Merrillville ... IN ... 170
Brown Mackie College-Michigan City ... IN ... 170
Harrison College - Fort Wayne Campus ... IN ... 172
Harrison College - Indianapolis East Campus ... IN ... 172
Ivy Tech Community College-Central Indiana IN ... 175
Ivy Tech Community College of Indiana-Columbus ... IN ... 176
Ivy Tech Community College of Indiana-East Central ... IN ... 176
Ivy Tech Community College of Indiana-Kokomo ... IN ... 176
Ivy Tech Community College of Indiana-Lafayette ... IN ... 176
Ivy Tech Community College of Indiana-Northwest ... IN ... 176
Ivy Tech Community College of Indiana-Southwest ... IN ... 177
Ivy Tech Community College of Indiana-Wabash Valley ... IN ... 177
National College ... IN ... 178
University of Saint Francis ... IN ... 181
Vincennes University ... IN ... 181
Des Moines Area Community College ... IA ... 183
Iowa Lakes Community College ... IA ... 186
Iowa Western Community College ... IA ... 186
Kirkwood Community College ... IA ... 187
Mercy College of Health Sciences ... IA ... 187
Western Iowa Tech Community College ... IA ... 190
Hutchinson Community College and Area Vocational School ... KS ... 193
Seward County Community College/Area Technical School ... KS ... 196
Wichita Area Technical College ... KS ... 197
Ashland Community and Technical College . KY ... 201
Bluegrass Community and Technical College KY ... 201
Bowling Green Technical College ... KY ... 201
Brown Mackie College-Louisville ... KY ... 199
Hazard Community and Technical College ... KY ... 202
Jefferson Community and Technical College KY ... 202
Madisonville Community College ... KY ... 202
National College ... KY ... 205
Owensboro Community and Technical College ... KY ... 203
St. Catharine College ... KY ... 206
Somerset Community College ... KY ... 203
Southeast Kentucky Community and Technical College ... KY ... 203
Spencerian College ... KY ... 206
West Kentucky Community and Technical College ... KY ... 203
Bossier Parish Community College ... LA ... 209
Career Technical College ... LA ... 208
Delgado Community College ... LA ... 210
Our Lady of the Lake College ... LA ... 214
South Central Louisiana Technical College Lafourche Campus ... LA ... 211
South Louisiana Community College Ardoin Campus ... LA ... 211
Southern University at Shreveport-Louisiana LA ... 215
Eastern Maine Community College ... ME ... 218
Baltimore City Community College ... MD ... 221
Chesapeake College ... MD ... 222
Community College of Baltimore County, The ... MD ... 222
Frederick Community College ... MD ... 222
Montgomery College ... MD ... 224
Bunker Hill Community College ... MA ... 239
Massachusetts Bay Community College ... MA ... 239
North Shore Community College ... MA ... 240
Quincy College ... MA ... 243
Quinsigamond Community College ... MA ... 240
Springfield Technical Community College ... MA ... 241
Baker College of Allen Park ... MI ... 247
Baker College of Cadillac ... MI ... 248
Baker College of Clinton Township ... MI ... 248
Baker College of Flint ... MI ... 248
Baker College of Jackson ... MI ... 248
Baker College of Muskegon ... MI ... 248
Baker College of Port Huron ... MI ... 248
Delta College ... MI ... 250
Henry Ford Community College ... MI ... 252
Lansing Community College ... MI ... 254
Macomb Community College ... MI ... 254
Northern Michigan University ... MI ... 256
Oakland Community College ... MI ... 256
Wayne County Community College District .. MI ... 259
Anoka Technical College ... MN ... 265
Lake Superior College ... MN ... 266
Minnesota West Community and Technical College ... MN ... 267
Northland Community and Technical College MN ... 268
Rasmussen College - St. Cloud ... MN ... 270
Rochester Community and Technical College ... MN ... 268
Saint Cloud Technical and Community College ... MN ... 269
Saint Mary's University of Minnesota ... MN ... 271
East Central Community College ... MS ... 274
Hinds Community College ... MS ... 274
Holmes Community College ... MS ... 274
Itawamba Community College ... MS ... 274
Meridian Community College ... MS ... 275
Mississippi Gulf Coast Community College .. MS ... 275
Pearl River Community College ... MS ... 276
Colorado Technical University, Kansas City . MO ... 279
Lincoln University ... MO ... 283
Metropolitan Community College - Penn Valley ... MO ... 285
Ozarks Technical Community College ... MO ... 287
Saint Louis Community College at Forest Park ... MO ... 288
Flathead Valley Community College ... MT ... 294
Great Falls College Montana State University ... MT ... 295
University of Montana - College of Technology, The ... MT ... 295
Nebraska Methodist College ... NE ... 299
Southeast Community College ... NE ... 300
College of Southern Nevada ... NV ... 302
Great Bay Community College ... NH ... 304
Atlantic Cape Community College ... NJ ... 307
Bergen Community College ... NJ ... 307
Eastwick College ... NJ ... 309
Sussex County Community College ... NJ ... 315
Central New Mexico Community College ... NM ... 317
San Juan College ... NM ... 320
City University of New York Kingsborough Community College ... NY ... 328
Long Island University Brooklyn Campus ... NY ... 338
Nassau Community College ... NY ... 342
New York University ... NY ... 344
Niagara County Community College ... NY ... 344
Onondaga Community College ... NY ... 345
Trocaire College ... NY ... 358
Asheville - Buncombe Technical Community College ... NC ... 368
Blue Ridge Community College ... NC ... 368
Cabarrus College of Health Sciences ... NC ... 362
Cape Fear Community College ... NC ... 368
Carolinas College of Health Sciences ... NC ... 363
Catawba Valley Community College ... NC ... 369
Central Piedmont Community College ... NC ... 369
Cleveland Community College ... NC ... 369
Coastal Carolina Community College ... NC ... 369
College of the Albemarle ... NC ... 369
Durham Technical Community College ... NC ... 370
Edgecombe Community College ... NC ... 370
Fayetteville Technical Community College ... NC ... 370
Guilford Technical Community College ... NC ... 371
Lenoir Community College ... NC ... 371
Miller-Motte Technical College ... NC ... 367
Robeson Community College ... NC ... 373
Rockingham Community College ... NC ... 373
Sandhills Community College ... NC ... 373
South College ... NC ... 376
South Piedmont Community College ... NC ... 374
Wake Technical Community College ... NC ... 374
Wilson Community College ... NC ... 375
Bismarck State College ... ND ... 382
Brown Mackie College-Akron ... OH ... 385
Brown Mackie College-Cincinnati ... OH ... 385

Institution	State	Page
Brown Mackie College-Findlay	OH	385
Central Ohio Technical College	OH	386
Cincinnati State Technical and Community College	OH	387
Columbus State Community College	OH	389
Cuyahoga Community College	OH	389
Fortis College	OH	390
Lakeland Community College	OH	394
Lorain County Community College	OH	395
Miami-Jacobs Career College	OH	396
Owens Community College	OH	400
Sinclair Community College	OH	401
University of Akron, Main Campus, The	OH	403
University of Cincinnati-Clermont College	OH	403
Brown Mackie College-Tulsa	OK	407
Community Care College	OK	407
Platt College-OKC Central	OK	411
Concorde Career College	OR	415
Mt. Hood Community College	OR	417
Community College of Allegheny County	PA	425
Delaware County Community College	PA	426
Harrisburg Area Community College	PA	430
Lackawanna College	PA	433
Lancaster General College of Nursing and Health Sciences	PA	433
Luzerne County Community College	PA	435
McCann School of Business & Technology	PA	435
McCann School of Business & Technology	PA	436
Montgomery County Community College	PA	436
Mount Aloysius College	PA	437
Northampton Community College	PA	437
Pennsylvania College of Technology	PA	440
Pittsburgh Technical Institute	PA	444
Sanford-Brown Institute-Wilkins Township	PA	447
New England Institute of Technology	RI	453
Aiken Technical College	SC	455
Central Carolina Technical College	SC	455
Florence - Darlington Technical College	SC	458
Greenville Technical College	SC	458
Horry-Georgetown Technical College	SC	458
Midlands Technical College	SC	459
Miller-Motte Technical College	SC	459
Piedmont Technical College	SC	460
Spartanburg Community College	SC	461
Technical College of the Lowcountry	SC	461
Tri-County Technical College	SC	461
York Technical College	SC	463
Presentation College	SD	465
Southeast Technical Institute	SD	466
Western Dakota Technical Institute	SD	466
Chattanooga State Community College	TN	474
Concorde Career College	TN	468
Fortis Institute	TN	468
Miller-Motte Technical College	TN	471
Nashville State Community College	TN	475
Northeast State Community College	TN	475
Amarillo College	TX	479
Angelina College	TX	480
Austin Community College District	TX	481
Baptist Health System School of Health Professions	TX	481
Cisco College	TX	482
College of Health Care Professions, The	TX	483
Collin County Community College District	TX	483
Del Mar College	TX	485
El Centro College	TX	485
El Paso Community College	TX	486
Galveston College	TX	486
Houston Community College	TX	487
Howard College	TX	488
Kilgore College	TX	489
Lamar State College-Port Arthur	TX	501
Lone Star College System	TX	490
McLennan Community College	TX	490
North Central Texas College	TX	491
Paris Junior College	TX	492
St. Philip's College	TX	479
San Jacinto College Central	TX	493
Sanford-Brown College-Houston	TX	494
South Plains College	TX	494
Tarrant County College District	TX	496
Temple College	TX	496
Texas State Technical College Harlingen	TX	500
Trinity Valley Community College	TX	502
Tyler Junior College	TX	503
Vernon College	TX	507
Virginia College at Austin	TX	508
Wharton County Junior College	TX	509
Dixie State College of Utah	UT	512
Everest College	UT	510
Salt Lake Community College	UT	512
Stevens-Henager College	UT	510
Miller-Motte Technical College	VA	521
National College	VA	521
National College	VA	522
Piedmont Virginia Community College	VA	528
Sentara College of Health Sciences	VA	524
Bellingham Technical College	WA	531
Clover Park Technical College	WA	532
Columbia Basin College	WA	532
Renton Technical College	WA	537
Seattle Central Community College	WA	537
Spokane Community College	WA	533
Yakima Valley Community College	WA	540
Southern West Virginia Community and Technical College	WV	543
West Virginia Northern Community College	WV	543
West Virginia University at Parkersburg	WV	545
Chippewa Valley Technical College	WI	553
Gateway Technical College	WI	554
Madison Area Technical College	WI	554
Mid-State Technical College	WI	554
Milwaukee Area Technical College	WI	554
Moraine Park Technical College	WI	554
Northcentral Technical College	WI	555
Northeast Wisconsin Technical College	WI	555
Waukesha County Technical College	WI	555
Western Technical College	WI	555
Laramie County Community College	WY	556

SURTEC: Accrediting Bureau of Health Education Schools: surgical technologist (C,A)

Institution	State	Page
Brown Mackie College-Phoenix	AZ	12
Brown Mackie College-Tucson	AZ	12
American Career College-Los Angeles	CA	27
American Career College-Ontario	CA	27
American Career College-Orange County	CA	28
CBD College	CA	38
Anthem College	CO	81
Central Florida Institute	FL	103
Herzing University	FL	110
Lincoln Tech Fern Park Orlando Campus	FL	113
MedVance Institute of Fort Lauderdale	FL	113
Sanford-Brown Institute	FL	117
Southwest Florida College	FL	118
Brown Mackie College-Atlanta	GA	126
Brown Mackie College-Boise	ID	143
Brown Mackie College-Fort Wayne	IN	170
Brown Mackie College-Louisville	KY	199
Herzing University	LA	209
MedVance Institute-Baton Rouge	LA	213
Anthem College	MO	278
Brown Mackie College-St. Louis	MO	279
Sanford-Brown College	MO	289
Mandl School	NY	339
Brown Mackie College-North Canton	OH	386
Brown Mackie College-Tulsa	OK	407
Heritage College	OK	408
Brown Mackie College-Greenville	SC	455
Baptist Health System School of Health Professions	TX	481
College of Health Care Professions, The	TX	483
Sanford-Brown College	TX	494
Sanford-Brown College-Houston	TX	494
Anthem College-Milwaukee	WI	546

SW: Council on Social Work Education: social work (B,M)

Institution	State	Page
Alabama Agricultural and Mechanical University	AL	1
Alabama State University	AL	1
Auburn University	AL	1
Jacksonville State University	AL	4
@Judson College	AL	5
Miles College	AL	5
Oakwood University	AL	6
Talladega College	AL	7
Troy University	AL	8
Tuskegee University	AL	8
University of Alabama at Birmingham	AL	8
University of Alabama, The	AL	8
University of Montevallo	AL	9
University of North Alabama	AL	9
University of South Alabama	AL	9
University of Alaska Anchorage	AK	10
University of Alaska Fairbanks	AK	10
Arizona State University	AZ	11
Northern Arizona University	AZ	16
Arkansas State University-Jonesboro	AR	20
Harding University Main Campus	AR	21
Philander Smith College	AR	23
Southern Arkansas University	AR	23
University of Arkansas at Little Rock	AR	24
University of Arkansas at Monticello	AR	25
University of Arkansas at Pine Bluff	AR	25
University of Arkansas Main Campus	AR	24
Azusa Pacific University	CA	30
California State University-Bakersfield	CA	34
California State University-Chico	CA	34
California State University-Dominguez Hills	CA	34
California State University-East Bay	CA	34
California State University-Fresno	CA	35
California State University-Fullerton	CA	35
California State University-Long Beach	CA	35
California State University-Los Angeles	CA	35
@California State University-Monterey Bay	CA	35
California State University-Northridge	CA	35
California State University-Sacramento	CA	36
California State University-San Bernardino	CA	36
California State University-Stanislaus	CA	36
Humboldt State University	CA	36
La Sierra University	CA	53
Loma Linda University	CA	54
Pacific Union College	CA	60
@Point Loma Nazarene University	CA	62
San Diego State University	CA	37
San Francisco State University	CA	37
San Jose State University	CA	37
University of California-Berkeley	CA	73
University of California-Los Angeles	CA	74
University of Southern California	CA	76
Whittier College	CA	79
Colorado State University	CO	83
Colorado State University-Pueblo	CO	83
Metropolitan State University of Denver	CO	86
University of Denver	CO	89
Central Connecticut State University	CT	90
Eastern Connecticut State University	CT	90
Sacred Heart University	CT	94
Southern Connecticut State University	CT	90
University of Connecticut	CT	94
University of Saint Joseph	CT	95
Western Connecticut State University	CT	91
Delaware State University	DE	96
Catholic University of America, The	DC	97
Gallaudet University	DC	98
Howard University	DC	98
University of the District of Columbia	DC	100
Barry University	FL	101
Florida Agricultural and Mechanical University	FL	118
Florida Atlantic University	FL	119
Florida Gulf Coast University	FL	119
Florida International University	FL	119
Florida Memorial University	FL	109
Florida State University	FL	119
Saint Leo University	FL	116
Southeastern University	FL	118
University of Central Florida	FL	120
University of South Florida	FL	121
University of West Florida	FL	121
@Warner University	FL	123
Albany State University	GA	124
Augusta State University	GA	125
Clark Atlanta University	GA	127
Dalton State College	GA	128
Georgia State University	GA	131
Kennesaw State University	GA	133
Savannah State University	GA	136
Thomas University	GA	138
University of Georgia	GA	138
Valdosta State University	GA	139
University of Guam	GU	559
Brigham Young University Hawaii	HI	140
Hawaii Pacific University	HI	140
University of Hawaii at Manoa	HI	141
Boise State University	ID	142
Brigham Young University-Idaho	ID	143
Idaho State University	ID	143
Lewis-Clark State College	ID	144
Northwest Nazarene University	ID	144
Aurora University	IL	145
Bradley University	IL	146
Chicago State University	IL	146
DePaul University	IL	149
Dominican University	IL	150
Governors State University	IL	151
Illinois State University	IL	153
@Lewis University	IL	156
Loyola University Chicago	IL	157
MacMurray College	IL	157
Northeastern Illinois University	IL	160
Olivet Nazarene University	IL	161
St. Augustine College	IL	163
Southern Illinois University Carbondale	IL	165
Southern Illinois University Edwardsville	IL	165
Trinity Christian College	IL	166
University of Chicago	IL	166
University of Illinois at Chicago	IL	167
University of Illinois at Springfield	IL	167
University of Illinois at Urbana-Champaign	IL	167
University of St. Francis	IL	167
Western Illinois University	IL	168
Anderson University	IN	169
Ball State University	IN	169
Goshen College	IN	171
Huntington University	IN	173
Indiana State University	IN	173
Indiana University-Purdue University Indianapolis	IN	174
Indiana Wesleyan University	IN	175
Manchester University	IN	177
Saint Mary's College	IN	179
Taylor University	IN	180
University of Indianapolis	IN	180
University of Saint Francis	IN	181
University of Southern Indiana	IN	181
Valparaiso University	IN	181
Briar Cliff University	IA	183
Buena Vista University	IA	183
@Clarke University	IA	183
Dordt College	IA	184
@Loras College	IA	187
Luther College	IA	187
Mount Mercy University	IA	187
Northwestern College	IA	188
St. Ambrose University	IA	188
University of Iowa	IA	182
University of Northern Iowa	IA	182
Wartburg College	IA	189
Bethel College	KS	191
Fort Hays State University	KS	192
Kansas State University	KS	194
Newman University	KS	195
Pittsburg State University	KS	196
University of Kansas Main Campus	KS	197
Washburn University	KS	197
Wichita State University	KS	198
Asbury University	KY	198
Brescia University	KY	199
Campbellsville University	KY	199
Eastern Kentucky University	KY	200
Kentucky Christian University	KY	201
Kentucky State University	KY	203
Morehead State University	KY	204
Murray State University	KY	205
Northern Kentucky University	KY	205
Spalding University	KY	206
Union College	KY	207
University of Kentucky	KY	207
University of Louisville	KY	207
@University of Pikeville	KY	207
Western Kentucky University	KY	208
Grambling State University	LA	215
Louisiana College	LA	209
Louisiana State University and Agricultural and Mechanical College	LA	212
Northwestern State University	LA	216
Southeastern Louisiana University	LA	216
Southern University and A&M College	LA	214
Southern University at New Orleans	LA	214
Tulane University	LA	215
University of Louisiana at Monroe	LA	216
University of Maine	ME	220
University of Maine at Presque Isle	ME	220
University of New England	ME	221
University of Southern Maine	ME	220
Bowie State University	MD	228
Coppin State University	MD	228
Frostburg State University	MD	228
Hood College	MD	223
McDaniel College	MD	224
Morgan State University	MD	224
Salisbury University	MD	228
@Sojourner-Douglass College	MD	226
University of Maryland Baltimore	MD	227
University of Maryland Baltimore County	MD	227
Anna Maria College	MA	230
Boston College	MA	232
Boston University	MA	232
Bridgewater State University	MA	237
College of Our Lady of the Elms	MA	233
Eastern Nazarene College	MA	234
Gordon College	MA	235
Regis College	MA	244
Salem State University	MA	238
Simmons College	MA	244
Smith College	MA	244
Springfield College	MA	244
Western New England University	MA	246
Westfield State University	MA	238
Wheelock College	MA	246
Adrian College	MI	246
Andrews University	MI	247
Calvin College	MI	249
Central Michigan University	MI	249
Cornerstone University	MI	250
Eastern Michigan University	MI	250
Ferris State University	MI	250
Grand Valley State University	MI	251
Hope College	MI	252
Kuyper College	MI	253
Madonna University	MI	254
Marygrove College	MI	254
Michigan State University	MI	255
Northern Michigan University	MI	256
Oakland University	MI	256
Saginaw Valley State University	MI	257
Siena Heights University	MI	258
Spring Arbor University	MI	258
University of Detroit Mercy	MI	258
University of Michigan-Ann Arbor	MI	259
University of Michigan-Flint	MI	259
Wayne State University	MI	260
Western Michigan University	MI	260
Augsburg College	MN	261
Bemidji State University	MN	265
Bethel University	MN	261
College of Saint Scholastica, The	MN	262
Concordia College	MN	262
Metropolitan State University	MN	267
Minnesota State University Moorhead	MN	267
Minnesota State University, Mankato	MN	267
@North Central University	MN	270
St. Catherine University	MN	270
St. Cloud State University	MN	269
St. Olaf College	MN	271
Southwest Minnesota State University	MN	269
University of Minnesota Duluth	MN	271
University of Minnesota-Twin Cities	MN	272
University of Saint Thomas	MN	272
Winona State University	MN	269
Alcorn State University	MS	272
Delta State University	MS	273
Jackson State University	MS	274
Mississippi College	MS	275
Mississippi State University	MS	275
Mississippi Valley State University	MS	276
Rust College	MS	276
University of Mississippi	MS	277
University of Southern Mississippi	MS	277
Avila University	MO	278
Evangel University	MO	281
@Fontbonne University	MO	281
Lindenwood University	MO	283
Missouri State University	MO	286
Missouri Western State University	MO	286
Park University	MO	287
Saint Louis University	MO	289
Southeast Missouri State University	MO	289

@Southwest Baptist University ... MO ... 290
University of Central Missouri ... MO ... 290
University of Missouri - Columbia ... MO ... 291
University of Missouri - Kansas City ... MO ... 291
University of Missouri - Saint Louis ... MO ... 291
Washington University in St. Louis ... MO ... 292
William Woods University ... MO ... 293
Salish Kootenai College ... MT ... 296
University of Montana - Missoula, The ... MT ... 294
Chadron State College ... NE ... 299
Creighton University ... NE ... 297
Nebraska Wesleyan University ... NE ... 299
Union College ... NE ... 300
University of Nebraska at Kearney ... NE ... 300
University of Nebraska at Omaha ... NE ... 301
University of Nevada, Las Vegas ... NV ... 302
University of Nevada, Reno ... NV ... 303
Plymouth State University ... NH ... 307
University of New Hampshire ... NH ... 306
Centenary College ... NJ ... 308
Georgian Court University ... NJ ... 310
Kean University ... NJ ... 311
Monmouth University ... NJ ... 311
Ramapo College of New Jersey ... NJ ... 313
Richard Stockton College of New Jersey, The ... NJ ... 313
Rutgers the State University of New Jersey New Brunswick Campus ... NJ ... 314
Rutgers the State University of New Jersey Newark Campus ... NJ ... 314
Seton Hall University ... NJ ... 315
Eastern New Mexico University Main Campus ... NM ... 318
New Mexico Highlands University ... NM ... 318
New Mexico State University Main Campus . NM ... 319
Western New Mexico University ... NM ... 321
Adelphi University ... NY ... 322
@City University of New York College of Staten Island ... NY ... 327
City University of New York Herbert H. Lehman College ... NY ... 327
City University of New York Hunter College . NY ... 327
@City University of New York Medgar Evers College ... NY ... 328
City University of New York York College ... NY ... 329
College of New Rochelle, The ... NY ... 330
College of Saint Rose, The ... NY ... 330
Columbia University in the City of New York NY ... 330
Concordia College ... NY ... 330
Daemen College ... NY ... 331
Dominican College of Blauvelt ... NY ... 332
Fordham University ... NY ... 334
Iona College ... NY ... 336
Keuka College ... NY ... 337
Long Island University Brooklyn Campus ... NY ... 338
Long Island University C.W. Post Campus ... NY ... 339
Marist College ... NY ... 340
Mercy College ... NY ... 340
Molloy College ... NY ... 341
Nazareth College of Rochester ... NY ... 342
New York University ... NY ... 344
Niagara University ... NY ... 344
Nyack College ... NY ... 344
Roberts Wesleyan College ... NY ... 347
Siena College ... NY ... 350
Skidmore College ... NY ... 351
State University of New York at Binghamton NY ... 351
State University of New York at Fredonia ... NY ... 352
State University of New York at Stony Brook NY ... 352
State University of New York College at Buffalo ... NY ... 353
State University of New York College at Plattsburgh ... NY ... 354
State University of New York, The College at Brockport ... NY ... 352
Syracuse University Main Campus ... NY ... 357
Touro College ... NY ... 358
University at Albany, SUNY ... NY ... 351
University at Buffalo-SUNY ... NY ... 351
Yeshiva University ... NY ... 361
Appalachian State University ... NC ... 377
Barton College ... NC ... 362
Bennett College ... NC ... 362
Campbell University ... NC ... 362
East Carolina University ... NC ... 377
Elizabeth City State University ... NC ... 377
Fayetteville State University ... NC ... 377
Johnson C. Smith University ... NC ... 366
Livingstone College ... NC ... 366
Mars Hill College ... NC ... 366
Meredith College ... NC ... 367
Methodist University ... NC ... 367
North Carolina Agricultural and Technical State University ... NC ... 378
North Carolina Central University ... NC ... 378
North Carolina State University ... NC ... 378
Shaw University ... NC ... 376
University of North Carolina at Chapel Hill ... NC ... 378
University of North Carolina at Charlotte ... NC ... 379
University of North Carolina at Greensboro .. NC ... 379
University of North Carolina at Pembroke ... NC ... 379
University of North Carolina Wilmington ... NC ... 379
Warren Wilson College ... NC ... 380
Western Carolina University ... NC ... 380
Winston-Salem State University ... NC ... 380
Minot State University ... ND ... 382
University of Mary ... ND ... 383
University of North Dakota Main Campus ... ND ... 381
Ashland University ... OH ... 384
Bluffton University ... OH ... 385
Bowling Green State University ... OH ... 385
Capital University ... OH ... 386
Case Western Reserve University ... OH ... 386
Cedarville University ... OH ... 386
Cleveland State University ... OH ... 388
College of Mount St. Joseph ... OH ... 388
Defiance College, The ... OH ... 389
Franciscan University of Steubenville ... OH ... 391
Lourdes University ... OH ... 395
Malone University ... OH ... 395
Miami University ... OH ... 396
Mount Vernon Nazarene University ... OH ... 396
Ohio Dominican University ... OH ... 398
Ohio State University Main Campus, The ... OH ... 398
Ohio University Main Campus ... OH ... 399
@Union Institute & University ... OH ... 402
University of Akron, Main Campus, The ... OH ... 403
University of Cincinnati Main Campus ... OH ... 403
University of Findlay, The ... OH ... 404
University of Rio Grande ... OH ... 404
University of Toledo ... OH ... 404
Ursuline College ... OH ... 405
Wright State University Main Campus ... OH ... 406
Xavier University ... OH ... 406
Youngstown State University ... OH ... 406
East Central University ... OK ... 407
Northeastern State University ... OK ... 409
Northwestern Oklahoma State University ... OK ... 409
Oral Roberts University ... OK ... 411
Southwestern Oklahoma State University ... OK ... 412
University of Oklahoma Norman Campus ... OK ... 413
Concordia University ... OR ... 415
George Fox University ... OR ... 415
Pacific University ... OR ... 419
Portland State University ... OR ... 418
University of Portland ... OR ... 420
Alvernia University ... PA ... 421
Bloomsburg University of Pennsylvania ... PA ... 441
Bryn Mawr College ... PA ... 423
Cabrini College ... PA ... 424
California University of Pennsylvania ... PA ... 441
Carlow University ... PA ... 424
Cedar Crest College ... PA ... 425
Chatham University ... PA ... 425
Eastern University ... PA ... 428
Edinboro University of Pennsylvania ... PA ... 442
Elizabethtown College ... PA ... 428
Gannon University ... PA ... 429
Juniata College ... PA ... 432
Kutztown University of Pennsylvania ... PA ... 443
La Salle University ... PA ... 432
Lock Haven University ... PA ... 443
Mansfield University of Pennsylvania ... PA ... 443
Marywood University ... PA ... 435
Mercyhurst University ... PA ... 436
Messiah College ... PA ... 436
Millersville University of Pennsylvania ... PA ... 443
Misericordia University ... PA ... 436
Philadelphia Biblical University ... PA ... 444
Saint Francis University ... PA ... 446
Seton Hill University ... PA ... 447
Shippensburg University of Pennsylvania ... PA ... 443
Slippery Rock University of Pennsylvania ... PA ... 443
Temple University ... PA ... 447
University of Pennsylvania ... PA ... 448
University of Pittsburgh ... PA ... 449
Valley Forge Christian College ... PA ... 450
West Chester University of Pennsylvania ... PA ... 444
Widener University ... PA ... 451
Inter American University of Puerto Rico Arecibo Campus ... PR ... 563
Inter American University of Puerto Rico Fajardo Campus ... PR ... 563
Inter American University of Puerto Rico Metropolitan Campus ... PR ... 563
Pontifical Catholic University of Puerto Rico, The ... PR ... 565
@Universidad del Este ... PR ... 565
University of Puerto Rico-Humacao ... PR ... 567
University of Puerto Rico-Rio Piedras Campus ... PR ... 568
University of the Sacred Heart ... PR ... 568
Providence College ... RI ... 453
Rhode Island College ... RI ... 454
Salve Regina University ... RI ... 454
Benedict College ... SC ... 455
Coker College ... SC ... 457
Columbia College ... SC ... 457
Limestone College ... SC ... 459
South Carolina State University ... SC ... 460
University of South Carolina Columbia ... SC ... 462
Winthrop University ... SC ... 463
Oglala Lakota College ... SD ... 465
Presentation College ... SD ... 465
University of Sioux Falls ... SD ... 466
University of South Dakota, The ... SD ... 465
Austin Peay State University ... TN ... 473
Belmont University ... TN ... 467
East Tennessee State University ... TN ... 473
Freed-Hardeman University ... TN ... 469
Lincoln Memorial University ... TN ... 470
Lipscomb University ... TN ... 470
Middle Tennessee State University ... TN ... 473
Southern Adventist University ... TN ... 473
Tennessee State University ... TN ... 474
@Trevecca Nazarene University ... TN ... 476
Union University ... TN ... 477
University of Memphis, The ... TN ... 474
University of Tennessee at Chattanooga ... TN ... 477
University of Tennessee at Martin ... TN ... 477
University of Tennessee, Knoxville ... TN ... 477
Abilene Christian University ... TX ... 478
@Angelo State University ... TX ... 480
Baylor University ... TX ... 482
Hardin-Simmons University ... TX ... 487
Howard Payne University ... TX ... 488
Lamar University ... TX ... 501
Lubbock Christian University ... TX ... 490
Midwestern State University ... TX ... 491
Our Lady of the Lake University ... TX ... 492
Prairie View A & M University ... TX ... 496
St. Edward's University ... TX ... 493
Stephen F. Austin State University ... TX ... 496
Tarleton State University ... TX ... 497
Texas A & M University - Commerce ... TX ... 498
Texas A & M University - Kingsville ... TX ... 498
Texas Christian University ... TX ... 499
Texas Southern University ... TX ... 500
Texas State University-San Marcos ... TX ... 501
Texas Tech University ... TX ... 502
Texas Woman's University ... TX ... 502
University of Houston ... TX ... 503
University of Houston - Clear Lake ... TX ... 503
University of Houston - Downtown ... TX ... 503
University of Mary Hardin-Baylor ... TX ... 504
University of North Texas ... TX ... 504
University of Texas at Arlington, The ... TX ... 505
University of Texas at Austin ... TX ... 505
University of Texas at El Paso ... TX ... 506
University of Texas at San Antonio ... TX ... 506
University of Texas of the Permian Basin ... TX ... 507
University of Texas - Pan American ... TX ... 506
West Texas A & M University ... TX ... 499
Brigham Young University ... UT ... 509
University of Utah, The ... UT ... 511
Utah State University ... UT ... 511
Weber State University ... UT ... 511
Castleton State College ... VT ... 515
@Champlain College ... VT ... 513
University of Vermont ... VT ... 514
Christopher Newport University ... VA ... 517
Eastern Mennonite University ... VA ... 518
Ferrum College ... VA ... 519
George Mason University ... VA ... 519
James Madison University ... VA ... 520
Longwood University ... VA ... 521
@Mary Baldwin College ... VA ... 521
Norfolk State University ... VA ... 522
Radford University ... VA ... 523
Virginia Commonwealth University ... VA ... 526
Virginia Intermont College ... VA ... 529
@Virginia State University ... VA ... 529
Virginia Union University ... VA ... 530
@Virginia Wesleyan College ... VA ... 530
Eastern Washington University ... WA ... 533
Heritage University ... WA ... 535
Pacific Lutheran University ... WA ... 536
Seattle University ... WA ... 538
University of Washington ... WA ... 539
Walla Walla University ... WA ... 539
Bethany College ... WV ... 540
Concord University ... WV ... 543
Marshall University ... WV ... 544
Mountain State University ... WV ... 541
Shepherd University ... WV ... 544
West Virginia State University ... WV ... 544
West Virginia University ... WV ... 545
Carthage College ... WI ... 546
Concordia University Wisconsin ... WI ... 547
Marian University ... WI ... 548
Mount Mary College ... WI ... 549
University of Wisconsin-Eau Claire ... WI ... 551
University of Wisconsin-Green Bay ... WI ... 551
University of Wisconsin-Madison ... WI ... 550
University of Wisconsin-Milwaukee ... WI ... 551
University of Wisconsin-Oshkosh ... WI ... 551
University of Wisconsin-River Falls ... WI ... 552
@University of Wisconsin-Stevens Point ... WI ... 552
University of Wisconsin-Superior ... WI ... 552
University of Wisconsin-Whitewater ... WI ... 553
Viterbo University ... WI ... 553
University of Wyoming ... WY ... 556

TEAC: Teacher Education Accreditation Council: teacher education (B,M,D)

@Northcentral University ... AZ ... 16
University of Phoenix ... AZ ... 19
Chapman University ... CA ... 39
Adams State University ... CO ... 80
Colorado State University ... CO ... 83
Colorado State University-Pueblo ... CO ... 83
Fort Lewis College ... CO ... 84
Regis University ... CO ... 87
@Western State Colorado University ... CO ... 89
@Strayer University ... DC ... 99
@Flagler College ... FL ... 107
@Jose Maria Vargas University ... FL ... 112
@University of Miami ... FL ... 122
@University of Hawaii at Hilo ... HI ... 141
@American InterContinental University ... IL ... 145
@Greenville College ... IL ... 151
@Knox College ... IL ... 155
@American College of Education ... IN ... 169
@Buena Vista University ... IA ... 183
St. Ambrose University ... IA ... 188
@Centenary College of Louisiana ... LA ... 208
Tulane University ... LA ... 215
University of Southern Maine ... ME ... 220
Boston College ... MA ... 232
@Cambridge College ... MA ... 233
Lesley University ... MA ... 236
@University of Massachusetts Boston ... MA ... 236
@Worcester State University ... MA ... 238
@Adrian College ... MI ... 246
Albion College ... MI ... 247
@Alma College ... MI ... 247
@Aquinas College ... MI ... 247
Baker College of Flint ... MI ... 248
@Calvin College ... MI ... 249
Central Michigan University ... MI ... 249
@Cornerstone University ... MI ... 250
@Ferris State University ... MI ... 250
@Hope College ... MI ... 252
@Lake Superior State University ... MI ... 253
@Marygrove College ... MI ... 254
Michigan State University ... MI ... 255
Michigan Technological University ... MI ... 255
Northern Michigan University ... MI ... 256
Oakland University ... MI ... 256
@Olivet College ... MI ... 257
@Robert B. Miller College ... MI ... 257
@Rochester College ... MI ... 257
@Siena Heights University ... MI ... 258
Spring Arbor University ... MI ... 258
@University of Detroit Mercy ... MI ... 258
University of Michigan-Ann Arbor ... MI ... 259
University of Michigan-Dearborn ... MI ... 259
@Wayne State University ... MI ... 260
Bethel University ... MN ... 261
College of Saint Scholastica, The ... MN ... 262
@Concordia College ... MN ... 262
@Rust College ... MS ... 276
@Lindenwood University ... MO ... 283
Rockhurst University ... MO ... 288
@University of Missouri - Columbia ... MO ... 291
William Woods University ... MO ... 293
Montana State University ... MT ... 295
University of Nebraska - Lincoln ... NE ... 300
University of New Hampshire ... NH ... 306
Bloomfield College ... NJ ... 307
Caldwell College ... NJ ... 308
Centenary College ... NJ ... 308
College of Saint Elizabeth ... NJ ... 308
@Drew University ... NJ ... 309
Fairleigh Dickinson University ... NJ ... 310
Felician College ... NJ ... 310
Georgian Court University ... NJ ... 310
New Jersey City University ... NJ ... 312
Princeton University ... NJ ... 312
Ramapo College of New Jersey ... NJ ... 313
Richard Stockton College of New Jersey, The ... NJ ... 313
Rutgers the State University of New Jersey Camden Campus ... NJ ... 314
Rutgers the State University of New Jersey New Brunswick Campus ... NJ ... 314
Rutgers the State University of New Jersey Newark Campus ... NJ ... 314
Saint Peter's College ... NJ ... 314
Thomas Edison State College ... NJ ... 316
Alfred University ... NY ... 322
Bard College ... NY ... 323
@Barnard College ... NY ... 323
@Cazenovia College ... NY ... 325
Colgate University ... NY ... 329
College of Mount Saint Vincent ... NY ... 330
@College of New Rochelle, The ... NY ... 330
@Cornell University ... NY ... 331
@Daemen College ... NY ... 331
Dominican College of Blauvelt ... NY ... 332
@Elmira College ... NY ... 332
Hartwick College ... NY ... 335
@Hobart and William Smith Colleges ... NY ... 335
Hofstra University ... NY ... 335
Houghton College ... NY ... 336
@Keuka College ... NY ... 337
Le Moyne College ... NY ... 338
LIU Riverhead ... NY ... 339
Long Island University Brooklyn Campus ... NY ... 338
Long Island University C.W. Post Campus ... NY ... 339
Long Island University Hudson Graduate Center at Westchester ... NY ... 339
Manhattan College ... NY ... 339
Medaille College ... NY ... 340
Nazareth College of Rochester ... NY ... 342
New York University ... NY ... 344
@Pratt Institute ... NY ... 346
@Roberts Wesleyan College ... NY ... 347
Rochester Institute of Technology ... NY ... 347
@St. Francis College ... NY ... 348
St. John's University ... NY ... 348
@Saint Joseph's College, New York ... NY ... 349
St. Lawrence University ... NY ... 349
@Sarah Lawrence College ... NY ... 350
@Skidmore College ... NY ... 351
State University of New York at Binghamton NY ... 351
State University of New York College at Plattsburgh ... NY ... 354
State University of New York Empire State College ... NY ... 355
@Touro College ... NY ... 358
Union Graduate College ... NY ... 358

TED: National Council for Accreditation of Teacher Education: teacher education (B,M,S,D)

University of Montana - Missoula, The ... MT ... 294
University of Montana Western, The ... MT ... 294
Chadron State College ... NE ... 299
Concordia University ... NE ... 297
Creighton University ... NE ... 297
Doane College ... NE ... 297
Hastings College ... NE ... 298
Nebraska Wesleyan University ... NE ... 299
Peru State College ... NE ... 299
Union College ... NE ... 300
University of Nebraska at Kearney ... NE ... 300
University of Nebraska at Omaha ... NE ... 301
Wayne State College ... NE ... 299
York College ... NE ... 301
University of Nevada, Reno ... NV ... 303
Keene State College ... NH ... 306
Plymouth State University ... NH ... 307
College of New Jersey, The ... NJ ... 308
Kean University ... NJ ... 311
Monmouth University ... NJ ... 311
Montclair State University ... NJ ... 311
New Jersey City University ... NJ ... 312
Rider University ... NJ ... 313
Rowan University ... NJ ... 314
Seton Hall University ... NJ ... 315
William Paterson University of New Jersey ... NJ ... 317
Eastern New Mexico University Main Campus ... NM ... 318
New Mexico Highlands University ... NM ... 318
New Mexico State University Main Campus ... NM ... 319
University of New Mexico Main Campus ... NM ... 321
Western New Mexico University ... NM ... 321
Adelphi University ... NY ... 322
Canisius College ... NY ... 325
City University of New York Brooklyn College ... NY ... 326
City University of New York College of Staten Island ... NY ... 327
City University of New York Herbert H. Lehman College ... NY ... 327
City University of New York Hunter College ... NY ... 327
City University of New York Medgar Evers College ... NY ... 328
City University of New York Queens College ... NY ... 328
City University of New York The City College ... NY ... 326
City University of New York York College ... NY ... 329
College of Saint Rose, The ... NY ... 330
Concordia College ... NY ... 330
Dowling College ... NY ... 332
Five Towns College ... NY ... 334
Fordham University ... NY ... 334
Iona College ... NY ... 336
Manhattanville College ... NY ... 339
Metropolitan College of New York ... NY ... 341
Molloy College ... NY ... 341
Mount Saint Mary College ... NY ... 342
New York City College of Technology/City University of New York ... NY ... 328
New York Institute of Technology ... NY ... 343
Niagara University ... NY ... 344
Nyack College ... NY ... 344
Pace University ... NY ... 345
Relay Graduate School of Education ... NY ... 347
Sage Colleges, The ... NY ... 348
St. Bonaventure University ... NY ... 348
St. John Fisher College ... NY ... 348
St. Thomas Aquinas College ... NY ... 349
Siena College ... NY ... 350
State University of New York at Fredonia ... NY ... 352
State University of New York at New Paltz ... NY ... 352
State University of New York at Stony Brook ... NY ... 352
State University of New York College at Buffalo ... NY ... 353
State University of New York College at Cortland ... NY ... 353
State University of New York College at Geneseo ... NY ... 353
State University of New York College at Old Westbury ... NY ... 353
State University of New York College at Oneonta ... NY ... 353
State University of New York College at Oswego ... NY ... 354
State University of New York College at Potsdam ... NY ... 354
State University of New York, The College at Brockport ... NY ... 352
Syracuse University Main Campus ... NY ... 357
Teachers College, Columbia University ... NY ... 357
University of Rochester ... NY ... 359
Wagner College ... NY ... 360
Appalachian State University ... NC ... 377
Barton College ... NC ... 362
Bennett College ... NC ... 362
Campbell University ... NC ... 362
Catawba College ... NC ... 363
Chowan University ... NC ... 363
Duke University ... NC ... 364
East Carolina University ... NC ... 377
Elizabeth City State University ... NC ... 377
Elon University ... NC ... 364
Fayetteville State University ... NC ... 377
Gardner-Webb University ... NC ... 364
Greensboro College ... NC ... 364
High Point University ... NC ... 365
Johnson C. Smith University ... NC ... 366
Lenoir-Rhyne University ... NC ... 366
Livingstone College ... NC ... 366
Mars Hill College ... NC ... 366
Meredith College ... NC ... 367
Methodist University ... NC ... 367
Montreat College ... NC ... 367
North Carolina Agricultural and Technical State University ... NC ... 378
North Carolina Central University ... NC ... 378
North Carolina State University ... NC ... 378
North Carolina Wesleyan College ... NC ... 375
Pfeiffer University ... NC ... 375
Queens University of Charlotte ... NC ... 376
St. Andrews University ... NC ... 376
Saint Augustine's University ... NC ... 376
Salem College ... NC ... 376
Shaw University ... NC ... 376
University of North Carolina at Asheville ... NC ... 378
University of North Carolina at Chapel Hill ... NC ... 378
University of North Carolina at Charlotte ... NC ... 379
University of North Carolina at Greensboro ... NC ... 379
University of North Carolina at Pembroke ... NC ... 379
University of North Carolina Wilmington ... NC ... 379
Wake Forest University ... NC ... 380
Western Carolina University ... NC ... 380
Wingate University ... NC ... 380
Winston-Salem State University ... NC ... 380
Dickinson State University ... ND ... 381
Mayville State University ... ND ... 381
Minot State University ... ND ... 382
North Dakota State University Main Campus ... ND ... 382
University of North Dakota Main Campus ... ND ... 381
Valley City State University ... ND ... 382
Antioch University Midwest ... OH ... 384
Ashland University ... OH ... 384
Baldwin Wallace University ... OH ... 384
Bluffton University ... OH ... 385
Bowling Green State University ... OH ... 385
Capital University ... OH ... 386
Cedarville University ... OH ... 386
Central State University ... OH ... 387
Cleveland State University ... OH ... 388
College of Wooster, The ... OH ... 388
Defiance College, The ... OH ... 389
Franciscan University of Steubenville ... OH ... 391
Heidelberg University ... OH ... 391
Hiram College ... OH ... 391
John Carroll University ... OH ... 392
Kent State University Main Campus ... OH ... 393
Malone University ... OH ... 395
Marietta College ... OH ... 395
Miami University ... OH ... 396
Mount Vernon Nazarene University ... OH ... 396
Muskingum University ... OH ... 397
Notre Dame College ... OH ... 397
Ohio Dominican University ... OH ... 398
Ohio Northern University ... OH ... 398
Ohio State University Main Campus, The ... OH ... 398
Ohio University Main Campus ... OH ... 399
Ohio Wesleyan University ... OH ... 400
Otterbein University ... OH ... 400
Shawnee State University ... OH ... 401
University of Akron, Main Campus, The ... OH ... 403
University of Cincinnati Main Campus ... OH ... 403
University of Dayton ... OH ... 404
University of Findlay, The ... OH ... 404
University of Mount Union ... OH ... 404
University of Rio Grande ... OH ... 404
University of Toledo ... OH ... 404
Ursuline College ... OH ... 405
Walsh University ... OH ... 405
Wittenberg University ... OH ... 406
Wright State University Main Campus ... OH ... 406
Youngstown State University ... OH ... 406
Cameron University ... OK ... 407
East Central University ... OK ... 407
Langston University ... OK ... 408
Northeastern State University ... OK ... 409
Northwestern Oklahoma State University ... OK ... 409
Oklahoma Baptist University ... OK ... 409
Oklahoma Christian University ... OK ... 409
Oklahoma Panhandle State University ... OK ... 410
Oklahoma State University ... OK ... 410
Oklahoma Wesleyan University ... OK ... 411
Oral Roberts University ... OK ... 411
Southeastern Oklahoma State University ... OK ... 412
Southern Nazarene University ... OK ... 412
Southwestern Oklahoma State University ... OK ... 412
University of Central Oklahoma ... OK ... 413
University of Oklahoma Norman Campus ... OK ... 413
University of Science and Arts of Oklahoma ... OK ... 413
George Fox University ... OR ... 415
Lewis and Clark College ... OR ... 416
Oregon State University ... OR ... 418
Pacific University ... OR ... 419
Portland State University ... OR ... 418
University of Portland ... OR ... 420
Western Oregon University ... OR ... 419
Willamette University ... OR ... 421
Bloomsburg University of Pennsylvania ... PA ... 441
California University of Pennsylvania ... PA ... 441
Clarion University of Pennsylvania ... PA ... 442
Duquesne University ... PA ... 428
East Stroudsburg University of Pennsylvania ... PA ... 442
Edinboro University of Pennsylvania ... PA ... 442
Indiana University of Pennsylvania ... PA ... 442
King's College ... PA ... 432
Kutztown University of Pennsylvania ... PA ... 443
Lock Haven University ... PA ... 443
Mansfield University of Pennsylvania ... PA ... 443
Marywood University ... PA ... 435
Millersville University of Pennsylvania ... PA ... 443
Penn State Harrisburg ... PA ... 439
Penn State University Park ... PA ... 438
Shippensburg University of Pennsylvania ... PA ... 443
Slippery Rock University of Pennsylvania ... PA ... 443
University of Scranton, The ... PA ... 450
West Chester University of Pennsylvania ... PA ... 444
Widener University ... PA ... 451
University of Puerto Rico-Aguadilla ... PR ... 566
University of Puerto Rico at Arecibo ... PR ... 567
University of Puerto Rico at Bayamon ... PR ... 567
University of Puerto Rico at Cayey ... PR ... 567
University of Puerto Rico at Ponce ... PR ... 568
University of Puerto Rico at Utuado ... PR ... 568
University of Puerto Rico-Humacao ... PR ... 567
University of Puerto Rico-Mayaguez Campus ... PR ... 567
University of Puerto Rico-Rio Piedras Campus ... PR ... 568
Rhode Island College ... RI ... 454
University of Rhode Island ... RI ... 454
Anderson University ... SC ... 455
Benedict College ... SC ... 455
Charleston Southern University ... SC ... 456
Citadel, The Military College of South Carolina, The ... SC ... 456
Claflin University ... SC ... 456
Clemson University ... SC ... 456
Coastal Carolina University ... SC ... 456
College of Charleston ... SC ... 457
Columbia College ... SC ... 457
Converse College ... SC ... 457
Erskine College ... SC ... 458
Francis Marion University ... SC ... 458
Furman University ... SC ... 458
Lander University ... SC ... 459
Limestone College ... SC ... 459
Morris College ... SC ... 459
Newberry College ... SC ... 459
North Greenville University ... SC ... 460
Presbyterian College ... SC ... 460
South Carolina State University ... SC ... 460
Southern Wesleyan University ... SC ... 461
University of South Carolina Aiken ... SC ... 462
University of South Carolina Beaufort ... SC ... 462
University of South Carolina Columbia ... SC ... 462
University of South Carolina Upstate ... SC ... 463
Winthrop University ... SC ... 463
Augustana College ... SD ... 464
Black Hills State University ... SD ... 465
Dakota State University ... SD ... 465
Northern State University ... SD ... 466
South Dakota State University ... SD ... 466
University of Sioux Falls ... SD ... 466
University of South Dakota, The ... SD ... 465
Austin Peay State University ... TN ... 473
Belmont University ... TN ... 467
Carson-Newman College ... TN ... 467
Christian Brothers University ... TN ... 467
Cumberland University ... TN ... 468
East Tennessee State University ... TN ... 473
Freed-Hardeman University ... TN ... 469
Lee University ... TN ... 470
LeMoyne-Owen College ... TN ... 470
Lipscomb University ... TN ... 470
Middle Tennessee State University ... TN ... 473
Milligan College ... TN ... 471
Southern Adventist University ... TN ... 473
Tennessee State University ... TN ... 474
Tennessee Technological University ... TN ... 474
Trevecca Nazarene University ... TN ... 476
Union University ... TN ... 477
University of Memphis, The ... TN ... 474
University of Tennessee at Chattanooga ... TN ... 477
University of Tennessee at Martin ... TN ... 477
University of Tennessee, Knoxville ... TN ... 477
Vanderbilt University ... TN ... 478
Angelo State University ... TX ... 480
Baylor University ... TX ... 482
Lamar University ... TX ... 501
Midwestern State University ... TX ... 491
Prairie View A & M University ... TX ... 496
Sam Houston State University ... TX ... 501
Stephen F. Austin State University ... TX ... 496
Texas Tech University ... TX ... 502
Trinity University ... TX ... 502
University of Houston ... TX ... 503
University of Houston - Clear Lake ... TX ... 503
University of North Texas ... TX ... 504
University of Texas at Arlington, The ... TX ... 505
University of Texas of the Permian Basin ... TX ... 507
Weber State University ... UT ... 511
Western Governors University ... UT ... 512
University of Vermont ... VT ... 514
College of William & Mary ... VA ... 518
Eastern Mennonite University ... VA ... 518
George Mason University ... VA ... 519
Hampton University ... VA ... 519
James Madison University ... VA ... 520
Liberty University ... VA ... 520
Longwood University ... VA ... 521
Marymount University ... VA ... 521
Norfolk State University ... VA ... 522
Old Dominion University ... VA ... 522
Radford University ... VA ... 523
Virginia Commonwealth University ... VA ... 526
Virginia Polytechnic Institute and State University ... VA ... 529
Virginia State University ... VA ... 529
Virginia Union University ... VA ... 530
Gonzaga University ... WA ... 534
Pacific Lutheran University ... WA ... 536
Seattle Pacific University ... WA ... 537
Seattle University ... WA ... 538
Western Washington University ... WA ... 539
Whitworth University ... WA ... 540
Bethany College ... WV ... 540
Bluefield State College ... WV ... 543
Concord University ... WV ... 543
Fairmont State University ... WV ... 543
Glenville State College ... WV ... 544
Marshall University ... WV ... 544
Shepherd University ... WV ... 544
West Liberty University ... WV ... 544
West Virginia State University ... WV ... 544
West Virginia University ... WV ... 545
West Virginia University at Parkersburg ... WV ... 545
West Virginia Wesleyan College ... WV ... 545
Alverno College ... WI ... 546
Cardinal Stritch University ... WI ... 546
Edgewood College ... WI ... 547
Marian University ... WI ... 548
Marquette University ... WI ... 548
University of Wisconsin-Platteville ... WI ... 552
University of Wisconsin-Stout ... WI ... 552
University of Wisconsin-Whitewater ... WI ... 553
Viterbo University ... WI ... 553
University of Wyoming ... WY ... 556

THEA: National Association of Schools of Theatre: theatre (C,A,B,M,D)

Alabama State University ... AL ... 1
Auburn University ... AL ... 1
Jacksonville State University ... AL ... 4
University of Alabama at Birmingham ... AL ... 8
University of Alabama, The ... AL ... 8
University of Arizona ... AZ ... 18
University of Arkansas at Little Rock ... AR ... 24
University of Central Arkansas ... AR ... 25
AMDA College and Conservatory of the Performing Arts ... CA ... 27
American Academy of Dramatic Arts, Los Angeles Campus ... CA ... 27
California Institute of the Arts ... CA ... 32
California State University-Chico ... CA ... 34
California State University-Dominguez Hills ... CA ... 34
California State University-Fresno ... CA ... 35
California State University-Fullerton ... CA ... 35
California State University-Long Beach ... CA ... 35
California State University-Northridge ... CA ... 35
California State University-San Bernardino ... CA ... 36
California State University-Stanislaus ... CA ... 36
Chapman University ... CA ... 39
Dell'Arte International School of Physical Theatre ... CA ... 44
Loyola Marymount University ... CA ... 56
San Diego State University ... CA ... 37
San Francisco State University ... CA ... 37
San Jose State University ... CA ... 37
Theatre of Arts ... CA ... 72
University of California-Los Angeles ... CA ... 74
Vanguard University of Southern California ... CA ... 77
Metropolitan State University of Denver ... CO ... 86
University of Hartford ... CT ... 95
Howard University ... DC ... 98
Florida International University ... FL ... 119
Florida State University ... FL ... 119
Miami Dade College ... FL ... 113
University of Florida ... FL ... 120
University of South Florida ... FL ... 121
Columbus State University ... GA ... 127
Georgia Southern University ... GA ... 131
Kennesaw State University ... GA ... 133
University of Georgia ... GA ... 138
University of West Georgia ... GA ... 139
Valdosta State University ... GA ... 139
Boise State University ... ID ... 142
Idaho State University ... ID ... 143
Bradley University ... IL ... 146
Eastern Illinois University ... IL ... 150
Illinois State University ... IL ... 153
Loyola University Chicago ... IL ... 157
Northern Illinois University ... IL ... 160
Southern Illinois University Carbondale ... IL ... 165
Southern Illinois University Edwardsville ... IL ... 165
University of Illinois at Urbana-Champaign ... IL ... 167
Western Illinois University ... IL ... 168
Ball State University ... IN ... 169
Butler University ... IN ... 170
Indiana University Bloomington ... IN ... 173
Indiana University-Purdue University Fort Wayne ... IN ... 174
Purdue University Main Campus ... IN ... 178
Vincennes University ... IN ... 181
University of Iowa ... IA ... 182
Kansas State University ... KS ... 194
Morehead State University ... KY ... 204
Murray State University ... KY ... 205
University of Kentucky ... KY ... 207
University of Louisville ... KY ... 207
Western Kentucky University ... KY ... 208
Grambling State University ... LA ... 215
Louisiana State University and Agricultural and Mechanical College ... LA ... 212

Northwestern State University LA 216
University of New Orleans LA 213
Community College of Baltimore County, The MD 222
Towson University MD 228
College of the Holy Cross MA 233
Salem State University MA 238
Hope College MI 252
Oakland University MI 256
Wayne State University MI 260
Western Michigan University MI 260
Normandale Community College MN 268
St. Cloud State University MN 269
St. Olaf College MN 271
University of Minnesota-Twin Cities MN 272
Winona State University MN 269
Belhaven University MS 273
University of Mississippi MS 277
University of Southern Mississippi MS 277
Missouri State University MO 286
University of Missouri - Kansas City MO 291
University of Montana - Missoula, The MT 294
University of Nebraska - Lincoln NE 300
University of Nevada, Las Vegas NV 302
Kean University NJ 311
Montclair State University NJ 311
Rowan University NJ 314
University of New Mexico Main Campus NM 321
AMDA College and Conservatory of the Performing Arts NY 322
American Academy of Dramatic Arts NY 322
Ithaca College NY 336
State University of New York at Fredonia NY 352
State University of New York at New Paltz NY 352
State University of New York College at Buffalo NY 353
State University of New York College at Oswego NY 354
State University of New York, The College at Brockport NY 352
Appalachian State University NC 377
East Carolina University NC 377
Lees-McRae College NC 366
Mars Hill College NC 366
North Carolina Agricultural and Technical State University NC 378
North Carolina Central University NC 378
University of North Carolina at Greensboro NC 379
Western Carolina University NC 380
North Dakota State University Main Campus ND 382
University of North Dakota Main Campus ND 381
Bowling Green State University OH 385
Kent State University Main Campus OH 393
Miami University OH 396
Ohio State University Main Campus, The OH 398
Ohio University Main Campus OH 399
Otterbein University OH 400
Sinclair Community College OH 401
University of Cincinnati Main Campus OH 403
Youngstown State University OH 406
Oklahoma State University OK 410
University of Oklahoma Norman Campus OK 413
Portland State University OR 418
University of Portland OR 420
Bloomsburg University of Pennsylvania PA 441
California University of Pennsylvania PA 441
Indiana University of Pennsylvania PA 442
Lehigh University PA 434
Messiah College PA 436
Penn State University Park PA 438
Slippery Rock University of Pennsylvania PA 443
Temple University PA 447
University of Pittsburgh PA 449
West Chester University of Pennsylvania PA 444
Coastal Carolina University SC 456
College of Charleston SC 457
Francis Marion University SC 458
University of South Carolina Columbia SC 462
Winthrop University SC 463
University of South Dakota, The SD 465
University of Memphis, The TN 474
University of Tennessee at Chattanooga TN 477
Baylor University TX 482
Del Mar College TX 485
KD Studio-Actors Conservatory TX 489
Southern Methodist University TX 495
Stephen F. Austin State University TX 496
Texas Tech University TX 502
University of Texas - Pan American TX 506
University of the Incarnate Word TX 504
Brigham Young University UT 509
Snow College UT 512
Christopher Newport University VA 517
James Madison University VA 520
Longwood University VA 521
Old Dominion University VA 522
Radford University VA 523
Virginia Commonwealth University VA 526
Virginia Polytechnic Institute and State University VA 529
Davis & Elkins College WV 541
West Virginia University WV 545
Marquette University WI 548
University of Wisconsin-Madison WI 550
University of Wisconsin-Stevens Point WI 552
University of Wisconsin-Whitewater WI 553
Casper College WY 556

THEOL: Association of Theological Schools: theology (M,FP,D)

@Amridge University AL 1
Samford University AL 6
Phoenix Seminary AZ 17
American Baptist Seminary of the West CA 27
Azusa Pacific University CA 30
Biola University CA 31
Church Divinity School of the Pacific CA 40
Claremont School of Theology CA 40
Dominican School of Philosophy and Theology CA 45
Franciscan School of Theology CA 47
Fresno Pacific Biblical Seminary CA 47
Fuller Theological Seminary CA 48
Golden Gate Baptist Theological Seminary CA 48
Graduate Theological Union CA 48
International Theological Seminary CA 51
@La Sierra University CA 53
Logos Evangelical Seminary CA 54
Loyola Marymount University CA 56
Pacific Lutheran Theological Seminary CA 60
Pacific School of Religion CA 60
Saint John's Seminary CA 64
Saint Patrick's Seminary & University CA 64
San Francisco Theological Seminary CA 66
Santa Clara University CA 68
@Shepherd University School of Theology CA 69
Starr King School for the Ministry CA 71
Westminster Theological Seminary in California CA 78
@World Mission University CA 79
Denver Seminary CO 84
Iliff School of Theology CO 85
St. John Vianney Theological Seminary CO 88
Hartford Seminary CT 93
Yale University CT 96
Catholic University of America, The DC 97
Howard University DC 98
Pontifical Faculty of the Immaculate Conception at the Dominican House of S tudies DC 99
Washington Theological Union DC 100
Wesley Theological Seminary DC 100
Barry University FL 101
Knox Theological Seminary FL 112
&Reformed Theological Seminary FL 115
St. Vincent De Paul Regional Seminary FL 117
Columbia Theological Seminary GA 127
Emory University GA 129
Interdenominational Theological Center GA 132
Mercer University GA 134
Catholic Theological Union IL 146
Chicago Theological Seminary IL 146
Garrett-Evangelical Theological Seminary IL 151
Lincoln Christian University IL 156
Lutheran School of Theology at Chicago IL 157
McCormick Theological Seminary IL 157
Meadville Lombard Theological School IL 158
Moody Bible Institute IL 159
North Park University IL 159
Northern Seminary IL 160
Seabury-Western Theological Seminary IL 164
Trinity International University IL 166
University of Chicago IL 166
University of Saint Mary of the Lake-Mundelein Seminary IL 167
Anabaptist Mennonite Biblical Seminary IN 169
Anderson University IN 169
Bethany Theological Seminary IN 169
Christian Theological Seminary IN 170
Concordia Theological Seminary IN 170
Earlham College and Earlham School of Religion IN 171
Grace College and Seminary IN 171
Mid-America Reformed Seminary IN 178
Oakland City University IN 178
Saint Meinrad School of Theology IN 180
University of Notre Dame IN 180
University of Dubuque IA 189
Wartburg Theological Seminary IA 190
Central Baptist Theological Seminary KS 191
Asbury Theological Seminary KY 198
Lexington Theological Seminary KY 204
Louisville Presbyterian Theological Seminary KY 204
Southern Baptist Theological Seminary, The KY 206
New Orleans Baptist Theological Seminary LA 213
Notre Dame Seminary, Graduate School of Theology LA 214
Bangor Theological Seminary ME 217
Mount St. Mary's University MD 225
Saint Mary's Seminary and University MD 226
Washington Bible College/Capital Bible Seminary MD 229
Andover Newton Theological School MA 230
Blessed John XXIII National Seminary MA 231
Boston College MA 232
Boston University MA 232
Episcopal Divinity School MA 234
Gordon-Conwell Theological Seminary MA 235
Harvard University MA 235
Hellenic College-Holy Cross Greek Orthodox School of Theology MA 235
Saint John's Seminary MA 244
Andrews University MI 247
Calvin Theological Seminary MI 249
Cornerstone University MI 250
Ecumenical Theological Seminary MI 250
Moody Theological Seminary-Michigan MI 255
Sacred Heart Major Seminary MI 257
SS. Cyril and Methodius Seminary MI 258
Western Theological Seminary MI 260
Bethel University MN 261
Luther Seminary MN 264
Saint John's University MN 271
United Theological Seminary of the Twin Cities MN 271
University of Saint Thomas MN 272
Reformed Theological Seminary MS 276
Wesley Biblical Seminary MS 278
Aquinas Institute of Theology MO 278
Assemblies of God Theological Seminary MO 278
Concordia Seminary MO 280
Covenant Theological Seminary MO 280
Eden Theological Seminary MO 281
Kenrick-Glennon Seminary-Kenrick School of Theology MO 283
Midwestern Baptist Theological Seminary MO 285
Nazarene Theological Seminary MO 286
Saint Paul School of Theology MO 289
Urshan Graduate School of Theology MO 292
Drew University NJ 309
Immaculate Conception Seminary of Seton Hall University NJ 310
New Brunswick Theological Seminary NJ 312
Princeton Theological Seminary NJ 312
Christ the King Seminary NY 325
Colgate Rochester Crozer Divinity School NY 329
General Theological Seminary NY 334
New York Theological Seminary NY 344
Northeastern Seminary NY 344
Nyack College NY 344
Saint Bernard's School of Theology & Ministry NY 348
Saint Joseph's Seminary NY 349
Saint Vladimir's Orthodox Theological Seminary NY 349
Seminary of the Immaculate Conception NY 350
Union Theological Seminary NY 358
Campbell University NC 362
Carolina Graduate School of Divinity NC 363
Duke University NC 364
Gardner-Webb University NC 364
Hood Theological Seminary NC 365
&Reformed Theological Seminary NC 376
Shaw University NC 376
Southeastern Baptist Theological Seminary NC 377
Wake Forest University NC 380
Ashland University OH 384
Athenaeum of Ohio OH 384
Bexley Hall Seminary OH 385
Cincinnati Christian University OH 387
Methodist Theological School in Ohio OH 396
Payne Theological Seminary OH 401
Pontifical College Josephinum OH 401
Saint Mary Seminary and Graduate School of Theology OH 401
Trinity Lutheran Seminary OH 402
United Theological Seminary OH 403
Winebrenner Theological Seminary OH 406
Oral Roberts University OK 411
Phillips Theological Seminary OK 411
George Fox University OR 415
Mount Angel Seminary OR 417
Multnomah University OR 417
Western Seminary OR 421
Biblical Theological Seminary PA 422
Byzantine Catholic Seminary of SS. Cyril and Methodius PA 424
Evangelical Theological Seminary PA 429
Lancaster Theological Seminary PA 433
Lutheran Theological Seminary at Gettysburg PA 435
Lutheran Theological Seminary at Philadelphia PA 435
Moravian College PA 437
Palmer Theological Seminary of Eastern University PA 438
Pittsburgh Theological Seminary PA 444
@Reformed Episcopal Seminary PA 445
Reformed Presbyterian Theological Seminary PA 445
Saint Charles Borromeo Seminary PA 446
St. Tikhon's Orthodox Theological Seminary PA 446
Saint Vincent Seminary PA 446
Trinity Episcopal School for Ministry PA 448
Westminster Theological Seminary PA 451
Dominican Study Center of the Caribbean PR 561
Evangelical Seminary of Puerto Rico PR 562
Columbia International University SC 457
Erskine College SC 458
Lutheran Theological Southern Seminary of Lenoir-Rhyne University SC 459
Sioux Falls Seminary SD 465
Emmanuel Christian Seminary TN 468
Harding School of Theology TN 469
Lipscomb University TN 470
Memphis Theological Seminary TN 471
Pentecostal Theological Seminary TN 472
Sewanee: The University of the South TN 472
Vanderbilt University TN 478
Abilene Christian University TX 478
Austin Presbyterian Theological Seminary TX 481
Baptist Missionary Association Theological Seminary TX 481
Baylor University TX 482
Brite Divinity School TX 482
Dallas Theological Seminary TX 485
Hardin-Simmons University TX 487
Houston Graduate School of Theology TX 488
Oblate School of Theology TX 491
@Redeemer Theological Seminary TX 492
Seminary of the Southwest TX 494
Southern Methodist University TX 495
Southwestern Baptist Theological Seminary TX 495
University of St. Thomas TX 505
Baptist Theological Seminary at Richmond VA 516
Eastern Mennonite University VA 518
John Leland Center for Theological Studies, The VA 520
Protestant Episcopal Theological Seminary in Virginia VA 522
&Reformed Theological Seminary VA 523
Regent University VA 523
Union Presbyterian Seminary VA 525
Virginia Union University VA 530
@Washington Baptist University VA 530
@Seattle School of Theology and Psychology, The WA 538
Seattle University WA 538
Nashotah House WI 549
Sacred Heart School of Theology WI 550

TRACS: Transnational Association of Christian Colleges and Schools: christian studies education (C,A,B,M,D)

International Baptist College AZ 14
@Shorter College AR 23
Bethesda University of California CA 30
California Christian College CA 32
Community Christian College CA 42
Epic Bible College CA 45
Evangelia University CA 46
Grace Mission University CA 48
King's University, The CA 53
Shasta Bible College and Graduate School CA 69
Southern California Seminary CA 70
@Veritas Evangelical Seminary CA 77
World Mission University CA 79
@Pensacola Christian College FL 115
Trinity Baptist College FL 122
University of Fort Lauderdale FL 122
Beulah Heights University GA 126
@Georgia Christian University GA 130
Luther Rice University GA 133
Pacific Islands University GU 559
New Saint Andrews College ID 144
Christian Life College IL 147
Mid-America Reformed Seminary IN 178
@Faith Theological Seminary MD 222
Maple Springs Baptist Bible College & Seminary MD 224
Boston Baptist College MA 232
Central Baptist Theological Seminary of Minneapolis MN 262
@Lutheran Brethren Seminary MN 264
Messenger College MO 284
Apex School of Theology NC 362
Heritage Bible College NC 365
New Life Theological Seminary NC 367
Piedmont Baptist College and Graduate School NC 375
Shepherds Theological Seminary NC 376
Southern Evangelical Seminary NC 377
Ohio Mid-Western College (Formerly Temple Baptist College) OH 398
Hillsdale Free Will Baptist College OK 408
Gutenberg College OR 416
Bob Jones University SC 455
Clinton Junior College SC 456
@Hiwassee College TN 469
Oxford Graduate School TN 472
Tennessee Temple University TN 476
Visible Music College TN 478
@Grace School of Theology TX 487
Paul Quinn College TX 492
Central Baptist Theological Seminary VA 517
Patrick Henry College VA 522
Virginia Baptist College VA 526
Virginia University of Lynchburg VA 530
Bakke Graduate University WA 531
Faith Evangelical College & Seminary WA 534
Seattle School of Theology and Psychology, The WA 538
Northland International University WI 549

VET: American Veterinary Medical Association: veterinary medicine (FP,D)

Auburn University AL 1
Tuskegee University AL 8
University of California-Davis CA 73
Western University of Health Sciences CA 78
Colorado State University CO 83
University of Florida FL 120
University of Georgia GA 138
University of Illinois at Urbana-Champaign IL 167
Purdue University Main Campus IN 178
Iowa State University IA 182
Kansas State University KS 194
Louisiana State University and Agricultural and Mechanical College LA 212
Tufts University MA 245

Michigan State University ..... MI 255
University of Minnesota-Twin Cities ..... MN 272
Mississippi State University ..... MS 275
University of Missouri - Columbia ..... MO 291
Cornell University ..... NY 331
North Carolina State University ..... NC 378
Ohio State University Main Campus, The ..... OH 398
Oklahoma State University ..... OK 410
Oregon State University ..... OR 418
University of Pennsylvania ..... PA 448
University of Tennessee, Knoxville ..... TN 477
Texas A & M University ..... TX 497
Virginia Polytechnic Institute and State University ..... VA 529
Washington State University ..... WA 539
University of Wisconsin-Madison ..... WI 550

WC: Western Association of Schools and Colleges, Accrediting Commission for Senior Colleges and Universities

@American Samoa Community College ..... AS 559
&Argosy University, Phoenix ..... AZ 11
@Academy for Jewish Religion ..... CA 26
Academy of Art University ..... CA 26
Alliant International University-Fresno & Sacramento ..... CA 27
Alliant International University-Irvine ..... CA 27
Alliant International University-Los Angeles ..... CA 27
Alliant International University-San Diego ..... CA 27
Alliant International University-San Francisco ..... CA 27
American Conservatory Theater ..... CA 28
American Film Institute Conservatory ..... CA 28
American Jewish University ..... CA 28
American University of Armenia ..... CA 28
&Argosy University, Inland Empire ..... CA 29
&Argosy University, Los Angeles ..... CA 29
Argosy University, Orange County ..... CA 29
&Argosy University, San Diego ..... CA 29
&Argosy University, San Francisco Bay Area ..... CA 29
Art Center College of Design ..... CA 29
&Art Institute of California, A College of Argosy University - Inland Em pire, The ..... CA 29
&Art Institute of California, A College of Argosy University - Los Angel es, The ..... CA 30
&Art Institute of California, A College of Argosy University - Orange Co unty, The ..... CA 30
&Art Institute of California, A College of Argosy University - Sacrament o, The ..... CA 30
&Art Institute of California, A College of Argosy University - San Franc isco, The ..... CA 30
Azusa Pacific University ..... CA 30
Biola University ..... CA 31
Brandman University ..... CA 31
@Brooks Institute ..... CA 31
California Baptist University ..... CA 31
California College of the Arts ..... CA 32
California Institute of Integral Studies ..... CA 32
California Institute of Technology ..... CA 32
California Institute of the Arts ..... CA 32
California Lutheran University ..... CA 33
California Maritime Academy ..... CA 33
California Northstate College of Pharmacy ..... CA 33
California Polytechnic State University-San Luis Obispo ..... CA 33
California State Polytechnic University-Pomona ..... CA 33
California State University-Bakersfield ..... CA 34
California State University-Channel Islands ..... CA 34
California State University-Chico ..... CA 34
California State University-Dominguez Hills ..... CA 34
California State University-East Bay ..... CA 34
California State University-Fresno ..... CA 35
California State University-Fullerton ..... CA 35
California State University-Long Beach ..... CA 35
California State University-Los Angeles ..... CA 35
California State University-Monterey Bay ..... CA 35
California State University-Northridge ..... CA 35
California State University-Sacramento ..... CA 36
California State University-San Bernardino ..... CA 36
California State University-San Marcos ..... CA 36
California State University-Stanislaus ..... CA 36
Cedars-Sinai Medical Center Graduate Program in Biomedical Sciences and Tra nslational Medicine ..... CA 38
Chapman University ..... CA 39
Charles R. Drew University of Medicine & Science ..... CA 39
City of Hope ..... CA 40
Claremont Graduate University ..... CA 40
Claremont McKenna College ..... CA 40
Claremont School of Theology ..... CA 40
Cogswell Polytechnical College ..... CA 41
Concordia University ..... CA 43
Dominican School of Philosophy and Theology ..... CA 45
Dominican University of California ..... CA 45
Fashion Institute of Design and Merchandising-Los Angeles ..... CA 46
Fielding Graduate University ..... CA 47
Franciscan School of Theology ..... CA 47
Fresno Pacific Biblical Seminary ..... CA 47
Fresno Pacific University ..... CA 48
Fuller Theological Seminary ..... CA 48
Golden Gate Baptist Theological Seminary ..... CA 48
Golden Gate University ..... CA 48
Graduate Theological Union ..... CA 48
Harvey Mudd College ..... CA 49
@High Tech High Graduate School of Education ..... CA 50
Holy Names University ..... CA 50
Hope International University ..... CA 50
Humboldt State University ..... CA 36
Humphreys College ..... CA 50
@International Technological University ..... CA 51
John F. Kennedy University ..... CA 52
@John Paul the Great Catholic University ..... CA 52
Keck Graduate Institute ..... CA 40
La Sierra University ..... CA 53
Laguna College of Art & Design ..... CA 53
Life Pacific College ..... CA 54
Logos Evangelical Seminary ..... CA 54
Loma Linda University ..... CA 54
Loyola Marymount University ..... CA 56
Marymount College ..... CA 56
Master's College and Seminary, The ..... CA 56
Menlo College ..... CA 57
Mills College ..... CA 57
Mount St. Mary's College ..... CA 57
National Hispanic University, The ..... CA 58
National University ..... CA 58
Naval Postgraduate School ..... CA 558
@NewSchool of Architecture and Design ..... CA 59
Notre Dame de Namur University ..... CA 59
Occidental College ..... CA 59
Otis College of Art and Design ..... CA 60
Pacific Oaks College ..... CA 60
Pacific School of Religion ..... CA 60
Pacific Union College ..... CA 60
Pacifica Graduate Institute ..... CA 60
Palo Alto University ..... CA 61
Pardee RAND Graduate School of Policy Studies ..... CA 61
#Patten University ..... CA 61
Pepperdine University ..... CA 61
Phillips Graduate Institute ..... CA 62
Pitzer College ..... CA 62
Point Loma Nazarene University ..... CA 62
Pomona College ..... CA 63
@Providence Christian College ..... CA 63
@Rudolf Steiner College ..... CA 64
Saint John's Seminary ..... CA 64
Saint Mary's College of California ..... CA 64
Saint Patrick's Seminary & University ..... CA 64
Samuel Merritt University ..... CA 64
San Diego Christian College ..... CA 65
San Diego State University ..... CA 37
San Francisco Art Institute ..... CA 65
San Francisco Conservatory of Music ..... CA 66
San Francisco State University ..... CA 37
San Francisco Theological Seminary ..... CA 66
San Joaquin College of Law ..... CA 66
San Jose State University ..... CA 37
@Sanford-Burnham Graduate School of Biomedical Sciences ..... CA 67
Santa Clara University ..... CA 68
Saybrook University ..... CA 68
Scripps College ..... CA 69
Scripps Research Institute, The ..... CA 69
Simpson University ..... CA 69
Sofia University (formerly Institute of Transpersonal Psychology) ..... CA 69
Soka University of America ..... CA 69
Sonoma State University ..... CA 37
Southern California College of Optometry ..... CA 70
Southern California Institute of Architecture ..... CA 70
Southern California University of Health Sciences ..... CA 71
Stanford University ..... CA 71
Teachers College of San Joaquin ..... CA 72
Thomas Aquinas College ..... CA 72
Touro College Los Angeles ..... CA 72
Touro University-California ..... CA 73
#Trident University International ..... CA 73
United States University ..... CA 73
University of California-Berkeley ..... CA 73
University of California-Davis ..... CA 73
University of California-Hastings College of the Law ..... CA 74
University of California-Irvine ..... CA 74
University of California-Los Angeles ..... CA 74
University of California-Merced ..... CA 74
University of California-Riverside ..... CA 74
University of California-San Diego ..... CA 74
University of California-San Francisco ..... CA 75
University of California-Santa Barbara ..... CA 75
University of California-Santa Cruz ..... CA 75
University of LaVerne ..... CA 75
University of Redlands ..... CA 76
University of San Diego ..... CA 76
University of San Francisco ..... CA 76
University of Southern California ..... CA 76
University of the Pacific ..... CA 76
University of the West ..... CA 77
Vanguard University of Southern California ..... CA 77
West Coast University ..... CA 78
&Western State University College of Law ..... CA 78
Western University of Health Sciences ..... CA 78
Westminster Theological Seminary in California ..... CA 78
Westmont College ..... CA 79
Whittier College ..... CA 79
William Jessup University ..... CA 79
Woodbury University ..... CA 79
Wright Institute, The ..... CA 79
&Argosy University, Denver ..... CO 81
&Art Institute of California, A College of Argosy University - Hollywood, Th ..... CA 29
&Art Institute of California, A College of Argosy University - San Diego, Th ..... CA 30
&Art Institute of California, A College of Argosy University - Sunnyvale, Th ..... CA 30
&Argosy University, Sarasota ..... FL 101
&Argosy University, Tampa ..... FL 101
&Argosy University, Atlanta ..... GA 124
University of Guam ..... GU 559
&Argosy University, Hawaii ..... HI 140
Brigham Young University Hawaii ..... HI 140
Chaminade University of Honolulu ..... HI 140
Hawaii Pacific University ..... HI 140
University of Hawaii at Hilo ..... HI 141
University of Hawaii at Manoa ..... HI 141
University of Hawaii Maui College ..... HI 142
University of Hawaii - West Oahu ..... HI 141
&Argosy University, Chicago ..... IL 145
&Argosy University, Schaumburg ..... IL 145
&Argosy University, Twin Cities ..... MN 260
Northern Marianas College ..... MP 560
&Argosy University, Nashville ..... TN 467
&Argosy University, Dallas ..... TX 480
&Argosy University, Salt Lake City ..... UT 509
&Argosy University, Washington DC ..... VA 516
&Argosy University, Seattle ..... WA 531

WJ: Western Association of Schools and Colleges, Accrediting Commission for Community and Junior Colleges

American Samoa Community College ..... AS 559
Allan Hancock College ..... CA 26
American River College ..... CA 56
Antelope Valley College ..... CA 28
Bakersfield College ..... CA 52
Barstow Community College District ..... CA 30
Berkeley City College ..... CA 62
Butte College ..... CA 31
Cabrillo College ..... CA 31
Cañada College ..... CA 67
&Carrington College California - Antioch ..... CA 38
&Carrington College California - Citrus Heights ..... CA 38
&Carrington College California - Emeryville ..... CA 38
&Carrington College California - Pleasant Hill ..... CA 38
Carrington College California - Sacramento ..... CA 38
&Carrington College California - San Jose ..... CA 38
&Carrington College California - San Leandro ..... CA 38
&Carrington College California - Stockton ..... CA 38
Cerritos College ..... CA 39
Cerro Coso Community College ..... CA 52
Chabot College ..... CA 39
Chaffey College ..... CA 39
Citrus College ..... CA 40
City College of San Francisco ..... CA 40
Coastline Community College ..... CA 41
College of Alameda ..... CA 62
College of Marin ..... CA 42
College of San Mateo ..... CA 67
College of the Canyons ..... CA 41
College of the Desert ..... CA 42
College of the Redwoods Community College District ..... CA 42
College of the Sequoias ..... CA 42
College of the Siskiyous ..... CA 42
Columbia College ..... CA 80
Contra Costa College ..... CA 43
Copper Mountain College ..... CA 43
Cosumnes River College ..... CA 56
Crafton Hills College ..... CA 65
Cuesta College ..... CA 43
Cuyamaca College ..... CA 49
Cypress College ..... CA 59
De Anza College ..... CA 47
Deep Springs College ..... CA 43
Defense Language Institute ..... CA 557
Diablo Valley College ..... CA 43
East Los Angeles College ..... CA 54
El Camino College ..... CA 45
&El Camino College Compton Center ..... CA 45
Evergreen Valley College ..... CA 67
Fashion Institute of Design and Merchandising-Los Angeles ..... CA 46
&Fashion Institute of Design and Merchandising-Orange County ..... CA 46
&Fashion Institute of Design and Merchandising-San Diego ..... CA 46
&Fashion Institute of Design and Merchandising-San Francisco ..... CA 47
Feather River College ..... CA 47
Folsom Lake College ..... CA 56
Foothill College ..... CA 47
Fresno City College ..... CA 72
Fullerton College ..... CA 59
Gavilan College ..... CA 48
Glendale Community College ..... CA 48
Golden West College ..... CA 41
Grossmont College ..... CA 49
Hartnell College ..... CA 49
&Heald College, Concord ..... CA 49
&Heald College, Fresno ..... CA 49
&Heald College, Hayward ..... CA 49
&Heald College, Milpitas ..... CA 49
&Heald College, Modesto ..... CA 49
&Heald College, Rancho Cordova ..... CA 50
&Heald College, Roseville ..... CA 50
&Heald College, Salinas ..... CA 50
&Heald College, San Francisco ..... CA 50
&Heald College, Stockton ..... CA 50
Imperial Valley College ..... CA 51
Irvine Valley College ..... CA 70
Lake Tahoe Community College ..... CA 53
Laney College ..... CA 62
Las Positas College ..... CA 39
Lassen Community College ..... CA 53
Long Beach City College ..... CA 54
Los Angeles City College ..... CA 54
Los Angeles County College of Nursing and Allied Health ..... CA 55
#Los Angeles Harbor College ..... CA 54
Los Angeles Mission College ..... CA 55
Los Angeles Pierce College ..... CA 55
#Los Angeles Southwest College ..... CA 55
Los Angeles Trade-Technical College ..... CA 55
Los Angeles Valley College ..... CA 55
Los Medanos College ..... CA 43
Mendocino College ..... CA 57
Merced College ..... CA 57
Merritt College ..... CA 62
MiraCosta Community College District ..... CA 57
Mission College ..... CA 78
#Modesto Junior College ..... CA 80
Monterey Peninsula College ..... CA 57
#Moorpark College ..... CA 77
Moreno Valley College ..... CA 63
Mt. San Antonio College ..... CA 58
Mt. San Jacinto College ..... CA 58
MTI College ..... CA 58
Napa Valley College ..... CA 58
Norco College ..... CA 63
Ohlone College ..... CA 59
Orange Coast College ..... CA 41
#Oxnard College ..... CA 77
#Palo Verde College ..... CA 61
Palomar College ..... CA 61
Pasadena City College ..... CA 61
Porterville College ..... CA 53
Reedley College ..... CA 72
Rio Hondo College ..... CA 63
Riverside City College ..... CA 64
Sacramento City College ..... CA 56
Saddleback College ..... CA 70
Salvation Army College for Officer Training at Crestmont, The ..... CA 64
San Bernardino Valley College ..... CA 65
San Diego City College ..... CA 65
San Diego Mesa College ..... CA 65
San Diego Miramar College ..... CA 65
San Joaquin Delta College ..... CA 66
&San Joaquin Valley College-Bakersfield ..... CA 66
&San Joaquin Valley College-Fresno ..... CA 66
&San Joaquin Valley College-Fresno Aviation Campus ..... CA 66
&San Joaquin Valley College-Hesperia ..... CA 66
&San Joaquin Valley College-Modesto ..... CA 66
&San Joaquin Valley College-Rancho Cordova ..... CA 66
&San Joaquin Valley College-Rancho Cucamonga ..... CA 67
San Joaquin Valley College, Inc. ..... CA 66
#San Jose City College ..... CA 67
Santa Ana College ..... CA 63
Santa Barbara City College ..... CA 68
Santa Monica College ..... CA 68
Santa Rosa Junior College ..... CA 68
Santiago Canyon College ..... CA 63
#Shasta College ..... CA 69
Sierra College ..... CA 69
Skyline College ..... CA 67
Solano Community College ..... CA 70
Southwestern College ..... CA 71
Taft College ..... CA 72
Ventura College ..... CA 77
#Victor Valley College ..... CA 77
West Hills College Coalinga ..... CA 78
West Hills College Lemoore ..... CA 78
West Los Angeles College ..... CA 55
West Valley College ..... CA 78
Woodland Community College ..... CA 80
Yuba College ..... CA 80
#College of Micronesia-FSM ..... FM 559
Guam Community College ..... GU 559
Hawaii Tokai International College ..... HI 140
&Heald College, Honolulu ..... HI 141
Kapiolani Community College ..... HI 141
University of Hawaii Hawaii Community College ..... HI 142
University of Hawaii Honolulu Community College ..... HI 142
University of Hawaii Kauai Community College ..... HI 142
University of Hawaii Leeward Community College ..... HI 142
University of Hawaii Windward Community College ..... HI 142
College of the Marshall Islands ..... MH 560
#Northern Marianas College ..... MP 560
&Heald College, Portland ..... OR 416
Palau Community College ..... PW 560

Index of FICE Numbers

Code	Institution	State	Page
001349	University of Northern Colorado	CO	89
001350	Colorado State University	CO	83
001352	Denver Seminary	CO	84
001353	Fort Lewis College	CO	84
001354	Iliff School of Theology	CO	85
001355	Lamar Community College	CO	86
001358	Colorado Mesa University	CO	82
001359	Colorado Northwestern Cmty College	CO	82
001360	Metropolitan State Univ Denver	CO	86
001361	Northeastern Junior College	CO	86
001362	Otero Junior College	CO	87
001363	Regis University	CO	87
001365	Colorado State University-Pueblo	CO	83
001368	Trinidad State Junior College	CO	88
001369	United States Air Force Academy	CO	558
001370	University of Colorado Boulder	CO	88
001371	University of Denver	CO	89
001372	Western State Colorado University	CO	89
001374	Albertus Magnus College	CT	90
001378	Central Connecticut State Univ	CT	90
001379	Connecticut College	CT	92
001380	Western Connecticut State Univ	CT	91
001385	Fairfield University	CT	92
001387	Hartford Seminary	CT	93
001389	Holy Apostles College and Seminary	CT	93
001392	Manchester Community College	CT	91
001393	Mitchell College	CT	93
001397	University of New Haven	CT	95
001398	Northwestern CT Cmty-Tech College	CT	92
001399	Norwalk Community College	CT	92
001401	Post University	CT	93
001402	Quinnipiac University	CT	93
001403	Sacred Heart University	CT	94
001406	Southern Connecticut State Univ	CT	90
001409	University of Saint Joseph	CT	95
001414	Trinity College	CT	94
001415	United States Coast Guard Academy	CT	558
001416	University of Bridgeport	CT	94
001417	University of Connecticut	CT	94
001422	University of Hartford	CT	95
001424	Wesleyan University	CT	95
001425	Eastern Connecticut State Univ	CT	90
001426	Yale University	CT	96
001428	Delaware State University	DE	96
001429	Goldey-Beacom College	DE	96
001431	University of Delaware	DE	96
001433	Wesley College	DE	97
001434	American University	DC	97
001436	Capitol College	MD	221
001437	The Catholic University of America	DC	97
001441	Univ of the District of Columbia	DC	100
001443	Gallaudet University	DC	98
001444	George Washington University	DC	98
001445	Georgetown University	DC	98
001448	Howard University	DC	98
001459	Strayer University	DC	99
001460	Trinity Washington University	DC	99
001462	Washington Bible Col/Cap Bible Sem	MD	229
001464	Wesley Theological Seminary	DC	100
001466	Barry University	FL	101
001467	Bethune Cookman University	FL	102
001468	St. Thomas University	FL	117
001469	Florida Institute of Technology	FL	108
001470	Brevard Community College	FL	102
001471	College of Central Florida	FL	103
001472	Chipola College	FL	103
001473	Clearwater Christian College	FL	103
001475	Daytona State College	FL	104
001477	Edison State College	FL	105
001478	Edward Waters College	FL	105
001479	Embry-Riddle Aeronautical Univ	FL	105
001480	Florida A and M University	FL	118
001481	Florida Atlantic University	FL	119
001482	Florida College	FL	108
001484	Florida State College Jacksonville	FL	109
001485	Florida Keys Community College	FL	108
001486	Florida Memorial University	FL	109
001487	Eckerd College	FL	105
001488	Florida Southern College	FL	109
001489	Florida State University	FL	119
001490	Gulf Coast State College	FL	110
001493	Indian River State College	FL	111
001495	Jacksonville University	FL	111
001497	Jones College	FL	112
001499	Everest Univ-North Orlando Campus	FL	106
001500	Broward College	FL	102
001501	Florida Gateway College	FL	108
001502	Lake-Sumter Community College	FL	112
001504	State Col of FL, Manatee-Sarasota	FL	118
001505	Lynn University	FL	113
001506	Miami Dade College	FL	113
001507	New College of Florida	FL	120
001508	North Florida Community College	FL	113
001509	Nova Southeastern University	FL	114
001510	Northwest Florida State College	FL	114
001512	Palm Beach State College	FL	114
001513	Pensacola State College	FL	115
001514	Polk State College	FL	115
001515	Rollins College	FL	116
001519	Santa Fe College	FL	117
001520	Seminole State College of Florida	FL	117
001521	Southeastern University	FL	118
001522	South Florida State College	FL	117
001523	St. Johns River State College	FL	116
001526	Saint Leo University	FL	116
001528	St. Petersburg College	FL	116
001531	Stetson University	FL	121
001533	Tallahassee Community College	FL	122
001534	Everest University-Tampa Campus	FL	107
001535	University of Florida	FL	120
001536	University of Miami	FL	122
001537	University of South Florida	FL	121
001538	University of Tampa	FL	123
001540	Webber International University	FL	123
001541	Abraham Baldwin Agricultural Coll	GA	123
001542	Agnes Scott College	GA	123
001543	Darton College	GA	128
001544	Albany State University	GA	124
001545	Andrew College	GA	124
001546	Armstrong Atlantic State University	GA	124
001547	Point University	GA	136
001552	Augusta State University	GA	125
001554	Berry College	GA	126
001555	Thomas University	GA	138
001556	Brenau University	GA	126
001557	Brewton-Parker College	GA	126
001558	College of Coastal Georgia	GA	127
001559	Clark Atlanta University	GA	127
001560	Columbia Theological Seminary	GA	127
001561	Columbus State University	GA	127
001562	Georgia Perimeter College	GA	131
001563	Emmanuel College	GA	129
001564	Emory University	GA	129
001566	Fort Valley State University	GA	129
001567	Gainesville State College	GA	129
001568	Interdenominational Theol Center	GA	132
001569	Georgia Institute of Technology	GA	130
001570	Southern Polytechnic State Univ	GA	137
001571	Georgia Military College	GA	131
001572	Georgia Southern University	GA	131
001573	Georgia Southwestern State Univ	GA	131
001574	Georgia State University	GA	131
001575	Gordon State College	GA	132
001577	Kennesaw State University	GA	133
001578	LaGrange College	GA	133
001579	Georgia Health Sciences University	GA	130
001580	Mercer University	GA	134
001581	Middle Georgia College	GA	134
001582	Morehouse College	GA	134
001585	North Georgia College & State Univ	GA	134
001586	Oglethorpe University	GA	135
001587	Paine College	GA	135
001588	Piedmont College	GA	136
001589	Reinhardt University	GA	136
001590	Savannah State University	GA	136
001591	Shorter University	GA	137
001592	South Georgia College	GA	137
001594	Spelman College	GA	138
001596	Toccoa Falls College	GA	138
001597	Truett McConnell College	GA	138
001598	University of Georgia	GA	138
001599	Valdosta State University	GA	139
001600	Wesleyan College	GA	139
001601	University of West Georgia	GA	139
001602	Georgia College & State University	GA	130
001604	Young Harris College	GA	140
001605	Chaminade University of Honolulu	HI	140
001606	Brigham Young University Hawaii	HI	140
001610	University of Hawaii at Manoa	HI	141
001611	University of Hawaii at Hilo	HI	141
001612	Univ of Hawaii Honolulu Cmty Col	HI	142
001613	Kapiolani Community College	HI	141
001614	Univ of Hawaii Kauai Cmty College	HI	142
001615	Univ of Hawaii Maui College	HI	142
001616	Boise State University	ID	142
001617	The College of Idaho	ID	143
001619	College of Southern Idaho	ID	143
001620	Idaho State University	ID	143
001621	Lewis-Clark State College	ID	144
001623	North Idaho College	ID	144
001624	Northwest Nazarene University	ID	144
001625	Brigham Young University-Idaho	ID	143
001626	University of Idaho	ID	144
001628	American Academy of Art	IL	145
001632	Aquinas Institute of Theology	MO	278
001633	Augustana College	IL	145
001634	Aurora University	IL	145
001636	Southwestern Illinois College	IL	165
001637	Bethany Theological Seminary	IN	169
001638	Black Hawk College	IL	145
001639	Blackburn College	IL	146
001640	Prairie State College	IL	161
001641	Bradley University	IL	146
001643	Spoon River College	IL	165
001647	City Colleges of Chicago	IL	147
001648	City Cols of Chicago Harry Truman	IL	147
001649	City Cols of Chicago RJ Daley Col	IL	147
001650	City Cols of Chicago Malcolm X	IL	147
001652	City Cols of Chicago Washington Col	IL	147
001654	City Cols of Chicago Kennedy-King	IL	147
001655	City Cols of Chicago W Wright Col	IL	147
001657	Midwestern University	IL	158
001659	Rosalind Franklin U of Med/Science	IL	163
001661	Chicago Theological Seminary	IL	146
001663	Spertus College	IL	165
001664	University of St. Francis	IL	167
001665	Columbia College Chicago	IL	148
001666	Concordia University Chicago	IL	148
001669	Danville Area Community College	IL	148
001671	DePaul University	IL	149
001672	DeVry University - Home Office	IL	149
001674	Eastern Illinois University	IL	150
001675	Elgin Community College	IL	150
001676	Elmhurst College	IL	150
001678	Eureka College	IL	151
001681	Highland Community College	IL	152
001682	Garrett-Evangelical Theol Seminary	IL	151
001684	Greenville College	IL	151
001685	Hebrew Theological College	IL	152
001688	Illinois College	IL	152
001689	Illinois College of Optometry	IL	152
001691	Illinois Institute of Technology	IL	153
001692	Illinois State University	IL	153
001693	Northeastern Illinois University	IL	160
001694	Chicago State University	IL	146
001696	Illinois Wesleyan University	IL	153
001698	John Marshall Law School	IL	154
001699	Joliet Junior College	IL	154
001700	Judson University	IL	154
001701	Kaskaskia College	IL	155
001703	Kendall College	IL	155
001704	Knox College	IL	155
001705	Illinois Valley Community College	IL	153
001706	Lake Forest College	IL	155
001707	Lewis University	IL	156
001708	Lincoln Christian University	IL	156
001709	Lincoln College	IL	156
001710	Loyola University Chicago	IL	157
001712	Lutheran School of Theology Chicago	IL	157
001716	MacCormac College	IL	157
001717	MacMurray College	IL	157
001721	McCormick Theological Seminary	IL	157
001722	McKendree University	IL	158
001723	Meadville Lombard Theol School	IL	158
001724	Millikin University	IL	158
001725	Monmouth College	IL	158
001727	Moody Bible Institute	IL	159
001728	Morton College	IL	159
001732	National Univ of Health Sciences	IL	159
001733	National-Louis University	IL	159
001734	North Central College	IL	159
001735	North Park University	IL	159
001736	Northern Seminary	IL	160
001737	Northern Illinois University	IL	160
001739	Northwestern University	IL	160
001741	Olivet Nazarene University	IL	161
001742	Illinois Eastern CC Olney Central	IL	152
001744	Principia College	IL	161
001745	Quincy University	IL	161
001746	Robert Morris University	IL	162
001747	Rock Valley College	IL	162
001748	Rockford College	IL	163
001749	Roosevelt University	IL	163
001750	Dominican University	IL	150
001752	Sauk Valley Community College	IL	164
001753	School of the Art Institute Chicago	IL	164
001754	Seabury-Western Theol Seminary	IL	164
001756	Shimer College	IL	164
001757	Southeastern Illinois College	IL	164
001758	Southern Illinois Univ Carbondale	IL	165
001759	Southern Illinois Univ Edwardsville	IL	165
001765	Univ of Saint Mary Lake-Mundelein	IL	167
001767	Benedictine University	IL	145
001768	Saint Xavier University	IL	163
001769	South Suburban Col of Cook County	IL	164
001771	Trinity Christian College	IL	166
001772	Trinity International University	IL	166
001773	Triton College	IL	166
001774	University of Chicago	IL	166
001775	Univ of Illinois Urbana-Champaign	IL	167
001776	University of Illinois at Chicago	IL	167
001778	VanderCook College of Music	IL	167
001779	Illinois Eastern CC Wabash Valley	IL	153
001780	Western Illinois University	IL	168
001781	Wheaton College	IL	168
001783	Worsham College of Mortuary Science	IL	168
001784	Ancilla College	IN	169
001785	Anderson University	IN	169
001786	Ball State University	IN	169
001787	Bethel College	IN	169
001788	Butler University	IN	170
001789	Christian Theological Seminary	IN	170
001792	DePauw University	IN	171
001793	Earlham Col/Earlham Sch of Rel	IN	171
001795	University of Evansville	IN	180
001798	Franklin College of Indiana	IN	171
001799	Goshen College	IN	171
001800	Grace College and Seminary	IN	171
001801	Hanover College	IN	172
001803	Huntington University	IN	173
001804	University of Indianapolis	IN	180
001805	Indiana Tech	IN	173
001807	Indiana State University	IN	173
001808	University of Southern Indiana	IN	181
001809	Indiana University Bloomington	IN	173
001811	Indiana University East	IN	173

Code	Institution	State	Page
002228	Wheelock College	MA	246
002229	Williams College	MA	246
002230	Woods Hole Oceanographic Inst	MA	246
002233	Worcester Polytechnic Institute	MA	246
002234	Adrian College	MI	246
002235	Albion College	MI	247
002236	Alma College	MI	247
002237	Alpena Community College	MI	247
002238	Andrews University	MI	247
002239	Aquinas College	MI	247
002240	Bay Noc Community College	MI	248
002241	Calvin College	MI	249
002242	Calvin Theological Seminary	MI	249
002243	Central Michigan University	MI	249
002246	Cleary University	MI	249
002247	Concordia University	MI	249
002248	Cranbrook Academy of Art	MI	250
002249	Davenport University	MI	250
002251	Delta College	MI	250
002259	Eastern Michigan University	MI	250
002260	Ferris State University	MI	250
002261	Mott Community College	MI	255
002262	Kettering University	MI	253
002263	Glen Oaks Community College	MI	251
002264	Gogebic Community College	MI	251
002265	Grace Bible College	MI	251
002266	Cornerstone University	MI	250
002267	Grand Rapids Community College	MI	251
002268	Grand Valley State University	MI	251
002269	Great Lakes Christian College	MI	251
002270	Henry Ford Community College	MI	252
002272	Hillsdale College	MI	252
002273	Hope College	MI	252
002274	Jackson Community College	MI	252
002275	Kalamazoo College	MI	252
002276	Kellogg Community College	MI	253
002277	Lake Michigan College	MI	253
002278	Lansing Community College	MI	254
002279	Lawrence Technological University	MI	254
002282	Madonna University	MI	254
002284	Marygrove College	MI	254
002288	Rochester College	MI	257
002290	Michigan State University	MI	255
002292	Michigan Technological University	MI	255
002293	Lake Superior State University	MI	253
002294	Monroe County Community College	MI	255
002295	Montcalm Community College	MI	255
002296	Baker College of Muskegon	MI	248
002297	Muskegon Community College	MI	256
002299	North Central Michigan College	MI	256
002301	Northern Michigan University	MI	256
002302	Northwestern Michigan College	MI	256
002303	Oakland Community College	MI	256
002307	Oakland University	MI	256
002308	Olivet College	MI	257
002310	St. Clair County Community College	MI	257
002311	Kuyper College	MI	253
002313	Sacred Heart Major Seminary	MI	257
002314	Saginaw Valley State University	MI	257
002315	Schoolcraft College	MI	258
002316	Siena Heights University	MI	258
002317	Southwestern Michigan College	MI	258
002318	Spring Arbor University	MI	258
002322	Finlandia University	MI	251
002323	University of Detroit Mercy	MI	258
002325	University of Michigan-Ann Arbor	MI	259
002326	University of Michigan-Dearborn	MI	259
002327	University of Michigan-Flint	MI	259
002328	Washtenaw Community College	MI	259
002329	Wayne State University	MI	260
002330	Western Michigan University	MI	260
002331	Western Theological Seminary	MI	260
002332	Anoka-Ramsey Community College	MN	265
002334	Augsburg College	MN	261
002335	Riverland Community College	MN	268
002336	Bemidji State University	MN	265
002337	Bethany Lutheran College	MN	261
002339	Central Lakes College	MN	265
002340	Carleton College	MN	261
002341	College of Saint Benedict	MN	262
002342	St. Catherine University	MN	270
002343	The College of Saint Scholastica	MN	262
002345	University of Saint Thomas	MN	272
002346	Concordia College	MN	262
002347	Concordia University, St. Paul	MN	263
002350	Vermilion Community College	MN	269
002353	Gustavus Adolphus College	MN	263
002354	Hamline University	MN	264
002355	Hibbing Community College	MN	266
002356	Itasca Community College	MN	266
002357	Luther Seminary	MN	264
002358	Macalester College	MN	264
002360	Minnesota State University, Mankato	MN	267
002361	Martin Luther College	MN	264
002362	Minneapolis Cmty & Tech College	MN	267
002365	Minneapolis College of Art Design	MN	265
002366	Crossroads College	MN	263
002367	Minnesota State University Moorhead	MN	267
002369	North Central University	MN	270
002370	North Hennepin Community College	MN	268
002371	Northwestern College	MN	270
002373	Rochester Community & Tech College	MN	268
002375	Southwest Minnesota State Univ	MN	269
002377	St. Cloud State University	MN	269
002379	Saint John's University	MN	271
002380	St Mary's University of Minnesota	MN	271
002382	St. Olaf College	MN	271
002383	Crown College	MN	263
002385	Northland Community & Tech College	MN	268
002386	United Theol Seminary-Twin Cities	MN	271
002388	University of Minnesota Duluth	MN	271
002389	University of Minnesota-Morris	MN	271
002391	William Mitchell College of Law	MN	272
002393	Minnesota State Col-Southeast Tech	MN	267
002394	Winona State University	MN	269
002396	Alcorn State University	MS	272
002397	Belhaven University	MS	273
002398	Blue Mountain College	MS	273
002401	Coahoma Community College	MS	273
002402	Copiah-Lincoln Community College	MS	273
002403	Delta State University	MS	273
002404	East Central Community College	MS	274
002405	East Mississippi Community College	MS	274
002407	Hinds Community College	MS	274
002408	Holmes Community College	MS	274
002409	Itawamba Community College	MS	274
002410	Jackson State University	MS	274
002411	Jones County Junior College	MS	274
002413	Meridian Community College	MS	275
002414	Millsaps College	MS	275
002415	Mississippi College	MS	275
002416	Mississippi Delta Community College	MS	275
002417	Mississippi Gulf Coast Cmty College	MS	275
002422	Mississippi University for Women	MS	276
002423	Mississippi State University	MS	275
002424	Mississippi Valley State University	MS	276
002426	Northeast Mississippi Cmty College	MS	276
002427	Northwest Mississippi Cmty College	MS	276
002430	Pearl River Community College	MS	276
002433	Rust College	MS	276
002435	Southeastern Baptist College	MS	277
002436	Southwest Mississippi Cmty College	MS	277
002439	Tougaloo College	MS	277
002440	University of Mississippi	MS	277
002441	University of Southern Mississippi	MS	277
002447	William Carey University	MS	278
002449	Avila University	MO	278
002450	Calvary Bible Col & Theol Seminary	MO	279
002452	Central Bible College	MO	279
002453	Central Methodist University	MO	279
002454	University of Central Missouri	MO	290
002455	DeVry University-Kansas City Campus	MO	281
002456	Columbia College	MO	280
002457	Concordia Seminary	MO	280
002458	Cottey College	MO	280
002459	Crowder College	MO	280
002460	Culver-Stockton College	MO	280
002461	Drury University	MO	281
002462	Eden Theological Seminary	MO	281
002463	Evangel University	MO	281
002464	Fontbonne University	MO	281
002466	Harris-Stowe State University	MO	282
002467	Conception Seminary College	MO	280
002468	Jefferson College	MO	283
002469	St Louis Cmty Col Center	MO	288
002470	St Louis Cmty Col Florissant Valley	MO	288
002471	St Louis Cmty Col Forest Park	MO	288
002472	St Louis Cmty Col Meramec	MO	289
002473	Kansas City Art Institute	MO	283
002474	Kansas City Univ of Med & BioSci	MO	283
002476	Kenrick-Glennon Seminary	MO	283
002477	A. T. Still Univ of Health Sciences	MO	278
002479	Lincoln University	MO	283
002480	Lindenwood University	MO	283
002482	Maryville University of Saint Louis	MO	284
002484	Metropolitan Cmty Col-Penn Valley	MO	285
002485	Midwestern Baptist Theol Seminary	MO	285
002486	Mineral Area College	MO	285
002488	Missouri Southern State University	MO	286
002489	Missouri Valley College	MO	286
002490	Missouri Western State University	MO	286
002491	Moberly Area Community College	MO	286
002494	Nazarene Theological Seminary	MO	286
002495	Truman State University	MO	290
002496	Northwest Missouri State University	MO	287
002498	Park University	MO	287
002499	Rockhurst University	MO	288
002500	College of the Ozarks	MO	279
002501	Southeast Missouri State University	MO	289
002502	Southwest Baptist University	MO	290
002503	Missouri State University	MO	286
002504	St. Louis College of Pharmacy	MO	288
002506	Saint Louis University	MO	289
002509	Saint Paul School of Theology	MO	289
002512	Stephens College	MO	290
002514	North Central Missouri College	MO	287
002515	Univ of Missouri System Admin	MO	291
002516	University of Missouri - Columbia	MO	291
002517	Missouri Univ of Science Tech	MO	291
002518	Univ of Missouri - Kansas City	MO	291
002519	Univ of Missouri - Saint Louis	MO	291
002520	Washington University in St. Louis	MO	292
002521	Webster University	MO	292
002522	Wentworth Military Academy/Jr Col	MO	293
002523	Westminster College	MO	293
002524	William Jewell College	MO	293
002525	William Woods University	MO	293
002526	Carroll College	MT	293
002527	University of Great Falls	MT	296
002528	Miles Community College	MT	294
002529	http://ehesDawson Community College	MT	294
002530	Montana State University - Billings	MT	295
002531	Montana Tech of the Univ of Montana	MT	296
002532	Montana State University	MT	295
002533	Montana State University - Northern	MT	295
002534	Rocky Mountain College	MT	296
002536	The University of Montana-Missoula	MT	294
002537	The University of Montana Western	MT	294
002539	Chadron State College	NE	299
002540	College of Saint Mary	NE	297
002541	Concordia University	NE	297
002542	Creighton University	NE	297
002544	Doane College	NE	297
002547	Grace University	NE	297
002548	Hastings College	NE	298
002551	University of Nebraska at Kearney	NE	300
002553	Midland University	NE	298
002554	University of Nebraska at Omaha	NE	301
002555	Nebraska Wesleyan University	NE	299
002557	Mid-Plains Community College	NE	298
002559	Peru State College	NE	299
002560	Western Nebraska Community College	NE	301
002563	Union College	NE	300
002565	University of Nebraska - Lincoln	NE	300
002566	Wayne State College	NE	299
002567	York College	NE	301
002568	University of Nevada, Reno	NV	303
002569	University of Nevada, Las Vegas	NV	302
002572	Colby-Sawyer College	NH	303
002573	Dartmouth College	NH	304
002575	Franklin Pierce University	NH	305
002579	New England College	NH	305
002580	Southern New Hampshire University	NH	305
002581	NHTI-Concord's Community College	NH	304
002582	Manchester Community College	NH	304
002583	Great Bay Community College	NH	304
002586	Rivier College	NH	305
002587	Saint Anselm College	NH	305
002589	University of New Hampshire	NH	306
002590	Keene State College	NH	306
002591	Plymouth State University	NH	307
002595	Assumption College for Sisters	NJ	307
002596	Atlantic Cape Community College	NJ	307
002597	Bloomfield College	NJ	307
002598	Caldwell College	NJ	308
002599	Centenary College	NJ	308
002600	College of Saint Elizabeth	NJ	308
002601	Cumberland County College	NJ	309
002603	Drew University	NJ	309
002607	Fairleigh Dickinson University	NJ	310
002608	Georgian Court University	NJ	310
002609	Rowan University	NJ	314
002610	Felician College	NJ	310
002611	Immaculate Conception Seminary	NJ	310
002613	New Jersey City University	NJ	312
002615	Middlesex County College	NJ	311
002616	Monmouth University	NJ	311
002617	Montclair State University	NJ	311
002619	New Brunswick Theological Seminary	NJ	312
002620	UMDNJ-New Jersey Medical School	NJ	316
002621	New Jersey Institute of Technology	NJ	312
002622	Kean University	NJ	311
002624	Ocean County College	NJ	312
002625	William Paterson University of NJ	NJ	317
002626	Princeton Theological Seminary	NJ	312
002627	Princeton University	NJ	312
002628	Rider University	NJ	313
002629	Rutgers State Univ Central Office	NJ	314
002631	Rutgers State Univ - Newark	NJ	314
002632	Seton Hall University	NJ	315
002638	Saint Peter's College	NJ	314
002639	Stevens Institute of Technology	NJ	315
002642	The College of New Jersey	NJ	308
002643	Union County College	NJ	316
002649	Santa Fe Univ of Art and Design	NM	320
002650	University of the Southwest	NM	321
002651	Eastern New Mexico University	NM	318
002653	New Mexico Highlands University	NM	318
002654	New Mexico Inst of Mining & Tech	NM	319
002655	New Mexico Junior College	NM	319
002656	New Mexico Military Institute	NM	319
002657	NM State University-Main Campus	NM	319
002658	NM State University-Alamogordo	NM	319
002659	NM State University-Carlsbad	NM	319
002660	San Juan College	NM	320
002661	Eastern New Mexico Univ - Roswell	NM	318
002663	Univ of New Mexico Main Campus	NM	321
002664	Western New Mexico University	NM	321
002665	Vaughn Col of Aeronautics & Tech	NY	359
002666	Adelphi University	NY	322
002667	Dowling College	NY	332
002668	Alfred University	NY	322
002669	Bank Street College of Education	NY	323
002670	Baptist Bible College and Seminary	PA	422
002671	Bard College	NY	323
002674	New York Theological Seminary	NY	344

Code	Institution	State	Page
003113	Pontifical College Josephinum	OH	401
003115	Rabbinical College of Telshe	OH	401
003116	University of Rio Grande	OH	404
003119	Sinclair Community College	OH	401
003121	Tiffin University	OH	402
003122	United Theological Seminary	OH	403
003123	The Univ of Akron, Main Campus	OH	403
003125	University of Cincinnati Main	OH	403
003127	University of Dayton	OH	404
003131	University of Toledo	OH	404
003133	Urbana University	OH	405
003134	Ursuline College	OH	405
003135	Walsh University	OH	405
003141	Wilberforce University	OH	405
003142	Wilmington College	OH	405
003143	Wittenberg University	OH	406
003144	Xavier University	OH	406
003145	Youngstown State University	OH	406
003146	Western Oklahoma State College	OK	414
003147	Bacone College	OK	407
003149	Southern Nazarene University	OK	412
003150	Cameron University	OK	407
003151	Oklahoma Wesleyan University	OK	411
003152	University of Central Oklahoma	OK	413
003153	Connors State College	OK	407
003154	East Central University	OK	407
003155	Eastern Oklahoma State College	OK	408
003156	Redlands Community College	OK	411
003157	Langston University	OK	408
003158	Murray State College	OK	408
003160	Northeastern Oklahoma A&M College	OK	408
003161	Northeastern State University	OK	409
003162	Northern Oklahoma College	OK	409
003163	Northwestern Oklahoma State Univ	OK	409
003164	Oklahoma Baptist University	OK	409
003165	Oklahoma Christian University	OK	409
003166	Oklahoma City University	OK	410
003167	Univ of Science & Arts of Oklahoma	OK	413
003168	Rogers State University	OK	411
003170	Oklahoma State University	OK	410
003172	Oklahoma State Univ - Okmulgee	OK	410
003174	Oklahoma Panhandle State University	OK	410
003176	Carl Albert State College	OK	407
003178	Seminole State College	OK	412
003179	Southeastern Oklahoma State Univ	OK	412
003180	Southwestern Christian University	OK	412
003181	Southwestern Oklahoma State Univ	OK	412
003183	St. Gregory's University	OK	412
003184	University of Oklahoma Norman	OK	413
003185	University of Tulsa	OK	413
003186	Blue Mountain Community College	OR	414
003188	Central Oregon Community College	OR	414
003189	Clatsop Community College	OR	415
003191	Concordia University	OR	415
003193	Eastern Oregon University	OR	418
003194	George Fox University	OR	415
003196	Lane Community College	OR	416
003197	Lewis and Clark College	OR	416
003198	Linfield College	OR	416
003199	Marylhurst University	OR	416
003203	Mount Angel Seminary	OR	417
003204	Mt. Hood Community College	OR	417
003206	Multnomah University	OR	417
003207	Pacific Northwest College of Art	OR	419
003208	Northwest Christian University	OR	417
003209	Western Oregon University	OR	419
003210	Oregon State University	OR	418
003211	Oregon Institute of Technology	OR	418
003212	Pacific University	OR	419
003213	Portland Community College	OR	419
003216	Portland State University	OR	418
003217	Reed College	OR	420
003218	Chemeketa Community College	OR	414
003219	Southern Oregon University	OR	419
003220	Southwestern Oregon Community Col	OR	420
003221	Treasure Valley Community College	OR	420
003222	Umpqua Community College	OR	420
003223	University of Oregon	OR	419
003224	University of Portland	OR	420
003225	Warner Pacific College	OR	421
003227	Willamette University	OR	421
003228	Bryn Athyn Col of the New Church	PA	423
003229	Albright College	PA	421
003230	Allegheny College	PA	421
003231	Community College of Allegheny Cty	PA	425
003233	Alvernia University	PA	421
003235	Arcadia University	PA	422
003237	Bryn Mawr College	PA	423
003238	Bucknell University	PA	423
003239	Bucks County Community College	PA	423
003240	Butler County Community College	PA	423
003241	Cabrini College	PA	424
003242	Carnegie Mellon University	PA	424
003243	Cedar Crest College	PA	425
003244	Chatham University	PA	425
003245	Chestnut Hill College	PA	425
003247	Misericordia University	PA	436
003249	Community College of Philadelphia	PA	426
003251	Curtis Institute of Music	PA	426
003252	Delaware Valley College	PA	426
003253	Dickinson College	PA	427
003254	The Penn State Dickinson Sch of Law	PA	439
003256	Drexel University	PA	427
003258	Duquesne University	PA	428
003259	Eastern University	PA	428
003260	Palmer Theol Sem of Eastern Univ	PA	438
003262	Elizabethtown College	PA	428
003263	Evangelical Theological Seminary	PA	429
003265	Franklin & Marshall College	PA	429
003266	Gannon University	PA	429
003267	Geneva College	PA	429
003268	Gettysburg College	PA	429
003269	Grove City College	PA	430
003270	Gwynedd-Mercy College	PA	430
003272	Harcum College	PA	430
003273	Harrisburg Area Community College	PA	430
003274	Haverford College	PA	430
003275	Holy Family University	PA	431
003276	Immaculata University	PA	431
003277	Indiana University of Pennsylvania	PA	442
003279	Juniata College	PA	432
003280	Keystone College	PA	432
003282	King's College	PA	432
003283	Lackawanna College	PA	433
003284	Lafayette College	PA	433
003285	Lancaster Bible College	PA	433
003286	Lancaster Theological Seminary	PA	433
003287	La Salle University	PA	432
003288	Lebanon Valley College	PA	434
003289	Lehigh University	PA	434
003290	Lincoln University	PA	434
003291	Lutheran Theol Seminary Gettysburg	PA	435
003292	Lutheran Theol Seminary at Phila	PA	435
003293	Lycoming College	PA	435
003294	Manor College	PA	435
003296	Marywood University	PA	435
003297	Mercyhurst University	PA	436
003298	Messiah College	PA	436
003300	Moore College of Art and Design	PA	436
003301	Moravian College	PA	437
003302	Mount Aloysius College	PA	437
003303	Carlow University	PA	424
003304	Muhlenberg College	PA	437
003305	Erie Business Center South	PA	428
003306	Valley Forge Christian College	PA	450
003309	Peirce College	PA	438
003311	Salus University	PA	446
003313	Widener University	PA	451
003315	Bloomsburg Univ of Pennsylvania	PA	441
003316	California University of PA	PA	441
003317	Cheyney University of Pennsylvania	PA	442
003318	Clarion University of Pennsylvania	PA	442
003319	Clarion University-Venango Campus	PA	442
003320	East Stroudsburg University of PA	PA	442
003321	Edinboro University of Pennsylvania	PA	442
003322	Kutztown University of Pennsylvania	PA	443
003323	Lock Haven University	PA	443
003324	Mansfield University of PA	PA	443
003325	Millersville University of PA	PA	443
003326	Shippensburg University of PA	PA	443
003327	Slippery Rock University of PA	PA	443
003328	West Chester University of PA	PA	444
003329	Penn State University Park	PA	438
003330	Penn State Lehigh Valley	PA	439
003331	Penn State Altoona	PA	438
003332	Penn State Beaver	PA	439
003333	Penn State Erie	PA	439
003334	Penn State Berks	PA	439
003335	Penn State DuBois	PA	439
003336	Penn State Fayette, The Eberly Camp	PA	439
003338	Penn State Hazleton	PA	439
003339	Penn State Greater Allegheny	PA	439
003340	Penn State Mont Alto	PA	440
003341	Penn State New Kensington	PA	440
003342	Penn State Abington	PA	438
003343	Penn State Schuylkill	PA	440
003344	Penn State Worthington-Scranton	PA	440
003345	Penn State Shenango	PA	440
003346	Penn State Wilkes-Barre	PA	440
003347	Penn State York	PA	440
003348	PA St Grt Vlly Sch of Grad Prof Std	PA	439
003350	The University of the Arts	PA	448
003351	Philadelphia Biblical University	PA	444
003352	Philadelphia Col of Osteopathic Med	PA	444
003353	Univ of Sciences in Philadelphia	PA	450
003354	Philadelphia University	PA	444
003356	Pittsburgh Theological Seminary	PA	444
003357	Point Park University	PA	445
003358	Reformed Presbyterian Theo Seminary	PA	445
003359	Robert Morris University	PA	445
003360	Rosemont College	PA	445
003362	Seton Hill University	PA	447
003364	Saint Charles Borromeo Seminary	PA	446
003366	Saint Francis University	PA	446
003367	Saint Joseph's University	PA	446
003368	Saint Vincent College	PA	446
003369	Susquehanna University	PA	447
003370	Swarthmore College	PA	447
003371	Temple University	PA	447
003376	Thiel College	PA	448
003378	University of Pennsylvania	PA	448
003379	University of Pittsburgh	PA	449
003380	Univ of Pittsburgh Bradford	PA	449
003381	Univ of Pittsburgh Greensburg	PA	449
003382	Univ of Pittsburgh at Johnstown	PA	449
003383	Univ of Pittsburgh Titusville	PA	450
003384	The University of Scranton	PA	450
003385	Ursinus College	PA	450
003386	Valley Forge Military College	PA	450
003388	Villanova University	PA	450
003389	Washington & Jefferson College	PA	451
003391	Waynesburg University	PA	451
003392	Westminster College	PA	451
003393	Westminster Theological Seminary	PA	451
003394	Wilkes University	PA	452
003395	Pennsylvania College of Technology	PA	440
003396	Wilson College	PA	452
003399	York College of Pennsylvania	PA	452
003401	Brown University	RI	453
003402	Bryant University	RI	453
003404	Johnson & Wales University	RI	453
003406	Providence College	RI	453
003407	Rhode Island College	RI	454
003408	Community College of Rhode Island	RI	453
003409	Rhode Island School of Design	RI	454
003410	Roger Williams University	RI	454
003411	Salve Regina University	RI	454
003413	Naval War College	RI	558
003414	University of Rhode Island	RI	454
003417	Allen University	SC	455
003418	Anderson University	SC	455
003419	Charleston Southern University	SC	456
003420	Benedict College	SC	455
003421	Bob Jones University	SC	455
003422	Southern Wesleyan University	SC	461
003423	The Citadel Military College of SC	SC	456
003424	Claflin University	SC	456
003425	Clemson University	SC	456
003426	University of South Carolina Sumter	SC	462
003427	Coker College	SC	457
003428	College of Charleston	SC	457
003429	Columbia International University	SC	457
003430	Columbia College	SC	457
003431	Converse College	SC	457
003432	Erskine College	SC	458
003434	Furman University	SC	458
003435	Lander University	SC	459
003436	Limestone College	SC	459
003437	Lutheran Theol Southern Seminary	SC	459
003438	Medical Univ of South Carolina	SC	459
003439	Morris College	SC	459
003440	Newberry College	SC	459
003441	North Greenville University	SC	460
003445	Presbyterian College	SC	460
003446	South Carolina State University	SC	460
003447	Spartanburg Methodist College	SC	461
003448	Univ of South Carolina-Columbia	SC	462
003449	University of South Carolina Aiken	SC	462
003450	Univ of South Carolina Beaufort	SC	462
003451	Coastal Carolina University	SC	456
003453	Univ of South Carolina Lancaster	SC	462
003454	Univ of South Carolina Salkehatchie	SC	462
003455	Voorhees College	SC	463
003456	Winthrop University	SC	463
003457	Wofford College	SC	463
003458	Augustana College	SD	464
003459	Black Hills State University	SD	465
003461	Dakota Wesleyan University	SD	464
003463	Dakota State University	SD	465
003465	Mount Marty College	SD	464
003466	Northern State University	SD	466
003467	Presentation College	SD	465
003469	University of Sioux Falls	SD	466
003470	South Dakota Sch of Mines & Tech	SD	466
003471	South Dakota State University	SD	466
003474	The University of South Dakota	SD	465
003477	Aquinas College	TN	467
003478	Austin Peay State University	TN	473
003479	Belmont University	TN	467
003480	Bethel University	TN	467
003481	Carson-Newman College	TN	467
003482	Christian Brothers University	TN	467
003483	Columbia State Community College	TN	475
003484	Covenant College	GA	128
003485	Cumberland University	TN	468
003486	Lipscomb University	TN	470
003487	East Tennessee State University	TN	473
003490	Fisk University	TN	468
003492	Freed-Hardeman University	TN	469
003494	Hiwassee College	TN	469
003495	Johnson University	TN	469
003496	King College	TN	470
003499	Lane College	TN	470
003500	Lee University	TN	470
003501	LeMoyne-Owen College	TN	470
003502	Lincoln Memorial University	TN	470
003504	Martin Methodist College	TN	471
003505	Maryville College	TN	471
003506	Meharry Medical College	TN	471
003507	Memphis College of Art	TN	471
003509	The University of Memphis	TN	474
003510	Middle Tennessee State University	TN	473
003511	Milligan College	TN	471
003517	Southern College of Optometry	TN	473
003518	Southern Adventist University	TN	473
003519	Rhodes College	TN	472

Code	Institution	State	Page
003944	Univ of Puerto Rico-Mayaguez	PR	567
003946	University of the Virgin Islands	VI	568
003947	Univ of California-Hastings Col Law	CA	74
003948	San Francisco Art Institute	CA	65
003954	University of Central Florida	FL	120
003955	University of West Florida	FL	121
003956	Dalton State College	GA	128
003961	Harper College	IL	151
003963	AIB College of Business	IA	181
003965	Bay State College	MA	231
003966	Boston Architectural College	MA	231
003969	University of Minnesota-Twin Cities	MN	272
003974	Mesivta Tifereth Jerusalem of Amer	NY	340
003976	Rabbin Academy Mesivta Rabbi Berlin	NY	346
003977	Rabbinical College Ch'san Sofer	NY	346
003978	Rabbinical Seminary of America	NY	347
003979	Teachers College, Columbia Univ	NY	357
003981	Univ of NC School of the Arts	NC	379
003982	Cleveland Institute of Art	OH	388
003985	Oral Roberts University	OK	411
003986	DeSales University	PA	427
003987	La Roche College	PA	432
003988	Neumann University	PA	437
003990	Florence-Darlington Tech College	SC	458
003991	Greenville Technical College	SC	458
003992	Piedmont Technical College	SC	460
003993	Midlands Technical College	SC	459
003994	Spartanburg Community College	SC	461
003995	Central Carolina Technical College	SC	455
003996	York Technical College	SC	463
003998	Chattanooga State Community College	TN	474
003999	Cleveland State Community College	TN	474
004003	Central Texas College	TX	482
004004	John Tyler Community College	VA	527
004007	Madison Area Technical College	WI	554
004027	Utah Valley University	UT	511
004033	Asheville-Buncombe Tech Cmty Col	NC	368
004049	Penn Foster College	AZ	17
004054	Hebrew Union Col-Jewish Inst of Rel	NY	335
004056	Sioux Falls Seminary	SD	465
004057	National American University	SD	464
004058	Gratz College	PA	430
004060	Winebrenner Theological Seminary	OH	406
004061	St Mary Seminary & Graduate School	OH	401
004062	Pitt Community College	NC	372
004069	University of Minnesota-Crookston	MN	271
004071	Walsh Col of Accountacy & Bus Admn	MI	259
004072	Northwood University	MI	256
004075	Eastern Iowa Cmty College District	IA	184
004076	Kirkwood Community College	IA	187
004080	Starr King School for the Ministry	CA	71
004081	Harding Graduate School of Religion	TN	469
004220	Kaplan University	IA	186
004283	Grantham University	MO	282
004431	M Lanning Healthcare Sch Radiology	NE	298
004452	Montgomery County Community College	PA	436
004453	El Centro College	TX	485
004463	South University	AL	7
004480	De Anza College	CA	47
004481	Ohlone College	CA	59
004484	John F. Kennedy University	CA	52
004490	Patten University	CA	61
004494	Everest College-San Bernardino	CA	46
004503	Everest College	CO	84
004506	Colorado Mountain College	CO	82
004507	Everest College	CO	84
004508	Univ of CO DenverlAnschultz Med Cam	CO	88
004509	Univ of Colorado at Colorado Spring	CO	88
004513	Housatonic Community College	CT	91
004546	Heald College, Honolulu	HI	141
004549	Univ of Hawaii Leeward Cmty Col	HI	142
004553	ITT Technical Institute	ID	144
004568	Midstate College	IL	158
004579	International Business College	IN	175
004583	Brown Mackie College-South Bend	IN	170
004586	Kaplan University	IA	186
004587	Northeast Iowa Community College	IA	188
004595	Hawkeye Community College	IA	185
004598	Iowa Western Community College	IA	186
004600	Northwest Iowa Community College	IA	188
004608	Barton County Community College	KS	190
004611	Kansas St Univ-Salina Col Tech/Avi	KS	194
004617	Natl College of Business & Tech	TN	472
004618	Spencerian College	KY	206
004619	Sullivan University	KY	206
004625	Delgado Community College	LA	210
004641	Dunwoody College of Technology	MN	263
004642	Globe University	MN	263
004645	Minneapolis Business College	MN	265
004646	Minnesota School of Business	MN	265
004648	Rasmussen College - Eagan	MN	270
004650	Chesapeake College	MD	222
004661	Hampshire College	MA	235
004666	Salter College	MA	244
004667	Sch of the Museum Fine Arts-Boston	MA	244
004673	Baker College of Flint	MI	248
004680	Baker College of Jackson	MI	248
004688	Univ of Mississippi Medical Center	MS	277
004697	San Mateo County CC District Office	CA	67
004703	Logan College of Chiropractic	MO	284
004707	Covenant Theological Seminary	MO	280
004711	Linn State Technical College	MO	284
004713	Three Rivers Community College	MO	290
004721	Kaplan University	NE	298
004729	Hesser College	NH	305
004731	Daniel Webster College	NH	304
004736	Bergen Community College	NJ	307
004740	Mercer County Community College	NJ	311
004741	Rutgers State Univ - Camden	NJ	314
004742	Central New Mexico Cmty College	NM	317
004743	Clovis Community College	NM	318
004749	Bryant & Stratton College	NY	324
004759	CUNY York College	NY	329
004762	Weill Cornell Medical College	NY	360
004765	CUNY Graduate Center	NY	327
004776	Central Yeshiva Tomchei Tmimim	NY	325
004779	Long Island U Brooklyn Campus	NY	338
004788	Herkimer County Community College	NY	335
004798	Mirrer Yeshiva Central Institute	NY	341
004799	Monroe College	NY	341
004804	New York Institute of Technology	NY	343
004811	Everest Institute	NY	333
004816	Suffolk Cty Cmty College Eastern	NY	356
004835	Caldwell Cmty College & Tech Inst	NC	368
004838	Guilford Technical Community Col	NC	371
004844	Wake Technical Community College	NC	374
004845	Wilson Community College	NC	375
004846	Rasmussen College - Fargo/Moorhead	ND	383
004852	Clark State Community College	OH	387
004853	Bradford School	OH	385
004855	Davis College	OH	389
004861	University of Northwestern Ohio	OH	404
004866	Stautzenberger College	OH	402
004868	Univ of Cincinnati-R. Walters Col	OH	403
004878	Clackamas Community College	OR	415
004882	Oregon Health & Science University	OR	418
004889	Cambria-Rowe Business College	PA	424
004890	Central Penn College	PA	425
004893	DuBois Business College	PA	428
004894	Erie Business Center, Main	PA	428
004898	McCann School of Business & Tech	PA	436
004901	Newport Business Institute	PA	437
004902	Penn Commercial Business/Tech Sch	PA	438
004910	Kaplan Career Institute	PA	432
004914	Newport Business Institute	PA	437
004920	Trident Technical College	SC	461
004922	South University Columbia Campus	SC	461
004923	Clinton Junior College	SC	456
004924	Forrest College	SC	458
004925	Horry-Georgetown Technical College	SC	458
004926	Tri-County Technical College	SC	461
004927	University of South Carolina Union	SC	463
004934	Daymar Institute	TN	468
004937	Jackson State Community College	TN	475
004938	South College	TN	473
004947	West Tennessee Business College	TN	478
004948	Texas A&M System Health Sci Center	TX	497
004949	Baylor College of Medicine	TX	481
004951	University of Texas HSC at Houston	TX	506
004952	The Univ of Texas Medical Branch	TX	507
004972	Galveston College	TX	486
004977	South Texas College of Law	TX	494
004988	Central Virginia Community College	VA	526
004992	Miller-Motte Technical College	VA	521
004996	Dabney S. Lancaster Community Col	VA	526
004999	Bellingham Technical College	WA	531
005000	Pierce College District	WA	536
005001	Edmonds Community College	WA	533
005006	Walla Walla Community College	WA	539
005007	West Virginia Junior College	WV	545
005008	Mountain State College	WV	541
005009	Bryant & Stratton College	WI	546
005015	University of Wisconsin-Parkside	WI	552
005019	Univ Adventista de las Antillas	PR	566
005022	Bayamon Central University	PR	560
005026	Inter Amer Univ of PR Arecibo	PR	563
005027	Inter Amer Univ of PR Barranquitas	PR	563
005028	Inter Amer Univ of PR Bayamon	PR	563
005029	Inter Amer Univ of PR Ponce	PR	564
005127	Brown Mackie College-Cincinnati	OH	385
005203	Remington College-Lafayette Campus	LA	214
005204	Beal College	ME	217
005208	The College of Westchester	NY	330
005210	Cleveland Institute of Electronics	OH	388
005220	Salt Lake Community College	UT	512
005223	New River Community College	VA	527
005245	Univ of Arkansas Cmty Col/Morrilton	AR	25
005252	Ridgewater College	MN	268
005254	Lanier Technical College	GA	133
005255	Moultrie Technical College	GA	134
005256	Wiregrass Georgia Tech College	GA	139
005257	GA Northwestern Technical College	GA	131
005258	Univ of Hawaii Cmty College	HI	142
005260	J.F. Drake State Technical College	AL	4
005263	Minnesota West Cmty & Tech College	MN	267
005264	Flint Hills Technical College	KS	192
005265	North Central Kansas Tech College	KS	195
005266	Highland Cmty Col-Technical Center	KS	193
005267	Northwest Kansas Technical College	KS	195
005271	Bowling Green Technical College	KY	201
005273	Gateway Cmty & Technical College	KY	202
005276	Central Maine Community College	ME	218
005277	Eastern Maine Community College	ME	218
005291	White Mountains Community College	NH	304
005294	Waukesha County Technical College	WI	555
005301	NE Wisconsin Technical College	WI	555
005304	Chippewa Valley Technical College	WI	553
005306	Bates Technical College	WA	531
005309	Lake Area Technical Institute	SD	464
005310	Pittsburgh Institute of Aeronautics	PA	444
005313	North Central State College	OH	397
005316	Coastal Carolina Community College	NC	369
005317	Forsyth Technical Community College	NC	370
005318	Catawba Valley Community College	NC	369
005320	Cape Fear Community College	NC	368
005363	Denmark Technical College	SC	457
005372	South Puget Sound Community College	WA	538
005373	Lake Washington Inst of Technology	WA	535
005378	Northeast State Community College	TN	475
005380	Mid-State Technical College	WI	554
005384	Nicolet Area Technical College	WI	555
005387	Northcentral Technical College	WI	555
005389	Gateway Technical College	WI	554
005390	Blackhawk Technical College	WI	553
005447	Randolph Community College	NC	373
005448	Durham Technical Community College	NC	370
005449	Central Carolina Community College	NC	369
005461	Salem Community College	NJ	315
005463	Alamance Community College	NC	368
005464	Richmond Community College	NC	373
005466	So LA Cmty Col T.H. Harris Campus	LA	212
005467	Sowela Technical Community College	LA	212
005469	NW LA Tech Col Shreveport Campus	LA	211
005471	NE LA Tech Col Delta-Ouachita Camp	LA	210
005475	NE LA Tech Col Northeast Campus	LA	210
005476	NE LA Tech Col Farmerville Campus	LA	210
005478	Capital Area Tech Col Jumonville	LA	210
005480	Centl LA Tech Col Huey P Long Camp	LA	210
005482	South LA Cmty Col Gulf Area Campus	LA	212
005488	Capital Area Tech Col Baton Rouge	LA	209
005489	Central LA Tech Community College	LA	210
005498	Wichita Area Technical College	KS	197
005499	Salina Area Technical College	KS	196
005500	Manhattan Area Technical College	KS	195
005511	Okefenokee Technical College	GA	135
005525	Southern Maine Community College	ME	219
005526	S Central LA Tech Col Young Mem Cam	LA	211
005528	South LA Cmty Col Teche Area Campus	LA	212
005533	St Paul Col A Cmty & Tech College	MN	269
005534	Saint Cloud Technical & Cmty Coll	MN	269
005535	Pine Technical College	MN	268
005537	South Central College	MN	269
005541	Minnesota State Cmty & Tech College	MN	267
005544	Alexandria Technical & Cmty Col	MN	265
005599	Augusta Technical College	GA	125
005600	Athens Technical College	GA	125
005601	Albany Technical College	GA	124
005615	Southwest Georgia Technical College	GA	138
005617	South Georgia Technical College	GA	137
005618	Savannah Technical College	GA	136
005619	North Georgia Technical College	GA	135
005621	Southern Crescent Technical College	GA	137
005622	Georgia Piedmont Technical College	GA	131
005624	Columbus Technical College	GA	128
005691	Shelton State Community College	AL	6
005692	Reid State Technical College	AL	6
005697	Northwest-Shoals Community College	AL	6
005699	George Wallace St Cmty Col-Selma	AL	4
005707	Southeast Arkansas College	AR	23
005732	Univ of Arkansas CC at Hope	AR	25
005733	Bevill State Community College	AL	2
005734	Trenholm State Technical College	AL	7
005739	Mesabi Range Cmty & Tech College	MN	266
005752	Clover Park Technical College	WA	532
005753	Owens Community College	OH	400
005754	Rowan-Cabarrus Community College	NC	373
005757	Lake Superior College	MN	266
005759	Northwest Technical College	MN	268
005760	Northern Maine Community College	ME	218
005761	L.E. Fletcher Technical Cmty Coll	LA	210
005763	Central Georgia Technical College	GA	127
005889	Univ Oklahoma Health Science Center	OK	413
006165	Los Angeles County Col of Nursing	CA	55
006191	St. Vincent's College	CT	94
006214	Blessing-Rieman College of Nursing	IL	146
006225	Trinity Col Nursing/Hlth Sci	IL	166
006228	Methodist College	IL	158
006240	St Francis Med Ctr Col of Nursing	IL	163
006250	Resurrection University	IL	162
006273	Mercy College of Health Sciences	IA	187
006305	Central ME Med Ctr Col Nur/Hlth Prf	ME	217
006324	Laboure College	MA	235
006385	Chamberlain Col of Nursing-St Louis	MO	279
006389	Goldfarb School of Nursing	MO	282
006392	Research College of Nursing	MO	287
006399	Bryan LGH Col of Health Sciences	NE	296
006404	Nebraska Methodist College	NE	299
006438	Phillip Beth Israel Sch of Nursing	NY	346
006443	Cochran School of Nursing	NY	329
006445	Crouse Hospital College of Nursing	NY	331
006448	Ellis School of Nursing	NY	332
006461	St. Elizabeth College of Nursing	NY	348
006467	St. Joseph's College of Nursing	NY	349
006477	Cabarrus College of Health Sciences	NC	362
006487	Aultman College Nursing/Health Sci	OH	384
006489	Christ Col of Nursing & Health Sci	OH	387

Code	Institution	State	Page
008613	Roanoke-Chowan Community College	NC	373
008614	Rab Col Bobover Yesh B'nei Zion	NY	346
008617	Rabbinical Seminary M'kor Chaim	NY	347
008635	IntelliTec Medical Institute	CO	85
008659	Lord Fairfax Community College	VA	527
008660	Germanna Community College	VA	526
008661	Southside Virginia Community Col	VA	528
008677	Northwest State Community College	OH	397
008694	Rasmussen College - St. Cloud	MN	270
008711	Coast Cmty College Dist Admin Ofc	CA	41
008788	SUNY System Office	NY	351
008843	Alaska Bible College	AK	10
008844	California Christian College	CA	32
008846	The Wright Institute	CA	79
008848	Warner University	FL	123
008849	Palm Beach Atlantic University	FL	114
008854	New Mexico State University Grants	NM	319
008855	Edgecombe Community College	NC	370
008859	John A. Gupton College	TN	469
008860	SIT	VT	514
008862	East Central College	MO	281
008863	Walters State Community College	TN	476
008871	Concorde Career College	CO	84
008878	Miami Int'l Univ of Art & Design	FL	113
008880	Morrison Institute of Technology	IL	159
008887	Concorde Career College	OR	415
008895	San Diego CC Dist Admin Offices	CA	65
008896	Pikes Peak Community College	CO	87
008902	Columbia Centro Universitario	PR	561
008903	College of the Canyons	CA	41
008904	Virginia Cmty College System Office	VA	526
008906	Macomb Community College	MI	254
008916	New England Law | Boston	MA	243
008918	Saddleback College	CA	70
008976	Clayton State University	GA	127
008988	Lurleen B. Wallace Cmty College	AL	5
009003	Olean Business Institute	NY	345
009009	Univ of New Hampshire at Manchester	NH	306
009010	Madisonville Community College	KY	202
009016	Univ of So Florida St. Petersburg	FL	121
009020	Foothill-De Anza Cmty Coll District	CA	47
009032	Empire College School of Business	CA	45
009043	Elmira Business Institute	NY	332
009047	Huntington Junior College	WV	541
009054	WV Northern Community College	WV	543
009058	Bethel University	MN	261
009077	USC The Business College	NY	359
009079	Everest College	OR	415
009082	International Business College	TX	486
009088	ITT Technical Institute	OH	392
009089	Hannibal-La Grange University	MO	282
009135	Illinois Eastern CC System Office	IL	152
009137	Metro CC-Kansas City Admin Ctr	MO	284
009139	Metropolitan Cmty Col-Maple Woods	MO	285
009140	Metropolitan Community Col-Longview	MO	285
009145	Governors State University	IL	151
009146	Yosemite Community College District	CA	80
009157	WyoTech	WY	557
009159	Paul D. Camp Community College	VA	528
009160	Rappahannock Community College	VA	528
009163	San Antonio College	TX	479
009169	Wright State University Lake Campus	OH	406
009185	Rose State College	OK	411
009186	Dean Institute of Technology	PA	426
009190	Oregon University System	OR	418
009192	Sierra Nevada College	NV	303
009193	Reformed Theological Seminary	MS	276
009194	Lakeshore Technical College	WI	554
009224	DeVry University - Decatur Campus	GA	128
009225	Texas State Tech College Harlingen	TX	500
009226	Francis Marion University	SC	458
009228	DeVry Univ - North Brunswick Campus	NJ	309
009230	Wayne County Community College Dist	MI	259
009231	Washington County Community College	ME	219
009232	Catholic Theological Union	IL	146
009236	Nashua Community College	NH	304
009248	Samaritan Hospital Sch of Nursing	NY	350
009256	Moraine Park Technical College	WI	554
009259	Laramie County Community College	WY	556
009267	Everest College	VA	519
009270	The Art Institute of Atlanta	GA	125
009272	Crafton Hills College	CA	65
009275	Northern Kentucky University	KY	205
009282	Highlands College of Montana Tech	MT	296
009292	Kaplan University-Maine	ME	218
009313	Daymar College-Owensboro	KY	200
009314	Great Falls Col Montana State Univ	MT	295
009322	Williamsburg Technical College	SC	463
009331	Dallas County Cmty Coll Dist Office	TX	484
009333	Univ of Illinois at Springfield	IL	167
009335	Mestiva Eastern Pkwy Rabbinical Sem	NY	340
009336	Johnston Community College	NC	371
009339	Utah System of Higher Education	UT	511
009343	Bryant & Stratton College	OH	386
009344	Ramapo College of New Jersey	NJ	313
009345	The Richard Stockton College of NJ	NJ	313
009346	Minnesota State Coll & Univ Sys Ofc	MN	265
009354	Medcenter One College of Nursing	ND	381
009401	Colorado Christian University	CO	82
009407	Lincoln College of New England	CT	93
009412	Fortis College	OH	390
009420	Sanford-Brown College-Tysons Corner	VA	524
009430	Tri-County Community College	NC	374
009449	Pennco Tech	PA	440
009451	Brown Mackie College-Tucson	AZ	12
009454	Griggs University	MI	252
009466	Kaplan College	TX	489
009479	St Paul's Sch of Nurs-Staten Island	NY	349
009507	Georgia Highlands College	GA	130
009542	Community College of Denver	CO	84
009543	Red Rocks Community College	CO	87
009544	Spokane Falls Community College	WA	533
009549	Western Texas College	TX	508
009618	Tulsa Welding School	OK	413
009621	Herzing University	WI	547
009629	Mountain Empire Community College	VA	527
009635	Florida International University	FL	119
009637	Southern Univ & A&M Col Sys Ofc	LA	214
009642	Texas State Tech College System	TX	500
009645	Bard College at Simon's Rock	MA	230
009646	Piedmont Community College	NC	372
009647	Oklahoma State Univ - Oklahoma City	OK	410
009651	Texas A&M International University	TX	497
009652	University of Puerto Rico at Ponce	PR	568
009684	Blue Ridge Community College	NC	368
009704	North Seattle Community College	WA	537
009706	South Seattle Community College	WA	537
009707	Bluegrass Cmty & Tech Col	KY	201
009721	Bradford School	PA	423
009740	Inver Hills Community College	MN	266
009741	The University of Texas at Dallas	TX	506
009742	North Orange Cty Cmty Col District	CA	59
009743	Bellevue University	NE	296
009744	Fox Valley Technical College	WI	554
009747	Gordon-Conwell Theological Seminary	MA	235
009748	Carrington College CA-Sacramento	CA	38
009756	Univ of Massachusetts Worcester	MA	237
009763	Tulsa Community College	OK	412
009764	Tunxis Community College	CT	92
009765	Three Rivers Community College	CT	92
009767	City Cols of Chicago Olive-Harvey	IL	147
009768	University of North Texas H.S.C.	TX	504
009769	Metropolitan College of New York	NY	341
009777	Kaplan College	IN	177
009782	Saint Luke's College of Health Sci	MO	289
009786	Illinois Eastern CC Lincoln Trail	IL	152
009795	Missouri College	MO	286
009797	Midland College	TX	491
009800	Rush University	IL	163
009826	Kennebec Valley Community College	ME	218
009837	ITT Technical Institute	OH	392
009841	University of North Florida	FL	120
009862	Clarkson College	NE	297
009863	Lancaster Genl Col Nursing/Hlth Sci	PA	433
009867	Univ of CT Health Center	CT	95
009892	Duluth Business University, Inc.	MN	263
009896	Oakton Community College	IL	160
009903	Vance-Granville Community College	NC	374
009910	Technical College of the Lowcountry	SC	461
009912	Volunteer State Community College	TN	476
009914	Roane State Community College	TN	476
009917	Ivy Tech Cmty Col-Central Indiana	IN	175
009923	Ivy Tech Cmty Coll of IN-Southeast	IN	177
009924	Ivy Tech Cmty Coll of IN-E. Central	IN	176
009925	Ivy Tech Cmty Coll of IN-Southwest	IN	177
009926	Ivy Tech Cmty Coll of IN-Northeast	IN	176
009928	Piedmont Virginia Community College	VA	528
009929	SUNY College of Optometry	NY	355
009930	Univ of Texas of the Permian Basin	TX	507
009932	Texas State Technical Col W. Texas	TX	500
009936	Middlesex Community College	MA	240
009941	Belmont College	OH	385
009942	Shawnee State University	OH	401
009962	Luna Community College	NM	318
009975	NW LA Tech Col Northwest Campus	LA	211
009976	College of the Ouachitas	AR	21
009981	Morgan Community College	CO	86
009982	Victory University	TN	478
009986	Seton Hall University School of Law	NJ	315
009987	St. Anthony College of Nursing	IL	163
009989	Santa Barbara Business College	CA	68
009992	Oak Hills Christian College	MN	270
009994	Passaic County Community College	NJ	312
010010	American Samoa Community College	AS	559
010013	Alliant Internatl Univ-Los Angeles	CA	27
010014	Garrett College	MD	222
010017	Payne Theological Seminary	OH	401
010019	University Texas SW Medical Center	TX	507
010020	Lewis and Clark Community College	IL	156
010027	James A. Rhodes State College	OH	392
010037	Ivy Tech Cmty Coll of IN-Richmond	IN	176
010038	Ivy Tech Cmty Coll of IN-Columbus	IN	176
010039	Ivy Tech Cmty Coll of IN-Lafayette	IN	176
010040	Ivy Tech Cmty Coll of IN-Northwest	IN	176
010041	Ivy Tech Cmty Coll of IN-Kokomo	IN	176
010043	Bon Secours Memorial Col of Nursing	VA	517
010051	La Guardia Community College/CUNY	NY	328
010056	Aiken Technical College	SC	455
010060	Vernon College	TX	507
010061	Bryant & Stratton College	VA	517
010065	Washington Theological Union	DC	100
010074	St Patrick's Seminary & University	CA	64
010097	CUNY Medgar Evers College	NY	328
010098	Morrison University	NV	302
010106	Seattle Community Colleges	WA	537
010109	Ivy Tech Cmty Coll of IN-Southern	IN	177
010111	Cerro Coso Community College	CA	52
010115	University of Texas at San Antonio	TX	506
010130	Wade College Infomart	TX	508
010139	DeVry University - Irving Campus	TX	486
010142	Touro College	NY	358
010148	Colorado Technical University	CO	83
010149	Pepperdine University	CA	61
010153	Helene Fuld College of Nursing	NY	335
010166	City Col Montana State Univ Billngs	MT	295
010170	Western Dakota Technical Institute	SD	466
010176	Westmoreland County Community Col	PA	451
010182	Rogue Community College	OR	420
010193	Herzing University	AL	4
010195	Art Institute of Fort Lauderdale	FL	101
010198	ECPI College of Technology	VA	518
010248	The Art Institutes International MN	MN	261
010256	Benedictine College	KS	191
010264	South College	NC	376
010266	Hillsdale Free Will Baptist College	OK	408
010279	Hickey College	MO	282
010286	SUNY Empire State College	NY	355
010298	Texas A & M University at Galveston	TX	497
010316	Lincoln College of Technology	IL	157
010338	Eastern Virginia Medical School	VA	518
010340	Los Medanos College	CA	43
010343	College of Micronesia-FSM	FM	559
010345	Cincinnati State Tech & Cmty Col	OH	387
010356	Everest Institute	WV	541
010362	College of Southern Nevada	NV	302
010363	Western Nevada College	NV	303
010364	Whatcom Community College	WA	540
010365	Charles Drew Univ of Med & Science	CA	39
010368	Fresno Pacific Biblical Sem	CA	47
010374	Metropolitan State University	MN	267
010378	Rabbinical College of Long Island	NY	346
010387	El Paso Community College	TX	486
010388	Reading Area Community College	PA	445
010391	Oklahoma City Community College	OK	409
010394	Univ of Medicine & Dentistry of NJ	NJ	316
010395	University of San Diego	CA	76
010402	Dakota County Technical College	MN	266
010405	Pinnacle Career Institute	MO	287
010410	TESST College of Technology	MD	226
010434	Renton Technical College	WA	537
010438	Haskell Indian Nations University	KS	193
010439	Southwest Tennessee Community Coll	TN	476
010441	Pardee RAND Grad Sch of Policy Stds	CA	61
010453	Washington State Community College	OH	405
010460	American Baptist College	TN	466
010474	Marymount College	CA	56
010487	West Georgia Technical College	GA	139
010489	National College	KY	205
010491	Hennepin Technical College	MN	266
010501	Lakeview College of Nursing	IL	156
010509	Hallmark College of Technology	TX	487
010529	Memphis Theological Seminary	TN	471
010530	Quinebaug Valley Community College	CT	92
010546	Century College	MN	266
010549	Kehilath Yakov Rabbinical Seminary	NY	337
010554	Concordia College Alabama	AL	2
010567	Colegio Universitario de San Juan	PR	561
010573	West Virginia Junior College	WV	545
010618	Mid-America College of Funeral Svc	IN	178
010627	ITT Technical Institute	MI	252
010633	Houston Community College	TX	487
010652	Pasco-Hernando Community College	FL	114
010674	Texas Tech University Health Sci Ct	TX	502
010684	Erie Community College City Campus	NY	333
010687	The Ohio State University AT Inst	OH	399
010724	Carlos Albizu University	PR	561
010727	DeVry University - Chicago Campus	IL	149
010736	Marion Technical College	OH	395
010761	Dallas Institute of Funeral Service	TX	485
010771	Gupton Jones Coll of Funeral Svc	GA	132
010784	Cmty Colleges of Spokane Dist 17	WA	533
010805	University of Cincinnati-Clermont	OH	403
010813	Amer Acad McAllister Inst Funeral	NY	322
010814	Pittsburgh Inst of Mortuary Science	PA	444
010818	The University of Akron-Wayne Col	OH	403
010819	Conservatory of Music Puerto Rico	PR	561
010832	Western State Univ College of Law	CA	78
010837	Simmons Inst of Funeral Service	NY	351
010854	Thomas Jefferson School of Law	CA	72
010861	West Virginia Business College	WV	542
010879	Richland Community College	IL	162
010880	Chatfield College	OH	387
010881	Stark State College	OH	402
010906	Cincinnati Col of Mortuary Science	OH	387
010913	Madison Media Inst-Col Media Arts	WI	548
010923	Union Institute & University	OH	402
010943	Rabbinical College Beth Shraga	NY	346
010975	Univ of Puerto Rico at Bayamon	PR	567
010997	East Georgia State College	GA	129
010998	Pennsylvania Institute of Tech	PA	441
011005	Kaplan College	OH	393
011009	Palau Community College	PW	560
011017	Herzing University	MN	264
011031	Technical Career Institutes	NY	357
011046	Central Ohio Technical College	OH	386
011074	Bainbridge College	GA	126

Index of Universities, Colleges and Schools

Institution	State	Page
Argosy University, Twin Cities	MINNESOTA	260
Argosy University, Washington DC	VIRGINIA	516
Arizona Christian University (formerly Southwestern College)	ARIZONA	11
Arizona College of Allied Health	ARIZONA	11
Arizona School of Acupuncture and Oriental Medicine	ARIZONA	11
Arizona State University	ARIZONA	11
Arizona Western College	ARIZONA	12
Arkansas Baptist College	ARKANSAS	19
Arkansas Northeastern College	ARKANSAS	20
Arkansas State University-Beebe	ARKANSAS	20
Arkansas State University-Jonesboro	ARKANSAS	20
Arkansas State University-Mountain Home	ARKANSAS	20
Arkansas State University-Newport	ARKANSAS	20
Arkansas State University System	ARKANSAS	20
Arkansas Tech University	ARKANSAS	20
Arlington Baptist College	TEXAS	480
Armstrong Atlantic State University	GEORGIA	124
Art Academy of Cincinnati	OHIO	384
Art Center College of Design	CALIFORNIA	29
Art Institute of Atlanta, The	GEORGIA	125
Art Institute of California, A College of Argosy University - Hollywood, Th	EALIFORNIA	29
Art Institute of California, A College of Argosy University - Inland Em pire, The	CALIFORNIA	29
Art Institute of California, A College of Argosy University - Los Angel es, The	CALIFORNIA	30
Art Institute of California, A College of Argosy University - Orange Co unty, The	CALIFORNIA	30
Art Institute of California, A College of Argosy University - Sacrament o, The	CALIFORNIA	30
Art Institute of California, A College of Argosy University - San Diego, Th	EALIFORNIA	30
Art Institute of California, A College of Argosy University - San Franc isco, The	CALIFORNIA	30
Art Institute of California, A College of Argosy University - Sunnyvale, Th	EALIFORNIA	30
Art Institute of Charlotte, The	NORTH CAROLINA	362
Art Institute of Cincinnati, The	OHIO	384
Art Institute of Colorado, The	COLORADO	81
Art Institute of Dallas	TEXAS	480
Art Institute of Fort Lauderdale, The	FLORIDA	101
Art Institute of Houston, The	TEXAS	480
Art Institute of Indianapolis, The	INDIANA	169
Art Institute of Las Vegas, The	NEVADA	301
Art Institute of Michigan, The	MICHIGAN	247
Art Institute of New York City, The	NEW YORK	323
Art Institute of Ohio-Cincinnati, The	OHIO	384
Art Institute of Philadelphia	PENNSYLVANIA	422
Art Institute of Phoenix, The	ARIZONA	12
Art Institute of Pittsburgh	PENNSYLVANIA	422
Art Institute of Portland, The	OREGON	414
Art Institute of Salt Lake City, The	UTAH	509
Art Institute of Seattle, The	WASHINGTON	531
Art Institute of Tucson, The	ARIZONA	12
Art Institute of York - Pennsylvania, The	PENNSYLVANIA	422
Art Institutes International - Kansas City, The	KANSAS	190
Art Institutes International Minnesota, The	MINNESOTA	261
ASA Institute of Business & Computer Technology	NEW YORK	323
Asbury Theological Seminary	KENTUCKY	198
Asbury University	KENTUCKY	198
Asheville - Buncombe Technical Community College	NORTH CAROLINA	368
Ashford University	IOWA	182
Ashland Community and Technical College	KENTUCKY	201
Ashland University	OHIO	384
Ashworth College	GEORGIA	125
Asian Institute of Medical Studies	ARIZONA	12
Asnuntuck Community College	CONNECTICUT	91
Aspen University	COLORADO	81
Assemblies of God Theological Seminary	MISSOURI	278
Assumption College	MASSACHUSETTS	230
Assumption College for Sisters	NEW JERSEY	307
ATA College	KENTUCKY	198
Atenas College	PUERTO RICO	560
Athenaeum of Ohio	OHIO	384
Athens State University	ALABAMA	1
Athens Technical College	GEORGIA	125
ATI Career Training Center	FLORIDA	101
ATI Career Training Center	TEXAS	480
Atlanta Metropolitan State College	GEORGIA	125
Atlanta Technical College	GEORGIA	125
Atlanta's John Marshall Law School	GEORGIA	125
Atlantic Cape Community College	NEW JERSEY	307
Atlantic Institute of Oriental Medicine	FLORIDA	101
Atlantic University	VIRGINIA	516
Atlantic University College	PUERTO RICO	560
ATS Institute of Technology	OHIO	384
Auburn University	ALABAMA	1
Auburn University at Montgomery	ALABAMA	1
Augsburg College	MINNESOTA	261
Augusta State University	GEORGIA	125
Augusta Technical College	GEORGIA	125
Augustana College	ILLINOIS	145
Augustana College	SOUTH DAKOTA	464
Aultman College of Nursing and Health Sciences	OHIO	384
Aurora University	ILLINOIS	145
Austin College	TEXAS	481
Austin Community College District	TEXAS	481
Austin Graduate School of Theology	TEXAS	481
Austin Peay State University	TENNESSEE	473
Austin Presbyterian Theological Seminary	TEXAS	481
Ave Maria School of Law	FLORIDA	101
Ave Maria University	FLORIDA	101
Averett University	VIRGINIA	516
Aviation Institute of Maintenance	VIRGINIA	516
Aviator College of Aeronautical Science & Technology	FLORIDA	101
Avila University	MISSOURI	278
Azure College	FLORIDA	101
Azusa Pacific University	CALIFORNIA	30
Babel University Professional School of Translation	HAWAII	140
Babson College	MASSACHUSETTS	230
Bacone College	OKLAHOMA	407
Bainbridge College	GEORGIA	126
Bainbridge Graduate Institute	WASHINGTON	531
Bais HaMedrash & Mesivta of Baltimore	MARYLAND	221
Bais Medrash Toras Chesed	NEW JERSEY	307
Baker College of Allen Park	MICHIGAN	247
Baker College of Auburn Hills	MICHIGAN	247
Baker College of Cadillac	MICHIGAN	248
Baker College of Clinton Township	MICHIGAN	248
Baker College of Flint	MICHIGAN	248
Baker College of Jackson	MICHIGAN	248
Baker College of Muskegon	MICHIGAN	248
Baker College of Owosso	MICHIGAN	248
Baker College of Port Huron	MICHIGAN	248
Baker College System	MICHIGAN	247
Baker University	KANSAS	190
Bakersfield College	CALIFORNIA	52
Bakke Graduate University	WASHINGTON	531
Baldwin Wallace University	OHIO	384
Ball State University	INDIANA	169
Baltimore City Community College	MARYLAND	221
Bangor Theological Seminary	MAINE	217
Bank Street College of Education	NEW YORK	323
Baptist Bible College	MISSOURI	278
Baptist Bible College and Seminary	PENNSYLVANIA	422
Baptist College of Florida, The	FLORIDA	101
Baptist Health System School of Health Professions	TEXAS	481
Baptist Memorial College of Health Sciences	TENNESSEE	467
Baptist Missionary Association Theological Seminary	TEXAS	481
Baptist Theological Seminary at Richmond	VIRGINIA	516
Baptist University of the Americas	TEXAS	481
Barclay College	KANSAS	190
Bard College	NEW YORK	323
Bard College at Simon's Rock	MASSACHUSETTS	230
Barnard College	NEW YORK	323
Barry University	FLORIDA	101
Barstow Community College District	CALIFORNIA	30
Barton College	NORTH CAROLINA	362
Barton County Community College	KANSAS	190
Baruch College/City University of New York	NEW YORK	326
Bastyr University	WASHINGTON	531
Bates College	MAINE	217
Bates Technical College	WASHINGTON	531
Baton Rouge College	LOUISIANA	208
Baton Rouge Community College	LOUISIANA	209
Baton Rouge School of Computers	LOUISIANA	208
Bauder College	GEORGIA	126
Bay Medical Center	FLORIDA	102
Bay Mills Community College	MICHIGAN	248
Bay Noc Community College	MICHIGAN	248
Bay Path College	MASSACHUSETTS	230
Bay State College	MASSACHUSETTS	231
Bayamon Central University	PUERTO RICO	560
Baylor College of Medicine	TEXAS	481
Baylor University	TEXAS	482
Beacon College	FLORIDA	102
Beal College	MAINE	217
Beaufort County Community College	NORTH CAROLINA	368
Becker College-Worcester	MASSACHUSETTS	231
Beckfield College	KENTUCKY	198
Beckfield College	OHIO	385
Be'er Yaakov Talmudic Seminary	NEW YORK	323
Beis Medrash Heichal Dovid	NEW YORK	323
Bel-Rea Institute of Animal Technology	COLORADO	81
Belhaven University	MISSISSIPPI	273
Bellarmine University	KENTUCKY	198
Bellevue College	WASHINGTON	531
Bellevue University	NEBRASKA	296
Bellin College, Inc.	WISCONSIN	546
Bellingham Technical College	WASHINGTON	531
Belmont Abbey College	NORTH CAROLINA	362
Belmont College	OHIO	385
Belmont University	TENNESSEE	467
Beloit College	WISCONSIN	546
Bemidji State University	MINNESOTA	265
Benedict College	SOUTH CAROLINA	455
Benedictine College	KANSAS	191
Benedictine University	ILLINOIS	145
Benjamin Franklin Institute of Technology	MASSACHUSETTS	231
Bennett College	NORTH CAROLINA	362
Bennington College	VERMONT	513
Bentley University	MASSACHUSETTS	231
Berea College	KENTUCKY	199
Bergen Community College	NEW JERSEY	307
Bergin University of Canine Studies	CALIFORNIA	30
Berkeley City College	CALIFORNIA	62
Berkeley College	NEW JERSEY	307
Berkeley College	NEW YORK	323
Berklee College of Music	MASSACHUSETTS	231
Berks Technical Institute	PENNSYLVANIA	422
Berkshire Community College	MASSACHUSETTS	239
Berry College	GEORGIA	126
Beth Benjamin Academy of Connecticut	CONNECTICUT	90
Beth Hamedrash Shaarei Yosher Institute	NEW YORK	323
Beth Hatalmud Rabbinical College	NEW YORK	324
Beth Medrash Govoha	NEW JERSEY	307

Institution	State	Page
Calvary Bible College and Theological Seminary	MISSOURI	279
Calvin College	MICHIGAN	249
Calvin Theological Seminary	MICHIGAN	249
Cambria-Rowe Business College	PENNSYLVANIA	424
Cambridge College	MASSACHUSETTS	233
Cambridge Institute of Allied Health & Technology	FLORIDA	102
Cambridge Junior College	CALIFORNIA	38
Camden County College	NEW JERSEY	308
Cameron College	LOUISIANA	208
Cameron University	OKLAHOMA	407
Campbell University	NORTH CAROLINA	362
Campbellsville University	KENTUCKY	199
Cañada College	CALIFORNIA	67
Canisius College	NEW YORK	325
Cankdeska Cikana Community College	NORTH DAKOTA	381
Cape Cod Community College	MASSACHUSETTS	239
Cape Fear Community College	NORTH CAROLINA	368
Capella University	MINNESOTA	261
Capital Area Technical College Baton Rouge Campus	LOUISIANA	209
Capital Area Technical College Folkes Campus	LOUISIANA	209
Capital Area Technical College Jumonville Campus	LOUISIANA	210
Capital Community College	CONNECTICUT	91
Capital University	OHIO	386
Capitol College	MARYLAND	221
Cardinal Stritch University	WISCONSIN	546
Career College of Northern Nevada	NEVADA	301
Career Point College	TEXAS	482
Career Technical College	LOUISIANA	208
Career Training Academy	PENNSYLVANIA	424
Career Training Solutions	VIRGINIA	517
Caribbean University	PUERTO RICO	560
Carl Albert State College	OKLAHOMA	407
Carl Sandburg College	ILLINOIS	146
Carleton College	MINNESOTA	261
Carlos Albizu University	PUERTO RICO	561
Carlos Albizu University Miami Campus	FLORIDA	102
Carlow University	PENNSYLVANIA	424
Carnegie Mellon University	PENNSYLVANIA	424
Carolina Bible College	NORTH CAROLINA	363
Carolina Christian College	NORTH CAROLINA	363
Carolina Graduate School of Divinity	NORTH CAROLINA	363
Carolinas College of Health Sciences	NORTH CAROLINA	363
Carrington College - Albuquerque	NEW MEXICO	317
Carrington College - Boise	IDAHO	143
Carrington College California - Administrative Office	CALIFORNIA	38
Carrington College California - Antioch	CALIFORNIA	38
Carrington College California - Citrus Heights	CALIFORNIA	38
Carrington College California - Emeryville	CALIFORNIA	38
Carrington College California - Pleasant Hill	CALIFORNIA	38
Carrington College California - Sacramento	CALIFORNIA	38
Carrington College California - San Jose	CALIFORNIA	38
Carrington College California - San Leandro	CALIFORNIA	38
Carrington College California - Stockton	CALIFORNIA	38
Carrington College - Mesa	ARIZONA	12
Carrington College - Phoenix	ARIZONA	13
Carrington College - Portland	OREGON	414
Carrington College - Spokane	WASHINGTON	532
Carrington College - Tucson	ARIZONA	13
Carrington College - Westside	ARIZONA	13
Carroll College	MONTANA	293
Carroll Community College	MARYLAND	221
Carroll University	WISCONSIN	546
Carson-Newman College	TENNESSEE	467
Carteret Community College	NORTH CAROLINA	369
Carthage College	WISCONSIN	546
Carver College	GEORGIA	126
Casa Loma College-Van Nuys	CALIFORNIA	38
Cascadia Community College	WASHINGTON	532
Case Western Reserve University	OHIO	386
Casper College	WYOMING	556
Castleton State College	VERMONT	515
Catawba College	NORTH CAROLINA	363
Catawba Valley Community College	NORTH CAROLINA	369
Catholic Distance University, The	VIRGINIA	517
Catholic Theological Union	ILLINOIS	146
Catholic University of America, The	DISTRICT OF COLUMBIA	97
Cayuga Community College	NEW YORK	325
Cazenovia College	NEW YORK	325
CBD College	CALIFORNIA	38
Cecil College	MARYLAND	222
Cedar Crest College	PENNSYLVANIA	425
Cedar Valley College	TEXAS	484
Cedars-Sinai Medical Center Graduate Program in Biomedical Sciences and Tra nslational Medicine	CALIFORNIA	38
Cedarville University	OHIO	386
Centenary College	NEW JERSEY	308
Centenary College of Louisiana	LOUISIANA	208
Center for Advanced Legal Studies	TEXAS	482
Center for Advanced Studies On Puerto Rico and the Caribbean	PUERTO RICO	561
Central Alabama Community College	ALABAMA	2
Central Arizona College	ARIZONA	13
Central Baptist College	ARKANSAS	21
Central Baptist Theological Seminary	KANSAS	191
Central Baptist Theological Seminary	VIRGINIA	517
Central Baptist Theological Seminary of Minneapolis	MINNESOTA	262
Central Bible College	MISSOURI	279
Central Carolina Community College	NORTH CAROLINA	369
Central Carolina Technical College	SOUTH CAROLINA	455
Central Christian College of Kansas	KANSAS	191
Central Christian College of the Bible	MISSOURI	279
Central College	IOWA	183
Central Community College	NEBRASKA	297
Central Connecticut State University	CONNECTICUT	90
Central Florida Institute	FLORIDA	103
Central Georgia Technical College	GEORGIA	127
Central Lakes College	MINNESOTA	265
Central Louisiana Technical College Avoyelles Campus	LOUISIANA	210
Central Louisiana Technical College Huey P. Long Campus	LOUISIANA	210
Central Louisiana Technical College Oakdale Campus	LOUISIANA	210
Central Louisiana Technical Community College	LOUISIANA	210
Central Maine Community College	MAINE	218
Central Maine Medical Center College of Nursing and Health Professions	MAINE	217
Central Methodist University	MISSOURI	279
Central Michigan University	MICHIGAN	249
Central New Mexico Community College	NEW MEXICO	317
Central Ohio Technical College	OHIO	386
Central Oregon Community College	OREGON	414
Central Penn College	PENNSYLVANIA	425
Central Piedmont Community College	NORTH CAROLINA	369
Central State University	OHIO	387
Central Texas College	TEXAS	482
Central Virginia Community College	VIRGINIA	526
Central Washington University	WASHINGTON	532
Central Wyoming College	WYOMING	556
Central Yeshiva Tomchei Tmimim Lubavitch America	NEW YORK	325
Centralia College	WASHINGTON	532
Centre College	KENTUCKY	199
Centro de Estudios Multidisciplinarios	PUERTO RICO	561
Centura College	VIRGINIA	517
Centura Institute	FLORIDA	103
Century College	MINNESOTA	266
Cerritos College	CALIFORNIA	39
Cerro Coso Community College	CALIFORNIA	52
Chabot College	CALIFORNIA	39
Chabot-Las Positas Community College District	CALIFORNIA	39
Chadron State College	NEBRASKA	299
Chaffey College	CALIFORNIA	39
Chamberlain College of Nursing - St. Louis	MISSOURI	279
Chaminade University of Honolulu	HAWAII	140
Champlain College	VERMONT	513
Chancellor University	OHIO	387
Chandler-Gilbert Community College	ARIZONA	15
Chapman University	CALIFORNIA	39
Charles R. Drew University of Medicine & Science	CALIFORNIA	39
Charleston School of Law	SOUTH CAROLINA	456
Charleston Southern University	SOUTH CAROLINA	456
Charlotte School of Law	NORTH CAROLINA	363
Charter College	ALASKA	10
Charter College-Oxnard	CALIFORNIA	39
Charter Oak State College	CONNECTICUT	90
Chatfield College	OHIO	387
Chatham University	PENNSYLVANIA	425
Chattahoochee Technical College	GEORGIA	127
Chattahoochee Valley Community College	ALABAMA	2
Chattanooga College	TENNESSEE	467
Chattanooga State Community College	TENNESSEE	474
Chemeketa Community College	OREGON	414
Chesapeake College	MARYLAND	222
Chestnut Hill College	PENNSYLVANIA	425
Cheyney University of Pennsylvania	PENNSYLVANIA	442
CHI Institute/Broomall Campus	PENNSYLVANIA	425
Chicago School of Professional Psychology	ILLINOIS	146
Chicago State University	ILLINOIS	146
Chicago Theological Seminary	ILLINOIS	146
Chief Dull Knife College	MONTANA	294
Chipola College	FLORIDA	103
Chippewa Valley Technical College	WISCONSIN	553
Chowan University	NORTH CAROLINA	363
Christ College of Nursing and Health Sciences, The	OHIO	387
Christ the King Seminary	NEW YORK	325
Christendom College	VIRGINIA	517
Christian Brothers University	TENNESSEE	467
Christian Life College	ILLINOIS	147
Christian Theological Seminary	INDIANA	170
Christie's Education, Inc.	NEW YORK	326
Christopher Newport University	VIRGINIA	517
Church Divinity School of the Pacific	CALIFORNIA	40
Cincinnati Christian University	OHIO	387
Cincinnati College of Mortuary Science	OHIO	387
Cincinnati State Technical and Community College	OHIO	387
Cisco College	TEXAS	482
Citadel, The Military College of South Carolina, The	SOUTH CAROLINA	456
Citrus College	CALIFORNIA	40
City College	FLORIDA	103
City College at Montana State University Billings	MONTANA	295
City College of San Francisco	CALIFORNIA	40
City Colleges of Chicago	ILLINOIS	147
City Colleges of Chicago Harold Washington College	ILLINOIS	147
City Colleges of Chicago Harry S Truman College	ILLINOIS	147
City Colleges of Chicago Kennedy-King College	ILLINOIS	147
City Colleges of Chicago Malcolm X College	ILLINOIS	147
City Colleges of Chicago Olive-Harvey College	ILLINOIS	147
City Colleges of Chicago Richard J. Daley College	ILLINOIS	147
City Colleges of Chicago Wilbur Wright College	ILLINOIS	147
City of Hope	CALIFORNIA	40
City University of New York	NEW YORK	326
City University of New York Borough of Manhattan Community College	NEW YORK	326
City University of New York Bronx Community College	NEW YORK	326
City University of New York Brooklyn College	NEW YORK	326
City University of New York College of Staten Island	NEW YORK	327
City University of New York Graduate Center	NEW YORK	327
City University of New York Herbert H. Lehman College	NEW YORK	327
City University of New York Hunter College	NEW YORK	327

Institution	State	Page
Concordia University Texas	TEXAS	483
Concordia University Wisconsin	WISCONSIN	547
Concordia University, St. Paul	MINNESOTA	263
Connecticut Board of Regents for Higher Education	CONNECTICUT	90
Connecticut College	CONNECTICUT	92
Connors State College	OKLAHOMA	407
Conservatory of Music of Puerto Rico	PUERTO RICO	561
Consolidated School of Business	PENNSYLVANIA	426
Contra Costa College	CALIFORNIA	43
Contra Costa Community College District Office	CALIFORNIA	43
Converse College	SOUTH CAROLINA	457
Conway School of Landscape Design	MASSACHUSETTS	233
Cooper Union	NEW YORK	331
Copiah-Lincoln Community College	MISSISSIPPI	273
Copper Mountain College	CALIFORNIA	43
Coppin State University	MARYLAND	228
Corban University	OREGON	415
Corcoran College of Art and Design	DISTRICT OF COLUMBIA	98
Cornell College	IOWA	183
Cornell University	NEW YORK	331
Cornerstone University	MICHIGAN	250
Corning Community College	NEW YORK	331
Cornish College of the Arts	WASHINGTON	533
Cossatot Community College of the University of Arkansas	ARKANSAS	25
Cosumnes River College	CALIFORNIA	56
Cottey College	MISSOURI	280
County College of Morris	NEW JERSEY	309
Court Reporting Institute of Dallas	TEXAS	484
Covenant College	GEORGIA	128
Covenant Theological Seminary	MISSOURI	280
Cowley County Community College	KANSAS	192
Cox College	MISSOURI	280
Coyne College	ILLINOIS	148
Crafton Hills College	CALIFORNIA	65
Cranbrook Academy of Art	MICHIGAN	250
Craven Community College	NORTH CAROLINA	370
Creative Center, The	NEBRASKA	297
Creighton University	NEBRASKA	297
Criswell College	TEXAS	484
Crossroads Bible College	INDIANA	171
Crossroads College	MINNESOTA	263
Crouse Hospital College of Nursing	NEW YORK	331
Crowder College	MISSOURI	280
Crowley's Ridge College	ARKANSAS	21
Crown College	MINNESOTA	263
Cuesta College	CALIFORNIA	43
Culinary Institute LeNotre	TEXAS	484
Culinary Institute of America	NEW YORK	331
Culinary Institute of America at Greystone, The	CALIFORNIA	43
Culver-Stockton College	MISSOURI	280
Cumberland County College	NEW JERSEY	309
Cumberland University	TENNESSEE	468
Curry College	MASSACHUSETTS	233
Curtis Institute of Music	PENNSYLVANIA	426
Cuyahoga Community College	OHIO	389
Cuyamaca College	CALIFORNIA	49
Cypress College	CALIFORNIA	59
Dabney S. Lancaster Community College	VIRGINIA	526
Dade Medical College	FLORIDA	104
Daemen College	NEW YORK	331
Dakota College at Bottineau	NORTH DAKOTA	382
Dakota County Technical College	MINNESOTA	266
Dakota State University	SOUTH DAKOTA	465
Dakota Wesleyan University	SOUTH DAKOTA	464
Dallas Baptist University	TEXAS	484
Dallas Christian College	TEXAS	484
Dallas County Community College District Office	TEXAS	484
Dallas Institute of Funeral Service	TEXAS	485
Dallas Theological Seminary	TEXAS	485
Dalton State College	GEORGIA	128
Daniel Webster College	NEW HAMPSHIRE	304
Danville Area Community College	ILLINOIS	148
Danville Community College	VIRGINIA	526
Daoist Traditions College of Chinese Medical Arts	NORTH CAROLINA	363
Dartmouth College	NEW HAMPSHIRE	304
Darton College	GEORGIA	128
Davenport University	MICHIGAN	250
Davidson College	NORTH CAROLINA	363
Davidson County Community College	NORTH CAROLINA	370
Davis & Elkins College	WEST VIRGINIA	541
Davis College	NEW YORK	331
Davis College	OHIO	389
Dawson Community College	MONTANA	294
Daymar College-Bellevue	KENTUCKY	200
Daymar College-Bowling Green	KENTUCKY	200
Daymar College-Chillicothe	OHIO	389
Daymar College-Jackson	OHIO	389
Daymar College-Lancaster	OHIO	389
Daymar College-Louisville	KENTUCKY	200
Daymar College-Louisville East	KENTUCKY	200
Daymar College-Madisonville	KENTUCKY	200
Daymar College-New Boston	OHIO	389
Daymar College-Owensboro	KENTUCKY	200
Daymar College-Paducah	KENTUCKY	200
Daymar College-Scottsville	KENTUCKY	200
Daymar Institute	TENNESSEE	468
Daytona College	FLORIDA	104
Daytona State College	FLORIDA	104
De Anza College	CALIFORNIA	47
Dean College	MASSACHUSETTS	233
Dean Institute of Technology	PENNSYLVANIA	426
Deep Springs College	CALIFORNIA	43
Defense Language Institute	US SERVICE SCHOOLS	557
Defiance College, The	OHIO	389
Del Mar College	TEXAS	485
Delaware College of Art and Design	DELAWARE	96
Delaware County Community College	PENNSYLVANIA	426
Delaware State University	DELAWARE	96
Delaware Technical Community College, Office of the President	DELAWARE	96
Delaware Technical Community College, Owens Campus	DELAWARE	96
Delaware Technical Community College, Stanton-Wilmington Campus	DELAWARE	96
Delaware Technical Community College, Terry Campus	DELAWARE	96
Delaware Valley College	PENNSYLVANIA	426
Delgado Community College	LOUISIANA	210
Dell'Arte International School of Physical Theatre	CALIFORNIA	44
Delta College	MICHIGAN	250
Delta College of Arts & Technology	LOUISIANA	208
Delta School of Business & Technology, DBA Delta Tech	LOUISIANA	208
Delta State University	MISSISSIPPI	273
Denison University	OHIO	389
Denmark Technical College	SOUTH CAROLINA	457
Denver School of Nursing	COLORADO	84
Denver Seminary	COLORADO	84
DePaul University	ILLINOIS	149
DePauw University	INDIANA	171
Des Moines Area Community College	IOWA	183
Des Moines University	IOWA	184
DeSales University	PENNSYLVANIA	427
Design Institute of San Diego	CALIFORNIA	44
DeVry College of New York	NEW YORK	332
DeVry University - Addison Campus	ILLINOIS	149
DeVry University - Alpharetta Campus	GEORGIA	128
DeVry University - Arlington Campus	VIRGINIA	518
DeVry University - Atlanta Buckhead Center	GEORGIA	128
DeVry University - Atlanta Cobb/Galleria Center	GEORGIA	128
DeVry University - Atlanta/Perimeter Center	GEORGIA	128
DeVry University - Austin	TEXAS	486
DeVry University - Bakersfield	CALIFORNIA	44
DeVry University - Bellevue Center	WASHINGTON	533
DeVry University - Bethesda Center	MARYLAND	222
DeVry University - Charlotte Center	NORTH CAROLINA	364
DeVry University - Chesapeake	VIRGINIA	518
DeVry University - Chicago Campus	ILLINOIS	149
DeVry University - Chicago Loop Center	ILLINOIS	149
DeVry University - Chicago O'Hare Center	ILLINOIS	149
DeVry University - Cincinnati	OHIO	390
DeVry University - Colorado Springs Center	COLORADO	84
DeVry University - Colton	CALIFORNIA	44
DeVry University - Columbus Campus	OHIO	390
DeVry University - Columbus North Center	OHIO	390
DeVry University - Daly City	CALIFORNIA	44
DeVry University - Dayton	OHIO	390
DeVry University - Decatur Campus	GEORGIA	128
DeVry University - Denver South Center	COLORADO	84
DeVry University - Downers Grove	ILLINOIS	149
DeVry University - Edina	MINNESOTA	263
DeVry University - Elgin Center	ILLINOIS	149
DeVry University - Federal Way Campus	WASHINGTON	533
DeVry University - Fort Lauderdale	FLORIDA	104
DeVry University - Fort Washington Campus	PENNSYLVANIA	427
DeVry University - Fort Worth	TEXAS	486
DeVry University - Fremont Campus	CALIFORNIA	44
DeVry University - Fresno	CALIFORNIA	44
DeVry University - Gurnee	ILLINOIS	149
DeVry University - Gwinnett Center	GEORGIA	128
DeVry University - Henderson	NEVADA	301
DeVry University - Henry County	GEORGIA	129
DeVry University - Home Office	ILLINOIS	149
DeVry University - Houston Campus	TEXAS	486
DeVry University - Indianapolis	INDIANA	171
DeVry University - Irving Campus	TEXAS	486
DeVry University - Jacksonville	FLORIDA	104
DeVry University - Kansas City Campus	MISSOURI	281
DeVry University - Kansas City Downtown Center	MISSOURI	281
DeVry University - King of Prussia	PENNSYLVANIA	427
DeVry University - Long Beach Campus	CALIFORNIA	44
DeVry University - Louisville	KENTUCKY	200
DeVry University - Manassas	VIRGINIA	518
DeVry University - Memphis	TENNESSEE	468
DeVry University - Merrillville Center	INDIANA	171
DeVry University - Mesa Center	ARIZONA	13
DeVry University - Miami Center	FLORIDA	104
DeVry University - Milwaukee Center	WISCONSIN	547
DeVry University - Miramar Campus	FLORIDA	104
DeVry University - Naperville Center	ILLINOIS	149
DeVry University - Nashville	TENNESSEE	468
DeVry University - North Brunswick Campus	NEW JERSEY	309
DeVry University - Northeast Phoenix Center	ARIZONA	13
DeVry University - Oakland Center	CALIFORNIA	44
DeVry University - Oklahoma City	OKLAHOMA	407
DeVry University - Orlando Campus	FLORIDA	104
DeVry University - Orlando North Center	FLORIDA	104
DeVry University - Palmdale	CALIFORNIA	44
DeVry University - Paramus	NEW JERSEY	309
DeVry University - Philadelphia	PENNSYLVANIA	427
DeVry University - Phoenix Campus	ARIZONA	13
DeVry University - Pittsburgh	PENNSYLVANIA	427
DeVry University - Pomona Campus	CALIFORNIA	44
DeVry University - Portland	OREGON	415
DeVry University - Raleigh/Durham	NORTH CAROLINA	364
DeVry University - Richardson	TEXAS	486
DeVry University - Sacramento	CALIFORNIA	44
DeVry University - St. Louis	MISSOURI	281
DeVry University - San Diego Campus	CALIFORNIA	44
DeVry University - San Jose	CALIFORNIA	44

Institution	State	Page
Illinois State University	ILLINOIS	153
Illinois Valley Community College	ILLINOIS	153
Illinois Wesleyan University	ILLINOIS	153
Immaculata University	PENNSYLVANIA	431
Immaculate Conception Seminary of Seton Hall University	NEW JERSEY	310
Imperial Valley College	CALIFORNIA	51
Independence Community College	KANSAS	193
Independence University	UTAH	510
Indian Hills Community College	IOWA	185
Indian River State College	FLORIDA	111
Indiana State University	INDIANA	173
Indiana Tech	INDIANA	173
Indiana University	INDIANA	173
Indiana University Bloomington	INDIANA	173
Indiana University East	INDIANA	173
Indiana University Kokomo	INDIANA	174
Indiana University Northwest	INDIANA	174
Indiana University of Pennsylvania	PENNSYLVANIA	442
Indiana University-Purdue University Fort Wayne	INDIANA	174
Indiana University-Purdue University Indianapolis	INDIANA	174
Indiana University South Bend	INDIANA	174
Indiana University Southeast	INDIANA	175
Indiana Wesleyan University	INDIANA	175
Infotech Career College	CALIFORNIA	51
Inste Bible College	IOWA	185
Institute for Clinical Social Work	ILLINOIS	154
Institute for Doctoral Studies in the Visual Arts	MAINE	218
Institute for the Psychological Sciences	VIRGINIA	520
Institute of American Indian Arts	NEW MEXICO	318
Institute of Business and Medical Careers	COLORADO	85
Institute of Business and Medical Careers	WYOMING	556
Institute of Clinical Acupuncture and Oriental Medicine	HAWAII	141
Institute of Design and Construction	NEW YORK	336
Institute of Production and Recording	MINNESOTA	264
Institute of Taoist Education and Acupuncture	COLORADO	85
Institute of Technology	CALIFORNIA	51
Institute of World Politics, The	DISTRICT OF COLUMBIA	99
Instituto de Banca y Comercio	PUERTO RICO	562
IntelliTec College	COLORADO	85
IntelliTec Medical Institute	COLORADO	85
Inter American University of Puerto Rico Aguadilla Campus	PUERTO RICO	563
Inter American University of Puerto Rico Arecibo Campus	PUERTO RICO	563
Inter American University of Puerto Rico Barranquitas Campus	PUERTO RICO	563
Inter American University of Puerto Rico Bayamon Campus	PUERTO RICO	563
Inter American University of Puerto Rico Central Office	PUERTO RICO	562
Inter American University of Puerto Rico Fajardo Campus	PUERTO RICO	563
Inter American University of Puerto Rico Guayama Campus	PUERTO RICO	563
Inter American University of Puerto Rico Metropolitan Campus	PUERTO RICO	563
Inter American University of Puerto Rico Ponce Campus	PUERTO RICO	564
Inter American University of Puerto Rico San German Campus	PUERTO RICO	564
Inter American University of Puerto Rico School of Law	PUERTO RICO	564
Inter American University of Puerto Rico School of Optometry	PUERTO RICO	564
Interactive College of Technology	GEORGIA	132
Interdenominational Theological Center	GEORGIA	132
Interface College	WASHINGTON	535
Interior Designers Institute	CALIFORNIA	51
International Academy of Design and Technology	CALIFORNIA	51
International Academy of Design and Technology	FLORIDA	111
International Academy of Design and Technology	ILLINOIS	154
International Academy of Design and Technology	MICHIGAN	252
International Academy of Design and Technology	TENNESSEE	469
International Academy of Design and Technology	TEXAS	488
International Academy of Design and Technology	WASHINGTON	535
International Academy of Design and Technology-Online	FLORIDA	111
International Academy of Design and Technology-Schaumburg	ILLINOIS	154
International Baptist College	ARIZONA	14
International Business College	INDIANA	175
International College of Broadcasting	OHIO	392
International Institute for Restorative Practices	PENNSYLVANIA	431
International Technological University	CALIFORNIA	51
International Theological Seminary	CALIFORNIA	51
Inver Hills Community College	MINNESOTA	266
Iona College	NEW YORK	336
Iowa Central Community College	IOWA	185
Iowa Lakes Community College	IOWA	186
Iowa State University	IOWA	182
Iowa Valley Community College District	IOWA	186
Iowa Wesleyan College	IOWA	186
Iowa Western Community College	IOWA	186
Irvine Valley College	CALIFORNIA	70
Island Drafting and Technical Institute	NEW YORK	336
Isothermal Community College	NORTH CAROLINA	371
Itasca Community College	MINNESOTA	266
Itawamba Community College	MISSISSIPPI	274
Ithaca College	NEW YORK	336
ITI Technical College	LOUISIANA	209
ITT Technical Institute	ALABAMA	4
ITT Technical Institute	ARIZONA	14
ITT Technical Institute	ARKANSAS	22
ITT Technical Institute	CALIFORNIA	51
ITT Technical Institute	CALIFORNIA	52
ITT Technical Institute	CALIFORNIA	51
ITT Technical Institute	CALIFORNIA	52
ITT Technical Institute	COLORADO	85
ITT Technical Institute	FLORIDA	111
ITT Technical Institute	GEORGIA	132
ITT Technical Institute	IDAHO	144
ITT Technical Institute	ILLINOIS	154
ITT Technical Institute	INDIANA	175
ITT Technical Institute	IOWA	186
ITT Technical Institute	KANSAS	194
ITT Technical Institute	KENTUCKY	201
ITT Technical Institute	LOUISIANA	209
ITT Technical Institute	MARYLAND	223
ITT Technical Institute	MASSACHUSETTS	235
ITT Technical Institute	MICHIGAN	252
ITT Technical Institute	MINNESOTA	264
ITT Technical Institute	MISSISSIPPI	274
ITT Technical Institute	MISSOURI	283
ITT Technical Institute	MISSOURI	282
ITT Technical Institute	MISSOURI	283
ITT Technical Institute	NEBRASKA	298
ITT Technical Institute	NEVADA	301
ITT Technical Institute	NEW MEXICO	318
ITT Technical Institute	NEW YORK	337
ITT Technical Institute	NORTH CAROLINA	365
ITT Technical Institute	OHIO	392
ITT Technical Institute	OKLAHOMA	408
ITT Technical Institute	OREGON	416
ITT Technical Institute	PENNSYLVANIA	431
ITT Technical Institute	SOUTH CAROLINA	458
ITT Technical Institute	TENNESSEE	469
ITT Technical Institute	TEXAS	488
ITT Technical Institute	TEXAS	489
ITT Technical Institute	UTAH	510
ITT Technical Institute	VIRGINIA	520
ITT Technical Institute	WASHINGTON	535
ITT Technical Institute	WEST VIRGINIA	541
ITT Technical Institute	WISCONSIN	547
Ivy Tech Community College-Central Indiana	INDIANA	175
Ivy Tech Community College of Indiana-Bloomington	INDIANA	175
Ivy Tech Community College of Indiana-Central Office	INDIANA	175
Ivy Tech Community College of Indiana-Columbus	INDIANA	176
Ivy Tech Community College of Indiana-East Central	INDIANA	176
Ivy Tech Community College of Indiana-Kokomo	INDIANA	176
Ivy Tech Community College of Indiana-Lafayette	INDIANA	176
Ivy Tech Community College of Indiana-North Central	INDIANA	176
Ivy Tech Community College of Indiana-Northeast	INDIANA	176
Ivy Tech Community College of Indiana-Northwest	INDIANA	176
Ivy Tech Community College of Indiana-Richmond	INDIANA	176
Ivy Tech Community College of Indiana-Southeast	INDIANA	177
Ivy Tech Community College of Indiana-Southern Indiana	INDIANA	177
Ivy Tech Community College of Indiana-Southwest	INDIANA	177
Ivy Tech Community College of Indiana-Wabash Valley	INDIANA	177
J. Sargeant Reynolds Community College	VIRGINIA	527
Jackson Community College	MICHIGAN	252
Jackson State Community College	TENNESSEE	475
Jackson State University	MISSISSIPPI	274
Jacksonville College	TEXAS	489
Jacksonville State University	ALABAMA	4
Jacksonville University	FLORIDA	111
James A. Rhodes State College	OHIO	392
James H. Faulkner State Community College	ALABAMA	5
James Madison University	VIRGINIA	520
James Sprunt Community College	NORTH CAROLINA	371
Jamestown Business College	NEW YORK	337
Jamestown College	NORTH DAKOTA	381
Jamestown Community College	NEW YORK	337
Jarvis Christian College	TEXAS	489
Jefferson College	MISSOURI	283
Jefferson College of Health Sciences	VIRGINIA	520
Jefferson Community and Technical College	KENTUCKY	202
Jefferson Community College	NEW YORK	337
Jefferson Davis Community College	ALABAMA	5
Jefferson State Community College	ALABAMA	5
Jewish Theological Seminary of America	NEW YORK	337
J.F. Drake State Technical College	ALABAMA	4
J.F. Ingram State Technical College	ALABAMA	4
JNA Institute of Culinary Arts	PENNSYLVANIA	431
John A. Gupton College	TENNESSEE	469
John A. Logan College	ILLINOIS	154
John Brown University	ARKANSAS	22
John Carroll University	OHIO	392
John Dewey College	PUERTO RICO	564
John F. Kennedy University	CALIFORNIA	52
John Leland Center for Theological Studies, The	VIRGINIA	520
John Marshall Law School	ILLINOIS	154
John Paul the Great Catholic University	CALIFORNIA	52
John Tyler Community College	VIRGINIA	527
John Wood Community College	ILLINOIS	154
Johns Hopkins University	MARYLAND	223
Johnson & Wales University	FLORIDA	112
Johnson & Wales University	RHODE ISLAND	453
Johnson & Wales University-Charlotte	NORTH CAROLINA	365
Johnson & Wales University - Denver Campus	COLORADO	85
Johnson C. Smith University	NORTH CAROLINA	366
Johnson College	PENNSYLVANIA	431
Johnson County Community College	KANSAS	194
Johnson State College	VERMONT	515
Johnson University	TENNESSEE	469
Johnston Community College	NORTH CAROLINA	371
Joliet Junior College	ILLINOIS	154
Jones College	FLORIDA	112
Jones County Junior College	MISSISSIPPI	274
Jones International University	COLORADO	85
Jose Maria Vargas University	FLORIDA	112
Judge Advocate General's Legal Center & School, The	US SERVICE SCHOOLS	557
Judson College	ALABAMA	5
Judson University	ILLINOIS	154

Institution	State	Page
Penn State Schuylkill	PENNSYLVANIA	440
Penn State Shenango	PENNSYLVANIA	440
Penn State University Park	PENNSYLVANIA	438
Penn State Wilkes-Barre	PENNSYLVANIA	440
Penn State Worthington-Scranton	PENNSYLVANIA	440
Penn State York	PENNSYLVANIA	440
Pennco Tech	PENNSYLVANIA	440
Pennsylvania Academy of the Fine Arts	PENNSYLVANIA	440
Pennsylvania College of Art & Design	PENNSYLVANIA	440
Pennsylvania College of Technology	PENNSYLVANIA	440
Pennsylvania Highlands Community College	PENNSYLVANIA	441
Pennsylvania Institute of Health and Technology	PENNSYLVANIA	441
Pennsylvania Institute of Technology	PENNSYLVANIA	441
Pennsylvania School of Business	PENNSYLVANIA	441
Pennsylvania State System of Higher Education, Office of the Chancellor	PENNSYLVANIA	441
Pensacola Christian College	FLORIDA	115
Pensacola State College	FLORIDA	115
Pentecostal Theological Seminary	TENNESSEE	472
Pepperdine University	CALIFORNIA	61
Peralta Community Colleges District Office	CALIFORNIA	62
Peru State College	NEBRASKA	299
Pfeiffer University	NORTH CAROLINA	375
Philadelphia Biblical University	PENNSYLVANIA	444
Philadelphia College of Osteopathic Medicine	PENNSYLVANIA	444
Philadelphia University	PENNSYLVANIA	444
Philander Smith College	ARKANSAS	23
Phillips Beth Israel School of Nursing	NEW YORK	346
Phillips Community College of the University of Arkansas	ARKANSAS	25
Phillips Graduate Institute	CALIFORNIA	62
Phillips Theological Seminary	OKLAHOMA	411
Phoenix College	ARIZONA	16
Phoenix Institute of Herbal Medicine and Acupuncture	ARIZONA	17
Phoenix School of Law	ARIZONA	17
Phoenix Seminary	ARIZONA	17
Piedmont Baptist College and Graduate School	NORTH CAROLINA	375
Piedmont College	GEORGIA	136
Piedmont Community College	NORTH CAROLINA	372
Piedmont Technical College	SOUTH CAROLINA	460
Piedmont Virginia Community College	VIRGINIA	528
Pierce College District	WASHINGTON	536
Pierpont Community & Technical College	WEST VIRGINIA	543
Pikes Peak Community College	COLORADO	87
Pima County Community College District	ARIZONA	17
Pima Medical Institute-Albuquerque	NEW MEXICO	320
Pima Medical Institute-Chula Vista	CALIFORNIA	62
Pima Medical Institute-Denver	COLORADO	87
Pima Medical Institute-Las Vegas	NEVADA	303
Pima Medical Institute-Mesa	ARIZONA	17
Pima Medical Institute-Seattle	WASHINGTON	536
Pima Medical Institute-Tucson	ARIZONA	17
Pine Manor College	MASSACHUSETTS	243
Pine Technical College	MINNESOTA	268
Pinnacle Career Institute	KANSAS	196
Pinnacle Career Institute	MISSOURI	287
Pioneer Pacific College	OREGON	419
Pitt Community College	NORTH CAROLINA	372
Pittsburg State University	KANSAS	196
Pittsburgh Institute of Aeronautics	PENNSYLVANIA	444
Pittsburgh Institute of Mortuary Science	PENNSYLVANIA	444
Pittsburgh Technical Institute	PENNSYLVANIA	444
Pittsburgh Theological Seminary	PENNSYLVANIA	444
Pitzer College	CALIFORNIA	62
Platt College	CALIFORNIA	62
Platt College	COLORADO	87
Platt College	OKLAHOMA	411
Platt College-OKC Central	OKLAHOMA	411
Plaza College	NEW YORK	346
Plymouth State University	NEW HAMPSHIRE	307
Point Loma Nazarene University	CALIFORNIA	62
Point Park University	PENNSYLVANIA	445
Point University	GEORGIA	136
Polk State College	FLORIDA	115
Polytechnic Institute of New York University	NEW YORK	346
Polytechnic University Puerto Rico	FLORIDA	115
Pomona College	CALIFORNIA	63
Ponce Paramedical College	PUERTO RICO	564
Ponce School of Medicine & Health Sciences	PUERTO RICO	565
Pontifical Catholic University of Puerto Rico-Arecibo Campus	PUERTO RICO	565
Pontifical Catholic University of Puerto Rico-Mayaguez Campus	PUERTO RICO	565
Pontifical Catholic University of Puerto Rico, The	PUERTO RICO	565
Pontifical College Josephinum	OHIO	401
Pontifical Faculty of the Immaculate Conception at the Dominican House of S tudies	DISTRICT OF COLUMBIA	99
Pontifical John Paul II Institute for Studies on Marriage and Family	DISTRICT OF COLUMBIA	99
Porterville College	CALIFORNIA	53
Portland Community College	OREGON	419
Portland State University	OREGON	418
Post University	CONNECTICUT	93
Potomac College	DISTRICT OF COLUMBIA	99
Potomac College	VIRGINIA	522
Potomac State College of West Virginia University	WEST VIRGINIA	545
Prairie State College	ILLINOIS	161
Prairie View A & M University	TEXAS	496
Pratt Community College	KANSAS	196
Pratt Institute	NEW YORK	346
Presbyterian College	SOUTH CAROLINA	460
Presbyterian Theological Seminary in America	CALIFORNIA	63
Prescott College	ARIZONA	17
Presentation College	SOUTH DAKOTA	465
Prince George's Community College	MARYLAND	225
Prince Institute-Rocky Mountains	COLORADO	87
Prince Institute - Southeast	ALABAMA	6
Prince William Sound Community College	ALASKA	11
Princeton Theological Seminary	NEW JERSEY	312
Princeton University	NEW JERSEY	312
Principia College	ILLINOIS	161
Prism Career Institute-Upper Darby Campus	PENNSYLVANIA	445
Professional Business College	NEW YORK	346
Professional Golfers Career College	CALIFORNIA	63
Professional Golfers Career College	FLORIDA	115
Professional Skills Institute	OHIO	401
Professional Training Center	FLORIDA	115
Protestant Episcopal Theological Seminary in Virginia	VIRGINIA	522
Providence Christian College	CALIFORNIA	63
Providence College	RHODE ISLAND	453
Provo College	UTAH	510
Pueblo Community College	COLORADO	87
Pulaski Technical College	ARKANSAS	23
Purchase College, State University of New York	NEW YORK	354
Purdue University Calumet	INDIANA	178
Purdue University Main Campus	INDIANA	178
Purdue University North Central Campus	INDIANA	179
Puritan Reformed Theological Seminary	MICHIGAN	257
Queens University of Charlotte	NORTH CAROLINA	376
Quincy College	MASSACHUSETTS	243
Quincy University	ILLINOIS	161
Quinebaug Valley Community College	CONNECTICUT	92
Quinnipiac University	CONNECTICUT	93
Quinsigamond Community College	MASSACHUSETTS	240
Rabbi Isaac Elchanan Theological Seminary	NEW YORK	346
Rabbi Jacob Joseph School	NEW JERSEY	313
Rabbinical Academy Mesivta Rabbi Chaim Berlin	NEW YORK	346
Rabbinical College Beth Shraga	NEW YORK	346
Rabbinical College Bobover Yeshiva B'nei Zion	NEW YORK	346
Rabbinical College Ch'san Sofer	NEW YORK	346
Rabbinical College of America	NEW JERSEY	313
Rabbinical College of Long Island	NEW YORK	346
Rabbinical College of Telshe	OHIO	401
Rabbinical College Ohr Shimon Yisroel	NEW YORK	346
Rabbinical Seminary M'kor Chaim	NEW YORK	347
Rabbinical Seminary of America	NEW YORK	347
Radford University	VIRGINIA	523
Radians College	DISTRICT OF COLUMBIA	99
Rainy River Community College	MINNESOTA	268
Ramapo College of New Jersey	NEW JERSEY	313
Rancho Santiago Community College District	CALIFORNIA	63
Randolph College	VIRGINIA	523
Randolph Community College	NORTH CAROLINA	373
Randolph-Macon College	VIRGINIA	523
Ranger College	TEXAS	492
Ranken Technical College	MISSOURI	287
Rappahannock Community College	VIRGINIA	528
Raritan Valley Community College	NEW JERSEY	313
Rasmussen College - Appleton	WISCONSIN	550
Rasmussen College - Aurora	ILLINOIS	161
Rasmussen College - Bismarck	NORTH DAKOTA	383
Rasmussen College - Blaine	MINNESOTA	270
Rasmussen College - Bloomington	MINNESOTA	270
Rasmussen College - Brooklyn Park	MINNESOTA	270
Rasmussen College - Eagan	MINNESOTA	270
Rasmussen College - Fargo/Moorhead	NORTH DAKOTA	383
Rasmussen College - Fort Myers	FLORIDA	115
Rasmussen College - Green Bay	WISCONSIN	550
Rasmussen College - Lake Elmo/Woodbury	MINNESOTA	270
Rasmussen College - Mankato	MINNESOTA	270
Rasmussen College - Mokena/Tinley Park	ILLINOIS	162
Rasmussen College - New Port Richey	FLORIDA	115
Rasmussen College - Ocala	FLORIDA	115
Rasmussen College - Rockford	ILLINOIS	162
Rasmussen College - Romeoville/Joliet	ILLINOIS	162
Rasmussen College - St. Cloud	MINNESOTA	270
Rasmussen College - Tampa/Brandon	FLORIDA	115
Rasmussen College - Wausau	WISCONSIN	550
Reading Area Community College	PENNSYLVANIA	445
Reconstructionist Rabbinical College	PENNSYLVANIA	445
Red Rocks Community College	COLORADO	87
Redeemer Theological Seminary	TEXAS	492
Redlands Community College	OKLAHOMA	411
Redstone College	COLORADO	87
Reed College	OREGON	420
Reedley College	CALIFORNIA	72
Reformed Episcopal Seminary	PENNSYLVANIA	445
Reformed Presbyterian Theological Seminary	PENNSYLVANIA	445
Reformed Theological Seminary	FLORIDA	115
Reformed Theological Seminary	MISSISSIPPI	276
Reformed Theological Seminary	NORTH CAROLINA	376
Reformed Theological Seminary	VIRGINIA	523
Refrigeration School, The	ARIZONA	18
Regent University	VIRGINIA	523
Regis College	MASSACHUSETTS	244
Regis University	COLORADO	87
Reid State Technical College	ALABAMA	6
Reinhardt University	GEORGIA	136
Relay Graduate School of Education	NEW YORK	347
Remington College	TENNESSEE	472
Remington College	TEXAS	492
Remington College-Baton Rouge Campus	LOUISIANA	214
Remington College Cleveland Campus	OHIO	401
Remington College-Colorado Springs	COLORADO	88
Remington College-Dallas Campus	TEXAS	493
Remington College-Fort Worth Campus	TEXAS	493
Remington College-Honolulu Campus	HAWAII	141

Index of Universities, Colleges and Schools

Index of Universities, Colleges and Schools

Institution	State	Page
University of Tennessee System Office	TENNESSEE	477
University of Tennessee, Knoxville	TENNESSEE	477
University of Texas at Arlington, The	TEXAS	505
University of Texas at Austin	TEXAS	505
University of Texas at Brownsville and Texas Southmost College, The	TEXAS	505
University of Texas at Dallas, The	TEXAS	506
University of Texas at El Paso	TEXAS	506
University of Texas at San Antonio	TEXAS	506
University of Texas at Tyler	TEXAS	506
University of Texas Health Science Center at Houston (UTHealth), The	TEXAS	506
University of Texas Health Science Center at San Antonio.	TEXAS	507
University of Texas M.D. Anderson Cancer Center, The	TEXAS	507
University of Texas Medical Branch, The	TEXAS	507
University of Texas of the Permian Basin	TEXAS	507
University of Texas - Pan American	TEXAS	506
University of Texas Southwestern Medical Center	TEXAS	507
University of Texas System Administration	TEXAS	505
University of the Arts, The	PENNSYLVANIA	448
University of the Cumberlands	KENTUCKY	207
University of the District of Columbia	DISTRICT OF COLUMBIA	100
University of the Incarnate Word	TEXAS	504
University of the Ozarks	ARKANSAS	26
University of the Pacific	CALIFORNIA	76
University of the Rockies	COLORADO	89
University of the Sacred Heart	PUERTO RICO	568
University of the Sciences in Philadelphia	PENNSYLVANIA	450
University of the Southwest	NEW MEXICO	321
University of the Virgin Islands	VIRGIN ISLANDS	568
University of the West	CALIFORNIA	77
University of Toledo	OHIO	404
University of Tulsa	OKLAHOMA	413
University of Utah, The	UTAH	511
University of Vermont	VERMONT	514
University of Virginia	VIRGINIA	525
University of Virginia's College at Wise, The	VIRGINIA	525
University of Washington	WASHINGTON	539
University of West Alabama, The	ALABAMA	9
University of West Florida	FLORIDA	121
University of West Georgia	GEORGIA	139
University of Western States	OREGON	421
University of Wisconsin Colleges	WISCONSIN	553
University of Wisconsin-Eau Claire	WISCONSIN	551
University of Wisconsin-Green Bay	WISCONSIN	551
University of Wisconsin-La Crosse	WISCONSIN	551
University of Wisconsin-Madison	WISCONSIN	550
University of Wisconsin-Milwaukee	WISCONSIN	551
University of Wisconsin-Oshkosh	WISCONSIN	551
University of Wisconsin-Parkside	WISCONSIN	552
University of Wisconsin-Platteville	WISCONSIN	552
University of Wisconsin-River Falls	WISCONSIN	552
University of Wisconsin-Stevens Point	WISCONSIN	552
University of Wisconsin-Stout	WISCONSIN	552
University of Wisconsin-Superior	WISCONSIN	552
University of Wisconsin System	WISCONSIN	550
University of Wisconsin-Whitewater	WISCONSIN	553
University of Wyoming	WYOMING	556
University System of Georgia Office	GEORGIA	139
University System of Maryland Office, The	MARYLAND	227
University System of New Hampshire	NEW HAMPSHIRE	306
Upper Iowa University	IOWA	189
Urban College of Boston	MASSACHUSETTS	245
Urbana University	OHIO	405
Urshan Graduate School of Theology	MISSOURI	292
Ursinus College	PENNSYLVANIA	450
Ursuline College	OHIO	405
U.S. Career Institute	COLORADO	89
USC The Business College	NEW YORK	359
U.T.A. Mesivta of Kiryas Joel	NEW YORK	359
Utah College of Dental Hygiene at Careers Unlimited, The	UTAH	511
Utah State University	UTAH	511
Utah State University-College of Eastern Utah	UTAH	512
Utah System of Higher Education	UTAH	511
Utah Valley University	UTAH	511
Utica College	NEW YORK	359
Valdosta State University	GEORGIA	139
Valencia College	FLORIDA	123
Valley City State University	NORTH DAKOTA	382
Valley College - Beckley Campus	WEST VIRGINIA	542
Valley College - Martinsburg Campus	WEST VIRGINIA	542
Valley Forge Christian College	PENNSYLVANIA	450
Valley Forge Military College	PENNSYLVANIA	450
Valor Christian College	OHIO	405
Valparaiso University	INDIANA	181
Van Andel Institute Graduate School	MICHIGAN	259
Vance-Granville Community College	NORTH CAROLINA	374
Vanderbilt University	TENNESSEE	478
VanderCook College of Music	ILLINOIS	167
Vanguard University of Southern California	CALIFORNIA	77
Vassar College	NEW YORK	359
Vatterott College-Cleveland	OHIO	405
Vatterott College-Des Moines	IOWA	189
Vatterott College-Joplin	MISSOURI	292
Vatterott College-Kansas City	MISSOURI	292
Vatterott College-Memphis	TENNESSEE	478
Vatterott College-NorthPark	MISSOURI	292
Vatterott College-O'Fallon	MISSOURI	292
Vatterott College-Oklahoma City	OKLAHOMA	414
Vatterott College-Omaha	NEBRASKA	301
Vatterott College-Quincy	ILLINOIS	168
Vatterott College-Saint Joseph	MISSOURI	292
Vatterott College-Springfield	MISSOURI	292
Vatterott College-Sunset Hills	MISSOURI	292
Vatterott College-Tulsa	OKLAHOMA	414
Vatterott College - Wichita	KANSAS	197
Vaughn College of Aeronautics and Technology	NEW YORK	359
Ventura College	CALIFORNIA	77
Ventura County Community College District	CALIFORNIA	77
Veritas Evangelical Seminary	CALIFORNIA	77
Vermilion Community College	MINNESOTA	269
Vermont College of Fine Arts	VERMONT	515
Vermont Law School	VERMONT	515
Vermont State Colleges System Office	VERMONT	515
Vermont Technical College	VERMONT	516
Vernon College	TEXAS	507
Vet Tech Institute	PENNSYLVANIA	450
Vet Tech Institute of Houston	TEXAS	508
Victor Valley College	CALIFORNIA	77
Victoria College	TEXAS	508
Victory University (formerly Crichton College)	TENNESSEE	478
Villa Maria College of Buffalo	NEW YORK	359
Villanova University	PENNSYLVANIA	450
Vincennes University	INDIANA	181
Virginia Baptist College	VIRGINIA	526
Virginia College	ALABAMA	3
Virginia College	FLORIDA	123
Virginia College	MISSISSIPPI	277
Virginia College	MISSISSIPPI	278
Virginia College at Austin	TEXAS	508
Virginia College School of Business and Health	TENNESSEE	478
Virginia Commonwealth University	VIRGINIA	526
Virginia Community College System Office	VIRGINIA	526
Virginia Highlands Community College	VIRGINIA	529
Virginia Intermont College	VIRGINIA	529
Virginia International University	VIRGINIA	529
Virginia Marti College of Art & Design	OHIO	405
Virginia Military Institute	VIRGINIA	529
Virginia Polytechnic Institute and State University	VIRGINIA	529
Virginia State University	VIRGINIA	529
Virginia Union University	VIRGINIA	530
Virginia University of Lynchburg	VIRGINIA	530
Virginia Wesleyan College	VIRGINIA	530
Virginia Western Community College	VIRGINIA	529
Visible Music College	TENNESSEE	478
Vista College	UTAH	512
Viterbo University	WISCONSIN	553
Volunteer State Community College	TENNESSEE	476
Voorhees College	SOUTH CAROLINA	463
Wabash College	INDIANA	181
Wade College Infomart	TEXAS	508
Wagner College	NEW YORK	360
Wake Forest University	NORTH CAROLINA	380
Wake Technical Community College	NORTH CAROLINA	374
Walden University	MINNESOTA	272
Waldorf College	IOWA	189
Walla Walla Community College	WASHINGTON	539
Walla Walla University	WASHINGTON	539
Wallace State Community College - Hanceville	ALABAMA	10
Walsh College of Accountancy and Business Administration	MICHIGAN	259
Walsh University	OHIO	405
Walters State Community College	TENNESSEE	476
Warner Pacific College	OREGON	421
Warner University	FLORIDA	123
Warren County Community College	NEW JERSEY	317
Warren Wilson College	NORTH CAROLINA	380
Wartburg College	IOWA	189
Wartburg Theological Seminary	IOWA	190
Washburn University	KANSAS	197
Washington & Jefferson College	PENNSYLVANIA	451
Washington Adventist University	MARYLAND	229
Washington and Lee University	VIRGINIA	530
Washington Baptist University	VIRGINIA	530
Washington Bible College/Capital Bible Seminary	MARYLAND	229
Washington College	MARYLAND	229
Washington County Community College	MAINE	219
Washington State Community College	OHIO	405
Washington State University	WASHINGTON	539
Washington Theological Union	DISTRICT OF COLUMBIA	100
Washington University in St. Louis	MISSOURI	292
Washtenaw Community College	MICHIGAN	259
Watkins College of Art, Design & Film	TENNESSEE	478
Waubonsee Community College	ILLINOIS	168
Waukesha County Technical College	WISCONSIN	555
Waycross College	GEORGIA	139
Wayland Baptist University	TEXAS	508
Wayne Community College	NORTH CAROLINA	375
Wayne County Community College District	MICHIGAN	259
Wayne State College	NEBRASKA	299
Wayne State University	MICHIGAN	260
Waynesburg University	PENNSYLVANIA	451
Weatherford College	TEXAS	508
Webb Institute	NEW YORK	360
Webber International University	FLORIDA	123
Weber State University	UTAH	511
Webster University	MISSOURI	292
Weill Cornell Medical College	NEW YORK	360
Wellesley College	MASSACHUSETTS	245
Wells College	NEW YORK	360
Wenatchee Valley College	WASHINGTON	539
Wentworth Institute of Technology	MASSACHUSETTS	245
Wentworth Military Academy and Junior College	MISSOURI	293
Wesley Biblical Seminary	MISSISSIPPI	278
Wesley College	DELAWARE	97
Wesley Theological Seminary	DISTRICT OF COLUMBIA	100

Index of Universities, Colleges and Schools